Abbreviations Used in this Dicti[onary]
Abréviations utilisées dans ce di[ctionnaire]

marketing	*Mktg*	marketing
masculine plural noun	*mpl*	nom masculin pluriel
music	*Mus*	musique
mythology	*Myth*	mythologie
noun	*n*	nom
shipping	*Naut*	nautisme
term used in Northern England	*NEng*	terme utilisé dans le nord de l'Angleterre
feminine noun	*nf*	nom féminin
feminine plural noun	*nfpl*	nom féminin pluriel
masculine noun	*nm*	nom masculin
masculine and feminine noun	*nmf*	nom masculin et féminin
masculine plural noun	*nmpl*	nom masculin pluriel
plural noun	*npl*	nom pluriel
proper noun	*npr*	nom propre
nuclear	*Nucl*	nucléaire
New Zealand English	*NZ*	anglais de Nouvelle-Zélande
obstetrics	*Obst*	obstétrique
officially recommended term	*Offic*	recommandation officielle
onomatopoeia	*onomat*	onomatopée
optics	*Opt*	optique
computing	*Ordinat*	informatique
birds	*Orn*	oiseaux
parliament	*Parl*	parlement
pejorative	*Pej, Péj*	péjoratif
petroleum industry	*Petr, Pétr*	industrie pétrolière
pharmacy	*Pharm*	pharmacie
philosophy	*Phil*	philosophie
photography	*Phot*	photographie
physics	*Phys*	physique
physiology	*Physiol*	physiologie
plural	*pl*	pluriel
politics	*Pol*	politique
past participle	*pp*	participe passé
predeterminer	*predet*	prédéterminant
prefix	*pref, préf*	préfixe
preposition	*prep, prép*	préposition
proper noun	*pr n*	nom propre
pronoun	*pron*	pronom
proverb	*Prov*	proverbe
psychology, psychiatry	*Psy*	psychologie, psychiatrie
past tense	*pt*	prétérit
something	*qch*	quelque chose
somebody	*qn*	quelqu'un
registered trademark	®	marque déposée
radio	*Rad*	radio
rail	*Rail*	chemins de fer

relig.		
South African English		
somebody	*sb*	
school	*Sch, Scol*	scola.
Scottish English	*Scot*	anglais d'Éco[sse]
term used in Southern England	*SEng*	terme utilisé dans le sud de l'Angleterre
singular	*sing*	singulier
formal	*Sout*	soutenu
specialist term	*Spec, Spéc*	vocabulaire de spécialité
Stock Exchange	*St Exch*	Bourse
something	*sth*	quelque chose
suffix	*suff*	suffixe
superlative	*superl*	superlatif
technology	*Tech*	technologie
telecommunications	*Tel, Tél*	télécommunications
textiles	*Tex*	textile
theatre	*Theat, Théât*	théâtre
transport	*Transp*	transports
television	*TV*	télévision
typography, printing	*Typ*	typographie, imprimerie
European Union	*UE*	Union européenne
university	*Univ*	université
verb	*v*	verbe
intransitive verb	*vi*	verbe intransitif
reflexive verb	*vpr*	verbe pronominal
transitive verb	*vt*	verbe transitif
transitive verb used with a preposition [eg **parvenir à** (to reach); ils sont **parvenus à** un accord (they reached an agreement)]	*vt ind*	verbe transitif indirect [par exemple: **parvenir à**; ils sont **parvenus à** un accord]
inseparable transitive verb [phrasal verb where the verb and the adverb or preposition cannot be separated, eg **look after**; he **looked after** the children]	*vt insep*	verbe transitif à particule inséparable [par exemple: **look after** (s'occuper de); he **looked after** the children (il s'occupait des enfants)]
separable transitive verb [phrasal verb where the adverb and preposition can be separated, eg **send back**; she **sent** the present **back** or she **sent back** the present]	*vt sep*	verbe transitif à particule séparable [par exemple: **send** back (rendre); she **sent** the present **back** *ou* she **sent** back the present (elle a rendu le cadeau)]
veterinary medicine	*Vet, Vét*	médecine vétérinaire
vulgar	*Vulg*	vulgaire
zoology	*Zool*	zoologie

HARRAP'S

UNABRIDGED

DICTIONARY
DICTIONNAIRE

Volume 2
French–English
Français–Anglais

HARRAP

This (second) edition first published in 2007
by Chambers Harrap Publishers Ltd
7 Hopetoun Crescent, Edinburgh EH7 4AY, UK

Previous edition published 2001

© Chambers Harrap Publishers Ltd 2007

Dépôt légal: novembre 2006

This volume
ISBN 978 0245 50585 7 (France)
ISBN 978 0245 60746 2 (UK)

Volume 1 (English – French)
ISBN 978 0245 50584 9 (France)
ISBN 978 0245 60745 5 (UK)

Designed and typeset by Chambers Harrap Publishers Ltd, Edinburgh
Printed and bound in Italy by Rotolito Lombarda SpA

Contributors (2nd edition)/ Collaborateurs (2e édition)

Managing Editor/Coordination éditoriale

Anna Stevenson

Editors/Rédacteurs

Nadia Cornuau
Stuart Fortey
Laurence Larroche
Kate Nicholson
Georges Pilard

with/avec

Lola Busuttil
Lynda Carey
Anne Convery
Guy Ferlin
Graham Frankland
Nadia Ghalem
Susan Howarth
Val McNulty
Ruth Noble

Prepress/Prépresse

Anne Benson
Isla MacLean
David Reid
Clair SImpson

CONTRIBUTORS/COLLABORATEURS

Contributors (1st edition)/
Collaborateurs (1re édition)

Editor–in–Chief / Rédacteur en chef

Patrick White

Managing Editor / Coordination éditoriale

Anna Stevenson

Senior Editors / Rédacteurs seniors

Gearóid Cronin
Laurence Larroche
Georges Pilard

Editors / Rédaction

Lola Busuttil	Lesley Johnston
Isabelle Elkaim	Stéphanie Marchand
Stuart Fortey	Françoise de Peretti
Frances Illingworth	Susan Steinberg

with / avec

Dougal Campbell	Claude Moureau-Bondy
Lynda Carey	Ruth Noble
Daniela Delas	Elaine O'Donoghue
Pat Dunn	Martine Pierquin
Gilla Evans	Rose Rociola
Kay L. Hawkins	Deborah Sanders
Lynn Hubble	Alan Seaton
Anne Kansau	Megan Thomson
David Kennedy	Sheilagh Wilson
Sophie Marin	

Canadian French Consultant / Spécialiste pour les canadianismes

Louis B. Mignault,
Associate Professor (retired),
University of Toronto

Swiss French Consultant / Spécialiste pour les helvétismes

André Thibault,
Université de Strasbourg

Reading Panel / Comité de lecture

Louis B. Mignault,
Associate Professor (retired),
University of Toronto

Philip O'Prey,
Université Catholique de l'Ouest,
Angers

Kathleen Shields,
University College of Maynooth

Computing Support / Informatique éditoriale

Siri Hansen

Prepress / Prépresse

Clair Good
David Reid

Contents / Table des matières

Preface   vii
Préface   ix

Introduction (English)   xi
Introduction (français)   xix

French Pronunciation   xxvii

French Conjugation Tables   xxix

FRENCH - ENGLISH DICTIONARY   1-1296
DICTIONNAIRE FRANÇAIS - ANGLAIS

Supplement / Appendice

Chronology   (3)
Chronologie

French Communication Guide   (29)

Nations of the World   (59)

Administrative Divisions (French)   (65)

French Legal System   (67)

Military Ranks   (69)
Grades militaires

French Allusions   (73)

Abréviations français-anglais   (81)
French-English Abbreviations

Acknowledgements

Acknowledgements are due to the Chambers editorial team for material used in the English chronology, to Martyn Back for the original idea for the inclusion of allusions, to Joe de Miribel for his advice on military ranks, to Mónica Tamariz for lists of biochemistry terminology, to Peter Walton for his help with financial terms, to Stewart Wittering for his help with scientific terms, to Scott Forbes and SULA for Australian and American material respectively, and to Emmanuelle Jowa for her advice on Belgian French.

Remerciements

L'éditeur tient à remercier l'équipe éditoriale des éditions Chambers pour les documents fournis lors de la rédaction de la chronologie du monde anglophone, Martyn Back, qui eut l'idée de créer des notes explicatives sur les allusions, Joe de Miribel pour l'aide apportée lors de la rédaction du tableau comparatif des grades militaires, Mónica Tamariz pour les termes de biochimie, Peter Walton pour les termes financiers, Stewart Wittering pour les termes scientifiques, Scott Forbes pour les termes australiens, SULA pour les termes américains et Emmanuelle Jowa pour les termes de français de Belgique.

Trademarks

Marques déposées

Preface

Gone are the days when a dictionary was just a long series of words arranged in alphabetical order, to be consulted hurriedly and closed afterwards with a smile of gratitude as soon as you had found the answer to your query. There were no such smiles, however, when the word being looked up did not feature in the dictionary because it was too old-fashioned, too specialized or too rare.

Fortunately, this problem was unlikely to occur with the four-volume Harrap *Standard* French dictionary. Its comprehensiveness guaranteed that users who had searched in vain through other bilingual dictionaries could be assured of finding the word in its pages. However, the *Standard* was a dictionary in the traditional mould. Although there was much to admire in the detailed way in which translations were presented, and the variety of illustrative examples and expressions shown, the entries were listed in a tried-and-tested sequence and according to a deliberately uniform model.

Harrap, the "grande dame" of British lexicography, has been publishing dictionaries which have been valued by students, translators and the general public for a century. Now, twenty years after the last revision of the *Standard,* Harrap is marking its centenary with the publication of the Harrap *Unabridged* French-English dictionary. This worthy successor to the *Standard* is published in two large volumes, whose contents are not only better presented and more accessible but also richer and enhanced by new distinctive features.

It is immediately apparent on opening the book that it represents a new concept of what a bilingual dictionary should be. This is made evident by the new layout which draws the attention to certain features, as if to underline the greater importance of certain words and to highlight interesting aspects of usage associated with them.

The impressive new look of the text could be seen as simply a presentation gimmick, designed to break up the monotony of the traditional dictionary page layout, but in fact the new design reflects a genuine desire to go beyond the scope of a traditional bilingual dictionary. In order to provide real help to a translator, a good bilingual dictionary should be more than just a collection of words with their matching equivalents in the other language. It should also constitute a means of discovering the associations of words and the ways in which they are used in the other culture.

So, for example, at the entry for **Carnaby Street**, a boxed note gives the user an added insight into the cultural connotations of this street, once a symbol of London in the swinging sixties and today a centre for second-hand clothes shops. On the French-English side of the dictionary, you can find, for example, information about **Canal+**, informing the user not only that this is a pay TV channel which can be viewed at certain hours by non-subscribers, but also that it plays a prominent role in funding international film-making. Such information, which the user will not necessarily expect to come across in a bilingual dictionary but is bound to find both welcome and useful, gives the dictionary an added encyclopedic dimension and at the same time makes it more interesting to browse through.

In this way the dictionary entertainingly reveals the associations of many proper names that the user may have often read or heard without knowing exactly to what they refer. The connotations of these words remain opaque as they are usually not translated. In a sense, the dictionary performs the role of a guide, charting a path through the cultural landscape of another country and arousing the curiosity of the reader who may previously have been unaware of these connotations.

The dictionary breaks further new ground in the notes in grey-tinted boxes that highlight phrases that are used allusively — often ones that have originated in literature, the cinema or popular culture. These are the kinds of phrases that we hear in everyday conversations and usually have little idea that they are in fact famous quotations. For example, we are reminded that the phrase "Qu'importe le flacon pourvu qu'on ait l'ivresse" is an allusion to a play by Alfred de Musset in which the protagonist argues that the fact of being in love is more important than the person you love. Similarly, on the English-French side of the dictionary, the note on the phrase "I have a dream" describes how this phrase was used by Martin Luther King in Washington in 1963, and his dream of an America where all citizens would be equal and would live together in harmony. Another example is the phrase "Smile, you're on Candid Camera", translated as "Souriez, c'est pour le caméra invisible", a reference to our own era where people's lives are so dominated by television.

The same concern with presenting language as it is used in real life is reflected in the prominent position given in this dictionary to the international dimension and the diversity of linguistic use. Comprehensive

coverage of the standard varieties of both languages is rightly complemented by extensive coverage of French as it is used in Belgium, Canada and Switzerland, and English as it is used not only in the United States but also in Scotland, Ireland and Australia.

Last but not least: what dictionary user has not been confronted with the difficulty of trying to guess what a shortened form is short for (for example **specs** for **spectacles** in English or **réa** for **réanimation** in French), or, even more cryptically, to decipher abbreviations? Shortened forms and abbreviations are equally impenetrable, in either language, for anyone who has not lived in the country concerned. The dictionary offers help in the form of supplements which contain list of these items. Browsing through these lists, it is striking to note at an entry like **ENT** (ear, nose and throat) how pragmatic and down-to-earth English is, while the French equivalent **ORL** (oto-rhino-laryngologiste) illustrates the tendency of French towards erudite abstraction. Fortunately, hundreds of shortened forms and abbreviations — so frequently criticized nowadays as a curse — are explained and translated here. The explanations may sometimes be surprising, but they are always enlightening.

An overview of this dictionary would not be complete without mentioning the fact that it also faithfully records terms from new technologies and the latest scientific discoveries, and includes the titles of numerous works of art from the fields of literature, painting, music and cinema. Taking all of this into account, it is fair to say that this centenary edition really does represent the dawn of a new era in lexicography. Dictionaries are no longer simply useful but rather off-putting weighty tomes to be consulted only in moments of dire necessity; as the *Unabridged* proves, they are now user-friendly books which have the additional merit of being enjoyable to read.

Henriette WALTER
Emeritus Professor of Linguistics,
Université de Haute–Bretagne,
Member of the Conseil Supérieur
de la langue française

Préface

Le temps n'est plus où un dictionnaire n'était qu'une longue suite de mots classés dans l'ordre alphabétique, que l'on consultait fébrilement à la recherche d'une précision et que l'on refermait avec un sourire de reconnaissance dès que l'on avait trouvé l'information recherchée. Il faut toutefois ajouter que la déception était grande quand le mot, trop désuet, trop spécialisé ou trop rare, n'y figurait pas.

Cette dernière expérience avait peu de chances de se produire avec le dictionnaire bilingue Harrap['s *Standard*], où la générosité de la nomenclature a toujours été un gage pour trouver ce que l'on avait cherché en vain dans les autres dictionnaires bilingues. Mais il demeurait un dictionnaire classique, où l'on appréciait, certes, l'abondance des précisions dans la traduction des formes et où l'on admirait la diversité des expressions retenues, mais où toutes les entrées se suivaient sagement, dans un ordre immuable et rassurant, et selon un modèle volontairement uniforme.

Après un siècle de publications de dictionnaires fort appréciés des étudiants, des traducteurs et du grand public, et vingt ans après les derniers remaniements, voici que nous est présenté, en cadeau d'anniversaire, le tout dernier enfant de cette grande dame de la lexicographie anglaise, aujourd'hui centenaire: le Harrap's *Unabridged,* en deux forts volumes où l'information est encore plus riche, plus diversifiée, mieux mise en valeur et plus accessible.

Cette fois, c'est dès le premier coup d'œil que l'on perçoit l'avènement d'une nouvelle conception lexicographique. Elle se signale d'abord visuellement par des espaces imprimés d'une façon un peu différente et qui se détachent clairement du reste, comme pour souligner l'importance plus grande de certains mots et pour attirer l'attention sur certains développements qui ne sont que leur prolongement naturel.

Cette nouvelle disposition spectaculaire du texte pourrait n'être qu'un artifice de présentation, uniquement destiné à rompre la monotonie de la page de dictionnaire traditionnelle. En fait, cette maquette originale répond à un véritable désir d'aller plus loin qu'un dictionnaire bilingue habituel. Pour apporter une aide plus efficace à la traduction, un dictionnaire bilingue, en effet, se doit de ne pas être seulement un répertoire de mots avec leurs équivalents dans l'autre langue mais de constituer aussi un meilleur moyen d'imaginer ce qui peut être évoqué derrière les mots.

C'est ainsi, par exemple, qu'à l'entrée **Carnaby Street**, un encadré permet à l'utilisateur d'entrer en quelque sorte dans cette rue de Londres, naguère haut-lieu des milieux branchés et aujourd'hui spécialisée dans la vente des vêtements d'occasion. Côté français-anglais, on trouve, entre autres, des informations sur **Canal+**, chaîne de télévision privée à péage, mais qui peut être captée en clair à certaines heures, et qui finance aussi la production cinématographique. Ces renseignements, inattendus mais bienvenus dans un dictionnaire bilingue, lui apportent de ce fait une dimension encyclopédique supplémentaire tout en lui donnant un surcroît de vie.

Derrière de nombreux noms propres, souvent lus ou entendus sans savoir exactement ce qu'ils recouvrent et qui risquent de n'évoquer aucune image puisqu'on ne les traduit généralement pas, se profilent ainsi des réalités que l'on prend plaisir à connaître : le dictionnaire joue alors d'une certaine manière le rôle d'un guide inattendu, qui ouvre une brèche enrichissante dans le paysage culturel du voisin et parvient à piquer la curiosité du lecteur resté jusque-là indifférent.

Un pas de plus est franchi avec d'autres encadrés, cette fois sur fond grisé, qui s'attardent sur certaines allusions littéraires, picturales ou cinématographiques. On les a souvent entendues dans des conversations familières et sans soupçonner la plupart du temps que ce sont des citations de phrases célèbres. Ainsi, par exemple, nous rappelle-t-on que la phrase «Qu'importe le flacon pourvu qu'on ait l'ivresse», est une allusion à une pièce de Musset où le personnage soutient que ce qui compte, c'est le sentiment amoureux et non pas la personne aimée. Dans la partie anglais-français, l'encadré «I have a dream» évoque Martin Luther King à Washington en 1963 et son rêve d'une Amérique où tous les citoyens seraient égaux et vivraient ensemble en bonne intelligence. Voici aussi, avec «Smile, you're on Candid Camera», traduit par «Souriez, c'est pour la caméra invisible», un clin d'œil à notre époque où la vie de chacun est plus ou moins rythmée par des émissions de télévision.

Dans le même désir de mieux coller à la réalité, la dimension géographique et la diversité des usages sont dans cet ouvrage maintes fois soulignées : à côté de la norme d'usage de plus large diffusion, une place légitime y a été consacrée, pour le français, aux variétés lexicales de Belgique, de Suisse et du Canada, et pour l'anglais, aux usages d'Écosse, d'Irlande, d'Australie et des États-Unis.

Enfin, qui ne s'est jamais trouvé confronté avec le redoutable problème d'avoir à deviner le mot suggéré

PRÉFACE

par une abréviation (par exemple **specs** pour **spectacles** en anglais ou **réa** pour **réanimation** en français), ou, question plus insoluble encore, d'essayer de comprendre ce qui se cache derrière les sigles ? Abréviations et sigles sont tout aussi impénétrables, dans l'une et l'autre langue, pour qui n'a pas vécu dans le pays. À parcourir les annexes très utiles qui leur sont consacrées dans cet ouvrage, il est piquant de retrouver, par exemple, sous **ENT** (ear, nose and throat) le côté pragmatique et toujours proche des gens de l'anglais, tandis qu'avec l'équivalent français **ORL** (oto-rhino-laryngologiste), c'est plutôt la tendance savamment abstraite de la langue française qui apparaît au grand jour. Fort heureusement, des centaines d'abréviations et de sigles — cette plaie si souvent dénoncée des temps modernes — sont ici développés et traduits : ils étonnent parfois et ils rassurent toujours.

Si l'on ajoute que ce dictionnaire se fait aussi très largement l'écho attentif des nouvelles techniques et des dernières découvertes scientifiques, et qu'il rappelle en outre les titres de nombreuses œuvres de littérature, de peinture, de musique ou de cinéma, on peut dire que cette édition du centenaire marque vraiment l'entrée de la lexicographie dans une ère nouvelle : celle des dictionnaires qui ne sont plus uniquement de gros volumes très savants, très utiles mais parfois un peu rébarbatifs, et que l'on consulte seulement par nécessité, mais des ouvrages accueillants, qu'on lit aussi vraiment pour le plaisir.

Henriette WALTER
*Professeur émérite de linguistique à
l'université de Haute-Bretagne,
Membre du Conseil Supérieur de la
langue française*

x

Introduction (English)

When the editors set out to produce a new large French-English English-French dictionary for publication in Harrap's centenary year, they were very aware of the illustrious footsteps in which they were following. Professor Jean Mansion's *Standard Dictionary*, conceived by George Harrap in the early years of the company and published in two parts in 1935 and 1939, was a monumental work that for many years enjoyed an enviable reputation and was much loved among students, academics and professional translators. The first edition of the *Unabridged*, published in 2001, preserved many of the characteristics which earned the *Standard* its high reputation whilst at the same time drawing on all the advances of modern bilingual lexicography in order to produce a book that was truly a product of the 21st century.

The first edition of the *Unabridged* enjoyed great acclaim and quickly became an essential dictionary for all those working with French at an advanced level, receiving highly favourable comments and reviews from all over the globe. Six years later, the time is ripe for a second edition, which benefits from extensive updating, several thousand new references and many additional features. With this book, the editors hope to continue to build on and extend the foundations laid down by Jean Mansion so many years ago by publishing this record of how English and French are continuing to evolve into languages ever richer and more diverse.

Writing the dictionary

The computerization of the editorial process, and the existence of texts in searchable databases, have allowed this dictionary to be produced in a fraction of the time required to write the *Standard*. If Professor Mansion were alive today, he would surely have relished the opportunities for rapid searching offered by the Internet, and for better communication with contributors and consultants through e-mail. At the same time, the Internet has spawned a host of new vocabulary, generously represented in this book, and has consolidated the international nature of both English and French. For example, in searching for a French term on the Internet one is just as likely to find oneself consulting a Canadian or Swiss website as one produced in France. This dictionary has responded to this trend by giving fuller international coverage of both languages than will be found in any other general bilingual available.

Much of this international coverage was supplied by consultants with specialist knowledge of the different varieties of each language. Consultants' input was also invaluable in the creation of the specialist language databases in such areas as IT, finance and slang which were exploited in the writing of this book. An experienced reading panel of university lecturers brought fresh insights to the text and made many valuable suggestions.

Whilst all those who contributed to the dictionary played a valuable role, particular credit must go to the in-house editorial team which laboured long and hard to ensure the successful completion of a project initiated four years ago, and to the prepress team for their design input and skilful handling of over 10,000 pages of proofs.

Comprehensive?

In producing a dictionary of the size of the *Unabridged*, the editors have sought to include as many terms and phrases as possible. It would, however, be wrong to assert that the *Unabridged* gives comprehensive coverage of the English and French languages, as such an achievement would be beyond a dictionary even twice as large. What can be reasonably claimed, however, is that the *Unabridged* gives a full and wide-ranging view of the two languages as they are spoken and written at the beginning of the 21st century.

Organization of entries

Headwords are presented in blue type in this dictionary and appear in alphabetical order. Note that it is the style in this dictionary to place a word beginning with an upper-case letter before one beginning with a lower-case one; thus **March** will precede **march**.

■ Grammatical divisions

The grammatical classification of an entry is marked with a label in blue capitals, eg **N, VI**, or **PRÉP**. All the abbreviated labels are included in the list of abbreviations at the front and back of the dictionary. When an entry has more than one part of speech, each part of speech appears on a new line.

> **malvoyant, -e** [malvwajã, -ãt] ADJ partially sighted
> NM,F partially sighted person; **les malvoyants** the partially sighted

■ **Semantic divisions**

The different senses of a word are each introduced by a number in bold type:

> **snood** [snuːd] ɴ **1** *(for hair)* résille *f* **2** *(hood)* cagoule *f* **3** *Fishing* empile *f* **4** *Scot Hist (headband)* = bandeau porté autrefois dans les cheveux par les jeunes femmes célibataires

Nuances of senses, or semantic splits required to show different translations for the same sense, are shown within the same sense category by using indicating material in brackets. This material may consist of a synonym or typical collocating words, eg the objects of a transitive verb, or the nouns with which an adjective is commonly used. In some cases, both are given, with an arrow preceding the collocating words:

> **debase** [dɪ'beɪs] ᴠᴛ **1** *(degrade → person, sport)* avilir, abaisser; *(→ reputation)* ternir; *(→ tradition, profession, politics)* dévaloriser **2** *(make less valuable → object)* dégrader, altérer; *(→ metal, currency, coinage)* déprécier

In some more complex entries with many senses, the senses are subdivided first into larger sense groups, each of which is then further divided. In these cases, a bold upper-case letter indicates the major sense division and indicating material in capitals describes it:

> **MIEUX** [mjø]
>
> **ADV** better **A, B, C** ■ best **B**
> **ADJ** better **1–3**
> **NM** improvement **1** ■ best **2**
>
> **ADV A.** *COMPARATIF DE "BIEN"* **1** *(d'une manière plus satisfaisante)* better; **tout va m.** things are better (now):...

■ **English compounds**

In this dictionary English compounds of two or more words have been presented under the entry for the first word of the compound. They appear in bold italic type in alphabetical order in a block at the end of the entry. The block is introduced by the symbol ▸▸.

> **editorial** [ˌedɪ'tɔːrɪəl] ᴀᴅᴊ *(decision, comment)* de la rédaction; *(job, problems, skills)* de rédaction, rédactionnel
>
> ɴ **1** *(article)* éditorial *m* **2** *(department)* service *m* de la rédaction, rédaction *f*
>
> ▸▸ *editorial changes* corrections *fpl*; *editorial column* colonne *f* rédactionnelle; *editorial conference* conférence *f* éditoriale; *editorial content* contenu *m* rédactionnel; *editorial department (in press)* service *m* de la rédaction, rédaction *f*, direction *f* de la rédaction;...

The rule of entering a compound under its first element means, for example, that **sedge warbler**, **melodious warbler** and **garden warbler** will be found under **sedge**, **melodious** and **garden** respectively, and not at the entry **warbler**.

Hyphenated words in both English and French, however, appear as entries in their own right, in the relevant alphabetical order.

Grammatical information

■ Plurals

When a French noun has an irregular plural, this is shown immediately after the headword, sometimes in brackets:

> **linteau, -x** [lɛ̃to] NM lintel

> **trullo** [trulo] (*pl* **trullos** *ou* **trulli**) NM *Archit* trullo

Note that the plural of hyphenated French nouns is always given, unless the noun does not change its form in the plural, in which case it is marked **inv**:

> **protège-tympan** [prɔtɛʒtɛ̃pɑ̃] NM INV earplug

Similarly, English irregular plurals are also given after the headword, placed in brackets:

> **salmon** ['sæmən] (*pl* **inv** *or* **salmons**) N *Ich* saumon
> *m*; **young s.** tacon *m*
> ►► *salmon farm* élevage *m* de saumons; *salmon*
> *fillet* filet *m* de saumon; *salmon ladder, salmon*
> *leap* échelle *f* à saumon(s); *salmon pink* (rose
> *m*) saumon *m*; *salmon steak* darne *f* de saumon;
> *Ich salmon trout* truite *f* saumonée

> **emissary** ['emɪsərɪ] (*pl* **emissaries**) N émissaire *m*

> **madwoman** ['mæd,wʊmən] (*pl* **madwomen**
> [-,wɪmɪn]) N folle *f*, aliénée *f*

■ English verb forms

Irregular forms of English verbs are given after the headword for that verb:

> **edify** ['edɪfaɪ] (*pt & pp* **edified**) VT *Formal* édifier

> **seek** [siːk] (*pt & pp* **sought** [sɔːt]) VT **1** (*search for →*
> *job, person, solution*) chercher, rechercher; **he**
> **constantly sought her approval** il cherchait
> constamment à obtenir son approbation; ...

■ French verb conjugations

A number in square brackets is given after each French verb in volume 2. Users should refer to the conjugation model indicated by this number in the list of French conjugations on page xxix in volume 2 in order to read the full conjugation of the verb.

Pronunciation

Pronunciation information has been given for all words using the International Phonetic Alphabet (IPA). An explanation of the symbols used can be found on page xxvii. In contrast to most bilingual dictionaries, a phonetic transcription has been given for all abbreviations, unless they are only used in written language. Thus it will be clear whether the abbreviation is an acronym or its letters are pronounced individually.

Register

The register of all words and phrases in the source language is clearly indicated in this dictionary. Register labels are used to indicate the level of language - whether formal (*Formal/Sout*), informal (*Fam*), very informal (*very/très Fam*), or vulgar (*Vulg*) - and also to indicate usage, showing whether a word is, for example, pejorative, ironic or euphemistic. All abbreviated labels are included in the list of labels on the inside cover of the book. As far as possible, the translations given match the register of the word in the source language and no register markers are therefore applied to translations, as the user can assume that the translation is a close register match of the source language item. For example:

> **macchabée** [makabe] NM *Fam (cadavre)* stiff

In cases where it has proved impossible to find an exact equivalent in terms of register for a word that is informal, or where it is considered desirable to include a neutral alternative translation, the neutral register of the translation is indicated by a superscript symbol (■) that comes immediately after the translation. For example:

> **adman** ['ædmæn] (*pl* **admen** [-men]) N *Fam* publicitaire■ *m*

> **quat'zyeux** [katzjø] **entre quat'zyeux** ADV *Fam* in private■

> **savater** [3] [savate] VT *Fam* to kick■ , to boot

Those French terms which are examples of verlan (the process of inverting syllables to create a slang word) have been labelled as such, with the original form indicated in brackets:

> **keuf** [kœf] NM *très Fam (verlan de* **flic***)* cop; **les keufs** the fuzz, the cops

Similarly, those British slang words which are examples of rhyming slang have been labelled, with both the full form of the original phrase and the word with which it rhymes indicated. Note that where, as in the example below, the term is not widely used in Britain but restricted to southern England, and particularly the London area, it is labelled *SEng*.

> **dustbin** ['dʌstbɪn] N **1** *Br (for rubbish)* poubelle *f* **2** *SEng Fam* **dustbins** (*rhyming slang* **dustbin lids** = **kids**) gosses *mpl*, mômes *mpl*
> ►► **dustbin lid** couvercle *m* de poubelle; *dustbin liner* sac-poubelle *m*; *Br* **dustbin man** éboueur *m*

Many terms from the Canadian French dialect joual have been included in this dictionary. They have all been labelled *CanJoual* but do not have any additional labelling as to the level of language. This labelling should be understood, however, to imply that the term is non-standard and of a colloquial level of language.

Register labels can occur in various combinations. A word can be either archaic or literary, old-fashioned or humorous, for example. In such cases the presentation is as follows:

> **abysm** [ə'bɪzəm] N *Arch or Literary* abîme *m*

> **enamouré, -e** [ãnamure], **énamouré, -e** [enamure] ADJ *Vieilli ou Hum (regard, sourire)* amorous; **être e. de qn** to be enamoured of sb

> **mater** ['meɪtə(r)] N *Br Old-fashioned or Hum* **(the) m.** ma mère, maman *f*

A word which is simultaneously informal and old-fashioned, or informal and euphemistic, will be presented as follows with the labels in sequence:

> **Mae West** [ˌmeɪ'west] N *Am Fam Old-fashioned* gilet *m* de sauvetage (gonflable)▪

> **untruth** [ˌʌn'truːθ] N *Euph Formal (lie)* mensonge *m*, invention *f*; **to tell an u.** mentir, dire un mensonge

In the cases of certain words belonging to a particular variety of slang such as drugs or crime slang, the register label *Fam* or *very Fam* etc is accompanied by labels indicating the variety to which the term in question belongs. For example:

> **coked up** [kəʊkt-] ADJ *Fam Drugs slang* défoncé à la coke

> **Poulaga** [pulaga] NF *Fam Arg crime* **la maison P.** the cops, *Br* the pigs, the fuzz

In instances where a term is given two translations, one technical and the other non-technical, the technical translation is placed second and preceded by the label *Spec* or *Spéc* in the English-French and French-English volumes respectively. The technical translation has been given in addition to the neutral one where the word being translated can be used in both technical and non-technical contexts.

> **drug** ...
> ... **drug dependency** dépendance *f* à l'égard des drogues, toxicomanie *f*, *Spec* pharmacodépendance *f*;

> **mastiquer**[1] [3] [mastike] VT *(pain, viande)* to chew, *Spéc* to masticate

Some French words in this dictionary are marked with the label *Offic*. This indicates that the word in question is an officially recommended form, used less commonly than an alternative term which is often derived from English:

> **caravanette** [kærəvə'net] N camping-car *m*, *Offic* autocaravane *f*

Specialist language

The *Unabridged* features a vast number of specialized items of vocabulary relating to areas as diverse as computing, finance, law, science and medicine. Many technical terms have been retained from the Harrap *Standard*, which was used as a source for this dictionary, while a great many new terms have been added, particularly terminology created by the growth of the Internet or connected with fast-evolving areas like the stock market or genetic engineering.

A full list of the abbreviated field labels used to mark these specialist terms is to be found on the inside cover of the book. Field labels are used primarily to indicate specialist vocabulary, or to differentiate the various meanings of the headword. In cases where a word has several meanings in different domains, all with the same translation, field labels are combined in sequence to show that the translation works for all the senses indicated. For example:

> **palette** ['pælət] N *Art & Comput* palette *f*
> ▸▸ *palette knife Art* couteau *m* (à palette); *Culin* spatule *f*, *Art* **palette knife painting** peinture *f* au couteau

> **hybride** [ibrid] ADJ 1 *Bot, Zool & Ling* hybrid 2 *(mêlé)* hybrid, mixed; **une solution un peu h.** a rather hybrid solution; **une architecture h.** a patchwork of architectural styles; **un album h.** a crossover album
> NM hybrid

Navigating long entries

Long entries, consisting as they do of large blocks of dense text, tend not to be very user-friendly. One innovation in this dictionary that should help the user is the inclusion of "menus" at the beginning of many such entries. The aim of these menus is twofold: (i) to summarize the main translations of the entry; and (ii) to make use of the knowledge that the user already has to help them find the sense they want more quickly. Experienced dictionary users will want to consult the entries for common words to look for phrases and examples, rather than to learn that, for example, "pour" is a translation of "for". Thus in consulting, for example, the entry **care** the user can refer to the menu to locate quickly the "souci" sense of the word, and hence the phrases given at that category.

> **CARE** [keə(r)]
> VI s'intéresser à **1** ▪ aimer **2** ▪ vouloir **3**
> N souci **1** ▪ soin **2, 3** ▪ charge **4**

International coverage

This dictionary differs from its competitors in giving very full coverage of the international varieties of both English and French. In the English-French volume of the dictionary, thorough treatment of English as it is used in Britain and in America is complemented by extensive coverage of Australian, Irish and Scottish English. Thus, terms which the user might search for in vain in other bilingual dictionaries — such as **beyond the Black Stump, gurrier** and **muckle** (Australian, Irish and Scottish, respectively) to cite but three — will be found within the pages of the Harrap *Unabridged*.

Similarly, in the French-English volume, Canadian French is well represented, as are Belgian French and Swiss French. This reflects the dictionary's policy of ensuring coverage of the French language as it is used outside France. While this coverage cannot claim to be exhaustive, the editors of the dictionary hope that they have succeeded in their aim of including a substantial quantity of words and expressions from each of these French-speaking countries. As mentioned above, Canadian French joual terms have been included, as have terms particular to Acadian, the dialect spoken in the Maritime Provinces (Nova Scotia, New Brunswick, Prince Edward Island). These latter terms have been labelled (*en acadien*). Likewise, when a term is specific to a certain French-speaking canton of Switzerland, it is labelled accordingly:

> **lambouri** [lãburi] NM *Can (en acadien)* navel

In all these cases, work done by a team of consultants from the countries concerned, combined with material drawn from monolingual sources, has formed the basis for a final selection of words and expressions associated with each country. Regional varieties of both languages are also covered, with terms from, for example, Southern France or Northern England featuring among the entries and expressions treated.

As far as target language is concerned, in the French-English volume of the dictionary, British and American variant translations are shown systematically, marked as *Br* and *Am* respectively:

> **sapeur-pompier** [sapœrpɔ̃pje] (*pl* **sapeurs-
> pompiers**) NM *Br* fireman, *Am* firefighter; **les
> sapeurs-pompiers** *Br* the fire brigade, *Am* the
> fire department

In the English-French volume, Belgian, Canadian and Swiss variant translations are also shown where appropriate:

> **mobile ...**
> **... *mobile phone*** (téléphone *m*) portable *m*, *Belg*
> GSM *m*, *Suisse* Natel® *m inv*, *Can* cellulaire *m*;

> **logjam** ['lɒgdʒæm] N **1** *(in river)* bouchon *m* de
> bois flottés, *Can* digue *f* **2** *Fig (deadlock)* im-
> passe *f*

Word-building boxes

A feature new to this edition of the Harrap *Unabridged* and unique to Harrap bilingual dictionaries is the inclusion of boxed notes integrated into the main text covering common prefixes and suffixes, designed to provide the user with an insight into word building and the generation of new words. More than 100 prefixes and suffixes have been selected for this feature and the notes cover the most common senses of the prefix or suffix and how it can be used to create new words.

> **ARCH-, ARCHI-** [arʃ, arʃi] PRÉF
> ● The prefixes **arch-** and **archi-**, like *arch-* in Eng-
> lish, have a non-colloquial use that denotes the
> HIGHEST RANK in a given hierarchy. Thus an
> **archevêque** (archbishop) has several *évêques* un-
> der his command, whereas an **archiduc**
> (archduke) was in fact a prince in the Austrian
> imperial dynasty.
> ● The colloquial use of **archi-** is a common and
> productive one, whereby virtually any adjective
> can be prefixed to indicate the HIGHEST DEGREE
> of a quality or a fault. This idea is often conveyed
> in the English translation by the use of an adverb
> like *very, totally, completely* etc:
> **archiconnu** very well known; **archidrôle** hilar-
> ious; **archifaux** totally wrong; **archinul** com-
> pletely useless

Cultural notes

The Harrap *Unabridged* contains over five hundred notes on cultural topics, where extra information that could not be conveyed in a conventional translation or gloss format is highlighted in a boxed entry integrated into the main text. Many of these notes concern "culture-specific" items, that is to say topics whose relevance or implications may not be immediately obvious to non-native speakers; other more encyclopedic-style notes provide the user with information on terms relating to the politics or history of the country. Examples in the English-French volume are the notes at **devolution, countryside debate** and **gun control**. In the French-English volume **bizutage, charentaises** and **cohabitation** are similarly explained for the non-native user. In line with the dictionary policy of comprehensive international coverage, the boxes include information on items of Canadian, Irish and Scottish relevance as well as French Canadian, Belgian and Swiss items.

> *Culture*
> **DEVOLUTION**
> Le projet de décentralisation pour l'Écosse et le
> pays de Galles ("devolution"), soumis à référen-
> dum dans les années 70, fut abandonné par le
> parti conservateur, à la tête de la Grande-Bre-
> tagne de 1979 à 1997. Cependant, à la suite de la
> victoire des travaillistes en 1997, Tony Blair ho-
> nora sa promesse électorale et organisa un nou-
> veau référendum dans les deux régions. Les
> Écossais se déclarèrent en faveur de la décen-
> tralisation à une écrasante majorité. Le "oui"
> l'emporta également au pays de Galles mais de
> façon moins convaincante. Moins de deux ans
> plus tard, le 6 mai 1999, l'Écosse retrouvait un
> parlement après 300 ans d'interruption et les
> Gallois disposaient d'une assemblée pour la
> première fois en 500 ans (voir aussi encadrés
> sous **Scottish Parliament** et **Welsh Assembly**).

Culture

LA COHABITATION
Originally, this term refers to the period (1986–1988) during which the socialist President (François Mitterrand) had a right-wing Prime Minister (Jacques Chirac), following the victory of the RPR in the legislative elections and Mitterrand's decision not to resign as President. It has since been used to refer to the similar situation which arose following the 1993 elections (with Édouard Balladur as Prime Minister) and also after the 1997 elections (with the left-wing government of Lionel Jospin co-ruling with the President Jacques Chirac).

Allusions

A major innovative feature of this dictionary is the inclusion of notes on allusions, explaining to non-native speakers how certain phrases are used allusively in the other language. The allusions are often literary but many also derive from areas such as advertisements and popular culture. These notes are designed to enable the user to decode areas of language which might otherwise remain opaque. In each case, the origin of the phrase is explained in addition to its contemporary usage. Examples in the English-French volume are **come up and see me some time**, **dark Satanic mills** and **magical mystery tour**, and in the French-English volume **le mot de Cambronne**, **le degré zéro** and **faire avancer le schmilblick**.

More than 250 allusions have been selected for the dictionary. Our selection has been guided by the degree to which the phrase is used in the language and its origin is recognized by native speakers.

Works of art

The dictionary contains around a thousand titles of works of art with their equivalents in the target language. Famous paintings as well as films, works of literature and music are covered. These are to be found at the end of the entry for the first important word in the title (for example Dickens' *Hard Times* is at the end of the entry **hard**, and Proust's *À l'ombre des jeunes filles en fleur* at **ombre**) and are preceded by an icon designating the genre to which the work of art belongs. While many of these items have perfectly straightforward translations, it will be found that others are translated in quite unexpected ways.

'Le Blé en herbe' *Colette* 'The Ripening Seed'

'À bout de souffle' *Godard* 'Breathless'

'The End of the Affair' *Greene, Jordan* 'La Fin d'une liaison'

The titles included are a selection of those judged to be either culturally significant or which generate interesting translations.

Introduction (français)

Au moment de se mettre à la tâche, les lexicographes qui travaillèrent à la rédaction d'un nouveau grand dictionnaire anglais-français français-anglais eurent une pensée émue pour leurs illustres prédécesseurs. En effet, le *Harrap's Standard* — dirigé par le professeur Jean Mansion, conçu par George Harrap peu après la création de sa maison d'édition et publié en deux parties en 1935 et 1939 — était un ouvrage monumental qui jouit pendant de nombreuses années d'une réputation sans égal auprès des étudiants, des universitaires et des traducteurs professionnels. La première édition du *Harrap's Unabridged*, dont la publication en 2001 coïncida avec le centenaire de la maison Harrap's, conserva les caractéristiques qui firent le succès du *Standard*, tout en tirant le meilleur parti des innovations technologiques qui révolutionnent le domaine de la lexicographie bilingue depuis quelques années.

La première édition du *Harrap's Unabridged* fut très bien accueillie, elle fit l'object d'excellentes critiques dans le monde entier et devint rapidement un ouvrage essentiel pour tous les anglicistes avertis. Six ans plus tard, il était temps de proposer au lecteur une deuxième édition remise à jour, et augmentée de plusieurs milliers d'articles ainsi que de nouveaux types de notes et d'aides à la traduction. Avec la présente édition, les rédacteurs entendent consolider les succès obtenus jusqu'ici en proposant un panorama toujours plus complet et toujours plus riche des langues anglaise et française.

L'élaboration du dictionnaire

Grâce à l'outil informatique et à l'existence de textes sur bases de données interrogeables, la rédaction de ce dictionnaire n'a nécessité qu'une fraction du temps qui fut consacré à l'élaboration du *Standard*. Nul doute que toutes les possibilités de recherche qu'offre l'Internet au lexicographe d'aujourd'hui auraient ravi le professeur Mansion, et que celui-ci aurait su faire bon usage du courrier électronique pour communiquer avec ses nombreux collaborateurs.

L'Internet a donné naissance à toute une nouvelle terminologie, très bien représentée dans le présent ouvrage, et a contribué à rendre accessible au plus grand nombre les différentes variétés de français et d'anglais. A titre d'exemple, lorsque l'on recherche un terme anglais sur l'Internet on peut être amené à consulter un site américain, canadien ou australien aussi bien que britannique. De même, lors d'une recherche de termes français, l'on peut consulter des sites canadiens, belges ou suisse au même titre que des sites franco-français. C'est pourquoi nous avons décidé de rendre compte de la richesse des deux langues au-delà de leur pays d'origine et l'*Unabridged* propose ainsi un panorama linguistique des mondes francophone et anglophone d'une richesse inégalée.

Des spécialistes ont assuré le traitement des diverses variétés de français et d'anglais qui figurent dans ce dictionnaire. Par ailleurs, nos consultants ont joué un rôle déterminant lors de l'élaboration de bases de données spécialisées dans des domaines tels que l'informatique, la finance et l'argot, bases de données largement exploitées lors de la conception de l'*Unabridged*. Enfin, un comité de lecture composé d'universitaires francophones et anglophones nous a fait part de ses remarques et suggestions tout au long de la rédaction de ce livre.

Pour finir, il convient de rendre hommage aux lexicographes de la société Harrap qui n'ont pas ménagé leurs efforts pour que soit mené à bien ce projet entamé il y a quatre ans, sans oublier l'équipe prépresse qui a assuré la composition de l'ouvrage et le traitement de plus de 10 000 pages d'épreuves.

Un dictionnaire complet?

Les rédacteurs se sont efforcés d'inclure autant de termes et d'expressions que possible dans les deux volumes de l'*Unabridged*. Cependant cet ouvrage ne peut prétendre à l'exhaustivité tant il est vrai que même un dictionnaire deux fois plus volumineux ne pourrait rendre compte des deux langues dans leur intégralité. Ce qui est indéniable, c'est que l'*Unabridged* présente un panorama complet et très large des deux langues telles qu'on les parle et qu'on les écrit en ce début de XXIème siècle.

La structure des entrées

Les entrées du dictionnaire apparaissent en bleu et sont classées par ordre alphabétique. Il faut noter que les homographes comportant une majuscule à l'initiale sont placés avant ceux dont la première lettre est une minuscule. Ainsi **Pépin (le Bref)** apparaît avant **pépin**.

■ Le classement en fonction des catégories grammaticales

Les différentes catégories grammaticales sont indiquées en lettres capitales bleues et en abrégé; par exemple: NM, NF, VI, PRÉP. La liste des abréviations des indicateurs de catégories grammaticales utilisées figure en début et en fin de dictionnaire. Lorsqu'un mot comporte plusieurs catégories grammaticales, ces dernières apparaissent à la ligne.

> **hand-knit** (*pt & pp* **handknitted,** *cont* **handknitting**) N pull *m/etc* tricoté à la main
> VT tricoter à la main

■ **Les divisions sémantiques**

Les différents sens du mot sont précédés d'un chiffre en gras:

> **snood** [snu:d] N **1** *(for hair)* résille *f* **2** *(hood)* cagoule *f* **3** *Fishing* empile *f* **4** *Scot Hist (headband)* = bandeau porté autrefois dans les cheveux par les jeunes femmes célibataires

Les nuances et les distinctions sémantiques qui nécessitent des traductions différentes au sein d'une même catégorie sont signalées par des indicateurs de sens qui apparaissent entre parenthèses. Ces indicateurs peuvent être des synonymes ou des collocations. Pour les verbes transitifs ces collocations sont des compléments d'objet typiques, pour les adjectifs il s'agit des noms qui leur sont associés le plus fréquemment. Dans certains cas figurent un indicateur synonymique ainsi que des collocations, ces dernières étant précédées d'une flèche.

> **debase** [dɪ'beɪs] VT **1** *(degrade → person, sport)* avilir, abaisser; *(→ reputation)* ternir; *(→ tradition, profession, politics)* dévaloriser **2** *(make less valuable → object)* dégrader, altérer; *(→ metal, currency, coinage)* déprécier

Lorsqu'un mot est particulièrement complexe, ses sens principaux sont divisés en grandes sous-catégories dont chacune est elle-même subdivisée. Une lettre majuscule en gras signale chaque grande sous-catégorie et est suivi d'explications en capitales d'imprimerie:

> **MIEUX** [mjø]
>
> | ADV | better **A, B, C** ■ best **B** |
> | ADJ | better **1–3** |
> | NM | improvement **1** ■ best **2** |
>
> ADV **A.** *COMPARATIF DE "BIEN"* **1** *(d'une manière plus satisfaisante)* better; **tout va m.** things are better (now):...

■ **Les mots composés anglais**

Dans ce dictionnaire, les noms composés anglais de deux éléments ou plus apparaissent dans l'article consacré au premier élément du mot composé. Ils sont présentés en italique à la fin de l'article et sont classés par ordre alphabétique. Pour les entrées concernées, la section des mots composés est signalée par le symbole ►►.

> **editorial** [ˌedɪ'tɔːrɪəl] ADJ *(decision, comment)* de la rédaction; *(job, problems, skills)* de rédaction, rédactionnel
> N **1** *(article)* éditorial *m* **2** *(department)* service *m* de la rédaction, rédaction *f*
> ►► *editorial changes* corrections *fpl*; *editorial column* colonne *f* rédactionnelle; *editorial conference* conférence *f* éditoriale; *editorial content* contenu *m* rédactionnel; *editorial department (in press)* service *m* de la rédaction, rédaction *f*, direction *f* de la rédaction;...

Puisque que les mots composés apparaissent sous le premier élément, il faut, à titre d'exemple, chercher les mots **sedge warbler**, **melodious warbler** et **garden warbler** respectivement aux articles **sedge**, **melodious** et **garden**, et non à l'article **warbler**.

Cependant, les mots composés avec trait d'union sont présentés en tant qu'entrées à part entière, selon l'ordre alphabétique.

Les informations d'ordre grammatical

■ Le pluriel

Dans le volume français-anglais, le pluriel irrégulier des noms est indiqué juste après l'intitulé de l'entrée.

> **linteau, -x** [lɛ̃to] NM lintel

> **trullo** [trulo] (*pl* **trullos** *ou* **trulli**) NM *Archit* trullo

Le pluriel des noms composés avec trait d'union est donné systématiquement, sauf pour les noms invariables ; dans ce cas la mention **inv** figure juste après l'abréviation qui indique la catégorie grammaticale.

> **protège-tympan** [prɔtɛʒtɛ̃pɑ̃] NM INV earplug

De même, dans le volume anglais-français, les pluriels irréguliers apparaissent entre parenthèses, à la suite de l'entrée :

> **salmon** ['sæmən] (*pl* **inv** *or* **salmons**) N *Ich* saumon
> *m*; **young s.** tacon *m*
> ▸▸ ***salmon farm*** élevage *m* de saumons; ***salmon***
> ***fillet*** filet *m* de saumon; ***salmon ladder, salmon***
> ***leap*** échelle *f* à saumon(s); ***salmon pink*** (rose
> *m*) saumon *m*; ***salmon steak*** darne *f* de saumon;
> *Ich* ***salmon trout*** truite *f* saumonée

> **emissary** ['emɪsərɪ] (*pl* **emissaries**) N émissaire *m*

> **madwoman** ['mæd,wʊmən] (*pl* **madwomen**
> [-,wɪmɪn]) N folle *f*, aliénée *f*

■ La conjugaison des verbes anglais

La forme irrégulière de chaque verbe anglais est donnée juste après l'entrée correspondante :

> **edify** ['edɪfaɪ] (*pt & pp* **edified**) VT *Formal* édifier

> **seek** [siːk] (*pt & pp* **sought** [sɔːt]) VT **1** (*search for* →
> *job, person, solution*) chercher, rechercher; **he**
> **constantly sought her approval** il cherchait
> constamment à obtenir son approbation; ...

■ La conjugaison des verbes français

Dans le volume français-anglais un numéro entre crochets apparaît à la suite de chaque verbe. Pour consulter la conjugaison complète d'un verbe, il faut se reporter au numéro correspondant du tableau des conjugaisons du volume 2 (pages xxix à xl).

La prononciation

La prononciation de toutes les entrées est donnée en alphabet phonétique international (API). La liste des symboles de l'API utilisés dans ce dictionnaire figure en page xxvii. Contrairement à la plupart des autres dictionnaires bilingues, notre ouvrage indique la phonétique de toutes les abréviations, sauf lorsqu'il s'agit d'abréviations utilisées uniquement à l'écrit. Ainsi, l'utilisateur sait s'il a à faire à un acronyme ou à une abréviation dont les lettres se prononcent séparément.

Les niveaux de langue

Le registre de toutes les expressions et tous les mots donnés en langue source est clairement indiqué dans le dictionnaire. Des indicateurs de registre sont donnés pour préciser le niveau de langue, qu'il soit soutenu (*Formal/Sout*), familier (*Fam*), très familier (*very Fam/très Fam*), ou vulgaire (*Vulg*). Les nuances d'emploi sont également indiquées lorsqu'un terme est employé en tant qu'euphémisme ou de façon péjorative ou ironique. La liste de toutes les abréviations utilisées comme indicateurs figure à l'intérieur de la couverture. D'une manière générale les traductions reflètent le niveau de langue des mots et expressions de la langue source et elles ne sont donc pas accompagnées d'indicateurs de registre, comme dans l'exemple suivant:

> **macchabée** [makabe] **NM** *Fam (cadavre)* stiff

Lorsqu'il s'est avéré impossible de trouver une traduction qui corresponde au registre familier d'un terme de la langue source, ou lorsqu'il est souhaitable de faire figurer également en traduction un terme de registre non familier, la traduction est accompagnée d'un symbole en exposant (■) qui indique qu'il ne s'agit pas d'un terme familier, comme dans les exemples suivants:

> **adman** ['ædmæn] (*pl* **admen** [-men]) **N** *Fam* publicitaire■ *m*

> **quat'zyeux** [katzjø] **entre quat'zyeux** **ADV** *Fam* in private■

> **savater** [3] [savate] **VT** *Fam* to kick■, to boot

Dans le volume français-anglais, les termes de verlan sont indiqués comme tels, et la forme originelle du mot est indiquée entre parenthèses:

> **keuf** [kœf] **NM** *très Fam (verlan de* **flic**) cop; **les keufs** the fuzz, the cops

De même, dans le volume anglais-français, les termes de "rhyming slang" sont clairement indiqués et sont accompagnés de leur forme complète ainsi que du terme avec lequel ils riment. Il faut noter que lorsqu'un terme n'est pas employé dans l'ensemble de la Grande-Bretagne mais uniquement dans le sud de l'Angleterre et particulièrement dans la région de Londres, il est accompagné de l'abréviation *SEng*, comme dans l'exemple suivant:

> **dustbin** ['dʌstbɪn] **N 1** *Br (for rubbish)* poubelle *f* **2** *SEng Fam* **dustbins** (*rhyming slang* **dustbin lids** = **kids**) gosses *mpl*, mômes *mpl*
> ▶▶ **dustbin lid** couvercle *m* de poubelle; ***dustbin liner*** sac-poubelle *m*; *Br* **dustbin man** éboueur *m*

De nombreux termes de joual figurent dans ce dictionnaire. Ils sont tous accompagnés de la mention *Can Joual*, sans indication supplémentaire de niveau de langue, car le joual est par définition une langue de registre familier.

Un terme peut comporter plusieurs indicateurs de registre. À titre d'exemple, un mot archaïque peut également être utilisé pour ses accents littéraires, et l'on peut choisir d'employer un terme vieilli de façon à produire un effet humoristique. La présentation est alors la suivante:

> **abysm** [ə'bɪzəm] N *Arch or Literary* abîme *m*

> **enamouré, -e** [ãnamure], **énamouré, -e** [enamure] ADJ *Vieilli ou Hum (regard, sourire)* amorous; **être e. de qn** to be enamoured of sb

> **mater** ['meɪtə(r)] N *Br Old-fashioned or Hum* **(the) m.** ma mère, maman *f*

Les termes qui sont à la fois familiers et vieillis, ou bien familiers et euphémistiques sont présentés comme suit, avec les indicateurs les uns à la suite des autres:

> **Mae West** [ˌmeɪ'west] N *Am Fam Old-fashioned* gilet *m* de sauvetage (gonflable)■

> **untruth** [ˌʌn'truːθ] N *Euph Formal (lie)* mensonge *m*, invention *f*; **to tell an u.** mentir, dire un mensonge

Lorsqu'un terme appartient à une variété d'argot particulier (comme l'argot de la drogue ou du milieu), les indicateurs de niveau de langue *Fam* ou *très Fam* sont suivis d'une mention où figure le type d'argot dont il s'agit, comme dans les exemples suivants:

> **coked up** [kəʊkt-] ADJ *Fam Drugs slang* défoncé à la coke

> **Poulaga** [pulaga] NF *Fam Arg crime* **la maison P.** the cops, *Br* the pigs, the fuzz

Dans le cas où un mot de la langue source comporte deux traductions, l'une de registre technique et l'autre qui s'utilise dans la langue de tous les jours, la traduction technique est placée en seconde position et précédée de l'abréviation *Spéc* dans le volume français-anglais et *Spec* dans le volume anglais-français. Une traduction technique est fournie en plus de la traduction habituelle lorsque le mot traduit s'utilise dans des contextes techniques et non techniques.

> **drug ...**
> ... ***drug dependency*** dépendance *f* à l'égard des drogues, toxicomanie *f*, *Spec* pharmacodépendance *f*;

> **mastiquer¹** [3] [mastike] VT *(pain, viande)* to chew, *Spéc* to masticate

Certains mots français sont accompagnés de la mention *Offic*. Cette abréviation indique que l'emploi du mot en question est recommandé à la place de l'anglicisme correspondant, pourtant souvent d'un usage plus courant:

> **caravanette** [kærəvə'net] N camping-car *m*, *Offic* autocaravane *f*

Le vocabulaire de spécialité

Le Harrap's *Unabridged* comporte un très grand nombre de termes techniques liés à toutes sortes de domaines tels que l'informatique, la finance, le droit, les sciences et la médecine. Un nombre non négligeable de termes proviennent du Harrap's *Standard*, qui est l'une des sources utilisées lors de la rédaction de l'*Unabridged*. De très nombreux termes nouveaux ont été ajoutés notamment dans des domaines dont la terminologie évolue rapidement, tels que l'Internet, la finance et le génie génétique.

La liste complète des abréviations des domaines de spécialité utilisés dans le dictionnaire figure à l'intérieur de la couverture. Les indicateurs de domaines de spécialité servent à signaler les termes techniques ou à distinguer les différentes acceptions d'un terme. Lorsqu'un mot s'utilise dans différents domaines et que sa traduction est la même dans tous les cas, les indicateurs sont présentés les uns à la suite des autres et précèdent la traduction, comme dans les exemples suivants:

> **palette** ['pælət] N *Art & Comput* palette *f*
> ▶▶ *palette knife Art* couteau *m* (à palette); *Culin*
> spatule *f*, *Art* **palette knife painting** peinture *f* au
> couteau

> **hybride** [ibrid] ADJ 1 *Bot, Zool & Ling* hybrid 2
> *(mêlé)* hybrid, mixed; **une solution un peu h.** a
> rather hybrid solution; **une architecture h.** a
> patchwork of architectural styles; **un album h.**
> a crossover album
>   NM hybrid

La consultation des articles longs

Les longs articles de dictionnaire se présentent souvent sous forme de blocs de texte particulièrement denses et rébarbatifs. Une des innovations de cet ouvrage consiste à faire figurer des "menus" en tête des articles longs pour faciliter la recherche de l'utilisateur. L'utilité de ces menus est double: 1/ ils présentent en résumé les traductions d'un terme suivant ses différentes acceptions 2/ ils permettent au lecteur de repérer facilement le sens qu'il recherche en faisant appel à ses connaissances. Les utilisateurs de dictionnaires chevronnés consultent les articles longs davantage pour trouver des expressions et des exemples qui illustrent les différents usages d'un terme, que pour apprendre que le mot "pour" se traduit par "for". Ainsi un lecteur qui consulte l'article **care**, par exemple, pourra trouver immédiatement le sens qui correspond au français "souci" et toutes les expressions qui s'y rapportent grâce au menu.

> **CARE** [keə(r)]
>
> VI s'intéresser à **1** ▪ aimer **2** ▪ vouloir **3**
> N souci **1** ▪ soin **2, 3** ▪ charge **4**

Le français et l'anglais d'ailleurs

Ce dictionnaire se distingue de ses concurrents par son traitement en profondeur des différentes variétés d'anglais et de français dans le monde. Dans le volume anglais-français, l'anglais de Grande-Bretagne et des États-Unis est traité de manière exhaustive, et les mots et expressions propres à l'anglais d'Australie, d'Irlande et d'Écosse sont également très bien représentés. À titre d'exemple, des termes tels que **gurrier**, **muckle** et **beyond the Black Stump**, qui proviennent respectivement de l'anglais d'Irlande, d'Écosse et d'Australie et que l'on chercherait en vain dans d'autres dictionnaires bilingues, se trouvent dans le Harrap's *Unabridged*.

De même, dans le volume français-anglais, le français du Canada est très bien représenté, tout comme le français de Suisse et de Belgique. Un des buts de ce dictionnaire bilingue est de donner droit de cité au français que l'on parle hors de France. Sans prétendre à l'exhaustivité, les rédacteurs du présent ouvrage ont inclus un nombre non négligeable de termes et expressions originaires des pays cités plus haut. Des termes de joual ont été inclus ainsi que des termes d'acadien (le parler franco-canadien utilisé dans les Provinces Maritimes) qui sont précédés de la mention (*en acadien*). De même, le fait que tel ou tel terme suisse est propre à un canton particulier est clairement indiqué.

> **lambouri** [lãburi] NM *Can (en acadien)* navel

La liste des mots et expressions de chacun des pays mentionnés a été établie par des consultants originaires des pays en question et s'est enrichie de termes issus de sources monolingues. Les variantes régionales des deux langues telles qu'on les parle en France et en Grande-Bretagne sont également représentées avec entre autres des termes et expressions originaires du sud de la France et du nord de l'Angleterre.

Dans le volume français-anglais, les variantes britanniques et américaines des traductions sont systématiquement données et clairement indiquées par les abréviations *Br* et *Am*:

> **sapeur-pompier** [sapœrpɔ̃pje] (*pl* **sapeurs-pompiers**) NM *Br* fireman, *Am* firefighter; **les sapeurs-pompiers** *Br* the fire brigade, *Am* the fire department

Dans le volume anglais-français, des traductions en français de Belgique, du Canada et de Suisse sont fournies lorsque nécessaire:

> **mobile ...**
> ... ***mobile phone*** (téléphone *m*) portable *m*, *Belg* GSM *m*, *Suisse* Natel® *m inv*, *Can* cellulaire *m*;

> **logjam** ['lɒgdʒæm] N **1** (*in river*) bouchon *m* de bois flottés, *Can* digue *f* **2** *Fig* (*deadlock*) impasse *f*

Les préfixes et les suffixes

Une des nouveautés de cette nouvelle édition du Harrap's *Unabridged* est la présence dans le texte de plus de cent encadrés sur les préfixes et les suffixes les plus fréquents et les plus générateurs en anglais et en français. Ceux-ci servent à expliquer les procédés de formation de nouveaux termes et comportent de très nombreux exemples. Les dictionnaires bilingues Harrap sont d'ailleurs les seuls à proposer ce type d'aide à l'utilisateur.

> **-ISH** [ɪʃ] SUFF
>
> ● Le suffixe **-ish** sert à produire des adjectifs à partir de noms et d'adjectifs. Certains d'entre eux, notamment les adjectifs de nationalité, sont fixes et n'ont aucune connotation particulière:
> **English** anglais; **Swedish** suédois; **Turkish** turc; **foolish** idiot; **childish** puéril; **feverish** fiévreux
> ● Mais dans de nombreux cas, ce suffixe exprime un caractère d'APPROXIMATION:
> **blueish** bleuâtre; **reddish** rougeâtre; **whitish** blanchâtre, etc.
> ● On peut ajouter **-ish** à de très nombreux adjectifs; il se traduit alors le plus souvent en employant les adverbes *plutôt* ou *assez*:
> **a biggish house** une maison plutôt grande; **a prettyish girl** une fille assez jolie; **a longish film** un film plutôt long; **shall we meet round eightish?** on se retrouve vers huit heures? C'est un suffixe très productif: par exemple, à partir du pronom **more**, on a créé l'adjectif **moreish**, qui désigne quelque chose qui a un goût de revenez-y, comme dans la phrase **this cake is very moreish**.
> ● Il est même possible d'utiliser **-ish** tout seul pour nuancer un jugement comme dans l'exemple suivant:
> **was the film funny? – ish...** est-ce que le film était amusant? – assez amusant...

Les encadrés culturels

Le Harrap's *Unabridged* contient plus de cinq cents encadrés intégrés au texte qui portent sur des points de culture; des explications y sont données lorsqu'une traduction ou une glose ne suffit pas à fournir les informations nécessaires. Ces encadrés culturels concernent le plus souvent des thèmes propres à une culture ou à un pays particuliers, qui ne sont pas nécessairement connus en dehors du pays en question. D'autres encadrés fournissent des informations de nature encyclopédique sur des termes liés à l'histoire et à la politique des différents pays concernés. À titre d'exemple, dans le volume français-anglais, des notes en anglais éclaireront les lecteurs anglophones sur des sujets tels que le **bizutage**, la **cohabitation** ou le **Pacs**, et dans le volume anglais-français, les utilisateurs francophones pourront lire des notes en français sur la **devolution**, le **countryside debate** et le problème des armes à feu aux États-Unis (**gun control**). Les encadrés culturels comprennent également des informations sur l'Irlande, l'Écosse, le Canada, la Belgique et la Suisse.

> **Culture**
> **DEVOLUTION**
> Le projet de décentralisation pour l'Écosse et le pays de Galles ("devolution"), soumis à référendum dans les années 70, fut abandonné par le parti conservateur, à la tête de la Grande-Bretagne de 1979 à 1997. Cependant, à la suite de la victoire des travaillistes en 1997, Tony Blair honora sa promesse électorale et organisa un nouveau référendum dans les deux régions. Les Écossais se déclarèrent en faveur de la décentralisation à une écrasante majorité. Le "oui" l'emporta également au pays de Galles mais de façon moins convaincante. Moins de deux ans plus tard, le 6 mai 1999, l'Écosse retrouvait un parlement après 300 ans d'interruption et les Gallois disposaient d'une assemblée pour la première fois en 500 ans (voir aussi encadrés sous **Scottish Parliament** et **Welsh Assembly**).

> **Culture**
> **LA COHABITATION**
> Originally, this term refers to the period (1986–1988) during which the socialist President (François Mitterrand) had a right-wing Prime Minister (Jacques Chirac), following the victory of the RPR in the legislative elections and Mitterrand's decision not to resign as President. It has since been used to refer to the similar situation which arose following the 1993 elections (with Édouard Balladur as Prime Minister) and also after the 1997 elections (with the left-wing government of Lionel Jospin co-ruling with the President Jacques Chirac).

Les allusions

L'une des grandes innovations de ce dictionnaire est la présence de notes explicatives qui portent sur de nombreuses expressions anglaises et françaises qui sont en fait des allusions culturelles. Les allusions sont souvent issues de la littérature mais nombreuses sont celles qui proviennent également de la culture populaire. Ces notes explicatives sont destinées à permettre à l'utilisateur de comprendre des expressions a priori impénétrables utilisées dans l'autre langue. Dans chaque cas, la note explicative éclaire le lecteur sur l'origine de l'expression et la façon dont on l'emploie. Parmi les allusions présentes dans le volume anglais-français notons **come up and see me some time**, **dark Satanic mills** et **magical mystery tour**, et dans le volume français-anglais **le mot de Cambronne**, **le degré zéro** et **faire avancer le schmilblick**.

Le dictionnaire compte plus de 250 allusions. Elles ont été retenues car elles sont d'un emploi relativement fréquent et sont reconnues comme allusions par la plupart de ceux qui les utilisent.

Les œuvres littéraires et les œuvres d'art

Ce dictionnaire compte environ mille titres d'œuvres littéraires et d'œuvres d'art avec leur équivalent dans l'autre langue. Les beaux-arts, la musique, le cinéma et la littérature sont représentés. Le titre d'une œuvre se trouve à la fin de l'article de dictionnaire correspondant au premier mot important du titre en question. Ainsi, *Hard Times*, de Dickens, est traité à la fin de l'article **hard**, et *À l'ombre des jeunes filles en fleurs* apparaît à la fin de l'article **ombre**. Les titres sont signalés par des symboles représentant le genre d'œuvre dont il s'agit. Souvent les traductions sont prévisibles, parfois elles le sont beaucoup moins…

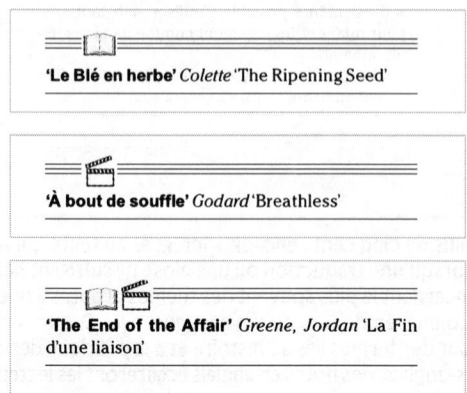

'Le Blé en herbe' *Colette* 'The Ripening Seed'

'À bout de souffle' *Godard* 'Breathless'

'The End of the Affair' *Greene, Jordan* 'La Fin d'une liaison'

Ont été inclus les titres d'œuvres jugées importantes d'un point de vue culturel, ou dont la traduction est particulièrement intéressante.

French Pronunciation

French pronunciation is shown in this dictionary using the symbols of the IPA (International Phonetic Alphabet). In the table below, examples of French words using these sounds are given, followed by English words which have a similar sound. Where there is no equivalent in English, an explanation is given.

IPA symbol	French example	English example
Consonants		
[b]	*bébé*	*b*ut
[d]	*d*onner	*d*oor
[f]	*f*orêt	*f*ire
[g]	*g*are	*g*et
[ʒ]	*j*our	plea*s*ure
[k]	*c*arte	*k*itten
[l]	*l*ire	*l*one*l*y
[m]	*m*a*m*an	*m*at
[n]	*n*i	*n*ow
[ŋ]	parki*ng*	si*ng*ing
[ɲ]	campa*gn*e	ca*ny*on
[p]	*p*atte	*p*at
[r]	*r*are	Like an English /r/ but pronounced at the back of the throat
[s]	*s*oir	*s*it
[ʃ]	*ch*ose	*sh*am
[t]	*t*able	*t*ap
[v]	*v*aleur	*v*alue
[z]	*z*éro	*z*ero
Vowels		
[a]	ch*a*t	c*a*t
[ɑ]	*â*ge	g*a*sp
[e]	*é*t*é*	b*ay*
[ɛ]	p*è*re	b*e*d
[ə]	l*e*	*a*mend
[ø]	d*eu*x	Does not exist in English: [e] pronounced with the lips rounded
[œ]	s*eu*l	c*ur*tain
[i]	v*i*te	b*ee* – not quite as long as the English [i:]
[ɔ]	d*o*nner	c*o*t – slightly more open than the English /o/
[o]	ch*au*d	d*au*ghter – but higher than its English equivalent
[u]	t*ou*t	y*ou* – but shorter than its English equivalent
[y]	v*oi*ture	Does not exist in English: [i] with lips rounded
[ã]	*en*f*an*t	Nasal sound pronounced lower and further back in the mouth than [ɔ̃]
[ɛ̃]	v*in*	Nasal sound: /a/ sound pronounced letting air pass through the nose
[ɔ̃]	b*on*jour	Nasal sound: closed /o/ sound pronounced letting air pass through the nose
[œ̃]	*un*	Nasal sound: like [ɛ̃] but with lips more rounded

IPA symbol	French example	English example
Semi-vowels		
[w]	v*oi*r	*w*eek
[j]	*y*oyo, pai*lle*	*y*ard
[ɥ]	n*ui*t	Does not exist in English: the vowel [y] elided with the following vowel

French Conjugation Tables

	1 avoir	2 être	3 chanter	4 baisser	5 pleurer
Present	j'ai	je suis	je chante	je baisse	je pleure
	tu as	tu es	tu chantes	tu baisses	tu pleures
	il, elle a	il, elle est	il, elle chante	il, elle baisse	il, elle pleure
	nous avons	nous sommes	nous chantons	nous baissons	nous pleurons
	vous avez	vous êtes	vous chantez	vous baissez	vous pleurez
	ils, elles ont	ils, elles sont	ils, elles chantent	ils, elles baissent	ils, elles pleurent
Imperfect	il, elle avait	il, elle était	il, elle chantait	il, elle baissait	il, elle pleurait
Past Historic	il, elle eut	il, elle fut	il, elle chanta	il, elle baissa	il, elle pleura
	ils, elles eurent	ils, elles furent	ils, elles chantèrent	ils, elles baissèrent	ils, elles pleurèrent
Future	j'aurai	je serai	je chanterai	je baisserai	je pleurerai
	il, elle aura	il, elle sera	il, elle chantera	il, elle baissera	il, elle pleurera
Conditional	j'aurais	je serais	je chanterais	je baisserais	je pleurerais
	il, elle aurait	il, elle serait	il, elle chanterait	il, elle baisserait	il, elle pleurerait
Present Subjunctive	que j'aie	que je sois	que je chante	que je baisse	que je pleure
	qu'il, elle ait	qu'il, elle soit	qu'il, elle chante	qu'il, elle baisse	qu'il, elle pleure
	que nous ayons	que nous soyons	que nous chantions	que nous baissions	que nous pleurions
	qu'ils, elles aient	qu'ils, elles soient	qu'ils, elles chantent	qu'ils, elles baissent	qu'ils, elles pleurent
Imperfect Subjunctive	qu'il, elle eût	qu'il, elle fût	qu'il, elle chantât	qu'il, elle baissât	qu'il, elle pleurât
	qu'ils, elles eussent	qu'ils, elles fussent	qu'ils, elles chantassent	qu'ils, elles baissassent	qu'ils, elles pleurassent
Imperative	aie	sois	chante	baisse	pleure
	ayons	soyons	chantons	baissons	pleurons
	ayez	soyez	chantez	baissez	pleurez
Present Participle	ayant	étant	chantant	baissant	pleurant
Past Participle	eu, eue	été	chanté, -e	baissé, -e	pleuré, -e

	6 jouer	7 saluer	8 arguer	9 copier	10 prier
Present	je joue	je salue	j'argue, arguë	je copie	je prie
	tu joues	tu salues	tu argues, arguës	tu copies	tu pries
	il, elle joue	il, elle salue	il, elle argue, arguë	il, elle copie	il, elle prie
	nous jouons	nous saluons	nous arguons	nous copions	nous prions
	vous jouez	vous saluez	vous arguez	vous copiez	vous priez
	ils, elles jouent	ils, elles saluent	ils, elles arguent, arguënt	ils, elles copient	ils, elles prient
Imperfect	il, elle jouait	il, elle saluait	il, elle arguait	il, elle copiait	il, elle priait
Past Historic	il, elle joua	il, elle salua	il, elle argua	il, elle copia	il, elle pria
	ils, elles jouèrent	ils, elles saluèrent	ils, elles arguèrent	ils, elles copièrent	ils, elles prièrent
Future	je jouerai	je saluerai	j'arguerai, arguërai	je copierai	je prierai
	il, elle jouera	il, elle saluera	il, elle arguera, arguëra	il, elle copiera	il, elle priera
Conditional	je jouerais	je saluerais	j'arguerais, arguërais	je copierais	je prierais
	il, elle jouerait	il, elle saluerait	il, elle arguerait, arguërait	il, elle copierait	il, elle prierait
Present Subjunctive	que je joue	que je salue	que j'argue, arguë	que je copie	que je prie
	qu'il, elle joue	qu'il, elle salue	qu'il, elle argue, arguë	qu'il, elle copie	qu'il, elle prie
	que nous jouions	que nous saluions	que nous arguions	que nous copiions	que nous priions
	qu'ils, elles jouent	qu'ils, elles saluent	qu'ils, elles arguent, arguënt	qu'ils, elles copient	qu'ils, elles prient
Imperfect Subjunctive	qu'il, elle jouât	qu'il, elle saluât	qu'il, elle arguât	qu'il, elle copiât	qu'il, elle priât
	qu'ils, elles jouassent	qu'ils, elles saluassent	qu'ils, elles arguassent	qu'ils, elles copiassent	qu'ils, elles priassent
Imperative	joue	salue	argue, arguë	copie	prie
	jouons	saluons	arguons	copions	prions
	jouez	saluez	arguez	copiez	priez
Present Participle	jouant	saluant	arguant	copiant	priant
Past Participle	joué, -e	salué, -e	argué, -e	copié, -e	prié, -e

FRENCH CONJUGATION TABLES

	11 payer[1]		12 grasseyer	13 ployer	14 essuyer
Present	je paie	je paye	je grasseye	je ploie	j'essuie
	tu paies	tu payes	tu grasseyes	tu ploies	tu essuies
	il, elle paie	il, elle paye	il, elle grasseye	il, elle ploie	il, elle essuie
	nous payons	nous payons	nous grasseyons	nous ployons	nous essuyons
	vous payez	vous payez	vous grasseyez	vous ployez	vous essuyez
	ils, elles paient	ils, elles payent	ils, elles grasseyent	ils, elles ploient	ils, elles essuient
Imperfect	il, elle payait	il, elle payait	il, elle grasseyait	il, elle ployait	il, elle essuyait
Past Historic	il, elle paya	il, elle paya	il, elle grasseya	il, elle ploya	il, elle essuya
	ils, elles payèrent	ils, elles payèrent	ils, elles grasseyèrent	ils, elles ployèrent	ils, elles essuyèrent
Future	je paierai	je payerai	je grasseyerai	je ploierai	j'essuierai
	il, elle paiera	il, elle payera	il, elle grasseyera	il, elle ploiera	il, elle essuiera
Conditional	je paierais	je payerais	je grasseyerais	je ploierais	j'essuierais
	il, elle paierait	il, elle payerait	il, elle grasseyerait	il, elle ploierait	il, elle essuierait
Present Subjunctive	que je paie	que je paye	que je grasseye	que je ploie	que j'essuie
	qu'il, elle paie	qu'il, elle paye	qu'il, elle grasseye	qu'il, elle ploie	qu'il, elle essuie
	que nous payions	que nous payions	que nous grasseyions	que nous ployions	que nous essuyions
	qu'ils, elles paient	qu'ils, elles payent	qu'ils, elles grasseyent	qu'ils, elles ploient	qu'ils, elles essuient
Imperfect Subjunctive	qu'il, elle payât	qu'il, elle payât	qu'il, elle grasseyât	qu'il, elle ployât	qu'il, elle essuyât
	qu'ils, elles payassent	qu'ils, elles payassent	qu'ils, elles grasseyassent	qu'ils, elles ployassent	qu'ils, elles essuyassent
Imperative	paie	paye	grasseye	ploie	essuie
	payons	payons	grasseyons	ployons	essuyons
	payez	payez	grasseyez	ployez	essuyez
Present Participle	payant	payant	grasseyant	ployant	essuyant
Past Participle	payé, -e	payé, -e	grasseyé, -e	ployé, -e	essuyé, -e

[1] According to some grammarians, the verb **rayer** should keep the **-y-** in all its conjugated forms.

	15 créer	16 avancer	17 manger	18 céder[1]	19 semer
Present	je crée	j'avance	je mange	je cède	je sème
	tu crées	tu avances	tu manges	tu cèdes	tu sèmes
	il, elle crée	il, elle avance	il, elle mange	il, elle cède	il, elle sème
	nous créons	nous avançons	nous mangeons	nous cédons	nous semons
	vous créez	vous avancez	vous mangez	vous cédez	vous semez
	ils, elles créent	ils, elles avancent	ils, elles mangent	ils, elles cèdent	ils, elles sèment
Imperfect	il, elle créait	il, elle avançait	il, elle mangeait	il, elle cédait	il, elle semait
Past Historic	il, elle créa	il, elle avança	il, elle mangea	il, elle céda	il, elle sema
	ils, elles créèrent	ils, elles avancèrent	ils, elles mangèrent	ils, elles cédèrent	ils, elles semèrent
Future	je créerai	j'avancerai	je mangerai	je céderai	je sèmerai
	il, elle créera	il, elle avancera	il, elle mangera	il, elle cédera	il, elle sèmera
Conditional	je créerais	j'avancerais	je mangerais	je céderais	je sèmerais
	il, elle créerait	il, elle avancerait	il, elle mangerait	il, elle céderait	il, elle sèmerait
Present Subjunctive	que je crée	que j'avance	que je mange	que je cède	que je sème
	qu'il, elle crée	qu'il, elle avance	qu'il, elle mange	qu'il, elle cède	qu'il, elle sème
	que nous créions	que nous avancions	que nous mangions	que nous cédions	que nous semions
	qu'ils, elles créent	qu'ils, elles avancent	qu'ils, elles mangent	qu'ils, elles cèdent	qu'ils, elles sèment
Imperfect Subjunctive	qu'il, elle créât	qu'il, elle avançât	qu'il, elle mangeât	qu'il, elle cédât	qu'il, elle semât
	qu'ils, elles créassent	qu'ils, elles avançassent	qu'ils, elles mangeassent	qu'ils, elles cédassent	qu'ils, elles semassent
Imperative	crée	avance	mange	cède	sème
	créons	avançons	mangeons	cédons	semons
	créez	avancez	mangez	cédez	semez
Present Participle	créant	avançant	mangeant	cédant	semant
Past Participle	créé, -e	avancé, -e	mangé, -e	cédé, -e	semé, -e

[1] The Académie française recommends **je cèderai** and **je cèderais** in the future and conditional tenses respectively.

	20 rapiécer[1]	21 acquiescer	22 siéger[1,2]	23 déneiger	24 appeler
Present	je rapièce	j'acquiesce	je siège	je déneige	j'appelle
	tu rapièces	tu acquiesces	tu sièges	tu déneiges	tu appelles
	il, elle rapièce	il, elle acquiesce	il, elle siège	il, elle déneige	il, elle appelle
	nous rapiéçons	nous acquiesçons	nous siégeons	nous déneigeons	nous appelons
	vous rapiécez	vous acquiescez	vous siégez	vous déneigez	vous appelez
	ils, elles rapiècent	ils, elles acquiescent	ils, elles siègent	ils, elles déneigent	ils, elles appellent
Imperfect	il, elle rapiéçait	il, elle acquiesçait	il, elle siégeait	il, elle déneigeait	il, elle appelait
Past Historic	il, elle rapiéça	il, elle acquiesça	il, elle siégea	il, elle déneigea	il, elle appela
	ils, elles rapiécèrent	ils, elles acquiescèrent	ils, elles siégèrent	ils, elles déneigèrent	ils, elles appelèrent
Future	je rapiécerai	j'acquiescerai	je siégerai	je déneigerai	j'appellerai
	il, elle rapiécera	il, elle acquiescera	il, elle siégera	il, elle déneigera	il, elle appellera
Conditional	je rapiécerais	j'acquiescerais	je siégerais	je déneigerais	j'appellerais
	il, elle rapiécerait	il, elle acquiescerait	il, elle siégerait	il, elle déneigerait	il, elle appellerait
Present Subjunctive	que je rapièce	que j'acquiesce	que je siège	que je déneige	que j'appelle
	qu'il, elle rapièce	qu'il, elle acquiesce	qu'il, elle siège	qu'il, elle déneige	qu'il, elle appelle
	que nous rapiécions	que nous acquiescions	que nous siégions	que nous déneigions	que nous appelions
	qu'ils, elles rapiècent	qu'ils, elles acquiescent	qu'ils, elles siègent	qu'ils, elles déneigent	qu'ils, elles appellent
Imperfect Subjunctive	qu'il, elle rapiéçât	qu'il, elle acquiesçât	qu'il, elle siégeât	qu'il, elle déneigeât	qu'il, elle appelât
	qu'ils, elles rapiéçassent	qu'ils, elles acquiesçassent	qu'ils, elles siégeassent	qu'ils, elles déneigeassent	qu'ils, elles appelassent
Imperative	rapièce	acquiesce	siège	déneige	appelle
	rapiéçons	acquiesçons	siégeons	déneigeons	appelons
	rapiécez	acquiescez	siégez	déneigez	appelez
Present Participle	rapiéçant	acquiesçant	siégeant	déneigeant	appelant
Past Participle	rapiécé, -e	acquiescé	siégé	déneigé, -e	appelé, -e

[1] The Académie française recommends **je rapiècerai; je siègerai** and **je rapiècerais; je siègerais** in the future and conditional tenses respectively.

[2] **Assiéger** conjugates like **siéger**, except that its past participle is variable.

	25 peler	26 interpeller	27 jeter	28 acheter	29 dépecer
Present	je pèle	j'interpelle	je jette	j'achète	je dépèce
	tu pèles	tu interpelles	tu jettes	tu achètes	tu dépèces
	il, elle pèle	il, elle interpelle	il, elle jette	il, elle achète	il, elle dépèce
	nous pelons	nous interpellons	nous jetons	nous achetons	nous dépeçons
	vous pelez	vous interpellez	vous jetez	vous achetez	vous dépecez
	ils, elles pèlent	ils, elles interpellent	ils, elles jettent	ils, elles achètent	ils, elles dépècent
Imperfect	il, elle pelait	il, elle interpellait	il, elle jetait	il, elle achetait	il, elle dépeçait
Past Historic	il, elle pela	il, elle interpella	il, elle jeta	il, elle acheta	il, elle dépeça
	ils, elles pelèrent	ils, elles interpellèrent	ils, elles jetèrent	ils, elles achetèrent	ils, elles dépecèrent
Future	je pèlerai	j'interpellerai	je jetterai	j'achèterai	je dépècerai
	il, elle pèlera	il, elle interpellera	il, elle jettera	il, elle achètera	il, elle dépècera
Conditional	je pèlerais	j'interpellerais	je jetterais	j'achèterais	je dépècerais
	il, elle pèlerait	il, elle interpellerait	il, elle jetterait	il, elle achèterait	il, elle dépècerait
Present Subjunctive	que je pèle	que j'interpelle	que je jette	que j'achète	que je dépèce
	qu'il, elle pèle	qu'il, elle interpelle	qu'il, elle jette	qu'il, elle achète	qu'il, elle dépèce
	que nous pelions	que nous interpellions	que nous jetions	que nous achetions	que nous dépecions
	qu'ils, elles pèlent	qu'ils, elles interpellent	qu'ils, elles jettent	qu'ils, elles achètent	qu'ils, elles dépècent
Imperfect Subjunctive	qu'il, elle pelât	qu'il, elle interpellât	qu'il, elle jetât	qu'il, elle achetât	qu'il, elle dépeçât
	qu'ils, elles pelassent	qu'ils, elles interpellassent	qu'ils, elles jetassent	qu'ils, elles achetassent	qu'ils, elles dépeçassent
Imperative	pèle	interpelle	jette	achète	dépèce
	pelons	interpellons	jetons	achetons	dépeçons
	pelez	interpellez	jetez	achetez	dépecez
Present Participle	pelant	interpellant	jetant	achetant	dépeçant
Past Participle	pelé, -e	interpellé, -e	jeté, -e	acheté, -e	dépecé, -e

	30 envoyer	31 aller[1]	32 finir	33 haïr	34 ouvrir
Present	j'envoie	je vais	je finis	je hais	j'ouvre
	tu envoies	tu vas	tu finis	tu hais	tu ouvres
	il, elle envoie	il, elle va	il, elle finit	il, elle hait	il, elle ouvre
	nous envoyons	nous allons	nous finissons	nous haïssons	nous ouvrons
	vous envoyez	vous allez	vous finissez	vous haïssez	vous ouvrez
	ils, elles envoient	ils, elles vont	ils, elles finissent	ils, elles haïssent	ils, elles ouvrent
Imperfect	il, elle envoyait	il, elle allait	il, elle finissait	il, elle haïssait	il, elle ouvrait
Past Historic	il, elle envoya	il, elle alla	il, elle finit	il, elle haït	il, elle ouvrit
	ils, elles envoyèrent	ils, elles allèrent	ils, elles finirent	ils, elles haïrent	ils, elles ouvrirent
Future	j'enverrai	j'irai	je finirai	je haïrai	j'ouvrirai
	il, elle enverra	il, elle ira	il, elle finira	il, elle haïra	il, elle ouvrira
Conditional	j'enverrais	j'irais	je finirais	je haïrais	j'ouvrirais
	il, elle enverrait	il, elle irait	il, elle finirait	il, elle haïrait	il, elle ouvrirait
Present Subjunctive	que j'envoie	que j'aille	que je finisse	que je haïsse	que j'ouvre
	qu'il, elle envoie	qu'il, elle aille	qu'il, elle finisse	qu'il, elle haïsse	qu'il, elle ouvre
	que nous envoyions	que nous allions	que nous finissions	que nous haïssions	que nous ouvrions
	qu'ils, elles envoient	qu'ils, elles aillent	qu'ils, elles finissent	qu'ils, elles haïssent	qu'ils, elles ouvrent
Imperfect Subjunctive	qu'il, elle envoyât	qu'il, elle allât	qu'il, elle finît	qu'il, elle haït	qu'il, elle ouvrît
	qu'ils, elles envoyassent	qu'ils, elles allassent	qu'ils, elles finissent	qu'ils, elles haïssent	qu'ils, elles ouvrissent
Imperative	envoie	va	finis	hais	ouvre
	envoyons	allons	finissons	haïssons	ouvrons
	envoyez	allez	finissez	haïssez	ouvrez
Present Participle	envoyant	allant	finissant	haïssant	ouvrant
Past Participle	envoyé, -e	allé, -e	fini, -e	haï, -e	ouvert, -e

[1] The imperative form of **aller** is **vas** in the construction **vas-y**. The imperative forms of **s'en aller** are **va-t'en, allons-nous-en** and **allez-vous-en**. In compound tenses, the verb **être** may be used instead of **aller**, for example **avoir été, j'ai été** etc. In compound tenses of the reflexive verb **s'en aller**, en is usually placed before the auxiliary verb, eg **je m'en suis allé(e)**, but in everyday language **je me suis en allé(e)** is becoming increasingly common.

	35 fuir	36 dormir[1]	37 mentir[2]	38 servir	39 acquérir
Present	je fuis	je dors	je mens	je sers	j'acquiers
	tu fuis	tu dors	tu mens	tu sers	tu acquiers
	il, elle fuit	il, elle dort	il, elle ment	il, elle sert	il, elle acquiert
	nous fuyons	nous dormons	nous mentons	nous servons	nous acquérons
	vous fuyez	vous dormez	vous mentez	vous servez	vous acquérez
	ils, elles fuient	ils, elles dorment	ils, elles mentent	ils, elles servent	ils, elles acquièrent
Imperfect	il, elle fuyait	il, elle dormait	il, elle mentait	il, elle servait	il, elle acquérait
Past Historic	il, elle fuit	il, elle dormit	il, elle mentit	il, elle servit	il, elle acquit
	ils, elles fuirent	ils, elles dormirent	ils, elles mentirent	ils, elles servirent	ils, elles acquirent
Future	je fuirai	je dormirai	je mentirai	je servirai	j'acquerrai
	il, elle fuira	il, elle dormira	il, elle mentira	il, elle servira	il, elle acquerra
Conditional	je fuirais	je dormirais	je mentirais	je servirais	j'acquerrais
	il, elle fuirait	il, elle dormirait	il, elle mentirait	il, elle servirait	il, elle acquerrait
Present Subjunctive	que je fuie	que je dorme	que je mente	que je serve	que j'acquière
	qu'il, elle fuie	qu'il, elle dorme	qu'il, elle mente	qu'il, elle serve	qu'il, elle acquière
	que nous fuyions	que nous dormions	que nous mentions	que nous servions	que nous acquérions
	qu'ils, elles fuient	qu'ils, elles dorment	qu'ils, elles mentent	qu'ils, elles servent	qu'ils, elles acquièrent
Imperfect Subjunctive	qu'il, elle fuît	qu'il, elle dormît	qu'il, elle mentît	qu'il, elle servît	qu'il, elle acquît
	qu'ils, elles fuissent	qu'ils, elles dormissent	qu'ils, elles mentissent	qu'ils, elles servissent	qu'ils, elles acquissent
Imperative	fuis	dors	mens	sers	acquiers
	fuyons	dormons	mentons	servons	acquérons
	fuyez	dormez	mentez	servez	acquérez
Present Participle	fuyant	dormant	mentant	servant	acquérant
Past Participle	fui, -e	dormi	menti	servi, -e	acquis, -e

[1] **Endormir** conjugates like **dormir**, except that its past participle is variable.

[2] **Démentir** conjugates like **mentir**, except that its past participle is variable.

	40 venir	41 cueillir	42 mourir	43 partir	44 revêtir
Present	je viens	je cueille	je meurs	je pars	je revêts
	tu viens	tu cueilles	tu meurs	tu pars	tu revêts
	il, elle vient	il, elle cueille	il, elle meurt	il, elle part	il, elle revêt
	nous venons	nous cueillons	nous mourons	nous partons	nous revêtons
	vous venez	vous cueillez	vous mourez	vous partez	vous revêtez
	ils, elles viennent	ils, elles cueillent	ils, elles meurent	ils, elles partent	ils, elles revêtent
Imperfect	il, elle venait	il, elle cueillait	il, elle mourait	il, elle partait	il, elle revêtait
Past Historic	il, elle vint	il, elle cueillit	il, elle mourut	il, elle partit	il, elle revêtit
	ils, elles vinrent	ils, elles cueillirent	ils, elles moururent	ils, elles partirent	ils, elles revêtirent
Future	je viendrai	je cueillerai	je mourrai	je partirai	je revêtirai
	il, elle viendra	il, elle cueillera	il, elle mourra	il, elle partira	il, elle revêtira
Conditional	je viendrais	je cueillerais	je mourrais	je partirais	je revêtirais
	il, elle viendrait	il, elle cueillerait	il, elle mourrait	il, elle partirait	il, elle revêtirait
Present Subjunctive	que je vienne	que je cueille	que je meure	que je parte	que je revête
	qu'il, elle vienne	qu'il, elle cueille	qu'il, elle meure	qu'il, elle parte	qu'il, elle revête
	que nous venions	que nous cueillions	que nous mourions	que nous partions	que nous revêtions
	qu'ils, elles viennent	qu'ils, elles cueillent	qu'ils, elles meurent	qu'ils, elles partent	qu'ils, elles revêtent
Imperfect Subjunctive	qu'il, elle vînt	qu'il, elle cueillît	qu'il, elle mourût	qu'il, elle partît	qu'il, elle revêtît
	qu'ils, elles vinssent	qu'ils, elles cueillissent	qu'ils, elles mourussent	qu'ils, elles partissent	qu'ils, elles revêtissent
Imperative	viens	cueille	meurs	pars	revêts
	venons	cueillons	mourons	partons	revêtons
	venez	cueillez	mourez	partez	revêtez
Present Participle	venant	cueillant	mourant	partant	revêtant
Past Participle	venu, -e	cueilli, -e	mort, -e	parti, -e	revêtu, -e

	45 courir	46 faillir[1]	47 défaillir[2]	48 bouillir	49 gésir[3]
Present	je cours	je faillis, faux	je défaille	je bous	je gis
	tu cours	tu faillis, faux	tu défailles	tu bous	tu gis
	il, elle court	il, elle faillit, faut	il, elle défaille	il, elle bout	il, elle gît
	nous courons	nous faillissons, faillons	nous défaillons	nous bouillons	nous gisons
	vous courez	vous faillissez, faillez	vous défaillez	vous bouillez	vous gisez
	ils, elles courent	ils, elles faillissent, faillent	ils, elles défaillent	ils, elles bouillent	ils, elles gisent
Imperfect	il, elle courait	il, elle faillissait, faillait	il, elle défaillait	il, elle bouillait	il, elle gisait
Past Historic	il, elle courut	il, elle faillit	il, elle défaillit	il, elle bouillit	
	ils, elles coururent	ils, elles faillirent	ils, elles défaillirent	ils, elles bouillirent	
Future	je courrai	je faillirai, faudrai	je défaillirai	je bouillirai	
	il, elle courra	il, elle faillira, faudra	il, elle défaillira	il, elle bouillira	
Conditional	je courrais	je faillirais, faudrais	je défaillirais	je bouillirais	
	il, elle courrait	il, elle faillirait, faudrait	il, elle défaillirait	il, elle bouillirait	
Present Subjunctive	que je coure	que je faillisse, faille	que je défaille	que je bouille	
	qu'il, elle coure	qu'il, elle faillisse, faille	qu'il, elle défaille	qu'il, elle bouille	
	que nous courions	que nous faillissions, faillions	que nous défaillions	que nous bouillions	
	qu'ils, elles courent	qu'ils, elles faillissent, faillent	qu'ils, elles défaillent	qu'ils, elles bouillent	
Imperfect Subjunctive	qu'il, elle courût	qu'il, elle faillît	qu'il, elle défaillît	qu'il, elle bouillît	
	qu'ils, elles courussent	qu'ils, elles faillissent	qu'ils, elles défaillissent	qu'ils, elles bouillissent	
Imperative	cours	faillis, faux	défaille	bous	
	courons	faillissons, faillons	défaillons	bouillons	
	courez	faillissez, faillez	défaillez	bouillez	
Present Participle	courant	faillissant, faillant	défaillant	bouillant	gisant
Past Participle	couru, -e	failli	défailli	bouilli, -e	

[1] The more common conjugation of the verb **faillir** is the one modelled on the verb **finir**. This verb is rarely found in its conjugated form.

[2] **Je défaillerai, tu défailleras** etc and **je défaillerais, tu défaillerais** etc are also used in the future and conditional tenses respectively. The same forms are also used for **tressaillir** and **assaillir**.

[3] **Gésir** is not used in other tenses and moods.

FRENCH CONJUGATION TABLES

	50 saillir[1]	51 ouïr[2]	52 recevoir	53 devoir	54 mouvoir
Present		j'ouïs, ois	je reçois	je dois	je meus
		tu ouïs, ois	tu reçois	tu dois	tu meus
	il, elle saille	il, elle ouït, oit	il, elle reçoit	il, elle doit	il, elle meut
		nous ouïssons, oyons	nous recevons	nous devons	nous mouvons
		vous ouïssez, oyez	vous recevez	vous devez	vous mouvez
	ils, elles saillent	ils, elles ouïssent, oient	ils, elles reçoivent	ils, elles doivent	ils, elles meuvent
Imperfect	il, elle saillait	il, elle ouïssait, oyait	il, elle recevait	il, elle devait	il, elle mouvait
Past Historic	il, elle saillit	il, elle ouït	il, elle reçut	il, elle dut	il, elle mut
	ils, elles saillirent	ils, elles ouïrent	ils, elles reçurent	ils, elles durent	ils, elles murent
Future		j'ouïrai, orrai	je recevrai	je devrai	je mouvrai
	il, elle saillera	il, elle ouïra, orra	il, elle recevra	il, elle devra	il, elle mouvra
Conditional		j'ouïrais, orrais	je recevrais	je devrais	je mouvrais
	il, elle saillerait	il, elle ouïrait, orrait	il, elle recevrait	il, elle devrait	il, elle mouvrait
Present Subjunctive		que j'ouïsse, oie	que je reçoive	que je doive	que je meuve
	qu'il, elle saille	qu'il, elle ouïsse, oie	qu'il, elle reçoive	qu'il, elle doive	qu'il, elle meuve
		que nous ouïssions, oyions	que nous recevions	que nous devions	que nous mouvions
	qu'ils, elles saillent	qu'ils, elles ouïssent, oient	qu'ils, elles reçoivent	qu'ils, elles doivent	qu'ils, elles meuvent
Imperfect Subjunctive	qu'il, elle saillît	qu'il, elle ouït	qu'il, elle reçût	qu'il, elle dût	qu'il, elle mût
	qu'ils, elles saillissent	qu'ils, elles ouïssent	qu'ils, elles reçussent	qu'ils, elles dussent	qu'ils, elles mussent
Imperative	not used	ouïs, ois	reçois	dois	meus
		ouïssons, oyons	recevons	devons	mouvons
		ouïssez, oyez	recevez	devez	mouvez
Present Participle	saillant	oyant	recevant	devant	mouvant
Past Participle	sailli, -e	ouï, -e	reçu, -e	dû, due, dus, dues	mû, mue, mus, mues

[1] This conjugation table refers to **saillir**[2] in the dictionary.

[2] In modern French, the verb **ouïr** is used only in the infinitive, in compound tenses and in the expressions **par ouï-dire** and **oyez, braves gens**.

	55 émouvoir	56 promouvoir[1]	57 vouloir	58 pouvoir[2]	59 savoir
Present	j'émeus	je promeus	je veux	je peux, puis	je sais
	tu émeus	tu promeus	tu veux	tu peux	tu sais
	il, elle émeut	il, elle promeut	il, elle veut	il, elle peut	il, elle sait
	nous émouvons	nous promouvons	nous voulons	nous pouvons	nous savons
	vous émouvez	vous promouvez	vous voulez	vous pouvez	vous savez
	ils, elles émeuvent	ils, elles promeuvent	ils, elles veulent	ils, elles peuvent	ils, elles savent
Imperfect	il, elle émouvait	il, elle promouvait	il, elle voulait	il, elle pouvait	il, elle savait
Past Historic	il, elle émut	il, elle promut	il, elle voulut	il, elle put	il, elle sut
	ils, elles émurent	ils, elles promurent	ils, elles voulurent	ils, elles purent	ils, elles surent
Future	j'émouvrai	je promouvrai	je voudrai	je pourrai	je saurai
	il, elle émouvra	il, elle promouvra	il, elle voudra	il, elle pourra	il, elle saura
Conditional	j'émouvrais	je promouvrais	je voudrais	je pourrais	je saurais
	il, elle émouvrait	il, elle promouvrait	il, elle voudrait	il, elle pourrait	il, elle saurait
Present Subjunctive	que j'émeuve	que je promeuve	que je veuille	que je puisse	que je sache
	qu'il, elle émeuve	qu'il, elle promeuve	qu'il, elle veuille	qu'il, elle puisse	qu'il, elle sache
	que nous émouvions	que nous promouvions	que nous voulions	que nous puissions	que nous sachions
	qu'ils, elles émeuvent	qu'ils, elles promeuvent	qu'ils, elles veuillent	qu'ils, elles puissent	qu'ils, elles sachent
Imperfect Subjunctive	qu'il, elle émût	qu'il, elle promût	qu'il, elle voulût	qu'il, elle pût	qu'il, elle sût
	qu'ils, elles émussent	qu'ils, elles promussent	qu'ils, elles voulussent	qu'ils, elles pussent	qu'ils, elles sussent
Imperative	émeus	promeus	veux, veuille	not used	sache
	émouvons	promouvons	voulons, veuillons		sachons
	émouvez	promouvez	voulez, veuillez		sachez
Present Participle	émouvant	promouvant	voulant	pouvant	sachant
Past Participle	ému, -e	promu, -e	voulu, -e	pu	su, -e

[1] This verb is rarely found in its conjugated forms.

[2] When the subject and verb are inverted in the interrogative, **puis-je** is the only possible conjugated form.

	60 valoir	61 prévaloir	62 voir	63 prévoir	64 pourvoir
Present	je vaux	je prévaux	je vois	je prévois	je pourvois
	tu vaux	tu prévaux	tu vois	tu prévois	tu pourvois
	il, elle vaut	il, elle prévaut	il, elle voit	il, elle prévoit	il, elle pourvoit
	nous valons	nous prévalons	nous voyons	nous prévoyons	nous pourvoyons
	vous valez	vous prévalez	vous voyez	vous prévoyez	vous pourvoyez
	ils, elles valent	ils, elles prévalent	ils, elles voient	ils, elles prévoient	ils, elles pourvoient
Imperfect	il, elle valait	il, elle prévalait	il, elle voyait	il, elle prévoyait	il, elle pourvoyait
Past Historic	il, elle valut	il, elle prévalut	il, elle vit	il, elle prévit	il, elle pourvut
	ils, elles valurent	ils, elles prévalurent	ils, elles virent	ils, elles prévirent	ils, elles pourvurent
Future	je vaudrai	je prévaudrai	je verrai	je prévoirai	je pourvoirai
	il, elle vaudra	il, elle prévaudra	il, elle verra	il, elle prévoira	il, elle pourvoira
Conditional	je vaudrais	je prévaudrais	je verrais	je prévoirais	je pourvoirais
	il, elle vaudrait	il, elle prévaudrait	il, elle verrait	il, elle prévoirait	il, elle pourvoirait
Present Subjunctive	que je vaille	que je prévale	que je voie	que je prévoie	que je pourvoie
	qu'il, elle vaille	qu'il, elle prévale	qu'il, elle voie	qu'il, elle prévoie	qu'il, elle pourvoie
	que nous valions	que nous prévalions	que nous voyions	que nous prévoyions	que nous pourvoyions
	qu'ils, elles vaillent	qu'ils, elles prévalent	qu'ils, elles voient	qu'ils, elles prévoient	qu'ils, elles pourvoient
Imperfect Subjunctive	qu'il, elle valût	qu'il, elle prévalût	qu'il, elle vît	qu'il, elle prévît	qu'il, elle pourvût
	qu'ils, elles valussent	qu'ils, elles prévalussent	qu'ils, elles vissent	qu'ils, elles prévissent	qu'ils, elles pourvussent
Imperative	vaux	prévaux	vois	prévois	pourvois
	valons	prévalons	voyons	prévoyons	pourvoyons
	valez	prévalez	voyez	prévoyez	pourvoyez
Present Participle	valant	prévalant	voyant	prévoyant	pourvoyant
Past Participle	valu, -e	prévalu, -e	vu, -e	prévu, -e	pourvu, -e

	65 asseoir[1]	66 surseoir	67 seoir[2]		68 pleuvoir[3]
Present	j'assieds	j'assois	je sursois		
	tu assieds	tu assois	tu sursois		
	il, elle assied	il, elle assoit	il, elle sursoit	il, elle sied	il pleut
	nous asseyons	nous assoyons	nous sursoyons		
	vous asseyez	vous assoyez	vous sursoyez		
	ils, elles asseyent	ils, elles assoient	ils, elles sursoient	ils, elles siéent	
Imperfect	il, elle asseyait	il, elle assoyait	il, elle sursoyait	il, elle seyait	il pleuvait
Past Historic	il, elle assit	il, elle assit	il, elle sursit	*not used*	il plut
	ils, elles assirent	ils, elles assirent	ils, elles sursirent		
Future	j'assiérai	j'assoirai	je surseoirai		
	il, elle assiéra	il, elle assoira	il, elle surseoira	il, elle siéra	il pleuvra
Conditional	j'assiérais	j'assoirais	je surseoirais		
	il, elle assiérait	il, elle assoirait	il, elle surseoirait	il, elle siérait	il pleuvrait
Present Subjunctive	que j'asseye	que j'assoie	que je sursoie		
	qu'il, elle asseye	qu'il, elle assoie	qu'il, elle sursoie	qu'il, elle siée	qu'il pleuve
	que nous asseyions	que nous assoyions	que nous sursoyions		
	qu'ils, elles asseyent	qu'ils, elles assoient	qu'ils, elles sursoient	qu'ils, elles siéent	
Imperfect Subjunctive	qu'il, elle assît	qu'il, elle assît	qu'il, elle sursît	*not used*	qu'il plût
	qu'ils, elles assissent	qu'ils, elles assissent	qu'ils, elles sursissent		
Imperative	assieds	assois	sursois	*not used*	*not used*
	asseyons	assoyons	sursoyons		
	asseyez	assoyez	sursoyez		
Present Participle	asseyant	assoyant	sursoyant	seyant	pleuvant
Past Participle	assis, -e	assis, -e	sursis	*not used*	plu

[1] In written French, the preferred spelling of the -oi- forms is -eoi-, eg **j'asseois, il, elle asseoira, que tu asseoies, ils, elles asseoiraient**.

[2] In this case, **seoir** has the sense of "to suit". When it means "to be located" it exists only in the past participle (**sis, -e**).

[3] The figurative use of the verb **pleuvoir** allows a conjugation in the third-person plural, eg **les insultes pleuvent, pleuvaient, pleuvront, plurent, pleuvraient**.

	69 falloir	70 échoir	71 déchoir	72 choir	73 vendre
Present			je déchois	je chois	je vends
			tu déchois	tu chois	tu vends
	il faut	il, elle échoit	il, elle déchoit	il, elle choit	il, elle vend
			nous déchoyons	*not used*	nous vendons
			vous déchoyez	*not used*	vous vendez
		ils, elles échoient	ils, elles déchoient	ils, elles choient	ils, elles vendent
Imperfect	il fallait	il, elle échoyait	*not used*	*not used*	il, elle vendait
Past Historic	il fallut	il, elle échut	il, elle déchut	il, elle chut	il, elle vendit
		ils, elles échurent	ils, elles déchurent	ils, elles churent	ils, elles vendirent
Future			je déchoirai	je choirai, cherrai	je vendrai
	il faudra	il, elle échoira, écherra	il, elle déchoira	il, elle choira, cherra	il, elle vendra
Conditional			je déchoirais	je choirais, cherrais	je vendrais
	il faudrait	il, elle échoirait, écherrait	il, elle déchoirait	il, elle choirait, cherrait	il, elle vendrait
Present Subjunctive	qu'il faille	qu'il, elle échoie	que je déchoie	*not used*	que je vende
			qu'il, elle déchoie		qu'il, elle vende
			que nous déchoyions		que nous vendions
		qu'ils, elles échoient	qu'ils, elles déchoient		qu'ils, elles vendent
Imperfect Subjunctive	qu'il fallût	qu'il, elle échût	qu'il, elle déchût	qu'il, elle chût	qu'il, elle vendît
		qu'ils, elles échussent	qu'ils, elles déchussent	*not used*	qu'ils, elles vendissent
Imperative	*not used*	*not used*	*not used*	*not used*	vends
					vendons
					vendez
Present Participle	*not used*	échéant	*not used*	*not used*	vendant
Past Participle	fallu	échu, -e	déchu, -e	chu, -e	vendu, -e

	74 répandre	75 répondre	76 mordre	77 perdre	78 rompre
Present	je répands	je réponds	je mords	je perds	je romps
	tu répands	tu réponds	tu mords	tu perds	tu romps
	il, elle répand	il, elle répond	il, elle mord	il, elle perd	il, elle rompt
	nous répandons	nous répondons	nous mordons	nous perdons	nous rompons
	vous répandez	vous répondez	vous mordez	vous perdez	vous rompez
	ils, elles répandent	ils, elles répondent	ils, elles mordent	ils, elles perdent	ils, elles rompent
Imperfect	il, elle répandait	il, elle répondait	il, elle mordait	il, elle perdait	il, elle rompait
Past Historic	il, elle répandit	il, elle répondit	il, elle mordit	il, elle perdit	il, elle rompit
	ils, elles répandirent	ils, elles répondirent	ils, elles mordirent	ils, elles perdirent	ils, elles rompirent
Future	je répandrai	je répondrai	je mordrai	je perdrai	je romprai
	il, elle répandra	il, elle répondra	il, elle mordra	il, elle perdra	il, elle rompra
Conditional	je répandrais	je répondrais	je mordrais	je perdrais	je romprais
	il, elle répandrait	il, elle répondrait	il, elle mordrait	il, elle perdrait	il, elle romprait
Present Subjunctive	que je répande	que je réponde	que je morde	que je perde	que je rompe
	qu'il, elle répande	qu'il, elle réponde	qu'il, elle morde	qu'il, elle perde	qu'il, elle rompe
	que nous répandions	que nous répondions	que nous mordions	que nous perdions	que nous rompions
	qu'ils, elles répandent	qu'ils, elles répondent	qu'ils, elles mordent	qu'ils, elles perdent	qu'ils, elles rompent
Imperfect Subjunctive	qu'il, elle répandît	qu'il, elle répondît	qu'il, elle mordît	qu'il, elle perdît	qu'il, elle rompît
	qu'ils, elles répandissent	qu'ils, elles répondissent	qu'ils, elles mordissent	qu'ils, elles perdissent	qu'ils, elles rompissent
Imperative	répands	réponds	mords	perds	romps
	répandons	répondons	mordons	perdons	rompons
	répandez	répondez	mordez	perdez	rompez
Present Participle	répandant	répondant	mordant	perdant	rompant
Past Participle	répandu, -e	répondu, -e	mordu, -e	perdu, -e	rompu, -e

	79 prendre	80 craindre	81 peindre	82 joindre	83 battre
Present	je prends	je crains	je peins	je joins	je bats
	tu prends	tu crains	tu peins	tu joins	tu bats
	il, elle prend	il, elle craint	il, elle peint	il, elle joint	il, elle bat
	nous prenons	nous craignons	nous peignons	nous joignons	nous battons
	vous prenez	vous craignez	vous peignez	vous joignez	vous battez
	ils, elles prennent	ils, elles craignent	ils, elles peignent	ils, elles joignent	ils, elles battent
Imperfect	il, elle prenait	il, elle craignait	il, elle peignait	il, elle joignait	il, elle battait
Past Historic	il, elle prit	il, elle craignit	il, elle peignit	il, elle joignit	il, elle battit
	ils, elles prirent	ils, elles craignirent	ils, elles peignirent	ils, elles joignirent	ils, elles battirent
Future	je prendrai	je craindrai	je peindrai	je joindrai	je battrai
	il, elle prendra	il, elle craindra	il, elle peindra	il, elle joindra	il, elle battra
Conditional	je prendrais	je craindrais	je peindrais	je joindrais	je battrais
	il, elle prendrait	il, elle craindrait	il, elle peindrait	il, elle joindrait	il, elle battrait
Present Subjunctive	que je prenne	que je craigne	que je peigne	que je joigne	que je batte
	qu'il, elle prenne	qu'il, elle craigne	qu'il, elle peigne	qu'il, elle joigne	qu'il, elle batte
	que nous prenions	que nous craignions	que nous peignions	que nous joignions	que nous battions
	qu'ils, elles prennent	qu'ils, elles craignent	qu'ils, elles peignent	qu'ils, elles joignent	qu'ils, elles battent
Imperfect Subjunctive	qu'il, elle prît	qu'il, elle craignît	qu'il, elle peignît	qu'il, elle joignît	qu'il, elle battît
	qu'ils, elles prissent	qu'ils, elles craignissent	qu'ils, elles peignissent	qu'ils, elles joignissent	qu'ils, elles battissent
Imperative	prends	crains	peins	joins	bats
	prenons	craignons	peignons	joignons	battons
	prenez	craignez	peignez	joignez	battez
Present Participle	prenant	craignant	peignant	joignant	battant
Past Participle	pris, -e	craint, -e	peint, -e	joint, -e	battu, -e

	84 mettre	85 moudre	86 coudre	87 absoudre[1]	88 résoudre[2]
Present	je mets	je mouds	je couds	j'absous	je résous
	tu mets	tu mouds	tu couds	tu absous	tu résous
	il, elle met	il, elle moud	il, elle coud	il, elle absout	il, elle résout
	nous mettons	nous moulons	nous cousons	nous absolvons	nous résolvons
	vous mettez	vous moulez	vous cousez	vous absolvez	vous résolvez
	ils, elles mettent	ils, elles moulent	ils, elles cousent	ils, elles absolvent	ils, elles résolvent
Imperfect	il, elle mettait	il, elle moulait	il, elle cousait	il, elle absolvait	il, elle résolvait
Past Historic	il, elle mit	il, elle moulut	il, elle cousit	il, elle absolut	il, elle résolut
	ils, elles mirent	ils, elles moulurent	ils, elles cousirent	ils, elles absolurent	ils, elles résolurent
Future	je mettrai	je moudrai	je coudrai	j'absoudrai	je résoudrai
	il, elle mettra	il, elle moudra	il, elle coudra	il, elle absoudra	il, elle résoudra
Conditional	je mettrais	je moudrais	je coudrais	j'absoudrais	je résoudrais
	il, elle mettrait	il, elle moudrait	il, elle coudrait	il, elle absoudrait	il, elle résoudrait
Present Subjunctive	que je mette	que je moule	que je couse	que j'absolve	que je résolve
	qu'il, elle mette	qu'il, elle moule	qu'il, elle couse	qu'il, elle absolve	qu'il, elle résolve
	que nous mettions	que nous moulions	que nous cousions	que nous absolvions	que nous résolvions
	qu'ils, elles mettent	qu'ils, elles moulent	qu'ils, elles cousent	qu'ils, elles absolvent	qu'ils, elles résolvent
Imperfect Subjunctive	qu'il, elle mît	qu'il, elle moulût	qu'il, elle cousît	qu'il, elle absolût	qu'il, elle résolût
	qu'ils, elles missent	qu'ils, elles moulussent	qu'ils, elles cousissent	qu'ils, elles absolussent	qu'ils, elles résolussent
Imperative	mets	mouds	couds	absous	résous
	mettons	moulons	cousons	absolvons	résolvons
	mettez	moulez	cousez	absolvez	résolvez
Present Participle	mettant	moulant	cousant	absolvant	résolvant
Past Participle	mis, -e	moulu, -e	cousu, -e	absous, -oute	résolu, -e

[1] The past historic and imperfect subjunctive forms are rarely used.

[2] The past participle **résous, -oute** may also be used when the verb means "to transform, to become", eg **un brouillard résous en pluie,** although this form is rare.

	89 suivre	90 vivre[1]	91 paraître	92 naître	93 croître[2]
Present	je suis	je vis	je parais	je nais	je croîs
	tu suis	tu vis	tu parais	tu nais	tu croîs
	il, elle suit	il, elle vit	il, elle paraît	il, elle naît	il, elle croît
	nous suivons	nous vivons	nous paraissons	nous naissons	nous croissons
	vous suivez	vous vivez	vous paraissez	vous naissez	vous croissez
	ils, elles suivent	ils, elles vivent	ils, elles paraissent	ils, elles naissent	ils, elles croissent
Imperfect	il, elle suivait	il, elle vivait	il, elle paraissait	il, elle naissait	il, elle croissait
Past Historic	il, elle suivit	il, elle vécut	il, elle parut	il, elle naquit	il, elle crût
	ils, elles suivirent	ils, elles vécurent	ils, elles parurent	ils, elles naquirent	ils, elles crûrent
Future	je suivrai	je vivrai	je paraîtrai	je naîtrai	je croîtrai
	il, elle suivra	il, elle vivra	il, elle paraîtra	il, elle naîtra	il, elle croîtra
Conditional	je suivrais	je vivrais	je paraîtrais	je naîtrais	je croîtrais
	il, elle suivrait	il, elle vivrait	il, elle paraîtrait	il, elle naîtrait	il, elle croîtrait
Present Subjunctive	que je suive	que je vive	que je paraisse	que je naisse	que je croisse
	qu'il, elle suive	qu'il, elle vive	qu'il, elle paraisse	qu'il, elle naisse	qu'il, elle croisse
	que nous suivions	que nous vivions	que nous paraissions	que nous naissions	que nous croissions
	qu'ils, elles suivent	qu'ils, elles vivent	qu'ils, elles paraissent	qu'ils, elles naissent	qu'ils, elles croissent
Imperfect Subjunctive	qu'il, elle suivît	qu'il, elle vécût	qu'il, elle parût	qu'il, elle naquît	qu'il, elle crût
	qu'ils, elles suivissent	qu'ils, elles vécussent	qu'ils, elles parussent	qu'ils, elles naquissent	qu'ils, elles crûssent
Imperative	suis	vis	parais	nais	croîs
	suivons	vivons	paraissons	naissons	croissons
	suivez	vivez	paraissez	naissez	croissez
Present Participle	suivant	vivant	paraissant	naissant	croissant
Past Participle	suivi, -e	vécu, -e	paru, -e	né, -e	crû, crue, crus, crues

[1] **Survivre** conjugates like **vivre**, except that its past participle is always invariable.

[2] The Académie française recommends that **crusse, crusses, crussions, crussiez** and **crussent** be used in the imperfect subjunctive.

	94 accroître[1]	95 rire	96 conclure[2]	97 nuire[3]	98 conduire
Present	j'accrois	je ris	je conclus	je nuis	je conduis
	tu accrois	tu ris	tu conclus	tu nuis	tu conduis
	il, elle accroît	il, elle rit	il, elle conclut	il, elle nuit	il, elle conduit
	nous accroissons	nous rions	nous concluons	nous nuisons	nous conduisons
	vous accroissez	vous riez	vous concluez	vous nuisez	vous conduisez
	ils, elles accroissent	ils, elles rient	ils, elles concluent	ils, elles nuisent	ils, elles conduisent
Imperfect	il, elle accroissait	il, elle riait	il, elle concluait	il, elle nuisait	il, elle conduisait
Past Historic	il, elle accrut	il, elle rit	il, elle conclut	il, elle nuisit	il, elle conduisit
	ils, elles accrurent	ils, elles rirent	ils, elles conclurent	ils, elles nuisirent	ils, elles conduisirent
Future	j'accroîtrai	je rirai	je conclurai	je nuirai	je conduirai
	il, elle accroîtra	il, elle rira	il, elle conclura	il, elle nuira	il, elle conduira
Conditional	j'accroîtrais	je rirais	je conclurais	je nuirais	je conduirais
	il, elle accroîtrait	il, elle rirait	il, elle conclurait	il, elle nuirait	il, elle conduirait
Present Subjunctive	que j'accroisse	que je rie	que je conclue	que je nuise	que je conduise
	qu'il, elle accroisse	qu'il, elle rie	qu'il, elle conclue	qu'il, elle nuise	qu'il, elle conduise
	que nous accroissions	que nous riions	que nous concluions	que nous nuisions	que nous conduisions
	qu'ils, elles accroissent	qu'ils, elles rient	qu'ils, elles concluent	qu'ils, elles nuisent	qu'ils, elles conduisent
Imperfect Subjunctive	qu'il, elle accrût	qu'il, elle rît	qu'il, elle conclût	qu'il, elle nuisît	qu'il, elle conduisît
	qu'ils, elles accrussent	qu'ils, elles rissent	qu'ils, elles conclussent	qu'ils, elles nuisissent	qu'ils, elles conduisissent
Imperative	accrois	ris	conclus	nuis	conduis
	accroissons	rions	concluons	nuisons	conduisons
	accroissez	riez	concluez	nuisez	conduisez
Present Participle	accroissant	riant	conluant	nuisant	conduisant
Past Participle	accru, -e	ri	conclu, -e	nui	conduit, -e

[1] **Recroître** conjugates like **accroître**, except that its past participle is **recrû, recrue, recrus, recrues**.

[2] **Inclure** and **occlure** conjugate like **conclure**, except that their past participles are **inclus, -e** and **occlus, -e** respectively.

[3] **Luire** and **reluire** conjugate like **nuire** but also have the alternative forms **je luis** etc in the past historic.

	99 écrire	100 suffire	101 confire[1]	102 dire	103 contredire
Present	j'écris	je suffis	je confis	je dis	je contredis
	tu écris	tu suffis	tu confis	tu dis	tu contredis
	il, elle écrit	il, elle suffit	il, elle confit	il, elle dit	il, elle contredit
	nous écrivons	nous suffisons	nous confisons	nous disons	nous contredisons
	vous écrivez	vous suffisez	vous confisez	vous dites	vous contredisez
	ils, elles écrivent	ils, elles suffisent	ils, elles confisent	ils, elles disent	ils, elles contredisent
Imperfect	il, elle écrivait	il, elle suffisait	il, elle confisait	il, elle disait	il, elle contredisait
Past Historic	il, elle écrivit	il, elle suffit	il, elle confit	il, elle dit	il, elle contredit
	ils, elles écrivirent	ils, elles suffirent	ils, elles confirent	ils, elles dirent	ils, elles contredirent
Future	j'écrirai	je suffirai	je confirai	je dirai	je contredirai
	il, elle écrira	il, elle suffira	il, elle confira	il, elle dira	il, elle contredira
Conditional	j'écrirais	je suffirais	je confirais	je dirais	je contredirais
	il, elle écrirait	il, elle suffirait	il, elle confirait	il, elle dirait	il, elle contredirait
Present Subjunctive	que j'écrive	que je suffise	que je confise	que je dise	que je contredise
	qu'il, elle écrive	qu'il, elle suffise	qu'il, elle confise	qu'il, elle dise	qu'il, elle contredise
	que nous écrivions	que nous suffisions	que nous confisions	que nous disions	que nous contredisions
	qu'ils, elles écrivent	qu'ils, elles suffisent	qu'ils, elles confisent	qu'ils, elles disent	qu'ils, elles contredisent
Imperfect Subjunctive	qu'il, elle écrivît	qu'il, elle suffit	qu'il, elle confit	qu'il, elle dît	qu'il, elle contredît
	qu'ils, elles écrivissent	qu'ils, elles suffissent	qu'ils, elles confissent	qu'ils, elles dissent	qu'ils, elles contredissent
Imperative	écris	suffis	confis	dis	contredis
	écrivons	suffisons	confisons	disons	contredisons
	écrivez	suffisez	confisez	dites	contredisez
Present Participle	écrivant	suffisant	confisant	disant	contredisant
Past Participle	écrit, -e	suffi	confit, -e	dit, -e	contredit, -e

[1] **Circoncire** conjugates like **confire**, except that its past participle is **circoncis, -e**.

	104 maudire	105 bruire[1]	106 lire	107 croire	108 boire
Present	je maudis	je bruis	je lis	je crois	je bois
	tu maudis	tu bruis	tu lis	tu crois	tu bois
	il, elle maudit	il, elle bruit	il, elle lit	il, elle croit	il, elle boit
	nous maudissons	*not used*	nous lisons	nous croyons	nous buvons
	vous maudissez		vous lisez	vous croyez	vous buvez
	ils, elles maudissent		ils, elles lisent	ils, elles croient	ils, elles boivent
Imperfect	il, elle maudissait	il, elle bruyait	il, elle lisait	il, elle croyait	il, elle buvait
Past Historic	il, elle maudit	*not used*	il, elle lut	il, elle crut	il, elle but
	ils, elles maudirent		ils, elles lurent	ils, elles crurent	ils, elles burent
Future	je maudirai	je bruirai	je lirai	je croirai	je boirai
	il, elle maudira	il, elle bruira	il, elle lira	il, elle croira	il, elle boira
Conditional	je maudirais	je bruirais	je lirais	je croirais	je boirais
	il, elle maudirait	il, elle bruirait	il, elle lirait	il, elle croirait	il, elle boirait
Present Subjunctive	que je maudisse	*not used*	que je lise	que je croie	que je boive
	qu'il, elle maudisse		qu'il, elle lise	qu'il, elle croie	qu'il, elle boive
	que nous maudissions		que nous lisions	que nous croyions	que nous buvions
	qu'ils, elles maudissent		qu'ils, elles lisent	qu'ils, elles croient	qu'ils, elles boivent
Imperfect Subjunctive	qu'il, elle maudît	*not used*	qu'il, elle lût	qu'il, elle crût	qu'il, elle bût
	qu'ils, elles maudissent		qu'ils, elles lussent	qu'ils, elles crussent	qu'ils, elles bussent
Imperative	maudis	*not used*	lis	crois	bois
	maudissons		lisons	croyons	buvons
	maudissez		lisez	croyez	buvez
Present Participle	maudissant	*not used*	lisant	croyant	buvant
Past Participle	maudit, -e	bruit	lu, -e	cru, -e	bu, -e

[1] **Bruire** is normally used only in the present indicative, imperfect (**je bruyais, tu bruyais** etc), future and conditional forms. **Bruisser** (see table 3) is often used instead of **bruire**, particularly for the forms in which the latter is defective.

	109 faire	110 plaire	111 taire	112 extraire	113 clore[1]
Present	je fais	je plais	je tais	j'extrais	je clos
	tu fais	tu plais	tu tais	tu extrais	tu clos
	il, elle fait	il, elle plaît	il, elle tait	il, elle extrait	il, elle clôt
	nous faisons	nous plaisons	nous taisons	nous extrayons	*not used*
	vous faites	vous plaisez	vous taisez	vous extrayez	*not used*
	ils, elles font	ils, elles plaisent	ils, elles taisent	ils, elles extraient	ils, elles closent
Imperfect	il, elle faisait	il, elle plaisait	il, elle taisait	il, elle extrayait	*not used*
Past Historic	il, elle fit	il, elle plut	il, elle tut	*not used*	*not used*
	ils, elles firent	ils, elles plurent	ils, elles turent		
Future	je ferai	je plairai	je tairai	j'extrairai	je clorai
	il, elle fera	il, elle plaira	il, elle taira	il, elle extraira	il, elle clora
Conditional	je ferais	je plairais	je tairais	j'extrairais	je clorais
	il, elle ferait	il, elle plairait	il, elle tairait	il, elle extrairait	il, elle clorait
Present Subjunctive	que je fasse	que je plaise	que je taise	que j'extraie	que je close
	qu'il, elle fasse	qu'il, elle plaise	qu'il, elle taise	qu'il, elle extraie	qu'il, elle close
	que nous fassions	que nous plaisions	que nous taisions	que nous extrayions	que nous closions
	qu'ils, elles fassent	qu'ils, elles plaisent	qu'ils, elles taisent	qu'ils, elles extraient	qu'ils, elles closent
Imperfect Subjunctive	qu'il, elle fît	qu'il, elle plût	qu'il, elle tût	*not used*	*not used*
	qu'ils, elles fissent	qu'ils, elles plussent	qu'ils, elles tussent		
Imperative	fais	plais	tais	extrais	clos
	faisons	plaisons	taisons	extrayons	*not used*
	faites	plaisez	taisez	extrayez	*not used*
Present Participle	faisant	plaisant	taisant	extrayant	closant
Past Participle	fait, -e	plu	tu, -e	extrait, -e	clos, -e

[1] **Déclore**, **éclore** and **enclore** conjugate like **clore**, although the Académie française recommends **il, elle éclot** and **il, elle enclot** in the present tense. The verb **enclore** also has the forms **nous enclosons, vous enclosez** in the present tense and **enclosons, enclosez** in the imperative.

	114 vaincre	115 frire	116 foutre
Present	je vaincs	je fris	je fous
	tu vaincs	tu fris	tu fous
	il, elle vainc	il, elle frit	il, elle fout
	nous vainquons	*not used*	nous foutons
	vous vainquez		vous foutez
	ils, elles vainquent		ils, elles foutent
Imperfect	il, elle vainquait	*not used*	il, elle foutait
Past Historic	il, elle vainquit	*not used*	*not used*
	ils, elles vainquirent		
Future	je vaincrai	je frirai	je foutrai
	il, elle vaincra	il, elle frira	il, elle foutra
Conditional	je vaincrais	je frirais	je foutrais
	il, elle vaincrait	il, elle frirait	il, elle foutrait
Present Subjunctive	que je vainque	*not used*	que je foute
	qu'il, elle vainque		qu'il, elle foute
	que nous vainquions		que nous foutions
	qu'ils, elles vainquent		qu'ils, elles foutent
Imperfect Subjunctive	qu'il, elle vainquît	*not used*	*not used*
	qu'ils, elles vainquissent		
Imperative	vaincs	fris	fous
	vainquons	*not used*	foutons
	vainquez		foutez
Present Participle	vainquant	*not used*	foutant
Past Participle	vaincu, -e	frit, -e	foutu, -e

A¹, a¹ NM INV **1** (*lettre*) A, a; **de A (jusqu')à Z** from A to Z; **A comme Anatole** ≃ A for Andrew **2** *Mus* (*note*) A

A² **1** *Élec* (*abrév écrite* **ampère**) A, Amp **2** *Météo* (*abrév écrite* **anticyclone**) anticyclone **3** (*abrév* **autoroute**) *Br* ≃ M, motorway, *Am* ≃ I, interstate **4** (*abrév écrite* **apprenti conducteur**) (*sur une voiture*) = indicates that the driver has recently obtained his or her licence, *Br* ≃ L

a² [a] *voir* **avoir²**

a³ (*abrév écrite* **are**) a

À [a]

> to A2, E, J3 ▪ at A1, B1 ▪ in A1, B1 ▪ on A1, B1 ▪ from A3 ▪ with C1, I ▪ of D ▪ by F2, G3

à + le contracts to form **au**, **à + les** contracts to form **aux** [o].

PRÉP **A.** *DANS L'ESPACE* **1** (*indiquant la position*) at; (*à l'intérieur de*) in; (*sur*) on; **il habite à la campagne** he lives in the country; **elle habite au Canada** she lives in Canada; **j'habite au Havre** I live in Le Havre; **je suis aux Bermudes** I'm in Bermuda; **j'aimerais vivre à la Martinique** I'd like to live in Martinique; **il est à l'hôpital** he's in *Br* hospital *or Am* the hospital; **elle travaille à l'hôpital** she works at the hospital; **au jardin** in the garden; **à l'orée du bois** at the edge of the wood; **au marché** at the market; **il fait 45°C au soleil** it's 45°C in the sun; **quand on est à 2000 mètres d'altitude** when you're 2,000 metres up; **au niveau de la mer** at sea level; **à l'intersection des deux droites** at the intersection of the two lines; **elle attendait à la porte** she was waiting at *or* by the door; **tenez-vous correctement à table** behave (properly) at the table; **au mur/plafond** on the wall/ceiling; **à terre** on the ground; **c'est au rez-de-chaussée** it's on the *Br* ground floor *or Am* first floor; **j'ai mal à la tête** I've got a headache; **j'ai une ampoule au pied** I've got a blister on my foot; **à ma droite** on *or* to my right; **vous tournez à gauche après le feu** you turn left after the traffic lights; **la gare est à 500 mètres d'ici** the station is 500 metres from here **2** (*indiquant la direction*) to; **aller à Paris/aux États-Unis/à la Jamaïque** to go to Paris/to the United States/to Jamaica; **aller au cinéma** to go to the movies *or Br* cinema; **aller à la piscine** to go swimming, to go to the swimming pool; **est-ce qu'elle est allée à l'université?** has she been to university?; **il a lancé le javelot à 74 mètres** he threw the javelin 74 metres; **lever les bras au ciel** to throw up one's arms **3** (*indiquant la provenance, l'origine*) **puiser de l'eau à la fontaine** to get water from the fountain; **retenir l'impôt à la source** to deduct tax at source; **remonter à l'origine d'une affaire** to get to the root of a matter; **je l'ai entendu à la radio** I heard it on the radio; **je l'ai vu à la télé** I saw it on TV; **on en a parlé aux informations** they mentioned it *or* it was mentioned on the news

B. *DANS LE TEMPS* **1** (*indiquant un moment précis*) at; (*devant une date, un jour*) on; (*indiquant une époque, une période*) in; **à 6 heures** at 6 o'clock; **il ne rentrera qu'à 8 heures** he won't be back before 8; **à Pâques** at Easter; **à Noël** at Christmas; **à l'aube/l'aurore/midi** at dawn/daybreak/midday; **au crépuscule** at dusk; **le 12 au soir** on the evening of the 12th; **à dater de ce**

jour from that day on *or* onwards; **à mon arrivée** on my arrival; **à ma naissance** when I was born; **à l'automne** in *Br* (the) autumn *or Am* the fall; **à la Renaissance** in the Renaissance; **au XVIIème siècle** in the 17th century; **à chaque fois** every time; **à chaque instant** every minute; **vous allez quelque part à Noël?** are you going somewhere for Christmas?; **je te le donnerai à ton anniversaire** I'll give it to you on your birthday; **à trois, tu pars!** when I count three, go! **2** (*indiquant un délai*) **à une semaine des élections, 35 pour cent des électeurs sont encore indécis** with only one week to go before election day, 35 percent of voters are still undecided; **nous sommes à deux semaines de Noël** there are only two weeks to go before Christmas, Christmas is only two weeks away; **il me tarde d'être à dimanche** I can't wait till Sunday; **à demain/la semaine prochaine/mardi** see you tomorrow/next week/(on) Tuesday

C. *MARQUANT LE MOYEN, LA MANIÈRE* **1** (*indiquant le moyen, l'instrument, l'accompagnement*) **peindre à l'eau/à l'huile** to paint in watercolours/oils; **marcher au fuel** to run off *or* on oil; **couper qch au couteau** to cut sth with a knife; **cousu à la main** hand-sewn; **cousu à la machine** machine-sewn; **des mots écrits à la craie** words written in chalk; **jouer qch à la guitare** to play sth on the guitar; **cuisiner au beurre** to cook with butter; **aller à pied/à bicyclette/à cheval** to go on foot/by bicycle/on horseback **2** (*indiquant la manière*) **à voix haute** out loud; **on a ri aux larmes** we laughed till we cried; **agir à son gré** to do as one pleases *or* likes; **tout fonctionne à merveille** everything works perfectly; **je l'aime à la folie** I love him/her to distraction; **nous pourrions multiplier les exemples à l'infini** we could cite an infinite number of examples; **il s'assit à califourchon sur la chaise** he sat astride the chair; **à toute vitesse** at full speed; **à petits pas** at a slow pace; **au ralenti** in slow motion; **au rythme de deux par semaine** at the rate of two a week; **à jeun** on *or* with an empty stomach; **faire qch à la russe/turque** to do sth the Russian/Turkish way; **la vie à l'américaine** the American way of life; **un film policier à la Hitchcock** a thriller in the style of *or* à la Hitchcock; *Fam* **encore une blague à la Marie** another one of Marie's little jokes

D. *MARQUANT L'APPARTENANCE* **je veux une chambre à moi** I want my own room *or* a room of my own; **à qui est ce livre? – à moi** whose book is it? – (it's) mine; **c'est un ami à moi qui m'a parlé de vous** it was a friend of mine who told me about you; *Fam* **encore une idée à Papa!** another of Dad's ideas!

E. *INDIQUANT L'ATTRIBUTION, LA DESTINATION* **je suis à vous dans une minute** I'll be with you in a minute; **c'est à moi de jouer/parler** it's my turn to play/to speak; **ce n'est pas à moi de le faire** it's not up to me to do it; **à l'attention de M. le directeur** (*dans la correspondance*) for the attention of the manager; **à Jacques** to *or* for Jacques; **à notre fille bien-aimée** (*sur une tombe*) in memory of our beloved daughter; **à toi pour toujours** yours for ever

F. *INTRODUISANT UNE ÉVALUATION, UN RAPPORT DISTRIBUTIF* **1** (*introduisant un prix*) **un livre à 30 euros** a book which costs 30 euros, a book which costs 30 euros; **un tableau à 100 000 euros** a painting worth 100,000 euros; **tout à**

cinq euros everything five euros; **ne fais pas la difficile pour une robe à 50 euros** don't make so much fuss about a 50-euro dress **2** (*indiquant un rapport, une mesure*) **vendus à la douzaine/au poids/au détail** sold by the dozen/by weight/individually; **payé à la page** paid by the page; **les promotions s'obtiennent au nombre d'années d'ancienneté** promotion is in accordance with length of service; **faites-les aligner deux à deux** line them up two by two **3** (*introduisant un nombre de personnes*) **ils ont soulevé le piano à quatre** it took four of them to lift the piano; **à deux, on aura vite fait de repeindre la cuisine** between the two of us, it won't take long to repaint the kitchen; **nous travaillons à sept dans la même pièce** there are seven of us working in the same room; **on peut dormir à six dans le chalet** the chalet can sleep six; **ils sont venus à plusieurs** several of them came **4** (*indiquant une approximation*) **je m'entraîne trois à cinq heures par jour** I practise three to five hours a day; **j'en ai vu 15 à 20** I saw 15 or 20 of them

G. *MARQUANT DES RAPPORTS DE CAUSE OU DE CONSÉQUENCE* **1** (*indiquant la cause*) **à ces mots, il s'est tu** on hearing these words, he fell silent; **à ces cris, je me suis retourné** when I heard the cries, I turned round; **on l'a distribué à sa demande** it was given out at his request **2** (*indiquant la conséquence*) **il lui a tout dit, à ma grande surprise** he told him/her everything, much to my surprise; **à la satisfaction générale** to the satisfaction of all concerned **3** (*d'après*) **je t'ai reconnu à ta voix/démarche** I recognized (you by) your voice/walk; **au tremblement de ses mains, je voyais bien qu'il avait peur** I could tell he was scared from *or* by the way his hands were shaking; **à sa mine, on voit qu'il est en mauvaise santé** you can tell from the way he looks that he's ill; **à ce que je vois/comprends** from what I see/understand; **à ce qu'elle dit, la lettre n'est jamais arrivée** according to her *or* to what she says, the letter never arrived

H. *SUIVI DE L'INFINITIF* **1** (*indiquant l'hypothèse, la cause*) **il s'est fait des ennemis à se conduire ainsi** he's made enemies by behaving that way; **tu vas te fatiguer à rester debout** you'll get tired standing up; **à t'entendre, on dirait que tu t'en moques** listening to you, I get the feeling you don't care; **une histoire à vous faire rougir** an embarrassing story; **à bien considérer les choses...** all things considered... **2** (*exprimant l'obligation*) **la somme est à régler avant le 10** the full amount has to *or* must be paid by the 10th; **le mur est à repeindre** the wall needs to be repainted; **à consommer avec modération** drink in moderation; **c'est une pièce à voir absolument** this play is really worth seeing; **un livre à lire et à relire** a book which can be read over and over again; **les vêtements à laver/repasser** the clothes to be washed/ironed; **la phrase à retenir** the sentence to be *or* which should be remembered **3** (*exprimant la possibilité*) **il n'y a rien à voir/à manger** there's nothing to see/to eat **4** (*en train de*) **il était assis là à bâiller** he was sitting there yawning; **j'étais sur la terrasse à lire** I was reading on the patio; **ne restez pas là à rêvasser** don't just sit there daydreaming **5** (*au point de*) **il en est à regretter ce qu'il a**

fait he's come to regret what he did; **ils en sont à se demander si ça en vaut la peine** they've got to the stage of wondering whether it's worth the effort

I. *MARQUANT LA CARACTÉRISATION* **une fille aux cheveux longs** a girl with long hair; **l'homme au pardessus** the man in *or* with the overcoat; **une bête à cornes** a horned animal, an animal with horns; **une chemise à manches courtes** a short-sleeved shirt, a shirt with short sleeves; **un pyjama à fleurs/rayures** flowery/stripy pyjamas; **une voiture à cinq vitesses** a five-gear car, a car with five gears; **une fugue à trois voix** a fugue in three parts; **des sardines à l'huile** sardines in oil; **concombre à la vinaigrette** cucumber in vinaigrette; **poulet aux épices** spicy chicken; **glace à la framboise** raspberry ice cream; **arme à feu** firearm; **avion à réaction** jet plane; **chauffage au charbon/gaz** coal/gas heating; **calculette à piles** battery-operated calculator; **tasse à thé** tea cup; **mousse à raser** shaving cream; **machine à coudre** sewing machine; **papier à lettres** writing paper; **bureau à louer** *(dans petite annonce, sur panneau)* office for rent

J. *SERVANT DE LIEN SYNTAXIQUE* **1** *(introduisant le complément du verbe)* **parler à qn** to talk to sb; **téléphoner à qn** to phone sb; **croire à qch** to believe in sth; **penser à qn** to think of *or* about sb; **convenir à qn** to suit sb; *Littéraire* **aimer à faire qch** to like to do sth, to like doing sth; **il consent à ce que nous y allions** he agrees to our going; **dire à qn de faire qch** to tell sb to do sth; **rendre qch à qn** to give sth back to sb, to give sb sth back; **dérober qch à qn** to steal sth from sb; **autoriser qn à faire qch** to authorize sb to do sth

2 *(introduisant le complément d'un nom)* **l'aspiration à la liberté** hopes for freedom; **l'appartenance à un parti** membership of a party; **son dévouement à notre cause** his/her devotion to our cause

3 *(introduisant le complément de l'adjectif)* **c'est difficile à dessiner** it's difficult to draw; **perpendiculaire à la droite B** perpendicular to line B; **dévoué à la cause** devoted to the cause; **agréable aux yeux** pleasant to look at; **doux au toucher** soft to the touch

---

Å *Phys (abrév écrite* **Angström***)* A, Å

A2 [ɑdø] NF *Anciennement (abrév* **Antenne 2***)* = French state-owned television channel (now France 2)

A3 [ɑtrwa] NM A3

A4 [ɑkatr] NM A4

AA [ɑɑ] NF *Banque & Bourse* **(notation) AA** AA (rating), double-A rating

AAA [ɑɑɑ] NF *Banque & Bourse* **(notation) A.** AAA (rating), triple-A rating

AAD *Électron (abrév écrite* **analogique analogique digital***)* AAD

Aaron [aarɔ̃] NPR *Bible* Aaron

AB *Scol (abrév écrite* **assez bien***)* = fair grade (as assessment of schoolwork), ≃ C+, ≃ B–

abaca [abaka] NM **1** *Bot* abaca **2** *Tex* manila *or* manilla hemp

abacule [abakyl] NM *Cér* abaculus

abaissable [abɛsabl] ADJ lowerable

abaissant, -e [abɛsɑ̃, -ɑ̃t] ADJ degrading, humiliating

abaisse [abɛs] NF *Culin (en pâtisserie)* piece of rolled-out pastry; **faites une a. de 3mm** roll the pastry to a thickness of 3mm

abaisse-langue [abɛslɑ̃g] NM INV *Méd Br* tongue spatula, *Am* tongue depressor

abaissement [abɛsmɑ̃] NM **1** *(d'une vitre)* lowering; *(d'un store)* pulling down; *(d'une manette → en tirant)* pulling down; *(→ en poussant)* pushing down **2** *(du niveau d'un fleuve etc)* lowering; *(de la température)* fall, drop **3** *Écon (des prix, des taux, d'un impôt)* lowering, reduction; *(d'une monnaie)* weakening **4** *Fig Vieilli & Littéraire* abasement, humbling

abaisser [4] [abese] VT **1** *(faire descendre → vitre)* to lower; *(→ store)* to pull down; *(→ voilette)* to let down; *(→ pont-levis)* to lower, to let down; **a. la manette** *(en tirant)* to pull the lever down; *(en poussant)* to push the lever down

2 *(réduire → température)* to lower

3 *(réduire → prix, taux, impôt)* to lower, to reduce; *(monnaie)* to weaken

4 *Fig Littéraire (individu, pays)* to abase, to humble

5 *Math (perpendiculaire)* to drop; *(chiffre)* to bring down, to carry

6 *Mus* to transpose down

7 *Culin* to roll out

8 *Cartes* to lay down

▸**s'abaisser** VPR **1** *(vitre, pont-levis)* to be lowered; *(voile, rideau)* to fall; *(paupière)* to droop

2 *(être en pente → champ)* to slope down; **le terrain s'abaisse vers le fleuve** the land drops away towards the river

3 s'a. à qch to stoop to sth; **s'a. à des compromissions** to stoop to compromise; **je ne m'abaisserais jamais à un tel niveau** I'd never stoop so low as that; **s'a. à faire qch** to stoop so low as to do sth; **il ne s'abaisserait pas à mentir** he wouldn't demean himself by lying, he wouldn't stoop so low as to lie

abaisseur [abesœr] ADJ **1** *Élec (transformateur)* step-down **2** *Anat* **muscle a.** depressor

NM *Anat* depressor; **a. de tension** depressor

abajoue [abaʒu] NF *Zool* cheek pouch

abandon [abɑ̃dɔ̃] NM **1** *(fait de rejeter)* abandonment, rejection; *Jur (de biens, de droit)* surrender; **son a. de toute ambition politique** the fact that he/she gave up all political ambition; **faire a. de qch à qn** to donate sth (freely) to sb; *Jur* **a. du domicile conjugal** desertion of the marital home; *Jur* **a. d'enfant** abandonment (of one's child); *Jur* **a. de famille** desertion; *Mil & Jur* **a. de poste** dereliction of duty

2 *(fait d'être rejeté)* **éprouver un sentiment d'a.** to feel abandoned

3 *(état négligé)* neglected state; **les lieux étaient dans un (état de) grand a.** the place was shamefully neglected

4 *(absence de contraintes)* abandon, freedom; **dans ses bras, elle avait connu un délicieux a.** she had experienced such sweet surrender in his arms; **une pose d'un a. fort séduisant** a most seductive pose; **avec a.** *(parler)* freely; *(danser, rire)* with gay abandon

5 *Sport* withdrawal; **il y a eu a. par Vigor au troisième round** Vigor threw in the towel in the third round; **il y a eu a. par Roger juste avant l'arrivée** Roger dropped out just before the finish

6 *Ordinat* abort

7 *Bourse* **a. de l'option** *ou* **de prime** relinquishment *or* abandonment of the option

□ **à l'abandon** ADJ **un potager à l'a.** a neglected kitchen garden ADV **laisser son affaire/ses enfants à l'a.** to neglect one's business/one's children

abandonnataire [abɑ̃dɔnatɛr] NMF *Jur* beneficiary

abandonné, -e [abɑ̃dɔne] ADJ **1** *(parc)* neglected; *(mine, exploitation)* disused; *(village)* deserted; *(maison, voiture)* abandoned; *(vêtement, chaussure)* discarded **2** *(enfant, animal)* abandoned

abandonner [3] [abɑ̃dɔne] VT **1** *(quitter → enfant, chien, voiture)* to abandon; *(→ épouse)* to leave, to desert; *(→ lieu)* to abandon, to leave; *Mil (→ poste)* to desert, to abandon; **abandonné de tous** forsaken by all; **ils ont abandonné la ville pour la campagne** they left city life behind and settled in the country; **les troupes abandonnèrent le village** the troops withdrew from the village

2 *(faire défaut à)* to fail, to desert, to forsake; *Littéraire* **mes forces m'abandonnent** my strength is failing me

3 *(renoncer à → projet, principe)* to discard, to abandon; *(→ hypothèse)* to abandon; *(→ espoir)* to give up, to abandon; *(→ cours)* to drop out of; *(→ études)* to give up; *(→ carrière)* to give up, to leave; *Jur (→ droit, privilège)* to relinquish, to renounce; **a. le pouvoir** to leave *or* to retire from *or* to give up office; **elle abandonne la géographie** she's dropping geography; **elle a abandonné l'enseignement** she's given up *or* left teaching; **a. la partie** to give up; *Fig* to throw in the sponge *or* towel; **il a abandonné sa part d'héritage à sa sœur** he gave up his share of the inheritance in favour of his sister

4 *(livrer)* **a. qn à** to leave *or* to abandon sb to; **il nous abandonne à notre destin** he's abandoning us to our fate; *Hum* **il vous a abandonné à votre triste sort** he's left you to your unhappy fate; **ils abandonnent le pays à la famine** they are condemning the country to starvation

5 *Naut (navire)* to abandon; *(homme)* to maroon

6 *Ordinat* to abort

7 *Bourse* **a. l'option** *ou* **la prime** to relinquish *or* abandon *or* surrender the option

USAGE ABSOLU *(dans une lutte, une discussion)* to give up; **il ne comprendra jamais, j'abandonne** he'll never understand, I give up; **discute le prix, n'abandonne pas!** haggle over the price, don't give in!

▸**s'abandonner** VPR **1** *(se laisser aller)* to let (oneself) go; **elle s'abandonna dans ses bras** she surrendered herself to him

2 *(s'épancher)* to open one's heart, to pour out one's feelings

3 s'a. à *(désespoir)* to give way to; *(rêverie)* to drift off into; *(plaisirs)* to give oneself up to

abandonnique [abɑ̃dɔnik] ADJ *Psy* **être a.** to have a fear of being abandoned

abaque [abak] NM **1** *(pour compter)* abacus **2** *Math* chart, graph **3** *Archit* abacus

abasie [abazi] NF *Méd* abasia

abasourdi, -e [abazurdi] ADJ stunned

abasourdir [32] [abazurdir] VT **1** *(stupéfier)* to stun; **la nouvelle nous a abasourdis** we were stunned by the news **2** *(sujet: bruit, clameur)* to stun, to deafen

abasourdissant, -e [abazurdisɑ̃, -ɑ̃t] ADJ *(bruit)* shattering, deafening; *(nouvelle)* stunning

abasourdissement [abazurdismɑ̃] NM amazement, *Sout* stupefaction

abasside [abasid] = **abbaside**

abat *etc voir* **abattre**

abatage [abataʒ] = **abattage**

abatant [abatɑ̃] NM *Vieilli* flap, drop-leaf

abâtardir [32] [abɑtardir] VT *(race, individu)* to cause to degenerate; *(valeur)* to debase; *Fig* **une version abâtardie de la pièce** a watered-down version of the play

▸**s'abâtardir** VPR to degenerate, to become debased

abâtardissement [abɑtardismɑ̃] NM *(d'une race)* degeneration; *(d'une valeur)* debasement

abatée [abate] NF **1** *Naut* beating **2** *Aviat* stall

abatis [abati] NM *Can Agr* = land which has been deforested in preparation for cultivation

abat-jour [abaʒur] NM INV lampshade, shade; *Fig* **elle a mis sa main en a.** she shaded her eyes with her hand

abats [aba] NMPL *Culin Br* offal *(UNCOUNT)*, *Am* variety meat; **a. de volaille** giblets

abat-son [abasɔ̃] *(pl* **abat-sons***)* NM *Archit* louvre

abattable [abatabl] ADJ *(arbre)* that can be felled

abattage [abataʒ] NM **1** *(d'arbres)* felling **2** *(d'animaux)* slaughter, slaughtering; **45 kilos à l'a.** 45 kilos at the time of slaughter **3** *Mines* cutting, working; **face d'a.** working face, coalface; **a. à l'explosif** blasting **4** *Naut* **a. en carène** careening **5** *Com* **vente à l'a.** sale at knock-down prices **6** *Fam (locution)* **avoir de l'a.** to slog one's guts out

abattant [abatɑ̃] NM flap, drop-leaf

abattée [abate] NF **1** *Naut* beating **2** *Aviat* stall

abattement [abatmɑ̃] NM **1** *(épuisement → physique)* exhaustion; *(→ mental)* despondency, dejection **2** *Fin (rabais)* reduction; *(d'impôts)* allowance; **donnant droit à a.** eligible for tax relief; **a. à la base** basic personal allowance; **a. fiscal** tax allowance; **a. forfaitaire** fixed-rate rebate

abatteur [abatœr] NM **1** *(d'arbres)* feller **2** *(d'animaux)* slaughterer, slaughterman **3** *Fam (de travail)* slogger, hard worker▪

abattis [abati] NM **1** *Mil* abatis, abattis **2** *(dans une forêt)* felled trees **3** *Can* = **abatis**

NMPL **1** *(de volaille)* giblets **2** *Fam (bras et jambes)* limbs▪, arms and legs▪; **t'as intérêt à numéroter tes a.!** start saying your prayers!

abattoir [abatwar] NM slaughterhouse, abattoir; *Fig* **envoyer des hommes à l'a.** to send men to the slaughter *or* to be slaughtered *or* butchered

abattre [83] [abatr] VT **1** *(faire tomber → arbre)* to cut down, to fell; *(→ mur)* to pull *or* to knock down; *(→ quille)* to knock down; *(→ adversaire)*

to bring down; *Fam Fig* **a. de la besogne** *ou* **du travail** to get through a lot of work■ ; *Fam* **on a abattu 20 kilomètres en une journée** we *Br* clocked up *or Am* racked up 20 kilometres in a day

2 *(sujet: vent, tempête etc)* to knock down; **l'arbre fut abattu par le vent** the tree was blown down

3 *(mettre à plat → main, battant)* to bring down; **elle a abattu son poing sur le buffet** she slammed her fist down on the sideboard; **a. ses cartes** *ou* **son jeu** to lay down one's cards; *Fig* to lay one's cards on the table, to show one's hand

4 *(faire retomber → blé, poussière)* to settle; *(→ vent)* to bring down

5 *(tuer → personne)* to shoot (down); *(→ avion)* to shoot *or* to bring down; *(→ lièvre)* to shoot; *(→ perdrix)* to shoot, to bring down; *(→ animal domestique)* to put down; *(→ animal de boucherie)* to slaughter; **c'est un homme à a.** this man is on the hit-list

6 *Fig (démoraliser)* to dishearten, to depress; *(épuiser)* to drain, to wear out; **la défaite l'a complètement abattu** *(moralement)* the defeat completely crushed him; **ne pas se laisser a.** to keep one's spirits up; **ne nous laissons pas a.** let's not let things get us down

7 *Mines* to break down, to stope

VI *Naut (bateau à moteur)* to pay off; *(voilier)* to bear away

►**s'abattre VPR 1** *(s'écrouler → maison)* to fall down; *(→ personne)* to fall (down), to collapse; **l'arbre s'est abattu** the tree came crashing down

2 s'a. sur *(pluie)* to come pouring down on; *(grêle)* to come pelting *or* beating down on; *(coups)* to rain down on; *(se jeter sur → oiseau, personne)* to swoop down on; **le malheur/la maladie venait de s'a. sur nous** suddenly we'd been struck by disaster/disease; *aussi Fig* **s'a. sur sa proie** to swoop down on one's prey

abattu, -e [abaty] **ADJ 1** *(démoralisé)* despondent, dejected, downcast; **d'un air a.** dejectedly, dispiritedly; **a. par la chaleur** limp with the heat **2** *(épuisé)* exhausted, worn-out

NM fusil à l'a. uncocked rifle

abat-vent [abavɑ̃] **NM INV 1** *(d'une cheminée)* (chimney) cowl **2** *Hort* windbreak

abat-voix [abavwa] **NM INV** *(d'une chaire à prêcher)* sounding-board

abbaside [abasid] *Hist* **ADJ** Abbasid, Abbaside

NMF Abbasid, Abbaside

abbatial, -e, -aux, -ales [abasjal, -o] **ADJ** abbey *(avant n)*

❑ **abbatiale NF** abbey

abbaye [abei] **NF** *(communauté, bâtiment)* abbey; **l'a. de Cîteaux** = the abbey where the Cistercian order was founded in 1098 by Robert de Molesmes; **l'a. de Clairvaux** = the most famous of the Cistercian monasteries founded by Saint Bernard; **l'a. de Thélème** = Rabelais' aristocratic utopia in 'Gargantua'

abbé [abe] **NM 1** *(d'une abbaye)* abbot **2** *(ecclésiastique)* = title formerly used in France for members of the secular clergy; *Vieilli* **monsieur l'a.** *(en s'adressant à lui)* Father; *(en parlant de lui)* the Reverend Father

> *Culture*
>
> **ABBÉ PIERRE**
>
> Abbé Pierre (born 1912) is a Catholic priest who is one of France's best-loved public figures. He was a member of the French Resistance during the Second World War and a member of parliament from 1947 to 1951. After the war, he created the charity Emmaüs (see that entry) to help the homeless. He is a fervent defender of human rights and a tireless fighter against poverty and injustice.

abbevillien, -enne [abviljɛ̃, -ɛn] **ADJ** Abbevillian

abc [abese] **NM INV 1** *(base)* basics, fundamentals; **elle ignore même l'a. du métier** she doesn't even know the basics of the job **2** *(livre)* primer, alphabet book

abcéder [18] [apsede] *Méd* **VI** to abscess; **la plaie a abcédé** the wound has abscessed

►**s'abcéder VPR** to abscess

abcès [apsɛ] **NM** *Méd* abscess; **a. à la gencive** gumboil; *Fig* **crever** *ou* **vider l'a.** to clear the air; **le Premier ministre a décidé de crever** *ou* **vider l'a. en affrontant directement ses critiques** the Prime Minister decided to bring things to a head *or* to resolve matters by confronting his critics directly; **a. de fixation** *Méd* fixation abscess; *Fig* focal point

Abdias [abdjas] **NPR** *Bible* Obadiah

abdicataire [abdikatɛr] **ADJ 1** *(qui va abdiquer)* abdicating **2** *(qui a abdiqué)* abdicated

NMF abdicator

abdication [abdikasjɔ̃] **NF** abdication

abdiquer [3] [abdike] **VT** *(pouvoir)* to abdicate, to surrender; *(responsabilité, opinion)* to abdicate, to renounce

VI to abdicate, to give in; **il abdique facilement devant ses enfants** he gives in easily to his children; **elle n'abdiquera jamais devant les syndicats** she'll never give way to the unions

abdomen [abdɔmɛn] **NM** *Anat* abdomen

abdominal, -e, -aux, -ales [abdɔminal, -o] **ADJ** *Anat* abdominal

❑ **abdominaux NMPL** *Anat* **1** *(muscles)* stomach *or* abdominal muscles **2** *(exercices)* **faire des abdominaux** to do exercises for the stomach muscles

abdominoplastie [abdɔminoplasti] **NF** *Méd* abdominoplasty

abdos [abdo] **NMPL** *Fam (abrév* **abdominaux**) **1** *(muscles)* abs, stomach *or* abdominal muscles■ **2** *(exercices)* **faire des a.** to do exercises for the stomach muscles■ , to do abs

abducteur [abdyktœr] **ADJ M 1** *Anat* abductor **2** *Chim (tube)* delivery *(avant n)*

NM *Anat* abductor muscle

abduction [abdyksjɔ̃] **NF** *Physiol* abduction

abécédaire [abesedɛr] **NM** primer, alphabet book

abeille [abɛj] **NF** *Entom* bee; *Fam* **avoir les abeilles** to be hacked off *or Br* cheesed off; **a. charpentière** carpenter bee; **a. coupeuse de feuilles** leafcutter bee; **a. maçonne** mason bee; **a. ouvrière** worker (bee)

Abel [abɛl] **NPR** *Bible* Abel

abélien, -enne [abeljɛ̃, -ɛn] **ADJ** *Math* abelian

aber [abɛr] **NM** (deep) estuary *(in Brittany)*

aberrance [abɛrɑ̃s] **NF** aberrance

aberrant, -e [abɛrɑ̃, -ɑ̃t] **ADJ 1** *(comportement)* deviant, aberrant; *(prix)* ridiculous; *(idée)* preposterous, absurd; **c'est a.!** it's absurd!, it's ridiculous! **2** *Biol* aberrant

aberration [abɛrasjɔ̃] **NF 1** *(absurdité)* aberration; **dans un moment d'a.** in a moment of aberration; **par quelle a. avait-elle dit oui?** whatever had possessed her to say yes?; **c'est une a.!** it's absurd!, it's ridiculous! **2** *Astron, Biol & Opt* aberration; *Biol* **a. chromosomique** chromosome abnormality

abêtir [32] [abetir] **VT** to dull the mind of; **abêti de fatigue** numb *or* dazed with fatigue

►**s'abêtir VPR** to become mindless *or* half-witted

abêtissant, -e [abetisɑ̃, -ɑ̃t] **ADJ** *(activité, tâche)* mind-numbing; *(émission)* moronic, mindless

abêtissement [abetismɑ̃] **NM 1** *(action)* **l'a. des enfants par la télévision** the mind-numbing effects of television on children; **l'a. lié au travail à la chaîne** the mind-numbing *or* stultifying effects of working on an assembly line **2** *(résultat)* dull-wittedness

abhorrer [3] [abɔre] **VT** *Littéraire* to loathe, to abhor

Abidjan [abidʒɑ̃] **NM** *Géog* Abidjan

abiétacée [abjetase] *Bot* **NF** fir (tree), *Spéc* abies

❑ **abiétacées NFPL** Abietineae

abiétin, -e [abjetɛ̃, -in] **ADJ** *Bot* pinaceous

abîme [abim] **NM 1** *Géog (gouffre)* abyss, chasm, gulf

2 *Fig (moral)* despair; *(financier)* ruin; **il est au bord de l'a.** *(moral)* he is on the brink *or* verge of despair; *(financier)* he is on the brink *or* verge of ruin; **être au fond de l'a.** to have reached rock bottom, to be at one's lowest ebb; *Littéraire* **l'a. appelle l'a.** deep calleth to deep

3 *Fig (distance mentale)* gulf, chasm; **il y avait comme un a. entre nous** a great abyss seemed to open up between us

❑ **abîmes NMPL** *Littéraire (infini)* depths; **les abîmes de son cœur** the depths of his/her heart; **plongé dans des abîmes de perplexité** utterly nonplussed

abîmé, -e [abime] **ADJ 1** *(vêtement)* ruined; *(livre, meuble)* damaged **2** *Fam (personne, visage)* beaten up; **il est bien a.** he was beaten up pretty badly, he's in a pretty bad state

abîmer [3] [abime] **VT 1** *(gâter → aliment, vêtement, livre)* to spoil; *(→ meuble)* to damage; *(→ yeux)* to ruin; **tu vas a. ta poupée!** you'll break your doll!

2 *Fam (meurtrir)* to injure■ ; **ils l'ont bien abîmé** they've made a right mess of him; **a. le portrait à qn** to smash sb's face in; **se faire a. le portrait** to get one's face smashed in

3 *Littéraire* **abîmé dans ses pensées** deep in thought; **abîmé dans le désespoir** in the depths of despair; **abîmée dans la contemplation du portrait, elle ne m'a pas vu venir** she was so absorbed in the portrait that she didn't see me coming

►**s'abîmer VPR 1** *(endommager)* to ruin; **tu t'abîmes les yeux** you're ruining your eyes *or* eyesight; **tu vas t'a. la peau avec ces crèmes** you'll ruin your skin with those creams; **s'a. la santé** to ruin one's health; *Fam Fig* **je ne vais pas m'a. la santé à l'aider** why should I break my neck to help him/her?

2 *(aliment)* to spoil, to go bad *or Br* off; *(livre, meuble)* to get damaged; *(vêtement, chaussures)* to wear out; **si tu portes ce pantalon sans arrêt, il va s'a.** if you keep on wearing those *Br* trousers *or Am* pants all the time, you'll ruin them

3 *Littéraire (navire)* to sink, to founder

4 *Littéraire* **s'a. dans qch** *(se plonger dans)* to be deeply absorbed in sth; **s'a. dans ses pensées** to be lost *or* deep in thought; **s'a. dans le désespoir** to be plunged in despair; **elle s'abîmait dans la contemplation de vieux manuscrits** she would become deeply absorbed in old manuscripts

ab intestat [abɛ̃tɛsta] *Jur* **ADV** intestate

ADJ INV intestate

abiogenèse [abjɔʒənɛz] **NF** *Biol* abiogenesis

abiotique [abjɔtik] **ADJ** *Biol* abiotic

abject, -e [abʒɛkt] **ADJ** despicable, contemptible; **il a été a. avec elle** he behaved despicably towards her; **d'une manière abjecte** abjectly

abjectement [abʒɛktəmɑ̃] **ADV** *Littéraire* abjectly

abjection [abʒɛksjɔ̃] **NF 1** *(état)* utter humiliation **2** *(caractère vil)* abjectness, vileness; **l'a. de son comportement** his vile behaviour **3** *(chose vile)* **ce film est une a.** this film is a complete outrage *or* a disgrace

abjuration [abʒyrasjɔ̃] **NF** recantation, abjuration

abjurer [3] [abʒyre] **VT** to abjure, to recant

VI to recant

Abkhazie [abkazi] **NF** *Géog* Abkhazia

abkhaze [abkaz] **ADJ** Abkhazian

NM *Ling (langue)* Abkhazian, Abkhaz

❑ **Abkhaze NMF** Abkhazian, Abkhaz, Abkhazi

ablactation [ablaktasjɔ̃] **NF** ablactation

ablater [3] [ablate] **s'ablater VPR** *Tech* to wear down *or* away

ablatif, -ive [ablatif, -iv] **ADJ** *Astron* ablative

NM *Gram* ablative (case); **à l'a.** in the ablative; **a. absolu** ablative absolute

ablation [ablasjɔ̃] **NF 1** *Méd* removal, *Spéc* ablation **2** *Géol & Tech* ablation **3** *Astron* ablation

ablative [ablativ] *voir* **ablatif**

-ABLE [abl] **SUFF**

• This very productive suffix expresses the idea of POSSIBILITY and is used to create adjectives, mainly from transitive verbs but also sometimes from intransitive verbs or nouns. Its equivalent in English is, in a lot of cases, *-able* or *-ible*. When there is no equivalent form in *-able*, the translation often includes an expression like "which can be..." or "easy to...":

payable payable; **mangeable** edible; **abordable** affordable; **maniable** easy to handle; **négligeable** negligible; **simplifiable** which can be made simpler; **variable** variable; **valable** valid; **effroyable** horrifying

• **-able** is often found in conjunction with a base and the prefix **in-** (or **im-**), with the idea of IMPOSSIBILITY, even if there is no equivalent positive form:

intolérable intolerable, unbearable; **inusable** which will never wear out; **immuable** unchanging; **impitoyable** merciless

• One recent trend is to use **-able** to create adjectives applied to people, meaning, in contexts of election or award-giving, "who can be elected..." or "who can be awarded...":
un nobélisable a potential Nobel prizewinner; **les oscarisables** potential Oscar winners, Oscar hopefuls; **les cardinaux papables** the cardinals who are likely candidates for the papacy; **les présidentiables** would-be presidential candidates; **il est considéré comme premier ministrable** he's considered Prime Minister material; **un académisable** a potential future member of the Académie française

---

ablégat [ablega] **NM** *Rel* ablegate

ableret [ablərɛ] **NM** *Pêche* square dip-net *or* dipping-net

ablette [ablɛt] **NF** *Ich* bleak

ablution [ablysjɔ̃] **NF 1** *Rel (du corps, du calice)* ablution **2** *Fam (toilette)* **faire ses ablutions** to perform one's ablutions

abnégation [abnegasjɔ̃] **NF** abnegation, self-denial; **avec a.** selflessly

aboi [abwa] **NM** *Chasse* bay
□ **aux abois** **ADJ 1** *Chasse* **être aux abois** to stand at bay **2** *Fig* **être aux abois** to have one's back against *or* to the wall **ADV 1** *Chasse* at bay **2** *Fig* **mettre qn aux abois** to have sb by the throat

aboie *etc voir* **aboyer**

aboiement [abwamɑ̃] **NM** *(d'un chien)* bark; **des aboiements** barking *(UNCOUNT)*; *Fig* **le vendeur/l'officier répondit par un a.** the salesman/the officer barked (out) an answer
□ **aboiements** **NMPL** *Fig Péj* ranting, raving; **les aboiements de la presse** the rantings of the press

aboiteau, -x [abwato] **NM** *Can (barrage)* aboiteau, = dyke with wooden sluices allowing excess fresh water to drain from the land and preventing salt water from entering at high tide

abolir [32] [abɔlir] **VT 1** *(une loi, la peine de mort)* to abolish **2** *Fig* **le téléphone abolit les distances** the telephone makes distance irrelevant

abolition [abɔlisjɔ̃] **NF** abolition

abolitionnisme [abɔlisjɔnism] **NM** abolitionism

abolitionniste [abɔlisjɔnist] **ADJ** abolitionist
NMF abolitionist

abominable [abɔminabl] **ADJ 1** *(désagréable → temps, odeur)* appalling, abominable **2** *(object → crime)* heinous, abominable, vile; **l'a. homme des neiges** the abominable snowman

abominablement [abɔminabləmɑ̃] **ADV** *(laid, cher)* horribly, frightfully; *(habillé)* abominably, hideously; **a. (mal) organisé** appallingly *or* abominably badly organized

abomination [abɔminasjɔ̃] **NF 1** *(acte, propos)* abomination; **cette soupe, c'est une a.** that soup is revolting; **il dit des abominations** he says appalling things **2** *(sentiment)* loathing, detestation, abomination; **avoir qch en a.** to abhor *or* to loathe sth

abominer [3] [abɔmine] **VT** *Littéraire* to loathe, to abhor, to abominate

abondamment [abɔ̃damɑ̃] **ADV** *(servir, saler)* copiously; *(manger, boire)* in copious amounts; *(rincer)* thoroughly; *(pleuvoir)* heavily; **elle a a. traité la question** she has amply *or* fully dealt with the question; **je vous l'ai a. répété** I have told you again and again; **a. illustré** lavishly illustrated

abondance [abɔ̃dɑ̃s] **NF 1** *(prospérité)* affluence; **vivre dans l'a.** to live in affluence **2** *(grande quantité)* **a. de qch** abundance *or* wealth of sth; **une a. de citations/détails** a wealth of quotations/details; **parler avec a.** to be eloquent; **parler d'a.** to extemporize; *Prov* **a. de biens ne nuit pas** = there's no harm in having too much
□ **en abondance** **ADV** in abundance, in plenty; **des fautes en a.** an abundance of mistakes

abondant, -e [abɔ̃dɑ̃, -ɑ̃t] **ADJ 1** *(en quantité → nourriture)* abundant, copious; *(→ récolte)* bountiful; *(→ vivres)* plentiful; *(→ végétation)* luxuriant, lush; *(→ larmes)* copious; *(→ chevelure)* luxuriant, thick; **peu a.** *(vivres)* scarce; *(récolte)* poor; *(végétation)* sparse; *(chevelure)* sparse, thin; **d'abondantes illustrations/recommandations** a wealth of illustrations/recommendations **2** *Littéraire (aisé → style)* lavish, fluent

abondement [abɔ̃dmɑ̃] **NM** *Fin* = employer's contribution to company savings scheme

abonder [3] [abɔ̃de] **VI 1** *(foisonner)* to be plentiful; **le raisin abonde cet automne** the grapes are plentiful this autumn; **a. en** to abound in, to be full of; **la rivière abonde en poissons** the river is teeming with fish; **son livre abonde en anecdotes** his/her book is rich in anecdotes
2 *Fig* **a. dans le sens de** to be in complete agreement with, to go along with; **ne me contredis pas, puisque j'abonde dans ton sens!** don't contradict me, I'm agreeing with you!

abonné, -e [abɔne] **NM,F 1** *(à un journal, à une revue, au téléphone etc)* subscriber; **abonnés au gaz/à l'électricité** gas/electricity consumers; **il n'y a pas d'a. au numéro que vous avez demandé** ≃ the number you have dialled has not been recognized; **se mettre aux abonnés absents** *Tél* to have one's phone calls rerouted to an answering service; *Fig* to be unavailable; *Fig* **pendant le mois d'août il sera aux abonnés absents** he won't be contactable during the month of August; **a. numérique** digital subscriber **2** *(pour un trajet, au théâtre, au concert, au stade)* season-ticket holder

abonnement [abɔnmɑ̃] **NM 1** *(à un journal, à une revue, au téléphone etc)* subscription; **prendre un a. à** to take out a subscription to **2** *(pour un trajet, au théâtre, au concert, au stade)* season ticket; **prendre un a.** to take out a season ticket **3** *(tarif → pour gaz, électricité)* standing charge; *Tél* line rental; **a. à un service en ligne** on-line subscription

abonner [3] [abɔne] **VT 1 a. qn à qch** *(journal)* to take out a subscription for sb to sth; *(théâtre, concert, stade)* to buy sb a season ticket for sth; **être abonné à un journal** to subscribe to a paper
2 *(pour un service)* **être abonné au gaz** to have gas; **être abonné au téléphone** to have a phone, *Br* to be on the phone; *Hum* **encore une contravention? décidément, tu es abonné!** another parking ticket? you're making rather a habit of this, aren't you?; *Hum* **je suis encore tombé à ski, à croire que je suis abonné!** I took another tumble on the ski slopes, story of my life!
▸**s'abonner** **VPR le trajet revient moins cher si l'on s'abonne** the journey works out cheaper with a season ticket; **s'a. à** *(journal)* to take out a subscription to; *(théâtre, concert, stade)* to buy a season ticket for

abonnir [32] [abɔnir] **VT** to improve
▸**s'abonnir** **VPR** to improve

abonnissement [abɔnismɑ̃] **NM** improvement

abord [abɔr] **NM 1** *(contact)* **elle est d'un a. déconcertant/chaleureux** she has an offputting/a warm manner; **être d'un a. facile/difficile** to be approachable/unapproachable
2 *(accès → à une côte)* approach; *(→ à une maison)* access; **d'un a. facile** *(demeure)* easy to get to; *(texte)* easy to understand *or* to get to grips with
□ **abords** **NMPL** *(alentours)* surroundings; *(d'une ville)* outskirts; **les abords de la tour** the area around the tower
□ **aux abords** **ADV** all around; **dans le château et aux abords** in and around the castle
□ **aux abords de** **PRÉP aux abords de la ville** on the outskirts of the town; **aux abords du château/de la maison** (in the area) around the castle/house
□ **d'abord** **ADV 1** *(en premier lieu)* first; **il vaut mieux en parler d'a.** it's better to talk about it first; **il faudrait (tout) d'a. avoir l'argent et le temps** first you'd need the money and the time; **nous irons (tout) d'a. à Rome** we'll go to Rome first; **pense d'a. à tes études!** think about your studies first!
2 *(au début)* at first, initially, to begin with; **d'a., elle a été gentille** at first *or* initially she was nice; **j'ai cru (tout) d'a. qu'il s'agissait d'une blague** at first *or* to begin with I thought it was a joke
3 *(introduisant une restriction)* to start with, for a start; **d'a., tu n'es même pas prêt!** to start with *or* for a start, you're not even ready!; **d'a., il ne dit jamais bonjour** for a start, he never says hello
4 *(de toute façon)* anyway; **je n'ai jamais aimé ça, d'a.** I've never liked it anyway; **et puis d'a., qu'est-ce que tu veux?** and anyway, what do you want?
5 *Suisse (tout de suite)* immediately; *(bientôt)* soon
□ **dès l'abord** **ADV** at the outset, from the (very) beginning
□ **de prime abord, au premier abord** **ADV** at first sight *or* glance
□ **en abord** **ADJ** *Naut* close to the side

abordabilité [abɔrdabilite] **ADJ** *Can* affordability

abordable [abɔrdabl] **ADJ 1** *(peu cher → prix)* reasonable; *(→ produit)* reasonably priced, affordable; **les fraises ne sont plus abordables** it's impossible even to think of buying strawberries now **2** *(ouvert → patron, célébrité)* approachable **3** *(facile → texte)* accessible; *(→ problème)* that can be discussed **4** *Naut (côte)* accessible; **le rivage n'était pas a.** the shore was not easy to approach

abordage [abɔrdaʒ] **NM** *Naut* **1** *(manœuvre → d'assaut)* boarding; *(→ avec un éperon)* grappling; **à l'a.!** stand by to repel boarders! **2** *(collision)* collision; **l'a. s'est produit à la sortie du chenal** the two boats collided as they came out of the fairway **3** *(approche → du rivage)* coming alongside; *(→ d'un quai)* berthing

aborder [3] [abɔrde] **VT 1** *(accoster → passant)* to accost, to walk up to, to approach; **on n'aborde pas les gens dans la rue!** you don't just walk up to people in the street!; **elle s'est fait a. dans la rue** she was accosted in the street; **quand le policier l'a abordé** when the detective came *or* walked up to him; **quand vas-tu l'a. pour cette augmentation?** when are you going to approach him about your pay rise?
2 *(arriver à l'entrée de)* to enter; **les chevaux abordent la dernière ligne droite** the horses are now entering the home straight; **je suis tombé de vélo au moment où j'abordais la dernière montée/le virage** I fell off my bike as I was coming up to the last climb/the bend
3 *(faire face à → nouvelle vie)* to embark on; *(→ tâche)* to tackle, to get to grips with; *(→ retraite)* to approach; **à 18 ans, on est prêt à a. la vie** when you're 18, you're ready to start out in life; **comment a. l'ascension?** how should one tackle the climb?
4 *(se mettre à examiner → texte, problème)* to approach; **on n'aborde Pascal qu'en dernière année** we only start studying Pascal in the final year; **chez nous, on n'abordait pas ces sujets-là** we never used to mention those topics in our house; **il n'a pas eu le temps d'a. le sujet** he didn't have time to get onto *or* to broach the subject; **11 heures, et nous n'avons même pas abordé la nouvelle motion!** 11 o'clock, and we haven't even got round to discussing the new motion!
5 *Naut (attaquer)* to board; *(percuter)* to collide with, to ram into
VI to touch *or* to reach land; **nous abordons à Gênes demain** we reach Genoa tomorrow

aborigène [abɔriʒɛn] **ADJ 1** *(autochtone)* aboriginal; *(d'Australie)* Aboriginal, native Australian **2** *Bot* indigenous
NMF *(autochtone)* aborigine; *(autochtone d'Australie)* Aborigine, Aboriginal; **les aborigènes d'Australie** the (Australian) Aborigines, native Australians

abortif, -ive [abɔrtif, -iv] **ADJ** abortive
NM *Méd* abortifacient, ecbolic

abot [abo] **NM** *(d'un cheval)* clog, hobble

abouchement [abuʃmɑ̃] **NM 1** *(de deux tubes)* butt-joining **2** *Méd* anastomosis

aboucher [3] [abuʃe] **VT 1** *(tuyaux)* to butt, to join up, to join end to end **2** *(gens)* to bring together; **a. qn avec qn** to put sb in touch *or* contact with sb
▸**s'aboucher** **VPR s'a. avec qn** *(se mettre en rapport avec qn)* to get in touch with sb; *(se lier avec qn)* to team up with sb

Abou Dhabi [abudabi] = **Abu Dhabi**

abouler [3] [abule] *Fam* **VT** to hand over▪, to give over▪; **aboule ton fric!** cough up!; **la clé, là, aboule!** sling us that key, will you!
▸**s'abouler** **VPR** to turn up, to show up, to roll up; **tu t'aboules?** you coming?

aboulie [abuli] **NF** *Psy* abulia, aboulia

aboulique [abulik] *Psy* **ADJ** abulic, aboulic
NMF abulia *or* aboulia sufferer

Abou-Simbel [abusimbɛl] **NM** *Géog* Abu Simbel

about [abu] NM Tech butt (of a beam)

aboutage [abutaʒ] NM Menuis (action, résultat) finger jointing

aboutement [abutmã] NM Tech (joint) butt or butted joint; (fait d'assembler) butt-joining, joining end-to-end

abouter [3] [abute] VT Tech to join end-to-end, to butt

abouti, -e [abuti] ADJ 1 (projet, démarche) successful 2 (œuvre) accomplished

aboutir [32] [abutir] VI 1 (réussir → projet, personne) to succeed; **l'entreprise n'a pas abouti** the venture fell through or never came to anything; **une enquête qui n'aboutira pas** an enquiry which will come to nothing; **faire a. des négociations** to bring talks to a satisfactory conclusion

2 (finir) **le chemin aboutit sur la berge du fleuve** the path leads to the river bank; **a. en prison** to end up in prison; **toi, tu vas a. en pension!** you'll end up being sent away to boarding school, you will!

▫ **aboutir à** VT IND 1 (voie, rue) to end at or in, to lead to; (fleuve) to end in; **cette route aboutit à la prison** this road ends at the prison; **où aboutit cette allée?** where does this lane go to or end up?

2 (avoir pour résultat) to lead to, to result in; **cela aboutira à une guerre** that will lead to a war; **de bonnes intentions qui n'aboutissent à rien** good intentions which come to nothing; **tu aboutiras au même résultat** you'll arrive at or get the same result; **j'ai abouti à la conclusion que...** I finally concluded or came to the conclusion that...; **a. à un compromis** to come to a compromise; **à quelle décision veux-tu nous faire a.?** which decision are you leading us up to?

aboutissant [abutisã] NM Littéraire (conclusion) (final) outcome, result; (résultat positif) success

▫ **aboutissants** NMPL abuttals; Fig **les tenants et les aboutissants** the ins and outs

aboutissement [abutismã] NM (conclusion) (final) outcome, result; (résultat positif) success

above the line [œbɔvzəlajn] ADJ (coûts, dépenses) above-the-line

aboyer [13] [abwaje] VI 1 (chien) to bark; (chien de meute) to bay 2 Fig (personne) to bark; **a. après ou contre qn** to yell at sb 3 (locution) **a. à la lune** to howl at the moon; Fig to complain to no avail

aboyeur, -euse [abwajœr, -øz] ADJ barking

abracadabra [abrakadabra] NM abracadabra

abracadabrant, -e [abrakadabrã, -ãt] ADJ Fam incredible

abracadabrantesque [abrakadabrãtɛsk] ADJ Fam Hum incredible, out of this world

Abraham [abraam] NPR Bible Abraham

abraser [3] [abraze] VT to wear off, Sout to abrade

abrasif, -ive [abrazif, -iv] ADJ abrasive
NM abrasive

abrasimètre [abrazimɛtr] NM abrasimeter, abrasion tester

abrasion [abrazjɔ̃] NF 1 (action de frotter) abrasion, wearing off; (résultat) abrasion 2 Géol abrasion

abrasive [abraziv] voir abrasif

abréaction [abreaksjɔ̃] NF Psy abreaction

abréagir [32] [abreaʒir] VI Psy to abreact

abrégé [abreʒe] NM 1 (d'un texte) summary; **faire un a. de qch** to make a summary of sth, to summarize sth 2 (livre) abstract; **un a. d'histoire de France** a short history of France; **un a. de philosophie** a short guide to philosophy

▫ **en abrégé** ADJ (mot, phrase) in abbreviated form ADV (écrire) in brief, in an abridged version; **en a., voici ce qui s'est passé** here's what happened in a nutshell

abrègement [abrɛʒmã] NM (d'un texte) shortening, abridgement; (d'un mot) abbreviation; (d'une syllabe) shortening 2 (d'un délai) shortening; (d'un congé) cutting short, curtailing

abréger [22] [abreʒe] VT 1 (interrompre → vacances) to curtail, to cut short, to shorten; (→ vie) to cut short, to put an (early) end to; **la pluie a abrégé le pique-nique** the rain put an early end to the picnic, the picnic was cut short by the rain; **pour a. votre attente** so as not to keep you waiting; Euph **a. les souffrances de qn** to put an end to sb's suffering

2 (tronquer → discours) to cut; (→ texte) to cut, to abridge; (→ conversation) to cut short; (→ mot) to abbreviate, Sout to truncate

USAGE ABSOLU Fam **abrège!** get to the point!

▫ **pour abréger** ADV **Catherine, ou Cath pour a.** Catherine, or Cath for short; **pour a., nous avons échoué** to cut a long story short, we failed

▫ **s'abréger** VPR to be abbreviated or shortened (à to)

abreuvement [abrœvmã] NM watering

abreuver [5] [abrœve] VT 1 (faire boire → animaux) to water 2 Fig **a. qn de critiques** to heap criticism upon sb; **a. qn d'insultes** to shower sb with abuse; **elle l'abreuvait d'éloges** she heaped praise upon him; **nous sommes abreuvés d'images de violence** we get swamped with violent images

▫ **s'abreuver** VPR 1 (animal) to drink 2 Fam (personne) to drink▪; Hum **c'est là qu'ils vont s'a.** it's their watering hole

abreuvoir [abrœvwar] NM 1 (bac) (drinking) trough; (plan d'eau) watering place; **mener les chevaux à l'a.** to lead the horses to water, to water the horses 2 Can Vieilli drinking fountain

abréviatif, -ive [abrevjatif, -iv] ADJ abbreviatory

abréviation [abrevjasjɔ̃] NF abbreviation

abréviative [abrevjativ] voir abréviatif

abri [abri] NM 1 (cabane, toit, refuge) shelter; **a. antiatomique ou antinucléaire** (nuclear) fallout shelter; **a. anti-aérien** air-raid shelter; **a. à vélos** bicycle shed

2 Fig refuge; **un a. contre la solitude** a refuge from or a protection against or a guard against loneliness

▫ **à l'abri** ADV 1 (des intempéries) **être à l'a.** to be sheltered; **mets ton vélo à l'a., il va se mouiller** put your bike away, it'll get wet; **mettre qn à l'a.** to find shelter for sb; **se mettre à l'a.** to take cover, to shelter

2 (en lieu sûr) in a safe place; **j'ai mis ma collection de verres à l'a.** I've put my collection of glasses away in a safe place; **mettre sa fortune à l'a. dans le pétrole** to invest one's money safely in oil

▫ **à l'abri de** PRÉP 1 **être à l'a. de** (pluie, chaleur) to be sheltered from; (obus) to be sheltered or shielded from; (regards) to be hidden from; **se mettre à l'a. de** (pluie, chaleur) to (take) shelter from; (obus) to take cover from

2 Fig **nos économies nous mettront à l'a. du besoin** our savings will shield us against poverty or will protect us from hardship; **à l'a. des contrôles** safe from checks; **à l'a. du danger** safe from danger; **à l'a. de tout soupçon** free from (all) suspicion; **personne n'est à l'a. d'une erreur/d'un maître-chanteur** anyone can make a mistake/fall victim to a blackmailer; **il l'a mis dans un tiroir à l'a. des regards indiscrets** he locked it in a drawer safe from prying eyes; **composez votre code confidentiel à l'a. des regards indiscrets** (message sur l'écran d'un distributeur automatique) ≃ please enter your PIN (number)

Abribus® [abribys] NM bus shelter

abricot [abriko] NM 1 Bot (fruit) apricot 2 (couleur) apricot
ADJ INV apricot, apricot-coloured

abricoté, -e [abrikɔte] ADJ apricot-flavoured

abricotier [abrikɔtje] NM Bot apricot tree

abricotine [abrikɔtin] NF Suisse apricot brandy

abrier [10] [abrije] Can VT to cover up (to protect from the cold)

▫ **s'abrier** VPR to wrap up (well)

abri-sous-roche [abrisurɔʃ] (pl **abris-sous-roche**) NM Géol rock-shelter

abrité, -e [abrite] ADJ (du soleil) shady; (du vent) sheltered

abriter [3] [abrite] VT 1 (protéger → de la pluie, des intempéries) to shelter; (→ du soleil) to shade, to shelter; **a. qn/qch de la pluie** to shelter sb/sth from the rain; **a. qn/qch du soleil** to shade sb/sth; **tu veux que je t'abrite sous mon parapluie?** do you want to shelter under my umbrella?; **abritant ses yeux avec un journal** shading her eyes with a newspaper; **cet auvent nous abrite des regards indiscrets** (des passants) the

awning gives us some privacy; (des intrus) the awning shields us from prying eyes

2 (loger → personnes) to house, to accommodate; (→ société, machine) to house

▫ **s'abriter** VPR **s'a. des tirs** to take cover; **s'a. de la pluie/du vent** to (take) shelter from the rain/ from the wind; **s'a. du soleil** to shade oneself from the sun; Fig **s'a. derrière la loi/ses parents** to hide behind the law/one's parents

abrivent [abrivã] NM windbreak

abrogatif, -ive [abrɔgatif, -iv] ADJ Jur abrogative

abrogation [abrɔgasjɔ̃] NF Jur repeal, rescinding, abrogation

abrogative [abrɔgativ] voir abrogatif

abrogatoire [abrɔgatwar] ADJ Jur abrogative

abrogeable [abrɔʒabl] ADJ Jur repealable

abroger [17] [abrɔʒe] VT Jur to repeal, to rescind, to abrogate

abroutissement [abrutismã] NM Zool (d'un animal sauvage) browsing

abrupt, -e [abrypt] ADJ 1 (raide → côte) steep, abrupt; (→ versant) sheer 2 (brusque → manières) abrupt, brusque; (→ refus) blunt, abrupt, curt; (→ personne) short, sharp, abrupt; (→ changement) abrupt, sudden, sharp
NM steep slope

abruptement [abryptəmã] ADV (répondre) abruptly, brusquely, curtly; (changer) abruptly, suddenly; **ne le lui dis pas trop a.** don't just blurt it out in front of him/her

abruti, -e [abryti] NM,F Fam idiot; **arrête de rire comme un a.** stop laughing like an idiot; **regarde où tu vas, a.!** look where you're going, you idiot!; **quelle abrutie, j'ai oublié ton livre** fool that I am or like a fool, I've forgotten your book

abrutir [32] [abrytir] VT 1 (abêtir) to turn into an idiot

2 (étourdir) to stupefy; **abruti de soleil** dazed by sunshine; **abruti de fatigue** numb or dazed with tiredness; **abruti par l'alcool** stupefied with drink; **après trois heures d'algèbre, je suis complètement abruti!** after three hours of algebra, I feel completely punch-drunk!

3 (accabler) **a. qn de travail** to overwork sb; **a. qn de conseils** to pester sb with endless advice

▫ **s'abrutir** VPR 1 (s'accabler) **s'a. de travail** to overwork oneself, to work oneself into the ground

2 (s'abêtir) to turn into an idiot; **on s'abrutit à trop regarder la télévision** too much television rots the brain

abrutissant, -e [abrytisã, -ãt] ADJ 1 (qui rend bête) mind-numbing 2 (qui étourdit) stupefying 3 (qui fatigue) wearing, exhausting

abrutissement [abrytismã] NM mindless state; **l'a. des enfants par la télévision** the mind-numbing effects of television on children

Abruzzes [abryz] NFPL **les A.** the Abruzzi

ABS [abeɛs] NM INV Aut (abrév **Antiblockiersystem**) ABS

Absalon [apsalɔ̃] NPR Bible Absalom

abscisse [apsis] NF Math abscissa

abscons, -e [apskɔ̃, -ɔ̃s] ADJ Littéraire abstruse

absence [apsãs] NF 1 (fait de n'être pas là) absence; **cette décision a été prise pendant mon a.** this decision was taken in my absence or while I was away; **sa troisième a.** (à l'école) the third time he's/she's been away from or missed school; (au travail) the third time he's/she's been off work; (à une réunion) the third time he's/she's stayed away from or not attended the meeting; **nous avons regretté votre a.** we were sorry that you weren't with us; **on a remarqué ses absences répétées** his/her persistent absenteeism didn't go unnoticed; **comment vais-je supporter ton a.?** how shall I cope with you not being there or around?

2 (de goût, d'imagination etc) lack, absence; **a. d'idéaux** lack of ideals; **une rassurante a. de préjugés** a reassuring lack of prejudice

3 (défaillance) **j'ai eu une a. ou un moment d'a.** my mind went blank; **elle a des absences ou des moments d'a.** her mind wanders at times, at times she can be absent-minded

4 Jur absence

5 Méd **a. (épileptique)** epileptic vertigo

▫ **en l'absence de** PRÉP in the absence of; **en mon a.** during or in my absence; **en l'a. de mon**

fils in my son's absence, while my son is/was away; **en l'a. de symptômes, il m'est difficile de me prononcer** since there are no symptoms, it is hard for me to say; **en l'a. de toute information** faced with a total lack of information, in the absence of any information

absent, -e [apsã, -ãt] **ADJ 1** (*personne → de l'école*) absent; (*→ du travail*) off work, absent; (*→ de son domicile*) away; **il était a. de la réunion** he was not present at the meeting; **il est a. de Paris en ce moment** he isn't in Paris at the moment

2 (*inattentif*) absent; **regard a.** vacant look; **d'un air a.** absent-mindedly

3 (*chose*) missing; (*sentiment*) lacking; **une plante absente de nos montagnes** a plant which cannot be found on our mountains; **un regard d'où toute tendresse est absente** a look entirely devoid of tenderness

NM,F (*du travail, de l'école*) absentee; (*dans une famille*) absent person; **on ne fait pas cours, il y a trop d'absents** we're not having a lesson today, there are too many pupils missing *or* away; **les Russes ont été les grands absents lors de la Coupe du Monde** the Russians were the most notable absentees from the World Cup; *Littéraire* **elle rêvait à l'a.** (*à une personne décédée*) she was dreaming of her dear departed

---

Allusion

Les absents ont toujours tort

This expression is used in two slightly different contexts. In the first, a speaker describes a delightful occasion that the listener has missed. The latter exclaims "If only I'd been there!", and the speaker rejoins **Les absents ont toujours tort**. This means literally "It is always a mistake to be absent" and more loosely "You really should have been there!". In the second usage, someone has failed to appear at a crucial gathering, where he had a role to play. By not attending, he has not only waived any right to criticize the proceedings, but laid himself open to blame if things go wrong. Here again, the literal meaning is "It is always a mistake to be absent", and more loosely in this context "The people who are not there always get blamed."

---

absentéisme [apsãteism] **NM** absenteeism; **a. scolaire** truancy

absentéiste [apsãteist] **ADJ** absentee

NMF absentee; **les absentéistes** (*au travail*) persistent absentees

absenter [3] [apsãte] **s'absenter VPR** to be absent; **s'a. de son travail** to be off *or* to stay away from work; **s'a. du lycée** to be away from *or* to miss school; **je ne m'étais absentée que quelques minutes** I'd only gone out for a few minutes

absidal, -e, -aux, -ales [apsidal, -o] **ADJ** *Archit* apsidal

abside [apsid] **NF** *Archit* apse

absidial, -e, -aux, -ales [apsidjal, -o] = **absidal**

absidiole [apsidjol] **NF** *Archit* apsidiole

absinthe [apsɛ̃t] **NF 1** (*alcool*) absinthe **2** *Bot* wormwood, absinthe

🕮

'L'Absinthe' *Degas* 'Absinthe'

absinthisme [apsɛ̃tism] **NM** *Méd* absinthism

absolu, -e [apsɔly] **ADJ 1** (*total → liberté*) absolute, complete; (*→ repos*) complete; (*→ silence*) total; **un dénuement a.** abject poverty; **en cas d'absolue nécessité** when absolutely necessary; **nous sommes dans l'impossibilité absolue de vous aider** we are quite unable to help you; **vous avez notre soutien a.** you have our unconditional support

2 *Pol* (*pouvoir, monarque, majorité*) absolute

3 (*sans nuances*) absolute; **elle voit les choses de manière absolue** she sees things in absolute terms *or* in black and white

4 (*intransigeant*) uncompromising, rigid; **refus a. d'obtempérer** outright refusal to comply

5 *Chim, Math & Phys* absolute

6 *Ling* (*ablatif, construction*) absolute; **l'emploi a. d'un verbe transitif** the absolute use of a transitive verb

NM 1 *Phil* **l'a.** the Absolute

2 *Ling* absolute construction

◻ **dans l'absolu ADV** in absolute terms

absoluité [apsɔlyite] **NF** absoluteness

absolument [apsɔlymã] **ADV 1** (*entièrement → croire, avoir raison*) absolutely, entirely; (*→ ravi, faux*) absolutely, completely; (*→ défendu*) strictly; **personne, a. personne ne doit sortir** no one, absolutely no one must go out; **a. pas** not at all; **a. rien** absolutely nothing, nothing whatsoever

2 (*à tout prix*) absolutely; **il faut a. leur parler** we (absolutely *or* simply) must speak to them, it's imperative that we speak to them; **elle veut a. venir avec moi** she insists on coming with me

3 (*oui*) absolutely; **vous y croyez? – a.!** do you believe in that? – absolutely *or* totally!; **il a raison! – a.!** he's right! – absolutely!

4 *Ling* absolutely; **employé a.** used absolutely *or* in an absolute construction

absolution [apsɔlysjɔ̃] **NF 1** *Rel* absolution; **donner l'a. à qn** to give sb absolution; **je vous donne l'a. de vos péchés** I absolve you of your sins **2** *Jur* acquittal

absolutisme [apsɔlytism] **NM** *Pol* absolutism

absolutiste [apsɔlytist] *Pol* **ADJ** absolutist

NMF absolutist

absolutoire [apsɔlytwar] **ADJ** *Jur* absolving, absolutory

absolvait *etc voir* **absoudre**

absorbable [apsɔrbabl] **ADJ** absorbable

absorbance [apsɔrbãs] **NF** *Phys* absorbance, optical density transmission

absorbant, -e [apsɔrbã, -ãt] **ADJ 1** (*tissu*) absorbent **2** (*lecture*) absorbing, gripping **3** *Phys* absorptive **4** *Bot* **poils absorbants** root hairs

absorber [3] [apsɔrbe] **VT 1** (*éponger → gén*) to absorb, to soak up; (*→ avec un buvard*) to blot; (*→ avec une éponge*) to sponge off

2 (*lumière*) to absorb; (*bruit*) to absorb, to deaden

3 (*consommer → aliment*) to take, to consume; (*→ boisson*) to drink; (*→ bénéfices, capitaux*) to absorb; *Écon* (*→ entreprise*) to take over, to absorb; **cette manœuvre vise à faire a. la Dalco par l'Imalux** this move is designed to allow Imalux to take over Dalco

4 (*préoccuper → sujet: travail*) to absorb, to engross, to occupy; (*→ sujet: pensée*) to absorb, to grip; **très absorbée par son activité politique** very much engrossed in her political activities; **être absorbé dans ses pensées** to be lost *or* deep in thought

5 (*faire s'intégrer → réfugiés, nouveaux élèves*) to absorb

▸ **s'absorber VPR** **s'a. dans** to become absorbed in; **s'a. dans un livre** to be engrossed in a book; **s'a. dans ses pensées** to be lost *or* deep in thought

absorbeur [apsɔrbœr] **NM** absorber

absorptiométrie [apsɔrpsjometri] **NF** *Méd* absorptiometry

absorption [apsɔrpsjɔ̃] **NF 1** (*ingestion*) swallowing, taking; **l'a. d'un somnifère n'est pas sans risques** taking a sleeping pill is not without risk **2** (*pénétration*) absorption; **masser jusqu'à a. complète par la peau** massage well into the skin **3** (*intégration*) assimilation; *Écon* (*d'une entreprise*) takeover **4** *Littéraire* (*concentration de l'esprit*) absorption, engrossment **5** *Physiol* absorption

absorption-fusion [apsɔrpsjɔ̃fyziɔ̃] (*pl* **absorptions-fusions**) **NF** *Écon* merger

absorptivité [apsɔrptivite] **NF** *Phys* absorbency

absoudre [87] [apsudr] **VT 1** *Rel* to absolve; **a. qn de ses péchés** to absolve sb from his/her sins, to forgive sb his/her sins **2** *Littéraire* (*pardonner*) to absolve; **je l'ai absous de ses erreurs de jeunesse** I forgave him his youthful indiscretions **3** *Jur* to dismiss

absoute [apsut] **NF** *Rel* final absolution

abstème [apstɛm] *Rel* **ADJ** abstaining

NMF abstainer

abstenir [40] [apstənir] **s'abstenir VPR 1** *Pol* to abstain

2 s'a. de (*éviter de*) to refrain *or* to abstain from; **s'a. de fumer** to refrain from smoking; **abstiens-toi de la critiquer** don't criticize her; **s'a. de tout commentaire** to refrain from comment

USAGE ABSOLU (*ne pas agir*) **dans ce cas, mieux vaut s'a.** in that case, it's better not to do

anything; **pas sérieux s'a.** (*dans une offre d'emploi*) serious applicants only; (*dans une petite annonce*) no timewasters, please; **agences s'a.** (*dans une petite annonce*) no agencies, please; *Prov* **dans le doute, abstiens-toi** when in doubt, don't

abstention [apstãsjɔ̃] **NF 1** *Pol* abstention; **a. électorale** abstention **2** (*renoncement*) abstention **3** *Jur* **a. délictueuse** failure to act

abstentionnisme [apstãsjonism] **NM** *Pol* abstention

abstentionniste [apstãsjonist] *Pol* **ADJ** abstentionist

NMF abstainer

abstenu, -e [apstəny] **PP** *voir* **abstenir**

abstient *etc voir* **abstenir**

abstinence [apstinãs] **NF 1** *Rel* abstinence; **faire a.** to refrain from eating meat **2** (*chasteté*) abstinence **3** (*tempérance*) abstemiousness

abstinent, -e [apstinã, -ãt] **ADJ 1** *Rel* abstinent **2** (*chaste*) abstinent, chaste **3** (*tempérant*) abstemious

NM,F 1 *Rel* abstinent person **2** (*chaste*) abstinent *or* chaste person **3** (*tempérant*) abstemious person

abstint *etc voir* **abstenir**

abstract [apstrakt] **NM** (*résumé*) abstract

abstraction [apstraksjɔ̃] **NF 1** (*notion*) abstraction, abstract idea; **se perdre dans des abstractions** to lose oneself in abstractions; **l'a.** the theoretical plane; **un esprit capable d'a.** a mind capable of abstract thought

2 (*fait d'isoler*) abstraction; **faire a. de** (*ignorer*) to take no account of, to ignore, to disregard; **a. faite de** apart from, leaving aside; **a. faite de la forme** style apart; **a. faite de son âge** disregarding his/her age

3 *Beaux-Arts* **l'a.** abstract *or* non-representational art; **l'a. lyrique** lyrical abstraction

Abstraction-Création [apstraksjɔ̃kreasjɔ̃] **NF** *Beaux-Arts* = influential group of artists, associated with the constructivist movement, active in Paris in the 1930s

abstractionnisme [apstraksjonism] **NM** *Phil* abstractionism

abstractionniste [apstraksjonist] *Phil* **ADJ** abstractionist

NMF abstractionist

abstraire [112] [apstrɛr] **VT 1** (*séparer*) to abstract **2** *Phil* to abstract

▸ **s'abstraire VPR** to cut oneself off

abstrait, -e [apstrɛ, -ɛt] **PP** *voir* **abstraire**

ADJ 1 (*conçu par l'esprit*) abstract

2 (*non appliqué → science, pensée*) theoretical, abstract, pure

3 (*ardu*) abstract, *Péj* obscure

4 *Beaux-Arts* abstract, non-representational

5 *Ling & Math* abstract

NM 1 *Phil* **l'a.** the abstract; (*notions*) abstract ideas, the theoretical plane

2 *Beaux-Arts* (*art*) abstract *or* non-representational art; (*artiste*) abstract *or* non-representational artist

◻ **dans l'abstrait ADV** in the abstract; **dans l'a., il est facile de critiquer** it's easy to be critical if you just look at things in the abstract

abstraitement [apstrɛtmã] **ADV** in the abstract, abstractly

abstrayait *etc voir* **abstraire**

abstrus, -e [apstry, -yz] **ADJ** abstruse

absurde [apsyrd] **ADJ 1** (*remarque, idée*) absurd, preposterous; (*personne*) ridiculous, absurd; **ne soyez pas a.!** don't be absurd!, don't talk nonsense!; **d'une manière a.** absurdly **2** (*oubli, contretemps*) absurd **3** *Phil* absurd

NM 1 (*absurdité*) absurd **2** *Littérature, Théât & Phil* **l'a.** the absurd

absurdement [apsyrdəmã] **ADV** absurdly, ludicrously

absurdité [apsyrdite] **NF 1** (*irrationalité*) absurdity **2** (*parole, action*) absurdity; **ne dis pas d'absurdités!** don't be absurd!, don't talk nonsense!; **cette réaction est une a.** this reaction is completely absurd

Abu Dhabi [abudabi] **NM** *Géog* Abu Dhabi

Abuja [abuʒa] **NM** *Géog* Abuja

abus [aby] **NM 1** (*excès → de café*) excess consumption; (*→ de stupéfiants, d'alcool*) abuse; **a. d'alcool** excessive drinking; **l'a. de**

somnifères taking too many sleeping pills; **faire des a.** to overindulge *(in food or drink)*; **il y a de l'a.** that's a bit much *or* over the top

2 *(injustice)* injustice; **une pratique qui a donné lieu à des a.** a practice which has given rise to abuse; **les a.** excesses

3 *Jur* misuse; **a. d'autorité** misuse *or* abuse of authority; **a. de biens sociaux** misappropriation of funds; **a. de confiance** breach of trust; **a. de droit** abuse of power; **a. de faiblesse** exploitation of a vulnerable person; **a. de jouissance** infringement of ownership; **a. de position dominante** abuse of dominant position; **a. de pouvoir** abuse of power

4 *Ling* **a. de langage** misuse of language

abuser [3] [abyze] VT *Littéraire* to deceive, to mislead

USAGE ABSOLU *(exagérer)* **je crains d'a.** I wouldn't like to impose; **je veux bien t'aider mais là, tu abuses!** I don't mind helping you but there is a limit!; **vraiment, il abuse!** he's going a bit far *or* pushing it a bit!; *Fam* **dites donc, la queue c'est pour tout le monde, faudrait pas a.!** hey, can you not queue up like everybody else?

❏ **abuser de** VT IND **1** *(consommer excessivement)* to overuse; **a. de la boisson** to drink too much; **a. des féculents** to eat too much starchy food; **il ne faut pas a. des bonnes choses** good things should be enjoyed in moderation, enough is as good as a feast; **n'abuse pas de ce médicament** don't take too much of this medicine, only take this medicine in small doses; **a. de ses forces** to overtax oneself

2 *(mal utiliser → pouvoir, privilège)* to abuse, to misuse; **le directeur abuse de son autorité** the manager is abusing his position

3 *(exploiter → ami, bonté, patience)* to take advantage of, to exploit; *(→ confiance)* to abuse; **tu abuses de lui** you take advantage of him; **elle abuse de la liberté que je lui donne** she takes advantage of the freedom I allow her; **je ne voudrais pas a. de votre gentillesse** I don't want to impose; **je ne veux pas a. de votre temps** I don't want to take up your time; **tu abuses de nos liens familiaux** you're exploiting *or* taking advantage of the fact that we're family; **a. de la situation** to take unfair advantage of the situation

4 *Euph (violer)* to abuse sexually

▸**s'abuser** VPR to be mistaken; **si je ne m'abuse** if I'm not mistaken, correct me if I'm wrong

abusif, -ive [abyzif, -iv] ADJ **1** *(immodéré)* excessive; **l'emploi a. de la force** excessive *or* unwarranted use of force; **l'usage a. des médicaments** the overprescribing *or* excessive use of prescription drugs; **100 euros, c'est a.!** 100 euros, that's a bit much! **2** *(outrepassant ses droits → père, mère)* domineering **3** *(incorrect → emploi)* incorrect; **l'emploi a. du mot "réaliser"** the misuse *or* the incorrect use of the word "réaliser"

Abu Simbel [abusimbɛl] = **Abou-Simbel**

abusive [abyziv] *voir* **abusif**

abusivement [abyzivmɑ̃] ADV **1** *(de façon injuste)* wrongly, unfairly **2** *(de façon incorrecte)* wrongly, improperly; **le terme "réaliser" est employé a.** the word "réaliser" is used incorrectly **3** *(de façon excessive)* excessively

abyme [abim] NM **tableau/film/pièce avec mise en a.** painting within a painting/film within a film/play within a play

abyssal, -e, -aux, -ales [abisal, -o] ADJ *Géog (faune, relief)* abyssal; **les fosses abyssales** deep-sea trenches

abysse [abis] NM **l'a.** the abyssal zone

abyssin, -e [abisɛ̃, -in] ADJ **1** *Hist* Abyssinian **2** *Zool (chat)* Abyssinian

    NM *Zool (chat)* Abyssinian (cat)

❏ **Abyssin, -e** NM,F Abyssinian

Abyssinie [abisini] NF **l'A.** Abyssinia

abyssinien, -enne [abisinjɛ̃, -ɛn] ADJ *Hist* Abyssinian

❏ **Abyssinien, -enne** NM,F Abyssinian

abzyme [abzim] NF *Chim* abzyme

AC 1 *(abrév écrite* **appellation contrôlée***)* appellation contrôlée *(official certification guaranteeing the quality of French produce, especially wines and cheeses)* **2** *Mktg (abrév écrite* **audience cumulée***)* cumulative audience

ac 1 *Fin (abrév écrite* **argent comptant***)* cash **2** *Compta (abrév écrite* **année courante***)* current year

acabit [akabi] NM *Péj* **de cet a.** of that type; **son amie est du même a.** he/she and his/her friend are two of a kind; **ils sont tous du même a.** they are all (pretty much) the same, *Br* they are all much of a muchness

acacia [akasja] NM *Bot* acacia; **faux a.** false acacia, robinia; **a. du Sénégal** gum arabic tree

académicien, -enne [akademisjɛ̃, -ɛn] NM,F *(membre → d'une académie)* academician; *(→ de l'Académie française)* member of the French Academy *or* the Académie française

    NM *Antiq* academic, academician

académie [akademi] NF **1** *(société savante)* learned society, academy; **l'A. Colarossi** = art school established in Paris in the nineteenth century as an alternative to the official "École des Beaux Arts"; **l'A. française** the French Academy, the Académie Française *(learned society of leading men and women of letters)*; **l'A. (des) Goncourt** = literary society whose members choose the winner of the "Prix Goncourt"; **l'A. Julian** = art school established in Paris in 1868 by Rodolphe Julian, as an alternative to the official "École des Beaux Arts"; **l'A. des sciences** the Academy of Science **2** *(école)* academy; **a. de danse/musique** school of dance/music **3** *(salle)* **a. de billard** billiard hall **4** *Admin & Scol Br* ≃ education authority area, *Am* ≃ school district **5** *Beaux-Arts* nude **6** *Fam (corps)* body■, figure■

❏ **d'académie** ADJ *Beaux-Arts* academic

Culture

ACADÉMIE FRANÇAISE

This was originally a group of men of letters who were encouraged by Cardinal Richelieu in 1635 to become an official body. Consisting of 40 distinguished writers ("les Quarante" or "les Immortels"), the Académie's chief task was, and is, to produce a definitive dictionary and to be the ultimate authority in matters concerning the French language.

---

académique [akademik] ADJ **1** *(d'une société savante)* academic; *(de l'Académie française)* of the French Academy *or* the Académie française; **elle occupe un fauteuil a.** *(à l'Académie française)* she is a member of the French Academy *or* the Académie française

2 *Péj (conventionnel)* academic; **danse a.** ballet dancing; **style a.** academic *or* pedantic style **3** *Belg, Suisse & Can Scol* **l'année a.** the academic year

4 *Phil* **philosophe a.** Platonic philosopher

académiquement [akademikmɑ̃] ADV academically

académisme [akademism] NM academicism

acadianisme [akadjanism] NM = word or phrase used in the Acadia region of Canada

Acadie [akadi] NF **l'A.** Acadia

Culture

ACADIE

This area of eastern Canada (now the Maritime Provinces of Nova Scotia and New Brunswick) was under French rule until the Treaty of Utrecht in 1713, when it passed into the hands of the English. Most of the French-speaking "Acadiens" were deported in 1755 (those in Louisiana became known as "Cajuns", a corruption of "Acadians"), but many later returned and today there is a lively French-speaking community in the Maritime Provinces. The Acadian dialect has remained very close to its origins (16th- and 17th-century French, reflecting regional usage at the time) but has also borrowed many words from English.

---

acadien, -enne [akadjɛ̃, -ɛn] ADJ Acadian

    NM *(dialecte)* Acadian

❏ **Acadien, -enne** NM,F Acadian

acagnardi, -e [akaɲardi] ADJ *Can Fam* **1** *(fatigué)* *Br* shattered, *Am* bushed **2** *(bourru)* gruff■, rough■

acajou [akaʒu] NM **1** *(arbre)* mahogany (tree); **a. d'Afrique** African mahogany; **a. d'Amérique**

Centrale *ou* **du Honduras** true mahogany, big-leaf mahogany, Honduras mahogany; **a. à pommes** *(anacardier)* cashew (tree); **a. du Sénégal** Senegal mahogany **2** *(bois)* mahogany

    ADJ INV *(couleur)* mahogany

acalculie [akalkyli] NF *Méd* acalculia

acalèphe [akalɛf] NM *Ich* jellyfish

acalorique [akalɔrik] ADJ noncaloric

acanthacée [akɑ̃tase] *Bot* NF member of the Acanthus family

❏ **acanthacées** NFPL Acanthaceae

acanthe [akɑ̃t] NF **1** *Bot* acanthus **2** *Archit* **(feuille d')a.** acanthus (leaf)

acanthocéphale [akɑ̃tosefal] *Zool* NM acanthocephalan

❏ **acanthocéphales** NMPL Acanthocephala

a cappella, a capella [akapela] *Mus* ADV a cappella

    ADJ INV a cappella

Acapulco [akapylko] NM Acapulco

acardiaque [akardjak] ADJ *Méd* acardiac

acariâtre [akarjɑtr] ADJ *(caractère)* sour; *(personne)* bad-tempered, cantankerous; **être d'humeur a.** to be bad-tempered

acaricide [akarisid] ADJ **un produit a.** an acaricide

    NM acaricide

acarien [akarjɛ̃] NM *Entom* mite, house dust mite, *Spéc* acarid

acariose [akarjoz] NF *Méd* acariasis

acarus [akarys] NM *Entom* mite, *Spéc* acarus; **a. sarcopte** *ou* **de la gale** itch mite

acaule [akol] ADJ *Bot* acaulescent

accablant, -e [akablɑ̃, -ɑ̃t] ADJ *(chaleur)* oppressive; *(preuve, témoignage, vérité)* damning; *(travail)* exhausting; *(douleur)* excruciating; *(chagrin)* overwhelming; **le poids a. des soucis** the heavy burden of worries; **il est d'une stupidité accablante** he's too stupid for words

accablement [akabləmɑ̃] NM **1** *(désespoir)* dejection, despondency; **saisi d'un grand a.** utterly dejected **2** *(dû à la chaleur)* (heat) exhaustion

accabler [3] [akable] VT **1** *(abattre → sujet: fatigue, chaleur)* to overcome, to overwhelm; *(→ sujet: soucis)* to overcome; *(→ sujet: chagrin, deuil, travail)* to overwhelm; **accablé de chagrin** grief-stricken; **accablé de fatigue/par la chaleur** overwhelmed *or* overcome with fatigue/with the heat; **accablé de soucis** careworn; **accablé de dettes** burdened with debts

2 *(accuser → sujet: témoignage)* to condemn; **je ne veux pas l'a. mais il faut reconnaître qu'elle a commis des erreurs** I don't want to be too hard on her but it has to be said that she made some mistakes

3 *(couvrir)* **a. qn d'injures** to heap abuse upon *or* to hurl insults at sb; **a. qn de mépris** to show utter contempt for sb; **a. qn de critiques** to be highly critical of sb; **a. la population d'impôts** to overtax the population; **a. qn de questions** to bombard sb with questions; **a. qn de conseils** to pester sb with advice; **a. qn de sa sollicitude** to be oversolicitous towards sb

accalmie [akalmi] NF *(du bruit, du vent, de la pluie, d'un combat, d'une crise politique)* lull; *(d'une maladie)* temporary improvement; *(de souffrances)* temporary relief *or* respite; *(du commerce)* slack period; *(dans le travail, l'agitation)* break; **pas un instant d'a. dans la journée** not a moment's respite throughout the day; **l'a. qui précède l'orage** the lull or calm before the storm

accaparant, -e [akaparɑ̃, -ɑ̃t] ADJ *(travail, études, enfant)* demanding

accaparement [akaparmɑ̃] NM **1** *Écon (spéculative)* hoarding **2** *(d'une conversation, d'une personne)* monopolization

accaparer [3] [akapare] VT **1** *Écon (marché)* to corner; **a. des marchandises** *(pour contrôler le marché)* to withhold goods from the market

2 *(monopoliser → conversation, personne)* to monopolize; *(→ victoires, récompenses)* to carry off; *(→ places)* to grab; **elle a tout de suite accaparé le fauteuil** she grabbed the armchair right away; **n'accapare pas le téléphone** don't monopolize the phone; **ne laisse pas les enfants t'a.** don't let the children monopolize you **3** *(absorber → sujet: travail, soucis)* to absorb; **il est complètement accaparé par ses études**

he's wrapped up *or* completely absorbed in his studies; **son travail l'accapare** his/her work takes up all his/her time

accapareur, -euse [akaparœr, -øz] NM,F *Péj* hoarder

accastillage [akastijaʒ] NM *Naut* **1** *(ensemble des structures)* superstructure **2** *(quincaillerie marine)* deck fittings

accastiller [3] [akastije] VT *Naut* **1** *(doter d'une structure)* to provide with a superstructure **2** *(équiper en quincaillerie)* to fit out

accédant, -e [aksedɑ̃, -ɑ̃t] NM,F **un a. à la propriété** a new home-owner

accéder [18] [aksede] **accéder à** VT IND **1** *(atteindre → trône)* to accede to; *(→ poste, rang)* to rise to; *(→ indépendance, gloire)* to gain, to attain; *(→ lieu)* to reach; **on accède à la maison par un petit chemin** you get to the house via a narrow path, access to the house is by a narrow path; **a. à la propriété** to become a home-owner; **a. à de hautes responsabilités** to acquire important responsibilities; **faire a. qn au pouvoir** to bring sb to power; **la résolution de l'ONU vise à les faire a. à l'indépendance** the UN resolution is aimed at allowing them to become independent

2 *(accepter → demande, requête)* to grant; *(→ désir)* to meet, to give in to

3 *(connaître → culture)* to attain a degree of; *(→ secrets, documents)* to gain access to

4 *Ordinat (programme)* to access

accelerando [akselerɑ̃do] ADV *Mus* accelerando

accélérateur, -trice [akseleratœr, -tris] ADJ accelerating

NM accelerator; *Chim* accelerant; **a. de bronzage** tanning accelerator; *Ordinat* **a. graphique** graphic *or* graphics accelerator; **a. de particules** particle accelerator

accélération [akselerasjɔ̃] NF **1** *Aut, Tech & Phys* acceleration; **avoir de l'a.** to have good acceleration; **a. de la pesanteur** acceleration of free fall *or* of gravity **2** *(accroissement du rythme → du cœur, du pouls)* acceleration; *(→ d'un processus, de travaux)* speeding up; **l'a. de l'histoire** the gathering pace of historical events

accélératrice [akseleratris] *voir* **accélérateur**

accéléré, -e [akselere] ADJ accelerated; **ils reprirent le travail à un rythme a./la marche à un pas a.** they started working/walking at a faster pace; **un stage a.** a crash course

NM fast motion

□ **en accéléré** ADJ speeded-up, accelerated ADV speeded-up; **montre-moi la scène en a.** show me the scene speeded-up

accélérer [18] [akselere] VT *(allure)* to accelerate; *(rythme cardiaque)* to raise, to increase; *(pouls)* to quicken; *(démarches, travaux)* to speed up; **a. le pas** to quicken one's pace; *Fam* **a. le mouvement** to get things moving; **le gouvernement a décidé de faire a. la réforme** the government has decided to speed up the reform process

VI **1** *Aut* to accelerate; **allez, accélère!** come on, step on it!

2 *Fam (se dépêcher)* **accélère un peu!** come on, get going *or* move!

▸**s'accélérer** VPR *(pouls, cœur)* to beat faster; *(rythme, mouvement)* to accelerate, to speed up

accélérographe [akselerɔgraf] NM accelerograph

accéléromètre [akselerɔmɛtr] NM *Phys* accelerometer

accent [aksɑ̃] NM **1** *(prononciation)* accent; **avoir un a.** to speak with *or* to have an accent; **il n'a pas d'a.** he doesn't have an accent; **elle a un bon a. (en anglais/chinois)** her (English/Chinese) accent is very good; **elle avait l'a. italien** she spoke with an Italian accent; **l'a. du Midi** a southern (French) accent

2 *(de la voix)* stress; **a. de hauteur** pitch; **a. d'intensité** tonic *or* main stress; **a. tonique** tonic accent; *(signe)* stress mark; **a. secondaire** secondary stress; **mettre l'a. sur** to stress; *Fig* to stress, to emphasize

3 *(signe graphique)* accent; **a. grave/circonflexe/aigu** grave/circumflex/acute (accent); **e a. grave/aigu** e grave/acute

4 *Fig (inflexion)* note, accent; **un a. de sincérité/d'émotion** a note of sincerity/of emotion; **avec un a. plaintif** in plaintive tones; **les accents du désespoir/de l'amour** the accents of despair/of love; **avoir l'a. de la vérité** to ring true; *Littéraire* **un poème aux accents baudelairiens** a poem with a Baudelairian flavour to it

□ **accents** NMPL *(son)* **les accents d'un accordéon** the strains of an accordion

accenteur [aksɑ̃tœr] NM *Orn* accentor; **a. alpin** alpine accentor; **a. mouchet** dunnock

accentuable [aksɑ̃tɥabl] ADJ *(voyelle, consonne)* that can take an accent; *(syllabe)* that can be accented *or* stressed

accentuation [aksɑ̃tɥasjɔ̃] NF **1** *(phonétique)* stressing, accentuation; **l'a., en anglais, se définit ainsi** the stress pattern of English is defined as follows; **les règles de l'a. espagnole** the stress rules in Spanish

2 *(système graphique)* use of accents; **faire des fautes d'a.** to put accents in the wrong place

3 *(intensification → d'une ressemblance, d'une différence, des traits)* emphasizing; *(→ d'un effort)* intensification, increase; *(→ du chômage, d'une crise)* increase, rise

accentué, -e [aksɑ̃tɥe] ADJ **1** *(son, syllabe)* stressed, accented; **voyelle non accentuée** unstressed vowel **2** *(dans l'écriture)* accented; **un e a.** an e with an accent, an accented e **3** *(exagéré → traits, défaut)* marked, pronounced; *(→ tendance)* increased, stronger

accentuel, -elle [aksɑ̃tɥɛl] ADJ accentual, stress *(avant n)*, accent *(avant n)*

accentuer [7] [aksɑ̃tɥe] VT **1** *(son, syllabe)* to stress, to accent

2 *(dans l'écriture)* to put an accent on

3 *(rendre plus visible → ressemblance, différence)* to accentuate, to bring out, to emphasize; *(→ forme, traits)* to emphasize, to accentuate, to highlight; **le maquillage accentue la forme de l'œil** make-up accentuates the outline of the eye

4 *(augmenter → efforts)* to increase, to intensify; *(→ chômage, crise)* to increase

▸**s'accentuer** VPR *(contraste, ressemblance)* to become more marked *or* apparent *or* pronounced; *(tendance)* to become more noticeable; *(chômage)* to rise, to increase; *(crise)* to increase in intensity

acceptabilité [aksɛptabilite] NF **1** *Ling* acceptability **2** *Mktg* **a. de la marque** brand acceptability, brand acceptance

acceptable [aksɛptabl] ADJ *(offre, condition)* acceptable; *(attitude)* decent, acceptable; *(travail)* fair, acceptable; *(repas)* decent; *(réponse)* satisfactory; *(prix)* fair, reasonable

acceptant, -e [aksɛptɑ̃, -ɑ̃t] ADJ acceptant

NM,F acceptant

acceptation [aksɛptasjɔ̃] NF **1** *(accord)* acceptance; **a. sous condition** conditional acceptance; **sous réserve d'a. du dossier** subject to a favourable report **2** *Fin & Jur* acceptance; **a. bancaire** banker's acceptance; **a. conditionnelle** qualified acceptance; **a. partielle** partial acceptance; **a. des risques** assumption of risk

accepter [4] [aksɛpte] VT **1** *(recevoir volontiers → cadeau, invitation)* to accept; *(s'engager volontiers dans → défi, lutte)* to take up; **j'accepte ton pari** I'll take you up on your bet

2 *(admettre → hypothèse, situation, excuse)* to accept; *(→ condition)* to agree to, to accept; *(→ mort, échec, sort)* to accept, to come to terms with; *(→ requête)* to grant; **j'accepte que cela soit difficile** I agree that it is *or* might be difficult; **j'accepte qu'il vienne** I agree to him coming; **a. de faire qch** to agree to do sth; **je n'ai pu leur faire a. votre proposition** I was unable to persuade them to accept your offer; **il ne trahira pas – acceptons-en l'augure** he won't betray us – let's take it on trust that he won't

3 *(tolérer → critique, hypocrisie)* to take, to stand for, to put up with; **il accepte tout de sa femme** he'd put up with anything from his wife; **il n'accepte pas l'échec** he refuses to acknowledge failure; **elle accepte qu'il lui parle** she puts up with him talking to her; **il n'a pas accepté qu'elle le quitte** he just couldn't take *or* accept her leaving him; **je n'accepte pas qu'on se moque de moi** I will not be made fun of; **a. de** to be prepared to; **j'accepte de ne rien dire** I'm prepared to say nothing

4 *(accueillir)* to accept; **elle a tout de suite été acceptée dans la famille** she was readily accepted *or* made welcome by the family; **a. qn comme associé** to take sb in as a partner; **il a du mal à se faire a. dans la famille** he's finding it hard to gain acceptance with the family; **acceptez-vous Jean-Guy Pierre pour époux?** do you take this man, Jean-Guy Pierre, to be your lawfully wedded husband?; **les animaux ne sont pas acceptés** *(sur vitrine)* no animals allowed, no pets; **acceptez-vous les cartes de crédit?** do you take credit cards?

5 *Fin (chèque, effet)* to accept, to sign, to honour

USAGE ABSOLU **ne fais pas tant d'histoires, accepte!** don't make such a fuss, say yes!

▸**s'accepter** VPR to accept oneself; **je me trouvais trop grosse, maintenant je m'accepte telle que je suis** I used to think I was too fat, now I've learned to accept myself the way I am

accepteur, -euse [aksɛptœr, -øz] NM,F *(gén)* accepter; *Fin (d'une facture, d'un effet)* acceptor, drawee

NM *Chim & Phys* acceptor

acception [aksɛpsjɔ̃] NF *Ling* meaning, sense; **dans toutes les acceptions du mot** *ou* **du terme** in every sense of the word

□ **sans acception de** PRÉP **1** *(gén)* without taking into account **2** *Jur* **sans a. de personne** without giving preference to anyone

Acces [aksɛs] NF *(abrév* **association des chaînes du câble et du satellite**) = association of French cable and satellite channels

accès [aksɛ] NM **1** *(entrée)* access; **un a. direct à** *ou* **sur la route** direct access to the road; **l'a. de la chambre t'est interdit** you're forbidden to enter the bedroom; **a. gratuit** *(sur panneau)* free admission; **a. interdit** *(sur panneau ou porte)* no entry, no admittance; **a. réservé aux voyageurs munis de billets** *(sur panneau)* ticket-holders only; **d'a. facile** *(lieu)* easy to get to; *(personne)* approachable; *(œuvre)* accessible; **d'a. difficile** *(lieu)* hard to get to; *(personne)* unapproachable; *(œuvre)* difficult; **facile/difficile d'a.** *(lieu)* easy/hard to get to; **avoir a. à** *(lieu, personne, études, profession)* to have access to; **donner a. à** *(lieu)* to lead to; *(musée, exposition)* to allow entry to; *(études, profession)* to lead to, to open the way to; **l'a. au statut de membre de l'Union européenne** entry into the European Union

2 *(chemin, voie)* way in, access, entrance; **les a. de la ville** the approaches to the town; **les a. de la maison** the ways in *or* entrances to the house; **a. aux trains** *ou* **quais** *(sur panneau)* to the trains

3 *(crise → de rhumatisme, de goutte)* attack; *(→ de folie, de jalousie)* fit; **a. de colère** fit of anger, angry outburst; **un a. de fièvre** a sudden high temperature; *Fig* a burst of intense activity; **un a. de toux** a fit of coughing, a coughing fit; **un a. de joie** a burst of happiness; **un a. de tristesse** a wave of sadness

4 *Ordinat* access; *(à une page Web)* hit; **avoir a. à** to be able to access; **a. aléatoire** random access; **a. commuté** dial-up access; **a. direct** direct access; **a. à distance** remote access; **a. par ligne commutée** dial-up access; **a. mémoire simultané** interleaving; **à a. multiple** multi-access; **a. sécurisé par mot de passe** password-protected access; **a. séquentiel** sequential access

□ **par accès** ADV in spurts, in fits and starts; **ça le prenait par a.** it came over him in waves

accessibilité [aksesibilite] NF accessibility

accessible [aksesibl] ADJ *(livre, œuvre)* accessible; *(personne)* approachable; *(lieu)* accessible; *(prix)* affordable; **a. au public** *(sur panneau)* open to the public; **les toilettes doivent être accessibles aux handicapés** toilets must have disabled access; **un luxe qui n'est pas a. à tous** a luxury that not everyone can afford; **être a. à la pitié** to be capable of pity; **être a. à la flatterie** to be susceptible to flattery

accession [aksɛsjɔ̃] NF **1** *(arrivée)* **a. au trône** accession *or* acceding to the throne; **depuis son a. au poste/rang de...** since he rose to the post/rank of...; **le pays fête son a. à l'indépendance** the country's celebrating becoming independent *or* achieving independence; **a. à la propriété** home ownership; **faciliter l'a. à la**

propriété to make it easier for people to become home-owners; **a. au statut de membre de l'Union européenne** entry into the European Union

2 *Jur* accession

accessit [aksesit] **NM** *Br* ≃ certificate of merit, *Am* ≃ Honorable Mention

accessoire [akseswar] **ADJ** *(détail, considération)* of secondary importance, less important; *(rôle)* subordinate; **des frais accessoires** incidentals, incidental expenses; **des avantages accessoires** fringe benefits

NM 1 *(considérations secondaires)* minor details; **laissons l'a. de côté** let's forget about the (minor) details for now

2 *(dispositif, objet)* accessory; **a. automobile/informatique/vestimentaire** car/computer/fashion accessory; *Can* **a. électrique** electrical fitting

3 *Cin, Théât & TV* prop; **a. cassable** breakaway

❑ **accessoires NMPL** *Jur* fittings, fixtures, appurtenances

accessoirement [akseswarmɑ̃] **ADV** 1 *(secondairement)* secondarily 2 *(éventuellement)* if necessary, if need be

accessoiriser [3] [akseswarize] **VT** *(voiture, tenue)* to accessorize

accessoiriste [akseswarist] **NMF** 1 *Cin, Théât & TV* props person, propman, *f* props girl; *(au générique)* props 2 *Aut* car accessories dealer

access prime time [aksɛsprajmtajm] **NM** *TV* early prime time

accident [aksidɑ̃] **NM** 1 *(chute, coup)* accident; *(entre véhicules)* crash, accident, collision; **un a. est si vite arrivé** accidents happen so easily; **la police est sur le lieu de l'a.** the police are at the scene of the accident; **a. mortel** fatal accident; **a. d'avion** plane crash; **a. de la circulation** road accident; **a. de chemin de fer** rail accident; *Jur* **a. avec délit de fuite** hit-and-run; **a. de mission** = accident that occurs while engaged in work-related activities outside work premises; **a. de la route** road accident; **a. de trajet** = accident on the way to or from work; **a. du travail** industrial accident; **a. de voiture** car crash

2 *(fait imprévu)* mishap, accident; **a. (de parcours)** hitch; **Anne a eu un petit a. avec la confiture** Anne had a little accident *or* mishap with the jam; **ce n'était pas prévu, c'est un a.** it wasn't planned, it was an accident

3 *Méd* **a. cardiaque** heart attack; **a. cérébro-vasculaire, a. vasculaire cérébral** stroke, *Spéc* cerebral vascular accident; **a. médical** medical accident; **a. de santé** (sudden) health problem

4 *Euph (incontinence)* accident; **à six ans, il a encore des accidents la nuit** although he's six, he still has accidents *or* wets the bed at night

5 *Géol* **un a. de terrain** an uneven piece of ground; **les accidents du relief** the unevenness *or* irregularity of the contours; **a. tectonique** tectonic shift

6 *Phil* accident

7 *Mus* accidental

❑ **par accident ADV** accidentally, by accident *or* chance

accidenté, -e [aksidɑ̃te] **ADJ** 1 *(endommagé → voiture, avion)* damaged 2 *(inégal → terrain)* uneven, broken, irregular 3 *(mouvementé → destin, vie)* eventful, chequered

NM,F injured person, casualty; **a. du travail** victim of an industrial injury; **a. de la route** person in a road accident

accidentel, -elle [aksidɑ̃tɛl] **ADJ** 1 *(dû à un accident)* accidental; *(dû au hasard)* incidental, accidental, *Sout* fortuitous; **je l'ai rencontré de façon totalement accidentelle** I met him quite by accident 2 *Phil* accidental 3 *Mus* **signes accidentels** accidentals

accidentellement [aksidɑ̃tɛlmɑ̃] **ADV** 1 *(dans un accident)* in an accident; *(par hasard)* incidentally, accidentally, by accident, *Sout* fortuitously 2 *Phil* accidentally

accidenter [3] [aksidɑ̃te] **VT** *(personne)* to injure, to wound; *(véhicule)* to damage

accidentologie [aksidɑ̃tɔlɔʒi] **NF** road accident research

accidentologue [aksidɑ̃tɔlɔg] **NMF** accident researcher, person who specializes in the study of road accidents

accipiens [aksipjɛ̃s] **NM** receiver *(of sum of money)*

accise [aksiz] *Fin* **NF** *Can* tax; *(sur produits importés)* excise duty

❑ **accises NFPL** *Belg* indirect tax

accisien [aksizjɛ̃] **NM** *Belg Fin* indirect taxes agent

acclamation [aklamasjɔ̃] **NF** cheering *(UNCOUNT)*, *Littéraire* acclamation; **être accueilli par les acclamations de la foule** to be greeted with cheers from the crowd; **son discours fut salué par des acclamations** his/her speech was greeted with cheers

❑ **par acclamation ADV** by popular acclaim, by acclamation; **motion adoptée par a.** motion carried by acclamation

acclamer [3] [aklame] **VT** to cheer, *Littéraire* to acclaim; **se faire a.** to be cheered

acclimatable [aklimatabl] **ADJ** acclimatizable, *Am* acclimatable

acclimatation [aklimatasjɔ̃] **NF** acclimatization, *Am* acclimation

acclimatement [aklimatmɑ̃] **NM** acclimatization, *Am* acclimation

acclimater [3] [aklimate] **VT** 1 *Bot & Zool* to acclimatize, *Am* to acclimate 2 *(adopter)* **a. un usage étranger** to adopt a foreign practice

▸**s'acclimater VPR** 1 *Bot & Zool* to acclimatize *or Am* acclimate, to become acclimatized *or Am* acclimated 2 *(personne)* to adapt; **il s'est bien acclimaté à la vie parisienne** he's adapted *or* taken to the Parisian way of life very well

accointances [akwɛ̃tɑ̃s] **NFPL** *Péj* contacts, links; **avoir des a. avec le milieu** to have contacts with *or* to be connected to the criminal underworld; **il a des a. en haut lieu** he has friends in high places

accointer [3] [akwɛ̃te] **s'accointer VPR** *Péj Vieilli* **s'a. avec** to take up with, to team up with

accolade [akɔlad] **NF** 1 *(embrassade)* embrace; **donner l'a. à qn** to embrace sb; **recevoir l'a.** to be embraced 2 *Hist* accolade; **recevoir l'a.** to be knighted 3 *(signe typographique)* brace, bracket 4 *Archit* ogee arch

accolage [akɔlaʒ] *nm Hort (de vigne, d'arbres)* tying up

accolement [akɔlmɑ̃] **NM** *Littéraire* association, bracketing (together)

accoler [3] [akɔle] **VT** 1 *(disposer ensemble)* to place *or* to put side by side; **a. deux photographies, a. une photographie à une autre** to put two photographs side by side; **le nom de l'épouse est accolé à celui du mari** the wife's surname is joined *or* added to that of the husband 2 *(joindre par une accolade)* to bracket together 3 *Hort (vigne, arbres)* to tie up

accommodant, -e [akɔmɔdɑ̃, -ɑ̃t] **ADJ** accommodating, obliging

accommodat [akɔmɔda] **NM** *Biol* acclimatization, *Am* acclimation

accommodation [akɔmɔdasjɔ̃] **NF** 1 *(acclimatement)* acclimatization, *Am* acclimation; *(adaptation)* adaptation 2 *Opt* focusing

accommodement [akɔmɔdmɑ̃] **NM** 1 *(accord)* arrangement; **trouver des accommodements avec sa conscience** to come to terms with one's conscience 2 *Pol* compromise; **propositions d'a. en vue d'une trêve** compromise proposals for a truce

accommoder [3] [akɔmɔde] **VT** 1 *(adapter)* to adapt, to adjust, to fit; **a. un produit aux désirs des clients** to adapt *or* to tailor a product to the clients' wishes

2 *Culin* to prepare; **a. une viande en ragoût** to make *or* to prepare a stew; **a. les restes** to use up the leftovers

3 *Can (convenir à)* to accommodate, to satisfy; **il fait semblant de ne pas comprendre quand cela l'accommode** he pretends not to understand whenever it suits him; **la société a tout fait pour nous a.** the company did everything they could to meet our needs

VI *Opt* to focus

▸**s'accommoder VPR** 1 **s'a. à qch** to adapt to sth; **il s'est accommodé à la vie à la campagne** he has adapted to country life

2 **s'a. avec qn** to come to an agreement with sb

3 **s'a. de qch** to put up with sth; **il s'accommode d'une modeste retraite** he's content *or* satisfied with a small pension

accompagnateur, -trice [akɔ̃paɲatœr, -tris] **NM,F** 1 *(de touristes)* guide, courier; *(d'enfants)* group leader, accompanying adult; *(de malades)* nurse 2 *Mus* accompanist 3 *Belg Rail* **a. de train** ticket inspector

accompagnement [akɔ̃paɲmɑ̃] **NM** 1 *Culin (d'un rôti) Br* trimmings, *Am* fixings; *(d'un mets)* garnish; **servi avec un a. de petits légumes** served with mixed vegetables 2 *Mus* accompaniment; **chanter sans a.** to sing unaccompanied 3 *Littéraire (escorte)* escort

❑ **d'accompagnement ADJ** *Mil voir* **tir**

accompagner [3] [akɔ̃paɲe] **VT** 1 *(aller avec)* to go with; *(venir avec)* to come with; **tu vas chez Paul? je t'accompagne** you're going to see Paul? I'll come along *or* I'll go with you; **a. qn à l'aéroport** to go to the airport with sb; *(en voiture)* to take sb to the airport; **a. qn en ville** *(à pied)* to walk into town with sb; *(en voiture)* to drive sb into town; **a. un groupe de touristes** to accompany a group of sightseers, to take some sightseers on a tour; **être accompagné de gardes du corps** to be followed around *or* accompanied by bodyguards; **elle vient toujours accompagnée** she never comes alone, she always brings somebody with her; **les enfants doivent être accompagnés** children must be accompanied by an adult; **je serai accompagné de ma cousine** I'll come with my cousin; *Prov* **il vaut mieux être seul que mal accompagné** you're better off alone than in bad company; *Fig* **a. un mourant** to be with a dying man to the end; **a. qn du regard** to follow sb with one's eyes; **nos vœux/pensées vous accompagnent** our wishes/thoughts are with you

2 *(compléter)* to go with; **un échantillon de parfum accompagne tout achat** a sample of perfume comes with every purchase; **ces mesures sont accompagnées d'un programme de réinsertion des prisonniers** these measures will be supported by a rehabilitation programme for prisoners; **le dictionnaire est accompagné d'un CD de prononciation** the dictionary comes with a pronunciation CD; **ce gratin accompagne agréablement toutes les viandes** this gratin goes well with any meat dish; **une sauce pour a. vos poissons** a sauce to complement your fish dishes; **il a accompagné ses mots d'un sourire** he said it with a smile; **un sourire accompagné d'un regard complice** a smile and a knowing glance; **accompagné de vin blanc, c'est un délice** served with white wine, it's delicious

3 *Mus* to accompany, to provide an accompaniment for; **a. qn au piano** to accompany sb on the piano

▸**s'accompagner VPR** 1 *Mus* **s'a. à un instrument** to accompany oneself on an instrument; **il chante et s'accompagne à l'accordéon** he sings and accompanies himself on the accordion

2 **s'a. de qch** to come with sth; **ses remarques s'accompagnaient d'une menace** his/her remarks contained a threat; **ces maux de tête s'accompagnent souvent de saignements de nez** these headaches are often accompanied by nose bleeds

accompli, -e [akɔ̃pli] **ADJ** 1 *(parfait)* accomplished 2 *(révolu)* **elle a 20 ans accomplis** she's turned *or* over 20 3 *Gram* perfective

NM *Gram* perfective

accomplir [32] [akɔ̃plir] **VT** 1 *(achever → mandat, obligation)* to fulfil; *(→ mission, travail)* to accomplish, to carry out; *(→ formalités)* to go through; **a. son devoir** to perform one's duty; **a. de bonnes actions** to do good (deeds); **a. de mauvaises actions** to commit evil (deeds); **il n'a rien accompli à ce jour** up to now he hasn't achieved *or* accomplished anything

2 *(réaliser → miracle)* to perform; *(→ souhait, promesse)* to fulfil; **a. un exploit technique** to perform a feat of engineering; **a. les dernières volontés de qn** to carry out sb's last wishes

▸**s'accomplir VPR** 1 *(être exécuté → vœu)* to come true, to be fulfilled; *(→ prophétie)* to come true; **ce qui s'accomplit autour de nous** the things happening all around us; **la volonté de Dieu s'accomplira** God's will shall be done

2 *(s'épanouir)* to blossom; **elle s'est accomplie en travaillant comme bénévole en Afrique** she

blossomed when she did voluntary work in Africa

accomplissement [akɔ̃plismɑ̃] **NM 1** *(exécution)* **cinq ans pour l'a. de ce travail** five years to carry out *or* to complete this work; **après l'a. de votre mission** after carrying out your mission **2** *(concrétisation)* **l'a. d'une prophétie** the realization of a prophecy; **l'a. d'un exploit sportif/d'un miracle** the performance of an athletic feat/of a miracle

accon [akɔ̃] **NM** *Naut* lighter, (flat-bottomed) barge

acconage [akɔnaʒ] **NM** *Naut* lighterage

acconier [akɔnje] **NM** *Naut* lighterman

accord [akɔr] **NM 1** *(entente)* agreement; *(harmonie)* harmony; **a. de l'expression et de la pensée** harmony between expression and thought; **il faut un bon a. entre les participants** the participants must all get on well with each other; **d'un commun a.** by common consent, by mutual agreement; **vivre en parfait a.** to live in perfect harmony; **vivre en a. avec ses principes** to live by one's principles; **être en a. avec soi-même** to be true to oneself; **la décision doit être prise en a. avec les différents intéressés** the decision must be made with the agreement *or* the consent of the different parties involved

2 *(convention)* & *Com* agreement; *(non formel)* understanding; *(pour résoudre un conflit)* settlement; **signer un a.** to sign an agreement; **conclure un a. avec** to come to an agreement with; **arriver** *ou* **parvenir à un a.** to come to an agreement, to reach (an) agreement; **a. d'achat et de vente** buy-sell agreement; **a. atypique** atypical contract; *Banque* **a. de clearing** clearing agreement; **a. collectif** collective agreement; **a. commercial** trade agreement; **a. de commercialisation** marketing agreement; *Écon* **a. de compensation** offset agreement; *Banque* **a. de crédit** credit agreement; **a. dérogatoire** derogatory agreement; **a. de distribution exclusive** exclusive distribution agreement; *Fin* **a. d'entreprise** *ou* **d'établissement** collective agreement; **a. d'exclusivité** exclusivity agreement; **a. en forme simplifié** executive agreement; **a. de franchise** franchise agreement; **a. de licence** licensing agreement; **a. de non-divulgation** non-disclosure agreement; **a. de paiement** payment agreement; **a. de partenariat** partnership agreement; **a. de principe** agreement in principle; **a. procédural** choice of law agreement; **a. régional** regional agreement; **a. de représentation** agency agreement; **a. de reprise** buyback agreement; **a. salarial** pay *or* wage agreement; **a. de siège** headquarters agreement; *Bourse* **a. de taux futur** Future Rate Agreement; *Bourse* **a. de taux à terme** Forward Rate Agreement; **les accords d'Évian** = the agreement signed on 18 March 1962, establishing a ceasefire in Algeria and recognizing the country's independence; **A. Général sur les Tarifs Douaniers et le Commerce** General Agreement on Tariffs and Trade; **les accords de Grenelle** = an agreement between the government and trade unions (27 May 1968) improving wages and working conditions and aimed at ending workers' support for student disturbances; **accords d'Helsinki** Helsinki Agreement; **A. de libre-échange nord-américain** North American Free Trade Agreement; *UE* **A. monétaire européen** European monetary agreement; **A. multilatéral sur l'investissement** multilateral investment agreement; **A. sur la réduction du temps de travail** = French agreement to reduce the working week to 35 hours

3 *(approbation)* consent, agreement; **demander l'a. de qn** to ask for sb's agreement *or* consent; **donner son a. à** to consent to; **donner son a. oralement** to give one's verbal consent

4 *Ling* agreement, concord; **a. en genre/nombre** gender/number agreement; **a. en genre et en nombre** agreement in number and in gender; **y a-t-il a. entre le sujet et le verbe?** does the verb agree with the subject?

5 *Mus (de sons)* chord, concord; *(d'un instrument)* tuning; **a. arpégé** broken chord; **a. parfait** triad *or* common chord; *Littéraire* **de doux accords** sweet strains

6 *Tech* tuning

❑ **d'accord** **ADV** OK; **tu viens? – d'a.** are you coming? – OK; **dix euros chacun, d'a.?** ten euros each, OK?; **(c'est) d'a. pour ce soir** it's OK for tonight; **tu avais dit que c'était d'a.!** you said (that) it was OK!; **d'a., puisque c'est comme ça, je n'irai pas!** OK *or* all right *or* I see, if that's the way it is I won't go!; **être d'a. (avec qn)** to agree (with sb); **ils ne sont pas d'a.** they don't agree, they disagree; **je suis d'a. pour qu'on lui dise** I agree to him/her being told *or* that he/she should be told; **(je ne suis) pas d'a.!** *(je refuse)* no (way)!; *(c'est faux)* I disagree!; **alors là, je ne suis plus d'a.!** now there I disagree!; *Sout* **nous en sommes** *ou* **demeurons d'a.** we are in agreement; **j'ai enfin réussi à les mettre d'a.** I've finally managed to get them to agree; **cessez de vous battre sinon c'est moi qui vais vous mettre d'a.!** stop fighting or I'll be the one to sort you out!; **se mettre d'a. (sur qch)** to agree (on sth); **ils n'arrivent pas à se mettre d'a.** they can't manage to agree *or* to reach an agreement; **mettez-vous d'a., je ne comprends rien à ce que vous dites** get your story straight, I can't understand a word of what you're saying; **mettons-nous bien d'a., c'est vous le responsable** let's get one thing straight, you're in charge; **tomber d'a.** to come to an agreement; **tomber d'a. sur qch** to agree on sth

❑ **en accord avec** **PRÉP 1** *(personne)* **en a. avec lui** in agreement with him

2 *(suivant)* **en a. avec les directives** according to the guidelines; **en a. avec notre politique commerciale** in line with *or* in keeping with our business policy

accordable [akɔrdabl] **ADJ 1** *(opinions)* which can be reconciled **2** *(faveur)* which can be granted **3** *Mus* tunable

accordage [akɔrdaʒ] **NM** *Mus* tuning

accordailles [akɔrdɑj] **NFPL** *Arch (fiançailles → engagement)* plighting of troths; *(→ célébration)* = party given for the signing of the marriage contract

accord-cadre [akɔrkadr] *(pl* **accords-cadres***)* **NM** framework *or* outline agreement

accordé, -e [akɔrde] **NM,F** *Arch* fiancé, *f* fiancée; **son a.** her betrothed

accordement [akɔrdəmɑ̃] **NM** *Mus* tuning

accordéon [akɔrdeɔ̃] **NM** *Mus* accordion; **a. diatonique/chromatique** diatonic/chromatic accordion; *Fig* **coup d'a.** sudden reversal

❑ **en accordéon** **ADJ** *(chaussettes)* wrinkled; *(voiture)* crumpled

Culture

ACCORDÉON

The accordion, also known as the "piano à bretelles" or "piano du pauvre", is associated in the French mind with the popular tradition of the "bal musette", where people would dance the "java" and the "valse musette" to accordion music. It has been fashionable again since the 1990s.

accordéoniste [akɔrdeɔnist] **NMF** *Mus* accordionist

accorder [3] [akɔrde] **VT 1** *(octroyer → congé, permission)* to give, to grant; *(→ faveur, pardon)* to grant; *(→ subvention)* to grant, to award; *(→ dommages-intérêts)* to award; *(→ découvert bancaire, remise)* to allow, to give; *(→ prêt)* to authorize, to extend; *(→ interview)* to give; **a. le droit de vote à qn** to give sb the right to vote, to enfranchise sb; **a. sa grâce à un condamné** to grant a condemned man a pardon, to extend a pardon to a condemned man; **a. la main de sa fille à qn** to give sb one's daughter's hand in marriage; **a. toute sa confiance à qn** to give sb one's complete trust; **a. de l'importance à qch** to attach importance to sth; **a. de la valeur aux objets** to set a value on things; **je vous accorde une heure, pas plus** I'll allow you one hour, no more; **voulez-vous m'a. cette danse?** may I have this dance?

2 *(concéder)* **a. à qn que** to admit to *or* to grant sb that; **vous m'accorderez que, là, j'avais raison** you must admit that on this point I was right; **ils sont un peu jeunes, je vous l'accorde, mais...** granted, they're a bit young, but..., they're a bit young I grant you, but...

3 *(harmoniser)* **a. les couleurs d'une pièce** to coordinate the colours in a room

4 *Gram* to make agree; **a. le verbe avec le sujet** to make the verb agree with the subject

5 *Mus* to tune; **les musiciens accordent leurs instruments** *(avant un concert)* the players are tuning up; *Fig* **a. ses violons** to agree; **il faudrait a. vos violons!** make your minds up!, get your stories straight!

▸**s'accorder** **VPR 1** *(être du même avis)* **tous s'accordent à dire que...** they all agree *or* concur that...; **ils se sont accordés pour baisser leurs prix** they agreed among themselves that they would drop their prices

2 *(se mettre d'accord)* to agree, to come to an agreement (**avec qn** with sb; **sur qch** on sth); **s'a. sur le prix** to agree on the price

3 *(s'entendre)* **on ne s'est jamais accordés (tous les deux)** we two never saw eye to eye *or* got along

4 *(être en harmonie → caractères)* to blend; *(→ opinions)* to match, to tally, to converge; **le moderne et l'ancien s'accordent parfaitement** old and new blend perfectly together; **ce qu'il dit ne s'accorde pas avec sa personnalité** he's saying things which are out of character

5 *Gram* to agree; **s'a. en genre avec** to agree in gender with

6 *Mus* to tune up

7 *(s'autoriser)* to allow oneself; **s'a. dix minutes de repos** to allow *or* to give oneself ten minutes' rest; **s'a. quelques jours de repos** to take a few days off

accordeur [akɔrdœr] **NM** *Mus* (piano) tuner

accordoir [akɔrdwar] **NM** *Mus* (piano) tuning key

accore [akɔr] **ADJ** *Géol* abrupt, sheer

NF *Naut* shore

accort, -e [akɔr, -ɔrt] **ADJ** *Littéraire* pleasant, comely; **une femme rondelette et accorte** an attractively buxom woman

accostable [akɔstabl] **ADJ** *Naut* **le rivage n'est pas a.** you can't get near the shore

accostage [akɔstaʒ] **NM 1** *Naut* drawing *or* coming alongside **2** *(d'une personne)* accosting

accoster [3] [akɔste] **VT 1** *(personne)* to go up to, to accost; **je me suis fait a. dans la rue** I got accosted in the street **2** *Naut* to come *or* to draw alongside

VI *Naut* to berth

accot [ako] **NM** *Hort (contre le gel)* protective covering

accoté, -e [akɔte] **ADJ** *Can Fam* living with a partner▪; **ils sont accotés depuis deux ans** they've been living together for two years

accotement [akɔtmɑ̃] **NM 1** *(d'une route)* shoulder, *Br* verge; **accotements stabilisés** *(sur panneau)* hard shoulders; **accotements non stabilisés** *(sur panneau)* soft shoulders, *Br* soft verges **2** *Rail (rail)* shoulder

accoter [3] [akɔte] **VT** to lean; **a. une échelle contre un mur** to lean a ladder against a wall; **maisons accotées à la colline** houses hugging the hillside

▸**s'accoter** **VPR** **s'a. à** *ou* **contre** to lean against

accotoir [akɔtwar] **NM** armrest

accouchée [akuʃe] **NF** = woman who has recently given birth

accouchement [akuʃmɑ̃] **NM** *Obst (travail)* childbirth, labour; *(expulsion)* delivery; **première/deuxième phase de l'a.** first/second stage of labour; **pendant mon a.** while I was giving birth *or* in labour; **procéder à un a.** to deliver a woman; **elle a eu un a. difficile** she had a difficult delivery; **on a dû provoquer l'a.** she had to be induced; **a. avant terme** premature delivery; **a. dirigé** induced delivery; **a. sans douleur** painless delivery *or* childbirth; **a. au forceps** forceps delivery; **a. naturel** natural childbirth; **a. prématuré** premature delivery; **a. par le siège** breech birth; **a. à terme** full term delivery

accoucher [3] [akuʃe] **VI 1** *Obst (avoir un bébé)* to have a baby, to give birth; **pendant qu'elle accouchait** while she was giving birth *or* in labour; **elle a accouché chez elle** she had a home birth *or* confinement; **Diane a accouché l'été dernier/avant terme** Diane had her child last summer/prematurely; **j'accouche en juin** my baby's due in June; **ils ont été obligés de la faire a. avant terme** they had to induce her

2 *Fam (parler)* **accouche!** spit it out!, let's have it!

VT c'est lui qui l'a accouchée he delivered her baby

❑ **accoucher de VT IND 1** *Obst (enfant)* to give birth to, to have; **a. d'une fille** to give birth to a girl; **a. de jumeaux** to have twins

2 *Fam (produire)* to come up with, to produce■; **six mois de travail pour a. d'une pièce aussi nulle!** six months of work to produce such a useless play!

accoucheur, -euse [akuʃœr, -øz] **NM,F** *Obst* obstetrician

accoudement [akudmɑ̃] **NM** leaning on one's elbows

accouder [3] [akude] **s'accouder VPR s'a. à** *ou* **sur qch** to lean (one's elbows) on sth; **s'a. à la fenêtre** to lean out of the window; **être accoudé à qch** to lean on sth; **il était accoudé au bar** he was leaning on the bar

accoudoir [akudwar] **NM** armrest

accouer [6] [akwe] **VT** *(chevaux)* to string

accouple [akupl] **NF** *Chasse* leash

accouplement [akupləmɑ̃] **NM 1** *(raccordement)* linking, joining; *Tech* coupling, connecting; *Élec* connecting; *Aut* **a. direct** direct drive; **a. à glissement** slip clutch; *Aviat* **a. à griffe** *ou* **à griffes** dog clutch, jaw clutch **2** *Agr* yoking, coupling **3** *Zool* mating

accoupler [3] [akuple] **VT 1** *(raccorder → mots)* to link *or* to join (together); *Tech* to couple, to connect; *Élec* to connect **2** *Agr (pour le trait)* to yoke *or* to couple together **3** *Zool* to mate

▸**s'accoupler VPR** *(animaux)* to mate

accourcir [32] [akursir] **VT** *Arch* to shorten

accourcissement [akursismɑ̃] **NM** *Arch* shortening

accourir [45] [akurir] **VI** to run, to rush; **elle est accourue pour le voir** she hurried *or* rushed to see him; **ils sont accourus (pour) m'annoncer la nouvelle** they came running to tell me the news; **elle l'appelle et il accourt** all she has to do is whistle and he comes running; **ses hurlements ont fait a. tout le voisinage** his/her screams brought all the neighbours rushing to the scene

accoutrement [akutrəmɑ̃] **NM** *Péj* outfit

accoutrer [3] [akutre] *Péj* **VT** to dress up; **comme te voilà accoutré!** you do look ridiculous in that outfit!; **accoutré d'une vieille capote** rigged out in an old army greatcoat

▸**s'accoutrer VPR** to get dressed up

accoutumance [akutymɑ̃s] **NF 1** *(adaptation)* habituation (**à** to) **2** *(d'un toxicomane)* addiction, dependency; **l'effet d'a. des drogues dures** the habit-forming effect of hard drugs

accoutumé, -e [akutyme] **ADJ** usual, customary

❑ **comme à l'accoutumée ADV** as usual, as always

accoutumer [3] [akutyme] **VT a. qn à qch/à faire qch** to accustom sb to sth/to doing sth, to get sb used to sth/to doing sth; **être accoutumé à qch/à faire qch** to be accustomed *or* used to sth/to doing sth

▸**s'accoutumer VPR s'a. à** to get used to; **il faudra vous a. à vous lever tôt** you'll have to get used to getting up early

accouvage [akuvaʒ] **NM** artificial incubation

accouver [3] [akuve] **VT** *(oiseau)* to set; *(œufs)* to incubate

VI *(oiseau)* to sit, to brood

accouveur, -euse [akuvœr, -øz] **NM,F** hatchery operator

Accra [akra] **NM** *Géog* Accra, Akkra

accréditation [akreditasjɔ̃] **NF** *Fin* accreditation

accrédité, -e [akredite] **ADJ** *Fin* accredited; **notre représentant dûment a.** our duly authorized agent

NM,F 1 *Banque (détenteur d'une lettre de crédit)* holder of a letter of credit **2** *Compta* beneficiary, payee

accréditer [3] [akredite] **VT** *(rumeur, nouvelle)* to substantiate, to give credence to; *(personne, représentant)* to accredit; *Banque (client)* to open an account for, to open credit facilities for; *Banque* **être accrédité auprès d'une banque** to have credit facilities at a bank

▸**s'accréditer VPR** *(rumeur)* to gain ground

accréditeur [akreditœr] **NM** *Jur* surety, guarantor

accréditif, -ive [akreditif, -iv] *Banque* **ADJ lettre accréditive** letter of credit

NM 1 *(lettre de crédit)* letter of credit; *Compta* credential **2** *(crédit)* credit; **loger un a. sur une banque** to open credit facilities with a bank; **a. permanent** permanent credit

accrescent, -e [akrɛsɑ̃, -ɑ̃t] **ADJ** *Bot* accrescent

accréter [18] [akrete] **VT** *Astron & Géol* to accrete

accrétion [akresjɔ̃] **NF** *Astron & Géol* accretion

accro [akro] *Fam* **ADJ** hooked; **être a. à qch** *(drogue)* to be hooked on sth; *Fig* to be hooked on *or* really into sth; **il va à tous les matchs de foot, il est vraiment a.** he goes to all the football matches, he's a real football junkie

NMF *(toxicomane)* addict■; *(passionné)* fanatic■; **les accros de la hi-fi** hi-fi fanatics; **c'est un a. du football** he's really mad on football

accroc [akro] **NM 1** *(déchirure)* tear, rip; **faire un a. à sa chemise** to tear *or* to rip one's shirt

2 *Fam (entorse)* breach, violation; **faire un a. au règlement** to bend the rules; **faire un a. à un contrat** to breach *or* to violate a contract

3 *(incident)* snag, hitch; **un voyage sans a.** *ou* **accrocs** an uneventful trip; **ce n'est qu'un petit a. à notre planning** it's just a minor hitch as far as our schedule is concerned

accrochage [akrɔʃaʒ] **NM 1** *(suspension → d'un tableau)* hanging; *Beaux-Arts* small exhibition

2 *(fixation → d'un wagon)* hitching (up), coupling; *(→ d'une remorque)* hitching (up)

3 *Aut (collision → entre véhicules)* collision; **en 30 ans de conduite, je n'ai jamais eu le moindre a.** in 30 years as a driver, I've never had an accident of any sort; **ce n'est qu'un tout petit a.** it's only a scratch

4 *(querelle)* quarrel, squabble; **avoir un a. avec qn** to clash with sb

5 *Mil* skirmish, engagement

6 *Sport (en boxe)* clinch; *(entre deux coureurs)* tangle

7 *Métal* scaffold, scaffolding

accroche [akrɔʃ] **NF** gimmick; *(slogan)* slogan

accroche-cœur [akrɔʃkœr] *(pl inv ou* **accroche-cœurs**) **NM** *Br* kiss-curl, *Am* spit curl; **se faire des accroche-cœurs** to put one's hair into kiss curls

accroche-plat [akrɔʃpla] *(pl inv ou* **accroche-plats**) **NM** plate-hanger

accrocher [3] [akrɔʃe] **VT 1** *(suspendre → tableau)* to hang; *(→ manteau, rideau)* to hang up; **un petit miroir accroché au moyen d'un clou** a small mirror hanging on *or* from a nail

2 *(saisir)* to hook; *Naut* **a. une embarcation avec une gaffe** to hook a boat in; *Fam Fig* **il a accroché une bonne commande** he landed a big order

3 *(relier)* **a. qch à** to tie sth (on) to; **a. un wagon à un train** to couple *or* to hitch a wagon to a train; **a. un pendentif à une chaîne** to attach a pendant to a chain

4 *Fam (aborder)* to corner, to buttonhole, to collar; **le curé m'a accroché à la sortie de l'église** the priest buttonholed me outside the church

5 *Fig (retenir l'intérêt de)* to grab the attention of; *(attirer → regard)* to catch; **il faut a. le lecteur dès les premières pages** we must make the reader sit up and take notice from the very beginning of the book; **qui accroche le regard** eye-catching; **ses bijoux accrochaient la lumière** her jewels caught the light

6 *(déchirer → collant, vêtement)* to snag, to catch; **a. sa robe à des ronces** to catch one's dress on brambles

7 *(heurter → piéton)* to hit; **il a accroché l'aile de ma voiture** he caught *or* scraped my wing; **elle m'a accroché en me dépassant** she scraped my bodywork as she overtook me; **elle a accroché le vase au passage et il est tombé** she knocked the vase as she went past and it crashed to the ground

8 *Mil* to engage in a skirmish with

9 *Rad* **a. une station** to tune in to a station

USAGE ABSOLU *Fig (attirer l'attention)* **un slogan qui accroche** a catchy slogan

VI 1 *(coincer → fermeture, tiroir)* to jam, to stick; *Fig (buter)* to be stuck; **des skis qui accrochent** skis that don't run smoothly; **farte tes skis, la neige accroche ce matin** wax your skis because the snow's sticky this morning; *Fig* **la discussion accroche sur la composition du comité** the discussion has got bogged down over the composition of the committee; *Fig* **j'accroche sur la traduction de ce mot** I just can't come up with a good translation for this word

2 *Fam (bien marcher)* **ça n'a pas accroché entre eux** they didn't hit it off; **je n'ai jamais accroché en physique** I never really got into physics; **en musique, il a tout de suite accroché** he took to music straight away

▸**s'accrocher VPR 1** *(emploi passif)* to hang, to hook on; **la médaille s'accroche au bracelet avec un fermoir** the medallion fixes *or* fastens on to the bracelet with a clasp; **la remorque s'accroche à la voiture** the trailer hooks *or* hitches on to the (back of the) car

2 *(emploi réciproque) (entrer en collision → voitures)* to crash (into each other), to collide; *(→ boxeurs)* to clinch; *(se disputer → personnes)* to clash; **les pédales des deux vélos se sont accrochées** the pedals on the two bicycles got tangled up; *Fam* **ils ne peuvent pas se supporter, ils vont s'a. tout de suite** they can't stand each other so they're bound to start arguing straight away; *Mil* **les deux divisions se sont accrochées** there was a skirmish between the two divisions

3 *Fam (persévérer → athlète, concurrent)* to apply oneself; **il faut s'a. pour suivre son explication** you've got to have your wits about you if you want to understand his explanation; **avec lui, il faut s'a.!** he's hard work!; **accroche-toi, tu n'as pas tout entendu!** brace yourself, you haven't heard everything yet!

4 **s'a. à** to hang *or* to cling on to; **accroche-toi à la poignée!** hang on (tight) to the handle!; *Fig* **s'a. au pouvoir/à la vie/à qn** to cling to power/to life/to sb; *Littéraire* **une bicoque s'accrochait à la falaise** a shack was clinging to the cliff

5 *Fam* **s'a. avec** to clash with

6 *très Fam (locution)* **tu peux te l'a.!** *(tu ne l'auras jamais)* you can whistle for it!; *(tu ne l'auras plus)* you can kiss it goodbye!

accrocheur, -euse [akrɔʃœr, -øz] **ADJ 1** *(attirant → titre, slogan, chanson)* catchy; *(→ sourire)* beguiling; **une publicité accrocheuse** an eye-catching advertisement **2** *(tenace → vendeur)* pushy

NM,F fighter

accroire [akrwar] **VT** *(à l'infinitif seulement) Littéraire* **faire** *ou* **laisser a. qch à qn** to mislead sb into believing sth; **en faire a. à qn** to try to deceive sb

accrois *voir* **accroître**

accroissait *etc voir* **accroître**

accroissement [akrwasmɑ̃] **NM 1** *(augmentation)* increase (**de** in); *(→ du capital)* accumulation; **l'a. de la population** population growth; **les nouveaux équipements ont permis un a. de la productivité** the new equipment has led to an increase in productivity; *Fin* **a. global net** aggregate net increment **2** *Math* increment

accroître [94] [akrwatr] **VT** *(fortune, sentiment)* to increase; *(domaine)* to add (on) to; *(popularité)* to enhance

▸**s'accroître VPR** *(fortune)* to increase; *(tension)* to rise; *(sentiment)* to grow, to increase; *(population)* to rise, to increase, to grow

accroupir [32] [akrupir] **s'accroupir VPR** to squat *or* to crouch (down); **il était accroupi** he was squatting *or* crouching

accroupissement [akrupismɑ̃] **NM 1** *(action)* squatting, crouching **2** *(position)* squatting position

accru, -e [akry] **PP** *voir* **accroître**

ADJ *(fortune)* increased, larger; *(sentiment)* deeper; *(popularité)* enhanced

NM *Bot* sucker

❑ **accrue NF** *Agr (extension)* = extension of forest by natural seeding

accu [aky] **NM** *Fam* battery; **les accus sont morts** the battery's dead

accueil [akœj] **NM 1** *(manière d'accueillir)* welcome, greeting; **nous avons reçu le plus chaleureux des accueils** we were given the heartiest of welcomes; **faire bon a. à qn** to give sb a warm welcome; **faire mauvais a. à qn** to give sb a cool reception; *Fig* **faire bon/mauvais**

a. à une proposition to receive a proposal warmly/coldly; *Fin* **faire (bon) a. à une traite** to meet *or* to honour a bill

2 *(bureau, comptoir)* desk, reception; **passez à l'a.** go to the reception desk, go to reception; **tenir l'a.** to be on reception

3 *Jur* **a. de l'embryon** embryo donation

❑ **d'accueil** ADJ *(discours, cérémonie)* welcoming; *(hôtesse, hall)* reception *(avant n)*; *(pays)* host *(avant n)*

accueillant, -e [akœjɑ̃, -ɑ̃t] ADJ *(peuple, individu)* welcoming, friendly; *(sourire)* warm, welcoming; *(maison)* hospitable; **peu a.** *(endroit)* inhospitable; *(personne)* unwelcoming, cold

accueillir [41] [akœjir] VT 1 *(aller chercher)* to meet; **a. qn à l'aéroport** to meet sb at the airport

2 *(recevoir)* **a. qn froidement** to give sb a cool reception; **être très bien/mal accueilli** to get a very pleasant/poor welcome; **il a été accueilli par des bravos** he was greeted with cheers; **ils m'ont accueilli avec un sourire gêné** they gave me an embarrassed smile as I came in; **elle a été accueillie par des huées** she was booed *or* hissed as she came in; **a. une idée avec scepticisme/enthousiasme** to greet an idea with scepticism/enthusiasm; **le projet a été très mal accueilli par la direction** the project got a frosty reception *or* response from the management; **le film a été mal accueilli par le public** the film was badly received by the public; *Fin* **a. une traite** to meet *or* to honour a bill

3 *(héberger)* to house, to accommodate; **l'hôpital peut a. 1000 malades** the hospital can accommodate 1,000 patients; **j'étais sans abri et ils m'ont accueilli** I was homeless and they took me in *or* gave me a home; **j'ai un ami qui pourrait vous a. pendant un certain temps** I have a friend who could put you up for a while

accul [aky] NM *Chasse* bottom of a fox's earth; **mettre un renard à l'a.** to run a fox to ground

acculé, -e [akyle] ADJ 1 *Équitation (cheval)* liable to throw itself on its haunches *(when reined in)* 2 *Hér (cheval)* cabré, rampant 3 *Naut (bateau)* down at the stern 4 *Archit* **varangues acculées** rising floor timbers

❑ **acculée** NF *Naut* sternway

acculer [3] [akyle] VT 1 *(bloquer)* **a. qn contre qch** to drive sb back against sth; *Chasse* **a. un animal** to bring an animal to bay; **tel un animal acculé** like an animal at bay 2 *(contraindre)* **a. qn à la faillite** to push sb into bankruptcy; **a. qn au désespoir** to drive sb to despair

VI *Naut* to list by the stern

acculturation [akyltyrasjɔ̃] NF acculturation

acculturé, -e [akyltyre] ADJ acculturated

acculturer [3] [akyltyre] VT to acculturate; **a. un groupe ethnique** to help an ethnic group adapt *or* adjust to a new cultural environment

accumulateur [akymylatœr] NM accumulator

accumulation [akymylasjɔ̃] NF 1 *(action)* accumulation, amassing, building up; *(collection)* mass; *(de marchandises → action)* stockpiling; *(→ résultat)* stockpile; *(de dettes)* accumulation; *(de stocks)* accumulation, build-up; *(d'erreurs)* series; **que vais-je faire de cette a. de vieux journaux?** what am I going to do with this pile of old newspapers?; **devant cette a. de preuves/démentis** faced with this mass of proof/with repeated denials; **a. de capital** capital accumulation; *Fin* **a. des intérêts** accrual of interest

2 *Élec* storage; **chauffage par a.** storage heating

accumulé, -e [akymyle] ADJ *Fin (intérêts)* accrued

accumuler [3] [akymyle] VT 1 *(conserver → boîtes, boutons)* to keep *or* to hoard (in large quantities), to accumulate; *(→ denrées)* to stockpile, to hoard; *(→ papiers)* to keep; *(marchandises)* to stockpile; *(stocks)* to accumulate, to build up; *(dettes)* to accumulate; *Fin* **intérêts accumulés** accrued interest

2 *(réunir → preuves)* to pile on, to accumulate; *(→ fortune, argent)* to amass; **a. les gaffes/erreurs** to make endless blunders/mistakes; *Fam* **mais tu les accumules!** *(les bêtises)* you never stop, do you?

▸**s'accumuler** VPR *(dettes, travail)* to accumulate, to mount (up), to pile up; *(nuages)* to gather, to build up; *Fin (intérêts)* to accrue; **le linge sale s'accumule** the dirty laundry is piling up; **les toxines s'accumulent dans l'organisme** there is a build-up of toxins in the body

accusateur, -trice [akyzatœr, -tris] ADJ *(silence, regard)* accusing; *(document)* incriminating; **il a pointé vers elle un index a.** he pointed an accusing finger at her

NM,F *(dénonciateur)* accuser

NM *Hist* **a. public** public prosecutor *(during the French Revolution)*

accusatif [akyzatif] NM *Ling* accusative; **à l'a.** in the accusative

accusation [akyzasjɔ̃] NF 1 *Jur* charge, indictment; **mettre qn en a.** to indict *or* to charge sb; **a. fondée** substantiated charge 2 *(reproche)* accusation, charge; **lancer** *ou* **porter une a. contre** to make an accusation against

accusatoire [akyzatwar] ADJ accusatory

accusatrice [akyzatris] *voir* **accusateur**

accusé, -e [akyze] ADJ *(traits)* sharp, pronounced; *(rides)* deep; *Écon & Fin (baisse, hausse)* sharp

NM,F *Jur* defendant; **l'a.** the accused; **a., levez-vous!** the accused will stand!

❑ **accusé (de) réception** NM *(d'une lettre)* acknowledgement (of receipt); *(d'un colis)* receipt; **envoyer qch en recommandé avec a. reception** to send sth by *Br* recorded delivery *or Am* certified mail; *Ordinat* acknowledge, acknowledgement

accuser [3] [akyze] VT 1 *(désigner comme coupable)* to accuse; **je ne t'accuse pas!** I'm not accusing you!; **tout l'accuse** everything points to his guilt; **a. qn de qch** to accuse sb of sth; **il a accusé le jury de favoritisme** he accused the jury of being biased; **on m'accuse d'avoir menti** I'm being accused of lying; **elle l'accuse de les avoir tués** she's accusing him/her of killing them; **il s'est fait a. injustement** he was unjustly accused; **"J'accuse"** = title of an open letter to the French President which appeared in "l'Aurore" in January 1898, in which Émile Zola insisted that Alfred Dreyfus had been unjustly incriminated; *Jur* **a. qn de meurtre/viol** to charge sb with murder/rape; **de quoi l'accuse-t-on?** what's the charge against him?; **toutes ces manigances visent à faire a. un innocent** all this scheming is designed to bring about the indictment of an innocent man

2 *(rejeter la responsabilité sur)* to blame, to put the blame on; **je ne t'accuse pas!** I'm not blaming you!

3 *(accentuer)* to highlight, to emphasize, to accentuate; **la lumière accuse les reliefs** sunlight emphasizes the outlines

4 *(indiquer)* **la Bourse accuse une forte baisse** the stock market is registering heavy losses; **son visage accuse une grande fatigue** you can see on his/her face how tired he/she is; **il accuse ses 50 ans** he's 50 and looks it; **le compteur accuse 130 km/h** the speedometer's reading 130 km/h

5 *(locutions)* **a. réception de** to acknowledge receipt of; **a. le coup** *Boxe* to reel with the punch; *Fig (de fatigue)* to show the strain; *(moralement)* to take it badly; *Fam* **il lui faut le temps d'a. le coup** he/she needs time to let it sink in

▸**s'accuser** VPR to confess; **la seule chose dont je peux m'a., c'est...** the only fault I would admit to is...; **il s'est accusé du crime pour protéger son frère** he confessed to the crime to protect his brother; **il s'est accusé d'avoir volé** he confessed to having committed a theft

ace [es, ɛs] NM *(au tennis)* ace

acellulaire [aselylɛr] ADJ *Biol* acellular

acéphale [asefal] ADJ acephalous

acéracée [aserase] *Bot* NF maple, *Spéc* Acer

❑ **acéracées** NFPL Aceraceae

acerbe [asɛrb] ADJ 1 *(parole, critique)* cutting, acerbic; **d'un ton a.** crisply 2 *Littéraire (goût)* bitter

acerbité [asɛrbite] NF 1 *(d'une parole, d'une critique)* acerbity; **répondre avec a.** to answer sharply 2 *Littéraire (du goût)* bitterness

acéré, -e [asere] ADJ 1 *(lame, pointe)* sharp 2 *Fig (critique, propos)* biting, caustic

acérer [18] [asere] VT to sharpen

acéricole [aserikɔl] ADJ *Can (industrie, production)* maple (sugar) *(avant n)*

acériculteur, -trice [aserikyltœr, -tris] NM,F *Can* maple producer

acériculture [aserikyltyr] NF *Can* maple production, maple sugaring

acescence [asɛsɑ̃s] NF *(d'un vin, d'une bière)* acescence, acescency; **tourner à l'a.** to sour, to begin to turn sour

acescent, -e [asɛsɑ̃, -ɑ̃t] ADJ *(vin, bière)* acescent

acétabulaire [asetabylɛr] ADJ *Anat* acetabular

acétabule [asetabyl] NF *Anat* acetabulum

acetabulum [asetabylɔm] NM *Anat* acetabulum

acétal [asetal] NM *Chim* acetal

acétaldéhyde [asetaldeid] NM *Chim* acetaldehyde

acétamide [asetamid] NM *Chim* acetamide

acétate [asetat] NM *Chim* acetate; **a. d'aluminium** aluminium acetate; **a. de cellulose** cellulose acetate

acéteux, -euse [asetø, -øz] ADJ *Chim* acetous

acétification [asetifikasjɔ̃] NF *Chim* acetification, acetifying

acétifier [9] [asetifje] VT *Chim* to acetify

acétimètre [asetimɛtr] NM acetimeter, acetometer

acétique [asetik] ADJ *Chim* acetic; **une odeur a.** a vinegary smell

acétobacter [asetɔbaktɛr] NM *Chim* acetobacter

acétocellulose [asetɔselyloz] NF *Chim* cellulose acetate

acétomètre [asetɔmɛtr] = **acétimètre**

acétone [asetɔn] NF *Chim* acetone

acétonémie [asetɔnemi] NF *Méd* acetonaemia

acétonémique [asetɔnemik] ADJ *Méd* acetonaemic

acétonurie [asetɔnyri] NF *Méd* acetonuria

acétylation [asetilasjɔ̃] NF *Chim* acetylation

acétylcellulose [asetilselyloz] NF *Chim* cellulose acetate

acétylcholine [asetilkɔlin] NF *Chim* acetylcholine

acétylcoenzyme A [asetilkɔɑ̃zimɑ] NF *Biol & Chim* acetyl coenzyme A, acetyl CoA

acétyle [asetil] NM *Chim* acetyl

acétylène [asetilɛn] NM *Chim* acetylene

acétylénique [asetilenik] ADJ *Chim* acetylenic

acétylsalicylique [asetilsalisilik] ADJ *Pharm* acetylsalicylic

acétylure [asetilyr] NM *Chim* acetylide

ACF [ɑseɛf] NM *Aut (abrév* **Automobile Club de France)** = French automobile association, *Br* ≃ AA, ≃ RAC, *Am* ≃ AAA

ACFAS [akfas] NF *(abrév* **Association canadienne-française pour l'avancement des sciences)** French-Canadian Association for the Advancement of Science

ach. *(abrév écrite* **achète, achètent)** *(dans une annonce)* **retraités a. maison en bord de mer** retired couple looking to buy seaside home

Achaïe [akai] NF *Géog* Achaia, Achaea

achaine [akɛn] = **akène**

achalage [aʃalaʒ] NM *Can Fam (situation)* pain (in the neck); **j'en ai assez de tes achalages** I've had enough of you bugging me

achalandage [aʃalɑ̃daʒ] NM *(clientèle)* custom, clientele

achalandé, -e [aʃalɑ̃de] ADJ **bien a.** *(bien approvisionné)* well-stocked; *(qui compte de nombreux clients)* with a large clientele; **mal a.** *(mal approvisionné)* poorly-stocked; *(qui compte peu de clients)* with a small clientele

achalander [3] [aʃalɑ̃de] VT *(magasin)* to stock

achalant, -e [aʃalɑ̃, -ɑ̃t] *Can Fam* ADJ **être a.** to be a pain (in the neck)

NM,F pain (in the neck)

achalasie [akalazi] NF *Méd* achalasia

achalé, -e [aʃale] ADJ *Can Fam* **pas a.** forward

achaler [3] [aʃale] VT *Can Fam* to bug

achards [aʃar] NMPL *Culin* achar, relish

acharisme [akarism] NM *Rel* Ash'arism

acharné, -e [aʃarne] ADJ *(combat, lutte, concurrence)* fierce; *(travail)* relentless; *(travailleur)* hard; *(joueur)* hardened; **il est a. à votre perte** *ou* **à vous perdre** he is set *or* bent *or* intent on ruining you

NM,F **un a. du travail** a workaholic

acharnement [aʃarnəmɑ̃] NM *(dans un combat)* fury; *(dans le travail)* relentlessness, perseverance; **son a. à détruire les preuves** his/her determination to destroy the proof; **son a. à**

réussir his/her determination to succeed; **a. au travail** dedication to work; *Méd* **a. thérapeutique** use of intensive treatment *(to keep a patient alive)*

▫ **avec acharnement** ADV *(combattre)* tooth and nail, furiously; *(travailler)* relentlessly; *(résister)* fiercely

acharner [3] [aʃarne] VT *Vieilli (chien)* to flesh, to blood

▸**s'acharner** VPR **1 s'a. sur** *ou* **contre** *ou* **après qn** *(le tourmenter)* to persecute *or* to hound sb; **les médias s'acharnent sur** *ou* **contre moi** I'm being hounded by the press; **ses créanciers s'acharnent sur elle** she's being hounded by her creditors, her creditors won't give her a moment's peace; **le meurtrier s'est acharné sur sa victime** the murderer savaged his victim; **les examinateurs se sont acharnés sur le candidat** the examiners had a real go at the candidate; **le sort s'acharne sur lui** he's dogged by bad luck

2 s'a. sur qch *(persévérer)* to work (away) at sth; **voilà deux jours que je m'acharne sur ces calculs** I've been working away at these calculations for two days now; **cesse de t'a. sur ce nœud!** just leave that knot alone!; **s'a. à faire qch** *(persévérer)* to strive to do sth; *(vouloir à tout prix)* to be determined to do sth; **il s'acharne à vous nuire** he is determined to do you harm, he is set on harming you; **je m'acharne à lui faire mettre son écharpe** I'm always on at him/her to wear his/her scarf

USAGE ABSOLU **inutile de t'a., tu ne la convaincras pas** you might as well give up, you won't convince her

achat [aʃa] NM **1** *(fait d'acheter)* purchase, purchasing, buying; **l'a. d'une voiture neuve** the purchasing of a new car; **faire un a.** to make a purchase; **faire un a. à crédit** to buy *or* to purchase something on credit; **faire l'a. de qch** to buy *or* to purchase sth; **aller faire ses achats** to go shopping; **a. sur catalogue** mail-order purchasing; **achats centralisés** centralized purchasing; **achats comparatifs** comparison shopping; **a. au comptant** cash purchase; **a. à crédit** credit purchase, purchase for the account; *(location-achat)* buying on hire purchase *or Am* on the installment plan; **achats directs** direct purchasing; **achats à domicile** teleshopping; *Mktg* **a. d'émotion** emotional purchase; **a. d'espace** media buying; **a. en espèces** cash purchase; **achats hors taxes** tax-free shopping; *Mktg* **a. impulsif, a. d'impulsion** impulse buy; *Fin* **achats institutionnels** institutional buying; *Mktg* **a. juste à temps** just-in-time purchasing; *Ordinat* **a. en ligne** on-line purchase; **a. à petit prix** low-cost purchase; *Mktg* **a. prévu** destination purchase; **achats regroupés** one-stop buying; *Mktg* **a. renouvelé** repeat purchase; **achats spéculatifs** speculative buying; *Mktg* **a. spontané** impulse buy; *Com* **a. de système** systems buying; *Bourse* **a. à terme** forward buying; *Pol* **a. de voix** vote-buying

2 *(article acheté)* purchase, buy; **réglez vos achats à la caisse** pay at the cash desk; **un sac rempli d'achats** a bag full of shopping; **montre-nous tes achats** show us what you've bought; **c'est un bon/mauvais a.** it's a good/bad buy

▫ **à l'achat** ADV **la livre vaut 1,50 euros à l'a.** the buying rate for sterling is 1.50 euros; **cette machine est chère à l'a. mais vous l'amortirez en quelques années** this machine involves a high initial outlay but it will pay for itself in a few years

ache [aʃ] NF *Bot* wild celery, water parsley; **a. des chiens** fools' parsley; **a. de montagne** *ou* **des montagnes** common lovage, Italian lovage; **a. d'eau** water parsnip

acheb [akɛb] NM *Bot* acheb

achéen, -enne [akeɛ̃, -ɛn] *Antiq* ADJ Achaian, Achaean; **la ligue Achéenne** the Achaean League

NM,F Achaian, Achaean

achéménide [akemenid] ADJ *Hist, Archéol & Beaux-Arts* Achaemenian, Achaemenid

acheminement [aʃminmɑ̃] NM **1** *(de marchandises)* conveying, forwarding, shipment; *(de troupes)* moving; *(de trains)* routing; **l'a. des marchandises se fait par Calais** the goods are routed through Calais; **a. du courrier** mail handling **2** *(progression)* progress

acheminer [3] [aʃmine] VT **1** *(marchandises)* to convey, to forward; *(courrier)* to handle; **a. des produits par avion** to ship products by plane; **a. un colis vers** to ship a parcel to

2 *Mil* to convey, to move; **a. des troupes vers** *ou* **sur le front** to move troops up to the front *or* up the line

3 *Rail* to route; **a. un train vers** *ou* **sur** to route a train to *or* towards

▸**s'acheminer** VPR **s'a. vers** *(endroit, succès)* to head for; *(accord, solution)* to move towards; **nous nous acheminons vers la résolution du conflit** we're moving towards a solution to the conflict

achetable [aʃtabl] ADJ purchasable

achète [akɛt] NM *Zool* hirudinid

acheter [28] [aʃte] VT **1** *(cadeau, objet d'art, denrée)* to buy, *Sout* to purchase; **où l'as-tu acheté?** where did you buy it?; **j'ai acheté ce livre cinq euros** I bought this book for five euros; **a. des actions** *ou* **une part dans une entreprise** to buy into a business; **il a acheté les terrains environnants** he bought up the surrounding land; **a. qch au kilo** to buy sth by the kilo; **a. qch comptant/en gros/d'occasion/à crédit** to buy sth cash/wholesale/second-hand/on credit; **a. qch à tempérament** to buy sth on hire purchase *or Am* on the installment plan; **a. qch au détail** to buy sth retail; *(à l'unité)* to buy sth individually; **a. qch par correspondance** to buy sth by mail order; **a. qch à qn** *(pour soi)* to buy sth from sb; *(pour le lui offrir)* to buy sb sth, to buy sth for sb; **je lui ai acheté sa vieille voiture** I bought his old car from *or* off him; **si ça te plaît, je te l'achète** I'll buy you it *or* it for you if you like it; *Bourse* **a. à terme** to buy forward

2 *(échanger → liberté, paix)* to buy

3 *(soudoyer → témoin, juge)* to bribe, to buy (off); *(→ électeurs)* to buy; **ne crois pas que tu pourras m'a.** you must understand I won't be bought; **ils ont été achetés** they were bribed; **il s'est fait a. par la Mafia** he was bought by the Mafia

4 *Can Vieilli (enfant)* to have

USAGE ABSOLU **1** *(gén)* to buy; **achetez français!** buy French (products)!

2 *Can Vieilli (accoucher)* to give birth

▸**s'acheter** VPR **1** *(emploi passif)* to be on sale; **où est-ce que ça s'achète?** where can you buy it?; **ces choses-là ne s'achètent pas** such things cannot be bought *or* are not for sale

2 s'a. qch to buy oneself sth; **s'a. une conduite** to turn over a new leaf

acheteur, -euse [aʃtœr, -øz] NM,F **1** *(client)* buyer, purchaser; **les acheteurs se font rares** there are fewer and fewer buyers *or* customers; **trouver un a. pour qch** to find a buyer for *or* to find somebody to buy sth; **on n'a pas pu trouver a. pour ce produit** there are no buyers for *or* there is no market for this product; **je suis a.!** I'm interested!; *Mktg* **a. anonyme** anonymous buyer; *Mktg* **a. cible** target buyer; **a. éventuel** potential buyer; *Mktg* **a. impulsif** impulse buyer; *Com* **a. industriel** business buyer; *Mktg* **a. non-identifié** anonymous buyer; **a. potentiel** potential buyer

2 *(professionnel)* buyer; **a. industriel** business buyer; **a. principal** head buyer

3 *Jur* vendee

acheuléen, -enne [aʃøleɛ̃, -ɛn] ADJ Acheulean, Acheulian

NM **l'a.** the Acheulean, the Acheulian

achevé, -e [aʃve] ADJ *(sportif, artiste)* accomplished; *(œuvre)* perfect; *(idiot)* downright, absolute; **c'est d'un ridicule a.** it's utterly preposterous

▫ **achevé d'imprimer** NM colophon

achèvement [aʃɛvmɑ̃] NM completion

achever [19] [aʃve] VT **1** *(finir → discours, lettre)* to finish, to end, to bring to a close *or* an end; *(→ repas)* to finish, to end; *(→ journal, livre)* to reach the end of, to finish; **a. sa vie à l'hôpital** to end one's days in hospital; **laisse-le a. sa phrase** let him finish what he's saying; **a. de faire qch** to finish doing sth; **ils avaient juste achevé de rembourser le crédit** they'd just finished paying off the debt; **a. de mettre au point une invention** to put the final touches to an invention; **cette remarque acheva de le décourager** this remark discouraged him completely

2 *(tuer → animal)* to destroy; *(→ personne)* to finish off

3 *Fam (accabler)* to finish off; **la mort de sa femme l'a achevé** his wife's death really finished him off; **toutes ces courses m'ont achevé** all this shopping has done me in

4 *Fam (ruiner)* to finish off, to clean out; **les frais d'avocat l'ont achevé** the lawyer's fees cleaned him out

USAGE ABSOLU *(finir de parler)* to finish (talking); **à peine avais-je achevé que...** I'd hardly finished (talking) *or* stopped talking when...

▸**s'achever** VPR *(vie, journée, vacances)* to come to an end, to draw to a close *or* an end; *(dîner, film)* to end, to finish; **le livre s'achève sur une note d'espoir/un chapitre consacré à la peinture** the book ends on a hopeful note/with a chapter on painting; **ainsi s'achève notre aventure** thus ends the story of our adventure; *Rad & TV* **ainsi s'achève notre journal** (and) that's the end of the news

'On achève bien les chevaux' *McCoy, Pollack*
'They Shoot Horses, Don't They?'

Achgabat [aʃgabat] NM Ashgabat, Ashkhabad

achigan [aʃigɑ̃] NM *Can Ich* black-bass

Achille [aʃil] NPR *Myth* Achilles

achillée [akile] NF *Bot* yarrow, milfoil; **a. sternutatoire** sneezewort

acholie [akɔli] NF *Méd* acholia

achondroplasie [akɔ̃drɔplazi] NF *Méd* achondroplasia

achoppement [aʃɔpmɑ̃] *voir* **pierre**

achopper [3] [aʃɔpe] VI *Vieilli* **a. au problème de...** to come up against the problem of...; *Vieilli* **a. sur** to stumble on *or* over; *Fig* to come up against; **elle achoppe sur les r** she can't pronounce her r's

Achoura [aʃura] NF *Rel* Ashura

achromat [akrɔma] NM *Opt* achromat

achromatique [akrɔmatik] ADJ *Opt* achromatic

achromatiser [3] [akrɔmatize] VT *Opt* to achromatize

achromatisme [akrɔmatism] NM *Opt* achromatism

achromatopsie [akrɔmatɔpsi] NF *Méd* achromatopsia

achrome [akrom] ADJ **1** *Phot* achromous, achromatous **2** *Méd* achromic

achromie [akrɔmi] NF *Méd* achromia

achromique [akrɔmik] ADJ *Méd* achromic

achylie [aʃili] NF *Méd* achylia (gastrica)

aciculaire [asikylɛr] ADJ *Bot & Minér* acicular

acide [asid] ADJ **1** *(goût, fruit)* sour, acidic; *(propos)* acid, cutting, caustic **2** *Chim & École* acid

NM **1** *Biol & Chim* acid; **a. acétylsalicylique** acetylsalicylic acid; **a. alphalinolénique** alpha-linolenic acid; **a. aminé** amino acid; **a. aminé essentiel** essential amino acid; **a. ascorbique** ascorbic acid; **a. aspartique** aspartic acid; **a. carbonique** carbonic acid; **a. carboxylique** carboxylic acid; **a. chlorhydrique** hydric chloride; **a. cholique** cholic acid; **a. désoxyribonucléique** deoxyribonucleic acid; **a. fluorhydrique** hydrofluoric acid; **a. folique** folic acid, folacin; **a. formique** formic acid, methanoic acid; **a. gras** fatty acid; **a. gras essentiel** essential fatty acid; **a. hyaluronique** hyaluronic acid; **a. nicotinique** niacin; **a. nucléique** nucleic acid; **a. œnolique** oenolin; **a. oxalique** oxalic acid; **a. palmitique** palmitic acid; **a. phénique** carbolic acid, phenol; **a. picrique** picric acid; **a. propanoïque** propanoic acid; **a. propionique** propionic acid; **a. ribonucléique** ribonucleic acid; **a. sialique** sialic acid; **a. sulfhydrique** hydrogen sulphide; **a. sulfurique** sulphuric acid; **a. tellureux** tellurous acid; **a. valérique** pentanoic acid **2** *Fam (LSD)* acid

acide-alcool [asidalkɔl] *(pl* **acides-alcools***)* NM *Chim* acid alcohol

acidifiable [asidifjabl] ADJ *Chim* acidifiable

acidifiant [asidifjɑ̃] *Chim* ADJ acidifying

NM acidifier

acidificateur [asidifikatœr] NM *Chim* acidifier, acidifying agent

acidification [asidifikasjɔ̃] NF *Chim* acidification

acidifier [9] [asidifje] *Chim* VT to acidify

▸**s'acidifier** VPR to acidify

acidimètre [asidimɛtr] NM **1** *(pour le lait ou le vin)* acidimeter **2** *Tech (pour les accumulateurs)* acidimeter, acidometer

acidimétrie [asidimetri] NF *Chim* acidimetry

acidiphile [asidifil] = **acidophile**

acidité [asidite] NF **1** *(d'un goût, d'un fruit)* acidity, sourness; *(d'un propos)* tartness, sharpness **2** *Chim, Géol & Méd* acidity; *Physiol* **a. gastrique** acid stomach

acid jazz [asiddʒaz] NM *Mus* acid jazz

acido-alcalimétrie [asidoalkalimetri] *(pl* **acido-alcalimétries***)* NF *Géol* acidoalkalimetry

acidobasique [asidobazik] ADJ *Chim* acidobasic

acidocétose [asidɔsetoz] NF *Méd* ketoacidosis

acidophile [asidɔfil] ADJ *Biol* acidophil

acidose [asidoz] NF *Méd* acidosis

acidulé, -e [asidyle] ADJ *(goût)* acidulous; *Fig (coloris)* vivid, (very) bright

aciduler [3] [asidyle] VT **1** *Culin* to acidulate **2** *Chim* to make *or* to render acid

acier [asje] NM *Métal* steel; **a. haute tension** high-tensile steel; **a. inoxydable/trempé** stainless/tempered steel

❑ **d'acier** ADJ steel *(avant n)*; *Fig (regard)* steely; **muscles/cœur d'a.** muscles/heart of steel

aciérage [asjeraʒ] NM **1** *Métal (fabrication)* steeling; *(durcissement)* case-hardening **2** *Typ* steel-engraving

aciéré, -e [asjere] ADJ *Métal* steely

aciérer [18] [asjere] VT **1** *Métal (fabriquer)* to steel; *(durcir)* to case-harden **2** *Typ* to engrave on steel

aciérie [asjeri] NF *Métal* steelworks *(singulier)*, steel plant

aciériste [asjerist] NMF *Métal* steel manufacturer

acinésie [asinezi] = **akinésie**

acineuse [asinøz] ADJ F *Biol* acinous

acinus [asinys] *(pl* **acini** [asini]*)* NM *Biol* acinus

aclinique [aklinik] ADJ aclinic

acmé [akme] NM OU NF **1** *Littéraire (apogée)* acme, summit, height **2** *Méd* climax

acméisme [akmeism] NM *Littérature* Acmeism

acné [akne] NF *Méd* acne; **avoir de l'a.** to suffer from *or* to have acne; **a. juvénile** teenage acne

acnéique [akneik] *Méd* ADJ acned

NMF acne sufferer

acœlomate [aselɔmat] *Zool* NM acoelomate

❑ **acœlomates** NMPL Acoelomata

acolytat [akɔlita] NM *Rel* acolythate

acolyte [akɔlit] NM **1** *Rel* acolyte **2** *(complice)* sidekick

acompte [akɔ̃t] NM **1** *(versement régulier)* instalment; *(avance sur → une commande, des travaux)* down payment; *(→ un salaire)* advance; *(→ un loyer)* deposit; **payer par** *ou* **en plusieurs acomptes** to pay by *or* in instalments; **donner** *ou* **verser un a. de 500 euros (sur), payer** *ou* **verser 500 euros en a. (sur)** *(achat)* to make a down payment of 500 euros (on), to pay a deposit of 500 euros (on); **recevoir un a. sur son salaire** to receive an advance on one's salary; **a. de** *ou* **sur dividende** interim dividend; *Fin* **a. provisionnel** interim *or* advance payment; *Fin* **a. provisionnel d'impôt** advance tax payment

2 *(avant-goût)* foretaste, preview; **j'ai pris un petit a.** I had a little foretaste (of how things would be)

acon [akɔ̃] NM *Naut* lighter, (flat-bottomed) barge

aconage [akɔnaʒ] NM *Naut* lighterage

aconier [akɔnje] NM lighterman

aconit [akɔnit] NM *Bot* aconite, monkshood

aconitine [akɔnitin] NF *Chim* aconite

a contrario [akɔ̃trarjo] ADJ INV converse

ADV conversely

acoquinement [akɔkinmɑ̃] NM *Péj* **son a. avec l'extrême-droite l'a complètement discrédité** his connections with the extreme right ruined his reputation

acoquiner [3] [akɔkine] **s'acoquiner** VPR *Péj* **s'a. à** *ou* **avec qn** to take up *or* to fall in with sb; *Fig* to cosy up to sb; **il s'est acoquiné avec Pierrot** he's taken up *or* fallen in with Pierrot

acore [akɔr] NM *Bot* sweet rush, sweet flag

Açores [asɔr] NFPL **les A.** the Azores

à-côté [akote] *(pl* **à-côtés***)* NM **1** *(aspect → d'une question)* side issue; *(→ d'une histoire, d'un événement)* side *or* secondary aspect **2** *Fam (gain)* bit of extra money▪; *(frais)* incidental expense▪; **se faire des à-côtés** to make a bit on the side; **les frais d'hôtel plus les à-côtés** hotel expenses plus incidentals

acotylédone [akɔtiledɔn] *Bot* ADJ acotyledonous

NF acotyledon

acotylédoné, -e [akɔtiledɔne] *Bot* ADJ acotyledonous

❑ **acotylédonée** NF acotyledon

acoumètre [akumɛtr] NM *Méd* acoumeter

à-coup [aku] *(pl* **à-coups***)* NM **1** *(secousse → d'un moteur, d'un véhicule)* cough, judder; *(→ d'une machine)* jerk, jolt; **le moteur a des à-coups** the engine judders; **sans à-coups** smoothly **2** *(de l'économie)* upheaval

❑ **par à-coups** ADV *(travailler)* in spurts; *(avancer)* in fits and starts

acouphène [akufɛn] NM *Méd* tinnitus

acousticien, -enne [akustisjɛ̃, -ɛn] NM,F acoustician

acoustique [akustik] ADJ acoustic; **appareil a.** hearing aid

NF *(science)* acoustics *(singulier)*; *(qualité sonore)* acoustics

ACP [ɑsepe] NM *(abrév* **Groupe des États d'Afrique, des Caraïbes et du Pacifique***)* ACP Group

acquéreur, -euse [akerœr, -øz] NM,F purchaser, buyer; *Jur* vendee; **se porter a. de qch** to offer to buy sth; **il s'est rendu** *ou* **il est devenu a. de...** he's become the owner of...; **elle a trouvé un a. pour sa voiture** she found a buyer for her car; **ton chat a trouvé a.?** have you found a (new) home for your cat?

ADJ **les pays acquéreurs de cette technologie** countries which buy *or* acquire this technology; *Com* **société acquéreuse** takeover company

acquérir [39] [akerir] VT **1** *(biens)* to buy, to purchase, to acquire; *(fortune)* to acquire; **a. qch dans des circonstances douteuses** to come by sth in dubious circumstances; **a. qch par héritage** to come into sth; *Prov* **bien mal acquis ne profite jamais** ill-gotten gains seldom prosper

2 *Fig (habitude)* to develop; *(célébrité)* to attain, to achieve; *(droit)* to obtain; *(expérience)* to gain; *(savoir-faire)* to acquire; *(information, preuve)* to obtain, to acquire, to get hold of; **a. de la valeur** to increase in value; **a. la conviction/la certitude que...** to become convinced/certain that...; **a. une immunité** to become immune, to acquire immunity; **sa réaction lui a acquis l'estime de tous** his/her reaction won him/her everybody's esteem; **ce stage est destiné à leur faire a. une expérience pratique** this placement is designed to give them practical experience; **l'expérience qu'il a acquise sur le terrain lui a été utile** the experience he gained on the job has been useful

3 *(au passif)* **il vous est entièrement acquis** he backs you fully; **mon soutien vous est acquis** you can be certain of my support; **ce droit lui est acquis** he/she has an established right in this respect; **l'électorat n'est pas encore acquis à cette idée** the electorate hasn't fully accepted *or* hasn't quite come round to that idea yet

▸**s'acquérir** VPR **1** *(emploi passif)* **cette habitude s'acquiert facilement** it's easy to get into the habit; **la souplesse s'acquiert par des exercices** you become supple by exercising

2 *(gagner)* **s'a. la confiance de qn** to gain *or* to win sb's trust

acquêt [akɛ] NM *Jur* marital property; **communauté réduite aux acquêts** = marriage settlement whereby only goods acquired since the marriage are deemed to be held in common

acquiert *etc voir* **acquérir**

acquiescement [akjɛsmɑ̃] NM *(accord)* agreement; *(consentement)* assent, agreement; **hocher la tête en signe d'a.** to nod one's agreement

❑ **d'acquiescement** ADJ *(geste, signe)* approving

acquiescer [21] [akjese] VI to agree, to approve; **a. d'un signe de tête** to nod (one's) approval; **a. à qch** to assent *or* to agree to sth

acquis, -e [aki, -iz] PP *voir* **acquérir**

ADJ **1** *(avantage, droit, fait)* established; *(fortune, titre)* acquired; *Psy* learnt; **je tiens votre soutien pour a.** I take it for granted that you'll support me; **nous tenons pour acquise l'égalité de l'homme et de la femme** we take it as an established fact that men and women are equals

2 *(tournure impersonnelle)* **il est a. que vous ne participerez pas aux frais** it's understood that you won't contribute financially; **il est a. que la loi sera votée** it's understood that the law will be passed; **il est a. que la couche d'ozone est en danger** it is an established fact that the ozone layer is at risk

NM **1** *(savoir)* knowledge; **fonctionner sur des a. anciens** to get by on what one already knows

2 *(expérience)* experience; **avoir de l'a.** to be experienced

3 *(avantages, droits)* established privileges, rights to which one is entitled; **considère ça comme un a.** you can take it for granted; *UE* **a. communautaire** acquis communautaire *(entire body of legislation ratified by the EU since its inception, to which all new member states must adhere)*; **les a. sociaux** social benefits

acquisitif, -ive [akizitif, -iv] ADJ *Jur* acquisitive

acquisition [akizisjɔ̃] NF **1** *(apprentissage)* acquisition **2** *(achat → gén)* purchase; *(d'entreprise)* acquisition; **faire l'a. d'une maison** to buy *or* to purchase a house; **faire l'a. d'une entreprise** to acquire a company; **regarde ma dernière a.** look at my latest buy; **nouvelle a.** *(achat)* new purchase; *(dans un musée)* new acquisition; *UE* **a. intracommunautaire** intra-Community acquisition **3** *Ordinat* **a. de données** data acquisition

acquisitive [akizitiv] *voir* **acquisitif**

acquit [aki] NM *Com* receipt; **donner a. de qch** to give a receipt for sth; **pour a.** *(sur facture, quittance)* received (with thanks), paid; **a. de paiement** receipt

❑ **par acquit de conscience** ADV in order to set my/his/*etc* mind at rest

acquit-à-caution [akiakosjɔ̃] *(pl* **acquits-à-caution** [akiakosjɔ̃]*)* NM *Com* bond note

acquittable [akitabl] ADJ **1** *Jur* liable to be acquitted **2** *Fin* payable

acquitté, -e [akite] NM,F *Jur* = person who has been acquitted

acquittement [akitmɑ̃] NM **1** *(règlement → d'une facture, d'un droit)* payment; *(→ d'une obligation)* discharge; *(→ d'une promesse)* fulfilment; *(→ d'une dette)* payment, discharge; *(→ d'une fonction, d'un travail)* performance; *(→ d'un engagement)* fulfilment **2** *Jur* acquittal

acquitter [3] [akite] VT **1** *(payer → facture, note)* to pay, to settle; *(→ dette)* to pay off, to discharge; *(→ droits)* to pay; *(→ lettre de change)* to receipt; *(→ chèque)* to endorse

2 *(libérer)* **a. qn d'une dette/d'une obligation** to release sb from a debt/from an obligation

3 *Jur* to acquit

▸**s'acquitter** VPR **s'a. de** *(obligation)* to discharge; *(promesse)* to carry out; *(dette)* to pay off, to discharge; *(facture, droits)* to pay; *(fonction, travail)* to perform; *(engagement)* to fulfil; **s'a. envers** to repay

acra [akra] NM *Culin* accra, akkra *(Caribbean salt codfish or vegetable fritter)*

acre [akr] NF **1** *Anciennement (en France)* ≃ 5200m^2 **2** *Can* acre *(= 4047m^2)*

âcre [ɑkr] ADJ **1** *(saveur, odeur)* acrid **2** *Littéraire (propos, ton)* bitter

âcreté [ɑkrəte] NF **1** *(d'une saveur, d'une odeur)* acridness, acridity **2** *Littéraire (d'un propos, d'un ton)* bitterness

acrididé [akridide], **acridien** [akridjɛ̃] *Entom* NM acridid, acridian

❑ **acrididés** NMPL Acrididae

acrimonie [akrimɔni] NF acrimony, acrimoniousness

acrimonieux, -euse [akrimɔnjø, -øz] ADJ acrimonious

acrobate [akrɔbat] NMF *(gén)* acrobat; *(au trapèze)* trapeze artist

NM *Zool (mammifère)* flying squirrel

acrobatie [akrɔbasi] NF **1** *Sport* acrobatics **2** *Fig* **faire des acrobaties pour obtenir un crédit** to turn cartwheels to get credit; **il a réussi à remonter son affaire par quelques acrobaties** he managed to save his business by doing some skilful manoeuvring **3** *Aviat* **a. aérienne** aerobatics

acrobatique [akrɔbatik] ADJ acrobatic

acrocéphale [akrɔsefal] ADJ acrocephalic, acrocephalous

acrocéphalie [akrɔsefali] NF acrocephaly

acrocyanose [akrɔsjanoz] NF *Méd* acrocyanosis

acrodynie [akrɔdini] NF *Méd* acrodynia

acroléine [akrɔlein] NF *Chim* acrolein

acromégalie [akrɔmegali] NF *Méd* acromegaly

acromégalique [akrɔmegalik] ADJ *Méd* acromegalic

acromion [akrɔmjɔ̃] NM *Anat* acromion

acronyme [akrɔnim] NM *Ling* acronym

acrophobie [acrɔfɔbi] NF *Psy* acrophobia

Acropole [akrɔpɔl] NF **l'A.** the Acropolis

acropole [akrɔpɔl] NF acropolis, citadel

acrosome [akrɔzɔm] NM *Biol* acrosome

acrosport [akrɔspɔr] NM *Sport* sports acrobatics

acrostiche [akrɔstiʃ] NM *Littérature* acrostic

acrotère [akrɔtɛr] NM *Archit* acroter, acroterion, acroterium

acrylique [akrilik] *Chim & Tex* ADJ acrylic; **en a.** acrylic *(avant n)*
NM acrylic

acrylonitrile [akrilɔnitril] NM *Chim* acrylonitrile

ACT [ɑsete] NMF *Belg Rail (abrév* **accompagnateur de train**) ticket inspector

actanciel, -elle [aktɑ̃sjɛl] ADJ *Littérature* **schéma a.** actantial model (of narrative analysis), model for the distribution of actants

actant [aktɑ̃] NM **1** *Ling* agent **2** *Littérature* actant *(character considered from the point of view of how he contributes to the narrative dynamic)*

acte [akt] NM **A.** *SÉQUENCE* **1** *Mus & Théât* act; **a. III, scène 2** Act III, scene 2; **un opéra en trois/cinq actes** an opera in three/five acts; **une pièce en un seul a.** a one-act play
2 *Fig* period, episode; **sa mort annonçait le dernier a. de la campagne d'Italie/de la Révolution** his death ushered in the last episode of the Italian campaign/the Revolution
B. *ACTION* **1** *(gén)* action, act; **nous ne voulons pas des promesses mais des actes** we don't want promises but action; **son premier a. a été d'ouvrir la fenêtre** the first thing he did was to open the window; **juger qn sur ses actes** to judge sb by his/her actions; **un a. irresponsable** an irresponsible act; **passer aux actes** to take action, to act; **le dossier est prêt, nous passerons aux actes vendredi** the plans are ready, we'll set things in motion on Friday; **faire a. de citoyen** to act in one's capacity as a citizen; **faire a. d'héritier** to come forward as a beneficiary; **faire a. de témoin** to act as a witness, to testify; **faire a. de candidature** *(chercheur d'emploi)* to submit one's application, to apply; *(maire) Br* to stand, *Am* to run; **faire a. d'autorité** to show one's authority; **faire a. de bonne volonté** to show willing *or* one's good will; **elle a fait a. de courage** she proved *or* showed her courage; **faire a. de présence** to put in a token appearance; **a. de banditisme** criminal act; **a. de bravoure** act of bravery, brave deed, courageous act; **a. de charité** act of charity; **a. criminel** criminal offence, crime; **un a. de Dieu** an act of God; **a. de folie** act of madness; **a. de guerre** act of war; **a. d'hostilité** hostile act; **a. manifeste** overt act; **un a. contre nature** an unnatural act; **a. de terrorisme** terrorist action, act of terrorism; **a. simulé** bogus deed; **a. de vandalisme** act of vandalism; **a. de vengeance** act of revenge
2 *Méd* **a. chirurgical** *ou* **opératoire** operation; **a. de laboratoire** laboratory test; **a. (médical)** *(consultation)* (medical) consultation; *(traitement)* (medical) treatment
3 *Physiol (mouvement)* **a. instinctif/réflexe** instinctive/reflex action; **a. volontaire/involontaire** voluntary/involuntary action
4 passer à l'a. *(gén)* to act; *Psy* to act out; *(sexuellement)* to do the deed
5 *Psy* **a. manqué** acte manqué; **c'était peut-être un a. manqué** maybe subconsciously I/he/*etc* did it deliberately; **tu parles d'un a. manqué!** how Freudian can you get!
6 *Rel* **a. d'amour** act of love; **a. de foi** act of faith; *Hist (pendant l'Inquisition)* auto-da-fé
7 *Phil* **a. gratuit** motiveless act, *Spéc* acte gratuit
C. *ACTION LÉGALE, POLITIQUE* **1** *Jur* act, action; **a. administratif** administrative act; **a. d'administration** administrative act; **a. bilatéral** bilateral act; **a. de commerce** commercial transaction; **a. judiciaire** judicial act; **a. juridictionnel** legal ruling; **a. juridique** legal transaction; **a. du Palais** ≃ act between *Br* two counsels *or Am* attorneys at law; **a. de procédure** procedure; **a. à titre gratuit** act without consideration; **a. à titre onéreux** act for valuable consideration; **a. translatif** deed of transfer; **a. unilatéral** act of benevolence
2 *Pol* **a. de gouvernement** *(en France)* act of State; **A. du Parlement** *(en Grande-Bretagne)* Act of Parliament; **c'est maintenant un A. du Parlement** it has now become law; *UE* **a. unique européen** Single European Act
D. *DOCUMENT ADMINISTRATIF, LÉGAL* **1** *Admin* certificate; *Jur* deed; **demander a. de qch** to ask for formal acknowledgement of sth; **je demande a. de cette remarque** I want this remark to be minuted; **je demande a. du fait que...** I want it on record that...; **donner a. de qch** *(constater légalement)* to acknowledge sth formally; *Fig* **donner a. à qn de qch** to acknowledge the truth of what sb said; **dont a.** duly noted *or* acknowledged; **prendre a. de qch** *(faire constater légalement)* to record sth; *(noter)* to take a note of *or* to note sth; **je prends a. de votre refus** I have taken note of *or* noted your refusal; **le comité prendra a.** the committee will note; **a. de cession** conveyance; **a. de décès** death certificate; **a. de l'état civil** ≃ certificate delivered by the Registrar of births, deaths and marriages; **a. hypothécaire** mortgage deed; **a. de mariage** marriage certificate; **a. de naissance** birth certificate; **a. de propriété** title deed; **a. de transfert** deed of assignment; **a. de renonciation** quitclaim deed
2 *(en droit pénal)* **a. d'accusation** (bill of) indictment, charge; **lire l'a. d'accusation** to read out the bill of indictment *or* the charge; **quel est l'a. d'accusation?** what is the defendant being charged with?, what is the charge?; **a. d'instruction** measure of enquiry; **a. de poursuite** initiation of legal proceedings; **actes préparatoires** preparation *(of a crime)*
3 *(en droit civil)* **a. apparent** act apparent; **a. d'appel** notice of appeal; **a. authentique** *ou* **notarié** notarial act; **a. d'avocat à avocat** ≃ act between two *Br* counsels *or Am* attorneys at law; **a. d'avoué à avoué** ≃ act between two *Br* counsels *or Am* attorneys at law; **a. en brevet** = contract delivered by a notary in the original; **a. à cause de mort** = instrument not taking effect until death; **a. consensuel** consensual contract, contract of mutual assent; **a. conservatoire** conservation measure; **a. constitutif** incorporation of legal status, recognition of right; **a. déclaratif** declaration of legal status, recognition of right; **a. de disposition** act of disposal; **a. de donation** deed of covenant, gift; **a. fictif** ficitious action; **a. extrajudiciaire** = document served by a "huissier" without legal proceedings; **a. d'huissier** writ; **a. de notoriété** sworn affidavit; **a. récognitif** deed of recognition; **a. de simple tolérance** = tolerated access to another's property which does not result in its acquisition; **a. sous seing privé** private agreement; **a. de succession** attestation of inheritance *or* will; **a. de suscription** (testamentary) superscription
4 *(en droit commercial)* **a. d'association** partnership agreement *or* deed, articles of partnership; **a. de commerce** act of merchant; **a. mixte** = bilateral action which is commercial for one party but private for the other; **a. de vente** bill of sale
5 *(dans la diplomatie)* **a. diplomatique** diplomatic instrument
❑ **actes** NMPL **1** *(procès-verbaux)* proceedings; *(annales)* annals; **les actes de l'Académie des sciences** the annals of the Academy of Science
2 *Rel* **les Actes des apôtres** the Acts of the Apostles; **les Actes des martyrs** the acts of the martyrs
❑ **en acte** ADV *Phil* in action

acte-condition [aktəkɔ̃disjɔ̃] *(pl* **actes-conditions**)
NM *Jur* = legal transaction making a legal rule or set of rules applicable to an individual

actée [akte] NF *Bot* baneberry

Actéon [akteɔ̃] NPR *Myth* Actaeon

actéon [akteɔ̃] NM *Zool (mollusque)* actaeon

acter [3] [akte] VT **1** *(noter)* to take a note of, to note; *Jur* to record **2** *Can Fam (jouer* → *rôle)* to play (the part of)▪, to act▪; *(*→ *pièce de théâtre)* to perform▪; *(faire semblant)* to pretend▪
VI *Can Fam* to act▪; **a. dans un film/une pièce** to be in a film/a play▪; **cette fille acte bien/mal** this girl is a good/bad actress▪

acte-règle [aktərɛgl] *(pl* **actes-règles**) NM = legal act the effect of which is to create, modify or eliminate an objective legal situation

acteur, -trice [aktœr, -tris] NM,F *Cin, Théât & TV* actor, *f* actress; **a. de cinéma/de théâtre** screen actor, movie *or Br* film/stage actor; **a. comique** comic actor; **actrice comique** comedienne, comic actress; **a. de composition** versatile actor; **a. enfant** child actor; **a. de genre** character actor; **a. virtuel** *ou* **de synthèse** virtual-reality actor, synthespian
NM *Fig* protagonist; **les acteurs du drame** the people involved in the drama; **les différents acteurs de la négociation** the different participants in *or* parties involved in the negotiations; **a. économique** economic agent *or* player; **a. du marché, a. sur le marché** market participant, market player; **les acteurs sociaux** = employer, workers and trade unions

ACTH [ɑseteaʃ] NF INV *Biol (abrév* **adreno-cortico-trophic-hormone**) ACTH

ac'theure [astœr] = **asteur**

actif, -ive [aktif, -iv] ADJ **1** *(qui participe* → *membre, militaire, supporter)* active; **être a. dans une organisation** to be active within an organization; **participer de façon** *ou* **prendre une part active à** to take part fully *or* an active part in; **a. sur le plan politique** politically active
2 *(dynamique* → *vie)* busy, active; *(*→ *personne)* active, lively, energetic; **les années les plus actives de ma vie** the busiest years of my life; **avoir une retraite très active** to have a very active *or* busy retirement
3 *(qui travaille* → *population)* working, active
4 *Écon (marché)* active; **balance commerciale active** favourable trade balance; **la Bourse a été très active aujourd'hui** trading on the stock market was brisk today
5 *(efficace* → *remède, substance)* active, potent; *(*→ *shampooing)* active; **le principe a. de ce détachant** the active ingredient in this stain-remover
6 *Élec & Opt* active
7 *Gram* active; **à la voix active** in the active voice
8 *Chim* active, activated
9 *Ordinat (fichier, fenêtre)* active
NM **1** *Gram* active voice; **à l'a.** in the active voice
2 *(travailleur)* member of the active *or* working population; **les actifs** the active *or* working population
3 *Com, Compta & Fin (patrimoine)* assets; *Jur (d'une succession)* estate; **mettre** *ou* **porter une somme à l'a. de qn** to add a sum to sb's assets; **excédent de l'a. sur le passif** excess of assets over liabilities; **a. brut** gross assets; **a. brut de succession** gross estate; **a. circulant** floating *or* current assets; **a. circulant net** net current assets; **a. corporel** tangible assets; **a. corporel net** net tangible assets; **a. différé** deferred asset; **a. disponible liquide** available assets; **a. d'exploitation** operating assets; **a. fictif** fictitious assets; **a. immobilisé** fixed *or* capital assets; **a. incorporel** intangible assets; **a. liquide** liquid assets; **a. net** net assets *or* worth; **a. net comptable** net accounting *or* book assets; **a. net réévalué** net revalued assets; **a. non-disponible immobilisé** illiquid assets; **a. principal** core assets; **a. réalisable** realizable assets; **a. réel** real assets; **a. de roulement** current assets; **a. sous-jacent** underlying asset
❑ **active** NF *Mil* **l'active** the regular army
❑ **à l'actif de** PRÉP **mettre qch à l'a. de qn** to credit sb with sth; **avoir qch à son a.** to have sth to one's credit; **elle a de nombreuses victoires à son a.** she has many achievements to her credit; **elle n'a que des échecs à son a.** she's never succeeded in anything; **à son a., on peut mettre la conception du nouveau musée** to his/her credit, it should be said that he/she was the creator of the new museum

actine [aktin] NF *Biol & Chim* actin

acting-out [aktiŋaut] NM INV *Psy* acting out

actinide [aktinid] NM *Chim* actinide

actinidia [aktinidja], **actinidie** [aktinidi] NM *Bot* kiwi plant

actinie [aktini] NF *Zool* sea anemone, *Spéc* actinia

actinique [aktinik] ADJ *Phys* actinic

actinisme [aktinism] NM *Phys* actinism

actinite [aktinit] NF *Méd* sunburn

actinium [aktinjɔm] NM *Chim* actinium

actinologie [aktinɔlɔʒi] NF *Phys* actinology

actinomètre [aktinɔmɛtr] NM *Phys* actinometer

actinométrie [aktinɔmetri] NF *Phys* actinometry

actinomycète [aktinɔmisɛt] NM *Biol* actinomycete

actinomycine [aktinɔmisin] NF *Méd & Vét* actinomycin

actinomycose [aktinɔmikoz] NF *Méd & Vét* actinomycosis

actinote [aktinɔt] NF *Minér* actinolite

actinothérapie [aktinɔterapi] NF *Méd* actinotherapy

action [aksjɔ̃] NF **1** *(acte)* act, action; **l'a. de marcher** the act of walking; **responsable de ses actions** responsible for his/her actions; **bonne/mauvaise a.** good/evil deed; **faire une bonne a.** to do a good deed; **faire une mauvaise a.** to commit an evil deed; **faire de bonnes actions** to do good (deeds); **faire de mauvaises actions** to commit evil (deeds); **une a. d'éclat** a brilliant feat; **une a. de grâces** an offering of thanks

2 *(actes)* action; **passer à l'a.** *(gén)* to take action; *Mil* to go into action; **assez parlé, il est temps de passer à l'a.** enough talking, let's get down to it *or* take some action; **dans le feu de l'a., en pleine a.** right in the middle *or* at the heart of the action; **l'a.** *(l'intrigue)* the action *or* plot; **l'a. se passe en Europe/l'an 2000** the action is set in Europe/the year 2000

3 *(intervention)* action; **un conflit qui nécessite une a. immédiate de notre part** a conflict necessitating immediate action on our part; **une a. syndicale est à prévoir** some industrial action is expected; **a. revendicative** *(des travailleurs)* industrial action; *(des étudiants)* protests; **a. directe** direct action; **A. directe** = right-wing terrorist organization; **l'A. française** = French nationalist and royalist group founded in the late 19th century

4 *(activités)* work, activities; *(mesures)* measures; *(campagne)* campaign; **l'a. gouvernementale en faveur des sans-abri** the government's measures to help the homeless; **l'a. du gouvernement a été de laisser les forces s'équilibrer** the government's policy *or* course of action was to let the various forces balance each other out; **elle a été louée pour son a. au sein de nombreuses œuvres caritatives** she was praised for the work she did as a member of numerous charitable organizations; **l'organisme a sensibilisé le public par le biais de différentes actions** the organization has raised public awareness of the issue through various campaigns; **l'a. de l'institut dépasse le cadre strict de la médecine** the institute's sphere of activities goes beyond the purely medical field; **il est chargé de l'a. culturelle dans l'association** he has responsibility for cultural affairs in the organization

5 *(effet)* action, effect; **cette campagne aura une a. psychologique sur les consommateurs** this campaign will have a psychological effect *or* influence on the consumer; **l'a. de l'acide sur le métal** the action of acid on metal; **l'a. de la morphine** the effect of morphine

6 *Bourse (titre, valeur)* share; *(document)* share certificate; **actions** shares, equity, *Am* stock; **avoir des actions dans une société, détenir des actions d'une société** to have shares *or* a shareholding in a company; **émettre des actions sur un marché** to issue shares on a market; **les actions Comtel sont en hausse/à la baisse** Comtel shares are up/down; *Fig Hum* **ses actions ont baissé/monté** his stock has fallen/risen; **capital en actions** equity capital; **dividende en actions** *Br* bonus issue, *Am* stock dividend; **a. d'apport** *(délivrée au fondateur d'une société)* founder's share; *(émise par une société en échange d'un apport en nature)* vendor's share; **a. d'attribution** bonus share; **a. de capital** ≃ ordinary share; **a. de capitalisation** capital share; **a. cotée (en Bourse)** quoted share; **actions cotées en Bourse** common stock; **a. différée** deferred stock; **a. de distribution** income share; **a. à dividende cumulatif** cumulative share; **a. à dividende prioritaire** preferred share; **a. gratuite** bonus share; **a. de jouissance** dividend share; **a. libérée** paid-up share; **a. nominative** registered stock; **a. nouvelle** new share; **a. ordinaire** *Br* ordinary share, *Am* common stock; **a. au porteur** bearer share; **a. de premier rang** *ou* **de priorité** *ou* **privilégiée** *Br* preference share, *Am* preferred stock; **a. privilégiée cumulative** cumulative *Br* preference share *or Am* preferred stock; **a. reflet** tracker share; **a. syndiquée** syndicated share

7 *Mktg* campaign; **a. commerciale** marketing campaign; **a. promotionnelle** promotional campaign; **a. de vente** sales campaign, sales drive

8 *Jur* action, lawsuit; **intenter une a. contre** *ou* **à qn** to bring an action against sb, to take legal action against sb, to take sb to court *or* to bring a lawsuit against sb; **a. civile** civil action; **a. collective** class action; **a. confessoire** action in recognition of easement; **a. contractuelle** action for breach of contract; **a. en contrefaçon** action for infringement of patent; **a. déclaratoire** action in definition of right; **a. en diffamation** libel action; **a. disciplinaire** disciplinary action; **a. en dommages-intérêts** action *or* claim for damages; **a. à fins de subsides** action for child maintenance; **a. immobilière** action concerning real property; **a. judiciaire** action; **a. en justice** legal action, lawsuit; **a. mixte** mixed real and personal action; **a. mobilière** action concerning movable property; **a. négatoire** negatory action; **a. en nullité** action for (a) voidance of contract; **a. oblique** derivative action; **a. paulienne** revocatory action; **a. personnelle** personal action, action in personam; **a. en pétition d'hérédité** = claim to succeed to an estate held by a third party; **a. pétitoire** claim of ownership; **a. possessoire** possessory action; **a. publique** = public prosecution initiated by the public prosecutor; **déclencher l'a. publique** to bring about a public prosecution; **a. en recherche de maternité naturelle** maternity suit; **a. en recherche de paternité naturelle** paternity suit; **a. récursoire** claim for contribution; **a. rédhibitoire** remedy for latent defect; **a. réelle** real action, action in rem; **a. rescisoire** rescissory action

9 *Mil, Mus & Phys* action; **à double/simple a.** *(arme à feu, détente)* double-/single-action

10 *Gram* action; **l'a. du verbe** the action of the verb

11 *Suisse (vente promotionnelle)* sale, special offer

12 *Sport* **une magnifique a.** a great bit of play; **il y a eu quelques belles actions lors de cette rencontre** there were some fine passages of play *or* there was some good play during the match; **l'équipe a gagné grâce à l'a. de Marchand** some neat play from Marchand won the game for the team; **on va revoir l'a. de Thierry Henry** let's see that bit of play from Thierry Henry again

13 *Admin* **a. sanitaire et sociale** health and social services

❑ **d'action** ADJ **1** *(mouvementé → roman)* action-packed, full of action; **film d'a.** action movie

2 *(entreprenant)* **homme/femme d'a.** man/woman of action

3 *Pol & Ind* **journée/semaine d'a.** day/week of action

❑ **en action** ADJ in action; **être en a.** to be in action; **ils sont déjà en a. sur les lieux** they're already busy at the scene ADV **entrer en a.** *(pompiers, police)* to go into action; *(loi, règlement)* to become effective, to take effect; **mettre qch en a.** to set sth in motion; **la sirène s'est/a été mise en a.** the alarm went off/was set off

❑ **sous l'action de** PRÉP due to, because of; **sous l'a. de la pluie** due to the effect *or* because of the rain

actionnable [aksjɔnabl] ADJ actionable

actionnaire [aksjɔnɛr] NMF *Bourse Br* shareholder, *Am* stockholder; **les petits actionnaires** small *Br* shareholders *or Am* stockholders; **a. majoritaire** majority *Br* shareholder *or Am* stockholder; **a. minoritaire** minority *Br* shareholder *or Am* stockholder; **a. de référence** major *Br* shareholder *or Am* stockholder

actionnariat [aksjɔnarja] NM *Bourse* **1** *(système) Br* shareholding, *Am* stockholding; **a. ouvrier** worker *Br* shareholding *or Am* stockholding, worker share ownership; **a. intermédiaire** nominee *Br* shareholding *or Am* stockholding; **a. des salariés** employee *Br* shareholding *or Am* stockholding, employee share ownership **2** *(actionnaires)* **l'a.** *Br* the shareholders, *Am* the stockholders

actionner [3] [aksjɔne] VT **1** *(mettre en marche → appareil)* to start up; *(→ sirène)* to set off; *(→ sonnette)* to ring; **le moteur est actionné par la vapeur** the engine is steam-powered *or* steam-driven; **actionné à la main** hand-operated **2** *Jur* **a. qn** to bring an action against *or* to sue sb

actionneur [aksjɔnœr] NM *Tech* actuator

actionnisme [aksyonism] NM **1** *(en sociologie)* action theory **2** *Beaux-Arts* **a. viennois** Viennese Actionism

action research [akʃənrizərtʃ] NF *(en psychosociologie)* action research

activateur, -trice [aktivatœr, -tris] ADJ *(substance)* activating; *(système)* activation *(avant n)*

NM activator, activation agent; *Biol & Chim* coenzyme

activation [aktivasjɔ̃] NF **1** *(d'un processus, de travaux)* speeding up *or* along, hastening **2** *Chim & Phys* activation

activatrice [aktivatris] *voir* **activateur**

active [aktiv] *voir* **actif**

activé, -e [aktive] ADJ **1** *Chim & Phys* activated **2** *Ordinat (fichier, fenêtre)* active; *(option)* enabled

activement [aktivmɑ̃] ADV actively; **participer a. à qch** to take an active part *or* to be actively engaged in sth

activer [3] [aktive] VT **1** *(feu)* to stoke (up); *(travaux, processus)* to speed up **2** *Fam (presser)* **active le pas!** get a move on! **3** *Chim & Phys* to activate **4** *Ordinat* to activate; **a. une option** to select an option

USAGE ABSOLU *Fam (se dépêcher)* **active un peu!** get a move on!

▸**s'activer** VPR **1** *(s'affairer)* to bustle about **2** *Fam (se dépêcher)* **il est tard, dis-leur de s'a.!** it's late, tell them to get a move on!

activeur [aktivœr] NM *Chim* activator

activisme [aktivism] NM activism

activiste [aktivist] ADJ activist, militant

NMF activist, militant

activité [aktivite] NF **1** *(animation)* activity *(UNCOUNT)*; **déborder d'a.** *(sujet: personne)* to be extraordinarily active; **le restaurant/l'aéroport débordait d'a.** the restaurant/airport was very busy; **elle déploie une grande a. au travail** she invests a lot of energy in her work; **période de grande a. diplomatique** period of intense diplomatic activity; *Bourse* **sans a.** *(marché)* slack, dull

2 *Admin & Écon* **avoir une a. professionnelle** to be actively employed; **mes activités professionnelles** my professional activities; **être sans a.** to be unemployed; **avoir une a. non rémunérée** to be in unpaid work; **a. bancaire** banking; **a. commerciale** business activity; **a. économique** economic activity; **a. industrielle** industrial activity; **a. lucrative** gainful employment; **a. politique** political activity; **a. primaire/secondaire/tertiaire** primary/secondary/tertiary-sector employment

3 *(occupation → d'une personne, d'un marché, d'une entreprise)* activity; **une a. différente leur est proposée tous les soirs** they can do a different activity every evening; **pensez-vous conserver une a. après la retraite?** do you intend to carry on some form of activity *or* occupation after retirement?; **activités dirigées** guided activities; **activités d'éveil** discovery classes

4 *Astron & Physiol* activity; **a. cérébrale** brain activity; **l'a. solaire** solar activity

❑ **en activité** ADJ *(fonctionnaire, militaire)* (currently) in post; *(médecin)* practising; *(volcan)* active, live; *Admin* **rester en a.** to remain in gainful employment

❑ **en pleine activité** ADJ *(industrie, usine)* fully operational; *(bureau, restaurant)* bustling; *(marché boursier, secteur)* active, brisk; **être en pleine a.** *(très affairé)* to be very busy; *(non retraité)* to be in the middle of one's working life

actrice [aktris] *voir* **acteur**

actuaire [aktɥɛr] NMF *Fin & Assur* actuary

actualisation [aktɥalizasjɔ̃] NF **1** *(mise à jour → d'un texte, d'un ouvrage)* updating; **faire l'a. d'un ouvrage** to update a work **2** *Phil* actualization **3** *Écon & Fin* discounting **4** *Ling* realization **5** *Ordinat (d'écran)* refresh; *(d'un logiciel)* update

actualiser [3] [aktɥalize] VT **1** *(texte, ouvrage)* to update, to bring up to date **2** *Phil* to actualize **3** *Écon* to discount **4** *Ling* to realize **5** *Ordinat (écran)* to refresh; *(logiciel)* to update

actualisme [aktɥalism] NM *Phil & Géol* actualism, methodological uniformitarianism

actualité [aktɥalite] NF **1** *(caractère actuel)* topicality

2 *(événements récents)* current developments; **l'a. médicale/scientifique** medical/scientific developments; **se tenir au courant de l'a. politique/théâtrale** to keep abreast of political/theatrical events; **il s'intéresse à l'a.** he's interested in current affairs; **une question d'une a. brûlante** a highly topical issue

3 *Phil* actuality, reality

❑ **actualités** NFPL **les actualités** *(les informations)* the news *(singulier)*; **les actualités télévisées** the television news; **il est passé aux actualités** he was on the news

❑ **d'actualité** ADJ *(film, roman, débat)* topical; **c'est un sujet d'a.** it's very topical (at the moment); **cette question est toujours d'a.** this is still a topical question

actuariat [aktɥarja] NM *Fin & Assur* **1** *(fonction)* **l'a.** the actuarial profession **2** *(corporation)* body of actuaries

actuariel, -elle [aktɥarjɛl] ADJ *Fin & Assur* actuarial

actuel, -elle [aktɥɛl] ADJ **1** *(présent)* present, current; **sous le gouvernement a.** under the present government; **l'a. président** the president in office; **dans les circonstances actuelles** under the present circumstances; **le monde a.** today's world; **à l'époque actuelle** nowadays, in this day and age; **le cours a. du dollar** the current (exchange) rate for the dollar **2** *(d'actualité)* topical **3** *Phil & Rel* actual

actuellement [aktɥɛlmã] ADV *(à présent)* at present, at the moment; *(de nos jours)* nowadays, currently

acuité [akɥite] NF **1** *(du son)* shrillness **2** *(intensité → de l'intelligence)* sharpness; *(→ d'une crise)* severity; *(→ du regard)* penetration; *(→ d'un chagrin)* keenness; *(→ d'une douleur)* intensity, acuteness **3** *Méd* acuity, acuteness; **a. visuelle** acuteness of vision

aculéate [akyleat] *Entom* ADJ aculeate

❑ **aculéates** NMPL Aculeata, aculeate Hymenoptera

acuminé, -e [akymine] ADJ *Bot* acuminate

acuponcteur, -trice [akypɔ̃ktœr, -tris] NM,F *Méd* acupuncturist

acuponcture [akupɔ̃ktyr] NF *Méd* acupuncture

acupressing [akupresiŋ] NM *Méd* acupressure

acupuncteur, -trice [akupɔ̃ktœr, -tris] = **acuponcteur, -trice**

acupuncture [akupɔ̃ktyr] = **acuponcture**

acutangle [akytãgl] ADJ *Géom* acute-angled

ACV [aseve] NM *Méd (abrév* **accident cérébrovasculaire)** stroke, *Spéc* cerebrovascular accident

acyclique [asiklik] ADJ acyclic

acylation [asilasjɔ̃] NF *Chim* acylation

acyle [asil] NM *Chim* acyl

Ada [ada] NM INV *Ordinat* Ada

ADAC [adak] NM *Aviat (abrév* **avion à décollage et atterrissage courts)** STOL

adage [adaʒ] NM **1** *(maxime)* adage, saying; **selon l'a.** as the saying goes **2** *(en danse)* adagio

adagio [adadʒjo] *Mus* NM adagio
 ADV adagio

Adam [adã] NPR *Bible* Adam

adamantin, -e [adamãtɛ̃, -in] ADJ *Anat & Littéraire* adamantine

adamique [adamik] ADJ Adamic

adamisme [adamism] NM *Rel* Adamatism

adamsite [adamsit] NF *Chim* adamsite

adaptabilité [adaptabilite] NF adaptability

adaptable [adaptabl] ADJ adaptable

adaptateur, -trice [adaptatœr, -tris] NM,F *(personne)* adapter, adaptor
 NM **1** *Élec (objet)* adapter, adaptor; *Phot* **a. graphique couleur** colour graphics adapter **2** *TV (pour TNT)* set-top box, digital receiver

adaptatif, -ive [adaptatif, -iv] ADJ adaptive

adaptation [adaptasjɔ̃] NF **1** *(flexibilité)* adaptation; **faculté d'a.** adaptability; **ils n'ont fait aucun effort d'a.** they didn't try to adapt **2** *Biol* adaptation **3** *Cin, Théât & TV* adaptation, adapted version; **a. scénique** *ou* **théâtrale/cinématographique** stage/screen adaptation **4** *Mus* arrangement, setting; **a. pour piano** arrangement for (the) piano

adaptative [adaptativ] *voir* **adaptatif**

adaptatrice [adaptatris] *voir* **adaptateur**

adapter [3] [adapte] VT **1** *(fixer)* **a. un embout à un tuyau/un filtre sur un objectif** to fit a nozzle on to a pipe/a filter on to a lens

2 *(ajuster)* **a. son discours à son public** to fit one's language to one's audience; **a. des illustrations à un texte** to select pictures to fit a text; **adapté aux circonstances** appropriate; **la méthode n'est pas vraiment adaptée à la situation** the method isn't very appropriate for this situation; **a. la main-d'œuvre aux nouvelles technologies** to adapt the workforce to new technology; **adapté aux besoins du client** adapted *or* tailored to the needs of the customer **3** *Cin, Théât & TV* to adapt; **a. un roman au théâtre** *ou* **à la scène/au cinéma** to adapt a novel for the stage/for the cinema; **a. une pièce pour la télévision** to adapt a play for TV; **adapté d'une nouvelle de...** adapted from a short story by...

4 *Mus* to arrange; **il a adapté le concerto pour le piano** he arranged the concerto for piano

▶**s'adapter** VPR **1** *(s'ajuster)* **s'a. à** to fit; **la clé s'adapte à la serrure** the key fits the lock; **s'a. sur** to fit on; **le couvercle s'adapte sur le bocal par un crochet/par un pas de vis** the lid clips/screws onto the jar

2 *(s'habituer)* to adapt (oneself); **tu t'adapteras!** you'll get used to it!; **savoir s'a.** to be adaptable; **elle n'a pas pu s'a. à ce milieu** she couldn't adjust to this social circle; **il s'est bien adapté/il a eu du mal à s'a. à sa nouvelle école** he has settled down well/he's had trouble settling down in his new school

adaptif, -ive [adaptif, -iv] ADJ *Biol* adaptive

ADAV [adav] NM *Aviat (abrév* **avion à décollage et atterrissage verticaux)** VTOL

ADD *Électron (abrév écrite* **analogique digital digital)** ADD

addax [adaks] NM *Zool* addax

addenda [adɛ̃da] NMPL addenda

addendum [adɛ̃dɔm] NM addendum

addictif, -ive [adiktif, -iv] ADJ *Méd* addictive

addiction [adiksjɔ̃] NF (drug) addiction

addictive [adiktiv] *voir* **addictif**

Addis-Ababa [adisababa], **Addis-Abeba** [adisabeba] NM *Géog* Addis Ababa

additif, -ive [aditif, -iv] ADJ *Math & Phot* additive
 NM **1** *(à un texte)* additional clause **2** *(ingrédient)* additive; **sans additifs** additive-free

addition [adisjɔ̃] NF **1** *(ajout)* addition; **l'a. d'une aile au bâtiment** the addition of a new wing to the building; **faire des additions à un texte** to add to a text **2** *Math* sum; **faire une a.** to add (figures) up, to do a sum **3** *(facture)* Br bill, Am check; *Fam* **l'a. est salée!** the bill's a bit steep!

additionnel, -elle [adisjɔnɛl] ADJ additional; *Ordinat* add-on

additionner [3] [adisjɔne] VT **1** *Math (nombres)* to add (up); **a. 15 et 57** to add 15 and 57, to add 15 to 57, to add together 15 and 57 **2** *(altérer)* **a. un alcool d'un peu d'eau** to add a little water to a drink; **du vin/lait additionné d'eau** watered-down wine/milk

▶**s'additionner** VPR to build up; **aux longues heures de travail s'additionnent celles passées dans le métro** along with the long working hours, there are those spent on the underground

additionneur [adisjɔnœr] NM *Électron* adder

additive [aditiv] *voir* **additif**

additivé, -e [aditive] ADJ treated with additives

adducteur [adyktœr] ADJ M *Anat (muscle)* adductor *(avant n)*; *(canal)* feeder *(avant n)*
 NM *Anat (muscle)* adductor; *(canal)* feeder *(canal)*

adduction [adyksjɔ̃] NF **1** *Physiol* adduction **2** *(en travaux publics)* **a. d'eau** water conveyance

adduit [adɥi] NM *Chim* adduct

-ADE [ad] SUFF

This suffix is used to form feminine nouns.

● In the majority of cases, the basis is a verb. The idea is that of an ACTION or the RESULT of an action, and the register is often colloquial:
une bousculade a scramble, a stampede; **une engueulade** a bawling out, a quarrel; **la rigolade** fun; **des embrassades** hugging and kissing; **une embuscade** an ambush

Occasionally, the basis for derivation is a noun:
des fanfaronnades (from *fanfaron*) boasting; **une œillade** (from *œil*) a wink

● Adding the suffix **-ade** to a noun can result in a COLLECTIVE noun:
une fusillade a volley of shots; **une arcade** arches; **une colonnade** a colonnade

● When added to a noun, **-ade** can also convey the idea of something MADE OF the ingredient that the noun refers to:
une orangeade an orange drink; **une persillade** chopped parsley; **une grillade** grilled meat

Adélaïde [adelaid] NM *Géog* Adelaide

Adélie [adeli] *voir* **terre**

ADEME [adɛm] NF *Écol (abrév* **Agence de l'environnement et de la maîtrise de l'énergie)** = French public body responsible for environmental and energy management

ademption [adãpsjɔ̃] NF *Jur* ademption

Aden [adɛn] NM *Géog* Aden

adénine [adenin] NF *Biol & Chim* adenine

adénite [adenit] NF *Méd* adenitis

adénocarcinome [adenokarsinɔm] NM *Méd* adenocarcinoma

adénogramme [adenogram] NM *Méd* lymph node biopsy

adénoïde [adenɔid] ADJ *Anat* adenoidal

adénoïdectomie [adenɔidɛktɔmi] NF *Méd* adenoidectomy

adénome [adenom] NM *Méd* adenoma

adénopathie [adenopati] NF *Méd* adenopathy

adénosine [adenozin] NF *Biol* adenosine

adénovirus [adenovirys] NM *Méd* adenovirus

adent [adã] NM *Menuis* dovetail

adepte [adɛpt] NMF **1** *Rel & Pol* follower; **un a. de la non-violence** a supporter of non-violence **2** *Fig* **faire des adeptes** to become popular; **la méthode Pilates a fait de nombreux adeptes** Pilates now has a big following; **les adeptes du tennis** tennis enthusiasts; **c'est une a. de romans policiers** she's an avid reader of detective novels

adéquat, -e [adekwa, -at] ADJ suitable, appropriate

adéquatement [adekwatmã] ADV suitably, appropriately

adéquation [adekwasjɔ̃] NF appropriateness; **l'a. entre l'offre et la demande favorise la stabilité des prix** the balance between supply and demand encourages stable prices; *Fin* **a. des fonds propres** capital adequacy

adextré, -e [adɛkstre] ADJ *Hér* dexterwise, dexterways; **a. d'une étoile** with a star dexterwise *or* dexterways

ad fundum [adfundum] *Fam Arg scol* = **à-fond**

adhérence [aderãs] NF **1** *(par la colle, le ciment)* adhesion **2** *(au sol)* adhesion, grip; **l'a. des skis sur la neige** the skis' grip on the snow; **le manque d'a. d'une voiture** a car's lack of *or* poor road-holding **3** *Littéraire (adéquation)* **a. de l'expression à la pensée** cohesion between expression and thought **4** *Anat* adhesion

adhérent, -e [aderã, -ãt] ADJ **1** *(gén)* adherent; **a. à la route** with good road-holding **2** *Bot* adherent, adnate
 NM,F member

adhérer [18] [adere] **adhérer à** VT IND **1** *(coller sur)* to adhere to; **a. à la route** to hold the road **2** *(se rallier à → opinion)* to adhere to, to support; *(→ cause)* to support; *(→ idéal)* to adhere to; *(→ association)* to join, to become a member of; **ils promettent n'importe quoi pour faire a. les gens à leur parti** they make all sorts of promises to get people to join their party

    USAGE ABSOLU **une colle qui adhère rapidement** a quick-setting glue; **pour une France moderne, adhérez!** join us in building a new France!

adhésif, -ive [adezif, -iv] ADJ adhesive, sticky

    NM **1** *(substance)* adhesive **2** *(ruban)* sticky tape, *Br* Sellotape®, *Am* Scotch® tape

adhésion [adezjɔ̃] NF **1** *(accord)* support, adherence; **donner son a. à un projet** to give one's support to *or* to support a project **2** *(inscription)* membership; **l'a. au club est gratuite** club membership is free; **de plus en plus d'adhésions** more and more members; **après leur a. à l'Union européenne** after joining the European Union

adhésive [adeziv] *voir* **adhésif**

adhésivité [adezivite] NF adhesiveness

ad hoc [adɔk] ADJ INV **1** *(approprié)* appropriate, suitable **2** *(destiné à tel usage → règle, raisonnement, commission)* ad hoc; **juge a.** specially appointed judge; **réunions a.** meetings (organized) on an ad hoc basis

ad hominem [adɔminɛm] ADJ INV ad hominem; **pas d'arguments a. s'il vous plaît!** no personal attacks please!

adiabatique [adjabatik] *Phys & Météo* ADJ adiabatic; **courbe a.** adiabat; **diagramme a.** adiabatic chart

    NF adiabat; **a. humide** condensation adiabat; **a. sèche** dry adiabat; **pseudo a., a. saturée** pseudo adiabat

adiabatisme [adjabatism] NM *Phys* adiabatism, adiabatic state *(of gas)*

adiante [adjɑ̃t], **adiantum** [adjɑ̃tɔm] NM *Bot* maidenhair (fern)

adieu, -x [adjø] NM goodbye, *Littéraire* farewell; **des adieux émouvants** an emotional farewell; **faire ses adieux à qn** to say goodbye *or* one's farewells to sb; **faire ses adieux à la scène/au music-hall** to make one's final appearance on stage/on a music-hall stage; **dire a. à qn** to say goodbye *or* farewell to sb; **tu peux dire a. à ta voiture/tes ambitions** you can say goodbye to your car/ambitions

    ❏ **adieu** EXCLAM **1** *(pour toujours)* goodbye, *Littéraire* farewell; *Fam* **a. Berthe!** that's the end of it!

    2 *(dans le Midi) & Suisse (bonjour)* hello, hi; *(au revoir)* bye

    ❏ **d'adieu** ADJ INV *(baiser)* farewell *(avant n)*; *(regard, cadeau)* parting *(avant n)*

‖══════‖▢‖══════‖

'L'Adieu aux armes' *Hemingway* 'A Farewell to Arms'

à-Dieu-va [adjøva], **à-Dieu-vat** [adjøvat] EXCLAM it's in God's hands

adipeux, -euse [adipø, -øz] ADJ **1** *(tissu, cellule)* adipose; *(visage)* puffed up, puffy **2** *Hum (personne)* podgy

---

adipique [adipik] ADJ *Chim* adipic

adipocyte [adipɔsit] NM *Physiol* adipocyte

adipolyse [adipɔliz] NF *Méd* lipolysis

adipopexie [adipɔpɛksi] NF *Physiol* lipopexia, adipopexia

adipose [adipoz] NF *Physiol* adiposis

adiposité [adipozite] NF *Physiol* adiposity

adiposo-génital, -e, -aux, -ales [adipozoʒenital, -o] ADJ *Méd* adipogenital, adiposo-genital

adipsie [adipsi] NF *Méd* adipsia

adja [adʒa] NF *Fam* **mettre l'a.** *ou* **les adjas** to beat it, to do a bunk

adjacent, -e [adʒasɑ̃, -ɑ̃t] ADJ adjoining, adjacent; *Math (angles)* adjacent; **a. à qch** adjoining sth, adjacent to sth

adjectif, -ive [adʒɛktif, -iv] ADJ adjective *(avant n)*, adjectival

    NM *Gram* adjective; **a. épithète** attributive adjective; **a. attribut** predicative adjective

adjectival, -e, -aux, -ales [adʒɛktival, -o] ADJ *Gram* adjectival

adjective [adʒɛktiv] *voir* **adjectif**

adjectivé, -e [adʒɛktive] ADJ *Gram* used as an adjective

adjectivement [adʒɛktivmɑ̃] ADV *Gram* adjectivally, as an adjective

adjectiver [3] [adʒɛktive], **adjectiviser** [3] [adʒɛktivize] VT *Gram* to use as an adjective

adjoindre [82] [adʒwɛ̃dr] VT **1** *(ajouter)* **a. à** to add to; **a. une véranda à une pièce** to add a conservatory on to a room; **a. des équipements à un ordinateur** to upgrade a computer with add-ons; **a. une pièce à une lettre** to enclose a document with a letter

    2 *(associer)* **on m'a adjoint un secrétaire/une assistante** I was given a secretary/an assistant

    ▸**s'adjoindre** VPR **s'a. qn** to take sb on; **ils se sont adjoint des collaborateurs** they've taken on some helpers

adjoint, -e [adʒwɛ̃, -ɛt] ADJ assistant, deputy *(avant n)*; *(directeur)* assistant, associate

    NM,F *(assistant)* assistant, deputy; **a. au maire** deputy mayor; **a. d'enseignement** assistant teacher

    NM *Mil* adjunct

adjonction [adʒɔ̃ksjɔ̃] NF **1** *(fait d'ajouter)* adding; **sans a. de sucre/sel** with no added sugar/salt; *(sur emballage)* no added sugar/salt **2** *(chose ajoutée)* addition; **faire une a./des adjonctions à un texte** to make an addition/additions to a text; **biffer les adjonctions** to cross out the addenda

adjudant [adʒydɑ̃] NM **1** *Mil (dans l'armée de terre)* *Br* ≃ staff sergeant, *Am* ≃ sergeant major; *(dans l'armée de l'air)* *Br* ≃ warrant officer, *Am* ≃ master sergeant **2** *Fam Hum* **bien, mon a.!** aye, aye, captain!

adjudant-chef [adʒydɑ̃ʃɛf] *(pl* **adjudants-chefs**) NM *Mil (dans l'armée de terre)* *Br* ≃ warrant officer 2nd class, *Am* ≃ warrant officer; *(dans l'armée de l'air)* *Br* ≃ warrant officer, *Am* ≃ senior master sergeant

adjudant-major [adʒydɑ̃maʒɔr] *(pl* **adjudants-majors**) NM *Mil (dans l'armée de terre)* *Br* ≃ warrant officer 1st class, *Am* ≃ warrant officer; *(dans l'armée de l'air)* *Br* ≃ warrant officer, *Am* ≃ chief master sergeant

adjudicataire [adʒydikatɛr] NMF **1** *Jur (aux enchères)* successful bidder **2** *Com (d'un appel d'offres)* successful *Br* tenderer *or Am* bidder

adjudicateur, -trice [adʒydikatœr, -tris] NM,F **1** *Jur (dans des enchères)* seller **2** *Com (dans un appel d'offres)* awarder *(of a contract)*

adjudicatif, -ive [adʒydikatif, -iv] ADJ *Jur & Com* = relating to a sale by auction or a tender

adjudication [adʒydikasjɔ̃] NF **1** *Jur (enchères)* auction sale; *(attribution)* auctioning (off); **a. forcée** compulsory sale

    2 *Com (appel d'offres)* invitation to *Br* tender *or Am* bid; *(attribution)* awarding, allocation

    ❏ **en adjudication** ADV **mettre une propriété en a.** to put a property up for (sale by) auction; **mettre un marché en a.** to put a contract out to tender

    ❏ **par adjudication, par voie d'adjudication** ADV **1** *Jur (aux enchères)* by auction

    2 *Com* by *Br* tender *or Am* bid

adjudicative [adʒydikativ] *voir* **adjudicatif**

adjudicatrice [adʒydikatris] *voir* **adjudicateur**

---

adjuger [17] [adʒyʒe] VT **1** *Jur (aux enchères)* **a. qch à qn** to knock sth down to sb; **a. un objet au plus offrant** to sell an item to the highest bidder; **la statuette a été adjugée pour 1000 euros** the statuette was knocked down for 1,000 euros; **une fois, deux fois, trois fois, adjugé, vendu!** going, going, gone!; *Fig* **adjugé, vendu!** gone!, done!

    2 *(attribuer)* **a. un contrat/marché à qn** to award a contract/market to sb; **a. une note à qn** to give sb a *Br* mark *or Am* grade; **a. une place à qn** to give sb a seat

    ▸**s'adjuger** VPR to take; **elle s'est adjugé la plus jolie chambre** she took *or* commandeered the nicest room; **s'a. la meilleure place** to take the best seat

adjuration [adʒyrasjɔ̃] NF plea, entreaty

adjurer [3] [adʒyre] VT to entreat, to implore; **a. qn de faire qch** to implore *or* to entreat sb to do sth

adjuvant, -e [adʒyvɑ̃, -ɑ̃t] ADJ adjuvant, auxiliary

    NM **1** *Méd & Pharm (médicament)* adjuvant **2** *(produit)* additive **3** *Littérature & Théât* companion, partner

adlérien, -enne [adlerjɛ̃, -ɛn] ADJ *Psy* Adlerian

ad lib [adlib], **ad libitum** [adlibitɔm] ADV *(gén) & Mus* ad lib

ad litem [adlitɛm] ADJ INV ad litem

ADM [adeɛm] NFPL *(abrév* **armes de destruction massive***)* WMD

admettre [84] [admɛtr] VT **1** *(laisser entrer → client, spectateur)* to allow *or* to let in; **le public sera admis après 8 heures** the public will be allowed in after 8; **les enfants de moins de dix ans ne sont pas admis** children under the age of ten are not admitted; **on nous admit dans le lieu saint** we were admitted into the holy place

    2 *Tech* to let in; **la soupape admet les liquides** the valve lets the fluid in

    3 *(recevoir)* **a. qn chez soi** to allow sb into one's house; **a. qn dans un groupe** to let *or* to allow sb into a group; **il m'a finalement admis parmi ses amis** *(introduit auprès d'eux)* he finally introduced me to his circle of friends; *(considéré comme l'un d'eux)* he finally allowed me to become a friend; **a. qn dans un club** to admit sb to (membership of) a club; **faire a. qn dans un club** to sponsor sb for membership of a club; **elle a été admise à l'Académie/à l'hôpital** she was elected to the Académie/admitted to hospital; **a. les femmes à** *ou* **dans la prêtrise** to admit women to the priesthood; *Bourse* **a. une société à la cote** to list a company

    4 *Scol & Univ* to pass; **être admis** to pass; **nous admettrons plus de candidats cette année** we will pass *or* let through more candidates this year; **il ne sera pas admis dans la classe supérieure** he won't be admitted to *or* allowed into the next *Br* year *or Am* class

    5 *(autoriser)* **il a été admis à passer les épreuves à la session de septembre** he was allowed *or* permitted to take the tests in September

    6 *(reconnaître)* to admit to; **a. un vol** to admit to a theft *or* to having stolen; **j'admets mon erreur** I admit I was wrong; **j'admets m'être trompé** I admit *or* accept that I made a mistake; **il faut a. que c'est un résultat inattendu** you've got to admit the result is unexpected

    7 *(accepter)* **il n'a pas reçu ta lettre, admettons** OK, so he didn't get your letter; **j'admets que les choses se sont/se soient passées ainsi** I accept that things did happen/may have happened that way; **il est difficile d'a. qu'il s'est/qu'il se soit trompé** it's difficult to accept that he made/may have made a mistake; **j'admets tes motifs, mais je ne suis pas d'accord sur ta façon d'agir** I accept your reasons, but I don't approve of the way you behaved

    8 *(permettre → sujet: personne)* to tolerate, to stand for; *(→ sujet: chose)* to allow, to admit, *Sout* to be susceptible of; **tout texte admet de multiples interprétations** any text can lend itself to many different readings; **un résultat qui admet deux types d'explication** a finding which admits of *or* allows two different explanations; **l'usage admis** the accepted custom; **ces insolences ne seront pas admises** this kind of rudeness won't be tolerated; **un ton qui n'admet pas la discussion** *ou* **réplique**

a tone brooking no argument; **sa mine n'admettait pas la réplique** his look didn't invite a reply; **le règlement n'admet aucune dérogation** there shall be no breach of the regulations; **je n'admets pas d'être accusé sans preuve** I refuse to let myself be accused without proof; **je n'admets pas qu'on me parle sur ce ton!** I won't tolerate *or* stand for this kind of talk!; **je n'admets pas qu'on soit en retard** I won't tolerate lateness *or* stand for people being late

9 (*supposer*) to assume; **si on admet qu'il gagne 1000 euros par mois** if one assumes he earns 1,000 euros a month

◻ **admettons que** CONJ let's suppose *or* assume, supposing, assuming; **admettons qu'il soit venu, pourquoi n'a-t-il pas laissé un message sur mon bureau?** assuming he did come, why didn't he leave a message on my desk?

◻ **en admettant que** CONJ supposing *or* assuming (that); **en admettant que je parte à 3 heures, je peux être à Nice dans la soirée** supposing I leave at 3, I could be in Nice by the evening; **en admettant que tu aies raison, tu pourrais quand même faire preuve d'indulgence** (even) supposing you're right, you could be a bit more tolerant

adminicule [adminikyl] NM *Jur* adminicle, corroboratory evidence

administrateur, -trice [administratœr, -tris] NM,F **1** *Admin* (*dans une société*) (non-executive) director; **il est l'a./elle est l'administratrice de l'entreprise** he's/she's the director of the firm; *Jur* **a. de biens** *Br* estate agent, *Am* real estate agent; **a. judiciaire** (official) receiver

2 *Admin* (*dans les affaires publiques*) administrator; **a. civil** senior civil servant; **a. délégué** associate administrator

3 *Admin* (*dans une institution, une fondation*) trustee; *Jur* **a. légal** (*de biens*) trustee; (*d'un enfant*) legal guardian

4 *Ordinat* **a. de réseau** network manager; **a. de serveur** server administrator

administrateur-séquestre, administratrice-séquestre [administratœrsekɛstr, administratrissekɛstr] (*mpl* **administrateurs-séquestres,** *fpl* **administratrices-séquestres**) NM,F receiver

administratif, -ive [administratif, -iv] ADJ *Admin* administrative

administration [administrasjɔ̃] NF **1** (*fait de donner*) **l'a. d'un remède/sédatif** administering a remedy/sedative; **l'a. d'un sacrement** administering a sacrament; **l'a. de la justice** applying the law; **l'a. d'une preuve** producing *or* adducing a proof

2 *Admin* (*gestion → d'une entreprise*) management; (*→ d'une institution*) administration; (*→ de biens*) management, administration; (*→ d'un pays*) government, running; (*→ d'une commune*) running; **la mauvaise a. d'une société** the mismanagement of a company; **les frais d'a.** spending on administration, administration costs; **a. économique** e-government; **a. fiscale** tax authorities; **a. légale** guardianship; **a. des ventes** sales management

3 *Admin* (*fonction publique*) **l'A.** ≃ the Civil Service; **entrer dans l'A.** ≃ to become a civil servant, to enter the Civil Service

4 *Admin* (*service public*) **a. communale** local government; **l'a. des Douanes** *Br* ≃ the Customs and Excise, *Am* ≃ the Customs Service; **l'a. des Eaux et Forêts** *Br* ≃ the Forestry Commission, *Am* ≃ the Forest Service; **l'a. de l'Enregistrement** the Registration Department; **l'a. des Impôts** *Br* ≃ the Inland Revenue, *Am* ≃ the Internal Revenue Service; **a. locale** local authority; **a. municipale** local government; **a. portuaire** port authorities; **a. privée** private administration; (*fonction*) ≃ Civil Service

5 (*équipe présidentielle*) **l'A. Bush** the Bush administration

6 *Ordinat* **a. de réseau** network management

administrative [administrativ] *voir* **administratif**

administrativement [administrativmã] ADV *Admin* administratively

administratrice [administratris] *voir* **administrateur**

administré, -e [administre] NM,F ≃ constituent; **le maire informera ses administrés** the mayor will

---

inform those people who come under his/her jurisdiction

administrer [3] [administre] VT **1** *Admin* (*diriger → entreprise*) to manage; (*→ institution, fondation, département*) to administer, to run; (*→ biens*) to manage; (*→ succession*) to be a trustee of; (*→ pays*) to govern, to run; (*→ commune*) to run

2 (*donner → remède, sacrement*) to administer; (*→ gifle, fessée*) to give; **on lui a administré les derniers sacrements** he/she was given the last rites; **a. un malade** to administer *or* to give the last rites to a sick person

3 *Jur* (*preuve*) to produce, to adduce; **a. la justice** to administer justice

admirable [admirabl] ADJ admirable; **elle a été a. de courage/volonté** she showed admirable courage/willpower

admirablement [admirabləmã] ADV wonderfully; **ils s'entendent a. bien** they get along wonderfully

admirateur, -trice [admiratœr, -tris] NM,F admirer

admiratif, -ive [admiratif, -iv] ADJ admiring; **son regard était a.** he looked impressed

admiration [admirasjɔ̃] NF admiration, wonder; **avoir** *ou* **éprouver de l'a. pour qn/qch** to admire sb/sth; **avoir** *ou* **éprouver une a. sans bornes pour qn/qch** to have the utmost admiration for sb/sth; **être a. devant qn/qch** to be filled with admiration for sb/sth; **faire l'a. de tous** to be universally admired; **susciter** *ou* **soulever l'a. de qn** to fill sb with admiration; **tomber en a. devant qch** to be stopped in one's tracks by the beauty of sth; **éperdu d'a. (pour)** lost in admiration (for); **un regard d'a.** an admiring look

admirative [admirativ] *voir* **admiratif**

admirativement [admirativmã] ADV admiringly

admiratrice [admiratris] *voir* **admirateur**

admirer [3] [admire] VT to admire; **je l'admire beaucoup, ça n'a pas dû être facile pour lui** I admire him enormously, it can't have been easy for him; **il m'a fait a. sa voiture** he showed off his car to me; **elle nous a fait a. la vue de la terrasse** she took us on to the terrace so that we could admire the view

admis, -e [admi, -iz] PP *voir* **admettre**

NM,F *Scol & Univ* (*à un examen*) successful candidate

admissibilité [admisibilite] NF **1** (*d'une proposition, d'un procédé*) acceptability **2** *Univ* (*après la première partie*) = eligibility to take the second part of an exam; (*après l'écrit*) = eligibility to take the oral exam **3** (*à un emploi*) eligibility

admissible [admisibl] ADJ **1** (*procédé, excuse*) acceptable; **il n'est pas a. que...** it is unacceptable that...

2 *Univ* (*après la première partie*) = eligible to take the second part of an exam; (*après l'écrit*) = eligible to take the oral exam

3 (*à un emploi*) eligible; **il faut remplir certaines conditions pour être a. à ce poste** you must meet certain requirements in order to be eligible for this job

NMF *Univ* (*après la première partie*) = student who is allowed to take the second part of an exam; (*après l'écrit*) = student who is allowed to take the oral exam

admission [admisjɔ̃] NF **1** (*accueil*) admission, admittance, entry; **l'a. des pays de l'Est dans l'Union européenne** the entry *or* admission of Eastern European countries into the European Union; **demande d'a.** (*à l'hôpital*) admission form; (*dans un club*) membership application

2 *Univ* (*à un examen*) passing an exam; **son a. à l'université** his admission to *or* his being admitted to the university; **a. sur concours** entry by competitive examination; **a. sur dossier** entry by written application

3 *Tech* intake; *Aut* induction

4 *Bourse* **a. à la cote** admission to quotation, listing; **faire une demande d'a. à la cote** to seek admission to quotation

5 *Com* (*en douane*) **a. temporaire** temporary entry

6 *Jur* **a. des créances** recognizance of debts

admittance [admitãs] NF *Phys* admittance

admixtion [admiksjɔ̃] NF *Pharm* admixture

admonestation [admɔnɛstasjɔ̃] NF *Littéraire* admonition, rebuke

admonester [3] [admɔnɛste] VT *Littéraire* to admonish

---

admonition [admɔnisjɔ̃] NF **1** *Littéraire* (*reproche*) admonition, rebuke **2** *Rel* admonition

ADN [adeɛn] NM *Biol* (*abrév* **acide désoxyribonucléique**) DNA; **A. mt** mtDNA; **A. recombinant** recombinant DNA

adné, -e [adne] ADJ *Bot* adnate

adnominal, -e, -aux, -ales [adnominal, -o] *Gram* ADJ adnominal
NM adnominal

ad nutum [adnytɔm] ADV instantaneously, immediately

ado [ado] NMF *Fam* teenager ®, teen

adobe [adɔb] NM *Constr* adobe

adolescence [adɔlesɑ̃s] NF adolescence; **je me souviens de mon a.** I remember when I was a teenager; **au seuil de l'a.** in early adolescence; **il a eu une a. difficile** he had a difficult adolescence

adolescent, -e [adɔlesɑ̃, -ɑ̃t] ADJ adolescent, teenage
NM,F adolescent, teenager

adon [adɔ̃] NM *Can* coincidence

adonide [adɔnid] NF *Bot* pheasant's eye, adonis

Adonis [adɔnis] NPR *Myth* Adonis

adonis [adɔnis] NM **1** (*bel homme*) Adonis; **ce n'est pas un a.!** he's no oil painting! **2** (*papillon*) adonis

adonner [3] [adɔne] V IMPERSONNEL *Can* to suit, to be convenient; **viens me voir quand ça t'adonnera** come and see me whenever it suits you

VI *Can* **a. avec qch** (*vêtements etc*) to go with sth

▶**s'adonner** VPR **1** **s'a. à** (*lecture, sport, loisirs*) to go in for; (*travail, études*) to devote oneself to; **s'a. à la boisson/au jeu** to take to drink/to gambling; **être adonné à qch** to be addicted to sth

2 *Can* **s'a. avec qn** to get on *or* along with sb

adoptable [adɔptabl] ADJ adoptable

adoptant, -e [adɔptɑ̃, -ɑ̃t] ADJ adopting
NM,F adopter

adopté, -e [adɔpte] ADJ adopted; **enfants adoptés** adopted children
NM,F adoptee

adopter [3] [adɔpte] VT **1** (*enfant*) to adopt; **ils ont pu le faire a. par une famille française** they managed to have him adopted by a French family; *Fig* **ses beaux-parents l'ont tout de suite adoptée** her in-laws took an instant liking to her

2 (*choisir → cause*) to take up; (*→ point de vue*) to adopt, to approve; (*→ politique*) to adopt, to take up; (*→ loi, projet*) to adopt, to pass; (*→ mode*) to follow, to adopt; (*→ produit*) to adopt; **le projet de loi a été adopté** the bill went through; **ils ont fait a. le projet de loi par l'Assemblée** they managed to get the bill through Parliament; **adopté à l'unanimité** carried unanimously

3 (*se mettre dans → position, posture*) to adopt, to assume; **a. la démarche de Charlot** to walk like Charlie Chaplin

4 (*emprunter → nom*) to assume; (*→ accent*) to put on; **a. un profil bas** to keep a low profile

adopteur [adɔptœr] NM *Mktg* (*d'un produit*) adopter; **a. précoce** early adopter; **les adopteurs précoces de notre nouveau produit représentent cinq pour cent du marché potentiel** the early adopters of our new product make up five percent of the potential market

adoptianisme [adɔpsjanism] NM *Rel* Adoptianism, Adoptionism

adoptif, -ive [adɔptif, -iv] ADJ (*enfant*) adopted; (*parent*) adoptive; (*patrie*) adopted

adoption [adɔpsjɔ̃] NF **1** (*d'un enfant*) adoption; **a. plénière** full adoption; **a. simple** simple adoption **2** (*d'une loi, d'un projet*) adoption, passing **3** *Mktg* (*d'un produit*) adoption

◻ **d'adoption** ADJ (*pays*) adopted; **c'est un Parisien d'a.** he's Parisian by adoption, he's adopted Paris as his home town

adoptive [adɔptiv] *voir* **adoptif**

adorable [adɔrabl] ADJ **1** (*charmant → personne*) adorable; (*→ endroit*) beautiful; (*→ sourire*) lovely; (*→ sourire*) charming; **une a. petite maison** an adorable little house **2** *Rel* worthy of adoration, adorable

adorablement [adɔrabləmã] ADV adorably

adorateur, -trice [adɔratœr, -tris] NM,F **1** *Rel* worshipper **2** (*admirateur* → *d'un chanteur*) fan, admirer; (→ *d'une femme*) admirer

adoration [adɔrasjɔ̃] NF **1** *Rel* worship, adoration **2** (*admiration*) adoration; **être en a. devant qn** to dote on *or* to worship sb

---

'L'Adoration des mages' *Botticelli* 'Adoration of the Magi'

---

adoratrice [adɔratris] *voir* **adorateur**

adorer [3] [adɔre] VT **1** (*aimer* → *personne*) to adore, to love; (→ *maison, robe, livre*) to love, to adore; **elle adore les roses/lire/qu'on lui écrive** she loves roses/to read/to get letters **2** *Rel* to adore, to worship

▸ **s'adorer** VPR to adore each other

ados [ado] NM *Agr* bank (*to protect crops against the wind*)

adossé, -e [adose] ADJ **elle était adossée au mur** she was leaning against the wall; **une maison adossée à la colline** a house built right up against the hillside; **la cabane adossée au garage** the shed backing on to the garage

adossement [adosmɑ̃] NM **l'a. d'un bâtiment à** *ou* **contre qch** a building leaning against sth

adosser [3] [adose] VT **a. qch à** *ou* **contre qch** to put sth (up) against sth; **a. une armoire à** *ou* **contre un mur** to put a wardrobe against a wall; **a. une échelle contre un mur** to put *or* to lean a ladder against a wall

▸ **s'adosser** VPR **s'a. à** *ou* **contre qch** to lean against sth

adoubement [adubmɑ̃] NM *Hist* dubbing (ceremony)

adouber [3] [adube] VT **1** *Hist* (*chevalier*) to dub **2** *Échecs* to adjust

adoucir [32] [adusir] VT **1** (*rendre plus doux* → *peau, regard, voix, eau*) to soften; (→ *amertume, caractère, acidité*) to take the edge off; **l'âge l'a beaucoup adouci** he's mellowed a lot with age; **du miel pour a. votre thé** honey to sweeten your tea; **a. une sauce** (*la sucrer*) to sweeten a sauce; (*la rendre plus veloutée*) to make a sauce smoother **2** (*atténuer* → *couleur, propos, dureté*) to tone down; (→ *difficulté, antagonisme*) to ease **3** (*rendre supportable* → *peine, punition*) to reduce, to lessen the severity of; (→ *chagrin*) to ease; **le tribunal a adouci la sentence** the court reduced the sentence; **ils s'efforcent d'a. les conditions de vie des prisonniers** they try to make the prisoners' living conditions less harsh; **seul le temps pourra a. les mauvais souvenirs** time alone will ease the painful memories **4** *Métal* to temper down, to soften **5** *Météo* (*temps, température*) to make warmer *or* milder

▸ **s'adoucir** VPR **1** (*devenir plus doux* → *peau, regard, voix, lumière*) to soften; (→ *personne, caractère*) to mellow **2** *Météo* (*temps, température*) to become milder **3** (*s'atténuer* → *pente*) to become less steep; (→ *accent*) to become less broad **4** *Agr* (→ *vin*) to mellow

adoucissant, -e [adusisɑ̃, -ɑ̃t] ADJ emollient; **crème adoucissante pour les mains** hand cream; **produit a. pour le linge** fabric softener

NM **1** *Méd* emollient **2** (*pour le linge*) fabric conditioner

adoucissement [adusismɑ̃] NM **1** (*de la peau, de l'eau*) softening; (*d'un caractère*) softening, mellowing; **un imperceptible a. de son regard/sa voix** an imperceptible softening in his look/voice **2** (*estompage* → *d'une couleur, d'un contraste*) softening, toning down **3** (*atténuation* → *d'une peine*) reduction **4** *Météo* **a. de la température** rise in temperature **5** *Métal* tempering, softening

adoucisseur [adusisœr] NM **a. (d'eau)** water softener

ADP [adepe] NF *Chim* (*abrév* **adénosine diphosphate**) ADP

ad patres [adpatres] ADV *Fam* **aller a.** to go to meet one's Maker; **envoyer qn a.** to send sb to (meet) his/her Maker

ad probationem [adprobasjɔnɛm] ADJ (*écrit*) evidentiary

adr. 1 (*abrév écrite* **adresse**) addr. **2** (*abrév écrite* **adresser**) addr.

adragante [adragɑ̃t] *voir* **gomme**

adrénaline [adrenalin] NF *Physiol* adrenalin, adrenaline

adrénergique [adrenɛrʒik] *Physiol* ADJ adrenergic

NM adrenergic

adrénolytique [adrenolitik] *Biol & Chim* ADJ adrenolytic

NM adrenolytic

adressable [adrɛsabl] ADJ *Ordinat* addressable

adressage [adrɛsaʒ] NM *Ordinat* addressing; **a. direct** direct addressing; **a. multiple** multiple selection; **mode d'a.** address mode

adresse [adrɛs] NF **1** (*domicile*) address; **parti sans laisser d'a.** gone without leaving a forwarding address; **a. bibliographique** imprint; **a. de facturation** invoicing address, address for invoicing; **a. du lieu de travail** business address; **a. de livraison** delivery address; (*d'objets volumineux*) shipping address; **une bonne a.** (*magasin*) a good *Br* shop *or Am* store; (*restaurant*) a good restaurant; (*hôtel*) a good hotel **2** (*discours*) formal speech, address **3** (*dans un dictionnaire*) headword **4** *Ordinat* address; **Can a. de courriel** e-mail address; **a. électronique** e-mail address; **a. Internet** Internet address; **a. IP** IP address; **a. URL** URL; **a. virtuelle** virtual address **5** (*dextérité*) skill, dexterity, deftness; **jongler avec a.** to juggle skilfully *or* with dexterity; **jeu d'a.** game of skill **6** (*subtilité*) cleverness, adroitness; **répondre avec a.** to give a tactful answer

▢ **à l'adresse de** PRÉP intended for, aimed at; **une observation à votre a.** a remark aimed at *or* intended for you; **je l'ai dit à l'a. de ceux qui…** I said it for the benefit of those who…

adresser [4] [adrese] VT **1** (*envoyer*) **a. qch à qn** (*gén*) to address *or* to direct sth to sb; (*par courrier*) to send *or* to forward sth to sb; **adressez toute requête au Bureau 402** direct *or* address all requests to Department 402; **a. CV détaillé à Monique Bottin** send detailed CV to Monique Bottin **2** (*destiner*) **a. qch à qn** (→ *remarque*) to address sth to *or* to direct sth at sb; (→ *geste, regard*) to aim sth at sb; (→ *paquet, enveloppe*) to address sth to sb; **le colis était mal adressé** the address on the parcel was wrong; **cette lettre vous est adressée** this letter is addressed to you; **il faudra a. vos remarques au président** please address your remarks to the chair; **a. des questions à qn** to ask sb questions, to direct questions at sb; **a. la parole à qn** to speak to sb; **elle ne m'adresse plus la parole** she won't talk *or* speak to me any more; **a. un compliment à qn** to pay sb a compliment; **a. un reproche à qn** to level a reproach at sb; **nous ne vous adressons aucun reproche** we don't blame you in any way; **à qui sont adressées ces allusions?** who are these hints meant for?; **a. des prières à Dieu** to pray to God; **adresse ta prière à la Vierge Marie** make your prayer to the Virgin Mary; **il leur adressa des regards furieux** he looked at them with fury in his eyes, he shot furious glances at them; **le clin d'œil m'était sans doute adressé** the wink was probably meant for *or* intended for *or* aimed at me; **a. un signe à qn** to wave at sb; **a. un signe de tête à qn** (*positif*) to nod at sb; (*négatif*) to shake one's head at sb; **a. un sourire à qn** to smile at sb **3** (*diriger* → *personne*) **a. un malade à un spécialiste** to refer a patient to a specialist; **on m'a adressé à vous** I've been referred to you **4** *Ordinat* to address

▸ **s'adresser** VPR **1** (*emploi réciproque*) **ils ne s'adressent plus la parole** they don't talk to each other any more; **s'a. à** (*parler à*) to speak to, to address; **c'est à vous que je m'adresse** I'm talking to you; **le ministre s'adressera d'abord aux élus locaux** the minister will first address the local councillors; **comment s'adresse-t-on à un archevêque?** how do you address an archbishop?; *Fig* **s'a. à la générosité de qn** to appeal to sb's generosity

2 s'a. à (*être destiné à*) to be meant for *or* aimed at; **à qui s'adresse cette remarque?** who's this remark aimed at?; **une émission qui s'adresse aux adolescents** a show aimed at a teenage audience

3 s'a. à (*pour se renseigner* → *personne*) to go and see; (→ *guichet, bureau*) to go to; **adressez-vous à la concierge** go and ask *or* see the porter; **il faut vous a. au syndicat d'initiative** you should ask at the tourist office; **je ne sais pas à qui m'a.** I don't know who to go to

adret [adrɛ] NM *Géog* (*dans les Alpes*) sunny side (*of a valley*)

Adriatique [adrijatik] ADJ Adriatic; **la mer A.** the Adriatic Sea

NF **l'A.** the Adriatic (Sea)

adroit, -e [adrwa, -at] ADJ **1** (*habile* → *gén*) deft, dexterous; (→ *apprenti, artisan, sportif*) skilful; **être a. de ses mains** to be clever with one's hands; **être a. au billard** to be very good at billiards; **je ne suis pas très adroite pour faire les ourlets** I'm not very good at doing hems; **a. comme un singe** as agile as a monkey

2 (*astucieux* → *manœuvre*) clever; (→ *diplomate*) skilful; (→ *politique*) clever; (→ *phrase*) neatly turned; **la remarque n'était pas bien adroite** it was a rather clumsy thing to say

adroitement [adrwatmɑ̃] ADV **1** (*avec des gestes habiles*) skilfully **2** (*astucieusement*) cleverly

ADSL [adeesɛl] NM *Ordinat & Tél* (*abrév* **Asymmetric Digital Subscriber Line**) ADSL; **est-ce que tu as l'A. chez toi?** have you got broadband at home?

adsorbant, -e [atsɔrbɑ̃, -ɑ̃t] *Phys & Biol* ADJ adsorbent

NM adsorbent

adsorber [3] [atsɔrbe] VT *Phys & Biol* to adsorb

adsorption [atsɔrpsjɔ̃] NF *Phys & Biol* adsorption

adstrat [adstra] NM *Ling* adstratum

adulaire [adylɛr] NF *Minér* adularia

adulateur, -trice [adylatœr, -tris] *Littéraire* ADJ adulatory

NM,F adulator

adulation [adylasjɔ̃] NF *Littéraire* adulation; *Fig* **il est complètement en a. devant elle** he completely idolizes her

adulatrice [adylatris] *voir* **adulateur**

aduler [3] [adyle] VT *Littéraire* to adulate, to fawn upon

adulescent, -e [adylɛsɑ̃, -ɑ̃t] NM,F *Fam* adultescent

adulte [adylt] ADJ **1** (*individu*) adult; (*attitude*) mature; **devenir a.** to become an adult, to grow up **2** *Zool* full-grown, adult; *Bot* full-grown

NMF adult; **livres/films pour adultes** adult books/films

adultération [adylterasjɔ̃] NF adulteration

adultère [adyltɛr] ADJ (*relation*) adulterous; **femme a.** adulteress; **homme a.** adulterer

NMF *Littéraire* adulterer, f adulteress

NM (*infidélité*) adultery; **commettre l'a. avec qn** to have an adulterous relationship with sb, to commit adultery with sb

adultérer [18] [adyltere] VT *Littéraire* to adulterate

adultérin, -e [adylterɛ̃, -in] ADJ adulterine

ad validitatem [advaliditatɛm] ADJ *Jur* (*écrit*) substantial

ad valorem [advalɔrɛm] ADJ INV *Jur* (*droit, taxe*) ad valorem

advection [advɛksjɔ̃] NF *Météo* advection

advenir [40] [advənir] V IMPERSONNEL to happen; **qu'est-il advenu de toutes tes belles idées?** what has become of all your wonderful ideas?; **qu'est-il advenu de lui?** what *or* whatever became of him?; **il advient que… it** (so) happens that…; **il advint que je tombai malade** it (so) happened that I fell ill, I happened to fall ill; **quoi qu'il advienne, quoi qu'il puisse a.** come what may, whatever may happen; **advienne que pourra** come what may; **je signe, allez, advienne que pourra!** I'll sign, and blow the consequences!

advenice [advɑ̃tis] ADJ **1** *Phil* adventitious **2** *Bot* adventitious

NF *Bot* adventitious plant

adventif, -ive [advɑ̃tif, -iv] ADJ **1** *Bot* (*racine*) adventitive **2** *Géol* (*cône, cratère*) adventive, parasitic

adventiste [advɑ̃tist] *Rel* ADJ Adventist

NMF Adventist; **les Adventistes du septième jour** the Seventh-Day Adventists

adventive [advɑ̃tiv] *voir* **adventif**

advenu, -e [advəny] PP *voir* **advenir**

adverbe [advɛrb] NM *Gram* adverb; **a. de lieu/ temps/quantité** adverb of place/time/degree

adverbial, -e, -aux, -ales [advɛrbjal, -o] ADJ *Gram* adverbial

adverbialement [advɛrbjalmɑ̃] ADV *(employer) Gram* adverbially

adversaire [advɛrsɛr] NMF adversary, opponent; *(dans un conflit, une guerre)* enemy, adversary; **je n'ai pas peur de l'a.** I'm not afraid of the opposition

adversatif, -ive [advɛrsatif, -tiv] ADJ *Ling* adversative

adverse [advɛrs] ADJ 1 *(camp, opinion)* opposing; **dans les rangs adverses, on ne croit pas aux privatisations** privatization isn't popular with the opposition 2 *Littéraire (circonstances)* adverse 3 *Jur* opposing

adversité [advɛrsite] NF adversity; **poursuivi par l'a.** the victim of many misfortunes; **conserver son optimisme dans l'a.** to remain optimistic in the face of adversity; **ne pas reculer devant l'a.** not to yield in the face of adversity

advertorial [advɛrtɔrjal] NM *Presse* advertorial

advient *etc voir* **advenir**

advint *etc voir* **advenir**

ad vitam æternam [advitamɛtɛrnam] ADV for ever

adynamie [adinami] NF *Méd* adynamia

AE [ɑə] NMF *Scol (abrév* **adjoint d'enseignement**) assistant teacher

aède [aɛd] NM poet *(in Ancient Greece)*

A-EF [ɑəɛf] NF *(abrév* **Afrique-Équatoriale française**) FEA

ægagropile [egagrɔpil] NM *Vét* hair-ball

ægyrine [eʒirin] NF *Minér* aegirine, aegirite

AELE [ɑələ] NF *UE (abrév* **Association européenne de libre-échange**) EFTA

AEN [ɑəɛn] NF *Nucl (abrév* **Agence pour l'énergie nucléaire**) = French atomic energy agency, ≃ AEA

æpyornis [epjɔrnis] NM aepyornis

aérage [aeraʒ] NM *Mines* ventilation, air supply

aérateur [aeratœr] NM 1 *Constr* ventilator 2 *Agr* aerator

aération [aerasjɔ̃] NF *Tech* ventilation; *Chim* aeration; *(d'une pièce)* airing, ventilation; **il faudrait un peu d'a. dans cette chambre** this room needs airing

aéraulique [aerolik] *Phys* ADJ *(système)* ventilation *(avant n)*
  NF study of ventilation, aeraulics *(singulier)*

aéré, -e [aere] ADJ 1 *(chambre)* well-ventilated, airy; *Chim* aerated; **bien a.** well-ventilated, airy; **mal a.** poorly-ventilated, stuffy 2 *(présentation, texte)* well-spaced

aérer [18] [aere] VT 1 *(ventiler → chambre, maison)* to air, to ventilate; *(→ voiture)* to let some air into; *Chim* to aerate 2 *(rendre moins dense → texte)* to space out
  ▶ **s'aérer** VPR to get some fresh air; **si on allait s'a.?** how about getting some fresh air?; **s'a. l'esprit/les idées** to clear one's mind/one's thoughts

aéricole [aerikɔl] ADJ *Bot* aerial

aérien, -enne [aerjɛ̃, -ɛn] ADJ 1 *Aviat (tarif, base, raid, catastrophe)* air *(avant n)*; *(combat, photographie)* aerial *(avant n)*; **nos forces aériennes** our air forces 2 *(à l'air libre → câble)* overhead 3 *(léger → mouvement, démarche)* light, floating; **d'une légèreté aérienne** as light as air 4 *Tél* overhead
  NM aerial

aérifère [aerifɛr] ADJ *Physiol (voie, conduit)* air-conducting; **canaux aérifères** air passages, air-conducting passages

aérium [aerjɔm] NM *Méd Br* sanatorium, *Am* sanatarium

aérobic [aerobik] NM *Sport* aerobics *(singulier)*

aérobie [aerobi] ADJ *Biol & Aviat* aerobic
  NM *Biol* aerobe, aerobium

aérobiologie [aerobjɔlɔʒi] NF *Biol* aerobiology

aérobiologique [aerobjɔlɔʒik] ADJ *Biol* aerobiologic

aérobiose [aerobjoz] NF *Biol* aerobiosis

aéro-club [aeroklœb] *(pl* **aéro-clubs**) NM *Aviat* flying club

aérocolie [aerocɔli] NF *Méd* wind

aérocondenseur [aerokɔ̃dɑ̃sœr] NM *Tech* aero-condenser

aérodrome [aerodrom] NM *Aviat* airfield

aérodynamique [aerodinamik] ADJ *(étude, soufflerie)* aerodynamic; *(ligne, profil, voiture)* streamlined
  NF aerodynamics *(singulier)*

aérodynamisme [aerodinamism] NM aerodynamics *(singulier)*

aérodyne [aerodin] NM *Aviat* aerodyne

aérofrein [aerofrɛ̃] NM air brake

aérogare [aerogar] NF *Aviat (pour les marchandises)* airport building; *(pour les voyageurs)* air terminal

aérogastrie [aerogastri] NF *Méd* aerogastria

aérogel [aeroʒɛl] NM *Chim* aerogel

aérogénérateur [aeroʒeneratœr] NM *Élec* aero-generator

aéroglisseur [aeroglisœr] NM *Transp* hovercraft

aérogramme [aerogram] NM *(lettre)* aero-gramme, air letter

aérographe [aerograf] NM airbrush

aérolite, aérolithe [aerolit] NM *Astron* aerolite

aérologie [aerolɔʒi] NF *Météo* aerology

aérologique [aerolɔʒik] ADJ *Météo* aerological

aéromobile [aeromɔbil] ADJ *Mil* airmobile

aéromobilité [aeromɔbilite] NF *Mil* airmobility

aéromodélisme [aeromɔdelism] NM aeromodelling

aéromodéliste [aeromɔdelist] NM aeromodeller

aéromoteur [aeromotœr] NM wind power engine

aéronaute [aeronot] NMF *Aviat* aeronaut

aéronautique [aeronotik] *Aviat* ADJ aeronautic, aeronautical
  NF aeronautics *(singulier)*

aéronaval, -e, -als, -ales [aeronaval] ADJ *(bataille)* air and sea *(avant n)*
  ▫ **aéronavale** NF **l'aéronavale** *Br* ≃ the Fleet Air Arm, *Am* ≃ Naval Aviation

aéronef [aeronɛf] NM *Aviat* aircraft

aéronomie [aeronɔmi] NF *Chim & Phys* aeronomy

aérophagie [aerofaʒi] NF *Méd* wind, *Spéc* aerophagia; **avoir** *ou* **faire de l'a.** to have wind

aérophysique [aerofizik] NF *Phys* aerophysics *(singulier)*

aérophobe [aerofɔb] NMF aerophobe

aéroplane [aeroplan] NM *Vieilli Br* aeroplane, *Am* airplane

aéroport [aeropɔr] NM *Aviat* airport

aéroporté, -e [aeropɔrte] ADJ *Mil* airborne

aéroportuaire [aeropɔrtɥɛr] ADJ *Aviat* airport *(avant n)*

aéropostal, -e, -aux, -ales [aeropɔstal, -o] ADJ *Aviat* airmail *(avant n)*
  ▫ **Aéropostale** NF *Hist* **l'Aéropostale** = first French airmail service between Europe and South America; *(filiale d'Air France)* = subsidiary of Air France

aéroréfrigérant, -e [aerorefriʒerɑ̃, -ɑ̃t] ADJ cooling; **tour aéroréfrigérante** cooling tower
  NM cooling tower

aéroscope [aeroskɔp] NM *Phys* aeroscope

aérosol [aerosɔl] NM aerosol
  ADJ INV **bombe a.** aerosol (can)
  ▫ **en aérosol** ADJ spray *(avant n)*; **nous l'avons aussi en a.** we also have it in spray form

aérospatial, -e, -aux, -ales [aerospasjal, -o] ADJ *Aviat & Astron* aerospace *(avant n)*
  ▫ **aérospatiale** NF 1 *(science)* aerospace science 2 *(industrie)* aerospace industries; **l'Aéro-spatiale** = important state-owned aerospace company based in Toulouse

aérostat [aerosta] NM *Aviat* aerostat

aérostation [aerostasjɔ̃] NF *Aviat* aerostation

aérostatique [aerostatik] ADJ *Aviat* aerostatic, aerostatical
  NF *Phys* aerostatics *(singulier)*

aérostier [aerostje] NM *Aviat* balloonist

aérotechnique [aerotɛknik] *Astron & Aviat* ADJ aerotechnical
  NF aerotechnics *(singulier)*

aéroterrestre [aeroterɛstr] ADJ *Mil* air and land *(avant n)*

aérothérapie [aeroterapi] NF *Méd* aerotherapeutics *(singulier)*

aérotherme [aerotɛrm] NM unit heater

aérothermique [aerotɛrmik] ADJ *Tech* aerothermic

aérothermodynamique [aerotɛrmodinamik] NF *Tech* aerothermodynamics *(singulier)*

Aérotrain® [aerotrɛ̃] NM *Transp* hovertrain

aérotransporté, -e [aerotrɑ̃sporte] ADJ *Mil* airborne

æschne [ɛskn] NF *Entom* great dragonfly

æthuse [etyz] NF *Bot* fool's parsley, lesser hemlock

aétite [aetit] NF *Minér* aetite, eagle stone

AF¹ 1 *(abrév écrite* **allocations familiales**) family allowance *(UNCOUNT)*, child benefit *(UNCOUNT)* 2 *Suisse (abrév écrite* **Assemblée fédérale**) (Swiss) federal assembly

AF² *(abrév écrite* **Air France**) Air France

Afars [afar] NMPL 1 *(peuple)* Afars 2 *Vieilli Géog* **Territoire français des A. et des Issas** Territory of the Afars and Issas

AFAT, Afat [afat] NF *Mil (abrév* **auxiliaire féminin de l'armée de terre**) = female member of the French army

AFB [ɑɛfbe] NF *Banque (abrév* **Association française des banques**) = French Bankers' Association

affabilité [afabilite] NF affability, friendliness; **avec a.** affably; **être d'une grande a.** to be very gracious *or* affable

affable [afabl] ADJ affable, friendly; **sous des dehors affables** behind a benign façade

affablement [afabləmɑ̃] ADV affably

affabulateur, -trice [afabylatœr, -tris] NM,F inveterate liar, storyteller; *Psy* mythomaniac, pathological liar

affabulation [afabylasjɔ̃] NF 1 *Littérature* plot construction 2 *Psy* mythomania

affabulatrice [afabylatris] *voir* **affabulateur**

affabuler [3] [afabyle] VI to invent stories
  VT *Littérature (intrigue)* to construct

affacturage [afaktyraʒ] NM *Com* factoring

affactureur [afaktyrœr] NM *Com* factor

affadir [32] [afadir] VT 1 *(aliments)* to make bland *or* tasteless 2 *(ternir → couleurs)* to make dull, to cause to fade; *(→ style, personnalité)* to make dull *or* uninteresting
  ▶ **s'affadir** VPR 1 *(aliments)* to become tasteless 2 *(couleur)* to fade; *(style, personnalité)* to become dull *or* uninteresting; **dans sa deuxième période, ses couleurs se sont affadies** in his second period, he paints in duller shades

affadissant, -e [afadisɑ̃, -ɑ̃t] ADJ *(adaptation, version)* bland, insipid

affadissement [afadismɑ̃] NM 1 *(d'un mets)* loss of taste, increased blandness 2 *(d'une couleur → par le soleil)* fading; *(→ par un pigment)* dulling

affaibli, -e [afebli] ADJ weakened; **utiliser un mot dans son sens a.** to use a word in its weaker sense

affaiblir [32] [afeblir] VT 1 *(personne)* to weaken; **sa maladie l'a beaucoup affaibli** his illness has weakened him a lot *or* sapped all his energy
  2 *(atténuer)* to weaken; **le brouillard affaiblit tous les sons** the fog muffles all sounds; **l'usage a affaibli le sens original du mot** the original meaning of the word has become weakened through use
  3 *(armée, institution)* to weaken, to undermine; **un pays affaibli par la guerre** a country weakened by war
  4 *(monnaie)* to weaken
  ▶ **s'affaiblir** VPR 1 *(dépérir)* to weaken, to become weaker; **elle s'est beaucoup affaiblie depuis le mois dernier** she has grown a lot weaker since last month; **s'a. de jour en jour** to get weaker and weaker every day, to get weaker by the day
  2 *(s'atténuer → signification, impact)* to weaken, to grow weaker; *(→ lumière)* to fade; *(→ son)* to grow fainter, to fade away; **la lumière du jour s'affaiblissait peu à peu** the daylight was fading gradually

affaiblissant, -e [afeblisɑ̃, -ɑ̃t] ADJ *(effet)* weakening, enfeebling, *(maladie)* debilitating

affaiblissement [afeblismɑ̃] NM *(d'une personne, d'un sentiment, du sens d'un mot)* weakening; *(d'une lumière, d'un bruit)* fading

affaiblisseur [afeblisœr] NM *Phot* reducer

affaire [afɛr] NF 1 *(entreprise)* business, firm, company; **monter une a.** to set up a business; **remonter une a.** to put a business back on its feet; **administrer** *ou* **gérer** *ou* **diriger une a.** to

run a business; **elle a une grosse a. de meubles** she's got a big furniture business; **faire entrer qn dans une a.** to bring sb into a firm; **l'a. familiale** the family business

2 *(transaction)* deal, transaction; **faire a. avec qn** to do a deal with sb; **conclure une a. (avec qn)** to clinch a deal (with sb); **faire beaucoup d'affaires** to do a lot of business; **(c'est une) a. conclue!, c'est une a. faite!** it's a deal!; **a. blanche** profitless *or* break-even deal; **l'a. ne s'est jamais faite** the deal was never clinched; **l'a. ne se fera pas** the deal's off; **l'a. n'est pas encore faite** the deal isn't clinched yet; *Fig* it's by no means a foregone conclusion; **c'est une a. entendue!** we agree on that!

3 *Fam (achat à bon marché)* **une a. (en or)** an unbeatable bargain; **faire une (bonne) a.** to get a (good) bargain; **à mon avis, ce n'est pas une a.!** I wouldn't exactly call it a bargain!; **en ce moment, chez Lépo tu as des affaires en or** there are great bargains to be had at Lépo's at the moment; **lui, c'est vraiment pas une a.!** he's no bright spark!

4 *(problème, situation délicate)* business; **une mauvaise** *ou* **sale a.** a nasty business; **ce n'est pas une mince a., c'est toute une a.** it's quite a business; *Ironique* **quelle** *ou* **la belle a.!** so what (does it matter)?; **c'est une autre a.** that's another story *or* a different proposition; **pour lui faire manger des légumes, c'est toute une a.!** we have a terrible time getting him to eat vegetables!; **je n'en fais pas toute une a.** I'm not making an issue of it; **c'est une a. de gros sous** it's a huge scam; **sortir** *ou* **tirer qn d'a.** *(par amitié)* to get sb out of trouble; *(médicalement)* to pull sb through; **être sorti** *ou* **tiré d'a.** *(après une aventure, une faillite)* to be out of trouble *or* in the clear; *(après une maladie)* to be off the danger list; **se sortir** *ou* **se tirer d'a.** *(après une aventure, une faillite)* to get oneself out of trouble; *(après une maladie)* to make a full recovery; **on n'est pas encore tirés d'a.** we're not out of the woods yet

5 *(scandale)* scandal *or* affair; *(crime)* murder; *(escroquerie)* business, job; **l'a. des pots-de-vin** the bribery scandal; **l'a. Dreyfus** the Dreyfus affair; *Pol* **a. d'État** affair of state; *Fig* **n'en fais pas une a. d'État!** don't blow it up out of all proportion!, *Am* don't make a federal case out of it!; **être sur une a.** to be in on a job

6 *(procès)* trial, lawsuit, case; **l'a. est jugée demain** the trial concludes tomorrow; **plaider/juger une a.** to act for one of the parties/to be a judge in a lawsuit; **saisir un tribunal d'une a.** to bring a case before a judge; **a. en cause** case before the court; **a. civile** civil action; **a. correctionnelle** criminal action; **a. en état** = case which is ready for trial; **a. politique** political scandal *or* affair

7 *Fam (ce qui convient)* **j'ai votre a.** I've got just the thing for you; **la mécanique, c'est pas/c'est son a.** car engines aren't exactly/are just his/her thing; **la vieille casserole fera l'a.** the old saucepan'll do; **leur maison ferait bien mon a.** I'd be quite happy with their house; **je vais lui faire son a.** I'll sort *or* straighten him out!

8 *(responsabilité)* **c'est mon/leur a.** it's my/their business; **l'a. d'autrui** other people's business; **fais ce que tu veux, c'est ton a.** do what you like, it's your business *or* problem; **en faire son a.** to take the matter in hand, to make it one's business; **l'architecte? j'en fais mon a.** I'll deal with *or* handle the architect

9 *(question)* **dis-moi l'a. en deux mots** tell me briefly what the problem is; **l'âge/l'argent/le temps ne fait rien à l'a.** age/money/time doesn't make any difference; **c'est l'a. d'une seconde** it can be done in a trice; *Fam* **c'est l'a. d'un coup de fil** all it takes is a phone call; **c'est une a. de vie ou de mort** it's a matter of life and death; **pour moi, c'est une a. d'honnêteté intellectuelle** for me, it's a matter of *or* it's a question of intellectual honesty; **a. de principe** matter of principle; **je ne le lui dirai jamais, a. de principe!** I'll never tell him/her, as *or* it's a matter of principle; **a. de goût** question of taste; **c'est (une) a. de goût** to each his own, it's a question of taste; **pour une a. de souveraineté territoriale** over some business to do with territorial sovereignty; **faut-il les emprisonner? – a. d'opinion** should they be sent to prison? – it's a matter of opinion

10 *(locutions)* **avoir a. à** to (have to) deal with; **avoir a. à forte partie** to have a strong *or* tough opponent; **avoir a. à plus fort/plus malin que soi** to be dealing with someone stronger/more cunning than oneself; **il vaut mieux ne pas avoir a. à lui** it's better to avoid having anything to do with him; **je n'ai eu a. qu'à sa femme** I only ever dealt with *or* had to do with his wife; **tu vas avoir a. à moi si tu tires la sonnette!** if you ring the bell, you'll have me to deal with!; **elle a eu a. à moi quand elle a voulu vendre la maison!** she had me to contend with when she tried to sell the house!; **à la cuisine, il est à son a.** when he's cooking, he's in his element; **tout à son a., il ne m'a pas vu entrer** he was so absorbed in what he was doing, he didn't see me come in; *Belg* **être tout en a.** *ou* **affaires** to be all of a flutter

❑ **affaires** NFPL **1** *Com & Écon (activités commerciales)* business *(UNCOUNT)*; **comment vont les affaires?** how's business?; **parler affaires** to talk business; **les affaires vont bien/mal** business is good/bad; **les affaires vont mal cet été** business is slow this summer; **être dans les affaires** to be in business; **les affaires sont les affaires!** business is business!; **pour affaires** *(voyager, rencontrer)* for business purposes, on business; **voyage/repas d'affaires** business trip/lunch

2 *Admin & Pol* affairs; **être aux affaires** to run the country, to be the head of state; **depuis qu'il est revenu aux affaires** since he's been back in power; **les affaires courantes** everyday matters; **les affaires de l'État** the affairs of state; **affaires étrangères** foreign affairs; **affaires intérieures** internal *or* domestic affairs; **affaires internationales** international affairs; **affaires publiques** public affairs; **les Affaires sociales** the Social Services (department); **les Affaires** *(scandale)* = financial scandals involving members of government

3 *(situation matérielle)* **ses affaires** his business affairs, his financial situation; **il connaît bien les affaires de son père** he's well acquainted with his father's business affairs; **mettre de l'ordre dans ses affaires (avant de mourir)** to put one's affairs in order (before dying)

4 *(situation personnelle)* **s'il revient, elle voudra le revoir et ça n'arrangera pas tes affaires** if he comes back, she'll want to see him and that won't help the situation; **mêle-toi de tes affaires!** mind your own business!, keep your nose out of this!; *Fam* **c'est mes affaires, ça te regarde pas!** that's MY business!; **affaires de cœur** love life

5 *(objets personnels)* things, belongings, (personal) possessions; **tes affaires de classe** your school things; **mes affaires de plage** my beach *or* swimming things; **range tes affaires** tidy up your things; *Hum* **ses petites affaires** his/her little things; *Péj* his/her precious belongings

❑ **en affaires** ADV when (you're) doing business, in business; **en affaires il faut avoir la tête froide** in business, one needs a cool head; **être dur en affaires** to drive a hard bargain, to be a tough businessman, *f* businesswoman

❑ **toutes affaires cessantes** ADV forthwith; **toutes affaires cessantes, ils sont allés chez le maire** they dropped everything and went to see the mayor

affairé, -e [afere] ADJ busy; **prends un air a.** look busy, pretend you've got a lot to do; **ils entraient et sortaient d'un air a.** they were bustling in and out; **être a. à faire qch** to be busy doing sth

affairement [afɛrmɑ̃] NM *Littéraire* bustle

affairer [4] [afere] **s'affairer** VPR to bustle; **il est toujours à s'a. dans la maison** he's always bustling about the house; **s'a. auprès de qn** to fuss around sb; **s'a. à faire qch** to be busy doing sth

affairisme [aferism] NM *Péj* wheeling and dealing

affairiste [aferist] NMF *Péj* wheeler-dealer

affaissé, -e [afese] ADJ **le sol était a.** the ground had subsided; **il était a. sur sa chaise** he was slumped in his chair

affaissement [afɛsmɑ̃] NM **1** *(effondrement → gén)* subsidence; *(→ du plancher, d'une poutre, d'un canapé)* sagging; **a. de sol** *ou* **de terrain** subsidence; **a. de la route/du terrain provoqué par des pluies diluviennes** road subsidence/subsidence due to torrential rain **2** *(relâchement → d'un muscle, des traits)* sagging **3** *(dépression)* collapse, breakdown

affaisser [4] [afese] VT *Géol (terrain, sol)* to cause to sink *or* to subside

▶**s'affaisser** VPR **1** *(se tasser → gén)* to subside, to collapse, to sink; *(→ bâtiment)* to collapse; *(→ plancher, poutre, canapé)* to sag; **la route s'est affaissée en plusieurs endroits** the road has subsided in several places; **à l'image, on voit la tour s'a. après l'explosion** on the screen, you can see the tower collapsing after the blast

2 *(s'affaler)* to collapse, to slump; **s'a. sur un canapé** to collapse *or* to slump onto a couch

3 *Écon (monnaie, marché)* to collapse, to slump

affaitage [afɛtaʒ], **affaitement** [afɛtmɑ̃] NM *(d'oiseaux de proie)* manning, training

affalé, -e [afale] ADJ **être a. dans un fauteuil** to be slumped in an armchair

affalement [afalmɑ̃] NM collapsing, slumping

affaler [3] [afale] VT *Naut (voile)* to haul down

▶**s'affaler** VPR **s'a. dans un fauteuil** to flop into an armchair; **s'a. sur le sol** to collapse on the ground; **s'a. sur un divan** to flop down onto a couch

affamé, -e [afame] ADJ famished, starving; *Littéraire* **a. de** hungry for; **a. d'honneurs** thirsting for glory

NM,F starving person; **les affamés** the starving

affamer [3] [afame] VT to starve

affameur, -euse [afamœr, -øz] NM,F starver

afféager [17] [afeaʒe] VT *Hist & Jur* to subfeu

affect [afɛkt] NM *Psy* affect

affectation [afɛktasjɔ̃] NF **1** *(manière)* affectation; **il n'y a aucune a. dans son langage** his/her language is not at all affected; **avec a.** affectedly

2 *(attribution → gén)* allocation; *Fin (→ d'une somme, de crédits)* assignment, allocation; **l'a. de crédits à la recherche** the allocation of funds to research; **l'a. de l'aile sud aux services administratifs** allocating the south wing to administration; *Écon & Compta* **affectations budgétaires** budget appropriations; **a. aux dividendes** sum available for dividend; **a. de fonds** appropriation of funds; **a. hypothécaire** mortgage charge

3 *(nomination → à une fonction)* appointment, nomination; *(→ à une ville, un pays)* posting

4 *Mil* posting; **il a reçu son a. en Allemagne** he was posted to Germany

5 *Ordinat (de touche)* assignment; **a. de mémoire** memory allocation

affecté, -e [afɛkte] ADJ *(personne)* affected, mannered; **parler d'une manière affectée** to speak affectedly

affecter [4] [afɛkte] VT **1** *(feindre)* to affect, to put on a show of; **a. une grande joie** to pretend to be overjoyed; **a. de faire qch** to pretend to do sth

2 *(présenter → une forme)* to assume; **a. l'apparence de** to take on *or* to assume the appearance of

3 *(assigner)* to allocate, to assign; **a. des crédits à la recherche** to allocate funds to research

4 *(nommer → à une fonction)* to appoint, to nominate; *(→ à une ville, un pays)* to post; **être affecté à un poste** to be appointed to a post; **être affecté à un bureau** *(venant de l'extérieur)* to be appointed to work in an office; *(d'un autre service)* to be transferred to an office; **son père l'a fait a. à Paris** his father got him a post in Paris

5 *Mil* to post

6 *(atteindre)* to affect; **la grève a affecté plusieurs usines** the strike has affected *or* hit several factories; **le virus a affecté les deux reins** both kidneys were affected by the virus; **il est affecté d'une timidité maladive** he's painfully shy

7 *(émouvoir)* to affect, to move; **il est très affecté par cette lettre/l'accident de ses parents** he's greatly affected by this letter/his parents' accident

8 *Math* to modify

▶**s'affecter** VPR *Littéraire* **s'a. de** to be affected *or* moved *or* stirred by

affectif, -ive [afɛktif, -iv] ADJ **1** *(problème, réaction)* emotional **2** *Psy* affective

affection [afɛksjɔ̃] NF **1** *(attachement)* affection, fondness, liking; **avoir de l'a. pour** to be fond of, to have a fondness for, to have a liking for; **je n'ai pas beaucoup d'a. pour son frère** I don't much care for his brother; **prendre qn en a.** to become fond of sb; **une marque** *ou* **un signe d'a.** a token of love *or* affection; **en manque d'a.** in need of affection

2 *Méd* disease, disorder

3 *Psy* affection

affectionné, -e [afɛksjɔne] ADJ *(dans une lettre)* loving, devoted; **votre petite-fille affectionnée** your loving *or* devoted granddaughter

affectionner [3] [afɛksjɔne] VT **1** *(objet, situation)* to be fond of **2** *(personne)* to like, to feel affection for

affective [afɛktiv] *voir* **affectif**

affectivité [afɛktivite] NF **1** *Psy (réactions)* **l'a.** emotionality, *Spéc* emotional life **2** *(caractère)* sensitivity

affectueuse [afɛktɥøz] *voir* **affectueux**

affectueusement [afɛktɥøzmɑ̃] ADV **1** *(tendrement)* affectionately, fondly **2** *(dans une lettre)* **bien a.** with love

affectueux, -euse [afɛktɥø, -øz] ADJ loving, affectionate; **c'est un enfant très a.** he's a very affectionate child; **elle le regardait d'un air a.** she was looking at him fondly *or* affectionately

affenage [afnaʒ] NM *Agr* foddering

afférent, -e [aferɑ̃, -ɑ̃t] ADJ **1** *Jur* **a. à** accruing to, relating to; **la part** *ou* **portion afférente à qn** the portion accruing to sb **2 a. à** *(qui se rapporte à)* relating *or* relevant to; **voici les renseignements afférents à l'affaire** here is information relating *or* relevant to the matter **3** *Physiol (nerf, vaisseau)* afferent

affermage [afɛrmaʒ] NM **1** *Jur (d'un bien rural)* tenant farming **2** *(d'un emplacement publicitaire)* contracting

affermer [3] [afɛrme] VT **1** *Jur (bien rural)* to lease (out), to rent (out) **2** *(emplacement publicitaire)* to contract for

affermir [32] [afɛrmir] VT **1** *Constr (consolider → mur)* to reinforce, to strengthen

2 *(rendre plus ferme)* to strengthen, to tone up, to firm up; **a. ses muscles par la natation** to strengthen one's muscles by swimming; **lotion tonique pour a. votre peau** firming lotion for your skin

3 *(assurer)* to strengthen; **a. sa position** to strengthen one's position; **a. sa voix** to steady one's voice

▸**s'affermir** VPR **1** *(puissance, influence)* to be strengthened; *(investissements, monnaie)* to strengthen

2 *(muscle, chair)* to firm up, to tone up, to get firmer

affermissement [afɛrmismɑ̃] NM *(d'un pont)* strengthening, consolidating; *(de la peau)* toning; *(des muscles)* strengthening, toning *or* firming up; *(d'une monnaie, du pouvoir)* strengthening

affété, -e [afete] ADJ *Arch* affected

afféterie [afetri] NF *Littéraire* affectation

affichage [afiʃaʒ] NM **1** *(sur une surface)* posting; **a. sauvage** fly posting; **a. interdit** *(sur panneau)* stick no bills, post no bills

2 *Mktg (activité)* bill-sticking, bill-posting; *(ensemble d'affiches)* posters; *(publicité)* poster advertising, display advertising; **a. transport** transport advertising

3 *Ordinat* display; **a. couleur** colour display; **a. à cristaux liquides** liquid crystal display, LCD; **a. graphique** graphics display; **a. numérique** *ou* **digital** digital display; **a. plasma** plasma display; **a. tel écran-tel écrit, a. tel-tel, a. Wysiwyg** WYSIWYG display

affiche [afiʃ] NF **1** *(annonce officielle)* public notice; *(image publicitaire)* advertisement, poster; *(d'un film, d'une pièce, d'un concert)* poster; **a. publicitaire** poster, advertisement; **a. électorale** election poster

2 *Cin & Théât* **en tête d'a., en haut de l'a.** at the top of the bill; **tenir l'a.** to run; **la pièce a tenu l'a. pendant plusieurs années** the play ran for several years; **quitter l'a.** to close

▫ **à l'affiche** ADV *Cin & Théât* **être à l'a.** to be on; **qu'est-ce qui est à l'a. en ce moment?** what's on at the moment?; **mettre une pièce à l'a.** to put a play on, to stage a play; **rester à l'a.** to run; **la pièce est restée à l'a. pendant deux ans** the play ran for two years

afficher [3] [afiʃe] VT **1** *(placarder → annonce, poster)* to post (up), to stick up; *(mettre en évidence → prix, produit)* to display, to put up; **le jugement a été affiché dans toutes les mairies** the judgment was posted up in all the city halls

2 *Cin & Théât (annoncer)* to bill, to have on the bill; **une des salles affichait du Mozart** one of the concert halls had Mozart on the bill; **on affiche complet pour ce soir** there's a full house tonight; **a. une vente** to advertise a sale, *Am* to post a sale

3 *Péj (exhiber)* to show off, to display, to flaunt; **a. son désespoir** to make one's despair obvious; **a. sa fortune/une liaison** to flaunt one's wealth/an affair

4 *Com (présenter)* to show; **a. un déficit/un excédent** to show a deficit/a surplus

5 *Ordinat (message)* to display; *(fichiers, articles)* to show; **l'écran affiche...** the on-screen message reads..., the screen displays the message...

▸**s'afficher** VPR **1** *Péj (s'exhiber)* **elle s'affiche avec lui** she makes a point of being seen with him

2 *Ordinat (sur un écran)* to be displayed

affichette [afiʃɛt] NF small poster

afficheur [afiʃœr] NM **1** *(personne)* billposter, billsticker; *(entreprise d'affichage)* poster advertising company **2** *Ordinat* visual display unit, VDU; **a. LCD** LCD display

affichiste [afiʃist] NMF poster designer

affidavit [afidavit] NM *Jur* affidavit

affidé, -e [afide] *Péj Littéraire* ADJ accomplice

NM,F accomplice

affilage [afilaʒ] NM *Tech (d'un couteau, d'une lame)* sharpening

affilé, -e [afile] ADJ *(aiguisé)* sharp; **un poignard bien a.** a well-sharpened dagger

▫ **d'affilée** ADV **il a pris plusieurs semaines de congé d'affilée** he took several weeks' leave in a row; **pendant deux/trois heures d'affilée** for two/three hours at a stretch

affiler [3] [afile] VT *(couteau, lame)* & *Can (crayon)* to sharpen

affiliation [afiljasjɔ̃] NF affiliation; **demander son a. à une organisation** to apply for membership of an organization

affilié, -e [afilje] ADJ affiliated; **non a.** non-affiliated

NM,F affiliate, affiliated member

affilier [9] [afilje] **s'affilier** VPR **s'a. à** to affiliate oneself to, to become affiliated to

affiloir [afilwar] NM *Tech* whetstone

affinage [afinaʒ] NM *(d'un fromage)* maturing; *(du coton)* fining; *(d'un métal, du sucre)* fining, refining

affine [afin] ADJ *Math & Géom (application, espace)* affine

affinement [afinmɑ̃] NM refinement

affiner [3] [afine] VT **1** *(purifier → verre, métal)* to refine

2 *(adoucir → traits)* to soften

3 *(raffiner → goût, sens)* to refine; *(→ esprit, jugement)* to sharpen, to make more acute

4 *(mûrir)* **a. du fromage** to allow cheese to mature

▸**s'affiner** VPR **1** *(se raffiner → traits, goûts)* to become more refined; *(→ esprit, jugement)* to become sharper *or* more acute

2 *(mincir)* to become thinner

affinerie [afinri] NF *Métal* refinery

affineur, -euse [afinœr, -øz] NM,F refiner

affinité [afinite] NF **1** *(sympathie)* affinity; **avoir des affinités avec qn** to have an affinity with sb; **ils ont de fortes affinités l'un avec l'autre** there's a strong rapport between them; **se sentir des affinités avec un lieu** to feel a sense of affinity with a place **2** *Chim* affinity

affiquet [afikɛ] NM *Couture* stitch holder

▫ **affiquets** NMPL trinkets *(fastened to clothing)*

affirmatif, -ive [afirmatif, -iv] ADJ **1** *(catégorique)* affirmative; **il a été très a. à ce sujet** he was quite positive about it; **parler d'un ton a.** to speak affirmatively; **faire un signe de tête a.** to nod in agreement

2 *Ling* affirmative

ADV *Mil & Tél* **a.!** affirmative!

▫ **affirmative** NF **répondre par l'affirmative** to answer yes *or* in the affirmative; **nous aimerions savoir si vous serez libre mercredi; dans l'affirmative, nous vous prions de...** we'd like to know if you are free on Wednesday; if you are *or* if so, please...

affirmation [afirmasjɔ̃] NF **1** *(gén)* affirmation; *(de la personnalité)* assertion **2** *Jur* solemn affirmation **3** *Ling* affirmation

affirmative [afirmativ] *voir* **affirmatif**

affirmativement [afirmativmɑ̃] ADV affirmatively

affirmer [3] [afirme] VT **1** *(assurer)* to assert, *Sout* to affirm; **rien ne permet encore d'a. qu'il s'agit d'un acte terroriste** there is no firm evidence as yet that terrorists were involved; **je ne pourrais pas l'a.** I couldn't swear to it, I can't be (absolutely) positive about it; **elle affirme ne pas l'avoir vu de la soirée** she maintains she didn't see him all evening; **le Premier ministre a affirmé son désir d'en finir avec le terrorisme** the Prime Minister stated his desire to put an end to terrorism; **"ça s'est passé la semaine dernière", affirma-t-il** "it happened last week," he said

2 *(exprimer → volonté, indépendance)* to assert

▸**s'affirmer** VPR *(personne)* to assert oneself; *(qualité, désir, volonté)* to assert *or* to express itself

affixal, -e, -aux, -ales [afiksal, -o] ADJ *Ling* affixable

affixe [afiks] NM *Ling* affix

affixé, -e [afikse] ADJ *Ling* affixed

affleurement [aflœrmɑ̃] NM **1** *Géol* outcrop **2** *Menuis* levelling

affleurer [5] [aflœre] VT *Menuis (étagère, planches)* to level

VI *(écueil)* to show on the surface; *Géol (filon)* to outcrop; *Fig* to show through; **l'espace d'une seconde, il laissa a. ses sentiments** for a second he let his feelings show through

afflictif, -ive [afliktif, -iv] ADJ *Jur* corporal

affliction [afliksjɔ̃] NF *Littéraire* affliction; **plongé dans l'a.** deeply distressed

afflictive [afliktiv] *voir* **afflictif**

affligé, -e [afliʒe] ADJ *(air, ton)* upset

affligeant, -e [afliʒɑ̃, -ɑ̃t] ADJ **1** *Littéraire (attristant)* distressing **2** *(lamentable)* appalling, pathetic; **des résultats affligeants** pathetic *or* appalling results; **d'une ignorance affligeante** appallingly ignorant

affliger [17] [afliʒe] VT **1** *(atteindre)* to afflict, to affect; **être affligé d'un handicap** to be afflicted with a handicap; *Fig Hum* **elle est affligée d'un prénom ridicule** she's cursed with a ridiculous first name **2** *Littéraire (attrister)* to aggrieve, to affect; **sa mort m'a beaucoup affligé** his/her death affected me greatly

▸**s'affliger** VPR *Littéraire* to be distressed, to feel grief; **s'a. de** to be distressed about, to grieve over

affluence [aflyɑ̃s] NF **1** *(foule)* crowd; **il y a a.** it's crowded; **il y a trop d'a.** it's too crowded **2** *Littéraire (abondance)* abundance

affluent, -e [aflyɑ̃, -ɑ̃t] ADJ *(fleuve, rivière)* tributary

NM tributary, affluent

affluer [7] [aflye] VI **1** *(couler)* to rush; **le sang afflua à son visage** blood rushed to his/her face; *Fig* **les capitaux affluent** money's flowing *or* rolling in **2** *(arriver)* to surge; **les manifestants affluaient vers la cathédrale** the demonstrators were flocking to the cathedral; **la nouvelle fit a. les curieux sur la place** the news brought people flooding into the square

afflux [afly] NM **1** *(de sang)* rush, *Sout* afflux **2** *(de voyageurs)* influx, flood; *(de capitaux)* inflow, influx; **a. de capitaux** *ou* **de fonds** capital inflow **3** *Élec* surge (of current)

affolant, -e [afɔlɑ̃, -ɑ̃t] ADJ **1** *(inquiétant)* frightening, terrifying; **des rumeurs affolantes parvenaient du front** terrifying rumours came from the front **2** *Fam (en intensif)* appalling; **c'est a. ce qu'il y a comme circulation** the traffic's appalling; **c'est a. ce qu'elle a grandi** it's frightening *or* scary how much she's grown

aff–afr

affolé, -e [afɔle] ADJ **1** *(bouleversé)* panic-stricken; **il avait l'air complètement a. au téléphone** he sounded totally panic-stricken *or* in a complete panic over the phone **2** *(boussole)* spinning

affolement [afɔlmɑ̃] NM **1** *(panique)* panic; **l'a. était si grand que nous avons oublié de fermer la porte** there was such a panic that we forgot to lock the door; **pas d'a.!** don't panic!; **sans a.** in a cool(, calm) and collected way **2** *(d'une boussole)* spinning **3** *Métal & Phys* perturbation

affoler [3] [afɔle] VT **1** *(terrifier)* to throw into a panic; *(bouleverser)* to throw into turmoil; **les hurlements de l'animal l'affolèrent complètement** the howling of the animal threw him/her into a total panic; **les poulains étaient affolés** the foals were running around panic-stricken **2** *Littéraire (sexuellement)* to drive wild with desire
▸**s'affoler** VPR **1** *(s'effrayer)* to panic; **ne t'affole pas, tout va bien!** don't panic, everything's OK!; **elle s'affole toujours à l'idée de partir** she always panics *or* gets frantic at the thought of going away; **l'animal s'affolait** the animal was getting distressed **2** *(boussole)* to spin

affouage [afwaʒ] NM **1** *(droit)* common of estovers **2** *(bois)* = firewood cut by "affouagistes"

affouagé, -e [afwaʒe] NM,F = holder of the privilege to cut firewood from a communal forest

affouager [17] [afwaʒe] VT *Jur* **a. une commune** = to draw up the list of inhabitants who have a right to take firewood from a communal forest; **a. un bois** to mark off estovers in a wood

affouagiste [afwaʒist] NMF = holder of the privilege to cut firewood from a communal forest

affouillement [afujmɑ̃] NM **1** *Géog* undermining, erosion; **force d'a.** scour **2** *Mil* scouring

affouiller [3] [afuje] VT *Géol (rive, fondation etc)* to undermine, to erode, to wash away

affouragement [afuraʒmɑ̃] NM **1** *Agr* foddering **2** *Chasse* (game) feeding

affourager [17] [afuraʒe] VT *Agr* to fodder

affourcher [3] [afurʃe] VT **1 a. qn sur qch** to seat sb astride sth **2** *Menuis* to join by tongue and groove *or* by open mortise **3** *Naut (bateau)* to moor (head-to-wind)

affranchi, -e [afrɑ̃ʃi] ADJ **1** *(esclave)* freed **2** *(émancipé)* emancipated, liberated
NM,F **1** *(esclave libéré)* freed slave **2** *Fam Arg crime* shady character

═══🎞═══

'Les Affranchis' *Scorsese* 'Goodfellas'

affranchir [32] [afrɑ̃ʃir] VT **1** *(libérer → esclave)* to (set) free; **a. qn de qch** to free *or* to release sb from sth **2** *(colis, lettre)* to stamp, to put a stamp *or* stamps on; **paquet insuffisamment affranchi** parcel with insufficient postage on it **3** *Fam Arg crime (renseigner)* **a. qn** to give sb the lowdown, to tip sb off **4** *Cartes* to clear
▸**s'affranchir** VPR **1** *(colonie)* to gain one's freedom; *(adolescent)* to gain one's independence; *(opprimé)* to become emancipated *or* liberated; **s'a. de la tutelle de ses parents** to free oneself from one's parents' supervision; **s'a. de la domination étrangère** to throw off foreign domination **2** *Belg (prendre de l'assurance)* to become self-confident

affranchissable [afrɑ̃ʃisabl] ADJ *(colis, lettre)* which must be stamped, non postage paid

affranchissement [afrɑ̃ʃismɑ̃] NM **1** *(libération)* freeing; **après leur a.** after they were set free **2** *(d'une lettre → action)* stamping; *(→ coût)* postage; **tarifs d'a. pour l'Afrique** postage *or* postal rates to Africa; **a. insuffisant** insufficient postage; **dispensé d'a.** post-free, postage paid

affres [afr] NFPL *Littéraire* pangs; **les a. de la jalousie** the pangs of jealousy; **les a. de la mort** the pangs *or* throes of death; **les a. de la création** the throes of creativity

affrètement [afrɛtmɑ̃] NM chartering

affréter [18] [afrete] VT *Transp (avion, navire)* to charter

affréteur [afretœr] NM *Transp* charterer, charter company

affreuse [afrøz] *voir* **affreux**

affreusement [afrøzmɑ̃] ADV **1** *(en intensif)* dreadfully, horribly, terribly; **elle a été a. mutilée** she was horribly mutilated; **ce tableau est a. laid** this painting is terribly ugly; **il parle a. mal l'anglais** his English is awful **2** *(laidement)* **a. habillé/décoré** hideously dressed/decorated

affreux, -euse [afrø, -øz] ADJ **1** *(répugnant)* horrible, ghastly; **quelle ville affreuse!** what a horrible city!
2 *(très désagréable)* dreadful, awful; **nous avons connu quelques années affreuses** we have been through a few dreadful years; **il a fait un temps a. pendant toute la semaine** the weather was awful all week long; **qu'est-ce que ça a augmenté, c'est a.!** it's dreadful *or* shocking how the price has gone up!
NM *Fam* **1** *(mercenaire)* (white) mercenary *(in Africa)*
2 *(en appellatif)* **tu viens, l'a.?** coming, you little terror *or* monster?

affriander [3] [afrijɑ̃de] VT *Littéraire* to allure, to entice

affriolant, -e [afrijɔlɑ̃, -ɑ̃t] ADJ alluring, appealing; **des dessous affriolants** sexy underwear; *Fig* **ce travail n'a rien d'a.** it's not the world's most exciting job

affrioler [3] [afrijɔle] VT to excite, to allure

affriquée [afrike] *Ling* ADJ F *(consonne)* affricative
NF affricate

affront [afrɔ̃] NM affront; **essuyer** *ou* **subir un a.** to be affronted *or* offended; **faire un a. à qn** to affront sb; **tu ne vas pas me faire l'a. de refuser?** you're not going to offend me by refusing?

affronté, -e [afrɔ̃te] ADJ **1** *Menuis (planche)* joined edgewise **2** *Hér* affrontee

affrontement [afrɔ̃tmɑ̃] NM **1** *(heurt)* confrontation; **les derniers affrontements ont fait plusieurs morts** the last confrontation claimed several casualties; **l'a. de deux idéologies** the clash *or* conflict of ideologies **2** *(mise de niveau) Menuis* joining edge to edge; *Méd* closing up

affronter [3] [afrɔ̃te] VT **1** *(ennemi, mort)* to face, to confront; *(problème)* to face (up to); *(équipe, adversaire)* to meet, to clash with; **il n'a pas hésité à a. le danger/l'incendie** he didn't hesitate to face danger/the fire; **a. la colère de qn** to brave sb's wrath
2 *Menuis (planche)* to butt-joint
3 *Méd* **a. les lèvres d'une plaie** to close up a wound
▸**s'affronter** VPR *(gén)* to confront one another; *(équipes, joueurs)* to meet, to clash; **deux thèses s'affrontent dans le débat sur la peine de mort** there are two opposing theories in the debate on the death penalty

affruiter [3] [afrɥite] *Hort* VT to plant with fruit trees
VI to bear fruit, to produce fruit

affublement [afybləmɑ̃] NM rig-out

affubler [3] [afyble] VT *Péj (habiller)* to attire; **affublé d'une veste rouge** attired in a red jacket; **qui l'a affublé ainsi?** who on earth dressed him like that?; *Fig* **on l'avait affublé d'un surnom idiot** he had been given a stupid nickname
▸**s'affubler** VPR *Péj* **s'a. de** to don; **elle s'était affublée d'une robe à froufrous** she had donned a flouncy dress

affusion [afyzjɔ̃] NF *Méd* affusion

affût [afy] NM **1** *Mil (d'un canon)* carriage, mount
2 *Opt (d'un télescope)* frame
3 *Chasse* hide, *Am* blind
❑ **à l'affût** ADV *Chasse* **se mettre à l'a.** to hide out; **être à l'a.** to be lying in wait; **chasse à l'a.** sitting up
❑ **à l'affût de** PRÉP **1** *Chasse* **être à l'a. de** to be lying in wait for **2** *(à la recherche de)* **il est toujours à l'a. des ragots/des articles les plus récents** he's always on the look-out for juicy bits of gossip/the latest articles; **à l'a. d'un sourire** begging for a smile

affûtage [afytaʒ] NM *Tech* **1** *(aiguisage)* grinding, sharpening **2** *(outils)* set of bench tools

affûter [3] [afyte] VT **1** *Tech (outils)* to grind, to sharpen **2** *Équitation* **a. un cheval** to bring a horse to the top of its form

affûteur [afytœr] NM *Tech* grinder

affûteuse [afytøz] NF *Tech* grinding machine

affûtiaux [afytjo] NMPL *Fam* **1** *(bijoux)* trinkets, knick-knacks **2** *(outils)* tools

afghan, -e [afgɑ̃, -an] ADJ Afghan
NM *(langue)* Afghan
❑ **Afghan, -e** NM,F Afghan, Afghani

afghani [afgani] NM afghani

Afghanistan [afganistɑ̃] NM **l'A.** Afghanistan; **vivre en A.** to live in Afghanistan; **aller en A.** to go to Afghanistan

afibrinogénémie [afibrinɔʒenemi] NF *Méd* afibrinogenaemia

aficionado [afisjonado] NM aficionado; **les aficionados du football** football enthusiasts

afin [afɛ̃] **afin de** PRÉP in order to, so as to; **il s'est levé tôt a. d'éviter les embouteillages** he got up early (in order) to avoid traffic jams
❑ **afin que** CONJ *(suivi du subjonctif)* in order *or* so that; **préviens-moi si tu viens a. que je puisse préparer ta chambre** tell me if you are coming so that I can prepare your bedroom

aflatoxine [aflatɔksin] NF *Méd* aflatoxin

AFLS [aɛfɛlɛs] NF *(abrév* **Agence française de lutte contre le sida**) = French Aids research and care agency

AFME [aɛfɛmø] NF *Anciennement (abrév* **Agence française pour la maîtrise de l'énergie**) = French agency for energy management

AFNOR, Afnor [afnɔr] NF *Ind (abrév* **Association française de normalisation**) = French industrial standards authority, *Br* ≃ BSI, *Am* ≃ ASA

afocal, -e, -aux, -ales [afɔkal, -o] ADJ *Opt* afocal

à-fond [afɔ̃] *(pl* **à-fonds**) NM *Belg* **faire un à.** to down one's drink in one
❑ **à-fonds** NMPL *Suisse* spring-cleaning *(UNCOUNT)*; **faire les à-fonds** to spring-clean, to do the spring-cleaning

a fortiori [afɔrsjɔri] ADV a fortiori, even more so, with all the more reason

AF-P [aɛfpe] NF *Presse (abrév* **Agence France-Presse**) Agence France-Presse *(French national news agency)*

AFPA [aɛfpea] NF *(abrév* **Association pour la formation professionnelle des adultes**) = government body promoting adult vocational training

AFR [aɛfɛr] NF *(abrév* **allocation de formation reclassement**) = allowance paid to employees requiring further training *or* new qualifications

africain, -e [afrikɛ̃, -ɛn] ADJ African
❑ **Africain, -e** NM,F African

africanisation [afrikanizasjɔ̃] NF Africanization, Africanizing

africaniser [3] [afrikanize] VT to Africanize
▸**s'africaniser** VPR to become Africanized

africanisme [afrikanism] NM Africanism

africaniste [afrikanist] NMF Africanist, specialist on Africa

afrikaander [afrikɑ̃dɛr] = **afrikaner**

afrikaans [afrikɑ̃s] NM *(langue)* Afrikaans

afrikaner [afrikanɛr], **afrikander** [afrikɑ̃dɛr] ADJ Afrikaner
❑ **Afrikaner, Afrikander** NM,F Afrikaner

Afrique [afrik] NF **l'A.** Africa; **l'A. australe** Southern Africa; **l'A. noire** Black Africa; **l'A. du Nord** North Africa; **l'A. du Sud** South Africa; **vivre en A. du Sud** to live in South Africa; **aller en A. du Sud** to go to South Africa

Afrique-Équatoriale française [afrikekwatɔrjalfrɑ̃sɛz] NF **l'A.** French Equatorial Africa

Afrique-Occidentale française [afrikɔksidɑ̃talfrɑ̃sɛz] NF **l'A.** *Géog* French West Africa

afro [afro] ADJ INV afro; **coiffure a.** afro hairstyle
NM afro

afro-américain, -e [afroamerikɛ̃, -ɛn] *(mpl* **afro-américains**, *fpl* **afro-américaines**) ADJ Afro-American
❑ **Afro-Américain, -e** NM,F Afro-American

afro-antillais, -e [afroɑ̃tije, -ɛz] *(mpl inv, fpl* **afro-antillaises**) ADJ Afro-Caribbean
❑ **Afro-Antillais, -e** NM,F Afro-Caribbean

afro-asiatique [afroazjatik] *(pl* **afro-asiatiques**) ADJ **1** *Géog* Afro-Asian **2** *Ling* Afro-Asiatic
❑ **Afro-Asiatique** NMF Afro-Asian

afro-brésilien, -enne [afrobreziljɛ̃, -ɛn] *(mpl* **afro-brésiliens**, *fpl* **afro-brésiliennes**) ADJ Afro-Brazilian
❑ **Afro-Brésilien, -enne** NM,F Afro-Brazilian

afro-cubain, -e [afrokybɛ̃, -ɛn] (*mpl* afro-cubains, *fpl* afro-cubaines) ADJ Afro-Cuban
❑ **Afro-Cubain, -e** NM,F Afro-Cuban

afropessimisme [afropesimism] NM compassion fatigue *(towards underdeveloped African countries)*, Africa fatigue

afro-rock [afrorɔk] NM *Mus* Afro-rock

after [aftœr] NM OU NF *Fam (soirée)* after-party; **on a décidé d'aller faire l'a. chez Alex** we finished the night off at Alex's place; **je fais un** *ou* **une a. après la soirée en boîte, d'accord?** everybody back to mine after the clubs shut, yeah?

after-shave [aftœrʃɛv] ADJ INV aftershave; **une lotion a.** aftershave (lotion)
NM INV aftershave (lotion)

AG [ɑʒe] NF *(abrév* **assemblée générale**) GM

ag. *(abrév écrite* **agence**) agcy

aga [aga] NM aga

agaçant, -e [agasɑ̃, -ɑ̃t] ADJ **1** *(irritant)* irritating, annoying; **ce qu'il peut être a.!** he can be so annoying! **2** *Littéraire (excitant)* exciting, titivating

agace [agas] NF *Arch Orn* magpie

agacement [agasmɑ̃] NM irritation, annoyance; **montrer de l'a.** to show irritation

agace-pissette [agaspisɛt] (*pl* **agace-pissettes**) NF *Can Vulg* pricktease, prickteaser

agacer [16] [agase] VT **1** *(irriter)* to irritate, to annoy; **ses plaisanteries m'agacent** his/her jokes get on my nerves; **il m'agace avec ses questions** he's getting on my nerves, asking all those questions **2** *(dents)* **le jus de citron agace les dents** lemon juice sets one's teeth on edge **3** *Littéraire (exciter)* to excite, to titivate

agacerie [agasri] NF piece of flirtatiousness *or* of coquettish behaviour; **faire de petites agaceries à qn** to tease sb

agaceur, -euse [agasœr, -øz], **agaceux, -euse** [agasø, -øz] ADJ *Can* irritating, annoying; **ce qu'il peut être a.!** he can be so annoying!

agada [agada] NF *Rel* **l'a.** the Aggadah, the Agada

agalactie, agalaxie [agalaksi] NF *Vét & Méd* agalactia, agalaxy

agame[1] [agam] NM *Zool (lézard)* agama

agame[2] [agam] ADJ *Biol & Bot* agamic

Agamemnon [agamɛmnɔ̃] NPR *Myth* Agamemnon

agami [agami] NM *Orn* agami, trumpeter

agamidé [agamide] *Zool* NM agamid
❑ **agamidés** NMPL Agamidae

agamie [agami] NF *Biol* agamogenesis

agammaglobulinémie [agamaglɔbylinemi] NF *Méd* agammaglobulinaemia

agapanthe [agapɑ̃t] NF *Bot* agapanthus

agape [agap] NF *Arch Rel* agape
❑ **agapes** NFPL *Hum* feast; **faire des agapes** to have a feast

agar-agar [agaragar] (*pl* **agars-agars**) NM *Biol & Pharm* agar, agar-agar

agaric [agarik] NM *Bot* agaric

agaricacée [agarikase] *Bot* NF mushroom, *Spéc* member of the Agaricaceae family
❑ **agaricacées** NFPL Agaricaceae

agaricale [agarikal] *Bot* NF mushroom of the Agaricales order
❑ **agaricales** NFPL Agaricales

agasse [agas] = **agace**

agassin [agasɛ̃] NM *Hort (d'une branche de vigne)* non-fruiting basal bud

agate [agat] NF **1** *Minér* agate **2** *(bille)* glass marble

agatisé, -e [agatize] ADJ *Minér* agate-like, agatized

agavacée [agavase] *Bot* NF century plant, plant of the agave family
❑ **agavacées** NFPL Agavaceae

agave [agav], **agavé** [agave] NM *Bot* agave; **a. americana** century plant

AGC [ɑʒese] NM *Phot (abrév* **adaptateur graphique couleur**) CGA

AGCS [ɑʒesees] NM *Écon (abrév* **Accord général sur le commerce des services**) GATS

AGE [ɑʒeœ] NF *(abrév* **assemblée générale extraordinaire**) EGM

age [aʒ] NM *Agr (de la charrue)* beam

âge [ɑʒ] NM **1** *(nombre d'années)* age; **quel â. as-tu?** how old are you?; **quand j'avais ton â.** when I was your age; **être du même â. que** to be the same age *or* as old as; **à ton â., je lisais beaucoup** when I was your age, I used to read a lot; **à ton â., on ne pleure plus** you're old enough not to cry now; **un garçon/une fille de ton â. ne doit pas parler comme ça** a boy/a girl (of) your age shouldn't talk like that; **d'un â. avancé** getting on *or* advanced in years; *Hum* **d'un â. canonique** ancient; *Euph* **d'un certain â.** *(dame, monsieur)* middle-aged; *Hum* **un canapé d'un certain â.** a couch which is past its best *or* prime; **d'â. mûr** middle-aged; **à cause de son jeune/grand â.** because he's/she's so young/old; **avancer en â.** to be getting on in years; **il veut se marier, c'est normal, il a l'â.** he wants to get married, it's normal at his age; **quand tu auras l'â.!** when you're old enough!; **je n'ai plus l'â.** *ou* **je ne suis plus en â. de grimper à la corde** I'm too old for climbing ropes; **j'ai passé l'â.!** I'm too old (for this kind of thing)!; **les boums, c'est de son â.** they all want to have parties at that age; **ce n'est pas de ton â.!** *(tu es trop jeune)* you're not old enough!; *(tu es trop vieux)* you're too old (for it)!; **ce sont des choses qui ne sont plus de mon â.** I'm too old for that sort of thing now; **tu es en â. de comprendre** you're old enough to understand; **ils ne sont pas en â. de se marier** they're not old enough to get married; **sans â.** ageless; **elle n'a pas d'â.** she seems ageless; **on ne lui donne vraiment pas son â.** he/she doesn't look his/her age at all; **quel â. me donnez-vous?** how old do you think I am?; **faire** *ou* **paraître son â.** to look one's age; **elle ne fait** *ou* **ne paraît pas son â.** she doesn't look her age, she looks younger than she actually is; **elle est bien pour son â.** she looks good for her age; **on a l'â. de ses artères** you're as old as you feel; **l'â. d'un arbre/vin** the age of a tree/wine; **un whisky 20 ans d'â.** a 20-year-old whisky

2 *(période)* age, time (of life); **la quarantaine, c'est l'â. des grandes décisions** forty is the time (of life) for making momentous decisions; **une fois passé l'â. des poupées** when one's too old for dolls; **c'est le bel â.!** these are the best years of one's life!; **ne te plains pas, c'est le bel â.!** don't complain, these are the best years of your life *or* you're in your prime!; **l'â. adulte** *(gén)* adulthood; *(d'un homme)* manhood; *(d'une femme)* womanhood; **l'â. ingrat** *ou Fam* **bête** the difficult *or* awkward age; **l'â. critique** the change of life; **l'â. mûr** maturity; **l'â. pubertaire** *ou* **de la puberté** the age of puberty; **l'â. de raison** the age of reason; **avoir l'â. de raison** to have reached the age of reason; **l'â. tendre** the tender years; **l'â. viril** manhood; **le premier â.** infancy; **le troisième â.** *(période)* old age; *(groupe social)* senior citizens; **le quatrième â.** *(période)* advanced old age; *(groupe social)* very old people

3 *(vieillissement)* ageing; **avec l'â., il s'est calmé** he became more serene with age *or* as he grew older; **les effets de l'â.** the effects of ageing; **prendre de l'â.** to age, to get older; **j'ai mal aux genoux – c'est l'â.!** my knees hurt – it's your age!

4 *Admin* age; **quel est l'â. de la retraite en France?** what's the retirement age in France?; **avoir l'â. légal (pour voter)** to be old enough to vote, to be of age; **l'â. scolaire** compulsory school age; **un enfant d'â. scolaire** a school-age child, a child of school age

5 *Archéol* age; **l'â. de bronze** the Bronze Age; **l'â. de fer** the Iron Age; *Fig & Myth* **l'â. d'or** the golden age; **l'â. néolithique** *ou* **de la pierre polie** the Neolithic Age; **l'â. paléolithique** *ou* **de la pierre taillée** the Palaeolithic Age; **c'est une tradition venue du fond des âges** it's a tradition which has come down through the ages

6 *Psy* **â. mental** mental age; **il a un â. mental de cinq ans** he has a mental age of five
❑ **à l'âge de** PRÉP **je l'ai connu à l'â. de 17 ans** *(j'avais 17 ans)* I met him when I was 17; *(il avait 17 ans)* I met him when he was 17; **on est majeur à l'â. de 18 ans** 18 is the age of majority
❑ **en bas âge** ADJ *(enfant)* very young *or* small
❑ **entre deux âges** ADJ *(personne)* middle-aged

âgé, -e [ɑʒe] ADJ **1** *(vieux)* old; **c'est un monsieur très â. maintenant** he's a very old man now; **elle est plus/moins âgée que moi** she's older/younger than I am **2 â. de** *(de tel âge)* aged; **être â. de 20 ans** to be 20 years old; **une jeune fille âgée de 15 ans** a 15-year-old girl, a girl of 15

Aged [aʒɛd] NF *(abrév* **allocation de garde d'enfant à domicile**) = allowance paid to working parents who employ a childminder at home

agence [aʒɑ̃s] NF **1** *(bureau)* agency, bureau; **a. commerciale** sales office; *Fin* mercantile agency; **a. conseil en communication** public relations agency, PR agency; **a. de coupures de presse** press cuttings agency; **a. de design** design agency; **a. de distribution** distribution agency; **a. immobilière** *Br* estate agent's, *Am* real-estate office; **a. d'intérim** temping agency; **a. maritime** shipping *or* forwarding agency; **a. de marketing direct** direct marketing agency; **a. matrimoniale** marriage bureau; **a. de notation** *Br* credit (rating) agency, *Am* credit bureau; **a. photographique** photographic agency; **a. de placement** employment agency *or* bureau; **a. de presse** press *or* news agency; **a. de promotion** promotions agency; **a. de promotion des ventes** sales promotion agency; **a. de publicité** advertising agency; **a. de recouvrements** debt collection agency; **a. de renseignements** information bureau; **a. de tourisme** tourist agency; **a. de voyages** travel agency *or* agent's; **A. pour l'énergie nucléaire** = French atomic energy agency, ≃ AEA; **A. de l'environnement et de la maîtrise de l'énergie** = French public body responsible for environmental and energy management; **A. française de lutte contre le sida** = French Aids research and care agency; *Anciennement* **A. française pour la maîtrise de l'énergie** = French agency for energy management; **A. France-Presse** = French national news agency; **A. internationale de l'énergie atomique** International Atomic Energy Agency; **A. nationale pour l'amélioration de l'habitat** = national agency responsible for housing projects and restoration grants; **A. nationale pour l'emploi** = national employment agency; **A. nationale de recherches sur le sida** = Aids research institute; **A. spatiale européenne** European Space Agency; *Anciennement* **l'a. Tass** Tass, the Tass news agency

2 *(succursale)* branch (office); **quand vous passerez à l'a.** when you next visit the branch; **a. bancaire** bank branch

agencé, -e [aʒɑ̃se] ADJ *Suisse (cuisine)* fitted

agencement [aʒɑ̃smɑ̃] NM *(d'un lieu)* layout, design; *(d'un texte)* layout; *(d'éléments)* order, ordering

agencer [16] [aʒɑ̃se] VT **1** *(aménager)* to lay out; **a. un musée** to lay out a museum; **a. une pièce** to arrange the furniture in a room; **un studio bien agencé** a well laid-out studio flat

2 *(organiser)* to put together, to construct; **a. les scènes d'une comédie** to construct the scenes of a comedy; **des phrases mal agencées** badly constructed sentences

▶**s'agencer** VPR **les parties du discours s'agencent bien/mal** the different parts of the speech go/don't hang well together

agencier [aʒɑ̃sie] NM *Journ* freelance journalist *(working for a press agency)*

agenda [aʒɛ̃da] NM **1** *(livre)* diary; **a. de bureau** desk diary; **a. électronique** personal organizer; **a. de poche** pocket diary; *Fig* **avoir un a. très chargé** to have a very full diary **2** *Ordinat* notebook **3** *Pol* **a. politique** political agenda; *UE* **A. 2000** Agenda 2000

agender [3] [aʒɑ̃de] VT *Suisse (rendez-vous, date)* to note down (in a *Br* diary *or Am* notebook)

agénésie [aʒenezi] NF *Méd* agenesis, agenesia

agenouillement [aʒnujmɑ̃] NM *Littéraire* kneeling

agenouiller [3] [aʒnuje] **s'agenouiller** VPR to kneel (down); **s'a. devant une statue** to kneel (down) before a statue; *Fig* **il refuse de s'a. devant le pouvoir** he refuses to bow to authority

agenouilloir [aʒnujwar] NM *(prie-dieu)* hassock, kneeling stool; *(planche)* kneeling plank

agent [aʒɑ̃] NM

> Note that it is no longer considered a mistake to feminize this word and to say **une agente** (with a final **e**) for senses 1, 2 and 3 but some French speakers nonetheless regard this form as unacceptable, especially in France. See also the entry **féminisation**.

1 *(employé)* **a. d'affaires** business agent; **a. artistique** agent; **a. d'assurances** insurance

agent; **a. attitré** appointed agent; *Bourse* **a. de change** stockbroker, exchange dealer *or* broker; **a. commercial** sales representative; **a. commercial exclusif** sole agent, sole representative; **a. commissionnaire** commission agent; **a. comptable** accountant; **a. de conduite** *(d'un train)* train driver; **a. consulaire** consular agent; **a. contractuel** *Admin* contract public servant; *(agent de police) Br* traffic warden, *Am* traffic policeman; *Com* **a. direct** commission agent; **a. de distribution** distribution agent; **a. double** double agent; **a. électoral** canvasser; **a. exclusif** sole agent; **a. exportateur** export agent; **a. du fisc** tax official; **a. de fret** freight forwarder, forwarding agent; **un a. du gouvernement** a government official; **a. immobilier** *Br* estate agent, *Am* real estate agent, realtor; **a. importateur** import agent; **a. indépendant** free agent; **a. intermédiaire** middleman; *Jur* **a. de justice** = officer of the court; *Mil* **a. de liaison** liaison officer; **a. lié** tied agent; **a. de ligne** forwarding agent; **a. littéraire** literary agent; **agents de maîtrise** lower management; **a. mandataire** authorized agent; **a. maritime** shipping agent; **a. provocateur** agent provocateur; **a. publicitaire**, **a. de publicité** advertising agent, publicity agent; *Belg* **a. de quartier** community policeman, policeman on the beat; **a. de recouvrement** *ou* **de recouvrements** debt collector; **a. secret** secret agent; **a. de sécurité** security officer; **a. souscripteur** underwriting *or* underwriter agent; **a. technico-commercial** sales technician, sales engineer; *Mil* **a. de transmission** dispatch rider; **a. du trésor** government broker

2 *(policier)* **a. (de police)** *(homme)* policeman, police officer *Br* constable, *Am* patrolman; *(femme)* policewoman, *Br* woman police constable, *Am* woman police officer; **a. de la circulation**, **a. contractuel** *Br* (male) traffic warden *or Am* traffic policeman; **a. de police administrative** = police officer in charge of crime prevention and keeping order; **a. de police judiciaire** = assistant police officer in the French Criminal Investigation Department; **a. verbalisateur** = police officer in charge of reporting petty offences; **s'il vous plaît, monsieur l'a.** excuse me, officer

3 *(émissaire)* agent, official; *Péj* **des agents de l'étranger** foreign agents

4 *(cause → humaine)* agent; *(→ non humaine)* factor; **elle a été l'un des principaux agents de la révolution** she was a prime mover in the revolution; **a. atmosphérique/économique** atmospheric/economic factor

5 *Méd* **a. asphyxiant** asphyxiant; *Méd* **a. carcinogène** *ou* **cancérogène** carcinogen; *Chim* **a. chimique** chemical agent; **a. conservateur** *ou* **de conservation** preservative; *Chim* **a. mouillant** wetting agent; *Med* **a. paralysateur** paralyser

6 *Gram & Phil* agent

7 *Ordinat* **a. intelligent** intelligent agent

agentif [aʒɑ̃tif] **NM** *Gram* agentive

agérate [aʒerat], **ageratum** [aʒeratɔm] **NM** *Bot* ageratum

Agétac [aʒetak] **NM** *Com* (*abrév* **Accord Général sur les Tarifs Douaniers et le Commerce**) GATT

aggadah [agada] = **agada**

aggiornamento [adʒɔrnamɛnto] **NM** *Rel & Fig* aggiornamento; **le parti doit faire son a.** the party has to move with the times

agglo [aglo] **NM** *Fam Constr* chipboard

agglomérant [aglɔmerɑ̃] **NM** *Constr* binder

agglomérat [aglɔmera] **NM** **1** *Géol* agglomerate **2** *Ling* cluster

agglomération [aglɔmerasjɔ̃] **NF** **1** *(ville et sa banlieue)* town; **l'a. parisienne** Paris and its suburbs, greater Paris **2** *Transp* built-up area; **en a.** in a built-up area **3** *Mines (de sable)* aggregation **4** *(assemblage)* conglomeration

aggloméré, -e [aglɔmere] **ADJ** agglomerate
NM 1 *Mines* briquet, briquette **2** *Constr* chipboard; **a. de liège** agglomerated cork **3** *Géol* conglomerate

agglomérer [18] [aglɔmere] **VT** *(pierre, sable)* to

aggregate; *(charbon)* to briquet; *(métal)* to agglomerate
▸**s'agglomérer** *VPR (sable, particules)* to agglomerate; **les populations pauvres s'agglomèrent dans les favelas** the poor are packed together in the shanty towns

agglutinant, -e [aglytinɑ̃, -ɑ̃t] **ADJ** *Ling & Méd* agglutinative
NM bond

agglutination [aglytinasjɔ̃] **NF 1** *Ling & Méd* agglutination **2** *Péj (masse)* mass

agglutiner [3] [aglytine] **VT** to mass *or* to pack together
▸**s'agglutiner** *VPR* to congregate; **ils s'agglutinaient à la fenêtre** they were all pressing up against the window; **les pucerons s'agglutinent sous chaque bourgeon** greenfly congregate in a dense mass under each bud

agglutinine [aglytinin] **NF** *Biol* agglutinin

agglutinogène [aglytinɔʒɛn] **NM** *Biol* agglutinogen

aggravant, -e [agravɑ̃, -ɑ̃t] **ADJ** aggravating; **et, fait a., il avait oublié l'argent** and he'd forgotten the money, which made things worse

aggravation [agravasjɔ̃] **NF 1** *(d'une maladie, d'un problème)* aggravation, worsening; *(de l'inflation)* increase; **son état de santé a connu une a.** his/her health has worsened; **l'a. du chômage le mois dernier** the increase in unemployment last month **2** *(d'une peine)* increase

aggraver [3] [agrave] **VT** *(mal, problème)* to aggravate, to make worse, to exacerbate; *(mécontentement, colère)* to increase; **ces mesures ne feront qu'a. l'inflation** these measures will only serve to worsen inflation; **n'aggrave pas ton cas** don't make your position worse than it is; **pour a. les choses** to make matters worse
▸**s'aggraver** *VPR* to get worse, to worsen; **son état s'est aggravé** his/her condition has worsened; **la situation s'aggrave** the situation is getting worse; *Fam Hum* **décidément, mon pauvre vieux, ça s'aggrave!** you get worse!

agha [aga] **NM** aga

agile [aʒil] **ADJ** nimble, agile; **un esprit a.** an agile mind

agilement [aʒilmɑ̃] **ADV** *(grimper, se mouvoir)* nimbly, agilely

agilité [aʒilite] **NF** agility

agio [aʒjo] **NM 1** *Fin (dans un échange de devises)* agio **2** *Banque* **agios** *(quand on est à découvert)* bank charges; *(d'un emprunt)* interest payments

a giorno [adʒjɔrno] **ADJ INV** *(éclairage)* like natural light
ADV *(éclairage)* like natural light

agiotage [aʒjɔtaʒ] **NM** *Bourse* speculating, speculation

agioter [3] [aʒjɔte] **VI** *Bourse* to speculate, to gamble

agioteur, -euse [aʒjɔtœr, -øz] **NM,F** *Bourse* speculator, gambler

agir [32] [aʒir] **VI A.** *AVOIR UNE ACTIVITÉ* **1** *(intervenir)* to act, to take action; **il faut a. rapidement pour enrayer l'épidémie** we have to act quickly *or* to take swift action to prevent the epidemic from developing; **en cas d'incendie, il faut a. vite** in the event of a fire, it is important to act quickly; **sur les ordres de qui avez-vous agi?** on whose orders did you act?; **est-ce la jalousie qui l'a fait a.?** was it jealousy that made her do it?; **c'est l'ambition qui le fait a.** he is motivated by ambition; **a. auprès de qn** *(essayer de l'influencer)* to try to influence sb; **a. auprès de qn pour obtenir qch** to approach sb for sth; **je vous en prie, agissez auprès de l'archevêque** please use your influence with the archbishop; **a. au nom de** *ou* **pour qn** to act on behalf of *or* for sb

2 *(passer à l'action)* to do something; **parler et a. sont deux choses différentes** there's quite a difference between talking and actually doing something; **elle parle, mais elle n'agit pas** she talks, but she doesn't do anything; **assez parlé, maintenant il faut a.!** enough talk, let's have some action!

3 *(se comporter)* to act, to behave; **elle agit bizarrement ces temps-ci** she's been acting or behaving strangely of late; **bien/mal a. envers qn** to behave well/badly towards sb; **tu n'as pas agi loyalement** you didn't play fair; **il a agi en**

bon citoyen he did what any honest citizen would have done; **a. à la légère** to act rashly; **a. selon sa conscience** to act according to one's conscience, to let one's conscience be one's guide

B. *AVOIR UN EFFET* **1** *(fonctionner → poison, remède)* to act, to take effect, to work; *(→ élément nutritif)* to act, to have an effect; *(→ détergent)* to work; **laisser a. un décapant** to allow a paint-stripper to work; **laisser a. la justice** to let justice take its course; **pour faire a. le médicament plus efficacement** to increase the efficiency of the drug

2 *(avoir une influence)* **a. sur** to work *or* to have an effect on; **tes larmes n'agissent plus sur moi** your tears don't have any effect on me *or* don't move me any more; *Bourse* **a. sur le marché** to manipulate the market

C. *DANS LE DOMAINE JURIDIQUE* to act in a court of law; **a. contre qn** *(en droit pénal)* to prosecute sb; *(en droit civil)* to sue sb; **a. en diffamation** to sue for libel; **a. en recherche de paternité** to bring a paternity suit

❑ **s'agir de v IMPERSONNEL 1** *(être question de)* **je voudrais te parler – de quoi s'agit-il?** I'd like to talk to you – what about?; **de qui s'agit-il?** who is it?; **je voudrais vous parler d'une affaire importante, voici ce dont il s'agit** I'd like to talk to you about an important matter, namely this; **le criminel dont il s'agit** the criminal in question; **l'affaire dont il s'agit** the matter at issue; **ne la mêle pas à cette affaire, il s'agit de toi et de moi** don't bring her into this, it's between you and me; **il ne s'est agi que de littérature toute la soirée** the only thing talked about all evening was literature; **mais enfin, il s'agit de sa santé!** but her health is at stake (here)!; **je peux te prêter de l'argent – il ne s'agit pas de ça** *ou* **ce n'est pas de ça qu'il s'agit** I can lend you some money – that's not the point *or* the question; **s'il ne s'agissait que de moi, la maison serait déjà vendue** if it were just up to me, the house would already be sold; **s'il ne s'agissait que d'argent, la solution serait simple!** if it were only a question of money, the answer would be simple!; *Ironique* **une augmentation? il s'agit bien de cela à l'heure où l'on parle de licenciements** a rise? that's very likely now there's talk of redundancies; **quand il s'agit d'aller à la chasse, il trouve toujours le temps!** when it comes to going hunting, he can always find time!; **quand il s'agit de râler, tu es toujours là!** you can always be relied upon to moan!; **une voiture a explosé, il s'agirait d'un accident** a car has exploded, apparently by accident; **il s'agirait d'une grande première scientifique** it is said to be an important first for science

2 *(falloir)* **maintenant, il s'agit de lui parler** now we must talk to her; **c'est qu'il s'agit de gagner ce match!** we must win this match!; **il s'agissait pour moi d'être convaincant** I had to be convincing; **il s'agit de savoir si...** the question is whether...; **il s'agirait d'obéir!** *(menace)* you'd better do as you're told!; **dis donc, il ne s'agit pas de se perdre!** come on, we mustn't get lost now!; **il s'agit bien de pleurer maintenant que tu l'as cassé!** you may well cry, now that you've broken it!; **il ne s'agit pas que tu ailles tout lui raconter!** you'd better not go and repeat everything to him/her!

❑ **s'agissant de PRÉP 1** *(en ce qui concerne)* as regards, with regard to; **s'agissant de lui, vous pouvez avoir toute confiance** as far as he's concerned, you've got nothing to worry about

2 *(puisque cela concerne)* **un service d'ordre ne s'imposait pas, s'agissant d'une manifestation pacifique** there was no need for a police presence, given that this was a peaceful demonstration

âgisme [aʒism] **NM** ageism, age discrimination

agissant, -e [aʒisɑ̃, -ɑ̃t] **ADJ 1** *(entreprenant)* active **2** *(efficace)* efficient, effective; **un remède a.** an effective remedy

agissements [aʒismɑ̃] **NMPL** machinations, schemes; **des a. louches** suspicious dealings

agitateur, -trice [aʒitatœr, -tris] **NM,F** *Pol* agitator
NM *Chim* beater, agitator

agitation [aʒitasjɔ̃] **NF 1** *(mouvement → de l'air)* turbulence; *(→ de l'eau)* roughness; *(→ de la rue)* bustle

2 *(fébrilité)* agitation, restlessness; **être dans un état d'a. extrême** to be extremely agitated; **l'a. régnait dans la salle** *(excitation)* the room was buzzing with excitement; *(inquiétude)* there was an uneasy atmosphere in the room 3 *Méd & Psy* agitated depression 4 *Pol* unrest; **a. parmi la population** civil unrest; **a. syndicale** industrial unrest 5 *(sur le marché de la Bourse)* activity

agitato [aʒitato] **ADV** *Mus* agitato

agitatrice [aʒitatris] *voir* **agitateur**

agité, -e [aʒite] **ADJ 1** *(mer)* rough, stormy 2 *(personne → remuante)* restless; *(→ angoissée)* agitated, worried; **c'était un enfant très a.** he was a very restless child 3 *(troublé → vie)* hectic; *(→ nuit, sommeil)* restless; *(→ esprit)* perturbed, troubled; *(→ époque)* unsettled **NM,F 1** *Méd & Psy* disturbed (mental) patient 2 *(excité)* **c'est un a.** he can't sit still for a minute; *Fam Hum* **a. du bocal** headcase, *Br* nutter, *Am* wacko

agiter [3] [aʒite] **VT 1** *(remuer → liquide)* to shake; *Chim* to agitate; *(→ mouchoir, journal, drapeau)* to wave about; *(sujet: vent → arbre, branches)* to sway; **a. les bras** to flap *or* to wave one's arms; **a. la queue** *(chien)* to wag its tail; *(cheval)* to flick its tail; **une petite brise agite la surface du lac** a soft breeze is ruffling the surface of the lake; **il agitait une facture sous mon nez en hurlant** he was yelling and waving a bill at me; **a. avant usage** *ou* **de s'en servir** *(sur mode d'emploi)* shake well before use 2 *(brandir)* to brandish; **a. le spectre de qch devant qn** to threaten sb with the spectre of sth 3 *(troubler)* to trouble, to upset; **cette nouvelle risque de l'a. encore plus** this news could upset him/her even more; **un besoin d'action agitait les étudiants** the students were longing for action; **une violente colère l'agitait** he/she was in the grip of a terrible rage; **a. le peuple contre le gouvernement** to incite the people to rise up against the government 4 *(débattre)* to debate, to discuss; **a. une question/un thème** to debate a question/a theme ▶**s'agiter VPR 1** *(bouger)* to move about; **s'a. dans son sommeil** to toss and turn in one's sleep; **cesse de t'a. sur ta chaise!** stop fidgeting about on your chair! 2 *(s'énerver)* to become agitated *or* excited, to get upset *or* worked up; **il ne faut pas que le malade s'agite** care should be taken not to upset *or* excite the patient; **tu t'agites trop, ne te fais donc pas tant de souci** you're getting too worked up, don't worry so much 3 *Fam* *(se dépêcher)* to move on; *(s'affairer)* to rush about; **il faut t'a. un peu si tu veux être à l'heure/avoir ton examen** you'd better get a move on if you want to be on time/to pass your exam 4 *(se révolter)* to be in a state of unrest 5 *(mer)* to become rough

agit-prop [aʒitprɔp] **NF INV** *Pol* agit-prop

aglossa [aglosa] **NM** *Entom* grease moth

agnat [agna] **NM** *Jur* agnate

agnathe [agnat] *Ich* **NM** agnathan ❑ **agnathes NMPL** Agnatha

agnation [agnasjɔ̃] **NF** *Jur* agnation

agnatique [agnatik] **ADJ** *Jur* agnatic

agneau, -x [aɲo] **NM 1** *Zool (animal)* lamb; *Fig* **il est doux comme un a.!** he's as meek *or* gentle as a lamb! **a. de lait** suckling lamb 2 *Culin* lamb (UNCOUNT); **l'a. est gras, la viande d'a. est grasse** lamb is fatty; **côtelettes d'a.** lamb chops 3 *(en appellatif)* **viens mon a. (joli)!** come on, my lamb!; **mes agneaux, vous allez me dire la vérité maintenant!** now, my little friends, you're going to tell me the truth! 4 *(fourrure)* lamb, lambskin; *(peau)* lambskin; **une veste en a.** a lambskin jacket 5 *Rel* **l'A. (de Dieu)** the Lamb (of God); **l'a. mystique** the mystic lamb; **l'a. pascal** the paschal lamb

'L'Agneau mystique' *Van Eyck* 'Adoration of the Holy Lamb'

agnelage [aɲəlaʒ] **NM** *Zool (naissance)* lambing; *(période)* lambing season *or* time

agnelée [aɲəle] **NF** *Zool* fall *(of lambs)*

agneler [24] [aɲəle] **VI** *Zool* to lamb

agnelet [aɲəlɛ] **NM** *Vieilli Zool* small lamb, lambkin

agnelin [aɲlɛ̃] **NM** *Tex* lambskin

agneline [aɲlin] *Tex* **ADJ** lambswool **NF** lambswool

agnelle [aɲɛl] **NF** *Zool* ewe lamb, young ewe

Agnès [aɲɛs] **NPR** = character in Molière's 'l'École des femmes', the archetype of the naive and innocent woman

agnosie [agnozi] **NF** *Méd* agnosia

agnosique [agnozik] *Méd* **ADJ** agnosic **NMF** person suffering from agnosia

agnosticisme [agnostisism] **NM** *Phil* agnosticism

agnostique [agnostik] *Phil* **ADJ** agnostic **NMF** agnostic

Agnus Dei [agnysdei, agnusdei] **NM INV** *Rel (prière)* Agnus Dei

agnus-Dei [agnysdei, agnusdei] **NM INV** *Rel (médaillon)* Agnus Dei

AGO [aʒeo] **NF** *(abrév* **assemblée générale ordinaire)** ordinary general meeting

agonie [agoni] **NF 1** death throes, pangs of death, death agony; **il a eu une longue a.** he died a slow and painful death; *Fig* **l'a. de l'empire** the death throes of the empire; **être à l'a.** to be at the point of death; *Fig* to suffer agonies; *Fig* **ne prolongez pas son a.** please put him/her out of his/her misery 2 *Vieilli Littéraire* anguish

agonir [32] [agonir] **VT a. qn d'injures** *ou* **d'insultes** to hurl abuse at sb; **elle s'est fait a.** she was reviled

agonisant, -e [agonizɑ̃, -ɑ̃t] **ADJ** dying **NM,F** dying person

agoniser [3] [agonize] **VI** to be dying

agoniste [agonist] *Physiol* **ADJ** **muscle a.** agonist; **substance a.** agonist **NM** agonist

agora [agora] **NF 1** *Antiq* agora 2 *(espace piétonnier)* concourse

agoraphobe [agorafob] *Psy* **ADJ** agoraphobic **NMF** agoraphobic

agoraphobie [agorafobi] **NF** *Psy* agoraphobia; **souffrir d'a.** to be agoraphobic

agouti [aguti] **NM** *Zool* agouti

Agra [agra] **NM** *Géog* Agra

agrafage [agrafaʒ] **NM 1** *(de papiers, de tentures)* stapling; *(de vêtements)* hooking, fastening 2 *(de bois ou de métal)* clamping, cramping 3 *Méd* clamping

agrafe [agraf] **NF 1** *(pour papier)* staple; *(pour vêtement)* hook, fastener; *(bijou)* clasp; *Com* **a. antivol** anti-theft *or* security tag 2 *(pour bois ou métal)* clamp 3 *Méd* clamp

agrafer [3] [agrafe] **VT 1** *(papiers)* to staple (together); *(vêtement)* to fasten (up) 2 *Méd* to clamp 3 *Fam Arg crime (arrêter) Br* to nick, *Am* to bust; **il s'est fait a.** he got *Br* nicked *or* *Am* busted

agrafeuse [agraføz] **NF** stapler

agrainage [agrɛnaʒ] **NM** *Chasse* feeding *(of birds with grain)*

agrainer [4] [agrene] **VT** *(animaux d'élevage, gibier)* to scatter grain for

agraire [agrɛr] **ADJ** *Agr (société)* agrarian; *(réforme, lois)* land *(avant n)*

agrammatical, -e, -aux, -ales [agramatikal, -o] **ADJ** *Gram* ungrammatical

agrammaticalité [agramatikalite] **NF** *Gram* ungrammaticality

agrammatisme [agramatism] **NM** *Méd* agrammatism

agrandir [32] [agrɑ̃dir] **VT 1** *(élargir → trou)* to enlarge, to make bigger; *(→ maison, jardin)* to extend; *(→ couloir, passage)* to widen; **ses yeux agrandis par la terreur** his/her eyes wide with fear; **a. le cercle de ses activités** to enlarge the scope of one's activities; **j'ai besoin de partenaires pour a. mon affaire** I need partners to expand my business 2 *Littéraire (exalter → âme, pensée)* to elevate, to uplift 3 *(faire paraître grand)* **un trait de crayon pour a. les yeux** a pencil line to make your eyes look bigger; **on avait agrandi la scène par des décors transparents** the stage had been made to

look bigger by the use of see-through sets 4 *Typ & Phot (cliché, copie)* to enlarge, to blow up; *(sur écran)* to magnify; *Ordinat (fenêtre)* to maximize ▶**s'agrandir VPR 1** *(s'élargir)* to grow, to get bigger; **la banlieue s'agrandit sans cesse** the suburbs never stop growing; **le cercle de famille s'agrandit** the family circle is widening; **quand elle le vit, ses yeux s'agrandirent** when she saw him, her eyes widened 2 *Écon* to expand; **le marché des logiciels s'agrandit** the software market is expanding 3 *(avoir plus de place)* **nous voudrions nous a.** we want more space for ourselves; **avec le troisième enfant, il faut s'a.** when the third child comes along, a family needs more living space

agrandissement [agrɑ̃dismɑ̃] **NM 1** *Phot* enlargement; **je voudrais faire un a. de cette photo** I'd like to get this photo blown up *or* enlarged 2 *(d'un appartement, d'une affaire)* extension

agrandisseur [agrɑ̃disœr] **NM** *Phot* enlarger

agranulocytose [agranylositoz] **NF** *Méd* agranulocytosis

agraphie [agrafi] **NF** *Méd* agraphia

agrarien, -enne [agrarjɛ̃, -ɛn] *Hist* **ADJ** agrarian **NM,F** agrarian

agréable [agreabl] **ADJ** pleasant, nice, agreeable; **une corvée pas très a.** a rather unpleasant chore; **il ne souhaite que vous être a.** he only wants to be nice to you; **il me serait bien a. de le revoir** I would love to see him again; **une couleur a. à l'œil** a colour (which is) pleasing to the eye; **a. au goût** pleasant to the taste; **être a. au toucher** to feel nice; **voilà quelqu'un qui est a. à vivre** he's/she's really easy to get on with; **a. à regarder** attractive **NM l'a., ici, c'est la grande terrasse** the nice thing *or* what's nice about this place is the big terrace

agréablement [agreabləmɑ̃] **ADV** pleasantly, agreeably

agréage [agreaʒ] **NM** *Com* = acceptance of goods tested before purchase

agréation [agreasjɔ̃] **NF** *Belg* approval, acceptance

agréé, -e [agree] **ADJ 1** *(organisme, agent)* recognized, authorized; *Jur* registered 2 *(produit)* approved; *Tél* **appareil a.** = France Télécom approved

agréer [15] [agree] **VT** to approve, to authorize; *(dans la correspondance)* **veuillez a., Madame/Monsieur, mes salutations distinguées** *(à une personne dont on connaît le nom) Br* yours sincerely, *Am* sincerely (yours); *(à une personne dont on ne connaît pas le nom) Br* yours faithfully, *Am* sincerely (yours) ❑ **agréer à VT IND** *Littéraire* to please, to suit; **si cela vous agrée, nous nous verrons la semaine prochaine** if it suits you, we shall meet next week

agrég [agreg] **NF** *Fam Univ (abrév* **agrégation)** = high-level competitive examination for teachers

agrégat [agrega] **NM 1** *(de roches, de substances)* aggregate; *Fig Péj* conglomeration, mish-mash 2 *Fin* **a. monétaire** monetary aggregate

agrégatif, -ive [agregatif, -iv] *Univ* **ADJ** *(candidat, étudiant)* = who is studying to take the "agrégation" **NM,F** "agrégation" candidate

agrégation [agregasjɔ̃] **NF 1** *Univ* = high-level competitive examination for teachers 2 *(assemblage)* agglomeration

agrégative [agregativ] *voir* **agrégatif**

agrégé, -e [agreʒe] **ADJ 1** *Univ* = who has passed the "agrégation" 2 *(assemblé)* agglomerated **NM,F** *Univ* = person who has passed the "agrégation"

agréger [22] [agreʒe] **VT 1** *(assembler)* to agglomerate (together) **2** *(intégrer)* **a. qn à** to incorporate sb into

▸**s'agréger VPR 1** *(s'assembler)* to form a mass **2 s'a. à** to incorporate oneself into

agrément [agremã] **NM 1** *(attrait)* charm, appeal, attractiveness; *(plaisir)* pleasure; **sa maison est pleine d'a.** his house is delightful *or* very attractive; **un visage sans a.** an unattractive face; **les agréments de la vie** the pleasures of life

2 *(accord)* approval, consent; *Mktg (du consommateur, du client)* approval; **agir avec l'a. de ses supérieurs** to act with one's superiors' approval *or* consent

3 *Fin (garantie financière)* bonding scheme

4 *Fin* **a. fiscal** tax approval

5 *Mus* ornament

❑ **d'agrément ADJ** *(jardin, voyage)* pleasure *(avant n)*

agrémenter [3] [agremãte] **VT a. qch avec** *ou* **de** to decorate sth with; **vous pouvez a. votre plat avec quelques feuilles de menthe** decorate *or* garnish the dish with a few sprigs of mint; **des balcons agrémentés de géraniums** balconies bedecked with geraniums; **une lettre agrémentée de quelques expressions à l'ancienne** a letter graced *or* adorned with a few quaint old phrases

agrès [agrɛ] **NMPL 1** *Sport* apparatus; **elle a eu 20 aux (exercices aux) a.** she got 20 for apparatus work **2** *Naut* lifting gear; *(sur un ballon)* tackle **3** *Can* **a. de pêche** fishing tackle

NM *Can Fam* unattractive person ▪, *Br* minger, *Am* skank

agresser [4] [agrese] **VT 1** *(physiquement)* to attack, to assault; *(pour voler)* to mug; **se faire a.** to be assaulted; *(pour son argent)* to be mugged

2 *(verbalement)* to attack; **pourquoi m'agresses-tu ainsi? je n'ai fait que dire la vérité!** why are you being so aggressive towards me? I only told the truth!; **je me suis sentie agressée** I felt I was being got at

3 *(psychologiquement)* to stress; **dans les grandes villes on se sent tout le temps agressé** big cities are very stressful places, you always feel stressed in big cities

4 *(avoir un effet nocif sur)* to damage

agresseur [agresœr] **ADJ M** *(État, pays)* attacking

NM *(d'une personne)* attacker, assailant, aggressor; *(d'un pays)* aggressor; **elle n'a pas pu voir son a.** she couldn't see her assailant *or* the person who assaulted her

agressif, -ive [agresif, -iv] **ADJ 1** *(hostile → personne)* aggressive, hostile, *Littéraire* belligerent; **ne sois pas si a.!** don't be so hostile *or* aggressive!

2 *(oppressant → musique, image)* aggressive; **la laideur agressive des monuments** the sheer ugliness of the buildings; **un maquillage a.** outrageous make-up

3 *(dynamique)* dynamic, aggressive; **une concurrence agressive** aggressive competitors; **il nous faut une politique commerciale agressive** we need a sales policy with some punch (to it)

4 *Psy (acte, pulsion)* aggressive

agression [agresjɔ̃] **NF 1** *(attaque → contre une personne)* attack, assault; *(→ pour voler)* mugging; *(→ contre un pays)* aggression; **être victime d'une** *ou* **subir une a.** to be assaulted; *(pour son argent)* to be mugged; **a. sexuelle** sexual assault; **le nombre des agressions a diminué** the number of attacks has decreased; *Fig* **les agressions de la vie moderne** the stresses and strains of modern life; **les agressions du soleil contre votre peau** the harm the sun does to your skin

2 *Psy* aggression

agressive [agresiv] *voir* **agressif**

agressivement [agresivmã] **ADV** aggressively

agressivité [agresivite] **NF** aggressivity, aggressiveness

agreste [agrɛst] **ADJ** *Littéraire* rustic

agricole [agrikɔl] **ADJ** *Agr (économie, pays)* agricultural; *(population)* farming *(avant n)*; *(produit)* farm *(avant n)*

agriculteur, -trice [agrikyltœr, -tris] **NM,F** *Agr* farmer

agriculture [agrikyltyr] **NF** *Agr* agriculture, farming; **a. raisonnée** integrated farming

agriffer [3] [agrife] **s'agriffer VPR** *Littéraire* **s'a. à** to clutch, to grip

Agrigente [agriʒɑ̃t] **NM** *Géog* Agrigento

agrile [agril] **NM** *Entom* agrilus

agrion [agrijɔ̃] **NM** *Entom* agrion, demoiselle

agriote [agrijɔt] **NM** *Entom* agriotes

agripaume [agripom] **NF** *Bot* motherwort

Agrippa [agripa] **NPR** Agrippa

agrippement [agripmã] **NM** gripping, grasping; *Méd* **réflexe d'a.** grasping reflex

agripper [3] [agripe] **VT 1** *(prendre)* to grab, to snatch **2** *(tenir)* to grip, to grasp, to clutch; **ne m'agrippe pas ainsi!** stop clutching me like that!

▸**s'agripper VPR** to hold on; **agrippe-toi, j'arrive** hold on tight, I'm coming; **s'a. à qch** to cling to *or* to hold on (tight) to sth; **elle s'agrippait à mon bras** she was gripping my arm

Agrippine [agripin] **NPR** Agrippina

agritourisme [agriturism] **NM** *Agr* agritourism

Agro [agro] **NF** *Fam Arg scol* = nickname for "ENSA"

agroalimentaire [agroalimãtɛr] *Agr* **ADJ** food-processing *(avant n)*

NM l'a. the food-processing industry, agribusiness

agrobiologie [agrobjɔlɔʒi] **NF** *Agr* agrobiology

agrochimie [agroʃimi] **NF** *Agr* agrochemistry

agrochimique [agroʃimik] **ADJ** *Agr* agrochemical, agrichemical; **produits agrochimiques** agrochemicals, agrichemicals

agrochimiste [agroʃimist] **NMF** *Agr* agrochemist

agroclimatologie [agroklimatɔlɔʒi] **NF** *Agr* agroclimatology

agro-économie [agroekɔnɔmi] **NF** agricultural economics

agroforesterie [agrofɔrɛstəri] **NF** *Agr* agroforestry

agro-industrie [agroɛ̃dystri] *(pl* **agro-industries)** **NF** *Agr* agro-industry, agribusiness

agro-industriel, -elle [agroɛ̃dystrijɛl] **ADJ** *(mpl* **agro-industriels,** *fpl* **agro-industrielles)** agro-industrial

agrologie [agrolɔʒi] **NF** *Agr* agrology

agronome [agrɔnɔm] **NMF** *Agr* agronomist, agriculturalist

agronomie [agrɔnɔmi] **NF** *Agr* agronomy

agronomique [agrɔnɔmik] **ADJ** *Agr* agronomic, agronomical

agropastoral, -e, -aux, -ales [agropastɔral, -o] **ADJ** *Agr* agricultural

agrostide [agrɔstid], **agrostis** [agrɔstis] **NF** *Bot* bent grass

agroterrorisme [agroterɔrism] **NM** agroterrorism

agrotide [agrɔtid], **agrotis** [agrɔtis] **NF** *Entom* dart-moth, *Spéc* agrotis; **a. des moissons** turnip-moth, common dart-moth

agrotourisme [agroturism] **NM** agrotourism

agrume [agrym] **NM** *Bot* citrus fruit

agrumiculture [agrymikyltyr] **NF** citrus fruit farming

aguardiente [agwardjɛnte] **NF** *(alcool)* aguardiente

aguerrir [32] [agerir] **VT** to harden, to toughen (up); *(troupes)* to train (for battle)

▸**s'aguerrir VPR** to become hardened *or* tougher; **s'a. à** *ou* **contre qch** to become hardened to sth

aguets [agɛ] **aux aguets ADV** **être aux a.** to be on watch *or* the lookout

agueusie [agøzi] **NF** *Méd* ageusia

agui [agi] **NM** *Naut* **1** *(ajut de cordages)* tying of bowlines **2** *(nœud de chaise)* bowline; **nœud d'a.** bowline knot

aguichage [agiʃaʒ] **NM** *(technique publicitaire)* teaser advertising

aguichant, -e [agiʃɑ̃, -ɑ̃t] **ADJ** seductive, enticing, alluring

aguiche [agiʃ] **NF** *(publicité)* teaser

aguicher [3] [agiʃe] **VT** to seduce, to entice, to allure

aguicheur, -euse [agiʃœr, -øz] **ADJ** seductive, enticing, alluring

NM,F tease

Ah *Élec (abrév écrite* **ampère-heure)** ah

ah [a] **EXCLAM 1** *(renforce l'expression d'un sentiment)* ah, oh; **ah, que cette tomate est bonne!** oh *or* ah *or* mmm, this tomato's delicious!; **ah, comme je vous plains!** oh, I feel so sorry for

you!; **ah, ne va pas croire cela!** oh please, you mustn't believe that!; **ah, ça y est, je l'ai trouvé!** ah *or* aha, here we are, I've found it!; **ah, je te l'avais bien dit!** aha, I told you so!; **ah, c'est un secret** aha, that's a secret; **ah là là, qu'est-ce qu'il m'énerve!** oh, he's a real pain in the neck!

2 *(dans une réponse)* **il est venu – ah bon?** he came – did he (really)?; **ils n'en ont plus en magasin – ah bon!** *(ton résigné)* they haven't got any more in stock – oh well!; **ah non alors!** certainly not!; **ah oui?** really?

NM INV ah; **pousser des oh et des ah** to ooh and ah

AHA [aaʃa] **NM** *Chim (abrév* **alpha-hydroxy-acide)** AHA

ahan [aã] **NM** *Vieilli & Littéraire* **à grand a.** with much puffing and panting

ahaner [3] [aane] **VI** *Littéraire* to puff and pant

ahuri, -e [ayri] **ADJ 1** *(surpris)* dumbfounded, amazed, stunned; **il a eu l'air a. quand je lui ai annoncé le prix/qu'il avait gagné** he looked dumbfounded when I told him the price/he'd won

2 *(hébété)* stupefied, dazed; **elle erra pendant des heures, l'air a.** she wandered about for hours looking dazed; **il avait l'air complètement a.** he looked as if he was in a daze

NM,F idiot; **espèce d'a.!** you idiot!

ahurir [32] [ayrir] **VT** to stun, to daze

ahurissant, -e [ayrisɑ̃, -ɑ̃t] **ADJ** stunning, staggering; **je trouve ça a.** I think it's staggering; **il a un culot a.** he's got one hell of a cheek

ahurissement [ayrismã] **NM** daze; **son a. était tel qu'il ne m'entendait pas** he was so stunned that he didn't even hear me

A.I., a.i. [ai] *Belg (abrév* **ad intérim)** **ADJ** *(président, trésorier)* interim *(avant n)*, acting *(avant n)*; *(secrétaire)* acting *(avant n)*; *(gouvernement)* caretaker *(avant n)*

ADV in a temporary capacity, temporarily

ai *voir* **avoir**²

aï [ai] **NM** *Zool* ai, three-toed sloth

aiche [ɛʃ] **NF** *Pêche* bait

aicher [4] [ɛʃe] **VT** *Pêche (appât, ligne)* to bait

AID [aide] **NF** *(abrév* **Association Internationale de Développement)** IDA

AIDA [aidea] **NM** *Mktg (abrév* **attention-intérêt-désir-action)** AIDA

aidant, -e [edɑ̃, -ɑ̃t] **NM,F** *Belg* = **aide**¹

aide¹ [ɛd] **NM 1** *(assistant → payé)* assistant; *(→ bénévole)* helper; **les aides du président** the presidential aides; **a. familial (étranger)** male au pair

2 *(comme adj; avec ou sans trait d'union)* assistant *(avant n)*

3 *Mil* **a. de camp** aide-de-camp

NF a. à domicile, a. familiale, a. ménagère home help

aide² [ɛd] **NF 1** *(appui)* help, assistance, aid; **avoir besoin d'a.** to need help; **avec l'a. de mon frère** with help from my brother *or* my brother's help; **avec l'a. de Dieu** with the help of God; **elle y est arrivée sans l'a. de personne** she succeeded with no help at all *or* unaided *or* without anyone's help; **à l'a.!** help!; **au secours, à l'a.!** help me, PLEASE!; **j'ai eu de l'a.** I had help; **il a demandé l'a. d'un prêtre** he asked for the help *or* aid *or* assistance of a priest; **appeler à l'a.** to call for help; **quand elle s'est retrouvée au chômage, elle a appelé ses parents à l'a.** when she found herself unemployed, she asked *or* turned to her parents for help; **offrir son a. à qn** to give sb help, to go to sb's assistance; **venir en a. à qn** to come to sb's aid; **que Dieu vous vienne en a.** may God help you

2 *(don d'argent)* aid; **recevoir l'a. de l'État** to receive government aid; **a. au développement économique (des pays du tiers-monde)** economic aid (to Third World countries); **a. financière** financial aid *or* assistance; **a. fiscale** tax credit; **a. humanitaire** humanitarian aid; **a. aux jeunes agriculteurs** = grant to young farmers; **a. juridictionelle** ≃ legal aid; **a. personnalisée au logement** ≃ housing benefit *(UNCOUNT)*; **A. publique au développement** Official Development Assistance; **a. à la reconversion des entreprises** industrial reconversion grants; **a. au retour** = policy aimed at discouraging immigration by giving support to foreign nationals

returning to their country of origin; **a. sociale** *Br* social security, *Am* welfare

3 *Ordinat* **a. à la césure** hyphenation help; **a. contextuelle** context-sensitive help; **a. en ligne** on-line help

□ **aides** NFPL *Équitation* aids

□ **à l'aide de** PRÉP 1 *(avec)* with the help of; **marcher à l'a. de béquilles** to walk with crutches

2 *(au secours de)* **aller/venir à l'a. de qn** to go/to come to sb's aid

aidé, -e [ede] ADJ *(emploi, contrat)* subsidized by the State

aide-comptable [ɛdkɔ̃tabl] *(pl* **aides-comptables)** NMF *Compta* junior accountant

aide-cuisinier [ɛdkɥizinje] *(pl* **aides-cuisiniers)** NMF kitchen assistant

aide-éducateur, -trice [ɛdedykatœr, -tris] *(mpl* **aides-éducateurs,** *fpl* **aides-éducatrices)** NM,F ≃ classroom assistant, *Am* ≃ teacher's assistant

aide-électricien [ɛdelektrisjɛ̃] *(pl* **aides-électriciens)** NM *Cin & TV* best boy

aide-infirmière [ɛdɛ̃firmjɛr] *(pl* **aides-infirmières)** NF *Br* healthcare assistant, auxiliary nurse, *Am* nurse's aid

Aïd-el-Adha [aidɛlada] NF INV *Rel* Id al-Adha, Eid al-Adha, Great Festival

Aïd-el-Fitr [aidɛlfitr] NF INV *Rel* Id al-Fitr, Eid ul-Fitr, Aïd-el-Fitr

Aïd-el-Kébir [aidɛlkebir] NF INV *Rel* Id al-Adha, Eid al-Adha, Great Festival

Aïd-el-Séguir [aidɛlsegir] NF INV *Rel* Id al-Fitr, Eid ul-Fitr, Aïd-el-Fitr

aide-mémoire [ɛdmemwar] NM INV notes

aide-monteur, -euse [ɛdmɔ̃tœr, -øz] *(mpl* **aides-monteurs,** *fpl* **aides-monteuses)** NM,F *Cin & TV* assistant film editor

aide-opérateur, -trice [ɛdɔperatœr, -tris] *(mpl* **aides-opérateurs,** *fpl* **aides-opératrices)** NM,F assistant cameraman, *f* assistant camerawoman

aider [4] [ede] VT 1 *(apporter son concours à)* to help; **elle l'a aidé toute sa vie** she helped him all her life; **que puis-je faire pour vous a.?** how may I help you?; *Ironique* **tu veux que je t'aide?** stop that!; **je me suis fait a. par mon frère** I got my brother to help me; **a. qn à faire qch** to help sb (to) do sth; **peux-tu m'a. à ranger mes affaires?** can you help me to put away my things?; **elle l'aide à tenir sa comptabilité** she helps him/her to keep his/her books; **il a aidé la vieille dame à monter/descendre** he helped the old lady up/down; **aide-moi à rentrer/sortir la table** help me move the table in/out

2 *(financièrement)* to help out, to aid, to assist; **il a fallu l'a. pour monter son affaire** he/she needed help to set up his/her business; **subventions pour a. l'industrie** subsidies to industry

USAGE ABSOLU to help (out); *(favoriser, être utile)* to help; **parfois, pour payer son déjeuner, il aide dans les cuisines** sometimes, to pay for his lunch, he helps out in the kitchens; *Fam* **ça aide** it's a help; *Fam* **avoir un père richissime, ça aide** it helps if your dad's loaded; **des diplômes, ça aide** qualifications come in handy; **la fatigue aidant, je me suis endormi tout de suite** helped by exhaustion, I fell asleep right away; **elle l'oubliera, le temps aidant** she'll forget him in time; *Fam* **il n'est pas aidé!** he hasn't got much going for him!; **Dieu aidant** with the help of God, God willing

□ **aider à** VT IND to aid, to help; **a. à la digestion** to aid digestion; **a. à la compréhension entre les peuples** to aid or to promote better understanding between peoples; **ça aide à passer le temps** it helps to pass the time

▸**s'aider** VPR 1 *(emploi réfléchi) Prov* **aide-toi, le ciel t'aidera** God helps those who help themselves

2 *(emploi réciproque)* to help each other; **entre femmes, il faut s'a.** we women should help each other

3 **s'a. de** to use; **elle s'est aidée de plusieurs ouvrages** she made use of or used several books; **marcher en s'aidant d'une canne** to walk with a stick

Aides [ɛd] NM = French Aids charity

aide-soignant, -e [ɛdswaɲɑ̃, -ɑ̃t] *(mpl* **aides-soignants,** *fpl* **aides-soignantes)** NM,F *Méd*

Br healthcare assistant, auxiliary nurse, *Am* nurse's aid

aie *etc voir* **avoir²**

aïe [aj] EXCLAM *(cri → de douleur)* ouch!; *(→ de surprise)* **a., la voilà!** oh dear or oh no, here she comes!; **a., a., a., qu'est-ce qu'on va faire?** oh dear, what are we going to do?; **a., a., a., il était dur, l'examen!** boy, was that exam tough!

AIEA [aiɛa] NF *Nucl (abrév* **Agence internationale de l'énergie atomique)** IAEA

aïeul, -e [ajœl] NM,F grandparent; *(grand-père)* grandfather; *(grand-mère)* grandmother

aïeux [ajø] NMPL *Littéraire* forefathers, ancestors; *Hum* **ah, mes a., travailler avec lui n'est pas une sinécure** heavens, working with him is no easy task!

aigail [ɛgaj] NM *Littéraire* dew

aigle [ɛgl] NM 1 *Orn* eagle; **a. d'Amérique** American eagle; **a. des mers** sea eagle; *Can* **a. pêcheur** fish hawk or *Am* eagle, *Br* osprey; **a. ravisseur** tawny eagle; **a. royal** golden eagle; **avoir des yeux** ou **un regard d'a.** to be eagle-eyed; *Hum* **ce n'est pas un a.** he's no rocket scientist; **l'A. de Meaux** = name given to Bossuet

2 *Ich* **a. de mer** eagle ray

3 *(lutrin)* lectern

NF 1 *Orn (female)* eagle

2 *Mil* eagle

3 *Hér* eagle

aiglefin [ɛglǝfɛ̃]** = **églefin**

aiglette [ɛglɛt] NF *Hér* eaglet

aiglon, -onne [ɛglɔ̃, -ɔn] NM,F *Orn* eaglet; **l'A.** = name given to Napoleon II

aigre [ɛgr] ADJ 1 *(acide → vin)* acid, sharp; *(→ goût, lait)* sour; **le vin a un goût a.** the wine tastes sour; **crème a.** sour cream; **le lait est devenu a.** the milk has turned or gone sour

2 *(perçant → voix, son)* shrill, sharp

3 *(vif → bise, froid)* bitter

4 *(méchant)* cutting, harsh, acid; **elle répondit d'un ton a.** she retorted acidly

NM **ton vin sent l'a.** your wine smells sour; **tourner à l'a.** *(lait)* to turn sour; *Fig (discussion)* to turn sour or nasty

aigre-doux, -douce [ɛgrǝdu, -dus] *(mpl* **aigres-doux,** *fpl* **aigres-douces)** ADJ *Culin* sweet-and-sour; *Fig* **ses lettres étaient aigres-douces** his/her letters were tinged with bitterness

aigrefin [ɛgrǝfɛ̃] NM swindler

aigrelet, -ette [ɛgrǝlɛ, -ɛt] ADJ *(odeur, saveur)* sourish; *(son, voix)* shrillish; *(propos)* tart, sour, acid

aigrement [ɛgrǝmɑ̃] ADV sourly, tartly, acidly

aigremoine [ɛgrǝmwan] NF *Bot* agrimony

aigret, -ette¹ [ɛgrɛ, -ɛt] ADJ *Littéraire* sourish

aigrette² [ɛgrɛt] NF 1 *Orn (oiseau)* egret, tufted heron; **a. garzette, petite a.** little egret 2 *(décoration → d'un héron)* aigrette; *(→ d'un perroquet)* crest; *(→ d'une chouette)* horn 3 *(panache)* aigrette, plume 4 *Bot* egret; *(du maïs)* tassel

aigretté, -e [ɛgrɛte] ADJ 1 *Orn (héron)* with an aigrette; *(perroquet)* crested; *(chouette)* horned 2 *Bot* with an egret; *(maïs)* tasselled

aigreur [ɛgrœr] NF 1 *(acidité)* sourness, acidity; **l'a. du lait** the sourness of the milk 2 *(animosité)* sharpness, bitterness; **ses propos étaient pleins d'a.** his remarks were very bitter

□ **aigreurs** NFPL **avoir des aigreurs (d'estomac)** to have heartburn or acid indigestion

aigri, -e [egri] ADJ bitter, embittered

NM,F embittered person; **ce n'est qu'un a.** he's just bitter

aigrin [egrɛ̃] NM *Hort* young wild pear-tree, young crab-tree

aigrir [32] [egrir] VT *(lait, vin)* to make sour; *(personne)* to embitter, to make bitter

VI *(lait)* to turn (sour), to go off; *(vin)* to turn sour

▸**s'aigrir** VPR *(lait)* to turn (sour), to go off; *(vin)* to turn sour; *(caractère)* to sour; *(personne)* to become embittered

aigrissement [egrismɑ̃] NM *Littéraire (d'une boisson)* turning sour; *(de relations)* souring

aigu, -ë [egy] ADJ 1 *(perçant → voix)* high-pitched, *Péj* shrill, piercing; *(→ glapissement, hurlement)* piercing, shrill; *Mus* high-pitched; **on entendait la sonnerie aiguë du téléphone** we could hear the shrill ringing of the telephone

2 *(effilé)* sharp; **ses petites dents aiguës** his/ her sharp little teeth

---

3 *(pénétrant → esprit, intelligence)* sharp, keen; **j'ai la conscience aiguë de lui avoir causé du tort** I am acutely aware of having done him/her wrong; **avoir un sens a. de l'observation** ou **un regard a.** to be an acute observer

4 *(grave → crise, douleur)* sharp, acute; *Méd (→ phase, appendicite)* acute; **au stade le plus a. du conflit** at the height of the conflict

5 *Math (angle)* acute

NM high-pitched; **l'a., les aigus** treble range; **dans les aigus** in treble

aiguail [ɛgaj] NM *Littéraire* dew

aiguë [egy] *voir* **aigu**

aigue-marine [ɛgmarin] *(pl* **aigues-marines)** NF *Minér* aquamarine

aiguière [ɛgjɛr] NF *Antiq* ewer

aiguillage [egɥijaʒ] NM 1 *Rail (manœuvre)* shunting, switching; *(dispositif)* shunt, switch 2 *Ordinat* switching 3 *Fig* orientation; **erreur d'a.** wrong turning

aiguillat [egɥija] NM *Ich* spiny dogfish, picked or piked dogfish

aiguille [egɥij] NF 1 *(pour coudre, pour tricoter)* needle; *Vieilli* **pousser** ou **tirer l'a.** to ply the needle; **a. à coudre/tricoter/repriser** sewing/ knitting/darning needle

2 *Méd* needle; **a. hypodermique** hypodermic needle

3 *(d'une montre, d'une pendule)* hand; *(d'un électrophone)* arm; *(d'une balance)* pointer; *(d'une boussole)* needle; **l'a. des secondes** the second hand; **la grande a., l'a. des minutes** the minute hand; **la petite a., l'a. des heures** the hour hand; **a. aimantée** magnetic needle

4 *Géog* needle, high peak

5 *Bot* needle; **a. de pin/de sapin** pine/fir tree needle

6 *Rail* switch, shunt, points

7 *Ich* **a. de mer** *(syngnathe)* pipefish; *(orphie)* needlefish

8 *(tour, clocher)* spire

aiguillée [egɥije] NF length of thread *(on a needle)*

aiguiller [3] [egɥije] VT 1 *Rail* to shunt, to switch 2 *(orienter → recherche)* to steer; **a. la police sur une fausse piste** to put the police on a false scent; **on l'a aiguillé vers une section scientifique** he was steered or guided towards the sciences; **il a été mal aiguillé dans ses études** he was badly advised about his studies

aiguilletage [egɥijtaʒ] NM 1 *(d'un tapis)* needling, needlebonding 2 *Naut* lashing, tying down

aiguilleté, -e [egɥijte] ADJ 1 *(tapis)* needled 2 *Naut* lashed, tied down

aiguilleter [27] [egɥijte] VT 1 *(tapis)* to needle 2 *Naut* to lash, to tie down

aiguillette [egɥijet] NF 1 *Tex* aglet 2 *Culin (de canard, d'oie)* strip of breast; *(de bœuf)* **a. (de rumsteck)** top of the rump (of beef) 3 *Ich* garfish, needlefish

□ **aiguillettes** NFPL *Mil* aglets

aiguilleur [egɥijœr] NM 1 *Rail Br* pointsman, *Am* switchman 2 *Aviat* **a. (du ciel)** air traffic controller

aiguillier [egɥije] NM *Couture* needlecase

aiguillon [egɥijɔ̃] NM 1 *Entom* sting 2 *Bot* prickle 3 *(bâton)* goad 4 *Littéraire (motivation)* incentive, stimulus, motivating force; **l'a. du remords** the pricks of remorse

aiguillonner [3] [egɥijɔne] VT 1 *(piquer → bœuf)* to goad 2 *(stimuler → curiosité)* to arouse; *(→ personne)* to spur on, to goad on; **aiguillonné par son ambition** goaded on by his ambition

aiguillot [egɥijo] NM *Naut* pintle

aiguisage [egiza3] NM sharpening, grinding

aiguise-crayon [egizkrɛjɔ̃] *(pl inv ou* **aiguise-crayons)** NM *Can Fam* pencil sharpener

aiguisement [egizmɑ̃] = **aiguisage**

aiguiser [3] [egize] VT 1 *(rendre coupant → couteau, lame)* to sharpen; *(→ faux)* to whet; **bien aiguisé** sharp 2 *(stimuler → curiosité)* to stimulate, to rouse; *(→ faculté, sens)* to sharpen; *(→ appétit)* to whet, to stimulate

aiguiseur, -euse [egizœr, -øz] NM,F *Tech* sharpener, grinder

aiguisoir [egizwar] NM 1 *Tech* sharpener 2 *Can* pencil sharpener

aïkido [ajkido] NM *Sport* aikido; **faire de l'a.** to do aikido

ail [aj] *(pl* **ails** ou **aulx** [o]) NM *Bot* garlic; *Can* **a. des**

bois wild leek; **a. des ours** ramsons, wild garlic
□ **à l'ail** ADJ garlic (avant n)

ailante [ɛlɑ̃t] NM Bot ailanthus

aile [ɛl] NF **1** Orn (d'un oiseau) wing; Fig **laissez-vous porter sur les ailes du rêve** let yourself be carried away as in a dream; **avoir des ailes** to run like the wind; Fam **avoir un petit coup dans l'a.** to be tipsy; Fam **il a un sacré coup dans l'a.** he's had one over the eight; **couper** ou **rogner les ailes à qn** to clip sb's wings; **donner des ailes à qn** to give or to lend sb wings; **c'est la peur qui lui donne des ailes** fear lends him wings; **prendre qn sous son a.** to take sb under one's wing
2 (d'un moulin) sail; (d'un avion) wing; **a. (delta), a. libre, a. volante** hang glider; Aviat **a. (en) delta** delta wing
3 Aut Br wing, Am fender
4 Anat **les ailes du nez** the nostrils
5 Archit wing; **rajouter une a. à une maison** to build a wing or a side extension onto a house
6 Sport wing
7 Mil wing, flank; **l'a. marchante** the wheeling flank; Fig the militants, the active elements
8 (d'un parti) wing
9 Culin wing; **a. de poulet** chicken wing

'Les Ailes du désir' Wenders 'Wings of Desire'

ailé, -e [ele] ADJ winged, Spéc alate
aileron [ɛlʁɔ̃] NM **1** Ich (d'un poisson, d'un requin) fin; Orn (d'un oiseau) pinion; **potage aux ailerons de requin** shark's fin soup **2** Aviat aileron **3** (d'une voiture de course) aerofoil **4** (de roue à eau) paddle board **5** (d'un sous-marin) fin keel; (d'une planche à voile) skeg
ailette [ɛlɛt] NF **1** (d'un radiateur) fin **2** (d'une turbine) blade **3** Tech fin
ailier [elje] NM Sport wing; (au football) winger
aillade [ajad] NF Culin (sauce) garlic sauce; (vinaigrette) garlic vinaigrette; (tranche de pain) = slice of bread rubbed with olive oil and garlic and then toasted
aille etc voir **aller²**

-AILLE [-aj] SUFF

This suffix is used to form feminine nouns.

● When added to a noun or a verb, it generates a COLLECTIVE noun. This noun can be of a neutral register:
 des broussailles undergrowth, scrub; **de la pierraille** loose stones, scree; **de la rocaille** loose stones; **une rocaille** a rockery
Very often, however, there are derogatory connotations, especially when the noun used as a basis is itself colloquial:
 ferraille scrap iron; **marmaille** kids; **flicaille** cops; **tripaille** guts; **boustifaille** (an alteration of boufaille, itself derived from bouffer) grub
● The resulting noun, when derived from a verb, can refer to an ACTION, often, but not exclusively, to do with a ritual or a celebration:
 fiançailles engagement, engagement party; **semailles** sowing, sowing season; **retrouvailles** reunion; **bataille** battle
● Again in conjunction with a verb, **-aille** refers to tools or instruments:
 des tenailles pincers; **une cisaille** shears

ailler [3] [aje] VT Culin (gigot, rôti) to put garlic in; (croûton) to rub garlic on
ailleurs [ajœʁ] ADV somewhere else, elsewhere; **et si on allait a.?** how about going somewhere else?; **allons voir a.** let's go and look somewhere else or elsewhere; **tu sais, ce n'est pas mieux a. qu'ici** you know, it's no better anywhere else than it is here; **on ne trouve ça nulle part a.** you won't find that anywhere else; **il fera beau partout a.** the weather will be fine everywhere else; **il a toujours l'air a.** he always looks as if he's miles away; **il est a.!** he's miles away!; **ils venaient d'a.** they came from another place; **l'erreur doit provenir d'a.** the mistake must come from somewhere else
 NM Littéraire **il rêvait d'un a. impossible** he was dreaming of a distant world he would never see
 □ **d'ailleurs** ADV **1** (de toute façon) besides, anyway; **je n'ai pas envie de sortir, d'a. il fait trop froid** I don't want to go out and anyway or

besides, it's too cold; **d'a. je sais bien que tu n'en veux pas** besides, I know quite well that you don't want any
 2 (de plus) what's more; **je n'en sais rien et d'a. je ne tiens pas à le savoir** I don't know anything about it and what's more I don't want to know
 3 (du reste) for that matter; **je ne les aime pas, elle non plus d'a.** I don't like them, nor does she for that matter
 4 (à propos) incidentally; **nous avons dîné dans un restaurant, très bien d'a.** we had dinner in a restaurant which, incidentally, was very good; **d'a., j'avais quelque chose à te dire à ce sujet** by the way or incidentally, I had something to tell you about this
 5 (bien que) although, while; **votre inquiétude – d'a. légitime – n'en est pas moins exagérée** your concern – although justified or justified as it is – is nonetheless exaggerated
 □ **par ailleurs** ADV **1** (d'un autre côté) otherwise; **il est charmant, mais pas très efficace par a.** he's charming but otherwise not very efficient; **je comprenais ses arguments, même si par a. je ne les approuvais pas** I understood what he was getting at, even though I didn't actually approve
 2 (de plus) besides, moreover; **par a., tu sais bien que je suis occupée ce jour-là** besides, you know I'm busy that day; **la pièce est trop longue et par a. pas très intéressante** the play's too long and not very interesting (either) for that matter; **par a. je voulais te dire que je prends mes congés au mois d'août** I also wanted to let you know I'll be taking my holidays in August
ailloli [ajɔli] = **aïoli**
aimable [ɛmabl] ADJ **1** (gentil) kind, pleasant, amiable; **il a dit quelques mots aimables avant de partir** he said a few kind words before leaving; **soyez assez a. de nous prévenir si vous ne venez pas** please be kind enough to let us know if you aren't coming; **peu a.** not very nice; **vous êtes trop a., merci beaucoup** you're most kind, thank you very much; **c'est très a. à vous** it's very kind of you; Ironique **c'est une a. plaisanterie!** you must be joking!; **nous prions notre a. clientèle de bien vouloir nous excuser du dérangement** (sur vitrine ou panneau) = we apologize for any inconvenience; Fam **il est a. comme une porte de prison** (en ce moment) he's like a bear with a sore head; (toujours) he's a miserable so-and-so
 2 (poli) nice
 3 Littéraire (digne d'amour) lovable; (séduisant) attractive; **elle le trouvait plutôt a.** she thought him rather attractive
aimablement [ɛmabləmɑ̃] ADV kindly, pleasantly, amiably
aimant¹ [ɛmɑ̃] NM **1** (instrument) magnet **2** (oxyde de fer) magnetite
aimant², -e [ɛmɑ̃, -ɑ̃t] ADJ loving, caring
aimantation [ɛmɑ̃tasjɔ̃] NF Tech magnetization
aimante [ɛmɑ̃t] voir **aimant²**
aimanter [3] [ɛmɑ̃te] VT Tech to magnetize
aimer [4] [eme] VT **1** (d'amour) to love; **a. qn d'amour véritable** to truly love sb; **il m'aime un peu, beaucoup, passionnément, à la folie** (en effeuillant une fleur) he loves me, he loves me not, he loves me, he loves me not
 2 (apprécier) to like, to be fond of; **je l'aime beaucoup** I'm very fond of him/her; **je l'aime bien** I like him/her; **je les aime bien mais sans plus** I quite like them but that's all; **je n'aime plus tellement le jazz** I'm not so keen on jazz now; **les chats aiment le canapé** the cats like the sofa; **jamais tu ne me feras a. la voile!** you'll never persuade me to like sailing!; **il a réussi à se faire a. de tous** he got everybody to like him; **nous aimions à nous promener au bord du lac** we used to enjoy walking by the lake; **j'aime à croire** ou **à penser que tu m'as dit la vérité cette fois** I'd like to think that you told me the truth this time; **il aime que ses enfants l'embrassent avant d'aller au lit** he loves his children to kiss him good night; **je n'aime pas qu'on me mente/que tu rentres si tard** I don't like being lied to/your coming home so late; Prov **qui aime bien châtie bien** spare the rod and spoil the child
 3 a. autant ou **mieux** (préférer) to prefer; **j'aime mieux la rouge** I prefer the red one; **pas de**

dessert, merci, j'aime autant ou **mieux le fromage** no dessert, thanks, I'd rather have or I'd prefer cheese; **j'aime autant** ou **mieux ça** (it's) just as well; **il aimerait autant** ou **mieux prendre son bain tout de suite** he'd rather have or he'd prefer to have his bath now; **elle aime autant** ou **mieux que tu y ailles** she'd rather you or she'd prefer it if you went; Fam **j'aime mieux pas** I'd rather not; Belg **a. mieux les talons de qn que ses pointes** to be happier when sb is not around
 4 (au conditionnel) (souhaiter) **j'aimerais un café, s'il vous plaît** I'd like a coffee, please; **j'aimerais bien te voir** I'd really like to see you; **j'aurais aimé le voir** I would like to have seen him; **j'aimerais tant te voir heureux** I'd so love to see you happy; **nous aimerions assez la rencontrer** we'd rather or quite like to meet her
 ▶ **s'aimer** VPR **1** (emploi réfléchi) to like oneself; **je ne m'aime pas** I don't like myself; **je m'aime bien habillé en bleu/avec les cheveux courts** I think I look good in blue/with short hair
 2 (emploi réciproque) (d'amour) to love each other; (s'apprécier) to like each other; **regarde ces deux-là comme ils s'aiment!** look at how those two love each other!; **les gens qui s'aiment** people in love; **un couple qui s'aime** a loving or devoted couple; **les trois frères ne s'aimaient pas** the three brothers didn't care for or like each other
 3 Littéraire (faire l'amour) to make love; **c'est là qu'ils s'étaient aimés pour la première fois** it was there that they had made love for the first time

Je t'aime, moi non plus

The title of a Serge Gainsbourg song, made famous by Jane Birkin, and also of a film, this means literally "I love you, nor do I". It conveys the idea that people's feelings cannot be perfectly synchronized, and that love is a constant ballet of the emotions, with one party or the other being inclined to move on. In everyday conversation or journalistic use, this expression describes a situation where things are apparently not working out, or relationships (eg between two senior members of government) are starting to deteriorate. The English equivalent might be "The love affair is starting to cool down."

Qui m'aime me suive

This rousing battle-cry ("Let him who loves me follow me!") is attributed to Philippe VI of the House of Valois, in 1328. The expression has become part of everyday language: if one suddenly decides to rush off and do something, one might say this to the company at large, inviting them to come too ("Anyone like to join me?").

Ain [ɛ̃] NM **l'A.** Ain

-AIN, -AINE [ɛ̃, ɛn] SUFF

● This suffix conveys the idea of ORIGIN or BELONGING.

(i) It appears in nouns and adjectives of nationality, or refers to inhabitants of regions, cities etc:
 africain(e), Africain(e) African; **américain(e), Américaine(e)** American; **lorrain(e)** of or from Lorraine; **toulousain(e)** of or from Toulouse; **napolitain(e), Napolitain(e)** Neapolitan
(ii) The idea can also be more general, ie that of "relating to...". It is translated in most cases by using the suffix -an:
 républicain(e) republican; **humain(e)** human; **élisabéthain(e)** Elizabethan
(iii) Following the idea of belonging or origin, nouns ending in **-ain(e)** can refer to social status, trade or membership of a particular group:
 châtelain(e) (person who comes from a château) lord or lady of the manor; **sacristain** (who looks after the sacristie) sacristan; **forain(e)** (who works on a foire) stallholder; **dominicain(e)** (member of a religious order founded by saint Dominique) Dominican
● When coupled with a number, **-ain** and **-aine** are used to form nouns referring to a group

of X units, or a quantity close to X units. The latter is conveyed only by the feminine suffix **-aine**:

une douzaine d'œufs a dozen eggs; **une douzaine de pages** roughly twelve pages; **un quatrain** a quatrain = (a stanza of four lines); **une centaine d'invités** a hundred or so guests; **sous huitaine** within a week; **il doit avoir la cinquantaine** he must be about fifty

aine [ɛn] NF *Anat* groin

aîné, -e [ene] ADJ **l'enfant a.** *(de deux)* the elder *or* older child; *(de plusieurs)* the eldest *or* oldest child; **la branche aînée de la famille** the senior branch of the family

NM,F **1** *(entre frères et sœurs)* **l'a.** *(de deux)* the elder *or* older boy; *(de plusieurs)* the eldest *or* oldest boy; **l'aînée** *(de deux)* the elder *or* older girl; *(de plusieurs)* the eldest *or* oldest girl; **notre aînée est étudiante** *(de deux)* our elder daughter's a student; *(de plusieurs)* our eldest (daughter) is a student

2 *(le plus âgé)* **l'a.** *(de deux)* the older man; *(de plusieurs)* the oldest man; **l'aînée** *(de deux)* the older woman; *(de plusieurs)* the oldest woman; **Pitt l'a.** Pitt the Elder; **il est mon a.** he is older than me; **il est mon a. de deux ans** he is two years older than me

❑ **aînés** NMPL *(d'une famille, d'une tribu)* **les aînés** the elders; *Hum* **respecte un peu tes aînés!** show some respect for your elders!

aînesse [ɛnɛs] *voir* **droit**[3]

ainsi [ɛ̃si] ADV **1** *(de cette manière)* this *or* that way; **je suis a. faite** that's the way I am; **puisqu'il en est a.** since that is the case, since that is the way things are; **s'il en était vraiment a.** if this were really so *or* the case; **c'est toujours a.** it's always like that; **c'est a. que cela s'est passé** this is how it happened; **on voit a. que...** in this way *or* thus we can see that...; **les sondages montrent a. la fragilité du parti au pouvoir** the polls thus highlight the governing party's fragility; **a. s'achève notre émission** this concludes our programme; **a. va le monde** it's the way of the world *or* the way things go; *Rel* **a. soit-il** amen; *Hum* so be it

2 *(par conséquent)* so, thus; **nous n'avons rien dérangé, a. vous retrouverez tout plus facilement** we didn't move anything, so you'll find everything again easily; **a. tu n'as pas réussi à le voir?** so you didn't manage to see him?; **a. (donc) tout est fini entre nous** so everything is over between us

3 *(par exemple)* for instance, for example; **je n'arrête pas de faire des bêtises: a., l'autre jour...** I keep doing silly things: for example, the other day...

❑ **ainsi que** CONJ **1** *(comme)* as; **tout s'est passé a. que je l'ai dit** everything happened as I said (it would); **a. que je l'ai fait remarquer...** as I pointed out...

2 *(et)* as well as; **mes parents a. que mes frères seront là** my parents will be there as well as my brothers

3 *Littéraire (exprimant une comparaison)* like; **il souriait dans son sommeil a. qu'un enfant** he smiled in his sleep just like a child

❑ **et ainsi de suite** ADV and so on, and so forth

❑ **pour ainsi dire** ADV **1** *(presque)* virtually; **nous ne nous sommes pour a. dire pas vus** we virtually didn't see each other

2 *(si l'on peut dire)* so to speak, as it were; **elle est pour a. dire sa raison de vivre** she's his/her reason for living, so to speak *or* as it were

AIO [aio] NM *Mktg* *(abrév* **activités, intérêts et opinions***)* AIO

aïoli [ajɔli] NM *Culin* **1** *(sauce)* aïoli, garlic mayonnaise **2** *(plat provençal)* = dish of cod and poached vegetables served with aïoli sauce

AIR [ɛr]

air **1, 4, 6** ▪ look **1** ▪ likeness **2** ▪ tune **3** ▪ atmosphere **7**

NM **1** *(apparence)* air, look; **"bien sûr", dit-il d'un a. guilleret/inquiet** "of course," he said, jauntily/looking worried; **elle l'écoute de l'a. de quelqu'un qui s'ennuie** when she listens to him/her, she looks bored; **il avait un a. angoissé/mauvais** he looked anxious/very nasty; **avoir bel** *ou* **bon a.** to look impressive; **avoir mauvais a.** to look shifty; **son fils a mauvais a.** his/her son has a shifty look about him; **ne te laisse pas prendre à son faux a. de gentillesse** don't be taken in by his/her apparent kindness; **son témoignage a un a. de vérité qui ne trompe pas** his/her testimony sounds unmistakably genuine; **Maria, tu as l'a. heureux** *ou* **heureuse** Maria, you look happy; **elle n'a pas l'a. satisfait** *ou* **satisfaite** she doesn't look as if she's pleased; **cette poire a l'a. mauvaise, jette-la** this pear looks (as though it's) rotten, throw it away; **l'armoire avait l'a. ancienne** the wardrobe looked like an antique *or* looked old; *Fam* **j'avais l'a. fin!** I looked a real fool!; **il a l'a. de t'aimer beaucoup** he seems to be very fond of you; **je ne voudrais pas avoir l'a. de lui donner des ordres** I wouldn't like (it) to look as though I were ordering him/her about; **ça a l'a. d'un** *ou* **d'être un scarabée** it looks like a beetle; *Fam* **ça m'a tout l'a. (d'être) traduit de l'anglais** it looks to me as though it's been translated from English; **il a peut-être la rougeole – il en a tout l'a.** he may have measles – it certainly looks like it; *aussi Ironique* **avoir un petit a. penché** *ou* **des petits airs penchés** to look pensive; **avec son a. de ne pas y toucher** *ou* **sans avoir l'a. d'y toucher, il arrive toujours à ses fins** though you wouldn't think it to look at him, he always manages to get his way; *Fam* **je me suis approchée, l'a. de rien** *ou* **de ne pas en avoir, et je lui ai flanqué ma main sur la figure** I walked up, all innocent, and gave him/her a slap in the face; **elle n'a l'a. de rien (comme ça), mais elle a une réputation internationale en biologie** she may look very unassuming, but she's an internationally known biologist; **ça n'a l'a. de rien comme ça, mais c'est une lourde tâche** it doesn't look much but it's quite a big job; *Fam* **elle n'a pas l'a. comme ça, mais elle sait ce qu'elle veut!** you wouldn't think it to look at her, but she knows what she wants!; **sans en avoir l'a., elle a tout rangé en une heure** she tidied up everything in an hour without even looking busy; **je suis arrivée au bout de mon tricot, sans en avoir l'a.!** I managed to finish my knitting, though it didn't seem that I was making any progress!; **prendre** *ou* **se donner des airs** to give oneself airs; **prendre de grands airs** to put on airs (*Br* and graces)

2 *(ressemblance)* likeness, resemblance; **un a. de famille** *ou* **parenté** a family resemblance *or* likeness; **il a un faux a. de James Dean** he looks a bit like James Dean; *Can* **avoir l'a. de qn** to look like sb

3 *Mus (mélodie)* tune; *(à l'opéra)* aria; **siffloter un petit a. joyeux** to whistle a happy little tune; **le grand a. de la Tosca** Tosca's great aria; *Fig Péj* **avec lui c'est toujours le même a.!** he should change his tune! **c'est l'a. qui fait la chanson** it's not what you say, it's the way you say it

4 *(qu'on respire)* air; **la pollution/température de l'a.** air pollution/temperature; **l'a. de la mer/des montagnes** (the) sea/mountain air; **l'a. était chargé d'une odeur de jasmin** a smell of jasmine filled the air; **ça manque d'a. ici** it's stuffy in here; **donne un peu d'a., on étouffe ici** let's have some air, it's stifling in here; **j'ouvre la porte pour faire de l'a.** I'll open the door to let some air in; **a. conditionné** *(système)* air-conditioning; **ils ont l'a. conditionné dans leur immeuble** their building is air-conditioned; **a. comprimé** compressed air; **outil à a. comprimé** pneumatic tool; **a. liquide** liquid air; **prendre l'a.** to get some fresh air, *Vieilli* to take the air; *Péj* **déplacer** *ou* **remuer beaucoup d'a.** to make a lot of noise; *Fam* **(allez,) de l'a.!** come on, beat it!; *Fam* **vous, les gosses, de l'a.!** come on you lot, scram!

5 *Fam (vent)* **il y a** *ou* **il fait de l'a. aujourd'hui** *(un peu)* it's breezy today; *(beaucoup)* it's windy today

6 *(ciel)* air; **dans l'a.** *ou* **les airs** (up) in the air *or* sky; **prendre l'a.** *(avion)* to take off, to become airborne, to take to the air; **transport par a.** air transport; **le musée de l'A. et de l'Espace** = air museum in Le Bourget, north of Paris

7 *(ambiance)* atmosphere; **de temps en temps, il me faut l'a. du pays natal** I need to go back to my roots from time to time; **c'est dans l'a. du temps** it's the in thing; **vivre de l'a. du temps** to live on (thin) air; **c'est bien joli d'être amoureux, mais on ne vit pas de l'a. du temps** love is all very well but you can't exist on love alone

❑ **à l'air** ADV **laisser qch à l'a.** to leave sth uncovered; **mets les draps à l'a. sur le balcon** put the sheets on the balcony to air; **j'ai mis tous les vêtements d'hiver à l'a.** I put all the winter clothes out for an airing; **mettre son derrière à l'a.** to bare one's bottom

❑ **à l'air libre** ADV out in the open

❑ **au grand air** ADV *(dehors)* (out) in the fresh air

❑ **dans l'air** ADV in the air; **il y a du printemps dans l'a.** spring is in the air; **il y a de la bouderie dans l'a.** somebody's sulking around here; *aussi Fig* **il y a de l'orage dans l'a.** there's a storm brewing; **influencé par les idées qui sont dans l'a.** influenced by current ideas; **la révolution est dans l'a.** revolution is in the air; **la maladie est dans l'a.** the disease is going around; **il y a quelque chose dans l'a.!** there's something going on!

❑ **en l'air** ADJ **1** *(levé)* in the air, up; **les pattes en l'a.** with its feet in the air; **les mains en l'a.!** hands up! **2** *(non fondé → promesse)* empty; **encore des paroles en l'a.!** more empty words!; **je ne fais pas de projets en l'a.** when I make a plan, I stick to it ADV **1** *(vers le haut)* (up) in the air; **jeter** *ou* **lancer qch en l'a.** to throw sth (up) in the air; **tirer en l'a.** to fire in the air; **regarde en l'a.** look up **2** *Fig (sans réfléchir)* **parler en l'a.** to say things without meaning them; **vous dites que vous montez votre affaire? – oh, nous parlions en l'a.** did you say you're setting up your own business? – oh, we were just tossing *or* kicking ideas around **3** *Fig (sens dessus dessous)* **mettre qch en l'a.** to make an awful mess of sth; *Fam* **flanquer** *ou très Fam* **foutre qch en l'a.** *(jeter)* to chuck sth out, to bin sth; *(gâcher)* to screw sth up

airain [ɛrɛ̃] NM *Littéraire* bronze; *Fig* **avoir un cœur d'a.** to have a heart of stone

air-air [ɛrɛr] ADJ INV *Mil* air-to-air

Airbag® [ɛrbag] NM **1** *(dispositif)* Airbag **2** *Fam* **airbags** *(seins)* boobs

Airbus® [ɛrbys] NM Airbus®

aire [ɛr] NF **1** *(terrain)* area; **a. de jeu** playground; **a. de pique-nique** picnic site *or* area; **aires de repos** rest areas *(along a road)*, *Br* ≃ lay-bys; **a. de stationnement** parking area

2 *(région → linguistique)* area; *(→ économique)* sphere

3 *Aviat & Astron* **a. d'atterrissage** landing area; **a. d'embarquement** boarding area; **a. de lancement** launching site

4 *Géol* **a. continentale** continental shield

5 *Math* area

6 *Agr* floor; **a. de battage** threshing floor

7 *(nid d'aigle)* eyrie

airedale [ɛrdɛl], **airedale-terrier** [ɛrdɛltɛrje] *(pl* **airedale-terriers***)* NM *(chien)* Airedale (terrier)

airelle [ɛrɛl] NF *Bot (myrtille)* blueberry, bilberry; *(rouge)* cranberry; **a. canneberge** cranberry

airer [4] [ɛre] VI to build an eyrie

air-sol [ɛrsɔl] ADJ INV *Mil* air-to-ground

-AIS, -AISE [ɛ, ɛz] SUFF

• Placed at the end of a place name, **-ais** and **-aise** denote the ORIGIN of a person, be it a country, a region or a city:

anglais(e) English; **un(e) Anglais(e)** an Englishman, an Englishwoman; **japonais(e), Japonais(e)** Japanese; **charentais(e)** of or from the Charente; **Bordelais(e)** inhabitant of or person from Bordeaux.

• Additionally, the masculine form ending in **-ais** can be used, without a capital, to refer to a language:

ils parlent anglais they speak English; **en français** in French

ais [ɛ] NM **1** *Arch* board, plank **2** *Typ* wetting

board; *(en reliure)* press-board **3** *Constr* **a. de contre-marche** riser

aisance [ɛzɑ̃s] **NF 1** *(naturel)* ease; **aller et venir avec a.** to walk back and forth with ease; **danser/jongler/s'exprimer avec a.** to dance/to juggle/to express oneself with great ease; **parler une langue avec a.** to speak a language fluently; **il est incroyable d'a. quand il saute** he jumps with amazing ease

2 *(prospérité)* affluence; **vivre dans l'a.** to live a life of ease

3 *Couture* **donner de l'a. à la taille** to let a garment out at the waist

4 *Jur* **aisances de voirie** public easement

aise [ɛz] *Littéraire* **ADJ** delighted; **je suis bien a. de vous revoir** I'm delighted to see you again

NF 1 *(plaisir)* pleasure, joy; **il ne se sentait plus d'a.** he was utterly contented; **son accueil nous a comblés d'a.** his/her welcome filled us with joy

2 *(locutions)* **je suis plus à l'a. avec mes vieilles pantoufles** I feel more comfortable with my old slippers on; **on est mal à l'a. dans ce fauteuil** this armchair isn't very comfortable; **être à l'a.** *(riche)* to be well-to-do *or* well-off; **nous sommes bien plus à l'a. depuis que ma femme travaille** we're much better off now my wife's working; **il se sent à l'a.** *ou* **à son a.** he feels at ease; *Fig* **il s'est senti mal à l'a. pendant toute la réunion** he felt ill-at-ease during the entire meeting; **il nous a mis tout de suite à l'a.** *ou* **à notre a.** he put us at (our) ease right away; **mettez-vous donc à l'a.** *ou* **à votre a.** make yourself comfortable; **à ton a.!** please yourself!; **à votre a.** as you please; **tu en parles à ton a.** it's easy for you to talk; **il en prend à son a. avec ses collègues** he takes his colleagues for granted; *Fam* **être à l'a. dans ses baskets** to be together; *Fam* **on y sera ce soir, à l'a.!** we'll be there tonight, no hassle *or* sweat!; *Fam* **le piano rentre à l'a.** you can get the piano in no problem; *Fam* **tu crois qu'on va y arriver? – à l'a.!** do you think we'll manage? – easily!; *Fam Ironique* **tu ne te gênes pas toi au moins, à l'a., Blaise!** you go right ahead, don't mind me!

▫ **aises NFPL** creature comforts; **il aime ses aises** he likes his creature comforts; *Ironique* **prends tes aises, surtout!** do make yourself comfortable, won't you?

aisé, -e [eze] **ADJ 1** *(facile)* easy; **ce n'est pas chose aisée que de le faire** it's no easy thing *or* not easy to do **2** *(prospère)* well-to-do, well-off; **une famille aisée** a well-to-do family **3** *(naturel → manières)* easy, free; *(→ style)* flowing

aisément [ezemɑ̃] **ADV** easily; **il est a. reconnaissable à cause de sa cicatrice** he's easy to recognize because of his scar

Aisne [ɛn] **NF l'A.** Aisne

aisseau, -x [ɛso] **NM** *Constr* **1** *(pour la toiture)* shingle **2** *(outil)* roofer's hammer

aisselle [ɛsɛl] **NF 1** *Anat* armpit **2** *Bot* axil

aisy [ɛzi] **NM** *(mot dialectal du Jura)* = bitter liquid produced during the fermentation of Gruyère cheese

Aix-en-Provence [ɛksɑ̃prɔvɑ̃s] **NF** Aix-en-Provence

Aix-la-Chapelle [ɛkslaʃapɛl] **NF** *Géog* Aachen

aixois, -e [ɛkswa, -az] **ADJ** = of/from Aix-en-Provence, Aix-la-Chapelle, Aix-les-Bains etc

▫ **Aixois, -e NM,F** = inhabitant of or person from Aix-en-Provence, Aix-la-Chapelle, Aix-les-Bains etc

AJ [aʒi] **NF** *(abrév* **auberge de jeunesse***)* youth hostel

AJA [aʒia] **NF** *Agr (abrév* **aide aux jeunes agriculteurs***)* = grant to young farmers

ajaccien, -enne [aʒaksjɛ̃, -ɛn] **ADJ** of/from Ajaccio

▫ **Ajaccien, -enne NM,F** = inhabitant of or person from Ajaccio

Ajaccio [aʒaksjo] **NM** *Géog* Ajaccio

Ajax [aʒaks] **NPR** *Myth* Ajax

ajiste [aʒist] **ADJ** = who is a member of the "Fédération des auberges de jeunesse"

NMF = member of the "Fédération des auberges de jeunesse", ≃ youth hosteller

ajointer [3] [aʒwɛ̃te] **VT** to join up; *(planches, tuyaux etc)* to fit end to end

ajonc [aʒɔ̃] **NM** *Bot* gorse *(UNCOUNT)*, furze *(UNCOUNT)*

ajour [aʒur] **NM 1** *(laissant passer la lumière)* opening, hole, orifice; *(en sculpture etc)* (ornamental) perforation, openwork **2** *Couture* **ajours** hemstitching *(UNCOUNT)*; *(dans une dentelle)* openwork *(UNCOUNT)*

ajouré, -e [aʒure] **ADJ 1** *Couture (nappe, napperon)* openwork *(avant n)*, hemstitched **2** *Archit* with an openwork design

ajourer [3] [aʒure] **VT 1** *Couture (nappe)* to hemstitch **2** *Archit* to decorate with openwork

ajourné, -e [aʒurne] **ADJ** *(date, élection, réunion)* postponed; *(candidat)* referred; *(soldat)* deferred

NM,F *(étudiant)* referred student; *(soldat)* deferred soldier

ajournement [aʒurnəmɑ̃] **NM 1** *(d'une réunion, d'une décision, d'un voyage)* postponement; *(après le début de la séance)* adjournment **2** *Jur* **a. du prononcé de la peine** deferment (of sentence) **3** *(d'un étudiant)* referral; *(d'un soldat)* deferment

ajourner [3] [aʒurne] **VT 1** *(réunion, décision, voyage etc)* to postpone, to put off; *(après le début de la séance)* to adjourn; **nous avons préféré a. notre voyage** we preferred to postpone our trip; **l'avocat a fait a. le procès** the lawyer requested a postponement of the trial *or* asked for the trial to be postponed **2** *Jur* to summon, to subpoena **3** *(étudiant)* to refer; *(soldat)* to defer

ajout [aʒu] **NM** *(à un texte)* addition; *(à un bâtiment)* extension; **quelques ajouts dans la marge** a few additions *or* addenda in the margin; *Mktg* **a. à la gamme** range addition; *Mktg* **a. à la ligne** line addition; *Ordinat* **a. de mémoire** memory upgrade

ajoute [aʒut] **NF** *Belg* addition

ajouté [aʒute] **NM** addition, addendum

ajouter [3] [aʒute] **VT 1** *(mettre)* to add; **ajoute donc une assiette pour ton frère** lay an extra place *or* add a plate for your brother

2 *Math* to add; **a. 500 euros de loyer** *(dans une colonne)* to add in 500 euros for the rent; **ils ont ajouté 15 pour cent de service** they added on 15 percent for the service; **a. 10 à 15** to add 10 and 15 (together), to add 10 to 15; **pour obtenir le résultat final, a. les deux sommes** to get the final result add both sums together

3 *(dire)* to add; **il est parti sans rien a.** he left without saying another word; **je n'ai plus rien à a.** I have nothing further to say *or* to add; **"venez aussi", ajouta-t-il** "you come too," he added; **ajoutez à cela qu'il est têtu** added to this, he's stubborn

4 a. foi à *(croire)* to believe, *Sout* to give credence to; **je refuse d'a. foi à ses dires** I refuse to believe what he/she said

5 *Ordinat (à une base de données)* to append

▫ **ajouter à VT IND** to add to; **ça ne fait qu'a. à mon embarras** it only adds to my confusion

▸**s'ajouter VPR** to be added; **vient s'a. là-dessus le loyer** the rent is added *or* comes on top; **mon licenciement s'ajoute à mes autres problèmes** losing my job just adds to my other problems

ajust [aʒyst] = **ajut**

ajustable [aʒystabl] **ADJ** adjustable

ajustage [aʒystaʒ] **NM 1** *Ind* fitting **2** *(des pièces de monnaie)* gauging

ajusté, -e [aʒyste] **ADJ** close-fitting

ajustement [aʒystəmɑ̃] **NM 1** *(modification → d'un projet)* adjustment, adaptation; *(→ des prix, des salaires, d'une monnaie, des statistiques)* adjusting, adjustment; **a. saisonnier** seasonal adjustment; **a. structurel** structural adjustment **2** *Ind* fitting

ajuster [3] [aʒyste] **VT 1** *(adapter)* to fit; *Couture* **a. un vêtement** to alter a garment; **a. qch à** *ou* **sur** to fit sth to *or* on; **a. la théorie à la réalité** to adapt the theory to reality, to make the theory fit reality; **a. l'offre à la demande** to adjust *or* adapt supply to demand, to match supply and demand

2 *(mécanisme, réglage)* to adjust

3 *Fin (salaires, prix, monnaie)* to adjust

4 *Chasse* **a. un lapin** to aim at a rabbit; **a. son coup** *ou* **tir** to aim one's shot; *Fig* **tu as bien ajusté ton coup** *ou* **tir** your aim was pretty accurate, you had it figured out pretty well

5 *(arranger → robe, coiffure)* to rearrange; *(→ cravate)* to straighten

6 *Équitation* to adjust

7 *Ind* to fit

8 *(en statistique)* to adjust

▸**s'ajuster VPR 1** *(s'adapter)* to fit; **l'embout s'ajuste sur le** *ou* **au tuyau** the nozzle fits onto the pipe

2 *(emploi réfléchi)* to straighten one's clothes, to tidy oneself up

ajusteur [aʒystœr] **NM** fitter

ajut [aʒy] **NM** *Naut* carrick bend

ajutage [aʒytaʒ] **NM** *Tech* adjutage, ajutage

akathisie [akatizi] **NF** *Méd* akathisia

akène [akɛn] **NM** *Bot* achene, akene

akinésie [akinezi] **NF** *Méd* akinesia

akkadien, -enne [akadjɛ̃, -ɛn] **ADJ** Akkadian, Accadian

NM *(langue)* Akkadian, Accadian

▫ **Akkadien, -enne NM,F** Akkadian, Accadian

akvavit [akwavit] = **aquavit**

ALA [aɛla] **NM** *Biol & Chem (abrév* **acide alphalinolénique***)* ALA

Alabama [alabama] **NM l'A.** Alabama; **en A.** in Alabama

alabandine [alabɑ̃din], **alabandite** [alabɑ̃dit] **NF** *Chim* alabandite

alabastrite [alabastrit] **NF** *Minér* gypseous alabaster

alacrité [alakrite] **NF** *Littéraire* alacrity, eagerness

Aladin [aladɛ̃] **NPR** *Littérature* Aladdin

Alains [alɛ̃] **NMPL** *Hist* Alans, Alani

alaire [alɛr] **ADJ** *Aviat* wing *(avant n)*

alaise [alɛz] **NF** drawsheet; **a. en caoutchouc** rubber sheet *or* undersheet

alaisé, -e [alɛze] = **alésé**

Alamans [alamɑ̃] **NMPL** *Hist* Alamans, Alemanni

alambic [alɑ̃bik] **NM** still *(for making alcohol)*

alambiqué, -e [alɑ̃bike] **ADJ** *Littéraire (style)* convoluted; *(explication)* involved, tortuous; *(esprit)* oversubtle

alambiquer [3] [alɑ̃bike] **VT** *Littéraire* to refine too much, to subtilize; **s'a. le cerveau (à approfondir quelque chose)** to puzzle *or* to rack one's brains (over something)

alambiqueur, -euse [alɑ̃bikœr, -øz] **NM,F** *Littéraire* **a. de phrases** spinner of fine sentences

Åland [olɑ̃d] **NM** *Géog* the Åland Islands

alandier [alɑ̃dje] **NM** *Cér* round kiln

alangui, -e [alɑ̃gi] **ADJ** languid

alanguir [32] [alɑ̃gir] **VT** *(sujet: chaleur, fatigue)* to make listless *or* languid *or* languorous; *(sujet: oisiveté, paresse)* to make indolent *or* languid; *(sujet: fièvre)* to make feeble, to enfeeble

▸**s'alanguir VPR** to grow languid; **elle s'alanguissait peu à peu** *(devenait triste)* her spirits gradually fell; *(n'offrait plus de résistance)* she was weakening gradually

alanguissement [alɑ̃gismɑ̃] **NM** languor

alanine [alanin] **NF** *Chim* alanine

Alaouites [alawit] **NMPL** *Hist & Rel* Alids

alarmant, -e [alarmɑ̃, -ɑ̃t] **ADJ** alarming; **son état est a.** his/her condition is giving serious cause for concern

alarme [alarm] **NF 1** *(dispositif)* **a. antivol** burglar alarm; *(d'une voiture)* car alarm; **a. incendie** fire alarm **2** *(alerte)* alarm; **donner l'a.** to give *or* to raise the alarm; *Fig* to raise the alarm; **sonner l'a.** to sound the alarm **3** *(inquiétude)* alarm, anxiety; **à la première a.** at the first sign of danger

▫ **d'alarme ADJ** *(dispositif, signal, sonnette)* alarm *(avant n)*

alarmer [3] [alarme] **VT 1** *(inquiéter → sujet: personne, remarque)* to alarm; *(→ sujet: bruit)* to startle **2** *(alerter → opinion, presse)* to alert

▸**s'alarmer VPR** to become alarmed; **il n'y a pas de quoi s'a.** there's no cause for alarm

alarmisme [alarmism] **NM** alarmism

alarmiste [alarmist] **ADJ** alarmist

NMF alarmist

Alaska [alaska] **NM l'A.** Alaska; **en A.** in Alaska; **la route de l'A.** the Alaska Highway

alastrim [alastrim] **NM** *Méd* alastrim

alaterne [alatɛrn] **NM** *Bot* buckthorn, *Spéc* alaternus

albacore [albakɔr] **NM** *Ich* albacore, long-finned tunny

albanais, -e [albanɛ, -ɛz] ADJ Albanian ▸ NM (*langue*) Albanian
◻ **Albanais, -e** NM,F Albanian

Albanie [albani] NF l'A. Albania; **vivre en A.** to live in Albania; **aller en A.** to go to Albania

albanophone [albanɔfɔn] ADJ Albanian-speaking ▸ NMF Albanian speaker

albâtre [albɑtr] NM **1** *Minér* alabaster **2** (*objet*) alabaster (object)
◻ **d'albâtre** ADJ *Littéraire* (*blanc*) **des épaules d'a.** alabaster shoulders, shoulders of alabaster

albatros [albatros] NM **1** *Orn* (*oiseau*) albatross; **a. hurleur** wandering albatross **2** *Golf* albatross

albédo [albedo] NM *Astron & Phys* albedo

alberge [albɛrʒ] NF *Bot* clingstone apricot

albergier [albɛrʒje] NM *Bot* clingstone apricot tree

Alberta [albɛrta] NF l'A. Alberta

albigeois, -e [albiʒwa, -az] ADJ of/from Albi
◻ **Albigeois, -e** NM,F = inhabitant of or person from Albi
◻ **albigeois** NMPL *Hist* Albigensians; **la croisade des a.** the Albigensian Crusade

---

Culture
LES ALBIGEOIS
The Albigensians were intransigent Cathar heretics of the Languedoc in the 12th and 13th centuries against whom two crusades were directed.

---

albinisme [albinism] NM *Méd & Vét* albinism

albinos [albinos] ADJ & NMF *Méd & Vét* albino

Albion [albjɔ̃] NF *Géog* Albion; *Littéraire* **la perfide A.** perfidious Albion

albite [albit] NF *Minér* albite

albizzia [albizja] NM *Bot* albizzia

albraque [albrak] NF *Mines* drainway

albuginé, -e [albyʒine] ADJ albugineous
◻ **albuginée** NF *Anat* tunica albuginea testis

albugo [albygo] NM *Méd* albugo

album [albɔm] NM **1** (*livre*) album; **a. à colorier** *ou* **de coloriage** colouring book; **a. (de) photos** photograph album; **a. de bandes dessinées** comic book **2** (*disque*) album, LP **3** *Ordinat* (*sur Macintosh*) scrapbook

albumen [albymɛn] NM *Biol & Bot* albumen

albumine [albymin] NF *Biol* albumin

albuminé, -e [albymine] ADJ *Bot* albuminous

albumineux, -euse [albyminø, -øz] ADJ *Biol* albuminous

albuminoïde [albyminɔid] *Biol* ADJ albuminoid ▸ NM albuminoid, scleroprotein

albuminurie [albyminyri] NF *Méd* albuminuria

albumose [albymoz] NF *Méd Br* proteose, *Am* albumose

alcade [alkad] NM alcade, alcalde

alcaïque [alkaik] ADJ *Littérature* Alcaic

alcalescence [alkalesɑ̃s] NF *Chim* alkalescence

alcalescent, -e [alkalesɑ̃, -ɑ̃t] ADJ *Chim* alkalescent

alcali [alkali] NM *Chim* alkali; **a. volatil** ammonia

alcalifiant, -e [alkalifjɑ̃, -ɑ̃t] ADJ alcalizing

alcalimètre [alkalimɛtr] NM *Chim* alkalimeter

alcalimétrie [alkalimetri] NF *Chim* alkalimetry

alcalin, -e [alkalɛ̃, -in] ADJ **1** *Chim* alkaline **2** *Méd* **médicament a.** antacid ▸ NM *Chim* alkali

alcalinisation [alkalinizasjɔ̃] NF *Chim* alkalinization

alcaliniser [3] [alkalinize] VT *Chim* to alkalinize

alcalinité [alkalinite] NF *Chim* alkalinity

alcalino-terreux [alkalinɔtɛrø] ADJ M *Chim* **métaux a.** alkaline earth metals

alcaloïde [alkalɔid] NM *Chim* alkaloid

alcalose [alkaloz] NF *Méd* alkalosis

alcane [alkan] NM *Chim* alkane

alcarazas [alkarazas] NM alcarraza

Alcatel Alsthom [alkatɛlalstɔm] NM = large French telecommunications and public transport engineering firm

alcazar [alkazar] NM *Archit* alcazar

alcène [alsɛn] NM *Chim* alkene, olefine

Alceste [alsɛst] NPR = main character in Molière's 'le Misanthrope', who shuns society

alchémille [alkemij] NF *Bot* alchemilla; **a. des champs** parsley-piert; **a. vulgaire** lady's mantle

alchimie [alʃimi] NF alchemy; *Fig* chemistry

alchimique [alʃimik] ADJ alchemical

alchimiste [alʃimist] NM alchemist

Alcibiade [alsibjad] NPR Alcibiades

alcidé [alside] *Orn* NM auk
◻ **alcidés** NMPL Alcidae

alcine [alsin] NM *Chim* alkene, olefine

alcolo [alkɔlo] = **alcoolo**

alcool [alkɔl] NM **1** (*boissons alcoolisées*) l'a. alcohol; **je ne touche pas à l'a.** I never touch alcohol, I don't drink; **l'a. au volant accroît considérablement les risques d'accidents** drink-driving greatly increases the risk of accidents; **boisson sans a.** non-alcoholic drink; **bière sans a.** alcohol-free beer
2 (*spiritueux*) **voulez-vous un petit a.?** would you like a digestif?; **a. de prune** plum brandy; **a. de fruit, a. blanc** = clear spirit made of distilled fruit wine
3 *Chim & Pharm* alcohol, spirit; **a. à 90°** *Br* surgical spirit, *Am* rubbing alcohol; **a. absolu** pure *or* absolute alcohol; **a. à brûler** methylated spirits; **a. camphré** *ou* **de camphre** camphorated alcohol; **a. dénaturé** methylated spirits; **a. déshydraté** pure *or* absolute alcohol; **a. éthylique** ethyl alcohol, ethanol; **a. de menthe** medicinal mint spirit; **a. méthylique** methyl alcohol, methanol; **a. propylique** propanol; **a. pur** raw spirits
◻ **à alcool** ADJ (*réchaud, lampe*) spirit (*avant n*)

alcoolat [alkɔla] NM *Chim & Pharm* medicinal spirit

alcoolature [alkɔlatyr] NF *Pharm* herbal tincture, alcoholature

alcoolé [alkɔle] NM (alcoholic) tincture

alcoolémie [alkɔlemi] NF presence of alcohol in the blood; **taux d'a.** blood alcohol concentration

alcoolification [alkɔlifikasjɔ̃] NF alcoholic fermentation, alcoholization

alcoolique [alkɔlik] ADJ alcoholic ▸ NMF alcoholic; **Alcooliques anonymes** Alcoholics Anonymous

alcoolisable [alkɔlizabl] ADJ that can be alcoholized

alcoolisation [alkɔlizasjɔ̃] NF **1** *Chim* alcoholization **2** *Méd* alcoholism

alcoolisé, -e [alkɔlize] ADJ **1** (*qui contient de l'alcool*) **boissons alcoolisées** alcoholic drinks *or* beverages, *Sout* intoxicating liquors; **non a.** non-alcoholic; **bière peu alcoolisée** low-alcohol beer **2** *Fam* (*personne*) drunk

alcooliser [3] [alkɔlize] VT **1** (*convertir en alcool*) to alcoholize, to convert to alcohol **2** (*additionner d'alcool*) to add alcohol to
▸ **s'alcooliser** VPR *Fam* (*s'enivrer*) to get drunk ■; (*être alcoolique*) to drink

alcoolisme [alkɔlism] NM *Méd* alcoholism

alcoolo [alkɔlo] NMF *Fam* alkie

alcoologie [alkɔlɔʒi] NF medical study of alcoholism

alcoologue [alkɔlɔg] NMF = specialist in the treatment of alcoholism

alcoolomanie [alkɔlɔmani] NF alcoholomania

alcoomètre [alkɔmɛtr] NM alcoholometer

alcoométrie [alkɔmetri] NF alcoholometry

alcopop [alkɔpɔp] NM alcopop

Alcotest®, Alcootest® [alkɔtɛst] NM **1** (*appareil*) breathalyser **2** (*vérification*) breath test; **subir un A.** to take a breath test; **soumettre qn à un A.** to give sb a breath test, to breath-test *or* to breathalyse sb

alcôve [alkov] NF *Archit* alcove, recess
◻ **d'alcôve** ADJ (*secret, histoire*) intimate

alcoylation [alkɔilasjɔ̃] NF *Chim* alkylation

alcoyle [alkɔil] NM *Chim* alkyl

alcyne [alsin] NM *Chim* alkyne

alcyon [alsjɔ̃] NM **1** *Myth* halcyon **2** *Ich* kingfisher, halcyon

alcyonaire [alsjɔnɛr] *Ich* NM alcyonarian
◻ **alcyonaires** NMPL Alcyonaria

aldéhyde [aldeid] NM *Chim* aldehyde; **a. formique** formaldehyde

aldéhydique [aldeidik] ADJ *Chim* aldehydic

al dente [aldɛnte] *Culin* ADJ INV al dente ▸ ADV al dente

aldin, -e [aldɛ̃, -in] ADJ *Typ* (*édition, caractère*) Aldine

aldol [aldɔl] NM *Chim* aldol

aldose [aldoz] NM *Chim* aldose

aldostérone [aldosteron] NF *Anat* aldosterone

ALE [aɛlø] NF *Com* (*abrév* **Association de libre-échange**) FTA

ale [ɛl] NF (*alcool*) ale

aléa [alea] NM unforeseen turn of events; **tenir compte des aléas** to take the unforeseen *or* unexpected into account; **les aléas de l'existence** the ups and downs of life; **ça fait partie des aléas du métier** (*risque*) it's one of the risks you have to take in this job; (*désagrément*) it's one of the disadvantages of the job

aléatoire [aleatwar] ADJ **1** (*entreprise, démarche*) risky, hazardous, chancy; **c'est a.** it's uncertain, there's nothing definite about it **2** *Jur* (*contrat*) aleatory **3** *Fin* **gain a.** chance *or* contingent gain; **marché/spéculation a.** risky market/speculation; **profit a.** contingent profit **4** *Mktg* (*sondage, échantillonnage*) random **5** *Math* random **6** *Mus* aleatory

aléatoirement [aleatwarmɑ̃] ADV **1** (*par hasard*) by chance, at random **2** (*de façon risquée*) riskily, in a risky *or* chancy manner

alémanique [alemanik] ADJ & NMF *Géog & Ling* Alemannic

ALENA [alena] NM *Com* (*abrév* **Accord de libre-échange nord-américain**) NAFTA

alène [alɛn] NF *Tech* awl

alénois [alenwa] ADJ M *Bot* **cresson a.** garden *or* golden cress

alentour [alɑ̃tur] ADV **dans la campagne a.** in the surrounding countryside; **les églises a.** the churches in the neighbourhood; **tout a.** all around
◻ **alentours** NMPL neighbourhood, vicinity, (surrounding) area; **les alentours de la ville** the area around the city; **les espaces verts des alentours de Londres** London's green belt; **surveille les alentours** (*d'un bâtiment*) keep an eye on the neighbourhood; **il doit être dans les alentours** (*tout près*) he's somewhere around (here); **il n'y avait personne aux alentours** there was no one around *or* in the vicinity; **aux alentours de** (*dans l'espace, le temps*) around; **aux alentours de Paris** near Paris; **aux alentours de 1815** around 1815; **aux alentours de minuit** round (about) *or* some time around midnight; **aux alentours de 50 m** around 50 m; **aux alentours de 500 euros** around 500 euros

aléoute [aleut], **aléoutien, -enne** [aleusjɛ̃, -ɛn] ADJ Aleutian; **les îles aléoutiennes** the Aleutian Islands
◻ **Aléoutien, -enne** NM,F Aleut, Aleutian

Aléoutiennes [aleusjɛn] NFPL **les A.** the Aleutian Islands

Alep [alɛp] NF *Géog* Aleppo

aleph [alɛf] NM INV aleph

alépine [alepin] NF *Tex* alepine

alérion [alerjɔ̃] NM *Hér* alerion, allerion

alerte[1] [alɛrt] ADJ (*démarche*) quick, alert; (*esprit*) lively, alert; (*style*) lively, brisk; (*personne*) spry

alerte[2] [alɛrt] NF **1** (*signal*) alarm; **donner l'a.** to give the alert; **a.!** (*aux armes*) to arms!; (*attention*) watch out! **fausse a.** false alarm; **a. aérienne** air raid *or* air strike warning; **a. à la bombe** bomb scare; **a. rouge** red alert; **fin d'a.** all clear
2 (*signe avant-coureur*) alarm, warning sign; **à la première a.** at the first warning; **je ne suis pas surpris de son hospitalisation, elle avait déjà eu une a. le mois dernier** I'm not surprised she's in hospital, she had a warning sign last month; **l'a. a été chaude** that was a close call
◻ **d'alerte** ADJ warning (*avant n*), alarm (*avant n*)
◻ **en alerte, en état d'alerte** ADV on the alert; **être en état d'a.** to be in a state of alert; **toutes les casernes de pompiers étaient en état d'a.** the entire fire service was on standby *or* the alert

alertement [alɛrtəmɑ̃] ADV alertly, briskly, in a lively manner

alerter [3] [alɛrte] VT **1** (*alarmer*) to alert; **un bruit insolite l'avait alerté** he'd been alerted by an unusual sound **2** (*informer → autorités*) to notify, to inform; (→ *presse*) to alert; **nous avons été alertés par les résidents eux-mêmes** the local residents themselves drew our attention to the problem; **a. qn de** to alert sb to; **a. qn des dangers de l'alcool** to alert *or* to awaken sb to the dangers of alcohol

alésage [aleza3] NM *Tech* **1** *(technique)* reaming, boring (out) **2** *(diamètre d'un cylindre, du canon d'un fusil)* bore

alésé, -e [aleze] ADJ *Hér (tête, membre d'animal)* couped, coupé; *(fasce, barre, burelle)* humetty

alèse [alɛz] = **alaise**

aléser [18] [aleze] VT *Tech* to ream, to bore

aléseur [alezœr] NM *Mines* (drill) reamer

aléseuse [alezøz] NF boring *or* reaming machine; **a. fraiseuse** milling machine

Alésia [alezja] NF *Géog* Alesia

> ### Culture
> ### ALÉSIA
> This is the site in the Côte-d'Or where, in 52 BC, Vercingetorix, leader of the coalition of the Gauls against Rome, was besieged by Julius Caesar. His surrender marked the end of Gaulish resistance to Rome.

alésoir [alezwar] NM *Tech* reamer

aléthique [aletik] ADJ *Phil* alethic

aleurite [alørit] NF *Bot* spurge

aleurode [alørɔd] NM *Entom* aleurodes, mealy-wings

aleurone [alørɔn] NF *Biol & Bot* aleurone, aleuron

alevin [alvɛ̃] NM *Ich* alevin, young fish

alevinage [alvina3] NM *Pêche* **1** *(pisciculture)* fish farming **2** *(repeuplement)* stocking with young fish

aleviner [3] [alvine] VT *Pêche* to stock (with young fish)

alevinier [alvinje] NM *Pêche* breeding-pond

alevinière [alvinjɛr] NF *Pêche* breeding-pond

alexandra [aleksɑ̃dra] NM *(cocktail)* brandy alexander

Alexandre [alɛksɑ̃dr] NPR **A. le Grand** Alexander the Great

Alexandrie [alɛksɑ̃dri] NF *Géog* Alexandria

alexandrin, -e [alɛksɑ̃drɛ̃, -in] ADJ **1** *Hist* Alexandrian **2** *Littérature* Alexandrine
◦ NM *Littérature* Alexandrine
□ **Alexandrin, -e** NM,F Alexandrian

> ### Culture
> ### ALEXANDRIN
> First favoured as the "vers héroïque" by sixteenth-century poets like Ronsard, the Alexandrine became the pre-eminent verse form of seventeenth-century classical French literature: it reached its highest development in the writings of Boileau, and in the classical tragedies of Corneille and Racine, who regarded it as being the form best suited to express the idea of "grandeur". The Alexandrine (based on a syllable count like all other French verse) consists of a line of twelve syllables with a medial caesura after the sixth syllable.

alexandrite [aleksɑ̃drit] NF *Minér* alexandrite

alexie [alɛksi] NF *Méd* acquired dyslexia, alexia

alexine [alɛksin] NF *Biol & Méd* alexin

alexithymie [alɛksitimi] NF *Psy* alexithymia

alezan, -e [alzɑ̃, -an] ADJ *(cheval)* chestnut; **a. clair** sorrel
◦ NM,F *(cheval)* chestnut; **a. clair** sorrel

alézé, -e [aleze] = **alésé**

alfa [alfa] NM **1** *Bot* esparto (grass) **2** *(papier)* esparto paper

alfange [alfɑ̃3] NF *Arch* Moorish scimitar

alfatier, -ère [alfatje, -ɛr] ADJ *Bot* esparto

alfénide [alfenid] NM = type of German silver alloy

Alfred [alfrɛd] NPR **A. le Grand** Alfred the Great

algarade [algarad] NF quarrel

Algarve [algarv] NF **l'A.** the Algarve

algazelle [algazɛl] NF *Zool* algazel

algèbre [alʒɛbr] NF *Math* algebra; *Fam* **pour moi, c'est de l'a.** it's all Greek to me, I can't make head nor tail of it

algébrique [alʒebrik] ADJ *Math* algebraic, algebraical

algébriquement [alʒebrikmɑ̃] ADV *Math* algebraically

algébriste [alʒebrist] NM,F *Math* algebraist

Algeco® [alʒeko] NM Portakabin®

Alger [alʒe] NM *Géog* Algiers

Algérie [alʒeri] NF **l'A.** Algeria; **vivre en A.** to live in Algeria; **aller en A.** to go to Algeria; *Hist* **la**

---

guerre d'A. the Algerian War; *Hist* **l'A. française** French Algeria

> ### Culture
> ### LA GUERRE D'ALGÉRIE
> This was the most bitter of France's post-colonial struggles, and lasted from 1954 to 1962. In a country dominated by a million white settlers, the **pieds noirs** (see box at this entry), the French government's attempts to crush the revolt of the "Front de libération nationale" (**FLN**) (see entry), and to put an end to their struggle for independence with massive military intervention, came to nothing. The return to power of General de Gaulle in 1958, and the Accords d'Évian in 1962, led to Algerian independence and the resettlement of the "pieds noirs" in France.

algérien, -enne [alʒerjɛ̃, -ɛn] ADJ Algerian
□ **Algérien, -enne** NM,F Algerian

algérois, -e [alʒerwa, -az] ADJ of/from Algiers
□ **Algérois, -e** NM,F = inhabitant of or person from Algiers

Algésiras [alʒeziras] NM *Géog* Algeciras

algide [alʒid] ADJ *Méd* algid

algidité [alʒidite] NF *Méd* algidity

algie [alʒi] NF *Méd* ache, pain

alginate [alʒinat] NM *Chim* alginate

algine [alʒin] NF *Chim* algin

alginique [alʒinik] ADJ *Chim* alginic; **acide a.** alginic acid

algique [alʒik] ADJ *Méd* pain-producing, *Spéc* algesic

algoculture [algokyltyr] NF *Agr* seaweed farming, *Spéc* algoculture

algol [algɔl] NM *Ordinat* ALGOL

algologie [algoloʒi] NF *Bot* algology

algonkien, -enne [algɔ̃kjɛ̃, -ɛn] *Géol* ADJ Algonkian
□ **Algonkien, -enne** NM,F Algonkian

algonkin, -e [algɔ̃kɛ̃, -in] ADJ Algonquin, Algonkian
◦ NM *Ling* Algonquin, Algonkian
□ **Algonkin, -e** NM,F Algonquin, Algonkian; **les Algonkins** the Algonquin

algonquien, -enne [algɔ̃kjɛ̃, -ɛn] ADJ Algonquian
◦ NM *Ling* Algonquian
□ **Algonquien, -enne** NM,F Algonquian; **les Algonquiens** the Algonquians

algonquin, -e [algɔ̃kɛ̃, -in] = **algonkin**

algorithme [algɔritm] NM *Math* algorithm

algorithmique [algɔritmik] ADJ *Math* algorithmic

algothérapie [algoterapi] NF *Méd* algotherapy

alguazil [algwazil] NM *Hist* alguazil, alguacil

algue [alg] NF *Bot* (piece of) seaweed, *Spéc* alga
□ **algues** NFPL seaweed *(UNCOUNT)*, *Spéc* algae; **algues bleues** blue-green algae

Alhambra [alɑ̃bra] NF **l'A.** the Alhambra

alias [aljas] NM *Ordinat (de courrier électronique, de bureau)* alias
◦ ADV alias, aka; **Frédo, a. le Tueur** Frédo, aka the Killer

aliassage [aljasa3] NM *Ordinat* aliasing

Ali Baba [alibaba] NPR **A. et les quarante voleurs** Ali Baba and the Forty Thieves

alibi [alibi] NM **1** *Jur* alibi; **un a. en or** a cast-iron alibi **2** *(prétexte)* alibi, excuse

aliboufier [alibufje] NM *Bot* styrax, storax

alicament [alikamɑ̃] NM nutraceutical, dietary supplement

alicante [alikɑ̃t] NM *(vin)* Alicante wine

Alice [alis] NPR Alice

□ **'Alice au pays des merveilles'** *Carroll* 'Alice in Wonderland'

'Alice dans les villes' *Wenders* 'Alice in the Cities'

alicylique [alisilik] ADJ *Chim* alicyclic

alidade [alidad] NF *Tech* alidad

aliénabilité [aljenabilite] NF *Jur* alienability

aliénable [aljenabl] ADJ *Jur* alienable

aliénant, -e [aljenɑ̃, -ɑ̃t] ADJ *Jur* alienating

aliénataire [aljenatɛr] NM,F *Jur* alienee

aliénateur, -trice [aljenatœr, -tris] NM,F *Jur* alienator

---

aliénation [aljenasjɔ̃] NF **1** *Phil & Pol* alienation **2** *Psy* **a. (mentale)** insanity, mental illness **3** *(perte → d'un droit, d'un bien)* loss, removal **4** *Jur* alienation, transfer of property; **a. de biens** disposal of property

aliénatrice [aljenatris] *voir* **aliénateur**

aliéné, -e [aljene] ADJ **1** *Phil & Pol* alienated **2** *Psy* insane, mentally disturbed
◦ NM,F *Psy* insane person, mentally disturbed person

aliéner [18] [aljene] VT **1** *(abandonner → indépendance, liberté, droit)* to give up; *Jur* to alienate
2 *(supprimer → droit, liberté, indépendance)* to remove, to confiscate
3 *(faire perdre)* **ce commentaire vous a aliéné la sympathie de l'auditoire** that comment lost you the audience's sympathy
4 *Phil & Pol* to alienate; **les dirigeants ont aliéné la base** the leadership has alienated the rank and file
▸**s'aliéner** VPR **s'a. qn** to alienate sb; **elle s'est aliéné la presse** she has alienated the press; **je me suis aliéné leur amitié** I caused them to turn away *or* to become estranged from me

aliéniste [aljenist] *Vieilli Psy* ADJ psychiatric
◦ NMF psychiatrist

Aliénor [aljenɔr] NPR **A. d'Aquitaine** Eleanor of Aquitaine

alifère [alifɛr] ADJ *Entom* aliferous

aliforme [alifɔrm] ADJ *Zool* aliform

aligné, -e [aliɲe] ADJ aligned, in alignment

alignement [aliɲmɑ̃] NM **1** *(rangée)* line, row; **d'interminables alignements d'arbres** line upon line of trees; **être à** *ou* **dans l'a.** to be *or* to stand in line; **ne pas être à** *ou* **dans l'a.** to be out of line; **mettre qch à** *ou* **dans l'a. de** to bring sth into line *or* alignment with; **se mettre à** *ou* **dans l'a.** to fall into line; **perdre l'a.** to get out of line *or* alignment
2 *Fig (gén)* aligning, bringing into alignment; *Com (des prix)* alignment (**sur** with); *(d'une monnaie, d'une économie)* alignment; **l'a. des salaires sur le coût de la vie** bringing salaries into line with the cost of living; **leur a. sur la politique des socialistes** their coming into line with the socialists' policy; **a. monétaire** monetary alignment *or* adjustment
3 *Jur* building line
4 *Compta (d'un compte)* making up, balancing
5 *Ordinat* alignment
□ **alignements** NMPL *(de menhirs)* standing stones *(arranged in a row)*, alignments

aligner [3] [aliɲe] VT **1** *(mettre en rang)* to line up, to align; **a. des dominos** to line up dominoes (end to end)
2 *Mil (soldats, tanks)* to line up, to form into lines; *(divisions)* to line up
3 *(présenter → preuves)* to produce one by one; *(→ en écrivant)* to string together; *(→ en récitant)* to string together, to reel off; **je passe ma journée à a. des chiffres** I spend my day producing lists of figures
4 *(mettre en conformité)* **a. qch sur** to line sth up with, to bring sth into line with; **chaque membre doit a. sa politique sur celle de la Communauté** each member state must bring its policies into line with those of the Community
5 *Ordinat* to align
6 *Compta (compte)* to make up, to balance
7 *Écon (prix)* to align, to bring into line (**sur** with)
8 *Écon (monnaie, économie)* to align
9 *Fam (réprimander)* **a. qn** to tell sb off; **il s'est fait a. par un flic en moto** a motorcycle cop slapped a fine on him
10 *très Fam (locution)* **les a.** *(payer)* to cough up, to fork out
▸**s'aligner** VPR **1** *(foule, élèves)* to line up, to form a line; *(soldats)* to fall into line
2 *très Fam (locutions)* **il peut toujours s'a.!** he's got no chance (of getting anywhere)!; **elle s'entraîne tous les jours, alors tu peux toujours t'a.!** she trains every day, so you don't stand a chance!
3 **s'a. sur** *(imiter → nation, gouvernement)* to fall into line *or* to align oneself with; **la Corée du Sud sera obligée de s'a. sur les prises de position nipponnes** South Korea will be forced to fall into line with the Japanese position

aligot [aligo] NM *Culin* = mashed potatoes blended with garlic and soft cheese, a speciality of the Auvergne region

aligoté [aligɔte] NM *(vin)* aligoté (wine)

aliment [alimã] NM 1 *(nourriture)* (type *or* kind of) food; *(portion)* (piece of) food; **citez trois aliments** list three types of food *or* three different foods; **l'eau n'est pas un a.** water is not (a) food *or* has no food value; **le chien salive si l'on met devant lui un a.** the dog salivates if you put food in front of him; **des aliments** food *(UNCOUNT)*, foodstuffs; **la plupart des aliments** most food *or* foodstuffs; **aliments pour bébé/chien** baby/dog food; **aliments congelés/diététiques** frozen/health food; **a. énergétique** energy-giving food; **aliments préparés** processed food

2 *Fig Littéraire* **l'a. de** *ou* **un a. pour l'esprit** food for thought

3 *(dans les assurances)* interest, risk

◻ **aliments** NMPL *Jur Br* maintenance *(UNCOUNT)*, *Am* alimony *(UNCOUNT)*

alimentaire [alimãtɛr] ADJ 1 *Com & Méd* food *(avant n)*; **sac/papier a.** bag/paper for wrapping food; **mauvaises habitudes alimentaires** bad eating habits

2 *(pour gagner de l'argent)* **œuvre a.** potboiler; **écrire un livre/tourner un film a.** to write/to shoot a potboiler; **je fais des enquêtes, mais c'est purement a.** I do surveys, but it's just to make ends meet

3 *(de la digestion)* alimentary

4 *Tech* feeding *(avant n)*, feeder *(avant n)*

5 *Jur (obligation)* maintenance *(avant n)*

alimentation [alimãtasjɔ̃] NF 1 *(fait de manger)* (consumption of) food; *(fait de faire manger)* feeding; **combien dépensez-vous pour l'a.?** how much do you spend on food?; *Méd* **a. par perfusion** drip-feeding

2 *(régime)* diet; **une a. carnée** a meat-based diet; **une a. saine** a healthy diet; **un insecte dont l'a. est à base de nectar** an insect that feeds on nectar

3 *Com (magasin) Br* grocer's (shop), *Am* grocery store; *(rayon)* groceries; **au fond à droite, après l'a.** on the right at the bottom, past the grocery shelves *or* groceries

4 *(activité)* **l'a.** food distribution, the food (distribution) trade

5 *Ordinat* **a. papier** paper feed; **a. feuille à feuille, a. page par page** cut sheet feed, single sheet feed

6 *(approvisionnement)* feed, supply; **assurer l'a. d'une pompe en électricité** to supply electricity to a pump; **l'a. d'une ville en eau** the water supply to a town

7 *Mil (d'une armée)* arms supply

alimenter [3] [alimãte] VT 1 *(nourrir → malade, bébé)* to feed

2 *(rivière, lac)* to flow into; *Tech (moteur, pompe)* to feed, to supply; *(ville)* to supply; **a. qn en eau** to supply sb with water; **a. un ordinateur en données** to feed data into a computer; *(dans l'imprimerie)* **alimenté par bobine** web-fed

3 *(approvisionner → compte)* to pay money into; **a. les caisses de l'État** to be a source of revenue *or* cash for the Government

4 *(entretenir → conversation)* to sustain; *(→ curiosité, intérêt)* to feed, to sustain; *(→ doute, désaccord)* to fuel

▶**s'alimenter** VPR 1 *(emploi réfléchi) (gén)* to eat; *(→ bébé)* to feed oneself; **elle ne s'alimente plus depuis une semaine** she hasn't had any solid food for a week; **s'a. bien/mal** to have a good/poor diet; **il a l'âge de s'a. tout seul** he's old enough to feed himself

2 **s'a. en** *(se procurer)* to be supplied with; **comment le village s'alimente-t-il en eau?** how does the village get its water?

alinéa [alinea] NM *(espace)* indent; *(paragraphe)* paragraph; **faire un a.** to indent

alios [aljɔs] NM *Géol* iron pan

aliphatique [alifatik] ADJ *Chim* aliphatic

aliquante [alikãt] ADJ F *Math* **partie a.** aliquant part

aliquote [alikɔt] *Arch Math* ADJ aliquot; **partie a.** aliquot part

NF aliquot

alise [aliz] NF *Bot* sorb-apple

alisier [alizje] NM *Bot* service tree; **a. blanc** white-beam

alisma [alisma] = **alisme**

alismacée [alismase] *Bot* NF water plantain, *Spéc* member of the Alismaceae family

◻ **alismacées** NFPL Alismaceae

alismatacée [alismatase] *Bot* NF water plantain, *Spéc* member of the Alismataceae family

◻ **alismatacées** NFPL Alismataceae

alisme [alism] NM *Bot* alisma, water plantain

alitement [alitmã] NM confinement *(to one's bed)*

aliter [3] [alite] VT to confine to bed

▶**s'aliter** VPR to take to one's bed; **rester alité** to be confined to one's bed, to be bedridden

alizarine [alizarin] NF alizarin, alizarine

alize [aliz] = **alise**

alizé [alize] ADJ M *(vent)* trade *(avant n)*

NM trade wind

alizier [alizje] = **alisier**

alkékenge [alkekãʒ] NM *Bot* strawberry tomato, physalis

alkermès [alkɛrmɛs] NM *(liqueur)* alkermes

al-Khalil [alkalil] NF *Géog* El Khalil

alkylation [alkilasjɔ̃] = **alcoylation**

alkyle [alkil] = **alcoyle**

allache [alaʃ] NF *Ich* sardinella

Allah [ala] NPR Allah

allaitement [alɛtmã] NM *(processus)* feeding, *Br* suckling, *Am* nursing; *(période)* breast-feeding period; **a. au biberon** *ou* **artificiel** bottle-feeding; **a. maternel** *ou* **au sein** breast-feeding; **a. mixte** mixed feeding

allaiter [4] [alete] VT *(enfant)* to breast-feed; *(sujet: animal)* to suckle; **à quelle heure est-ce que tu l'allaites?** what time do you feed him/her?

allant, -e [alã, -ãt] ADJ *Littéraire* lively, active

NM energy, drive; **être plein d'a.** to have plenty of drive

allantoïde [alãtɔid] NF *Anat* allantois

allantoïdien, -enne [alãtɔidjɛ̃, -ɛn] ADJ *Anat* allantoid, allantoic

allantoïne [alãtɔin] NF *Physiol* allantoin

alléchant, -e [aleʃã, -ãt] ADJ 1 *(plat, odeur)* mouthwatering, appetizing 2 *(proposition, projet, offre)* enticing, tempting

allécher [18] [aleʃe] VT 1 *(sujet: odeur, plat)* **a. qn** to give sb an appetite; **l'odeur du pain chaud allèche les enfants** the smell of hot bread makes the children's mouths water 2 *(sujet: offre, proposition, projet → gén)* to tempt, to seduce, to entice; *(→ dans le but de tromper)* to lure

allée [ale] NF 1 *(à la campagne)* footpath, lane; *(dans un jardin)* alley; *(dans un parc)* walk, path; *(en ville)* avenue; *(devant une maison, une villa)* drive, driveway; *(dans un cinéma, un train, un magasin)* aisle; **les allées du pouvoir** the corridors of power

2 *Archéol* **a. couverte** = series of dolmens, arranged to form a covered walkway

3 *Golf* fairway

◻ **allées et venues** NFPL comings and goings; **toutes ces allées et venues pour rien** all this running around *or* about for nothing; **des allées et venues de la cave au grenier** endless trips from attic to cellar; **nous faisons des allées et venues entre Québec et Toronto** we go *or* we shuttle back and forth between Quebec and Toronto

allégation [alegasjɔ̃] NF allegation, (unsubstantiated) claim

allégé, -e [aleʒe] ADJ *Culin (yaourt, chips)* low-fat; *(confiture)* low-sugar; **vinaigrette allégée** low-calorie *or* low-fat vinaigrette

allège [alɛʒ] NF 1 *Constr (d'une fenêtre)* basement; *(mur)* dwarf wall 2 *Naut* barge, lighter

allégeance [aleʒãs] NF 1 *Hist* allegiance; **a. politique** political allegiance 2 *Naut* handicap

allégement, allègement [alɛʒmã] NM 1 *(diminution → d'un fardeau)* lightening; *(→ d'une douleur)* relief, alleviation, soothing

2 *Écon (d'impôts, de charges, de dépenses)* reduction; **ils sont en faveur de l'a. des charges sociales pour les entreprises** they are in favour of reducing employers' national insurance contributions; **a. fiscal** tax relief

3 *Scol* **a. de l'effectif** reduction in class size; **a. des programmes** streamlining of the curriculum

4 *Sport (des skis)* lifting (the weight off the skis)

alléger [22] [aleʒe] VT 1 *(rendre moins lourd → malle, meuble)* to make lighter, to lighten; **il va falloir a. le paquet de 10 grammes** we'll have to take 10 grams off the parcel; **pour a. votre silhouette** to make your body look trimmer

2 *Écon (impôts, charges, dépenses)* to reduce; **a. les impôts de 10 pour cent** to reduce tax by 10 percent, to take 10 percent off tax

3 *(soulager → douleur)* to relieve, to soothe; **je me suis senti allégé d'un grand poids** *ou* **fardeau** I felt (that) a great weight had been taken off my shoulders

4 *(faciliter → procédure, texte)* to simplify, to trim (down); **les formalités ont été allégées** some of the red tape was done away with

5 *Scol* **a. le programme** to trim the curriculum

Alleghany, Allegheny [alegani] NM *Géog* 1 **l'A.** the Allegheny (river) 2 **les monts A.** the Allegheny Mountains, the Alleghenies

allégorie [alegɔri] NF *Littérature* allegory

allégorique [alegɔrik] ADJ *Littérature* allegorical

allégoriquement [alegɔrikmã] ADV *Littérature* allegorically

allègre [alɛgr] ADJ cheerful, light-hearted; **d'un ton a.** cheerfully, light-heartedly; **marcher d'un pas a.** to walk with a light step

allègrement, allégrement [alɛgrəmã] ADV 1 *(joyeusement)* cheerfully, light-heartedly 2 *Hum (carrément)* heedlessly, blithely; **il s'est a. moqué de nous** he has been blithely making fools of us

allégresse [alegrɛs] NF cheerfulness, liveliness; **des cris d'a.** cries of joy; *Littéraire* **le cœur plein d'a.** with a light heart, light-heartedly; **accueillir qn avec a.** to give sb a cheerful welcome; **a. générale** general rejoicing

allegretto [alegreto] ADV *Mus (tempo)* allegretto

allégretto [alegreto] NM *Mus (morceau de musique)* allegretto

allegro [alegro] ADV *Mus (tempo)* allegro

allégro [alegro] NM *Mus (morceau de musique)* allegro

alléguer [18] [alege] VT 1 *(prétexter)* to argue; **a. comme excuse/prétexte que** to put forward as an excuse/a pretext that; **il allégua que personne ne l'avait informé de ce projet** he alleged that no one had informed him of the plan; **alléguant du fait que** arguing that; **a. l'ignorance** to plead ignorance, to argue that one didn't know 2 *(citer)* to cite, to quote; **a. un texte de loi** to quote a legal text

allèle [alɛl] NM *Biol* allele, allel, allelomorph

allélomorphe [alelɔmɔrf] ADJ *Biol* allelomorphic

alléluia [aleluja] NM *Rel* alleluia, hallelujah

Allemagne [alman] NF **l'A.** Germany; **vivre en A.** to live in Germany; **aller en A.** to go to Germany; *Anciennement* **l'A. de l'Est/de l'Ouest** East/West Germany

allemand, -e [almã, -ãd] ADJ German

NM *(langue)* German

◻ **Allemand, -e** NM,F German; *Anciennement* **A. de l'Est/de l'Ouest** East/West German

◻ **allemande** NF *(danse, musique)* allemande

allène [alɛn] NM *Chim* allene

aller[1] [ale] NM 1 *(voyage)* outward journey; **je suis passé les voir à l'a.** I dropped in to see them on the way (there); **à l'a., nous sommes passés par Anchorage** on the flight out, we went via Anchorage; **l'avion était en retard à l'a. et au retour** the flight was delayed both ways; **un a. (et) retour** a round trip; **l'a. est plus long que le retour** *(gén)* the outward journey is longer than the return journey; *(en avion)* flying out takes longer than flying back; **faire des allers et retours** *(personne, document)* to go back and forth, to shuttle back and forth; **je fais plusieurs allers et retours par jour entre l'hôpital et la maison** I go back and forth between the hospital and home several times a day; **je vais à la banque, mais je ne fais qu'un a. et retour** I'm going to the bank, but I'll be right back

2 *(billet)* **a. (simple)** *Br* single (ticket), *Am* one-way ticket; **viens donc nous voir, je t'offre l'a.** come and see us, I'll pay half the price of the trip; **a. (et) retour** *Br* return *or* *Am* round-trip (ticket); **deux allers et retours pour Paris** *Br* two returns *or* *Am* round-trip tickets to Paris;

c'est combien l'a. retour? how much is the *Br* return *or Am* round-trip (ticket)?

3 *Fam* **a. et retour** *(gifle)* slap■

4 *Bourse* **a. et retour** bed and breakfasting

ALLER² [31] [ale]

> **V AUX** to be going to **1** ■ to go **2**
> **VI** to go **A1–7, B1–3** ■ to be **D** ■ to be right **E3** ■ to fit **A6, E1** ■ to run **A5**
> **VPR** *(s'en aller)* to go **1** ■ to come undone **2** ■ to die **3** ■ to come off **4** ■ to fade **4**

V AUX 1 *(suivi de l'infinitif) (exprime le futur proche)* to be going *or* about to; **tu vas tomber!** you're going to fall!, you'll fall!; **attendez-le, il va arriver** wait for him, he'll be here any minute now; **attends, tu vas comprendre!** wait, all will become clear *or* will be revealed!; **j'allais justement te téléphoner** I was just going to phone you, I was on the point of phoning you; **fais vite, la pièce va commencer** be quick, the play is about *or* is going to start; **il va être cinq heures** it's going on five; **il va pleuvoir, on dirait** it looks like rain *or* as if it's going to rain; **est-ce que ça va durer longtemps?** is it going to be long?; **tu vas faire ce que je te dis, oui ou non?** will you do as I say or won't you?

2 *(suivi de l'infinitif) (en intensif)* to go; **pourquoi es-tu allé tout lui raconter?** why did you go and tell him/her everything?; *Ironique* **je voudrais apprendre à skier – c'est ça, va te casser une jambe!** I'd like to learn how to ski – that's right, go and break your leg!; **pour a. me faire tuer?** why should I go and get killed?; **ne va pas croire/penser que...** don't go and believe/think that...; **tu ne vas pas me faire croire que tu ne savais rien!** you can't fool me into thinking that you didn't know anything!; **pourvu qu'elle n'aille pas se trouver mal!** let's hope she doesn't go and faint!; **qu'est-ce que tu vas t'imaginer!** you know me/him/her/*etc* better than that!; **que n'iront-ils pas s'imaginer!** God knows what they'll think!; **où est-elle? – allez savoir!** where is she? – God knows!; **allez expliquer ça à un enfant de cinq ans!** try and explain *or* try explaining that to a five-year-old!

3 *(exprime la continuité)* **a. en s'améliorant** to get better and better, to improve; **a. en empirant** to get worse and worse, to worsen; **a. en augmentant** to keep increasing; **le bruit allait en diminuant** the noise was getting fainter and fainter; **a. croissant** *(tension)* to be rising; *(nombre)* to be rising *or* increasing

VI A. *EXPRIME LE MOUVEMENT* **1** *(se déplacer)* to go; **qui va là?** who goes there?; *Vieilli* **tu sais a. à cheval?** can you ride a horse?; **va vite!** hurry up!; *(à un enfant)* run along (now)!; **a. à grands pas** to stride along; **vous alliez à plus de 90 km/h** *(en voiture)* you were driving at *or* doing more than 90 km/h; **va moins vite!** drive more slowly!, slow down!; **a. çà et là** to flit about; **a. (et) venir** *(de long en large)* to pace up and down; *(entre deux destinations)* to come and go, to go to and fro; **je vais et viens entre la France et la Suisse** I go *or* I shuttle back and forth between France and Switzerland; **je n'ai fait qu'a. et venir toute la matinée** I was in and out all morning; **il allait et venait dans la pièce** he was pacing up and down the room

2 *(se rendre* → *personne)* **a. à** to go to; **en allant à Limoges** on the way to Limoges; **a. à la mer/à la montagne** to go to the seaside/mountains; **il n'ira pas aux jeux Olympiques** he won't go to the Olympic Games; **son film ira au festival de Cannes** his/her film will go to *or* be shown at the Cannes festival; **a. à l'université** *(bâtiment)* to go to the university; *(institution)* to go to university *or* college; **a. à l'école** *(bâtiment)* to go to the school; *(institution)* to go to school; **a. à l'église** *(bâtiment)* to go to the church; *(institution)* to go to church, to be a churchgoer; **les gens qui vont à l'église/au concert** *(gén)* the people who go to church/to the concert; *(habitués)* churchgoers/concertgoers; **a. à la messe** to go to *or* to attend mass; *(être pratiquant)* to be a churchgoer; **a. à la chasse/pêche** to go hunting/fishing; **a. aux champignons** to go mushroom-picking; **a. aux escargots** to go snail-collecting; **où vas-tu?** where are you going?; **comment y va-t-on?** how do you get there?; **il y est allé en courant** he ran there; **on y va!** let's go!; **je n'irai pas** I won't go; **j'irai en avion/voiture** I'll fly/drive, I'll go by plane/car; **j'irai à** *ou* **en vélo** I'll go (there) by bike, I'll cycle (there); **a. chez un ami** to go to see a friend, to go to a friend's; **a. chez le dentiste** to go to the dentist's; **tu n'iras plus chez eux, tu m'entends?** you will not visit them again, do you hear me?; **je vais toujours chez Burthot pour mes chocolats** I always go to Burthot for my chocolates *or* buy my chocolates from Burthot; **il a peur d'a. dans l'eau** he's afraid to go into the water; **je vais dans les Pyrénées** I'm going to the Pyrenees; **a. en Autriche** to go *or* to travel to Austria; **a. en Avignon/Arles** to go to Avignon/to Arles; **a. en haut/bas** to go up/down; **j'allais vers le nord** I was heading *or* going north

3 *(suivi de l'infinitif) (pour se livrer à une activité)* **a. faire qch** to go and do sth, *Am* to go do sth; **je vais faire mes courses tous les matins** I go shopping every morning; **va ramasser les poires dans le jardin** go and pick the pears in the garden; *très Fam* **va voir là-bas si j'y suis!** push off!, clear off!; *très Fam* **va te faire voir!**, *Vulg* **va te faire foutre!** go to hell!, get lost *or Br* stuffed!

4 *(mener* → *véhicule, chemin)* to go; **ce train ne va pas à Pau** this train doesn't go to Pau; **cette route ne va pas à Bruges** this road doesn't go to Bruges; **cette rue va vers le centre** this street leads towards the city centre; **a. droit au cœur de qn** to go straight to sb's heart; **il choisit des mots qui vont droit au cœur** he uses words which speak to the heart

5 *(fonctionner* → *machine)* to go, to run; *(*→ *moteur)* to run; *(*→ *voiture, train)* to go; **le manège allait de plus en plus vite** the roundabout was going faster and faster; **son pouls va trop vite** his/her pulse (rate) is too fast

6 *(se ranger* → *dans un contenant)* to go, to belong; *(*→ *dans un ensemble)* to fit; **où vont les tasses?** where do the cups go?; **les poupées russes vont l'une dans l'autre** Russian dolls fit one inside the other; **ton morceau de puzzle ne va pas ici** your piece of jigsaw doesn't fit *or* belong here

7 *(être remis)* **a. à** to go to; **l'argent collecté ira à une œuvre** the collection will go *or* be given to (a) charity; **le prix d'interprétation masculine est allé à Jean Dufour** Jean Dufour was awarded the prize for best actor, the prize for best actor went to Jean Dufour; **la médaille d'or est allée à la Chine** China won *or* got the gold medal, the gold medal went to China

B. *S'ÉTENDRE* **1** *(dans l'espace)* **leur propriété va de la rivière à la côte** their land stretches from the river to the coast; **le passage qui va de la page 35 à la page 43** the passage which goes from page 35 to page 43; **a. jusqu'à** *(vers le haut)* to go *or* to reach up to; *(vers le bas)* to go *or* to reach down to; *(en largeur, en longueur)* to go to, to stretch as far as; **la tapisserie va jusqu'au plafond** the tapestry goes up to the ceiling

2 *(dans le temps)* **a. de... à...** to go from... to...; **sa période productive va de 1867 à 1892** his/her most productive period was from 1867 to 1892; **a. jusqu'à** *(bail, contrat)* to run till; **mon congé maladie va jusqu'au 15 janvier** my sick leave runs till 15 January; **jusqu'à quand vont les congés de février?** when does the February break finish?

3 *(dans une série)* **a. de...à...** to go *or* to range from... to...; **vos notes vont de 11 à 18** your *Br* marks *or Am* grades go *or* range from 11 to 18; **avec des températures allant de 10°C à 15°C** with temperatures (of) between 10°C and 15°C *or* ranging from 10°C to 15°C; **les prix vont jusqu'à 5000 euros** prices go as high as 5,000 euros; **sa voix va jusqu'au do** his/her voice reaches *or* goes up to C; **désolée, madame, nous n'allons pas jusqu'à la taille 50** sorry, Madam, we don't stock *or* go up to size 50

C. *PROGRESSER* **1** *(se dérouler)* **a. vite/lentement** to go fast/slow; **la course va trop vite/lentement pour elle** the race is too fast/slow for her; **arrêtez-moi si je vais trop vite** *(en parlant)* stop me if I'm going too fast; **à partir de ce moment-là, le divorce est allé très vite** from that moment onwards, the divorce proceedings went very fast; **plus ça va, moins je comprends la politique** the more I see of politics, the less I understand it; **plus ça va, plus je l'aime** I love him/her more each day

2 *(personne)* **j'irai jusqu'à 300 euros pour le fauteuil** I'll pay *or* go up to 300 euros for the armchair; **a. jusqu'à faire** to go as far as doing, to go so far as to do; **il est allé jusqu'à publier le tract** he went as far as publishing the pamphlet; **j'irais même jusqu'à dire que...** I would even go so far as to say that...; **sans a. jusque-là** without going that far; **il va sur** *ou* **vers la cinquantaine** he's getting on for *or* going on fifty; **elle va sur ses cinq ans** she's nearly *or* almost five, she'll be five soon; **a. à la faillite/l'échec** to be heading for bankruptcy/failure; **a. à sa ruine** to be on the road to ruin; **où va-t-on** *ou* **allons-nous s'il faut se barricader chez soi?** what's the world coming to if people have to lock themselves in nowadays?; **allons (droit) au fait** let's get (straight) to the point; **a. au plus pressé** to do the most urgent thing first

D. *ÊTRE DANS TELLE OU TELLE SITUATION* **1** *(en parlant de l'état de santé)* **bonjour, comment ça va? – ça va** hello, how are you? – all right; **comment vas-tu? – ça va** how are you? – fine; **comment va ta mère?** how's your mother?; *Fam* **comment va la santé?, comment va?** how are you keeping?; **ça va?** *(après un choc)* are you all right?; **ça ne va pas du tout** I'm not at all well; **je vais bien** I'm fine *or* well; **ça va bien?** are you OK?; **mon cœur ne va plus trop bien** my heart's not as good as it used to be; **elle va beaucoup mieux** she's (feeling) much better; **ton genou va mieux?** is your knee better?, does your knee feel (any) better?; **bois ça, ça ira mieux** drink this, you'll feel better; **il va mal** he's not at all well, he's very poorly; *Fam* **ça va pas (bien)** *ou* **la tête!, ça va pas, non?** you're off your head!, you must be mad!■ ; *Fam* **ça va? – on fait a.** how are you? – mustn't grumble *or* muddling along

2 *(se passer)* **comment vont les affaires? – elles vont bien** how's business? – (it's doing) OK *or* fine; **ça va de moins en moins bien entre eux** things have gone from bad to worse between them; **ça a l'air d'a. beaucoup mieux avec son mari** things seem to be much better between her and her husband; **les choses vont** *ou* **ça va mal** things aren't too good *or* aren't going too well; **ça va mal dans le sud du pays** there's trouble in the south of the country; **obéis-moi ou ça va mal a. (pour toi)!** do as I say or you'll be in trouble!; **comment ça va dans ton nouveau service?** how are you getting on *or* how are things in the new department?; **ça a l'air d'a.** you seem to be coping; **et le lycée, ça va?** and how's school?; **quelque chose ne va pas?** is there anything wrong *or* the matter?; **il y a quelque chose qui ne va pas dans l'imprimante** there's something wrong with the printer; **ça ne va pas tout seul** *ou* **sans problème** it's not an *or* it's no easy job; *Fam* **et le travail, ça va comme tu veux?** is work going all right?; *Fam* **faire a.** *(commerce)* to run, to manage■

E. *EXPRIME L'ADÉQUATION* **1** *(être seyant)* **a. (bien) à qn** *(taille d'un vêtement)* to fit sb; *(style d'un vêtement)* to suit sb; **le bleu lui va** blue suits him/her, he/she looks good in blue; **rien ne me va** I don't look good in anything, nothing suits me; **mon manteau te va mieux qu'à moi** my coat looks much better on you (than on me), my coat suits you better than (it does) me; **ça ne te va pas de parler vulgairement** coarse language doesn't suit *or* become you; *Ironique* **ça te va bien de donner des conseils!** you're a fine one to give advice!; **cela te va à ravir** *ou* **à merveille** that looks wonderful on you, you look wonderful in that

2 *(être en harmonie)* **a. avec qch** to go with sth, to match sth; **j'ai acheté un chapeau pour a. avec ma veste** I bought a hat to go with *or* to

match my jacket; **a. ensemble** *(couleurs, styles)* to go well together, to match; *(éléments d'une paire)* to belong together; **ils vont bien ensemble, ces deux-là!** those two make quite a pair!; **je trouve qu'ils vont très mal ensemble** I think (that) they're an ill-matched couple *or* they make a very odd pair

3 *(convenir)* **le ton de ta voix ne va pas, reprends à la ligne 56** your tone isn't right, do it again from line 56; **la clé de 12 devrait a.** spanner number 12 should do (the job); **nos plats vont au four** our dishes are oven-proof; **tu veux de l'aide? – non, ça ira** do you want a hand? – no, I'll manage *or* it's OK; **tu ne rajoutes pas de crème? – ça ira comme ça** don't you want to add some cream? – that'll do (as it is) *or* it's fine like this; **ça ira pour aujourd'hui** that'll be all for today, let's call it a day; **pour un studio, ça peut a.** as far as studio apartments go, it's not too bad; **la robe ne va pas à la taille** the dress isn't right at the waist; **on dînera après le spectacle – ça me va** we'll go for dinner after the show – that's all right *or* fine by me *or* that suits me (fine); **je vous fais un rabais de 10 pour cent, ça vous va?** I'll give you a 10 percent discount, is that all right?; **je vous ai mis un peu plus de la livre, ça (vous) va?** it's a bit over a pound, is that all right?

F. *LOCUTIONS* **allez, un petit effort** come on, put some effort into it; **allez, ne pleure plus** come on (now), stop crying; **allons, pose cette arme!** come on (now), put that gun down!; **allez, je m'en vais!** right, I'm going now!; **zut! j'ai cassé un verre! – et allez (donc), le troisième en un mois!** damn! I've broken a glass! – well done, that's the third in a month!; **allez** *ou* **allons donc!** *(tu exagères)* go on *or* get away (with you)!, come off it!; **allez-y!** go on!, off you go!; **vas-y, lance-toi!** go on then, do it!; **allons-y!** let's go!; *Fam Hum* **allons-y Alonzo!** let's go!, *Am* let's go Cisco!; **allons-y, après la troisième mesure!** let's take it from the third bar!; *Ironique* **allons-y, ne nous gênons pas!** don't mind me!; **allons bon, j'ai perdu ma clef maintenant!** oh no, now I've lost my key!; **allons bon, voilà qu'il recommence à pleurer!** here we go, he's crying again!; **il n'est pas encore rentré – allons bon!** he's not home yet – oh no *or* dear!; **c'est mieux comme ça, va!** it's better that way, you know!; **tu ne seras pas en retard, va, tu as une heure devant toi!** you won't be late, you know, you've got an hour to go yet!; *Fam* **(espèce de) frimeur, va!** you show-off!; *Fam* **sale bête, va!** you disgusting creature!; *Fam* **va donc, eh, chauffard!** roadhog!; *Fam* **va donc, eh, minable!** get lost, you little creep!; *Fam* **ça va, ça va bien, ça va comme ça** OK; **je t'aurai prévenu! – ça va, ça va!** don't say I didn't warn you! – OK, OK!; **c'est toujours moi qui fais la vaisselle – oh, eh, ça va!** it's always me who does the dishes – give it a rest!; **ça va comme ça, hein! j'en ai assez de tes jérémiades!** just shut up, will you! I'm fed up with your moaning!; *Fam* **une fois que tu es sur le plongeoir, il faut y a.!** once you're on the diving board, you've got to jump!; *Fam* **quand faut y a., faut y a.** when you've got to go, you've got to go; *Fam* **vas-y doucement, c'est fragile** gently *or* easy does it, it's fragile; *Fam* **vas-y mollo avec le vin!** go easy on the wine!; **ils n'y sont pas allés doucement avec les meubles** they were a bit rough with the furniture; **ils n'y sont pas allés doucement avec les grévistes** they didn't exactly handle the strikers with kid gloves; *Fam* **j'en veux 500 euros – comme tu y vas!** I want 500 euros for it – isn't that a bit steep?; **c'est un fasciste – comme vous y allez!** he's a fascist – that's going a bit far!; *Fam* **où tu vas?** are you mad?▪, have you got a screw loose?, *Br* are you off your head?; *Fam* **ça y va, les billets de 50 euros!** 50-euro notes are going as if there was no tomorrow!; **ça y allait, les bouteilles de champagne!** champagne flowed like water!; **aux réunions de famille, il y va toujours d'une** *ou* **de sa chansonnette** every time there's a family gathering, he sings a little song; *Hum* **elle y est allée de sa petite larme** she had a little cry; **il** *ou* **cela** *ou* **ça va de soi (que)** it goes without saying (that); **il va de soi que je vous paierai** it goes without saying that I'll pay you; **il** *ou* **cela** *ou* **ça va sans dire (que)** it goes without saying (that); **il y va de ta vie/carrière/réputation** your life/career/reputation is at stake; **il n'y va pas seulement de sa dignité** his/her dignity isn't the only thing at stake here; **il en va de la littérature comme de la peinture** it's the same with literature as with painting; **il n'en va pas de même pour toi** the same doesn't apply to you; **il en irait autrement si ta mère était encore là** things would be very different if your mother was still here; *Fam* **va pour le saint-émilion!** all right *or* OK then, we'll have the Saint-Émilion!; **je vous en donne 50 euros – va pour 50 euros!** I'll give you 50 euros for it – very well *or* all right, 50 euros (it is)!; **si tu vas par là, si vous allez par là** on those grounds, on that account; **tout le monde est égoïste, si tu vas par là!** everybody's selfish, if you look at it like that!

▸**s'en aller** VPR **1** *(partir → personne)* to go; **il faut que je m'en aille** I must be off, I must go; **je lui donnerai la clé en m'en allant** I'll give him/her the key on my way out; **ne t'en va pas** don't go; **va-t'en!** go away!; **s'en a. discrètement** to slip away (quietly); **les employés qui ont 58 ans sont encouragés à s'en a.** employees who are 58 are encouraged to leave; **les voisins s'en vont** the neighbours are moving; **tous les jeunes s'en vont du village** all the young people are leaving the village; **va-t'en de là!** get away from there!; **il regarda le bateau s'en a.** he watched the boat leaving *or* leave

2 *(se défaire, se détacher)* to come undone; **attention! ta barrette s'en va!** careful, your hair slide is coming out!

3 *(mourir → personne)* to die, to pass away; **si je m'en vais avant toi** if I die before you; *Hum* **il s'en va de la poitrine** his cough will carry him off

4 *(disparaître → tache)* to come off, to go (away); *(→ son)* to fade away; *(→ forces)* to fail; *(→ jeunesse)* to pass; *(→ lumière, soleil, couleur)* to fade (away); *(→ peinture, vernis)* to come off; **ça s'en ira au lavage/avec du savon** it'll come out in the wash/wash out with soap; **leur dernière lueur d'espoir s'en est allée** their last glimmer of hope has gone *or* vanished; **la morale, la politesse, tout s'en va!** morals and good manners just don't exist any more!

5 *(suivi de l'infinitif) (en intensif)* **il s'en alla trouver le magicien** off he went to find the wizard; *Fam* **je m'en vais lui dire ses quatre vérités!** I'm going to tell him/her a few home truths!; *Fam* **je m'en vais vous faire la démonstration** let me demonstrate▪

---

allergène [alɛrʒɛn] NM *Méd* allergen

allergénique [alɛrʒenik] ADJ *Méd* allergenic

allergide [alɛrʒid] NF *Méd* = skin infection caused by an allergy

allergie [alɛrʒi] NF **1** *Méd* allergy; **avoir** *ou* **faire une a. à** to be allergic to **2** *Fam Fig* allergy; **avoir une a. à** to be allergic to

allergique [alɛrʒik] ADJ **1** *Méd (réaction)* allergic; **être a. à qch** to be allergic to sth **2** *Fam Fig* allergic; **je suis a. au sport** I'm allergic to sport

allergisant, -e [alɛrʒizɑ̃, -ɑ̃t] ADJ *Méd* allergenic

allergologie [alɛrgɔlɔʒi] NF *Méd* diagnosis and treatment of allergies

allergologiste [alɛrgɔlɔʒist], **allergologue** [alɛrgɔlɔg] NMF *Méd* allergist

aller-retour [alerətur] *(pl* **allers-retours***)* NM **1** *(voyage)* round trip; **faire des allers-retours** *(personne, document)* to go back and forth, to shuttle back and forth; **je fais plusieurs allers-retours par jour entre l'hôpital et la maison** I go back and forth between the hospital and home several times a day; **je vais à la banque, mais je ne fais qu'un a.** I'm going to the bank, but I'll be right back **2** *(billet) Br* return *or Am* round-trip (ticket)

alleu, -x [alø] NM *Hist & Jur* **(franc) a.** allodium, alodium

alleutier [aløtje] NM *Hist* allodialist, allodiary

alliacé, -e [aljase] ADJ *Culin* alliaceous

alliage [aljaʒ] NM **1** *Métal & Tech* alloy; **structure en a. léger** alloy structure **2** *Littéraire (ajout)* adjunct

alliaire [aljɛr] NF *Culin* garlic mustard

alliance [aljɑ̃s] NF **1** *(pacte)* alliance, pact, union; **l'a. entre socialistes et communistes** *ou* **les socialistes et les communistes** the alliance between *or* of Socialists and Communists; **conclure une a. avec un pays** to enter into *or* to forge an alliance with a country; **conclure une a. avec qn** to ally oneself with sb; **faire a. avec/contre qn** to ally *or* to team up with/against sb; *Mktg* **a. de marque** co-branding; **l'A. française** = organization promoting French language and culture abroad; **a. stratégique** strategic alliance

2 *(mariage)* union, marriage

3 *(combinaison)* union, blending, combination; *Ling* **a. de mots** oxymoron

4 *(bague)* wedding ring

5 *Rel* covenant

❑ **par alliance** ADJ by marriage

Culture

L'ALLIANCE FRANÇAISE

In many respects, the activities of the Alliance française are similar to those of the British Council, although it is a private body. It organizes classes in French language and civilization and has branches all over the world.

allié, -e [alje] ADJ **1** *(nation, pays)* allied **2** *(dans une famille)* related by marriage

NM,F **1** *(pays, gouvernement)* ally; *Hist* **les Alliés** the Allies **2** *Jur* relation by marriage; **parents et alliés** immediate family and close relatives **3** *(ami)* ally, supporter

Allier [alje] NM **l'A.** Allier

allier [9] [alje] VT **1** *(unir → pays, gouvernements, chefs)* to unite, to ally (together); *(→ familles)* to relate *or* to unite by marriage

2 *(combiner → efforts, moyens, qualités)* to combine; *(→ sons, couleurs, parfums)* to match, to blend (together); **elle allie l'intelligence à l'humour** she combines intelligence and humour

3 *Tech* to (mix into an) alloy

▸**s'allier** VPR **1** *(pays)* to become allied; **s'a. avec un pays** to ally oneself to a country, to form an alliance with a country; **s'a. contre** to unite against

2 *(par le mariage → personnes)* to marry; *(→ familles)* to become allied *or* related by marriage; **s'a. à une famille** to marry into a family; **les aristocrates s'alliaient entre eux** aristocrats used to intermarry

3 *(se combiner → couleurs, sons, parfums)* to match, to blend (together); *(→ qualités, talents, arts)* to combine, to unite

4 *Tech* to (become mixed into an) alloy

alligator [aligatɔr] NM *Zool* alligator

allitération [aliterasjɔ̃] NF *Ling* alliteration; **a. en s** alliteration of the letter s

allô [alo] EXCLAM hello, hullo; **a., qui est à l'appareil?** hello, who's speaking?; **a., je voudrais parler à Damien** hello, I'd like to speak to Damien

Allobroges [alɔbrɔʒ] NMPL *Hist* Allobroges

alloc [alɔk] NF *Fam (abrév* **allocation***)* benefit▪; **les allocs** *(allocations familiales)* child benefit▪ *(UNCOUNT)*

allocataire [alɔkatɛr] NMF beneficiary

allocation [alɔkasjɔ̃] NF **1** *(attribution → d'argent)* allocation; *(→ de dommages-intérêts, d'une indemnité)* awarding; *Fin & Bourse (→ de titres)* allocation, allotment

2 *Admin (prestation financière)* allowance, *Br* benefit, *Am* welfare; **avoir** *ou* **toucher des allocations** to be on *Br* benefit *or Am* welfare; **a. (de) chômage** *Br* unemployment benefit, *Am* welfare; **allocations familiales** family allowance *(UNCOUNT)*, child benefit *(UNCOUNT)*; **a. de formation reclassement** = allowance paid to employees requiring further training or new qualifications; **a. de garde d'enfant à domicile** = allowance paid to working parents who employ a childminder at home; **a. (de) logement, a.-logement** *Br* housing benefit, *Am* rent subsidy *or* allowance; **je touche une a.-logement** I get *Br* housing benefit *or Am* a rent subsidy; **a. (de) maternité** maternity allowance; **a. de parent isolé** = allowance paid to single parents; **a.**

de rentrée scolaire = allowance paid to parents to help cover costs incurred at the start of the school year; **a. de solidarité spécifique** = allowance paid to long-term unemployed people who are no longer entitled to unemployment benefit; **a. unique dégressive** = unemployment allowance that gradually decreases over time, the sum depending on age, previous salary and amount of national insurance paid; **a. vieillesse** old-age pension

❑ **allocations** NFPL *Fam* **les allocations** *(service) Br* social security■, *Am* welfare■; *(bureau)* the social security office■

allocentrisme [alɔsɑ̃trism] NM *Psy* allocentrism

allochtone [alɔktɔn] ADJ & NMF *Géol & Écol* immigrant

allocutaire [alɔkytɛr] NMF *Ling* addressee

allocution [alɔkysjɔ̃] NF *(discours)* (formal) speech

allodial, -e, -aux, -ales [alɔdjal, -o] ADJ *Hist & Jur* allodial, alodial

allogamie [alɔgami] NF *Bot* allogamy

allogène [alɔʒɛn] ADJ *(gén)* foreign; *(population)* non-native

NMF alien

allogreffe [alɔgrɛf] NF *Méd* allograft, homograft

allométrie [alɔmetri] NF *Biol* allometry

allomorphe [alɔmɔrf] NM *Ling* allomorph

allomorphie [alɔmɔrfi] NF *Ling* allomorphism

allonge [alɔ̃ʒ] NF **1** *(rallonge → gén)* extension; *(→ d'une table)* leaf **2** *(crochet)* (butcher's) hook **3** *Fin* rider **4** *Sport* reach; **avoir une bonne a.** to have a long reach

allongé, -e [alɔ̃ʒe] ADJ **1** *(forme, silhouette)* elongated **2** *(couché)* **il était a. sur le canapé** he was lying on the sofa; **il est resté a. pendant trois mois** he was bedridden for three months

allongement [alɔ̃ʒmɑ̃] NM **1** *(extension → d'une route, d'un canal)* extension; *(→ d'une distance)* increasing, lengthening; *(→ d'une durée, de la vie)* lengthening, extension; *(→ des jours)* lengthening; **l'a. du temps de loisir** the increased time available for leisure pursuits; **a. de l'espérance de vie des femmes** increase in women's life expectancy; **l'a. de la durée de la vie active** working for longer

2 *Aviat* aspect ratio

3 *Tech (déformation)* stretching; *Métal* elongation

4 *Ling* lengthening

allonger [17] [alɔ̃ʒe] VT **1** *(rendre plus long → robe, route, texte)* to lengthen, to make longer; *(→ espérance de vie, délai)* to prolong; **le dernier chapitre allonge inutilement le récit** the last chapter just drags the story out pointlessly; **la coupe vous allonge la silhouette** the cut of the garment makes you look thinner; **a. le pas** to take longer strides

2 *(étirer → bras, jambe)* to stretch out; **a. le cou** to stretch one's neck; **a. le bras pour prendre qch** *(devant soi)* to stretch out one's hand to get sth; *(en l'air)* to stretch up to reach sth; *(par terre)* to bend down to pick up sth

3 *(coucher → blessé, malade)* to lay down; *très Fam (assommer)* to knock down■, to floor; **vite, allongez-la par terre** quick, lay her down on the floor

4 *très Fam (donner → argent)* to produce■, to come up with; **a. un pourboire au coiffeur** to slip the hairdresser a tip; **cette fois-ci, il a fallu qu'il les allonge** this time, he had to cough up *or* to fork out; **a. une taloche à qn** to give sb a slap■; **a. un coup à qn** to fetch sb a blow

5 a. la sauce *Culin* to make the sauce thinner; *Fig* to spin things out

6 *Équitation (allure)* to lengthen

VI **les jours allongent** the days are drawing out *or* getting longer

▶**s'allonger** VPR **1** *(se coucher)* to stretch out; **allongez-vous!** lie down!; **il/le chien s'allongea sur le tapis** he/the dog stretched out on the rug; **allonge-toi un peu** have a little lie-down

2 *(se prolonger → visite, récit)* to drag on; *(→ vie, période)* to become longer

3 *(grandir → enfant)* to get taller, to grow

4 *(se renfrogner)* **son visage s'allongea** his/her face fell, he/she made *or Br* pulled a long face

allopathe [alɔpat] *Méd* ADJ allopathic

NMF allopathist, allopath

allopathie [alɔpati] NF *Méd* allopathy

allopathique [alɔpatik] ADJ *Méd* allopathic

allophone [alɔfɔn] *Ling* ADJ **les résidents allophones** foreign-language speaking residents

NMF = person whose native language is not that of the community in which he/she lives

allosaure [alɔzɔr] NM *Zool (en paléontologie)* allosaur, allosaurus

allosome [alɔsɔm] NM *Biol* allosome

allostérie [alɔsteri] NF *Biol & Chim* allostery

allostérique [alɔsterik] ADJ *Biol & Chim* allosteric

allotir [32] [alɔtir] VT **1** *Jur* **a. des héritiers** to share *or* to apportion an inheritance among heirs **2** *Com (magasins)* to group, to sort out

allotissement [alɔtismɑ̃] NM **1** *Jur* allotment; **l'a. des héritiers** the apportionment of an inheritance among heirs **2** *Com (magasins)* grouping

allotropie [alɔtrɔpi] NF *Chim & Phys* allotropy

allotropique [alɔtrɔpik] ADJ *Chim & Phys* allotropic

allouchier [alyʃje] NM *Bot* whitebeam

allouer [6] [alwe] VT **1** *(attribuer → argent)* to allocate; *(→ dommages-intérêts, indemnité)* to award, to grant; *(→ dépense, budget)* to allow, to pass; *Fin & Bourse (→ actions)* to allocate, to allot; *Admin (→ salaire, pension)* to grant, to award **2** *(temps)* to allot, to allow; **au terme du temps alloué** at the end of the allotted time; **le temps alloué à ces activités** the time allotted *or* allocated to these activities

allouf [aluf] NF *Fam* match■ *(for lighting fire)*

alluchon [alyʃɔ̃] NM *Tech* cog, tooth

allumage [alymaʒ] NM **1** *(d'un feu, d'une chaudière)* lighting; *(du gaz)* lighting, turning on **2** *(d'une ampoule, d'un appareil électrique)* turning *or* switching on **3** *Aut & Tech* ignition; **régler l'a.** to set *or* to adjust the timing; **avance/retard à l'a.** advanced/retarded ignition; **a. électronique/à induction** electronic/coil ignition **4** *Astron* ignition **5** *Tech* firing *(of a mine)*

allumé, -e [alyme] ADJ **1** *(feu, chaudière)* alight, burning; *(haut-fourneau)* in blast **2** *Fam (ivre)* trashed, wasted **3** *Fam (dingue)* crazy, off one's head *or* rocker

NM,F *Fam* **1** *(fou)* crackpot, crank **2** *(fanatique)* fanatic■; **c'est un a. de l'informatique/du cinéma** he's mad *or* crazy about computers/the cinema

allume-cigare, allume-cigares [alymsigar] *(pl* **allume-cigares***)* NM cigarette lighter

allume-feu [alymfø] *(pl* **inv** *ou* **allume-feux***)* NM **1** *(bois)* kindling wood **2** *(à alcool)* firelighter

allume-gaz [alymgaz] NM INV gas lighter

allumer [3] [alyme] VT **1** *(enflammer → bougie, réchaud, cigarette, torche, gaz)* to light; *(→ bois, brindille)* to light, to kindle; *(→ feu, incendie)* to light, to start

2 *(mettre en marche → lampe, appareil, lumière)* to turn on, to switch on, to put on; *(→ phare)* to put on, to turn on; *Ordinat* to power up; **laisse la pièce allumée** leave the lights on in the room; **j'ai laissé la radio allumée!** I forgot to turn off the radio!; **le bureau est allumé** there's a light on in the office, the lights are on in the office

3 *Littéraire (commencer → guerre)* to start; *(→ passion, haine)* to stir up

4 *Fam (sexuellement)* to turn on, to make horny

5 *Fam (battre)* to beat up, *Br* to do over; **se faire a.** to get beaten up *or Br* done over

6 *Fam (tuer)* to kill■, *Br* to do in

USAGE ABSOLU **allume!** turn the light on!; **comment est-ce qu'on allume?** how do you turn *or Br* switch it on?; **où est-ce qu'on allume?** where's the switch?

▶**s'allumer** VPR **1** *(s'éclairer)* **leur fenêtre vient de s'a.** a light has just come on at their window

2 *Fig (visage, œil, regard)* to light up

3 *(se mettre en marche → appareil, radio)* to switch on, to turn on; *(→ lumière)* to come on; *Ordinat* to power up; **ça ne s'allume pas** the light's not working; **où est-ce que ça s'allume?** where's the light switch?

4 *(prendre feu → bois, brindille)* to catch (fire); *(→ incendie)* to start, to flare up

5 *Littéraire (commencer → haine, passion)* to be aroused; *(→ guerre)* to break out

allumette [alymɛt] NF **1** *(pour allumer)* match, matchstick; **l'os s'est cassé comme une a.** the bone snapped like a twig; **ne joue pas avec les allumettes** don't play with matches; **a. suédoise** *ou* **de sûreté** safety match; **être gros** *ou* **épais comme une a.** to be as thin as a rake; **avoir des jambes comme des allumettes** to have legs like matchsticks **2** *Culin (gâteau)* allumette

allumettier, -ère [alymetje, -ɛr] NM,F **1** *(industriel)* match manufacturer **2** *(ouvrier)* worker in a match factory

allumeur [alymœr] NM **1** *Tech* igniter **2** *Aut* (ignition) distributor **3** *(lampiste)* **a. de réverbères** lamplighter

allumeuse [alymøz] NF *Fam Péj* tease

allure [alyr] NF **1** *(vitesse d'un véhicule)* speed; **à grande/faible a.** at (a) high/low speed; **rouler à petite a.** *ou* **à une a. réduite** to drive at a slow pace *or* slowly; **aller** *ou* **rouler à toute a.** to go at (top *or* full) speed; **le train filait à toute a. dans la nuit** the train sped through the night

2 *(vitesse d'un marcheur)* pace; **il accélérait l'a.** he was quickening his pace; **marcher à vive a.** to walk at a brisk pace; **courir à toute a.** to run as fast as one can; *Fig* **à cette a., tu n'auras pas fini avant demain** at that speed *or* rate, you won't have finished before tomorrow

3 *(apparence → d'une personne)* look, appearance; **avoir de l'a., avoir grande a.** to have style; **une femme d'a. élégante entra** an elegant-looking woman came in; **avoir fière a.** to cut a fine figure; **avoir piètre a.** to cut a shabby figure; **il a une drôle d'a.** he looks odd *or* weird; **un personnage à l'a.** *ou* **d'a. suspecte** a suspicious-looking character; **je n'aime pas l'a. qu'elle a** I don't like the look of her; **un château d'a. médiévale** a medieval-looking castle; **le projet prend une mauvaise a.** the project is taking a turn for the worse; **prendre des allures de** to take on an air of

4 *Belg (élégance)* **n'avoir pas d'a.** to be totally lacking in sophistication, to be unsophisticated; **être sans a.** *(manquer d'élégance → gén)* to be shabby-looking; *(→ femme)* to be dowdy; *(manquer de savoir-vivre)* to be totally lacking in sophistication

5 *Can* **avoir d'a.** *(être vraisemblable)* to be likely

6 *Can* **avoir de l'a.** *(être sensé)* to make sense

❑ **allures** NFPL *Équitation* paces; *Naut* reach

alluré, -e [alyre] ADJ stylish

allusif, -ive [alyzif, -iv] ADJ allusive; **il est resté très a.** he wasn't very specific

allusion [alyzjɔ̃] NF **1** *(référence)* allusion, reference; **faire a. à qch** to allude to sth, to refer to sth; **il n'y a fait a. qu'en passant** he only made passing reference to it; **par a. à** alluding to; **"veni, vidi, vici", dit-il, par a. à Jules César** "veni, vidi, vici," he said, alluding to Julius Caesar

2 *(sous-entendu)* hint; **une a. cousue de fil blanc** a heavy hint; **c'est une a.?** are you hinting at something?; **l'a. m'échappe** I don't get it; **s'exprimer par allusions** to express oneself obliquely *or* allusively

allusive [alyziv] *voir* **allusif**

allusivement [alyzivmɑ̃] ADV allusively

alluvial, -e, -aux, -ales [alyvjal, -o] ADJ *Géol* alluvial

alluvion [alyvjɔ̃] *Géol* NF *Arch* alluviation

❑ **alluvions** NFPL alluvion *(UNCOUNT)*, alluvium *(UNCOUNT)*

alluvionnaire [alyvjɔnɛr] ADJ *Géol* alluvial

alluvionnement [alyvjɔnmɑ̃] NM *Géol* alluviation

alluvionner [3] [alyvjɔne] VI *Géol* to deposit alluvion *or* alluvium

allyle [alil] NM *Chim* allyl

allylique [alilik] ADJ *Chim* allyl *(avant n)*; **alcool a.** allyl alcohol

alma mater [almamatɛr] NM OU NF *Belg, Can & Suisse* alma mater

almanach [almana] NM almanac

almandin [almɑ̃dɛ̃] NM *Minér* almandine

almée [alme] NF alma, almah, alme, almeh

almicantarat [almikɑ̃tara] NM *Astron* almucantar, almacantar

aloès [alɔɛs] NM *Bot* aloe; *Pharm* bitter aloes

alogique [alɔʒik] ADJ *Ling* alogical

aloi [alwa] NM **1 de bon a.** *(marchandise, individu)* of sterling *or* genuine worth; *(plaisanterie)* in good taste; *(succès)* well-deserved, worthy; **de**

mauvais a. *(marchandise)* worthless; *(individu)* worthless, no-good *(avant n)*; *(plaisanterie)* in bad taste; *(succès)* cheap **2** *Arch (titre)* = proportion of precious metal in an alloy

alopécie [alɔpesi] NF *Méd* alopecia

alors [alɔr] ADV **1** *(à ce moment-là)* then; **j'étais jeune a.** I was young then; **Rome était a. à la tête d'un grand empire** at that time Rome was at the head of a great empire, Rome was then at the head of a great empire; **le cinéma d'a. était encore muet** films were still silent in those days; **le Premier ministre d'a. refusa de signer les accords** the then Prime Minister refused to sign the agreement; **jusqu'a.** until then; **a. seulement, il se rendit compte de la situation** it was only then that he understood the situation; **et a. il a déclaré...** and then he declared...; **venez la semaine prochaine, j'aurai plus de temps a.** come next week, I'll have more time then
2 *(en conséquence)* so; **il s'est mis à pleuvoir, a. nous sommes rentrés** it started to rain, so we came back in; **a., il n'y a pas d'autre solution?** so there's no other solution then?
3 *(dans ce cas)* then, so, in that case; **s'il mourait, a. elle devrait reprendre son travail** if he died, then she would have to go back to work; **je préfère renoncer tout de suite, a.!** in that case, I'd just as soon give up straight away!; **n'en parlons plus a.** let's say no more about it then; **mais a., ça change tout!** but that changes everything!
4 *(emploi expressif)* **et a.?** so?, so what?; **il va se mettre en colère, et a.?** if he gets angry, so what?; **et a., qu'est-ce qui s'est passé?** so what happened then?; **a., qu'est-ce qu'on fait?** so what are we going to do?, what are we going to do, then?; **a., tu viens, oui ou non?** so are you coming or not?, are you coming or not, then?; **dites-le-lui, ou a. je ne viens pas** tell him/her, otherwise *or* or else I'm not coming; **a. là, il exagère!** he's going a bit far there!; **a. là, je ne sais plus quoi dire!** well then, I don't know what to say!; **a. quoi, t'as un problème?** what do you mean you've got a problem?; **ça a., je ne l'aurais jamais cru!** my goodness, I would never have believed it!; **non mais a., pour qui vous vous prenez?** well really, who do you think you are?
❑ **alors que** CONJ **1** *(au moment où)* while, when; **l'orage éclata a. que nous étions encore loin de la maison** the storm broke while *or* when we were still a long way from the house
2 *(bien que, même si)* even though; **il a parlé tout le temps, a. qu'on ne lui avait rien demandé** he talked non-stop, even though no one had asked him anything; **elle est sortie, a. que c'était interdit** she went out, even though she wasn't supposed to; **a. même qu'il ne nous resterait que ce moyen, je refuserais de l'utiliser** even if this were the only means left to us, I wouldn't use it
3 *(tandis que)* while; **il part en vacances, a. que je reste ici tout l'été** he's going on holiday, while I stay here all summer

alose [aloz] NF *Ich* shad

alouate [alwat] NM *Zool* howler (monkey)

alouette [alwɛt] NF **1** *Orn* lark; **a. des bois** woodlark; **a. calandrelle** calandra lark; **a. des champs** skylark; **a. hausse-col, a. oreillarde** shore lark; **a. de mer** sealark; **a. pispolette** lesser short-tailed lark; *Fam* **il attend que les alouettes lui tombent toutes cuites dans le bec** he's waiting for things to just fall into his lap
2 *Culin* **a. sans tête** ≃ veal olive

alourdir [32] [alurdir] VT **1** *(ajouter du poids à)* to weigh down, to make heavy *or* heavier; **l'emballage alourdit le paquet de 200 g** the wrapping makes the parcel heavier by 200 g; **alourdi par la fatigue** heavy with exhaustion
2 *(style, allure, traits)* to make heavier *or* coarser; *(impôts)* to increase; **la grossesse commençait à a. sa démarche** her pregnancy was beginning to make her walk more heavily; **cette répétition alourdit la phrase** the repetition makes the sentence unwieldy
▶ **s'alourdir** VPR **1** *(grossir → personne)* to put on weight; *(→ taille)* to thicken, to get thicker
2 *(devenir lourd)* to become heavy *or* heavier; **ses paupières s'alourdissaient** his/her eyelids were beginning to droop *or* were getting heavy;

sa démarche s'est alourdie he/she walks more heavily
3 *(devenir plus grossier)* to get coarser; **ses traits s'alourdissent** his/her features are getting coarser; **durant cette période, son trait de pinceau s'alourdit** in this period, his/her brushwork becomes heavier
4 *(augmenter → charges, impôts)* to increase

alourdissement [alurdismã] NM **1** *(d'un paquet, d'un véhicule)* increased weight **2** *(d'un style)* heaviness; *(des impôts)* increase; **seul l'a. de sa silhouette laissait deviner sa maladie** the only sign of her illness was that she had put on a little weight

aloyau [alwajo] NM *Culin* sirloin

alpaga [alpaga] NM *Zool* alpaca

alpage [alpaʒ] NM **1** *(pâturage)* high (mountain) pasture **2** *(saison)* grazing season *(spent by livestock in high pastures)*
❑ **d'alpage** ADJ *(fromage, produit)* mountain *(avant n)*; **lait d'a.** = milk from cattle grazing in mountain pastures

alpaguer [3] [alpage] VT *très Fam* **1** *(arrêter)* to nab, *Am* to bust; **se faire a.** to get nabbed *or Am* busted **2** *(accaparer)* to nab

Alpax® [alpaks] NM *Métal* Alpax

alpe [alp] NF (high) alpine pasture

alpenstock [alpɛnstɔk] NM alpenstock

alper [3] [alpe] VI *Suisse* = to move cattle up to higher mountain pastures at the beginning of summer

Alpes [alp] NFPL **les A.** the Alps; **les A. dinariques** the Dinaric Alps; **les A. du Sud** the Southern Alps; **les A. suisses** the Swiss Alps; **les A. de Transylvanie** the Transylvanian Alps

Alpes-de-Haute-Provence [alpdəotprɔvãs] NFPL **les A.** Alpes-de-Haute-Provence

Alpes-Maritimes [alpmaritim] NFPL **les A.** Alpes-Maritimes

alpestre [alpɛstr] ADJ alpine; **plante a.** alpine plant

alpha [alfa] NM INV alpha; *Fig* **l'a. et l'oméga de** the beginning and the end of

alphabarre [alfabar] NF alphabar

alphabet [alfabɛ] NM **1** *(d'une langue)* alphabet; **a. arabe/cyrillique/grec/romain** Arab/Cyrillic/Greek/Roman alphabet **2** *(abécédaire)* spelling *or* ABC book, alphabet **3** *(code)* **a. Morse** Morse code; **a. phonétique** phonetic alphabet; **a. phonétique international** International Phonetic Alphabet

alphabète [alfabɛt] ADJ literate
NMF person who can read and write

alphabétique [alfabetik] ADJ alphabetic, alphabetical

alphabétiquement [alfabetikmã] ADV alphabetically

alphabétisation [alfabetizasjɔ̃] NF elimination of illiteracy; **campagne/taux d'a.** literacy campaign/rate; **l'a. de la population** teaching the population to read and write

alphabétisé, -e [alfabetize] ADJ literate
NM,F person who has learned to read and write as an adult

alphabétiser [3] [alfabetize] VT to teach to read and write

alphabétisme [alfabetism] NM alphabetical writing (system)

alpha-hydroxy-acide [alfaidrɔksiasid] NM *Chim* alpha-hydroxy acid

alphanumérique [alfanymerik] ADJ alphanumeric

Alphapage® [alfapaʒ] NM = radiopaging system run by France Télécom

alpha-test [alfatɛst] NM *Ordinat* alphatest; **alpha-tests** *(procédure)* alpha testing

Alphée [alfe] NM *Myth* Alpheus

alpheus [alfeys] NM *Zool* **(crevette) a.** alpheus

alpin, -e [alpɛ̃, -in] ADJ **1** *Biol, Bot & Géol* alpine **2** *Sport (club)* mountaineering *(avant n)*, mountain-climbing *(avant n)*; *(ski)* downhill

alpinisme [alpinism] NM *Sport* mountaineering, mountain-climbing; **faire de l'a.** to climb, to go mountain-climbing

alpiniste [alpinist] NMF *Sport* mountaineer, climber

alpiste [alpist] NM *Bot* canary grass; **a. panaché** gardener's garters

alque [alk] NM *Can Orn* auk

alquifoux [alkifu] NM *Chim & Cér* alquifoux, potters' lead

Alsace [alzas] NF **l'A.** Alsace
NM Alsace (wine)

Alsace-Lorraine [alzaslɔrɛn] NF **l'A.** Alsace-Lorraine

ALSACE-LORRAINE
The chief subjects, and victims, of the long-standing conflict between Germany and France, these two provinces were seized by the Germans at the end of the Franco-Prussian War in 1871, becoming part of the German Reich. They reverted to France after the First World War, were seized by Germany again in 1940, and were finally restored to France at the end of the Second World War.

alsacien, -enne [alzasjɛ̃, -ɛn] ADJ Alsatian
NM *(dialecte)* Alsatian
❑ **alsacien, -enne** NM,F Alsatian; **les Alsaciens** the people of Alsace

L'ALSACIEN
Alsatian, which includes several Germanic dialects, remains a living language and is still widely spoken by young and old alike in many parts of Alsace.

Altaï [altai] NM *Géog* **l'A.** the Altai Mountains

altaïque [altaik] ADJ *Géog & Ling* Altaic

alter [alter] NMF *Fam (abrév* **altermondialiste***)* alterglobalist

ALTER- [alter] PRÉF
● This prefix, from the Latin *alter* meaning *other*, has emerged in recent years to refer to the anti-globalization movement or **altermondialisme**. The idea in French, unlike the English, is not strictly that of opposition but rather of a possible alternative to globalization. The prefix has also given rise to **altermondialiste** (adjective and noun), as in:
le mouvement altermondialiste the anti-globalization movement; **les idées altermondialistes** antiglobalization ideas; **les altermondialistes** those in favour of antiglobalization, supporters of antiglobalization
● **Alter-** has become a very productive prefix, which can be seen and heard in neologisms such as **alterconsommation, alterconsommateurs, alteréconomie, altereuropéen** etc. In order to translate these, a periphrasis would probably have to be used: *an alternative to mass consumption/the liberal economy* or *a new form of consumption/economy, people looking for an alternative to mass consumption* or *new consumers, which offers a new vision of Europe* etc.
● Due to its relatively recent coinage (the late 1990s), the prefix **alter-** does not yet have a fixed grammatical status, as evidenced by the occurrence of, variously, **alter** or **alters** as a plural adjective.
● As is often the case with prefixes and suffixes, there is some uncertainty as to the use of the hyphen, even if the unhyphenated forms seem to be outweighing their hyphenated equivalents (**altermondialisme** rather than **alter-mondialisme**, but **alter-européen** rather than **altereuropéen**, maybe for greater ease of reading).

altérabilité [alterabilite] NF *(d'aliment, de matériel)* liability to deteriorate; *(de couleur → à l'usage)* liability to fade; *(→ au lavage)* liability to run; *Tech (→ en peinture)* liability to degrade

altérable [alterabl] ADJ *(aliment, matériel)* liable to deteriorate *or* be damaged; *(couleur → à l'usage)* liable to fade; *(→ au lavage)* liable to run; *Tech (→ en peinture)* liable to degrade

altéragène [alteraʒen] ADJ *Biol (substance)* harmful to the environment, noxious

altérant, -e [alterã, -ãt] ADJ **1** *(qui modifie)* altering **2** *(qui donne soif)* thirst-inducing

altération [alterasjɔ̃] NF **1** *(dégradation → d'aliments, de matériel, de la santé)* deterioration; *(→ de couleurs → à l'usage)* fading; *(→ au lavage)* running; *Tech (→ en peinture)* degrading; **sans aucune a. de la qualité de l'image et du son** *(sur*

emballage de cassette vidéo) without deterioration of picture and sound quality

2 *(falsification → de monnaie, de document)* falsification; *(→ de texte)* garbling; *(dilution → du vin)* adulteration

3 *Mus (dièse)* sharp (sign); *(bémol)* flat (sign)

4 *Géol* weathering

5 *Ordinat (d'un fichier)* corruption

altercation [altɛrkasjɔ̃] NF quarrel, altercation; **j'ai eu une violente a. avec elle** I had a violent quarrel *or* a huge row with her

alterconsommateur [altɛrkɔ̃sɔmatœr] NM ethical consumer

alterconsommation [altɛrkɔ̃sɔmasjɔ̃] NF ethical consumption, ethical purchasing

altéré, -e [altere] ADJ **1** *(aliments)* spoiled, damaged; *(couleurs)* faded; *Tech (→ en peinture)* degraded; *(santé, amitié)* impaired, affected; *(traits)* drawn, distorted **2** *(falsifié → faits)* altered, falsified; *(dilué → vin)* adulterated **3** *(assoiffé)* thirsty **4** *Ordinat* corrupted

alter ego [alterego] NM INV **1** *Hum (ami)* alter ego **2** *(homologue)* counterpart, alter ego

altérer [18] [altere] VT **1** *(dégrader → couleur)* to fade; *Tech (→ en peinture)* to degrade; *(→ denrée)* to affect *or* to impair the quality of; *(→ amitié)* to affect

2 *(falsifier → fait, histoire)* to distort; *(→ vérité)* to distort, to twist; *(→ monnaie)* to falsify; *(→ document)* to tamper with, to falsify; *(diluer → vin)* to adulterate

3 *(changer → composition, équilibre)* to change, to alter, to modify; **les traits altérés par le chagrin/la fatigue/la maladie** his/her face pinched with grief/drawn with tiredness/drawn with illness; **la peur lui altérait le visage** *ou* **les traits** fear had transformed his/her features; **la voix altérée par l'angoisse** his/her voice strained with anxiety

4 *Ordinat* to corrupt

5 *Littéraire (assoiffer)* to make thirsty; **altéré de** thirsty *or* thirsting for; **altéré de gloire** thirsting for glory; **altéré de sang** bloodthirsty

6 *Mus (accord)* to alter; *(note)* to inflect

►**s'altérer** VPR **1** *(se dégrader → denrée)* to spoil; *(→ sentiment, amitié)* to deteriorate; *(→ couleurs)* to fade; *(→ voix)* to be distorted; **leurs rapports se sont altérés** their relationship has deteriorated; **sa santé s'est altérée** his/her health has got worse

2 *Ordinat* to corrupt

3 *(se transformer → substance, minéral)* to alter, to (undergo a) change

altérite [alterit] NF *Minér* altered rock

altérité [alterite] NF otherness

altermondialisation [altɛrmɔ̃djalizasjɔ̃] NF alter-globalization, ethical globalization

altermondialisme [altɛrmɔ̃djalism] NM alterglobalism, ethical globalization movement

altermondialiste [altɛrmɔ̃djalist] ADJ alterglobalist

NMF alterglobalist

alternance [altɛrnɑ̃s] NF **1** *(succession)* alternation; **l'a. des saisons** the alternating *or* changing seasons; **a. des cultures** crop rotation

2 *Pol* **a. (du pouvoir)** changeover of political power; **pratiquer l'a.** to take turns running a country; **l'A.** = transfer of power

3 *Ling* **a. vocalique** vowel gradation

4 *Élec* alternation

❑ **en alternance** ADV **ils donnent** *ou* **programment 'Manon' et 'la Traviata' en a.** they're putting on 'Manon' and 'la Traviata' alternately; **jouer en a. avec un autre comédien** to alternate with another actor; **faire qch en a. avec qn** to take turns with sb to do sth

alternant, -e [altɛrnɑ̃, -ɑ̃t] ADJ alternating

alternat [altɛrna] NM **1** *Agr* crop rotation **2** *Pol (en diplomatie)* alternat

alternateur [altɛrnatœr] NM *Élec* alternator

alternatif, -ive [altɛrnatif, -iv] ADJ **1** *(périodique)* alternate, alternating

2 *(à option)* alternative; **modèle a. de croissance** alternative model of growth; **rock a.** alternative rock

❑ **alternative** NF **1** *(choix)* alternative, option; **se trouver devant une pénible alternative** to be faced with a difficult choice, to be in a difficult dilemma

2 *(solution de remplacement)* alternative; **l'alternative écologiste** the green alternative; **alternatives économiques** economic alternatives

3 *Phil* alternative *or* disjunctive (proposition)

4 *(en tauromachie)* = ceremony which gives a novice bullfighter the opportunity to take his place among experienced fighters

❑ **alternatives** NFPL *(succession)* alternating phases

alternativement [altɛrnativmɑ̃] ADV (each) in turn, alternately

alterne [altɛrn] ADJ *Bot & Géom* alternate

alterné, -e [altɛrne] ADJ **1** *Transp (stationnement)* (authorized) on alternate sides of the street; **circulation alternée** = ban imposed on city-centre traffic during periods of heavy pollution, with cars whose registration plates have even numbers and those with odd numbers being barred from the roads on alternate days **2** *Littérature* alternate **3** *Math (application)* alternate; *(série)* alternating **4** *Jur* **résidence alternée** *(pour la garde des enfants)* alternating residence; **garde alternée** *(d'enfant)* alternating custody

alterner [3] [altɛrne] VT **1** *(faire succéder)* to alternate **2** *Agr* to rotate

VI *(se succéder → phases)* to alternate; *(→ personnes)* to alternate, to take turns; **faire a.** to alternate

altesse [altɛs] NF Highness; **Son A. Royale** *(prince)* His Royal Highness; *(princesse)* Her Royal Highness; **Son A. Sérénissime** *(prince)* His Most Serene Highness; *(princesse)* Her Most Serene Highness

althæa [altea], **althée** [alte] NM *Bot* althaea

altier, -ère [altje, -ɛr] ADJ haughty, arrogant; **avoir un port a.** to carry oneself proudly; **avoir une démarche altière** to walk proudly

altimètre [altimɛtr] NM altimeter

altimétrie [altimetri] NF altimetry

altiport [altipɔr] NM *Aviat* (ski-resort) airfield

altise [altiz] NF *Entom* flea-beetle; **a. potagère** turnip-fly

altiste [altist] NMF *Mus* viola player, violist

altitude [altityd] NF altitude; **a. au-dessus du niveau de la mer** height above sea level; **à une a. de 4500 m, à 4500 m d'a.** at an altitude of 4,500 m; **à haute/basse a.** at high/low altitude; **prendre de l'a.** to gain altitude, to climb; **perdre de l'a.** to lose altitude

❑ **d'altitude** ADJ *(restaurant, station)* mountain-top

❑ **en altitude** ADV high up, at high altitude

alto [alto] NM *Mus* **1** *(instrument à cordes)* viola; *(saxophone)* alto **2** *(voix)* contralto *or* alto (voice); *(chanteuse)* contralto, alto; **je suis a.** I sing alto *or* contralto

altocumulus [altokymylys] NM *Météo* altocumulus

altostratus [altostratys] NM *Météo* altostratus

altruisme [altrɥism] NM altruism

altruiste [altrɥist] ADJ altruistic

NMF altruist

Altuglas® [altyglas] NM *Br* ≃ Perspex®, *Am* ≃ Plexiglas®

alu [aly] NM *Fam Br* aluminium■, *Am* aluminum■; **papier a.** *Br* tinfoil■, aluminium foil■, *Am* aluminum foil

alucite [alysit] NF *Entom* plume moth, *Spéc* alucita, **a. (des céréales)** corn-moth

aluette [alyɛt] NF *Cartes* = card game, originally from Spain, using 48 special cards and in which the players use a system of sign language

alule [alyl] NF *Orn* alula

aluminage [alyminaʒ] NM *Métal* alumination, aluming

aluminate [alyminat] NM *Chim* aluminate

alumine [alymin] NF *Chim* alumina, *Br* aluminium *or Am* aluminum oxide

aluminé, -e [alymine] ADJ *Chim* aluminized

aluminer [3] [alymine] VT *Métal* to aluminate, to alum

aluminerie [alyminri] NF *Ind Br* aluminium *or Am* aluminum works

alumineux, -euse [alyminø, -øz] ADJ *Chim* aluminous

aluminiage [alyminjaʒ] NM *Métal* aluminizing

aluminisation [alyminizasjɔ̃] NF *Métal* aluminizing

aluminium [alyminjɔm] NM *Br* aluminium, *Am* aluminum

aluminosilicate [alyminɔsilikat] NM *Chim* aluminosilicate

aluminothermie [alyminɔtɛrmi] NF *Métal* aluminothermy

aluminure [alyminyr] NF *Métal* aluminizing

alun [alœ̃] NM *Chim* alum

alunage [alynaʒ] NM **1** *Métal* aluming **2** *Phot (de négatifs)* alum-hardening, hardening

aluner [3] [alyne] VT **1** *Métal* to alum **2** *Phot* to harden; **bain aluné** hardening bath

alunir [32] [alynir] VI *Astron* to land (on the moon)

alunissage [alynisaʒ] NM *Astron* (moon *or* lunar) landing

alunite [alynit] NF *Chim* alunite

alvéolaire [alveɔlɛr] ADJ *Anat & Ling* alveolar

alvéole [alveɔl] NF **1** *(d'une ruche)* cell, *Spéc* alveolus **2** *Anat* **a. dentaire** tooth socket, *Spéc* alveolus; **a. pulmonaire** air cell, *Spéc* alveolus **3** *Géol* cavity, pit

alvéolé, -e [alveɔle] ADJ honeycombed, *Spéc* alveolate

alvéolite [alveɔlit] NF *Méd* alveolitis

alysse [alis] NF *Bot* alyssum

alyte [alit] NM *Zool* midwife toad, *Spéc* alytes

AM *(abrév écrite* **Assurance maladie***)* health insurance

amabilité [amabilite] NF *(qualité)* kindness, friendliness, amiability; **un homme plein d'a.** a very kind man; **ils ont eu l'a. de...** they were kind enough to...; **d'un ton sans a.** rather curtly; **veuillez avoir l'a. de...** please be so kind as to...

❑ **amabilités** NFPL *(politesses)* polite remarks; **faire des amabilités à qn** to be polite to sb; **trêve d'amabilités, passons aux choses sérieuses** enough of the pleasantries, let's get down to business

amadou [amadu] NM *Bot* touchwood, tinder

amadouer [6] [amadwe] VT **1** *(enjôler)* to cajole; **elle essaie de l'a. pour qu'il accepte** she's trying to cajole *or* to coax him into agreeing **2** *(adoucir)* to mollify, to soften (up); **c'est pour m'a. que tu me dis ça?** are you saying this to soften me up?

►**s'amadouer** VPR to mellow; **s'a. avec l'âge** to mellow with age

amadouvier [amaduvje] NM *Bot* tinder fungus, tinder agaric

amaigri, -e [amegri] ADJ *(visage)* gaunt; *(trait)* (more) pinched; **je le trouve très a.** he looks a lot thinner *or* as if he's lost a lot of weight

amaigrir [32] [amegrir] VT **1** *(sujet: maladie, régime)* to make thin *or* thinner; **son séjour en prison l'a beaucoup amaigri** he's lost a lot of weight while he's been in prison; **le visage amaigri par la maladie** his/her face emaciated from illness **2** *Tech (épaisseur)* to reduce; *(pâte)* to thin down **3** *Agr (sol)* to impoverish

►**s'amaigrir** VPR to lose weight

amaigrissant, -e [amegrisɑ̃, -ɑ̃t] ADJ slimming, *Am* reducing

amaigrissement [amegrismɑ̃] NM **1** *(perte de poids → du corps)* weight loss; *(→ des cuisses, de la silhouette)* weight reduction; **un a. de 10 kg** a weight reduction of 10 kg **2** *Tech (de l'épaisseur)* reducing; *(d'une pâte)* thinning down

Amalécites [amalesit] NMPL *Bible* Amalekites

amalgamation [amalgamasjɔ̃] NF *Chim* amalgamation

amalgame [amalgam] NM **1** *Métal* amalgam **2** *(mélange)* mixture, amalgam; **il ne faut pas faire l'a. entre ces deux questions** the two issues must not be confused **3** *Hist & Mil* amalgamation

amalgamer [3] [amalgame] VT **1** *Métal* to amalgamate **2** *(mélanger → ingrédients)* to combine, to mix up **3** *(réunir → services, sociétés)* to amalgamate; **les deux unités ont été amalgamées** the two units have been amalgamated

►**s'amalgamer** VPR **1** *Métal* to amalgamate **2** *(s'unir)* to combine, to amalgamate **3** *(se mélanger)* to get mixed up

Amalthée [amalte] NPR *Myth* Amaltheia, Amalthea

aman [amɑ̃] NM *Littéraire* safe-conduct; *Arch* **demander l'a.** to surrender

amanché, -e [amɑ̃ʃe] ADJ *Can Fam* **1** *(habillé)* **bien a.** well dressed■; **mal a.** badly dressed■; **être a. comme la chienne de Jacques** to be dressed like a dog's dinner **2 être a.** *(dans une*

mauvaise passe) to be up the creek; **je la plains d'être amanchée avec cette ivrogne** I feel really sorry for her being stuck with that drunk

amancher [3] [amɑ̃ʃe] **VT** *Can* **1** *(disposer)* to arrange **2** *Fam* **se faire a.** *(se faire rouler)* to be had *or* conned; *(devenir enceinte)* to get knocked up

amandaie [amɑ̃dɛ] **NF** almond grove

amande [amɑ̃d] **NF** **1** *(fruit)* almond; **chocolat aux amandes** almond chocolate; **a. douce/amère** sweet/bitter almond **2** *(noyau)* kernel
▫ **d'amande(s)** **ADJ** almond *(avant n)*
▫ **en amande** **ADJ** *(yeux)* almond-shaped

amandier [amɑ̃dje] **NM** *Bot* almond tree

amandine [amɑ̃din] **NF** *Culin* almond tartlet

amanite [amanit] **NF** *Bot* amanita; **a. panthère** false blusher; **a. phalloïde** death-cap; **a. tue-mouches** fly agaric; **a. vaginée** grisette; **a. vineuse** blushing amanita, blushing mushroom

amant [amɑ̃] **NM** (male) lover; **prendre un a.** to take a lover
▫ **amants** **NMPL** lovers; **devenir amants** to become lovers; **les amants de Vérone** Romeo and Juliet

'L'Amant' *Duras* 'The Lover'

'L'Amant de lady Chatterley' *Lawrence* 'Lady Chatterley's Lover'

'Les Amants' *Malle* 'The Lovers'

'Les Amants du Pont-Neuf' *Carax* 'Les Amants du Pont-Neuf' (UK), 'The Lovers on the Bridge'

'Les Amants magnifiques' *Molière* 'Love's the Best'

amante [amɑ̃t] **NF** *Littéraire* lover, mistress

amarantacée [amarɑ̃tase] *Bot* **NF** member of the Amaranthaceae family
▫ **amarantacées** **NFPL** Amaranthaceae

amarante [amarɑ̃t] **ADJ INV** *(couleur)* amaranthine
NF 1 *Bot* amaranth, love-lies-bleeding **2** *Menuis* amaranth (wood)

amaretto [amarɛto] **NM** *(boisson)* amaretto

amareyeur, -euse [amarɛjœr, -øz] **NM,F** *Pêche* oyster-bed worker

amaril, -e [amaril] **ADJ** *Méd* amaril; **fièvre amarile** yellow fever

amarinage [amarinaʒ] **NM** *Naut* **1** *(habitude)* getting used to the sea, finding one's sea legs **2** *(remplacement)* manning *(of a captured vessel)*

amariner [3] [amarine] **VT** *Naut* **1** *(habituer à la mer)* to accustom to life at sea **2** *(navire)* to take over
▫ **s'amariner** **VPR** to find one's sea legs

amarnien, -enne [amarnjɛ̃, -ɛn] **ADJ** *Géog & Hist* Amarnian; **les lettres amarniennes** the Amarna letters

amarrage [amaraʒ] **NM 1** *Naut (dans un port)* mooring **2** *Naut (à un objet fixe)* lashing **3** *Aviat (d'un ballon)* mooring; *Astron* docking **4** *Naut (amarres)* ropes
▫ **à l'amarrage** **ADJ** *Naut & Aviat* moored

amarre [amar] **NF** *Naut* mooring line *or* rope; **larguer les amarres** to cast off, to slip the moorings; *Fig* to set off; **rompre les amarres** to break its moorings; *Fig* to break off all links

amarrer [3] [amare] **VT 1** *Naut (cordages)* to fasten, to make fast; *(navire)* to hitch, to moor **2** *(bagages)* to tie down; **nous avons amarré les valises sur le toit de la voiture** we tied the luggage to the car roof **3** *Astron* to dock
USAGE ABSOLU *Naut* **a. à quai** to wharf
▫ **s'amarrer** **VPR** *Naut (à une berge)* to moor; *(dans un port)* to dock, to berth **2** *Astron* to dock

amaryllidacée [amarilidase] *Bot* **NF** amaryllid, *Spéc* member of the Amaryllidaceae family
▫ **amaryllidacées** **NFPL** Amaryllidaceae

amaryllis [amarilis] **NF** *Bot* amaryllis

amas [amɑ] **NM 1** *(tas)* heap, mass, jumble **2** *Astron* cluster; **a. globulaire/ouvert** globular/open cluster **3** *Minér* mass

amasser [3] [amase] **VT 1** *(entasser → vivres, richesses)* to amass, to hoard; **a. une fortune** to amass a fortune; **après avoir amassé un petit pécule** having got together a bit of money **2** *(rassembler → preuves, information)* to amass
▫ **s'amasser** **VPR** *(foule, troupeau)* to gather *or* to mass (in large numbers); *(preuves)* to accumulate, to pile up

amateur [amatœr] **ADJ 1** *(avec ou sans trait d'union) (non professionnel)* amateur *(avant n)*; *Sport* amateur, non-professional; **théâtre a.** amateur theatre; **photographe/peintre a.** amateur photographer/painter; *Sport* **rencontre a.** amateur event
2 *(friand, adepte)* **être a. de qch** to be very interested in sth; **elle est a. de concerts** she's a keen *or* dedicated concert-goer; **il est a. de bonne chère** he's very fond of good food
NM

> Note that the feminine noun **amatrice** is now quite commonly used but some French speakers nonetheless regard this form as unacceptable. French Canadians tend to use the form **amateure**. See also the entry **féminisation**.

1 *(non professionnel → gén)* & *Sport* amateur
2 *Péj (dilettante)* dilettante, mere amateur
3 *(connaisseur)* **a. de** connoisseur of; **a. d'art** art lover *or* enthusiast
4 *Fam (preneur)* taker; **il y a des amateurs?** any takers?; **je ne suis pas a.** I'm not interested▪, I don't go in for that sort of thing
▫ **d'amateur** **ADJ** *Péj* amateurish; **c'est du travail d'a.** it's a shoddy piece of work
▫ **en amateur** **ADV** non-professionally; **je fais de la compétition en a.** I compete non-professionally *or* as an amateur; **s'intéresser à qch en a.** to have an amateur interest in sth

amateurisme [amatœrism] **NM 1** *(gén)* & *Sport* amateurism, amateur sport **2** *Péj (dilettantisme)* amateurism, amateurishness; **c'est de l'a.** it's amateurish

amatir [32] [amatir] **VT** *(surface)* to mat, to dull; *(or, argent)* to deaden

amaurose [amoroz] **NF** *Méd* amaurosis

Amazone [amazon] **NPR** *Myth* Amazon
NF *Géog* **l'A.** the Amazon (river)

amazone [amazon] **NF 1** *(cavalière)* horsewoman **2** *(tenue)* (woman's) riding habit; *(jupe)* riding skirt **3** *Fam Arg crime (prostituée)* = prostitute operating from a car **4** *Orn* Amazon parrot
▫ **en amazone** **ADV** **monter en a.** to ride side-saddle

Amazonie [amazoni] **NF** **l'A.** the Amazon (Basin)

amazonien, -enne [amazɔnjɛ̃, -ɛn] **ADJ** Amazonian; **la forêt amazonienne** the Amazon Forest
▫ **Amazonien, -enne** **NM,F** Amazonian

amazonite [amazɔnit] **NF** *Minér* amazonite

ambages [ɑ̃baʒ] **sans ambages** **ADV** without beating about the bush

ambassade [ɑ̃basad] **NF 1** *(bâtiment)* embassy; **l'a. du Canada** the Canadian Embassy **2** *(fonction)* ambassadorship **3** *(personnel)* embassy (staff) **4** *(mission)* mission; **être envoyé en a. auprès de qn** to be sent on a mission to sb

ambassadeur, -drice [ɑ̃basadœr, -dris] **NM,F 1** *(diplomate)* ambassador; **c'est l'a. du Canada** he's the Canadian Ambassador; **a. auprès de** ambassador to; **a. extraordinaire** ambassador extraordinary
2 *Fig (représentant)* representative, ambassador; **vous êtes les ambassadeurs de votre pays** you are ambassadors for your country
▫ **ambassadrice** **NF** *(femme d'ambassadeur)* ambassador's wife; *(diplomate)* (woman) ambassador, ambassadress

ambassadorial, -e, -aux, -ales [ɑ̃basadɔrjal, -o] **ADJ** ambassadorial

ambiance [ɑ̃bjɑ̃s] **NF 1** *(atmosphère)* mood, atmosphere; **l'a. qui règne à Paris** the general atmosphere *or* mood in Paris; **l'a. générale du marché** the prevailing mood of the market; **comment créer une a. intime** how to create an intimate atmosphere
2 *(cadre)* surroundings, ambiance; *(éclairage)* lighting effects
3 *Fam (animation)* **il y a de l'a. ici!** it's pretty lively in here!; **mettre de l'a.** to liven things up; **il**

va y avoir de l'a. quand elle saura ça! there'll be hell to pay when she hears this!
▫ **d'ambiance** **ADJ** *(éclairage)* soft, subdued; *(musique)* mood *(avant n)*

ambiancer [16] [ɑ̃bjɑ̃se] **VI** *(en Afrique francophone)* to liven things up

ambianceur [ɑ̃bjɑ̃sœr] **NM** *(en Afrique francophone)* party animal

ambiant, -e [ɑ̃bjɑ̃, -ɑ̃t] **ADJ** **température ambiante** room temperature; *Tech* ambient temperature; **les préjugés ambiants** the reigning *or* prevailing prejudices; **la médiocrité ambiante** the all-pervading mediocrity

ambidextre [ɑ̃bidɛkstr] **ADJ** ambidextrous
NMF ambidexter

ambient [ambjɛnt] **NM** *Mus* ambient, ambient music

ambigu, -ë [ɑ̃bigy] **ADJ 1** *(à deux sens)* ambiguous, equivocal; **l'expression est ambiguë** the phrase has two possible meanings *or* is ambiguous; **de façon ambiguë** ambiguously, equivocally **2** *(difficile à cerner)* ambiguous; **c'est un personnage a.** he/she is an ambiguous character

ambiguïté [ɑ̃biguite] **NF 1** *(équivoque)* ambiguity; **réponse sans a.** unequivocal *or* unambiguous answer; **répondre sans a.** to answer unequivocally *or* unambiguously **2** *Ling* ambiguity

ambigument [ɑ̃bigymɑ̃] **ADV** ambiguously

ambiophonie [ɑ̃bjɔfɔni] **NF** *Tech* Ambisonics® *(singulier)*

ambisexué, -e [ɑ̃bisɛksɥe] **ADJ** ambisexual, bisexual

ambitieuse [ɑ̃bisjøz] *voir* **ambitieux**

ambitieusement [ɑ̃bisjøzmɑ̃] **ADV** ambitiously

ambitieux, -euse [ɑ̃bisjø, -øz] **ADJ** ambitious; **trop a.** overambitious
NM,F ambitious man, *f* ambitious woman

ambition [ɑ̃bisjɔ̃] **NF 1** *(désir)* ambition, aspiration; **une seule a. l'anime** he/she has but one ambition; **j'ai l'a.** *ou* **mon a. est de...** it's my ambition to...
2 *(désir de réussite)* ambition; **avoir de l'a.** to be ambitious; **je n'ai pas beaucoup d'a.** I'm not particularly ambitious; **être plein d'a.** to be very ambitious; **manquer d'a.** to lack ambition; **un homme sans a.** an unambitious man

ambitionner [3] [ɑ̃bisjɔne] **VT** *(poste)* to have one's heart set on; **elle ambitionne de monter sur les planches** her ambition is to go on the stage
VI *Can (exagérer)* to overdo it; *Fig* **a. sur le pain béni** to take undue advantage
▫ **s'ambitionner** **VPR** *Can* to drive oneself hard

ambitus [ɑ̃bitys] **NM** *Mus* range

ambivalence [ɑ̃bivalɑ̃s] **NF** ambivalence

ambivalent, -e [ɑ̃bivalɑ̃, -ɑ̃t] **ADJ** ambivalent

amble [ɑ̃bl] **NM** *(chameau, cheval)* amble; **aller l'a.** to amble

ambler [3] [ɑ̃ble] **VI** *Arch* to amble

ambleur, -euse [ɑ̃blœr, -øz] *Équitation* **ADJ** ambling
NM,F ambler

amblyope [ɑ̃blijɔp] *Opt* **ADJ** amblyopic
NMF amblyopia sufferer

amblyopie [ɑ̃blijɔpi] **NF** *Opt* amblyopia

amblyoscope [ɑ̃blijɔskɔp] **NM** *Opt* amblyoscope

amblystome [ɑ̃blistɔm] = **ambystome**

ambon [ɑ̃bɔ̃] **NM** *Archit* ambo

ambre [ɑ̃br] **ADJ INV** amber
NM **a. (gris)** ambergris; *Bot* **a. (jaune)** amber

ambré, -e [ɑ̃bre] **ADJ** *(couleur)* amber; *(parfum)* amber-scented; **un vin a.** an amber-coloured wine

ambréine [ɑ̃brein] **NF** *Chim* ambrein

ambrer [3] [ɑ̃bre] **VT** to scent with amber

ambrette [ɑ̃brɛt] **NF 1** *Bot* abel-musk, musk-mallow (of India); *(en parfumerie)* musk-seed, ambrette **2** *Hort* sweet sultan; **poire d'a.** ambrette

ambroisie [ɑ̃brwazi] **NF 1** *Myth* ambrosia **2** *Bot* ragweed, ambrosia; **a. à feuille d'Armoise** common *or* short ragweed

ambroisien, -enne [ɑ̃brwazjɛ̃, -ɛn] **ADJ** ambrosial

ambrosiaque [ɑ̃brɔzjak] **ADJ** ambrosial

ambrosien, -enne [ɑ̃brɔzjɛ̃, -ɛn] **ADJ** *Rel* Ambrosian

ambulacraire [ɑ̃bylakrɛr] **ADJ** *Zool* ambulacral

ambulacre [ɑ̃bylakr] **NM** *Zool* ambulacrum

ambulance [ɑ̃bylɑ̃s] NF ambulance; **en a.** in an ambulance; *Fig* **on ne tire pas sur une a.** you shouldn't kick a man when he's down

ambulancier, -ère [ɑ̃bylɑ̃sje, -ɛr] NM,F **1** *(chauffeur)* ambulance driver **2** *(infirmier)* ambulance man, *f* ambulance woman

ambulant, -e [ɑ̃bylɑ̃, -ɑ̃t] ADJ itinerant, travelling; *Fam* **c'est un dictionnaire a.** he's/she's a walking dictionary

ambulatoire [ɑ̃bylatwar] ADJ *Méd & Jur* ambulatory

ambystome [ɑ̃bistɔm] *Zool* NM ambystomid (salamander)
□ **ambystomes** NMPL Ambystoma, Amblystoma

AME [ɑɛmø] NM *Écon* (*abrév* **Accord monétaire européen**) EMA

âme [ɑm] NF **1** *(vie)* soul; **avoir l'â. chevillée au corps** to hang on grimly to life; **rendre l'â.** to pass away
2 *(personnalité)* soul, spirit; **avoir** *ou* **être une â. généreuse** to have great generosity of spirit; **avoir une â. de chef** to be a born leader
3 *(principe moral)* **en mon â. et conscience** in all conscience
4 *(cœur)* soul, heart; **faire qch avec/sans â.** to do sth with/without feeling; **sans â.** *(personne)* unfeeling; *(tableau, ville)* soulless, that has no soul; **touché jusqu'au fond de l'â.** deeply moved; **de toute mon â.** with all my heart *or* soul; **c'est un artiste dans l'â.** he's a born artist
5 *(personne)* soul; **un village de cinq cents âmes** a village of five hundred souls; **mon â., ma chère â.** *(en appellatif)* (my) dearest; **â. charitable, bonne â.** kind soul; *Ironique* **il y a toujours de bonnes âmes pour conseiller quand c'est trop tard!** there are always plenty of people ready with helpful advice when it's too late!; **son â. damnée** the person who does his/her evil deeds *or* dirty work for him/her; **aller** *ou* **errer comme une â. en peine** to wander around like a lost soul; **â. sensible** sensitive person; **âmes sensibles, s'abstenir** not for the squeamish; **â. sœur** kindred spirit, soul mate; **chercher/trouver l'â. sœur** to seek/to find a soul mate; **il n'y a pas â. qui vive** there isn't a (living) soul around
6 *Littéraire (inspirateur)* soul; *Fig* **c'était elle, l'â. du groupe** she was the inspiration of the group; **celui qui était l'â. du dadaïsme** he who was the moving spirit behind Dadaism
7 *(d'une arme)* bore; **â. rayée** rifled bore
8 *(centre → d'un aimant, d'une statue)* core; *(→ d'un câble)* heart, core; *(d'une poutre)* web
9 *(d'un violon)* soundpost

===============================

'Les Âmes mortes' *Gogol* 'Dead Souls'

----

amélanchier [amelɑ̃ʃje] NM *Bot* amelanchier, shadbush, snowy mespil; **a. à grappes** Juneberry

améliorable [ameljɔrabl] ADJ improvable, that can be improved

améliorant, -e [ameljɔrɑ̃, -ɑ̃t] ADJ soil-improving

amélioration [ameljɔrasjɔ̃] NF **1** *(action)* improving, bettering; **assurer l'a. des conditions de travail** to ensure that working conditions are improved; *Agr* **a. des sols** soil improvement
2 *(résultat)* improvement; *Ordinat (d'image, de qualité)* enhancement; **apporter des améliorations à qch** to improve on sth, to carry out improvements to sth; **on observe une nette a. de son état de santé** his/her condition has improved considerably; **a. (du temps)** better weather; **pas d'a. prévue cet après-midi** no improvement expected in the weather this afternoon; *Bourse* **a. des cours** improvement in prices; *Mktg* **a. du produit** product augmentation, product improvement
□ **améliorations** NFPL *Jur* improvements; **apporter des améliorations à qch** to carry out improvements to sth

améliorer [3] [ameljɔre] VT **1** *(changer en mieux → sol)* to improve; *(→ relations)* to improve, to make better; *(→ productivité)* to increase, to improve
2 *(perfectionner → technique)* to improve, to better; **a. son anglais** to improve one's (knowledge of) English
3 *Sport (record, score)* to better, to improve on

4 *Ordinat (logiciel)* to upgrade; *(image, qualité)* to enhance
▸**s'améliorer** VPR to improve; **le vin s'améliore en vieillissant** wine improves with age; **l'état de la malade s'est un peu amélioré** there's been some improvement in the patient's condition; **le temps s'améliore** the weather's getting better, the weather's improving; **ça ne s'améliore pas** it's not getting any better

amen [amɛn] NM INV *Rel* amen; **tu dis a. à tout ce qu'elle fait** you agree with everything she does

aménageable [amenaʒabl] ADJ **1** *(bureau, logement)* convertible; **un espace a. en garage** space which can be converted into a garage **2** *(emploi du temps)* flexible

aménagement [amenaʒmɑ̃] NM **1** *(d'une pièce, d'un local)* fitting (out); *(d'un parc)* laying out, designing; *(d'un terrain)* landscaping; **on prévoit l'a. d'un des bureaux en salle de réunion** we're planning to convert one of the offices into a meeting room
2 *Admin* **a. foncier** improvement of land; **a. rural** rural development *or* planning; **a. du territoire** town and country planning, regional development; **a. urbain** urban planning; **a. urbain et rural** town and country planning
3 *(refonte → d'un texte)* redrafting, adjusting
4 *(assouplissement)* **a. du temps de travail** flexibility of working hours; **il a obtenu des aménagements d'horaire** he managed to get his timetable rearranged; **a. fiscal** tax adjustment
□ **aménagements** NMPL **aménagements intérieurs** (fixtures and) fittings

aménager [17] [amenaʒe] VT **1** *(parc)* to design, to lay out; *(terrain)* to landscape; *(région)* to develop; **a. une sortie sur une autoroute** to build an exit onto a motorway
2 *(équiper)* to fit out, to equip; **grenier aménagé** loft conversion; **camping aménagé** fully equipped camping site; **plage aménagée** beach with full amenities
3 *(transformer)* **a. une pièce en atelier** to convert a room into a workshop
4 *(installer)* to install, to fit; **a. un placard sous un escalier** to fit or to install a cupboard under a staircase; **il aménagea une cachette dans le grenier** he made a place to hide things in the attic
5 *(assouplir → horaire)* to plan, to work out
6 *(refaire → texte)* to adapt, to redraft

aménageur, -euse [amenaʒœr, -øz] NM,F planner

aménagiste [amenaʒist] NMF *(d'une forêt)* forest manager

amendable [amɑ̃dabl] ADJ **1** *Jur & Pol (texte)* amendable **2** *Agr* improvable **3** *Suisse* liable to be fined

amende [amɑ̃d] NF fine; **une a. de 30 euros, 30 euros d'a.** a 30-euro fine; **avoir une a. de 30 euros** to be fined 30 euros; **être condamné à une grosse a.** to be heavily fined; **défense d'entrer sous peine d'a.** *(sur panneau)* trespassers will be fined *or* prosecuted; **a. forfaitaire** on-the-spot fine; **mettre qn à l'a.** to fine sb; *Fig* to penalize sb; **faire a. honorable** to make amends

amendement [amɑ̃dmɑ̃] NM **1** *Jur & Pol* amendment; **a. constitutionnel** constitutional amendment; **a. européen** European amendment **2** *Agr (incorporation)* fertilizing, enrichment; *(substance)* fertilizer

amender [3] [amɑ̃de] VT **1** *Jur & Pol* to amend **2** *Agr* to fertilize **3** *Littéraire (corriger)* to amend **4** *Suisse (infliger d'une amende)* to fine
▸**s'amender** VPR to mend one's ways, to turn over a new leaf

amène [amɛn] ADJ *Littéraire* affable, amiable; **d'une façon peu a.** in a very unpleasant manner

amenée [amne] *d'amenée* ADJ supply *(avant n)*

amener [19] [amne] VT **1** *(faire venir → personne)* to bring (along); **a. qn chez soi** to bring sb round to one's place, to bring sb home; **amenez vos amis!** (do) bring your friends!; **qu'est-ce qui vous amène?** what brings you here?; **a. des capitaux** to attract capital; **a. l'eau à ébullition** to bring the water to the boil; **a. la conversation sur un sujet** to bring the conversation round to a subject; *Fig* **qu'est-ce qui vous a amené à la musique/à Dieu?** what got you involved with music/made you turn to God?

2 *Fam (apporter)* to bring (along)■; **amène les couteaux** bring *or* get the knives; **j'amènerai mon travail** I'll bring some work along
3 *(acheminer)* to bring, to convey; *(conduire → sujet: véhicule, chemin)* to take; **le pipeline amène le pétrole au terminal** the pipeline brings the oil to the terminal; **les journaux sont amenés par avion** the papers are brought (over) by air; **la petite route vous amène à la plage** the path will take you to the beach; **dans le taxi qui les amenait au bureau** in the taxi taking them to the office
4 *(provoquer → perte, ruine)* to bring about, to cause; *(→ guerre, maladie, crise)* to bring (on) *or* about, to cause; *(→ paix)* to bring about
5 *(entraîner)* **mon métier m'amène à voyager** my job involves a lot of travelling; **son travail l'amène à rencontrer beaucoup de monde** he/she meets a lot of people through his/her work; **la police a été amenée à interroger des centaines de personnes au cours de l'enquête** the police ended up having to question hundreds of people during the investigation; **et ceci nous amène à parler de la ponctualité** which brings us to the question of punctuality
6 *(inciter)* **a. qn à faire qch** to lead sb to do sth; *(en lui parlant)* to talk sb into doing sth
7 *(introduire → sujet)* to introduce; **un bon auteur sait a. le dénouement de son récit** a good author knows how to bring his/her story to a conclusion
8 *Cartes* to throw
9 *Naut (drapeau)* to strike; *Mil* **a. les couleurs** to strike the colours
10 *(tirer → filets)* to draw in
▸**s'amener** VPR *Fam* to come along■, to turn up, to show up; **alors, tu t'amènes?** are you coming or aren't you?; **elle s'est amenée avec deux types** she showed up with two blokes; **faut s'a. avec une cravate?** do you have to wear a tie?

aménité [amenite] NF *(caractère)* amiability, affability; **sans a.** ungraciously, somewhat curtly
□ **aménités** NFPL *Ironique* insults, cutting remarks

aménorrhée [amenɔre] NF *Méd* amenorrhoea

amentales [amɑ̃tal] NFPL *Bot* amentiferae

amentifère [amɑ̃tifɛr] *Bot* ADJ amentiferous
□ **amentifères** NFPL amentiferae

amenuisement [amənɥizmɑ̃] NM *(de rations, de l'espoir)* dwindling; *(des chances)* lessening

amenuiser [3] [amənɥize] VT **1** *(amincir → planche, bande)* to thin down **2** *(diminuer → économies, espoir)* to diminish, to reduce
▸**s'amenuiser** VPR *(rations, espoir)* to dwindle, to run low; *(chances)* to grow *or* to get slimmer; *(distance)* to grow smaller

amer[1] [amɛr] NM *Naut* seamark

amer[2], **-ère** [amɛr] ADJ **1** *(fruit)* bitter; **orange amère** bitter orange, Seville orange; **a. comme (du) chicotin** as bitter as wormwood **2** *Fig (déception)* bitter
NM *(alcool)* bitters

amérasien, -enne [amerazjɛ̃, -ɛn] ADJ Amerasian
□ **Amérasien, -enne** NM,F Amerasian

amère [amɛr] *voir* **amer**[2]

amèrement [amɛrmɑ̃] ADV bitterly

américain, -e [amerikɛ̃, -ɛn] ADJ American
NM **1** *Ling* American English
2 *Belg Fam Culin (steak tartare)* steak tartare■; *(bifteck de viande crue et maigre)* steak■
□ **Américain, -e** NM,F American
□ **américaine** NF **1** *(voiture)* American car; **une grosse américaine** a big American car
2 *(course cycliste)* track relay (race)
□ **à l'américaine** ADJ **1** *Archit* American-style
2 *Culin* à l'américaine *(cooked with tomatoes)*

américanisation [amerikanizasjɔ̃] NF Americanization

américaniser [3] [amerikanize] VT to Americanize
▸**s'américaniser** VPR to become Americanized

américanisme [amerikanism] NM **1** *(science)* American studies **2** *(tournure)* Americanism

américaniste [amerikanist] ADJ *(étudiant)* specializing in American studies
NMF Americanist

américanocentriste [amerikanosɑ̃trist] ADJ American-centric

américium [amerisjɔm] NM *Chim* americium

amérindianisme [amerɛ̃djɛ̃nism] NM *Can* Amerindianism, = Canadian word derived from an Amerindian language

amérindien, -enne [amerɛ̃djɛ̃, -ɛn] ADJ Amerindian, American Indian
□ **Amérindien, -enne** NM,F Amerindian, American Indian

Amérique [amerik] NF **l'A.** America; **l'A. centrale/latine/du Nord/du Sud** Central/Latin/North/South America

amerlo [amɛrlo] NMF *Fam Vieilli* Yank, Yankee

amerloque [amɛrlɔk] NMF *Fam* Yank, Yankee

amerlot [amɛrlo] = **amerlo**

amerrir [32] [amerir] VI *Aviat* to land (on the sea), to make a sea landing; *Astron* to splash down; **faire a. un hydravion** to land a seaplane

amerrissage [amerisaʒ] NM *Aviat* sea landing; *Astron* splashdown; *Aviat* **faire un a. forcé** to make an emergency landing at sea

amertume [amɛrtym] NF bitterness; **être plein d'a.** to be very bitter; **avec a.** bitterly; **remplir d'a.** to embitter, to fill with bitterness

amétabole [ametabɔl] ADJ *Entom* ametabolic, ametabolous

améthyste [ametist] NF *Minér* amethyst

amétrope [ametrɔp] *Opt* ADJ ametropic
NMF ametropia sufferer

amétropie [ametrɔpi] NF *Opt* ametropia

ameublement [amœbləmɑ̃] NM **1** *(meubles)* furniture; **articles d'a.** furnishings **2** *(installation)* furnishing; *(décoration)* (interior) decoration **3** *(activité)* furniture trade

ameublir [32] [amœblir] VT **1** *Agr (sol)* to loosen, to break down **2** *Jur & Fin (biens immobiliers)* to convert into personalty

ameublissement [amœblismɑ̃] NM **1** *Agr (du sol)* loosening, breaking up **2** *Jur & Fin (biens immobiliers)* conversion into personalty, inclusion in the communal estate

ameuter [4] [amœte] VT **1** *(attirer l'attention de)* **le bruit a ameuté les passants** the noise drew a crowd of passers-by; **il a ameuté toute la rue** he got the whole street out; **a. l'opinion publique sur qch** to awaken public opinion to sth; **il faut a. la presse** we must get the press onto this **2** *(chiens)* to form into a pack
► **s'ameuter** VPR to gather, to band together

AMF [aɛmɛf] NF **1** *(abrév* **Association des maires de France***)* = French association of mayors **2** *Bourse* *(abrév* **Autorité des marchés financiers***)* = French Stock Exchange authority

amharique [amarik] NM *(langue)* Amharic

AMI [aɛmi] NM *Fin (abrév* **Accord multilatéral sur l'investissement***)* MAI

ami, -e[1] [ami] ADJ *(voix, peuple, rivage)* friendly; **un pays a.** a friendly country, an ally; **dans une maison amie** in the house of friends
NM,F **1** *(camarade)* friend; **c'est un de mes amis/une de mes amies** he's/she's a friend of mine; *Fam* **des amis à nous** friends of ours; **mes voisins sont des amis** I'm friendly with the people next door; **Tom et moi sommes restés amis** I stayed friends with Tom; **un médecin de mes amis** a doctor friend of mine; **un a. de la famille** *ou* **maison** a friend of the family; **se faire un a. de qn** to make friends with sb; **je m'en suis fait une amie** she became my friend *or* a friend (of mine); **devenir l'a. de qn** to become friends *or* friendly with sb; **ne pas avoir d'amis** to have no friends; **être entre amis** to be among friends; **nous sommes entre amis (ici)** we're among *or* we're all friends (here); **amis d'enfance** childhood friends; **les amis de mes amis sont mes amis** any friend of yours is a friend of mine
2 *(amoureux)* boyfriend; *(amoureuse)* girlfriend; **petit** *ou Vieilli* **bon a.** boyfriend; **petite** *ou Vieilli* **bonne amie** girlfriend
3 *(bienfaiteur)* **l'a. des pauvres/du peuple** the friend of the poor/of the people; **un a. des arts** a patron of the arts; **les amis de la nature/des bêtes** nature/animal lovers
4 *(partisan)* **club des amis de Shakespeare** Shakespeare club *or* society
5 *(comme interjection)* **mon pauvre a.!** you poor fool!; **écoutez, mon jeune a.!** now look here, young man!; **mon a.!** *(entre amis)* my friend!; *(entre époux)* (my) dear!; *Vieilli* **eh, l'a.!** hey, you (over) there!

6 *Fam (locution)* **il a essayé de faire a.-a. avec moi** he came on all buddy-buddy with me
□ **en ami** ADV *(par amitié)* as a friend; *(en non-professionnel)* as a friend, on a friendly basis; **je te le dis en a.** I'm telling you as a friend *or* because I'm your friend; **vous êtes là professionnellement ou en a.?** are you here in your professional capacity or as a friend?

amiable [amjabl] ADJ *(accord, compromis)* amicable, friendly; *Jur* **a. compositeur** = arbitrator who makes a decision in accordance with what is fair rather than in accordance with the law
□ **à l'amiable** ADV privately, amicably; **régler qch à l'a.** *(gén)* to reach an amicable agreement about sth; *(sans procès)* to settle sth out of court ADJ **divorce à l'a.** no-fault divorce

amiante [amjɑ̃t] NM *Minér* asbestos

amiante-ciment [amjɑ̃tsimɑ̃] *(pl* **amiantes-ciments***)* NM *Constr* asbestos cement

amibe [amib] NF *Biol* amoeba

amibiase [amibjaz] NF *Méd* amoebiasis

amibien, -enne [amibjɛ̃, -ɛn] ADJ *Méd* amoebic
NM *Biol* member of the Amoebae

amiboïde [amibɔid] *Biol* ADJ amoeboid, amoeba-like
NM amoeba

amical, -e, -aux, -ales [amikal, -o] ADJ friendly; **peu a.** unfriendly; **un match a.** a friendly (match)
□ **amicale** NF association, club

amicalement [amikalmɑ̃] ADV in a friendly manner; **il lui répondit a.** he answered him in a friendly tone; **discuter a.** to have a friendly chat; **bien a.** *(en fin de lettre)* yours

amict [ami] NM amice

amide [amid] NM *Chim* amide

amidon [amidɔ̃] NM *Chim* starch

amidonnage [amidɔnaʒ] NM *Tex* starching

amidonner [3] [amidɔne] VT *Tex* to starch

amidonnerie [amidɔnri] NF *Chim* starch factory

amidonnier, -ère [amidɔnje, -ɛr] ADJ *Chim* starch *(avant n)*
NM,F *Ind* **1** *(ouvrier)* worker in a starch factory **2** *(fabricant)* starch manufacturer
NM *Bot* emmer; **a. sauvage** wild emmer

amidopyrine [amidɔpirin] NF *Méd* amidopyrine

amie[2] [ami] NF *Ich* bowfin

amiénois, -e [amjenwa, -az] ADJ of/from Amiens
□ **Amiénois, -e** NM,F = inhabitant of or person from Amiens
□ **Amiénois** NM **l'A.** = district of ancient France, with Amiens as its capital

amieuter [3] [amjøte] **s'amieuter** VPR *Can* to improve, to get better

amigne [amiɲ] NF *Suisse* = grape variety from the Valais canton, or white wine produced from these grapes

Amigo [amigo] NM *Belg* **l'A.** = nickname given to the central police station in Brussels

amimie [amimi] NF *Méd* amimia

amimique [amimik] ADJ *Méd (personne)* suffering from amimia

amincir [32] [amɛ̃sir] VT **1** *(amaigrir)* to make thin *or* thinner; *(rendre svelte)* to slim down; **cette veste t'amincit** this jacket makes you look slimmer; **je cherche une coiffure qui amincisse le visage** I'm looking for a hairstyle that'll make my face look thinner **2** *(planche)* to fine down, to thin down
► **s'amincir** VPR to get thin *or* thinner

amincissant, -e [amɛ̃sisɑ̃, -ɑ̃t] ADJ slimming, *Am* reducing

amincissement [amɛ̃sismɑ̃] NM *(d'une épaisseur)* thinning down; *(d'une personne, de la taille, des hanches)* slimming; **après deux mois de régime, elle a constaté un a. de la taille de 2 cm** after dieting for two months, she found that she had lost 2 cm from around the waist; **ce régime favorise l'a.** this diet helps you to lose weight

amine [amin] NF *Chim* amine

aminé, -e [amine] *voir* **acide**

aminoacide [aminoasid] NM *Chim* amino acid

aminogène [aminoʒɛn] NM *Chim* aminogen

aminoplaste [aminoplast] NM *Chim* aminoplastic, aminoplast

amiral, -e, -aux, -ales [amiral, -o] ADJ **vaisseau** *ou* **navire a.** flagship
NM admiral; **a. de la flotte** Admiral of the Fleet
□ **amirale** NF admiral's wife

amirauté [amirote] NF *Naut & Mil (corps des amiraux)* admiralty; *(grade)* admiralship, admiralty; **accéder à l'a.** to become an admiral

amish [amiʃ] ADJ INV *(culture, histoire)* Amish
NMF INV *Rel* Amish

amitié [amitje] NF **1** *(sentiment)* friendship; **faire qch par a.** to do sth out of friendship; **se lier d'a. avec qn** to make friends *or* to strike up a friendship with sb; **prendre qn en a., se prendre d'a. pour qn** to befriend sb, to make friends with sb; **avoir de l'a. pour qn** to be fond of sb; **l'a. qui lie nos deux pays** the friendship between our two countries
2 *(relation)* friendship; **lier** *ou* **nouer une a. avec qn** to strike up a friendship with sb; *Euph* **a. particulière** homosexual relationship, special relationship
3 *(faveur)* kindness, favour; **faites-moi l'a. de rester** please do me the kindness or favour of staying
□ **amitiés** NFPL *(salutations, compliments)* **faites-lui** *ou* **présentez-lui mes amitiés** give him/her my best regards *or* wishes; **il vous fait** *ou* **vous transmet toutes ses amitiés** he sends you his best regards *or* wishes; **mes amitiés à vos parents** best regards to your parents; **(toutes) mes amitiés** *(en fin de lettre)* best regards *or* wishes; **amitiés, Marie** *(en fin de lettre)* love or yours, Marie

amitieux, -euse [amitjø, -øz] ADJ *Belg* friendly, affectionate

amitose [amitoz] NF *Biol* amitosis

AMM [aɛmɛm] NF *Pharm (abrév* **autorisation de mise sur le marché***)* = official authorization for marketing a pharmaceutical product

Amman [aman] NM *Géog* Amman

ammocète [amɔsɛt] NF *Zool* ammocoete

ammodyte [amɔdit] NF **1** *Ich* ammodyte **2** *Zool (vipère)* ammodyte, sand viper

ammonal [amɔnal] NM ammonal

ammoniac, -aque [amɔnjak] ADJ *Chim* ammoniac; **gaz a.** ammonia; **gomme ammoniaque** gum ammoniac; **sel a.** salt ammoniac
NM *Chim* ammonia
□ **ammoniaque** NF *Chim* ammonia (water), aqueous ammonia

ammoniacal, -e, -aux, -ales [amɔnjakal, -o] ADJ *Chim* ammoniacal

ammoniaque [amɔnjak] *voir* **ammoniac**

ammoniaqué, -e [amɔnjake] ADJ *Chim* ammoniated

ammonification [amɔnifikasjɔ̃] NF *Chim* ammonification, ammonization

ammonisation [amɔnizasjɔ̃] NF *Chim* ammonization, ammonification

ammonite [amɔnit] NF *Zool & Géol* ammonite

ammonium [amɔnjɔm] NM *Chim* ammonium

ammoniurie [amɔnjyri] NF *Méd* ammoniuria

ammophile[1] [amɔfil] ADJ ammophilous
NF *Entom* **(guêpe) a.** digger wasp, *Spéc* ammophila

ammophile[2] [amɔfil] NM *Bot* sand reed, *Spéc* ammophila

amnésie [amnezi] NF *Méd* amnesia; **souffrir d'a.** to have amnesia

amnésique [amnezik] *Méd* ADJ *(patient)* amnesic; **être a.** to have amnesia
NMF amnesic, amnesiac

amniocentèse [amnjosɛ̃tɛz] NF *Méd* amniocentesis

amnios [amnjos] NM *Anat & Obst* amnion

amnioscopie [amnjoskɔpi] NF *Méd* amnioscopy

amniote [amnjɔt] *Zool* NM amniote
□ **amniotes** NMPL Amniota

amniotique [amnjotik] ADJ *Anat & Obst* amniotic

amnistiable [amnistjabl] ADJ *Jur* eligible for amnesty

amnistiant, -e [amnistjɑ̃, -ɑ̃t] ADJ *Jur* amnestying

amnistie [amnisti] NF *Jur* amnesty; **accorder une a. à qn** to grant sb amnesty; **l'a. des contraventions** = traditional waiving of parking fines by the French president after a presidential election; **loi d'a.** amnesty law

---

Culture
AMNISTIE
Parking fines as well as some prison sentences are traditionally waived by the French president immediately after a presidential election. The latter is known as "la grâce présidentielle".

amnistié, -e [amnistje] *Jur* **ADJ** amnestied
NM,F *(prisonnier)* amnestied prisoner; *(exilé)* amnestied exile

amnistier [9] [amnistje] **VT** *Jur (personne)* to grant an amnesty to, to amnesty; *(délit)* to grant amnesty for

amoché, -e [amɔʃe] **ADJ** *Fam* **1** *(voiture)* wrecked **2** *(personne, visage)* smashed *or* messed up

amocher [3] [amɔʃe] *Fam* **VT** *(meubles, vêtements)* to ruin▪, to mess up; *(voiture)* to bash up; *(adversaire, boxeur)* to smash up; *(visage, jambe)* to mess up; **se faire a.** to get smashed up; *très Fam* **il s'est fait a. le portrait** he got his face smashed in
▸**s'amocher** **VPR** to get badly bashed; **il s'est salement amoché le genou en tombant de vélo** he fell off his bike and really messed up his knee

amodiataire [amɔdjatɛr] **NMF** *Jur (de terres)* lessee; *(d'une mine)* sublessee

amodiateur, -trice [amɔdjatœr, -tris] **NM,F** *Jur (de terres)* lessor; *(d'une mine)* sublessor

amodiation [amɔdjasjɔ̃] **NF** *Jur (de terre)* leasing; *(d'une mine)* subleasing

amodier [9] [amɔdje] **VT** *Jur* to lease

amoindrir [32] [amwɛ̃drir] **VT 1** *(faire diminuer → valeur, importance)* to diminish, to reduce; *(→ forces)* to weaken; *(→ autorité, faculté)* to weaken, to lessen, to diminish; *(→ réserves)* to diminish
2 *(rendre moins capable)* to weaken, to diminish; **il est sorti de son accident très amoindri** *(physiquement)* his accident left him physically much weaker; *(moralement)* his accident left him psychologically impaired; **se sentir amoindri** to feel weakened
▸**s'amoindrir** **VPR** *(autorité, forces)* to weaken, to grow weaker; *(réserves)* to diminish, to dwindle

amoindrissement [amwɛ̃drismɑ̃] **NM** *(d'une autorité, de facultés)* weakening; *(de forces)* diminishing, weakening; *(de réserves)* reduction, diminishing

amok [amɔk] **ADJ** **être a.** to be running amok
NM *(accès de folie)* frenzy

amollir [32] [amɔlir] **VT** *(beurre, pâte)* to soften, to make soft; *(volonté, forces)* to weaken, to diminish; **a. qn** *(l'adoucir)* to soften sb; *(l'affaiblir)* to weaken sb
▸**s'amollir** **VPR 1** *(beurre, pâte, plastique)* to soften, to become soft; *(jambes)* to go weak **2** *(s'affaiblir → énergie, courage)* to weaken

amollissant, -e [amɔlisɑ̃, -ɑ̃t] **ADJ** enervating

amollissement [amɔlismɑ̃] **NM** debilitation

amome [amɔm] **NM** *Bot* amomum

amonceler [24] [amɔ̃sle] **VT 1** *(entasser → boîtes, livres, chaussures)* to heap up, to pile up; *(→ neige, sable, feuilles)* to bank up; *(→ vivres, richesses)* to amass, to hoard; **a. une fortune** to build up *or* to amass a fortune
2 *(rassembler → documents, preuves, informations)* to amass
▸**s'amonceler** **VPR** *(papiers, boîtes, feuilles)* to heap up, to pile up; *(preuves)* to accumulate, to pile up; *(dettes)* to mount, to pile up; *(neige, sable, nuages)* to bank up

amoncellement [amɔ̃sɛlmɑ̃] **NM** *(d'objets divers, d'ordures)* heap, pile; *(de neige, de sable, de feuilles, de nuages)* heap; *(de richesses)* hoard; **devant cet a. de preuves** faced with this wealth of evidence

amoncellerai *etc voir* **amonceler**

Amon-Rê [amɔ̃re] **NPR** Amen-Ra

amont [amɔ̃] **NM** *(d'une rivière)* upstream water; *(d'une montagne)* uphill slope; **vent d'a.** land breeze; **vers l'a.** *(d'une rivière)* upstream
ADJ INV *(ski, skieur)* uphill *(avant n)*
❑ **en amont** **ADV** *aussi Fig* upstream
❑ **en amont de** **PRÉP** *(rivière)* upstream from; *(montagne)* uphill from, above; **la Tamise en a. de Londres** the Thames upstream from London; *Fig* **les étapes en a. de la production** the stages upstream of production, the pre-production stages

amontillado [amɔ̃tijado] **NM** *(vin)* Amontillado

amoral, -e, -aux, -ales [amɔral, -o] **ADJ** amoral

amoralisme [amɔralism] **NM** *(gén)* & *Phil* amorality

amoralité [amɔralite] **NF** amorality

amorçage [amɔrsaʒ] **NM 1** *Tech (d'une pompe, d'une cartouche)* priming; *Élec (d'une dynamo)* energizing; *(d'un arc électrique)* striking **2** *Pêche* baiting **3** *Ordinat* booting

amorce [amɔrs] **NF 1** *Tech (détonateur)* primer, detonator; *(d'un obus)* percussion cap; *(d'une balle)* cap, primer; *(pétard)* cap; **pistolet à amorces** cap gun **2** *Pêche* bait **3** *(début)* beginning; **l'a. d'une réforme** the beginnings of a reform; *Cin* **a. de début** start leader, head leader; *Cin* **a. de fin** tail leader

amorcer [16] [amɔrse] **VT 1** *(commencer → travaux)* to start, to begin; *(→ réforme)* to initiate, to begin; *(→ discussion, réconciliation)* to start, to begin, to initiate; *(→ virage)* to go into; *(→ descente)* to start, to begin; **ils ont amorcé la dernière tranche des travaux** they're into the final phase of the building work; **les travaux sont bien amorcés** the work is well under way; **elle amorça un pas vers la porte** she made as if to go to the door
2 *Tech (pompe, cartouche)* to prime; *Élec (dynamo)* to energize; *(arc)* to strike
3 *Pêche* to bait
4 *Ordinat* to boot (up); **a. de nouveau** to reboot
USAGE ABSOLU *Pêche* **a. au pain** to use bread as ground bait
▸**s'amorcer** **VPR 1** *(commencer)* to begin; **le processus ne fait que s'a.** the process has only just begun *or* got under way
2 *Ordinat* to boot (up)

amorceur [amɔrsœr] **NM 1** *Élec* igniter **2** *(d'une pompe)* primer

amorçoir [amɔrswar] **NM 1** *Pêche* bait box **2** *Tech (arme)* gunpowder container

amorphe [amɔrf] **ADJ 1** *Fam (indolent)* lifeless▪, passive▪; **cette chaleur me rend totalement a.** this heat is making me lethargic *or* listless▪ **2** *Biol* & *Chim* amorphous

amorphie [amɔrfi] **NF** *Biol* & *Chim* amorphousness

amorti [amɔrti] **NM 1** *Ftbl* **faire un a.** to trap the ball **2** *Tennis* drop shot

amortie [amɔrti] **NF** *Ftbl* & *Tennis* drop shot

amortir [32] [amɔrtir] **VT 1** *(absorber → choc)* to cushion, to absorb; *(→ son)* to deaden, to muffle; *(→ douleur)* to deaden; **l'herbe a amorti sa chute** the grass broke his/her fall; **a. le coup** to cushion *or* to soften the blow; *Fig* to soften the blow
2 *(rentabiliser)* **il a amorti sa nouvelle voiture en six mois** he recouped the cost of his new car in six months; **le matériel a été amorti dès la première année** the equipment paid for itself by the end of the first year, the cost of the equipment was written off by the end of the first year
3 *Fin (dette)* to pay off, to amortize; *(prêt)* to repay; *(équipement)* to depreciate, to write off, to amortize; *(investissement)* to amortize; *Bourse (obligation)* to redeem; **a. des actions** to call in shares
4 *Ftbl (ballon)* to trap; *Tennis (balle)* to kill
▸**s'amortir** **VPR 1** *(dépenses, investissement)* to pay for itself; **un achat qui s'amortit en deux ans** *Écon* a purchase that can be paid off in two years; *Bourse* a purchase that can be redeemed in two years
2 *(s'affaiblir → bruit)* to fade (away)

amortissable [amɔrtisabl] **ADJ** *(dette)* redeemable

amortissement [amɔrtismɑ̃] **NM 1** *(adoucissement → d'un choc)* absorption, cushioning; *(→ d'un coup)* cushioning; *(→ d'un son)* deadening, muffling
2 *Fin (d'une dette)* paying *or* writing off; *(d'un titre)* redemption; *(d'un emprunt)* paying off, amortization
3 *Compta (perte de valeur)* depreciation; **l'a. d'un équipement est plus rapide si on emprunte à court terme** equipment pays for itself faster if it's paid for with a short-term loan; **a. accéléré** accelerated depreciation; **a. annuel** annual depreciation; **a. anticipé** redemption before due date; **a. du capital** depreciation of capital; **a. dégressif** declining balance depreciation, sliding scale depreciation; **a. linéaire** straightline depreciation, diminishing balance (method)
4 *Archit* amortizement

amortisseur [amɔrtisœr] **NM** shock absorber; **a. de vibrations** vibration damper; **a. à gaz** gas strut; **a. hydraulique** hydraulic shock absorber, hydraulic damper; **a. pneumatique** air cushion

Amou Daria [amudarja] **NM** *Géog* Amu Darya

amouillante [amujɑ̃t] **ADJ** *(vache)* about to calve
NF cow about to calve

Amour [amur] **NM** *Géog* **l'A.** the (River) Amur; **la Côte d'A.** = the French Atlantic coast near la Baule
NPR *Myth* **(le dieu) A.** Cupid, Eros

amour [amur] **NM 1** *(sentiment)* love; **une vie sans a.** a loveless life; **son a. des** *ou* **pour les enfants** his/her love of *or* for children; **l'a. de ma mère** *(qu'elle a pour moi)* my mother's love; *(que j'ai pour elle)* my love for my mother; **le grand a.** true love; **éprouver de l'a. pour qn** to feel love for sb; **aimer qn d'a.** to be in love with sb; **être fou d'a. pour qn** to be madly in love with sb; *Can* **être/tomber en a. (avec qn)** to be/fall in love (with sb); *Fam* **ce n'est pas** *ou* **plus de l'a., c'est de la rage!** it's not so much love, it's an obsession!; **l'a. filial** *(d'un fils)* a son's love; *(d'une fille)* a daughter's love; **l'A. Médecin** Doctor Cupid; **l'a. libre** free love; **l'a. maternel/paternel** motherly/fatherly love, a mother's/father's love; **l'a. du prochain** love of one's neighbour
2 *(amant)* lover, love; **un a. de jeunesse** an old flame
3 *(liaison)* (love) affair, romance; **ils ont vécu un grand a.** they had a passionate affair
4 *(acte sexuel)* love-making; **faire l'a. à** *ou* **avec qn** to make love to *or* with sb; **pendant/après l'a.** while/after making love
5 *(vif intérêt)* love; **l'a. de la nature** love of nature; **l'a. de la justice** passion for justice; **faire qch avec a.** to do sth with loving care *or* with love
6 *(terme affectueux)* **mon a.** my love *or* darling; **oui, mon a.!** yes, my love!; **un a. de petite fille** a delightful little girl; **apporte les glaçons, tu seras un a.** be a darling and bring the ice
7 *Beaux-Arts* cupid
❑ **amours** **NFPL 1** *Hum (relations amoureuses)* love life; **comment vont tes amours?** how's your love life (these days)?; **à vos amours!** *(pour trinquer)* cheers!, here's to you!; *(après un éternuement)* bless you! **2** *Zool* courtship and mating **NMPL** *Suisse (vin)* **les amours** = the last drops of wine in a bottle
❑ **d'amour** **ADJ** *(chagrin, chanson)* love *(avant n)*
❑ **par amour** **ADV** out of *or* for love; **par a. pour qn** for the love of sb
❑ **pour l'amour de** **PRÉP** for the love *or* sake of; **pour l'a. de Dieu!** *(ton suppliant)* for the love of God!; *(ton irrité)* for God's sake!; **pour l'a. du ciel!** for heaven's sake!; **faire qch pour l'a. de l'art** to do sth for the sake of it

♫
'L'Amour sorcier' *de Falla* 'Love, the Magician'

🎬
'A nos amours' *Pialat* 'To Our Loves'

📖
'Les Amours jaunes' *Corbière* 'These Jaundiced Loves'

Allusion

Amour, amour, quand tu nous tiens (on peut bien dire: Adieu Prudence!)
This is a quotation from La Fontaine's fable *Le lion amoureux* ("The lion in love"), which was addressed to Mme de Sévigné, with whom he was in love. In its entirety, the quotation means "Love, when you have us in your power, well may we bid farewell to sense!" It is a reflection on the absolute sway of passionate love, which can cause near-insanity. The first two words of the quotation are often dropped, and La Fontaine's conclusion changed thus: **Argent, argent, quand tu nous tiens...** or **Pouvoir, pouvoir, quand tu nous tiens...**, the idea being that one can become utterly enslaved by wealth or power, and engaged in a frenzied pursuit of one's goal.

J'ai deux amours, mon pays et Paris
This is the title of a song made famous by Josephine Baker, the American-born music-hall artiste who was the darling of Paris in the 1920s and 1930s. The French public warmed to this declaration, which means "I have two loves, my own country and Paris", delivered in Josephine Baker's American-accented voice. In modern variants, people will substitute other terms, for example, **J'ai deux amours, la science et la voile** ("I have two loves, science and sailing").

amouracher [3] [amuraʃe] **s'amouracher** VPR **s'a. de qn** to become infatuated with sb

amour-en-cage [amurãkaʒ] (*pl* **amours-en-cage**) NM *Bot* ground *or* winter cherry, Chinese lantern

amourette¹ [amurɛt] NF **1** (*liaison*) casual love affair **2** *Can Vulg* **amourettes** balls, nuts, *Br* bollocks
▫ **amourettes** NFPL *Culin* marrowbone jelly (UNCOUNT)

amourette² [amurɛt] NF *Bot* quaking-grass; **bois d'a.** snakewood, letterwood

amoureuse [amurøz] *voir* **amoureux**

amoureusement [amurøzmã] ADV lovingly; **il la regardait a.** he watched her lovingly *or* with love in his eyes

amoureux, -euse [amurø, -øz] ADJ **1** (*tendre → regard, geste*) loving, tender; (*vie, exploit*) love (*avant n*)
2 (*épris*) **un homme a.** a man in love; **être a. de qn** to be in love with sb; **ils sont a.** (*l'un de l'autre*) they're in love (with each other); **tomber a. de qn** to fall in love with sb; **être éperdument** *ou* **follement a. de qn** to be head over heels *or* madly in love with sb; **être fou a.** *ou* **a. fou** to be madly in love
3 (*amateur*) **elle est amoureuse de la montagne** she has a passion for mountains
NM,F **1** (*amant*) lover; **un couple d'a.** a pair of lovers; **la transi** lovesick hero; *Théât* **jouer les a.** to play lovers' parts
2 (*adepte*) lover; **a. des beaux-arts** a lover of fine arts; **les a. de la nature** nature-lovers
▫ **en amoureux** ADV **si nous sortions en a. ce soir?** how about going out tonight, just the two of us?

amour-propre [amurprɔpr] (*pl* **amours-propres**) NM pride; **elle est blessée dans son a.** her pride is hurt

amovibilité [amɔvibilite] NF removability

amovible [amɔvibl] ADJ (*housse, doublure, couvercle, manche*) removable, detachable; (*col*) detachable; *Ordinat* (*disque dur*) removable

AMP [ɑɛmpe] NF **1** *Chim & Biol* (*abrév* **adénosine monophosphate**) AMP **2** *Méd* (*abrév* **assistance médicale à la procréation**) (medically) assisted conception

ampélidacée [ãpelidase] *Bot* NF vitaceous plant, *Spéc* member of the Ampelidaceae family
▫ **ampélidacées** NFPL vitaceous plants, *Spéc* Ampelidaceae

ampélologie [ãpelɔlɔʒi] NF study of the vine

ampélopsis [ãpelɔpsis] NM *Bot* ampelopsis

ampérage [ãperaʒ] NM *Élec* amperage

ampère [ãpɛr] NM *Élec* ampere

ampère-heure [ãpɛrœr] (*pl* **ampères-heures**) NM *Élec* ampere hour

ampèremètre [ãpɛrmɛtr] NM *Élec* ammeter, amperometer

ampère-tour [ãpɛrtur] (*pl* **ampères-tours**) NM *Électron* ampere turn

amphé [ãfe] NF *Fam Pharm* (*amphétamine*) speed

amphétamine [ãfetamin] NF *Pharm* amphetamine

amphétaminique [ãfetaminik] *Pharm* ADJ amphetamine-like
NM amphetamine-like drug

amphi [ãfi] NM *Fam* (*abrév* **amphithéâtre**) lecture hall ▪ *or Br* theatre ▪

amphiarthrose [ãfiartroz] NF *Méd* amphiarthrosis

amphibie [ãfibi] ADJ *Aviat & Mil* amphibious
NM *Écol* amphibian

amphibien [ãfibjɛ̃] *Zool* NM amphibian
▫ **amphibiens** NMPL Amphibia

amphibole [ãfibɔl] NF *Minér* amphibole
ADJ *Méd* amphibolic

amphibolite [ãfibolit] NF *Minér* amphibolite

amphibologie [ãfibɔlɔʒi] NF *Ling* amphibology, amphiboly

amphibologique [ãfibɔlɔʒik] ADJ *Ling* amphibological

amphictyon [ãfiktjɔ̃] NM *Hist* amphictyon; **le Conseil des Amphictyons** the Amphictyonic Council

amphictyonie [ãfiktjɔni] NF *Hist* amphictyony

amphictyonique [ãfiktjɔnik] ADJ *Hist* amphictyonic

amphigouri [ãfiguri] NM *Ling* nonsense; *Littéraire* amphigory

amphigourique [ãfigurik] ADJ *Ling* overblown; *Littéraire* amphigoric

amphimixie [ãfimiksi] NF *Biol* amphimixis, karyogamy

amphineure [ãfinœr] *Zool* NM mollusc of the Amphineura class
▫ **amphineures** NMPL Amphineura

amphioxus [ãfjoksys] NM *Zool* lancelet

amphipathique [ãfipatik] ADJ *Biol & Chim* amphipatic

amphiphile [ãfifil] ADJ *Chim* amphipathic, amphiphilic

amphipode [ãfipɔd] *Zool* NM amphipod
▫ **amphipodes** NMPL Amphipoda

amphisbène [ãfizbɛn] NM *Zool* amphisbaena

amphithéâtre [ãfiteatr] NM **1** *Antiq* amphitheatre; *Univ* lecture hall *or* theatre; (*d'un théâtre*) amphitheatre, (upper) gallery; (*salle de dissection*) dissection room **2** *Géol* **a. morainique** morainic cirque *or* amphitheatre

Amphitryon [ãfitrijɔ̃] NPR *Myth* Amphitryon
▫ **amphitryon** NM host

ampholyte [ãfolit] NM *Chim* ampholyte

amphore [ãfɔr] NF *Antiq* amphora

amphotère [ãfɔtɛr] ADJ *Chim* amphoteric

ampicilline [ãpisilin] NF *Pharm* ampicillin

ample [ãpl] ADJ **1** (*large → pull*) loose, baggy; (*→ cape, jupe*) flowing, full **2** (*mouvement, geste*) wide, sweeping; (*style*) rich; (*voix*) sonorous **3** (*abondant → stock, provisions*) extensive, ample; **de plus amples renseignements** further details *or* information

amplectif, -ive [ãplɛktif, -iv] ADJ *Bot* amplexicaul

amplement [ãplemã] ADV fully, amply; **gagner a. sa vie** to make a very comfortable living; **il y a a. de quoi les nourrir** there's more than enough to feed them; **ça suffit a., c'est a. suffisant** that's more than enough; **nous avons a. le temps** we have plenty of time

ampleur [ãplœr] NF **1** (*largeur → d'un pull*) looseness; (*→ d'une cape, d'une jupe*) fullness; **coupez en biais pour donner plus d'a.** cut on the bias to give more fullness
2 (*rondeur → d'un mouvement, d'un geste*) fullness
3 (*importance → d'un projet*) scope; (*→ d'un stock, de ressources*) abundance; **l'a. des dégâts** the extent of the damage; **l'a. de la crise** the scale *or* extent of the crisis; **des événements d'une telle a.** events of such magnitude; **prendre de l'a.** to gain in importance

ampli [ãpli] NM *Fam* (*abrév* **amplificateur**) amp

ampliatif, -ive [ãplijatif, -iv] ADJ *Jur* (*mémoire*) amplifying; (*acte*) duplicate (*avant n*)

ampliation [ãplijasjɔ̃] NF **1** *Jur* (*d'un acte*) certified copy; (*d'un document archivé*) exemplification; **pour a.** (*sur document*) certified true copy **2** *Physiol* (*de la cage thoracique*) expansion

ampliative [ãplijativ] *voir* **ampliatif**

amplifiant, -e [ãplifjã, -ãt] ADJ **1** *Élec & Phys* amplifying; *Opt* magnifying; *Phot* enlarging **2** (*d'un raisonnement*) **induction amplifiante** ampliative inference

amplificateur, -trice [ãplifikatœr, -tris] ADJ *Élec & Phys* amplifying; *Opt* magnifying; *Phot* enlarging
NM **1** *Élec & Rad* amplifier; **a. de puissance** power amplifier **2** *Phot* enlarger
▫ **amplificatrice** NF *Phot* enlarger

amplification [ãplifikasjɔ̃] NF **1** *Élec & Phys* amplification, amplifying; *Phot* (*action*) enlarging, enlargement; *Opt* magnifying
2 (*développement → d'un courant, d'une tendance*) development, increase; (*→ d'un conflit*) deepening; (*→ de tensions, de revendications,*

**d'une hausse*) increase; (*→ d'une différence*) widening; (*→ d'échanges, de relations*) development, expansion
3 *Péj* (*exagération*) exaggeration, magnification

amplificatrice [ãplifikatris] *voir* **amplificateur**

amplifier [9] [ãplifje] VT **1** *Élec & Phys* to amplify; *Opt* to magnify; *Phot* to enlarge
2 (*développer → courant, tendance*) to develop, to increase; (*→ conflit*) to deepen; (*→ tensions, revendications, hausse*) to increase; (*→ différence*) to widen; (*→ échanges, relations*) to develop, to expand
3 *Péj* (*exagérer*) to exaggerate, to magnify; **les médias ont amplifié le scandale** the scandal has been blown up out of all proportion by the media
▸**s'amplifier** VPR (*augmenter → courant, tendance*) to develop, to increase; (*→ conflit*) to deepen; (*→ tensions, revendications, hausse*) to increase; (*→ différence*) to widen; (*→ échanges, relations*) to develop, to expand

ampliforme [ãplifɔrm] ADJ **soutien-gorge a.** padded bra
NM (*soutien-gorge*) padded bra

amplitude [ãplityd] NF **1** *Astron, Math & Phys* amplitude **2** *Météo* range; **a. thermique** temperature range **3** *Écon* **a. des fluctuations** amplitude of fluctuations **4** *Littéraire* (*étendue*) magnitude, extent

ampli-tuner [ãplitynɛr] (*pl* **amplis-tuners**) NM amplifier-tuner deck

ampoule [ãpul] NF **1** *Élec* bulb; **a. à baïonnette/vis** bayonet/screw-in bulb; *Phot* **a. de flash** flashbulb, flashlight **2** (*récipient*) phial, vial; **a. autocassable** break-open phial *or* vial **3** (*cloque*) blister; *Fam Hum* **toi, tu ne vas pas attraper** *ou* **te faire des ampoules!** don't strain yourself, will you!

ampoulé, -e [ãpule] ADJ *Péj* pompous, bombastic

amputation [ãpytasjɔ̃] NF **1** *Méd* amputation **2** *Fig* (*suppression*) removal, cutting out; **ce texte a subi de nombreuses amputations** this text has been heavily cut

amputé, -e [ãpyte] NM,F *Méd* amputee

amputer [3] [ãpyte] VT **1** *Méd* (*membre*) to amputate, to remove; **a. un bras à qn** to amputate sb's arm; **elle a été amputée d'un pied** she had a foot amputated
2 (*ôter une partie de → texte*) to cut (down), to reduce; (*→ budget*) to cut back; **l'article a été amputé d'un tiers** the article was cut by a third; **le pays a été amputé de deux provinces** the country lost two provinces; **le palais a été amputé de son aile sud** the south wing of the palace was demolished

Amritsar [amritsar] NM *Géog* Amritsar

amstellodamois, -e [amstɛlodamwa, -az] ADJ of/from Amsterdam
▫ **Amstellodamois, -e** NM,F = inhabitant of or person from Amsterdam

Amsterdam [amstɛrdam] NM *Géog* Amsterdam

amuïr [32] [amɥir] **s'amuïr** VPR *Ling* **le s s'est amuï** the s became mute

amuïssement [amɥismã] NM *Ling* = disappearance of a (voiced) phoneme

amulette [amylɛt] NF amulet

amure [amyr] NF *Naut* tack; **naviguer tribord/bâbord amures** to sail on the starboard/port tack; **changer d'a.** to change tack

amurer [3] [amyre] *Naut* VT (*voile*) to tack, to board the tack of
USAGE ABSOLU **a. à bâbord** to tack to port

amusant, -e [amyzã, -ãt] ADJ **1** (*drôle*) funny, amusing; **les gags ne sont même pas amusants** the jokes aren't even funny; **le plus a., c'est que...** the funniest *or* most amusing thing is that...
2 (*divertissant*) entertaining; **je vais t'apprendre un petit jeu a.** I'm going to teach you an entertaining little game
3 (*curieux*) funny; **tiens, c'est a., je n'avais pas remarqué...** that's funny, I hadn't noticed...

amuse-bouche [amyzbuʃ] (*pl inv ou* **amuse-bouches**) NM *Culin* appetizer; **des a.** *ou* **amuse-bouches** appetizers, *Br* nibbles

amuse-gueule [amyzgœl] (*pl inv ou* **amuse-gueules**) NM *Culin* appetizer; **des a.** *ou* **amuse-gueules** appetizers, *Br* nibbles

amusement [amyzmɑ̃] NM **1** *(sentiment)* amusement; **écouter qn/sourire avec a.** to listen to sb with/to smile in amusement; **à son grand a.** much to his/her amusement **2** *(chose divertissante)* entertainment; *(jeu)* recreational activity, pastime; *Ironique* **tu parles d'un a.!** this isn't exactly my idea of fun!

amuser [3] [amyze] VT **1** *(faire rire)* to make laugh, to amuse; **elle m'amuse** she makes me laugh; **cela ne m'amuse pas du tout** I don't find that in the least bit funny; **ah, ça t'amuse, toi!** you think that's funny, do you?; **il nous a regardés d'un air amusé** he looked at us in amusement; *Fam* **a. la galerie** to play to the gallery **2** *(plaire à)* to appeal to; **ça ne l'amuse pas de travailler chez eux** he/she doesn't enjoy *or* like working there; **tu crois que ça m'amuse d'être pris pour un imbécile?** do you think I enjoy being taken for a fool?; **si ça t'amuse, fais-le** do it if that's what you want, if it makes you happy, do it **3** *(divertir)* to entertain **4** *(détourner l'attention de)* to divert, to distract **5** *Littéraire (tromper)* to delude, to deceive; **il m'a amusé pendant un an avec ses promesses** for a whole year he led me a merry dance with his promises

▸**s'amuser** VPR **1** *(jouer → enfant)* to play; **elle s'amuse dehors avec son cousin** she's outside playing with her cousin; **à cet âge-là, on s'amuse avec presque rien** at that age, they amuse themselves very easily; **s'a. avec** *(manipuler)* to fiddle *or* to play with **2** *(se divertir)* to have fun; **je ne me suis jamais autant amusé** I've never had so much fun; **ils se sont bien amusés** they really had a good time; **amusez-vous bien!** enjoy yourselves!, have a good time!; **qu'est-ce qu'on s'est amusés!** we had so much fun!; *Fam* **on s'amusait comme des petits fous** we were having a whale of a time; **elles ont construit une hutte pour s'a.** they built a hut, just for fun; **mais, papa, c'était pour s'a.!** but, dad, we were only having fun!; **ils ne vont pas s'a. avec le nouveau colonel** they won't have much fun with the new colonel; **s'a. aux dépens de qn** to make fun of sb **3** *(perdre son temps)* **s'a. en route** *ou* **en chemin** to dawdle on the way; *Fig* to waste time needlessly; **on n'a pas le temps de s'a.** there's no time for fooling around **4** **s'a. à faire qch** *(jouer à)* to have fun doing sth; *(s'occuper à)* to be busy doing sth; **ils s'amusaient à imiter le professeur** they were having fun imitating the teacher; **on s'amusait à la marelle** we used to play hopscotch; **ils s'amusent à dessiner** they're busy drawing; **il s'amuse à faire des avions en papier en cours** he spends his time making paper aeroplanes in class; **si tu crois que je vais m'a. à ça!** if you think I have nothing better to do!; **Fam si je dois m'a. à tout lui expliquer, j'ai pas fini!** if I've got to go and explain everything to him/her, I'll still be there next week!; **ne t'amuse pas à toucher ce fil!** don't you (go and) touch *or* go touching that wire!

amusette [amyzɛt] NF **1** *(distraction)* idle amusement **2** *Belg (personne frivole)* frivolous person

amuseur, -euse [amyzœr, -øz] NM,F **1** *(artiste)* entertainer **2** *Péj (personne peu sérieuse)* smooth talker

amusie [amyzi] NF *Méd* amusia; **a. (sensorielle)** sensory amusia; **atteint d'a.** tone-deaf

amygdale [amidal] NF *Anat* tonsil; **se faire opérer des amygdales** to have one's tonsils removed *or* out

amygdalectomie [amidalɛktɔmi] NF *Méd* tonsillectomy

amygdalien, -enne [amigdaljɛ̃, -ɛn] ADJ **angine amygdalienne** tonsillitis

amygdaline [amidalin] NF *Chim* amygdalin

amygdalite [amidalit] NF *Méd* tonsillitis

amygdalotomie [amidalɔtɔmi] NF *Méd* tonsillotomy

amylacé, -e [amilase] ADJ *Biol* amylaceous

amylase [amilaz] NF *Biol & Chim* amylase

amyle [amil] NM *Chim* amyl

amylène [amilɛn] NM *Chim* amylene

amylique [amilik] ADJ *Chim* amyl *(avant n)*

amyloïde [amilɔid] ADJ *Chim (substance, matière)* starchy, *Spéc* amyloid, amylaceous; *Méd* **maladie a.** amyloidosis

amylose [amiloz] NF *Méd (gén)* amyloidosis; *(du foie, de la rate)* amyloid *or* waxy degeneration **NM** *Chim* amylose

amyotrophie [amjɔtrɔfi] NF *Méd* amyotrophy, amyotrophia

an [ɑ̃] NM **1** *(durée de douze mois)* year; **dans un an** one year from now; **encore deux ans et je m'arrête** two more years and then I'll stop; **j'ai cinq ans de métier** I have five years' experience in this field; **une amitié de 20 ans** a friendship of 20 years' standing; **un prêt sur 20 ans** a loan over 20 years; **un an plus tard** *ou* **après** one year later; **voilà deux ans qu'elle est partie** she's been gone for two years now; **par an** a year; **deux fois par an** twice a year; **je gagne tant par an** I earn so much a year *or* per year; **tous les ans** *(gén)* every *or* each year; *(publier, réviser)* yearly, on a yearly basis; **bon an mal an, je dois gagner dans les 20 000 euros** in an average year, I earn 20,000 euros, on average, I earn 20,000 euros a year **2** *(avec l'art déf) (division du calendrier)* (calendar) year; **l'an dernier** *ou* **passé** last year; **l'an prochain** next year; **en l'an 10 apr. J.-C.** in (the year) 10 AD; **en l'an 200 avant notre ère** in (the year) 200 BC; **en l'an 2000** in the year 2000; *Hist* **l'an Un/Deux de la Révolution** Year One/Two of the (French) Revolution; **le jour** *ou* **le premier de l'an** New Year's Day; *Arch* **en l'an de grâce 1624** in the Year of Our Lord 1624; *Fam* **je m'en fiche** *ou* **moque comme de l'an quarante!** I don't give two hoots! **3** *(pour exprimer l'âge)* **à trois ans** at three (years of age); **elle a cinq ans** she's five (years old); **on fête ses vingt ans** we're celebrating his/her twentieth birthday; **un enfant de cinq ans** a five-year-old (child) ▫ **ans** NMPL *Littéraire* advancing *or* passing years; **un visage que les ans ne semblent pas avoir touché** a face seemingly untouched by the passing (of the) years

anabaptisme [anabatism] NM *Rel* Anabaptism

anabaptiste [anabatist] ADJ & NMF *Rel* Anabaptist

anabas [anabas] NM *Ich* climbing fish, *Spéc* anabas

anabiose [anabjoz] NF *Bot* anabiosis

anableps [anablɛps] NM *Ich* anableps

anabolique [anabolik] ADJ *Biol* anabolic

anabolisant, -e [anabolizɑ̃, -ɑ̃t] *Biol* ADJ anabolic **NM** anabolic steroid

anabolisme [anabolism] NM *Physiol* anabolism

anabolite [anabolit] NM *Physiol* anabolite

anacarde [anakard] NM *Bot* cashew (nut), *Spéc* anacard

anacardiacée [anakardjase] *Bot* NF member of the Anacardiaceae family ▫ **anacardiacées** NFPL Anacardiaceae

anacardier [anakardje] NM *Bot* cashew (tree)

anachorète [anakɔrɛt] NM *Rel* anchorite; *Fig* **il mène une vie d'a.** he lives the life of a recluse

anachorétique [anakɔretik] ADJ *Rel* anchoretic, anchoritic

anachorétisme [anakɔretism] NM *Rel* anchoretism

anachronique [anakrɔnik] ADJ anachronistic, anachronic

anachronisme [anakrɔnism] NM anachronism

anaclinal, -e, -aux, -ales [anaklinal, -o] ADJ *Géol (cours d'eau, versant)* anaclinal

anaclitique [anaklitik] ADJ *Psy* anaclitic

anacoluthe [anakɔlyt] NF *Ling* anacoluthon

anaconda [anakɔ̃da] NM *Zool* anaconda, eunectes

Anacréon [anakreɔ̃] NPR Anacreon

anacréontique [anakreɔ̃tik] ADJ *Littérature* Anacreontic

anacréontisme [anakreɔ̃tism] NM *Littérature* imitation of Anacreon

Anacroisés® [anakrwaze] NMPL anagram crossword

anacrouse [anakruz] NF *Mus* anacrusis

anacyclique [anasiklik] ADJ palindromic **NM** palindrome

anadrome [anadrom] ADJ *Ich* anadromous

anaérobie [anaerɔbi] *Biol* ADJ anaerobic **NM** anaerobe

anaérobiose [anaerɔbjoz] NF *Biol* anaerobiosis

anaglyphe [anaglif] NM *Typ, Beaux-Arts & Phot* anaglyph

anaglyptique [anagliptik] ADJ embossed **NF** embossed print

anagogie [anagɔʒi] NF *Rel* anagoge, anagogy

anagogique [anagɔʒik] ADJ *Rel* anagogic, anagogical

anagrammatique [anagramatik] ADJ anagrammatic(al)

anagrammatisme [anagramatism] NM anagrammatism

anagramme [anagram] NF *Ling* anagram

ANAH [ana, aɛnɑaʒ] NF *(abrév* **Agence nationale pour l'amélioration de l'habitat)** = national agency responsible for housing projects and restoration grants

anal, -e, -aux, -ales [anal, -o] ADJ *Anat & Psy* anal

analectes [analɛkt] NMPL *Littérature* analects, analecta

analepse [analɛps] NF *Littérature & Ling* analepsis

analeptique [analɛptik] *Méd* ADJ analeptic **NM** analeptic

analgésie [analʒezi] NF *Méd* analgesia

analgésique [analʒezik] *Pharm* ADJ analgesic **NM** analgesic

analité [analite] NF *Psy* anality

anallergique [analɛrʒik] ADJ *Méd* hypoallergenic

analogie [analɔʒi] NF analogy; **il y a une a. entre ces deux histoires** there's an analogy between the two stories; **trouver une a. entre deux choses** to draw an analogy between two things ▫ **par analogie** ADV by analogy; **par a. avec** by analogy with

analogique [analɔʒik] ADJ **1** *(présentant un rapport)* analogical; **dictionnaire a.** thesaurus **2** *Ordinat* analog; **calculateur a.** analog computer; **convertisseur a. numérique** analog-to-digital converter

analogiquement [analɔʒikmɑ̃] ADV analogically

analogue [analɔg] ADJ analogous, similar; **a. par la forme** analogous in shape; **une histoire a. à une autre** a story similar to another one **NM** analogue; **ce mot anglais n'a pas d'a. en français** this English word has no equivalent in French

analphabète [analfabɛt] ADJ & NMF illiterate

analphabétisme [analfabetism] NM illiteracy

analycité [analisite] NF *Ling* analyticity

analysable [analizabl] ADJ **1** *(que l'on peut examiner)* analysable **2** *Ordinat* scannable

analysant, -e [analizɑ̃, -ɑ̃t] NM,F *Psy* analysand

analyse [analiz] NF **1** *(étude)* analysis; **cet argument ne résiste pas à l'a.** this argument doesn't stand up to analysis; **l'a. des faits montre que...** an examination of the facts shows that...; **en dernière a.** in the last *or* final analysis, when all is said and done, all things considered; *Com* **a. des besoins** needs analysis; *Com & Mktg* **a. conjointe** conjoint analysis, trade-off analysis; *Compta & Fin* **a. des coûts** cost analysis; *Compta & Fin* **a. coûts-bénéfices** cost-benefit analysis; *Compta & Fin* **a. de coût et d'efficacité** cost-effectiveness analysis; *Compta & Fin* **a. coût-profit** cost-benefit analysis; *Compta & Fin* **a. des coûts et rendements** cost-benefit analysis; **a. démographique** demographic analysis; **a. des écarts** variance analysis; **a. économique** economic analysis; **a. de faisabilité** feasibility study; *Compta & Fin* **a. fondamentale** fundamental analysis; *Mktg* **a. des forces et faiblesses** strengths and weaknesses analysis; *Mktg* **a. des forces, faiblesses, opportunités et menaces** SWOT analysis; **a. de marché** market survey *or* research; **a. du marché** market analysis; **a. des marchés** market research; **a. des médias** media analysis; *Mktg* **a. des opportunités et des menaces** opportunity and threat analysis; *Compta & Fin* **a. du point mort** break-even analysis; **a. de portefeuille** portfolio analysis; **a. des postes de travail** job analysis; *Compta & Fin* **a. du prix de revient** cost analysis; **a. de produit** product analysis; *Compta & Fin* **a. du rendement** rate of return analysis; **a. des résultats** processing of results; *Compta & Fin* **a. des résultats financiers** bottom-line analysis; **a. des risques** risk analysis; **a. par secteur d'activité** segment reporting; *Mktg* **a. par segment** cluster analysis; **a. du style de vie** lifestyle analysis; *Compta & Fin* **a. technique** technical analysis; **a. des**

tendances trend analysis; **a. de valeur** value analysis *or* engineering; **a. des ventes** sales analysis

2 *Scol* analysis; **faire l'a. d'un texte** to analyse a text; **a. de texte** textual analysis; *Gram* **a. logique/grammaticale** sentence/grammatical analysis; **faire une a. grammaticale** to parse; **faites l'a. grammaticale de cette phrase** parse this sentence

3 *Biol* analysis; **a. de sang** blood analysis *or* test; **faire une a. de sang** to have a blood test **4** *Psy* analysis, psychoanalysis; **être en a.** to be in analysis; **faire une a.** to undergo analysis **5** *Ordinat* analysis; *Électron* scan, scanning; **a. de données** data analysis; **a. factorielle** factor analysis; **a. fonctionnelle** functional *or* systems analysis; **a. lexicale** lexical scan; **a. numérique** numerical analysis; **a. organique** systems design; **a. des performances du système** system evaluation; *Ordinat* **a. de système, a. systémique** systems analysis

6 *Chim & Math* analysis

7 *Mines* essaying; **a. des minerais** ore essaying

analysé, -e [analize] **NM,F** *Psy* analysand

analyser [3] [analize] **VT 1** (*étudier*) to analyse **2** *Gram* to parse; **a. une phrase en constituants** to parse a sentence into its constituents **3** (*résumer*) to summarize, to make an abstract *or* a précis of **4** *Biol & Chim* to analyse, to test **5** *Psy* to analyse; **se faire a.** to undergo analysis

▶**s'analyser VPR elle s'analyse trop** she goes in for too much self-analysis

analyseur [analizœr] **NM 1** *Ordinat* analyser; **a. logique/différentiel** logic/differential analyser; **a. syntaxique** parser **2** *Électron* scanner, analyser **3** *Élec* analyser **4** *Chim* analyst

analyste [analist] **NMF 1** (*gén*) analyst; **a. financier** financial analyst; **a. du marché** market analyst; **a. des médias** media analyst; **a. en placements** investment analyst **2** *Psy* analyst, psychoanalyst

analyste-programmeur, -euse [analistprogramœr, -øz] (*mpl* **analystes-programmeurs,** *fpl* **analystes-programmeuses**) **NM,F** *Ordinat* systems analyst

analyticité [analitisite] = **analycité**

analytique [analitik] **ADJ** analytic, analytical; **géométrie/philosophie a.** analytical geometry/philosophy

NM abstract

NF analytics (*singulier*)

analytiquement [analitikmã] **ADV** analytically

anamnèse [anamnɛz], **anamnésie** [anamnezi] **NF** *Psy & Rel* anamnesis

anamorphique [anamɔrfik] **ADJ** *Cin & TV* anamorphic

anamorphose [anamɔrfoz] **NF** *Zool & Opt* anamorphosis

ananas [anana(s)] **NM** *Bot* pineapple

anapeste [anapɛst] **NM** *Littérature* anapaest

anaphase [anafaz] **NF** *Biol* anaphase

anaphore [anafɔr] **NF** *Littérature & Ling* anaphora

anaphorèse [anafɔrɛz] **NF** *Chim & Phys* anaphoresis

anaphorique [anafɔrik] **ADJ** *Ling* anaphoric, anaphorical

anaphrodisiaque [anafrɔdizjak] **ADJ** anaphrodisiac

NM anaphrodisiac

anaphrodisie [anafrɔdizi] **NF** *Méd* anaphrodisia

anaphylactique [anafilaktik] **ADJ** *Méd* anaphylactic

anaphylaxie [anafilaksi] **NF** *Méd* anaphylaxis

anaplasie [anaplazi] **NF** *Biol & Méd* anaplasia

anaplastie [anaplasti] = **autoplastie**

anaplastique [anaplastik] **ADJ** *Biol & Méd* anaplastic

anar [anar] **NMF** *Fam* (*abrév* **anarchiste**) anarchist ▪

anarchie [anarʃi] **NF 1** *Pol* anarchy **2** (*désordre*) anarchy, lawlessness

anarchique [anarʃik] **ADJ** anarchic, anarchical

anarchiquement [anarʃikmã] **ADV** anarchically

anarchisant, -e [anarʃizã, -ãt] **ADJ** *Pol & Hist* anarchistic

anarchiser [3] [anarʃize] **VT** *Pol* to anarchize

anarchisme [anarʃism] **NM** *Pol & Hist* anarchism

anarchiste [anarʃist] **ADJ** anarchist, anarchistic

NMF anarchist

anarcho-syndicalisme [anarkosɛ̃dikalism] **NM** *Ind* anarchosyndicalism

anarcho-syndicaliste [anarkosɛ̃dikalist] (*pl* **anarcho-syndicalistes**) **ADJ & NMF** *Ind* anarcho-syndicalist

anarthrie [anartri] **NF** *Psy* anarthria

anasarque [anazark] **NF** *Méd* anasarca

ANASE [anaz] **NF** (*abrév* **Association des nations de l'Asie du Sud-Est**) ASEAN

Anastase [anastɑz] **NPR** Anastasius

Anastasie [anastazi] **NPR 1** *Rel* Anastasia **2** *Littéraire* censorship

anastatique [anastatik] **ADJ** anastatic

anastigmat(e) [anastigmat], **anastigmatique** [anastigmatik] *Opt* **ADJ M** anastigmatic

NM anastigmat, anastigmatic lens

anastigmatisme [anastigmatism] **NM** *Opt* anastigmatism

anastomose [anastɔmoz] **NF** *Anat, Bot & Méd* anastomosis

anastomoser [3] [anastɔmoze] **VT** *Méd* to anastomose

▶**s'anastomoser VPR 1** *Anat* to anastomose **2** *Géog* (*fleuve*) to become braided

anastrophe [anastrɔf] **NF** *Gram* anastrophe

anastylose [anastiloz] **NF** *Archit* anastylosis

anatexie [anateksi] **NF** *Géol* anatexis

anathématisation [anatematizasjɔ̃] **NF** anathematization

anathématiser [3] [anatematize] **VT 1** *Littéraire* (*condamner*) to censure **2** *Rel* to anathematize

anathème [anatɛm] **NM 1** (*condamnation*) anathema; **jeter l'a. sur** to pronounce an anathema upon, to anathematize **2** *Rel* anathema

anatidé [anatide] **Orn NM** anatine bird

▫ **anatidés NMPL** Anatidae

anatife [anatif] **NM** *Zool* (*crustacé*) barnacle

anatocisme [anatɔsism] **NM** *Fin* anatocism, compound interest

Anatolie [anatɔli] **NF l'A.** Anatolia

anatolien, -enne [anatɔljɛ̃, -ɛn] **ADJ** Anatolian

▫ **Anatolien, -enne NM,F** Anatolian

anatomie [anatɔmi] **NF** *Anat* **1** (*étude, structure*) anatomy; **a. pathologique** pathological anatomy **2** *Fam* (*corps*) body ▪; **une belle a.** a gorgeous figure; *Euph* **son pantalon révélait tous les détails de son a.** his/her trousers didn't leave much to the imagination; *Euph* **dans la partie la plus charnue de son a.** in his/her posterior

anatomique [anatɔmik] **ADJ** *Anat* anatomical; **faire l'étude a. d'un corps** to anatomize *or* to dissect a body

anatomiquement [anatɔmikmã] **ADV** *Anat* anatomically

anatomiste [anatɔmist] **NMF** *Anat* anatomist

anatomopathologie [anatɔmopatɔlɔʒi] **NF** *Méd* anatomicopathology

anatoxine [anatɔksin] **NF** *Méd* anatoxin, toxoid

anavenin [anavənɛ̃] **NM** *Méd* antivenin

Anaxagore [anaksagɔr] **NPR** Anaxagoras

Anaximandre [anaksimɑ̃dr] **NPR** Anaximander

Anaximène [anaksimɛn] **NPR** Anaximenes

ANC [ɑɛnse] **NM** (*abrév* **African National Congress**) ANC

ancestral, -e, -aux, -ales [ɑ̃sɛstral, -o] **ADJ 1** (*venant des ancêtres*) ancestral **2** (*ancien → tradition, coutume*) ancient, age-old, time-honoured

ancêtre [ɑ̃sɛtr] **NMF 1** (*ascendant*) ancestor, forefather; **c'était mon a.** he/she was an ancestor of mine; **la maison de ses ancêtres** his/her family home **2** (*précurseur → personne, objet*) ancestor, forerunner, precursor **3** *Fam* (*vieille personne*) *Br* old boy, *f* old girl, *Am* old-timer

▫ **ancêtres NMPL** ancestors, forebears

anche [ɑ̃ʃ] *Mus* **NF** reed

▫ **anches NFPL les anches** reed instruments, the reeds

Anchise [ɑ̃ʃiz] **NPR** *Myth* Anchises

anchoïade [ɑ̃ʃɔjad] **NF** *Culin* anchoyade, anchovy and olive oil paste (*speciality of the South of France*)

anchois [ɑ̃ʃwa] **NM** *Ich* anchovy

anchorman [ɑ̃kɔrman] **NM** *TV* anchorman, anchor

anchoyade [ɑ̃ʃɔjad] = **anchoïade**

ancien, -enne [ɑ̃sjɛ̃, -ɛn] **ADJ 1** (*vieux → coutume, tradition, famille*) old, ancient, time-honoured; (*→ amitié, relation*) old, long-standing; (*→ bague,*

châle) old, antique; **un meuble a.** an antique; **livres anciens** antiquarian books; **une de nos règles déjà ancienne stipule que...** one of our long-standing rules stipulates *or* states that...

2 *Antiq* (*langue, histoire, civilisation*) ancient; **la Grèce ancienne** ancient *or* classical Greece **3** (*avant le nom*) (*ex → président, époux, employé*) former, ex-; (*→ stade, église*) former; **mon a. patron** my former boss *or* ex-boss; **ses anciens camarades** his/her old *or* former comrades; **c'est une ancienne infirmière** she used to work as a nurse; **l'a. aéroport** the old *or* former airport; **mon ancienne école** my old school; **une ancienne colonie française** a former French colony; **l'ancienne rue de la Gare** what used to be rue de la Gare; **un a. combattant** a (war) veteran, an ex-serviceman; **un a. élève** a former pupil, *Br* an old boy, *Am* an alumnus; **une ancienne élève** a former pupil, *Br* an old girl, *Am* an alumna

4 (*passé*) former; **dans les temps anciens, dans l'a. temps** in former times, in olden *or* bygone days

5 (*qui a de l'ancienneté*) senior; **vous n'êtes pas assez a. dans la profession** you've not been in the job long enough; **ils sont plus anciens que moi dans la fonction** they're senior to me (in the job)

6 *Ling* **a. français** Old French

NM,F 1 (*qui a de l'expérience*) old hand **2** (*qui est plus vieux*) elder; **respectez les anciens** have some respect for your elders **3** (*qui a participé*) **un a. de l'ÉNA** a former student of the "ÉNA"; **un a. du parti communiste** an ex-member of the Communist Party; **un a. de la guerre de Corée** a Korean War veteran, a veteran of the Korean War

4 *Hist* **la querelle des Anciens et des Modernes** = famous controversy in the 17th century, in which artists and writers debated the relative merits of classical and contemporary art and writing

NM 1 (*objets*) **l'a.** antiques; **meublé entièrement en a.** entirely furnished with antiques **2** (*construction*) **l'a.** old *or* older buildings; **les murs sont plus épais dans l'a.** walls are thicker in old *or* older buildings

▫ **Anciens NMPL** *Antiq & Littérature* Ancients

▫ **à l'ancienne ADJ** old-fashioned; **des fiançailles à l'ancienne** an old-fashioned *or* old-style engagement; **bœuf à l'ancienne** beef in the traditional style; **bague à l'ancienne** traditional-style ring

▫ **Ancien Régime NM l'A. Régime** the "Ancien Régime"

▫ **Ancien Testament NM l'A. Testament** the Old Testament

'L'Ancien et le Nouveau Testament' *Giotto* 'Scenes from the Old and New Testament'

anciennement [ɑ̃sjɛnmɑ̃] **ADV** previously, formerly

ancienneté [ɑ̃sjɛnte] **NF 1** (*d'une chose*) oldness **2** (*d'une personne*) length of service; (*avantages acquis*) seniority; **elle a beaucoup d'a. chez nous** she's been with us for a long time; **avoir 15 ans d'a. dans une entreprise** to have 15 years' service with a firm; **avancer** *ou* **être promu à l'a.** to be promoted by seniority

▫ **de toute ancienneté ADV** from time immemorial

ancillaire [ɑ̃siler] **ADJ** (*avec une servante*) **les amours ancillaires** love affairs with servants

ancolie [ɑ̃kɔli] **NF** *Bot* columbine, aquilegia

Ancône [ɑ̃kon] **NM** *Géog* Ancona

ancrage [ɑ̃kraʒ] **NM 1** *Tech* (*fixation*) anchorage;

a. des câbles d'un pont suspendu cable anchorage of a suspension bridge; **a. mécanique** mechanical bond; **a. à scellement** permanent soil anchor

2 *Naut (arrêt)* moorage, anchorage; *(droits)* anchorage *or* moorage *or* berthing (dues)

3 *(enracinement)* **l'a. d'un parti dans l'électorat** a party's electoral base; **l'action de la pièce n'a aucun a. dans la réalité** the plot of the play has no basis in reality

4 *Ordinat & Typ* justification; **a. à droite/gauche** right/left justification

ancre [ãkr] NF **1** *Naut* **a. (de marine)** anchor; **a. de corps-mort** mooring anchor; **a. flottante** drag anchor; **a. à jet** kedge anchor; *Fig* **a. de salut** last resort; **elle est mon a. de salut** she's my last hope; **a. de terre** shore anchor; **être à l'a.** to ride *or* to lie at anchor; **jeter l'a.** to cast *or* to drop anchor; *Fig* to put down roots; **lever l'a.** to weigh anchor; *Fig* **allez, on lève l'a.!** come on, let's go!

2 *Constr* **a. de mur** cramp (iron); **a. de tête/voûte** wall/tie anchor

3 *(d'une horloge)* pallet; **a. à chevilles** pin pallet, lever fork

4 *Ordinat* anchor

ancrer [3] [ãkre] VT **1** *Naut* to anchor **2** *(attacher)* to anchor; **a. un câble** to anchor a cable **3** *Fig* to root; **la propagande a ancré le parti dans la région** propaganda has established the party firmly in this area; **c'est une idée bien ancrée** it's a firmly rooted idea

▶**s'ancrer** VPR **1** *Naut* to drop *or* to cast anchor **2** *(se fixer)* to settle; **sa famille s'est ancrée dans la région** his/her family has settled in the area

andain [ãdɛ̃] NM *Agr* swath *(of cut grass, hay etc)*

andalou, -se [ãdalu, -uz] ADJ Andalusian

NM *(dialecte)* Andalusian

❏ **Andalou, -se** NM,F Andalusian

Andalousie [ãdaluzi] NF **l'A.** Andalusia

andalousite [ãdaluzit] NF *Minér* andalusite

andante [ãdãt(e)] *Mus* ADV *(tempo)* andante

NM *(morceau de musique)* andante

andantino [ãdãtino] *Mus* ADV *(tempo)* andantino

NM *(morceau de musique)* andantino

Andes [ãd] NFPL **les A.** the Andes; **la cordillère des A.** the Andes Mountain Ranges; **le climat des A.** the climate of the Andes, the Andean climate

andésite [ãdezit] NF *Géol* andesite

andin, -e [ãdɛ̃, -in] ADJ Andean

❏ **Andin, -e** NM,F Andean

andorran, -e [ãdɔrã, -an] ADJ Andorran

❏ **Andorran, -e** NM,F Andorran

Andorre [ãdɔr] NF **(la principauté d')A.** (the principality of) Andorra; **vivre à A.** to live in Andorra; **aller à A.** to go to Andorra

Andorre-la-Vieille [ãdɔrlavjɛj] NM *Géog* Andorra la Vella

andouille [ãduj] NF **1** *Culin* chitterlings sausage *(eaten cold)* **2** *Fam (imbécile)* dummy; **faire l'a.** to fool around; **espèce d'a.!** you great dummy!; **fais pas l'a., touche pas la prise!** watch out, don't touch the socket!; **fais pas l'a., tu sais bien qu'elle t'aime!** don't do anything stupid, you know she loves you!

andouiller [ãduje] NM *Zool (d'un cerf)* tine, antler; **a. de massacre** brow tine, brow antler

andouillette [ãdujɛt] NF *Culin* chitterlings sausage *(for grilling)*

andrène [ãdrɛn] NM *Entom* andrena

andrinople [ãdrinɔpl] NF *Tex* Turkey red *(cotton fabric)*

androcée [ãdrose] NM *Bot* androecium

androcéphale [ãdrosefal] ADJ *Beaux-Arts* androcephalous

Androclès [ãdrɔklɛs] NPR Androcles

androgène [ãdrɔʒɛn] *Biol* ADJ androgenic

NM androgen

androgenèse [ãdrɔʒɛnɛz], **androgénie** [ãdrɔʒeni] NF *Biol* androgenesis

androgyne [ãdrɔʒin] *Biol & Bot* ADJ androgynous

NM androgyne

androgynie [ãdrɔʒini] NF *Biol & Bot* androgyny

androïde [ãdrɔid] NMF android

andrologie [ãdrɔlɔʒi] NF *Méd* andrology

andrologique [ãdrɔlɔʒik] ADJ *Méd* andrological

andrologue [ãdrɔlɔg] NMF *Méd* andrologist

Andromaque [ãdrɔmak] NPR *Myth* Andromache

Andromède [ãdrɔmɛd] NPR *Myth* Andromeda

Andronic [ãdrɔnik] NPR *Hist* Andronicus

andropause [ãdrɔpoz] NF *Méd* male menopause

androstérone [ãdrɔsteron] NF *Biol* androsterone

âne [an] NM **1** *(animal)* donkey, ass; **il est comme l'â. de Buridan** he can't make up his mind; **être mauvais** *ou* **méchant comme un â. rouge** to be vicious *or* nasty; **il y a plus d'un** *ou* **il n'y a pas qu'un â. (à la foire) qui s'appelle Martin** that's a very common name, lots of people are called that; **â. sauvage** wild ass

2 *(imbécile)* idiot, fool; **faire l'â.** to play the fool; **c'est un â. bâté** he's a complete idiot; **faire l'â. pour avoir du son** to play the fool to achieve one's ends

anéantir [32] [aneãtir] VT **1** *(détruire → armée, ville)* to annihilate, to destroy, to wipe out; *(→ rébellion, révolte)* to quell, to crush; *(→ espoir)* to dash, to destroy; *(→ succès, effort)* to ruin, to wreck; *(→ amour, confiance)* to destroy; **leur équipe a été anéantie** their team was annihilated *or* routed

2 *(accabler → sujet: nouvelle, événement)* to overwhelm, to crush; **ça l'a anéanti** it was a tremendous blow to him; **être anéanti par le chagrin** to be overcome by grief; **elle est anéantie** she's devastated

3 *(épuiser)* to exhaust; **elle est anéantie par la chaleur/fatigue** she's overwhelmed by the heat/utterly exhausted

▶**s'anéantir** VPR to disappear, to vanish; **s'a. dans l'oubli** to sink into oblivion; **tous nos espoirs se sont anéantis** all our hopes were dashed

anéantissement [aneãtismã] NM **1** *(destruction)* ruin, annihilation, destruction; **c'est l'a. d'un mois de travail** it's a whole month's work lost; **cette nouvelle fut l'a. de tous mes espoirs** this news dashed all my hopes **2** *(accablement)* prostration; **être dans l'a. le plus total** to be completely devastated

anecdote [anɛkdɔt] NF anecdote; *Péj* **tout cela, c'est de l'a.** this is all trivial detail, this is just so much trivia

anecdotier, -ère [anɛkdɔtje, -ɛr] NM,F *Littéraire* anecdotist

anecdotique [anɛkdɔtik] ADJ **1** *(qui contient des anecdotes)* anecdotal **2** *(sans intérêt)* trivial

anéchoïque [anekɔik] ADJ *Tech* anechoic

anélasticité [anelastisite] NF *Tech* lack of elasticity

anélastique [anelastik] ADJ *Tech* unelastic

anémiant, -e [anemjã, -ãt] ADJ *Méd* causing anaemia

anémie [anemi] NF **1** *Méd* anaemia; **faire de l'a.** to have anaemia; **a. aplasique** aplastic anaemia; **a. falciforme, a. à hématies falciformes** sickle cell anaemia; **a. pernicieuse** pernicious anaemia **2** *Fig* **nous constatons une a. de la production** we can see that output has slowed to a trickle

anémié, -e [anemje] ADJ **1** *Méd* anaemic **2** *(affaibli)* weakened, anaemic

anémier [9] [anemje] VT **1** *Méd* to make anaemic **2** *(affaiblir)* to weaken, *Littéraire* to enfeeble

anémique [anemik] ADJ **1** *Méd* anaemic **2** *(faible → personne)* feeble, ineffectual; *(→ plante)* spindly, weedy; *(→ économie, industrie)* weak, slow, sluggish; **un texte plutôt a.** a rather colourless piece of writing

anémochore [anemokɔr] ADJ *Bot* anemochorous

anémographe [anemograf] NM *Météo* anemograph

anémomètre [anemomɛtr] NM *Météo* anemometer

anémone [anemɔn] NF **1** *Bot* anemone; **a. des bois** wood anemone **2** *Zool* **a. de mer** sea anemone

anémophile [anemofil] ADJ *Bot* anemophilous

anémophilie [anemofili] NF *Bot* anemophily

anencéphale [anãsefal] ADJ *Méd* anencephalic

anencéphalie [anãsefali] NF *Méd* anencephaly

anépigraphe [anepigraf] ADJ *Archéol* anepigraphic, anepigraphous

anérection [anerɛksjɔ̃] NF *Méd* impotence

anergie [anɛrʒi] NF *Méd* anergy

ânerie [anri] NF **1** *(caractère stupide)* stupidity; **tu es d'une â.!** you are so stupid!, you're such an idiot! **2** *(parole)* stupid *or* silly remark; **dire des âneries** to make stupid *or* silly remarks, to talk

rubbish **3** *(acte)* stupid blunder *or* mistake; **faire des âneries** to make stupid mistakes

anéroïde [aneroid] ADJ *Météo* aneroid

ânesse [anɛs] NF *Zool* she-ass, jenny; **lait d'â.** ass's milk

anesthésiant, -e [anɛstezjã, -ãt] = **anesthésique**

anesthésie [anɛstezi] NF *Méd* anaesthesia; **faire une a. à qn** to anaesthetize sb, to give sb an anaesthetic; **être sous a.** to be anaesthetized *or* under an anaesthetic; **a. épidurale** epidural (anaesthesia); **a. générale** general anaesthesia; **a. locale** local anaesthesia; **a. péridurale** epidural (anaesthesia); **a. tronculaire** nerve-blocking anaesthesia, nerve block

anesthésier [9] [anɛstezje] VT **1** *Méd* to anaesthetize; **docteur, allez-vous m'a.?** doctor, are you going to give me an anaesthetic?

2 *(insensibiliser → bras, jambe)* to numb, to deaden; **le glaçon m'a anesthésié la gencive** the ice cube numbed *or* took all the feeling out of my gum

3 *Fig (opinion publique)* to anaesthetize; *Hum* **on ressort de ses cours complètement anesthésié** your brain is numb with boredom when you come out of his/her lectures

anesthésiologie [anɛstezjɔlɔʒi] NF *Méd Br* anaesthetics *(singulier)*, *Am* anesthesiology

anesthésiologiste [anɛstezjɔlɔʒist] NMF *Méd Br* anaesthetist, *Am* anesthesiologist

anesthésique [anɛstezik] *Méd* ADJ anaesthetic

NM anaesthetic; **un a. local** a local anaesthetic

anesthésiste [anɛstezist] NMF *Méd (médecin) Br* anaesthetist, *Am* anesthesiologist; *(infirmière) Br* anaesthetic nurse, *Am* anesthetist

anesthésiste-réanimateur [anɛstezistreanimatœr] *(pl* **anesthésistes-réanimateurs**) NMF *Méd Br* anaesthetist, *Am* anesthesiologist

aneth [anɛt] NM *Bot* dill

aneurine [anœrin] NF aneurin

anévrismal, -e, -aux, -ales [anevrismal, -o] ADJ *Méd* aneurismal, aneurysmal

anévrisme [anevrism] NM *Méd* aneurism, aneurysm

anévrysmal, -e, -aux, -ales [anevrismal, -o] = **anévrismal**

anévrysme [anevrism] = **anévrisme**

anfractuosité [ãfraktɥozite] NF **1** *Géol (cavité)* crevice, crack **2** *Méd* anfractuosity

angarie [ãgari] NF *Jur* angary

ange [ãʒ] NM **1** *Rel* angel; **c'est mon bon a.** he's/she's my guardian angel; **c'est mon mauvais a.** he's/she's a bad influence on me; **a. déchu/gardien** fallen/guardian angel; **un a. passa** there was a sudden silence, there was a lull in the conversation; **ah, un a. passe!** hasn't anybody got anything to say?, don't all talk at once!; **discuter du sexe des anges** to engage in pointless intellectual arguments, to argue about how many angels can fit on the end of a pin; **être aux anges** to be beside oneself with joy; **elle était aux anges quand je le lui ai dit** when I told her, she was ecstatic; **il riait** *ou* **souriait aux anges dans son sommeil** he was smiling happily in his sleep

2 *(personne parfaite)* angel; **passe-moi le pain, tu seras un a.** be an angel and pass me the bread; **c'est un a. de douceur** he's/she's sweetness itself; **mon a.** my darling *or* angel

3 *Ich* **a. (de mer)** monkfish, angel shark

angéiographie [ãʒeiografi] = **angiographie**

angéiologie [ãʒeiolɔʒi] = **angiologie**

angéite [ãʒeit] NF *Méd* angiitis

angélique [ãʒelik] ADJ *Rel & Fig* angelic; **un sourire a.** an angelic smile

NF *Bot & Culin* angelica; **a. sauvage** wild angelica

NM *(bois)* basralocus wood

angéliquement [ãʒelikmã] ADV angelically

angélisme [ãʒelism] NM **1** *(refus des réalités charnelles et physiques)* otherworldliness **2** *(naïveté)* blissful naivety, refusal to face up to reality; **certains élus font preuve d'a. en trouvant toujours des excuses aux délinquants** certain people in power just refuse to face up to reality; they're always finding excuses for delinquents; **sans vouloir faire de l'a., je ne pense pas que la répression soit la solution** without wishing to be naive, I don't think repression is the answer

ang-ang

angelot [ãʒlo] NM *Beaux-Arts* cherub
angélus [ãʒelys] NM *Rel* Angelus

'L'Angélus' *Millet* 'The Angelus'

Angers [ãʒe] NM *Géog* Angers
angevin, -e [ãʒvɛ̃, -in] ADJ 1 *(d'Angers)* of/from Angers 2 *(de l'Anjou)* of/from Anjou
  □ **Angevin, -e** NM,F 1 *(d'Angers)* = inhabitant of or person from Angers 2 *(de l'Anjou)* = inhabitant of or person from Anjou
angiectasie [ãʒjɛktazi] NF *Méd* angiectasis
angine [ãʒin] NF *Méd* 1 *(infection → des amygdales)* tonsillitis; *(→ du pharynx)* pharyngitis; **avoir une a.** to have a sore throat; **a. catarrhale** catarrhal *or* acute pharyngitis; **a. couenneuse** diphtheria 2 *(douleur cardiaque)* angina; **a. de poitrine** angina (pectoris)
angineux, -euse [ãʒinø, -øz] ADJ *Méd* anginal, anginous
angio- [ãʒjo] PRÉF angio-
angiocardiographie [ãʒjokardjografi] NF *Méd* angiocardiography
angiocholite [ãʒjokolit] NF *Méd* angiocholitis
angiogenèse [ãʒjoʒɛnɛz] NF *Méd* angiogenesis
angiogramme [ãʒjogram] NM *Méd* angiogram
angiographie [ãʒjografi] NF *Méd* angiography
angiographique [ãʒjografik] ADJ *Méd* angiographic
angiologie [ãʒjolɔʒi] NF *Méd* angiology
angiomatose [ãʒjomatoz] NF *Méd* angiomatosis
angiome [ãʒjom] NM *Méd* angioma
angioneurotique [ãʒjonørɔtik] ADJ *Méd* angioneurotic
angioplastie [ãʒjoplasti] NF *Méd* angioplasty
angiosperme [ãʒjospɛrm] *Bot* NF angiosperm
  □ **angiospermes** NFPL Angiospermae
angiotensine [ãʒjotãzin] NF *Méd* angiotensin
Angkor [ãkor] NM *Géog* Angkor
anglais, -e [ãglɛ, -ɛz] ADJ *(d'Angleterre)* English; *(de Grande-Bretagne)* British; **l'équipe anglaise** the England team
  NM *(langue)* English; **a. américain/britannique** American/British English
  □ **Anglais, -e** NM,F *(d'Angleterre)* Englishman, *f* Englishwoman; *(de Grande-Bretagne)* Briton; **les A.** *(d'Angleterre)* English people, the English; *(de Grande-Bretagne)* British people, the British; *Fam* **les A. ont débarqué** I have my period■
  □ **anglaise** NF 1 *(écriture)* italic longhand 2 *Bot* morello cherry
  □ **anglaises** NFPL ringlets; **elle était coiffée avec des anglaises** her hair was in ringlets
  □ **à l'anglaise** ADJ 1 *Culin* boiled 2 *Hort* **jardin/parc à l'anglaise** landscaped garden/park 3 *Menuis* **escalier/limon à l'anglaise** open staircase/stringboard ADV **se sauver** *ou* **filer à l'anglaise** to slip away
anglaiser [4] [ãglɛze] VT **a. un cheval** to nick a horse's tail
angle [ãgl] NM 1 *(coin → d'un meuble, d'un mur, d'une pièce)* corner, angle; *(→ d'une rue, d'une table)* corner; **faire un a.** *(chemin)* to bend, to turn; *(maison)* to be L-shaped, to form an angle; **la maison qui est à** *ou* **qui fait l'a.** the house on the corner; **la statue est à l'a. de deux rues** the statue stands at a crossroads; **le buffet a des angles arrondis/pointus** the dresser has rounded/sharp corners; **a. saillant/rentrant** salient/re-entrant angle; **a. vif** sharp angle; *Fig* **arrondir les angles** to smooth things over
  2 *Géom* angle; **a. aigu/droit/obtus** acute/right/obtuse angle; **la rue fait un a. droit avec l'avenue** the street is at right angles to the avenue; **les rues se coupent à a. droit** the roads cross at right angles; **a. alterne interne/plat** interior/exterior alternate angle; **a. mort** *(en voiture)* blind spot; **a. ouvert** wide angle; **a. plat** straight angle; **a. plein** 360-degree angle; **angles opposés/supplémentaires** opposite/supplementary angles; **angles opposés par le sommet** vertical and opposite angles
  3 *(aspect)* angle, point of view; **je ne vois pas cela sous cet a.** I don't see it quite in that light *or* from that angle; **quel que soit l'a. qu'on choisisse, le résultat est le même** you get the same result whichever way you go about it; **présenter les choses sous un certain a.** to present things

from a certain point of view; **sous quel a. avez-vous abordé le sujet?** how did you approach the subject?; **vu sous cet a.** seen from that angle; **vu sous l'a. économique/du rendement, cette décision se comprend** from an economic/a productivity point of view, the decision makes sense
  4 *Opt* angle; **a. d'incidence/de réflexion/de réfraction** angle of incidence/of reflection/of refraction; **a. d'ouverture** aperture angle, beam width
  5 *Tech* angle; **a. d'attaque/d'affûtage/de coupe** working/lip/cutting angle
  6 *Cin* **a. de prise de vue** camera angle; **a. du regard** point of view
  □ **d'angle** ADJ 1 *Constr* quoin *(avant n)*, cornerstone *(avant n)*
  2 *(table)* corner *(avant n)*
angledozer [ãgledozer] NM angledozer
Angles [ãgl] NMPL *Hist* Angles
anglet [ãglɛ] NM *Archit* mitre joint
Angleterre [ãglətɛr] NF **l'A.** England; *(Grande-Bretagne)* (Great) Britain; **vivre en A.** to live in England/Great Britain; **aller en A.** to go to England/Great Britain; *Hist* **la bataille d'A.** the Battle of Britain
anglican, -e [ãglikã, -an] ADJ *Rel* Anglican
  NM,F Anglican
anglicanisme [ãglikanism] NM *Rel* Anglicanism
angliche [ãgliʃ] *Fam* ADJ *(d'Angleterre)* English■; *(de Grande-Bretagne)* Brit
  NM,F *(d'Angleterre)* Englishman■, *f* Englishwoman■; *(de Grande-Bretagne)* Brit
anglicisant, -e [ãglisizã, -ãt] ADJ *(étudiant)* specializing in English
anglicisation [ãglisizasjɔ̃] NF anglicization, anglicizing
angliciser [3] [ãglisize] VT to anglicize
  ►**s'angliciser** VPR to become anglicized
anglicisme [ãglisism] NM *Ling* anglicism
angliciste [ãglisist] NMF 1 *(étudiant)* student of English 2 *(enseignant)* teacher of English 3 *(spécialiste)* Anglicist, expert in English language and culture
anglo [ãglo] NMF *Can Fam Péj* English-speaking Quebecker■
anglo- [ãglo] PRÉF Anglo-
anglo-américain, -e [ãgloamerikɛ̃, -ɛn] *(mpl* **anglo-américains,** *fpl* **anglo-américaines)** ADJ Anglo-American
  NM *(langue)* American English
  □ **Anglo-Américain, -e** NM,F Anglo-American
anglo-arabe [ãgloarab] *(pl* **anglo-arabes)** ADJ *(cheval)* anglo-arab
  NM anglo-arab horse
anglo-canadien, -enne [ãglokanadjɛ̃, -ɛn] *(mpl* **anglo-canadiens,** *fpl* **anglo-canadiennes)** ADJ Anglo-Canadian
  NM *(langue)* Canadian English
  □ **Anglo-Canadien, -enne** NM,F English Canadian
anglo-français, -e [ãglofrãsɛ, -ɛz] *(mpl inv, fpl* **anglo-françaises)** ADJ Anglo-French
  □ **Anglo-Français, -e** NM,F Anglo-Frenchman, *f* Anglo-Frenchwoman
anglo-irlandais, -e [ãgloirlãdɛ, -ɛz] *(mpl inv, fpl* **anglo-irlandaises)** ADJ Anglo-Irish
  □ **Anglo-Irlandais, -e** NM,F Anglo-Irishman, *f* Anglo-Irishwoman; **les A.** the Anglo-Irish
anglomane [ãgloman] NMF Anglomaniac
anglomanie [ãglomani] NF Anglomania
anglo-normand, -e [ãglonɔrmã, -ãd] *(mpl* **anglo-normands,** *fpl* **anglo-normandes)** ADJ 1 *Hist* Anglo-Norman 2 *Géog* of/from the Channel Islands; **les îles anglo-normandes** the Channel Islands
  NM *(langue)* Anglo-Norman
anglophile [ãglofil] ADJ Anglophilic, Anglophiliac
  NMF Anglophile
anglophilie [ãglofili] NF Anglophilia
anglophobe [ãglofɔb] ADJ Anglophobic
  NMF Anglophobe
anglophobie [ãglofɔbi] NF Anglophobia
anglophone [ãglofɔn] ADJ English-speaking, Anglophone
  NMF English speaker, Anglophone
anglo-saxon, -onne [ãglosaksɔ̃, -ɔn] *(mpl* **anglo-saxons,** *fpl* **anglo-saxonnes)** ADJ 1 *(culture, civilisation, littérature)* Anglo-American, British and

American, Anglo-Saxon; **les coutumes anglo-saxonnes** customs in English-speaking countries 2 *Hist* Anglo-Saxon
  NM *(langue)* Old English, Anglo-Saxon
  □ **Anglo-Saxon, -onne** NM,F Anglo-Saxon; **les Anglo-Saxons** *(peuples)* British and American people; *Hist* the Anglo-Saxons

angoissant, -e [ãgwasã, -ãt] ADJ 1 *(expérience)* distressing, harrowing, agonizing; *(nouvelle, livre, film)* distressing, harrowing; **il a vécu trois jours très angoissants** he lived through three harrowing days 2 *(sens affaibli)* **j'ai trouvé l'attente très angoissante** the wait was a strain on my nerves; **une période angoissante** an anxious time
angoisse [ãgwas] NF *(inquiétude)* anxiety; *(tourment)* anguish; **l'a. de la mort** the fear of death; **être** *ou* **vivre dans l'a.** to live in a (constant state of) anxiety; **vivre dans l'a. de qch** to live in dread of *or* to dread sth; **avec elle, je vis dans l'a. d'une fugue** I live in constant fear that she'll run away; **l'a. de devoir faire un choix** the anguish of having to make a choice; **a. existentielle** (existential) angst; *Fam* **c'est l'a.!, bonjour l'a.!** what a pain *or* drag *or* bummer!
  □ **angoisses** NFPL **avoir des angoisses** to suffer from anxiety attacks

'L'Angoisse du gardien du but au moment du penalty' *Wenders* 'The Goalkeeper's Fear of the Penalty'

angoissé, -e [ãgwase] ADJ *(personne)* anxious; *(regard)* haunted, anguished, agonized; *(voix, cri)* agonized, anguished; **être a. avant un examen** to feel anxious before an exam
  NM,F anxious person; **c'est un grand a.** he's the anxious type *or* a terrible worrier
angoisser [3] [ãgwase] VT **a. qn** *(inquiéter)* to cause sb anxiety, to cause anxiety to sb; *(tourmenter)* to cause sb anguish; **ça m'angoisse de devoir parler en public** I get very nervous if I have to speak in public, I find speaking in public a real ordeal
  VI *Fam* to worry■; **j'angoisse à mort pour l'examen de demain** I'm worried sick about tomorrow's exam
  ►**s'angoisser** VPR *Fam* to get worked up; **elle s'angoisse pour un rien** she gets worked up over nothing
Angola [ãgola] NM **l'A.** Angola; **vivre en A.** to live in Angola; **aller en A.** to go to Angola
angolais, -e [ãgolɛ, -ɛz] ADJ Angolan
  □ **Angolais, -e** NM,F Angolan
angon [ãgɔ̃] NM 1 *(arme)* angon 2 *Pêche* hook, spear
angor [ãgor] NM *Méd* angina (pectoris)
angora [ãgora] ADJ angora; **chat/chèvre/lapin a.** Angora cat/goat/rabbit; **de la laine a.** angora wool
  NM 1 *(chat, lapin)* Angora 2 *(laine)* angora
  □ **en angora** ADJ angora *(avant n)*
Angoulême [ãgulɛm] NM *Géog* Angoulême; **le festival d'A.** = festival of comic strip art held in Angoulême
angoumoisin, -e [ãgumwazɛ̃, -in] ADJ of/from Angoulême
  □ **Angoumoisin, -e** NM,F = inhabitant of or person from Angoulême
angrois [ãgrwa] = engrois
angstrœm, angström [ãgstrœm] NM *Phys* angstrom
anguiforme [ãgiform] ADJ snake-like, *Spéc* anguine
Anguilla [ãgija] NF *Géog* Anguilla
anguille [ãgij] NF *Ich* eel; **a. de mer/électrique** conger/electric eel; **mince comme une a.** thin as a reed; **souple comme une a.** supple as a reed; *Fig* **il y a a. sous roche** there's something fishy going on

ang-ann

anguillère [ãgijɛr] NF **1** (*vivier*) eel-pond, eel-preserve **2** *Pêche* eel-pot

anguillidés [ãgijide] NMPL *Ich* Anguillidae

anguilliforme [ãgijifɔrm] ADJ eel-like, *Spéc* anguilliform

anguillule [ãgijyl] NF eelworm, *Spéc* anguillula; **a. du blé** wheatworm

angulaire [ãgylɛr] ADJ angular

anguleux, -euse [ãgylø, -øz] ADJ (*objet*) angular; (*visage*) bony, sharp-featured, angular; (*personne*) skinny, bony; (*esprit, caractère*) stiff

angusticlave [ãgystiklav] NM *Antiq* angusticlave

angustifolié, -e [ãgystifɔlje] ADJ *Bot* angustifoliate

angustura [ãgystyra] NF *Bot* angostura

anharmonique [anarmɔnik] ADJ *Math* anharmonic

anhélation [anelasjɔ̃] NF *Méd* anhelation

anhéler [18] [anele] VI *Littéraire* to breathe with difficulty, to gasp

anhidrose [anidroz] NF *Méd* anidrosis, anhidrosis

anhydre [anidr] ADJ *Chim* anhydrous

anhydride [anidrid] NM *Chim* anhydride; **a. carbonique** carbon dioxide; **a. sulfureux** sulphur dioxide; **a. tellureux** tellurium dioxide

anhydrite [anidrit] NF *Minér* anhydrite

anhydrobiose [anidrɔbjoz] NF *Biol & Écol* anhydrobiosis

anhypothétique [anipotetik] ADJ *Phil* (*théorie, idée*) = which has not been formulated before

anicroche [anikrɔʃ] NF hitch, snag; **il n'y a pas eu d'anicroches** there were no hitches, all went smoothly; **il pourrait bien y avoir des anicroches** there might well be a few snags or hitches; **sans a.** smoothly, without a hitch

anidrose [anidroz] = **anhidrose**

ânier, -ère [ɑnje, -ɛr] NM,F donkey driver

anilide [anilid] NF *Chim* anilide

aniline [anilin] NF *Chim* aniline

animadversion [animadvɛrsjɔ̃] NF *Littéraire* animadversion, censure

animal, -e, -aux, -ales [animal, -o] ADJ *Zool* animal (*avant n*); **l'instinct a.** the animal instinct; **il répondit par un grognement a.** he gave an animal grunt by way of reply
NM **1** (*gén*) animal; **les animaux de la ferme** (*dans les livres d'enfants*) farm animals; **ils ont vendu tous les animaux de l'exploitation** they sold all the livestock on the farm; **a. familier** ou **domestique** pet; **a. de boucherie** animal bred for meat; **animaux de laboratoire** laboratory animals; **grands animaux** larger animals
2 *Fam* (*personne*) dope, oaf; **c'est qu'il a encore raison, cet a.-là** ou **l'a.!** the devil's right again!; **qu'est-ce qu'il a encore fait, ce grand a.(-là)?** what's that great oaf been up to this time?; **quel a.!** what a brute!, what a beast!

animalcule [animalkyl] NM *Zool* animalcule

animale [animal] *voir* **animal**

animalerie [animalri] NF **1** (*de laboratoire*) breeding farm (*for laboratory animals*) **2** (*magasin*) pet shop

animalier, -ère [animalje, -ɛr] ADJ (*peintre, sculpteur*) animal (*avant n*)
NM **1** *Beaux-Arts* animalier **2** (*employé*) animal keeper (*in a laboratory*)

animaliser [3] [animalize] VT to animalize

animalisme [animalism] NM *Phil* animalism

animaliste [animalist] NMF *Phil* animalist

animalité [animalite] NF animality, animal nature

animateur, -trice [animatœr, -tris] NM,F **1** (*responsable → de maison de jeunes, de centre sportif*) youth leader, coordinator; (*→ de groupe*) leader; (*→ d'entreprise, de service*) coordinator
2 *Rad & TV* (*gén*) presenter; (*de jeux, de variétés*) host; (*d'un débat*) moderator
3 (*élément dynamique*) moving spirit, driving force
4 *Cin* animator
5 *Mktg* (*d'une réunion de groupe*) leader, moderator; **a. des ventes** marketing executive

animation [animasjɔ̃] NF **1** (*entrain*) life, liveliness, excitement; **mettre un peu d'a. dans une réunion** to liven up a meeting; **son arrivée a créé beaucoup d'a.** his/her arrival caused a great deal of excitement
2 (*vivacité*) liveliness, vivacity, animation; **elles discutaient de politique avec a.** they were having a lively discussion about politics

3 (*d'un quartier, d'une ville*) life; **il y a de l'a. dans les rues le soir** the streets are very lively or full of life at night
4 (*coordination → d'un groupe*) running; (*→ d'un débat*) chairing; **chargé de l'a. culturelle** in charge of cultural activities; **responsable de l'a. de l'équipe** responsible for coordinating the team; **faire de l'a., travailler dans l'a.** (*dans un centre aéré, dans une maison des jeunes, dans une colonie de vacances*) to be a youth leader, to run activities; **organiser des animations de rue** to organize street shows; **il y aura une petite a. pour les enfants** some activities will be organized for the children
5 (*promotion → d'un produit*) promotion; **faire des animations dans les supermarchés** to promote products in supermarkets; **a. commerciale** marketing campaign; **a. des ventes** sales drive, sales promotion
6 *Cin* animation; **a. de cellos** cel animation; **a. d'objets** object animation; **a. par ordinateur** computer animation
7 *Météo* **a. satellite** satellite picture

animatrice [animatris] *voir* **animateur**

animatique [animatik] NF *Ordinat* board test

animé, -e [anime] ADJ **1** (*doué de vie*) animate; **les êtres animés** animate beings **2** (*doté de mouvement*) moving, animated; **les vitrines animées de Noël** moving or animated window displays at Christmas **3** (*plein de vivacité → personne, discussion*) lively, animated; (*→ marché, ville, rue*) busy, bustling; (*→ quartier*) lively, busy **4** *Fin & Bourse* (*marché*) brisk, buoyant **5** *Ling* animate

animelles [animɛl] NFPL *Culin* animal testicles

animer [3] [anime] VT **1** (*doter de mouvement → mécanisme, robot*) to move, to actuate; **le piston est animé d'un mouvement de va-et-vient** the piston is driven back and forth
2 (*inspirer*) to prompt, to motivate; **c'est la générosité qui l'anime** he's prompted or motivated by generous feelings; **être animé de qch** to be motivated or prompted by sth; **être animé des meilleures intentions** to have the best of intentions; **être animé d'un nouvel espoir** to be buoyed up by new hope
3 (*égayer → soirée, repas*) to bring some life to, to liven up; (*→ quartier*) to liven up; (*→ pièce*) to brighten up; (*→ regard*) to light up; **le plaisir animait son visage** his face was lit up with joy; **a. un personnage** to make a character come to life
4 *Rad & TV* (*présenter → débat*) to chair; (*→ émission d'actualité*) to present; (*→ émission de variétés*) to host
5 (*faire fonctionner → atelier*) to run
6 *Sport* **a. une course** to set the pace for a race
►**s'animer** VPR (*personne, conversation*) to become animated; (*quartier, rue, visage, yeux*) to come alive; (*pantin, poupée*) to come to life

animisme [animism] NM *Phil & Rel* animism

animiste [animist] *Phil & Rel* ADJ animistic
NMF animist

animosité [animozite] NF animosity, hostility, resentment; **avoir de l'a. contre qn** to feel resentment or hostility towards sb; **un regard plein d'a.** a hostile look

animus [animys] NM *Psy* animus

anion [anjɔ̃] NM *Phys* anion

anionique [anjɔnik] ADJ *Phys* anionic

anis [ani(s)] NM **1** *Bot* anise **2** *Culin* aniseed; **à l'a.** aniseed (*avant n*), aniseed-flavoured

anisé, -e [anize] ADJ *Culin* aniseed-flavoured

aniser [3] [anize] VT *Culin* to flavour with aniseed

anisette [anizɛt] NF (*alcool*) anisette

anisogamie [anizogami] NF *Biol* anisogamy

anisole [anizɔl] NM *Chim* anisole

anisotrope [anizɔtrɔp] ADJ *Phys* anisotropic, aeolotropic

anisotropie [anizɔtrɔpi] NF *Phys* anisotropy, aeolotropy

Anjou [ãʒu] NM **l'A.** *Géog* **(l')A.** Anjou

Ankara [ãkara] NM *Géog* Ankara

ankylosaure [ãkilosɔr] NM *Zool* (*en paléontologie*) ankylosaur, ankylosaurus

ankylose [ãkiloz] NF **1** *Méd* ankylosis **2** (*engourdissement*) stiffness, numbness

ankylosé, -e [ãkiloze] ADJ **1** *Méd* ankylosed **2** (*engourdi*) numb; **mon bras est complètement a.** my arm's gone completely numb

ankyloser [3] [ãkiloze] VT to ankylose
►**s'ankyloser** VPR **1** *Méd* to ankylose **2** (*devenir engourdi → bras, jambe*) to become numb; (*→ personne*) to go stiff **3** *Fig* (*dans un métier*) to get into a rut

ankylostome [ãkilostɔm] NM *Entom* hookworm

ankylostomiase [ãkilostɔmjaz] NF *Méd* ankylostomiasis

'Anna Karénine' *Tolstoï* 'Anna Karenina'

annal, -e, -aux, -ales [anal, -o] ADJ valid for one year, yearly

annales [anal] NFPL **1** (*chronique*) annals; **rester dans les a.** to go down in history **2** (*d'examen*) past examination papers (*with annotations*) **3** (*revue*) review

annaliste [analist] NMF annalist

annalité [analite] NF yearly nature

Annam [anam] NM *Géog* Annam

annamite [anamit] ADJ Annamese
❑ **Annamite** NMF Annamese

Annapurna [anapyrna] NM **l'A.** Annapurna

annate [anat] *Rel & Hist* NF annat
❑ **annates** NFPL annates, first fruits

Anne [an] NPR **A. d'Autriche** Anne of Austria; **A. Boleyn** Anne Boleyn; **A. de Clèves** Anne of Cleves

Allusion

Anne, ma sœur Anne, ne vois-tu rien venir?
In Charles Perrault's story *Bluebeard*, Bluebeard's wife and her sister, Anne, are imprisoned in a castle, hoping their brother will come and rescue them. Each time Bluebeard's wife asks "Sister Anne, can't you see anything coming?", the answer is the same: "No, I can see only the high road shimmering and the green grass growing." In modern idiom, this expression is used jokingly while waiting for someone who is late, or for something which is late in starting.

anneau, -x [ano] NM **1** (*gén*) ring; **l'a. de ma bague est trop grand** the hoop of my ring is too large; **un simple a. d'or** a plain band of gold; **en forme d'a.** ring-shaped, *Sout* annular; **a. épiscopal/nuptial** bishop's/wedding ring; **l'a. du pêcheur** the fisherman's ring
2 (*pour rideaux*) ring; (*maillon*) link; (*boucle → de ficelle*) loop
3 *Math* ring
4 *Bot & Géom* annulus
5 *Zool* (*d'un ver*) metamere, somatite; (*d'un serpent*) coil
6 *Anat* ring; **a. inguinal/crural** inguinal/crural ring
7 *Astron* ring; **les anneaux de Saturne** the rings of Saturn
8 *Sport* **a. de vitesse** (*pour patinage*) rink; (*pour bicyclette*) racetrack
9 *Opt* ring; **anneaux colorés** coloured rings
❑ **anneaux** NMPL *Sport* rings; (*jeu*) hoopla; **exercices aux anneaux** ring exercises
❑ **en anneau** ADJ **1** (*gén*) ring-shaped, *Sout* annular
2 *Électron* ring (*avant n*)

'L'Anneau du Nibelung' *Wagner* 'The Ring of the Nibelung'

annecien, -enne [ansjɛ̃, -ɛn] ADJ of/from Annecy
❑ **Annecien, -enne** NM,F = inhabitant of or person from Annecy

Annecy [ansi] NM *Géog* Annecy; **le festival d'A.** = annual cartoon film festival in Annecy

année [ane] NF **1** (*division du calendrier*) year; **a. bissextile** leap year; *Fin* **a. budgétaire** *Br* financial year, *Am* fiscal year; **a. civile** calendar or civil year; **a. comptable** accounting year; **a. en cours** current year; **a. d'exercice** *Br* financial year, *Am* fiscal year; **a. fiscale** tax year, *Am* fiscal year; **a. d'imposition** year of assessment
2 (*date*) year; **quelle est son a. de naissance?** what year was he/she born?; **l'a. 1789** the year 1789; **l'a. prochaine/dernière** next/last year; **a. de fabrication** year of manufacture; *Com* **a.**

record peak *or* record year; **l'a. de référence** the base year

3 *(durée)* year; **il y a des années que je ne l'ai pas vue** I haven't seen her for years; **ce projet durera toute l'a.** this project will last the whole year; **d'a. en a.** from year to year; **d'une a. à l'autre** from one year to the next; **tout au long de l'a., toute l'a.** all year long *or* round; **j'ai encore deux années à faire** I have two more years to do; **j'ai cinq années de métier** I have five years' experience in this field; **entrer dans sa trentième a.** to enter one's thirtieth year; **elle entre dans sa trentième a.** she'll be thirty (on her) next birthday; **années d'abondance** prosperous years; **la première a. de la guerre** the first year of the war; **les plus belles années de ma vie** the best years of my life; *Univ* **première a.** *Br* first year, *Am* freshman year; *Univ* **dernière a.** *Br* final year, *Am* senior year; **c'est une étudiante de troisième a.** *Br* she's a third-year student, *Am* she's in her junior year; **elle est en troisième a. de médecine** she's in her third year at medical school; **l'a. scolaire/universitaire/judiciaire** the school/academic/legal year; **une a. sabbatique** a sabbatical (year); **l'a. sidérale** the sidereal year; *Fam* **années de vaches maigres/grasses** lean/prosperous years ■; **années de plomb** dark years; **les années de plomb de l'Occupation** the dark years of the Occupation

4 *(célébration)* **l'a. de** the Year of; **l'a. du Dragon** the Year of the Dragon; **l'a. de l'Enfance** the Year of the Child; **l'a. de la Femme** International Women's Year

5 *(nouvel an)* **bonne a.!** happy New Year!; **souhaiter la bonne a. à qn** to wish sb a happy New Year; **carte/souhaits de bonne a.** New Year card/wishes

6 *Belg (locution)* **être de la bonne a.** to be naive

❑ **années** NFPL **les années soixante/soixante-dix** the sixties/seventies; **les Années folles** the roaring twenties

❑ **à l'année** ADV *(louer, payer)* annually, on a yearly basis

'L'Année dernière à Marienbad' Robbe-Grillet, Resnais 'Last Year at Marienbad'

'L'Année de tous les dangers' Weir 'The Year of Living Dangerously'

Allusion

L'année de tous les dangers
The name of the Peter Weir film (see above) is also used allusively as an expression to describe any situation where everything is going wrong or when there are problems and potential risks ahead, for example **Pour l'équipe de France, c'est l'année de tous les dangers**, ie "Things are looking dangerous for the French team." Other words can be substituted for "année". In the example **Pour le pays, ce sont les élections de tous les dangers**, the meaning would be "These elections could be crucial for the country."

---

année-lumière [anelymjɛr] *(pl* **années-lumière)** NF *Astron* light year; *Fig* **à des années-lumière de** light years away from; **mon cousin et moi, nous sommes à des années-lumière l'un de l'autre** my cousin and I are poles apart

annelé, -e [anle] ADJ **1** *(gén)* ringed **2** *Archit & Bot* annulate, annulated

anneler [24] [anle] VT to ring

annelet [anlɛ] NM **1** *(anneau)* small ring **2** *Archit* annulet

annélide [anelid] *Zool* NF annelid

❑ **annélides** NFPL Annelida

annexe [anɛks] ADJ **1** *(accessoire → tâche, détail, fait)* subsidiary, related; *(sans importance)* minor; **des considérations annexes** side issues; **ne parlons pas de cela, c'est tout à fait a.** let's forget about this, it's very much a minor point *or* it's not relevant to the matter in hand

2 *(dossier)* additional; **les documents** *ou* **pièces annexes** the attached documents

3 **bâtiment a.** annexe

4 *(revenus, frais)* supplementary

NF **1** *(bâtiment)* annexe; *(d'une ferme, d'un château)* outbuilding; *(d'une église)* chapel of ease; **l'a. de l'école** the school annexe

2 *(supplément → d'un document)* annexe; *(→ d'un dossier)* appendix; *(→ d'un contrat)* rider; *(→ d'un bilan)* schedule; *Jur (→ d'une loi)* rider, annexe; **mettre qch en a. à** to append sth to; **les détails du sondage sont en a.** the details of the survey are in the appendix; **en a. à ma lettre** enclosed with my letter; **en a. veuillez trouver…** *(dans une lettre)* please find enclosed…; *(dans un e-mail)* please find attached…

3 *Méd* appendage; **annexes de l'utérus** adnexa

4 *(d'un bateau)* dinghy

❑ **annexes** NFPL **1** *Compta* notes to the accounts

2 *Jur* **annexes de propres** = clause in a prenuptial agreement contract allowing the two partners to keep their separate estates

annexer [4] [anɛkse] VT **1** *(joindre)* to annex, to append, to attach; **pièces annexées** *(à une lettre)* enclosures; *(à un dossier)* appended documents, appendices; **a. un témoignage à un dossier** to append a testimony to a file **2** *Hist & Pol* to annex

►**s'annexer** VPR *Fam* **s'a. qch** *(le monopoliser)* to hog sth; *Euph (le voler)* to filch sth, to purloin sth

annexion [anɛksjɔ̃] NF annexation

annexionnisme [anɛksjɔnism] NM annexationism

annexionniste [anɛksjɔnist] ADJ annexational
NMF annexationist

annexite [anɛksit] NF *Méd* adnexitis

annihilation [aniilasjɔ̃] NF **1** *Sout (destruction)* annihilation, destruction **2** *Phys* annihilation

annihiler [3] [aniile] VT *Sout (efforts, révolte)* to annihilate, to destroy; *(personne)* to crush, to destroy

anniversaire [anivɛrsɛr] ADJ anniversary *(avant n)*; **le jour** *ou* **la date a. de leur rencontre** the anniversary of the day they first met
NM **1** *(d'une naissance)* birthday; **c'est arrivé le jour de son a.** it happened on his/her birthday; **une fête d'a.** a birthday party; **bon** *ou* **joyeux a.!** happy birthday!

2 *(d'un mariage, d'une mort, d'un événement)* anniversary; **le cinquantième a. de leur mariage** their fiftieth wedding anniversary

3 *(fête)* birthday party

annonacée [anɔnase] *Bot* NF anonaceous plant
❑ **annonacées** NFPL Anonaceae

annonce [anɔ̃s] NF **1** *(nouvelle)* notice, notification; *(fait de dire)* announcement; **tu as lu l'a. de sa nomination?** did you read the notification of his/her appointment?; **faire une a.** *(gén)* to make an announcement; **faire l'a. de la sortie d'un disque** to announce the release of a new record

2 *(texte → d'information)* notice; *(→ pour une transaction)* advert, ad; **mettre** *ou* **passer une (petite) a. dans un journal** to put an advertisement *or* an ad in a paper; **annonces classées** classified advertisements *or* ads, *Br* small ads; **a. judiciaire** legal notice; **a. publicitaire** advertisement; **les petites annonces** *(de location, de vente)* classified advertisements *or* ads, *Br* small ads, *Am* want ads; *(courrier du cœur)* personal ads *or* column

3 *Can (publicité)* advert, ad

4 *Cartes* declaration; **faire une a.** to declare

5 *(présage)* sign; *Littéraire* portent; **cet incident était en fait l'a. de la guerre** this incident was really a portent of the forthcoming war; **le retour des hirondelles est l'a. du printemps** it's a sign that the spring is on its way when the swallows return

6 *Rad & TV* **a. de continuité** continuity announcement

annoncé, -e [anɔ̃se] ADJ predictable

annoncer [16] [anɔ̃se] VT **1** *(communiquer → renseignement)* to announce; *(→ mauvaise nouvelle)* to announce, to break; *(→ météo)* to predict, to forecast; **je n'ose pas le lui a.** I daren't break it to him/her; **a. la naissance d'un enfant** to announce the birth of a child; **ils annoncent du soleil pour demain** sunshine is forecast for tomorrow, the forecast for tomorrow is sunny; **on annonce des réductions d'impôts** tax reductions have been announced; **a.**

qch à qn to inform sb of sth, to tell sb sth; **on m'a annoncé sa mort hier** I was told *or* informed of his/her death yesterday; **a. à qn que** to inform sb that; **je vous annonce que je me marie** I'd like to inform you that I'm getting married; **je leur ai annoncé que je m'en allais** I told them I was leaving; **le gouvernement a fait a. sa décision par son porte-parole** the decision was announced by a government spokesman

2 *Com (proposer)* to quote; **a. un prix** to quote a price

3 *(présenter → visiteur)* to announce; *(→ projet, changement)* to introduce, to usher in; **qui dois-je a.?** what name shall I say?; **se faire a.** to give one's name; **elle est arrivée sans se faire a.** she came unannounced; **a. un nouveau disque** to announce *or* to introduce a new record

4 *(présager)* to announce, to foreshadow, *Littéraire* to herald; *(être signe de)* to be a sign *or* an indication of; **ça n'annonce rien de bon** it doesn't bode well, it isn't a very good sign; **le tremblement de ses mains annonçait toujours une violente colère** the tremor in his hands was a sure sign of imminent wrath

5 *Cartes* to declare; *Fam Fig* **a. la couleur** to lay one's cards on the table

►**s'annoncer** VPR **1** *(prévenir de sa visite)* to notify *or* to warn (that one will come); **viens quand tu veux, ce n'est pas la peine de t'a.** come whenever you like, there's no need to let me know beforehand

2 *(se profiler)* to be looming *or* on the horizon; **une grave crise s'annonce** a serious crisis is looming

3 *(dans des constructions attributives)* **la journée s'annonce très belle** it looks like it's going to be a beautiful day; **le vent s'annonce violent** it looks as though there's going to be a gale; **cela s'annonce très bien** things are looking very promising *or* good; **mes premiers oraux s'annoncent bien** I seem to have done all right in my first orals; **cela s'annonce plutôt mal** it doesn't look very promising, the picture doesn't look *or* isn't too good; **voilà un anniversaire qui s'annonce mal** my/your/*etc* birthday has got off to a bad start

annonceur, -euse [anɔ̃sœr, -øz] NM,F *(présentateur)* announcer
NM **a. (publicitaire)** advertiser

annonciateur, -trice [anɔ̃sjatœr, -tris] ADJ announcing, heralding, foreshadowing; **bourgeons annonciateurs du printemps** buds heralding spring; **les secousses annonciatrices d'un tremblement de terre** the tremors that are the warning signs of an earthquake; **des nuages noirs annonciateurs de pluie** black clouds which are the harbingers of rain
NM **1** *Électron* signal; **a. de couplage** interlocking signal

2 *Tél* annunciator board; **a. de fin de communication** supervisory indicator

Annonciation [anɔ̃sjasjɔ̃] NF *Bible* **l'A.** the Annunciation **2** *(fête)* Annunciation *or* Lady Day

annonciatrice [anɔ̃sjatris] *voir* **annonciateur**

annoncier, -ère [anɔ̃sje, -ɛr] *Journ* NM,F *(personne)* publicity editor
NM *Can (feuille d'annonces)* advertisements page

annone [anɔn] NF **1** *Bot* Anona, Annona **2** *Antiq* annona

annotateur, -trice [anɔtatœr, -tris] NM,F annotator

annotation [anɔtasjɔ̃] NF **1** *(note explicative)* annotation **2** *(note personnelle)* note; **faire des annotations dans un texte** *(gén)* to write notes in the margins of a text; *(éditeur, correcteur)* to annotate a text

annotatrice [anɔtatris] *voir* **annotateur**

annoter [3] [anɔte] VT **1** *(commenter)* to annotate **2** *(de remarques personnelles)* to write notes on; **entièrement annoté** *(livre)* covered with notes; *(édition)* fully annotated

annuaire [anɥɛr] NM *(recueil → d'une association, d'une société)* yearbook, annual; *(liste d'adresses)* directory; **a. (téléphonique)** telephone directory *or* book; **je suis dans l'a.** I'm in the (phone) book; **a. électronique** = telephone directory available on Minitel; **a. des marées** tide table

annualisation [anɥalizasjɔ̃] NF annualization; **l'a. du temps de travail permettra de répondre à une demande saisonnière** calculating working hours across the year will enable us to meet seasonal demand

annualiser [3] [anɥalize] VT to annualize

annualité [anɥalite] NF yearly recurrence; **l'a. budgétaire** the yearly or annual voting of the budget

annuel, -elle [anɥɛl] ADJ **1** (qui revient chaque année) yearly, annual; **budget a.** annual budget; **congé a.** annual leave; **chiffre d'affaires a.** annual or yearly turnover; **consommation annuelle** yearly or annual consumption **2** (qui dure un an) annual; **une plante annuelle** an annual

annuellement [anɥɛlmɑ̃] ADV annually, yearly, on a yearly basis

annuitaire [anɥitɛr] ADJ Compta & Fin (dette) redeemable by yearly payments

annuité [anɥite] NF **1** Fin (dans le remboursement d'un emprunt) annual instalment or repayment; **remboursement par annuités** repayment by annual payments or yearly instalments; Compta **a. d'amortissement** annual depreciation or writedown; Compta **a. constante** (de remboursement) fixed annual payment; **a. réversible** reversionary annuity **2** Can & Suisse (rente) annuity; **a. différée** deferred annuity **3** (année de service) year

annulabilité [anylabilite] NF Jur (d'un contrat, d'une action) voidableness; (d'une loi, d'un jugement) revocability

annulable [anylabl] ADJ **1** (gén) cancellable, annullable **2** Jur (contrat) voidable, cancellable, revocable; (loi, jugement) revocable, repealable

annulaire [anylɛr] ADJ **1** (circulaire) annular, ring-shaped **2** Méd annular
NM Anat (doigt) third or ring finger

annulatif, -ive [anylatif, -iv] ADJ revocatory, annulling

annulation [anylasjɔ̃] NF **1** (d'un ordre, d'un rendez-vous, d'un projet) cancellation, calling off; (d'une réservation) cancellation; (d'une commande) cancellation, withdrawal; (d'une proposition) withdrawal; (d'une dette) cancellation, writing off; Banque (d'un chèque) cancellation
2 Jur (d'un décret, d'un acte judiciaire) revocation, annulment; (d'un jugement, d'un verdict) quashing; (d'une loi) revocation, rescindment; (d'un contrat) annulment, invalidation; (d'un mariage) annulment; (d'un testament) setting aside; (d'un droit) abolition, defeasance
3 Ordinat deletion; **a. d'entrée** (commande) cancel entry; **a. des révisions** (commande) undo changes

annulative [anylativ] voir **annulatif**

annuler [3] [anyle] VT **1** (ordre, rendez-vous, projet) to cancel, to call off; (réservation) to cancel; (commande) to cancel, to withdraw; (dette) to cancel, to write off; Banque (chèque) to cancel
2 Jur (décret, acte judiciaire) to revoke, to annul; (jugement, verdict) to quash; (loi) to rescind, to revoke; (contrat) to annul, to render null and void, to invalidate; (mariage) to annul; (testament) to set aside, to nullify; (droit) to abolish
3 (remplacer) to supersede, to cancel; **ce catalogue annule les précédents** this catalogue supersedes all previous issues
4 Ordinat to cancel; (opération) to undo; **a. les révisions** (commande) undo changes
5 Sport (but) to disallow
▸**s'annuler** VPR to cancel each other out; **les deux forces s'annulent** the two forces cancel each other out

anoa [anɔa] NM Zool anoa

anobie [anɔbi], **anobion** [anɔbjɔ̃] NM Entom anobium; **a. roux** deathwatch beetle; **a. ponctué** furniture beetle

anobli, -e [anɔbli] ADJ ennobled

anoblir [32] [anɔblir] VT to ennoble, to confer a title on

anoblissement [anɔblismɑ̃] NM ennoblement; **lettres d'a.** letters patent of nobility

anode [anɔd] NF Chim & Électron anode

anodin, -e [anɔdɛ̃, -in] ADJ **1** (inoffensif → remarque, plaisanterie) harmless; (→ blessure) slight, minor **2** (insignifiant → personne, propos)

ordinary, commonplace; (→ détail) trifling, insignificant; (→ événement) meaningless, insignificant

anodique [anɔdik] ADJ Chim & Électron anodic, anodal, anode (avant n); **polarisation a.** anodic polarization; **pulvérisation/tension a.** anode sputtering/voltage; **traitement a.** anodizing

anodisation [anɔdizasjɔ̃] NF Métal anodization

anodiser [3] [anɔdize] VT Métal to anodize

anodonte [anɔdɔ̃t] Zool ADJ edentate
❑ **anodontes** NMPL Anodonta

anodontie [anɔdɔ̃si] NF Méd anodontia

anomal, -e, -aux, -ales [anɔmal, -o] ADJ anomalous

anomalie [anɔmali] NF **1** (bizarrerie → d'une expérience, d'une attitude) anomaly; (→ d'une procédure, d'une nomination) irregularity **2** Astron & Ling anomaly **3** Biol abnormality

anomalure [anɔmalyr] NM Zool scaly-tailed squirrel

anomère [anɔmɛr] Chim ADJ anomeric
NM anomer

anomie [anɔmi] NF anomie

anomique [anɔmik] ADJ anomic

anomoure [anɔmur] Zool NM anomuran
❑ **anomoures** NMPL Anomura

ânon [ɑnɔ̃] NM Zool (ass's) foal, young donkey or ass

anon. (abrév écrite **anonyme**) anon

anonacée [anɔnase] = **annonacée**

anone [anɔn] NF Bot Anona, Annona

ânonnement [anɔnmɑ̃] NM (balbutiement) les ânonnements des enfants qui apprennent à lire the faltering tones of children learning to read

ânonner [3] [anɔne] VT to stumble through; **â. sa leçon** to recite one's lesson falteringly; **â. son rôle** to stumble through one's lines
VI to stammer out one's words; **il lisait en ânonnant** he read haltingly

anonymat [anɔnima] NM anonymity; **conserver ou garder l'a.** to remain anonymous; **l'a. le plus total est garanti** confidentiality is guaranteed; **sous le couvert de** ou **en gardant l'a.** anonymously; **sortir de l'a.** (devenir célèbre) to come to public attention, to emerge from obscurity

anonyme [anɔnim] ADJ **1** (sans nom → manuscrit, geste, appel) anonymous; **rester a.** to remain unnamed or anonymous
2 (inconnu → auteur, attaquant) anonymous, unknown
3 (sans personnalité → vêtement, meuble) drab, nondescript; (→ maison, appartement) anonymous, soulless, drab; **perdu dans la foule a.** lost in the crowd
NMF anonym; **c'était signé "a."** it was signed "anon"

anonymement [anɔnimmɑ̃] ADV anonymously

anophèle [anɔfɛl] NM Entom anopheles

anorak [anɔrak] NM anorak

anordir [32] [anɔrdir] VI (vent) to veer round to the North

anorexie [anɔrɛksi] NF Méd anorexia; **faire de l'a.** to suffer from anorexia; Psy **a. mentale** anorexia nervosa

anorexigène [anɔrɛksiʒɛn] Pharm ADJ anorectic
NM appetite suppressant

anorexique [anɔrɛksik] ADJ anorexic
NMF Méd anorexic

anorganique [anɔrganik] ADJ Méd non-organic

anorgasmie [anɔrgasmi] NF Méd anorgasmia, anorgasmy

anormal, -e, -aux, -ales [anɔrmal, -o] ADJ **1** (inhabituel → événement) abnormal, unusual; (→ comportement) abnormal, Sout aberrant; **à son âge, c'est a.** it's not normal at his/her age; **il fait une chaleur anormale** it's abnormally hot
2 (non réglementaire) irregular; **la procédure que vous avez utilisée est tout à fait anormale** it was most irregular for you to proceed in that way
3 (injuste) unfair, unjustified; **il est parfaitement a. qu'ils ne vous aient pas payé** it's intolerable that they didn't pay you
4 (handicapé) mentally handicapped
5 Biol abnormal, anomalous
NM,F mentally handicapped person

anormalement [anɔrmalmɑ̃] ADV **1** (inhabituellement) unusually, abnormally **2** Biol abnormally, aberrantly

anormalité [anɔrmalite] NF abnormality

anosmie [anɔsmi] NF Méd anosmia

anoure [anur] Zool ADJ anuran, anurous
NM anuran
❑ **anoures** NMPL Anura, Salienta

anovulation [anɔvylasjɔ̃] NF Méd anovulation

anovulatoire [anɔvylatwar] ADJ Méd anovulatory, anovular

anoxémie [anɔksemi] NF Méd anoxemia, anoxaemia

anoxie [anɔksi] NF Méd anoxia

ANP [ɑɛnpe] NM (abrév **assistant numérique personnel**) PDA

ANPE [ɑɛnpeə] NF (abrév **Agence nationale pour l'emploi**) = national employment agency; **s'inscrire à l'A.** to sign on

ANRS [ɑɛnɛrɛs] NF (abrév **Agence nationale de recherches sur le sida**) = Aids research institute

anse [ɑ̃s] NF **1** (poignée) handle; Fig **faire danser ou valser l'a. du panier** to fiddle the books **2** Électron ear **3** Géog cove, bight **4** Anat ansa, loop **5** Méd snare **6** Math compound curve **7** Archit **a. (de panier)** basket-handle arch

ansé, -e [ɑ̃se] ADJ (vase) with a handle; Hér **croix ansée** ansate or ansated cross, crux ansata, ankh

ANSEA [ɑ̃sea] NF (abrév **Association des nations du Sud-Est asiatique**) ASEAN

ansée [ɑ̃se] voir **ansé**

ansériforme [ɑ̃serifɔrm] Orn NM anserine bird
❑ **ansériformes** NMPL Anseriformes

ansérine [ɑ̃serin] ADJ F Méd **peau a.** anserine skin
NF Bot goose-foot, pigweed; **a. à balais** belvedere

antabuse® [ɑ̃tabyz] NM Pharm Antabuse®, disulfiram
ADJ **effet a.** disulfiram effect

antagonique [ɑ̃tagɔnik] ADJ (forces, personnes) antagonistic; (intérêts, influences) conflicting

antagonisme [ɑ̃tagɔnism] NM antagonism

antagoniste [ɑ̃tagɔnist] ADJ (attitude, relation, forces, personnes) antagonistic; **avoir des positions antagonistes** to have opposing or conflicting opinions; **les partis antagonistes** the opposing parties; **les muscles antagonistes** antagonistic muscles
NMF antagonist

antalgie [ɑ̃talʒi] NF Méd analgesia

antalgique [ɑ̃talʒik] Méd ADJ analgesic
NM analgesic

Antalya [ɑ̃talja] NM Géog Antalya

antan [ɑ̃tɑ̃] ❑ **d'antan** ADJ of yesteryear; **visiter le Paris d'a.** to visit the Paris of yesteryear; **mes amis d'a.** my erstwhile friends, my friends from the old days

---

Allusion

Mais où sont les neiges d'antan?

This famous refrain is from La ballade des Dames du temps jadis by François Villon (1431–63), an elegiac lament for passing time and fading beauty. It is translated into English as "Where are the snows of yesteryear?" In everyday conversation or newspaper articles, the expression is used to contrast a present-day state of affairs with a better one in times gone by. With Villon's refrain one can either express a truly nostalgic reaction or poke fun at others who are overly nostalgic, so the expression is used both sincerely and ironically. The word "neiges" can be replaced by another, eg **Où sont les grands sportifs d'antan?** ("Where are the great sportsmen of yesteryear?")

Antananarivo [ɑ̃tananarivo] NM Géog Antananarivo

Antarctide [ɑ̃tarktid] NF **l'A.** Antarctica

antarctique [ɑ̃tarktik] ADJ Antarctic; **le cercle polaire a.** the Antarctic Circle
❑ **Antarctique** NM Géog **l'A.** Antarctica

Antarès [ɑ̃tarɛs] NM Astron Antares

ante [ɑ̃t] NF Archit anta

antebois [ɑ̃təbwa] NM chair rail

antécédence [ɑ̃tesedɑ̃s] NF Géol antecedence

antécédent, -e [ɑ̃tesedɑ̃, -ɑ̃t] ADJ **1** (précédent → élément) antecedent; (→ événement) prior, previous; **a. à** prior to
2 Géol antecedent
NM Gram, Ling & Math antecedent

ant-ant

◻ **antécédents** NMPL 1 *(faits passés)* antecedents, past *or* previous history; **avoir de bons/ mauvais antécédents** to have a good/bad record; **vérifier les antécédents judiciaires de qn** to check if sb has a criminal record
2 *Méd* **antécédents (médicaux)** past *or* previous (medical) history, case history; **il y a des antécédents cancéreux dans ma famille** my family has a history of cancer
Antéchrist [ɑ̃tekrist] NM *Bible* Antichrist
antécime [ɑ̃tesim] NF subsidiary peak
antédiluvien, -enne [ɑ̃tedilyvjɛ̃, -ɛn] ADJ 1 *Bible* antediluvian 2 *Fam (vieux)* antiquated, ancient; **un frigo a.** an ancient fridge
Antée [ɑ̃te] NPR *Myth* Antaeus
antéfixe [ɑ̃tefiks] NF antefix
antéhypophyse [ɑ̃teipofiz] NF *Physiol* anterior pituitary
antéislamique [ɑ̃teislamik] ADJ pre-Islamic
antémémoire [ɑ̃tememwar] NF *Ordinat* cache (memory); **mettre en a.** to cache
antenais, -e [ɑ̃tənɛ, -ɛz] ADJ **agneau a.** teg, tegg
anténatal, -e, -aux, -ales [ɑ̃tenatal, -o] ADJ *Méd Br* antenatal, *Am* prenatal
antennaire [ɑ̃tenɛr] NM *Ich* frogfish
antennate [ɑ̃tenat] *Entom* NM antennata
◻ **antennates** NMPL Antennata
antenne [ɑ̃tɛn] NF 1 *Zool & Entom* antenna, feeler; *Fam* **avoir des antennes** *(avoir de l'intuition)* to be very intuitive■; *(avoir des contacts)* to know all the right people
2 *Électron Br* aerial, *Am* antenna; **a. cadre** loop *Br* aerial *or Am* antenna; **a. collective** shared aerial; **a. directive** beam *Br* aerial *or Am* antenna; **a. parabolique** satellite dish, dish *Br* aerial *or Am* antenna; **mini a. parabolique** mini-dish; **a. télescopique** telescopic mast
3 *Rad & TV* **à vous l'a.** over to you; **être à l'a.** to be on (the air); **passer à l'a.** to go on the air; **garder l'a.** to stay on the air; **je passe l'a. à notre prochain invité** I'll hand you over to our next guest; **prendre l'a.** to come on the air; **rendre l'a.** to hand back to the studio; **sur notre a.** *Rad* on this frequency *or* station; *TV* on this channel; *Anciennement* **A. 2** = French state-owned television channel (now called France 2); **temps d'a.** air time
4 *(agence, service)* office; **notre a. à Genève** our agent in Geneva, our Geneva office; **a. chirurgicale** surgical unit
antenniste [ɑ̃tenist] NMF *Électron* aerial engineer
antépénultième [ɑ̃tepenyltjɛm] ADJ antepenultimate; **l'a. fois** the time before last
NF *Ling* antepenult
antéposé, -e [ɑ̃tepoze] ADJ *Ling (mot, verbe, nom)* preceding; **dans certains cas le mot "mère" est a., par exemple dans "mère patrie"** in some cases the word "mère" is placed before the noun, for example in "mère patrie"
antéposer [3] [ɑ̃tepoze] VT *Ling* **dans les phrases suivantes il faut a. l'épithète** in the following sentences the adjective must be placed before the noun
antéposition [ɑ̃tepozisjɔ̃] NF *Ling* anteposition
antéprédicatif, -ive [ɑ̃tepredikatif, -iv] ADJ *Ling* antepredicative
antérieur, -e [ɑ̃terjœr] ADJ 1 *(précédent)* anterior, prior; **la situation antérieure** the previous *or* former situation; **à une date antérieure** at an earlier date; **une vie antérieure** a former life; **a. à** prior to, before; **être a. à** to predate; **c'était bien a. à cette époque** it was long before that time; **la période antérieure à la révolution** the period before the revolution; **la période antérieure à l'ovulation** the period preceding ovulation
2 *Anat (de devant)* anterior
3 *Ling* front *(avant n)*
NM *(d'un cheval)* foreleg, forelimb
antérieurement [ɑ̃terjœrmɑ̃] ADV previously
◻ **antérieurement à** PRÉP prior to, previous to, before
antériorité [ɑ̃terjorite] NF 1 *(d'un événement)* anteriority, antecedence, precedence 2 *Gram* anteriority
antérograde [ɑ̃terograd] ADJ *Méd* anterograde
antéversion [ɑ̃teversjɔ̃] NF *Anat* anteversion
anthémis [ɑ̃temis] NF *Bot* anthemis

anthère [ɑ̃tɛr] NF *Bot* anther
anthéridie [ɑ̃teridi] NF *Bot* antheridium
anthérozoïde [ɑ̃terozoid] NM *Bot* antherozoid
anthèse [ɑ̃tɛz] NF *Bot* anthesis
anthologie [ɑ̃tɔlɔʒi] NF *Littérature* anthology
anthonome [ɑ̃tɔnɔm] NM *Entom* anthonomus
anthozoaire [ɑ̃tozoɛr] NM *Zool* NM anthozoan
◻ **anthozoaires** NMPL Anthozoa
anthracène [ɑ̃trasɛn] NM *Chim* anthracene
anthracite [ɑ̃trasit] ADJ INV charcoal grey
NM *Minér* anthracite, hard coal
anthraciteux, -euse [ɑ̃trasitø, -øz] ADJ *Minér* anthracitic
anthracnose [ɑ̃traknoz] NF *Bot* anthracnose, anthracnosis
anthracose [ɑ̃trakoz] NF *Méd* miner's lung, *Spéc* anthracosis
anthraquinone [ɑ̃trakinɔn] NF *Chim* anthraquinone
anthrax [ɑ̃traks] NM *Méd* carbuncle, anthrax *(sore)*
anthrène [ɑ̃trɛn] NM *Entom* carpet-beetle
anthropique [ɑ̃trɔpik] ADJ anthropogenic
anthropobiologie [ɑ̃trɔpɔbjɔlɔʒi] NF anthropobiology
anthropocentrique [ɑ̃trɔpɔsɑ̃trik] ADJ *Phil* anthropocentric
anthropocentrisme [ɑ̃trɔpɔsɑ̃trism] NM *Phil* anthropocentrism
anthropogenèse [ɑ̃trɔpɔʒənɛz], **anthropogénie** [ɑ̃trɔpɔʒeni] NF anthropogenesis, anthropogeny
anthropoïde [ɑ̃trɔpoid] *Zool* ADJ anthropoid
NM anthropoid ape
anthropologie [ɑ̃trɔpɔlɔʒi] NF anthropology
anthropologique [ɑ̃trɔpɔlɔʒik] ADJ anthropological
anthropologue [ɑ̃trɔpɔlɔg], **anthropologiste** [ɑ̃trɔpɔlɔʒist] NMF anthropologist
anthropométrie [ɑ̃trɔpɔmetri] NF anthropometry
anthropométrique [ɑ̃trɔpɔmetrik] ADJ anthropometric, anthropometrical; **service a.** criminal anthropometry department, *Br* ≃ Criminal Records Office; **fiche a.** = record containing fingerprints and details of height, weight etc
anthropomorphe [ɑ̃trɔpɔmɔrf] ADJ anthropomorphous, anthropomorphic
anthropomorphique [ɑ̃trɔpɔmɔrfik] ADJ anthropomorphic
anthropomorphisme [ɑ̃trɔpɔmɔrfism] NM anthropomorphism
anthropomorphiste [ɑ̃trɔpɔmɔrfist] ADJ anthropomorphist
NMF anthropomorphist
anthroponyme [ɑ̃trɔponim] NM *Ling* anthroponym
anthroponymie [ɑ̃trɔponimi] NF *Ling* anthroponymy
anthropophage [ɑ̃trɔpɔfaʒ] ADJ cannibal *(avant n)*, cannibalistic, *Spéc* anthropophagous
NMF cannibal, *Spéc* anthropophagite
anthropophagie [ɑ̃trɔpɔfaʒi] NF cannibalism, *Spéc* anthropophagy
anthropophile [ɑ̃trɔpɔfil] ADJ *Zool & Bot* anthropophilic, anthropophilous
anthropopithèque [ɑ̃trɔpɔpitɛk] NM *Zool* anthropopithecus
anthroposophie [ɑ̃trɔpɔzɔfi] NF *Phil* anthroposophy
anthropotechnique [ɑ̃trɔpɔtɛknik] NF *Tech* anthropotechnics *(singulier)*
anthropozoïque [ɑ̃trɔpɔzoik] *Géol* ADJ anthropozoic
NM anthropozoic
anthurium [ɑ̃tyrjɔm] NM *Bot* anthurium
anthyllide [ɑ̃tilid], **anthyllis** [ɑ̃tilis] NF *Bot* anthyllis; **a. vulnéraire** kidney vetch
anti-¹ [ɑ̃ti] PRÉF *(contre, qui s'oppose à)* anti-; **être anti-télévision** to be anti-television, to be against television; **être anti-sport** not to like sport
anti-² [ɑ̃ti] PRÉF *(qui précède)* ante-
antiacarien, -enne [ɑ̃tiakarjɛ̃, -ɛn] ADJ anti-dust mite, *Spéc* antiacarid
NM anti-dust mite spray
antiacide [ɑ̃tiasid] ADJ 1 *Chim* antacid 2 *Tech* acid-fast, acid-resistant
antiacnéique [ɑ̃tiakneik] ADJ anti-acne
NM acne treatment

antiacridien, -enne [ɑ̃tiakridjɛ̃, -ɛn] ADJ anti-locust, locust-control *(avant n)*; **lutte antiacridienne** anti-locust *or* locust-control campaign
antiadhésif, -ive [ɑ̃tiadezif, -iv] ADJ antiadhesive *(avant n)*; *(poêle)* nonstick
NM antiadhesive
antiaérien, -enne [ɑ̃tiaerjɛ̃, -ɛn] ADJ *Mil* anti-aircraft
anti-âge [ɑ̃tiaʒ] ADJ INV **crème a.** anti-ageing cream
antiagrégeant [ɑ̃tiagreʒɑ̃] NM *Biol* anticoagulant
antialcoolique [ɑ̃tialkɔlik] ADJ anti-alcohol *(avant n)*
antialcoolisme [ɑ̃tialkɔlism] NM anti-alcoholism
anti-aliassage [ɑ̃tialjasaʒ] *(pl* **anti-aliassages)** NM *Ordinat* anti-aliasing
antiallergique [ɑ̃tialɛrʒik] *Méd* ADJ antiallergenic
NM antiallergen
antiamaril, -e [ɑ̃tiamaril] ADJ *Méd* yellow fever *(avant n)*; **vaccin a.** yellow fever vaccine
antiaméricain, -e [ɑ̃tiamerikɛ̃, -ɛn] ADJ anti-American
antiaméricanisme [ɑ̃tiamerikanizm] NM anti-Americanism
antiangineux [ɑ̃tiaʒinø], **antiangoreux** [ɑ̃tiaʒɔrø] NM *Méd* antianginal drug
antiapartheid [ɑ̃tiapartɛd] ADJ *Hist & Pol* anti-apartheid
antiasthmatique [ɑ̃tiasmatik] *Méd* ADJ anti-asthmatic
NM antiasthmatic
antiatome [ɑ̃tiatɔm] NM *Phys* antiatom
antiatomique [ɑ̃tiatɔmik] ADJ *Mil* antiatomic
antiautoritaire [ɑ̃tiotoritɛr] ADJ antiauthoritarian
antiavortement [ɑ̃tiavɔrtəmɑ̃] ADJ INV pro-life, anti-abortion
antibactérien, -enne [ɑ̃tibakterjɛ̃, -ɛn] ADJ *Biol* antibacterial
antibalistique [ɑ̃tibalistik] ADJ *Astron* antiballistic
antibélier [ɑ̃tibelje] NM *Tech* water hammer arrester
antibiogramme [ɑ̃tibjɔgram] NM *Biol* antibiogram
antibiorésistance [ɑ̃tibjɔrezistɑ̃s] NF *(d'une bactérie)* antibioresistance, resistance to antibiotics
antibiothérapie [ɑ̃tibjɔterapi] NF *Méd* antibiotic therapy
antibiotique [ɑ̃tibjɔtik] ADJ antibiotic
NM antibiotic; **prendre des antibiotiques** to take antibiotics; **être sous antibiotiques** to be on antibiotics; **mettre qn sous antibiotiques** to put sb on antibiotics
antiblocage [ɑ̃tiblɔkaʒ] ADJ *Aut* antilock *(avant n)*
antibois¹, -e [ɑ̃tibwa, -az] ADJ of/from Antibes
◻ **Antibois, -e** NM,F = inhabitant of or person from Antibes
antibois² [ɑ̃tibwa] NM chair rail
antibourgeois, -e [ɑ̃tiburʒwa, -az] ADJ antibourgeois
antibrouillage [ɑ̃tibrujaʒ] NM *Électron* antijamming
antibrouillard [ɑ̃tibrujar] ADJ INV *Aut* fog *(avant n)*; **phare** *ou* **dispositif a.** fog *Br* lamp *or Am* light
antibruit [ɑ̃tibrɥi] ADJ INV 1 *(matériau)* soundproof; **mur a.** antinoise barrier 2 *Aut* anti-drumming, antisqueak
antibuée [ɑ̃tibɥe] *Aut* ADJ INV demisting, antimisting
NM 1 *(dispositif)* demister 2 *(produit)* antimist agent, clear vision agent
anticabrage [ɑ̃tikabraʒ] ADJ *Tech (système, dispositif)* anti-squat
anticalcaire [ɑ̃tikalkɛr] ADJ antiliming, antiscale *(avant n)*
anticancéreux, -euse [ɑ̃tikɑ̃serø, -øz] ADJ *Méd* 1 *(centre, laboratoire)* cancer *(avant n)* 2 *(médicament)* anticancer *(avant n)*, *Spéc* carcinostatic
anticapitalisme [ɑ̃tikapitalism] NM *Pol* anticapitalism
anticapitaliste [ɑ̃tikapitalist] *Pol* ADJ anticapitalist
NMF anticapitalist
anticasseurs [ɑ̃tikasœr] *voir* **loi**
anticathode [ɑ̃tikatɔd] NF *Électron* anticathode

anticellulite [ɑ̃tiselulit] ADJ INV anti-cellulite

anticernes [ɑ̃tisɛrn] NM concealer (to hide shadows under the eyes)

antichambre [ɑ̃tiʃɑ̃br] NF anteroom, antechamber; **dans les antichambres du pouvoir** on the fringes of power; **faire a.** to wait quietly (to be received)

antichar [ɑ̃tiʃar] ADJ Mil antitank

antichoc [ɑ̃tiʃɔk] ADJ shockproof

anticholinergique [ɑ̃tikɔlinɛrʒik] Chim ADJ anticholinergic
  NM anticholinergic

antichômage [ɑ̃tiʃomaʒ] ADJ INV (politique, mesure) that aims to reduce unemployment

antichrèse [ɑ̃tikrɛz] NF Jur antichresis

anti-chute [ɑ̃tiʃyt] ADJ INV **traitement a.** treatment to stop hair loss

anticipatif, -ive [ɑ̃tisipatif, -iv] ADJ **1 paiement a.** prepayment **2** Belg = anticipé

anticipation [ɑ̃tisipasjɔ̃] NF **1** (prévision) anticipation; **a. des résultats** anticipation or forecasting of the results; Écon **anticipations** expectations
  2 Com **a. de paiement** (somme) advance payment; (action) paying in advance
  3 (science-fiction) science-fiction
  ◻ **d'anticipation** ADJ **1** (roman, film) science-fiction (avant n), futuristic; **littérature d'a.** science fiction
  2 Com & Fin **achat d'a.** hedge purchase
  ◻ **par anticipation** ADJ Fin advance (avant n); **paiement par a.** advance payment, prepayment ADV (payer, régler) in advance

anticipative [ɑ̃tisipativ] voir anticipatif

anticipativement [ɑ̃tisipativmɑ̃] ADV Belg in advance

anticipatoire [ɑ̃tisipatwar] ADJ anticipatory

anticipé, -e [ɑ̃tisipe] ADJ **1** (avant la date prévue → retraite, départ) early; (→ remboursement) before due date; (→ dividende, paiement) advance; (→ ventes) expected; **faire le règlement a. d'une facture** to pay a bill in advance **2** (fait à l'avance) **avec nos remerciements anticipés** thanking you in advance or anticipation

anticiper [3] [ɑ̃tisipe] VT **1** Com & Fin **a. un paiement** to pay or to settle a bill in advance; **a. un paiement de dix jours** to pay ten days early
  2 (prévoir) to anticipate; **il a bien anticipé la réaction de son adversaire** he anticipated or foresaw his opponent's reaction
  USAGE ABSOLU **il a bien anticipé** he anticipated his opponent's moves; **mais j'anticipe!** but I'm getting ahead of myself!; **n'anticipons pas!** let's just wait and see!, all in good time!
  ◻ **anticiper sur** VT IND **a. sur ce qui va se passer** (deviner) to guess what's going to happen; (raconter) to explain what's going to happen

anticlérical, -e, -aux, -ales [ɑ̃tiklerikal, -o] Rel ADJ anticlerical
  NM,F anticlerical

anticléricalisme [ɑ̃tiklerikalism] NM Rel anticlericalism

anticlinal, -e, -aux, -ales [ɑ̃tiklinal, -o] ADJ Géol & Biol anticlinal
  NM Géol anticline

anticoagulant, -e [ɑ̃tikoagylɑ̃, -ɑ̃t] ADJ **1** Méd anticoagulating **2** Chim anticlotting
  NM **1** Méd anticoagulant **2** Chim anticlotting agent

anticodon [ɑ̃tikodɔ̃] NM Biol & Chim anticodon

anticolonialisme [ɑ̃tikɔlɔnjalism] NM anticolonialism

anticolonialiste [ɑ̃tikɔlɔnjalist] ADJ anticolonialist
  NMF anticolonialist

anticommercial, -e, -aux, -ales [ɑ̃tikɔmɛrsjal, -o] ADJ Com (attitude) unbusinesslike

anticommunisme [ɑ̃tikɔmynism] NM Pol anticommunism; **a. primaire** crude anticommunism; **faire de l'a. primaire** to be fiercely anticommunist

anticommuniste [ɑ̃tikɔmynist] ADJ anticommunist
  NMF Pol anticommunist

anticonceptionnel, -elle [ɑ̃tikɔ̃sɛpsjɔnɛl] ADJ (pilule, méthode, mesures) contraceptive, birth-control (avant n)

anticoncurrentiel, -elle [ɑ̃tikɔ̃kyrɑ̃sjɛl] ADJ Écon anticompetitive

anticonformisme [ɑ̃tikɔ̃fɔrmism] NM nonconformism

anticonformiste [ɑ̃tikɔ̃fɔrmist] ADJ nonconformist
  NMF nonconformist

anticonjoncturel, -elle [ɑ̃tikɔ̃ʒɔ̃ktyrɛl] ADJ Écon corrective

anticonstitutionnel, -elle [ɑ̃tikɔ̃stitysjɔnɛl] ADJ Jur unconstitutional

anticonstitutionnellement [ɑ̃tikɔ̃stitysjɔnɛlmɑ̃] ADV Jur unconstitutionally

anticorps [ɑ̃tikɔr] NM Physiol antibody

anticorrosif, -ive [ɑ̃tikɔrozif, -iv] ADJ anticorrosive; **traitement a.** rust-proofing

anticorrosion [ɑ̃tikɔrozjɔ̃] ADJ INV anticorrosive, rust-resistant

anticorrosive [ɑ̃tikɔroziv] voir anticorrosif

anti-crénelage [ɑ̃tikrenalaʒ] (pl anti-crénelages) NM Ordinat anti-aliasing

anti-crevaison [ɑ̃tikrœvɛzɔ̃] ADJ INV (pneu) puncture-proof, anti-puncture; **système a.** puncture-proofing system

anticryptogamique [ɑ̃tikriptogamik] ADJ fungicidal
  NM fungicide

anticyclique [ɑ̃tisiklik] ADJ Écon anticyclic

anticyclonal, -e, -aux, -ales [ɑ̃tisiklɔnal, -o] ADJ Météo anticyclonic

anticyclone [ɑ̃tisiklon] NM Météo anticyclone

anticyclonique [ɑ̃tisiklɔnik] ADJ Météo anticyclonic

antidate [ɑ̃tidat] NF antedate

antidater [3] [ɑ̃tidate] VT to antedate, to predate

antidéflagrant, -e [ɑ̃tideflagrɑ̃, -ɑ̃t] ADJ Mines explosion-proof

antidémarrage [ɑ̃tidemaraʒ] NM Aut engine immobilizer; **a. codé** security-coded immobilizer

antidémocratique [ɑ̃tidemɔkratik] ADJ Pol antidemocratic

antidépresseur [ɑ̃tideprɛsœr] Pharm ADJ M antidepressant
  NM antidepressant

antidérapant, -e [ɑ̃tiderapɑ̃, -ɑ̃t] ADJ **1** (surface, tapis) nonslip **2** Aut nonskid, antiskid
  NM non-slip coating

antidétonant, -e [ɑ̃tidetonɑ̃, -ɑ̃t] ADJ antiknock (avant n)
  NM antiknock (compound)

antidiphtérique [ɑ̃tidifterik] ADJ Méd diphtheria (avant n); **sérum a.** diphtheria serum

anti-discriminatoire [ɑ̃tidiskriminatwar] ADJ (mesures, politique) anti-discriminatory

antidiurétique [ɑ̃tidjyretik] Méd ADJ antidiuretic
  NM antidiuretic

antidopage [ɑ̃tidopaʒ], **antidoping** [ɑ̃tidopiŋ] ADJ INV **contrôle/mesure a.** drug detection test/measure

antidote [ɑ̃tidɔt] NM antidote; **l'a. de l'arsenic** the antidote to arsenic; **un a. contre la tristesse** a remedy for sadness

antidouleur [ɑ̃tidulœr] ADJ INV Méd painkilling; **centre a.** pain clinic
  NM Pharm painkiller, analgesic

antidrogue [ɑ̃tidrɔg] ADJ INV drug-prevention (avant n)

antidumping [ɑ̃tidœmpiŋ] ADJ INV Jur (loi, législation) anti-dumping

anti-éblouissant, -e [ɑ̃tieblɥisɑ̃, -ɑ̃t] (mpl anti-éblouissants, fpl anti-éblouissantes) ADJ anti-dazzle; **écran a.** anti-glare screen; **rétroviseur a.** anti-dazzle rear-view mirror

antiéconomique [ɑ̃tiekɔnɔmik] ADJ Com contrary to economic principles, uneconomic

antieffraction [ɑ̃tiɛfraksjɔ̃] ADJ INV (dispositif) burglarproof

antiémétique [ɑ̃tiemetik], **antiémétisant, -e** [ɑ̃tiemetizɑ̃, -ɑ̃t] Pharm ADJ antiemetic
  NM antiemetic

antiémeute [ɑ̃tiemøt] ADJ antiriot

antienne [ɑ̃tjɛn] NF **1** Mus & Rel antiphon **2** Fig refrain; **chanter toujours la même a.** to be always harping on about the same thing

antienzyme [ɑ̃tiɑ̃zim] NF Biol antienzyme

antiesclavagisme [ɑ̃tiɛsklavaʒism] NM Pol opposition to slavery; Hist (aux États-Unis) abolitionism

antiesclavagiste [ɑ̃tiɛsklavaʒist] ADJ antislavery (avant n); Hist (aux États-Unis) abolitionist

NMF Pol opponent of slavery; Hist (aux États-Unis) abolitionist

antiétatique [ɑ̃tietatik] ADJ Pol opposed to state intervention, noninterventionist

antifading [ɑ̃tifediŋ] NM Élec & Rad automatic gain control, automatic volume control

antifascisme [ɑ̃tifaʃism] NM Pol antifascism

antifasciste [ɑ̃tifaʃist] Pol ADJ antifascist
  NMF antifascist

antiferromagnétisme [ɑ̃tiferomaɲetism] NM Minér antiferromagnetism

antifongique [ɑ̃tifɔ̃ʒik] Méd ADJ antifungal, fungicidal
  NM fungicide

antifriction [ɑ̃tifriksjɔ̃] ADJ INV Métal antifriction; **alliage a.** antifriction metal, white metal

antifumée [ɑ̃tifyme] Pétr ADJ INV (masque) anti-smoke; **cagoule a.** smoke hood
  NM non-smoke-producing substance

anti-g [ɑ̃tiʒe] ADJ INV Aviat anti-G

antigang [ɑ̃tigɑ̃g] voir brigade

antigel [ɑ̃tiʒel] NM **1** Aut antifreeze **2** Chim antigel

antigélif [ɑ̃tiʒelif] NM Constr antifreeze

antigène [ɑ̃tiʒɛn] NM Biol antigen

antigénique [ɑ̃tiʒenik] ADJ Biol antigenic

antigivrant, -e [ɑ̃tiʒivrɑ̃, -ɑ̃t] ADJ Aviat anti-ice (avant n)
  NM anti-icer

antigivreur [ɑ̃tiʒivrœr] NM anti-icer

antiglisse [ɑ̃tiglis] ADJ INV Ski antislip, nonslip

Antigone [ɑ̃tigɔn] NPR Myth Antigone

antigoutte [ɑ̃tigut] ADJ INV (peinture) nondrip

antigouvernemental, -e, -aux, -ales [ɑ̃tiguvɛrnəmɑ̃tal, -o] ADJ Pol antigovernment (avant n)

antigrève [ɑ̃tigrɛv] ADJ INV antistrike (avant n)

antigrippal, -e, -aux, -ales [ɑ̃tigripal, -o] ADJ Méd & Pharm (médicament, traitement) flu (avant n)

antigrippe [ɑ̃tigrip] ADJ INV Méd (vaccin) flu (avant n)

Antigua [ɑ̃tigwa] NF Géog Antigua; **A. et Barbuda** Antigua and Barbuda

antiguais, -e [ɑ̃tigwɛ, -ɛz] ADJ Antiguan
  ◻ **Antiguais, -e** NM,F Antiguan; **les A. et Barbudiens** Antiguans and Barbudans

antiguerre [ɑ̃tigɛr] NMF INV person opposed to the war; **les a.** the people opposed to the war

antihalo [ɑ̃tialo] Phot ADJ INV antihalation
  NM antihalation

antihausse [ɑ̃tios] ADJ INV Écon regulating price increases, anti-inflationary

antihéros [ɑ̃tiero] NM Littérature antihero

antihistaminique [ɑ̃tiistaminik] Chim ADJ antihistamine
  NM antihistamine

antihygiénique [ɑ̃tiiʒjenik] ADJ unhygienic

anti-impérialisme [ɑ̃tiɛ̃perjalism] (pl anti-impérialismes) NM Pol anti-imperialism

anti-impérialiste [ɑ̃tiɛ̃perjalist] (pl anti-impérialistes) ADJ anti-imperialist
  NMF Pol anti-imperialist

anti-infectieux, -euse [ɑ̃tiɛ̃fɛksjø, -øz] Pharm ADJ anti-infective
  NM anti-infective agent

anti-inflammatoire [ɑ̃tiɛ̃flamatwar] (pl anti-inflammatoires) Méd ADJ anti-inflammatory
  NM anti-inflammatory agent

anti-inflationniste [ɑ̃tiɛ̃flasjɔnist] (pl anti-inflationnistes) ADJ Écon anti-inflationary

antijeu [ɑ̃tiʒø] NM (contraire aux règles) breaking the rules; (à l'esprit) unsporting behaviour; **faire de l'a.** (contre les règles) to break the rules; (contre l'esprit) to be unsporting

antillais, -e [ɑ̃tijɛ, -ɛz] ADJ West Indian
  ◻ **Antillais, -e** NM,F West Indian

Antilles [ɑ̃tij] NFPL **les A.** the Antilles, the West Indies; **aux A.** in the West Indies; **les Grandes/Petites A.** the Greater/Lesser Antilles; **les A. françaises/néerlandaises** the French/Dutch West Indies; **la mer des A.** the Caribbean Sea

Culture
ANTILLES
The French West Indies include the overseas "départements" of Martinique and Guadeloupe, the latter including the islands of La Désirade, Marie-Galante, Saint-Barthélemy (Saint Bart), Les Saintes and part of Saint-Martin.

antilocapre [ãtilɔkapr] NF *Zool* pronghorn (antelope)

antilogarithme [ãtilɔgaritm] NM *Math* antilogarithm

antilogie [ãtilɔʒi] NF antilogy

antilope [ãtilɔp] NF *Zool* antelope; **a. d'Amérique** pronghorn (antelope); **a. cervicapre** blackbuck; **a. noire** sable antelope; **a. pygmée** pygmy antelope; **a. rouanne** roan antelope; **a. royale** royal antelope; **a. saïga** saiga antelope

antimaçonnique [ãtimasɔnik] ADJ antimasonic

antimatière [ãtimatjɛr] NF *Phys* antimatter

antimigraineux, -euse [ãtimigrɛnø, -øz] *Méd* ADJ anti-migraine
   NM anti-migraine drug

antimilitarisme [ãtimilitarism] NM *Mil* antimilitarism

antimilitariste [ãtimilitarist] *Mil* ADJ antimilitarist
   NMF antimilitarist

antimissile [ãtimisil] ADJ INV *Mil* antimissile

antimite [ãtimit] ADJ INV **boules a.** mothballs; **produit a.** moth repellent
   NM mothproofing agent, moth repellent

antimitotique [ãtimitɔtik] *Biol & Méd* ADJ antimitotic
   NM antimitotic

antimoine [ãtimwan] NM *Chim* antimony

antimonarchique [ãtimɔnarʃik] ADJ *Pol* antimonarchical

antimonarchiste [ãtimɔnarʃist] *Pol* ADJ antimonarchist
   NMF antimonarchist

antimondialisation [ãtimɔ̃djalizasjɔ̃] NF *Pol* antiglobalization

antimondialiste [ãtimɔ̃djalist] ADJ antiglobalist
   NMF antiglobalist

antimoniate [ãtimɔnjat] NM *Chim* antimoniate

antimonié, -e [ãtimɔnje] ADJ *(plomb)* antimoniated, antimonial; **hydrogène a.** hydrogen antimonide

antimoniure [ãtimɔnjyr] NM *Chim* antimonide

antimycosique [ãtimikɔzik] *Méd* ADJ antimycotic
   NM antimycotic

antinataliste [ãtinatalist] ADJ *(politique, campagne, mesures)* aimed at reducing the birth rate

antinational, -e, -aux, -ales [ãtinasjɔnal, -o] ADJ *Pol* antinational

antinationalisme [ãtinasjɔnalism] NM *Pol* antinationalism

antinazi, -e [ãtinazi] *Pol* ADJ anti-Nazi
   NM,F anti-Nazi

antineutrino [ãtinøtrino] NM *Phys* antineutrino

antineutron [ãtinøtrɔ̃] NM *Phys* antineutron

antinévralgique [ãtinevralʒik] ADJ *Pharm* antineuralgic

antinomie [ãtinɔmi] NF *Ling* antinomy

antinomique [ãtinɔmik] ADJ *Ling* antinomic

Antinoüs [ãtinɔys] NPR *Hist* Antinous

antinucléaire [ãtinykleɛr] *Nucl* ADJ antinuclear
   NMF supporter of antinuclear policies

Antioche [ãtjɔʃ] NM *Géog* Antioch

antioncogène [ãtiɔ̃kɔʒɛn] NM *Méd* antioncogene

Antiope [ãtjɔp] NPR *Myth* Antiope

Antiope® [ãtjɔp] NM *Tél* = information system available via the French television network, *Br* ≃ Teletext

antioxydant [ãtiɔksidã] NM *Biol & Chim* antioxidant, oxidation inhibitor

antipaludéen, -enne [ãtipalydeɛ̃, -ɛn], **antipaludique** [ãtipalydik] *Méd* ADJ antimalarial, antipaludal
   NM antimalarial, antipaludal

antipanique [ãtipanik] ADJ **porte a.** door equipped with a panic bar; **barre a.** panic bar

antipape [ãtipap] NM *Rel* antipope

antiparallèle [ãtiparalɛl] ADJ *Géom & Phys* antiparallel

antiparasitage [ãtiparazitaʒ] NM *Élec* interference suppression

antiparasitaire [ãtiparazitɛr] ADJ pest control *(avant n)*
   NM pesticide

antiparasite [ãtiparazit] *Élec* ADJ INV anti-interference *(avant n)*

NM interference suppressor, interference eliminator, *Br* noise blanker

antiparasiter [3] [ãtiparazite] VT *Élec* to suppress interference in

antiparlementaire [ãtiparləmãtɛr] ADJ *Pol* antiparliamentary

antiparlementarisme [ãtiparləmãtarism] NM *Pol* antiparliamentarism

antiparti [ãtiparti] ADJ INV *Pol* antiparty

antiparticule [ãtipartikyl] NF *Phys* antiparticle

antipathie [ãtipati] NF antipathy; **avoir** *ou* **éprouver de l'a. pour qn** to dislike sb

antipathique [ãtipatik] ADJ unpleasant; **je le trouve assez a., il m'est plutôt a.** I don't like him much

antipatinage [ãtipatinaʒ] ADJ *Tech (système, dispositif)* antiskid *(avant n)*

antipatriotique [ãtipatriɔtik] ADJ *Pol* unpatriotic

antipatriotisme [ãtipatriɔtism] NM antipatriotism

antipelliculaire [ãtipɛlikylɛr] ADJ *(shampooing, traitement)* dandruff *(avant n)*, anti-dandruff *(avant n)*

antipéristaltique [ãtiperistaltik] ADJ *Méd* antiperistaltic; **contraction a.** antiperistalsis

antipersonnel [ãtipɛrsɔnɛl] ADJ INV *Mil* antipersonnel; **mine a.** anti-personnel mine

antiperspirant, -e [ãtipɛrspirã, -ãt] ADJ *Physiol* antiperspirant

antiphlogistique [ãtiflɔʒistik] ADJ *Méd* anti-inflammatory

antiphonaire [ãtifɔnɛr] NM *Mus & Rel* antiphonary

antiphrase [ãtifraz] NF *Ling* antiphrasis
   ❏ **par antiphrase** ADV ironically; **il a dit ça par a.** he was being ironic; **cette absence de discussion appelée par a. débat** this lack of discussion ironically referred to as a debate

antipode [ãtipɔd] NM antipode; **les antipodes** the antipodes; **la Nouvelle-Zélande est aux antipodes de la France** New Zealand is at the opposite point of the globe from France; *Fig* **c'est aux antipodes de ce que je pensais** it's light years away from what I imagined; **nous sommes aux antipodes l'un de l'autre** we are light years away from each other, we are poles apart

antipodisme [ãtipɔdism] NM foot juggling

antipodiste [ãtipɔdist] NMF foot juggler

antipoétique [ãtipɔetik] ADJ *Littérature* unpoetic

antipoison [ãtipwazɔ̃] ADJ INV **centre a.** emergency poisons unit; **service téléphonique a.** poison emergency telephone service

antipoliomyélitique [ãtipɔljomjelitik] ADJ *Méd* antipolio, polio *(avant n)*

antipollution [ãtipɔlysjɔ̃] ADJ INV antipollution *(avant n)*; **contrôle/mesure a.** pollution control/measure

antiprotéase [ãtiprɔteaz] NF *Pharm* protease inhibitor, antiprotease

antiprotectionniste [ãtiprɔtɛksjɔnist] *Écon* ADJ antiprotectionist, free trade *(avant n)*
   NMF antiprotectionist, free-trader

antiproton [ãtiprɔtɔ̃] NM *Phys* antiproton

antiprurigineux, -euse [ãtipryriʒinø, -øz] *Pharm* ADJ antipruritic
   NM antipruritic

antipsychiatrie [ãtipsikjatri] NF *Psy* antipsychiatry

antipsychiatrique [ãtipsikjatrik] ADJ *Psy* antipsychiatric

antipsychotique [ãtipsikɔtik] *Pharm* ADJ antipsychotic
   NM antipsychotic

antipub [ãtipyb] ADJ INV anti-advertising *(avant n)*
   NMF *(personne)* = supporter of the anti-advertising movement

antiputride [ãtipytrid] ADJ antiputrefactive

antipyrétique [ãtipiretik] *Méd* ADJ antipyretic, antifebrile
   NM antipyretic, antifebrile

antipyrine [ãtipirin] NF *Pharm* antipyrine

antiquaille [ãtikaj] NF *Péj (worthless)* antique, piece of bric-a-brac

antiquaire [ãtikɛr] NMF antique dealer

antiquark [ãtikwark] NM *Phys* antiquark

antique [ãtik] ADJ **1** *(d'époque → meuble, bijou,*

châle) antique, old **2** *(démodé)* antiquated, ancient; *Fam* **un a. frigo** an ancient fridge **3** *Littéraire (ancien)* former, belonging to the past; **son a. prouesse** his/her former prowess
   NM **l'a.** *(œuvres)* antiquities; *(art)* classical art

antiquisant, -e [ãtikizã, -ãt] ADJ *(style, décoration)* inspired by antiquity

antiquité [ãtikite] NF **1** *(objet)* antique; **des antiquités** antiques; **magasin d'antiquités** antique shop; *Fig Hum* **sa voiture, c'est une a.!** his/her car is ancient *or* an old wreck!
   2 *Antiq (période)* **l'a.** ancient times, antiquity; **l'A. (grecque et romaine)** Ancient Greece and Rome
   3 *(ancienneté)* great age; **ça remonte à la plus haute a.** that goes back *or* dates back to time immemorial
   ❏ **antiquités** NFPL *Beaux-Arts* antique art
   ❏ **de toute antiquité** ADV from time immemorial

antirabique [ãtirabik] ADJ *Méd* anti-rabies *(avant n)*

antirachitique [ãtiraʃitik] ADJ *Méd* antirachitic

antiracisme [ãtirasism] NM *Pol* antiracism

antiraciste [ãtirasist] ADJ antiracist
   NMF antiracist

antiradar [ãtiradar] *Mil* ADJ INV antiradar
   NM anti-radar device

antiradiation [ãtiradjasjɔ̃] ADJ INV *Nucl* antiradiation

antirationnel, -elle [ãtirasjɔnɛl] ADJ antirational

antiréalisme [ãtirealism] NM *Cin* anti-realism

antiréaliste [ãtirealist] ADJ *Cin* anti-realist

antireflet [ãtirəflɛ] ADJ INV coated, *Spéc* bloomed; *Ordinat* non-reflecting, antiglare; **verre a.** non-reflecting glass

antiréglementaire [ãtiregləmãtɛr] ADJ against regulations

antirejet [ãtirəʒɛ] ADJ INV *Méd (traitement, médicament)* anti-rejection *(avant n)*, that prevents organ rejection

antireligieux, -euse [ãtirəliʒjø, -øz] ADJ *Rel* antireligious

antirépublicain, -e [ãtirepyblikɛ̃, -ɛn] *Pol* ADJ antirepublican
   NM,F antirepublican

antirétroviral, -e, -aux, -ales [ãtiretrɔviral, -o] ADJ *(molécule, traitement)* antiretroviral

antirévolutionnaire [ãtirevɔlysjɔnɛr] *Pol* ADJ antirevolutionary
   NMF antirevolutionary

antirides [ãtirid] ADJ anti-wrinkle *(avant n)*

antiroi [ãtirwa] NM *Hist* anti-king

antiroman [ãtirɔmã] NM *Littérature* anti-novel

antirouille [ãtiruj] ADJ INV antirust *(avant n)*, rust-resistant
   NM *(pour protéger de la rouille)* rust inhibitor; *(pour enlever la rouille)* rust remover

antiroulis [ãtiruli] ADJ INV *Aut & Naut* anti-roll *(avant n)*

antisalissure [ãtisalisyr] ADJ INV *Naut & Tex* stain-resistant

antisatellite [ãtisatɛlit] ADJ INV *Mil* antisatellite

antiscientifique [ãtisjãtifik] ADJ antiscientific

antiscorbutique [ãtiskɔrbytik] ADJ *Méd* antiscorbutic

antisèche [ãtisɛʃ] NF *Fam Arg scol Br* crib, *Am* cheat sheet

antiségrégationniste [ãtisegregasjɔnist] ADJ & NMF *Pol* antisegregationist

antisémite [ãtisemit] *Rel* ADJ anti-Semitic
   NMF anti-Semite

antisémitisme [ãtisemitism] NM *Rel* anti-Semitism

antisepsie [ãtisɛpsi] NF *Méd* antisepsis

antiseptique [ãtisɛptik] *Méd & Pharm* ADJ antiseptic
   NM antiseptic

antisérotoninergique [ãtiserɔtɔninɛrʒik] ADJ *Biol & Chim* antiserotoninergic

antisérum [ãtiserɔm] NM *Physiol* antiserum

antisida [ãtisida] ADJ INV *Méd (vaccin, campagne)* Aids *(avant n)*; *(traitement)* Aids *(avant n)*, for Aids

antisismique [ãtisismik] ADJ *Constr* antiseismic

antisocial, -e, -aux, -ales [ãtisɔsjal, -o] ADJ anti-social

anti-sous-marin, -e [ãtisumarɛ̃, -in] *(mpl* **anti-sous-marins**, *fpl* **anti-sous-marines**) ADJ *Mil* anti-submarine

ant-ape

antisoviétique [ɑ̃tisɔvjetik] ADJ *Pol* anti-Soviet

antispasmodique [ɑ̃tispasmɔdik] *Pharm* ADJ antispasmodic
 NM antispasmodic

antisportif, -ive [ɑ̃tispɔrtif, -iv] ADJ *Sport* **1** *(hostile au sport)* anti-sport **2** *(contraire à l'esprit sportif)* unsporting, unsportsmanlike

antistatique [ɑ̃tistatik] ADJ *Élec* antistatic

Antisthène [ɑ̃tistɛn] NPR *Phil* Antisthenes

antistress [ɑ̃tistrɛs] ADJ INV anti-stress

antistrophe [ɑ̃tistrɔf] NF *Littérature* antistrophe

antisudoral, -e, -aux, -ales [ɑ̃tisydɔral, -o] ADJ *Physiol* antiperspirant

antisymétrique [ɑ̃tisimetrik] ADJ *Math* antisymmetrical

antisyndical, -e, -aux, -ales [ɑ̃tisɛ̃dikal, -o] ADJ *Ind* antiunion

antisyndicalisme [ɑ̃tisɛ̃dikalism] NM union-bashing

antisyphilitique [ɑ̃tisifilitik] ADJ *Méd* antisyphilitic

antitabac [ɑ̃titaba] ADJ INV *(campagne, lutte)* anti-smoking

antitache [ɑ̃titaʃ] NM INV stain remover

antiterroriste [ɑ̃titɛrɔrist] ADJ antiterrorist

antitétanique [ɑ̃titetanik] ADJ *Méd* antitetanic

antithéâtre [ɑ̃titeatr] NM *Littérature* anti-theatre

antithermique [ɑ̃titɛrmik] *Méd* ADJ antithermic
 NM antithermic, febrifuge

antithèse [ɑ̃titɛz] NF *Ling* antithesis; *Fig* **je suis l'a. de ma sœur** I'm the complete opposite of my sister

antithétique [ɑ̃titetik] ADJ *Ling* antithetical, antithetic

antithyroïdien, -enne [ɑ̃titirɔidjɛ̃, -ɛn] ADJ *Méd* antithyroid

antitout [ɑ̃titu] ADJ INV *Fam* systematically opposed to everything■, anti-everything

antitoxine [ɑ̃titɔksin] NF *Biol & Pharm* antitoxin

antitoxique [ɑ̃titɔksik] ADJ *Biol & Pharm* antitoxic

antitragus [ɑ̃titragys] NM *Anat* antitragus

antitrust [ɑ̃titrœst] ADJ INV *Br* anti-monopoly, *Am* antitrust

antitrypsine [ɑ̃titripsin] NF *Biol & Chim* antitrypsin

antituberculeux, -euse [ɑ̃titybɛrkylø, -øz] ADJ *Méd* antitubercular, antituberculous; **centre a.** tuberculosis centre

antitussif, -ive [ɑ̃titysif, -iv] ADJ *Pharm* cough *(avant n)*, *Spéc* antitussive; **produit/sirop a.** cough preparation/syrup

antiulcéreux, -euse [ɑ̃tiylserø, -øz] *Pharm* ADJ antiulcer
 NM antiulcer drug

antiunitaire [ɑ̃tiynitɛr] ADJ disruptive

antivariolique [ɑ̃tivarjɔlik] ADJ **vaccin a.** smallpox vaccine

antivénéneux, -euse [ɑ̃tivenenø, -øz] ADJ *Méd* antidotal

antivénérien, -enne [ɑ̃tivenerjɛ̃, -ɛn] ADJ *Méd* antivenereal

antivenimeux, -euse [ɑ̃tivənimø, -øz] ADJ *Méd* antivenin

antivieillissement [ɑ̃tivjɛjismɑ̃] NM *(produit qui ralentit le vieillissement)* anti-ageing product; **traitement a.** anti-ageing treatment

antiviral, -e, -aux, -ales [ɑ̃tiviral, -o] *Méd & Pharm* ADJ antiviral, antivirus *(avant n)*
 NM antiviral

antivirus [ɑ̃tivirys] NM *Ordinat* antivirus

antivol [ɑ̃tivɔl] ADJ INV antitheft
 NM **1** *Aut* theft protection; *(sur la direction)* steering (wheel) lock **2** *(de vélo)* (bicycle) lock

Antoine [ɑ̃twan] NPR **A. de Padoue** Anthony of Padua; **(Marc) A.** (Mark) Antony

antoinisme [ɑ̃twanism] NM *Rel* = theosophic religion founded by Louis Antoine

antonomase [ɑ̃tɔnɔmaz] NF *Ling* antonomasia

antonyme [ɑ̃tɔnim] NM *Ling* antonym

antonymie [ɑ̃tɔnimi] NF *Ling* antonymy

antonymique [ɑ̃tɔnimik] ADJ *Ling* antonymous

antre [ɑ̃tr] NM **1** *(abri)* cavern, cave **2** *(repaire → d'un fauve, d'un ogre)* lair, den; *(→ d'un brigand)* hideout **3** *Fig* den **4** *Anat* antrum

antrustion [ɑ̃trystjɔ̃] NM *Hist* antrustion

anuité, -e [anɥite] ADJ *Littéraire* benighted

anurie [anyri] NF *Méd* anuria

anus [anys] NM *Anat* anus; **a. artificiel** colostomy

anuscopie [anyskɔpi] NF *Méd* anoscopy

Anvers [ɑ̃vɛr(s)] NM *Géog (ville)* Antwerp; **la province d'A.** Antwerp province

anversois, -e [ɑ̃vɛrswa, -az] ADJ of/from Antwerp
 ▫ **Anversois, -e** NM,F = inhabitant of or person from Antwerp

anxiété [ɑ̃ksjete] NF anxiety, worry; **attendre qch avec a.** to wait anxiously for sth; **être en proie à l'a.** to be very anxious or worried; *Psy* **a. névrotique** anxiety neurosis

anxieuse [ɑ̃ksjøz] *voir* **anxieux**

anxieusement [ɑ̃ksjøzmɑ̃] ADV anxiously, worriedly; **ils se regardèrent a.** they exchanged worried or anxious looks

anxieux, -euse [ɑ̃ksjø, -øz] ADJ *(inquiet → attente)* anxious, worried; *(→ regard, voix, personne)* anxious, worried; **être a. de qch** to be anxious or impatient about sth; **être a. de réussir** to be impatient to succeed or for success
 NM,F worrier; **c'est un grand a.** he's the anxious type, he's a dreadful worrier

anxiogène [ɑ̃ksjɔʒɛn] ADJ *Psy* anxiety-provoking

anxiolytique [ɑ̃ksjɔlitik] ADJ anxiolytic
 NM tranquillizer

AOC [aose] NF *(abrév* **appellation d'origine contrôlée***)* appellation (d'origine) contrôlée *(official certification guaranteeing the quality of French produce, especially wines and cheeses)*

A-OF [aoɛf] NF *Géog (abrév* **Afrique-Occidentale française***)* FWA

aoriste [aɔrist] NM *Ling* aorist

aorte [aɔrt] NF *Anat* aorta

aortique [aɔrtik] ADJ *Anat* aortic, aortal

aortite [aɔrtit] NF *Méd* aortitis

Aoste [aost] NM *Géog* Aosta

août [u(t)] NM August; **la journée du 10 a. 1792** = the day on which a popular uprising led to the fall of the king and the creation of the "Commune insurrectionnelle" to replace the "Commune de Paris", marking the beginning of the Terror *(see box at* **terreur***)*; **la nuit du 4 a. 1789** = the night during which feudal privileges were abolished by the "Assemblée Constituante" (considered to be one of the starting points of the French Revolution); **le 15 a.** = national holiday in France, well-known as a time of heavy traffic congestion; *voir aussi* **mars**

aoûtat [auta] NM *Entom* harvest mite, *Am* chigger, red mite

aoûté, -e [aute, ute] ADJ *Bot (fruit, rameau)* ripened by the August sun

aoûtement [autmɑ̃] NM *Bot* **1** *(de fruits)* ripening **2** *(de rameaux)* lignification

aoûtien, -enne [ausjɛ̃, -ɛn] NM,F August *Br* holidaymaker or *Am* vacationer

AP [ape] NF *Presse (abrév* **Associated Press***)* AP

apache¹ [apaʃ] ADJ Apache
 ▫ **Apache** NMF Apache

apache² [apaʃ] NM *Vieilli* hooligan *(in turn-of-the-century Paris)*

apadana [apadana] NF *Archéol* apadana

apagogie [apagɔʒi] NF apagoge

apaisant, -e [apɛzɑ̃, -ɑ̃t] ADJ **1** *(qui calme la douleur)* soothing **2** *(qui calme la colère → paroles, voix)* soothing; *(→ influence)* calming

apaisement [apɛzmɑ̃] NM **1** *(fait de calmer → soif)* quenching; *(→ faim, désir)* assuaging; *(→ chagrin)* easing, alleviation; *(→ douleur)* soothing, alleviation; **une politique d'a.** a policy of appeasement; **attendre l'a. d'une tempête** to wait for a storm to die down; **j'attendais l'a. de ses colères** I would wait for him/her to calm down after his/her angry outbursts **2** *(fait de se calmer)* quietening down; **chercher l'a. auprès de qn** to go to sb for reassurance
 ▫ **apaisements** NMPL *(paroles)* assurances; **donner des apaisements à qn** to give sb assurances

apaiser [4] [apɛze] VT *(calmer → opposants, mécontents)* to calm down, to pacify, to appease; *(→ soif)* to quench, to slake; *(→ faim, désir)* to assuage; *(→ chagrin)* to ease, to alleviate; *(→ douleur)* to soothe, to alleviate; **je ne savais pas quoi dire pour a. sa colère** I didn't know what to say to calm him/her down; **ses excuses apaisèrent quelque peu leur colère** his/her

apologies made them a bit less angry, his/her apologies mollified them somewhat; **a. les esprits** to calm things down; **son visage était enfin apaisé** his/her face bore a look of peace at last
 ▫ **s'apaiser** VPR *(se calmer → personne)* to calm down; *(→ bruit, dispute, tempête, vent)* to die down, to subside; *(→ colère, chagrin, douleur)* to subside; *(→ faim, désir)* to be assuaged; *(→ soif)* to be quenched

apanage [apanaʒ] NM prerogative, privilege; **avoir l'a. de qch** to have a monopoly on sth; **être l'a. de qn** to be sb's privilege

aparté [aparte] NM **1** *(discussion)* private conversation **2** *Théât* aside
 ▫ **en aparté** ADV as an aside; **il me l'a dit en a.** he took me aside to tell me

apartheid [aparted] NM *Hist & Pol* apartheid

apathie [apati] NF apathy, listlessness

apathique [apatik] ADJ apathetic, listless

apathiquement [apatikmɑ̃] ADV apathetically, listlessly

apatite [apatit] NF *Minér* apatite

apatosaure [apatozɔr] NM *Zool (en paléontologie)* apatosaurus, brontosaurus

apatride [apatrid] *Jur* ADJ stateless
 NMF stateless person

apatridie [apatridi] NF *Jur* statelessness

apax [apaks] = **hapax**

APD [apede] NF *(abrév* **Aide publique au développement***)* ODA

APE [apea] NF *UE (abrév* **Assemblée parlementaire européenne***)* EP

APEC [apɛk] NF *(abrév* **Association pour l'emploi des cadres***)* = agency providing information and employment and training opportunities for professionals

Apennin [apenɛ̃] NM **l'A., les Apennins** the Apennines

apepsie [apɛpsi] NF *Méd* apepsy

aperception [apɛrsɛpsjɔ̃] NF *Phil* apperception

apercevoir [52] [apɛrsəvwar] VT **1** *(voir brièvement)* to glimpse, to catch sight of; **il était pressé, je n'ai fait que l'a.** he was in a hurry, so I just caught a glimpse of him
 2 *(distinguer)* to make out; **on apercevait le phare au loin** you could (just) make out the lighthouse in the distance
 3 *(remarquer)* to see, to notice; **elle seule avait aperçu la contradiction** she alone had noticed the contradiction; **elle cherche à ne pas laisser a. sa fatigue** she's trying not to let her tiredness show; **si on y pense bien, on aperçoit des difficultés** if you think about it, you start to see difficulties
 ▫ **s'apercevoir** VPR **1** *(emploi réfléchi)* to catch sight of oneself
 2 *(emploi réciproque)* to catch a glimpse of one another
 3 **s'a. de** *(voir)* to notice, to see; *(réaliser)* to become aware of, to realize; **il ne s'est aperçu de rien** he didn't notice or see anything; **la couleur est différente mais on s'en aperçoit à peine** the shade isn't the same but you can hardly see it or it's hardly noticeable; **sans s'en a.** inadvertently, without realizing it; **s'a. que** to realize or to understand that; **je m'aperçois que c'est plus difficile que je ne croyais** I now realize it's more difficult than I thought; **il s'en est aperçu peu à peu** it gradually dawned on him; **cet incident nous a fait nous a. de notre vulnérabilité** this incident made us realize how vulnerable he/she was

aperçu [apɛrsy] NM **1** *(idée générale)* outline, idea; **avoir un a. de la situation** to have a general idea of the situation; **donner un a. de la situation à qn** to give sb a general idea or outline of the situation; **un a. du sujet en deux mots** a quick survey or a brief outline of the subject; *Ordinat* **a. avant impression** print preview **2** *(observation)* insight

aperçut *etc voir* **apercevoir**

apériodique [aperjɔdik] ADJ aperiodic

apériteur, -trice [aperitœr, -tris] *Assur* ADJ **compagnie apéritrice** *(gén)* leading insurer or office; *(en assurance maritime)* leading underwriter
 NM *(gén)* leading insurer or office; *(en assurance maritime)* leading underwriter

apéritif, -ive [aperitif, -iv] ADJ **faire une promenade apéritive** to take a walk to work up an appetite; **prendre une boisson apéritive** to have an aperitif

NM drink, aperitif; **venez à 19 heures pour l'a.** come round for drinks at 7; **prendre l'a.** to have a drink *(before lunch or dinner)*, to have an aperitif

---

Culture

L'APÉRITIF

In France, the "apéritif", or "apéro", is an informal social ritual. It is quite usual to invite people for before-dinner drinks without actually providing dinner, or to arrange to meet someone in a café "pour l'apéritif" before going out for a meal.

---

apéritrice [aperitris] *voir* **apériteur**

apéro [apero] NM *Fam* aperitif■, drink■ *(before lunch or dinner)*

aperture [apɛrtyr] NF *Ling* aperture

apesanteur [apəzɑ̃tœr] NF *Astron & Phys* weightlessness; **en état d'a., en a.** in weightless conditions

apétale [apetal] *Bot* ADJ apetalous

NF apetalous plant

à-peu-près [apøprɛ] NM INV **1** *(approximation)* approximation; **il y a trop d'à. dans votre rapport** your report is too vague **2** *Vieilli (plaisanterie)* dreadful pun

apeuré, -e [apœre] ADJ scared, frightened

apeurer [apœre] VT to frighten, to scare

APEX [apɛks] NM *(ticket)* APEX

apex [apɛks] NM **1** *Anat & Astron* apex **2** *(accent)* macron

aphagie [afaʒi] NF *Méd* aphagia

aphasie [afazi] NF *Méd* aphasia

aphasique [afazik] *Méd* ADJ aphasic

NMF aphasic

aphélandra [afelɑ̃dra] NM *Bot* aphelandra

aphélie [afeli] NM *Astron* aphelion

aphérèse [aferɛz] NF **1** *Ling* aphaeresis **2** *Am Méd* apheresis

aphidé [afide], **aphidien** [afidjɛ̃] *Entom* NM aphis, aphid, aphidian

❑ **aphidés, aphidiens** NMPL Aphididae

aphone [afɔn] ADJ **1** *(sans voix)* hoarse; **j'étais complètement a.** I'd lost my voice; **il est devenu a., tellement il a crié** he's shouted himself hoarse **2** *Méd* aphonic

aphonie [afɔni] NF *Méd* aphonia

aphorisme [afɔrism] NM *Ling* aphorism; *Péj* **s'exprimer par aphorismes** to speak in platitudes

aphrodisiaque [afrɔdizjak] ADJ aphrodisiac

NM aphrodisiac

Aphrodite [afrɔdit] NPR *Myth* Aphrodite

aphrodite [afrɔdit] NF *Zool* sea mouse

aphte [aft] NM mouth ulcer, *Spéc* aphtha

aphteux, -euse [aftø, -øz] ADJ aphthous

aphylle [afil] ADJ *Bot* aphyllous

API [apei] NM *Ling (abrév* **alphabet phonétique international)** IPA

NF *(abrév* **allocation de parent isolé)** = allowance paid to single parents

api [api] NM *Bot* **pomme d'a.** = type of small apple

à-pic [apik] NM INV steep rock face, sheer cliff

apical, -e, -aux, -ales [apikal, -o] ADJ *Bot & Géom* apical

❑ **apicale** NF *Ling* apical consonant

apico-alvéolaire [apikoalveɔlar] *Ling* ADJ *(consonne)* apico-alveolar

NF apico-alveolar

apico-dental, -e, -aux, -ales [apikodɑ̃tal, -o] *Ling* ADJ *(consonne)* apico-dental

❑ **apico-dentale** NF apico-dental

apicole [apikɔl] ADJ beekeeping *(avant n)*, *Spéc* apiarian; **exploitation a.** honey farm

apiculteur, -trice [apikyltœr, -tris] NM,F beekeeper, *Spéc* apiculturist, apiarist

apiculture [apikyltyr] NF beekeeping, *Spéc* apiculture

apidé [apide] *Entom* NM member of the Apidae family

❑ **apidés** NMPL Apidae

apiéceur, -euse [apjesœr, -øz] NM,F *Arch* piece worker *(in the clothing trade)*

apifuge [apifyʒ] ADJ **produit a.** bee repellent

apiol [apjɔl] NM *Pharm* apiol

---

apion [apjɔ̃] NM *Entom* apion, gorse-weevil, seed-weevil

apiquage [apikaʒ] NM *Naut* **1** *(d'une vergue)* peaking **2** *(du beaupré)* steeve, steeving, angle

apiquer [3] [apike] VT *Naut* **1** *(vergue)* to peak, to cockbill; **vergue apiquée** yard apeak **2** *(beaupré)* to steeve

apisiopèse [apisiopɛz] NF aposiopesis

apitoie *etc voir* **apitoyer**

apitoiement [apitwamɑ̃] NM pity, compassion; **pas d'a.!** *(ne sois pas indulgent)* don't feel sorry for him/her/*etc*!; *(sois sans pitié)* show no mercy!

apitoyer [13] [apitwaje] VT to arouse the pity of; **il veut m'a.** he's trying to make me feel sorry for him
▶ **s'apitoyer** VPR **s'a. sur qn** to feel sorry for *or* to pity sb; **s'a. sur soi-même** *ou* **sur son sort** to feel sorry for oneself

apivore [apivɔr] *Zool* ADJ apivorous, bee-eating

NM *(oiseau)* apivorous *or* bee-eating bird; *(animal)* apivorous *or* bee-eating animal

ap. J.-C. *(abrév écrite* **après Jésus-Christ)** AD

APL [apeɛl] NF *(abrév* **aide personnalisée au logement)** ≃ housing benefit

aplacental [aplasɛ̃tal] *Zool* ADJ aplacental

NM aplacental animal

aplanat [aplana] *Phot* ADJ M **objectif a.** aplanatic lens

NM aplanat, aplanatic lens

aplanétique [aplanetik] ADJ *Opt & Phot* aplanatic

aplanétisme [aplanetism] NM *Opt & Phot* aplanatism

aplanir [32] [aplanir] VT **1** *(niveler → terrain)* to level (off), to grade; *(→ surface)* to smooth, to level off

2 *Fig (difficulté)* to smooth out *or* over, to iron out; *(obstacle)* to remove
▶ **s'aplanir** VPR *(surface)* to level out *or* off
2 *(difficulté, obstacle)* **les difficultés se sont peu à peu aplanies** the difficulties gradually smoothed themselves out

aplanissement [aplanismɑ̃] NM **1** *(d'un jardin, d'une surface)* levelling (off); *Fig* **nous lui devons l'a. de toutes nos difficultés** we have him/her to thank for ironing out all our problems **2** *Géol* peneplanation

aplasie [aplazi] NF *Méd* aplasia

aplasique [aplazik], **aplastique** [aplastik] ADJ *Méd* aplastic

aplat, à-plat[1] [apla] *(pl* **à-plats)** NM *(couleur)* flat tint, solid colour

à-plat[2] [apla] *(pl* **à-plats)** NM *(d'une feuille de papier)* flatness, smoothness

aplati, -e [aplati] ADJ *(gén)* flattened; *(nez)* flat; **la Terre est aplatie aux pôles** the Earth is flat at the poles *or Spéc* oblate

aplatir [32] [aplatir] VT **1** *(rendre plat → tôle, verre, surface)* to flatten (out); *(→ métal)* to beat flat; *(→ terre, sol)* to roll, to crush; *(→ rivet)* to clench, to close; *(→ couture, pli)* to press (flat), to smooth (out); *(→ cheveux)* to smooth *or* to plaster down; **aplatissez le morceau de pâte avec votre main** flatten out the piece of dough with your hand; **a. qch à coups de marteau** to hammer sth flat

2 *(écraser)* to flatten, to squash, to crush; **a. son nez contre la vitre** to flatten *or* to squash one's nose against the window

3 *Fam (vaincre)* to crush, to flatten; **encore un mot et je t'aplatis!** one more word and I'll flatten you!

4 *Sport* **a. le ballon** *(au rugby)* to score a try, to ground the ball; *Can (au football américain)* to touch the ball down; **a. un essai** to score a try, to ground the ball

USAGE ABSOLU *Sport (en rugby)* to score a try
▶ **s'aplatir** VPR **1** *(être plat)* to be flat; *(devenir plat → terrain)* to flatten (out), to become flat; *(→ cheveux)* to go flat; *(→ chapeau)* to get flattened; **son crâne s'aplatit au sommet** his/her head is flat at the top; **après la rivière, le relief commence à s'a.** the contours flatten out *or* get flatter beyond the river

2 *(se coller)* **s'a. par terre** to lie flat on the ground; **s'a. contre le mur** to flatten oneself against the wall; **aplatissez-vous contre la voiture** press yourself flat against the car; **sa voiture s'est aplatie contre un arbre** his/her car smashed into a tree

---

3 *Fam (s'humilier)* to crawl; **s'a. devant qn** to go crawling to sb; **s'a. comme une carpette** to crawl

4 *Fam (tomber)* to fall flat on one's face

aplatissage [aplatisaʒ] NM *(de la tôle, du verre, d'une surface)* flattening; *(du métal)* beating flat; *(de la terre, du sol)* rolling, crushing; *(d'un rivet)* clenching, closing; *(d'une couture, d'un pli)* pressing (flat), smoothing (out)

aplatissement [aplatismɑ̃] NM **1** *Astron & Géom* **l'a. de la Terre** the flattening of the Earth; **l'a. d'une courbe** the oblateness of a curve **2** *(fait de rendre plat)* flattening **3** *Fam (servilité)* crawling

aplatisseur [aplatisœr] NM *Tech* roller crusher

aplatissoir [aplatiswar] NM *Métal* **1** *(marteau)* flatting hammer **2** *(laminoir)* flatting mill

aplatissoire [aplatiswar] NF = **aplatissoir**

aplite [aplit] NF *Minér* aplite

aplomb [aplɔ̃] NM **1** *(verticalité)* perpendicularity; **à l'a. de** *(au-dessus de)* directly above; *(au-dessous de)* directly below

2 *(confiance en soi)* self-assurance, self-possession; **avoir de l'a.** ≃ to be self-possessed, to be self-assured; **répondre avec a.** to answer with self-assurance *or* self-possession

3 *Péj (insolence)* nerve; **avoir l'a. de faire qch** to have the nerve to do sth; **il ne manque pas d'a.** he really has a nerve

❑ **aplombs** NMPL *Équitation* stand

❑ **d'aplomb** ADJ **1** *(vertical)* perpendicular; **être d'a.** to be vertical; *Constr* **ne pas être d'a.** to be out of plumb *or* off plumb; *(en déséquilibre)* to be askew; **être bien d'a. sur ses jambes** to be steady on one's feet **2** *(en bonne santé)* well; **être d'a.** to be well *or* in good health; **ne pas être d'a.** to feel unwell *or* out of sorts ADV **1** *(à la verticale)* *Constr* **mettre qch d'a.** to plumb sth (up); *(redresser)* to straighten sth up **2** *(en bonne santé)* **remettre qn d'a.** to put sb back on his/her feet, to make sb better **3** *Can Fam (complètement)* totally, big time; **se faire avoir d'a.** to be had big time

aplomber [3] [aplɔ̃be] *Can* VT *(verticalement)* to make straight; *(horizontalement)* to make level
▶ **s'aplomber** VPR to straighten up

apnée [apne] NF apnoea; **descendre** *ou* **plonger en a.** to dive without breathing apparatus

apnéiste [apneist] NMF apnoea diver, breath-holding diver

apoastre [apoastr] NM *Astron* apastron

apocalypse [apokalips] NF *(catastrophe)* apocalypse; **une a. nucléaire** a nuclear holocaust

❑ **Apocalypse** NF *Rel* **l'A.** the Apocalypse, (Book of) Revelation; **la Tenture de l'A.** = important series of 14th century narrative tapestries kept at the castle in Angers

❑ **d'apocalypse** ADJ *(vision)* apocalyptic; *(récit)* doom-laden; **un paysage d'a.** a scene of total devastation

apocalyptique [apokaliptik] ADJ apocalyptic, cataclysmic; *Fig* **un paysage a.** a scene of total devastation; **un silence a.** a doom-laden silence

apocope [apokɔp] NF *Ling* apocope

apocopé, -e [apokope] ADJ *Ling* apocopated

apocrine [apokrin] ADJ *Physiol* apocrine

apocryphe [apokrif] ADJ apocryphal

NM *Littérature* apocryphal text; **les apocryphes (de la Bible)** the Apocrypha

apocynacée [aposinase] *Bot* NF apocynaceous plant

❑ **apocynacées** NFPL Apocynaceae

apode [apɔd] *Zool* ADJ apodal

NM apode

apodictique [apodiktik] ADJ *Phil* apodictic, apodeictic

apodose [apodoz] NF *Gram* apodosis

apoenzyme [apoɑ̃zim] NM OU NF *Biol & Chim* apoenzyme

apogamie [apogami] NF *Bot* apogamy

apogée [apoʒe] NM **1** *Astron* apogee **2** *(sommet)* peak, summit, apogee; **l'a. de la réussite** the pinnacle *or* the peak of achievement; **à l'a. de sa carrière** at the height *or* at the peak of his/her career; **atteindre son a.** to reach one's peak

apogonidé [apogonide] *Ich* NM cardinal fish

❑ **apogonidés** NMPL cardinal fish, *Spéc* Apogonidae

apolipoprotéine [apɔlipɔprɔtein] NF *Méd* apolipoprotein

apolitique [apɔlitik] *Pol* ADJ *(sans convictions politiques)* apolitical; *(non affilié)* nonpolitical ▪ NMF apolitical person

apolitisme [apɔlitism] NM *Pol (refus de s'engager)* apolitical stance; *(engagement sans affiliation)* nonpolitical stance

apollinien, -enne [apɔlinjɛ̃, -ɛn] ADJ *Myth & Phil* Apollonian

Apollodore [apɔlɔdɔr] NPR *A. de Damas* Apollodorus of Damascus

Apollon [apɔlɔ̃] NPR *Myth* Apollo; **l'A. du Belvédère** the Apollo Belvedere
□ **apollon** NM 1 *(bel homme)* Adonis; **un jeune a.** a young Adonis; **c'est un véritable a.** he's like a Greek god; **ce n'est pas un a.** he's no oil painting 2 *Entom* apollo butterfly

Apollonios [apɔlɔnjɔs] NPR Apollonius

apologétique [apɔlɔʒetik] ADJ apologetic ▪ NF*Rel* apologetics *(singulier)*

apologie [apɔlɔʒi] NF *(défense)* apologia (**de** for); *(éloge)* encomium, eulogy (**de** of); **faire l'a. de qn/qch** *(défendre)* to (seek to) justify sb/sth; *(louer)* to eulogize sb/sth

apologiste [apɔlɔʒist] NMF apologist

apologue [apɔlɔg] NM *Littérature* apologue

apolune [apɔlyn] NM *Astron* apolune

apomixie [apɔmiksi] NF *Biol* apomixis

apomorphe [apɔmɔrf] NF *Biol* apomorph

apomorphie [apɔmɔrfi] NF *Biol* apomorphy

apomorphine [apɔmɔrfin] NF *Pharm* apomorphine, apomorphia

aponévrectomie [apɔnevrɛktɔmi] NF *Méd* aponeurectomy

aponévrose [apɔnevroz] NF *Anat* aponeurosis

aponévrotique [apɔnevrɔtik] ADJ *Anat (membrane)* aponeurotic, fascial

apophantique [apɔfɑ̃tik] ADJ *Phil* apophantic

apophonie [apɔfɔni] NF *Ling* ablaut, vowel gradation

apophtegme [apɔftɛgm] NM *Ling* apophthegm

apophysaire [apɔfizɛr] ADJ *Anat* apophyseal

apophyse [apɔfiz] NF *Anat* apophysis

apoplectique [apɔplɛktik] *Méd* ADJ apoplectic ▪ NMF apoplectic

apoplexie [apɔplɛksi] NF *Méd* apoplexy; **attaque d'a.** stroke; *Fig* **il était au bord de l'a.** he nearly had a fit

apoprotéine [apɔprɔtein] NF *Biol* apoprotein

apoptose [apɔptɔz] NF *Biol* apoptosis

aporétique [apɔretik] ADJ *Phil* aporetic

aporie [apɔri] NF *Phil* aporia

aposélène [apɔselɛn] NM *Astron* apolune

apothéose [apɔteoz] NF 1 *(apogée)* summit; **l'a. du courage** the height of bravery; **ce concert a été l'a. du festival** the concert was the highlight of the festival 2 *Théât* (grand) finale; **cela s'est terminé en a.** it ended in grand style 3 *Antiq* apotheosis

apothicaire [apɔtikɛr] NM *Arch* apothecary

apôtre [apotr] NM 1 *Rel* apostle, disciple 2 *(avocat)* advocate; **se faire l'a. d'une idée** to champion *or* to speak for an idea; **un a. de la tolérance** an advocate *or* a champion of tolerance; *Péj* **faire le bon a.** to be holier-than-thou

Appalaches [apalaʃ] NMPL **les A.** the Appalachian Mountains, the Appalachians

appalachien, -enne [apalaʃjɛ̃, -ɛn] ADJ Appalachian

apparaître [91] [aparɛtr] VI 1 *(à la vue)* to appear; **des nuages menaçants apparaissaient dans le ciel** menacing clouds were appearing in the sky; **après le bosquet, on voit a. le village** after you pass the copse, the village comes into view; **a. à qn en songe** *ou* **rêve** to appear *or* to come to sb in a dream
2 *(à l'esprit)* to appear, to transpire, to emerge; **ce qui apparaît, c'est surtout sa méchanceté** what emerges above all is his/her wickedness; **la vérité m'est apparue un beau jour** the truth came to *or* dawned on me one day; **il apparaît enfin tel qu'il est** he's showing his true self at last; **la voir dans un contexte professionnel la fait a. sous un jour complètement nouveau** seeing her in a professional context shows her in a completely new light; **faire a. la vérité** to bring the truth to light
3 *(surgir)* to appear, to materialize; **il est apparu tout d'un coup au coin de la rue** he appeared suddenly at the street corner; **la fée est apparue** the fairy appeared *or* materialized; **le chat est apparu au milieu des couvertures** the cat emerged from the blankets
4 *(figurer)* to appear, to feature; **la liste des ingrédients doit a. sur le paquet** the list of ingredients must appear *or* feature on the packet; **le nom du traducteur n'apparaît pas sur la page de titre** the translator's name doesn't appear on the title page; **Marilyn n'apparaît qu'une fois dans la première bobine** Marilyn appears only once in the first reel
5 *(se manifester → symptôme, bouton)* to appear; *(→ maladie)* to develop; *(→ préjugé, habitude)* to develop, to surface; **quand apparaissent les premières rides** when the first wrinkles appear; **une coutume apparue en Europe** a custom which first developed in Europe; **faire a.** to reveal
6 *(sembler)* to seem, to appear; **cette histoire m'apparaît bien dérisoire aujourd'hui** the whole thing strikes me as ridiculous now; **il m'apparaît comme le seul capable d'y parvenir** he seems to me to be the only person capable of doing it
7 *(tournure impersonnelle)* **il apparaît impossible de faire...** it appears to be *or* it seems impossible to do...; **il apparaît que...** it appears *or* emerges that...

apparat [apara] NM 1 *(cérémonie)* pomp; **en grand a.** with great pomp (and ceremony); **sans a.** without pomp, simply; **tenue/discours d'a.** ceremonial dress/speech 2 *Littérature* **a. critique** critical apparatus, apparatus criticus

APOSTROPHES
This former weekly television programme about books, which ran from 1975 to 1990, had a significant influence on the reading habits of people in France, and an invitation by its host, Bernard Pivot, was considered by authors to be a great honour. "Passer à Apostrophes" and "passer chez Pivot" became well-known catchphrases. It was then replaced by "Bouillon de culture", still hosted by Pivot but with a wider perspective, addressing other aspects of modern-day culture such as cinema and social problems.

apostropher [3] [apɔstrɔfe] VT to shout at
▪ **s'apostropher** VPR to shout at each other

apothécie [apɔtesi] NF *Bot* apothecium

apothème [apɔtɛm] NM *Géom* apothegm

apparatchik [aparatʃik] NM *Pol* apparatchik

apparaux [aparo] NMPL 1 *Naut* handling gear, tackle; **a. de bord** equipment on board 2 *Gym* apparatus

appareil [aparɛj] NM 1 *(dispositif)* apparatus, device; **a. acoustique** hearing aid; **a. de chauffage** heater; **a. de contrôle** tester; **a. dentaire** *(prothèse)* dentures, (dental) plate; *(pour corriger)* brace, plate; *Tél* **a. mains libres** hands-free device; **a. ménager** household appliance; **a. de mesure** measuring device *or* apparatus; **a. orthopédique** orthopedic device; **a. photo** camera; **a. photo APS** APS camera; **a. photo autofocus** autofocus camera; **a. photo compact** compact camera; **a. photo à instantanés** candid camera; **a. photo jetable** disposable camera; **a. photo monoculaire** single-lens camera; **a. photo numérique** digital camera; **a. plâtré** plaster cast; **a. de projection** film projector; **a. de prothèse** surgical appliance; **a. reflex** reflex camera; **a. photo reflex à deux objectifs** twin-lens reflex camera; **a. TENS** TENS machine; **a. (téléphonique)** telephone; **qui est à l'a.?** who's speaking?; **Berlot à l'a.!** Berlot speaking!
2 *Aviat* craft, aircraft; **une fois dans l'a.** once on board the aircraft
3 *Anat* apparatus, system; **a. digestif** digestive apparatus *or* system; **a. respiratoire** respiratory apparatus
4 *Gym (agrès)* apparatus; **exercices aux appareils** apparatus work, exercises on the apparatus
5 *Constr* bond
6 *(système)* apparatus; **l'a. du parti** the party apparatus *or* machinery; *Littérature* **a. critique** critical apparatus; *Pol* **a. étatique** machinery of state, state apparatus; *Pol* **a. idéologique d'État** ideological state apparatus; **l'a. législatif** the machinery of the law; **a. de production** production facilities; **a. psychique** psychic *or* mental apparatus
7 *Littéraire (cérémonial)* trappings; **l'a. somptueux du couronnement** the pomp and circumstance *or* sumptuous trappings of the coronation
8 *Culin* mixture

appareillable [aparɛjabl] ADJ *Méd (personne)* who can wear *or* be fitted with a prosthesis

appareillade [aparɛjad] NF *Orn* mating

appareillage [aparɛjaʒ] NM 1 *Naut* casting off, weighing anchor 2 *Tech* equipment 3 *Méd* fitting with a prosthesis 4 *Constr* bonding

appareillement [aparɛjmɑ̃] NM *(d'animaux)* matching, pairing

appareiller [4] [aparɛje] VT 1 *Constr* to bond 2 *Méd (personne)* to fit with a prosthesis 3 *Naut (bateau)* to rig out; *(filet)* to spread 4 *(assortir)* to match, to pair 5 *Zool* to mate
▪ VI *Naut* to cast off, to get under way

apparemment [aparamɑ̃] ADV apparently; **a., tout va bien** everything seems to be *or* apparently everything's all right

apparence [aparɑ̃s] NF 1 *(aspect → d'une personne)* appearance; *(→ d'un objet, d'une situation)* appearance, look; **ça a l'a. du bois** it looks like wood; **avoir une a. de sagesse** to have an air of wisdom; **avoir belle a.** to look impressive; **avoir une a. maladive** to look sickly, to be sickly-looking; **à l'a. soignée** *(personne)* well-groomed; **un homme à l'a. négligée** an untidy-looking *or* an unkempt(-looking) man; **il a l'air gentil, mais ce n'est qu'une (fausse) a.** he seems nice, but it's only a façade; **sous l'a. du** *ou* **une a. de libéralisme** in the guise of *or* behind a façade of liberalism; **les apparences** appearances; **il a les apparences contre lui** everything points against him; **il va très bien, malgré les apparences** he's perfectly well, contrary to all appearances; **juger sur** *ou* **d'après les apparences** to judge *or* to go by appearances; **les apparences sont trompeuses, il ne faut pas se fier aux apparences** *(en jugeant une personne)* looks are deceptive; *(en jugeant une situation)* there's more to it than meets the eye, appearances can be deceptive; **faire qch pour sauver les apparences** to do sth for appearances' sake; **heureusement pour nous, les apparences sont sauvées** fortunately, we've been able to save face

apostasie [apɔstazi] NF *Rel* apostasy

apostasier [9] [apɔstazje] *Rel* VT to apostatize
▪ VI to apostatize

apostat, -e [apɔsta, -at] *Rel & Littéraire* ADJ apostate, renegade *(avant n)* ▪ NM,F apostate, renegade

aposter [3] [apɔste] VT *Vieilli* to post as a watchman

a posteriori [aposterjɔri] ADJ INV a posteriori ▪ ADV afterwards; **il est facile de juger a.** it's easy to be wise after the event; **je m'en suis aperçu a.** I realized later *or* afterwards

apostille [apɔstij] NF *Jur* apostil

apostiller [3] [apɔstije] VT *Jur* 1 *(demande, pétition)* to add a marginal recommendation to 2 *(document)* to add a marginal note to

apostolat [apɔstɔla] NM 1 *Rel* apostolate, discipleship 2 *(prosélytisme)* evangelism, proselytism 3 *(vocation)* dedication, vocation; **pour lui, l'enseignement est un a.** he is whole-heartedly devoted to teaching, teaching is his mission in life

apostolicité [apɔstɔlisite] NF *Rel* apostolicity

apostolique [apɔstɔlik] ADJ *Rel* apostolic

apostoliquement [apɔstɔlikmɑ̃] ADV apostolically

apostrophe [apɔstrɔf] NF 1 *(interpellation)* invective 2 *Gram* apostrophe; **mis en a.** used in apostrophe; **le vocatif est le cas de l'a.** the vocative is the case of direct address 3 *(signe)* apostrophe; **s a.** s apostrophe

2 *(trace)* semblance, vestige; **elle n'a plus la moindre a. de respect pour lui** she no longer has the slightest semblance of respect for him

❑ **en apparence ADV** apparently, by *or* to all appearances; **en a. il travaille, mais comment le savoir vraiment?** it may look as though he's working, but how can one be sure?; **le calme était revenu dans la ville, du moins en a.** calm had been restored in the city, at least that was the impression

apparent, -e [aparɑ̃, -ɑ̃t] **ADJ 1** *(visible)* visible; **devenir a.** to become apparent, to surface, to emerge; **il n'y a aucun danger a.** there's no apparent *or* visible danger; **installation apparente** surface installation; **avec poutres apparentes** with exposed beams; **couture apparente** topstitched seam

2 *(évident)* obvious, apparent, evident; **sans raison apparente** for no obvious *or* apparent reason

3 *(superficiel)* apparent; **un danger plus a. que réel** a danger that is more apparent than real *or* not as bad as it seems; **une tranquillité apparente** outward *or* surface calm; **sous cette apparente bonté se cache un grand égoïsme** beneath that kind exterior there lies great selfishness

apparenté, -e [aparɑ̃te] **ADJ 1** *(parent)* related **2** *(allié)* allied; **des listes apparentées** grouped electoral lists *(in proportional elections)*; **la construction et industries apparentées** building and allied trades; **les socialistes et apparentés** the socialists and their allies **3** *(ressemblant)* similar; **deux styles apparentés** two similar *or* closely related styles **4** *Ling* cognate

apparentement [aparɑ̃tmɑ̃] **NM 1** *(lien)* link; **son a. à la bourgeoisie** his/her links to the bourgeoisie **2** *Pol (alliance)* alliance; **a. à un groupe parlementaire** alliance with a parliamentary group; **a. de listes électorales** grouping of electoral lists *(in proportional elections)*

apparenter [3] [aparɑ̃te] **s'apparenter VPR 1** *(emploi réciproque) Pol* to enter into an alliance **2 s'a. à** *(ressembler à)* to be like; *(s'allier à → un parti)* to enter into an alliance with; *(→ une famille)* to marry into; **cette histoire s'apparente à une aventure que j'ai vécue** this story is similar to *or* is like an experience I once had

appariement [aparimɑ̃] **NM** matching, pairing

apparier [10] [aparje] **VT 1** *(chaussures, gants)* to match, to pair **2** *Zool* to mate

▸**s'apparier VPR** to mate

appariteur [aparitœr] **NM 1** *Jur (huissier)* usher **2** *Univ Br* porter, *Am* campus policeman

apparition [aparisjɔ̃] **NF 1** *(arrivée → d'une personne, d'une saison)* arrival, appearance; **avec l'a. du printemps** with the coming *or* arrival of spring; **faire une a.** to put in *or* to make an appearance; **faire son a.** *(maladie)* to develop; *(soleil)* to come out; **la star a finalement fait son a. vers 18 heures** the star finally appeared *or* made his/her appearance around 6 o'clock; **brèves apparitions du soleil cet après-midi** brief sunny spells *or* intervals this afternoon; **les nuages feront leur a. dans la soirée** the sky will cloud over in the evening; *TV* **a. graduelle** fade-in

2 *(première manifestation)* (first) appearance; **l'a. de la religion** the first appearance *or* the birth of religion; **dès l'a. des premiers symptômes** as soon as the first symptoms appear

3 *(vision)* apparition, vision; **avoir une a.** to be visited by an apparition; **avoir des apparitions** to have visions; **l'a. de la Vierge à sainte Bernadette** Saint Bernadette's vision of the Virgin Mary, the apparition of the Virgin Mary to Saint Bernadette

apparoir [aparwar] **V IMPERSONNEL** *Jur* **il appert de ces témoignages que...** it appears *or* it is evident from these statements that...

appart [apart] **NM** *Fam Br* flat■, *Am* apartment■

appartement [apartəmɑ̃] **NM 1** *(logement) Br* flat, *Am* apartment; **a. de fonction** company *Br* flat *or Am* apartment; **a. témoin** *ou* **modèle** *Br* show flat, *Am* model apartment; **a. thérapeutique** sheltered accommodation *(UNCOUNT)* **2** *Can Fam Vieilli (pièce)* room■; **ils ont une nouvelle maison à six appartements** they have a new house with six rooms

❑ **appartements NMPL** *(d'un château)* apartments; *Hum* **se retirer dans ses appartements** to withdraw *or* to retire to one's quarters

appartenance [apartənɑ̃s] **NF 1** *(statut de membre)* **son a. à la tendance symboliste** his/her links *or* his/her association with the Symbolist group; **en raison de son a. à la communauté juive** because he/she belongs/belonged to the Jewish community; **a. à un groupe/club** membership of a group/club; **a. à un parti** affiliation to *or* membership of a party; **a. à une communauté** membership of a community **2** *Math* membership

appartenir [40] [apartənir] **appartenir à VT IND 1** *(être la propriété de)* to belong to; **à qui appartient la voiture verte?** whose is the green car?; **cet argent m'appartient en propre** this money is my own

2 *(faire partie de → groupe)* to belong to, to be part of; *(→ professorat, syndicat)* to belong to; **il appartient à la même section que toi** he's a member of *or* he belongs to the same group as you; **elle appartient à une famille très riche** she comes from a very wealthy family; **l'araignée n'appartient pas à la famille des insectes** spiders do not belong to *or* are not members of the insect family

3 *(dépendre de)* **la décision t'appartient** it's up to you, it's for you to decide; **pour des raisons qui m'appartiennent** for my own reasons; **l'éducation des enfants appartient aux deux parents** bringing up children is the responsibility of both parents

4 *(tournure impersonnelle)* **il appartient à chacun de faire attention** it's everyone's responsibility to be careful; **il ne vous appartient pas d'en décider** it's not for you to decide, the decision is not yours (to make)

5 *Math* to be a member of

▸**s'appartenir VPR** *(être libre)* **avec tout ce travail, je ne m'appartiens plus** I have so much work, my time isn't my own any more

apparu, -e [apary] **PP** *voir* **apparaître**

appas [apɑ] **NMPL** *Littéraire* charms

appassionato, -a [apasjonato, -a] *Mus* **ADJ** appassionato; **la 'Sonate appassionata' de Beethoven** Beethoven's 'appassionata sonata'

❑ **appassionato ADV** appassionato

appât [apɑ] **NM 1** *Chasse & Pêche* bait *(UNCOUNT)*; *(pour attirer le gros gibier)* kill; **mordre à l'a.** to take the bait; *Fig* to rise to the bait **2** *(attrait)* **l'a. de** the lure of; **l'a. du gain** the lure *or* attraction of money; **la récompense était un a. de taille** the reward was a tempting bait

appâter [3] [apɑte] **VT 1** *(attirer → poisson, animal)* to lure; *(→ personne)* to lure, to entice; **a. qn par des promesses** to entice sb with promises **2** *(nourrir → oiseau)* to feed **3** *(engraisser → volaille)* to forcefeed

appauvrir [32] [apovrir] **VT** *(rendre pauvre → personne)* to impoverish, to make poor; *(→ pays)* to impoverish, to drain; *(→ terre)* to impoverish, to drain, to exhaust; *(→ sang)* to make thin, to weaken; *(→ langue)* to impoverish

▸**s'appauvrir VPR** *(personne, famille, pays)* to get *or* to grow poorer; *(sol)* to become exhausted; *(sang)* to become thin; *(langue)* to become impoverished, to lose its vitality

appauvrissement [apovrismɑ̃] **NM** *(gén)* impoverishment; *(du sang)* thinning

appeau, -x [apo] **NM** *Chasse* **1** *(sifflet)* birdcall **2** *(oiseau)* decoy (duck), stool pigeon; *Fig* **servir d'a. à qn** to act as a decoy for sb

appel [apɛl] **NM 1** *(cri)* call; **un a. au secours** a shout *or* cry for help; **tu n'as pas entendu mes appels?** didn't you hear me calling (out)?; **le mâle répond à l'a. de la femelle** the male answers the call of the female; **l'a. des sens/du large** the call of the senses/of the sea; **l'a. de la nature** the call of the wild; **a. à l'insurrection** call to insurrection; **a. aux armes** call to arms; **un a. à la grève** a call for strike action; **a. au peuple** appeal to the people; **a. au rassemblement** call for unity; **l'a. du 18 juin 1940** = appeal for resistance made from London by General de Gaulle to the French during World War II; **a. de détresse** *Naut* distress signal, call for help; *(d'une personne)* call for help; **faire un a. de phares (à qn)** to flash one's lights (at sb); **faire un a. du pied à qn** to make covert advances *or* approaches *or* overtures to sb; **a. radio** radio message

2 *(coup de téléphone)* **a. (téléphonique)** (telephone) *or* phone call; *Mktg* **a. à froid** cold call; **a. gratuit** *Br* Freefone® call, *Am* toll-free call; **a. interurbain** long-distance call; **a. en PCV** *Br* reverse charge call, *Am* collect call; **a. avec préavis** person-to-person call; **a. de réveil** wake-up *or* alarm call

3 *(demande)* request; **lancer un a. pour l'aide aux sinistrés** to launch an appeal for the disaster victims; **il est resté sourd aux appels (à l'aide) de sa famille** he ignored his family's calls *or* appeals *or* pleas (for help); **faire a. à** *(clémence, générosité)* to appeal to; *(courage, intelligence, qualité)* to summon (up); *(souvenirs)* to summon (up); **faire a. à la générosité publique** to appeal to public generosity; **faire a. à tout son courage** to summon (up) all one's courage, to take one's courage in both hands; **cela fait a. à des notions complexes** it involves complex notions; **faire a. à la force** to resort to force; **faire a. à l'armée** to call in the army, to call the army out; **faire a. à un spécialiste** to call in a specialist; **il a fait a. à elle pour son déménagement** he asked her to help him when he moved house

4 *Écon* call; **a. de fonds** call for funds; **faire un a. de fonds** to call up capital; **a. d'offres** invitation to tender; **répondre à un a. d'offres** to make a bid; *Bourse* **a. de couverture** *ou* **de garantie** *ou* **de marge** margin call

5 *Jur* appeal; **en a.** on appeal; **faire a.** to appeal; **faire a. d'un jugement** to appeal against a decision; **aller en a.** to appeal, to go to appeal; **a. des causes** preliminary hearing; **a. en garantie** claim for contribution; **a. incident** cross-appeal; **a. à maxima/minima** appeal by the Prosecution against the severity/leniency of the sentence; **a. principal** appeal by the defendant; **a. provoqué par l'a. principal** = form of cross-appeal by an opposing party against whom no appeal has been lodged; **a. à témoins** appeal for witnesses (to come forward)

6 *(liste de présence)* roll call; *Mil (mobilisation)* call-up; **faire l'a.** *Scol Br* to call the register, *Am* to call (the) roll; *Mil* to call the roll; **répondre à l'a.** to be present; **a. d'une classe** call-up *or* calling up of a class

7 *Typ* **a. de note** reference mark

8 *Ordinat* call; **a. par référence/valeur** call by reference/value; **programme/séquence d'a.** call routine/sequence

9 *Cartes* **faire un a. à cœur/carreau** to ask for a hearts/diamonds return

10 *Sport* take-off; *Escrime* appel; **prendre son a.** to take off

11 *Tech* **a. d'air** draught

❑ **sans appel ADJ 1** *Jur* without (the possibility of an) appeal

2 *(irrévocable)* irrevocable; **c'est sans a.** there's no going back on it, it's final; **une décision sans a.** an irrevocable *or* a final decision; **répondre d'un ton sans a.** to reply dismissively

appelant, -e [aplɑ̃, -ɑ̃t] **ADJ** *Ordinat* calling

NM,F *Jur* appellant

NM *Chasse (appeau)* birdcall; *(leurre)* decoy (duck)

appelé, -e [aple] **NM,F il y a beaucoup d'appelés et peu d'élus** many are called but few are chosen

NM *Mil* conscript

appeler [24] [aple] **VT 1** *(interpeller)* to call (out) to, to shout to; **appelle-le, il a oublié sa lettre** give him a shout, he's left his letter behind; **attendez que je vous appelle** wait till I call you; **a. qn par la fenêtre** to call out to sb from the window; **a. le nom de qn** to call out sb's name; **a. au secours** to shout "help", to call for help; *Fig* to call for help

2 *(au téléphone)* to call (up); **appelle-moi demain** call me tomorrow; **appelez ce numéro en cas d'urgence** dial this number in an emergency; **elle appelle Londres** she's on the phone to London; **on vous appelle de Bonn** there's a call for you from Bonn; **je vais a. le bureau pour dire que je ne viendrai pas** I'll call the office to say I won't be coming in

3 *(faire venir → médecin)* to call, to send for;

(→ *police)* to call; (→ *renforts)* to call up *or* out; (→ *ascenseur)* to call; **a. du secours** to go for help; **a. qn à l'aide** to call to sb for help; **a. un taxi** *(dans la rue)* to hail a taxi; *(par téléphone)* to phone for *or* to call a taxi; **a. le garçon** to call the waiter; **le patron m'a appelé pour me faire signer le contrat** the boss called me in to get me to sign the contract; **a. qn à qch** to call sb to sth; **a. qn à une fonction importante** to call *or* to appoint sb to a high office; **être appelé sous les drapeaux** to be called up *or* conscripted; **faire a. qn** to send for sb, to summon sb; *Littéraire* **Dieu/le devoir vous appelle** God/your duty is calling you; *Hum* **le devoir m'appelle!** duty calls!; **une affaire m'appelle en ville** I have to go to town on business

4 *Jur* to summon; **être appelé à comparaître** to be summoned *or* issued with a summons; **être appelé à la barre** to be called *or* summoned to the witness stand; **être appelé devant le juge** to be called up before the magistrate

5 *(désirer)* **a. qch (de tous ses vœux)** to yearn (passionately) for sth; **une réconciliation que nous appelons de tous nos vœux** a reconciliation which we most ardently desire

6 *(nécessiter)* to require, to call for; **la situation appelle des mesures immédiates** the situation calls for *or* requires immediate action; **sa conduite appelle une punition** his/her attitude calls for *or* deserves punishment; **un acte qui appelle une condamnation immédiate** an act which calls for immediate censure

7 *(entraîner)* to lead to; **un coup en appelle un autre** one blow leads to another

8 *(inviter)* **a. qn à qch** to call sb to sth; **a. (des travailleurs) à la grève** to call a strike, to put out a strike call; **a. les gens à la révolte** to incite people to rebel; **a. aux armes** to call to arms; **il faut a. les gens à voter** *ou* **aux urnes** people must be urged to vote

9 *(destiner)* **être appelé à faire qch** to be bound to do sth; **ce quartier est appelé à disparaître** this part of town is due to be demolished (eventually); **il va être appelé à revenir souvent** he will have to come back often; **j'étais appelée à devenir religieuse** I had a vocation to become a nun

10 *(nommer)* to call; **comment on appelle ça en chinois?** what's (the word for) this in Chinese?; **ici, on appelle tout le monde par un surnom** here we give everybody a nickname; **appelez-moi Jo** call me Jo; **je l'appelle par son prénom** I call him/her by his/her first name; **nous appellerons le bébé Marie** we'll call *or* name the baby Marie; **elle se fait a. Jaspe** she wants to be called Jaspe; *Fam* **se faire a. Arthur** to catch it, *Br* to get it in the neck

11 *Ordinat (programme, fichier)* to call (up); *(réseau)* to dial

12 *Fin* **capital appelé** called-up capital

USAGE ABSOLU **la pauvre, elle a appelé toute la nuit** the poor thing called out all night; **écoute, il appelle!** listen, he's calling out!

▫ **en appeler à** VT IND to appeal to; **j'en appelle à votre bon cœur** I'm appealing to your generosity; **j'en appelle à vous en dernier recours** I'm appealing to you as a last resort

▸**s'appeler** VPR **1** *(emploi passif)* to be called; **comment s'appelle-t-il?** what's his name?, what's he called?; **voilà ce qui s'appelle une gaffe!** that's what's called *or* that's what I call putting your foot in it!; *Fam* **ça s'appelle revient** make sure you give it back

2 *(emploi réciproque)* to call one another; **vous vous appelez par vos prénoms?** are you on first-name terms?

3 *(au téléphone)* **on s'appelle demain?** talk to you tomorrow

appelette [aplɛt] NF *Ordinat* applet

appellatif, -ive [apɛlatif, -iv] *Ling* ADJ appellative
NM appellative

appellation [apɛlasjɔ̃] NF appellation, designation; **une a. injurieuse** an insulting name **a. d'origine contrôlée** appellation (d'origine) contrôlée *(official certification guaranteeing the quality of French produce, especially wines and cheeses)*; **c'est une a. bordeaux contrôlée** it's a Bordeaux appellation contrôlée; **a. d'origine** label of quality; **un vin sans a.** a non-vintage wine

appellative [apɛlativ] *voir* **appellatif**

appelle *etc voir* **appeler**

appendice [apɛ̃dis] NM **1** *(supplément)* appendix **2** *(prolongement)* appendage **3** *Hum (nez)* snout **4** *Anat* appendix

appendicectomie [apɛ̃disɛktɔmi] NF *Méd* appendicectomy, appendectomy; **j'ai eu une a.** I had my appendix out

appendicite [apɛ̃disit] NF appendicitis; **crise d'a.** appendicitis; **se faire opérer de l'a.** to have one's appendix removed

appendiculaire [apɛ̃dikylɛr] ADJ *Anat* appendicular

appendre [73] [apɑ̃dr] VT *Littéraire* to hang, to affix

appentis [apɑ̃ti] NM **1** *(bâtiment)* lean-to **2** *(toit)* lean-to, sloping roof

Appenzell [apɛnzɛl] NM **1** *(ville)* Appenzell **2** *(région)* **l'A.** Appenzell
▫ **appenzell** NM *Culin (fromage)* Appenzell *(type of Swiss cheese)*

appert *voir* **apparoir**

appertisation [apɛrtizasjɔ̃] NF sterilization *(by thermal processing in hermetically sealed cans)*

appertiser [3] [apɛrtize] VT to sterilize *(by thermal processing in hermetically sealed cans)*

appesantir [32] [apəzɑ̃tir] VT *(rendre pesant* → *démarche)* to slow down; (→ *tête, corps)* to weigh down; (→ *facultés)* to dull; **les paupières appesanties par le sommeil** eyes heavy with sleep; *Fig* **a. son bras** *ou* **autorité sur un pays** to strengthen one's authority over a country

▸**s'appesantir** VPR **1** *(devenir lourd* → *tête)* to become heavier; (→ *gestes, démarche)* to become slower; (→ *esprit)* to grow duller; *Fig* **la main de fer de l'Inquisition s'appesantit sur eux** the iron fist of the Inquisition weighed down on them

2 *(insister)* **s'a. sur un sujet** to concentrate on *or* to dwell at length on a subject

appesantissement [apəzɑ̃tismɑ̃] NM *(de l'esprit)* (growing) dullness; *(des gestes, de la démarche)* increased heaviness

appétence [apetɑ̃s] NF *Littéraire* appetence, appetency; **une a. d'aventure** an appetence for adventure

appétissant, -e [apetisɑ̃, -ɑ̃t] ADJ **1** *(odeur, mets)* appetizing, mouthwatering; **peu a.** unappetizing **2** *Fam (attirant)* attractive; **une femme aux rondeurs appétissantes** a curvaceous woman

appétit [apeti] NM **1** *(envie de manger)* appetite; **avoir de l'a.** *ou* **bon a.** to have a good *or* hearty appetite; **je n'ai plus d'a.** I've lost my appetite, I'm off my food; **manger avec a.** *ou* **de bon a.** to eat heartily; **manger sans a.** to pick at one's food; **la promenade m'a donné de l'a.** *ou* **m'a ouvert l'a.** *ou* **m'a mis en a.** the walk has given me an appetite; **des amuse-gueule pour ouvrir l'a. de vos invités** little snacks as appetizers for your guests; *Fig* **quelques diapositives d'abord, pour vous ouvrir l'a.** first, a few slides, to whet your appetite; **ça va te couper l'a.** it'll spoil your appetite; **perdre l'a.** to lose one's appetite; **bon a.!** enjoy your meal!; **avoir un a. d'oiseau** to eat like a bird; **avoir un a. de loup** *ou* **d'ogre** to eat like a horse; *Prov* **l'a. vient en mangeant** = the more you have, the more you want

2 *(désir)* **a. de** appetite for; **un insatiable a. de vivre/de connaissances** an insatiable thirst for life/for knowledge; **a. sexuel** sexual appetite
▫ **appétits** NMPL *(instincts)* appetites

applaudimètre [aplodimɛtr] NM *Br* clapometer, *Am* applause meter

applaudir [32] [aplodir] VT **1** *(acteur, orateur)* to applaud, to clap; *(discours, pièce)* to applaud; **et on l'applaudit encore une fois!** let's give him/her another big hand!, let's hear it for him/her one more time!; **ils se sont fait a. pendant un bon quart d'heure** they were applauded for a good quarter of an hour; **il a longuement fait a. le pianiste** he led a long round of applause for the pianist

2 *Fig Littéraire (approuver)* to applaud, to praise; **la décision du gouvernement a été vivement applaudie** the government's decision has been much praised

VI to clap, to applaud; **les gens applaudissaient à tout rompre** there was thunderous applause; *Fig* **a. à une initiative** to praise *or* to applaud an initiative; **a. des deux mains à qch** to approve of *or* to welcome sth heartily

▸**s'applaudir** VPR **s'a. de qch/d'avoir fait qch** to congratulate oneself on sth/on having done sth

applaudissement [aplodismɑ̃] NM *(approbation)* approval
▫ **applaudissements** NMPL applause *(UNCOUNT)*, clapping *(UNCOUNT)*; **un tonnerre** *ou* **une tempête d'applaudissements** thunderous applause; **sous les applaudissements** amidst *or* in the midst of applause; **soulever des applaudissements** to be applauded

applaudisseur, -euse [aplodisœr, -øz] NM applauder

applet [aplɛ] NM *Can Ordinat* applet

applicabilité [aplikabilite] NF applicability; **a. directe** immediate effect

applicable [aplikabl] ADJ applicable; **cette règle est a. à tous les cas** this rule applies to all cases; **loi a. à partir du 1er mars** law to be applied *or* to come into force as of 1 March; **règlement a. immédiatement** ruling effective forthwith

applicage [aplikaʒ] NM *Tech* application

applicateur [aplikatœr] ADJ M applicator *(avant n)*
NM applicator; **tampon avec a.** applicator tampon

application [aplikasjɔ̃] NF **1** *(pose)* application; **laisser sécher après a. de la première couche** allow to dry after applying the first coat of paint

2 *(mise en pratique* → *d'une loi)* application, enforcement; (→ *d'une sentence)* enforcement; **mesures prises en a. de la loi** measures taken to enforce the law, law-enforcement measures; **mettre qch en a.** *(théorie)* to put sth into practice; *(loi, règlement)* to enforce sth, to implement sth; **entrer en a.** to come into force

3 *Tech* application; **les applications pratiques des voyages dans l'espace** the practical applications of space travel

4 *(soin)* application; **travailler avec a.** to work diligently, to apply oneself (to one's work); **il y mettait une a. inhabituelle** he was doing it with unusual application *or* zeal

5 *Math* mapping, function; **a. bijective** bijective mapping, bijection; **a. surjective** surjective mapping, surjection

6 *Couture* **a. de dentelle** (piece of) appliqué lace

7 *Ordinat* application, *Fam* app; **a. bureautique** business application; **a. graphique** graphics application; **a. phare** killer app; **a. en service** current application

applique [aplik] NF **1** *(lampe)* wall lamp **2** *Couture* piece of appliqué work; **l'a.** appliqué work

appliqué, -e [aplike] ADJ **1** *(personne)* assiduous, hard-working; *(écriture)* careful **2** *Univ* applied; **informatique appliquée à la gestion** computer technology applied to management

appliquer [3] [aplike] VT **1** *(poser* → *masque, crème, ventouse)* to apply; (→ *enduit)* to apply, to lay on; **a. sur le cou et le visage** *(sur mode d'emploi)* apply to neck and face; **a. son oreille contre la porte** to put one's ear to the door

2 *(mettre en pratique* → *décret)* to enforce, to apply; (→ *peine)* to enforce; (→ *sanctions, règlement, mesures)* to enforce, to apply; (→ *idée, réforme)* to put into practice, to implement; (→ *recette, méthode)* to use; (→ *théorie, invention)* to apply, to put into practice; **la règle de l'accord du participe n'est pas toujours appliquée** the rule for participle agreement is not always applied; **a. une loi à un cas particulier** to apply a law to a particular case; **je ne fais qu'a. la consigne!** I don't make the rules, I'm just following orders!; **vous devez faire a. le règlement** you must make sure the rules are obeyed; **ces juges sont chargés de faire a. les peines** these judges are responsible for ensuring that sentences are carried out

3 *(donner* → *sobriquet, gifle)* to give; (→ *baiser)* to plant; **un coup de pied bien appliqué** a powerful kick; **elle lui fit une bise bien appliquée** she planted a kiss on his/her cheek

4 *(consacrer)* **a. qch à** to devote sth to; **a. toute son énergie à son travail** to devote all one's energy to one's work; **a. son esprit à ses études** to apply one's mind to one's studies

►**s'appliquer** VPR **1** *(se poser)* **s'a. sur** *(sujet: objet)* to be laid *or* to fit over; *(sujet: enduit)* to go over, to be applied on; **le pansement s'applique directement sur la lésion** the dressing is applied directly to the wound itself; **s'applique sur toutes sortes de surfaces** *(produit)* may be applied on many different surfaces

2 *(être utilisé)* to apply; **le terme s'applique uniquement aux plantes** the term only applies to plants; **à qui s'applique cette remarque?** who is that remark intended for?; **cela ne s'applique pas dans notre cas** it doesn't apply in *or* it's not applicable to our case

3 *(être attentif → élève, apprenti)* to take care (over one's work), to apply oneself (to one's work); **tu ne t'appliques pas assez!** you don't take enough care over your work!, you don't apply yourself enough!; **s'a. à ses devoirs** to apply oneself to one's homework

4 *(s'acharner)* **s'a. à faire qch** to try to do sth; **je me suis appliqué à faire ce qu'on attendait de moi** I took the trouble to do what was expected of me; **elle s'applique à me contredire** she is making a point of contradicting me

appliquette [aplikɛt] NF *Ordinat* applet

appoggiature, appogiature [apɔʒjatyr] NF *Mus* appoggiatura

appoint [apwɛ̃] NM **1** *(argent)* **faire l'a.** to give the exact money *or* change; **prière de faire l'a.** *(sur panneau)* exact money only, please, no change given **2** *(revenu supplémentaire)* extra *or* additional income; **ce travail à mi-temps lui fait un petit a.** this part-time job brings him/her a little extra income **3** *Littéraire (aide)* assistance, contribution; **apporter son a. à qch** to contribute to sth

◻ **d'appoint** ADJ extra; **radiateur d'a.** extra radiator; **salaire d'a.** extra income

appointage [apwɛ̃taʒ] NM *Tech* shaping into a point

appointé [apwɛ̃te] NM *Suisse Mil Br* ≃ lance corporal, *Am* ≃ private 1st class

appointements [apwɛ̃tmɑ̃] NMPL salary; **toucher ses a.** to draw one's salary

appointer [3] [apwɛ̃te] VT **1** *(rémunérer)* to pay a salary to; **être appointé à la semaine** to be paid weekly *or* by the week **2** *Tech* to sharpen

appondre [75] [apɔ̃dr] VT *Suisse* to join (together)

apponse [apɔ̃s] NF *Suisse Fam* **1** *(point de rencontre)* join■ **2** *(d'une table)* flap■ **3** *(d'un bâtiment)* annexe■

appontage [apɔ̃taʒ] NM *Aviat* landing *(on an aircraft carrier)*

appontement [apɔ̃tmɑ̃] NM *Naut* wharf, landing stage

apponter [3] [apɔ̃te] VI *Aviat* to land *(on an aircraft carrier)*

apponteur [apɔ̃tœr] NM *Aviat* landing officer

apport [apɔr] NM **1** *(fait d'apporter)* contribution; **l'a. culturel des immigrés** the cultural contribution of immigrants; **a. journalier recommandé** recommended daily intake; **l'a. journalier en fer et en calcium** *(fourni)* the daily supply of iron and calcium; *(reçu)* the daily intake of iron and calcium

2 *Fin (fait d'apporter)* contribution; *Écon* inflow, influx; *(dans une entreprise)* initial share; **cette région bénéficie de l'a. (en devises) du tourisme** this area benefits from the financial contribution made *or* the money brought in by tourism; **sans a. extérieur nous étions perdus** without outside financial help we'd have been ruined; **un a. d'argent frais** an injection of new money; **a. en capital** capital contribution; **apports en communauté** = goods contributed by spouses to the joint estate; **a. en espèces** cash contribution; **a. de gestion** management buy-in; **apports en numéraire/en nature** cash contribution/contribution in kind; **apports en société** = contribution made by each partner to the start-up of a company

apporter [3] [apɔrte] VT **1** *(objet)* to bring; **apporte-le ici** bring it over here; **apporte-le à papa dans la cuisine** take it to Dad in the kitchen; **je t'ai apporté un cadeau** I've brought you a present *or* a present for you; **apportez vos livres avec vous** bring your books along, bring your books with you; **on lui apporte ses repas au lit** he/she has his/her meals brought to him/her in bed; **Marie, apportez une chaise** Marie, bring *or* fetch a chair; **apporte le plateau que j'ai laissé dehors** bring in the tray that I left outside; **faut-il a. à boire?** should we bring a bottle?; **les marins qui ont apporté le virus en Europe** the sailors who brought *or* carried the virus (with them) to Europe; *Fig* **a. sa pierre à l'édifice** to make one's contribution

2 *(fournir → message, nouvelle)* to give; *(→ preuve)* to give, to provide, to supply; *(→ résultat)* to produce; *(→ capitaux)* to bring in, to contribute; *(→ soulagement, satisfaction)* to bring; *(→ modification)* to introduce; **a. de l'attention** *ou* **du soin à qch/à faire qch** to exercise care in sth/doing sth; **elle apporte à ce projet l'enthousiasme de la jeunesse** she brings the enthusiasm of youth to the project; **il apporte à 'Don Juan' un éclairage particulier** he brings an individual interpretation to 'Don Juan'; **vous avez des qualités à a. à notre société** you have skills to bring to our company; **a. de l'aide à qn** to help sb; **il apporte un peu de soleil dans notre vie** he brings a little sunshine into our lives; **cette expérience lui a beaucoup apporté** the experience has been very beneficial for him/her; **ce travail ne m'apporte pas grand-chose** I don't get very much out of this work; **qu'est-ce que ça peut t'a.?** what good can that do you?

apporteur [apɔrtœr] NM **1** *(gén)* bearer **2** *Fin (de capitaux)* contributor; **a. d'affaires** business provider

apposer [3] [apoze] VT **1** *(ajouter → cachet, signature)* to affix, to append; *Jur (insérer → clause)* to insert **2** *(poser → affiche, plaque)* to put up; *Jur* **a. les scellés sur une porte** to affix the seals on a door

apposition [apozisjɔ̃] NF **1** *(ajout)* affixing, appending **2** *(pose)* putting up; *Jur (des scellés)* affixing **3** *Gram* apposition; **un substantif en a.** a noun in apposition

appréciabilité [apresjabilite] NF *Littéraire* appreciability

appréciable [apresjabl] ADJ **1** *(perceptible → changement)* appreciable, noticeable; **de manière a.** appreciably **2** *(considérable → somme, effort)* appreciable **3** *(précieux)* **il a des qualités appréciables** he has some good qualities; **c'est a. de pouvoir se lever une heure plus tard** it's nice to be able to get up an hour later

appréciateur, -trice [apresjatœr, -tris] NM,F appreciator (**de** of); *Com* appraiser, valuer; **un a. du talent** a good judge of talent

appréciatif, -ive [apresjatif, -iv] ADJ **1** *(estimatif)* evaluative; **état a. du mobilier** evaluation *or* estimate of the value of the furniture **2** *(admiratif)* appreciative

appréciation [apresjasjɔ̃] NF **1** *(estimation → d'un poids, d'une valeur)* estimation, assessment; *(→ d'une situation)* assessment, appreciation, grasp; **je laisse cela à votre a.** I leave it to your judgement; **le pourboire est laissé à votre a.** *(sur carte)* gratuities to be given at your discretion; **son a. du problème laisse à désirer** his/her grasp of the problem isn't all it should be; *Fin* **a. des investissements** investment appraisal; **a. des risques** risk assessment

2 *(observation)* remark, comment; *Scol* **il a obtenu d'excellentes appréciations** he got a very good report from his teachers

3 *(augmentation → d'une devise)* appreciation; **a. monétaire** currency appreciation

appréciative [apresjativ] *voir* **appréciatif**

appréciatrice [apresjatris] *voir* **appréciateur**

apprécier [9] [apresje] VT **1** *(évaluer → poids, valeur)* to estimate, to assess; *(→ distance)* to estimate, to judge; **je ne crois pas que tu m'apprécies/que tu apprécies mon travail à sa juste valeur** I don't think you appreciate just how good I am/my work is; **il est impossible d'a. l'étendue des dégâts** it's impossible to estimate *or* assess the extent of the damage

2 *(discerner → ironie, subtilités)* to appreciate; **a. l'importance de qch** to appreciate the significance of sth

3 *(aimer)* to appreciate; **a. qn pour qch** to appreciate sb for sth, to like sb because of sth; **on l'apprécie pour son humour** he's/she's appreciated for his/her sense of humour; **j'ai beaucoup apprécié cette soirée** I liked *or* enjoyed the evening very much; **un vin très apprécié des connaisseurs** a wine much appreciated by connoisseurs; **vous apprécierez son goût relevé** you'll like its spicy taste; **je n'apprécie pas du tout ce genre de blagues** I don't care for *or* like that sort of joke at all; *Fam* **le sel dans son café, il n'a pas apprécié!** he was not amused when he found his coffee had salt in it!; **il a moyennement apprécié** he was not amused; *Fam* **les premières chaleurs à la sortie de l'hiver, on apprécie!** the first spell of mild weather after the winter is really welcome!

►**s'apprécier** VPR **1** *Fin (monnaie)* to appreciate (in value), to rise; **l'euro s'est apprécié par rapport au dollar** the euro has risen against the dollar

2 *(emploi réciproque)* to like each other

appréhender [3] [apreɑ̃de] VT **1** *(craindre → examen, réaction)* to feel apprehensive about; **j'appréhende mon opération** I am apprehensive *or* worried about my operation; **elle appréhendait de partir** she was apprehensive about leaving

2 *(comprendre)* to comprehend, to grasp; **une situation difficile à a. dans son ensemble** a situation which is difficult to grasp in its entirety

3 *Jur (arrêter)* to arrest, to apprehend

appréhensif, -ive [apreɑ̃sif, -iv] ADJ apprehensive

appréhension [apreɑ̃sjɔ̃] NF **1** *(crainte)* fear, apprehension; **avoir** *ou* **éprouver de l'a.** to feel apprehensive, to have misgivings; **l'a. de l'échec/d'une catastrophe** fear of failure/of a catastrophe; **avec a.** apprehensively; **je n'y pense pas sans une certaine a.** I'm a little apprehensive about it **2** *Phil (compréhension)* apprehension

appréhensive [apreɑ̃siv] *voir* **appréhensif**

apprenant, -e [aprœnɑ̃, -ɑ̃t] NM,F learner

apprendre [79] [aprɑ̃dr] VT **1** *(s'initier à)* to learn; **j'apprends le russe** I'm learning Russian; **ils ont décidé de lui faire a. l'anglais** they've decided that he/she should have English lessons; **a. qch de qn** to learn sth from sb, to be taught sth by sb; **a. qch par cœur** to learn sth (off) by heart; **a. à faire qch** to learn (how) to do sth; **a. à nager/à faire du vélo** to learn (how) to swim/to ride a bike; **a. à être patient** to learn patience, to learn to be patient; **a. à connaître qn/une ville** to get to know sb/a town

2 *(enseigner)* **a. qch à qn** to teach sb sth *or* sth to sb; **a. à qn à faire qch** to teach sb (how) to do sth; **elle m'a appris le français/à nager** she taught me French/(how) to swim; *Fig* **je t'apprendrai à fouiller dans mon sac!** I'll teach you to go through my bag!; **ça t'apprendra à faire l'imbécile** that'll teach you (not) to fool around; **il/ça va lui a. à vivre!** he'll/it'll teach him/her a thing or two!

3 *(donner connaissance de)* to tell; **a. qch à qn** to tell sb sth; **qui te l'a appris?** who told you?; **vous ne m'apprenez rien!** tell me something new!

4 *(être informé de → départ, mariage)* to learn *or* to hear of; *(→ nouvelle)* to hear; **j'ai appris sa mort à la radio** I heard of his/her death on the radio; **on apprend à l'instant qu'un prisonnier s'est échappé** we've just heard that a prisoner has escaped; **qu'est-ce que j'apprends, vous démissionnez?** what's this I hear about you resigning?; **apprenez** *ou* **vous apprendrez qu'ici on ne fait pas ce genre de choses** you'll have to learn that we don't do things like that here; *Fam* **tiens, tiens, on en apprend des choses!** well, well, who'd have thought such a thing?; *Hum* **on en apprend tous les jours!** you learn something new every day!

5 *Belg (former)* to train

USAGE ABSOLU **il apprend facilement/avec difficulté** learning comes/doesn't come easily to him; **a. lentement/vite** to be a slow/fast learner; **on apprend à tout âge** it's never too late to learn; **ça lui apprendra!** that'll teach him/her!; *Prov* **on n'apprend pas à un vieux singe à faire la grimace** don't teach your grandmother to suck eggs

►**s'apprendre** VPR to be learnt; **le style, ça ne s'apprend pas** style isn't something you can

learn; **ça ne s'apprend pas du jour au lendemain** you can't learn it overnight; **ça s'apprend vite** it's easy to learn, it can be learned quickly; **le chinois ne s'apprend pas facilement** it isn't easy to learn Chinese

apprenti, -e [aprɑ̃ti] NM,F apprentice; **a. maçon** builder's apprentice; **a. imprimeur** printer's devil; **être placée comme apprentie chez une couturière** to be apprenticed to a seamstress; **il a mis son fils a chez un boucher** he apprenticed his son to a butcher; *Fig* **jouer les apprentis sorciers** *ou* **à l'a. sorcier** to play at being God

'L'Apprenti sorcier' *Dukas* 'The Sorcerer's Apprentice'

apprentissage [aprɑ̃tisaʒ] NM 1 *(fait d'apprendre)* **l'a. des langues** language learning, learning languages; *Fig* **faire l'a. de qch** to learn one's first lessons in sth; **faire l'a. de la vie** to gain some experience of life 2 *(durée)* (period of) apprenticeship 3 *Mktg (expérience de consommation)* learning

❑ **d'apprentissage** ADJ *(centre, école)* training; *(contrat)* of apprenticeship

❑ **en apprentissage** ADV **être en a. chez qn** to be apprenticed to *or* to be serving one's apprenticeship with sb; **mettre qn en a. chez un artisan** to apprentice sb to a craftsman

apprêt [apre] NM 1 *(affectation)* affectation, affectedness; **un style sans a.** an unaffected style; **parler sans a.** to speak unaffectedly *or* without affectation 2 *Tech (préparation → du cuir, d'un tissu)* dressing; *(→ du papier)* dressing; *(→ d'un plafond, d'un mur)* sizing; *(produit → pour cuir, tissu)* dressing; *(→ pour papier)* finish; *(→ pour plafond, mur)* size

❑ **apprêts** NMPL *Littéraire (préparatifs)* preparations; **les apprêts du bal** preparations for the ball

apprêtage [apretaʒ] NM *Tech (d'un cuir, d'un tissu)* dressing, finishing; *(d'un papier)* finishing; *(d'un plafond, d'un mur)* sizing

apprêté, -e [aprete] ADJ affected, fussy

apprêter [4] [aprete] VT 1 *Tech (cuir, tissu)* to dress, to finish; *(papier)* to finish; *(plafond, mur)* to size 2 *Littéraire (préparer → repas)* to get ready, to prepare; *(habiller)* to get ready, to dress

▸ **s'apprêter** VPR 1 *Littéraire (emploi réfléchi)* to prepare *or* to dress oneself 2 **s'a. à faire qch** to be getting ready to do sth

apprêteur, -euse [apretœr, -øz] NM,F *Tech (d'un tissu, d'un papier)* finisher

appris, -e [apri, -iz] PP *voir* **apprendre**

apprivoisable [aprivwazabl] ADJ tameable, which can be tamed; **difficilement a.** difficult to tame

apprivoisé, -e [aprivwaze] ADJ tame

apprivoisement [aprivwazmɑ̃] NM taming

apprivoiser [3] [aprivwaze] VT *(animal)* to tame, to domesticate; *(enfant, peur)* to tame; **apprivoisez votre corps** get to know your body

▸ **s'apprivoiser** VPR 1 *(animal)* to become tame; *(personne)* to become more sociable 2 *Littéraire* **s'a. à** *(se familiariser avec)* to get used *or* accustomed to

approbateur, -trice [aprobatœr, -tris] ADJ *(regard, sourire)* approving; *(commentaire)* supportive; **faire un signe de tête a.** to give an approving nod, to nod (one's head) in approval

NM,F *Littéraire* approver, applauder

approbatif, -ive [aprobatif, -iv] ADJ approving

approbation [aprobasjɔ̃] NF 1 *(assentiment)* approval, approbation; **il sourit en signe de a.** he gave a smile of approval, he smiled approvingly; **recevoir/gagner l'a. de qn** to meet with/to win sb's approval; **recevoir l'a. générale** to meet with general approval; **donner son a. à un projet** to approve a plan

2 *(autorisation)* approval; **soumettre qch à l'a. de qn** to submit sth to sb for approval; **je ne peux rien faire sans son a.** I can't do anything without his/her approval

approbativement [aprobativmɑ̃] ADV approvingly

approbatrice [aprobatris] *voir* **approbateur**

approchable [aprɔʃabl] ADJ approachable, accessible; **une vedette difficilement a.** an inaccessible *or* unapproachable star

approchant, -e [aprɔʃɑ̃, -ɑ̃t] ADJ similar; **voici quelque chose d'a.** here's something quite similar; **rien d'a.** nothing like that; **il a dû le traiter d'escroc ou quelque chose d'a.** he must have called him a crook or something like that *or* something of the sort

ADV *Suisse* about, around; **gagner a. 500 euros, gagner 500 euros a.** to earn about 500 euros

approche [aprɔʃ] NF 1 *(venue)* approach; **l'a. des examens** the approaching exams; **il sentait l'a. de la mort** he felt that death was approaching *or* upon him

2 *(accès)* approachability; **il est d'a. facile/difficile** he is approachable/unapproachable; **sa fiction est plus facile d'a. que son théâtre** his/her novels are more accessible than his/her plays

3 *(manière d'aborder)* approach; **une a. écologique du problème** an ecological approach to the problem; **cette étude a nécessité un long travail d'a.** the study required a great deal of preliminary work; *Mktg* **a. directe** cold calling; *Mktg* **a. personnalisée** person-to-person approach

4 *Typ (espacement)* spacing; *(erreur)* spacing error; *(signe)* close-up mark

5 *Aviat* approach; **être en a. (finale)** to be on one's final approach

6 *Sport* approach (shot)

7 *Chasse* **chasser à l'a.** to stalk; **chasse à l'a.** stalking; **chasse au cerf à l'a.** deer-stalking

❑ **approches** NFPL **les approches de l'aéroport** the area surrounding the airport, the vicinity of the airport

❑ **à l'approche de** PRÉP 1 *(dans le temps)* **tous les ans, à l'a. de l'été** every year, as summer draws near; **à l'a. de l'épreuve, j'ai commencé à m'inquiéter** as the contest drew near, I started to worry; **à l'a. de la trentaine** as one nears *or* approaches (the age of) thirty

2 *(dans l'espace)* **à l'a. de son père, il s'est enfui** he ran away as his father approached

❑ **aux approches de** PRÉP 1 *(dans le temps)* **tous les ans, aux approches de l'été** every year, as summer draws near; **aux approches de l'épreuve, j'ai pris peur** as the test drew near, I panicked; **aux approches de la trentaine elle a voulu avoir des enfants** as she approached thirty she wanted to have children

2 *(dans l'espace)* **aux approches de la frontière, il y avait davantage de soldats** there were more soldiers as we approached *or* neared the border; **il y a plusieurs centres commerciaux aux approches de la ville** there are several shopping centres on the outskirts of the town

approché, -e [aprɔʃe] ADJ *(idée, calcul)* approximate

approcher [3] [aprɔʃe] VT 1 *(mettre plus près → lampe, chaise)* to move *or* to draw nearer, to move *or* to draw closer; **approche un peu ton tabouret** draw *or* bring your stool a bit nearer *or* closer; **approche la table du mur** move *or* draw the table closer to the wall; **a. une tasse de ses lèvres** to lift *or* to raise a cup to one's lips; **elle approcha ses lèvres des miennes** she put her lips close to mine; **n'approche pas ta main de la flamme** don't put your hand near the flame

2 *(aller près de)* to go near, to approach; *(venir près de)* to come near, to approach; **ne l'approchez/m'approchez surtout pas!** please don't go near him/her/come near me!

3 *(côtoyer → personnalité)* to approach; **il n'est pas facile de l'a.** he's/she's not very approachable; **il approche les grands de ce monde** he rubs shoulders with the people at the top

4 *(faire des démarches auprès de) (personne)* to approach; **il a été approché par diverses sociétés** he was approached by various companies

VI 1 *(dans l'espace)* to come *or* to get nearer, to approach; **toi, approche!** you, come over here!; **faire a. qn** *(d'un signe)* to beckon to sb; **on approche de Paris** we're getting near *or* we're nearing Paris; **comme nous approchions de notre destination** as we were nearing our

destination; **a. de la sainte table** *ou* **des sacrements** *Rel* to partake of the Sacrament; *Fig* to be close; **enfin nous approchons du but!** at last we're nearing our goal!; **a. de la perfection** to be *or* to come close to perfection; **tu approches de la vérité** you're getting close to the truth; **nous approchions alors des 200 km/heure** we were going at almost 200 km an hour

2 *(dans le temps → nuit, aube)* to draw near; *(→ événement, saison)* to approach, to draw near; **l'heure** *ou* **le moment approche** it will soon be time; **on approchait de l'hiver** winter was drawing near; **il approche de la fin** he's nearing his end; **quand on approche de la cinquantaine** when you're *Br* getting on for fifty *or Am* going on fifty

▸ **s'approcher** VPR 1 *(venir)* to come near, to approach; *(aller)* to go near, to approach; **approche-toi** come here *or* closer; **je me suis approché pour voir** I went closer to have a look; **elle le tira par la manche pour le faire s'a.** she took him by the sleeve and pulled him closer

2 **s'a. de qn** *(venir)* to come up to sb, to approach sb; *(aller)* to go up to sb, to approach sb; **s'a. de qch** *(venir)* to go near sth, to approach sth; *(aller)* to go up to sth, to approach sth; *(correspondre à)* to be *or* to come close to sth; **qu'elle ne s'approche pas trop du bord** see that she doesn't go too near the edge; **on s'approche de la côte** we're nearing *or* approaching the coast; **leurs thèses s'approchent beaucoup des nôtres** their ideas are very close to ours; **vos descriptions ne s'approchent pas du tout de la réalité** your descriptions bear no resemblance to the facts; **s'a. de la perfection** to be *or* to come close to perfection

approfondi, -e [aprɔfɔ̃di] ADJ thorough, detailed, extensive; **une connaissance approfondie de la langue** a thorough command *or* knowledge of the language; **traiter qch de façon approfondie** to go into sth thoroughly

approfondir [32] [aprɔfɔ̃dir] VT 1 *(creuser → puits)* to deepen, to dig deeper

2 *(détailler davantage → sujet, étude)* to go deeper *or* more thoroughly into; **il faut a. la question** the question needs to be examined in more detail; **il semblait réticent, je n'ai pas voulu a. la question** he seemed reluctant, so I avoided pressing the matter; **tu n'approfondis jamais (les choses)** you only ever skim the surface of things; **sans a.** superficially

3 *(parfaire → connaissances)* to improve, to deepen; **a. sa connaissance de qch** to improve one's knowledge of sth, to acquire a deeper knowledge of sth

approfondissement [aprɔfɔ̃dismɑ̃] NM 1 *(d'un puits)* increasing the depth of, deepening 2 *(des connaissances)* extending; **l'a. de l'enquête pourrait le compromettre** a more thorough investigation might compromise him; **l'a. de la question est réservé au deuxième volume** there will be a more thorough examination of the issue in volume two

appropriation [aprɔprijasjɔ̃] NF 1 *Jur (saisie)* appropriation; **a. de fonds** misappropriation of funds, embezzlement; **a. par violence** forcible seizure 2 *(adéquation)* appropriateness, suitability 3 *Belg (nettoyage)* cleaning

approprié, -e [aprɔprije] ADJ *(solution, technique)* appropriate, suitable, *Sout* apposite; *(tenue)* proper, right; **peu a.** inappropriate; **de manière peu appropriée** inappropriately; **mots appropriés s'il en fut!** how appropriate those words were!; **un discours a. aux circonstances** a speech appropriate *or* suited to the circumstances; **on ne peut pas entrer si on n'a pas la tenue appropriée** they won't let you in if you're not wearing the proper *or* right clothes

approprier [10] [aprɔprije] VT 1 *(adapter)* to adapt, to suit; **il a su a. son style à un public d'adolescents** he's managed to adapt his style to a teenage audience 2 *Belg (nettoyer)* to clean

▸ **s'approprier** VPR 1 *(biens, invention)* to appropriate; *(pouvoir)* to seize 2 **s'a. à** *(s'adapter à)* to be suitable *or* appropriate for, to be in keeping with

approuvable [apruvabl] ADJ approvable, commendable

approuver [3] [apruve] VT 1 *(être d'accord avec*

→ *méthode, conduite)* to approve of; **je n'approuve pas la manière dont tu les traites** I don't approve *or* I disapprove of the way you treat them; **elle m'a approuvé de ne pas avoir cédé** she approved of my not giving in; **nous vous approuvons dans votre choix** we approve of your choice; **je vous approuve entièrement** I think you're entirely right; **elle approuve tout ce qu'il dit/fait** she agrees with everything he says/does; **la proposition a été approuvée par tout le monde** the proposition met with *or* received general approval; **a. et contre-argumenter** to agree and counter

2 *(autoriser* → *alliance, fusion)* to approve, to agree to; (→ *médicament, traitement)* to approve; (→ *facture)* to pass; (→ *contrat)* to ratify; (→ *projet de loi)* to approve, to pass; **le transfert de fonds n'a pas encore été approuvé** the transfer of funds has not yet been approved *or* authorized

approvisionné, -e [aprɔvizjɔne] **ADJ bien a.** *(magasin, rayon)* well-stocked

approvisionnement [aprɔvizjɔnmɑ̃] **NM 1** *(action)* supplying (**en** with); *(d'un magasin)* stocking (**en** with); **assurer l'a. d'un haut-fourneau en coke** to feed a blast furnace with coke; **faire un a. de qch** to stock up with sth; **l'approvisionnement du pays en pétrole/en matières premières est compromis par l'embargo** the supply of oil/raw materials to the country has been jeopardized by the embargo

2 *(provisions)* supply, provision, stock; **a. en eau/gaz** water/gas supply; **approvisionnements de réserve** reserve stocks

3 *Com* procurement

approvisionner [3] [aprɔvizjɔne] **VT 1** *(village, armée)* to supply; *(magasin)* to supply; **être approvisionné en électricité** to be supplied with electricity; **a. qn en qch** to supply sb with sth; **a. l'armée en équipement** to supply the army with equipment, to supply equipment to the army

2 *(arme)* to load

3 *Banque (compte)* to pay money *or* funds into; **son compte n'a pas été approvisionné depuis six mois** no funds have been paid into his/her account for six months

▸**s'approvisionner VPR** *(personne)* to shop; *(commerce, entreprise)* to stock up; **où est-ce que vous vous approvisionnez?** *(individu)* where do you do your shopping?; *(commerce, entreprise)* where do you get your supplies from?; **s'a. en qch** *(stocker)* to stock up on sth, to get in supplies of sth

approvisionneur, -euse [aprɔvizjɔnœr, -øz] **NM,F** supplier

approximatif, -ive [aprɔksimatif, -iv] **ADJ** *(coût, évaluation)* approximate, rough; *(traduction)* rough; *(réponse)* vague; **nous nous sommes exprimés dans un anglais a.** we expressed ourselves in broken English; **ce chiffre est très a.** this figure is only a rough estimate

approximation [aprɔksimasjɔ̃] **NF 1** *(estimation)* approximation; **ce chiffre n'est qu'une a.** this is only an approximate figure *or* a rough estimate

2 *Péj (à-peu-près)* generality, (vague) approximation; **à l'examen, le jury ne se contentera pas d'approximations** at the exam, the examiners won't be satisfied with generalities

3 *Math* approximation; **calcul par approximations successives** calculus by continual approach

approximative [aprɔksimativ] *voir* **approximatif**

approximativement [aprɔksimativmɑ̃] **ADV** *(environ)* approximately, roughly; *(vaguement)* vaguely

appt *(abrév écrite* **appartement**) apt.

appui [apɥi] **NM 1** *Constr (d'un balcon, d'un garde-fou)* support; **à hauteur d'a.** elbow high; **a. de fenêtre** windowsill, window ledge

2 *(dans les positions du corps)* **prendre a. sur qch** to lean (heavily) on sth; **prenant a. sur les épaules de son partenaire** leaning *or* resting on his/her partner's shoulders; **prendre a. sur le pied gauche** *(pour sauter)* to take off from the left foot; **trouver un a.** *(pied)* to gain *or* to get a hold; *(alpiniste)* to get a purchase

3 *(soutien)* support, backing; *Mil* support; **a. moral** moral support; **apporter son a. à une initiative** to back *or* to support an initiative; **avoir l'a. de qn** to have sb's support *or* backing; **ai-je votre a.?** do I have your support?; **avoir des appuis en haut lieu** to have friends in high places; **a. aérien/naval** air/naval support; **a. financier** (financial) backing; **la société ne bénéficie pas d'un a. financier suffisant** the company does not have sufficient financial backing

❑ **à l'appui ADV il a lu, à l'a., une lettre datée du 24 mai** in support of this *or* to back this up, he read out a letter dated 24 May; **preuves à l'a.** with supporting evidence; **accusation sans preuves/témoignages à l'a.** charge not supported by any evidence/testimony

❑ **à l'appui de PRÉP** in support of, supporting; **à l'a. de ses dires** in support of *or* to support what he/she was saying

❑ **d'appui ADJ 1** *Ling (consonne)* supporting; *(voyelle)* support *(avant n)*

2 **point d'a.** *(d'un levier)* fulcrum

appui-bras [apɥibra] *(pl* **appuis-bras**) **NM** armrest

appuie *etc voir* **appuyer**

appuie-bras [apɥibra] **NM INV** = **appui-bras**

appuie-tête [apɥitɛt] **NM INV** = **appui-tête**

appui-main [apɥimɛ̃] *(pl* **appuis-main**) **NM** *(d'un peintre)* maulstick

appui-tête [apɥitɛt] *(pl* **appuis-tête**) **NM** headrest

appuyé, -e [apɥije] **ADJ** *(allusion)* heavy, laboured; *(regard)* insistent

appuyer [14] [apɥije] **VT 1** *(faire reposer)* to lean, to rest; **a. son bras/sa main sur le dos d'une chaise** to rest one's arm/hand on the back of a chair; **le vélo était appuyé contre la grille** the bicycle was resting *or* leaning against the railings

2 *(faire peser)* to press; **appuie ta main sur le couvercle** press down on the lid

3 *(étayer)* to support; **mur appuyé sur des contreforts** wall supported by buttresses

4 *(donner son soutien à* → *candidat, réforme)* to back, to support; (→ *proposition)* to second; **la police, appuyée par l'armée** the police, backed up *or* supported by the army

5 *Fin (apporter un soutien financier)* to back, to support; **a. qn financièrement** to back sb (financially), to give sb financial backing

6 *(fonder)* to ground, to base; **a. son raisonnement sur des faits** to base one's argument on *or* to ground one's argument in facts

VI 1 *(exercer une pression)* to press, to push down; **il faut a. de toutes ses forces** you have to press as hard as you can; **a. sur qch** *(avec le doigt)* to press sth, to push sth; *(avec le pied)* to press down on sth; **appuyez délicatement sur l'endroit sensible** press gently on the sore spot; **a. sur son stylo** to press on one's pen; **a. sur la gâchette** to pull the trigger; *Fam* **appuie sur le 3ème étage** *(dans un ascenseur)* press *or* push the button for the third floor; **il faut a. dessus de toutes tes forces** you have to press down on it as hard as you can; **a. sur la chanterelle** to harp on

2 *(insister)* **a. sur** *(mot, urgence, argument, aspect)* to stress, to emphasize; *(note)* to sustain; **il a beaucoup appuyé sur l'aspect pratique du stage/sur les qualités nécessaires pour ce poste** he put great emphasis on the practical aspect of the course/on the qualities necessary for the job; **inutile d'a. là-dessus, on a compris** you don't need to keep going on about it, we understand

3 *Aut* **a. sur la** *ou* **à droite/gauche** to bear right/left; **a. sur la pédale de frein** to brake; **a. sur l'accélérateur** *(aller vite) Br* to put one's foot down, *Am* to step on the gas

4 *Équitation* **a. sur le mors** to hang on the bit

▸**s'appuyer VPR 1** *Fam* to have to put up with; **s'a. qn** to get stuck *or Br* landed *or* lumbered with sb; **je me suis appuyé cinq heures de voiture pour te voir** I had to drive for five hours just to see you■ ; **qui c'est qui va encore s'a. le ménage?** guess who's going to get stuck with the housework again?

2 **s'a. à** *(physiquement)* to lean *or* to rest on; **il entra, s'appuyant à son bras** he came in leaning on his/her arm

3 **s'a. contre** to lean against; **s'a. contre la rampe** to lean against the banister

4 **s'a. sur** *(se soutenir sur)* to lean on; *(s'en remettre à* → *ami)* to lean *or* to depend *or* to rely on; (→ *amitié, aide)* to count *or* to rely on; (→ *témoignage)* to rely on; *(se fonder sur)* to be based on; **le voilà, appuyé sur sa canne** there he is, leaning on his stick; **ce récit s'appuie sur une expérience vécue** this story is based on a real-life experience

apr. *(abrév écrite* **après**) after; **a. J.-C.** AD

apragmatique [apragmatik] **ADJ** *Psy* apragmatic

apragmatisme [apragmatizm] **NM** *Psy* apragmatism

apraxie [apraksi] **NF** *Méd* apraxia

apraxique [apraksik] *Méd* **ADJ** apraxic

NMF apraxia sufferer

âpre [apr] **ADJ 1** *(âcre* → *goût)* sour; (→ *vin)* rough **2** *(rude* → *voix, ton)* harsh, rough; (→ *hiver)* harsh; (→ *froid)* bitter, biting; (→ *reproche)* bitter, harsh; *(féroce* → *concurrence, lutte)* bitter, fierce; *Péj* **â. au gain** greedy, money-grabbing

aprème [aprɛm] **NM OU NF** *Fam* afternoon■ ; **à c't' a.!** see you this afternoon!■

âprement [aprəmɑ̃] **ADV** *(sévèrement)* bitterly, harshly; **on me l'a â. reproché** I was harshly *or* bitterly criticized for it; **se battre â.** to fight bitterly; **cette victoire fut â. disputée** it was a fiercely contested victory

après [aprɛ] **PRÉP 1** *(dans le temps)* after; **a. le départ de Paul** after Paul left; **a. (le) dîner** after dinner; **je prendrai un café a. le déjeuner** I'll have a coffee after lunch; **le but a été marqué a. deux minutes de jeu** the goal was scored two minutes into the game *or* after kick-off; **530 a. Jésus-Christ** 530 AD; **c'était peu a. 3 heures** it was shortly *or* soon after 3 o'clock; **c'était bien a. son départ** it was a long time *or* a good while after he/she left; **a. toutes ses promesses, voilà qu'elle change d'avis!** after all her promises, now she's changed her mind!; *Fam* **qu'est-ce qu'il fait froid aujourd'hui, a. le beau temps qu'on a eu hier!** it's so cold today, after the nice weather we had yesterday!; **a. cela, que prendrez-vous?** what would you like after that?; **tu le contredis en public, et a. ça tu t'étonnes qu'il s'énerve!** you contradict him in public (and) then you're surprised that he's annoyed!; **a. ça, il ne te reste plus qu'à aller t'excuser** the only thing you can do now is apologize; **a. quoi, nous verrons** then we'll see; **a. ce qu'il m'a fait, je ne lui parlerai plus jamais** after what he did to me, I'll never speak to him again; **a. avoir dîné, ils bavardèrent** after dining *or* after dinner they chatted; **a. avoir salué l'assistance, elle prit la parole** having bowed *or* after bowing, she spoke to the audience; **jour a. jour** day after day; **page a. page, le mystère s'épaissit** the mystery gets deeper with every page *or* by the page

2 *(dans l'espace)* after; **a. le pont, la route bifurque** after the bridge the road forks; **la gare est a. le parc** the station is past *or* after the park; **a. la fontaine, tournez à gauche** turn left after the fountain; *Fam* **son foulard est resté accroché a. les ronces** his/her scarf got caught on the brambles■

3 *(dans un rang, un ordre, une hiérarchie)* after; **a. les livres, il aime la musique** after books, music is his second love; **a. vous, je vous en prie** after you; **vous êtes a. moi** *(dans une file d'attente)* you're after me; **il était juste a. moi dans la file** he was just behind me in the queue; **quelle lettre vient a. w?** which letter comes after w?; **il fait passer ma carrière a. la sienne** my career comes after his *or* takes second place to his, according to him; **le travail passe a. la santé** your health is more important than your work

4 *(indiquant un mouvement de poursuite, l'attachement, l'hostilité)* **courir a. qn** to run after sb; **le chien aboie a. les passants** the dog barks at the passers-by; **crier a. qn** to shout at sb; **il est furieux a. toi** he's furious with you; **s'énerver a. qch** to get angry with sth; **il est constamment a. moi** *(me surveille)* he's always breathing down my neck; *(me harcèle)* he's always nagging *or* going on at me; **ils sont a. une invitation, c'est évident** it's obvious they're angling for *or* they're after an invitation; **être a. une bonne affaire** to be onto a bargain; **demander a. qn** to ask after sb

ADV 1 *(dans le temps)* **un mois a.** a month later; **aussitôt a.** straight *or* immediately after *or* afterwards; **bien a.** a long *or* good while after, much later; **longtemps a.** a long time after *or* afterwards; **peu a.** shortly after *or* afterwards; **garde tes forces pour a.** conserve your strength for afterwards *or* later; **nous sommes allés au cinéma et a. au restaurant** we went to the movies *or Br* cinema and then to a restaurant; **a. on ira dire que je suis avare!** and then people will say I'm mean!; **a., tu ne viendras pas te plaindre!** don't come moaning to me afterwards!; **et a.?** *(pour demander la suite)* and then what?; *(marquant l'indifférence)* so what?; **et a.? qu'a-t-il fait?** and then what did he do?; *Fam* **et a.? qu'est-ce que ça peut faire?** so what? who cares?; **il menace de démissionner? et a.?** so he's threatening to resign, so what?

2 *(dans l'espace)* after; **vous tournez au feu, c'est tout de suite a.** you turn at the lights, and it's just after that

3 *(dans un rang, un ordre, une hiérarchie)* next; **qui est a.?** *(dans une file d'attente)* who's next?; **et qu'est-ce qui vient a.?** and what's next?

❑ **après coup** ADV afterwards, later; **c'est a. coup que j'ai compris** it was only later *or* afterwards that I understood; **il n'a réagi qu'a. coup** it wasn't until afterwards *or* later that he reacted; **laissez les journalistes parler, nous démentirons a. coup** let the press talk, we'll deny it all afterwards *or* later; **n'essaie pas d'inventer une explication a. coup** don't try to invent an explanation after the event

❑ **après que** CONJ after; **a. qu'il eut terminé...** after he had finished...; **je te dirai ce que j'en pense a. que tu auras décidé** I'll tell you what I think after you've made a decision; **je me suis couché a. que tu aies téléphoné** I went to bed after you phoned

❑ **après tout** ADV **1** *(introduisant une justification)* after all; **a. tout, ça n'a pas beaucoup d'importance** after all, it's not particularly important

2 *(emploi expressif)* then; **il peut bien venir, a. tout, s'il veut** he can come, then, if he wants *or* likes; **débrouille-toi tout seul, a. tout!** sort it out yourself then!

❑ **d'après** PRÉP **1** *(introduisant un jugement)* according to; **d'a. moi** in my opinion; **d'a. eux** in their opinion, according to them; **alors, d'a. vous, qui va gagner?** so who do you think is going to win?; **d'a. les informations qui nous parviennent** from *or* according to the news we're getting; **d'a. ce que je sais** from what I know; **d'a. ce qu'elle dit** from what she says; **d'a. mon expérience** in my experience **2** *(introduisant un modèle, une citation)* **d'a. Tolstoï** *(adaptation)* adapted from Tolstoy; **peint d'a. nature** painted from life; **d'a. une idée originale de...** based on *or* from an original idea by... ADJ **1** *(dans le temps)* following, next; **le jour d'a., il était là** the following *or* next day, he was there; **l'instant d'a.** the next moment **2** *(dans l'espace)* next; **je descends à la station d'a.** I'm getting off at the next station; **la maison d'a. est la nôtre** the next house is ours; **la poste? c'est juste la rue d'a.** the post office? it's the next street along

❑ **par après** ADV *Belg (dans le passé)* afterwards, later; *(dans le futur)* later

après-coup [aprɛku] *(pl* **après-coups**) NM *Psy* aftereffect

après-demain [aprɛdmɛ̃] ADV the day after tomorrow; **a. matin/soir** the day after tomorrow in the morning/evening

après-dîner [aprɛdine] *(pl* **après-dîners**) NM evening; **discours d'a.** after-dinner speech

après-guerre [aprɛgɛr] *(pl* **après-guerres**) NM OU NF post-war era *or* period; **le théâtre d'a.** post-war drama; **l'a. froide** the post-Cold War period

après-midi [aprɛmidi] NM INV OU NF INV afternoon; **en début/fin d'a.** early/late in the afternoon; **à 2 heures de l'a.** at 2 (o'clock) in the afternoon, at 2 p.m.; **je le ferai dans l'a.** I'll do it this afternoon

après-rasage [aprɛrazaʒ] *(pl* **après-rasages**) ADJ INV aftershave *(avant n)*
NM aftershave (lotion)

après-shampoing, après-shampooing [aprɛʃɑ̃pwɛ̃] NM conditioner

après-ski [aprɛski] *(pl* **après-skis**) NM *(botte)* snow boot

après-soleil [aprɛsɔlɛj] *(pl* **après-soleils**) NM aftersun (cream)

après-vente [aprɛvɑ̃t] ADJ INV *Com* after-sales

âpreté [aprəte] NF **1** *(âcreté → d'un goût)* sourness; *(→ d'un vin)* roughness **2** *(dureté → d'une voix, d'un ton)* harshness, roughness; *(→ de l'hiver)* harshness; *(→ du froid)* bitterness; *(→ d'un reproche)* bitterness, harshness; **combattre avec â.** to struggle bitterly *or* grimly; **défendre avec â. son territoire** to fight for one's territory to the bitter end

a priori [apriɔri] ADJ INV *Phil* a priori
ADV in principle, on the face of it; **a., c'est une bonne idée** on the face of it *or* in principle it's a good idea; **a., je ne vois pas d'inconvénient** in principle I can't see any reason why not
NM INV *(préjugé)* preconception, preconceived idea; **avoir un a. favorable envers qn** to be biased *or* prejudiced in favour of sb; **avoir des a.** to be biased *or* prejudiced; **être sans a.** to be impartial

apriorique [apriɔrik] ADJ based on preconceptions, biased

apriorisme [apriɔrism] NM *Phil* apriorism

aprioriste [apriɔrist] ADJ based on preconceptions, biased
NMF = person with preconceived ideas

apriorité [apriɔritik] = **apriorique**

à-propos [apropo] NM INV aptness, relevance; **votre remarque manque d'à.** your remark is not relevant *or* to the point; **intervenir avec à.** to intervene opportunely *or* at the right time; **répondre avec à.** to give a suitable *or* an appropriate reply; **quelle que soit la situation, il réagit avec à.** whatever the situation, he always does *or* says the right thing; **faire preuve d'à.** to show presence of mind

APS [apɛɛs] *(abrév* **advanced photo system**) ADJ INV *(appareil photo)* APS
NM INV APS

apsara, apsaras [apsara] NF *Rel* apsara, upsara

apside [apsid] NF *Astron* apsis; **les apsides** the apsides

apte [apt] ADJ **a. à qch** *(par sa nature)* fit for *or* suited to sth; *(par ses qualifications)* qualified for sth; **a. (au service militaire)** fit (for military service); **a. à faire qch** *(par sa nature)* suited to doing sth; *(par ses qualifications)* qualified to do sth; **être a. à remplir une fonction** to be suited to a position; **est-elle a. à conduire un autobus?** is she qualified to drive a bus?

aptère [aptɛr] ADJ **1** *Zool* apterous, wingless **2** *Archit* apteral

aptérygote [apteriɡɔt] *Entom* NM apterygote
❑ **aptérygotes** NMPL Apterygota

aptéryx [apteriks] NM *Orn* apteryx, kiwi

aptitude [aptityd] NF *(capacité)* ability, aptitude; **a. à assimiler les langues** ability to learn *or* aptitude for learning foreign languages; **il n'a aucune a. dans ce domaine** he has *or* shows no aptitude in that direction; **avoir une a. au bonheur/à la patience** to have a capacity for happiness/for patience
❑ **aptitudes** NFPL **aptitudes (intellectuelles)** abilities; **avoir/montrer des aptitudes en langues** to have/to show a gift for languages

Apulée [apyle] NPR *Littérature* Apuleius

Apulie [apyli] NF *Géog* **l'A.** Apulia

apurement [apyrmɑ̃] NM *Compta* **1** *(des comptes)* auditing **2** *(d'une dette, du passif)* discharge

apurer [3] [apyre] VT *Compta* **1** *(comptes)* to audit **2** *(dette, passif)* to discharge

apyre [apir] ADJ *Tech* refractory

apyrétique [apiretik] ADJ *Méd* apyretic

apyrexie [apirɛksi] NF *Méd* apyrexia

apyrogène [apirɔʒɛn] ADJ *Méd* apyrogenic

aquacole [akwakɔl] ADJ aquacultural, aquicultural; **établissement a.** fish farm

aquaculteur, -trice [akwacyltœr, -tris] NM,F aquaculturalist, aquiculturalist

aquaculture [akwakyltyr] NF aquaculture, aquiculture

aquafortiste [akwafɔrtist] NMF *Typ* etcher

Aquagym® [akwaʒim] NF *Sport* aquarobics *(singulier)*

aquamanile [akwamanil] NM *Hist* aquamanile

aquanaute [akwanot] NMF aquanaut

aquaplanage [akwaplanaʒ] NM *Aut* aquaplaning

aquaplane [akwaplan] NM *Sport* **1** *(activité)* aquaplaning **2** *(planche)* aquaplane

aquaplaning [akwaplaniŋ] = **aquaplanage**

aquarelle [akwarɛl] NF *Beaux-Arts (tableau)* watercolour; **peindre à l'a.** to paint in watercolours

aquarellé, -e [akwarɛle] ADJ *Beaux-Arts* touched up in watercolours

aquareller [26] [akwarɛle] VT to touch up in watercolours

aquarelliste [akwarelist] NMF *Beaux-Arts* watercolourist

aquariophile [akwarjɔfil] NMF aquarist

aquariophilie [akwariɔfili] NF = the breeding of fish for aquaria

aquarium [akwarjɔm] NM **1** *(décoratif)* fish tank, aquarium **2** *(au zoo)* aquarium; **a. d'eau de mer** oceanarium

aquatinte [akwatɛ̃t] NF *Beaux-Arts* aquatint

aquatintiste [akwatɛ̃tist] NMF *Beaux-Arts* aquatinter

aquatique [akwatik] ADJ aquatic, water *(avant n)*

aquatubulaire [akwatybylɛr] ADJ *Tech* **chaudière a.** water-tube boiler

aquavit [akwavit] NM *(alcool)* aquavit

aquazole® [akwazɔl] NM Aquazole®

aqueduc [akdyk] NM **1** *(conduit)* aqueduct **2** *Anat* duct

aqueux, -euse [akø, -øz] ADJ **1** *Anat & Chim* aqueous **2** *(plein d'eau)* watery

à quia [akɥija] ADV *Littéraire Vieilli* **être à.** to be dumbfounded *or* nonplussed; **réduire qn à.** to leave sb dumbfounded *or* nonplussed

aquicole [akɥikɔl] = **aquacole**

aquiculteur, -trice [akɥikyltœr, -tris] = **aquaculteur**

aquiculture [akɥikyltyr] = **aquaculture**

aquifère [akɥifɛr] *Géol* ADJ water-bearing, *Spéc* aquiferous
NM aquifer

aquilin [akilɛ̃] ADJ M *(nez)* aquiline

aquilon [akilɔ̃] NM *Littéraire* north wind

aquitain, -e [akitɛ̃, -ɛn] ADJ of/from Aquitaine, Aquitaine *(avant n)*
❑ **Aquitain, -e** NM,F = inhabitant of or person from Aquitaine
❑ **Aquitaine** NF **l'Aquitaine** Aquitaine

aquitanien, -enne [akitanjɛ̃, -ɛn] *Géol* ADJ Aquitanian
NM Aquitanian

aquosité [akozite] NF aquosity, aqueousness

AR¹ [aɛr] NM *(abrév* **accusé de réception**) acknowledgement (of receipt); **envoyer qch en recommandé avec AR** to send sth by *Br* recorded delivery *or Am* certified mail

AR² **1** *(abrév écrite* **arrière**) back **2** *(abrév écrite* **aller-retour**) R

ara [ara] NM *Orn* macaw

arabe [arab] ADJ *(cheval)* Arab, Arabian; *(pays)* Arab, Arabic; *(langue, littérature)* Arabic; *(civilisation)* Arab; **chiffres arabes** Arabic numerals, Arabics
NM *(langue)* Arabic; **a. dialectal/littéral** vernacular/written Arabic
❑ **Arabe** NMF Arab

Culture

ARABE

Note that in a French context this word usually refers to people from the former colonies of North Africa, who make up the largest ethnic minority in France.

arabesque [arabɛsk] NF arabesque

arabica [arabika] NM *Bot* arabica

Arabie [arabi] NF **l'A.** Arabia; **l'A. Saoudite** Saudi Arabia; **vivre en A. Saoudite** to live in Saudi Arabia; **aller en A. Saoudite** to go to Saudi Arabia

arabique [arabik] ADJ Arabic

arabisant, -e [arabizɑ̃, -ɑ̃t] ADJ Arabic
NM,F Arabist, Arabic scholar

arabisation [arabizasjɔ̃] NF Arabization

arabiser [3] [arabize] VT to Arabize, to Arabicize

arabisme [arabism] NM Arabism

arabité [arabite] NF Arab identity

arable [arabl] ADJ *Agr* arable

arabo-islamique [araboislamik] *(pl* **arabo-islamiques**) ADJ Arab-Islamic

arabophone [arabɔfɔn] ADJ Arabic-speaking
NMF Arabic speaker

arac [arak] = **arak**

aracée [arase] *Bot* NF aroid

□ **aracées** NFPL Araceae

arachide [araʃid] NF *Bot* peanut, *Spéc* groundnut

arachnéen, -enne [arakneɛ̃, -ɛn] ADJ **1** *Littéraire (dentelle)* gossamer *(avant n)*, gossamery **2** *Zool* arachnidan

arachnide [araknid] *Zool* NM arachnid

□ **arachnides** NMPL Arachnida

arachnoïde [araknɔid] NF *Anat* arachnoid

arachnoïdien, -enne [araknɔidjɛ̃, -ɛn] ADJ *Anat* arachnoid

arachnoïdite [araknɔidit] NF *Méd* arachnoiditis

arack [arak] = **arak**

Aragon [aragɔ̃] NM **l'A.** Aragon

aragonais, -e [aragɔnɛ, -ɛz] ADJ Aragonese

□ **Aragonais, -e** NM,F Aragonese; **les A.** the Aragonese

aragonite [aragɔnit] NF *Minér* aragonite

araignée [areɲe] NF **1** *Zool* spider; **a. d'eau** water spider; **a. de mer** spider crab, sea spider; **a. rouge** red spider; **a. à toile en entonnoir** funnel-web spider; *Fam Hum* **avoir une a. au plafond** to have bats in the belfry; *Prov* **a. du matin, chagrin, a. du soir, espoir** = seeing a spider in the morning brings bad luck, seeing one in the evening brings good luck

2 *Pêche* gill net

3 *Ordinat* crawler

araignée-crabe [areɲekrab] *(pl* **araignées-crabes**) NF *Zool* crab spider

araignée-loup [areɲelu] *(pl* **araignées-loups**) NF *Zool* wolf spider

araire [arɛr] NM *Agr* swing-plough

arak [arak] NM *(alcool)* arak, arrack

Aral [aral] NF **la mer d'A.** the Aral Sea

aralia [aralja] NM *Bot* Aralia

araliacée [araljase] *Bot* NF araliaceous plant

□ **araliacées** NFPL Araliaceae

araméen, -enne [arameɛ̃, -ɛn] ADJ Aramaic, Aramean, Aramaean

NM *(langue)* Aramaic

□ **Araméen, -enne** NM,F Aramean, Aramaean

aramide [aramid] ADJ *Tex* aramid

aramon [aramɔ̃] NM *(cépage)* aramon

aranéide [araneid] *Zool* NM araneid

□ **aranéides** NMPL Araneida

arapaïma [arapaima] NM *Ich* arapaima

Ararat [ararat] NM **le mont A.** Mount Ararat

arasement [arazmɑ̃] NM **1** *Constr (égalisation → d'un mur)* levelling; *(→ d'une planche)* planing down; *(assise)* levelling course **2** *Géol* erosion

araser [3] [araze] VT **1** *Constr (égaliser → mur)* to level, to make level *or* flush; *(→ planche)* to plane down **2** *Géol* to erode

aratoire [aratwar] ADJ *Agr* ploughing

araucaria [arɔkarja] NM *Bot* araucaria; **a. du Chili** monkey puzzle tree, Chilean pine

arawak [arawak] NM *Ling* Arawakan

arbalète [arbalɛt] NF crossbow

arbalétrier [arbaletrije] NM **1** *(soldat)* crossbowman **2** *Ich* triggerfish **3** *Constr* rafter

arbalétrière [arbaletriɛr] NF *Archit* arrowslit, crossbow slit (window)

arbitrable [arbitrabl] ADJ arbitrable

arbitrage [arbitraʒ] NM **1** *Jur* arbitration; **a. international** international arbitration; **recourir à l'a.** to go to arbitration; **soumettre un différend à un a.** to refer a dispute to arbitration; **trancher par a.** to settle by arbitration

2 *Sport (gén)* refereeing; *(au volley-ball, au tennis, au cricket)* umpiring

3 *Bourse* arbitrage; **a. à la baisse** bear closing; **a. de change** arbitration of exchange; **a. comptant-terme** cash and carry arbitrage; **a. sur indice** index arbitrage; **a. risque** risk arbitrage

arbitragiste [arbitraʒist] NM *Bourse* arbitrageur, arbitrager

arbitraire [arbitrɛr] ADJ **1** *(choix, décision)* arbitrary **2** *(gouvernement, pouvoir, action)* arbitrary, despotic

NM arbitrariness, arbitrary nature

arbitrairement [arbitrɛrmɑ̃] ADV arbitrarily

arbitral, -e, -aux, -ales [arbitral, -o] ADJ **1** *Jur* arbitral; **tribunal a.** tribunal, court of arbitration **2** *Sport* **décision arbitrale** *(gén)* referee's decision; *(au volley-ball, au tennis, au cricket)* umpire's decision

arbitralement [arbitralmɑ̃] ADV *Jur & Sport* by arbitration

arbitre [arbitr] NM

> Note that it is no longer considered a mistake to feminize this word and to say **une arbitre** in the sport sense. Nevertheless, some French speakers still regard this form as unacceptable, especially in France. See also the entry **féminisation**.

1 *Jur* arbiter, arbitrator; **exercer un rôle d'a.** to act as arbitrator, to arbitrate; *Fig* **elle va devenir l'a. de la situation** she will hold the key to the situation; **a. rapporteur** referee *(in commercial suit)*; **l'a. de l'élégance** the arbiter of style

2 *Sport (gén)* referee; *(au volley-ball, au tennis, au cricket)* umpire

3 *Phil* **libre a.** free will

4 *Fin* **a. financier** financial ombudsman

arbitrer [3] [arbitre] VT **1** *(différend)* to arbitrate, to settle by arbitration; **il ne reste plus qu'à faire a. votre différend par le directeur** the only option left is to ask the director to settle your dispute **2** *Sport (gén)* to referee; *(au volley-ball, au tennis, au cricket)* to umpire **3** *Bourse (valeurs)* to carry out an arbitrage operation on

arboré, -e [arbɔre] ADJ *École* planted with trees, wooded, *Spéc* arboreous

arborer [3] [arbɔre] VT **1** *(porter → veste, insigne)* to sport, to wear; *(→ drapeau)* to bear, to display **2** *(afficher → sourire, air)* to wear; *(→ idées)* to parade; *(→ manchette, titre)* to carry

arborescence [arbɔresɑ̃s] NF **1** *Bot* arborescence **2** *Ordinat (structure)* tree diagram, directory structure; *(chemin)* directory path

arborescent, -e [arbɔresɑ̃, -ɑ̃t] ADJ **1** *Bot* arborescent **2** *Ordinat* **structure arborescente** tree diagram, directory structure

arboretum [arbɔretɔm] NM *École* arboretum

arboricole [arbɔrikɔl] ADJ **1** *Hort* arboricultural **2** *Zool* tree-dwelling, *Spéc* arboreal

arboriculteur, -trice [arbɔrikyltœr, -tris] NM,F *Hort* tree grower, *Spéc* arboriculturist

arboriculture [arbɔrikyltyr] NF *Hort* arboriculture; **a. fruitière** cultivation of fruit trees

arborisation [arbɔrizasjɔ̃] NF arborization

arborisé, -e [arbɔrize] ADJ **1** *(qui présente des arborisations)* dendritic **2** *Suisse (boisé)* planted with trees

arbouse [arbuz] NF *Bot* arbutus berry

arbousier [arbuzje] NM *Bot* strawberry tree, *Spéc* arbutus

arbovirose [arbovirɔz] NF *Méd* arbovirus infection

arbovirus [arbovirys] NM *Méd* arbovirus

arbre [arbr] NM **1** *Bot* tree; **jeune a.** sapling; *Prov* **entre l'a. et l'écorce il ne faut pas mettre le doigt** = one shouldn't get involved in other people's family quarrels; **a. d'agrément** *ou* **d'ornement** ornamental tree; **a. d'amour** Judas tree; **a. à caoutchouc** rubber tree; *Bible* **l'a. de la Croix** the Rood; **a. à feuille(s) caduque(s)** deciduous tree; **a. feuillu** hardwood (tree); **a. aux fraises** strawberry tree; **a. fruitier** fruit tree; *Rel & Beaux-Arts* **a. de Jessé** tree of Jesse; **a. de Josué** Joshua tree; **a. de Judée** Judas tree, (Eastern) redbud; *Hist* **a. de la liberté** tree of liberty; **a. de Moïse** pyracantha; **a. nain** dwarf tree; **a. de Noël** Christmas tree; **a. à pain** breadfruit tree; **a. à perruque** wig tree, Venetian sumach; **a. résineux** softwood (tree); *Bible* **l'a. de la science du bien et du mal** the tree of knowledge; **a. vert** evergreen (tree); **a. de vie** *Bot* thuya; *Anat* arbor vitae; *Bible* tree of life; **a. du voyageur** traveller's tree, ravenala

2 *Fig* **faire l'a. fourchu** to do a headstand *(with one's legs apart)*; **a. généalogique** family tree; **faire son a. généalogique** to draw up one's family tree

3 *Tech* shaft; **a. d'accouplement** coupling shaft; *Aut* **a. arrière** back axle shaft; **a. à cames** camshaft; **a. à cames en tête** overhead camshaft; *Aut* **a. à cardan** cardan shaft; *Aut* **a. de commande** driveshaft; *Naut* **a. de couche** engine shaft; **a. coudé** crankshaft; **a. creux** hollow shaft; *Aut* **a. de distribution** distributor shaft, camshaft; **a. d'entraînement** driveshaft; **a. d'entrée** input *or* primary shaft; *Aut* **a. d'essieu** axle shaft; **a. à excentrique** *ou* **d'excentrique** eccentric shaft; *Naut* **a. d'hélice, a. porte-hélice** propeller shaft; *Élec* **a. d'induit** armature shaft; **a. intermédiaire** intermediate shaft, layshaft, countershaft; **a. manivelle** crankshaft; **a. mené** driven shaft; **a. moteur** driving shaft; **a. de pompe** pump shaft; **a. primaire** primary *or* input shaft; **a. principal** main shaft; **a. de renvoi** jackshaft; *Aut* **a. de roue** axle shaft; **a. secondaire** secondary shaft, layshaft, countershaft; **a. de sortie** output shaft; **a. de transmission** driveshaft

4 *Anat* **a. respiratoire** respiratory system

5 *(diagramme)* tree; *Mktg* **a. de décision** decision tree

6 *(locutions)* **abattre** *ou* **couper l'a. pour avoir le fruit** to kill the goose that lays the golden eggs; **les arbres cachent la forêt** you can't see the *Br* wood *or Am* forest for the trees

arbre-de-Noël [arbrœdœnoɛl] *(pl* **arbres-de-Noël**) NM Christmas tree

arbrisseau, -x [arbriso] NM *Bot* shrub; **plantation** *ou* **parterre d'arbrisseaux** shrubbery

arbuste [arbyst] NM *Bot* shrub, bush; **plantation d'arbustes** shrubbery

arbustif, -ive [arbystif, -iv] ADJ *Bot* shrubby

ARC [ark] NF *(abrév* **Association de recherche sur le cancer**) = French national cancer research charity

NM *(abrév* **Aids-related complex**) ARC

arc [ark] NM **1** *(arme)* bow

2 *Géom* arc; **a. de cercle** arc of a circle; **être assis en a. de cercle** to be seated in a semicircle

3 *Anat* arch; **a. aortique** arch of the aorta

4 *Physiol* **a. réflexe** reflex arc

5 *Électron* **a. électrique** electric arc

6 *Archit* arch; **a. brisé** pointed arch; **a. en fer à cheval/en plein cintre** horseshoe/semicircular arch; **a. en ogive** ogee arch; **a. surbaissé/surhaussé** depressed/raised arch; **l'a. de triomphe du Carrousel** = triumphal arch in the Tuileries gardens in Paris; **a. de triomphe** triumphal arch; **l'a. de triomphe (de l'Étoile)** the Arc de Triomphe

□ **à arc** ADJ *(lampe, soudure)* arc *(avant n)*

arcade [arkad] NF **1** *Archit* archway; **des arcades** arches, an arcade; **une a. de verdure** a leafy vault **2** *Anat* arch; **a. dentaire** dental arch; **a. sourcilière** arch of the eyebrows; **il s'est ouvert l'a. sourcilière** he was cut above the eye **3** *Suisse (dans le canton de Genève) (boutique) Br* shop, *Am* store

Arcadie [arkadi] NF **l'A.** Arcadia

arcadien, -enne [arkadjɛ̃, -ɛn] ADJ Arcadian

□ **Arcadien, -enne** NM,F Arcadian

arcane [arkan] NM *(secret)* mystery, *Littéraire* arcanum; **les arcanes de la politique/de la science** the mysteries of politics/of science

□ **arcanes** NMPL *(cartes de tarot)* arcana

arcanne [arkan] NF *Tech* ruddle, red ochre

arcanson [arkɑ̃sɔ̃] NM colophony, rosin

Arcat-Sida [arkatsida] NM = association promoting Aids care and research

arcature [arkatyr] NF *Archit* arcature, blind arcade

arc-boutant [arkbutɑ̃] *(pl* **arcs-boutants**) NM *Archit* flying buttress

arc-boutement [arkbutmɑ̃] *(pl* **arcs-boutements**) NM *Archit* buttressing *(UNCOUNT)*

arc-bouter [3] [arkbute] VT *Archit (mur)* to buttress

▸ **s'arc-bouter** VPR to brace oneself; **s'arc-boutant des deux jambes** bracing himself/herself with both legs; **s'a. contre un mur** to brace one's back against a wall

arc-doubleau [arkdublo] *(pl* **arcs-doubleaux**) NM *Archit* transverse rib

arceau, -x [arso] NM **1** *Archit* arch (of vault) **2** *(de croquet)* hoop; *(d'une voiture)* roll bar **3** *Méd* cradle

arc-en-ciel [arkɑ̃sjɛl] *(pl* **arcs-en-ciel**) NM rainbow

ARCH-, ARCHI- [arʃ, arʃi] PRÉF

● The prefixes **arch-** and **archi-**, like *arch-* in English, have a non-colloquial use that denotes the HIGHEST RANK in a given hierarchy. Thus an **archevêque** (archbishop) has several *évêques* under his command, whereas an **archiduc** (archduke) was in fact a prince in the Austrian imperial dynasty.

● The colloquial use of **archi-** is a common and productive one, whereby virtually any adjective can be prefixed to indicate the HIGHEST DEGREE of a quality or a fault. This idea is often conveyed in the English translation by the use of an adverb like *very, totally, completely* etc:
archiconnu very well known; **archidrôle** hilarious; **archifaux** totally wrong; **archinul** completely useless

archaïque [arkaik] ADJ **1** (*vieux*) archaic, outmoded, antiquated **2** *Beaux-Arts & Ling* archaic
archaïsant, -e [arkaizɑ̃, -ɑ̃t] ADJ archaistic ▸ NM,F archaist
archaïsme [arkaism] NM (*mot*) archaism, archaic term; (*tournure*) archaism, archaic turn of phrase
archange [arkɑ̃ʒ] NM archangel
archangélique [arkɑ̃ʒelik] ADJ archangelic
arche [arʃ] NF **1** *Archit* arch; **la Grande A. (de la Défense)** = large office block at la Défense near Paris, shaped like a square archway **2** *Rel* ark; **l'a. d'alliance** the Ark of the Covenant; **l'a. de Noé** Noah's Ark; **l'a. sainte** the Holy Ark
archée [arʃe] NF bowshot
archéen, -enne [arkeɛ̃, -ɛn] *Géol* ADJ Archaean ▸ NM Archaean
archégone [arkegɔn] NM *Bot* archegonium
archelle [arʃɛl] NF *Belg* wall-mounted rack (*for hanging utensils*)
archéobactérie [arkeobakteri] NF *Biol* archaebacterium
archéologie [arkeɔlɔʒi] NF archaeology
archéologique [arkeɔlɔʒik] ADJ *Archéol* archaeological
archéologue [arkeɔlɔg] NMF *Archéol* archaeologist
archéomagnétisme [arkeomaɲetizm] NM *Archéol* archaeomagnetism
archéoptéryx [arkeɔpteriks] NM *Orn* archaeopteryx
archer [arʃe] NM **1** (*tireur à l'arc*) archer, bowman **2** *Ich* **a. cracheur** archer fish
archère [arʃɛr] NF *Archit* arrow slit, loophole
archerie [arʃœri] NF **1** *Sport* (*technique*) archery; (*matériel*) archer's equipment **2** *Arch Mil* (*troupe*) archery
archet [arʃe] NM **1** *Mus* bow; **avoir un excellent coup d'a.** to be an outstanding violonist **2** *Tech* bow-saw
archèterie [arʃɛtri] NF *Mus* bow-making (*UNCOUNT*)
archetier, -ère [arʃǝtje, -ɛr] NM,F *Mus* bow-maker
archétypal, -e, -aux, -ales [arketipal, -o] ADJ archetypal
archétype [arketip] NM **1** (*symbole*) archetype; **c'est l'a. du père de famille** he is the archetypal family man **2** *Biol* prototype
archétypique [arketipik] ADJ archetypical
archevêché [arʃǝveʃe] NM *Rel* **1** (*fonction, territoire*) archbishopric **2** (*palais*) archbishop's palace
archevêque [arʃǝvɛk] NM *Rel* archbishop
archi [arʃi] *Fam Archit* NF (*abrév* **architecture**) archit ▸ NMF (*abrév* **architecte**) archt
archi- [arʃi] PRÉF *voir* ARCH-
archiatre [arkiatr] NM *Ancienneté* archiater
archichancelier [arʃiʃɑ̃sǝlje] NM *Hist* archchancellor (*dignitary in the court of Napoleon I*)
archichlamydée [arʃiklamide] *Bot* NF archichlamydeous plant ▫ **archichlamydées** NFPL Archichlamydeae
archiconfrérie [arʃikɔ̃freri] NF *Rel* archconfraternity
archiconnu, -e [arʃikɔny] ADJ *Fam* very well known ■; **c'est a.!** everybody knows that!, that's common knowledge!
archicube [arʃikyb] NM *Fam Scol* = graduate of the "École normale supérieure"
archidiaconat [arʃidjakona] NM *Rel* archdeaconship, archdeaconry
archidiaconé [arʃidjakone] NM *Rel* archdeaconry
archidiacre [arʃidjakr] NM *Rel* archdeacon
archidiocésain, -e [arʃidjoseɛ̃, -ɛn] ADJ *Rel* archdiocesan
archidiocèse [arʃidjosɛz] NM *Rel* archdiocese
archidrôle [arʃidrol] ADJ *Fam* hilarious ■
archiduc [arʃidyk] NM archduke

archiduché [arʃidyʃe] NM archduchy
archiduchesse [arʃidyʃɛs] NF archduchess

ARCHIDUCHESSE
This word is familiar to many French people as part of a famous tongue twister: "les chaussettes de l'archiduchesse sont-elles sèches ou archisèches?"

Archie [arʃi] NM *Ordinat* Archie
archiépiscopal, -e, -aux, -ales [arʃiepiskɔpal, -o] ADJ *Rel* archiepiscopal
archiépiscopat [arʃiepiskɔpa] NM *Rel* archiepiscopate
archière [arʃiɛr] NF *Archit* arrow slit, loophole
archifaux, -fausse [arʃifo, -fos] ADJ *Fam* totally wrong; **c'est faux et a.** it couldn't be more wrong
Archiloque [arʃilɔk] NPR *Littérature* Archilochis
archimandrite [arʃimɑ̃drit] NM *Rel* archimandrite
Archimède [arʃimɛd] NPR Archimedes
archimédien, -enne [arʃimedjɛ̃, -jɛn] ADJ *Math* Archimedean
archipel [arʃipɛl] NM *Géol* archipelago; **l'a. frison** the Frisian Islands; **l'a. de la Nouvelle-Sibérie** the New Siberian Islands; **l'a. de la Sonde** the Sunda Islands

'L'Archipel du Goulag' Soljenitsyne 'The Gulag Archipelago'

archiphonème [arʃifɔnɛm] NM *Ling* archiphoneme
archiplein, -e [arʃiplɛ̃, -ɛn] ADJ *Fam* (*train, salle*) jam-packed; **la salle était pleine et archipleine** the room was bursting at the seams
archipresbytéral, -e, -aux, -ales [arʃiprɛsbiteral, -o] ADJ *Rel* archpriestly
archiprêtre [arʃiprɛtr] NM *Rel & Hist* archpriest
archiréussi, -e [arʃireysi] ADJ *Fam* **c'était a.** it was a fantastic success
archisec, -sèche [arʃisɛk, -sɛʃ] ADJ *Fam* bone-dry
architecte [arʃitɛkt] NMF **1** (*gén*) architect; **avoir un diplôme d'a.** to have a degree in architecture; **a. d'intérieur** interior designer; **a. naval** naval architect; **a. paysagiste** landscape architect; **a. urbaniste** *Br* town planner, *Am* city planner
2 *Fig* (*d'une réforme, d'une politique*) architect
3 *Ordinat* **a. de réseaux** network architect
architectonie [arkitektɔni] NF architectonics (*singulier*)
architectonique [arʃitɛktɔnik] ADJ architectonic ▸ NF architectonics (*singulier*)
architectural, -e, -aux, -ales [arʃitɛktyral, -o] ADJ architectural
architecture [arʃitɛktyr] NF **1** *Archit* (*art, style*) architecture; **a. d'intérieur** interior design; **a. navale** naval architecture
2 (*structure → d'une œuvre d'art*) structure, architecture
3 *Ordinat* architecture
architecturer [3] [arʃitɛktyre] VT to structure; **un exposé bien architecturé** a well-structured talk; *Ordinat* **architecturé autour de...** with its architecture built around...
architrave [arʃitrav] NF *Archit* architrave
architravée [arʃitrave] NF *Archit* architraved cornice
archivage [arʃivaʒ] NM filing *or* storing (away)
archive [arʃiv] NF archive; *Ordinat* **a. autodécompactable** self-extracting archive
archiver [3] [arʃive] VT **1** (*document, revue*) to file *or* to store (away) **2** *Ordinat* to archive
archives [arʃiv] NFPL **1** (*documents*) archives, records; *Ordinat* archive; **a. audiovisuelles/sonores** audiovisual/sound archives; **a. cinématographiques** movie *or Br* film archives; **a. familiales** family records **2** (*lieu*) record office; **les A. nationales** the French Historical Archives, *Br* ≃ the Public Record Office, *Am* ≃ the National Archives
▫ **d'archives** ADJ library (*avant n*); *TV* **document/images d'a.** library document/pictures; *Ordinat* **copie d'a.** archive file

LES ARCHIVES NATIONALES
The French Historical Archives were created in 1789 to house all legal documents concerning the history of France. They are open to the public and are located in the Marais in Paris and in special buildings outside the capital.

archiviste [arʃivist] NMF archivist; (*dans une entreprise*) filing clerk; (*dans la fonction publique*) keeper of public records
archiviste-paléographe [arʃivistpaleɔgraf] (*pl* **archivistes-paléographes**) NMF palaeographer (*with diploma from the "École des Chartes"*)
archivistique [arʃivistik] NF science of archiving
archivolte [arʃivɔlt] NF *Archit* archivolt
archontat [arkɔ̃ta] NM *Antiq* **1** (*dignité*) archonship **2** (*durée*) archontate
archonte [arkɔ̃t] NM *Antiq* archon
arçon [arsɔ̃] NM **1** (*de selle*) saddletree; **être ferme sur ses arçons** to be steady in the saddle; *Fig Vieilli* to have fixed opinions **2** *Tex* bow
arçonner [3] [arsɔne] VT *Tex* to card *or* to clean with a bow
arctique [arktik] ADJ Arctic; **le cercle polaire a.** the Arctic Circle
▫ **Arctique** NM **l'A.** the Arctic
arcure [arkyr] NF *Hort* bending (*of a vine shoot or branch of a fruit tree*)

-ARD, -ARDE [ar, ard] SUFF

● These two suffixes are applied to adjectives, nouns and verbs, and serve mostly to describe people in a DEROGATORY way. The register is often colloquial as the basic word to which they are attached is itself colloquial:
trouillard(e) (from *trouille*) lily-livered, chicken; **connard** (from *con*) stupid bastard [note that the feminine is *connasse*; see **-ASSE**]; **nullard(e)** (from *nul*) thick, stupid; **braillard(e)** (from *brailler*) bawler
● **-ard** and **-arde** can also simply refer to the idea of BELONGING, without any pejorative connotations. This is the case for adjectives and nouns relating to places or to political or social concepts:
banlieusard(e) suburban, suburbanite; **soixante-huitard(e)** veteran of the 1968 students' revolt; **smicard(e)** minimum-wage earner

Ardèche [ardɛʃ] NF **l'A.** the Ardèche
ardéchois, -e [ardeʃwa, -az] ADJ of/from the Ardèche
▫ **Ardéchois, -e** NM,F = inhabitant of or person from the Ardèche
ardéiformes [ardeifɔrm] NMPL *Orn* Ciconiiformes
ardemment [ardamɑ̃] ADV ardently, fervently, passionately; **désirer qch a.** to yearn for *or* to crave sth; **désirer a. faire qch** to yearn to do sth
ardennais, -e [ardɛnɛ, -ɛz] ADJ of/from the Ardennes
▫ **Ardennais, -e** NM,F = inhabitant of or person from the Ardennes
Ardennes [ardɛn] NFPL **les A.** the Ardennes; **la bataille des A.** the Battle of the Bulge; **noix des A.** Ardennes ham
ardent, -e [ardɑ̃, -ɑ̃t] ADJ **1** (*brûlant → chaleur*) burning, scorching; (*→ soleil*) blazing, scorching; (*→ fièvre*) burning, raging; (*→ soif*) raging; **un rouge a.** a fiery red
2 (*vif → tempérament*) fiery, passionate; (*→ désir*) ardent, eager, fervent; (*→ imagination*) vivid, fiery; (*→ conviction*) deep-seated; (*→ lutte*) fierce
3 (*passionné → amant*) ardent, eager, hot-blooded; (*→ révolutionnaire, admirateur*) ardent, fervent
ardeur [ardœr] NF **1** (*fougue*) passion, ardour, fervour; **soutenir une cause avec a.** to support a cause passionately *or* ardently *or* fervently; **il n'a jamais montré une grande a. au travail** he's never shown much enthusiasm for work; *Hum* **modérez vos ardeurs!** control yourself! **2** *Littéraire* (*chaleur*) (burning) heat
ardillon [ardijɔ̃] NM tongue (*of a belt buckle*)
arditi [arditi] NMPL *Mil & Hist* = irregular troops in the Italian army during World War I
ardoise [ardwaz] NF **1** *Géol* (*matière, tuile*) slate; **crayon d'a.** slate pencil
2 (*objet*) slate; **a. magique** magic slate

3 *Fam (compte)* bill, slate; **mets-le sur mon a.** put it on my bill *or* on the slate; **on a une a. de 50 euros chez le boucher** we've run up a bill of 50 euros at the butcher's; **il a des ardoises dans tous les bars de la ville** he owes money in all the bars in town

4 *Ordinat* **a. électronique** notepad computer
▫ **d'ardoise, en ardoise** ADJ slate *(avant n)*

ardoisé, -e [ardwaze] ADJ slate-grey

ardoisier, -ère [ardwazje, -ɛr] ADJ **1** *(contenant de l'ardoise)* slaty **2** *(ressemblant à l'ardoise)* slate-like **3** *(industrie, production)* slate *(avant n)*
▪ NM **1** *(exploitant)* slate-quarry owner **2** *(ouvrier)* slate-quarry worker **3** *Belg (couvreur)* roofer
▫ **ardoisière** NF slate quarry

ardoisier-zingueur [ardwazjezɛ̃gœr] *(pl* **ardoisiers-zingueurs)** NM = roofer laying zinc roofs

ardt *Admin (abrév écrite* **arrondissement) 1** *(dans une ville)* = administrative subdivision of major French cities such as Paris, Lyons or Marseilles **2** *(au niveau départemental)* = administrative subdivision of a "département", governed by a "sous-préfet"

ardu, -e [ardy] ADJ *(difficile → problème, question)* tough, difficult; *(→ tâche)* arduous, hard

are [ar] NM are, $=100m^2$

aréage [areaʒ] NM land surveying *(measured in ares)*

arec [arɛk] NM *Bot* areca

arécacée [arekase] *Bot* NF palm tree
▫ **arécacées** NFPL Arecaceae

aréflexie [arefleksi] NF *Méd* areflexia

aréique [areik] ADJ *Géol* with no permanent river system

aréisme [areism] NM *Géol (d'une région)* absence of a permanent river system

areligieux, -euse [arəliʒjø, -øz] ADJ *Rel* not religious

aréna [arena] NM OU NF *Can* = sports centre with skating rink, *Am* arena

arénacé, -e [arenase] ADJ *Géol (roche)* arenaceous

arène [arɛn] NF **1** *(d'amphithéâtre)* arena; *(pour la corrida)* bullring; *Fig* **l'a. politique** the political arena; *Fig* **descendre** *ou* **entrer dans l'a.** to enter the fray *or* the arena **2** *Géol (sable)* arenite, sand; **a. granitique** granitic sand **3** *Orn* lek
▫ **arènes** NFPL *(amphithéâtre)* amphitheatre; *(pour la corrida)* bullring

arénicole [arenikɔl] *Zool* ADJ sand-dwelling, *Spéc* arenicolous
▪ NF sandworm; **a. des pêcheurs** lobworm, lugworm

arénisation [arenizasjɔ̃] NF *Géol* granular disintegration

arénite [arenit] NF *Géol* arenite, sandstone

aréographie [areografi] NF *Astron* areography

aréolaire [areɔlɛr] ADJ **1** *Anat* areolar **2** *Géol* **érosion a.** areal *or* surface erosion

aréole [areɔl] NF *Anat, Bot & Méd* areola

aréomètre [areɔmɛtr] NM *Phys* hydrometer

aréométrie [areɔmetri] NF *Phys* hydrometry

aréopage [areɔpaʒ] NM learned assembly *or* gathering
▫ **Aréopage** NM *Antiq* **l'A.** the Areopagus

aréostyle [areɔstil] NM *Archit* areostyle, araeostyle

aréquier [arekje] NM *Bot* areca

arête [arɛt] NF **1** *Ich (de poisson)* bone; **cabillaud sans arêtes** boneless cod fillet; **enlever les arêtes d'un poisson** to bone a fish; **poisson plein d'arêtes** fish full of bones, bony fish **2** *Archit (angle → d'un toit)* arris; *(→ d'un cube)* edge; *(→ d'une voûte)* groin; *(→ d'un comble)* hip **3** *Anat* **l'a. du nez** the bridge of the nose **4** *Géog* crest, ridge **5** *Bot* beard

arêtier [aretje] NM *Constr* hip *(of roof)*

arêtière [aretjɛr] NF *Constr* arris *or* hip tile

areu [arø] EXCLAM *(en langage enfantin)* **a. a.!** goo-goo!

argali [argali] NM *Zool* argali

arganier [arganje] NM *Bot* argan

argas [argas] NM *Entom* argas

argent [arʒɑ̃] NM **1** *Minér (métal)* silver
2 *(richesse)* money; **avoir de l'a.** to have money, to be wealthy; **une famille qui a de l'a.** a well-to-do family; *Fin* **placer son a.** to invest

one's money; *Fin* **trouver de l'a.** to raise money; **(se) faire de l'a.** to make money; **pour de l'a.** for money; **l'a. lui fond dans les mains** money just runs through his/her fingers; **tu en auras pour ton a.** you'll get your money's worth, you'll get value for money; **je n'en ai pas vraiment eu pour mon a.** I didn't get my money's worth, I felt rather short-changed; **en être pour son a.** to end up out of pocket; **jeter l'a. par les fenêtres** to throw money down the drain, to squander money; *Prov* **l'a. n'a pas** *ou* **point d'odeur** = it's all money!; *Prov* **l'a. ne fait pas le bonheur** money can't buy happiness; *Prov* **l'a. (trouvé) n'a pas de maître** money knows no master; *Prov* **le temps, c'est de l'a.** time is money; *Fin* **a. à bon marché** cheap money; *Compta* **a. en caisse** cash in hand; *(recettes)* takings; **a. comptant** cash; **payer** *ou* **régler en a. comptant** to pay cash; **accepter** *ou* **prendre qch pour a. comptant** to take sth at face value; *Ordinat* **a. électronique** e-cash, electronic money; **a. frais** new money; *Fin* **a. au jour le jour** call money, day-to-day money; **a. liquide** ready cash *or* money; *Fin* **a. mal acquis** dirty money; *Fin* **a. mort** dead money; *Fin* **a. non alloué** unallocated cash; **a. de poche** pocket money; **se faire de l'a. de poche** to make a bit of extra money; *Écon* **a. rare** tight money; **l'a. sale** dirty money; *Ordinat* **a. virtuel** e-cash, electronic money; *Fin* **a. à vue** call money

3 *(couleur)* silver (colour); **la surface du lac était du plus pur a.** the surface of the lake was the purest silver
4 *Hér* argent
▪ ADJ INV silver, silver-coloured; **robe en lamé a.** silver lamé dress
▫ **d'argent** ADJ **1** *(en métal)* silver *(avant n)*
2 *(couleur)* silver, silvery, silver-coloured; **des reflets d'a.** silvery reflections
3 *(pécuniaire)* money *(avant n)*
4 *(intéressé)* **homme/femme d'a.** man/woman for whom money matters
▫ **en argent** ADJ silver *(avant n)*

argentage [arʒɑ̃taʒ] NM *(d'un miroir)* silvering; *(d'un couvert)* silver-plating

argentan [arʒɑ̃tɑ̃] NM German *or* nickel silver

argenté, -e [arʒɑ̃te] ADJ **1** *(renard)* silver *(avant n)*; *(tempes)* silver, silvery; *(reflet)* silvery **2** *(plaqué)* silver-plated, silver *(avant n)*; **métal a.** silver plate **3** *Fam (fortuné)* well-heeled; **on n'était pas très argentés à l'époque** we weren't very well-off *or* we were rather hard up at the time

argenter [arʒɑ̃te] VT **1** *(miroir)* to silver; *(cuillère)* to plate, to silver-plate **2** *Littéraire (faire briller)* **la lune argentait la mer** the moon turned the sea silver

argenterie [arʒɑ̃tri] NF silver, silverware

argenteur [arʒɑ̃tœr] NM silverer

argentier [arʒɑ̃tje] NM **1** *(meuble)* silver cabinet **2** *Hist* **le Grand a.** = the superintendent of the Royal Household; *Fam (ministre)* the Finance Minister

argentifère [arʒɑ̃tifɛr] ADJ *Minér* silver-bearing, *Spéc* argentiferous

argentin¹, -e¹ [arʒɑ̃tɛ̃, -in] ADJ *(son)* silvery
▫ **argentine** NF *Bot* silverweed

argentin², -e² [arʒɑ̃tɛ̃, -in] ADJ Argentinian, Argentine
▫ **Argentin, -e** NM,F Argentinian, Argentine

Argentine [arʒɑ̃tin] NF **l'A.** Argentina; **vivre en A.** to live in Argentina; **aller en A.** to go to Argentina

argentino [arʒɑ̃tino] NM *(monnaie)* argentino

argentique [arʒɑ̃tik] ADJ **1** *Chim* argentic, silver **2** *Phot* **image a.** silver image

argentite [arʒɑ̃tit] NF *Minér* argentite

argenton [arʒɑ̃tɔ̃] NM = **argentan**

argenture [arʒɑ̃tyr] NF silvering

argien, -enne [arʒjɛ̃, -jɛn] ADJ Argive
▫ **Argien, -enne** NM,F Argive

argilacé, -e [arʒilase] ADJ *Minér* argillaceous

argile [arʒil] NF *Minér* clay; **a. grasse** fat clay; **a. réfractaire** fire clay

argileux, -euse [arʒilø, -øz] ADJ *Minér* clayey, clayish

arginine [arʒinin] NF *Chim* arginine

argiope [arʒjɔp] NF *Zool* garden spider, *Spéc* Argiope (spider)

Argolide [argɔlid] NF *Géog* **l'A.** Argolis

argon [argɔ̃] NM *Chim* argon

argonaute [argɔnot] NM *Zool (mollusque)* argonaut, paper nautilus

Argonautes [argɔnot] NMPL *Myth* **les A.** the Argonauts

argonide [argɔnid] NM *Chim* **les argonides** the inert gases

Argos [argɔs] NPR *Myth Géog* Argus

argot [argo] NM *Ling* slang; **parler a.** to talk (in) slang; **un mot d'a.** a slang word; **l'a. scolaire** school slang; **a. de métier** jargon

ARGOT

This term can refer to both **la langue verte** (the slang of the underworld) and the jargon of particular social or professional groups (such as butchers, soldiers, students etc). Some "argot" has evolved from being part of the secret language of a select group to becoming part of everyday speech, while other terms have become obsolete, supplanted by **verlan** (see box at this entry), the slang used by young people in the suburbs of big cities.

argoteur, -euse [argɔtœr, -øz], **argotier, -ère** [argɔtje, -ɛr] NM,F talker of slang

argotique [argɔtik] ADJ **1** *(propre à l'argot)* slang *(avant n)* **2** *(familier)* slangy

argotisme [argɔtism] NM *Ling (mot)* slang word; *(tournure)* slang expression

argotiste [argɔtist] NMF *Ling* expert in slang

argousier [arguzje] NM *Bot* sallow thorn, sea buckthorn

argousin [arguzɛ̃] NM *Vieilli Péj* cop

Argovie [argɔvi] NF *Géog* Aargau

argovien, -enne [argɔvjɛ̃, -ɛn] ADJ of/from Aargau
▫ **Argovien, -enne** NM,F = inhabitant of or person from Aargau

arguer [8] [argɥe] VT **1** *(conclure)* to deduce; **que peut-on a. de ces écrits?** what can we deduce from *or* what conclusion can be drawn from these writings?
2 *(prétexter)* **a. que...** to put forward the fact that...; **arguant qu'il avait une mauvaise vue** pleading his poor eyesight
3 *Jur* **a. une pièce de faux** to assert a deed to be forged
▫ **arguer de** VT IND to use as an excuse, to plead; **elle argua d'une migraine pour se retirer** she pleaded a headache in order to retire; **il s'est tiré en arguant de son ignorance** he got away with it by pleading ignorance

argument [argymɑ̃] NM **1** *Ling (raison)* argument; **ses arguments** his reasoning; **les arguments pour/contre la réforme** the arguments supporting/opposing *or* for/against the reform; **présenter ses arguments** to state one's case; **avoir de bons/solides arguments** to have a good/strong case; **tirer a. de qch** to use sth as an argument
2 *Com* **a. de vente** selling point
3 *Littérature (sommaire)* general description, outline
4 *Math* argument

argumentaire [argymɑ̃tɛr] NM **1** *Com* promotion leaflet; **l'a. est très convaincant** the sales pitch is very convincing **2** *Ling (arguments)* arguments

argumentateur, -trice [argymɑ̃tatœr, -tris] *Péj* ADJ argumentative
▪ NM,F arguer

argumentatif, -ive [argymɑ̃tatif, -iv] ADJ *Ling* argumentative

argumentation [argymɑ̃tasjɔ̃] NF *Ling* **1** *(raisonnement)* argumentation, rationale **2** *(fait d'argumenter)* reasoning

argumentative [argymɑ̃tativ] *voir* **argumentatif**

argumentatrice [argymɑ̃tatris] *voir* **argumentateur**

argumenter [3] [argymɑ̃te] *Ling* VI **1** *(débattre)* to argue; **a. en faveur de/contre qch** to argue for/against sth; **a. de qch** *(en tirer des conséquences)* to base an argument on sth; **a. de qch avec qn** to argue with sb about sth
2 *(ergoter)* to be argumentative, to quibble
▪ VT *(texte, démonstration)* to support with (relevant) arguments; **motion bien/mal argumentée** impressively/poorly argued motion

Argus [argys] = **Argos**

argus [argys] **NM 1** *(publication)* **l'a. de l'automobile** the price guide for used cars; **ta voiture vaut à peine 1000 euros à l'a.** the book price for your car would only be 1,000 euros; **acheter/vendre qch à l'a.** to buy/sell sth for the book price **2** *Orn* argus pheasant **3** *Littéraire (gardien)* guardian

argutie [argysi] **NF** *Ling* quibble; **arguties** quibbling, hairsplitting

argyrisme [arʒirism] **NM** *Méd* silver poisoning, *Spéc* argyria

argyronète [arʒirɔnɛt] **NF** *Zool* water spider

argyrose [arʒiroz] **NF 1** *Minér* argentite, argyrose, argyrite **2** *Méd* silver poisoning, *Spéc* argyria

aria [arja] **NF** *Mus* aria
   NM *Vieilli (souci, tracas)* nuisance

Ariane [arjan] **NPR** *Myth* Ariadne; **le fil d'A.** Ariadne's clew

arianisme [arjanism] **NM** *Rel* arianism

aride [arid] **ADJ 1** *(sec → terre, région)* arid, barren; *(→ climat)* arid; *(→ vent)* dry; *(→ cœur)* unfeeling **2** *(difficile → sujet)* arid, dull, uninteresting

aridité [aridite] **NF 1** *(de la terre, d'une région)* aridity, barrenness; *(du climat)* aridity; **son a. de cœur** his/her heartlessness **2** *(d'un sujet)* dullness, *Sout* aridity

Ariège [arjɛʒ] **NF l'A.** the Ariège

ariégeois, -e [arjeʒwa, -az] **ADJ** of/from the Ariège
   □ Ariégeois, -e NM,F = inhabitant of or person from the Ariège

arien, -enne [arjɛ̃, -ɛn] **ADJ** Aryan
   □ Arien, -enne NM,F Aryan

ariette [arjɛt] **NF** *Mus* arietta, ariette

arille [arij] **NM** *Bot* aril, arillus

arillé, -e [arije] **ADJ** *Bot* arillate, arillated

arioso [arjozo] **NM** *Mus* arioso

Arioste [arjɔst] **NPR l'A.** Ariosto

ariser [3] [arize] **VT** *Naut (voile)* to reef

Aristarque [aristark] **NPR** Aristarchus
   □ aristarque NM *Littéraire* severe critic

Aristide [aristid] **NPR** Aristides

aristo [aristo] *Fam* **ADJ** *(abrév* **aristocratique)** aristocratic■
   NMF *(abrév* **aristocrate)** aristocrat■, *Br* toff; **les aristos** the upper crust, *Br* the toffs

aristocrate [aristɔkrat] **ADJ** aristocratic
   NMF aristocrat; **des manières d'a.** aristocratic manners; **une famille d'aristocrates** an aristocratic family

aristocratie [aristɔkrasi] **NF** aristocracy

aristocratique [aristɔkratik] **ADJ** aristocratic; **avoir du sang a. (dans les veines)** to have aristocratic blood (in one's veins), to be blue-blooded

aristocratiquement [aristɔkratikmɑ̃] **ADV** aristocratically

aristocratisme [aristɔkratism] **NM** *Pol* elitism

aristoloche [aristɔlɔʃ] **NF** *Bot* birthwort

Aristophane [aristɔfan] **NPR** Aristophanes

Aristote [aristɔt] **NPR** Aristotle

aristotélicien, -enne [aristɔtelisjɛ̃, -ɛn] *Phil* **ADJ** Aristotelian
   NM,F Aristotelian

aristotélisme [aristɔtelism] **NM** *Phil* Aristotelianism

arithméticien, -enne [aritmetisjɛ̃, -ɛn] **NM,F** *Math* arithmetician

arithmétique [aritmetik] **ADJ 1** *Math (moyenne, progression)* arithmetical **2** *Tech* **machine a.** adding machine
   NF 1 *(matière)* arithmetic; **faire de l'a.** to do arithmetic **2** *(livre)* arithmetic book

arithmétiquement [aritmetikmɑ̃] **ADV** *Math* arithmetically

arithmomancie [aritmɔmɑ̃si] **NF** arithmomancy

arithmomanie [aritmɔmani] **NF** *Psy* arithmomania

arithmomètre [aritmɔmɛtr] **NM** arithmometer

Arizona [arizɔna] **NM l'A.** Arizona; **en A.** in Arizona

Arkansas [arkɑ̃sas] **NM l'A.** Arkansas; **dans l'A.** in Arkansas

Arkhangelsk [arkɑ̃gɛlsk] **NM** *Géog* Arkhangelsk, *Formerly* Archangel

arkose [arkoz] **NF** *Minér* arkose

Arlequin [arlǝkɛ̃] **NPR** Harlequin
   □ arlequin NM Harlequin

arlequinade [arlǝkinad] **NF 1** *Théât* harlequinade **2** *Fig Péj* (piece of) buffoonery

Arles [arl] **NM** *Géog* Arles; **à** *ou* **en A.** in Arles

arlésien, -enne [arlezjɛ̃, -ɛn] **ADJ** of/from Arles
   □ Arlésien, -enne NM,F = inhabitant of or person from Arles

---

Allusion

C'est l'Arlésienne

L'Arlésienne was a play by Alphonse Daudet, which Bizet turned into the better-known opera in 1872. The character known as l'Arlésienne ("the woman from Arles") never appears on stage at any point. The expression is used about someone or something that one believes may not exist at all, eg **Sa copine, c'est l'Arlésienne!** ("Does this much talked-about girlfriend really exist?") In addition, one can greet the re-appearance of a long-lost acquaintance by saying **C'est le retour de l'Arlésienne!**, ie "Well, well! it's the famous disappearing man/woman!"

---

armada [armada] **NF 1** *(quantité)* **une a. de touristes** an army of tourists; **toute une a. de motos est arrivée tout à coup** a whole fleet of motorbikes suddenly appeared **2** *Hist* **l'(Invincible) A.** the Spanish Armada

armagnac [armaɲak] **NM** *(alcool)* Armagnac (brandy)

armailli [armaji] **NM** *Suisse* shepherd *(in Fribourg)*

armateur [armatœr] **NM** *Naut (propriétaire → d'un navire)* ship owner; *(→ d'une flotte)* fleet owner; *(locataire)* shipper

armature [armatyr] **NF 1** *(cadre → d'une fenêtre, d'une tente, d'un abat-jour)* frame; *(structure → d'un exposé, d'une théorie)* structure, framework **2** *Constr (de charpente)* framework; *(dans le béton)* reinforcement; *(d'un câble)* armouring **3** *Couture* underwiring; **soutien-gorge à a.** underwired bra **4** *Phys (d'un condensateur)* plate; *(d'un aimant)* armature **5** *Mus* key signature

arme [arm] **NF 1** *(objet)* arm, weapon; *(arsenal)* weapons; **l'a. du crime** the murder weapon; **porter une a. sur soi** to carry a weapon; **il chargea son a.** he loaded his gun; **l'a. biologique** biological weapons, bioweapons; **a. blanche** knife; **l'a. chimique** chemical weapons; *Jur* **a. par destination** = ordinary object used as an offensive weapon; **armes de destruction massive** weapons of mass destruction; **a. à feu** firearm; *Jur* **a. par nature** lethal weapon; **l'a. nucléaire** nuclear weapons; *Jur* **a. simulée** replica weapon; **rester l'a. au pied** to be ready for action; *Fam* **passer l'a. à gauche** *(mourir)* to kick the bucket

   2 *(emploi)* force, service; **dans quelle a. est-il?** which service *or* which branch of the army is he in?; **l'a. de l'artillerie** the artillery

   3 *(instrument)* weapon; **contre ses accusations, j'ai l'a. absolue** I have the perfect response to his/her accusations; **une bonne a. psychologique** a good psychological weapon; **son sourire est une a. fatale** his/her smile is a deadly weapon; *Fig* **une a. à double tranchant** a double-edged sword; **le pouvoir est une a. à double tranchant** power is a double-edged sword; **tu lui as donné une a. contre toi** you've given him/her a stick to beat you with

   □ armes NFPL 1 *(matériel de guerre)* arms, weapons, weaponry; **le métier des armes** the military profession, soldiering; **prendre les armes** to take up arms; **porter les armes** to be a soldier; **portez/présentez/reposez armes!** shoulder/present/order arms!; **aux armes!** to arms!; **une nation en armes** a nation in arms; **régler** *ou* **résoudre qch par les armes** to settle sth by force; *Fig* **tourner ses armes contre qn** to turn (one's weapons) against sb; **passer qn par les armes** to send sb to the firing squad; **il a été passé par les armes ce matin** he died before the firing squad this morning; **mettre bas** *ou* **déposer les armes** to lay down one's arms; **partir avec armes et bagages** to leave with bag and baggage; **armes conventionnelles** conventional weapons; **armes de dissuasion** deterrent; **armes de guerre** weapons of war, weaponry; **armes de jet** projectiles, missiles
   2 *Escrime* fencing
   3 *Hér* coat of arms

□ à armes égales ADV on equal terms

□ aux armes de PRÉP *Hér* bearing the arms of

□ d'armes ADJ **frère d'armes** brother-in-arms; *Hist* **homme d'armes** man-at-arms

armé, -e¹ [arme] **ADJ 1** *(personne)* armed **(de)**; **attention, il est a.!** watch out, he's armed *or* he's carrying a weapon!; **il sort toujours a.** he always carries a weapon when he goes out; **a. jusqu'aux dents** armed to the teeth; *Fig* **a. de ses lunettes/d'une loupe, il explorait la paroi rocheuse** armed with his glasses/a magnifying glass, he examined the rock face; **a. de pied en cap** *Hist* in full armour; *Fig* (well) prepared, fully armed; **bien/mal a. contre le froid** well-protected/defenceless against the cold; **je suis a. contre ce genre de sarcasme** I have become inured to this kind of sarcasm; **pas encore a. contre les déceptions amoureuses** as yet unprepared for coping with unhappy love affairs; **mal a. (pour lutter) contre la concurrence** defenceless in the face of the competition
   2 *Constr (béton)* reinforced; *(poutre)* trussed; *(verre)* wired
   NM *(position)* cock

armée² [arme] **NF 1** *(forces militaires)* *Mil* army; **être dans l'a.** to be in the army; **être à l'a.** to be doing one's military service; **a. active** *ou* **régulière** regular army; **l'a. de l'air** the Air Force; **l'a. de mer** the Navy; **a. de métier** professional army; **a. nationale** conscript army; **a. d'occupation** army of occupation; **a. de réserve** reserves; **l'A. rouge** the Red Army; **l'A. du Salut** the Salvation Army; **l'a. de terre** the Army; **le musée de l'A.** = army museum at les Invalides in Paris
   2 *Fig* army, host; **une a. de figurants/sauterelles** an army of extras/grasshoppers

'**L'Armée des ombres'** Melville 'The Army in the Shadows'

armeline [armǝlin] **NF** *(peau)* ermine, armeline

armement [armǝmɑ̃] **NM 1** *Mil (militarisation → d'un pays, d'un groupe)* arming **2** *Naut* commissioning, fitting-out **3** *(d'un appareil photo)* winding (on); *(d'un pistolet)* cocking **4** *(armes)* arms, weapons, weaponry; **limitation** *ou* **réduction des armements stratégiques** strategic arms limitation

Arménie [armeni] **NF l'A.** Armenia; **vivre en A.** to live in Armenia; **aller en A.** to go to Armenia

arménien, -enne [armenjɛ̃, -ɛn] **ADJ** Armenian
   NM *(langue)* Armenian
   □ Arménien, -enne NM,F Armenian

armer [3] [arme] **VT 1** *Mil (guérilla, nation)* to arm, to supply with weapons *or* arms; **a. qn chevalier** to knight sb, to dub sb a knight
   2 *Fig (préparer)* to equip, to arm; **a. qn contre les difficultés de la vie** to equip sb to deal with the difficulties of life
   3 *(arme)* to cock
   4 *Phot* to wind (on)
   5 *Naut* to commission, to fit out
   6 *Constr (béton, ciment)* to reinforce; *(poutre)* to truss
   7 *Tech (câble)* to sheathe
   ► s'armer VPR 1 *(prendre une arme → policier, détective)* to arm oneself; *(→ nation)* to arm
   2 **s'a. de qch** *(s'équiper de → arme)* to arm oneself with sth; *(→ instrument)* to equip oneself with sth; *Fig (prendre)* **s'a. de courage/patience** to muster *or* to summon up one's courage/patience; **ils se sont armés de chaînes de vélo** they armed themselves with bicycle chains; **m'étant armé d'un magnétophone** having equipped myself with a tape-recorder

armet [armɛ] **NM** *(casque)* armet

Armide [armid] **NPR** Armida

armillaire [armilɛr] **ADJ** *Astron* **sphère a.** armillary sphere

armille [armij] **NF** *(bracelet)* armlet
   □ armilles NFPL *Archit* annulets

arminianisme [arminjanism] **NM** Arminianism

arminien, -enne [arminjɛ̃, -ɛn] **ADJ** Arminian
   NM,F Arminian

armistice [armistis] **NM** armistice; **(l'anniversaire de) l'A.** Armistice Day, *Br* Remembrance Day, *Am* Veteran's Day

armoire [armwar] **NF** *(placard)* *Br* cupboard, *Am*

closet; (pour vêtements) Br wardrobe, Am closet; **a. frigorifique** cold room or store; **a. à glace** mirrored wardrobe; Fig Hum **c'est une véritable a. à glace** he's/she's built like the side of a house; **a. à linge** linen cupboard; **a. normande** large wardrobe; **a. à pharmacie** medicine cabinet or chest; **a. réfrigérante** chill cabinet; **a. de toilette** bathroom cabinet; **a. sèche-linge** drying cupboard

armoiries [armwari] NFPL Hér coat of arms, armorial bearings
▫ **aux armoiries de** PRÉP bearing the arms of

armoise [armwaz] NF 1 Bot artemisia, Am sagebrush; **a. absinthe** ou **amère** wormwood; **a. commune** mugwort; **a. en épi** spicate wormwood 2 Tex sarcenet

armoisin [armwazɛ̃] NM Tex sarcenet

armon [armɔ̃] NM futchel

armorial, -e, -aux, -ales [armɔrjal, -o] Hér ADJ armorial
▪ NM armorial

armoricain, -e [armɔrikɛ̃, -ɛn] ADJ Armorican; Littérature **le cycle a.** the Breton cycle
▫ **Armoricain, -e** NM,F Armorican
▫ **à l'armoricaine** ADJ Culin in a tomato and garlic sauce

armorier [10] [armɔrje] VT Hér to emblazon (**de** with)

Armorique [armɔrik] NF **l'A.** Armorica

armure [armyr] NF 1 Hist armour; **vêtu de son a.** armour-clad 2 (protection) defence; **cette insolence est une a.** he/she/etc uses insolence as a defence mechanism 3 Tex weave, pattern, design; **a. toile** plain weave 4 (d'un câble) sheathing 5 Mus key signature

armurerie [armyrri] NF 1 (activité) arms trade 2 (magasin) armourer's, gunsmith's 3 (usine) arms factory

armurier [armyrje] NM 1 (fabricant) gunsmith, armourer; (vendeur) gun dealer 2 Mil armourer

ARN [αɛrɛn] NM Biol (abrév acide ribonucléique) RNA; **A. messager** messenger RNA; **A. de transfert** t-RNA

arnaque [arnak] NF Fam swindle▪, rip-off; **c'est de l'a.!** what a rip-off!

arnaquer [3] [arnake] VT 1 Fam (duper) to rip off; **a. qn de 100 euros** to do sb out of 100 euros; **il nous a joliment arnaqués** he really ripped us off; **je me suis fait a. en achetant cette voiture** I was conned or I got ripped off when I bought this car 2 Fam Arg crime (arrêter) to nab; **se faire a. par les flics** to get nabbed by the cops

arnaqueur [arnakœr] NM Fam swindler▪, rip-off merchant

Arnhem [arnɛm] NM Arnhem

arni [arni] NM Zool Asiatic buffalo, arni

arnica [arnika] NM OU NF Bot arnica

Arnoul [arnul] NPR Hist Arnold

arobas [arobas], **arobase** [arobaz] NF Ordinat (dans une adresse électronique) at (sign)

arobe [arɔb] NF (mesure) arroba

arole, arolle [arɔl] NM Suisse Bot Swiss stone pine, arolla pine

aromate [arɔmat] NM (herbe) herb; (condiment) spice; **aromates** seasoning

aromathérapeute [arɔmaterapøt] NMF aromatherapist

aromathérapie [arɔmaterapi] NF aromatherapy

aromatique [arɔmatik] ADJ aromatic, fragrant
▪ NM Chim aromatic compound

aromatisant, -e [arɔmatizɑ̃, -ɑ̃t] ADJ aromatic
▪ NM flavouring, seasoning

aromatisation [arɔmatizasjɔ̃] NF flavouring

aromatiser [3] [arɔmatize] VT to flavour; **chocolat aromatisé au rhum** chocolate flavoured with rum, rum-flavoured chocolate

arôme [arom] NM (parfum) aroma, fragrance; (goût) flavour; **crème glacée a. vanille** vanilla-flavoured ice-cream; **a. artificiel** artificial flavouring

aronde [arɔ̃d] NF voir **queue**

ARP [aɛrpe] NMF Cin (abrév auteur-réalisateur-producteur) writer-director-producer

arpège [arpɛʒ] NM Mus arpeggio

arpégé, -e [arpeʒe] ADJ Mus spreaded, arpeggiated

arpégement [arpeʒmɑ̃] NM Mus spreading

arpéger [22] [arpeʒe] VT Mus (accord) to play as an arpeggio, to spread, to arpeggiate

arpent [arpɑ̃] NM Arch ≃ acre; **un petit a. de terre** a few acres of or a patch of land

arpentage [arpɑ̃taʒ] NM land-surveying, land-measuring

arpenter [3] [arpɑ̃te] VT 1 (parcourir → couloir) to pace up and down; **a. un quai** to pace up and down a platform 2 (mesurer) to survey, to measure

arpenteur [arpɑ̃tœr] NM surveyor, land-surveyor

arpenteur-géomètre [arpɑ̃tœrʒeɔmɛtr] NM surveyor, land-surveyor

arpenteuse [arpɑ̃tøz] NF Entom looper, measuring worm

arpète, arpette [arpɛt] Fam (apprenti) apprentice
▫ **arpète, arpette** NF (apprentie couturière) seamstress's apprentice

arpion [arpjɔ̃] NM Fam (pied) foot▪, Br plate, Am dog; (orteil) toe▪

arqué, -e [arke] ADJ (sourcils) arched; (nez) hooked; (jambes) bandy, bow (avant n); **aux jambes arquées** bandy-legged, bow-legged

arquebusade [arkəbyzad] NF Mil arquebusade

arquebuse [arkəbyz] NF Mil arquebus, harquebus

arquebusier [arkəbyzje] NM Mil arquebusier, harquebusier

arquer [3] [arke] VT (courber → planche) to bend, to curve; **a. le dos** to arch one's back
▪ VI 1 (fléchir → poutre) to sag 2 Fam (marcher) to walk▪; **il peut plus a.** he can't walk any more
▸**s'arquer** VPR to bend, to curve

arr (abrév écrite **arrondissement**) 1 (dans une ville) = administrative subdivision of major French cities such as Paris, Lyons or Marseilles 2 (au niveau départemental) = administrative subdivision of a ''département'', governed by a ''sous-préfet''

arrachage [araʃaʒ] NM (d'une plante) pulling up, uprooting; (de pommes de terre) lifting; (d'une dent, d'un clou) pulling out, extraction; **l'a. des mauvaises herbes** weeding

arraché [araʃe] NM Sport snatch; Fig **gagner à l'a.** to snatch a victory; **une victoire à l'a.** a hard-won victory; **ils ont obtenu le contrat à l'a.** it was a struggle for them to get the contract

arrache-agrafes [araʃagraf] NM INV staple remover

arrache-clou [araʃklu] (pl **arrache-clous**) NM nail claw

arrachement [araʃmɑ̃] NM 1 (fait d'enlever → plante) uprooting, pulling up; (→ feuille) ripping or tearing out; (→ papier peint) ripping or tearing off 2 Fig (déchirement) wrench; **l'a. des adieux** the wrench of saying goodbye; **quitter notre pays fut un véritable a.** it was a wrench or it was heart-rending to leave our country

arrache-pied [araʃpje] **d'arrache-pied** ADV (travailler) flat out, relentlessly

arracher [3] [araʃe] VT 1 (extraire → clou, cheville) to pull out, to draw out; (→ arbuste) to pull up, to root up; (→ pommes de terre, betteraves) to lift; (→ mauvaises herbes, liseron) to pull out, to root out; (→ poil, cheveu) to pull out; (→ dent) to pull out, to draw, to extract; **se faire a. une dent** to have a tooth out; **il a eu un bras arraché dans l'explosion** he had an arm blown off in the explosion; Fam Fig **ça arrache la gorge!** (alcool fort, piment) it blows your head off!; **elle t'arracherait les yeux si elle savait** she'd scratch your eyes out if she knew; **des images à vous a. le cœur** a heart-rending spectacle; **a. son masque à qn** to unmask sb; très Fam **ça t'arracherait la gueule de dire merci/de t'excuser?** it wouldn't kill you to say thanks/to apologize
2 (déchirer → papier peint, affiche) to tear off, to rip off; (→ page) to tear out, to pull out; **la dernière page de mon agenda a été arrachée** the last page was torn out of my diary
3 (prendre → sac, billet) to snatch, to grab; **j'ai réussi à lui a. le pistolet des mains** (très vite) I managed to snatch the gun away or to grab the gun from him/her; (après une lutte) I managed to wrest the gun from his/her grip
4 (obtenir → victoire) to snatch; **a. des aveux/une signature à qn** to wring a confession/a signature out of sb; **a. des larmes à qn** to bring tears to sb's eyes; **a. un sourire à qn** to force a smile out of sb; **a. une parole à qn** to get or to squeeze a word out of sb; **pas moyen de lui a. le**

moindre commentaire it's impossible to get him/her to say anything
5 (enlever → personne) **a. qn à son lit** to drag sb out of or from his/her bed; **comment l'a. à son ordinateur?** how can we get or drag him/her away from his/her computer?; **arraché très jeune à sa famille** torn from the bosom of his/her family at an early age; **a. un bébé à sa mère** to take a child from its mother; **a. qn au sommeil** to force sb to wake up; **l'arrivée de sa sœur l'arracha à ses rêveries** he/she was awoken from his/her daydreams by the arrival of his/her sister; **a. qn à** (le sauver de) to snatch or to rescue sb from; **a. qn à la mort** to snatch sb from (the jaws of) death; **a. qn à l'enfer du jeu** to rescue sb from the hell of gambling

USAGE ABSOLU Fam **ça arrache!** (alcool fort, piment) it blows your head off!
▪ VI Can **en a.** to have a hard time (of it)
▸**s'arracher** VPR 1 (s'écorcher) **je me suis arraché la peau du genou en tombant** I fell (over) and scraped my knee; Fam **c'est à s'a. les cheveux** it's enough to drive you crazy; **s'a. les yeux** to scratch each other's eyes out
2 (se disputer → personne, héritage) to fight over; **les gens s'arrachaient les taxis** people were fighting over the available taxis; **on s'arrache les droits d'adaptation du roman** people are fighting over the film rights to the novel
3 très Fam (partir) **allez, on s'arrache!** come on, let's be off!▪
4 **s'a. à, s'a. de** to tear oneself away from; **s'a. au sommeil** to tear oneself from sleep; **s'a. à ses rêveries** to snap out of one's daydreams; **s'a. à son travail/à son ordinateur/de son fauteuil** to tear oneself away from one's work/one's computer/out of one's armchair; **elle s'arracha à son étreinte** she tore herself away or she wrenched herself free from his/her embrace

arracheur, -euse [araʃœr, -øz] Agr NM,F (pommes de terre, de betteraves) lifter; Arch **a. de dents** tooth-puller
▫ **arracheuse** NF lifter, grubber

arrachis [araʃi] NM 1 (arrachage) uprooting 2 (arbre arraché) uprooted tree 3 (ensemble des arbres arrachés) uprooted trees

arrachoir [araʃwar] NM Agr (de pommes de terre) (potato) lifter; (de betteraves) (beet) puller

arrageois, -e [araʒwa, -az] ADJ of/from Arras
▫ **Arrageois, -e** NM,F = inhabitant of or person from Arras

arraisonnement [arɛzɔnmɑ̃] NM Naut boarding (for inspection)

arraisonner [3] [arɛzɔne] VT Naut (navire) to board (for inspection)

arrangeable [arɑ̃ʒabl] ADJ (difficulté) which can be settled; (projet, voyage) which can be fixed or arranged

arrangeant, -e [arɑ̃ʒɑ̃, -ɑ̃t] ADJ accommodating, obliging

arrangement [arɑ̃ʒmɑ̃] NM 1 (fait de disposer) arrangement, laying out; (résultat) arrangement, layout; **modifier l'a. d'une pièce** to change the layout of a room; **l'a. des vers dans un sonnet** the order of lines in a sonnet
2 (accord) arrangement, settlement; **parvenir à un a.** to reach an agreement, to come to an arrangement; **a. à l'amiable** amicable settlement; **nous avons un a.** we have an understanding; **c'était un a. entre nous** we'd agreed it between ourselves; **sauf a. contraire** unless otherwise agreed; Jur **a. de famille** family settlement (in financial disputes)
3 Mus arrangement, setting; **a. pour piano** arrangement for (the) piano

arranger [17] [arɑ̃ʒe] VT 1 (mettre en ordre → chignon) to tidy up; (→ tenue) to straighten; (→ bouquet) to lay out; (→ pièce) to lay out, to arrange; **c'est bien arrangé, chez toi** your place is nicely decorated
2 (organiser → rencontre, entrevue) to arrange, to fix; (→ emploi du temps) to arrange; **c'est Paul qui a arrangé la cérémonie/l'exposition** Paul organized the ceremony/put the exhibition together; **a. qch à l'avance** to prearrange sth; **ils ont arrangé ça entre eux** they've fixed it up between them
3 (résoudre → dispute, conflit) to settle, to sort out; **je vais a. ça avec ton professeur** I'll sort

this out with your teacher; **c'est arrangé, tu peux partir** it's all settled, you're free to leave now; **et mes rhumatismes n'arrangent pas les choses** *ou* **n'arrangent rien à l'affaire** my rheumatism doesn't help matters either; **voilà qui n'arrange pas mes affaires!** that's all I needed!

4 *Mus* to arrange; **a. un morceau pour la guitare** to arrange a piece for (the) guitar

5 *(convenir à)* to suit; **ce soir ou demain, comme ça t'arrange** tonight or tomorrow, as it suits you *or* whichever is convenient for you; **mardi? non, ça ne m'arrange pas** Tuesday? no, that's no good for me; **ça m'arrange (à merveille)** it suits me (down to the ground); **on ne peut pas a. tout le monde** you can't please *or* satisfy everybody; **ce n'est pas parce que ça t'arrange de le croire que c'est vrai** just because it suits you to think so doesn't mean that it's true

6 *Fam (réparer → radio, réveil)* to fix■; *(→ chaussures)* to repair■, to mend■; *(→ robe)* to alter■; **je vais t'a. ça en moins de deux** I'll fix this for you in no time

7 *(modifier → traduction, présentation)* to alter, to modify; **je ne t'ai jamais rien promis, tu arranges l'histoire (à ta façon)** I never promised you anything, you're just twisting things; **Bonaparte n'a jamais dit cela, il arrange l'histoire (à sa façon)** Bonaparte never said that, he's rewriting history (to suit himself)

8 *Fam (maltraiter) Br* to sort out, *Am* to work over; **eh bien, on t'a joliment arrangé!** well, they certainly gave you a good going over!

▸**s'arranger VPR 1** *(emploi réfléchi)* **va donc t'a.!** go and tidy yourself up!; **elle sait s'a.** she knows how to make the best of herself; *Fam Ironique* **tu t'es encore bien arrangé/bien arrangé la figure!** you've made a fine mess of yourself/of your face again!

2 *(emploi réciproque) (se mettre d'accord)* to come to an agreement; **on trouvera bien un moyen de s'a.** we'll come to some sort of an arrangement; **elle et moi, nous nous arrangeons pour la garde des enfants** she and I have an arrangement whereby we look after each other's children; **on s'était arrangé pour que ce soit une surprise** we'd arranged it so that it would be a surprise

3 *(se débrouiller)* to manage; **je m'arrangerai, ne t'en fais pas** I'll find a way *or* work something out, don't worry; **arrangez-vous pour avoir l'argent, sinon...** make sure *or* see that you have the money, or else...; **je me suis arrangé pour vous faire tous inviter** I've managed to get an invitation for all of you; **il s'arrange toujours pour partir plus tôt** he always manages to leave early

4 *(s'améliorer)* to improve, to get better; **les choses s'arrangeront d'elles-mêmes** things'll sort themselves out *or* take care of themselves; **ça ne risque pas de s'a. tout seul** things are hardly likely to work themselves out on their own; **tout a fini par s'a.** everything worked out fine in the end; *Hum* **tu ne t'arranges pas avec les années!** you're not getting any better in your old age!; **et Louis? – ça ne s'arrange pas!** what about Louis? – he's no better!; *Fam* **et maintenant il veut faire construire, ça s'arrange pas!** now he wants to build a house, he's completely off his head!

5 *(se dérouler)* to turn out; *Fam* **comment ça s'est arrangé, tes histoires de bagnole?** how did things turn out in the end after all that trouble you had with your car?

6 s'a. avec to come to an agreement with; **on s'est arrangé avec les voisins** we sorted something out with the neighbours; **je m'arrangerai avec lui pour qu'il garde les enfants** I'll arrange for him to look after the children; **il s'est arrangé à l'amiable avec ses créanciers** he came to an amicable agreement with his creditors; **arrange-toi avec ma mère pour les meubles** see my mother about the furniture; **arrange-toi avec lui** you'll have to sort it out with him, you'll have to come to an agreement with him; **je m'arrangerai avec ce que j'ai** I'll make do with what I've got

7 s'a. de to put up with, to make do with; **ce n'est peut-être pas la couleur que tu préfères, mais tu t'en arrangeras!** it may not be your favourite colour but you'll just have to put up with it!; **ce n'est pas confortable, mais on s'en arrange** it's not comfortable, but we make do with it; **il s'arrange de tout** he's very easy-going

arrangeur, -euse [arɑ̃ʒœr, -øz] **NM,F** *Mus* arranger

Arras [aras] **NM** *Géog* Arras

arrdt *(abrév écrite* **arrondissement***)* **1** *(dans une ville)* = administrative subdivision of major French cities such as Paris, Lyons or Marseilles **2** *(au niveau départemental)* = administrative subdivision of a "département", governed by a "sous-préfet"

arrenter [3] [arɑ̃te] **VT** *Jur* to rent

arrérager [17] [areraʒe] *Jur* **VI** to be in arrears
▸**s'arrérager VPR** to fall into arrears

arrérages [areraʒ] **NMPL** *Jur* arrears

arrestation [arɛstasjɔ̃] **NF** arrest; **procéder à une a.** to make an arrest; **procéder à l'a. de qn** to arrest sb; **être en état d'a.** to be under arrest; **mettre qn en état d'a.** to place sb under arrest

arrêt [arɛ] **NM 1** *(interruption)* stopping; **il a décidé l'a. du match** he decided to put a stop to *or* to call a halt to *or* to stop the match; **a. momentané des programmes** temporary blackout; **annoncer l'a. des poursuites** to announce that there will be no more prosecutions; **l'a. se fait automatiquement** it stops automatically; **appuyer sur le bouton "a."** press the "stop" button; **temps d'a.** pause; **marquer un temps d'a.** to stop *or* to pause for a moment; *Ordinat* **a. de fin de session** shutdown; **a. des hostilités** cessation of hostilities; **a. de paiement** stoppage of pay; **a. de travail** *(grève)* stoppage; *(congé)* sick leave; *(certificat)* doctor's *or* medical certificate; **être en a. de travail** to be on sick leave

2 *Transp (pause)* stop, halt; **avant l'a. complet de l'appareil** before the aircraft has come to a complete stop *or* standstill; **ce train est sans a. jusqu'à Arcueil** this train is non-stop *or* goes straight through to Arcueil; **en cas d'a. entre deux gares** if the train stops between stations; **Brive, Brive, deux minutes d'a.** this is Brive, there will be a two-minute stop; **arrêts fréquents** *(sur véhicule de livraison)* slow deliveries; **a. demandé** *(dans un autobus)* stop requested

3 *(lieu)* **a. (d'autobus)** bus stop; **je descends au prochain a.** I'm getting off at the next stop

4 *Ftbl* **faire un a. du pied gauche** to make a save with one's left foot; **a. de jeu** stoppage; **jouer les arrêts de jeu** to play injury time; **faire un a. de volée** to make a mark

5 *Cin & TV* **a. sur image** freeze frame; **faire un a. sur image** to freeze a frame

6 *Méd* **a. cardiaque** *ou* **du cœur** cardiac arrest, cardiac failure; **a. cardiocirculatoire** asystole

7 *Couture* **faire un a.** to fasten off; **faire un a. de mailles** to cast off

8 *Jur (décision)* judgment, ruling; **a. de mise en accusation** committal for trial on indictment; **a. de mort** death sentence; *Fig* **signer son a. de mort** to sign one's own death warrant; **a. de non-lieu** dismissal of the charges; **rendre un a. de non-lieu** to dismiss a case for lack of evidence **a. de règlement** = judgment setting a binding precedent; **a. de renvoi** committal for trial at the Criminal Court; **rendre un a.** to deliver *or* to pronounce a judgment; *Littéraire* **les arrêts de la Providence** the decrees of Fate

9 *(arrestation)* arrest; **faire a. sur des marchandises** to seize *or* to impound goods

❑ **arrêts NMPL** *Mil* arrest; **mettre qn aux arrêts** to place sb under arrest; **être aux arrêts** to be under arrest; **arrêts forcés** *ou* **de rigueur** close arrest

❑ **à l'arrêt ADJ** *(véhicule)* stationary; **l'appareil est à l'a. sur la piste** the aircraft is at a standstill on the runway

❑ **d'arrêt ADJ 1** *Tech (dispositif)* stopping, stop *(avant n)*

2 *Couture* **point d'a.** finishing-off stitch

❑ **en arrêt ADV rester en a. devant qch** to stop dead *or* short before sth; **tomber en a.** *(chien)* to point; **je suis tombé en a. devant un magnifique vaisselier** I stopped to admire a splendid dresser

❑ **sans arrêt ADV** *(sans interruption)* non-stop; *(à maintes reprises)* constantly

arrêté¹ [arete] **NM 1** *Jur (décret)* order, decree; **a. ministériel** ministerial order; **a. municipal** *Br* ≃ bylaw, *Am* ≃ ordinance; **a. préfectoral** *Br* ≃ bylaw, *Am* ≃ ordinance *(issued by a prefecture)*; **par a. royal** by royal decree **2** *Banque* **a. de compte** *(bilan)* statement of account; *(fermeture)* settlement of account

arrêté², -e [arete] **ADJ** *(opinion)* fixed, set; *(intention)* firm

arrête-bœuf [arɛtbœf] **NM INV** *Bot* rest-harrow, cammock

arrêter [4] [arete] **VT 1** *(empêcher d'avancer → passant, taxi)* to stop; **arrêtez-le! il a volé mon portefeuille!** stop that man, he's stolen my wallet!; **tu arrêteras la voiture devant l'entrée** you'll stop the car in front of the entrance; **la circulation est arrêtée sur la N7** traffic is held up *or* has come to a standstill on the N7 (road); *Fam* **arrête-moi à la gare** drop me off at the station; *Sport* **a. un ballon** to make a save, to save a goal; *Fam Hum* **arrête ton char!** *(je ne te crois pas)* come off it!; *(arrête de te vanter)* stop showing off!

2 *(retenir → personne)* to stop; *(→ regard)* to catch, to fix; **qu'est-ce qui t'arrête?** what's stopping you?; **rien ne peut plus l'a.** nothing can stop him/her now

3 *(interrompre)* to interrupt; **arrêtez-moi si je parle trop vite** stop me if I'm speaking too fast

4 *(éteindre → radio, télévision)* to turn off; *(→ moteur)* to stop, to switch off; *Ordinat (système)* to shut down

5 *(mettre fin à → élan)* to stop, to check; *(→ écoulement, saignement)* to stem, to stop; *(→ croissance, chute)* to stop, to arrest, to bring to a halt; *Fam Hum* **on n'arrête pas le progrès!** what will they think of next!; **a. les frais** to stop messing about

6 *(abandonner → construction, publication, traitement)* to stop; *(→ sport, chant)* to give up; *(cesser de fabriquer)* to discontinue (the manufacture of); **j'ai arrêté le piano/ma carrière d'acteur** I've given up the piano/my acting career

7 *(sujet: police)* to arrest; **se faire a.** to get *or* to be arrested

8 *(déterminer → date, lieu)* to appoint, to decide on, to fix; *(→ plan, procédure)* to decide on, to settle on, to settle upon; **a. sa décision** to make up one's mind; **a. son choix** to make one's choice

9 *(sujet: médecin)* **a. qn** to put sb on sick leave; **ça fait un mois que je suis arrêté** I've been on sick leave for a month

10 *Banque (compte)* to close, to settle; *Compta (comptes de l'exercice)* to close

11 *Couture (point)* to fasten off; **a. les mailles** to cast off

12 *(gibier)* to point

VI arrête, tu me fais mal! stop it, you're hurting me!; **vous allez a. un peu, tous les deux!** stop it, the pair of you!; **quatre albums en un an! mais vous n'arrêtez pas!** four albums in a year! you never stop *or* you don't ever take a break, do you?; **a. de faire qch** to stop doing sth; **arrête de pleurer** stop crying; **il a arrêté de travailler l'an dernier** he retired last year; **j'ai arrêté de fumer** I've given up *or* stopped smoking; **a. de se droguer** to give up *or* to come off drugs; *(tournure impersonnelle)* **il n'a pas arrêté de neiger** it hasn't stopped snowing, it's been snowing non-stop

▸**s'arrêter VPR 1** *(cesser → bruit, pluie, saignement)* to stop; **notre histoire ne s'arrête pas là** this isn't the end of our story; **les émissions s'arrêtent à 4 heures** broadcasting stops *or* ends at 4 a.m.; **s'a. de faire qch** *(cesser de)* to stop doing sth; *(renoncer à)* to give up doing sth, to stop doing sth; **elle s'est arrêtée de jouer en me voyant** she stopped playing when she saw me; **s'a. de composer/fumer** to stop writing music/smoking; **il s'est arrêté de travailler après son accident** he stopped working after his accident; **le monde ne va pas s'a. de tourner pour autant** that won't stop the world from turning

2 *(s'immobiliser → montre)* to stop; *(→ ascenseur, véhicule)* to stop, to come to a stop *or* halt; *(→ système)* to shut down; **dites au chauffeur de s'a.** tell the driver to stop; **une voiture vint s'a. à ma hauteur** a car pulled up alongside me; **s'a. net** to stop dead *or* short

3 *(faire une halte, une pause)* to stop; **passer**

sans s'a. devant qn to pass by sb without stopping; on va s'a. à un Restoroute we'll stop at a *Br* motorway *or Am* highway café; on s'est arrêtés plusieurs fois en route we made several stops on the way; s'a. chez qn to call at sb's; tu peux t'a. chez l'épicier en venant? could you stop off at the grocer's on your way here?; on va s'a. un quart d'heure we'll stop for fifteen minutes, we'll take a fifteen-minute break; aujourd'hui, je m'arrête à midi today I'm stopping work at noon; nous nous étions arrêtés à la page 56 we'd left off at page 56

4 *(se fixer)* son regard s'arrêta sur leur ami his/her gaze fell on their friend; notre choix s'est arrêté sur le canapé en cuir we decided *or* settled on the leather couch

5 s'a. à *(faire attention à)* to pay attention to; il ne faut pas s'a. aux apparences one mustn't go by appearances; s'a. à des vétilles to pay attention to the smallest of details

arrêtiste [arɛtist] NM *Jur* legal commentator

arrêt-maladie [arɛmaladi] *(pl* **arrêts-maladies**) NM *(congé)* sick leave; *(certificat)* medical certificate; être en a. to be on sick leave

arrêtoir [arɛtwar] NM *Tech (dans un mécanisme)* stop

arrhes [ar] NFPL *Fin* deposit; verser des a. to pay a deposit; verser 300 euros d'a. to leave 300 euros as a deposit *or* a deposit of 300 euros

Arrien [arjɛ̃] NPR Arrian

arriération [arjerasjɔ̃] NF *Vieilli Psy* backwardness, retardation

arrière [arjɛr] ADJ INV 1 *Aut (roue, feu)* rear; *(siège)* back

2 *Sport* backward; roulade a. backward roll

NM 1 *(d'une maison)* back, rear; *(d'un véhicule)* rear (end), back (end); à l'a. du véhicule at the rear of the vehicle; asseyez-vous à l'a. sit in the back

2 *Sport (au basket-ball)* guard; *(au football, au rugby)* back; *(au volley-ball)* rearline player; *Ftbl* jouer a. droit/gauche to play right/left back; a. central centre-back; a. intercalé = full-back who has come up into the line; a. latéral side back; a. volant sweeper; la ligne des arrières, les arrières the back line, the backs

3 *Naut* stern; à l'a. astern; à l'a. de at the stern of

4 *Mil* les blessés ont été transportés à l'a. the wounded were carried behind the lines

EXCLAM (stand) back!

▫ **arrières** NMPL *Mil* rear; assurer *ou* protéger ses arrières to protect one's rear; *Fig* to leave oneself a way out *or* an escape route

▫ **en arrière** ADV 1 *(regarder)* back; *(se pencher, tomber)* backward, backwards; revenir en a. *(sur une route)* to retrace one's steps; *(avec un magnétophone)* to rewind (the tape); reviens en a., je n'ai pas vu le début du film rewind (the tape), I didn't see the beginning of the film; se balancer d'avant en a. to rock to and fro; ramener ses cheveux en a. to sweep one's hair back; rester en a. *(d'un convoi, d'un défilé)* to stay at the back *or* rear; ne restez pas en a., rapprochez-vous don't stay at the back, come closer; *Naut* en a. toute! full astern!

2 *(dans le temps)* back; revenir en a. to go back in time; cela nous ramène plusieurs mois en a. this takes us back several months; *Suisse* il y a un siècle en a. a century ago; *Suisse* il date de cent ans en a. it dates back a hundred years

▫ **en arrière de** PRÉP behind; *Mil* rester en a. de la colonne to fall behind (in the line); il reste en a. des autres élèves he's fallen behind the other pupils; se tenir en a. de qn to stand behind sb

arriéré, -e [arjere] ADJ 1 *Fin (impayé → loyer, intérêt)* overdue, in arrears; *(→ dette)* outstanding

2 *(mentalement retardé)* backward, (mentally) retarded

3 *(archaïque → idée, technologie)* outdated; *(→ pays, région)* backward; ils sont un peu arriérés dans sa famille they're a bit old-fashioned *or* behind the times in his/her family; le pays est économiquement a. the country is economically backward

NM,F *(retardé mental)* backward *or* mentally retarded person

NM 1 *Fin (dette)* arrears; avoir des arriérés to be in arrears; a. d'impôts tax arrears, back taxes; avoir 400 euros d'a. de loyer/d'impôts to be 400 euros in arrears with one's rent/taxes; solder un a. to pay off arrears

2 *(retard)* backlog; j'ai beaucoup d'a. dans mon travail I have a big backlog of work *or* a lot of work to catch up on

arrière-ban [arjɛrbɑ̃] *(pl* **arrière-bans**) NM *Hist (levée)* arrière-ban *(summons to the king's vassals to do military service)*; *(vassaux)* vassals

arrière-bec [arjɛrbɛk] *(pl* **arrière-becs**) NM *Archit (d'une pile de pont)* cutwater

arrière-bouche [arjɛrbuʃ] *(pl* **arrière-bouches**) NF *Anat* back of the mouth

arrière-boutique [arjɛrbutik] *(pl* **arrière-boutiques**) NF *Br* back-shop, *Am* back-store; dans mon a. at the back of my *Br* shop *or Am* store

arrière-cerveau [arjɛrsɛrvo] *(pl* **arrière-cerveaux**) NM *Anat (rhombencéphale)* hind-brain, *Spéc* rhombencephalon

arrière-chœur [arjɛrkœr] *(pl* **arrière-chœurs**) NM retrochoir

arrière-corps [arjɛrkɔr] NM INV *Archit* retreating part *(of building)*

arrière-cour [arjɛrkur] *(pl* **arrière-cours**) NF *Br* backyard

arrière-cousin, -e [arjɛrkuzɛ̃, -in] *(mpl* **arrière-cousins**, *fpl* **arrière-cousines**) NM,F distant cousin

arrière-cuisine [arjɛrkɥizin] *(pl* **arrière-cuisines**) NF scullery

arrière-fleur [arjɛrflœr] *(pl* **arrière-fleurs**) NF 1 *(floraison tardive)* late flower 2 *(seconde floraison)* second efflorescence *or* flowering

arrière-fond [arjɛrfɔ̃] *(pl* **arrière-fonds**) NM innermost depths

arrière-garde [arjɛrgard] *(pl* **arrière-gardes**) NF *Mil* rearguard; *Fig* d'a. *(idées)* old-fashioned

arrière-gorge [arjɛrgɔrʒ] *(pl* **arrière-gorges**) NF *Anat* back of the throat

arrière-goût [arjɛrgu] *(pl* **arrière-goûts**) NM aftertaste; ça vous laisse un a. d'amertume one is left with a bitter aftertaste; le vin a un petit a. de cassis there's an aftertaste of blackcurrant to the wine

arrière-grand-mère [arjɛrgrɑ̃mɛr] *(pl* **arrière-grands-mères**) NF great-grandmother

arrière-grand-oncle [arjɛrgrɑ̃tɔ̃kl] *(pl* **arrière-grands-oncles**) NM great-great-uncle, great-granduncle

arrière-grand-père [arjɛrgrɑ̃pɛr] *(pl* **arrière-grands-pères**) NM great-grandfather

arrière-grands-parents [arjɛrgrɑ̃parɑ̃] NMPL great-grandparents

arrière-grand-tante [arjɛrgrɑ̃tɑ̃t] *(pl* **arrière-grands-tantes**) NF great-great-aunt, great-grandaunt

arrière-main [arjɛrmɛ̃] *(pl* **arrière-mains**) NM 1 *Tennis* (coup d')a. backhand (stroke) 2 *(d'un cheval)* (hind)quarters

arrière-neveu [arjɛrnəvø] *(pl* **arrière-neveux**) NM great-nephew, grandnephew; *Littéraire* nos arrière-neveux our children's children

arrière-nièce [arjɛrnjɛs] *(pl* **arrière-nièces**) NF great-niece, grandniece

arrière-pays [arjɛrpei] NM INV hinterland; dans l'a. in the hinterland; aller dans l'a. to go inland

arrière-pensée [arjɛrpɑ̃se] *(pl* **arrière-pensées**) NF ulterior motive; son acceptation cachait une a. de revanche behind his/her acceptance lay a lurking idea of revenge; sans arrière-pensées without any ulterior motives

arrière-petite-fille [arjɛrpətitfij] *(pl* **arrière-petites-filles**) NF great-granddaughter

arrière-petite-nièce [arjɛrpətitnjɛs] *(pl* **arrière-petites-nièces**) NF great-great-niece

arrière-petit-fils [arjɛrpətifis] *(pl* **arrière-petits-fils**) NM great-grandson

arrière-petit-neveu [arjɛrpətinəvø] *(pl* **arrière-petits-neveux**) NM great-great-nephew

arrière-petits-enfants [arjɛrpətizɑ̃fɑ̃] NMPL great-grandchildren

arrière-plan [arjɛrplɑ̃] *(pl* **arrière-plans**) NM *(gén) & Ordinat* background; on la voit à l'a. sur la photo she's in the background of the picture; une vallée profonde, avec les Alpes en a. a deep valley with the Alps in the background; *Fig* être à l'a. to remain in the background; ce projet est passé à l'a. this plan has been put on the back burner; *Fig* se trouver relégué à l'a. to be upstaged

arrière-port [arjɛrpɔr] *(pl* **arrière-ports**) NM *Naut* inner harbour

arriérer [18] [arjere] VT *Fin (paiement)* to postpone, to delay, to defer

arrière-saison [arjɛrsɛzɔ̃] *(pl* **arrière-saisons**) NF 1 *(fin de l'automne)* end of the *Br* autumn *or Am* fall 2 *Agr* end of the season

arrière-salle [arjɛrsal] *(pl* **arrière-salles**) NF inner room, back room

arrière-train [arjɛrtrɛ̃] *(pl* **arrière-trains**) NM 1 *Zool* hindquarters 2 *Hum (fesses)* hindquarters, behind

arrière-vassal, -e [arjɛrvasal,-o] *(mpl* **arrière-vassaux**, *fpl* **arrière-vassales**) NM,F rear vassal, under-vassal

arrière-voussure [arjɛrvusyr] *(pl* **arrière-voussures**) NF *Archit* rear-vault, arrière-voussure

arrimage [arimaʒ] NM 1 *Naut* stowage 2 *Astron (d'une navette spatiale)* docking

arrimer [3] [arime] VT 1 *Naut* to stow 2 *(attacher)* to secure, to fasten; a. un chargement sur le toit d'une voiture to secure *or* to fasten a load to the roof of a car 3 *Astron* to dock

arrimeur [arimœr] NM *Naut* stevedore

arriser [3] [arize] VT *Naut (voile)* to reef

arrivage [arivaʒ] NM 1 *(de produits)* delivery, consignment; nous venons d'avoir un a. we've just had a (fresh) consignment in; prix selon a. *(dans une poissonnerie)* price according to availability

2 *Fin (de fonds)* accession

3 *Hum (de personnes)* influx; il y a encore eu un a. de touristes ce matin another horde of tourists arrived this morning, there was another influx of tourists this morning

arrivant, -e [arivɑ̃, -ɑ̃t] NM,F newcomer, new arrival; il y a dix nouveaux arrivants there are ten newcomers *or* new arrivals

arrivé, -e [arive] ADJ 1 *(qui a réussi)* être a. to have made it, to have arrived

2 le dernier/premier a. the last/first (person) to arrive

▫ **arrivée** NF 1 *(venue → d'une saison, du froid)* arrival, coming; *(→ d'un avion, d'un ami)* arrival; l'arrivée de nouveaux produits sur le marché the arrival of new products onto the market; on attend son arrivée pour le mois prochain we're expecting him/her to arrive *or* he's/she's expected to arrive next month; à mon arrivée à la gare on *or* upon my arrival at the station, when I arrived at the station; quelques mois après son arrivée au pouvoir a few months after he/she came to power; on viendra t'attendre à l'arrivée du train we'll be waiting for you at the station; heure d'arrivée *(d'un train)* time of arrival; *(du courrier)* time of delivery

2 *Sport* finish

3 *Tech* arrivée d'air/de gaz *(robinet)* air/gas inlet; *(passage)* inflow of air/gas

arriver [3] [arive] VI *(aux être)* A. *DANS L'ESPACE* 1 *(parvenir à destination → voyageur, véhicule, courrier)* to arrive; a. à l'école to arrive at school, to get to school; a. chez qn to arrive at sb's house; a. chez soi to get *or* to arrive home; a. au sommet to reach the summit; elle doit a. à Paris vers midi she should arrive *or* be in Paris at around twelve; dès que je suis arrivé au Canada as soon as I arrived in *or* got to Canada; Colomb croyait être arrivé aux Indes Columbus thought he'd reached the Indies; le bateau arrive à quai the ship's coming alongside the quay; j'étais à peine arrivé que le téléphone sonna no sooner had I arrived than the phone rang; on arrive à quelle heure? what time do we get there?; nous sommes bientôt *ou* presque arrivés we're almost there; les invités vont bientôt a. the guests will be arriving soon; qui est arrivé après l'appel? *(en classe)* who came in after I *Br* called the register *or Am* called roll?; je serai chez toi dans un quart d'heure, qui est déjà arrivé? I'll be at your place in fifteen minutes, who's already there?; puis la police est arrivée then the police arrived *or* came; le courrier est-il arrivé? has the mail *or Br* post arrived *or* come yet?; être bien arrivé *(personne,

colis) to have arrived safely; **vous voilà enfin arrivés, je m'inquiétais** *(ici)* here you are *or* you've arrived at last, I was getting worried; *(là-bas)* you got there at last, I was getting worried; **si tu n'arrives pas à l'heure, je pars sans toi** *(ici)* if you aren't here on time, I'll go without you; *(là-bas)* if you don't get there on time, I'll go without you; **par où es-tu arrivé?** *(ici)* which way did you come?; *(là-bas)* which way did you take to get there?; **a. de** to have (just) come from; **ils arrivent de Tokyo** they've just arrived *or* come from Tokyo; **d'où arrives-tu pour être si bronzé?** where did you get that tan?; **j'arrive tout juste de vacances** I'm just back from my holidays; **y aller sans réserver? t'arrives d'où, toi?** go there without booking? you must be joking!; **même en roulant vite ça nous fait a. après minuit** even if we drive fast we won't get there before midnight

2 *(finir → dans un classement)* to come (in); **a. le premier** *(coureur)* to come in first, to take first place; *(invité)* to arrive first, to be the first to arrive; **a. le dernier** *(coureur)* to come in last, to take last place; *(invité)* to be the last to arrive; **il est arrivé cinquième au marathon** he took (the) fifth place *or* came in fifth in the marathon; **ils sont arrivés dans un mouchoir** it was a close finish

3 *(venir)* to come, to approach; **je l'ai vu a.** I saw him approaching *or* coming; **les voilà qui arrivent** here they come; **tu es prêt? – j'arrive tout de suite/dans une minute** are you ready? – I'm coming/I'll be with you in a minute; **j'arrive, j'arrive!** I'm coming!; **je n'ai pas vu la voiture a.** I didn't see the car (coming); **ils sont arrivés en voiture** they came by car; **l'express arrivait en gare** the express train was pulling in; **une odeur de chocolat arrivait de la cuisine** a smell of chocolate wafted in *or* came from the kitchen; **le courant/l'eau n'arrive plus** there's no more power/no more water coming through

B. *DANS LE TEMPS* **1** *(événement, jour, moment)* to come; **Noël arrive bientôt** it'll soon be Christmas; **le jour arrivera où...** the day will come when...; **la soixantaine/retraite est vite arrivée** sixty/retirement is soon upon us; **le printemps est arrivé** spring is here *or* has come; **juillet est enfin arrivé!** July is here at last!; **le grand jour est arrivé!** the big day's here at last!; **l'aube arriva enfin** dawn broke at last

2 *(se produire)* to happen; **comment est-ce arrivé?** how did it happen?; **un accident est si vite arrivé!** accidents will happen!; **ce sont des choses qui arrivent** these things happen; **ça n'arrive pas dans la vie** it doesn't happen in real life; **a. à qn** to happen to sb; **il s'est fait renvoyer – ça devait lui a.** he got fired – it was bound to happen; **ce genre d'histoires n'arrive qu'à moi!** these things only happen to me!; **ça peut a. à tout le monde** it could happen to anyone; **ça peut a. à tout le monde de se tromper!** everybody makes mistakes!; **un malheur lui est arrivé** something bad's happened to him/her; **ça n'arrive pas qu'aux autres** it's easy to think it'll never happen to you; **ça ne t'arrive jamais d'être de mauvaise humeur?** aren't you ever in a bad mood?; **tu ne te décourages jamais? – si, ça m'arrive** don't you ever get discouraged? – yes, from time to time; **tu es encore en retard? que cela ne t'arrive plus!** late? don't let it happen again!

V IMPERSONNEL 1 *(venir)* **il est arrivé des dizaines de photographes** dozens of photographers arrived; **il arrive un train toutes les heures** there's a train every hour

2 *(aventure, événement)* **il est arrivé un accident** there's been an accident; **il est arrivé tant de choses depuis deux semaines** so many things have happened during the last two weeks; **comme il arrive souvent en pareilles circonstances** as is often the case in such circumstances; **il m'est arrivé une histoire incroyable!** something incredible happened to me!; **s'il m'arrivait quelque chose, prévenez mon père** if anything happens *or* should anything happen to me, let my father know; **pourvu qu'il ne lui soit rien arrivé!** let's hope nothing's happened to him/her!

3 *(se produire parfois)* **ne peut-il pas a. que l'ordinateur se trompe?** couldn't the computer ever make a mistake?; **il arrive bien qu'ils se disputent mais...** they do quarrel sometimes *or* from time to time but...; **il m'arrive parfois de le rencontrer dans la rue** sometimes I meet him in the street; **il m'arrive rarement de me mettre en colère** I don't get angry very often; **il lui arrivait de s'enfermer des heures dans sa bibliothèque** sometimes he'd/she'd spend hours shut away in his/her library; **s'il arrivait que je sois** *ou* **fusse absent** if I happened to be away

❑ **arriver à VT IND 1** *(niveau, taille, lieu)* **le bas du rideau arrive à 20 cm du sol** the bottom of the curtain is 20 cm above the ground; **on arrive au carrefour, tu vas tourner à droite** we're coming up to *or* approaching the crossroads, you want to turn right; **le fil du téléphone n'arrive pas jusqu'à ma chambre** the phone cord doesn't reach *or* isn't long enough to reach my room; **l'eau arrive au canal par ce tuyau** the water reaches the channel through this pipe; **des bruits de conversation arrivaient jusqu'à nous** the sound of people chatting reached us; **ses cheveux lui arrivent à la taille** his/her hair comes down to his/her waist; **ma nièce m'arrive à l'épaule** my niece comes up to my shoulder; **la boue m'arrivait jusqu'aux genoux** the mud came up to my knees, I was knee-deep in mud; **la neige nous arrivait à mi-corps** the snow came up to our waists

2 *(étape, moment, conclusion)* to come to, to reach; **nous arrivons à une phase cruciale du projet** we're reaching a crucial stage in our project; **où (en) étions-nous arrivés la semaine dernière?** *(dans une leçon)* where did we get up to *or* had we got to last week?; **arrivée à la fin de son discours** when she reached the end of her speech; **maintenant qu'il est arrivé au terme de son mandat** now that he's come to *or* reached the end of his term of office; **arrivée à la fin de sa carrière/vie** having reached the end of her career/life; **j'arrive à un âge où...** I've reached an age when...; **je suis arrivé à la conclusion suivante** I've come to *or* reached the following conclusion; **arrivez-en au fait** get to the point; **et ses tableaux? – j'y arrive/arrivais** what about his/her paintings? – I'm/I was coming to that

3 *(rang, résultat)* to get; *(succès)* to achieve; **pour a. à une meilleure rentabilité** to get better results; **tu as refait l'addition? – oui, j'arrive au même total que toi** did you redo the calculations? – yes, I get the same result as you; **alors, tu es arrivé à ce que tu voulais?** so, did you manage to get *or* to achieve what you wanted?; **si tu veux a.** if you want to get on *or* to succeed in life

4 *(pouvoir, réussir à)* **a. à faire qch** to manage to do sth, to succeed in doing sth; **tu arrives à nager le crawl?** can you do the crawl?; **tu n'arriveras jamais à la convaincre** you'll never succeed in convincing her, you'll never manage to convince her; **je n'arrive pas à m'y habituer** I just can't get used to it; **je n'arrive pas à comprendre son refus** I can't understand why he/she said no; **il n'arrive pas à prononcer ce mot** he can't pronounce this word; **je ne suis pas encore arrivé à lui écrire ce mois-ci** I still haven't got round to writing to him/her this month; **je parie que tu n'y arriveras pas!** I bet you won't be able to do it!; **tu m'aides? je n'y arrive pas!** can you help me? I can't do *or* manage it!; **tu n'arriveras jamais à rien** you'll never get anywhere; **je n'arriverai jamais à rien avec lui!** I'll never be able to do anything with him!

5 *(locutions)* **(en) a. à qch** *(en venir à)* **comment peut-on en a. au suicide?** how can anybody get to the point of contemplating suicide?; **j'en arrive à penser que...** I'm beginning to think that...; **j'en arrive parfois à me demander si...** sometimes I (even) wonder if...; **elle en arrive même à ne plus le souhaiter** she's even starting to hope it won't happen; **je ne veux pas me faire opérer – il faudra pourtant bien en a. là** I don't want to have an operation – you have no choice; **depuis, je ne lui parle plus – c'est malheureux d'en a. là** since then, I haven't spoken to him/her – it's a shame when it comes to that

USAGE ABSOLU *(réussir socialement)* to succeed, to arrive

'C'est arrivé près de chez vous' *Belvaux, Bonzel & Poelvoorde* 'Man Bites Dog'

arrivisme [arivism] **NM** pushiness, ambitiousness; **elle n'est entrée au comité que par a.** for her, joining the committee was just a way of furthering her career *or* ambitions

arriviste [arivist] **ADJ** self-seeking, careerist

NMF careerist

arrobas [arɔbas] = **arobas**

arrobase [arɔbaz] = **arobas**

arrobe [arɔb] = **arobe**

arroche [arɔʃ] **NF** *Bot* orach; **a. des jardins** mountain spinach

arrogamment [arɔgamɑ̃] **ADV** arrogantly

arrogance [arɔgɑ̃s] **NF** arrogance; **parler avec a.** to speak arrogantly

arrogant, -e [arɔgɑ̃, -ɑ̃t] **ADJ** arrogant; **prendre un air a.** to take on an arrogant *or* haughty air

NM,F arrogant person

arroger [17] [arɔʒe] **s'arroger VPR** to assume, to arrogate (to oneself); **s'a. le droit de faire qch** to assume the right to do sth

arroi [arwa] **NM** *Arch* array; **arriver en grand a.** to arrive with great pomp and ceremony; **être en mauvais a.** to be in a sad *or* a sorry state

Arromanches-les-Bains [arɔmɑ̃ʃlebɛ̃] **NM** *Géog* = coastal town in Normandy famous for being the site of the first Allied landings of June 1944

arrondi, -e [arɔ̃di] **ADJ 1** *(objet, forme)* rounded, round; *(visage)* round **2** *(voyelle)* rounded

NM 1 *Couture* hemline **2** *(forme → d'une sculpture)* rounded form *or* shape; *(→ du visage)* round shape, roundness; *(→ d'un parterre)* circular line *or* design **3** *Aviat* flaring out, flattening out **4** *Ordinat & Math* rounding

arrondir [32] [arɔ̃dir] **VT 1** *(rendre rond)* to make into a round shape, to round (off); *(incurver)* to round off; **le potier arrondit son bloc d'argile** the potter rounds off his lump of clay; **arrondissez les gestes, Mesdemoiselles** round out the movement, ladies; **cette coiffure lui arrondit le visage** that haircut makes his/her face look round; **a. les lignes d'un dessin** to make the lines of a drawing rounder; **a. un angle de table** to round off a table corner

2 *(augmenter → capital, pécule)* to increase; *(→ patrimoine, domaine)* to extend; *Fam* **a. ses fins de mois** to make a little extra on the side; *Fam* **cela m'aide à a. mes fins de mois** it keeps the wolf from the door

3 *Math* to round off; *(vers le haut)* to round up; *(vers le bas)* to round down; **a. un total à l'euro supérieur/inférieur** to round a sum up/down to the nearest euro

4 *Couture* to level (off)

5 *(dégrossir → style, phrase)* to refine, to polish; *(→ parfum, goût, personnalité)* to make smoother, to round out

▸**s'arrondir VPR 1** *(grossir → femme enceinte, ventre)* to get bigger *or* rounder; *(→ visage)* to become rounder, to fill out; *(→ somme)* to mount up; **mes économies se sont arrondies!** my nest-egg is a nice size now!

2 *(devenir rond → voyelle)* to become rounded

arrondissage [arɔ̃disaʒ] **NM** *Tech* rounding

arrondissement [arɔ̃dismɑ̃] **NM** *Admin* **1** *(dans une ville)* = administrative subdivision of major French cities such as Paris, Lyons or Marseilles **2** *(au niveau départemental)* = administrative subdivision of a "département", governed by a "sous-préfet"

Culture

ARRONDISSEMENT

In Paris, Lyons and Marseilles, the number of the "arrondissement" corresponds to the last two figures in a postcode: thus, you can tell from the postcode 75012 that it refers to the 12th arrondissement of Paris.

arrondissure [arɔ̃disyr] **NF** *Typ (du dos d'un livre)* rounding

arrosable [arɔzabl] **ADJ** that can be watered

arrosage [arozaʒ] **NM 1** *(d'un jardin, de plantes)* watering; *(de la chaussée)* spraying **2** *Fam (corruption)* bribing **3** *(par les médias)* bombardment **4** *Mil (avec des bombes)* heavy bombing;

(avec des obus) heavy shelling; *(avec des balles)* spraying

arrosé, -e [aroze] **ADJ 1** *(pluvieux)* **la région est bien arrosée** the area has a high rainfall **2** *(accompagné d'alcool)* **café a.** coffee laced with alcohol; *Fam* **le repas a été plutôt bien a.** there was plenty to drink with the meal; *Fam* **après un dîner un peu trop a.** after having had a bit too much to drink at dinner

arrosement [arɔzmɑ̃] **NM** *Géog* watering

arroser [3] [aroze] **VT 1** *(asperger → plante, jardin, pelouse)* to water; **arrosez légèrement le dessus des feuilles** sprinkle some water on the surface of the leaves; **a. une voiture au jet** to hose down *or* to spray a car; **arrête, tu m'arroses!** stop it, you're spraying water (all) over me *or* I'm getting wet!; *Fam* **se faire a.** *(par la pluie)* to get drenched *or* soaked

2 *(inonder)* to soak; **attention les enfants, vous allez a. mon parquet!** careful, children, you'll get my floor all wet!; **a. qn de qch** to pour sth over sb, to drench sb in sth

3 *Culin (gigot, rôti)* to baste

4 *(repas)* **une mousse de saumon arrosée d'un bon sauvignon** a salmon mousse washed down with a fine Sauvignon; *Fam* **(bien) a. son déjeuner** to drink (heavily) with one's lunch

5 *Fam (fêter)* to drink to; **tu as été reçu premier, on va a. ça!** you came first, this calls for a celebration!; **a. une naissance** to drink to a new baby, *Br* to wet a baby's head

6 *Géog (couler à travers)* to water, to irrigate; **la Seine arrose Paris** the river Seine flows through Paris

7 *Mil (avec des bombes, des obus)* to bombard; *(avec des balles)* to spray

8 *Fam (corrompre)* to grease the palm of; **il avait arrosé des notables** he'd greased the palm of some VIPs

9 *(sujet: médias)* to bombard

▶**s'arroser VPR** *Fam* **une nouvelle comme ça, ça s'arrose!** a piece of news like that calls for a celebration!

arroseur [arozœr] **NM 1** *(personne)* waterer **2** *(dispositif)* sprinkler

Allusion

C'est l'arroseur arrosé

This expression comes from a short silent film (1895) by the Lumière brothers. The title was *L'arroseur arrosé* (literally "the waterer gets soaked" but known in English as "Hoist by his own Petard") or alternatively *Le jardinier et le petit espiègle* ("the gardener and the little imp"). It is a comical vignette, in which a gardener, busy watering his plants, manages to turn the hose on himself and gets drenched to the skin within the space of a few minutes. The expression is used in contemporary French to describe a situation where the tables are turned on someone. For example, it could be used if a politician who had championed family values is revealed to be an adulterer, and is vilified by the press and his colleagues. The English expression "now the boot is on the other foot" conveys a similar idea; more rarely, one speaks of "the biter bit".

arroseuse [arozøz] **NF** water cart

arrosoir [arozwar] **NM** watering *Br* can *or Am* pot

arrow-root [arorut] **NM** arrowroot

arroyo [arɔjo] **NM** *Géol* arroyo

arrt *Admin (abrév écrite* **arrondissement**) **1** *(dans une ville)* = administrative subdivision of major French cities such as Paris, Lyons or Marseilles **2** *(au niveau départemental)* = administrative subdivision of a "département", governed by a "sous-préfet"

ARS [aɛrɛs] **NF** *(abrév* **allocation de rentrée scolaire**) = allowance paid to parents to help cover costs incurred at the start of the school year

ars [ar, ars] **NM** *Anat* stifle (joint)

arsenal, -aux [arsənal, -o] **NM 1** *Mil & Naut* arsenal; **ils ont découvert un véritable a.** *(armes)* they've stumbled on a major arms cache; *(bombes)* they've stumbled on a bomb factory; **a. maritime** naval dockyard **2** *Fam (panoplie)* equipment, gear; **l'a. législatif** *ou* **des lois** the might of the law; **elle est arrivée avec l'a. du parfait chasseur** she came with all the right hunting gear

Arsène Lupin [arsɛnlypɛ̃] **NPR** = the gentleman thief in the detective novels of Maurice Leblanc (1864–1941)

arséniate [arsenjat] **NM** *Chim & Minér* arsenate, arseniate; **a. diplombique** *ou* **de plomb** acid lead arsenate; **a. basique de plomb** *ou* **triplombique** basic lead arsenate

arsenic [arsənik] **NM** *Chim* arsenic

'Arsenic et vieilles dentelles' *Capra, Kesselring* 'Arsenic and Old Lace'

arsenical, -e, -aux, -ales [arsənikal, -o], **arsénié, -e** [arsenje] **ADJ** *Chim* arsenical

arsénieux, -euse [arsenjø, -øz] **ADJ M** *Chim* arsenious; **acide** *ou* **anhydride a.** arsenious oxide

arsénique [arsenik] **ADJ M** *Chim* arsenic *(avant n)*

arsénite [arsenit] **NM** *Chim* arsenite

arséniure [arsenjyr] **NM** *Minér & Chim* arsenide

arsin [arsɛ̃] **ADJ M bois a.** wood damaged by fire

arsine [arsin] **NF** *Chim* arsine

arsouille [arsuj] *très Fam Vieilli* **ADJ** *(allure, genre)* loutish

NMF *Br* yob, *Am* roughneck

ART [aɛrte] **NF** *Tél (abrév* **autorité de régulation des télécommunications**) French telecommunications watchdog, *Br* ≃ Oftel

art [ar] **NM 1** *Beaux-Arts* art; **l'a. de Cézanne** Cézanne's art; **l'a. pour l'a.** art for art's sake; **a. abstrait** abstract art; **a. académique** academic art; *Ordinat* **a. ASCII** ASCII art; **a. brut** art brut; **a. cinétique** kinetic art; **a. conceptuel** conceptual art; **a. contemporain** contemporary art; **a. concret** Concrete Art; **a. cybernétique** cybernetic art; **a. déco** art deco; **a. environnemental** environmental art; **a. féministe** feminist art; **a. figuratif** figurative art; **l'a. grec** Greek art; **a. informel** informal art; **a. minimal** minimalist art; **l'a. moderne** modern art; **a. multimédia** multimedia art; **a. naïf** naive art; **a. non figuratif** nonfigurative art; **A. nouveau** Art nouveau; **a. numérique** digital art; **a. pauvre** process art; **a. primitif** primitive art; **a. sacré** *ou* **religieux** religious art; **a. vidéo** video art; **cinéma** *ou* **salle d'a. et d'essai** art house; **regardez cette pyramide de fruits, c'est du grand a.!** look at this pyramid of fruit, it's a work of art!; **vos graffiti dans le couloir, ce n'est pas du grand a.!** your graffiti in the corridor is hardly a work of art!; **le Musée national d'a. moderne** = the Paris Museum of Modern Art, in the Pompidou Centre

2 *(goût)* art, taste, artistry; **une maison décorée avec/sans a.** a house decorated with/ without taste

3 *(technique)* art; *Fig* **découper un poulet, c'est tout un a.!** carving a chicken is quite an art!; **l'a. culinaire** the art of cooking; **l'a. dramatique** dramatic art, dramatics; **cours d'a. dramatique** *(classe)* drama class; *(école)* drama school; **a. floral** flower arranging, floral art; **l'a. de la guerre** the art of warfare; **l'a. oratoire** the art of public speaking; **l'a. poétique** poetics; **l'a. sacré, le grand a.** (the art of) alchemy

4 *(don)* art, talent; **l'a. d'aimer** the art of loving; **avoir l'a. du compromis** to have mastered the art of compromise; **il a l'a. de m'énerver** he has a knack of getting on my nerves; **l'a. de vivre** the art of living; **l'Orient nous apprend un nouvel a. de vivre** from the East, we are learning a new way of living; **je voulais juste le prévenir! – oui, mais il y a l'a. et la manière** I didn't want to offend him, just to warn him! – yes, but there are ways of going about it

❑ **arts NMPL** arts; **être un ami des arts** to be a friend of the arts; **arts appliqués** ≃ art and design; **Arts Déco** = nickname of the "École nationale des arts décoratifs"; **arts décoratifs** decorative arts; **arts graphiques** graphic arts; **arts martiaux** martial arts; *Scol* **arts ménagers** home economics; *Univ* **les arts et métiers** = college for the advanced education of those working in commerce, manufacturing, construction and design; **les arts plastiques** the visual arts; **les arts premiers** ethnic art; **les arts du spectacle** the performing arts; **arts et traditions populaires** arts and crafts; **le musée des Arts d'Afrique et d'Océanie** = the museum of African and Oceanian Art in Vincennes near Paris; **le musée des Arts décoratifs** = the museum of decorative arts in the Louvre; **le musée des Arts et Traditions populaires** = the museum of arts and crafts in the Bois de Boulogne in Paris

'L'Art de la fugue' *Bach* 'The Art of Fugue'

'L'Art poétique' *Boileau* 'Ars Poetica'

'L'Art d'aimer' *Ovide* 'Ars Amatoria' *or* 'The Art of Love'

art. *(abrév écrite* **article**) art.

Artaban [artabɑ̃] **NPR fier comme A.** as proud as Punch

Artaxerxès [artagzɛrsɛs] **NPR** *Hist* Artaxerxes

Arte [arte] **NF** *TV* = Franco-German cultural television channel created in 1992

artefact [artefakt] **NM** artefact, artifact

artel [artɛl] **NM** *Hist* artel

artémia [artemja] **NF** *Zool* brine shrimp, fairy shrimp

Artémis [artemis] **NPR** *Myth* Artemis

Artémise [artemiz] **NPR** Artemisia

Arte Povera [artepɔvɛra] **NF** *Beaux-Arts* Arte Povera

artère [artɛr] **NF 1** *Anat* artery; **a. coronaire** coronary artery **2** *(route)* (main) road; *(rue)* (main) street *or* thoroughfare; **les grandes artères** the main roads

artérialisation [arterjalizasjɔ̃] **NF** *Physiol* aeration

artériectomie [arterjɛktɔmi] **NF** *Méd* arteriectomy

artériel, -elle [arterjɛl] **ADJ** *Anat* arterial

artériographie [arterjɔgrafi] **NF** *Méd* arteriography

artériole [arterjɔl] **NF** *Anat* arteriole

artériopathie [arterjɔpati] **NF** *Méd* arteriopathy

artérioscléreux, -euse [arterjɔsklerø, -øz] *Méd* **ADJ** arteriosclerotic

NM,F arteriosclerosis sufferer

artériosclérose [arterjɔskleroz] **NF** *Méd* arteriosclerosis

artériotomie [arterjɔtɔmi] **NF** *Méd* arteriotomy

artério-veineux, -euse [arterjɔvenø, -øz] *(mpl* **artério-veineux,** *fpl* **artério-veineuses**) **ADJ** *Anat* arteriovenous

artérite [arterit] **NF** *Méd* arteritis

artéritique [arteritik] **ADJ** *Méd* arteritic

artésien, -enne [artezjɛ̃, -ɛn] **ADJ** *(langue, patois)* of/from Artois

❑ **Artésien, -enne NM,F** = inhabitant of or person from Artois

arthralgie [artralʒi] **NF** *Méd* arthralgia

arthrite [artrit] **NF** *Méd* arthritis; **a. déformante** rheumatoid arthritis

arthritique [artritik] *Méd* **ADJ** arthritic

NMF arthritis sufferer

arthritisme [artritism] **NM** *Méd* arthritism, arthritic diathesis

arthrodèse [artrɔdɛz] **NF** *Méd* arthrodesis

arthrodie [artrɔdi] **NF** *Anat* arthrodia

arthrographie [artrɔgrafi] **NF** *Méd* arthrography

arthropathie [artrɔpati] **NF** *Méd* arthropathy

arthroplastie [artrɔplasti] **NF** *Méd* arthroplasty

arthropode [artrɔpɔd] *Zool & Entom* **NM** arthropod

❑ **arthropodes NMPL** the Arthropoda

arthroscopie [artrɔskɔpi] **NF** *Méd* arthroscopy

arthrose [artroz] **NF** *Méd* arthrosis

Arthur [artyr] **NPR** *Myth* Arthur; **la légende du roi A.** Arthurian legend; *Fam* **se faire appeler A.** to get one's head bitten off, to get bawled out

artichaut [artiʃo] **NM** artichoke; **a. d'Espagne** pattypan squash

artichautière [artiʃotjɛr] **NF** *Hort* artichoke bed

artiche [artiʃ] **NM** *Fam (argent)* dough, *Br* dosh, *Am* bucks

article [artikl] **NM 1** *Com* article, item; **nous ne suivons** *ou* **faisons plus cet a.** we don't stock that item any more; **articles d'alimentation** foodstuffs; **a. d'appel** loss leader, traffic builder; **a. bas de gamme** bottom-of-the-range item; **a. de base** staple; **articles de bureau** office equipment and stationery; **articles de consommation courante** consumer goods; **a.**

démarqué mark-down; **articles d'exportation** export goods, exports; **a. en fin de série** discontinued item; **a. à forte rotation** fast mover; **articles de grande consommation** consumables, consumer goods; **a. haut de gamme** top-of-the-range item; **articles d'importation** import goods, imports; **articles de luxe** luxury goods; **a. de marque** branded article; **articles de mercerie** *Br* haberdasher's goods, *Am* notions; **articles de mode** fashion accessories; **a. de première nécessité** basic commodity; **articles en promotion** *(sur vitrine)* special offers; **a. de rebut** reject; **a. en réclame** special offer; **articles de réexportation** re-export goods, re-exports; **articles sans suite** discontinued line; **articles de toilette** toiletries; **articles de voyage** travel goods; **faire l'a. pour** to do a sales pitch for; *Fig* to praise; *Fam* **elle a fait l'a. pour son bouquin toute la soirée** she went on about her book all evening

2 *Compta & Fin (d'une facture)* item; *(d'un compte)* entry; **facture détaillée par articles** itemized bill; **a. de contre-passation** transfer entry; **articles de dépense** items of expenditure; **articles divers** sundries

3 *Journ* article; *(d'un dictionnaire, d'un guide)* entry; **a. de fond** leading article, *Br* leader; **a. de tête** leading article, *Br* leader

4 *(sujet)* point; **elle dit qu'on lui doit trois millions, et sur cet a., tu peux lui faire confiance!** she says she's owed three million, and you can believe what she says on that score *or* point

5 *Rel* **articles de foi** articles of faith; *Fig* **le socialisme, pour moi, c'est un a. de foi** socialism is an article of faith for me

6 *(paragraphe)* article, clause; **les articles de la Constitution** the articles *or* clauses of the Constitution; **l'a. 10 du contrat** point *or* paragraph *or* clause 10 of the contract; **a. de loi** article of law; **A. 16** = article of the French Constitution entitling the President to assume overall power in an emergency

7 *Gram* article; **a. défini/indéfini** definite/indefinite article; **a. élidé** elided article

8 *Ordinat (d'un menu)* command; *(dans des groupes de discussion)* article; *(dans une base de données)* record

9 *(locution)* **à l'a. de la mort** at death's door, on the point of death

articulaire [artikylɛr] **ADJ** articular; **douleurs articulaires** joint pain, sore joints

articulateur [articylatœr] **NM** *Physiol* articulator

articulation [artikylasjɔ̃] **NF 1** *Anat* joint; **a. du coude/du genou/de la hanche** elbow/knee/hip joint; **a. immobile/mobile** fixed/hinge joint; **a. temporomandibulaire** temporomandibular joint; **j'ai mal aux articulations** my joints ache

2 *(prononciation)* articulation; **lieu** *ou* **point d'a.** point of articulation

3 *(liaison)* link, link-up; *(structure)* structure; **l'a. des deux parties** the link between the two parts; **l'a. des idées dans le texte** the structuring of ideas in the text

4 *Jur* enumeration, setting forth *or* out

5 *Tech* connection, joint

articulatoire [artikylatwar] **ADJ** *Ling* articulatory

articulé, -e [artikyle] **ADJ 1** *(mobile)* articulated **2** *Anat* articulated, jointed **3** *Tech* hinged, jointed; **jouet a.** jointed toy; **poupée articulée** jointed doll **4** *Ling* articulated

NM 1 *Zool* arthropod **2** *Méd* articulate

articuler [3] [artikyle] **VT 1** *(prononcer)* to articulate

2 *(dire)* to utter; **j'étais si ému que je ne pouvais plus a. un seul mot** I was so moved that I couldn't utter *or* say a single word

3 *(enchaîner → démonstration, thèse)* to link up *or* together; *(→ faits)* to connect

4 *Tech* to joint

5 *Jur (accusations)* to enumerate, to set forth *or* out

USAGE ABSOLU *(parler clairement)* **articule, je ne comprends rien** speak more clearly, I don't understand; **il articule mal** he doesn't speak clearly; **bien a.** to pronounce clearly

▶**s'articuler VPR 1** *(former une articulation)* to be joined together; **la façon dont les os s'articulent** the way the bones are joined together; **ces deux parties s'articulent assez bien** the two parts of the text hang together well

2 s'a. autour de to hinge *or* to turn on; **son article s'articule autour d'une idée originale** his/her article hinges on an original idea

3 *Anat, Tech & Zool* **s'a. sur** to be articulated *or* jointed with

articulet [artikyle] **NM** *Fam Journ* short article■

artifice [artifis] **NM 1** *(stratagème)* (clever) device *or* trick; **ils ont réussi à dissimuler la situation financière par des artifices de calcul** they managed to hide the financial situation by tweaking the figures; **ils ont usé de tous les artifices pour faire passer la proposition** they used every trick in the book to get the motion through; **beauté sans artifices** artless beauty

2 *Littéraire (adresse)* skill; **la scène est peinte avec tant d'a. que l'œil s'en trouve ébloui** the scene is depicted so skilfully that it is a wonder to behold

3 *(explosif)* firework

artificialité [artifisjalite] **NF** artificiality

artificiel, -elle [artifisjɛl] **ADJ 1** *(colorant, fleur, lumière, intelligence, insémination)* artificial; *(lac, soie)* artificial, man-made; *(perle)* artificial, imitation *(avant n)*; *(dent)* false; *(bras, hanche)* replacement *(avant n)*

2 *(factice → besoin, plaisir)* artificial

3 *(affecté → manières)* artificial; *(→ sourire)* false, artificial; *(→ rire)* forced; **je le trouve totalement a.** I find him totally artificial; **le style est très a.** the style is very contrived *or* artificial

4 *(arbitraire)* artificial; **la comparaison est totalement artificielle** it's a very artificial comparison

artificiellement [artifisjɛlmɑ̃] **ADV 1** *(fabriqué, créé)* artificially **2** *(arbitrairement)* arbitrarily

artificier [artifisje] **NM 1** *(en pyrotechnie)* fireworks expert **2** *Mil (soldat)* blaster; *(spécialiste)* bomb disposal expert

artificieuse [artifisjøz] *voir* **artificieux**

artificieusement [artifisjøzmɑ̃] **ADV** *Littéraire* deceitfully

artificieux, -euse [artifisjø, -øz] **ADJ** *Littéraire* deceitful

artillerie [artijri] **NF** *Mil* artillery; **a. anti-aérienne** anti-aircraft artillery; **a. anti-chars** anti-tank artillery; **a. d'assaut** assault artillery *or* guns; **a. de campagne** field artillery; **a. légère/lourde** light/heavy artillery; *Fig* **ils ont envoyé la grosse a.** *ou* **l'a. lourde** they used drastic measures; **pièce/tir d'a.** artillery cannon/fire

artilleur [artijœr] **NM** *Mil* artilleryman

artimon [artimɔ̃] **NM** *Naut (mât)* mizzen, mizzenmast; *(voile)* mizzen; **mât d'a.** mizzenmast

artiodactyle [artjɔdaktil] *Zool* **NM** artiodactyl

❑ **artiodactyles NMPL** Artiodactyla

artisan, -e [artizɑ̃, -an] **NM,F 1** *(travailleur)* craftsman, *f* craftswoman, artisan; **a. ébéniste** cabinet-maker; **a. verrier** (skilled) glassmaker **2** *(responsable)* architect, author; **Churchill fut l'a. de la défense nationale** Churchill was the architect of national defence; **l'a. de la paix** the peacemaker; **être l'a. de sa propre chute/ruine** to bring about one's own downfall/ruin

artisanal, -e, -aux, -ales [artizanal, -o] **ADJ 1** *(des artisans → classe, tradition)* artisan *(avant n)*; **métier a.** craft

2 *(traditionnel → méthode, travail)* traditional; **ils font toujours leur pain de façon artisanale** they still make their bread in the traditional way; **un fauteuil fabriqué de façon artisanale** a hand-made armchair; **une bombe de fabrication artisanale** a home-made bomb

3 *(rudimentaire)* basic, crude; **leur production est restée à un niveau a.** their production has remained small-scale

artisanalement [artizanalmɑ̃] **ADV ils savent encore travailler a. dans cette région** they still use traditional work methods in this area; **produire des fromages a.** to make cheese on a small scale

artisanat [artizana] **NM 1** *(profession)* **l'a.** the craft industry, the crafts **2** *(ensemble des artisans)* artisans **3** *(produits)* arts and crafts; **exposition d'a.** arts and crafts exhibition; **a. d'art** *(sur panneau)* arts and crafts; **le travail du cuir fait partie de l'a. local** leatherwork is part of local industry

artiste [artist] **ADJ 1** *(personne)* artistic

2 *(bohème → genre, vie)* bohemian

NMF 1 *Beaux-Arts (créateur)* artist; **mener une vie d'a.** to lead an artist's life; **a. peintre** painter; **représentation** *ou* **vue d'a.** artist's impression

2 *Cin & Théât (interprète)* performer; *(comédien)* actor; *(chanteur)* singer; *(de music-hall)* artiste, entertainer; **a. de cabaret** cabaret entertainer; **a. comique** comedian; **a. dramatique** actor, *f* actress

3 *(personne habile)* artist; **notre boulanger est un véritable a.** our baker is a true artist; **voilà ce que j'appelle un travail d'a.!** now that's what I call the work of an artist!; *Ironique* **quel est l'a. qui a réalisé cette merveille au tableau?** which of you lot created this masterpiece on the blackboard?

artistement [artistəmɑ̃] **ADV** *Littéraire* artistically

artistique [artistik] **ADJ** *(enseignement, richesses)* artistic; **elle a un certain sens a.** she has a certain feeling for art; **genre a.** art form

artistiquement [artistikmɑ̃] **ADV** artistically

artocarpe [artɔkarp], **artocarpus** [artɔkarpys] **NM** *Bot* artocarpus

Artois [artwa] **NM l'A.** Artois

artothèque [artɔtɛk] **NF** art lending library

arum [arɔm] **NM** *Bot* arum; **a. maculé** lords and ladies

aruspice [aryspis] = **haruspice**

arvale [arval] *Antiq* **NM** member of the Arval Brethren

ADJ Arval

arvine [arvin] **NF** *Suisse* = grape variety from the Valais canton, and white wine produced from these grapes

aryen, -enne [arjɛ̃, -ɛn] **ADJ** Aryan

❑ **Aryen, -enne NM,F** Aryan

arylamine [arilamin] **NF** *Chim* arylamine

aryle [aril] **NM** *Chim* aryl

aryténoïde [aritenɔid] *Anat* **ADJ** arytenoid

NM arytenoid

arythmie [aritmi] **NF** *Méd* arrhythmia

arythmique [aritmik] **ADJ** *Méd* arrhythmic, arrhythmical

AS [ɑɛs] **NF 1** *Sport (abrév* **association sportive***)* sports club **2** *(abrév* **assistante (de service) sociale***)* social worker

as[1] [a] *voir* **avoir**[2]

as[2] [as] **NM 1** *(carte, dé, domino)* ace; *(aux courses)* number one; **l'as de cœur/pique** the ace of hearts/spades; *Fam* **t'es fagoté** *ou* **ficelé** *ou* **fichu comme l'as de pique** you look as if you've been dragged through a hedge backwards; *Fam* **et mon sandwich, alors, il passe à l'as?** what about my sandwich, then?; **mon augmentation est passée à l'as** I might as well forget the idea of getting a pay rise

2 *Fam (champion)* ace, champ, wizard; **Delphine, t'es un as!** Delphine, you're a marvel!; **un as du traitement de texte** a word-processing wizard; **un as de la route** *ou* **du volant** a crack driver; **un as de la gâchette** a crack shot

3 *Antiq (poids, monnaie)* as

a/s *(abrév écrite* **aux soins de***)* c/o

ASA, Asa [aza] **NM INV** *Phot (abrév* **American Standards Association***)* ASA, Asa; **une pellicule 100 A.** a 100 ASA film

asa fœtida [azafetida] **NF INV** *Bot & Pharm* asafoetida, asafetida

asana [azana] **NF** *(yoga)* asana

asbeste [asbɛst] **NF** *Minér* asbestos

asbestose [asbɛstoz] **NF** *Méd* asbestosis

ASBL [ɑɛsbeɛl] **NF** *(abrév* **association sans but lucratif***)* *Br* non-profit-making *or Am* not-for-profit organization

asc. *(abrév écrite* **ascenseur***)* *Br* lift, *Am* elevator

ascaride [askarid] *Zool* **NM** roundworm, *Spéc* ascarid

❑ **ascarides NMPL** Ascaridae

ascaridiase [askaridjaz], **ascaridiose** [askaridjoz] **NF** *Méd* ascariasis

ascaris [askaris] = **ascaride**

ascendance [asɑ̃dɑ̃s] **NF 1** *(ancêtres)* ancestry **2** *(extraction)* **être d'a. allemande** to be of German descent; **être d'a. paysanne** to be of peasant origin **3** *Astron* ascent, rising **4** *Aviat & Météo* ascending current

ascendant, -e [asɑ̃dɑ̃, -ɑ̃t] **ADJ 1** *(mouvement)* rising, ascending; *(courbe)* rising; *(série)* ascending

2 *Anat (aorte, côlon)* ascending

NM 1 (*emprise*) influence, ascendancy; **avoir de l'a. sur qn** to have influence over sb; **je n'ai aucun a. sur eux** I have no influence over them; **subir l'a. de qn** to be under the influence of sb **2** *Astrol* ascendant; **Verseau a. Cancer** Aquarius with Cancer as the rising sign *or* with Cancer in the ascendant

□ **ascendants** NMPL *Jur* (*parents*) ascendants, ancestors

ascender [3] [asɑ̃de] **ascender à** VT IND *Suisse* (*prix, dépense, devis*) to amount to

ascenseur [asɑ̃sœr] **NM 1** (*dans un bâtiment*) *Br* lift, *Am* elevator; **il habite au quatrième sans a.** *Br* he lives on the fourth floor of a building with no lift, *Am* he lives in a fifth-floor walk-up **2** *Ordinat* scroll box

'L'Ascenseur pour l'échafaud' *Malle* 'Lift to the Scaffold'

ascension [asɑ̃sjɔ̃] **NF 1** (*montée → d'un ballon*) ascent; (*→ d'un avion*) climb, ascent **2** (*escalade → d'un alpiniste*) ascent, climb; **faire l'a. d'un pic** to climb a peak; **il a fait plusieurs ascensions dans les Alpes** he did several climbs in the Alps **3** (*progression*) ascent, rise; **ses affaires connaissent une a. rapide** his/her business is booming; **l'a. des Dumot dans le monde de la finance** the rising fortunes of the Dumot family in the world of finance; **a. professionnelle** climb up the professional ladder; **a. sociale** social climbing **4** *Rel* **l'A.** (*élévation du Christ*) the Ascension; **l'A., le jeudi de l'A.** Ascension Day **5** *Astron* ascension; **a. droite d'un astre** right ascension of a heavenly body

Culture
L'ASCENSION
Ascension Day is on the fortieth day after Easter and is a public holiday in France. Many people take an extended weekend break during this period.

ascensionnel, -elle [asɑ̃sjɔnɛl] ADJ (*mouvement*) upward

ascensionner [3] [asɑ̃sjɔne] *Vieilli* VT to climb VI to climb

ascensionniste [asɑ̃sjɔnist] NMF *Vieilli* (*en montagne ou en ballon*) ascensionist

ascensoriste [asɑ̃sɔrist] NMF *Br* lift *or Am* elevator engineer

ascèse [asɛz] NF *Rel* asceticism, ascetic lifestyle

ascète [asɛt] NMF *Rel* ascetic; **vivre en a.** to live an ascetic life

ascétique [asetik] ADJ *Rel* ascetic

ascétisme [asetism] NM *Rel* asceticism

ascidie [asidi] NF **1** *Bot* ascidium **2** *Zool* ascidian □ **ascidies** NFPL *Zool* ascidians, *Spéc* Ascidiacaea

ASCII [aski] NM *Ordinat* (*abrév* **American Standard Code for Information Interchange**) ASCII

ascite [asit] NF *Méd* ascites

ascitique [asitik] *Méd* ADJ ascitic, ascitical NMF patient suffering from ascites

asclépiadacée [asklepjadase] *Bot* NF asclepiad □ **asclépiadacées** NFPL Asclepiadaceae

asclépiade[1] [asklepjad] NF *Bot* asclepias, milkweed

asclépiade[2] [asklepjad] *Littérature* ADJ asclepiadean, asclepiadic NM asclepiad

asclépias [asklepjas] = **asclépiade**[1]

ascomycète [askɔmisɛt] *Bot* NM ascomycete □ **ascomycètes** NMPL Ascomycetes

ascorbique [askɔrbik] ADJ *Méd* ascorbic

ascospore [askɔspɔr] NF *Bot* ascospore

asdic [asdik] NM *Naut* asdic

ASE [ɑɛsə] NF *Astron* (*abrév* **Agence spatiale européenne**) ESA

ase [az] NF *Méd* **a. fétide** asafoetida

aséismique [aseismik] = **asismique**

aselle [azɛl] NM *Zool* (*crustacé*) asellus; **a. aquatique** water-slater

asémantique [asemɑ̃tik] ADJ *Ling* asemantic

asepsie [asɛpsi] NF *Méd* asepsis

aseptique [asɛptik] ADJ *Méd* aseptic

aseptisation [asɛptizasjɔ̃] NF (*d'une blessure, d'un pansement*) sterilization, asepsis; (*d'une pièce*) disinfection

aseptisé, -e [asɛptize] ADJ (*ambiance*) clinical; (*univers*) sterile, sanitized

aseptiser [3] [asɛptize] VT (*blessure*) to sterilize; (*pièce*) to disinfect

asexualité [asɛksɥalite] NF asexuality

asexué, -e [asɛksɥe] ADJ (*plante, reproduction*) asexual; (*individu*) asexual, sexless

ashkénase [aʃkenaz] ADJ **juif a.** Ashkenazi NMF Ashkenazi; **les ashkénases** the Ashkenazim

ashram [aʃram] NM *Rel* ashram

ashtanga yoga [aʃtɑ̃gajɔga] NM ashtanga (yoga)

ASI [aɛsi] NF (*abrév* **association de solidarité internationale**) international aid organization

asiadollar [azjadɔlar] NM Asiadollar

asiago [asjago] NM *Culin* (*fromage*) asiago (*Italian grating cheese made from cow's milk*)

asialie [asjali] NF *Méd* asialia, aptyalism

asiate [azjat] *Péj* ADJ Oriental □ **Asiate** NMF = offensive term used to refer to an Oriental

asiatique [azjatik] ADJ **1** (*d'Extrême-Orient*) Oriental; **un restaurant a.** = a restaurant serving Oriental cuisine **2** (*de l'Asie en général*) Asian □ **Asiatique** NMF **1** (*d'Extrême-Orient*) Oriental **2** (*de l'Asie en général*) Asian

Culture
ASIATIQUE
This word tends to refer to Oriental people (ie from countries such as China, Japan, Laos etc), rather than Asia as a whole. Note that it does not refer to the British English sense of "Asian" meaning someone from the Indian subcontinent.

Asie [azi] NF *Géog* Asia; **l'A. centrale** Central Asia; *Hist* **l'A. Mineure** Asia Minor; **l'A. du Sud-Est** Southeast Asia

asiento [asjɛnto] NM *Hist* asiento (*contract given by the Spanish crown granting a trade monopoly, especially in the slave trade*)

asilage [azilaʒ] NM *Com & Mktg* cross-marketing

asilaire [azilɛr] ADJ *Littéraire* **séjour/traitement a.** stay/treatment at a mental hospital

asile [azil] NM **1** (*abri*) refuge; **offrir à qn un a. pour la nuit** to give sb shelter for the night; **chercher/trouver a.** to seek/to find refuge; **votre jardin est un a. de paix et de verdure** your garden is a haven of peace and greenery; *Littéraire* **le dernier a.** the final resting place, the grave **2** *Hist & Pol* asylum; **demander l'a. diplomatique/politique** to seek diplomatic protection/political asylum **3** (*établissement → gén*) home; **a. d'aliénés** *ou* **de fous** mental home, *Vieilli* (lunatic) asylum; **a. de nuit** night shelter; *Fam* **il est bon pour l'a.!** he ought to be locked up! **4** *Entom* robberfly, *Spéc* asilus **5** *Mktg* (*document publicitaire*) stuffer, insert

asinien, -enne [azinjɛ̃, -ɛn] ADJ *Zool* asinine

asismique [asismik] ADJ *Géol* aseismic

Asmara [asmara] NM *Géog* Asmara

Asmodée [asmɔde] NPR Asmodeus

Asmonéens [asmɔneɛ̃] NMPL *Hist* Hasmoneans

asociabilité [asɔsjabilite] NF asociability

asocial, -e, -aux, -ales [asɔsjal, -o] ADJ antisocial, *Sout* asocial NM,F dropout, social outcast

asocialité [asɔsjalite] NF asociality

asomatognosie [asɔmatɔgnɔzi] NF *Psy* asomatognosia

asparagine [asparaʒin] NF *Chim* asparagine

asparagus [asparagys] NM *Bot* asparagus fern

aspartam, aspartame [aspartam] NM *Chim* aspartame; **yaourt à l'a.** yoghurt sweetened with aspartame

aspartique [aspartik] ADJ *Chim* aspartic

Aspasie [aspazi] NPR *Hist* Aspasia

aspe [asp] NM *Tex* silk reel *or* winder

aspect [aspɛ] NM **1** (*apparence*) appearance, look; **un bâtiment d'a. imposant** an imposing-looking building; **des fromages d'un bel a.** fine-looking cheeses; **tu ne trouves pas que la viande a un a. bizarre?** don't you think the meat looks odd?; **donner l'a. de qch à qn** to give sb the appearance of sth, to make sb look like sth; **ces couleurs sombres donnent à la pièce un a. bien terne** all those dark colours make the room look very dull; **prendre l'a. de qch** (*ressembler à quelque chose*) to take on the appearance of sth; (*se métamorphoser en quelque chose*) to turn into sth; **offrir** *ou* **présenter l'a. de qch** to look like *or* to resemble sth **2** (*point de vue*) aspect, facet; **envisager** *ou* **examiner une question sous tous ses aspects** to consider a question from all angles; **vu sous cet a.** seen from this angle *or* point of view; **sous un a. nouveau** in a new light **3** *Astrol & Ling* aspect □ **à l'aspect de** PRÉP at the sight of, upon seeing; **elle s'est évanouie à l'a. du sang** she fainted at the sight of the blood

aspectuel, -elle [aspɛktɥɛl] ADJ *Ling* aspectual

asperge [aspɛrʒ] NF **1** (*plante*) asparagus; **des asperges** asparagus **2** *Fam* (*personne*) **une (grande) a.** a beanpole

asperger [17] [aspɛrʒe] VT **1** (*légèrement*) to sprinkle; **a. le linge avant de le repasser** to spray clothes with water before ironing; **a. qn d'eau** *ou* **avec de l'eau** to spray sb with water **2** (*tremper*) to splash, to splatter; **se faire a.** to get splashed; **on s'est fait copieusement a.** we got drenched *or* soaked; **a. qn/qch de qch** to splash sb/sth with sth, to splash sth on sb/sth ▶**s'asperger** VPR **1** (*emploi réfléchi*) **s'a. de qch** to splash oneself with sth, to splash sth on oneself **2** (*emploi réciproque*) to splash *or* to spray one another

aspergès [aspɛrʒɛs] NM *Rel* **1** (*goupillon*) aspergillum, holy-water sprinkler **2** (*rite*) Asperges

aspergille [aspɛrʒil] NF *Biol* aspergillus

aspergillose [aspɛrʒiloz] NF *Méd* aspergillosis

aspergillus [aspɛrʒilys] = **aspergille**

aspérité [asperite] NF **1** (*proéminence*) rough bit; **les aspérités de la roche** the rough edges of the rock; **les aspérités d'une surface** the roughness of a surface **2** *Littéraire* (*rudesse*) asperity, harshness

aspermatisme [aspɛrmatism] NM *Méd* aspermia

asperme [aspɛrm] ADJ *Bot* seedless

aspermie [aspɛrmi] NF *Méd* aspermia

asperseur [aspɛrsœr] NM sprinkler

aspersion [aspɛrsjɔ̃] NF **1** (*d'eau*) sprinkling, spraying **2** *Rel* sprinkling, aspersion

aspersoir [aspɛrswar] NM **1** *Rel* (*goupillon*) aspersorium **2** (*pomme d'arrosoir*) rose

aspérule [asperyl] NF *Bot* **a. à l'esquinancie** squinancywort; **a. odorante** woodruff

asphaltage [asfaltaʒ] NM asphalting

asphalte [asfalt] NM **1** (*bitume*) asphalt **2** *Fam* (*chaussée*) street■

asphalter [3] [asfalte] VT to asphalt

asphaltier [asfaltje] NM *Naut* asphalt carrier

asphodèle [asfɔdɛl] NM *Bot* asphodel; **a. blanc** king's spear

asphyxiant, -e [asfiksjɑ̃, -ɑ̃t] ADJ **1** (*obus, vapeur*) asphyxiating, suffocating **2** (*oppressant → ambiance*) stifling, suffocating

asphyxie [asfiksi] NF **1** *Méd* asphyxia; **mourir par a.** to die of asphyxiation; **a. par submersion** drowning **2** *Fig* paralysis; **la guerre conduit le pays à l'a.** war is paralysing the country; **a. économique** economic paralysis *or* strangulation

asphyxié, -e [asfiksje] ADJ **1** (*personne → par manque d'air*) suffocated; (*→ au gaz*) asphyxiated **2** *Fig* (*personne*) oppressed; (*pays, économie*) paralysed NM,F (*personne → par manque d'air*) suffocated person; (*→ au gaz*) asphyxiated person

asphyxier [9] [asfiksje] VT **1** (*priver d'air*) to suffocate; (*faire respirer du gaz à*) to asphyxiate; **mourir asphyxié** to die of asphyxiation **2** *Fig* (*personne*) to oppress; (*pays, économie*) to paralyse ▶**s'asphyxier** VPR **1** (*volontairement, au gaz*) to gas oneself **2** (*accidentellement*) to suffocate; **un enfant peut s'a. avec un sac en plastique** a child could suffocate (itself) with a plastic bag **3** *Fig* (*pays, économie*) to become paralysed

aspic [aspik] NM **1** *Zool* asp **2** *Bot & Culin* aspic

aspidistra [aspidistra] NM *Bot* aspidistra

aspirant, -e [aspirã, -ãt] **ADJ** sucking, pumping
NM,F candidate; **un a. à un poste** a job candidate, a candidate for a post
NM *Mil* (*dans l'armée de terre, de l'air*) officer cadet; (*dans la marine*) midshipman

aspirateur [aspiratœr] **NM 1** (*domestique*) vacuum cleaner, *Br* Hoover®; **passer l'a.** to do the vacuuming *or Br* hoovering; **j'ai passé l'a. dans la chambre** I vacuumed *or Br* hoovered the bedroom **2** *Méd & Tech* aspirator

aspirateur-balai [aspiratœrbalɛ] (*pl* **aspirateurs-balais**) **NM** upright vacuum cleaner *or Br* Hoover®

aspirateur-traîneau [aspiratœrtrɛno] (*pl* **aspirateurs-traîneaux**) **NM** cylinder vacuum cleaner *or Br* Hoover®

aspiration [aspirasjɔ̃] **NF 1** (*ambition*) aspiration, ambition **2** (*souhait*) yearning, longing, craving **3** (*absorption → d'air*) sucking up **4** *Tech* induction **5** *Ling* (*d'une voyelle*) aspiration **6** *Méd* **a. endo-utérine, IVG par a.** abortion by vacuum extraction

aspiratoire [aspiratwar] **ADJ** aspiratory

aspiré, -e [aspire] **ADJ** (*voyelle*) aspirate
❏ **aspirée** **NF** aspirate

aspirer [3] [aspire] **VT 1** (*inspirer*) to inhale, to breathe in; **il aspira goulûment l'air frais** he took long deep breaths of *or* he gulped in the fresh air; **j'aspirais avec précaution l'air glacé** I was breathing the icy air in cautiously
2 (*pomper*) to suck up; **a. une boisson avec une paille** to suck a drink through a straw; **a. de l'air/des gaz d'une conduite** to pump air/gas out of a main
3 (*avec un aspirateur*) to vacuum, *Br* to hoover; **a. la poussière d'un tapis** to vacuum *or Br* to hoover a carpet
4 *Ling* (*voyelle*) to aspirate
❏ **aspirer à VT IND** (*paix, repos*) to crave, to long for, to yearn for; (*rang, dignité*) to aspire to; **a. à faire qch** to long to do sth

aspirine [aspirin] **NF** *Pharm* aspirin; **un comprimé ou cachet d'a.** an aspirin; **prenez deux aspirines** take two aspirin(s)

aspiro-batteur [aspirobatœr] (*pl* **aspiro-batteurs**) **NM** beating vacuum cleaner *or Br* Hoover®

asple [aspl] **NM** *Tex* silk reel *or* winder

asplénium [asplenjɔm] **NM** *Bot* asplenium

asque [ask] **NM** *Bot* ascus

asram [aʃram] = **ashram**

ASS [aɛsɛs] **NF** (*abrév* **allocation de solidarité spécifique**) = allowance paid to long-term unemployed people who are no longer entitled to unemployment benefit

assa-fœtida [asafetida] = **asa fœtida**

assagir [32] [asaʒir] **VT** *Littéraire* **1** (*apaiser → personne*) to quieten down; (→ *passion, violence*) to soothe, to allay; **l'âge assagit les passions** passions wane *or* become less intense with age; **un visage aux traits assagis** a face with composed features; **l'expérience l'a assagie** experience has made her a wiser person
2 (*faire se ranger*) to cause to settle down; **c'est un homme assagi maintenant** he's calmed down a lot
▶**s'assagir VPR 1** (*se calmer → enfant*) to calm down, to *Br* quieten *or Am* quiet down; (*se ranger → adulte*) to settle down
2 *Fig* **la passion s'assagit avec l'âge** passions wane *or* become less intense with age

assagissement [asaʒismã] **NM** settling *or* quietening down

assai [asaj] **ADV** *Mus* assai

assaillant, -e [asajã, -ãt] **ADJ** *Mil* (*armée, troupe*) assailing, assaulting, attacking
NM assailant, attacker

assaillir [47] [asajir] **VT** *Mil* to attack; (*esprit, imagination*) to beset; **le doute m'assaillit** I was beset with doubt; **le bureau est assailli de demandes** the office is swamped *or* besieged with inquiries; **à mon retour j'ai été assailli de questions** when I came back I was bombarded with questions

assainir [32] [asenir] **VT 1** (*nettoyer → quartier, ville*) to clean up, to improve; (→ *logement*) to clean up; (→ *air*) to purify
2 (*assécher → plaine, région*) to improve the drainage of; (→ *marécage*) to drain

3 (*stabiliser → situation*) to clear up; (→ *bilan*) to balance; (→ *budget, monnaie, économie*) to stabilize; **a. ses finances** to put one's finances in order; **a. le climat social** to put an end to social strife
▶**s'assainir VPR** to improve, to become healthier; **la situation s'est assainie** the situation has improved

assainissant, -e [asenisã, ãt] **ADJ** cleansing, purifying

assainissement [asenismã] **NM 1** (*nettoyage → d'un quartier, d'une ville*) cleaning-up, improvement; (→ *d'un logement, d'un appartement*) cleaning up; (→ *de l'air*) purification; **un nouveau projet d'a. pour notre quartier** a new project for improving our district
2 (*assèchement*) draining
3 (*d'un budget, d'une monnaie, de l'économie*) stabilization; (*d'un bilan*) balancing; (*des finances*) putting in order; **a. monétaire** stabilization of the currency

assainisseur [aseniscœr] **NM** air-freshener

assaisonnement [asɛzɔnmã] **NM** *Culin* **1** (*processus*) dressing, seasoning **2** (*condiments*) seasoning; (*sauce*) dressing

assaisonner [3] [asɛzɔne] **VT 1** *Culin* (*plat, sauce*) to season; (*salade*) to dress; **ta salade est trop assaisonnée** there's too much dressing on your salad; **a. des poireaux avec de la *ou* à la vinaigrette** to give leeks a vinaigrette dressing
2 *Fig* (*agrémenter*) **a. qch de** to spice *or* to lace sth with
3 *Fam* (*malmener*) **a. qn** to tell sb off; **on va l'a., celui-là!** we'll certainly take care of HIM!; **elle m'a drôlement assaisonné quand je suis arrivé en retard!** she (certainly) let me have it when I turned up late!
4 *Fam* (*escroquer*) to sting, to rip off; **un restaurant où on se fait a.** a restaurant where you get ripped off
USAGE ABSOLU *Culin* **assaisonnez et servez immédiatement** season and serve immediately

Assam [asam] **NM 1** (*état*) Assam **2** (*thé*) Assam (tea)

assamais, -e [asamɛ, -ɛz] **ADJ** Assamese
NM (*langue*) Assamese
❏ **Assamais, -e NM,F** Assamese; **les A.** the Assamese

assassin, -e [asasɛ̃, -in] **ADJ** *Littéraire Hum* **1** (*méchant → regard*) murderous; (→ *remarque*) crushing **2** (*provocant → sourire*) provocative; (→ *œillade*) provocative, smouldering; **jeter une œillade assassine à qn** to give someone a smouldering look
NM (*gén*) murderer, killer; (*d'une personnalité connue*) assassin; **à l'aide, à l'a.!** help, murder!

assassinat [asasina] **NM** (*gén*) murder; (*d'une personnalité connue*) assassination; *Fig* **l'a. de la liberté** the assassination of liberty

assassine [asasin] *voir* **assassin**

assassiner [3] [asasine] **VT 1** (*tuer → gén*) to murder; (→ *personnalité connue*) to assassinate; **se faire a.** to be murdered
2 *Fam Péj* (*malmener → musique, symphonie*) to murder, to slaughter
3 *Fam* (*ruiner*) to bleed; **on assassine le contribuable!** the taxpayer is being bled dry!
4 *Fam* (*critiquer → livre, film*) to slate, to pan; **il s'est fait a. par la presse de droite** he got crucified by the right-wing press; **si je dis ce que je pense vraiment, je vais me faire a.** if I say what I really think I'll get crucified

assaut [aso] **NM 1** *Mil* assault, attack, onslaught; **un a. contre** an assault on *or* against; *aussi Fig* **aller *ou* monter à l'a.** to attack; **à l'a.!** charge!; **donner l'a.** to launch *or* to mount an attack; **donner l'a. à** to launch *or* mount an attack on, to storm; **se lancer à l'a. d'une ville** to launch an attack *or* to mount an onslaught on a town; **ils se sont lancés à l'a. de la face nord** they launched *or* mounted an assault on the north face; *Fig* **ils se sont lancés à l'a. du marché japonais** they set out to capture the Japanese market; **résister aux assauts de l'ennemi** to withstand enemy attacks; **prendre d'a. un palais** to storm a palace; *Fig* **à la chute de la Bourse, les banques ont été prises d'a. par les petits porteurs** when the Stock Exchange crashed, the banks were stormed by small

shareholders; **le bar était pris d'a.** the bar was mobbed; **les otages libérés ont subi les assauts de la presse** the released hostages had to put up with press harassment; **les assauts répétés de la maladie** the repeated attacks *or* onslaughts of the disease; *Littéraire* **elles font a. de politesse/gentillesse** they're falling over each other to be polite/nice; **troupes d'a.** storm troops
2 *Escrime* bout

─────────────

-ASSE [as] **SUFF**
● The main connotation of this suffix is a DEROGATORY one, when coupled with a noun, an adjective or a verb:
vinasse cheap wine, plonk; **paperasse** paperwork, forms; **blondasse** yellowish, blondish; **connasse** stupid bitch; **la chiasse** the runs
● Note that the resulting nouns are always feminine (**la vinasse, la paperasse**), whereas the adjectives are masculine or feminine (**des cheveux blondasses, un style fadasse**).

─────────────

asseau [aso] **NM** *Constr* tiler's hammer

assèchement [asɛʃmã] **NM** draining, drying-up

assécher [18] [aseʃe] **VT** (*drainer → terre, sol*) to drain (the water off); (*vider → étang, réservoir*) to empty
VI (*à marée basse*) to become dry, to dry up
▶**s'assécher VPR** to become dry, to dry up

ASSEDIC, Assedic [asedik] **NFPL** (*abrév* **Association pour l'emploi dans l'industrie et le commerce**) = French unemployment insurance scheme, *Br* ≃ Unemployment Benefit Office, *Am* ≃ Unemployment Office; **toucher les A.** to get unemployment benefit

assemblage [asãblaʒ] **NM 1** (*fait de mettre ensemble*) assembling, constructing, fitting together; *Couture* sewing together; (*d'un tricot*) making up; *Menuis* joining; **procéder à l'a. de pièces** to assemble parts; **a. par soudage** soldering together; **a. par tenons et mortaises** tenon and mortise joining
2 *Aut & Ind* assembly
3 (*ensemble*) assembly; *Constr* framework, structure; *Menuis* joint; **a. à tenon et mortaise** mortise-and-tenon joint
4 *Beaux-Arts* assemblage
5 *Typ* gathering
6 *Péj* (*amalgame*) collection, concoction; **son livre n'est qu'un a. d'idées bizarres** his/her book is just a collection of weird ideas thrown together
7 *Ordinat* assembly; **langage d'a.** assembly language

assemblé [asãble] **NM** (*pas de danse*) assemblé

assemblée[1] [asãble] **NF 1** (*groupe*) gathering; (*auditoire*) audience; **en présence d'une nombreuse a.** in front of a large audience; *Rel* **l'a. des fidèles** the congregation
2 (*réunion*) meeting; **a. des actionnaires** shareholders' meeting; **a. générale** general meeting; **a. générale d'actionnaires** general meeting of shareholders; **a. générale annuelle** annual general meeting; **la fédération a tenu son a. annuelle à Lille** the federation held its annual meeting in Lille; **a. (générale) ordinaire/ extraordinaire** ordinary/extraordinary (general) meeting
3 *Pol* (*élus*) **la Haute A.** the (French) Senate; **a. constituante** constituent assembly; **a. fédérale** (*en Suisse*) (Swiss) federal assembly; *Hist* **l'A. législative** the Legislative Assembly; **l'A. (nationale)** the (French) National Assembly; **A. parlementaire européenne** European Parliament
4 (*bâtiment*) **l'A.** ≃ the House

Culture

ASSEMBLÉE NATIONALE

The French parliament has two chambers: the National Assembly and the Senate. The members of the National Assembly (the "députés") are elected in the "élections législatives" held every five years.

assemblée² [asɑ̃ble] = **assemblé**

assembler [3] [asɑ̃ble] **VT 1** *(monter)* to assemble, to put *or* to fit together; *Menuis* to joint; **elle a tout assemblé elle-même à partir d'un kit** she put it together herself from a kit; **assemblez le dos et le devant du tricot** sew the back and the front of the sweater together; **a. des poutres bout à bout** to butt beams; **a. deux pièces par collage/soudure** to glue/to solder two parts together

2 *(combiner → pensées)* to gather (together); *(→ documents)* to collate

3 *Vieilli (personnes)* to call together, to assemble

4 *Ordinat* to assemble

►**s'assembler VPR** *(foule, badauds)* to gather; *(députés, actionnaires)* to gather, to assemble

assembleur, -euse [asɑ̃blœr, -øz] **NM,F** *(ouvrier)* fitter

NM *Ordinat* assembler (language)

❑ **assembleuse NF** *Typ* gathering machine

assener [19], **asséner** [18] [asene] **VT** *(coup)* to deliver, to strike; *Fig* **je lui ai asséné quelques vérités bien senties** I hurled a few home truths at him/her; **on nous assène des publicités toute la journée** we're bombarded with adverts all day long; **c'est là qu'il lui a asséné l'argument final** that's when he produced the argument that clinched matters

assentiment [asɑ̃timɑ̃] **NM** assent, agreement; **donner/refuser son a. (à qch)** to give/withhold one's assent (to sth); **hocher la tête en signe d'a.** to nod one's head (in agreement)

asseoir [65] [aswar] **VT 1** *(mettre en position assise)* **a. qn** *(le mettre sur un siège)* to sit sb down; *(le redresser dans son lit)* to sit sb up; **il assit les enfants sur un banc** he placed *or* sat the children on a bench; **huit personnes seront là pour dîner, où vais-je les a.?** there will be eight people at dinner, where am I going to put them all?; **assois-le-bien, il va tomber** sit him up properly, he's going to fall over; **a. qn sur le trône** *(le couronner)* to put sb on the throne

2 *(consolider)* to establish; **a. son autorité** to establish *or* to strengthen one's authority; **a. sa réputation sur qch** to base one's reputation on sth

3 *(faire reposer → statue)* to sit, to rest; **veillez à bien a. l'appareil sur son pied** make sure the camera is resting securely on its stand

4 *Fam (étonner)* to stun, to astound▪; **son insolence nous a tous assis** we were stunned by his/her insolence; **j'en suis resté assis** I was flabbergasted

5 *Fin (impôt, taxe)* to base, to calculate the basis for; **a. l'impôt sur le revenu** to base taxation on income

6 *Équitation* to sit

VI faire a. qn to ask sb to sit down; **je vous en prie, faites a. tout le monde** please have everyone sit down *or* get everyone to sit down; **je n'ai pas pu le faire a.** I couldn't get him to sit down

►**s'asseoir VPR 1** *(s'installer)* to sit down; **elle s'est assise** she sat down; **asseyez-vous donc** please, do sit down; **asseyons-nous par terre** let's sit on the floor; **venez vous a. à table avec nous** come and sit at the table with us; **tu devrais t'a. un peu dans ton lit, tu serais mieux** you should sit up a bit in bed, you'd be more comfortable; **s'a. en tailleur** to sit cross-legged; **il s'assit sur ses talons** he sat down on his heels

2 *très Fam (locution)* **ton opinion, je m'assois dessus** I couldn't give a damn about your opinion; **votre dossier, vous pouvez vous a. dessus** you know what you can do with your file

assermentation [asɛrmɑ̃tasjɔ̃] **NF** *Can & Suisse* swearing in, taking of an oath

assermenté, -e [asɛrmɑ̃te] **ADJ 1** *(fonctionnaire, médecin)* sworn (in); *(expert, témoin)* on *or* under oath **2** *Hist* **prêtre a.** juror *(who, in 1790, swore allegiance to the constitution regarding the French clergy)*; **prêtre non a.** non-juror *(who, in 1790, refused to swear allegiance to the constitution regarding the French clergy)*

NM,F person on *or* under oath

assermenter [3] [asɛrmɑ̃te] **VT** *Jur (fonctionnaire, médecin)* to swear in; *(expert, témoin)* to put on *or* under oath

assertif, -ive [asɛrtif, -iv] **ADJ** *(affirmatif)* assertive

assertion [asɛrsjɔ̃] **NF** assertion

assertive [asɛrtiv] *voir* **assertif**

assertorique [asɛrtɔrik] **ADJ** *Phil* assertoric, assertorial

asservir [32] [asɛrvir] **VT 1** *(assujettir → gén)* to enslave; *(→ nation)* to reduce to slavery, to enslave; **être asservi à une cause** to be in thrall to a cause; *Vieilli* **a. ses instincts** to control one's instincts, to keep one's instincts under control **2** *Tech* to put under servo *or* remote control; **moteur asservi** servomotor

►**s'asservir à VPR** to submit *or* to bow to

asservissant, -e [asɛrvisɑ̃, -ɑ̃t] **ADJ** enslaving; **avoir un emploi a.** to be a slave to one's job

asservissement [asɛrvismɑ̃] **NM 1** *(assujettissement)* enslavement (**de** of); **on note un a. de plus en plus grand à la mode** people are following fashion more and more slavishly **2** *Tech* servomechanism

asservisseur [asɛrvisœr] **ADJ M** controlling

NM control unit, *Br* control system, *Am* controlling means

assesseur [asesœr] **NM** assessor

assette [asɛt] **NF** *Constr* tiler's hammer

asseyait *etc voir* **asseoir**

assez [ase] **ADV 1** *(suffisamment)* enough; **je suis a. fatigué comme ça** I'm tired enough as it is; **la maison est a. grande pour nous tous** the house is big enough for all of us; **il roule a. vite comme ça** he drives fast enough as it is; **tu n'as pas crié a. fort** you didn't shout loud enough; **j'ai a. travaillé pour aujourd'hui** I've done enough work for today; **il n'a pas a. fait attention** he didn't pay (careful) enough attention; **est-ce que c'est a.?** is that enough?; **c'est bien a.** that's plenty; **c'est plus qu'a.** that's more than enough; **ça a a. duré!** it's gone on long enough!; **a. parlé, agissons!** that's enough talk *or* talking, let's DO something!; **en voilà** *ou* **c'(en) est a.!** that's enough!, enough's enough!; **elle est a. grande pour s'habiller toute seule** she's old enough to dress herself; **il est a. bête pour le croire** he's stupid enough to believe it

2 *(plutôt, passablement)* quite, rather; **disons qu'elle est a. jolie, sans plus** let's say she's quite pretty, no more than that; **j'aime a. sa maison** I quite like his house; **c'est un a. bon exemple de ce qu'il ne faut pas faire** it's a pretty good example of what not to do; **je suis a. contente de moi** I'm quite pleased with myself; **la situation est a. grave** the situation is quite serious; **ils sont arrivés a. tard** they arrived rather late; **ils se connaissent depuis a. longtemps** they've known each other for quite a long time; **j'ai a. peu mangé aujourd'hui** I haven't eaten much today; **il y a a. peu de monde** there aren't many people, it isn't very busy

❑ **assez de ADJ** enough; **il y a a. de monde** there are enough people; **nous n'aurons pas a. de temps** we won't have enough time; **il y en a a.** there is/are enough; **il en reste juste a.** there is/are just enough left; **il n'a pas besoin de venir, nous sommes (bien) a. de deux** he doesn't need to come, two of us will be (quite) enough; **j'aurai bien a. d'une couverture** one blanket will be quite enough *or* sufficient; **j'ai a. d'argent pour vivre** I have enough money to live on; **j'ai juste a. d'essence pour finir le trajet** I've got just enough petrol to last the journey; *Fam* **j'en ai a. de vous écouter râler** I've had enough of (listening to) your moaning; **j'en ai (plus qu')a. de toutes ces histoires!** I've had (more than) enough of all this fuss!

assibilation [asibilasjɔ̃] **NF** *Ling* assibilation, sibilation

assidu, -e [asidy] **ADJ 1** *(zélé)* assiduous, diligent, hard-working; **élève a.** hard-working pupil; **il n'est pas très brillant mais au moins il est a.** he's not very bright but at least he's conscientious; **un amoureux a.** a persistent lover; **il lui faisait une cour assidue** he courted her assiduously

2 *(constant)* unflagging, unremitting, untiring; **grâce à un travail a.** by dint of hard work; **elle a fourni des efforts assidus** she made unremitting efforts

3 *(fréquent)* regular, constant; **un visiteur a. des expositions** a frequent *or* dedicated exhibition-goer

assiduité [asidɥite] **NF 1** *(zèle)* assiduity; **travailler avec a. (à qch)** to work assiduously *or* zealously (at sth)

2 *(régularité)* regular attendance; **l'a. aux répétitions est essentielle** regular attendance at rehearsals is vital; **je fréquente les musées avec a.** I visit museums regularly

❑ **assiduités NFPL** attentions; **importuner** *ou* **poursuivre qn de ses assiduités** to force one's attentions upon sb

assidûment [asidymɑ̃] **ADV 1** *(avec zèle)* assiduously; **il y travaille a.** he is hard at work on it **2** *(régulièrement)* assiduously, unremittingly, untiringly

assied *etc voir* **asseoir**

assiégé, -e [asjeʒe] **NM,F** besieged person; **les assiégés** the besieged

assiégeant, -e [asjeʒɑ̃, -ɑ̃t] **ADJ** besieging

NM besieger

assiégée [asjeʒe] *voir* **assiégé**

assiéger [22] [asjeʒe] **VT 1** *Mil (ville, forteresse)* to lay siege to, to besiege

2 *(se présenter en foule à)* to besiege, to mob; **la maison fut assiégée par les journalistes** the house was besieged by journalists; **les guichets ont été assiégés** the ticket office was stormed by the public; **la ville est assiégée par les touristes** the town is overrun with *or* by tourists

3 *Littéraire (importuner → sujet: personne)* to harass, to plague, to pester; *(→ sujet: pensées)* to beset

assiéra *etc voir* **asseoir**

assiette [asjɛt] **NF 1** *(récipient)* plate; **grande a.** dinner plate; **petite a.** dessert *or* side plate; *Belg* **a. profonde** soup dish; **a. en carton** paper plate; **a. creuse** *ou* **à soupe** soup dish; **a. à dessert** dessert plate; **a. plate** (dinner) plate; *Fam* **c'est l'a. au beurre** it's a cushy number

2 *(contenu)* plate, plateful; **une (pleine) a. de soupe** a (large) plateful of soup; **finis d'abord ton a.** eat up what's on your plate first; **faire une a. de légumes** to prepare a dish of (mixed) vegetables; **a. anglaise** assorted cold meats

3 *(assise)* foundation, basis; *(d'une voie ferrée, d'une route)* bed

4 *Fin (d'un impôt, d'un taux)* base; *(d'une hypothèque)* = property or funds on which a mortgage is secured; **a. de l'amortissement** depreciation, depreciable base; **a. fiscale** *ou* **de l'impôt** taxable income

5 *Équitation* seat; **avoir une bonne a.** to have a good seat

6 *Naut* trim

7 *(locution)* **je ne suis pas** *ou* **je ne me sens pas dans mon a.** I don't feel too well, I'm feeling (a bit) out of sorts

assiettée [asjete] **NF 1** *(mesure)* **une a. de** a plate *or* plateful of **2** *(contenu)* **il a jeté toute l'a. par terre** he threw all the contents of the plate on the floor

assignable [asiɲabl] **ADJ 1** *(attribuable)* ascribable, attributable **2** *Jur* liable to be subpoenaed

assignat [asiɲa] **NM** *Hist* paper money *(issued during the French Revolution)*

assignataire [asiɲatɛr] **NMF** *Jur* beneficiary of an allocation

assignation [asiɲasjɔ̃] **NF 1** *(attribution → d'une tâche, d'un poste)* allocation, assignment **2** *Jur* **a. (à comparaître)** *(d'un témoin)* subpoena; *(d'un accusé)* summons; **a. à résidence** *ou* **à domicile** house arrest; **a. à toutes fins** summons to the "tribunal d'instance" *(to resolve the dispute either by arbitration or by a court ruling)* **3** *Fin (de parts, de fonds)* allotment, allocation (**de** to) **4** *Bourse* exercise notice

assigner [3] [asiɲe] **VT 1** *(attribuer → tâche, poste)* to allocate, to assign; *(→ valeur)* to attach, to

ascribe; *(→ délai)* to set; **a. un délai de deux mois à un projet** to set a deadline of two months for a project; **a. un même objectif à deux projets** to set the same goal for two projects

2 *Jur* **a. un témoin (à comparaître)** to subpoena a witness; **a. le prévenu** to summon the defendant; **a. qn à résidence** to put sb under house arrest; **être assigné à résidence** to be under house arrest; **a. qn (en justice) pour diffamation** to issue a writ for libel against sb

3 *Fin (part, fonds, crédits)* to allocate; **a. des crédits à la recherche** to allocate funds for *or* to research

assimilable [asimilabl] **ADJ 1** *Physiol* assimilable, easily absorbed *or* assimilated

2 *(abordable)* easily acquired *or* assimilated; **l'informatique est a. à tout âge** computer skills are easy to acquire at any age

3 *(population)* easily assimilated *or* integrated; **des populations difficilement assimilables** groups of people difficult to integrate

4 *(similaire)* comparable (**à** to); **son travail est souvent a. à celui d'un médecin** his/her work can often be compared to that of a doctor

assimilateur, -trice [asimilatœr, -tris] **ADJ** assimilative, assimilatory

assimilation [asimilasjɔ̃] **NF 1** *Physiol* assimilation

2 *Bot* **a. chlorophyllienne** photosynthesis

3 *(fait de comprendre)* **avoir un grand pouvoir d'a.** to acquire knowledge very easily; **l'a. des connaissances se fait à un rythme différent selon les élèves** pupils assimilate knowledge at different rates

4 *(intégration)* assimilation, integration; **politique d'a.** policy of assimilation

5 *(identification)* comparison; **l'a. de ses théories au marxisme** the way his/her theories have been likened to Marxism; **l'a. des postes de maîtrise à des postes de cadres** placing supervisory positions in the same category as executive positions

6 *(d'une voyelle)* assimilation

assimilatrice [asimilatris] *voir* **assimilateur**

assimilé, -e [asimile] **ADJ** comparable, similar; **talc pour bébé et produits assimilés** baby powder and similar products

NM cadres et assimilés executives and their equivalent

assimiler [3] [asimile] **VT 1** *Physiol* to assimilate, to absorb, to metabolize; *(digérer)* to digest; **son organisme n'assimile pas le fer** his/her body can't metabolize iron; **il assimile mal le lait** he can't digest milk properly

2 *(comprendre)* to assimilate, to take in; **il n'assimile rien** he doesn't take anything in; **j'ai du mal à a. les logarithmes** I have trouble mastering logarithms; **c'est du freudisme mal assimilé** it's ill-digested Freudianism

3 *(intégrer)* to assimilate, to integrate

4 *(une voyelle)* to assimilate

❑ **assimiler à VT IND** to compare to; **il n'est pas question d'a. les infirmières aux aides-soignantes** there's no question of placing the nurses in the same category as auxiliaries; **être assimilé à un cadre supérieur** to be given equivalent status to an executive

▸**s'assimiler VPR 1** *Physiol* to become absorbed *or* metabolized; *(être digéré)* to be assimilated *or* digested; **les aliments riches en fibres s'assimilent plus facilement** high-fibre food is easier to digest

2 *(s'intégrer)* to become assimilated

3 *(se comparer)* to compare oneself (**à** to *or* with); *(être comparable)* to be comparable (**à** with)

assis, -e [asi, -iz] **PP** *voir* **asseoir**

ADJ 1 *(établi)* stable; **position bien assise** well-established position

2 *(non debout)* sitting (down); **il est plus à l'aise dans la position assise que dans la position couchée** he feels more comfortable sitting than lying down; **j'étais assise sur un tabouret** I was sitting on a stool; **nous étions a. au premier rang** we were seated in the first row; **êtes-vous bien a.?** are you sitting comfortably?; **être a. en tailleur** to be sitting cross-legged; **je préfère être assise pour repasser** I prefer doing the ironing sitting down; **je vous en prie, restez a.** please don't get up; **tout le monde est resté a.** everyone remained seated; **se tenir a.** to be sitting up; **a.!** *(à un chien)* sit!

❑ **assise NF 1** *(fondement)* foundation, basis

2 *Constr* course; *(d'une route)* bed

3 *Anat, Bot & Géol* stratum

❑ **assises NFPL 1** *Jur* Assize Court, *Br* ≃ crown court; **être envoyé aux assises** to be committed for trial

2 *(réunion → gén)* meeting; *(→ d'un parti, d'un syndicat)* conference; **la fédération tient ses assises à Nice** a meeting of the federation is being held *or* is taking place in Nice

Assise [asiz] **NM** *Géog* Assisi

assistanat [asistana] **NM 1** *Scol* (foreign) assistant exchange scheme **2** *Univ* assistantship **3** *(secours → privé)* aid; *(→ public)* state aid

assistance [asistɑ̃s] **NF 1** *(aide)* assistance; **prêter a. à qn** to lend *or* to give assistance to sb, to assist sb; **trouver a. auprès de qn** to get help from sb; **a. éducative** = measure ordered by a judge to protect a child's physical, psychological or educational wellbeing; **a. judiciaire** legal aid; **a. médicale pour les pays du tiers-monde** medical aid for Third World countries; *Jur* **a. des plaideurs** legal assistance, legal advice; **l'A. (publique)** *(à Paris et Marseille)* = authority which manages the social services and state-owned hospitals; *Vieilli* **c'est un enfant de l'A.** he was brought up in an institution; **a. sociale** *(aux pauvres)* welfare; *(métier)* social work; *Ordinat* **a. technique** technical support; *Ordinat* **a. technique téléphonique** support line; *Ordinat* **a. à l'utilisateur** user support

2 *Méd* **a. médicale à la procréation** assisted conception; **a. respiratoire** artificial respiration

3 *(spectateurs → d'une pièce, d'un cours)* audience; *(→ d'une messe)* congregation; **la remarque a ému toute l'a.** the entire audience was moved by the remark; **y a-t-il quelqu'un dans l'a. qui souhaiterait intervenir?** does anyone in the audience wish to speak?

4 *(présence)* attendance (**à** at); at; **l'a. aux conférences n'est pas obligatoire** attendance at lectures is not compulsory

assistant, -e [asistɑ̃, -ɑ̃t] **NM,F 1** *(second)* assistant; **l'a. du directeur** the director's assistant; **a. de direction** personal assistant, PA; *Cin & TV* **a. du directeur artistique** assistant artistic director; *Cin & TV* **a. de réalisation** assistant director; *Cin & TV* **a. du producteur** assistant producer; *Cin & TV* **a. du régisseur de plateau** assistant floor manager; *Cin & TV* **a. de production** production assistant; *Cin & TV* **a. de plateau** floor assistant

2 *Scol* (foreign language) assistant

3 *Univ Br* lecturer, *Am* assistant teacher

4 *(aide)* **a. maternel** *(à son domicile)* childminder; *(en collectivité) Br* crèche *or Am* daycare center worker; **a. social** social worker

NM *Ordinat (programme)* assistant; **a. numérique personnel** personal digital assistant, PDA; **a. personnel** personal assistant

❑ **assistante NF assistante de police** policewoman, *Br* WPC *(in charge of minors)*

assistant-réalisateur, assistante-réalisatrice [asistɑ̃realizatœr, asistɑ̃trealizatris] *(mpl* **assistants-réalisateurs**, *fpl* **assistantes-réalisatrices)** **NM,F** *Cin & TV* assistant director

assisté, -e [asiste] **ADJ 1** *Admin (aidé)* **enfants assistés** children in *Br* care *or Am* custody; **chômeurs assistés** unemployed people receiving state aid; **être a.** to receive state aid; **je ne veux pas être a.!** I don't want charity!

2 *Ordinat* **a. par ordinateur** computer-aided, computer-assisted

NM,F *Admin* **les assistés** recipients of state aid; **ils ont une mentalité d'assistés** they expect everything to be done for them

assister [3] [asiste] **VT** *(aider)* to assist, to aid; *(soutenir financièrement)* to help (financially); **je l'ai assisté pendant l'opération/dans son travail** I assisted him during the operation/in his work; **le prêtre est assisté d'un enfant de chœur** the priest is attended by a choirboy; **nous vous ferons a. par un avocat** we will make sure you get a lawyer to assist you; **se faire a. par qn** to be assisted by sb; **a. qn dans ses derniers moments** *ou* **dernières heures** to comfort sb in his/her last hours; **que Dieu vous assiste!** (may) God be with you *or* help you!; *Jur* **a. (qn) d'office** to be appointed by the court (to defend sb)

❑ **assister à VT IND 1** *(être présent à → messe, gala)* to attend; *(→ concert de rock, enregistrement de télévision)* to be at

2 *(être témoin de)* to witness, to be a witness to; **il a assisté à l'accident** he was a witness to *or* he witnessed the accident

3 *(remarquer)* to note, to witness; **on assiste à une recrudescence de la criminalité/du chômage** we are witnessing a new increase in crime/unemployment

assoce [asɔs] **NF** *Fam* association■, organization■

associatif, -ive [asɔsjatif, -iv] **ADJ** *(règle, activité)* of an association *or* organization; *(militant, regroupement)* organized; **la vie associative est très développée dans ce pays** a lot of people in this country belong to clubs and associations; **le mouvement syndical et le mouvement a.** trade unions and organizations

association [asɔsjasjɔ̃] **NF 1** *(groupement)* society, association; *(organisation)* organization; **protéger la liberté d'a.** to protect freedom of association; **a. des anciens élèves** association of *Br* former pupils *or Am* alumni; **a. d'avocats** ≃ chambers; **a. de bienfaisance** charity, charitable organization; **a. à but non lucratif** *ou* **sans but lucratif** *Br* non-profit-making *or Am* not-for-profit organization; **a. de consommateurs** consumer association; **a. de défense des consommateurs** consumer protection association; **A. pour l'emploi des cadres** = agency providing information and employment and training opportunities for professionals; **A. européenne de libre-échange** European Free Trade Association; **A. pour la formation professionnelle des adultes** = government body promoting adult vocational training; **A. française des banques** French Bankers' Association; **A. française de normalisation** = French industrial standards authority, *Br* ≃ British Standards Institution, *Am* ≃ American Standards Association; **a. humanitaire** charity organization; **A. de libre-échange** Free Trade Association; **a. loi 1901** = type of non-profit-making organization; **a. de malfaiteurs** criminal conspiracy; **a. de parents d'élèves** *Br* ≃ Parent-Teacher Association, *Am* ≃ Parent-Teacher Organization; **A. de recherche sur le cancer** = French national cancer research charity; **a. sportive** sports club; *Anciennement* **A. du sport scolaire et universitaire** = former schools and university sports association

2 *(collaboration)* partnership, association; **notre a. n'a pas duré longtemps** we weren't partners for long; **travailler en a. avec l'État** to work in association with the state; **un opéra produit en a. avec une chaîne italienne** an opera produced in association with an Italian TV channel; *Fin* **a. capital-travail** profit-sharing scheme

3 *(d'images)* association; *(de couleurs)* combination; **l'a. de nos intérêts devrait nous être profitable à tous les deux** combining our interests should be profitable to us both; **a. d'idées** association of ideas; *Psy* **a. libre** free association; *Psy* **associations verbales** free associations

4 *Bot* **a. végétale** plant association

associationnisme [asɔsjasjɔnism] **NM** *Phil* associationism

associationniste [asɔsjasjɔnist] *Phil* **ADJ** associationist

NMF associationist

associative [asɔsjativ] *voir* **associatif**

associativité [asɔsjativite] **NF** *Math* associativity

associé, -e [asɔsje] **ADJ** associate; **directeur/membre a.** associate director/member

NM,F *Com & Fin* associate, partner; **je l'ai pris comme a.** I took him into partnership; **a. commanditaire** *Br* sleeping partner, *Am* silent partner; **a. commandité** active partner; **a. fictif** nominal partner; **a. fondateur** founding partner; **a. gérant** active partner; **a. majoritaire** senior partner; **a. minoritaire** junior partner; **associés à part égale** equal partners; **a. passif** sleeping partner; **a. principal** senior partner; **a. en second** junior partner

associer [9] [asɔsje] **VT 1** *(idées, images, mots)* to

associate; **a. qn/qch à** to associate or to connect or to link sb/sth with; **elle a toujours associé la ville de Nice à une enfance heureuse** she has always associated the city of Nice with her happy childhood; **on associe souvent rhumatismes et humidité** rheumatism and damp conditions are frequently associated

2 (faire participer) **il m'a associé à son projet** he included me in his project; **son entreprise est associée au projet** his/her company is taking part in the project; **a. les travailleurs aux profits de leur entreprise** to allow workers to share in their company's profits; **j'aurais voulu l'a. à mon bonheur** I would have liked to share my happiness with him/her

3 (saveurs, couleurs) to combine (**qch à** sth with)

▸**s'associer** VPR **1** (s'allier) to join forces (**à** with); Com to enter or to go into partnership, to become partners (**à** ou **avec** with); (prendre part **à**) to share (**à** in); **associons-nous pour réussir** let us join forces in order to succeed; **la France et l'Allemagne se sont associées pour le projet Hermès** France and Germany are partners in the Hermes project; **il s'est associé à** ou **avec son frère pour monter une petite société d'ingénierie** he went into partnership with his brother and set up a small engineering company; **je m'associe pleinement à votre malheur** I share your grief; **s'a. à une entreprise criminelle** to be an accomplice or to take part in a crime

2 (s'harmoniser) to be combined

3 s'a. qn to take sb on as a partner

assoiffé, -e [aswafe] ADJ thirsty; **a. de sang** bloodthirsty; **a. de savoir/de vengeance** thirsty or hungry for knowledge/for revenge

assoiffer [3] [aswafe] VT to make thirsty; **a. une ville** to cut off the water supply to a town

assoit etc voir **asseoir**

assolement [asɔlmã] NM Agr crop rotation; **a. triennal** three-course system

assoler [3] [asɔle] VT Agr (terres) to rotate crops on

assombrir [32] [asɔ̃brir] VT **1** (rendre sombre) to darken, to make dark or darker; **l'orage assombrit le ciel** the sky's getting dark with the impending storm; **sous un ciel assombri** under darkened skies; **le mur brun assombrit la pièce** the brown wall makes the room look darker

2 (rendre triste) to cast a shadow or a cloud over, to mar; **la mort de son père a bien assombri notre séjour** his/her father's death cast a shadow over our stay; **aucun incident n'a assombri la cérémonie** no incident marred the ceremony

▸**s'assombrir** VPR **1** (s'obscurcir) to darken, to grow dark; **à l'approche du cyclone, le ciel s'est assombri** with the approaching hurricane, the sky grew very dark

2 (s'attrister → visage) to become gloomy, to cloud over; (→ personne, humeur) to become gloomy

assombrissement [asɔ̃brismã] NM Littéraire darkening

assommant, -e [asɔmã, -ãt] ADJ Fam **1** (ennuyeux) boring, tedious; **j'ai passé une demi-heure assommante** I spent an excruciatingly boring half-hour **2** (fatigant) **les enfants ont été assommants toute la matinée!** the children were unbearable all morning!; **tu es a., à la fin, avec tes questions!** all these questions are getting really annoying!

assommer [3] [asɔme] VT **1** (frapper) to knock out; **se faire a.** to be knocked out

2 (tuer) **a. un bœuf** to fell an ox; Fam **à a.** ou **qui assommerait un bœuf** powerful■ ; Fam **l'eau-de-vie de sa grand-mère, elle assommerait un bœuf** his/her grandmother's brandy could kill a horse

3 Fam (ennuyer) **a. qn** to bore sb stiff or to tears; **ils m'assomment avec leurs statistiques** they bore me to tears with their statistics

4 Fam (importuner) to harass■ , to wear down■

5 (abrutir) to stun

assommeur, -euse [asɔmœr, -øz] NM,F slaughterer

assommoir [asɔmwar] NM Arch **1** (matraque) club **2** Fam (bar) gin palace

assomption [asɔ̃psjɔ̃] NF **1** Rel **l'A.** the Assumption **2** (hypothèse) assumption

---

L'ASSOMPTION
The Feast of the Assumption, on the 15th of August, is a Catholic feast day and an important holiday in France.

assomptionniste [asɔ̃psjɔnist] NM Rel Assumptionist

assonance [asɔnãs] NF Littérature assonance

assonancé, -e [asɔnãse] ADJ Littérature assonant; **vers assonancés** assonant verse

assonant, -e [asɔnã, -ãt] ADJ Littérature assonant

assorti, -e [asɔrti] ADJ **1** (en harmonie) **un couple bien a.** a well-matched couple; **un couple mal a.** an ill-matched or ill-assorted couple; **les deux couleurs sont très bien assorties** the two colours match (up) or blend (in) perfectly; **pantalon avec veste assortie** Br trousers or Am pants with matching jacket

2 (chocolats) assorted; **fromages assortis** choice of cheeses

3 (approvisionné) **un magasin bien/mal a.** a well-stocked/poorly-stocked shop

assortiment [asɔrtimã] NM **1** (ensemble) assortment, selection; **a. de charcuterie** selection of or assorted cold meats; **a. d'outils** set of tools, tool kit; **voulez-vous les mêmes gâteaux pour tout le monde ou un a.?** would you like the same cakes for everybody or would you prefer an assortment?

2 (harmonisation) arrangement, matching

3 Com (choix) selection, range, stock; **nous avons un vaste a. de jupes** we stock a large selection of skirts; **nous avons un vaste a. de desserts** we offer a large selection or a wide range of desserts; Mktg **a. de produits** product mix

assortir [32] [asɔrtir] VT **1** (teintes, vêtements) to match; **j'ai acheté le couvre-lit assorti au papier peint** I bought a bedspread to match the wallpaper; **a. ses chaussures à sa ceinture** to match one's shoes with or to one's belt

2 (personnes) to match, to mix

3 Com (approvisionner) to supply, to stock

4 (accompagner) **il a assorti son discours d'un paragraphe sur le racisme** he included a paragraph on racism in his speech; **une peine de prison assortie d'une amende de 1000 euros** a prison sentence accompanied by a fine of 1,000 euros

▸**s'assortir** VPR **1** (s'harmoniser) to match, to go together well; **sa manière de s'habiller s'assortit à sa personnalité** the way he/she dresses matches or reflects his/her personality

2 (être complété) **son étude s'assortit de quelques remarques sur la situation actuelle** his/her study includes a few comments on the present situation

3 Com to buy one's stock; **il s'assortit dans les magasins de gros** he buys his stock wholesale

Assouan [aswã] NM Géog Aswan, Assouan; **le barrage d'A.** the Aswan (High) Dam

assoupi, -e [asupi] ADJ **1** (endormi → personne) asleep, sleeping, dozing **2** Littéraire (calme → ville) sleepy; (→ passion) dormant

assoupir [32] [asupir] VT **1** (endormir) to make drowsy or sleepy **2** Littéraire (atténuer → soupçon, douleur) to soften

▸**s'assoupir** VPR **1** (s'endormir) to doze off, to fall asleep **2** Littéraire (s'affaiblir → crainte, douleur) to be dulled

assoupissant, -e [asupisã, -ãt] ADJ soporific

assoupissement [asupismã] NM **1** (sommeil léger) doze; (état somnolent) drowsiness; **tomber dans un léger a.** to doze off **2** Littéraire (atténuation → des soupçons, de la douleur) dulling, numbing; **l'a. de tous ses sens** the numbing of all his/her senses

assouplir [32] [asuplir] VT **1** (rendre moins dur → corps) to make supple, to loosen up; (→ linge, cuir) to soften; **ajoutez du lait pour a. la pâte** add milk until the dough is pliable

2 (rendre moins strict → règlement) to relax; **a. ses positions** to take a softer line; **l'âge n'a pas assoupli son caractère** he/she hasn't mellowed with age, age hasn't made him/her more tractable or any easier; **le règlement de l'école a été considérablement assoupli** the school rules have been considerably relaxed

---

▸**s'assouplir** VPR **1** (devenir moins strict) to become looser or more supple, to loosen up

2 (caractère, règlement) to become more flexible

assouplissant [asuplisã] NM (fabric) softener

assouplissement [asuplismã] NM **1** Sport warming-up; **des exercices** ou **une séance d'a.** warming-up exercises **2** (d'un linge, d'un cuir) softening **3** (d'une position) softening; Écon (de la réglementation, du contrôle) relaxing; (du crédit) easing; **demander l'a. d'un règlement** to ask for regulations to be relaxed

assouplisseur [asuplisœr] = **assouplissant**

assourdir [32] [asurdir] VT **1** (personne) to deafen; (bruit, son) to dull, to deaden, to muffle **2** Ling to make voiceless or unvoiced

▸**s'assourdir** VPR Ling to become voiceless or unvoiced

assourdissant, -e [asurdisã, -ãt] ADJ deafening, ear-splitting

assourdissement [asurdismã] NM **1** (d'un bruit) deadening, dulling, muffling **2** (d'une personne → processus) deafening; (→ résultat) temporary deafness **3** Ling devoicing

assouvir [32] [asuvir] VT (désir, faim) to appease, Sout to assuage; (soif) to quench; (curiosité) to satisfy; **a. sa vengeance** to satisfy one's desire for revenge

assouvissement [asuvismã] NM (d'une passion, de la faim) appeasing, Sout assuaging; (de la soif) quenching; (de la curiosité) satisfying

assoyait etc voir **asseoir**

ASSU, Assu [asy] NF Anciennement (abrév **Association du sport scolaire et universitaire**) = former schools and university sports association

Assuérus [asɥerys] NPR Ahasuerus

assuétude [asɥetyd] NF Méd addiction

assujetti, -e [asyʒeti] ADJ **1** Littéraire (population, prisonnier) subjugated **2** Jur **être a. à l'impôt** to be liable for tax

NM,F Jur = person liable for tax; **les assujettis** those who are liable for tax

assujettir [32] [asyʒetir] VT **1** (astreindre) **a. qn à qch** to subject sb to sth; **être assujetti à un contrôle médical très strict** to be subjected to very strict medical checks; Jur **être assujetti à l'impôt** to be liable for tax

2 (arrimer) to fasten, to secure; **a. une porte avec une chaîne** to secure a door with a chain

3 Littéraire (asservir → nation, peuple) to subjugate, to hold under a yoke

▸**s'assujettir à** VPR to submit (oneself) to

assujettissant, -e [asyʒetisã, -ãt] ADJ demanding

assujettissement [asyʒetismã] NM **1** Littéraire (asservissement) subjection **2** Littéraire (contrainte) tie **3** Jur **a. à l'impôt** liability to taxation

assumer [3] [asyme] VT **1** (endosser) to take on, to take upon oneself, to assume; **j'en assume l'entière responsabilité** I take or I accept full responsibility for it; **il assume la charge de directeur depuis la mort de son père** he's been director since his father died; **nous assumerons toutes les dépenses** we'll meet all the expenses; **elle assume à la fois les fonctions de présidente et de trésorière** she acts both as chairperson and treasurer; **j'ai assumé ces responsabilités pendant trop longtemps** I held that job for too long

2 (accepter) to accept; **il assume mal ses origines** he's never been able to come to terms with his background

USAGE ABSOLU Fam **ils font des gosses et après ils n'assument pas!** they have kids and then they don't face up to their responsibilities as parents!; **j'assume!** I don't care what other people think!

▸**s'assumer** VPR **il a du mal à s'a. en tant que père** he's finding it hard to come to terms with his role as father; Fam **il serait temps que tu t'assumes!** it's time you accepted yourself as you are!

assurable [asyrabl] ADJ Assur insurable

assurage [asyraʒ] NM Sport (alpinisme) belaying

assurance [asyrãs] NF **1** (contrat) insurance (policy); **placer des assurances** to sell insurance (policies); **les assurances** insurance companies; Fam **il est dans les assurances** he's in insurance■ ; Fam **je vais écrire à mon a.** I'll write to my insurance company■ ; **a. contre les**

ass-ast

accidents *Br* insurance against (personal) accidents, accident insurance; **a. auto** *ou* **automobile** car *or Am* automobile insurance; **a. bagage** baggage insurance; *Suisse* **a. casco** comprehensive insurance, all-risks insurance; **a. chômage** *(payée par le patron et le salarié)* ≃ unemployment insurance; *(reçue par le chômeur)* ≃ unemployment benefit(s); **a. crédit** loan repayment insurance; **a. contre l'incendie** insurance against fire, fire insurance; **a. invalidité** *Br* critical illness cover, *Am* disability insurance; **a. maritime** marine insurance; **a. maternité** maternity benefit; **a. mixte** endowment policy; **a. multirisque** comprehensive insurance; **a. personnelle** private health insurance *or* cover; **a. de portefeuille** portfolio insurance; **a. responsabilité civile** *ou* **au tiers** third party insurance; *Com* **a. de responsabilité du produit** product liability insurance; **a. tous risques** comprehensive insurance; **les assurances sociales** *Br* ≃ National Insurance, *Am* ≃ Welfare; **a. vieillesse** retirement pension; *Suisse* **a. vieillesse et survivants** = Swiss pension scheme; **a. contre le vol** insurance against theft; **a. volontaire** private health insurance *or* cover

2 *(promesse)* assurance; **j'ai reçu l'a. formelle que l'on m'aiderait financièrement** I was assured I would receive financial help

3 *(garantie)* guarantee (**de** of); **je vous donne l'a. que tout sera fait d'ici demain** I assure you *or* I guarantee (you) that everything will be done by tomorrow; **demander/recevoir des assurances** to ask for/to receive assurance; **le retour à la démocratie constitue une a. de paix pour le pays** the return of democracy will guarantee peace for the country

4 *(aisance)* self-confidence, assurance; **manque d'a.** insecurity; **manquer d'a.** to be insecure; **s'exprimer avec a.** to speak with assurance; **elle a perdu toute sa belle a.** she's lost all her cockiness; **je chantonnais pour me donner un peu d'a.** I was singing to give myself some confidence; **elle a de l'a. dans la voix** she sounds confident

5 *(certitude)* **avoir l'a. que...** to feel certain *or* assured that...; **j'ai l'a. qu'il viendra** I'm sure he'll come

6 *(dans la correspondance)* **veuillez croire à l'a. de ma considération distinguée** *(à quelqu'un dont on connaît le nom) Br* yours sincerely, *Am* sincerely (yours); *(à quelqu'un dont on ne connaît pas le nom) Br* yours faithfully, *Am* sincerely (yours)

7 *Sport (en alpinisme)* **(point d')a.** belay

assurance-crédit [asyrãskredi] *(pl* **assurances-crédits)** NF loan repayment insurance

assurance-décès [asyrãsdesε] *(pl* **assurances-décès)** NF *Assur* life insurance *or Br* assurance

assurance-incendie [asyrãsε̃sãdi] *(pl* **assurances-incendie)** NF *Assur* insurance against fire, fire insurance

assurance-maladie [asyrãsmaladi] *(pl* **assurances-maladie)** NF *Assur* health insurance

assurance-vie [asyrãsvi] *(pl* **assurances-vie)** NF *Assur* life insurance *or Br* assurance

assuré, -e [asyre] ADJ **1** *(incontestable)* certain, sure; **succès a. pour son nouvel album!** his/her new album is sure to be a hit!; **discrétion assurée** confidentiality guaranteed

2 *(résolu)* assured, self-confident; **marcher d'un pas a.** to walk confidently; **d'une voix mal assurée** quaveringly, in an unsteady voice; **avoir un air a.** to look self-confident

NM,F **1** *(qui a un contrat d'assurance)* insured person, policyholder; **les assurés** the insured

2 *Admin* **a. social** *Br* ≃ contributor to the National Insurance scheme, *Am* ≃ contributor to Social Security

assurément [asyremã] ADV assuredly, undoubtedly, most certainly; **a. non!** certainly *or* indeed not!; **a. (oui)!** yes, indeed!, (most) definitely!

assurer [3] [asyre] VT **1** *(certifier)* to assure; **il m'a assuré qu'il viendrait** he assured me he'd come; **je t'assure qu'elle est sincère** I assure you she's sincere; **mais si, je t'assure!** yes, I swear!; **il faut de la patience avec elle, je t'assure!** you need a lot of patience when dealing with her, I'm telling you!

2 *(rendre sûr)* to assure; **je l'assurai qu'il**

pouvait signer I assured him he could sign; **laissez-moi vous a. de ma reconnaissance** let me assure you of my gratitude

3 *(procurer)* to maintain, to provide; **a. le ravitaillement des populations sinistrées** to provide disaster victims with supplies; **une permanence est assurée le samedi après-midi** there is someone on duty on Saturday afternoons; **a. la surveillance de qch** to guard sth; **pour mieux a. la sécurité de tous** to ensure greater safety for all; **a. une liaison aérienne/ferroviaire** to operate an air/a rail link; **a. le ramassage scolaire** to operate a school bus service; **a. à qn un bon salaire** to secure a good salary for sb

4 *(mettre à l'abri)* to ensure, to secure; **a. l'avenir** to make provision *or* provide for the future; **a. ses arrières** *Mil* to protect one's rear; *Fig* to leave oneself a way out *or* something to fall back on

5 *(arrimer)* to secure, to steady; **a. le chargement d'une voiture avec des cordes** to secure the load on a car with ropes

6 *Com* to insure; **a. ses bagages/sa voiture** to insure one's luggage/one's car; **j'ai fait a. mes bijoux** I had my jewellery insured; **être mal assuré contre le vol** to be under-insured in case of theft; **a. qch pour 10 000 euros** to insure sth for 10,000 euros

7 *Sport (en alpinisme)* to belay

8 *Naut (bout)* to belay, to make fast

9 *Littéraire* **a. son visage** *ou* **sa contenance** to put on a firm countenance

VI *Fam* **il assure en physique/anglais** he's good at physics/English■; **elle a beau être nouvelle au bureau, elle assure bien** she may be new to the job but she's certainly doing OK; **les femmes d'aujourd'hui, elles assurent!** modern women can do anything!■; **il va falloir a.!** we'll have to show that we're up to it!; **tu as encore oublié ton rendez-vous! t'assures pas** you missed your appointment again! you're useless!; **il assure pas une cacahuète** *ou* **un clou quand il s'agit de draguer** he hasn't got a clue when it comes to *Br* chatting up *or Am* hitting on women

▶**s'assurer** VPR **1** *(par contrat d'assurance)* to insure oneself; **s'a. contre le vol/l'incendie** to insure oneself against theft/fire; **il est obligatoire pour un automobiliste de s'a.** by law, a driver must be insured

2 *(s'affermir)* to steady oneself

3 *(se fournir → revenu)* to secure, to ensure

4 **s'a. de qch** *(contrôler)* to make sure of sth; **assurez-vous de la validité de votre passeport** make sure your passport is valid; **je vais m'en a. immédiatement** I'll check right away; **s'a. que** to make sure (that), to check (that); **assure-toi que tout va bien** make sure everything's OK; **pouvez-vous vous a. qu'elle est bien rentrée?** could you check she got back all right?

assureur [asyrœr] NM *Assur* underwriter; *(agent)* insurance agent; *(compagnie)* insurance company; *(courtier)* insurance broker

assureur-conseil [asyrœrkɔ̃sεj] *(pl* **assureurs-conseils)** NM *Assur* insurance adviser

Assyrie [asiri] NF l'A. Assyria

assyrien, -enne [asirjɛ̃, -ɛn] ADJ Assyrian

NM *(langue)* Assyrian

❑ **Assyrien, -enne** NM,F Assyrian

assyriologie [asirjolɔʒi] NF Assyriology

assyriologue [asirjolɔg] NMF Assyriologist

astaciculture [astasikyltyr] NF crayfish farming

Astana [astana] NM *Géog* Astana

Astarté [astarte] NPR *Myth* Astarte

astasie [astazi] NF *Méd* astasia

astate [astat] NM *Chim* astatine

astatique [astatik] ADJ *Phys* astatic

aster [astεr] NM **1** *Bot* aster; **a. (d'automne)** Michaelmas daisy; **a. maritime** sea aster **2** *Biol* aster

astéracée [asterase] NF *Bot* composite

astéréognosie [astereɔgnozi] NF *Méd* astereognosis

astéride [asterid] *Zool* NM member of the Asteroidea

❑ **astérides** NMPL Asteroidea

astérie [asteri] *Zool* NF asteroid, asteroidean

❑ **astéries** NFPL Asteroidea

astérisque [asterisk] NM asterisk

Astérix [asteriks] NPR Asterix; **le parc A.** = large theme park north of Paris

astéroïde [asterɔid] NM *Astron* asteroid

asteur, asteure [astœr] *Can Fam* ADV now■

❑ **asteur que, asteure que** CONJ now that■

asthénie [asteni] NF *Méd* asthenia

asthénique [astenik] *Méd* ADJ asthenic

NMF asthenia sufferer

asthénosphère [astenɔsfεr] NF *Géol* asthenosphere

astheur, astheure [astœr] = **asteur**

asthmatique [asmatik] *Méd* ADJ asthmatic

NMF asthmatic

asthme [asm] NM *Méd* asthma; **avoir de l'a.** to suffer from asthma; **crise d'a.** attack of asthma, asthma attack

asti [asti] NM *(vin)* Asti Spumante

asticot [astiko] NM **1** *Entom (ver)* maggot; *Pêche* gentle **2** *Fam (individu) Br* bloke, *Am* guy; **qu'est-ce qu'il veut, cet a.?** what's wrong with HIM?

asticoter [3] [astikote] VT *Fam* to bug

astigmate [astigmat] *Opt* ADJ astigmatic

NMF astigmatic

astigmatique [astigmatik] ADJ *Opt* astigmatic

astigmatisme [astigmatism] NM *Opt* astigmatism

astiquage [astikaʒ] NM polishing, shining

astiquer [3] [astike] VT to polish, to shine

astragale [astragal] NM **1** *Anat* astragalus, talus **2** *Archit* astragal **3** *Bot* astragalus

Astrakan [astrakã] NM *Géog* Astrakhan

astrakan [astrakã] NM astrakhan (fur); **un manteau en a.** an astrakhan coat

Astrakhan [astrakã] *voir* **Astrakan**

astral, -e, -aux, -ales [astral, -o] ADJ *Astrol & Astron* astral

astre [astr] NM *Astrol & Astron* star; *Littéraire* **l'a. du jour** the sun; *Littéraire* **l'a. de la nuit** the moon; **beau comme un a.** radiantly handsome *or* beautiful; **né sous un a. favorable** born under a lucky star

Astrée [astre] NPR *Myth* Astraea

astreignait *etc voir* **astreindre**

astreignant, -e [astrɛɲã, -ãt] ADJ demanding, exacting; **un programme a.** a punishing schedule

astreindre [81] [astrɛ̃dr] VT **a. qn à qch** to tie sb down to sth; **il est astreint à un régime sévère** he's on a very strict diet; **a. qn à faire qch** to compel *or* to force *or* to oblige sb to do sth; **je l'astreins à faire ses comptes** I force him/her to check his/her accounts

▶**s'astreindre** VPR **s'a. à faire qch** to compel *or* to force oneself to do sth; **il s'astreint à un régime sévère** he sticks to a strict diet

astreinte [astrɛ̃t] NF **1** *Jur* = daily penalty for delay in payment of debt **2** *(contrainte)* obligation, constraint

astrild [astrild] NM *Orn* waxbill

astringence [astrɛ̃ʒãs] NF *Méd* astringency, astringence

astringent, -e [astrɛ̃ʒã, -ãt] ADJ astringent; *(vin)* sharp

NM astringent

astrobiologie [astrɔbjolɔʒi] NF *Astrol & Biol* astrobiology

astroblème [astrɔblεm] NM *Géog* astrobleme

astrolabe [astrɔlab] NM *Astron* astrolabe

astrolâtrie [astrɔlatri] NF *Astrol* astrolatry

astrologie [astrɔlɔʒi] NF *Astrol* astrology

astrologique [astrɔlɔʒik] ADJ *Astrol* astrological

astrologue [astrɔlɔg] NMF *Astrol* astrologer

astrométrie [astrɔmetri] NF *Astron* astrometry

astrométrique [astrɔmetrik] ADJ *Astron* astrometric, astrometrical

astrométriste [astrɔmetrist] NMF *Astron* astrometrist

astronaute [astrɔnot] NMF *Astron* astronaut

astronautique [astrɔnotik] NF *Astron* astronautics *(singulier)*

astronef [astrɔnεf] NM *Vieilli* spaceship

astronome [astrɔnɔm] NMF *Astron* astronomer

astronomie [astrɔnɔmi] NF *Astron* astronomy; **a. infrarouge** infrared astronomy

astronomique [astrɔnɔmik] ADJ **1** *Astron* astronomic, astronomical **2** *Fam (somme)* astronomic, astronomical; **ça a atteint des prix**

astronomiques! it's become ridiculously expensive!

astronomiquement [astrɔnɔmikmɑ̃] ADV astronomically

astrophotographie [astrofotografi] NF *Phot & Astron* astrophotography

astrophysicien, -enne [astrofizisjɛ̃, -ɛn] NM,F *Astron* astrophysicist

astrophysique [astrofizik] *Astron* ADJ astrophysical

  NF astrophysics *(singulier)*

astuce [astys] NF **1** *(ingéniosité)* astuteness, shrewdness; **il est plein d'a.** he's a shrewd individual

  2 *Fam (plaisanterie)* joke■, gag■; *(jeu de mots)* pun■; **je n'ai pas compris l'a.!** I didn't get it!; **encore une de tes astuces vaseuses!** another one of your awful puns!

  3 *Fam (procédé ingénieux)* trick■; *(conseil)* tip■; **en page 23, notre rubrique "astuces"** our tips are on page 23; **je n'arrive pas à l'ouvrir – attends, il doit y avoir une a.** I can't open it – wait, there must be some knack *or* trick (to it); **comment fais-tu tenir le loquet? – ah, ah, c'est l'a.!** how do you get the latch to stay on? – aha, wouldn't you like to know!; **j'ai trouvé une a. formidable pour ne pas avoir à attendre** I've hit upon a great trick to avoid waiting; **les astuces du métier** the tricks of the trade

astucieuse [astysjøz] *voir* **astucieux**

astucieusement [astysjøzmɑ̃] ADV shrewdly, cleverly

astucieux, -euse [astysjø, -øz] ADJ *(personne)* shrewd, clever; *(solution, méthode)* clever

asturien, -enne [astyrjɛ̃, -ɛn] ADJ Asturian

  ❏ **Asturien, -enne** NM,F Asturian

Asturies [astyri] NFPL **les A.** Asturias; **le prince des A.** the Prince of Asturias

Astyage [astjaʒ] NPR *Hist* Astyages

Asuncion [asunsjɔn] NM *Géog* Asuncion

asymbolie [asɛ̃bɔli] NF *Méd* asymbolia

asymétrie [asimetri] NF asymmetry, lack of symmetry

asymétrique [asimetrik] ADJ asymmetric, asymmetrical

asymptomatique [asɛ̃ptɔmatik] ADJ *Méd (maladie)* asymptomatic; *(porteur)* without symptoms

asymptote [asɛ̃ptɔt] *Géom* ADJ *(courbe, plan)* asymptotic, asymptotical

  NF asymptote

asymptotique [asɛ̃ptɔtik] ADJ *Géom* asymptotic, asymptotical

asynchrone [asɛ̃kron] ADJ *Phys & Ordinat* asynchronous

asynchronisme [asɛ̃kronism] NM *Phys & Ordinat* asynchronism

asyndète [asɛ̃dɛt] NF *Ling* asyndeton

asynergie [asinɛrʒi] NM *Méd* asynergy, asynergia

asyntaxique [asɛ̃taksik] ADJ *Ling* asyntactic

asystolie [asistɔli] NF *Méd* asystole

asystolique [asistɔlik] ADJ *Méd* asystolic

ataca [ataka] = **atoca**

Atalante [atalɑ̃t] NPR *Myth* Atalanta

ataraxie [ataraksi] NF *Phil* ataraxia

ataraxique [ataraksik] ADJ *Phil* ataractic

atavique [atavik] ADJ *Biol* atavistic, atavic

atavisme [atavism] NM *Biol* atavism; **ils sont prudents, c'est un vieil a. paysan** they're very cautious, it's an old peasant instinct; **faire qch par a.** to do sth because it's in one's genes

ataxie [ataksi] NF *Méd* ataxia; **a. locomotrice** locomotor ataxia

ataxique [ataksik] *Méd* ADJ ataxic

  NMF person who suffers from ataxia

atchoum [atʃum] EXCLAM atishoo!

atèle [atɛl] NM *Zool* spider monkey

atélectasie [atelɛktazi] NF *Méd* atelectasis

atelier [atəlje] NM **1** *(d'un bricoleur, d'un artisan)* workshop; *(d'un peintre, d'un photographe)* studio; *(d'un couturier)* workroom; **a. d'artiste** artist's studio; **les Ateliers Nationaux** = workshops created after the 1848 revolution to provide work for the unemployed; **a. de stylisme** designer's studio

  2 *(d'une usine)* shop; **l'a. s'est mis en grève** the shopfloor has gone on strike; **il est devenu contremaître après cinq ans d'a.** he became a foreman after five years on the factory *or* shop floor; **a. d'assemblage** assembly shop; *Aut* **a. de**

carrosserie bodyshop; **a. de montage** assembly room; **a. naval** shipyard; **a. protégé** sheltered workshop; **a. de réparations** repair shop

  3 *(cours)* workshop; *Beaux-Arts* class; **a. chorégraphique** dance workshop; **un a. de peinture sur soie** a silk painting workshop, a workshop on silk painting; *Théât* **l'A.** = innovative theatre company founded by Charles Dullin in 1921

  4 *(groupe de travail)* group, workgroup; **les enfants travaillent en ateliers** the children work in groups

  5 *(de francs-maçons)* lodge

atellanes [atɛllan] NFPL *Antiq & Théât* atellans

atémi [atemi] NM *Sport (arts martiaux)* atemi

atemporel, -elle [atɑ̃pɔrel] ADJ timeless

ater [atɛr] NMF *Univ (abrév* **attaché temporaire d'enseignement et de recherche***)* = holder of, or candidate for, a doctorate with a temporary university teaching post, who must then sit a competitive entry examination to qualify for a full-time post

atérien, -enne [aterjɛ̃, -ɛn] *Archéol* ADJ Aterian

  NM **l'a.** Aterian culture

atermoie *etc voir* **atermoyer**

atermoiement [atɛrmwamɑ̃] NM *Com & Jur* = arrangement with creditors for extension of time for payment

  ❏ **atermoiements** NMPL *(hésitations)* procrastination, delaying

atermoyer [13] [atɛrmwaje] VI to procrastinate, to delay; **ayant atermoyé deux mois, ils ont fini par dire oui** having held back from making a decision for two months, they finally said yes

---

-ATEUR, -ATRICE [atœr, atris] SUFF

● These suffixes are usually attached to the radical of a noun in **-ation** minus its ending or to the radical of a verb. The idea conveyed is that of an AGENT, whether it is a person or a thing (such as a machine or a tool). The equivalent suffix in English is often *-er* or *-or* :

  aviateur, aviatrice pilot, aviator; **admirateur, admiratrice** admirer; **décorateur, décoratrice** interior designer; **commentateur, commentatrice** commentator; **aspirateur** vacuum cleaner; **calculatrice** calculator

---

ATF [ɑteɛf] NM *Bourse (abrév* **accord de taux futur***)* forward rate agreement, future rate agreement

Athalie [atali] NPR *Antiq* Athaliah

Athanase [atanaz] NPR *Antiq* Athanasius; **le symbole de saint A.** the Athanasian Creed

athanor [atanɔr] NM athanor

athée [ate] *Rel* ADJ atheistic, atheist *(avant n)*

  NMF atheist

athéisme [ateism] NM *Rel* atheism

athématique [atematik] ADJ *Ling* athematic

Athéna [atena] NPR *Myth* Athena, Athene

athénée [atene] NM **1** *Antiq* Atheneum **2** *Belg Br* secondary school, *Am* high school

Athènes [atɛn] NM *Géog* Athens

athénien, -enne [atenjɛ̃, -ɛn] ADJ Athenian

  ❏ **Athénien, -enne** NM,F Athenian; *Hum* **c'est là que les Athéniens s'atteignirent** that was when things started to get complicated

athérine [aterin] NF *Ich* sand smelt

athermane [atɛrman] ADJ *Tech* athermanous, impervious to radiant heat

athermique [atɛrmik] ADJ *Tech* athermic, athermous

athérome [aterom] NM *Méd* **1** *(kyste sébacé)* encysted tumour, wen **2** *(maladie des artères)* degeneration of the arteries, atherosclerosis

athérosclérose [ateroskleroz] NF *Méd* atherosclerosis

athérure [ateryr] NM *Zool* brush-tailed porcupine

athétose [atetoz] NF *Méd* athetosis

athétosique [atetozik] *Méd* ADJ athetotic, athetosic

  NMF *(personne)* person suffering from athetosis

athlète [atlɛt] NMF athlete; **un corps/une carrure d'a.** an athletic body/build

athlétique [atletik] ADJ athletic

athlétisme [atletism] NM *Sport* athletics *(singulier)*; **épreuves d'a.** athletic events, track and field events

Athos [atos] *voir* **mont**

athrepsie [atrɛpsi] NF *Méd* athrepsia

athymie [atimi], **athymormie** [atimɔrmi] NF *Psy* athymia

atique [atik] = **attique**

atlante [atlɑ̃t] NM *Beaux-Arts* Atlas

Atlantide [atlɑ̃tid] NM *Myth* **l'A.** Atlantis

atlantique [atlɑ̃tik] ADJ Atlantic; **l'Arc a.** the Atlantic arc; **la côte a.** the Atlantic coast; **l'océan a.** the Atlantic ocean; **le Pacte a.** the Atlantic Charter

  ❏ **Atlantique** NM **l'A.** the Atlantic (Ocean)

atlantisme [atlɑ̃tism] NM *Pol* Atlanticism

atlantosaure [atlɑ̃tosɔr] NM atlantosaurus

Atlas [atlas] NPR *Myth* Atlas

  NM *Géog* **l'A.** the Atlas Mountains; **le Haut** *ou* **Grand A.** the High Atlas; **le Moyen A.** the Middle Atlas

atlas [atlas] NM **1** *(livre)* atlas **2** *Anat* atlas

ATM [ɑteɛm] NM *(abrév* **asynchronous transfer mode***)* ATM

atm *Phys (abrév écrite* **atmosphère***)* atm

atman [atmɑ̃] NM *Rel* atman

atmosphère [atmosfɛr] NF **1** *Géog* atmosphere; **la haute a.** the upper atmosphere **2** *(ambiance)* atmosphere, ambiance; **avoir besoin de changer d'a.** to need a change of scene **3** *(air que l'on respire)* air; **l'a. humide du littoral** the dampness of the air on the coast **4** *Phys (unité)* atmosphere

---

Allusion

Atmosphère, atmosphère, est-ce que j'ai une gueule d'atmosphère?

In Marcel Carné's 1938 film, *Hôtel du Nord*, scripted by the Prévert brothers, the French actress Arletty plays the female lead (a prostitute). At one point, in a comical scene, Arletty's screen partner (her pimp) speaks of "feeling like a change of scene" ("vouloir changer d'atmosphère") from the dreary canal-side Parisian hotel where they are staying. She replies with this phrase "Do I look like an atmosphere?" because she doesn't know the word "atmosphere" and thinks it refers pejoratively to her. People will sometimes use this famous phrase **avoir une gueule d'atmosphère** for humorous effect and in an allusion to the film.

---

atmosphérique [atmosferik] ADJ *(condition, couche, pression)* atmospheric

atoca [atɔka] NM *Can Bot* cranberry

atocatière [atokatjɛr] NF *Can Bot* cranberry bog

atoll [atɔl] NM *Géog* atoll

atome [atom] NM *Phys* atom; **l'ère de l'a.** the atomic age; *Fig* **pas un a. de** not an ounce of; *Fam* **avoir des atomes crochus avec qn** to have things in common with sb; **je n'ai pas d'atomes crochus avec elle** I don't have much in common with her

atome-gramme [atomgram] *(pl* **atomes-grammes***)* NM *Phys* gram-atom

atomicité [atomisite] NF *Phys* atomicity

atomique [atomik] ADJ *(masse, bombe)* atomic; *(énergie)* atomic, nuclear; *(explosion)* nuclear

atomisation [atomizasjɔ̃] NF *Phys* atomization, atomizing; *Fig (du pouvoir, de forces politiques)* dispersal

atomisé, -e [atomize] ADJ *Phys* atomized

  NM,F person suffering from the effects of radiation

atomiser [3] [atomize] VT **1** *Phys* to atomize **2** *Nucl* to destroy with an atom bomb, to blast with a nuclear device **3** *Fig* to pulverize

atomiseur [atomizœr] NM spray; **parfum en a.** spray perfume

atomisme [atomism] NM *Phys & Phil* atomism

atomiste [atomist] ADJ **1** *Phys* atomic **2** *Phil* atomistic, atomistical, atomist

  NMF **1** *Phys* atomic scientist **2** *Phil* atomist

atomistique [atomistik] ADJ *Phil* atomistic, atomistical, atomist

  NF *Phys* atomic science

atonal, -e, -aux, -ales [atonal, -o] ADJ *Mus* atonal

atonalité [atonalite] NF *Mus* atonality

atone [aton] ADJ **1** *(expression, œil, regard)* lifeless, expressionless **2** *Écon (croissance)* very sluggish **3** *Ling* atonic, unaccented, unstressed **4** *Méd* atonic

atonie [atoni] NF **1** *(inertie)* lifelessness **2** *Méd* atony

atonique [atɔnik] ADJ *Méd* atonic

atours [atur] NMPL *Arch* attire, array; *Hum* **elle avait revêtu ses plus beaux a.** she was dressed in all her finery

atout [atu] NM **1** *Cartes* trump; **jouer a.** to play a trump; *(en ouvrant le jeu)* to lead trump *or* trumps; **il a joué a. carreau** diamonds were trumps; **l'a. est à pique** spades are trumps; **quel est l'a.?** what's trump *or* trumps?; **prendre avec de l'a.** to trump; **jouer trois sans a.** to play three no trumps; **a. maître** master trump; *Fig* trump card

2 *(avantage)* asset, *Fig* trump; **la connaissance d'une langue étrangère est un a.** knowledge of a foreign language is an asset *or* an advantage; **il a tous les atouts dans son jeu** *ou* **en main** he has all the trumps *or* all the winning cards; **mettre tous les atouts dans son jeu** to maximize one's chances of success

3 *Fam (coup)* clout, thump; **prendre un a.** to get clouted *or* thumped

atoxique [atɔksik] ADJ *Méd* non-poisonous, non-toxic

ATP [atepe] NF **1** *Tennis* (*abrév* **Association des tennismen professionnels**) ATP **2** *Biol & Chim* (*abrév* **adénosine triphosphate**) ATP

NMPL (*abrév* **Arts et traditions populaires**) arts and crafts; **musée des A.** arts and crafts museum

atrabilaire [atrabilɛr] *Littéraire* ADJ cantankerous, atrabilious

NMF cantankerous person

atrabile [atrabil] NF *(dans la médecine ancienne)* black bile

atractyligénine [atraktiliʒenin] NF *Chim* atractyligenin

âtre [atr] NM *Littéraire* hearth; **au coin de l'â.** by *or* round the fireplace

Atrée [atre] NPR *Myth* Atreus

atrésie [atrezi] NF *Méd* atresia

atriau, -x [atri(j)o] NM *Suisse Culin* = circular sausagemeat patty

Atrides [atrid] NPR *Myth* **les A.** the Atreids, the Atridae

atriqué, -e [atrike] ADJ *Can Fam* **bien a.** well dressed▪; **mal a.** badly dressed▪; **être a. comme la chienne de Jacques** to be dressed like a dog's dinner

atrium [atrijɔm] NM *Antiq & Archit* atrium

atroce [atrɔs] ADJ **1** *(cruel)* atrocious, foul; **des scènes atroces** horrifying *or* gruesome scenes; **leur vengeance fut a.** their revenge was awesome

2 *(insupportable)* excruciating, dreadful, atrocious; **il est mort dans d'atroces souffrances** he died in dreadful pain

3 *(en intensif)* **sa maison est d'un mauvais goût a.** his house is horribly tasteless; **d'une laideur a.** hideously ugly

4 *Fam* atrocious, foul; **il est a. avec son père** he's really awful to his father; **il fait un temps a.** the weather's dreadful; **les haricots étaient atroces!** the beans were foul!

atrocement [atrɔsmɑ̃] ADV **1** *(cruellement)* atrociously, horribly; **a. mutilé** horribly *or* hideously mutilated **2** *(en intensif)* atrociously, dreadfully, horribly; **elle a a. mal** she's in dreadful *or* terrible pain; **a. ennuyeux** excruciatingly boring; **j'ai a. froid** I'm frozen to death; **j'ai a. faim** I'm starving; **j'ai a. soif** I'm dying of thirst

atrocité [atrɔsite] NF **1** *(caractère cruel)* atrociousness; **le repentir n'excuse pas l'a. de ses crimes** repentance does not excuse the horror of his/her crimes

2 *(crime)* atrocity; **les atrocités de la guerre** the atrocities committed in wartime

3 *(chose horrible)* **on m'a raconté des atrocités sur votre compte** I have been hearing dreadful things about you; **ce tableau est une a.** this picture is a real horror *or* an atrocity

atrophie [atrɔfi] NF *Méd* atrophy

atrophié, -e [atrɔfje] ADJ *Méd* atrophied

atrophier [9] [atrɔfje] *Méd & Fig* VT to atrophy

▸**s'atrophier** VPR to atrophy

atrophique [atrɔfik] ADJ atrophic

atropine [atrɔpin] NF *Méd* atropin, atropine

Atropos [atrɔpɔs] NPR *Myth* Atropos

atropos [atrɔpɔs] NM *Entom* **1** *(papillon)* **(sphinx) a.** death's-head hawk-moth **2** *(psoque)* death-watch

attabler [3] [atable] **s'attabler** VPR to sit down (at the table); **tous les convives sont déjà attablés** all the guests are already seated at the table; **venez donc vous a. avec nous** do come and sit at our table

attachant, -e [ataʃɑ̃, -ɑ̃t] ADJ *(personnalité)* engaging, lovable; *(livre, spectacle)* captivating; **c'est un enfant très a.** he's such a lovable child

attache [ataʃ] NF **1** *(lien → gén)* tie; *(→ en cuir, en toile)* strap; *(→ en ficelle)* string; *(→ d'un vêtement)* clip, fastener; *(→ d'un rideau)* tie-back

2 *(ami)* tie, friend; *(parent)* relative, family tie; **il n'a plus aucune a. en France** he doesn't have any ties left in France; **elle a des attaches en Normandie** she has relatives in Normandy; **un homme sans attaches** *(sans partenaire)* an unattached man; *(sans relations)* a man without family or friends; **tous les ans ils séjournaient à Monteau, ils s'y étaient fait des attaches** they went back to Monteau every year, they'd made friends there

3 *Anat* **a. de la main/du pied** wrist/ankle joint

4 *Bot* tendril

5 *Rail* **a. de rail** rail fastening

▫ **attaches** NFPL *Anat* joints; **avoir des attaches fines** to be small-boned

▫ **à l'attache** ADJ *(chien, cheval)* tied up

attaché, -e [ataʃe] ADJ *(affectivement)* **être a. à** to be attached to *or* fond of

NM,F attaché; **a. d'administration** administrative assistant; **a. d'ambassade** embassy attaché; **a. commercial** *(d'une ambassade)* commercial attaché; *(d'une entreprise)* sales representative; **a. culturel** cultural attaché; **a. militaire** military attaché; **a. de presse** press officer; *(dans le corps diplomatique)* press attaché; *Univ* **a. temporaire d'enseignement et de recherche** = holder of, or candidate for, a doctorate with a temporary university teaching post, who must then sit a competitive entry examination to qualify for a full-time post

attaché-case [ataʃekɛz] (*pl* **attachés-cases**) NM attaché case

attachement [ataʃmɑ̃] NM **1** *(affection)* affection, attachment; **son a. pour sa mère** his/her affection for *or* attachment to his/her mother **2** *Mktg* **a. à la marque** brand bonding **3** *Constr* daily statement *(to record progress and costs)*

attacher [3] [ataʃe] VT **1** *(accrocher)* to tie, to tie up; **a. son chien** to tie up one's dog; **a. les mains d'un prisonnier** to tie a prisoner's hands together; **a. qn/qch à** to tie sb/sth to; **a. un chien à une corde/à sa niche** to tie a dog to a rope/to his kennel; **pauvre bête, il l'a attachée à une chaîne** he's chained the poor thing up; **la barque est attachée à une chaîne** the boat's moored on the end of a chain *or* chained up; **a. qn à une chaise** to tie sb to a chair; **une photo était attachée à la lettre** *(avec un trombone)* a picture was clipped to the letter; *(avec une agrafe)* a picture was stapled to the letter; *Fam* **il n'attache pas son chien avec des saucisses** he's as mean as hell

2 *(pour fermer)* to tie; **a. un colis avec une ficelle** to tie up a parcel; **une simple ficelle attachait la valise** the suitcase was held shut with a piece of string

3 *(vêtement)* to fasten; **peux-tu m'aider à a. ma robe?** can you help me do up my dress?; **a. ses lacets** to tie one's shoelaces; **attachez votre ceinture** fasten your seatbelt

4 *(accorder)* to attach; **j'attache beaucoup de prix** *ou* **de valeur à notre amitié** I attach great value to *or* set great store by our friendship; **elle attache trop d'importance à son physique** she attaches too much importance to the way she looks

5 *(fixer)* **a. ses yeux** *ou* **son regard sur qn** to fix one's eyes upon sb

6 *(associer)* to link, to connect; **le scandale auquel son nom est/reste attaché** the scandal with which his/her name is/remains linked; **plus rien ne l'attache à Paris** he/she has no ties in Paris now; **qu'est-ce qui m'attache à la vie maintenant?** what is there for me to live for now?

7 *(comme domestique, adjoint)* **a. un apprenti à un maître** to apprentice a young boy to a master; **elle est attachée à mon service depuis dix ans** she has been working for me for ten years

VI *Culin* to stick; **le riz a attaché** the rice has stuck; **poêle/casserole qui n'attache pas** non-stick pan/saucepan

▸**s'attacher** VPR **1** *(emploi réfléchi)* to tie oneself (up); **il s'est attaché avec une corde** he tied himself (up) with a rope

2 *(emploi passif)* to fasten, to do up; **la robe s'attache sur le côté** the dress does up *or* fastens at the side; **s'a. avec une fermeture Éclair®/des boutons** to zip/to button up

3 s'a. (les services de) qn to take sb on; **il s'est attaché les services d'un garde du corps** he's hired a bodyguard

4 s'a. à *(se lier avec)* to become fond of *or* attached to; *(s'efforcer de)* to devote oneself to; **s'a. aux pas de qn** to follow sb closely; **je m'attache à le rendre heureux** I try (my best) to make him happy; **elle s'est attachée à reproduire les fresques fidèlement** she took great pains to reproduce the frescoes faithfully

attagène [ataʒɛn] NM *Entom* (two-spotted) carpet beetle

attagis [ataʒi] NM *Orn* seedsnipe

attaquable [atakabl] ADJ **1** *Mil* open to attack **2** *(discutable)* contestable; **son système/testament n'est pas a.** his/her system/will cannot be contested; **ses déclarations seront difficilement attaquables** his/her statements will be difficult to contest

attaquant, -e [atakɑ̃, -ɑ̃t] ADJ attacking, assaulting, assailing

NM,F **1** *(assaillant)* attacker, assailant **2** *Sport* striker

attaque [atak] NF **1** *(agression)* attack, assault; *(d'une voiture, d'un train)* hold-up; **à l'a.!** attack!; **passer à l'a.** to attack; *Fig* to attack, to go on the offensive; **a. aérienne** air attack *or* raid; **a. à main armée** *(contre une banque)* armed robbery; **a. préventive** pre-emptive strike

2 *(diatribe)* attack, onslaught; **il a été victime d'odieuses attaques dans les journaux** he was subjected to scurrilous attacks in the newspapers; **pas d'attaques personnelles, s'il vous plaît** let's not get personal, please

3 *Méd (d'apoplexie)* stroke; *(cardiaque)* heart attack; *(crise)* fit, seizure; **a. d'épilepsie** epileptic fit

4 *Sport* attack; *(en alpinisme)* start

5 *Mktg (sur un marché)* attack; **a. frontale** head-on attack; **a. latérale** flank attack

6 *Mus* attack; **ton a. n'est pas assez nette** your attack is too weak

▫ **d'attaque** ADJ *Fam* **être** *ou* **se sentir d'a.** to be on top form; **je ne me sens pas d'a. pour aller à la piscine** I don't feel up to going to the swimming pool; **te sens-tu d'a. pour un petit tennis?** do you feel up to a game of tennis?; **je ne me sens pas tellement d'a. ce matin** I don't really feel up to much this morning

attaquer [3] [atake] VT **1** *(assaillir → ennemi, pays, forteresse, marché)* to attack, to launch an attack on; *(→ passant, touriste)* to attack; **il s'est fait a. par deux hommes** he was attacked *or* assaulted by two men; **madame, c'est lui qui m'a attaqué!** please, Miss, he started it!; **nous avons été attaqués par les moustiques** we were attacked by mosquitoes; **a. une place par surprise** to make a surprise attack on a fort; **a. le mal à la racine** to tackle the root of the problem

2 *(abîmer → sujet: rouille)* to damage, to corrode, to eat into; **l'humidité a même attaqué l'abat-jour** the damp even damaged the lampshade

3 *(critiquer)* to attack, to condemn; **il a été attaqué par tous les journaux** he was attacked by all the newspapers; **j'ai été personnellement attaqué** I suffered personal attacks; **le projet a été violemment attaqué** the project came in for some fierce criticism; *Jur* **a. qn en justice** to bring an action against sb, to take sb to court; **a. qn en diffamation** to bring a libel action against sb; **a. un testament** to contest a will

4 *(entreprendre → tâche)* to tackle, to attack, to get started on; **j'ai attaqué ma pile de dossiers vers minuit** I got started on my pile of files around midnight; **prêt à a. le travail?** ready to get *or* to settle down to work?

5 *Fam (commencer → repas, bouteille)* **a. le petit déjeuner** to dig into breakfast; **on attaque le beaujolais?** shall we have a go at that Beaujolais?

6 *Méd* to affect; **le poumon droit est attaqué** the right lung is affected

7 *Mus* to attack

8 *Cartes* **a. à l'atout** to lead trumps; **a. à carreau** to lead diamonds

USAGE ABSOLU *(commencer)* **bon, on attaque?** right, shall we get going?; **quand l'orchestre attaque** when the orchestra strikes up

▸**s'attaquer à** VPR **1** *(combattre)* to take on, to attack; **il ne faut pas s'a. à plus faible que soi** pick on somebody your own size!; **elle s'est attaquée aux institutions** she took on the establishment; **s'a. aux préjugés** to attack *or* to fight *or* to tackle prejudice; **il s'est tout de suite attaqué au problème** he tackled the problem right away

2 *(agir sur)* to attack; **cette maladie ne s'attaque qu'aux jeunes enfants** only young children are affected by this disease; **les bactéries s'attaquent à vos gencives** bacteria attack your gums

attardé, -e [atarde] ADJ **1** *(qui traîne)* **il ne restait plus que quelques passants attardés** there were only a few people still about **2** *Vieilli (anormal)* backward, (mentally) retarded **3** *(démodé)* old-fashioned

NM,F *Vieilli (malade)* (mentally) retarded person

attarder [3] [atarde] **s'attarder** VPR **1** *(rester tard → dans la rue)* to linger; *(→ chez quelqu'un)* to stay late; *(→ au bureau, à l'atelier)* to stay on *or* late; **ne nous attardons pas, la nuit va tomber** let's not stay any longer, it's almost nightfall; **je me suis attardée près de la rivière** I lingered by the river; **rentre vite, ne t'attarde pas** be home early, don't stay out too late; **ils se sont attardés ici bien après minuit** they stayed around here long after midnight; **s'a. à des détails** to get bogged down in detail; **elles s'attardaient à boire leur café** they were lingering over their coffee

2 s'a. sur *(s'intéresser à)* to linger over, to dwell on; **s'a. sur des détails** to get bogged down in detail; **attardons-nous quelques minutes sur le cas de cette malade** let's consider the case of this patient for a minute; **vous vous êtes trop attardé sur l'aspect technique** you spent too much time discussing the technical side; **l'image contenue dans la strophe vaut que l'on s'y attarde** the image in the stanza merits further consideration; **encore un mélodrame qui ne vaut pas que l'on s'y attarde** another forgettable melodrama

atteindre [81] [atɛ̃dr] VT **1** *(lieu)* to reach, to get to; *Rad & TV* to reach; **aucun son ne nous atteignait** no sound reached us; **des émissions qui atteignent un large public** programmes reaching a wide audience

2 *(situation, objectif)* to reach, *Sout* to attain; **a. la gloire** to attain glory; **il a atteint son but** he's reached his goal *or* achieved his aim; **leur propagande n'atteint pas son but** their propaganda misses its target; **avez-vous atteint vos objectifs de vente?** have you reached *or* fulfilled your sales targets?; **les taux d'intérêt ont atteint un nouveau record** interest rates have reached a record high

3 *(âge, valeur, prix)* to reach; **a. 70 ans** to reach the age of 70; **le sommet atteint plus de 4000 mètres** the summit is over 4,000 metres high; **les dégâts atteignent 200 000 euros** 200,000 euros' worth of damage has been done

4 *(communiquer avec)* to contact, to reach; **il est impossible d'a. ceux qui sont à l'intérieur de l'ambassade** the people inside the embassy are incommunicado

5 *(toucher)* to reach, to get at, to stretch up to; **je n'arrive pas à a. le dictionnaire qui est là-haut** I can't reach the dictionary up there

6 *(frapper)* to hit; **a. la cible** to hit the target; **a. la cible en plein centre** to hit the bull's eye; **la balle/le policier l'a atteint en pleine tête** the bullet hit/the policeman shot him in the head; **atteint à l'épaule** wounded in the shoulder

7 *(blesser moralement)* to affect, to move, to stir; **il peut dire ce qu'il veut à mon sujet, ça ne m'atteint pas** he can say what he likes about me, it doesn't bother me at all; **rien ne l'atteint** nothing affects *or* can reach him/her

8 *(affecter → sujet: maladie, fléau)* to affect; **les tumeurs secondaires ont déjà atteint le poumon** the secondary tumours have already spread to the lung; **être atteint d'un mal incurable** to be suffering from an incurable disease; **les pays atteints par la folie de la guerre** countries in the grip of war mania

□ **atteindre à** VT IND *Littéraire* to achieve, to attain

atteint, -e [atɛ̃, -ɛ̃t] ADJ **1** *(d'une maladie, d'un fléau)* affected; **quand le moral est a.** when depression sets in; **la partie gauche de la façade est atteinte** the left side of the façade is affected

2 *Fam (fou)* touched; **il est plutôt a.** he's not quite right in the head

□ **atteinte** NF *(attaque)* attack; **je considère que c'est une atteinte à mon honneur** I consider it an attack on my honour; **atteinte aux bonnes mœurs** offence against public decency; **atteinte à la liberté individuelle** infringement of personal freedom; **atteinte aux droits de l'homme** violation of human rights; **atteinte à la sûreté de l'État** high treason; **atteinte à la vie privée** violation of privacy; **porter atteinte au pouvoir de qn** to undermine sb's power; **porter atteinte à la réputation de qn** to damage sb's reputation; **porter atteinte à l'ordre public** to commit a breach of the peace, to disturb the peace; **hors d'atteinte** out of reach

□ **atteintes** NFPL *(effets nocifs)* effects; **les premières atteintes du mal se sont manifestées quand il a eu 20 ans** *(épilepsie, diabète)* he first displayed the symptoms of the disease at the age of 20; *(alcoolisme, dépression)* the first signs of the problem came to light when he was 20

attelage [atlaʒ] NM **1** *(fait d'attacher → un cheval)* harnessing; *(→ un bœuf)* yoking; *(→ une charrette, une remorque)* hitching up **2** *(plusieurs animaux)* team; *(paire d'animaux)* yoke **3** *(véhicule)* carriage **4** *Rail (processus, dispositif)* coupling

atteler [24] [atle] VT **1** *(cheval)* to harness; *(bœuf)* to yoke; *(charrette, remorque)* to hitch up; **a. une voiture** to attach horses to a carriage **2** *Rail* to couple

▸**s'atteler** VPR **s'a. à** to get down to, to tackle; **il va falloir que tu t'attelles à ces révisions!** you'll have to get down to that revision!

attelle [atɛl] NF **1** *Méd* splint **2** *(pour un cheval)* hame

attellera *etc voir* **atteler**

attenant, -e [atnɑ̃, -ɑ̃t] ADJ adjoining, adjacent; **cour attenante à la maison** back yard adjoining the house

ATTENDRE [73] [atɑ̃dr] VT **A. 1** *(rester jusqu'à la venue de → retardataire, voyageur)* to wait for; **je l'attends pour partir** I'm waiting till he/she gets here before I leave, I'll leave as soon as he/she gets here; **il va falloir t'a. encore longtemps?** are you going to be much longer?; **attendez-moi après le travail** wait for me after work; **a. qn à la sortie** to wait for sb outside; **(aller) a. qn à l'aéroport/la gare** to (go and) meet sb at the airport/the station; **le train ne va pas vous a.** the train won't wait (for you); **l'avion l'a attendu** they delayed the plane for him; *Fig* **a. qn au passage** *ou* **au tournant** to wait for a chance to pounce on sb; **elle se trompera, et je l'attends au tournant** she'll make a mistake and that's when I'll get her; *Can Fig* **a. qn avec une brique et un fanal** to wait angrily for sb; **le film est attendu avec une brique et un fanal par les critiques** the critics are already getting their knives out for this film

2 *(escompter l'arrivée de → facteur, invité)* to wait for, to expect; *(→ colis, livraison)* to expect, to await; *(→ réponse, événement)* to wait for, to await; **je ne t'attendais plus!** I'd given up waiting for you!; **a. qn d'une minute à l'autre** to expect sb any minute; **a. qn à** *ou* **pour dîner** to expect sb for dinner; **vous êtes attendu, le docteur va vous recevoir immédiatement** the doctor's expecting you, he'll see you straightaway; **j'attends un coup de téléphone** I'm expecting a telephone call; **qu'est-ce que tu attends?** *(ton interrogatif ou de reproche)* what are you waiting for?; **qu'est-ce qu'il attend pour les renvoyer?** why doesn't he just fire them?; **qu'attendez-vous pour déjeuner?** why don't you go ahead and have lunch?; **ils n'attendent que ça, c'est tout ce qu'ils attendent** that's exactly *or* just what they're waiting for; **il attend le grand jour avec impatience** he's eagerly looking forward to the big day; **a. fiévreusement des résultats** to be anxiously waiting for results; **nous attendons des précisions** we're awaiting further details; **a. son tour** to wait one's turn; **a. son heure** to bide one's time; **a. le bon moment** to wait for the right moment (to come along); **a. demain pour faire qch** to delay *or* to put off doing sth till *or* until tomorrow; **cela peut a. demain** that can wait till *or* until tomorrow; **je lui ai prêté 100 euros et je les attends toujours** I lent him/her 100 euros and I still haven't got it back *or* I'm still waiting for it; **se faire a.** to keep others waiting; **désolé de m'être fait a.** sorry to have kept you waiting; **les hors-d'œuvre se font a.** the starters are taking a long time to come; **la réforme se fait a.** the reform is taking a long time to materialize; **les résultats ne se sont pas fait a.** *(après une élection)* the results didn't take long to come in; *(conséquences d'une action)* there were immediate consequences; *Fam* **alors, tu attends le dégel?** are you going to hang around here all day?; **a. qn comme le Messie** to wait eagerly for sb

3 *(sujet: femme enceinte)* **a. un bébé** *ou* **un enfant,** *Belg* **a. famille** to be expecting (a child), to be pregnant; **a. des jumeaux** to be pregnant with *or* expecting twins; **j'attends une fille** I'm expecting a girl; **elle attend son bébé pour le 15 avril** her baby's due on 15 April; *Euph* **a. un heureux événement** to be expecting

4 *(être prêt pour)* to await, to be ready for; **ta chambre t'attend** your room's ready (for you); **la voiture vous attend** the car's ready, the car's waiting for you; **venez, le dîner nous attend** come along, dinner's ready *or* dinner is served

5 *(sujet: destin, sort, aventure)* to await, to be *or* to lie in store for; **une mauvaise surprise l'attendait** there was an unpleasant surprise in store for him/her; **c'est là que la mort l'attendait** that's where he/she was to meet his/her death; **une nouvelle vie vous attend là-bas** a whole new life awaits you there; **il ne sait pas quel sort l'attend** he doesn't know what fate has in store for him; **si tu savais** *ou* **tu ne sais pas ce qui t'attend!** you haven't a clue what you're in for, have you?; **avant de me porter volontaire, je voudrais savoir ce qui m'attend** before I volunteer, I'd like to know what I'm letting myself in for

6 *(espérer)* **a. qch de qn/qch** to expect sth from sb/sth; **qu'attendez-vous de moi?** what do you expect of me?; **j'attendais mieux d'elle** I expected better of her, I was expecting better things from her; **j'attends de lui une réponse** I expect him to answer *or* an answer from him; **nous attendons beaucoup de la réunion** we expect a lot (to come out) of the meeting; **sa réponse, je n'en attends pas grand-chose** I'm not expecting too much (to come) out of his/her response

7 *(avoir besoin de)* to need; **le document attend encore trois signatures** the document needs another three signatures; **le pays attend encore l'homme qui sera capable de mettre fin à la guerre civile** the country is still waiting for the man who will be able to put an end to the civil war

B. *AVEC COMPLÉMENT INTRODUIT PAR "QUE"* **nous attendrons qu'elle soit ici** we'll wait till she gets here *or* for her to get here; **j'attends qu'il réponde** I'm waiting till he answers, I'm waiting for his answer *or* for him to answer; **elle attendait toujours qu'il rentre avant d'aller se coucher** she would always wait up for him; **attends (un peu) que je le dise à ton père!** just you wait until I tell your father!

C. *AVEC COMPLÉMENT INTRODUIT PAR "DE"* **attends d'être grand** wait until you're older; **nous attendions de sortir** we were waiting to go out; **j'attends avec impatience de la revoir** I can't wait to see her again; **nous attendons de**

voir la suite des événements we're waiting to see what happens next

VI 1 *(patienter)* to wait; **les gens n'aiment pas a.** people don't like to be kept waiting *or* to have to wait; **je passe mon temps à a.** I spend all my time waiting around; **il est en ligne, vous attendez?** he's on the other line, will you hold?; **faites-les a.** ask them to wait; **si tu crois qu'il va t'aider, tu peux toujours a.!** if you think he's going to help you, don't hold your breath!; **il peut toujours a.!** he'll have a long wait!; **attends, je vérifie** hold on, I'll check!; **mais enfin attends, je ne suis pas prêt!** wait a minute, will you, I'm not ready!; **elle s'appelle, attends, comment déjà?** her name is, hold on, what is it again?; **c'était en, attendez un peu, 1986** it was in, just a minute, 1986; **et attends, tu ne sais pas le plus beau!** wait (for it) *or* hold on, the best part's yet to come!; **attendez voir, je crois me souvenir…** let's see *or* let's think *or* let me see, I seem to remember…; **et alors là, attendez, il s'est mis à tout avouer** and at that point, wait for it *or* would you believe it, he started to come clean; *Fam* **attends voir, je vais demander** hold *or* hang on, I'll ask; *Fam* **attends voir, toi!** *(menace)* just you wait!; *Prov* **tout vient à point à qui sait a.** all things come to he who waits

2 *(sujet: plat chaud, soufflé)* to wait; *(sujet: vin, denrée)* to keep; **les spaghetti ne doivent pas a.** spaghetti must be served as soon as it's ready; **il fait trop a. ses vins** *(les sert trop vieux)* he keeps his wines too long

3 *(être reporté)* to wait; **votre projet attendra** your plan'll have to wait

❑ **attendre après VT IND** *Fam* **1** *(avoir besoin de)* **a. après qch** to be in desperate need of sth▪; **garde le livre, je n'attends pas après** keep the book, I'm not desperate *or* in a hurry for it

2 *(compter sur)* **a. après qn** to rely *or* to count on sb▪; **je n'ai pas attendu après toi pour me l'expliquer** I didn't exactly rely on you to explain it to me; **si tu attends après lui, tu n'auras jamais tes renseignements** if you're counting on him *or* if you leave it up to him, you'll never get the information you want; **elle est assez grande, elle n'attend plus après toi!** she's old enough to get along (perfectly well) without you!▪

❑ **en attendant ADV 1** *(pendant ce temps)* **finis ton dessert, en attendant je vais faire le café** finish your dessert, and in the meantime I'll make the coffee; **le train aura un retard de 20 minutes – en attendant, allons boire un café** the train's going to be 20 minutes late – let's go and have a coffee while we wait

2 *Fam (malgré cela)* **oui mais, en attendant, je n'ai toujours pas mon argent** that's as may be but I'm still missing my money; **ris si tu veux mais, en attendant, j'ai réussi à mon examen** you can laugh if you like, but I still passed my exam

❑ **en attendant que CONJ** until (such time as); **en attendant qu'il s'explique, on ne sait rien** until (such time as) he's explained himself *or* as long as he hasn't provided any explanations, we don't know anything

▸**s'attendre VPR 1** *(emploi réciproque)* **les enfants, attendez-vous pour traverser la rue** children, wait for each other before you cross the road

2 s'a. à to expect; **on ne s'attendait pas à sa mort** his/her death was unexpected; **il faut s'a. à des embouteillages** traffic jams are expected; **il faut s'a. à tout** we should be prepared for anything; **s'a. au pire** to expect the worst; **savoir à quoi s'a.** to know what to expect; **je ne m'attendais pas à cela de votre part** I didn't expect this from you; **nous ne nous attendions pas à ce que la grève réussisse** we weren't expecting the strike to succeed, we hadn't anticipated that the strike would succeed; **il fallait s'y a.** that was to be expected; **comme il fallait s'y a.** as was to be expected, predictably enough; **tu aurais dû t'y a.** you should have known; **je m'y attendais** I expected as much

---

'En attendant Godot' *Beckett* 'Waiting for Godot'

Allusion

J'ai failli attendre

This is a quotation attributed to Louis XIV, and it means "I almost waited". According to the story, the king's coach arrived exactly on time, and this was his ironic comment. When one is kept waiting for something or someone, this is sometimes said; as a reproach to a friend who turns up late, it has the flavour of "So you finally decided to show up!"

---

attendri, -e [atɑ̃dri] **ADJ 1** *(ému → regard)* fond, tender **2** *(amolli → viande)* tenderized

attendrir [32] [atɑ̃drir] **VT 1** *(émouvoir)* to move to tears *or* pity

2 *(apitoyer)* to move to pity; **s'il espère m'a. avec ses cadeaux, il se trompe** if he's hoping to soften me up with his presents, he's mistaken; **se laisser a.** to give in to pity

3 *(viande)* to tenderize

▸**s'attendrir VPR 1** *(être ému)* to be moved *or* touched (**sur** by); **ne nous attendrissons pas!** let's not get emotional!; **il s'attendrit facilement** he gets emotional easily, he is easily moved; **s'a. sur un bébé** to gush over a baby

2 *(être apitoyé)* to feel compassion; **s'a. sur le sort de qn** to feel pity *or* sorry for sb; **s'a. sur soi-même** to indulge in self-pity, to feel sorry for oneself

attendrissant, -e [atɑ̃drisɑ̃, -ɑ̃t] **ADJ** moving, touching; **regarde-le essayer de s'habiller, c'est a.!** look at him trying to dress himself, how sweet!; **il est d'une naïveté attendrissante** his naivety is touching; **de façon attendrissante** touchingly

attendrissement [atɑ̃drismɑ̃] **NM 1** *(tendresse)* emotion *(UNCOUNT)*; **pas d'a.!** let's not get emotional!; **l'a. le gagnait** he was getting emotional; **je ne suis pas porté aux attendrissements** I don't tend to get emotional, I'm not the emotional type **2** *(pitié)* pity, compassion; **a. sur soi-même** self-pity

attendrisseur [atɑ̃drisœr] **NM** *(pour viande)* tenderizer; **passer de la viande à l'a.** to tenderize meat

attendu[1] [atɑ̃dy] **PRÉP** considering, given

❑ **attendu que CONJ** since, considering *or* given that; *Jur* whereas

attendu[2] [atɑ̃dy] **NM** *Jur* **les attendus d'un jugement** the reasons adduced for a verdict

attendu[3]**, -e** [atɑ̃dy] **PP** *voir* **attendre**

ADJ le train est a. pour cinq heures the train is expected at five o'clock; **très a.** eagerly-awaited; **la princesse, très attendue, descend de voiture** the eagerly-awaited princess is now getting out of the car; **un mariage a. avec impatience** an eagerly-awaited wedding

attentat [atɑ̃ta] **NM 1** *(assassinat)* assassination attempt; **commettre un a. contre qn** to make an attempt on sb's life

2 *(explosion)* attack; **a. à la bombe** bomb attack, bombing; **a. à la voiture piégée** car bomb attack *or* explosion; **l'ambassade a été hier la cible d'un a.** the Embassy was bombed yesterday

3 *(atteinte)* **a. aux libertés constitutionnelles** violation of constitutional liberties; **a. contre la sécurité de l'État** acts harmful to State security; *Jur* **a. aux mœurs** indecent behaviour; **a. à la pudeur** indecent assault

attentatoire [atɑ̃tatwar] **ADJ** *Jur* **a. à la dignité de l'homme** detrimental *or* prejudicial to human dignity

attentat-suicide [atɑ̃tasɥisid] *(pl* **attentats-suicides)** **NM** suicide (bomb) attack

attente [atɑ̃t] **NF 1** *(fait d'attendre)* waiting; *(période)* wait; **l'a. est longue** it's a long time to wait; **vous devez compter une a. de quatre heures** you should expect a four-hour wait; **le plus dur, c'est l'a.** the toughest part is the waiting; **j'étais là depuis 40 minutes et l'a. se prolongeait** I'd been there for 40 minutes and I was still waiting; **pendant l'a. du verdict/des résultats** while awaiting the verdict/the results; **deux heures d'a.** a two-hour wait

2 *(espérance)* expectation; **répondre à l'a. de qn** to come up to sb's expectations; **si la marchandise ne répond pas à votre a.** should the goods not meet your requirements

❑ **dans l'attente de PRÉP 1** *(dans le temps)* **être dans l'a. de qch** to be waiting for *or* awaiting sth; **il vit dans l'a. de ton retour** he lives for the moment when you return

2 *(dans la correspondance)* **dans l'a. de vous lire/de votre réponse/de vous rencontrer** looking forward to hearing from you/to your reply/to meeting you

❑ **en attente ADV laisser qch en a.** to leave sth pending **ADJ** *(dossier, affaire)* pending; **le projet est en a.** the project is on hold; *Ordinat* **liste de fichiers à imprimer en a.** print queue

attenter [3] [atɑ̃te] **attenter à VT IND 1** *(commettre un attentat contre)* **a. à la vie de qn** to make an attempt on sb's life; **a. à ses jours** *ou* **à sa vie** to attempt suicide

2 *(porter atteinte à)* **a. à l'honneur/à la réputation de qn** to undermine sb's honour/reputation; **a. à la liberté de qn** to infringe upon sb's liberty; **a. aux libertés civiles** to violate civil rights

attentif, -ive [atɑ̃tif, -iv] **ADJ 1** *(concentré → spectateur, public, élève)* attentive; **l'auditoire était très a.** the audience was very attentive; **soyez attentifs!** pay attention!; **écouter qn d'une oreille attentive** to listen to sb attentively, to listen to every word sb says

2 *(prévenant → présence)* watchful; *(→ gestes, comportement, parole)* solicitous, thoughtful; **avoir besoin de soins attentifs** to be in need of tender loving care

3 *(scrupuleux)* **un examen a.** a close *or* careful examination

4 il était a. au moindre bruit/mouvement he was alert to the slightest sound/movement; **être a. à ce qui se dit** to pay attention to *or* to listen carefully to what is being said; **être a. aux autres/aux besoins de qn** to be attentive to others/to sb's needs; **être a. à sa santé** to be mindful of one's health; **être a. à son travail** to be careful *or* painstaking in one's work; **a. à ne pas être impliqué** anxious not to be involved; **il était a. à ne blesser personne** he was careful not to upset anyone

attention [atɑ̃sjɔ̃] **NF 1** *(concentration)* attention; **appeler** *ou* **attirer l'a. de qn sur qch** to call sb's attention to sth, to point sth out to sb; **mon a. a été attirée sur le fait que…** it has come to my attention *or* notice that…; **avoir l'a. de qn** to have sb's attention; **vous avez toute mon a.** you have my undivided attention; **consacrer toute son a. à un problème** to devote one's attention to *or* to concentrate on a problem; **écouter qn avec a.** to listen to sb attentively, to listen hard to what sb's saying; **lire qch avec a.** to read sth carefully *or* attentively; **manque d'a.** carelessness; **porter son a. sur qch** to turn one's attention to sth; **faire a.** to pay attention; **faites bien a.** *(écoutez)* listen carefully, pay attention; *(regardez)* look carefully; **faire a. à** to pay attention to, to heed; **fais particulièrement a. au dernier paragraphe** pay special attention to the last paragraph; **faites a. à ces menaces** bear these threats in mind; **fais a. (à ce) qu'ils soient tous à l'heure** make sure (that) they're all on time

2 *(égard)* attention *(UNCOUNT)*, attentiveness *(UNCOUNT)*, thoughtfulness *(UNCOUNT)*; **elle avait eu l'a. délicate de mettre des géraniums dans ma chambre** she'd kindly put geraniums in my bedroom; **je n'ai jamais droit à la moindre petite a.** nobody ever does nice things for me; **les mille et une attentions de la vraie tendresse** the thousand and one ways in which people express their love for each other; **entourer qn d'attentions, être plein d'attentions pour qn** to lavish attention on sb

3 *(capacité à remarquer)* attention; **attirer l'a.** to attract attention; **arrête, tu vas attirer l'a.!** stop, people will start looking!; **attirer l'a. de qn** to catch *or* to attract sb's attention; **tu as fait a. au numéro de téléphone?** did you get the phone number?; **quand il est entré, je n'ai d'abord pas fait a. à lui** when he came in I didn't notice him at first; **ne fais pas a. à lui, il dit n'importe quoi** don't mind him *or* pay no attention to him, he's talking nonsense

4 faire a. à qn/qch *(surveiller, s'occuper de)* to pay attention to sb/sth; **faire a. à sa santé** to take care of *or* to look after one's health; **faire a.**

à soi to look after *or* to take care of oneself; **faire a. à sa ligne** to watch one's weight; **il ne fait pas assez a. à sa femme** he doesn't pay enough attention to his wife; **elle fait trop a. aux autres hommes** she's too interested in other men

5 faire a. *(être prudent)* to be careful *or* cautious; **fais bien a. en descendant de l'escabeau** do be careful when you come off the stepladder; **fais a. aux voitures** watch out for the cars; **fais a. à ce que tu dis!** watch what you're saying!; **fais a. à toi** take care; **a. à la marche/porte** mind the step/door; **a. à tes bottes sales sur le tapis!** watch your muddy boots on that carpet!; **a. à la voiture!** mind the car!; **a. au départ!** stand clear of the doors!

EXCLAM 1 *(pour signaler un danger)* watch *or* look out!; **a., il est armé!** watch *or* look out, he's got a gun!; **a., a., tu vas le casser!** gently *or* easy (now), you'll break it!; **a. chien méchant** *(sur panneau)* beware of the dog; **a. fragile** *(sur emballage)* handle with care; **a. peinture fraîche** *(sur panneau)* wet paint; **a. travaux** *(sur panneau)* men at work

2 *(pour introduire une nuance)* **a., ce n'est pas cela que j'ai dit** now look, that's not what I said
❑ **à l'attention de PRÉP** *(sur une enveloppe)* **à l'a. de Madame Chaux** for the attention of Madame Chaux

attentionné, -e [atɑ̃sjɔne] **ADJ** considerate, thoughtful; **être a. envers qn** to be considerate *or* attentive towards sb; **comme mari, il était très a.** he was a very attentive *or* caring husband

attentionnel, -elle [atɑ̃sjɔnɛl] **ADJ** *Psy* attentional; *(déficit, trouble)* attention *(avant n)*

attentisme [atɑ̃tism] **NM** wait-and-see policy

attentiste [atɑ̃tist] **ADJ attitude a.** wait-and-see attitude; **politique a.** waiting game, wait-and-see policy; **pratiquer une politique d'a.** to play a waiting game

NMF les attentistes those who play a waiting game

attentive [atɑ̃tiv] *voir* **attentif**

attentivement [atɑ̃tivmɑ̃] **ADV** *(en se concentrant → écouter)* carefully, attentively; *(→ lire, regarder)* closely

atténuant, -e [atenɥɑ̃, -ɑ̃t] **ADJ** *(excuse, circonstance)* mitigating

atténuateur [atenɥatœr] **NM** *Élec* attenuator

atténuation [atenɥasjɔ̃] **NF 1** *(d'une douleur)* easing; *(du chagrin)* relief; *(d'une couleur)* toning down, softening; *(d'un bruit)* muffling; *(de la lumière)* dimming, subduing; *(d'un choc)* cushioning; softening; *(d'un contraste)* softening

2 *(d'une responsabilité)* reduction, lightening; *(de propos, d'une accusation)* toning down; *(d'une faute)* mitigation

atténué, -e [atenye] **ADJ** *Méd (virus)* attenuated

atténuer [7] [atenɥe] **VT 1** *(rendre moins perceptible → douleur)* to relieve, to soothe; *(→ chagrin)* to ease; *(→ couleur)* to tone down, to soften; *(→ bruit)* to muffle; *(→ lumière)* to dim, to subdue; *(→ choc)* to cushion, to soften; *(→ contraste)* to soften; **le temps a atténué les souvenirs** the memories have faded over time

2 *(rendre moins important, moins grave → responsabilité)* to reduce, to lighten, to lessen; *(→ propos, accusation)* to tone down; **le remords n'atténue pas la faute** remorse does not lessen the blame

►**s'atténuer VPR** *(chagrin, cris, douleur)* to subside, to die down; *(effet)* to subside, to fade, to wane; *(lumière)* to fade, to dim; *(bruit)* to diminish, to tone down; *(couleur)* to dim

atterrage [atɛraʒ] **NM** *Naut* landfall

atterrant, -e [atɛrɑ̃, -ɑ̃t] **ADJ** appalling, shocking

atterrer [4] [atere] **VT** to dismay, to appal; **sa réponse m'a atterré** I was appalled at his/her answer; **je l'ai trouvé atterré par la nouvelle** I found him reeling from the shock of the news; **il les regarda d'un air atterré** he looked at them aghast *or* in total dismay

atterrir [32] [aterir] **VI 1** *Aviat* to land, to touch down; **l'avion allait a.** the plane was coming in to land; **a. en catastrophe** to make an emergency landing; **a. sur le ventre** to make a belly landing; **a. trop court** to undershoot; **a. trop long** to overshoot; **faire a. un avion** to land an aircraft

2 *Fam (retomber)* to land, to wind up, *Br* to fetch up; **la voiture a atterri dans un champ** the car ended up *or* landed in a field; **tous ses vêtements ont atterri dans la cour** all his/her clothes ended up in the yard

3 *Fam (se retrouver)* to end up, to wind up, to land up; **a. en prison** to end up *or* to land up in jail; **le dossier finit par a. sur son bureau** the file eventually landed up *or* wound up on his/her desk; **j'ai finalement atterri comme réceptionniste dans un cabinet dentaire** I ended up as a receptionist in a dentist's surgery

4 *Naut (voir la terre)* to make *or* sight land, to make a landfall; *(toucher terre)* to reach *or* to hit land

5 *Fam* **atterris, mon vieux!** what planet have you been on?

atterrissage [aterisaʒ] **NM 1** *Aviat* landing; **prêt à l'a.** ready to touch down *or* to land; **après l'a.** after touchdown *or* landing; **a. en catastrophe** emergency landing; **a. en douceur** soft landing; **a. forcé** emergency landing; **a. aux instruments** instrument landing; **a. raté** bad landing; **a. sur le ventre** belly landing; **a. sans visibilité** blind landing; **a. à vue** visual landing

2 *Naut (en voyant la terre)* making land, landfall; *(en touchant terre)* reaching *or* hitting land
❑ **d'atterrissage ADJ** landing *(avant n)*

atterrissement [aterismɑ̃] **NM** *Géol* alluvial deposit

atterrisseur [aterisœr] **NM** *Aviat* undercarriage

attestation [atɛstasjɔ̃] **NF 1** *(document)* certificate; **a. d'assurance** insurance certificate; **a. de conformité** certificate of conformity; **a. médicale** doctor's *or* medical certificate **2** *Scol (diplôme)* certificate (of accreditation) **3** *Jur* attestation **4** *(preuve)* proof; **son échec est une nouvelle a. de son incompétence** his/her failure further demonstrates his/her incompetence

attesté, -e [atɛste] **ADJ** *Ling* attested; **formes attestées dans la littérature du XIIème siècle** forms attested *or* occurring in 12th-century literature

attester [3] [atɛste] **VT 1** *(certifier)* to attest; **il atteste que sa femme était bien chez elle** he attests that his wife was at home; **ce document atteste que...** this is to certify that...

2 *(témoigner)* to attest *or* to testify to, to vouch for; **cette version des faits est attestée par la presse** this version of the facts is borne out by the press; **ce mot n'est attesté dans aucun dictionnaire** this word isn't attested *or* doesn't occur in any dictionary
❑ **attester de VT IND** to prove, to testify to, to show evidence of; **sa réponse atteste de sa sincérité** his/her answer shows evidence of *or* testifies to *or* demonstrates his/her sincerity; **ainsi qu'en attesteront ceux qui me connaissent** as those who know me will testify

atticisme [atisism] **NM 1** *Beaux-Arts & Littérature* atticism **2** *(esprit)* attic salt

atticiste [atisist] **NMF** *Beaux-Arts & Littérature* atticist

attiédir [32] [atjedir] *Littéraire* **VT 1** *(refroidir → air)* to cool; *(→ liquide)* to make lukewarm **2** *(réchauffer)* to warm (up) **3** *Fig (sentiment)* to cool

►**s'attiédir VPR 1** *(se refroidir)* to cool (down), to become cooler **2** *(se réchauffer)* to warm up, to become warmer **3** *Fig (sentiment)* to cool, to wane

attiédissement [atjedismɑ̃] **NM 1** *(refroidissement)* cooling down **2** *(réchauffement)* warming up **3** *Fig (des sentiments)* cooling

attifement [atifmɑ̃] **NM** *Fam* (weird) get-up *or* gear

attifer [3] [atife] *Fam* **VT** *Péj* to get up, to rig out; **elle attife ses enfants n'importe comment** she dresses her children any old how; **être attifé de qch** to be got up *or* rigged out in sth

►**s'attifer VPR** to get oneself up, to rig oneself out; **comment tu t'es attifé!** what DO you look like!

attiger [17] [atiʒe] **VI** *très Fam Vieilli* to go over the top, to go a bit far; **là, il attigeait!** he went a bit far there!

Attila [atila] **NPR** Attila (the Hun)

attique[1] [atik] **ADJ** Attic
❑ **Attique NF** Attica

attique[2] [atik] **NM 1** *Archit* attic **2** *Suisse (appartement luxueux)* penthouse

NF *Belg Menuis (d'une porte, d'une fenêtre) Br* fanlight, *Am* transom

attirable [atirabl] **ADJ** attractable

attirail [atiraj] **NM** equipment *(UNCOUNT)*; **a. de pêche** fishing tackle; **il a tout un a. pour la pêche** he's got a full set of fishing tackle; **a. de plombier** plumber's tool kit; *Fam* **on emporte l'ordinateur et tout son a.** let's take the computer and all the bits that go with it; *Péj* **qu'est-ce que c'est que (tout) cet a.?** what's all this paraphernalia for?

attirance [atirɑ̃s] **NF** attraction; **l'a. entre nous deux a été immédiate** we were attracted to each other straight away; **éprouver de l'a. pour qn/qch** to feel attracted to sb/sth; **l'a. du vice** the lure of vice

attirant, -e [atirɑ̃, -ɑ̃t] **ADJ** attractive

attirer [3] [atire] **VT 1** *(tirer vers soi)* to draw; **elle a attiré l'enfant contre elle/sur son cœur** she drew the child to her/to her bosom; **il m'a attiré vers le balcon pour me montrer le paysage** he drew me towards the balcony to show me the view; **l'aimant attire le fer/les épingles** iron is/pins are attracted to a magnet

2 *(inciter à venir → badaud)* to attract; *(→ proie)* to lure; **couvre ce melon, il attire les guêpes** cover that melon up, it's attracting wasps; **a. les foules** to attract *or* to draw (in) the crowds; **les requins, attirés par l'odeur du sang** sharks attracted *or* drawn by the smell of blood; **le coup de feu les a attirés sur les lieux** the shot drew them to the scene; **a. qn dans un coin/un piège** to lure sb into a corner/a trap; **après l'avoir attirée derrière un paravent, il l'a embrassée** he kissed her after luring her behind a screen; **a. qn avec** *ou* **par des promesses** to lure *or* to entice sb with promises

3 *(capter → attention, regard)* to attract, to catch; **a. l'attention de qn** to catch *or* to attract sb's attention; **a. l'attention de qn sur qch** to call sb's attention to sth, to point sth out to sb; **a. l'intérêt de qn** to attract sb's interest; **essayant d'a. l'œil du serveur** trying to catch the waiter's eye; **une affiche qui attire les regards** an eye-catching poster

4 *(plaire à)* to attract, to seduce; **les femmes mariées l'attirent, il est attiré par les femmes mariées** he's attracted to married women; **se sentir attiré par qn** to feel attracted to sb; **il a une façon de sourire qui attire les femmes** women find the way he smiles attractive; **son originalité attire les hommes** his/her originality appeals to men; **ce qui m'attire dans ce projet** what attracts me *or* what I find attractive about this project; **la musique classique ne m'attire pas beaucoup** classical music doesn't appeal to me much

5 *(avoir comme conséquence)* to bring, to cause; **a. des ennuis à qn** to cause trouble for sb, to get sb into trouble; **sa démission lui a attiré des sympathies** his/her resignation won *or* earned him/her some sympathy; **a. sur soi la colère/haine de qn** to incur sb's anger/hatred

6 *Astron & Phys* to attract

►**s'attirer VPR 1** *(emploi réciproque)* to attract one another; **les contraires s'attirent** opposites attract (each other)

2 s'a. des ennuis to get oneself into trouble, to bring trouble upon oneself; **s'a. la colère de qn** to incur sb's anger; **s'a. les bonnes grâces de qn** to win *or* to gain sb's favour; **s'a. des ennemis** to make enemies

attisement [atizmɑ̃] **NM** *Littéraire (de colère, de haine, de désir)* arousal

attiser [3] [atize] **VT 1** *(flammes, feu)* to poke; *(incendie)* to fuel **2** *Littéraire (colère, haine, désir)* to stir up, to rouse

attitré, -e [atitre] **ADJ 1** *(accrédité)* accredited, appointed **2** *(habituel → fournisseur, marchand)* usual, regular **3** *(favori → fauteuil, place)* favourite

attitude [atityd] **NF 1** *(comportement)* attitude; *Péj (affectation)* attitude; **son a. envers moi/les femmes** his/her attitude towards me/women; **elle a eu une a. irréprochable** her attitude was beyond reproach; **prendre une a.** to strike an attitude; **prendre des attitudes** to put on airs; **il prend des attitudes de martyr** he puts on a

martyred look; **il a l'air indigné, mais ce n'est qu'une a.** he looks indignant but he's only putting it on

2 *(point de vue)* standpoint; **adopter une a. ambiguë** to adopt an ambiguous standpoint *or* attitude

3 *(maintien)* bearing, demeanour; *(position)* position, posture; **avoir une a. gauche** to move clumsily; **surpris dans une a. coupable** caught in a compromising position

4 *Belg (locution)* **prendre a.** to make *or* take a decision

attitudinal, -e, -aux, -ales [atitydinal, -o] **ADJ** *Psy* attitudinal

attorney [atɔrnɛ] **NM** *Jur* attorney; **a. général** Attorney-General

attouchement [atuʃmɑ̃] **NM 1** *(sexuel)* **se livrer à des attouchements sur qn** to fondle sb, to interfere with sb **2** *(pour guérir)* laying on of hands

attracteur [atraktœr] **NM** *Phys* attractor

attractif, -ive [atraktif, -iv] **ADJ 1** *Phys* attractive **2** *(plaisant)* attractive, appealing

attraction [atraksjɔ̃] **NF 1** *Astron & Phys* attraction; **a. terrestre** earth's gravity; **a. universelle** gravity

2 *(attirance)* attraction, appeal; **l'a. qu'il éprouve pour elle/la mort** his attraction to her/death; **exercer une a. sur qn/qch** to attract sb/sth; **la religion exerce-t-elle encore une a. sur les jeunes?** does the younger generation still feel drawn towards religion?; **les automobiles allemandes suscitent une a. très marquée chez les Britanniques** German cars are very popular with the British

3 *(centre d'intérêt)* attraction; **la grande a. de la soirée** the chief attraction of the evening; **les attractions touristiques de la région** the area's tourist attractions

4 *(distraction)* attraction; **a. numéro un** *ou* **principale** star attraction; **il y aura des attractions pour les enfants** entertainment will be provided for children; **les attractions** *(dans un gala etc)* the show; **les attractions passent à 21 heures** the show starts at 9 o'clock

5 *Ling* attraction

attractive [atraktiv] *voir* **attractif**

attractivité [atraktivite] **NF** attractiveness

attraire [112] [atrɛr] **VT** *Jur* **a. qn en justice** to institute proceedings against someone

attrait [atrɛ] **NM 1** *(beauté → d'un visage, d'une ville, d'une idéologie)* attraction, attractiveness; *(intérêt → d'un produit)* attraction, appeal; **elle trouve beaucoup d'a. à ses romans** she finds his/her novels very appealing; **un des attraits du célibat** one of the attractions of celibacy; **un village sans (grand) a.** a rather charmless village; **a. commercial** market appeal; **ce produit présente un a. commercial certain** this product has definite market appeal

2 *(fascination)* attraction, appeal; **éprouver un a. pour qch** to feel an attraction towards sth

□ **attraits NMPL** *Euph Littéraire* charms; **sans qu'elle cherche à dissimuler ses attraits** making no attempt to hide what nature has endowed her with

attrapade [atrapad], **attrapage** [atrapaz] **NF** *Fam* telling-off

attrape [atrap] **NF** catch, trick; **il doit y avoir une a. là-dessous** there must be a catch in it somewhere

attrape-couillon [atrapkujɔ̃] *(pl* **attrape-couillons)** **NM** *très Fam* con trick

attrape-mouche [atrapmuʃ] *(pl* **attrape-mouches)** **NM 1** *Bot* flytrap **2** *(papier collant)* flypaper

attrape-nigaud [atrapnigo] *(pl* **attrape-nigauds)** **NM** confidence trick

attraper [3] [atrape] **VT 1** *(prendre)* to pick up; **a. un timbre délicatement avec des pinces** to pick a stamp up carefully with tweezers; **la chatte attrape ses chatons par la peau du cou** the cat picks up her kittens by the scruff of the neck; **elle attrapa sa guitare sur le sol** she picked up her guitar from the floor; **attrape la casserole par le manche** hold *or* grasp the pan by the handle

2 *(saisir au passage → bras, main, ballon)* to grab; **a. qn par le bras** to grab sb by the arm; **a. qn par la taille** to grab sb round the waist; **il m'a attrapé par les épaules et m'a secoué** he took me by the shoulders and shook me; **il a attrapé un stylo et a couru répondre au téléphone** he grabbed a pen and ran to answer the phone; **attrape Rex, attrape!** come on Rex, get it!

3 *(saisir par force, par ruse)* to capture, to catch

4 *(surprendre → voleur, tricheur)* to catch; *(→ bribe de conversation, mot)* to catch; **a. qn à faire qch** to catch sb doing sth; **attends que je t'attrape!** just you wait till I get hold of you!; **si tu veux le voir, il faut l'a. au saut du lit/à la sortie du conseil** if you want to see him, you have to catch him as soon as he gets up/as soon as he comes out of the board meeting; **que je ne t'attrape plus à écouter aux portes!** don't let me catch you listening at doors again!

5 *(réprimander)* to tell off; **papa m'a attrapé!** Daddy told me off!; **je vais l'a. quand il va rentrer** he'll catch it from me when he gets home; **se faire a.** to get a telling-off

6 *(prendre de justesse → train)* to catch

7 *Fam (avoir)* to get; **a. une contravention** to get a ticket; **a. un coup de soleil** to get sunburnt; *Vieilli* **a. froid** *ou* **un rhume** *ou* **du mal** to catch *or* to get a cold; **elle a attrapé la rubéole de son frère** she got *or* caught German measles off *or* from her brother; **ferme la fenêtre, tu vas nous faire a. un rhume!** close the window or we'll all catch cold!; **tiens, attrape!** *(à quelqu'un qui vient d'être critiqué)* that's one in the eye for you!, take that!

8 *(tromper → naïf, gogo)* to catch (out), to fool

▸**s'attraper VPR 1** *(emploi passif) (être contracté → maladie, mauvaise habitude)* to be catching; **le cancer ne s'attrape pas** you can't catch cancer; **la rougeole s'attrape facilement** measles is very contagious

2 *(emploi réciproque) (se disputer)* to fight, to squabble; **tu les as entendus s'a.?** did you hear them squabbling?

attrape-touristes [atrapturist] **NM INV** tourist trap

attrape-tout [atraptu] **ADJ INV** catch-all *(avant n)*; **une catégorie a.** a catch-all category

attrapeur de rêves [atrapørdərɛv] **NM** dreamcatcher

attrayant, -e [atrɛjɑ̃, -ɑ̃t] **ADJ** *(homme, femme)* good-looking, attractive; *(suggestion)* attractive, appealing; **peu a.** unattractive, unappealing; **j'avoue que la perspective est attrayante** I must say the idea is appealing

attrempage [atrɑ̃paʒ] **NM** *Tech* bringing to the required temperature

attremper [3] [atrɑ̃pe] **VT** *Tech* to bring to the required temperature

attribuable [atribɥabl] **ADJ a. à** attributable to

attribuer [7] [atribɥe] **VT 1** *(distribuer → somme, bien)* to allocate; *(→ titre, privilège)* to grant; *(→ fonction, place, salaire, prime)* to allocate, to assign; *(→ prix, récompense)* to award; *Fin & Bourse (→ actions, dividendes)* to allocate, to allot; *Ordinat (mémoire)* to allocate; **nous ne sommes pas ici pour a. des blâmes** it is not up to us to lay the blame; *Théât* **a. un rôle à qn** to cast sb for a part; *Fig* to cast sb in a role

2 *(imputer)* **a. qch à qn** to ascribe *or* to attribute sth to sb; **ses contemporains ne lui attribuaient aucune originalité** his/her contemporaries did not credit him/her with any originality; **a. la paternité d'un enfant/d'une œuvre à qn** to consider sb to be the father of a child/author of a work; **un sonnet longtemps attribué à Shakespeare** a sonnet long thought to have been written by Shakespeare; **ces mots ont été attribués à Marat** these words were attributed to Marat, Marat is supposed to have said these words; **on attribue cette découverte à Pasteur** this discovery is attributed to Pasteur, Pasteur is credited with this discovery; **j'attribue sa réussite à son environnement** I put his/her success down *or* I attribute his/her success to his/her background; **un divorce qu'il faut a. à l'alcoolisme** a divorce which alcoholism must take the blame for; **attribue leur conduite à la stupidité plus qu'à la méchanceté** you must put their behaviour down to stupidity rather than to evil intent; **à quoi a. cette succession de catastrophes?** what could account for this series of disasters?

3 *(accorder)* **a. de l'importance à qch** to attach importance to sth; **a. de la valeur à qch** to find value in sth; **a. de l'intérêt à qch** to find sth interesting

▸**s'attribuer VPR s'a. qch** to claim sth for oneself; **il s'est attribué la plus grande chambre** he claimed the largest room for himself; **s'a. un titre** to give oneself a title; **s'a. une fonction** to appoint oneself to a post; **s'a. tout le mérite de qch** to claim all the credit for sth

attribut [atriby] **NM 1** *(caractéristique)* attribute, (characteristic) trait; *Euph* **attributs (virils** *ou* **masculins)** (male) privates **2** *Gram* predicate; **adjectif a.** predicative adjective

attributaire [atribytɛr] **NMF 1** *Écon* allottee **2** *Jur* beneficiary **3** *(d'un prix)* winner

attributif, -ive [atribytif, -iv] **ADJ 1** *Gram* predicative, attributive **2** *Jur* assignment *(avant n)*

attribution [atribysjɔ̃] **NF 1** *(distribution → d'une somme, d'un bien)* allocation; *(→ d'un titre, d'un privilège)* granting; *(→ d'une place, d'une fonction, d'une part)* allocation, assignment; *(→ d'un prix, d'une récompense)* awarding; *(→ d'un salaire, d'une prime)* assigning, allocation; *Fin & Bourse (→ d'actions, de dividendes)* allocation, allotment; *Ordinat (→ de mémoire)* allocation; *Jur* **a. préférentielle** preferential distribution; *Cin & TV* **attribution des rôles** casting

2 *(reconnaissance → d'une œuvre, d'une responsabilité, d'une découverte)* attribution; **toiles d'a. douteuse** paintings of doubtful origin; **l'a. de la figurine à Rodin a été contestée** doubts have been cast on whether Rodin actually sculpted the figurine; *Jur* **a. de paternité** affiliation

□ **attributions NFPL** responsibilities; **cela n'est pas** *ou* **n'entre pas dans mes attributions** that doesn't come within my remit, that's not part of my responsibilities

attributive [atribytiv] *voir* **attributif**

attriqué, -e [atrike] = **atriqué, -e**

attristant, -e [atristɑ̃, -ɑ̃t] **ADJ** saddening, depressing; **il est a. de voir que...** it's such a pity to see that...; **comme c'est a.!** it's so depressing!

attristé, -e [atriste] **ADJ** *(visage, regard)* sad; **contempler qch d'un œil a.** to gaze sadly at sth

attrister [3] [atriste] **VT** to sadden, to depress; **sa mort nous a tous profondément attristés** we were all greatly saddened by his/her death; **cela m'attriste de voir que...** it makes me sad *or* I find it such a pity to see that...

▸**s'attrister VPR s'a. de qch** to be saddened by sth, to be sad about sth; **je m'attriste d'apprendre qu'il est parti** I'm sad *or* it grieves me to hear that he's gone

attrition [atrisjɔ̃] **NF** *Méd & Rel* attrition

attroupement [atrupmɑ̃] **NM** crowd; **un a. s'est formé** a crowd gathered; **provoquer un a.** to draw a crowd; *Jur* **a. illégal** unlawful assembly, rout

attrouper [3] [atrupe] **VT** *(foule)* to draw, to attract; **arrêtez de crier, vous allez a. les passants** stop shouting, you'll draw a crowd

▸**s'attrouper VPR** *(gén)* to gather

atypie [atipi] **NF** atypia

atypique [atipik] **ADJ** atypical

atypisme [atipism] = **atypie**

au [o] *voir* **à**

aubade [obad] **NF** *Mus* dawn serenade, aubade; **donner une a.** *ou* **l'a. à qn** to serenade sb (at dawn)

aubain [obɛ̃] **NM** *Hist* alien resident *(in France)*

aubaine [obɛn] **NF** *(argent)* windfall; *(affaire)* bargain; *(occasion)* godsend, golden opportunity; **quelle a.!** what a godsend!; **c'est une véritable a. pour notre usine** it comes as *or* it is a godsend to our factory; **profiter de l'a.** to take advantage *or* to make the most of a golden opportunity; *Can* **à prix d'a.** at a reduced price

Aube [ob] **NF l'A.** Aube

aube [ob] **NF 1** *(aurore)* dawn; **à l'a.** at dawn, at daybreak; **il se leva à l'a.** he rose at dawn; **l'a. pointait quand il se leva** dawn was about to break when he got up; *Fig* **l'a. d'une ère nouvelle** the dawn *or* dawning of a new era **2** *Rel* alb **3** *Naut (en bois)* paddle; *(en métal)* blade **4** *(d'un moulin à vent)* vane, blade; *(pale)* blade

aubépine [obepin] **NF** *Bot* hawthorn; **fleur d'a.** may blossom

aubère [obɛr] **ADJ** *(cheval)* red roan

NM red roan (horse)

auberge [obɛrʒ] **NF** inn; *Fam* **tu prends la maison pour une a.?** you treat this house like a hotel!; **c'est un peu l'a. espagnole** you get out of it

what you put in it in the first place; **a. de jeunesse** youth hostel; *Fam* **il n'est pas sorti/on n'est pas sortis de l'a.** he's/we're not out of the woods yet

===📽===

'L'Auberge espagnole' *Klapisch* 'Pot Luck' (UK), 'The Spanish Apartment' (US)

aubergine [obɛrʒin] NF **1** *Bot* (*légume*) *Br* aubergine, *Am* eggplant **2** *Fam* (*contractuelle*) *Br* (female) traffic warden, *Am* meter maid
ADJ INV (*couleur*) aubergine
aubergiste [obɛrʒist] NMF inn-keeper
aubette [obɛt] NF *Belg* **1** (*kiosque à journaux*) news stand **2** (*abri*) bus shelter
aubier [obje] NM *Bot* sapwood
aubin [obɛ̃] NM *Équitation* hobbling gait
aubois, -e [obwa, -az] ADJ of/from the Aube
□ **Aubois, -e** NM,F = inhabitant of or person from the Aube
auburn [obœrn] ADJ INV auburn
Aubusson [obysɔ̃] NM *Géog* = town in central France famous as a centre for tapestry-making
aucuba [okyba] NM *Bot* Aucuba
aucun, -e [okœ̃, -yn] ADJ **INDÉFINI 1** (*avec une valeur négative*) no, not any; **il ne fait a. effort** he doesn't make any effort; **aucune décision n'a encore été prise** no decision has been reached yet; **a. article n'est encore prêt** none of the articles is ready yet; **a. mot ne sortit de sa bouche** he/she didn't utter a single word; **il n'y a aucune raison de croire que...** there's no reason *or* there isn't any reason to think that...; **il n'y a a. souci à se faire** there is nothing to worry about; **ils n'eurent a. mal à découvrir la vérité** they had no trouble (at all) finding out the truth; **elle n'en prend a. soin** she doesn't look after it at all; **je ne vois a. inconvénient à ce que vous restiez** I don't want your staying at all; **en aucune façon** in no way; **sans aucune exception** without any exception; **sans a. doute** undoubtedly, without any doubt; **sans a. remords** quite remorselessly; **aucune idée!** no idea!
2 (*avec une valeur positive*) any; **il est plus rapide qu'a. autre coureur** he's faster than any other runner; **avez-vous aucune intention de le faire?** have you any intention of doing it?
PRON INDÉFINI 1 (*avec une valeur négative*) none; **a. d'entre eux n'a pu répondre** none of them could answer; **je sais qu'a. n'a menti** I know that none *or* not one of them lied; **je n'ai lu a. de ses livres** I haven't read any of his/her books; **a. (des deux)** neither (of them)
2 (*servant de réponse négative*) none; **combien d'entre eux étaient présents? – a.!** how many of them were present? – none!
3 (*avec une valeur positive*) any; **j'ai apprécié son dernier livre plus qu'a. de ses films** I enjoyed his/her last book more than any of his/her films; **il est plus fort qu'a. de vos hommes** he's stronger than any of your men; **d'aucuns** some; **d'aucuns pensent que la guerre est inévitable** some (people) think *or* there are those who think that war is unavoidable
aucunement [okynmɑ̃] ADV **1** (*dans des énoncés négatifs avec "ne" ou "sans"*) in no way, not in the least *or* slightest; **il n'avait a. envie d'y aller** he didn't want to go there in the slightest; **il agissait sans a. se soucier des autres** he behaved without the slightest regard for others; **je n'ai a. l'intention de me laisser insulter** I certainly have no *or* I haven't the slightest intention of letting myself be insulted
2 (*servant de réponse négative*) not at all; **a-t-il été question de cela? – a.** was it a question of that? – not at all; **je vous dérange? – a.!** am I disturbing you? – not at all *or* by no means!
AUD [ayde] NF (*abrév* **allocation unique dégressive**) = unemployment allowance that gradually decreases over time, the sum depending on age, previous salary and amount of national insurance paid

---

-AUD, -AUDE [o, od] SUFF
● This suffix is added to adjectives or nouns to form new adjectives or nouns with a DEROGATORY emphasis, always applied to people and referring to physical appearance or character

traits. It has no direct equivalent in English and so in order to translate it accurately, a similarly negative word has to be used:
  rougeaud(e) ruddy; **courtaud(e)** short-legged, squat; **lourdaud(e)** oafish/oaf; **rustaud(e)** uncouth/yokel; **salaud** bastard

audace [odas] NF **1** (*courage*) daring, boldness, audaciousness; **il faut beaucoup d'a. pour réussir** you need to be very daring to succeed; **avec a.** audaciously; **ils ont eu l'a. de nous attaquer par le flanc droit** they were bold enough to attack our right flank; **elle a toutes les audaces** she's daring
2 (*impudence*) audacity; **il a eu l'a. de dire non** he dared (to) *or* he had the audacity to say no; **tu ne manques pas d'a.!** you've got some cheek!
3 (*innovation*) innovation; **les audaces de l'architecture moderne** the bold innovations of modern architecture
audacieuse [odasjøz] *voir* **audacieux**
audacieusement [odasjøzmɑ̃] ADV audaciously
audacieux, -euse [odasjø, -øz] ADJ **1** (*courageux*) daring, bold, audacious **2** (*impudent*) bold, audacious, impudent **3** (*innovateur*) bold, audacious, innovative
  NM,F bold man, *f* bold woman; **c'était un a.** he was very daring
Aude [od] NF **l'A.** Aude
au-deçà [odœsa] ADV on this side
□ **au-deçà de** PRÉP on this side of
au-dedans [odədɑ̃] ADV **1** (*à l'intérieur*) inside; **vert a., rouge au-dehors** green (on the) inside, red (on the) outside
2 (*mentalement*) inwardly; **elle a l'air confiante mais a. elle a des doutes** she looks confident but deep within herself *or* but inwardly she has doubts
□ **au-dedans de** PRÉP inside, within; *Fig* **a. d'elle-même, elle regrette son geste** deep down *or* inwardly, she regrets what she did
au-dehors [odəɔr] ADV **1** (*à l'extérieur*) outside; **il fait bon ici, mais a. il fait froid** it's warm in here, but outside *or* outdoors it's cold
2 (*en apparence*) outwardly; **elle est généreuse même si a. elle paraît dure** she's generous even if she looks cold *or* if she's outwardly cold
□ **au-dehors de** PRÉP outside, *Littéraire* without; **a. de ces murs, personne ne sait rien** nobody knows anything outside these walls
au-delà [odəla] NM **l'a.** the hereafter, the next world
  ADV beyond; **a. il y a la mer** beyond *or* further on there is the sea; **tu vois le monument? l'école est un peu a.** can you see the monument? the school is a little further (on) *or* just beyond (that); **le désir d'aller a.** the desire to go further; **500 euros, et je n'irai pas a.** 500 euros and that's my final offer; **surtout ne va pas a.** (*d'une somme*) whatever you do, don't spend any more; **il a obtenu tout ce qu'il voulait et bien a.** he got everything he wanted and more
□ **au-delà de** PRÉP (*dans l'espace*) beyond; (*dans le temps*) after; **a. de la frontière** on the other side of *or* beyond the border; **a. de 300 euros, vous êtes imposable** above 300 euros you must pay taxes; **ne va pas a. de 100 euros** don't spend more than 100 euros; **a. des limites du raisonnable** beyond the limits of what is reasonable, beyond what's reasonable; **réussir a. de ses espérances** to succeed beyond one's expectations; **c'est a. de sa juridiction** it is beyond *or* outside his/her jurisdiction; **a. de ses forces/moyens** beyond one's strength/means

===📖===

'Au-delà du principe de plaisir' *Freud* 'Beyond the Pleasure Principle'

===📖===

'Au-delà du bien et du mal' *Nietzsche* 'Beyond Good and Evil'

au-dessous [odsu] ADV **1** (*dans l'espace*) below, under, underneath; **il habite à l'étage a.** he lives one floor below; **il n'y a personne (à l'étage) a.** there's no one on the floor below
2 (*dans une hiérarchie*) under, below; **les**

enfants âgés de dix ans et a. children aged ten and below; **la taille a.** the next size down; *Mus* **un ton a.** one tone lower
□ **au-dessous de** PRÉP **1** (*dans l'espace*) below, under, underneath; **elle habite a. de chez moi** she lives downstairs from me; **a. du genou** below the knee; **juste a. de la corniche** right under the cornice
2 (*dans une hiérarchie*) below; **a. du niveau de la mer** below sea level; **a. de zéro** below zero; **température a. de zéro** sub-zero temperature; **a. de la moyenne** below average; **a. de 65 ans** under 65; **les paquets a. de 10 kg** parcels of less than 10 kg; **a. d'un certain prix** under *or* below a certain price; **le commandant est a. du colonel** a major is ranked lower than a colonel; **c'est a. de lui de supplier** it's beneath him to beg; **je suis a. de la tâche** I'm not up to the job; **il est vraiment a. de tout!** he's really useless!; **le service est a. de tout** the service is an absolute disgrace
au-dessus [odsy] ADV **1** (*dans l'espace*) above; **il habite a.** he lives upstairs; **il n'y a rien a.** (*dans une maison*) there is nothing upstairs or (up) above; **il y a une croix a.** there's a cross above it; **là-haut, il y a le hameau des Chevrolles, et il n'y a rien a.** up there is Chevrolles village, and there's nothing beyond it
2 (*dans une hiérarchie*) above; **les enfants de dix ans et a.** children aged ten and over; **la taille a.** the next size up; *Mus* **un ton a.** one tone higher
□ **au-dessus de** PRÉP **1** (*dans l'espace*) above; **le placard est a. de l'évier** the cupboard is above the sink; **a. du genou** above the knee; **il habite a. de chez moi** he lives upstairs from me; **un avion passa a. de nos têtes** a plane flew overhead
2 (*dans une hiérarchie*) above; **a. du niveau de la mer** above sea level; **a. de 5000 pieds** above 5,000 feet; **10 degrés a. de zéro** 10 degrees above zero; **les paquets a. de 10 kg** parcels weighing more than 10 kg; **a. d'un certain prix** above a certain price; **a. de la moyenne** above average; **a. de 15 ans** over 15 years old; **le colonel est a. du commandant** a colonel is ranked higher than a major; **vivre a. de ses moyens** to live beyond one's means; **a. de tout soupçon** above all *or* beyond suspicion; **elle est a. de ça** she's above all that; **c'était a. de mes forces** it was too much for *or* beyond me; **se situer a. des partis** to be politically neutral
au-devant [odvɑ̃] **au-devant de** PRÉP **aller** *ou* **se porter a. de qn** to go and meet sb; **courir** *ou* **se précipiter a. de qn** to run to meet sb; **aller a. des désirs de qn** to anticipate sb's wishes; **aller a. de ses obligations** to do more than what's expected of one; **il va a. de graves ennuis/d'une défaite** he's heading for serious trouble/for failure; **aller a. du danger** to court danger
audibilité [odibilite] NF audibility
audible [odibl] ADJ audible; **règle ton micro, tu es à peine a.** adjust your microphone, we can barely hear you
audience [odjɑ̃s] NF **1** (*entretien*) audience; **donner a.** *ou* **accorder une a. à qn** to grant sb an audience
2 *Jur* hearing; **l'a. est suspendue** the case is adjourned; **A. de la Chambre** (*à la Cour de Cassation*) = group of five judges who sit in each division of the "Cour de Cassation"
3 (*public touché → par un livre*) readership; (*→ par un film, une pièce, un concert*) public; (*→ pour des idées, un parti*) following; **un livre dont l'a. a dépassé tous les espoirs** a book with an unexpectedly large readership; **une émission à large a.** a very popular programme; **cette proposition a trouvé a. auprès de la population française** this proposal met with a favourable reception from the French population
4 (*public → à la radio*) listeners; (*→ à la télévision*) viewers; (*→ chiffres*) ratings
5 *Mktg* audience; **a. captive** captive audience; **a. cible** target audience; **a. cumulée** cumulative audience; **a. globale** global audience; **a. instantanée** instantaneous audience; **a. télévisuelle** television audience; **a. utile** addressable audience
audiencer [16] [odjɑ̃se] VT *Jur* to submit for hearing

audiencier [odjɑ̃sje] *voir* **huissier**

audiencia [odjɑ̃sja] NF *Hist* audience, audiencia

Audimat® [odimat] NM *TV (appareil)* = device used for calculating viewing figures for French television, installed for a period of time in selected households; *(résultats)* audience ratings, audience viewing figures; **la dictature de l'A.** the pressure to get good ratings

audimètre [odimɛtr] NM *TV* audience rating device; **victime de l'a.** victim of the ratings

audimétrie [odimetri] NF *TV* = calculation of audience ratings

audimutité [odimytite] NF *Méd* (congenital) mutism *(not accompanied by deafness)*

audio [odjo] ADJ INV audio; **cassette a.** audio cassette

audiocassette [odjokasɛt] NF (audio) cassette

audioconférence [odjokɔ̃ferɑ̃s] NF *Tél* audio conference

audiodisque [odjodisk] NM record

audioélectronique [odjoelɛktrɔnik] ADJ audio-electronic

  NF **l'a.** audioelectronics *(singulier)*

audiofréquence [odjofrekɑ̃s] NF *Tech* audio frequency

audiogramme [odjogram] NM *Tech* audiogram

audioguide [odjogid] NF audioguide, headset *(providing recorded commentary on exhibit etc)*

audiologie [odjolɔʒi] NF *Méd* audiology

audiomètre [odjomɛtr] NM *Tech* audiometer

audiométrie [odjometri] NF *Tech* audiometry

audionumérique [odjonymerik] ADJ **disque a.** compact disc

audio-oral, -e [odjoɔral, -o] *(mpl* **audio-oraux**, *fpl* **audio-orales)** ADJ *Scol* audio-oral

audiophone [odjofɔn] NM **1** *(de malentendant)* hearing aid **2** *(lors d'une visite de musée)* audioguide, headset *(providing recorded commentary on exhibit etc)*

audioprothésiste [odjoprotezist] NMF *Méd* hearing aid specialist

Audiotex® [odjoteks] NM *Tél* Audiotex®, audiotext

audiotypie [odjotipi] NF audio-typing

audiotypiste [odjotipist] NMF audio-typist

audiovisuel, -elle [odjovizɥɛl] ADJ *(dans l'enseignement)* audiovisual; *(des médias)* broadcasting

  NM **1** *(matériel)* **l'a.** *(des médias)* radio and television equipment *(UNCOUNT)*; *(dans l'enseignement)* audiovisual aids **2** *(médias)* **l'a.** broadcasting **3** *(techniques)* **l'a.** media techniques

audiphone [odifɔn] NM *Tél* pre-recorded telephone message service

audit [odit] NM *Admin & Compta* **1** *(service)* audit; **être chargé de** *ou* **faire l'a. d'une société** to audit a company; **a. d'acquisition** due diligence; **a. consommateur** consumer audit; **a. des détaillants** retail audit; **a. environnemental** environmental audit; **a. externe** external audit; **a. interne** internal audit; **a. marketing** marketing audit; **a. opérationnel** operational audit; **a. de vente** sales audit **2** *(personne, entreprise)* auditor; **a. des détaillants** retail auditor; **a. externe** external auditor; **a. interne** internal auditor; **a. marketing** marketing auditor

auditer [3] [odite] VT to audit

auditeur, -trice [oditœr, -tris] NM,F **1** *(d'une radio, d'un disque)* listener; **les auditeurs** the audience

  2 *Ling* hearer

  3 *(chargé de l'audit)* auditor; **a. à la Cour des comptes** junior official at the "Cour des comptes"; **a. des détaillants** retail auditor; **a. externe** external auditor; **a. interne** internal auditor; **a. marketing** marketing auditor

  4 *Scol & Univ* **a. libre** unregistered student, *Am* auditor; **j'y vais en a. libre** *Br* I go to the lectures but I'm not officially on the course, *Am* I audit the lectures

  5 *Jur* **A. à la Cour de cassation** = assistant judge at the "Cour de cassation"; **a. de justice** = student at the "École nationale de la magistrature"; **a. de première classe** Legal Assistant Grade I; **a. de deuxième classe** Legal Assistant Grade II

auditif, -ive [oditif, -iv] ADJ hearing, *Spéc* auditory; **troubles auditifs** hearing disorder

audition [odisjɔ̃] NF **1** *Cin, Mus & Théât* audition; **passer une a.** to audition; **faire passer une a. à qn** to audition sb **2** *Jur* **pendant l'a. des témoins** while the witnesses were being heard **3** *Physiol* hearing **4** *(fait d'écouter)* listening; **l'a. est meilleure dans cette salle** the sound is better in this room; **ne pas toucher pendant l'a.** do not touch while listening

auditionner [3] [odisjɔne] VT **a. qn** to audition sb, to give sb an audition
  VT to audition

auditive [oditiv] *voir* **auditif**

auditoire [oditwar] NM **1** *(public)* audience **2** *Belg & Suisse (salle de conférences)* conference hall; *(salle de cours)* lecture hall, lecture theatre

auditorat [oditɔra], **auditoriat** [oditɔrja] NM *Jur* function of auditor

auditorium [oditɔrjɔm] NM auditorium; *Rad & TV* recording studio

auditrice [oditris] *voir* **auditeur**

audomarois, -e [odomarwa, -az] ADJ of/from Saint-Omer

  ❑ **Audomarois, -e** NM,F = inhabitant of or person from Saint-Omer

audonien, -enne [odonjɛ̃, -ɛn] ADJ of/from Saint-Ouen

  ❑ **Audonien, -enne** NM,F = inhabitant of or person from Saint-Ouen

AUE [ayœ] NM *(abrév* **Acte unique européen)** SEA

auge [oʒ] NF **1** *Constr* trough **2** *Géog & Géol* **a. glaciaire, vallée en a.** U-shaped valley **3** *Tech (d'un moulin)* channel **4** *(mangeoire)* trough; *Fam Hum* **amène ton a.** pass your plate‼ **5** *(d'un concasseur)* hopper

augée [oʒe] NF troughful, mangerful

augeron, -onne [oʒœrɔ̃, -ɔn] ADJ of/from the Auge region

  ❑ **Augeron, -onne** NM,F = inhabitant of or person from the Auge region

auget [oʒɛ] NM bucket *(of waterwheel)*

augette [oʒɛt] NF small trough

Augias [oʒjas] NPR *Myth* Augeas; *Littéraire* **nettoyer les écuries d'A.** to cleanse the Augean stables

augment [ogmɑ̃] NM *Ling* augment

augmentable [ogmɑ̃tabl] ADJ augmentable

augmentatif, -ive [ogmɑ̃tatif, -iv] *Ling* ADJ augmentative

  NM augmentative suffix

augmentation [ogmɑ̃tasjɔ̃] NF **1** *(fait d'augmenter)* increase *(de* in); **une a. de 3 pour cent** a 3 percent increase; **l'a. des cas d'hépatite** the increase in the number of hepatitis cases; **constater l'a. des salaires/impôts** to note the increase in salaries/taxes; **en a.** rising, increasing; **a. des bénéfices** earnings growth; **a. de capital** increase in capital; **a. de prix** price increase; **a. du prix de vente** mark-up

  2 *(action d'augmenter)* **l'a. de qch** the raising of sth; **l'a. des prix par les producteurs** the raising of prices by producers

  3 *(majoration de salaire) Br* (pay) rise, *Am* raise; **demander une a.** to ask for a rise; **quand vas-tu toucher ton a.?** when will your rise come through?

  4 *Ordinat* **a. de puissance** upgrade, upgrading

  5 *Mus* augmentation

  6 *(en tricot)* **faire une a.** to make a stitch, to make one

augmenter [3] [ogmɑ̃te] VT **1** *(porter à un niveau plus élevé → impôt, prix, nombre, taux d'intérêt)* to put up, to increase, to raise; *(→ durée, dépenses)* to increase; *(→ tarif)* to step up; *(→ salaire)* to increase, to raise; **a. le pain** *ou* **le prix du pain** to put up bread prices; **la crise a fait a. le prix du pétrole** the crisis has pushed up the price of oil; *Fam* **elle a été augmentée** she got a *Br* (pay) rise *or Am* raise; **a. le temps passé au bureau** to increase the time spent in the office; **a. les impôts de 5 pour cent** to put up *or* to raise *or* to increase taxes by 5 percent; **nous voulons a. les ventes de 10 pour cent** we want to boost sales by 10 percent; *Fam* **ils ont augmenté les employés de 20 euros** they put up the employees' pay by 20 euros

  2 *(intensifier → tension, difficulté)* to increase, to step up, to make worse; **ces déclarations n'ont fait qu'a. la peur du peuple** these remarks only added to *or* fuelled the people's fear

  3 *Mus* to augment; **en augmentant** crescendo

  VI **1** *(dette, population)* to grow, to increase, to get bigger; *(quantité, poids, dépenses)* to increase; *(prix, impôt, taux d'intérêt, salaire)* to increase, to go up, to rise; **tout ou la vie augmente!** everything's going up!; **achetez maintenant, ça va a.!** buy now, prices are going up!; **le prix a augmenté de 10 pour cent** the price has gone up by 10 percent; **le chiffre d'affaires a augmenté de 10 pour cent par rapport à l'année dernière** the turnover has increased by 10 percent *or* is 10 percent up on last year; **a. de valeur** to increase in value; **les salaires n'ont pas augmenté depuis 1998** salaries have been pegged at the same level since 1998; *Fam* **la viande a augmenté, le prix de la viande a augmenté** meat's gone up, meat has increased in price; **ça va faire a. la viande** it'll put the price of meat up

  2 *(difficulté, tension)* to increase, to grow; **la violence augmente dans les villes** urban violence is on the increase

  ▸ **s'augmenter** VPR **s'a. de** to increase by; **la famille s'est augmentée de deux jumeaux** a set of twins has joined the family; **notre société s'est augmentée de trois nouveaux cadres** our company has acquired three new managers

Augsbourg [ogsbur] NM *Géog* Augsburg

augural, -e, -aux, -ales [ogyral, -o] ADJ augural

augure [ogyr] NM **1** *Antiq* augur; *(voyant)* prophet, soothsayer; **consulter les augures** to consult the oracle **2** *(présage)* omen; *Antiq* augury

  ❑ **de bon augure** ADJ auspicious; **c'est de bon a.** it's auspicious, it augurs well, it bodes well

  ❑ **de mauvais augure** ADJ ominous, inauspicious; **c'est de mauvais a.** it's ominous, it doesn't augur well, it bodes ill

augurer [3] [ogyre] VT to foresee; **sa visite ne laisse pas a. de progrès significatif** no significant progress can be expected as a result of his/her visit; **sa réponse augure mal/bien de notre prochaine réunion** his/her answer doesn't augur well/augurs well for our next meeting; **je n'augure rien de bon de tout cela** I don't see any good coming of all this; **que peut-on a. de cette rencontre prochaine?** what does this next meeting hold in store?

Auguste [ogyst] NPR *(empereur)* Augustus; **le siècle d'A.** the Augustan Age

auguste [ogyst] ADJ **1** *(personnage)* august **2** *(majestueux → geste, pas, attitude)* majestic, noble

  NM clown

augustin, -e [ogystɛ̃, -in] NM,F *Rel* Augustinian

augustinien, -enne [ogystinjɛ̃, -ɛn] *Rel* ADJ Augustinian

  NM,F Augustinian

augustinisme [ogystinism] NM *Rel* Augustinianism

aujourd'hui [oʒurdɥi] ADV **1** *(ce jour)* today; **je l'ai vu a.** I've seen him today; **le journal d'a.** today's paper; **nous sommes le trois a.** today's the third; **ce sera tout pour a.** that'll be all for today; **il y a huit jours a.** a week ago today; **dès a.** today; *Fam* **qu'est-ce qu'il est paresseux! — c'est pas d'a.!** he's so lazy! — tell me something new!; *Fam* **alors! c'est pour a. ou pour demain?** come on, we haven't got all day!

  2 *(à notre époque)* today, nowadays; **la France d'a.** modern *or* present-day France, the France of today

  3 *Belg (locutions)* **a. matin** this morning; **a. soir** this evening, tonight

aula [ola] NF *Suisse* hall

aulacode [olakɔd] NM *Zool* great cane rat

Aulide [olid] NPR Aulis

aulique [olik] ADJ *Hist* Aulic

aulnaie [onɛ] NF *Bot* alder plantation, alder grove

aulne [on] NM *Bot* alder; **a. blanc** grey alder; **a. glutineux** common alder; **a. rouge** red alder; **g. vert** green alder

auloffée [olɔfe] NF *Naut* luffing; **faire une a.** to luff

aulx [o] *pl de* **ail**

aumône [omon] NF charity, alms; **faire l'a. à qn** to give alms to sb; **demander l'a.** to ask for charity; **je ne demande pas l'a., uniquement ce qui m'est dû** I'm not asking for any handouts, only for what's rightly mine; **vivre d'aumônes** to live

on charity; *Littéraire* **il lui fit l'a. d'un regard** he spared him/her a glance

aumônerie [omonri] NF *Rel* chaplaincy

aumônier [omonje] NM *Rel* chaplain

aumônière [omonjɛr] NF *Hist* purse

aunaie [onɛ] = **aulnaie**

aune[1] [on] NF ell; **un visage long** *ou* **une tête longue d'une a.** a face as long as a fiddle; *Littéraire* **savoir ce qu'en vaut l'a.** to know the value of things (through experience); **c'est moi qui l'ai écrit – alors vous savez ce qu'en vaut l'a.!** I wrote it – so you should know what it's worth!; **tout est mesuré à l'a. de la rentabilité** everything is assessed using profitability as the only criterion

aune[2] [on] = **aulne**

aunée [one] NF 1 *(mesure)* ell 2 *Bot* **a. (hélène)** elecampane

auparavant [oparavɑ̃] ADV 1 *(avant)* before, previously; **dix ans a.** ten years before *or* previously; **il avait a. vécu à l'étranger** he had previously lived abroad 2 *(tout d'abord)* beforehand, first; **vous signerez là, mais a. j'aimerais faire une photocopie** you'll sign here but before you do *or* but first I'd like to make a photocopy

auprès [oprɛ] ADV *Littéraire* nearby

▫ **auprès de** PRÉP 1 *(à côté de)* close to, near, by; **assis a. du feu** sitting by the fire; **rester a. de qn** to stay with *or* close to sb

2 *(dans l'opinion de)* **avoir de l'influence a. de qn** to have some influence with sb; **il passe pour un fin connaisseur a. de ses amis** he's considered a connoisseur by his friends

3 *(en s'adressant à)* **chercher du réconfort a. d'un ami** to seek comfort from a friend; **se renseigner a. de qn** to ask sb; **faire une demande a. d'un organisme** to make an application *or* to apply to an organization; **demander une autorisation a. de qn** to ask permission of sb; **agir a. de qn** to use one's influence with sb

4 *(comparé à)* compared with *or* to; **ce n'est rien a. de ce qu'il a gagné** it's nothing compared to *or* with what he made

5 *(dans un titre)* **ambassadeur a. du roi du Danemark** ambassador to the King of Denmark

auquel [okɛl] *voir* **lequel**

aura [ora] NF aura

aurantiacées [ɔrɑ̃tjase], **aurantiées** [ɔrɑ̃tje] NFPL *Bot* Aurantiaceae

aurélie [oreli] NF *Zool* Aurelia

Aurélien [oreljɛ̃] NPR Aurelian

auréole [oreɔl] NF 1 *Beaux-Arts* halo; *Fig* **ils aiment à se parer de l'a. du sacrifice** they like to wear the crown of sacrifice; **il a toujours nimbé sa mère d'une a.** he's always worshipped his mother 2 *(tache)* ring; **produit détachant qui ne laisse pas d'a.** product that removes stains without leaving a mark 3 *Astron* halo

auréoler [3] [oreɔle] VT 1 *(parer)* **a. qn de toutes les vertus** to turn sb into a saint; **tout auréolée de ses victoires américaines, elle vient se mesurer aux basketteuses européennes** basking in the glory of her American victories, she's come to challenge the European basketball teams 2 *Beaux-Arts* to paint a halo around the head of; *Fig* **tête auréolée de cheveux roux** head with a halo of red hair

▸**s'auréoler** VPR to be crowned with (**de** with); **elle aime à s'a. de mystère** she likes to wreathe *or* shroud herself in mystery; **il s'était auréolé de gloire sur les champs de bataille** he had won his laurels on the battlefield

auréomycine [oreomisin] NF *Pharm* aureomycin

aureus [ɔreys] NM *Antiq* aureus

auriculaire [orikylɛr] ADJ auricular

NM *Anat* little finger

auricule [orikyl] NF *Anat* auricle

auriculé, -e [ɔrikyle] ADJ *Anat* auriculate

auriculothérapie [ɔrikyloterapi] NF *Méd* auriculotherapy

aurifère [orifɛr] ADJ gold-bearing, *Spéc* auriferous

aurification [ɔrifikasjɔ̃] NF *(en odontologie)* filling of teeth with gold, *Spéc* aurification

aurifier [9] [orifje] VT to fill with gold

aurige [ɔriʒ] NM *Antiq* charioteer

aurignacien, -enne [ɔriɲasjɛ̃, -ɛn] ADJ aurignacian

NM aurignacian

Aurigny [ɔriɲi] NF *Géog* Alderney

auripare verdin [oriparvɛrdɛ̃] NM *Orn* verdin

aurique[1] [orik] ADJ *Naut* **voile a.** gaffsail

aurique[2] [orik] NF *Chim* auric

aurochs [orɔk] NM *Zool* aurochs

auroral, -e, -aux, -ales [ɔrɔral, -o] ADJ 1 *Littéraire (de l'aurore)* dawn *(avant n)* 2 *Astron & Météo* auroral

aurore [ɔrɔr] NF 1 *(matin)* daybreak, dawn; **avant l'a.** before daybreak; *Fig* **nous voici à l'a. d'une ère nouvelle** we are witnessing the dawn *or* dawning of a new era; *Presse* **l'A.** = former French newspaper

2 *Astron* aurora; **a. australe** aurora australis; **a. boréale** aurora borealis; **a. polaire** northern lights, aurora polaris

ADJ INV golden (yellow)

▫ **aux aurores** ADV *Hum* at the crack of dawn

Auschwitz [ɔʃvits] NM Auschwitz

auscitain, -e [ositɛ̃, -ɛn] ADJ of/from Auch

▫ **Auscitain, -e** NM,F = inhabitant of or person from Auch

auscultation [oskyltasjɔ̃] NF *Méd* listening with a stethoscope, *Spéc* auscultation

auscultatoire [ɔscyltatwar] ADJ *Méd* auscultatory

ausculter [3] [oskylte] VT *Méd* to listen to *or* to sound the chest of, *Spéc* to auscultate; **il t'a ausculté?** did he listen to your chest?

Ausone [ozɔn] NPR Ausonius

auspices [ospis] NMPL 1 *(parrainage)* **faire qch sous les a. de qn** to do sth under the patronage *or* auspices of sb 2 *(présage)* **sous de bons/mauvais a.** under favourable/unfavourable auspices 3 *Antiq* auspices

aussi [osi] ADV 1 *(également)* too, also; **tu y vas? j'y vais a.** are you going? I'm going too *or* as well; **j'y étais moi a.** I was there too *or* as well; **elle a. travaille à Rome** she too works in Rome, she works in Rome as well; **il a faim, moi a.** he's hungry, and so am I *or* me too; **elle parle russe, moi a.** she speaks Russian and so do I; **c'est a. leur avis** they think so too; **joyeux Noël! – vous a.!** merry Christmas! – the same to you!

2 *(en plus)* too, also; **il parle anglais et a. espagnol** he speaks English and also Spanish; **le talent ne suffit pas, il faut a. travailler** it's not enough to be talented, you also have to work *or* you have to work too; **j'ai a. une maison à Paris** I also have a house in Paris; **elle travaille a. à Rome** she also works in Rome, she works in Rome too *or* as well

3 *(terme de comparaison) (devant adj)* **il est a. grand que son père** he's as tall as his father; **il est loin d'être a. riche qu'elle** he's far from being as rich as she is *or* as her; **elle est a. belle qu'intelligente** *ou* **qu'elle est intelligente** she is as beautiful as she is intelligent; **ils sont a. bons l'un que l'autre** they're (both) equally good

4 *(terme de comparaison)* **il ne s'attendait pas à être payé a. rapidement que cela** he didn't expect to be paid as quickly as that *or* that quickly; **il se conduit a. mal qu'autrefois** he behaves just as badly as before; **a. souvent/tard/cher que...** as often/late/expensive as...; **a. doucement que possible** as quietly as possible; **il ne s'est jamais senti a. bien que depuis qu'il a arrêté de fumer** he's never felt so well since he stopped smoking; **il peut a. bien rentrer chez lui** he might just as well go home; **je ferais a. bien de partir** I might as well leave; *Fam* **a. sec** right away

5 *(tellement)* so; *(avec un adjectif épithète)* such; **je n'ai jamais rien vu d'a. beau** I've never seen anything so beautiful; **as-tu déjà mangé quelque chose d'a. bon?** have you ever eaten anything so delicious?; **je ne le savais pas a. têtu** I didn't know he was so stubborn; **d'a. beaux cheveux** such lovely hair; **une a. bonne occasion ne se représentera plus** such a good opportunity won't come up again; **a. léger qu'il soit** *ou* **a. léger soit-il, je ne pourrai pas le porter** light as it is, I won't be able to carry it; **a. curieux que cela puisse paraître** strange as *or* though it may seem

CONJ 1 *(indiquant la conséquence)* therefore, and so; **il était très timide, a. n'osa-t-il rien répondre** he was very shy, and so he didn't dare reply; **j'avais confiance en elle, a. n'avais-je pas fait de copie du contrat** I trusted her, and so I hadn't made a copy of the contract

2 *(d'ailleurs)* **on ne lui a rien dit, a. pourquoi n'a-t-il pas demandé?** we didn't tell him anything, but in any case, why didn't he ask?; *Littéraire* **a. bien est-ce ma faute, je ne l'avais pas prévenu** but it's my fault, I didn't warn him

aussière [osjɛr] NF *Naut* hawser; **a. de halage** warp; **a. de touée** stream-cable; **cordage commis en a.** hawser-laid rope

aussitôt [osito] ADV immediately; **il vint a.** he came right away *or* immediately; **a. après son départ** immediately *or* right after he/she left; **je suis tombé malade a. après avoir acheté la maison** right after buying *or* as soon as I'd bought the house I was taken ill; **il est arrivé a. après** he arrived immediately after *or* afterwards; **a. rentré chez lui, il se coucha** as soon as he got home, he went to bed; **a. votre lettre reçue, je...** as soon as I received your letter, I...; **a. dit, a. fait** no sooner said than done

▫ **aussitôt que** CONJ as soon as; **a. que possible** as soon as possible; **il l'appela a. qu'il l'aperçut** he called out the moment *or* as soon as he saw her

austénite [ɔstenit] NF *Métal* austenite

austénitique [ɔstenitik] ADJ *Métal* austenitic

austère [ostɛr] ADJ *(architecture, mode de vie)* austere, stark; *(paysage)* bleak, austere; *(style)* dry; *(personnalité)* stern, austere; *(expression)* stern; *(vêtement)* plain, severe

austèrement [ostɛrmɑ̃] ADV austerely

austérité [osterite] NF 1 *(dépouillement → d'une architecture, d'un mode de vie)* austerity, starkness; *(→ d'un style)* dryness; *(→ d'une personnalité)* sternness, austerity; *(→ d'une expression)* sternness; **l'a. de leur vêtements reflète leur religion** their religious views are reflected in their austere dress

2 *Écon* austerity; **mesures d'a.** austerity measures; **politique d'a.** policy of austerity

▫ **austérités** NFPL *Rel* **les austérités** the austerities

Austerlitz [ostɛrlits] NM *Géog* Austerlitz

> *Culture*
>
> **AUSTERLITZ**
>
> Austerlitz is a town in the region of Moravia in the Czech Republic. It was the site of Napoleon's decisive victory over the Russian and Austrian forces in Moravia on 2 December 1805. The presence in the field of the Emperors of the three powers involved led to its being called the Battle of the Three Emperors.

austral, -e, -als *ou* **-aux, -ales** [ostral, -o] ADJ *(hémisphère)* southern; *(pôle)* south *(avant n)*; *(constellation)* austral

australanthropien [ostralɑ̃trɔpjɛ̃] NM *Archéol* Australopithecus

Australasie [ostralazi] NF **l'A.** Australasia

australasien, -enne [ostralazjɛ̃, -ɛn] ADJ Australasian

▫ **Australasien, -enne** NM,F Australasian

australe [ɔstral] *voir* **austral**

Australie [ostrali] NF **l'A.** Australia; **vivre en A.** to live in Australia; **aller en A.** to go to Australia; **l'A.-Méridionale** South Australia; **l'A.-Occidentale** Western Australia

australien, -enne [ostraljɛ̃, -ɛn] ADJ Australian

▫ **Australien, -enne** NM,F Australian

australopithèque [ostralɔpitɛk] NM *Archéol* Australopithecus

Austrasie [ɔstrazi] NF *Hist* Austrasia *(former region in eastern Gaul)*

austro-asiatique [ostroazjatik] ADJ *Ling* Austro-Asiatic

austro-hongrois, -e [ostroɔ̃grwa, -az] ADJ Austro-Hungarian

▫ **Austro-Hongrois, -e** NM,F Austro-Hungarian

austronésien, -enne [ostronezjɛ̃, -ɛn] *Ling* ADJ Austronesian

NM **l'a.** the Austronesian family of languages

autan [otɑ̃] NM southerly wind

AUTANT [otɑ̃] ADV 1 *(marquant l'intensité)* **je ne le hais plus a.** I don't hate him as much as I did; **j'ignorais que tu l'aimais a.** I didn't know that you loved him/her so much; **s'entraîne-t-il toujours a.?** does he still train as much (as he used to)?; **pourquoi attendre a.?** why wait that *or* so long?

2 *(en corrélation avec "que")* as much as; **les chaussures valent a. que la robe** the shoes are worth as much as the dress; **rien ne me déplaît a. que d'être en retard** there's nothing I dislike so much as being late; **tu peux le nier a. que tu voudras** you can deny it as much as you like; **la patiente doit prendre du repos a. que faire se peut** the patient must have as much rest as (is) possible; **je l'aime a. que toi** *(que tu l'aimes)* I like him/her as much as you do; *(que je t'aime)* I like him/her as much as (I like) you; **j'ai travaillé a. que lui** I worked as much *or* as hard as he did; **cela me concerne a. que vous** it's of as much concern to me as it is to you

3 *(indiquant la quantité)* **je ne pensais pas qu'ils seraient a.** I didn't think there would be so many of them; **elle boit toujours a.** she still drinks just as much (as she used to); **on lui en remboursera a.** he'll/she'll get the same amount back; **ils sont a. que nous** there are as many of them as (there are of) us; **a. pour moi!** my mistake!

4 *(avec "en") (la même chose)* **tu devrais en faire a.** you should do the same; **pourriez-vous en faire a.?** could you do as much *or* the same?; **j'en aurais fait a. pour toi** I'd have done the same *or* as much for you; **tâchez d'en faire a.** try to do the same; **il a fini son travail, je ne peux pas en dire a.** he's finished his work, I wish I could say as much *or* the same; **elle est honnête, tout le monde ne peut pas en dire a.** she's honest, and not everyone can say that *or* as much; **ce n'est pas toi qui pourrais en dire a.** you certainly couldn't say that *or* as much, could you?; *Fam* **j'en ai a. à votre service!** same to you!, likewise!

5 *(avec l'infinitif) (mieux vaut)* **a. revenir demain** I/you/*etc* might as well come back tomorrow; **a. manger le reste** I/you/*etc* might as well eat up what's left; **a. dire la vérité** I/you/*etc* might as well tell the truth; **a. y aller tant qu'il ne pleut pas** I/you/*etc* might as well go while it's not raining

6 *(mieux)* **j'aurais a. fait de rester chez moi** I might as well have stayed at home, I'd have done as well to stay at home; **tu aurais a. fait de passer par Le Mans** you'd have done as well to go via Le Mans; **a. aurait valu demander à sa sœur** it'd have been as well to ask his/her sister

7 *Belg (tant)* **il gagne a. par mois** he earns so much a month

❑ **autant..., autant** ADV **a. il est cultivé, a. il est nul en mathématiques** he's highly educated, but he's no good at mathematics; **a. il est gentil avec moi, a. il est désagréable avec elle** he's very nice to me, but he's horrible to her; **a. j'aime le vin, a. je déteste la bière** I hate beer as much as I love wine

❑ **autant de** ADJ *(avec un nom non comptable)* as much; *(avec un nom comptable)* as many; **il y a a. d'eau ici** there's as much water here; **il y a a. de sièges ici** there are as many seats here; **je ne pensais pas qu'il aurait a. de patience** I didn't think he'd have so much patience; **je n'avais jamais vu a. d'eau/d'oliviers** I'd never seen so much water/so many olive trees; **ces livres sont a. de chefs-d'œuvre** every last one of these books is a masterpiece; **a. d'hommes, a. d'avis** as many opinions as there are men; **a. de lecteurs, a. de lectures** as many readings as there are readers; **il y a a. de femmes que d'hommes** there are as many women as (there are) men; **je lis a. de romans que de nouvelles** I read as many novels as short stories; **(c'est) a. de gagné** *ou* **de pris** at least that's something, we've got that much out of it anyway; **c'est a. de perdu** that's that (gone); **c'est a. de fait** that's that done at least

❑ **autant dire** ADV in other words; **j'ai été payé 300 euros, a. dire rien** I was paid 300 euros, in other words a pittance

❑ **autant dire que** CONJ **trois heures dans le four, a. dire que le poulet était carbonisé!** after three hours in the oven, needless to say the chicken was burnt to a cinder!; **l'ambassade ne répond plus, a. dire que tout est perdu** the embassy's phones are dead, a sure sign that all is lost

❑ **autant que** CONJ **1** *(dans la mesure où)* as far as; **a. que possible** as far as (is) possible; **a. que je me souvienne** as far as I can remember; **a. que je (le) sache** as far as I know

2 *(il est préférable que)* **a. que je vous le dise tout de suite...** I may as well tell you straightaway...

❑ **d'autant** ADV **si le coût de la vie augmente de deux pour cent, les salaires seront augmentés d'a.** if the cost of living goes up by two percent, salaries will be raised accordingly; **cela augmente d'a. mon intérêt pour cette question** it makes me all the more interested in this question; **si l'on raccourcit la première étagère de cinq centimètres, il faudra raccourcir la deuxième d'a.** if we shorten the first shelf by five centimetres, we'll have to shorten the second one by the same amount

❑ **d'autant mieux** ADV all the better, much better; **pars à la campagne, tu te reposeras d'a. mieux** you'll have a much better rest if you go to the country; **c'est d'a. mieux ainsi** it's much better like that

❑ **d'autant mieux que** CONJ **il a travaillé d'a. mieux qu'il se sentait encouragé** he worked all the better for feeling encouraged

❑ **d'autant moins que** CONJ **je le vois d'a. moins qu'il est très occupé en ce moment** I see even less of him now that he's very busy

❑ **d'autant moins... que** CONJ **elle est d'a. moins excusable qu'on l'avait prévenue** what she did is all the less forgivable as she'd been warned; **la promenade a été d'a. moins agréable que j'étais un peu souffrant** the walk wasn't very pleasant, particularly as *or* since I wasn't feeling well

❑ **d'autant plus** ADV all the more reason; **mais je ne l'ai jamais fait! – eh bien d'a. plus!** but I've never done it before! – so *or* well, all the more reason!

❑ **d'autant plus que** CONJ especially as; **il vous écoutera d'a. plus qu'il vous connaît** he'll listen to you, especially as *or* particularly as he knows you

❑ **d'autant plus... que** CONJ **c'est d'a. plus stupide qu'il ne sait pas nager** it's particularly *or* all the more stupid given (the fact) that he can't swim

❑ **d'autant que** CONJ *(vu que, attendu que)* especially as, particularly as; **il faut rentrer – oui, d'a. que je n'ai pas encore préparé le dîner** it's time to go home – yes particularly *or* especially as I haven't got dinner ready yet; **c'est une bonne affaire, d'a. que le crédit est très avantageux** it's a good deal, especially as the terms of credit are very advantageous

❑ **pour autant** ADV **la situation n'est pas perdue pour a.** the situation isn't hopeless for all that, it doesn't necessarily mean all is lost; **n'en perds pas l'appétit pour a.** don't let it put you off your food; **il t'aime bien, mais il ne t'aidera pas pour a.** just because he's fond of you (it) doesn't mean that he'll help you; **fais-le-lui remarquer sans pour a. le culpabiliser** point it out to him, but don't make him feel guilty about it

❑ **pour autant que** CONJ as far as; **pour a. que je (le) sache** as far as I know; **tu n'es pas inscrit, pour a. que je sache?** you're not on the register, as far as I know?; **pour a. qu'on puisse prévoir** as far as we can foresee *or* predict; **pour a. qu'on puisse faire la comparaison** inasmuch as a comparison can be made; **pour a. qu'il ait pu être coupable** guilty though he might have been

---

'Autant en emporte le vent' *Mitchell, Fleming* 'Gone with the Wind'

---

autarcie [otarsi] NF *Écon* self-sufficiency, *Spéc* autarky; **vivre en a.** to be self-sufficient

autarcique [otarsik] ADJ *Écon* self-sufficient, *Spéc* autarkic

autécologie [otekɔlɔʒi] NF *Écol* autecology

autécologique [otekɔlɔʒik] ADJ *Écol* autecological

autel [otɛl] NM **1** *Rel* altar; **conduire** *ou* **mener qn à l'a.** to take sb to the altar *or* down the aisle; *Fig* **être immolé sur l'a. de** to be sacrificed on the altar of **2** *Littéraire* **l'A.** the Church

Auteuil [otøj] NM *Géog & Courses de chevaux* = upper-class district of Paris well-known for its racecourse

auteur [otœr] NM

> Note that it is no longer considered a mistake to feminize this word and to say **une auteur** or even **une auteure** (with a final **e**) but some French speakers nonetheless regard these forms as unacceptable, especially in France. See also the entry **féminisation**.

1 *(créateur → d'un livre, d'un article, d'une chanson)* writer, author; *(→ d'une toile)* painter; *(→ d'un décor, d'un meuble, d'un vêtement)* designer; *(→ d'un morceau de musique)* composer; *(→ d'une statue)* sculptor; *(→ d'un film, d'un clip)* director; **on retrouve cette expression chez plusieurs auteurs** several writers use that phrase; **une marine d'un a. inconnu** a seascape by an unknown artist; **quelle jolie chanson, qui en est l'a.?** what a lovely song, who wrote it?; **Léonard de Vinci a été l'a. de nombreuses inventions** Leonardo da Vinci invented many things; **un a. dramatique** a playwright; **a. de gags** gagman; **a. à sensation** sensationalist writer; **un a. à succès** a popular writer

2 *(responsable)* **l'a. d'un accident** the person who caused an accident; **l'a. du meurtre** the murderer; **le meurtre dont il est l'a.** the murder he committed; **les auteurs de ce crime** those who committed that crime; **les auteurs présumés de l'attentat** those suspected of having planted the bomb; **qui est l'a. de cette farce?** who's behind *or* who thought up this prank?; **l'a. de la victoire/défaite** the person who brought about victory/defeat; *Littéraire & Hum* **l'a. de mes jours** my progenitor

auteur-compositeur [otœrkɔ̃pozitœr] *(pl* **auteurs-compositeurs**) NM *Mus* composer and lyricist; **a. interprète** singer-songwriter; **je suis a. interprète** I write and sing my own material

auteur-réalisateur [otœrrealizatœr] *(pl* **auteurs-réalisateurs**) NM writer-director

authenticité [otɑ̃tisite] NF **1** *(d'un document, d'un tableau, d'un tapis)* authenticity; *(d'un sentiment)* genuineness; **l'a. de son chagrin** his/her heartfelt grief **2** *Jur* authenticity

authentification [otɑ̃tifikasjɔ̃] NF *(gén) & Ordinat* authentication

authentifier [9] [otɑ̃tifje] VT *(gén) & Ordinat* to authenticate

authentique [otɑ̃tik] ADJ **1** *(document, tableau, tapis, objet d'art)* genuine, authentic; *(sentiment)* genuine, heartfelt **2** *Jur* authentic; *(copie)* certified

authentiquement [otɑ̃tikmɑ̃] ADV authentically, genuinely

autisme [otism] NM *Méd* autism

autiste [otist] *Méd* ADJ autistic
NMF autistic person

autistique [otistik] ADJ *Méd* autistic

auto [oto] NF car, *Am* automobile; **en a., il faut être prudent** one should be careful when driving; **petite a.** toy car

auto- [oto] PRÉF *(de soi-même)* self-

auto-accusateur, -trice [otoakyzatœr, -tris] *(mpl* **auto-accusateurs,** *fpl* **auto-accusatrices**) ADJ self-accusatory

auto-accusation [otoakyzasjɔ̃] *(pl* **auto-accusations**) NF self-accusation

auto-adhésif, -ive [otoadezif, -iv] ADJ self-adhesive

auto-alarme [otoalarm] *(pl* **auto-alarmes**) NM auto-alarm

auto-alimenter [3] [otoalimɑ̃te] **s'auto-alimenter** VPR to be self-perpetuating

auto-allumage [otoalymaʒ] *(pl* **auto-allumages**) NM *Aut* spontaneous combustion

auto-amorçage [otoamɔrsaʒ] *(pl* **auto-amorçages**) NM *Tech* automatic priming

auto-amputation [otoɑ̃pytasjɔ̃] *(pl* **auto-amputations**) NF *Zool* autotomy, self-amputation

auto-analyse [otoanaliz] *(pl* **auto-analyses**) NF *Psy* self-analysis

autoanticorps [otoɑ̃tikɔr] NM INV *Biol* autoantibody

autoantigène [otoɑ̃tiʒɛn] NM autoantigen

autoberge [otobɛrʒ] NF **(voie) a.** *Br* embankment road, *Am* expressway *(along riverbank)*

autobiographe [otobjɔgraf] **NMF** autobiographer

autobiographie [otobjɔgrafi] **NF** autobiography

autobiographique [otobjɔgrafik] **ADJ** autobiographical

autobloqueur [otoblɔkœr] **NM** *Sport* jammer

autobronzant, -e [otobrɔ̃zɑ̃, -ɑ̃t] **ADJ** self-tanning **NM 1** *(crème)* self-tanning cream, fake tan **2** *(cachet)* tanning pill

autobus [otobys] **NM** *Transp* bus; **a. à impériale** double-decker (bus); **a. à soufflet** articulated bus, *Br* bendy bus; *Can* **a. scolaire** school bus

autocar [otokar] **NM** *Transp* bus, *Br* coach; **a. pullman** luxury coach

autocaravane [otokaravan] **NF** *Aut Br* camper van, *Am* motor home

autocariste [otokarist] **NMF** *(propriétaire)* coach operator; *(conducteur)* coach driver

autocassable [otokasabl] *voir* **ampoule**

autocélébration [otoselebrasjɔ̃] **NF** self-congratulation; **la cérémonie a tourné à l'a.** the ceremony turned into an exercise in self-congratulation

autocélébrer [18] [otoselebre] **s'autocélébrer VPR** to sing one's own praises

autocensure [otosɑ̃syr] **NF** self-censorship, self-regulation; **pratiquer l'a.** to censor oneself

autocensurer [3] [otosɑ̃syre] **s'autocensurer VPR** to censor oneself

autocentré, -e [otosɑ̃tre] **ADJ** *Écon* autocentric

autocéphale [otosefal] **ADJ** *Rel* autocephalous

autochenille [otoʃnij] **NF** *Aut* half-track

autochrome [otokrom] *Phot* **ADJ** autochrome **NF** autochrome

autochromie [otokromi] **NF** *Phot* autochromy

autochtone [ɔtɔkton, otokton] **ADJ** native **NMF** native; *Hum* **les autochtones sont arrivés en masse** the locals turned up in droves

autocinétique [otosinetik] **ADJ** *Psy* autokinetic

autocinétisme [otosinetizm] **NM** *Psy* autokinesis

autoclave [otoklav] **ADJ** pressure-sealed, autoclave *(avant n)* **NM** *Tech* autoclave; *Culin & Vieilli* pressure cooker

autocoat [otokot] **NM** car coat

autocollant, -e [otokolɑ̃, -ɑ̃t] **ADJ** self-adhesive; *(enveloppe)* self-sealing **NM** sticker

autocommutateur [otokomytatœr] **NM** *Ordinat* autoswitch; **a. privé** private branch exchange, PBX

autoconcurrence [otokɔ̃kyrɑ̃s] **NF** internal competition

autoconduction [otokɔ̃dyksjɔ̃] **NF** *Électron* mutual induction

autoconsommation [otokɔ̃sɔmasjɔ̃] **NF** **les légumes qu'ils cultivent sont destinés à l'a.** the vegetables they grow are meant for their own consumption; **économie d'a.** subsistence economy

autocopiant, -e [otokɔpjɑ̃, -ɑ̃t] **ADJ** carbonless, self-copying

autocopie [otokɔpi] **NF 1** *(procédé)* duplication **2** *(document)* duplicate copy

autocorrecteur, -trice [otokɔrɛktœr, -tris] **ADJ** *Ordinat* self-correcting

autocorrectif, -ive [otokɔrɛktif, -iv] **ADJ** self-correcting

autocorrection [otokɔrɛksjɔ̃] **NF** self-correcting

autocorrective [otokɔrɛktiv] *voir* **autocorrectif**

autocorrectrice [otokɔrɛktris] *voir* **autocorrecteur**

autocouchette [otokuʃɛt] = **autos-couchettes**

autocrate [otokrat] **NM** *Pol* autocrat

autocratie [otokrasi] **NF** *Pol* autocracy

autocratique [otokratik] **ADJ** *Pol* autocratic

autocratiquement [otokratikmɑ̃] **ADV** *Pol* autocratically

autocritique [otokritik] **NF** self-criticism; **faire son a.** to make a thorough criticism of oneself

autocuiseur [otokɥizœr] **NM** pressure cooker

autodafé [otodafe] **NM** *Hist* auto-da-fé; **faire un a. de livres** to burn books

autodéfense [otodefɑ̃s] **NF** self-defence ❑ **d'autodéfense ADJ** *(arme)* defensive; **groupe d'a.** vigilante group

autodérision [otoderizjɔ̃] **NF** self-mockery

autodestructeur, -trice [otodɛstryktœr, -tris] **ADJ** self-destructive

autodestruction [otodɛstryksjɔ̃] **NF** self-destruction

autodestructrice [otodɛstryktris] *voir* **autodestructeur**

autodétermination [otodetɛrminasjɔ̃] **NF** self-determination

autodéterminé, -e [otodetɛrmine] **ADJ** self-determined

autodétruire [98] [otodetrɥir] **s'autodétruire VPR** to self-destruct

autodiagnostic [otodjagnɔstik] **NM** self-diagnosis

autodiagnostique [otodjagnɔstik] **ADJ** self-diagnostic

autodictée [otodikte] **NF** *Scol* rewriting from memory

autodidacte [otodidakt] **ADJ** self-taught, self-educated **NMF** autodidact

autodirecteur, -trice [otodirɛktœr, -tris] **ADJ** self-guiding **NM** self-guiding device

autodiscipline [otodisiplin] **NF** self-discipline

autodrome [otodrom] **NM** *Aut* motor-racing track; *(pour les essais)* car-testing track

auto-école [otoekɔl] *(pl* **auto-écoles)** **NF** driving-school; **voiture a.** driving-school car

autoécologie [otoekɔlɔʒi] **NF** *Écol* autecology

autoécologique [otoekɔlɔʒik] **ADJ** *Écol* autecological

auto-édition [otoedisjɔ̃] **NF** self-publishing

auto-élévateur, -trice [otoelevatœr, -tris] *(mpl* **auto-élévateurs,** *fpl* **auto-élévatrices)** **ADJ** self-adjusting

auto-érotique [otoerɔtik] *(pl* **auto-érotiques)** **ADJ** autoerotic, onanistic

auto-érotisme [otoerɔtism] **NM** autoeroticism, onanism

autoexcitateur, -trice [otoɛksitatœr, -tris] **ADJ** self-exciting

autofécondant, -e [otofekɔ̃dɑ̃, -ɑ̃t] **ADJ** *Biol* self-fertilizing

autofécondation [otofekɔ̃dasjɔ̃] **NF** *Biol* self-fertilization, self-fertilizing

autofiction [otofiksjɔ̃] **NF** *Littérature* autofiction

autofinancé, -e [otofinɑ̃se] **ADJ** self-financed; **3 milliards d'euros autofinancés à un tiers seulement** 3 billion euros, only a third of which was self-financed

autofinancement [otofinɑ̃smɑ̃] **NM** self-financing; **capacité d'a.** cash flow

autofinancer [16] [otofinɑ̃se] **s'autofinancer VPR 1** *(entreprise)* to be self-financing **2** *(personne)* to be self-supporting

autofocus [otofɔkys] *Phot* **ADJ** autofocus **NM 1** *(système)* autofocus system **2** *(appareil)* autofocus camera

autogame [otogam] **ADJ** *Biol* autogamous

autogamie [otogami] **NF** *Biol* autogamy, self-fertilization

autogène [otoʒɛn] **ADJ** *Méd & Tech* autogenous

autogenèse [otoʒənɛz] **NF** *Biol* autogenesis

autogéré, -e [otoʒere] **ADJ** self-managed, self-run

autogérer [18] [otoʒere] **VT** *(entreprise, commune)* to self-manage ►**s'autogérer VPR** *(collectivité)* to be self-managing

autogestion [otoʒɛstjɔ̃] **NF** (workers') self-management; **entreprise/université en a.** self-managed company/university

autogestionnaire [otoʒɛstjɔnɛr] **ADJ** based on workers' self-management **NMF** advocate of workers' self-management

autogire [otoʒir] **NM** *Astron* autogiro

autogoal [otogol] **NM** *Suisse aussi Fig* own goal

autogonfler [3] [otogɔ̃fle] **s'autogonfler VPR** to self-inflate

autogouverner [3] [otoguvɛrne] **s'autogouverner VPR** to be self-governing

autographe [otograf] **ADJ** handwritten, autograph *(avant n)* **NM** autograph

autographie [otografi] **NF** autolithography

autographier [9] [otografje] **VT** to make a facsimile of using transfer-ink

autographique [otografik] **ADJ** autographic; **encre a.** transfer-ink

autogreffe [otogrɛf] **NF** *Méd* autograft; **faire une a.** to carry out an autograft

autoguidage [otogidaʒ] **NM** homing guidance

autoguidé, -e [otogide] **ADJ** *(avion)* remotely-piloted; *(missile)* guided

auto-hypnose [otoipnoz] **NF** autohypnosis

auto-immun, -e [otoimœ̃, -yn] *(mpl* **auto-immuns,** *fpl* **auto-immunes)** **ADJ** *Méd* autoimmune

auto-immunisation [otoimynizasjɔ̃] *(pl* **auto-immunisations)** **NF** *Méd* autoimmunity

auto-immunitaire [otoimynitɛr] *(pl* **auto-immunitaires)** **ADJ** *Méd* autoimmune

auto-immunité [otoimynite] *(pl* **auto-immunités)** = **auto-immunisation**

auto-inductance [otoɛ̃dyktɑ̃s] *(pl* **auto-inductances)** **NF** *Phys* self-inductance

auto-induction [otoɛ̃dyksjɔ̃] *(pl* **auto-inductions)** **NF** *Élec* self-induction

auto-infection [otoɛ̃fɛksjɔ̃] *(pl* **auto-infections)** **NF** *Méd* autoinfection

auto-intoxication [otoɛ̃tɔksikasjɔ̃] *(pl* **auto-intoxications)** **NF** *Méd* self-poisoning, autointoxication

autolimitation [otolimitasjɔ̃] **NF** setting of voluntary limits

autolimiter [3] [otolimite] **VT** to set voluntary limits to; **les Japonais autolimitent leurs exportations de voitures** the Japanese set voluntary limits to their car exports

autolubrifiant, -e [otolybrifjɑ̃, -ɑ̃t] **ADJ** self-lubricating

autolubrification [otolybrifikasjɔ̃] **NF** self-lubrication

autolysat [otoliza] **NM** *Biol* substance resulting from autolysis

autolyse [otoliz] **NF** *Biol* autolysis

automate [ɔtɔmat] **NM 1** *(robot)* automaton, robot; **comme un a.** like a robot **2** *Suisse (machine)* vending machine; *(à billets)* *Br* cash dispenser, *Am* ATM

automaticien, -enne [ɔtɔmatisjɛ̃, -ɛn] **NM,F** automation *or* robotics specialist

automaticité [ɔtɔmatisite] **NF** automaticity

automation [ɔtɔmasjɔ̃] **NF** automation

automatique [ɔtɔmatik] **ADJ** automatic; **de façon a.** automatically; **il est absent tous les lundis, c'est a.** he's off every Monday without fail **NM 1** *(téléphone)* **l'a.** direct dialling **2** *(arme)* automatic **NF 1** *Aut* automatic (car) **2** *(science)* automation, cybernetics *(singulier)*

automatiquement [ɔtɔmatikmɑ̃] **ADV** automatically

automatisable [ɔtɔmatizabl] **ADJ** automatable

automatisation [ɔtɔmatizasjɔ̃] **NF** automation

automatiser [3] [ɔtɔmatize] **VT** to automate ►**s'automatiser VPR** to become automated

automatisme [ɔtɔmatism] **NM 1** *(habitude)* automatism; **j'éteins toutes les lampes, c'est un a.** I always switch lamps off, I do it without thinking *or* it's automatic with me; **fermer la porte à double tour est devenu un a.** double-locking the door has become automatic **2** *(dispositif)* automatic device

automédication [otomedikasjɔ̃] **NF** *Méd* self-medication

automédon [otomedɔ̃] **NM** *Vieilli Hum* cabby, coachman

automitrailleuse [otomitrajøz] **NF** *Mil* armoured car

automnal, -e, -aux, -ales [otɔnal, -o] **ADJ** *Br* autumnal, autumn *(avant n)*, *Am* fall *(avant n)*; **des teintes automnales** autumnal hues

automne [otɔn] **NM** *Br* autumn, *Am* fall; *Littéraire* **l'a. de sa vie** the autumn of his/her life

automobile [otomɔbil] **NF 1** *Aut (véhicule)* *Br* motor car, *Am* automobile **2** *Sport* driving, *Br* motoring **3** *(industrie)* car industry **ADJ 1** *(des voitures → accessoire, industrie)* car *(avant n)*; *(→ club)* automobile *(avant n)*; *(bateau, engin)* automotive, self-propelled; **A. Club de France** = French automobile association, *Br* ≃ AA, RAC, *Am* ≃ AAA **2** *Admin (vignette)* car *(avant n)*; *(assurance)* car, automobile *(avant n)*

automobilisme [otomɔbilism] **NM** *Aut* driving, *Br* motoring

automobiliste [otomɔbilist] **NMF** *Aut* driver, *Br* motorist

automorphisme [otomɔrfism] **NM** *Math* automorphism

aut-aut

automoteur, -trice [otomɔtœr, -tris] **ADJ** automotive, motorized, self-propelled
  NM 1 *Mil* self-propelled gun **2** *Naut* self-propelled barge
  ❑ **automotrice** NF electric railcar
automouvant, -e [otomuvɑ̃, -ɑ̃t] **ADJ** self-propelled
automutilation [otomytilasjɔ̃] NF self-mutilation
autoneige [otonɛʒ] NF *Can* snowmobile *(used to carry several passengers)*
autonettoyant, -e [otonɛtwajɑ̃, -ɑ̃t] **ADJ** self-cleaning
autonettoyer [13] [otonɛtwaje] **s'autonettoyer** VPR to self-clean
autonome [otɔnom, otonom] **ADJ 1** *(autogéré → territoire, organisme)* autonomous, self-governing; *(→ gouvernement)* autonomous; **gestion a.** managerial autonomy **2** *(non affilié → syndicat)* independent **3** *(libre → personne, caractère, personnalité)* self-sufficient, independent **4** *(appareil)* self-contained; *Ordinat* stand-alone **5** *Biol & Physiol* autonomic, autonomous
  ❑ **autonomes** NMPL = unaffiliated political extremist group in France in the 1970s
autonomie [otɔnɔmi, otonomi] NF **1** *(d'une personne)* autonomy, independence; *(d'un État, d'un pays)* autonomy, self-government **2** *(d'un véhicule, d'un avion)* range; *(d'une batterie)* life; **ce rasoir a une a. de 30 minutes** this razor will run for 30 minutes before it needs recharging; **a. de vol** flight range
autonomisation [otɔnɔmizasjɔ̃, otonomizasjɔ̃] NF *(fait de devenir autonome)* attainment of autonomy
autonomiste [otɔnɔmist, otonomist] *Pol* **ADJ** separatist
  NMF separatist
autopalpation [otopalpasjɔ̃] NF *Méd* self-examination *(of breasts)*
auto-patrouille [otopatruj] *(pl* **autos-patrouilles***)* NF *Can* patrol car
autoplastie [otoplasti] NF *Méd* autoplasty
autopompe [otopɔ̃p] NF *Br* fire engine, *Am* fire truck
autopont [otopɔ̃] NM *Br* flyover, *Am* overpass
autoportant, -e [otoportɑ̃, -ɑ̃t] **ADJ** *Constr* self-supporting
autoportrait [otoportrɛ] NM self-portrait; **faire son a.** to paint a self-portrait; **en réalité, dans cette nouvelle, elle fait son a.** this short story is in fact her self-portrait

▱

'Autoportrait à l'oreille coupée' *Van Gogh* 'Self-portrait with Bandaged Ear'

autoproclamer [3] [otoprɔklame] **s'autoproclamer** VPR to proclaim *or* declare oneself to be; **il s'autoproclama président** he declared himself president
autoproclamé, -e [otoprɔklame] **ADJ** self-proclaimed
autoproduction [otoprɔdyksjɔ̃] NF *Écon* self-supply
autopropulsé, -e [otoprɔpylse] **ADJ** self-propelled
autopropulseur [otoprɔpylsœr] **ADJ M** self-propelling
  NM self-propulsion apparatus *or* system
autopropulsion [otoprɔpylsjɔ̃] NF self-propulsion
autopsie [ɔtɔpsi, otopsi] NF **1** *Méd* autopsy, *Br* post mortem (examination); **pratiquer une a.** to perform an autopsy *or Br* a post mortem (examination) **2** *(analyse)* critical analysis, autopsy, post mortem; **faire l'a. d'un conflit** to go into the causes of a conflict
autopsier [9] [ɔtɔpsje, otopsje] VT *Méd* to perform an autopsy *or Br* a post mortem (examination) on
autopunitif, -ive [otopynitif, -iv] **ADJ** *Psy* self-punishing
autopunition [otopynisjɔ̃] NF *Psy* self-punishment
autopunitive [otopynitiv] *voir* **autopunitif**
autoradio [otoradjo] NM car radio
autoradiographie [otoradjografi] NF autoradiography
auto-rafraîchissement [otorafrɛʃismɑ̃] NM *Ordinat* auto-refresh

autorail [otoraj] NM *Rail* railcar
autoréférence [otoreferɑ̃s] NF *Ling* self-reference
autoréglage [otoreglaʒ] NM *Tech* automatic control
autorégulateur, -trice [otoregylatœr, -tris] **ADJ** *Tech* self-regulating
autorégulation [otoregylasjɔ̃] NF **1** *Biol & Physiol* self-regulation **2** *Tech* automatic regulation
autorégulatrice [otoregylatris] *voir* **autorégulateur**
autoréparable [otoreparabl] **ADJ** self-repairing
auto-reverse [otorivœrs], **auto-réversible** [otoreversibl] **ADJ** auto-reverse
autorisation [ɔtɔrizasjɔ̃] NF **1** *(consentement → d'un parent)* permission, consent; *(→ d'un supérieur)* permission, authorization; *(→ d'un groupe)* authorization; **demander l'a. de faire qch** to ask permission to do sth; **donner son a. à qch** to consent to sth; **donner à qn l'a. de faire qch** to give sb permission to do sth; **qui t'a donné l'a. de prendre ces pommes?** who said you could have these apples?; **je n'ai pas eu l'a. de sortir ce soir** I didn't get permission to go out tonight; **faire qch sans a.** to do sth without permission; **a. maritale** husband's authorization; **a. de vol** flight clearance
  2 *Admin (acte officiel)* authorization, licence, permit; **avoir l'a. de vendre qch** to be licensed to sell sth; **a. d'exporter** export permit; *Pharm* **a. de mise sur le marché** = official authorization for marketing a pharmaceutical product; **a. de sortie** *(d'un lycée)* (special) pass; **a. de sortie du territoire** parental authorization *(permitting a minor to leave a country)*
  3 *Banque* **une a. de 1000 euros** a temporary overdraft of up to 1,000 euros; **a. de crédit** credit line, line of credit; **a. de découvert** overdraft facility; **a. d'émettre des billets de banque** note issuance facility; **a. de prélèvement** direct debit mandate
  4 *Ordinat* **a. d'accès** access authorization
autorisé, -e [ɔtɔrize] **ADJ 1** *Journ* official; **de source autorisée, le président aurait déjà signé l'accord** sources close to the President say that he's already signed the agreement; **les milieux autorisés** official circles **2** *(agréé → aliment, colorant)* permitted **3** *(qui a la permission)* **personnes autorisées** authorized persons
autoriser [3] [ɔtɔrize] VT **1** *(permettre → manifestation, réunion, publication)* to authorize, to allow; *(→ emprunt)* to authorize, to approve; **le défilé n'avait pas été autorisé** no permission *or* authorization had been given for the march (to be held); **une pétition pour faire a. la sortie d'un film** a petition to have a film passed for release; **une tournure autorisée par l'usage** a turn of phrase sanctioned *or* hallowed by usage
  2 *(donner l'autorisation à)* **a. qn à** to allow sb *or* to give sb permission to; **je ne t'ai pas autorisé à utiliser ma voiture** I never said you could use my car; **je ne t'autorise pas à me parler sur ce ton** I won't have you talk to me like that; **a. qn à faire** *(lui en donner le droit)* to entitle sb *or* to give sb the right to do; **vous êtes mes parents mais cela ne vous autorise pas à ouvrir mon courrier** you may be my parents but that doesn't give you the right to open my letters; **sa réponse nous autorise à penser que...** from his/her reply we may deduce that..., his/her reply leads us to conclude that...; **rien ne nous autorise à le croire** nothing entitles us to believe that
  3 *(justifier)* to justify, *Sout* to permit of; **la jeunesse n'autorise pas tous les débordements** being young isn't an excuse for uncontrolled behaviour; **cette dépêche n'autorise plus le moindre espoir** this news spells the end of any last remaining hopes
  ▸**s'autoriser** VPR **1** *(s'offrir)* **je m'autorise un petit verre de vin le soir** I allow myself a small glass of wine in the evening
  2 s'a. de *(se servir de)* to use as a pretext, to take advantage of; **elle s'autorise de sa confiance** she exploits his/her confidence in her; **ils s'autorisent de cette guerre pour justifier les exactions commises** they're using the war as a pretext to justify committing such acts of violence

autoritaire [ɔtɔritɛr] **ADJ** authoritarian; **il est très a.** he's very overbearing
  NMF authoritarian
autoritairement [ɔtɔritɛrmɑ̃] **ADV** in an authoritarian way, with (excessive) authority
autoritarisme [ɔtɔritarism] NM authoritarianism
autorité [ɔtɔrite] NF **1** *(pouvoir)* authority, power; **l'a. de la loi** the authority *or* power of the law; **un territoire soumis à l'a. de...** an area within the jurisdiction of...; **par a. de justice** by order of the court; **avoir de l'a. sur qn** to be in *or* to have authority over sb; **il n'a aucune a. sur ses élèves** he can't keep order over *or* he has no control over his pupils; **être sous l'a. de qn** to be *or* to come under sb's authority; **se mettre sous l'a. de qn** to place oneself under sb's authority; **exercer son a. sur qn** to exercise authority over sb; **faire qch de sa propre a.** to do sth on one's own authority; **avoir a. pour faire qch** to have authority to do sth; **l'a. parentale** *(droits)* parental rights; *(devoirs)* parental responsibilities
  2 *(fermeté)* authority; **ses parents n'ont aucune a.** his/her parents have no control over him/her; **faire preuve d'a. envers un enfant** to show some authority towards a child; **il a besoin d'un peu d'a.** he needs to be taken in hand; **avec de l'a. dans la voix** with a note of authority in his voice
  3 *(compétence)* authority; *(expert)* authority, expert; **dire qch en invoquant l'a. de qn** to say sth on sb's authority; **parler de qch avec a.** to talk authoritatively about sth; **édition qui fait a.** authoritative edition; **version qui fait a.** definitive version; **essai qui fait a.** seminal essay; **il fait a. en matière de physique nucléaire** he is an authority on nuclear physics; **c'est une a. en matière de...** he's/she's an authority *or* expert on...
  4 *Admin (pouvoir établi)* authority; **l'a., les autorités** *(personnel)* the authorities; **a. administrative indépendante** = independent government agency with specific regulatory powers; **les autorités françaises** the French authorities; **a. judiciaire** judicial power, judiciary; **les autorités militaires/religieuses** the military/religious authorities; **s'adresser à l'a. compétente** to apply to the appropriate authority; **a. de régulation** regulating body; *Tél* **l'a. de régulation des télécommunications** the French telecommunications watchdog, *Br* ≃ Oftel; **un agent** *ou* **représentant de l'a.** an official; **les autorités ont dû intervenir** the authorities had to intervene
  ❑ **d'autorité** **ADV** without consultation; **si tu ne me le donnes pas, je le prendrai d'a.** if you won't give it to me I'll take it without asking you; **d'a., j'ai décidé de fermer la bibliothèque le mercredi** I decided on my own authority to close the library on Wednesdays; **ils ont gelé les crédits d'a.** they unilaterally stopped the funding
autoroute [otorut] NF **1** *Aut Br* motorway, *Am* freeway; **conduite sur a.** *Br* motorway *or Am* freeway driving; **a. à péage** *Br* toll motorway, *Am* turnpike; **l'a. du Soleil** = the motorway linking Paris, Lyons and Marseilles, famously congested during the "grands départs" of July and August **2** *Ordinat* **l'a. de l'information** the information superhighway

┌─ *Culture* ─┐
AUTOROUTE
The construction of many of France's motorways is funded by consortia of both private and public companies. They are privately run and operate a toll system ("péage").

autoroutier, -ère [otorutje, -ɛr] *Aut* **ADJ** *Br* motorway *(avant n)*, *Am* freeway *(avant n)*
  ❑ **autoroutière** NF = car particularly suited to motorway driving conditions; **c'est une bonne autoroutière** it's ideal for *Br* motorway *or Am* freeway driving
auto sacramental [otosakramɛtal] *(pl* **auto sacramentals** *ou* **auto sacramentales***)* NM *Hist & Théât* auto sacramental *(Spanish allegorical religious drama performed in the streets)*
autosatisfaction [otosatisfaksjɔ̃] NF self-satisfaction

auto-scooter [otoskutɛr] (*pl* **auto-scooters**) NF OU NM *Belg* bumper car, dodgem

autoscopie [otoskɔpi] NF 1 (*en parapsychologie*) autoscopy; *Psy (hallucination)* out-of-body experience, *Spéc* autoscopy 2 (*outil pédagogique*) = training in public speaking during which students are filmed and then analyse the playback of their performance

autos-couchettes [otokuʃɛt] ADJ INV train a. carsleeper train

autosécurité [otosekyrite] NF *Belg Aut* test of roadworthiness

autosexable [otosɛksabl] ADJ *Orn (race)* autosexing

auto-skooter [otoskutɛr] (*pl* **auto-skooters**) = **auto-scooter**

autosome [otozom] NM *Biol* autosome

autosomique [otozomik] ADJ *Biol* autosomal

autostéréoscopique [otostereoskɔpik] ADJ autostereoscopic

auto-stop [otostɔp] NM hitch-hiking, hitching; **faire de l'a.** to hitch-hike, to hitch; **elle a fait de l'a. jusqu'à Chicago** she hitch-hiked to *or* she hitched (a ride) to Chicago; **nous allons faire le tour de l'Europe en a.** we're going to hitch-hike around Europe; **prendre qn en a.** to give sb a lift *or* a ride

auto-stoppeur, -euse [otostɔpœr, -øz] (*mpl* **auto-stoppeurs**, *fpl* **auto-stoppeuses**) NM,F hitch-hiker; **prendre un a.** to pick up a hitch-hiker

autosubsistance [otosybzistɑ̃s] NF *Écon* (economic) self-sufficiency

autosuffisance [otosyfizɑ̃s] NF *Écon* self-sufficiency

autosuffisant, -e [otosyfizɑ̃, -ɑ̃t] ADJ *Écon* self-sufficient

autosuggestion [otosygʒɛstjɔ̃] NF *Psy* autosuggestion

autosurveillance [otosyrvɛjɑ̃s] NF *Méd* self-monitoring

auto-tamponneuse [ototɑ̃pɔnøz] (*pl* **autos-tamponneuses**) NF bumper car, dodgem

autotest [ototɛst] NM *Ordinat* self-test

autotester [3] [ototɛste] **s'autotester** VPR *Ordinat* to self-test

autotomie [ototomi] NF *Zool* autotomy

autotour [ototur] NM (*en tourisme*) = motoring holiday prebooked through a travel agent

autotracté, -e [ototrakte] ADJ *Tech* self-propelled

autotransformateur [ototrɑ̃sformatœr] NM *Élec* autotransformer

autotransfusion [ototrɑ̃sfyzjɔ̃] NF *Méd* autotransfusion, autologous transfusion

autotrempant, -e [ototrɑ̃pɑ̃, -ɑ̃t] ADJ *Métal* self-hardening

autotrophe [ototrof] *Biol* ADJ autotrophic ■ NM autotroph

autotrophie [ototrofi] NF *Biol* autotrophy

autour[1] [otur] NM *Orn* goshawk

autour[2] [otur] ADV around, round; **mets du papier de soie a.** wrap it up in tissue paper; **tout a.** all around; **il y avait un arbre et les enfants couraient (tout) a.** there was a tree and the children were running round it; **une nappe avec des broderies tout a.** a tablecloth with embroidery all around *or* round the edges
□ **autour de** PRÉP 1 (*dans l'espace*) around; **a. du village** around the village; **il observait les gens a. de lui** he looked at the people around him; **discuter qch a. d'un verre** to discuss sth over a drink
2 (*indiquant une approximation*) around; **il gagne a. de 12 000 euros** he earns around 12,000 euros; **elle a a. de 20 ans** she's about 20; **il a fait beaucoup de films a. des années 30** he made a lot of films around the 1930s; **ils sont arrivés a. de 20 heures** they arrived (at) around 8 p.m.

autovaccin [otovaksɛ̃] NM *Méd* autogenous vaccine

AUTRE [otr]

ADJ	different **1, 3** ■ another **1, 2** ■ other **5, 7**
PRON	other **1–3** ■ another **3** ■ else **1, 2**
NM	other

ADJ indéfini 1 (*distinct, différent*) **un a. homme** another *or* a different man; **il a rencontré une a. femme** he's met another woman; **vous avez cette jupe dans une a. taille?** do you have this skirt in another *or* in a different size?; **donnez-moi une a. tasse, celle-ci est ébréchée** give me another *or* a new cup, this one's chipped; **j'ai une a. idée** I've got another idea; **en d'autres lieux** elsewhere; **dans d'autres circonstances...** in other circumstances..., had the circumstances been different...; **tu veux a. chose?** do you want anything else?; **il n'y a que du fromage, je n'ai pas a. chose** there's only cheese, I haven't got anything else; **toute a. réaction m'aurait surpris** any other reaction would've surprised me; **la vérité est tout a.** the truth is quite *or* very *or* altogether different; **je me faisais une tout a. idée de la question** I had quite a different concept of the matter; *Fam* **ça c'est une a. histoire** *ou* **affaire** *ou* **paire de manches** that's something else altogether, that's another story *or* kettle of fish (altogether); **autres temps, autres mœurs** other days, other ways

2 (*supplémentaire*) **voulez-vous un a. café?** would you like another coffee?; **il n'y a pas d'autres verres?** aren't there any other glasses?; **une a. bière, s'il vous plaît** another beer please; **un a. mot sur le sujet** another *or* one more word on the subject; **vous avez le droit à une a. réponse** you may give one more answer; **elle est partie sans autres explications** she left without further explanation; **il nous faut une a. chaise** we need one more *or* an extra *or* another chair; **essaie une a. fois** try again *or* one more time

3 (*devenu différent*) different; **c'est un a. appartement maintenant!** it's quite a different *Br* flat *or Am* apartment now!, the *Br* flat *or Am* apartment is completely transformed now!; **je me sens un a. homme** I feel a different *or* new man; **je me sens, comment dire, a.** I feel, how can I put it, different; **un tout a. homme** a completely different man; **avec des fines herbes, ça a un tout a. goût!** it tastes completely different with some mixed herbs added!; **elle est tout a. désormais** she's completely different now

4 (*marquant la supériorité*) **leur ancien appartement avait un a. cachet!** their old *Br* flat *or Am* apartment had far more character!; **leurs émissions sont d'une a. qualité!** their programmes are far better!; **la cuisine d'Éric, c'est a. chose!** you should taste Éric's cooking!; **le Japon, ah c'est a. chose!** Japan, now that's really something else!; **Marc est bon en maths, mais Jean c'est a. chose!** Marc is good at maths, but Jean is in a different class altogether!

5 (*restant*) other, remaining; **les autres passagers ont été rapatriés en autobus** the other passengers were taken home by bus

6 (*avec les pronoms "nous" et "vous"*) **nous autres consommateurs...** we consumers...; **vous autres Français...** you French people...; *Fam* **écoutez-le, vous autres!** listen to him, you lot!

7 (*dans le temps*) other; **on y est allés l'a. jour** we went there the other day; **on ira une a. année** we'll go another year; **l'a. fois** the other time; **d'autres fois** other times; **en d'autres temps** in other times; (*dans le passé*) in days gone by; **l'a. matin** the other morning; **je l'ai vu l'a. dimanche** I saw him the other Sunday; **un a. jour** some other day; **je reviendrai à un a. moment** I'll come back some other time; **dans l'a. vie** in the next world; **dans une a. vie** in another life

8 (*en corrélation avec "l'un"*) **l'une et l'a. hypothèses sont valables** both hypotheses are valid; **l'un ou l'a. projet devra être accepté** one of the two projects will have to be accepted; **ni l'une ni l'a. explication n'est plausible** neither explanation is plausible

PRON 1 (*désignant des personnes*) **un a.** someone else, somebody else; **d'autres** other people, others; **on n'attend pas les autres?** aren't we going to wait for the others?; **d'autres que moi vous donneront les explications nécessaires** others will give you the necessary explanations; **plus que tout a., tu aurais dû prévoir que...** you of all people should have foreseen that...; **tout** *ou* **un a. que lui aurait refusé** anyone else but him would have refused; **quelqu'un d'a.** someone else; **aucun a., nul a.** no one else, nobody else, none other; **personne d'a.** no one else, nobody else; **bien d'autres ont essayé** a lot of other people have tried; **elle est plus futée que les autres** she's cleverer than (any of) the others; **comme dit** *ou* **dirait l'a.** as they say; *Fam* **à d'autres!** go on with you!, come off it!; *Fam* **et l'a. qui n'arrête pas de pleurer!** now the other one won't stop crying!; *Fam* **eh l'a., il est fou!** listen to that one *or* him, he's mad!

2 (*désignant des choses*) **un a.** another one; **d'autres** other ones, others; **une maison semblable à une a.** a house like any other; **le restaurant ne me disait rien, nous en avons cherché un a.** the restaurant didn't appeal to me, (so) we looked for another one; **ce livre ou l'a.** this book or the other one; **mes chaussures sont sales, il faut que je mette les autres** my shoes are dirty, I'll have to wear the other ones; **je n'en ai pas besoin d'autres** I don't need any more; **quelque chose d'a.** something else; **rien d'a.** nothing else; *Suisse* **sans a.** (*sans plus*) without further ado; (*facilement*) easily

3 (*en corrélation avec "l'un"*) **l'une chante, l'a. danse** one sings, the other dances; **l'un et l'a.** both of them; **l'un ou l'a.** (either) one or the other, either one; **je l'ai su par l'une ou l'a. de ses collègues** I heard it through one or other of his colleagues; **l'un après l'a.** one after another *or* the other; **ils marchaient l'un derrière l'a./l'un à côté de l'a.** they were walking one behind the other/side by side; **ni l'un ni l'a. n'est venu** neither (of them) came; **je n'ai pu les joindre ni l'un ni l'a.** I couldn't get hold of either (one) of them; **on ne peut pas les distinguer l'un de l'a.** you can't tell one from the other, you can't tell them apart; **on les prend souvent l'un pour l'a.** people often mistake one for the other; **les uns le détestent, les autres l'adorent** he's loathed by some, loved by others; **aimez-vous les uns les autres** love one another; **aidez-vous les uns les autres** help each other *or* one another; **n'écoute pas ce que disent les uns et les autres** don't listen to what people say; **l'un ne va pas sans l'a.** you can't have one without the other; **présente-les l'un à l'a.** introduce them to each other; **ils sont tout l'un pour l'a.** they mean everything to each other; **vous êtes des brutes les uns comme les autres!** you're (nothing but) beasts, all of you!; **l'un dans l'a.** all in all, at the end of the day; **c'est plus cher, mais plus solide: l'un dans l'a. on s'y retrouve** it's more expensive, but it's stronger: all in all *or* at the end of the day it amounts to the same; **l'un dans l'a., nous avons recouvré nos frais** at the end of the day we broke even
■ NM *Phil* **l'a.** the other

autrefois [otrəfwa] ADV in the past, in former times *or* days; **je l'ai bien connu a.** I knew him well once; **a. s'élevait ici un château médiéval** there used to be a medieval castle here; **d'a.** of old, of former times; **les maisons d'a. n'avaient aucun confort** in the past *or* in the old days, houses were very basic; **sa vie d'a.** his/her past life; **des chants d'a.** old-time songs

autrement [otrəmɑ̃] ADV 1 (*différemment*) another *or* some other way; **la banque est fermée, je vais me débrouiller a.** the bank's closed, I'll find some other way (of getting money); **il est habillé a. que d'habitude** he hasn't got his usual clothes on; **comment pourrait-il en être a.** how could things be different?; **il n'en a jamais été a.** things have always been this way *or* have never

aut–ava

been any other way or have never been any different; **nous ne les laisserons pas construire la route ici, il faudra qu'ils fassent a.** we won't let them build the road here, they'll have to find another or some other way; **il n'y a pas moyen de faire a.** there's no other way or no alternative; **j'ai accepté, je n'ai pas pu faire a.** I had no alternative but to say yes; **je n'ai pu faire a. que de les entendre** I couldn't help but overhear them; **il n'a pas pu faire a. que de rembourser** he had no alternative but to pay the money back; **on ne peut faire a. que d'admirer son audace** one can't but admire his/her daring **2** (sinon) otherwise, or else; **payez car a. vous aurez des ennuis** pay up or else you'll get into trouble; **les gens sont désagréables, a. le travail est intéressant** the people are unpleasant, but otherwise or apart from that the work's interesting; **c'est dommage, a. on aurait pu partir à minuit** it's a shame, because otherwise we could have left at midnight **3** (beaucoup) far; (beaucoup plus) far more; **c'est a. plus grave cette fois-ci** it's far more serious this time; **elle est a. plus jolie que sa sœur** she's far prettier than her sister; **c'est a. moins cher au marché** it's far cheaper if you buy it at the market; **il est a. moins intelligent que son premier mari** he's much less bright than her first husband; **elle est a. intelligente** she is far more intelligent, she is more intelligent by far

□ **autrement dit** ADV in other words; **a. dit tu me quittes?** in other words, you're leaving me?
□ **pas autrement** ADV not particularly; **cela ne me surprend pas a.** that does not particularly surprise me

Autriche [otriʃ] NF **l'A.** Austria; **vivre en A.** to live in Austria; **aller en A.** to go to Austria
Autriche-Hongrie [otriʃɔ̃gri] NF **l'A.** Austria-Hungary
autrichien, -enne [otriʃjɛ̃, -ɛn] ADJ Austrian
□ **Autrichien, -enne** NM,F Austrian; Hist **l'Autrichienne** (Queen) Marie-Antoinette
autruche [otryʃ] NF Orn ostrich; **des chaussures en a.** ostrich-skin shoes; **un sac en a.** an ostrich-skin handbag; **faire l'a.** to bury one's head in the sand
autruchon [otryʃɔ̃] NM Orn young ostrich
autrui [otrɥi] PRON INDÉFINI others, other people; **peu m'importe l'opinion d'a.** other people's opinion or the opinion of others means little to me; **la liberté d'a.** other people's freedom, the freedom of others; Prov **ne fais pas à a. ce que tu ne voudrais pas qu'on te fît** do as you would be done by
autunite [otynit] NF Minér autunite
auvent [ovɑ̃] NM **1** (en dur) porch roof; **un toit en a.** a sloping roof **2** (en toile) awning, canopy
auvergnat, -e [ovɛrɲa, -at] ADJ of/from the Auvergne
□ NM Ling = dialect spoken in the Auvergne
□ **Auvergnat, -e** NM,F = inhabitant of or person from the Auvergne
Auvergne [ovɛrɲ] NF **l'A.** the Auvergne
aux [o] voir à
auxerrois, -e [ɔksɛrwa, -az] ADJ of/from Auxerre
□ **Auxerrois, -e** NM,F = inhabitant of or person from Auxerre
auxiliaire [oksiljɛr] ADJ **1** Ling auxiliary **2** (personnel) auxiliary, extra; **services auxiliaires de l'armée** non-combatant services **3** Tech auxiliary, standby
□ NMF **1** (employé temporaire) temporary worker; **ce n'est qu'un a.** he's only temporary **2** Jur **a. de justice** representative of the law **3** Méd **a. médical** paramedic; **les auxiliaires médicaux** the paramedical profession **4 a. de vie sociale** ≃ social worker **5** (aide) helper, assistant; **elle m'a été une a. infatigable** she was a constant help to me **6** Mil **a. féminin de l'armée de terre** = female member of the French army
□ NM **1** Ling auxiliary **2** (outil, moyen) aid; **le magnétoscope est l'a. précieux de mon enseignement** I find a Br video recorder or Am VCR to be an invaluable teaching aid
□ **auxiliaires** NMPL **1** Antiq = foreign troops of the Roman Army

2 Naut (moteurs) auxiliary engines; (équipement) auxiliary equipment (UNCOUNT)
auxiliairement [oksiljɛrmɑ̃] ADV **1** Ling **verbe utilisé a.** verb used as an auxiliary **2** (accessoirement) secondarily; **a., cela peut servir d'abri** it can also, if necessary, be used as a shelter
auxiliariat [oksiljarja] NM Scol (status of the) assistant teachers
auxiliateur, -trice [oksiljatœr, -tris] Rel ADJ who helps
□ NM,F person who helps
auxine [ɔksin] NF Bot auxin
auxquels, auxquelles voir lequel
AV 1 Banque (abrév écrite **avis de virement**) (bank) transfer advice **2** (abrév écrite **avant**) front
Av., av. (abrév écrite **avenue**) Ave.
avachi, -e [avaʃi] ADJ **1** (sans tenue → vêtement) crumpled, rumpled, shapeless; (→ sommier, canapé) sagging; (→ chaussures) shapeless, down-at-heel; (→ cuir) limp; (→ gâteau, soufflé) collapsed; (→ chapeau) shapeless; **mon vieux pantalon a.** my baggy old trousers **2** (indolent) flabby, spineless; **la génération avachie que nous a léguée la guerre** the flabby or Littéraire supine post-war generation; **être a. dans un fauteuil** to be slumped in an armchair
avachir [32] [avaʃir] VT (personne, muscles) to make flabby; **la chaleur m'avachit** the heat makes me feel quite limp or floppy
▸**s'avachir** VPR **1** (s'affaisser → vêtement, chaussures) to become shapeless; (→ sommier, canapé) to start sagging; (→ cuir) to go limp; (→ gâteau, soufflé) to collapse **2** (s'affaler) **s'a. dans un fauteuil/sur une table** to slump into an armchair/over a table **3** (se laisser aller) to let oneself go
avachissement [avaʃismɑ̃] NM **1** (perte de tenue → d'un vêtement) becoming limp, losing (its) shape; (→ de chaussures) wearing out; (→ d'un sommier, d'un canapé) starting to sag; **lutter contre l'a. des tissus musculaires** to prevent the slackening of muscles **2** (état déformé) limp or worn-down appearance **3** (perte de courage → physique) going limp; (→ moral) loss of moral fibre **4** (état physique → temporaire) limpness; (→ permanent) flabbiness; (découragement) loss of moral fibre; (veulerie) spinelessness
aval, -als [aval] NM **1** Fin & Jur (d'un effet de commerce) endorsement, guarantee; **donner son a. à une traite/un billet** to guarantee or to endorse a draft/a bill; **a. bancaire** bank guarantee **2** (soutien) support; **donner son a. à qn** to back sb (up) **3** (autorisation) authorization; **avoir l'a. des autorités** to have (an) official authorization; **donner son a. à qn/qch** to give sb/sth one's approval; **pour a.** (sur document) for approval **4** (d'une rivière) downstream water **5** (d'une pente) downhill side (of a slope); **faites face à l'a.** face the valley; **regardez vers l'a.** look down the slope
□ ADJ **ski/skieur a.** downhill ski/skier
□ **en aval de** PRÉP **1** (en suivant une rivière) downstream or downriver from **2** (en montagne) downhill from **3** (après) following on from; **les étapes qui se situent en a. de la production** the post-production stages
avalanche [avalɑ̃ʃ] NF **1** Géol avalanche **2** Fig (quantité → de courrier, de protestations, de compliments, de lumière) flood; (→ de coups, d'insultes) shower; **il y eut une a. de réponses** the answers came pouring in
avalancheux, -euse [avalɑ̃ʃø, -øz] ADJ Géol avalanche-prone
avalant, -e [avalɑ̃, -ɑ̃t] ADJ Naut (bateau) going downstream
avalement [avalmɑ̃] NM swallow, swallowing (UNCOUNT)
avaler [3] [avale] VT **1** (consommer → nourriture) to swallow; (→ boisson) to swallow, to drink; **a. qch d'un (seul) coup** ou **d'un trait** to swallow sth in one gulp; **j'ai dû a. quelque chose de travers** something went down the wrong way; **je n'ai rien avalé depuis deux jours** I haven't had a

thing to eat for two days; **a. du lait à petites gorgées** to sip milk; **a. sa salive** to swallow; **à midi, elle prend à peine le temps d'a. son déjeuner** at lunchtime, she bolts her meal **2** Fig **le distributeur a avalé ma carte!** the Br cash machine or Am ATM has eaten or swallowed my card!; **tu as avalé ta langue?** have you lost your tongue?, has the cat got your tongue?; **a. les obstacles/les kilomètres** to make light work of any obstacle/of distances; **a. ses mots** to swallow one's words; **vouloir tout a.** to be hungry or thirsty for experience; **a. qn tout cru** to eat sb alive; Fam **a. son bulletin** ou **son acte de naissance** ou **sa chique** to kick the bucket, to go and meet one's maker; **comme quelqu'un qui aurait avalé son** ou **un parapluie** (raide) stiffly, with his/her back like a rod; (manquant d'adaptabilité) stiffly, starchily **3** (inhaler → fumée, vapeurs) to inhale, to breathe in; **a. la fumée** to inhale **4** (lire → roman, article) to devour; **une petite anthologie que vous avalerez en un après-midi** a short anthology which you will read or get through in one afternoon **5** Fam (croire → mensonge) to swallow, to buy; **vous croyez que je vais a. ça?** do you think I'll buy that?; **il a avalé mon histoire (toute crue)** he swallowed my story hook, line and sinker; **je lui ai fait a. que j'étais malade** I got him/her to believe that I was sick; **on ne nous le fera pas a.** it won't wash (with us); **elle lui ferait a. n'importe quoi** he/she believes anything she says **6** Fam (accepter → insulte) to swallow; Fig **pilule difficile à a.** hard or bitter pill to swallow; Fig **a. la pilule** to swallow the bitter pill; **a. des couleuvres** (insultes) to swallow insults; (mensonges) to be taken in; **faire a. des couleuvres à qn** (insultes) to humiliate sb; (mensonges) to take sb in
USAGE ABSOLU (manger, boire) to swallow
avaleur [avalœr] NM **a. de sabres** sword swallower
avalisé, -e [avalize] ADJ Jur (effet de commerce) endorsed, guaranteed
avaliser [3] [avalize] VT **1** Jur (effet de commerce) to endorse, to guarantee; (signature) to guarantee **2** (donner son accord à) to back, to condone, to support; **nous n'avalisons pas ces comportements barbares** we do not condone such barbaric behaviour
avaliseur [avalizœr], **avaliste** [avalist] NM Jur endorser, guarantor, backer
avaloir [avalwar] NM **1** (de conduit) head; (de cheminée) hood **2** Pêche fish trap **3** Fam throat, gullet **4** Belg (bouche d'égout) manhole, inspection chamber
à-valoir [avalwar] NM INV advance (payment)
avaloire [avalwar] NF (pièce de harnachement) breeching

AVANCE [avɑ̃s]

| advance 4–6 | ▪ ahead 1 | ▪ lead 3 | ▪ early 1 |

NF **1** (par rapport au temps prévu) **prendre de l'a. dans ses études** to get ahead in one's studies; **j'ai pris de l'a. sur le** ou **par rapport au planning** I'm ahead of schedule; **avoir de l'a. sur** ou **par rapport à ses concurrents** to be ahead of the competition or of one's competitors; **arriver avec dix minutes/jours d'a.** to arrive ten minutes/days early; **le livreur a une heure d'a.** the delivery man is an hour early; **le maillot jaune a pris 37 secondes d'a.** the yellow jersey's 37 seconds ahead of time **2** (d'une montre, d'un réveil) **sa montre prend de l'a.** her watch is fast; **ma montre a une minute d'a.** my watch is one minute fast; **ma montre prend une seconde d'a. toutes les heures** my watch gains a second every hour **3** (avantage → d'une entreprise) lead; (→ d'une armée) progress, advance; **l'a. prise par notre pays en matière de génétique** our country's lead in genetics; **perdre son a. sur un marché/dans une discipline scolaire** to lose one's lead in a market/school subject; **conserver son a. sur ses concurrents** to retain one's lead over one's competitors; **ralentir l'a. de qn** to slow sb's progress; **avoir dix points d'a. sur qn** to have a ten-point lead over sb; **elle a une a. de**

dix mètres sur la Britannique she leads the British girl by ten metres, she has a ten-metre lead over the British girl; **avoir une demi-longueur d'a.** to lead by half a length

4 *(dans un approvisionnement)* **prends ce beurre, j'en ai plusieurs paquets d'a.** have this butter, I keep several packs in reserve; **de la sauce tomate? j'en fais toujours d'a.** tomato sauce? I always make some in advance

5 *Fin (acompte)* advance; **donner à qn une a. sur son salaire** to give sb an advance on his/her salary; **faire une a. de 100 euros à qn** to advance 100 euros to sb; **avances** sums advanced; **a. bancaire** bank advance; **a. à découvert** unsecured *or* uncovered advance; **avances en devises** foreign currency loan; **a. de fonds** advance, loan; **a. sur honoraires** retainer; **a. en numéraire** cash advance; **a. sur recette** loan to a producer *(to be recouped against box-office takings)*; **a. sur titre** collateral loan; **a. de trésorerie** cash advance

6 *Aut* **a. à l'allumage** ignition advance

7 *Tech* **a. rapide** fast forward

8 *Ordinat* **a. automatique** automatic feed

▫ **avances** NFPL *(propositions → d'amitié, d'association)* overtures, advances; *(→ sexuelles)* advances; **faire des avances à qn** *(sujet: séducteur)* to make advances to sb; *(sujet: entreprise)* to make overtures to sb; **ils nous ont fait quelques avances mais rien n'a été signé** they made a few overtures but there was no actual deal

▫ **à l'avance** ADV *(payer, informer)* in advance, beforehand; **vous le saurez à l'a.** you'll know beforehand; **dites-le-moi bien à l'a.** tell me well in advance, give me plenty of notice; **je n'ai été averti que deux minutes à l'a.** I was only warned two minutes beforehand, I only got two minutes' notice; **acheter un billet deux mois à l'a.** to buy a ticket two months in advance; **réservez longtemps à l'a.** book early; **je savais à l'a. qu'il allait mentir** I knew in advance *or* I could tell beforehand that he would lie; **je me réjouis/j'ai peur à l'a. de voir la tête qu'elle fera quand elle l'apprendra** I'm looking/I'm not looking forward to seeing her face when she hears about it

▫ **d'avance, par avance** ADV *(payer, remercier)* in advance; **d'a. merci** thanking you in advance; **savourant d'a. sa revanche** already savouring his/her planned revenge; **c'est joué d'a.** it's a foregone conclusion; *Fam* **c'est tout combiné d'a.** it's a put-up job; **d'a. je peux te dire qu'il n'est pas fiable** I can tell you right away *or* now that he's not reliable

▫ **en avance** ADJ **elle est en a. sur le reste de la classe** she's ahead of the rest of the class; **être en a. sur son temps** *ou* **époque** to be ahead of one's time; **être en a. sur la concurrence** to be ahead of the competition; **techniquement, ils sont en a. par rapport à nous** they're technologically ahead of us ADV *(avant l'heure prévue)* early; **arriver en a.** to arrive early; **elle arrive** *ou* **elle est toujours en a.** she's always early; **être en a.** to be early; **être en a. de dix minutes/jours** to be ten minutes/days early; **je me dépêche, je ne suis pas en a.!** I must rush, I'm (rather) late!

avancé, -e [avɑ̃se] ADJ **1** *(dans le temps → heure)* late; **à une heure avancée** late at night; **à une date avancée de la colonisation romaine** at a late stage in the colonization by Rome; **la saison est avancée** it's late in the season; **les pommiers sont bien avancés cette année** the apple trees are early this year; **à un âge a.** late (on) in life; **arriver à un âge a.** to be getting on in years

2 *(pourri → poisson, viande)* bad, *Br* off; *(→ fruit)* overripe; **des pêches un peu avancées** peaches that are past their best

3 *(développé → intelligence, économie)* advanced; **un garçon a. pour son âge** a boy who's mature for *or* ahead of his years; **pays parvenus à un stade/état a. de la technologie** countries that have reached an advanced stage/state of technological development; **à un stade peu a.** at an early stage; **je ne suis pas assez a. dans mon travail pour pouvoir sortir ce soir** I'm not far enough ahead with my work to be able to go out tonight; *Ironique* **te voilà bien a.!** a (fat) lot of good that's done you!

4 *Mil (division, élément)* advance *(avant n)*; **ouvrage a.** outwork

▫ **avancée** NF **1** *(marche)* advance; *Fig (progression)* progress

2 *(d'un toit)* overhang

3 *Pêche* trace, cast, leader

avancement [avɑ̃smɑ̃] NM **1** *(promotion)* promotion, advancement; **avoir** *ou* **obtenir de l'a.** to get (a) promotion, to get promoted **2** *(progression)* progress; **y a-t-il de l'a. dans les travaux?** is the work progressing? **3** *Jur* **a. d'hoirie** = gift of part of an inheritance given in advance **4** *Ordinat* **a. par friction** friction feed; **a. du papier** sheet feed

AVANCER [16] [avɑ̃se]

VT to move forward **1** ▪ to bring forward **1, 3** ▪ to stick out **2** ▪ to put forward **3, 4** ▪ to advance **6**

VI to move forward **1** ▪ to advance **1** ▪ to progress **1–3** ▪ to be getting on **2** ▪ to stick out **5**

VPR to move forward **1** ▪ to make progress **2** ▪ to commit oneself **3** ▪ to stick out **4**

VT **1** *(pousser vers l'avant)* to push *or* to move forward; *(amener vers l'avant)* to bring forward; **tu es trop loin, avance ta chaise** you're too far away, move *or* bring your chair forward; **a. un siège à qn** to draw up a seat for sb; **il m'avança un siège et me demanda de m'asseoir** he pulled up a chair for me and asked me to sit down; **a. son assiette** *(vers le plat de service)* to push one's plate forward; **a. les aiguilles d'une horloge** to put the hands of a clock forward; *Hum* **la voiture de Madame/Monsieur est avancée** Madam/Sir, your carriage awaits

2 *(allonger)* **a. la tête** to stick one's head out; **a. le cou** to crane one's neck; **a. sa** *ou* **la main vers qch** *(pour l'attraper)* to reach towards sth; *(pour qu'on vous le donne)* to hold out one's hand for sth

3 *(dans le temps)* to bring *or* to put forward, *Am* to move up; **ils ont dû a. la date de leur mariage** they had to bring the date of their wedding forward; **l'heure du départ a été avancée de dix minutes** the starting time was put forward ten minutes; **la réunion a été avancée à demain/lundi** the meeting was brought forward to tomorrow/Monday; **a. sa montre (d'une heure)** to put one's watch forward (by an hour)

4 *(proposer → explication, raison, opinion)* to put forward, to suggest, to advance; *(→ argument, théorie, plan)* to put forward; **être sûr de ce que l'on avance** to be certain of what one is saying; **si ce qu'il avance est vrai** if his allegations are true

5 *(faire progresser)* **a. qn** to help sb along; **je vais rédiger les étiquettes pour vous a.** I'll write out the labels to make it quicker for you *or* to help you along; **trêve de bavardage, tout cela ne m'avance pas** that's enough chatting, all this isn't getting my work done; **voilà qui n'avance pas mes affaires** this isn't much good *or* help (to me), that doesn't get me very far; *Fam* **ça t'avance à quoi de mentir?** what do you gain by lying?; **voilà à quoi ça t'avance de tricher** this is where cheating gets you; **les insultes ne t'avanceront à rien** being abusive will get you nowhere

6 *(prêter → argent, somme, loyer)* to lend, to advance

7 *Hort (plante)* to push, to force

VI **1** *(se déplacer dans l'espace)* to move forward, to proceed, to progress; *Mil* to advance, to progress; **a. d'un pas** to take one step forward; **a. à grands pas** to stride forward *or* along; **a. avec difficulté** to plod along; **a. vers** *ou* **sur qn d'un air menaçant** to advance on *or* towards sb threateningly; **avoir du mal à a.** to make slow progress, to be slowed down in one's progress; **le bus avançait lentement** the bus was moving slowly; **ne restez pas là, avancez!** don't just stand there, move on!; **avance!** *(en voiture)* move!; **faire a. qn/une mule** to move sb/a mule along; **a. vers un objectif** *(armée)* to advance toward *or* on a target; *(entreprise)* to make good progress in trying to fulfil an objective

2 *(progresser → temps, action)* to be getting on, to progress; **l'heure avance** time's getting on, it's getting late; **l'été/l'hiver avance** we're well into the summer/winter; **au fur et à mesure que la nuit avançait** as the night wore on; **le jeu avançait, je n'avais plus que cinq cartes devant moi** the game was progressing *or* we were well on into the game and I only had five cards left in front of me; **ça avance?** how's it going?; **alors, ce tricot, ça avance?** how's this knitting of yours coming along?; **ça avance bien** it's coming along nicely; **les réparations n'avançaient pas/avançaient** the repair work was getting nowhere/was making swift progress; **le projet n'avance plus** the project's come to a halt *or* standstill; **faire a.** *(cause)* to promote; *(connaissances)* to further, to advance; **faire a. les choses** *(accélérer une action)* to speed things up; *(améliorer la situation)* to improve matters

3 *(personne)* to (make) progress, to get further forward; **tu n'avanceras pas en remâchant tes idées noires** you won't get very far by going over the same depressing thoughts again and again; **j'ai l'impression de ne pas a.** I don't feel I'm getting anywhere *or* I'm making any headway; **a. dans une enquête/son travail** to (make) progress in an investigation/one's work; **les peintres avancent vite/lentement** the decorators are making good/slow progress; **a. en âge** *(enfant)* to grow up, to get older; *(personne mûre)* to be getting on in years; **a. en grade** to go up the promotion ladder

4 *(montre, réveil)* **votre montre avance** *ou* **vous avancez de dix minutes** your watch is *or* you are ten minutes fast; **pendule qui avance d'une seconde toutes les heures** clock that gains a second every hour

5 *(faire saillie → nez, menton)* to jut out, to stick out, to protrude; *(→ piton, promontoire)* to jut out, to stick out

▸**s'avancer** VPR **1** *(approcher)* to move forward *or* closer; **avancez-vous, les enfants** move forward *or* come closer, children; **elle s'avançait discrètement vers les gâteaux** she was discreetly making her way toward the cakes; **il s'avança vers moi** he came towards me

2 *(prendre de l'avance)* **s'a. dans son travail** to make progress *or* some headway in one's work

3 *(prendre position)* to commit oneself; **je ne voudrais pas m'a., mais il est possible que...** I can't be positive, but it might be that...; **il s'est avancé à la légère** he committed himself rather rashly; **je me suis trop avancé pour me dédire** I've gone too far *or* I'm in too deep to pull out now; **je m'avance peut-être un peu trop en affirmant cela** it might be rash of me to say this

4 *(faire saillie)* to jut out, to stick out, to protrude; **la jetée s'avance dans la mer** the jetty sticks out into the sea

avanie [avani] NF *Littéraire* snub; **faire (subir) des avanies à qn** to snub sb; **subir des avanies** to be snubbed

AVANT [avɑ̃]

PRÉP before **1–3** ▪ until **1**

ADV before **1** ▪ far **2** ▪ first **3**

ADJ INV forward, front

NM front **1, 3** ▪ forward **2**

PRÉP **1** *(dans le temps)* before; **a. le lever du soleil** before sunrise; **il est arrivé a. la nuit/le dîner** he arrived before nightfall/dinner; **je voudrais te voir a. mon départ** I'd like to see you before I leave; **a. son élection** prior to his/her election, before being elected; **a. la guerre** in the pre-war period, before the war; **200 ans a. Jésus-Christ** 200 (years) BC; **je ne serai pas prêt a. une demi-heure** I won't be ready for another half-hour; **ne me réveille pas a. onze heures** don't wake me up before eleven; **quand mon manteau sera-t-il prêt? – pas a. mardi** when will my coat be ready? – not before Tuesday; **nous n'ouvrons pas a. dix heures** we don't open until ten; **le contrat sera signé a. deux**

mois the contract will be signed within two months; **vous recevrez votre livraison a. la fin du mois** you'll get your delivery before the end *or* by the end of the month; **il faut que je termine a. ce soir** I've got to finish by this evening; **il faut que tu y sois bien a./un peu a. onze heures** you have to be there well before/a bit before eleven; **peu a. les élections** a short while *or* time before the elections

2 *(dans l'espace)* before; **vous tournez à droite juste a. le feu** you turn right just before the lights; **il est tombé a. la ligne d'arrivée** he fell before the finishing line

3 *(dans un rang, un ordre, une hiérarchie)* before; **vous êtes a. moi** *(dans une file d'attente)* you're before me; **il était juste a. moi dans la file** he was just in front of me in the queue; **leur équipe est maintenant a. la nôtre dans le classement général** their team is now ahead of us in the league; **je place le travail a. tout le reste** I put work above *or* before everything else; **ta santé passe a. ta carrière** your health is more important than *or* comes before your career

ADV 1 *(dans le temps)* before; **quelques jours a.** some days before; **il fallait (y) réfléchir a.** you should have thought (about it) before; **a./après** *(légende de photo)* before/after; **a., j'avais plus de patience avec les enfants** I used to be more patient with children; **a., il n'y avait pas de machines à laver** before *or* in the old days, there weren't any washing machines; **la maison est comme a.** the house has remained the same *or* is the same as it was (before); **peu de temps a.** shortly before *or* beforehand; **quand j'ai un rendez-vous, j'aime arriver un peu a.** when I'm due to meet someone, I like to get there a little ahead of time; **bien** *ou* **longtemps a.** well *or* long before; **c'était bien a., tu n'étais pas encore né** it was well before that, you weren't born then; **on n'a aucune chance de le rattraper, il est parti bien a.** there's no chance of catching up with him, he left well ahead of us; **il est parti quelques minutes a.** he left a few minutes before *or* earlier; **un jour/mois/an a.** a day/month/year earlier; **très a. dans la saison** very late in the season; **discuter/lire bien a. dans la nuit** to talk/to read late into the night

2 *(dans l'espace)* **vous voyez le parc? il y a un restaurant juste a.** see the park? there's a restaurant just before it *or* this side of it; **allons plus a.** let's go further; **il s'était aventuré trop a. dans la forêt** he'd ventured too far into the forest; *Fig* **sans entrer** *ou* **aller plus a. dans les détails** without going into any further *or* more detail; **il est allé trop a. dans les réformes** he went too far with the reforms; **on m'a empêché d'aller plus a. dans mon enquête** I was prevented from carrying my investigations further

3 *(dans un rang, un ordre, une hiérarchie)* **est-ce que je peux passer a.?** can I go first?; **lequel met-on a.?** which one do you put first?; **il y a quelqu'un a.?** *(dans une file d'attente)* is someone else before me?; **tu sortiras cet été, mais tes examens, ça passe a.!** you can go out this summer, but your exams come first!

ADJ INV *(saut périlleux, roulade)* forward; *(roue, siège, partie)* front; **la partie a. du véhicule** the front part of the vehicle

NM 1 *(d'un véhicule)* front; *Naut* bow, bows; **tout l'a. de la voiture a été enfoncé** the front of the car was all smashed in; **il s'est porté vers l'a. du peloton** he moved to the front of the bunch; *Naut* **de l'a. à l'arrière** fore and aft; **à l'a.** in the front; **montez à l'a.** sit in the front; *aussi Fig* **aller de l'a.** to forge ahead; *Can* **mettre qch de l'a.** to put sth forward

2 *Sport* forward; *(au volley)* front-line player; **il est a. dans son équipe de foot** he's a forward in his football team; **jouer a. droit/gauche** to play right/left forward; **la ligne des avants, les avants** the forward line, the forwards

3 *Mil* **l'a.** the front

❑ **avant de PRÉP** before; **a. de partir, il faudra...** before leaving, it'll be necessary to...; **écoute-moi a. de crier** listen to me before you start shouting; **je ne signerai rien a. d'avoir vu les locaux** I won't sign anything until *or* before I see the premises; **a. d'arriver au pont, il y a un feu rouge** there is a set of traffic lights before you come to the bridge

❑ **avant que CONJ ne dites rien a. qu'il n'arrive** don't say anything until he arrives; **je viendrai la voir a. qu'elle (ne) parte** I'll come and see her before she leaves; **a. qu'il comprenne, celui-là!** by the time he's understood!

❑ **avant que de PRÉP** *Littéraire* before; **a. que de mourir...** before dying...; **a. que de donner mon avis, j'entendrai chacun d'entre vous** before I state my opinion, I'll hear what each of you has to say

❑ **avant tout ADV 1** *(surtout)* **c'est une question de dignité a. tout** it's a question of dignity above all (else)

2 *(tout d'abord)* first; **a. tout, je voudrais vous dire ceci** first (and foremost), I'd like to tell you this

❑ **avant toute chose ADV** first of all; **a. toute chose, je voudrais que vous sachiez ceci** first of all, I'd like you to know this; **a. toute chose, je vais prendre une douche** I'll have a shower before I do anything else

❑ **d'avant ADJ le jour/le mois d'a.** the previous day/month, the day/month before; **je vais essayer de prendre le train d'a.** I'll try to catch the earlier train; **les locataires d'a. étaient plus sympathiques** the previous tenants were much nicer

❑ **en avant ADV** *(marcher)* in front; *(partir)* ahead; *(se pencher, tomber, bondir)* forward; **envoyer qn en a.** to send sb on ahead *or* in front; **je pars en a., je t'attendrai là-bas** I'm going on ahead, I'll wait for you there; **il s'élança en a.** he rushed forward; **en a.!** forward!; *Mil* **en a., marche!** forward march!; *Naut* **en a., toute!** full steam ahead!; *Fig* **mettre qn en a.** *(pour se protéger)* to use sb as a shield; *(pour le faire valoir)* to push sb forward *or* to the front; **mettre qch en a.** to put sth forward; **se mettre en a.** to push oneself forward *or* to the fore

❑ **en avant de PRÉP il marche toujours en a. des autres** he always walks ahead of the others; **être en a. d'un convoi** *(dans les premiers)* to be at the front of a procession; *(en premier)* to be leading a procession; **le barrage routier a été installé en a. de Dijon** the roadblock was set up just before Dijon

---

avantage [avɑ̃taʒ] **NM 1** *(supériorité)* advantage; **sa connaissance du danois est un a. par rapport aux autres candidats** his/her knowledge of Danish gives him/her an advantage *or* the edge over the other candidates; **avoir un a. sur qn/qch** to have an advantage over sb/sth; **le nouveau système a des avantages sur l'ancien** the new system has advantages over the old one; **cela vous donne un a. sur eux** this gives you an advantage over them; **garder/perdre l'a.** to keep/to lose the upper hand; **prendre l'a.** *ou* **un a. sur qn** to gain the upper hand over sb; **avoir l'a. sur qn** to have the advantage over sb; **avoir l'a. de** to have the advantage of; **ils nous ont battus, mais ils avaient l'a. du nombre** they defeated us, but they had the advantage of numbers; **j'ai sur toi l'a. de l'âge** I have age on my side; **elle a l'a. d'avoir 20 ans/d'être médecin** she's 20/a doctor, which is an advantage; *Mktg* **a. absolu** absolute advantage; *Mktg* **a. comparatif** *ou* **comparé** comparative advantage; *Mktg* **a. concurrentiel** competitive advantage; *Mktg* **avantages et coûts comparatifs** comparative advantages and costs

2 *(intérêt)* advantage; **les avantages et les inconvénients d'une solution** the advantages and disadvantages *or* pros and cons of a solution; **cette idée présente l'a. d'être simple** the idea has the advantage of being simple; **à mon/son a.** in my/his/her interest; **c'est (tout) à ton a.** it's in your (best) interest; **exploiter une idée à son a.** to exploit an idea to one's own advantage; **avoir a. à faire qch** to be better off doing sth; **vous auriez a. à apprendre la comptabilité** it would be to your advantage *or* you'd do well to learn accounting; **tu as tout a. à l'acheter ici** you'd be much better off buying it here; **elle aurait a. à se taire** she'd be well-advised to keep quiet; **quel a. as-tu à déménager?** what do you gain from moving house?; **tirer a. de** to derive an advantage from, to take advantage of; **ne tirez pas a. de sa naïveté** don't take advantage of his/her naivety; **tirer a. de la situation** to turn the situation to (one's) advantage; **la réforme ne doit pas tourner à l'a. des privilégiés** the reform mustn't be allowed to work in favour of the wealthy; **notre lien de parenté a tourné à mon a.** our family relationship worked to my advantage; **il tournera même ce divorce à son a.** he'll even turn this divorce to his advantage

3 *Fin (bénéfice)* benefit; **elle ne tire de sa participation aucun a. matériel** she derives no material benefit *or* gain from her contribution; **avantages accessoires** financial benefits; **avantages acquis** long-service benefits; **avantages collectifs** social welfare; **avantages complémentaires** perks; **avantages en espèces** cash benefits; **avantages financiers** financial benefits; **a. fiscal** tax benefit, tax incentive; **avantages en nature** benefits *or* payments in kind; **avantages sociaux** *(dans une entreprise)* fringe benefits; *(au sein de l'État)* welfare benefits

4 *(plaisir)* **je n'ai pas l'a. de vous avoir été présenté** I haven't had the privilege *or* pleasure of being introduced to you; **j'ai (l'honneur et) l'a. de vous annoncer que...** I am pleased *or* delighted to inform you that...

5 *Sport* advantage; **a. (à) Rops!** advantage Rops!

6 *(locutions)* **être à son a.** *(avoir belle allure)* to look one's best; *(dans une situation)* to be at one's best; **changer à son a.** to change for the better

avantager [17] [avɑ̃taʒe] **VT 1** *(favoriser)* to advantage, to give an advantage to; **ils ont été avantagés par rapport aux étudiants étrangers** they were given an advantage over the foreign students; **être avantagé dès le départ par rapport à qn** to have a head start on *or* over sb; **être avantagé par la nature** to be favoured by nature; **il n'a pas été avantagé par la nature!** nature hasn't been particularly kind to him!

2 *(mettre en valeur)* to show off, to show to advantage; **son uniforme l'avantage** he looks his best in (his) uniform; **cette coupe ne t'avantage pas** that hairstyle doesn't flatter you

avantageuse [avɑ̃taʒøz] *voir* **avantageux**

avantageusement [avɑ̃taʒøzmɑ̃] **ADV 1** *(peu cher)* at *or* for a good price

2 *(favorablement)* **il s'en est tiré a.** he got away lightly; **vous pourriez a. remplacer ces deux hommes par une machine** you could usefully replace these two operatives with a machine; **l'opération se solde a. pour elle** the transaction has worked to her advantage; **parler de qn a.** to speak favourably of sb

avantageux, -euse [avɑ̃taʒø, -øz] **ADJ 1** *(contrat, affaire)* profitable; *(prix)* attractive; *(conditions, situation)* favourable; **c'est une offre très avantageuse** it's an excellent bargain; **les cerises sont avantageuses en ce moment** cherries are a good buy at the moment

2 *(flatteur → pose, décolleté, uniforme)* flattering; **parler de qn en termes a.** to speak favourably of sb; **il a une idée un peu trop avantageuse de lui-même** he's got too high an opinion of himself; **prendre des airs a.** to look self-satisfied; **un sourire a.** a superior smile, a smirk

avant-après [avɑ̃aprɛ] **NM INV** *(d'une personne, d'une maison)* makeover

avant-bassin [avɑ̃basɛ̃] *(pl* **avant-bassins)** **NM** *Naut* outer basin, dock

avant-bec [avɑ̃bɛk] *(pl* **avant-becs)** **NM** *Archit (d'un pont)* pier-head

avant-bras [avɑ̃bra] **NM INV** *Anat* forearm

avant-cale [avɑ̃kal] *(pl* **avant-cales)** **NF** *Naut* fore hold

avant-centre [avɑ̃sɑ̃tr] *(pl* **avants-centres)** **NM** *Sport* centre-forward

avant-clou [avɑ̃klu] *(pl* **avant-clous)** **NM** (fine) gimlet

avant-contrat [avɑ̃kɔ̃tra] *(pl* **avant-contrats)** **NM** *Jur* preliminary contract

avant-corps [avɑ̃kɔr] **NM INV** *Archit (d'un bâtiment)* projecting part

avant-cour [avɑ̃kur] (*pl* **avant-cours**) NF forecourt

avant-coureur [avɑ̃kurœr] (*pl* **avant-coureurs**) *voir* **signe**

avant-creuset [avɑ̃krøzɛ] (*pl* **avant-creusets**) NM *Métal* fore-hearth *(of blast furnace)*

avant-dernier, -ère [avɑ̃dɛrnje, -ɛr] (*mpl* **avant-derniers**, *fpl* **avant-dernières**) ADJ second last, last but one; **l'avant-dernière fois** the time before last

NM,F second last, last but one; **arriver a.** to be second last *or* last but one

avant faire droit [avɑ̃fɛrdrwa] NM INV *Jur* interim order

avant-garde [avɑ̃gard] (*pl* **avant-gardes**) NF **1** *Mil* vanguard **2** *(élite)* avant-garde; **peinture/architecture d'a.** avant-garde painting/architecture; **être à l'a. de la mode/du progrès** to be in the vanguard *or* at the forefront of fashion/progress

avant-gardisme [avɑ̃gardism] (*pl* **avant-gardismes**) NM avant-gardism

avant-gardiste [avɑ̃gardist] (*pl* **avant-gardistes**) ADJ avant-garde

NMF avant-gardist

avant-goût [avɑ̃gu] (*pl* **avant-goûts**) NM foretaste

avant-guerre [avɑ̃gɛr] (*pl* **avant-guerres**) NM OU NF *Hist* pre-war years *or* period; **les voitures d'a.** pre-war cars

avant-hier [avɑ̃tjɛr] ADV the day before yesterday; **a. au soir** the evening before last; **a. matin** two mornings ago

avant-main [avɑ̃mɛ̃] (*pl* **avant-mains**) NM **1** *(de cheval)* forequarters, forehand **2** *Sport (au tennis)* **coup d'a.** forehand (stroke)

avant-midi [avɑ̃midi] NM INV OU NF INV *Belg & Can* morning

avant-mont [avɑ̃mɔ̃] (*pl* **avant-monts**) NM *Géog* foothill(s)

avant-papier [avɑ̃papje] (*pl* **avant-papiers**) NM *Presse* advance story

avant-pays [avɑ̃pei] NM INV *Géog* foreland

avant-plan [avɑ̃plɑ̃] (*pl* **avant-plans**) NM *Belg* foreground

avant-port [avɑ̃pɔr] (*pl* **avant-ports**) NM *Naut* outer harbour

avant-poste [avɑ̃pɔst] (*pl* **avant-postes**) NM **1** *Mil* outpost **2** *(lieu de l'action)* **il est toujours aux avant-postes** he's always where the action is

avant-première [avɑ̃prəmjɛr] (*pl* **avant-premières**) NF **1** *Théât* dress rehearsal **2** *Cin* preview; **présenter qch en a.** to preview sth

avant-programme [avɑ̃prɔgram] (*pl* **avant-programmes**) NM *(d'un événement)* synopsis of events

avant-projet [avɑ̃prɔʒɛ] (*pl* **avant-projets**) NM pilot study; *Jur* **a. de contrat** draft contract; *Jur* **a. de loi** draft bill

avant-propos [avɑ̃prɔpo] NM INV foreword

avant-scène [avɑ̃sɛn] (*pl* **avant-scènes**) NF *Théât* **1** *(partie de la scène)* apron, proscenium **2** *(loge)* box

avant-soirée [avɑ̃sware] (*pl* **avant-soirées**) NF *TV* early evening television

avant-spectacle [avɑ̃spɛktakl] (*pl* **avant-spectacles**) NM *Belg & Can* pre-show performance; **en a.** as a curtain-raiser

avant-texte [avɑ̃tekst] (*pl* **avant-textes**) NM preliminary notes

avant-titre [avɑ̃titr] (*pl* **avant-titres**) NM *(d'un livre)* half-title

avant-toit [avɑ̃twa] (*pl* **avant-toits**) NM *Archit* **l'a.** the eaves

avant-train [avɑ̃trɛ̃] (*pl* **avant-trains**) NM **1** *Zool* forequarters **2** *Aut* front-axle unit **3** *Mil* limber

avant-trou [avɑ̃tru] (*pl* **avant-trous**) NM *Tech* preliminary hole

avant-veille [avɑ̃vɛj] (*pl* **avant-veilles**) NF two days before *or* earlier; **l'a. de son mariage** two days before he/she got married; *Fig* **à l'a. de la révolution** on the eve of the revolution

avare [avar] ADJ **1** *(pingre)* mean, miserly, tight-fisted **2** *Fig* **être a. de** to be sparing of; **elle est plutôt a. de sourires** she doesn't smile much; **il n'a pas été a. de compliments/de conseils** he was generous with his compliments/advice; **il n'est pas a. de son temps** he gives freely of his time

NMF miser; **un vieil a.** an old miser *or* skinflint

'L'Avare' *Molière* 'The Miser'

avarice [avaris] NF miserliness, avarice

avaricieux, -euse [avarisjø, -øz] *Arch* ADJ miserly, stingy

NM,F miser, skinflint

avarie [avari] NF damage *(sustained by vehicle, ship, cargo)*; **subir des avaries** to sustain damage; **avaries communes/particulières/simples** general/particular/ordinary damage; **avaries de mer** sea damage; **avaries de route** damage in transit

avarié, -e [avarje] ADJ **1** *(aliment, marchandise)* spoilt, damaged; **de la viande avariée** tainted meat; **cette viande est avariée** this meat has gone off **2** *Naut* **navire a.** damaged ship

avarier [10] [avarje] VT to damage; **la chaleur a avarié les aliments** the food has gone off in the heat

▸**s'avarier** VPR *(denrée alimentaire)* to rot, to go bad *or Br* off

avatar [avatar] NM **1** *Rel* avatar **2** *(changement)* change, metamorphosis **3** *(mésaventure)* misadventure, mishap; **les avatars de la vie politique** the vicissitudes of political life **4** *Ordinat* avatar

AVC [avese] NM *Méd* (*abrév* **accident vasculaire cérébral**) stroke, *Spec* cerebral vascular accident

Ave [ave] NM INV *Rel* Ave Maria, Hail Mary

AVEC [avɛk]

with **1–9** ■ to, towards **2** ■ despite **7**

PRÉP **1** *(indiquant la complémentarité, l'accompagnement, l'accord)* with; **et a. la viande, quels légumes voulez-vous?** what vegetables would you like with your meat?; **et a. ceci?** *(dans un magasin)* anything else?; **je ne prends jamais de sucre a. mon café** I never take sugar in my coffee; **une maison a. jardin** a house with a garden; **une chambre a. vue sur le lac** a room with a view over the lake; **un homme a. une blouse blanche** a man in a white coat *or* with a white coat on; **je viendrai a. ma femme** I'll come with my wife, I'll bring my wife along; **habiter a. qn** to live with sb; **j'ai réalisé le catalogue a. lui** I designed the catalogue with him; **a. les encouragements de...** encouraged by..., with the encouragement of...; **a. la collaboration de...** with contributions from *or* by...; **tous les résidents sont a. moi** all the residents support me *or* are behind me *or* are on my side; **là-dessus, je suis a. vous** I'm with you on that point; **a. les écologistes, je pense que...** like the greens, I think that...; **a., dans le rôle principal/dans son premier rôle, X** starring/introducing X; **un film a. Gabin** a film featuring Gabin

2 *(envers)* **être patient/honnête a. qn** to be patient/honest with sb; **être gentil a. qn** to be kind *or* nice to sb; **se comporter bien/mal a. qn** to behave well/badly towards sb

3 *(en ce qui concerne)* **a. lui, c'est toujours la même chose** it's always the same with him; **ce qu'il y a a. eux, c'est qu'ils ne comprennent rien** the problem with them is that they don't understand anything; **a. lui, tout est toujours simple** everything is always simple according to him; **a. ça, il faut compter les frais d'assurance** the cost of insurance should also be added on top of that; **il est compétent, et a. ça il ne prend pas cher** he's very competent and he's cheap as well; **et a. ça, il n'est pas content!** *(en plus)* and on top of that *or* and what's more, he's not happy!; *(malgré tout)* with all that, he's still not happy!; **a. tout ça, j'ai oublié de lui téléphoner** with all that, I forgot to call him/her; **et a. ça que je me gênerais!** I should worry!

4 *(indiquant la simultanéité)* **se lever a. le jour** to get up at the crack of dawn; **se coucher a. les poules** to go to bed early; **le paysage change a. les saisons** the countryside changes with the seasons

5 *(indiquant une relation d'opposition)* with; **se battre a. qn** to fight with sb; **être en guerre a. un pays** to be at war with a country; **se disputer a. qn** to quarrel with sb; **rivaliser a. qn** to compete with sb

6 *(indiquant une relation de cause)* with; **a. le temps qu'il fait, je préfère ne pas sortir** I prefer not to go out in this weather; **ils ne pourront pas venir a. cette pluie** they won't be able to come with (all) this rain; **a. tout le chocolat que tu as mangé, tu vas être malade** you're going to be ill with all that chocolate you've eaten; **a. ce nouveau scandale, le ministre va tomber** this new scandal will mean the end of the minister's career; **a. sa force de caractère, elle s'en sortira** with her strength of character she'll come through; **au lit a. la grippe** in bed with (the) flu; **ils ont compris a. le temps** in time, they understood; **s'améliorer a. l'âge** to improve with age; **ne m'embête pas a. toutes ces histoires** don't bother me with all that

7 *(malgré)* **a. tous ses diplômes, Pierre ne trouve pas de travail** even with all his qualifications, Pierre can't find work; **a. ses airs aimables, c'est une vraie peste** despite his/her pleasant manner, he's/she's a real pest

8 *(indiquant la manière)* with; **elle est habillée a. goût** she is dressed tastefully *or* with taste; **faire qch a. plaisir** to do sth with pleasure, to take pleasure in doing sth; **faire qch a. beaucoup de soin** to do sth with great care, to take great care in doing sth; **regarder qn a. passion/mépris** to look at sb passionately/contemptuously; **ce n'est pas a. colère que je le fais** I'm not doing it in anger

9 *(indiquant le moyen, l'instrument)* with; **marcher a. une canne** to walk with a stick, to use a walking-stick; **couper qch a. un couteau** to cut sth with a knife; **fonctionner a. des piles** to run on batteries, to be battery-operated; **c'est fait a. de la laine** it's made of wool; **a. un peu de chance** with a bit of luck; **a. un peu plus d'argent...** with a little more money...; **elle est partie a. un bateau de pêche** she left on a fishing boat; **nous avons continué a. cinq litres de carburant** we carried on with five litres of fuel; **tu peux conduire un poids lourd a. ton permis?** can you drive a heavy goods vehicle with *or* on your licence?; **voyager a. un faux passeport** to travel with *or* on a forged passport

ADV **1** *Fam* **il a pris la clef et il est parti a.** he took the key and went off with it■; **ôtez vos chaussures, vous ne pouvez pas entrer a.** take off your shoes, you can't come in with them on■; **je vous mets le poisson a.?** shall I put the fish in with the rest?■

2 *Belg* **je vais faire des courses, tu viens a.?** I'm going shopping, are you coming (with me)?

❑ **d'avec** PRÉP **distinguer qch d'a. qch** to distinguish sth from sth; **divorcer d'a. qn** to divorce sb; **se séparer d'a. qn** to separate from sb

aveline [avlin] NF *Bot* filbert, cobnut

avelinier [avlinje] NM *Bot* filbert, cob

Ave Maria [avemarja] NM INV *Rel* Ave Maria, Hail Mary

aven [avɛn] NM *Géol* sinkhole, *Br* swallow hole

avenant¹ [avnɑ̃] NM *Jur* **1** *(gén)* amendment; **a. à un contrat** amendment to a contract

2 *(dans les assurances)* endorsement, additional clause; **a. d'augmentation de la garantie** endorsement for an increase in cover

❑ **à l'avenant** ADV **un exposé sans intérêt et des questions à l'a.** a boring lecture with equally boring questions; **il se levait de mauvaise humeur, boudait toute la matinée, et le reste à l'a.** he was in a foul mood when he got up, he sulked all morning and he carried on like that for the rest of the day; **toutes les unes de journaux sont à l'a.** all the front pages carry the same story

❑ **à l'avenant de** PRÉP in accordance with; **ils se sont conduits à l'a. de leurs principes** they behaved according to their principles

avenant², -e [avnɑ̃, -ɑ̃t] ADJ pleasant; **le personnel est compétent mais peu a.** the staff are competent but not very pleasant; **une hôtesse avenante accueille les visiteurs** a gracious hostess greets the visitors; **son visage arborait un air faussement a.** his/her face wore a deceptively welcoming look

avènement [avɛnmɑ̃] NM **1** *(d'un souverain)* accession; *Rel (du Messie)* advent, coming **2** *(d'une époque, d'une mode)* advent; **l'a. d'une ère nouvelle** the advent of a new era

avenir [avnir] NM **1** *(période future)* future; **dans un a. indéterminé** sometime in the future; **dans un a. proche/lointain** in the near/distant future; **pas dans un a. proche** not in the foreseeable future; **il est temps de songer à l'a.** it's time to think of the future; **ce que nous réserve l'a.** what the future holds (for us); **l'a. dira si j'ai raison** time will tell if I'm right; **espérer dans/croire en un a. meilleur** to hope for/to believe in a better future; **l'a. est à nous** the future is ours; **les moyens de transport de l'a.** the transport systems of the future

2 *(générations futures)* future generations

3 *(situation future)* future; **nous devons nous préoccuper de l'a. de notre fils** we should start thinking about our son's future; **tu as devant toi un brillant a.** you have a promising future ahead (of you); **assurer l'a. de qn** to make provision for sb

4 *(chances de succès)* future, (future) prospects; **une invention sans a.** an invention with no future; **avoir de l'a.** to have a future; **les nouveaux procédés techniques ont de l'a.** the new technical processes are promising *or* have a good future; **découverte d'un matériau d'a.** discovery of a promising new material; **les professions d'a.** up-and-coming professions

5 *Jur* writ of summons *(to opposing counsel)*

□ **à l'avenir** ADV in future; **à l'a., vous êtes priés d'arriver à l'heure** in future, you are requested to be on time

Allusion

La femme est l'avenir de l'homme

Originally, this came from a Louis Aragon poem, and it means "Woman is the future of man". Aragon dedicated his 1963 collection of poems, *Le Fou d'Elsa*, to his wife, the writer Elsa Triolet. The poems were set to music and sung by Jean Ferrat. The cycle is a celebration of love, and speaks of its revitalizing effects. In modern French, any other term can be substituted for "la femme" and said to be the future of man: for example, **La science est l'avenir de l'homme** ("Science is the future of man").

Avent [avɑ̃] NM *Rel* advent; **l'A.** Advent; **calendrier de l'A.** Advent calendar

Aventin [avɑ̃tɛ̃] NM **le mont A.** the Aventine Hill

aventure [avɑ̃tyr] NF **1** *(incident → gén)* experience, incident; *(→ extraordinaire)* adventure; **il m'est arrivé une drôle d'a. ce matin** a strange thing happened to me this morning; **le récit d'une a. en mer** the tale of an adventure at sea; **pour trouver un taxi le samedi soir, c'est tout une a.** finding a taxi on a Saturday night is quite a performance

2 *(risque)* adventure, venture; **l'a. est au coin de la rue** the unexpected is always round the corner; **adopter un tel projet, c'est se lancer dans l'a.** accepting such a project is a bit risky; **la grande a.** great adventure; **se lancer dans une grande a.** to set off on a big adventure; **dire la bonne a. à qn** to tell sb's fortune

3 *(liaison)* (love) affair

□ **à l'aventure** ADV at random, haphazardly; **marcher/rouler à l'a.** to walk/to drive aimlessly; **partir à l'a.** to go off in search of adventure

□ **d'aventure(s)** ADJ *(roman, film)* adventure *(avant n)*

□ **d'aventure, par aventure** ADV by chance; **si d'a. tu le vois, transmets-lui mon message** if by any chance you see him, give him my message

aventuré, -e [avɑ̃tyre] ADJ *(hypothèse, théorie)* risky; *(démarche)* chancy, risky, *Littéraire* venturesome

aventurer [3] [avɑ̃tyre] VT **1** *(suggérer → hypothèse, analyse)* to venture

2 *(risquer → fortune, réputation, bonheur)* to risk, to chance

▸**s'aventurer** VPR **1** *(aller)* to venture; **il n'avait pas peur de s'a. le soir dans des ruelles obscures** he wasn't afraid of venturing out into dark alleys at night

2 s'a. à faire to venture to do; **je ne m'aventure plus à faire des pronostics** I no longer venture or dare to make any forecasts; **téléphone-lui si tu veux, moi je ne m'y aventurerais pas** call him/her if you like, I wouldn't chance it myself

aventureuse [avɑ̃tyrøz] *voir* **aventureux**

aventureusement [avɑ̃tyrøzmɑ̃] ADV **1** *(hardiment)* adventurously **2** *(dangereusement)* riskily

aventureux, -euse [avɑ̃tyrø, -øz] ADJ **1** *(hardi → héros)* adventurous **2** *(dangereux → projet)* risky, chancy

aventurier [avɑ̃tyrje] NM **1** *(explorateur)* adventurer; *(aimant le risque)* risk-taker **2** *Péj (escroc)* rogue

aventurière [avɑ̃tyrjɛr] NF *Péj* adventuress

aventurine [avɑ̃tyrin] NF *Minér* aventurin, aventurine

aventurisme [avɑ̃tyrism] NM *Pol* adventurism

aventuriste [avɑ̃tyrist] ADJ adventurist

NMF adventurist

avenu, -e[1] [avny] ADJ *Jur* **nul et non a.** null and void

avenue[2] [avny] NF *(de ville)* avenue; *(menant à une maison)* drive(way); **sur l'a. Foch** on the Avenue Foch; *Fig* **les avenues du pouvoir** the paths to power

avéré, -e [avere] ADJ *(fait, information)* known, established; **c'est un fait a. que..., il est a. que...** it is a known fact that...

avérer [18] [avere] VT *(affirmer)* **a. un fait** to vouch for the accuracy of a fact

▸**s'avérer** VPR **1** *(être prouvé)* to be proved (correct); **cette hypothèse ne s'est jamais avérée** this hypothesis was never proved correct

2 *(se révéler)* to prove (to be); **la solution s'est avérée inefficace** the solution turned out *or* proved (to be) inefficient; **les jeunes vendeurs se sont avérés plus performants que les anciens** the younger salesmen showed *or* proved themselves to be more efficient than their seniors

3 *(tournure impersonnelle)* **il s'avère difficile d'améliorer les résultats** it's proving difficult to improve on the results; **il s'avère que mon cas n'est pas prévu par le règlement** it turns out *or* it so happens that my situation isn't covered by the regulations

Averne [avɛrn] NM **1** *Géog* **le lac A.** Lake Avernus

2 *Littéraire* **l'A.** the infernal regions, Hades

Averroès [avɛrɔɛs] NPR Averroës

averroïsme [avɛrɔism] NM *Phil* Averroism

avers [avɛr] NM obverse

averse [avɛrs] NF shower *(rain)*; **sous l'a.** in the rain; *Fig* **laisser passer l'a.** to wait until the storm blows over; **une a. d'injures s'abattit sur moi** I was assailed by a string *or* stream of insults; **a. météorique** meteorite shower

aversion [avɛrsjɔ̃] NF aversion, dislike; **sa laideur m'inspirait de l'a.** his/her ugliness filled me with loathing; **avoir de l'a. pour** to have an aversion to *or* for, to have a dislike for; **il les a pris en a.** he took a violent dislike to them

averti, -e [avɛrti] ADJ (well-)informed; **un critique a. en matière de musique** a critic well-informed about music; **le consommateur est de plus en plus a.** consumers are better and better informed; *Euph* **à dix ans, c'était déjà une jeune fille avertie** even at ten, she knew the facts of life; **pour lecteurs avertis seulement** for adult readers only; *Prov* **un homme a. en vaut deux** forewarned is forearmed

avertir [32] [avɛrtir] VT **1** *(informer)* to inform; **avertis-moi dès que tu (le) sauras** let me know as soon as you know; **l'avez-vous averti de votre départ?** have you informed him that *or* did you let him know that you are leaving?; **il faut l'a. que le spectacle est annulé** he/she must be informed *or* told that the show's off; **nous n'avons pas été avertis du danger** we were not warned about the danger

2 *(par menace, par défi)* to warn; **je t'avertis que la prochaine fois la punition sera sévère** I'm warning you that the next time the punishment will be severe; **tiens-toi pour averti!** be warned!; **vous voilà avertis!** I give you fair warning!, don't say I haven't warned you!

avertissement [avɛrtismɑ̃] NM **1** *(signe)* warning, warning sign; **il est parti sans le moindre a.** he left without any warning

2 *(appel à l'attention)* notice, warning; **il n'a pas tenu compte de mon a.** he didn't take any notice of my warning

3 *(blâme)* warning, reprimand; *Sport (de l'arbitre)* warning, caution; *Admin (lettre)* warning letter; **donner un a. à qn** to give sb a warning, to warn sb; **premier et dernier a.!** I'm telling you now and I won't tell you again!

4 *(en début de livre)* **a. (au lecteur)** foreword

5 *Rail* warning signal

6 *Ordinat* **a. de réception** *(de message)* acknowledgement; **a. à réception d'un courrier** mail received message

avertisseur, -euse [avɛrtisœr, -øz] ADJ warning

NM alarm, warning signal; **a. lumineux** warning light; **a. sonore** *(gén)* alarm; *Aut* horn; **a. d'incendie** fire alarm

avestique [avɛstik] NM *(langue)* Avestan, Avestic

aveu, -x [avø] NM **1** *(confession)* confession; **faire un a.** to acknowledge *or* to confess *or* to admit something; **je vais vous faire un a., j'ai peur en voiture** I must confess that I'm scared travelling in cars; **obtenir les aveux d'un criminel** to make a criminal confess; **recueillir les aveux d'un criminel** to take down a criminal's confession; **faire des aveux complets** *(à la police)* to make a full confession; *Fig Hum* to confess all; *aussi Fig* **passer aux aveux** to confess; **faire l'a. de qch** to own up to sth; **faire l'a. de son inexpérience/amour** to confess to being inexperienced/in love; **(faire) l'a. de son ignorance lui a été pénible** he/she found it difficult to admit *or* to acknowledge his/her ignorance

2 *Hist* = recognition between a vassal and his overlord; *Fig* **c'était un homme sans a.** *(vagabond)* he was a vagabond *or* vagrant; *(sans scrupules)* he was a dishonourable man, he was not a man of his word

3 *(autorisation)* permission, consent; **nous ne pouvons rien faire sans l'a. de l'intéressé** we can do nothing without the consent of the party concerned

4 *Belg (locution)* **être/entrer en a.** *ou* **aveux** to acknowledge *or* to confess *or* to admit something

□ **de l'aveu de** PRÉP according to; **de l'a. des participants, il ressort que...** according to the participants, it seems that...; **la tour ne tiendra pas, de l'a. même de l'architecte** the tower will collapse, even the architect says so; **de son propre a.** by his/her own reckoning

aveuglant, -e [avœglɑ̃, -ɑ̃t] ADJ *(éclat, lueur)* blinding, dazzling; *(évidence, preuve)* overwhelming; *(vérité)* self-evident, glaring; **soudain, une vérité aveuglante lui est apparue** the truth came to him/her in a blinding flash

aveugle [avœgl] ADJ **1** *(privé de la vue)* blind; **un enfant a. de naissance** a child born blind *or* blind from birth; **a. d'un œil** blind in one eye; **devenir a.** to go blind; **l'accident qui l'a rendu a.** the accident which blinded him *or* deprived him of his sight; **je ne suis pas a., je vois bien tes manigances** I'm not blind, I can see what you're up to; **la passion la rend a.** she's blinded by passion; **il faudrait être a. pour ne pas voir qu'elle souffre** you'd have to be blind not to see that she's in pain

2 *(extrême → fureur, passion)* blind, reckless

3 *(absolu → attachement, foi, soumission)* blind, unquestioning; **avoir une confiance a. en qn** to trust sb implicitly *or* unreservedly

4 *Constr (mur, fenêtre)* blind

NMF blind man, *f* woman; **les aveugles** the blind; **parler de/juger qch comme un a. des couleurs** to speak of/to judge sth blindly

□ **en aveugle** ADV **faire qch en a.** to do sth blindly; **faire un test en a.** to do a blind test; **se lancer en a. dans une entreprise** to take a leap in the dark

aveuglement [avœgləmɑ̃] NM blindness, blinkered state; **dans son a., il est capable de tout** in his blindness, he's capable of anything

aveuglément [avœglemɑ̃] ADV *(inconsidérément)* blindly; **elle lui faisait a. confiance** she trusted him implicitly

aveugle-né, -e [avœgləne] *(mpl* **aveugles-nés**, *fpl* **aveugles-nées**) NM,F *Méd* = person blind from birth; **c'est un a.** he was born blind, he's been blind from birth

aveugler [5] [avœgle] VT **1** *(priver de la vue, éblouir)* to blind; **l'accident qui l'a aveuglée**

the accident which blinded her *or* deprived her of her sight; **la lueur des phares m'aveuglait** the glare of the headlights blinded *or* dazzled me; *Fig* **la haine/l'amour l'aveugle** he's/she's blinded by hatred/love

2 *Naut* **a. une voie d'eau** to stop a leak

3 *(fenêtre)* to wall up, to block

▸**s'aveugler VPR** to delude oneself; **il ne faut pas t'a., ça ne sera pas facile** don't delude yourself, it won't be easy; **s'a. sur** to close one's eyes to; **ne vous aveuglez pas sur vos chances de réussite** don't overestimate your chances of success

aveuglette [avœglɛt] **à l'aveuglette ADV 1** *(sans voir)* blindly; **il m'a fallu marcher à l'a. le long d'un tunnel** I had to grope my way through a tunnel; **elle conduisait à l'a. dans un brouillard épais** she drove blindly through a thick fog

2 *Fig* **choisir qch à l'a.** to choose sth at random *or* in the dark *or* blindly; **lancer des coups à l'a.** to hit out blindly; **je ne veux pas agir à l'a.** I don't want to act without first weighing up the consequences; **leur projet n'a pas été entrepris à l'a.** they did their homework before undertaking their project

aveulir [32] [avølir] *Littéraire* **VT** to enervate

▸**s'aveulir VPR** to become enervated

aveulissement [avølismɑ̃] **NM** *Littéraire* enervation

Aveyron [avɛrɔ̃] **NM l'A.** the Aveyron

aveyronnais, -e [avɛrɔnɛ, -ɛz] **ADJ** of/from the Aveyron

❑ **Aveyronnais, -e NM,F** = inhabitant of or person from the Aveyron

aviaire [avjɛr] **ADJ** *Orn* avian; *Méd* **grippe a.** bird flu, *Spéc* avian flu; **peste a.** fowl pest

aviateur, -trice [avjatœr, -tris] **NM,F** *Aviat* pilot, *Vieilli* aviator; **elle a été l'une des premières aviatrices** she was one of the first women pilots

aviation [avjasjɔ̃] **NF** *Aviat* **1** *(transport)* aviation; **a. civile** civil aviation; **a. marchande** *ou* **commerciale** commercial aviation; **a. de tourisme** civil aviation **2** *(activité)* flying; **faire de l'a.** to go flying; **elle était destinée à l'a.** she was meant to fly **3** *(fabrication)* aircraft industry **4** *Mil (armée de l'air)* air force; *(avions)* aircraft, air force; **l'a. ennemie a attaqué nos bases** enemy aircraft attacked our bases

aviatrice [avjatris] *voir* **aviateur**

avicole [avikɔl] **ADJ 1** *(d'oiseaux → élevage)* bird *(avant n)*; *(de volailles → ferme, producteur, élevage)* poultry *(avant n)* **2** *(parasite)* avicolous

aviculteur, -trice [avikyltœr, -tris] **NM,F** *(éleveur → d'oiseaux)* bird breeder *or* farmer, *Spéc* aviculturist; *(→ de volailles)* poultry breeder *or* farmer

aviculture [avikyltyr] **NF** *(élevage → d'oiseaux)* bird breeding, *Spéc* aviculture; *(→ de volailles)* poultry farming *or* breeding

avide [avid] **ADJ 1** *(cupide)* greedy, grasping; **un homme a.** a greedy man; **des mains avides se tendaient vers l'or** greedy *or* grasping hands reached towards the gold

2 *(enthousiaste)* eager, avid; **écouter d'une oreille a.** to listen eagerly *or* avidly; **a. de** greedy *or* avid for; **un produit a. d'oxygène** an oxygen-hungry product; **a. de louanges** hungry for praise; **a. de nouveauté** eager *or* avid for novelty; **a. de savoir** eager to learn, thirsty for knowledge; **un candidat a. de succès** a candidate hungry for success; **a. de connaître le monde** eager *or* anxious *or* impatient to discover the world

avidement [avidmɑ̃] **ADV 1** *(voracement → manger)* greedily, ravenously; *(→ boire)* greedily **2** *(avec enthousiasme)* eagerly, avidly, keenly; **regardant a. ce que faisaient les aînés** watching keenly what the older ones were doing; **écouter qn a.** to listen to sb eagerly **3** *(par cupidité)* greedily, covetously

avidité [avidite] **NF 1** *(voracité)* voracity, greed, *Péj* gluttony; **manger avec a.** to eat greedily *or* ravenously **2** *(enthousiasme)* eagerness, enthusiasm; **écouter avec a.** to listen eagerly **3** *(cupidité)* greed, cupidity, covetousness

avifaune [avifon] **NF** *Écol* avifauna

Avignon [aviɲɔ̃] **NM** *Géog* Avignon; **à** *ou* **en A.** in Avignon; *Théât* **le festival d'A.** the Avignon festival

> *Culture*
>
> **LE FESTIVAL D'AVIGNON**
>
> Founded by Jean Vilar in 1947 and held every summer in Avignon in the South of France, this arts festival is a showcase for new theatre and dance performances: "La pièce sera donnée d'abord en Avignon". Along with the programme of official shows ("le in") performed in prestigious venues such as the Court of Honour of the "Palais des Papes", a programme comprising numerous fringe shows, referred to as "le off", has also been performed since the 1970s.

avignonnais, -e [aviɲɔnɛ, -ɛz] **ADJ** of/from Avignon

❑ **Avignonnais, -e NM,F** = inhabitant of or person from Avignon

avilir [32] [avilir] **VT 1** *(personne)* to debase, to shame; **vos mensonges vous avilissent** your lies are unworthy of you

2 *(monnaie)* to cause to depreciate, to devalue; *(marchandise)* to cause to depreciate; **l'inflation a avili l'euro** inflation has devalued the euro

▸**s'avilir VPR 1** *(emploi réfléchi)* to demean *or* to debase *or* to disgrace oneself; **il s'avilit dans l'alcoolisme** he's sunk into alcoholism

2 *(monnaie, marchandise)* to depreciate

avilissant, -e [avilisɑ̃, -ɑ̃t] **ADJ** degrading, demeaning; **mon métier n'a rien d'a.** there is nothing shameful about my job

avilissement [avilismɑ̃] **NM 1** *(d'une personne)* degradation, debasement; **le roman décrit l'a. d'un homme par le jeu** the novel describes a man's downfall through gambling **2** *(d'une monnaie)* depreciation, devaluation

aviné, -e [avine] **ADJ** *(qui a trop bu)* drunken, intoxicated; *(qui sent le vin → souffle)* wine-laden; *(altéré par la boisson → voix)* drunken; **une brute avinée** a drunken brute

aviner [3] [avine] **VT** *(fût, futaille)* to season

avion [avjɔ̃] **NM 1** *(véhicule)* plane, *esp Br* aeroplane, *Am* airplane; **a. bimoteur/quadrimoteur** twin-engined/four-engined plane; **a. charter** charter plane; **a. de chasse** fighter plane; **a. civil** civil aircraft; **a. commercial** commercial aircraft; **a. à décollage et atterrissage courts** short take-off and landing aircraft; **a. à décollage vertical** jump-jet; **a. furtif** stealth aircraft; **a. de guerre** warplane; **a. à hélices** propeller plane; **a. hôpital** hospital plane; **a. de ligne** airliner; **a. militaire** military plane; **a. de ravitaillement (en vol)** refuelling aircraft; **a. à réaction** jet(plane); **a. de reconnaissance** reconnaissance aircraft; **a. sans pilote** pilotless aircraft; **a. de tourisme** private aircraft; **a. de transport** transport aircraft

2 *(mode de transport)* **l'a.** flying; **irez-vous en a. ou en train?** are you flying or going by train?; **j'ai fait une partie du trajet en a.** I flew part of the way; **je déteste (prendre) l'a.** I hate flying; **elle n'a jamais pris l'a.** she's never been on a plane, she's never flown; **courrier par a.** air mail

avion-cargo [avjɔ̃kargo] *(pl* **avions-cargos)** **NM** freight plane

avion-cible [avjɔ̃sibl] *(pl* **avions-cibles)** **NM** *Mil* target-practice aircraft, drone

avion-citerne [avjɔ̃sitɛrn] *(pl* **avions-citernes)** **NM** (air) tanker, supply plane

avion-école [avjɔ̃ekɔl] *(pl* **avions-écoles)** **NM** training plane *or* aircraft

avion-espion [avjɔ̃ɛspjɔ̃] *(pl* **avions-espions)** **NM** spy plane

avionique [avjɔnik] **NF** avionics *(singulier)*

avionnerie [avjɔnri] **NF** *Can (usine)* aircraft factory; *(industrie)* aircraft industry

avionneur [avjɔnœr] **NM** aircraft constructor

avion-suicide [avjɔ̃sɥisid] *(pl* **avions-suicide)** **NM** suicide plane

avion-taxi [avjɔ̃taksi] *(pl* **avions-taxis)** **NM** charter aircraft

aviron [avirɔ̃] **NM 1** *(rame)* oar; *Can* paddle; **tirer sur les avirons** to row; **coup d'a.** stroke; **en trois coups d'a. vous serez de l'autre côté** you'll row to the other side in no time at all **2** *Sport (activité)* rowing; **faire de l'a.** to row

avironner [3] [avirɔne] **VI** *Can* to paddle

avis [avi] **NM 1** *(point de vue)* opinion, viewpoint; **les a. sont partagés au sein du parti** opinions within the party are divided; **avoir son** *ou* **un a. sur qch** to have views on sth; **je n'ai pas d'a. sur la question** I have nothing to say *or* no opinion on the matter; **ne décide pas pour elle, elle a son a.!** don't decide for her, she knows her own mind!; **j'aimerais avoir votre a.** I'd like to hear your views *or* to know what you think (about it); **demande** *ou* **prends l'a. d'un second médecin** ask the opinion of another doctor; **toi, je ne te demande pas ton a.!** I didn't ask for your opinion!; **donner son a.** to give *or* to contribute one's opinion; **si vous voulez (que je vous donne) mon a.** if you ask me *or* want my opinion; **donner** *ou* **émettre un a. favorable** *(à une demande)* to give the go-ahead; *(à une proposition)* to give a positive response, to come out in favour; **après a. favorable, vous procéderez à l'expulsion** having obtained permission (from the authorities), you will start the eviction procedure; **émettre un a. défavorable** to give a negative response; **prendre l'a. de qn** to seek sb's advice; **je vais prendre des a. et je vous contacterai** I'll seek further advice before contacting you; **à mon a.** in my opinion; **à mon a., c'est un mensonge** in my opinion, it's a lie, I think it's a lie; *Hum* **à mon humble a.** in my humble opinion; **être d'a. que...** to be of the opinion that...; **elle est d'a. qu'il est trop tard** she's of the opinion that it's too late; **je ne suis pas d'a. qu'on l'envoie en pension** I don't agree with his/her being sent away to boarding school; **de l'a. de** *(selon)* according to; **de l'a. des experts** according to the experts; **de l'a. général, ce film est un chef-d'œuvre** the general view is that the film is a masterpiece; **je suis de votre a.** I agree with you; **il n'est pas de ton a.** he doesn't agree with you; **lui et moi ne sommes jamais du même a.** he and I don't see eye to eye *or* never agree on anything; **je suis du même a. que toi** I agree with you; **il n'est pas du même a. que son père** he disagrees with his father; *Hum* **m'est a. que...** it seems to me that..., methinks...; **sur l'a. de** on the advice *or* at the suggestion of; **c'est sur leur a. que j'ai fait refaire la toiture** I had the roof redone on their advice; *Presse* **a. éditorial** editorial opinion

2 *(information)* announcement; *(sommation → légale)* notice; *(→ fiscale)* notice, demand; **j'ai reçu un a. du percepteur** I had a tax demand; **jusqu'à nouvel a.** until further notice; **nous irons sauf a. contraire** *(de votre part)* unless we hear otherwise *or* to the contrary, we'll go; *(de notre part)* unless you hear otherwise *or* to the contrary, we'll go; **il reste encore quelques parts de gâteau, a. aux amateurs** there's still some cake left if anyone's interested; **a. au lecteur** foreword; **a. au public** *(sur panneau)* public notice; *Fin* **a. d'appel de fonds** call letter; *Bourse* **a. d'attribution** allotment letter; **a. de la banque** bank notification *or* advice; *Jur* **a. consultatif** advisory opinion; *Jur* **a. contraire** dissent; *Banque* **a. de crédit** credit advice; *Banque* **a. de débit** debit advice; **a. de décès** death notice; *Jur* **a. défavorable** unfavourable verdict; **en cas d'a. défavorable du jury** should the jury return an unfavourable verdict; *Banque* **a. de domiciliation** notice of payment by banker's order; *Bourse* **a. d'exécution** contract note; *Fin* **a. d'imposition** tax assessment; **a. de licenciement** redundancy notice; *Jur* **a. motivé** counsel's opinion; *Fin* **a. de non-imposition** tax exemption document; *Bourse* **a. d'opération sur titres, a. d'opéré** trade ticket, contract note; **a. de paiement** payment advice; *Banque* **a. de prélèvement** direct debit advice; **a. de rappel** reminder; **a. de réception** acknowledgement of receipt; **a. de recherche** *(d'un criminel)* wanted (person) poster; *(d'un disparu)* missing person poster; *Banque* **a. de rejet** notice of returned cheque; *Banque* **a. de remise** remittance advice; *Banque* **a. de retrait (de fonds)** notice of withdrawal; *Jur* **a. à tiers-détenteur** = seizure of money by the Treasury; *Fin* **a. de vérification** notice of audit; *Banque* **a. de virement** (bank) transfer advice

avisé, -e [avize] **ADJ** shrewd, prudent; **un conseiller très a.** a shrewd counsellor; **bien a.** well-advised; **mal a.** ill-advised

aviser [3] [avize] **VT 1** *(informer)* to inform, to

notify; **a. qn de qch** to inform *or* to notify sb of sth; **vous serez avisé par lettre** you will be notified *or* informed by letter; **avez-vous été avisé?** have you been informed?; **il m'a avisé que ma candidature était retenue** he informed me that my application had been accepted

2 *Littéraire (voir)* to notice, to glimpse, to catch sight of; **il avisa dans la foule un de ses amis** he caught sight of one of his friends in the crowd

VI to decide, to see (what one can do); **maintenant nous allons devoir a.** we'll have to see what we can do now; **s'il n'est pas là dans une heure, j'aviserai** I'll have another think if he isn't here in an hour; **avisons au plus pressé** let's attend *or* see to the most urgent matters

▸**s'aviser de** **VPR** 1 *(remarquer)* to notice, to become aware of; **je me suis avisé de sa présence quand elle a ri** I suddenly noticed her presence when she laughed; **il s'est avisé trop tard (de ce) qu'il n'avait pas sa clé** he realized too late that he didn't have his key

2 *(oser)* to dare to; **ne t'avise pas de l'interrompre quand elle parle** don't think of interrupting her while she's speaking; **et ne t'avise pas de recommencer!** and don't you dare do that again!; **le premier qui s'avise de tricher sera puni** the first one who takes it into his head to cheat will be punished; **il s'est avisé de sortir malgré l'interdiction du médecin** he decided to go out despite the doctor's orders

aviso [avizo] **NM** *Mil* sloop

avitaillement [avitajmɑ̃] **NM** 1 *Naut* victualling, refuelling 2 *Aviat* refuelling

avitailler [3] [avitaje] **VT** *Aviat & Naut* to refuel

avitailleur [avitajœr] **NM** 1 *Naut* refuelling tanker 2 *Aviat* air tanker

avitaminose [avitaminoz] **NF** *Méd* vitamin deficiency, *Spéc* avitaminosis; **a. C** vitamin C deficiency

avivage [avivaʒ] **NM** 1 *Tex* touching up *(of colours)* 2 *Métal* burnishing

avivé [avive] **NM** sawn timber

avivement [avivmɑ̃] **NM** *Méd* revivification

aviver [3] [avive] **VT** 1 *(intensifier → flammes)* to fan, to stir up; *(→ feu)* to revive, to rekindle; *(→ couleur)* to brighten, to revive; *(→ sentiment)* to stir up; *(→ désir)* to excite, to arouse; *(→ blessure)* to irritate; *(→ querelle)* to stir up, to exacerbate; *(→ crainte)* to heighten 2 *Menuis* to square off 3 *(métal)* to burnish; *(marbre)* to polish 4 *Méd* to open up

av. J.-C. *(abrév écrite* **avant Jésus-Christ***)* BC

avocaillon [avɔkajɔ̃] **NM** *Fam Péj* pettifogger, pettifogging lawyer

avocasserie [avɔkasri] **NF** *Fam Vieilli* chicanery, pettifoggery

avocassier, -ère [avɔkasje, -ɛr] **ADJ** *Fam Vieilli* pettifogging

avocat[1] [avɔka] **NM** *(fruit)* avocado

avocat[2], **-e** [avɔka, -at] **NM,F** 1 *Jur* lawyer, *Am* attorney(-at-law); *(à la barre) Br* barrister, *Am* trial lawyer *or* attorney, *Scot* advocate; **mon a.** my lawyer *or* counsel; **mes avocats** my counsel; *Fam* **je lui mettrai mes avocats sur le dos!** I'll take him/her to court!■; **a. d'affaires** business lawyer; **a. consultant** *Br* ≃ counsel in chamber, ≃ consulting barrister, *Am* ≃ attorney; **a. de la défense** counsel for the defence, *Br* ≃ defending counsel, *Am* ≃ defense counsel; **a. général** *Br* ≃ counsel for the prosecution, *Am* ≃ prosecuting attorney

2 *(porte-parole)* advocate, champion; **se faire l'a. d'une mauvaise cause** to advocate *or* to champion a lost cause; **je serai votre a. auprès de lui** I'll plead with him on your behalf; **a. du diable** devil's advocate; **se faire l'a. du diable** to be devil's advocate

avocat-avoué [avɔkaavue] *(pl* **avocats-avoués***)* **NM** *Jur Br* ≃ lawyer, *Am* ≃ attorney

avocat-conseil, avocate-conseil [avɔkakɔ̃sɛj, avɔkatkɔ̃sɛj] *(mpl* **avocats-conseils,** *fpl* **avocates-conseils***)* **NM,F** *Jur* legal adviser

avocatier [avɔkatje] **NM** *Bot* avocado (tree)

avocat-plaidant, avocate-plaidante [avɔkaplɛdɑ̃, avɔkatplɛdɑ̃t] *(mpl* **avocats-plaidants,** *fpl* **avocates-plaidantes***)* **NM,F** *Br* ≃ barrister, *Am* ≃ trial attorney

avocette [avɔsɛt] **NF** *Orn* avocet

avodiré [avodire] **NM** *Bot (arbre)* avodire (pyramide); *(bois)* avodire, African white mahogany

avoine [avwan] **NF** 1 *Bot (plante)* oat; *(grains)* oats; **a. commune** common oats; **a. élevée** tall oat-grass 2 *très Fam (locution)* **passer une a. à qn** to beat sb up

avoir[1] [avwar] **NM** 1 *Com (attestation de crédit)* credit note; *(en comptabilité)* credit side; **la fleuriste m'a fait un a.** the florist gave me a credit note; **j'ai un a. de 20 euros à la boucherie** I've got 20 euros' credit at the butcher's

2 *Écon & Fin (capital)* capital; **avoirs** assets, holdings; **a. en banque** bank credit; **avoirs en caisse** cash holdings; **a. en devises** foreign currency holding; **avoirs numéraires** cash holdings; **avoirs disponibles** liquid assets; **a. fiscal** tax credit

3 *Littéraire (possessions)* assets, worldly goods; **vivre d'un petit a. personnel** to live off a small personal income; **dépouillé de tout son a.** stripped of all his/her worldly goods

AVOIR[2] [1] [avwar]

> **VT** to have **A1–4, 6, 9, B1, 2, C1, 4, D2, E** ■ to have on **B3** ■ to own **A1** ■ to be **B5, 6** ■ to make **C2** ■ to get **A5, 8, 10, D1** ■ to feel **C3** ■ to give **C2** ■ to catch **A11** ■ to take in **D3**
> **V AUX** to have **A1, 2** ■ to have to **B2, 3**

V AUX A. 1 *(avec des verbes transitifs)* **as-tu lu sa lettre?** did you read *or* have you read his/her letter?; **les deux buts qu'il avait marqués** the two goals he had scored; **j'aurais voulu vous aider** I'd have liked to help you; **non content de les a. humiliés, il les a jetés dehors** not content with humiliating them, he threw them out

2 *(avec des verbes intransitifs)* **j'ai maigri** I've lost weight; **as-tu bien dormi?** did you sleep well?; **tu as dû rêver** you must have been dreaming

3 *(avec le verbe "être")* **j'ai été surpris** I was surprised; **il aurait été enchanté** he would've *or* would have been delighted

B. 1 *(exprime la possibilité)* **tu as à manger dans le réfrigérateur** there's something to eat in the fridge for you; **je n'ai rien à boire** I haven't got anything *or* I have nothing *or* I've got nothing to drink; **ils n'ont qu'à écrire au directeur** *(conseil)* all they have to do *or* all they've got to do is write to the manager; *(menace)* just let them (try and) write to the manager; **s'il vous manque quelque chose, vous n'avez qu'à me le faire savoir** if you're missing anything, just let me know; **tu n'as qu'à le recoller** all you've got to do is glue it back together; *Fam* **t'as qu'à leur dire!** why don't you (just) tell them!; *Fam* **t'as qu'à la mettre à la porte!** just throw her out!; *Fam* **t'as qu'à me frapper, pendant que tu y es!** why don't you hit me while you're at it?

2 *(exprime l'obligation)* **a. à** to have to; **partez, j'ai à travailler** go away, I've got to work; **j'ai à ajouter une petite précision** I must add one point, I must just say one thing; **je n'ai pas à me justifier auprès de vous** I don't have to justify myself to you; **un jour, tu auras à t'expliquer** one day, you'll have to account for yourself; **et voilà, je n'ai plus qu'à recommencer!** so now I've got to start all over again!

3 *(exprime le besoin)* **a. à** to have to; **il a à te parler** he's got something to *or* there's something he wants to tell you; **j'ai à réfléchir** I need to think (it over); **tu n'as pas à t'inquiéter** you shouldn't worry, you have nothing to worry about; **tu n'as pas à te plaindre** you shouldn't complain, you have nothing to complain about

4 *(locutions)* **je n'ai que faire de tes états d'âme** I couldn't care less about your moods; **la démocratie, ils n'en ont que faire** they couldn't care less about democracy

VT A. 1 *(être propriétaire de → action, bien, domaine etc)* to have, to own, to possess; *(→ chien, hôtel, voiture)* to have, to own; **a. de l'argent** to have money; **tu n'aurais pas un stylo en plus?** have you got *or* do you happen to have a spare pen?; **je n'ai plus de sucre** I've run out of sugar

2 *Com* to have; **a. un article en magasin** to have an item in stock; **a. un article en vitrine** to display an item in the window; **nous avons plus grand si vous préférez** we have it in a larger size if you prefer; **j'ai encore quelques places à 25 euros/un vol à 17 heures 30** I still have some 25 euro seats/a flight at five thirty p.m. (available)

3 *(ami, collègue, famille etc)* to have; **il a encore sa grand-mère** his grandmother's still alive; **je n'ai plus ma mère** my mother's dead; **voilà sept ans qu'il n'a plus sa femme** he lost his wife *or* his wife died seven years ago; **elle a trois enfants** she has three children; **elle a eu des jumeaux** she had twins; **il n'a jamais eu d'enfants** he never had any children; **elle a un mari qui fait la cuisine** she's got the sort *or* kind of husband who does the cooking; **j'avais un père qui jouait avec ses enfants** I had the kind of father who played with his children; *Fam* **j'ai la chaîne de mon vélo qui est cassée** the chain on my bike is broken■; *Fam* **il a sa tante qui est malade** his aunt's ill■

4 *(détenir → permis de conduire, titre)* to have, to hold; *(→ droits, privilège)* to have, to enjoy; *(→ emploi, expérience, devoirs, obligations)* to have; *(→ documents, preuves)* to have, to possess; *Sport* to have; **quand nous aurons le pouvoir** when we're in power; **a. l'arme nucléaire est devenu une de leurs priorités** possession of nuclear weapons has become one of their priorities; **a. l'heure** to have the time; **quelle heure avez-vous?** what time do you make it?; **a. le ballon** to be in possession of *or* to have the ball

5 *(obtenir → amende, article)* to get; *(→ information, rabais, récompense)* to get, to obtain; *(→ au téléphone)* to get through to; **où as-tu eu tes chaussettes?** where did you get *or* buy your socks?; **elle a ses renseignements par Mirna** she gets her information from Mirna; **je pourrais vous a. des places gratuites** I could get you free tickets; **tu auras la réponse/le devis demain** you'll get the answer/estimate tomorrow; *Fam* **il a toutes les filles qu'il veut** he gets all the girls he wants; **j'ai essayé de t'a. toute la journée** I tried to get through to you *or* to contact you all day; **je l'ai eu au téléphone** I got him on the phone; **je n'arrive même pas à a. leur standard** I can't even get through to their switchboard; **pour a. Besançon, composez le 8513** for Besançon *or* to get through to Besançon, dial 8513

6 *(jouir de → beau temps, bonne santé, liberté, bonne réputation)* to have, to enjoy; *(→ choix, temps, mauvaise réputation)* to have; **a. la confiance de qn** to be trusted by sb; **a. l'estime de qn** to be held in high regard by sb; **vous avez toute ma sympathie** you have all my sympathy; **j'ai une heure pour me décider** I have an hour (in which) to make up my mind; **il a tout pour lui et il n'est pas heureux!** he's got everything you could wish for and he's still not happy!; **tu veux tout a.!** you want (to have) everything!

7 *(recevoir chez soi)* **il a son fils tous les dimanches** his son stays with him every Sunday; **a. de la famille/des amis à dîner** to have relatives/friends over for dinner; **j'aurai ma belle-famille au mois d'août** my in-laws will be staying with me in August

8 *Rad & TV (chaîne, station)* to receive, to get; **bientôt, nous aurons les chaînes européennes** soon, we'll be able to get the European channels

9 *(attraper → otage, prisonnier)* to have; *Fam* **les flics ne l'auront jamais** the cops'll never catch him/her

10 *(atteindre → cible)* to get, to hit; **vise la pomme – je l'ai eue!** aim at the apple – (I) got it!; **tu peux m'a. le pot de confiture?** can you reach the pot of jam for me?

11 *(monter à bord de → avion, bus, train)* to catch; **je n'ai pas pu a. le train de cinq heures** I couldn't catch *or* get the five o'clock train; **j'ai eu le dernier avion** I caught *or* got the last plane

B. 1 *(présenter → tel aspect)* to have (got); **elle a un joli sourire** she's got *or* she has a nice smile; **tu as de petits pieds** you've got *or* you have small feet; **il a les yeux verts** he's got *or* he has green eyes; **elle a le nez de sa mère** she's got *or* she has her mother's nose; **un monstre qui a**

sept têtes a seven-headed monster, a monster with seven heads; **je cherche un acteur qui ait un grand nez** I'm looking for an actor with a big nose; **elle a une jolie couleur de cheveux** her hair's a nice colour; **elle a beaucoup de sa mère** she really takes after her mother; **il a tout de l'aristocrate** he's the aristocratic type; **tu as tout d'un fou avec cette coiffure** you look like a madman with that hairstyle; **les ordinateurs qui ont un disque dur** computers with a hard disk; **la méthode a l'avantage d'être bon marché** this method has the advantage of being cheap; **ton père a le défaut de ne pas écouter ce qu'on lui dit** your father's weakness is not listening to what people tell him; **l'appareil a la particularité de s'éteindre automatiquement** the machine's special feature is that it switches itself off automatically

2 *(avec pour complément une partie du corps)* to have; **a. l'estomac vide** to have an empty stomach; **j'ai la tête lourde** my head aches; **j'ai le bras ankylosé** my arm's stiff; **j'ai les jambes qui flageolent** my legs are shaking; **il a les yeux qui se ferment** he can't keep his eyes open; *très Fam* **en a.** to have a lot of balls; *très Fam* **ne pas en a.** to have no balls

3 *(porter sur soi → accessoire, vêtement, parfum)* to have on, to wear; **tu vois la dame qui a le foulard?** do you see the lady with the scarf?; **faites attention, il a une arme** careful, he's got a weapon *or* he's armed

4 *(faire preuve de)* **a. de l'audace** to be bold; *Fam* **a. du culot** to be cheeky■, to have a nerve; *Fam* **il a eu le culot de me le dire** he had the cheek■ *or* the nerve to tell me; **a. du talent** to have talent, to be talented; **ayez la gentillesse de...** would you *or* please be kind enough to...; **aie la politesse de laisser parler les autres** please be polite enough to let the others talk; **il a eu la cruauté de lui dire** he was cruel enough to tell him

5 *(exprime la mesure)* to be; **le voilier a 4 m de large** *ou* **largeur** the yacht is 4 m wide; **j'ai 70 cm de tour de taille** I'm 70 cm round the waist, I have a 70 cm waist; **le puits a 2 m de profondeur** the well's 2 m deep; **la porte a 1,50 m de haut** *ou* **hauteur** the door is 1 m 50 cm high; **j'en ai pour 200 euros** it's costing me 200 euros; **tu en as pour 12 jours/deux heures** it'll take you 12 days/two hours; **j'ai pour 300 euros de frais!** I have 300 euros worth of expenses!; **j'en ai eu pour 27 euros** I had to pay *or* it cost me 27 euros; **on en a bien pour trois heures pour aller jusqu'à Lille** it's going to take us *or* we'll need at least three hours to get to Lille; *Fam* **si la police l'attrape, il en aura pour 20 ans!** if the police catch him, he'll get *or* cop 20 years!

6 *(exprime l'âge)* to be; **quel âge as-tu?** how old are you?; **j'ai 35 ans** I'm 35 (years old); **nous avons le même âge** we're the same age; **il a deux ans de plus que moi** he's two years older than me; **il vient d'a. 74 ans** he's just turned 74

C. 1 *(subir → symptôme)* to have, to show, to display; *(→ maladie, hoquet, mal de tête etc)* to have; *(→ accident, souci, ennuis)* to have; *(→ difficultés)* to have, to experience; *(→ opération)* to undergo, to have; *(→ crise)* to have, to go through; **a. de la fièvre** to have *or* to be running a temperature; **a. un cancer** to have cancer; **a. des migraines** to suffer from *or* to have migraines; **a. des contractions** to have contractions; **j'ai une rougeur au coude** I have a red blotch on my elbow; **je ne sais pas ce que j'ai aujourd'hui** I don't know what's the matter *or* what's wrong with me today; **qu'as-tu? tu es affreusement pâle** what's wrong? you're deathly pale; **sa sœur n'a rien eu** his/her sister escaped unscathed; *Fam* **le car n'a rien eu du tout, mais la moto est fichue** there wasn't a scratch on the bus, but the motorbike's a write-off; *Fam* **qu'est-ce qu'elle a encore, cette voiture?** NOW what's wrong with this car?■; **il a des souris chez lui** he's got mice; **un enfant/chaton qui a des vers** a child/kitten with worms

2 *(émettre, produire → mouvement)* to make; *(→ ricanement, regard, soupir)* to give; **a. un sursaut** to (give a) start; **elle eut un pauvre sourire** she smiled faintly *or* gave a faint smile; **elle eut cette phrase devenue célèbre** she said *or* uttered those now famous words; **il eut une moue de dédain** he pouted disdainfully

3 *(ressentir)* **a. faim** to be *or* to feel hungry; **a. peur** to be *or* to feel afraid; **a. des scrupules** to have qualms; **a. des remords** to feel remorse; **a. du chagrin** to feel *or* to be sad; **a. un pressentiment** to have a premonition; **a. de l'amitié pour qn** to regard *or* to consider sb as a friend; **a. de l'admiration pour qn** to admire sb; **je n'ai que mépris pour lui** I feel only contempt for him; **a. du respect pour qn** to have respect for *or* to respect sb; *Fam* **en a. après** *ou* **contre qn** to be angry with sb■; **après** *ou* **contre qui en as-tu?** who are you angry with?; **ce chien/cette guêpe en a après toi!** this dog/wasp has got it in for you!; **en a. après** *ou* **contre qch** to be angry about sth; **moi, j'en ai après** *ou* **contre la pollution!** pollution really makes me angry!

4 *(élaborer par l'esprit → avis, idée, suggestion)* to have; **j'ai mes raisons** I have my reasons; **elle a toujours réponse à tout** she's got an answer for everything

D. *Fam* **1** *(battre, surpasser)* to get, to beat■; **ne t'inquiète pas, on les aura dans la descente!** don't worry, we'll get them going downhill!; **tu essaies d'accaparer le marché, mais je t'aurai!** you're trying to corner the market, but I'll get the better of you!; **il m'a eu au cinquième set** he got *or* beat me in the fifth set; **il va se faire a. dans la dernière ligne droite** he's going to get beaten in the final straight

2 *(escroquer)* to have, to do, to con; **500 euros pour ce buffet? tu t'es fait a.!** 500 euros for that dresser? you were conned *or* had *or* done!; **les touristes, on les a facilement** tourists are easily conned

3 *(duper)* to take in, to take for a ride, to have; **je t'ai bien eu!** I took you in *or* I had you there, didn't I?; **il m'a eu** he led me up the garden path, I was taken in by him; **tu t'es fait a.!** you've been had *or* taken in *or* taken for a ride!; **tu essaies de m'a.!** you're having *or* putting me on!; **n'essaie pas de m'a.** don't try it on with me

E. *(devoir participer à → débat, élection, réunion)* to have, to hold; *(→ rendez-vous)* to have; **j'ai (un) cours de chimie ce matin** I've got a chemistry lesson this morning; **avons-nous une réunion aujourd'hui?** is there *or* do we have a meeting today?

❑ **il y a** V IMPERSONNEL **1** *(dans une description, une énumération → suivi d'un singulier)* there is; *(→ suivi d'un pluriel)* there are; **il y avait trois chanteurs** there were three singers; **il n'y a pas de lit** there is no bed; **il y a du soleil** the sun is shining; **qu'est-ce qu'il y a dans la malle?** what's in the trunk?; **il n'y a qu'ici qu'on en trouve** this is the only place (where) you can find it/them; **il n'y a pas que moi qui le dis** I'm not the only one to say so; **il y a juste de quoi faire une jupe** there is just enough to make a skirt; **avoue qu'il y a de quoi être énervé!** you must admit it's pretty irritating!; **merci – il n'y a pas de quoi!** thank you – don't mention it *or* you're welcome!; **il n'y a rien à faire, la voiture ne démarre pas** it's no good, the car won't start; **il n'y a pas à dire, il sait ce qu'il veut** there's no denying he knows what he wants; **il n'y a que lui pour dire une chose pareille!** trust him to say something like that!; **circulez, il n'y a rien à voir,** *Fam* **y a rien à voir** move along, there's nothing to see; *Fam* **qu'est-ce qu'il y a? – il y a que j'en ai marre!** what's the matter? – I'm fed up, that's what!; **il y a voiture et voiture** there are cars and cars; *Fam* **il n'y en a que pour lui!** he's the one who gets all the attention!■; *Fam* **il y en a** *ou* **il y a des gens, je vous jure!** some people, honestly *or* really!; *Fam* **quand il n'y en a plus, il y en a encore!** there's plenty more where that came from!

2 *(exprimant la possibilité, l'obligation etc)* **il n'y a plus qu'à payer les dégâts** we'll just have to pay for the damage; **il n'y a qu'à lui dire** you/we/*etc* just have to tell him; **il n'y a qu'à commander pour être servi** you only have to order to get served

3 *(indiquant la durée)* **il y a 20 ans de ça** 20 years ago; **il y a une heure que j'attends** I've been waiting for an hour

4 *(indiquant la distance)* **il y a bien 3 km d'ici au village** it's at least 3 km to the village

5 *(à l'infinitif)* **il va y a. de la pluie** there's going to be some rain; **il pourrait y a. un changement** there could be a change; **il doit y a. une raison** there must be a *or* some reason

---

avoir-client [avwarklijɑ̃] NM *Compta* customer credit

avoirdupoids, avoirdupois [avwardypwa] NM avoirdupois (weight)

avoir-fournisseur [avwarfurnisœr] NM *Compta* supplier credit

avoisinant, -e [avwazinɑ̃, -ɑ̃t] ADJ neighbouring, nearby; **les quartiers avoisinants ont été évacués** the surrounding streets were evacuated

avoisiner [3] [avwazine] VT **1** *(dans l'espace)* to be near *or* close to, to border on; **la propriété avoisine la rivière** the land borders on the river; *Fig* **son attitude avoisine l'insolence** his/her attitude verges on insolence **2** *(en valeur)* to be close on, to come close to; **les dégâts avoisinent le million** damages come close to one million; **une somme avoisinant les 80 euros** a sum in the region of 80 euros

Avoriaz [avɔrjaz] NF **le festival d'A.** = former festival of science-fiction and horror films held annually at Avoriaz in the French Alps

avorté, -e [avɔrte] ADJ *(réforme, tentative)* failed, abortive; **une initiative avortée** an abortive move

avortement [avɔrtəmɑ̃] NM *Obst* abortion; **être contre l'a.** to be against abortion; *Fig* **l'a. d'une tentative** the failure of an attempt; **a. spontané** miscarriage; **a. thérapeutique** termination *(for medical reasons)*

avorter [3] [avɔrte] VI **1** *Obst (faire une fausse couche)* to miscarry; *(subir une IVG)* to abort, to have an abortion; *Zool* to abort; **faire a. qn** *(médicament, piqûre)* to induce a miscarriage in sb **2** *(plan, réforme, révolution)* to miscarry, to fall through

VT to abort, to carry out an abortion on; **se faire a.** to have an abortion

avorteur, -euse [avɔrtœr, -øz] NM,F *Obst* abortionist

avorton [avɔrtɔ̃] NM **1** *(personne → chétive)* runt; *(→ monstrueuse)* freak, monster; **espèce d'a.!** you little runt! **2** *(plante)* stunted plant

avouable [avwabl] ADJ worthy, respectable; **un motif a.** a worthy motive; **des mobiles peu avouables** disreputable motives

avoué[1] [avwe] NM *Jur Br* ≃ solicitor, *Am* ≃ attorney

avoué[2], -e [avwe] ADJ *(partisan, auteur)* confessed; **il est allé là-bas dans le but a. de se venger** he went there with the declared aim of taking revenge

avouer [6] [avwe] VT **1** *(erreur, forfait)* to admit, to confess (to), to own up to; **elle a avoué voyager sans billet/tricher aux cartes** she owned up to travelling without a ticket/to cheating at cards

2 *(doute, sentiment)* to admit *or* to confess to; **elle refuse d'a. ses angoisses/qu'elle a des ennuis** she refuses to acknowledge her anxiety/to admit that she has problems; **je t'avoue que j'en ai assez** I must admit that I've had all I can take; **ceci me surprend, je l'avoue** this surprises me, I must confess *or* admit *or* say; **il faut a. qu'elle a de la patience** you have to admit (that) she's patient; **tu avoueras que ce n'était pas facile** you'll admit that it wasn't easy

USAGE ABSOLU **il a avoué** *(à la police)* he owned up, he made a full confession; **si personne n'avoue, tout le monde sera puni** if no one owns up, then everyone will be punished; **allez, avoue, elle te plaît** go on, admit it, you like her

▶**s'avouer** VPR **elle ne s'avoue pas encore battue** *ou* **vaincue** she won't admit defeat yet; **je m'avoue complètement découragé** I confess *or* admit to feeling utterly discouraged; **s'a. coupable** to admit one's guilt

avril [avril] NM April; *Prov* **en a., ne te découvre pas d'un fil** ≃ ne'er cast a clout till May is out; *voir aussi* **mars**

AVS [ɑvεεs] NF **1** (*abrév* **auxiliaire de vie sociale**) ≃ social worker **2** *Suisse Assur* (*abrév* **assurance vieillesse et survivants**) = Swiss pension scheme

avulsion [avylsjɔ̃] NF **1** *Méd* extraction **2** *Jur* avulsion

avunculaire [avɔ̃kylεr] ADJ avuncular

avunculat [avɔ̃kyla] NM (*en anthropologie*) avunculate

AWACS [awaks] NM *Aviat* (*abrév* **airborne warning and control system**) (*système*) AWACS; (*avion*) AWACS plane

awalé [awale] NM (*en Afrique francophone*) awari (*African dice game played with pebbles*)

axe [aks] NM **1** *Géom* axis; **a. des abscisses** x-axis; **a. optique** principal axis; **a. des ordonnées** y-axis; **a. de rotation** axis of rotation; **a. de symétrie** axis of symmetry; **a. des X** x-axis; **a. des Y** y-axis; **a. des Z** z-axis

2 (*direction*) direction, line; **deux grands axes de développement** two major directions of development; **développer de nouveaux axes de recherche** to open up new areas of research; **sa politique s'articule autour de deux axes principaux** his/her policy revolves around two main themes *or* issues; **il est dans l'a. du parti** (*membre*) he's in the mainstream of the party; *Ftbl* **dans l'a. (du terrain)** down the middle

3 (*voie*) **ils vont ouvrir un nouvel a. Paris–Bordeaux** they're going to open up a new road link between Paris and Bordeaux; *Rail* **l'a. Lyon-Genève** the Lyons-Geneva line; **(grand) a.** *Br* major road, *Am* main highway; **tous les (grands) axes routiers sont bloqués par la neige** all major roads are snowed up; **a. rouge** = section of the Paris road system where parking is prohibited to avoid congestion, *Br* ≃ red route; **l'A. historique** (*à Paris*) = series of historical landmarks which form an uninterrupted perspective from the Louvre to the Grande Arche at La Défense

4 *Tech* axle

5 *Hist* **l'A.** the Axis

▫ **dans l'axe de** PRÉP (*dans le prolongement de*) in line with; **la perspective s'ouvre dans l'a. du palais** the view opens out from the palace; **le Louvre s'inscrit dans l'a. des Champs-Élysées** the Louvre is directly in line with the Champs-Élysées

axel [aksεl] NM (*en patinage artistique*) axel

axénique [aksenik] ADJ *Biol* axenic

axer [3] [akse] VT **il est très axé sur le spiritisme** he is very keen on spiritualism; **toute sa vie est axée là-dessus** his whole life revolves around it; **a. une campagne publicitaire sur les enfants** to build an advertising campaign around children; **le premier trimestre sera axé autour de Proust** the first term will be devoted to Proust; **une modernisation axée sur l'importation des meilleures techniques étrangères** modernization based on importing the best foreign techniques; **une visite touristique axée sur...** a guided tour focusing on...

axérophtol [akserɔftɔl] NM (*vitamine A*) axerophthol

axial, -e, -aux, -ales [aksjal, -o] ADJ **1** (*d'un axe*) axial **2** (*central*) central; **éclairage a.** central overhead lighting (*in a street*)

axile [aksil] ADJ *Bot* axile

axillaire [aksilεr] ADJ *Anat* axillary

axiologie [aksjɔlɔʒi] NF *Phil* axiology

axiologique [aksjɔlɔʒik] ADJ *Phil* axiological

axiomatique [aksjɔmatik] ADJ *Ling* axiomatic ■ NF *Math* axiomatics (*singulier*)

axiomatisation [aksjɔmatizasjɔ̃] NF *Ling* axiomatization

axiomatiser [3] [aksjɔmatize] VT *Ling & Math* to axiomatize

axiome [aksjom] NM *Ling & Math* axiom

axis [aksis] NM *Anat & Zool* axis

axisymétrique [aksisimetrik] ADJ *Géom* axisymmetric, axisymmetrical

axolotl [aksɔlɔtl] NM *Zool* axolotl

axone [akson] NM *Anat* axon, axone

axonge [aksɔ̃ʒ] NF **1** *Pharm* lard, hog's fat **2** *Mil* rifle grease, axle grease

axonométrie [aksɔnɔmetri] NF *Géom* axonometry

axonométrique [aksɔnɔmetrik] ADJ *Géom* **perspective a.** axonometric projection

ay [aj] NM (*alcool*) = champagne from Ay

ayant *voir* **avoir**²

ayant cause [εjɑ̃koz] (*pl* **ayants cause**) NM *Jur* beneficiary, legal successor; **a. universel** universal legatee; **a. à titre particulier** specific legatee; **a. à titre universel** residuary legatee

ayant-compte [εjɑ̃kɔ̃t] (*pl* **ayants-comptes**) NM *Banque* account holder

ayant droit [εjɑ̃drwa] (*pl* **ayants droit**) NM *Jur* (*gén*) beneficiary; (*à une propriété*) rightful owner; (*à un droit*) eligible party

ayatollah [ajatɔla] NM *Rel* ayatollah; *Fam Fig* **les ayatollahs du libéralisme** fanatical advocates of the free market, those who preach the gospel of the free market

aye-aye [ajaj] (*pl* **ayes-ayes**) NM *Zool* aye-aye

ayons *etc voir* **avoir**²

ayuntamiento [ajuntamjεnto] NM *Admin* (*en Espagne*) = municipal council in Spain

azalée [azale] NF *Bot* azalea

Azay-le-Rideau [azεlərido] NM *Géog* = one of the most famous of the sixteenth-century châteaux of the Loire Valley

azéotrope [azeɔtrɔp] *Chim & Phys* ADJ azeotropic ■ NM azeotrope

azéotropique [azeɔtrɔpik] ADJ *Chim & Phys* azeotropic

Azerbaïdjan [azεrbajdʒɑ̃] NM **l'A.** Azerbaijan; **vivre en A.** to live in Azerbaijan; **aller en A.** to go to Azerbaijan

azerbaïdjanais, -e [azεrbaidʒanε, -εz] ADJ Azerbaijani ■ NM (*langue*) Azerbaijani

▫ **Azerbaïdjanais, -e** NM,F Azerbaijani; **les A.** the Azerbaijanis *or* Azerbaijani

azéri, -e [azeri] ADJ Azeri

▫ **Azéri, -e** NM,F Azeri

azerole [azrɔl] NF *Bot* azarole, = fruit of the Neapolitan medlar

azerolier [azrɔlje] NM *Bot* azarole, Neapolitan medlar

azidothymidine [azidɔtimidin] NF *Méd* AZT

azilien, -enne [aziljε̃, -εn] *Archéol* ADJ Azilian ■ NM Azilian

azimut [azimyt] NM azimuth; *Fam* **partir dans tous les azimuts** to be all over the place; **la discussion partait dans tous les azimuts** the discussion was all over the place

▫ **tous azimuts** *Fam* ADJ all-out, full-scale■; **une attaque tous azimuts** an all-out attack; **publicité tous azimuts** comprehensive advertising campaign■ ADV all over (the place); **prospecter tous azimuts** to canvass all over; **la jeune société se développe tous azimuts** the new firm is really taking off

azimutal, -e, -aux, -ales [azimytal, -o] ADJ azimuthal

azimuté, -e [azimyte] ADJ *Fam* crazy■, *Br* round the bend

Azincourt [azε̃kur] NM Agincourt

azobé [azɔbe] NM *Bot* azobe

azoïque¹ [azɔik] ADJ *Biol* azoic

azoïque² [azɔik] *Chim* ADJ **colorants azoïques** azo dyes; **composés azoïques** azo compounds ■ NM azo compound

azolla [azɔla] NF *Bot* Azolla

azonal, -e, -aux, -ales [azonal, -o] ADJ *Météo* azonal

azoospermie [azɔɔspεrmi] NF *Biol* azoospermia

azotate [azɔtat] NM *Chim* nitrate; **a. de potasse** nitre, saltpetre

azote [azɔt] NM *Chim* nitrogen

azoté, -e [azɔte] ADJ *Chim* nitrogenous, azotic

azotémie [azɔtemi] NF *Méd* azotaemia

azotémique [azɔtemik] ADJ *Méd* azotaemic

azoter [3] [azɔte] VT *Chim* to nitrogenize

azoteux, -euse [azɔtø, -øz] ADJ *Chim* nitrous

azothydrique [azɔtidrik] ADJ *Chim* hydrazoic

azotique [azɔtik] ADJ *Chim* nitric

azotite [azɔtit] NM *Chim* nitrite

azotobacter [azɔtɔbaktεr] NM azotobacter

azoture [azɔtyr] NM *Chim* azide

azoturie [azɔtyri] NF *Méd* azoturia

azotyle [azɔtil] NM *Chim* nitryl

Azov [azɔv] *voir* **mer**

AZT® [ɑzεdte] NM *Méd* (*abrév* **azidothymidine**) AZT

aztèque [astεk] ADJ Aztec

▫ **Aztèque** NMF Aztec

azulejo [azuleχo] NM *Cér* azulejo tile

azulène [azylεn] NM *Chim* Azulene

azur [azyr] NM **1** (*couleur*) azure, sky-blue; **la Côte d'A.** the French Riviera, the Côte d'Azur **2** *Littéraire* (*ciel*) skies ■ ADJ INV azure, sky-blue

azurage [azyraʒ] NM *Tech* blueing

azurant [azyrɑ̃] NM *Tech* fluorescent brightening agent

azuré, -e [azyre] ADJ *Littéraire* azure, sky-blue

azuréen, -enne [azyreε̃, -εn] ADJ **1** *Littéraire* (*bleu*) azure, sky-blue **2** (*de la Côte d'Azur*) of the Côte d'Azur *or* French Riviera

azurer [3] [azyre] VT to blue, to tinge with blue

azurite [azyrit] NF *Minér* azurite

azygos [azigos] *Anat* ADJ (*veine*) azygous, unpaired ■ NF azygous vein

azyme [azim] *voir* **pain**

B

B¹, b [be] NM INV **1** *(lettre)* B, b; **B comme Berthe** ≃ B for Bob **2** *Mus (note)* B

B² **1** *Scol (abrév écrite* **bien)** = good grade (as assessment of schoolwork), ≃ B **2** *Phys (abrév écrite* **Bel**) B

B2B [bitubi] ADJ *(abrév* **business to business)** B2B

B2C [bitusi] ADJ *(abrév* **business to consumer)** B2C

BA [bea] NF *Fam (abrév* **bonne action)** = good deed; **faire une BA** to do a good deed; **j'ai fait ma BA pour aujourd'hui** I've done my good deed for the day

Baal [baal] *(pl* **Baals** *ou* **Baalim)** NM *Rel* Baal

baba [baba] ADJ *Fam* **en être** *ou* **rester b.** to be flabbergasted
▪ NM **1** *Culin* **b. (au rhum)** (rum) baba **2** *Fam (locution)* **l'avoir dans le b.** to be let down; **après ils partiront en congé et c'est toi qui l'auras dans le b.!** then they'll go off on holiday and you'll be left holding the baby!
▪ NMF *(hippie)* hippyish person; *(personne relax)* laid-back person

b.a.-ba [beaba] NM ABCs, rudiments; **apprendre le b. du métier** to learn the ABCs *or* basics of the trade

baba cool [babakul] *(pl* **babas cool)** *Fam* ADJ *(hippie)* hippyish; *(relax)* laid-back; **elle est très b.** she's a bit of a hippy
▪ NMF *(hippie)* hippyish person; *(personne décontractée)* laid-back person

Babel [babɛl] *voir* **tour¹**

babeleer [babəlɛr] NM *Belg Fam* chatterbox

babélisme [babelism] NM babel

babeurre [baboer] NM buttermilk

babiche [babiʃ] NF *Can* babiche, = strips of rawhide or sinew often used for webbing snowshoes

babil [babil] NM *(des enfants, du ruisseau)* babbling; *(des oiseaux)* twittering

babillage [babijaʒ] NM *(des enfants)* babble, babbling; *(d'un bavard)* chatter

babillard, -e [babijar, -ard] ADJ *Littéraire (personne)* chattering; *(ruisseau)* babbling
▪ NM,F *Littéraire (personne)* chatterbox
▪ NM **1** *Offic Ordinat* bulletin board, BBS **2** *Chasse (chien)* babbler, mouthy hound
□ **babillarde** NF *Fam* letter▪

babillement [babijmɑ̃] = **babil**

babiller [3] [babije] VI *(oiseau)* to twitter; *(ruisseau)* to murmur, to babble; *(enfant)* to babble, to chatter; *(bavard)* to prattle (on), to chatter (away)

babines [babin] NFPL **1** *Zool* chops **2** *Fam (lèvres)* lips▪; **se lécher** *ou* **pourlécher les b.** to lick one's chops; **d'avance, je m'en lèche les b.** my mouth's watering in anticipation

babiole [babjɔl] NF **1** *(objet)* knick-knack, trinket; **je voudrais lui acheter une b. pour marquer son anniversaire** I would like to buy him/her a little something for his/her birthday **2** *(incident)* trifle

babiroussa [babirusa] NM *Zool* babirusa

babisme [babism] NM *Rel* Babism

baboler [3] [babole] VI *Suisse* to mumble; *(enfant)* to babble, to chatter

bâbord [babɔr] NM *Naut* port; **à b.** on the port side

bâbordais [babɔrdɛ] NM *Naut* member of the port watch; **les b.** the port watch

babos [babos] NMF *Fam* hippyish person

babouche [babuʃ] NF *(oriental)* slipper

babouchka [babyʃka] NF babushka

babouin [babwɛ̃] NM *Zool* baboon

baboune [babun] NF *Can (moue)* **faire la b.** to sulk▪
□ **babounes** NFPL *(lèvres)* big or full lips▪

babouvisme [babuvism] NM *Pol* babouvism

---

baby [bebi] ADJ INV **taille b.** baby-size(d); **whisky b.** small whisky
▪ NM small whisky

baby-beef [bebibif] *(pl* **baby-beefs)** NM feeder

baby-boom [bebibum, babibum] *(pl* **baby-booms)** NM baby boom; **les enfants du b.** the baby boomers

baby-boomer [bebibumœr] *(pl* **baby-boomers)** NMF baby boomer; **la génération des baby-boomers** the baby-boom generation

baby-foot [babifut] NM INV *(jeu)* table football; *(table)* football table

Babylone [babilɔn] NM *Géog* Babylon

babylonien, -enne [babilɔnjɛ̃, -ɛn] ADJ Babylonian
□ **Babylonien, -enne** NM,F Babylonian

baby-sitter [bebisitœr] *(pl* **baby-sitters)** NMF baby-sitter

baby-sitting [bebisitiŋ] *(pl* **baby-sittings)** NM baby-sitting; **faire du b.** to baby-sit

baby-test [bebitɛst] *(pl* **baby-tests)** NM developmental test *(for young children)*

bac¹ [bak] NM **1** *Naut* (small) ferry *or* ferryboat **2** *(dans un réfrigérateur)* compartment, tray; **b. à glace** ice-cube tray; **b. à légumes** vegetable compartment **3** *(dans un bureau) Ordinat* **b. d'alimentation (papier)** *(d'une imprimante)* sheet feed; **b. mobile pour dossiers suspendus** *Br* filing trolley, *Am* movable file cabinet; *Ordinat* **b. de** *ou* **à papier, b. de** *ou* **à feuilles** *(d'imprimante)* paper tray **4** *(pour plantes)* **b. (à fleurs)** plant holder; **b. à réserve d'eau** self-watering planter **5** *Com (présentoir)* dumpbin **6** *(fosse, réserve → pour liquides)* tank, vat; *(→ pour stockage de pièces)* container; **b. à douche** shower tray; **b. à sable** *(d'enfant) Br* sandpit, *Am* sandbox; *(pour routes)* grit bin; **b. à sel** salt bin *(for roads)* **7** *Phot (cuvette → vide)* tray; *(→ pleine)* bath
□ **bacs** NMPL **bacs (des disquaires)** = containers holding items in a record store, *Fig* record stores; **son nouvel album est maintenant dans les bacs** his/her new album is out now

bac² NM *Fam Scol (abrév* **baccalauréat)** *(diplôme)* = final secondary school examination, qualifying for university entrance, *Br* ≃ A-levels, *Am* ≃ high school diploma; **b. + 3** *(dans une annonce)* = three years of higher education required

bacante [bakɑ̃t] = **bacchante**

baccalauréat [bakalɔrea] NM *Scol* = final secondary school examination, qualifying for university entrance, *Br* ≃ A-levels, *Am* ≃ high school diploma; **b. international** international baccalaureate; **b. L** *ou* **littéraire** = arts-based baccalauréat; **b. S** *ou* **scientifique** = science-based baccalauréat

---

Culture

BACCALAURÉAT

The "baccalauréat", or "bac", is taken by pupils who have completed their final year at the "lycée"; successful candidates may go to university. Depending on which subjects pupils choose to study at "lycée", they prepare for a "baccalauréat général", "technologique" (vocational) or "professionnel" (vocational and including professional training). Since the last major reform, in 1995, there have been three main types of "baccalauréat général", each corresponding to a specific field: "bac L" (arts subjects), "bac ES" (economics and social studies) and "bac S" (sciences). Pupils study all major subjects for the "bac", each subject being given a particular **coefficient** (see box at this entry) depending on the "baccalauréat" chosen.

---

baccara [bakara] NM *Cartes* baccara, baccarat

Baccarat [bakara] NM *Géog* = town in eastern France, famous for its fine crystalware

baccarat [bakara] NM Baccarat (crystal); **un vase en b.** a Baccarat crystal vase

bacchanale [bakanal] NF *Littéraire (débauche)* drunken revel, bacchanal; *(danse)* bacchanalian dance
□ **bacchanales** NFPL *Antiq & Myth* bacchanalia

bacchante [bakɑ̃t] NF **1** *Antiq & Myth* bacchante, bacchanal **2** *Littéraire Péj (femme)* bacchante
□ **bacchantes** NFPL *Fam Hum* moustache▪, whiskers

Bacchus [bakys] NPR *Myth* Bacchus

baccifère [baksifɛr] ADJ *Bot* bacciferous

bacciforme [baksifɔrm] ADJ *Bot* bacciform

Bach [bak] NPR **Jean-Sébastien** *ou* **Johann Sebastian B.** Johann Sebastian Bach

bâchage [baʃaʒ] NM covering over with a tarpaulin

bâche [baʃ] NF **1** *(toile)* transport cover, canvas sheet, tarpaulin; **bâches imperméables** waterproof tarpaulin **2** *Tech (réservoir)* tank, cistern

bâchée [baʃe] NF *(en Afrique francophone)* canvas-backed van

bachelier, -ère [baʃəlje, -ɛr] NM,F *Scol* = student who has passed the baccalauréat

bâcher [3] [baʃe] VT to cover (with a tarpaulin)
▸ **se bâcher** VPR *Fam* to hit the sack *or* the hay

bachi-bouzouk [baʃibuzuk] *(pl* **bachi-bouzouks)** NM *Fam Hist* Bashi-Bazouk

bachique [baʃik] ADJ Bacchic; **chanson b.** drinking song

bachot [baʃo] NM **1** *(barque)* wherry, skiff **2** *Fam Vieilli Scol* = **baccalauréat**

bachotage [baʃɔtaʒ] NM *Fam Scol & Univ* cramming; **faire du b.** to cram, *Br* to swot up, *Am* to bone up

bachoter [3] [baʃɔte] VI *Fam Scol & Univ* to cram, *Br* to swot up, *Am* to bone up; **il a été obligé de b. dans toutes les matières** he had to cram all the subjects

bachoteur, -euse [baʃɔtœr, -øz] NM,F *Fam Scol & Univ* crammer

bacillaire [basilɛr] *Biol & Méd* ADJ bacillar, bacillary; **malade b.** tubercular patient
▪ NMF tubercular patient

bacillariophycée [basilarjɔfise] NF *Bot* diatom

bacille [basil] NM **1** *Biol & Méd (bactérie)* bacillus; **b. de Koch** Koch's bacillus **2** *Entom* stick insect

bacilliforme [basilifɔrm] ADJ *Biol & Méd* bacilliary

bacilloscopie [basilɔskɔpi] NF *Méd* bacilloscopy

bacillose [basiloz] NF *Méd* pulmonary tuberculosis

bacillurie [basilyri] NF *Méd* bacilluria

backbone [bakbɔn] NM *Ordinat* backbone

backer [3] [bake] VT *Can Joual (aider)* to back

backgammon [bakgamɔn] NM *(jeu)* backgammon

background [bakgrawnd] NM background

back-office [bakɔfis] *(pl* **back-offices)** NM *Banque* back office

bâclage [baklaʒ] NM *Fam (action)* botching; **cette toiture, c'est du b.!** they/you/*etc* made a really shoddy job of that roof!

bâcle [bakl] NF bar *(across a door or window)*

bâclé, -e [bakle] ADJ *Fam* botched; **c'est du travail b.** *(réparation)* it's a botched job; *(devoir)* it's slapdash work

bâcler [3] [bakle] VT *Fam* to botch; **nous avons bâclé les formalités en deux jours** we pushed through the red tape in a couple of days; **on bâcle le ménage et on arrive** we'll give the

house a quick clean and be right there; **b. sa toilette** to give oneself a quick wash▪; **je vais b. les comptes vite fait** I'll throw the accounts together in no time

bacon [bekɔn] NM **1** *(lard)* bacon; *(porc fumé)* smoked loin of pork, Canadian bacon **2** *Can Fam* **avoir du b.** to be loaded

baconien, -enne [bakɔnjɛ̃, -ɛn] ADJ *Phil* Baconian; **induction baconienne** Baconian method

baconisme [bakɔnism] NM *Phil* Baconianism

baconiste [bakɔnist] NMF *Phil* Baconian

bactéricide [bakterisid] *Biol* ADJ bactericidal ▪ NM bactericide

bactérie [bakteri] NF *Biol* bacterium; **bactéries** bacteria

bactériémie [bakterjemi] NF *Méd* bacteraemia

bactérien, -enne [bakterjɛ̃, -ɛn] ADJ *Biol* bacterial

bactériologie [bakterjɔlɔʒi] NF *Biol* bacteriology

bactériologique [bakterjɔlɔʒik] ADJ *Biol* bacteriological

bactériologiste [bakterjɔlɔʒist] NMF *Biol* bacteriologist

bactériolyse [bakterjɔliz] NF *Biol* bacteriolysis

bactériophage [bakterjɔfaʒ] *Biol* ADJ bacteriophage ▪ NM bacteriophage

bactériostatique [bakterjɔstatik] ADJ *Biol* bacteriostatic

badaboum [badabum] ONOMAT *(bruit de chute)* crash!, bang!

badamier [badamje] NM *Bot* Indian almond tree

badaud, -e [bado, -od] NM,F **1** *(curieux)* curious onlooker; *(promeneur)* stroller; **un attroupement de badauds** a crowd of gaping onlookers; **attirer les badauds** to draw a crowd **2** *Ordinat (sur Internet)* lurker

badauder [3] [badode] VI *Littéraire* to stroll about full of idle curiosity

badauderie [badodri] NF *Littéraire* idle curiosity

Bade [bad] NM *Géog* Baden

bader [3] [bade] VT *Fam Arg crime* to check out▪, to scope

baderne [badɛrn] NF *très Fam* **une vieille b.** an old fogy, an old stick-in-the-mud

Bade-Württemberg [badvyrtɛbɛr] NM **le B.** Baden-Württemberg

badge [badʒ] NM **1** *(insigne)* badge; **passer son b. de secouriste** to get one's first-aid badge **2** *(carte magnétique)* swipe card

badger [17] [badʒe] VI to swipe one's card

badgeuse [badʒøz] NF swipe card reader

badiane [badjan] NF *Bot (arbre)* Chinese anise tree; *(fruit)* star anise

badigeon [badiʒɔ̃] NM *Constr (pour l'extérieur)* whitewash; *(pour l'intérieur)* distemper; *(pigmenté)* coloured distemper, *Br* colourwash; **passer du b.** *(pour l'extérieur)* to whitewash sth; *(pour l'intérieur)* to distemper sth

badigeonnage [badiʒɔnaʒ] NM **1** *Constr (de l'extérieur)* whitewashing; *(de l'intérieur)* distempering; *(avec un badigeon pigmenté)* painting with coloured distemper, colourwashing **2** *Méd* painting; **le b. d'une plaie avec de l'alcool** painting a wound with surgical spirit

badigeonner [3] [badiʒɔne] VT **1** *Constr (intérieur)* to distemper; *(extérieur)* to whitewash; *(en couleur)* to paint with coloured distemper, *Br* to colourwash **2** *Méd* to paint; **b. la plaie d'alcool** paint *or* dab surgical spirit liberally onto the wound **3** *Culin* to brush; **b. la pâte de jaune d'œuf** brush the pastry with egg yolk

badigeonneur, -euse [badiʒɔnœr, -øz] NM,F *Constr* painter, whitewasher **2** *Péj Vieilli (peintre amateur)* dauber

badigoinces [badigwɛ̃s] NFPL *très Fam* lips▪; **se lécher les b.** to lick one's lips *or* chops; **se caler les b.** to have a blow-out *or Am* a chow-down

badin¹ [badɛ̃] NM *Aviat* airspeed indicator

badin², -e¹ [badɛ̃, -in] ADJ *(gai)* light-hearted; *(plaisant)* playful; **tenir des propos badins** to (indulge in light-hearted) banter; **répondre d'un ton b.** to answer playfully *or* jokingly

badinage [badinaʒ] NM banter, jesting, badinage

badine² [badin] NF switch, stick

badiner [3] [badine] VI to jest, to banter, to tease;

ne **badine pas avec ta santé** don't trifle with your health; **elle ne badine pas sur le chapitre de l'exactitude** she's very strict about *or* she's a stickler for punctuality

'On ne badine pas avec l'amour' *Musset* 'You Can't Trifle with Love'

Allusion

On ne badine pas avec l'amour

Alfred de Musset's play of this name was written in 1834, after the end of his affair with George Sand. De Musset suffered from his mistress's inconstancy, and the play's title is a warning that lovers have a responsibility to tread carefully, as people can get seriously hurt. In modern French, another word can be substituted for "l'amour", in alluding to anything that should be taken seriously.

badinerie [badinri] NF *Littéraire* jest, badinage

bad-lands [badlɑ̃ds] NFPL *Géol* badlands

badloqué, -e [badloke] ADJ *Can Joual* **être b.** to be unlucky▪

badminton [badmintɔn] NM *Sport* badminton

bâdrage [badraʒ] NM *Can Joual* pain (in the neck)

bâdrant, -e [badrɑ̃, -ɑ̃t] *Can Joual* ADJ annoying▪ NM,F annoying person▪, pain (in the neck)

bâdrer [3] [badre] VT *Can Fam* **b. qn** to bug sb, *Am* to give sb a pain (in the neck)

baes [bas], **baesine** [bazin] NM,F *Belg* **1** *(patron de café)* café owner **2** *(logeur)* landlord of student lodgings

BAFA, Bafa [bafa] NM *(abrév* **brevet d'aptitude aux fonctions d'animation)** = diploma for youth leaders and workers

baffe [baf] NF *Fam* slap▪, clout, smack; **coller une b. à qn** to give sb a smack in the face; **recevoir/ donner une paire de baffes** to get/to give a couple of slaps

baffer [3] [bafe] VT *Fam* to clout, to cuff

Baffin [bafɛ̃] *voir* **terre**

baffle [bafl] NM *(enceinte)* speaker; *Tech* baffle

bafouer [6] [bafwe] VT *(personne)* to ridicule, to jeer at; *(autorité, loi)* to flout, to defy; *(sentiment)* to ridicule, to scoff at

bafouillage [bafujaʒ] NM **1** *(bredouillage)* sputtering, stammering **2** *(propos → incohérents)* gibberish; *(→ inaudibles)* mumblings

bafouille [bafuj] NF *très Fam* letter▪, missive▪

bafouiller [3] [bafuje] VI *(bégayer)* to stutter, to stammer; **la peur le faisait b.** he was so frightened he couldn't talk properly; **tellement embarrassé qu'il en bafouillait** stammering with embarrassment
▪ VT to stammer; **"euh... oui, euh... non", bafouilla-t-elle** "well... yes, well... no", she stammered; **b. des propos incohérents** to talk (a lot of) gibberish

bafouilleur, -euse [bafujœr, -øz] NM,F *(bégayeur)* stammerer; *(personne incohérente)* mumbler

bâfrer [3] [bafre] *très Fam* VT to gobble, to wolf (down); **il a bâfré trois douzaines d'huîtres** he wolfed down three dozen oysters; **elle a tout bâfré** she polished off the lot
▪ VI to stuff one's face, to make a pig of oneself

bâfreur, -euse [bafrœr, -øz] NM,F *très Fam* glutton, greedy guts, *Am* chowhound

bagad [bagad] NM *Mus (formation musicale bretonne)* = group of Breton folk musicians

bagage [bagaʒ] NM **1** *(pour voyager)* baggage (UNCOUNT), luggage (UNCOUNT); **mes bagages** my luggage; **chacun de mes bagages** *(sacs)* each (one) of my bags; *(valises)* each (one) of my suitcases; **il avait pour tout b. un sac et un manteau** he was carrying only a bag and a coat; **faire ses bagages** to pack one's bags; *Fig* **il a fait ses bagages sans demander son reste** he left without further ado; **en b. accompagné** *(expédier, voyager)* as registered baggage; **un seul b. est autorisé en cabine** only one piece of hand-baggage *or* hand-luggage is allowed; **un b. à main** a piece of hand-baggage *or* hand-luggage; **bagages de soute** registered

baggage *(in an aeroplane)* **2** *(formation)* background (knowledge); **son b. scientifique était insuffisant pour faire des études de médecine** his scientific knowledge was insufficient for studying medicine; **en musique, elle a déjà un bon b.** she already has a good grounding in music

bagagerie [bagaʒri] NF luggage room

bagagiste [bagaʒist] NMF **1** *(dans un hôtel)* porter; *(dans un aéroport)* baggage handler **2** *(fabricant)* travel goods manufacturer

bagarre [bagar] NF **1** *(échange de coups)* fight, brawl; **une b. entre ivrognes** a drunken brawl; **la b. est devenue générale** the fight degenerated into a free-for-all; **des bagarres ont éclaté dans la rue** scuffles *or* fighting broke out in the street; **il va y avoir de la b.** there's going to be a fight; **aimer la b.** to like a fight
2 *Fig* battle, fight; **se lancer dans la b. politique** to join the political fray; *Sport* **la b. a été très dure pendant la deuxième mi-temps/le deuxième set** it was a close fight during the second half/set

bagarrer [3] [bagare] VI *(physiquement)* to fight; *(verbalement)* to argue; **elle a bagarré dur pour arriver là où elle est** she fought hard to get where she is; **pour les convaincre, il faut b.** you have to work hard at convincing them
▶ **se bagarrer** VPR **1** *(se combattre)* to fight, to scrap; **ils n'arrêtent pas de se b.** they're always fighting
2 *(se quereller)* to quarrel, to have a scene; **mes parents se bagarraient** my parents used to quarrel
3 *(combattre)* to fight; **il adore se b.** he loves a good fight
4 *Fig* to fight, to struggle; **se b. pour que justice soit faite** to fight *or* to struggle in order to see justice done

bagarreur, -euse [bagarœr, -øz] *Joual* ADJ aggressive▪; **elle a des enfants bagarreurs** her kids are always ready for a scrap
▪ NM,F brawler

bagasse [bagas] NF **1** *(de canne à sucre)* bagasse **2** *(marc de raisin)* marc

bagatelle [bagatɛl] NF **1** *(chose → sans valeur)* trinket, bauble; *(→ sans importance)* trifle, bagatelle; **se fâcher pour une b.** to take offence over nothing; *Ironique* **ça m'a coûté la b. de 5000 euros** it cost me a mere 5,000 euros
2 *Mus* bagatelle
3 *Fam (sexe)* **il est porté/elle est portée sur la b.** he/she likes to play around
▫ **Bagatelle** NF **le parc de B.** = park near Paris famous for its rose gardens

Bagdad [bagdad] NM *Géog* Baghdad

bagel [bagɛl] NM *Can* bagel

bagnard [baɲar] NM *Hist* convict

bagne [baɲ] NM *(prison)* prison; *Hist* penal colony; **condamné à cinq ans de b.** sentenced to five years' penal servitude; *Fig* **c'est le b., ici!** they work you to death in this place!; **son travail, c'est pas le b.!** he's not exactly overworked!

bagnole [baɲɔl] NF *Fam* car▪; **une vieille b.** an old car *or Br* banger

bagou [bagu] = **bagout**

bagouse [baguz] NF *Fam* ring▪

bagout [bagu] NM *Fam* glibness▪; **il a du b.** he has the gift of the gab, he can talk the hind legs off a donkey

bagouze [baguz] = **bagouse**

baguage [bagaʒ] NM **1** *Hort* girdling **2** *Orn* ringing

bague [bag] NF **1** *(bijou)* ring; **passer la b. au doigt à qn** to marry sb; **b. de fiançailles** engagement ring **2** *(d'un champignon)* ring; *(d'un cigare)* band; *(d'une boîte de conserve)* ring-pull **3** *Tech* collar, ring; *Élec* **b. collectrice** collector ring; **b. de roulement** ball race, bearing race; **b. de serrage** jubilee clip

bagué, -e [bage] ADJ **1** *(orné)* ringed, beringed; **doigts bagués d'or** gold-ringed fingers **2** *Archit* ringed; **colonne baguée** ringed column

baguenaude [bagnod] NF *Bot* bladder senna pod

baguenauder [3] [bagnode] *Fam* VI to amble *or* to stroll *or* to drift along

▸**se baguenauder** VPR to amble *or* to stroll *or* to drift along

baguenaudier [bagnodje] NM *Bot* bladder senna

baguer [3] [bage] VT **1** *(oiseau)* to ring; *(doigt)* to put a ring on **2 un cigare bagué d'or** a cigar with a gold band **3** *Tech* to collar **4** *Couture* to baste, to tack

baguette [bagɛt] NF **1** *(petit bâton)* switch, stick; **b. de coudrier** hazel stick *or* switch; **b. divinatoire** *ou* **de sourcier** divining rod; **b. magique** magic wand; *Fig* **d'un coup de b. magique** as if by magic; **elle a les cheveux raides comme des baguettes (de tambour)** her hair is poker straight

2 *Culin (pain)* baguette, French loaf *or Br* stick; *(pour manger)* chopstick; **manger avec des baguettes** to eat with chopsticks

3 *Mus (pour diriger)* baton; **sous la b. du jeune chef** under the baton of the young conductor; **b. de tambour** drumstick; **mener** *ou* **faire marcher qn à la b.** to rule sb with an iron hand *or* a rod of iron

4 *Aut* **b. de protection latérale** side trim

5 *(d'une chaussure)* foxing; *(sur des bas, un collant)* clock

6 *Menuis* length of beading; **cacher les câbles avec des baguettes** to bead in the wires

baguettisant [bagetizɑ̃] NM sorcerer, wizard

baguier [bagje] NM ring case

baguio [bagjo] NM *Météo* typhoon

bah [ba] EXCLAM *(marque l'indifférence)* who cares!; **b., on verra bien!** oh well, we'll have to see!

bahaï [baaj] *Rel* ADJ Bahai

NMF INV Bahai

bahaïsme [baaism] NM *Rel* Bahaism

Bahamas [baamas] NFPL **les B.** the Bahamas; **vivre aux B.** to live in the Bahamas; **aller aux B.** to go to the Bahamas

bahamien, -enne [baamjɛ̃, -ɛn] ADJ Bahamian

❑ **Bahamien, -enne** NM,F Bahamian

Bahreïn [barɛjn], **Bahrayn** [barajn] NM *Géog* Bahrain, Bahrein; **vivre à B.** to live in Bahrain; **aller à B.** to go to Bahrain

bahreïni, -e [barejni] ADJ Bahraini, Bahreini

❑ **Bahreïni, -e** NM,F Bahraini, Bahreini

baht [bat] NM *Fin* baht

bahut [bay] NM **1** *(buffet → gén)* sideboard, buffet; *(→ ancien)* trunk **2** *Fam (collège, lycée)* school▪; **à quelle heure tu retournes au b.?** what time are you going back to school? **3** *Fam (taxi)* taxi▪, cab▪; *(camion)* lorry▪, truck▪; **avance ton b.!** get that heap of junk out of my way!

bai, -e[1] [bɛ] ADJ bay

baie[2] [bɛ] NF **1** *Bot* berry **2** *Archit* opening; **b. vitrée** picture *or* bay window **3** *Géog* bay; **le b. de Baffin** Baffin Bay; **la b. du Biafra** Bight of Biafra; **la b. de Cardigan** Cardigan Bay; **la b. de Chesapeake** Chesapeake Bay; *Hist* **la b. des Cochons** the Bay of Pigs; **la b. de Gdansk** the Gulf of Gdansk; **la b. d'Hudson** Hudson Bay; **la b. de James** James Bay; **la b. de San Francisco** San Francisco Bay **4** *Électron & Tél* rack **5** *Ordinat* bay

baignade [bɛɲad] NF **1** *(activité)* swimming, *Br* bathing; **à l'heure de la b.** at swimming time; **b. interdite** *(sur panneau)* no swimming **2** *(lieu)* swimming *or Br* bathing place; **aménager une b.** to lay out an area for swimming; *(pour bébés)* to lay out an area for paddling

baigner [4] [beɲe] VT **1** *(pour laver) Br* to bath, *Am* to bathe; **c'est l'heure de b. les enfants** it's time *Br* to bath *or Am* to bathe the children; *(pour soigner)* to bathe; **baigne ton doigt malade dans de l'eau chaude** bathe your sore finger in hot water

2 *Littéraire (sujet: fleuve, mer)* to wash, to bathe; **la Seine baigne Paris** the Seine bathes *or* washes Paris; **un rayon de lumière baignait la pièce** light suffused the room, the room was bathed in light; **la clairière était baignée de soleil** the clearing was bathed *or* flooded with sunlight

3 *(mouiller)* to soak, to wet; **un visage baigné de larmes** a face bathed in tears; **il était baigné de sueur après sa course** he was soaked with sweat after the race

VI **1** *(être immergé → dans l'eau, dans le lait)* to soak; *(→ dans l'alcool, dans le vinaigre)* to steep; **des cerises baignant dans l'alcool** cherries steeping *or* soaking in alcohol; **les pommes de terre baignaient dans la sauce** the potatoes were swimming in sauce; **il faut que le tissu baigne complètement dans la teinture** the material must be fully immersed in the dye; **il baignait dans son sang** he was lying in a pool of his own blood

2 *Littéraire (être environné → de brouillard, de brume)* to be shrouded *or* swathed; **le paysage baignait dans la brume** the countryside was shrouded in mist

3 *Fig* **nous baignons dans le mystère** we're deep in mystery; **il baigne dans la joie** he is overwhelmed with joy, he's overjoyed; **elle baigne dans la musique depuis sa jeunesse** she's been immersed in music since she was young

4 *Fam (locution)* **ça** *ou* **tout baigne (dans l'huile)!** everything's great!

▸**se baigner** VPR **1** *(emploi réfléchi)* **se b. les yeux/le visage** to bathe one's eyes/face

2 *(dans une baignoire)* to have *or Am* to take a bath; *(dans un lac, la mer, une piscine)* to have a swim, to go swimming; **je me suis baigné dans la mer Morte** I went swimming in the Dead Sea; **à quelle heure on va se b.?** when are we going swimming?, when are we having a swim?

baigneur, -euse [bɛɲœr, -øz] NM,F swimmer, *Br* bather

NM baby doll

'Les Grandes baigneuses' *Cézanne* 'The Large Bathers'

baignoire [bɛɲwar] NF **1** *(dans une salle de bains)* bathtub, *Br* bath; **b. encastrée** sunken bath; **b. sabot** hip bath; **supplice** *ou* **torture de la b.** torture by immersion **2** *Théât* ground floor box **3** *Mil & Naut* conning tower

Baïkal [baikal] *voir* **lac**

bail [baj] *(pl* **baux** [bo]*)* NM **1** *Jur (de location)* lease; **donner qch à b.** to lease (out) sth; **prendre qch à b.** to take out a lease on sth; **faire/passer un b.** to draw up/to enter into a lease; **renouveler un b.** to renew a lease; **résilier un b.** to cancel a lease; **b. commercial/professionnel/rural** commercial/professional/rural lease; **b. à construction** construction lease; **b. emphytéotique** long lease; **b. à ferme** farm lease; **b. d'habitation** *Br* house-letting lease, *Am* rental lease; **b. à long terme** long-term lease *(18–25 years)*; **b. à loyer** rental agreement, lease; **b. à nourriture** = undertaking to maintain a person for life in return for consideration; **b. à réhabilitation** = contract for the purchase and renovation of private real estate by a housing association

2 *Fam (locution)* **il y a** *ou* **ça fait un b. que...** it's been ages since...; **ça fait un b. qu'il ne m'a pas téléphoné** it's been ages since he last phoned me, he hasn't phoned me for ages

> *Culture*
> **BAIL**
> In France, the usual duration of the "bail", or lease, for private rented accommodation is three years. The expression "bail à céder", often seen on signs in shop windows, means that the lease on the shop or office is for sale.

baille [baj] NF **1** *Naut (baquet, mauvais bateau)* tub **2** *très Fam (eau)* water▪; **tomber** *ou* **se retrouver à la b.** to fall into the drink

❑ **Baille** NF = nickname of the naval academy in Brest

bâillement [bajmɑ̃] NM **1** *(action)* yawn; **étouffer un b.** to stifle a yawn; **des bâillements** yawning *(UNCOUNT)* **2** *(ouverture)* gap

bailler [3] [baje] VT *Arch* to give; **la b. belle** *ou* **bonne à qn** to try to hoodwink sb

bâiller [3] [baje] VI **1** *(ouvrir la bouche)* to yawn; **b. de sommeil/d'ennui/de fatigue** to yawn drowsily/with boredom/with tiredness; **b. à s'en décrocher la mâchoire** *ou* **comme une carpe** to yawn one's head off; **ses discours me font b.** his speeches send me to sleep

2 *(être entrouvert → porte, volet)* to be ajar *or* half-open; *(→ col)* to gape; **son chemisier bâille aux emmanchures** her blouse gapes at the armholes

bailleresse [bajrɛs] *voir* **bailleur**

bâilleuse [bajøz] *voir* **bâilleur**

bâilles [baj] NFPL *Belg* **faire des b.** to yawn

bailleur, -eresse [bajœr, bajrɛs] NM,F *Jur* lessor; **b. de fonds** *(investisseur)* (financial) backer, sponsor; *(associé passif) Br* sleeping partner, *Am* silent partner; **b. de licence** licenser

bâilleur, -euse [bajœr, -øz] NM,F yawner; *Prov* **un bon b. en fait bâiller deux** = one person yawning sets off everyone else

bailli [baji] NM *Hist* bailiff

bailliage [bajaʒ] NM *Hist (circonscription)* bailiwick; *(tribunal)* bailiff's court

bâillon [bajɔ̃] NM *(sur une personne)* gag; **mettre un b. à qn** to gag sb; *Fig* **mettre un b. à l'opposition** to gag *or* to muzzle the opposition

bâillonnement [bajɔnmɑ̃] NM gagging

bâillonner [3] [bajɔne] VT *(otage, victime)* to gag; *Fig (adversaire, opposant)* to gag, to muzzle

bain [bɛ̃] NM **1** *(pour la toilette)* bath, bathing; **donner un b. à qn** to bath sb, to give sb a bath; **prendre un b.** to have *or Am* to take a bath; **vider/faire couler un b.** to empty/to run a bath; **mon b. refroidit** my bath's *or* bathwater's getting cold; **je préfère le b. à la douche** I prefer baths to showers; **b. de bouche** mouthwash, mouth rinse; **b. de boue** mudbath; **b. moussant** bubble bath; **b. parfumé** scented bath; **b. de pieds** footbath; **prendre un b. de pieds** to soak *or* to bathe one's feet (in warm soapy water); **b. de siège** sitz-bath, hip bath; **faire des bains de siège** to take a sitz-bath *or* a hip bath; *Can* **b. tourbillon** whirlpool bath; **b. turc** Turkish bath; **b. de vapeur** steam bath; *Fig* **être dans le b.** *(s'y connaître)* to be in the swing of things; *(être compromis)* to be in it up to one's neck; *Fig* **quand on n'est plus dans le b.** when you've got out of the habit of things; **être dans le même b. (que)** to be in the same boat (as); **mettre deux choses dans le même b.** to lump two things together; **mettre qn dans le b.** *(l'initier)* to put sb in the picture; *(le compromettre)* to drag sb into it; **se mettre** *ou* **se remettre dans le b.** to get (back) into the swing of things *or* the routine

2 *Can (baignoire)* bathtub, *Br* bath

3 b. à remous Jacuzzi®

4 *(activité)* bathing, swimming; **prendre un b.** *(nager)* to have a swim; *(patauger)* to have a paddle; **b. de minuit** midnight swim *or* dip

5 *(à la piscine)* **grand b.** *(bassin)* big pool; *(côté)* deep end; **petit b.** *(bassin)* children's pool; *(côté)* shallow end

6 *Fig (immersion)* **b. de culture** feast of culture; **ce séjour à Paris était un véritable b. de culture** this stay in Paris was a complete cultural experience; **b. de foule** walkabout; **prendre un b. de foule** to go on a walkabout; **b. de jouvence** rejuvenating *or* regenerating experience; **cela a été pour moi un b. de jouvence** it's taken years off me; **b. linguistique** *ou* **de langue** immersion in a language; **b. de sang** bloodbath; **la manifestation s'est terminée dans un b. de sang** the demonstration ended in a bloodbath; **b. de soleil** sunbathing; **prendre un b. de soleil** to sunbathe

7 *(substance pour trempage)* bath; *Phot* **b. d'arrêt** stop bath; *Phot* **b. de développement** developing bath; *Phot* **b. de fixage** fixing bath; *Culin* **b. de friture** deep fat; *Métal* **b. de fusion** (welding) puddle; *Phot* **b. révélateur** developing bath; *Chim* **b. de sable** sandbath; **b. de sels** salt bath; **b. de trempe** quenching bath; *(cuve)* vat

❑ **bains** NMPL *(établissement)* baths; **bains douches** public baths (with showers); **bains turcs** Turkish baths

❑ **de bain** ADJ *(sels, serviette)* bath *(avant n)*

bain-marie [bɛ̃mari] *(pl* **bains-marie***)* *Culin* NM **1** *(processus)* bain-marie cooking **2** *(casserole)* bain-marie

❑ **au bain-marie** ADV in a bain-marie

baïonnette [bajɔnɛt] NF bayonet; **b. au canon** fix bayonet; **ampoule à b.** bulb with a bayonet fitting

baïram [bairam] NM *Rel* Bairam

baisable [bɛzabl] ADJ *Vulg* fuckable, *Br* shaggable

baise [bɛz] NF **1** *Belg (baiser)* kiss **2** *Vulg* **la b.** *(sexe)* sex▪, *Br* shagging

baise-en-ville [bɛzɑ̃vil] **NM INV** *Fam Hum Vieilli* overnight case *or* bag■

baise-la-piastre [bɛzlapjas] **NMF** *Can Fam* skinflint, tightwad

baisemain [bɛzmɛ̃] **NM faire le b. à qn** to kiss sb's hand

baisement [bɛzmɑ̃] **NM** kissing; **le b. de la Croix** the kissing of the Cross

baiser[1] [beze] **NM** kiss; **donner** *ou* **faire/envoyer un b. à qn** to give/to blow sb a kiss; **gros baisers** *(dans une lettre)* love and kisses; **b. d'adieu** parting *or* goodbye *or* farewell kiss; **b. de Judas** kiss of Judas; **b. de paix** kiss of peace

'Le Baiser' *Klimt, Rodin* 'The Kiss'

'Le Baiser au lépreux' *Mauriac* 'The Kiss to the Leper'

'Baisers volés' *Truffaut* 'Stolen Kisses'

baiser[2] [4] [beze] **VT 1** *Littéraire (embrasser)* to kiss; **b. le front/la main de qn** to kiss sb's forehead/hand; **b. la terre** to kiss the ground; *Can Fig Vulg* **b. le cul de la vieille** to come home empty-handed■ *(from a fishing or hunting trip)* **2** *Vulg (coucher avec)* to screw, to fuck; **il est mal baisé** he needs to get laid; **c'est une mal baisée** she's a frustrated old cow **3** *Vulg (tromper)* to shaft, to con; *(vaincre)* to outdo■ ; **se faire b.** to get conned; **on les a baisés à la deuxième mi-temps** we finally got the buggers in the second half **4** *(prendre)* to nab; **ils se sont fait b. par le contrôleur** they got nabbed by the ticket inspector

VI *Vulg* to fuck; **il baise bien** he's a good fuck; **on a bien baisé** we had a good fuck; **b. avec qn** to screw sb

baiseur, -euse [bezœr, -øz] **NM,F** *Vulg* **c'est un sacré b./une sacrée baiseuse** he/she screws around; **c'est un bon b./une bonne baiseuse** he/she's good in bed

baisoter [3] [bɛzɔte] **VT** *Vieilli* to kiss all over

baisse [bɛs] **NF 1** *(des prix, du chômage, du taux de l'inflation)* fall, drop, decline (**de** in); **la b. du dollar** the fall in the value of the dollar; **b. des prix** *(résultat)* fall in prices; *(action)* price cutting; **b. de la production** drop in production

2 *Bourse (des cours, des valeurs)* fall; **le marché des obligations a connu une b. sensible** the bond market has dropped considerably

3 *(de la température, de la tension)* fall, drop (**de** in)

❑ **à la baisse ADJ spéculations à la b.** bear speculations; **le marché est à la b.** the market is falling *or* is bearish **ADV** on the downswing *or* downturn *or* decline; **jouer** *ou* **spéculer à la b.** to bear, to go a bear, to speculate for a fall; **revoir** *ou* **réviser à la b.** to revise downwards

❑ **en baisse ADJ être en b.** *(crédits, fonds)* to be sinking *or* decreasing; *(actions)* to be falling; *(température, nombre d'adhésions)* to be falling *or* dropping; *(popularité)* to be on the decline *or* the wane; **acheter en b.** to buy on a falling market

BAISSER [4] [bese] **VT 1** *(vitre de voiture)* to lower, to wind *or* to let down; *(store)* to lower, to take *or* to let down; *(tableau)* to lower; **il faudra b. l'étagère de deux crans** the shelf will have to be taken down two pegs; *Théât* **le rideau est baissé** the curtain's down; *(boutique)* the iron curtain's down; **b. son pantalon/sa culotte** to pull down one's trousers/knickers; *aussi Fig* **b.** *Fam* **son pantalon** *ou très Fam* **sa culotte (devant qn)** to climb *or* to back down

2 *(main, bras)* to lower; **b. les yeux** *ou* **paupières** to lower one's eyes, to look down, to cast one's eyes down; **b. les yeux (sur qn/qch)** to look down (at sb/sth); **faire b. les yeux à qn** to stare sb out *or* down; **marcher les yeux baissés** *(de tristesse)* to walk with downcast eyes; *(en cherchant)* to walk with one's eyes to the ground; **b. le nez dans/sur son journal** to bury one's head in/to look down at one's newspaper; **il gardait le nez baissé sur sa soupe** he was hunched over his soup; **b. son chapeau sur ses yeux** to pull *or* to tip one's hat over one's eyes; **attention, baisse la tête!** look out, duck!; **les fleurs baissent la tête** the flowers are drooping; **en baissant la tête** *(posture)* with one's head down *or* bent; *(de tristesse)* head bowed (with sorrow); *Fig* **b. la tête** *ou* **le nez (de honte)** to hang one's head (in shame); *Fig* **b. les bras** to throw in the towel

3 *(en intensité, en valeur)* to lower, to turn down; **b. la radio/lumière** to turn the radio/light down; **b. la voix** to lower one's voice; **b. un prix/le loyer** to bring down *or* to lower *or* to reduce a price/the rent; **la concurrence fait b. les prix** competition brings prices down; **faire b. le coût de la vie** to lower *or* reduce *or* bring down the cost of living; **b. le ton** to calm down; *Fam* **baisse le ton!** cool it!, pipe down!

VI *(espoir, lumière)* to fade; *(marée)* to go out; *(soleil)* to go down, to sink; *(température)* to go down, to drop, to fall; *(prix, action boursière)* to drop, to fall; *(stocks)* to be running low; *(santé, faculté)* to decline; *(pouvoir)* to wane, to dwindle, to decline; **la crue baisse** the waters are subsiding; **l'eau a baissé (d'un mètre) dans le bassin** the water level in the pond has gone down (by one metre); **le jour baisse** the daylight's fading; **la qualité baisse** the quality's deteriorating; **nos réserves de sucre ont baissé** our sugar reserves have run low, we're low on sugar; **le dollar a baissé** the dollar has weakened; **ces mesures visent à faire b. les prix du mètre carré** these measures are intended to bring down the price per square metre; **sa vue baisse** his eyesight's fading *or* getting weaker *or* failing; **sa mémoire baisse** her memory's failing; **son travail baisse** his/her work's deteriorating; **il a beaucoup baissé depuis sa maladie** he's deteriorated *or* declined considerably since his illness; **sa voix baissa, et il s'arrêta au milieu de la phrase** his voice trailed off in mid-sentence; **b. dans l'estime de qn** to go down in sb's estimation; **on l'a fait b. à 50 euros** we beat him/her down to 50 euros

►**se baisser VPR 1** *(personne)* to bend down; **il faut se b. pour passer** you have to bend down *or* to stoop to go through; **se b. pour éviter un coup** to duck in order to avoid a blow; **il n'y a qu'à se b. pour les prendre** *ou* **les ramasser** they're *Br* two a penny *or Am* a dime a dozen

2 *(store, vitre)* to go down; **la poignée ne se baisse plus** the handle won't go down now

baissier, -ère [besje, -ɛr] *Bourse* **ADJ** bear *(avant n)*, bearish

NM,F bear

baissière [bɛsjɛr] **NF 1** *Agr* depression, dip *(where rain collects)* **2** *(en viticulture)* lee

bajoue [baʒu] **NF** *Zool* chop, chap

❑ **bajoues NFPL** *Hum* jowls; **il avait des bajoues** he had great big jowls

bajoyer [baʒwaje] **ADJ** *Tech* **mur b.** *(d'écluse)* chamber wall, lateral wall *(of a lock)*; *(de rivière)* river wall

NM 1 *Tech (d'écluse)* chamber wall, lateral wall *(of a lock)*; *(de rivière)* river wall **2** *(d'échelle à poissons)* side *(of fish ladder)*

bakchich [bakʃiʃ] **NM** *Fam (pourboire)* tip■ ; *(pot-de-vin)* bribe■ , *Br* backhander

Bakélite [bakelit] **NF** Bakelite

baklava [baklava] **NM** *Culin* baklava

Bakou [baku] **NM** *Géog* Baku

bakufu [bakufu] **NM** *Hist* Bakufu

BAL, Bal [bal, beaɛl] **NF** *Ordinat (abrév* **boîte aux lettres (électronique)**) e-mail

bal, -als [bal] **NM 1** *(réunion → populaire)* dance; *(→ solennelle)* ball, dance; **b. en plein air** open-air dance; **la tradition des bals de rue** the tradition of dancing in the streets; **aller au b.** to go dancing *or* to a dance; **donner un b.** to give a ball; **b. costumé** fancy-dress ball; **b. masqué** masked ball; **b. musette** dance (with accordion music); **b. populaire** = (local) dance open to the public; **b. travesti** costume ball; **mener le b.** to lead off (at a dance); *Fig* to have the upper hand; **ouvrir le b.** *(être le premier à danser)* to open the ball; *Fig (être le premier à faire quelque chose)* to start the ball rolling

2 *(lieu)* dance hall

'Le Bal du comte d'Orgel' *Radiguet, Allégret* 'Count d'Orgel's Ball' (book), 'The Ball of Count Orgel' (film)

balade [balad] **NF** *Fam* **1** *(promenade → à pied)* walk■ , stroll, ramble; *(→ en voiture)* drive■ , spin; *(→ à vélo, à moto, à cheval)* ride■ ; **faire une b.** *(à pied)* to go for a walk; *(en voiture)* to go for a drive; *(à vélo, à moto, à cheval)* to go for a ride; **être/partir en b.** *(à pied)* to be out for/go (out) for a walk; *(en voiture)* to be out for/go (out) for a drive; *(à vélo, à moto, à cheval)* to be out for/go (out) for a ride

2 *(voyage)* jaunt, trip; **une jolie b. à travers l'Italie** a delightful jaunt across Italy

balader [3] [balade] *Fam* **VT 1** *(promener → enfant, chien)* to take (out) for a walk■ ; *(→ touriste, visiteur)* to take *or* to show around■ ; **je les ai baladés en voiture** I took them (out) for a drive■

2 *(emporter)* to carry■ *or Péj* to cart about; **b. le téléphone d'une pièce à l'autre** to carry the telephone from room to room■

►**se balader VPR 1** *(se promener → à pied)* to stroll *or* to amble along; **se b. sans but** to drift (aimlessly) along; **se b., aller se b.** *(à pied)* to go for a walk■ ; *(en voiture)* to go for a drive■ ; *(à vélo, à moto, à cheval)* to go for a ride■

2 *(voyager)* to go for a trip *or* jaunt; **aller se b. en Espagne** to go for a trip around Spain

3 *(traîner)* to lie around■ ; **ses vêtements se baladent partout** his/her clothes are lying around all over the place; **je n'aime pas les fils électriques qui se baladent** I hate trailing wires; **qu'est-ce que c'est que cette fourchette qui se balade?** what's this fork doing lying around?

baladeur, -euse [baladœr, -øz] **ADJ** *Fam* **être de tempérament b.** to have wanderlust; **il est d'humeur baladeuse ce matin** he just can't stay in one place today; **avoir la main baladeuse** *ou* **les mains baladeuses** to have wandering hands

NM 1 *(Walkman®)* Walkman®, personal stereo; **b. numérique** portable digital music player **2** *Aut* sliding shaft **3** *Tech* sliding gear wheel

❑ **baladeuse NF 1** *(lampe)* inspection *or* portable lamp **2** *Aut* trailer

baladin [baladɛ̃] **NM** *Arch* wandering player, travelling artist

balafon [balafɔ̃] **NM** *Mus* balafo

balafre [balafr] **NF 1** *(entaille)* slash, gash, cut **2** *(cicatrice)* scar; *Hum* **Jojo la B.** ≃ Scarface Joe

balafré, -e [balafre] **ADJ** scarred; **un visage b.** a scarred face

NM,F scarface

balafrer [3] [balafre] **VT** to slash, to gash, to cut

balai [balɛ] **NM 1** *(de ménage)* broom; **b. éponge** mop; **b. mécanique** carpet sweeper; *Fam* **du b.!** scram! **2** *Élec* brush **3** *Aut* **b. d'essuie-glace** *Br* windscreen *or Am* windshield wiper blade **4** *Fam (autobus)* last bus■ ; *(métro)* last underground *or Am* subway train■ **5** *très Fam (année)* year■ ; **il a 50 balais** he's 50■

balai-brosse [balɛbrɔs] *(pl* **balais-brosses**) **NM** (long-handled) *Br* scrubbing *or Am* scrub brush

balaie *etc voir* **balayer**

balais [balɛ] **ADJ M rubis b.** balas *or* spinel ruby

balaise [balɛz] = **balèze**

balalaïka [balalaika] **NF** *Mus* balalaika

balan [balɑ̃] **NM** *Suisse* **être sur le b.** *(être sur le point de tomber)* to be tottering; *(hésiter)* to be indecisive; *(être inquiet quant à son sort)* to wait nervously

Balance [balɑ̃s] **NF 1** *Astron* Libra **2** *Astrol* Libra; **être B.** to be Libra *or* a Libran

balance [balɑ̃s] **NF 1** *(instrument de mesure → gén)* (pair of) scales; *(→ pour pesées délicates)* balance; **monter sur la b.** to stand on the scales; **b. à bascule** weighing machine; **b. électronique** electronic scales; **b. à fléau** beam balance; **b. de ménage** kitchen scales; **b. de précision** precision balance; **b. de Roberval** Roberval's balance; **b. romaine** steelyard; *Fig* **jeter qch dans la b.** to take sth into account, to take account of sth; *Fig* **mettre tout son poids** *ou* **tout mettre dans la b.** to use (all of) one's influence to tip the scales; *Fig* **tenir la b. égale**

entre deux personnes/opinions to strike a balance between two people/opinions

2 *(équilibre)* balance; *Pol* **b. électorale** electoral balance; **b. des forces** *ou* **des pouvoirs** balance of power;

3 *Écon & Compta* balance; **la b. est en excédent** there is a surplus; **faire la b.** to make up the balance sheet; **b. de l'actif et du passif** credit and debit balance, balance of assets and liabilities; **b. âgée** aged debtors; **b. de caisse** cash balance; **b. commerciale** *ou* **du commerce** balance of trade; **b. commerciale déficitaire** trade deficit; **b. commerciale excédentaire** trade surplus; **b. courante** current balance; **b. (générale) des comptes, b. des paiements** balance of payments; **balances sterling** sterling balances *or* holdings

4 *Pêche* crayfish net

5 *Électron* balance; **b. électrodynamique** current balance *or* weigher

6 *Cin & TV* **b. des blancs** white balance

7 *Fam Arg crime (dénonciateur)* squealer, *Br* grass, *Am* rat

❑ **en balance** ADV **mettre deux arguments en b.** to balance two arguments; **mettre en b. toutes les données** to weigh up all the information; **mettre en b. les avantages et les inconvénients** to weigh (up) the pros and cons

❑ **balances** NFPL balances; **balances dollars** dollar balances *or* holdings

balancé, -e [balɑ̃se] ADJ *Fam* **être bien b.** to have a stunning figure; **tout bien b.** all things considered■, taking one thing with another■

balancelle [balɑ̃sɛl] NF **1** *(siège)* swing chair **2** *Naut* balancelle **3** *Tech* swing tray **4** *Belg* footrest

balancement [balɑ̃smɑ̃] NM **1** *(mouvement → d'un train)* sway, swaying; *(→ d'un navire)* pitching, roll, rolling; *(→ de la tête)* swinging; *(→ des hanches)* swaying; *(→ d'une jupe)* swinging **2** *(équilibre)* balance, equilibrium, symmetry **3** *Littéraire (hésitation)* wavering, hesitation

balancer [16] [balɑ̃se] VT **1** *(bras, hanches)* to swing; *(bébé)* to rock; *(personne → dans un hamac)* to push

2 *(compenser)* to counterbalance, to counteract, to cancel out

3 *Fam (se débarrasser de → objet)* to throw away■, to chuck out; **je ne trouve plus sa lettre, j'ai dû la b.** I can't find his/her letter, I must have chucked it out; **b. qch par la fenêtre** to throw *or* to chuck *or* to pitch sth out of the window; **tout b.** to chuck it all in

4 *Fam (se débarrasser de → personne)* **b. qn** to get rid of sb; **ils ont balancé le corps dans la rivière** they dumped the body in the river; **elle a balancé son mec** she's dumped *or* ditched her boyfriend

5 *Fam (donner → coup)* to give■; **b. une gifle à qn** to give sb a slap■, to smack sb in the face; **il lui a balancé un coup de poing** he socked him/her one

6 *(lancer → livre, clefs)* to chuck *or* to toss (over); **balance le journal** can you chuck *or* sling me the paper?

7 *Fam (dire → insulte)* to hurl; **elle n'arrête pas de me b. des trucs vraiment durs** she's always making digs at me; **elle m'a balancé ça en pleine figure** she came out with it just like that

8 *Fam Arg crime (dénoncer → bandit)* to squeal on, *Br* to shop; *(→ complice)* to rat on

9 *Fin (budget, compte)* to balance; **b. les comptes** to balance *or* to make up the books

VI **1** *Littéraire (hésiter)* to waver, to dither; **sans b.** unhesitatingly, unreservedly; *Hum* **entre les deux, mon cœur balance** I can't choose between them

2 *Fam Vieilli* **ça balance** *(boîte de nuit, musique)* it's groovy; **balance, mec!** groove on, man!

►**se balancer** VPR **1** *(osciller → personne)* to rock, to sway; *(→ train)* to roll, to sway; *(→ navire)* to roll, to pitch; *(→ branche)* to sway; **se b. d'un pied sur l'autre** to shift from one foot to the other; **se b. sur sa chaise** to tip back one's chair; *Naut* **se b. sur ses ancres** to ride at anchor

2 *(sur une balançoire)* to swing; *(sur une bascule)* to seesaw; *(au bout d'une corde)* to swing, to dangle; **quand on l'a retrouvé, il se balançait au bout d'une corde** *(pendu)* when they found him, he was swinging from the end of a rope

3 *(se compenser)* to balance; **profits et pertes se balancent** profits and losses cancel each other out, the account balances

4 *Fam (locution)* **je m'en balance** *(je m'en fous)* I don't give a damn; **tes opinions, tout le monde s'en balance!** who gives a damn about what you think?

balancier [balɑ̃sje] NM **1** *(de moteur)* beam, rocker arm; *(d'horloge)* pendulum; *(de montre)* balance wheel; *(autour d'un axe)* walking beam; **retour de b.** backlash **2** *(de funambule)* pole **3** *Zool* balancer, haltere

balancine [balɑ̃sin] NF **1** *Aviat & Naut* topping lift **2** *Can Fam (balançoire)* swing■

balançoire [balɑ̃swar] NF **1** *(suspendue)* swing; **faire de la b.** to have a (go on the) swing, to play on the swing **2** *(bascule)* seesaw

balane [balan] NF *Zool (crustacé)* acorn barnacle, acorn shell

balanite [balanit] NF *Méd* balanitis

balanoglosse [balanoglɔs] NM *Zool* Balanoglossus

balata [balata] NM *Bot* balata-tree, bully-tree

NF balata (gum); **courroie en b.** balata belt

Balaton [balatɔ̃] *voir* **lac**

balayage [balɛjaʒ] NM **1** *(d'un sol, d'une pièce)* sweeping; *(d'épluchures, de copeaux)* sweeping up

2 *(avec un projecteur, un radar)* scanning, sweeping; **b. d'une zone/du ciel avec un faisceau lumineux** scanning an area/the sky with a light beam

3 *(de la chevelure)* highlighting; **se faire faire un b.** to get one's hair highlighted, to get highlights in one's hair

4 *Électron* scanning, sweep, sweeping; **circuit/fréquence/vitesse de b.** sweep current/frequency/speed

5 *Ordinat* scanning; **b. de ligne** row scanning; **b. télévision** *ou* **de trame** raster scan

balayer [11] [baleje] VT **1** *(nettoyer → sol, pièce)* to sweep (up *or* out); *(→ tapis)* to brush, to sweep; **le sol a besoin d'être balayé** the floor could do with a sweep

2 *(pousser → feuilles, nuages)* to sweep (along *or* away *or* up); *(→ poussière, épluchures, copeaux)* to sweep up *or* away; **le vent balayait les feuilles** the wind swept the leaves along *or* away; **balayé par le vent** windswept; **balayant les jetons de la main** *(pour les ramasser)* sweeping up the tokens with his/her hand; *(pour les éloigner)* sweeping the tokens away with his/her hand

3 *(parcourir → sujet: vent, tir)* to sweep (across *or* over); *(→ sujet: faisceau, regard)* to sweep, to scan; *(→ sujet: caméra)* to pan across; **les vagues balayaient la jetée** the waves were sweeping (over) the jetty; **ses grandes ailes balayaient le sol** its large wings swept the ground; **ses yeux balayèrent l'assemblée** he scanned the audience; **les branches/les avirons balayaient l'eau** the branches brushed/the oars trailed on the surface of the water

4 *(détruire → obstacles, préjugés)* to sweep away *or* aside; *(repousser → objections, critiques)* to brush aside; **la monarchie a été balayée par la révolution** the monarchy was swept aside by the revolution; **b. l'ennemi hors de ses positions** to sweep the enemy out of its positions; **les ouragans balaient tout sur leur passage** the hurricanes sweep away everything in their path

5 *Fam (renvoyer)* to push out, to get rid of; **il va falloir me b. ces incapables!** these incompetents have got to go!

6 *Électron* to scan

VI to sweep up; **il faudra b. ici** this place needs a good sweep; *Fig* **b. devant chez soi** *ou* **sa porte** to set one's own house in order

balayette [balɛjɛt] NF brush

balayeur, -euse [balɛjœr, -øz] NM,F street *or* road sweeper

❑ **balayeuse** NF **1** *(machine)* road-sweeping machine **2** *Can (aspirateur)* vacuum cleaner, *Br* Hoover®

balayures [balejyr] NFPL sweepings

balboa [balboa] NM *(monnaie)* balboa

balbutiant, -e [balbysjɑ̃, -ɑ̃t] ADJ **1** *(hésitant)* stuttering, stammering; **il répondit, tout b.** he stammered an answer **2** *(récent)* **c'est une technique encore balbutiante** it's a technique that's still in its infancy

balbutiement [balbysimɑ̃] NM stammer, stutter; **balbutiements** *(d'un bègue)* stammering, stuttering; *(d'un ivrogne)* slurred speech; *(d'un bébé)* babbling

❑ **balbutiements** NMPL *(d'une technique, d'un art)* early stages, beginnings, infancy; **l'informatique n'en était alors qu'à ses (premiers) balbutiements** IT was then only in its infancy *or* in its early stages

balbutier [9] [balbysje] VI **1** *(bègue)* to stammer, to stutter; *(ivrogne)* to slur (one's speech); *(bébé)* to babble; **la timidité le fait b.** he's so shy he stammers; **j'en balbutiais d'ahurissement** I was so astonished (that) I was stuck for words

2 *(débuter)* to be just starting *or* in its early stages *or* in its infancy

VT to stammer (out); **b. des remerciements** to stammer out one's thanks; **b. une prière** to mumble a prayer

balbuzard [balbyzar] NM *Orn Br* osprey, *Am* fish eagle *or* hawk

balcon [balkɔ̃] NM **1** *(plate-forme)* balcony **2** *(balustrade)* railings, railing **3** *Théât* balcony; **premier b.** dress circle; **deuxième b.** upper circle; **dernier b.** gallery

balconnet [balkɔnɛ] NM **1** *(balustrade)* overhanging railing **2 (soutien-gorge à) b.** half-cup bra

balconville [balkɔ̃vij] NM *Can Hum* **passer les vacances en b.** to spend one's holidays at home

baldaquin [baldakɛ̃] NM **1** *(sur un lit)* canopy, tester **2** *(sur un autel, un trône)* canopy, baldachin, baldachino

Bâle [bal] NM *Géog* Basel, Basle; **le canton de B.** Basel; **le demi-canton de B.-Ville** Basel-Stadt; **le demi-canton de B.-Campagne** Basel-Land

bale [bal] NF *Bot & Agr* **la b.** the chaff, the husks

Baléares [balear] NFPL *Géog* Baleares; **les (îles) B.** the Balearic Islands; **aux B.** in the Balearic Islands

baleine [balɛn] NF **1** *Zool* whale; **b. blanche** beluga (whale); **b. bleue** blue whale; **b. à bosse** humpback whale; **b. franche** right whale; *Fam* **rire** *ou* **rigoler** *ou* **se tordre comme une b.** to split one's sides laughing **2** *(fanon)* whalebone, baleen **3** *(de parapluie)* rib **4** *(de corset → en plastique)* bone, stay; *(→ en métal)* steel; *(→ en fanon)* (whalebone) stay **5** *(pour un col)* collar stiffener

baleiné, -e [balene] ADJ **1** *(corset, gaine)* boned **2** *(col)* stiffened

baleineau, -x [balɛno] NM *Zool* whale calf

baleinier, -ère [balenje, -ɛr] ADJ whaling; **industrie baleinière** whaling (industry); **port b.** whaling station

NM **1** *(navire)* whaling ship, whaler **2** *(chasseur)* whaler

❑ **baleinière** NF **1** *Naut* lifeboat **2** *Pêche* whaleboat, whaler, whale catcher

balénoptère [balenɔptɛr] *Zool* NM finback (whale), rorqual (whale)

❑ **balénoptères** NMPL Balaenopteridae

balestron [balɛstrɔ̃] NM *Naut* sprit

balèvre [balɛvr] NF *Constr* lip

balèze [balɛz] *Fam* ADJ **1** *(grand)* hefty, huge■; **un type b.** a great hulk (of a man) **2** *(doué)* great■, brilliant■; **b. en physique** ace *or Br* dead good at physics **3** *(difficile)* tough, tricky

NMF *(homme)* big guy; *(femme)* big woman■; **un gros** *ou* **grand b.** a great hulk (of a man)

Bali [bali] NF *Géog* Bali; **à B.** in Bali

balier [9] [balje] *Can Fam* VT *(nettoyer → sol, pièce)* to sweep (up *or* out)■; *(→ tapis)* to brush■, to sweep■

VI to sweep up■

balinais, -e [balinɛ, -ɛz] ADJ Balinese

❑ **Balinais, -e** NM,F Balinese; **les B.** the Balinese

balisage [balizaʒ] NM **1** *(signaux → en mer)* markers, beacons, buoyage; *(→ aériens)* lights, markers; *(→ sur route)* markers, road markers; **b. d'aéroport** airport lights; **b. d'entrée de piste** airway markers; **b. maritime** navigational markers; *Aviat* **b. des bords de piste** runway lights; **b. des pistes d'approche** landing area lights

2 *(pose → de signaux, de signes)* marking out; *Ordinat (d'un texte)* tagging; **b. par radars** beacon signalling

balise [baliz] NF **1** *Naut* beacon, (marker) buoy; **b. de guidage** radar beacon; *(sur route)* road marker cone, police cone; *(sur sentier)* waymark; **b. maritime** navigational marker; **b. radio** (radio) beacon; *Aviat* marker, beacon **2** *Ordinat (d'un texte)* tag; **b. de début** opening tag; **b. de fin** closing tag **3** *Bot* canna fruit

baliser [3] [balize] VT **1** *Naut* to mark out, to buoy
2 *Aviat* **b. une piste** to mark out a runway with lights
3 *(trajet)* to mark out *or* off; **b. une voie (pour l'interdire à la circulation)** to cone off a lane (from traffic); **balisé de drapeaux/piquets** marked out with flags/poles; **sentier balisé** waymarked path
4 *Ordinat (texte)* to tag
VI *très Fam* to be scared stiff; **ça me fait b. rien que d'y penser** the very thought of it scares me stiff

baliseur [balizœr] NM *Naut* **1** *(navire)* buoy *or* lighthouse tender, *Br* Trinity House boat **2** *(personne)* buoy keeper

balisier [balizje] NM *Bot* canna

baliste[1] [balist] NF *Antiq* ballista

baliste[2] [balist] NM *Ich* triggerfish, filefish

balisticien, -enne [balistisjɛ̃, -ɛn] NM,F ballistics expert

balistique [balistik] ADJ ballistic
NF ballistics *(singulier)*

balivage [balivaʒ] NM staddling

baliveau, -x [balivo] NM **1** *Constr* scaffold *or* scaffolding pole **2** *(arbre)* sapling

balivernes [balivɛrn] NFPL **1** *(propos)* nonsense (UNCOUNT); **ce sont des b.** it's all nonsense; **raconter des b.** to talk nonsense **2** *(bagatelles)* trivia *(pl)*, trifles; **s'inquiéter pour des b.** to worry over trivial details

balkanique [balkanik] ADJ Balkan

balkanisation [balkanizasjɔ̃] NF **1** *Pol* Balkanization **2** *(fragmentation)* parcelling off into tiny units

balkaniser [3] [balkanize] VT **1** *Pol* to Balkanize **2** *(fragmenter)* to parcel off into tiny units

Balkans [balkɑ̃] NMPL **les B.** the Balkans; **vivre aux B.** to live in the Balkans; **aller aux B.** to go to the Balkans

ballade [balad] NF *Littérature & Mus* **1** *(poème narratif, chanson)* ballad **2** *(poème court à forme fixe, pièce musicale)* ballade

═══════════════

'La Ballade de Bruno' *Herzog* 'Stroszek'

───────────────

ballant, -e [balɑ̃, -ɑ̃t] ADJ *(jambes)* dangling; *(poitrine)* wobbling; **il était debout, les bras ballants** he stood with his arms dangling at his sides; **ne reste pas là, les bras ballants** don't just stand there like an idiot
NM **1** *(mouvement) (d'un véhicule)* sway, roll **2** *Naut (d'un cordage)* slack; **donner du b. à un câble** to give a cable some slack, to slacken off a cable

ballast [balast] NM **1** *Naut* ballast tank *or* container **2** *Constr & Rail* ballast

ballastage [balastaʒ] NM *Naut & Rail* ballasting

ballaster [3] [balaste] VT *Naut & Rail* to ballast

ballastière [balastjɛr] NF gravel pit, stone quarry

balle [bal] NF **1** *(d'arme)* bullet; **tirer à balles réelles** to shoot with real bullets; **se tirer une b. dans la bouche/tête** to shoot oneself in the mouth/head; **tué par balles** shot dead; **b. à blanc** blank; **b. en caoutchouc** rubber bullet; **b. dum-dum** dum-dum bullet; **b. perdue** stray bullet; **b. traçante** tracer bullet
2 *(pour jouer)* ball; **jouer à la b.** to play with a ball; **la b., la b.!** *(dans les jeux d'équipe)* over here, over here!; *Fig* **la b. est dans son camp** the ball's in his/her court; **b. de caoutchouc** rubber ball; **b. de golf** golf ball; *Can* **b. molle** *(sport)* softball; **b. au mur** handball; *Can* **b. de neige** snowball; **b. de tennis** tennis ball
3 *(point, coup)* stroke, shot; **une belle b.** a fine stroke *or* shot; *Tennis* **faire des balles** to practise, *Br* to knock up; *Tennis* **b. de jeu/match** game/match point; **b. nulle** no-ball
4 *(paquet)* bale
5 *Bot & Agr* **la b.** the chaff, the husks
6 *Fam (visage)* face■; **avoir une bonne b.** to have a friendly face

7 *Fam (locutions)* **c'est de la b.!** *Br* it's absolutely wicked!, *Am* it's totally awesome!; **trop de la b., ce film** *Br* that film's wicked!, *Am* that movie's awesome!
❑ **balles** NFPL **1** *Anciennement Fam* **t'as pas cent balles?** *(un ancien franc)* have you got one franc?■; *(monnaie)* can you spare some change?■; **j'ai dépensé cent balles aujourd'hui** I've spent a tenner today; **200 balles** 200 francs■
2 *Fam* **à deux balles** *(médiocre)* pathetic, lame; **une excuse à deux balles** a lame excuse; **de la philosophie/psychologie à deux balles** pop philosophy/psychology

baller [3] [bale] VI *Littéraire (bras, jambe)* to dangle

ballerine [balrin] NF **1** *(danseuse)* ballerina, ballet dancer **2** *(chaussure → de danse)* ballet *or* dancing shoe; *(→ de ville)* pump

ballet [balɛ] NM *Mus & Théât* **1** *(genre)* ballet (dancing)
2 *(œuvre)* ballet (music); *(spectacle)* ballet; **le b. blanc** classical ballet *(in white tutus)*; *Hist* **b. de cour** court entertainment *(danced by the monarch and courtiers)*; *Euph* **ballets roses/bleus** = sexual orgies between adults and female/male minors; *Fig* **l'incident a donné lieu à tout un b. diplomatique** the incident has given rise to intense diplomatic activity; **les Ballets russes** the Ballets Russes
3 *(troupe)* ballet company
4 *Sport* **b. aquatique** aquashow, *Am* aquacade

balletomane [balɛtɔman] NMF ballet lover, *Sout* balletomane

ballet-pantomime [balɛpɑ̃tɔmim] *(pl* **ballets-pantomimes**) NM *Mus & Théât* pantomime ballet

ballon [balɔ̃] NM **1** *Sport* ball; **jouer au b.** to play with a ball; **b. de basket** basketball; **b. de foot** *ou* **football** football; **b. de rugby** rugby ball; **le b. ovale** *(le rugby)* rugby; **le b. rond** *(le foot)* soccer, *Br* football; **son premier b.** the first time that he's/she's touched the ball
2 *(sphère)* **b. (de baudruche)** (party) balloon; **b. d'hélium** helium balloon; **b. d'oxygène** *Méd* oxygen tank; *Fig* life-saver
3 *Aviat (hot-air)* balloon; **monter en b.** *(ascension)* to go up in a balloon; **b. de barrage** barrage balloon; **b. captif** captive balloon; **b. dirigeable** airship, dirigible; **b. d'essai** pilot balloon; *Fig* test; **lancer un b. d'essai** *(se renseigner)* to put out feelers; *(faire un essai)* to do a trial run, to run a test; **b. libre** free balloon
4 *Chim* round-bottomed flask, balloon; *(pour l'Alcotest®)* (breathalyser) bag; *Fam* **on m'a fait souffler dans le b.** I was breathalysed■, I was made to blow into the bag
5 *(verre)* (round) wine glass, balloon glass; *(contenu)* glassful; **b. de rouge** glass of red wine; **il boit son b. de blanc tous les matins** he has a little glass of white wine every morning
6 *(réservoir)* **b. (d'eau chaude)** hot water tank
7 *Géog* **les ballons** the (rounded tops of the) Vosges mountains; **le b. d'Alsace/de Guebwiller** the Ballon d'Alsace/de Guebwiller
8 *Suisse (petit pain)* (bread) roll
9 *Suisse (de vin)* = decilitre of wine
10 *très Fam (location)* **avoir le b.** to have a bun in the oven

ballonné, -e [balɔne] ADJ bloated; **être b.** to feel bloated

ballonnement [balɔnmɑ̃] NM **1** *Méd* distension (UNCOUNT), flatulence (UNCOUNT); **j'ai des ballonnements** I feel bloated **2** *Vét* bloat

ballonner [3] [balɔne] VT to swell

ballonnet [balɔnɛ] NM **1** *Aviat* ballonet **2** small balloon

ballon-panier [balɔ̃panje] NM INV *Can Sport* basketball

ballon-sonde [balɔ̃sɔ̃d] *(pl* **ballons-sondes**) NM *Météo* sounding balloon

ballot [balo] NM **1** *(paquet)* bundle, package **2** *Fam (sot)* nitwit, blockhead; **cette espèce de b. n'avait rien compris** the poor fool hadn't got the idea at all

ballote [balɔt] NF *Bot* black *or* stinking horehound

ballotin [balɔtɛ̃] NM *Br* sweet *or Am* candy box; **un b. de chocolats** a small box of chocolates

ballottage [balɔtaʒ] NM *Pol* **il y a b. à Tours** there will be a second ballot in Tours; **être en b.** to

have to *Br* stand *or Am* run again in a second round

ballottement [balɔtmɑ̃] NM *(d'un véhicule)* rocking, swaying, shaking; *(d'un navire)* tossing (about); *(d'un passager, d'un sac)* shaking about, tossing about; *(d'un radeau)* tossing, bobbing about

ballotter [3] [balɔte] VT *(véhicule)* to rock, to sway, to shake; *(navire)* to toss (about); *(passager, sac)* to shake about, to toss about; *(radeau)* to toss, to bob about; **les détritus ballottés par les vagues** refuse bobbing up and down in the waves; *Fig* **être ballotté entre deux endroits** to be shifted *or* shunted around constantly from one place to the other; **être ballotté entre deux personnes** to waver between two people; **être ballotté par les événements** to be carried along by events
VI *(tête)* to loll, to sway; *(valise)* to bang *or* to shake about, to rattle around; *(poitrine)* to bounce (up and down)

ballottine [balɔtin] NF *Culin* stuffed and boned meat roll, ballottine

balloune [balun] NF *Can Joual* balloon■; *(de savon)* bubble■; **souffler dans la b.** to be breathalysed, to blow into the bag; *Fig* **prendre** *ou* **virer une b., partir en b.** to get trashed; **être en b.** *(enceinte)* to be knocked up *or* in the club

ball-trap [baltrap] *(pl* **ball-traps**) NM **1** *(tir → à une cible)* trapshooting, clay-pigeon shooting; *(→ à deux cibles)* skeet, skeet shooting **2** *(appareil)* trap

balluchon [balyʃɔ̃] NM bundle; *aussi Fig* **faire son b.** to pack one's bags

balnéaire [balneɛr] ADJ seaside *(avant n)*

balnéothérapie [balneɔterapi] NF *Méd* balneotherapy

BALO [beaɛlo] NM *(abrév* **Bulletin des Annonces Légales et Obligatoires)** = publication in which listed companies must make compulsory legal announcements, such as accounts and notice of annual general meetings

baloche [balɔʃ] NM *Fam* local dance■

bâlois, -e [balwa, -az] ADJ of/from Basel
❑ **Bâlois, -e** NM,F = inhabitant of or person from Basel

baloney [balɔni] NM *Can Joual* baloney (sausage)

balourd, -e [balur, -urd] ADJ *(physiquement)* clumsy; *(dans ses paroles, son comportement)* awkward; **qu'il est b. quand il veut demander un service!** he's so awkward when he wants to ask a favour!
NM,F *(physiquement)* clumsy person; *(dans ses paroles, son comportement)* awkward person
NM *Tech* unbalance

balourdise [balurdiz] NF **1** *(caractère → physiquement)* clumsiness; *(→ dans ses paroles, son comportement)* awkwardness **2** *(parole, acte)* blunder, gaffe; **dire des balourdises** to say the wrong thing

baloutchi [balutʃi] NM *(langue)* Baluchi

Baloutchistan [balutʃistɑ̃], **Béloutchistan** [belutʃistɑ̃] NM **le B.** Baluchistan

balsa [balza] NM *Bot* balsa, balsawood

balsamier [balzamje] NM *Bot* balsam tree

balsamine [balzamin] NF *Bot* balsam, busy Lizzie

balsamique [balzamik] ADJ **1** *Bot & Méd* balsamic **2** *Littéraire (odorant)* fragrant, scented
NM balsam

balte [balt] ADJ Baltic; **les pays Baltes** the Baltic states; **les républiques baltes** the Baltic republics
NM *Ling* Baltic
❑ **Balte** NMF Balt

Balthazar [baltazar] NPR *Bible* Balthazar

balthazar [baltazar] NM *(bouteille)* Balthazar

baltique [baltik] ADJ Baltic
NM *Ling* Baltic
❑ **Baltique** NF **la B.** the Baltic (Sea); **les ports de la B.** the Baltic ports

baluchithérium [balyʃiterjɔm] NM *Zool (en paléonthologie)* indricotherium, baluchitherium

baluchon [balyʃɔ̃] = **balluchon**

balustrade [balystrad] NF *(d'un balcon)* balustrade; *(d'un pont)* railing

balustre [balystr] NM **1** *(pilier → de balustrade, de siège)* baluster **2** *(compas)* pair of compasses *(with spring bow dividers)* **3** *Can (dans une église)* = railing separating the chancel from

the nave; *Fam Fig Péj* **mangeur de b.** *(homme)* Holy Joe; *(femme)* Holy Mary

balzacien, -enne [balzasjɛ̃, -ɛn] **ADJ un héros b.** *Littérature* a hero in a Balzac novel; *Fig* a hero reminiscent of Balzac; **une description balzacienne** *Littérature* a description from a Balzac novel; *Fig* a description reminiscent of Balzac

balzan, -e [balzɑ̃, -an] **ADJ** white-stockinged
□ **balzane NF** *(d'un cheval)* white stocking (of a horse)

Bamako [bamako] **NM** *Géog* Bamako

bambin [bɑ̃bɛ̃] **NM** *Fam* toddler, tot

bambochade [bɑ̃bɔʃad] **NF** *Beaux-Arts* bambocciade

bambochard, -e [bɑ̃bɔʃar, -ard] = **bambocheur**

bamboche [bɑ̃bɔʃ] **NF** *Fam Vieilli* partying; **c'est la b. ce soir!** it's party-time tonight!; **faire b.** to party

bambocher [3] [bɑ̃bɔʃe] **VI** *Fam Vieilli* to party; **à l'époque où je bambochais** in the days when I was always partying; **il adore b.** he's always ready for a good night out

bambocheur, -euse [bɑ̃bɔʃœr, -øz] *Fam Vieilli* **ADJ être b.** to enjoy partying; **c'est un type très b.** he really enjoys partying **NM,F** partygoer, reveller▪

bambou [bɑ̃bu] **NM** *Bot* bamboo; *Fam* **attraper un coup de b.** to get sunstroke▪; *Fam* **avoir le coup de b.** *(devenir fou)* to crack up, to go nuts; *(être fatigué)* to be wiped or *Br* shattered or *Am* pooped; *Fam* **c'est le coup de b. dans ce restaurant!** *(très cher)* this restaurant costs an arm and a leg or *Br* a packet
□ **en bambou ADJ** *(meuble, cloison)* bamboo *(avant n)*

bamboula [bɑ̃bula] **NF** *très Fam (fête)* wild party; **faire la b.** to party

bambouseraie [bɑ̃buzrɛ] **NF** bamboo plantation

ban [bɑ̃] **NM** **1** *(applaudissements)* **un b. pour...!** three cheers or a big hand for...!
2 *(roulement de tambour)* drum roll; *Fig* **fermer le b.** to bring the proceedings to a close; *Fig* **ouvrir le b.** to open the proceedings; *(sonnerie de clairon)* bugle call
3 *Hist (condamnation)* banishment, banning; *(convocation)* ban; *(vassaux)* vassals; *Fig* **le b. et l'arrière-b.** the world and his wife; **convoquer le b. et l'arrière-b.** to summon the (entire) family
4 *Arch (proclamation)* (public) proclamation
□ **bans NMPL** *(de mariage)* banns; **les bans sont affichés** ou **publiés** the banns have been posted or published
□ **à ban ADV** *Suisse* **mettre qch à b.** to forbid access to sth
□ **au ban ADV** **mettre qn au b.** to banish sb
□ **au ban de PRÉP** **être au b. de la société** to be an outcast or a pariah; **mettre un pays au b. des nations** to boycott a country; **mettre qn au b. d'un club** to blackball sb

banal, -e, -als, -ales [banal] **ADJ 1** *(courant)* commonplace, ordinary, everyday *(avant n)*; **ce n'est vraiment pas b.** it's most unusual, it's really strange
2 *(sans originalité → idée, histoire, situation)* trite, banal; *(→ objet)* everyday *(avant n)*; *(→ argument)* standard, well-worn; *(→ vie)* humdrum, mundane; *(→ événement)* everyday *(avant n)*; *(→ événement)* everyday **ce que je vais vous dire là est très b.** there's nothing original or unusual about what I'm going to say
3 *Ordinat* general-purpose
4 *Hist (moulin, fournil)* communal

banalement [banalmɑ̃] **ADV** in an ordinary way; **nous nous sommes rencontrés fort b.** we met in very ordinary or unremarkable circumstances

banalisation [banalizasjɔ̃] **NF 1** *(généralisation)* spread; *Péj (perte d'originalité)* trivialization; **la b. des transports aériens** the fact that air travel has become commonplace or has become an everyday phenomenon; **son exposé est une b. des idées de Lacan** his account trivializes Lacan's ideas
2 *(d'un véhicule)* **la b. des voitures de police** the use of unmarked police cars
3 *Rail (d'une voie)* signalling for two-way working; *(d'une locomotive)* use of engine by several crews

banalisé, -e [banalize] **ADJ 1** *(véhicule)* unmarked
2 *Ordinat* general-purpose

banaliser [3] [banalize] **VT 1** *(rendre courant → pratique)* to trivialize, to make commonplace; **maintenant que la téléphonie sans fil est banalisée** now that cordless phones have become commonplace
2 *Péj (œuvre)* to deprive or to rob of originality; *(idée)* to turn into a commonplace
3 *(véhicule)* to remove the markings from; *(marque déposée)* to turn into a household name
4 *Rail (voie)* to signal for two-way working; *(locomotive)* to man with several crews
▶**se banaliser VPR** to become commonplace or a part of (everyday) life; **les achats en-ligne se sont banalisés** online shopping is now part of everyday life

banalité [banalite] **NF 1** *(d'une idée, d'une histoire, d'une situation)* triteness, banality; *(d'un objet, d'un événement)* everydayness; *(d'un argument)* triteness, banality, triviality; *(de la vie)* mundanity; *(d'une tenue)* ordinariness **2** *(propos, écrit)* platitude, commonplace, cliché **3** *Hist (d'un moulin, d'un fournil)* communalism

banana split [bananasplit] **NM INV** *Culin* banana split

banane [banan] **NF 1** *Bot (fruit)* banana; **b. plantain** ou **jaune** plantain; **b. verte** green banana **2** *Fam (pare-chocs)* overrider▪ **3** *Fam (coiffure) Br* quiff **4** *Fam (hélicoptère)* chopper **5** *Fam (décoration)* medal▪; *Br* gong **6** *(sac) Br* bum bag, *Am* fanny pack **7** *Élec* banana plug **8** *très Fam (idiot)* nitwit, *Br* twit, *Am* dumbbell
ADJ INV banana-shaped

bananeraie [bananrɛ] **NF** *Bot* banana plantation or grove

bananier, -ère [bananje, -ɛr] **ADJ** banana *(avant n)*
NM 1 *Bot* banana, banana tree **2** *Naut* banana boat

banat [bana] **NM** *Hist* Banat, Banate

banc [bɑ̃] **NM 1** *(siège)* bench, seat; *Jur* **b. des accusés** dock; **au b. des accusés** in the dock; *Jur* **le b. des avocats** the lawyers' bench; **b. d'église** pew; **b. des joueurs** *Sport* player's bench; **sur le b. des ministres** on the government bench; **b. des pénalités** penalty box; **b. public** park bench; **b. des punitions** penalty box; *Jur* **(au) b. des témoins** *Br* (in the) witness box, *Am* (on the) witness stand; **sur les bancs de l'école** in one's schooldays; **ils se sont connus sur les bancs de l'école** they got to know each other at school
2 *Menuis & Tech (établi)* bench, workbench; *(bâti)* frame, bed
3 *Cin & TV* **b. de montage** editing desk
4 *Ordinat* bank; **b. de mémoire** memory bank
5 *Naut* (oarsman's) bench, thwart
6 *(de poissons)* shoal, school; **b. de harengs** herring shoal; **b. de maquereaux** school of mackerel; **b. de morues** cod bank or shoal; **b. de sardines** school or shoal of sardines; **b. d'huîtres** *(dans la mer)* oyster bed; *(dans un restaurant)* display of oysters; **b. de homards** lobster ground; **b. de pêche** fishing bank or ground
7 *(amas)* bank; **b. de boue** mudbank, mudflats; **b. de brume** fog patch; **b. de glace** ice floe; **b. de gravier** gravel bank; *Can* **b. de neige** snowdrift; *(entassé mécaniquement)* bank of snow; **b. de sable** sandbank, sandbar
8 *Géol (couche)* bed, layer; *(au fond de la mer)* bank, shoal
□ **banc d'essai NM** *Ind* test rig, test bed; *Mktg* benchtest; *Ordinat* benchmark; *Fig* test; **faire un b. d'essai** *(un test en action)* to have a trial run; **mettre qn au b. d'essai** to give sb a test; **mettre une idée au b. d'essai** to test out an idea; *Aut* **b. d'essai à rouleaux** road simulator

bancable [bɑ̃kabl] **ADJ** *Com (effet)* bankable; **non b.** unbankable

bancaire [bɑ̃kɛr] **ADJ** *Banque (commission, crédit, dépôt, frais, prêt)* bank *(avant n)*; *(opération)* banking

bancal, -e, -als, -ales [bɑ̃kal] **ADJ 1** *(meuble)* rickety, wobbly; *(personne)* lame **2** *(peu cohérent → idée, projet)* unsound; *(→ raisonnement)*

weak, unsound; **la proposition est un peu bancale** the proposal doesn't really stand up to examination

bancarisation [bɑ̃karizasjɔ̃] **NF** *Banque* **le taux de b.** the number of bank account holders; **la b. de l'économie** the growing role of banks in the economy; **la b. de la population française** the growing number of bank account holders in France

bancarisé, -e [bɑ̃karize] **ADJ** *Banque* **être b.** to have an account with a bank, to use the banking system

bancassurance [bɑ̃kasyrɑ̃s] **NF** *Banque* bancassurance

bancassureur [bɑ̃kasyrœr] **NM** *Banque* insurance banker, bancassurer

bancatique [bɑ̃katik] **NF** *Banque* electronic or computerized banking *(UNCOUNT)*

banchage [bɑ̃ʃaʒ] **NM** *Constr* placing concrete in forms

banche [bɑ̃ʃ] **NF** *Constr* form, shutter *(for moulding concrete)*

bancher [3] [bɑ̃ʃe] **VT** *Constr* to place in forms; **béton banché** = concrete moulded with timber or steel forms

banco [bɑ̃ko] **NM** banco; **faire b.** to go banco

bancomat [bɑ̃koma] **NM** *Suisse Br* cashpoint, *Am* ATM

bancoulier [bɑ̃kulje] **NM** *Bot* candleberry tree, candlenut (tree)

bancroche [bɑ̃krɔʃ] **ADJ** *Fam* lame▪, *Am* gimpy

banc-titre [bɑ̃titr] *(pl* **bancs-titres)** **NM** *Cin & TV* rostrum camera

bandage [bɑ̃daʒ] **NM 1** *Méd (pansement)* bandage, dressing; **il faut resserrer le b.** the bandage should be tightened; **b. abdominal** abdominal bandage or binder; **b. fenêtré** fenestrated bandage; **b. herniaire** truss **2** *(fait de panser)* bandaging, binding (up) **3** *(fait de tendre → un ressort)* stretching, tensing; *(→ un arc)* bending, drawing **4** *Aut & Rail (en caoutchouc)* tyre; *(en métal)* hoop, band

bandagiste [bɑ̃daʒist] **NMF** bandage manufacturer

bandana [bɑ̃dana] **NM** *Tex* bandana, bandanna

bandant, -e [bɑ̃dɑ̃, -ɑ̃t] **ADJ** *Vulg* exciting▪; **elle est bandante** she's a real turn-on; *Hum (sens affaibli)* **pas très b. comme boulot!** this job's hardly the most exciting thing going!

BANDE [bɑ̃d]

gang, group **A1** ▪ band **A1, B1, 3, 5, 8, 12–14** ▪ bunch **A2** ▪ strip **B1, 2** ▪ reel **B4** ▪ bandage **B7** ▪ cushion **B11** ▪ list, heel **C**

NF A. 1 *(groupe → de malfaiteurs)* gang; *(→ d'amis)* group; *(→ d'enfants)* troop, band; *(→ d'animaux)* herd; *(→ de chiens, de loups)* pack; **faire partie de la b.** to be one of the group; **b. armée** armed gang or band; **la b. à Bonnot** = group of anarchists led by Jules Joseph Bonnot who carried out terrorist attacks on several banks in the 1900s; **la B. noire** the Bande Noire group *(group of early 20th Century naturalist painters who depicted scenes of harsh Breton life)*; **b. organisée** organized (criminal) gang; **la B. des Quatre** the Gang of Four; *Péj* **une b. de** a pack or bunch of; *Fam* **une b. de menteurs/voleurs** a bunch of liars/crooks; *très Fam* **vous y comprenez rien, b. de cons!** you just don't get it, do you, you *Br* bloody or *Am* goddamn idiots!
2 *(locutions)* **il fait toujours b. à part** he keeps (himself) to himself; **il a encore décidé de faire b. à part** he's decided yet again to go it alone; **ceux de Bel-Air font b. à part** those who come from Bel-Air stick together

B. 1 *(d'étoffe, de papier etc)* strip, band; **b. gommée** gummed binding strip; **b. de journal** newspaper wrapper; **b. molletière** puttee, putty; **b. publicitaire** *(autour d'un livre)* belly band; *Aut* **b. de roulement** tyre tread
2 *(de territoire)* strip; *Transp* **b. d'arrêt d'urgence** emergency lane, hard shoulder; **b. de sable** strip or spit or tongue of sand; **b. de terrain** strip of land
3 *(sur une route)* band, stripe; **b. blanche** white line
4 *Cin* reel; *Cin & Phot* **b. amorce** start or head

leader; **b. audionumérique** digital audio tape, DAT; **b. démo** demo tape; **b. latérale** sideband; **b. (magnétique)** (magnetic) tape; **b. magnétique audio** audio tape; **b. mère** master tape; **b. originale** soundtrack; **b. parole** dialogue track; **b. son magnétique** magnetic soundtrack; **b. sonore** soundtrack; **b. vidéo** videotape

5 *Électron & Rad* band; **b. de fréquence** frequency band; **b. (de fréquence) publique** Citizens' Band, CB; **sur la b. FM** on FM; **b. passante** pass-band

6 *Ordinat* **b. de défilement** scroll bar; **b. perforée** perforated tape, *Br* punched paper tape

7 *Méd* bandage; **b. Velpeau** crêpe bandage, *Am* Ace bandage®

8 *Archit* band

9 *Littérature* **b. dessinée** *(dans un magazine)* comic strip, *Br* (strip) cartoon; *(livre)* comic book; **la b. dessinée** *(genre)* comic strips, *Br* (strip) cartoons; **l'auteur d'une b. dessinée célèbre** the author of a well-known comic book; **magazine** *ou* **revue de bandes dessinées** comic

10 *Mil* **b. de mitrailleuse** machinegun belt

11 *(au billard)* cushion; **jouer la b.** to play off the cushion

12 *Biol* **b. chromosomique** chromosome band

13 *Phys* **b. de fréquences** frequency band

14 *Fin (d'une monnaie)* **b. de fluctuation** fluctuation band

C. *Naut* list, heel; **donner de la b.** to heel over, to list.

❏ **en bande** ADV as *or* in a group, all together; **ils ne se déplacent qu'en b.** they always go around in a gang

❏ **par la bande** ADV in a roundabout way; **apprendre qch par la b.** to learn sth through the grapevine; **faire qch par la b.** to do sth underhandedly

bandé, -e [bɑ̃de] ADJ **1** *(recouvert)* bandaged; **avoir les yeux bandés** to be blindfolded; **pieds bandés** bound *or* bound-up feet **2** *Hér* bendy **3** *(tendu)* stretched, tensed

bande-annonce [bɑ̃danɔ̃s] *(pl* **bandes-annonces)** NF *Cin* trailer; **la b. de son dernier film** the trailer for his/her last film

bandeau, -x [bɑ̃do] NM *(serre-tête)* headband

2 *(coiffure)* coiled hair; **avoir les cheveux en b., porter des bandeaux** = to wear one's hair parted in the middle and swept back round the sides

3 *(sur les yeux)* blindfold; *(sur un œil)* eye patch; **avoir un b. sur les yeux** to be blindfolded; *Fig* to be blind to reality

4 *Archit* string *or* belt course

5 *Journ (titre)* streamer

6 *Mktg (espace publicitaire)* advertising space *(in the shape of a band around a vehicle)*; *Ordinat (dans un site Web)* banner; **b. publicitaire** banner advertisement

7 *Aut* (piece of) capping

bandelette [bɑ̃dlɛt] NF **1** *(bande)* strip; **les bandelettes d'une momie** the wrappings of a mummy **2** *Anat* **b. optique** optic tract **3** *Archit* bandelet

bander [3] [bɑ̃de] VT **1** *(panser → main, cheville)* to bandage (up); **b. les yeux à qn** *(pour qu'il ne voie pas)* to blindfold sb; **avoir les yeux bandés** *Méd* to have one's eyes bandaged; *(avec un bandeau)* to be blindfolded

2 *(tendre → arc)* to draw, to bend; *(→ ressort, câble)* to stretch, to tense; *Littéraire (muscle)* to tense, to tauten; **b. ses forces** to gather up *or* to muster one's strength; **bandant toutes ses forces vers ce seul but** his/her whole being directed towards that goal

3 *Archit* to arch, to vault

VI *Vulg* to have a hard-on; **ça me fait b.** it gives me a hard-on; **il bande pour elle** he's got the hots for her, she really turns him on *or* gives him the horn; *(sens affaibli)* **ça me fait pas b.** it doesn't turn me on

bandera [bɑ̃dera] NF *Mil* bandera

banderille [bɑ̃drij] NF banderilla

banderillero [bɑ̃derijero] NM banderillero

banderole [bɑ̃drɔl] NF **1** *(bannière → sur un mât, une lance)* banderole; *(→ en décoration)* streamer; *(→ dans une manifestation)* banner **2** *Archit* banderole

bande-son [bɑ̃dsɔ̃] *(pl* **bandes-son)** NF soundtrack

bandicoot [bɑ̃dikut] NM *Zool* bandicoot rat

bandit [bɑ̃di] NM **1** *(brigand)* bandit; *(gangster)* gangster; **b. de grand(s) chemin(s)** highwayman **2** *(escroc)* crook, conman; **b., va!** *(dit avec affection)* you rogue *or* rascal!

banditisme [bɑ̃ditism] NM crime; *Fig* **c'est du b.!** it's daylight robbery!; **grand b.** organized crime

bandonéon [bɑ̃dɔneɔ̃] NM *Mus* bandoneon

bandothèque [bɑ̃dɔtɛk] NF tape library

bandouiller [3] [bɑ̃duje] VI *Vulg* to have a semi

bandoulière [bɑ̃duljɛr] NF **1** *(d'une arme)* sling; *(à cartouches)* bandolier

2 *(d'un sac)* shoulder strap

❏ **en bandoulière** ADV **porter un sac en b.** to carry a shoulder bag; **porter une guitare en b.** to carry a guitar slung across one's back; **on peut aussi le mettre en b.** you can also wear it over your shoulder; **son fusil en b.** his gun slung across his chest

bang¹ [bɑ̃] NM *(franchissement du mur du son)* sonic boom

EXCLAM bang!, crash!; **b., b., t'es mort!** bang, bang, you're dead!; **et b., tout est tombé par terre!** and then crash, everything was on the floor!

bang² [bɑ̃] NM *Fam Arg drogue (pipe à eau)* bong

bangiée [bɑ̃ʒje] *Bot* NF Bangiophyte

❏ **bangiées** NFPL Bangiophycidae

bangiophycée [bɑ̃ʒjofise] *Bot* NF Bangiophyte

❏ **bangiophycées** NFPL Bangiophycidae

Bangkok [bɑ̃kɔk] NM *Géog* Bangkok

bangladais, -e [bɑ̃gladɛ, -ɛz] ADJ Bangladeshi

❏ **Bangladais, -e** NM,F Bangladeshi

Bangladesh [bɑ̃gladɛʃ] NM **le B.** Bangladesh; **vivre au B.** to live in Bangladesh; **aller au B.** to go to Bangladesh

Bangladeshi [bɑ̃gladɛʃi] = **bangladais**

Bangui [bɑ̃gi] NM *Géog* Bangui

banian [banjɑ̃] NM *Bot* banyan

banjo [bɑ̃(d)ʒo] NM *Mus* banjo

banjoïste [bɑ̃(d)ʒɔist] NMF *Mus* banjoist

Banjul [bɑ̃ʒul] NM *Géog* Banjul

banlieue [bɑ̃ljø] NF suburb; **la b.** the suburbs; **la maison est en b.** the house is on the outskirts of the town *or* in the suburbs; **vivre en b.** to live in the suburbs; **une b. de Londres** a suburb of London; **une b. cossue** a prosperous suburb; **b. pavillonnaire** = suburb with lots of little houses of uniform appearance; **la b. rouge** = towns in the Paris suburbs with Communist mayors; **b. verte** garden suburb; **grande b.** = outer suburbs; **proche b.** inner suburbs; *Fam* **des loubards de b.** *Br* yobs *or* *Am* hoods from the suburbs

NM *Belg Transp* commuter train

> ### Culture
> **BANLIEUE**
> In France the word "banlieue" often refers not to the upmarket areas of a city – as the word "suburbia" suggests in English-speaking countries – but to the impoverished suburban areas on the outskirts of some cities. These neighbourhoods are culturally and ethnically diverse and are frequently associated with social problems such as delinquency, unemployment and unrest. In November 2005, following the accidental death of two youths who were being chased by the police, unprecedented rioting erupted in many French cities, with gangs of youths burning cars and fighting the police for nearly three weeks running. The riots highlighted issues of discrimination and lack of opportunity among people from immigrant backgrounds in French society.

---

banlieusard, -e [bɑ̃ljøzar, -ard] ADJ *Péj* suburban

NM,F *(gén)* suburbanite; *Transp* commuter; **les banlieusards** = people who live in the suburbs

banne [ban] NF **1** *(auvent)* awning, tilt **2** *(charrette)* cart **3** *(panier)* (wicker) basket

banneret [banrɛ] NM *Hist* banneret

banneton [bantɔ̃] NM **1** *(de boulanger)* (baker's) bread-basket **2** *Pêche* corf

bannette [banɛt] NF **1** *(panier)* small hamper, basket **2** *Naut (couchette)* bunk

banni, -e [bani] ADJ banished, exiled

NM,F exile

bannière [banjɛr] NF **1** *(étendard)* banner; **la b. étoilée** the Star-spangled Banner; **combattre** *ou* **lutter sous la b. de qn** to fight on sb's side; **se ranger sous la b. de** to join the ranks of **2** *Vieilli (de chemise)* shirt-tail; **se balader en b.** to go about in one's shirt-tails **3** *Ordinat (dans un site Web)* banner; **b. publicitaire** banner advertisement

bannir [32] [banir] VT **1** *(expulser)* to banish, to exile

2 *Littéraire (éloigner)* to reject, to cast out; **b. qn de sa présence** to cast sb from one's presence; **banni à jamais de mes relations** forever banished from my circle of friends

3 *(supprimer → idée, pensée)* to banish; *(→ aliment)* to cut out; **j'ai banni cette idée** I banished *or* dismissed the idea from my mind; **bannissez la violence de vos comportements** banish all violence from your behaviour; **il a complètement banni la cigarette** he has completely given up smoking; **vous devez b. le sucre de votre alimentation** you must exclude sugar from your diet, you must cut sugar out of your diet

bannissement [banismɑ̃] NM banishment

banon [banɔ̃] NM = cheese made from unpasteurized goat's *or* ewe's milk and wrapped in chestnut leaves, produced in Provence

banquable [bɑ̃kabl] = **bancable**

banque [bɑ̃k] NF *Banque* **1** *(établissement)* bank; **avoir une somme à la** *ou* **en b.** to have some money in the bank; **mettre une somme à la b.** to bank a sum of money; **passer à la b.** to go to the bank; **b. d'acceptation** *Br* accepting *or* *Am* acceptance house; **b. d'affaires** investment bank, *Br* merchant bank; **b. centrale** central bank; **b. de clearing** clearing bank; **b. commerciale** commercial bank; **b. de compensation** clearing bank; **b. confirmatrice** confirming bank; **b. de crédit** credit bank; **b. de dépôt** deposit bank; **b. de détail** retail bank; **b. émettrice** *ou* **d'émission** issuing bank *or* house; **b. d'épargne** savings bank; **b. d'escompte** discount house *or* bank; **b. de gestion de patrimoine** trust bank; **b. de gros** wholesale bank; **b. hypothécaire** mortgage bank; **b. industrielle** industrial bank; **b. d'investissement** investment bank, *Br* merchant bank; **b. notificatrice** advising bank; **b. de placement** issuing bank *or* house; **b. privée** private bank; **b. de recouvrement** collecting agency *or* bank; **la B. d'Angleterre** the Bank of England; **B. centrale européenne** European Central Bank; **B. européenne d'investissement** European Investment Bank; **B. européenne pour la reconstruction et le développement** European Bank for Reconstruction and Development; **la B. de France** the Banque de France, = French issuing bank; **B. française du commerce extérieur** French foreign trade bank; **B. internationale pour la reconstruction et le développement** International Bank for Reconstruction and Development; **la B. mondiale** the World Bank; **B. des règlements internationaux** Bank for International Settlements

2 *(activité, secteur)* banking; **travailler dans la b.** to be *or* work in banking; *Vieilli* **la haute b.** high finance; **b. à distance** remote banking; **b. à domicile** telebanking, home banking; **b. électronique** e-banking; **b. d'entreprise** corporate banking; **b. en ligne** e-banking; **b. universelle** global banking

3 *(centre de collecte)* bank; **b. alimentaire** food bank; **b. d'organes** organ bank; **b. du sang/du sperme** blood/sperm bank; **b. des yeux** eye bank

4 *Ordinat, Rad & TV* **b. de données** data bank; **b. d'images** picture data bank; **b. de programmes** programme library, programme archives

5 *(à un jeu → réserve)* bank; **tenir la b.** to be the banker, to keep the bank; **faire sauter la b.** to break the bank

banquer [3] [bɑ̃ke] VI *très Fam* to fork out; **qui va b.?** who's going to foot the bill?; **à toi de b.** your turn to cough up

banqueroute [bɑ̃krut] NF *Fin (faillite)* bankruptcy; **faire b.** to go bankrupt; **b. frauduleuse** fraudulent bankruptcy; **b. simple** bankruptcy *(with irregularities amounting to a breach of the law)* **2** *(échec)* failure; **la b. d'une politique** the

utter failure of a policy; **critiquant la b. de notre société** criticizing our bankrupt society

banqueroutier, -ère [bɑ̃krutje, -ɛr] NM,F *Fin* bankrupt; *(frauduleux)* fraudulent bankrupt

banquet [bɑ̃kɛ] NM banquet; **donner un b.** to give a banquet; **faire un b.** to have *or* to hold a banquet; **la campagne des banquets** = Guizot's ban on reformist banquets in 1848 which was the prelude to the revolution

'Le Banquet' *Platon* 'The Symposium'

banqueter [27] [bɑ̃ktə] VI 1 *(bien manger)* to feast, to eat lavishly 2 *(prendre part à un banquet)* to banquet

banquette [bɑ̃kɛt] NF 1 *(siège → de salon)* seat, *Am* banquette; *(→ de piano)* (duet) stool; *(→ de restaurant)* wall seat; *(→ de voiture, de métro)* seat; **b. avant/arrière** front/back seat; *Fig* **jouer devant les banquettes** to play to an empty house 2 *Archit* window seat 3 *Tech* berm; **b. de halage** towpath 4 *(sur une route)* = kerb separating a bus lane from the rest of the roadway 5 *Rail* track bench 6 *Mil* **b. de tir** banquette

banquette-lit [bɑ̃kɛtli] *(pl* **banquettes-lits)** NF studio couch

banquier, -ère [bɑ̃kje, -ɛr] NM,F banker; **b. d'affaires** investment banker, *Br* merchant banker; **b. escompteur** discounting banker; **b. prêteur** lending banker

banquise [bɑ̃kiz] NF *Géol (côtière)* ice, ice shelf; *(dérivante)* pack ice, ice field *or* floe

banquiste [bɑ̃kist] NM *(forain)* barker

banteng [bɑ̃tɛn] NM *Zool* banteng

bantou, -e [bɑ̃tu] ADJ Bantu
  NM *(langue)* Bantu
  ❏ **Bantou, -e** NM,F Bantu; **les Bantous** the Bantu *or* Bantus

bantoustan [bɑ̃tustɑ̃] NM *Hist* Bantustan, Bantu Homeland

banyuls [baɲuls] NM *(vin)* Banyuls (wine)

baobab [baɔbab] NM *Bot* baobab

Bapaume [bapom] NM *Géog* = scene of General Faidherbe's victory over the Prussians in 1871

baptême [batɛm] NM 1 *Rel* baptism; *(cérémonie)* christening, baptism; **donner le b. à qn** to baptize *or* to christen sb; **recevoir le b.** to be baptized *or* christened; **b. civil** civil baptism, ≃ naming ceremony
  2 *(d'un bateau)* christening, naming; *(d'une cloche)* blessing, dedication
  3 *(première expérience)* **b. de l'air** first *or* maiden flight; *Mil & Fig* **b. du feu** baptism of fire; **maintenant que tu as eu ton b. du feu** now you've been blooded; **b. de la ligne** (first) crossing of the line
  4 *Belg* = **bizutage**
  EXCLAM *Can Fam* goddammit!

baptisé, -e [batize] ADJ *Rel* baptized

baptiser [3] [batize] VT 1 *Rel* to christen, to baptize 2 *(personne, animal → nommer)* to name, to call; *(→ surnommer)* to nickname, to christen, to dub; **elle a baptisé son chien Victor** she named her dog Victor 3 *(bateau)* to christen, to name; *(cloche)* to bless, to dedicate 4 *Fam (diluer → vin, eau)* to water down

baptismal, -e, -aux, -ales [batismal, -o] ADJ baptismal

baptisme [batism] NM *Rel* Baptist doctrine

baptistaire [batistɛr] ADJ *Rel* **registre b.** register of baptisms; **extrait b.** certificate of baptism

baptiste [batist] ADJ *Rel* baptist
  NM,F *Rel* Baptist; **les baptistes** the Baptists 2 *Can Fam (Canadien français)* = nickname given to French Canadians (from their patron saint, John the Baptist)

baptistère [batistɛr] NM *Rel* baptistery

baquais, -e [bakɛ, -ɛz] = **baquet²**

baquer [3] [bake] VT *Can Joual (aider)* to back
  ▸ **se baquer** VPR *Fam* to go for a dip

baquèse, baquesse [bakɛs] *voir* **baquet²**

baquet¹ [bakɛ] NM 1 *(récipient)* tub 2 *(siège)* bucket seat

baquet², -èsse *ou* **-esse** [bakɛ, -ɛz, -ɛs] *Can Fam* NM,F *(homme trapu)* stubby man; *(femme trapue)* stubby woman
  ❏ **baquèse, baquesse** NF *Hum* 1 *(épouse)* other half 2 *(partenaire de danse)* partner■

bar [bar] NM 1 *(café)* bar; *Suisse* **b. à café** café; **b. à thème** theme bar; **b. à vin** wine bar 2 *(comptoir)* bar; **le prix au b. n'est pas le même que le prix en salle** the price for eating or drinking at the bar is not the same as the price in the rest of the establishment 3 *Ich* (European) sea bass; **b. tacheté** spotted sea bass 4 *Phys* bar

Barabbas [barabas] NPR *Bible* Barabbas

barachois [baraʃwa] NM *Can* sandbar *(at river mouth)*

baragouin [baragwɛ̃] NM *Fam* 1 *(langage incompréhensible)* jargon, gobbledegook, *Br* double-Dutch 2 *Péj (langue étrangère)* lingo

baragouinage [baragwinaʒ] NM *Fam* 1 *(manière de parler)* jabbering, gibbering 2 *(jargon)* jargon, gobbledegook

baragouiner [3] [baragwine] *Fam* VT *(langue)* to speak badly■; *(discours)* to gabble; **je baragouine l'espagnol** I can barely put two words of Spanish together; **qu'est-ce qu'elle baragouine?** *(langue étrangère)* what's that language she's jabbering in?; *(propos incompréhensibles)* what's she jabbering on about?
  VI *(de façon incompréhensible)* to jabber, to gibber, to talk gibberish; *(dans une langue étrangère)* to jabber away

baragouineur, -euse [baragwinœr, -øz] NM,F *Fam* jabberer, gabbler

baraka [baraka] NF 1 *Rel (dans l'Islam)* baraka 2 *Fam (chance)* luck■; **avoir la b.** to be lucky■ *or Br* jammy; **il a la b. en ce moment** he's on a winning streak at the moment

baraque [barak] NF *Archit* 1 *(cabane → à outils)* shed; *(→ d'ouvriers, de pêcheurs)* shelter, hut; *(→ de forains)* stall; *(→ de vente)* stall, stand, booth
  2 *Fam (maison)* shack, shanty; **une vieille b.** an old shack; **une b. minuscule** a rabbit hutch of a house; **t'en as une belle b.!** you've got a great place!; **une grande b. au bord de la mer** a big place by the sea; **qui commande dans cette b.?** who the hell's in charge around here?; **j'en ai marre de cette b.!** I've had enough of this place!

baraqué, -e [barake] ADJ *Fam* muscular■, hefty, *Péj* beefy; **un type b.** a great hulk of a man

baraquement [barakmɑ̃] NM 1 *(baraques)* shacks 2 *Mil* camp

baraquer [3] [barake] VI *(chameau)* to kneel down

barasingha [barasiŋga] NM *Zool* barasingha, swamp deer

baraterie [baratri] NF *Jur (criminelle)* barratry; *(simple)* fault

baratin [baratɛ̃] NM *Fam (pour vendre)* sales talk, patter, spiel; **b. publicitaire** sales pitch; *(pour convaincre)* flannel; *(pour draguer)* sweet *or* smooth talk, *Br* patter; **avoir du b.** to be a smooth talker; **faire du b. à qn** *(pour convaincre)* to flannel sb; *(pour draguer) Br* to chat sb up, *Am* to hit on sb

baratiner [3] [baratine] *Fam* VI *(parler beaucoup)* to chatter; *(mentir)* to flannel
  VT **b. qn** *(pour vendre)* to give sb the sales pitch *or* patter *or* spiel; *(pour convaincre) Br* to flannel sb; *(pour séduire) Br* to chat sb up, *Am* to hit on sb

baratineur, -euse [baratinœr, -øz] *Fam* ADJ *(menteur, séducteur)* smooth-talking; **il est très b.** he's a real smooth talker
  NM,F 1 *(séducteur)* smooth talker 2 *(menteur)* fibber

barattage [barataʒ] NM churning

baratte [barat] NF churn

baratter [3] [barate] VT to churn

barbacane [barbakan] NF 1 *Constr* weep hole, weeper 2 *Hist (construction)* barbican; *(meurtrière)* loophole

Barbade [barbad] NF **la B.** Barbados; **vivre à la B.** to live in Barbados; **aller à la B.** to go to Barbados; **de la B.** Barbadian

barbant, -e [barbɑ̃, -ɑ̃t] ADJ *Fam* boring■; **il est b.** he's a drag *or* bore; **l'émission était barbante** the programme was boring■ *or* a drag

barbaque [barbak] NF *très Fam (viande)* meat■; *Péj* tough meat■

barbare [barbar] ADJ 1 *Hist (primitif)* barbarian, barbaric 2 *(terme, emploi)* incorrect 3 *(cruel)* barbaric
  NM,F barbarian

barbarée [barbare] NF *Bot* winter cress

barbaresque [barbarɛsk] *Hist* ADJ Barbary *(avant n)*; **les États barbaresques** the Barbary states; **les pirates barbaresques** the Barbary Coast pirates
  ❏ **Barbaresque** NMF = inhabitant of or person from Barbary

Barbarie [barbari] NF *Hist* **la B.** Barbary

barbarie [barbari] NF 1 *(cruauté)* barbarity, barbarousness; **acte de b.** barbarous act 2 *Hist (état primitif)* barbarism

barbarisme [barbarism] NM barbarism

barbe¹ [barb] NM *(cheval)* barb

barbe² [barb] NF 1 *(d'homme → drue)* (full) beard; *(→ clairsemée)* stubble; *(→ en pointe)* goatee; **avoir de la b.** *(homme)* to need a shave; *(adolescent)* to have some hairs on one's chin; **porter la b.** to have a beard; **se faire la b.** to (have a) shave; **se raser/se tailler la b.** to shave off/to trim one's beard; **un homme à la b. rousse** a red-bearded man, a man with a red beard; **sans b.** *(rasé)* beardless, clean-shaven; *(imberbe)* beardless, smooth-chinned; **b. de deux jours** two days' stubble *or* growth; **b. à papa** *Br* candy floss, *Am* cotton candy; **fausse b.** false beard; **femme à b.** bearded woman; *Littéraire* **du côté de la b.** on the male side; **vieille b.** (old) stick-in-the-mud, old fogy; *Fam* **rien que des vieilles barbes** a bunch of *Br* wrinklies *or Am* greybeards; *Fam* **il n'a pas encore de b. au menton** he's still wet behind the ears; *Fam Hum* **elle a une longue b. blanche, cette plaisanterie!** that joke's got whiskers!; *Fam* **c'est la b.!, quelle b.!** what a drag *or* bore!; *Fam* **la b.!** *(pour faire taire)* shut up!, shut your mouth!, shut your trap!; *(pour protester)* damn!, hell!, blast!; **parler dans sa b.** to mutter under one's breath; **il a marmonné quelque chose dans sa b.** he muttered something under his breath; **rire dans sa b.** to laugh up one's sleeve; **faire qch à la b. de qn** to do sth under sb's very nose
  2 *(d'animal)* tuft of hairs, beard
  3 *Bot* beard, awn
  4 *(filament → de plume)* barb; *(→ de coton)* tuft; *(→ de métal, de plastique)* burr
  5 *Tech* beard, bolt toe
  ❏ **barbes** NFPL *(de papier)* ragged edge; *(d'encre)* smudge
  ❏ **en barbe** ADV *Naut* **mouiller en b.** to moor with two anchors ahead

barbeau, -x [barbo] NM 1 *Ich* barbel 2 *très Fam (souteneur)* pimp 3 *Bot* cornflower, bluebottle

Barbe-Bleue [barbəblø] NPR Bluebeard

barbecue [barbəkju] NM 1 *(appareil)* barbecue (set); **faire cuire de la viande au b.** to barbecue meat 2 *(repas)* barbecue; **faire un b.** to have a barbecue; *Can* **poulet b.** barbecued chicken

barbe-de-capucin [barbdəkapysɛ̃] *(pl* **barbes-de-capucin)** NF *Bot* wild chicory

barbelé, -e [barbəle] ADJ barbed
  NM *Br* barbed wire, *Am* barbwire; **derrière les barbelés** behind the *Br* barbed wire *or Am* barbwire

barbelure [barbəlyr] NF 1 *Bot* awn, beard *(of wheat)* 2 *(d'une flèche)* barb

barber [3] [barbe] *Fam* VT 1 *(lasser)* to bore■; **je vais lui écrire, mais ça me barbe!** I'll write to him/her, but what a drag! 2 *(importuner)* to hassle; **ne me barbe pas avec ces histoires!** don't hassle me with this stuff!
  ▸ **se barber** VPR to be bored stiff *or* to tears *or* to death; **qu'est-ce qu'on se barbe ici!** this place is so boring *or* a total drag!■

Barberousse [barbərus] NPR Barbarossa

Barbès [barbɛs] NM *Géog* = district in north Paris with a large North African immigrant population

barbet, -ette [barbɛ, -ɛt] NM,F *Zool (chien)* water spaniel
  NM *Ich voir* **rouget**
  ❏ **barbette** NF 1 *(vêtement)* barb 2 *Mil* barbette

barbeuc, barbeuk [barbœk] NM *Fam (barbecue)* BBQ, *Br & Austr* barbie

barbeux, -euse [barbø, -øz] *Can Fam* ADJ **être b.** to be a pain (in the neck)
  NM pain (in the neck)

barbiche [barbiʃ] NF goatee

barbichette [barbiʃɛt] NF (small) goatee

barbichu, -e [barbiʃy] *Fam* ADJ bearded■, with a goatee (beard)■
NM man with a goatee (beard)■

barbier [barbje] NM *Can & Vieilli* barber

'Le Barbier de Séville' *Beaumarchais, Rossini* 'The Barber of Seville'

barbifier [9] [barbifje] VT *Fam* **1** *Vieilli (raser)* to shave■ **2** *(ennuyer)* to bore■

barbillon [barbijɔ̃] NM **1** *Zool & Ich (poisson)* barbel; **barbillons** *(replis → de poisson)* barbels; *(→ de cheval, de bœuf)* barbs **2** *très Fam (souteneur)* (young) pimp

barbital, -als [barbital] NM *Pharm* barbitone, *Am* barbital

barbiturique [barbityrik] *Pharm* ADJ barbituric
NM barbiturate

barbiturisme [barbityrism] NM *Méd* barbiturate poisoning; *(dépendance)* barbiturate addiction, barbiturism

barbituromanie [barbityrɔmani] NF *Méd* barbiturate addiction, barbiturism

Barbizon [barbizɔ̃] NM **l'école de B.** = the Barbizon school (landscape painters of the mid-19th century, including Millet, Corot and Diaz)

barbon [barbɔ̃] NM *Littéraire* **(vieux) b.** *(homme → âgé)* old man, greybeard; *(→ aux idées dépassées)* (old) stick-in-the-mud

barbot [barbo] NM *Can* ink stain; *Fig (écriture)* scrawl

barbotage [barbɔtaʒ] NM **1** *Fam (baignade)* paddling■, splashing about **2** *Chim* bubbling (through a liquid)

barbote [barbɔt] NF *Ich (loche)* loach

barboter [3] [barbɔte] VI **1** *(s'ébattre)* to paddle, to splash around *or* about; **b. dans son bain** to splash around in one's bath
2 *(patauger)* to wade
3 *Chim* **faire b. un gaz** to bubble a gas (through a liquid)
VT *Fam (dérober)* to pinch, to swipe; **quelqu'un m'a barboté mon stylo** someone's pinched my pen
▫ **barboter dans** VT IND *Fam* **1** *(être impliqué dans)* to have a hand in; **b. dans des affaires louches** to be mixed up in some shady business; **un scandale où barbotent quelques ministres** a scandal several ministers are mixed up in
2 *(être empêtré dans)* to be embroiled in; **je barbote dans ces histoires de divorce** I'm embroiled in this divorce business

barboteur, -euse [barbɔtœr, -øz] ADJ *Fam* light-fingered
NM,F *Fam (voleur)* pilferer
NM *Chim* bubbler, wash bottle
▫ **barboteuse** NF **1** *(vêtement)* (pair of) rompers *or* crawlers, playsuit **2** *Can (gonflable) Br* paddling pool, *Am* wading pool; *(dans une piscine)* children's pool, wading pool

barbotin [barbɔtɛ̃] NM *Tech* sprocket-wheel; *Naut* cable wheel

barbotine [barbɔtin] NF *Cér* slip

barbotte [barbɔt] = **barbote**

barbouillage [barbujaʒ] NM **1** *(application de couleur, de boue)* daubing **2** *(fait d'écrire)* scribbling, scrawling; *(écrit)* scribble, scrawl **3** *(tableau → de mauvais artiste) Péj* daub; *(→ d'enfant)* scribbled picture; **à l'âge des premiers barbouillages** when a child first learns to draw

barbouille [barbuj] NF *Fam Péj* daub

barbouiller [3] [barbuje] VT **1** *(salir)* **tu as barbouillé ton tablier!** you've dirtied your apron!; **b. qch de qch** to smear sth with sth; **son menton était barbouillé de confiture** his chin was smeared with jam; **il avait le visage barbouillé de larmes** his face was tear-stained
2 *(peindre)* to daub; **b. des toiles** to mess about *or* around with paint; **à son âge, elle ne fait encore que b. du papier** at her age, all she does is splash paint on paper; **b. qch de peinture** to slap paint on sth, to daub sth with paint; **les lèvres barbouillées de rouge vif** her lips smeared with bright red lipstick
3 *(gribouiller)* to scrawl, to scribble; **il barbouille du papier** he's scribbling away; *Fig Péj* he's just a scribbler
4 *Fam (donner la nausée à)* to nauseate■; **ça me barbouille (l'estomac** *ou* **le cœur)** it turns my stomach; **avoir l'air barbouillé** to look green around the gills; **avoir l'estomac** *ou* **se sentir barbouillé** to feel queasy *or* nauseated
USAGE ABSOLU *(peinturlurer)* **je ne peins pas, je barbouille** I'm not really a painter, I just mess about with colours

barbouilleur, -euse [barbujœr, -øz] NM,F *Péj (écrivain)* scribbler; *(peintre)* dauber

barbouillis [barbuji] = **barbouillage**

barbouze [barbuz] NF *très Fam* **1** *(espion)* secret agent■ **2** *(garde du corps)* heavy, minder■; *(intermédiaire)* minder■ **3** *(barbe)* beard■

barbu, -e[1] [barby] ADJ bearded
NM **1** *(homme)* bearded man, man with a beard; *Fam* Islamic fundamentalist■ **2** *Orn* barbet **3** *très Fam (poils pubiens de la femme)* bush

Barbuda [barbyda] NM Barbuda

barbue[2] [barby] NF *Ich* brill

barbule [barbyl] NF **1** *Orn (d'une plume)* barbule **2** *Bot* Barbula

barcarolle [barkarɔl] NF *Mus* barcarolle

barcasse [barkas] NF *Péj Naut* boat■, tub

barcelonais, -e [barsəlɔnɛ, -ɛz] ADJ Barcelonese
▫ **Barcelonais, -e** NM,F = inhabitant of or person from Barcelona

Barcelone [barsəlɔn] NM *Géog* Barcelona

barco® [barko] NM data projector

bard [bar] NM **1** *(sans roues)* hand-barrow **2** *(avec roues)* hand-trolley

barda [barda, *Can* bardɑ] NM *Fam* **1** *Mil* gear, *Br* kit **2** *(chargement)* stuff, gear, paraphernalia **3** *Can (pagaille)* shambles *(singulier)*; **petit b.** household chores; **grand b.** big clean-up **4** *Can (bruit)* **faire du b.** to make a racket

bardaf [bardaf] EXCLAM *Belg* crash!

bardage [bardaʒ] NM **1** *Constr (revêtement de maison) Br* weatherboarding, *Am* siding **2** *(autour d'un tableau)* (protective) boarding **3** *(transport de matériaux lourds)* hand transport

bardane [bardan] NF *Bot* burdock

bardas [bardas] NM *Can (pagaille)* shambles *(singulier)*; **être de b.** *(déranger)* to be a nuisance

bardasser [3] [bardase] *Can* VI **1** *(faire des besognes)* to do chores **2** *(perdre son temps)* to waste one's time **3** *(montrer sa mauvaise humeur en faisant du bruit)* to bang about in a temper
VT **1** *(cogner)* to bang **2** *(secouer)* to shake up **3** *(traiter sans ménagement)* to be rough with

barde [bard] NM *Littérature (poète)* bard
NF **1** *Culin* bard **2** *Arch (protection pour cheval)* bard

bardeau, -x [bardo] NM **1** *Constr (pour toiture)* shingle; **un toit de bardeaux** a shingle roof **2** *Constr (pour façade) Br* weatherboard, *Am* clapboard **3** *Constr (pour carrelage)* lath **4** *Zool* hinny **5** *Can Fam* **manquer un b.** to be not quite right in the head, to have a slate loose

barder [3] [barde] VT **1** *Culin* to bard
2 *Arch (cuirasser)* to bard
3 *Fig* **être bardé de** *(être couvert de)* to be covered in *or* with; **coffre bardé de ferrures** chest bound with iron bands; **être bardé de diplômes** to have a string of academic titles
V IMPERSONNEL *Fam* **ça barde!** all hell's broken loose!; **ça barde chez les voisins!** the neighbours are having a hell of a *Br* row *or Am* spat!; **quand il a dit ça, ça a bardé!** things really turned nasty when he said that!; **ça va b. si elle le retrouve!** there'll be hell to pay if she finds him!; **si je le retrouve, ça va b.!** if I find him, I'll give him something to remember me by!; **si tu ne te dépêches pas, ça va b.!** you'll get it *or* be for it if you don't hurry up!

bardis [bardi] NM *Naut* shifting boards

bardolino [bardolino] NM *(vin)* Bardolino

bardot [bardo] NM *Zool* hinny

bare-foot [bɛrfyt] NM INV *Sport* barefoot waterskiing, *Am* barefooting

barème [barɛm] NM **1** *(tableau)* ready reckoner **2** *Fin (tarification)* scale; **b. fiscal** *ou* **d'imposition** tax rate schedule *or* structure, tax scale; **b. des prix** price list, schedule of prices; **b. des salaires** wage scale, variable sliding scale

barémique [baremik] ADJ *Belg* **le salaire b. du secteur** the official salary scale in the sector; **augmentation b.** incremental salary increase; **cette majoration est applicable à tous les échelons barémiques** this increase is applicable at all points on the scale; *Fig* **le niveau b. des candidats était trop bas** the average level of the applicants was too low

Barents [barɛ̃s] *voir* **mer**

baresthésie [barɛstezi] NF *Méd* baresthesia

baréter [18] [barete] VI *(éléphant)* to trumpet

barge[1] [barʒ] NF **1** *Naut* barge, lighter **2** *Orn* godwit; **b. égocéphale, b. à queue noire** black-tailed godwit; **b. rousse** bar-tailed godwit

barge[2] [barʒ] ADJ *Fam (fou)* nuts, bananas, *Br* off one's head

barguigner [3] [bargiɲe] VI *Fam* **sans b.** without hesitation *or* shillyshallying

barguiner [3] [bargine] VI *Can Fam* **1** *(hésiter)* to dither **2** *(marchander)* to bargain■, to haggle

Bari [bari] NM *Géog* Bari

baribal, -als [baribal] NM *Zool* American black bear

barigoule [barigul] **à la barigoule** ADJ *Culin* **artichauts à la b.** = artichokes stuffed with mushrooms and ham

baril [baril] NM *(de vin)* barrel, cask; *(de pétrole)* barrel; *(de lessive)* drum; **b. de poudre** powder keg

barillet [barijɛ] NM **1** *(baril)* small barrel *or* cask **2** *Tech (d'un revolver, d'une serrure)* cylinder; *(d'une horloge)* spring box, spring drum

barine [barin] NM *(terme respectueux utilisé dans la Russie tsariste)* gentleman, sir, my lord

bariolage [barjɔlaʒ] NM **1** *(action)* daubing with bright colours **2** *(motif)* gaudy colour scheme

bariolé, -e [barjɔle] ADJ *(tissu)* multicoloured; *(foule)* colourful

barioler [3] [barjɔle] VT to cover with gaudy colours, to splash bright colours on

bariolure [barjɔlyr] NF garish *or* gaudy colours

barjaque [barʒak] NF *Suisse & (en Savoie, Provence) Fam* chatterbox

barjaquer [3] [barʒake] VI *Suisse & (en Savoie, Provence) Fam* to ramble

barjo(t) [barʒo] *Fam* ADJ nuts, bananas
NMF nut, *Br* nutter

barkhane [barkan] NF *Géol* barchan(e), barkhan

barlong, -longue [barlɔ̃, -lɔ̃g] ADJ *Archit* having the shape of an unequal-sided quadrilateral

barlotière [barlɔtjɛr] NF *(d'un vitrail)* iron window-bar, saddle-bar

barmaid [barmɛd] NF barmaid

barman [barman] *(pl* **barmans** *ou* **barmen** [-mɛn]*)* NM barman, *Am* bartender

Barmécide [barmesid] NPR Barmecide; **festin de B.** Barmecide feast

bar-mitsva [barmitsva] NF INV *Rel* bar mitzvah

barn [barn] NM *Phys* barn

Barnabé [barnabe] NPR Barnabas

barnabite [barnabit] NM *Rel* Barnabite

barnache [barnaʃ] = **bernache**

barographe [barɔgraf] NM *Phys* barograph

barolo [barolo] NM *(vin)* Barolo

baromètre [barɔmɛtr] NM *Phys* barometer, glass; **le b. est au beau fixe** the barometer is set *or* reads fair; **le b. est à la pluie** the barometer is set on rain; *Fig* **b. de l'opinion publique** barometer *or* indicator of public opinion; **b. anéroïde** aneroid barometer; *Mktg* **b. de clientèle** customer barometer; **b. enregistreur** recording barometer; *Mktg* **b. d'image** image barometer; *Mktg* **b. de marque** brand barometer

barométrie [barɔmetri] NF *Phys* barometry

barométrique [barɔmetrik] ADJ *Phys* barometric, barometer *(avant n)*

baron, -onne [barɔ̃, -ɔn] NM,F **1** *(noble)* baron, *f* baroness **2** *(magnat)* **b. de la finance** tycoon **3** *Culin* **b. d'agneau** baron of lamb **4** *Fam Arg crime (compère)* plant

baronet, baronnet [barɔnɛ] NM *Hist* baronet

baronnage [barɔnaʒ] NM *Hist* baronage

baronnie [barɔni] NF *Hist* barony

baronne [barɔn] *voir* **baron**

baroque [barɔk] ADJ **1** *(gén)* baroque **2** *(étrange → idée)* weird; *Fam* **son short avec ses escarpins, ça fait un peu b.** her shorts and her court shoes look a bit weird together **3** *(perle)* tear-shaped
NM Baroque

baroqueux, -euse [barɔkø, -øz] NM,F *Mus* = advocate of the use of period instruments

baroquisant, -e [barɔkizɑ̃, -ɑ̃t] ADJ tending towards the Baroque

baroquisme [barɔkism] **NM** tendency towards the Baroque

baroscope [barɔskɔp] **NM** baroscope

barothérapie [barɔterapi] **NF** *Méd* hyperbaric therapy

barotraumatisme [barɔtromatism] **NM** *Méd* barotrauma

baroud [barud] **NM** *Fam* battle■; **b. d'honneur** last stand; **pour moi, c'est un b. d'honneur** it's my way of going out in style

baroudeur [barudœr] **NM** *Fam (qui aime le combat)* fighter■; **c'est un b.** *(voyageur)* he's knocked about a bit

barouf [baruf] **NM** *très Fam* racket, din; **faire du b.** *(bruit)* to kick up a racket; *(scandale)* to make a fuss

barque [bark] **NF** *Naut* small boat; **b. de pêcheur** small fishing boat; *Littéraire* **la b. fatale** *ou* **de Charon** Charon's bark, Charon's ferry; *Fig* **mener sa b.** to look after oneself; **il est assez grand pour mener sa b.** he's old enough to look after himself; **il a bien/mal mené sa b.** he managed/didn't manage his affairs well; **c'est elle qui mène la b.** she's the boss, she's in charge; **charger la b.** to overdo it

barquette [barkɛt] **NF 1** *Culin* = boat-shaped tartlet **2** *(récipient → pour plat à emporter)* container; *(→ de fraises, de framboises)* punnet

barracuda [barakuda] **NM** *Ich* barracuda

barrage [baraʒ] **NM 1** *Archit (réservoir)* dam; *(régulateur)* weir, barrage; **b. (de retenue)** dam; *Fig* **faire b. à** to stand in the way of, to obstruct, to hinder; **b. flottant** floating dam; **b. mobile** movable dam; **le b. de Grand Coulee** the Grand Coulee Dam; **le b. Hoover** the Hoover dam; **le b. de Kariba** the Kariba dam **2** *(dispositif policier)* **b. (de police)** police cordon; **b. routier** roadblock **3** *Mil* **b. roulant** creeping *or* rolling barrage **4** *Sport* **(match de) b.** play-off

barrage-poids [baraʒpwa] *(pl* **barrages-poids***)* **NM** *Archit* gravity dam

barrage-voûte [baraʒvut] *(pl* **barrages-voûtes***)* **NM** *Archit* arch *or* arched dam

barragiste [baraʒist] **NMF** *Sport (équipe)* play-off team; *(joueur)* play-off player

barramunda [baramunda] **NM** *Ich* barramunda

barramundi [baramundi] **NM** *Ich* barramundi

barranco [barɑ̃ko] **NM** *Géog* barranca, volcanic gorge

BARRE [bar]

> bar **1, 2, 6–8** ■ helm, tiller **3** ■ line **4** ■ level **5**

NF 1 *(tige → de bois)* bar; *(→ de métal)* bar, rod; **b. de fer** iron bar; **j'ai une b. sur l'estomac/au-dessus des yeux** *(douleur)* I have a pain across my stomach/eyes; *Aut* **b. d'accouplement** tie-rod; *Naut* **b. antiroulis** anti-roll bar; **b. d'appui** handrail; **b. de céréales** *Br* cereal bar, *Am* granola bar; **une b. de chocolat** a bar of chocolate; **b. chocolatée** *Br* chocolate bar, *Am* candy bar; **b. à mine** digging bar; *Élec* **b. omnibus** busbar; **b. de réaction** radius arm; **b. de remorquage** tow bar; *Aut* **b. de torsion** torsion bar

2 *Sport* **barres asymétriques/parallèles** asymmetric/parallel bars; **b. à disques** barbell; **b. fixe** high *or* horizontal bar; *(en danse)* barre; **exercices à la b.** barre work *or* exercises; *Fig* **avoir b. sur qn** to have an advantage over sb

3 *Naut* **b. (de gouvernail)** *(gén)* helm; *(sur un voilier)* tiller; *(sur un navire)* wheel; **prendre la b.** to take the helm; *Fig* to take charge; **être à la b.** to be at the helm, to steer; *Fig* to be at the helm *or* in charge

4 *(trait)* line; **faire des barres** to draw lines; **mets la b. sur ton T** cross your T; **b. de soustraction/fraction** subtraction/fraction line; **b. oblique** slash; **b. oblique inversée** backslash; **double b.** double bar; **avoir b. sur qn** to have a hold over *or* on sb

5 *(niveau)* level; **le dollar est descendu au-dessous de la b. des 0,50 euros** the dollar fell below the 0.50 euro level; **pour l'examen de physique, la b. a été fixée à 12** the *Br* pass mark *or Am* passing grade for the physics exam was set at 12; **mettre** *ou* **placer la b. trop haut** to set too high a standard; **à chaque fois, ils mettent la b. plus haut** they keep making it harder to meet the target

6 *Mus* **b. (de mesure)** bar line; **double b.** double bar

7 *Jur* **b. (du tribunal)** bar; **b. des témoins** *Br* witness box, *Am* witness stand; **appeler qn à la b.** to call sb to the *Br* witness box *or Am* witness stand; **comparaître à la b.** to appear as a witness

8 *Ordinat* **b. de défilement** scroll bar; **b. d'espacement** space bar; **b. d'état** status bar; **b. d'icônes** icon bar; **b. de lancement rapide** quick launch bar; **b. de menu** menu bar; **b. de navigation** navigation bar; **b. d'outils** tool bar; **b. de sélection** menu bar; **b. des tâches** taskbar; **b. de titre** title bar

9 b. HLM *Br* ≃ large block of council flats, *Am* ≃ large public housing unit

10 *Can* **la b. du jour** dawn, daybreak

11 *Can Joual* **b. de savon** bar of soap

12 *Géog (crête)* ridge; *(banc de sable)* sandbar; *(houle)* race

13 *Nucl & Phys* **b. de contrôle** control rod

14 *Hér* bar; **b. de bâtardise** bend sinister

barré, -e [bare] **ADJ 1** *Banque (chèque)* crossed; **chèque non b.** open cheque

2 *(dent)* impacted

3 *Fam (locutions)* **on est mal barrés pour y être à huit heures** we haven't got a hope in hell *or* we don't stand a chance of being there at eight; *Ironique* **on est bien barrés!, on est mal barrés!** (that's) great!, (that's) marvellous!; **c'est mal b.** it's got off to a bad start; **entre eux deux, c'est mal b.** they started off on the wrong foot with each other; **il est bien b., ce mec-là** that guy's completely nuts; **c'est un film bien b.** *(loufoque)* it's a really wacky film; *(étrange)* it's a really weird *or* freaky film; *Can* **ne pas être b.** to be a live wire

NM *Mus* barré

barreau, -x [baro] **NM 1** *(de fenêtre, de cage)* bar; *(d'échelle)* rung; *(de chaise)* rung, crosspiece; *Fam Hum* **b. de chaise** fat cigar; **être derrière les barreaux** to be behind bars **2** *Jur* **le b.** the Bar; **être admis** *ou* **reçu au b.** to be called to the Bar; **être radié du b.** to be disbarred

barrement [barmɑ̃] **NM** *Banque (sur un chèque)* crossing

barrens [barœns] **NMPL** *Géog* barren land

barrer [3] [bare, *Can* bɑre] **VT 1** *(bloquer → porte, issue)* to bar; *(→ voie, route)* to block, to obstruct; **les grévistes barrent la voie de chemin de fer** strikers are blocking the railway track; **des éboulements barrent le torrent** fallen boulders are blocking the stream; **la rue est temporairement barrée** the street has been temporarily closed; **b. le passage à qn** to block sb's way; *aussi Fig* **b. la route à qn** to stand in sb's way

2 *Can & (régional en France) (fermer à clef)* to lock

3 *(rayer → chèque)* to cross; *(→ erreur, phrase)* to cross out, to score out; **b. ses T** to cross one's Ts; **une profonde tranchée barrait le paysage** a deep trench scarred the landscape; **un pli lui barrait le front** he/she had a deep line running right across his/her forehead; **l'écharpe tricolore qui lui barrait la poitrine** the tricolour sash he/she wore across his/her chest

4 *Naut* to steer

VI *Naut* to steer, to be at the helm; *Sport (à l'aviron)* to cox

▸**se barrer VPR** *Fam* **1** *(partir)* to beat it, to clear off; **on se barre d'ici!** let's get out of here!; **barre-toi de là, tu me gênes!** shift, you're in my way!

2 *(se détacher)* to come off■

barrette [barɛt] **NF 1** *(pince)* **b. (à cheveux)** *Br* (hair) slide, *Am* barrette; **b. de médaille** medal bar **2** *Couture* collar pin **3** *Élec* **b. de connexion** connecting strip **4** *Rel* biretta; **recevoir la b.** to be made a cardinal **5** *Mines* helmet **6** *Fam (de haschisch)* thin strip **7** *Ordinat* **b. de mémoire vive** RAM module

barreur, -euse [barœr, -øz] **NM,F 1** *Naut (gén)* helmsman, *f* helmswoman **2** *Sport (en aviron)* coxswain; **avec b.** coxed; **sans b.** coxless

barricade [barikad] **NF** barricade; **nous avons conquis ces libertés sur les barricades** we won those freedoms by going out in the streets and fighting for them; *Fig* **être du même côté de la b.** to be on the same side of the fence; **les journées des Barricades** = insurrections where barricades were erected in the streets

> *Culture*
>
> **LES JOURNÉES DES BARRICADES**
>
> This expression refers to two distinct episodes in French history: the first, during which barricades were erected in the streets of Paris, occurred in 1588 during religious riots, and the second took place in the streets of the capital when riots broke out during the **Fronde** (see box at this entry) in 1648.

barricader [3] [barikade] **VT** *(porte, rue)* to barricade

▸**se barricader VPR 1** *(se retrancher)* to barricade oneself **2** *(s'enfermer)* to lock *or* to shut oneself away; **il s'est barricadé dans sa chambre** he's locked *or* shut himself in his room

barrière [barjɛr] **NF 1** *(clôture)* fence; *(porte)* gate; **b. de dégel** = closure of road to heavy traffic during thaw; *Belg* **b. Nadar** crowd barrier; **b. de passage à niveau** *Br* level *or Am* grade crossing gate; **b. de sécurité** guardrail

2 *(obstacle)* barrier; **la b. de la langue** the language barrier; **dresser** *ou* **mettre une b. entre...** to raise a barrier between...; **faire tomber une b./les barrières** to break down a barrier/the barriers

3 *Géog* **b. de corail** barrier reef; **b. écologique** ecological barrier; **b. naturelle** natural barrier; **la Grande B.** the Great Barrier Reef

4 *Écon* **b. commerciale** trade barrier; **barrières douanières** trade *or* tariff barrier; **b. à l'entrée** entry barrier; **b. non tarifaire** non-tariff barrier; **b. tarifaire** tariff barrier

barrique [barik] **NF** barrel, cask

barrir [32] [barir] **VI** *(éléphant)* to trumpet

barrissement [barismɑ̃] **NM** *(de l'éléphant)* trumpeting *(UNCOUNT)*

barrot [baro] **NM** *Naut (poutrelle)* beam

bar-tabac [bartaba] *(pl* **bars-tabacs***)* **NM** = bar where tobacco, stamps and lottery tickets are also sold over the counter

bartavelle [bartavɛl] **NF** *Orn* rock partridge

barter [bartœr], **bartering** [bartœriŋ] **NM** *Rad & TV* bartering

Barthélemy [bartelemi] **NPR** Bartholomew

bartholinite [bartɔlinit] **NF** *Méd* bartholinitis

barycentre [barisɑ̃tr] **NM** *Astron & Phys* barycentre

barycentrique [barisɑ̃trik] **NM** *Astron & Phys* barycentric

baryon [barjɔ̃] **NM** *Phys* baryon

baryonique [barjɔnik] **ADJ** *Phys* baryonic

barysphère [barisfɛr] **NF** *Géol* barysphere

baryte [barit] **NF** *Chim* baryta, barium hydroxide

baryté, -e [barite] **ADJ** *Méd* **bouillie barytée** barium meal

barytine [baritin], **barytite** [baritit] **NF** *Minér* barytes, barytine, barytite

barytique [baritik] **ADJ** *Chim* baric

baryton [baritɔ̃] **NM** *Mus (voix)* baritone (voice); *(chanteur)* baritone; **saxophone b.** baritone saxophone

baryum [barjɔm] **NM** *Chim* barium; **sulfate de b.** barium meal

barzoï [barzɔj] **NM** *Zool* borzoi, Russian wolfhound

BAS [beaɛs] **NM** *Admin (abrév* **Bureau d'aide sociale***)* welfare office

bas[1] [ba] **NM 1** *(de femme)* stocking; **le visage dissimulé sous un b.** wearing a stocking mask; **des b. avec/sans couture** seamed/seamless stockings; **b. fins** sheer stockings; **b. de laine** woollen stockings; *Fig* savings, nest egg; *Fig* **qu'y a-t-il dans son b. de laine?** how much money has he got under the mattress?, how big is his nest egg?; **le b. de laine des Français** the savings of small-time French investors; **b. (de) Nylon®** nylon stockings; **b. résille** fishnet stockings; **b. de soie** silk stockings; **b. à varices** support stockings

2 *Can (chaussette)* sock; **marcher en pied de b.** to walk around in stockinged feet

bas-bas

BAS², BASSE [ba, bas]

> **ADJ** low A1, 2, B1–6 ■ short A1 ■ lower A4, 5 ■ quiet B5 ■ mean B6 ■ crude B7 ■ bass B4
> **ADV** low 1, 3
> **NM** bottom, lower part 1

ADJ A. *DANS L'ESPACE* **1** *(de peu de hauteur → bâtiment, mur)* low; *(→ herbes)* low, short; *(→ nuages)* low; **une petite maison basse** a squat little house; **une chaise basse** a low chair; **le tableau est trop b., remonte-le un peu** the painting is too low *or* far down, move it up a bit; **avoir le front b.** to be low-browed; **attrape les branches basses** grasp the lower *or* bottom branches; **le soleil était b. sur l'horizon** the sun was low on the horizon; **à basse altitude** at (a) low altitude; **la partie basse du buffet** the lower part of the dresser

2 *(peu profond)* low; **les eaux sont basses** the water level's low *or* down; **la Seine est basse** the (level of the) Seine is low; **aux basses eaux** *(de la mer)* at low tide; *(d'une rivière)* when the water level is low; *Fig* at a time of stagnation; **c'est la basse mer** *ou* **marée basse** it's low tide, the tide is low

3 *(incliné vers le sol)* **être assis la tête basse** to sit with one's head down; **marcher la tête basse** to hang one's head as one walks; **le chien s'enfuit, la queue basse** the dog ran away with its tail between its legs

4 *Naut* **basses voiles, voiles basses** lower sails *or* courses; **basses vergues** lower yards

5 *Géog* **les basses terres** the lowlands; **la basse Bretagne** the western part of Brittany; **les basses Alpes** the foothills of the Alps; **la basse vallée du Rhône** the lower Rhone valley; **la basse Loire/Seine** the lower Loire/Seine (valley)

B. *DANS UNE HIÉRARCHIE* **1** *(en grandeur → prix, fréquence, pression etc)* low; **à b. prix** cheap, for a low price; **acheter/vendre qch à b. prix** to buy/sell sth cheap; **les b. salaires** low salaries; **à basse température** *(laver)* at low temperatures; **le thermomètre est b.** temperatures are low; **la note la plus basse est 8** the lowest mark is 8; **les enchères sont restées très basses** the bidding didn't get off the ground; **le moral de l'équipe est b.** the team's in low spirits, morale in the team is low; **son moral est très b.** he's down, he's in very low spirits

2 *(médiocre → intérêt, rendement)* low, poor; *(→ dans les arts)* inferior, minor, crude; **le niveau de la classe est très b.** the (achievement) level of the class is very low; **c'est du b. comique** it's low comedy; **c'est de la basse littérature** it's inferior literature; *Cartes* **les basses cartes** the small *or* low cards; **les b. morceaux** *(en boucherie)* the cheap cuts

3 *(inférieur dans la société)* low, humble, *Littéraire* lowly; **de basse origine** of humble origin; **de basse condition** from a poor family; **le b. clergé** the minor clergy; **le b. peuple** the lower classes *or Péj* orders

4 *Mus (grave → note)* low, bottom *(avant n)*; *(→ guitare, flûte)* bass *(avant n)*; **sa voix tremble dans les notes basses** her voice quavers in the bottom of the range; **le ton est trop b., je ne pourrai pas le chanter** the piece is pitched too low, I won't be able to sing it; **une voix basse** a deep voice

5 *(peu fort)* low, quiet; **parler à voix basse** to speak in a low *or* quiet voice; **sur un ton b.** in hushed tones

6 *Péj (abject, vil → âme)* low, mean, villainous; *(→ acte)* low, base, mean; *(→ sentiment)* low, base, abject; **de basses compromissions** shabby compromises; **à moi toutes les basses besognes** I get stuck with all the dirty work

7 *Péj (vulgaire → terme, expression)* crude, vulgar

8 *Ling* **b. allemand** Low German; **b. breton** Breton *(as spoken in southern Brittany)*

9 *(le plus récent)* **le B.-Empire** the late Empire; **la basse latinité** late Roman times; **le b. Moyen Âge** the late Middle Ages

ADV 1 *(à faible hauteur, à faible niveau)* low; **les oiseaux sont passés très b.** the birds flew very low; **la dernière étagère est placée trop b.** the last shelf is too low; **je mettrais l'étagère plus b.** I'd put the shelf lower down; **le thermomètre est descendu** *ou* **tombé très b. cette nuit** temperatures dropped very low last night; **les prix ne descendront pas plus b.** prices won't come down any further; **leurs actions sont au plus b.** their shares have reached an all-time low; **elle est bien b.** *(physiquement)* she's very poorly; *(moralement)* she's very low *or* down; **vous êtes tombé bien b.** *(financièrement)* you've certainly gone down in the world; *(moralement)* you've sunk really low; **il est tombé bien b. dans mon estime** he's gone down a lot in my estimation; **plus b., vous trouverez la boulangerie** *(plus loin)* you'll find the baker's a little further on; **j'habite deux maisons plus b. que lui** I live two houses down from his place; **plus b.** *(dans un document)* below, further down *or* on; **voir plus b.** see below; **je sais tout maintenant, alors b. les masques** I know everything now, so you can stop pretending; *Fam* **b. les pattes!** hands off!

2 *(d'une voix douce)* in a low voice; *(d'une voix grave)* in a deep voice; **mets le son plus b.** turn the sound down; **mets la musique tout b.** turn the music right down; **il dit tout haut ce que les autres pensent tout b.** he voices the thoughts which others keep to themselves

3 *Mus* **tu prends la deuxième mesure un peu trop b.** *(à un chanteur, à un musicien)* you're taking the second bar a bit flat

4 *Vét* **mettre b.** to give birth; **elle a mis b. quatre chiots** she gave birth to four puppies

5 *Naut* **mettre pavillon b.** to lower *or* to strike the colours; **haler b.** to haul in *or* down; **mettre b. les feux** to draw the fires

NM 1 *(partie inférieure → d'un pantalon, d'un escalier, d'une hiérarchie etc)* bottom; *(→ d'un visage)* lower part; **le b. d'une robe** *(partie inférieure)* the bottom of a dress; **elle a le b. du visage de son père** the bottom *or* lower part of her face is like her father's; **le b. du dos** the small of the back; *Typ & Ordinat* **b. de page** footer; **b. de pyjama** pyjama bottoms

2 *Culin* **b. de carré** prime chops (of veal)

3 *Naut* **le b. de l'eau** low tide

4 *Pêche* **b. de ligne** trace, cast

5 *Mktg (du marché)* low end

6 *Can (appartement → au rez-de-chaussée) Br* ground-floor flat, *Am* first-floor apartment; *(→ en sous-sol) Br* basement flat, *Am* basement apartment

7 *Littéraire (ignominie)* baseness, vileness; **se complaire dans le b. et le vulgaire** to revel in base and vulgar things

▫ **basse NF 1** *Mus (partie)* bass (part *or* score); **basse chiffrée** figured bass; **basse continue** basso continuo; **basse contrainte** basso ostinato; **basse noble** basso profundo; **basse obstinée** basso ostinato

2 *(voix d'homme)* bass (voice); **basse chantante** basso cantante; **basse profonde** basso profundo; *(chanteur)* bass; **la basse intervient à la sixième mesure** the bass comes in on the sixth bar

3 *(instrument → gén)* bass (instrument); *(→ violoncelle)* (double) bass

4 *Géog* shoal, flat, sandbank

▫ **à bas ADV mettre qch à b.** to pull sth down; **ils ont mis à b. tout le quartier** they razed the whole district to the ground; **à b. la dictature!** down with dictatorship!

▫ **à bas de PRÉP se jeter/sauter à b. de son cheval** to throw oneself/to jump off one's horse

▫ **au bas de PRÉP au b. des escaliers** at the foot *or* bottom of the stairs; **au b. de la page** at the foot *or* bottom of the page; **au b. de la hiérarchie/liste** at the bottom of the hierarchy/list; **au b. du jardin** at the bottom (end) *or* far end of the garden

▫ **de bas en haut ADV** from bottom to top, from the bottom up; **regarder qn de b. en haut** to look sb up and down

▫ **d'en bas ADJ les voisins d'en b.** the people downstairs; **la porte d'en b. est fermée** the downstairs door is shut; *Fig* **la France d'en b.** the French underclass **ADV** *(dans une maison)* from downstairs; *(d'une hauteur)* from the bottom; *Fig* **elle est partie d'en b.** she worked her way up, she started from nowhere

▫ **du bas ADV 1** *(de l'étage inférieur)* **l'appartement du b.** the flat underneath *or* below *or* downstairs

2 *(du rez-de-chaussée)* downstairs *(avant n)*; **les chambres du b.** the downstairs rooms; **les volets du b.** the downstairs shutters

3 *(de l'endroit le moins élevé)* lower; **le carreau du b. est cassé** the lower pane is broken

▫ **en bas ADV 1** *(à un niveau inférieur → dans un bâtiment)* downstairs, down; *Fam* **je vais** *ou* **descends en b.** I'm going down *or* downstairs; **passe par en b., c'est plus court** *(par l'étage inférieur)* cut through downstairs, it's quicker; *(par le jardin en contrebas)* cut through the bottom of the garden, it's quicker; **la maison a deux pièces en b. et deux en haut** the house has two rooms downstairs and two upstairs

2 *(dans la partie inférieure)* **prends le carton par en b.** take hold of the bottom of the box

3 *(vers le sol)* **je ne peux pas regarder en b., j'ai le vertige** I can't look down, I feel dizzy; **le village semblait si petit tout en b.** the village looked so small down there *or* below; **suspendre qch la tête en b.** to hang sth upside down

▫ **en bas de PRÉP en b. de la côte** at the bottom *or* foot of the hill; **en b. des marches** at the bottom *or* foot of the stairs; **signez en b. du contrat** sign at the bottom of the contract; **j'ai rangé les draps en b. de l'armoire** I've put the sheets at the bottom of the wardrobe; **ils se retrouvent en b. du classement général** they're now (at the) bottom of the league; **il s'est laissé glisser jusqu'en b. de l'échelle** he slid down (to the bottom of) the ladder

basal, -e, -aux, -ales [bazal, -o] **ADJ** *Physiol* basal

basalte [bazalt] **NM** *Géol* basalt

basaltique [bazaltik] **ADJ** *Géol* basaltic

basane [bazan] **NF 1** *(peau de mouton)* sheepskin **2** *très Fam (peau)* hide■, skin■ **3** *Fam Arg mil (cavalerie)* cavalry■

basané, -e [bazane] **ADJ 1** *(bronzé → touriste)* suntanned; *(→ navigateur)* tanned, weather-beaten **2** *très Fam (connotation raciste)* swarthy■, dark-skinned■ **3** *Can (en acadien)* freckled
NM,F *très Fam* darky, = offensive term used to refer to dark-skinned people

basaner [3] [bazane] **VT** to tan

basanite [bazanit] **NF** *Minér* basanite

bas-bleu [bablø] *(pl* **bas-bleus** *)* **NM** *Péj* bluestocking

bas-breton, -onne [babrǝtɔ̃, -ɔn] *(mpl* **bas-bretons,** *fpl* **bas-bretonnes** *)* **ADJ** of/from Western *or* Lower Brittany
NM *(langue)* the language of Lower Brittany
▫ **Bas-breton, -onne NM,F** = inhabitant of *or* person from Western *or* Lower Brittany

Bas-Canada [bakanada] **NM** *Hist* Lower Canada

> *Culture*
>
> **BAS-CANADA**
> After Canada became a British colony in 1763, mounting difficulties between the French and British settlers prompted England to divide Canada into two separate parts: Upper Canada (roughly equivalent to modern-day Ontario) and Lower Canada (roughly equivalent to modern-day Quebec). Through the Constitutional Act of 1791, each entity was granted an elected Assembly. Difficulties arose when the French-Canadians, who in 1770 had been granted the right to their religion and their "code civil" and who dominated the Assembly of Lower Canada, became frustrated with the actions of the Executive Council (dominated by British Canadians). The political climate led to the creation of the "Parti des Patriotes", led by Louis-Joseph Papineau, and, eventually, the rebellion of 1837. Lower and Upper Canada were abolished in 1841 as a result of recommendations made by the Durham Report.

bas-côté [bakote] (pl **bas-côtés**) NM (de route) side, verge; (d'église) aisle

basculant, -e [baskylã, -ãt] voir **benne, pont**

bascule [baskyl] NF 1 (balance) weighing machine; (pèse-personne) scales 2 (balançoire) seesaw; **mouvement de b.** seesaw motion; **pratiquer une politique de b.** to change allies frequently 3 Tech bascule; Électron **b. bistable** flip-flop 4 Ordinat toggle 5 Can **donner la b. à qn** Br to give sb the bumps

basculement [baskylmã] NM (d'une pile) toppling over; (d'un récipient) tipping out or over; **pour empêcher le b. de l'électorat vers les verts** to prevent a swing to the green party

basculer [3] [baskyle] VI 1 (personne) to topple, to fall over; (vase) to tip over; (benne) to tip up; **un peu plus et il faisait b. la voiture dans le vide** it would only have taken a little push to send the car over the edge; **le levier fait b. le wagonnet dans la benne** the lever tips the contents of the truck into the skip

2 Fig **son univers a basculé** his/her world collapsed; **nous étions heureux, et puis tout a basculé** we were happy, then everything turned upside down; **la pièce bascule soudain dans l'horreur** the mood of the play suddenly switches to horror; **b. dans l'opposition** to go over to the opposition

3 Ordinat to toggle

VT 1 (renverser → chariot) to tip up; (→ chargement) to tip out; **b. son vote sur** to switch one's vote to

2 Tél (appel) to transfer

basculeur [baskylœr] NM 1 Tech rocker switch 2 Ordinat (touche) toggle key

basculis [baskyli] NM Can Géol = blocks of ice which pile up at the mouths of rivers

bas-de-casse [badɑkas] NM INV Typ lower case; **en b.** lower-case, in lower case; **mettre en b.** to put in lower case

bas-de-chausses [badɑʃos] NM INV Arch breeches, leggings, (full-length) hose

bas-du-fleuve [badyflœv] NM Can = lower reaches of the St Lawrence River (below Quebec City)

base [baz] NF 1 (support) base; **à la b. du cou** at the base of the neck; **b. de maquillage** make-up base

2 (fondement) basis, groundwork (UNCOUNT), foundations; **établir qch/reposer sur une b. solide** to set sth up/to rest on a sound basis; **quelle est votre b. de départ?** what's or where's your starting point?; Jur **b. légale** legal basis

3 (centre) **b. de plein air (et de loisirs)** outdoor recreation centre

4 Mil **b. (aérienne/militaire/navale)** (air/army/naval) base; **b. arrière** rear base; **b. de lancement** launch or launching site; **b. d'opérations/de ravitaillement** operations/supply base; **rentrer à la b.** to go back to base

5 Astron **b. de lancement** launching site

6 Pol **la b.** the grass roots, the rank and file

7 Fin & Compta **sur une b. nette** on a net basis; **b. amortissable** basis for depreciation; **b. de calcul** basis of calculations; **b. hors taxe** amount exclusive of Br VAT or Am sales tax; **b. d'imposition** taxable base; **b. monétaire** monetary base

8 Géom, Ordinat & Math base; **b. d'un système numérique** base or radix of a numeration system; **système de b. cinq/huit** base five/eight system; **b. de données** database; **mettre qch dans une b. de données** to enter sth into a database; **b. de données client-serveur** client-server database; **b. de données relationnelles** relational database

9 Mktg **b. de clientèle** customer base; **b. de consommateurs** customer base; **b. de données de consommateurs** customer database; Écon **b. de sondage** sample base

10 Ling (en diachronie) root; (en synchronie) base, stem; (en grammaire générative) base component

11 Culin (d'un cocktail, d'une sauce) basic ingredient

12 Électron **b. de temps** clock

13 Chim base

❑ **bases** NFPL 1 (fondations) foundations, basis; **les bases de la sémiotique** the basis of semiotics; **établir ou jeter les bases d'une alliance**

to lay the foundations of or for an alliance

2 (acquis) basic knowledge; **votre enfant n'a pas les bases** your child lacks basic knowledge; **avoir de bonnes bases en arabe/musique** to have a good grounding in Arabic/music

❑ **à base de** PRÉP **à b. de café** coffee-based; **une boisson à b. de gin** a gin-based drink

❑ **à la base** ADV 1 (en son fondement) **le raisonnement est faux à la b.** the basis of the argument is false

2 (au début) at the beginning, to begin or to start off with; **à la b., nous étions un groupe de rock** to begin with or originally, we were a rock band

❑ **à la base de** PRÉP **être à la b. de qch** (à la source de) to be at the root or heart of sth

❑ **de base** ADJ 1 (fondamental → vocabulaire, industrie) basic; (→ principe) basic, fundamental; **militant de b.** grass-roots militant

2 (de référence → prix, salaire, traitement) basic; (→ documents, données) source (avant n)

3 Ling base (avant n)

❑ **sur la base de** PRÉP on the basis of; **je suis payée sur la b. de 13 euros de l'heure** I am paid at a basic rate of 13 euros an hour

base-ball [bɛzbol] (pl **base-balls**) NM Sport baseball

baselle [bazɛl] NF Bot basella, Malabar nightshade

baser [3] [baze] VT 1 (fonder) **b. qch sur qch** to base sth on sth; **b. une affirmation sur les faits** to base or to ground an assertion on facts or in fact; **tes soupçons ne sont basés sur rien** there are no grounds for your suspicions, your suspicions are groundless; **b. une doctrine sur le libéralisme** to base a doctrine on liberalism

2 Mil & Com (installer) to base; **être basé à** to be based at/in; **les soldats basés à Berlin** the soldiers based in Berlin, the Berlin-based soldiers; **aviation basée à terre** ground-based air force; **l'entreprise est basée à Lyon** the firm's based in Lyons

▶ **se baser** VPR **se b. sur** to base one's judgement on, to go by or on; **sur quoi te bases-tu?** what's your basis for that?, what are you going on?; **je me base sur les chiffres de l'année dernière** I'm going by last year's figures, I've taken last year's figures as the basis for my calculations

bas-fond [bafɔ̃] (pl **bas-fonds**) NM 1 Géog (dans la mer, la rivière) shallow, shoal 2 Géog (dans le terrain) low ground, hollow

❑ **bas-fonds** NMPL Littéraire **les bas-fonds de New York** the seedy parts of New York; **les bas-fonds de la société** the dregs of society

Basic [bazik] NM Ordinat BASIC

basicité [bazisite] NF Chim basicity

baside [bazid] NF Bot basidium

basidiomycète [bazidjɔmisɛt] Bot NM basidiomycete

❑ **basidiomycètes** NMPL Basidiomycetes

basilaire [baziler] ADJ Anat & Bot (sillon, placenta) basilar

basileus [bazileøs] NM Hist = official title of the Byzantine emperor

basilic [bazilik] NM 1 Bot basil 2 Myth & Zool basilisk

basilical, -e, -aux, -ales [bazilikal, -o] ADJ Archit basilical

Basilicate [bazilikat] NF Géog **la B.** Basilicata

basilique¹ [bazilik] NF Archit basilica; **la b. Saint-Pierre** Saint Peter's Basilica

basilique² [bazilik] Anat ADJ basilic

     NF basilic vein

basin [bazɛ̃] NM Tex dimity

basiphile [bazifil] ADJ Bot basophilous

basique [bazik] ADJ basic

basir [32] [bazir] Can (en acadien) VT to hide

     VI (disparaître) to disappear; (mourir) to die

bas-jointé, -e [baʒwɛ̃te] (mpl **bas-jointés**, fpl **bas-jointées**) ADJ low-pasterned

basket [baskɛt] NF (chaussure) Br trainer, Am sneaker; Fam **être bien dans ses baskets** to be very together or Br sorted

     NM Sport basketball

basket-ball [baskɛtbol] (pl **basket-balls**) NM Sport basketball

basketteur, -euse [baskɛtœr, -øz] NM,F Sport basketball player

bas-mât [bama] (pl **bas-mâts**) NM Naut lower mast

basmati [basmati] NM Bot basmati; **riz b.** basmati rice

basoche [bazɔʃ] NF Jur & Hist body of clerks attached to the courts of justice 2 Péj & Vieilli legal fraternity; **termes de b.** legal jargon

basophile [bazɔfil] ADJ Biol basophile, basophilic

basquaise [baskɛz] ADJ F Basque

     NF Basque

❑ **(à la) basquaise** ADJ Culin basquaise, with a tomato and ham sauce

basque¹ [bask] NF Couture basque; **s'accrocher ou se pendre aux basques de qn** to dog sb's footsteps, to stick to sb like glue; **cet enfant est toujours pendu à mes basques** that child just won't let go of me

basque² [bask] ADJ Basque; **le Pays b.** the Basque Country; **vivre au Pays b.** to live in the Basque Country; **aller au Pays b.** to go to the Basque Country

     NM (langue) Basque

❑ **Basque** NMF Basque

> **Culture**
> **BASQUE**
> The area covered by the Basque Country includes the far south-western corner of France. The French portion shares with its Spanish counterpart a common language and a strong sense of separate identity. Nevertheless, nationalist sentiment is much less radical there and Basque is not as widely spoken as it is on the other side of the Pyrenees. Basque, or "Euskera", stands out as one of the very few non-Indo-European languages surviving in Europe.

basquine [baskin] NF Arch basquine, vasquine

bas-relief [barəljɛf] (pl **bas-reliefs**) NM Beaux-Arts bas-relief, low relief

Bas-Rhin [barɛ̃] NM **le B.** Bas-Rhin

bas-rouge [baruʒ] (pl **bas-rouges**) NM (chien) Beauceron (dog)

bassari [basari] NM Zool cacomistle, ringtail (cat)

basse [bas] voir bas

Basse-Autriche [basotriʃ] NF **la B.** Lower Austria; **en B.** in Lower Austria

Basse-Californie [baskalifɔrni] NF **la B.** Lower California; **en B.** in Lower California

basse-cour [baskur] (pl **basses-cours**) NF 1 (lieu) farmyard 2 (volaille) (animaux de) **b.** poultry; **toute la b. était en émoi** the hens and chickens were extremely agitated

basse-fosse [basfos] (pl **basses-fosses**) NF Archit dungeon

bassement [basmã] ADV (agir) basely, meanly; **sa visite était b. intéressée** his/her visit was motivated by mere self-interest; **parlons de choses b. matérielles** let's talk money; Hum **question b. intéressée, as-tu de quoi payer mon repas?** I hate to mention this, but have you got enough to pay for my meal?

Basse-Normandie [basnɔrmãdi] NF **la B.** Basse-Normandie; **en B.** in Basse-Normandie

bassesse [bases] NF 1 (caractère vil) baseness; (servilité) servility; **il ne poussera pas la b. jusque-là** he won't stoop that low 2 (action → mesquine) base or despicable act; (→ servile) servile act; **il ne reculera devant aucune b.** he will stoop to anything; **faire des bassesses** to behave despicably

basset [base] NM (chien) basset (hound)

basse-taille [bastaj] (pl **basses-tailles**) NF 1 Mus basso cantante, singing bass 2 (en orfèvrerie) **émaux de ou sur b.** basse-taille enamelling

Basseterre [basetɛr] NM Géog Basseterre

Basse-terre [basetɛr] NM Géog Basse-terre

bassin [basɛ̃] NM 1 Anat pelvis

2 (piscine) pool; (plan d'eau) ornamental lake; (plus petit) pond; **petit b.** (de la piscine) small or children's pool; **grand b.** (de la piscine) main pool

3 (récipient) basin, bowl; (d'une balance) pan; **b. hygiénique** ou **de lit** bedpan

4 Écol **b. de décantation** settling tank

5 Géog basin; **b. houiller** coal basin; **b. hydrographique** drainage area; **b. minier** mining

area; **b. sédimentaire** sedimentary basin; **b. versant** watershed; **le B. d'Aquitaine** the Aquitaine Basin; **le B. du Congo** the Congo Basin; **le B. de Foxe** Foxe Basin; **le B. parisien** the Paris Basin; **le B. rouge** the Red Basin

6 *Naut* dock; **b. de radoub** dry dock

7 *Rad & TV* **b. d'audience** audience pool

'Le Bassin aux nymphéas' *Monet* 'The Water Lily Pond'

---

bassinant, -e [basinɑ̃, -ɑ̃t] **ADJ** *Fam* boring■; **elle est vraiment bassinante** she's a real pain in the neck

bassine [basin] **NF** basin, bowl; **b. à confiture** preserving pan; **une b. de confiture** a panful of jam

bassiner [3] [basine] **VT 1** *(chauffer)* to warm *(with a warming pan)* **2** *(humecter)* to moisten **3** *Fam (ennuyer)* to bore■; **il nous bassine avec ses histoires de cœur** we're bored stiff hearing about his love affairs; **tu nous bassines avec ça!** stop going on and on about it!

bassinet [basinɛ] **NM 1** *Anat* renal pelvis **2** *Hist* bascinet, basinet

bassinette [basinɛt] **NF** *Can Br* carrycot, *Am* bassinet

bassinoire [basinwar] **NF 1** *Arch (à lit)* warming pan **2** *Fam (importun)* old bore, pain in the neck, crashing bore

bassin-versant [basɛ̃vɛrsɑ̃] *(pl* **bassins-versants)** **NM** *Géog* catchment basin *or* area

bassiste [basist] **NMF** *Mus* **1** *(guitariste)* bass guitarist **2** *(contrebassiste)* double-bass player

basson [basɔ̃] **NM** *Mus* **1** *(instrument)* bassoon **2** *(musicien)* bassoonist

bassoniste [basɔnist] **NMF** *Mus* bassoonist

Bassora [basɔra] **NM** *Géog* Basra, Basrah

basta [basta] **EXCLAM** *Fam* (that's) enough!; **je la rembourse et puis b.!** I'll give her her money back and then that's it!; **je termine la page 14 et b.!** I'll finish page 14 and then that's it!

bastaing [bastɛ̃] **NM** *Menuis* batten

bastaque [bastak] **NF** *Naut* runner and tackle

baste [bast] **EXCLAM 1** *(assez)* enough of that! **2** *(pour exprimer le mépris)* pooh!, nonsense! **3** *Naut* hold hard! avast!

baster [3] [baste] **VI** *Suisse* to give in

bastiais, -e [bastjɛ, -ɛz] **ADJ** of/from Bastia

□ **Bastiais, -e** **NM,F** = inhabitant of or person from Bastia

bastide [bastid] **NF 1** *Archit (maison)* Provençal cottage; *(ferme)* Provençal farmhouse **2** *Hist* walled town *(in south-west France)*

bastidon [bastidɔ̃] **NM** *(en Provence)* small country house

bastille [bastij] **NF 1** *Archit (fort)* fortress **2** *(à Paris)* **la B.** *(forteresse)* the Bastille; *(quartier)* Bastille, the Bastille area; **la prise de la B.** the storming of the Bastille; **l'Opéra B.** the Bastille opera house

---

Culture

BASTILLE

The Bastille, a state prison and a symbol of "Ancien Régime" tyranny, fell to the people of Paris on 14 July 1789, marking the beginning of the Revolution. The square where the Bastille once stood is now the home of the Paris opera house, known as "l'Opéra-Bastille".

---

bastillé, -e [bastije] **ADJ** *Hér* **bande bastillée** bend battled *or* embattled

bastingage [bastɛ̃gaʒ] **NM 1** *Naut* rail; **par-dessus le b.** overboard **2** *Hist* bulwark

bastion [bastjɔ̃] **NM 1** *Archit* bastion **2** *(d'une doctrine, d'un mouvement)* bastion; **b. du socialisme** socialist stronghold, bastion of socialism; **les derniers bastions de la chrétienté** the last outposts *or* bastions of Christianity

bastionné, -e [bastjɔne] **ADJ** *Archit* bastioned

Bastoche [bastɔʃ] **NF** *Fam* **la B.** = the Bastille area of Paris

baston [bastɔ̃] **NF** *Fam* **il y a eu de la b.** there was a bit of a scuffle *or* Br punch-up *or* Am fist fight

bastonnade [bastɔnad] **NF** beating

bastonner [3] [bastɔne] *Fam* **se bastonner VPR** to fight■

V IMPERSONNEL **ça a bastonné** there was a scuffle *or Br* a punch-up *or Am* a fist fight

bastos [bastos] **NF** *Fam Arg* crime bullet■, slug

bastringue [bastrɛ̃g] **NM** *Fam* **1** *(attirail)* stuff, gear, *Br* clobber; **et tout le b.** and the whole caboodle *or* shebang **2** *(bal)* (sleazy) dance hall **3** *(orchestre)* dance band■ **4** *(bruit)* din, racket **5** *Can (danse)* = type of folk dance

Basutoland [basytɔlɑ̃d] **NM** Basutoland

bas-ventre [bavɑ̃tr] *(pl* **bas-ventres)** **NM** *Anat* (lower) abdomen, pelvic area

BAT [beate] **NM** *(abrév* **bon à tirer)** press proof, final corrected proof; **donner le B.** to pass for press

bat *etc voir* **battre**

bât [ba] **NM** packsaddle; **cheval de b.** packhorse; *Fig* **c'est là que** *ou* **où le b. blesse** that's where the shoe pinches

bât. *(abrév écrite* **bâtiment)** *(dans une adresse)* building

bataclan [bataklɑ̃] **NM** *Fam (attirail)* stuff, junk, *Br* clobber; **et tout le b.** and the whole caboodle *or* shebang

bataille [bataj] **NF 1** *(combat)* battle, fight; **une b. d'idées** a battle of ideas; **une b. politique/électorale** a political/an electoral contest; **b. aérienne** *(à grande échelle)* air battle; *(isolée)* dogfight; **b. aéronavale** sea-air battle; **b. de boules de neige** snowball fight; **b. électorale** electoral contest; **b. de polochons** pillow fight; **b. rangée** pitched battle; **b. de rue** street fight *or* brawl; *Fig* **arriver après la b.** to arrive when it's all over bar the shouting

2 *Cartes* ≃ beggar-my-neighbour; **b. navale** *(jeu)* battleships

□ **en bataille ADJ 1** *Mil* in battle order

2 *(en désordre)* **avoir les cheveux en b.** to have tousled hair; **avoir les sourcils en b.** to have bushy eyebrows, to be beetle-browed

batailler [3] [bataje] **VI 1** *(physiquement)* to fight, to battle; **il est toujours prêt à b.** he's always spoiling *or* ready for a fight

2 *Fig* to struggle, to fight; **on a bataillé dur pour avoir ce contrat** we fought *or* struggled hard to win this contract; **j'ai dû b. pendant une heure pour ouvrir la porte** I had to struggle for an hour to get the door open; **je bataille contre leur désordre** I wage a constant battle against their untidiness

batailleur, -euse [batajœr, -øz] **ADJ** *(agressif)* quarrelsome, ready

NM,F fighter; **c'est un b.** *(agressif)* he's always spoiling *or* ready for a fight

bataillon [batajɔ̃] **NM 1** *Mil* battalion; **le b. d'Afrique** = disciplinary battalion originally stationed in Africa **2** *(foule)* **un b. de** scores of, an army of

bâtard, -e [batar, -ard] **ADJ 1** *(enfant)* illegitimate; *(animal)* crossbred; **chien b.** mongrel **2** *(genre, œuvre)* hybrid; *(solution)* half-baked, ill-thought-out

NM,F *(chien)* mongrel; *(enfant)* illegitimate child; *Péj* bastard

NM *(pain)* = short French stick

EXCLAM *Can Fam* goddammit!

□ **bâtarde NF** slanting round-hand writing

bâtardeau, -x, batardeau, -x [batardo] **NM** *Tech* cofferdam

bâtardise [batardiz] **NF** illegitimacy, *Péj Littéraire* bastardy

Bataves [batav] **NMPL** *Hist* **les B.** the Batavi

batavia [batavja] **NF** batavia lettuce

batayole [batjɔl] **NF** *Naut* stanchion

Bat d'Af [batdaf] **NM** *Hist* = the "bataillon d'Afrique", a disciplinary battalion originally stationed in North Africa (or, by extension, someone serving in it)

bâté, -e [bate] **ADJ** *âne b.* *Zool* dunce, numbskull

bateau, -x [bato] **NM 1** *Naut (navire, embarcation)* boat; *(grand)* ship; **je prends le b. à Anvers/à dix heures** I'm sailing from Antwerp/at ten; **faire du b.** *(en barque, en vedette)* to go boating; *(en voilier)* to go sailing; **b. à aubes** paddle steamer; **b. de guerre** warship, battleship; **b. hôtel** boatel; **b. à moteur** motor boat; **b. de pêche** fishing boat; **b. de plaisance** pleasure boat *or* craft; **b. pneumatique** rubber boat, dinghy; **b. à rames** *Br* rowing boat, *Am* rowboat; **b. à roues** paddle steamer; **b. à vapeur** steam-

boat, steamer; **b. à voiles** yacht *or* sailing boat; *Fam* **mener** *ou* **conduire qn en b.** to lead sb up the garden path, to take sb for a ride; *Fam* **monter un b. à qn** to set sb up; *Can Fig* **manquer le b.** to miss the boat

2 *(charge)* **un b. de charbon** a boatload of coal

3 *(sur le trottoir)* dip (in the pavement)

□ **bateau ADJ INV 1** *Couture* **col** *ou* **encolure b.** boat neck

2 *(banal)* hackneyed; **un sujet b.** an old chestnut

'Le Bateau ivre' *Rimbaud* 'The Drunken Boat'

'Céline et Julie vont en bateau' *Rivette* 'Céline and Julie Go Boating' (UK), 'Phantom Ladies over Paris' (US)

---

bateau-citerne [batositɛrn] *(pl* **bateaux-citernes)** **NM** *Transp* tanker

bateau-école [batoekɔl] *(pl* **bateaux-écoles)** **NM** *Naut* training ship

bateau-feu [batofø] *(pl* **bateaux-feux)** **NM** *Naut* lightship

bateau-lavoir [batolavwar] *(pl* **bateaux-lavoirs)** **NM** washhouse *(on a river)*

□ **Bateau-Lavoir NM le B.** = building in Montmartre where Picasso took up residence in 1904 and which became famous as a meeting-place for artists and writers

bateau-mouche [batomuʃ] *(pl* **bateaux-mouches)** **NM** *Naut* river boat *(on the Seine)*

bateau-phare [batofar] *(pl* **bateaux-phares)** **NM** *Naut* lightship

bateau-pilote [batopilɔt] *(pl* **bateaux-pilotes)** **NM** *Naut* pilot ship *or* boat

bateau-pompe [batopɔ̃p] *(pl* **bateaux-pompes)** **NM** *Naut* fireboat

bateau-porte [batopɔrt] *(pl* **bateaux-portes)** **NM** *Naut* floating dam, caisson

batée [bate] **NF** *Tech (récipient)* wash-trough

batelage [batlaʒ] **NM** *Naut* **1** *(transport)* ferry transport **2** *(salaire)* lighterage

batelet [batlɛ] **NM** *Littéraire* little boat

bateleur, -euse [batlœr, -øz] **NM,F** tumbler, street entertainer

batelier, -ère [batəlje, -ɛr] *Naut* **ADJ** inland waterways *(avant n)*

NM,F *(marinier)* boatman, *f* boatwoman; *(sur un bac)* ferryman, *f* ferrywoman

batellerie [batɛlri] **NF** *Naut* **1** *(activité)* inland waterways transport **2** *(flotte)* inland *or* river fleet

bâter [3] [bate] **VT** *(âne)* to put a packsaddle on

bat-flanc [baflɑ̃] **NM INV** *Constr (cloison → de dortoir)* wooden partition; *(→ d'écurie)* bail

bath [bat] **ADJ INV** *Fam Vieilli* super, super-duper, great

batholite [batɔlit] **NM** *Géol* batholith

bathyal, -e, -aux, -ales [batjal, -o] **ADJ** *Géol* bathyal

bathymètre [batimɛtr] **NM** *Phys* bathometer, bathymeter

bathymétrie [batimetri] **NF** *Phys* bathymetry

bathymétrique [batimetrik] **ADJ** *Phys* bathymetric

bathyscaphe [batiskaf] **NM** *Phys* bathyscaph, bathyscaphe

bathysphère [batisfɛr] **NF** *Phys* bathysphere

bâti, -e [bati] **ADJ 1** *(personne)* **être bien b.** to be well-built; **être b. en force** to have a powerful build, to be powerfully built **2** *(terrain)* built-up, developed

NM 1 *Couture (technique)* basting, tacking; *(fil)* tacking; **défais le b.** take out the tacking **2** *(cadre)* frame; **b. d'assemblage** assembly jig

batifolage [batifɔlaʒ] **NM** *Fam* **1** *(amusement → de personnes)* romping about, *Br* larking about; *(→ d'animaux)* frolics, *Br* larking about **2** *(flirt)* flirting

batifoler [3] [batifɔle] **VI** *Fam* **1** *(s'amuser → personnes)* to romp about, *Br* to lark about; *(→ animaux)* to frolic, *Br* to lark about **2** *(flirter)* to flirt■

batifoleur, -euse [batifɔlœr, -øz] **NM,F** *Fam* **1** *(personne frivole)* **c'est un grand b.** he loves romping *or Br* larking about **2** *(flirt)* flirt■

batik [batik] **NM** *Tex* batik; **en b.** batik *(avant n)*

batillage [batijaʒ] **NM** *Naut* backwash, wake *(against river banks)*

bâtiment [batimɑ̃] **NM 1** *Archit (édifice)* building; **bâtiments de ferme/d'usine** farm/factory buildings; **les bâtiments d'exploitation** the sheds and outhouses *(of a farm)* **2** *Constr (profession)* **le b., l'industrie du b.** the building trade, the construction industry; **bâtiments et travaux publics** building and civil engineering; **être dans le b.** to be a builder *or* in the building trade; *Fig* **il est du b.** *(il est du métier)* he's in the same line of business; *(il s'y connaît)* he knows what he's doing; **quand le b. va, tout va** a busy building trade is the sign of a healthy economy **3** *Naut* ship, (sea-going) vessel; **b. de charge** freighter; **b. de guerre** warship; **b. de haut bord** ship of the line; **b. léger** light craft; **b. de soutien** support vessel

bâtir [32] [batir] **VT 1** *Constr* to build; **se faire b. une maison** to have a house built; **b. (qch) sur le sable** to build (sth) on sand; *Fig* **b. des châteaux en Espagne** to build castles in the air

2 *(créer → fortune)* to build up; *(→ foyer)* to build; *(→ théorie, hypothèse)* to build up, to develop; **bâtissons l'avenir ensemble** let's work together to build our future

3 *Couture* to baste, to tack

❑ **à bâtir ADJ 1** *Constr (pierre, terrain)* building *(avant n)*

2 *Couture* basting *(avant n)*, tacking *(avant n)*

▸**se bâtir VPR 1** *(ville, maisons)* to be built

2 se b. une réputation (de) to build up a reputation (as)

bâtisse [batis] **NF 1** *aussi Péj Archit (bâtiment)* building; **une grande b.** a big barn of a place **2** *Constr (partie en maçonnerie)* masonry

bâtisseur, -euse [batisœr, -øz] **NM,F** *Constr* builder; *Fig* **b. d'empires** empire-builder

batiste [batist] **NF** *Tex* batiste, cambric

bâton [batɔ̃] **NM 1** *(baguette → gén)* stick; *(→ d'agent de police) Br* truncheon, *Am* nightstick; *(→ de berger)* staff, crook; *(→ de skieur)* pole; **donner des coups de b. à qn** to beat sb with a stick; **b. lumineux** glow stick; **b. de maréchal** marshal's baton; *Fig* **cette nomination, c'est son b. de maréchal** this appointment is the high point of his/her career; **b. de pèlerin** pilgrim's staff; *Fig* **prendre son b. de pèlerin** to go on a crusade; **être le b. de vieillesse de qn** to be the staff of sb's old age; *Vulg* **b. merdeux** *(personne)* shit; *(situation)* shitty situation; **mettre des bâtons dans les roues à qn** *(continuellement)* to impede sb's progress; *(une fois)* to throw a *Br* spanner *or Am* wrench in the works for sb

2 *(barreau)* **b. de chaise** chair rung

3 *(de craie, de dynamite, de réglisse)* stick; **b. de rouge à lèvres** lipstick

4 *Scol (trait)* (vertical) line; **faire des bâtons** to draw vertical lines; **à l'âge où les enfants font des bâtons** at the age when children are in the earliest stages of learning to write

5 *Can & Suisse* **b. (de hockey)** *Br* ice hockey stick, *Am* hockey stick

6 *Anciennement Fam (10 000 francs)* 10,000 francs▪; **10 bâtons** 100,000 francs▪

7 *(en baseball)* home plate

❑ **à bâtons rompus ADJ 1** *Menuis* **parquet à bâtons rompus** herringbone flooring **2** *(conversation)* idle **ADV parler à bâtons rompus** to make casual conversation

bâtonnat [batɔna] **NM** *Jur* ≃ office of President of the Bar

bâtonner [3] [batɔne] **VT** to beat with a stick

bâtonnet [batɔnɛ] **NM 1** *(petit bâton)* stick; **b. de manucure** orange stick **2** *Anat* **b. de la rétine** retinal rod

bâtonnier [batɔnje] **NM** *Jur* ≃ President of the Bar

batoude [batud] **NF** circus trampoline

batracien [batrasjɛ̃] *Zool* **NM** batrachian

❑ **batraciens NMPL** frogs and toads, *Spéc* batrachians, Batrachia

battage [bataʒ] **NM 1** *(du blé)* threshing; *(de l'or, d'un tapis)* beating; *(du beurre)* churning **2** *Fam* **b. médiatique** media hype; **b. (publicitaire)** hype, *Am* ballyhoo; **faire du b. autour de qch** to hype sth (up), *Am* to ballyhoo sth; **ils font tout un b. pour sa pièce** his/her play is getting a lot of hype

battant, -e [batɑ̃, -ɑ̃t] **ADJ porte battante** *(bruyante)* banging door; *(laissée ouverte)* swinging door; *(à battant libre)* swing door; **le cœur b.** with beating heart; **sous une pluie battante** in the driving *or* pelting rain; **à onze heures battantes** on the stroke of eleven

NM,F *Fig* fighter; **c'est une battante!** she's a real fighter!

NM 1 *(d'une cloche)* clapper, tongue

2 *(d'une table)* leaf; **le b. droit de la porte était ouvert** the right half of the double door was open; **porte à deux battants** double door; **ouvrir la porte à deux battants** to open both sides *or* halves of the door

3 *Naut (d'un drapeau)* fly

4 *Fam (cœur)* ticker

batte [bat] **NF 1** *Sport* bat; **b. de base-ball/cricket** baseball/cricket bat **2** *Culin* **b. à beurre** dasher **3** *(outil → maillet)* mallet; *(→ tapette)* beater

battée [bate] **NF 1** *(de laine etc)* amount beaten at one time **2** *Constr (de porte, fenêtre)* jamb **3** *Tech (récipient)* wash-trough

battellement [batɛlmɑ̃] **NM** *Constr* = double thickness of tiles along the lower edge of a roof

battement [batmɑ̃] **NM 1** *(mouvement → des ailes)* flapping *(UNCOUNT)*; *(→ des paupières)* flutter; **battements de mains** clapping *(UNCOUNT)*, applause *(UNCOUNT)* **2** *(en danse)* battement; **b. de jambes** *(d'un nageur)* leg movement **3** *(d'une porte)* banging *(UNCOUNT)*, beating *(UNCOUNT)*; **des battements de tambour** drumbeats **4** *(rythme du cœur, du pouls)* beating *(UNCOUNT)*, throbbing *(UNCOUNT)*, beat; **je sens les battements de son cœur** I can feel his/her heart beating; **chaque b. de cœur** every heartbeat; **j'ai des battements de cœur** *(palpitations)* I suffer from palpitations; *(émotion)* my heart's beating *or* pounding **5** *(pause)* break; **un b. de dix minutes** a ten-minute break **6** *(attente)* wait; **il y a un b. de cinq minutes entre les deux trains** there's a five-minute wait between the two trains; **j'ai une heure de b. entre la réunion et le déjeuner** I have an hour between the meeting and lunch **7** *(sur une fenêtre)* shutter catch

batterie [batri] **NF 1** *Mil* battery; **mettre une arme en b.** to put a gun in battery; **b. antichars** anti-tank battery; **b. de canons** battery of artillery *or* guns

2 *Aut, Élec & Phys* battery; **ça fonctionne sur b.** it's battery-operated *or* battery-powered; **b. d'accumulateurs** battery of accumulators; **b. de cellules solaires** solar-powered battery; *Fig* **recharger** *ou* **regonfler ses batteries** to recharge one's batteries

3 *Mus (en jazz, rock, pop)* drums, drum kit; *(en musique classique)* percussion instruments; *(roulement)* drum roll; **tenir la b.** to play the *or* to be on drums; **Harvey Barton à la b.** Harvey Barton on drums

4 *(série)* battery; **b. de piles** batteries; **b. de tests/mesures** battery of tests/of measures; **b. de cuisine** set of kitchen utensils; *Hum* **les officiers avec leur b. de cuisine** the officers with all their decorations *or Br* gongs

5 *Agr* **poulet de b.** battery hen; **élevage en b.** battery farming

6 *(en danse)* batterie

batteur [batœr] **NM 1** *Mus* drummer **2** *(ustensile de cuisine)* mixer **3** *(ouvrier)* beater; *Agr* thresher **4** *(au cricket)* batsman; *(au base-ball)* batter **5** *Agr (rouleau d'une batteuse)* beater drum

batteuse [batøz] **NF 1** *Agr* thresher, threshing machine **2** *Métal* beater

battitures [batityr] **NFPL** *Métal* hammer-scales, anvil-dross

battle-dress [batœldrɛs] **NM INV** battledress

battoir [batwar] **NM** *Arch (pour laver)* beetle, battledore

❑ **battoirs NMPL** *Fam* (great) paws, mitts

BATTRE [83] [batr]

> **VT** to beat **1–5, 8** ▪ to defeat **2** ▪ to churn **5** ▪ to whisk, to whip **5** ▪ to shuffle **7**
> **VI** to bang **1** ▪ to beat **1**
> **VPR** to fight **1, 2** ▪ to struggle **2**

VT 1 *(brutaliser → animal)* to beat; *(→ personne)* to batter; **b. qn à mort** to batter sb to death; **il m'énerve tellement que je le battrais!** he annoys me so much that I could hit him!; **b. en brèche** *(mur)* to breach; *(gouvernement)* to topple; *(politique)* to demolish, *Br* to drive a coach and horses through; **b. qn comme plâtre** to beat sb severely

2 *(vaincre → adversaire)* to beat, to defeat; **Bordeaux s'est fait b. 2 à 0** Bordeaux were beaten *or* defeated 2 nil; **b. qn aux échecs** to defeat *or* to beat sb at chess; **se tenir pour** *ou* **s'avouer battu** to admit defeat; **b. qn à plate couture** *ou* **à plates coutures** to beat sb hollow

3 *(surpasser → record)* to beat; *aussi Fig* **b. tous les records** to set a new record; **j'ai battu tous les records de vitesse pour venir ici** I must have broken the record getting here; **cet hiver, nous battrons tous les records de froid** this winter will be the coldest on record

4 *(frapper → tapis, or)* to beat (out); *(→ blé, grain)* to thresh; **b. qch à froid** to cold-hammer sth; **b. froid à qn** to cold-shoulder sb; **b. la semelle** to stamp one's feet *(to keep warm)*; **b. monnaie** to mint (coins); *Prov* **il faut b. le fer quand il est chaud** strike while the iron is hot

5 *Culin (remuer → beurre)* to churn; *(→ blanc d'œuf)* to beat, to whip (up), to whisk; **œufs battus en neige ferme** stiffly beaten egg whites; **battez le sucre avec le beurre** cream together the sugar and the butter; *Fig* **b. l'air de ses bras** to beat the air with one's arms

6 *(sillonner)* **b. le secteur** to scour *or* to comb the area; **ils ont battu les bois pour retrouver l'enfant** they combed (every inch of) the woods to find the missing child; **b. le pavé parisien** to roam the streets of Paris; *Chasse* **b. les buissons** to beat the bushes; **b. la campagne** *ou* **le pays** to comb the countryside; *Fig* to be in one's own little world

7 *Cartes* **b. les cartes** to shuffle the cards *or* pack

8 *Mus (mesure)* to beat (out); *Mil & Mus (tambour)* to beat (on); *Mil* **b. la générale** to sound the call to arms; *Mil* **b. le rappel** to drum up troops; *Fig* **b. le rappel de la famille/du parti** to gather the family/party round; *Fam* **b. (le) tambour** *ou* **la grosse caisse** to make a lot of noise; **mon cœur bat la chamade** my heart's racing

9 *Naut* **b. pavillon** to sail under *or* to fly a flag; **un navire battant pavillon britannique** a ship flying the British flag

10 *(locution)* **b. son plein** *(fête)* to be in full swing

VI 1 *(cœur, pouls)* to beat, to throb; *(pluie)* to lash, to beat down; *(porte)* to rattle, to bang; *(store)* to flap; **l'émotion faisait b. mon cœur** my heart was beating *or* racing with emotion; **le vent faisait b. les volets** the shutters were banging in the wind

2 *(locutions)* **b. en retraite** to retreat; *Fig* to beat a retreat; *très Fam* **j'en ai rien à b.** I don't give a shit *or Br* a toss *or Am* a rat's ass

❑ **battre de VT IND b. des mains** to clap (one's hands); **b. des paupières** *(d'éblouissement)* to blink; **b. des cils** *(pour séduire)* to flutter one's eyelashes; **l'oiseau bat des ailes** *(lentement)* the bird flaps its wings; *(rapidement)* the bird flutters its wings; *Fig* **b. de l'aile** to be in a bad way

▸**se battre VPR 1** *(emploi réciproque)* to fight, to fight (with) one another; **se b. à mains nues** to fight with one's bare hands; **se b. à l'épée/au couteau** to fight with swords/knives; **se b. en duel** to fight (each other in) a duel; *Fig* **ne vous battez pas, il y en a pour tout le monde** don't get excited, there's enough for everyone; **on se bat pour assister à ses cours** people are falling over each other to get into his/her classes; *Ironique* **surtout ne vous battez pas pour m'aider!** don't all rush to help me!

2 *(lutter)* to fight; *Fig* to fight, to struggle; **se b. avec/contre qn** to fight with/against sb; **se b. contre des moulins à vent** to tilt at windmills; **j'ai dû me b. pour pouvoir entrer/sortir** I had to fight my way in/out; **il faut se b. pour le faire coucher à huit heures!** it's a real struggle to get him to bed at eight!; **je me suis battu pour qu'il accepte** I had a tough time getting him to accept; **nous nous battons pour la paix/contre l'injustice** we're fighting for peace/against

injustice; **se b. contre la maladie** to struggle or to fight against disease; *Hum* **je suis obligé de me b. avec la serrure chaque fois que je rentre** I have to struggle or to do battle with the lock every time I come home

3 *(frapper)* **se b. les flancs** to struggle pointlessly; *très Fam* **je m'en bats l'œil** I don't give a tinker's cuss

'De battre mon cœur s'est arrêté' *Audiard* 'The Beat that my Heart Skipped'

battu, -e[1] [baty] ADJ **1** *(maltraité)* battered **2** *(vaincu)* beaten, defeated; **on est battus d'avance** we've got no chance **3 avoir les yeux battus** to have rings or circles round one's eyes **4** *(or, fer)* beaten

battue[2] [baty] NF **1** *Chasse* battue, beat **2** *(recherche)* search *(through an area)*

batture [batyr] NF *Can* **1** *(estran)* sandbank **2** *(glaces)* batture ice, = ice which builds up along the sides of a river

bau, -x [bo] NM *Naut* beam

baud [bo] NM *Ordinat & Tél* baud; **à (une vitesse de) 28 800 bauds** at 28,800 baud

baudelairien, -enne [bodlɛrjɛ̃, -ɛn] ADJ of Baudelaire, Baudelairean

baudet [bodɛ] NM **1** *Zool (âne)* donkey, ass **2** *Menuis* sawhorse, trestle

baudrier [bodrije] NM **1** *(bandoulière)* baldric **2** *Sport* harness

baudroie [bodrwa] NF *Ich* monkfish, anglerfish

baudruche [bodryʃ] NF **1** *(peau)* bladder **2** *Fam (personne)* wimp

bauge [boʒ] NF **1** *(du cochon, du sanglier)* wallow **2** *(lieu sale)* pigsty **3** *Constr* clay and straw mortar

Bauhaus [boos] NM **le B.** the Bauhaus

bauhinie [boini] NF *Bot* bauhinia

baume [bom] NM *Bot & Pharm* balsam, balm; **b. de benjoin** friar's balsam; **b. du Canada** Canada balsam; **b. démêlant** hair conditioner; **b. du Pérou** Peru balsam, balsam of Peru; **b. du tigre** tiger balm; **b. de Tolu** tolu; *Fig* **mettre un peu de b. au cœur de qn** to soothe sb's aching heart; *Fig* **si ça peut te mettre du b. au cœur** if it's any consolation (to you)

baumé [bome] NM Baumé scale

baumier [bomje] NM *Bot* balsam tree

bauquière [bokjɛr] NF *Archit* beam-shelf, shelfpiece

baux [bo] **1** *voir* **bail 2** *voir* **bau**

bauxite [boksit] NF *Géol* bauxite

bavard, -e [bavar, -ard] ADJ *(personne → qui parle beaucoup)* talkative; *(→ indiscret)* indiscreet; *(roman, émission)* wordy, long-winded; **elle n'était pas bien bavarde ce soir** she hardly said a word or she wasn't in a talkative mood tonight; **il est b. comme une pie** he's a real chatterbox

  NM,F **quelle bavarde, celle-là!** she's a real chatterbox!; **attention, c'est une bavarde!** watch out, she can't keep quiet!; **les bavards, on leur règle leur compte!** *(délateurs)* we know how to deal with informers!

  NM *Fam Arg crime (avocat)* lawyer■, brief
  ◻ **bavarde** NF *Fam (langue)* tongue■; **tenir sa bavarde** to hold one's tongue, to keep one's mouth shut

bavardage [bavardaʒ] NM **1** *(action de parler)* chatting, chattering; *Scol* **puni pour b.** punished for talking in class **2** *Ordinat (sur Internet)* chat
  ◻ **bavardages** NMPL *(conversation)* chatter *(UNCOUNT)*; *Péj (racontars)* gossip *(UNCOUNT)*

bavarder [3] [bavarde] VI **1** *(parler)* to chat, to talk; **b. avec qn** to have a chat with sb; **on bavardait des heures au téléphone** we used to talk for hours on the phone; **avec qui tu bavardes?** who are you chatting to? **2** *(médire)* to gossip **3** *(être indiscret)* to talk **4** *Ordinat (sur Internet)* to chat

bavardoir [bavardwar] NM *Can Ordinat* chat room

bavarois, -e [bavarwa, -az] ADJ Bavarian
  NM *Ling* Bavarian
  ◻ **Bavarois, -e** NM,F Bavarian
  ◻ **bavaroise** NF *Culin* Bavarian cream

bavasser [3] [bavase] VI *Fam Péj (parler)* to natter, to yack; *(médire)* to gossip■

bavasseux, -euse [bavasø, -øz] NM,F *Can Fam Péj (bavard)* chatterbox; *(indiscret)* gossip(monger)

bave [bav] NF *(d'un bébé)* dribble; *(d'un chien)* slobber, slaver; *(d'un malade, d'un chien enragé)* foam, froth; *(d'un escargot)* slime; *(d'un crapaud)* spittle; *Prov* **la b. du crapaud n'atteint pas la blanche colombe** sticks and stones may break my bones, but names will never hurt me

baver [3] [bave] VI **1** *(bébé)* to dribble, to drool, to slobber; *(chien)* to slaver, to slobber; *(malade, chien enragé)* to foam or to froth at the mouth; **b. d'envie à la vue de qch** to drool over sth; *Fam Fig* **j'avais des bottes neuves, tous les copains en bavaient!** I had a pair of brand-new boots, all my friends were green with envy!; **b. d'admiration devant qn** to worship the ground sb walks on

  2 *(encre, stylo)* to leak

  3 *Fam (locutions)* **en b.** *(souffrir)* to have a rough or hard time of it; **on va t'en faire b. à l'armée** they'll make you sweat blood or they'll put you through it in the army; **tu n'as pas fini d'en b.!** you've got a hard road or *Br* slog ahead of you!; **en b. des ronds de chapeau** *(être étonné)* to have eyes like saucers; *(souffrir)* to go through the mill, to have a rough time of it

  VT **1** *Fam (dire)* **qu'est-ce que tu baves?** what are you rambling or jabbering or *Br* wittering on about?

  2 *Can très Fam (contrarier)* to mess around, *Br* to wind up; **se faire b.** to be messed around, *Br* to be wound up
  ◻ **baver sur** VT IND *Fam (médire de) Br* to slag off, *Am* to badmouth

bavette [bavɛt] NF **1** *(bavoir)* bib **2** *(viande)* **b. (d'aloyau)** top of sirloin **3** *Aut* mudguard

baveux, -euse [bavø, -øz] ADJ *(bouche, enfant)* dribbling; *(baiser)* wet; *(omelette)* runny
  NM,F *Can très Fam* jerk; **petit b.** *(enfant)* little devil
  NM *Fam* **1** *(savon)* soap■ **2** *(journal)* newspaper■, rag **3** *(baiser)* sloppy kiss■

Bavière [bavjɛr] NF **la B.** Bavaria

bavocheux, -euse [bavoʃø, -øz] ADJ *Typ* mackled

bavoir [bavwar] NM bib

bavolet [bavolɛ] NM **1** *(coiffe)* (peasant's) bonnet **2** *(voile)* curtain *(of woman's bonnet)* **3** *(drap)* valance, side-apron

bavure [bavyr] NF **1** *Typ* smudge, ink stain **2** *Ind* burr **3** *(erreur)* mistake; **un spectacle sans b.** a faultless or flawless show; **b. (policière)** police error; **il y a eu une b.** the police have made a serious blunder

baxter [bakstɛr] NM *Belg Méd Br* drip, *Am* IV

bayadère [bajadɛr] NF *(danseuse)* bayadere
  ADJ *Tex (rayé)* bayadere *(avant n)*, striped

bayer [3] [baje] VI **b. aux corneilles** to stand gaping; *(être inactif)* to stargaze

Bayeux [bajø] NM Bayeux

bayonnais, -e [bajɔnɛ, -ɛz] ADJ of/from Bayonne
  ◻ **Bayonnais, -e** NM,F = inhabitant of or person from Bayonne

bayou [baju] NM *Géog* bayou

bayram [bɛram] NM *Rel* Bairam

Bayreuth [bajrøt] NM Bayreuth

bazar [bazar] NM **1** *(souk)* bazaar, bazar; *(magasin)* general store, *Am* dime store

  2 *Fam (désordre)* clutter, shambles *(singulier)*; **quel b., cette chambre!** what a shambles or mess this room is!; **il a mis un sacré b. dans mes papiers** he made a hell of a mess of my papers

  3 *Fam (attirail)* stuff, junk, *Br* clobber; **et tout le b.** and the whole caboodle

  4 *Belg Fam (chose)* thing■, thingy
  ◻ **de bazar** ADJ *Péj (psychologie, politique)* halfbaked, *Am* two-bit *(avant n)*

bazarder [3] [bazarde] VT *Fam (jeter)* to dump, to chuck (out); *(vendre)* to sell off■, *Br* to flog

Bazeilles [bazɛj] NM *Géog* Bazeilles *(town in the Ardennes where, during the Franco-Prussian War, French marines were defeated by the Bavarians)*

bazooka [bazuka] NM *Mil* bazooka

bazou [bazu] NM *Can Fam* old pile of junk, rustbucket; *Ironique* **un beau b.** nice wheels

BB [bebe] NPR = nickname of Brigitte Bardot

BBS [bebeɛs] NM *Ordinat (abrév* **bulletin board system***)* BBS

BBZ [bebezɛd] NM *Compta (abrév* **budget base zéro***)* ZBB

BCBG [besebeʒe, besbeʒe] ADJ INV *(abrév* **bon chic bon genre***)* = term used to describe an uppermiddle-class lifestyle reflected especially in expensive but conservative clothes; **elle est très B.** *Br* ≃ she's really Sloaney, *Am* ≃ she's a real preppie type; **ils ont une clientèle plutôt B.** they have a largely upper-middle-class clientele

BCE [beseə] NF *(abrév* **Banque centrale européenne***)* European central bank

BCG® [beseʒe] NM *Méd (abrév* **bacille Calmette-Guérin***)* BCG®

bcp *(abrév écrite* **beaucoup***)* many, a lot

BD [bede] NF **1** *Littérature (abrév* **bande dessinée***) (dans un magazine)* comic strip, *Br* cartoon (strip); *(livre)* comic book **2** *Ordinat (abrév* **base de données***)* dbase

bd *(abrév écrite* **boulevard***)* Blvd.

bdc *Typ (abrév écrite* **bas de casse***)* lc

BDF [bedeɛf] NF *(abrév* **Bibliothèque de France***)* = the new French national library building

B. de F. NF *(abrév écrite* **Banque de France***)* the Banque de France, = French issuing bank

beach-volley [bitʃvɔlɛ] NM *Sport* beach volleyball

beagle [bigœl] NM *Zool (chien)* beagle

béance [beɑ̃s] NF *Littéraire* wide opening, yawning gap

béant, -e [beɑ̃, -ɑ̃t] ADJ *(gouffre)* gaping, yawning; *(plaie)* gaping, open; **b. d'étonnement** gaping in surprise; **être b. d'admiration** to be openmouthed or *Littéraire* agape with admiration

béarnais, -e [bearnɛ, -ɛz] ADJ of/from the Béarn
  ◻ **Béarnais, -e** NM,F = inhabitant of or person from the Béarn
  ◻ **béarnaise** NF *Culin* **(sauce à la) béarnaise** béarnaise sauce

beat [bit] NM *Mus* beat

béat, -e [bea, -at] ADJ *(heureux)* blissfully happy; *Péj (niais → air, sourire)* vacant, vacuous; *(→ optimisme)* smug; *(→ admiration)* blind; **être b. d'admiration** to be open-mouthed or *Littéraire* agape with admiration; **elle nous observait d'un air b.** she watched us open-mouthed

béatement [beatmɑ̃] ADV *Péj (idiotement)* **il la regardait b.** he looked at her with a blissfully stupid expression

béatification [beatifikasjɔ̃] NF *Rel* beatification

béatifier [9] [beatifje] VT *Rel* to beatify

béatifique [beatifik] ADJ *Rel* beatific

béatitude [beatityd] NF **1** *Rel* beatitude; **les béatitudes** the Beatitudes **2** *(bonheur)* bliss, *Littéraire* beatitude

beatnik [bitnik] NMF *Littérature* beatnik; **les beatniks** the Beat Generation

BEAU, BELLE [bo, bɛl]

ADJ	beautiful A1–4 ■ good-looking A1 ■ fine A3, 4, B1, 3, C6 ■ smart B4 ■ nice C1 ■ good A3, C3, 4 ■ Ironic use D ■ Emphatic use C2
ADV fine, warm, nice 1

bel is used before masculine singular nouns beginning with a vowel or h mute.

ADJ A. 1 *(bien fait, joli → femme)* beautiful, good-looking; *(→ homme)* good-looking, handsome; *(→ enfant, physique, objet, décor)* beautiful, lovely; **c'est très b.** it's gorgeous *or* exquisite *or* beautiful; **un b. chat** a beautiful *or* handsome cat; **de la tour, on a une belle vue** *ou* **la vue est belle** there's a lovely *or* beautiful view from the tower; **elle est belle fille** she's a good-looking *or* beautiful girl; *Fam* **il est b. garçon** *ou* **gosse** he's good-looking, he's a good-looking guy; **ils forment un b. couple** they make a lovely couple; **elle est assez belle** she's fairly good-looking; **se faire b./belle** to get dressed up, to do oneself up; **ça, c'est une belle moto!** that's a terrific-looking bike!; **la robe a une très belle coupe** the dress is beautifully cut; *Fam* **ce n'était pas b. à voir** it wasn't a pretty sight; *Fam* **son cadavre n'était pas b. à voir** his/her body wasn't a pretty sight; **il est b. comme l'amour** *ou* **un ange** *ou* **un astre** *ou* **le jour** *(homme)* he's a very handsome *or* good-looking man; *(petit garçon)* he's a very handsome *or* good-looking boy; **il est b. comme un dieu** he looks like a Greek god; **elle est belle comme un ange** *ou* **le jour** she's a real beauty

2 *(attrayant pour l'oreille → chant, mélodie, voix)* beautiful, lovely; **quelques beaux accords** some fine chords; **le russe est une belle langue** Russian is a beautiful language

3 *(remarquable, réussi → poème, texte)* fine, beautiful; *(→ chanson, film)* beautiful, lovely; **de beaux vêtements** fine clothes; **de belles paroles de Brel** some fine lyrics by Brel; **le boucher a de la belle marchandise** the butcher's got nice meat; **le plus b. moment du match** the finest moment in the match; **il y a eu quelques beaux échanges** there were a few good *or* fine rallies; **quel b. coup!** what a magnificent shot!; **son cheval a fait une belle course** his/her horse ran a very good race; **nous avons fait un b. voyage** we had a wonderful trip

4 *Météo* fine, beautiful; **il y aura un b. soleil sur tout le pays** the whole country will enjoy bright sunshine; **la mer sera belle** the sea will be calm; **temps froid mais b. sur tout le pays** the whole country will enjoy cold but sunny weather; **du b. temps** nice *or* good weather; **on a eu du très b. temps** we had beautiful weather, the weather was beautiful; **une belle après-midi** a beautiful afternoon; **les derniers beaux jours** the last days of summer

B. 1 *(digne)* noble, fine; **une belle âme** a noble nature; **elle a eu un b. geste** she made a noble gesture; **je suis chirurgien – vous faites un b. métier** I'm a surgeon – yours is a fine profession

2 *(convenable)* nice; **ce n'est pas b. de tirer la langue!** it's not nice to stick your tongue out (at people)!; **ce n'est pas b. de mentir!** it's very naughty *or* it's not nice to lie!

3 *(brillant intellectuellement)* wonderful, fine; **c'est un b. sujet de thèse** it's a fine topic for a thesis; **en une belle expression, il résume le dilemme** he encapsulates the dilemma in one apt phrase

4 *(d'un haut niveau social)* smart; **faire un b. mariage** *(financièrement)* to marry into money *or* a fortune; *(socialement)* to marry into a very good family; *Fam* **le b. monde** *ou* **linge** the upper crust, the smart set

C. 1 *(gros, important → gains, prime, somme)* nice, handsome, tidy; **donnez-moi un b. melon/poulet** give me a nice big melon/chicken; **il a un bel appétit** he has a good *or* hearty appetite; **manger avec un bel appétit** to eat heartily; **c'est un b. cadeau qu'il t'a fait là!** that's a nice *or* that's quite a present he gave you!; **un b. coup en Bourse** a spectacular deal on the Stock Exchange

2 *(en intensif)* **il a une belle cicatrice dans le dos** he's got quite a (big) scar on his back; **je me suis fait une belle bosse** I got a great big bump; *Fam* **elle lui a mis une belle raclée** she gave him/her a good hiding; *Fam* **il y a un b. bazar dans ta chambre!** your room's in a fine *or* real mess!; **il y a eu un b. scandale** there was a huge scandal; **c'était une belle bêtise de lui faire confiance** it was a stupid *or* big mistake to trust him/her; **tu m'as fait une belle peur** you gave me a real scare; **quel b. vacarme!** what a terrible noise!; **un bel hypocrite** a real hypocrite; *très Fam* **t'es un b. salaud!** you're a right bastard!; *Fam* **il y a b. temps de ce que je te dis là** what I'm telling you now happened ages ago

3 *(agréable)* good; **présenter qch sous un b. jour** to show sth in a good light; **ce serait trop b.!** that'd be too good to be true!; **c'est trop b. pour être vrai** it's too good to be true; **c'est b., l'amour!** love's a wonderful thing!; **un b. coup de dés** a lucky throw of the dice

4 *(prospère)* good; **après la guerre, ils croyaient à un bel avenir** after the war, they thought they had a wonderful future ahead of them; **tu as encore de belles années devant toi** you still have quite a few good years ahead of you; **avoir une belle situation** *(financière)* to have a very well-paid job; *(prestigieuse)* to have a high-flying job; **il a fait une très belle carrière dans les textiles** he carved out a brilliant career for himself in textiles

5 *(dans des appellations)* **venez, ma belle amie** do come along, darling; **mais oui, mon bel ami, je vous accorde que...** yes, my friend, I'll grant you that...; *Fam* **alors, (ma) belle enfant, qu'en dis-tu?** what do you think about that, my dear?; **mon b. monsieur, personne ne vous a rien demandé!** my friend, this is none of your business!

6 *(certain)* **un b. jour/matin** one fine day/morning

7 *Can Fam (locution)* **c'est beau!** *(c'est d'accord)* OK!; **si vous n'êtes pas d'accord avec lui, vous pouvez lui écrire – c'est beau, je le ferai** if you don't agree with him, you can write to him – alright, I will!

D. *Ironique* **belle demande!** *(saugrenue)* what a question!; **que voilà un b. langage!** language, please!; **c'est du b. travail!** a fine mess this is!; **en voilà, une belle excuse!** that's a good excuse!, what an excuse!; **je vais le lui faire comprendre, et de la belle manière!** I'll make him/her understand, and in no uncertain terms!; **ils ont oublié tous leurs beaux discours** they've forgotten all their fine *or* fine-sounding words; **garde tes belles promesses** *ou* **tes beaux serments!** you can keep your promises!; **belles paroles** fine words; **assez de belles paroles!** enough fine words!; *Hum* **sur ces belles paroles, il faut que je m'en aille** on that note, I must go now; **il lui en a dit de belles!** the things he told him/her (you wouldn't believe)!; **j'en ai appris** *ou* **entendu de belles sur toi!** I heard some fine *or* right things about you!; **il est sorti de voiture et il m'en a dit de belles!** he got out of his car and gave me a right earful!; **il en a fait de belles quand il était petit!** he didn't half get up to some mischief when he was little!; *Fam* **elle en a vu de belles avec son mari!** her husband's led her a merry dance!; **nous voilà beaux!** we're in a fine mess now!; **c'est bien b., tout ça, mais...** that's all very fine *or* well, but...; **c'est bien b. de critiquer les autres, mais toi, que fais-tu?** it's all very well to criticize, but what do YOU ever do?; *Fam* **et tu ne sais pas le plus b.!** and you haven't heard the best part (yet)!, and the best part's still to come!; *Fam* **le plus b., c'est que sa femme n'en savait rien!** the best part (of it) is that his wife knew nothing about it!; *Fam* **ça, c'est le plus b.!** that crowns it all!, that (really) takes the biscuit!

ADV 1 *Météo* **il fait b.** the weather's *or* it's fine; **il fera b. et chaud** it'll be warm and sunny; **il n'a pas fait très b. l'été dernier** the weather wasn't very nice *or* good last summer

2 *(locutions)* **il ferait b. voir (cela)!** that'll be the day!; **il ferait b. voir qu'elle me donne des ordres!** her, boss me around? that'll be the day!; **elle le fera quand même – il ferait b. voir (cela)!** she'll do it all the same – just let her try!; **j'avais b. tirer, la porte ne s'ouvrait pas** however hard I pulled, the door wouldn't open; **j'ai eu b. le lui répéter plusieurs fois, il n'a toujours pas compris** I have told him and told him but he still hasn't understood; **j'avais b. me raisonner, j'avais peur** however hard I tried to reason with myself, I was frightened; **on a b. dire...** whatever you say..., say what you like...; *Fam* **on a b. dire, on a b. faire, les jeunes s'en vont un jour de la maison** whatever you do or say, young people eventually leave home; **tu auras b. faire, la pelouse ne repoussera plus ici** whatever you do, the lawn won't grow here again; **vous avez b. dire, elle a quand même tout financé elle-même** say what you like *or* you may criticize, but she's paid for it all herself; *Prov* **a b. mentir qui vient de loin** = it's easy to lie when there's nobody around to contradict you; **voir tout en b.** to see the world through rose-coloured spectacles; **alors, vous signez? – hé, tout b. (tout b.)!** you will sign then? – hey, steady on *or* not so fast!

NM 1 *(esthétique)* **elle aime le b.** she likes beautiful things

2 *(objets de qualité)* **pour les meubles du salon, je veux du b.** I want really good *or* nice furniture for the living room

3 *(homme)* beau, dandy; *Can* **faire le b.** to strut about

4 *(locutions)* **le temps est au b.** the weather looks fine; **le temps/baromètre est au b. fixe** the weather/barometer is set fair; *Fam* **nos relations sont au b. fixe** things between us are looking rosy; *Fam* **il a le moral au b. fixe** he's in high spirits; *Fam* **elle a dit un gros mot – c'est du b.!** she said a rude word! – how naughty!; *Fam* **il m'a pincé – c'est du b.!** he pinched me – that was naughty *or* that wasn't a nice thing to do!; **faire le b.** *(chien)* to sit up and beg

❑ **belle NF 1** *(jolie femme)* beauty; *(dame)* lady; **il se plaisait en compagnie de ces belles** he liked the company of these fair ladies

2 *Fam (en appellatif)* **bonjour ma belle!** good morning, beautiful!; **tu te trompes, ma belle!** you're quite wrong, my dear!

3 *Hum ou Littéraire (amie, amante)* lady friend, beloved; **sa belle l'a quitté** his lady (friend) has left him; **il chantait sous les fenêtres de sa belle** he was singing beneath the windows of his beloved

4 *Sport* decider, deciding match; *(jeux)* decider, deciding game; **on fait** *ou* **joue la belle?** shall we play the decider?

5 *(locutions) Fam* **(se) faire la belle** *Br* to do a runner, *Am* to cut and run; *Can (chien)* to stand up on its back legs; *Can Fig* **faire la belle devant qn** to suck up to sb

6 *Belg Fam (locutions)* **avoir belle à faire qch** to have no trouble doing sth▪, to find it easy to do sth▪; **en avoir une belle avec qn** to go through some hard times with sb; **en faire une (bien) belle** to do something really silly *or* stupid; **ne jamais en faire une belle** to be always putting one's foot in it; **ne pas en faire une belle** to be a total disaster

❑ **belle de Fontenay NF** Belle de Fontenay potato

❑ **belle page NF** *Typ* right-hand page, odd-number page; **chaque chapitre commence en belle page** each chapter starts on the right-hand page

❑ **au plus beau de PRÉP au plus b. de la fête** when the party is/was in full swing; **au plus b. du discours** right in the middle of the speech

❑ **bel et bien ADV** well and truly; **il m'aurait bel et bien frappé si tu n'avais pas été là** he really would have hit me if you hadn't been there; **elle s'est bel et bien échappée** she got away and no mistake; *Fam* **ils nous ont bel et bien eus** they well and truly conned us; **il est bel et bien mort** he's dead all right, he's well and truly dead

❑ **bel et bon, bel et bonne ADJ** fine; *Ironique* **tout ceci est bel et bon, mais...** this is all very fine, but...

❑ **de plus belle ADV** *(aboyer, crier)* louder than ever, even louder; *(frapper)* harder than ever, even harder; *(taquiner, manger)* more than ever, even more; **la pluie a recommencé de plus belle** it started to rain again harder than ever; **le combat a repris de plus belle** the fight resumed with renewed violence; **il s'est mis à**

bea–bec

travailler de plus belle he went back to work with renewed energy

'La Belle et la Bête' *Madame Leprince de Beaumont, Cocteau* 'Beauty and the Beast'

'La Belle au bois dormant' *Perrault, Tchaïkovski* 'Sleeping Beauty'

'Le Beau Danube bleu' *Johann Strauss* 'The Blue Danube'

Culture

LA BELLE ÉPOQUE

This refers to the period of apparent stability and prosperity from the closing years of the 19th century to the beginning of the First World War, which found its expression in café and theatre society, fashion, art and architecture. Its chief surviving monument is the area on the south side of the Champs-Élysées containing the "Petit Palais" and the "Grand Palais", erected at the time of the Universal Exhibition of 1900.

Allusion

La belle et la bête

This expression means "Beauty and the Beast" in English, and is used in a similar way in the two languages. The 18th-century tale by Madame Leprince de Beaumont became a famous French film classic in the hands of Jean Cocteau (1946). The phrase is applied, somewhat unkindly, to an ill-assorted couple, one of whom appears more personable and charming at first sight.

Allusion

Sois belle et tais-toi

This means "Look pretty and keep your mouth shut". Originally the title of a 1958 film by Marc Allégret, and a Serge Gainsbourg song, it was an archetypal male chauvinist expression. However, it is now used ironically to ridicule anyone who treats women as sex objects. One can substitute any other adjective for "belle", and use the phrase rudely to someone annoying.

Beaubourg [bobur] **NM** *Géog* = name commonly used to refer to the Pompidou Centre

---

Culture

BEAUBOURG

This term officially refers to the area surrounding the Pompidou Centre but it has come to mean the museum itself. Its very unusual design – bare coloured pipes on the outside and an escalator tube snaking along the front – was the subject of much controversy when it was built in 1977, but today it is the second most visited building in France (only recently overtaken by the Louvre). It houses a modern art gallery, a cinema, an open-stack library and other cultural exhibits.

---

beauceron, -onne [bosrɔ̃, -ɔn] **ADJ** of/from the Beauce area
NM *Zool* (chien) Beauceron (dog)
❏ **Beauceron, -onne NM,F** = inhabitant of or person from the Beauce area

BEAUCOUP [boku]

a lot **1–3** ■ a great deal **1** ■ much **1, 2** ■ many **3**

ADV 1 *(modifiant un verbe)* a lot, a great deal; *(dans des phrases interrogatives ou négatives)* much, a lot, a great deal; **il boit b.** he drinks a lot *or* a great deal; **il travaille b.** he works a lot *or* a great deal; **il ne mange pas b.** he doesn't eat much *or* a great deal *or* a lot; **il sort b.** he goes out a lot *or* a great deal; **elle voyage b.** she travels a lot *or* a great deal; **je ne l'ai pas b. vu** I

---

didn't see much of him; **je vous remercie b.** thank you very much (indeed); **on s'aimait b.** we liked each other a lot *or* a great deal; **il compte b. pour moi** he means a lot *or* a great deal to me; **ils ne s'apprécient pas b.** they don't like each other much; **dix bouteilles, ça ne fait pas b.?** ten bottles, isn't that a bit much?

2 *(modifiant un adverbe)* much, a lot; **c'est b. mieux comme ça** it's much *or* a lot better like that; **b. moins intéressant** much *or* a lot less interesting; **b. plus bête** much *or* a lot more stupid; **b. plus grand** much *or* a lot bigger; **b. trop fort** much *or* far too loud; **il parle b. trop** he talks far too much; **en faire b. trop** to overdo it

3 *(de nombreuses personnes)* many, a lot; *(de nombreuses choses)* a lot; **b. pensent que...** a lot of people *or* many people think that...; **nous sommes b. à penser cela** there are a lot *or* many of us who think that; **il n'y en a pas b. qui réussissent** not a lot of people *or* not many succeed; **nous étions b. à le croire** many *or* a lot of us believed it; **elle a b. à faire/à dire** she has a lot to do/to say; **c'est b.** that's a lot; **c'est déjà b. qu'il y soit allé!** at least he went!; **ça compte pour b.** that counts for a lot; **il est pour b. dans son succès** he played a large part in *or* he had a great deal to do with his/her success; **c'est b. dire** that's a bit of an overstatement

4 *(modifiant un adjectif)* **imprudent, il l'est même b.** he's really quite careless
❏ **beaucoup de ADJ** *(suivi d'un nom comptable)* many, a lot of; *(suivi d'un nom non comptable)* much, a lot of, a great deal of; **b. de monde** a lot of people; **b. de gens pensent que...** a lot of people *or* many people think that...; **j'ai b. de choses à dire** I've got many *or* a lot of things to say; **il n'a pas b. d'amis** he doesn't have many *or* a lot of friends, he has few friends; **b. d'entre nous** many *or* a lot of us; **il faut b. de courage** it takes a lot of *or* a great deal of courage; **elle a b. de goût** she has a lot of *or* a great deal of taste; **je n'ai pas b. de patience** I don't have much *or* a lot of *or* a great deal of patience; **il ne nous reste plus b. de temps** we've not got much time left; **il n'y a plus b. de lait** there isn't much milk left; **il y en a b.** there is/are a lot
❏ **de beaucoup ADV 1** *(avec un comparatif ou un superlatif)* by far; **il est de b. le plus jeune** he is the youngest by far, he is by far the youngest; **elle est de b. la plus douée** she's the most talented by far, she is by far the most talented; **il est mon aîné de b.** he's considerably older than I am

2 *(avec un verbe)* **il a gagné de b.** he won easily; **il te dépasse de b.** he's far *or* much taller than you; **je préférerais de b. rester** I'd much rather stay; **je préfère de b. le sien** I much prefer his/hers; **as-tu raté ton train de b.?** did you miss your train by much?; **je la préfère, et de b.** I much prefer her

---

'Beaucoup de bruit pour rien' *Shakespeare* 'Much Ado about Nothing'

---

beauf [bof] *très Fam* **NM 1** *(beau-frère)* brother-in-law■ **2** *Fig Péj* = archetypal lower-middle-class Frenchman
ADJ *Fig Péj* = typical of the archetypal lower-middle-class Frenchman

---

Allusion

Beauf

The cartoonist Cabu invented a character he called "mon beauf" ("my brother-in-law"). This **beauf** is reactionary, narrow-minded, ultra-conventional and something of a redneck, and the sense has come to enter the French language in its own right. The word can be used as an adjective: for example, the idea that women should do all the cooking and child-care could be described as **beauf**.

---

beau-fils [bofis] *(pl* **beaux-fils**) **NM 1** *(gendre)* son-in-law **2** *(fils du conjoint)* stepson
Beaufort [bofɔr] *voir* échelle
beaufort [bofɔr] **NM** *(fromage)* Beaufort cheese

---

beau-frère [bofrɛr] *(pl* **beaux-frères**) **NM** brother-in-law
Beaujolais [boʒɔlɛ] **NM le B.** (the) Beaujolais (region)
beaujolais [boʒɔlɛ] **NM** *(vin)* Beaujolais (wine)

Allusion

Le beaujolais nouveau est arrivé

This is an advertising slogan seen everywhere at the time of year when Beaujolais nouveau wine comes on sale; the campaign has even crossed the Channel. The slogan has been adapted, with other words substituted for **beaujolais nouveau**, and has become part of everyday French. Thus one might hear **L'impôt nouveau est arrivé** ("The new tax has come into force") or **Le Depardieu nouveau est arrivé** ("The latest Depardieu film is out").

---

beaujolpif [boʒɔlpif] **NM** *Fam* Beaujolais■
beau-papa [bopapa] *(pl* **beaux-papas**) **NM** *Fam* **1** *(père du conjoint)* father-in-law■ **2** *(conjoint de la mère)* stepdad
beau-parent [boparɑ̃] *(pl* **beaux-parents**) **NM** *(conjoint de la mère ou du père)* step-parent
beau-père [bopɛr] *(pl* **beaux-pères**) **NM 1** *(père du conjoint)* father-in-law **2** *(conjoint de la mère)* stepfather
beaupré [bopre] **NM** *Naut* bowsprit
beauté [bote] **NF 1** *(d'une femme, d'une statue)* beauty, loveliness; *(d'un homme)* handsomeness; **avoir la b. du diable** to have a youthful glow
2 *(femme)* beauty, beautiful woman; **je vous offre un verre, b.?** can I get you a drink, darling?
3 *(élévation → de l'âme)* beauty; *(→ d'un raisonnement)* beauty, elegance; **pour la b. du geste** *ou* **de la chose** for the beauty of it; **je lui ai cédé mon tour, pour la b. du geste** I let him/her have my turn, just because it was a nice thing to do
❏ **beautés NFPL** *(d'un paysage)* beauties, beauty spots; *(d'une œuvre)* beauties
❏ **de beauté ADJ** *(concours, reine)* beauty *(avant n)*
❏ **de toute beauté ADJ** magnificent, stunningly beautiful
❏ **en beauté ADV** **être en b.** to look stunning; **gagner une course en b.** to win a race handsomely; **finir en b.** to end with a flourish *or* on a high note; **pour terminer votre repas en b.** as a splendid finishing touch to your meal
Beauvau [bovo] **NF** *Géog* **la place B.** = square in Paris where the Ministry of the Interior is situated
beaux-arts [bozar] **NMPL 1** *(genre)* fine arts; **musée des B.** museum of fine art **2** *(école)* **les B.** art school; **être aux B., faire les B.** to be at art school
beaux-parents [boparɑ̃] **NMPL** father-in-law and mother-in-law, in-laws
bébé [bebe] **NM 1** *(nourrisson)* baby; **avoir un b.** to have a baby; **elle a eu son b. hier** she had her baby *or* she gave birth yesterday; **attendre un b.** to be expecting a baby; *Péj* **faire le b.** to act like *or* to be a baby; *Can Joual Fig* **c'est mon b.** *(projet)* it's my baby
2 *Zool* baby; **la lionne s'occupe de ses bébés** the lioness looks after her babies *or* young *or* cubs; **b. phoque/lapin** baby seal/rabbit
3 *Can Joual (jolie fille)* **un beau b.** a babe
ADJ INV *Péj* babyish, baby-like; **elle est restée b.** she's still very much a baby
bébé-éprouvette [bebeepruvɛt] *(pl* **bébés-éprouvette**) **NM** test-tube baby
bébelle [bebɛl] **NF** *Can* toy; *Péj (babiole)* trinket
bébert [bebɛr] **NM** *Fam* = stereotypical reactionary Frenchman
bébête [bebɛt] **ADJ** silly
NF *(en langage enfantin)* little insect, *Br* creepy-crawly; *TV* **le B. Show** = former satirical television puppet show, in which French political figures are represented as animals
bébite [bebit] *Can* = **bibite**
be-bop [bibɔp] **NM** *Mus & (danse)* bebop
bec [bɛk] **NM 1** *(d'oiseau)* beak, bill; *(de tortue)* beak; **au b. long/court** long/short-billed; **donner des coups de b. à** to peck (at); **nez en b. d'aigle** hook nose; **avoir b. et ongles** to be

well-equipped and ready to fight; **se défendre b. et ongles** to fight tooth and nail

  2 *Fam (bouche)* mouth■; **ferme ton b.!** shut up!, pipe down!; **ouvre le b.!** *(en nourrissant un enfant)* open wide!; **il n'a pas ouvert le b. de la journée** he hasn't opened his mouth all day; **ça lui a bouclé** *ou* **cloué** *ou* **clos le b.** it shut him/her up; **avoir toujours la cigarette/pipe au b.** to have a cigarette/pipe always stuck in one's mouth; **se retrouver le b. dans l'eau** to be left high and dry; **être un b. sucré** to have a sweet tooth

  3 *(d'une plume)* nib

  4 *(de casserole)* lip; *(de bouilloire, de théière)* spout

  5 *Mus (de saxophone, de clarinette)* mouthpiece

  6 *Géog* bill, headland

  7 *Belg, Suisse & Can Fam (baiser)* kiss■, peck; **donner un b. à qn** to give sb a kiss *or* peck; *Can* **b. pincé** snob

  8 *(d'un vêtement)* **faire un b.** to pucker

  9 *Fam (locution)* **tomber sur un b.** to run into *or* to hit a snag

  ❑ **bec à gaz** NM gas burner

  ❑ **bec de gaz** NM lamppost, gaslight

  ❑ **bec fin** NM gourmet; *Can* **avoir le b. fin** to be picky

bécane [bekan] NF *Fam* **1** *(moto, vélo)* bike **2** *Hum (ordinateur)* computer■, puter; *(machine à écrire)* typewriter■

bécard [bekar] NM *Ich* **1** *(saumon)* grilse, male salmon *(coming up to spawn)* **2** *(brochet)* adult pike

bécarre [bekar] *Mus* ADJ **la b.** A natural
  NM natural

bécasse [bekas] NF **1** *Orn* woodcock; **b. américaine** American woodcock **2** *Fam (sotte)* silly goose, *Br* twit

bécasseau, -x [bekaso] NM *Orn* **1** *(échassier)* sandpiper; **b. maritime** purple sandpiper; **b. maubèche** knot; **b. minuscule** least sandpiper; **b. minute** little stint; **b. sanderling** sanderling; **b. variable** dunlin **2** *(petit de la bécasse)* young woodcock

Bécassine [bekasin] NPR = early cartoon character representing a naive but optimistic Breton housekeeper

bécassine [bekasin] NF **1** *Orn* snipe; **b. double** great snipe; **b. des marais** common snipe; **b. sourde** jack snipe **2** *Fam (sotte)* silly goose, nincompoop, ninny

because [bikoz] *Fam* CONJ because■, coz
  PRÉP because of■; **elle est pas revenue b. sa maladie** she never came back coz she was ill

bec-croisé [bɛkkrwaze] *(pl* **becs-croisés**) NM *Orn* crossbill

bec-de-cane [bɛkdəkan] *(pl* **becs-de-cane**) NM **1** *(poignée)* door handle **2** *(serrure)* spring lock

bec-de-corbeau [bɛkdəkɔrbo] *(pl* **becs-de-corbeau**) NM **1** *Méd* curved dressing-forceps **2** *(outil)* rave-hook

bec-de-corbin [bɛkdəkɔrbɛ̃] *(pl* **becs-de-corbin**) NM **1** *(outil)* rave-hook **2** *Hist* halberde en b. halberd **3** *(forme)* **canne à b.** crutch-handled walking-stick; **nez en b.** hooked nose

bec-de-lièvre [bɛkdəljɛvr] *(pl* **becs-de-lièvre**) NM *Méd* harelip

bec-de-perroquet [bɛkdəperɔkɛ] *(pl* **becs-de-perroquet**) NM *Méd* osteophyte

bec-en-ciseaux [bɛkɑ̃sizo] *(pl* **becs-en-ciseaux**) NM *Orn* skimmer, scissor bill

bec-en-fourreau [bɛkɑ̃furo] *(pl* **becs-en-fourreau**) NM *Orn* sheathbill

bec-en-sabot [bɛkɑ̃sabo] *(pl* **becs-en-sabot**) NM *Orn* shoebill

becfigue [bɛkfig] NM *Orn (dans le Midi) (oiseau)* (garden) warbler; *(fauvette)* blackcap; *(jaseur)* waxwing; *(pipi)* pipit

bec-fin [bɛkfɛ̃] *(pl* **becs-fins**) NM *Orn* warbler

béchage [beʃaʒ] NM *Agr* digging (up)

béchamel [beʃamɛl] NF *Culin* **(sauce) b.** white sauce, béchamel (sauce)

bêche [bɛʃ] NF spade

bêche-de-mer [bɛʃdəmɛr] *(pl* **bêches-de-mer**) NF *Zool* trepang, sea-cucumber, bêche-de-mer
  NM *(langue)* beach-la-mar

bêcher [beʃe] VT **1** *Agr (sol)* to dig (over); *(pommes de terre)* to dig (up *or* out) **2** *Fam*

(critiquer) to run down, to pull apart *or* to pieces
  VI *Fam (faire le snob)* to put on airs

bêcheur, -euse [beʃœr, -øz] NM,F *Fam* **1** *(critiqueur)* knocker **2** *Péj (prétentieux)* stuck-up person, snooty person; **quelle bêcheuse, celle-là!** she's so stuck-up *or* snooty!

bêcheveter [28] [beʃvəte] VT *Arch (gén)* to place head to tail; *(bouteilles)* to store alternate ways up

bécosses [bekɔs] NFPL *Can Joual Br* bog, *Am* john, can

bécot [beko] NM *Fam (bise)* kiss■, peck; **gros b.** smacker

bécoter [3] [bekɔte] *Fam* VT *Br* to snog, *Am* to neck
  ▶ **se bécoter** VPR *Br* to snog, *Am* to neck

becquée [beke] NF *Orn* beakful; **donner la b.** *(oiseau)* to feed; *Hum* **sa maman lui donne la b.** his/her mummy's feeding him/her little bits of food

becquerel [bɛkrɛl] NM *Nucl* becquerel

becquet [bekɛ] NM **1** *Aut* spoiler **2** *Typ (papier)* = slip of paper, showing the position of a query or addition in copy prepared for print **3** *Théât* = change made to a play by its author during rehearsals

becquetance [bɛktɑ̃s] NF *très Fam* grub, nosh, *Am* chow

becqueter [27] [bekte] VT **1** *(picoter)* to peck (at) **2** *très Fam (manger)* to eat■; **il n'y avait rien à b.** there was no grub

bectance [bɛktɑ̃s] NF *très Fam* grub, nosh, *Am* chow

becter [4] [bɛkte] VT *très Fam (manger)* to eat■; **il n'y avait rien à b.** there was no grub

bécune [bekyn] NF *Ich* barracuda

bedaine [bədɛn] NF paunch, pot belly; **prendre de la b.** to develop a paunch *or* a pot belly; **un homme qui a de la b.** a man of ample girth

bedainer [4] [bədɛne] VI *Can* to be getting a paunch

bédane [bedan] NM *(outil)* mortise chisel

Bède [bɛd] NPR **B. le Vénérable** the Venerable Bede

bédé [bede] NF *Fam* **la b.** comic strips■, *Br* (strip) cartoons; **une b.** a comic strip *or Br* (strip) cartoon

bedeau, -x [bədo] NM *Rel* beadle, verger

bédégar [bedegar] NM *Bot* bedeguar

bédéiste [bedeist] NMF *Littérature* comic strip artist, *Br* (strip) cartoonist

bédéphile [bedefil] NMF comics fan

bédo [bedo] NM *Fam (cigarette de cannabis)* joint, spliff

bedon [bədɔ̃] NM *Vieilli (d'enfant)* tummy; *(gros ventre)* paunch

bedonnant, -e [bədɔnɑ̃, -ɑ̃t] ADJ paunchy

bedonner [3] [bədɔne] VI to get paunchy

bédouin, -e [bedwɛ̃, -in] ADJ Bedouin, Beduin
  ❑ **Bédouin, -e** NM,F Bedouin, Beduin

BEE [beəə] NM *(abrév* **Bureau européen de l'environnement**) EEB

bée [be] ADJ F **être bouche b. devant** to gape at; **j'en suis restée bouche b.** I was flabbergasted

beefsteak [biftɛk] = **bifteck**

beeper [3] [bipe] VT to beep

béer [15] [bee] VI *Littéraire* to be wide open; **la valise béait à ses pieds** the case lay wide open at his/her feet; **b. d'admiration** to gape with *or* to be lost in admiration

Beethoven [betɔvɛn] NPR Beethoven

beffroi [befrwa] NM *Archit* belfry

before [bifɔr] NM *ou* NF *(soirée)* = party attended before spending the night clubbing; **où est-ce qu'on va faire le** *ou* **la b. ce soir?** where are we going to go to start things off this evening?

bégaie *etc voir* **bégayer**

bégaiement [begɛmɑ̃] NM *(trouble de la parole)* stammer, stutter; **bégaiements** *(d'un bègue)* stammering *(UNCOUNT)*, stuttering *(UNCOUNT)*; *(d'embarras, d'émotion)* faltering *(UNCOUNT)*; *Fig* **les premiers bégaiements d'une industrie nouvelle** the first hesitant steps of a new industry

bégard [begar] NM *Rel* beghard, beguin

bégayant, -e [begɛjɑ̃, -ɑ̃t] ADJ *(discours)* stammering, stuttering

bégayer [11] [begeje] VI *(hésiter → bègue)* to

stammer, to stutter; *(→ ivrogne)* to slur (one's speech); **la colère la faisait b.** she was so angry she was stammering
  VT to stammer (out); **b. des excuses** to stammer out an apology

bégonia [begɔnja] NM *Bot* begonia

bégu, -ë [begu] ADJ *Zool* with a retrusive lower jaw, *Spéc* retrognathic; **être b.** to have parrot mouth, *Spéc* to be retrognathic

bègue [bɛg] ADJ stammering, stuttering; **être b.** to (have a) stammer
  NMF stammerer, stutterer

bégueule [begœl] *Fam* ADJ prudish; **elle n'est pas b.** she's no prude
  NF prude

bégueulerie [begœlri] NF *Fam* prudishness

béguin [begɛ̃] NM **1** *Fam (attirance)* **avoir le b. pour qn** to have a crush on sb **2** *Fam (amoureux)* crush **3** *(coiffe)* bonnet

béguinage [beginaʒ] NM *Rel* beguine convent

béguine [begin] NF *Rel* beguine (nun)

bégum [begɔm] NF begum

béhaï [beaj] = **bahaï**

béhaïsme [beaism] = **bahaïsme**

béhaviorisme [beavjɔrism] NM *Psy* behaviourism

béhavioriste [beavjɔrist] *Psy* ADJ behaviourist
  NMF behaviourist

Behring [beriŋ] = **Béring**

BEI [beəi] NF *(abrév* **Banque européenne d'investissement**) EIB

beige [bɛʒ] ADJ beige
  NM beige

beigeasse [bɛʒas], **beigeâtre** [bɛʒatr] ADJ *Péj* yellowish *or* greyish beige

beigne [bɛɲ] NF *très Fam (gifle)* slap■, clout; **filer une b. à qn** to slap sb■, to give sb a smack; **tu veux une b.?** do you want a thick ear?
  NM *Can Culin (beignet)* doughnut; *Fig* **se faire passer les beignes** to get a spanking

beignerie [bɛɲəri] NF *Can* doughnut shop

beignet [bɛɲɛ] NM *Culin (gén)* fritter; *(au sucre, à la confiture)* doughnut; **b. aux pommes** apple doughnut; **b. de crevettes** *(chips)* prawn cracker; *(avec de la pâte)* prawn fritter

Beijing [bejʒiŋ] NM *Géog* Beijing

beïram [beiram] = **baïram**

béjaune [beʒon] NM **1** *Orn (bec)* yellow beak; *(oisillon)* young bird, nestling **2** *Chasse* eyas **3** *Littéraire* novice; *(idiot)* fool, simpleton; **montrer son b.** to reveal one's ignorance

bêk [bɛk] EXCLAM *Belg* ugh!

béké [beke] NMF Caribbean creole *(with white ancestry)*

bel [bɛl] ADJ *voir* **beau**
  NM *(unité d'intensité du son)* bel

bêlant, -e [bɛlɑ̃, -ɑ̃t] ADJ **1** *(mouton)* bleating **2** *(chevrotant → voix)* bleating, shaky

Belarus [belarys] NF **la république de B.** the Republic of Belarus

bel cantiste, belcantiste [bɛlkɑ̃tist] ADJ *Mus* bel canto *(avant n)*; **répertoire b.** bel canto (opera) repertory

bel canto [bɛlkɑ̃to] NM INV *Mus* bel canto

Belém [belɛm] NM *Géog* Belém

bêlement [bɛlmɑ̃] NM bleat; **les bêlements des moutons** the bleating of the sheep

bélemnite [belɛmnit] NF *Zool & Géol* belemnite

bêler [4] [bele] VI to bleat
  VT *(chanson)* to bleat out

bel-étage, bel étage [bɛletaʒ] *(pl* **beaux(-)étages** [bozetaʒ]) NM *Belg* **1** *(rez-de-chaussée surélevé)* mezzanine *Br* ground *or Am* first floor **2** *(maison)* = house with mezzanine ground/first floor

belette [bəlɛt] NF **1** *Zool* weasel **2** *Fam (jeune femme) Br* bird, *Am* chick

Belfast [belfast] NM *Géog* Belfast

Belfort [belfɔr] NM *Géog* Belfort; **le Territoire de B.** the Territory of Belfort

Belga [bɛlga] NF *Journ* = Belgian press agency

belge [bɛlʒ] ADJ Belgian
  ❑ **Belge** NMF Belgian

belgicain, -e [bɛlʒikɛ̃, -ɛn] *Belg Péj* ADJ **être b.** *(partisan de l'unité belge)* to be in favour of a united Belgium; *(attaché aux traditions nationales)* to be attached to conservative (Belgian) tradition
  NM,F *(partisan de l'unité belge)* Belgian nationalist *(in favour of national unity)*; *(personne*

bel–ben

attachée aux traditions nationales) conservative (Belgian)

belgicisme [bɛlʒisism] **NM** Ling (mot) Belgian-French word; (tournure) Belgian-French expression

Belgique [bɛlʒik] **NF** la B. Belgium; **vivre en B.** to live in Belgium; **aller en B.** to go to Belgium

belgitude [bɛlʒityd] **NF** Belg aussi Hum Belgian identity, Belgianness

Belgrade [bɛlgrad] **NM** Géog Belgrade

Bélier [belje] **NM** 1 Astron Aries 2 Astrol Aries; **être B.** to be Aries or an Arian

bélier [belje] **NM** 1 Zool ram 2 Tech **b. (hydraulique)** hydraulic ram 3 Hist battering ram 4 Constr pile driver, ram(mer)

bélière [beljɛr] **NF** 1 (d'une cloche) clapper ring; (d'une montre) ring 2 (du bélier qui conduit le troupeau) (sheep) bell

bélinogramme [belinɔgram] **NM** Phot = document sent by Belinograph

bélinographe [belinɔgraf] **NM** Phot Belinograph (early type of facsimile machine)

bélître [belitr] **NM** 1 (mendiant) beggar 2 (homme de rien) good-for-nothing

Belize [beliz] **NM** le B. Belize; **vivre au B.** to live in Belize; **aller au B.** to go to Belize

bélizien, -enne [belizjɛ̃, -ɛn] **ADJ** Belizean
  □ **Bélizien, -enne NM,F** Belizean

belladone [beladɔn] **NF** Bot belladonna, deadly nightshade

bellâtre [bɛlatr] **NM** Péj fop

belle [bɛl] voir **beau**

Bellecour [bɛlkur] **NF** Géog **la place B.** = square in Lyons

belle-dame [bɛldam] (pl **belles-dames**) **NF** 1 Bot belladonna 2 Entom painted lady

belle-de-jour [bɛldəʒur] (pl **belles-de-jour**) **NF** Bot convolvulus, morning-glory

belle-de-nuit [bɛldənɥi] (pl **belles-de-nuit**) **NF** 1 Bot marvel of Peru, four-o'clock 2 (prostituée) lady of the night

belle-doche [bɛldɔʃ] (pl **belles-doches**) **NF** Fam mother-in-law▪

belle-famille [bɛlfamij] (pl **belles-familles**) **NF** sa **b.** (de l'épouse) her husband's family, her in-laws; (de l'époux) his wife's family, his in-laws

belle-fille [bɛlfij] (pl **belles-filles**) **NF** 1 (bru) daughter-in-law 2 (fille du conjoint) stepdaughter

belle-maman [bɛlmamɑ̃] (pl **belles-mamans**) **NF** Fam 1 (mère du conjoint) mother-in-law▪ 2 (conjointe du père) Br stepmum, Am stepmom

bellement [bɛlmɑ̃] **ADV** 1 (joliment) nicely, finely 2 (vraiment) well and truly, in no uncertain manner; **il l'a b. remis à sa place** he really took him/her down a peg or two

belle-mère [bɛlmɛr] (pl **belles-mères**) **NF** 1 (mère du conjoint) mother-in-law 2 (conjointe du père) stepmother

belles-lettres [bɛlɛtr] **NFPL** literature, Sout belles-lettres

belle-sœur [bɛlsœr] (pl **belles-sœurs**) **NF** sister-in-law

Belleville [bɛlvil] **NM** Géog = area of Paris with a large immigrant population

bellicisme [belisism] **NM** warmongering, Sout bellicosity

belliciste [belisist] **ADJ** warmongering, Sout bellicose
  NMF warmonger

belligérance [beliʒerɑ̃s] **NF** belligerence, belligerency

belligérant, -e [beliʒerɑ̃, -ɑ̃t] **ADJ** belligerent, warring
  NM,F belligerent
  □ **bélligérants NMPL les bélligérants** the belligerents, the warring nations

belliqueux, -euse [belikø, -øz] **ADJ** (peuple) warlike; (ton, discours) aggressive, belligerent; (enfant, humeur) quarrelsome, Sout bellicose

bellot, -otte [bɛlo, -ɔt] **ADJ** Arch comely, sweetly pretty

belluaire [belɥɛr] **NM** 1 Antiq beast-fighter 2 Littéraire (dompteur) wild-beast tamer

Belmopan [bɛlmɔpã] **NM** Géog Belmopan

belon [bəlɔ̃] **NF** Zool (huître) Belon oyster

belote [bəlɔt] **NF** Cartes belote (card game); **faire une b.** to play a game of belote

below the line [bilozəlajn] **NM** Compta below-the-line costs

béluga [belyga], **bélouga** [beluga] **NM** 1 Zool white or beluga whale 2 Culin (caviar) beluga (caviar)

belvédère [belvedɛr] **NM** Archit (pavillon) belvedere, gazebo; (terrasse) panoramic viewpoint

Belzébuth [bɛlzebyt] **NPR** Beelzebub

bémol [bemɔl] Mus **ADJ INV** mi b. E flat
  NM flat; **double b.** double flat; **mettre un b.** (parler moins fort) to pipe down; (modérer ses propos) to climb down

bémoliser [3] [bemɔlize] **VT** Mus to flatten, Am to flat; Fig to tone down

ben [bɛ̃] **ADV** Fam 1 (pour renforcer) **b. quoi?** so what?; **b. non** well, no; **b. voilà, euh...** yeah, well, er...; **b. voyons (donc)!** what next! 2 (bien) pt'êt b. qu'oui, pt'êt b. qu'non maybe yes, maybe no

bénard, -e [benar, -ard] **ADJ** double-sided; **serrure bénarde** double-sided lock; **clé bénarde** key to a double-sided lock
  NM Fam Br keks, trousers▪, Am pants▪
  □ **bénarde NF** pin key lock, double-sided lock

Bénarès [benarɛs] **NM** Géog Benares

benchmarking [bɛnʃmarkiŋ] **NM** Mktg benchmarking

bendir [bɛndir] **NM** Mus bendir (type of large Moroccan drum)

bène [bɛn] **NM** Fam Br trousers▪, keks, Am pants▪

bénédicité [benedisite] **NM** Rel grace; **dire le b.** to say grace

bénédictin, -e [benediktɛ̃, -in] Rel **ADJ** Benedictine
  □ **Bénédictin, -e NM,F** Benedictine

Bénédictine® [benediktin] **NF** (liqueur) Benedictine

bénédiction [benediksjɔ̃] **NF** 1 Rel benediction, blessing; (d'une église) consecration; **recevoir la b. papale** to be given or to receive the Pope's blessing; **donner la b. à qn** to pronounce the blessing on or to bless sb; **la b. nuptiale leur sera donnée à...** the marriage ceremony will take place or Sout the marriage will be solemnized at...
  2 (accord) blessing; **donner sa b. à qch** to give sth one's blessing; **vous avez ma b.** you have my blessing; Fam **il peut déguerpir dès demain, et avec ma b.!** he can get lost tomorrow, with my blessing!
  3 (aubaine) blessing, godsend; **c'est une b. qu'il soit vivant/qu'elle se porte volontaire** it's a blessing that he's alive/a godsend that she's volunteering to do it

bénef [benɛf] **NM** Fam profit▪; **c'est tout b. pour elle** she gets quite a deal out of this

bénéfice [benefis] **NM** 1 Écon, Com & Fin profit; **faire du b.** to make a profit; **faire ou enregistrer un b. brut/net de 200 euros** to gross/to net 200 euros; **donner un b.** to show a profit; **réaliser ou dégager un b.** to make a profit; **b. de ou pour l'exercice 2007** profits for the year 2007; **rapporter des bénéfices** to yield a profit; **vendre qch à b.** to sell sth at a profit; Fam **c'est tout b. à ce prix-là** at that price, you make a 100 percent profit on it; Fig **il leur apprend l'anglais en les amusant, c'est tout b.!** he teaches them English while entertaining them, what better way is there?; **b. par action** earnings per share; **b. brut/net** gross/net profit; **b. brut avant impôts** pre-tax profit; **b. consommateur** (d'un produit) consumer benefit; **b. cumulé** cumulative profit; **b. à distribuer, bénéfices distribuables** distributable profits; **b. escompté** desired profit; **bénéfices exceptionnels** excess or windfall profits; **bénéfices de l'exercice** current earnings; **b. d'exploitation** operating or trading profit; **bénéfices financiers** interest received; **b. fiscal** taxable profit; **b. imposable** taxable profit; **b. avant/après impôt** pre-tax/after-tax profit; **bénéfices industriels et commerciaux** business profits; **b. marginal** marginal profit; **b. net dilué par action** fully diluted earnings per share; **bénéfices non commerciaux** non-commercial profits (earned from activities such as the liberal professions, the arts, sport or holding certain official posts); **bénéfices non distribués** undistributed profits, retained profit; **b. par action** earnings per share; **b. transféré** profit transferred

2 (avantage) benefit, advantage; **il n'y a pas de b. à mentir** there's nothing to gain by lying; **tirer (un) b. de qch** to derive some benefit or an advantage from sth; **c'est le b. que l'on peut tirer de cette conduite** that's the reward for such behaviour; **laisser à qn le b. du doute** to give sb the benefit of the doubt; **il a eu le b. du doute** he was given the benefit of the doubt; Hist **b. du clergé** benefit of clergy

3 Jur **b. de discussion** right of seizure and sale; **b. de division** benefit of division; **b. d'émolument** = principle whereby a spouse is liable for the other's debts only to the extent of his/her share of the common assets; **b. d'inventaire** = an heir's lack of liability for debts beyond inherited assets; **sous b. d'inventaire** = without liability to debts beyond inherited assets; Fig **j'accepte, sous b. d'inventaire** everything else being equal, I accept

4 Rel living, benefice

5 Hist benefice

6 Psy **b. primaire/secondaire** primary/secondary gain

7 Can **concert-repas-b.** fundraising concert/dinner

□ **à bénéfice ADV** (exploiter, vendre) at a profit

□ **au bénéfice de PRÉP** 1 (en faveur de) for (the benefit of); **match au b. de l'enfance handicapée** benefit match for handicapped children

2 Jur **au b. de l'âge** by prerogative of age

bénéficiaire [benefisjɛr] **ADJ** (opération) profitable; (entreprise) profit-making; (marge) profit (avant n); (compte) in credit; (bilan) showing a profit
  NMF (d'une mesure) beneficiary; (d'un mandat, d'un chèque) payee, recipient; **qui en seront les principaux bénéficiaires?** who will benefit by it most?; (d'un compte) joint beneficiary

bénéficier [9] [benefisje] □ **bénéficier de VT IND** 1 (avoir) to have, to enjoy; **b. de conditions idéales/d'avantages sociaux** to enjoy ideal conditions/welfare benefits; **cette carte d'abonnement vous fait b. d'une remise de 20 pour cent** this season ticket entitles you to a 20 percent reduction; Jur **b. de circonstances atténuantes** to have the benefit of or to be granted extenuating circumstances; Jur **il a bénéficié d'une ordonnance de non-lieu** he was discharged

2 (profiter de) to benefit by or from; **b. d'une forte remise** to get a big reduction; **b. d'une mesure** to benefit by or to profit from a measure; **faire b. qn de ses connaissances** to allow sb to benefit by or to give sb the benefit of one's knowledge

□ **bénéficier à VT IND** to benefit; **à qui vont b. ces mesures?** who are these measures going to benefit?, who is going to benefit from these measures?

bénéfique [benefik] **ADJ** 1 (avantageux) beneficial, advantageous; **ce séjour à la montagne vous sera b.** this stay in the mountains will do you good or will be beneficial to you 2 Astrol favourable

Benelux [benelyks] **NM** le B. Benelux; **les pays du B.** the Benelux countries

benêt [bənɛ] Péj **ADJ M** simple-minded, idiotic, silly
  NM simpleton; **son grand b. de fils** his great fool of a son

bénévolat [benevɔla] **NM** (travail) voluntary work; (système) system of voluntary work

bénévole [benevɔl] **ADJ** (aide, conseil) voluntary, free; (association) voluntary; (médecin) volunteer (avant n); **être employé à titre b.** to do voluntary work
  NMF volunteer, voluntary worker

bénévolement [benevɔlmɑ̃] **ADV** voluntarily; **travailler b. pour qn** to do voluntary work for sb

Bengale [bɛ̃gal] **NM** le B. Bengal; **vivre au B.** to live in Bengal; **aller au B.** to go to Bengal

bengali [bɛ̃gali] **ADJ** Bengali
  NM 1 (langue) Bengali 2 Orn waxbill; **b. rouge** avadavat
  □ **Bengali NMF** Bengali

Benghazi [bɛngazi] **NM** Géog Benghazi

bénichon [beniʃɔ̃] **NF** Suisse = celebration (with large banquets and dancing) held in the canton

of Fribourg to mark the end of summer and beginning of harvest time

bénigne [beniɲ] *voir* **bénin**

bénignité [beniɲite] NF **1** *Méd (d'une maladie)* mildness; *(d'une tumeur)* non-malignancy **2** *Littéraire (mansuétude)* benignancy, kindness

Bénin [benɛ̃] NM **le B.** Benin; **vivre au B.** to live in Benin; **aller au B.** to go to Benin

bénin, -igne [benɛ̃, -iɲ] ADJ **1** *Méd (maladie)* minor; *(tumeur)* non-malignant, benign; **une forme bénigne de rougeole** a mild form of measles **2** *(accident)* slight, minor; *(sanction)* mild **3** *Littéraire (gentil)* benign, kindly

béninois, -e [beninwa, -az] ADJ Beninese
□ **Béninois, -e** NM,F Beninese; **les B.** the Beninese

béni-oui-oui [beniwiwi] NMF INV *Péj* yes-man, *f* yes-woman

bénir [32] [benir] VT **1** *Rel (fidèles)* to bless, to give one's blessing to; *(eau, pain, église)* to consecrate; *(union)* to solemnize

2 *(remercier)* **je bénis le passant qui m'a sauvé la vie** I'll be eternally thankful to the passer-by who saved my life; **béni soit le jour où je t'ai rencontré** blessed be the day I met you; **elle bénit le ciel de lui avoir donné un fils** she thanked God for giving her a son; *Ironique* **toi, je te bénis d'avoir perdu mes clés!** thanks a lot for losing my keys!

bénisseur, -euse [benisœr, -øz] ADJ *Fam* blessing▪

bénit, -e [beni, -it] ADJ consecrated, blessed

bénitier [benitje] NM **1** *Rel (dans une église)* stoup, font **2** *Zool (mollusque)* giant clam

Benjamin [bɛ̃ʒamɛ̃] NPR *Bible* Benjamin

benjamin, -e [bɛ̃ʒamɛ̃, -in] NM,F **1** *(d'une famille)* youngest child; **mon b.** my youngest (child) **2** *Sport* junior *(10 to 12 years old)*

benjoin [bɛ̃ʒwɛ̃] NM *Chim & Pharm* benzoin, benjamin

benne [bɛn] NF *Mines* tub, truck; *(de camion)* tipping *or* dump body; *(de grue)* scoop; *(de téléphérique)* (cable) car; **b. basculante** tipper; **b. à ordures** *(partie du camion) Br* skip, *Am* dumpster; **b. preneuse** clamshell

benoît, -e [bənwa, -at] ADJ **1** *Vieilli* kind, gentle; **b. lecteur** gentle reader **2** *Péj (doucereux)* bland, ingratiating
□ **benoîte** NF *Bot* herb bennet, wood avens; **benoîte des ruisseaux** water avens

benoîtement [bənwatmã] ADV *Péj* blandly, ingratiatingly

benthamisme [bɛ̃tamism] NM *Phil* Benthamism

benthique [bɛ̃tik] ADJ *Géol* benthic

benthos [bɛ̃tɔs] NM *Écol* benthos

bentonite [bɛ̃tɔnit] NF *Minér* bentonite

benzaldéhyde [bɛ̃zaldeid] NM *Chim* benzaldehyde

Benzédrine® [bɛ̃zedrin] NF *Pharm* Benzedrine®

benzène [bɛ̃zɛn] NM *Chim* benzene

benzénique [bɛ̃zenik] ADJ *Chim* benzene *(avant n)*

benzidine [bɛ̃zidin] NF *Chim* benzidine

benzine [bɛ̃zin] NF **1** *Chim* benzin, benzine **2** *Suisse (essence) Br* petrol, *Am* gas

benzoate [bɛ̃zwat] NM *Chim* benzoate

benzodiazépine [bɛ̃zɔdjazepin] NF *Pharm* benzodiazepine

benzoïque [bɛ̃zɔik] ADJ *Chim & Pharm* benzoic

benzol [bɛ̃zɔl] NM *Chim* benzol, benzole

benzolisme [bɛ̃zɔlism] NM *Méd* benzol poisoning

benzonaphtol [bɛ̃zɔnaftɔl] NM *Pharm* sodium benzoate, benzoate of soda

benzopyrène [bɛ̃zopirɛn] NM *Chim* benzopyrene

benzoyle [bɛ̃zwal] NM *Chim* benzoyle

benzyle [bɛ̃zil] NM *Chim* benzyl

benzylique [bɛ̃zilik] ADJ *Chim* benzyl *(avant n)*

béotien, -enne [beɔsjɛ̃, -ɛn] ADJ **1** *Antiq* Boeotian
2 *Péj (inculte)* uncultured, philistine
NM,F *Péj (rustre)* philistine
□ **Béotien, -enne** NM,F *Antiq* Boeotian

béotisme [beɔtism] NM philistinism

BEP [beøpe] NM *Scol (abrév* **brevet d'études professionnelles)** = vocational diploma (taken after two years of study at a "lycée professionnel")

BEPC [beøpese] NM *Ancienment Scol (abrév* **brevet d'études du premier cycle)** = former

school certificate taken after four years of secondary education

béquée [beke] = **becquée**

béquet [bekɛ] = **becquet**

béqueter [27] [bɛkte] = **becqueter**

béquillard, -e [bekijar, -ard] NM,F *Fam* person (walking) on crutches▪

béquille [bekij] NF **1** *(canne)* crutch; **marcher avec des béquilles** to walk on *or* with crutches **2** *(de moto)* stand **3** *Fig (soutien)* prop **4** *Naut* shore, prop **5** *Aviat* tail skid **6** *(d'une serrure)* handle **7** *(d'une arme)* stand **8** *Fam (coup de genou dans la cuisse)* **faire une b. à qn** to give sb a dead leg

béquiller [3] [bekije] VI to hobble (along) on crutches
VT *Naut* to shore up, to prop up

ber [bɛr] NM *Naut* cradle

berbère [bɛrbɛr] ADJ Berber
NM *(langue)* Berber
□ **Berbère** NMF Berber

□ **berbéridacée** [bɛrberidase] *Bot* NF member of the Berberidaceae family
□ **berbéridacées** NFPL Berberidaceae

berbéris [bɛrberis] NM *Bot* berberis; **b. commun** barberry

berbérophone [bɛrberɔfɔn] ADJ Berber-speaking
NMF Berber speaker

bercail [bɛrkaj] NM sheepfold; **ramener au b. la brebis égarée** to bring the lost sheep back to the fold; **rentrer** *ou* **revenir au b.** *(à la maison)* to get back home; *Rel* to return to the fold

berçante [bɛrsãt] NF *Can* **(chaise) b.** rocking chair

berce [bɛrs] NF **1** *Bot* hogweed **2** *Belg (berceau)* cradle

berceau, -x [bɛrso] NM **1** *(lit)* cradle; **du b. à la tombe** from the cradle to the grave; **on se connaît depuis le b.** we've known each other since we were babies; *Fam* **il/elle les prend au b.** *(séducteur)* he's/she's a cradle-snatcher; *Fam* **ils les prennent au b., les flics, maintenant** policemen seem to get younger and younger these days; **prendre qn au b. pour lui apprendre qch** to teach sb sth right from the earliest age; *Can* **la revanche des berceaux** the revenge of the cradle *(period in Canadian history – roughly from the 1850s to the 1940s – when the birth rate among French Canadians was far higher than that of English-speaking Canadians)*
2 *(lieu d'origine)* cradle, birthplace; **le b. de la civilisation** the cradle of civilization
3 *Archit* **(voûte en) b.** barrel vault
4 *(tonnelle)* arbour, bower
5 *(d'un moteur, d'un canon)* cradle

bercelonnette [bɛrsəlɔnɛt] NF rocking cradle

bercement [bɛrsəmã] NM rocking *or* swaying movement

bercer [16] [bɛrse] VT **1** *(bébé)* to rock, to cradle; **b. un bébé dans ses bras** to cradle or to rock a baby in one's arms; **il faut la b. pour qu'elle s'endorme** you have to rock her to sleep; **un bateau bercé par la houle** a boat rocked by the waves; **les chansons qui ont bercé mon enfance** the songs I was brought up on
2 *(calmer → douleur)* to lull, to soothe
3 *(tromper)* **b. qn de (belles) paroles/(vaines) promesses** to fob sb off with fine words/empty promises
▶ **se bercer** VPR **1 se b. de qch** to delude oneself with sth; **se b. d'illusions** to delude oneself, to entertain illusions; **ne nous berçons pas d'illusions** let's not be under any illusions
2 *Can (se balancer)* to rock (back and forth) *(in a rocking chair)*

berceur, -euse¹ [bɛrsœr, -øz] ADJ lulling, soothing

berceuse² [bɛrsøz] NF **1** *(chanson d'enfant)* lullaby; *Mus* berceuse **2** *Can* rocking chair

Bercy [bɛrsi] NM *Géog* **1** *Fin (ministère)* = the French Ministry of Finance **2** *(stade)* = large sports and concert hall in Paris

BERD, Berd [bɛrd] NF *Banque & UE (abrév* **Banque européenne pour la reconstruction et le développement)** EBRD

béret [berɛ] NM **b. (basque)** (French) beret

Bérézina [berezina] NF *Géog* **la B.** = Napoleon's retreat over the River Berezina in Bielorussia in 1812

bergamasque [bɛrgamask] NF *(danse)* bergamask

Bergame [bɛrgam] NM *Géog* Bergamo

bergamote [bɛrgamɔt] NF *Bot* bergamot orange
□ **à la bergamote** ADJ *(savon)* bergamot-scented; *(thé)* with bergamot, bergamot-flavoured

bergamotier [bɛrgamɔtje] NM *Bot* bergamot (tree)

berge [bɛrʒ] NF **1** *Géog (rive)* bank; **route** *ou* **voie sur b.** *(dans une grande ville)* embankment road **2** *très Fam (an)* year▪; **à 25 berges, elle a monté sa boîte** when she was 25, she set up her own business

Bergen [bɛrgɛn] NM *Géog* Bergen

berger, -ère [bɛrʒe, -ɛr] NM,F **1** *(pâtre)* shepherd, *f* shepherdess; **des histoires de bergers et de bergères** pastoral stories
2 *(guide)* shepherd; **bon/mauvais b.** good/bad shepherd
NM *Zool (chien)* sheepdog; **b. allemand, b. d'Alsace**, German shepherd; **b. de Beauce** Beauceron (dog); **b. d'Écosse** collie (dog); **b. des Pyrénées** Pyrenean mountain dog, Pyrenean shepherd
□ **bergère** NF *(fauteuil)* bergère

bergerie [bɛrʒəri] NF **1** *Agr* sheepfold **2** *Beaux-Arts (peinture)* pastoral (painting); *(tapisserie)* pastoral tapestry; *Littérature (poème)* pastoral **3** *Com* counter

bergeronnette [bɛrʒərɔnɛt] NF *Orn* wagtail; **b. printanière flavéole** yellow wagtail; **b. des ruisseaux** grey wagtail; **b. de Yarrell** pied wagtail

bergsonien, -enne [bɛrksɔnjɛ̃, -ɛn] ADJ *Phil* Bergsonian

béribéri [beriberi] NM *Méd* beriberi

bérimbau [berimbo] NM *Mus* berimbau

Béring [beriŋ] NM *voir* **détroit, mer**

berk [bɛrk] EXCLAM *Fam* ugh!, yuk!

berkélium [bɛrkeljɔm] NM *Chim* berkelium

berlander [3] [bɛrlãde] VI *Can (hésiter)* to dither; *(fainéanter)* to waste one's time

Berlin [bɛrlɛ̃] NM *Géog* Berlin; *Ancienment* **B.-Est** East Berlin; *Ancienment* **B.-Ouest** West Berlin; *Hist* **le mur de B.** the Berlin Wall

berline [bɛrlin] NF **1** *Aut Br* saloon car, *Am* sedan; **grosse b.** *Br* big saloon (car), *Am* full-size sedan; **moyenne b.** compact car **2** *Hist* berlin, berline; *Can (voiture)* = horse-drawn cart formerly used to deliver bread and milk **3** *Mines* truck, tub

berlinette [bɛrlinɛt] NF *Aut* Berlinette

berlingot [bɛrlɛ̃go] NM **1** *(bonbon) Br* ≃ boiled sweet, *Am* ≃ hard candy **2** *(emballage → de lait)* carton; *(→ de produit d'entretien)* pack

berlinois, -e [bɛrlinwa, -az] ADJ of/from Berlin
□ **Berlinois, -e** NM,F Berliner; *Ancienment* **B. de l'Est/l'Ouest** East/West Berliner

berloque [bɛrlɔk] NF *Belg* **battre la b.** to beat *or* to pound wildly

berlot [bɛrlo] NM *Can Hist* = horse-drawn sled with a rectangular body and two seats, formerly used for transporting people

berlue [bɛrly] NF **avoir la b.** to be seeing things; **si je n'ai pas la b., c'est bien Paul là-bas** if my eyes don't deceive me, that's Paul over there

berme [bɛrm] NF **1** *(autour d'un château fort)* berm; *(le long d'un canal, d'un fossé etc)* (tow-)path, verge **2** *Belg & Suisse* **b. centrale** *(terre-plein) Br* central reservation, *Am* median (strip)

bermuda [bɛrmyda] NM **un b.** (a pair of) Bermuda shorts, Bermudas

Bermudes [bɛrmyd] NFPL **les B.** Bermuda; **vivre aux B.** to live in Bermuda; **aller aux B.** to go to

Bermuda; **le triangle des B.** the Bermuda Triangle

bermudien, -enne [bɛrmydjɛ̃, -ɛn] **ADJ** *Naut* Bermuda *(avant n)*; **gréement b.** Bermuda rig

bernache [bɛrnaʃ], **bernacle** [bɛrnakl] **NF 1** *Orn* barnacle goose; **b. du Canada** Canada goose; **b. à cou roux** red-breasted goose; **b. cravant** brent (goose); **b. d'Hawaï, b. néné** Hawaiian goose, nene; **b. nonnette** barnacle goose **2** *Zool (crustacé)* (goose) barnacle

bernardin, -e [bɛrnardɛ̃, -in] **NM,F** *Rel* Bernardine

bernard-l'ermite, bernard-l'hermite [bɛrnarlɛrmit] **NM INV** *Zool (crustacé)* hermit crab

Berne [bɛrn] **NM** *Géog* Bern; **le canton de B.** Bern

berne [bɛrn] ❑ **en berne ADV** *(gén) & Mil & Naut* at half-mast; **mettre les drapeaux en b.** to half-mast the flags, to lower the flags to half-mast

berner [3] [bɛrne] **VT** *(tromper)* to fool, to dupe, to take in; **on s'est fait b.** we were taken in *or* duped; **je ne vais pas me laisser b. cette fois** I won't be made a fool of this time; **n'essaie pas de me b.** don't try to fool me

bernicle [bɛrnikl] **NF** *Zool (mollusque)* limpet

Bernin [bɛrnɛ̃] **NPR Le B.** Bernini

bernique [bɛrnik] **NF** *Zool (mollusque)* limpet
EXCLAM *Arch* nothing doing!

bernois, -e [bɛrnwa, -az] **ADJ** Bernese
❑ **Bernois, -e NM,F** Bernese

berrichon, -onne [beriʃɔ̃, -ɔn] **ADJ** of/from Berry
NM *(dialecte)* Berry dialect
❑ **Berrichon, -onne NM,F** = inhabitant of or person from Berry

berruyer, -ère [beryje, -ɛr] **ADJ** of/from Bourges
❑ **Berruyer, -ère NM,F** = inhabitant of or person from Bourges

Berry [beri] **NM le B.** Berry *(region in central France)*

bersaglier [bɛrsaglije, bɛrsalje] **NM** *Mil* bersaglieri

Bertha [bɛrta] **NF** *Hist* **la grosse B.** *(canon)* Big Bertha

Berthe [bɛrt] **NPR** Bertha; *Littéraire* **du temps où B. filait** *(référence à Berthe de Bourgogne)* in olden times, in the days of yore

berthe [bɛrt] **NF** *(col)* bertha

bertillonnage [bɛrtijɔnaʒ] **NM** *(en anthropométrie)* Bertillon system

berwette [bɛrwɛt] **NF** *Belg* **faire b.** to draw a blank, to be out of luck

béryl [beril] **NM** *Géol* beryl

béryllium [beriljɔm] **NM** *Chim* beryllium, glucinium

berzingue [bɛrzɛ̃g] ❑ **à tout(e) berzingue ADV** *Fam* at full speed▪, double-quick

besace [bəzas] **NF** *(de mendiant)* bag; *(de pèlerin)* scrip; **sac b.** = large, soft handbag

besaiguë [bəzegy] **NF 1** *Menuis* mortise axe **2** *(d'un vitrier)* glazier's hammer

besant [bəzɑ̃] **NM 1** *Archit* bezant, byzant **2** *Hér (meuble)* bezant **3** *(monnaie)* bezant

bésef [bezɛf] **ADV** *très Fam* **pas b.** *(non comptable)* not much▪, not a lot▪; *(comptable)* not many▪, not a lot; **de la patience, j'en ai pas b.** I don't have tons of patience; **il n'y en avait pas b., des clients** there weren't tons of customers

bésicles [bezikl], **besicles** [bəzikl] **NFPL** *Arch* spectacles; *Hum* specs

bésigue [bezig] **NM** *Cartes* bezique

besogne [bəzɔɲ] **NF** *(travail)* task, job, work; **se mettre à la b.** to get down to work; **c'est de la belle** *ou* **bonne b.** it's a fine piece of work, it's a neat job; **une rude b.** a hard task

besogner [3] [bəzɔɲe] **VI** *Péj (travailler)* to drudge, to slave away, to toil away
VT *Vulg* to hump, to screw

besogneux, -euse [bəzɔɲø, -øz] **ADJ 1** *(travailleur)* plodding **2** *Littéraire (pauvre)* needy, poor
NM,F drudge

besoin [bəzwɛ̃] **NM 1** *(nécessité)* need; **un b. de chaleur humaine** a need for human warmth; **il a de gros besoins d'argent** he needs lots of money; **nos besoins en pétrole/ingénieurs** our oil/engineering requirements; **quels sont ses besoins?** what are his/her (basic) needs?; **tous vos besoins seront satisfaits** all your needs will be answered *or* satisfied; *Compta* **besoins de caisse** cash requirements; *Compta* **besoins de crédit** borrowing requirements; *Compta* **besoins en fonds de roulement** working capital requirements; **besoins (éducatifs) particuliers** special needs; **un enfant à besoins (éducatifs) particuliers** a child with special needs; *Compta* **besoins de trésorerie** cash requirements; **ressentir** *ou* **éprouver le b. de faire qch** to feel the need to do sth; **il n'est pas b. de vous le dire** you hardly need to be told; **si b. est** if necessary, if needs be; **si le b. s'en faisait sentir** if the need *or* necessity arose; **il n'est pas b. de mentir** there's no need to lie; **sans qu'il soit b. de prévenir les parents** without it being necessary to let the parents know; *Euph* **b. (naturel), petit b., b. pressant** call of nature; **faire ses besoins** *(personne)* to attend to *or* to answer the call of nature; *(animal)* to do its business; **être pris d'un b. pressant** to be taken *or* caught short; **avoir un b. pressant d'argent** to be pressed for money

2 *(pauvreté)* need; **dans le b.** in need; **ceux qui sont dans le b.** the needy; *Prov* **c'est dans le b. qu'on connaît le véritable ami** *ou* **ses vrais amis** a friend in need is a friend indeed

3 *(locutions)* **avoir b. de qn/qch** to need sb/sth; **avoir b. de faire qch** to need to do sth; **je n'en ai aucun b.** I have no need of it whatsoever; **j'ai b. d'oublier** I need to forget; **il a b. qu'on s'occupe de lui** he needs looking after; **elle n'a pas b. qu'on le lui répète** she doesn't need *or* have to be told twice; **je n'ai pas b. de vous rappeler que...** I don't need to *or* I needn't remind you that...; **mon agenda a b. d'être mis à jour** my *Br* diary *or Am* datebook needs updating *or* to be updated; **avoir bien** *ou* **grand b. de qch** to be in dire need of sth, to need sth badly; **tu aurais bien b. d'un shampooing** your hair's badly in need of a wash; *Ironique* **un pneu crevé! on en avait bien b.** *ou* **on en avait bien b. de ça!** a flat tyre, that's all we needed!; **tu avais bien b. de lui dire!** you WOULD have to go and tell him!, what did you (want to) tell him for?

❑ **au besoin ADV** if necessary, if needs *or* need be

❑ **pour les besoins de PRÉP pour les besoins de la cause** for the purpose in hand; **pour les besoins du direct** for the purpose of the live broadcast

Bessarabie [bɛsarabi] **NF** *Géog* Bessarabia

Bessemer [bɛsmɛr] **NM** *Métal* **convertisseur B.** Bessemer converter; **procédé B.** Bessemer process

besson, -onne [besɔ̃, -ɔn] **NM,F 1** *Zool (agneau)* twin lamb **2** *Arch (jumeau)* twin

bessonnière [besɔnjɛr] **NF** *Zool (brebis)* = sheep which has twin lambs

bestiaire [bɛstjɛr] **NM 1** *(recueil)* bestiary **2** *Antiq* gladiator

bestial, -e, -aux, -ales [bɛstjal, -o] **ADJ** *(instinct, acte)* bestial, brutish

bestialement [bɛstjalmɑ̃] **ADV** bestially, brutishly

bestialité [bɛstjalite] **NF 1** *(brutalité)* bestiality, brutishness **2** *(zoophilie)* bestiality

bestiau, -x [bɛstjo] **NM** *Fam (animal)* beast▪, creature▪
❑ **bestiaux NMPL** *(d'une exploitation)* livestock; *(bovidés)* cattle; **traités/entassés comme des bestiaux** treated/penned in like cattle

bestiole [bɛstjɔl] **NF** *Fam (insecte) Br* creepy-crawly, *Am* creepy-crawler; *(petit animal)* creature▪

best of [bɛstɔf] **NM INV** greatest hits compilation; **un b. des Rolling Stones** a compilation of the greatest hits of the Rolling Stones

best-seller [bɛstsɛlœr] *(pl* **best-sellers***)* **NM** best-seller

bêta, -asse [bɛta, -as] **ADJ** *Fam (stupide)* silly, *Br* daft
NM,F *Fam (idiot)* blockhead, numbskull; **espèce de gros b.!** you blockhead!
NM INV 1 *(lettre)* beta
2 *Bourse* beta (coefficient)
❑ **bêta ADJ INV** *Géol & Électron* beta *(avant n)*

bêtabloquant, -e [bɛtablɔkɑ̃, -ɑ̃t] **ADJ** *Méd* beta-blocker *(avant n)*
NM beta-blocker

bétail [betaj] **NM** *Agr* **le b.** *(gén)* livestock; *(bovins)* cattle; **cent têtes de b.** a hundred head of cattle; **traiter les gens comme du b.** to treat people like cattle; **gros b.** (big) cattle; **petit b.** small livestock; **b. d'engraissement** fat stock

bétaillère [betajɛr] **NF** *Br* cattle truck, *Am* stock car

bêtasse [bɛtas] *voir* **bêta**

bêtastimulant, -e [betastimylɑ̃, -ɑ̃t] *Méd* **ADJ** beta-stimulating
NM beta-stimulant

bêta-test [betatɛst] *(pl* **bêta-tests***)* **NM** *Ordinat* beta test; **bêta-tests** *(procédure)* beta testing

bêtathérapie [bɛtaterapi] **NF** *Méd* beta ray therapy

bêtatron [bɛtatrɔ̃] **NM** *Phys* betatron

bête [bɛt] **ADJ 1** *(peu intelligent)* stupid, idiotic; **il est plus b. que méchant** he's not wicked, just (plain) stupid; **mais non, cela ne me dérange pas, ce que tu peux être b.!** of course you're not putting me out, how silly (can you be *or* of you)!; **c'est encore moi qui vais payer, je suis bien b., tiens!** I'll end up paying again, like an idiot!; **mais oui, je me souviens maintenant, suis-je b.!** ah, now I remember, how stupid of me!; **je ne suis pas b. au point de...** I know better than to...; **il faudrait être b. pour dépenser plus** it would be foolish *or* you'd have to be an idiot to spend more; **loin d'être b.** far from stupid; **pas si b., j'ai pris mes précautions** I took some precautions, I'm not a complete idiot; **pas si b., la petite!** she's no fool, that girl!; **ce n'est pas b., ton idée!** that's quite a good idea you've got there!; **être b. comme ses pieds** *ou* **comme une cruche** *ou* **comme une oie** *ou* **à manger du foin** *Br* to be as thick as two short planks, *Am* to be as dumb as they come; **c'est b. à pleurer** it's ridiculously stupid; **je suis b. et discipliné, moi, je fais ce qu'on me dit de faire!** I'm just carrying out orders!

2 *(regrettable)* **je n'ai pas su le retenir, comme c'est b.!** I didn't know how to keep him, what a pity *or* waste!; **c'est b. de ne pas y avoir pensé** it's silly *or* stupid not to have thought of it; **ce serait trop b. de laisser passer l'occasion** it would be a pity not to take advantage of the occasion

3 *(simple)* **c'est tout b., il suffisait d'y penser!** it's so simple, we should have thought of it before!; *Fam* **c'est b. comme tout** *ou* **chou** it's simplicity itself *or* (as) easy as pie *or* (as) easy as falling off a log

4 *(stupéfait)* **en être** *ou* **rester tout b.** to be struck dumb *or* dumbfounded

5 *Can (de mauvaise humeur)* grumpy; **avoir l'air b.** to look grumpy; **être b. comme ses (deux) pieds** to be a nasty piece of work

NF 1 *Zool (animal → gén)* animal; *(→ effrayant)* beast; **mener les bêtes aux champs** to take the herd off to graze; **aimer les bêtes** to be an animal-lover; *Antiq* **jeté** *ou* **livré (en pâture) aux bêtes** thrown to the lions; *Fig* **b. curieuse** strange-looking creature; **cessez de me dévisager, je ne suis pas une b. curieuse!** stop staring at me as if I had two heads!; **ils nous regardaient comme des bêtes curieuses** they were staring at us as if we were from Mars; **b. à cornes/poils/plumes** horned/furry/feathered animal; **b. de compagnie** *(sanglier)* pig of the sounder; **b. fauve** *(gén)* wild animal *or* beast; *(félin)* big cat; **b. féroce** *ou* **sauvage** wild animal *or* beast; **b. noire** *(sanglier)* wild boar; *Can* **b. puante** (striped) skunk; **b. de race** pedigree animal; **b. rousse** *(sanglier)* squeaker; **b. de somme** *ou* **de charge** beast of burden; **je ne veux pas être la b. de somme du service** I don't want to do all the dirty work in this department; **la b. du Gévaudan** = a large animal (probably a wolf), believed to be responsible for the disappearance of over 50 people in the Lozère in the 1760s; **b. de trait** draught animal; *Fam* **malade comme une b.** sick as a dog; *Fam* **travailler comme une b.** to work like a slave *or* dog; *Fam* **s'éclater comme une b.** to have a great time; *Arch ou Hum* **faire la b. à deux dos** to make the beast with two backs

2 *(insecte)* **(petite) b.** insect, creature; **b. à bon Dieu** *Br* ladybird, *Am* ladybug; *Can* **b. à patates** Colorado *or* potato beetle

3 *(personne)* **grosse b., va!** you silly fool!; **tu n'es qu'une grande b.** you're a great fool; *Fam* **c'est une bonne** *ou* **brave b.** *(généreux)* he's a good sort; *(dupe)* he's a bit of a sucker

4 *Fam (expert)* **c'est une vraie b. en physique!** he's/she's brilliant at physics!▪; **b. à concours** *Br* swot, *Am* grind *(who sits many competitive exams)*; **b. de scène/télévision** great live/television performer▪

5 *Rel* **la b. de l'Apocalypse** the beast of the Apocalypse

6 la b. immonde = Nazism

7 *(locutions)* **ma b. noire** my bugbear *or* pet hate; **un ministre qui est la b. noire des étudiants** a minister students love to hate; **le latin, c'était ma b. noire** Latin was my pet hate; **se payer** *ou* **se servir sur la b.** to get one's payment in kind *(by docking it off a man's pay or by demanding a woman's sexual favours)*

'**Que la bête meure**' *Chabrol* 'This Man Must Die'

'**La Bête humaine**' *Zola* 'The Beast in Man' *or* 'The Human Beast'

Allusion

Bête et méchant

In 1960, a group of French cartoonists brought out a satirical magazine called *Hara-Kiri*, with the subtitle "un journal bête et méchant" ("a stupid and vicious publication"), which is itself an allusion to a Voltaire quotation ("en ville on devient bête et méchant"); in fact, it was caustic and original. The two adjectives are often run together and translated as "nasty" in English. Anything can be described as **bête et méchant** – a person, a situation or a story.

bétel [betɛl] NM *Bot* betel

Bételgeuse [betɛlgøz] NF *Astron* Betelgeuse

bêtement [bɛtmã] ADV **1** *(stupidement)* foolishly, stupidly, idiotically; **rire b.** to giggle; **mourir b.** to die senselessly **2** *(simplement)* **tout b.** purely and simply, quite simply

Béthanie [betani] NM *Géog & Bible* Bethany

Bethléem [bɛtleɛm] NM *Géog & Bible* Bethlehem

Bethsabée [bɛtsabe] NPR *Bible* Bathsheba

bêtifiant, -e [betifjã, -ãt] ADJ idiotic, stupid

bêtifier [9] [betifje] VI to talk nonsense; **elle bêtifie quand elle parle à son enfant** she uses baby-talk to talk to her child

bêtise [betiz] NF **1** *(stupidité)* idiocy, foolishness, stupidity; **il est d'une rare b.** he's exceptionally stupid; **j'ai eu la b. de ne pas vérifier** I was foolish enough not to check; **c'est de la b. d'y aller seul** going there alone is sheer stupidity; **il n'y a pas de limite à la b. humaine** human folly knows no bounds

2 *(remarque)* silly *or* stupid remark; **dire une b.** to say something stupid; **dire des bêtises** to talk nonsense

3 *(action)* stupid thing, piece of foolishness *or* idiocy; **bêtises de jeunesse** youthful pranks; **le chat a encore fait des bêtises** the cat has been up to some mischief again; **ne recommencez pas vos bêtises** don't start your stupid tricks again; **faire une b.** to do something silly *or* stupid; **je viens de faire une grosse b.** I've just done something very silly; **tu as fait une b. en refusant** it was stupid *or* foolish of you to refuse, you were a fool to refuse

4 *(vétille)* trifle, small detail; **pleurer pour des bêtises** to cry over the smallest thing; **on se dispute toujours pour des bêtises** we're always arguing over trifles *or* having petty squabbles; **dépenser tout son argent en bêtises** to fritter away one's money; **elle achète énormément de bêtises** she buys lots of rubbish *or Am* trash

5 *Culin* **b. de Cambrai** *Br* ≃ humbug, *Am* ≃ (hard) mint candy

6 *Can* **bêtises** *(injures)* insults

bêtisier [betizje] NM *(écrit)* collection of howlers; *(à la télévision)* collection of humorous TV outtakes; *Journ* **le b. de la semaine** gaffes of the week

bétoine [betwan] NF *Bot* betony; **b. d'eau** water betony; **b. des montagnards** *ou* **des Vosges** arnica

bétoire [betwar] NM **1** *Géol* small swallow hole *or* sinkhole **2** *(puisard)* steep-sided stone well *(for collecting rainwater)*

béton [betɔ̃] NM **1** *Constr* concrete; *Péj* **maintenant, il y a du b. partout** the place is just a vast expanse of concrete now; **b. armé/précontraint** reinforced/pre-stressed concrete

2 *Ftbl* **faire le b.** to pack the defence

3 *Fam (locution)* **laisse b.!** forget it!, drop it!

ADJ *Fam (solide → argument)* cast-iron; **un dossier de candidature b.** an extremely thorough application■

❑ **en béton** ADJ **1** *Constr* concrete *(avant n)*

2 *Fam (solide → estomac, alibi, argument)* cast-iron; *(→ défense, garantie)* watertight, surefire; **la défense a un dossier en b.** the defence has a watertight case

bétonnage [betɔnaʒ] NM **1** *Constr* concreting; *Fig Péj* **ils s'insurgent contre le b. du littoral** they are protesting against the way the coastline is being built up by property developers **2** *Ftbl* defensive play

bétonner [3] [betɔne] VT **1** *Constr* to concrete; *Fig* **les promoteurs immobiliers qui bétonnent le littoral** the property developers who are building all along the coast **2** *Fam (préparer avec soin)* to work hard on■ ; **il a bétonné son discours/dossier** he's worked really hard on his speech/application

VI *Ftbl* to pack the defence, to play defensively

bétonneur [betɔnœr] NM *Péj* = ruthless property developer who builds with no thought for the environment

bétonneuse [betɔnøz], **bétonnière** [betɔnjɛr] NF *Constr* cement mixer

betôt [bɛto] ADV *Can Vieilli (bientôt)* soon; *(il y a peu de temps)* just a while ago

bette [bɛt] NF *Bot (Swiss)* chard

betterave [bɛtrav] NF *Bot* **b. (potagère)** beet; **b. fourragère** mangel-wurzel; **b. (rouge)** *Br* beetroot, *Am* red beet; **b. sucrière** sugar beet

betteravier, -ère [bɛtravje, -ɛr] ADJ beet *(avant n)*

NM beet grower

bétulacée [betylase] *Bot* NF birch, *Spéc* member of the Betulaceae family

❑ **bétulacées** NFPL birches, *Spéc* Betulaceae

bétulinée [betyline] *Arch* = **bétulacée**

bétyle [betil] NM *Archéol* baetyl, baetulus

beu [bø] NF *Fam Arg drogue* grass, weed, herb

beuglant [bøglã] NM *Fam Vieilli* sleazy nightclub

beuglante [bøglãt] NF *Fam (chanson)* song■ ; *(cri)* yell; **pousser une b.** *(chanter)* to belt out a song; *(crier)* to give a yell

beuglement [bøglmã] NM **1** *(cri → de la vache)* moo; *(→ du taureau)* bellow; *(→ d'une personne)* bellow, yell; **des beuglements** *(de vache)* mooing *(UNCOUNT)*, lowing *(UNCOUNT)*; *(de taureau)* bellowing *(UNCOUNT)*; *(d'une personne)* bellowing *(UNCOUNT)*, yelling *(UNCOUNT)*, bawling *(UNCOUNT)*; **pousser des beuglements** *(vache)* to moo, to low; *(taureau)* to bellow; *(personne)* to bellow, to yell, to bawl **2** *(bruit → de la radio)* blaring noise

beugler [5] [bøgle] VI **1** *(crier → vache)* to moo, to low; *(→ taureau)* to bellow; *(→ chanteur, ivrogne)* to bellow, to bawl **2** *(être bruyant → radio)* to blare

VT *(chanson)* to bawl out, to bellow out

beur [bœr] *Fam* ADJ *(culture, mode, musique)* = of people born in France of North African parents; *(personne)* = born in France of North African parents

❑ **Beur** NMF = person born in France of North African immigrant parents

Culture

BEUR

The **verlan** (see box at this entry) word for "arabe" is not derogatory and is frequently used by second-generation Arabs in France.

Beurette [bœrɛt] NF *Fam* = young woman born in France of North African immigrant parents

beurk [bœrk] = **berk**

beurre [bœr] NM *Culin* **1** *(de laiterie)* butter; **au b.** *(biscuits)* (all-)butter *(avant n)*; **faire la cuisine au b.** to cook with butter; **du b. fondu** *Br* melted *or Am* drawn butter; **b. de baratte** butter from the churn; **b. clarifié** clarified butter; **b. demi-sel** slightly salted butter; **b. laitier** dairy butter; **b. à la motte** loose butter; **b. non salé** unsalted butter; **b. roux** brown butter; **b. salé** salted butter; **b. de yack** *ou* **yak** (Tibetan) ghee; **entrer dans qch comme dans du b.** to slice through sth like a hot knife through butter; *Fam* **faire son b.** to make money hand over fist; *Fam* **ils font leur b. sur le dos des touristes** they get rich pickings by fleecing the tourists; *Fam* **ça met du b. dans les épinards** it's a nice little earner; **vouloir le b. et l'argent du b.** to want to have one's cake and eat it; **il n'y en a pas plus que de b. en branche** *(introuvable)* it's nowhere to be found

2 *(sauce, pâte)* **b. blanc/noir** white/black butter sauce; **b. d'anchois** anchovy paste; **b. de cacahuètes** peanut butter; **b. de cacao/de muscade** cocoa/nutmeg butter; **b. composé** beurre composé; **b. d'escargot** = flavoured butter used in the preparation of snails; **b. manié** beurre manié

3 *Belg (locutions) Fam* **battre le b.** to get nowhere; *Fam* **le chat a mangé le b.** the game's up; *très Fam* **être le cul dans le b.** to be in clover

beurré, -e [bœre] ADJ **1** *Culin* **du pain b.** buttered bread; **tartine beurrée** piece of bread and butter **2** *très Fam (ivre)* plastered, *Br* pissed; **b. (comme un petit Lu)** *Br* pissed as a newt, *Am* stewed to the gills

NM butter-pear, beurré

❑ **beurrée** NF *très Fam (ivresse)* **prendre une beurrée** to get plastered, *Br* to get pissed **2** *Can (tartine)* piece of bread and butter; *Fam* **coûter une b.** to cost a bomb *or* an arm and a leg; **elle m'a servi une b. de critiques** she heaped criticism on me

beurre-frais [bœrfrɛ] ADJ INV buttercup-yellow

beurrer [5] [bœre] VT *Culin (tartine, moule)* to butter

VI *Can Fam (exagérer)* to lay it on a bit thick; **quand il parle de sa fortune, je trouve qu'il beurre pas mal épais** I think he lays it on a bit thick *or* stretches it a bit when he talks about how much money he's got

▶**se beurrer** VPR *très Fam* to get plastered, *Br* to get pissed

beurrerie [bœrri] NF **1** *(laiterie)* (butter-producing) dairy **2** *(industrie)* butter industry

beurrier, -ère [bœrje, -ɛr] ADJ *(production, industrie)* butter *(avant n)*; *(région)* butter-producing

NM *(récipient)* butter dish

beuverie [bœvri] NF *Fam* drinking binge, bender

bévatron [bevatrɔ̃] NM *Phys* bevatron

bévue [bevy] NF *(gaffe)* blunder, gaffe; **commettre une b.** to make a gaffe

bey [bɛ] NM *Hist* bey

beylical, -e, -aux, -ales [belikal, -o] ADJ *Hist* beylical

beylicat [belika], **beylik** [belik] NM *Hist* beylic

beylisme [belism] NM *Littérature* attitude of a Stendhalian hero

Beyrouth [berut] NM *Géog* Beirut, Beyrouth; **de B.** Beiruti; **B.-Est** East Beirut; **B.-Ouest** West Beirut

bézef [bezɛf] = **bésef**

bézoard [bezɔar] NM *Zool* bezoar

BF [beɛf] NF *(abrév* **Banque de France***)* the Banque de France, = French issuing bank

BFCE [beɛfsea] NF *(abrév* **Banque française du commerce extérieur***)* French foreign trade bank

bharal [baral] NM *Zool* bharal

BHL [beaʃɛl] NPR *(abrév* **Bernard-Henri Lévy***)* = initials commonly used to refer to the philosopher and journalist Bernard-Henri Lévy

Bhopal [bɔpal] NM *Géog* Bhopal

Bhoutan, Bhutan [butã] NM **le B.** Bhutan; **vivre au B.** to live in Bhutan; **aller au B.** to go to Bhutan

BHV [beaʃve] NM *(abrév* **Bazar de l'Hôtel de Ville***)* = large department store in central Paris, now part of a nationwide chain

bi¹ [bi] NM *Can* **donner** *ou* **faire un bi** to lend a hand, to muck in

bi² [bi] ADJ INV *Fam (bisexuel)* bi

bi- [bi] PRÉF bi-; **bilatéral** bilateral; **bipartisan** bipartisan

biacide [biasid] *Chim* ADJ diacidic

NM diacid

Biafra [bjafra] NM **le B.** Biafra; **vivre au B.** to live in Biafra; **aller au B.** to go to Biafra

biafrais, -e [bjafrɛ, -ɛz] ADJ Biafran

❑ **Biafrais, -e** NM,F Biafran

biais, -e [bjɛ, bjɛz] ADJ *(oblique)* slanting; **voûte biaise** skew arch

NM **1** *(obliquité)* slant; **le b. d'un mur** the slant of a wall

2 *Couture (bande)* bias binding; *(sens)* bias; **travailler dans le b.** to cut on the bias *or* cross

bia–bid

3 *(moyen)* way; **j'ai trouvé un b. pour ne pas payer** I found a way of not paying; **elle cherche un b. pour se faire connaître** she is trying to find a way of making herself known; **par le b. de qch** through, via, by means of sth; **par le b. de qn** through sb

4 *(aspect)* angle; **je ne sais pas par quel b. le prendre** I don't know how or from what angle to approach him; **prendre le b.** to go off at a tangent

5 *(dans des statistiques)* bias

▫ **de biais** ADV *(aborder)* indirectly, *Sout* tangentially; **regarder qn de b.** to give sb a sidelong glance

▫ **en biais** ADV sideways, slantwise, at an angle; **regarder qn en b.** to give sb a sidelong glance; **traverser la rue en b.** to cross the street diagonally

biaisé, -e [bjeze] ADJ *(statistiques, raisonnement)* distorted

biaiser [4] [bjeze] VI to prevaricate, to equivocate; **il va falloir b. pour avoir des places pour l'opéra** we'll have to be a bit clever to get tickets for the opera
  VT *(résultats)* to distort

biarrot, -e [bjaro, -ɔt] ADJ of/from Biarritz
  ▫ **Biarrot, -e** NM,F = inhabitant of or person from Biarritz

biathlète [bijatlɛt] NMF *Sport* biathlete

biathlon [biatlɔ̃] NM *Sport* biathlon

biauriculaire [bjɔrikylɛr] ADJ *Physiol* biauricular

biaxe [bjaks] ADJ *Opt & Minér* biaxial

bibande [bibãd] *Tél* ADJ dual-band
  NM *(téléphone portable)* dual-band *Br* mobile phone or *Am* cellphone

bibasique [bibazik] ADJ *Chim* dibasic

bibelot [biblo] NM *(précieux)* curio, bibelot; *(sans valeur)* trinket, knick-knack

biberon [bibrɔ̃] NM *Br* feeding or *Am* baby bottle; **l'heure du b.** feeding time; **donner le b. à un bébé/agneau** to bottle-feed a baby/lamb; **enfant nourri** ou **élevé au b.** bottle-fed baby; **il est encore au b.?** is he still being bottle-fed?; **prendre son b.** to have one's bottle; **il prend trois biberons par jour** he has three bottles or feeds a day; **prendre qn au b.** to start sb from the earliest possible age

biberonner [3] [bibrɔne] VI *Fam Hum* to tipple, to booze

bibi¹ [bibi] NM *Fam (chapeau)* (woman's) hat■

bibi² [bibi] PRON *Fam Hum (moi)* yours truly; **les corvées, c'est pour b.** yours truly gets stuck or *Br* lumbered with the chores

bibiche [bibiʃ] NF *Fam (terme d'affection)* sweetheart

Bibi Fricotin [bibifrikɔtɛ̃] NPR = comic strip character from the interwar years

bibine [bibin] NF *Fam* **c'est de la b.** *(boisson, bière)* it's dishwater; *(c'est facile)* it's a piece of cake

bibite [bibit] NF *Can Fam* **1** *(insecte)* bug; *(doryphore)* *Br* creepy-crawly, *Am* creepy-crawler; *(animal)* animal■ **2 il fait froid en b.** it's really cold■, it's freezing; **être en b. (contre qn)** to be teed off (with sb)

bibitif, -ive [bibitif, -iv] *Belg* ADJ Bacchic
  ▫ **bibitive** NF *Fam Arg scol* drunken revel

bible [bibl] NF **1** *Rel* **la B.** the Bible; **une b. de poche** a pocket Bible **2** *(référence)* bible; **la b. des mélomanes** the music lover's bible

bibli [bibli] NF *Fam (bibliothèque)* library■

bibliobus [biblijɔbys] NM *Br* mobile library, *Am* bookmobile

bibliographe [biblijɔgraf] NMF bibliographer

bibliographie [biblijɔgrafi] NF bibliography

bibliographique [biblijɔgrafik] ADJ bibliographic, bibliographical

bibliologie [biblijɔlɔʒi] NF bibliology

bibliomane [biblijɔman] NMF book lover, *Sout* bibliomaniac

bibliomanie [biblijɔmani] NF bibliomania

bibliophile [biblijɔfil] NMF book lover, *Spéc* bibliophile

bibliophilie [biblijɔfili] NF *(amour des livres)* bibliophily; *(science du bibliophile)* bibliophilism

bibliothécaire [biblijɔtekɛr] NMF librarian

bibliothéconomie [biblijɔtekɔnɔmi] NF library science

bibliothèque [biblijɔtɛk] NF **1** *(lieu)* library; *(meuble)* bookcase; **la b. de l'Arsenal** = library in Paris with an important collection of documents on theatre; **b. de dépôt** legal copyright deposit library; **la B. de France** = the new French national library building; **b. municipale** public library; **la B. nationale** = the former French national library building, now containing only archive material and coins, medals etc; **la B. nationale de France** = French national library, comprising the ''Bibliothèque de France'' and the ''Bibliothèque nationale''; **b. de prêt** lending library; **b. universitaire** university library

2 *(collection)* collection; **sa b. de livres d'art** his/her collection of art books; **c'est une b. ambulante** he's a walking encyclopedia; **b. de logiciels** software library; **la B. rose** = collection of books for very young children; *Hum* **tu en es resté à la B. rose!** ≃ you're still reading *Br* Janet and John stories or *Am* Jon and Jane books!; **la B. verte** = collection of books for older children

3 *Ordinat (de programmes)* library

4 *Com* **b. de gare** station *Br* bookstall or *Am* newsstand

---

Culture

BIBLIOTHÈQUE NATIONALE

Situated in the rue de Richelieu in Paris, the "Bibliothèque nationale" (also known as the "BN" or "Bibliothèque Richelieu") used to be a large copyright deposit library comparable to the British Library in London and the Library of Congress in Washington. This role has now been taken on by the "Bibliothèque nationale de France", which includes the "Bibliothèque Richelieu" and the new "Bibliothèque de France". This brand-new library (also known as the "Bibliothèque François-Mitterrand"), created in 1989 and situated in the south-east of Paris, stands as the last of the large-scale public works of the Mitterrand era. Fully computerized, it contains both a public library and a research library.

Culture

BIBLIOTHÈQUE ROSE, BIBLIOTHÈQUE VERTE

In France, these two series of illustrated stories for children have had an enduring success for some 150 years and form part of every French child's early reading experience. Among the lasting successes of "la Bibliothèque rose" (books with large print for young readers who have just learnt to read) are the stories by the Comtesse de Ségur, while "la Bibliothèque verte" remains famous for publishing *Le Club des cinq*, its translated version of Enid Blyton's Famous Five series, as well as simplified versions of classic works of literature.

---

biblique [biblik] ADJ *Rel* biblical

bibliste [biblist] NMF *Rel* Biblist, Biblicist

Bi-bop® [bibɔp] NM *Tél* = mobile telephone system run by France Télécom

Bic® [bik] NM ballpoint (pen), *Br* ≃ Biro®, *Am* ≃ Bic®

bicaméral, -e, -aux, -ales [bikameral, -o] ADJ *Pol* two-chamber, *Sout* bicameral

bicamérisme [bikamerism], **bicaméralisme** [bikameralism] NM *Pol* two-chamber (political) system, *Sout* bicameralism

bicarbonate [bikarbɔnat] NM *Chim* bicarbonate; **b. de soude** bicarbonate of soda

bicarbonaté, -e [bikarbɔnate] ADJ *Chim* bicarbonate *(avant n)*

bicarburation [bikarbyrasjɔ̃] NF *Aut* = dual-fuel (petrol and LPG) system

bicarré, -e [bikare] ADJ *Math* biquadratic

bicaténaire [bikatenɛr] ADJ *Biol* bicatenary

bicentenaire [bisãtnɛr] ADJ bicentenary, bicentennial
  NM bicentenary, bicentennial

bicéphale [bisefal] ADJ two-headed, *Sout* bicephalous

biceps [bisɛps] NM *Anat* biceps; *Fam* **avoir des b.** to have big biceps

Bichat [biʃa] *voir* **entretien**

biche [biʃ] NF **1** *Zool* doe, hind **2** *Fam (en appellatif)* **ma b.** darling, sweetheart

biche-cochon [biʃkɔʃɔ̃] *(pl* **biches-cochons)** NF *Zool* duiker

bicher [3] [biʃe] VI *Fam* **1** *(être satisfait)* to be tickled pink; **ça nous faisait b. de le voir s'empêtrer dans ses mensonges** it was really gratifying to see him getting tangled in his lies **2** *(tournure impersonnelle)* **ça biche?** how's it going?, how's things?

bichette [biʃɛt] NF **1** *Zool* hind calf, young hind or doe **2** *Fam (en appellatif)* **ma b.** darling, sweetheart

bichir [biʃir] NM *Ich* bichir

Bichkek [biʃkek] NM *Géog* Bishkek

bichlamar [biʃlamar] NM *(langue)* beach-la-mar

bichlorure [biklɔryr] NM *Chim* bichloride, dichloride

bichof [biʃɔf] NM *(boisson)* bishop

bichon, -onne [biʃɔ̃, -ɔn] NM,F *(chien)* Maltese (terrier)

bichonnage [biʃɔnaʒ] NM *Fam* **1** *(action de choyer)* pampering■ **2** *(action de pomponner)* sprucing up

bichonner [3] [biʃɔne] *Fam* VT **1** *(choyer)* to pamper■; **il aime se faire b.** he loves to be pampered **2** *(pomponner)* to spruce up
  ►**se bichonner** VPR *(se pomponner)* to spruce oneself up

bichromate [bikrɔmat] NM *Chim* bichromate, dichromate

bichromie [bikrɔmi] NF *Typ* two-colour process

bicipital, -e, -aux, -ales [bisipital, -o] ADJ *Anat* bicipital

Bickford [bikfɔrd] *voir* **cordeau**

biclic [biklik] NM *Ordinat* double click

bicliquer [3] [biklike] VI *Ordinat* to double-click

biclo [biklo], **biclou** [biklu] NM *Fam* bike

bicolore [bikɔlɔr] ADJ two-coloured

biconcave [bikɔ̃kav] ADJ biconcave

biconvexe [bikɔ̃vɛks] ADJ biconvex

bicoque [bikɔk] NF shack

bicorne [bikɔrn] NM cocked or two-pointed hat

bicorps [bikɔr] *Aut* ADJ hatchback
  NM hatchback (vehicle)

bicot [biko] NM **1** *Fam Zool (biquet)* kid■ **2** *très Fam* = offensive term used to refer to a North African Arab

bicouche [bikuʃ] NF *Biol & Chim* bilayer

bicross [bikrɔs] NM *Sport* cyclo-cross bicycle; **faire du b.** to do cyclo-cross

biculturalisme [bikyltyralism] NM biculturalism

biculturel, -elle [bikyltyrɛl] ADJ bicultural

bicuspide [bikyspid] ADJ *Anat* bicuspid

bicycle [bisikl] NM **1** *(à roues inégales)* *Br* pennyfarthing, *Am* ordinary **2** *Can* bicycle; *Can Joual* **b. à gaz** motorbike; *Can Joual* **b. à trois roues** tricycle

bicyclette [bisiklɛt] NF **1** *(engin)* bicycle; **faire de la b.** to cycle; **apprendre à faire de la b.** to learn cycling or how to ride a bicycle; **monter à b.** to ride a bicycle; **allons-y** ou **en b.** let's cycle, let's go there by bicycle; **b. de course** racer, racing bike; **b. de route** roadster, touring bike **2** *Sport* **la b.** cycling

bidasse [bidas] NM *Fam Mil (soldat)* *Br* squaddie, *Am* grunt

bide [bid] NM *Fam* **1** *(ventre)* belly, gut; **avoir/prendre du b.** to have/develop a belly **2** *(échec)* flop, washout; **ça a été** ou **fait un b.** it was a complete flop or washout

bident [bidã] NM two-pronged pitchfork

bidet [bidɛ] NM **1** *(de toilette)* bidet **2** *Fam (cheval)* nag

bidimensionnel, -elle [bidimãsjɔnɛl] ADJ bidimensional

bidirectionnel, -elle, bi-directionnel, -elle [bidirɛksjɔnɛl] ADJ bidirectional; *Tél* **b. simultané** full duplex

bidoche [bidɔʃ] NF *très Fam* meat■

bidon [bidɔ̃] ADJ INV *Fam (histoire, excuse, société)* phoney; *(numéro, adresse, information)* false■, bogus; *(élections)* rigged
  NM **1** *(récipient)* can, tin; *Mil* water bottle, canteen; **b. d'essence** petrol can; **b. d'huile** oilcan; **b. de lait** *Br* milk churn, *Am* milk can **2** *Fam (ventre)* belly, gut

3 *Fam (mensonge)* **tout ça, c'est du b.** that's a load of garbage *or Br* rubbish; **je te jure que ce n'est pas du b.** I swear that's the honest truth
❑ **bidons** NMPL *Belg Fam (frusques)* togs, gear, threads; *(affaires)* things■ , stuff

bidonnage [bidɔnaʒ] NM *Fam* falsifying■ ; *(d'élections)* rigging; **b. d'un questionnaire** filling in a questionnaire with false information■

bidonnant, -e [bidɔnɑ̃, -ɑ̃t] ADJ *Fam* side-splitting, hysterical; **elle est bidonnante** she's a scream *or* a hoot; **c'était b.** it was a scream *or* a hoot

bidonner [3] [bidɔne] **se bidonner** VPR *Fam* to kill oneself (laughing), to laugh one's head off; **qu'est-ce qu'on se bidonne avec eux!** it's a laugh a minute with them!

bidonville [bidɔ̃vil] NM shantytown

bidouillage [bidujaʒ], **bidouille** [biduj] NM *Fam* tinkering; *Ordinat (d'un logiciel)* patching; **ce n'est pas vraiment réparé, c'est du b.** it hasn't really been fixed, it's just a patch-up job

bidouiller [3] [biduje] VT *Fam* to tinker with; *Ordinat (logiciel)* to patch

bidouilleur, -euse [bidujœr, -øz] NM,F *Fam Ordinat* hacker, expert user■

bidous [bidu] NMPL *Can Fam* cash, dough; **avoir des b.** to be loaded, *Br* to be rolling in it

bidule [bidyl] NM *Fam* **1** *(objet)* thingy, whatsit **2** *(personne)* thingy, what's-his-name, *f* what's-her-name; **eh, B., t'as pas vu ma sœur?** hey, you *or Am* buddy, seen my sister?

bief [bjɛf] NM *(de cours d'eau)* reach; *(de moulin)* race; **b. d'aval/d'amont** tail/mill race

bielle [bjɛl] NF *Tech* connecting rod; *Aut* **b. d'accouplement** coupling rod; **tête de b.** connecting rod end; *Aut* big end; **pied de b.** connecting rod small end; *Aut* small end; *Aut* **b. de connexion** connecting rod; *Aut* **b. pendante** drop arm

biellette [bjɛlɛt] NF *Tech* rod

biélorusse [bjelɔrys] ADJ Belarusian, *Anciennement* Belorussian, Byelorussian
NM *(langue)* Belarusian, *Anciennement* Belorussian, Byelorussian
❑ **Biélorusse** NMF Belarusian, *Anciennement* Belorussian, Byelorussian

Biélorussie [bjelɔrysi] NF **la B.** Belarus, *Anciennement* Belorussia, Byelorussia; **vivre en B.** to live in Belarus; **aller en B.** to go to Belarus

BIEN [bjɛ̃]

> **ADV** well **1–3** ■ good **1** ■ right, correctly **4** ■ very **6** ■ really **6, 7, 9** ■ a lot **8** ■ at least **12** ■ quite a lot of **15**
> **ADJ** good **1, 2** ■ good-looking **3** ■ nice **3, 4, 6** ■ well **5**
> **NM** good **1, 2** ■ good thing **3** ■ possession, property **4, 5**
> **EXCLAM** OK

ADV **1** *(de façon satisfaisante)* well; **tout allait b.** everything was going well *or* fine; **ça te va b.** *(aspect)* it suits you; *(taille)* it fits you; *Ironique* **ça te va b. de te plaindre!** you're a fine one to complain!; **il s'est b. remis de son opération** he recovered well *or* made a good recovery from his operation; **il s'en est b. tiré** he came out of it well; **elle se débrouille b. sans moi** she manages very well without me; **la pièce est très b. jouée** the acting in the play's very good; **il cuisine b.** he's a good cook; **elle écrit b.** *(style)* she writes well; *(calligraphie)* she has beautiful writing; **il parle b. (le) grec** his Greek is good, he speaks Greek well; **du travail b. fait** a job well done; **la pièce finit b.** the play has a happy ending; **ça commence b.!** it's got off to a good start!; *Ironique* here we go!; **on mange b. ici** the food is good here; **le grille-pain ne marche pas très b.** the toaster doesn't work very well; **la vis tient b.** the screw is secure *or* is in tight; **dors b.!** sleep well!; **il gagne b. sa vie** he earns a good living; **ils vivent b.** they have a comfortable life; **b. payé** well paid; **faire b.** to look good; **ce vase fait très b. sur la cheminée** the vase looks very good on the fireplace; **b. prendre qch** to take sth well; **il s'y est b. pris** he tackled it well; **il s'y est b. pris pour interviewer le ministre** he did a good job of interviewing the minister; **vivre b. qch** to have a positive experience of sth; **b. se tenir** to behave oneself; **tiens-toi b.!** *(à la rambarde)* hold on tight!; *(sur la chaise)* sit properly!; *(à table)* behave yourself!; **tu tombes b.!** you've come at (just) the right time!

2 *(du point de vue de la santé)* **aller** *ou* **se porter b.** to feel well *or* fine; **elle ne va pas très b. ces jours-ci** she's not very well at the moment; *Hum* **il se porte plutôt b.!** he doesn't look as if he's starving!

3 *(conformément à la raison, à la loi, à la morale)* well, decently; **b. agir envers qn** to do the proper *or* right *or* correct thing by sb; **b. se conduire** to behave well *or* decently; **tu as b. fait** you did the right thing, you did right; **j'ai cru b. faire** I thought it was the right thing to do; **tu fais b. de ne plus les voir** you're right not to see them any more; **tu fais b. de me le rappeler** thank you for reminding me, it's a good thing you reminded me (of it); **il ferait b. de se faire oublier!** he'd be well advised to *or* he'd do well to *or* he'd better keep a low profile!; **tu ferais b. de partir plus tôt** you'd do well to leave earlier; **pour b. faire, nous devrions partir avant 9 heures** ideally, we should leave before 9; **il faudrait lui acheter un cadeau pour b. faire** we really ought to buy him/her a present

4 *(sans malentendu)* right, correctly; **si je vous comprends b.** if I understand you correctly *or* properly; **ai-je b. entendu ce que tu viens de dire?** did I hear you right?; **comprenez-moi b., je ne veux pas interférer, mais...** don't misunderstand me, I don't want to interfere but...; **si je me souviens b.** if I remember right *or* correctly

5 *(avec soin)* **écoute-moi b.** listen (to me) carefully; **as-tu b. vérifié?** did you check properly?; **fais b. ce que l'on te dit** do exactly *or* just as you're told; **mélangez b.** stir well; **soigne-toi b.** take good care of yourself

6 *(suivi d'un adjectif) (très)* really, very; **c'est b. agréable** it's really *or* very nice; **elle est b. belle** she's really *or* very beautiful; **b. déçu** really *or* terribly disappointed; **b. mûr** really *or* very ripe; **tu es b. sûr?** are you quite certain *or* sure?; **c'est b. bon** it's very *or* really good; **bois un thé b. chaud** have a nice hot cup of tea; **cette robe est b. chère** that dress is a bit on the expensive side *or* rather expensive; **cela me paraît b. risqué!** that seems pretty *or* rather risky to me!

7 *(suivi d'un adverbe)* **tu habites b. loin** you live a long way away; **c'était il y a b. longtemps** it was a very long time ago; **embrasse-le b. fort** give him a big hug; **il est b. tard pour sortir** it's a bit late to go out; **b. souvent** (very) often; **b. avant/après** well before/after; **b. trop tôt** far *or* much too early; **c'est b. mieux** it's much better; **c'est b. plus joli comme ça** it looks much nicer like that

8 *(suivi d'un verbe) (beaucoup)* **on a b. ri** we had a good laugh, we laughed a lot; **hier soir, on a b. discuté** we had a good (long) discussion last night; **je t'aime b., tu sais** I like you a lot *or* I'm very fond of you, you know

9 *(véritablement)* **j'ai b. l'impression que...** I really have the feeling that...; **j'ai b. cru que...** I really thought that...; **il a b. failli se noyer** he very nearly drowned; **sans b. se rendre compte de ce qu'il faisait** without being fully aware of *or* without fully realizing what he was doing

10 *(pour renforcer, insister)* **qui peut b. téléphoner à cette heure-ci?** who could that be calling at this hour?; **où peut-il b. être?** where on earth is he?; **je sais b. que tu dis la vérité** I know very well that you're not lying; **veux-tu b. te taire?** will you please be quiet?; **c'est b. lui** it IS him; **ce n'est pas lui, mais b. son associé que j'ai eu au téléphone** it wasn't him, but rather his partner I spoke to on the phone; **c'est b. ça** that's it, that's right; **c'est b. ce que je disais/pensais** that's just what I was saying/thinking; *Ironique* **c'est b. le moment d'en parler!** it's hardly the right time to talk about it!; **c'est b. ce qui me préoccupe!** that's (just) what's worrying me!; **vous vous appelez b. Anne, n'est-ce pas?** your name IS Anne, isn't it?; **j'ai pourtant b. entendu frapper** I'm sure I heard a knock at the door; **je le vois b. médecin** I can (quite) see him as a doctor; **tu vas lui dire? – je pense b.!** are you going to tell him/her? – you bet I am!; **je vais me plaindre – je comprends** *ou* **pense b.!** I'm going to complain – I should think so too!; **il ne m'aidera pas, tu penses b.!** he won't help me, you can be sure of that!; **c'est b. de lui, ça!** that's typical of him!, that's just like him!

11 *(volontiers)* **j'irais b. avec toi** I'd really like to go with you; **je te dirais b. quelque chose, mais je suis poli** I could say something rude but I won't; **je boirais b. quelque chose** I could do with *or* I wouldn't mind a drink; **j'irais b. nager un peu** I fancy *or* I wouldn't mind going for a little swim; **je t'aurais b. accompagné, mais...** I'd have been happy to go with you, but...; **je l'aurais b. tué!** I could have killed him!

12 *(au moins)* at least; **ça fait b. vingt fois qu'on lui dit** he's/she's been told at least twenty times; **ils étaient b. 30** there were at least 30 of them; **il est b. 10 heures** it must be 10 o'clock at least; **il a b. 50 ans** he must be at least 50

13 *(exprimant la supposition, l'éventualité)* **tu verras b.** you'll see; **ça lui passera b.** he'll/she'll grow out of it; **je l'entendrai b. venir** I'll hear him/her coming; **ils pourraient b. refuser** they might well refuse; **ça se pourrait b.** it's perfectly possible

14 *(pourtant)* **mais il fallait b. le lui dire!** but he/she had to be told (all the same)!; **il faut b. le faire** it's got to be done

15 b. de, b. des *(suivi d'un nom)* quite a lot of; **j'ai eu b. du souci** I've had a lot to worry about; **elle a b. du courage!** isn't she brave!, she's got a great deal of courage!; **b. des fois...** more than once...; **b. des gens** lots of *or* quite a lot of *or* quite a few people; **j'ai reçu b. des lettres** I received quite a lot of *or* a good many letters

16 *(dans la correspondance)* **b. à toi** love; **b. à vous** yours

ADJ INV **1** *(qui donne satisfaction)* good; **comment trouves-tu mon dessin? – très b.!** how do you like my drawing? – it's very nice *or* good!; **il est b., ton médecin?** is your doctor (any) good?; **elle serait b. dans le rôle de Turandot** she'd be *or* make a good Turandot; **c'est b. de s'amuser mais il faut aussi travailler** it's all right to have fun but you have to work too; *Fam* **je recule? – non, vous êtes b. là** shall I move back? – no, you're all right *or* OK *or* fine like that; *Fam* **qu'est-ce qu'il est b. dans son dernier film!** he's great *or* really good in his new film!

2 *Scol (sur un devoir)* good; **assez b.** fair; **très b.** very good

3 *(esthétique → personne)* good-looking, attractive; *(→ chose)* nice, lovely; **je ne me trouve jamais de chaussures b.** I can never find (any) nice shoes; **tu es très b. en jupe** *(cela te sied)* you look very nice in a skirt; *(c'est acceptable pour l'occasion)* a skirt is perfectly all right; **elle est drôlement b., ta sœur!** *(jolie)* your sister's really good-looking!; **il est b. de sa personne** he's a good-looking man; **elle est b. de sa personne** she's a good-looking woman

4 *(convenable → personne)* decent, nice; **ce ne sont pas des gens b.** they aren't decent people; **on ne rencontre pas que des gens b. par petites annonces** the people you meet through ads aren't always the right sort; *Fam* **adresse-toi à lui, c'est un type b.** go and see him, he's a decent guy; **ce serait b. de lui envoyer un peu d'argent** it'd be a good idea to send him/her some money; **ils se sont séparés et c'est b. comme ça** they've split up and it's better that way; **chacun a ses idées et c'est b. ainsi** everybody's got their own ideas and that's how it should be; **tout ça c'est très b., mais...** that's all well and good *or* all very well, but...; **c'est très b. à vous de n'avoir rien dit** it's very good of you not to have said anything; **ce n'est pas b. de tirer la langue** it's naughty *or* it's not nice to stick out your tongue; **ce n'est pas b. de montrer (les gens) du doigt** it's not nice to point *or* you shouldn't point (at people); **ce n'est pas b. de tricher** you shouldn't cheat

5 *(en forme)* well; **elle n'est pas/est très b. en**

ce moment she's not doing/she's doing well right now; **je n'étais pas b. hier** I wasn't feeling well yesterday; **se sentir b.** to feel fine *or* well; **se sentir b. dans sa peau** to feel at ease *or* happy with oneself; **vous ne vous sentez pas b.?** aren't you feeling well?; *(mentalement)* are you crazy?; *Fam* **il n'est pas b., celui-là!** he's got a problem, he has!; **me/te/***etc* **voilà b.!** NOW I'm/you're/*etc* in a fine mess!; *Fam* **là, on (n')est pas b.!** we're really in trouble now!

6 *(à l'aise)* **on est b. ici** it's nice here; **on est vraiment b. dans ce fauteuil** this armchair is really comfortable; **je suis b. avec toi** I like being with you

7 *(en bons termes)* **être b. avec qn** to be well in with sb; **ils sont b. ensemble** they're happy together; **se mettre b. avec qn** to get in with sb, to get into sb's good books

NM 1 *Phil & Rel* **le b.** good; **la différence entre le b. et le mal** the difference between good and evil *or* right and wrong; **faire le b.** to do good; **elle fait du b. autour d'elle** she does good (works) wherever she goes; **rendre le b. pour le mal** to return good for evil

2 *(ce qui est agréable, avantageux)* **c'est pour son b.** it's for his/her good; **c'est pour ton b. que je dis ça** I'm saying this for your own good *or* benefit; **c'est ton b. que je veux** I only want what's best for you; **en tout b. tout honneur** *(proposition, affaire)* (fair and) above-board; **le b. commun** *ou* **général** the common good; **c'est pour le b. de tous/de l'entreprise** it's for the common good/the good of the firm; **pour le b. public** in the public interest; **vouloir du b. à qn** to wish sb well; **elle ne te voulait pas que du b.** her motives weren't entirely honourable; **dire/penser du b. de** to speak/to think well of; **si tu savais le b. qu'on dit de toi** you should hear the wonderful things people say about you; **on ne m'a dit que du b. de votre cuisine** I've only heard good things about your cooking; **continue à me masser, ça fait du b.** carry on massaging me, it's doing me good; **cela fait du b. de se dégourdir les jambes** it's nice to be able to stretch your legs; *Fam* **les piqûres, ça ne fait pas de b.!** injections are no fun!; *Fam* **je me suis cogné l'orteil, ça fait pas du b.!** I banged my toe, it's quite painful!; **faire du b.** *ou* **le plus grand b. à qn** *(médicament, repos)* to do sb good, to benefit sb; **la promenade m'a fait du b.** the walk did me good; **le dentiste ne m'a pas fait du b.!** the dentist really hurt me!; **un peu de pluie ferait du b. aux plantes** some rain would do the plants good *or* wouldn't hurt the plants; **cela m'a fait du b. de te parler** it did me good to talk to you; **une subvention ferait du b. aux agriculteurs** a subsidy would be of great help to the farming community; *Fam* **laisser tomber les livres par terre, ça ne leur fait pas du b.** you don't do a book too much good by dropping it on the floor; **la séparation leur fera le plus grand b.** being apart will do them a lot *or* a world of good; **le repos m'a fait (un) grand b.** the rest did me the world *or* a power of good; *Ironique* **grand b. te/lui fasse!** much good may it do you/him/her!; **b. m'en a pris** it was just as well I did it; **b. leur en a pris de ne pas l'écouter** how right they were not to listen to him/her, it was just as well they didn't listen to him/her; *Fam* **ça fait du b. par où ça passe!** aah, I feel better for that!

3 *(bienfait)* good *or* positive thing, benefit; **la restructuration sera un b. pour l'entreprise** reorganization will be a positive move for the firm; **cette décision a été un b. pour tout le monde** the decision was a good thing for all *or* everyone concerned

4 *(propriété personnelle)* possession, piece *or* item of property; *(argent)* fortune; **mon b. t'appartient** what's mine is yours; **il a mangé tout son b. en trois mois** he squandered his fortune in three months; *Fam* **ils ont un petit b. en Ardèche** they have a bit of land in the Ardèche; **la jeunesse est un b. précieux** youth is a precious asset; **tous mes biens** all my worldly goods, all I'm worth; **les biens temporels** *ou* **de ce monde** material possessions, worldly goods; *Fam* **avoir du b. au soleil** to be well-off *or* rich

5 *Écon* possession; *Jur* assets; **biens** possessions, property; **biens capitaux** capital goods *or* items; **biens communs** marital property; **biens communaux** communal lands; **biens de consommation** consumer products, consumer goods; **biens de consommation courante** consumer goods; **biens de consommation durables** consumer durables; **biens de consommation non durables** disposable goods; **biens corporels** tangible assets; **biens dotaux** dowry; **biens durables** consumer durables, durable goods; **biens d'équipement** capital equipment *or* goods; **biens d'équipement ménager** consumer durables; **biens de famille** family property; **biens fonciers** (real) property, real estate; **biens immédiatement disponibles** off-the-shelf goods; **biens immeubles, biens immobiliers** real assets; **biens incorporels** intangible property; **biens en indivision** jointly-owned goods; **biens insaisissables** non-seizable property; **biens intermédiaires** intermediate goods; **biens marchands** commodities; **biens meubles, biens mobiliers** personal property *or* estate, movables; **biens d'occasion** second-hand goods; **biens personnels** personal property; **biens de première nécessité** staples; **biens présents et à venir** = all present and future property of an estate; **biens privés/publics** private/public property; **biens propres** = spouse's separate property; **biens de production** producer *or* capital goods; **biens saisis** distress; **biens et services** goods and services; *Compta* **biens sociaux** corporate assets *or* funds; **biens vacants** ownerless property

6 *Hist* **biens nationaux** = property confiscated from nobles during the Revolution and resold

EXCLAM 1 *(indiquant une transition)* OK, right (then); **b., je t'écoute** right *or* OK, I'm listening; **b., c'est fini pour aujourd'hui** right *or* OK, that's it for today; **b.! où en étions-nous?** right! where were we?

2 *(marquant l'approbation)* **je n'irai pas! – b., n'en parlons plus!** I won't go! – very well *or* all right (then), let's drop the subject!; **c'est décidé! – b.!** we've decided! – good *or* fine!; **je reviens dans une heure – b.** I'll be back in an hour – (all) right *or* fine; **très b., je vais avec toi** fine *or* very well, I'll go with you; **fort b.** fine; **b., b., on y va** all right, all right *or* OK, OK, let's go

❑ **bien entendu** ADV of course; **tu m'aideras? – b. entendu!** will you help me? – of course *or* that goes without saying!

❑ **bien entendu que** CONJ of course; **b. entendu que j'aimerais y aller** of course I'd like to go

❑ **bien que** CONJ despite the fact that, although, though; **b. que je comprenne votre problème, je ne peux vous aider** although *or* though I understand your problem, I can't help you; **b. qu'ayant travaillé cette question, je serais en peine d'en parler** although I've studied this question, I would be hard put to speak about it; **b. que malade, il a tenu à y aller** although (he was) ill, he insisted on going; **sa maison, b. que petite, est agréable** small though it is, his/her house is nice

❑ **bien sûr** ADV of course; **viendras-tu? – b. sûr!** will you come? – of course (I will)!; **puis-je le prendre? – b. sûr** may I take it? – of course *or* please do *or* by all means

❑ **bien sûr que** CONJ of course; **b. sûr qu'elle n'avait rien compris!** of course she hadn't understood a thing!; **c'est vrai? – b. sûr que oui!** is it true? – of course it is!

---

bien-aimé, -e [bjɛ̃neme] (*mpl* **bien-aimés,** *fpl* **bien-aimées**) **ADJ** beloved

NM,F beloved

bien-dire [bjɛ̃dir] **NM** elegance of speech, eloquence; **être** *ou* **se mettre sur son b.** to speak carefully, to choose one's words carefully

biénergie [bienɛrʒi] **NF** *Tech (chauffage)* **système b.** bi-energy system

bien-être [bjɛ̃nɛtr] **NM INV 1** *(aise)* well-being; **une agréable sensation de b.** a wonderful feeling of well-being **2** *(confort matériel)* (material) well-being **3** *Can* **b. social** *Br* social security, *Am* welfare

bienfacture [byɛ̃faktyr] **NF** *Suisse* high quality

bienfaisance [bjɛ̃fəzɑ̃s] **NF 1** *(charité)* charity **2** *Littéraire (générosité)* benevolence

❑ **de bienfaisance ADJ** *(bal)* charity *(avant n)*; **association** *ou* **œuvre de b.** charity, charitable organization; **travailler pour les œuvres de b.** to do charity work

bienfaisant, -e [bjɛ̃fəzɑ̃, -ɑ̃t] **ADJ 1** *(bénéfique → effet, climat)* beneficial, *Sout* salutary **2** *(indulgent → personne)* kind, kindly, *Sout* beneficent

bienfait [bjɛ̃fɛ] **NM 1** *Littéraire (acte de bonté)* kindness; **combler qn de bienfaits** to shower sb with kindness; *Prov* **un b. n'est jamais perdu** = a good deed will be rewarded **2** *(effet salutaire)* benefit; **les bienfaits d'un séjour à la montagne** the benefits *or* beneficial effects of a stay in the mountains; **les bienfaits de la civilisation** the advantages *or* benefits of civilization

bienfaiteur, -trice [bjɛ̃fɛtœr, -tris] **NM,F** benefactor, *f* benefactress; **l'association fonctionne grâce à des bienfaiteurs** the association keeps going *or* running thanks to its benefactors; **b. du genre humain** great man, *f* great woman

bien-fondé [bjɛ̃fɔ̃de] (*pl* **bien-fondés**) **NM** *(d'une revendication)* rightfulness; *(d'un argument)* validity; **établir le b. de qch** to substantiate sth

bien-fonds [bjɛ̃fɔ̃] **NM** *Jur* real estate

bienheureux, -euse [bjɛ̃nørø, -øz] **ADJ 1** *Rel* blessed; **b. les pauvres d'esprit** blessed are the poor in spirit **2** *(heureux → personne, vie)* happy, blissful; *(→ hasard)* fortunate, lucky

NM,F *Rel* **les b.** the blessed *or* blest; **dormir comme un b.** to sleep the sleep of the just

bien-jugé [bjɛ̃ʒyʒe] (*pl* **bien-jugés**) **NM** *Jur* just and lawful decision

biennal, -e, -aux, -ales [bjenal, -o] **ADJ** biennial

❑ **biennale NF** biennial arts festival

Bienne [bjɛn] **NM** *Géog* Biel

bien-pensant, -e [bjɛ̃pɑ̃sɑ̃, -ɑ̃t] (*mpl* **bien-pensants,** *fpl* **bien-pensantes**) *Péj* **ADJ** *(conformiste)* conservative, conformist

NM,F conservative person, conformist

bienséance [bjɛ̃seɑ̃s] **NF** decorum, propriety; **les bienséances** the proprieties

bienséant, -e [bjɛ̃seɑ̃, -ɑ̃t] **ADJ** decorous, proper, becoming; **il n'est pas b. d'élever la voix** it is unbecoming *or* it isn't proper *or* it isn't done to raise one's voice

bientôt [bjɛ̃to] **ADV 1** *(prochainement)* soon, before long; **on est b. arrivés?** are we nearly there?, will we soon be there?; **à (très) b.!** see you soon!; **je reviens b.** I'll be back soon; **il sera b. de retour** he'll soon be back, he'll be back before long; **j'ai b. fini** I've almost finished; **il est b. midi** it's nearly midday; **b., ce ne sera plus qu'un mauvais souvenir** it'll soon be nothing but a bad memory; **tu vas b. être plus grand que moi!** you'll be taller than me soon *or* before you know it!; **l'accord de paix n'est pas pour b.** it is unlikely that the peace agreement will be signed soon; **c'est pour b.?** will it be long?; *(naissance)* is it *or* is the baby due soon?; *Fam* **c'est pas b. fini ce vacarme?** have you quite finished (making all that racket)?

2 *(rapidement)* soon, quickly, in no time; **il eut b. fait de reprendre ses esprits** he came around in no time; **cela est b. dit** that's easier said than done

bienveillamment [bjɛ̃vɛjamɑ̃] **ADV** kindly, benevolently

bienveillance [bjɛ̃vejɑ̃s] **NF 1** *(qualité)* benevolence, kindliness; **parler de qn avec b.** to speak favourably of sb **2** *(dans des formules de politesse)* **je sollicite de votre b. un entretien** I beg to request an interview

bienveillant, -e [bjɛ̃vejɑ̃, -ɑ̃t] **ADJ** *(personne)* benevolent, kindly; *(regard, sourire)* kind, kindly, gentle

bienvenir [bjɛ̃vnir] **VI** *(à l'infinitif seulement) Littéraire* **se faire b. de qn** to ingratiate oneself with sb

bienvenu, -e [bjɛ̃vny] **ADJ** *(remarque)* opportune, apposite; *(repas, explication)* welcome

NM,F être le b. to be welcome; **soyez les bienvenus dans notre ville** welcome to our city; **tu seras toujours la bienvenue chez nous** you'll always be welcome here, we'll always be pleased to have you with us; **cet argent était**

vraiment le b. that money was most welcome
□ **bienvenue** NF welcome; **souhaiter la bienvenue à qn** to welcome sb EXCLAM welcome!; *Can (de rien)* you're welcome!; **bienvenue à toi, ami!** welcome to you, my friend!
□ **de bienvenue** ADJ *(discours)* welcoming; *(cadeau)* welcome *(avant n)*

bière [bjɛr] NF **1** *(alcool)* beer; **b. blanche** wheat beer; **b. blonde** lager; **b. brune** *Br* brown ale, *Am* dark beer; *Can* **b. d'épinette** spruce beer; **b. (à la) pression** draught beer; *Fam* **c'est de la petite b.** it's small beer; *Fam* **ce n'est pas de la petite b.** it's quite something **2** *(cercueil)* coffin, *Am* casket; **mettre qn en b.** to place sb in his/her *Br* coffin *or Am* casket; **assister à la mise en b.** to be present when the body is placed in the *Br* coffin *or Am* casket

biergol [bjɛrgɔl] NM diergol

bièvre [bjɛvr] NM **1** *Arch Zool* beaver **2** *Orn* **harle b.** goosander, *Am* American merganser

biface [bifas] NM biface

biffage [bifaʒ] NM crossing *or* scoring out

biffe [bif] *Fam Arg mil* NF infantry
□ **Biffe** NF **la B.** = nickname of the French infantry

biffement [bifmɑ̃] NM crossing *or* scoring out

biffer [3] [bife] VT to cross out, to score out; **tu peux b. ce nom de ta liste** you can cross *or* score this name off your list

biffeton [biftɔ̃] = **bifton**

biffin [bifɛ̃] NM **1** *Fam Arg mil* foot soldier, footslogger **2** *Fam (chiffonnier)* ragman, *Br* rag-and-bone man

biffure [bifyr] NF crossing out, stroke; **faire des biffures sur une lettre** to cross things out in a letter

bifide [bifid] ADJ bifid

bifidus [bifidys] NM *Biol* bifidus; **yaourt au b.** live yoghurt

bifilaire [bifilɛr] ADJ *Phys* bifilar

biflèche [biflɛʃ] NM *Mil* double trail, bipod

bifocal, -e, -aux, -ales [bifɔkal, -o] ADJ *Opt* bifocal; **lunettes bifocales** bifocals

bifolié, -e [bifɔlje] ADJ *Bot* bifoliate

bifoliolé, -e [bifɔljɔle] ADJ *Bot* bifoliolate

bifteck [biftɛk] NM **1** *(tranche)* (piece of) steak; **un b. dans le filet** a piece of fillet steak; **un b. dans la hampe** a (piece of) steak cut off the flank; **un b. haché** a beefburger; **défendre/gagner son b.** to look after/to earn one's bread and butter **2** *(catégorie de viande)* steak; **du b. haché** *Br* (best) mince, *Am* lean ground beef

bifton [biftɔ̃] NM *Fam (billet de banque)* note■, *Am* greenback; *(de transport, de spectacle)* ticket■

bifurcation [bifyrkasjɔ̃] NF **1** *(intersection)* junction, turning **2** *(changement)* change (of course)

bifurquer [3] [bifyrke] VI **1** *(route)* to branch off, *Sout* to bifurcate; *(conducteur)* to turn off; **on a alors bifurqué sur Lyon** we then turned off towards Lyons; **b. à gauche** to turn left **2** *(changer)* **b. vers** to branch off into, to switch to; **il a bifurqué vers la politique** he branched out into politics

bigame [bigam] ADJ bigamous
NMF bigamist

bigamie [bigami] NF bigamy

bigarade [bigarad] NF *Bot* bitter *or* Seville orange

bigaradier [bigaradje] NM *Bot* bitter *or* Seville orange tree

bigarré, -e [bigare] ADJ *(fleur)* variegated, multicoloured; *(vêtement)* multicoloured; *(foule)* colourful

bigarreau, -x [bigaro] NM *Bot (cerise)* bigarreau (cherry)

bigarrer [3] [bigare] VT *Littéraire (colorer)* to variegate, to colour in many shades

bigarrure [bigaryr] NF variegation, multicoloured effects

big band [bigbɑ̃d] *(pl* **big bands***)* NM *Mus* big band

big(-)bang [bigbɑ̃g] NM *Phys & Fin* big bang

Bige® [biʒ] ADJ INV *Rail (abrév* **billet individuel de groupe étudiant***)* **billet B.** = cut-price student travel ticket

Big Five [bigfajv] NFPL *Cin* **les B.** the Big Five

bigle [bigl] *Fam Vieilli* ADJ *(myope)* short-sighted■; *(qui louche)* cross-eyed■
NMF *(myope)* short-sighted person■; *(qui louche)* cross-eyed person■

bigler [3] [bigle] *Fam* VI to squint
VT *(observer)* to eye, to check out, *Br* to clock
□ **bigler sur** VT IND to eye (with greed)

bigleux, -euse [biglø, -øz] *Fam* ADJ *(myope)* short-sighted■; *(qui louche)* cross-eyed■
NM,F *(myope)* short-sighted person■; *(qui louche)* cross-eyed person■

bignone [biɲɔn] NF, **bignonia** [biɲɔnja] NM *Bot* bignonia

bignoniacées [biɲɔnjase] NFPL *Bot* Bignoniaceae

bigophone [bigɔfɔn] NM *Fam (téléphone)* phone, *Br* blower, *Am* horn; **passe-moi un coup de b.** give me a buzz *or Br* a bell

bigophoner [3] [bigɔfɔne] VI *Fam* to make a phone call■; **b. à qn** to give sb a buzz *or Br* a bell

bigorne [bigɔrn] NF anvil *(with two pointed ends)*

bigorneau, -x [bigɔrno] NM *Zool (mollusque)* periwinkle, winkle

bigorner [3] [bigɔrne] *très Fam* VT *(défoncer → moto, voiture)* to smash up
▸ **se bigorner** VPR to scrap, to fight■

bigot, -e [bigo, -ɔt] *Rel* ADJ *(dévot)* sanctimonious, holier-than-thou
NM,F religious zealot

bigoterie [bigɔtri] NF *Rel* (religious) bigotry

bigotisme [bigɔtism] NM = **bigoterie**

bigouden [bigudɛn] ADJ from the Bigouden area (of Brittany)
NM Bigouden (woman's) headgear
NF Bigouden woman

bigoudi [bigudi] NM curler, roller; **(se) mettre des bigoudis** to put one's hair into curlers *or* rollers; **elle est sortie en bigoudis** she went out with her hair in curlers *or* rollers

bigre [bigr] EXCLAM *Vieilli* gosh!, my!

bigrement [bigrəmɑ̃] ADV *(très) Br* jolly, *Am* mighty; **il fait b. froid ici** it's *Br* jolly *or Am* mighty cold in here; **il faut être b. culotté** you have to have a hell of a nerve; **il était b. surpris** he was dead surprised; **ça a b. changé** it has changed a heck of a lot

bigrille [bigrij] ADJ **lampe b.** double-grid valve

biguanide [bigwanid] NF *Chim* biguanide

bigue [big] NF **1** *Constr* hoisting-gin, sheers **2** *Naut* mast-crane, heavy lift derrick
□ **bigues** NFPL sheer-legs

biguine [bigin] NF *Mus & (danse)* beguine

bihebdomadaire [biɛbdɔmadɛr] ADJ biweekly, twice-weekly

bihoreau, -x [biɔro] NM *Orn* **(héron) b.** night heron

bijectif, -ive [biʒɛktif, -iv] ADJ *Math* bijective

bijection [biʒɛksjɔ̃] NF *Math* bijection

bijou, -x [biʒu] NM **1** *(parure)* jewel; **bijoux** jewellery, jewels; **bijoux de famille** family jewels *or* jewellery; *très Fam Fig (sexe masculin)* family jewels, *Br* wedding tackle; **bijoux fantaisie** costume jewellery **2** *(fleuron)* gem; **un b. de l'art rococo** a gem of Rococo art; **cette montre est un b. de précision** this watch is a marvel of precision **3** *Fam (en appellatif)* **bonjour, mon b.** hello, precious *or* my love

bijouterie [biʒutri] NF **1** *(bijoux)* jewels, jewellery **2** *(magasin) Br* jeweller's (shop), *Am* jeweler's (store) **3** *(industrie)* jewellery business **4** *(fabrication)* jewellery-making

bijoutier, -ère [biʒutje, -ɛr] NM,F jeweller

bijumeau, -x [biʒymo] *voir* **muscle**

Bikini® [bikini] NM bikini

bilabiale [bilabjal] *Ling* ADJ F bilabial
NF bilabial (consonant)

bilabié, -e [bilabje] ADJ *Bot* bilabiate

bilame [bilam] NM *Tech* bimetallic strip

bilan [bilɑ̃] NM **1** *Fin & Compta* statement (of accounts); *(de l'actif, des responsabilités)* schedule; *Banque (d'un compte)* balance; **dresser** *ou* **établir** *ou* **faire le b.** to draw up the balance sheet; **déposer le** *ou* **son b.** to file one's petition (in bankruptcy); **b. annuel** annual accounts; **b. commercial** market report; **b. (comptable)** balance sheet; **b. condensé** summary balance sheet; **b. consolidé** consolidated balance sheet; **b. de l'exercice** end-of-year balance sheet; **b. financier** financial statement; **b. de groupe** consolidated balance sheet; **b. intérimaire** interim statement; **b. de liquidation** statement of affairs; **b. d'ouverture** opening balance sheet; **b. prévisionnel** forecast balance sheet; **b. social** social report
2 *(appréciation)* appraisal, assessment; *(résultats)* results; **faire le b. de qch** to take stock of *or* to assess sth; **arrivé à 40 ans, on fait souvent le b.** you often stop to take stock when you reach 40; **b. de carrière** = summary of one's employment record; **b. de compétence** = summary of one's skills; **quel est le b. de ces discussions?** what is the end result of these talks?, what have these talks amounted to?; **le b. définitif fait état de 20 morts** the final death toll stands at 20; **accident sur l'autoroute, b.: quatre morts** *(dans un journal)* motorway accident, four dead; **un b. économique positif** positive economic results
3 *Méd* **b. (de santé)** (medical) check-up; **se faire faire un b. (de santé)** to have a check-up; *Fig* **faire le b. de santé d'une entreprise** to assess *or* to evaluate the state of a company

bilatéral, -e, -aux, -ales [bilateral, -o] ADJ bilateral, two-way

bilatéralement [bilateralmɑ̃] ADV bilaterally

bilatéralisme [bilateralism] NM *Pol* bilateralism

bilatéralité [bilateralite] NF bilateralism

Bilbao [bilbao] NM Bilbao

bilboquet [bilbɔkɛ] NM **1** *(jeu)* cup-and-ball game **2** *Typ* small job

bile [bil] NF **1** *Physiol* bile; *Arch & Littéraire* choler **2** *Fam (locutions)* **décharger** *ou* **épancher sa b. sur qn** to vent one's spleen on sb; **se faire de la b.** to fret; **je me suis fait beaucoup de b. pour toi** I was worried sick about you; **te fais pas de b.** don't you fret *or* worry

biler [3] [bile] **se biler** VPR *Fam (s'inquiéter)* to fret, to worry■; **te bile pas pour lui** don't worry about him

bileux, -euse [bilø, -øz] ADJ *Fam* easily worried■; **je n'ai jamais été du genre b.** I never was one to worry about things, I never was much of a worrier

bilharzia [bilarzia], **bilharzie** [bilarzi] NF *Biol (parasite)* bilharzia, schistosome

bilharziose [bilarzjoz] NF *Méd (maladie)* bilharzia, bilharziasis, bilharziosis, schistosomiasis

biliaire [biljɛr] ADJ *Physiol (vaisseaux)* biliary; *Méd* **calcul b.** gallstone, *Spéc* biliary calculus; *Anat* **vésicule b.** gall bladder; *Méd* **cirrhose b.** cirrhosis (of the liver)

bilié, -e [bilje] ADJ *Méd* bilious

bilieux, -euse [biljø, -øz] ADJ **1** *(pâle → teint)* bilious, sallow, yellowish **2** *(colérique → personne, tempérament)* testy, irascible **3** *(inquiet)* anxious

biligenèse [biliʒənɛz] NF *Physiol* biliation

biligénèse [biliʒenɛz], **biligénie** [biliʒeni] NF *Physiol* biligenesis, bilification

bilinéaire [bilineɛr] ADJ bilinear

bilingue [bilɛ̃g] ADJ **1** *Ling* bilingual **2** *Can Fam (bisexuel)* bi
NMF **1** *Ling* bilingual speaker **2** *Can Fam (bisexuel)* bi

bilinguisme [bilɛ̃gɥism] NM bilingualism

bilirubine [bilirybin] NF *Physiol* bilirubin

biliverdine [bilivɛrdin] NF *Physiol* biliverdin

bill [bil] NM *Pol* bill

billage [bijaʒ] NM *Métal* ball testing *(for hardness)*

billard [bijar] NM **1** *(jeu)* billiards *(singulier)*; **faire un b.** to play a game of billiards; **b. américain** pool; **b. anglais** snooker; **b. russe** bar billiards
2 *(salle → gén)* billiard room; *(→ pour billard anglais)* snooker room; *(→ pour billard américain)* pool room
3 *(meuble → gén)* billiard table; *(→ pour billard anglais)* snooker table; *(→ pour billard américain)* pool table; **b. électrique** *(jeu)* pinball; *(machine)* pinball machine
4 *Fam (table d'opération)* **une fois qu'on est sur le b.** once you're under the knife■; **monter** *ou* **passer sur le b.** to go under the knife; **faire passer qn sur le b.** to open sb up; **quand est-ce que tu passes sur le b.?** when are you going under the knife?

billbergia [bilbɛrʒja] NM *Bot* billbergia

bille[1] [bij] NF **1** *(de verre)* marble; *Fig* **placer ses billes** to get oneself in; *Fig* **reprendre ses billes** to pull out *(of a deal)*; *Fam* **toucher sa b. en** to be *Br* bloody *or Am* darned good at; **en mécanique, je touche pas ma b.** I haven't got a clue about mechanics
2 *(de billard)* ball; **être chauve comme une b.**

de billard to be bald *Br* as a coot *or Am* as an egg **3** *Ind & Tech* ball; **b. de roulement** ball bearing **4** *Fam (tête)* mug; **avoir une bonne b.** to look a good sort; **avoir une b. de clown** to have a funny face

5 *Fam (niais)* mug

◽ **à bille** ADJ *(crayon, stylo)* ballpoint *(avant n)*; *(déodorant)* roll-on *(avant n)*

◽ **bille en tête** ADV straight, straightaway; **il est allé b. en tête se plaindre à la direction** he went shooting off to complain to the management

bille² [bij] NF *(tronçon de bois)* saw log

biller [3] [bije] VT *Métal* to ball-test

billet [bijɛ] NM **1** *(gén)* ticket; **b. d'avion/de train/de concert/de loterie** plane/train/concert/lottery ticket; **voyageurs munis de billets** ticket holders; **retenez** *ou* **réservez les billets à l'avance** book ahead; **b. aller** *ou* **simple** *Br* single (ticket), *Am* one-way ticket; **b. aller-retour** *Br* return *or Am* roundtrip ticket; **b. circulaire** *Br* day return (ticket), *Am* roundtrip ticket; **b. électronique** e-ticket; **b. de faveur** complimentary ticket; **b. de retour** return ticket

2 *(argent)* **b. (de banque)** *Br* note, banknote, *Am* bill; **le nouveau b. de 50 euros** the new 50-euro *Br* note *or Am* bill; **le b. est un faux** this note is a forgery; *Vieilli* **un b. (dix francs)** ten francs; **le b. vert** the dollar, the US currency; **faux b.** forged banknote

3 *Com & Fin (effet)* note, bill; **b. de complaisance** accommodation bill; **b. à ordre** promissory note, note of hand; **b. au porteur** bearer bill; **b. de reconnaissance de dettes** IOU; **b. du Trésor** Treasury bill; *Banque* **b. de trésorerie** commercial paper

4 *(message)* note; **b. doux** *ou* **galant** billet doux, love letter; *Journ* **b. d'humeur** column

5 *Mil* **b. de logement** billet

6 *(locutions)* **je te fiche mon b. que tu te trompes** I'd bet my bottom dollar *or* my boots that you're wrong; **elle est enceinte, je t'en fiche mon b.** I bet you anything she's pregnant

billeté, -e [bijte] ADJ *Hér* billety

billétique [bijetik] NF *Banque & Ordinat* cash dispenser technology

billette [bijɛt] NF **1** *(morceau de bois)* billet, piece of firewood **2** *(lingot d'acier)* billet **3** *Archit* billet **4** *Hér* billet

billetterie [bijɛtri] NF **1** *(opérations)* ticket distribution; *(guichet)* ticket office; **b. automatique** ticket machine **2** *Banque (distributeur)* Br cashpoint, *Am* ATM

billettiste [bijetist] NMF **1** *(vendeur)* ticket seller **2** *(journaliste)* columnist

billevesées [bijvəze] NFPL *Littéraire* nonsense, twaddle

billion [biljɔ̃] NM **1** *(million de millions)* trillion, *Br Vieilli* billion **2** *Arch (milliard)* billion, *Br Vieilli* milliard

billon [bijɔ̃] NM **1** *(de bois)* balk **2** *(en viticulture)* vine-plant *(cut very short)* **3** *Agr* ridge of earth *(formed by two plough furrows)*; **b. de délimitation** *(entre deux champs)* balk; **labourer en billons** to rafter **4** *(alliage)* alloy of precious metal with copper **5** *(monnaie)* **(monnaie de) b.** copper *or* nickel coinage

billonnage [bijɔnaʒ] NM **1** *Agr* ridging **2** *Jur* uttering of base coin

billot [bijo] NM *(de bourreau, d'enclume)* block; **finir** *ou* **périr sur le b.** to be beheaded

bilobé, -e [bilɔbe] ADJ bilobate, bilobed

biloculaire [bilɔkylɛr] ADJ bilocular

biloquer [3] [bilɔke] VT *Agr* to plough deeply

bimane [biman] *Zool* ADJ bimanous
　NMF bimane

bimbeloterie [bɛ̃blɔtri] NF **1** *(babioles)* knickknacks **2** *(commerce)* fancy goods business

bimbelotier, -ère [bɛ̃blɔtje, -ɛr] NM,F **1** *(fabricant)* fancy goods manufacturer **2** *(vendeur)* fancy goods dealer

bimbo [bimbo] NF *Fam Péj* bimbo

bi-média [bimedja] ADJ bi-media

bimensuel, -elle [bimɑ̃sɥɛl] ADJ twice monthly, *Br* fortnightly, *Am* semimonthly
　NM *Journ (revue)* Br fortnightly, *Am* semimonthly

bimensuellement [bimɑ̃sɥɛlmɑ̃] ADV twice a month, *Br* every fortnight

bimestre [bimɛstr] NM period of two months

bimestriel, -elle [bimɛstrijɛl] ADJ bimonthly
　NM *(revue)* bimonthly

Bimétal® [bimetal] NM Bimetal

bimétallique [bimetalik] ADJ bimetallic

bimétallisme [bimetalism] NM bimetallism

bimétalliste [bimetalist] *Écon* ADJ bimetallist
　NM bimetallist

bimillénaire [bimilenɛr] ADJ bimillenary
　NM bimillenary

bimoteur [bimɔtœr] *Aviat* ADJ M twin-engined
　NM twin-engined plane *or* aircraft

binage [binaʒ] NM *Agr* hoeing

binaire [binɛr] ADJ **1** *Math & Ordinat* binary; **langage b.** binary notation **2** *Littérature & Mus* binary; **mesure b.** binary rhythm
　NF *Astron* binary (star)

binard, binart [binar] NM dray *(for carting stone)*

binational, -e, -aux, -ales [binasjɔnal, -o] ADJ with dual nationality

bine [bin] NF *Can* **1** *Fam (visage)* mug **2** *Can Joual* **bines au lard** *Am* pork beans, *Br* beans with pork; **être dans les bines** to be out to lunch; **faire qch en criant b.** to do sth in a flash

biner¹ [3] [bine] VT *Agr* to hoe

biner² [3] [bine] VI *Rel* = to say mass twice a day

binerie [binəri] NF *Can Joual* = snack bar serving pork beans; *Fig Péj* greasy spoon

binette [binɛt] NF **1** *Agr* hoe **2** *Fam (visage)* mug **3** *Can Ordinat* smiley, emoticon

bineur, -euse [binœr, -øz] NM,F *Agr* cultivator

bing [biŋ] ONOMAT thwack!, smack!

bingo [biŋgo] NM **1** *(jeu)* bingo; **jouer au b.** to play bingo **2** *Can Fam (révolte)* prison riot▪
　EXCLAM bingo!

BinHex *Ordinat (abrév écrite* **Binary Hexadecimal)** BinHex

biniou [binju] NM **1** *Mus (instrument de musique)* (Breton) bagpipes **2** *Fam (téléphone)* phone, *Br* blower, *Am* horn; **filer un coup de b. à qn** to give sb a buzz *or Br* a bell

binoclard, -e [binɔklar, -ard] *Fam Péj* ADJ **être b.** to wear glasses▪ *or Br* specs
　NMF four-eyes, *Br* speccy

binocle [binɔkl] NM *(lorgnon)* pince-nez
◽ **binocles** NMPL *OU* NFPL *Fam (lunettes)* glasses▪, *Br* specs

binoculaire [binɔkylɛr] ADJ *Opt* binocular

binôme [binom] NM **1** *Math* binomial; **le b. de Newton** the binomial theorem **2** *Fam (étudiant)* partner▪; **travailler en b.** to work in twos▪

binomial, -e, -aux, -ales [binɔmjal, -o] ADJ *Math* binomial

binominal, -e, -aux, -ales [binɔminal, -o] ADJ *Biol* binominal

binouze [binuz] NF *Fam (bière)* beer▪; **on va se boire une b.?** *Br* fancy a pint?, *Am* want to go for a beer?

bintje [bintʃ] NF *Bot (pomme de terre)* bintje potato

binucléaire [binykleɛr] ADJ *Biol* binuclear

binz [bins] NM **1** *(chose compliquée)* **quel b. pour trouver sa maison!** it was a real performance *or* hassle *or Br* carry-on finding his/her house! **2** *(désordre)* shambles *(singulier)*

bio [bjo] ADJ INV *(nourriture, aliment)* organic
　NF *Fam* **1** *(abrév* **biographie)** biog **2** *(abrév* **biologie)** biology▪; *Scol & Univ* **faire de la b.** to do biology

bio- [bjo] PRÉF bio-

bioactif, -ive [bjoaktif, -iv] ADJ *Biol* bioactive

bioastronomie [bjoastrɔnɔmi] NF *Astron & Biol* bioastronomy

biobibliographie [bjobiblijɔgrafi] NF biobibliography

biocarburant [bjokarbyrɑ̃] NM *Écol* biofuel

biocatalyseur [bjokatalizœr] NM *Biol* biocatalyst

biocénose [bjosenoz] NF *Écol* biocoenosis, biocenosis

biochimie [bjoʃimi] NF biochemistry

biochimique [bjoʃimik] ADJ biochemical

biochimiste [bjoʃimist] NMF biochemist

biocide [bjosid] *Chim* ADJ biocidal
　NM biocide

bioclimat [bjoklima] NM bioclimate

bioclimatique [bjoklimatik] ADJ bioclimatic

bioclimatologie [bjoklimatɔlɔʒi] NF bioclimatology

biocœnose [bjosenoz] = **biocénose**

biocompatible [bjokɔ̃patibl] ADJ *Méd* biocompatible

bioconversion [bjokɔ̃vɛrsjɔ̃] NF *Chim & Ind* bioconversion

biodégradabilité [bjodegradabilite] NF *Écol* biodegradability

biodégradable [bjodegradabl] ADJ *Écol* biodegradable

biodégradation [bjodegradasjɔ̃] NF *Écol* biodegradation

biodégrader [3] [bjodegrade] VI *Écol* to biodegrade

biodesign [bjodizajn] NM bio-design

biodiesel [bjodjezɛl] NM *Chim* biodiesel

biodisponibilité [bjodisponibilite] NF *Pharm* bio-availability

biodiversité [bjodivɛrsite] NF *Biol* biodiversity

bioélectricité [bjoelɛktrisite] NF *Physiol* bioelectricity

bioélectrique [bjoelɛktrik] ADJ *Physiol* bioelectric

bioélément [bjoelemɑ̃] NM *Biol* bioelement

bioénergétique [bjoenɛrʒetik] ADJ *Biol & Psy* bioenergetic

bioénergie [bjoenɛrʒi] NF *Biol & Psy* bioenergetics

bioéthanol [bjoetanɔl] NM *Chim* bioethanol

bioéthique [bjoetik] NF *Méd* bioethics *(singulier)*

biofeedback [bjofidbak] NM *Méd & Psy* biofeedback

biogaz [bjogaz] NM *Chim* biogas

biogène [bjoʒɛn] NM *Géol* biogen

biogenèse [bjoʒənɛz] NF *Biol* biogenesis

biogénétique [bjoʒenetik] ADJ *Biol* biogenetic

biogéographie [bjoʒeɔgrafi] NF *Biol* biogeography

biogéographique [bjoʒeɔgrafik] ADJ *Biol* biogeographical

biographe [bjograf] NMF biographer

biographie [bjografi] NF biography; **b. officielle** authorized biography; **b. romancée** fictionalized biography, biographical novel

biographique [bjografik] ADJ biographical

bio-industrie [bjoɛ̃dystri] NF biotechnology industry

bio-informatique [bjoɛ̃fɔrmatik] NF bioinformatics *(singulier)*

biologie [bjolɔʒi] NF biology

biologique [bjolɔʒik] ADJ **1** *Biol* biological **2** *(naturel → produit, aliment)* organic

biologisant, -e [bjolɔʒizɑ̃, -ɑ̃t] ADJ *Biol* biology-based

biologiste [bjolɔʒist] NMF biologist

bioluminescence [bjolyminesɑ̃s] NF *Biol, Entom & Ich* bioluminescence

bioluminescent, -e [bjolyminesɑ̃, -ɑ̃t] ADJ *Biol, Entom & Ich* bioluminescent

biomagnétisme [bjomaɲetism] NM *Biol* biomagnetism

biomasse [bjomas] NF *Biol* biomass

biomatériau, -x [bjomaterjo] NM *Méd* biomaterial

biomathématiques [bjomatematik] NFPL *Biol & Math* biomathematics *(UNCOUNT)*

biome [bjom] NM *Écol* biome

biomécanique [bjomekanik] NF *Biol* biomechanics *(UNCOUNT)*

biomédecine [bjomedsin] NF biomedicine

biomédical, -e, -aux, -ales [bjomedikal, -o] ADJ biomedical

biométrie [bjometri] NF *Biol & Math* biometry, biometrics *(singulier)*

biométrique [bjometrik] ADJ biometric

biomoléculaire [bjomolekylɛr] ADJ *Biol* biomolecular

biomolécule [bjomolekyl] NF *Biol* biomolecule

biomorphique [bjomorfik] ADJ *Beaux-Arts* biomorphic

biomorphisme [bjomorfism] NM *Beaux-Arts* biomorphism

bionique [bjonik] *Biol & Électron* ADJ bionic
　NF bionics *(singulier)*

biophysicien, -enne [bjofizisjɛ̃, -ɛn] NM,F biophysicist

biophysique [bjofizik] NF biophysics *(singulier)*

biopiratage [bjopirataʒ] NM biopiracy

biopiraterie [bjopiratri] NF biopiracy

biopsie [bjopsi] NF *Biol & Méd* biopsy

biopuce [bjopys] NF biochip

biorémédiation [bjoremediasjɔ̃] NF *Écol* bioremediation

biorythme [bjoritm] NM *Biol & Physiol* biorhythm

BIOS [bjɔs] NM *Ordinat (abrév* **Basic Input/Output System***)* BIOS

biosécurité [bjɔsekyrite] NF biosafety, biosecurity

biosphère [bjɔsfɛr] NF biosphere

biostasie [bjɔstazi] NF *Géog* biostasy

biosynthèse [bjɔsɛ̃tɛz] NF *Biol & Chim* biosynthesis

biosynthétique [bjɔsɛ̃tetik] ADJ *Biol* biosynthetic

biotechnique [bjɔtɛknik], **biotechnologie** [bjɔtɛknɔlɔʒi] NF *Biol* biotechnology

biotechnologique [bjɔtɛknɔlɔʒik] ADJ biotechnological

bioterrorisme [bjɔterɔrism] NM bioterrorism

bioterroriste [bjɔterɔrist] ADJ bioterrorist
  NMF -e bioterrorist

biothérapie [bjɔterapi] NF *Biol & Méd* biotherapy

biotine [bjɔtin] NF *Chim* biotin

biotique [bjɔtik] ADJ *Biol* biotic

biotite [bjɔtit] NF *Minér* biotite

biotope [bjɔtɔp] NM *Écol* biotope

biotype [bjɔtip] NM *Biol* biotype

biotypologie [bjɔtipɔlɔʒi] NF *Biol* biotypology

biovigilance [bjɔviʒilɑ̃s] NF 1 *(en ce qui concerne les biotechnologies)* GM monitoring 2 *(en ce qui concerne les prélèvements biologiques)* = monitoring the health and safety of biological samples, removed organs etc

bioxyde [bjɔksid] NM *Chim* dioxide

bip [bip] NM 1 *(signal sonore)* beep; **"parlez après le b. (sonore)"** ''please speak after the beep or tone''; **faire b.** to bleep; **b. de censure** censor bleep 2 *(appareil)* pager, beeper

bipale [bipal] ADJ twin-bladed

bipare [bipar] ADJ *Bot & Zool* biparous

biparti, -e [biparti] ADJ 1 *Bot* bipartite 2 *Pol* bipartite, two-party *(avant n)*

bipartisme [bipartism] NM *Pol* bipartism, two-party system

bipartite [bipartit] ADJ 1 *Bot* bipartite 2 *Pol* bipartite, two-party *(avant n)*

bipartition [bipartisjɔ̃] NF bipartition

bipasse [bipas] NM *Tech* by-pass

bip-bip [bipbip] *(pl* **bips-bips***)* NM bleep, bleeping sound or tone; **faire b.** to bleep
  ◦ **Bip-Bip** NM *(personnage de dessin animé)* Road Runner

Bipe [bip] NM *(abrév* **Bureau d'informations et de prévisions économiques***)* = French economic information and forecasting office

bipède [biped] ADJ *(personne, animal)* biped
  NM 1 *(deux pattes du cheval)* = any two legs of a horse; **b. antérieur** forelegs; **b. postérieur** hind legs; **b. diagonal** = foreleg and its opposite back leg 2 *Fam Hum (individu)* two-legged creature

bipédie [bipedi] NF bipedalism

bipenne [bipɛn], **bipenné, -e** [bipɛne] ADJ 1 *Zool* two-winged 2 *Bot (feuille)* bipinnate, double compound
  ◦ **bipenne** NF 1 *Zool* two-winged insect 2 *Antiq* double axe

biper [bipe] VT to page

bipeur [bipœr] NM *(appareil)* pager, beeper

biphasé, -e [bifaze] ADJ *Élec* diphasic, two-phase *(avant n)*

biphényle [bifenil] NM *Chim* diphenyl, biphenyl

bipied [bipje] NM *(d'une arme)* bipod

biplace [biplas] ADJ two-seater *(avant n)*
  NM two-seater

biplan [biplɑ̃] NM *Aviat* biplane

bipolaire [bipɔlɛr] ADJ bipolar

bipolarisation [bipɔlarizasjɔ̃] NF *Pol* bipolarization

bipolarisé, -e [bipɔlarize] ADJ bipolarized

bipolarité [bipɔlarite] NF bipolarity

bipoutre [biputr] ADJ *Aviat* twin-boom

biquadratique [bikwadratik] *Math* ADJ *(équation)* biquadratic
  NF biquadratic (equation)

bique [bik] NF 1 *Zool* nanny-goat 2 *Fam Péj (femme)* **vieille b.** old bag or cow

biquet, -ette [bikɛ, -ɛt] NM,F 1 *Zool* kid 2 *Fam (en appellatif)* **mon b.** my pet

biquotidien, -enne [bikɔtidjɛ̃, -ɛn] ADJ twice-daily

birapport [birapɔr] NM *Math* anharmonic ratio

birbe [birb] NM *Littéraire Péj* **vieux b.** old fuddy-duddy or stick-in-the-mud

bircher [birʃɛr] NM *Suisse* muesli

BIRD [bœrd] NF *(abrév* **Banque internationale pour la reconstruction et le développement***)* IBRD

birdie [bœrdi] NM *Golf* birdie

biréacteur [bireaktœr] NM *Aviat* twin-engined jet

biréfringence [birefrɛ̃ʒɑ̃s] NF *Opt* birefringence

biréfringent, -e [birefrɛ̃ʒɑ̃, -ɑ̃t] ADJ *Opt* birefringent

birème [birɛm] NF *Hist* bireme

Bir Hakeim [birakɛm] NF *Hist* = scene of the heroic resistance of the free French forces against Rommel during the North African Campaign (June 1942)

biribi [biribi] NM *Fam Arg mil* = company consisting of convicted soldiers

birman, -e [birmɑ̃, -an] ADJ Burmese
  NM *(langue)* Burmese
  ◦ **Birman, -e** NM,F Burmese; **les Birmans** the Burmese

Birmanie [birmani] NF **la B.** Burma; **vivre en B.** to live in Burma; **aller en B.** to go to Burma

birotor [birɔtɔr] *Tech* ADJ INV *(aéronef)* dual-rotor
  NM dual-rotor aircraft

biroute [birut] NF 1 *Aviat* windsock, wind cone or sleeve 2 *Vulg (pénis)* cock, prick

bis¹ [bis] ADV 1 *Mus* repeat, twice 2 *(dans une adresse)* **13 b.** 13A
  EXCLAM *(à un spectacle)* encore!; **chanter une chanson en b.** to sing or to give an encore

bis², -e¹ [bi, biz] ADJ *(couleur)* greyish-brown; *(toile)* unbleached

bisaïeul, -e [bizajœl] NM,F great-grandfather, *f* great-grandmother

bisaiguë [bizegy] NF 1 *Menuis* mortise axe 2 *(d'un vitrier)* glazier's hammer

bisannuel, -elle [bizanɥɛl] ADJ *(tous les deux ans)* biennial

bisbille [bizbij] *Fam* NF tiff
  ◦ **en bisbille** ADV at loggerheads or odds; **être en b. avec qn** to be at loggerheads with sb; **on est longtemps restés en b.** we were at loggerheads for a long time

bisbrouille [bisbruj] NF *Belg* tiff

biscaïen, -enne, biscayen, -enne [biskajɛ̃, -jɛn] ADJ = of/from the Basque province of Vizcaya
  ◦ **Biscaïen, -enne** NM,F = inhabitant of or person from the Basque province of Vizcaya

Biscaye [biskaj] NM *Géog* Biscay

bischof [biʃɔf] NM = **bichof**

biscôme [biskom] NM *Suisse* = Swiss gingerbread

biscornu, -e [biskɔrny] ADJ 1 *(irrégulier → forme)* irregular, misshapen 2 *(étrange → idée)* cranky, queer, weird; *(→ esprit, raisonnement)* twisted, tortuous

biscoteaux [biskoto] NMPL *Fam* biceps■

biscotin [biskɔtɛ̃] NM crisp *Br* biscuit or *Am* cookie

biscotos [biskoto] = **biscoteaux**

biscotte [biskɔt] NF *Culin* = piece of toasted bread sold in packets and often eaten for breakfast

biscotterie [biskɔtri] NF = factory where ''biscottes'' are made

biscuit [biskɥi] NM 1 *Culin (gâteau sec) Br* biscuit, *Am* cookie; **b. pour chien** dog biscuit; **b. à la cuiller** *Br* sponge finger, *Am* ladyfinger; **b. fourré** filled biscuit; **b. de mer** cuttlefish bone; **b. salé** cracker, *Br* savoury biscuit; **b. soda** soda cracker 2 *(gâteau)* **b. glacé** Neapolitan ice cream; **b. roulé** Swiss roll; **b. de Savoie** sponge cake 3 *(porcelaine)* biscuit, bisque
  ADJ INV biscuit-coloured

biscuiter [biskɥite] VT *Ind* to make into biscuit

biscuiterie [biskɥitri] NF 1 *(usine) Br* biscuit or *Am* cookie factory 2 *(commerce) Br* biscuit or *Am* cookie trade 3 *(fabrication) Br* biscuit or *Am* cookie making

bise² [biz] NF 1 *(vent)* North or northerly wind 2 *Littéraire (hiver)* **la b.** the icy blast of winter

bise³ [biz] NF *(baiser)* kiss; **donner** ou **faire une b. à qn** to give sb a kiss; **se faire la b.** to kiss each other on both cheeks; **grosses bises** *(dans une lettre)* love and kisses

biseau, -x [bizo] NM *Tech (bord, outil)* bevel; **en b.** bevelled; **taillé en b.** bevelled

biseautage [bizotaʒ] NM 1 *Tech (du bois, du verre)* bevelling 2 *(de cartes à jouer)* marking

biseauter [bizote] VT 1 *Tech (bois, verre)* to bevel 2 *Cartes* **b. les cartes** to mark the cards

biser¹ [3] [bize] VI *Agr (du grain)* to darken, to deteriorate

biser² [3] [bize] VT *Fam* to kiss■

biset [bizɛ] NM *Orn* rock pigeon or dove

bisexualité [bisɛksɥalite] NF bisexuality, *Am* bisexualism

bisexué, -e [bisɛksɥe] ADJ *Biol* bisexual

bisexuel, -elle [bisɛksɥɛl] ADJ bisexual
  NM,F bisexual

bishop [biʃɔp] = **bichof**

Bismarck [bismark] NPR Bismarck

bismuth [bismyt] NM *Chim* bismuth

bismuthine [bismytin] NF *Chim* bismuthinite, bismuth glance

bison [bizɔ̃] NM *Zool* 1 *(d'Amérique)* American buffalo or bison 2 *(d'Europe)* European bison, wisent

Bison Futé [bizɔ̃fyte] NM = organization giving details of road conditions, traffic congestion etc

bisou [bizu] NM *Fam* kiss■ ; **donner** ou **faire un b. à qn** to give sb a kiss■

bisoune [bizun] NF *Can Fam* 1 *(petite fille)* sweetheart, sweetie 2 *(pénis) Br* willy, *Am* weener

bisque [bisk] NF *Culin* bisque; **b. de homard** lobster bisque

bisquer [3] [biske] VI *Fam* to be riled or nettled; **bisque, bisque, rage!** I win! *(gloating exclamation of victory)*; **faire b. qn** to rile or nettle sb

Bissau [bisao] NM *Géog* Bissau

bisse [bis] NM *Suisse* irrigation canal *(in the Valais canton)*

bissecteur, -trice [bisɛktœr, -tris] *Géom* ADJ bisecting
  ◦ **bissectrice** NF bisector, bisectrix

bissection [bisɛksjɔ̃] NF *Géom* bisection, bisecting

bissel [bisɛl] NM *Rail* pony-truck *(of engine)*

bisser [3] [bise] VT 1 *(sujet: artiste)* to do again; **b. qn** to ask sb to do an encore 2 *Belg Scol (redoubler)* to repeat

bisseur, -euse [bisœr, -øz] NM,F *Belg Scol* pupil repeating a *Br* year or *Am* grade

bissexte [bisɛkst] NM odd day *(of leap year)*, 29 February

bissextile [bisɛkstil] *voir* **année**

bissexué, -e [bisɛksɥe] = **bisexué**

bissexuel, -elle [bisɛksɥɛl] = **bisexuel**

bistandard [bistɑ̃dar] ADJ *TV* dual-standard

bistorte [bistɔrt] NF *Bot* bistort

bistouille [bistuj] NF *Fam* 1 *(alcool)* raw spirits■ , rot-gut 2 *(dans le nord de la France)* = coffee laced with spirits 3 *(absurdité)* nonsense, bosh

bistouquette [bistukɛt] NF *Fam Br* willy, *Am* peter

bistouri [bisturi] NM *Méd* bistoury, lancet

bistournage [bisturnaʒ] NM castration *(by twisting of the testicular cord)*

bistourner [3] [bisturne] VT 1 *(lame)* to wring, to wrench 2 *(castrer)* to castrate *(by twisting the testicular cord)*

bistre [bistr] ADJ INV bistre; *(teint, peau)* swarthy, dark
  NM bistre

bistré, -e [bistre] ADJ brownish; *(teint, peau)* swarthy, dark

bistrer [3] [bistre] VT to colour with bistre

bistro, bistrot [bistro] NM ≃ café, *Br* ≃ pub, *Am* ≃ bar; **chaise/table b.** bistrot-style chair/table

---
Culture

BISTROT

This word can refer either to a small café or to a cosy restaurant, especially one frequented by regulars. These establishments are usually less classy than bistros in English-speaking countries. The "style bistrot" refers to a style of furnishing inspired by the chairs, tables and zinc countertops typical of the traditional "bistrot".

---

bistrotier, -ère [bistrotje, -ɛr] NM,F *Fam* bistrot owner

bisulfate [bisylfat] NM *Chim* bisulphate

bisulfite [bisylfit] NM *Chim* bisulphite

bisulfure [bisylfyr] NM *Chim* disulphide, bisulphide

bisynchrone [bisɛ̃kron] ADJ *Ordinat* bisynchronous, bisync

BIT [beite] NM *(abrév* **Bureau international du travail***)* ILO

bit [bit] NM *Ordinat* bit; **bits par pouce/seconde**

bits per inch/second; **b. d'arrêt** stop bit; **b. de contrôle** control bit; **b. de départ** start bit

bite [bit] NF *Vulg* prick, cock

bitension [bitãsjɔ̃] NF *Élec* dual voltage

biter [3] [bite] VT *Vulg* **j'y bite rien** I don't understand fuck-all

biterrois, -e [biterwa, -az] ADJ of/from Béziers
  □ **Biterrois, -e** NM,F = inhabitant of or person from Béziers

bitmap [bitmap] *Ordinat* ADJ bitmap
  NM bitmap

bitonal, -e, -aux, -ales [bitɔnal, -o] ADJ *Mus* bitonal; **Tél sonnerie bitonale** two-tone ring

bitoniau, -x [bitɔnjo] NM *Fam* thingy, whatsit

bitord [bitɔr] NM *Naut* spun-yarn; **b. en trois** three-yarn spun-yarn

bitos [bitos] NM *Fam* hat▪

bitte [bit] NF **1** *Naut* bitt; **b. d'amarrage** bollard **2** *Vulg (pénis)* prick, cock

bitter [biter] NM *(boisson)* bitters

bitture [bityr] NF **1** *très Fam (soûlerie)* **prendre une b.** to get plastered; **il (se) tenait une de ces bittures!** he got really plastered! **2** *Naut* range of cable
  □ **à toute bitture** ADV *Fam* at full speed▪

bitturer [3] [bityre] **se bitturer** VPR *très Fam* to get plastered

bitu, -e [bity] ADJ *Belg très Fam* wasted, *Br* pissed

bitumage [bitymaʒ] NM asphalting, bituminizing

bitumé, -e [bityme] ADJ asphalted, bituminized

bitume [bitym] NM **1** *Chim & Constr* bitumen **2** *(revêtement)* asphalt, bitumen **3** *Fam (trottoir) Br* pavement▪, *Am* sidewalk▪; **arpenter le b.** to walk the streets; **sur le b.** *(sans abri)* out on the street; *(sans ressources)* on skid row

bitumer [3] [bityme] VT *Chim & Constr* to asphalt, to bituminize

bitumeux, -euse [bitymø, -øz], **bitumineux, -euse** [bityminø, -øz] ADJ *Chim* bituminous

biture [bityr] = **bitture**

biturer [bityre] = **bitturer**

biunivoque [biynivɔk] ADJ *Math* **correspondance b.** one-to-one mapping

bivalence [bivalãs] NF *Chim* bivalence, bivalency

bivalent, -e [bivalã, -ãt] ADJ *Chim* bivalent

bivalve [bivalv] *Bot & Zool* ADJ bivalve
  NM bivalve

biveau, -x [bivo] NM *Constr* bevel

bivitellin, -e [bivitelɛ̃, -in] ADJ *Biol* dizygotic

bivouac [bivwak] NM bivouac; **feu de b.** watchfire

bivouaquer [3] [bivwake] VI to bivouac, to set up camp overnight

biwa [biwa] NM *Mus* biwa

bizarde [bizard] ADJ F *Chasse & Zool* **tête b.** abnormal antlers

bizarre [bizar] ADJ *(comportement, personne, idée, ambiance)* odd, peculiar, strange; **tu ne le trouves pas b.?** don't you think he's strange?; **je l'ai trouvé b. ce matin-là** I thought he was behaving oddly that morning; *Fam* **c'est un type vraiment b.** he's a real weirdo; **c'est b., ce n'est pas ce qu'elle m'avait dit** that's odd or strange, that's not what she told me; **elle s'habille de manière b.** she has strange dress sense; **se sentir b.** to feel (a bit) funny
  NM **le b. dans l'histoire, c'est que...** what's really strange is that...

Allusion

Bizarre, bizarre, vous avez dit bizarre? Comme c'est bizarre...
This is a line of dialogue from Marcel Carné's 1937 film *Drôle de drame*. The actors Louis Jouvet and Michel Simon star in scenes that are now some of the most famous in French cinema. The allusion means "strange, strange, did you say strange? That's very strange", and has passed into everyday use, so the reaction to some strange occurrence might well be to murmur **bizarre, bizarre**...

bizarrement [bizarmã] ADV oddly, strangely, peculiarly; **b., ce matin-là, il ne s'était pas rasé** for some strange reason, he hadn't shaved that morning

bizarrerie [bizarri] NF **1** *(caractère bizarre)* strangeness; **la b. de son comportement** the strangeness of his/her behaviour **2** *(action bizarre)* eccentricity; **ses bizarreries ne me surprennent plus** his/her eccentricities no longer surprise me

bizarroïde [bizarɔid] ADJ *Fam* odd, weird, bizarre

bizet [bizɛ] NM *Zool (mouton)* = breed of sheep

bizou [bizu] = **bisou**

bizoune [bizun] = **bisoune**

bizut [bizy] NM *Fam Arg scol Br* fresher, *Am* freshman

bizutage [bizytaʒ] NM *Fam Arg scol* = practical jokes played on new arrivals in a school or college, *Br* ≃ ragging, *Am* ≃ hazing

Culture

BIZUTAGE
In some French schools and colleges, students in fancy-dress take to the streets and play practical jokes, sometimes of a very cruel nature, on each other and on passers-by at the beginning of the school year. This is part of the traditional initiation ceremony known as "bizutage". As a consequence of the excessive behaviour to which it has often led, a law was passed in 1998 to make it an offence.

bizuter [3] [bizyte] VT *Fam Arg scol Br* ≃ to rag, *Am* ≃ to haze; **se faire b.** *Br* ≃ to be ragged, *Am* ≃ to be hazed

bizuth [bizy] = **bizut**

bla-bla(-bla) [blabla(bla)] NM INV *Fam* blah, claptrap; **arrête ton b.!** stop talking *Br* rubbish or *Am* garbage!; **c'est du b.** that's just a lot of baloney or *Br* waffle

blablater [3] [blablate] VI *Fam* to waffle on, *Br* to witter on

Black [blak] NM,F *Fam (personne de race noire)* Black▪

black [blak] ADJ *(personne de race noire)* Black▪
  NM **travailler au b.** *(clandestinement)* = to work without declaring one's earnings; *(en plus de son travail habituel)* to moonlight

black-bass [blakbas] NM INV *Ich* black bass

blackboulage [blakbulaʒ] NM *(dans des élections)* blackballing; *(à un examen)* failing

blackbouler [3] [blakbule] VT *(candidat → dans des élections)* to blackball; *(→ à un examen)* to fail; **se faire b.** *(dans des élections)* to be blackballed; *(à un examen)* to fail; **il s'est fait b. à son examen** they failed him at his exam

black jack [blak(d)ʒak] NM *Cartes* blackjack

black-out [blakaut] NM INV blackout; **faire le b. sur qch** to hush up or cover up sth; **b. partiel** brownout

black-rot [blakrɔt] *(pl black-rots)* NM *(maladie de la vigne)* black rot

blad [blad] NM *Typ* blad

blafard, -e [blafar, -ard] ADJ pallid, wan

blaff [blaf] NM *Culin (plat antillais)* = dish consisting of fish marinated in lime juice then cooked in court-bouillon

blague [blag] NF **1** *(histoire)* joke; **il est toujours à dire des blagues** he's always joking
  2 *(duperie)* hoax, *Br* wind-up; **c'est une b.?** are you kidding?, you can't be serious!; **raconter des blagues** to lie; **elle dit qu'elle va démissionner mais c'est de la b.** she says she'll resign but that's all guff or hot air; *Fam* **elle a eu des triplés – sans b.!** she had triplets – never or no kidding!; *Fam* **vous allez arrêter, non mais, sans b.!** will you PLEASE give it a rest!; **b. à part** kidding or joking apart, in all seriousness; **b. à part, c'est un homme très agréable** seriously though, or joking apart, he's a very nice man
  3 *(farce)* (practical) joke, trick; **il m'a fait une mauvaise** ou **sale b.** he played a nasty trick on me
  4 *(maladresse)* blunder, *Br* boob, *Am* blooper; **faire une b.** *Br* to boob, *Am* to make a blooper
  5 *(sottise)* silly or stupid thing (to do); **je vous laisse seuls deux minutes, pas de blagues!** I'm leaving you alone for two minutes, so no funny business!
  □ **blague à tabac** NF tobacco pouch

blaguer [3] [blage] *Fam* VI to joke▪; **je ne blague plus!** I'm serious!; **j'aime bien b.** I like a joke; **tu blagues?** you're kidding!
  VT to tease▪; **b. qn sur qch** to tease sb about sth

blagueur, -euse [blagœr, -øz] *Fam* ADJ *(enfant,*

expression) joking▪, teasing▪; **il est très b.** he really likes a joke
  NM,F joker▪

blair [blɛr] NM *Fam* nose▪, *Br* conk, *Am* schnozz

blaireau, -x [blɛro] NM **1** *Zool* badger **2** *(pour se raser)* shaving brush **3** *Beaux-Arts* (badger-hair) brush **4** *Fam (imbécile)* jerk, prat

blairer [4] [blɛre] VT *très Fam* **personne ne peut le b.** no one can stand or *Br* stick him

blairisme [blɛrism] NM *Pol* Blairism

blâmable [blamabl] ADJ blameworthy

blâme [blam] NM **1** *(condamnation)* disapproval; **rejeter le b. sur qn** to put the blame on sb; **s'attirer** ou **encourir le b. de qn** to incur sb's disapproval **2** *Admin & Scol* reprimand; **recevoir un b.** to be reprimanded; **donner un b. à qn** to reprimand sb

blâmer [3] [blame] VT **1** *(condamner)* to blame; **je ne le blâme pas d'avoir agi ainsi** I don't blame him for having acted that way; **il ne faut pas l'en b.** he/she should not be blamed for it **2** *Admin & Scol (élève, fonctionnaire)* to reprimand

blanc, blanche [blã, blãʃ] ADJ **1** *(couleur)* white; **avoir les cheveux blancs** to have grey hair, to be grey-haired; **un vieillard à cheveux blancs** a white-haired old man; **à 40 ans, j'étais déjà toute blanche** at 40 years of age I was already grey or all my hair had already turned grey; **que tu es b.!** how pale you look!; **être b. de peau** to be white-skinned or pale-skinned; **être b. de rage** to be white or livid with rage; *Fam Hum* **être b. comme un cachet d'aspirine** ou **un lavabo** *(malade, de peur)* to be as white as a sheet; *(pas bronzé)* to be completely white▪; **b. comme un linge** white as a sheet; **b. comme le lis** lily-white; **b. comme neige** snow-white, (as) white as snow, (as) white as the driven snow; *Fig* (as) pure as the driven snow; **elle est sortie du procès blanche comme neige** she came out of the trial as pure as the driven snow or with her reputation intact; **le pouvoir se veut b. comme neige** the authorities are trying to look as innocent as the lamb
  2 *(race)* white, Caucasian; *(personne)* white, white-skinned, Caucasian; **les quartiers blancs de la ville** the white areas of town
  3 *(vierge)* blank; **elle a remis (une) copie blanche** she handed in a blank sheet of paper; **écrire sur du papier b.** to write on plain or unlined paper; **vote b.** blank vote
  4 *(voix)* monotone
  5 *(examen)* mock
  6 *(innocent)* innocent, pure; **il n'est pas aussi b. qu'il en a l'air** he's not as innocent as he looks; **il n'est pas sorti tout b. de l'affaire** he hasn't come out of this business untarnished
  7 *Culin (sauce, viande)* white
  8 *(verre)* plain
  9 *Littérature (vers)* blank
  10 *Élec* white
  NM **1** *(couleur)* white; **le b. lui va bien** he/she looks good in white; **b. cassé** off-white; **aller du b. au noir, passer du b. au noir** to go from one extreme to the other
  2 *(matière → blanche) (fard)* white make-up powder; **b. de baleine** spermaceti; **b. de chaux** whitewash; **b. d'Espagne** ou **de Meudon** whiting
  3 *(cornée)* **b. de l'œil** white of the eye; **regarder qn dans le b. de l'œil** ou **des yeux** to look sb straight in the face or eye
  4 *Culin* **b. de poulet** chicken breast; **dans le poulet, je préfère le b.** when I have chicken, I like the white meat or the breast best; **b. d'œuf** egg white, white of an egg; **blancs d'œufs battus** beaten egg whites; **b. de cuisson** = mixture of water, lemon juice and flour used for blanching food
  5 *(linge)* **le b.** household linen; **un magasin de b.** a linen shop; **faire une machine de b.** to do a machine-load of whites
  6 *(vin)* white wine; **boire du b.** to drink white wine; **un b. sec** a dry white wine; *Fam* **un petit b.** *(verre)* a (nice) little glass of white wine; **b. de blancs** blanc de blancs *(white wine from white grapes)*; **b. cassis** kir *(made with blackcurrant cordial rather than crème de cassis)*
  7 *(espace libre)* blank space, blank, space; *(dans une conversation)* blank; **laissez un b.** leave a blank or space
  8 *Bot* mildew

9 *Can & Suisse (trou de mémoire)* blank; **avoir un b.** to have a blank

10 *Typ* **b. de grand fond** gutter, fore-edge; **b. de petit fond** gutter, back margin

ADV **il a gelé b. la semaine dernière** there was some white frost last week; **voter b.** to return a blank vote; **un jour il dit b., l'autre il dit noir** one day he says yes, the next day he says no; **il dit b. aux uns et noir aux autres** he says one thing to one person and another thing to someone else; **l'un dit b., l'autre dit noir** one (of them) says one thing, the other says the opposite

❏ **Blanc, Blanche** NM,F **1** *(homme)* white man, Caucasian; *(femme)* white woman, Caucasian; **les Blancs** white people; **petit B.** poor white; *Péj* **les petits Blancs** white trash

2 *Hist (en Russie)* White Russian; *(en France)* Bourbon supporter *(in post-revolutionary France)*; **les Blancs et les Bleus** = Chouan insurgents and Republican soldiers during the French Revolution

❏ **blanche** NF **1** *Mus Br* minim, *Am* half note

2 *(bille)* white (ball)

3 *Fam Arg drogue (héroïne)* **la blanche** smack

4 *(eau-de-vie)* colourless spirit

❏ **à blanc** ADJ *(cartouche)* blank; **tir à b.** firing blanks ADV **1 tirer à b.** to fire blanks **2** *(à un point extrême)* **chauffer à b.** to make white-hot

❏ **en blanc** ADJ **1** *(chèque, procuration)* blank **2** *(personne)* **une mariée en b.** a bride wearing white; **les hommes en b.** (hospital) doctors ADV *(peindre, colorer)* white; *(s'habiller, sortir)* in white; **laisser une ligne/page en b.** to leave a line/page blank; **tu vas te marier en b.?** will you have a white wedding?, will you get married in white?

blanc-bec [blɑ̃bɛk] *(pl* **blancs-becs***)* NM greenhorn; **jeune b.** young whippersnapper

blanc-étoc, blanc-estoc [blɑ̃etɔk] *(pl* **blancs-étocs, blancs-estocs***)* NM complete clearing of woodland

blanchaille [blɑ̃ʃaj] NF **1** *(poisson)* small fry, bait **2** *Culin* whitebait

blanchâtre [blɑ̃ʃatr] ADJ *(mur)* offwhite, whitish; *(nuage)* whitish; *(teint)* pallid

blanche [blɑ̃ʃ] *voir* **blanc**

Blanche-Neige [blɑ̃ʃnɛʒ] NPR Snow White

'Blanche-Neige et les sept nains' Grimm, Disney 'Snow White and the Seven Dwarfs'
---

blanchet [blɑ̃ʃɛ] NM *Typ* blanket

blancheur [blɑ̃ʃœr] NF **1** *(couleur)* whiteness; **ces draps sont d'une b. douteuse** these sheets aren't very white; **ses mains avaient la b. du lis** she had lily-white hands **2** *Littéraire (pureté)* purity, innocence

blanchiment [blɑ̃ʃimɑ̃] NM **1** *(décoloration, nettoyage→ d'un mur)* whitewashing; *(→ d'un tissu)* bleaching **2** *(d'argent)* laundering **3** *Hort (industrial)* blanching **4** *Culin (de légumes)* blanching

blanchir [32] [blɑ̃ʃir] VT **1** *(couvrir de blanc)* to whiten, to turn white; **b. à la chaux** to whitewash; **le gel a blanchi les champs** the frost has turned the fields white

2 *(décolorer)* to turn white, to bleach; **le temps a blanchi ses cheveux** time has turned his/her hair white

3 *(linge → nettoyer)* to launder; *(→ à l'eau de Javel)* to bleach; **donner ses draps à b.** to take one's sheets to be laundered or cleaned; **être logé, nourri et blanchi** to get bed and board and to have one's laundry done

4 *(innocenter)* to exonerate, to clear; **il est sorti complètement blanchi des accusations portées contre lui** he was cleared of the charges laid against him

5 *(argent)* to launder; **b. l'argent de la drogue** to launder money made from drug trafficking; **ces sommes sont blanchies dans l'immobilier** this money is laundered by investing it in real estate

6 *Culin* to blanch; *Hort (légumes, salade)* to blanch (industrially)

7 *Typ (texte, page)* to space, to space out

VI *(barbe, cheveux)* to turn grey; **elle a blanchi très jeune** her hair turned grey when she was still very young; **b. de rage** to turn ashen-faced

with rage; *Littéraire* **b. sous le harnais** ou **harnois** to go grey in the saddle

▸**se blanchir** VPR to exonerate oneself, to clear one's name; **se b. d'une accusation** to clear one's name of an allegation

blanchissage [blɑ̃ʃisaʒ] NM **1** *(nettoyage)* laundering; **porter ses draps au b.** to take one's sheets to the laundry **2** *(raffinage)* refining

blanchissant, -e [blɑ̃ʃisɑ̃, -ɑ̃t] ADJ **1** *(barbe, cheveux)* greying; *(peau etc)* paling; **l'aube blanchissante** the brightening dawn **2** agent **b.** whitener

blanchissement [blɑ̃ʃismɑ̃] NM *(des cheveux)* whitening

blanchisserie [blɑ̃ʃisri] NF laundry; **envoyer ses draps à la b.** to send one's sheets away to be laundered or cleaned

blanchisseur, -euse [blɑ̃ʃisœr, -øz] NM,F launderer, laundryman, *f* laundrywoman

blanchon [blɑ̃ʃɔ̃] NM *Can Zool* whitecoat *(baby seal)*

blanc-manger [blɑ̃mɑ̃ʒe] *(pl* **blancs-mangers***)* NM *Culin* = almond milk jelly

blanc-seing [blɑ̃sɛ̃] *(pl* **blancs-seings***)* NM *Jur* signature to a blank document; *aussi Fig* **donner son b. à qn** to give sb carte blanche

blandices [blɑ̃dis] NFPL *Littéraire* blandishments

blanquette [blɑ̃kɛt] NF **1** *(vin)* **b. de Limoux** = sparkling white wine **2** *Culin* blanquette; **b. de veau** blanquette of veal

blanquisme [blɑ̃kism] NM *Pol* Blanquism

blaps [blaps] NM *Entom* blaps, churchyard beetle

blase [blaz] NM *très Fam* **1** *(nom)* handle, moniker **2** *(nez)* beak, *Br* hooter, *Am* schnozz

blasé, -e [blaze] ADJ blasé; **être b. de qch** to be indifferent to sth

NM,F blasé person; **jouer les blasés** to act as if one's seen it all

blasement [blazmɑ̃] NM *Littéraire* boredom

blaser [3] [blaze] VT to make blasé

▸**se blaser** VPR to become blasé

blason [blazɔ̃] NM **1** *(écu)* arms, blazon; **salir** ou **ternir son b.** to tarnish one's reputation, *Br* to blot one's copy-book; **redorer son b.** *(ses finances)* to restore the family fortune *(by marrying into money)*; *(son prestige)* to polish up one's image **2** *(héraldique)* heraldry **3** *(genre poétique)* blazon

blasonner [3] [blazone] VT to blazon

blasphémateur, -trice [blasfematœr, -tris] ADJ *(personne)* blaspheming; *(acte, parole)* blasphemous

NM,F blasphemer

blasphématoire [blasfematwar] ADJ blasphemous

blasphème [blasfɛm] NM blasphemy; **dire des blasphèmes** to blaspheme

blasphémer [18] [blasfeme] VI to blaspheme

VT *Littéraire* **b. le nom de Dieu** to take God's name in vain

blastème [blastɛm] NM *Biol* blastema

blastocyste [blastosist] NM *Biol* blastocyst

blastoderme [blastodɛrm] NM *Biol* blastoderm

blastogenèse [blastoʒɛnɛz] NF *Biol* blastogenesis

blastomère [blastomɛr] NM *Biol* blastomere

blastomycète [blastomisɛt] NM *Bot* member of the Blastomycetes

blastomycose [blastomikoz] NF *Méd* blastomycosis

blastopore [blastopɔr] NM *Biol* blastopore

blastula [blastyla], **blastule** [blastyl] NF *Biol* blastula, blastule

blatérer [18] [blatere] VI *(bélier)* to bleat; *(chameau)* to bray

blatte [blat] NF cockroach

blaze [blaz] = **blase**

blazer [blazɛr] NM blazer

bld *(abrév écrite* **boulevard***)* Blvd.

blé [ble] NM **1** *Bot* wheat; **b. dur** durum wheat; **b. d'hiver** winter wheat; *Can* **b. d'Inde** *Br* maize, *Am* (Indian) corn; **b. noir** buckwheat; **b. en herbe** wheat in the blade; *Fig* **manger son b. en herbe** to spend one's money as soon as one has it; *Littéraire* **blés** *(champs)* wheatfields **2** *très Fam (argent)* dough, *Br* dosh

---
'Le Blé en herbe' Colette 'The Ripening Seed'
---

blèche [blɛʃ] ADJ *Fam* **1** *(mauvais)* bad■ **2** *(moche)* ugly■, *Br* minging

bled [blɛd] NM **1** *Fam (petit village)* small village■; *Péj* dump, hole; **un petit b. paumé** a little place out in the sticks or the middle of nowhere **2** *(en Afrique du Nord)* **le b.** the interior of the country; **aller au b.** to go up-country

❏ **Bled** NM **le B.** = book used to teach French language in primary schools

blédard [bledar] NM *Hist* **1** *(colon)* = settler in North Africa, living in the interior of the country **2** *(soldat)* = French soldier in North Africa, living in the interior of the country

blème [blɛm] NM *Fam* problem■, *Br* prob

blême [blɛm] ADJ **1** *(personne)* pale, ashen-faced, wan; *(visage, teint)* pale, wan; **b. de peur/rage** ashen-faced with fear/rage; **elle est devenue b. quand je le lui ai dit** she went pale or she blanched when I told her **2** *(lueur)* pale, wan; *(matin)* pale

blêmir [32] [blemir] VI to blanch, to (turn) pale; **b. de peur/rage** to blanch or go white with fear/rage

blêmissement [blemismɑ̃] NM paling, blanching

blende [blɛd] NF *Minér* blende

blennie [bleni] NF *Ich* blenny

blennorragie [blenoraʒi] NF *Méd* blennorrhagia, gonorrhoea

blennorragique [blenoraʒik] ADJ *Méd* blennorrhagic, gonorrhoeal

blennorrhée [blenore] NF *Méd* blennorrhoea

blépharite [blefarit] NF *Méd* blepharitis

blépharoptose [blefaroptoz] NF *Méd* ptosis

blèsement [blɛzmɑ̃] NM lisping

bléser [18] [bleze] VI to lisp

blésité [blezite] NF lisping

blésois, -e [blezwa, -az] ADJ of/from Blois

❏ **Blésois, -e** NM,F = inhabitant of or person from Blois

blessant, -e [blɛsɑ̃, -ɑ̃t] ADJ *(propos)* hurtful, cutting; **se montrer b. envers qn** to hurt sb's feelings

blessé, -e [blese] ADJ **1** *(soldat)* wounded; *(accidenté)* injured; **b. au genou** hurt in the knee **2** *(vexé → amour-propre, orgueil, personne)* hurt

NM,F *(victime → d'un accident)* injured person; *(→ d'une agression)* wounded person; **un mort et trois blessés** one dead and three wounded/injured; **les blessés de la route** road casualties; **b. léger/grave** slightly/severely injured person; **grand b.** severely injured person; **b. de la face** person with facial wounds/injuries; **b. de guerre** *(en service)* wounded soldier; *(après la guerre)* wounded veteran

blesser [4] [blese] VT **1** *(au cours d'un accident)* to injure, to hurt; *(au cours d'une agression)* to injure, to wound; **vous êtes blessé?** are you hurt?; **il a été blessé par balle** he was hit by a bullet, he sustained a bullet-wound; **b. qn avec un couteau** to wound sb with a knife, to inflict a knife-wound on sb; **être blessé d'un coup de couteau** to be stabbed or knifed; **elle est blessée à la jambe** she has a leg injury, her leg's hurt; **être blessé dans un accident de voiture** to be injured in a car accident; **il a été blessé à la guerre** he was wounded in the war, he has a war-wound

2 *(partie du corps)* to hurt, to make sore; **b. la vue** to offend the eye; **b. l'oreille** to grate on the ear

3 *(offenser)* to offend, to upset; **tu l'as blessé avec tes questions** you hurt his feelings with your questions; **tes paroles m'ont blessé** I felt hurt by what you said; **b. qn dans son amour-propre** to hurt sb's pride

4 *Littéraire (aller contre → convenances, vérité)* to offend; *(→ intérêts)* to harm

USAGE ABSOLU to hurt; **des chaussures qui blessent** *(par compression)* shoes that pinch; *(par frottement)* shoes that rub

▸**se blesser** VPR to injure or to hurt oneself; **elle s'est blessée au bras** she injured or hurt her arm

blessure [blesyr] NF **1** *Méd (dans un accident)* injury; *(par arme)* wound; **infliger une b. à qn** to wound sb; **b. grave/légère/mortelle** severe/slight/fatal injury; **b. par balle** gunshot wound; *Jur* **blessures par imprudence** (non-malicious) wounding; **b. pénétrante** puncture wound; **b.**

en séton seton wound; **b. superficielle** flesh wound; **nettoyer une b.** to clean out a wound; **c'était avant ma b.** it was before I was injured **2** *Fig (offense)* wound; **une b. d'amour-propre** a blow to one's pride *or* self-esteem

blet, -ette[1] [blɛ, -ɛt] **ADJ** *(fruit)* mushy, overripe

blètse [blɛts] **NM** *Suisse (pour rapiécer)* patch

blette[1] [blɛt] *voir* **blet**

blette[2] **NF** *Bot* Swiss chard

blettir [32] [bletir] **VI** *(fruit)* to become mushy *or* overripe

blettissement [bletismɑ̃] **NM pour empêcher le b. des poires** to stop pears going mushy *or* becoming overripe

blettissure [blɛtisyr] **NF** = **blettissement**

bletz [blɛtz] = **blètse**

bleu, -e [blø] **ADJ 1** *(coloré)* blue; **avoir les yeux bleus** to have blue eyes, to be blue-eyed; *Fig* **avoir le menton b.** to have a five o'clock shadow

2 *(meurtri, altéré)* blue, bruised; **avoir les lèvres bleues** *(meurtries)* to have bruised lips; *(de froid, de maladie)* to have blue lips; **son bras était tout b.** his/her arm was black and blue; *Méd* **enfant b.** blue baby, hole-in-the-heart baby; **b. de froid** blue with cold; *Can* **un froid b.** extreme cold; **il fait un froid b.** it's freezing (cold)

3 *Culin* very rare; **le steak doit être servi b.** you should serve the steak very rare

4 *Belg* **être b. de qn/qch** *(être passionné)* to be crazy about sb/sth

5 *(locution)* **j'en suis resté b.** I was flabbergasted

NM,F *(gén)* newcomer, greenhorn; *Mil* rookie, raw recruit; *Scol* new boy, *f* new girl

NM 1 *(couleur)* blue; **peindre un mur en b.** to paint a wall blue; **admirer le b. du ciel/de la mer** to admire the blueness of the sky/sea; **b. clair** light blue; **b. foncé** dark blue; **b. acier** steel blue; **b. ardoise** slate blue; **b. canard** peacock blue; **b. ciel** sky blue; **b. (de) cobalt** cobalt blue; **b. horizon** sky blue; **b. lavande** lavender blue; **b. marine** navy blue; *Méd* **b. de méthylène** methylene blue; **b. noir** blue black; **b. nuit** midnight blue; **b. outremer** ultramarine; **b. pastel** powder blue; **b. pervenche** periwinkle blue; **b. pétrole** petrol blue; **b. de Prusse** Prussian blue; **b. roi** royal blue; **b. rouan** blue roan; **b. turquoise** turquoise; **b. vert** blue green; *Fam* **il n'y a vu que du b.** he didn't notice a thing *or* was none the wiser

2 *(ecchymose)* bruise; **se faire un b.** to get a bruise; **se faire un b. à la cuisse** to bruise one's thigh; **être couvert** *ou* **plein de bleus** to be black and blue

3 *(vêtement)* **b. (de travail)** (worker's) overalls; **b. de chauffe** work overalls, *Br* boiler suit

4 *Suisse Fam (permis de conduire) Br* driving licence▪, *Am* driver's license▪

5 *(fromage)* blue cheese; **b. de Bresse** = creamy blue cheese from the Bresse region in the east of France

6 *Hist* soldier of the Republic *(during the French Revolution)*

7 *Can Pol* Conservative

8 *(pour la lessive)* blue, blueing; **passer du linge au b.** to blue laundry

9 *Vieilli* **petit b.** telegram

❑ **bleue NF 1 la grande bleue** the Mediterranean (sea)

2 *Suisse (liqueur)* absinthe

3 *(locution)* **en voir de bleues** to go through a lot

❑ **bleus NMPL** *Can Fam* **1 avoir/prendre les bleus** *(être/devenir triste)* to have/get the blues; **prendre les bleus** *(voir rouge)* to go crazy

2 être dans les bleus *(ivre)* to be wasted

❑ **au bleu** *Culin* **ADJ truite au b.** trout au bleu **ADV cuire** *ou* **faire un poisson au b.** to cook a fish au bleu

bleuâtre [bløatr] **ADJ** bluish, bluey

bleuet [bløɛ] **NM** *Bot* **1** *(fleur)* cornflower **2** *Can (fruit)* blueberry; *(buisson)* blueberry bush; *Fam* **les Bleuets** = nickname given to residents of the Lac St-Jean area of Quebec

bleuetière [bløɛtjɛr] **NF** *Can Hort* blueberry field

bleuir [32] [bløir] **VI** to turn *or* to go blue

VT to turn blue

bleuissement [bløismɑ̃] **NM empêcher le b. des chairs** to stop the flesh turning *or* going blue

bleusaille [bløzaj] **NF** *Fam Arg mil* **la b.** the rookies

bleuté, -e [bløte] **ADJ** *(pétale, aile)* blue-tinged; *(lentille, verre)* blue-tinted

blindage [blɛ̃daʒ] **NM 1** *(revêtement)* armour plate *or* plating; *(fait de blinder)* armouring **2** *Élec* screening, shielding **3** *(d'une porte → revêtement)* reinforcement; *(→ fait de blinder)* reinforcing **4** *Mines* timbering

blinde [blɛ̃d] **NF** blind

❑ **à toute blinde ADV** *Fam* at full speed▪, like lightning, *Br* like the clappers

❑ **blindes NFPL** wooden frame *(to support planks, fascines)*

blindé, -e [blɛ̃de] **ADJ 1** *(voiture, tank, train)* armoured, armour-clad, armour-plated; *(brigade, division)* armoured **2** *(renforcé → paroi)* reinforced; **porte blindée** steel security door **3** *Élec* screened, shielded **4** *Fam (insensible)* hardened; **b. contre qch** hardened to sth **5** *très Fam (ivre)* blitzed, plastered **6** *Fam* **être b. (de monde)** to be packed *or Br* heaving (with people)

NM *Mil* **1** *(véhicule)* armoured vehicle; **les blindés** the armour **2** *(soldat)* = member of a tank regiment

blinder [3] [blɛ̃de] **VT 1** *(contre les agressions)* to armour, to armour-plate **2** *(renforcer → porte)* to reinforce **3** *Élec* to screen, to shield **4** *Mines* to timber **5** *Fam (endurcir)* to toughen (up), to harden; **le genre d'éducation qui vous blinde pour la vie** the sort of education that gives you a thick skin for the rest of your life; **b. qn contre qch** to harden sb to sth

▸**se blinder VPR** *Fam* **1** *(s'enivrer)* to get blitzed *or* plastered **2** *(s'endurcir)* to toughen oneself up; **se b. contre qch** to harden oneself to sth

blind trust [blaɪndtrœst] **NM** *Fin* blind trust

blini [blini] **NM** *Culin* blini

blinquer [3] [blɛ̃ke] *Belg Fam* **VT** to polish▪

VI to shine▪

blister [blistɛr] **NM** blister pack; **marchandise vendue sous b.** goods sold in blister packs

Blitz [blits] **NM** *Hist* **le B.** the Blitz

blizzard [blizar] **NM** blizzard

bloblote [blɔblɔt] **NF** *Fam* **avoir la b.** to have the shakes

bloc [blɔk] **NM 1** *(masse → de pierre)* block; *(→ de bois, de béton)* block, lump; **le fronton a été fait dans un seul b.** the pediment was hewn from a single block; **être tout d'un b.** *(en un seul morceau)* to be made of a single block; *(trapu)* to be stockily built; *(direct)* to be simple and straightforward; *(inflexible)* to be unyielding; **elle s'est retournée tout d'un b. et l'a giflé** she swivelled round and slapped him in the face

2 *(de papier)* pad; **b. de bureau** desk pad; **b. calendrier** tear-off calendar; **b. à dessin** sketch block; **b. à en-tête** headed notepad; **b. de papier** writing pad

3 *(installation)* **b. frigorifique** refrigeration unit; **b. opératoire** *(salle) Br* operating theatre, *Am* operating room; *(locaux)* surgical unit; **b. sanitaire** toilet block

4 *(maisons)* block

5 *(ensemble)* block; *(d'actions, de titres)* block, parcel; *(groupe d'actionnaires)* shareholding; **deux blocs adverses** two opposing factions *or* blocks; **former un b.** *(sociétés)* to form a grouping; *(amis, alliés)* to stand together; *(composants)* to form a single whole; **faire b.** to form a block; **faire b. avec/contre qn** to stand (together) with/against sb; *Fin* **b. de contrôle** controlling shareholding; **le B. national** = the centre-right group which governed France from November 1919 until May 1924; **le B. Québecois** = sovereignist political party in Quebec; **b. sièges** block of seats

6 *Suisse (immeuble)* block

7 *Géog, Écon & Fin (zone)* bloc; *Hist* **le b. des pays de l'Est** the Eastern bloc; **b. monétaire** monetary bloc; **le b. des pays de l'Ouest** *ou* **occidental** the Western Alliance; *Hist* **le b. soviétique** the Soviet bloc; **b. sterling** sterling bloc

8 *Géol* **b. erratique** erratic (block)

9 *Jur* **b. de constitutionnalité** = full set of constitutional regulations

10 *Fam Arg crime (prison)* slammer, *Br* nick; **allez, au b.!** lock him up!

11 *Ordinat* block; **b. d'alimentation secteur** mains power unit; **b. de calcul** arithmetic unit; **b. de données** data block; **b. de mémoire** memory bank; **b. de touches** keypad

12 *Can Fam (tête)* nut, head▪

13 *Belg Fam* awful weather▪

❑ **à bloc ADV visser une vis à b.** to screw a screw down hard; **fermer une manette à b.** to turn a tap hard off; **serrer le frein à b.** to pull the brakes on hard; **gonfler un pneu à b.** to blow a tyre all the way up; **remonter une pendule à b.** to wind a clock all the way up; *Fam* **il est gonflé** *ou* **remonté à b.** he's on top form *or* full of beans; **ne le provoque pas, il est remonté à b.!** leave him alone, he's already wound up!

❑ **en bloc ADV** as a whole; **j'ai tout rejeté en b.** I rejected it lock, stock and barrel, I rejected the whole thing; **condamner une politique en b.** to condemn a policy outright

blocage [blɔkaʒ] **NM 1** *(arrêt → des freins)* locking, jamming on; *(→ d'un écrou)* tightening (up)

2 *Écon (des loyers, des tarifs, du crédit)* freeze; *(d'un compte bancaire)* freezing; **b. des prix** price freeze; **b. des salaires** wage freeze

3 *Sport (de la balle)* trapping

4 *Méd* blockage

5 *Psy* block, blockage; **avoir** *ou* **faire un b.** to have a (mental) block; **faire un b. sur qch** to block sth off

6 *Constr* rubble, infill

7 *Ordinat (dans réseau)* lockout; **b. majuscule** caps lock

8 *Pol* **b. institutionnel** institutional deadlock

blocaille [blɔkaj] **NF** *Constr* rubble

bloc-appartement [blɔkapartəmɑ̃] *(pl* **blocs-appartements***)* **NM** *Can Br* block of flats, *Am* apartment building

bloc-cuisine [blɔkkɥizin] *(pl* **blocs-cuisines***)* **NM** kitchen unit

bloc-cylindres [blɔksilɛ̃dr] *(pl* **blocs-cylindres***)* **NM** cylinder block

bloc-diagramme [blɔkdjagram] *(pl* **blocs-diagrammes***)* **NM** *Géog* block diagram

bloc-eau [blɔko] *(pl* **blocs-eaux***)* **NM** plumbing unit

bloc-évier [blɔkevje] *(pl* **blocs-éviers***)* **NM** sink unit

block [blɔk] **NM** *Rail* block system

blockbuster [blɔkbœstœr] **NM** *Cin* blockbuster

blockhaus [blɔkos] **NM 1** *Mil* blockhouse; *(de petite taille)* pillbox **2** *Naut* armoured tower

bloc-moteur [blɔkmɔtœr] *(pl* **blocs-moteurs***)* **NM** *Aut* engine block

bloc-notes [blɔknɔt] *(pl* **blocs-notes***)* **NM** notepad, memo pad, *Am* scratchpad; *Ordinat (pour texte supprimé)* clipboard; *Ordinat* **b. électronique** electronic notepad

blocus [blɔkys] **NM 1** *Mil* blockade; **faire le b. d'une ville** to blockade a city; **lever/forcer le b.** to raise/to run the blockade; *Hist* **le B. continental** the Continental System; **b. économique** economic blockade **2** *Belg Fam* awful weather▪

blog [blɔg] **NM** *Ordinat (abrév* **weblog***)* blog; **b. vidéo** vlog, video blog

blogging [blɔgiŋ] **NM** *Ordinat* blogging

blogosphère [blɔgɔsfɛr] **NF** *Ordinat* blogosphere

blogueur, -euse [blɔgør, -øz] **NM,F** *Ordinat* blogger

bloke [blok] **NMF** *Can Joual* = pejorative name for an English-speaking Canadian

blond, -e [blɔ̃, blɔ̃d] **ADJ 1** *(chevelure)* blond, fair; *(personne)* blond, fair-haired; **b. platine** *ou* **platiné** platinum blond; **b. ardent** *ou* **roux** *ou* **vénitien** strawberry blond; **b. cendré** ash blond; **des cheveux b. cendré** ash blond hair; **b. filasse** flaxen-haired; **b. comme les blés** golden-haired

2 *(jaune pâle)* pale yellow, golden, honey-coloured

NM,F blonde (person); **une blonde incendiaire** a blonde bombshell; **une blonde décolorée** a peroxide blonde; **une blonde platine** a platinum blonde

NM *(couleur → des cheveux)* blond colour; *(→ du sable)* golden colour; **se teindre (les cheveux) en b.** to dye one's hair blond; **ses cheveux sont d'un b. très clair** she has light blond hair

❑ **blonde** NF **1** *(cigarette)* Virginia cigarette **2** *(bière)* lager **3** *Can (amie)* girlfriend

blondasse [blɔ̃das] *Péj* ADJ *(cheveux)* yellowish; **elle est b.** she's blondish

NF *(personne)* brassy blonde

blondeur [blɔ̃dœr] NF *(des cheveux, d'une personne)* fairness, blondness, blondeness; *(du sable, des blés)* goldenness, gold

blondin[1], **-e** [blɔ̃dɛ̃, -in] NM,F fair-haired child

blondin[2] [blɔ̃dɛ̃] NM *Tech* cableway

blondinet, -ette [blɔ̃dinɛ, -ɛt] ADJ blond-haired, fair-haired

NM,F little blond-haired *or* fair-haired child

blondir [32] [blɔ̃dir] VI **1** *(personne, cheveux)* to go fairer **2** *Culin* **faire b. des oignons** to sweat onions gently until transparent; **faites b. le roux avant d'ajouter le bouillon** wait until the roux turns golden before adding the stock **3** *Littéraire (feuille, blé)* to turn gold

VT to bleach; **b. ses cheveux** *(à l'eau oxygénée)* to bleach one's hair; *(par mèches)* to put (blonde) highlights in one's hair; **l'eau de mer blondit les cheveux** sea water bleaches the hair

bloom [blum] NM *Métal* bloom

bloomer [blymœr] NM *Vieilli* bloomers

bloque [blɔk] NF *Belg Fam* awful weather■

bloqué, -e [blɔke] ADJ *Ordinat (écran)* frozen

bloquer [3] [blɔke] VT **1** *(caler → table)* to wedge, to stop wobbling; *(empêcher de fonctionner)* to jam; **bloque la porte** *(ouverte)* wedge the door open; *(fermée)* wedge the door shut; **c'est le tapis qui bloque la porte** the carpet's jamming the door; **b. une roue** *(avec une cale)* to put a block under *or* to chock a wheel; *(avec un sabot de Denver)* to clamp a wheel; **la roue est bloquée** the wheel is locked *or* jammed; **la porte est bloquée** the door is stuck *or* jammed

2 *(serrer fort → vis)* to screw down hard, to overtighten; *(→ frein)* to jam on, to lock

3 *(entraver)* **b. le passage** *ou* **la route** to block the way; **pousse-toi, tu me bloques le passage** move, you're (standing) in my way; **être bloqué dans l'ascenseur** to be stuck in the *Br* lift *or Am* elevator; **je suis bloqué à la maison avec un gros rhume** I'm stuck at home with a bad cold; **les pourparlers sont bloqués** the negotiations are at a standstill *or* have reached an impasse

4 *(empêcher l'accès à → ville, point stratégique)* to block, to seal off; **la neige bloque les routes** the roads are blocked by the snow; **bloqué par la neige** snowbound; **bloqué par les glaces** icebound

5 *Fam (retenir → une personne)* to hold up

6 *Écon (loyers, prix, salaires, crédits)* to freeze; *Fin (compte bancaire)* to freeze, to stop; *(chèque)* to stop; *Pol (mesure, vote)* to block; **le ministre a fait b. les crédits** the minister imposed a restriction on funding

7 *(réunir)* to group together; **les cours sont bloqués sur six jours** the classes are grouped together over six days; **on va b. les activités sportives le matin** all sport will be done in the morning

8 *Psy* to cause *or* to produce a (mental) block in; **ça la bloque** she has a mental block about it; **ça me bloque de me sentir observé** I get a (mental) block if I feel I'm being watched; **il est bloqué sur le plan sexuel** he's sexually repressed

9 *Ftbl* **b. la balle** to trap the ball

10 *Belg Fam (étudier → examen)* to cram for, *Br* to swot for, *Am* to grind away for; *(→ matière)* to cram, *Br* to swot up, *Am* to grind away at

11 *Can Fam (échouer à → examen)* to fail■, to flunk

12 *Constr* to fill (with rubble)

▸**se bloquer** VPR **1** *(clef)* to jam, to stick, to get stuck; *(machine, mécanisme)* to jam, to get stuck; *(frein, roue)* to jam, to lock

2 *(personne → ne pas communiquer)* to close in on oneself; *(→ se troubler)* to have a mental block; **je me bloque quand on me parle sur ce ton** my mind goes blank *or* I freeze when somebody speaks to me like that

bloqueur, -euse [blɔkœr, -øz] ADJ *Belg Fam* hardworking■, *Br* swotty

NM,F *Belg Fam* hardworking student■, *Br Péj* swot, *Am Péj* grind

NM *Sport* **1** *(en football américain)* tackle; *(en volley-ball)* blocker **2** *(en alpinisme)* ascender

blottir [32] [blɔtir] VT **1** *(poser)* **b. sa tête contre l'épaule de qn** to lay one's head on sb's shoulder **2** *Fig* **une ferme blottie au fond de la vallée** a farmhouse nestling in the bottom of the valley; **blottis les uns contre les autres** huddled up *or* snuggled up together

▸**se blottir** VPR to curl up, to snuggle up; **se b. contre qn** to snuggle up to sb; **blotti sous mes couvertures** snug in my blankets

blousage [bluzaʒ] NM *(au billard)* pot

blousant, -e [bluzɑ̃, -ɑ̃t] ADJ loose, loose-fitting; **la tunique se porte blousante** the tunic is worn tucked loosely into the waist

blouse [bluz] NF **1** *(courte → à l'école)* = smock formerly worn by French schoolchildren; *(→ à l'ancienne, de paysan)* smock; *(→ chemisier)* blouse **2** *(longue → pour travailler)* overalls; *(→ d'un médecin)* white coat; *(→ d'un chimiste, d'un laborantin)* lab coat; **les blouses blanches** doctors and nurses; **b. stérile** scrubs **3** *(au billard)* pocket

blouser [3] [bluze] VT **1** *Vieilli (au billard)* to pot, to pocket **2** *Fam (tromper)* to con, to trick; **je me suis fait b.** I've been conned, I was had

VI to be loose-fitting, to fit loosely; **faire b. un chemisier** to pull a blouse out a bit at the waist

blouson [bluzɔ̃] NM (short) jacket; **b. d'aviateur** bomber jacket; *Vieilli* **les blousons dorés** rich young thugs; *Vieilli* **les blousons noirs** = young louts in black leather jackets

blousse [blus] NF *Tex* noil, combings

blue chip [bluʃip] *(pl* **blue chips***)* NM *Bourse* blue chip

bluegrass [blugras] NM *Mus* bluegrass

bluejacking [bludʒakiŋ] NM *Tél* bluejacking

blue-jean [bludʒin] *(pl* **blue-jeans***)* NM, **blue-jeans** [bludʒins] NM INV *Vieilli* (pair of) jeans

blues [bluz] NM **1** *Mus (musique)* blues *(singulier)*; **chanter le b.** to sing the blues **2** *Fam (cafard)* **avoir le b.** to have the blues, to be feeling blue *or* down; **j'ai un coup de b.** I'm feeling a bit blue *or* down

bluet [blyɛ] NM *Bot* cornflower

Bluetooth® [blutuθ] ADJ *Électron* Bluetooth®

bluette [blyɛt] NF **1** *Péj Littérature* pretty little story **2** *Littéraire* sparklet

bluff [blœf] NM bluff; **ne le crois pas, c'est du b.!** don't believe him, he's just bluffing!; **il faut y aller au b.** you'll have to try and bluff

bluffer [3] [blœfe] VT **1** *(tromper)* to bluff **2** *Fam (impressionner)* to blow away; **ils m'ont vraiment bluffé lors du concert qu'ils ont donné à Paris** they really blew me away when they played Paris

VI to bluff

bluffeur, -euse [blœfœr, -øz] ADJ **il est très b.** he's always bluffing

NM,F bluffer

blush [blœʃ] NM blusher

blutage [blytaʒ] NM *(tamisage)* bolting, boulting

bluter [3] [blyte] VT *(tamiser → farine)* to bolt, to boult

bluterie [blytri] NF **1** *(machine)* bolting-machine, bolter **2** *(lieu)* bolting-room

blutoir [blytwar] NM bolting-machine, bolter

BM [beɛm] NF *(abrév* **Banque mondiale***)* World Bank

BMPT [beɛmpete] NM *Beaux-Arts (abrév* **Buren, Mosset, Parmentier, Toroni***)* **le groupe B.** the BMPT group

BMTN [beɛmteɛn] NM *Fin (abrév* **bon à moyen terme négociable***)* MTN

BN [beɛn] NF *(abrév* **Bibliothèque nationale***)* = the former French national library building, now containing only archive material and coins, medals etc

BNF [beɛnɛf] NF *(abrév* **Bibliothèque nationale de France***)* = French national library, comprising the "Bibliothèque de France" and the "Bibliothèque nationale"

BNP [beɛnpe] NF *Banque (abrév* **Banque nationale de Paris***)* = the second largest French clearing bank

BNPA [beɛnpea] NM *Bourse (abrév* **bénéfice net par action***)* earnings per share

BNT [beɛnte] NF *(abrév* **barrière non tarifaire***)* NTB

BO [beo] NM *Admin (abrév* **Bulletin officiel***)* = official listing of all new laws and decrees

NF *Cin (abrév* **bande originale***) (d'un film)* (original) soundtrack

boa [bɔa] NM **1** *Zool* boa; **b. constricteur** boa constrictor **2** *(tour de cou)* boa

Boadicée [bɔadise] NPR *Hist* Boadicea

boat people [botpipœl] NM INV (South East Asian) refugee; **les b.** the boat people

bob [bɔb] NM **1** *(chapeau)* sun hat, bucket hat **2** *Sport* bobsleigh, *Am* bobsled

bobard [bɔbar] NM *Fam* fib; **raconter des bobards** to fib, to tell fibs

bobèche [bɔbɛʃ] NF *(d'un bougeoir)* candle ring; *Fam Vieilli* **se monter la b.** to get all worked up

bobet [bɔbɛ] *Suisse Fam* ADJ stupid■, *Am* dumb

NM twit, *Am* jerk

bobettes [bɔbɛt] NFPL *Can Fam (caleçon)* boxers

bobeur [bɔbœr] NM *Sport* bobsleigh racer

bobinage [bɔbinaʒ] NM **1** *(enroulage)* winding, reeling **2** *Élec* coil

bobinard [bɔbinar] NM *très Fam* whorehouse, *Br* knocking shop

bobine [bɔbin] NF **1** *(de ruban, de fil)* reel; *Couture (dans une machine à coudre)* bobbin; **une b. de fil** a reel of thread

2 *Élec* coil; **b. d'allumage** ignition coil; **b. de dérivation** shunt coil; **b. d'induction** induction coil

3 *Cin & Phot* reel; **une b. de pellicule** a roll of film

4 *Fam (visage)* face■, mug; **elle a fait une drôle de b.** she pulled a (funny) face; **quand je pense à la b. qu'il va faire!** I can hardly wait to see (the look on) his face!

❑ **en bobine** ADV **rester en b.** to be left in the lurch

bobineau, -x [bɔbino] = **bobinot**

bobiner [3] [bɔbine] VT **1** *Couture & Tex* to reel, to spool, to wind **2** *Élec* to coil **3** *Pêche* to reel in

bobinette [bɔbinɛt] NF *Arch* wooden latch

bobineur, -euse [bɔbinœr, -øz] *Couture* NM,F winder, winding operative

NM *(d'une machine à coudre)* bobbin winder

❑ **bobineuse** NF winding machine, coiler

bobinier [bɔbinje] NM *(personne, machine)* coil winder

bobinoir [bɔbinwar] NM winding machine

bobinot [bɔbino] NM **1** *Tex* (small) spool, bobbin **2** *(de bobine à papier)* offcut **3** *Cin & TV* reel

bobo[1] [bɔbo] NM *(en langage enfantin) (égratignure)* scratch, *Am* boo-boo; *(bosse)* bump; **faire b. (à qn)** to hurt (sb); **se faire b.** to hurt oneself; **j'ai un b. au doigt** my finger hurts; **il n'y a pas de b., tout le monde va bien?** no one hurt, everybody OK?

bobo[2] [bɔbo] *Fam (abrév* **bourgeois bohème***)* ADJ bobo

NMF bobo

bobonne [bɔbɔn] NF **1** *Fam Péj* the old lady, *Br* the missus; **il va partout avec b.** his old lady goes everywhere with him; **sa femme, c'est une vraie b.** his wife's the real housewife-in-curlers type; **b., t'es prête?** ready, Missus? **2** *Belg Fam* grandma

bobsleigh [bɔbslɛg] NM *Sport* bobsleigh, *Am* bobsled

bobtail [bɔbtɛjl] NM *Zool (chien)* Old English sheepdog

boc [bɔk] NM *Suisse* goatee (beard)

bocage [bɔkaʒ] NM **1** *Géog* bocage *(countryside with small fields and many hedges)* **2** *Littéraire (bois)* copse, coppice, thicket

bocager, -ère [bɔkaʒe, -ɛr] ADJ **pays/paysage b.** country/landscape of small fields and hedges

bocal, -aux [bɔkal, -o] NM **1** *(pour les conserves)* jar, bottle; **manger des fruits en bocaux** to eat bottled *or* preserved fruit; **mettre des haricots verts en bocaux** to preserve *or* to bottle green beans **2** *(aquarium)* fishbowl, bowl **3** *Fam (locution)* **se remplir/se rincer le b.** to stuff/to drink oneself silly

bocard [bɔkar] NM *Métal* ore crusher, stamping mill

bocardage [bɔkardaʒ] NM *Métal* crushing, stamping *(of ore)*

bocarder [3] [bɔkarde] VT *Métal* to crush, to stamp *(ore)*

Boccace [bɔkas] NPR Boccaccio

BOCE [beosea] NM *UE (abrév* **Bulletin officiel des**

communautés européennes) = official listing of all new EC directives

boche [bɔʃ] *très Fam Vieilli* ADJ Boche, Kraut
NMF Boche, Kraut, = offensive term used to refer to German people; **les boches** the Boche, the Krauts

Bochiman [bɔʃimɑ̃] NMPL Bushmen

bock [bɔk] NM *(récipient)* ≃ (half-pint) beer glass; *(contenu)* glass of beer

bodhi [bɔdi] NF *Rel* bodhi

bodhisattva [bɔdisatva] NM *Rel* bodhisattva

body [bɔdi] NM *(justaucorps)* bodystocking, body

Bodyboard® [bɔdibɔrd] NM *Sport* **1** *(planche)* bodyboard **2** *(sport)* bodyboarding

bodybuildé, -e [bɔdibilde] ADJ muscular

body-building [bɔdibildiŋ] NM **le b.** body building; **faire du b.** to do body building

Boèce [bɔɛs] NPR Boëthius

boentje [buntjə] NM OU NF *Belg Fam Hum (attirance)* **avoir un b. pour qn** to have a crush on sb

Boer [bur] NM Boer; **les Boers** the Boers

boësse [bwɛs] NF **1** *(de sculpteur)* (chasing) chisel **2** *(de doreur)* wire brush, burnishing brush

boëte, boette, boëtte [bwɛt] NF *Pêche* bait

bœuf [bœf, *pl* bø] NM **1** *Zool (de trait)* ox; *(de boucherie)* bullock, steer; **b. musqué** musk ox; **il a un b. sur la langue** *(on l'a payé)* somebody's bought his silence; *(il ne veut rien dire)* he's keeping his own counsel; **fort comme un b.** as strong as an ox; **saigner comme un b.** to bleed profusely; **souffler comme un b.** to wheeze *or* to pant (heavily); *Fam* **on n'est pas des bœufs** you can't treat us like slaves **2** *Culin* beef; **b. bourguignon** bœuf *or* beef bourguignon; **b. à braiser** braising steak *or* beef; **b. gros sel** ≃ boiled beef and vegetables (with sea salt); **b. (à la) mode** beef à la mode **3** *Fam* jam session; **faire un b.** to have a jam session, to jam **4** [bø] *Can Fam (policier)* cop, *Br* pig
ADJ INV *Fam* **elle a fait un effet b.** she made quite a splash; **il a eu un succès b.** he was incredibly successful■

BOF [beoɛf] NM *Hist (abrév* **Beurre, Œufs, Fromages**) = name given to black market profiteers during the Occupation of France

bof [bɔf] EXCLAM = term expressing lack of interest or enthusiasm; **tu as aimé la pièce? – b.!** did you like the play? – it was all right, I suppose; **ça te dirait de venir avec nous? – b.** would you like to come with us? – I don't know *or* I'm not bothered; **la b. génération** = in the 1970s, young people who showed little interest in anything

bogey [bɔgɛ] NM *Golf* bogey

boggie [bɔgi] = **bogie**

boghead [bɔgɛd] NM *Minér* boghead coal

boghei [bɔgɛ] NM buggy *(carriage)*

bogie [bɔʒi] NM *Rail* bogie, bogy

bogomile [bɔgɔmil] NMF *Hist & Rel* Bogomil

Bogota [bɔgɔta] NM *Géog* Bogota

bogue¹ [bɔg] NF *Bot* chestnut bur

bogue² [bɔg] NM *Ordinat* bug; **le b. de l'an 2000** the millennium bug; **b. de logiciel** software bug

bogué, -e [bɔge] ADJ *Ordinat* bug-ridden

boguet [bɔgɛ] NM **1** *Suisse (cyclomoteur)* moped **2** = **boghei**

Bohême [bɔɛm] NF **la B.** Bohemia

bohème [bɔɛm] ADJ bohemian; **lui, c'est le genre b.** he's the artistic type
NMF bohemian; **mener une vie de b.** to lead a bohemian *or* an unconventional life
NF **la b.** the bohemian *or* artistic way of life

'La Bohème' *Puccini* 'La Bohème'

bohémien, -enne [bɔemjɛ̃, -ɛn] ADJ Bohemian
❑ **Bohémien, -enne** NM,F **1** *(de Bohême)* Bohemian **2** *Péj (nomade)* gipsy, traveller

'La Bohémienne' *Hals* 'The Gypsy Girl'

bohrium [bɔrjɔm] NM *Chim* bohrium

boille [bɔj] NF *Suisse* **1** *Br* churn, *Am* milk pail **2** *(pour la vendange)* grape tub

boire [108] [bwar] VT **1** *(avaler)* to drink; **b. qch à petits coups** *ou* **à petites gorgées** to sip sth; **b. de l'eau/de la bière** to drink water/beer; *Fam* **b. un coup** *ou* **pot** *ou* **verre** to have a drink; **elle a tout bu d'un coup** she gulped it all down; **b. un coup de trop** to have one too many; **donnenous quelque chose à b.** give us a drink *or* something to drink; **b. du lait** *ou* **du petit-lait** to lap it up; **il buvait ses paroles** he was lapping up everything he/she said; *Fam* **b. la tasse** *ou* **un bouillon** *(en nageant)* to swallow water; *(perdre de l'argent)* to lose a lot of money; *(faire faillite)* to go under
2 *(absorber)* to absorb, to soak up; **les géraniums ont bu toute l'eau** the geraniums soaked up *or* drank all the water
VI **1** *(s'hydrater)* to drink; **vous ne buvez pas assez** you don't drink enough fluids; **il buvait à petits coups** *ou* **à petites gorgées** he was sipping his drink; **b. à la bouteille** to drink from the bottle; **commander à b.** to order a drink; **manger salé fait b.** eating salty things makes you thirsty; **fais-le b.** *(malade, enfant, animal)* give him a drink *or* something to drink; **s'arrêter pour faire b. les chevaux** to stop and water the horses; **tant qu'elle a de la fièvre, faites-la b. abondamment** if she's feverish make sure she gets plenty of liquid; **il y a à b. et à manger là-dedans** *(dans un verre)* there are bits floating in the glass; *Fig* it's a bit of a mixed bag; **b. jusqu'à plus soif** to drink one's fill
2 *(pour fêter un événement)* **b. à** to toast, to drink to; **nous buvons à ta santé** we're drinking to *or* toasting your health
3 *(pour s'enivrer)* to drink; **il boit trop** he drinks too much, he has a drink problem; **il a toujours aimé b.** he's always enjoyed a drink; **elle s'est mise à b. après la mort de son mari** she started drinking after her husband died; *Fam* **il boit bien** *ou* **sec** he's a rather heavy drinker; **elle l'a fait b. pour qu'il avoue** she got him drunk so that he'd confess; *Fam* **b. comme une éponge** *ou* **un tonneau** *ou* **un trou** to drink like a fish
4 *(plante)* to soak up *or* absorb water
5 *Can (bébé)* to feed; **donner à b. à un bébé** to breastfeed a baby
NM **1 le b. et le manger** eating and drinking; **il en oublie** *ou* **perd le b. et le manger** he's becoming totally distracted
2 *Can* **le b. du bébé** the feeding of the baby
▶**se boire** VPR **se boit frais/chambré** should be drunk chilled/at room temperature; **ça se boit comme du petit-lait** it goes down like silk *or Br* a treat

bois [bwa] NM **1** *(forêt → de grands arbres)* wood, wooded area; *(→ de jeunes ou petits arbres)* thicket, copse, coppice; *(→ d'arbres plantés)* grove; **un b. de pins** a pine grove; **un b. de chênes** an oak wood; **le B. de Boulogne** the Bois de Boulogne; *Chasse* **faire le b.** to scout the area; *Fig* **sortir du b.** *(se révéler tel qu'on est)* to show one's true colours
2 *(matière)* wood *(UNCOUNT)*; *(pour la construction)* timber, *Am* lumber; **en b.** wooden; **b. blanc** whitewood; **b. à brûler** firewood; **b. de charpente** timber; **b. de chauffage** firewood; *Can* **b. de corde** firewood; **b. debout** standing timber; **b. dur** hardwood; **b. d'ébène** ebony; *Fig* black gold; **b. exotique** imported wood; **b. de fer** ironwood; *Suisse* **b. de feu** firewood; **b. flottants** driftwood; *Can* **b. franc** hardwood; **b. des îles** tropical hardwood; **b. mort** deadwood; *Can* **b. mou** softwood; **b. d'œuvre** timber; **b. de papeterie,** *Can* **b. de papier** pulpwood; **b. à pâte** pulpwood; *Can* **b. de poêle** firewood; *Can* **b. rond** log, roundwood; **une cabane en b. rond** a log cabin; **b. de rose** rosewood; **b. de sappan** sappanwood; **b. tendre** softwood; **b. de violette** kingwood; **petit b.** kindling; **il est du b. dont on fait les flûtes** he's very easy-going; **il est du b. dont on fait les héros** he's got the stuff of heroes; **faire feu** *ou* **flèche de tout b.** to use all available means; **dans un tel cas, il faut faire feu de tout b.** this is a case of all's fair in love and war; **ils font flèche de tout b. pour faire tomber le ministère** they're pulling out all the stops to bring down the government; **touchons** *ou* **je touche du b.** touch wood; *Fam* **je vais leur montrer de quel b. je me chauffe!** I'll show them what I'm made of!; *Fam* **ça envoie le** *ou* **du b.** it rocks, *Br* it's the business; *Fam* **ce guitariste envoie du b.** the guitarist rocks
3 *(partie en bois → d'une raquette)* frame; *Fam* **faire un b.** *(au tennis)* to hit the ball off the wood; **b. de lit** bedstead
4 *Beaux-Arts* **b. (gravé)** woodcut
5 *(club de golf)* wood
❑ **bois** NMPL **1** *Zool* antlers
2 *Ftbl* goalposts
3 *Mus* woodwind section *or* instruments
4 *Hist* **les b. de justice** the guillotine
❑ **de bois** ADJ **1** *(charpente, jouet, meuble)* wooden
2 *(impassible)* **je ne suis pas de b.** I'm only human

boisage [bwazaʒ] NM *Mines (action)* timbering; *(soutènement)* timber work

boisé, -e [bwaze] ADJ **1** *(région, terrain)* wooded, woody **2** *Constr* panelled
NM *Can* coppice, wooded area

boisement [bwazmɑ̃] NM *Hort* afforestation

boiser [3] [bwaze] VT **1** *Hort* to afforest **2** *Mines* to timber **3** *Constr* to panel

boiserie [bwazri] NF piece of decorative woodwork; **des boiseries** panelling

boiseur [bwazœr] NM *Mines* timberman

bois-métal [bwametal] (*pl* **bois-métaux**) NM *Golf* metal wood

boisseau, -x [bwaso] NM **1** *(mesure)* bushel; **garder** *ou* **mettre** *ou* **tenir qch sous le b.** to keep sth hidden *or* a secret **2** *Tech (tuyau)* drain tile; *(de cheminée)* chimney (flue) tile

boisselier [bwasəlje] NM bushel-maker

boissellerie [bwasɛlri] NF **1** *(activité)* bushel making **2** *(récipients)* hollow ware

Boisserie [bwasri] NF **la B.** = home of General de Gaulle in the village of Colombey-les-Deux-Églises in the east of France

boisson [bwasɔ̃] NF **1** *(liquide à boire)* drink; **j'aimerais une b. fraîche** I'd like a cool drink; **je m'occupe de la b.** I'll take care of the drinks; **et pour la b.?** *(au restaurant)* and what would you like to drink?; **b. alcoolisée** alcoholic drink; **la consommation de boissons alcoolisées est interdite dans l'enceinte du stade** drinking alcohol is forbidden inside the stadium; **b. chaude** hot drink; **b. gazeuse** *Br* fizzy drink, *Am* soda
2 *(alcool)* **la b.** drink, drinking; **c'est la b. qui l'a tué** it's the drink that killed him; **être pris de b.** to be inebriated *or* intoxicated
3 *Can (spiritueux)* alcohol, alcoholic drinks; **b. forte** hard liquor, spirits; **être/se mettre en b.** to be/get drunk

boîte [bwat] NF **1** *(récipient → à couvercle, à fente)* box; **b. d'allumettes** *(pleine)* box of matches; *(vide)* matchbox; **b. à chaussures** shoebox; **b. de couleurs** paintbox; **b. à idées** suggestions box; *Can Joual* **b. à lunch** lunchbox; *Can Joual* **b. à malle** mailbox; **b. à ordures** *Br* dustbin, *Am* trash can; *aussi Ordinat* **b. à outils** tool box, toolkit; **b. à ouvrage** sewing box; **b. à pain** bread bin; **b. de peinture** paintbox, box of paints; **b. à pharmacie** first aid box *or* kit; **b. à pilules** pillbox; **b. à thé** tea caddy; *Fam* **c'est dans la b.!** *(à un tournage de film)* it's in the can!; *Fam* **et toi, b. à malice?** what about you, you clever little monkey?; **b. de Pandore** Pandora's box; *Fam* **ferme ta b. (à camembert, tu l'ouvriras au dessert)** shut your trap *or* mouth
2 *(pour aliments)* **b. (de conserve)** can, *Br* tin; **acheter une b. de haricots** to buy a can *or Br* tin of beans; **il ne mange que des boîtes** he eats nothing but canned *or Br* tinned food
3 *(pour boissons)* can; **une b. de limonade** a can of lemonade
4 *(contenu → d'un récipient à couvercle, à fente)* box, boxful; *(→ d'une conserve)* canful, *Br* tinful; **manger une b. de haricots** to eat a canful *or Br* tinful of beans; **dévorer une b. entière de chocolats** to eat one's way through a *or* to eat a whole box of chocolates
5 *(pour le courrier)* **b. à** *ou* **aux lettres** *(dans la rue) Br* postbox, letterbox, *Am* mailbox; *(chez soi) Br* letterbox, *Am* mailbox; **mettre qch à la b. aux lettres** to mail *or Br* post sth; **servir de b. aux lettres** to be a go-between; *Ordinat* **b. aux lettres électronique** electronic mailbox, e-mail; **b. postale** PO box; **b. vocale** voice mail
6 *Ordinat* **b. de dialogue** dialogue box
7 *Aviat & Aut* **b. noire** black box
8 *Fam (entreprise)* firm; **b. d'intérim** temping

agency; **j'ai changé de b.** I got a job with a new firm; **il a été renvoyé de sa b.** he got the sack

9 *Fam (discothèque)* **b. (de nuit)** club, night-club; **aller** *ou* **sortir en b.** to go to a nightclub, to go clubbing; **b. de jazz** jazz club

10 **Can b. à chanson** *(cabaret)* = small bar or coffee house with live music

11 *Fam (lycée)* school▪; *Péj* **b. à bac** *ou* **à bachot** *Br* crammer

12 *Anat* **b. crânienne** cranium

13 *Aut* **b. à gants** glove compartment; **b. de vitesses** gearbox

14 *Élec* **b. de dérivation** junction box

15 *Menuis* **b. à onglets** mitre box

16 *Mus* **b. à musique** musical box; **b. à rythmes** beatbox

▫ **en boîte** ADJ canned, *Br* tinned ADV **1** *Ind & Culin* **mettre des fruits en b.** to can *or Br* to tin fruit; **mettre des petits pois en b.** to can *or Br* to tin peas **2** *Fam (location)* **mettre qn en b.** to pull sb's leg, *Br* to wind sb up

boîte-boisson [bwatbwasɔ̃] *(pl* **boîtes-boissons)** NF can *(of drink)*

boitement [bwatmɑ̃] NM limp, limping; **être affecté d'un léger b.** to limp a little

boîte-pont [bwatpɔ̃] *(pl* **boîtes-ponts)** NF *Aut* transaxle

boiter [3] [bwate] VI **1** *(en marchant)* to limp, to be lame; **b. du pied droit** *ou* **de la jambe droite** to have a lame right leg **2** *(être bancal → chaise, table)* to wobble, to be rickety **3** *(être imparfait → projet, raisonnement)* to be shaky **4** *Littérature* **vers qui boitent** halting verse

boiterie [bwatri] NF lameness

boiteux, -euse [bwatø, -øz] ADJ **1** *(cheval, personne)* lame; *(meuble, table)* rickety; **il est b.** he walks with a limp, he limps **2** *(imparfait → paix, alliance)* fragile, shaky; *(→ comparaison, raisonnement)* unsound, shaky; *(→ traduction, phrase)* iffy; *(→ vers)* limping; **ton premier paragraphe est b.** your first paragraph doesn't hang together very well

NM,F lame man, *f* woman

boîtier [bwatje] NM **1** *(gén)* case, casing; *(d'une lampe de poche)* battery compartment; **b. de montre** watchcase **2** *Phot* camera body; **détacher l'objectif du b.** take the lens off (the camera) **3** *Ordinat* **b. de commande** command box; **b. commutateur** data switch; **b. vertical** tower **4** *Aut* **b. de direction** steering box; *Élec* **b. de raccordement** connecting box

boitillant, -e [bwatijɑ̃, -ɑ̃t] ADJ hobbling

boitillement [bwatijmɑ̃] NM slight limp, hobble

boitiller [3] [bwatije] VI to limp slightly, to be slightly lame, to hobble; **elle est rentrée/sortie en boitillant** she hobbled in/out

boiton [bwatɔ̃] NM *Suisse Fam* pigsty

boit-sans-soif [bwasɑ̃swaf] NMF INV *Fam* drunk, lush

boitte [bwat] = **boëte**

boivent *etc voir* **boire**

bol [bɔl] NM **1** *(récipient)* bowl; **le B. d'or** = French motorcycle racing trophy

2 *(contenu)* bowl, bowlful; **prendre un b. d'air** *(se promener)* to (go and) get some fresh air; *(changer d'environnement)* to get a change of air

3 *Fam (chance)* luck▪; **avoir du b.** to be a lucky devil; **il a un de ces bols!** he's got the luck of the devil!; **pas de b.!** what rotten luck!

4 *Vieilli (pilule)* bolus

5 *Can Fam (tête)* nut, head▪

6 *Can Joual* **b. de toilette** toilet bowl

▫ **au bol** ADJ *(coupe de cheveux)* bowl *(avant n)*, *Br* pudding-bowl *(avant n)*

▫ **bol alimentaire** bolus

bolchevik, bolchevique [bɔlʃəvik] ADJ Bolshevik, Bolshevist

NM,F Bolshevik, Bolshevist

bolchevisme [bɔlʃəvism] NM *Pol* Bolshevism

boldo [bɔldo] NM *Bot* boldo

bolduc [bɔldyk] NM ribbon *(used for gift wrapping)*

bolé, -e¹ [bɔle] NM,F *Can Joual Péj* egghead, brainbox; **c'est un b. d'informatique** he's a computer geek

bolée² [bɔle] NF **b. de cidre** bowl *or* bowlful of cider *(in North-West France, cider is often served in bowls)*

boléro [bɔlero] NM **1** *Mus & (danse)* bolero **2** *(veste)* bolero

bolet [bɔlɛ] NM *Bot* boletus

boletale [bɔlɛtal] NF *Bot* member of the Boletus genus

bolide [bɔlid] NM **1** *(voiture de course)* fast (racing) car; *Hum* **où vas-tu avec ton b.?** where are you going with that fiendish machine of yours?; **entrer dans une/sortir d'une pièce comme un b.** to hurtle into a/out of a room **2** *Astron* meteor, fireball, *Spéc* bolide

bolier [bɔlje] NM *Pêche* bag-net, wing-net

bolivar [bɔlivar] NM **1** *(monnaie)* bolivar **2** *(chapeau)* = tall, wide-brimmed hat

boliviano [bɔlivjano] NM *(monnaie)* boliviano

Bolivie [bɔlivi] NF **la B.** Bolivia; **vivre en B.** to live in Bolivia; **aller en B.** to go to Bolivia

bolivien, -enne [bɔlivjɛ̃, -ɛn] ADJ Bolivian

▫ **Bolivien, -enne** NM,F Bolivian

bollandiste [bɔlɑ̃dist] NM *Rel* Bollandist

bollard [bɔlar] NM *Naut* bollard

bolognaise [bɔlɔɲɛz] ADJ F *Culin* **sauce b.** bolognese sauce; **spaghettis (à la) b.** spaghetti bolognese

Bologne [bɔlɔɲ] NM *Géog* Bologna

bolomètre [bɔlɔmɛtr] NM *Phys* bolometer

bolonais, -e [bɔlɔnɛ, -ɛz] ADJ Bolognese

▫ **Bolonais, -e** NM,F Bolognese; **les B.** the Bolognese

bolson [bɔlsɔ̃] NM *Géol* bolson

bombage [bɔ̃baʒ] NM **1** *(action)* spray-painting; *(graffiti)* (aerosol) graffiti **2** *(en verrerie)* bending

bombance [bɔ̃bɑ̃s] NF feast; **faire b.** to feast

bombard [bɔ̃bar] NM *Can Ordinat* mail bomb

bombarde [bɔ̃bard] NF **1** *Mus (jeu d'orgues)* bombarde, bombardon; *(de Bretagne)* shawm **2** *Hist (machine de guerre)* bombarde

bombardement [bɔ̃bardəmɑ̃] NM **1** *Mil (avec des obus)* shelling (UNCOUNT); *(avec des bombes)* bombing (UNCOUNT); **b. aérien** air raid; **le b. atomique d'Hiroshima** the dropping of the atomic bomb on Hiroshima; **b. en piqué** dive-bombing **2** *(lancement de projectiles)* showering, pelting; *Fig (de questions)* flood; *Phys* **b. atomique** atomic bombardment

bombarder [3] [bɔ̃barde] VT **1** *Mil (avec des obus)* to shell; *(avec des bombes)* to bomb **2** *(avec des projectiles)* to shower, to pelt; *Phys* to bombard; **être bombardé de boules de neige** to be pelted with snowballs; *Fig* **b. qn de questions** to bombard sb with questions; **être bombardé de lettres/coups de téléphone** to be inundated with letters/phone calls; **elle s'est fait b. de critiques** she came in for a volley of criticism **3** *(suivi d'un nom) Fam (promouvoir)* **il a été bombardé responsable du projet** he found himself catapulted into the position of project manager; **il a réussi à la faire b. directrice** he managed to pitchfork her into the position of director

VI *Fam (fumer beaucoup)* to smoke like a chimney

bombardier [bɔ̃bardje] NM **1** *Aviat & Mil (avion)* bomber; *(pilote)* bombardier **2** *Entom* bombardier (beetle)

bombardon [bɔ̃bardɔ̃] NM *Mus* bombardon

bombax [bɔ̃baks] NM *Bot* bombax, silk-cotton tree

Bombay [bɔ̃bɛ] NM *Géog* Bombay, Mumbai

bombe [bɔ̃b] NF **1** *Mil & Nucl* bomb; **b. A** A bomb; **b. atomique** atom *or* atomic bomb; **la b. atomique** the Bomb; **b. à billes** cluster bomb; **b. à eau** water bomb; **b. à fragmentation** fragmentation bomb; **b. à guidage laser** laser-guided bomb; **b. H** H bomb; **b. à hydrogène** hydrogen bomb; **b. incendiaire** firebomb; **b. intelligente** intelligent *or* smart bomb; **b. à neutrons** neutron bomb; **b. radioactive** radioactive *or* dirty bomb; *aussi Fig* **b. à retardement** time bomb; **b. sale** dirty bomb; **b. volante** flying bomb; **arriver comme une b.** to come like a bolt out of the blue; **la nouvelle est arrivée comme une** *ou* **a fait l'effet d'une b.** the news came like a bolt out of the blue

2 *Géol* **b. volcanique** volcanic bomb

3 *(aérosol)* spray; **en b.** in a spray can; **peinture en b.** spray paint; **déodorant en b.** deodorant

spray; **chantilly en b.** aerosol cream; **b. anticrevaison** instant puncture sealant; **b. insecticide** *Br* fly *or Am* bug spray; **b. lacrymogène** *ou Fam* **lacrymo** *(utilisée par la police)* tear-gas canister; *(pour l'auto-défense)* mace spray; **b. serpentin** Silly String®

4 *Équitation* riding hat *or* cap

5 *Culin* **b. glacée** bombe; **b. glacée au chocolat** chocolate bombe

6 *Méd* **b. au cobalt** cobalt bomb, cobalt therapy unit

7 *très Fam (personne)* **b. sexuelle** sex kitten *or* bomb

8 *Fam (fête)* feast, spree; **faire la b.** to whoop it up, to have a riotous old time; **on a fait une de ces bombes!** we had a ball!

9 *Fam* **c'est de la b. (de balle)!** *Br* it's absolutely wicked!, *Am* it's totally awesome!

10 *Can (bouilloire)* kettle

▫ **à toute bombe** ADV *Fam* at full speed▪, like lightning; **aller à toute b.** to bomb along, to belt along

bombé, -e [bɔ̃be] ADJ **1** *(renflé → paroi)* bulging; *(→ front)* bulging, domed; *(→ poitrine, torse)* thrown out, stuck out; *(→ forme)* rounded **2** *(convexe → route)* cambered

bombement [bɔ̃bmɑ̃] NM **1** *(renflement)* bulge **2** *(convexité → route)* camber

bomber [3] [bɔ̃be] VT **1** *(rendre convexe → route, chaussée)* to camber **2** *(gonfler)* **b. le torse** to stick out one's chest; *Fig* to swagger about **3** *(slogan)* to spray, to spray-paint

VI **1** *(route)* to camber **2** *Fam (se dépêcher)* to belt along, *Br* to bomb along; **va falloir b.!** we'll have to get a move on!

bombeur, -euse [bɔ̃bœr, -øz] NM,F graffiti artist *(who uses spray paint)*

bombinette [bɔ̃binɛt] NF *Fam* **1** *(petite bombe)* little bomb **2** *(petite voiture très nerveuse)* nippy little car

bombonne [bɔ̃bɔn] = **bonbonne**

bombyx [bɔ̃biks] NM *Entom* bombyx; **b. du mûrier** silk moth

bôme [bom] NF *Naut* boom

bomme [bɔm] NM *Can Joual* bum

bommer [3] [bɔme] VI *Can Joual* to bum about

Bon [bɔ̃] *voir* **cap**

BON, BONNE¹ [bɔ̃, bɔn]

ADJ good A1–5, B1-4, C3, D1–3, E1, 3 ▪ valid A4 ▪ nice B1, 2 ▪ correct, right C1 ▪ right, appropriate C2 ▪ OK C4 ▪ kind D2

NM,F good person 1 ▪ right one 2

NM goodie 1 ▪ voucher, coupon 5 ▪ bond 6

ADV nice, warm 1

EXCLAM so 1 ▪ right 1, 2 ▪ OK 2

ADJ **A.** *QUI CONVIENT, QUI DONNE SATISFACTION* **1** *(en qualité → film, récolte, résultat, connaissance)* good; **les hôteliers ont fait une bonne saison** it was a good season for the hotel trade; **très bonne idée!** very good *or* excellent idea!; **viande de bonne qualité** good-quality meat; **de très bonne qualité** of superior *or* very good quality; **elle parle un b. espagnol** she speaks good Spanish, her Spanish is good; **il a un b. accent en russe** he has a good accent in Russian *or* a good Russian accent; *Scol* **de bonnes notes** good *or* high *Br* marks *or Am* grades; *Tennis* **il a un b. service** he has a good serve, his serve is good, he serves well

2 *(qui remplit bien sa fonction → matelas, siège, chaussures)* good, comfortable; *(→ éclairage, hygiène)* good, adequate; *(→ freins)* good, reliable; *(→ cœur, veines, charpente, gestion, investissement)* good, sound; **il a une bonne santé** he's in good health, his health is good; **de bonnes jambes** a strong pair of legs; **une bonne vue, de bons yeux** good eyesight

3 *(au tennis)* good; **la balle est bonne** the ball's in, the ball is good; **son service était b.** his serve was good *or* in; *Ftbl* **la remise en jeu n'était pas bonne** it was a foul throw

4 *(qui n'est pas périmé → nourriture)* good; *(→ document, titre de transport)* valid; **le lait n'est plus b.** the milk has turned *or Br* has gone off; **l'eau du robinet n'est pas bonne** the water

from the *Br* tap *or Am* faucet isn't drinkable *or* isn't fit to drink; **ta carte d'identité n'est plus bonne** your identity card is no longer valid; **l'ampoule n'est plus bonne** the bulb's gone; **la colle n'est plus bonne** the glue isn't usable any more

5 *(compétent → acteur, conducteur, comptable)* good; *(→ politique)* fine, good; **b. père et b. époux** a good father and husband; **comme toute bonne journaliste, elle ne veut pas révéler ses sources** like all good journalists, she's not prepared to name her sources; **en b. professeur, il me reprend lorsque je fais des fautes** he corrects my mistakes, as any good teacher would; **être/ne pas être b. en musique** to be good/bad at music; **nos bons clients** our good *or* regular customers

6 b. à *(digne de)* **les poires/piles sont bonnes à jeter** the pears/batteries can go straight in the *Br* bin *or Am* trash can; **la table est tout juste bonne à faire du petit bois** the table is only good for firewood; **je ne suis bonne qu'à repasser tes chemises!** I'm only fit to iron your shirts!; **tu n'es b. qu'à critiquer!** all you ever do is criticize!; **il y a un restaurant là-bas – c'est b. à savoir** there's a restaurant there – that's worth knowing *or* good to know; **à quoi b.?** what for?; **à quoi b. insister** there's no point in insisting; **je pourrais lui écrire, mais à quoi b.?** I could write to him/her, but what would be the point?

7 *(condamné à)* **il est b. pour 15 ans (de prison)** he's going to get 15 years in prison; **je suis bonne pour recommencer** I'll have to do it (all over) again; *Mil* **b. pour le service** fit for (national) service; *Fam* **on est bons pour une amende** we stand to get a fine; *Fam* **les motards nous suivent – on est bons!** the cops are following us – we've had it *or* we're in for it!

B. *PLAISANT* **1** *(pour les sens)* good, nice; **ton ragoût était très b.** your casserole was very good *or* nice; **il y a une bonne odeur de café ici** there's a nice smell of coffee in here; **avoir une bonne odeur** to smell good *or* nice; **viens te baigner, l'eau est bonne!** come for a swim, the water's lovely and warm!; **elle est bonne?** *(l'eau)* what's the water like?

2 *(atmosphère, compagnie, semaine)* good, nice, pleasant; **c'est si b. de ne rien faire!** it feels so good to be doing nothing!; **je me souviens des bons moments** I remember the good *or* happy times; **vous avez passé un b. Noël?** did you enjoy your Christmas?, did you have a good *or* nice Christmas?; **b. anniversaire!** happy birthday!; **bonne (et heureuse) année!** happy New Year!; **b. appétit!**, *Fam* **b. app'!** enjoy your meal!, *Am* enjoy!; **bonne chance!** good luck!; **bonne journée!** have a nice day!; **b. voyage!** *(plaisant)* have a nice *or* good trip!; *(sans incident)* have a safe journey!; **passe une bonne soirée** enjoy yourself (tonight)

3 *(en intensif)* **un b. grog bien chaud** a nice hot toddy; **b. vieux, bonne vieille** good old; **les bonnes vieilles méthodes** the good old methods; **elle est bien bonne celle-là!** that's a good one (that)!; *Ironique* that's a bit much!; **prendre** *ou* **se donner** *ou* **se payer du b. temps** to have fun, to have a great *or* good time; **c'était le b. temps!** those were the (good old) days!; **le b. vieux temps** the good old days

4 *(favorable, optimiste → prévisions, présage)* good, favourable; *(→ nouvelle)* good; **c'est (un) b. signe** it's a good sign; **la météo est bonne** the weather forecast is good

C. *JUSTE, ADÉQUAT* **1** *(correct → numéro de téléphone)* right; *(→ réponse, solution)* correct, right; **c'est la bonne rue** it's the right street

2 *(opportun)* right, convenient, appropriate; **ce n'est pas la bonne époque** it isn't the right time; **l'héritage est arrivé au b. moment pour elle** the inheritance came at the right time *or* at a convenient time for her; **je suis arrivé au b. moment pour les séparer** I got there in time to separate them; **ce n'est pas le b. jour pour demander une augmentation** it's not the right day *or* an appropriate moment to ask for a pay rise; **ayez le b. geste** *(en sauvetage)* do the right thing; *(honnête)* do the decent thing; **tout lui est b. pour se faire remarquer** he'll/she'll stop at nothing to attract attention; **juger** *ou* **trouver b. de** to think it appropriate *or* fitting to; **elle n'a pas jugé b. de s'excuser** she didn't see fit to apologize; **juger** *ou* **trouver b. que** to think it appropriate *or* fitting that; **il n'est pas toujours b. de dire ce que l'on pense** it's not always a good *or* wise thing to say what's on one's mind; **il serait b. de préciser l'heure de la réunion** it would be a good idea to say what time the meeting is; **il est b. qu'un bébé dorme l'après-midi** a baby should sleep in the afternoon; **il ne serait pas b. que l'on nous voie ensemble** it wouldn't be a good thing for us to be seen together; **il serait b. que tu te fasses oublier** you'd do well to keep *or* you'd better keep a low profile; **comme/où/quand/si b. vous semble** as/wherever/whenever/if you see fit

3 *(bénéfique, salutaire)* good, beneficial; **c'est b. pour les plantes** it's good for the plants; **c'est b. contre** *ou* **pour le mal de mer** it's good for seasickness; **b. pour la santé** good for you, good for your health; **le b. air de la campagne** the good *or* fresh country air; **attention, le virage n'est pas b.!** careful, this bend's nasty *or* dangerous!

4 *Fam (locutions)* **c'est b.!** *(c'est juste)* that's right!; *(ça suffit)* that'll do!; *(c'est d'accord)* OK!; **c'est b., c'est b., je m'en occupe!** OK, OK, I'll do it!; **c'est b.?** OK?

D. *MORALEMENT* **1** *(décent, honnête → conduite)* good, proper; *(→ influence, mœurs)* good; **avoir de bonnes lectures** to read the right kind of books; **avoir de bonnes fréquentations** to mix with the right sort of people; **ils n'ont pas bonne réputation** they don't have a good reputation; **un b. Français n'aurait pas accepté la défaite** a good *or* proper Frenchman wouldn't have admitted defeat

2 *(bienveillant, amical → personne)* good, kind, kindly; *(→ sourire)* kind, warm; *Rel* **Dieu est b.** God is merciful; **avoir une bonne tête** *ou Fam* **bouille** to have a nice *or* a friendly face; **son frère a une bonne tête** her brother looks nice; **avoir l'air b.** to look kind *or* kindly; **je suis déjà bien b. de te prêter ma voiture!** it's kind *or* decent enough of me to lend you my car as it is!; *Fam* **dites-lui plein de bonnes choses de ma part** give him/her my love; **avoir de bons rapports avec qn** to be on good terms with sb; **avoir b. cœur** to be kind-hearted; **de b. cœur** willingly; **tenez, prenez, c'est de b. cœur** please have it, I'd love you to; **à votre b. cœur, Messieurs-Dames, à vot' b. cœur M'sieurs-Dames** spare some change, ladies and gents?; **le B. Dieu** the (good) Lord

3 *(brave)* good; **c'est un b. garçon** he's a good lad *or* sort; **c'est une bonne petite** she's a nice *or* good girl; **et en plus ils boivent, mon b. Monsieur!** and what's more they drink, my dear man!; **alors ma bonne dame, qu'est-ce qu'il vous faut aujourd'hui?** well, madam, what do you need today?

E. *EN INTENSIF* **1** *(grand, gros)* good; **un b. mètre de tissu** at least one metre *or* a good metre of material; **une bonne averse** a heavy shower (of rain); **une bonne tranche** a thick slice; **donnez-moi une bonne livre de raisin** give me a pound of grapes or a little over; **elle fait un b. 42** she's a 42 or a 44, she's a large 42; **ça a duré une bonne minute** it lasted a good minute or so; **une bonne cuillère à soupe de farine** a heaped tablespoon *or* tablespoonful of flour

2 *(fort, violent)* **un b. coup** *(heurt)* a hefty *or* full blow; **un b. coup de pied** a powerful kick; **un b. coup de bâton** a mighty crack with a stick; **une bonne fessée** a good *or* sound spanking; *Fam* **pleurer un b. coup** to have a good cry; *Fam* **en prendre un b. coup** to get a real hammering

3 *(complet, exemplaire)* good; **le mur a besoin d'un b. lessivage** the wall needs a good scrub; **arriver** *ou* **être b. deuxième** to finish a strong second; **arriver** *ou* **être b. dernier** to bring up the rear; **une bonne fois pour toutes** once and for all

ADJ F *Fam (belle)* gorgeous, stunning, *Br* fit; **elle est bonne, la sœur à Frédo** Frédo's sister is a real babe *or Br* cracker

NM,F 1 *(personne vertueuse)* good person; **les bons** the good

2 *(personne idéale, chose souhaitée)* right one; *Fam* **je crois que c'est enfin le b.** *(lors d'un recrutement)* I think we've got our man at last; *(lors d'une rencontre amoureuse)* I think it's Mr Right at last; **je ferai toutes les agences jusqu'à ce que je trouve la bonne** I'll visit all the agencies until I find the right one

3 *(personne, chose de qualité)* **c'est un b./une bonne!** he's/she's good!; **on m'en soumet beaucoup mais je ne publie que les bons** I get a lot of them sent to me but I only publish the good ones

4 *(par affection)* **mon b.** *(à un jeune homme)* my dear boy; *(à un homme mûr)* my dear man; **ma bonne** *(à une jeune femme)* my dear girl; *(à une femme mûre)* my dear; **mais mon b./ma bonne, personne ne dit le contraire!** but my dear man/woman, nobody's saying anything different!

NM 1 *Cin (dans les films)* goody, goodie; **jouer le rôle du b.** to play the good guy; **les bons et les méchants** the goodies and the baddies, the good guys and the bad guys

2 *(chose de qualité)* **n'acheter que du b.** to buy only good quality; **il y a du b. dans votre dissertation** there are some good points in your essay; **il y a du b. et du mauvais dans ses propositions** his/her proposals have some good points *or* their merits; **avoir du b.** to have something good about it; **cette solution a cela de b. qu'elle est moins chère que les autres** this solution is interesting insofar as it is less expensive than the others

3 *(ce qui est moral)* **le b.** good

4 *(ce qui est plaisant)* **le b. de l'histoire, c'est que...** the funniest *or* best part of the story is that...

5 *(coupon)* voucher, coupon; **b. d'achat** discount voucher *(for future purchases)*; **b. de caisse** cash voucher; *Compta* interest-bearing note; **b. de commande** order form, purchase order; **b. à délivrer** freight release; **b. d'expédition** dispatch note, consignment note; *Anciennement* **b. pour francs** *(sur chèque)* = letters printed on cheque before amount to be written in figures; **b. de garantie** guarantee, guarantee slip; **b. de livraison** delivery note; *Fin* **b. à moyen terme négociable** medium term note; **b. de petite caisse** petty cash voucher; **b. de réduction** money-off coupon *or* voucher; **b. de remboursement** money-off voucher

6 *Bourse* **b. d'épargne** savings bond *or* certificate; **b. nominatif** registered bond; **b. de participation** participation certificate; **b. au porteur** bearer bond; **b. de souscription d'actions** equity *or* subscription warrant; **b. de souscription de parts de créateurs d'entreprise** = stock option in start-up company with tax privileges; **b. du Trésor** Treasury bill; *(obligation à terme)* Treasury bond

ADV 1 *Météo* **il fait b. ici** it's nice and warm here; **il fait b. ce soir** it's a nice evening

2 *(suivi d'un infinitif)* **il ne fait pas b. la déranger** you'll be ill-advised to disturb her; **il ne fait pas b. se promener seul dans les rues** walking the streets alone is not to be recommended; **il ne faisait pas b. être communiste alors** it wasn't advisable to be a communist in those days

EXCLAM 1 *(marque une transition)* right, so, well now; **b., eh bien je m'en vais** right, I'm off now; **b., où en étais-je?** right *or* so, where was I?

2 *(en réponse)* right, OK, fine; **je n'ai vraiment pas le temps – b., b., j'irai seul!** I really don't have the time – all right, all right, I'll go on my own then!; **sors d'ici! – b., b., c'est pas la peine de crier!** get out of here! – OK, OK, no need to shout!

□ **bon à rien, bonne à rien ADJ 1** *(inutile)* **je suis trop vieux, je ne suis plus b. à rien** I'm too old, I'm useless *or* no good now **2** *(incompétent)* useless, hopeless **NM,F** *(personne sans*

valeur) good-for-nothing; (*personne incompétente*) useless individual

❑ **bon à tirer** NM press proof, final corrected proof; **donner le b. à tirer** to pass for press

❑ **bonne femme** NF *Fam* **1** (*femme*) woman▪ ; **une vieille bonne femme** an old biddy **2** (*petite fille*) **une petite bonne femme adorable** a lovely little girl **3** (*épouse*) wife▪ , *Br* missus ADJ **1** *Culin* = cooking term used in the names of simple country dishes **2** *Couture* **des rideaux bonne femme** = old-fashioned curtains with tie-backs and frilled edges

❑ **bonnes feuilles** NFPL (*dans l'édition*) press proofs, final corrected proofs

═══ 🎭 ═══

'La Bonne âme de Setchouan' *Brecht* 'The Good Woman of Setzuan'

═══ 🎬 ═══

'Le Bon, la brute et le truand' *Leone* 'The Good, the Bad and the Ugly'

bonance [bɔnas] NF *Naut* lull, calm (*before or after a storm*)

bonamia [bɔnamja] NF *Zool* (*parasite de l'huître*) Bonamia ostreae

Bonaparte [bɔnapart] NPR Bonaparte

bonapartism [bɔnapartism] NM Bonapartism

bonapartiste [bɔnapartist] ADJ Bonapartist NMF Bonapartist

bonasse [bɔnas] ADJ *Péj* too easy-going, soft; **répondre d'un ton b.** to answer mildly

bonasserie [bɔnasri] NF *Littéraire Péj* **faire preuve de b.** to be too easy-going

bonbon [bɔ̃bɔ̃] NM **1** (*sucrerie*) *Br* sweet, *Am* candy; **b. acidulé** acid drop; **b. anglais** fruit drop; **b. à la menthe** mint **2** *Belg* (*biscuit*) *Br* biscuit, *Am* cookie **3** *très Fam* **casser les bonbons à qn** to piss sb off, *Br* to get on sb's tits, *Am* to break sb's balls

ADV *Fam* **coûter b.** to cost an arm and a leg *or* the earth *or Br* a bomb

bonbonne [bɔ̃bɔn] NF (*pour le vin*) demijohn; (*pour des produits chimiques*) carboy; **b. de gaz** gas canister

bonbonnière [bɔ̃bɔnjɛr] NF **1** (*boîte*) *Br* sweet *or Am* candy box **2** (*appartement*) bijou *Br* flat *or Am* apartment

bon-chrétien [bɔ̃kretjɛ̃] (*pl* **bons-chrétiens**) NM (*poire*) William's (Bon Chrétien) pear

bond [bɔ̃] NM **1** (*d'une balle*) bounce; **prendre** *ou* **saisir l'occasion au b.** to seize the opportunity; **prendre** *ou* **saisir une remarque au b.** to pounce on a remark; **prendre** *ou* **saisir la balle au b.** to catch the ball on the bounce *or* re-bound; *Fig* to seize the opportunity

2 (*saut*) jump, leap; **faire un b.** (*d'effroi, de surprise*) to leap up; **faire des bonds** to jump up and down; *Fig* to go up and down; **faire un b. en avant** (*économie*) to boom; (*prix, loyer*) to soar; (*recherche*) to leap forward; **je n'ai fait qu'un b. jusqu'à chez vous quand j'ai su la nouvelle** I rushed round to your place as soon as I heard the news; **se lever d'un b.** to leap up; **franchir un ruisseau d'un b.** to clear a stream at one jump, to leap across a stream; **avancer** *ou* **progresser par bonds** to come on *or* to progress in leaps and bounds; *Hist* **le grand b. en avant** the Great Leap Forward

3 *Sport* jump; **il a remporté l'épreuve avec un b. de 2,03 m** he won the competition with a jump of 2.03 m

4 (*locution*) **faire faux b. à qn** (*ne pas se présenter*) to leave sb high and dry; (*décevoir*) to let sb down; **demain à 11 heures, je vous fais faux b.** tomorrow at 11 I'll have to love you and leave you

bonde [bɔ̃d] NF **1** (*ouverture* → *d'un tonneau*) bunghole; (→ *d'un lavabo*) plughole **2** (*système de fermeture* → *d'un tonneau*) bung, stopper; (→ *d'un lavabo*) plug; (→ *d'un bassin*) sluice gate

bondé, -e [bɔ̃de] ADJ packed, jam-packed; **le train était b.** the train was packed (with people)

bondelle [bɔ̃dɛl] NF *Suisse Ich* = type of whitefish found in Lake Neuchâtel

bondérisation [bɔ̃derizasjɔ̃] NF *Métal* bonderization, bonderizing

bondérisé, -e [bɔ̃derize] ADJ *Métal* bonderized

bondériser [3] [bɔ̃derize] VT *Métal* to bonderize

bondieusard, -e [bɔ̃djøzar, -ard] *Fam Péj* ADJ churchy, sanctimonious▪

NM,F sanctimonious person▪ , holy Joe

bondieuserie [bɔ̃djøzri] NF *Fam Péj* **1** (*objet*) religious trinket▪ **2** (*bigoterie*) religiosity▪

bondir [32] [bɔ̃dir] VI **1** (*sauter*) to bounce, to bound, to leap (up); **le chat bondit sur la souris** the cat pounced *or* leapt on the mouse; **la moto bondit en avant** the motorbike leapt forward; **b. de joie** to leap for joy; **b. sur** (*pour importuner, semoncer*) to pounce on; **pareille inconscience me fait b.** such recklessness makes my blood boil; **ça va le faire b.** (*d'indignation, de colère*) he'll hit the roof, he'll go mad

2 (*courir*) to dash, to rush; **quand il a appris l'accident, il a bondi jusqu'à l'hôpital/chez elle** when he heard about the accident, he rushed (over) to the hospital/her place

bondissant, -e [bɔ̃disɑ̃, -ɑ̃t] ADJ leaping, bounding

bondissement [bɔ̃dismɑ̃] NM *Littéraire* (*d'un poulain*) bouncing, bounding; (*d'un agneau*) gambolling

bondon [bɔ̃dɔ̃] NM (*bonde*) bung

bondrée [bɔ̃dre] NF *Orn* **b. apivore** honey buzzard

bon enfant [bɔnɑ̃fɑ̃] ADJ INV (*caractère, personne*) good-natured, easy-going; (*atmosphère*) relaxed, informal

bongo [bɔ̃go] NM **1** *Zool* (*antilope*) bongo **2** *Mus* bongo (drum)

bonheur [bɔnœr] NM **1** (*chance*) luck; **par b.** fortunately, luckily; **avoir le b. de faire qch** to be lucky enough *or* to have the good fortune to do sth; **j'ai eu le b. de la connaître** I was lucky enough to know her; **tu ne connais pas ton b.!** you don't know when you're lucky *or* how lucky you are!; **jouer de b.** to have a lucky run; **porter b. à qn** to bring sb luck; **ça ne lui a pas porté b.!** he lived to regret it!, he had cause to bemoan the fact later!; **ça ne te portera pas b.!** don't think you'll get away with it!

2 (*contentement*) happiness; **quel b. de vous revoir!** how marvellous to see you again!; **b. total** bliss; **connaître le b.** to know what it's like to be happy, to experience happiness; **faire le b. de qn** (*le contenter*) to make sb happy, to bring sb happiness; **si cette robe peut faire ton b., prends-la** if this dress is any good *or* use to you, then take it; **trouver le b.** to find happiness; **as-tu trouvé ton b.?** did you find what you were looking for?

❑ **au petit bonheur (la chance)** ADV haphazardly

❑ **avec bonheur** ADV *Littéraire* **le salé et le sucré s'allient avec b.** savoury and sweet combine happily *or* are a happy combination; **il fait revivre avec b. la comédie musicale** he has breathed new life into musical comedy

bonheur-du-jour [bɔnœrdyʒur] (*pl* **bonheurs-du-jour**) NM escritoire, writing table

bonhomie [bɔnɔmi] NF geniality, bonhomie; **avec b.** good-naturedly

bonhomme [bɔnɔm] (*pl* **bonshommes** [bɔ̃zɔm]) *Fam* NM **1** (*homme*) fellow, *Br* chap; **un grand b.** a (great) big man; **un sale b.** a nasty piece of work

2 (*partenaire*) old man, *Vieilli* fellow; (*garçon*) lad; **allez viens, mon petit b.** come along, little man

3 (*figure*) man; **dessiner des bonshommes** to draw little men *or* people; *Can* **b. Carnaval** = jolly snowman character, symbol of the Quebec winter carnival; *Suisse* **B. Hiver** = effigy symbolizing winter that is paraded through the streets and burnt during the ''Brandons'' festival; **b. de neige** snowman; **le b. Noël** Father Christmas, Santa Claus; **b. de pain d'épice** gingerbread man; *Can* **b. Sept Heures** *Br* bogeyman, *Am* boogie man; *Can* **vas au b.!** go to blazes!

4 (*locutions*) **aller** *ou* **suivre son petit b. de chemin** to go *or* to carry on at one's own pace; **l'idée faisait son petit b. de chemin** the idea was slowly but surely gaining ground

ADJ (*air, caractère*) good-natured, good-tempered; (*atmosphère*) relaxed, informal; **..., dit-il d'un ton b.** ..., he said good-naturedly

boni [bɔni] NM *Com* **1** (*bénéfice*) profit; **faire un** *ou*

du b. to make a profit; **b. de liquidation** liquidation surplus **2** (*dépense*) balance in hand **3** (*bonus, prime*) bonus

boniche [bɔniʃ] = **bonniche**

bonichon [bɔniʃɔ̃] NM *Fam* woman's cap

Boniface [bɔnifas] NPR *Rel* Boniface

bonification [bɔnifikasjɔ̃] NF **1** *Agr* improvement **2** *Sport* bonus points; (*en cyclisme*) time bonus **3** (*somme allouée*) profit **4** (*rabais*) discount, reduction **5** (*prime*) bonus **6** *Écon* **b. d'intérêts** interest relief

bonifié, -e [bɔnifie] ADJ **1** *Agr* improved **2** *Banque* (*prêt*) soft, at a reduced rate of interest; *Fin* (*taux*) reduced

bonifier [9] [bɔnifje] VT **1** *Agr* to improve **2** (*adoucir* → *caractère*) to improve, to mellow **3** (*payer*) to pay as a bonus **4** *Écon* to credit

▸**se bonifier** VPR **1** (*vin*) to improve **2** (*caractère*) to mellow, to improve

boniment [bɔnimɑ̃] NM **1** *Com* sales talk *or* patter; **faire du** *ou* **son b.** to deliver the sales patter *or* spiel; *Fam* **faire du b. à qn** (*pour convaincre*) to sweet-talk sb; (*pour séduire*) *Br* to chat sb up, *Am* to hit on sb **2** *Fam* (*mensonge*) tall story; **tout ça, c'est des boniments** that's a load of claptrap *or* guff; **arrête tes boniments** stop fibbing

bonimenter [3] [bɔnimɑ̃te] VI *Fam* to deliver the sales talk *or* the patter

bonimenteur, -euse [bɔnimɑ̃tœr, -øz] NM,F *Péj* (*menteur*) smooth talker

bonite [bɔnit] NF *Ich* bonito; **b. à dos rayé** Atlantic bonito; **b. à ventre rayé** skipjack tuna

bonitou [bɔnitu] NM *Ich* frigate mackerel

bonjour [bɔ̃ʒur] NM **1** (*salutation* → *gén*) hello; (→ *le matin*) good morning; (→ *l'après-midi*) good afternoon; *Can* (*au revoir* → *pendant la journée*) goodbye, bye, see you later; **b., comment allez-vous?** hello, how are you?; **va dire b. à la dame** go and say hello to the lady; **vous lui donnerez le b.** *ou* **vous lui direz b. de ma part** say hello for me; **vous avez le b. de Martin** Martin sends his love; **bien le b. chez vous** regards to everybody (back home); *Fam* **t'as le b. d'Alfred!** get lost!

2 *Fam* (*exprime la difficulté*) **pour le faire aller à l'école, b.!** no way can you get him to go to school!; **je n'ai pas fait de gym depuis un mois, b. les courbatures!** I haven't done any exercise for a month, I'm going to ache, let me tell you!; **b. l'odeur! what a smell!**▪ ; **si mes parents l'apprennent, b. l'ambiance!** if my parents find out, there'll be one hell of an atmosphere!; **b. la liberté d'expression!** so much for freedom of expression!; **b. les dégâts!** what a mess!; (*ça va aller mal*) there'll be trouble!

Allusion

Chers amis, bonjour!

With this catchphrase, Lucien Jeunesse, radio game show host, introduced *Le Jeu des 1000 francs*, one of the longest-running French radio programmes and still going strong – albeit with a new host and the updated title *Le Jeu des 1000 euros*. A cheery greeting to all and sundry, it is still used today by anyone coming into a bar or café and seeing familiar friends.

Allusion

Bonjour les dégâts

This was originally part of a slogan in a "don't drink and drive" campaign (the full slogan was **Un verre ça va! deux verres, bonjour les dégâts!** "One drink is fine, two means a mess!"). The shorter phrase is used today as a comment on any disastrous situation, whether used seriously or ironically.

bon marché [bɔ̃marʃe] ADJ INV cheap, inexpensive

Bonn [bɔn] NM *Géog* Bonn

bonnard [bɔnar] ADJ *Fam* great, *Am* neat; (*personne*) nice▪

bonne² [bɔn] ADJ *voir* bon

NF **1** (*domestique*) maid; **b. d'enfants** nanny, nursemaid; **b. à tout faire** servant, maid of all work; **c'est moi la b. à tout faire ici** I'm the servant around here

2 *Fam* (*chose plaisante*) **je vais t'en raconter une b.** I've got a good one for you; **il m'en a dit** *ou* **raconté une bien b.** he told me a good one

3 *(locutions)* **avoir qn à la b.** to like sb, *Am* to be in (solid) with sb; **le patron m'a à la b.!** I'm in the boss's good books!, the boss likes me!; **la petite Julie t'a à la b.!** Julie's really sweet on you!; **il prend tout à la b.** *(sans façons)* he takes things as they come; *(avec optimisme)* he always looks on the bright side; **tu en as de bonnes!** are you kidding?

'Les Bonnes' *Genet* 'The Maids'

Bonne-Espérance [bɔnɛsperɑ̃s] *voir* **cap**[1]

bonne-main [bɔnmɛ̃] (*pl* **bonnes-mains**) **NF** *Suisse* tip

bonne-maman [bɔnmamɑ̃] (*pl* **bonnes-mamans**) **NF** *Vieilli* grand-mama

bonnement [bɔnmɑ̃] **ADV tout b.** (quite) simply; **je lui ai dit tout b. ce que je pensais** I quite simply told him what I thought

bonnet [bɔnɛ] **NM 1** *(coiffe → de femme, d'enfant)* hat, bonnet; *(→ de soldat, de marin)* hat; **gros b.** bigshot, bigwig; **b. d'âne** dunce's cap; **b. de bain** swimming cap; **b. de douche** shower cap; *Fig* **b. d'évêque** parson's nose; **b. de nuit** nightcap; *Fig Péj* wet blanket; **b. à poils** busby, bearskin; *Vieilli* **b. de police** forage cap; **b. phrygien** cap of liberty, Phrygian cap; **b. de ski** ski cap; **c'est b. blanc et blanc b.** it's six of one and half a dozen of the other, *Br* it's all much of a muchness; **jeter son b. par-dessus les moulins** to throw caution to the winds; **parler à son b.** to talk to oneself; **prendre qch sous son b.** to take the initiative of doing sth; **il a pris sous son b. de le faire** he did it off his own bat; *Fam* **te casse pas le b.!** don't worry about it!▪, don't let it bother you!▪; *Fam* **se monter le b.** to get worked *or* het up

2 *Zool* reticulum

3 *(d'un soutien-gorge)* cup; **quelle profondeur de b.?** what cup size?

bonnet-de-prêtre [bɔnɛdəprɛtr] (*pl* **bonnets-de-prêtre**) **NM** *(pâtisson)* pattypan squash

bonneteau, -x [bɔnto] **NM** *Cartes* three-card trick

bonneterie [bɔnɛtri] **NF 1** *(commerce)* hosiery business *or* trade **2** *(industrie)* hosiery-making (industry) **3** *(magasin)* hosier's (shop) **4** *(articles)* hosiery

bonneteur [bɔntœr] **NM** *Cartes* three-card trick player

bonnetier, -ère [bɔntje, -ɛr] **NM,F 1** *(fabricant)* hosier **2** *(ouvrier)* hosiery worker

bonnetière [bɔntjɛr] **NF** *Arch* linen cupboard

bonnette [bɔnɛt] **NF** *Tech (objectif)* positive supplementary lens; **b. (anti-vent)** *(d'un microphone)* windscreen, windshield

bonniche [bɔniʃ] **NF** *Fam Péj* maid▪, *Br* skivvy; **faire la b.** to do all the dirty work, *Br* to skivvy; **je ne suis pas ta b.!** I'm not here to clean up your mess!

Bonnot [bɔno] *voir* **bande**

bonobo [bɔnɔbɔ] **NM** *Zool* bonobo

bon-papa [bɔ̃papa] (*pl* **bons-papas**) **NM** *Vieilli* grand-papa

bonsaï [bɔnzaj] **NM** *Hort* bonsai

bonshommes [bɔ̃zɔm] *voir* **bonhomme**

bonsoir [bɔ̃swar] **NM 1** *(en arrivant → le soir)* good evening; *(en partant → le soir)* good night; *Can (en partant → le soir)* goodbye; **viens dire b. à maman** come and say good night to mummy; **je vous souhaite le b.** I wish you a good night

2 *Fam Vieilli (exprime la difficulté)* **pour lui faire faire le ménage, b.!** no way can you get him to help around the house!; **ils sont efficaces, mais pour ce qui est de l'amabilité, b.!** they're efficient, but they're hardly the friendliest people in the world; **mais b. (de b.), où est-il passé?** where on earth has he got to now?

bonté [bɔ̃te] **NF** *(bienveillance)* kindness, goodness; **une femme d'une grande b.** a very kind *or* good woman; **un sourire plein de b.** a kind(ly) *or* benevolent smile; **elle l'a fait par pure b. d'âme** she did it out of the goodness of her heart; **il a eu la b. de passer nous voir** he was kind enough to come for a visit; **ayez la b. de...** please be so kind as to...; **b. divine!, b. du ciel!** good gracious!

❑ **bontés NFPL** *Littéraire* kindness, kindnesses; **comment vous remercier de toutes vos bontés?** how could I thank you for your kindness *or* kindnesses?; *Euph* **avoir des bontés pour qn** to bestow one's favours on sb

bonus [bɔnys] **NM 1** *Assur* no-claims bonus **2** *Mktg* bonus; **b. produit** product bonus **3** *(sur un DVD)* special feature **4** *Fig* bonus

bonus-malus [bɔnysmalys] **NM INV** *Assur* no-claims bonus system

bonze [bɔ̃z] **NM 1** *Rel* Buddhist monk, bonze **2** *Fam Fig Péj* big cheese; **un vieux b.** a pompous old fool

bonzerie [bɔ̃zri] **NF** *Rel* Buddhist monastery

bonzesse [bɔ̃zɛs] **NF** *Rel* Buddhist nun

boogie-woogie [bugiwugi] **NM** *Mus & (danse)* boogie-woogie

book [buk] **NM** pressbook, portfolio

booké, -e [buke] **ADJ** *Fam* booked-up, busy▪

bookmaker [bukmɛkœr] **NM** bookmaker

bookmark [bukmark] **NM** *Ordinat* bookmark

booléen, -enne [buleɛ̃, -ɛn], **boolien, -enne** [buljɛ̃, -ɛn] **ADJ** *Math & Ordinat* Boolean; *Ordinat* **opérateurs booléens** Boolean operators

boom [bum] **NM 1** *(développement)* boom, expansion; **il y a eu un b. sur les actions des sociétés privatisées** the shares of the privatized companies boomed; **le b. de la natalité** the baby boom; **le b. des fours à micro-ondes** the booming microwave oven market **2** *Bourse* boom

boomer [bumœr] **NM** *(haut-parleur)* woofer

boomerang [bumrɑ̃g] **NM** *(arme, jeu)* boomerang; *Fig* **faire b., avoir un effet b.** to boomerang

booster[1] [bustœr] **NM 1** *(d'une fusée)* booster **2** *(d'une radio, du son)* booster

booster[2] [3] [buste] **VT** *Fam (stimuler)* to boost

booter [3] [bute] **VI** *Ordinat* **b. (sur le lecteur B)** to boot (off the B drive)

bootlegger [butlɛgœr] **NM** *Hist* bootlegger

boots [buts] **NMPL OU NFPL** (desert) boots

bop [bɔp] **NM** *Mus & (danse)* = in France, the favoured dance of the "rats de cave" in Saint-Germain cellar nightclubs in the late 1940s and 1950s

boqueteau, -x [bɔkto] **NM** coppice, copse

bora [bɔra] **NF** bora

Bora Bora [bɔrabɔra] **NF** *Géog* Bora Bora

boraginacées [bɔraʒinase] = **borraginacées**

borain, -e [bɔrɛ̃, -ɛn] = **borin**

borane [bɔran] **NM** *Chim* borane

borasse [bɔras], **borassus** [bɔrasys] **NM** *Bot* borassus

borate [bɔrat] **NM** *Chim* borate

boraté, -e [bɔrate] **ADJ** *Chim* borated

borax [bɔraks] **NM** *Chim* borax, tincal

borborygme [bɔrbɔrigm] **NM 1** *(gargouillement)* rumble, gurgle, *Spéc* borborygmus **2** *Péj (paroles)* **borborygmes** mumbling

borchtch [bɔrtʃ] = **bortsch**

bord [bɔr] **NM 1** *(côté → d'une forêt, d'un domaine)* edge; *(→ d'une route)* side; **sur le b. de** on the edge of; **dessine sur le b. de ta feuille** draw on the edge of your paper; **sur le b. de la route** by the roadside; **sur le b. de la Seine** on the embankment (in Paris), next to the Seine; **sur les bords du fleuve** *(gén)* on the river bank; *(en ville)* on the waterfront; **sur les bords de Seine** on the embankment (in Paris), on the banks of the Seine; **regagner le b.** *(de la mer)* to get back to the shore *or* beach; *(d'une rivière)* to get back to the bank; *(d'une piscine)* to get back to the side; **le b. du trottoir** the kerb; **le b. de mer** the seafront; *Ordinat* **b. de reliure** inside margin; *Can* **l'autre b.** *(outre-Atlantique)* Europe

2 *(pourtour → d'une plaie)* edge; *(→ d'une assiette, d'une baignoire)* rim, edge; *(→ d'un verre)* rim; **remplir un verre jusqu'au b.** to fill a glass to the brim *or* to the top

3 *Couture (non travaillé)* edge; *(replié et cousu)* hem; *(décoratif)* border; **chapeau à larges bords** wide-brimmed *or* broad-brimmed hat; **b. ourlé/festonné** rolled/festooned hem

4 *Naut (côté, bastingage)* side; **jeter qch/tomber par-dessus b.** to throw sth/to fall overboard; **tirer des bords** to tack; **les hommes du b.** the crew; **prendre qn à son b.** to take sb on board *or* aboard

5 *(opinion)* side; **nous sommes du même b.** we're on the same side; *Can Pol* **être du bon b.** to be on the side of the majority; *Can Pol* **voter du bon b.** to vote for the winning side

6 *Can Fam* **prendre le b.** *(être éliminé)* to get the chop *or* the push; *(disparaître)* to fall by the wayside; **elle a pris le b. car son patron n'était pas satisfait de son travail** she got the chop because her boss wasn't happy with her work; **les valeurs humaines ont pris le b.** human values have fallen by the wayside

❑ **à bord ADV** *Aut* on board; *Aviat & Naut* aboard, on board; **il y avait toute une famille à b.** there was an entire family on board *or* in the vehicle; **avant de monter à b.** before boarding *or* going aboard; **assurez-vous que vous n'oubliez rien à b.** make sure you do not leave any of your belongings on board; **être seul maître à b.** to be the one in charge

❑ **à bord de PRÉP** on board; **à b. d'un navire/d'une voiture** on board a ship/car; **monter à b. d'un bateau/avion** to board a boat/plane

❑ **au bord de PRÉP 1** *(en bordure de)* **une maison au b. de la mer** a house by the sea, a seaside house; **se promener au b. de l'eau/la mer** to walk at the water's edge/the seaside; **aller au b. de la mer** to go to the seaside; **je l'ai trouvé au b. de la rivière** I found it on the river bank; **s'arrêter au b. de la route** to stop by the roadside

2 *(à la limite de)* on the brink *or* verge of, very close to; **au b. des larmes/de la dépression** on the verge of tears/of a nervous breakdown; **au b. de la défaillance** very close to fainting; **être au b. de l'abîme** to be on the verge of ruin; **il est au b. de la tombe** he's got one foot in the grave

❑ **bord à bord ADV** edge to edge

❑ **de bord ADJ** *(journal, livre, commandant)* ship's

❑ **de haut bord ADJ** rated

❑ **sur les bords ADV** slightly, a touch; **il est un peu radin sur les bords** he's a bit tight-fisted

bordage [bɔrdaʒ] **NM 1** *Couture* edging **2** *Naut (en bois)* planking; *(en métal)* plating

borde [bɔrd] **NF** *Hist* = small farm in the south-west of France

bordé [bɔrde] **NM 1** *Naut (en bois)* planking; *(en fer)* plating **2** *Couture* (piece of) trimming

Bordeaux [bɔrdo] **NM** Bordeaux; **B. métropole** = syndicate of local authorities in the Bordeaux area

bordeaux [bɔrdo] **ADJ INV** *(grenat)* burgundy *(avant n)*, claret *(avant n)*

NM *(vin)* Bordeaux (wine); **un b. rouge** a red Bordeaux, a claret; **un b. blanc** a white Bordeaux

bordée [bɔrde] **NF 1** *Naut (canons, salve)* broadside; *(distance)* tack; **lâcher une b.** to let fly a broadside; **tirer des bordées** to tack; *Fam Fig* **tirer une b.** to paint the town red; *Fam* **être en b.** to be on a binge **2** *Naut (partie de l'équipage)* watch **3** *Fig (série)* **une b. d'insultes** a torrent *or* stream of abuse **4** *Can* **b. de neige** heavy snowfall; **b. des oiseaux** spring snowfall

bordel [bɔrdɛl] *très Fam* **NM 1** *(hôtel de passe)* brothel, whorehouse, *Arch* bawdy-house

2 *(désordre)* shambles *(singulier)*, mess; **range ton b.!** clean up your (damn) mess!; **c'est toujours un vrai b. chez toi!** your place is always a shambles!; **foutre le b. dans une pièce/réunion** to turn a room into a pigsty/a meeting into a shambles; **ils sont venus foutre le b.** they only came to mess things up; **et tout le b.** and the whole damn lot

3 *(vacarme)* racket; **foutre le b.** to make a hell of a racket

EXCLAM dammit!, hell!; **mais qu'est-ce qu'il fout, b.!** what the bloody hell is he doing?; *Vulg* **b. de merde!** fuck!, fucking hell!

bordelais, -e [bɔrdəlɛ, -ɛz] **ADJ 1** *(de Bordeaux)* of/from Bordeaux **2** *(du Bordelais)* of/from the Bordeaux area

❑ **Bordelais, -e 1 NM,F** = inhabitant of or person from Bordeaux **2 NM le B.** the Bordeaux area

❑ **bordelaise NF** *(bouteille)* Bordeaux bottle; *(futaille)* = cask of about 225 litres

❑ **à la bordelaise ADJ** *Culin* in shallots and red wine

bordélique [bɔrdelik] **ADJ** *très Fam (chambre)* messy; *(écriture, esprit)* chaotic; **c'est plutôt b. chez toi** your place is a total shambles; **il est vraiment b.!** he leaves such a mess everywhere!; **quelle réunion b.!** what a chaotic meeting!

bor-bot

border [3] [bɔʀde] VT **1** *(garnir)* to edge, to trim; **b. qch de** to trim *or* to edge sth with; **un jupon bordé de dentelle** a lace-edged petticoat
  2 *(en se couchant)* **as-tu bien bordé ton lit?** did you tuck the blankets in properly?; **va te coucher, je viendrai te b.** go to bed, I'll come and tuck you in
  3 *(délimiter)* to line; **les troènes qui bordent la clôture** the privet lining the fence; **la route est bordée de haies** the road is lined with hedges
  4 *Naut (de planches)* to plank; *(de tôles)* to plate; *(voile)* to haul on

bordereau, -x [bɔʀdəʀo] NM **1** *Fin & Com* note, slip; *(de marchandises)* invoice, account; *(formulaire)* form; **suivant b. ci-inclus** as per enclosed statement; **b. d'achat** purchase note; *Compta* **b. de caisse** cash statement; **b. de cession de créances professionnelles** transfer deed for the assignment of debt(s); *Compta* **b. de compte** statement of account; **b. Dailly** transfer deed for the assignment of debt(s); **b. de débit** debit note; **b. de dépôt** paying-in slip; **b. de droits** royalty statement; *Banque* **b. d'encaissement** paying-in slip; **b. d'escompte** list of bills for discount; **b. d'expédition** *ou* **d'envoi** dispatch note, consignment note; **b. de livraison** delivery note; **b. (des) prix** price list; *Banque* **b. de remise (d'espèces** *ou* **de chèques)** paying-in slip; *Banque* **b. de retrait** withdrawal slip; *Compta* **b. de saisie** accounting entry sheet; **b. de salaire** salary advice, wages slip; **b. de vente** sales slip; *Banque* **b. de versement** *Br* paying-in slip, *Am* deposit slip
  2 *Jur* **b. des pièces** docket

borderie [bɔʀdœʀi] NF *Hist* = small farm in the south-west of France

borderline [bɔʀdœʀlajn] NM INV *Psy* borderline case

bordier, -ère [bɔʀdje, -ɛʀ] ADJ **1** *Naut* **navire b.** lopsided ship, lopsider **2** *Géog* **mer bordière** epicontinental sea
  NM **1** *Naut* lop-sided ship, lopsider **2** *Suisse (riverain)* local resident

bordigue [bɔʀdig] NF *Pêche* crawl

bordure [bɔʀdyʀ] NF **1** *(bord→ d'un évier)* edge; *(→ d'un verre)* edge, rim; *(→ d'une plate-bande)* border, edge; *(→ d'une cheminée)* *Br* surround, *Am* border; **une b. de trottoir** a *Br* kerb *or Am* curb stone; **la b. du trottoir** *Br* the kerb, *Am* the curb
  2 *(bande décorative)* border; **des assiettes à b. dorée** plates with a gold border *or* edged in gold **3** *(d'un vêtement)* border, edge; *(d'un chapeau)* brim; **foulard à b. bleue** scarf trimmed with blue *or* edged with blue *or* with a blue border
  4 *Typ & Ordinat (d'un paragraphe, d'une cellule)* border
  ◻ **en bordure de** PRÉP **habiter une maison en b. de mer** to live in a house by the sea; **le parc est juste en b. de la ville** the park is on the edge of the town

bordurette [bɔʀdyʀɛt] NF = kerb separating a bus lane from the rest of the roadway

bore [bɔʀ] NM *Chim* boron

boréal, -e, -als *ou* **-aux, -ales** [bɔʀeal, -o] ADJ North *(avant n)*

Borée [bɔʀe] NPR *Myth* Boreas
  ◻ **borée** NM *Littéraire* the North wind

borgne [bɔʀɲ] ADJ **1** *(personne)* one-eyed; **un homme b.** a one-eyed man, a man who's blind in one eye **2** *(fenêtre, mur)* obstructed **3** *(mal fréquenté → hôtel)* shady
  NMF one-eyed person

borie [bɔʀi] NF = small dry-stone Provençal house

borin, -e [bɔʀɛ̃, -in] ADJ of/from the Borinage region of Belgium
  ◻ **Borin, -e** NM,F = inhabitant of or from the Borinage region of Belgium

borique [bɔʀik] ADJ *Chim* boracic, boric; **acide b.** boric acid

boriqué, -e [bɔʀike] ADJ *Pharm* **pommade boriquée** boracic ointment; **compresse en coton b.** boracic lint compress

bornage [bɔʀnaʒ] NM *Jur* boundary marking; **procéder au b. d'un terrain** to mark the boundaries of a plot

borne [bɔʀn] NF **1** *(pour délimiter)* boundary stone, landmark; **b. kilométrique** milepost; **b.**

milliaire (Roman) milestone; **ne reste pas planté là comme une b.!** don't just stand there!
  2 *(point)* *Ordinat* **b. d'accès** *(à Internet)* access point; **b. d'appel d'urgence** emergency call box; **b. d'information** information point; **b. d'incendie** (fire) hydrant, *Am* fireplug; *Ordinat* **b. interactive** *ou* **multimédia** interactive terminal
  3 *(pour marquer un emplacement)* bollard; **b. d'amarrage** bollard
  4 *Fam (kilomètre)* kilometre■; **on a fait les 10 bornes à pied** we walked the 10 kilometres
  5 *Élec* terminal
  6 *Math* bound; **b. inférieure** lower bound; **b. supérieure** upper bound
  7 *Suisse (cheminée)* = large chimney used to smoke pork
  ◻ **bornes** NFPL *Fig* bounds, limits; **sans bornes** *(patience, ambition)* boundless; **faire reculer les bornes de la science** to roll back the frontiers of science; **dépasser** *ou* **passer les bornes** to go too far; **son ambition n'a** *ou* **ne connaît pas de bornes** his/her ambition knows no bounds

borné, -e [bɔʀne] ADJ **1** *(individu)* narrow-minded; *(esprit)* narrow; **tu es vraiment b.** you're so narrow-minded! **2** *Math* bounded

borne-fontaine [bɔʀnfɔ̃tɛn] *(pl* **bornes-fontaines)** NF **1** *(fontaine)* public drinking fountain **2** *Can (bouche d'incendie)* (fire) hydrant, *Am* fireplug

Bornéo [bɔʀneo] NF *Géog* Borneo; **à B.** in Borneo

borner [3] [bɔʀne] VT **1** *(délimiter → champ, terrain)* to mark off *or* out, to mark the boundary of
  2 *(restreindre)* to limit, to restrict
  ► **se borner** VPR **1 se b. à** *(se limiter à)* to be limited *or* restricted to; **son rôle se borne à recevoir les clients** his/her role is limited to welcoming the clients; **nos relations se sont bornées à quelques échanges sur le palier** our relationship was never more than the odd conversation on the landing
  2 se b. à *(se contenter de)* to limit *or* to restrict oneself to; **bornez-vous à l'essentiel** keep to the essentials; **se b. à faire qch** to limit *or* to restrict oneself to doing sth; **je me bornerai à quelques commentaires** I'll just make a few comments; **je me borne à vous mettre en garde** I'm just warning you

Bornholm [bɔʀnɔlm] NM *Géog* Bornholm

bornoyer [13] [bɔʀnwaje] VT *(jalonner)* to stake off, to mark off
  VI *(regarder)* = to look along an edge or surface with one eye closed so as to judge its straightness or levelness

Borodine [bɔʀɔdin] NPR Borodin

borosilicate [bɔʀɔsilikat] NM *Chim* borosilicate

borosilicaté, -e [bɔʀɔsilikate] ADJ *Chim* borosilicate

borough [bɔʀo] NM *Admin* borough

borraginacées [bɔʀaʒinase], **borraginées** [bɔʀaʒine] NFPL *Bot* Borraginaceae

borréliose [bɔʀeljoz] NF *Méd* Lyme disease, Lyme borreliosis

bort [bɔʀt] NM *(diamant)* bort

bortsch [bɔʀtʃ] NM *Culin* borsch, borscht

boruration [bɔʀyʀasjɔ̃] NF *Métal* boriding

borure [bɔʀyʀ] NM *Chim* boride

Bosch [bɔʃ] NPR **Jérôme B.** Hieronymus Bosch

bosco [bɔsko] NM *Fam Naut* bosun■, boatswain■

boscot, -otte [bɔsko, -ɔt] *Vieilli* ADJ hunchbacked
  NM,F hunchback

boskoop [bɔskɔp] NF *Bot (pomme)* Boskoop apple

bosniaque [bɔsnjak] ADJ Bosnian
  ◻ **Bosniaque** NMF Bosnian

Bosnie [bɔsni] NF **la B.** Bosnia

Bosnie-Herzégovine [bɔsnjɛʀzegɔvin] NF **la B.** Bosnia-Herzegovina; **vivre en B.** to live in Bosnia-Herzegovina; **aller en B.** to go to Bosnia-Herzegovina

bosnien, -enne [bɔsnjɛ̃, -ɛn] ADJ Bosnian
  ◻ **Bosnien, -enne** NM,F Bosnian

boson [bɔzɔ̃] NM *Phys* boson

Bosphore [bɔsfɔʀ] NM **le B.** the Bosphorus, the Bosporus

bosquet [bɔskɛ] NM coppice, copse

boss [bɔs] NM *Fam* boss; **à la maison, c'est elle le b.!** she's the boss at home!

bossage [bɔsaʒ] NM *Archit & Tech* boss

bossa-nova [bɔsanɔva] *(pl* **bossas-novas)** NF *Mus* bossa nova

bosse [bɔs] NF **1** *(à la suite d'un coup)* bump, lump; **se faire une b.** to get a bump
  2 *Anat & Zool (protubérance)* hump; **b. de bison** dowager's hump; *Fam* **rouler sa b.** to knock about
  3 *(du sol)* bump; *(en ski)* mogul; **un terrain plein de bosses** a bumpy piece of ground
  4 *Naut* painter; **b. d'amarrage** mooring rope; **b. de remorque** towrope; **b. de ris** reef point
  5 *Rail* **b. de débranchement, b. de triage** hump *(in gravity yard)*
  6 *(locution)* **avoir la b. des maths/du commerce** to be a born mathematician/businessman, *f* businesswoman
  ◻ **en bosse** ADJ *Beaux-Arts* embossed

bosselage [bɔslaʒ] NM *Beaux-Arts* embossing

bosselé, -e [bɔsle] ADJ **1** *(carrosserie)* dented **2** *(ouvrage)* embossed

bosseler [24] [bɔsle] VT **1** *(carrosserie)* to dent **2** *(ouvrage)* to emboss

bossellement [bɔslmã] NM denting

bossellera *etc voir* **bosseler**

bosselure [bɔslyʀ] NF *(irregular)* bumps

bosser¹ [3] [bɔse] *Fam* VI to work■; **j'ai bossé toute la nuit pour cet examen** I stayed up all night working for that exam; **il bosse en usine depuis l'âge de 14 ans** he's been working in a factory since the age of 14; **b. dur** to work hard, to graft
  VT *Br* to swot up on, *Am* to bone up on; **tu ferais mieux de b. ta physique** you should *Br* swot up on *or Am* bone up on your physics

bosser² [3] [bɔse] VT *Naut* to tie up with a painter

bosser³ [3] [bɔse] VT *Can Joual* to boss around

bossette [bɔsɛt] NF **1** *Aut* boss **2** *(d'un cheval)* boss, stud **3** *(d'une arme)* swell, boss **4** *Suisse (tonneau)* wheeled barrel *(used for transporting grapes to the press)*; **b. à purin** slurry barrel

bosseur, -euse [bɔsœʀ, -øz] *Fam* ADJ **être b.** to work hard■, to be hardworking■
  NM,F hard worker■, slogger

bossoir [bɔswaʀ] NM *Naut (pour hisser un bateau)* davit; *(pour manœuvrer l'ancre)* cathead

bossu, -e [bɔsy] ADJ humpbacked, hunchbacked; **être b.** to be humpbacked, to have a hump *or* humpback
  NM,F humpback, hunchback; *Fam* **rire** *ou* **rigoler** *ou* **se marrer comme un b.** to laugh fit to burst, to laugh oneself silly

'Le Bossu' *Féval* 'The Hunchback'

bossuer [7] [bɔswye] VT **1** *(carrosserie)* to dent **2** *(ouvrage)* to emboss

Boston [bɔstɔn] NM *Géog* Boston

boston [bɔstɔ̃] NM *Cartes, Mus & (danse)* boston

bostonner [3] [bɔstɔne] VI **1** *Cartes* to play boston
  2 *(danser)* to do the boston (two-step)

bostryche [bɔstʀiʃ] NM *Entom* bark beetle

bot¹ [bɔt] NM *Ordinat* bot

bot², -e [bo, bɔt] ADJ **pied b.** club foot

botanique [bɔtanik] ADJ botanical
  NF botany

botaniste [bɔtanist] NMF botanist

botcher [3] [bɔtʃe] VT *Can Joual* to mess up

bothriocéphale [bɔtʀijɔsefal] NM *Zool* Asian fish tapeworm, *Spéc* bothriocephalus

Botnie [bɔtni] *voir* **golfe**

Botox® [bɔtɔks] NM *Pharm* Botox®; **se faire faire des injections de B.** to have Botox® (injections), *Fam* to get Botoxed

Botrange [bɔtʀãʒ] NM **le signal de B.** = the highest point in Belgium (694m)

botrytis [bɔtʀitis] NM *Bot* botrytis

Botswana [bɔtswana] NM **le B.** Botswana; **vivre au B.** to live in Botswana; **aller au B.** to go to Botswana

botswanais, -e [bɔtswanɛ, -ɛz] ADJ Botswanan, Botswanian
  ◻ **Botswanais, -e** NM,F Botswanan, Botswanian

botte [bɔt] NF **1** *(chaussure)* (high) boot; **bottes en caoutchouc** *Br* wellington boots, *Am* rubber boots; **bottes de cavalier** riding boots; **bottes de cow-boy** cowboy boots; **bottes d'égoutier** waders; **bottes de sept lieues** seven-league

boots; **haut comme une** *ou* **ma b.** knee-high to a grasshopper; **être à la b. de qn** to be sb's puppet; **avoir qn à sa b.** to have sb under one's thumb; *Fam* **cirer** *ou* **lécher les bottes de qn** to lick sb's boots; **sous la b. de l'ennemi** beneath the enemy's heel

2 *(de fleurs, de radis)* bunch; *(de paille)* sheaf, bundle; *Fam* **il n'y en a pas des bottes** there isn't much *or* a lot of it; *Fam* **elle chante bien? – pas des bottes** is she a good singer? – not really

3 *Escrime* thrust; **allonger une b.** to thrust; **porter une b. à qn** to make a thrust at sb; *Fig* to hit out *or* to have a dig at sb; **b. secrète** secret weapon

4 *Fam (à Polytechnique)* = students who leave the "École Polytechnique" with the highest marks; **sortir dans la b.** to be among the best students in one's year

5 *très Fam* **il lui a proposé la b.** he asked her straight out to sleep with him

6 *Belg Fam* **être bien dans ses bottes** to have a fair bit (of money) tucked away; **être/se sentir droit dans ses bottes** to have an easy conscience; **avoir une pièce dans ses bottes** to have had one too many

> *Allusion*
>
> **Les bottes de sept lieues**
>
> The Charles Perrault fairy tale *Puss in Boots* tells the story of a cat with seven-league boots, which allow it to cover great distances in no time at all. In modern French, **chausser les bottes de sept lieues** ("to have one's seven-league boots on") means to have accomplished a great deal in relatively little time, or, more simply, to have got to a destination very quickly.

bottelage [bɔtlaʒ] NM trussing, tying up *(of hay, straw)*

botteler [24] [bɔtle] VT *(foin, paille)* to sheaf

botteleur, -euse [bɔtlœr, -øz] NM,F trusser

◻ **botteleuse** NF straw binder

botter [3] [bɔte] VT 1 *(chausser → enfant)* to put boots on; *(→ client)* to provide boots for, to sell boots to; **botté de cuir** wearing leather boots 2 *Sport* to kick; **b. la balle en touche** to kick the ball into touch; *Fig* to dodge the issue 3 *(locutions) Fam* **ça me botte!** I like that!; *Fam* **ça te botterait d'y aller?** do you fancy going?; **b. le train** *ou* **les fesses** *ou* **le derrière** *ou très Fam* **le cul à qn** to kick sb in the pants; **se faire b. les fesses** *ou* **le derrière** *ou très Fam* **le cul** to get a kick up the *Br* arse *or Am* ass

VI *Sport* to kick the ball

botteur [bɔtœr] NM *Sport* kicker

bottier, -ère [bɔtje, -ɛr] NM,F *(fabricant → de bottes)* bootmaker; *(→ de chaussures)* shoemaker

bottillon [bɔtijɔ̃] NM ankle boot

Bottin® [bɔtɛ̃] NM telephone directory, phone book; **le B. mondain** = directory of famous people, ≃ Who's Who

bottine [bɔtin] NF ankle boot; **b. à boutons** button boot; *Can Fam Fig* **avoir les deux pieds dans la même b.** to be all (fingers and) thumbs

botulinique [bɔtylinik], **botulique** [bɔtylik] ADJ *Méd* **toxine b.** botulin

botulisme [bɔtylism] NM *Méd* botulism

boubou [bubu] NM boubou, bubu

boubouler [3] [bubule] VI to hoot

bouc [buk] NM 1 *Zool* goat, he-goat, billy goat; **sentir le b., puer comme un b.** to stink to high heaven; **b. émissaire** scapegoat 2 *(barbe)* goatee (beard)

boucan[1] [bukɑ̃] NM *Fam* din, racket; **faire du b.** to kick up a din, to make a racket; **les voisins ont fait un de ces boucans!** the neighbours really kicked up a din!; **tu ne l'as pas entendu? il a pourtant fait assez de b.** didn't you hear him? he was making enough noise

boucan[2] [bukɑ̃] NM *Culin* = smoked meat from the West Indies

boucanage [bukanaʒ] NM smoking *(of meat, fish)*

boucane [bukan] NF *Can* smoke; *Fam* **faire de la b.** to have a smoke

boucaner [3] [bukane] VT *Culin (viande, poisson)* to smoke, to cure; **un teint boucané** a tanned *or* weatherbeaten complexion

boucanier [bukanje] NM buccaneer

boucau [buko] NM *(dans le Midi)* harbour entrance

boucaud [buko] NM shrimp

bouchage [buʃaʒ] NM 1 *(d'une bouteille)* corking 2 *(d'une fuite)* plugging, stopping 3 *(d'un trou)* filling up

bouchain [buʃɛ̃] NM *Naut* bilge; **b. vif** hard bilge

boucharde [buʃard] NF *Tech* bush-hammer

boucharder [3] [buʃarde] VT *Tech* to roughen

bouche [buʃ] NF 1 *(gén)* mouth; **j'ai la b. sèche** my mouth feels dry; **avoir la b. pleine** to have one's mouth full; **ne parle pas la b. pleine** don't talk with your mouth full; **une pipe à la b.** with a pipe in his/her mouth; *Littéraire* **elle me donna sa b.** she offered me her lips; **dans ta b. le mot prend toute sa valeur** when you say it *or* coming from you, the word takes on its full meaning; **ce n'est pas joli dans la b. d'un petit garçon!** that doesn't sound nice, coming from a little boy!; **ce sont toutes les mères qui s'expriment par sa b.** she's speaking for all mothers; **il a six bouches à nourrir** he has six mouths to feed (at home); **je n'ai pas l'intention de nourrir des bouches inutiles** I won't have loafers around here; **ça c'est pour** *ou* **je le garde pour la bonne b.** *(nourriture)* I'm keeping this as a treat for later; *(nouvelle)* I'm keeping the best until last; **de b. en b.** from person to person; **b. à oreille** grapevine; **par le b. à oreille** through the grapevine, by word of mouth; **de b. à oreille** confidentially; **être** *ou* **rester b. bée** to stand open-mouthed; **rester b. cousue** to keep one's lips sealed; *Péj* **avoir la** *ou* **faire sa b. en cœur** to simper; **il m'a annoncé la b. en cœur qu'il ne venait plus** he gaily announced to me that he was no longer coming; **c'est une fine b.** he's/she's a gourmet; **faire la fine b.** to be fussy *or* choosy; **faire la b. en cul-de-poule** to purse one's lips; **ouvrir la b.** to open one's mouth; *Fig* **elle n'a pas ouvert la b. de la soirée** she didn't say a word *or* open her mouth all evening; **il n'a que ce mot/nom à la b.** he only ever talks about one thing/person; **des insultes, tu n'as que ça à la b.** insults, that's all you ever come out with; **son nom est sur toutes les bouches** his/her name is on everyone's lips, he's/she's the talk of the town

2 *(orifice → d'un cratère)* mouth; *(→ d'un canon)* muzzle; **b. d'aération** air vent; **b. d'air chaud** hot-air vent; **b. d'arrosage** water pipe, standpipe; **b. de chaleur** hot-air vent; **b. d'eau** fire hydrant, *Am* fireplug; **b. d'égout** manhole, inspection chamber; **b. d'incendie** fire hydrant, *Am* fireplug; **b. de métro** metro entrance, underground entrance

3 *(d'un vin)* full-bodiedness, richness; **un vin bien en b.** a full-bodied wine

◻ **bouches** NFPL *Géog (d'un fleuve, d'un détroit)* mouth

bouché, -e[1] [buʃe] ADJ 1 *(nez)* blocked, *Med* congested; *(oreilles)* blocked up; **j'ai le nez b.** my nose is blocked 2 *Météo (ciel, horizon, temps)* cloudy, overcast 3 *Fam (idiot)* stupid, *Br* thick; **il est vraiment b.** he's really stupid!; **b. à l'émeri** *Br* as thick as two short planks, *Am* as dumb as they come 4 *(sans espoir → avenir)* hopeless; *(→ filière, secteur)* oversubscribed 5 *(bouteille)* corked; *(cidre, vin)* bottled

bouche-à-bouche [buʃabuʃ] NM INV mouth-to-mouth (resuscitation); **faire du b. à qn** to give sb mouth-to-mouth (resuscitation) *or* the kiss of life

bouche-à-oreille [byʃaorɛj] NM INV word-of-mouth; *Mktg (publicité)* word-of-mouth advertising; **le b. a très bien fonctionné** the news travelled fast, the news spread like wildfire; **son restaurant a très bien marché grâce au b.** word got around about how good his new restaurant was and it was a big success

bouchée[2] [buʃe] NF 1 *(contenu)* mouthful; **ne prends pas de si grosses bouchées** don't put such big pieces into your mouth; **il n'a fait qu'une b. du petit pain** he swallowed the roll whole; **elle n'a fait qu'une b. de ses rivales** she made short work of her rivals; **je n'en ferai qu'une b.!** I'll eat him for breakfast!; **mettre les bouchées doubles** to work twice as hard, to put on a spurt; **pour une b. de pain** for a song *or* next to nothing; **il a acheté ce tableau pour une b. de pain** he bought this painting for next to nothing 2 *Culin* (vol-au-vent) case; **b. à la reine** chicken vol-au-vent; *(friandise)* **b. (au chocolat)** chocolate bouchée

bouche-pores [buʃpɔr] NM INV *Tech* filler

boucher[1] [3] [buʃe] VT 1 *(fermer → trou)* to fill up; *(→ fuite)* to plug, to stop; *(→ bouteille)* to cork; *Fig* **b. un trou** to fill a gap; *Fam* **je parie que ça t'en bouche un coin!** I bet you're impressed!

2 *(entraver)* to obstruct, to block; **tu me bouches le passage** you're in *or* blocking my way; **la tour nous bouche complètement la vue** the tower cuts off *or* obstructs our view totally

▸**se boucher** VPR 1 *(s'obstruer → tuyau, narine)* to get blocked

2 *Météo (temps)* to become overcast

3 **se b. le nez** to hold one's nose; **se b. les oreilles** to put one's fingers in *or* to plug one's ears; *Fig* to refuse to listen; **se b. les yeux** to hide one's eyes; *Fig* to refuse to see

boucher[2], **-ère**[1] [buʃe, -ɛr] NM,F butcher; *Fam* **ce chirurgien est un vrai b.** that surgeon is a real butcher

'Le Boucher' *Chabrol* 'The Butcher'

bouchère[2] [buʃɛr] NF *Suisse* cold sore

boucherie [buʃri] NF 1 *(boutique)* butcher's *Br* shop *or Am* store; **viande de b.** butcher's meat; **b. chevaline** horse-butcher's (*Br* shop *or Am* store) 2 *(métier)* butchery 3 *Can & Suisse (abattage)* butchering *(of pigs)* 4 *Fig (massacre)* slaughter, butchery

Bouches-du-Rhône [buʃdyron] NFPL **les B.** the Bouches-du-Rhône

bouche-trou [buʃtru] (*pl* **bouche-trous**) NM *Fam (personne)* stand-in, stopgap; *(objet)* makeshift replacement

boucholeur [buʃɔlœr] NM mussel-farmer

bouchon [buʃɔ̃] NM 1 *(en liège)* cork; *(d'un bidon, d'une bouteille en plastique)* cap; *(d'une bouteille en verre, d'une carafe, d'un tonneau)* stopper; **vin qui sent le b.** corked wine; *Fam* **un b. de carafe** a huge diamond▪ *or* rock; **b. (du réservoir) d'essence** petrol cap; *Aut* **b. de vidange** blow-off; *Fam* **tu pousses le b. un peu loin** you're going a bit far *or* pushing it a bit; *Fam* **prendre du b.** to be getting on (in years)

2 *(bonde)* plug; **b. de cérumen** earwax plug

3 *(poignée de paille, de foin)* wisp

4 *Fam Aut (embouteillage)* traffic jam; *(à une intersection)* gridlock; **trois kilomètres de b.** a three-kilometre tailback

5 *Pêche* float

6 *(de paille)* = twist of straw used to rub down a horse

7 *(à Lyon)* = small restaurant serving traditional Lyonnaise food

bouchonnage [buʃɔnaʒ] NM *(d'un cheval)* rubbing down *(of a horse)*

bouchonné, -e [buʃɔne] ADJ *(vin)* corked

bouchonner [3] [buʃɔne] VT *(cheval)* to rub down

VI *Fam* **ça bouchonne à partir de 5 heures** traffic is nose-to-tail from 5 p.m. onwards▪

bouchonnier [buʃɔnje] NM *(fabricant)* maker of corks; *(marchand)* dealer in corks

bouchot [buʃo] NM mussel bed

bouchoteur [buʃɔtœr] NM mussel-farmer

bouclage [buklaʒ] NM 1 *Journ (d'un article)* finishing off; *(d'un journal)* putting to bed; **c'est mardi le b.** the paper's going to bed *or* to press on Tuesday 2 *Fam (d'un coupable)* locking up▪; *(d'un quartier)* surrounding▪, sealing off▪ 3 *(d'une ceinture)* fastening, buckling 4 *(des cheveux)* curling 5 *Tech* **b. acoustique** acoustic feedback

boucle [bukl] NF 1 *(de cheveux)* curl; **Boucles d'or** Goldilocks 2 *(d'une ceinture)* buckle; *(d'un lacet)* loop; *(d'un cours d'eau)* loop, meander; **elle ne fait pas de boucles à ses lettres** she doesn't put any loops on her letters; **faire une b. à un ruban** to loop a ribbon; **faire une b.** *(en marchant, en voiture)* to loop back 3 *Ordinat* loop; *Tél* **b. locale** local loop; **b. locale radio** wireless local loop 4 *Sport (en course)* lap; **la Grande b.** *(le Tour de France cycliste)* the Tour de France

◻ **boucle d'oreille** NF earring

bouclé, -e [bukle] **ADJ** *(cheveux, barbe)* curly; *(personne)* curly-haired

bouclement [bukləmɑ̃] **NM 1** *(de taureau, de porc)* ringing **2** *Suisse (des comptes, d'un budget)* closing

boucler [3] [bukle] **VT 1** *(fermer → ceinture)* to buckle, to fasten; *(→ chambre, maison etc)* to lock (up); **b. sa ceinture en voiture** to fasten one's seat belt; **b. sa valise** to shut one's suitcase; *Fig* to pack one's bags; *Fam* **toi, tu la boucles!** not a word out of you!

2 *(dans une opération policière)* **b. une avenue/un quartier** to seal off an avenue/area

3 *Fam (fermer → porte)* to lock▪; *(enfermer)* to shut away▪, to lock up▪; **si tu continues, je te boucle dans ta chambre** any more of this and you'll go to your room; **je suis bouclé à la maison avec la grippe** I'm stuck at home with the flu; **il s'est fait b. pour six mois** he's been put away for six months

4 *(mettre un terme à → affaire)* to finish off, to settle; *(→ programme de révisions)* to finish (off); *Journ* **b. un journal/une édition** to put a paper/an edition to bed

5 *(équilibrer)* **b. son budget** to make ends meet; **il a du mal à b. ses fins de mois** he's always in the red at the end of the month

6 *Aviat* **b. la boucle** to loop the loop; *Fig* to come full circle; *Fig* **la boucle est bouclée, on a bouclé la boucle** we're back to square one

7 *(cheveux, mèches)* to curl

8 *(taureau, porc)* to ring

VI 1 *(cheveux)* to curl, to be curly; **il boucle naturellement** he has naturally curly hair

2 *Ordinat* to get stuck in a loop, to loop round and round

▸**se boucler VPR 1 se b. chez soi** to shut oneself away▪

2 *Ordinat (lignes)* to wrap

bouclette [buklɛt] **NF 1** *(de cheveux)* small curl; *(de laine, de moquette)* curl **2** *(comme adj) Tex (fil, laine)* bouclé

bouclier [buklije] **NM 1** *(protection de soldat)* shield; *(de policier)* riot shield; *Fig* **elle lui a fait un b. de son corps** she shielded him/her with her body; **b. humain** human shield **2** *(protection)* shield; *Astron* **b. thermique** thermal *or* heat shield; **b. antimissile** missile shield; **b. atomique** atomic shield **3** *Géol* shield; **le b. canadien** the Canadian shield

boucot [buko] **NM** shrimp

Bouddha [buda] **NPR** Buddha

bouddha [buda] **NM** *(statue)* buddha

bouddhique [budik] **ADJ** *Rel* Buddhist, Buddhistic

bouddhisme [budism] **NM** *Rel* Buddhism

bouddhiste [budist] *Rel* **ADJ** Buddhist

NMF Buddhist

bouder [3] [bude] **VI** to sulk; **elle est partie b.** she's gone off in a sulk

VT *(ami)* to refuse to talk to; *(dessert)* to refuse; *(dessert, cadeau)* to refuse to accept; *(élection)* to refuse to vote in; *(fournisseur)* to stay away from; **le public a boudé son film** hardly anyone went to see his/her film; **en été les Parisiens boudent les salles de cinéma** Parisians stay away from *or* don't go to the cinema in summer; **b. son plaisir** to deny oneself

▸**se bouder VPR** not to talk to each other, to refuse to have anything to do with each other

bouderie [budri] **NF** sulking *(UNCOUNT)*; **je ne supporte plus ses bouderies** I'm fed up with his/her sulking

boudeur, -euse [budœr, -øz] **ADJ** sulky, sullen

NM,F sulky person

▫ **boudeuse NF** *(siège)* courting couch

Boudin [budɛ̃] **NM** *Mil* = regimental march of the French Foreign Legion

boudin [budɛ̃] **NM 1** *Culin* **b. (noir)** *Br* black pudding, *Am* blood sausage; **b. blanc** *Br* white pudding, *Am* white sausage; *Fam* **faire du b.** to sulk **2** *(cylindre)* roll **3** *Fam Péj (femme)* dog, *Br* boot, *Am* beast; **sa sœur est un vrai b.!** his sister looks like *Br* the back of a bus *or Am* a Mack truck! **4** *(doigt)* fat finger **5** *Belg (traversin)* bolster **6** *Archit* torus **7** *Rail (d'une roue)* flange

boudinage [budinaʒ] **NM** *Tex* slubbing

boudiné, -e [budine] **ADJ** *(doigt, main) Br* podgy, *Am* pudgy; **je me sens boudinée dans cette robe** this dress is too tight for me; **il a l'air b. dans ses vêtements** he looks as though his clothes are a size too small

boudiner [3] [budine] **VT 1** *(sujet: vêtement)* **cette jupe la boudine** this skirt shows all her bulges **2** *Ind (fil de métal)* to coil; *Tex* to rove; *(tuyau)* to extrude

▸**se boudiner VPR se b. dans une jupe** to squeeze oneself into a skirt (that is too tight)

boudineuse [budinøz] **NF** *Ind (pour les fils métalliques)* coiler; *(pour les tuyaux et les matières plastiques)* extruder, extrusion machine; *Tex* rover

boudoir [budwar] **NM 1** *(pièce)* boudoir **2** *Culin (biscuit) Br* sponge finger, *Am* ladyfinger

boue [bu] **NF 1** *Géol (terre détrempée)* mud; **couvert de b.** muddy **2** *(dépôt)* sludge; *Méd* **boues activées** activated sludge; **boues d'épuration** sewage sludge

bouée [bwe] **NF 1** *Naut (en mer)* buoy; **b. d'amarrage** mooring buoy; **b. à cloche** bell buoy; **b. de corps-mort** anchor buoy; **b. lumineuse** light buoy, floating light; **b. sonore** sonobuoy **2** *(pour nager)* rubber ring; **b. de sauvetage** lifebelt, lifebuoy; **il s'est raccroché à elle comme à une b. de sauvetage** he hung onto her as if his life depended on it

bouette [bwɛt] = **boëte**

boueux, -euse [buø, -øz] **ADJ 1** *(sale → trottoir)* muddy; *(→ tapis)* mud-stained **2** *Typ* smudged

NM *Fam Br* bin man, *Am* garbage collector

bouffant, -e [bufɑ̃, -ɑ̃t] **ADJ** *(coiffure)* bouffant; *(manche)* puffed out; *(pantalon)* baggy

NM *(d'une manche)* puff; *(des cheveux)* body

bouffarde [bufard] **NF** *Fam* pipe▪

bouffe [buf] **NF** *Fam (aliments)* food▪, grub, nosh; **aimer la bonne b.** to like one's food; **on se fait une b.?** do you fancy getting together for a meal?

ADJ opéra b. comic opera

'La Grande bouffe' *Ferreri* 'Blow-out'

bouffée [bufe] **NF 1** *(exhalaison)* puff; **envoyer des bouffées de fumée** to puff (out) smoke; **tirer des bouffées d'une pipe** to draw on one's pipe; **une b. d'air** a puff *or* a breath of wind; *aussi Fig* **une b. d'air frais** a breath of fresh air; **une b. de parfum** a whiff of perfume; **des odeurs de cuisine m'arrivaient par bouffées** the smell of cooking wafted over to me

2 *(accès)* fit, outburst; **une b. de colère** a fit of rage; **une b. de tendresse** a sudden burst of tenderness; *Méd* **avoir des bouffées de chaleur** to have hot *Br* flushes *or Am* flashes; *Psy* **b. délirante** delirious fit

bouffer [3] [bufe] **VT** *Fam* **1** *(manger)* to eat▪; *(manger voracement)* to guzzle; *Fig* **je l'aurais bouffé!** I could have killed him!; **il ne va pas te b.** he won't eat you; **il a bouffé du lion aujourd'hui** he's full of beans today

2 *(gaspiller)* to be heavy on, to soak up; **b. de l'essence** to be heavy on *Br* petrol *or Am* gas; **il a bouffé toute sa fortune** he blew all his money

3 *(accaparer)* **les enfants me bouffent tout mon temps** the kids take up every minute of my time; **tu te laisses b. par ta mère** you're letting your mother walk all over you

4 *(locutions)* **b. du curé** to be a priest-hater; **b. du communiste** to be a commie-basher; **b. du kilomètre** *ou* **des kilomètres** to eat up the miles

USAGE ABSOLU *Fam (manger)* **b. au restaurant** to eat out; **on a bien/mal bouffé** the food was great/terrible; **je vais les faire b. et on sera tranquilles** I'll give them something to eat and then we'll have some peace

VI *(gonfler)* to puff (out); **faire b. ses manches** to puff out one's sleeves; **faire b. ses cheveux** to give one's hair more volume

▸**se bouffer VPR** *Fam* **se b. le nez** *(une fois)* to have a go at one another; *(constamment)* to be at daggers drawn

bouffetance [buftɑ̃s] **NF** *très Fam (aliments)* food▪, grub, nosh

bouffette [bufɛt] **NF** *(ruban)* rosette

bouffeur, -euse [bufœr, -øz] **NM,F** *Fam* guzzler; **un gros b. de viande** a great meat-eater▪, a real carnivore; **c'est un b. de curé** he's very anticlerical▪

bouffi, -e [bufi] **ADJ** *(yeux)* puffed-up, puffy; *(visage)* puffed-up, puffy, bloated; **les yeux bouffis de sommeil** eyes puffy with sleep; *Fig* **être b. d'orgueil** to be bloated with pride; **tu l'as dit, b.!** you said it!

NM *Culin (hareng)* bloater

bouffir [32] [bufir] **VT 1** *(visage, yeux)* to puff up **2** *Culin (hareng)* to bloat

VI to become swollen *or* bloated, to puff up

bouffissage [byfisaʒ] **NM** *Culin (des harengs)* bloating

bouffissure [bufisyr] **NF** *(d'un visage, d'un corps)* puffy *or* swollen state; *(d'un style)* turgidness

bouffon, -onne [bufɔ̃, -ɔn] **ADJ** *(scène)* comical, farcical

NM 1 *Théât* buffoon; *Hist* **le b. du roi** the king's jester; *Hist* **la querelle des Bouffons** = mid-eighteenth century quarrel between the partisans of Italian and French music **2** *Fam (personne ridicule)* buffoon, clown

bouffonnement [byfɔnmɑ̃] **ADV** like a buffoon *or* clown

bouffonner [3] [bufɔne] **VI** *Fam Vieilli* to play *or* to act the buffoon

bouffonnerie [bufɔnri] **NF 1** *(acte)* piece of buffoonery; *(parole)* farcical remark; **faire des bouffonneries** to play *or* act the buffoon **2** *(caractère)* buffoonery

bougainvillée [bugɛ̃vile] **NF, bougainvillier** [bugɛ̃vilje] **NM** *Bot* bougainvillaea

bouge [buʒ] **NM 1** *(logement)* hovel; *(café)* cheap *or* sleazy bar **2** *(d'un tonneau)* widest part **3** *Naut* camber

bougé [byʒe] **NM** *Phot* camera shake

bougeoir [buʒwar] **NM** candleholder, candlestick

bougeotte [buʒɔt] **NF** *Fam* fidgets; **avoir la b.** *(remuer)* to have the fidgets; *(voyager)* to have itchy feet

bouger [17] [buʒe] **VI 1** *(remuer)* to move; **rien ne bouge** nothing's stirring; **j'ai une dent qui bouge** I have a loose tooth; **rester sans b.** to stay still; **ne bougeons plus!** hold it!; **le vent fait b. les branches des arbres** the branches of the trees are swaying in the wind; **il sait faire b. ses oreilles** he can wiggle his ears

2 *(se déplacer)* to move; **je n'ai pas bougé de la maison** I never stirred from the house; **un métier où on bouge beaucoup** a job involving a lot of travel

3 *(se modifier → couleur d'un tissu)* to fade; **les prix n'ont pas bougé** prices haven't changed *or* altered

4 *(s'activer)* to move, to stir; **les syndicats commencent à b.** the unions are on the move; **ce projet a fait b. les habitants du quartier** the project has spurred the local inhabitants into action; *Fam* **ça bouge pas mal, dans cette ville** there's a lot going on *or* happening in this town

VT to move, to shift

▸**se bouger VPR** *Fam* **bouge-toi de là!** shift yourself!; **si on se bougeait un peu?** come on, let's get moving *or* let's get a move on!; **tu ne t'es pas beaucoup bougé pour trouver un nouveau boulot** you didn't try very hard to find a new job▪

bougie [buʒi] **NF 1** *(en cire)* candle; **s'éclairer à la b.** to use candles for lighting **2** *Aut Br* spark plug, *Am* sparking plug **3** *Méd (sonde)* bougie

bougillon, -onne [byʒijɔ̃, -ɔn] *Suisse* **ADJ** fidgety

NM,F fidget; **faire le b.** to fidget

bougnat [buɲa] **NM** *Vieilli* = owner of a small café also selling coal, usually from the Auvergne

bougnoul, bougnoule [buɲul] **NM** *Fam* = racist term used to refer to a North African

bougon, -onne [bugɔ̃, -ɔn] *Fam* **ADJ** grouchy, grumpy

NM,F grumbler, grouch

bougonnement [bugɔnmɑ̃] **NM** grouching *(UNCOUNT)*, grumbling *(UNCOUNT)*

bougonner [3] [bugɔne] **VI** *Fam* to grouch, to grumble

bougonneur, -euse [bugɔnœr, -øz] *Fam* **ADJ** grouchy, grumpy

NM,F grumbler, grouch

bougonneux, -euse [bugɔnø, -øz] *Can* = **bougonneur**

bougran [bugrɑ̃] **NM 1** *Tex* buckram **2** *Couture* foundation

bougre [bugr] *Fam Vieilli* **NM 1** *(homme)* chap,

fellow; **c'est un bon b.!** he's a decent chap; **un pauvre b.** a poor chap **2** *Péj* **b. d'imbécile** *ou* **d'andouille!** you stupid idiot!

EXCLAM 1 *(marque la colère)* damn! **2** *(marque la surprise)* I'll be dashed!, cripes!

bougrement [bugrəmɑ̃] **ADV** *Fam Vieilli* damn, *Br* dashed; **il fait b. froid** it's damn cold

bougresse [bugrɛs] **NF** *Fam Vieilli* wretched woman; **elle sait s'y prendre, la b.!** *(ton admiratif)* that one certainly knows what she's about!

boui-boui [bwibwi] *(pl* **bouis-bouis)** **NM** *Fam (restaurant)* greasy spoon, *Br* caff; **au b. du coin** at the local caff

bouif [bwif] **NM** *Fam* cobbler ■

bouillabaisse [bujabɛs] **NF** *Culin* bouillabaisse, = type of fish soup, typical of Provence

bouillant, -e [bujɑ̃, -ɑ̃t] **ADJ 1** *(qui bout)* boiling; *(très chaud)* boiling hot; **j'aime boire mon café b.** I like my coffee to be boiling hot **2** *(ardent)* fiery, passionate; **b. de colère** seething with anger; **b. d'impatience** bursting with impatience

bouillasse [bujas] **NF** *Fam (boue)* muck, mud; *(de neige)* slush

Bouillaud [bujo] **NPR** *Méd* **maladie de B.** rheumatic fever

bouille¹ [buj] **NF** *Fam (figure)* face ■, mug; **il a une bonne b.** *(sympathique)* he looks (like) a nice guy *or Br* bloke

bouille² [buj] **NF** *Suisse* **1** *Br* churn, *Am* milk pail **2** *(pour la vendange)* grape tub

bouilleur [bujœr] **NM 1** *(distillateur)* distiller; **b. de cru** home distiller **2** *Tech (d'une chaudière)* heating *or* fire tube

bouilli, -e [buji] **ADJ** *Culin (eau, lait, viande)* boiled

NM *Culin (viande)* boiled meat; *(bœuf)* boiled beef; *Can* = stew of beans, cabbage, carrots, potatoes, salt pork and ham cooked together for several hours

□ **bouillie** **NF 1** *(pour enfants)* baby food *or* cereal; **bouillie bordelaise** Bordeaux mixture; **avoir de la bouillie dans la bouche** to mumble; **c'est de la bouillie pour chats** it's a dog's breakfast **2** *Méd* **bouillie barytée** barium meal

□ **en bouillie** **ADJ** crushed **ADV** crushed; **réduire qch en bouillie** *(légumes, fruits)* to mash *or* to pulp sth; **mettre** *ou* **réduire qn en bouillie** to beat sb to a pulp; **les voitures ont été réduites en bouillie** the cars were completely smashed up

bouillir [48] [bujir] **VI 1** *(arriver à ébullition)* to boil; **faire b. de l'eau pour le thé** to boil water for tea; **faire b. des légumes** to boil vegetables; **faire b. des instruments** *Méd* to sterilize *or* to boil instruments; **faire b. la marmite** to keep the pot boiling

2 *(s'irriter)* to boil; **ça me fait b.** it makes my blood boil; **b. d'impatience** to be bursting with impatience; **b. de colère** to seethe with anger

VT to boil; **b. du linge** to boil washing

bouilloire [bujwar] **NF** kettle; **b. électrique** electric kettle

bouillon [bujɔ̃] **NM 1** *Culin* broth, stock; **b. gras/maigre** meat/clear stock; **b. cube** stock cube; **b. de légumes** vegetable stock; **b. de onze** *ou* **d'onze heures** poisoned drink; *Fam* **boire** *ou* **prendre un b.** *(en nageant)* to swallow water; *Fig* to suffer heavy losses

2 *Biol* **b. de culture** culture medium; *Fig* **ces quartiers sont un véritable b. de culture pour la délinquance** these areas are a perfect breeding-ground for crime

3 *(remous)* **éteindre le feu dès le premier b.** turn off the heat as soon as it boils; **couler à gros bouillons** to gush out *or* forth; **bouillir à gros bouillons** to boil fast *or* hard; **cuire à gros bouillons** to bubble fiercely

4 *Couture* puff

5 *Journ* unsold copies

6 *(dans un métal)* blowhole

7 *Can (sève d'érable)* = partly evaporated maple sap, during the process of producing maple syrup

bouillon-blanc [bujɔ̃blɑ̃] *(pl* **bouillons-blancs)** **NM** *Bot* great *or* common mullein, Aaron's rod

bouillonnant, -e [bujɔnɑ̃, -ɑ̃t] **ADJ** bubbling, foaming, seething; **b. de vie/d'idées** bubbling over with life/ideas

bouillonné [bujɔne] **NM** *Couture* ruffle, ruffled border

bouillonnement [bujɔnmɑ̃] **NM** bubbling, foaming, seething; *Fig* **b. d'idées** ferment of ideas

bouillonner [3] [bujɔne] **VI 1** *(liquide)* to bubble; *(source)* to foam, to froth; *Fig* **ils bouillonnent d'idées** they're full of ideas **2** *(s'agiter)* **b. d'impatience** to be bursting with impatience; **b. de colère** to seethe with anger

bouillotte [bujɔt] **NF** hot-water bottle

bouillotter [3] [bujɔte] **VI** to boil gently, to simmer

boukha [byra] **NF** boukha *(Tunisian brandy made from figs)*

boul. *(abrév écrite* **boulevard)** Blvd.

boulaie [bulɛ] **NF** *Bot* birch plantation

boulange [bulɑ̃ʒ] **NF** *Fam (métier)* bakery trade *or* business ■; **il est dans la b.** he works as a baker ■

boulanger¹ [17] [bulɑ̃ʒe] **VT** **b. de la farine** to make bread

VI to make bread

boulanger², -ère [bulɑ̃ʒe, -ɛr] **NM,F** baker

ADJ bakery; **pommes boulangères** = thinly-sliced potatoes and onions baked in the oven

boulangerie [bulɑ̃ʒri] **NF 1** *(boutique)* bakery, *Br* baker's (shop); **b. pâtisserie** baker's and confectioner's, bread and cake *Br* shop *or Am* store **2** *(industrie)* bakery trade *or* business

boulangisme [bulɑ̃ʒism] **NM** *Hist* = 19th-century movement supporting General Boulanger

BOULANGISME

General Boulanger was a French army officer who started an anti-parliamentary anti-German movement. His supporters came close to overthrowing the government in 1889.

boulangiste [bulɑ̃ʒist] *Hist* **ADJ** *(mouvement, parti)* of General Boulanger

NMF supporter of General Boulanger

boulder [buldœr] **NM** *Géol* boulder

boule [bul] **NF 1** *(sphère)* ball; *(de machine à écrire)* golf ball; **b. de billard** billiard ball; **il a le crâne comme une b. de billard** he's (as) bald as a coot; *Ordinat* **b. de commande** trackball; **b. de cristal** crystal ball; **regarder dans sa b. de cristal** to look into one's crystal ball; **b. doseuse** *(pour la lessive)* detergent ball; **b. de feu** fireball; **b. de gomme** gumdrop; **b. de loto** lottery ball; **avoir les yeux en boules de loto** *(de surprise)* to be wide-eyed; **b. à neige** *(objet décoratif)* snowdome, snowglobe; **b. de neige** snowball; *Fig* **faire b. de neige** to snowball; **b. de poils** *(dans l'estomac d'un animal)* hairball; **une petite b. de poils** *(chaton)* a little fluffy ball, a little ball of fluff; **b. puante** stinkbomb; **boules Quiès®** = earplugs made of wax; **b. à thé** tea ball; **avoir une b. dans la gorge** to have a lump in one's throat; **avoir une b. sur l'estomac** to have a heavy stomach

2 *Fam (tête)* head ■, nut; **avoir la b. à zéro** to have a shaved head; **coup de b.** headbutt ■; **donner un coup de b. à qn** to headbutt ■ *or* nut sb; **perdre la b.** to crack up, to lose one's marbles, *Br* to lose the plot

3 *(jeux)* **b. (de pétanque)** = steel bowl used in playing boules; **jouer aux boules** to play boules *(popular French game played on bare ground with steel bowls)*

4 *Belg (bonbon)* boiled sweet

5 *Suisse (saucisson)* **b. de Bâle** = large saveloy

6 *Suisse (pâtisserie)* **b. de Berlin** doughnut

□ **boules** **NFPL** *très Fam* **1 avoir les boules** *(être effrayé)* to be scared stiff; *(être furieux)* to be pissed off; *(être déprimé)* to be feeling down; **tu me fous les boules** *(tu me fais peur)* you're scaring me; *(tu me déprimes)* you're really getting me down; **les boules!** nightmare!

2 *(testicules)* balls, nuts

3 *Can (seins)* boobs, tits

□ **en boule** **ADJ** *Fam (en colère)* **être en b.** to be mad *or* livid; **ça me met en b.** it makes me mad *or* livid **ADV** **se mettre en b.** *(en rond)* to curl up into a ball; *Fam (en colère)* to fly off the handle, to go mad

boulé [bule] **NM** □ **au boulé** *Culin* at the hardball stage

boulê [bulɛ] **NF** *Antiq* Boulê, Athenian Council

bouleau, -x [bulo] **NM** *Bot* **1** *(arbre)* birch; **b. argenté** silver birch **2** *(bois)* birch

boule-de-neige [buldənɛʒ] *(pl* **boules-de-neige)** **NF** *Bot (arbuste)* guelder rose

Boule-de-Suif [buldəsɥif] **NM** = the best known of Maupassant's tales, about the Franco-Prussian War

bouledogue [buldɔg] **NM** *Zool (chien)* bulldog

bouléguer [18] [bulege] **VT** *(en français régional) (remuer)* to shake

bouler [3] [bule] **VI** to roll along; **b. au bas de l'escalier** to tumble down the stairs; *Fam* **envoyer b. qn** to send sb packing

boulet [bulɛ] **NM 1** *(projectile)* cannonball; *(de prisonnier)* ball (and chain); *Fig* **c'est un b. qu'il traînera toute sa vie** it will be a millstone round his neck all his life; **arriver comme un b. dans une pièce** to come crashing into a room; **tirer à boulets rouges sur qn** to lay into sb **2** *Mines* (coal) nut **3** *Zool* fetlock

bouletage [bylta3] **NM** *Minér* balling

bouleté, -e [bulte] **ADJ** *Vét (cheval)* with overshot fetlock

boulette [bulɛt] **NF 1** *Culin* **b. (de viande)** meatball; **b. (pour chien)** croquette; **b. empoisonnée** poison ball **2** *(de papier)* pellet **3** *Fam (erreur)* blunder, *Am* blooper; **faire une b.** to blunder, *Am* to goof

boulevard [bulvar] **NM 1** *(avenue)* boulevard; **les grands boulevards** *(à Paris)* the main boulevards *(with many theatres, restaurants and nightclubs)*; **les boulevards extérieurs** *ou* **des maréchaux** the (Paris) outer boulevards *(following the old town wall)*; **le b. du crime** = nickname given to the boulevard du Temple in Paris in the 19th century because of its theatres, where crimes often featured in the melodramas of the day; **le b. des Italiens** = boulevard in Paris where the offices of 'Le Monde' used to be; **le b. périphérique** (the Paris) *Br* ring road *or Am* beltway; *Fig* **ouvrir un b. à qn/qch** to leave the way open for sb/sth

2 *Théât* **le b.** light comedy

□ **de boulevard** **ADJ** *Théât* **pièce de b.** light comedy

'Boulevard du crépuscule' Wilder 'Sunset Boulevard'

THÉÂTRE DE BOULEVARD

This term originally referred to the style of plays produced at the theatres found on the "Grands Boulevards" of north-central Paris. It has come to mean any light vaudevillian comedy.

boulevardier, -ère [bulvardje, -jɛr] **ADJ** *Théât (humour)* facile

bouleversant, -e [bulvɛrsɑ̃, -ɑ̃t] **ADJ** *(émouvant)* deeply moving; *(pénible)* upsetting, distressing; **elle est bouleversante dans ce rôle** she gives a profoundly *or* deeply moving performance

bouleversement [bulvɛrsəmɑ̃] **NM** upheaval, upset; **son divorce a été un grand b. dans sa vie** his/her divorce drastically changed *or* was a great upheaval in his/her life; **le b. de toutes mes habitudes** the disruption of my entire routine; **des bouleversements politiques** political upheavals

bouleverser [3] [bulvɛrse] **VT 1** *(émouvoir)* to move deeply; **bouleversé par la naissance de son fils** deeply moved by his son's birth

2 *(affliger)* to upset, to distress; **bouleversé par la mort de son ami** shattered *or* very distressed by the death of his friend; **bouleversé par la souffrance des prisonniers** distressed *or* profoundly upset by the prisoners' suffering

3 *(désorganiser → maison, tiroir)* to turn upside down; *(→ habitudes, vie, plan)* to turn upside down, to disrupt, to change drastically

boulgour [bulgur] **NM** bulghur (wheat)

boulier¹ [bulje] **NM** abacus

boulier² [bulje] **NM** *Pêche* bag-net, wing-net

boulimie [bulimi] **NF** bulimia; **être atteint de b.**, **faire de la b.** to be bulimic; *Fig* **avoir une b. de connaissance** to have an unquenchable thirst for knowledge

boulimique [bulimik] **ADJ** bulimic
NMF bulimic
boulin [bulɛ̃] **NM** *Constr* putlog
bouline [bulin] **NF** *Naut* bowline; **naviguer** *ou* **aller à la b.** to sail close-hauled *or* close to the wind; **nœud de b.** bowline-knot; **courir la b.** to run the gauntlet
boulingrin [bulɛ̃grɛ̃] **NM** lawn *(in a formal garden)*
boulinier, -ère [bulinje, -ɛr] *Naut* **ADJ** weatherly; **navire mauvais b.** leewardly ship
NM ship that sails well to windward
boulisme [bulism] **NM** *(jeu)* boules
bouliste [bulist] **NMF** boules player
boulle [bul] **NM** **INV** *Beaux-Arts* boulle furniture *(style of highly ornamented furniture associated with Henri-Charles Boulle (1642–1732))*
Boul'Mich' [bulmiʃ] **NM** **le B.** = le Boulevard Saint-Michel (in Paris)
boulochage [buloʃaʒ] **NM** *Tex* pilling
boulocher [3] [buloʃe] **VI** *Tex* to pill
boulodrome [bulodrom] **NM** bowling alley
Boulogne-Billancourt [bulɔɲbijɑ̃kur] **NM** = town in the Paris suburbs, the site until recently of the state-run Renault car factory, well-known for its enlightened approach to labour relations
bouloir [bulwar] **NM** *Constr* larry
boulomane [buloman] **NMF** = person who loves playing boules
boulon [bulɔ̃] **NM** bolt; **b. avec écrou** nut and bolt; **b. à vis** screw bolt; *Fam Fig* **serrer** *ou* **resserrer les boulons** to tighten the screws; *Fam* **il lui manque un b., à ce type!** that guy's got a screw loose!
boulonnage [bulonaʒ] **NM** *Tech* bolting (on)
boulonnais, -e [bulonɛ, -ɛz] **ADJ** *(de Boulogne-sur-Mer)* of/from Boulogne-sur-Mer; *(de Boulogne-sur-Seine)* of/from Boulogne-sur-Seine
▫ **Boulonnais, -e** **NM,F** *(de Boulogne-sur-Mer)* = inhabitant of or person from Boulogne-sur-Mer; *(de Boulogne-sur-Seine)* = inhabitant of or person from Boulogne-sur-Seine
NM 1 *Géog* **le B.** = the Boulonnais area of the Pas-de-Calais département **2** *(cheval)* = heavy draught-horse of the Boulogne region
boulonner [3] [bulone] **VT** *Tech* to bolt (on)
VI *Fam* to work■, to plug away; **il boulonne dur** he works really hard
boulonnerie [bulonri] **NF 1** *(fabrique)* nut-and-bolt manufacture **2** *(industrie)* nut-and-bolt trade **3** *(dans une quincaillerie)* nut-and-bolt section
boulot¹ [bulo] **NM** *Fam* **1** *(fait de travailler)* **le b.** work■; *Péj* **elle est très b. b.** she's a workaholic **2** *(ouvrage réalisé)* piece of work■, job■; **il s'est coupé les cheveux tout seul, t'aurais vu le b.!** he cut his own hair, you should have seen the mess! **3** *(travail à faire)* **du b.** a lot of work■; **il y a encore du b. dessus!** it needs loads more work doing on it!; **tout le monde au b.!** come on everybody, let's get cracking! **4** *(emploi, poste)* job■; **un petit b.** a casual job■; **faire des petits boulots** to do casual work■ **5** *(lieu)* work■; **j'ai appelé le b. pour dire que j'étais malade** I called in sick; **aller au b.** to go to work; **je déjeune au b.** I have lunch at work
boulot², -otte [bulo, -ɔt] *Fam* **ADJ** plump, tubby; **une petite bonne femme boulotte** a tubby little woman
NM,F plump *or* tubby person
boulotter [3] [bulɔte] *Fam* **VT** *(manger)* to eat■
USAGE ABSOLU **elle n'arrête pas de b.** she just won't stop eating
VI *Vieilli (travailler)* to work■, to slave away; **il a passé sa vie à b.** he slaved away all his life
boum [bum] **EXCLAM** bang!; **faire b.** to go bang; **ça a fait b.!** *(attentat)* it went bang!; *(ballon)* it went pop!; **bébé a fait b.** *(en langage enfantin)* baby's had a tumble
NM 1 *(bruit)* bang; **il y a eu un grand b. et tout s'est effondré** there was a loud bang and everything collapsed **2** *Fam (succès)* **le b. des portables** the *Br* mobile phone boom, *Am* the cellphone boom, the boom in *Br* mobile phones *or Am* cellphones; **faire un b.** to be a great success story *or* a runaway success; **être en plein b.** *(dans une boutique, une entreprise)* to have a rush on; *(dans*

des préparations) to be rushed off one's feet
NF *Fam* party■ *(for teenagers)*
boumer [3] [bume] **VI** *Fam* **alors, ça boume?** so, how's tricks?; **ça boume pas très fort pour lui** he's having a rough time of it; **ça boume!** things are (going) fine!
bountche [buntʃə], **bountje** [buntjə] *Belg* = **boentje**
bounty [bunti] **NM** *Fam Péj* = black person who has adopted the lifestyle and values of a white person, *Br* Bounty bar, *Am* oreo (cookie)
bouquet [bukɛ] **NM 1** *(fleurs → gén)* bunch; *(→ grand, décoratif)* bouquet; *(→ petit)* sprig, spray; **le b. de la mariée** the wedding *or* bride's bouquet **2** *Bot (groupe → d'arbres)* clump, cluster **3** *(dans un feu d'artifice)* **b. (final)** crowning *or* final piece, (grand) finale; *Fam* **alors ça, c'est le b.!** that's the limit!, that takes the *Br* biscuit *or Am* cake! **4** *Culin* **b. garni** bouquet garni **5** *(arôme → d'un vin)* bouquet, nose **6** *Zool (crustacé)* (common) prawn **7** *TV* **b. numérique** *ou* **de programmes** multichannel digital TV package, multiplex; **b. satellitaire, b. satellite** satellite package
bouqueté, -e [bukte] **ADJ** *(vin)* with a good bouquet *or* nose
bouquetière [buktjɛr] **NF** flower girl
bouquetin [buktɛ̃] **NM** *Zool* ibex
bouquin [bukɛ̃] **NM 1** *Fam (livre)* book■ **2** *Chasse & Zool (lapin)* buck rabbit; *(lièvre)* male hare **3** *Vieilli Zool (bouc)* (old) billy-goat
bouquinage [bukinaʒ] **NM** *Chasse & Zool (de lapins, de lièvres)* bucking, mating
bouquiner [3] [bukine] **VT** *Fam* to read■
VI 1 *Fam* to read■ **2** *Chasse & Zool (lapin, lièvre)* to buck, to mate
bouquinerie [bukinri] **NF 1** *(commerce)* secondhand book trade **2** *(boutique)* secondhand *Br* bookshop *or Am* bookstore
bouquineur [bukinœr] **NM 1** *(amateur de vieux livres)* lover of old books **2** *(bibliophile)* bookhunter
bouquiniste [bukinist] **NMF** secondhand bookseller

Culture
LES BOUQUINISTES
In Paris, this term can refer specifically to the people who sell books, prints, cards etc from small wooden or metal stalls fixed to the top of the wall running along the banks of the Seine.

bour [bur] **NM** *Suisse* = jack of trumps in "yass" (Swiss card game)
bourbe [burb] **NF** *(gén)* mud, *Littéraire* mire; *(dans l'eau)* sludge
bourbeux, -euse [burbø, -øz] **ADJ** muddy; **eau bourbeuse** muddy *or* sludgy water
bourbier [burbje] **NM 1** *Géol (marécage)* quagmire **2** *Fig (situation difficile)* mess, quagmire
bourbillon [burbijɔ̃] **NM** *Méd (d'un abcès, d'un furoncle etc)* core
Bourbon [burbɔ̃] **NPR** Bourbon; **les Bourbons** = the royal dynasty which ruled France from 1589 to 1792 and from 1814 to 1830
bourbon [burbɔ̃] **NM** *(alcool)* bourbon
bourbonien, -enne [burbɔnjɛ̃, -ɛn] **ADJ** of the Bourbon dynasty; **nez b.** hooked *or* aquiline nose
bourbonnais, -e [burbɔnɛ, -ɛz] **ADJ** of/from the Bourbonnais region
▫ **Bourbonnais, -e** **NM,F** = inhabitant of or person from the Bourbonnais region
NM le B. = region of central France, with capital Moulins
bourbouille [burbuj] **NF** *Méd* prickly heat, heat rash, *Spéc* miliaria
bourdaine [burdɛn] **NF** *Bot* alder buckthorn
bourde [burd] **NF** *Fam* **1** *(bêtise)* blunder, *Br* bloomer, *Am* blooper; **faire une b.** *(gaffer)* to blunder, to put one's foot in it; *(faire une erreur)* to make a mistake■, to mess (things) up, *Am* to goof (up) **2** *Vieilli (mensonge)* fib; **raconter des bourdes** to tell fibs
bourdigue [burdig] = **bordigue**
bourdon [burdɔ̃] **NM 1** *Entom* bumblebee; **faux b.** drone **2** *Mus (jeu d'orgue)* bourdon; *(son de*

basse) drone **3** *(cloche)* great bell **4** *Typ* omission, out **5** *(bâton)* pilgrim's staff **6** *Fam (locution)* **avoir le b.** to feel down, to be down in the dumps
bourdonnant, -e [burdonɑ̃, -ɑ̃t] **ADJ** *(ruche, insecte)* humming, buzzing, droning
bourdonnement [burdonmɑ̃] **NM** *(vrombissement → d'un insecte, d'une voix)* hum, buzz, drone; *(→ d'un ventilateur, d'un moteur)* hum, drone; **j'ai des bourdonnements d'oreilles** my ears are ringing
bourdonner [3] [burdone] **VI** *(insecte, voix)* to hum, to buzz, to drone; *(moteur)* to hum; *(oreilles)* to ring; *(lieu)* to buzz; **la salle bourdonnait du bruit des conversations** the room was buzzing with the sound of conversation
boure [bur] = **bour**
bourg [bur] **NM** (market) town; **aller au b.** to go (up) to town
bourgade [burgad] **NF** (large) village, small town
bourge [burʒ] *Fam Péj* **ADJ** upper-class■, *Br* posh
NMF upper-class person■, *Br* toff; **chez les bourges** in upper-class circles■
bourgeois, -e [burʒwa, -az] **ADJ 1** *(dans un sens marxiste)* of the bourgeoisie, bourgeois **2** *(dans un sens non marxiste)* middle-class **3** *Péj (caractéristique de la bourgeoisie)* bourgeois; **goûts b.** bourgeois taste; **presse bourgeoise** bourgeois *or* capitalist press **4** *(aisé, confortable)* **intérieur b.** comfortable middle-class home; **quartier b.** comfortable residential area; **cuisine bourgeoise** good plain home cooking
NM,F 1 *(dans un sens marxiste)* bourgeois **2** *(dans un sens non marxiste)* member of the middle class; **grand b.** member of the upper-middle class; **petit b.** member of the lower middle class **3** *Hist (au Moyen Âge)* burgher; *(avant la Révolution)* member of the third estate; *(roturier)* commoner **4** *Suisse (citoyen)* citizen; **les b.** the townspeople **5** *Péj (béotien)* Philistine
▫ **bourgeoise** **NF** *Fam* **ma bourgeoise** my old lady, *Br* the wife
▫ **en bourgeois** **ADV** *Vieilli* **habillé en b.** out of uniform, (dressed) in civvies

'Le Bourgeois gentilhomme' *Molière* 'The Would-be Gentleman'

'Les Bourgeois de Calais' *Rodin* 'The Burghers of Calais'

bourgeoisement [burʒwazmɑ̃] **ADV 1** *(conventionnellement)* conventionally, respectably; **vivre b.** to lead a respectable life; **une maison meublée b.** a comfortably furnished house **2** *Jur* **occuper b. un local** to use premises for residential purposes only
bourgeoisial, -e, -aux, -ales [burʒwazjal, -o] **ADJ** *Suisse* town *(avant n)*
bourgeoisie [burʒwazi] **NF 1** *(dans un sens marxiste)* bourgeoisie; **la petite b.** the petty bourgeoisie **2** *(classe aisée, professions libérales)* middle class; **la petite/moyenne b.** the lower middle/the middle class; **la grande** *ou* **haute b.** the upper-middle class; *(en France)* the haute bourgeoisie **3** *Hist (au Moyen Âge)* burghers; *(avant la Révolution)* bourgeoisie, third estate **4** *Suisse (citoyenneté)* citizenship *(at "commune" level)*
bourgeon [burʒɔ̃] **NM** *Bot & Méd* bud; **en bourgeons** in bud; **b. gustatif** taste bud, *Spéc* gustatory bud
bourgeonnement [burʒonmɑ̃] **NM 1** *Bot* budding **2** *Méd* granulation **3** *Biol* budding
bourgeonner [3] [burʒone] **VI 1** *Bot* to bud **2** *(visage, nez)* to break out in spots
bourgeron [burʒərɔ̃] **NM** *(gén)* workman's blouse, overall; *Mil* fatigue coat; *Naut* jumper
Bourges [burʒ] **NM le printemps de B.** = annual music festival in Bourges
bourgmestre [burgmɛstr] **NM** *Belg* burgomaster
Bourgogne [burgɔɲ] **NF la B.** Burgundy

bourgogne [burgɔɲ] NM (vin) Burgundy (wine)

bourgueil [burgœj] NM (vin) Bourgueil

bourguignon, -onne [burgiɲɔ̃, -ɔn] ADJ **1** Géog & Hist Burgundian **2** Culin (sauce) bourguignonne

■ NM (dialecte) Burgundy dialect

❑ **Bourguignon, -onne** NM,F **1** Burgundian **2** Hist **les Bourguignons** the supporters of the Dukes of Burgundy (in the Hundred Years War)

❑ **bourguignonne** NF (bouteille) Burgundy wine bottle

❑ **à la bourguignonne** ADJ Culin with a bourguignonne sauce, cooked in red wine

bourlingue [burlɛ̃g] NF Fam (voyage) perilous journey■; (vie) adventurous life■

bourlinguer [3] [burlɛ̃ge] VI **1** Naut (voyager par mer) to sail (around) **2** Fam (se déplacer) to get around, to kick about; **elle a bourlingué dans le monde entier** she's been all over the world **3** Naut to labour

bourlingueur, -euse [burlɛ̃gœr, -øz] ADJ Fam adventurous

■ NM,F **1** (marin) old salt **2** Fam (aventurier) wanderer■, rover; **c'est un b.** he's always on the move

bouronner [3] [burɔne] VI Suisse (dans le canton du Vaud) to smoulder

bourrache [buraʃ] NF Bot borage

bourrade [burad] NF (de la main) push, shove; (du coude) poke, dig; **donner une b. amicale à qn** to give sb a friendly shove; **repousser qn d'une b.** to shove sb away; **une b. dans les côtes** a poke or a dig in the ribs

bourrage [buraʒ] NM **1** (remplissage → d'un coussin) stuffing; (→ d'une chaise) filling, padding; (→ d'une pipe, d'un poêle) filling; Fam **b. de crâne** (propagande) brainwashing; Scol cramming **2** Ordinat (dans une imprimante) jam; **b. (de cartes)** (card) jam; Cin **b. du film** piling up or buckling of the film; **b. papier** paper jam **3** (matériau) stuffing, filling

bourrasque [burask] NF **1** (coup de vent) squall, gust or blast (of wind); **b. de neige** snow flurry; **souffler en b.** to blow in gusts, to gust; Fig **une b. d'injures** a flurry of insults **2** (incident) storm, crisis; **sous la b.** in the midst of the crisis or storm

bourrasser [3] [burase] VT Can to push around, to bully

bourratif, -ive [buratif, -iv] ADJ Fam filling■, Péj stodgy; **des aliments bourratifs** stodge (UNCOUNT)

bourre[1] [bur] NM Fam Arg crime cop; **les bourres** the cops, the fuzz

bourre[2] [bur] NF **1** (rembourrage) filling, stuffing, wadding

2 Tex flock; **b. de laine** (déchet) flock of wool; (rembourrage) flock wool; **b. de papier** fluff; **b. de soie** flock or floss or waste silk

3 Bot down

4 (de fusil, de cartouche) wad

5 (d'un animal) underfur

6 (locutions) Fam **de première b.** great, excellent; Fam **raconter des bourres** to tell whoppers or Br porkies; Fam **le vendredi, c'est le coup de b. au bureau** Fridays are manic at work; Vulg **bonne b.!** I hope you get your oats!

❑ **à la bourre** ADV Fam **être à la b.** (être en retard) to be late■; (dans son travail) to be behind; (être pressé) to be in a rush; **il est toujours à la b.** (en retard) he's always late for everything; (dans son travail) he always leaves everything until the last minute

bourré, -e[1] [bure] ADJ **1** (plein → théâtre, bus) packed; (→ valise) crammed; **le coffre est b.** the Br boot or Am trunk is crammed full; **b. de** packed or crammed with; **les kiwis sont bourrés de vitamines** kiwi fruit are packed or crammed with vitamins; **un texte b. de fautes** a text full of or riddled with mistakes; **être b. de complexes** to be full of or a mass of hang-ups; **b. à craquer** full to bursting **2** très Fam (ivre) Br pissed, Am bombed

bourreau, -x [buro] NM **1** (exécuteur → gén) executioner; (→ qui pend) hangman **2** (tortionnaire) torturer; Fig (oppresseur) oppressor; **b. d'enfants** child beater; **b. des cœurs** heartbreaker; **b. de travail** workaholic

bourrée[2] [bure] NF Suisse **1** (grande affluence)

---

crowd **2** (grande quantité) **une b. de** masses of, loads of

bourrée[3] NF (danse) bourrée

bourrelé, -e [burle] ADJ **b. de remords** full of remorse, racked with guilt

bourrèlement [burɛlmã] NM Littéraire anguish, torment

bourrelet [burlɛ] NM **1** (isolant) weather strip, Br draught excluder **2** (de graisse) fold; **b. de chair** roll of flesh; **des bourrelets autour de la taille** a spare tyre **3** (petit coussin) pad, cushion

bourrelier [burəlje] NM saddler

bourrellerie [burɛlri] NF saddlery

bourre-pif [burpif] (pl **bourre-pifs**) NM Fam punch on the nose■

bourrer [3] [bure] VT **1** (rembourrer) to fill, to stuff **2** (remplir → pipe) to fill; (→ poche) to fill, to cram, to stuff; (→ valise, tiroir) to cram (full), to pack tightly; **b. un poêle de papier, b. du papier dans un poêle** to stuff a stove full of paper; Fam **b. le crâne** ou **le mou à qn** Br to have or Am to put sb on; **b. les urnes** to rig the vote (by producing large numbers of false ballot papers) **3** (gaver → sujet: aliment) to fill up; **b. qn de** to cram or to stuff sb with; **tu le bourres de sucreries/principes surannés** you're stuffing him full of sweets/outmoded principles **4** (frapper) très Fam **b. la gueule à qn** to kick sb's head or teeth in; **b. qn de coups** to beat sb up, Br to do sb over **5** Vulg (posséder sexuellement) to hump, Br to shag

USAGE ABSOLU **les bananes, ça bourre** bananas are very filling or fill you up

■ VI Fam (se hâter) to hurry■; **allez, bourrez un peu!** come on, get a move on!

▸ **se bourrer** VPR **1** Fam (manger) to stuff oneself or one's face; **se b. de** to stuff one's face with **2** très Fam (locution) **se b. la gueule** to get Br pissed or Am bombed

bourrette [burɛt] NF Tex bourette

bourriche [buriʃ] NF **1** (panier) hamper, wicker case **2** Pêche (filet) keepnet

bourrichon [buriʃɔ̃] NM Fam **monter le b. à qn** Br to have or Am to put sb on; **se monter le b.** to get (all) worked up; **elle s'était monté le b.** she'd imagined all sorts of things■

bourricot [buriko] NM donkey, Am burro

bourride [burid] NF Culin bourride (fish stew with garlic mayonnaise)

bourrin, -e [burɛ̃, burin] Fam ADJ **1** (qui manque de raffinement) oafish■; **il est un peu b. avec ses blagues de cul, mon cousin** he's a bit of a Neanderthal, my cousin, what with his dirty jokes **2** (agressif → personne, méthode) rough; (→ musique) heavy, hardcore; **leur équipe a joué de manière assez bourrine** their team played pretty rough

■ NM **1** (cheval) (old) nag **2** (policier) cop

■ NM,F (personne brusque) brute■; **il conduit comme un b.** he drives like a maniac; **c'est de la musique de b.** it's real headbanging music

bourrique [burik] NF **1** Zool donkey **2** Fam (personne obstinée) pig-headed individual; **elle ne voudra pas, la b.!** she's so pig-headed she won't want to! **3** (locution) **faire tourner qn en b.** to drive sb crazy or up the wall

bourriquet [burikɛ] NM **1** (ânon) ass's colt **2** (treuil) windlass, winch

bourroir [burwar] NM Mines tamping-bar, tamper

bourru, -e [bury] ADJ **1** (rude → personne, manières) gruff, rough; **d'un ton b.** gruffly **2** Tex rough **3** (jeune → vin) fermented; (→ lait) raw

Bourse [burs] NF Bourse **1** (marché) stock exchange, stock market; **la B. de Londres** the London Stock Exchange; **la B. de Paris** the Paris Bourse or Stock Exchange; **B. de** ou **du commerce, B. de(s) marchandises** commodity or commodities exchange; **B. coulisse** unlisted market; **B. d'instruments financiers à terme** financial futures exchange; **B. maritime** ou **des frets** shipping exchange; **B. du travail** (réunion) = meeting of local trade unions for the purpose of reaching agreement on how best to defend their interests and provide community services; (endroit) = local trade union centre; **la B. des valeurs** the stock exchange or market; **coup de B.** (spectacular) deal on the stock exchange

---

2 (cours) market; **la B. est calme/animée/en hausse** the market is quiet/is lively/has risen

❑ **à la Bourse, en Bourse** ADV on the stock exchange or market; **jouer à la** ou **en B.** to speculate on the stock exchange or market; **entrer en B.** (entreprise) to go live

bourse [burs] NF **1** (porte-monnaie) purse; **avoir la b. bien garnie** to have money in one's pocket; **faire b. commune** to pool one's money; **faire b. à part** to keep one's money separate; **sans b. délier** without paying a penny or Am cent; **la b. ou la vie!** stand and deliver!, your money or your life!; **ouvrir sa b.** to put one's hand in one's pocket; **ouvrir sa b. à qn** to lend sb money

2 Scol & Univ (allocation) scholarship, grant; **b. d'études** bursary; **avoir une b.** to be on or to have a grant

3 (vente d'occasion) **b. aux vêtements/aux jouets** second-hand clothes/toy sale

❑ **bourses** NFPL Anat scrotum

bourse-à-pasteur [bursapastœr] (pl **bourses-à-pasteur**) NF Bot shepherd's purse

boursicotage [bursikɔtaʒ] NM Bourse dabbling or speculating on the stock market

boursicoter [3] [bursikɔte] VI Bourse to dabble (on the stock market)

boursicoteur, -euse [bursikɔtœr, -øz], **boursicotier, -ère** [bursikɔtje, -ɛr] NM,F Bourse small-time investor; **il était b. à ses heures** he used to dabble from time to time on the stock market

boursier, -ère [bursje, -ɛr] ADJ **1** Scol & Univ **un étudiant b.** a grant or scholarship holder **2** Bourse (de la Bourse) stock exchange (avant n), (stock) market (avant n)

■ NM,F **1** Scol & Univ grant or scholarship holder; **les boursiers doivent remplir le formulaire ci-joint** students who receive a grant or scholarship should fill in the accompanying form **2** Bourse operator **3** Suisse treasurer

boursouflage [bursuflaʒ] NM (gonflement → du visage) swelling, puffiness; (→ de la peinture) blistering

boursouflé, -e [bursufle] ADJ **1** (gonflé → visage) swollen, puffy; (→ peinture) blistered; (→ plaie) swollen **2** (ampoulé) bombastic, pompous, turgid

boursouflement [bursufləmã] NM (gonflement → du visage) swelling, puffiness; (→ de la peinture) blistering

boursoufler [3] [bursufle] VT (gonfler → visage) to swell, to puff up; (→ peinture) to blister

▸ **se boursoufler** VPR (visage) to become swollen or puffy; (peinture) to blister; (surface) to swell (up)

boursouflure [bursuflyr] NF **1** (bouffissure) swelling, puffiness; (cloque) blister **2** (emphase) pomposity, turgidity

bouscueil [buskœj] NM Can (en acadien) pile-up of ice, break-up of ice

bousculade [buskylad] NF **1** (agitation) crush, pushing and shoving; **pas de b.!** no jostling or shoving!; **une b. vers la sortie** a scramble or stampede towards the exit; **j'ai perdu mon parapluie dans la b.** I lost my umbrella in the confusion **2** Fam (précipitation) rush; **ça a été la b. toute la journée** it's been one mad rush all day (long)

bousculer [3] [buskyle] VT **1** (pousser → voyageur, passant) to jostle, to push, to shove; (→ chaise, table) to bump or to knock into; **il l'a bousculée au passage** he bumped into her as he went past; **se faire b. par qn** to be jostled by sb

2 Fig (changer brutalement) to upset, to turn on its head, to turn upside down; **b. les traditions** to turn tradition on its head, to upset tradition; **b. les habitudes de qn** to upset sb's routine

3 (presser) to rush, to hurry; **j'ai été très bousculé** I've had a lot to do or a very busy time; **laisse-moi le temps de réfléchir, ne me bouscule pas** don't rush me, I need time to think

▸ **se bousculer** VPR **1** (dans une cohue) to jostle, to push and shove; **tout le monde se bousculait pour arriver à la caisse** everybody was shoving to get to the cash desk

2 (venir en foule) to rush; **les idées se bousculaient dans sa tête** his/her head was a jumble of ideas; **on se bouscule pour aller voir l'exposition** there's a rush to see the new exhibition; **on se bouscule pour avoir son livre** everybody's

clamouring for his/her book; *Ironique* **ne vous bousculez surtout pas pour m'aider** don't all rush to help me at once, will you?; *Fam* **ça se bouscule au portillon!** *(il y a affluence)* there's a huge crowd trying to get in!; *(il/elle bafouille)* he/she can't get his/her words out; *Hum* **ça ne se bouscule pas au portillon** people aren't exactly turning up in droves

bouse [buz] NF **b. (de vache)** *(matière)* cow dung; *(motte)* cowpat

bouseux, -euse [buzø, -øz] NM,F *très Fam Péj* yokel, country bumpkin, *Am* hick; **les b. du coin** the local yokels

bousier [buzje] NM *Entom* dung beetle, dung chafer

bousillage [buzijaʒ] NM **1** *Fam (gâchis)* botch, botch-up **2** *Constr* cob

bousiller [3] [buzije] VT **1** *Fam (mal faire)* to bungle, to botch (up) **2** *Fam (casser)* to bust, to wreck; **ma montre est bousillée** my watch is bust **3** *Fam (gâcher)* to spoil, to ruin; **tu as tout bousillé** you've spoilt it all *or* ruined the whole thing **4** *très Fam (tuer)* to bump off, to do in, to waste **5** *Constr* to cob (up)

▶**se bousiller** VPR *Fam* **se b. les yeux/la santé** to ruin one's eyes/health■

bousilleur, -euse [buzijœr, -øz] NM,F *Fam* botcher, bungler

bousin [buzɛ̃] NM **1** *(tourbe)* low-grade peat **2** *(terre)* dirt, earth *(clinging to quarried stone)*

boussole [busɔl] NF **1** *(instrument)* compass; **b. de marine** mariner's compass; **b. de poche** pocket compass **2** *Fam (locution)* **il a complètement perdu la b.** *(vieillard)* he's lost his marbles, he's gone gaga; *(fou)* he's off his head *or* rocker; **il s'agit de ne pas perdre la b.** let's keep our wits about us

boustifaille [bustifaj] NF *très Fam* grub, *Br* nosh, *Am* chow

boustrophédon [bustrɔfedɔ̃] NM **inscriptions en b.** boustrophedon inscriptions

BOUT [bu]

tip **1** ▪ toe **1** ▪ end **1, 2** ▪ piece **4** ▪ scrap **4** ▪ part, bit **4**

NM **1** *(extrémité → d'un couteau, d'un crayon)* tip; *(→ d'une botte, d'une chaussette)* toe; *(→ d'une table, d'une ficelle)* end; **le b. est arrondi** it's got a round tip; **à bouts ronds** round-tipped; **à bouts carrés** square-tipped; **tiens bien ton b., je tire** hold on to your end while I pull; **b. du doigt** fingertip, tip of the finger; **b. du nez** tip of the nose; **b. du sein** nipple; **b. filtre** filter tip; **à b. filtre** filter-tipped; *Fig* **prendre qch par le bon b.** to deal with sth in the right way; **prendre qn par le bon b.** to approach sb the right way; **plus que 40 pages à écrire, je tiens le bon b.** only another 40 pages to write, I can see the light at the end of the tunnel; **je ne sais pas par quel b. le prendre** *(personne)* I don't know how to handle *or* to approach him; *(article, travail)* I don't know how to tackle *or* to approach it; **aborder** *ou* **considérer** *ou* **voir les choses par le petit b. de la lorgnette** to take a narrow view of things; **il a accepté du b. des lèvres** he accepted reluctantly *or* half-heartedly; **je l'ai sur le b. de la langue** it's on the tip of my tongue; **sur le b. des doigts** perfectly, by heart; **il connaît** *ou* **sait ses verbes sur le b. des doigts** he knows his verbs by heart *or Br* off pat *or Am* down pat; **je connais son œuvre sur le b. des doigts** I know his/her work by heart *or* inside out; **s'asseoir du b. des fesses** to sit down gingerly; **s'en aller par tous les bouts** to fall *or* to come to pieces; **enfin, on en voit le b.** at last, we're beginning to see the light at the end of the tunnel; **on n'en voit pas le b.** there's no end to it

2 *(extrémité → d'un espace)* end; **le b. du tunnel** the end of the tunnel; *Fig* **on voit enfin le b. du tunnel** at last we can see the light at the end of the tunnel; **le b. du monde** the back of beyond; **ce n'est pas le b. du monde!** it won't kill you!; **ce serait bien le b. du monde si ça prenait plus de deux jours** it'll take two days at the very most

3 *(portion de temps)* **un b. de temps** a while; *Fam* **ça fait un bon b. de temps de ça** it was quite a long time ago *or* a while back; **il faudra attendre un bon b. de temps** you'll have to wait for quite some time

4 *(morceau → de pain, de bois, de terrain)* piece, a bit; *(→ de papier)* scrap, piece; **un vieux b. de chewing-gum** an old piece of chewing gum; **un b. de ciel bleu** a patch of blue sky; **donne-m'en un b.** give me some *or* a piece *or* a bit; *Fam* **un (petit) b. d'homme/de femme** a little man/woman; *Fam* **b. de chou** *ou* **zan** *(enfant)* toddler; *(en appellatif)* sweetie, *Br* poppet; **b. d'essai** screen test; **ça fait un bon b. de chemin** it's quite some *or* a way; **faire un b. de chemin avec qn** to go part of the way with sb; **faire un b. de conduite à qn** to walk sb part of the way; *Théât & Cin* **b. de rôle** walk-on *or* bit part; *Fam* **discuter** *ou* **tailler le b. de gras** to chew the fat; *très Fam* **mettre les bouts** to make oneself scarce; **la vie avec lui était intolérable, alors elle a mis les bouts** life with him was intolerable, so *Br* she did a bunk *or Am* she split

5 *Naut* **être b. au vent** to be head to the wind

6 [but] *Can Fam* **dans mon b.** in my neck of the woods; *Fam* **c'est le b. du b.!** that takes *Br* the biscuit *or Am* the cake!; *très Fam* **c'est le b. de la marde!** that takes *Br* the biscuit *or Am* the cake!

❑ **à bout** ADV **être à b.** to be at the end of one's tether; **ma patience est à b.!** I've run out of patience!; **mettre** *ou* **pousser qn à b.** to push sb to the limit; **ne me pousse pas à b.!** don't push me (too far)!

❑ **à bout de** PRÉP **1 être à b. de** *(ne plus avoir de)* **être à b. d'arguments** to have run out of arguments; **être à b. de course** to be worn out *or* done in; **il est à b. de forces** *(physiquement)* he's got no strength left in him; *(psychologiquement)* he can't cope any more; **être à b. de nerfs** to be on the verge of a breakdown; **être à b. de patience** to have run out of patience

2 *(locutions)* **porter un paquet à b. de bras** to carry a parcel (in one's outstretched arms); *Fig* **porter qn/une entreprise à b. de bras** to carry sb/a business; **venir à b. de** *(adversaire, obstacle)* to overcome; *(travail)* to see the end of; **je ne suis pas venu à b. de ces taches** I couldn't get rid of these stains

❑ **à bout portant** ADV point-blank; **tirer (sur) qn/qch à b. portant** to shoot sb/sth at point-blank range

❑ **à tout bout de champ** ADV all the time, non-stop; **elle me pose des questions à tout b. de champ** she never stops asking me questions; **on cite son nom à tout b. de champ** his/her name is constantly being quoted

❑ **au bout** [but] *Can Fam* ADJ excellent, great ADV **bon au b.** excellent, great

❑ **au bout de** PRÉP **1** *(après)* after; **au b. d'un moment** after a while; **au b. d'une heure** after an hour

2 *(à la fin de)* **j'arrive au b. de mon contrat** my contract's nearly up; **le succès est au b. de nos efforts** our efforts will lead to success; **pas encore au b. de ses peines** not out of the woods yet

3 *(dans l'espace)* **au b. de la rue** at the bottom *or* end of the road; *Fig* **leur couple est arrivé au b. du chemin** the two of them have come to the end of the road; **le mot est resté au b. de ma plume** I didn't write the word in the end; **la conclusion a dû rester au b. de sa plume** he must have forgotten to put in the conclusion; **être au b. de son** *ou* **du rouleau** *(épuisé)* to be completely washed out; *(presque mort)* to be at death's door

❑ **au bout du compte** ADV at the end of the day, in the end

❑ **bout à bout** ADV end to end; **disposez les montants b. à b. avant de les assembler** lay the struts end to end before assembling; **un ramassis de citations mises b. à b.** a whole mishmash of quotations

❑ **de bout en bout** ADV *(lire)* from cover to cover; **parcourir un couloir de b. en b.** to pace up and down a corridor; **tu as raison de b. en b.** you're completely *or* totally right; **elle a mené la course de b. en b.** she led the race from start to finish

❑ **d'un bout à l'autre** ADV **la pièce est drôle d'un b. à l'autre** the play's hilarious from beginning to end *or* from start to finish; **il m'a contredit d'un b. à l'autre** he contradicted me all the way

❑ **d'un bout de... à l'autre** PRÉP **d'un b. de l'année à l'autre** all year round; **d'un b. à l'autre du pays, les militants s'organisent** (right) throughout the country, the militants are organizing themselves

❑ **en bout de** PRÉP at the end of; **en b. de course** at the end of the race; *Fig* **le régime est en b. de course** the regime is running out of steam; **en b. de piste** at the end of the runway

❑ **jusqu'au bout** ADV to the very end; **il est resté jusqu'au b.** he stayed to the very end; **il va toujours jusqu'au b. de ce qu'il entreprend** he always sees things through to the very end; **j'irais jusqu'au b. du monde avec toi** I'd follow you to the end *or* ends of the earth; **il est toujours soigné jusqu'au b. des ongles** he's always immaculately turned out; **elle est artiste jusqu'au b. des ongles** she's an artist through and through

'À bout de souffle' *Godard* 'Breathless'

bout-à-bout [butabu] NM *Cin & TV* rough cut, rough edit

boutade [butad] NF *(plaisanterie)* joke, *Sout* sally; **faire une b.** to make *or* to crack a joke; **c'est une b.!** you're joking!; **c'était une b.!** (I was) only joking!; **s'en tirer par une b.** to joke one's way out of it

boutanche [butɑ̃ʃ] NF *Fam* bottle■

boutargue [butarg] NF *Culin* botargo

bout-dehors [budəɔr] (*pl* **bouts-dehors**) NM *Naut* boom

boute-en-train [butɑ̃trɛ̃] NM INV *(amuseur)* funny man, joker; **le b. de la bande** the life and soul of the group

boutefas [butfa] NM *Suisse Culin* = large pork sausage, encased in a pig's large intestine, a speciality of the Vaud canton

boutefeu, -x [butfø] NM **1** *(en pyrotechnie)* linstock **2** *Mil* shot firer **3** *Vieilli* troublemaker

boute-hors [butœɔr] NM INV *Naut* boom

bouteille [butɛj] NF **1** *(récipient → pour un liquide)* bottle; *(→ pour un gaz)* bottle, cylinder; **une b. de vin** *(pleine)* a bottle of wine; *(vide)* a wine bottle; **un casier à bouteilles** a bottle rack; **b. d'oxygène** cylinder of oxygen; **b. Thermos** Thermos® (*Br* flask *or Am* bottle); **avoir de la b.** to be an old hand; *Fam* **prendre de la b.** to be getting *or Br* knocking on a bit; **elle a pris de la b.** she's not getting any younger, she's getting on a bit; **c'est la b. à l'encre** the whole thing's a muddle; **jeter** *ou* **lancer une b. à la mer** to send a message in a bottle; *Fig* to send out an SOS

2 *(contenu)* bottle, bottleful; **boire une b. de rouge** to drink a bottle of red wine; **vendu en litres ou en bouteilles** sold in litres or in (75 cl) bottles; **boire une bonne b.** to drink a good bottle of wine; **être porté sur** *ou* **aimer** *ou* **caresser la b.** to like one's drink

❑ **bouteilles** NFPL *Naut* heads, toilets

❑ **en bouteille** ADJ *(gaz, vin)* bottled ADV **mettre du vin en b.** to bottle wine; **vieilli en b.** aged in the bottle

bouteiller [butɛje] NM *Hist* king's butler

bouteillerie [butɛjri] NF *(usine)* bottle factory; *(fabrication)* bottle industry

bouteillon [butɛjɔ̃] NM *Vieilli Mil* dixie

bouter [3] [bute] VT **1** *Littéraire Vieilli* to drive out, to chase out; **b. hors de France** to drive *or* chase out of France **2** *Belg & Suisse* **b. le feu à qch** to set fire to sth, to set sth on fire

bouterolle [butrɔl] NF **1** *(de fourreau)* chape **2** *(de serrure)* ward, snap; *(de clé)* ward **3** *(outil)* rivet-set, rivet-snap, riveting-die **4** *Pêche* shrimping-net

bouteroue [butru] NF *Vieilli Constr* spur post

boute-selle [butsɛl] NM INV *Mil* bugle call *(summoning cavalry to mount)*, *Am* boots-and-saddles

bouteur [butœr] NM *Mil (engin)* bulldozer

boutillier [butije] NM *Hist* king's butler

boutiquaire [butikɛr] **ADJ niveau b.** (dans un aéroport) shopping level or concourse

boutique [butik] **NF 1** Com (magasin) Br shop, Am store; **b. de mode** boutique; **b. franche** duty-free shop; **b. franchisée** franchise outlet; **b. hors taxe** duty-free shop; **tenir b.** to have a shop **2** Fam (lieu de travail) place, dump; **j'en ai marre de cette b.!** I've had enough of this dump!; **changer de b.** to get a new job; **parler b.** to talk shop

boutiquier, -ère [butikje, -ɛr] **NM,F** Com Br shopkeeper, Am storekeeper

boutis [buti] **NM 1** (technique) = Provençal embroidery style featuring embossed designs as in quilting **2** (dessus de lit etc) = bedspread, throw etc made using the Provençal "boutis" embroidery technique

boutisse [butis] **NF** Constr header, bonder; **assise de boutisses** heading course

boutoir [butwar] **NM 1** Zool (du sanglier) snout **2** (locution) **coup de b.** cutting remark

bouton [butɔ̃] **NM 1** Bot bud; **b. d'œillet** carnation bud; **b. de rose** rosebud
2 Couture button; **b. de bottine** boot stud; **avoir des yeux en boutons de bottine** to have beady eyes; **b. de col** collar stud; **b. de manchette** cuff link
3 (poignée de porte, de tiroir) knob
4 (de mise en marche) & Ordinat button; (interrupteur) switch; TV **b. de commande de synchronisme vertical** vertical hold; **b. de contraste** contrast button; Ordinat **b. de défilement** scroll button; Ordinat **b. de navigation** navigation button; Ordinat **b. d'option, b. radio** radio button; **b. de réglage** dial; **b. de réglage du volume** volume control; Ordinat **b. de réinitialisation** reset button; **b. de sonnette** bell-push; Ordinat **b. de souris** mouse button
5 Méd spot, pimple; **avoir des boutons** (pustules) to have spots; (petits, rouges) to have a rash; **b. d'acné** spot caused by acne; **b. de chaleur** heat bump; **b. de fièvre** fever blister, cold sore
6 (bijou) **b. d'oreille** stud (earring)
▫ **en bouton** ADJ Bot in bud

bouton-d'argent [butɔ̃darʒɑ̃] (pl **boutons-d'argent**) **NM** Bot yarrow

bouton-d'or [butɔ̃dɔr] (pl **boutons-d'or**) **NM** Bot buttercup

boutonnage [butɔnaʒ] **NM 1** (action de boutonner) buttoning (up) **2** (mode de fermeture) buttons; **à b. de haut en bas** button-through (avant n); **une veste à double b.** a double-buttoning jacket

boutonner [butɔne] **VT 1** (vêtement) to button (up), to do up **2** Escrime to button
▸ **VI** Bot to bud (up)
▸ **se boutonner** VPR **1** (se fermer) to button (up) **2** Fam (s'habiller) to button oneself up

boutonneux, -euse [butɔnø, -øz] **ADJ** (peau, visage, adolescent) spotty, pimply

boutonnier, -ère[1] [butɔnje, -jɛr] **NM,F 1** (fabricant) button manufacturer, button maker **2** (marchand) button dealer

boutonnière[2] [butɔnjɛr] **NF 1** Couture buttonhole; **point de b.** blanket stitch
2 Méd buttonhole; **faire une b. à qn** to make a buttonhole in sb
3 Fam (blessure) gash
4 Géol inlier
▫ **à la boutonnière** ADV on one's lapel; **avoir une fleur à la b.** to wear a flower on one's lapel or in one's buttonhole, to wear a Br buttonhole or Am boutonniere; **ils défilent, la décoration à la b.** they're marching with their medals on

bouton-poussoir [butɔ̃puswar] (pl **boutons-poussoirs**) **NM** push button

bouton-pression [butɔ̃presjɔ̃] (pl **boutons-pression**) **NM** snap (fastener), Br press stud

boutre [butr] **NM** Naut dhow

bout-rimé [butrime] (pl **bouts-rimés**) Littérature **NM** poem in set rhymes
▫ **bouts-rimés** NMPL bouts-rimés, rhymed endings

boutte [but] voir **bout 6**

bouturage [butyraʒ] **NM** Hort propagation by cuttings

bouture [butyr] **NF** Hort cutting; **faire des boutures** to take cuttings

bouturer [3] [butyre] **VT** Hort **1** (reproduire) to propagate (by cuttings) **2** (couper) to take cuttings from
▸ **VI** Bot to grow suckers

Bouvard et Pécuchet [buvarepekyʃe] **NPR** = characters from a novel of the same name by Flaubert; two middle-aged men whose naïve quest for scientific knowledge leads them into comic situations

bouverie [buvri] **NF** byre, cowshed

bouvet [buvɛ] **NM** Menuis grooving plane

bouveteuse [buvtøz] **NF** Menuis match plane

bouvier, -ère [buvje, -ɛr] **NM,F** bullock driver, cowherd
NM Zool (chien) bouvier, sheepdog; **b. des Flandres** bouvier des Flandres
▫ **bouvière** NF Orn bitterling

bouvillon [buvijɔ̃] **NM** Zool young bullock

bouvreuil [buvrœj] **NM** Orn bullfinch; **b. githagine** trumpeter finch

bouvril [buvril] **NM** lair (in a slaughterhouse)

Bouygues [buig] **NM** = large French building firm with investments in the media, especially television

bouzouki [buzuki] **NM** Mus bouzouki

Bovary [bovari] **NPR Emma** ou **Madame B.** = heroine of Flaubert's novel 'Madame Bovary', after whom the term "bovarysme" was coined to describe the feeling that romantic happiness is just round the corner

bovarysme [bovarism] **NM** romantic daydreaming

bovidé [bovide] **NM** Zool bovid; **les bovidés** the Bovidae

bovin, -e [bovɛ̃, -in] **ADJ 1** Zool (espèce) bovine; (élevage) cattle; (regard) **2** Péj (stupide) bovine
NM bovine; **les bovins** Zool bovines; Agr cattle; **bovins d'embouche** beef cattle; **bovins laitiers** dairy cattle

boviné [bovine] **NM** Zool bovine; **les bovinés** bovines

bowette [bovɛt] **NF** Mines cross-cut

bowling [bulin] **NM 1** (jeu) (tenpin) bowling; **aller faire un b.** to go bowling **2** (salle) bowling alley

bow-string [bostrin] (pl **bow-strings**) **NM** (poutre) bowstring girder

bow-window [bowindo] (pl **bow-windows**) **NM** Archit bow window

box[1] [bɔks] **NM INV** (cuir) box calf

box[2] [bɔks] (pl **inv** ou **boxes**) **NM 1** (enclos → pour cheval) stall, Br loose box **2** (garage) lock-up garage **3** (compartiment → à l'hôpital, au dortoir, dans un bureau) cubicle **4** Jur **b. des accusés** dock; aussi Fig **au b. des accusés** in the dock

box-calf [bɔkskalf] (pl **inv** ou **box-calfs**) **NM** (cuir) box calf

boxe [bɔks] **NF** Boxe boxing; **gants/match de b.** boxing gloves/match; **faire de la b.** to box; **b. américaine** full-contact karate, full-contact kick boxing; **b. anglaise** boxing; **b. française** kick or French boxing; **b. thaï** Thai boxing

boxer[1] [bɔksɛr] **NM** (chien) boxer

boxer[2] [3] [bɔkse] **VI** Boxe to box, to fight; **b. contre qn** to box against or fight sb
▸ **VT** Fam to punch ▪, to thump

boxer-short [bɔksœrʃɔrt] (pl **boxer-shorts**) **NM** boxer shorts

boxeur, -euse [bɔksœr, -øz] **NM,F** Boxe boxer

box-office [bɔksɔfis] (pl **box-offices**) **NM** box office; **être en tête du b.** to be a box-office hit

boxon [bɔksɔ̃] **NM** très Fam **1** (maison close) brothel, whorehouse **2** (désordre) mess; **foutre le b. dans qch** to make a mess of sth; **il fout le b. en classe** he creates havoc in the classroom; **quel b. dans sa chambre!** his room is a complete shambles!

boy [bɔj] **NM 1** (serviteur) boy **2** (danseur) (music-hall) dancer

boyard [bɔjar] **NM** Arch boyar

boyau, -x [bwajo] **NM 1** Culin length of casing **2** Mus **b. (de chat)** catgut, gut **3** (passage → de mine) gallery, tunnel; (→ souterrain) narrow tunnel; (→ tranchée) trench; (→ rue) narrow alleyway **4** (pneu) racing bike tyre **5** Can **b. d'arrosage** (garden) hose, hosepipe
▫ **boyaux** NMPL Zool guts, entrails; Fam (d'une personne) innards, guts

boyauderie [bwajodri] **NF** (activité) casing processing

boyaudier, -ère [bwajodje, -jɛr] **NM,F** gut-dresser

boyauter [3] [bwajote] **se boyauter** VPR Fam Vieilli to split one's sides with laughter

boycott [bɔjkɔt], **boycottage** [bɔjkɔtaʒ] **NM** boycott, boycotting

boycotter [3] [bɔjkɔte] **VT** to boycott; **les syndicats veulent faire b. les élections** the unions want people to boycott the elections; **se faire b.** to be boycotted

boycotteur, -euse [bɔjkɔtœr, -øz] **ADJ** boycotting (avant n)
NM,F boycotter

boy-scout [bɔjskut] (pl **boy-scouts**) **NM** Vieilli boy scout; Fig & Péj **mentalité de b.** boy-scout mentality

BP [bepe] **NF** (abrév **boîte postale**) PO box

BPA [bepea] **NM** Fin (abrév **bénéfice par action**) EPS

BPAL [bepeaɛl] **NF** (abrév **base de plein air et de loisirs**) outdoor recreation centre

BPF Anciennement Banque (abrév écrite **bon pour francs**) = abbreviation printed on cheques and invoices before amount to be written in figures

BPI[1] [bepei] **NM INV** Ordinat (abrév **bits per inch**) bpi

BPI[2] [bepei] **NF** (abrév **Bibliothèque publique d'information**) = library at the Centre Pompidou in Paris

bpp [bepepe] **NMPL** Ordinat (abrév **bits par pouce**) bpi

bps [bepeɛs] **NMPL** Ordinat (abrév **bits par seconde**) bps

brabançon, -onne [brabɑ̃sɔ̃, -ɔn] **ADJ** of/from Brabant
▫ **Brabançon, -onne** NM,F = inhabitant of or person from Brabant

Brabançonne [brabɑ̃sɔn] **NF** = Belgian national anthem

Brabant [brabɑ̃] **NM** le B. Brabant

brabant [brabɑ̃] **NM** Arch Agr metal plough

bracelet [braslɛ] **NM 1** (gén) bracelet; (rigide) bangle; **b. de cheville** (bijou) anklet; (pour criminel) electronic tag; **b. de détention** ou **électronique** electronic tag; **b. de montre** watchband, watchstrap **2** (pour faire du sport) wristband; **b. de force** leather wristband; **b. éponge** sweatband **3** (lien) band; **b. élastique** rubber band
▫ **bracelets** NMPL Fam Arg crime (menottes) bracelets, cuffs

bracelet-montre [braslɛmɔ̃tr] (pl **bracelets-montres**) **NM** wristwatch

brachial, -e, -aux, -ales [brakjal, -o] **ADJ** Anat brachial

brachiation [brakjasjɔ̃] **NF** (d'un singe) brachiation

brachiocéphalique [brakjosefalik] **ADJ** Anat brachiocephalic

brachiopode [brakjɔpɔd] Zool **NM** brachiopod, lampshell
▫ **brachiopodes** NMPL Brachiopoda

brachiosaure [brakjɔzɔr] **NM** Zool (en paléontologie) brachiosaur, brachiosaurus

brachycéphale [brakisefal] **ADJ** brachycephalic
NMF brachycephalic person

brachycéphalie [brakisefali] **NF** brachycephalism, brachycephaly

brachycère [brakisɛr] Entom **ADJ** brachycerous
▫ **brachycères** NMPL Brachycera

brachydactyle [brakidaktil] **ADJ** brachydactylic, brachydactylous

brachyoure [brakjur] Zool **NM** crab, Spéc member of the Brachyura family
▫ **brachyoures** NMPL Brachyura

braconnage [brakɔnaʒ] **NM** Chasse poaching

braconner [3] [brakɔne] **VI** Chasse to poach

braconnier, -ère [brakɔnje, ɛr] **NM,F** Chasse poacher

bractéaire [brakteɛr], **bractéal, -e, -aux, -ales** [brakteal, -o] **ADJ** Bot bracteal

bractée [brakte] **NF** Bot bract

bradage [bradaʒ] **NM** Com clearance sale

bradé, -e [brade] **ADJ** cut-price

Bradel [bradɛl] **NM** ou **NF** (reliure) B. Bradel binding

brader [3] [brade] **VT** Com to sell off cheaply; **on brade** (sur vitrine) clearance sale

braderie [bradri] **NF** Com **1** (vente → en plein air,

dans une salle) *Br* ≃ jumble sale, *Am* ≃ rummage sale **2** (*soldes*) clearance sale

bradeur, -euse [bradœr, -øz] NM,F *Com* discounter

bradycardie [bradikardi] NF *Méd* bradycardia

bradykinine [bradikinin] NF *Biol* bradykinin

bradype [bradip] NM *Zool* sloth

bradypsychie [bradipsiʃi] NF *Psy* bradypsychia

Bragance [bragɑ̃s] NM Braganza

braguette [bragɛt] NF *Br* flies, *Am* fly (*on trousers*)

Brahma [brama] NPR *Rel* Brahma

brahmane [braman] NM *Rel* Brahman

brahmanique [bramanik] ADJ *Rel* Brahmanic

brahmanisme [bramanism] NM *Rel* Brahmanism

Brahmapoutre [bramaputr], **Brahmaputra** [bramaputra] NM *Rel* **le B.** the Brahmaputra

brahmi [brami] NF *Rel* Brahmi

brahmine [bramin] NF *Rel* Brahmani

brai [brɛ] NM (*goudrons*) pitch

braies [brɛ] NFPL *Arch* breeches

braillage [brajaʒ] NM *Can Péj* bawling

braillard, -e [brajar, -ard] *Péj* ADJ **un bébé b.** a bawler

    NM,F bawler, squaller; **fais taire ton b.!** keep that squalling brat of yours quiet!

braille [braj] NM Braille; **apprendre le b.** to learn (to read) Braille; **un livre en b.** a book in Braille; **lire en b.** to read Braille

braillement [brajmɑ̃] NM bawl, howl; **les braillements d'un bébé** the crying *or* howling of a baby

brailler [3] [braje] VI **1** (*pleurer bruyamment*) to wail, to bawl, to howl **2** (*crier → mégère, ivrogne*) to yell, to bawl; (→ *radio*) to blare (out) **3** (*chanter*) to roar, to bellow **4** *Can* (*pleurer*) to cry

    VT to bawl (out), *Am* to holler (out)

brailleur, -euse [brajœr, -øz] *Péj* ADJ **un bébé b.** a bawler

    NM,F bawler, squaller; **fais taire ton b.!** keep that squalling brat of yours quiet!

braiment [brɛmɑ̃] NM (*d'un âne*) bray, braying

brainstorming [brɛnstɔrmiŋ] NM brainstorming; **un b.** a brainstorming session

brain-trust [brɛntrœst] (*pl* **brain-trusts**) NM *Br* brains trust, *Am* brain trust

braire [112] [brɛr] VI **1** (*âne*) to bray **2** *Fam* (*crier*) to yell, to bellow **3** *Fam* (*location*) **tu me fais b.!** you're getting on my wick!

braisage [brɛzaʒ] NM *Culin* braising

braise [brɛz] NF **1** (*charbons*) (glowing) embers; **cuire qch sur/sous la b.** to cook sth over/in the embers; *Fig* **un regard de b.** a smouldering look; *Fig* **être sur la b.** to be on tenterhooks **2** *Fam Arg crime* (*argent*) dough, moolah

braiser [4] [brɛze] VT *Culin* to braise

braisette [brɛzɛt] NF small ember

braisière [brɛzjɛr] NF **1** (*cocotte*) braising-pan, stew-pan **2** (*étouffoir pour la braise*) extinguishing box (*for charcoal*)

brame [bram] NF *Tech* (plate) slab

    NM (*d'un cerf*) bell (*of rutting stag*)

bramement [bramɑ̃] NM **1** (*d'un cerf*) bell **2** *Fam* (*cri*) wail

bramer [3] [brame] VI **1** (*cerf*) to bell **2** *Fam* (*pleurer*) to wail

bran [brɑ̃] NM **1** (*partie du son*) bran; **b. de scie** sawdust **2** *Vulg Vieilli* (*excrément*) shit

brancard [brɑ̃kar] NM **1** (*civière*) stretcher **2** (*limon d'attelage*) shaft

brancarder [3] [brɑ̃karde] VT to carry on a stretcher

brancardier [brɑ̃kardje] NM stretcher-bearer

branchage [brɑ̃ʃaʒ] NM (*ramure*) boughs, branches

    ❑ **branchages** NMPL (cut) branches

branche [brɑ̃ʃ] NF **1** *Bot* (*d'arbre*) branch, bough; (*de céleri*) stick; **grosse b.** limb, large branch; **b. fruitière** fruit-bearing branch; *Hum Vieilli* **vieille b.** old chum, old stick; *Fam* **s'accrocher** *ou* **se raccrocher** *ou* **se rattraper aux branches** to hang on by one's fingernails; *Fam* **accroche-toi aux branches!** brace yourself for a shock!

    2 *Anat* ramification

    3 *Électron* leg, branch; **circuit à deux branches** two-legged circuit

    4 (*tige → de lunettes*) *Br* sidepiece, *Am* bow; (→

d'un compas, d'un aimant) arm, leg; (→ *de ciseaux*) blade; (→ *de tenailles*) handle; (→ *d'un chandelier*) branch

    5 (*secteur*) field; **vous êtes dans quelle b.?** what's your line *or* field?; **les différentes branches de la physique** the different branches of physics

    6 (*d'une famille*) side; **par la b. maternelle** on the mother's side (of the family); **la b. aînée de la famille** the senior branch of the family; *Vieilli* **avoir de la b.** to have breeding

    7 *Suisse Univ* subject; **b. primaire** main subject, *Am* major; **b. secondaire** secondary subject, *Am* minor

    8 *Suisse* (*chocolat*) = cylindrical bar of chocolate

    ❑ **en branches** ADJ *Bot* (*épinards*) leaf (*avant n*); **céleri en branches** celery

branché, -e [brɑ̃ʃe] *Fam* ADJ trendy, hip; **être b. cinéma/jazz** to be into movies/jazz

    NM,F trendy person; **tous les branchés viennent dans ce café** you get all the trendy people in this café

branchement [brɑ̃ʃmɑ̃] NM **1** *Élec & Électron* (*sur un réseau*) connection; (*sur une prise*) plugging in; **b. d'appareil** (*tuyau*) connecting branch; (*liaison*) connection, installation; **b. de conduits** branch-off point; **b. d'égout** connection to the sewage system; **faire un b. d'égout** to be connected to the sewage system; **b. électrique** electric power supply; **b. au réseau électrique** network branch; **faire un b. au** *ou* **sur le réseau** to be connected to the mains (power supply); **faire un b. sur un tuyau** to be connected to a pipe

    2 *Rail Br* points, *Am* switch

brancher [3] [brɑ̃ʃe] VT **1** *Élec & Électron* (*sur un réseau*) to connect; (*sur une prise*) to plug in; **b. qch sur une prise** to plug sth in; *Fam* **je me branche où?** where is there a plug?; **être branché** (*appareil*) to be plugged in; (*canalisation*) to be connected to the system; **assurez-vous que l'appareil n'est pas branché** make sure the appliance is unplugged; **il faut que je fasse b. le téléphone** I've got to have the telephone installed

    2 *Fam* (*faire parler*) **b. qn sur** to start sb off *or* to get sb going on; **je l'ai branché sur le reggae et il ne s'est plus arrêté** I got him into reggae and after that there was no stopping him

    3 *Fam* (*mettre en rapport*) **b. qn avec** to put sb in touch with▪; **je vais te b. avec ma sœur, elle sait ce qu'il faut faire** I'll put you in touch with my sister, she knows what to do

    4 *Fam* (*intéresser*) **ça me branche bien!** that's great!; **ce type ne me branche pas des masses** that guy's really not my type; **l'acupuncture, ça me branche** I'm into acupuncture; **il est très branché (sur les) voyages** he's really into travelling▪; **ça vous brancherait d'y aller?** how do you fancy going there?

    5 *Fam* (*séduire*) **se faire b. par qn** *Br* to be chatted up by sb, *Am* to be hit on by sb

    VI (*se percher*) to roost, to sit

    ► **se brancher** VPR **1** *Can Fam* to decide▪, to make up one's mind▪

    2 **se b. sur** (*appareil*) to plug into; *Rad* to tune into; (*canalisation*) to connect up to; **se b. sur les grandes ondes** to tune into long wave; *Fam Fig* **il s'est branché sur l'informatique** he's got into computers

branchette [brɑ̃ʃɛt] NF *Littéraire* twig, sprig

branchial, -e, -aux, -ales [brɑ̃ʃjal, -o] ADJ *Zool* branchial

branchie [brɑ̃ʃi] NF *Zool* gill; **branchies** gills, *Spéc* branchiae

branchiopode [brɑ̃kjɔpɔd] NM *Zool* (*crustacé*) branchiopod

branchitude [brɑ̃ʃityd] NF *Fam* hipness, trendiness; **cette boîte est l'un des hauts lieux de la b. parisienne** this club is one of the coolest *or* hippest in Paris

branchouille [brɑ̃ʃuj] *Fam* ADJ hip, trendy

    NMF trendy person

branchu, -e [brɑ̃ʃy] ADJ *Bot* branchy

brandade [brɑ̃dad] NF **b. (de morue)** brandade, salt cod puree

brande [brɑ̃d] NF **1** *Bot* (*plantes*) heather, heath **2** *Écol* (*terrain*) heath, moor

Brandebourg [brɑ̃dbur] NM *Géog* Brandenburg; **la porte de B.** the Brandenburg Gate

brandebourg [brɑ̃dbur] *Couture* NM frog, frogging

    ❑ **à brandebourgs** ADJ frogged

brandebourgeois, -e [brɑ̃dburʒwa, -az] ADJ of/from Brandenburg

    ❑ **Brandebourgeois, -e** NM,F = inhabitant of or person from Brandenburg

brandir [32] [brɑ̃dir] VT (*arme*) to brandish; (*une menace*) to hold up

brandon [brɑ̃dɔ̃] NM (*pour allumer*) firebrand; **b. de discorde** (*objet, situation*) bone of contention; (*personne*) troublemaker

    ❑ **brandons, Brandons** NMPL *Suisse* **les brandons** *ou* **Brandons** = celebration of the end of winter in French-speaking Switzerland

---

Culture
LES BRANDONS
A traditional celebration in French-speaking Switzerland, the "Brandons" or "Dimanche des Brandons" takes place on the first Sunday in Lent, either as part of the Mardi-Gras Carnival or separately. The highlight of the festivities occurs when the revellers parade through the streets an effigy of a character called "Bonhomme Hiver" which is then burnt on a large bonfire to symbolize the end of winter.

---

brandy [brɑ̃di] NM (*alcool*) brandy

branlant, -e [brɑ̃lɑ̃, -ɑ̃t] ADJ **1** (*vieux → bâtiment, véhicule*) ramshackle, rickety **2** (*instable → pile d'objets*) unsteady, wobbly, shaky; (→ *échelle, chaise*) rickety, shaky; (→ *démarche*) tottering; (→ *dent*) loose; (→ *résolution, réputation*) shaky

branle [brɑ̃l] NM **1** (*mouvement*) pendulum motion **2** (*impulsion*) impulse, propulsion; **donner le b. à qch** (*procédure, situation*) to set sth going *or* in motion; **être en b.** to be on the move; **mettre en b.** (*cloche*) to set going; (*mécanisme, procédure*) to set going *or* in motion; **se mettre en b.** (*voyageur*) to set off, to start out; (*mécanisme*) to start going, to start moving; (*voiture*) to start (moving) **3** (*danse*) branle

branle-bas [brɑ̃lba] NM INV **1** (*agitation*) pandemonium, commotion; **dans le b. du départ** in the commotion of setting off; *Naut & Fig* **b. de combat!** action stations!; **quand ma tante arrivait, c'était le b. de combat** when my aunt arrived, it was action stations all round **2** *Naut* clearing of the decks

branlée [brɑ̃le] NF *Fam* thrashing; **prendre** *ou* **recevoir une b.** to get a thrashing, to get thrashed

branlement [brɑ̃lmɑ̃] NM (*dodelinement*) wagging (of the head)

branler [3] [brɑ̃le] VI (*échelle, pile d'objets*) to be shaky *or* unsteady; (*fauteuil*) to be rickety; (*dent*) to be loose; **b. dans le manche** (*outil*) to have a loose handle; *Can Fam Fig* to hum and haw; **b. du chef** (*de haut en bas*) to nod; (*de droite à gauche*) to shake one's head

    VT **1 b. la tête** (*de haut en bas*) to nod; (*de droite à gauche*) to shake one's head

    2 *Vulg* (*faire*) **j'en ai rien à b.** I don't give a (flying) fuck *or* a shit; **mais qu'est-ce qu'il branle?** (*il est en retard*) where the fuck is he?; (*il fait une bêtise*) what the fuck's he up to?

    3 *Vulg* (*masturber*) to jerk off, *Br* to wank

    ► **se branler** VPR *Vulg* to jerk off, *Br* to (have a) wank; *Fig* **je m'en branle** I don't give a shit *or* fuck

branlette [brɑ̃lɛt] NF *Vulg* hand-job, *Br* wank; **se faire une (petite) b.** to jerk off, *Br* to have a wank

branleur, -euse [brɑ̃lœr, -øz] NM,F *Vulg* **1** (*bon-à-rien*) loser, *Br* waster, *Am* slacker **2** (*fanfaron*) show-off, *Am* hotshot

branleux, -euse [brɑ̃lø, -øz] *Can Fam* ADJ (*qui hésite*) dithering; (*lâche*) chicken, cowardly▪

    NM,F (*qui hésite*) ditherer; (*lâche*) chicken

branque [brɑ̃k], **branquignol** [brɑ̃kiɲɔl] *Fam* ADJ (*fou*) crazy, nuts

    NMF (*imbécile*) dope, jerk; (*fou*) headcase, *Br* nutter, *Am* wacko

brante [brɑ̃t] NF *Suisse* = grape-picker's basket

braquage [brakaʒ] NM **1** *Aut* (steering) lock **2** *Aviat* deflection **3** *Fam* (*vol*) holdup, stickup

braque [brak] **ADJ** *Fam* crazy, nuts
NM *Zool (chien)* pointer

braquemart [brakmar] **NM 1** *Hist (épée)* cutlass **2** *très Fam* dick, prick, *Br* knob

braquement [brakmɑ̃] **NM** *Vieilli Aut* (steering) lock

braquer [3] [brake] **VT 1** *(pointer → fusil)* to point, to aim, to level; *(→ projecteur, télescope)* to train; **b. son revolver sur qn** to level *or* to point one's gun at sb; **b. une lunette sur** to train a telescope on
2 *(concentrer)* **son regard était braqué sur moi** he/she was staring straight at me, his/her gaze was fixed on me; **b. son attention sur qch** to fix one's attention on sth
3 *Aut & Aviat* to turn
4 *(rendre hostile)* to antagonize; **ne le braquez pas** don't antagonize him *or* put his back up; **b. qn contre** to set sb against; **elle est braquée contre ses collègues/ce mariage** she's totally opposed to her colleagues/dead set against this marriage
5 *Fam (attaquer → banque)* to hold up; *(→ caissier)* to hold at gunpoint
VI *(conducteur)* to turn the steering wheel; **b. bien/mal** to have a good/poor turning circle; **b. à droite/gauche** to turn hard to the right/left; **braque à fond!** *(vers la droite)* (turn) hard right!; *(vers la gauche)* (turn) hard left!
▸**se braquer VPR** to dig one's heels in; **il s'est braqué, il n'y a rien à faire** he's dug his heels in *or* he's set (his face) against it, there's nothing we can do

braquet [brakɛ] **NM** transmission ratio; **changer de b.** to change gear; **mettre le petit b.** to shift to first gear

braqueur, -euse [brakœr, -øz] **NM,F** armed robber

bras [bra] **NM 1** *(membre)* arm; *Anat* upper arm; **blessé au b.** wounded in the arm; **avoir qn à son b.** to have sb on one's arm; **son panier/épouse au b.** his basket/wife on his arm; **avoir qch dans les b.** to be carrying sth in one's arms; **porter un enfant dans les** *ou* **ses b.** to carry a child (in one's arms); **tomber dans les b. de qn** to fall into sb's arms; **ils sont tombés dans les b. l'un de l'autre** they fell into each other's arms; *Fig* **il l'a jetée dans les b. de Robert** he drove her into Robert's arms; **sous le b.** under one arm; **donner le b. à qn** to give sb one's arm; **prendre le b. de qn** to grab sb's arm; **offrir son b. à qn** to offer sb one's arm; **serrer qn dans ses b.** to hold sb in one's arms, to hug sb; **tendre** *ou* **allonger le b.** to stretch one's arm out; **les b. croisés** with one's arms folded, with folded arms; **rester les b. croisés** *(ne pas travailler)* to twiddle one's thumbs; *(être passif)* to stand idly by; **les b. en croix** (with) arms outstretched *or* outspread; *Fig* **b. droit** right-hand man, *f* woman; **faire un b. de fer avec qn** to arm-wrestle with sb; *Fig* to have a tussle with sb; **faire un b. d'honneur à qn** ≃ to give sb the finger; **jouer les gros b.** to throw one's weight around; *Fig Fam* **jouer petits b.** to hold back; **tomber à b. raccourcis sur qn** *(gén)* to lay into sb; *(physiquement)* to beat sb to a pulp; **avoir le b. long** to be influential; **se jeter dans les b. de qn** to throw oneself into sb's arms; *Fig* to fall an easy prey to sb; **les b. m'en tombent** I'm astounded, I'm flabbergasted; **lever les b.** *(d'impuissance)* to throw up one's arms (helplessly); **lever les b. au ciel** to throw up one's arms in indignation; **tu n'avais qu'à lui ouvrir les b.!** all you had to do was open up to him/her!; **tendre les b. à qn** to hold out one's arms to sb; *Fig* to offer sb (moral) support; **tendre les b. vers qn** to hold out one's arms to sb; *Fig* to turn to sb for help; *Can Fam* **coûter un b.** to cost a bomb *or Br* an arm and a leg
2 *Zool (du cheval)* arm; *(tentacule)* arm, tentacle
3 *(partie → d'une ancre, d'un électrophone, d'un moulin)* arm; *(→ d'une charrette)* arm, shaft; *(→ d'une grue)* arm, jib; *(→ d'un fauteuil)* arm, armrest; *(→ d'une brouette)* handle; *(→ d'une manivelle)* web, arm; *(→ d'un brancard)* pole; *(→ d'une croix)* arm; *Can* **b. d'escalier** banister; **b. de lecture** *(d'un électrophone)* pickup arm; **b. de levier** lever arm *or* crank; **b. manipulateur** computer-operated arm; **b. télémanipulateur** remote-control computer-operated arm; *Can* **b. de vitesse** *Br* gear lever, *Am* stick shift
4 *(pouvoir)* **le b. séculier** the secular arm; **le b. de la justice** the (long) arm of the law
5 *Géog (d'un delta)* arm; **b. abandonné** *ou* **mort** dead channel; **b. de mer** sound, arm of the sea; **b. de rivière** arm *or Am* branch of a river; **petit b. d'eau** armlet
6 *Naut* (anchor) arm
7 b. de lumière sconce
NMPL *(main-d'œuvre)* workers; **on a besoin de b.** we're short-handed *or* short-staffed; **le manque de b.** the shortage of manpower
❑ **à bras ouverts ADV** *(accueillir)* with open arms
❑ **au bras de PRÉP** on the arm of, arm in arm with
❑ **bras dessus, bras dessous ADV** arm in arm
❑ **sur les bras ADV avoir qn/qch sur les b.** to be stuck with sb/sth; **je me suis retrouvé avec le projet sur les b.** I got landed with the project; **je n'ai plus mes enfants sur les b.** my children are off my hands now; **le loyer m'est resté sur les b.** I was left with the rent to pay; **les libraires craignent que cette anthologie ne leur reste sur les b.** booksellers are worried that this anthology might not sell

brasage [brazaʒ] **NM** *Métal* brazing, soldering

braser [3] [braze] **VT** *Métal* to solder

brasero [brazero] **NM** brazier

brasier [brazje] **NM 1** *(incendie)* blaze, fire; **il retourna dans le b.** he went back into the blaze *or* inferno; **la maison n'était plus qu'un b.** the house was now a blazing mass, the fire was now raging through the house **2** *(tumulte)* fire; **le b. de ses passions** the (consuming) fire of his/her passions; **le pays est maintenant un véritable b.** the whole country's ablaze

Brasilia [brazilja] **NM** *Géog* Brasilia

brasiller [3] [brazije] **VI** to glitter, to sparkle

bras-le-corps [bralkɔr] ❑ **à bras-le-corps ADV prendre** *ou* **saisir qn à b.** to catch hold of *or* to seize sb around the waist; *Fig* **prendre un problème à b.** to tackle a problem head on

brasque [brask] **NF** *Tech* lute *(of crucible)*

bras-robot [brarobo] *(pl* **bras-robots***)* **NM** robot arm

brassage [brasaʒ] **NM 1** *(de la bière)* brewing; *(du malt)* mashing **2** *(de liquides)* mixing, swirling together; *(des cultures, des peuples)* intermixing, intermingling **3** *Naut (de la vergue)* bracing

brassard [brasar] **NM** armband; **b. de deuil** black armband

brasse [bras] **NF 1** *Sport* breaststroke; **tu sais nager la b.?** can you do the breaststroke?; **elle traverse la piscine en dix brasses** she can cross the swimming pool in ten strokes *(doing the breaststroke)*; **b. coulée** = breaststroke in which the face is submerged; **b. papillon** butterfly (stroke) **2** *(mesure)* = five feet; *Naut* fathom

brassée [brase] **NF** armful
❑ **par brassées ADV** by the armful; **on m'apportait des télégrammes par brassées** I was getting telegrams by the armful

brasser [3] [brase] **VT 1** *(bière)* to brew; *(malt)* to mash
2 *Cartes* to shuffle
3 *(populations)* to intermingle
4 *(agiter → air)* to fan; *(→ feuilles mortes)* to toss about, to stir; *Fig* **b. de l'air** *ou* **du vent** to work without getting anything done
5 *(manier → argent, sommes)* to handle; **b. des affaires** to handle a lot of business; **b. des millions** to handle millions
6 *Can & (régional en France) (remuer → soupe, sauce)* to stir; *(→ salade)* to toss; *Can Fam* **se faire b. la cage** to get an earful
7 *Naut (vergue)* to brace
▸**se brasser VPR 1** *(populations)* to intermingle
2 *(argent)* to be handled; **beaucoup d'argent se brasse dans ces milieux-là** large sums of money change hands in those circles

brasserie [brasri] **NF 1** *(fabrique de bière)* brewery; *(industrie)* brewing, beer-making (industry) **2** *(café)* = large café serving light meals

brasseur, -euse [brasœr, -øz] **NM,F 1** *Sport* breaststroker; **c'est un bon b.** he's good at the breaststroke **2** *(fabricant de bière)* brewer
❑ **brasseur d'affaires NM** *Com* big businessman

brassicole [brasicɔl] **ADJ** brewing *(avant n)*

brassière [brasjɛr] **NF 1** *(vêtement de bébé)* (baby's) *Br* vest *or Am* undershirt **2** *Naut* **b. de sauvetage** life jacket **3** *(soutien-gorge)* crop top; *Can Fam* bra■

brassin [brasɛ̃] **NM** brew, gyle

brasure [brazyr] **NF** *Métal* **1** *(soudure)* soldering joint *or* surface *or* seam **2** *(alliage)* brazing alloy

Bratislava [bratislava] **NM** *Géog* Bratislava

bravache [bravaʃ] **ADJ** swaggering, blustering; **d'un air b.** blusteringly
NM swaggerer, *Littéraire* braggart; **faire le b.** to brag

bravade [bravad] **NF** *(ostentation)* bravado; *(défi)* defiance; **faire qch par b.** *(ostentation)* to do sth out of bravado; *(défi)* to do sth in a spirit of defiance

brave [brav] **ADJ 1** *(courageux)* brave, bold **2** *(avant le nom) (bon)* good, decent; **de braves gens** good *or* decent people; *Fam* **un b. type** a nice guy *or Br* bloke **3** *(ton condescendant)* **ma b. dame/mon b. monsieur, personne ne dit le contraire!** my dear lady/my dear fellow, nobody's saying anything to the contrary!; **il est bien b. mais il ne comprend rien** he means well but he doesn't understand a thing
NM 1 *(héros)* brave man, *f* woman; **faire le b.** to act brave; **un b. parmi les braves** a hero amongst heroes **2** *(guerrier indien)* brave **3** *Vieilli* **mon b.** my good man

bravement [bravmɑ̃] **ADV 1** *(courageusement)* bravely, courageously **2** *(sans hésitation)* boldly, resolutely; **il s'est b. mis au travail** he set to work with a will

braver [3] [brave] **VT 1** *(affronter → danger, mort)* to defy, to brave; *(→ conventions)* to go against, to challenge **2** *(défier → autorité, personne)* to defy, to stand up to; *(→ ordres, lois)* to go against, to defy

bravissimo [bravisimo] **EXCLAM** bravissimo!

bravo [bravo] **EXCLAM 1** *(applaudissement)* bravo! **2** *(félicitations)* well done!, bravo!; **b.! bien parlé!** hear! hear!; **b., tu as raison!** good thinking!; *Ironique* **eh bien b., tu as réussi ton coup!** congratulations, you did a really great job there!
NM bravo; **un grand b. pour nos candidats** let's have a big hand for our contestants; **entrer/partir sous les bravos** to be cheered in/out

bravoure [bravur] **NF** bravery, courage; *Vieilli Mus* **air de b.** bravura; *Littérature* **morceau de b.** purple passage

brayer [breje] **NM 1** *Constr* truss, belt **2** *(d'une cloche)* thong **3** *Mil* flag-bearer's belt

brayon [brejɔ̃] **NM** *Can (en acadien)* floorcloth

Brazzaville [brazavil] **NM** *Géog* Brazzaville

BRB [beɛrbe] **NF** *(abrév* **brigade de répression du banditisme***)* organized crime division

break [brɛk] **NM 1** *Aut Br* estate car, *Am* station wagon **2** *(voiture à cheval)* break **3** *Mus* break **4** *Sport* **faire le b.** to break away **5** *(au tennis)* **balle de b.** break, break point **6** *(à la boxe)* break

breakdance [brɛkdɛns] **NF** breakdancing

breakfast [brɛkfast] **NM** cooked breakfast, full English breakfast

brebis [brəbi] **NF 1** *Zool* ewe; **lait/fromage de b.** ewe's milk/ewe's-milk cheese; **b. galeuse** black sheep **2** *Rel* sheep; **b. égarée** lost sheep; **les b. de Dieu** the faithful

brèche[1] [brɛʃ] **NF 1** *(ouverture)* breach, gap, break **2** *Mil* breach; **faire une b. dans un front** to breach open *or* to breach an enemy line; **être toujours sur la b.** to be always on the go **3** *Fig* hole, dent; **faire une b. à son capital** to make a hole *or* a dent in one's capital

brèche[2] [brɛʃ] **NF** *Géol* breccia

bréchet [breʃɛ] **NM** *Orn* wishbone

brechtien, -enne [brɛʃtjɛ̃, -ɛn] **ADJ** Brechtian

bredouillage [brədujaʒ] **NM** mumbling, muttering

bredouille [brəduj] **ADJ** empty-handed; **rentrer b.** *Chasse & Pêche* to come home empty-handed *or* with an empty bag; *Fig* to come back empty-handed

bredouillement [brədujmɑ̃] **NM** mumbling, muttering

bredouiller [3] [brəduje] **VI** to mumble, to mutter
VT to mumble, to mutter

bredouilleur, -euse [brədujœr, -øz] **ADJ** mumbling, muttering
NM,F mumbler, mutterer

bredouillis [brəduji] **NM** mumbling, muttering

bredzon [brɛdzɔ̃] **NM** *Suisse* = embroidered jacket with short puffed sleeves, traditional costume of shepherds in the canton of Fribourg

bref, brève [brɛf, brɛv] **ADJ 1** *(court → moment, vision)* brief, fleeting; *(concis → lettre, discours)* brief, short; **une brève histoire d'amour** a brief love affair; **soyez b.** be brief; **soyez plus b.** come to the point; **d'un ton b.** curtly
2 *Ling (syllabe, voyelle)* short
ADV in short, in a word; **enfin b., je n'ai pas envie d'y aller** well, basically, I don't want to go; **b., ce n'est pas possible** anyway, it's not possible
NM *Rel* (papal) brief
❑ **brève NF 1** *Ling (voyelle)* short vowel; *(syllabe)* short syllable
2 *Journ, Rad & TV* news in brief; **brèves de comptoir** bar talk
❑ **en bref ADV 1** *(en résumé)* in short, in brief
2 *Journ, Rad & TV* **les nouvelles en b.** the news in brief

breffage [brɛfaʒ] **NM** *Can* briefing
bregma [brɛgma] **NM** *Anat* bregma
bregmatique [brɛgmatik] **ADJ** *Anat* bregmatic
bréhaigne [breeɲ] **ADJ** *Zool (jument, biche)* barren
breitschwanz [brɛtʃvɑ̃ts] **NM** broadtail
Brejnev [brɛʒnɛf] **NPR** Brezhnev
brelan [brəlɑ̃] **NM** *Cartes* = three of a kind; **b. de rois** three kings
brêle [brɛl] **NF** *Fam* **1** *(imbécile)* cretin, jerk, *Br* tosspot **2** *(personne médiocre)* **je suis une b. en anglais** *Br* I'm totally crap at English, *Am* I suck at English
brêler [4] [brɛle] **VT** *Tech* to strap together
breloque [brəlɔk] **NF 1** *(bijou)* charm **2** *Mil* break-off **3** *(locution)* **battre la b.** to sound the dismiss; *Fig (montre)* to be on the blink; *(intellectuellement)* to wander; **mon cœur bat la b.** *(bat vite)* my heart is racing; *(fonctionne mal)* my heart is playing me up
Brême [brɛm] **NM** *Géog* Bremen
brème [brɛm] **NF 1** *Ich* bream **2** *Fam Arg crime* (playing) card■
bren [brɑ̃] **NM** *Vulg Vieilli (excrément)* shit
Brésil [brezil] **NM le B.** Brazil; **vivre au B.** to live in Brazil; **aller au B.** to go to Brazil
brésil [brezil] **NM** *Bot* brazilwood
brésilien, -enne [breziljɛ̃, -ɛn] **ADJ** Brazilian; **maillot/slip b.** high-cut swimsuit/briefs
NM *(langue)* Brazilian Portuguese
❑ **Brésilien, -enne NM,F** Brazilian
brésiller [3] [brezije] **VT** *Littéraire & Tech* to break into small pieces; *(broyer)* to crumble, to pulverize
VI to crumble
▸**se brésiller VPR** *Littéraire & Tech* to crumble
brésillet [brezijɛ] **NM** *Bot* braziletto; **b. des Indes** sapan-wood
bressan, -e [brɛsɑ̃, -an] **ADJ** of/from the Bresse region
❑ **Bressan, -e NM,F** = inhabitant of or person from the Bresse region
Bresse [brɛs] **NF la B.** Bresse *(region in eastern France famous for its poultry)*
brestois, -e [brɛstwa, -az] **ADJ** of/from Brest
❑ **Brestois, -e NM,F** = inhabitant of or person from Brest
Bretagne [brətaɲ] **NF la B.** Brittany; **la B. bretonnante** the Breton-speaking part of Brittany
bretèche [brətɛʃ] **NF** *Archit* bartizan
bretelle [brətɛl] **NF 1** *(bandoulière)* (shoulder) strap; **b. de fusil** gun sling; **porter l'arme à la b.** to carry one's weapon slung over one's shoulder
2 *(de robe)* shoulder strap; *(de soutien-gorge)* (bra) strap; **sans bretelles** strapless
3 *Rail* double crossover
4 *Transp* access road, *Br* slip road; **b. d'accès** access road; **b. d'autoroute** *Br* motorway slip road, *Am* highway on/off ramp; **b. de contournement** bypass; **b. de raccordement** *Br* motorway *or Am* highway junction; **b. de sortie** exit road
❑ **bretelles NFPL** *Br* braces, *Am* suspenders; *Fig* **se faire remonter les bretelles** to be told to pull one's socks up
bretesse [brətɛs] **NF** *Archit* bartizan
bretessé, -e [brətese] **ADJ** *Hér* bretessé, crenellated on both sides
breton, -onne [brətɔ̃, -ɔn] **ADJ** Breton; *Littérature* **le cycle b.** the Arthurian cycle of romance
NM *(langue)* Breton
❑ **Breton, -onne NM,F** Breton

> *Culture*
> **BRETON**
> Breton is a member of the Celtic family of languages and is related to Welsh and Gaelic. For many generations it was banned in favour of French before coming back into favour in recent decades with the revival of the Celtic identity and culture. However, despite efforts made to promote its use, Breton is still spoken principally by the older generations of Western Brittany.

bretonnant, -e [brətɔnɑ̃, -ɑ̃t] **ADJ** = relating to the preservation of Breton traditions and language
brette [brɛt] **NF** long sword, rapier
bretteler [24] [brɛtle] **VT** *(pierre etc)* to tool, to tooth; *(bijoux)* to hatch, to chase
bretter [3] [brɛte] **VI** *Can Fam* to dawdle; **qu'est-ce que tu brettes?** stop dawdling!
bretteur [brɛtœr] **NM** *Vieilli* swordsman, dueller
bretteux, -euse [brɛtø, -øz] *Can Fam* **ADJ** *(musard)* dawdling; *(fainéant)* lazy■
NM,F *(musard)* *Br* slowcoach, *Am* slowpoke; *(fainéant)* *Br* waster, *Am* slacker
bretzel [brɛtzɛl] **NM** *Culin* pretzel
breuvage [brœvaʒ] **NM 1** *(boisson)* beverage, drink; **un drôle de b.** a strange concoction **2** *(potion)* potion, beverage
brève[1] [brɛv] *voir* **bref**
brève[2] [brɛv] **NF** *Orn* pitta
brevet [brəvɛ] **NM 1** *Jur* **b. (d'invention)** patent; **accorder un b.** to grant a patent; **exploiter un b.** to work a patent; **prendre un b.** to take out a patent; **titulaire d'un b.** patentee; **(acte en) b.** contract delivered by a notary in the original
2 *Scol* diploma; **décerner** *ou* **délivrer un b. à qn** to award a diploma to sb; **le b. (des collèges)** = exam taken at 14 years of age; **b. d'aptitude aux fonctions d'animation** = diploma for youth leaders and workers; *Anciennement* **b. d'études du premier cycle** = former school certificate taken after four years of secondary education; **b. d'études professionnelles** = vocational diploma (taken after two years of study at a "lycée professionnel"); **brevets militaires** ≃ staff college qualifications; **b. professionnel** = vocational diploma; **b. de technicien** = vocational training certificate taken at 17 after three years' technical training; **b. de technicien agricole** = agricultural training certificate (taken at age 18); **b. de technicien hôtelier** = diploma in hotel and catering management; **b. de technicien supérieur** = advanced vocational training certificate (taken at the end of a two-year higher education course)
3 *Aviat* **b. de pilote** pilot's licence; **avoir son b. de pilote** to be a qualified pilot *or* qualified as a pilot
4 *(certificat)* certificate; **b. de secourisme** first-aid certificate; **décerner à qn un b. de moralité** to testify to *or* to vouch for sb's character
brevetabilité [brəvtabilite] **NF** patentability
brevetable [brəvtabl] **ADJ** patentable
breveté, -e [brəvte] **ADJ 1** *(diplômé)* qualified; **officier b. (d'état-major)** = officer who has passed staff college **2** *(invention)* patented; **inventeur b.** inventor holding letters patent
NM,F patentee
breveter [27] [brəvte] **VT** to patent; **faire b. qch** to take out a patent for sth
brévétoxine [brevetɔksin] **NF** *Méd* brevitoxin
bréviaire [brevjɛr] **NM** *Rel* breviary; *Fig* bible; **dire son b.** to read one's breviary
bréviligne [breviliɲ] **ADJ** *(personne)* squat, thick-set
brévité [brevite] **NF** *Ling (d'une voyelle, d'une syllabe)* shortness
BRGM [beɛrʒeɛm] **NM** *Géol & Minér (abrév* **Bureau de recherches géologiques et minières**) = French geological and mining research agency
BRI [beɛri] **NF** *Banque (abrév* **Banque des règlements internationaux**) BIS
Briansk [briɑ̃sk] **NM** *Géog* Bryansk
briard, -e [brijar, -ard] **ADJ** of/from the Brie region
NM *(chien)* briard (dog)
❑ **Briard, -e NM,F** = inhabitant of or person from the Brie region
bribes [brib] **NFPL 1** *(restes → d'un gâteau, d'un repas)* scraps, crumbs **2** *(fragments → de discours, de conversation)* snatches, scraps; *(→ d'information, de connaissances)* scraps, bits; **je ne connais que des b. de finlandais** I only know a few bits of Finnish
❑ **par bribes ADV** in snatches, bit by bit; **je connais l'histoire par b.** I've heard bits and pieces of the story
bric-à-brac [brikabrak] **NM INV 1** *(tas d'objets)* clutter, jumble, bric-à-brac; **c'est là que je mets tout mon b.** that's where I put all my odds and ends *or* bits and pieces **2** *(d'idées)* jumble, *Br* hotchpotch, *Am* hodgepodge **3** *(boutique)* *Br* junk shop, *Am* secondhand store
bricelet [brislɛ] **NM** *Suisse Culin* = thin crisp waffle
bric et de broc [brikedbrɔk] **de bric et de broc ADV** haphazardly; **meublé de b.** furnished with bits and pieces
bricheton [briʃtɔ̃] **NM** *Fam* bread■
brick [brik] **NM 1** *Naut* brig **2** *Culin* brik, = deep-fried filled filo-pastry parcel; **feuille de b.** = filo-type pastry used in North African cuisine **3** *(carton)* carton
brick-goélette [brikgɔelɛt] *(pl* **bricks-goélettes**) **NM** *Naut* schooner brig
bricolage [brikɔlaʒ] **NM 1** *(travail manuel)* do-it-yourself, *Br* DIY; **aimer le b.** to like do-it-yourself *or Br* DIY **2** *(réparation)* makeshift repair; **c'est du bon b.** it's good work **3** *(mauvais travail)* **c'est du b.** it's just been thrown together
❑ **de bricolage ADJ** *(magasin, manuel, rayon)* do-it-yourself *(avant n)*, *Br* DIY *(avant n)*
bricole [brikɔl] **NF 1** *(petit objet)* **des bricoles** things, bits and pieces; **je dois acheter quelques bricoles** I must buy a few things *or* a few bits and pieces
2 *(article de peu de valeur)* trifle; **je vais lui offrir une b.** I'm going to give him/her a little something; *Fam* **...et des bricoles** ...and a bit; **20 euros et des bricoles** 20-odd euros
3 *(chose sans importance)* piece of trivia; **des bricoles** trivia
4 *Fam (ennui)* trouble *(UNCOUNT)*; **il va t'arriver des bricoles** you're heading for trouble
5 *(harnais)* breast harness
6 *(bretelle)* carrying girth *or* strap
7 *Pêche* double hook
bricoler [3] [brikɔle] **VI 1** *(faire des aménagements)* to do odd jobs, *Br* to do DIY; **elle adore b.** she's a real do-it-yourself enthusiast; **j'ai passé la matinée à b. dans la maison** I spent the morning doing odd jobs about the house
2 *(avoir de petits emplois)* to do odd jobs; **jusqu'à 24 ans, j'ai bricolé** until I was 24, I never had a serious job
3 *Fam Péj (mauvais artisan, praticien ou étudiant)* to produce shoddy work
VT 1 *(confectionner)* to make; **c'est moi qui ai bricolé ça** it's all my own work; **j'ai bricolé une poignée pour la porte** I improvised a new handle for the door
2 *(réparer)* to fix (up), to mend, to carry out makeshift repairs to; **j'ai bricolé la radio et elle a l'air de marcher** I've tinkered with the radio a bit and it seems to be working
3 *(manipuler)* to tinker *or* to tamper with; **qui a bricolé le grille-pain?** who's been tinkering with the toaster?; **b. un moteur** to soup up an engine
bricoleur, -euse [brikɔlœr, -øz] **NM,F 1** *(qui construit ou répare soi-même)* handyman, *f* handywoman, *Br* DIY enthusiast **2** *Péj (dilettante)* amateur, dilettante
ADJ il est très b. he's good with his hands; **il n'est pas b.** he's no handyman
bride [brid] **NF 1** *Équitation* bridle; **tenir son cheval en b.** to curb *or* to rein in a horse; *Fig* **tenir ses passions en b.** to keep a tight rein on one's emotions; **rendre la b. à un cheval** to give a horse its head; **à b. abattue, à toute b.** at full speed, like greased lightning; **avoir la b. sur le cou** to be given a free hand; **laisser la b. sur le cou à qn** to give sb a free rein; **tenir la b. haute à qn** to keep sb on a tight rein; **tourner b.** to turn tail
2 *Couture (de boutonnière)* bar; *(pour un bouton)* loop; *(en dentelle)* bride, bar
3 *Méd* adhesion; **b. amniotique** amniotic band *or* adhesion
4 *Tech* strap, tie; *(d'un cylindre, d'un tuyau)* flange, collar
bridé, -e [bride] **ADJ 1 yeux bridés** slanting eyes;

avoir les yeux bridés to have slanting eyes **2** *Aut* **moteur b.** governed engine

NM,F *très Fam Br* slant-eye, *Am* gook, = offensive term used to refer to an Oriental

brider [3] [bride] VT **1** *Équitation* to bridle

2 *(serrer)* to constrict; **ma veste me bride aux emmanchures** my jacket is too tight under the arms

3 *(émotion)* to curb, to restrain; *(personne)* to keep in check; **b. son enthousiasme** to keep a check on *or* to curb one's enthusiasm; **b. les passions de qn** to curb *or* to dampen sb's passions

4 *Couture* to bind

5 *Culin* to truss

6 *Naut* to lash together

7 *(tuyaux)* to flange, to clamp

bridge [bridʒ] NM **1** *(dent)* bridge, bridgework **2** *Cartes* bridge; **faire un b.** to have *or* play a game of bridge; **b. contrat** contract bridge; **b. aux enchères** auction bridge

bridger [17] [bridʒe] VI *Cartes* to play bridge

Bridgetown [bridʒtaun] NM Bridgetown

bridgeur, -euse [bridʒœr, -øz] NM,F *Cartes* bridge player

bridon [bridɔ̃] NM *Équitation* snaffle (bridle)

Brie [bri] NF **la B.** the Brie region

brie [bri] NM *(fromage)* Brie

brief [brif] NM brief

briefer [3] [brife] VT to brief

briefing [brifiŋ] NM briefing

Brienne-le-Château [brijɛnləʃato] NF *Géog* = site of the military school where Napoléon studied (1779-1784) in the Champagne-Ardenne region

brièvement [brijɛvmɑ̃] ADV **1** *(pendant peu de temps)* briefly, fleetingly, for a short time **2** *(avec concision)* briefly, in a few words

brièveté [brijɛvte] NF *(courte durée)* brevity, briefness; *(du style, d'une réponse)* brevity

brifer [3] [brife] VT **1** *Fam (manger)* to eat■, *Am* to chow **2** *Vieilli (manger voracement)* to devour, to gobble

USAGE ABSOLU *Fam* to eat■, *Am* to chow

brigade [brigad] NF **1** *Mil (détachement)* brigade; **b. aérienne** group, *Am* wing; **b. de gendarmerie** squad of gendarmes; **b. des sapeurs-pompiers** *Br* fire brigade, *Am* fire department

2 *(équipe d'ouvriers)* gang, team

3 *(corps de police)* squad; **b. anti-émeute** riot squad; **b. antigang** organized crime division; *Hist* **les Brigades internationales** the International Brigades; **b. des mineurs** juvenile division; **b. mobile** flying squad; **b. des mœurs** vice squad; **b. de répression du (grand) banditisme** organized crime division; *Fam* **b. des stupéfiants** *ou* **des stups** drug squad; **b. volante** flying squad

4 *(en Italie)* **les Brigades rouges** the Red Brigades

brigadier [brigadje] NM **1** *(de police)* sergeant **2** *Mil* corporal **3** *Hist* brigadier **4** *Théât* = wooden baton used to give the three knocks at the beginning of a French theatre performance

brigadier-chef [brigadjeʃɛf] *(pl* **brigadiers-chefs***)* NM *Mil* lance-sergeant

brigand [brigɑ̃] NM **1** *(bandit)* bandit, *Littéraire* brigand **2** *(escroc)* crook, thief **3** *Fam (avec affection)* **b., va!** you rogue *or* imp *or* rascal!

brigandage [brigɑ̃daʒ] NM **1** *(vol à main armée)* armed robbery **2** *(acte malhonnête)* **c'est du b.** it's daylight robbery

brigander [3] [brigɑ̃de] VT *Suisse* **1** *(maltraiter)* to mistreat **2** *(abîmer)* to ruin

brigandine [brigɑ̃din] NF brigandine, brigantine

brigantin [brigɑ̃tɛ̃] NM *Naut* brigantine

brigantine [brigɑ̃tin] NF *Naut* spanker

brignolet [briɲɔlɛ] NM *Fam* bread■

brigue [brig] NF *Littéraire* intrigue; **avoir une place par (la) b.** to get a job by pulling strings

briguer [3] [brige] VT *(emploi)* to angle for; *(honneur)* to seek, to pursue, to aspire to; *(suffrage)* to seek

brillamment [brijamɑ̃] ADV brilliantly, magnificently; **réussir b. un examen** to pass an exam with flying colours

brillance [brijɑ̃s] NF *(du regard)* brilliance; *(des cheveux)* shine, sheen, gloss

brillant, -e [brijɑ̃, -ɑ̃t] ADJ **1** *(luisant → parquet)* shiny, polished; *(→ peinture)* gloss *(avant n)*; *(→ cheveux, lèvres, chaussures)* shiny, glossy; *(→ soie)* lustrous; *(→ pierre précieuse, cristal)* sparkling, glittering; *(→ yeux)* bright, shining; **yeux brillants de malice** eyes sparkling with mischief; **yeux brillants de fièvre** eyes bright with fever

2 *(remarquable → esprit, intelligence)* brilliant, outstanding; *(→ personne)* outstanding; *(→ succès, carrière, talent)* brilliant, dazzling, outstanding; *(→ conversation)* brilliant, sparkling; *(→ hommage)* superb, magnificent; *(→ représentation, numéro)* brilliant, superb; **il a été b.** he did very well indeed *or* brilliantly; **faire un mariage b.** to marry very well; **il est promis à un b. avenir** he has a brilliant future ahead of him; **c'est un b. parti** he/she'll be a good catch; **ce n'est pas b.** it's not brilliant; **sa santé n'est pas brillante** he's/she's not well, his/her health is not too good; **les résultats ne sont pas brillants** the results aren't too good *or* aren't all they should be

NM **1** *(éclat → d'un métal, d'une surface)* gloss, sheen; *(→ de chaussures, des cheveux)* shine; *(→ d'une peinture)* gloss; *(→ d'un tissu)* sheen; *(→ d'un diamant, d'un regard)* sparkle

2 *(brio)* brio, sparkle; **malgré le b. de sa conversation/son œuvre** in spite of his/her brilliant conversation/impressive work

3 *(diamant)* brilliant; **monté/taillé en b.** mounted/cut as a brilliant

▫ **brillant à lèvres** NM *(cosmétique)* lip gloss

brillantage [brijɑ̃taʒ] NM *(du cuir, de l'acier)* polishing; *(de pierre précieuse)* brillianteering

brillanté [brijɑ̃te] NM dimity

brillanter [3] [brijɑ̃te] VT **1** *Littéraire* to give glitter *or* sparkle to **2** *(pièce précieuse)* to cut into a brilliant **3** *Tex* to gloss **4** *(un métal)* to brighten

brillanteur [brijɑ̃tœr] ADJ M **agent b.** brightener

NM brightener

brillantine [brijɑ̃tin] NF *(pour les cheveux)* brilliantine

brillantiner [3] [brijɑ̃tine] VT *(cheveux, moustache)* to brilliantine, to put brilliantine on

briller [3] [brije] VI **1** *(luire → chaussure, soleil, lumière, regard)* to shine; *(→ acier)* to glint, to gleam; *(→ chandelle)* to glimmer; *(→ étoile)* to twinkle, to shine; *(→ lune)* to gleam, to shine; *(→ diamant)* to shine, to glitter, to sparkle; *(→ satin, soie)* to shimmer, to shine; *(→ dents)* to sparkle; *(→ eau)* to shimmer, to sparkle; *(→ feuille)* to shine, to glisten; **tout brille dans sa cuisine** his/her kitchen's gleaming; **il a le nez qui brille** he's got a shiny nose; **faire b. qch** to polish sth; **faire b. ses chaussures** to shine one's shoes; **faire b. un meuble/l'argenterie** to polish a piece of furniture/the silver; **la joie faisait b. ses yeux** his/her eyes were shining with joy; **sa bague en diamant brillait de tous ses feux** his/her diamond ring glittered brightly; **des yeux qui brillent de colère** eyes ablaze with anger; **des yeux qui brillent de plaisir/d'envie** eyes sparkling with pleasure/glowing with envy; **des yeux qui brillent de fièvre** eyes bright with fever; *Prov* **tout ce qui brille n'est pas (d')or** all that glitters is not gold

2 *(exceller)* to shine, to excel, to be outstanding; **b. à un examen** to do very well in an exam; **b. au tennis/en biologie** to be very good at tennis/at biology

3 *(se distinguer)* to stand out; **avoir le désir de b.** to be anxious to stand out; **b. en société** to be a social success; **b. dans une conversation** to shine in a conversation; **b. par son savoir/son intelligence** to be extraordinarily knowledgeable/intelligent; **b. par son absence** to be conspicuous by one's absence; **b. par son incompétence** to be remarkably incompetent; **elle ne brille pas par sa ponctualité** she's not noted for her punctuality; **faire b. les avantages d'une situation** to point out the advantages of a situation

brimade [brimad] NF **1** *(vexation)* bullying (incident), (incident of) victimization; **faire subir des brimades à qn** to victimize sb, to bully sb **2** *Fam Arg scol* initiation ceremony■, *Br* ragging, *Am* hazing

brimbaler [brɛ̃bale] = **bringuebaler**

brimborion [brɛ̃bɔrjɔ̃] NM *Littéraire* bauble, trinket

brimer [3] [brime] VT **1** *(faire subir des vexations à)* to victimize; **il se sent brimé** he feels victimized **2** *Fam Arg scol* to initiate■, *Br* to rag, *Am* to haze

brin [brɛ̃] NM **1** *(filament)* strand; *Tex* fibre; **câble à un b.** single-strand *or* single-stranded cable; **corde/laine à trois brins** three-ply rope/wool

2 *(tige → d'herbe)* blade; *(→ d'osier)* twig; *(→ de muguet, de persil, de bruyère, d'aubépine)* sprig

3 *(morceau → de laine, de fil)* piece, length; **b. de paille** (piece of) straw

4 *(parcelle)* **un b. de** a (tiny) bit of; **un b. de génie** a touch of genius; **il faut avoir un b. d'inconscience pour faire ça** you need to be a bit foolhardy to do that; **il n'a pas un b. de bon sens** he hasn't an ounce *or* a shred of common sense; **il n'y a pas un b. de vent** there isn't a breath of wind; **il n'y a pas un b. de vérité là-dedans** there isn't a grain of truth in it; **faire un b. de causette (à** *ou* **avec qn)** to have a quick chat (with sb); **faire un b. de cour à** to have a little flirt with; **faire un b. de toilette** to have a quick wash

5 *(locution)* **un beau b. de fille** a good-looking girl

▫ **un brin** ADV *Fam* a trifle, a touch; **il était un b. dépité** he was a trifle disappointed; **lève ton bras un b. plus haut** raise your arm a shade *or* fraction higher; **rigoler** *ou* **s'amuser un b.** to have a bit of fun

brindezingue [brɛ̃dzɛ̃g] ADJ *Fam* crazy, loopy

brindille [brɛ̃dij] NF *Bot* twig

brinell [brinɛl] NM *Métal* **1** *(machine)* Brinell test machine **2** *(essai)* Brinell test; **essai de dureté B.** Brinell hardness test

bringé, -e [brɛ̃ʒe] ADJ *(animal)* brindled

bringeure [brɛ̃ʒœr] NF brindling

bringue [brɛ̃g] NF *Fam* **1** *Péj (personne)* **une grande b.** a beanpole **2** *(noce)* **faire la b.** to live it up, to party **3** *Suisse (querelle)* row■; *(rengaine)* refrain■

bringuebalant, -e [brɛ̃gbalɑ̃, -ɑ̃t] ADJ shaky; **une voiture bringuebalante** a shaky old car

bringuebaler [3] [brɛ̃gbale] VT to joggle, to jiggle, to shake

VI to rattle; **c'est fragile, il ne faut pas que ça bringuebale dans la valise** it's fragile and mustn't rattle around in the suitcase; **une carriole qui bringuebale** a cart that rattles along

bringuer [3] [brɛ̃ge] *Suisse* VI **arrête de b.!** stop going on about it!

VT to go on at

►**se bringuer** VPR **ils se bringuaient** they were having a row

brinquebalant, -e [brɛ̃kbalɑ̃, -ɑ̃t] = **bringuebalant**

brinquebaler [brɛ̃kbale] = **bringuebaler**

brio [brijo] NM brio, verve

▫ **avec brio** ADV **parler avec b.** *(en une occasion)* to make a brilliant speech; *(naturellement)* to be a dazzling speaker; **il s'en est tiré avec b.** he carried it off with style; **passer une épreuve avec b.** to pass an exam with flying colours

brioche [brijɔʃ] NF **1** *Culin* brioche **2** *Fam (ventre)* paunch; **avoir de la b.** to be potbellied; **prendre de la b.** to be getting a paunch *or* potbelly

Allusion

(S'ils n'ont pas de pain,) qu'ils mangent de la brioche!

This phrase ("Let them eat cake!" in English) is usually attributed to Queen Marie-Antoinette of France, who allegedly said it when told that a crowd of people outside the royal palace were complaining about the price of bread. However, the expression undoubtedly predates Marie-Antoinette and the French Revolution as it can be found in Rousseau's *Confessions*, where it is attributed to a princess. The expression literally means "if they don't have any bread, let them eat brioche" and it is used ironically to convey a lack of concern for and understanding of the plight of others, as anyone living in the real world would know that if you can't afford bread it is highly unlikely that you would be able to afford brioche. The phrase is essentially used to express one's (or comment on someone else's) indifference towards the hardship suffered by others.

brioché, -e [brijɔʃe] ADJ that tastes like brioche

briochin, -e [brijoʃɛ̃, -in] ADJ of/from St-Brieuc
▫ **Briochin, -e** NM,F = inhabitant of or person from St-Brieuc

brion [briɔ̃] NM *Naut* forefoot

brique [brik] NF **1** *Constr* brick; **un mur de b.** *ou* **briques** a brick wall; **b. creuse** air brick; **b. pleine** solid brick; **b. réfractaire** firebrick; *très Fam* **bouffer des briques** to have nothing to eat **2** *(morceau)* piece; **b. de jeu de construction** building block **3** *(emballage → de lait, de jus de fruit)* carton **4** *Anciennement Fam (dix mille francs)* 10,000 francs ▪ **5** *Suisse (fragment)* fragment, splinter
  ADJ INV brick-red
▫ **en brique** ADJ brick *(avant n)*, made of brick

briquer [3] [brike] VT **1** *(pont de navire)* to scrub; *(maison)* to clean from top to bottom; **tout avait été briqué** everything had been scrubbed **2** *Suisse (briser)* to break, to smash

briquet [brikɛ] NM **1** *(appareil)* lighter; *(à amadou)* tinder box; **battre le b.** to strike a light **2** *(chien)* beagle

briquetage [briktaʒ] NM *Constr* **1** *(maçonnerie)* brickwork **2** *(enduit)* imitation brickwork

briqueter [27] [brikte] VT **1** *Constr (pavement, surface)* to face in imitation brickwork **2** *(transformer en briquettes)* to briquette

briqueterie [brikɛtri] NF brickworks *(singulier)*, brickyard

briqueteur [briktœr] NM *Constr* bricklayer

briquetier [briktje] NM **1** *(ouvrier)* brickmaker **2** *(dirigeant)* brickyard manager

briquette [brikɛt] NF **1** *Constr* small brick **2** *(de combustible)* briquette

bris [bri] NM **1** *(fragment)* piece, fragment; **des b. de glace** shards, fragments of glass; **être assuré contre les b. de glace** to be insured for plate glass risk **2** *Jur* **b. de clôture** breach of close; **b. de scellés** breaking of seals

brisance [brizɑ̃s] NF *Tech* brisance, shattering effect

brisant, -e [brizɑ̃, -ɑ̃t] ADJ **explosif b.** high explosive; **obus b.** high-explosive shell
  NM *(haut-fond)* reef, shoal
▫ **brisants** NMPL *(vagues)* breakers

Brisbane [brisban] NM Brisbane

briscard [briskar] NM **1** *Mil* old soldier, veteran **2** *(vétéran)* veteran, old hand; **un vieux b.** a veteran

brise [briz] NF breeze; **bonne b.** fresh breeze

brisé, -e [brize] ADJ **1** *(détruit)* broken; **un homme b.** *(par la fatigue)* a run-down *or* worn-out man; *(par les ennuis, le chagrin)* a broken man; **b. de fatigue** exhausted, tired out; **b. de chagrin** crushed by grief, brokenhearted **2** *Géom* broken **3** *Archit (arc)* broken
  NM *(danse)* brisé

brise-béton [brizbetɔ̃] NM INV *Tech* jackhammer

brise-bise [brizbiz] NM INV half curtain *(on the bottom half of a window)*

brise-copeaux [brizkɔpo] NM INV *Tech* chip breaker

brisées [brize] NFPL **1** *Chasse* broken branches *(to mark the way)* **2** *(locutions)* **aller** *ou* **marcher sur les b. de qn** to poach on sb's territory; **suivre les b. de qn** to follow in sb's footsteps, to follow sb's lead *or* example

brise-fer [brizfɛr] NM INV *Fam Vieilli* vandal

brise-glace(s) [brizglas] NM INV **1** *Naut* icebreaker **2** *(sur un pont)* icebreaker, ice apron *or* guard **3** *(outil)* hammer

brise-jet [brizʒɛ] NM INV tap swirl

brise-lames [brizlam] NM INV *Naut* breakwater, groyne, mole

brisement [brizmɑ̃] NM *Littéraire* breaking

brise-mottes [brizmɔt] NM INV harrow

briser [3] [brize] VT **1** *(mettre en pièces → verre, assiette)* to break, to smash; *(→ vitre)* to break, to shatter, to smash; *(→ motte de terre)* to break up; **b. qch en mille morceaux** to smash sth to pieces *or* smithereens, to shatter sth; **cela me brise le cœur** it breaks my heart; **la voix brisée par l'émotion** his/her voice choked with emotion; *Fig* **b. les tabous** to break taboos **2** *(séparer en deux → canne, branche)* to break, to snap; *(→ liens, chaînes)* to break; **b. la glace** to break the ice **3** *(assouplir)* **b. des chaussures** to break shoes in

4 *(défaire → réputation, carrière)* to wreck, to ruin; *(→ résistance, rébellion)* to crush, to quell; *(→ contrat)* to break; *(→ grève)* to break (up); **b. un mariage/une amitié/une famille** to break up a marriage/friendship/family; **b. l'élan de qn** to make sb stumble; *Fig* to clip sb's wings; *Littéraire* **b. ses liens** to burst one's bonds asunder **5** *(soumettre)* to break; **je le briserai** I'll break him **6** *(épuiser → sujet: soucis, chagrin)* to break, to crush; *(→ sujet: exercice, voyage)* to exhaust, to tire out; **brisé par la maladie** broken by illness **7** *(locutions) Littéraire* **brisons là!** not another word!, that's enough!; *très Fam* **tu me les brises!** you're really pissing me off!
▫ **briser avec** VT IND *(ami, tradition)* to break with
► **se briser** VPR **1** *(se casser → verre)* to shatter, to break; **se b. en mille morceaux** to break *or* to smash into pieces, to shatter; **son cœur s'est brisé** he was heartbroken *or* brokenhearted **2** *(être altéré → espoir)* to be shattered; *(→ voix)* to break, to falter **3** *(déferler → vagues)* to break **4** *(échouer → attaque, assaut)* to fail

brise-soleil [brizsɔlɛj] NM INV *Archit* brise-soleil

brise-tout [briztu] NM INV *Fam Vieilli* vandal

briseur, -euse [brizœr, -øz] NM,F **1** *Littéraire (casseur)* vandal **2** *Fig* **b. de grève** strikebreaker

brise-vent [brizvɑ̃] NM INV *Hort* windbreak

brisis [brizi] NM *Constr* break, lower slope *(of mansard roof)*

briska [briska] NM britzska

brisolée [brizɔle] NF *Suisse* = meal consisting of roast chestnuts, cheese and new wine, usually eaten outdoors in the countryside

brisquard [briskar] = **briscard**

brisque [brisk] NF **1** *Cartes (au bésigue)* ace or ten; *(jeu)* brisque, matrimony **2** *Mil* long-service badge, stripe **3** *Fam Mil* **une vieille b.** an old soldier ▪, a vet

Bristol [bristɔl] NM *Géog* Bristol

bristol [bristɔl] NM **1** *(carton)* Bristol board **2** *(carte de visite) Br* visiting *or Am* calling card **3** *(fiche)* index card

brisure [brizyr] NF **1** *(fêlure)* crack, break **2** *(fragment)* splinter, fragment **3** *(d'un gond)* break; *(d'un volet)* folding joint **4** *Hér* mark of cadency
▫ **brisures** NFPL **brisures de riz** broken rice

Britannicus [britanikys] NPR Britannicus

britannique [britanik] ADJ British
▫ **Britannique** ADJ **les îles Britanniques** the British Isles NMF Briton, *Am* Britisher; **les Britanniques** the British

brittonique [britɔnik] *Ling* ADJ Brythonic, Brittonic
  NM Brythonic, Brittonic

brize [briz], **briza** [briza] NF *Bot* briza, quaking-grass

broc [bro] NM *(gén)* pitcher; *(pour la toilette)* ewer

brocante [brɔkɑ̃t] NF **1** *(objets)* **la b.** second-hand goods; **faire de la b.** to deal in second-hand goods **2** *Com (commerce)* second-hand trade; *(marché)* = market selling second-hand goods; **magasin de b.** second-hand *Br* shop *or Am* store; **il y a une b. près d'ici** there's a second-hand market near here

brocanter [3] [brɔkɑ̃te] VI *Com* to deal in second-hand goods

brocanteur, -euse [brɔkɑ̃tœr, -øz] NM,F *Com* second-hand dealer

brocard [brɔkar] NM **1** *Littéraire (moquerie)* gibe, taunt **2** *Zool* roebuck

brocarder [3] [brɔkarde] VT *Littéraire* to gibe at, to mock

brocart [brɔkar] NM *Tex* brocade

brocatelle [brɔkatɛl] NF **1** *Tex* coarse brocade, brocatelle **2** *(marbre)* clouded marble brocatelle

broccio [brɔtʃjo] NM broccio cheese *(from Corsica)*

Brocéliande [brɔseljɑ̃d] NF *Myth* = former name for the Forêt de Paimpont in Brittany, known as the legendary forest in the Romance of the Round Table where Merlin is supposed to have lived

brochage [brɔʃaʒ] NM **1** *Typ* stitching, sewing **2** *Tex* brocade **3** *Tech* broaching

brochant, -e [brɔʃɑ̃, -ɑ̃t] ADJ *Hér* brochant, brouchant
▫ **brochant sur le tout** ADV and to crown *or* cap it all

broche [brɔʃ] NF **1** *Culin* spit, skewer, broach **2** *(bijou)* brooch **3** *(en alpinisme)* piton; **b. à glace** ice screw **4** *Électron & Méd* pin **5** *Tech* broaching tool, broach **6** *Tex* spindle **7** *(d'une serrure)* broach, hinge pin **8** *Zool (du cerf)* spike
▫ **à la broche** ADV *Culin* on a spit; **cuit à la b.** roasted on a spit, spit-roasted

broché, -e [brɔʃe] ADJ **1** *Tex* brocaded, broché **2** *(livre)* paperback *(avant n)*
  NM **1** *(tissu)* brocade, broché *or* swivel fabric **2** *(procédé)* brocading, swivel weaving

brocher [3] [brɔʃe] VT **1** *Typ* to stitch, to sew **2** *Tech* to broach **3** *Tex* to brocade, to figure; **tissu broché d'or** gold brocade

brochet [brɔʃɛ] NM *Ich* pike; **b. de mer** barracuda

brocheton [brɔʃtɔ̃] NM *Ich* pickerel, young pike, jack

brochette [brɔʃɛt] NF **1** *Culin (broche)* skewer; *(mets)* brochette, kebab; **du mouton en brochettes** lamb kebabs; **brochettes de fruits de mer** seafood kebabs **2** *(assemblée)* lot; **une jolie b. d'hypocrites** a fine lot of hypocrites **3** *(ribambelle)* **b. de décorations** row of decorations

brocheur, -euse [brɔʃœr, -øz] NM,F **1** *Typ* stitcher, sewer **2** *Tex* brocade weaver
  NM brocade loom
▫ **brocheuse** NF *Typ* binding machine; **brocheuse automatique sans couture** perfect binder

brochure [brɔʃyr] NF **1** *(livret)* pamphlet, booklet, brochure; **j'ai pris toutes les brochures sur Capri** I took all the brochures on Capri; **b. publicitaire** advertising brochure, publicity brochure **2** *Typ (technique)* stitching, sewing **3** *Tex* brocaded design, figured pattern

brocoli [brɔkɔli] NM broccoli *(UNCOUNT)*; **des brocolis** broccoli

brodequin [brɔdkɛ̃] NM **1** *(chaussure)* (laced) boot **2** *Antiq (bottine)* brodekin, buskin; *Littéraire* **chausser le b.** *(écrire)* to write tragedies; *(jouer)* to tread the boards
▫ **brodequins** NMPL *(pour torture)* **les brodequins** the boot

broder [3] [brɔde] VT **1** *Couture* to embroider; **brodé à la main** hand-embroidered; **brodé d'or** embroidered in gold thread; **un mouchoir brodé de fleurs** a handkerchief embroidered with flowers **2** *Littéraire (embellir)* to embellish, to embroider
  VI *(exagérer)* to use poetic licence; **b. sur qch** to embroider *or* to embellish sth

broderie [brɔdri] NF **1** *Couture (technique)* embroidery; **b. à l'aiguille** needlework, embroidery; **faire de la b.** to do embroidery *or* needlework; **b. anglaise** broderie anglaise; **b. mécanique** machine embroidery **2** *(ouvrage)* (piece of) embroidery, embroidery work; **des broderies** embroidery **3** *(industrie)* embroidery trade

brodeur, -euse [brɔdœr, -øz] *Couture* NM,F embroiderer
▫ **brodeuse** NF embroidering machine

broie etc voir **broyer**

broiement [brwamɑ̃] = **broyage**

brol, broll [brɔl] NM *Belg (tas d'objets, bric-à-brac)* clutter, jumble, bric-à-brac

bromate [brɔmat] NM *Chim* bromate

brome [brom] NM **1** *Chim* bromine **2** *Bot* brome grass, brome

bromé, -e [brome] ADJ *Chim* brominated

broméliacée [bromeljase] *Bot* NF bromeliad
▫ **broméliacées** NFPL Bromeliaceae

bromhydrique [brɔmidrik] ADJ *Chim* hydrobromic

bromique [brɔmik] ADJ *Chim* bromic

bromisme [brɔmism] NM *Méd* bromism

bromoforme [bromoform] NM *Chim* bromoform

bromure [brɔmyr] NM *Chim* bromide; *Pharm* **b. de potassium** potassium bromide

bronca [brɔ̃ka] NF **1** *(à une corrida)* = audience attending a bullfighting event **2** *(tollé)* outcry

bronche [brɔ̃ʃ] NF *Anat* bronchus; **les bronches** the bronchial tubes

bronchectasie [brɔ̃ʃɛktazi] NF *Méd* bronchiectasis

broncher [3] [brɔ̃ʃe] **VI** **1** *(réagir)* to react, to respond; **il n'a pas bronché** he didn't bat an eyelid; **tu n'as pas intérêt à b.!** not a word out of you!; **le premier qui bronche...** the first one to move a muscle... **2** *(cheval)* to stumble
❑ **sans broncher ADV** without batting an eye *or* an eyelid, without turning a hair *or* flinching
bronchiectasie [brɔ̃ʃjɛktazi] **NF** *Méd* bronchiectasis
bronchiole [brɔ̃ʃjɔl] **NF** *Anat* bronchiole
bronchiolite [brɔ̃ʃjɔlit] **NF** *Méd* bronchiolitis
bronchique [brɔ̃ʃik] **ADJ** bronchial
bronchite [brɔ̃ʃit] **NF** *Méd* bronchitis; **faire** *ou* **avoir une b.** to have bronchitis
bronchiteux, -euse [brɔ̃ʃitø, -øz] *Méd* **ADJ** bronchitic
NM,F bronchitis sufferer
bronchitique [brɔ̃ʃitik] *Méd* **ADJ** bronchitic; **être b.** to have chronic bronchitis
NMF chronic bronchitis patient
bronchodilatateur [brɔ̃kodilatatœr] **NM** *Méd* bronchodilator
broncho-pneumonie [brɔ̃kɔpnømɔni] (*pl* **broncho-pneumonies**), **broncho-pneumopathie** [brɔ̃kɔpnømopati] (*pl* **broncho-pneumopathies**) **NF** *Méd* bronchopneumonia
bronchorrhée [brɔ̃kore] **NF** *Méd* bronchorrhea
bronchoscope [brɔ̃kɔskɔp] **NM** *Méd* bronchoscope
bronchoscopie [brɔ̃kɔskɔpi] **NF** *Méd* bronchoscopy
Brongniart [brɔ̃ɲar] **NM le palais B.** = name by which the Paris Stock Exchange is sometimes known
brontosaure [brɔ̃tɔzɔr] **NM** *Zool* brontosaur, brontosaurus
bronzage [brɔ̃zaʒ] **NM** **1** *(de la peau → action)* tanning; *(→ hâle)* suntan, tan; **avoir un beau b.** to have a nice tan; **b. intégral** all-over tan **2** *Tech (d'une statue)* bronzing; *(d'une surface métallique)* blueing
bronzant, -e [brɔ̃zɑ̃, -ɑ̃t] **ADJ** suntan *(avant n)*
bronze [brɔ̃z] **NM** *Beaux-Arts & Métal* bronze; *Littéraire* **un homme au cœur de b.** a cold-hearted man
ADJ INV bronze, bronze-coloured
bronzé, -e [brɔ̃ze] **ADJ** **1** *(hâlé)* suntanned, tanned **2** *Tech* bronze, bronzed
bronzer [3] [brɔ̃ze] **VT** **1** *(hâler)* to tan **2** *(statue)* to bronze; *(surface métallique)* to blue
VI to tan, to go brown; **se faire b.** to sunbathe; **pour ceux qui ne veulent pas b. idiot** for those people who don't just want to lie on the beach
bronzette [brɔ̃zɛt] **NF** *Fam* sunbathing session■; **faire b.** to lie in the sun, to sunbathe for a while
bronzeur, -euse [brɔ̃zœr, -øz] **NM,F** **1** *Beaux-Arts* maker of bronzes **2** *Ind* bronzer
bronzier, -ère [brɔ̃zje, -jɛr] **NM,F** *Beaux-Arts* bronzesmith
brook [bruk] **NM** *Courses de chevaux* water jump
broquart [brɔkar] = **brocard**
broquelin [brɔklɛ̃] **NM** = left-over shreds of tobacco leaves used for making cigarettes
broquette [brɔkɛt] **NF** *(clou)* (tin)tack
brossage [brɔsaʒ] **NM** **1** *(de chaussures, de vêtements)* brushing **2** *(d'un cheval)* brushing down
brosse [brɔs] **NF** **1** *(ustensile)* brush; **laver le sol à la b.** to give the floor a scrub, to scrub the floor; **donner un coup de b. à qch** *(pour dépoussiérer)* to brush sth; *(pour laver)* to give sth a scrub; **b. à chaussures** shoe brush; **b. à cheveux** hairbrush; **b. en chiendent** *Br* scrubbing *or Am* scrub brush; **b. à dents** toothbrush; **b. à habits** clothes brush; **b. métallique** wire brush; **b. à ongles** nailbrush; **b. à reluire** brush *(for buffing)*; *Fam* **passer la b. à reluire à qn** to butter sb up, to soft-soap sb
2 *Beaux-Arts (pinceau)* brush
3 *(coiffure)* brush cut; **se faire couper les cheveux en b.** to have a brush cut
4 *(d'un renard)* brush; *(d'une abeille)* scopa
5 *Can Fam (locutions)* **être en b.** to be wasted *or Br* pissed; **prendre une b.** to get wasted *or Br* pissed
6 *Belg Fam (locution)* **faire b.** to draw a blank■, to be out of luck■
brosser [3] [brɔse] **VT** **1** *(épousseter → miettes)* to brush (off); *(→ pantalon, jupe)* to brush (down); *(→ tapis, cheveux)* to brush
2 *(frictionner)* to brush, to scrub; **b. un cheval** to rub a horse down
3 *Beaux-Arts (paysage, portrait)* to paint; **b. le portrait de qn** to paint sb's portrait, *Fig* to describe sb; **il m'a brossé un tableau idéal de son travail** he painted me a glowing picture of his job; **je vais vous b. un tableau de la situation** I'll give you a brief outline of the situation
4 *Belg Fam* **b. un cours** to skip a class, *Br* to skive (off), *Am* to cut a class
5 *Sport* to cut, to give spin to
▸**se brosser VPR** **1** *(se nettoyer)* to brush oneself (down); **brosse-toi, tu as de la poussière sur ton manteau** brush yourself down, you've got dust on your coat; **se b. les dents/les cheveux** to brush one's teeth/hair
2 *Fam (locution)* **il peut toujours se b., il n'aura jamais mon livre** he can whistle for my book
brosserie [brɔsri] **NF** **1** *(usine)* brush factory **2** *(commerce)* brushmaking industry
brosseur, -euse [brɔsœr, -øz] **NM,F** *Belg Fam* pupil who skips school, truant■
brossier [brɔsje] **NM** *(fabricant)* brushmaker; *(marchand)* dealer in brushes
brou [bru] **NM** *Bot* husk, *Am* shuck
❑ **brou de noix NM** walnut stain; **passer qch au b. de noix** to stain sth with walnut
broue [bru] **NF** *Can Fam* foam■, froth■; *Fig* **faire** *ou* **péter de la b.** to talk big, to show off; *Fig* **avoir de la b. dans le toupet** to be rushed off one's feet
brouet [bruɛ] **NM** *Hum ou Littéraire Culin* (coarse) gruel; **un noir b.** a foul brew
brouettage [bruɛtaʒ] **NM** carting, barrowing, wheel barrowing
brouette [bruɛt] **NF** barrow, wheelbarrow
brouettée [bruete] **NF** barrowful, wheelbarrowful
brouetter [4] [bruete] **VT** to cart *(in a wheelbarrow)*, to barrow, to wheelbarrow
brouhaha [bruaa] **NM** hubbub, (confused) noise; **un b. de voix** a hubbub of voices
brouillage [brujaʒ] **NM** *Rad (accidentel)* interference; *(intentionnel)* jamming; **b. électronique** electronic jamming
brouillamini [brujamini] **NM** *Fam Vieilli* confusion■, tangle■
brouillard [brujar] **NM** **1** *Météo (léger)* mist; *(épais)* fog; **il y a du b.** it's misty/foggy; **un b. à couper au couteau** a very thick fog, a pea-souper; **b. givrant** freezing fog; **b. matinal** early-morning fog; **il est dans le b.** he's not with it
2 *(voile)* mist; **avoir un b. devant les yeux** to have blurred vision; **voir à travers un b.** to see things through a haze *or* mist
3 *Phys* aerosol
4 *Bot* baby's breath, gypsophila
5 *Compta (livre de comptes)* daybook; **b. de caisse** cash book
brouillasse [brujas] **NF** drizzle
brouillasser [3] [brujase] **V IMPERSONNEL il brouillasse** it's drizzling
brouille [bruj] **NF** tiff, quarrel; **leur b. dure toujours** they're still not speaking *or* on speaking terms; **leur b. est irrémédiable** they've fallen out (with each other) for good
brouillé, -e [bruje] **ADJ** **1** *(terne)* **avoir le teint b.** to look off-colour **2** *(ciel)* cloudy **3** *Cartes* shuffled **4** *Culin* scrambled
brouille-ménage [brujmenaʒ] **NM** *Fam* red wine■, *Br* plonk
brouiller [3] [bruje] **VT** **1** *Culin (œuf)* to scramble
2 *(mélanger → cartes)* to shuffle; *Fam* **b. la cervelle à qn** to get sb muddled *or* confused; **ça m'a brouillé les idées** it confused *or* befuddled me; *Fig* **b. les cartes** to confuse the issue; **b. les pistes** *(dans un roman)* to confuse the reader; *(dans une poursuite)* to cover one's tracks, to put sb off one's scent; *(dans un débat)* to put up a smokescreen; *Vieilli Littéraire* **b. du papier** to scribble
3 *(dérégler)* to jumble; **b. la combinaison d'un coffre** to jumble the combination of a safe
4 *(troubler → liquide)* to cloud; **b. la vue à qn** to cloud *or* to blur sb's eyesight; **b. un miroir** to blur a mirror; **l'alcool brouille le teint** alcohol ruins your complexion; **les lettres étaient brouillées devant mes yeux** the letters were a blur before my eyes; **il avait les yeux brouillés par les larmes** his eyes were blurred with tears
5 *Rad (accidentellement)* to cause interference to; *(intentionnellement → signal)* to scramble; *(→ transmission, circuit)* to jam
6 *(amis, parents)* to turn against each other, to cause a disagreement between; **ça l'a brouillé avec sa famille** it's turned him against *or* estranged him from his family; *Fig* **ce professeur m'a brouillé avec les mathématiques** that teacher spoiled *or* ruined mathematics for me; **être b. avec qn** to be on bad terms with sb, to have fallen out with sb; **je suis brouillé avec les ordinateurs** I'm no good with computers; **ils sont brouillés** they're on bad terms *or* they've fallen out (with each other)
▸**se brouiller VPR** **1** *(se fâcher)* to quarrel, to fall out (with one another); **se b. avec qn** to fall out with sb
2 *(se mélanger → idées)* to get confused *or* muddled *or* jumbled; *(se troubler → vue)* to blur, to become blurred
3 *Météo (ciel)* to become cloudy, to cloud over; **le temps se brouille** it's clouding over
brouillerie [brujri] **NF** tiff
brouilleur [brujœr] **NM** *Rad & Ordinat* jammer
brouillon, -onne [brujɔ̃, -ɔn] **ADJ** **1** *(travail)* untidy, messy **2** *(personne)* muddleheaded, unmethodical; **avoir l'esprit b.** to be muddleheaded
NM,F muddler
NM **1** *(ébauche)* (rough) draft; **faire un b.** to make a (rough) draft; **faire une lettre au b.** to draft a letter, to write a first draft of a letter; **faire un exercice au b.** to do an exercise in rough; *Ordinat* **version b.** draft version **2 (papier) b.** rough paper, *Br* scrap *or Am* scratch paper
brouillonner [3] [brujɔne] **VT** to jot down
brouilly [bruji] **NM** *(vin)* Brouilly
broum [brum] **EXCLAM** brum, brum!
broussaille [brusaj] **NF** *(touffe)* clump of brushwood
❑ **broussailles NFPL** *Géog (sous-bois)* undergrowth; *(dans un champ)* scrub
❑ **en broussaille ADJ** *(cheveux)* tousled, dishevelled; *(sourcils, barbe)* bushy, shaggy
broussailleux, -euse [brusajø, -øz] **ADJ** **1** *Géog (terrain)* brushy, scrubby, covered with brushwood **2** *(sourcils, barbe)* shaggy, bushy; *(cheveux)* tousled, dishevelled
broussard, -e [brusar, -ard] **NM** bushman, *f* bushwoman
brousse [brus] **NF** **1** *Géog (type de végétation)* **la b.** the bush **2** *(étendue)* **la b.** *(en Afrique)* the bush; *(en Australie)* the outback; *Fam Fig* **vivre en pleine b.** to live in the backwoods *or* out in the sticks *or Am* in the boondocks
❑ **de brousse ADJ** **1** *(chaussures)* desert *(avant n)* **2** *(feux)* bush *(avant n)*
broussin [brusɛ̃] **NM** *Bot* gnarl *(on tree)*
brout [bru] **NM** *Bot* tender shoots, browse
broutage [brutaʒ] **NM** **1** *(du bétail)* grazing; *(d'un animal sauvage)* browsing **2** *Tech (d'une machine, d'un outil)* jerking, *Br* juddering; *(d'un embrayage)* slipping
broutard, broutart [brutar] **NM** *Zool (veau)* store calf
broutement [brutmɑ̃] **NM** **1** *(du bétail)* grazing; *(d'un animal sauvage)* browsing **2** *Tech (d'une machine, d'un outil)* jerking, *Br* juddering; *(d'un embrayage)* slipping
brouter [3] [brute] **VT** **1** *(sujet: bétail)* to graze, to feed on; *(sujet: animal sauvage)* to browse, to feed on; **b. des feuilles** to nibble at leaves **2** *Vulg* **b. qn** to go down on sb; **il nous les broute** he's being a pain in the arse
VI **1** *(bétail)* to graze, to feed; *(animal sauvage)* to browse, to feed; **elle fait b. ses chèvres dans le pré du voisin** she grazes her goats in her neighbour's field **2** *Tech (machine-outil)* to chatter, to jerk, *Br* to judder; *(embrayage)* to slip
brouteur [brutœr] **NM** *Ordinat* browser
brouteuse [brutøz] **NF** *Vulg* **b. (de minou)** dyke
broutille [brutij] **NF** *(chose futile)* trifle, trifling matter; **il s'inquiète pour des broutilles** he's worrying over nothing; **broutilles que tout cela!** what a lot of trivial nonsense!
brownie [brɔni] **NM** *Culin* brownie
brownien [bronjɛ̃] **ADJ M** *Phys* Brownian

browning [broniŋ] NM Browning (automatic rifle)

broyage [brwajaʒ] NM (des aliments par les dents) crushing, grinding; (pulvérisation → d'une couleur) grinding; (→ de la pierre, du sucre) crushing; (→ d'une fibre) breaking, crushing; (→ d'un grain) milling, grinding, crushing

broyat [brɔja] NM ground remains

broyer [13] [brwaje] VT 1 (écraser → couleur, matériau friable, nourriture) to grind; (→ pierre, sucre, ail) to crush; (→ grain) to mill, to grind; (→ fibre) to break, to crush; (→ main, pied) to crush; **b. dans un mortier** to pound in a mortar; **se faire b.** to be or get crushed 2 (locution) **b. du noir** to be in the doldrums, to think gloomy thoughts

broyeur, -euse [brwajœr, -øz] ADJ grinding
NM,F grinder, crusher; (de chanvre) hemp braker or dresser
NM (pulvérisateur → à minerai, à sable) grinder, crusher, mill; (→ à paille) bruiser; (→ à fibre) brake; (→ à déchets) disintegrator, grinder; **b. d'ordures** (dans un évier) waste disposal unit; **b. sanitaire** Saniflo®, macerator unit

bru [bry] NF Vieilli daughter-in-law

bruant [bryɑ̃] NM Orn (corn) bunting; **b. jaune** yellowhammer; **b. des neiges** snow bunting; **b. des roseaux** reed bunting

brucella [brysɛla] NF Biol brucella

brucelles [brysɛl] NFPL Suisse (pair of) tweezers

brucellose [bryseloz] NF Méd brucellosis

bruche [bryʃ] NM Entom **b. des pois** pea beetle, weevil

brucine [brysin] NF Chim brucine

Bruegel [brœgɛl] NPR Brueghel; **B. l'Ancien** Brueghel the Elder

brugeois, -e [bryʒwa, -az] ADJ of/from Bruges
□ **Brugeois, -e** NM,F = inhabitant of or person from Bruges

Bruges [bryʒ] NM Géog Bruges

brugnon [bryɲɔ̃] NM Bot nectarine

brugnonier [bryɲɔnje] NM Bot nectarine (tree)

bruine [bryin] NF Météo drizzle; **petite b.** fine drizzle

bruiner [3] [bryine] V IMPERSONNEL Météo **il bruine** it's drizzling

bruineux, -euse [bryinø, -øz] ADJ Météo drizzly

bruire [105] [bryir] VI Littéraire (feuilles, vent) to rustle, to whisper; (étoffe) to rustle; (eau) to murmur; (insecte) to hum, to buzz, to drone; **le vent faisait b. les arbres** the trees were rustling in the wind

bruissement [bryismɑ̃] NM (des feuilles, du vent, d'une étoffe) rustle, rustling; (de l'eau) murmuring; (d'un insecte) hum, humming, buzzing; (d'ailes) flapping

bruisser etc voir **bruire**

bruisser [3] [bryse] VI Littéraire (feuilles, vent) to rustle, to whisper; (étoffe) to rustle; (eau) to murmur; (insecte) to hum, to buzz, to drone; **le vent faisait bruire les arbres** the trees were rustling in the wind

bruit [bryi] NM 1 (son) sound, noise; **des bruits de pas** the sound of footsteps; **des bruits de voix** the hum of conversation; **les bruits de la maison/rue** the (everyday) sounds of the house/street; **un b. métallique** a clang; **un b. de vaisselle** a clatter of dishes; **un b. sec** a snap; **un b. sourd** a thud; **faire un b.** to make a sound or noise; **il y a un bruit** there's a faint sound; **c'est très calme, il n'y a pas un b.** it's very quiet, there's not a sound; **b. blanc** white noise; **b. de fond** background noise; **en b. de fond** in the background; **avec les jérémiades du père en perpétuel b. de fond** with the father's perpetual moaning in the background
2 (vacarme) noise; **j'ai horreur d'expliquer quelque chose dans le b.** I hate explaining something against a background of noise; **lutte contre le b.** noise abatement campaign; **un b. d'enfer** a terrible racket; **faire du b.** to be noisy; **ne fais pas de b.** be quiet; **la machine ne fait pas de b.** the machine doesn't make any noise; **sans faire de b.** noiselessly; **il est entré sans (faire de) b.** he came in without (making) a sound; **faire beaucoup de b.** to be very loud or noisy; Fig **il fait beaucoup de b. mais il n'agit pas** he makes a lot of noise but he does nothing; **beaucoup de b. pour rien** much ado about nothing

3 (retentissement) sensation, commotion, furore; **ça va faire du b.** it'll cause a sensation, we haven't heard the last of it; **sa démission a fait beaucoup de b.** his/her resignation caused quite a commotion; **on a fait beaucoup de b. autour de cet enlèvement** the kidnapping caused a furore; **on a fait grand b. autour de sa déclaration** his/her statement caused a great sensation or commotion; **cela fera du b. dans Landerneau** it will be the talk of the town

4 (rumeur) rumour, piece of gossip; **le b. court que...** rumour has it or it is rumoured that...; **répandre** ou **faire courir un b.** to spread a rumour; **se faire l'écho d'un b.** to spread a rumour; Littéraire **il n'est b. que de son mariage/nouveau livre** his/her marriage/new book is the talk of the town; **des bruits de bottes** rumours of impending war, the sound of jackboots; **c'est un b. de couloir** it's a rumour; **faux b.** false rumour; **faire circuler des faux bruits** to spread false rumours

5 Méd sound, noise; **b. cardiaque** ou **du cœur** heart or cardiac sound; **b. respiratoire** rattle; **b. de souffle** (heart) murmur

6 Rad & Tél noise; **bruits ambiants** background noise; **bruits parasites** interference; **b. solaire** solar (radio) noise
□ **sans bruit** ADV noiselessly, without a sound; **il s'avance sans b.** he moves forward without a sound

'Le Bruit et la fureur' Faulkner 'The Sound and the Fury'

bruitage [bryitaʒ] NM Rad & Théât sound effects; Cin foley

bruiter [3] [bryite] VT Cin, Rad & Théât to do the sound effects for

bruiteur, -euse [bryitœr, -øz] NM,F Rad & Théât sound effects engineer; Cin foley artist

brûlage [brylaʒ] NM (des herbes) burning; (d'une peinture) burning (off); (des cheveux) singeing; (du café) roasting; **se faire faire un b.** to have one's hair singed; **b. des terres** scorching

brûlant, -e [brylɑ̃, -ɑ̃t] ADJ 1 (chaud → lampe, assiette) burning (hot); (→ liquide) boiling (hot), scalding; (→ nourriture) burning (hot), piping hot; (→ soleil, température) blazing (hot), scorching, blistering; (→ personne, front) feverish; **avoir les mains brûlantes** to have hot hands
2 (animé) **yeux brûlants de curiosité** eyes gleaming with curiosity; **un regard b. de désir** a look of burning desire
3 (actuel, dont on parle) **sujet/dossier b.** burning issue; **c'est dire l'actualité brûlante de ce livre** this shows how very topical this book is
4 (ardent → regard, sentiment) ardent, impassioned; (→ imagination, récit, secret) passionate
NM Belg **avoir le b.** to have heartburn

brûlé, -e [bryle] ADJ 1 (calciné) burnt; **terre de Sienne brûlée** burnt sienna 2 Fam **être b.** (être compromis) to be finished, to have had it
NM,F Méd **un grand b.** a patient suffering from third-degree burns; **service pour les grands brûlés** burns unit
NM burnt part; Can (d'une forêt) burnt-out area, burn; **enlever le b. sur un gâteau** to scrape the burnt bits off a cake; **une odeur de b.** a smell of burning; **avoir un goût de b.** to taste burnt; **ça sent le b.** (odeur) there's a smell of burning; Fam Fig there's trouble brewing

brûle-gueule [brylgœl] NM INV (short) pipe

brûle-parfum, brûle-parfums [brylparfœ̃] (pl **brûle-parfums**) NM perfume burner

brûle-pourpoint [brylpurpwɛ̃] □ **à brûle-pourpoint** ADV 1 (sans détour) point-blank, without beating about the bush 2 (inopinément) out of the blue; **...demanda-t-elle à b.** ...she asked, out of the blue

brûler [3] [bryle] VT 1 (détruire → feuilles, corps, objet) to burn, to incinerate; **il a brûlé la moquette en jouant avec des allumettes** he burnt the carpet while playing with matches; **on a brûlé Jeanne d'Arc** Joan of Arc was burnt (at the stake); **b. qn vif/sur le bûcher** to burn sb alive/at the stake; Fig **b. ce qu'on a adoré** to turn against one's former love or loves; **b. le pavé** to tear along; **b. les planches** to give an

outstanding performance; **b. ses dernières cartouches** to shoot one's bolt; **b. ses vaisseaux** to burn one's boats or bridges
2 (consommer → électricité, fioul) to burn (up), to use, to consume; Fig **b. la chandelle par les deux bouts** to burn the candle at both ends; **elle brûle un cierge à la Vierge deux fois par an** she lights a candle to the Virgin Mary twice a year; Fig **b. un cierge à qn** to show one's gratitude to sb
3 (trop cuire) to burn; **mon gâteau est complètement brûlé** my cake is burnt to a cinder
4 (trop chauffer → tissu) to burn, to scorch, to singe; (→ cheveux, poils) to singe; (→ acier) to spoil; Littéraire **la chaleur de midi brûlait la plage** the midday heat had turned the beach into an inferno; **un paysage brûlé par le soleil** a landscape scorched by the sun
5 (irriter → partie du corps) to burn; **la fumée me brûle les yeux** the smoke is making my eyes smart or sting; **le froid me brûle les oreilles** the cold is making my ears burn; **le piment me brûle la langue** the chilli is burning my tongue; Fig **b. la cervelle à qn** to blow sb's brains out; Fig **l'argent lui brûle les doigts** money burns a hole in his/her pocket
6 (endommager → sujet: gel) to nip, to burn; (→ sujet: acide) to burn; **brûlé par le gel** frost-damaged; **le soleil brûle l'herbe** the sun scorches the grass
7 (dépasser) **b. son arrêt** (bus, personne) to go past or to miss one's stop; **b. un feu** to go through a red light; **b. un stop** to fail to stop at a stop sign; **b. la consigne** (l'oublier) to forget instructions; (y désobéir) to ignore instructions; **b. la politesse à qn** (passer devant lui) to push in front of sb (in the queue); (partir sans le saluer) to leave without saying goodbye to sb; **b. les étapes** (progresser rapidement) to advance by leaps and bounds; Péj to cut corners, to take short cuts
8 (café) to roast
9 (animer) to burn; **le désir qui le brûle** the desire that consumes him
10 Méd (verrue) to burn off
11 Fam Arg crime (tuer) to waste; **pas un geste ou je te brûle!** don't move or I'll blow your brains out!
VI 1 (flamber) to burn (up), to be on fire; (lentement) to smoulder; **le pin brûle bien** pine wood burns well; **b. sur le bûcher** to be burnt at the stake; **b. vif** to be burnt alive or to death; **la forêt a brûlé** the forest was burnt down or to the ground; **mon dîner a brûlé** my dinner's burnt; **ses vêtements brûlaient** his/her clothes were on fire
2 (se consumer → charbon, essence) to burn; **laisser b. la lumière** to leave the light burning or on; **faire b. le rôti** to burn the roast
3 (être chaud) to be burning; **avoir le front/la gorge qui brûle** to have a burning forehead/a burning sensation in the throat; **ça brûle** (plat, sol) it's boiling hot or burning; (eau) it's scalding; (feu) it's burning; **les yeux me brûlent** my eyes are stinging or smarting
4 Fig Littéraire **b. pour qn** to be in love with sb, to have a burning passion for sb
5 (jeux) to be close; **je brûle?** am I getting warm?
□ **brûler de** VT IND 1 (être animé de) **b. de colère** to be burning or seething with anger; **b. d'impatience/de désir** to be burning with impatience/desire
2 (désirer) to be dying or longing to; **b. de parler à qn** to be dying to talk to sb; **je brûle de te revoir** I'm longing or I can't wait to see you again
▶ **se brûler** VPR to burn oneself; **se b. avec du thé** to burn or to scald oneself with some tea; **se b. la main** to burn one's hand; Fam **se b. la cervelle** to blow one's brains out; **se b. les ailes** to get one's fingers burnt

brûlerie [brylri] NF 1 (pour le café) coffee roasting plant 2 (pour l'eau-de-vie) distillery

brûleur [brylœr] NM burner; **b. à gaz** gas burner or ring; **b. à mazout** oil burner

brûlis [bryli] NM 1 (mode de culture) slash-and-burn farming; **culture sur b.** slash-and-burn cultivation 2 (terrain) patch of burn-baited land

brûloir [brylwar] NM coffee roaster

brûlon [bryl5] NM *Suisse (d'un aliment)* burnt bit; **avoir un goût de b.** to taste burnt; **ça sent le b.** there's a smell of burning

brûlot [brylo] NM **1** *Naut (bateau)* fireship **2** *(écrit)* fierce *or* blistering attack **3** *(eau-de-vie flambée)* burnt brandy **4** *Can Entom (biting)* midge

brûlure [brylyr] NF **1** *(lésion)* burn; **se faire une b. au poignet** to burn oneself on the wrist; *Méd* **b. au premier/second/troisième degré** first-/second-/third-degree burn; **b. de cigarette** cigarette burn **2** *(sensation)* burning sensation; *Fig* **la b. de la honte** the burning sensation of shame; **brûlures d'estomac** heartburn **3** *(trace)* burnt patch

brumaire [brymɛr] NM = 2nd month of the French revolutionary calendar (from 23 October to 21 November)

brumasse [brymas] NF *Météo* thin mist, haze

brumasser [3] [brymase] V IMPERSONNEL *Météo* **il brumasse** there's a light mist

brume [brym] NF **1** *Météo (brouillard)* mist; **b. de chaleur** heat haze; **b. de mer** sea mist **2** *Naut* fog **3** *(confusion)* daze, haze; **il est encore dans les brumes du sommeil** he's still half asleep; **être dans les brumes de l'alcool** to be in a drunken stupor

brumer [3] [bryme] V IMPERSONNEL *Naut* to be foggy, to be hazy

brumeux, -euse [brymø, -øz] ADJ **1** *Météo* misty, foggy, hazy **2** *(vague)* hazy, vague; **un souvenir b.** a hazy *or* dim recollection

Brumisateur® [brymizatœr] NM = atomizer containing Evian® mineral water

brun, -e [brœ̃, bryn] ADJ **1** *(au pigment foncé → cheveux, peau)* brown, dark; *(→ tissu, couleur)* brown; *Can (→ yeux)* brown; **il est b. de peau** he's dark-skinned; **b. cuivré** tawny; *Can* **il fait b.** it's getting dark **2** *(bronzé)* brown, tanned ▪ NM,F dark-haired man, *f* dark-haired woman, brunette ▪ NM brown (colour) □ **brune** NF **1** *(cigarette)* brown tobacco cigarette **2** *(bière)* dark beer, *Br* ≃ brown ale □ **à la brune** ADV *Littéraire* at dusk

brunante [brynɑ̃t] NF *Can* dusk; **à la b.** at dusk

brunâtre [brynatr] ADJ brownish

brunch [brœntʃ] NM brunch

bruncher [3] [brœntʃe] VI to have brunch

Brunei [bryni] NM **le B.** Brunei; **vivre au B.** to live in Brunei; **aller au B.** to go to Brunei

brunéien, -enne [brynejɛ̃, -ɛn] ADJ Bruneian, of/from Brunei □ **Brunéien, -enne** NM,F Bruneian

brunelle [brynɛl] NF *Bot* self-heal

brunet, -ette [brynɛ, -ɛt] NM,F brown-haired boy, *f* girl

bruni [bryni] NM *Tech* burnish

brunir [32] [brynir] VI **1** *(foncer → cheveux, couleur)* to get darker, to darken; *(→ peau)* to get brown *or* browner; *(bronzer)* to tan **2** *Culin (sauce, oignons)* to brown; *(sucre)* to caramelize; **laissez b.** cook until golden; **faites b. les oignons** brown the onions ▪ VT *(hâler)* to tan; *(foncer → cheveux)* to darken **2** *Tech (polir → métal)* to burnish; *(→ acier)* to brown, to burnish

brunissage [brynisaʒ] NM *Tech* burnishing

brunissement [brynismɑ̃] NM tanning

brunisseur, -euse [brynisœr, -øz] NM,F *Tech* burnisher ▪ ADJ M **plat b.** browning dish

brunissoir [bryniswar] NM *Tech* burnisher, burnishing tool

brunissure [brynisyr] NF *Tex* burnish

Brunswick [brœzvik] NM *Géog* Brunswick

Brushing® [brœʃiŋ] NM blow-dry; **faire un B. à qn** to blow-dry sb's hair; **se faire faire un B.** to have a blow-dry

brusque [brysk] ADJ **1** *(bourru → ton)* curt, abrupt; *(→ personne)* abrupt, brusque, blunt; *(→ geste)* abrupt, rough; **un mouvement b.** a jerk, a sudden movement **2** *(imprévu)* abrupt, sudden; **un virage b.** a sharp bend; **une b. baisse de température** a sudden drop in temperature

brusquement [bryskəmɑ̃] ADV **1** *(soudainement)* suddenly, abruptly **2** *(sans ménagements)* abruptly, brusquely, curtly

brusquer [3] [bryske] VT **1** *(personne → malmener)* to be rough with; *(→ presser)* to rush **2** *(hâter → dénouement)* to rush; *(→ adieux)* to cut short; **b. les choses** to rush things

brusquerie [bryskəri] NF **1** *(brutalité)* abruptness, brusqueness, sharpness; **avec b.** abruptly **2** *(soudaineté)* abruptness, suddenness

brut, -e¹ [bryt] ADJ **1** *(non traité → pétrole, métal)* crude, untreated; *(→ laine, soie, charbon, brique)* untreated, raw; *(→ bois)* undressed; *(→ sucre, or)* unrefined; *(→ pierre précieuse)* rough, uncut; *(→ minerai)* raw; **bois b. de machine** machine-dressed timber; **b. de coulée** as cast; **b. de décoffrage** *(béton)* unsurfaced, exposed; *Fam (personne)* rough and ready; **b. de forge** as forged; **b. de laminage** as rolled **2** *Fig (non encore peaufiné)* rough and ready, no-frills *(avant n)*; *(personne)* unrefined **3** *(émotion, qualité)* naked, pure, raw; *(donnée)* raw; *(fait)* simple, plain; **à l'état b.** in the rough **4** *(sauvage)* brute; **la force brute** brute force **5** *Com & Fin (bénéfice, marge, valeur, salaire)* gross **6** *(poids)* gross **7** *(champagne)* brut, dry; *(cidre)* dry ▪ NM **1** *(salaire)* gross income **2** *(pétrole)* crude oil; **b. léger** light crude **3** *(champagne)* brut *or* dry champagne ▪ ADV *Com & Fin* gross; **gagner 2000 euros b.** to earn 2,000 euros gross; **ballot qui pèse 200 kilos b.** packet weighing 200 kilos gross (including packaging)

brutal, -e, -aux, -ales [brytal, -o] ADJ **1** *(violent → personne)* brutal, violent; *(→ enfant)* rough; *(→ choc)* strong, violent; *(→ coup)* brutal, savage; *(→ force)* brute; *(→ jeu)* rough; **être b. avec qn** to treat sb brutally, to be violent with sb **2** *(franc)* brusque, blunt; **il a été très b. en lui annonçant la nouvelle** he broke it to him/her very unfeelingly *or* harshly; **ils se parlèrent avec une franchise brutale** they had a very blunt and frank conversation **3** *(non mitigé)* brutal, raw; **cette vérité était trop brutale pour elle** the truth was too shocking for her **4** *(soudain → changement, arrêt)* sudden, abrupt; *(→ transition)* abrupt; *(→ mort)* sudden; **cela a été très b.** it was very sudden ▪ NM,F brute, violent individual

brutalement [brytalmɑ̃] ADV **1** *(violemment)* brutally, violently, savagely; **pousser qn b. contre qch** to shove sb brutally *or* roughly against sth **2** *(franchement)* brusquely, bluntly; **il lui annonça b. la nouvelle** he broke the news to him/her bluntly **3** *(tout d'un coup)* suddenly; **le vent peut changer b. de direction** the wind can change direction very suddenly; **s'arrêter b.** to come to an abrupt halt

brutaliser [3] [brytalize] VT **1** *(maltraiter)* to ill-treat; **b. qn** to knock sb about, to manhandle sb; **se faire b. par la police** to be manhandled by the police, to be a victim of police brutality **2** *(brusquer)* to rush; **il ne faut pas me b.** don't rush me

brutalisme [brytalism] NM **1** *(violence, brusquerie)* brutality **2** *Archit* Brutalism

brutalité [brytalite] NF **1** *(violence, brusquerie)* brutality; **il lui a parlé avec b.** he spoke to him/her harshly *or* very aggressively; **des brutalités** acts of brutality, violent acts; **brutalités policières** police brutality **2** *(soudaineté)* suddenness; **surpris par la b. de la crise** startled by the sudden onset of the crisis

brute² [bryt] NF **1** *(personne violente)* brute; **comme une b.** with all one's might, like mad; **frapper comme une b.** to hit sth with full force, to hammer away at sth; **ne tire pas comme une b., c'est fragile** don't pull so hard, it's delicate; **c'est une b. épaisse** he's nothing but a brute; **une grande** *ou* **grosse b.** a big brute

(of a man) **2** *(personne fruste)* boor, lout **3** *Littéraire (animal)* brute

brution [brysjɔ̃] NM *Fam Arg scol* = pupil or former pupil of the military academy at La Flèche

Brutus [brytys] NPR Brutus

Bruxelles [brysɛl] NM *Géog* Brussels

bruxellois, -e [brysɛlwa, -az] ADJ of/from Brussels □ **Bruxellois, -e** NM,F = inhabitant of or person from Brussels

bruxisme [bryksism] NM bruxism

bruxomanie [bryksɔmani] NF = **bruxisme**

bruyamment [brɥijamɑ̃] ADV *(parler, rire, protester)* loudly; *(manger, jouer)* noisily

bruyant, -e [brɥijɑ̃, -ɑ̃t] ADJ *(enfant, rue)* noisy; *(rire)* loud; **un quartier peu b.** a quiet neighbourhood

bruyère [brɥijɛr] NF **1** *Bot* heather; **(racine de) b.** briar; **b. cendrée** bell heather; **b. des marais** cross-leaved heath **2** *(lande)* moor, heath

bryologie [brijɔlɔʒi] NF *Bot* bryology

bryone [brijon] NF *Bot* bryony

bryophyte [brijɔfit] NF *Bot* bryophyte

bryozoaires [brijɔzɔɛr] NMPL *Biol* bryozoa

BSPCE [beɛspeseø] NM *Bourse (abrév* **bon de souscription de parts de créateurs d'entreprise**) = stock option in a start-up company with tax privileges

BT¹ [bete] NM *Scol (abrév* **brevet de technicien**) = vocational training certificate taken at 17 after three years' technical training

BT² *Élec (abrév écrite* **basse tension**) LT

BTA [betea] NM *Scol (abrév* **brevet de technicien agricole**) = agricultural training certificate (taken at age 18)

BTH [beteaʃ] NM *Scol (abrév* **brevet de technicien hôtelier**) = diploma in hotel and catering management

BTP [betepe] NMPL *Constr (abrév* **bâtiments et travaux publics**) = building and public works sector

BTS [beteɛs] NM *Univ (abrév* **brevet de technicien supérieur**) = advanced vocational training certificate (taken at the end of a two-year higher education course)

BTU [betey] NM *(abrév* **British thermal unit**) BTU

BU [bey] NF *(abrév* **bibliothèque universitaire**) university library

bu, -e [by] PP *voir* **boire**

buanderette [bɥɑ̃drɛt] NF *Can Joual Br* launderette, *Am* Laundromat®

buanderie [bɥɑ̃dri] NF **1** *(pièce, local → à l'intérieur)* laundry, utility room; *(→ à l'extérieur)* washhouse **2** *Can (laverie)* (coin-operated) cleaner's, laundry

buandier, -ère [bɥɑ̃dje, -jɛr] NM,F **1** *Tex* bleacher **2** *(blanchisseur)* laundryman, *f* laundrywoman

Buba [byba] NF *Banque (abrév* **Bundesbank**) **la B.** the Bundesbank

bubale [bybal] NM *Zool* hartebeest

bubble-gum [bœbœlgɔm] NM bubble-gum

bubon [bybɔ̃] NM *Méd* bubo

bubonique [bybɔnik] ADJ *Méd* bubonic

Bucarest [bykarɛst] NM *Géog* Bucharest

buccal, -e, -aux, -ales [bykal, -o] ADJ mouth *(avant n)*, *Spéc* buccal

buccin [byksɛ̃] NM **1** *Zool (mollusque)* whelk **2** *Antiq & Mus* trumpet

buccinateur [byksinatœr] NM **1** *Anat* buccinator **2** *Antiq & Mus* trumpet player

bucco-dentaire [bykodɑ̃tɛr] ADJ mouth *(avant n)*; **hygiène b.** oral hygiene

bucco-génital, -e [bykoʒenital] *(mpl* **bucco-génitaux** [-o]*, fpl* **bucco-génitales**) ADJ **rapports bucco-génitaux** oral sex

Bucéphale [bysefal] NPR Bucephalus

bûche [byʃ] NF **1** *(morceau de bois)* log **2** *Fam (personne apathique)* lump; **ne reste pas là comme une b.** don't just stand there *Br* like a lemon *or Am* like a lump on a log **3** *Culin & Hist* **b. glacée** Yule log *(with an ice-cream filling)*; **b. de Noël** Yule log **4** *Fam (locution)* **prendre** *ou* **ramasser une b.** to take a tumble, *Br* to come a cropper

bûcher¹ [3] [byʃe] VT **1** *Fam (travailler)* **b. un examen** to cram for an exam; **b. sa physique** to *Br* to swot up *or Am* to bone up on one's physics **2** *Can (arbre)* to fell, to cut down

VI **1** *Fam (travailler) Br* to swot, *Am* to grind **2** *Can (couper du bois)* to fell trees

bûcher[2] [byʃe] NM **1** *(supplice)* **le b.** the stake; **être condamné au b.** to be sentenced to be burnt at the stake; **monter** *ou* **mourir sur le b.** to be burnt at the stake **2** *(funéraire)* pyre **3** *(remise)* woodshed

bûcheron, -onne [byʃrɔ̃, -ɔn] NM,F woodcutter, lumberjack

bûchette [byʃɛt] NF **1** *(petit bois)* twig, stick **2** *(pour compter)* stick

bûcheur, -euse [byʃœr, -øz] *Fam* ADJ hardworking■

NM,F *(étudiant)* hardworking student■, *Br Péj* swot, *Am Péj* grind; *(travailleur)* hard worker■

bûchille [byʃij] NF *Suisse* **1** *(copeau)* wood shaving **2** *(écharde)* splinter

bucolique [bykɔlik] ADJ bucolic, pastoral

NF *Littérature* bucolic, pastoral poem

'Les Bucoliques' *Virgile* 'The Eclogues' *or* 'The Bucolics'

bucrane [bykran] NM *Archit* bucranium, bucrane

Budapest [bydapɛst] NM *Géog* Budapest

buddleia, buddleya [bydleja] NM *Bot* buddleia

budget [bydʒɛ] NM **1** *(d'une personne, d'une entreprise)* budget; **avoir un petit b.** to be on a (tight) budget; **des prix pour les petits budgets** budget prices; **se fixer un b. loisirs** to decide on a budget for one's leisure activities; **b. temps** *(délai)* allowance; *(en sociologie)* time budget

2 *Fin, Compta & Pol* budget; **le B.** ≃ the Budget; **inscrire qch au b.** to budget for sth; **le b. de l'éducation** the education budget; **b. annuel** annual budget; **b. des approvisionnements** purchase budget; **b. base zéro** zero-base budgeting; **b. des charges** overhead *or* cost budget; **b. commercial** sales budget; *UE* **b. communautaire européen** European Community budget; **b. des dépenses** expense budget; **b. équilibré** balanced budget; *Écon* **b. de l'État** state budget; **b. d'exploitation** operating budget; **b. de fonctionnement** operating budget; **b. glissant** rolling budget; **b. global** master *or* overall budget; **b. des investissements** capital budget; **b. marketing** marketing budget; **b. prévisionnel** provisional budget; **b. de production** production budget; **b. promotionnel** promotional *or* publicity budget; **b. publicitaire** *ou* **de publicité** advertising budget, publicity budget; **b. des recettes** revenue budget; **b. renouvelable** continuous budget; **b. social de la nation** national welfare budget; **b. de trésorerie** cash budget; **b. des ventes** sales budget

3 *(dans la publicité, dans le marketing)* account; **l'agence s'est assuré le b. Brook** the agency has secured the Brook account

budgétaire [bydʒetɛr] ADJ *(contrainte, dépenses, contrôle)* budgetary; *(déficit, excédent)* budget *(avant n)*; *(année) Br* financial, *Am* fiscal

budgéter [18] [bydʒete] VT **b. qch** to include sth in the budget, to budget for sth

budgétisation [bydʒetizasjɔ̃] NF *Compta* budgeting; **b. base zéro** zero-base budgeting

budgétiser [3] [bydʒetize] VT *Compta* to budget for

budgétivore [bydʒetivɔr] *Hum* ADJ wasteful of State resources

NMF big spender (of State resources)

buée [bɥe] NF condensation; **il y a de la b. sur les carreaux** the windows are covered in condensation *or* misted up; **plein** *ou* **couvert de b.** misted *or* steamed up; **mes lunettes se couvrent de b.** my glasses are getting steamed up

Buenos Aires [bɥenozɛr] NM *Géog* Buenos Aires

buffer [bœfœr] NM *Ordinat* buffer

buffet [byfɛ] NM **1** *(meuble → de salle à manger)* sideboard; **b. (de cuisine)** kitchen cabinet *or* dresser

2 *(nourriture)* buffet; **il y aura un b. pour le déjeuner** there will be a buffet lunch; **b. campagnard** buffet *(mainly with country-style cold meats)*; **b. froid** (cold) buffet

3 *(salle)* **b. (de gare)** (station) café *or* buffet *or* cafeteria

4 *(comptoir roulant)* refreshment *Br* trolley *or Am* cart

5 *(d'un orgue)* case

6 *très Fam (ventre)* belly; **ne rien avoir dans le b.** *(être à jeun)* to have an empty belly; *(être lâche)* to have no guts; **se remplir le b.** to stuff one's face, to pig out

buffetier, -ère [byftje, -jɛr] NM,F *Fam Vieilli (d'un buffet de gare etc)* buffet manager■

bufflage [byflaʒ] NM *Métal* buffing

buffle [byfl] NM **1** *Zool* buffalo; **b. d'Afrique** African buffalo; **b. d'Asie** Asian *or* Indian buffalo, water buffalo; **b. de Cafrerie, b. du Cap** Cape buffalo **2** *(cuir)* buffalo hide **3** *(pour polir)* buffer

bufflesse [byflɛs] NF *Zool* cow buffalo

buffleterie [byflətri, byflɛtri] NF *Mil* leather equipment

buffletin [byflətɛ̃] NM **1** *Zool* buffalo calf **2** *(cuir)* buffalo-calf hide **3** *(vêtement)* jerkin

bufflon [byflɔ̃] NM *Zool* young buffalo

bufflonne [byflɔn] NF *Zool* cow buffalo

bug [bœg] NM *Ordinat* bug

buggy [bygi] NM buggy

bugle[1] [bygl] NM *Mus* bugle

bugle[2] [bygl] NF *Bot* bugle

buglosse [byglɔs] NF *Bot* bugloss, alkanet

bugne [byɲ] NF *Culin* = strip of fried dough sprinkled with sugar, speciality of the Lyons region

bugrane [bygran] NF *Bot* restharrow

building [bildiŋ] NM high-rise (building)

buire [bɥir] NF ewer, flagon

buis [bɥi] NM **1** *Bot* box, boxtree; *Rel* **b. bénit** (blessed) palm **2** *Menuis* box, boxwood

buisson [bɥisɔ̃] NM **1** *Bot* bush; *Chasse* **faire b. creux** to draw a blank **2** *Culin* **b. d'écrevisses** crayfish en buisson **3** *Bible* **b. ardent** burning bush

buisson-ardent [bɥisɔ̃ardɑ̃] *(pl* **buissons-ardents)** NM *Bot* pyracantha

buissonnant, -e [bɥisɔnɑ̃, -ɑ̃t] ADJ growing in the shape of a bush, bushy

buissonneux, -euse [bɥisɔnø, -øz] ADJ **1** *Géog (terrain)* shrub-covered, covered with bushes **2** *(arbre, végétation)* bushy

buissonnier, -ère [bɥisɔnje, -jɛr] ADJ **1** *(animal)* bush-dwelling **2** *voir* **école**

Bujumbura [buʒumbura] NM *Géog* Bujumbura

Bulawayo [bulawajo] NM *Géog* Bulawayo

bulb [bœlb] NM *Naut* bulge, bulb

bulbaire [bylbɛr] ADJ *Méd* bulbar

bulbe [bylb] NM **1** *Bot* bulb, corm **2** *Anat* **b. pileux** hair bulb; **b. rachidien** medulla oblongata **3** *Archit* **b. (byzantin)** onion dome **4** *Naut* bulb **5** *(comme adj) Élec* **groupe b.** bulb turbine generator set

bulbeux, -euse [bylbø, -øz] ADJ *Bot* bulbous

bulbiculture [bylbikyltyr] NF *Bot* bulb growing

bulbille [bylbij] NF *Bot* bulbil, bulblet

bulbul [bylbyl] NM *Orn* bulbul

bulgare [bylgar] ADJ Bulgarian

NM *(langue)* Bulgarian

❑ **Bulgare** NMF Bulgarian

Bulgarie [bylgari] NF **la B.** Bulgaria; **vivre en B.** to live in Bulgaria; **aller en B.** to go to Bulgaria

bulge [bœlʒ] NM *Archit* bulge

bullaire [bylɛr] NM *Rel* **1** *(recueil)* collection of papal bulls **2** *(scribe)* engrosser of papal bulls

bulldog [byldɔg] NM *Zool (chien)* bulldog

bulldozer [byldozɛr] NM **1** *(machine)* bulldozer **2** *Fam (fonceur)* bulldozer; **c'est un b., cette femme!** that woman bulldozes her way through life!

bulle [byl] NF **1** *(d'air, de gaz, de bain moussant)* bubble; **b. d'air** *(dans un tuyau)* airlock; **b. de savon** soap bubble; **des bulles** bubbles, froth; **il n'y a plus de bulles dans le Coca®** the Coke® has gone flat; **faire des bulles** *(de savon)* to blow bubbles; *(bébé)* to dribble

2 *(de bande dessinée)* balloon, speech bubble; *Ordinat* **b. d'aide** help pop-up

3 *Fam Arg scol (zéro)* zero■; **avoir la b.** to get nought *or* (a) zero; **j'ai encore eu la b. en maths** I got a zero again in *Br* maths *or Am* math

4 *Méd (enceinte stérile)* bubble; **enfant b.** = child brought up in a sterile bubble

5 *(emballage)* blister

6 *Rel* bull

7 *Bourse* **b. boursière** stock market bubble, surge on the Stock Market; **b. immobilière** housing bubble; **b. Internet** Internet bubble; **b. spéculative** speculative bubble

NM **(papier) b.** Manila paper

bullé, -e [byle] ADJ *(feuille)* bullate; *(papier)* blistered

buller [3] [byle] VI *très Fam* to laze about *or* around■

bulletin [byltɛ̃] NM **1** *Rad & TV (communiqué)* bulletin; *(d'entreprise)* newsletter; **b. d'informations** news bulletin; **b. météorologique** weather forecast *or* report; **b. spécial** newsflash

2 *Admin* **b. de greffe** = document issued by the registrar; **b. de naissance** birth certificate; **le B. officiel** = official listing of all new laws and decrees; **B. officiel des communautés européennes** = official listing of all new EU directives; **b. de recensement** census return; **b. de santé** medical report

3 *Scol* **b. (scolaire** *ou* **de notes)** *Br* (school) report, *Am* report card; **b. mensuel/trimestriel** monthly/end-of-term *Br* report *or Am* report card; **avoir un bon/mauvais b.** to get a good/bad *Br* school report *or Am* report card

4 *Bourse* **B. de la Cote Officielle** Stock Exchange Daily Official List; **b. des cours** official (Stock Exchange) price list; **b. des oppositions** list of stopped bonds; **b. de souscription d'actions** share subscription *or* share application form

5 *Pol* **b. de vote** ballot paper; **b. blanc** blank ballot paper; **b. nul** spoiled ballot paper; **b. secret** secret ballot

6 *(revue)* bulletin, annals; *(→ d'entreprise)* newsletter

7 *(ticket, formulaire)* form; *Com* **b. de commande** order form; **b. de consigne** *Am* checkroom *or Br* left luggage ticket; *Com* **b. d'expédition** dispatch note, consignment note; *Com* **b. de garantie** guarantee (certificate); *Com* **b. de paie** *ou* **de salaire** pay (advice) slip, salary advice note; **b. de participation** entry form; *Com* **b. de vente** sales note; *Suisse Banque* **b. de versement** money order

bulletin-réponse [byltɛ̃repɔ̃s] *(pl* **bulletins-réponse)** NM *(gén)* reply form *or* coupon; *(pour un concours)* entry form

bulleux, -euse [bylø, -øz] ADJ *Méd* blistered

bull-finch [bulfinʃ] *(pl* **bull-finches** *ou* **bull-finchs)** NM *Équitation* bullfinch

bullionisme [byljɔnism] NM *Écon & Hist* bullionism

bullpack® [bylpak] NM bubble wrap

bull-terrier [bultɛrje] *(pl* **bull-terriers)** NM *(chien)* bull-terrier

bulot [bylo] NM *Zool (mollusque)* whelk

bun [bœn] NM *Culin* bun

bungalow [bœ̃galo] NM *(maison → sans étage)* bungalow; *(→ de vacances)* chalet

bunker [bunkœr] NM **1** *Sport* bunker, *Am* sand trap **2** *Mil* bunker; **b. enterré** underground bunker

Bunsen [bœ̃zɛn] NPR **bec B.** Bunsen burner

buplèvre [byplɛvr] NM *Bot* hare's ear; **b. à feuilles rondes** thorow-wax

bupreste [byprɛst] NM *Entom* buprestid

buraliste [byralist] NMF *(de bureau de tabac) Br* tobacconist, *Am* tobacco dealer *(licensed to sell stamps)*; *(de bureau de poste)* clerk; *(d'impôts)* receiver of taxes

bure[1] [byr] NF **1** *Tex* homespun **2** *(vêtement)* frock, cowl; **la b. du moine** monk's habit

bure[2] [byr] NM *Mines* staple shaft

bureau, -x [byro] NM **1** *(meuble → gén)* desk; *(→ à rabat)* bureau; *Can (→ pour vêtements)* chest of drawers; **b. à cylindre** roll top desk; **b. ministre** pedestal desk

2 *(pièce d'une maison)* study; *(meubles de cette pièce)* set of furniture *(for a study)*

3 *(lieu de travail)* office; **aller au b.** to go to the office; **travailler dans un b.** to do office work; **le centre de Londres est envahi par les bureaux** central London has been taken over by offices; **elle est dans son b.** she's in her office; **b. informatisé** electronic office, paperless office; **b. paysager** open-plan office

4 *(agence)* office; **b. d'aide sociale** welfare office *or* centre; **b. de change** *(banque)* bureau de change, foreign exchange office; *(comptoir)* bureau de change, foreign exchange counter; **b. de cotation ou d'évaluation** credit *Br* agency

or Am bureau; **b. de douane** customs house; **b. d'études** *(entreprise)* research consultancy; **b. d'expédition** forwarding office, shipping office; **b. d'exportation** export office; **b. des objets trouvés** *Br* lost property *or Am* lost-and-found office; **b. de perception** tax office; **b. de placement** employment agency *(for domestic workers)*; **b. de poste** post office; **b. de publicité** advertising agency; **b. de renseignements** information desk *or* point *or* centre; **b. de style** design consultancy; **b. de tabac** *Br* tobacconist's, *Am* tobacco dealer's; **b. de tri** sorting office; **b. de vote** polling station

5 *(service interne)* **b. d'achat** purchase department; **b. commercial** commercial department; **b. d'études** *(dans une entreprise)* research department *or* unit

6 *Théât* booking office; **jouer à bureaux fermés** to be fully booked

7 *(commission)* committee; **bureaux internationaux** international bureaux; **le syndicat réuni en b. confédéral** the union meeting at federal committee level; **b. politique** Politburo; **B. européen de l'environnement** European Environmental Bureau; **B. international du travail** International Labour Organization; **B. de recherches géologiques et minières** = French geological and mining research agency; **B. de vérification de la publicité** = French advertising standards authority, *Br* ≃ ASA

8 *Journ* office (abroad)

9 *Ordinat (écran)* desktop; **b. actif** active desktop; **b. électronique** electronic desktop

10 *Jur* **b. de conciliation** *(prud'hommes)* conciliation panel; **b. de jugement** *(prud'hommes)* adjudication panel

❑ **bureaux** NMPL *(locaux)* office, offices; **nos bureaux sont transférés au 10, rue Biot** our office has *or* our premises have been transferred to 10 rue Biot; **les bureaux du ministère** the Ministry offices

❑ **de bureau** ADJ *(travail, heures)* office *(avant n)*; *(articles, fournitures)* office *(avant n)*; stationery *(avant n)*; *(employé)* office *(avant n)*, white-collar

bureaucrate [byrokrat] NMF bureaucrat

bureaucratie [byrokrasi] NF **1** *(système)* bureaucracy **2** *(fonctionnaires)* officials, bureaucrats **3** *(tracasseries)* red tape, bureaucracy

bureaucratique [byrokratik] ADJ bureaucratic, administrative

bureaucratisation [byrokratizasjɔ̃] NF bureaucratization

bureaucratiser [3] [byrokratize] VT to bureaucratize

bureauticien, -enne [byrɔtisjɛ̃, -ɛn] NM,F specialist in office IT

Bureautique® [byrotik] ADJ **système/méthode B.** office IT system/method

NF **1** *(système)* office IT **2** *(matériel)* computerized office equipment

burelé, -e [byrle] ADJ **1** *Hér* barry; **b. de dix pièces** barry of ten pieces **2** *(timbre)* burelé

burèle, burelle [byrɛl] NF *Hér* barrulet

burette [byrɛt] NF **1** *(bidon)* **b. (d'huile)** oilcan **2** *Chim* burette **3** *Rel* cruet

❑ **burettes** NFPL *Vulg* nuts, balls, *Br* bollocks; **il me casse les burettes** he's pissing me off, *Am* he's breaking my balls

burgau [byrgo] NM *Zool (mollusque)* burgau, burgao

burgaudine [byrgodin] NF burgaudine

burger [bœrgœr] NM *Culin* burger

burgo [byrgo] = **burgau**

burgrave [byrgrav] NM *Mil & Hist* burgrave

burin [byrɛ̃] NM **1** *Tech* cold chisel **2** *(outil de graveur)* burin, graver **3** *(gravure)* engraving, print

burinage [byrinaʒ] NM *Tech* chiselling, chipping

buriné, -e [byrine] ADJ *(traits)* strongly marked; *(visage)* craggy, furrowed

buriner [3] [byrine] VT **1** *Beaux-Arts* to engrave **2** *Tech* to chisel **3** *Littéraire (visage)* to carve deep lines into

burineur [byrinœr] NM *Tech* chiseller, chipper

buriniste [byrinist] NMF *Beaux-Arts* engraver

burka [burka] = **burqa**

Burkina [byrkina] NM **le B.** Burkina; **vivre au B.** to live in Burkina; **aller au B.** to go to Burkina

burkinabé [byrkinabe] ADJ of/from Burkina

❑ **Burkinabé** NMF = inhabitant of or person from Burkina

burlat [byrla] NF *Bot (cerise)* Burlat *(variety of cherry)*

burle [byrl] NF = cold wind in the Massif Central

burlesque [byrlɛsk] ADJ **1** *(très drôle → accoutrement)* comic, comical, droll; *(→ plaisanterie)* funny **2** *Péj (stupide → idée)* ludicrous, ridiculous **3** *Cin, Littérature & Théât* burlesque

NM *Cin, Littérature & Théât* **le b.** the burlesque

burlesquement [byrlɛskəmɑ̃] ADV in a burlesque manner, comically

burlingue [byrlɛ̃g] NM *Fam* office■

burnes [byrn] NFPL *Vulg* balls, nuts, *Br* bollocks; **casser les b. à qn** to piss sb off, *Am* to break sb's balls

burnous [byrnu] NM *(arabe)* burnous, burnouse; *(de bébé)* hooded coat

buron [byrɔ̃] NM *(en Auvergne)* = shepherd's hut where cheese is made

burqa [burka] NF burka, burkha, burqa

burséracée [byrserase] *Bot* NF = member of the Buxaceae family, buxaceous plant

❑ **burséracées** NFPL Buxaceae

bursite [byrsit] NF *Méd* bursitis

burundais, -e [burundɛ, -ɛz] ADJ Burundian

❑ **Burundais, -e** NM,F Burundian

Burundi [burundi] NM **le B.** Burundi; **vivre au B.** to live in Burundi; **aller au B.** to go to Burundi

bus [bys] NM **1** *Transp (véhicule)* bus; **on y va en b.** *ou* **par le b.** we're going there by bus; **il était dans le b.** he was on the bus; **monter dans le/descendre du b.** to get on/off the bus **2** *Ordinat* bus; **b. d'adresses** address bus; **b. de contrôle** control bus; **b. de données** data bus; **b. multimédia** multimedia bus

busard [byzar] NM *Orn* harrier; **b. de Montagu** Montagu's harrier; **b. des roseaux** marsh harrier; **b. Saint-Martin** hen harrier

busc [bysk] NM **1** *(d'un corset)* busk, steel; *Couture* whalebone **2** *(d'une écluse)* locksill, mitresill **3** *(d'une arme)* shoulder *(of rifle-butt)*

buse [byz] NF **1** *Orn* buzzard **2** *Fam Péj* fool, dolt; **quelle b.!** what a fool! **3** *(conduit)* duct; **b. d'aérage** ventilation duct, air shaft **4** *Aut* **b. de carburateur** choke tube; **b. d'injection** injector nozzle **5** *Belg (échec)* failure

buser [3] [byze] VT *Belg* **1** *(blackbouler)* to blackball **2** *(étudiant)* to fail, *Am* to flunk

bush [buʃ] *(pl* **bushes)** NM *Géog* **le b.** the bush

bushido [buʃido] NM Bushido

business [biznɛs] NM *Fam* **1** *(affaires)* business; **parler b.** to talk business; **b. angel** *(commanditaire)* angel **2** *Vieilli (embrouillamini)* **qu'est-ce que c'est que ce b.?** what's this mess?; **c'est tout un b. pour démonter le moteur** it's a hell of a job taking the engine apart **3** *Vieilli (objet)* whatsit, thingamajig

businessman [biznɛsman] *(pl* **businessmen** [-men] *ou* **businessmans)** NM businessman

busqué, -e [byske] ADJ *(nez)* hook *(avant n)*, hooked

busquer [3] [byske] VT **1** *Vieilli (corset)* to busk; **b. un enfant** to put a child into stays **2** *(cintrer)* to curve

busserole [bysrɔl] NF *Bot* **b. raisin d'ours** bearberry; **b. des Alpes** Alpine bearberry

buste [byst] NM **1** *Anat (haut du corps)* chest; *(seins)* bust **2** *Beaux-Arts (sculpture)* bust; **un b. de Mozart** a bust of Mozart; **peindre qn en b.** to paint a half-length portrait of sb

bustier, -ère [bystje, -ɛr] NM,F *Beaux-Arts* bust sculptor

NM **1** *(soutien-gorge)* strapless bra **2** *(corsage)* bustier; **robe/maillot b.** strapless dress/*Br* swimming costume *or Am* bathing suit

but [byt] NM **1** *(dessein)* aim, purpose; **je vous ai blessé, ce n'était pas mon b.** I've hurt you, but it wasn't my intention *or* I didn't mean to; **quel est le b. de votre visite?** what's the purpose *or* object of your visit?; **quel est le b. de la manœuvre** *ou* **de l'opération?** what's the point of such a move?; **j'aimerais vous voir – dans quel b.?** I'd like to see you – what for?; **avoir pour b. de** to aim to; **j'avais pour b. de vous connaître** I was aiming to *or* my aim was to get to know you; **la réforme a un b. bien précis** the purpose of the reform is quite precise; **dans un b. (bien) précis** with a specific aim in mind; **dans le b. de faire...** for the purpose of doing..., with the aim of doing...; **je lui ai parlé dans le seul b. de t'aider** my sole aim in talking to him/her was to help you; **dans ce b.** with this end *or* aim in view; **aller** *ou* **frapper droit au b.** to get straight to the point; **à b. industriel** industrial; **à b. lucratif** profit-making; **association à b. non lucratif** non profit-making organization, *Am* not-for-profit organization

2 *(ambition)* aim, ambition, objective; **ils n'ont aucun b. dans la vie** they have no aim *or* purpose in life; **je suis encore loin du b.** I still have a long way to go; **nous sommes tout près du b.** we don't have far to go; **toucher au** *ou* **le b.** to have nearly achieved one's aim, to have nearly finished; **on touche au b.** we're nearly there, we've nearly finished; **je n'ai d'autre b. que de bien faire mon travail** my only ambition is to do my work well

3 *(destination)* **le b. de notre voyage leur était inconnu** our destination was unknown to them; **aujourd'hui, le b. de la promenade sera le monastère** today, we'll walk as far as *or* to the monastery; **sans b.** aimlessly

4 *Sport (limite, point)* goal; *(cible)* target, mark; **jouer dans les buts** to be (the) goalkeeper; **gagner/perdre (par) 5 buts à 2** to win/to lose by 5 goals to 2; *Fam* **marquer** *ou* **rentrer un b.** to score a goal; **un b. égalisateur** an equalizer, an equalizing goal; **b. en argent** silver goal; **b. en or** golden goal

5 *Gram* purpose

❑ **de but en blanc** ADV *(demander)* point-blank, suddenly; *(rétorquer)* bluntly; **répondre à qn de b. en blanc** to give sb a blunt answer, to answer sb bluntly; **demanda-t-elle de b. en blanc** she suddenly asked

butadiène [bytadiɛn] NM *Chim* butadiene

Butagaz® [bytagaz] NM Calor® gas

butane [bytan] NM *Chim (gaz)* **b.** butane; *(dans la maison)* Calor® gas

butanier [bytanje] NM *Naut* tanker, butane carrier

buté, -e[1] [byte] ADJ stubborn; **elle est complètement butée** she's as stubborn as a mule

butée[2] [byte] NF **1** *Tech* stop; *(de ski)* toe-piece **2** *Archit* abutment, buttress

butène [bytɛn] NM *Chim* butene, butylene

buter [3] [byte] VI **1** *(trébucher)* to stumble, to trip; **b. contre une pierre** to trip over a stone

2 b. contre qch *(cogner → sujet: personne)* to walk *or* to bump into sth

3 *(achopper)* **b. sur une difficulté** to come across a problem; **b. sur un mot** *(en parlant)* to trip over a word; *(en lisant pour soi)* to have trouble understanding a word

4 *Constr* **b. contre** to rest against, to be supported by

VT **1** *(braquer)* **b. qn** to put sb's back up, to make sb dig his/her heels in

2 *(mur)* to prop up, to buttress, to shore up

3 *Fam Arg crime (tuer)* to bump off, to waste; **se faire b.** to be bumped off *or* done in

▶**se buter** VPR **1** *(se braquer)* to dig one's heels in

2 *(se heurter)* **se b. dans** *ou* **contre** to bump into

buteur, -euse [bytœr, -øz] NM,F **1** *Sport* striker; *(au rugby)* kicker **2** *Fam Arg crime (assassin)* killer■

butin [bytɛ̃] NM **1** *(choses volées → par des troupes)* spoils, booty; *(→ par un cambrioleur)* loot **2** *(trouvailles)* finds **3** *Suisse Vieilli, Can Fam (affaires personnelles)* things, stuff; *Can Vieilli* **b. de corps** underwear

butiner [3] [bytine] VI *(insectes)* to gather nectar and pollen

VT **1** *(pollen, nectar)* to gather; *(fleurs)* to gather pollen and nectar from **2** *(rassembler → idées)* to glean, to gather

butineur, -euse [bytinœr, -øz] ADJ *Entom* pollen-gathering

NM *Ordinat* browser

butô [byto] NM *(danse japonaise)* buto

butoir [bytwar] NM **1** *Rail* buffer **2** *(de porte)* door stop **3 (date) b.** limit

butome [bytɔm] NM *Bot* butomus; **b. à ombelles** flowering rush, water-gladiole

butor [bytɔr] NM **1** *Péj (malotru)* boor, lout **2** *Orn* bittern; **b. d'Amérique** American bittern; **b. blongois** little bittern

buttage [bytaʒ] NM *Hort & Agr* earthing *or* banking up

butte [byt] NF **1** *(monticule)* hillock, knoll; *Géog* **la B. (Montmartre)** Montmartre; **habiter sur la B.** to live up on the hill *(in Montmartre)* **2** *Mil* **b. de tir** butts **3** *Hort & Agr* mound **4** *Géog* **b. témoin** outlier
▫ **en butte à** PRÉP **être en b. à** to be exposed to, to be faced with; **en b. aux quolibets** exposed to *or* prey to jeers

butter [3] [byte] VT **1** *Hort & Agr* to earth *or* to bank up **2** *Fam Arg crime (tuer)* to bump off, to waste

Buttes-Chaumont [bytʃomɔ̃] NFPL **le parc des B.** = landscaped park in Paris

butteur [bytœr] NM **1** *Agr* ridge-plough, ridging-plough **2** *Fam Arg crime (assassin)* killer▪

buttoir [bytwar] NM *Agr* ridge-plough, ridging-plough

butyle [bytil] NM *Chim* butyl

butylène [bytilɛn] NM *Chim* butylene

butylique [bytilik] ADJ *Chim* butylic

butyrate [bytirat] NM *Chim* butyrate

butyreux, -euse [bytirø, -øz] ADJ **1** *(qui a l'apparence du beurre)* buttery **2** *Chim* butyrous

butyrine [bytirin] NF *Chim* butyrin

butyrique [bytirik] ADJ butyric

butyromètre [bytirɔmɛtr] NM butyrometer

buvable [byvabl] ADJ **1** *(qui n'est pas mauvais à boire)* drinkable; *Hum* **il est b., ce petit vin!** this is a very drinkable little wine! **2** *Pharm (ampoule)* to be taken orally

buvait *etc voir* **boire**

buvant [byvɑ̃] NM = edge of a drinking glass

buvard [byvar] NM **1** *(morceau de papier)* piece of blotting paper; **(papier) b.** blotting paper **2** *(sous-main)* blotter

buvée [byve] NF *Agr* bran mash *(used as cattle feed)*

buvetier, -ère [byvtje, -jɛr] NM,F *Vieilli* tavern-keeper, bar-keeper

buvette [byvɛt] NF **1** *(dans une foire, une gare)* refreshment stall **2** *(de station thermale)* pump room

buveur, -euse [byvœr, -øz] NM,F **1** *(alcoolique)* drinker, drunkard; **c'est un gros b.** he's a heavy drinker **2** *(client de café)* customer **3** *(consommateur)* **nous sommes de grands buveurs de café** we're great coffee drinkers; **je ne suis pas un gros b. de lait** I don't drink much milk

buxacées [byksase] NFPL *Bot* the box family, *Spéc* Buxaceae

buzuki [buzuki] = **bouzouki**

buzz [bœz] NM buzz; **leur nouvel album génère un bon b.** their new album is causing a stir

BVA [beveɑ] NF *(abrév* **Brulé Ville Associés***)* = French market research company

BVP [bevepe] NM *(abrév* **Bureau de vérification de la publicité***)* = French advertising standards authority, *Br* ≃ ASA

byline [bilin] NF *Littérature* = epic song of old Russia

by-pass [bajpas] NM INV **1** *Élec* bypass **2** *Méd* bypass operation

byronien, -enne [bajrɔnjɛ̃, -ɛn] ADJ *(mélancolie, perspective)* Byronic; *(vers)* Byronian

byssinose [bisinoz] NF *Méd* byssinosis

byssus [bisys] NM *Zool* byssus

byte [bajt] NM *Ordinat* byte

Byzance [bizɑ̃s] NF **1** *Géog* Byzantium **2** *Fam (locutions)* **c'est B.!** it's the last word in luxury!; **c'est pas B.** it's not exactly luxurious

byzantin, -e [bizɑ̃tɛ̃, -in] ADJ **1** *Hist* Byzantine **2** *Péj* byzantine
▫ **Byzantin, -e** NM,F Byzantine

byzantinisme [bizɑ̃tinism] NM hair-splitting, argumentativeness

byzantiniste [bizɑ̃tinist], **byzantinologue** [bizɑ̃tinɔlɔg] NMF Byzantinist, specialist in Byzantine art

byzantinologie [bizɑ̃tinɔlɔʒi] NF Byzantinology

BZH *(abrév écrite* **Breizh***)* = Brittany (as nationality sticker on a car)

C

C¹, c¹ [se] NM INV **1** (lettre) C, c; **C comme Célestin** ≃ C for Charlie; **c cédille** c cedilla **2** Mus (note) C

C² **1** (abrév écrite **Celsius, centigrade**) C **2** Élec (abrév écrite **coulomb**) C

c² **1** (abrév écrite **centime**) c **2** (abrév écrite **con**) **c...** = abbreviation in polite texts for the word ''con''

C++ [seplysplys] NM Ordinat C++

C4 [sekatr] NM INV Belg = official document given to an employee who is being laid off by his or her employer, Br ≃ P45

c' [s] voir **ce²**

ç' [s] voir **ce²**

CA [sea] NM **1** Élec (abrév **courant alternatif**) AC **2** Com (abrév **chiffre d'affaires**) turnover **3** (abrév **conseil d'administration**) board of directors **4** Mil (abrév **corps d'armée**) army corps **5** Can (abrév **comptable agréé**) Br ≃ CA, Am ≃ CPA **NF** (abrév **chambre d'agriculture**) = farmers' association

ca (abrév écrite **centiare**) sq. m.

ça¹ [sa] NM Psy id

ÇA² [sa] PRON DÉMONSTRATIF **1** (désignant un objet → proche) this, it; (→ éloigné) that, it; **donne-moi ça** give me that, give it to me; **ça se trouve où?** where is it or that?; **laisse ça!** hands off!, leave that or it (alone)!; **c'est qui/quoi ça?** who's/what's that?; **qu'est-ce que tu veux? – ça, là-bas** what do you want? – that, over there; **ça sent bon** that or it smells nice; **il y avait ça entre moi et l'autobus** there was this or that much between me and the bus; **il y a ça de différence de taille entre eux** there is this or that much difference in height between them; Fam **il ne m'a pas donné ça!** he didn't give me a thing or a bean!; Fam **regarde-moi ça!** just look at that!; Fam **écoute-moi ça!** just listen to this!; Euph **il ne pense qu'à ça!** he's got a one-track mind!

2 (désignant → ce dont on vient de parler) this, that; (→ ce dont on va parler) this; **qu'est-ce que tu dis de ça?** what do you say to that?; **je n'ai jamais dit ça!** I never said that or any such thing!; **la liberté, c'est ça qui est important** freedom, that's what matters; **pas de ça chez nous** we don't want any of that here; **il y a un peu de ça, c'est vrai** it's true, there's an element of or a bit of that; **à part ça, tout va bien** apart from that, everything's fine; **il est parti il y a un mois/une semaine de ça** he left a month/a week ago; **écoutez, ça va vous étonner...** this will surprise you, listen...

3 Fam (servant de sujet indéterminé) **et ton boulot, comment ça se passe?** how's your job going?; **je voudrais m'inscrire, comment ça se passe?** I'd like to join, what do I have to do or how do I go about it?; **ça souffle!** there's quite a wind (blowing)!; **ça fait deux kilos/trois mètres** that's two kilos/three metres; **ça vous fera 15 euros** that'll be 15 euros; **ça fait deux heures que j'attends** I've been waiting for two hours; **ça me fait de la peine de le voir malade** it upsets me to see him ill; **ça vaut mieux** it's just as well; **qu'est-ce que ça peut faire?** what does it matter?; **qu'est-ce que ça veut dire?** what does it or that mean?; (c'est ridicule) where's the sense in it?; (ton menaçant) what do you mean by that?, what's that supposed to mean?; **les enfants, ça comprend tout** children understand everything; **ça bavarde dans le fond de la classe** there's talking going on at the back of the classroom; Péj **et ça n'arrête pas de se**

plaindre! and he's/they're/etc forever complaining!; **ça ira comme ça** that'll do; **ça y est, j'ai fini!** that's it, I'm finished!; **ça y est, ça devait arriver!** now look what's happened!; **ça y est, ça commence!** here we go!; **ça y est, tu es prêt?** so are you ready now?; **ça y est, c'est de ma faute!** that's it, it's all my fault!; **c'est ça!** that's right; Ironique right!; **c'est ça, dites que je suis folle** so I'm crazy, is that it or am I?; **c'est ça, moquez-vous de moi!** that's right, have a good laugh at my expense!; **c'est ça les hommes!** that's men for you!

4 (emploi expressif) **pourquoi ça?** why?, what for?; **qui ça?** who?, who's that?; **où ça?** where?, whereabouts?; **quand ça?** when?; **comment ça, c'est fini?** what do you mean it's over?; **ah ça oui!** you bet!; **ah ça non!** certainly not!

çà [sa] **çà et là** ADV here and there

caatinga [kaatiŋa] NF Bot caatinga

cab [kab] NM hansom, hansom cab

cabale [kabal] NF **1** (personnes) cabal; (intrigue) cabal, intrigue; **monter une c. contre qn** to plot against sb **2** Rel cabala, cabbala, kabbala

cabaler [3] [kabale] VI **1** Littéraire to intrigue, to cabal **2** Can Fam Pol to campaign▪

cabaliste [kabalist] NMF Rel cabalist, cabbalist, kabbalist

cabalistique [kabalistik] ADJ Rel (science) cabalistic, cabbalistic, kabbalistic; Fig (signes, formules) arcane

caban [kabã] NM (longue veste) car coat; (de marin) reefer jacket; (d'officier) pea jacket

cabane [kaban] NF **1** (hutte) hut, cabin; (pour animaux, objets) shed; **c. de** ou **en rondins** log cabin; **c. à outils** toolshed **2** Fam (maison) dump; **j'en ai marre de cette c.!** I'm fed up with this dump! **3** Fam (prison) clink; **il a fait huit ans de c.** he did or spent eight years in the clink or inside **4** Suisse (refuge) mountain refuge **5** Can **c. à sucre** sugar (and maple syrup) refinery, sap or sugar house

cabaner [3] [kabane] VI (bateau) to capsize
VT c. un bateau to turn a boat over for repairs

cabanon [kabanɔ̃] NM **1** (abri) shed, hut; (en Provence) (country) cottage **2** (chalet de plage) beach hut **3** Vieilli (pour fou) padded cell; Fam **il est bon pour le c.** he should be put away

cabaret [kabarɛ] NM **1** (établissement) nightclub, cabaret **2** (activité) **le c.** cabaret; **il a débuté au c.** he started off doing cabaret; **un spectacle de c.** a floorshow **3** (meuble) liqueur cabinet **4** Vieilli (auberge) tavern

cabaretier, -ère [kabartje, -ɛr] NM,F Vieilli innkeeper

cabas [kaba] NM **1** (pour provisions) shopping bag **2** (pour figues, raisins) basket

cabèche [kabɛʃ] NF Fam Vieilli nut, head▪

cabernet [kabɛrnɛ] NM (cépage) cabernet (grape)

cabestan [kabɛstã] NM Naut capstan; **c. horizontal** windlass; **grand c.** main capstan; **virez au c.!** heave!

cabiai [kabjɛ] NM Zool capybara

cabillaud [kabijo] NM Ich cod

cabillot [kabijo] NM Naut toggle

cabine [kabin] NF **1** Naut cabin

2 Aviat (des passagers) cabin; **c. (de pilotage)** cockpit; **personnel de c.** cabin crew

3 (de laboratoire de langues) booth; (de piscine, d'hôpital) cubicle; **c. (de bain)** (hutte) bathing or beach hut; (serviette) beach towel (for changing); **c. de bronzage** tanning booth; **c. de douche** shower cubicle; **c. d'essayage** Br changing or fitting room, Am dressing room; **c.**

Internet Internet booth; Cin **c. de projection** projection room; **c. de régie** control room

4 Tél **c. téléphonique** phone booth or Br box

5 (d'ascenseur) cage, Am car; (de camion, de tracteur, de grue, de train) cab; **c. (de téléphérique)** cablecar

6 Rail **c. d'aiguillage** signal box, points control box

cabinet [kabinɛ] NM **1** (de dentiste) Br surgery, Am office; (de magistrat) chambers; (d'avocat, de notaire) firm; (de médecin) Br surgery, Am office; **c. de consultation** (de médecin) consulting room

2 (réduit) **c. de débarras** Br boxroom, Am storage room; **c. noir** walk-in cupboard

3 (petite salle) Arch **cabinets d'aisances** toilet, privy; **c. de lecture** reading room; **c. particulier** (de restaurant) private dining room; **c. de toilette** bathroom; **c. de travail** study

4 (clientèle → de médecin, de dentiste) practice; **monter un c.** to set up a practice

5 (agence) **c. d'affaires** business consultancy; **c. d'architectes** firm of architects; **c. d'assurances** insurance firm or agency; **c. d'audit** firm of auditors; **c. conseil** consulting firm, consultancy firm; **c. de conseil en gestion** management consultancy; Mktg **c. d'études** market research firm; **c. d'expertise comptable** accounting firm; **c. d'experts-conseils** consultancy; **c. immobilier** Br estate agent's or Am realtor's office; **c. juridique** law firm; **c. de recrutement** recruitment agency; Pol **c. restreint** kitchen cabinet

6 Pol (gouvernement) cabinet; (d'un ministre) departmental staff; **faire partie du c.** to be in or a member of the Cabinet; **le c. du Premier ministre** the Prime Minister's departmental staff; **c. fantôme** shadow cabinet; **c. ministériel** minister's advisers, departmental staff

7 (d'un musée) (exhibition) room; **c. des estampes/médailles** prints/medals room; **c. des dessins** prints and drawings room

8 (meuble) cabinet

9 (d'horloge) (clock) case

□ **cabinets** NMPL Fam toilet▪, Br loo, Am bathroom▪

---

câblage [kɑblaʒ] NM **1** TV (pose du réseau) cable (TV) installation, cabling; **le c. d'une rue/ville** cabling a street/a town **2** Élec (opération) wiring; (fils) cables **3** (torsion) cabling **4** (d'un message) cabling

câble [kɑbl] NM **1** (cordage → en acier) cable, wire rope; (→ en fibres végétales) line, rope, cable; Aut **c. d'accélérateur** accelerator cable; Naut **c. d'amarrage** mooring line or cable; Aut **c. de démarreur** ou **de démarrage** jump lead; Aut **c. de frein** brake cable; Naut **c. de halage** ou **de remorquage** towrope, towline

2 Élec cable; **c. d'alimentation** supply or feed or power cable; **c. coaxial** coaxial cable; **c. électrique** electric cable; Tél **c. hertzien** radio link

cab-cac

(by hertzian waves); *Ordinat* **c. d'imprimante** printer cable; *Ordinat* **c. modem** modem cable; **c. optique** optical fibre; **c. à paires** paired cable; **c. parallèle** parallel cable; **c. (à courant) porteur** carrier cable; **c. à quartes** quad *or* quadded cable; **c. série** serial cable; *Fam* **péter un c.** *(craquer)* to crack up

3 *TV* **le c.** cable (TV); **avoir le c.** to have cable (TV); **transmettre par c.** to cablecast; **c. péritel®** SCART cable; **c. en fibres optiques** fibre-optic cable

4 *Tél (télégramme)* cable, cablegram

câblé, -e [kable] **ADJ 1** *TV (ville, région)* with cable (TV); *(émission)* cabled; **l'immeuble est c.** the building has cable (TV); *TV* **réseau c.** cable television network **2** *Ordinat* hard-wired **3** *Fam (à la mode)* switched on

NM cord

câbleau, -x [kablo] **NM 1** *Naut (cable)* cablet, small cable; *(d'amarrage)* mooring-rope; *(pour péniche)* tow-rope **2** *Rail* electric cable *(connecting two carriages)*

câbler [3] [kable] **VT 1** *TV (ville, région)* to link to a cable television network, to wire for cable; *(émission)* to cable **2** *Élec* to cable **3** *Élec (fils)* to twist together (into a cable), to cable **4** *Tél (message)* to cable

câblerie [kabləri] **NF** *Élec* cable *or* cable-manufacturing plant

câbleur, -euse [kablœr, -øz] **NM,F** *Élec* cable-layer

câblier [kablije] **NM 1** *Naut* cable-ship **2** *(fabricant)* cable-maker

câbliste [kablist] **NMF** *Cin & TV (personne)* cable operator

câblo [kablo] **NM** *Fam* TV cable operator, cable company

câblodistributeur [kablodistribytœr] **NM** *TV* cable operator, cable company

câblodistribution [kablodistribysjɔ̃] **NF** *TV* cable television, cablevision

câblogramme [kablogram] **NM** *Tél* cablegram

câblo-opérateur [kablooperatœr] *(pl* **câblo-opérateurs)** **NM** *TV* cable operator, cable company

câblot [kablo] = **câbleau**

cabochard, -e [kabɔʃar, -ard] *Fam* **ADJ** pig-headed, stubborn■

NM,F c'est un c. he's pigheaded *or* as stubborn as a mule

caboche [kabɔʃ] **NF 1** *Fam (tête)* nut, *Br* noddle; **mets-toi (bien) ça dans la c.!** get that into your thick head!; **avoir la c. dure** to be pigheaded **2** *(clou)* hob-nail

cabochon¹ [kabɔʃɔ̃] **NM 1** *(pierre)* cabochon **2** *(clou)* stud

cabochon², -onne [kabɔʃɔ̃, -ɔn] **NM,F** *Can (têtu)* stubborn person; *(incompétent)* bad worker

cabosse [kabɔs] **NF 1** *Fam Vieilli (bosse)* bruise■, bump■; **se faire une c.** to bump oneself **2** *Bot* cacao-pod, chocolate-nut

cabosser [3] [kabɔse] **VT** *(carrosserie, couvercle)* to dent; **une voiture cabossée** a battered car; **un chapeau cabossé** a battered hat

cabot [kabo] **NM 1** *Fam (chien)* dog■, *Péj* mutt **2** *Fam Arg mil* corporal■ **3** *(mulet)* common grey mullet **4** *(acteur)* ham (actor)

cabotage [kabɔtaʒ] **NM** *Naut* coastal navigation; *Naut* **petit/grand c.** inshore/seagoing navigation

caboter [3] [kabɔte] **VI** *Naut (gén)* to sail *or* to ply along the coast; *(ne pas s'éloigner)* to hug the shore

caboteur [kabɔtœr] **NM** *Naut (navire)* coaster, tramp

cabotin, -e [kabɔtɛ̃, -in] **ADJ** *(manières, personne)* theatrical

NM,F 1 *(personne affectée)* show-off, poseur **2** *Péj (acteur)* ham (actor)

cabotinage [kabɔtinaʒ] **NM** *(d'un poseur)* affectedness, theatricality; *(d'un artiste)* ham acting; **faire du c.** to ham it up

cabotiner [3] [kabɔtine] **VI** *Fam Péj* to play to the gallery, to showboat

caboulot [kabulo] **NM** *Fam* seedy pub, dive

cabrage [kabraʒ] **NM** *Aviat* nose-lift

cabré, -e [kabre] **ADJ 1** *(cheval)* rearing **2** *Aviat (avion)* tail down

cabrer [3] [kabre] **VT 1** *(cheval)* **il cabra son cheval** he made his horse rear up **2** *Aviat* to nose up **3** *(inciter à la révolte)* **c. qn** to put sb's

back up; **c. qn contre qn** to turn *or* to set sb against sb

▸**se cabrer** **VPR 1** *(cheval)* to rear up **2** *Aviat* to nose up **3** *(se rebiffer)* to balk, to jib; **se c. contre** to rebel against

cabrette [kabrɛt] **NF** *(en Auvergne)* bagpipes

cabri [kabri] **NM** *Zool* kid

cabriole [kabrijɔl] **NF 1** *(bond → d'un enfant)* leap; *(→ d'un animal)* prancing *(UNCOUNT)*, cavorting *(UNCOUNT)*; *(acrobatie)* somersault; **faire des cabrioles** *(clown)* to do somersaults; *(chèvre)* to prance *or* to cavort (about); *(enfant)* to dance *or* to leap about

2 *Fig (manœuvre)* clever manoeuvre; **il a éludé la question/refusé l'invitation par une c.** he managed to dodge the question/to duck out of having to accept the invitation; **elle s'en est tirée par une c.** she cleverly manoeuvred her way out of it

3 *(danse)* cabriole

4 *Équitation* capriole

cabrioler [3] [kabrijɔle] **VI** *(enfant)* to leap (about); *(animal)* to prance *or* to cavort (about)

cabriolet [kabrijɔlɛ] **NM 1** *Aut (véhicule → automobile)* convertible; *(→ hippomobile)* cabriolet **2** *(meuble)* cabriole chair

cab-signal [kabsiɲal] *(pl* **cab-signaux** [-o]) **NM** *Rail* cab signalling

cabus [kaby] **NM** *Bot* white cabbage

CAC, Cac [kak] **NM 1** *Bourse (abrév* **cotation assistée en continu)** automated quotation; *Bourse* **l'indice C.-40, le C.-40** the CAC-40 (index) *(Paris Stock Exchange Index)* **2** *Fin (abrév* **Compagnie des agents de change)** Institute of stockbrokers

caca [kaka] **NM** *Fam* **du c.** *(excrément)* poo, poop; *Fig* **c'est du c.!** it's yucky!; **du c. de chien** some dog dirt *or* poo; **faire c.** to do *or Br* to have a poo; **il nous fait un c. nerveux, l'autre!** he's having kittens!, he's having a fit!

▫ **caca d'oie** **NM** **INV** greenish-yellow **ADJ** **INV** greenish-yellow

cacaber [3] [kakabe] **VI** *(perdrix)* to call

cacahouète, cacahuète [kakawɛt] **NF 1** *Bot* peanut **2** *Fam (locutions)* **ce film ne vaut pas une c.** the film's a load of garbage *or Br* rubbish; **il n'assure pas une c.** he hasn't got a clue!; **il n'assure pas une c. avec les filles, il ne dit jamais ce qu'il faut** he hasn't got a clue when it comes to girls, he never says the right thing

cacaille [kakaj] **NF** *Belg Fam* piece of junk

cacao [kakao] **NM 1** *Bot (graine)* cocoa bean **2** *Culin* **(poudre de) c.** cocoa (powder); **au c.** cocoa-flavoured; *(boisson)* cocoa

cacaoté, -e [kakaɔte] **ADJ** *Culin* cocoa-flavoured

cacaotier [kakaɔtje] **NM** *Bot* cocoa tree

cacaotière [kakaɔtjɛr] **NF** *Agr* cocoa plantation

cacaoyer [kakaɔje] = **cacaotier**

cacaoyère [kakaɔjɛr] = **cacaotière**

cacaouette [kakawɛt] **NF** *Can (en acadien)* sled

cacaoui [kakawi], **cacaouite** [kakawit] **NM** *Can Orn* long-tailed duck

cacarder [3] [kakarde] **VI** *(oie)* to cackle

cacasser [3] [kakase] **VI** *Can Fam* **1** *(poule)* to cackle■; *(oiseau)* to chirp■ **2** *(tenir des propos → futiles)* to prattle (on); *(→ indiscrets)* to gossip■

cacatoès [kakatɔɛs] **NM** *Orn* cockatoo

cacatois [kakatwa] **NM** *Naut (voile)* royal; **grand/petit c.** main/fore royal; **(mât de) c.** royal mast

cachalot [kaʃalo] **NM** *Zool* sperm whale

cache [kaʃ] **NF** *(d'armes, de drogue)* cache

NM 1 *(pour œil, pour texte)* cover card; *(de machine à écrire)* cover **2** *Cin & Phot* mask; **c. latéral** slide matte; **c. d'avant-plan** foreground matte **3** *Ordinat* cache; **c. du disque dur** hard disk cache; **c. externe** external cache

caché, -e [kaʃe] **ADJ 1** *(dans une cachette → butin, or)* hidden **2** *(secret → sentiment)* secret; *(→ signification)* hidden, secret; *(→ talent)* hidden

cache-brassière [kaʃbrasjɛr] *(pl* **inv** *ou* **cache-brassières)** **NM** *Vieilli* bib

cache-cache [kaʃkaʃ] **NM** **INV** hide-and-seek; *aussi Fig* **jouer à c. (avec qn)** to play hide and seek (with sb)

cache-cœur [kaʃkœr] **NM** **INV** wrapover top

cache-col [kaʃkɔl] **NM** **INV** scarf

cachectique [kaʃɛktik] *Méd* **ADJ** cachectic

NMF person suffering from cachexia

cache-flamme [kaʃflam] *(pl* **inv** *ou* **cache-flammes)** **NM** *Mil* flash reducer, flash concealer

Cachemire [kaʃmir] **NM** *Géog* **le C.** Kashmir; **au C.** in Kashmir

cachemire [kaʃmir] **NM** *Tex* **1** *(tissu, poil)* cashmere; **en c.** cashmere *(avant n)* **2** *(châle)* cashmere shawl; *(pullover)* cashmere sweater; *(gilet)* cashmere cardigan **3** *(comme adj) (motif, imprimé)* paisley *(avant n)*

cache-misère [kaʃmizɛr] **NM** **INV 1** *(vêtement)* coat or wrap hiding shabby appearance **2** *Fig (destiné à cacher des défauts)* **cette mesure n'est qu'un c.** this is just a cosmetic measure designed to distract attention from the real problem

cache-nez [kaʃne] **NM** **INV** scarf, *Br* comforter

cache-oreilles [kaʃɔrɛj] **NM** **INV** earmuffs

cache-pot [kaʃpo] **NM** **INV** (flower *or* plant) pot holder

cache-poussière [kaʃpusjɛr] **NM** **INV** dust coat

cache-prise [kaʃpriz] **NM** **INV** socket cover

cacher¹ [kaʃer] = **kascher**

cacher² [3] [kaʃe] **VT 1** *(prisonnier, réfugié)* to hide; *(trésor, jouet)* to hide, to conceal

2 *(accroc, ride)* to hide, to conceal (from view); **il cache son jeu** he's not showing his hand; *Fig* he's keeping his plans to himself, he's playing his cards close to his chest

3 *(sujet: niche, grenier)* to hide, to conceal

4 *(faire écran devant)* to hide, to obscure; *Opt* **c. un œil** *(chez l'oculiste)* to cover one eye (with one's hand); **c. la lumière** *ou* **le jour à qn** to be in sb's light; **pousse-toi, tu caches ta sœur!** *(en prenant une photo)* get out of the way, you're right in front of your sister!; **tu me caches la vue!** you're blocking my view!

5 *(ne pas révéler → sentiment, vérité)* to hide, to conceal, to cover up; **c. son âge** to keep one's age (a) secret; **c. qch à qn** to conceal *or* to hide sth from sb; **toi, tu me caches quelque chose!** you're keeping something from me!; **je ne cache pas que...** I must say *or* admit that...; **je ne (te) cacherai pas que je me suis ennuyé** to be frank with you, (I must say that) I was bored; **pour ne rien te c.** to be completely open with you; **il l'aime, il ne l'a jamais caché** he loves him/her, he's never made any secret of it; **il n'a pas caché son soulagement** his relief was plain for all to see

▸**se cacher** **VPR 1** *(aller se dissimuler → enfant, soleil)* to hide; **se c. derrière des rideaux/dans un bois** to hide behind curtains/in the woods; **se c. de ses parents pour fumer, fumer en se cachant de ses parents** to smoke behind one's parents' back; **il me plaît, je ne m'en cache pas!** I like him, it's no secret!; **sans se c.** openly

2 *(être dissimulé → fugitif)* to be hiding; *(→ objet)* to be hidden; **le village se cache dans la vallée** the village lies tucked away at the bottom of the valley; **sa timidité se cache derrière une certaine rudesse** his/her shyness is hidden behind a bluff exterior

3 *(dissimuler quelque chose)* **je me cachais la tête sous les draps** I hid my head under the sheets; **cachez-vous un œil** cover one eye

---

---

cache-radiateur [kaʃradjatœr] **NM** **INV** radiator cover

cachère [kaʃɛr] = **kascher**

cache-sexe [kaʃsɛks] **NM** **INV** *(string)* G-string, thong; *(d'indigène)* apron

cachet [kaʃɛ] **NM 1** *Pharm* tablet; **un c. d'aspirine** an aspirin (tablet)

2 *(sceau)* seal; *(empreinte)* stamp; *Tél* **c. de la poste** postmark; **porter le c. de Nice** to be postmarked Nice, to bear a Nice postmark; **le c. de la poste faisant foi** date of postmark will be taken as proof of postage; *Mktg* **c. de fabrique** maker's trademark; *Tél* **c. d'oblitération** postmark

3 *(rémunération d'un artiste)* fee

4 *(charme → d'un édifice, d'une ville)* character; *(→ d'un vêtement)* style; **avoir du c.** *(édifice, village)* to be full of character; *(vêtements)* to be stylish; **donner du c. à** *ou* **faire le c. de qch** to give sth its charm *or* character; **n'avoir aucun c.** to be utterly lacking in character

cachetage [kaʃtaʒ] **NM** 1 *(d'une lettre)* sealing 2 *Constr* = reinforcement of slow hardening concrete with a quick hardening layer

cache-tampon [kaʃtɑ̃pɔ̃] *(pl* **inv** *ou* **cache-tampons)** **NM** *(jeu)* ≃ hunt-the-thimble

cacheté, -e [kaʃte] **ADJ** *(enveloppe)* sealed; **vin c.** *(avec un bouchon de cire)* sealed bottle of wine; *(vin fin)* vintage wine

cacheter [27] [kaʃte] **VT** *(enveloppe, vin)* to seal; **c. un billet à la cire** to seal a letter with wax

cacheton [kaʃtɔ̃] **NM** *Fam* 1 *(médicament)* tablet■, pill■; **il prend des cachetons pour dormir** he takes sleeping pills *or* tablets■ 2 *(cachet d'artiste)* fee■; **courir le c.** = to try to get little jobs here and there

cachetonner [3] [kaʃtɔne] **VI** *Fam (artiste)* to try to get little jobs here and there■

cachette [kaʃɛt] **NF** *(d'un enfant, pour un objet)* hiding place; *(d'un malfaiteur, d'un réfugié)* hideout; **sors de ta c.!** *(à un enfant)* come out!; *Can* **jouer à la c.** to play hide-and-seek

❑ **en cachette** **ADV** *(fumer, lire, partir)* secretly, in secret; *(rire)* to oneself, up one's sleeve; **il me l'a donné en c.** he gave it to me secretly *or* without anybody noticing; **ils faisaient circuler le livre en c.** the book was circulated in secret; **boire en c.** *(habituellement)* to be a secret drinker; **en c. de qn** *(boire, fumer)* behind sb's back, while sb's back is turned; *(préparer, décider)* without sb knowing, unbeknownst to sb

cachettera *etc voir* **cacheter**

cachexie [kaʃɛksi] **NF** 1 *Méd* cachexia 2 *Vét* rot

cachot [kaʃo] **NM** 1 *(cellule)* dungeon 2 *(isolement)* solitary confinement; **il a fait une semaine de c.** he spent a week in solitary (confinement)

cachotterie [kaʃɔtri] **NF** (little) secret; **elle aime faire des cachotteries** she likes to make a mystery of everything; **faire des cachotteries à qn** to keep secrets from sb

cachottier, -ère [kaʃɔtje, -ɛr] *Fam* **ADJ** secretive■; **il est c.** he's full of little mysteries *or* secrets

NM,F **c'est un c.** he's secretive; **tu ne me l'avais pas dit, petite cachottière!** you never told me, you secretive little thing!

cachou [kaʃu] **NM** 1 *(bonbon)* cachou 2 *(substance, teinture)* catechou, cachou, cutch

cachucha [katʃytʃa] **NF** *(danse)* cachucha

cacique [kasik] **NM** 1 *(notable)* cacique 2 *Fam Arg scol* **le c.** *(à un concours)* = student graduating in first place (especially from the "École normale supérieure") 3 *Fam (personne importante)* big shot, bigwig

cacochyme [kakɔʃim] *Littéraire* **ADJ** *Hum* doddery, doddering

NMF dodderer

cacographe [kakɔgraf] **NMF** *Littéraire* cacographer

cacographie [kakɔgrafi] **NF** *Littéraire* cacography

cacophonie [kakɔfɔni] **NF** cacophony

cacophonique [kakɔfɔnik] **ADJ** cacophonous

cacosmie [kakɔsmi] **NF** *Méd* cacosmia

cacou [kaku] **NMF** *Fam* **faire le c.** to act smart

cactacée [kaktase], **cactée** [kakte] **NF** *Bot* member of the cactus family *or* of the Cactaceae

cactus [kaktys] **NM** *Bot* cactus

CAD [seade] **NM** *(abrév* **Comité d'aide au développement)** DAC

c.-à-d. *(abrév écrite* **c'est-à-dire)** ie

CADA [kada] **NF** *(abrév* **Commission d'accès aux documents administratifs)** Commission for Access to Administrative Documents

cadastrage [kadastraʒ] **NM** *Admin* land registration

cadastral, -e, -aux, -ales [kadastral, -o] **ADJ** *Admin* cadastral

cadastre [kadastr] **NM** *Admin* 1 *(plans)* cadastral register, ≃ land register; **c. parcellaire** cadastral survey 2 *(service)* **le c.** cadastral survey (office), ≃ land registry

cadastrer [3] [kadastre] **VT** *Admin* ≃ to register with the land registry

cadavéreux, -euse [kadaverø, -øz] **ADJ** *(teint)* livid, deathly pale; *(fixité)* corpse-like

cadavérique [kadaverik] **ADJ** 1 *(du cadavre)* of a corpse; **rigidité c.** rigor mortis 2 *(blancheur)* deathly, cadaverous; *(teint)* deathly pale; *(fixité)* corpse-like

cadavre [kadavr] **NM** 1 *(d'une personne → gén)* corpse, body; *(→ à disséquer)* cadaver; *(d'un animal)* body, carcass; **c'est un c. ambulant** he's a walking corpse; *Fig* **il y a un c. entre eux** they share a guilty secret 2 *Fam Hum (bouteille)* empty, *Br* dead man

❑ **cadavre exquis** **NM** *(jeu)* ≃ consequences; *Littérature* cadavre exquis

Caddie® [kadi] **NM** 1 *(chariot) Br* (supermarket) trolley, *Am* (grocery) cart 2 *Ordinat (pour des achats en ligne) Br* shopping basket, *Am* shopping cart

caddie, caddy [kadi] **NM** *(au golf)* caddie, caddy

cade [kad] **NM** *Bot* cade

cadeau, -x [kado] **NM** 1 *(don)* present, gift; *Com* free gift, freebie; **recevoir un c. de qn** to get a present from *or* to be given a present by sb; **faire un c. à qn** to give sb a present; **faire c. de qch à qn** *(le lui offrir)* to make sb a present of sth, to give sb sth as a present; **je vous fais c. du kiwi** I'll give you *or* throw in the kiwi fruit for free; **je te dois cinq euros – je t'en fais c.!** I owe you five euros – forget it!; *Euph* **ils ne font pas c. des places!** the tickets aren't exactly cheap!; **il ne m'a pas fait de c.** *(dans une transaction, un match)* he didn't do me any favours; *(en me critiquant)* he didn't spare me; **dans la vie, on ne vous fait pas de c.** you can't expect things to be easy!; **ils ne font pas de c.!** *(gendarmes, examinateurs, employeurs)* they're not out to do anybody any favours!; *Fam* **ce n'est pas un c.!** *(personne insupportable)* he's a real pain!; *(personne bête)* he's no bright spark!; *Hum* **tiens, c.!** here's a little present for you!; **c. d'anniversaire/de Noël** birthday/Christmas present; **c. empoisonné** poisoned chalice; **c'est un c. empoisonné** it's more trouble than it's worth; **il m'a fait un c. empoisonné en me nommant à ce poste** he wasn't doing me any favours by appointing me to that job; **c. de noces** *ou* **de mariage** wedding present; **c. d'entreprise** giveaway *or* free gift; **c. publicitaire** free gift, freebie; *Prov* **les petits cadeaux entretiennent l'amitié** = gifts oil the wheels of friendship

2 *(comme adj; avec ou sans trait d'union)* **shampooing c.** free bottle of shampoo *(with a purchase)*

❑ **en cadeau** **ADV** *Com* free; **je l'ai eu en c.** I got it free *or* for nothing

cadeauter [3] [kadote] **VT** *(en Afrique francophone)* **c. qch a qn** to give sth to sb as a present

cadenas [kadna] **NM** padlock; **fermer au c.** to padlock

cadenasser [3] [kadnase] **VT** 1 *(fermer)* to padlock 2 *Fam (emprisonner)* to lock up■, to put away

cadence [kadɑ̃s] **NF** 1 *Mus & (en danse → rythme)* rhythm; *(accords)* cadence; *(passage de soliste)* cadenza; **marquer la c.** to beat out the rhythm

2 *Littérature* cadence

3 *Sport (d'un marcheur)* pace; *(d'un rameur)* rate; **à une bonne c.** at quite a pace; **tenir la c.** to keep in step; **c. de nage** *(en aviron)* stroke rate

4 *Ind* rate; **c. de production** rate of production; **c. de travail** work rate; **la direction nous impose des cadences infernales** the management wants us to work at an impossible speed; **non aux cadences infernales!** no speed-up!

5 *Mil* **c. de tir** rate of fire

❑ **à la cadence de** **PRÉP** at the rate of

❑ **en cadence** **ADV** **taper des mains en c.** to clap in time; **marcher en c.** to march

cadencé, -e [kadɑ̃se] **ADJ** 1 *(marche, musique)* rhythmical; *(gestes, démarche)* swinging; *Mil* **au pas c.** in quick time 2 *Ordinat* **c. à** running at

cadencer [16] [kadɑ̃se] **VT** *(vers, phrase)* to give rhythm to; **c. son pas** to march in rhythm

cadène [kadɛn] **NF** 1 *Hist (de forçat)* convict's chain 2 *Naut* chainplate

cadenette [kadnɛt] **NF** *Mil* = tress of hair worn by French soldiers in certain regiments as a mark of distinction

cadet, -ette [kadɛ, -ɛt] **ADJ** *(plus jeune)* younger; *(dernier-né)* youngest; **la branche cadette** the younger branch

NM,F 1 *(dans une famille → de deux)* younger (one); *(→ de plus de deux)* youngest (one); **son c.** *(fils)* his/her youngest son *or* boy; *(frère)* his/her youngest brother

2 *(frère, sœur plus jeune)* **mon c.** my younger brother; **ma cadette** my younger sister

3 *(entre personnes non apparentées)* **être le c. de qn** to be younger than sb; **je suis son c. de quatre ans** I'm four years his/her junior *or* four years younger than he/she is

4 *Sport* junior *(16 to 18 years old)*

NM 1 *Mil (élève)* cadet; *Can (dans la marine)* ≃ midshipman

2 *Hist (futur militaire)* cadet

3 *(locution)* **c'est le c. de mes soucis** it's the least of my worries

cadi [kadi] **NM** *Jur & Rel* cadi

Cadix [kadiks] **NM** *Géog* Cadiz

cadmiage [kadmjaʒ] **NM** *Métal* cadmium-coating

cadmie [kadmi] **NF** *Métal* zinc oxide residue

cadmier [9] [kadmje] **VT** *Métal* to coat with cadmium

cadmium [kadmjɔm] **NM** *Chim* cadmium

cadogan [kadɔgɑ̃] = **catogan**

cador [kadɔr] **NM** 1 *(chien)* mutt 2 *Fam (personne influente)* big cheese, big shot; *Fam Arg crime (d'une bande)* leader■, boss

cadrage [kadraʒ] **NM** 1 *Cin & Phot* centring; *(plan)* frame; *Cin & TV* **c. oblique** canted shot, (Dutch) angle shot 2 *Mines* framing 3 *Typ (des dimensions)* cropping; *(des couleurs)* masking 4 *Ordinat (d'objets)* positioning; *(de caractères)* alignment

cadran [kadrɑ̃] **NM** 1 *(d'une montre, d'une pendule)* face, dial; *(d'un instrument de mesure, d'une boussole)* face; *(d'un téléphone)* dial; **c. lumineux** luminous dial; **c. solaire** sundial 2 *Can Vieilli (réveille-matin)* alarm clock

cadrat [kadra] **NM** *Typ* quadrat, quad

cadratin [kadratɛ̃] **NM** *Typ* em quadrat, em quad; **demi-c.** en quad

CADRE [kadr]

executive **A1** ■ officer **A2** ■ grade **B1** ■ corps **B2** ■ frame **C1, 4** ■ setting **C2** ■ scope **C3** ■ box **C4**

NM **A.** 1 *(responsable → dans une entreprise)* executive; *(→ dans un parti, dans un syndicat)* cadre; **les cadres** the managerial staff, the management; **un poste de c.** an executive *or* a managerial post; **c. commercial** sales executive; **c. d'entreprise** executive manager; **c. supérieur** senior executive, member of (the) senior management; **c. moyen** middle manager; **l'école a été fondée pour les enfants des ouvriers et des cadres moyens** the school was founded for the children of working-class and lower middle-class families; **femme c.** woman executive; *Hum* **jeune c. dynamique** whizz kid

2 *Mil* officer, member of the officer corps; **les cadres** the (commissioned and non-commissioned) officers

B. 1 *Admin (catégorie)* grade, category *(within the Civil Service)*; **le c. (de la fonction publique)** *(toutes catégories)* the Civil Service

2 *Mil* corps; **c. d'active** ≃ active list; **c. de réserve** ≃ reserve list; **le C. noir** = military riding school in Saumur

C. 1 *(encadrement → d'un tableau, d'une porte, d'une ruche etc)* frame; **c. de bicyclette** bicycle frame

2 *(environnement)* setting, surroundings; **habiter dans un c. agréable/de verdure** to live in pleasant surroundings/a leafy setting; **le c. de** the scene of; **c'était le c. de mes amours enfantines** it was the scene of my childhood loves; **c. de travail** working environment; **c. de vie** (living) environment

3 *(portée, limites → d'accords, de réformes)*

scope, framework; loi c. outline law; **plan c.** blueprint (project); **réforme c.** general outline of reform; **sortir du c. de ses fonctions** to exceed (the scope of) one's duties

4 *Typ* box, space; *Ordinat (pour graphique)* box; *(sur l'Internet)* frame; *Admin* **c. réservé à l'administration** *(dans un formulaire)* for official use only

5 *(emballage)* crate, packing case

6 *Élec (de radio)* frame aerial

7 *Mines* casing

8 *(d'un livre)* outline, skeleton, plan

9 *Naut* berth

▫ **cadres** NMPL **1** *(contrainte)* **cadres sociaux** social structures; **cadres de la mémoire** structures of the memory

2 *Admin* staff list; **être sur les cadres** to be a member of staff; **rayé des cadres** dismissed; **hors c.** seconded, on secondment

▫ **dans le cadre de** PRÉP within the framework or scope of; **dans le c. de mes fonctions/de ce programme** as part of my job/of this programme; **s'inscrire dans le c. de** to come within the framework of; **cela n'entre pas dans le c. de mes fonctions** it falls outside the scope of my responsibilities

cadré, -e [kadre] ADJ *Cin & Phot* in-frame, on-frame

cadrer [3] [kadre] VI **1** *(correspondre → témoignages)* to tally, to correspond; **les deux notions ne cadrent pas ensemble** the two ideas don't go together; **c. avec** to be consistent with; **sa déposition cadre bien avec les premiers témoignages** his/her statement is consistent with the earlier testimonies; **il faudrait faire c. nos déclarations avec les siennes** we must make sure that what we say tallies with what he/she says; **les chiffres que vous nous avez communiqués ne cadrent pas avec les nôtres** the figures you gave us don't tally with or are not consistent with ours; **un aqu'un cadre pas du tout avec sa personnalité** he's/she's not the sort of person who would ever contemplate suicide

2 *Compta* **faire c. un compte** to square an account

VT **1** *Cin & Phot* to centre; *(plan)* to frame

2 *Ordinat (objets)* to position; *(caractères)* to align

cadreur, -euse [kadrœr, -øz] NM,F *Cin & TV* cameraman, *f* camerawoman

caduc, caduque [kadyk] ADJ **1** *Bot (feuille)* deciduous; **à feuilles caduques** deciduous

2 *Physiol (dent)* deciduous; *(membrane)* decidual

3 *Ling* mute; **le schwa est c.** the schwa falls or disappears

4 *Jur (accord, loi)* null and void; *(police d'assurances)* lapsed; **devenir c.** *(accord, contrat, loi)* to lapse; **rendre c.** *(accord, loi)* to make null and void

5 *(qui n'est plus fondé → théorie)* outmoded, obsolete

▫ **caduque** NF *Physiol* decidua, decidual membrane

caducée [kadyse] NM **1** *(de médecin, de pharmacien)* caduceus, doctor's badge; **avoir le c. sur son pare-brise** to display a doctor's badge on one's *Br* windscreen or *Am* windshield **2** *Myth* Caduceus

caducifolié, -e [kadysifolje] ADJ*Bot* deciduous

caducité [kadysite] NF*Jur (d'un accord, d'une loi)* = state of being null and void

caduque [kadyk] *voir* **caduc**

cadurcien, -enne [kadyrsjɛ̃, -ɛn] ADJ of/from Cahors

▫ **Cadurcien, -enne** NM,F = inhabitant of or person from Cahors

---

cæcal, -e, -aux, -ales [sekal, -o] ADJ *Anat & Vét* caecal

cæcum [sekɔm] NM*Anat & Vét* caecum

CAEM [seaɛm] NM *(abrév* **Conseil d'assistance économique mutuelle)** Comecon

caennais, -e [kane, -ɛz] ADJof/from Caen

▫ **Caennais, -e** NM,F = inhabitant of or person from Caen

cæsium [sezjɔm] = **césium**

CAF [kaf] NF *Admin (abrév* **Caisse d'allocations familiales)** *Br* Child Benefit office, *Am* Aid to Dependent Children office

ADJ INV *Com (abrév* **coût, assurance, fret)** cif

ADV *Com (abrév* **coût, assurance, fret)** cif; **vente C.** sale on cif basis

cafard¹ [kafar] NM **1** *Entom* cockroach, *Am* roach **2** *Fam (locutions)* **avoir le c.** to feel low, to feel down; **donner le c. à qn** to get sb down; **j'ai eu un coup de c. hier** I felt a bit down yesterday

cafard², -e [kafar, -ard] NM,F *Fam* **1** *(dénonciateur)* sneak, *Am* snitch **2** *(faux dévot)* (religious) hypocrite▪

ADJ*(air)* hypocritical▪, sanctimonious▪

cafardage [kafardaʒ] NM *Fam* sneaking, *Am* snitching

cafarder [3] [kafarde] *Fam* VI **1** *(rapporter)* to sneak, *Am* to snitch **2** *(être déprimé)* to feel down; **l'arrivée de l'automne me fait toujours c.** the arrival of autumn always gets me down

VT to sneak on, to tell on, *Am* to snitch on

cafardeur, -euse¹ [kafardœr, -øz] NM,F *Fam* sneak, *Am* snitch

cafardeux, -euse² [kafardø, -øz] ADJ *Fam (air, tempérament)* gloomy▪; *(endroit, temps)* miserable▪, depressing▪; **je suis** ou **je me sens c. en ce moment** I'm feeling low or down at the moment

caf'conc' [kafkɔ̃s] NM INV *Fam* = café where music-hall performances are given

café [kafe] NM **1** *(boisson, graine)* coffee; **faire du c.** to make coffee; **garçon, deux cafés** waiter, two coffees; **c. allongé** = coffee diluted with hot water; **c. crème** coffee with cream; **c. filtre** filter coffee; **c. frappé** ou **glacé** iced coffee; **c. en grains** coffee beans; **j'achète mon c. en grains** I buy coffee beans; **c. instantané** ou **soluble** ou **en poudre** instant coffee; **c. au lait** *Br* white coffee, *Am* coffee with milk; *Culin* **c. liégeois** coffee ice cream sundae; **c. moulu** ground coffee; **c. nature** ou **noir** black coffee; **c. turc** Turkish coffee; **c. vert** unroasted coffee; **c. viennois** Viennese coffee

2 *(fin du repas)* coffee, coffee-time; *Belg* = early evening meal (served with coffee), *Br* ≃ high tea; **au c., il n'avait toujours pas terminé son histoire** he still hadn't finished his story by the time we got to the coffee; **venez pour le c.** come and have coffee with us *(after the meal)*

3 *(établissement)* (licensed) café; **c. littéraire** literary café; **c. tabac** = cafe cum tobacconist's; *Péj* **quand on les entend parler, on se croirait au c. du Commerce** their conversation is nothing but bar-room philosophizing; **le C. de Flore** = historic café on the boulevard Saint-Germain, formerly a meeting place for writers and artists

ADJ **c. (au lait)** coffee-coloured

▫ **au café** ADJ *Culin (glace, entremets)* coffee, coffee-flavoured; **chou au c.** choux bun with coffee-flavoured or coffee-cream filling; **éclair au c.** coffee eclair

---

'**Café, le soir**' *Van Gogh*'Café, Night'

café-chantant [kafeʃɑ̃tɑ̃] *(pl* **cafés-chantants)** NM *Vieilli* = café providing evening entertainment by artistes

café-concert [kafekɔ̃sɛr] *(pl* **cafés-concerts)** NM = café where music-hall performances are given

caféier [kafeje] NM*Bot* coffee tree

caféière [kafejɛr] NF*Hort* coffee plantation

caféine [kafein] NF caffeine; **sans c.** decaffeinated, caffeine-free

caféisme [kafeism] NMexcessive coffee-drinking

cafet [kafɛt] NF*Fam* cafeteria

cafetan [kaftɑ̃] NM caftan, kaftan

cafeter [28] [kafte] = **cafter**

cafétéria [kafeterja] NFcafeteria

café-théâtre [kafeteatr] *(pl* **cafés-théâtres)** NM **1** *(café avec spectacle)* = café where theatre performances take place **2** *(petit théâtre)* alternative theatre

cafetier [kaftje] NM café owner

cafetière [kaftjɛr] NF **1** *(machine)* coffee maker; *(récipient)* coffee pot; **c. à pression** percolator **2** *Fam (tête)* nut, *Br* noddle

cafouillage [kafujaʒ] NM *Fam* **1** *(désordre)* shambles *(singulier)*, muddle; **il y a eu un c. devant les buts** there was a scramble in front of the goal **2** *Aut* misfiring▪

cafouiller [3] [kafuje] VI*Fam* **1** *(projet, service)* to get into a muddle; *(décideur, dirigeant)* to dither around or about; *(présentateur, orateur)* to get mixed up or into a muddle; **il a cafouillé dans ses explications** he tied himself in knots (in his explanations); *Sport* **c. avec le ballon** to fumble the ball **2** *Aut* to misfire▪

cafouilleur, -euse¹ [kafujœr, -øz] *Fam* ADJ*(personne)* **il est c.** he's totally disorganized▪

NM,F bungler

cafouilleux, -euse² [kafujø, -øz] ADJ *Fam (explications)* muddled; *(service)* chaotic, *Br* shambolic; **le départ de la course a été assez c.** the start of the race was rather chaotic

cafouillis [kafuji] NM*Fam* **1** *(désordre)* shambles *(singulier)*, muddle **2** *Aut* misfiring▪

cafre [kafr] ADJkafir, kaffir

NMFkafir, kaffir

caftan [kaftɑ̃] = **cafetan**

cafter [3] [kafte] *Fam* VIto sneak, *Am* to snitch

VT **c. qn** to sneak or *Am* to snitch on sb; **elle a cafté que j'étais pas à l'école** she sneaked or *Am* snitched on me and said I wasn't at school

cafteur, -euse [kaftœr, -øz] NM,F*Fam* sneak, *Am* snitch

NM*Ordinat* cookie

cage [kaʒ] NF **1** *(pour animaux)* cage; **un animal en c.** a caged animal; **mettre un animal en c.** to cage an animal; *Fig* **une c. dorée** a gilded cage; **c. à lapins** rabbit hutch; *Fig* **habiter dans des cages à lapins** to live in shoeboxes; **c. aux lions** lions' cage; **c. à oiseau** ou **oiseaux** cage, birdcage; **c. à poules** hen coop; *Fig* **habiter dans une c. à poules** to live in a shoebox

2 *Anat* **c. thoracique** rib cage

3 *Constr* **c. d'ascenseur** *Br* lift or *Am* elevator shaft; **c. d'escalier** stairwell

4 *(structure, enceinte)* **c. d'écureuil** *Br* climbing frame, *Am* jungle gym; *Élec* **c. de Faraday** Faraday cage

5 *Tech* **c. de roulement** ball-bearing casing

6 *Mines* **c. (d'extraction)** cage

7 *Fam Sport* goal▪; **dans la c.** in the net▪

8 *Fam (prison)* slammer, *Br* nick

9 *Ordinat* scroll box

'**La Cage aux folles**' *Molinaro*'Birds of a Feather'

cageot [kaʒo] NM **1** *(contenant)* crate; *(contenu)* crate, crateful **2** *Fam Péj (laideron)* dog, *Br* boot, *Am* beast; **quel c., sa femme!** his wife looks like *Br* the back of a bus or *Am* a Mack truck

cagerotte [kaʒrɔt] NF cheese-basket, cheese-drainer

caget [kaʒe] NMcheese-basket, cheese-drainer

cagette [kaʒɛt] NF *(contenant)* crate; *(contenu)* crate, crateful

cagibi [kaʒibi] NM*Br* boxroom, *Am* storage room

cag-cai

Cagliari [kaljari] NM Cagliari

cagna [kaɲa] NF **1** *Fam Arg mil* dug-out▪ **2** *Fam Vieilli (logement)* digs

cagnard, -e [kaɲar, -ard] ADJ *Fam Vieilli* lazy▪, idle▪
  NM,F *Fam Vieilli* lazybones
  NM **1** *(dans le Midi → endroit)* sunny and sheltered corner; *(→ soleil)* blazing sunshine▪; **quel c.!** what a scorcher!, *Br* it's roasting! **2** *Naut* dodger

cagne [kaɲ] = **khâgne**

cagneux, -euse [kaɲø, -øz] ADJ *(jambes)* crooked; *(cheval, personne)* knock-kneed; **genoux c.** knock knees
  NM,F = **khâgneux**

cagnotte [kaɲɔt] NF **1** *(caisse, somme)* jackpot; **la c. est maintenant de 2 millions d'euros** the jackpot is now 2 million euros **2** *Fam (fonds commun)* kitty **3** *Fam (économies)* nest egg

cagot, -e [kago, -ɔt] ADJ *Littéraire (air, personne)* sanctimonious, holier-than-thou
  NM,F **1** *(hypocrite)* hypocrite **2** *Hist* outcast *(presumed descendant of lepers under the Ancien Régime)*

cagou [kagu] NM *Orn* kagu

cagouille [kaguj] NF *(en Charente et dans le Bordelais)* snail

cagoulard [kagular] NM **1** *Rel* person wearing a penitent's hood **2** *Hist & Pol* cagoulard **3** *Fam (conspirateur)* conspirator▪

cagoule [kagul] NF **1** *(capuchon → d'enfant)* balaclava; *(→ de voleur)* hood, *(→ de pénitent)* hood, cowl **2** *(manteau → de moine)* cowl **3** *Fam (préservatif)* condom▪, rubber

cahier [kaje] NM **1** *Scol* notebook; **c. de maths/géographie** maths/geography copybook; **c. de brouillon** notebook *(for drafts)*, *Br* roughbook; **c. de correspondance** = notebook used by schoolteachers to write notes to pupils' parents, *Br* ≃ homework diary; **c. d'exercices** exercise book; **c. de textes** *(d'élève)* homework notebook; *(de professeur)* (work) record book; **c. de travaux pratiques** lab book
  2 *(recueil) Compta* **c. des achats** purchase ledger; **c. des charges** *(de matériel)* specifications; *(dans un contrat)* terms and conditions; **c. de revendications** claims register
  3 *(d'un journal)* section
  4 *Typ* gathering
  ❑ **cahiers** NMPL **1** *Littérature (mémoires)* diary, memoirs
  2 *Hist* **cahiers de doléances** book of grievances
  3 *Journ* review, journal

cahin-caha [kaɛ̃kaa] ADV **aller c.** *(marcheur)* to hobble along; *(entreprise, projet)* to struggle along; **comment va-t-il? – c.** how is he? – struggling along; **les affaires vont c.** business is slow *or* slack

cahors [kaɔr] NM Cahors (wine)

cahot [kao] NM jolt, judder

cahotant, -e [kaɔtɑ̃, -ɑ̃t] ADJ *(chemin)* bumpy, rough; *(voiture)* jolting, juddering

cahotement [kaɔtmɑ̃] NM *(fait de cahoter)* jolting, juddering; *(secousse)* jolt, judder

cahoter [kaɔte] VI *(véhicule)* to jolt (along)
  VT *(passagers)* to jolt, to bump about; *(voiture)* to jolt

cahoteux, -euse [kaɔtø, -øz] ADJ bumpy, rough

CAHT [seaaʃte] NM *Com (abrév* **chiffre d'affaires hors taxes***)* pre-tax turnover

cahute [kayt] NF **1** *(abri)* shack, hut **2** *Péj (foyer)* hovel

caïd [kaid] NM **1** *Fam (dans une matière)* wizard; *(en sport)* ace; *(d'une équipe)* star **2** *Fam (chef → de bande)* gang leader; *(→ d'une entreprise, d'un parti)* big shot, bigwig; **un c. de la drogue** a drug(s) baron; **jouer au c., faire son c.** to act tough **3** *Hist* caid, local governor *(of indigenous origin, under French rule)*

caïdat [kaida] NM **1** *(en Afrique du Nord)* kaidship **2** *Fam (d'un chef de bande)* gang leadership

caïeu, -x [kajø] NM *Hort (de tulipe)* off-set bulb; *(d'ail)* clove

caïlcédrat [kailsedra] NM *(arbre, bois)* Senegal mahogany

caillage [kajaʒ] NM *(du lait)* curdling; *Physiol (du sang)* coagulation, clotting

caillant, -e [kajɑ̃, -ɑ̃t] ADJ *Belg Fam* freezing

(cold); **il fait c.** it's freezing (cold) *or Br* baltic

caillassage [kajasaʒ] NM *(acte de vandalisme)* throwing stones

caillasse [kajas] NF **1** *(éboulis)* loose stones, scree **2** *Fam Péj (mauvais sol)* stones▪; **je ne peux rien planter, c'est de la c.** I can't plant anything, the ground's nothing but stones **3** *Géol (gravelly)* marl **4** *Fam (argent)* dough, *Br* dosh, *Am* bucks

caillasser [3] [kajase] VT to throw stones at

caille [kaj] NF **1** *Orn* quail **2** *Fam (en appellatif)* **ma (petite) c.** pet, sweetheart

caillé [kaje] NM curds
  ADJ M *(lait)* curdled

caillebotis [kajbɔti] NM *Tech* **1** *(grille)* grating **2** *(plancher)* duckboard

caillebotte [kajbɔt] NF curds

caille-lait [kajlɛ] NM INV *Bot* bedstraw

caillement [kajmɑ̃] NM *(du lait)* curdling; *Physiol (du sang)* coagulation, clotting

cailler [3] [kaje] VI *(lait)* to curdle; *Physiol (sang)* to coagulate, to clot; **faire c. du lait** to curdle milk
  V IMPERSONNEL *Fam* **ça caille ici!** it's freezing *or Br* baltic here!
  VT *(lait)* to curdle; *(sang)* to coagulate, to clot
  ►**se cailler** VPR **1** *Fam (avoir très froid)* to be freezing
  2 *très Fam* **se c. les miches, se les c.** to be freezing one's *Br* arse *or Am* ass off; **on se les caille dehors!** it's *Br* bloody *or Am* goddamn freezing outside!

caillera [kajra] NF *Fam Péj (verlan de* **racaille***)* **1** *(voyous)* trash, *Br* yobs **2** *(voyou)* lout, *Br* yob

cailleteau, -x [kajto] NM *Orn* quail chick, baby quail

caillette [kajɛt] NF *Zool & Vét* rennet stomach, abomasum

caillot [kajo] NM *(de lait)* (milk) curd; *Physiol & Méd* **c. (de sang)** bloodclot

caillou, -x [kaju] NM **1** *(gén)* stone **2** *Constr* **cailloux d'empierrement** road metal **3** *(en joaillerie)* stone; **c. du Rhin** rhinestone **4** *Fam (diamant)* rock, sparkler **5** *Minér* feldspar **6** *Fam (tête)* head▪, nut; **elle en a dans le c.** she's a smart cookie; **avoir le c. déplumé** to be bald▪; **il n'a plus un cheveu** *ou* **un poil sur le c.** he's as bald as a coot **7** *Fam* **le C.** *(la Nouvelle-Calédonie)* New Caledonia▪

cailloutage [kajutaʒ] NM **1** *Constr (empierrement → d'une route)* metalling; *(→ d'une voie ferrée)* ballasting **2** *Constr (pierres → d'une route)* road metal; *(→ d'une voie ferrée)* ballast **3** *(pâte de faïence)* hard paste

caillouter [3] [kajute] VT *Constr (route)* to metal; *(voie ferrée)* to ballast

caillouteux, -euse [kajutø, -øz] ADJ *(chemin, champ)* stony; *(plage)* pebbly, shingly

cailloutis [kajuti] NM *Constr* gravel, *Br* chippings; *(de route)* road metal

caïman [kaimɑ̃] NM *Zool* caiman, cayman; **c. à lunettes** spectacled caiman

Caïn [kaɛ̃] NPR *Bible* Cain

cainri [kɛ̃ri] ADJ *(verlan de* **ricain***)* Yank, *Br* Yankee
  ❑ **Cainri** NM *(verlan de* **Ricain***)* Yank, *Br* Yankee, = pejorative or humorous term used with reference to Americans

caïon [kajɔ̃] NM = **cayon**

caïque [kaik] NM *Naut* caïque

Caire [kɛr] NM *Géog* **Le C.** Cairo; **au C.** in Cairo

cairn [kɛrn] NM cairn

cairote [kɛrɔt] ADJ of/from Cairo
  ❑ **Cairote** NMF Cairene

CAISSE [kɛs]

case **A1, 2, B3** ▪ crate **A1** ▪ box **A1, 3** ▪ cylinder **B1** ▪ bodywork **C1** ▪ car **C2** ▪ till **E1, 2** ▪ check-out **E2** ▪ cash **E3** ▪ bank **E4** ▪ fund **F**		

NF **A. 1** *(pour marchandises → gén)* case; *(→ à claire-voie)* crate; *(de rangement)* box, chest; *(à thé etc)* chest; **mettre en c.** to box; **c. américaine** cardboard box; **c. d'emballage** packing crate; **c. à outils** toolbox; *très Fam Fig* **lâcher** *ou* **larguer une c.** to fart, *Br* to let off, *Am* to lay one
  2 *(boîte de 12 bouteilles)* case; **on a bu deux**

caisses de champagne we drank two cases of champagne
  3 *Hort* box, tub; **mettre un arbuste en c.** to plant a shrub in a tub
  B. 1 *Mus (fût de tambour)* cylinder; **c. claire** side *or* snare drum; **c. de résonance** resonance chamber, resonating body; **c. roulante** side drum; **grosse c.** *(tambour)* bass drum; *(musicien)* bass drummer
  2 *Mus (corps de violon)* belly, sounding board
  3 *(d'horloge)* case, casing
  4 *(de poulie)* shell
  C. 1 *(carrosserie)* body, bodywork
  2 *Fam Aut (voiture)* car▪; **vieille c.** old banger; **t'es venu en c.?** did you come by car?▪
  3 *Rail* water tank
  D. 1 *Anat* **c. du tympan** middle ear, *Spéc* tympanic cavity
  2 *Fam (locution)* **il part** *ou* **s'en va de la c.** his lungs are wearing out
  E. 1 *(tiroir)* till; *(petit coffre)* cashbox; **c. (enregistreuse)** till *or* cash register; **tenir la c.** to be the cashier; **partir avec la c.** to run off with the takings; *aussi Fig* **on l'a pris en train de se servir dans la c.** he was caught helping himself from *or* with his hand in the till; **faire une c. commune** to put one's money together, to have a kitty; *Écon* **les caisses de l'État** the State coffers
  2 *Com (lieu de paiement → d'un supermarché)* check-out, till; *(→ d'un cinéma, d'un casino, d'un magasin)* cash desk; *(→ d'une banque)* cashier's desk; **c.** *(sur panneau)* please pay here; **passer à la c.** *(dans un magasin)* to go to the cash desk; *(dans un supermarché)* to go through the check-out; *(dans une banque)* to go to the cashier's desk; *(se faire payer)* to be paid; *(recevoir son salaire)* to collect one's wages; *Fam* **après ce qu'il a dit au patron, il n'a plus qu'à passer à la c.!** after what he said to the boss, he'll be getting his *Br* cards *or Am* pink slip!; *Com* **c. éclair** *(distributeur) Br* cashpoint, *Am* ATM; *Com* **c. rapide** *(dans un supermarché)* express checkout
  3 *(argent → d'un commerce)* cash (in the till), takings; **faire la** *ou* **sa c.** to balance the cash, to do the till, *Br* to cash up
  4 *Banque* **c. de crédit** credit union; **c. d'épargne** ≃ savings bank; **c. d'épargne-logement** *Br* ≃ building society, *Am* ≃ savings and loan association; **C. nationale d'épargne** ≃ National Savings Bank; **c. régionale** ≃ local (bank) branch
  F. 1 *Admin (organisme chargé de la gestion des fonds)* fund; *(bureau)* office; **C. d'allocations familiales** *Br* Child Benefit office, *Am* Aid to Dependent Children office; **c. d'amortissement** sinking fund; **c. de chômage** unemployment fund; **c. de compensation** = equalization fund for payments such as child benefit, sickness benefit, pensions; **la C. des dépôts et consignations** Deposit and Consignment Office *(national French savings and banking institution which manages National Savings Bank funds and local community funds)*; **c. des écoles** = local schools' fund for extra-curricular activities, school meals etc; **C. nationale d'assurance vieillesse** = French government department dealing with benefit payments relating to old age; *Can* **c. populaire** = type of credit union; **c. de prévoyance** provident fund; **c. primaire d'assurance maladie** = French Social Security department in charge of medical insurance; **c. de retraite** pension fund; **c. de Sécurité sociale** Social Security office
  2 *(fonds)* fund, funds; **nous avons une c. pour les cas sociaux** we have a fund for needy individuals; **c. noire** slush fund
  ❑ **en caisse** ADJ **1** *Com* **argent en c.** cash **2** *Hort* **arbuste en c.** boxed shrub ADV **avoir 500 euros en c.** *Com* to have 500 euros in the till; *Fig* to have 500 euros in hand; **je n'ai plus rien en c.** *Com* my till's empty; *Fig* I'm broke

caisserie [kɛsri] NF *Ind* case *or* crate manufacture

caissette [kɛsɛt] NF **1** *(contenant)* small box **2** *(contenu)* small boxful

caissier, -ère [kesje, -ɛr] NM,F *Com (d'une boutique, d'un casino, d'une banque)* cashier; *(d'un*

supermarché) *Br* check-out operator *or Am* clerk; *(de cinéma)* cashier, *Br* box-office assistant

caisson [kɛsɔ̃] NM **1** *Constr (pour fondation)* caisson, cofferdam; **c. de pont** caisson *(for underwater work)* **2** *Archit (pour plafond)* coffer, caisson, lacunar **3** *Naut* caisson, cofferdam; **c. étanche** *ou* **de flottabilité** buoyancy tank **4** *Tech* **c. hyperbare** bathysphere; *Méd* **la maladie** *ou* **le mal des caissons** decompression sickness, the bends **5** *Tech* **c. de graves** subwoofer; **c. d'insonorisation** blimp **6** *Nucl* (nuclear reactor) casing **7** *Hist & Mil* caisson, ammunition wagon **8** *Fam* **se faire sauter le c.** to blow one's brains out

caitya [ʃaitja] NM *Rel* chaitya, caitya

cajoler [3] [kaʒɔle] VT *(enfant)* to cuddle

cajolerie [kaʒɔlri] NF *(manifestation de tendresse)* cuddle; **faire des cajoleries à qn** to cuddle sb
❑ **cajoleries** NFPL *Péj (flatteries)* flattery, cajolery

cajoleur, -euse [kaʒɔlœr, -øz] ADJ **1** *(affectueux → parent, ton)* affectionate, loving **2** *Péj (flatteur)* coaxing, wheedling
NM,F *Péj (flatteur)* wheedler, flatterer

cajou [kaʒu] *voir* **noix**

cajun [kaʒœ̃] ADJ Cajun
❑ **Cajun** NMF Cajun

cake [kɛk] NM *Culin* fruit cake

cake-walk [kɛkwok] NM INV *(musique, danse)* cake-walk

cakos [kɛkɔs] NMF *Fam Péj* **1** *(ringard)* useless idiot, *Br* prat **2** *(locution)* **faire le c.** to show off, to pose▪

cal[1] [kal] NM **1** *Méd (durillon → à la main)* callus; *(→ au pied)* corn **2** *Bot* callus

cal[2] *(abrév écrite* **calorie***)* cal

calabrais, -e [kalabrɛ, -ɛz] ADJ Calabrian
NM *(dialecte)* Calabrian dialect
❑ **Calabrais, -e** NM,F Calabrian

Calabre [kalabr] NF *Géog* **la C.** Calabria

caladium [kaladjɔm] NM *Bot* caladium

calage [kalaʒ] NM *Tech* **1** *(de pied de chaise)* wedging; *(de roue)* chocking **2** *(fait d'appuyer)* propping (up) **3** *(de manivelle à un axe)* wedging, keying; *(de roue à un axe)* fixing; *(de valve)* jamming, locking **4** *Aut (de moteur)* stalling **5** *(réglage)* adjustment; *(de valve, moteur)* tuning; *Aut* **c. d'allumage** ignition timing **6** *Typ* setting

Calais [kalɛ] NM *Géog* Calais

calaisien, -enne [kalɛzjɛ̃, -ɛn] ADJ of/from Calais
❑ **Calaisien, -enne** NM,F = inhabitant of or person from Calais

calaison [kalɛzɔ̃] NF *Naut* draught

calamar [kalamar] = **calmar**

calambac [kalɑ̃bak], **calambouc** [kalɑ̃buk], **calambour** [kalɑ̃bur] NM *Bot* agalloch, agalwood, eaglewood

calame [kalam] NM **1** *Bot* calamus **2** *Archéol* reed pen, calamus

calaminage [kalaminaʒ] NM *Tech* carbonizing

calamine [kalamin] NF **1** *Chim* calamine **2** *Aut* carbon deposit

calaminer [3] [kalamine] **se calaminer** VPR *Tech* to get covered with soot

calamistré, -e [kalamistre] ADJ brilliantined

calamite [kalamit] NF **1** *Bot (fossile)* calamite **2** *Vieilli Bot* liquid amber
NM *Zool* natterjack (toad)

calamité [kalamite] NF **1** *(événement)* calamity, catastrophe, disaster **2** *Fam Hum (personne)* walking disaster

calamiteux, -euse [kalamitø, -øz] ADJ calamitous, disastrous, catastrophic

calamus [kalamys] NM **1** *Bot* calamus **2** *Anat* calamus; **c. scriptorius** calamus scriptorius

calancher [3] [kalɑ̃ʃe] VI *Fam* to croak, *Br* to snuff it

calandrage [kalɑ̃draʒ] NM *Tex & Typ* calendering

calandre [kalɑ̃dr] NF **1** *Aut* radiator grille **2** *Tex & Typ* calender **3** *Orn* calandra lark; **c. nègre** black lark **4** *Agr* **c. du blé/riz** wheat/rice weevil

calandré, -e [kalɑ̃dre] ADJ *Typ* calendered

calandrer [3] [kalɑ̃dre] VT *Tex & Typ* to calender

calanque [kalɑ̃k] NF *Géol* (Mediterranean) creek

calao [kalao] NM *Orn* hornbill

calathéa [kalatea] NM *Bot* calathea

calbar [kalbar], **calbute** [kalbyt] NM *Fam Br* boxers, *Am* shorts, skivvies

calcaire [kalkɛr] ADJ *Géol & Chim (roche, relief)* limestone *(avant n)*; *(sol)* chalky, *Spéc* calcareous; *(sel)* calcium *(avant n)*; *(eau)* hard
NM **1** *Géol* limestone **2** *Chim (dans une casserole) Br* fur, *Am* sediment

calcanéum [kalkaneɔm] NM *Anat* calcaneum

calcareux, -euse [kalkarø, -øz] ADJ *Belg Chim* **eau calcareuse** hard water

calcédoine [kalsedwan] NF *Minér* chalcedony

calcémie [kalsemi] NF *Physiol* blood calcium content

calcéolaire [kalseɔlɛr] NF *Bot* calceolaria

calcicole [kalsikɔl] ADJ *Bot* calcicolous

calcif [kalsif] NM *Fam Br* boxers, *Am* shorts, skivvies

calcifère [kalsifɛr] ADJ *Biol & Chim* calciferous

calciférol [kalsiferɔl] NM *Biol & Chim* calciferol

calcification [kalsifikasjɔ̃] NF *Chim* calcification

calcifié, -e [kalsifje] ADJ *Chim* calcified

calcifier [10] [kalsifje] VT *Chim* to calcify

calciforme [kalsifɔrm] ADJ *Bot & Méd* cup-shaped, *Spéc* calciform

calcifuge [kalsifyʒ] ADJ *Bot* calcifuge, calcifugous

calcin [kalsɛ̃] NM *Tech* cullet

calcination [kalsinasjɔ̃] NF *Tech* calcination

calciné, -e [kalsine] ADJ *(bois, corps, viande)* charred, burned to a cinder; *(mur, maison)* charred

calciner [3] [kalsine] VT **1** *(transformer en chaux)* to calcine **2** *(brûler)* to burn to a cinder, to char **3** *(chauffer → brique, minerai)* to calcine; **désert calciné par le soleil** sun-baked desert
▶**se calciner** VPR **1** *(viande)* to burn to a cinder **2** *(être chauffé → brique, minerai)* to calcine

calciothermie [kalsjɔtɛrmi] NF *Métal* metallothermic reduction with calcium

calcique [kalsik] ADJ *Chim* calcic

calcite [kalsit] NF *Minér* calcite

calcitonine [kalsitɔnin] NF *Physiol* calcitonin

calcium [kalsjɔm] NM *Chim* calcium

calciurie [kalsjyri] NF calcium content of urine

calcschiste [kalkʃist] NM *Géol* calcareous schist, calc-schist

calcul[1] [kalkyl] NM **1** *Math (suite d'opérations)* calculation; **faire un c.** to do *or* make a calculation; **je fais des calculs à longueur de journée** I handle figures all day long; **ça reviendra moins cher, fais le c.!** it'll be cheaper, just work it out!; **faire le c. de qch** to work sth out, to calculate sth; **il suffit d'un rapide c. pour voir que...** a quick calculation is all that's needed to see that...; **le raisonnement est correct, mais le c. est faux** the method's right but the calculations are wrong; **erreur de c.** miscalculation; *Math* **c. différentiel/intégral/vectoriel** differential/integral/vector calculus; *Math* **c. algébrique** calculus; *Math* **c. des probabilités** probability theory
2 *Scol* **le c.** sums, arithmetic; **être mauvais en c.** to be bad at sums *or* arithmetic; **apprendre le c.** to learn (how) to count; **c. mental** *(matière)* mental arithmetic; *(opération)* mental calculation
3 *(estimation)* calculation, computation; **d'après mes calculs** according to my calculations; **tous calculs faits, le piano devrait pouvoir passer** if I've/we've/*etc* worked it out properly, we should get the piano through; **ça a été un bon c. de notre part** it was a good move on our part; **ce n'est pas un bon c.** it's not a good way of going about things; **un mauvais** *ou* **faux c.** a bad move
4 *Péj (manœuvre)* scheme; **par c.** out of (calculated) self-interest, from selfish *or* ulterior motives; **sans c.** without any *or* with no ulterior motive

calcul[2] [kalkyl] NM *Méd* stone, *Spéc* calculus; **c. biliaire** gall stone; **c. urinaire** *ou* **rénal** kidney stone, *Spéc* renal calculus

calculabilité [kalkylabilite] NF calculability

calculable [kalkylabl] ADJ *(prix)* calculable; *(dégâts)* estimable; **c'est c. de tête** you can work it out *or* calculate it in your head

calculateur, -trice [kalkylatœr, -tris] ADJ *Péj* calculating, scheming
NM,F **1** *(qui compte)* **c'est un bon/mauvais c.** he's good/bad at figures *or* sums
2 *Péj (personne intéressée)* **un fin c.** a shrewd operator; **un ignoble c.** a scheming character
NM **1** *Vieilli Ordinat (ordinateur)* computer; **c. digital** *ou* **numérique** digital computer; **c. électronique** electronic computer
2 *Aut* **c. embarqué** on-board computer
❑ **calculatrice** NF *Math (machine)* calculator; **calculatrice de bureau** desktop calculator; **calculatrice imprimante** print-out calculator; **calculatrice de poche** pocket calculator

calculatoire [kalkylatwar] ADJ *Math* calculative

calculatrice [kalkylatris] *voir* **calculateur**

calculé, -e [kalkyle] ADJ *(risque)* calculated; *(méchanceté)* premeditated, calculated; *(insolence)* deliberate; **"ça ne m'étonne pas de toi", lui dit-il avec une méchanceté calculée** "that doesn't surprise me coming from you," he said with deliberate malice; **sa générosité est calculée** his/her generosity is prompted by self-interest, he/she has an ulterior motive in being generous

calculer [3] [kalkyle] VT **1** *(dépenses, dimension, quantité etc)* to calculate, to work out; **on n'a pas encore calculé le montant de la facture** the bill hasn't been calculated yet; **c. qch de tête** *ou* **mentalement** to work sth out in one's head; **c. vite** to be quick at figures, to calculate quickly
2 *(avec parcimonie → pourboire, dépenses)* to work out to the last penny, to budget carefully
3 *(évaluer → avantages, inconvénients, chances, risque)* to calculate, to weigh up; **mal c. qch** to miscalculate sth; **c. que...** to work out *or* to calculate that...; **j'ai calculé qu'il me faudrait deux heures pour aller à Toulouse** I've worked out that it'll take me two hours to get to Toulouse; **tout bien calculé** taking everything into account
4 *(préparer → gestes, effets, efforts)* to calculate, to work out; **j'ai tout calculé** I have it all worked out; *Sport* **c. son élan** to work out one's run-up; *Fam* **c. son coup** to plan one's moves carefully▪; **tu as bien calculé ton coup!** you had it all figured out!; **tu as mal calculé ton coup!** you got it all wrong!
VI *Math* to calculate; **il calcule vite et bien** he's quick at arithmetic

calculette [kalkylɛt] NF **1** *Math* pocket calculator **2** *Fam (personne souffrant d'acné)* pizza-face

calculeux, -euse [kalkylø, -øz] ADJ **1** *Math (relatif aux calculs)* calculous, calculary **2** *(affecté de calculs)* calculous

Calcutta [kalkyta] NM *Géog* Calcutta

caldarium [kaldarjɔm] NM *Antiq* caldarium

caldeira [kaldɛra], **caldère** [kaldɛr] NF *Géol* caldera

caldoche [kaldɔʃ] ADJ = relating to the white inhabitants of New Caledonia
❑ **Caldoche** NMF = white inhabitant of New Caledonia

cale [kal] NF **1** *(pour bloquer → un meuble)* wedge; *(→ une roue)* wedge, chock; **mettre une voiture sur cales** to put a car on blocks
2 *Menuis (d'ébéniste)* **c. à poncer** sanding block
3 *(sur rails)* chock
4 *Naut (d'un bateau)* hold; **c. à charbon** bunker
5 *Naut (d'un quai)* slipway; **mettre sur cales** to lay down; **le bateau est sur cales** the boat is on the stocks; **c. de construction** *ou* **de lancement** slip, slipway; **c. de radoub** graving *or* dry dock; **c. sèche** dry dock; **être en c. sèche** to be in dry dock

calé, -e [kale] ADJ *Fam* **1** *(instruit)* **il est c. en histoire/maths** he's brilliant at history/*Br* maths *or Am* math **2** *(difficile → problème)* tough **3** *Belg (prêt)* ready▪

calebasse [kalbas] NF **1** *Bot (fruit, récipient)* calabash, gourd **2** *Fam (tête)* nut, *Br* noddle

calebassier [kalbasje] NM *Bot* calabash tree

calèche [kalɛʃ] NF barouche, calash; **une promenade en c.** a ride in a horse-drawn carriage

calecif [kalsif] = **calcif**

caleçon [kalsɔ̃] NM **1** *(sous-vêtement)* boxer shorts; **c. long, caleçons longs** long johns **2** *(pour nager)* **c. de bain** *Br* swimming trunks, *Am* swim shorts **3** *(pantalon)* leggings

caleçonnade [kalsɔnad] NF bedroom farce

Calédonie [kaledɔni] NF *Géog* **la C.** Caledonia

calédonien, -enne [kaledɔnjɛ̃, -ɛn] ADJ Caledonian
❑ **Calédonien, -enne** NM,F Caledonian

cale-étalon [kaletalɔ̃] (*pl* **cales-étalons**) NF *Tech* stop-measure

caléfaction [kalefaksjɔ̃] NF **1** *(fait de chauffer)* heating, warming **2** *Phys* film boiling

calembour [kalɑ̃bur] NM play on words, pun; **faire un c.** to make a pun; **faire des calembours** to play with words

calembredaine [kalɑ̃brədɛn] NF *(plaisanterie)* joke
❑ **calembredaines** NFPL *(sornettes)* balderdash, nonsense; **dire** *ou* **débiter des calembredaines** to talk a lot of (stuff and) nonsense

calendaire [kalɑ̃dɛr] NM *Rel* = register of memorial services

calendes [kalɑ̃d] NFPL **1** *Antiq* calends **2** *(locution)* **renvoyer** *ou* **remettre qch aux c. grecques** to put sth off *or* to postpone sth indefinitely

calendos [kalɑ̃dos] NM *Fam* Camembert®

calendrier [kalɑ̃drije] NM **1** *(tableau, livret, système)* calendar; *Hist* **c. grégorien/républicain** Gregorian/Republican calendar; **c. perpétuel/à effeuiller** perpetual/tear-off calendar
2 *(emploi du temps)* timetable, schedule; *(plan → de réunions)* schedule, calendar; *(→ d'un festival)* calendar; *(→ d'un voyage)* schedule; **j'ai un c. très chargé** I have a very busy schedule *or* timetable; **établir un c.** to draw up a timetable *or* schedule; **le c. de ses visites officielles n'a pas encore été établi** the timetable for his/her official visits hasn't been fixed yet; **c. de campagne** campaign schedule; *Mktg* media schedule; *Bourse* **c. des émissions** calendar of issues; *Bourse* **c. de remboursement** repayment schedule; *Sport* **c. des rencontres** *Br* fixture list, *Am* match schedule

> *Culture*
> **CALENDRIER DES POSTES**
> The "calendrier des Postes", also known as "l'almanach du facteur", is something of an institution in France. The tradition of postmen giving people calendars at New Year dates back some three centuries and to this day postmen sell their calendars door-to-door at the end of December and get to keep the proceeds of the sale. The "calendrier des postes" includes many extras such as pictures, maps, a list of the départements, useful telephone numbers and, very importantly, the names of the saints associated with each day of the year, which is often the first source of inspiration for future parents looking for a name for their unborn child.

> *Culture*
> **CALENDRIER RÉPUBLICAIN**
> The Republican calendar was first used in 1793. The year began on 22 September and was divided into twelve months of thirty days each, the remaining days being given over to celebrations. The names of the months were inspired by the changing seasons, the weather and the harvest: vendémiaire, brumaire, frimaire, nivôse, pluviôse, ventôse, germinal, floréal, prairial, messidor, thermidor, fructidor. The calendar was officially replaced by the Gregorian calendar in 1806.

calendula [kalɑ̃dyla] NM *Bot* calendula

cale-pied [kalpje] (*pl* **cale-pieds**) NM *Cyclisme* toe-clip

calepin [kalpɛ̃] NM **1** *(carnet)* notebook **2** *Belg (serviette)* briefcase

cale-porte [kalpɔrt] (*pl* **cale-portes**) NM door-stop

caler [3] [kale] VT **1** *(armoire, pied de chaise)* to wedge, to steady with a wedge; *(roue)* to chock, to wedge; *(chargement)* to secure; *Can (casquette, chapeau)* to jam on; **c. une porte** *(pour la fermer)* to wedge a door shut; *(pour qu'elle reste ouverte)* to wedge a door open
2 *(installer)* to prop up; **c. qn sur des coussins** to prop sb up on cushions; **le pied doit être bien calé dans la chaussure** the foot must be firmly held in the shoe; **bien calé dans son fauteuil** comfortably settled *or* ensconced in his armchair
3 *Fam (remplir)* **ça cale (l'estomac)** it fills you up, it's filling; **je suis calé** I'm full (up)
4 *(soupape)* to jam, to lock
5 *Naut (mât)* to house; *(voile)* to strike
6 *Can (boire → verre)* to down, to empty
VI **1** *Aut (moteur, voiture)* to stall; **j'ai calé** I've stalled
2 *(s'arrêter → devant un problème)* to give up; *(→ dans un repas)* to be full; **prends mon gâteau, je cale** have my cake, I'm full
3 *Naut* **c. 15 pieds** to draw 15 feet, to have a draught of 15 feet; **c. trop** to be too deep in water
4 *Can (enfoncer)* to sink
5 *Can (se dégarnir)* to have a receding hairline
▸**se caler** VPR **1** *(s'installer)* **se c. dans un fauteuil** to settle oneself comfortably in an armchair
2 *Fam (locution)* **se c. les joues, se les c.** *(bien manger)* to stuff one's face

caleter [28] [kalte] = **calter**

calf [kalf] NM box calf

calfat [kalfa] NM *Naut (ouvrier)* calker, caulker

calfatage [kalfataʒ] NM *Naut* calking, caulking

calfater [3] [kalfate] VT *Naut* to calk, to caulk

calfeutrage [kalføtraʒ], **calfeutrement** [kalføtrəmɑ̃] NM *(d'une fenêtre, d'une porte)* draught-proofing; *(d'une ouverture)* stopping up, filling

calfeutrer [3] [kalføtre] VT *(ouverture)* to stop up, to fill; *(fenêtre, porte → gén)* to make draught-proof; *(→ avec un bourrelet)* to weatherstrip
▸**se calfeutrer** VPR **1** *(s'isoler du froid)* to make oneself snug **2** *Fig (s'isoler)* to shut oneself up *or* away

Calgary [kalgari] NM Calgary

calibrage [kalibraʒ] NM **1** *(d'une pièce, d'un obus, d'un tube)* calibration **2** *Com (de fruits, d'œufs)* grading **3** *Typ* cast-off

calibration [kalibrasjɔ̃] NF *Archéol* calibration

calibre [kalibr] NM **1** *Ind & Tech* gauge; **c. d'épaisseur** feeler gauge, set of feelers
2 *Constr* template
3 *Mil (d'un canon, d'une arme)* bore, calibre; *(d'une balle)* calibre, size; **un canon de 70 calibres** a 70-millimetre gun; **fusil de c. 8 mm** 8-mm calibre rifle; *Sport* 8-mm gauge gun; **de gros c.** large-bore; **de petit c.** small-bore
4 *Com* grade, (standardized *or* standard) size
5 *Tech & Ind (pour la reproduction)* template
6 *Fam Arg crime (revolver) Br* shooter, *Am* rod
7 *Fig (type)* class, calibre; **de ce c.** of this calibre *or* class; **il est d'un autre c.** he's not in the same league

calibrer [3] [kalibre] VT **1** *(usiner → obus, revolver, tube)* to calibrate **2** *Com* to grade **3** *Typ* to cast off

calibreur [kalibrœr] NM **1** *Tech & Ind* calibrator; *Aut* **c. d'air** air bleed jet, air correction jet **2** *Cér* jiggerer

calibreuse [kalibrøz] NF *Tech & Ind* sizer, grader

calice [kalis] NM **1** *Bot & Physiol* calyx **2** *Rel* chalice

câlice [kɑlis] *Can Joual* NM bastard, jerk; **mon c.!** you bastard!
EXCLAM shit!
❑ **en câlice** ADV **1** *(beaucoup)* a lot, very much **2** **être en c. (contre qn)** to be fuming mad (with sb)

câlicer [3] [kɑlise] VT *Can Joual (laisser)* to chuck (down); **je vais te c. mon poing dans la face** I'm going to sock *or* smack you one

caliche [kaliʃ] NM *Minér* caliche

calicoba [kalikoba] NM *Ich* pumpkinseed (sunfish)

calicot [kaliko] NM **1** *Tex* calico **2** *(bande)* banner **3** *Vieilli (commis)* draper's assistant

calicule [kalikyl] NM *Bot* calicle, caliculus

califat [kalifa] NM caliphate

calife [kalif] NM caliph; **vouloir être c. à la place du c.** to want to be top dog

> *Allusion*
> **Vouloir être calife à la place du calife**
> A 1960s cartoon strip with a Persian flavour, *Iznogoud*, gave rise to this expression. In the cartoon, the grand vizir Iznogoud is obsessed with deposing the caliph and taking over his position. The expression is used today of someone who is displaying naked ambition and trying to oust his or her superior. For example, one might say of a pushy new recruit, **Regarde le nouveau, il veut être calife à la place du calife** ("Look at that new one, he's determined to push and shove his way to the top.")

Californie [kalifɔrni] NF *Géog* **la C.** California; **en C.** in California

californien, -enne [kalifɔrnjɛ̃, -ɛn] ADJ Californian
❑ **Californien, -enne** NM,F Californian

californium [kalifɔrnjɔm] NM *Chim* californium

califourchon [kalifurʃɔ̃] NM *Can* crotch
❑ **à califourchon** ADV astride; **être à c. sur qch** to be astride sth, to bestride sth; **monter** *ou* **s'asseoir** *ou* **se mettre à c. sur qch** to sit astride *or* to straddle sth; *Équitation* **monter à c.** *(à cheval)* to ride astride

Caligula [kaligyla] NPR Caligula

câlin, -e [kalɛ̃, -in] ADJ **1** *(regard, voix)* tender **2** *(personne)* affectionate
NM cuddle; **faire un c. à qn** to give sb a cuddle; **faire des câlins à qn** to (kiss and) cuddle sb

câliner [3] [kaline] VT to (kiss and) cuddle, to pet; **se faire c.** to be cuddled
▸**se câliner** VPR to cuddle

câlinerie [kalinri] NF *(qualité)* tenderness; *(geste)* caress, cuddle; **faire des câlineries à qn** to kiss and cuddle sb

caliorne [kaljɔrn] NF *Naut* purchase tackle

calisson [kalisɔ̃] NM *Culin* **c. (d'Aix)** = lozenge-shaped sweet made of iced marzipan

calla [kala] NF *Bot* arum lily

caller [kɔlœr] NM *Can (d'une danse carrée)* caller

calleux, -euse [kalø, -øz] ADJ **1** *(main, peau)* callous, horny **2** *Méd (ulcère)* callous

call-girl [kɔlgœrl] (*pl* **call-girls**) NF call girl

calligramme [kaligram] NM calligramme

calligraphe [kaligraf] NMF calligrapher

calligraphie [kaligrafi] NF calligraphy

calligraphier [9] [kaligrafje] VT **1** to calligraph **2** *(écrire avec soin)* **c. qch** to write sth in a beautiful hand

calligraphique [kaligrafik] ADJ calligraphic

callionyme [kaljɔnim] NM *Ich* sculpin

Calliope [kaljɔp] NPR *Myth* Calliope

callipyge [kalipiʒ] ADJ *Beaux-Arts* callipygian, callipygous; **la Vénus c.** the Callipygian Venus

callosité [kalozite] NF *Physiol* callosity, callus

calmant, -e [kalmɑ̃, -ɑ̃t] ADJ **1** *Pharm (contre l'anxiété)* tranquillizing, sedative; *(contre la douleur)* painkilling **2** *(propos)* soothing
NM *Pharm* **1** *(contre l'anxiété)* tranquillizer, sedative; **des calmants** tranquillizers; **prendre des calmants** to be on tranquillizers; **je voudrais m'arrêter de prendre des calmants** I want to come off tranquillizers **2** *(contre la douleur)* painkiller

calmar [kalmar] NM *Zool (mollusque)* squid

calme [kalm] ADJ **1** *(sans agitation → quartier, rue, moment)* quiet, peaceful; *(→ sans tension)* calm; **nous avons passé trois jours calmes** we had three quiet days; **le malade a passé une nuit c.** the patient had a peaceful night
2 *(sans mouvement → eau, étang, mer)* still, calm; *(→ air)* still; **par temps c.** when there's no wind
3 *(maître de soi)* calm, self-possessed; *(tranquille)* quiet; **parler d'une voix c.** to talk calmly; **c'est un enfant très c.** he's a very placid child; **rester c.** to stay calm
4 *Com (peu productif → marché)* quiet, dull, slack; **les affaires sont calmes en ce moment** business is slack *or* quiet at the moment
NMF *(personne)* calm *or* placid person
NM **1** *(absence d'agitation)* peace, quiet, calm; *(de l'air, de la nuit)* stillness; **avec c.** calmly; **du c.!** *(ne vous agitez pas)* keep quiet!; *(ne paniquez pas)* keep cool!; **un moment de c.** a lull; **je n'ai pas eu un moment de c. de toute la journée!** I haven't had a minute's peace all day!; **le c.** peace and quiet; **j'ai besoin de c. pour réfléchir** I need quiet *or* peace and quiet to think; **être au c.** to have *or* to enjoy peace and quiet; **il faut rester au c.** you should avoid excitement; **manifester dans le c.** to hold a peaceful demonstration; **ramener le c.** *(dans une assemblée)* to restore order; *(dans une situation)* to calm things down; **c'est le c. avant la tempête** this is the calm before the storm
2 *(silence)* silence; **faire qch dans le c.** to do sth quietly; **allons les enfants, on rentre dans le c.!** come on children, let's go back in quietly now!
3 *(sang-froid)* composure, calm; **du c.!** calm

down!; **une femme d'un grand c.** a very composed woman; **garder son c.** to keep calm; **perdre son c.** to lose one's composure; **retrouver son c.** to calm down, to regain one's composure

4 *(vent)* calm; **c'est le c. plat** *(en mer)* there's no wind; *(il ne se passe rien)* there's nothing happening; *(à la Bourse)* the Stock Exchange is in the doldrums; **c'est le c. plat dans ma vie sentimentale** my love life is in the doldrums, there's nothing happening in my love life

□ **calmes** NMPL *Météo* **calmes équatoriaux** doldrums

calmement [kalməmɑ̃] ADV calmly, quietly

calmer [3] [kalme] VT **1** *(rendre serein → enfant, opposant, foule)* to calm down; **essaie de c. les enfants** try and get the children to calm down; **nous devons c. les esprits** *(dans un groupe)* we must put everybody's mind at rest; *(dans la nation)* we must put the people's minds at rest; **c. le jeu** *Sport* to calm the game down; *Fig* to calm things down; *Fam* **je vais le c., moi!** I'll shut him up!

2 *(dépassionner → mécontentement)* to soothe, to calm; *(→ colère)* to calm, to appease; *(→ querelle)* to pacify, to defuse; *(→ débat)* to restore order to

3 *(diminuer → fièvre, inflammation)* to bring down; *(→ douleur)* to soothe, to ease; *(→ faim)* to satisfy, to appease; *(→ soif)* to quench; *(→ désespoir, crainte)* to ease, to allay; *(→ désir, passion, enthousiasme)* to dampen; *(→ impatience)* to relieve; **pour c. sa frayeur** to dispel or to allay his fear; **ça devrait leur c. les nerfs** that should soothe their (frayed) nerves

▶**se calmer** VPR **1** *(devenir serein)* to calm down; **attends que les choses se calment** wait for things to calm down

2 *(se taire)* Br to quieten or Am to quiet down

3 *(s'affaiblir → dispute, douleur)* to die down or away, to ease off or up; *(→ fièvre)* to die or to go down; *(→ anxiété)* to fade; *(→ passion)* to fade away, to cool; *(→ faim, soif)* to die down, to be appeased; **la douleur s'est calmée brusquement/peu à peu** the pain died away abruptly/eased up gradually

4 *Météo (averse)* to ease off; *(mer)* to become calm; *(vent)* to die down, to drop; *(tempête)* to die down, to blow over, to abate

calmir [32] [kalmir] VI *Naut (mer)* to become calm; *(vent)* to drop, to abate

calmos [kalmos] EXCLAM *Fam* chill (out)!, take it easy!

calo [kalo] NM *Ling* Calo

calomel [kalɔmɛl] NM *Chim & Pharm* calomel

calomniateur, -trice [kalɔmnjatœr, -tris] ADJ *(propos)* slanderous; *(écrit)* libellous
    NM,F slanderer; *(par écrit)* libeller

calomnie [kalɔmni] NF *(oralement)* slander, calumny; *(par écrit)* libel; **ce ne sont que des calomnies** it's all lies; **répandre des calomnies sur qn** to cast aspersions on sb; **être en butte à la c.** to be a victim of slander/libel, to be slandered/libelled

calomnier [9] [kalɔmnje] VT *(dénigrer → oralement)* to slander, *Sout* to calumniate; *(→ par écrit)* to libel

calomnieuse [kalɔmnjøz] *voir* **calomnieux**

calomnieusement [kalɔmnjøzmɑ̃] ADV *(oralement)* slanderously; *(par écrit)* libellously

calomnieux, -euse [kalɔmnjø, -øz] ADJ *(propos)* slanderous; *(écrit)* libellous

caloporteur [kalɔpɔrtœr] *Tech & Ind* ADJ M **fluide** *ou* **liquide c.** coolant
    NM coolant

calorie [kalɔri] NF *Phys & Physiol* calorie; **riche en calories** high in calories; **attention aux calories!** watch the calories!; **un régime basses calories** a low-calorie diet; **grande c.** kilocalorie, large calorie

calorifère [kalɔrifɛr] ADJ **1** *(produisant de la chaleur)* heat-giving **2** *(transportant de la chaleur)* heat-conveying
    NM **1** *(poêle)* stove **2** *Can (radiateur)* heater

calorifique [kalɔrifik] ADJ *Phys (perte)* heat *(avant n)*; *Physiol (valeur)* calorific

calorifuge [kalɔrify3] ADJ heat-insulating; **le bois est c.** wood is a poor conductor of heat

NM heat insulator; *(pour chaudière, pour tuyau)* lagging

calorifugeage [kalɔrify3a3] NM (heat) insulation; *(de chaudière, de tuyau)* lagging

calorifuger [17] [kalɔrify3e] VT to insulate; *(chaudière, tuyau)* to lag

calorimètre [kalɔrimɛtr] NM *Phys* calorimeter

calorimétrie [kalɔrimetri] NF *Phys* calorimetry

calorimétrique [kalɔrimetrik] ADJ *Phys* calorimetric, calorimetrical

caloriporteur [kalɔripɔrtœr] = **caloporteur**

calorique [kalɔrik] ADJ *Phys & Physiol* calorific, caloric; **ration c.** calorie intake

calorisation [kalɔrizasjɔ̃] NF *Métal* calorization

calot [kalo] NM **1** *Mil (coiffure militaire)* (forage) cap **2** *(bille)* big marble
    □ **calots** NMPL *Fam (yeux)* peepers

calotin [kalɔtɛ̃] NMF *Fam Péj* holy Joe

calotte [kalɔt] NF **1** *(petit bonnet)* skullcap; *Rel (de prêtre)* calotte, skullcap; *(partie du chapeau)* crown; *Fam* **la c.** the clergy■

2 *Fam (tape)* clout; *(sur la joue)* slap■; **flanquer une c. à qn** to clout sb (in the face); *(sur la joue)* to give sb a slap; **(se) prendre** *ou* **recevoir une c.** to get a clout; *(sur la joue)* to get a slap

3 *Anat* **c. du crâne** *ou* **crânienne** top of the skull

4 *Archit (voûte)* calotte

5 *Astron* **c. polaire** polar region

6 *Littéraire* **la c. des cieux** the dome or vault of heaven

7 *Math* **c. sphérique** portion of a sphere

8 *Géog* **c. glaciaire** icecap

calotter [3] [kalɔte] VT *Fam* to clout; *(sur la joue)* to slap■

caloyer, -ère [kalɔje, -ɛr] NM,F *Rel* caloyer

calquage [kalka3] NM **1** *(reproduction)* tracing **2** *Fam (imitation → d'une œuvre d'art)* imitating■

calque [kalk] NM **1** *(feuille)* piece of tracing paper; *(matériau)* tracing paper **2** *(dessin)* tracing, traced design; **prendre** *ou* **faire un c. de** to trace **3** *(copie → d'un tableau, d'un texte)* exact copy, replica **4** *(répétition → d'une attitude, d'une erreur)* carbon copy **5** *Ling* calque, loan translation

calquer [3] [kalke] VT **1** *(motif)* to trace **2** *(imiter → manières, personne)* to copy exactly; **il calque sa conduite sur celle de son frère** he models his behaviour on his brother's **3** *Ling* to translate literally; **calqué sur** *ou* **de l'espagnol** translated literally from Spanish

calter [3] [kalte] *Fam* VI to beat it, *Br* to clear off, *Am* to split
    ▶**se calter** VPR to beat it, *Br* to clear off, *Am* to split

caluger [17] [kaly3e] VI *Suisse (dans le Vaud)* to fall out of a toboggan; *Fig (échouer)* to fail

calumet [kalymɛ] NM peace pipe; **fumer le c. de la paix** to smoke the pipe of peace; *Fig* to make peace

calure [kalyr] NF *Suisse Fam (personne calée)* brainbox, brain

calva [kalva] NM *Fam* Calvados■

Calvados [kalvados] NM **le C.** Calvados

calvados [kalvados] NM *(alcool)* Calvados

calvaire [kalvɛr] NM **1** *Rel (crucifixion)* **le C. (de Jésus)** the suffering of Jesus on the Cross; **le C. (Mount)** Calvary

2 *(monument → à plusieurs croix)* calvary; *(→ à une croix)* wayside cross

3 *Beaux-Arts* calvary, road to Calvary

4 *Fig (souffrance)* ordeal; **sa maladie a été un long c.** his/her illness was a long ordeal

5 *Can Joual (juron)* bastard; **mon c.!** you bastard!
    EXCLAM *Can Joual* shit!

□ **en calvaire** ADV *Can Joual* **1** *(beaucoup)* a lot■, very much■; **c'est beau en c.** it's really nice

2 **être en c. (contre qn)** to be fuming mad (with sb)

calvairienne [kalverjɛn] NF *Rel (religieuse)* = nun belonging to the Congregation of Our Lady of Calvary

calville [kalvil] NF *Bot* calville apple, queening apple

Calvin [kalvɛ̃] NPR **Jean C.** John Calvin

calvinisme [kalvinism] NM *Rel* Calvinism

calviniste [kalvinist] *Rel* ADJ Calvinist, Calvinistic
    NMF Calvinist

calvitie [kalvisi] NF **1** *(absence de cheveux)* baldness; **c. naissante** incipient baldness; **c. précoce** premature baldness **2** *Fam (emplacement)* bald spot■

Calypso [kalipso] NPR *Myth* Calypso

calypso [kalipso] NM *Mus & (danse)* calypso

cama [kama] NM *Belg Fam (camarade)* pal, *Br* mate, *Am* buddy

camaïeu, -x [kamajø] NM *Beaux-Arts* **1** *(tableau)* monochrome painting **2** *(gravure)* monochrome engraving **3** *(technique)* **le c.** monochrome, monotint; **en c.** *(tableau)* monochrome; **un c. de bleus** a monochrome in blue **4** *(couleurs)* shades; **le c. du couchant** the shades of sunset

camail [kamaj] NM **1** *Zool (d'un cheval)* neck guard **2** *Rel (d'un ecclésiastique)* (ecclesiastical) cape, cope **3** *Orn (du coq)* neck feathers, hackles **4** *Hist* camail

camaldule [kamaldyl] NM *Rel* camaldolite

camarade [kamarad] NMF **1** *(ami)* friend; **c. de chambrée** roommate; **c. de classe** classmate; **c. d'école** schoolmate; **c. de jeu** playmate; **c. de régiment** comrade (in arms); **c. de travail** workmate, colleague **2** *Pol* comrade; **le c. Gorbatchev** comrade Gorbachev **3** *(en appellatif)* comrade

camaraderie [kamaradri] NF *(entre deux personnes)* good fellowship, friendship; *(dans un club, dans un groupe)* companionship, camaraderie; **il n'y a que de la c. entre eux** they're just (good) friends

camard, -e [kamar, -ard] ADJ *Vieilli (nez)* pug; *(personne)* pug-nosed
    □ **Camarde** NF *Littéraire* **la Camarde** the Grim Reaper

camarguais, -e [kamargɛ, -ɛz] ADJ of/from the Camargue
    □ **Camarguais, -e** NM,F = inhabitant of or person from the Camargue

Camargue [kamarg] NF **la C.** the Camargue

camarilla [kamarija] NF *Hist & Pol* camarilla

camber [3] [kɑ̃be] VT *Suisse* to stride over

cambial, -e, -aux, -ales [kɑ̃bjal, -o] ADJ *Fin* exchange *(avant n)*, currency *(avant n)*

cambiste [kɑ̃bist] *Fin & Banque* ADJ **banquier c.** = bank with a bureau de change or foreign exchange counter; **marché c.** currency or foreign exchange market
    NMF **1** *Bourse* exchange broker **2** *(de bureau de change)* bureau de change or foreign exchange dealer

cambium [kɑ̃bjɔm] NM *Bot* cambium

Cambodge [kɑ̃bɔd3] NM **le C.** Cambodia; **vivre au C.** to live in Cambodia; **aller au C.** to go to Cambodia

cambodgien, -enne [kɑ̃bɔd3jɛ̃, -ɛn] ADJ Cambodian
    NM *(langue)* Cambodian
    □ **Cambodgien, -enne** NM,F Cambodian

cambouis [kɑ̃bwi] NM dirty oil or grease

cambrage [kɑ̃bra3] NM *Tech (d'une barre, d'une poutre)* cambering

cambré, -e [kɑ̃bre] ADJ *Physiol (dos)* arched; *(pied)* with a high instep; *Zool (cheval)* bowlegged; **avoir la taille cambrée, être c.** to have a curved spine

cambrement [kɑ̃brəmɑ̃] NM *Physiol (du dos, du pied)* arching

cambrer [3] [kɑ̃bre] VT **1** *Physiol (pied)* to arch; **c. le dos** *ou* **les reins** to arch one's back **2** *Tech (barre, poutre)* to camber
    ▶**se cambrer** VPR to arch one's back

cambrésien, -enne [kɑ̃brezjɛ̃, -jɛn] ADJ **1** *(de Cambrai)* of/from Cambrai **2** *(du Cambrésis)* of/from the Cambrésis region
    □ **Cambrésien, -enne** NM,F **1** *(de Cambrai)* = inhabitant of or person from Cambrai **2** *(du Cambrésis)* = inhabitant of or person from the Cambrésis region

Cambrésis [kɑ̃brezi] NM **le C.** the Cambrésis region

cambrien, -enne [kɑ̃brijɛ̃, -ɛn] *Géol* ADJ Cambrian
    NM Cambrian (period)

cambriolage [kɑ̃brijɔla3] NM **1** *(coup)* burglary, break-in **2** *(activité)* **le c.** burglary, housebreaking

cambrioler [3] [kɑ̃brijɔle] VT *(propriété)* Br to

burgle, *Am* to burglarize; *(personne)* to burgle; **se faire c.** to be burgled

cambrioleur, -euse [kɑ̃brijɔlœr, -øz] **NM,F** burglar, housebreaker

Cambronne [kɑ̃brɔn] **NPR le mot de C.** = euphemism for the word "merde"

> *Allusion*
>
> **Le mot de Cambronne**
>
> At the Battle of Waterloo, the English called on General Cambronne to surrender; his comment was apparently **Merde!** ("Shit!"). Since "merde" is not used in polite society, **le mot de Cambronne** ("Cambronne's famous phrase") is used as a euphemism, as is "le mot de cinq lettres" – "the five-letter word".

cambrousard, -e [kɑ̃bruzar, -ard] *Fam Péj* **ADJ** countrified, awkward
NM,F yokel, peasant

cambrousse [kɑ̃brus], **cambrouse** [kɑ̃bruz] **NF** *Fam Péj (campagne)* country▪ ; **en pleine c.** in the sticks, in the middle of nowhere; **il arrive** *ou* **débarque de sa c.** he's just up from the sticks *or Am* the boondocks

cambrure [kɑ̃bryr] **NF 1** *Physiol (posture → du dos)* curve; *(→ du pied, d'une semelle)* arch **2** *Tech (d'une chaussée, d'une pièce de bois)* camber **3** *Opt* curve **4** *Physiol (partie → du pied)* instep; *(→ du dos)* small **5** *(support de semelage)* instep; **des chaussures à forte c.** shoes with a high instep

cambuse [kɑ̃byz] **NF 1** *Naut* storeroom **2** *Fam Péj (chambre, maison)* dump, *Br* tip

cambusier [kɑ̃byzje] **NM** *Naut* storekeeper

came [kam] **NF 1** *Tech* cam; *Aut* **c. de frein** expander; **à c. unique** single-cam **2** *Fam (drogue)* dope, stuff **3** *Fam (marchandises)* stuff, junk

camé, -e[1] [kame] *Fam* **ADJ** high; **il est c.** he's on something; **elle est complètement camée** she's as high as a kite
NM,F junkie, druggie

camée[2] [kame] **NM** *(en joaillerie)* cameo

caméléon [kameleɔ̃] **NM** *Zool & Fig* chameleon

caméléonesque [kameleɔnɛsk] **ADJ** chameleon-like

camélia [kamelja] **NM** *Bot* camellia

camélidé [kamelide] *Zool* **NM** = member of the camel family *or Spéc* the Camelidae
❑ **camélidés NMPL** Camelidae

cameline [kamlin], **caméline** [kamelin] **NF** *Bot* camelina, gold-of-pleasure

camelle [kamɛl] **NF** salt-pile

camellia [kamelja] = **camélia**

camelot [kamlo] **NM 1** *(dans la rue)* street peddler, hawker **2** *Pol* **c. du roi** Royalist supporter *(in France)*

camelote [kamlɔt] **NF** *Fam* **1** *(marchandise)* stuff, goods; **c'est de la bonne c.** it's good stuff **2** *Péj (mauvaise qualité)* **c'est de la c.** it's junk *or* trash; **leurs bagues, c'est de la c.** their rings are cheap and nasty

camembert [kamɑ̃bɛr] **NM 1** *Culin (fromage)* Camembert (cheese) **2** *(graphique)* pie chart

camer [3] [kame] **se camer VPR** *Fam* to do drugs; **se c. à la cocaïne** to be on coke; **il s'est jamais camé à l'héroïne** he's never done heroin

caméra [kamera] **NF 1** *Cin & TV* movie *or Br* film camera; **il s'est expliqué devant les caméras** he gave an explanation in front of the (television) cameras; **c. cachée** hidden camera; **c. à l'épaule** hand-held camera; **c. espionne** spy camera; **c. fixe** fixed camera; **c. infrarouge** infrared camera; *Ordinat* **c. Internet** web cam; **c. invisible** hidden camera; **C. d'or** = important prize awarded at the Cannes Film Festival to a director's debut full-length film; **c. portative** press camera; **c. sans film** filmless camera; **c. sonore** sound camera; **c. super-8** super 8 camera; **c. de télévision** television camera; **c. thermique** thermal cameral; **c. vidéo** video camera; **c. vidéo numérique** digital video camera
2 *Opt* **c. électronique** *ou* **électronographique** electronic camera

caméra-film [kamerafilm] *(pl* **caméras-film)** **NF** movie *or Br* film camera

cameraman [kameraman] *(pl* **cameramans** *ou* **cameramen** [-mɛn]) **NM** *Cin & TV* cameraman, camera operator

camérier [kamerje] **NM** *Rel (du Pape, d'un cardinal)* chamberlain

camériste [kamerist] **NF 1** *Hist (dame d'honneur)* lady-in-waiting **2** *Littéraire (femme de chambre)* lady's maid, personal maid

camerlingue [kamɛrlɛ̃g] **NM** *Rel* camerlengo

Cameroun [kamrun] **NM le C.** Cameroon; **vivre au C.** to live in Cameroon; **aller au C.** to go to Cameroon

camerounais, -e [kamrunɛ, -ɛz] **ADJ** Cameroonian
❑ **Camerounais, -e NM,F** Cameroonian

Caméscope® [kameskɔp] **NM** camcorder; **C. numérique** digital camcorder

camion[1] [kamjɔ̃] **NM 1** *Aut Br* lorry, *Am* truck; **interdit aux camions** *(sur panneau) Br* no HGVs, *Am* no trucks; **c. bâché** curtainsider; **c. benne** dumper truck; **c. de déménagement** *Br* removal van, *Am* moving van; **c. de dépannage** breakdown truck, *Am* wrecker; **c. des éboueurs** *Br* dustcart, *Am* garbage truck; **c. réfrigéré** refrigerated *Br* lorry *or Am* truck; **c. à remorque** *Br* lorry *or Am* truck with trailer; **c. à semi-remorque** *Br* articulated lorry, *Am* trailer truck
2 *(de peintre)* (paint) pail

camion[2] [kamjɔ̃] **NM** *(de dentellière)* minikin (pin)

camion-benne [kamjɔ̃bɛn] *(pl* **camions-bennes)** **NM** dumper truck

camion-citerne [kamjɔ̃sitɛrn] *(pl* **camions-citernes)** **NM** *Br* tanker (lorry), *Am* tank truck

camionnage [kamjɔnaʒ] **NM** *Com (prix, service)* haulage, carriage, *Am* truckage; **une entreprise de c.** a haulage firm, *Am* a trucking business

camionner [3] [kamjɔne] **VT** *Com* to haul, to transport by *Br* lorry *or Am* truck

camionnette [kamjɔnɛt] **NF** *Aut* van; **c. de livraison** delivery van

camionneur [kamjɔnœr] **NM 1** *(conducteur) Br* lorry *or Am* truck driver **2** *(entrepreneur)* (road) haulage contractor, (road) *Br* haulier *or Am* hauler

camisard [kamizar] **NM** *Hist* Calvinist partisan *(in the Cévennes uprising of 1702)*

camisole [kamizɔl] **NF 1** *Vieilli Can & Suisse (sous-vêtement féminin)* camisole; *Can & Suisse (sous-vêtement masculin) Br* vest, *Am* undershirt **2** *Psy* **c. chimique** chemical straitjacket *or* cosh; **c. de force** straitjacket

camomille [kamɔmij] **NF 1** *Bot* camomile; **grande c.** feverfew; **c. allemande** scented mayweed; **c. inodore** scentless mayweed; **c. puante** stinking camomile **2** *Culin (infusion)* camomile tea; **prendre une c.** to have a cup of camomile tea

camorra [kamɔra] **NF** camorra

camouflage [kamuflaʒ] **NM 1** *Mil (procédé)* camouflaging; *(matériel)* camouflage **2** *(de la vérité)* hiding, concealing; *(d'une erreur)* covering up **3** *(d'un message)* coding **4** *Zool* camouflage, mimicry

camoufler [3] [kamufle] **VT 1** *Mil* to camouflage
2 *(cacher → passage, gêne)* to conceal; *(→ bavure)* to cover up; *(→ vérité)* to hide, to conceal
3 *(déguiser)* **de nombreux crimes sont camouflés en suicides** murders are often made to look like suicide
4 *Compta* **c. un bilan** to window-dress the accounts
▸**se camoufler VPR 1** *Mil* to camouflage oneself
2 *Zool* to camouflage itself, to mimic its environment

camouflet [kamuflɛ] **NM 1** *Littéraire (affront)* snub, insult, affront; **essuyer un c.** to be snubbed **2** *Mil* camouflet, stifler

camp [kɑ̃] **NM 1** *Mil* (army) camp; **établir un c.** to set up *or* pitch camp; **c. de base** base camp; **c. militaire** military camp; **c. de prisonniers** prisoner of war camp; **c. retranché** fortified camp; **c. volant** temporary camp; *Fig* **vivre en c. volant** *(en situation changeante)* to be always on the move; *(en déménageant souvent)* to live out of a suitcase; **lever le c.** to break camp; *Fig* to make tracks
2 *Hist & Pol* camp; **c. (de concentration)** concentration camp; **la vie dans les camps** life in the concentration camps; **c. de déportation** deportation camp; **c. d'extermination** *ou* **de la mort** death camp; **c. d'internement** internment camp; **c. de réfugiés** refugee camp; **c. de travail (forcé)** forced labour camp; *Hist* **C. David** Camp David; *Hist* **le C. du Drap d'or** the Field of (the) Cloth of Gold *(meeting between François I of France and Henry VIII of England in 1520)*
3 *(de loisirs) Br* campsite, camping site, *Am* campground; **je fais un c. à Pâques avec ma classe** I'm going on a camping trip at Easter with my class; **j'envoie les enfants en c. cet été** I'm sending the children off to summer camp this year; **c. de scouts** scout camp
4 *Sport & (dans un jeu)* team, side; **faire deux camps** to form two teams
5 *(faction)* camp, side; **il faut choisir son c.** you must decide which side you're on; **passer dans l'autre c., changer de c.** to change sides, to go over to the other side
6 [kamp] *Can Joual* camp; *(maison de campagne)* holiday cottage; **c. de bûcherons/de chasse** lumberjacks'/hunting camp
7 *(locutions) Fam* **ficher le c.** to clear off, to beat it; *très Fam* **foutre le c.** *(personne)* to go to hell, *Br* to bugger off; **fous le c.!** go to hell!, *Br* bugger off!; **mon pansement fout le c.** my plaster's coming off▪ ; **tout fout le c.!** what the hell is the world coming to?

campagnard, -e [kɑ̃paɲar, -ard] **ADJ** *(accent, charme, style, vie)* country *(avant n)*, rustic
NM,F countryman, *f* countrywoman; **les campagnards** countryfolk

campagne [kɑ̃paɲ] **NF 1** *(habitat)* country; *(paysage)* countryside; **les travaux de la c.** farm *or* agricultural work; **la c. environnante** the surrounding country *or* countryside; **une c. plate** flat *or* open country; **une c. vallonnée** rolling countryside; **à la c.** in the country *or* countryside
2 *(activité)* campaign; **faire c. pour/contre** to campaign for/against; **lancer une c. pour/contre** to launch a campaign for/against
3 *Com & Pol* campaign; **c. d'affichage** poster campaign; **c. commerciale** sales campaign; *Mktg* **c. de dénigrement** countermarketing campaign; **c. de diffamation** smear campaign; **c. électorale** election campaign; *Mktg* **c. d'image de marque** branding campaign; **c. d'information** publicity campaign; *Mktg* **c. intensive** saturation campaign; **c. de presse** press campaign; **c. de promotion** promotional campaign; **c. publicitaire** *ou* **de publicité** advertising campaign; *Mktg* **c. de publicité directe** direct mail campaign; **c. de recrutement** recruitment drive; *Mktg* **c. de saturation** saturation campaign; **c. télévisée** *ou* **télévisuelle** television campaign; *Mktg* **c. de vente** sales drive
4 *Mil* campaign; **faire c.** to campaign, to fight; **la c. d'Italie** the Italian campaign; **les campagnes napoléoniennes** Napoleon's campaigns
5 *Archéol* **c. de fouilles** excavation plan
❑ **de campagne ADJ 1** *(rural → chemin, médecin, curé)* country *(avant n)*
2 *Culin (pain, saucisson)* country *(avant n)*
3 *Mil (tenue, artillerie)* field *(avant n)*
❑ **en campagne ADV** in the field, on campaign; *Fig* **être en c.** to be on the warpath; *aussi Fig* **entrer** *ou* **se mettre en c.** to go into action

campagnol [kɑ̃paɲɔl] **NM** *Zool* (field) vole

campane [kɑ̃pan] **NF 1** *Vieilli* bell **2** *Archit* campana **3** *(meuble)* tasselled fringe **4** *Bot* pasque flower **5** *Vét* capped hock

campaniforme [kɑ̃panifɔrm] **ADJ** *Archéol* bell-shaped, campaniform

Campanie [kɑ̃pani] **NF la C.** Campania

campanile [kɑ̃panil] **NM** *(d'une église)* bell-tower; *(isolé)* campanile

campanulacée [kɑ̃panylase] *Bot* **NF** member of the Campanulae
❑ **campanulacées NFPL** Campanulae

campanule [kɑ̃panyl] **NF** *Bot* bellflower, *Spéc* campanula; **c. à feuilles rondes** harebell

campé, -e [kɑ̃pe] **ADJ bien c.** *(robuste)* well-built; **bien c. sur ses jambes** standing firmly on his feet; *Littérature* **des personnages bien campés** *(bien décrits)* well-drawn characters; *Théât (bien interprétés)* well-played characters; **un**

récit bien c. a well-constructed story; **un portrait bien c.** a well-sketched portrait

campêche [kɑ̃pɛʃ] NM **1** *Bot (bois)* logwood, *Am* campeachy wood **2** *(colorant)* haematoxylin

campement [kɑ̃pmɑ̃] NM **1** *(installation)* camp, encampment; *(terrain)* camping place *or* ground; *(de bohémiens)* caravan site; **c. interdit** *(sur panneau)* no camping; **établir un c.** to set up camp; **replier le c.** to break camp **2** *Mil (détachement)* detachment of scouts

camper [3] [kɑ̃pe] VI **1** *(faire du camping)* to camp **2** *Mil* to camp (out); **c. sur ses positions** to stand one's ground, *Fig* to stand one's ground, to stick to one's guns

3 *(habiter temporairement)* **je campe chez un copain en attendant** meanwhile, I'm camping (out) at a friend's

VT **1** *Théât (personnage)* to play the part of

2 *Beaux-Arts (par un dessin → silhouette)* to draw, to sketch out

3 *Littérature (par un écrit → personnage)* to portray

4 *(placer)* **c. son chapeau sur l'oreille** to tilt one's hat over one's ear; **c. son chapeau sur sa tête** to stick one's hat on one's head

5 *Mil (troupes)* to encamp

▸**se camper** VPR **se c. devant qn** to plant oneself in front of sb

campeur, -euse [kɑ̃pœr, -øz] NM,F camper

camphorate [kɑ̃fɔrat] NM *Chim* camphorate

camphre [kɑ̃fr] NM *Chim* camphor

camphré, -e [kɑ̃fre] ADJ *Chim* camphorated

camphrier [kɑ̃frije] NM *Bot* camphor tree

camping [kɑ̃piŋ] NM **1** *(activité)* camping; **on a fait du c. l'été dernier** we went camping last summer; **j'aime faire du c.** I like camping; **c. à la ferme** farm camping; **c. sauvage** *(non autorisé)* camping on non-authorized sites; *(en pleine nature)* camping in the open, wilderness camping **2** *(terrain)* *Br* camp *or* camping site, *Am* campground; *(pour caravanes)* *Br* caravan *or* *Am* trailer site; **c. aménagé** camp site with facilities

❏ **de camping** ADJ *(avant n)* camping

camping-car [kɑ̃piŋkar] *(pl* **camping-cars***)* NM camper, *Br* camper van

camping-caravaning [kɑ̃piŋkaravaniŋ] NM INV *Br* caravanning, *Am* camping in a trailer

Camping-Gaz® [kɑ̃piŋgaz] NM INV camping stove

campo [kɑ̃po] NM *Géog (au Brésil)* campo

campos [kɑ̃po] NM *Fam* **donner c. à qn** to give sb a day/an afternoon/*etc* off ■

campus [kɑ̃pys] NM *Univ* campus; **sur le c.** on campus

camus, -e [kamy, -yz] ADJ *(nez)* pug *(avant n)*; *(personne)* pug-nosed

Canada [kanada] NM **le C.** Canada; **vivre au C.** to live in Canada; **aller au C.** to go to Canada

canada [kanada] NF *Bot* Canada apple

Canadair® [kanadɛr] NM *Aviat* fire-fighting plane, *Am* tanker plane

canadianisme [kanadjanism] NM *Ling* Canadianism

canadianité [kanadjanite] NF *Can* Canadianness

canadien, -enne [kanadjɛ̃, -ɛn] ADJ Canadian

❏ **Canadien, -enne** NM,F **1** *(gén)* Canadian; **C. français** French Canadian **2** *Can (d'origine française)* = descendant of the original French (as opposed to British) settlers in Canada

❏ **canadienne** NF **1** *(tente)* (ridge) tent **2** *(veste)* sheepskin-lined jacket **3** *(pirogue)* (Canadian) canoe

canadien-français, canadienne-française [kanadjɛ̃frɑ̃se, kanadjɛnfrɑ̃sɛz] *(mpl* **canadiens-français,** *fpl* **canadiennes-françaises***)* ADJ *Can* French-Canadian

canaille [kanaj] ADJ **1** *(polisson)* roguish **2** *(vulgaire)* coarse, vulgar

NF **1** *(crapule)* scoundrel, crook; *Vieilli* **la c.** the rabble **2** *(ton affectueux)* **petite c.!** you little devil *or* rascal!

canaillerie [kanajri] NF *Littéraire* **1** *(acte)* low trick **2** *(malhonnêteté)* crookedness **3** *(vulgarité)* coarseness, vulgarity

canal, -aux [kanal, -o] NM **1** *Naut & Géog* canal; *(bras de mer)* channel; **sur les canaux et rivières** on the inland waterways; **c. de dérivation** diversion *or* bypass channel; **c. de jonction** junction canal; **c. latéral** lateral canal; **c.**

maritime *ou* **de navigation** ship canal; **le c. Calédonien** the Caledonian Canal; **le c. du Midi** = canal linking the Garonne estuary to the Mediterranean; **le c. de Mozambique** the Mozambique Channel; **le c. du Nord** the North Channel; **le c. de Panama** the Panama Canal; **le c. Saint-Georges** St George's Channel; **le c. de Suez** the Suez Canal

2 *Constr* duct, channel; **c. d'amenée** feed *or* feeder channel; **c. de fuite** waste pipe

3 *Agr* channel; **c. de drainage/d'irrigation** drainage/irrigation canal

4 *Tél & Ordinat* channel; *Can (chaîne)* (TV) channel; **c. d'accès** access channel; **c. de dialogue en direct** IRC channel; **c. IRC** IRC channel; **c. mosaïque** multiscreen channel; **C.+, C. Plus** = French TV pay channel

5 *Archit* flute

6 *Anat* duct, canal; **c. auditif** auditory canal; **c. biliaire** bile duct; **c. déférent** vas deferens; **c. éjaculateur** ejaculatory canal; **c. inguinal** inguinal canal; **c. lacrymal** tear duct, *Spéc* lacrymal canal; **c. médullaire** medullary canal *or* cavity

7 *Bot* duct, canal

8 *Com & Mktg* **c. de communication** communications channel; **c. de communication commerciale** marketing communications channel; **c. de distribution** distribution channel

9 *Astron* canal

❏ **par le canal de** PRÉP through, via

canalicule [kanalikyl] NM *Anat & Archit* canaliculus

canalisable [kanalizabl] ADJ *(eau, énergie, pensées, efforts)* which can be channelled

canalisation [kanalizasjɔ̃] NF **1** *Constr (conduit)* pipe; *Pétr (pour pétrole)* pipeline; **canalisations** *(système)* pipes, pipework, piping **2** *Élec* wiring **3** *Constr (travaux → d'une rivière)* channelling; **la c. de la région** equipping the area with a canal system **4** *(rassemblement → d'énergies, d'une foule, de pensées)* channelling

canaliser [3] [kanalize] VT **1** *Constr (cours d'eau)* to channel; *(région)* to provide with a canal system **2** *(énergies, foule, pensées, ressources)* to channel; **la police canalisait les manifestants vers la sortie** the police were channelling the demonstrators towards the exit

cananéen, -enne [kananeɛ̃, -ɛn] *Bible* ADJ Canaanite

NM *Ling* Canaanite

❏ **Cananéen, -enne** NM,F Canaanite

canapé [kanape] NM **1** *(siège)* settee, sofa; **c. deux places** two-seater sofa, *Am* loveseat; **c. trois places** three-seater sofa; **c. clic-clac** = spring-action *or* metal-action sofa bed; **c. convertible** sofa bed, bed settee **2** *Culin* canapé

canapé-lit [kanapeli] *(pl* **canapés-lits***)* NM sofa bed, bed settee

canaque [kanak] ADJ Kanak

❏ **Canaque** NMF Kanak *(native or inhabitant of New Caledonia who seeks independence from France)*

canard [kanar] NM **1** *Orn* duck; **c. mâle** drake; **c. chipeau** gadwall; **c. garrot** goldeneye; **c. mandarin** mandarin duck; **c. de Miquelon** long-tailed duck; **c. musqué** Muscovy duck; **c. noir** black duck; **c. nyorca** ferruginous duck; **c. sauvage** wild duck; **c. siffleur** wigeon; **c. siffleur d'Amérique** American wigeon; *Fig* **c. boiteux** lame duck

2 *Culin* duck; **c. laqué** Peking duck; *Culin* **c. à l'orange** duck in orange sauce, duck à l'orange

3 *(terme affectueux)* **mon petit c.** sweetie, sweetie-pie

4 *Fam Journ (journal)* paper, rag; *Presse* **le C. enchaîné** = French satirical weekly newspaper, famous for its investigative journalism

5 *Fam (informations)* rumour

6 *Mus (couac)* false note; **faire un c.** to hit a false note, to go off key

7 *Fam (sucre → au café)* sugar lump dipped in coffee ■; *(→ à l'eau-de-vie)* sugar lump dipped in eau-de-vie ■; *(→ au rhum)* sugar lump dipped in rum ■; **faire un c.** = to dip a lump of sugar into one's drink

8 *Méd (bol)* feeding cup

9 *Can (bouilloire)* kettle

❏ **en canard** ADV **marcher en c.** to walk with one's feet turned out

canardeau, -x [kanardo] NM *Orn* duckling

canarder [3] [kanarde] VT *(avec une arme à feu)* to snipe at, to take potshots at; *(avec des projectiles)* to pelt; **se faire c.** *(au fusil)* to be sniped at; **se faire c. à coup de boules de neige** to be pelted with snowballs

VI **1** *Fam Mus (faire des fausses notes)* to sing off key ■; *(faire une fausse note)* to hit a false note ■, to go off key ■ **2** *Naut (navire)* to pitch

canardière [kanardjɛr] NF **1** *(mare)* duck-pond **2** *Chasse (appât)* duck shoot; *(fusil)* punt gun

canari¹ [kanari] NM *Orn* canary; *Ftbl* **les Canaris** = the Nantes football team

ADJ INV **(jaune) c.** canary-yellow

canari² [kanari] NM *(vase)* = earthenware jar for drinking water

Canarie [kanari] NF *Géog* **la Grande C.** Gran Canaria

canarien, -enne [kanarjɛ̃, -ɛn] ADJ Canarian

❏ **Canarien, -enne** NM,F Canarian

Canaries [kanari] NFPL **les (îles) C.** the Canary Islands, the Canaries; **aller aux C.** to go to the Canaries; **vivre aux C.** to live in the Canaries

canasson [kanasɔ̃] NM *Fam Zool* horse ■, *Péj* nag

canasta [kanasta] NF *Cartes* canasta

Canberra [kɑ̃bɛra] NM Canberra

cancale [kɑ̃kal] NF *Ich* (Cancale) oyster

cancan [kɑ̃kɑ̃] NM **1** *(cri du canard)* quack **2** *(danse)* (French) cancan **3** *(bavardage)* piece of gossip; **des cancans** gossip *(UNCOUNT)*; **n'écoute pas les cancans** don't listen to gossip *or* to what people say

cancaner [3] [kɑ̃kane] VI **1** *(canard)* to quack **2** *(médire)* to gossip; **leur divorce a beaucoup fait c.** their divorce caused a lot of gossip

cancanier, -ère [kɑ̃kanje, -ɛr] ADJ gossipy

NM,F gossip

cancellé, -e [kɑ̃sele] ADJ *Can Joual (annulé)* cancelled

Cancer [kɑ̃sɛr] NM **1** *Astron* Cancer **2** *Astrol* Cancer; **être C.** to be Cancer *or* a Cancerian

cancer [kɑ̃sɛr] NM **1** *Méd* cancer; **avoir un c.** to have cancer; **mourir d'un c.** to die of cancer; **atteint d'un c. rare** suffering from a rare form of cancer; **c. du foie/de la peau** liver/skin cancer; **c. du côlon** cancer of the bowel **2** *(fléau)* cancer, canker

cancéreux, -euse [kɑ̃serø, -øz] *Méd* ADJ *(cellule, tumeur)* malignant, cancerous; *(malade)* cancer *(avant n)*

NM,F cancer victim *or* sufferer; **les c. en phase terminale** terminal cancer patients, people with terminal cancer

cancérigène [kɑ̃seriʒɛn] ADJ *Méd* carcinogenic; **produit c.** carcinogen

cancérisation [kɑ̃serizasjɔ̃] NF *Méd* **pour empêcher la c. des cellules** to prevent cells from becoming malignant

cancérisé, -e [kɑ̃serize] ADJ *Méd* cancerated, cancered

cancériser [3] [kɑ̃serize] **se cancériser** VPR *Méd* to become cancerous *or* malignant

cancérogène [kɑ̃serɔʒɛn] *Méd* ADJ carcinogenic; **produit c.** carcinogen

NM carcinogen

cancérogenèse [kɑ̃serɔʒənɛz] NF *Méd* carcinogenesis

cancérologie [kɑ̃serɔlɔʒi] NF *Méd* oncology

cancérologique [kɑ̃serɔlɔʒik] ADJ *Méd* oncological

cancérologue [kɑ̃serɔlɔg] NMF *Méd* cancerologist; *(médecin)* oncologist

cancérophobie [kɑ̃serɔfɔbi] NF *Psy* cancerophobia

canche [kɑ̃ʃ] NF *Bot* hair-grass; **c. touffue** tussock(-grass)

cancoillotte [kɑ̃kwajɔt] NF *Culin* Cancoillotte

(strong-tasting soft cheese, from the Franche-Comté region)

cancre [kɑ̃kr]NM dunce

cancrelat [kɑ̃krəla] NM *Entom* cockroach, *Am* roach

cancroïde [kɑ̃krɔid]ADJ *Méd* cancroid

candela [kɑ̃dela]NF *Phys* candela

candélabre [kɑ̃delabr] NM **1** *(flambeau)* candelabra **2** *Archit (colonne ornementée)* ornate column **3** *Vieilli (réverbère)* street lamp, lamppost

candeur [kɑ̃dœr] NF ingenuousness, naivety; **un regard plein de c.** a guileless look; **il l'a raconté en toute c.** he recounted it quite candidly *or* ingenuously

candi [kɑ̃di]ADJ M *Culin* **fruits candis** crystallized *or* candied fruit; **sucre c.** sugar candy, rock candy

candida [kɑ̃dida]NM *Biol* candida

candidat, -e [kɑ̃dida, -at] NM,F **1** *Pol* candidate; **être c. aux élections** to be a candidate in the elections, to run *or Br* to stand in the elections; **être c. à la présidence** to run *or Br* to stand for president; *Can* **c. parachuté** parachuted candidate

　2 *(à un examen, à une activité)* candidate; *(à un emploi)* applicant, candidate; **les candidats à l'examen d'entrée** entrance examination candidates; **être c. à un poste** to be a candidate for a post; **se porter c. à un poste** to apply for a post; *Hum* **il y a des candidats à la vaisselle?** any volunteers *Br* for the washing-up *or Am* for doing the dishes?; **les candidats à l'aventure** adventure-seekers

candidature [kɑ̃didatyr]NF **1** *(gén)* candidature, candidacy; **poser sa c.** to declare oneself a candidate, *Br* to stand; **retirer sa c.** to stand down; **il a retiré sa c. à la présidence** he has stood down as a presidential candidate; **elle soigne sa c. au poste de trésorière** she's working on her election to the post of treasurer; **c. multiple** running *or Br* standing for election in several constituencies; **c. officielle** running *or Br* standing as official candidate

　2 *(pour un emploi)* application; **poser sa c. (à)** to apply (for); **retirer sa c.** to withdraw one's application; **c. en-ligne** e-mail *or* on-line application; **c. spontanée** unsolicited application

Candide [kɑ̃did]NPR Candide

Allusion

Jouer au/être le Candide

Candide, in Voltaire's story of the same name, is a naive young innocent, forced to experience all the horrors of human existence. This expression, which simply means "to play at being Candide" could be applied to anyone who knowingly plays the innocent in a given situation, usually with the aim of getting information or proving a point, or to anyone representing the point of view of the layman in a technical debate.

---

candide [kɑ̃did]ADJ ingenuous, naive

candidement [kɑ̃didmɑ̃] ADV ingenuously, naively

candidose [kɑ̃didoz]NF **1** *Biol (bactérie)* candida **2** *Méd (infection)* candidiasis

candir [32] [kɑ̃dir]VT *(sucre, bonbon)* to candy
　▸se **candir** VPR to candy

candisation [kɑ̃dizasjɔ̃] NF *(du sucre)* crystallizing, candying

candomblé [kɑ̃dɔ̃ble] NM *Rel (culte, lieu)* candomblé

cane [kan]NF *Orn (female)* duck

cané, -e [kane]ADJ *Fam* dead■

Canebière [kanbjɛr] NF **la C.** = large avenue in Marseilles

canéficier [kanefisje]NM *Bot* cassia (tree)

canepetière [kanpətjɛr]NF *Orn (little)* bustard

canéphore [kanefɔr] NF *Antiq & Archit* canephoros, canephorus, canephora

caner [3] [kane]VI *Fam* **1** *(de peur)* to chicken out **2** *(mourir)* to croak, to kick the bucket **3** *(s'enfuir)* to beat it, *Br* to leg it, *Am* to bug out

canetage [kantaʒ] NM *Tex* weft winding, pirn winding

canetière [kantjɛr]NF *Tex* spooler

caneton [kantɔ̃] NM **1** *Orn* duckling **2** *Culin* **c. à l'orange** duckling à l'orange

---

canette¹ [kanɛt]NF *Orn* duckling

canette² [kanɛt] NF **1** *(bouteille)* (fliptop) bottle; **c. (de bière)** bottle (of beer) **2** *(boîte)* can; **la rue était jonchée de canettes de bière vides** the street was littered with empty beer cans **3** *Tex (bobine)* spool

canevas [kanva]NM **1** *(d'un roman, d'un exposé)* framework **2** *Tex* canvas; **broderie sur c.** tapestry (work) **3** *Géog (d'une carte)* graticule

canezou [kanzu]NM *Vieilli* canezou

cangue [kɑ̃g]NF cang, cangue

caniche [kaniʃ]NM **1** *Zool* poodle **2** *Péj (personne)* lapdog, poodle

caniculaire [kanikylɛr]ADJ *Météo* scorching, blistering

canicule [kanikyl] NF **1** *(grande chaleur)* scorching heat; **la c.** *(en plein été)* the midsummer heat; **une semaine de c.** a weeklong heatwave; **quelle c.!** what a scorcher! **2** *Antiq & Astron* caniculars, canicular days
　▫ **canicules** NFPL *Belg (grande chaleur)* scorching heat

canidé [kanide]*Zool*NM canine
　▫ **canidés** NMPL **les canidés** the dog family, *Spéc* the Canidae

canier [kanje]NM *Géog (mot provençal)* reed bed

canif [kanif] NM penknife, pocket knife; *Fam Fig* **donner un coup de c. dans le contrat** to have the occasional fling

canin, -e¹ [kanɛ̃, -in]ADJ *Zool* canine; **exposition canine** dog show; **société canine** kennel club

canine² [kanin] NF *Anat* canine tooth

caninette [kaninɛt]NF = motorized scooter with an attachment for cleaning up dog dirt in the street

canisse [kanis] = **cannisse**

canitie [kanisi]NF *Méd* canities

caniveau, -x [kanivo] NM **1** *(le long du trottoir)* gutter **2** *(conduit)* gutter, drainage channel **3** *(pour câbles)* trough, conduit

canna [kana]NM *Bot* canna; **les cannas** the Cannaceae

cannabacée [kanabase] *Bot* NF member of the Cannabiaceae family
　▫ **cannabacées** NFPL Cannabiaceae

cannabique [kanabik]ADJ cannabis *(avant n)*, cannabic

cannabis [kanabis] NM *Bot (chanvre, drogue)* cannabis

cannabisme [kanabism] NM cannabis dependency

cannage [kanaʒ] NM **1** *(activité)* caning **2** *(produit)* canework

cannaie [kanɛ] NF *(de cannes à sucre)* sugar cane plantation; *(de roseaux)* reed plantation

canne [kan]NF **1** *(d'un élégant)* cane; *(d'un vieillard)* walking stick; **c. (anglaise)** crutch; **marcher avec des cannes** to be on crutches; **c. blanche** white *Br* stick *or Am* cane; **les cannes blanches** the visually disabled
　2 *Pêche* **c. à pêche** fishing rod
　3 *Bot* **c. à sucre** sugar cane
　4 *Escrime* **c. à épée** swordstick, sword cane
　5 *Suisse (au hockey sur glace) Br* ice hockey stick, *Am* hockey stick
　6 *(rotin)* cane *(UNCOUNT)*
　7 *Tech* **c. de souffleur** blowpipe
　▫ **cannes** NFPL *Fam (jambes)* legs■ , *Br* pins■; *Sport* ski-poles■ , poles■

canné, -e [kane]ADJ **1** *(en rotin)* cane *(avant n)* **2** *très Fam (mort)* dead as a doornail

canne-béquille [kanbekij] *(pl* **cannes-béquilles)** NF crutch

canneberge [kanbɛrʒ]NF *Bot* cranberry

canne-épée [kanepe] *(pl* **cannes-épées)** NF swordstick

cannelé, -e [kanle]ADJ **1** *(qui présente des cannelures → colonne)* fluted; *(→ pneu)* grooved; *(→ ongle)* ridged **2** *Opt* fluted **3** *(à gouttière)* grooved

canneler [24] [kanle]VT *(colonne)* to flute; *(pneu)* to groove

cannelier [kanəlje]NM *Bot* cinnamon tree

cannelle [kanɛl] NF **1** *(épice)* cinnamon; **c. de Ceylan/Chine** Ceylon/China cinnamon **2** *(robinet)* spigot **3** *Tex (de métier à tisser)* fluted roller
　ADJ INV pale brown, cinnamon-coloured
　▫ **à la cannelle** ADJ cinnamon-flavoured; **thé à la c.** cinnamon tea

---

cannelloni [kanelɔni] *(pl* inv *ou* **cannellonis)** NM *Culin* cannelloni

cannelure [kanlyr] NF **1** *Archit (d'un vase, d'un pilier)* flute, fluting **2** *(d'une vis, d'une pièce de monnaie)* groove, grooving **3** *Bot* stria; *Géol* **cannelures** striae

canner [3] [kane]VT **1** *(chaise)* to cane **2** *Can Joual (mettre en conserve)* to can
　VI = **caner 2, 3**

cannerie [kaneri]NF *Can Joual* cannery

Cannes [kan]NM *Géog* Cannes; *Cin* **le festival de C.** the Cannes film festival

cannetage [kantaʒ] = **canetage**

cannetière [kantjɛr] = **canetière**

cannetille [kantij]NF purl *(of gold or silver)*

cannette [kanɛt] = **canette²**

canneur, -euse [kanœr, -øz]NM,F cane worker

cannibale [kanibal] ADJ *(pratiques, rites)* cannibalistic; **tribu de c.** tribe of cannibals
　NMF *aussi Fig* cannibal
　NM *Belg Culin* steak tartare on toast

cannibalesque [kanibalɛsk]ADJ cannibal-like

cannibalique [kanibalik]ADJ cannibalistic

cannibalisation [kanibalizasjɔ̃] NF *Mktg & Tech (de machine, de produit)* cannibalization

cannibaliser [3] [kanibalize]VT *Mktg & Tech (machine, produit)* to cannibalize

cannibalisme [kanibalism] NM **1** *(anthropophagie)* cannibalism **2** *(férocité)* cannibalism, savagery **3** *Mktg & Tech* cannibalization

cannier, -ère [kanje, -jɛr]NM,F cane worker

cannisse [kanis] NF **1** *(coupe-vent)* rush fence **2** *Can Joual (bidon)* canister

cannois, -e [kanwa, -az]ADJ of/from Cannes
　▫ **Cannois, -e** NM,F = inhabitant of or person from Cannes

canoë [kanɔe] NM *Sport* canoe; **faire du c.** to go canoeing; **ils ont remonté le fleuve en c.** they canoed up the river

canoéisme [kanɔeism]NM *Sport* canoeing

canoéiste [kanɔeist]NMF *Sport* canoeist

canoë-kayak [kanɔekajak] *(pl* **canoës-kayaks)** NM *Sport* **faire du c.** to go canoeing

canon [kanɔ̃]NM **1** *Mil (pièce → moderne)* gun; *(→ ancienne)* cannon; *(tube d'une arme à feu)* barrel; **à c. double** double-barrelled; **à c. scié** *Br* sawn-off, *Am* sawed-off; **c. antiaérien** anti-aircraft gun; **c. antichar** anti-tank gun; **c. automatique** machine-gun; **c. lance-harpon** harpoon gun; **c. mitrailleur** heavy machine-gun; **c. rayé** rifled barrel
　2 *Naut* **c. de chasse/retraite** fore/aft gun
　3 *Électron* **c. électronique** *ou* **à électrons** electron gun
　4 *Agr* **c. arroseur** irrigation cannon
　5 *Sport* **c. à neige** snow-making machine
　6 *Météo* **c. paragrêle** cloud seeder
　7 *(de clé, de serrure)* barrel; *(de seringue)* body
　8 *Mus* canon; **c. à trois voix** canon for three voices; **chanter en c.** to sing a *or* in canon
　9 *Beaux-Arts* canon
　10 *(modèle)* model, *Sout* canon; **les canons de la beauté/du bon goût** the canons of beauty/good taste
　11 *Rel* canon
　12 *Zool* shank
　13 *Arch (mesure)* = wine measure equivalent to 0.058 l.
　14 *(verre → de vin)* glass (of wine); *(→ d'eau-de-vie)* shot (of spirits)
　15 *Fam (personne très belle)* babe, hottie
　ADJ INV **1** *Rel* **droit c.** canonic law
　2 *Fam (beau)* gorgeous, stunning, *Br* fit; **il est vraiment c.!** he's drop-dead gorgeous!, he's a total babe!

cañon [kanjɔ̃] = **canyon**

canon-harpon [kanɔ̃arpɔ̃] *(pl* **canons-harpons)** NM harpoon gun

canonial, -e, -aux, -ales [kanɔnjal, -o]ADJ *Rel (réglé par les canons)* canonic, canonical **2** *(du chanoine)* of a canon

canonicat [kanɔnika]NM *Rel* canonry

canonicité [kanɔnisite]NF *Rel* canonicity

canonique [kanɔnik]ADJ **1** *(conforme aux règles)* classic, canonic, canonical **2** *Rel* canonic, canonical **3** *Math* canonical
　NF canon

canoniquement [kanɔnikmɑ̃] ADV **1** *Rel* canonically **2** *Fam* conventionally■

canonisable [kanɔnizabl] **ADJ** *Rel* that merits canonization

canonisation [kanɔnizasjɔ̃] **NF** *Rel* canonization, canonizing

canoniser [3] [kanɔnize] **VT** *Rel* to canonize

canoniste [kanɔnist] **NM** *Rel* canonist

canonnade [kanɔnad] **NF** *Mil* heavy gunfire, cannonade; **une c.** a burst of gunfire

canonnage [kanɔnaʒ] **NM** *Mil* shelling

canonner [3] [kanɔne] **VT** *Littéraire Mil* to shell, to cannonade

canonnier [kanɔnje] **NM** *Mil* gunner

canonnière [kanɔnjɛr] **NF 1** *Naut* gunboat **2** *(meurtrière)* loophole

canope [kanɔp] **ADJ** canopic
  NM *(urne)* canopic jar

canopée [kanɔpe] **NF** *Écol* canopy

Canossa [kanɔsa] **NM** *(locution)* **aller à C.** to eat humble pie

canot [kano] **NM 1** *Naut (embarcation)* dinghy; **c. automobile** motorboat; **c. de pêche** fishing boat; **c. pneumatique** rubber *or* inflatable dinghy; **c. de sauvetage** lifeboat **2** *Can Sport (canoë)* canoe **3** *Can Fam (couvre-chaussure)* rubber overshoe ▪

canotage [kanɔtaʒ] **NM** *Naut & Sport* boating; *Can (en canoë)* canoeing; **faire du c.** to go boating; *Can Sport* to go canoeing

canot-camping [kanokɑ̃piŋ] **NM INV** *Can* canoe-camping *(travelling by canoe and stopping to camp along the way)*; **faire du c.** to go canoe-camping, to go on a canoe-camping trip

canoter [3] [kanɔte] **VI** *Naut & Sport* **1** *(se promener → en canot)* to go boating; *Can (→ en canoë)* to go canoeing **2** *(manœuvrer)* to handle a boat

canoteur, -euse [kanɔtœr, -øz] **NM,F 1** *Naut* rower *(in a dinghy)* **2** *Can Sport (personne qui fait du canoë)* canoeist

canotier [kanɔtje] **NM 1** *(chapeau)* (straw) boater **2** *Naut & Sport (rameur)* rower, oarsman

Canson® [kɑ̃sɔ̃] **NM** *Beaux-Arts* **papier C.** drawing paper

cant [kɑ̃t] **NM** *Littéraire* cant

cantabile [kɑ̃tabile] *Mus* **ADV** cantabile
  ADJ cantabile
  NM cantabile

Cantabriques [kɑ̃tabrik] *voir* **mont**

Cantal [kɑ̃tal] **NM le C.** Cantal, the Cantal area

cantal [kɑ̃tal] **NM** Cantal (cheese)

cantaloup [kɑ̃talu] **NM** *Bot* cantaloup (melon)

cantate [kɑ̃tat] **NF** *Mus* cantata

cantatille [kɑ̃tatij] **NF** *Mus* chamber cantata

cantatrice [kɑ̃tatris] **NF** *(d'opéra)* (opera) singer; *(de concert)* (concert) singer

▬▬▬▬ ▓ ▬▬▬▬

'La Cantatrice chauve' *Ionesco* 'The Bald Primadonna'

canter¹ [kɑ̃tɛr] **NM** *Équitation* cantering *(up to the weighing enclosure)*

canter² [3] [kɑ̃te] *Can Fam* **VI** to lean ▪, to be slanted ▪
  ►**se canter VPR** to rest ▪, to have a snooze

cantharellale [kɑ̃tarelal] *Bot* **NF** = mushroom of the Cantharellaceae family
  ❑ **cantharellales NFPL** Cantharellaceae

cantharide [kɑ̃tarid] **NF 1** *Entom* blister beetle **2** *Pharm* **poudre de c.** cantharides

cantharidine [kɑ̃taridin] **NF** *Chim & Pharm* cantharidin(e)

cantilène [kɑ̃tilɛn] **NF** *Littérature & Mus* cantilena

cantilever [kɑ̃tilevœr] **ADJ 1** *Constr (poutre, pont)* cantilever **2** *Aviat* cantilever
  NM *Constr (poutre)* cantilever

cantine [kɑ̃tin] **NF 1** *(dans une école)* dining hall, canteen; *(dans une entreprise)* canteen; **les élèves qui mangent à la c.** pupils who have school meals *or* school dinners; **je les mets à la c. à la rentrée** they're going to start having school meals next term; **c'est bon à la c.?** are the school dinners good?
  2 *(malle)* (tin) trunk
  3 *Suisse (boîte)* lunchbox
  4 *Suisse (tente)* marquee

cantiner [3] [kɑ̃tine] **VI** *Fam Arg crime* to buy goods in prison ▪

cantinier, -ère [kɑ̃tinje, -jɛr] **NM,F** canteen attendant

cantique [kɑ̃tik] **NM** *Rel & Mus* canticle; **c. de Noël** Christmas carol; **le C. des cantiques** The Song of Songs, The Song of Solomon

cantoche [kɑ̃tɔʃ] **NF** *Fam* canteen ▪

Canton [kɑ̃tɔ̃] **NM** Canton

canton [kɑ̃tɔ̃] **NM 1** *Admin (en France)* division of an "arrondissement", canton; *(en Suisse)* canton; *(au Luxembourg)* administrative unit, canton; *(au Canada)* township **2** *(de route, de voie ferrée)* section **3** *Archit* canton **4** *Hér* canton

┌─────────────┐
│ *Culture* │
└─────────────┘
CANTON

In the French system of local government, this administrative unit is managed by the local members of the "Conseil général". There are between 11 and 70 "cantons" in each "département". In Switzerland, a "canton" refers to each of the states which make up the Swiss Confederation. Each "canton" is a semi-autonomous region: it has internal sovereignty as well as a constitution. "Cantons" elect the "Conseil des États", which, together with the "Conseil national", forms the Swiss Federal Parliament.

cantonade [kɑ̃tɔnad] **à la cantonade ADV 1** *(sans interlocuteur précis)* to all present, to the company at large; **crier qch à la c.** to call *or* to shout sth (out); **"téléphone!", cria-t-il à la c.** "phone!" he called out; **il a perdu mais ce n'est pas la peine de le crier ou de l'annoncer à la c.** he's lost but there's no need to proclaim *or* to shout it from the rooftops
  2 *Théât* **parler à la c.** *(depuis les coulisses)* to speak off stage; *(à une personne qui est dans les coulisses)* to speak to the wings

cantonais, -e [kɑ̃tɔnɛ, -ɛz] **ADJ** Cantonese; *Culin* **riz c.** (special) fried rice
  NM *(langue)* Cantonese
  ❑ **Cantonais, -e NM,F** Cantonese; **les C.** the Cantonese

cantonal, -e, -aux, -ales [kɑ̃tɔnal, -o] *Pol* **ADJ** local
  ❑ **cantonales NFPL** = election held every six years for the "conseil général", ≃ local elections

cantonalisation [kɑ̃tɔnalizasjɔ̃] **NF** cantonalization

cantonaliser [3] [kɑ̃tɔnalize] **VT** to cantonalize

cantonalisme [kɑ̃tɔnalism] **NM** cantonalism

cantonaliste [kɑ̃tɔnalist] **NMF** cantonalist

cantonnement [kɑ̃tɔnmɑ̃] **NM 1** *(à une tâche, à un lieu)* confinement, confining *(UNCOUNT)* **2** *Mil (lieu)* billet; *(action)* billeting *(UNCOUNT)*

cantonner [3] [kɑ̃tɔne] **VT 1** *(isoler)* **c. qn dans un lieu** to confine sb to a place
  2 *Fig* **c. qch à** *ou* **dans** *(activité, explication)* to limit *or* to confine sth to; **si la discussion reste cantonnée au taux de chômage** if the discussion remains confined to the rate of unemployment
  3 *Mil* to billet; **c. un soldat chez qn** to billet a soldier on sb
  VI to be billeted; **c. chez qn** to be billeted on sb
  ►**se cantonner VPR 1 se c. dans** *(s'enfermer)* to confine oneself to; **il se cantonnait dans sa solitude** he took refuge in solitude
  2 se c. à *ou* **dans** *(être limité)* to be confined *or* limited *or* restricted to; *(se restreindre à)* to confine *or* to limit oneself to

cantonnier [kɑ̃tɔnje] **NM 1** *Constr (sur une route)* roadman, road mender **2** *Rail Br* platelayer, *Am* trackman

cantonnière [kɑ̃tɔnjɛr] **NF** *(de lit)* valance; *(rideau)* pelmet

Cantorbéry [kɑ̃tɔrberi] **NM** Canterbury

cantre [kɑ̃tr] **NM** *Tex* (warp) creel

canulant, -e [kanylɑ̃, -ɑ̃t] **ADJ** *Fam Vieilli* annoying ▪, maddening

canular [kanylar] **NM** hoax; **faire un c. à qn** to play a hoax on sb; **monter un c.** to set up a hoax

canularesque [kanylarɛsk] **ADJ** *Fam (exagéré)* over-the-top; *(impertinent)* irreverent ▪; *(extravagant)* outlandish ▪

canule [kanyl] **NF** *Méd* cannula

canuler [3] [kanyle] **VT** *Fam Vieilli* **1** *(agacer)* **c. qn** to drive sb mad *or* up the wall **2** *(tromper)* to hoax

canuse [kanyz] *voir* **canut¹**

Canut [kany(t)] **NPR** Canute, Cnut

canut¹, -use [kany, -yz] **NM,F** *Tex (à Lyon)* silk weaver *or* worker

canut² [kany] **NM** *Orn* knot

canyon [kanjon, kanjɔ̃] **NM** canyon

canyoning [kanjoniŋ], **canyonisme** [kanjonism] **NM** *Sport* canyoning

canyoniste [kanjonist] **NMF** *Sport* canyoner

canzone [kandzone] *(pl* **canzoni** [-ni]*)* **NF** *Mus & Littérature* canzone

canzonette [kɑ̃dzonɛt] **NF** *Mus & Littérature* canzonet

CAO [seao] **NF** *Ordinat (abrév* **conception assistée par ordinateur***)* CAD

caodaïsme [kaodaism] **NM** *Rel* Caodaism

caoua [kawa] **NM** *Fam* coffee ▪

caouanne [kawan] **NF** *Zool* loggerhead (turtle)

caoutchouc [kautʃu] **NM 1** *Bot* (natural *or* India) rubber
  2 *Chim* (synthetic) rubber; **c. butyle** Butyl®; **c. Mousse** foam rubber; **c. synthétique** synthetic rubber
  3 *Fam (élastique)* rubber *or* elastic band ▪
  4 *(soulier)* galosh
  5 *(manteau)* waterproof (coat), raincoat
  6 *Bot (ficus)* rubber plant
  ❑ **de caoutchouc, en caoutchouc ADJ** rubber *(avant n)*

caoutchoutage [kautʃutaʒ] **NM 1** *(processus)* coating with rubber, rubberizing **2** *(enduit)* rubberized coating

caoutchouter [3] [kautʃute] **VT** to cover *or* to overlay with rubber, to rubberize

caoutchouteux, -euse [kautʃutø, -øz] **ADJ** *(viande)* rubbery, chewy; *(fromage)* rubbery

CAP [seape] **NM** *Scol* **1** *(abrév* **certificat d'aptitude professionnelle***)* = vocational training certificate (taken at secondary school), *Br* ≃ City and Guilds examination **2** *(abrév* **certificat d'aptitude pédagogique***)* teaching diploma

Cap [kap] **NM Le C.** *(ville)* Cape Town; *(province)* Cape Province; **au C.** in Cape Town

Cap. *(abrév écrite* **capitaine***)* Capt

cap¹ [kap] **NM 1** *Géog* cape, headland, promontory; *Naut* **doubler** *ou* **passer un c.** to round a cape; **le c. des Aiguilles** Cape Agulhas; **le c. Blanc** Cap Blanc; **le c. Bon** Cape Bon; **le c. de Bonne-Espérance** the Cape of Good Hope; **c. Canaveral** Cape Canaveral; **c. Cod** Cape Cod; **le c. Finisterre** Cape Finisterre; **le c. Horn** Cape Horn; **le c. Nord** North Cape; **c. Kennedy** Cape Kennedy
  2 *Aviat, Aut & Naut* course; *Aviat* **c. au compas** magnetic *or* compass course; *Aviat* **c. magnétique** magnetic course *or* heading; *Naut* **c. au vent** head on to the wind; **changer de** *ou* **le c.** to alter one's *or* to change course; *Naut* **mettre le c. sur** to steer *or* to head for; *Aut* to head for; *Naut* **mettre le c. au large** to set out to sea; *Naut* **suivre un c.** to steer a course
  3 *(étape)* milestone, hurdle; **passer** *ou* **franchir le c. de** *(dans une situation difficile)* to get over, to come through; *(dans une gradation, des statistiques)* to pass the mark of; **il a passé le c. de la cinquantaine** he's in his fifties; **l'adolescence est un c. difficile à passer** adolescence is a difficult time to live through; **la revue a dépassé le c. des 2000 lecteurs** the readership of the magazine has passed the 2,000 mark
  4 *Can Aut* **c. de roue** hubcap

cap² [kap] **ADJ** *Fam* **t'es pas c. de…!** bet you can't…!; **même pas c.!** bet you can't!

capable [kapabl] **ADJ 1** *(compétent)* capable, competent, able; **un architecte très c.** a very capable *or* able architect
  2 *Jur* competent
  3 **être c. de** *(physiquement)* to be able to, to be capable of; *(psychologiquement)* to be capable of; **c. de porter 30 kilos** capable of lifting *or* able to lift 30 kilos; **te sens-tu c. de te lever?** do you feel able to get up?; **c. de mentir** capable of lying; **il n'est pas c. de se maîtriser** he's unable to control himself; **je n'en suis pas c.** I can't do it; **c. de générosité** capable of generosity *or* of being generous; **c. de tout** capable of (doing) anything; **c. du meilleur comme du pire** capable of the best as well as the worst; **il est c. de nous oublier!** I wouldn't put it past him to forget us!

capacimètre [kapasimɛtr] NM *Élec* faradmeter

capacitaire [kapasitɛr] NMF *Univ* **1** *(diplômé)* = holder of the "capacité en droit" qualification
2 *(étudiant)* = student preparing for the "capacité en droit" examination

capacitance [kapasitɑ̃s] NF *Élec* capacitance

capacité [kapasite] NF **1** *(aptitude)* ability, capability; **avoir la c. de faire qch** to have the ability to do sth, to be capable of doing sth; **diriger? il n'en a pas la c.** managing? he hasn't got the ability for it; **avoir une grande c. de travail** to be capable of *or* to have a capacity for hard work; **c. de concentration** attention span; **j'ai perdu toute c. de concentration** I'm no longer able to concentrate
2 *(d'un récipient, d'une salle, d'un véhicule)* capacity; **sac d'une grande c.** roomy bag; **c. d'accueil** *(d'un hôtel)* accommodation capacity, available beds; *Mktg* **c. linéaire** shelf space; *Physiol* **c. vitale** *ou* **thoracique** vital capacity
3 *Phys* capacity; **c. calorifique** heat capacity
4 *Élec* capacitance
5 *Ordinat & Tél* capacity
6 *Jur* capacity; **avoir c. pour** to be (legally) entitled to; *Fig* **je n'ai pas c. pour vous répondre** it's not up to me to give you an answer; **c. civile** civil capacity; *Pol* **c. électorale** (electoral) franchise; **c. d'ester en justice** standing to sue, *Br* locus standi; **c. d'exercice** = entitlement to exercise rights; **c. de jouissance** legal entitlement (to a piece of property); **c. matrimoniale** capacity to contract marriage
7 *Univ (diplôme)* **c. en droit** = law diploma leading to a degree course in law
8 *Écon* capacity; *Mktg* **c. d'achat** purchasing power; **c. contributive** ability to pay; **c. de crédit, c. d'emprunter** borrowing power *or* capacity; **c. d'endettement** borrowing *or* debt capacity; **c. de financement** financing capacity; *Fin* **c. d'imposition** ability to pay tax; **c. de production** manufacturing capacity; **c. productrice** maximum possible output *or* capacity
9 *Ordinat* **c. d'adressage** address capability; **c. de disque/disquette** disk capacity; **c. de mémoire** memory capacity; **c. de stockage** storage capacity; **c. de traitement** throughput
❑ **capacités** NFPL ability; **utiliser au mieux les capacités de qn** to make the best use of sb's ability; **un élève ayant des capacités mais paresseux** a pupil with ability but inclined to be lazy; **ses capacités d'organisateur** his/her abilities as an organizer; **capacités intellectuelles** intellectual capacity

capacitif, -ive [kapasitif, -iv] ADJ *Élec* capacitive

caparaçon [kaparasɔ̃] NM caparison

caparaçonner [3] [kaparasɔne] VT **1** *(cheval)* to caparison **2** *(protéger)* to cover from top to bottom
▸**se caparaçonner** VPR to deck oneself out, to bedeck oneself

cape [kap] NF **1** *(pèlerine)* cloak, cape; *Littéraire* **quitter la c. pour l'épée** to give up the gown for the sword
2 *(d'un cigare)* wrapper, outer leaf
3 *(de torero)* capa
4 *Naut* **être à la c.** to lie to; **mettre à la c.** to heave to
❑ **de cape et d'épée** ADJ swashbuckling; **une histoire/un film de c. et d'épée** a swashbuckler, a swashbuckling story/film
❑ **sous cape** ADV **rire sous c.** to laugh up one's sleeve

capéer [15] [kapee] = **capeyer**

capelage [kaplaʒ] NM *Naut (action)* rigging; *(partie du mât)* masthead; *(support)* hounds

capelan [kaplɑ̃] NM *Ich* capelin, poor cod

capeler [24] [kaple] VT *Naut* **1** *(cordage)* to reeve **2** *(vague)* **c. une lame par l'avant** to take a wave head-on

capelet [kaplɛ] NM *Vét* capped hock

capeline [kaplin] NF wide-brimmed hat, capeline

capella [kapela] *voir* **a cappella**

caper [3] [kape] VT **1** *Sport* to cap **2** *(cigare)* to wrap

CAPES, Capes [kapɛs] NM *Univ (abrév* **certificat d'aptitude au professorat de l'enseignement du second degré**) = secondary school teaching qualification, *Br* ≃ PGCE

> *Culture*
> **CAPES**
> This is a required qualification for state teachers in France. Candidates who pass this competitive exam become "professeurs certifiés" and are entitled to teach in secondary education.

capésien, -enne [kapesjɛ̃, -ɛn] NM,F *Univ* **1** *(étudiant)* student preparing to take the "CAPES" **2** *(diplômé)* holder of the "CAPES"

Cap-Est [kapɛst] NM Eastern Cape

CAPET, Capet[1] [kapɛt] NM *Univ (abrév* **certificat d'aptitude au professorat de l'enseignement technique**) = secondary school teaching qualification for technical subjects

Capet[2] [kapɛ] NPR **Hugues C.** Hugues Capet

capet [kapɛ] NM *Suisse (de berger)* shepherd's cap

capétien[1], **-enne**[1] [kapesjɛ̃, -ɛn] *Hist* ADJ Capetian *(dynasty of French kings, 987–1328)*
❑ **Capétien, -enne** NM,F Capetian

capétien[2], **-enne**[2] [kapetjɛ̃, -ɛn] NM,F *Univ* **1** *(étudiant)* student preparing to take the CAPET **2** *(diplômé)* holder of the CAPET

capeyer [12] [kapeje] VI *Naut* to lie to

capharnaüm [kafarnaɔm] NM *(chaos)* shambles *(singulier)*; **leur maison est un vrai c.** their house is a real shambles; **je n'y retrouve rien, dans ce c.!** I can't find a thing in all this clutter!

cap-hornier [kapɔrnje] *(pl* **cap-horniers**) NM *Naut (marin)* sailor who has travelled the Cape Horn route, Cape Horner; *(navire)* ship that has sailed the Cape Horn route, Cape Horner

capillaire [kapilɛr] ADJ *Biol* **1** *(relatif aux cheveux)* hair *(avant n)* **2** *(très fin → tube, vaisseau)* capillary *(avant n)*
NM **1** *Biol (vaisseau)* capillary **2** *Biol (tube)* capillary (tube) **3** *Bot* maidenhair (fern)

capillarite [kapilarit] NF *Méd* capillaritis

capillarité [kapilarite] *Physiol* NF capillarity, capillary action
❑ **par capillarité** ADV by *or* through capillary action

capilliculteur, -trice [kapilikyltœr, -tris] NM,F *Hum* hairdresser

capilliculture [kapilikyltyr] NF hair care

capillicultrice [kapilikyltris] *voir* **capilliculteur**

capilotade [kapilɔtad] **en capilotade** ADJ *(écrasé)* in a pulp; *(fatigué et douloureux)* aching; **j'ai les jambes en c.** my legs are aching; **mettre qch en c.** *(en morceaux)* to smash sth to pieces *or* to smithereens; **une infection lui a mis le genou en c.** his/her knee flared up because of an infection; *Fig* **la démocratie dans ce pays est en c.** democracy in this country is in ruins *or* tatters

capitaine [kapitɛn] NM **1** *Naut (dans la marine marchande)* captain, master; *(dans la navigation de plaisance)* captain, skipper; **oui, mon c.** yes, sir; *Mil* **c. de corvette** ≃ lieutenant commander; *Mil* **c. de frégate** ≃ commander; *Naut* **c. au long cours** master mariner; *Admin & Naut* **c. de port** harbour master; *Mil* **c. de vaisseau** ≃ captain
2 *Mil (dans l'armée → de terre)* captain; *(→ de l'air) Br* ≃ flight lieutenant, *Am* ≃ captain; *Littéraire* leader of men, military commander; **c. de gendarmerie** = captain of the "gendarmerie"; **les capitaines d'industrie** the captains of industry
3 *Sport* captain
4 c. des pompiers *Br* chief fire officer, *Am* fire chief
5 *Ich* threadfin

capitaine-commandant NM *Belg Mil (dans l'armée de terre)* = rank between major and captain; *(dans l'armée de l'air)* = rank between *Br* squadron leader and flight lieutenant *or Am* major and captain

capitainerie [kapitɛnri] NF *Naut* harbour master's office

capital[1], **-e, -aux**[1], **-ales** [kapital, -o] ADJ **1** *(détail)* vital; *(question, aide)* fundamental, crucial, vital; *(témoignage)* vital, crucial; *(argument, point)* fundamental; **c'est c.** it's essential *or* crucial; **c'est d'une importance capitale** it's of the utmost importance; **n'en fais pas une affaire capitale!** don't blow it up out of all proportion!; **il est c. que nous prenions des mesures** it is absolutely essential that we take action
2 *(œuvre, projet)* major
3 *(lettre → imprimée)* capital; *(→ manuscrite)* (block) capital
4 *Jur (crime, sentence)* capital; *Jur* **la peine capitale** capital punishment, the death penalty
❑ **capitale** NF **1** *Admin (ville)* capital (city); **la capitale** *(Paris)* the capital, Paris; **capitale régionale** regional capital; **la capitale des Gaules** = the city of Lyons; *Fig* **la capitale de la mode** the fashion capital
2 *Typ* capital (letter); **petite capitale** small capital
❑ **en capitales** ADV *Typ* in capitals, in block letters; **écrivez votre nom en capitales (d'imprimerie)** write your name in block capitals, print your name

capital[2], **-aux**[2] [kapital, -o] NM **1** *Écon & Fin (avoir → personnel)* capital *(UNCOUNT)*; *(→ d'une société)* capital *(UNCOUNT)*, assets; **une société au c. de 500 000 euros** a firm with assets of 500,000 euros; **il détient 5 pour cent du c. de la société** he has a 5 percent shareholding in the company, he holds 5 percent of the company's shares; **c. actions** share capital, equity (capital); **c. appelé** called-up capital; **c. d'apport** initial capital; **c. autorisé** authorized (share) capital; **c. circulant** circulating *or* floating capital; **c. déclaré** registered capital; **c. de départ** start-up capital; **c. disponible** available capital; *Bourse* **c. émis** issued capital; **c. d'emprunt** loan capital; **c. engagé** tied-up capital, capital employed; **c. d'établissement** invested capital; *Compta* **c. exigible** current liabilities; **c. existant** physical capital; **c. d'exploitation** *Br* working capital, *Am* operating capital; **c. financier** finance capital; **c. fixe** fixed *or* capital assets; **c. foncier** land; **c. humain** *(d'une entreprise)* manpower; **c. improductif** idle capital, unproductive capital; **c. initial** start-up capital; **capitaux investis** invested capital; **c. libéré** fully paid capital; **c. nominal** nominal capital; **c. d'origine** original capital; **c. réel** paid-up capital; **c. roulant** circulating capital; **c. de roulement** *Br* working capital, *Am* operating capital; *Bourse* **c. social** share capital; *Bourse* **c. social autorisé** authorized capital; **c. souscrit** subscribed capital; **c. technique** (technical) equipment; **c. variable** variable capital; **c. versé** paid-up capital
2 *(compensation)* **c. décès** death benefit; **c. départ** severance money *or* pay
3 *(monde de l'argent, des capitalistes)* **le c.** capital; **le grand c.** big business
4 *(ressources, accumulation)* **ces jeunes diplômés représentent un véritable c. pour notre entreprise** these qualified young people are an asset to our company; **notre c. de confiance auprès des usagers** the stock of goodwill we have built up among users; **un c. de connaissances** a fund of knowledge; **le c. culturel du pays** the nation's cultural wealth; **le c. intellectuel** intellectual resources; **le c. forêt de la planète** the forest reserves of the planet; **n'entamez pas votre c. santé** don't overtax your health
❑ **capitaux** NMPL *Écon & Fin (valeurs disponibles)* capital; **circulation des capitaux** circulation of capital; **fuite des capitaux** flight of capital; **capitaux flottants** floating capital; **capitaux fébriles** hot money; **capitaux frais** new capital; **capitaux gelés** frozen assets; **capitaux permanents** capital employed, long-term capital; **capitaux propres** equity, shareholders' equity *or* funds

'Le Capital' *Marx* 'Das Kapital' *or* 'Capital'

capital-développement [kapitaldevlɔpmɑ̃] NM *Fin* development capital

capitalisable [kapitalizabl] ADJ *Fin* capitalizable

capitalisation [kapitalizasjɔ̃] NF *Fin* capitalization; **c. boursière** market capitalization

capitaliser [3] [kapitalize] VT **1** *Fin (capital)* to capitalize; *(intérêts)* to add; *(revenu)* to turn into capital; **une fois que les intérêts ont été capitalisés** once the accrued interest has been calculated

2 *(amasser → argent)* to save up, to accumulate **3** *(accumuler)* to accumulate; **c. des heures supplémentaires** to accrue *or* to accumulate overtime; **c. des connaissances** to accumulate knowledge
VI *(économiser)* to save
❏ **capitaliser sur VT IND** *Fam (tirer profit de)* to capitalize on ▪

capitalisme [kapitalism] **NM** *Écon* capitalism; **c. de copinage** crony capitalism; **c. d'État** state capitalism; **c. monopolistique d'État** state monopoly capitalism; **c. sauvage** ruthless capitalism

capitaliste [kapitalist] **ADJ** *Écon* capitalist, capitalistic
NMF capitalist

capitalistique [kapitalistik] **ADJ** *Fin* capital-intensive

capital-marque [kapitalmark] *(pl* **capitaux-marques)** **NM** *Com* brand equity

capital-risque [kapitalrisk] *(pl* **capitaux-risques)** **NM** *Fin* venture *or* risk capital

capital-risqueur [kapitalriskœr] *(pl* **capitaux-risqueurs)** **NM** *Fin* venture capitalist

capitan [kapitɑ̃] **NM** *Littéraire & Vieilli* swashbuckler, braggadocio; **faire le c.** to swagger, to bluster

capitation [kapitasjɔ̃] **NF** *Hist & Fin* capitation, poll tax

capite [kapit] **NF** *Suisse (dans un vignoble, dans un jardin)* shed

capiteux, -euse [kapitø, -øz] **ADJ 1** *(fort → alcool, senteur)* heady **2** *(excitant → charme, blonde)* sensuous

Capitole [kapitɔl] **NM 1** *(à Toulouse)* **le C.** = main square in Toulouse **2** *(à Rome)* **le C.** the Capitol **3** *(à Washington)* **le C.** Capitol Hill, the Capitol

capitolin, -e [kapitɔlɛ̃, -in] **ADJ** *Antiq* Capitoline
❏ **Capitolin** *voir* **mont**

capiton [kapitɔ̃] **NM 1** *(matériau)* padding **2** *(section rembourrée)* boss, padded section **3** *Méd* subcutaneous fat

capitonnage [kapitɔnaʒ] **NM** padding

capitonner [3] [kapitɔne] **VT** to pad

capitoul [kapitul] **NM** *Hist* municipal magistrate *(of Toulouse)*

capitulaire [kapitylɛr] **ADJ** *Rel* capitular; **salle c.** chapter house
NM *Jur & Hist* capitulary

capitulard, -e [kapitylar, -ard] *Péj* **ADJ** defeatist
NM,F defeatist; **espèce de c.!** you quitter!, you defeatist!

capitulation [kapitylasjɔ̃] **NF 1** *Mil (action)* surrender, capitulation; *(traité)* capitulation; **c. sans conditions** unconditional surrender **2** *Fig (fait de céder)* surrendering

capitule [kapityl] **NM** *Bot* capitulum

capituler [3] [kapityle] **VI 1** *Mil* to surrender, to capitulate **2** *Fig (céder)* to surrender, to give in

caplan [kaplɑ̃] **NM** /ch **c. de Terre-Neuve** caplin

Cap-Nord [kapnɔr] **NM** Northern Cape

capodastre [kapodastr] **NM** *Mus* capo (tasto)

capon, -onne [kapɔ̃, -ɔn] *Fam Vieilli* **ADJ** cowardly ▪, yellow
NM,F coward ▪

caponière, caponnière [kapɔnjɛr] **NF 1** *(refuge)* shelter, refuge **2** *Archit & Mil* caponier(e); *Mil* **en c.** in a masked flanking emplacement

caporal, -aux [kapɔral, -o] **NM 1** *Mil (dans l'armée de terre)* Br ≃ lance corporal, Am ≃ private first class; **c. d'ordinaire** mess corporal **2** *Mil (dans l'armée de l'air)* Br ≃ senior aircraftman, Am ≃ airman first class **3** *(tabac)* Caporal tobacco **4** *Hist* **le Petit C.** = nickname used to refer to Napoleon Bonaparte

🎬 **'Le Caporal épinglé'** *Renoir* 'The Elusive Corporal'

caporal-chef [kapɔralʃɛf] *(pl* **caporaux-chefs** [kapɔroʃɛf])** **NM** *Mil (dans l'armée de terre)* ≃ corporal; *(dans l'armée de l'air)* Br ≃ corporal, Am ≃ senior airman

caporaliser [3] [kapɔralize] **VT** to set petty rules for

caporalisme [kapɔralism] **NM 1** *(autoritarisme)* petty officiousness, bossiness **2** *(régime politique)* military rule

capot [kapo] **NM 1** *Aut Br* bonnet, *Am* hood **2** *Naut (bâche)* tarpaulin; *(tôle)* cover; *(ouverture)* companion hatchway **3** *(d'une machine)* hood; *Ordinat* **c. d'imprimante** printer hood **4** *Can Vieilli (manteau)* loose woollen coat; *Fig* **virer** *ou* **changer son c. (de bord)** to switch allegiances; *Fam* **en avoir plein le c.** to be fed up, to have had it up to here
ADJ INV *Cartes* **être c.** to have made no tricks at all

capotage [kapɔtaʒ] **NM 1** *(d'une machine, d'un moteur)* hooding **2** *(culbute → d'une voiture)* overturning; *(→ d'un bateau)* capsizing

capote [kapɔt] **NF 1** *Fam (préservatif)* condom ▪, rubber; *Vieilli* **c. anglaise** condom ▪, *Br* French letter **2** *Aut (d'une voiture) Br* hood, *Am* top **3** *(manteau)* greatcoat **4** *(chapeau)* bonnet

capoté, -e [kapɔte] *Can Fam* **ADJ** crazy
NM,F wacko

capoter [3] [kapɔte] **VT** to fit with a hood
VI 1 *(voiture)* to overturn, to roll over; *(bateau)* to capsize, to turn turtle **2** *Fam (projet)* to fall through ▪, to collapse ▪; *(transaction)* to fall through ▪; **il a tout fait c.** he messed everything up; **leur veto a fait c. la négociation** their veto overturned *or* upset the negotiation process ▪; **son entêtement va faire c. le projet** his/her obstinacy is going to ruin the project **3** *Can Fam (perdre la tête)* to flip, to lose it; **c. sur qch/qn** to go mad for sth/sb

Capoue [kapu] **NM** Capua

Cap-Ouest [kapwɛst] **NM** Western Cape

cappa [kapa] **NF INV** *Rel* cope

Cappadoce [kapadɔs] **NF la C.** Cappadocia

cappadocien, -enne [kapadɔsjɛ̃, -jɛn] **ADJ** Cappadocian
❏ **Cappadocien, -enne NM,F** Cappadocian

cappa magna [kapamagna] **NF INV** *Rel* cope

cappella [kapɛla] *voir* **a cappella**

cappuccino [kaputʃino] **NM** cappuccino

câpre [kapr] **NF** caper

capricant, -e [kaprikɑ̃] **ADJ 1** *Méd (pouls)* caprizant **2** *Littéraire* bounding, leaping

capriccio [kapritʃjo] **NM** *Mus* capriccio

caprice [kapris] **NM 1** *(fantaisie)* whim, passing fancy; **elle lui passe tous ses caprices** she indulges his/her every whim; **rien n'est réfléchi, il n'agit que par c.** he doesn't think things through, he just acts on impulse; **par un c. du destin** by a whim of fate; **les caprices de la mode** the vagaries of fashion
2 *(colère)* tantrum; **faire des caprices** to throw tantrums; **elle n'a pas mal, c'est un c.** she's not in pain, she's just being awkward *or* difficult
3 *(irrégularité)* **c'est un véritable c. de la nature** it's a real freak of nature
4 *(engouement)* (sudden) infatuation
5 *Mus* capriccio, caprice

capricieuse [kaprisjøz] *voir* **capricieux**

capricieusement [kaprisjøzmɑ̃] **ADV** capriciously

capricieux, -euse [kaprisjø, -øz] **ADJ 1** *(coléreux)* temperamental; **un enfant c.** an awkward child **2** *(fantaisiste)* capricious, fickle; *Fig (ruisseau)* meandering; **le vol c. d'un papillon** the flitting of a butterfly **3** *(peu fiable → machine, véhicule)* unreliable, temperamental; *(→ saison, temps)* unpredictable
NM,F capricious person; **un petit c.** a spoilt child

Capricorne [kaprikɔrn] **NM 1** *Astron* Capricorn **2** *Astrol* Capricorn; **être C.** to be Capricorn *or* a Capricornean

capricorne [kaprikɔrn] **NM 1** *Entom* capricorn beetle **2** *Zool* serow

câprier [kaprije] **NM** *Bot* caper (plant)

caprification [kaprifikasjɔ̃] **NF** *Hort* caprification

caprifoliacée [kaprifɔljase] *Bot* **NF** caprifoil
❏ **caprifoliacées NFPL** Caprifoliaceae

caprin¹, -e [kaprɛ̃, -in] **ADJ** *Zool* goat *(avant n)*, *Spéc* caprine

caprin², -e [kaprɛ̃], **capriné** [kaprine] *Zool* **NM** member of the goat family
❏ **caprins NMPL** Capra, Caprinae

caprique [kaprik] **ADJ** *Chim* capric

caprolactame [kaprɔlaktam] **NM** *Chim* caprolactam

capron [kaprɔ̃] **NM** *Bot* hautboy *or* hautbois strawberry

caprylique [kaprilik] **ADJ** *Chim* caprylic

capsage [kapsaʒ] **NM** *Tech* straight-laying

capselle [kapsɛl] **NF** *Bot* cassweed, shepherd's purse

capside [kapsid] **NF** *Biol* capsid

capsien, -enne [kapsjɛ̃, -jɛn] **ADJ** *Archéol* Capsian

capsulage [kapsylaʒ] **NM 1** *(de bouteilles)* capping **2** *Pharm* encapsulation

capsulaire [kapsylɛr] **ADJ** *Bot* capsular

capsule [kapsyl] **NF 1** *(d'une bouteille)* top, cap **2** *Astron* **c. (spatiale)** (space) capsule **3** *Mil* cap, primer **4** *Pharm* capsule **5** *Bot* capsule **6** *Anat* capsule; **c. interne** internal capsule; **capsules surrénales** adrenal *or* suprarenal gland **7** *Chim* dish

capsule-congé [kapsylkɔ̃ʒe] *(pl* **capsules-congés)** **NF** = proof of duty paid on wine *or* spirits in the form of a cap placed on a bottle

capsuler [3] [kapsyle] **VT** *(des bouteilles)* to put a cap *or* top on

captage [kaptaʒ] **NM 1** *Rad & Tél* picking up, receiving **2** *Phys* harnessing **3** *Élec (du courant)* picking up **4** *(des eaux)* catchment; *(d'une source)* tapping **5** *Mines* **c. de grisou** degassing

captateur, -trice [kaptatœr, -tris] **NM,F** *Jur* inveigler; **c. de succession** legacy *or* inheritance hunter

captatif, -ive [kaptatif, -iv] **ADJ** *Psy* attention-seeking

captation [kaptasjɔ̃] **NF 1** *Jur* inveiglement **2** *Élec (d'une source, d'un courant)* harnessing

captative [kaptativ] *voir* **captatif**

captatoire [kaptatwar] **ADJ** *Jur* inveigling

captatrice [kaptatris] *voir* **captateur**

capté, -e [kapte] **NM,F** victim of inveiglement

capter [3] [kapte] **VT 1** *(attention, intérêt)* to capture **2** *Phys* to harness **3** *(eaux)* to collect, to catch; *(source)* to tap **4** *Rad & Tél* to pick up, to receive **5** *Élec (du courant)* to pick up **6** *Jur* to inveigle **7** *Fam (comprendre)* to get; **répète, j'ai pas capté** say that again, I didn't get it

capte-suies [kaptsɥi] **NM INV** extractor (fan)

capteur [kaptœr] **NM 1** *Écol* **c. (solaire)** solar panel **2** *(pour mesurer)* sensor; *(pour commander)* probe; *Ordinat* **c. photosensible** photosensitive *or* light-sensitive sensor

captieux, -euse [kapsjø, -øz] **ADJ** *Littéraire* specious, misleading

captif, -ive [kaptif, -iv] **ADJ 1** *(emprisonné)* captive; *Fig Littéraire* **être c. de son propre plaisir** to be a slave to pleasure **2** *Écon (marché)* captive **3** *(ballon)* captive
NM,F *Littéraire* captive

captivant, -e [kaptivɑ̃, -ɑ̃t] **ADJ** *(personne)* captivating; *(spectacle, livre, histoire)* captivating, enthralling, riveting

captive [kaptiv] *voir* **captif**

captiver [3] [kaptive] **VT** *(personne)* to captivate; *(spectacle, livre, histoire)* to captivate, to enthral

captivité [kaptivite] **NF** captivity; **vivre en c.** to be in captivity; **garder un animal en c.** to keep an animal in captivity

capture [kaptyr] **NF 1** *(de biens)* seizure, seizing, confiscation; *(d'un navire, d'un tank)* capture **2** *(arrestation)* capture; **après sa c., il a déclaré...** after he was captured *or* caught, he said... **3** *Chasse & Pêche* catching **4** *(biens ou animaux capturés)* catch, haul **5** *Géog & Phys* capture **6** *Ordinat* **c. d'écran** screen capture, screen dump, screen shot; **c. vidéo** video capture

capturer [3] [kaptyre] **VT 1** *(faire prisonnier)* to capture, to catch **2** *Chasse & Pêche* to catch **3** *(navire, tank)* to capture **4** *Ordinat* to capture

capuche [kapyʃ] **NF** hood; **c. en plastique** rain hood; **une veste/un haut à c.** a hooded jacket/top

capuchon [kapyʃɔ̃] **NM 1** *(bonnet)* hood; *(manteau)* hooded coat; *(de moine)* cowl **2** *(d'un stylo)* cap, top; *(d'un tube de dentifrice)* top **3** *(d'une cheminée)* cowl **4** *Zool* hood
❏ **à capuchon ADJ** hooded

capuchonné, -e [kapyʃɔne] **ADJ** hooded

capucin, -e [kapysɛ̃, -in] **NM,F** *Rel* Capuchin (Friar), *f* Capuchin nun; **les capucins** the Capuchins

NM 1 *Zool* capuchin (monkey) **2** *Chasse* hare, puss **3** *Orn* mannikin

□ **capucine ADJ INV** *(couleur)* orangey-red **NF 1** *Bot* nasturtium **2** *(danse)* (children's) round

capucinade [kapysinad] **NF** *Littéraire & Vieilli* dull sermon *or* lecture

capverdien, -enne [kapvɛrdjɛ̃, -ɛn] **ADJ** Cape Verdean

□ **Capverdien, -enne NM,F** Cape Verdean

Cap-Vert [kapvɛr] **NM le C.** Cape Verde; **au C.** in Cape Verde

capybara [kapibara] **NM** *Zool* capybara

caque [kak] **NF** herring barrel; *Prov* **la c. sent toujours le hareng** what is bred in the bone will come out in the flesh

caquelon [kaklɔ̃] **NM** *Culin* fondue pot

caquer [3] [kake] **VT 1** *(harengs)* to cure and barrel **2** *(poudre)* to barrel

caquet [kakɛ] **NM 1** *(gloussement)* cackle, cackling *(UNCOUNT)* **2** *Fam (bavardage)* yakking *(UNCOUNT)*; **il a un de ces caquets!** he yaks on and on!; **rabattre** *ou* **rabaisser le c. à qn** to take sb down a peg or two, to put sb in his/her place

caquetage [kaktaʒ], **caquètement** [kakɛtmɑ̃] **NM 1** *(de poules)* cackle, cackling *(UNCOUNT)* **2** *Fam (bavardage → futile)* prattle *(UNCOUNT)*; *(→ indiscret)* gossip *(UNCOUNT)*

caquetant, -e [kaktɑ̃, -ɑ̃t] **ADJ** cackling

caqueter [27] [kakte] **VI 1** *(poule)* to cackle **2** *(tenir des propos → futiles)* to prattle (on); *(→ indiscrets)* to gossip

car[1] [kar] **NM 1** *(autobus)* bus, *Br* coach; **c. de police** police van; **c. de ramassage (scolaire)** school bus **2** *TV & Rad* **c. régie** mobile unit, *Br* outside broadcasting van, OB van; **c. de reportage** mobile unit, *Br* outside broadcast *or* OB van; **c. de transmission** transmitter van **3** *TV* **c. monocaméra** single-camera unit; **c. multicaméra** multi-camera unit

car[2] [kar] **CONJ** because, for; **il est efficace, c. très bien secondé** he is efficient because he has very good back-up; **c. voyez-vous, je n'ai jamais pu me résoudre à…** (for *or* because) you see, I have never been able to bring myself to…; **c. enfin, à quoi vous attendiez-vous?** I mean, what did you expect?

carabe [karab] **NM** *Entom* ground beetle

carabidé [karabide] *Entom* **NM** ground beetle, *Spéc* carabid

□ **carabidés NMPL** Carabidae

carabin [karabɛ̃] **NM** *Fam Arg scol (étudiant en médecine)* medic

carabine [karabin] **NF** *Mil, Chasse & Sport* rifle; **c. à air comprimé** air rifle *or* gun

carabiné, -e [karabine] **ADJ** *Fam (note à payer, addition)* stiff, steep; *(rhume)* filthy, stinking; *(migraine)* blinding; *(fièvre)* violent, raging; **une grippe carabinée** a dreadful dose of the flu; **j'ai une gueule de bois carabinée** I've got one hell of a hangover

carabinier [karabinje] **NM 1** *(en Italie)* carabiniere, policeman **2** *(en Espagne)* carabinero, customs officer **3** *Hist & Mil* carabineer, carabinier **4** *(locution)* **il arrive toujours comme les carabiniers** he always turns up too late

carabistouille [karabistuj] **NF** *Belg Fam* **raconter des carabistouilles** to talk nonsense

Carabosse [karabɔs] *voir* **fée**

caracal, -als [karakal] **NM** *Zool* caracal, Persian lynx

Caracas [karakas] **NM** Caracas

caraco [karako] **NM** camisole

caracole [karakɔl] **NF** *Équitation & Archit* caracole; **escalier en c.** spiral staircase, caracole

caracoler [3] [karakɔle] **VI 1** *(sautiller)* to skip about, to gambol **2** *Équitation* to caracole **3** *Fig* **c. en tête** to be top dog, to be top of the league; **ils caracolent en tête du hit-parade** they're way up there *or* they're riding high at the top of the charts

caractère [karaktɛr] **NM 1** *(nature)* character, nature, temperament; **ce n'est pas dans son c. d'être agressif** it's out of character for him to be *or* it's not in his nature to be aggressive

2 *(tempérament)* temper; **quel c.!** what a temper!; *Fam* **quel fichu c.!** what a bad-tempered so-and-so!; **avoir bon c.** to be good-natured; **avoir mauvais** *ou* **(un) sale c.** to be bad-tempered; *Fam* **avoir un c. de chien** *ou* **de cochon** to have a foul temper

3 *(volonté, courage)* character; **avoir du c.** to have character; **elle manque de c.** she's not very strong-willed

4 *(type de personne)* character; **les caractères doux sont souvent mal compris** gentle people are often misunderstood

5 *(particularité)* nature, character; **le c. religieux de la cérémonie** the religious nature of the ceremony; **pour donner un c. d'authenticité à son œuvre** to give his/her work a stamp of authenticity; **une maladie sans c. de gravité** an illness not considered to be serious; **sa conversation a le c. d'une confession** he/she talks as if he/she were making a confession; **à c. officiel** of an official nature

6 *(trait)* characteristic, feature, trait; *(dans des statistiques)* characteristic; **tous les caractères d'une crise économique** all the characteristics of an economic crisis

7 *(originalité)* character; **un édifice qui a du c.** a building with character; **sans aucun c.** characterless

8 *Biol* character; **c. acquis** acquired trait *or* characteristic; **c. héréditaire** hereditary trait *or* characteristic

9 *Typ* character; **le choix des caractères** the choice of typeface; **en gros/petits caractères** in large/small print; **caractères étroits** condensed print; **en caractères étroits** in condensed print; **caractères gras** bold (type); **en caractères gras** in bold (type); **caractères d'imprimerie** block letters; **écrivez en caractères d'imprimerie** please write in block letters; **caractères romains** roman (type); **en caractères romains** in roman (type)

10 *Ordinat* character; **caractères par pouce** characters per inch; **caractères par seconde** characters per second; **caractères alphanumériques** alphanumeric characters; **c. de changement de ligne** line feed character; **c. de changement de page** page break character; **c. de contrôle** control character; **c. d'effacement** delete character; **c. imprimable** printable character; **c. d'interruption** break character; **c. joker** wildcard character; **c. majuscule** upper-case character; **c. minuscule** lower-case character; **c. en mode point** bit-mapped character, bitmap character; **c. de retour arrière** backspace character; **c. à sept bits** seven-bit character

□ **de caractère ADJ appartement/maison de c.** flat/house with character; **une femme de c.** a woman of character

caractériel, -elle [karakterjɛl] **ADJ 1** *(d'humeur changeante)* moody **2** *Psy (adolescent)* maladjusted, (emotionally) disturbed; *(troubles)* emotional **3** *(du caractère)* character *(avant n)*

NM,F *(enfant)* problem child; *(adulte)* maladjusted person

caractérisation [karakterizasjɔ̃] **NF** characterization

caractérisé, -e [karakterize] **ADJ** *(méchanceté)* blatant; *(indifférence)* pointed; **une rougeole caractérisée** a typical *or* clear *or* unmistakable case of measles

caractériser [3] [karakterize] **VT 1** *(constituer le caractère de)* to characterize; **avec la générosité qui le caractérise** with characteristic generosity; **qu'est-ce qui caractérise son art?** what are the main characteristics *or* features of his/her work?; **les symptômes qui caractérisent cette maladie** the characteristic symptoms of this illness **2** *(définir)* to characterize, to define

▸**se caractériser VPR se c. par** to be characterized by

caractéristique [karakteristik] **ADJ** characteristic, typical; **observez la rougeur c.** note the characteristic red hue; **c'est c. de sa façon d'agir** it's typical of his/her way of doing things

NF 1 *(trait)* characteristic, (distinguishing) feature *or* trait; **caractéristiques techniques** specifications **2** *Math* characteristic

caractérologie [karakterɔlɔʒi] **NF** characterology

caractérologique [karakterɔlɔʒik] **ADJ** characterological

caracul [karakyl] **NM** *Zool* caracul, karakul

carafe [karaf] **NF 1** *(récipient → ordinaire)* carafe; *(→ travaillé)* decanter **2** *(contenu)* jugful; *(de vin)* carafe; **une demi-c.** half a carafe (of wine) **3** *Fam (tête)* nut **4** *Fam (locution)* **rester** *ou* **tomber en c.** *(véhicule)* to break down■; *(voyageur)* to be stranded■

carafon [karafɔ̃] **NM 1** *(récipient → ordinaire)* small jug *or* carafe; *(→ travaillé)* small decanter **2** *(contenu)* (small) jugful; *(de vin)* small carafe **3** *Fam (tête)* nut; **il a rien dans le c.!** he's got nothing between his ears, *Br* he's as thick as two short planks, *Am* he's got rocks in his head

caraïbe [karaib] **ADJ** *(personne)* Caribbean

NM *(langue)* Carib

□ **Caraïbe NMF** Carib

□ **Caraïbe NF** *(chaîne montagneuse)* **la C.** the Caribbean

□ **Caraïbes NFPL les (îles) Caraïbes** the Caribbean, the West Indies; **la mer des Caraïbes** the Caribbean (Sea)

Caraïte [karait] **NM** *Rel* Karaite

carambolage [karɑ̃bɔlaʒ] **NM 1** *(de voitures)* pile-up, multiple crash **2** *(au billard) Br* cannon, *Am* carom

carambole [karɑ̃bɔl] **NF 1** *(boule)* red (billiard) ball **2** *Bot* star fruit, *Spéc* carambola

caramboler [3] [karɑ̃bɔle] **VI** *(au billard) Br* to cannon, *Am* to carom

VT to crash into; **onze voitures carambolées** an eleven-car pile-up

▸**se caramboler VPR dix voitures se sont carambolées sur l'autoroute** there has been a ten-car pile-up on the *Br* motorway *or Am* freeway

carambolier [karɑ̃bɔlje] **NM** *Bot* carambola (tree); **c. cylindrique** cucumber-tree

carambouillage [karɑ̃bujaʒ] **NM** fraudulent selling of goods bought on credit

carambouille [karɑ̃buj] **NF** fraudulent selling of goods bought on credit

carambouilleur, -euse [karɑ̃bujœr, -øz] **NM,F** swindler *(who fraudulently sells goods bought on credit)*

caramel [karamɛl] **NM 1** *(pour napper)* caramel **2** *(bonbon → dur)* toffee, caramel; *(→ mou)* toffee, fudge

ADJ INV caramel colour

caramélé, -e [karamele] **ADJ** *(aspect)* caramel-like; *(goût)* caramel-flavoured

caramélisation [karamelizasjɔ̃] **NF** caramelization

caramélisé, -e [karamelize] **ADJ** *(mets, sucre)* caramelized; *(glace)* caramel-flavoured

caraméliser [3] [karamelize] **VT 1** *(mets, moule)* to coat with caramel; *(glace)* to flavour with caramel **2** *(sucre)* to caramelize

VI to caramelize; **faire c. du sucre** to caramelize sugar

▸**se caraméliser VPR** *(sucre)* to caramelize; *(oignons)* to brown, to caramelize

carangue [karɑ̃g] **NF** *Ich* caranx

carapace [karapas] **NF 1** *Zool* shell, *Spéc* carapace **2** *Fig* shell; **il est difficile de percer sa c.** it's difficult to get through to him/her; **la voiture était recouverte d'une c. de boue** the car was encrusted with mud

carapater [3] [karapate] **se carapater VPR** *Fam* to skedaddle, to scram, to make oneself scarce; **c'est le moment de se c.!** it's time we made ourselves scarce!; **l'arrivée des flics les a fait se c.** they took to their heels when the cops arrived

caraque [karak] **ADJ porcelaine c.** fine Chinese porcelain

NF *Naut* carrack

carassin [karasɛ̃] **NM** *Ich* crucian carp; **c. doré** goldfish

carat [kara] **NM 1** *(d'un métal, d'une pierre)* carat; **chaîne de 22 carats** 22-carat (gold) chain; **or (à) 18 carats** 18-carat gold; **c. métrique** carat (weight); *Fam* **je te donne jusqu'à trois heures, dernier c.** I'll give you till three o'clock at the latest■ *or* tops **2** *Fam (année)* **il a dépassé les 60 carats** he's over 60■

Caravage [karavaʒ] **NPR** *Beaux-Arts* **le C.** Caravaggio; **un tableau du C.** a painting by Caravaggio

caravagesque [karavaʒɛsk] **ADJ** *Beaux-Arts* Caravaggist, of the Caravaggio school

caravagisme [karavaʒism] **NM** *Beaux-Arts* Caravaggism

caravagiste [karavaʒist] = **caravagesque**

caravanage [karavanaʒ] NM *Offic Br* caravanning, *Am* trailer camping; **faire du c.** *Br* to go caravanning, *Am* to go trailer camping

caravane [karavan] NF **1** (*véhicule → de vacancier*) *Br* caravan, *Am* trailer; (→ *de nomade*) caravan **2** (*convoi*) caravan; **la c. du Tour de France** the caravan following the Tour de France cyclists; **c. publicitaire** following vehicles

caravanier, -ère [karavanje, -ɛr] NM,F **1** (*nomade*) caravanner **2** (*vacancier*) *Br* caravanner, *Am* camper (*in a trailer*)
▸ ADJ **chemin c.** caravan route *or* track

caravaning [karavaniŋ] NM *Br* caravanning, *Am* trailer camping; **faire du c.** to go *Br* caravanning *or Am* trailer camping

caravansérail [karavãseraj] NM caravanserai, caravansary

Caravelle® [karavɛl] NF *Aviat* Caravelle®

caravelle [karavɛl] NF *Naut* caravel

carbamate [karbamat] NM *Chim* carbamate

carbamide [karbamid] NF *Chim* carbamide

carbamique [karbamik] ADJ *Chim* carbamic

carbet [karbɛ] NM *(aux Antilles et en Guyane)* hut

carbocation [karbɔkasjɔ̃] NM *Chim* carbocation

carbochimie [karbɔʃimi] NF organic chemistry

carbogène [karbɔʒɛn] NM **1** *Phys* seltzogene powder **2** *Pétr* carbogen

carbohémoglobine [karbɔemɔglɔbin] NF *Biol & Chim* carbohaemoglobin

carbonade [karbɔnad] NF *Culin* carbonade, carbonnade; **c. flamande** beef stew with beer

carbonado [karbɔnado] NM *Minér* carbonado

carbonarisme [karbɔnarism] NM *Hist & Pol* Carbonarism

carbonaro [karbɔnaro] NM *Hist & Pol* Carbonaro

carbonatation [karbɔnatasjɔ̃] NF *Chim* carbonatation

carbonate [karbɔnat] NM *Chim* carbonate

carbonaté, -e [karbɔnate] ADJ **1** *Géol (rocher)* carbonate **2** *Chim (eau)* carbonated

carbonater [3] [karbɔnate] VT *Chim* to carbonate

carbone [karbɔn] NM **1** *(papier)* carbon paper; *(feuille)* sheet of carbon paper **2** *Chim* carbon; *Archéol* **c. 14** carbon-14; **dater qch au c. 14** to carbon-date sth, to date sth with carbon-14 **3** *Écol* carbon; **bilan du c.** carbon balance; **émissions de c.** carbon emissions

carboné, -e [karbɔne] ADJ **1** *Chim* carbonaceous **2** *Minér* carboniferous

carbonifère [karbɔnifɛr] *Géol* ADJ carboniferous ▸ NM Carboniferous (period)

carbonique [karbɔnik] ADJ *Chim (acide)* carbonic

carbonisage [karbɔnizaʒ] NM *Tex* carbonizing

carbonisation [karbɔnizasjɔ̃] NF *Chim* carbonization

carboniser [3] [karbɔnize] VT **1** *(brûler → viande)* to burn to a cinder; (→ *édifice, forêt)* to burn to the ground; **des corps carbonisés** charred bodies **2** *Chim (transformer en charbon)* to carbonize, to turn into charcoal

carbonnade [karbɔnad] = **carbonade**

carbonyle [karbɔnil] NM *Chim* carbonyl

carbonylé, -e [karbɔnile] ADJ *Chim* carbonylic

carborane [karbɔran] NM *Chim* carborane

carborundum® [karbɔrɔ̃dɔm] NM *Chim* Carborundum®

carbosulfure [karbɔsylfyr] NM *Chim* carbon disulphide

carboxyhémoglobine [karbɔksiemɔglɔbin] NF *Biol & Chim* carboxyhaemoglobin

carboxylase [karbɔksilaz] NF *Biol* carboxylase

carboxyle [karbɔksil] NM *Chim* carboxyl

carboxylique [karbɔksilik] ADJ *Chim* carboxylic

carburant [karbyrã] ADJ M **mélange c.** mixture of air and *Br* petrol *or Am* gas ▸ NM fuel

carburateur [karbyratœr] NM *Tech* carburettor; **c. double corps** twin carburettor

carburation [karbyrasjɔ̃] NF **1** *Tech* carburation **2** *Métal* carburization, carburizing

carbure [karbyr] NM *Chim* carbide; **c. de calcium** calcium carbide

carburé, -e [karbyre] ADJ **1** *Métal* carburized **2** *Tech* carburetted

carburéacteur [karbyreaktœr] NM *Aviat* jet fuel

carburer [3] [karbyre] VT **1** *Aut* to carburate **2** *Métal* to carburize
▸ VI **1** *Aut* **le moteur carbure mal** the mixture is wrong **2** *Fam (aller vite)* **fais tes valises, et que ça carbure!** pack your bags, and be quick about it! **3** *Fam (travailler dur)* to work flat out; **alors, ça carbure?** are you working hard, then?▪ **4** *Fam (fonctionner)* **ça carbure?** how are things?; **il carbure au whisky/au café** whisky/coffee keeps him going

carburol [karbyrɔl] NM *Chim* gasohol, gazohol

carbylamine [karbilamin] NF *Chim* carbylamine

carcailler [3] [karkaje] VI *(caille)* to call

carcajou [karkaʒu] NM *Zool* wolverine

carcan [karkɑ̃] NM **1** *Hist (collier)* collar shackle; *Fig* **pris dans les règlements comme dans un c.** hemmed in by regulations **2** *(sujétion)* yoke, shackles; **pour moi, la famille est un c.** for me, the family is a bind; **le c. des horaires** scheduling constraints **3** *(pour bétail)* yoke

carcasse [karkas] NF **1** *(d'un animal)* carcass **2** *Fam Fig* **amène ta c.!** get yourself over here!; **promener** *ou* **traîner sa (vieille) c.** to drag oneself along **3** *(armature → d'un édifice, d'un bateau)* shell; (→ *d'un meuble)* carcass; (→ *d'un véhicule)* shell, body; (→ *d'un parapluie)* frame **4** *Élec* yoke ring **5** *Métal* casing, frame **6** *(d'un pneu)* carcass; **c. diagonale** cross-ply carcass; **c. radiale** radial-ply carcass; **pneu à c. diagonale/radiale** cross-ply/radial-ply tyre

---
Allusion

Tu trembles, carcasse
This expression relates to an anecdote about Henri de la Tour d'Auvergne, vicomte de Turenne (1611–75), a doughty warrior. In old age, still fighting, the vicomte felt himself tremble with fear, and addressed his body as if it were a disobedient servant: "You tremble, feeble frame, but you would tremble even harder if you knew where I am taking you." This spirited remark is used today, out of context, whenever one shivers, or a person near one shivers.

---

carcassonnais, -e [karkasɔnɛ, -ɛz] ADJ of/from Carcassonne
▫ **Carcassonnais, -e** NM,F = inhabitant of or person from Carcassonne

carcéral, -e, -aux, -ales [karseral, -o] ADJ prison *(avant n)*

carcinogène [karsinoʒɛn] *Méd* ADJ carcinogenic; **produit c.** carcinogen ▸ NM carcinogen

carcinogenèse [karsinoʒənɛz] NF *Méd* carcinogenesis

carcinoïde [karsinoid] *Méd* ADJ carcinoid ▸ NM carcinoid, carcinoid tumour

carcinologie [karsinɔlɔʒi] NF **1** *Ich (étude des crustacés)* carcinology **2** *Méd (étude du cancer)* oncology

carcinomateux, -euse [karsinomatø, -øz] ADJ *Méd* carcinomatous

carcinome [karsinom] NM *Méd* carcinoma; **c. glandulaire** glandular carcinoma

cardage [kardaʒ] NM *Tex* carding

cardamine [kardamin] NF *Bot* cardamine; **c. des prés** lady's smock, cuckoo flower

cardamome [kardamɔm] NF *Bot & Culin* cardamon, cardamum, cardamom

cardan [kardɑ̃] NM *Tech & Aut* **(joint de) c.** universal joint

carde [kard] NF **1** *Bot (d'une bette, d'un cardon)* leaf stalk **2** *Tex* card, carding brush

cardé [karde] NM *Tex* **1** *(fil)* carded yarn **2** *(étoffe)* carded cloth

carder [3] [karde] VT *Tex* to card

cardère [kardɛr] NF *Bot* teasel, fuller's teasel; **c. poilue** shepherd's rod

cardeur, -euse [kardœr, -øz] *Tex* NM,F carder, carding operator
▫ **cardeuse** NF carding machine

cardia [kardja] NM *Anat* cardia

cardial, -e, -aux, -ales [kardjal, -o] ADJ *Physiol* cardiac

cardialgie [kardjalʒi] NF *Méd* cardialgia

cardiaque [kardjak] ADJ heart *(avant n)*, cardiac; **une maladie c.** a heart disease; **elle est c.** she has a heart condition
▸ NMF cardiac *or* heart patient

cardigan [kardigɑ̃] NM cardigan

cardinal, -e, -aux, -ales [kardinal, -o] ADJ **1** *Astrol & Math* cardinal **2** *(essentiel)* essential, fundamental; **vertus cardinales** cardinal virtues **3** *Géog* **points cardinaux** points of the compass ▸ NM **1** *(apéritif)* = kir made with red wine **2** *Math* cardinal number, cardinal **3** *Rel* cardinal **4** *Orn* **c. (rouge)** cardinal

cardinalat [kardinala] NM *Rel* cardinalate, cardinalship

cardinalice [kardinalis] ADJ *Rel* of a cardinal

cardiogramme [kardjogram] NM *Méd* cardiogram

cardiographe [kardjograf] NM *Méd* cardiograph

cardiographie [kardjografi] NF *Méd* cardiography

cardioïde [kardioid] NF *Géom* cardioid

cardiologie [kardjolɔʒi] NF *Méd* cardiology

cardiologique [kardjolɔʒik] ADJ *Méd* cardiological

cardiologue [kardjolɔg] NMF *Méd* heart specialist, *Spéc* cardiologist

cardiomégalie [kardjomegali] NF *Méd* megalocardia, cardiomegaly

cardiomyopathie [kardjomjopati] NF *Méd* cardiomyopathy

cardiopathie [kardjopati] NF *Méd* heart disease, *Spéc* cardiopathy

cardio-pulmonaire [kardjopylmɔnɛr] *(pl* **cardio-pulmonaires**) ADJ *Méd* cardiopulmonary; **maladie c.** heart and lung disease

cardio-rénal, -e, -aux, -ales [kardjorenal, -o] ADJ *Méd* cardiorenal; **maladie cardio-rénale** heart and kidney disease

cardio-respiratoire [kardjorɛspiratwar] *(pl* **cardio-respiratoires**) ADJ *Méd* cardiorespiratory; **maladie c.** disease of the heart and respiratory system

cardiotomie [kardjotomi] NF *Méd* cardiotomy

cardiotonique [kardjotɔnik] *Pharm* ADJ cardiotonic ▸ NM cardiotonic

cardio-training [kardjotrɛniŋ] NM INV *Sport* cardio-training, CV training

cardio-vasculaire [kardjovaskylɛr] *(pl* **cardio-vasculaires**) ADJ *Méd* cardiovascular

cardite [kardit] NF *Méd* carditis

cardon [kardɔ̃] NM *Bot & Culin* cardoon

Carélie [kareli] NF **la C.** Karelia

carême [karɛm] NM **1** *Rel* **le c.** *(abstinence)* fasting; *(époque)* Lent; **faire c.** to fast for *or* to observe Lent; **face** *ou* **figure de c.** sad *or* long face **2** *(saison)* dry season *(in the West Indies)*

carême-prenant [karɛmprənɑ̃] *(pl* **carêmes-prenants**) NM *Arch* Shrovetide

carénage [karenaʒ] NM **1** *Naut (opération, lieu)* careenage **2** *Aviat & Aut* streamlined body

carence [karɑ̃s] NF **1** *Méd* deficiency; **c. en zinc** zinc deficiency; **avoir une c. alimentaire** to suffer from a nutritional deficiency **2** *(d'une administration, d'une œuvre, d'une méthode)* shortcoming, failing **3** *Psy* **c. affective** emotional deprivation **4** *Jur* insolvency
▫ **de carence, par carence** ADJ deficiency *(avant n)*

carencé, -e [karɑ̃se] ADJ **1** *Méd* suffering from a nutritional deficiency **2** *Psy* emotionally deprived

carencer [16] [karɑ̃se] VT *Méd* to cause a nutritional deficiency in

carène [karɛn] NF **1** *Naut* hull; **abattre un navire en c.** to careen a ship **2** *Aviat & Aut* streamlined body **3** *Bot & Orn* carina

caréner [18] [karene] VT **1** *Naut* to careen **2** *Aut & Aviat* to streamline

carentiel, -elle [karɑ̃sjɛl] ADJ *Méd* deficiency-related

caressant, -e [karɛsɑ̃, -ɑ̃t] ADJ **1** *(personne)* affectionate, loving; **un enfant c.** an affectionate child **2** *Littéraire (voix, sourire)* warm, caressing; *(vent)* caressing

caresse [karɛs] NF **1** *(attouchement)* caress, stroke; **faire des caresses à** *(chat)* to stroke; *(personne)* to caress **2** *Littéraire (d'un sourire)* tenderness; *(du vent, du soleil)* caress, kiss; **sous la c. du soleil** kissed by the sun

caresser [4] [karese] **VT 1** *(toucher → affectueuse-ment)* to stroke; *(→ sensuellement)* to caress; **c. un enfant** to pet a child; **le chat aime se faire c. derrière les oreilles** the cat likes being stroked behind the ears; **c. les cheveux de qn** to stroke sb's hair; *Fig* **c. qn des yeux** *ou* **du regard** to gaze lovingly at sb; **c. qn dans le sens du poil** to stroke sb's ego; **il faut le c. dans le sens du poil** don't rub him (up) the wrong way

2 *Littéraire (effleurer → tissu, papier)* to touch lightly; **c. les touches d'un piano** to tinkle away on the piano

3 *(avoir, former)* **c. le dessein de faire qch** to be intent on doing sth; **c. l'espoir de faire qch** to cherish the hope of doing sth; **c. le rêve de faire qch** to dream of doing sth

4 *Fam (battre)* **c. les oreilles à qn** to clout sb round the ear

▸**se caresser VPR 1** *(emploi réfléchi)* to caress oneself

2 *(emploi réciproque)* to cuddle

3 se c. qch to stroke sth

caret¹ [karɛ] **NM** *Zool (tortue à écailles)* hawksbill (turtle); *(caouanne)* loggerhead (turtle)

caret² [karɛ] **NM** *Naut & Tex* rope maker's reel; **fil de c.** rope yarn

carex [karɛks] **NM** *Bot* carex, sedge

car-ferry [karferi] *(pl* **car-ferrys** *ou* **car-ferries** [-ri]) **NM** ferry, car-ferry

cargaison [kargɛzɔ̃] **NF 1** *(marchandises)* cargo, freight **2** *Fam (quantité)* **load** *(de* of)

cargneule [karɲøl] **NF** *Minér* cellular dolomite

cargo [kargo] **NM** freighter; **c. mixte** cargo and passenger vessel

cargue [karg] **NF** *Naut (de voile)* brail

carguer [3] [karge] **VT** *Naut (voile)* to take in, to brail (up)

cari [kari] **NM 1** *(épice)* curry powder **2** *(plat)* curry □ **au cari** *ADJ* **poulet au c.** chicken curry, curried chicken

cariacou [karjaku] **NM** *Zool* Virginia deer

cariant, -e [karjã, -ãt] *ADJ* *Méd* cariogenic

cariatide [karjatid] = **caryatide**

caribe [karib] *ADJ (personne)* Caribbean □ **Caribe NMF** Carib

caribéen, -enne [karibeɛ̃, -ɛn] *ADJ* Caribbean **NM** Caribbean

caribou [karibu] **NM 1** *Zool* caribou, reindeer **2** *Can* = traditional Quebec drink of wine mixed with spirits

caricatural, -e, -aux, -ales [karikatyral, -o] *ADJ* **1** *(récit, explication)* distorted; **un féminisme c.** a mockery *or* travesty of feminism **2** *(visage)* grotesque **3** *(dessin, art)* caricatural *(exagéré)* typical, caricature *(avant n)*; **il a tout du vieux militaire c.** he's a typical old soldier

caricature [karikatyr] **NF 1** *(dessin)* caricature; **c. politique** (political) cartoon **2** *(déformation)* caricature; **c'est une c. de ce que j'ai dit** it makes a mockery of *or* it's a complete distortion of what I said **3** *(personne)* **c'est une vraie c.!** *(physiquement)* he/she looks grotesque!; *(dans son comportement)* he's/she's totally ridiculous!

caricaturer [3] [karikatyre] **VT 1** *(dessiner)* to caricature **2** *(déformer)* to distort

caricaturiste [karikatyrist] **NMF** caricaturist

caricole [karikɔl] **NF** *Belg Zool (mollusque)* periwinkle, winkle

CARICOM [karikɔm] **NF** *(abrév* **Communauté des Caraïbes)** CARICOM

carie [kari] **NF 1** *Méd* caries; **c. dentaire** tooth decay, *Spéc* dental caries; **elle n'a pas de caries** she doesn't have any bad teeth **2** *Bot (du blé)* bunt, smut; *(des arbres)* blight

carié, -e [karje] *ADJ* **1** *Méd (dent)* decayed, bad, *Spéc* carious; *(os)* decayed, *Spéc* carious **2** *Bot (blé)* smutty; *(arbre)* blighted

carier [10] [karje] *Méd* **VT** to decay, to cause decay in

▸**se carier VPR** to decay

carillon [karijɔ̃] **NM 1** *(cloches)* (set of) bells **2** *(sonnerie → d'une horloge)* chime; *(→ d'entrée)* chime; *(→ de cloches)* (peal of) bells; **on entendit un c. dans le lointain** bells could be heard ringing in the distance **3** *(horloge)* chiming clock

carillonné, -e [karijɔne] *ADJ* **fête carillonnée** high festival

carillonnement [karijɔnmã] **NM 1** *(action)* ringing **2** *(son)* chiming

carillonner [3] [karijɔne] **VI 1** *(cloches)* to ring, to chime; **c. à toute volée** to peal out; **on a fait c. les cloches pour la victoire** the bells were sounded in celebration of the victory **2** *(à la porte)* to ring (the doorbell) loudly

VT 1 *(heures)* to chime **2** *Péj (rumeur)* to broadcast, to shout from the roof tops **3** *(festival)* to announce with a peal of bells

carillonneur, -euse [karijɔnœr, -øz] **NM,F** bell ringer

carinate [karinat] **NM** *Orn* carinate

Carinthie [karɛ̃ti] **NF la C.** Carinthia

carioca [karjɔka] *ADJ* of/from Rio de Janeiro □ **Carioca NMF** Cariocan, Carioca

cariogène [karjɔʒɛn] *ADJ* *Méd* cariogenic

cariste [karist] **NM** forklift truck operator

caritatif, -ive [karitatif, -iv] *ADJ* charity *(avant n)*; **association caritative** charity

carlin [karlɛ̃] **NM** *(chien)* pug (dog)

carline [karlin] **NF** *Bot* carlina, carline; **c. vulgaire** carline thistle

carlingue [karlɛ̃g] **NF 1** *Aviat* cabin **2** *Naut* keelson

carlisme [karlism] **NM** *Hist & Pol* Carlism

carliste [karlist] *Pol* *ADJ* Carlist **NMF** Carlist

carmagnole [karmaɲɔl] **NF** *Hist (veste)* carmagnole □ **Carmagnole NF la C.** the Carmagnole *(song and dance popular during the French Revolution)*

carme [karm] **NM** *Rel* Carmelite, White Friar; **les carmes** the Carmelites

carmel [karmɛl] **NM** *Rel* **1** *(de carmélites)* carmel, Carmelite convent; *(de carmes)* carmel, Carmelite monastery **2** *(ordre)* **le c.** the Carmelite order

carmélite [karmelit] **NF** *Rel* Carmelite

carmin [karmɛ̃] *ADJ INV* crimson, carmine **NM** crimson, carmine; *Littéraire* **lèvres de c.** ruby lips

carminatif, -ive [karminatif, -iv] *ADJ* *Méd* carminative

carminé, -e [karmine] *ADJ* *Littéraire* crimson, carmine

Carnac [karnak] **NF** *(en Bretagne)* Carnac; **les alignements de C.** = lines of standing stones at Carnac **NM** *(en Égypte)* Karnak

carnage [karnaʒ] **NM 1** *(massacre)* slaughter, carnage; *Fig* **à l'examen, ça a été le c.!** they went down like ninepins in the exam!; **s'ils n'arrêtent pas, je fais un c.** if they don't stop, I'll kill them **2** *Can (en acadien)* din, loud noise

carnassier, -ère [karnasje, -ɛr] *ADJ (animal)* carnivorous; *(dent)* carnassial; *Fig (regard, sourire)* predatory **NM** carnivore □ **carnassière NF 1** *Zool (dent)* carnassial **2** *Chasse (sac)* game bag

carnation [karnasjɔ̃] **NF** *Littéraire (teint)* complexion; *(en peinture)* flesh tint

carnaval, -als [karnaval] **NM 1** *(fête)* carnival; **pendant le c.** during carnival, at carnival time **2** *(mannequin)* **(Sa Majesté) C.** King Carnival

🎵

'Le Carnaval des animaux' *Saint-Saëns* 'Carnival of the Animals'

carnavalesque [karnavalɛsk] *ADJ* **1** *(de carnaval)* carnival *(avant n)* **2** *(burlesque)* grotesque

Carnavalet [karnavalɛ] **NM** **le musée C.** = museum of Parisian history

carne [karn] **NF** *Fam* **1** *(viande)* tough meat **2** *Vieilli (cheval)* **(vieille) c.** old nag **3** *(terme d'injure)* swine; **petite c., va!** you little swine!; **vieille c.!** old bag!

carné, -e [karne] *ADJ* **1** *(en diététique)* meat-based **2** *(rosé)* flesh-toned, flesh-coloured

carneau, -x [karno] **NM** *Tech* flue

carnet [karnɛ] **NM 1** *(cahier)* notebook; **c. à dessins** sketchbook

2 *(registre) aussi Ordinat* **c. d'adresses** address book; *Douanes* **c. ATA** ATA carnet; **c. de bal** dance card; **c. de bord** logbook; *Belg* **c. de mariage** family record book *(in which dates of births and deaths are registered)*; **c. de route** logbook; **c. de santé** child's health record

3 *(à feuilles détachables)* **c. de chèques** cheque book; **c. à souches** counterfoil book; **c. de tickets (de métro)** = book of ten metro tickets; **c. de timbres** book of stamps

4 *Com* **c. de commandes** order book; **avoir un bon c. de commandes** to have a full order book; **c. de dépenses** account book

5 *Journ (rubrique)* **c. blanc** marriages column; **c. mondain** court and social; **c. rose** births column

6 *Scol* **c. de correspondance** = school report book; **c. de notes** *Br* school report, *Am* report card; **elle a eu un bon c. (de notes)** she got *Br* a good report *or Am* good grades

7 *Banque* **c. de banque** bank book, *Br* savings book; **c. de dépôt** deposit book; **c. de versements** paying-in book; *Belg & Suisse* **c. (d'épargne)** savings account

8 *Rad & TV* **c. d'écoute** = questionnaire in which a radio listener or TV viewer notes the programmes he or she has listened to or watched

carnier [karnje] **NM** *Chasse* game bag

carnification [karnifikasjɔ̃] **NF** *Méd* carnification

carnivore [karnivɔr] *ADJ* carnivorous **NM** carnivore, meat-eater □ **carnivores NMPL** carnivores, *Spéc* Carnivora

carnotzet, carnotset [karnotsɛt] **NM** *Suisse* = room set aside for drinking with friends, usually in a cellar

Carnutes [karnyt] **NMPL** *Hist* Carnutes

Caroline [karɔlin] **NF la C. du Nord/Sud** North/South Carolina; **en C. du Nord/Sud** in North/South Carolina

Carolines [karɔlin] **NFPL les (îles) C.** the Caroline Islands

carolingien, -enne [karɔlɛ̃ʒjɛ̃, -ɛn] *Hist* *ADJ* Carolingian *(dynasty of Frankish kings, 751–987)* □ **Carolingien, -enne NM,F** Carolingian

caroms [karɔm] **NM** = game in which a flat stone is used to knock smaller stones into the holes on a board

Caron [karɔ̃, karɔ] **NPR** *Myth* Charon

caronade [karɔnad] **NF** *(canon)* carronade

caroncule [karɔ̃kyl] **NF** *Anat, Bot & Orn* caruncle; *(de dindon)* wattle

carotène [karɔtɛn] **NM** *Biol & Chim* carotene, carotin

caroténoïde [karɔtenɔid] *Biol & Chim* *ADJ* carotenoid **NM** carotenoid

carotide [karɔtid] **NF** *Anat* carotid

carotidien, -enne [karɔtidjɛ̃, -ɛn] *ADJ* *Anat* carotid

carottage [karɔtaʒ] **NM 1** *Géol & Mines* core boring **2** *Fam (d'une somme)* pinching, *Br* nicking; *(d'une permission)* wangling; *(escroquerie)* swindling, diddling

carotte [karɔt] **NF 1** *Bot* carrot; *Fam* **les carottes sont cuites** the game's up; *Suisse* **c. rouge** beetroot; **c. sauvage** wild carrot

2 *Fam (récompense)* carrot; **la c. et le bâton** the carrot and the stick

3 *Géol & Mines* core

4 *(tabac)* plug

5 *(enseigne)* tobacconist's sign

6 *Fam Vieilli* **tirer une c. à qn** to swindle *or* to diddle sb

ADJ INV **(rouge) c.** red, carrot-coloured, *Péj* carroty

carotter [3] [karɔte] **VT** *très Fam* **1** *(argent, objet)* to pinch, *Br* to nick; *(permission)* to wangle; **c. qch à qn** to swindle *or* to diddle sb out of sth; **elle s'est fait c. une grosse somme par un prétendu assureur** she got diddled out of a lot of money by a bogus insurance agent **2** *Géol & Mines* to take a core (sample) of

carotteur, -euse¹ [karɔtœr, -øz] **NM,F** *Fam (escroc)* crook

carotteuse² [karɔtøz] **NF** core drill

carottier¹, -ère [karɔtje, -ɛr] = **carotteur, -euse**

carottier² [karɔtje] **NM** core drill

caroube [karub] **NF** *Bot* carob

caroubier [karubje] **NM** *Bot* carob (tree)

carouge¹ [karuʒ] **NF** *Bot* carob

carouge² [karuʒ] **NM** *Orn* cowbird; **c. à épaulettes rouges** redwing

carpaccio [karpatʃjo] **NM** *Culin* carpaccio

Carpates [karpat] **NFPL les C.** the Carpathian

Mountains, the Carpathians; **dans les C.** in the Carpathians

carpatique [karpatik] ADJ Carpathian

carpe¹ [karp] NF Ich carp

carpe² [karp] NM Anat carpus

carpeau, -x [karpo] NM Ich young carp

carpelle [karpɛl] NM Bot carpel

Carpentras [karpɑ̃tra(s)] NM = town in Southern France where a Jewish cemetery was vandalized in 1990, causing a public outcry

carpetbagger [karpɛtbagœr] NM Hist carpetbagger

carpette [karpɛt] NF 1 (petit tapis) (small) rug 2 Fam Péj (personne) doormat; **s'aplatir** ou **être (plat) comme une c. devant qn** to grovel in front of sb

carpiculture [karpikyltyr] NF carp farming

carpien, -enne [karpjɛ̃, -ɛn] ADJ Anat carpal

carpillon [karpijɔ̃] NM Ich very small carp

carpocapse [karpokaps] NF Entom carpocapsa; **c. des pommes** codling moth

carpophage [karpofaʒ] ADJ fruit-eating, Spéc carpophagous
▫ **carpophages** NMPL 1 Zool Carpophaga 2 Orn fruit pigeons, Spéc Carpophaga

carpophore [karpofor] NM Bot carpophore

carquois [karkwa] NM quiver

Carrache [karaʃ] NPR Carracci

carre [kar] NF 1 Sport (d'un ski, d'un patin à glace) edge; **lâcher les carres** to flatten the skis; **reprendre de la c.** to go back on one's edges 2 (d'une planche) crosscut 3 (sur un pin) notch (for extracting resin)

Carré [kare] NPR Vét **maladie de C.** canine distemper; **virus de C.** canine distemper virus

carré, -e [kare] ADJ 1 (forme, planche) square; **avoir les épaules carrées** to be square-shouldered; Can **danse carrée** square dance
2 Géom & Math square
3 (sans détours) straight, straightforward; **être c. en affaires** to have a forthright business manner; **il est un peu trop c.** he's a bit blunt
4 Naut (mât) square-rigged; (voile) square
NM 1 (gén) & Géom square; **un petit c. de ciel bleu** a little patch of blue sky; Anciennement **c. blanc** = white square in the corner of the screen indicating that a television programme is not recommended for children
2 Math square; **le c. de six** six squared, the square of six; **élever un nombre au c.** to square a number
3 Hort **c. de choux** cabbage patch
4 (foulard) (square) scarf; **c. de coton** cotton square; **c. Hermès** = designer headscarf made by Hermès (a status symbol in France)
5 (coiffure) bob
6 (viande) **c. d'agneau/de mouton/de porc/de veau** loin of lamb/mutton/pork/veal
7 (fromage) **c. de l'Est** = type of soft cheese
8 Cartes **c. d'as** four aces
9 Mil square; **former le c.** to get into square formation
10 Naut **c. (des officiers)** wardroom
11 Anat quadrate muscle
12 Fam Arg scol (élève) = second year student in certain "grandes écoles"
13 Can Vieilli (place) (public) square
▫ **carrée** NF Fam pad; **un peu d'ordre dans la carrée!** get this place tidied up!

carreau, -x [karo] NM 1 (sur du papier) square; (sur du tissu) check; **papier à carreaux** squared paper, graph paper; **mettre un motif au c.** to square up a design; **veste à carreaux** check or checked jacket; **draps à petits carreaux** sheets with a small check design or pattern
2 (plaque de grès, de marbre) tile
3 (sol) tiled floor; Fam **se retrouver sur le c.** (par terre) to end up on the floor; (pauvre) to wind up on skid row; Fam **rester sur le c.** (être assommé) to be laid out; (être tué) to be bumped off; (échouer) Br to come a cropper, Am to take a spill; Anciennement **le c. des Halles** (à Paris) the (floor of the) market; **c. de mine** pithead
4 (vitre) window-pane; (fenêtre) window; **regarder à travers les carreaux** to look through the window; **un c. cassé** a broken window
5 Cartes **du c.** diamonds; **dame/dix de c.**

queen/ten of diamonds; **jouer à** ou **du c.** to play diamonds
6 Suisse (jardin) (square) garden
7 Fam (locution) **tiens-toi à c.!** watch your step!; **il s'est tenu à c.** he kept a low profile
▫ **carreaux** NMPL Fam (lunettes) specs; **t'as vu l'autre là-bas avec ses carreaux?** look at old four-eyes over there!

carreauté, -e [karote] ADJ Can (chemise, nappe) Br check(ed), Am checkered

carrefour [karfur] NM 1 (de rues) crossroads (singulier), junction; Fig **nous arrivons à un c.** we've come to a crossroads; **c. ferroviaire** Br railway or Am railroad junction 2 (point de rencontre) crossroads (singulier); **Hong Kong, c. de l'Asie** Hong Kong, crossroads of Asia; **un c. d'idées** a forum of ideas 3 (rencontre) forum, symposium

carrelage [karlaʒ] NM 1 (carreaux) tiles, tiling; **poser un c.** (au sol) to lay tiles or a tiled floor 2 (opération) tiling 3 (sol) tiled floor 4 (mur) tiled wall

carreler [24] [karle] VT 1 (mur, salle de bains) to tile 2 (feuille de papier) to draw squares on, to square

carrelet [karlɛ] NM 1 Ich plaice 2 Naut (filet) square fishing net 3 Tech (aiguille) half-moon needle 4 (règle) square ruler

carreleur [karlœr] NM tiler

carrelle etc voir **carreler**

carrément [karemɑ̃] ADV 1 (dire) straight out, bluntly; (agir) straight; **elle a c. téléphoné au maire** she got straight on the phone to the mayor; **je vais le quitter! – ah, c.?** I'm going to leave him! – it's as serious as that, is it?; **y aller c.** to get on with it
2 Fam (en intensif) downright■; **c. bête** downright stupid; **t'as c. raison** you're absolutely right■; **il est c. en retard** he's well and truly late; **on gagne c. un mètre** you gain a whole metre■; **c'est du vol/de la corruption** it's daylight robbery/blatant corruption■; **tourne c. à gauche** take a sharp left; **c., mec!** Br absolutely, mate!, Am totally, man!
3 (poser) squarely, firmly

carrer [3] [kare] VT to square
▸**se carrer** VPR 1 (s'installer) to settle, Sout to ensconce oneself 2 (locutions) très Fam **tu peux te le c. où je pense!** you know what you can do with it!; Vulg **tu peux te le c. dans le cul** ou **dans l'oignon!** you can shove or stick it up your Br arse or Am ass!

carrick [karik] NM Vieilli coachman's heavy coat, box-coat

carrier¹ [karje] NM quarryman; **maître c.** quarry master

carrier² [karje] NM Orn carrier pigeon

carrière [karjɛr] NF 1 Mines (d'extraction) quarry; **c. de craie** chalkpit; **c. à ciel ouvert** open quarry
2 (profession) career; **la C.** (diplomatie) the diplomatic service; **la c. des armes** a military career
3 (parcours professionnel) career; **faire c. dans** to pursue a career in; **l'accident a brisé sa c.** the accident ruined or wrecked his/her career; **en début/en fin de c.** at the beginning/end of one's career
4 Littéraire (de la vie, du soleil) course; **la c. de la gloire** the path to glory; **donner (libre) c. à** to give free rein to
▫ **de carrière** ADJ (militaire) regular; (diplomate) career (avant n)

'La Carrière du roué' Hogarth 'The Rake's Progress'

---

carriérisme [karjerism] NM careerism

carriériste [karjerist] NMF careerist, career-minded person

carriole [karjol] NF 1 (à deux roues) cart 2 Can (traineau) (horsedrawn) sled, (horsedrawn) sleigh

carron [karɔ̃] NM Suisse Constr large brick

carrossable [karosabl] ADJ suitable for motor vehicles

carrossage [karosaʒ] NM Tech (angle) camber

carrosse [karos] NM 1 (véhicule) coach; **c. d'apparat** state coach 2 (panier) wine basket 3 Can

(voiture d'enfant) Br pram, Am baby carriage

'Le Carrosse d'or' Renoir 'The Golden Coach'

---

carrosser [3] [karose] VT 1 (voiture) to fit a body to 2 très Fam (locution) **elle est bien carrossée** she's got a good figure■, she's got curves in all the right places

carrosserie [karosri] NF 1 Aut (structure) body; (habillage) bodywork; **atelier de c.** body shop 2 (d'un appareil ménager) cover, case 3 très Fam (d'une personne) **belle c.!** nice bod!■ 4 (métier) coachwork, coach-building

carrossier [karosje] NM coachbuilder

carrousel [karuzɛl, karusɛl] NM 1 Équitation carousel 2 (de voitures, de personnes) merry-go-round; **le c. ministériel** the comings and goings at the Ministry 3 (à bagages) carousel 4 Phot (pour diapositives) carousel 5 Can, Belg & Suisse (manège) merry-go-round, carousel

carroyage [karwajaʒ] NM Tech (en dessin) squaring

carroyer [13] [karwaje] VT Tech to square

carrure [karyr] NF 1 (corps) build; **avoir une c. d'athlète** to have an athletic build 2 (qualité) stature, calibre; **une présidente d'une c. exceptionnelle** an exceptionally able chairwoman; **il a la c. d'un cadre supérieur** he's senior management material 3 (d'un vêtement) breadth across the shoulders

carry [kari] = **cari**

cartable [kartabl] NM 1 (à bretelles) satchel; (à poignée) schoolbag 2 Can (classeur à anneaux) ring binder

---

CARTE [kart]

| card A1, 3–6, C ■ menu A2 ■ map B ■ chart B |

NF A. 1 (pour la correspondance) card; Can **c. d'affaires** business card; **c. d'anniversaire** birthday card; **donner** ou **laisser c. blanche à qn** to give sb carte blanche or a free hand; **c. d'invitation** invitation card; **c. de Noël** Christmas card; **c. postale** postcard; Mktg **c. de publicité** mailing card; Mktg **c. de publicité directe** self-mailer; Mktg & Tél **c. T** reply-paid card; **c. de visite** (personnelle) Br visiting or Am calling card; (professionnelle) business card; **laisser sa c. à qn** to leave one's card with sb; **c. de vœux** greetings card (sent at Christmas and New Year)
2 (de restaurant) menu; (menu à prix non fixe) à la carte menu; **c. des desserts** dessert menu; **c. des vins** wine list; **ils ont une belle/petite c.** they have an impressive/a limited menu; **choisissez dans la c.** choose one of the à la carte dishes
3 (document officiel) card; **il a la c. du parti écologiste** he's a card-carrying member of the green party; **fille** ou **prostituée en c.** registered prostitute; **c. d'abonnement** Transp season ticket or pass; Mus & Théât season ticket; **c. d'adhérent** membership card; **c. d'alimentation** ration card; **c. de débarquement** landing card; **c. de don d'organe** donor card; **c. d'électeur** voting or Br polling card, Am voter registration card; **c. d'embarquement** boarding card, boarding pass; **c. d'entrée** pass; **c. d'étudiant** student card; **C. européenne d'assurance maladie** European Health Insurance Card; **c. de famille nombreuse** discount card (for families with at least three children); **c. de fidélité** loyalty card; **c. grise** car registration papers; **c. d'identité** identity card, ID card; **c. d'identité professionnelle** (de représentant) (official) ID card; **c. d'invalidité** = handicapped person's travel pass; **c. de lecteur** library or Br reader's card; **c. de membre** membership card; **c. nationale d'identité** (national) identity card or ID card; **c. nationale de priorité** = card giving priority in queues and on public transport; **C. Orange** = pass for travel on the Paris transport system; **c. de presse** press card; **c. de rationnement** ration card; **c. de réduction** discount card; **c. de représentant** = sales representative's official identity card; **c. de résident** (long term)

residence permit; **c. sanitaire** prostitute's registration papers; **c. de Sécurité sociale** *ou* **d'assuré social** ≃ National Insurance Card; **c. de séjour (temporaire)** (temporary) residence permit; **c. de sortie** pupil's pass *(showing entitlement to leave school at certain times)*; **C. Vermeil** = card entitling senior citizens to reduced rates in cinemas, on public transport etc; *Assur* **c. verte** green card; **c. VITALE** = smart card on which information about a patient is recorded, used when making payments to a doctor or chemist for purposes of reclaiming medical expenses

4 *Fin & Banque (autorisant une transaction)* card; **c. accréditive** charge card; **c. American Express®** American Express® card; **c. bancaire** bank card, cheque card; **c. bancaire à puce** smart card *(used as a bank card)*; **C. Bleue®** = bank card with which purchases are debited directly from the customer's bank account, *Br* ≃ debit card; **c. de crédit** credit card; **c. de crédit professionnelle** corporate (credit) card; **c. d'identité bancaire** bank card; **c. Mastercard®** Mastercard®; **c. de paiement** debit card; *Tél* **c. Pastel** phone card *(use of which is debited to one's own phone number)*; **c. de retrait** bank card; *Tél* **c. SIM** SIM card; **c. de téléphone** phonecard; **c. Visa®** Visa® card

5 *Ordinat* (circuit) card, (circuit) board; **c. accélérateur graphique** graphics accelerator card; **c. accélératrice** accelerator card *or* board; **c. d'affichage** display card; **c. bus** bus board; **c. de circuits** circuit board; **c. de circuit(s) intégré(s)** integrated circuit board, IC board; **c. contrôleur de disque** disk controller card; **c. d'extension** expansion card; **c. d'extension mémoire** memory card; **c. fax** fax card; **c. graphique** graphics card; **c. graphique numérique** digital graphics card; **c. magnétique** magnetic card; **c. à mémoire** smart card; **c. mère** motherboard; **c. modem** modem card; **c. perforée** punch card; **c. à pistes magnétiques** magnetic stripe card; **c. à puce** smart card; **c. réseau** network card; **c. RNIS** ISDN card; **c. SCSI** SCSI card; **c. son** sound card; **c. de télécopie** fax card; **c. unité centrale** CPU board; **c. vidéo** video board, video card; **c. vidéo accélératrice** video accelerator card

6 *Com* **c. de coloris** shade card; **c. d'échantillons** sample card, showcard

7 *Mktg* **c. perceptuelle** perceptual map; **c. de positionnement** positioning map

8 *Belg (au football, au rugby)* **c. jaune** yellow card; **c. rouge** red card

B. *Géog & Géol* map; *Astron, Météo & Naut* chart; **dresser une c. de la région** to map (out) the area; **c. du ciel** sky *or* celestial chart; **c. cognitive** cognitive map; **c. d'état-major** *Br* ≃ Ordnance Survey map, *Am* ≃ Geological Survey map; *Biol* **c. du génome humain** map of the human genome; **c. marine** nautical chart; **c. routière** road map; *Littérature* **la c. de** *ou* **du Tendre** map of the amorous sentiments *(from de Scudéry's novel 'Clélie', 1660)*; **c. topographique** contour map

C. *Cartes* **c. (à jouer)** (playing) card; **jouer aux cartes** to play cards; *Fam* **tirer** *ou* **faire les cartes à qn** to read sb's cards[*] ; *Fam* **se faire tirer les cartes** to have one's cards read[*] ; **jeu de cartes** *(activité)* card game; *(paquet)* pack *or* deck of cards; **c. forcée** forced card; *Fig* Hobson's choice; **c. maîtresse** master card; *Fig* master *or* trump card; *Fig* **une bonne c.** an asset; *aussi Fig* **montrer ses cartes** to show one's hand; *Fig* **jeter des cartes/une c. sur la table** to put proposals/a proposal on the table; *Fig* **jouer cartes sur table** to lay one's cards on the table; **il n'a pas joué toutes ses cartes** he hasn't played his last card; *Fig* he still has a trick *or* a card up his sleeve; *aussi Fig* **jouer sa dernière c.** to play one's last card; **jouons la c. de l'honnêteté/la qualité** let's go for honesty/quality; *Belg Fam (locution)* **taper la c.** to play cards[*]

❏ **à cartes** ADJ card-programmed, card *(avant n)*

❏ **à la carte** ADJ **1** *(au restaurant)* à la carte **2** *(programme, investissement)* customized; *(horaire)* flexible; **horaires à la c.** flexitime; **vacances à la c.** customized *Br* holidays *or Am* vacation ADV **manger à la c.** to eat à la carte

❏ **de grande carte** ADJ *(restaurant, établissement)* first-class

carte-adaptateur [kartadaptatœr] *(pl* **cartes-adaptateurs)** NF *Ordinat* adapter card; **c. réseau** network adaptor card

carte-clé [kartəkle] *(pl* **cartes-clés)** NF keycard; **c. électronique** electronic keycard

carte-fiche [kartəfiʃ] *(pl* **cartes-fiches)** NF index card

carte-guide [kartəgid] *(pl* **cartes-guides)** NF *(pour séparer des fiches)* file separator *or* divider

cartel [kartɛl] NM **1** *Écon* cartel; **c. de l'acier/de la drogue** steel/drug cartel; **c. de prix** price cartel; **se rassembler en c.** to form a cartel

2 *Pol* coalition, cartel

3 *Mil* cartel

4 *(pendule)* (decorative) wall clock

5 *(plaque)* name and title plaque *(on a painting, a statue)*

❏ **Cartel** NM **1** *Théât* **le C.** = group of four theatre companies directed by Baty, Dullin, Jouvet and Pitoëff from 1927 to 1940, influential in the development of modern French stagecraft

2 *Pol & Hist* **le C. des gauches** = a radical-socialist group formed in 1924 in opposition to the "bloc national" and gaining power in the same year under Édouard Herriot

carte-lettre [kartəlɛtr] *(pl* **cartes-lettres)** NF letter card

cartellisation [kartelizasjɔ̃] NF *(d'entreprises)* cartelization

cartelliser [3] [kartelize] VT to cartelize

carter [kartɛr] NM **1** *Élec* case, casing **2** *Aut* **c. d'engrenages** gearbox casing; **c. à l'huile** *Br* sump, *Am* oilpan; **c. du moteur** crankcase **3** *(de vélo)* chain guard

carte-réponse [kartrepɔ̃s] *(pl inv ou* **cartes-réponses)** NF reply card

Carterie® [kartəri] NF card shop

cartésianisme [kartezjanism] NM Cartesianism

cartésien, -enne [kartezjɛ̃, -ɛn] ADJ Cartesian NM,F Cartesian

carte-vue [kartəvy] *(pl* **cartes-vues)** NF *Belg* (picture) postcard

Carthage [kartaʒ] NM Carthage

Carthagène [kartaʒɛn] NF Carthagena

carthaginois, -e [kartaʒinwa, -az] ADJ Carthaginian

❏ **Carthaginois, -e** NM,F Carthaginian

carthame [kartam] NM *Bot* safflower

cartier [kartje] NM playing card manufacturer

cartilage [kartilaʒ] NM **1** *Anat (substance)* cartilage *(UNCOUNT)* **2** *(du poulet)* gristle

cartilagineux, -euse [kartilaʒinø, -øz] ADJ **1** *Anat* cartilaginous **2** *(poulet)* gristly

cartogramme [kartɔgram] NM cartogram

cartographe [kartɔgraf] NMF cartographer

cartographie [kartɔgrafi] NF cartography; *Biol* **c. du génome** gene *or* genetic mapping

cartographier [9] [kartɔgrafje] VT to chart, to make a map of

cartographique [kartɔgrafik] ADJ cartographic

cartomancie [kartɔmɑ̃si] NF cartomancy, fortune-telling *(with cards)*

cartomancien, -enne [kartɔmɑ̃sjɛ̃, -ɛn] NM,F fortune-teller *(with cards)*

carton [kartɔ̃] NM **1** *(matière)* cardboard; *(feuille)* piece of cardboard, (piece of) card; **c. ondulé** corrugated cardboard

2 c. (d'invitation) invitation (card)

3 *(boîte → grande)* cardboard box; *(→ petite)* carton; **c. à chapeaux** hatbox; **c. à chaussures** shoebox; **faire des cartons** to pack one's things up in cardboard boxes

4 *(contenu → d'une grande boîte)* cardboard boxful; *(→ d'une petite boîte)* cartonful

5 *(rangement → pour dossiers)* (box) file; *(→ pour dessins)* portfolio; **c. à dessin** portfolio; *Fig* **le projet est resté dans les cartons** the project never saw the light of day, the project was shelved

6 *Beaux-Arts* sketch, cartoon; **c. de tapisserie** (tapestry) cartoon

7 *Géog* inset map

8 *(au football, au rugby)* **c. jaune** yellow card; **c. rouge** red card

9 *Fam (locutions)* **taper le c.** to play cards[*] ; **faire un c.** *(au ball-trap)* to take a potshot; *Fig (réussir)* to hit the jackpot; **faire un c. sur qn** to shoot sb down[*] ; **prendre un c.** *(défaite)* to get thrashed; *(mauvaise note)* to get a bad mark[*]

10 *Cin & TV* **c. aide-mémoire** cue card

❏ **en carton** ADJ cardboard *(avant n)*

carton-feutre [kartɔ̃føtr] *(pl* **cartons-feutres)** NM *Constr* roofing felt

cartonnage [kartɔnaʒ] NM **1** *Typ (reliure)* board-binding; **c. pleine toile** *(couverture)* cloth boards **2** *(boîte)* cardboard box **3** *(empaquetage)* cardboard packing **4** *(fabrication)* cardboard industry

cartonné, -e [kartɔne] ADJ *(livre, volume)* case-bound, hardback

cartonner [3] [kartɔne] VT *Typ (livre)* to bind in boards; **livre cartonné** hardback (book)

VI *Fam* **1** *(réussir)* to hit the jackpot; *(avoir une bonne note)* to pass with flying colours; **ils ont cartonné avec leur dernier album** their last album was a huge hit **2** *(locutions)* **garé dans un couloir d'autobus, ça va c. (sec)!** he's parked in a bus lane, he's really going to catch it!; **ça cartonne!** *(musique)* it's mind-blowing!

cartonnerie [kartɔnri] NF **1** *(industrie)* cardboard industry **2** *(commerce)* cardboard trade **3** *(usine)* cardboard factory

cartonneux, -euse [kartɔnø, -øz] ADJ cardboard-like; **du fromage c.** cheese that tastes like cardboard

cartonnier, -ère [kartɔnje, -ɛr] NM,F **1** *Beaux-Arts* tapestry designer, mosaic designer **2** *(fabricant)* cardboard manufacturer

NM *Br* filing *or Am* file cabinet *(for cardboard files)*

carton-paille [kartɔ̃paj] *(pl* **cartons-pailles)** NM strawboard

carton-pâte [kartɔ̃pat] *(pl* **cartons-pâtes)** NM pasteboard; *Péj* **de c., en c.** *(décor)* cardboard *(avant n)*; *(personnage, intrigue)* cardboard cut-out *(avant n)*

cartoon [kartun] NM *(dessin, film)* cartoon; *(bande dessinée)* comic strip, *Br* (strip) cartoon

cartophile [kartɔfil] NMF cartophile, cartophilist

cartophilie [kartɔfili] NF cartophily

cartothèque [kartɔtɛk] NF map library

cartouche [kartuʃ] NF **1** *Mil & Chasse (projectile, charge)* cartridge; **c. à blanc** blank cartridge; **c. de chasse** sporting cartridge

2 *(recharge → d'un stylo)* cartridge; *Ordinat* **c. Bernoulli®** Bernoulli® disk; *Ordinat* **c. DAT** DAT cartridge; **c. d'encre** ink cartridge; *Ordinat* **c. d'enregistrement sur bande audionumérique** DAT cartridge; *Ordinat* **c. Jaz®** Jaz® disk; **c. de polices** font cartridge; **c. de toner** toner cartridge; **c. vidéo** video cartridge; *Ordinat* **c. Zip®** zip® disk

3 *(de cigarettes)* carton

4 *Phot* cartridge, cassette, magazine

5 *Élec* cartridge

NM **1** *Antiq & Beaux-Arts* cartouche

2 *Typ (sur un plan)* box; *Presse* **c. de titre** masthead

cartoucherie [kartuʃri] NF **1** *(fabrique)* cartridge factory **2** *(dépôt)* cartridge depot

cartouchière [kartuʃjɛr] NF **1** *(de soldat)* cartridge pouch **2** *(de chasseur → étui)* cartridge case; *(→ ceinture)* cartridge belt

cartulaire [kartylɛr] NM *Hist* cartulary, chartulary

carvi [karvi] NM *Bot & Culin* caraway

cary [kari] = **cari**

caryatide [karjatid] NF *Archit* caryatid

caryer [karje] NM *Bot* hickory

caryocinèse [karjɔsinɛz] NF *Biol* karyokinesis, mitosis

caryogamie [karjɔgami] NF *Biol* karyogamy

caryokinèse [karjɔkinez] = **caryocinèse**

caryologie [karjɔlɔʃi] NF *Biol* karyology

caryolytique [karjɔlitik] ADJ karyolytic NM karyolytic substance *or* drug

caryophyllée [karjɔfile], **caryophyllacée** [karjɔfilase] *Bot* NF member of the Caryophyllacea family

❏ **caryophyllées** NFPL Caryophyllacea

caryopse [karjɔps] NM *Bot* caryopsis

caryotype [karjɔtip] NM *Biol* karyotype

CAS [ka] NM **1** (hypothèse) **dans le premier c.** in the first instance; **dans le meilleur des c.** at best; **dans le pire des c.** at worst; **dans l'un des c.** in one case; **dans certains c., en certains c.** in some or certain cases; **en aucun c.** under no circumstances, on no account; **en pareil c.** in such a case; **auquel c., en ce c., dans ce c.** in which case, in that case, this being the case; **dans un c. comme dans l'autre, dans l'un ou l'autre c., dans les deux c.** either way; **c. de figure** case, instance; **envisageons ce c. de figure** let us consider that possibility; **le c. échéant** if necessary, if need be, should the need arise; **selon le c.** as the case may be

2 (situation particulière) case, situation; **c'est également mon c.** I'm in the same situation; **j'ai expliqué mon c.** I stated my case or position; **certains animaux sont presque aveugles; c'est le c. de la taupe** some animals, such as the mole, are almost blind; **ce n'est pas le c.** that's not the case; **il parle plusieurs langues étrangères mais ce n'est pas mon c.** he speaks several foreign languages but I don't; **c'est un c. très rare** it's a very rare occurrence; **c. particulier** special case; **c'est un c. particulier, elle n'a pas de ressources** she's a special case, she has no income; **se mettre dans un mauvais c.** to paint oneself into a corner; **c. de conscience** matter of conscience; **poser un c. de conscience à qn** to put sb in a (moral) dilemma; **c. d'école** textbook case; **c. d'espèce** special or particular case; **c. de force majeure** Jur event of force majeure; Fig case of absolute necessity; Jur **c. fortuit** act of God; **c. limite** borderline case; **ce n'est pas un c. pendable** it's not a hanging offence; **c. urgent** emergency or urgent case; **c'est le c. de le dire!** you said it!, you can say that again!

3 Méd case; **il y a eu trois c. de varicelle** there have been three cases of chickenpox; **ce malade est un c. désespéré** this patient is a hopeless case; **c. index** Br propositus, Am proband

4 Fam (personne) **ce garçon est un c.!** that boy is something else or a real case!

5 Gram (construction) **grammaire des** ou **de c.** case grammar; **langue à c.** inflected language; **les c. particuliers en grammaire française** exceptions in French grammar

6 (locutions) **faire grand c. de** (événement) to attach great importance to; (argument, raison) to set great store by; (invité, ami) to make a great fuss or much of; **on fit grand c. du jeune romancier** much was made of the young novelist; **ne faire aucun c. de** to pay no attention to, to take no notice of; **faire peu de c. de** (argument, raison) to pay scant attention to; (invité, ami) to ignore

☐ **au cas où** CONJ in case; **au c. où il ne viendrait pas** in case he doesn't come; Fam **prends un parapluie au c. où** take an umbrella just in case

☐ **dans le cas de** PRÉP **mettre qn dans le c. de faire** ou **d'avoir à faire qch** to put sb in the position of having to do sth

☐ **dans tous les cas** ADV in any case or event, anyway

☐ **en cas de** PRÉP in case of; **en c. de besoin** if need be, if the need should arise; **en c. d'incendie** in the event of a fire; **en c. d'urgence** in an emergency; **en c. de perte de la carte** should the card be lost

☐ **en tout cas** ADV in any case or event, anyway

☐ **cas social** NM = person needing social worker's assistance; **il y a beaucoup de c. sociaux dans son école** there are a lot of children from problem families at his/her school

Casablanca [kazablɑ̃ka] NM Casablanca

casanier, -ère [kazanje, -ɛr] ADJ home-loving, Péj stay-at-home
NM,F homebody, Péj stay-at-home

casaque [kazak] NF (d'un jockey) silks; (de mousquetaire) paletot (with wide sleeves); (blouse) paletot; Fig **tourner c.** (fuir) to turn and run; (changer d'opinion) to do a volte-face

casaquin [kazakɛ̃] NM **1** Vieilli jacket, blouse **2** Fam (human) body■; **tomber** ou **donner sur le c. à qn** to set about sb, to beat sb up; **avoir quelque chose dans le c.** to be a bit off-colour; **donner sur le c.** (vin) to go to one's head

casbah [kazba] NF **1** (dans les pays arabes) casbah, kasbah **2** Fam (maison) place, pad

cascabelle [kaskabɛl] NF Zool (du crotale) rattle

cascade [kaskad] NF **1** (chute d'eau) waterfall, Littéraire cascade

2 (abondance) **une c. de** (tissu, boucles) a cascade of; (compliments) a stream of; (sensations) a rush of, a gush of; **des cascades d'applaudissements** thundering applause

3 (acrobatie → au cirque) stunt; (→ au cirque) acrobatic trick; **faire de la c.** (au cinéma) to do stunts; (au cirque) to do acrobatics

☐ **en cascade** ADJ **1** (applaudissements) tumultuous; (rires) ringing; **ils ont connu des catastrophes en c.** they experienced a whole string or chain of disasters **2** Élec **montage en c.** cascade or tandem connection ADV **ses cheveux tombaient en c. sur ses épaules** his/her hair cascaded around his/her shoulders; Ordinat **ouvrir des fenêtres en c.** to cascade windows

cascader [3] [kaskade] VI Littéraire to cascade (down)

cascadeur, -euse [kaskadœr, -øz] NM,F (au cinéma) stuntman, f stuntwoman; (au cirque) acrobat

cascara [kaskara] NF Pharm cascara

cascatelle [kaskatɛl] NF Littéraire small cascade

casco [kasko] NF Suisse Assur comprehensive insurance, all-risks insurance

case [kaz] NF **1** (d'un damier, de mots croisés) square; (d'un formulaire) box; **retournez** ou **retour à la c. départ** return to go; Fig **retour à la c. départ!** back to square one!

2 (d'un meuble, d'une boîte) compartment; (pour le courrier) pigeonhole; Fam **il a une c. (de) vide** ou **il lui manque une c.** he's not all there, he's got a screw loose

3 Suisse **c. (postale)** postbox

4 Ordinat button; (en forme de boîte) box; **c. d'aide** help button; **c. "annuler"** cancel button; **c. de dimensionnement** size box; **c. de fermeture** close box; **c. d'option** ou **de pointage** check box, option box; **c. de redimensionnement** size box; **c. de saisie** input box; **c. zoom** zoom box

5 Rad & TV slot

6 (hutte) hut

'La Case de l'oncle Tom' Beecher Stowe 'Uncle Tom's Cabin'

caséation [kazeasjɔ̃] = **caséification**

caséeux, -euse [kazeø, -øz] ADJ **1** (rappelant le fromage) caseous **2** Méd caseous

caséification [kazeifikasjɔ̃] NF Méd caseation

caséine [kazein] NF Chim casein

casemate [kazmat] NF Mil **1** (d'une fortification) casemate **2** (ouvrage fortifié) blockhouse

caser [3] [kaze] Fam VT **1** (faire entrer) **c. qch dans qch** to fit sth in sth; **tu peux y c. un canapé** you can fit a sofa in; **peux-tu c. ça dans ta valise?** can you find room for this in your suitcase?

2 (dire → phrase, histoire) to get in

3 (loger → invités) to put up; **les enfants sont casés chez la grand-mère** the children are staying at their grandma's

4 (dans un emploi) to fix up; **elle est bien casée** she's fixed up nicely

5 (marier) to marry off; **il est enfin casé** he's settled down at last

► **se caser** VPR **1** (dans un emploi) to get fixed up with a job

2 (se marier) to settle down■

3 (se loger) to find somewhere to live■

caserne [kazɛrn] NF **1** Mil barracks (singulier ou pluriel); **c. de pompiers** fire station; **des plaisanteries de c.** barrack-room or locker-room jokes **2** Péj (logements) soulless high-rise Br flats or Am apartments

casernement [kazɛrnəmɑ̃] NM **1** (action) quartering in barracks **2** (locaux) barrack buildings

caserner [3] [kazɛrne] VT to barrack

casette [kazɛt] NF **1** Vieilli little house, hut **2** Tech sagger, seggar

cash [kaʃ] ADV cash; **payer c.** to pay cash; Fam **je te le vends, mais c.!** I'll sell it to you but it's cash on the nail!

cash and carry [kaʃɛndkari] NM INV cash-and-carry

casher [kaʃɛr] = **kasher**

cash-flow [kaʃflo] (pl **cash-flows**) NM Fin & Compta cash flow; **c. actualisé** discounted cash flow; **c. courant** current cash flow; **c. disponible** operating cash flow; **c. marginal** incremental cash flow; **c. net** net cash flow

cashmere [kaʃmir] NM cashmere

casier [kazje] NM **1** (case → ouverte) pigeonhole; (→ fermée) compartment; (→ dans une consigne, dans un gymnase) locker; **c. de consigne automatique** luggage locker

2 (meuble → à cases ouvertes) pigeonholes; (→ à tiroirs) Br filing or Am file cabinet; (→ à cases fermées) compartment; (→ à cases fermant à clef) locker

3 (pour ranger → des livres) unit; (→ dans un réfrigérateur) compartment; **c. à bouteilles** bottle rack

4 (pour transporter) crate

5 Admin & Jur record; **c. civil** civil register; **c. fiscal** tax record; **c. judiciaire** police or criminal record; **un c. judiciaire vierge** a clean (police) record; **maintenant, il a un c. (judiciaire)** now he's got a (criminal) record

6 Pêche pot

casing [kasiŋ] NM **1** Pétr (tubage) casing, piping **2** (de chaudière) casing

casino [kazino] NM casino

casinotier [kazinɔtje] NM casino operator

casoar [kazɔar] NM **1** Orn cassowary **2** (plumet) plume (on hats worn by Saint-Cyr cadets)

Caspienne [kaspjɛn] NF **la (mer) C.** the Caspian Sea

casque [kask] NM **1** (pour protéger) helmet; **le port du c. est obligatoire** (sur un chantier) hard hats must be worn; **c. colonial** pith helmet; **c. intégral** full face helmet; **c. de moto** crash helmet; **c. à pointe** spiked helmet; **c. de protection** (pour moto) crash helmet; (d'ouvriers) hard hat; **c. bleu** member of the UN peace-keeping force, Blue Beret; **les casques bleus** the UN peace-keeping force, the Blue Berets

2 (de coiffeur) hood hairdrier

3 (pour écouter) **c. (à écouteurs)** headphones, headset, earphones; **écouter un disque au c.** to listen to a record on headphones

4 [kas] Can Vieilli (chapeau) hat; Fig **en avoir plein le c.** to be fed up, to have had enough

5 Littéraire (cheveux) **un c. roux** a crown of red hair

6 Bot helmet, galea

7 Zool casque

casqué, -e [kaske] ADJ helmeted

casquer [3] [kaske] Fam VT (payer) to cough up
VI to cough up, to come up with the cash; **il va falloir c.** we're going to have to cough up

casquette [kaskɛt] NF cap; **c. d'officier** officer's peaked cap; Fig **avoir plusieurs casquettes** (responsabilités) to wear several hats; Fam **avoir la c. (de plomb)** to be hungover■, to have a hangover■

cassable [kasabl] ADJ breakable

cassage [kasaʒ] NM (d'assiettes) breaking; (de cailloux) crushing; (d'un syndicat) crushing; très Fam **c. de gueule** fist-fight, Br punch-up

Cassandre [kasɑ̃dr] NPR Myth & Fig Cassandra; **jouer les C.** to spread doom and gloom; **cela donne raison aux C. de l'économie** that bears out what the doom merchants were predicting for the economy; **la voix de C.** the voice of doom

cassant, -e [kasɑ̃, -ɑ̃t] ADJ **1** (cheveux, ongle) brittle; (métal) short **2** (réponse) curt; **être c. avec qn** to be short or curt with sb; **d'un ton c.** crisply **3** Fam (fatigant) tiring■; **c'est pas vraiment c.** it's not exactly tiring

cassate [kasat] NF Culin cassata

cassation[1] [kasasjɔ̃] NF **1** Jur annulment, Spéc cassation **2** Mil reduction to the ranks

cassation[2] [kasasjɔ̃] NF Mus cassation

casse[1] [kas] NF Typ case; **bas/haut de c.** lower/upper case; **lettre bas-/haut-de-c.** lower-case/upper-case letter

casse[2] [kas] NF **1** (bris, dommage) breakage; **est-ce qu'il y a eu de la c.?** was anything broken?, were there any breakages?

2 Fam (bagarre) **de la c.** a fist-fight or Br

cas–cas

punch-up; **il va y avoir de la c.** there's going to be trouble

3 *(de voitures)* scrapyard; **mettre** *ou* **envoyer à la c.** to scrap; **aller** *ou* **partir à la c.** to go for scrap; **vendre une voiture à la c.** to sell a car for scrap; *Fig* **une idéologie bonne pour la c.** an ideology fit for the scrapheap

casse³ [kas] NF *Bot (arbuste)* cassia

casse⁴ [kas] NM *Fam (d'une banque)* bank robbery■ ; *(d'une maison)* break-in■ ; **faire un c. chez un bijoutier** *Br* to do over *or Am* to boost a jeweller's

cassé, -e ADJ *Fam* **1** [kase] *(drogué)* stoned, high; *(ivre)* wasted, *Br* pissed; *(épuisé) Br* knackered, *Am* beat **2** [kase] *Can (sans argent)* broke; **c. comme un clou** *Br* stony *or Am* flat broke

  NM [kase] *Culin* **gros c.** large crack; **petit c.** small crack

casseau, -x [kaso] NM **1** *Typ* half-case **2** *Can (contenant)* box *(for fruit)*

casse-bonbons [kasbɔ̃bɔ̃] *Fam* ADJ INV **être c.** to be a pain (in the neck)

  NMF INV pain (in the neck)

casse-cou [kasku] ADJ INV *(personne)* daredevil; *(projet)* risky; *(endroit)* dangerous

  NMF INV **1** *(personne)* daredevil **2** *(endroit)* danger *or* dangerous spot; **crier c. à qn** to warn sb *(of a danger)*

casse-couilles [kaskuj] *Vulg* ADJ INV **être c.** to be a pain in the *Br* arse *or Am* ass

  NMF INV pain in the *Br* arse *or Am* ass

casse-croûte [kaskrut] NM INV **1** *Fam (repas léger)* snack■ ; *(sandwich)* sandwich■ , *Br* butty, sarnie **2** *Can (snack)* snack bar■

casse-cul [kasky] *très Fam* ADJ INV **1** *(sans intérêt)* boring as hell; **ses cours sont c.** his/her lectures are a complete pain in the *Br* arse *or Am* ass **2** *(agaçant)* **être c.** to be a pain in the *Br* arse *or Am* ass

  NMF INV pain in the *Br* arse *or Am* ass

casse-dalle [kasdal] NM INV *Fam* sandwich■ , *Br* butty, sarnie

casse-graine [kasgrɛn] NM INV *Fam (repas léger)* snack■

casse-gueule [kasgœl] *Fam* ADJ INV *(endroit)* dangerous■ , *Br* dodgy; *(projet)* risky■ , *Br* dodgy

  NMF INV daredevil■

  NM INV *(endroit)* dangerous spot■ ; *(entreprise)* risky undertaking■

cassement [kasmɑ̃] NM *Fam Vieilli* **1 c. de tête** *(souci)* headache, worry■ **2** *(cambriolage)* break-in■ , burglary■

Casse-Noisette [kasnwazɛt] NM

'Casse-Noisette' *Tchaïkovski* 'The Nutcracker (Suite)'

casse-noisettes [kasnwazɛt] NM INV *Br* (pair of) nutcrackers, *Am* nutcracker

casse-noix [kasnwa] NM INV **1** *(instrument) Br* (pair of) nutcrackers, *Am* nutcracker **2** *Orn* nutcracker

casse-pattes [kaspat] NM INV *Fam Vieilli (alcool)* rotgut

casse-pieds [kaspje] *Fam* ADJ INV *(sans intérêt)* boring■ ; *(agaçant)* annoying■ ; **c'est c. à faire** it's a drag; **un peu c. à préparer** a bit of a hassle to prepare

  NMF INV pain (in the neck)

casse-pierre, casse-pierres [kaspjɛr] *(pl* **casse-pierres)** NM **1** *Tech (masse)* stonebreaker's hammer; *(machine)* stone crusher **2** *Bot* meadow saxifrage

casse-pipe, casse-pipes [kaspip] NM INV *Fam Mil* **le c.** the front■ ; **aller au c.** to go to the front■

CASSER [3] [kase]

> | VT | to break **1, 2, 4** ■ to demolish **3** ■ to damage **5** |
> | VI | to break **1** ■ to break up **2** |
> | VPR | to break **1, 5, 6** ■ to push off **2** ■ to break down **3** ■ to crack **4** |

VT 1 *(mettre en pièces → assiette, jouet, table)* to break; *(→ porte)* to break down; *(→ poignée)* to break off; *(→ noix)* to crack (open); **c. qch en mille morceaux** to smash sth to bits *or* smithereens; **c. qch en deux** to break *or* to snap

sth in two; *Fig* **un homme que la douleur a cassé** a man broken by suffering; **avoir envie de tout c.** to feel like smashing everything up; **c. sa tirelire** to break into one's piggybank; **c. du bois** to chop wood; *Fam Fig* to crash-land; *Fam* **c. du sucre sur le dos de qn** to badmouth *or Br* to bitch about sb; *Fam* **un journal où on casse du coco** a commie-bashing paper; *Fam* **c. de l'arabe** to beat up Arabs, *Br* ≃ to go Pakibashing; *Fam* **c. du pédé** to go gay-bashing; *aussi Fig* **c. la banque** to break the bank; *Fam* **c. la baraque** to bring the house down; *(faire échouer un plan)* to ruin it all; **ne me casse pas la baraque en le lui disant** don't ruin it all for me by telling him/her; *Fam* **c. sa pipe** to kick the bucket; *Fam* **ça ne casse pas des briques, ça ne casse pas trois pattes à un canard** it's no great shakes *or* no big deal

2 *(interrompre → fonctionnement, déroulement, grève)* to break; **le mécanisme est cassé** the mechanism is broken; **c. le rythme** to break the rhythm; **c. l'ambiance** to ruin *or* to spoil the atmosphere

3 *(démolir)* to demolish; **on a dû c. le mur** we had to knock down *or* to demolish the wall

4 *(en parlant de parties du corps)* to break; **avoue ou je te casse le bras!** own up or I'll break your arm!; **c.** *Fam* **la figure** *ou très Fam* **la gueule à qn** to smash sb's face in; *Fam* **c. les oreilles à qn** *(avec de la musique)* to deafen sb■ ; *(en le harcelant)* to give sb a lot of hassle; *Fig* **c. les reins à qn** to put a stop to sb's career; *Fam* **c. les pieds à qn** to get on sb's nerves *or Br* wick; **ça fait deux mois qu'elle me casse les pieds pour que je t'en parle** she's been on at me for two months now to talk to you about it; *Vulg* **c. les bonbons** *ou* **les couilles à qn** *Br* to get on sb's tits *or* wick, *Am* to break sb's balls; *très Fam* **tu nous les casses** you're a *Br* bloody *or Am* goddamn pain in the neck

5 *(abîmer → voix)* to damage, to ruin; **ça m'a cassé la voix de chanter toute la nuit** I ruined my voice singing all night; **elle a la voix cassée** *(rauque)* she has a husky voice; *(éraillée)* she has a croaky voice

6 *(annihiler → espoir)* to dash, to destroy; *(→ moral)* to break, to crush; **la religion, la famille, ils veulent tout c.** religion, family values, they want to smash everything

7 *Jur (jugement)* to quash; *(arrêt)* to nullify; to annul; *(mariage)* to annul, to dissolve

8 *(rétrograder → officier)* to break, to reduce to the ranks; *(→ fonctionnaire)* to demote

9 *Com* **c. les prix** to slash prices; **c. le métier** to operate at unfairly competitive rates

10 *très Fam (cambrioler)* to do a job on, *Br* to do over

11 *Fam (voiture)* to take to bits *(for spare parts)*, to break, to cannibalize■

12 *Can Joual (billet de banque)* to change, to break

13 *Can Joual* **c. le français** to speak bad French, to murder the French language

VI 1 *(verre, chaise)* to break; *(fil)* to snap; *(poignée)* to break off; **la tige a cassé** *(en deux)* the stem snapped; *(s'est détachée)* the stem snapped off; **cela casse comme du verre** it's as fragile as glass; *Prov* **tout passe, tout lasse, tout casse** = nothing lasts forever

2 *Fam (se séparer)* to break up, to split up

▶ **se casser** VPR **1** *(se briser → assiette)* to break; *(→ poignée)* to break off; **se c. net** *(en deux)* to snap in two; *(se détacher)* to break clean off

2 *très Fam (partir)* to push off, to clear off; **casse-toi!** get lost!, push off!; **le voilà, casse-toi!** he's coming, get the hell out of here!; **tu viens? on se casse** we're out of here, are you coming?; **elle s'est cassée de chez ses parents** she cleared out of her parents' place

3 *(cesser de fonctionner → appareil, véhicule)* to break down

4 *(être altéré → voix)* to crack, to falter

5 *(tissu)* to break (off); **votre pli de pantalon doit se c. sur la chaussure** the crease of your *Br* trouser leg *or Am* pant leg must break over the shoe

6 se c. qch to break sth; **elle s'est cassé la**

jambe she's broken her leg; **se c. le cou** to break one's neck; *Fig* to take a tumble, *Br* to come a cropper; **se c.** *Vulg* **le cul** *ou Fam* **les reins** *(au travail)* to bust a gut, to kill oneself; **je me suis cassé le cul pour lui trouver cette adresse** I really went out of my way■ *or* bust a gut to find him/her that address; **se c.** *Fam* **la figure** *ou très Fam* **la gueule** *(personne)* to take a tumble, *Br* to come a cropper; *(livre, carafe)* to crash to the ground; *(projet)* to bite the dust, to take a dive; *Fam* **se c. la tête** *ou* **la nénette** to rack one's brains; **ne te casse pas la tête, fais une omelette** don't put yourself out, just make an omelette; *Fam* **tu donc, tu ne t'es pas cassé la tête!** well, you didn't exactly strain yourself, did you!; *Fam* **se c. le nez** *(ne trouver personne)* to find no one in; *(échouer) Br* to come a cropper, *Am* to bomb; **tu vas te c. la voix si tu continues à crier** you'll ruin your voice if you keep shouting; *Fam* **ça vaut mieux que de se c. une jambe** it's better than a poke in the eye with a sharp stick

7 *Fam (se donner du mal)* **il ne s'est pas cassé pour m'aider** he didn't overstrain himself helping me

❑ **à tout casser** *Fam* ADJ *(endiablé → fête)* fantastic; *(→ succès)* runaway; **une soirée à tout c.** one hell of a party ADV **1** *(tout au plus)* at the (very) most; **cela vaut 100 euros à tout c.** it's worth 100 euros at the very most■ ; **ça prendra un quart d'heure à tout c.** it'll take a quarter of an hour at the very most *or* at the outside■ , it'll take a quarter of an hour max *or* tops **2 applaudir à tout c.** to bring the house down

casserole [kasrɔl] NF **1** *(ustensile, contenu)* pan, saucepan **2** *Fam (instrument de musique)* flat *or* off-key instrument; *(voix)* flat *or* off-key voice; **chanter comme une c.** to sing off key **3** *Cin* spot (light)

❑ **la casserole** ADJ braised ADV **faire** *ou* **cuire à la c.** to braise; *Fam* **passer à la c.** *(être tué)* to get bumped off; *(subir une épreuve)* to go through it; *très Fam* **elle est passée à la c.** *(sexuellement)* she got screwed *or* laid, *Br* she got a good seeing-to

casse-tête [kastɛt] NM INV **1** *(jeu)* puzzle, brainteaser; **c. chinois** Chinese puzzle; *Fig* **c'est un vrai c. chinois** it's totally baffling, it's a complete mystery **2** *(préoccupation)* headache; **ç'a été un c. pour placer tout le monde à table** it was a headache seating everyone at the table **3** *(massue)* club

cassetin [kastɛ̃] NM **1** *Typ* box **2** *Métal* crucible *(of furnace)*

casse-tout [kastu] *Fam* ADJ INV butterfingered

  NMF INV butterfingers

cassette [kasɛt] NF **1** *(magnétique)* cassette, tape; **enregistrer qch sur c.** to tape sth; **c. audio** audio cassette *or* tape; **c. de démonstration** demo (tape); **c. pirate** pirate tape; **c. vidéo** video (cassette)

2 *Ordinat* cassette; **c. d'alimentation** *(de copieuse, d'imprimante)* paper tray; **c. à bande magnétique** mag tape cassette; **c. compacte numérique** digital compact cassette; **c. de fontes** font cassette; **c. numérique** digital audio tape; **c. de polices de caractères** font cassette

3 *(coffret)* casket

4 *(trésor royal)* privy purse

cassettothèque [kasɛtɔtɛk] NF cassette library

casseur, -euse [kasœr, -øz] NM,F **1** *(dans une manifestation)* rioting demonstrator **2** *Fam (cambrioleur)* burglar **3** *(ferrailleur)* scrap dealer, *Br* scrap merchant **4 c. de pierres** stonebreaker

cassie [kasi] NF *Bot (acacia)* sponge tree

cassier¹ [kasje] NM *Bot* **1** *(arbuste)* cassia **2** *(acacia)* sponge tree

cassier² [kasje] NM *Typ* case-rack

Cassin [kasɛ̃] *voir* **mont**

cassine [kasin] NF *Arch (petite maison)* small house

Cassiopée [kasjɔpe] NPR *Myth & Astron* Cassiopeia

cassis [kasis] NM **1** *(baie)* blackcurrant **2** *(plante)* blackcurrant bush **3** *(liqueur)* blackcurrant liqueur, cassis **4** *Fam (tête)* nut **5** *(dos d'âne)* dip

cassissier [kasisje] NM *Bot* blackcurrant bush

cassitérite [kasiterit] NF *Minér* cassiterite, tinstone

Cassius [kasjys] NPR Cassius

cassolette [kasɔlɛt] NF **1** *Culin* small baking dish **2** *(brûle-parfum)* incense-burner

cassonade [kasɔnad] NF light brown sugar

cassoulet [kasulɛ] NM *Culin* cassoulet, haricot bean stew *(with pork, goose or duck)*

cassure [kasyr] NF **1** *(fissure)* crack **2** *(rupture dans la vie, dans le rythme)* break **3** *(d'un tissu)* fold; **la c. de son pantalon** where his/her trousers rest on his/her shoes **4** *Géol* break; *(faille)* fault

castagne [kastaɲ] NF *Fam (coup)* clout, wallop; **aimer la c.** to like fighting■, *Br* to like a good scrap; **chercher la c.** to be looking for a fight■; **va y avoir de la c.** there's going to be a fist fight *or Br* punch-up

castagner [3] [kastaɲe] *Fam* VT to clout, to wallop
▸**se castagner** VPR to have a fist fight *or Br* a punch-up

castagnettes [kastaɲɛt] NFPL castanets; **ses dents jouaient des c.** his/her teeth were chattering; **ses genoux jouaient des c.** his/her knees were knocking

castagnole [kastaɲɔl] NF *Ich* damselfish

castard, -e [kastar, -ard] *Belg* = **costaud**

caste [kast] NF caste; **avoir l'esprit de c.** to be class conscious; **esprit de c.** class consciousness

castel [kastɛl] NM *Littéraire* small castle

castelperronien [kastɛlperɔnjɛ̃] NM *Hist* Castelperronian, Chatelperronian

castillan, -e [kastijã, -an] ADJ Castilian
■ NM *(dialecte)* Castilian
❑ **Castillan, -e** NM,F Castilian

Castille [kastij] NF **la C.** Castile; **en C.** in Castile; **C.-La Manche** La Mancha; **C.-León** Leon

castine [kastin] NF *Métal* limestone flux

casting [kastiŋ] NM *Cin & Théât (distribution)* casting; *(acteurs)* cast; **passer un c.** to go to an audition

castonguette [kastɔ̃gɛt] NF *Fam* medical insurance card■

Castor [kastɔr] NPR *Myth* **C. et Pollux** Castor and Pollux

castor [kastɔr] NM **1** *(animal)* beaver **2** *(fourrure)* beaver; **c. du Canada** Canadian beaver fur

castorette [kastɔrɛt] NF imitation beaver fur

castoréum [kastɔreɔm] NM *Pharm & (en parfumerie)* castoreum

castramétation [kastrametasjɔ̃] NF *Antiq & Mil* castrametation

castrat [kastra] NM **1** *Mus* castrato **2** *(homme castré)* castrated man, eunuch

castrateur, -trice [kastratœr, -tris] ADJ *Psy* castrating; *Fig (autoritaire)* repressive

castration [kastrasjɔ̃] NF **1** *(d'un homme, d'une femme)* castration; *Psy* **complexe de c.** castration complex; **c. chimique** chemical castration **2** *(d'un animal mâle)* castration; *(d'un cheval)* gelding; *(d'un animal domestique → mâle)* neutering; *(→ femelle)* spaying, neutering **3** *Bot* castration

castratrice [kastratris] *voir* **castrateur**

castrer [3] [kastre] VT **1** *(homme, femme)* to castrate **2** *(animal mâle)* to castrate; *(cheval)* to geld; *(animal domestique → mâle)* to neuter; *(→ femelle)* to spay, to neuter **3** *Bot* to castrate

Castries [kastri] NPR *Géog* Castries

castrisme [kastrism] NM *Pol* Castroism

castriste [kastrist] *Pol* ADJ Castroist
■ NMF Castroist, Castro supporter

castrum [kastrɔm] NM *Antiq* castrum

casuarina [kazɥarina] NM *Bot* casuarina

casuel, -elle [kazɥɛl] ADJ **1** *(éventuel)* fortuitous **2** *Ling* case *(avant n)* **3** *Belg (fragile)* fragile

casuellement [kazɥɛlmã] ADV *Arch & Littéraire* fortuitously, accidentally

casuiste [kazɥist] NM casuist

casuistique [kazɥistik] NF casuistry

casus belli [kazysbeli] NM INV casus belli

CAT [seate] NF *(abrév* **Confédération autonome du travail***)* = French trade union
■ NM *(abrév* **Centre d'aide par le travail***)* = day centre which helps disabled people to find work and become more independent

cata[1] [kata] NF *Fam* **c'est la c.** it's a disaster■

cata[2] [kata] NF *(abrév* **catamaran***)* cat

catabatique [katabatik] ADJ *Météo* katabatic

catabolique [katabɔlik] ADJ *Biol & Chim* catabolic

catabolisme [katabɔlism] NM *Biol & Chim* catabolism

catabolite [katabɔlit] NM *Biol & Chim* catabolite

catachrèse [katakrɛz] NF *Ling* catachresis

cataclysmal, -e, -aux, -ales [kataklismal, -o] ADJ **1** *Géog* cataclysmal, cataclysmic **2** *(bouleversant)* catastrophic, disastrous, cataclysmic

cataclysme [kataklism] NM **1** *Géog* natural disaster, cataclysm **2** *(bouleversement)* cataclysm, catastrophe, disaster

cataclysmique [kataklismik] ADJ **1** *Géog* cataclysmal, cataclysmic **2** *(bouleversant)* catastrophic, disastrous, cataclysmic

catacombes [katakɔ̃b] NFPL catacombs

Culture

LES CATACOMBES

The catacombs of Paris (usually simply referred to as "les Catacombes") are disused underground quarries linked by a network of tunnels and were used at the end of the 18th century to store the human remains of around six million people that were moved there in order to relieve the "overpopulation" of various Parisian cemeteries. During the Second World War, the French resistance had hideouts there, and for years the catacombs have remained popular for illicit meetings, concerts and parties and have attracted people looking for an interesting and spooky experience. Visitors can walk through the tunnels of the catacombs, past the millions of carefully stacked skulls, in the Denfert-Rochereau district of the 14th arrondissement of Paris.

---

catadioptre [katadjɔptr] NM **1** *(sur une voiture, sur un vélo)* reflector **2** *(sur une route)* cat's eye

catadioptrique [katadjɔptrik] ADJ *Opt & Phot* catadioptric

catafalque [katafalk] NM catafalque

cataire [katɛr] NF *Bot* catmint

catalan, -e [katalã, -an] ADJ Catalan
■ NM *(langue)* Catalan
❑ **Catalan, -e** NM,F Catalan

catalanisme [katalanism] NM *Pol* Catalanism

catalepsie [katalɛpsi] NF *Méd* catalepsy; **tomber en c.** to have a cataleptic fit

cataleptique [katalɛptik] *Méd* ADJ cataleptic
■ NMF cataleptic

catalogage [katalɔgaʒ] NM cataloguing

Catalogne [katalɔɲ] NF **la C.** Catalonia; **en C.** in Catalonia

catalogne [katalɔɲ] NF *Can Tex* = material woven from strips of coloured fabric, used for rugs and bedspreads

catalogue [katalɔg] NM **1** *(liste → de bibliothèque, d'exposition)* catalogue; **faire le c. des toiles exposées** to catalogue *or* to itemize the exhibits; *Beaux-Arts* **c. raisonné** catalogue raisonné **2** *Com (illustré)* catalogue; *(non illustré)* price list; **c. d'échantillons** sample book; **c. électronique** electronic catalogue; **c. en ligne** on-line catalogue; **c. illustré** illustrated catalogue; **c. des prix** price list; **c. de vente par correspondance** mail-order catalogue; **je n'achète jamais rien sur c.** I never buy anything from a catalogue **3** *Péj (énumération)* (long) list

cataloguer [3] [katalɔge] VT **1** *(livre)* to list, to catalogue; *(bibliothèque)* to catalogue; *(œuvre, marchandise)* to catalogue, to put into a catalogue **2** *Fam (juger)* to label, to categorize, to pigeonhole; **j'ai horreur d'être catalogué** I hate people putting labels on me; **il s'est fait c. comme dilettante** he was labelled a dilettante

catalpa [katalpa] NM *Bot* catalpa

catalyse [kataliz] NF *Chim* catalysis

catalyser [3] [katalize] VT **1** *(provoquer → forces, critiques)* to act as a catalyst for **2** *Chim* to catalyse

catalyseur [katalizœr] NM **1** *(personne, journal)* catalyst; **il a été le c. de...** he acted as a catalyst for... **2** *Chim* catalyst

catalytique [katalitik] ADJ *Chim* catalytic

catamaran [katamarã] NM *Naut* **1** *(voilier)* catamaran **2** *(flotteurs)* floats

Catane [katan] NM Catania

cataphore [katafɔr] NF *Med* cataphora

cataphorèse [kataforez] NF *Phys & Méd* cataphoresis

Cataphote® [katafɔt] NM **1** *(sur une voiture, sur un vélo)* reflector **2** *(sur une route)* cat's eye

cataplasme [kataplasm] NM **1** *Méd* poultice, cataplasm **2** *Fam (aliment)* **j'ai encore ce c. sur l'estomac** I can still feel that lead weight in my stomach

cataplectique [kataplɛktik] ADJ *Méd* cataplectic

cataplexie [kataplɛksi] NF *Méd* cataplexy **2** *Zool* cataplexis

catapultage [katapyltaʒ] NM **1** *Aviat & Mil* catapulting **2** *Fig (d'un employé)* rapid promotion

catapulte [katapylt] NF **1** *Aviat* catapult launcher **2** *Mil* catapult

catapulter [3] [katapylte] VT **1** *Tech & Aviat* to catapult **2** *Fig (employé)* **il a été catapulté directeur** he was catapulted into the manager's job; **elle s'est fait c. chef de cabinet** she got herself promoted over everybody else to principal private secretary

cataracte [katarakt] NF **1** *Méd* cataract; **se faire opérer de la c.** to have a cataract operation **2** *(chute d'eau)* waterfall, cataract

cataractopièse [kataraktɔpjez] NF *Méd* couching

catarhinien [katarinjɛ̃] *Zool* NM member of the Catarrhina family
❑ **catarhiniens** NMPL Catarrhina

catarrhal, -e, -aux, -ales [kataral, -o] ADJ *Méd* catarrhal

catarrhe [katar] NM *Méd* catarrh

catarrheux, -euse [katarø, -øz] *Méd* ADJ catarrhal, catarrhous
■ NM,F catarrh sufferer

catastase [katastaz] NF *Littérature* catastasis

catastrophe [katastrɔf] NF **1** *(désastre → en avion, en voiture)* disaster; *(→ dans une vie, dans un gouvernement)* catastrophe, disaster; **c. ferroviaire/aérienne** rail/air disaster; **c. naturelle** natural disaster; **éviter la c.** to avoid a catastrophe; **frôler la c.** to come close to disaster; **ce n'est pas une c.** it's not the end of the world; **c'est la c.!** it's a disaster!; **une c., la soirée chez Claude!** Claude's party was a total disaster!; *Fam* **une c., ce type!** the guy's a walking disaster!; **c., il nous manque deux chaises!** disaster, we're two chairs short!
2 *Théât* catastrophe, denouement
❑ **en catastrophe** ADV **partir en c.** to rush off; **s'arrêter en c.** to make an emergency stop; **atterrir en c.** to make a forced *or* an emergency landing

catastrophé, -e [katastrɔfe] ADJ *Fam* stunned; **un air c.** a stunned look; **il était c. de l'apprendre** he was stunned when he heard

catastropher [3] [katastrɔfe] VT to shatter, to stun

catastrophique [katastrɔfik] ADJ catastrophic, disastrous

catastrophisme [katastrɔfism] NM **1** *(pessimisme)* pessimism; **ne fais pas de c.!** don't be so pessimistic! **2** *Géol* catastrophism

catastrophiste [katastrɔfist] ADJ **1** *Fam (pessimiste)* pessimistic■, gloomy■; **être c.** to be full of doom and gloom **2** *Géol (relatif au catastrophisme)* catastrophist

catatonie [katatɔni] NF *Psy* catatonia, catatonic schizophrenia

catatonique [katatɔnik] *Psy* ADJ catatonic
■ NMF catatonic

cat-boat [katbot] *(pl* **cat-boats***)* NM *Naut* catboat

catch [katʃ] NM *Boxe (all-in)* wrestling; **faire du c.** to wrestle

catcher [3] [katʃe] VI *Boxe* to wrestle
■ VT *Can Joual* **1** *(attraper)* to catch■ **2** *(comprendre)* to get, to understand■

catcheur, -euse [katʃœr, -øz] NM,F *Boxe* (all-in) wrestler

catéchèse [kateʃɛz] NF *Rel* catechesis

catéchisation [kateʃizasjɔ̃] NF **1** *Rel* catechization, catechizing **2** *Péj* indoctrination

catéchiser [3] [kateʃize] VT **1** *Rel* to catechize **2** *Péj (endoctriner)* to indoctrinate; *(sermonner)* to preach at, to lecture

catéchisme [kateʃism] NM **1** *Rel (enseignement, livre)* catechism; **aller au c.** to go to catechism, ≃ to go to Sunday school **2** *Fig* doctrine, creed; **cela fait partie de leur c.** it's Gospel truth to them

catéchiste [katefist] NMF *Rel (gén)* catechist; *(pour enfants)* Sunday-school teacher

catécholamine [katekɔlamin] NF *Biol & Chim* catecholamine

catéchuménat [katekymena] NM *Rel* catechumenate

catéchumène [katekymɛn] NMF **1** *Rel* catechumen **2** *(que l'on initie)* novice

catégorie [kategɔri] NF **1** *(pour classifier → des objets, des concepts)* category, class, type; *(→ des employés)* grade; **mettre dans la même c.** to put in the same category, to lump together; **il appartient à cette c. de gens qui…** he belongs to that category *or* group of people who…; **c. d'âge** age group; **c. de produits** product category; **c. sociale** social class; **c. socio-économique** socioeconomic class; **c. socio-professionnelle** socioprofessional group **2** *(qualité → dans les transports, dans les hôtels)* class; **hôtel de seconde c.** second-class hotel; **morceau de première/deuxième/troisième c.** *(viande)* prime/second/cheap cut **3** *Sport* class; **premier dans sa c.** first in his class; **toutes catégories** for all comers **4** *Physiol* category

catégoriel, -elle [kategɔrjɛl] ADJ **1** *(d'une catégorie)* category *(avant n)*; **classement c.** classification by category **2** *(d'une catégorie socio-professionnelle)* **revendications catégorielles** sectional claims *(relating to one category of workers only)* **3** *Ling & Phil* category *(avant n)*

catégorique [kategɔrik] ADJ **1** *(non ambigu → refus)* flat, categorical, point-blank; *(→ réponse)* categorical **2** *(décidé)* adamant; **il a été c.** he was adamant; **elle a été c. sur ce point** she was adamant *or* categorical on this point; **là-dessus, je serai c.** I'm not prepared to budge on that; **je suis c.** *(j'en suis sûr)* I'm positive **3** *Phil* categorical

catégoriquement [kategɔrikmã] ADV *(nettement → affirmer)* categorically; *(→ refuser)* categorically, flatly, point-blank

catégorisation [kategɔrizasjɔ̃] NF categorization

catégoriser [3] [kategɔrize] VT *(ranger)* to categorize

catelle [katɛl] NF *Suisse* ceramic tile

caténaire [katenɛr] *Rail* ADJ **suspension c.** catenary
NF catenary

catgut [katgyt] NM *Méd* catgut

cathare [katar] *Rel & Hist* ADJ Cathar
❏ **Cathare** NMF Cathar

catharisme [katarism] NM *Rel & Hist* Catharism

catharomètre [katarɔmɛtr] NM *Chim* katharometer

catharsis [katarsis] NF *Psy & Théât* catharsis

cathartique [katartik] ADJ *Psy & Théât* cathartic

Cathay [katɛ] NM Cathay

cathédral, -e, -aux, -ales [katedral, -o] ADJ *Rel* cathedral *(avant n)*
❏ **cathédrale** NF *(édifice)* cathedral

cathèdre [katɛdr] NF cathedra

Catherine [katrin] NPR **C. d'Aragon** Catherine of Aragon; **C. de Médicis** Catherine de Medici; **C. de Russie** Catherine the Great

catherinette [katrinɛt] NF = woman who is still single and aged 25 on St Catherine's Day

cathéter [katetɛr] NM *Méd* catheter, can(n)ula

cathétérisme [kateterism] NM *Méd* catheterization

cathétomètre [katetɔmɛtr] NM cathetometer

catho [kato] *Fam* ADJ Catholic▪
NMF Catholic▪
❏ **Catho** NF **la c. d'Angers/de Paris** = the private Catholic university in Angers/Paris

cathode [katɔd] NF *Élec & Chim* cathode

cathodique [katɔdik] ADJ *Élec* cathodic; *Fig* **l'univers c.** the world of television

cathodoluminescence [katɔdɔlyminɛsɑ̃s] NF *Électron* cathodoluminescence

catholiciser [3] [katɔlisize] VT *Rel* to convert to Roman Catholicism

catholicisme [katɔlisism] NM *Rel* (Roman) Catholicism

catholicité [katɔlisite] NF *Rel (caractère)* catholicity; **la c.** *(église)* the (Roman) Catholic Church; *(fidèles)* the (Roman) Catholic community

catholicos [katɔlikɔs] NM *Rel* catholicos

catholique [katɔlik] ADJ **1** *Rel* (Roman) Catholic; **une institution c.** a Catholic *or* an RC school **2** *Fam (locution)* **pas très c. comme façon de faire** *(peu conventionnel)* not a very orthodox way of doing things; *(malhonnête)* not a very kosher way of doing things; **un individu pas très c.** a rather shady individual
NMF *Rel* (Roman) Catholic

catholiquement [katɔlikmã] ADV *Rel* catholically, according to the ways of the (Roman) Catholic church

catiche [katif] NF *Can Péj* sissy

catilinaire [katilinɛr] NF *Littéraire* **1** *(oraison)* Catilinarian oration **2** *(satire)* diatribe, outburst

catimini [katimini] ❏ **en catimini** ADV on the sly *or* quiet; **arriver/partir en c.** to sneak in/out

catin [katɛ̃] NF **1** *Vieilli (prostituée)* trollop **2** *Can (poupée)* doll **3** *Can (pansement)* finger bandage

catiner [3] [katine] VI *Can* to play with dolls; *Fig* to spoil a child

cation [katjɔ̃] NM *Chim* cation

cationique [katjɔnik] ADJ *Chim* cationic

catir [32] [katir] VT *Tex* to press; **c. à chaud/à froid** to hot-press/cold-press

catissage [katisaʒ] NM *Tex* pressing

catoblépas [katɔblepas] NM *Myth* catoblepas

catogan [katɔgã] NM = large bow holding the hair at the back of the neck

Caton [katɔ̃] NPR Cato

catoptrique [katɔptrik] *Opt* ADJ catoptric, catoptrical
NF catoptrics *(singulier)*

Cattégat [kategat] NM *Géog* **le C.** the Kattegat

cattleya [katleja] NM *Bot* cattleya

Catulle [katyl] NPR Catullus

Caucase [kokaz] NM **1** *(montagnes)* **le C.** the Caucasus **2** *(région)* **le C.** Caucasia; **dans le C.** in Caucasia

caucasien, -enne [kokazjɛ̃, -ɛn] ADJ Caucasian; **les langues caucasiennes** the Caucasian languages
❏ **Caucasien, -enne** NM,F Caucasian

caucasique [kokazik] ADJ *(peuple, langue)* Caucasian; **les langues caucasiques** the Caucasian languages

cauchemar [koʃmar] NM **1** *(mauvais rêve)* nightmare; **faire un c.** to have a nightmare; **ça me donne des cauchemars rien que d'y penser** it gives me nightmares just thinking about it **2** *(situation)* nightmare; **c'était un c. pour moi d'apprendre les verbes irréguliers** learning irregular verbs was a real nightmare for me; **une vision de c.** a nightmare vision **3** *(personne assommante)* nuisance

cauchemarder [3] [koʃmarde] VI to have nightmares; **la perspective d'une semaine avec eux me fait c.** the prospect of spending a week with them is a real nightmare

cauchemardesque [koʃmardɛsk], **cauchemardeux, -euse** [koʃmardø, -øz] ADJ **1** *(sommeil)* nightmarish **2** *Fig (horrifiant)* nightmarish, hellish

cauchois, -e [koʃwa, -az] ADJ of/from the Caux region
❏ **Cauchois, -e** NM,F = inhabitant of or person from the Caux region

caucus [kokys] NM *Belg Pol* caucus

caudal, -e, -aux, -ales [kodal, -o] ADJ *Zool* tail *(avant n)*, *Spéc* caudal

caudataire [kodatɛr] NM **1** *(du Pape, d'un roi)* train-bearer **2** *Fam* toady, flatterer▪

caudé, -e [kode] ADJ *Anat* tailed, *Spéc* caudate
NM *(dans la Beauce)* soup made with milk

caudebec [kodbɛk] NM *Vieilli* felt hat

caudillo [kaɔdijo] NM *Hist* caudillo; **le C.** General Franco

Caudine [kodin] ADJ *Antiq* **les Fourches Caudines** the Caudine Forks; *Fig* **passer sous les Fourches Caudines** to be forced to accept humiliating terms

caudrette [kodrɛt] NF *Pêche* lobster-net, bow-net

caulerpe [kolɛrp] NF *Bot* caulerpa

caulinaire [kolinɛr] ADJ *Bot* cauline, caulinary

cauri [kori], **cauris** [kori] NM *Zool* cowrie (shell)

causal, -e, -als *ou* **-aux, -ales** [kozal, -o] ADJ **1** *(lien)* causal **2** *Gram* causal

causalgie [kozalʒi] NF *Méd* causalgia

causalisme [kozalism] NM *Phil* doctrine of causality

causalité [kozalite] NF causality; **rapport de c.** causal relation; *Phil* **principe de c.** causal principle; *Jur* **c. adéquate** factual causation;

causant, -e [kozã, -ãt] ADJ *Fam* chatty; **il n'est pas très c.** *(coopératif)* he's not exactly forthcoming

causatif, -ive [kozatif, -iv] ADJ *Gram* causative

CAUSE [koz] NF **1** *(origine, motif)* cause, reason; **remonter jusqu'aux causes** to go back to the origins; **la c. profonde de sa tristesse** the underlying reason for his/her sadness; **quelle est la c. de son départ?** what caused him/her to leave?; **on ne connaît pas la c. de sa mort** the cause of death is unknown; **être (la) c. de qch** to be the cause of sth, to cause sth; **les enfants sont souvent c. de soucis** children are often a cause of worry; **c'est elle qui en est la c.** it's her fault, she's to blame; *Littéraire* **le mauvais temps est c. que je n'ai pu aller vous rendre visite** I wasn't able to come and see you on account of the bad weather; **relation de c. à effet** causal relationship; *Prov* **à petite c. grands effets** great oaks from little acorns grow; **il s'est fâché, et non sans c.** he got angry, and with good reason; **et pour c.!** and for a very good reason!; **il n'est pas venu, et pour c.!** no wonder he didn't come!; **elle est malheureuse, et pour c.!** she's unhappy, and with good reason *or* as well she might be!

2 *Phil* cause; **la c. première/seconde/finale** the first/second/final cause

3 *Jur (affaire → gén)* case, (law)suit; *(→ à plaider)* brief; *(motif)* cause; **un avocat sans causes** a briefless barrister; **la c. est entendue** each side has put forward its case; *Fig* it's an open and shut case; **c. adéquate** adequate cause; *aussi Fig* **c. célèbre** cause célèbre; **c. civile** civil action; **c. criminelle** criminal proceedings; **c. dirimante de mariage** diriment impediment to marriage; *aussi Fig* **c. étrangère** = cause for which the promisor is not liable; **c. évocable** = case that may be transferred to a superior court; **c. illicite** unjust cause; **c. immédiate** proximate cause; **c. licite** just cause; **plaider la c. de qn** to plead sb's case

4 *(parti que l'on prend)* cause; **la c. des mineurs** the miners' cause; **faire c. commune avec qn** to join forces with sb; **une c. perdue** a lost cause; **une bonne c.** a good cause; **pour la bonne c.** *(pour un bon motif)* for a good cause; *Hum (en vue du mariage)* with honourable intentions; **je suis tout acquis à sa c.** I support him/her wholeheartedly

❏ **à cause de** PRÉP **1** *(par la faute de)* because *or* on account of, due *or* owing to; **j'ai perdu mon temps à c. de toi** I wasted my time because of you

2 *(en considération de)* because *or* on account of, due *or* owing to; **acceptée à c. de ses diplômes** taken on on account of her qualifications

3 *(par égard pour)* for the sake *or* because of; **ils sont venus à c. de votre amitié** they came because of your friendship

❏ **en cause** ADJ **1** *(concerné)* in question; **la voiture en c. était à l'arrêt** the car involved *or* in question was stationary; **la somme/l'enjeu en c.** the amount/the thing at stake **2** *(que l'on suspecte)* **les financiers en c.** the financiers involved; **certains ministres sont en c.** some ministers are implicated **3** *(contesté)* **être en c.** *(talent)* to be in question; **votre honnêteté n'est pas en c.** your honesty is not in question *or* in doubt; *Jur* **affaire en c.** case before the court
ADV **1** *(en accusation)* **mettre qn en c.** to implicate sb; **mettre qch en c.** to call sth into question **2** *(en doute)* **remettre en c.** *(principe)* to question, to challenge; **son départ remet tout en c.** his/her departure reopens the whole question *or* debate

❏ **en tout état de cause** ADV in any case, at all events, whatever happens; **en tout état de c., nous ne pouvons partir que mardi** whatever happens, we can only leave on Tuesday

❏ **pour cause de** PRÉP owing to, because of; **fermé pour c. de décès** *(magasin)* closed owing to bereavement; **démissionner pour c. de maladie** to resign owing to ill-health *or* on grounds of health

causer [3] [koze] **VT** (*provoquer* → *peine, problème*) to cause; **c. des ennuis à qn** to make trouble for sb; **son départ nous a causé beaucoup de chagrin** his/her departure distressed us greatly *or* caused us great distress; **cela m'a causé de graves ennuis** it got me into a lot of trouble

VI *Fam* **1** (*bavarder*) **c. (à** *ou* **avec qn)** to chat (to sb); **je ne lui cause plus!** (*je suis fâché*) I'm not talking to him/her!; **c. de** to talk about; **c. de la pluie et du beau temps, c. de choses et d'autres** to talk about this and that; **cause toujours (, tu m'intéresses)!** (*je fais ce que je veux*) yeah, yeah (whatever)!; (*tu pourrais m'écouter*) don't mind me!; **je l'avais prévenu, mais cause toujours!** I'd warned him but I might as well have been talking to the wall!

2 (*médire*) to gossip, to prattle; **ça a fait c. dans le quartier** it set tongues wagging in the neighbourhood

3 (*suivi d'un nom sans article*) (*parler*) **c. politique** to talk about politics, to talk politics

> *Allusion*
>
> **Tu causes, tu causes, c'est tout ce que tu sais faire**
> The novel *Zazie dans le métro* (Raymond Queneau, 1959), filmed under the same title by Louis Malle in 1960, tells the story of a cheeky young girl who comes to Paris to visit her uncle. This quote "You talk and talk, but you don't actually do anything" is today used to someone as a reproach, and it can be loosely translated as "You just talk a lot of hot air."

causerie [kozri] **NF 1** (*discussion*) chat, talk **2** (*conférence*) informal talk (*in front of an audience*)

causette [kozɛt] **NF 1** *Fam* **faire la c. à qn** to chat to sb; **faire un brin de c.** to chew the fat, *Br* to have a chinwag **2** *Ordinat* chat

causeur, -euse [kozœr, -øz] **ADJ** chatty, talkative
  NM,F talker, conversationalist
  ❏ **causeuse NF** love seat

causse [kos] **NM** *Géog* limestone plateau

caussenard, -e [kosənar, -ard] **ADJ** of/from the Causses
  ❏ **Caussenard, -e NM,F** = inhabitant of or person from the Causses

Causses [kos] **NMPL les C.** the Causses (*area to the south and south-west of the Massif Central*)

causticité [kostisite] **NF** *Chim & Fig* causticity

caustique [kostik] **ADJ 1** *Chim* caustic **2** *Fig* (*mordant*) caustic, biting, sarcastic
  NM *Chim* caustic
  NF *Opt* caustic (curve)

cautèle [kotɛl] **NF** *Littéraire* wiliness, cunning

cauteleux, -euse [kotlø, -øz] **ADJ** *Littéraire* wily, cunning

cautère [kotɛr] **NM 1** *Méd* cautery **2** (*locution*) **c'est un c. sur une jambe de bois** it's as much use as a poultice on a wooden leg

cautérisation [koterizasjɔ̃] **NF** *Méd* cauterization, cauterizing

cautériser [3] [koterize] **VT** *Méd* to cauterize

caution [kosjɔ̃] **NF 1** *Jur* bail; **se porter c. pour qn** to go *or* stand bail for sb; **payer la c. de qn** to bail sb out, *Am* to post bail for sb
  2 (*garant*) surety, guarantor; **se porter c. pour qn** to stand security *or* surety *or* guarantee for sb; **les locataires étudiants doivent fournir une c. parentale** student tenants must provide proof that their parents will stand guarantor *or* surety for them; **c. solidaire** = statement signed by a third party guaranteeing payment of rent in the event of non-payment by the tenant
  3 (*garantie morale*) guarantee; (*soutien*) support, backing; **avec la c. du ministre** with the support *or* the backing of the minister; **donner** *ou* **apporter sa c. à** to support, to back; **c. juratoire** guarantee given on oath
  4 *Com & Fin* (*security*) deposit; **verser une c. de 50 euros** to pay 50 euros as security, to put down a 50-euro deposit (as security); **c. d'adjudication** bid bond; **c. bancaire** *ou* **de banque** bank guarantee; **c. de soumission** bid bond
  ❏ **sous caution ADV** (*libérer*) on bail

cautionnement [kosjonmɑ̃] **NM 1** (*contrat*) surety *or* security bond **2** (*somme*) security; *Jur* bail; **c. réel** collateral security **3** (*soutien*) support, backing

cautionner [3] [kosjone] **VT 1** *Jur* **c. qn** (*se porter caution*) to bail sb out, *Am* to post bail for sb; (*se porter garant*) to stand *or* to go bail for sb
  2 (*soutenir*) to support, to back; **je tiens à faire c. cette décision par le directeur des ventes** I want to get the sales director to back me up on this decision; **se faire c. par ses parents pour la location d'un appartement** to provide a parental guarantee when renting a flat

Caux [ko] **NM le pays de C.** the Caux region; **dans le pays de C.** in the Caux region

cavage [kavaʒ] **NM** *Constr* excavation

cavaillon¹ [kavajɔ̃] **NM** balk (*between rows of vine*)

cavaillon² [kavajɔ̃] **NM** Cavaillon melon

cavalcade [kavalkad] **NF 1** (*défilé*) cavalcade **2** (*course*) stampede; **pas de c. dans l'escalier, s'il vous plaît!** please, no stampeding down the stairs!; **c'est tout le temps la c.** we're always in such a rush

cavalcader [3] [kavalkade] **VI** to scamper around

cavale [kaval] **NF 1** *Littéraire* (*jument*) mare **2** *Fam Arg crime* jailbreak■; **être en c.** to be on the run

cavaler [3] [kavale] **VI** *Fam* **1** (*courir*) to run *or* to rush (around); **j'ai cavalé toute la journée pour trouver un cadeau** I ran around all day looking for a present; **je cavale tout le temps** I'm on the go the whole time
  2 (*se hâter*) to get a move on; **il va falloir c. si tu veux avoir ton train** you'll have to get a move on if you want to catch your train
  3 (*à la recherche de femmes*) to chase women; (*à la recherche d'hommes*) to chase men; **il ne pense qu'à c. après les femmes** chasing women is all he (ever) thinks about
  VT *très Fam* (*agacer*) **il commence à me c.** *Br* he's starting to get right up my nose, *Am* he's starting to tick me off
  ► **se cavaler VPR** *Fam* to clear off

cavalerie [kavalri] **NF 1** *Mil* cavalry; **c. légère** light (cavalry *or* horse) brigade; **c. lourde, grosse c.** armoured cavalry; *Fig* **la grosse c.** the run-of-the-mill stuff **2** *Com* **effets** *ou* **papiers de c.** accommodation bills *or* notes

cavaleur, -euse [kavalœr, -øz] *Fam* **ADJ** (*homme*) philandering■, womanizing; (*femme*) man-eating; **il est c.** he's a womanizer; **elle est cavaleuse** she'll go for anything in trousers
  NM philanderer■, womanizer
  ❏ **cavaleuse NF** man-eater

cavalier, -ère [kavalje, -ɛr] **ADJ 1** *Équitation* **allée** *ou* **piste cavalière** bridle path, bridleway
  2 *Péj* (*désinvolte* → *attitude*) offhand, cavalier; (→ *réponse*) curt, offhand; **agir de façon cavalière** to act in an offhand manner
  NM,F 1 *Équitation* rider **2** (*danseur*) partner
  NM 1 *Hist* Cavalier
  2 *Mil* cavalryman, mounted soldier
  3 *Bible* **les (quatre) Cavaliers de l'Apocalypse** the (Four) Horsemen of the Apocalypse
  4 (*pour aller au bal*) escort; **faire c. seul** (*dans une entreprise*) to go it alone; *Pol* to be a maverick
  5 *Échecs* knight
  6 *Can* (*amoureux*) boyfriend
  7 (*sur un dossier*) tab
  8 (*clou*) staple
  9 (*surcharge*) rider
  10 *Ordinat* jumper

cavalièrement [kavaljɛrmɑ̃] **ADV** casually, in a cavalier *or* an offhand manner

cavatine [kavatin] **NF** *Mus* cavatina

cave¹ [kav] **ADJ 1** *Littéraire* (*creux*) hollow, sunken
  2 *Anat voir* **veine**

cave² [kav] **NM 1** *Fam Arg crime* (*étranger au milieu*) outsider■
  2 *Fam* (*dupe*) sucker, *Br* mug, *Am* patsy
  ADJ *Can Fam* (*idiot*) stupid■, *Am* dumb; **c'est tellement c. comme film!** it's such a stupid film!

cave³ [kav] **NF 1** (*pièce*) cellar; *Fig* **de la c. au grenier** (*ranger, nettoyer*) from top to bottom; **c. à charbon** coal cellar; **c. à vin** wine cellar
  2 (*vins*) (wine) cellar; **avoir une bonne c.** to keep a good cellar
  3 *Can* (*sous-sol*) basement, cellar

4 (*cabaret*) *Br* cellar *or Am* basement nightclub
  5 (*coffret*) **c. à cigares** cigar box; **c. à liqueurs** cellaret

> **'Les Caves du Vatican'** *Gide* 'The Vatican Cellars'

cave⁴ [kav] **NF** *Cartes* (*gén*) stake; (*au poker*) ante

caveau, -x [kavo] **NM 1** (*sépulture*) vault, tomb, burial chamber **2** (*cabaret*) club (*in a cellar*)

caveçon [kavsɔ̃] **NM** *Équitation* cavesson; *Littéraire* **donner un coup de c. à qn** to humiliate sb

cavée [kave] **NF** *Belg* **1** *Géol* dry limestone valley **2** (*chemin creux*) sunken lane

caver¹ [3] [kave] **VT** *Littéraire* (*creuser*) to hollow *or* to dig (out)

caver² [3] [kave] *Cartes* **VT** to put up
  VI to put up a sum of money; **c. au plus fort** = to put up an amount equal to the highest on the table; *Fig* to carry things to extremes; *Fig* **c. sur la bêtise humaine** to count upon *or* bank on human stupidity

caverne [kavɛrn] **NF 1** (*grotte*) cave, cavern; **une c. de brigands** a den of thieves; **la c. d'Ali Baba** Ali Baba's cave; *Fig* **c'est une véritable c. d'Ali Baba** it's a real treasure-trove **2** *Méd* cavity

> *Allusion*
>
> **La Caverne d'Ali Baba**
> This expression means "Ali Baba's Cave". Although the story of Ali Baba and the Forty Thieves is equally familiar in English (Ali Baba seeing the thieves' treasure from his hiding-place in a jar), we are more apt to speak of a place where riches are displayed as an Aladdin's cave in English. The French will speak, for example, of a wonderful bookshop as **une vraie caverne d'Ali Baba** whereas we might speak of a "treasure-trove" in that context, reserving "Aladdin's Cave" for a display of something bright and glittering. In short, though the idea is similar in both languages, the usage varies slightly.

caverneux, -euse [kavɛrnø, -øz] **ADJ 1** (*voix*) sepulchral **2** *Méd* (*souffle, râle*) cavernous **3** *Anat* (*tissu*) cavernous

cavernicole [kavɛrnikol] *Zool* **ADJ** cave-dwelling, *Spéc* cavernicolous
  NM cave-dwelling *or Spéc* cavernicolous animal

cavet [kavɛ] **NM** *Archit* cavetto, hollowed moulding

caviar [kavjar] **NM 1** *Culin* caviar, caviare; **c. rouge** salmon roe; **c. d'aubergines** *Br* aubergine *or Am* eggplant caviar(e); *Littéraire* **c'est du c. pour le peuple** it is caviar to the general **2** *Typ* blue pencil; **passer au c.** to blue-pencil, to censor

caviardage [kavjardaʒ] **NM** blue-pencilling, censoring; **après un bon c.** after a thorough going-over with the blue pencil

caviarder [3] [kavjarde] **VT** to blue-pencil, to censor

cavicorne [kavikorn] **NM** *Zool* cavicorn animal

caviste [kavist] **NM** cellarman

cavitaire [kavitɛr] **ADJ** *Méd* cavitary

cavitation [kavitasjɔ̃] **NF** *Phys, Tech & Métal* cavitation

cavité [kavite] **NF 1** (*trou*) cavity; **une c. entre deux roches** a cavity *or* gap between two rocks **2** *Anat* cavity; **c. articulaire** socket; **c. buccale** oral cavity; **c. cotyloïde** acetabulum; **c. dentaire** pulp cavity **3** *Électron* **c. résonante** resonant cavity, cavity resonator

Cayenne [kajɛn] **NM** Cayenne

cayeu, -x [kajø] **NM** *Hort* (*de tulipe*) off-set bulb

cayon [kajɔ̃] **NM** *Suisse Fam* (*cochon*) pig■; (*viande*) pork■

cazagot [kazago] **NM** *Can* papoose

cazette [kazɛt] = **casette**

CB¹ [sibi] **NF** *Rad* (*abrév* citizen's band, canaux banalisés) CB

CB² [sebe] **NF** *Banque* (*abrév écrite* **Carte Bleue**®) = bank card with which purchases are debited directly from the customer's bank account, *Br* ≃ debit card

CBV [sebeve] **NM** *Bourse* (*abrév* **conseil des bourses de valeurs**) = regulatory body of the Paris Stock Exchange

CC *Pol* (*abrév écrite* **corps consulaire**) CC
C/C [sese] **NM** *Banque & Compta* (*abrév* **compte chèque, compte courant**) C/A
cc 1 (*abrév écrite* **cuillère à café**) tsp **2** (*abrév écrite* **charges comprises**) inclusive of maintenance costs
CCB [sesebe] **NM** *Banque* (*abrév* **compte de chèque bancaire**) C/A
CCE [seseə] **NF** *UE* (*abrév* **Commission des communautés européennes**) ECC
CCI [sesei] **NF 1** (*abrév* **Chambre de commerce et d'industrie**) CCI **2** (*abrév* **Chambre de commerce internationale**) ICC
CCNUCC [seseɛnysese] **NF** (*abrév* **Convention-cadre des Nations Unies sur les changements climatiques**) UNFCCC
CCP [sesepe] **NM** *Banque* (*abrév* **compte chèque postal, compte courant postal**) = post office account, *Br* ≃ Giro account, *Am* ≃ Post Office checking account
CCR [seseɛr] **NM** *Fin* (*abrév* **coefficient de capitalisation des résultats**) p/e ratio
CD[1] [sede] **NM** (*abrév* **Compact Disc**) CD; (*CD-ROM*) CD, CD-ROM; **CD audio** audio CD; **CD réinscriptible** CD-RW; **CD vidéo** CD video, CDV
CD[2] **1** (*abrév écrite* **chemin départemental**) minor road **2** (*abrév écrite* **comité directeur**) steering committee **3** (*abrév écrite* **corps diplomatique**) CD
cd *Phys* (*abrév écrite* **candela**) cd
CDD [sedede] **NM** (*abrév* **contrat à durée déterminée**) fixed term contract; **elle est en C.** she's on a fixed term contract
CD-E [sedeə] **NM** (*abrév* **Compact Disc Erasable**) CD-E
CdF [sedeɛf] **NMPL** (*abrév* **Charbonnages de France**) = the French Coal Board
CDI [sedei] **NM 1** (*abrév* **centre de documentation et d'information**) ≃ school library **2** (*abrév* **contrat à durée indéterminée**) permanent (employment) contract; **elle est en C.** she's got a permanent contract
CD-I NM (*abrév écrite* **Compact Disc interactif**) CDI, interactive CD
CD-Photo [sedefoto] **NM** photo CD
CD-R [sedeɛr] **NM** (*abrév* **Compact Disc recordable**) CD-R
CD-ROM, CD-Rom [sederɔm] **NM INV** *Ordinat* (*abrév* **Compact Disc read-only memory**) CD-ROM; **C. d'installation** installation CD-ROM
CD-RW NM *Ordinat* (*abrév écrite* **Compact Disc Rewritable**) CD-RW
CDS [sedeɛs] **NM** *Pol* (*abrév* **Centre des démocrates sociaux**) = French political party
CDthèque [sedetɛk] **NF** CD library
CDU [sedey] **NF** (*abrév* **classification décimale universelle**) DDC
CDV [sedeve] **NM** (*abrév* **Compact Disc Video**) CDV
CE [seə] **NM 1** (*abrév* **comité d'entreprise**) works council **2** *Scol* (*abrév* **cours élémentaire**) = two-year subdivision of primary-level education in France (ages 7 to 9); **CE1** = second year of primary school, *Br* ≃ year 3; **CE2** = third year of primary school, *Br* ≃ year 4 **3** *UE* (*abrév* **conseil de l'Europe**) Council of Europe
NF *UE* (*abrév* **Communauté européenne**) EC

CE[1], CET, CETTE, CES [sə, sɛt, se]

cet is used before a masculine singular noun or adjective beginning with a vowel or mute h.

ADJ DÉMONSTRATIF 1 (*dans l'espace → proche*) (*singulier*) this; (*pluriel*) these; (*→ éloigné*) (*singulier*) that; (*pluriel*) those; **cet homme qui vient vers nous** the man (who's) coming towards us; **tiens, prends cette canne** here, take this walking-stick; **tu vois cet immeuble?** you see that building?; **regarde de ce côté-ci** look over here; **cette veste, là-bas en vitrine** that jacket, over there in the window; **cet homme qui gesticule là-bas** that man over there (who's) waving his arms about; **je ne connais pas cette région-là** I don't know that region; **ces arbres, ces fleurs, ces jardins lui rappelaient son enfance** these trees, these flowers, these gardens reminded him/her of his/her childhood
2 (*dans le temps → à venir*) (*singulier*) this; (*pluriel*) these; (*→ passé*) last; **vas-y ce matin** go this morning; **cette nuit nous mettrons le chauffage** tonight we'll put *or* turn the heating on; **cette nuit j'ai fait un rêve étrange** last night I had a strange dream; **cette semaine je n'ai rien fait** I haven't done a thing this *or* this past *or* this last week; **cette année-là** that year; **ces jours-ci** these days, lately; **un de ces jours** one of these days; **fait ce jour à Blois** witnessed by my hand this day in Blois
3 (*désignant → ce dont on a parlé*) (*singulier*) this, that; (*pluriel*) these, those; (*→ ce dont on va parler*) (*singulier*) this; (*pluriel*) these; **je t'ai déjà raconté cette histoire** I've told you that story before; **enfin, ces personnes se sont rencontrées** these people finally met; **cette remarque traduit son incompréhension** this *or* that remark shows that he/she doesn't understand; **écoute cette histoire et tu vas comprendre** listen to this story and you'll understand
4 (*suivi d'une proposition relative*) **voici ce pont dont je t'ai parlé** here's the *or* that bridge I told you about; **cet air que tu fredonnais** that *or* the tune you were humming; **il était de ces comédiens qui...** he was one of those actors who...
5 (*emploi expressif*) **cette douleur dans son regard!** such grief in his/her eyes!; *Fam* **ce peuple!** what a crowd!; *Fam* **ce culot!** what a nerve!, the cheek of it!; **cette idée!** what an idea!, the very idea!; **cet enfant est un modèle de sagesse!** this *or* that child is so well behaved!; **mais c'est qu'elle a grandi, cette petite!** hasn't she grown into a big girl!; *Fam* **et cette bière, elle vient?** so is that beer on its way or what?; **et ce roman, tu le commences quand?** when will you get started on that novel of yours?; *Fam* **et ces douleurs/cette grippe, comment ça va?** how's the pain/the flu doing?; **ce roquet n'entrera pas chez moi!** I won't have that nasty little dog in my house!; **et pour ces messieurs, ce sera?** now what will the *or* you gentlemen be having?; **ces dames sont au salon** the ladies are in the drawing room

CE[2] [sə]

ce becomes **c'** before a vowel.

PRON DÉMONSTRATIF 1 (*sujet du verbe "être"*) **c'est à Paris** it's in Paris; **c'est sur votre bureau** it's on your desk; **c'était hier** it was yesterday; **demain c'est dimanche** tomorrow is Sunday, it's Sunday tomorrow; **ce n'est pas un hôtel ici!** this is not a hotel!; **c'est toi!** it's you!; **qui a dit ça? – c'est moi/lui** who said that? – me/him, I/he did; **c'est exact!** that's right!; **c'est un escroc** he's a crook; **ce sont mes frères** they are my brothers; **ce doit être son mari** it must be her husband; **dire oui, c'est renoncer à sa liberté** saying yes means *or* amounts to giving up one's freedom; **tes amis, ce sont** *ou Fam* **c'est des gens bien sympathiques** your friends are really nice people; **ce ne sont pas mes chaussures** they *or* these *or* those aren't my shoes; **c'est tout à fait possible** it's quite possible; **c'est rare qu'il pleuve en juin** it doesn't often rain in June; **c'est encore loin, la mer?** is the sea still far away?, is it still a long way to the sea?; **c'est à toi, ce livre?** is this book yours?; **qui est-ce?,** *Fam* **c'est qui?** who is it?; **où est-ce?,** *Fam* **c'est où?** where is it?; **qu'est-ce que c'est?,** *Fam* **c'est quoi?** what is it?, what's that?; **à qui est-ce?,** *Fam* **c'est à qui?** whose is it?; **c'est à toi?** is this *or* is it yours?; **serait-ce que tu as oublié?** have you forgotten, by any chance?
2 (*pour insister*) **c'est la robe que j'ai achetée** this is the dress (that) I bought; **c'est l'auteur que je préfère** he's/she's my favourite writer; **c'est elles qui me l'ont dit** it was they who told me; **c'est toi qui le dis!** that's what you say!, says you!; **c'est à vous, monsieur, que je voudrais parler** it was you I wanted to speak to, sir; **c'est à elle que je dois ma réussite** she's the one I owe my success to, *Sout* it is to her that I owe my success; **c'est à lui/à toi de décider** it's up to him/you to decide; **c'est à pleurer de rage** it's enough to make you weep with frustration
3 (*"c'est que" introduisant une explication*) **si je te le demande, c'est que j'en ai besoin** I wouldn't be asking you for it if I didn't need it; **s'il ne parle pas beaucoup, c'est qu'il est timide** if he doesn't say much, it's because he's shy; **c'est que maman est malade** Mum's ill, you see, the thing is Mum's ill; **ce n'est pas qu'il n'y tienne pas** it's not that he isn't keen on it, it isn't that he's not keen on it
4 (*comme antécédent du pronom relatif*) **ce qui, ce que** what; **ce qui m'étonne, c'est que...** what surprises me is that...; **ce qui est arrivé était à prévoir** what happened was foreseeable; **demande-lui ce qui lui ferait plaisir** ask him/her what he'd/she'd like; **voici ce que l'on me propose** here's what I've been offered; **je sais ce que c'est que la pauvreté** I know what poverty is; **il y a du vrai dans ce qu'il dit** there's some truth in what he says; **dis-moi ce que tu as fait** tell me what you did; **voici ce à quoi j'avais pensé** this is what I had thought of; **ce dont je ne me souviens pas, c'est l'adresse** what I can't remember is the address; **ce pour quoi j'ai démissionné** the reason (why) I resigned; **ce en quoi je croyais s'est effondré** the thing I believed in has collapsed
5 (*reprenant la proposition*) **ce qui, ce que** which; **cette action provoquerait une rupture, ce qui serait catastrophique** such an action would cause a split, which would be disastrous; **il dit en avoir les moyens, ce que je crois volontiers** he says he can afford it, which I'm quite prepared to believe
6 (*introduisant une complétive*) **je m'étonne de ce qu'il n'ait rien dit** I'm surprised (by the fact that) he didn't say anything; **veille à ce que tout soit prêt** make sure everything's ready; **il insiste sur ce que le travail doit être fait en temps voulu** he insists that the work must be done in the specified time
7 (*emploi exclamatif*) **ce que tu es naïf!** you're so naive!, how naive you are!; **ce qu'elle joue bien!** she's such a good actress!, what a marvellous actress she is!; **ce qu'il peut être pénible!** he can be really tiresome!; **tu vois ce que c'est que de mentir!** you see what happens when you lie!, you see where lying gets you!; **ce que c'est (que) d'être instruit, tout de même!** it must be wonderful to be educated!
8 (*locutions*) *Littéraire ou Hum* **ce me semble** it seems to me, I think, *Littéraire ou Hum* methinks; **vous êtes pressé, ce me semble** it seems to me (that) *or* you look like you're in a hurry; **je n'ai rien reçu, ce me semble** I don't think I've received anything, I don't appear to have received anything; **ce faisant** in so doing; **il l'a radiée de la liste, ce faisant il la prive de ses droits** he has struck her off the list, and in so doing he is depriving her of her rights; **ce disant** so saying, with these words; **il n'a rien dit, et ce malgré toutes les menaces** he said nothing, (and this) in spite of all the threats; **j'arrive et sur ce, le téléphone sonne** I arrive and just then the phone rings; **sur ce, je vous salue** and now, I take my leave; **sur ce, elle se leva** with that *or* thereupon *or* on that note, she got up; **pour ce faire** to this end, in order to do this; **ils veulent construire et pour ce faire ils ont pris contact avec des entrepreneurs** they want to start building and to this end they have contacted a firm of contractors

CEA [seəa] **NM** (*abrév* **Commissariat à l'énergie atomique**) = French atomic energy commission, *Br* ≃ AEA, *Am* ≃ AEC
CEAM [seəaɛm] **NF** (*abrév* **Carte européenne d'assurance maladie**) EHIC
céans [seɑ̃] **ADV** *Arch* here, within *or* in this house
cébidé [sebide] *Zool* **NM** member of the Cebidae family
▫ **cébidés NMPL** Cebidae
cébiste [sebist] **NMF** CB user
CEC [seəse] **NF** *Pol* (*abrév* **Confédération européenne des cadres**) CEC, European Confederation of Executives and Managerial Staff
CECA, Ceca [seka] **NF** *UE* (*abrév* **Communauté européenne du charbon et de l'acier**) ECSC

CECEI [səseəi] NM *(abrév* **comité des établissements de crédit et des entreprises d'investissement**) = French public authority empowered to authorize suppliers of financial services

ceci [səsi] PRON DÉMONSTRATIF this; **c. n'est pas très loin de nos préoccupations actuelles** this is not unrelated to our present concerns; **c. pour vous dire que...** all this to tell you that...; **c. (étant) dit** having said this *or* that; **à c. près que** except *or* with the exception that; **retenez bien c....** now, remember this...; **c. va vous étonner, écoutez...** this will surprise you, listen...; **son rapport a c. d'étonnant que...** his/her report is surprising in that...; **c. ne me concerne pas** this is nothing to do with me; **c. n'explique pas cela** one thing doesn't explain the other

cécidie [sesidi] NF *Bot* cecidium, gall

cécilie [sesili] NF *Zool* caecilian

cécité [sesite] NF blindness, *Sout* cecity; **être frappé de c.** to be struck blind; **être atteint de c.** to be blind; **c. nocturne/des neiges/des rivières** night/snow/river blindness; **c. verbale** word blindness, *Spéc* alexia

cédant, -e [sedɑ̃, -ɑ̃t] ADJ *Jur* assigning, granting
NM,F assignor, grantor

cédé, -e [sede] ADJ *(biens)* transferred, assigned, granted
NM,F *(débiteur)* person whose debt has been transferred

CEDEAO [sedeao] NF *(abrév* **Communauté économique des États d'Afrique de l'Ouest**) ECOWAS

céder [18] [sede] VT **1** *(donner)* to give (up); **il est temps de c. l'antenne** our time is up; **nous cédons maintenant l'antenne à Mélanie** we're now going to hand over to Mélanie; **cédez le passage** *(sur panneau) Br* give way, *Am* yield; **c. le passage à qn** to let sb through, to make way for sb; **c. du terrain** *Mil* to give ground, to fall back; *Fig* to back down *or* off; **c. le pas à qn** to give way to sb; *Fig* to let sb have precedence; **c. sa place à qn** to give up one's seat to sb; *Fig* to give up one's place to sb; **il ne le cède à personne en ambition** as far as ambition is concerned, he's second to none; **des gens qui ne le cèdent à personne en ténacité** people who are as tenacious as the best of them; **il ne le cède en rien à nos plus grands peintres** he can take his place alongside our greatest painters
2 *(vendre)* to sell; *(faire cadeau de)* to give away, to donate; **c. qch à bail** to lease sth; **il a cédé son fonds de commerce pour rien** he gave up *or* sold his business for next to nothing; **je ne céderai jamais le verger** I'll never part with *or* sell the orchard; **à c.** *(dans une annonce, sur panneau)* for sale; **c. ses biens à une fondation** to donate *or* to transfer one's assets to a foundation
3 *Jur* to transfer, to make over, to assign; *(bail)* to dispose of, to sell
VI **1** *(à la volonté d'autrui)* to give in; **je ne céderai pas!** I won't give in!, I won't back down!; **tu n'arriveras jamais à le faire c.** you'll never get him to back down; **c. devant les menaces** to give in *or* to yield to threats
2 *Mil* **c. sous l'assaut de l'ennemi** to be overpowered *or* overwhelmed by the enemy
3 *(casser → étagère, plancher)* to give way; *(→ câble, poignée)* to break off; *(→ couture)* to come unstitched
❑ **céder à** VT IND **1** *(ne pas lutter contre → sommeil, fatigue)* to succumb to; *(→ tentation, caprice, menace, exigences)* to give in *or* to yield to; **la fièvre a cédé aux médicaments** the fever responded to medication; **cette hypothèse cédera à la première analyse** this hypothesis won't stand up to analysis
2 *(être séduit par)* **c. à la facilité** to take the easy way out; **c. à qn** to give in to sb

cédérom [sederɔm] NM *Ordinat* CD-ROM

cédétiste [sedetist] ADJ CFDT *(avant n)*
NMF member of the CFDT

CEDEX®, Cedex® [sedɛks] NM *(abrév* **courrier d'entreprise à distribution exceptionnelle**) = accelerated postal service for bulk users

CEDH [seədeaʃ] NF *(abrév* **Cour européenne des droits de l'homme**) ECHR

cedi [sedi] NM cedi

cédille [sedij] NF *Ling* cedilla; **c c.** c cedilla

cédraie [sedrɛ] NF cedar plantation

cédrat [sedra] NM *Bot & Culin* citron

cédratier [sedratje] NM *Bot* citron (tree)

cèdre [sɛdr] NM **1** *(arbre)* cedar (tree), *Can* arborvitae; **c. de l'Atlas** Atlas cedar; **c. blanc** white cedar; **c. bleu** blue cedar; **c. déodar, c. de l'Himalaya** deodar cedar; **c. du Liban** cedar of Lebanon; **c. rouge** red cedar; **2** *(bois)* cedar, cedarwood

cédrière [sedrijɛr] NF *Can* cedar grove

cédule [sedyl] NF **1** *Vieilli Jur* note of hand, promise to pay; **c. de citation** = authority given by the "juge de paix" to issue a summons **2** *Admin (classification des taxes)* schedule; **c. d'impôts** tax bracket **3** *Fin* (Argentine) cedula **4** *Can Joual (horaire)* schedule

CEE [seəə] NF *UE (abrév* **Communauté économique européenne**) EEC

CEEA [seəəa] NF *(abrév* **Communauté européenne de l'énergie atomique**) Euratom

CEG [seəʒe] NM *Scol (abrév* **collège d'enseignement général**) = former junior secondary school

CÉGEP, cégep [seʒɛp] NM *Can Scol (abrév* **collège d'enseignement général et professionnel**) = college of further education

cégépien, -enne [seʒepjɛ̃, -ɛn] NM,F *Can Scol* = student at a "CEGEP"

cégétiste [seʒetist] ADJ CGT *(avant n)*
NMF member of the CGT

CEI [seəi] NF *(abrév* **Communauté des États indépendants**) CIS

ceindre [81] [sɛ̃dr] *Littéraire* VT **1** *(entourer)* **un cercle de fer ceignait son front** he/she had a band of iron around his/her head; **son bras ceignant ma taille** his/her arm around my waist; **c. sa tête d'une couronne** to place a crown upon one's head; **la tête ceinte d'une couronne de lauriers** with his/her head crowned with a laurel wreath; **un château ceint de hautes murailles** a castle surrounded by high walls
2 *(porter)* **c. la couronne** to assume the crown; **c. la tiare** to assume the papal crown; **c. l'écharpe tricolore** to don the mayoral (tricolour) sash
▸**se ceindre** VPR **se c. les reins** to gird one's loins; **se c. les reins d'une écharpe** to tie a sash round one's waist

ceint, -e [sɛ̃, sɛ̃t] PP *voir* **ceindre**

ceinturage [sɛ̃tyraʒ] NM *Hort* girdling

ceinture [sɛ̃tyr] NF **1** *(en cuir, en métal)* belt; *(fine et tressée)* cord; *(large et nouée)* sash; *(gaine, corset)* girdle; **c. cartouchière** cartridge belt; **c. de chasteté** chastity belt; **c. coulissante** drawstring belt; *Can* **c. fléchée** Assumption sash, = woven sash with an arrow pattern, the traditional Quebec costume; **c. de grossesse** maternity girdle; **c. orthopédique** surgical corset; **c. de sauvetage** life belt; *Aut* **c. de sécurité** seat *or* safety belt; *Aut* **c. de sécurité à enrouleur** inertia-reel seat belt; *Aut* **c. de sécurité trois points** lap and shoulder belt, three-point seat belt; **attachez votre c.** fasten your seat belt; **faire c., se serrer la c.** *(se priver)* to tighten one's belt, to go without; *Fam* **on a trop dépensé ces derniers temps, maintenant c.!** we've been overspending lately, we're going to have to tighten our belts now; *Fam* **ce soir, mon vieux, c.!** you'll have to go without tonight!
2 *Sport (à la lutte)* waistlock; *(au judo, au karaté)* belt; **elle est c. blanche/noire** she's a white/black belt; **il est c. noire de judo** he's a black belt in judo
3 *(taille)* waistband; *Anat* waist; **de l'eau jusqu'à la c.** with water up to one's waist; **nu jusqu'à la c.** naked from the waist up; *aussi Fig* **frapper au-dessous de la c.** to hit below the belt; **c'est un coup au-dessous de la c.!** that's a bit below the belt!
4 *Anat* **c. pelvienne/scapulaire** pelvic/pectoral girdle
5 *Transp* **chemin de fer de c.** circle line; **petite c.** *(à Paris → périphérique)* = inner ring road in Paris that runs alongside the "boulevard périphérique"; *(→ bus)* = bus that operates on this route; *(à Bruxelles)* = inner ring road; **grande c.** *(à Bruxelles)* outer ring road
6 *Archit* cincture
7 *Astron* **c. de rayonnement** *ou* **radiations** *ou* **Van Allen** Van Allen belt
8 *(enceinte)* belt, ring; *(de fortifications)* circle; **une c. de peupliers** a belt of poplars; **une c. montagneuse** a belt of mountains; **c. verte** green belt

ceinturer [3] [sɛ̃tyre] VT **1** *(porter avec une ceinture)* **vous pouvez la c.** *(robe)* you can wear it with a belt **2** *(saisir par la taille)* to grab round the waist **3** *(lieu)* to surround, to encircle; **les remparts ceinturent la ville** the town is surrounded by ramparts **4** *Hort* to girdle

ceinturon [sɛ̃tyrɔ̃] NM **1** *(ceinture)* (broad) belt **2** *Mil & Chasse (gén)* belt; *(à cartouches)* cartridge belt; *(à sabre)* sword belt

CEJ [seəʒi] NF *(abrév* **Cour européenne de justice**) ECJ

CEL [sɛl] NM *Banque (abrév* **compte épargne logement**) = savings account for purchasing a property

cela [səla] PRON DÉMONSTRATIF **1** *(désignant un objet éloigné)* that; **regardez c., là-bas!** look at that (over there)!
2 *(désignant → ce dont on vient de parler)* this, that; *(→ ce dont on va parler)* this; **c. (étant) dit...** having said this *or* that...; **je n'ai pas dit c.** I didn't say that; **c., je ne pouvais pas le prévoir** I couldn't have foreseen that; **c. mérite qu'on s'y intéresse** that *or* this is worth studying; **c. prouve que j'avais raison** that proves I was right; **je ne m'attendais pas à c.** I wasn't expecting that; **à part c.** apart from that; **après c., on n'en entendit plus parler** after that, nothing more was heard of it; **malgré c. il est resté fidèle à ses amis** in spite of (all) that, he remained loyal to his friends; **c'est pour c. que je viens** that's what I've come for *or* why I've come; **ce n'est quand même pas pour c. que vous vous êtes disputés?** you didn't argue over a little thing like that, did you?; **sans c. je ne serais pas venu** if it wasn't for that *or* otherwise I wouldn't have come; **qu'est-ce que c'est que c.?** what is that?; **c. n'explique pas ce qu'il a dit hier** this *or* that doesn't explain what he said yesterday; **il me l'a expliqué très clairement, et c. sans s'énerver le moins du monde** he explained it to me very clearly, and without getting the least bit annoyed; **il est parti il y a un mois/une semaine de c.** he left a month/a week ago; **c. va vous étonner, écoutez...** this'll surprise you, listen...; **son histoire a c. d'extraordinaire que...** his/her story is extraordinary in that...; *Ironique* **c'est c.!** that's right!; **c'est c., moquez-vous de moi!** that's right, have a good laugh (at my expense)!; **je suis folle, c'est (bien) c.?** so I'm out of my mind, is that it *or* am I?
3 *(remplaçant "ce")* **c. n'est pas très étonnant** that is not very surprising; **c. est mieux ainsi** it's better this way
4 *(dans des tournures impersonnelles)* it; **c. ne fait rien** it doesn't matter; **c. fait une heure que j'attends** I've been waiting for an hour; **c. fait longtemps que nous ne nous sommes vus** it's been a long time since we've seen each other
5 *(emploi expressif)* **pourquoi c.?** why?, what for?; **qui c.?** who?, who's that?; **où c.?** where?, whereabouts?; **quand c.?** when?

céladon [seladɔ̃] ADJ INV *(couleur)* pale green, celadon
NM **1** *Cér* celadon **2** *Arch & Littéraire* sentimental lover

céladonique [seladɔnik] ADJ *Littéraire* sentimental

céladonisme [seladɔnism] NM *Littéraire* affected sentimentality

célastracée [selastrase] *Bot* NF member of the Celastraceae family
❑ **célastracées** NFPL Celastraceae

Célèbes [selɛb] NF *Géog* Celebes; **à C.** in Celebes

célébrant, -e [selebrɑ̃, -ɑ̃t] *Rel* ADJ officiating
NM celebrant

célébration [selebrasjɔ̃] NF celebration; **la c. du mariage se fera à...** the marriage ceremony will take place at...

célèbre [selɛbr] ADJ famous, famed; **c. par** *ou* **pour qch** famous for sth; **devenir c.** to become famous; **se rendre c. par qch** to become famous for sth; **tristement c.** notorious; **c. dans le monde entier** world-famous

célébrer [18] [selebre] **VT 1** *(fête)* to observe; *(anniversaire, messe, mariage)* to celebrate; *(rite)* to perform; *(funérailles)* to hold **2** *(glorifier → personne)* to extol the virtues of; *(→ exploit)* to toast, to celebrate; *(→ courage)* to praise, to pay tribute to

celebret [selebrɛt] **NM INV** *Rel* celebret

célébrité [selebrite] **NF 1** *(gloire)* fame, celebrity **2** *(personne)* celebrity, personality

celer [25] [səle] **VT** *Arch & Littéraire* **c. qch à qn** to conceal sth from sb; **à ne vous rien c.** to tell you the truth
▶**se celer VPR** *Littéraire* to hide

céleri [sɛlri] **NM** celery; **pied de c.** head of celery; **c. en branches** celery; **c. rémoulade** celeriac salad

célérifère [selerifɛr] **NM** *Hist* = early bicycle without pedals or handlebars *(invented in France in the 17th century)*

céleri-rave [sɛlrirav] *(pl* **céleris-raves)** **NM** celeriac

célérité [selerite] **NF** *Littéraire* swiftness, speed, celerity; **avec c.** swiftly, rapidly

célesta [selɛsta] **NM** *Mus* celesta

céleste [selɛst] **ADJ 1** *(du ciel)* celestial **2** *(du paradis)* celestial, heavenly; *Littéraire* **la voûte c.** the vault of heaven **3** *(de Dieu)* divine **4** *Littéraire (surnaturel → beauté, voix, mélodie)* heavenly, sublime **5** *Hist* **le C. Empire** the Celestial Empire

célestement [selɛstəmã] **ADV** *Littéraire* celestially

célestin [selɛstɛ̃] **NM** *Rel* = monk of the Celestine order

célibat [seliba] **NM 1** *(vie de célibataire → d'un prêtre)* celibacy; *(→ d'un homme)* celibacy, bachelorhood; *(→ d'une femme)* spinsterhood, celibacy; **elle a choisi le c.** she decided to remain single or not to marry; **vivre dans le c.** *(homme)* to remain a bachelor; *(femme)* to remain single; *(prêtre)* to be celibate **2** *(chasteté)* celibacy

célibataire [selibatɛr] **ADJ 1** *(homme, femme)* single, unmarried; *(prêtre)* celibate; **il est encore c.** he's still a single man or a bachelor; **elle est c.** she is single or unmarried **2** *Admin* single
NM single man; *Admin* bachelor; **les célibataires paient davantage d'impôts que les hommes mariés** single men pay more tax than married men; **un c. endurci** a confirmed bachelor; **un club pour célibataires** a singles club
NF single woman

Célimène [selimɛn] **NPR** = character in Molière's 'le Misanthrope', a brilliant and beautiful socialite with many admirers

célimène [selimɛn] **NF** *Littéraire* coquette, flirt

cella [sella] **NF** *Antiq* cella, naos

celle [sɛl] *voir* **celui**

celle-ci [sɛlsi], **celle-là** [sɛlla] *voir* **celui**

cellérier, -ère [selerje, -ɛr] *Rel* **ADJ** = relating to the duties of a cellarer
NM,F cellarer

cellier [selje] **NM** *(pour nourriture)* storeroom, pantry; *(pour vin)* cellar

cello [sɛlo] **NM** *Cin* cel

celloïdin, -e [selɔidɛ̃, -in] **ADJ** *Phot* collodion-coated

Cellophane® [selɔfan] **NF** Cellophane®; **sous C.** Cellophane®-wrapped

cellulaire [selylɛr] **ADJ 1** *Biol (de la cellule)* cell *(avant n)*; *(formé de cellules)* cellular **2** *Mines* porous, poriferous **3** *Tech (béton)* cellular; *(matériau, mousse)* expanded **4** *(carcéral)* **emprisonnement** ou **régime c.** solitary confinement; **voiture c.** *Br* prison or police van, *Am* police wagon **5** *(gestion)* divisional
NM *Can Tél Br* mobile (phone), *Am* cellphone

cellular [selylar] **NM** *Tex* cellular linen

cellulase [selylaz] **NF** *Biol* cellulase

cellule [selyl] **NF 1** *Biol* cell; **c. donneuse** donor cell; **c. épithéliale** epithelial cell; **c. nerveuse** nerve cell; **c. de peau** skin cell; **c. sanguine** blood cell; **c. somatique** somatic cell; **c. souche** stem cell; **c. souche embryonnaire** embryonic stem cell; **c. spumeuse** foam cell
2 *(d'un prisonnier, d'un religieux)* cell; **deux par c.** two to a cell; *Mil* **dix jours de c.** ten days in the cells; *Hum* **il a passé la nuit en c. de**

dégrisement he spent a night in the cells to sober up
3 *(élément constitutif)* basic element or unit; *Pol* cell; **c. du parti communiste** Communist party cell; *Com* **c. d'achat** purchasing unit; **c. (terroriste) dormante** ou **en sommeil** sleeper cell; **c. de crise** crisis centre; **c. familiale** family unit or group; **c. de réflexion** think tank
4 *(d'une ruche)* cell
5 *Aviat* airframe
6 *Phot* **c. photoélectrique** photoelectric cell
7 *(de tourne-disque)* cartridge
8 *Ordinat (dans un tableur)* cell; **c. (de) mémoire** storage cell
9 *Tech* **c. photovoltaïque** photovoltaic cell

cellulite [selylit] **NF 1** *Physiol* cellulite **2** *Méd (inflammation)* cellulitis

cellulitique [selylitik] **ADJ 1** *Physiol* cellulite *(avant n)* **2** *Méd (relatif à l'inflammation)* cellulitis *(avant n)*

cellulo [selylo] **NM** *Cin* cel

Celluloïd® [selylɔid] **NM** celluloid®

cellulose [selyloz] **NF** *Chim* cellulose

cellulosique [selylozik] **ADJ** *Chim* cellulosic

Celsius [sɛlsjys] **NPR** Celsius

celte [sɛlt] **ADJ** Celtic
❏ **Celte NMF** Celt

Celtibères [sɛltibɛr] **NMPL** *Hist* Celtiberi

celtique [sɛltik] **ADJ** Celtic; **les langues celtiques** the Celtic languages
NM *Ling* Celtic

CELUI, CELLE [səlɥi, sɛl] *(mpl* **ceux** [sø], *fpl* **celles** [sɛl]) **PRON DÉMONSTRATIF 1** *(suivi de la préposition "de")* **le train de 5 heures est parti, prenons c. de 6 heures** we've missed the 5 o'clock train, let's get the 6 o'clock; **vous ajouterez à vos frais ceux de janvier** add January's expenses to the current ones; **j'ai comparé mon salaire avec c. d'Ève** I compared my salary with Eve's; **les hommes d'aujourd'hui et ceux d'autrefois** the men of today and those of former times; **le robinet de la cuisine fuit et c. de la salle de bain aussi** the tap in the kitchen's leaking and so is the one in the bathroom; **ceux d'entre vous qui veulent s'inscrire** those of you who wish to register
2 *(suivi d'un pronom relatif)* **c., celle** the one; **ceux, celles** those, the ones; **prête-moi ceux que tu as lus** lend me those or the ones you have read; **c'est celle que j'ai achetée** that's the one I bought; **c'est c. qui a réparé ma voiture** he's the one who fixed my car; **prends la rouge, c'est celle qui te va le mieux** take the red one, it's the one that suits you best; **tous les plats sont sales, prends c. qui est dans le lave-vaisselle** all the dishes are dirty, take the one in the dishwasher; **celle à qui j'ai écrit** the one I wrote to; **c. dont je t'ai parlé** the one I told you about
3 *(quiconque)* he, she; **heureux c. qui peut vivre de son art** happy (is) he who can make a living from his art
4 *(suivi d'un adjectif, d'un participe)* the one; **achetez celle conforme aux normes** buy the one that complies with the standard; **toutes les maisons sont en bois sauf celles voisines de l'église** all the houses are built of wood except the ones or those near the church; **tous ceux désirant participer à l'émission** all those wishing or who wish to take part in the show; **tous ceux ayant la même idée** all those with the same idea
❏ **celui-ci, celle-ci** *(mpl* **ceux-ci**, *fpl* **celles-ci)* **PRON DÉMONSTRATIF 1** *(désignant une personne ou un objet proches)* **c.-ci, celle-ci** this one (here); **ceux-ci, celles-ci** these ones, these (here); **donne-moi c.-ci** give me this one (here); **c'est c.-ci que je veux** this is the one I want, I want this one; **passe-moi le pinceau, non, pas c.-là, c.-ci** pass me the brush, no, not that one, this one
2 *(désignant ce dont on va parler ou ce dont on vient de parler)* **son inquiétude était celle-ci…** his/her worry was as follows…; **elle voulait voir Anne, mais celle-ci était absente** she wanted to see Anne, but she was out; **ah c.-ci, il me fera toujours rire!** now he always makes me laugh!
❏ **celui-là, celle-là** *(mpl* **ceux-là**, *fpl* **celles-là)* **PRON DÉMONSTRATIF 1** *(désignant une personne ou*

un objet éloignés) **c.-là, celle-là** that one (there); **ceux-là, celles-là** those ones, those (over there); **donne-moi c.-là** give me that one (there); **c'est c.-là que je veux** that's the one I want, I want that one; **il n'y a aucun rapport entre les deux décisions, c.n'explique pas celle-là** the two decisions are unconnected, the latter doesn't follow on from the former; **autre exemple, plus technique c.-là** another example, a more technical one this time
2 *(emploi expressif)* **il a toujours une bonne excuse, c.-là!** he's always got a good excuse, that one!

CEMAC [semak] **NF** *(abrév* **Communauté économique et monétaire de l'Afrique centrale)** CEMAC

cément [semã] **NM 1** *Métal* carburizing powder **2** *Anat* cement, cementum

cémentation [semãtasjɔ̃] **NF** *Métal* case-hardening

cémenter [3] [semãte] **VT** *Métal* to case-harden

cémentite [semãtit] **NF** *Métal* cementite

CEN [seən] **NM** *UE (abrév* **Comité européen de normalisation)** European Standards Commission

cénacle [senakl] **NM 1** *Rel* cenacle **2** *Littéraire (comité)* literary coterie or group; **admis au c.** admitted into the company of the select few
❏ **Cénacle NM** *Littérature* **le C.** = group of young Romantic writers who met at the homes of Victor Hugo and Charles Nodier between 1823 and 1830

cendar [sãdar] **NM** *Fam* ashtray▪

cendre [sãdr] **NF 1** *(résidu → gén)* ash, ashes; *(→ de charbon)* cinders; **c. de bois/de cigarette** wood/cigarette ash; **une viande au goût de c.** meat with a smoky taste; **un visage couleur de c.** an ashen face; **faire cuire des marrons sous la c.** to roast chestnuts in the ashes or embers; **mettre** ou **réduire en cendres** *(objet)* to reduce to ashes; *(maison, ville)* to burn to the ground; *Littéraire* **les cendres d'une passion mourante** the embers of a dying passion; *Littéraire* **troubler la c. des morts** to speak ill of the dead
2 *Géol* (volcanic) ash; **cendres volcaniques** volcanic ash
❏ **cendres NFPL** *Littéraire (dépouille)* ashes, remains
❏ **Cendres NFPL** *Rel* **les Cendres, le mercredi des Cendres** Ash Wednesday
ADJ INV ashy

cendré, -e [sãdre] **ADJ 1** *(gris)* ashen, ash *(avant n)*, ash-coloured **2** *(couvert de cendres)* ash-covered; **fromage c.** cheese matured in wood ash
NM cheese matured in wood ash
❏ **cendrée NF 1** *Chasse & Pêche* dust shot **2** *(revêtement)* cinders; *(piste)* cinder track; **sur la cendrée** (out) on the track

cendrer [3] [sãdre] **VT 1** *(chemin, piste)* to cinder **2** *Littéraire (rendre couleur de cendres)* to turn ash-grey

cendreux, -euse [sãdrø, -øz] **ADJ 1** *(plein de cendres)* full of ashes **2** *(gris → écorce, roche)* ash-coloured; *(→ teint)* ashen, ashy **3** *Métal* grainy, granular; *(sol)* ashy

cendrier [sãdrije] **NM** *(de fumeur)* ashtray; *(de fourneau)* ash pit; *(de poêle)* ashpan; *(de locomotive)* ash box

Cendrillon [sãdrijɔ̃] **NPR** Cinderella

════════════════

'Cendrillon' Perrault 'Cinderella'

cendrillon [sãdrijɔ̃] **NF** *Littéraire (servante)* drudge

cène [sɛn] *Rel* **NF** *(communion)* Holy Communion, Lord's Supper
❏ **Cène NF la C.** the Last Supper

cenelle [sənɛl] **NF** *Bot (baie)* haw

cenellier [sənɛlje] **NM** *Can & (dans le centre de la France)* Bot hawthorn

cénesthésie [senɛstezi] **NF** *Physiol* cenesthesia, cenesthesis

cénesthésique [senɛstezik] **ADJ** *Physiol* cenesthetic

cénesthopathie [senɛstɔpati] **NF** *Psy* cenesthopathy

cenne [sɛn] **NF** *Can Joual* cent

cénobite [senɔbit] NM *Rel* coenobite

cénobitique [senɔbitik] ADJ *Rel* coenobitic, monastic

cénobitisme [senɔbitism] NM *Rel* coenobitism

cénotaphe [senɔtaf] NM cenotaph

cénozoïque [senɔzɔik] ADJ *Géol* cenozoic

cens [sɑ̃s] NM 1 *Antiq (recensement)* census 2 *Hist (féodal)* quitrent; **c. électoral** = minimum tax quota for voting rights

censé, -e [sɑ̃se] ADJ supposed to; **être c. faire qch** to be supposed to do sth; **tu n'es pas c. le savoir** you're not supposed to know; **vous êtes c. arriver à 9 heures** *(indication)* you're supposed to arrive at 9 o'clock; *(rappel à l'ordre)* we expect you to arrive at 9 o'clock

censément [sɑ̃semɑ̃] ADV apparently, seemingly

censeur [sɑ̃sœr] NM 1 *Anciennement Scol Br* deputy head (teacher), *Am* assistant principal; **Madame le c.** *Br* the deputy headmistress or head teacher, *Am* the assistant principal 2 *(responsable de la censure)* censor 3 *(critique)* critic 4 *Antiq* censor

censier [sɑ̃sje] NM *Hist* rent roll

censitaire [sɑ̃siter] *Hist* ADJ poll-tax based
  NM eligible voter *(who has paid enough tax to gain voting rights)*

censive [sɑ̃siv] NF *Hist* fief, manor

censorat [sɑ̃sɔra] NM 1 *Anciennement Scol Br* deputy headship, *Am* position of assistant principal 2 *Antiq* censorship

censorial, -e, -aux, -ales [sɑ̃sɔrjal, -o] ADJ censorial

censurable [sɑ̃syrabl] ADJ censurable

censure [sɑ̃syr] NF 1 *(interdiction, examen)* censorship; **face à la c. paternelle** faced with his/her father's instruction that he/she shouldn't do it; **la c.** *(commission)* the censors 2 *Pol* censure 3 *Rel* censure; **les censures de l'Église** the censure of the Church 4 *Psy & Antiq* censorship

censurer [3] [sɑ̃syre] VT 1 *(film, livre)* to censor 2 *Pol* to pass a vote of censure or of no confidence; *Rel* to censure 3 *Psy* to exercise censorship on 4 *(critiquer)* to criticize, to censure

cent[1] [sɑ̃] ADJ 1 *(gén)* a or one hundred; **c. mille** a hundred thousand; **deux cents filles** two hundred girls; **trois c. quatre rangs** three hundred and four rows; **elle est aux c. coups** *(affolée)* she's frantic; **je te l'ai dit c. fois** I've told you a hundred times; **elle a eu c. fois l'occasion de le faire** she's had every chance to do it; **tu as c. fois raison** you're a hundred percent right; **je préfère c. fois celle-ci** I prefer this one a hundred times over; **c. fois mieux** a hundred times better; **faire les c. pas** to pace up and down; **à c. pieds sous terre** dead and buried; *Fam* **il y a c. sept ans que...** it's been ages since...; *Fam* **je ne vais pas attendre c. sept ans** I'm not going to wait forever (and a day); *Fam* **je m'embête** ou **m'ennuie à c. sous de l'heure** I'm bored stiff or to death; *Fam* **on se faisait suer à c. sous de l'heure** it was as exciting as watching paint dry; *Hist* **les C.-Jours** the Hundred Days

  2 *(dans des séries)* hundredth; **chambre c.** room one hundred; **page deux c. (six)** page two hundred (and six); **l'an neuf c.** the year nine hundred

  3 *Sport* **le c. mètres** the hundred metres; **le quatre c. mètres haies** the four hundred metres hurdle or hurdles; **le c. mètres nage libre** the hundred metres freestyle

  PRON hundred
  NM 1 *(gén)* hundred
  2 *(numéro d'ordre)* number one hundred
  3 *(chiffre écrit)* hundred
  4 *(centaine)* hundred; **un c. d'huîtres** a hundred oysters
  5 *(locutions)* **pour c.** percent; **20 pour c.** 20 percent; *Chim* **une solution à 30 pour c.** a 30 percent solution; **c. pour c. coton** a or one hundred percent pure cotton; **il est c. pour c. anglais** he's a hundred percent English; **je suis c. pour c. contre** I'm a hundred percent against it; **je te le donne en c.** guess, I'll give you three guesses; *voir aussi* **cinquante**

▭▭▭▭▭ 📖 ▭▭▭▭▭

'Cent Ans de solitude' *García Márquez* 'One Hundred Years of Solitude'

LES CENT-JOURS
This refers to the period in history between Napoleon's attempt to regain power on his return from Elba on 20 March 1815, and his defeat at Waterloo on 18 June, marking his second and final exile to St Helena.

cent[2] [sɛnt] NM *(monnaie)* cent

centaine [sɑ̃tɛn] NF 1 *(cent unités)* hundred; **la colonne des centaines** the hundreds column
  2 *(quantité)* **une c.** around or about a hundred, a hundred or so; **une c. de voitures** around or about a hundred cars; **elle a une c. d'années** she's around or about a hundred (years old)
  3 *(âge)* **avoir la c.** to be around or about a hundred; **quand on arrive à** ou **atteint la c.** when you reach a hundred
  ❑ **par centaines** ADV by the hundreds; **les gens arrivent par centaines** people are arriving by the hundreds or in their hundreds

centaure [sɑ̃tɔr] NM *Myth* centaur

centaurée [sɑ̃tɔre] NF *Bot* **c. (noire)** (common) knapweed; **petite c.** centaury; **c. scabieuse** greater scabweed

centavo [sɛntavo] NM centavo

centenaire [sɑ̃tner] ADJ 1 *(qui dure cent ans)* hundred-year *(avant n)*
  2 *(personne)* **ma grand-mère est c.** *(elle a cent ans)* my grandmother is a hundred (years old); *(elle a plus de cent ans)* my grandmother is over a hundred (years old)
  3 *(bâtiment)* over a hundred years old
  NMF *(vieillard)* centenarian
  NM *(anniversaire)* centenary, *Am & Can* centennial

centennal, -e, -aux, -ales [sɑ̃tenal, -o] ADJ centennial

centésimal, -e, -aux, -ales [sɑ̃tezimal, -o] ADJ centesimal; *Méd* **dilution centésimale** dilution to one part per hundred

cent-garde [sɑ̃gard] *(pl* **cent-gardes)** NM *Hist* = member of Napoleon III's household cavalry; **les cent-gardes** the household cavalry

centiare [sɑ̃tjar] NM centiare, square metre

centième [sɑ̃tjɛm] ADJ hundredth
  NMF 1 *(personne)* hundredth 2 *(objet)* hundredth (one)
  NM 1 *(partie)* hundredth 2 *(étage) Br* hundredth floor, *Am* hundred and first floor 3 *(location)* **ce n'est pas le c. de ce qu'il m'a fait** it doesn't even come close to what he did to me; **je n'ai pas compris le c. de ce qu'il disait** I didn't understand a fraction of what he was saying
  NF *Théât* hundredth performance; *voir aussi* **cinquième**

centièmement [sɑ̃tjɛmmɑ̃] ADV in hundredth place

centigrade [sɑ̃tigrad] ADJ centigrade

centigramme [sɑ̃tigram] NM centigram

centilage [sɑ̃tilaʒ] NM *(en statistiques)* percentile distribution

centile [sɑ̃til] NM *(en statistiques)* centile

centilitre [sɑ̃tilitr] NM centilitre

centime [sɑ̃tim] NM 1 *(centième d'euro)* cent; *Anciennement (centième de franc)* centime; **pas un c.** not a *Br* penny or *Am* cent; **ça ne m'a pas coûté un c.** it didn't cost me *Br* a penny or *Am* one cent; **je n'ai plus un c.** I haven't a penny to my name 2 *Fin* **centimes additionnels** additional tax

centimètre [sɑ̃timɛtr] NM 1 *(unité de mesure)* centimetre; **c. carré/cube** square/cubic centimetre 2 *(ruban)* tape measure, *Am* tape line

centimétrique [sɑ̃timetrik] ADJ centimetric

centon [sɑ̃tɔ̃] NM *Mus & Littérature* cento

centrafricain, -e [sɑ̃trafrikɛ̃, -ɛn] ADJ Central African; **République centrafricaine** Central African Republic
  ❑ **Centrafricain, -e** NM,F Central African

centrage [sɑ̃traʒ] NM centring

central, -e, -aux, -ales [sɑ̃tral, -o] ADJ 1 *(du milieu d'un objet)* middle *(avant n)*, central; **le trou c.** the central or middle hole
  2 *(du centre d'une ville)* central; **mon bureau est très c.** my office is very central
  3 *Admin & Pol* central, national
  4 *(principal)* main, crucial; **le point c. de votre**

---

exposé the main or crucial or key point in your thesis
  5 *Ling* centre *(avant n)*
  NM 1 *Tél* **c. (téléphonique)** (telephone) exchange; **c. numérique** digital exchange
  2 *Sport (de tennis)* **(court) c.** centre court
  ❑ **centrale** NF 1 *(usine)* **centrale (électrique)** power station; **centrale hydraulique/nucléaire/thermique** hydroelectric/nuclear/thermal station; **centrale surgénératrice** fast-breeder power station
  2 *Pol* **centrale ouvrière** ou **syndicale** *Br* trade or *Am* labor union confederation
  3 *(prison)* county jail, *Am* penitentiary
  4 *Com* **centrale d'achat(s)** central purchasing office; *(au sein d'une entreprise)* central purchasing department; **centrale de réservation(s)** central reservations unit, central reservations office

Centrale [sɑ̃tral] NF *Univ* = "grande école" which trains engineers

centralien, -enne [sɑ̃traljɛ̃, -ɛn] NM,F *Univ* = student or ex-student of "Centrale"

centralisateur, -trice [sɑ̃tralizatœr, -tris] ADJ centralizing

centralisation [sɑ̃tralizasjɔ̃] NF centralization

centralisatrice [sɑ̃tralizatris] *voir* **centralisateur**

centralisé, -e [sɑ̃tralize] ADJ centralized

centraliser [3] [sɑ̃tralize] VT to centralize

centralisme [sɑ̃tralism] NM *Pol* centralism

centraliste [sɑ̃tralist] *Pol* ADJ centralist
  NMF centralist

centraméricain, -e [sɑ̃tramerikɛ̃, -ɛn] ADJ Central American
  ❑ **Centraméricain, -e** NM,F Central American

centration [sɑ̃trasjɔ̃] NF *Psy* centration; **loi** ou **effet de c.** centration effect

CENTRE [sɑ̃tr] NM 1 *(milieu → gén)* middle, centre; *(→ d'une cible)* bull's eye, centre; **le c.** *(d'une ville) Br* the (city) centre, *Am* downtown; **aller au c.** *Br* to go into the (city) centre, *Am* to go downtown; **elle était le c. de tous les regards** all eyes were fixed on her; **il se prend pour le c. du monde** ou **de l'univers** he thinks the world revolves around him; **pour elle, je suis le c. du monde** I'm the centre of her world
  2 *(concentration)* **c. industriel** industrial area; **c. urbain** town; **les grands centres urbains** large conurbations
  3 *(organisme)* centre; **c. d'accueil** reception centre; **c. d'accueil de jour** daycare centre; *Can Joual* **c. d'achats** *Br* shopping centre, *Am* (shopping) mall; **c. aéré** = holiday activity centre for schoolchildren; **c. d'affaires** business centre; *(dans un aéroport, dans un hôtel)* business lounge; **c. d'aide par le travail** = day centre which helps disabled people to find work and become more independent; *Compta* **c. d'analyse** cost centre; *Compta* **c. (d'analyse) auxiliaire/principal** secondary/main cost centre; *Compta* **c. d'analyse opérationnel** operational cost centre; *Com* **c. d'appels** call centre; **c. de chèques postaux** PO cheque account centre; **c. commercial** *Br* shopping centre, *Am* (shopping) mall; **c. de conférences** conference centre; **c. de contrôle** *(spatial)* mission control; *Fin* **c. de coût** cost centre; **c. culturel** art or arts centre; **c. de dépistage du cancer/SIDA** centre for cancer/Aids screening; **c. de détention** = long-term detention centre where the emphasis is on resocialization; **c. de documentation** information centre; **c. de documentation et d'information** ≃ school library; **c. éducatif fermé** ≃ young offenders' institution; **c. éducatif renforcé** ≃ secure young offenders' institution; **c. d'évaluation** assessment centre; **c. pour femmes battues** women's refuge; **c. de formation continue** ou **permanente** = centre for continuing education; **c. d'hébergement pour les sans-abri** hostel for the homeless; **c. d'hébergement d'urgence** emergency refuge; **c. hospitalier** hospital (complex); **c. hospitalier spécialisé** psychiatric hospital; **c. hospitalo-universitaire** teaching hospital; **c. des impôts** tax centre or office; **c. d'information** information centre; **c. d'information et d'orientation** careers advisory centre; **c. d'instruction** military academy; **c. de loisirs** leisure or recreation centre; **c. médical** clinic; **c. médico-social**

health centre; **C. national de la recherche scientifique** = French national organization for scientific research, *Br* ≃ Science Research Council; **C. national de transfusion sanguine** = national blood transfusion centre; **c. pénitentiaire** = prison with sections incorporating different kinds of prison regime; *Fin* **c. de profit** profit centre; *Belg* **c. public d'aide sociale** welfare office *or* centre; **c. régional** = regional prison centre for prisoners serving three years or less; **c. régional de documentation pédagogique** = local centre for educational resources; **c. régional de formation professionnelle d'avocats** = regional centre for professional legal training; **c. de renseignements (téléphoniques)** *Br* directory enquiries, *Am* information; *Fin* **c. de revenus** revenue centre; **c. de semi-liberté** = semi-custodial centre from which the prisoner may be released to engage in certain activities; **c. social** social services office; **c. sportif** sports centre; **c. de tri** sorting office; **c. universitaire** university; **c. de vacances** holiday centre

4 *(point essentiel)* main *or* key point, heart, centre; **le c. du débat** the heart *or* the crux of the matter; **être au c. de** to be the key point of, to be at the heart *or* the centre of; **la sécurité est au c. de nos préoccupations** safety is at the centre of our concerns; **c. d'intérêt** centre of interest; **centres d'intérêt** *(sur un CV)* other interests; **c. d'intérêt touristique** tourist *or* visitor attraction

5 *Anat & Physiol* centre; *aussi Fig* **c. de gravité** centre of gravity; **c. nerveux** nerve centre; **c. phrénique** central tendon of the diaphragm; **c. vital** vital organs; *Fig* nerve centre

6 *Tech* **c. optique** optical centre

7 *Pol* middle ground, centre; **il est du c.** he's middle-of-the-road; **c. droit/gauche** moderate right/left; **il est (de) c. droit** he's right-of-centre; **il est (de) c. gauche** he's left-of-centre

8 *(au basketball)* centre

9 *Ftbl (position)* centre-forward; *(passe)* centre

10 *(au rugby → position)* centre

11 *Ind* **c. d'usinage** turning shop

❑ **Centre** NM *(région)* **le C.** Centre

---

centré, -e [sɑ̃tre] ADJ *Suisse (magasin, appartement)* central

centre-avant [sɑ̃travɑ̃] *(pl* **centres-avants**) NM *Belg Sport* centre-forward

centrer [3] [sɑ̃tre] VT 1 *(gén) & Tech* to centre

2 *(orienter)* **centrons le débat** let's give the discussion a focus, let's concentrate on one issue; **être centré sur** to be centred *or* focussed around; **le documentaire était centré sur l'enfance de l'artiste** the documentary was focused around the artist's childhood; **nos préoccupations sont centrées sur...** our number one concern is...; **être trop centré sur soi-même** to be too self-centred

3 *Typ (texte)* to centre

4 *Sport (ballon)* to centre

centre-répéteur [sɑ̃trərepetœr] *(pl* **centres-répéteurs**) NM *TV & Rad* relay station

centreur [sɑ̃trœr] NM = plastic adaptor for singles on a record-player

centre-ville [sɑ̃trəvil] *(pl* **centres-villes**) NM *Br* town centre, *Am* downtown; *(d'une grande ville) Br* city centre, *Am* downtown; **les boutiques du c.** *Br* the shops in the town/city centre, *Am* the downtown stores; **aller au c.** *Br* to go into the town/city centre, *Am* to go downtown

centrifugation [sɑ̃trifygasjɔ̃] NF *Tech* centrifugation

centrifuge [sɑ̃trifyʒ] ADJ *Tech* centrifugal

centrifuger [17] [sɑ̃trifyʒe] VT *Tech* to centrifuge

centrifugeur [sɑ̃trifyʒœr] NM 1 *Méd & Tech* centrifuge 2 *Culin* juice extractor, juicer

centrifugeuse [sɑ̃trifyʒøz] NF 1 *Méd & Tech* centrifuge 2 *Culin* juice extractor, juicer

centriole [sɑ̃triɔl] NM *Biol* centriole

centripète [sɑ̃tripɛt] ADJ *Phys* centripetal

centrisme [sɑ̃trism] NM *Pol* centrism

centriste [sɑ̃trist] *Pol* ADJ centrist

NMF centrist; **les centristes** the centre

centromère [sɑ̃trɔmɛr] NM *Biol* centromere

centrosome [sɑ̃trozom] NM *Biol* centrosoma, centrosome

cent-suisse [sɑ̃sɥis] *(pl* **cent-suisses**) NM *Hist* Swiss Guard *(responsible for guarding the Kings of France between 1481 and 1792)*

centuple [sɑ̃typl] ADJ **1000 est un nombre c. de 10** 1,000 is a hundred times 10

NM **le c. de 20 est 2000** a hundred times 20 is 2,000; **il a gagné le c. de sa mise** his bet paid off a hundredfold

❑ **au centuple** ADV a hundredfold; **je te le rendrai au c.** I'll repay you a hundred times over *or* a hundredfold

centupler [3] [sɑ̃typle] VT to increase a hundredfold *or* a hundred times, to multiply by a hundred

VI to increase a hundredfold; **quelques placements heureux ont fait c. sa fortune** a few lucky investments have increased his/her fortune one hundredfold

centurie [sɑ̃tyri] NF *Antiq & Mil* century

centurion [sɑ̃tyrjɔ̃] NM *Antiq & Mil* centurion

cénure [senyr] NM *Vét* coenourus

CEP [seəpe] NM *Anciennement Scol (abrév* **certificat d'études primaires**) = basic examination taken at the end of primary education

cep [sɛp] NM *Bot* **c. (de vigne)** vine stock

cépage [sepaʒ] NM grape variety

cèpe [sɛp] NM 1 *Bot* boletus 2 *Culin* cep

cépée [sepe] NF 1 *(rejet)* clump of shoots 2 *(bois)* young wood, coppice

cependant [səpɑ̃dɑ̃] CONJ 1 *(néanmoins)* however, nevertheless, yet; **il n'avait pas très envie de sortir ce soir-là; c. il se laissa entraîner** he didn't really want to go out that night, nevertheless he let himself be dragged along; **je suis d'accord avec vous, j'ai c. une petite remarque à faire** I agree with you, however I have one small comment to make; **il parle très bien, avec un léger accent c.** he speaks very well, albeit with a slight accent

2 *Littéraire (pendant ce temps)* meanwhile, in the meantime

❑ **cependant que** CONJ *Littéraire* while

céphalée [sefale], **céphalalgie** [sefalalʒi] NF *Méd* headache, *Spéc* cephalgia

céphalique [sefalik] ADJ *Anat* cephalic

Céphalonie [sefaloni] NF Cephalonia, Kefalonia

céphalophe [sefalɔf] NM *Zool* duiker

céphalopode [sefalɔpɔd] *Zool* NM *(mollusque)* cephalopod

❑ **céphalopodes** NMPL Cephalopoda

céphalo-rachidien, -enne [sefalɔraʃidjɛ̃, -ɛn] *(mpl* **céphalo-rachidiens**, *fpl* **céphalo-rachidiennes**) ADJ *Anat* cerebrospinal, *Spéc* cephalorachidian

céphalosporine [sefalɔsporin] NF *Pharm* cephalosporin

céphalothorax [sefalɔtɔraks] NM *Zool* cephalothorax

céphéide [sefeid] NF *Astron* Cepheid

cépole [sepɔl] NF *Ich* red band fish

cérambycidé [serɑ̃biside] *Entom* NM long-horned beetle, *Spéc* cerambycid

❑ **cérambycidés** NMPL Cerambycidae

cérame [seram] *Archéol* ADJ **grès c.** Grecian urn

NM Grecian urn

céramide [seramid] NM *Biol & Chim* ceramide

céramique [seramik] ADJ ceramic

NF 1 *(art)* ceramics *(singulier)*, pottery 2 *(objet)* piece of ceramic 3 *(matière)* ceramic; **des carreaux de c.** ceramic tiles 4 *Méd* dental ceramics *or* porcelain

céramiste [seramist] NMF ceramist

céramologue [seramɔlɔg] NMF ceramics expert

céraste [serast] NM *Zool* cerastes, horned viper

cérat [sera] NM *Pharm* cerate

Cerbère [sɛrbɛr] NPR *Myth* Cerberus

cerbère [sɛrbɛr] NM *Littéraire* 1 *(concierge)* ill-tempered doorkeeper 2 *(geôlier)* jailer

CERC [serk] NM *(abrév* **Centre d'études sur les revenus et les coûts**) = government body carrying out research into salaries and the cost of living

cercaire [sɛrkɛr] NF *Entom* cercaria

cerce [sɛrs] NF *Tech* curved template, hoop

cerceau, -x [sɛrso] NM *(d'enfant, d'acrobate, de tonneau, de jupon)* hoop; *(de tonnelle)* half-hoop; **faire rouler un c.** to bowl a hoop

cerclage [sɛrklaʒ] NM 1 *(action de cercler)* hooping 2 *Méd* **c. (du col de l'utérus)** cerclage 3 *(cercles d'une futaille)* hooping

cercle [sɛrkl] NM 1 *Géom* circle; *(forme)* circle, ring; **tracer un c.** to draw a circle; **décrire des cercles dans le ciel** *(avion, oiseau)* to fly around in circles, to wheel round, to circle; **faire c.** *ou* **former un c. autour de qn** to stand *or* to gather round sb in a circle; **entourer qch d'un c.** to put a ring round *or* to circle sth; **en c.** in a circle; **un village entouré d'un c. de collines** a village ringed with hills; **c. vicieux** vicious circle, catch-22; **se retrouver** *ou* **tomber dans un c. vicieux** to be caught in a vicious circle *or* in a catch-22 situation; **c. vertueux** virtuous circle; *Beaux-Arts* **le c. chromatique** the colour wheel

2 *(gamme, étendue → d'activités, de connaissances)* range, scope

3 *(groupe)* circle, group; **c. d'amis** circle *or* group of friends; **c. de famille** family (circle); **c. de lecture** book club *or* group; **c. littéraire** literary circle

4 *(club)* club; **un c. militaire** an officer's club

5 *(objet circulaire)* hoop; **c. d'arpenteur** protractor; **c. de roue** (wheel) tyre

6 *Astron & Math* circle; **grand c.** great circle; **c. horaire** horary circle

7 *Géog* **c. polaire** polar circle; **c. polaire arctique/antarctique** Arctic/Antarctic Circle

8 *Mktg* **c. de qualité** quality circle

9 *Beaux-Arts* **C. et Carré** = group of French abstract artists founded in Paris in 1929, later becoming part of the Abstraction-Création group

---

'Le Cercle de craie caucasien' *Brecht* 'The Caucasian Chalk Circle'

---

cercler [3] [sɛrkle] VT 1 *(emballage)* to ring; *(tonneau)* to hoop; **une caisse cerclée de fer** an iron-bound crate 2 *(entourer)* **des doigts cerclés d'or** gold-ringed fingers; **des lunettes cerclées d'écaille** horn-rimmed spectacles 3 *Méd* to wire

cercocèbe [sɛrkɔsɛb] NM *Zool* mangabey

cercope [sɛrkɔp] NM *Entom* froghopper, spittle bug; **c. sanguinolent** black and red froghopper

cercopithèque [sɛrkɔpitɛk] NM *Zool* guenon, *Spéc* cercopithecid

cercueil [sɛrkœj] NM *Br* coffin, *Am* casket

céréale [sereal] NF 1 *Bot & Agr* cereal; **ils cultivent des céréales** they grow cereals *or* grain 2 *Culin* **des céréales** (breakfast) cereal

céréaliculture [serealikyltyr] NF cereal farming

céréalier, -ère [serealje, -ɛr] ADJ cereal *(avant n)*

NM 1 *(producteur)* cereal farmer *or* grower 2 *(navire)* grain ship

cérébelleux, -euse [serebelø, -øz] ADJ *Anat* cerebellar

cérébral, -e, -aux, -ales [serebral, -o] ADJ 1 *Anat* cerebral 2 *Méd* brain *(avant n)* 3 *(intellectuel → activité, travail)* intellectual, mental; *(→ film, livre, personne)* cerebral, intellectual

NM,F intellectual

cérébralité [serebralite] NF mental ability

cérébrosclérose [serebrɔskleroz] NF cerebrosclerosis

cérébro-spinal, -e [serebrospinal] *(mpl* **cérébro-spinaux** [-o], *fpl* **cérébro-spinales**) ADJ *Anat* cerebrospinal

cérébro-vasculaire [serebrovaskylɛr] *(pl* **cérébro-vasculaires**) ADJ *Anat* cerebrovascular

cérémonial, -als [seremɔnjal] NM *(règles, livre)* ceremonial; **c. de cour** court etiquette

cérémonie [seremɔni] NF 1 *Rel* ceremony

2 *(fête)* ceremony, solemn *or* formal occasion; **c. d'ouverture/de clôture** opening/closing ceremony; **c. nuptiale** wedding ceremony; **la c. de remise des prix** the award ceremony

3 *(rituel)* ceremony, rites; **c. d'initiation** initiation rites; **c. du thé** tea ceremony; **avant qu'il ne s'endorme, c'est tout une c.** it's quite a performance getting him to go to sleep

❑ **cérémonies** NFPL *Péj (manières)* fuss, palaver; **ne fais pas tant de cérémonies** don't make such a fuss

❑ **avec cérémonie** ADV ceremoniously

❑ **de cérémonie** ADJ *Mil (tenue)* ceremonial; **uniforme de c.** (full) dress uniform

❑ **en grande cérémonie** ADV *(apporter, présenter)* with great formality, very ceremoniously

❑ **sans cérémonie** ADV **1** *(simplement)* casually, informally; **pas besoin de te changer, c'est sans c.** just come as you are, it's an informal occasion; **venez dîner ce soir, sans c.** come and have dinner tonight, it won't be anything special
2 *Péj (abruptement)* unceremoniously, without so much as a by-your-leave

cérémoniel, -elle [seremɔnjɛl] ADJ *Rel* ceremonial

cérémonieuse [seremɔnjøz] *voir* **cérémonieux**

cérémonieusement [seremɔnjøzmɑ̃] ADV ceremoniously, formally

cérémonieux, -euse [seremɔnjø, -øz] ADJ ceremonious, formal

CERES [serɛs] NM *Anciennement (abrév* **Centre d'études, de recherches et d'éducation socialiste**) = the intellectual section of the French socialist party, now independent

cerf [sɛr] NM *Zool* stag; **jeune c.** staggard, young stag; **grand c., vieux c.** hart; **grand vieux c.** royal (stag *or* hart); **c. du Canada** North American elk, wapiti; **c. commun** *ou* **d'Europe** red deer; **c. mulet** mule deer; **c. sika** sika deer; **c. des tourbières** Irish elk, megaceros, megaloceros; **c. en velours** stag in velvet; **c. de Virginie** (Virginian) white-tailed deer

cerf-cochon [sɛrkɔʃɔ̃] *(pl* **cerfs-cochons**) NM *Zool* hog deer

cerfeuil [sɛrfœj] NM *Bot* chervil; **c. sauvage** wild parsley

cerf-volant [sɛrvɔlɑ̃] *(pl* **cerfs-volants**) NM **1** *(jeu)* kite; **jouer au c.** to fly a kite **2** *Entom* stag beetle

cerf-voliste [sɛrvɔlist] *(pl* **cerfs-volistes**) NMF kite-flyer

cérifère [serifɛr] ADJ *Minér* cerium-bearing

cerisaie [sərizɛ] NF cherry orchard

'La Cerisaie' *Tchekhov* 'The Cherry Orchard'

cerise [səriz] NF **1** *(fruit)* cherry; **c. sauvage** wild cherry; *Can* **c. de France** cherry *(cultivated)*; *Fig* **la c. sur le gâteau** the icing on the cake; *Can Joual Vulg* **faire perdre la c. à qn** to pop sb's cherry **2** *Fam (tête)* head▪, nut
ADJ INV **(rouge) c.** cherry, cherry-red, cerise

cerisier [sərizje] NM **1** *(arbre)* cherry (tree); **c. acide** morello cherry, sour cherry; **c. (à fleurs) du Japon** Japanese cherry; **c. à grappes** (European) bird cherry **2** *(bois)* cherry (wood)

cérithe [serit], **cerithium** [seritjɔm] NM *Zool (mollusque)* cerithium

cérium [serjɔm] NM *Chim* cerium; **oxyde de c.** ceria

cermet [sɛrmɛ] NM ceramal, cermet

CERN, Cern [sɛrn] NM *(abrév* **Conseil européen pour la recherche nucléaire**) CERN

cerne [sɛrn] NM **1** *(sous les yeux)* shadow, (dark) ring *or* circle; **elle a des cernes** she's got dark rings *or* circles under her eyes **2** *Tex* ring; **faire un c.** to leave a ring **3** *Bot* (annual) ring **4** *Beaux-Arts* outline

cerné, -e [sɛrne] ADJ **avoir les yeux cernés** to have (dark) rings *or* circles under one's eyes

cerneau, -x [sɛrno] NM *(chair)* (shelled) walnut; **cerneaux de noix** walnut halves, halved walnuts

cerner [3] [sɛrne] VT **1** *(entourer)* to surround, to lie around; **les lacs qui cernent la ville** the lakes dotted around the *or* surrounding the town
2 *(assiéger → ville)* to surround, to seal off; *(→ armée, population)* to surround; **rendez-vous, vous êtes cernés!** give yourselves up, you are surrounded!
3 *(définir → question, problème)* to define, to determine; **ceci nous a permis de c. le problème de près** this has enabled us to home in on the problem
4 *(→ comprendre)* **il est difficile à c.** it's hard to say what kind of person he is
5 *(ouvrir → noix)* to crack open, to shell
6 *Hort* to ring

cernier [sɛrnje] NM *Ich* wreck fish, stone bass

cerque [sɛrk] NM (USU PL) *Entom* cercus, anal appendages

CERS [seəɛrɛs] NF *(abrév* **Commission européenne de recherches spatiales**) ESRO

cers [sɛrs] NM = strong westerly or south-westerly wind in the south of France

CERTAIN, -E [sɛrtɛ̃, -ɛn]

ADJ definite **1** ▪ certain **2–4** ▪ sure **3**
ADJ INDÉFINI certain **1, 2**

ADJ **1** *(incontestable → amélioration)* definite; *(→ preuve)* definite, positive; *(→ avantage, rapport)* definite, clear; *(→ décision, invitation, prix)* definite; **le médicament a des effets secondaires certains** the drug has definite side-effects; **avec un enthousiasme c.** with real *or* obvious enthusiasm; **tenir qch pour c.** to know sth for certain, have no doubt about sth; **je tiens son accord pour c.** I have no doubt that he'll agree; **c'est c.** *(pour confirmer)* undoubtedly, that's for certain *or* sure; **le projet a beaucoup de retard – c'est c., mais...** the project is a long way behind schedule – that's certainly true but...; **j'aurais préféré attendre, c'est c.** I'd have preferred to wait, of course; **il viendra, c'est c.** he'll definitely come; **il devrait venir, mais ce n'est pas c.** he should come, but it's not certain *or* definite; **une chose est certaine** one thing's for certain *or* sure; **elle démissionne, c'est maintenant c.** it's now certain *or* definite that she's resigning
2 *(inéluctable → échec, victoire)* certain; **devant un renvoi c./une mort certaine** faced with certain dismissal/death; **on nous avait présenté son départ comme c.** we'd been told he was certain to go
3 *(persuadé)* sure, certain; **être c. de ce qu'on avance** to be sure *or* certain about what one is saying; **il n'est pas très c. de sa décision** he's not sure he's made the right decision; **êtes-vous c. de votre bon droit?** are you sure (that) you're in the right?; **être c. d'avoir fait qch** to be sure *or* to be positive one has done sth; **il est c. de revenir** he's sure *or* certain to return; **si tu pars battu, tu es c. de perdre!** if you think you're going to lose, (then) you're bound *or* sure *or* certain to lose!; **êtes-vous sûr que c'était lui? – j'en suis c.!** are you sure it was him? – I'm positive!, I'm sure *or* certain (of it)!; **ils céderont – n'en sois pas si c.** they'll give in – don't be so sure; **j'étais c. que cela recommencerait** I was sure *or* I knew it would happen again; **si j'étais c. qu'il vienne** if I knew (for sure) *or* if I was certain that he was coming; **il me semble que c'est demain, mais je n'en suis pas certaine** I think it's tomorrow, but I'm not sure
4 *Math* certain
ADJ INDÉFINI *(avant le nom)* **1** *(exprimant l'indétermination)* certain; **à remettre à une certaine date** to be handed in on a certain date; **à un c. moment** at one point; **un c. nombre d'entre eux** some of them; **je voudrais vous poser un c. nombre de questions** I'd like to ask you a number of *or* some questions; **j'y ai cru un c. temps** I believed it for a while; **un c. temps après/avant** a while later/earlier; **d'un c. point de vue, tu as raison** in some ways *or* in a sense, you're right; **d'une certaine façon** *ou* **manière** in a way; **dans** *ou* **en un c. sens** in a sense; **jusqu'à un c. point** up to a (certain) point
2 *(exprimant une quantité non négligeable)* certain; **il a fait preuve d'une certaine intelligence** he has shown a certain amount of *or* some intelligence; **il a un c. charme, c'est indéniable** he has a certain charm, that's undeniable; **il a un c. talent** he has a certain *or* some talent; **il a eu une certaine influence sur elle** he had some influence on her; **il faut un c. courage!** you certainly need some pluck!; **elle a un c. culot!** she's got some nerve!; **c'est quand même à une certaine distance d'ici** it is quite a distance away
3 *(devant un nom de personne)* **un c. Christophe a téléphoné** someone called Christophe phoned; **les dialogues sont l'œuvre d'un c....** the dialogue is by someone called... *or* by one...; **si un c. M. Martin appelle, dites-lui que...** if a (certain) Mr Martin calls, tell him...; *Péj* **il voit souvent un c. Robert** he sees a lot of some character called Robert
NM *Bourse* fixed *or* direct rate of exchange; **le c. de la livre est de 1,46 euros** the rate of exchange for the pound is 1.46 euros
ADV *Can Fam* for sure, certainly▪; **il va neiger aujourd'hui c.** it's going to snow today for sure
❑ **certains, certaines** ADJ INDÉFINI PL *(quelques)* some, certain; **certaines fois** sometimes, on some occasions; **dans certaines circonstances** in certain *or* some circumstances; **certains jours** sometimes, on some days; **certains indices retrouvés chez lui...** certain clues found at his home...; **on retrouve cette tradition dans certains pays** this tradition can be found in a number of *or* in certain countries; **j'ai certaines idées sur la question** I have some *or* a few ideas on the subject; **je connais certaines personnes qui n'auraient pas hésité** I can think of some *or* a few people who wouldn't have thought twice about it PRON INDÉFINI PL *(personnes)* some (people); *(choses)* some; *(d'un groupe)* some (of them); **certains pensent que...** some people think that...; *aussi Hum* **je travaille, moi, je ne suis pas comme certains!** I work, unlike some people!; **certains d'entre vous semblent ne pas avoir compris** some of you seem not to have understood; **parmi ces gens, certains n'avaient jamais navigué** some of these people had never sailed before; **il a de nombreux amis et certains sont très influents** he has a lot of friends and some of them are very influential; **il vend des gravures et certaines sont très jolies** he sells engravings, and some (of them) are very pretty

certainement [sɛrtɛnmɑ̃] ADV **1** *(sans aucun doute)* certainly, surely, no doubt; **il va c. échouer** he is bound to fail
2 *(probablement)* (most) probably; **il y a c. une solution à ton problème** there must be a way to solve your problem; **elle va c. t'appeler** she'll probably call you; **tu te souviens c. de Paul?** surely you remember Paul?, you remember Paul, surely?; **il sera c. le vainqueur** he'll most probably win; **je reviendrai c. mardi** I'll very likely come back on Tuesday
3 *(dans une réponse)* certainly; **je peux? – c.!** may I? – certainly *or* of course!; **c. pas!** certainly not!

certes [sɛrt] ADV **1** *(assurément)* certainly, indeed; **vous n'ignorez c. pas quelle est la situation** I'm sure you are not unaware of the situation; **c., je ne pouvais pas lui dire la vérité** certainly, I couldn't tell him/her the truth
2 *(servant de réponse)* certainly; **acceptez-vous? – c.!** do you accept? – certainly!; **l'avez-vous lu? – c.!** did you read it? – I certainly did *or* I did indeed!; **m'en voulez-vous? – c. non!** are you angry with me? – of course not *or* certainly not!
3 *(indiquant la concession)* of course, certainly; **c., sa situation n'est pas enviable, mais que faire?** his/her situation is certainly not to be envied, but what can be done?; **je ne veux c. pas la décourager, mais...** I certainly wouldn't want to discourage her, but...; **il est beau, c., mais il n'est pas sympathique** he's handsome, I grant you, but he's not very nice; **il ne pouvait rien faire d'autre, c., mais il fallait qu'il nous en parle** he couldn't do anything else, granted, but he should have spoken to us about it

certif [sɛrtif] NM *Fam Anciennement Scol* = basic examination sat at the end of primary education

certificat [sɛrtifika] NM **1** *(attestation)* certificate; *Bourse* **c. d'actions provisoire** share certificate, (provisional) scrip; **c. d'arrêt de travail** *(pour cause de maladie)* medical certificate; **c. d'assurance** insurance certificate; *Jur* **c. de bonne vie et de bonnes mœurs** character reference; **c. de capacité** *(d'employé)* certificate of proficiency; *Jur* **c. complémentaire de protection** supplementary protection certificate; **c. de concubinage** = official document stating that two people are cohabiting; *Jur* **c. de coutume** = attestation of a foreign legal rule; *Com* **c. de dépôt** *(de marchandises)* warehouse warrant; *Bourse* **c. de dividende provisoire** scrip dividend; *Com* **c. d'entrepôt** warehouse warrant; *Com* **c. de garantie** certificate of guarantee, guarantee certificate, warranty; *Jur* **c. d'hérédité** proof of title; *Fin* **c. d'investissement** investment certificate; *Fin* **c. d'investissement privilégié** preferential investment certificate;

cer–cer

Com **c. de jaugeage** tonnage certificate; **c. médical** medical certificate; *Admin* **c. de naissance** birth certificate; *Jur* **c. de nationalité** certificate of (French) nationality; **c. de navigabilité** *(aérienne)* certificate of airworthiness; *(maritime)* certificate of seaworthiness; *Bourse* **c. nominatif d'action(s)** registered share certificate; *Fin* **c. de non-paiement** *(de chèque)* notification of unpaid cheque; *(de lettre de change)* certificate of dishonour; *Com* **c. d'origine** certificate of origin; *Jur* **c. de propriété** title deed; *Bourse* **c. provisoire** share certificate, (provisional) scrip; *Assur* **c. provisoire d'assurance** cover note; *Com* **c. de qualité** certificate of quality; *Admin* **c. de résidence** certificate of residence; **c. sanitaire** health certificate; **c. de scolarité** *Scol* school attendance certificate; *Univ* university attendance certificate; *Ordinat* **c. de sécurité** security certificate; *Fin* **c. de titres** share certificate; *Jur* **c. de travail** attestation of employment, *Br* ≃ P45; *Fin* **c. de trésorerie** treasury bond; **c. de vaccination** vaccination certificate; *Com* **c. de valeur** certificate of value

2 *(diplôme)* diploma, certificate; **c. d'aptitude pédagogique** teaching diploma; *Jur* **c. d'aptitude à la profession d'avocat** = qualifying certificate required in order to be admitted as a trainee barrister; **c. d'aptitude professionnelle** = vocational training certificate (taken at secondary school), *Br* ≃ City and Guilds examination; **c. d'aptitude au professorat de l'enseignement secondaire** *ou* **du second degré** = secondary school teaching qualification, *Br* ≃ PGCE; **c. d'aptitude au professorat de l'enseignement technique** = secondary school teaching qualification for technical subjects; *Anciennement* **c. d'études (primaires)** = basic examination sat at the end of primary education; *Anciennement* **c. (d'études supérieures) de licence** *(unité de valeur)* = each of the four examinations for the "licence"; **c. de formation professionnelle** vocational training certificate

certificateur [sɛrtifikatœr] *Jur* **ADJ M** certifying, guaranteeing

NM *(gén)* certifier, guarantor; *(de caution)* counter-security

certification [sɛrtifikasjɔ̃] **NF** *Jur* **1** *(authentification)* certification, authentication; **c. conforme** certification **2** *(garantie)* (bank) guarantee **3** *(assurance, attestation)* attestation, witnessing; **c. de signature** *ou* **des signatures** witnessing of signatures

certifié, -e [sɛrtifje] *Scol* **ADJ** *(professeur)* holding the "CAPES"

NM,F "CAPES" holder, ≃ qualified *Br* secondary school *or Am* high school teacher

certifier [9] [sɛrtifje] **VT 1** *(assurer)* to assure; **il m'a certifié que rien n'avait été vendu** he assured me nothing had been sold **2** *Jur (garantir → caution)* to guarantee, to counter-secure; *(→ signature)* to witness, to authenticate; *(→ document)* to authenticate, to certify; **une copie certifiée conforme (à l'original)** a certified copy of the original document

certitude [sɛrtityd] **NF** certainty; **ce n'est pas une hypothèse, c'est une c.** it's not a possibility, it's a certainty; **avoir la c. de qch** to be convinced of sth; **il viendra, j'en ai la c.** I'm convinced *or* certain *or* quite sure he'll come; **je sais avec c. que...** I know for a certainty that...

cérulé, -e [seryle], **céruléen, -enne** [seryleɛ̃, -ɛn] **ADJ** *Littéraire* cerulean

cérumen [serymɛn] **NM** *Physiol* earwax, *Spéc* cerumen

cérumineux, -euse [serymino, -øz] **ADJ** *Physiol* ceruminous

céruse [seryz] **NF** ceruse; **blanc de c.** white lead

cérusé, -e [seryze] **ADJ** *(bois, meuble)* limed, whitewashed, *Am* pickled

Cervantès [sɛrvɑ̃tɛs] **NPR** Cervantes

cerveau, -x [sɛrvo] **NM 1** *Anat* brain; **c. antérieur** forebrain; **c. moyen** midbrain; **c. postérieur** hindbrain; *Fam* **c. brûlé** hothead; *Fam* **il a le c. malade** *ou* **dérangé** *ou* **fêlé** he's got a screw loose, he's cracked

2 *(esprit)* mind, intellect, brains; **faire travailler son c.** to use one's brain

3 *Fam (génie)* brain, brainy person; **c'est un c.** he's a real brain, he's brainy

4 *(instigateur)* brains; **être le c. de qch** to be the brains behind sth

5 *Ordinat* **c. électronique** electronic brain

cervelas [sɛrvəla] **NM** *Culin* ≃ saveloy

cervelet [sɛrvəlɛ] **NM** *Anat* cerebellum

cervelle [sɛrvɛl] **NF 1** *Anat* brain

2 *Fam (intelligence)* brain; **une fille sans c.** a brainless *or* dimwitted girl; **se mettre qch dans la c.** to get sth into one's head; **il faudrait te le mettre dans la c.** get it into your head; **il n'a** *ou* **il n'y a rien dans sa petite c.** he's got nothing between his ears; **quand elle a quelque chose dans la c.** when she gets an idea into her head; **avoir une c. d'oiseau** *ou* **une tête sans c.** to be bird-brained; **se mettre la c. à l'envers** to rack one's brains

3 *Culin* brains; **de la c. de mouton** sheep's brains; **c. de canut** = fromage frais with herbs

cervical, -e, -aux, -ales [sɛrvikal, -o] **ADJ** *Anat* cervical

cervicalgie [sɛrvikalʒi] **NF** *Méd* neck pain

cervicite [sɛrvisit] **NF** *Méd* cervicitis

cervico-vaginal, -e, -aux, -ales [sɛrvikɔvaʒinal, -o] **ADJ** *Anat* cervicovaginal, of the cervix and vagina

cervidé [sɛrvide] *Zool* **NM** member of the deer family *or Spéc* Cervidae, *Spéc* cervid

▫ **cervidés NMPL** Cervidae

Cervin [sɛrvɛ̃] **NM le (mont) C.** the Matterhorn

cervoise [sɛrvwaz] **NF** *Antiq* barley ale

CES [seəɛs] **NM 1** *(abrév* **collège d'enseignement secondaire***)* = former secondary school **2** *Anciennement (abrév* **contrat emploi-solidarité***)* = short-term contract subsidized by the government

ces [se] *voir* **ce**

césalpiniacée [sezalpinjase], **césalpinée** [sezalpine], **césalpiniée** [sezalpinje] *Bot* **NM** caesalpiniaceous plant

▫ **césalpiniacées NMPL** Caesalpiniaceae

César [sezar] **NPR** Caesar; **rendez à C. ce qui appartient à C.** render unto Caesar that which is Caesar's

césar [sezar] **NM 1** *(despote)* tyrant, dictator **2** *Cin* = French cinema award

Césarée [sezare] **NM** *Géog* Cesarea

césarien, -enne [sezarjɛ̃, -ɛn] **ADJ 1** *Antiq* Caesarean **2** *(régime)* despotic

▫ **césarienne NF** *Obst* Caesarean (section); **on lui a fait une césarienne** she had a Caesarean; **elle est née par césarienne** she was born by Caesarean

césariser [3] [sezarize] **VT** *Obst* to perform a Caesarean (section) on

césarisme [sezarism] **NM** caesarism, imperialism

césium [sezjɔm] **NM** *Métal & Chim* caesium

CESP [seəɛspe] **NM** *(abrév* **Conseil européen des syndicats de police***)* CESP, European Council of Police Trade Unions

cespiteux, -euse [sɛspitø, -øz] **ADJ** *Bot* caespitose, cespitose

cessant, -e [sɛsɑ̃, -ɑ̃t] *voir* **affaire**

cessation [sɛsasjɔ̃] **NF 1** *Mil* **c. des hostilités** ceasefire **2** *(d'une activité)* cessation, stopping; **c. du travail** stoppage **3** *Com* **c. de paiement** suspension of payments; **être en c. de paiement** to have suspended (all) payments; **c. d'activité** termination of business; **pour cause de c. de commerce** due to closure

cesse [sɛs] **NF elle n'aura de c. qu'elle n'ait trouvé la réponse** she will not rest until she finds the answer

▫ **sans cesse ADV** continually, constantly; **elle se plaint sans c.** she's constantly complaining, she complains all the time

cesser [4] [sese] **VI** *(pluie)* to stop, *Sout* to cease; *(vent)* to die down, to drop, *Sout* to abate; *(combat)* to (come to a) stop; *(bruit, mouvement)* to stop, *Sout* to cease; **il y a trop d'absentéisme, il faut que cela cesse!** too many people are staying away from work, this must stop!; **faire c. qch** to put a stop to sth; **c. de faire qch** to stop doing sth; **cesse de pleurer** stop crying; **c. de fumer** to give up *or* to stop smoking; **il n'a pas cessé de pleuvoir aujourd'hui** it hasn't stopped raining today, it's rained non-stop today; **il ne cesse pas de gémir** he never stops moaning, he's always *or* forever moaning; **ne c. de faire qch** to keep doing, to persist in doing sth; **je ne cesse d'y penser** I can't stop thinking about it, I keep thinking about it; **les prix ne cessent d'augmenter** prices keep rising

VT 1 *(arrêter)* to stop, to halt; **c. le travail** to down tools, to walk out; **les chantiers navals cessent le travail** *(dans un titre)* stoppage at the shipyards; **c. toutes relations avec qn** to break off all relations with sb; **cessez ces cris!** stop that shouting!

2 *Mil* **c. le combat** to stop fighting; **c. le feu** to cease fire

cessez-le-feu [seselfø] **NM INV** *Mil* ceasefire

cessibilité [sesibilite] **NF** *Jur* assignability, transferability

cessible [sesibl] **ADJ** *Jur* assignable, transferable; *(pension, retraite)* negotiable

cession [sɛsjɔ̃] **NF** *Jur* assignment, transfer; **c. d'actifs** sale of assets; **c. de bail** lease transfer; *Jur* **c. de créance** assignment of receivables; *Jur* **c. de dettes** assignment of debts; *Jur* **c. de droits litigieux** assignment of contested debts; *Jur* **c. de droits successifs** assignment of inheritance rights; *Com* **c. de licence** licensing; *Com* **c. de licence de marque** corporate licensing; *Com* **c. de licence de nom** name licensing; *Fin* **c. de parts** sale *or* disposal of securities

cession-bail [sesjɔ̃baj] *(pl* **cessions-bails** *ou* **cessions-baux***)* **NF** *Jur* leaseback

cessionnaire [sɛsjɔnɛr] **NMF** *Jur (de biens)* assignee, transferee; *(d'un effet de commerce, d'une créance)* holder; *(d'un chèque)* endorser

c'est-à-dire [setadir] **ADV 1** *(introduisant une explication)* that is (to say), i.e., in other words; **toute la famille, c. mes parents et mes sœurs** all the family, i.e. *or* that is, my parents and my sisters

2 *(pour demander une explication)* **c.?** what do you mean?

3 *(introduisant une rectification)* or rather; **il est venu hier, c. plutôt avant-hier** he came yesterday, I mean *or* or rather the day before yesterday

4 *(introduisant une hésitation)* **tu penses y aller? – eh bien, c....** are you thinking of going? – well, you know *or* I mean...

▫ **c'est-à-dire que CONJ 1** *(introduisant une excuse, une hésitation)* actually, as a matter of fact; **voulez-vous nous accompagner? – c. que je suis un peu fatigué** do you want to come with us? – I'm afraid *or* actually I'm a bit tired; **elle m'en veut – c. qu'elle t'a attendue deux heures** she's annoyed with me – well, you DID keep her waiting for two hours; **tu m'en veux? – c. que oui, un peu** are you angry with me? – well, actually, I am a bit

2 *(introduisant une explication)* which means; **il a acheté une maison, c. qu'il s'est endetté** he bought a house, which means he got himself into debt

3 *(introduisant une rectification)* or rather; **je ne sais pas ce qu'il veut, c. que je préfère ne pas le savoir** I don't know what he wants, or rather I don't want to know

ceste [sɛst] **NM** *Antiq* caestus

cestode [sɛstɔd] *Entom* **NM** cestode

▫ **cestodes NMPL** Cestoda

césure [sezyr] **NF 1** *Littérature* caesura **2** *Ordinat* break, hyphenation; **c. automatique** soft hyphen; **c. imposée** hard hyphen

CET [seəte] **NM 1** *(abrév* **compte épargne temps***)* = scheme which allows employees to save up the hours of overtime they accumulate under the "RTT" system (see entry "RTT") for up to five years, eventually being compensated either financially or with additional holidays **2** *Anciennement (abrév* **collège d'enseignement technique***)* = technical school

cet [sɛt] *voir* **ce**

C&A *Com (abrév écrite* **coût et assurance***)* C&I

cétacé [setase] *Zool* **NM** cetacean

▫ **cétacés NMPL** Cetacea

cétane [setan] **NM** *Chim* cetane

céteau, -x [seto] **NM** *Ich* wedge sole

cétène [setɛn] **NM** *Chim* cetene, ketene

C&F *Com (abrév écrite* **coût et fret***)* C&F

cétoine [setwan] **NF** *Entom* beetle; **c. dorée** rose beetle

cétone [setɔn]NF *Chim* ketone

cétonémie [setɔnemi]NF *Chim* ketonaemia

cétonique [setɔnik]ADJ *Chim* ketonic

cétonurie [setɔnyri]NF *Méd* ketonuria

cétose [setoz]NM *Biol & Chim* ketose
 NF *Méd* ketosis

cétoxime [setɔksim]NF *Biol & Chim* ketoxime

cette [sɛt] *voir* **ce**

ceusses [søs]PRON *Fam Hum* **les c. qui...** them who...

ceux [sø] *voir* **celui**

ceux-ci [søsi], **ceux-là** [søla] *voir* **celui**

Cévennes [sevɛn]NFPL **les C.** the Cévennes

cévenol, -e [sevnɔl]ADJ of/from the Cévennes
 ❑ **Cévenol, -e** NM,F = inhabitant of or person from the Cévennes

Ceylan [selɑ̃]NM *Anciennement* Ceylon

ceylanais, -e [selanɛ, -ɛz] *Anciennement* ADJ Ceylonese
 ❑ **Ceylanais, -e** NM,F = inhabitant of or person from Ceylon

cézannien, -enne [sezanjɛ̃, -ɛn] ADJ = of or like Cézanne

cézig, cézigue [sezig]PRON *Fam* his lordship, *Br* his nibs

cf. *(abrév écrite* **confer***)* cf

CFA [seɛfa] NF *(abrév* **Communauté financière africaine***)* African Financial Community; **franc C.** = currency used in former French African colonies
 NM *(abrév* **Centre de formation des apprentis***)* = centre for apprenticeship training

CFAO [seɛfao]NF *(abrév* **conception et fabrication assistées par ordinateur***)* CAD/CAM

CFC [seɛfse] NM 1 *Chim (abrév* **chlorofluorocarbure***)* CFC 2 *(abrév* **centre de formation continue***)* = centre for continuing education

CFDT [seɛfdete] NF *(abrév* **Confédération française démocratique du travail***)* = French trade union

CFE–CGC [seɛfəseʒese] NF *(abrév* **Confédération française de l'encadrement–Confédération générale des cadres***)* = French trade union for engineers and middle and lower management staff

CFES [seɛfɛs] NM *Anciennement Scol (abrév* **certificat de fin d'études secondaires***)* = school-leaving certificate

CFF [seɛfɛf] NMPL *Suisse (abrév* **Chemins de fer fédéraux***)* = Swiss railways

CFL [seɛfɛl] NMPL *(abrév* **Chemins de fer luxembourgeois***)* = Luxembourg railways

CFP [seɛfpe]NF 1 *(abrév* **Compagnie française des pétroles***)* = French oil company 2 *(abrév* **Communauté française du Pacifique***)* **franc C.** = currency used in former French colonies in the Pacific area
 NM 1 *(abrév* **Centre de formation permanente***)* = centre for ongoing training and education 2 *(abrév* **Certificat de formation professionnelle***)* vocational training certificate

CFR [seɛfɛr] *(abrév* **cost and freight***)* CFR

CFTC [seɛftese]NF *(abrév* **Confédération française des travailleurs chrétiens***)* = French trade union

CGA [seʒea] NM *Ordinat (abrév* **colour graphics adaptor***)* CGA

CGC [seʒese] NF *(abrév* **Confédération générale des cadres***)* = French management union

CGI [seʒei] NM *Admin (abrév* **Code général des impôts***)* general tax code
 NF *Ordinat (abrév* **common gateway interface***)* CGI

CGPME [seʒepeɛmə] NF *(abrév* **Confédération générale des petites et moyennes entreprises***)* = French small business employers' organization

CGT [seʒete]NF *(abrév* **Confédération générale du travail***)* = major association of French trade unions (affiliated to the Communist Party)

CH *(abrév écrite* **Confédération helvétique***)* = Swiss nationality sticker on a car

ch *Aut (abrév écrite* **cheval-vapeur***)* hp

ch. 1 *(abrév écrite* **charges***)* bills **2** *(abrév écrite* **chauffage***)* heating **3** *(abrév écrite* **cherche***)* **architecte c. co-locataire** architect seeks *Br* flatmate or *Am* roommate; **JH c. JF** male WLTM female

chabichou [ʃabiʃu]NM *Culin* = kind of goat's milk cheese

châble [ʃɑbl]NM *Suisse* = steep gully on a forested mountainside, down which logs are rolled

chabler [3] [ʃɑble]VT to beat

chablis [ʃabli]NM *(vin)* Chablis

chablon [ʃablɔ̃]NM *Suisse (pochoir)* stencil

chabot [ʃabo] NM *Ich (de mer)* sea scorpion, bullhead; *(d'eau douce)* chub

chabraque [ʃabrak] NF 1 *Mil* shabrack 2 *Fam (femme laide)* dog, *Br* boot; *(femme de mœurs légères)* tramp, *Br* slag; *(femme bête)* stupid idiot

chabrol [ʃabrɔl], **chabrot** [ʃabro]NM *(dans le Sud-Ouest de la France)* **faire c.** = to add red wine to the last few spoonfuls of soup in one's bowl

chacal, -als [ʃakal]NM 1 *Zool* jackal 2 *Péj (personne)* vulture, jackal

cha-cha-cha [tʃatʃatʃa]NM INV cha-cha, cha-cha-cha

chachlik [ʃaʃlik]NM *Culin* shashlik, shashlick

chacone, chaconne [ʃakɔn] NF *Mus & (danse)* chaconne

chacote [ʃakɔt] NF *Can (en acadien)* quarrel, fight

chacun, -e [ʃakœ̃, -yn] PRON INDÉFINI 1 *(chaque personne, chaque chose)* each; **c. à sa façon** each in his own way; **c. à sa façon, ils ont raison** each one is right in his own way; **je vous donne 10 minutes c.** I'll give you 10 minutes each; **je les vends 15 euros c.** I'm selling them for 15 euros each *or* apiece; **ils ont pris c. son** *ou* **leur chapeau** each of them took their *or* his hat, they each took their hat; **ils sont partis c. de son** *ou* **de leur côté** they (each *or* all) went their separate ways; **c. de** (one) of; **c. d'entre nous** each of us; **c. des employés a une tâche à remplir** each employee has a job to do; **c. de ses gestes** each of his gestures; **Madame, c. son tour** please wait your turn, Madam; **alors comme ça tu pars en vacances? – eh oui, c. son tour!** so you're off on holiday, are you? – well, it's my turn now!; **nous y sommes allés c. à notre tour** we each went in turn
 2 *(tout le monde)* everyone, everybody; **c. le dit** everyone says so; **à c. (selon) son dû** each according to his/her merits; **à c. ses goûts** to each his own; **à c. son métier** every man to his own trade; **c. pour soi** every man for himself; **tout un c.** everybody, each and every person; *Fam* **à c. sa chacune** every Jack has his Jill

chadburn [tʃadbœrn]NM *Naut* chadburn, engine-room telegraph

chadouf [ʃaduf]NM well-sweep, shadoof

chaebol [kebɔl]NM *Écon* chaebol

chænichthys [keniktys]NM *Ich* Antarctic ice fish

chafiisme [ʃafiism]NM *Rel* Shafi'ism

chafouin, -e [ʃafwɛ̃, -in] ADJ *Péj (visage)* sly, cunning; **un homme à la mine chafouine** a sly-looking man

chagagnac [ʃagaɲak] ADJ *Can (en acadien → temps)* changeable; *(→ personne)* tired

chagatte [ʃagat]NF *Vulg* pussy, snatch, *Br* fanny

chagrin¹ [ʃagrɛ̃] NM *(peine)* sorrow, grief; **avoir du c.** to be upset; **il a un gros c.** *(enfant)* he's very unhappy; **causer** *ou* **faire du c. à qn** to cause distress to *or* to distress sb; **avoir un c. d'amour** to be disappointed in love

'Le Chagrin et la pitié' Ophuls 'The Sorrow and the Pity'

chagrin², -e [ʃagrɛ̃, -in]ADJ *Littéraire* 1 *(triste)* sad, sorrowful, woeful 2 *(revêche)* ill-tempered, quarrelsome; **esprits chagrins** malcontents

chagrin³ [ʃagrɛ̃]NM *(cuir)* shagreen

chagrinant, -e [ʃagrinɑ̃, -ɑ̃t] ADJ grievous, distressing

chagriner¹ [3] [ʃagrine]VT 1 *(attrister)* to grieve, to distress 2 *(contrarier)* to worry, to bother, to upset
 ►**se chagriner** VPR *Can* **le temps se chagrine** it's clouding over, it's getting cloudy

chagriner² [3] [ʃagrine] VT *(cuir)* to shagreen, to grain

chah [ʃa] = **shah**

chahut [ʃay] NM *Fam* rumpus, hullaballoo, uproar; **faire du c.** to make a racket, to kick up a rumpus

chahuter [3] [ʃayte] *Fam*VI 1 *(être indiscipliné)* to kick up a rumpus, to make a racket
 2 *(remuer)* **ça chahutait ferme sur le bateau!** it was a bit rough on the boat!
 VT 1 *(houspiller → professeur)* to rag, to bait; *(→ orateur)* to heckle; **un professeur chahuté** a teacher who can't control his/her pupils; **il se fait c. en classe** he can't keep (his class in) order; **le Premier ministre s'est fait c. à l'Assemblée** the Prime Minister was heckled in Parliament
 2 *(remuer)* to knock about, to bash around

chahuteur, -euse [ʃaytœr, -øz] *Fam* ADJ rowdy, boisterous
 NM,F rowdy (person); *(dans un meeting politique)* heckler

chai [ʃɛ]NM wine and spirits storehouse

Chaillot [ʃajo]NM **(le palais de) C.** = architectural complex built in 1937 on the site of the Trocadéro in Paris

chaînage [ʃenaʒ]NM 1 *Constr (action)* clamping, tying; *(armature)* clamps, ties; *(mesurage)* chaining 2 *Ordinat* chaining; *(de commandes)* piping

chaîne [ʃɛn]NF 1 *(attache, bijou)* chain; **le chien était attaché à sa niche par une c.** the dog was chained to its kennel; **une c. en or** a gold chain; **former une c. de solidarité** to create a network of support; **c. d'arpenteur** surveyor's chain; **c. de bicyclette** bicycle chain; **c. de montre** watch chain; **c. de sûreté** *(sur un bijou)* safety chain; *(sur une porte)* (door) chain; *Fig* **faire la c.** to form a (human) chain; **briser ses chaînes** to cast off one's chains *or* shackles; **le peuple a brisé ses chaînes** the people shook off their chains
 2 *(suite)* chain, series; **une c. d'événements** a chain of events; *Écol* **la c. alimentaire** the food chain; **c. de montagnes** (mountain) range; *Ling* **c. parlée** (speech) utterances; *Mktg* **c. de valeur** value chain
 3 *TV* channel; **je regarde la première c.** I'm watching channel one; **c. à la carte** pay-per-view channel; **c. de cinéma** cinema channel, movie channel; **c. commerciale** commercial channel; **c. généraliste** general-interest channel; **c. hertzienne** terrestrial channel; **c. d'information continue** news channel; **c. musicale** music channel; **c. numérique** digital channel; **c. payante** *ou* **à péage** subscription *or* pay channel; **c. publique** public *or* state-owned channel; **c. par satellite** satellite channel; **c. de télé-achat** shopping channel; **c. de télévision** television channel; **c. thématique** specialized channel
 4 *(stéréo)* hi-fi, music system; **c. compacte** compact system; **c. hi-fi** hi-fi; **c. laser** CD system; **c. stéréo** stereo
 5 *Com (de restaurants, de supermarchés)* chain; **c. de détail** retail chain; **c. de journaux** newspaper group; **c. volontaire** voluntary chain; **c. volontaire de détaillants** voluntary retailer chain
 6 *Ind* **c. de fabrication** production line; **c. du froid** cold chain; **c. de montage** assembly line
 7 *Aut* **c. de distribution** timing *or* camshaft chain
 8 *Ordinat* string; **c. vide/de caractères** null/character string; **c. de recherche** search string
 9 *Chim & Phys* chain; **à longue c.** long-chain
 10 *Tex* warp
 11 *(danse)* chain; **faites la c.!** *(dans une ronde)* hold hands and make a circle!
 12 *Can* **c. du trottoir** kerb
 13 *Constr (barre)* I-beam, tie-beam, tie-iron; *(pilier)* pier
 14 *Pêche* **c. à chalut** trawl grommet
 ❑ **chaînes** NFPL *Aut* (snow) chains
 ❑ **à la chaîne** ADJ *(travail)* assembly-line *(avant n)*, production-line *(avant n)* ADV *(travailler, produire)* on the production line; **faire qch à la c.** to mass-produce sth; **ils ont été faits à la c.** *(gén)* they're off the production line; *Péj* they've been churned out (in their hundreds); **des objets produits à la c.** mass-produced items
 ❑ **en chaîne** ADJ *(réaction)* chain *(avant n)*; **des catastrophes en c.** a whole catalogue of disasters

chaîner [4] [ʃene] VT 1 *Constr* to chain, to tie 2

(mesurer) to chain **3** *Aut (pneu)* to put chains on; *(voiture)* to fit with chains **4** *Ordinat* to chain; *(commandes)* to pipe

chaînetier, -ère [ʃɛntje, -ɛr] **NMF** chain maker

chaînette [ʃɛnɛt] **NF 1** *(bijou)* small chain **2** *Couture* **(point de) c.** chain stitch **3** *(attache)* **c. de sûreté** safety chain
 ▫ **en chaînette** **ADJ** *Archit & Géom* catenary

chaîneur [ʃɛnœr] **NM** *Tech* chainman, one of a line of men forming a chain

chaînier [ʃɛnje] **NM** chain maker, chainsmith

chaîniste [ʃɛnist] **NMF** chain maker

chaînon [ʃɛnɔ̃] **NM 1** *(élément → d'une chaîne, d'un raisonnement)* link; *aussi Fig* **le c. manquant** the missing link **2** *Géog* secondary chain *or* range (of mountains) **3** *Ordinat* **c. de données** data link

chaïote [ʃajɔt] = **chayote**

chair [ʃɛr] **NF 1** *(chez les humains, chez les animaux)* **la c., les chairs** the flesh; **c. à canon** cannon fodder; **il aime la c. fraîche** *(ogre)* he likes to eat children; **avoir la c. de poule** *(avoir froid, avoir peur)* to have goose pimples; **quelle horreur! ça me donne** *ou* **j'en ai la c. de poule!** how awful! it gives me goose pimples!; **bien en c.** chubby; **un être de c. et de sang** a creature of flesh and blood; **voir qn en c. et en os** to see sb in the flesh; **c. à saucisse** sausage meat; *Fam Fig* **je vais en faire de la c. à saucisse** *ou* **à pâté!** I'm going to make mincemeat out of him/her!
 2 *(de fruit)* flesh, pulp
 3 *Rel & Littéraire* flesh; **souffrir dans sa c.** to suffer in the flesh; **la c. est faible** the flesh is weak; **la c. de sa c.** his/her own flesh and blood; **le péché de c.** the sin of the flesh
 ADJ INV (couleur) c. flesh-coloured
 ▫ **chairs** **NFPL** *Beaux-Arts* flesh tones *or* tints

chairant, -e [ʃɛrɑ̃, -ɑ̃t] **ADJ** *Can (en acadien)* chubby

chaire [ʃɛr] **NF 1** *(estrade)* rostrum; **monter en c.** to go up on the rostrum; *Fig* to start one's speech **2** *Rel (siège)* throne, cathedra; *(tribune)* pulpit; **la c. apostolique** the Holy See **3** *Univ* chair; **être titulaire d'une c. de linguistique** to hold a chair in linguistics

chais [ʃɛ] = **chai**

chaise [ʃɛz] **NF 1** *(siège)* chair; **prenez donc une c.** have *or* take a seat; *Fig* **être assis entre deux chaises,** *très Fam* **avoir le cul entre deux chaises** to be in a difficult position▪; **c. à bascule,** *Can* **c. berçante, c. berceuse** rocking chair; **c. de cuisine/de jardin** kitchen/garden chair; **c. haute** *ou* **d'enfant** *ou* **de bébé** high-chair; **c. électrique** electric chair; **passer à la c. électrique** to go to the (electric) chair; **c. longue** *(d'extérieur)* deck chair; *(d'intérieur)* chaise longue; *Fam* **faire de la c. longue** to lounge about in a deckchair; **c. percée** commode; **c. pliante** folding chair; **c. à porteurs** sedan (chair); **c. de poste** post chaise; **c. roulante** wheelchair
 2 *(jeu)* **chaises musicales** musical chairs
 3 *Constr* wooden frame
 4 *Naut* **nœud de c.** bowline

chaisier, -ère [ʃezje, -ɛr] **NM,F 1** *(fabricant)* chair maker **2** *(gardien)* chair attendant *(in gardens or church)*

chakra [ʃakra] **NM** chakra

chaland[1] [ʃalɑ̃] **NM** *Naut* barge

chaland[2], **-e** [ʃalɑ̃, -ɑ̃d] **NM,F** *Vieilli* regular customer; **attirer le c.** to attract customers *or* custom

chalandage [ʃalɑ̃daʒ] **NM** *Com* shopping

chaland-citerne [ʃalɑ̃sitɛrn] *(pl* **chalands-citernes) NM** bunkering barge

chalandise [ʃalɑ̃diz] **NF** *Com* **zone de c.** customer catchment area

chalaze [kalɑz] **NF 1** *Biol & Bot* chalaza **2** *Méd* chalazion

chalazion [ʃalazjɔ̃] **NM** *Méd* chalazion

chalcocite [ʃalkɔsit] **NM** *Minér* chalcocite, chalcosine, copper glance

chalcographie [kalkɔgrafi] **NF** *Beaux-Arts* **1** *(art)* chalcography **2** *(lieu)* chalcography room

chalcolithique [kalkɔlitik] *Géol* **ADJ** Chalcolithic; **période c.** Chalcolithic period *or* age, Copper-Stone age
 NM Chalcolithic

chalcopyrite [kalkɔpirit] **NF** *Chim* chalcopyrite, copper pyrites

chalcosine [kalkɔzin], **chalcosite** [kalkɔzit] **NF** *Minér* chalcocite, chalcosine, copper glance

chaldaïque [kaldaik] **ADJ** Chaldean
 ▫ **Chaldaïque** **NMF** Chaldean

Chaldée [kalde] **NF** *Anciennement* **la C.** Chaldea

chaldéen, -enne [kaldeɛ̃, -ɛn] **ADJ** Chaldean
 NM *(langue)* Chaldee, Chaldean
 ▫ **Chaldéen, -enne** **NM,F** Chaldean

châle [ʃal] **NM** shawl

chalet [ʃalɛ] **NM 1** *(maison → alpine)* chalet; *(→ de plaisance)* wooden cottage **2** *Can* (holiday) cottage *(normally in the mountains or by the sea/lake)* **3** *Arch* **c. de nécessité** public convenience

chaleur [ʃalœr] **NF 1** *Météo* heat; **c. sèche/humide** dry/humid heat; **c. douce** warmth; **il fait une c. lourde** it's very muggy; **il fait une c. terrible dans ces dortoirs** it's terribly hot in these dormitories; **quelle c.!** what a scorcher!; **craint** *ou* **ne pas exposer à la c.** *(sur mode d'emploi)* store in a cool place; **c. animale** body heat
 2 *Phys* heat; **c. atomique** atomic heat; **c. latente** latent heat; **c. massique** *ou* **spécifique** specific heat
 3 *(sentiment)* warmth; **leur accueil manquait de c.** their welcome lacked warmth *or* wasn't very warm; **il y avait une certaine c. dans sa voix** his/her voice was warm (and welcoming); **plaider une cause avec c.** to plead a case fervently *or* with fervour; **c. humaine** human warmth
 4 *Beaux-Arts (d'une couleur)* warmth
 ▫ **chaleurs** **NFPL 1** *Météo* **les grandes chaleurs** the hottest days of the summer
 2 *Zool* heat; **la jument a ses chaleurs** the mare's *Br* on *or Am* in heat
 ▫ **en chaleur** **ADJ 1** *Zool Br* on heat, *Am* in heat
 2 *Vulg (homme, femme)* horny

chaleureuse [ʃalœrøz] *voir* **chaleureux**

chaleureusement [ʃalœrøzmɑ̃] **ADV** warmly

chaleureux, -euse [ʃalœrø, -øz] **ADJ** *(remerciement)* warm, sincere; *(accueil)* warm, cordial, hearty; *(applaudissements)* enthusiastic; *(approbation)* hearty, sincere; *(voix)* warm; *(ami)* warm-hearted; **remercier qn en termes c.** to thank sb warmly

châlit [ʃali] **NM** bedstead

challenge [ʃalɑ̃ʒ, tʃalɑ̃ʒ] **NM 1** *(défi)* challenge **2** *Sport (épreuve)* sporting contest; *(trophée)* trophy

challenger, challengeur [ʃalɑ̃dʒœr, tʃalɛndʒœr] **NM** *Sport* challenger; *Mktg* (market) challenger

chaloir [ʃalwar] [69] **V IMPERSONNEL** *Arch & Littéraire* **peu me** *ou* **peu m'en chaut** it matters (but) little to me, I care not

chaloupe [ʃalup] **NF 1** *Naut (à moteur)* launch; *(à rames) Br* rowing boat, *Am* rowboat; **c. de sauvetage** lifeboat **2** *Can (couvre-chaussure)* rubber overshoe, galosh

chaloupé, -e [ʃalupe] **ADJ 1** *(danse)* gliding, swaying **2** *(démarche)* rolling

chalouper [3] [ʃalupe] **VI 1** *(danser)* to sway, to glide **2** *(marcher)* to waddle

chalumeau, -x [ʃalymo] **NM 1** *Tech Br* blowlamp, *Am* blowtorch; **chauffer un métal au c.** to heat a piece of metal with a blowlamp; **c. oxhydrique/oxyacétylénique** oxyhydrogen/oxyacetylene torch **2** *Mus* pipe **3** *Vieilli (paille)* straw **4** *Can* spout *(for collecting sap of maple tree)*

chalut [ʃaly] **NM** *Pêche* trawl; **pêcher au c.** to trawl

chalutage [ʃalytaʒ] **NM** *Pêche* trawling

chalutier [ʃalytje] **NM 1** *(pêcheur)* trawlerman **2** *(bateau)* trawler; **petit c.** dragger

chamade [ʃamad] **NF** **battre la c.** to beat *or* to pound wildly

chamæcyparis [kamesiparis] **NM** *Bot* false cedar, *Spéc* chamaecyparis

chamærops [kamerɔps] = **chamérops**

chamaille [ʃamaj] **NF** *Fam* squabble, tiff; **des chamailles** squabbling

chamailler [3] [ʃamaje] **se chamailler** **VPR** *Fam (emploi réciproque)* to bicker, to squabble; **se c. avec qn** to bicker with sb

chamaillerie [ʃamajri] **NF** *Fam* squabble, tiff; **des chamailleries** squabbling

chamailleur, -euse [ʃamajœr, -øz] *Fam* **ADJ** quarrelsome
 NM,F bickerer, squabbler

chamaillis [ʃamaji] **NM** *Arch & Littéraire* fray, brawl

chaman [ʃaman] **NM** shaman

chamanisme [ʃamanism] **NM** shamanism

chamarré, -e [ʃamare] **ADJ** richly-coloured, brightly-coloured; **c. d'or** with gold brocade; *Littéraire* **montagne chamarrée de fleurs** mountainside decked *or* spangled with flowers

chamarrer [3] [ʃamare] **VT** to decorate, to adorn, to ornament

chamarrures [ʃamaryr] **NFPL** trimmings, adornments; **elle adore les c.** she loves a glittery style of dress; *Littéraire* **une chapelle toute or et c.** a chapel all in gold and heavily decorated

chambard [ʃɑ̃bar] **NM** *Fam (bruit)* din, racket, rumpus; *(bouleversement)* upset, upheaval; **faire du c.** *(faire du bruit)* to kick up (a din), to make a rumpus; *(protester)* to kick up (a fuss), to raise a stink

chambardement [ʃɑ̃bardəmɑ̃] **NM** *Fam* upheaval; **le grand c., le c. général** the revolution

chambarder [3] [ʃɑ̃barde] **VT** *Fam (endroit, objets)* to mess up, to turn upside down; *(projets)* to upset, to overturn, to turn upside down; *(société, conventions)* to turn upside down

chambellan [ʃɑ̃belɑ̃] **NM** chamberlain

chambertin [ʃɑ̃bɛrtɛ̃] **NM** Chambertin (wine)

chamboulement [ʃɑ̃bulmɑ̃] **NM** *Fam* **1** *(désordre)* mess, shambles **2** *(changement)* total change, upheaval; **il y a eu un c. complet dans nos projets** our plans were turned upside down

chambouler [3] [ʃɑ̃bule] **VT** *Fam (endroit, objets)* to mess up, to turn upside down; *(projets)* to mess up; **cette réunion imprévue a chamboulé mon emploi du temps** this last-minute meeting has messed up my schedule

chambranle [ʃɑ̃brɑ̃l] **NM** *(de cheminée)* mantelpiece; *(de porte)* (door) frame *or* casing; *(de fenêtre)* (window) frame *or* casing

chambranler [3] [ʃɑ̃brɑ̃le] **VI** *Can (personne)* to totter, to stagger; *(table)* to wobble

chambray [ʃɑ̃brɛ] **NM** *Tex* chambray

chambre [ʃɑ̃br] **NF 1** *(pièce)* bedroom; *(à l'hôtel)* room; **dans ma c.** in my room *or* bedroom; **une maison de cinq chambres** a five-bedroomed house; **avoir une c. en ville** *(étudiant)* to have a place in town; **faire c. à part** to sleep in separate rooms; **faire c. commune** to share the same room *or* bedroom; **réserver une c. d'hôtel** to book a hotel room; **vous auriez une c. (de) libre?** do you have any vacancies?; **c. individuelle** *ou* **pour une personne** single (room); **c. double** *ou* **pour deux personnes** double room; **c. d'hôte** bed and breakfast; **chambres d'hôte** *(sur panneau)* rooms available; **chambres à louer** rooms available; **c. avec ou sans pension** bed and breakfast or full board; **c. d'amis** guest *or* spare room; **c. de bonne** maid's room; *(louée à un particulier)* attic room; **c. à coucher** *(pièce)* bedroom; *(mobilier)* bedroom furniture; **c. d'enfant** child's room; *(pour tout-petits)* nursery; **c. meublée** furnished room, *Br* bedsit; **c. de service** servant's room; **camarade de c.** roommate
 2 *(local)* **c. de décontamination** decontamination chamber; **c. forte** strongroom; **c. froide** cold room; **c. à gaz** gas chamber; *Suisse* **c. à lessive** laundry room
 3 *Pol* House, Chamber; **la C.** the House; **siéger à la C.** to sit in the House; **la C. des communes** the House of Commons; *Anciennement* **la C. des députés** the (French) Chamber of Deputies; **la C. haute/basse** the Upper/Lower Chamber; **la C. des lords** *ou* **des pairs** the House of Lords; **la C. des représentants** the House of Representatives
 4 *Jur (subdivision d'une juridiction)* chamber; *(section)* Court; **première c.** upper chamber *or* court; **deuxième c.** lower chamber *or* court; **c. d'accusation** *(à la cour d'appel)* Indictment Division; **c. des appels correctionnels** District Court; **c. civile** *(à la cour d'appel)* Civil Division; **c. commerciale** *(à la cour d'appel)* Commercial Division; **c. commerciale et financière** *(à la Cour de cassation)* Commercial and Financial Division; **c. du conseil** court chambers; **c. correctionnelle** Criminal Division *(of the "tribunal de grande instance")*; **c. criminelle** *(à la Cour de cassation)* Criminal Division; **c. détachée**

= local branch of the "Cour de Cassation"; **c. de discipline** = professional disciplinary panel; **c. de l'instruction** Investigative Division; **c. des mineurs** (à la cour d'appel) Juvenile Division; **c. des mises en accusation** Court of criminal appeal; **c. mixte** (à la Cour de Cassation) joint bench, composite bench; **c. régionale des comptes** regional audit board; **c. des requêtes** appeal court; **c. sociale** (à la cour d'appel) Social Division

5 (organisme) **c. d'agriculture** = farmers' association; Fin **c. de clearing** clearing house; **c. de commerce** Chamber of Commerce; **c. de commerce et d'industrie** Chamber of Commerce and Industry; **c. de commerce internationale** International Chamber of Commerce; Fin **c. de compensation** clearing house; Fin **c. de compensation automatisée** automated clearing house; **c. des métiers** Guild Chamber; **c. syndicale** Employer's Syndicate; **c. syndicale des agents de change** stock exchange committee

6 Naut (local) **c. des cartes** ou **de navigation** chart house; **c. de chauffe** stokehold; **c. des machines** engine room; (cabine) cabin

7 Astron **c. de Schmidt** Schmidt telescope

8 Mil chamber

9 Tech & Aut chamber; **c. à air** inner tube; **sans c. à air** tubeless; **c. d'alimentation** feed chamber; **c. de carburation** mixing chamber; **c. de mélange** mixing chamber; **c. de résonance** resonating chamber; **c. de turbulence** swirl chamber, turbulence combustion chamber

10 Phys chamber; **c. à bulles** bubble chamber; **c. de combustion** combustion chamber

11 Phot **c. noire** darkroom

12 Opt **c. claire/noire** camera lucida/obscura

13 Anat **c. antérieure** ou **de l'œil** anterior chamber of the eye; **c. pulpaire (d'une dent)** (tooth) pulp chamber

14 Belg & Suisse (pièce quelconque) room; **une maison de six chambres** a six-roomed house
▫ **en chambre** ADJ **1** Hum (stratège, athlète) armchair (avant n) **2** (à domicile) **couturière en c.** dressmaker working from home ADV (travailler) at or from home

---

'La Chambre de Vincent à Arles' Van Gogh 'Vincent's Room, Arles'

Culture
LA CHAMBRE DES DÉPUTÉS
This was the official name for the French parliamentary assembly from 1814 to 1940. The name "l'Assemblée nationale" was adopted in 1946.

---

chambré, -e [ʃɑ̃bre] ADJ (vin) at room temperature

chambrée [ʃɑ̃bre] NF Mil **1** (pièce) (barrack) room **2** (soldats) **toute la c.** all the soldiers in the barrack room

chambrer [3] [ʃɑ̃bre] VT **1** (vin) to allow to breathe, to bring to room temperature **2** Fam (se moquer de) **c. qn** to make fun of sb , Br to wind sb up, to take the mickey out of sb
VI Can Joual to rent a room, to room

chambrette [ʃɑ̃brɛt] NF small room

chambreur, -euse [ʃɑ̃brœr, -øz] NM,F Can & Suisse Br lodger, Am roomer

chambrier [ʃɑ̃brije] NM Hist & Mil chief chamberlain

chambrière [ʃɑ̃brijɛr] NF **1** (servante) chambermaid **2** (fouet) lunging whip **3** (béquille) cartprop

chameau, -x [ʃamo] NM **1** (animal) camel; **c. de Bactriane** Bactrian camel **2** Fam Péj **quel c.!** (homme) he's a real swine!; (femme) she's a real cow!
ADJ Fam **ce qu'il/elle est c.!** what a swine he is/cow she is!; **ce qu'il peut être c. avec elle!** he can be such a swine to her!

chamelier [ʃaməlje] NM camel driver

chamelle [ʃamɛl] NF Zool she-camel

chamelon [ʃamlɔ̃] NM Zool young camel, camel colt

chamérops [kamerɔps] NM Bot European fan palm

chamito-sémitique [kamitɔsemitik] (pl **chamito-sémitiques**) ADJ Hamito-Semitic
NM Ling Hamito-Semitic language group

---

chamois [ʃamwa] NM **1** (animal) chamois **2** Ski = skiing proficiency grade
ADJ INV (couleur) buff, fawn

chamoisage [ʃamwazaʒ] NM (en tannerie) buffing

chamoiser [3] [ʃamwaze] VT to buff

chamoiserie [ʃamwazri] NF **1** (manufacture) chamois-leather factory **2** (secteur) chamois-leather industry **3** (peau) chamois leather

chamoisette [ʃamwazɛt] NF Belg duster

chamoiseur, -euse [ʃamwazœr, -øz] NM,F (en tannerie) chamois-leather dresser

chamoisine [ʃamwazin] NF soft (yellow) duster

chamoniard, -e [ʃamɔnjar, -ard] ADJ of/from Chamonix
▫ **Chamoniard, -e** NM,F = inhabitant of or person from Chamonix

chamotte [ʃamɔt] NF Cér chamotte, grog

champ [ʃɑ̃] NM **1** Agr field; **c. de blé** field of wheat; **c. de maïs** cornfield; **mener les bêtes aux champs** to take the herd to the fields; **en plein c.** ou **pleins champs** in the open (fields); **un c. de neige** a snowfield, a field of snow

2 (périmètre réservé) **c. d'aviation** airfield; **c. de courses** racecourse; **c. de foire** fairground; Mil & Sport **c. de tir** (terrain) rifle range; (portée d'une arme) field of fire

3 (domaine, étendue) field, range; **le c. de la psychanalyse/conscience** the field of psychoanalysis/consciousness; **élargir le c. de ses activités** to widen the range or scope of one's activities; **un vaste c. d'action** a broad field of activity; **avoir le c. libre** to have a free hand; **laisser le c. libre à qn** to leave the field open for sb; **il a du c. devant lui** he's got an open field in front of him; **prendre du c.** (pour observer) to step back; (pour réfléchir) to stand back; (pour sauter) to take a run-up; Mktg **c. concurrentiel** competitive scope; **c. d'expérimentation** field of experimentation

4 Cin & Phot **être dans le c.** to be in shot; **sortir du c.** to go out of shot; **hors c.** off camera

5 Opt (d'un télescope) field

6 Élec & Phys field; **c. électrique/magnétique** electric/magnetic field; **c. de pesanteur** gravitational field

7 Sport **c. (de jeu)** playing area

8 Hér field

9 Ordinat field; **c. d'action** sensitivity; **c. mémo** memo field; **c. numérique** numeric field; **c. de texte** text field; **c. variable** variable field

10 Ling & Math field; **c. lexical** lexical field; **c. sémantique** semantic field

11 Méd field; **c. opératoire/visuel** field of operation/view

12 Mil **aux champs** general salute; **c. de bataille** battlefield, battleground; Fig war zone; **la cuisine avait l'air d'un c. de bataille** the kitchen looked like a bomb had hit it; **c. clos** battleground; **c. d'honneur** field of honour; **il est mort** ou **tombé au c. d'honneur** he died for his country; **c. de manœuvre** parade ground; **c. de mines** minefield

13 Myth **les champs Élysées** ou **Élyséens** the Elysian Fields
▫ **champs** NMPL (campagne) country, countryside; **la vie aux champs** country life; **se promener dans les champs** to go for a walk in the country
▫ **sur le champ** ADV immediately, at once, right away

'Les Champs d'honneur' Rouaud 'Fields of Glory'

---

champ' [ʃɑ̃p] NM Fam bubbly, Br champers

Champagne [ʃɑ̃paɲ] NF **la C.** Champagne

champagne [ʃɑ̃paɲ] NM Champagne; **c. brut/rosé** extra dry/pink Champagne
ADJ INV **1** (couleur) champagne (avant n) **2** (alcool) voir **fine** NF

Champagne-Ardenne [ʃɑ̃paɲardɛn] NF **la C.** Champagne-Ardenne

champagnisation [ʃɑ̃paɲizasjɔ̃] NF sparkling wine production (according to the Champagne method)

champagniser [3] [ʃɑ̃paɲize] VT **c. le vin** to make sparkling wine (by using the Champagne method); **vins champagnisés** Champagne method wines

---

champart [ʃɑ̃par] NM **1** Hist champart **2** Agr cereal fodder

Champ-de-Mars [ʃɑ̃dmars] NM **le C.** = the esplanade where the Eiffel Tower stands

champenois, -e [ʃɑ̃pənwa, -az] ADJ of/from Champagne; **méthode champenoise** Champagne method
▫ **Champenois, -e** NM,F = inhabitant of or person from the Champagne region
▫ **champenoise** NF = bottle designed for Champagne

champêtre [ʃɑ̃pɛtr] ADJ Littéraire (vie, plaisirs, travaux) country (avant n), rustic; (bal) village (avant n); **déjeuner c.** picnic in the country; **travaux champêtres** working in the fields

champi, -isse [ʃɑ̃pi, -is] Arch ADJ **enfant c.** foundling (found in a field)
NM,F foundling (found in a field)

champignon [ʃɑ̃piɲɔ̃] NM **1** Bot mushroom, fungus; Culin mushroom; **c. de Paris** ou **de couche** button mushroom; **c. hallucinogène** magic mushroom; **c. noir** dried mushroom; **c. vénéneux** poisonous mushroom, toadstool; **grandir** ou **pousser comme un c.** (enfant) to grow fast, to shoot up; (ville, installations) to mushroom

2 Méd **un c., des champignons** a fungus, a fungal infection

3 (nuage) **c. (atomique)** mushroom cloud

4 Fam accelerator (pedal) ; **appuyer sur le c.** to put one's foot down, to step on it

champignonneur [ʃɑ̃piɲɔnœr] NM Suisse mushroom picker

champignonnière [ʃɑ̃piɲɔnjɛr] NF mushroom bed

champignonniste [ʃɑ̃piɲɔnist] NMF mushroom grower

champion, -onne [ʃɑ̃pjɔ̃, -ɔn] NM,F **1** Sport champion; **le c. du monde d'aviron** the world rowing champion; Fam **c'est un c. de la triche** he's a first-rate or prize cheat; **je suis vraiment le c. de la gaffe** I'm a great one for putting my foot in it

2 (défenseur) champion; **se faire le c. de qch** to champion sth
ADJ **1** Sport **l'équipe championne du monde** the world champions

2 Fam **pour les bêtises, il est c.!** he's a great one for getting up to stupid things!; **c'est c.!** it's terrific!

championnat [ʃɑ̃pjɔna] NM championship; **c. du monde de course de fond** world cross-country running championship

champis, -isse [ʃɑ̃pi, -is] = **champi**

champlever [19] [ʃɑ̃lve] VT (gravure) to cut away; (émail) to chase

champlure [ʃɑ̃plyr] NF Can (robinet) Br tap, Am faucet

Champs-Élysées [ʃɑ̃zelize] NMPL **les C.** (avenue) the Champs-Elysées

Champs-sur-Marne [ʃɑ̃syrmarn] NM **le château de C.** = château near Paris where foreign guests on state visits often stay

chamsin [kamsin] = **khamsin**

chançard, -e [ʃɑ̃sar, -ard] Fam ADJ lucky , Br jammy
NM,F lucky dog or devil, Br jammy devil

chance [ʃɑ̃s] NF **1** (aléa, hasard) luck; **bonne c.!** good luck!; **souhaiter bonne c. à qn** to wish sb good luck

2 (hasard favorable) (good) luck; **c'est une c. que je sois arrivée à ce moment-là!** it's a stroke of luck that I arrived then!; **quelle c. j'ai eue!** lucky me!; **avoir de la/ne pas avoir de c.** to be lucky/unlucky; **c'est bien ma c.!** just my luck!; **j'ai eu la c. de le rencontrer** I was lucky or fortunate enough to meet him; **votre génération aura peut-être plus de c. que la nôtre** your generation will perhaps have more luck than ours; **avec un peu de c., on pourra le faire** with a bit of luck, we'll be able to do it; **tenter sa c.** to try one's luck; très Fam **avoir une c. de cocu** ou **de pendu** to have the luck of the devil; Fam **c'est la faute à pas de c.** it's just bad luck ; **pas de c.!** bad or hard luck!

3 (sort favorable) luck, (good) fortune; **la c. lui sourit** fortune favours him/her; **la c. a voulu que sa lettre se soit égarée** luckily his/her letter got lost; **la c. est avec nous** our luck's in; **jour de c.** lucky day; **sa c. tourne** his/her luck is changing; **porter c.** to bring (good) luck; **son**

intransigeance ne lui a pas porté c. his/her intransigence has not brought him/her luck; **pousser sa c.** to push one's luck

4 *(possibilité)* chance; **tu n'as pas une c. sur dix de réussir** you haven't got a one-in-ten chance of succeeding; *Can* **participez et courez la c. de gagner une voiture** enter for your chance to win a car; **on pourrait lui donner encore une c.** we could give him/her another chance; **donner** *ou* **laisser sa c. à qn** to give sb his/her chance; **c'est ta dernière c.** it's your last chance; **sa dernière c. de salut** his/her last chance of salvation; **négociations de la dernière c.** last-ditch negotiations; **ce qu'il dit a toutes les chances d'être faux** the chances are that what he is saying is wrong; **quelles sont mes chances d'être nommé à ce poste?** what are my chances of being appointed to this post?; **il y a peu de chances qu'on te croie** there's little chance (that) you'll be believed; **son projet a de fortes** *ou* **grandes chances d'être adopté** his/her plan stands a good chance of being adopted; **il a compris qu'il fallait mettre toutes les chances de son côté** he realised he had to leave nothing to chance; **je cherche à évaluer mes chances de succès** I'm trying to evaluate my chances of success; **n'hésite pas, tu as tes chances** don't hesitate, you've got *or* you stand a chance; *Fam* **tu assisteras au débat? – il y a des chances** will you be present at the debate? – maybe

▫ **par chance** ADV luckily, fortunately; **par c., le courant était coupé** luckily the current was turned *or* switched off

chancel [ʃɑ̃sɛl] NM *Archit* chancel

chancelant, -e [ʃɑ̃slɑ̃, -ɑ̃t] ADJ **1** *(vacillant →démarche, pas)* unsteady, faltering; *(→ pile)* wobbly, tottering **2** *(faiblissant → santé)* failing, fragile; *(→ mémoire)* shaky, failing; *(→ courage, détermination)* wavering; *(→ autorité)* faltering, flagging

chanceler [24] [ʃɑ̃sle] VI **1** *(vaciller → personne)* to totter, to stagger; *(→ pile d'objets)* to wobble, to totter; **avancer/sortir en chancelant** to stagger *or* to totter forward/out; **l'uppercut le fit c.** the uppercut sent him reeling **2** *(faiblir → pouvoir, institution, autorité)* to falter, to flag; *(→ santé, mémoire)* to be failing; **les émeutes ont fait c. le pouvoir** the riots rocked the government

chancelier [ʃɑ̃səlje] NM **1** *(d'ambassade)* (embassy) chief secretary, *Br* chancellor; *(de consulat)* first secretary **2** *Pol (en Allemagne, en Autriche)* chancellor; *(en Grande-Bretagne)* **c. de l'Échiquier** Chancellor of the Exchequer **3** *Hist* chancellor

chancelière [ʃɑ̃səljɛr] NF **1** *(épouse)* chancellor's wife **2** *(chausson)* foot muff

chancelle *etc voir* **chanceler**

Chancellerie [ʃɑ̃sɛlri] NF *Pol* = all departments of the Ministry of Justice

chancellerie [ʃɑ̃sɛlri] NF **1** *Pol* chancery, chancellery **2** *Rel* apostolique Chancery

chanceux, -euse [ʃɑ̃sø, -øz] ADJ lucky, fortunate; *Littéraire* happy
NM,F lucky man, *f* woman

chanci [ʃɑ̃si] *Vieilli* ADJ mouldy
NM mould, mildew

chancir [32] [ʃɑ̃sir] *Vieilli* VI to go mouldy, to become mildewed
▸ **se chancir** VPR to go mouldy, to become mildewed

chancre [ʃɑ̃kr] NM **1** *Méd* chancre, canker; **c. induré** *ou* **syphilitique** hard *or* infective *or* true chancre; **c. mou** chancroid, soft chancre; *Fam* **bouffer comme un c.** to stuff oneself *or* one's face **2** *Bot* canker **3** *Littéraire (fléau)* plague

chancrelle [ʃɑ̃krɛl] NF *Méd* chancroid, soft chancre

chancreux, -euse [ʃɑ̃krø, -øz] ADJ *Méd* cankerous

chancroïde [ʃɑ̃krɔid] NM *Méd* chancroid, soft chancre

chandail [ʃɑ̃daj] NM **1** *(gén)* pullover, sweater **2** *Can* **c. (de hockey)** *Br* ice hockey shirt, *Am* hockey shirt

Chandeleur [ʃɑ̃dlœr] NF *Rel* **la C.** Candlemas

LA CHANDELEUR

This Catholic feast is celebrated on 2 February and commemorates the presentation of Jesus in the Temple after the completion of Mary's purification. Traditionally, crêpes with sweet fillings are eaten on this day, making it popular with children in particular.

chandelier [ʃɑ̃dəlje] NM *(à une branche)* candlestick; *(à plusieurs branches)* candelabrum, candelabra

chandelle [ʃɑ̃dɛl] NF **1** *(bougie)* candle; **s'éclairer à la c.** to use candlelight; **le jeu n'en vaut pas la c.** the game's not worth the candle; **brûler la c. par les deux bouts** to burn the candle at both ends; **devoir une fière c. à qn** to be deeply indebted to sb; **tenir la c.** *Br* to play gooseberry, *Am* to be a fifth wheel *or* the third wheel

2 *(feu d'artifice)* **c. romaine** Roman candle

3 *Fam (morve)* trickle of snot

4 *Aviat* chandelle; **monter en c.** to chandelle, to climb vertically

5 *(au tir, au rugby)* up-and-under; *Ftbl* high ball; **faire une c.** *Tennis* to lob the ball; *Ftbl* to loft the ball; **botter une c.** *(au rugby)* to play an up-and-under

6 *(position de gymnastique)* **faire la c.** to do a shoulder stand

7 *Constr* prop, stay

▫ **aux chandelles** ADJ *(dîner, repas)* candlelit
ADV *(dîner)* by candlelight

chanfrein [ʃɑ̃frɛ̃] NM **1** *Zool* nose, forehead **2** *(pièce d'armure)* chamfron, chamfrain **3** *Archit* chamfer, bevel edge

chanfreiner [4] [ʃɑ̃frene] VT *Archit* to chamfer, to bevel

change [ʃɑ̃ʒ] NM **1** *Fin (transaction)* exchange; *(taux)* exchange rate; **quel est le c.?** what's the rate of exchange *or* the exchange rate?; **faire le c.** to deal in foreign exchange; **c. du dollar** dollar exchange; **c. (ouvert de 9 h à 11 h)** *(sur panneau)* bureau de change (open from 9 a.m. till 11 a.m.); **donner le c. à qn** *(le duper)* to hoodwink sb, to put sb off the track; **gagner/perdre au c.** to be better/worse off because of the exchange rate; *Fig* to come out a winner/loser on the deal; **je perds au c. du point de vue salaire** I'm worse off as far as my pay goes

2 *(couche)* **c. complet** disposable *Br* nappy *or* *Am* diaper; **c. jetable** *Br* nappy *or* *Am* diaper liner

3 *Chasse* **donner le c.** to put hounds on the wrong scent; *Fig* **donner le c. à qn** to hoodwink sb, to put sb off the track

4 *Can Joual (petit)* **c.** *(monnaie)* change; **as-tu du c. pour un vingt?** have you got change for a twenty?; *Fig* **prendre tout son (petit) c.** to take all one's courage *or* strength

changeable [ʃɑ̃ʒabl] ADJ *(caractère, ordre)* changeable, alterable

changeant, -e [ʃɑ̃ʒɑ̃, -ɑ̃t] ADJ **1** *(moiré)* shot **2** *(inconstant → fortune)* fickle, unpredictable; *(→ humeur)* fickle, volatile, shifting; **être d'humeur changeante** to be moody **3** *Météo (temps)* unsettled, changeable; **un ciel c.** changing skies

changement [ʃɑ̃ʒmɑ̃] NM **1** *(substitution)* change (de of); **après le c. d'entraîneur/de régime** after the new trainer/regime came in; **c. d'adresse** change of address; **signaler son c. d'adresse** to give out one's new address; **en cas de c. de domicile** in case of a change of address; **c. de direction** *(dans une entreprise)* under new management; *Mktg* **c. de marque** brand switching; **c. de propriétaire** *(dans un magasin)* under new ownership

2 *(modification)* change; **un c. très net s'est produit** there's been a definite change; **apporter des changements à qch** to alter sth; **des changements sont intervenus** there have been changes; **comment va-t-il? – pas de** *ou* **aucun c.** how is he? – stable *or* no change; **c. de température/de temps** change in temperature/ (the) weather; **c. de cap** *ou* **de direction** change of course; **c. de programme** *TV* change in the (published) schedule; *Fig* change of plan *or* in the plans; **c. de programme, on ne va plus chez Paul** there's been a change of plan, we're not going to Paul's any more; *Écon* **c. structurel** structural change

3 *(évolution)* **le c.** change; **pour le c., votez Poblon!** for a new future, vote Poblon!; **je voudrais bien un peu de c.** I'd like things to change a little; **il va y avoir du c.** there are going to be some changes, things are going to change; **quand les enfants seront partis, ça fera du c.** things will be different after the children have gone

4 *Transp* change; **j'ai trois changements/je n'ai pas de c. pour aller chez elle** I have to change three times/I don't have to change to get to her place; **le voyage est sans c. jusqu'à Paris** the train goes straight through to Paris; **le c. est au bout du quai** change (lines) at the end of the platform

5 *Théât* **c. à vue** set change in full view of the audience; **c. de décor** scene change *or* shift; *Fig* **avoir besoin d'un c. de décor** to be in need of a change of scenery

6 *Sport* **c. de joueurs** change of players, changeover; *Tennis* **c. de balles!** new balls!

7 *Aut* **c. de vitesse** *(levier)* gear lever, *Am* gear shift; *(action → en voiture)* gear change *or* shift; *(→ à bicyclette)* gear change

8 *Ordinat* **c. de ligne** line feed; **c. de page** page break

9 *Cin & TV* **c. de plan** cutaway shot, cutaway

Le changement dans la continuité

In 1969, Georges Pompidou used this slogan in his electoral campaign for the presidency. "Change, with continuity" was supposed to be a pledge that he would follow through on various measures initiated by his predecessor. However, the expression is used ironically, the implication being that things will go on exactly as before.

CHANGER [17] [ʃɑ̃ʒe] VT *(aux avoir)* **1** *(modifier → apparence, règlement, caractère)* to change, to alter; *(→ testament)* to alter; **je désire faire c. l'ordre du jour de la réunion** I would like to propose some changes to the agenda of today's meeting; **cette expérience l'a beaucoup changée** the experience has changed her a lot; **on ne le changera pas** he'll never change; **cette coupe la change vraiment** that haircut makes her look really different; *Fam* **ça vous change un homme!** it changes a man!; **mais ça change tout!** ah, that changes everything!; **ça ne change rien** it makes no difference *or* *Br* odds; **qu'est-ce que ça change?** what difference does it make?; **je n'ai pas changé un mot à ton texte** I didn't alter a single *or* one word of your text; **il ne veut rien c. à ses habitudes** he won't alter his ways one jot *or* iota; **cela ne change rien au fait que...** that doesn't change *or* alter the fact that...; **tu n'y changeras rien** there's nothing you can do about it; **les règles du jeu** to alter the rules of the game; *Fig* to move the goalposts, to change the rules; **il est bien changé depuis son accident** he's changed a lot since his accident

2 *(remplacer → installation, personnel)* to change, to replace; *(→ roue, ampoule, draps)* to change; **ne change pas les assiettes** don't lay new plates; **j'ai fait c. les freins** I had new brakes put in; **on change les balles tous les six jeux** new balls are used every sixth game; **c. l'eau d'un vase** to change the water in a vase; **le directeur a été changé** there's been a change of manager; *Théât* **c. le décor** to change the set

3 *Fin (en devises, en petite monnaie)* to change; **c. de l'argent** to change money; **c. un billet pour avoir de la monnaie** to change a *Br* note *or* *Am* bill in order to get small change; **c. des euros en dollars** to change euros into dollars

4 *(troquer)* **c. qch pour qch** to change *or* exchange sth for sth; **elle changerait bien sa place contre** *ou* **pour la tienne** she'd happily swap places with you

5 *(transformer)* **c. qch en qch** to turn sth into sth; **elle a changé le prince en grenouille** she changed the prince into a frog; **je veux bien être changé en pierre si...** I'll eat my hat if...

6 *(transférer)* **c. qch de place** to move sth; **c. les meubles de place** to change *or* move the

furniture around; **c. une cassette de face** to turn a tape over; **c. qn de poste/service** to transfer sb to a new post/department; **c. son fusil d'épaule** to have a change of heart

7 *Fam (désaccoutumer)* **pars en vacances, ça te changera un peu** you should go away somewhere, it'll be a change for you; **mets-toi en jupe, ça te changerait** wear a skirt for a change; **enfin un bon spectacle, ça nous change des inepties habituelles!** a good show at last, that makes a change from the usual nonsense!; **viens, ça te changera les idées** come along, it'll take your mind off things; **ça change de l'ordinaire** it makes a change

8 *(bébé)* to change; **c. un malade** to put fresh clothes on a patient

USAGE ABSOLU *(échanger)* **j'aime mieux ton écharpe, on change?** I like your scarf better, shall we swap?; *Fam* **je ne voudrais pas c. avec elle** I'd hate to be in her shoes

VI *(aux avoir)* **1** *(se modifier → personne, temps, tarif etc)* to change; **sa personnalité a changé** he's/she's become different; **tu n'as pas changé** you've not changed, you're still the same; **les horaires de train vont c.** there's going to be a new train timetable; **le corps change à ton âge** at your age, bodily *or* physical changes occur; **c. en bien/mal** to change for the better/worse; *Fam* **plus ça change plus c'est la même chose** the more things change the more they stay the same

2 *Transp (de métro, de train)* to change

3 *(être remplacé)* to change; **le président change tous les trois ans** there's a change of chairperson every three years

❏ **changer de** VT IND **c. d'adresse** *(personne)* to move to a new address; *(commerce)* to move to new premises; **c. de nom/nationalité** to change one's name/nationality; **c. de rouge à lèvres** to switch lipsticks, to use a different lipstick; **c. de fournisseur** to use a different supplier; **le magasin a changé de propriétaire** the shop is under new management; **c. de partenaire** *(en dansant, dans un couple)* to change partners; **c. de chaussettes** to change one's socks; **c. de vêtements** to get changed; **c. de coiffure** to get a new hairstyle, to change one's hairstyle; **c. de style** to adopt a new style; **c. de chaîne** *(une fois)* to change channels; *(constamment)* to zap; **je dois c. d'avion à Athènes** I have to get a connecting flight in Athens; **c. de vie** to embark on a new life; **c. d'avis** *ou* **d'idée** to change one's mind; **elle m'a fait c. d'avis** she changed *or* made me change my mind; **c. d'avis comme de chemise** to keep changing one's mind; **c. de sujet** to change the subject; **tu vas c. de ton, dis!** don't take that tone with me!; **c. de direction** *(gén)* to change direction; *(vent)* to change; **c. de place** to move; **c. de place avec qn** to change seats with sb; **changez de côté** *(au tennis, au ping-pong)* change *or* switch sides; *(dans un lit)* turn over; **c. d'aspect** to begin to look different; **c. de forme** to change shape; **en chauffant, la sauce change de consistance** as it heats up, the sauce changes its consistency; **le courant a changé d'intensité** the intensity of the current has changed; **c. de peau** *(serpent)* to change *or* to shed *or* to slough its skin; *Aut* **c. de vitesse** to change gear; **c. d'air** to have a break; *Théât* **c. de décor** to change the set; *Fig* **j'ai besoin de c. de décor** I need a change of scenery; *aussi Fig* **c. de cap** to change *or* to alter course; *Fam* **c. de crémerie** to take one's custom *or* business elsewhere; *Fam* **change de disque!** give it a rest!, change the subject!

▸ **se changer** VPR **1** *(emploi réfléchi → s'habiller)* to get changed, to change (one's clothes)

2 se c. en to change *or* to turn into; **la grenouille se changea en prince** the frog turned into a prince

3 je broie du noir, il faut que je sorte pour me c. les idées I'm brooding, I must get out to take my mind off things

❏ **pour changer** ADV for a change

❏ **pour ne pas changer** ADV as usual; **et toi, tu ne fais rien, pour ne pas c.!** and you do nothing, as usual!

changeur [ʃɑ̃ʒœr] NM **1** *(personne)* money changer **2** *(dispositif)* **c. de billets** change machine;

c. de disques record changer; *Rad* **c. de fréquence** frequency changer; **c. de monnaie** change machine

chanlate, chanlatte [ʃɑ̃lat] NF *Constr* eavesboard, chantlate

channe [ʃan] NF *Suisse* pewter jug

chanoine [ʃanwan] NM *Rel* canon

chanoinesse [ʃanwanɛs] NF *Rel* canoness

chanson [ʃɑ̃sɔ̃] NF **1** *Mus* song; **mettre un texte en c.** to set a text to music; **la c. française** French songs; **c. d'amour/populaire** love/popular song; **c. à boire** drinking song; **c. enfantine** children's song, nursery rhyme; **c. de marins** *Br* shanty, *Am* chantey; *Fig* **c'est toujours la même c.** it's always the same old story; **ça va, on connaît la c.** enough of that, we've heard it all before; **ça, c'est une autre c.** that's another story

2 *Littérature* **c. courtoise** courtly love song; **c. de geste** chanson de geste, epic poem

3 *Vieilli* **chansons que tout cela!** nonsense!

✍

'La Chanson de Roland' 'The Song of Roland'

Culture

LA CHANSON POPULAIRE

French Canada has long had a strong tradition of folk singing and dancing. During the Great Depression, the singer Madame Bolduc gained renown with a new style of moralistic popular songs. Later, poets such as Félix Leclerc and Raymond Lévesque gave an impetus to an artistic form which was to become one of the significant vehicles of Quebec's cultural, social and political awakening, combining poetry and humour with political and social commentary. Gilles Vigneault, Pauline Julien and Robert Charlebois were among the leading artists of the 1960s and 1970s.

---

chansonnette [ʃɑ̃sɔnɛt] NF ditty, simple song; *Fam* **pousser la c.** to sing a song

chansonnier, -ère [ʃɑ̃sɔnje, -ɛr] NM,F = satirical cabaret singer or entertainer

NM **1** *Vieilli* songwriter **2** *(recueil)* songbook

chant [ʃɑ̃] NM **1** *(chanson)* song; *(mélodie)* melody; **c. funèbre** dirge; **c. grégorien** Gregorian chant; **c. de guerre** battle hymn; **c. de Noël** Christmas carol; **c. nuptial** wedding song; **écouter le c. des sirènes** to listen to the siren's *or* mermaid's song; **'le C. du départ'** = French revolutionary song written by Méhul

2 *(action de chanter)* singing

3 *(art de chanter)* singing; **apprendre le c.** to learn singing; **prendre des leçons de c.** to take singing lessons; **c. choral** choral singing

4 *(sons → d'un oiseau)* singing, chirping; *(→ d'une cigale)* chirping; *(→ d'un coq)* crowing; *(→ d'un violon)* sound; *Littéraire* **le c. des vagues/de la source** the song of the waves/of the spring; **son c. du cygne** his/her swan song

5 *(forme poétique)* ode, lyric; *(division de poème)* canto

6 *Constr* edge; **posés de c.** *ou* **sur c.** set edgewise *or* on edge

❏ **au chant du coq** ADV at cockcrow

🎵

'Le Chant de la Terre' *Mahler* 'The Song of the Earth'

---

chantable [ʃɑ̃tabl] ADJ singable

chantage [ʃɑ̃taʒ] NM blackmail; **faire du c. à qn** to blackmail sb; **il lui fait du c. au suicide** he's using suicide threats to blackmail him/her; **c. affectif** *ou* **au sentiment** emotional blackmail

chantant, -e [ʃɑ̃tɑ̃, -ɑ̃t] ADJ **1** *(langue)* musical; *(voix, accent)* lilting, singsong **2** *(aisément retenu → air)* tuneful; **un opéra très c.** an opera full of easily remembered tunes

chanté, -e [ʃɑ̃te] ADJ sung

chanteclair, chantecler [ʃɑ̃tklɛr] NM chanticleer

chantefable [ʃɑ̃tfabl] NF *Littérature* chantefable

chantepleure [ʃɑ̃tplœr] NF *Constr (de mur)* weephole; *(de gouttière)* spout

chanter [3] [ʃɑ̃te] VI **1** *(personne)* to sing; **c. juste/faux** to sing in tune/out of tune; **elle chantait accompagnée à la guitare** she was singing to the accompaniment of a guitar; **c. à tue-tête** to

sing at the top of one's voice; *Fam* **c'est comme si tu chantais** it's like talking to a brick wall, you're wasting your breath

2 *(oiseau)* to sing, to chirp; *(cigale)* to chirp; *(coq)* to crow; *Littéraire (rivière, mer)* to murmur; *(bouilloire)* to whistle; **écouter c. les oiseaux** to listen to the birds singing

3 *(être mélodieux → accent, voix)* to lilt; **avoir une voix qui chante** to have a singsong voice

4 *(locutions)* **faire c. qn** to blackmail sb; **si ça te chante** if you fancy it; **viens quand ça te chante** come whenever you feel like it *or* whenever the mood takes you; **ça te chante d'aller au concert?** how do you fancy (going to) a concert?

VT **1** *Mus (chanson, messe)* to sing; *Fig* **qu'est-ce que tu me chantes là?** what are you talking about?; **elle le chante sur tous les tons** she's always going on about it

2 *(célébrer)* to sing (of); **c. les exploits d'un héros** to sing (of) a hero's exploits; **c. victoire** to crow (over one's victory); **c. les louanges de qn** to sing sb's praises

3 *Can Fam (locution)* **c. la pomme à qn** *Br* to chat sb up, *Am* to hit on sb

---

🎬

'Chantons sous la pluie' *Donen & Kelly* 'Singin' in the Rain'

---

chanterelle [ʃɑ̃trɛl] NF **1** *Bot & Culin* chanterelle **2** *Mus* E-string **3** *Chasse* decoy (bird)

chanteur, -euse [ʃɑ̃tœr, -øz] NM,F **1** *(personne)* singer; **c. de charme** crooner; **c. folk** folk singer; **c. de rock** rock singer; **c. des rues** street singer **2** *Can Fam* **c. de pomme** flirt

ADJ **oiseau c.** songbird

chantier [ʃɑ̃tje] NM **1** *(entrepôt)* yard, depot

2 *(terrain)* *(working)* site; *Can (en sylviculture)* tree felling site; **sur le c.** on the site; **c. d'équarrissage** rendering plant; *Naut* **c. naval** shipyard

3 *Constr* **c. (de construction)** building site; **c. de démolition** demolition site *or* area; **c. interdit au public** *(sur panneau)* no admittance to the public

4 *(sur la route)* roadworks

5 *(projet d'envergure)* major project *or* piece of work; **ce projet de dictionnaire est un de nos grands chantiers pour les années à venir** this dictionary will be one of our major projects over the next few years

6 *Fam (désordre)* mess, shambles *(singulier)*; **quel c.!** what a mess!, what a shambles!; **ta chambre, c'est un vrai c.** your bedroom is a total shambles *or* looks like a bomb's hit it

❏ **en chantier** ADJ **la maison est en c.** I'm/we're *etc* still doing *or* Am fixing up the house ADV **il a plusieurs livres en c.** he has several books on the stocks *or* in the pipeline; **mettre un ouvrage en c.** to get a project started

chantignole, chantignolle [ʃɑ̃tiɲɔl] NF *Constr* purlin-cleat, bracket

chantilly [ʃɑ̃tiji] ADJ INV *voir* **crème**

NF INV sweetened chilled whipped cream, Chantilly cream

chantoir [ʃɑ̃twar] NM *Belg* sinkhole, *Br* swallow hole

chantonnement [ʃɑ̃tɔnmɑ̃] NM humming *(UNCOUNT)*, crooning *(UNCOUNT)*

chantonner [3] [ʃɑ̃tɔne] VT to hum, to croon, to sing softly

VI to hum, to croon, to sing softly

chantoung [ʃɑ̃tuŋ] NM = shantung

chantournement [ʃɑ̃turnəmɑ̃] NM *Tech* jigsawing

chantourner [3] [ʃɑ̃turne] VT *Tech* to jigsaw

chantre [ʃɑ̃tr] NM **1** *Rel* cantor; **grand c.** precentor

2 *Littéraire (poète)* poet, bard; **les chantres des bois** the woodland chorus; **le c. de** the eulogist of *or* apologist for; **il s'était fait le c. de la république** he had championed the cause of the republic

chanvre [ʃɑ̃vr] NM *Bot & Tex* hemp; **c. de Manille** abaca, Manila hemp; *Bot* **c. indien** Indian hemp

chanvrier, -ère [ʃɑ̃vrije, -ɛr] ADJ hemp *(avant n)*

NM,F **1** *(cultivateur)* hemp grower **2** *(ouvrier)* hemp dresser

chaos [kao] NM **1** *(confusion)* chaos; **un c. de ruines** a tangled heap of ruins **2** *Rel* **le C.** Chaos

chaotique [kaɔtik] ADJ chaotic

chaouch [ʃauʃ] NM (*en Afrique du Nord*) chaouch

chaource [ʃaurs] NM = type of cheese made from cow's milk

chap. (*abrév écrite* **chapitre**) ch

chapardage [ʃapardaʒ] NM *Fam* petty theft; **des chapardages répétés** pilfering (*UNCOUNT*)

chaparder [3] [ʃaparde] VT *Fam* to pinch, to swipe; **il s'est fait c. sa montre** he had his watch pinched *or Br* nicked; **on chapardait des fruits à l'étalage** we used to pinch fruit from shops

chapardeur, -euse [ʃapardœr, -øz] *Fam* ADJ sticky-fingered

  NM,F (*casual*) thief ▪; **un c. invétéré** a habitual pilferer

chape [ʃap] NF 1 *Rel* (*de prêtre*) cope 2 *Constr* screed; (*d'un pont, d'une chaussée*) coping; **comme une c. de plomb** like a lead weight 3 (*d'un pneu*) tread 4 (*d'une poulie*) shell; (*d'une bielle*) case; (*d'un cardan*) fork

chapé [ʃape] NM *Hér* chapé

chapeau, -x [ʃapo] NM 1 (*couvre-chef*) hat; **c. claque** opera hat; **c. cloche** cloche (hat); **c. de cow-boy** cowboy hat; **c. de feutre** felt hat; **c. de gendarme** paper hat; **c. haut-de-forme** top hat; **c. melon** *Br* bowler (hat), *Am* derby; **c. mou** *Br* trilby, *Am* fedora; **c. de paille** straw hat; **c. de pluie** rain hat; **c. de soleil** sunhat; **mettre** *ou* **porter la main au c.** to raise one's hat; *Fig* **faire porter le c. à qn** *Br* to force sb to carry the can, *Am* to leave sb holding the bag; *Fig* **si je me trompe je veux bien manger mon c.!** if I'm wrong I'll eat my hat!; *Fig* **tirer son c. à qn, donner un coup de c. à qn** to take one's hat off to sb; *Fig* **saluer qn c. bas** to doff one's hat to sb; **c. bas!** hats off!; **je te dis c.!** I take my hat off to you!, well done!, bravo!; *Fam* **travailler du c.** to have a screw loose, to be off one's rocker, *Br* to be not all there; *Can Fam* **parler à travers son c.** to talk through one's hat; *Can Fam* **faire le tour du c.** to score a hat-trick (*in an ice hockey game*)

  2 *Bot* (*d'un champignon*) cap

  3 *Culin* (*d'un vol-au-vent, d'une bouchée à la reine*) lid, top

  4 (*de texte, d'article*) introductory paragraph; *Rad & TV* introduction

  5 (*partie supérieure → d'un tuyau de cheminée*) cowl; **c. de lampe** lampshade; **c. de roue** hubcap; **prendre un virage sur les chapeaux de roue** to take a turning on two wheels; **démarrer sur les chapeaux de roue** to shoot off; (*film, réception, relation*) to get off to a great start

  ❏ **chapeau chinois** NM 1 *Mus* crescent

  2 *Zool* (*mollusque*) limpet

'Chapeau melon et bottes de cuir' 'The Avengers'

chapeauté, -e [ʃapote] ADJ **femme bien gantée et bien chapeautée** a woman with nice gloves and a nice hat on

chapeauter [3] [ʃapote] VT 1 *Fam* (*superviser*) to oversee, to supervise; **il a décidé de faire c. les deux services par un secrétaire général** he decided to put both departments under the control of a general secretary 2 (*article, texte*) to write an introductory piece for

chapelain [ʃaplɛ̃] NM chaplain

chapelet [ʃaplɛ] NM 1 *Rel* (*collier*) rosary, beads; (*prières*) rosary; **réciter** *ou* **dire son c.** to say the rosary, *Am* to tell one's beads; *Fam* **débiter** *ou* **dévider son c.** to tell all 2 (*d'îles, de saucisses*) string; (*d'insultes*) string, stream; **un c. de bombes** a stick of bombs

chapelier, -ère [ʃapəlje, -ɛr] ADJ (*commerce, industrie*) hat (*avant n*)

  NM,F hatter

chapelle [ʃapɛl] NF 1 *Rel* (*bâtiment*) chapel; (*chanteurs et musiciens*) choir and orchestra; (*objets liturgiques*) ornaments and plate; **c. ardente** chapel of rest; **transformer une salle en c. ardente** to turn a room into a temporary mortuary 2 *Fig* (*cercle*) clique, coterie 3 *Belg* (*café*) café

chapellenie [ʃapɛlni] NF chaplaincy

chapellerie [ʃapɛlri] NF 1 (*activité*) hat trade 2 (*industrie*) hat trade *or* hat-making industry 3 (*magasin*) hatshop

chapelure [ʃaplyr] NF breadcrumbs; **passer qch dans la c.** to coat sth with breadcrumbs

chaperon [ʃaprɔ̃] NM 1 (*surveillant*) chaperon, chaperone; **servir de c. à qn** to chaperon *or* to chaperone sb 2 *Constr* (*d'un mur*) coping 3 (*de faucon*) hood

'Le Petit chaperon rouge' *Perrault* 'Little Red Riding Hood'

chaperonner [3] [ʃaprɔne] VT 1 (*jeune fille, groupe*) to chaperon, to chaperone 2 *Constr* to cope 3 (*faucon*) to hood

chapiteau, -x [ʃapito] NM 1 *Archit* capital, chapiter; (*d'une armoire*) cornice 2 (*cirque*) big top; **nous vous accueillons ce soir sous le plus grand c. du monde** we welcome you tonight under the world's biggest top; **sous c.** in a marquee 3 (*d'un alambic*) head

chapitral, -e, -aux, -ales [ʃapitral, -o] ADJ (*assemblée, délibération*) capitular

chapitre [ʃapitr] NM 1 (*d'un livre*) chapter

  2 *Fin & Compta* (*d'un budget*) item; **inscrire une somme au c. des recettes/dépenses** to enter a sum under (the heading of) revenue/expenditure

  3 (*question*) matter, subject; **le c. est clos** that's the end of the matter, subject closed; **et maintenant, au c. des faits divers…** and now for the news in brief…; **il est exigeant sur le c. des vins** he's hard to please in the matter of *or* as regards wines; **tu as raison, au moins sur un c.** you're right, at least on one score

  4 *Rel* (*assemblée*) chapter; (*lieu*) chapterhouse

chapitrer [3] [ʃapitre] VT (*sermonner*) to lecture; (*tancer*) to admonish; **je l'ai dûment chapitré sur ses responsabilités** I gave him the appropriate lecture about his responsibilities; **se faire c. par qn** to be *or* to get told off by sb

chapka [ʃapka] NF shapka (*round brimless fur hat worn in Russia*)

chaplinesque [ʃaplinɛsk] ADJ (*comique, personnage*) Chaplinesque

chapon [ʃapɔ̃] NM capon

chaponnage [ʃaponaʒ] NM caponizing, caponization

chaponner [3] [ʃapone] VT to caponize

chapska [ʃapska] NM *Hist & Mil* lancer cap

chaptalisation [ʃaptalizasjɔ̃] NF chaptalization, chaptalizing

chaptaliser [3] [ʃaptalize] VT to chaptalize

chaque [ʃak] ADJ **INDÉFINI** 1 (*dans un groupe, dans une série*) each, every; **c. enfant a reçu un livre** each *or* every child received a book; **c. femme doit pouvoir travailler et élever ses enfants** every woman *or* all women should be able to work as well as bring up their children; **à c. pas** at every *or* each step; **c. hiver** every *or* each winter; **la distance est de trois mètres entre c. poteau** there is a distance of three metres between each pole; **je pense à elle à c. instant** I think about her all the time; **c. chose en son temps!** all in good time!; *Prov* **à c. jour suffit sa peine** sufficient unto the day (is the evil thereof)

  2 (*chacun*) each; **on a gagné 200 euros c. au Loto** we won 200 euros each on the lottery; **les disques sont vendus 13 euros c.** the records are sold at 13 euros each *or* a piece

char [ʃar] NM 1 *Mil* tank; **c. léger/moyen/lourd** light/medium/heavy tank; **c. d'assaut** *ou* **de combat** tank; **fait comme un c. d'assaut** built like a tank

  2 (*de carnaval*) float

  3 *Sport* **c. à voile** sand yacht; **faire du c. à voile** to go sand yachting

  4 (*voiture*) **c. à bancs** = open wagon with seats for passengers; **c. à bœufs** ox cart; **c. funèbre** hearse

  5 *Antiq* chariot; *Littéraire* **le c. de l'État** the ship of State; *Fam* **arrête ton c.(, Ben Hur)!** come off it!, yeah right!

  6 *Can Fam* (*voiture*) car ▪

  7 *très Fam* = **charre**

  8 *Suisse* (*jeu*) = type of board game for two players, each player having nine pieces which can be placed on concentric circles

  ❏ **chars** NMPL *Can* **les (gros) chars** *Br* the railway, *Am* the railroad; **les petits chars** the trams; *Fam* **ça vaut pas les chars** it's not up to much

charabia [ʃarabja] NM *Fam* gobbledegook, gibberish

characidé [ʃaraside] *Ich* NM characid

  ❏ **characidés** NMPL Characidae

characin [ʃarasɛ̃] NM *Ich* characin

charade [ʃarad] NF 1 (*devinette*) riddle 2 (*mime*) (game of) charades

charadriidé [karadriide] *Orn* NM = member of the Charadriidae family

  ❏ **charadriidés** NMPL Charadriidae

charadriiforme [karadriiform] *Orn* NM = member of the order Charadriiforme

  ❏ **charadriiformes** NMPL Charadriiformes

charançon [ʃarɑ̃sɔ̃] NM *Entom* weevil, snout beetle; **c. du blé/de la vigne** grain/vine weevil

charançonné, -e [ʃarɑ̃sone] ADJ weevilled, weevily

charango [tʃarãgo] NM *Mus* charango

charbon [ʃarbɔ̃] NM 1 *Mines* coal; **le rôti n'est plus qu'un morceau de c.** the roast is burnt to a cinder; **se passer le visage au c.** to black one's face; **chauffage au c.** coal-fired heating; **c. aggloméré** briquette; **c. de bois** charcoal; **grillades au c. de bois** barbecued meat; *Fam* **aller au c.** (*au travail*) to go to work; (*s'y mettre*) to do one's bit; **être** *ou* **marcher sur des charbons ardents** to be on tenterhooks, to be like a cat on *Br* hot bricks *or Am* a hot tin roof

  2 *Beaux-Arts* (*crayon*) charcoal (pencil); (**dessin au**) **c.** charcoal drawing

  3 (*maladie → chez l'animal, chez l'homme*) anthrax; (*→ des céréales*) smut, black rust

  4 *Pharm* charcoal; **c. actif** *ou* **activé** active *or* activated carbon, activated charcoal

  5 *Élec* carbon

charbonnage [ʃarbonaʒ] NM coalmining

  ❏ **charbonnages** NMPL coalmines, *Br* collieries; **les Charbonnages de France** the French Coal Board

charbonner [3] [ʃarbone] VT 1 *Beaux-Arts* (*croquis, dessin*) to (draw with) charcoal 2 (*noircir → visage*) to charcoal

  VI 1 (*mèche*) to char 2 *Naut* to bunker, to coal

charbonnerie [ʃarbonri] NF 1 *Anciennement* coal depot 2 *Hist* **la C.** the Carbonari

charbonneux, -euse [ʃarbonø, -øz] ADJ 1 (*noir*) coal-black, coal-like 2 (*souillé*) sooty black; **un dépôt c.** a sooty deposit, a carbon deposit; *Péj* **avoir les yeux c.** to wear heavy black eye makeup 3 (*brûlé*) charred 4 *Méd* anthracoid; **mouche charbonneuse** anthrax-carrying fly 5 *Bot* smutty

charbonnier, -ère [ʃarbonje, -ɛr] ADJ (*commerce, industrie*) coal (*avant n*); **navire c.** coaler, collier

  NM,F (*vendeur*) coaler, coalman; (*fabricant de charbon de bois*) charcoal-burner; *Prov* **c. est maître dans sa maison** *ou* **chez soi** *Br* an Englishman's *or Am* a man's home is his castle

  NM *Naut* coaler, collier

  ❏ **charbonnière** NF 1 (*lieu*) charcoal kiln *or* stack 2 *Belg* (*seau à charbon*) coal bucket 3 *Orn* great tit

charcutage [ʃarkytaʒ] NM *Fam Péj* (*opération chirurgicale*) butchering; (*travail mal fait*) hacking about; **c. électoral** gerrymandering; **faire du c. électoral** to gerrymander

charcuter [3] [ʃarkyte] *Fam* VT *Péj* 1 (*opérer*) to butcher, to hack about; **se faire c.** to be hacked to pieces 2 (*couper → volaille, texte*) to hack to pieces *or* about

  ▸ **se charcuter** VPR **je me suis charcutée en essayant de m'enlever l'écharde** I made a real mess of my finger trying to get the splinter out; **je me suis charcuté un doigt/le pied** I mangled one of my fingers/my foot

charcuterie [ʃarkytri] NF 1 (*magasin*) ≃ delicatessen 2 (*produits*) cooked meats; **assiette de c.** plate of assorted cooked meats 3 (*fabrication*) cooked meats trade

Culture

CHARCUTERIE

A "charcuterie" sells mainly food prepared with pork: sausages, pâtés, ham etc, collectively also known as "charcuterie". Ready-prepared dishes to take away are usually also sold.

charcutier, -ère [ʃarkytje, -ɛr] NM,F 1 (*commerçant*) pork butcher; **chez votre c. habituel** ≃ at

your local delicatessen **2** *Fam Péj (chirurgien)* butcher

chardon [ʃardɔ̃] **NM 1** *Bot* thistle; **c. bénit** knapweed **2** *(sur un mur)* spike

chardonay, chardonnais [ʃardɔnɛ] **NM** Chardonay *or* Chardonnay (wine)

chardonneret [ʃardɔnrɛ] **NM** *Orn* goldfinch

charentais, -e [ʃarɑ̃tɛ, -ɛz] **ADJ** of/from the Charente
⎯ **Charentais, -e NM,F** = inhabitant of or person from the Charente
⎯ **charentaises NFPL** *(pantoufles)* carpet slippers

Charente [ʃarɑ̃t] **NF la C.** the Charente (region)

Charente-Maritime [ʃarɑ̃tmaritim] **NF la C.** Charente-Maritime

Charenton [ʃarɑ̃tɔ̃] **NM** = suburb of Paris, with a famous psychiatric hospital

CHARGE [ʃarʒ]

> **NF** load **1, 2** ▪ burden **1, 3** ▪ responsibility **4** ▪ office **5** ▪ charge **6, 7, 14** ▪ cost **11**
> **NFPL** costs

NF 1 *(cargaison → d'un animal)* burden; *(→ d'un camion)* load; *(→ d'un navire)* cargo, freight; *Mil* payload; **plier sous une lourde c.** to be weighed down by a heavy burden; **camion en pleine c.** fully laden lorry; *Mil* **c. marchande** commercial payload; **c. utile** capacity load, payload; **c. à vide** empty weight

2 *(poussée)* load; *Aviat* **facteur de c.** load factor; **c. admissible** safe load; **c. de rupture** breaking *or* shearing stress; **c. de sécurité** safe load

3 *(gêne)* burden, *Fig* weight; **je ne veux pas devenir une c. pour eux** I don't want to become a burden to them

4 *(responsabilité)* responsibility; **à qui revient la c. de le faire?** who has *or* carries the responsibility for doing it?; **elle a (la) c. de réorganiser le service** she's got the job of reorganizing the department; **toutes les réparations sont à sa c.** he/she will pay for the repair work, all the repair work will be done at his/her cost; **à c. pour toi d'apporter le vin** you'll be responsible for bringing *or* it'll be up to you to bring the wine; **avoir c. d'âmes** *(prêtre)* to have the cure of souls; *(parent)* to have children in one's care; **enfants confiés à ma c.** children entrusted to me *or* in my charge *or* in my care; **nous prenons tous les frais médicaux en c.** we pay for *or* take care of all medical expenses; **elle a pris son neveu en c.** she took on responsibility for her nephew; **prendre un client en c.** *(taxi)* to pick up a fare; **être pris en c. à cent pour cent par la Sécurité sociale** to have one's medical expenses fully paid for by Social Security; **à ton âge, tu dois te prendre en c.** at your age, you should take yourself in hand *or* take responsibility for yourself; **enfants à c.** dependent children; **avoir qn à (sa) c.** *(gén)* to be responsible for supporting sb; *Admin* to have sb as a dependant; **ses enfants sont encore à sa c.** his/her children are still his/her dependants; **prendre les frais/un orphelin à sa c.** to take on the expenditure/an orphan

5 *Admin (fonction)* office; **c. élective** elective office; **c. de greffier** registrarship; **c. de notaire** notary's office

6 *(d'une mine, d'explosifs)* charge; **il a reçu toute la c. dans la poitrine** his chest took the full impact of the blast; **c. creuse** hollow charge; **c. d'explosifs** explosive charge; **c. nucléaire** nuclear charge

7 *Élec* **mettre une batterie en c.** to charge a battery; **c. électrique** electric charge; **c. négative/positive** minus/positive charge; **c. spatiale** space charge

8 *Fin (d'une dette) Br* servicing, *Am* service

9 *(portée)* **c. affective** *ou* **émotionnelle** emotive power; **avoir une forte c. symbolique** to have strong symbolic power *or* resonance; **une c. psychologique impossible à supporter** an unbearable mental strain

10 *Jur (présomption)* serious suspicion; **de très lourdes charges pèsent sur lui** very serious suspicions are hanging over him; **c. de la preuve** burden of proof

11 *Fin (coût)* cost; **c. fictive** fictitious cost; **c. opérationnelle** operating cost; **c. à payer** sum payable

12 *(satire)* caricature

13 *Méd* **c. virale** viral load

14 *Mil (assaut)* charge; **donner la c.** to charge; **sonner la c.** to sound the charge; **reculer devant une c. de police** to retreat when the police charge; **au pas de c.** at the double; **retourner** *ou* **revenir à la c.** to mount a fresh attack; *Fig* to go back onto the offensive; **je t'ai déjà dit non, tu ne vas pas revenir à la c.!** I've already said no, don't keep on at me!

15 *Beaux-Arts & Littérature (d'un personnage, d'un portrait)* caricature, burlesque; *Théât (d'un rôle)* overacting; *(genre)* skit; **jouer un rôle en c.** to overact a part
⎯ **charges NFPL** *(frais → gén)* costs, expenses; *(→ de locataire)* service *or* maintenance charges; *Compta* **charges constatées d'avance** prepaid expenses, prepayments; *Fin* **charges courantes** current expenses; **charges déductibles** deductible expenses; **charges de famille** dependants; **charges financières** financial expenses; **charges fiscales** tax; **charges fixes** fixed costs; **charges (locatives)** maintenance charges; **charges du mariage** marital expenses; **charges patronales** employer's contributions; *Compta* **charges payées d'avance** prepaid expenses, prepayments; *Compta* **charges à payer** accrued expenses, accruals; **charges salariales** wage costs; **charges sociales** *Br* ≃ national insurance contributions *(paid by the employer)*, *Am* ≃ social security charges *(paid by the employer)*; *Compta* **charges terminales** terminal charges
⎯ **à charge de PRÉP j'accepte, à c. de revanche** I accept, provided you'll let me do the same for you; **à c. de preuve** pending production of proof

'**La Charge héroïque**' Ford 'She Wore a Yellow Ribbon'

chargé, -e [ʃarʒe] **ADJ 1** *(occupé → journée)* busy, full; *(→ programme)* full

2 *(tissu, motif)* overelaborate; *(style)* (over)ornate

3 *Fig* **avoir la conscience chargée** to have a guilty conscience; **un gangster au passé c.** a gangster with a past; **il a un casier judiciaire c.** he has a long (criminal) record

4 *(plein)* **une pièce chargée de décorations de mauvais goût** a room cluttered with tasteless decorations; **un mur c. de tableaux** a wall covered in paintings; **l'air est c. du parfum des fleurs** the air is heavy with the scent of flowers; **un regard c. de reconnaissance** a look full of gratitude; *Littéraire* **c. d'ans** *ou* **d'années** stricken in years; **mourir c. d'ans** to die at a ripe old age, to die full of years

5 *Méd* **estomac c.** overloaded stomach; **avoir la langue chargée** to have a furred tongue

6 *Phys (particule)* charged; **particule chargée négativement/positivement** negatively/positively-charged particle

7 *Fam (ivre)* loaded, wrecked, wasted

NM *(responsable)* **c. d'affaires** chargé d'affaires; **c. de budget** account executive; *Com* **c. de clientèle** account manager; **c. de comptes** account manager; *Univ* **c. de cours** ≃ part-time lecturer; *Mktg* **c. d'étude de marché** market researcher; **c. de famille** person supporting a family; **c. de mission** *Admin* project leader *or* manager; *Pol* ≃ (official) representative; *Com & Mktg* **c. de relations clients** customer relations manager; *Univ* **c. de TD** tutor

chargement [ʃarʒəmɑ̃] **NM 1** *(marchandises → d'un camion)* consignment, shipment; *(→ d'un navire)* cargo, freight

2 *(fait de charger → un navire, un camion)* loading; *(→ une chaudière)* stoking; *(→ une arme)* loading; **à c. automatique** self-loading; **machine à laver à c. frontal** front-loading washing machine

3 *Élec* charging (up)

4 *(de lettre, de colis)* registration; *(lettre)* registered letter; *(colis)* registered parcel

CHARGER [17] [ʃarʒe]

> **VT** to load **1, 4** ▪ to pick up **2** ▪ to overload **3** ▪ to charge **4, 9** ▪ to put in charge of **5** ▪ to overdo **7**
> **VPR** to load **2** ▪ to take care of **3**

VT 1 *(véhicule, marchandises)* to load (**dans/sur** into/onto); **tes livres chargent un peu trop l'étagère** the shelf is overloaded with your books; **être chargé** to be loaded; **il est entré, les bras chargés de cadeaux** he came in loaded down with presents; **les arbres sont chargés de fruits** the trees are loaded down *or* groaning with fruit; **table chargée de mets** table laden with food; **navire chargé de blé** ship laden with wheat; **la voiture est trop chargée** the car is overloaded; *Méd* **c. son estomac** to overload one's stomach; **être chargé comme un bourricot** *ou* **un mulet** *ou* **un baudet** to be weighed down

2 *(prendre en charge → sujet: taxi)* to pick up

3 *(alourdir, encombrer)* to overload; **les notes dont il charge les marges de ses cahiers** the notes that fill the margins of his notepads; **ces meubles chargent trop la pièce** this furniture makes the room look (too) cluttered; **c. qn de qch** to overload sb with sth; **c. sa mémoire de détails** to clutter up one's mind with details

4 *(arme, caméra, appareil photo)* to load (up); *Élec* to charge (up); *Ordinat* to load (up)

5 *(d'une responsabilité)* **c. qn de qch** to put sb in charge of sth; **on l'a chargée d'un cours à l'université** she was assigned to teach *or* given a class at the university; **je vous charge d'un travail important** I'm giving you *or* entrusting you with an important job; **il est chargé de l'entretien** he's in charge of *or* responsible for maintenance; **être chargé de famille** to have family responsibilities; **c. qn de faire qch** to give sb the responsibility for doing sth; **il m'a chargé de vous transmettre un message** he asked me to give you a message; **j'étais chargé de faire tout le courrier du service** I was in charge of *or* responsible for the department's mail

6 *(amplifier)* to inflate, to put up

7 *(exagérer → rôle)* to camp up, to overdo; **dans son article, il charge un peu le portrait du Premier ministre** in his article, he caricaturizes the prime minister; **ne charge pas ainsi ton rôle, joue plus en finesse** don't overact, be more subtle; **elle n'est pas si idiote, tu charges un peu la description!** she's not that stupid, you're overdoing it a bit!

8 *(incriminer)* **c. qn** to make sb appear guiltier; **certains témoins ont essayé de le c. au maximum** some witnesses tried to strengthen the prosecution's case against him

9 *(attaquer)* to charge (at); **chargez!** charge!; **la police n'a pas chargé (les manifestants)** the police didn't charge (at the demonstrators)

10 c. une lettre = to send valuables by post; *(l'affranchir)* to register a letter

11 *Banque (compte)* to overcharge (on)

VI *Can Joual* **c. cher** to charge a lot of money

▸**se charger VPR 1** *(s'alourdir)* to weigh oneself down

cha-cha

2 *Ordinat* to load; **se c. automatiquement** to load automatically, to autoload

3 se c. de *(responsabilité)* to take on, to take care of; *(élève, invité)* to take care of, to look after; **je me charge de tout** I'll take care of everything; **quant à lui, je m'en charge personnellement** I'll personally take good care of him; **je me charge de le prévenir** I'll make sure to let him know; **je me charge de lui remettre votre lettre** I'll see to it personally that he/she gets your letter; **qui va se c. du travail?** who's going to take the job on?

chargeur [ʃaʀʒœʀ] NM **1** *Phot* cartridge, magazine **2** *(d'arme)* cartridge clip **3** *Élec* charger **4** *(ouvrier)* loader **5** *Naut* shipper **6** *Ordinat* feeder

chargeuse [ʃaʀʒøz] NF **1** *(distributrice)* distributor **2** *Mines* loading machine **3** *Métal* charging *or* loading machine

chargeuse-pelleteuse [ʃaʀʒøzpɛltøz] *(pl* **chargeuses-pelleteuses)** NF backhoe loader

charia [ʃaʀja] NF *Rel* sharia

charibotée [ʃaʀibɔte] NF *Fam* **une c. de** heaps *or* piles of; **une c. d'injures** a stream of abuse

chariboter [3] [ʃaʀibɔte] VI *Fam* **1** *(travailler)* to work unmethodically, to muddle through one's work **2** *(mettre du désordre)* to create disorder, to make a mess **3** *(exagérer)* to exaggerate, to spread it on thick

chariot [ʃaʀjo] NM **1** *(véhicule → gén)* wagon, *Br* waggon; *(→ dans un supermarché, à bagages) Br* trolley, *Am* cart; *(→ d'hôpital) Br* (hospital) trolley, *Am* gurney; **le c. des desserts/à liqueurs** the dessert/drinks trolley; **c. élévateur** fork-lift truck; **c. élévateur à fourche** fork-lift truck

2 *Astron* **le Grand C.** *Br* the Great Bear, *Am* the Big Dipper; **le Petit C.** *Br* the Little Bear *or Am* Dipper

3 *(de machine à écrire)* carriage

4 *Cin & TV* dolly; **c. omnidirectionnel** crab *or* crabbing dolly

5 *Aviat* **c. d'atterrissage** landing gear, undercarriage

chariotage [ʃaʀjɔtaʒ] NM *Tech & Ind* turning; **c. longitudinal** sliding; **c. transversal** cross-traverse; **barre de c.** feed-rod; **rectification par c.** traverse grinding

chariot-crabe [ʃaʀjokʀab] *(pl* **chariots-crabes)** NM *Cin & TV* crab *or* crabbing dolly

charioter [3] [ʃaʀjɔte] VT *Tech & Ind* to turn on a lathe

charismatique [kaʀismatik] ADJ **1** *Rel* charismatic **2** *(séduisant)* charismatic; **être c.** to have charisma

charisme [kaʀism] NM **1** *Rel* charisma, charism **2** *(pouvoir de séduction)* charisma

charitable [ʃaʀitabl] ADJ **1** *(généreux)* charitable; **se montrer c. envers qn** to be charitable *or* to exercise charity towards sb; *Ironique* **avis** *ou* **conseil c.** so-called friendly piece of advice **2** *(association, mouvement)* charitable, charity *(avant n)*

charitablement [ʃaʀitabləmɑ̃] ADV charitably, generously; *Hum* **je lui ai c. conseillé d'abandonner le chant** I advised him/her in the nicest possible way to give up singing

charité [ʃaʀite] NF **1** *(altruisme)* charity, love; **aurais-tu la c. de leur rendre visite?** would you be kind enough to go and visit them?; **faites-moi** *ou* **ayez la c. d'écouter mon histoire** please be kind enough to listen to my story; *Prov* **bien ordonnée commence par soi-même** charity begins at home

2 *(aumône)* charity; **demander la c.** to beg (for charity); **faire la c. (à)** to give a handout (to), *Vieilli* to give alms (to); *Fig* **je n'ai nul besoin qu'on me fasse la c.** I don't need anybody's help, I'll manage on my own; **la c., s'il vous plaît!** can you spare some change, please?
▫ **de charité** ADJ **fête de c.** benefit event; **œuvres de c.** charities; **vente de c.** charity sale

charivari [ʃaʀivaʀi] NM hurly-burly, hullabaloo

charlatan [ʃaʀlatɑ̃] NM *Péj* **1** *(médecin)* charlatan, quack; **remède de c.** quack remedy; **tous ces psys sont des charlatans** all these shrinks are quacks **2** *(vendeur)* conman, swindler **3** *(réparateur)* cowboy

charlatanerie [ʃaʀlatanʀi] NF *Péj* charlatanism

charlatanesque [ʃaʀlatanɛsk] ADJ *Péj* **1** *(médecine)* quackish **2** *(pratiques)* phoney, bogus

charlatanisme [ʃaʀlatanism] NM *Péj* charlatanism

Charlemagne [ʃaʀləmaɲ] NPR Charlemagne

charlemagne [ʃaʀləmaɲ] NM *Cartes* **faire c.** = to leave the card table when one is ahead

Charleroi [ʃaʀlərwa] NM Charleroi

Charles [ʃaʀl] NPR **C. Martel** Charles Martel; **C. Quint** Charles V, Charles the Fifth; **C. le Téméraire** Charles the Bold

charleston [ʃaʀlɛstɔn] NM charleston

Charlie Hebdo [ʃaʀliɛbdɔ] NM *Presse* = French satirical magazine

Charlot [ʃaʀlo] NPR Charlie Chaplin

charlot [ʃaʀlo] NM *Fam* clown, joker; **jouer les charlots** to fool around

charlotte [ʃaʀlɔt] NF *Culin* charlotte; **c. aux pommes** apple charlotte

Charlus [ʃaʀly] NPR **le baron de C.** = one of the characters in the Belle Époque society of Proust's novel 'À la recherche du temps perdu', described by Proust as "l'homme-femme"

charmant, -e [ʃaʀmɑ̃, -ɑ̃t] ADJ charming, engaging, delightful; **nous étions en charmante compagnie** we were in delightful company; **vous avez eu là une charmante attention** how very thoughtful of you; *Ironique* **charmante soirée!** what a great evening!; *Ironique* **c'est c.!** charming!

charme[1] [ʃaʀm] NM **1** *(attrait)* charm; **faire le c. de qch** to be the most attractive *or* greatest asset of sth; **c'est ce qui fait tout son c.** that's what is so appealing *or* charming about him/her; **leur maison ne manque pas de c.** their house is not without charm; **cette proposition ne manque pas de c.** the suggestion is not without a certain appeal

2 *(d'une femme, d'un homme)* charm, attractiveness; **elle a beaucoup de c.** she has great charm, she's very charming; **elle n'est pas belle, mais elle a du c.** she's not beautiful, but she is attractive; **les femmes lui trouvent du c.** women find him attractive; **faire du c. à qn** to try to charm sb

3 *(enchantement)* spell; **être/tomber sous le c. de** to be/to fall under the spell of; **tenir qn/un public sous le c.** to hold sb/an audience spellbound; **le c. est rompu** the spell's broken

4 *(locution)* **se porter comme un c.** to be in excellent health *or* as fit as a fiddle; **comment vous portez-vous? – comme un c.!** how do you feel? – never better!
▫ **charmes** NMPL *Euph (d'une femme)* charms; **vivre** *ou* **faire commerce de ses charmes** to trade on one's charms
▫ **de charme** ADJ **1** *Mus* **chanson de c.** sentimental ballad

2 *Euph (érotique → presse)* soft-porn; **magazine de c.** soft-porn magazine; **mannequin de c.** glamour model; **hôtesse de c.** escort (girl)

'**Le Charme discret de la bourgeoisie**' Buñuel 'The Discreet Charm of the Bourgeoisie'

charme[2] [ʃaʀm] NM *Bot* hornbeam; **c. de Caroline** ironwood

charmer [3] [ʃaʀme] VT **1** *(plaire à)* to delight, to enchant; **son sourire l'a charmé** he was enchanted by his/her smile **2** *(envoûter → auditoire)* to cast *or* to put a spell on; *(→ serpent)* to charm **3** *(dans des formules de politesse)* **je suis charmé de vous revoir** I'm delighted to see you again; **charmé de vous avoir rencontré** (it's been) very nice meeting you

charmeur, -euse [ʃaʀmœʀ, -øz] ADJ *(air, sourire)* charming, engaging
   NM,F *(séducteur)* charmer; **méfie-toi de ce c.** watch out, he'll try and use his charm on you; **c. de serpents** snake charmer

charmille [ʃaʀmij] NF **1** *(berceau de verdure)* bower, arbour **2** *(allée)* tree-covered walk *or* path

charmoie [ʃaʀmwa] NF hornbeam plantation

charnel, -elle [ʃaʀnɛl] ADJ **1** *(sexuel)* carnal; **l'amour c.** carnal love **2** *(physique → beauté)* physical, bodily; **nous parlons d'eux en tant qu'êtres charnels** we're talking about them as

human beings made of flesh and blood

charnellement [ʃaʀnɛlmɑ̃] ADV carnally; **connaître qn c.** to have carnal knowledge of sb

charnier [ʃaʀnje] NM **1** *(fosse)* mass grave **2** *(ossuaire)* charnel house **3** *(lieu de massacre)* scene of carnage

charnière [ʃaʀnjɛʀ] NF **1** *Anat & Menuis* hinge **2** *(transition)* junction, turning point; **Goethe est à la c. du XVIIIème et du XIXème siècle** Goethe lived during the transition from the 18th to the 19th century; **marquer la c. entre deux périodes** to be a turning point between two eras **3** *Mil* (point of) junction **4** *(comme adj; avec ou sans trait d'union)* **moment/siècle c.** moment/century of transition **5** *(au rugby)* half-back partnership

charnu, -e [ʃaʀny] ADJ **1** *(corps)* plump, fleshy; *(lèvres)* full, fleshy; *(fruit)* pulpy **2** *Anat* fleshy, flesh-covered; *Hum* **la partie charnue de son anatomie** his/her posterior **3** *(vin)* ropy

charognard [ʃaʀɔɲaʀ] NM **1** *Zool & Orn* carrion feeder **2** *Fam (exploiteur)* vulture

charogne [ʃaʀɔɲ] NF **1** *(carcasse)* **une c.** a decaying carcass; **ces animaux se nourrissent de c.** these animals feed off carrion **2** *très Fam (homme)* bastard; *(femme)* bitch; **espèce de c.!** *(homme)* you bastard!; *(femme)* you bitch!

charolais, -e [ʃaʀɔlɛ, -ɛz] ADJ of/from the Charolais area
   NM Charolais bull; **les c.** Charolais cattle
▫ **Charolais, -e** NM,F = inhabitant of or person from the Charolais area
▫ **Charolais** NM Charolais area
▫ **charolaise** NF Charolais cow

Charon [kaʀɔ̃] NPR *Myth* Charon

Charonne [ʃaʀɔn] NM Charonne *(metro station where in 1962 police charged a group of demonstrators, resulting in casualties)*

Culture

CHARONNE

On 8 February 1962, Paris police charged a crowd of demonstrators protesting against the OAS (a clandestine organization opposed to Algerian independence, then conducting a terrorist campaign in Paris), forcing them towards the closed gates of the metro station "Charonne". Over a hundred people were injured and eight were crushed to death. Half a million people attended their funerals, and the incident is remembered as one of the most tragic events of the period.

charophyte [kaʀɔfit] *Bot* NM charophyte
▫ **charophytes** NMPL Charophyta

charpentage [ʃaʀpɑ̃taʒ] NM carpentry *or* timber work

charpente [ʃaʀpɑ̃t] NF **1** *Constr* skeleton, framework; **c. en bois** *Br* timber *or Am* lumber work; **maison à c. de bois** wood frame house; **c. métallique** steel frame **2** *Anat* **il a la c. d'un boxeur** he's built like a boxer; **une c. d'athlète** an athlete's build; **c. osseuse** skeleton **3** *(schéma → d'un projet)* structure, framework; *(→ d'un roman)* outline

charpenté, -e [ʃaʀpɑ̃te] ADJ **bien** *ou* **solidement c.** *(personne)* well-built; *(film, argument)* well-structured

charpenter [3] [ʃaʀpɑ̃te] VT **1** *Constr* to carpenter **2** *(structurer → œuvre, discours)* to structure

charpenterie [ʃaʀpɑ̃tʀi] NF *(métier)* carpentry; *(chantier) Br* timberyard, *Am* lumber yard

charpentier [ʃaʀpɑ̃tje] NM *(ouvrier)* carpenter; *(entrepreneur)* (master) carpenter; **c. du bord** shipwright

charpentière [ʃaʀpɑ̃tjɛʀ] *voir* **abeille**

charpie [ʃaʀpi] NF *(pansement)* lint, shredded linen
▫ **en charpie** ADV **mettre** *ou* **réduire qch en c.** to tear sth to shreds; *Fig* **je vais le mettre** *ou* **réduire en c.** I'll make mincemeat (out) of him; **il a servi de la viande en c.** he served meat that was cooked to shreds

charre [ʃaʀ] NM *très Fam* **c'est pas du c.** *ou* **des charres!** no kidding!

charret [ʃaʀɛ] NM *Suisse (jeu)* = type of board game for two players, each player having nine pieces which can be placed on concentric circles

charretée [ʃarte] NF **1** *(contenu)* cartful, cartload; **une c. de blé** a cartload of wheat; **par charretées entières** by the cartload **2** *Fam (grande quantité)* **une c. d'insultes** loads *or* a heap of insults; **des charretées de vieux machins** piles of old junk, old junk by the crateful

charretier, -ère [ʃartje, -ɛr] ADJ *(chemin, voie)* cart *(avant n)*
   NM,F carter

charretin [ʃartɛ̃], **charreton** [ʃartɔ̃] NM small cart *(without sides)*

charrette [ʃarɛt] NF **1** *Agr* cart
   2 *Hist* **la c. des condamnés** the tumbrel *or* tumbril
   3 *Fam (travail intensif)* **se mettre en c.** to work against the clock
   4 *(licenciements)* **faire partie de la première/ dernière c.** to be included in the first/last wave of redundancies; **on ne sait pas qui va faire partie de la prochaine c.** you don't know where the axe is going to fall next time
   5 *Fam (voiture)* car, wheels, *Br* motor
   6 *Belg (locutions)* **ça ne veut pas dire c.** that's not saying much; **le chef du mouvement hésite, mais les militants poussent à la c.** the leader of the movement is hesitating, but the militants are egging him on *or* urging him to take action
   ADJ INV *Fam* **être c.** to be working against the clock *or* flat out
   EXCLAM *Suisse Fam* blast!, *Am* shoot!; **cette c. de Paul!** that *Br* blasted *or Am* darn Paul!

charriage [ʃarjaʒ] NM **1** *Transp* carriage, haulage **2** *Géol* overthrust

charrié, -e [ʃarje] ADJ *Géol* displaced *(as the result of an overthrust)*

charrier [10] [ʃarje] VT **1** *(sujet: personne)* to cart *or* to carry (along)
   2 *(sujet: fleuve, rivière)* to carry *or* to wash along; **la Néva charrie d'énormes glaçons** the Neva carries great blocks of ice
   3 *Fam (railler)* **c. qn** *Br* to take the mickey out of sb, *Am* to goof with sb; **il s'est fait c.** he got made fun of, *Br* he got the mickey taken out of him
   VI *Fam* **c. (dans les bégonias)** *(exagérer)* to go too far *or* (way) over the top; **cinq euros d'augmentation, ils charrient!** five euros on the price, they've got a nerve!; **cette fois, tu charries vraiment!** you're going too far this time!; **je veux bien aider mais faut pas c.** I don't mind lending a hand, but this is a bit over the top

charroi [ʃarwa] NM cartage

charron [ʃarɔ̃] NM **1** *(fabricant)* cartwright, wheelwright **2** *(réparateur)* wheelwright

charronnage [ʃarɔnaʒ] NM cartwright's *or* wheelwright's work

charroyer [13] [ʃarwaje] VT to cart

charrue [ʃary] NF **1** *(pour labourer)* plough; **c. polysoc** multiple plough; **mettre la c. avant les bœufs** to put the cart before the horse **2** *Can* snowplough

charte [ʃart] NF **1** *(document)* charter; **c. des droits fondamentaux** Charter of Fundamental Rights; **la c. des droits de l'homme** the Charter of Human Rights; **c. commerciale** commercial charter; **Fin c. du contribuable vérifié** taxpayer's charter; *Journ & Typ* **c. graphique** *ou* **rédactionnelle** house-style book; **C. sociale** Social Charter; **c. des valeurs** statement of principles **2** *Hist* charter; **la Grande C.** Magna Carta **3** *(plan)* **c. d'aménagement** development plan
   ▫ **chartes** *voir* **école**

charte-partie [ʃartəparti] *(pl* **chartes-parties***)* NF *Naut* charter-party

charter [ʃartɛr] NM *(avion)* chartered plane; *(vol)* charter flight

chartisme [ʃartism] NM *Hist* chartism

chartiste [ʃartist] NMF **1** *Pol (en Grande-Bretagne)* Chartist **2** *Univ* = student or former student of the "École des chartes" **3** *Bourse* chartist
   ADJ **1** *Pol (en Grande-Bretagne)* Chartist **2** *Univ* = relating to the "École des chartes" **3** *Bourse* **analyse c.** chart analysis

chartre [ʃartr] = **charte**

chartreux, -euse [ʃartrø, -øz] NM,F *Rel (moine)* Carthusian monk; *(religieuse)* Carthusian nun
   NM *(chat)* British blue (cat)
   ▫ **chartreuse** NF **1** *Rel (de moines)* Charterhouse, Carthusian monastery; *(de religieuses)* Carthusian convent **2** *(liqueur)* Chartreuse

---

≈≡≡▭≡≡≈
'La Chartreuse de Parme' *Stendhal* 'The Charterhouse of Parma'

---

chartrier [ʃartri(j)e] NM **1** *(personne)* custodian of charters **2** *(recueil)* cartulary, collection of charters **3** *(salle)* charter-room

Charybde [karibd] NPR **1** *Myth* Charybdis **2** *(locution)* **tomber de C. en Scylla** to jump out of the frying pan into the fire

chas [ʃa] NM eye *(of a needle)*

chasme [kasm] NM *Arch & Littéraire* chasm

chassant, -e [ʃasɑ̃, -ɑ̃t] ADJ *Mines* longitudinal

chasse [ʃas] NF **1** *(activité)* hunting; *(occasion)* hunt; **cette région a toujours été un pays de c.** this has always been a good area for hunting; **c. au daim/renard/tigre** deer/fox/tiger hunting; **c. à courre** *(activité)* hunting (with hounds); *(occasion)* hunt; **c. au faucon** falconry; **c. au furet** ferreting; **c. au lapin** rabbit shooting, rabbiting; **c. au lièvre** *(gén)* hare hunting; *(avec lévriers)* hare coursing; **c. aux papillons** butterfly catching; **c. au phoque** sealing, seal culling; **aller à la c.** *(à courre)* to go hunting; *(au fusil)* to go shooting; **dresser un chien pour la c.** *(à courre)* to train a dog for hunting *or* the hunt; *(au fusil)* to train a dog for shooting *or* the shoot; **c. sous-marine** underwater fishing; *Prov* **qui va à la c. perd sa place** = if somebody takes your place it serves you right for leaving it empty
   2 *(domaine → de chasse à courre)* hunting grounds; *(→ de chasse au fusil)* shooting ground; **louer une c.** to rent a shoot; **les chasses du roi** the royal hunting grounds; **c. gardée** *(sur panneau)* private, poachers will be prosecuted; *Fig* **les États Unis considèrent que l'Amérique latine est leur c. gardée** the US considers Latin America to be its backyard; *Fam* **laisse-la tranquille, c'est c. gardée** leave her alone, she's spoken for
   3 *(butin)* game; **la c. a été bonne** we got a good bag; **faire bonne c.** to get a good bag
   4 *(période)* hunting season, shooting season; **la c. est ouverte/fermée** it's open/close(d) season, the shooting season has begun/is over
   5 *(chasseurs)* hunters; **la c. vient de passer** the hunters have just gone by; *(à courre)* the hunt has just gone by
   6 *(poursuite)* chase, hunt; **faire** *ou* **donner la c. à un cambrioleur** to chase after a burglar; **prendre en c. une voiture** to chase a car
   7 *(recherche)* **c. à** search for; **la c. au faciès** = harassment of ethnic minorities by the police; **c. à l'homme** manhunt; **c. au trésor** treasure hunt; **c. aux sorcières** witch hunt; **faire la c. à** to search for, to (try to) track down; **faire la c. aux abus** to root out abusers *(of a system)*; *Fam* **faire la c. au mari** to be looking for a husband; *Zool & Fig* **en c.** *Br* on *or Am* in heat; **se mettre en c. pour trouver qch** to go out hunting for sth; **se mettre en c. pour trouver un emploi/une maison** to go job-hunting/house-hunting
   8 *Aviat* **la c.** fighter planes
   9 *(d'eau)* flush; **tirer la c. (d'eau)** to flush the toilet
   10 *Typ (épaisseur de la lettre)* width; *(d'une page)* overrun
   11 *Aut* caster

chassé [ʃase] NM *(pas de danse)* chassé

châsse [ʃas] NF **1** *(coffre)* shrine; **orné** *ou* **paré comme une c.** *(personne)* extravagantly overdressed **2** *Opt (de lunettes)* frame **3** *(d'un bijou)* setting

chasse-clou [ʃasklu] *(pl* **chasse-clous***)* NM *Tech* nail punch, nail set

chassé-croisé [ʃasekrwaze] *(pl* **chassés-croisés***)* NM **1** *(confusion)* **le c. ministériel/de limousines** the comings and goings of ministers/of limousines; **le c. des vacanciers sur les routes** the busy flow of holidaymakers on the roads **2** *(pas de danse)* set to partners

chasséen, -enne [ʃaseɛ̃, -ɛn] *Archéol* ADJ Chasséen
   NM Chasséen culture

chasse-galerie [ʃasgaleri] NF INV *Can* = French-Canadian legend in which witches or werewolves transport people through the air at night in a birch canoe

---

chasse-goupille [ʃasgupij] *(pl* **chasse-goupilles***)* NM *Tech* pin punch

chasselas [ʃasla] NM *(cépage)* **du c.** Chasselas grapes

chasse-marée [ʃasmare] NM INV *(bateau)* coasting lugger

chasse-mouches [ʃasmuʃ] NM INV flyswatter

chasse-neige [ʃasnɛʒ] NM INV **1** *(véhicule)* snowplough **2** *Ski (position du skieur)* snowplough; **descendre/tourner en c.** to snowplough down/ round; **virage en c.** snowplough turn

chasse-pierres [ʃaspjɛr] NM INV *Rail* cowcatcher

chassepot [ʃaspo] NM *Mil* chassepot

chasser [3] [ʃase] VT **1** *(animaux)* to hunt; **il chasse le daim** he hunts deer; **c. le phoque** to seal
   2 *(expulser)* to drive out, to expel; **c. qn du pays** to drive sb from the country; **il a été chassé de chez lui** he was made to leave home; **elle l'a chassé de la maison** she sent him packing; **c. qn/qch de son esprit** to dismiss sb/ sth from one's mind *or* thoughts; **je ne veux pas vous c. mais il est tard** I'm not trying to get rid of you but it's getting late
   3 *(congédier → employé)* to dismiss
   4 *(faire partir)* to dispel, to drive away, to get rid of; **le mauvais temps a chassé les touristes** the bad weather drove away the tourists; **pour c. les mauvaises odeurs** to get rid of bad smells; **sortez pour c. les idées noires** go out and forget your worries; **chassez le naturel, il revient au galop** the leopard can't change its spots
   5 *(pousser)* to drive (forward); **c. une mouche (du revers de la main)** to brush away a fly; **le vent chasse le sable/les nuages** the wind is blowing the sand/the clouds along
   6 *Bourse* **c. le découvert** to raid the bears
   VI **1** *(aller à la chasse → à courre)* to go hunting; *(→ au fusil)* to go shooting; **c. au furet** to ferret; *Fig* **c. sur les terres d'autrui** to poach on somebody's preserve *or* territory
   2 *Naut (déraper)* to skid; **le navire chasse sur son ancre** the ship is dragging its anchor
   3 *(venir)* to drive; **nuages qui chassent du nord** clouds driving from the north
   4 *Typ (caractère)* to drive out; *(texte)* to overrun

chasseresse [ʃasrɛs] ADJ F *Myth* **Diane c.** Diana the huntress
   NF *Littéraire* huntress

chasse-roue [ʃasru] *(pl* **chasse-roues***)* NM spur stone, guard stone *(to protect wall etc from impact of vehicles)*

châsses [ʃas] NMPL *Fam* eyes, peepers

chasseur, -euse [ʃasœr, -øz] NM,F **1** *(d'animaux)* hunter, huntsman, *f* huntress; **un très bon c.** *(de gibier à plumes)* an excellent shot; **c. de daims** deerhunter; **c. au marais** *ou* **à la sauvagine** wildfowler
   2 *(chercheur)* **c. d'autographes** autograph hunter; **c. d'images** (freelance) photographer; **c. de prime** bounty hunter; *aussi Fig* **c. de têtes** headhunter; **elle a été recrutée par un c. de têtes** she was headhunted
   ▫ **chasseur** NM **1** *Aviat & Mil* fighter (plane); **c. à réaction** jet fighter; *Naut* **c. de sous-marins** submarine hunter
   2 *Mil* chasseur; **c. alpin** Alpine chasseur
   3 *(dans un hôtel)* messenger (boy), *Am* bellboy
   ADJ INV *Culin* chasseur

chasseur-bagagiste [ʃasbagaʒist] *(pl* **chasseurs-bagagistes***)* NM luggage porter, porter

chasseur-bombardier [ʃasbɔ̃bardje] *(pl* **chasseurs-bombardiers***)* NM *Mil* fighter-bomber

chasseur-cueilleur [ʃasœrkœjœr] *(pl* **chasseurs-cueilleurs***)* NM hunter-gatherer

chassie [ʃasi] NF rheum; **avoir de la c. dans les yeux** to have rheumy eyes

chassieux, -euse [ʃasjø, -øz] ADJ *(œil)* rheumy; *(personne)* rheumy-eyed; **avoir les yeux c.** to have rheumy eyes
   NM,F rheumy-eyed person

châssis [ʃasi] NM **1** *Constr* frame; **c. dormant** fixed frame; **c. à guillotine** sash (frame); **c. mobile** sash; **c. à tabatière** skylight frame
   2 *Beaux-Arts* stretcher; *Phot* (printing) frame; *Typ* **c. d'imprimerie** chase
   3 *Aut* chassis, steel frame; **c. treillis** box section

chassis; **c. tubulaire** box section chassis, space frame chassis

4 *Hort (de jardin)* (cold) frame; **culture sous c.** forcing

5 *très Fam (corps féminin)* body■, bod, chassis; *Hum* **quel beau c.!** what a bod!

6 *Can (fenêtre)* window; **c. double** storm window

châssis-presse [ʃɑsiprɛs] (*pl* **châssis-presses**) **NM** *Phot* printing frame

chassoir [ʃaswar] **NM** *Tech* hoop driver

chaste [ʃast] **ADJ** chaste, innocent; *Hum* **ce n'est pas une plaisanterie pour vos chastes oreilles** this joke isn't for your innocent *or* delicate ears

chastement [ʃastəmɑ̃] **ADV** chastely, innocently

chasteté [ʃastəte] **NF** chastity

chasuble [ʃazybl] **NF 1** *Rel* chasuble **2** *(vêtement)* **robe c.** *Br* pinafore dress, *Am* jumper

chat[1], chatte [ʃa, ʃat] **NM,F 1** *(animal → gén)* cat; *(→ mâle)* tomcat; *(→ femelle)* she-cat; **un petit c.** a kitten; **regarde le petit c.** look at the little pussycat; **c. angora** Angora cat; **c. de Birmanie** Burmese cat; **c. doré** golden cat; **c. européen** tabby (cat); **c. de gouttière** alley cat; **c. margay** margay (cat); **c. pêcheur** fishing cat; **c. persan** Persian cat; **c. sauvage** *(félin)* wildcat; *Can (raton laveur)* raccoon; **c. siamois** Siamese cat; **c. viverrin** fishing cat; **appeler un c. un c.** to call a spade a spade; **avoir un c. dans la gorge** to have a frog in one's throat; **acheter c. en poche** to buy a pig in a poke; **écrire comme un c.** to scrawl; **il n'y a pas de quoi fouetter un c.** it's nothing to make a fuss about; **j'ai d'autres chats à fouetter** I've got better things to do, I've got other fish to fry; *Fam* **il n'y avait pas un c.** there wasn't a soul about; *Prov* **il ne faut pas réveiller le c. qui dort** let sleeping dogs lie; *Prov* **quand le c. n'est pas là, les souris dansent** when the cat's away, the mice will play; *Prov* **à bon c., bon rat** = it's tit for tat; *Prov* **c. échaudé craint l'eau froide** once bitten, twice shy

2 *Fam (terme d'affection)* **mon petit c., ma petite chatte** pussycat, sweetie, sweetheart

3 *(jeu)* tag, *Br* tig; **jouer à c.** to play tag *or Br* tig; **c'est Sonia le c.** Sonia's it; **jouer à c. perché** to play off-ground tag *or Br* tig; *Fig* **jouer au c. et à la souris avec qn** to play cat-and-mouse with sb

4 *(fouet)* **c. à neuf queues** cat-o'-nine-tails

5 *Belg (locution)* **acheter un c. dans un sac** to buy a pig in a poke

▫ **chatte NF** *Vulg* pussy, *Br* fanny; **avoir de la chatte** to be lucky *or Br* jammy

'Le Chat botté' *Perrault* 'Puss in Boots'

chat[2] [tʃat] **NM** *Ordinat (sur Internet)* chat

châtaigne [ʃatɛɲ] **NF 1** *Bot* chestnut; **c. d'eau** water chestnut **2** *très Fam (coup)* clout, thump; **il s'est pris une de ces châtaignes!** *(il a été frappé)* he got a real thump!; *(il s'est cogné)* he gave himself a nasty knock!; **je me suis pris une c.** *(choc électrique)* I got a shock **3** *Zool* **c. de mer** sea urchin

châtaigner [4] [ʃatɛɲe] *Fam* **VT** to whack, to clout

▸**se châtaigner VPR** to exchange blows■, to lay into each other

châtaigneraie [ʃatɛɲərɛ] **NF** chestnut grove

châtaignier [ʃateɲe] **NM 1** *Bot* chestnut tree **2** *(bois)* chestnut

châtain [ʃatɛ̃] **ADJ M** *(cheveux)* chestnut (brown); **c. clair** light brown; **c. doré** *ou* **roux** auburn; **être c.** to have brown hair

NM chestnut brown

chataire [ʃatɛr] = **cataire**

château, -x [ʃato] **NM 1** *(forteresse)* castle; **c. fort** fortified castle

2 *(palais)* castle, palace; *(manoir)* mansion, manor (house); **le c. de Versailles** the palace of Versailles; **les châteaux de la Loire** the Châteaux of the Loire; **c. de cartes** house of cards; **ses illusions se sont écroulées comme un c. de cartes** his/her illusions collapsed like a house of cards; **c. de sable** sandcastle; *Fig* **bâtir** *ou* **faire des châteaux en Espagne** to build castles in the air *or* the sky; *Fam* **le C.** *(la présidence de la République)* = humorous term referring to the French presidency

3 *(exploitation vinicole)* château; **mis en bouteilles au c.** château bottled

4 *Naut* **c. d'arrière** *ou* **de poupe** aftercastle; **c. d'avant** *ou* **de proue** forecastle, fo'c's'le, fo'c'sle

▫ **château d'eau NM** water tower

chateaubriand, châteaubriant [ʃatobrijɑ̃] **NM** *Culin* Chateaubriand (steak)

Château-la-Pompe [ʃatolapɔ̃p] **NM** *Fam Hum* water■; **accompagné d'un verre de C.** washed down with a glass of good old tapwater

châtelain, -e [ʃatlɛ̃, -ɛn] **NM,F 1** *(propriétaire)* lord of the manor, *f* lady of the manor, chatelaine **2** *Hist* (feudal) lord

▫ **châtelaine NF** *(chaîne de ceinture, bijou)* chatelaine

châtelet [ʃatlɛ] **NM** small (fortified) castle

châtellenie [ʃatɛlni] **NF** *Hist* castellany

châtelperronien, -enne [ʃatɛlperɔnjɛ̃, -jɛn] *Hist* **ADJ** Chatelperronian

NM Chatelperronian

chat-huant [ʃaɥɑ̃] (*pl* **chats-huants**) **NM** *Orn* brown owl

châtié, -e [ʃatje] **ADJ** *(style)* polished; **en langage c.** in refined language

châtier [9] [ʃatje] **VT** *Littéraire* **1** *(punir)* to chastise, to castigate; **c. son corps** to mortify the flesh; **c. l'audace de qn** to punish sb for his/her impudence **2** *(affiner)* to polish, to refine

chatière [ʃatjɛr] **NF 1** *(pour un chat)* cat door *or* flap **2** *(dans un toit)* ventilation hole **3** *(passage étroit)* narrow underground passage

châtieur [ʃatjœr] **NM** punisher, chastiser, *Littéraire* chastener, scourger

châtiment [ʃatimɑ̃] **NM** punishment, *Sout* chastisement; **c. corporel** corporal punishment; **il a reçu un c. sévère** he was severely punished

chatoie *etc voir* **chatoyer**

chatoiement [ʃatwamɑ̃] **NM** *(sur du métal, du verre)* gleam, shimmer; *(sur de la soie)* (soft) glimmer

chaton[1] [ʃatɔ̃] **NM 1** *Zool* kitten **2** *Bot* catkin, *Spéc* ament, amentum **3** *(poussière)* ball of fluff, *Am* dust bunny **4** *(terme d'affection)* **mon c.** darling

chaton[2] [ʃatɔ̃] **NM** *(tête d'une bague)* bezel; *(pierre enchâssée)* stone

chatou [ʃatu] *voir* **chatrou**

chatouille [ʃatuj] **NF 1** *Fam* tickle; **faire des chatouilles à qn** to tickle sb; **elle adore les chatouilles** she loves being tickled; **elle craint les chatouilles** she's ticklish **2** *Belg (locution)* **avoir c. à la tête/aux jambes** to have an itchy head/itchy legs

chatouillement [ʃatujmɑ̃] **NM** tickle; **je ressens encore un c. dans les oreilles mais je n'ai plus mal** my ears still tickle but it doesn't hurt any more

chatouiller [3] [ʃatuje] **VT 1** *(pour faire rire)* to tickle; **ah! ça chatouille!** oh! that tickles!; *Fam* **c. les côtes à qn** to give sb a thrashing **2** *(irriter)* to tickle **3** *(exciter → odorat, palais)* to titillate; *(→ curiosité)* to arouse **4** *(heurter → amour-propre, sensibilité)* to prick

VI *(démanger)* to itch

Allusion

Ça vous chatouille ou ça vous gratouille?

This expression comes from a play by Jules Romains, Knock, ou le triomphe de la médecine (1923) about a very doubtful doctor, newly arrived in a village. The play was filmed with Louis Jouvet as Dr Knock. At one point, the doctor (who recalls Molière's doctors) asks a patient suffering with a cough to define his symptoms: **Ça vous chatouille ou ça vous gratouille?** ("Is it a tickly kind of cough or a scratchy kind of cough?") Today when people complain of vague symptoms, they can be teased with this question.

chatouilleux, -euse [ʃatujø, -øz] **ADJ 1** *(physiquement)* ticklish **2** *(pointilleux)* sensitive, touchy; **il a un caractère c.** he's rather touchy; **c. sur qch** overparticular about sth; **elle est très chatouilleuse sur ce qu'elle appelle le bon goût** she's very sensitive *or* particular about what she calls good taste

chatouillis [ʃatuji] **NM** *Fam* tickle; **faire des c. à qn** to tickle sb; **aimer les c.** to love being tickled; **craindre les c.** to be ticklish

chatoyant, -e [ʃatwajɑ̃, -ɑ̃t] **ADJ** *(étoffe, plumage, couleur)* shimmering; *(pierre)* glistening, sparkling; *Fig (style)* sparkling

chatoyer [13] [ʃatwaje] **VI** *(étoffe, plumage, couleur)* to shimmer; *(pierre)* to glisten, to sparkle; **la lumière des bougies faisait c. les tissus précieux** the precious fabrics shimmered in the candlelight

châtrer [3] [ʃatre] **VT 1** *(étalon, verrat)* to geld, to castrate; *(homme, taureau)* to castrate; *(chat)* to neuter, *Am* to fix **2** *(article)* to make innocuous **3** *Hort (plante)* to cut back; *(fleur)* to castrate

chatrou [ʃatru] **NM** *(aux Antilles)* = small octopus eaten in the Caribbean

chatte [ʃat] *voir* **chat[1]**

chattemite [ʃatmit] **NF** *Littéraire Péj* **faire la c.** to be all sweetness and light

chatter [3] [tʃate] **VI** *Ordinat (sur l'Internet)* to chat

chatterie [ʃatri] **NF 1** *(câlinerie)* coaxing; **faire des chatteries à qn** to pamper sb **2** *(friandise)* delicacy

chatterton [ʃatɛrtɔn] **NM** *Élec Br* insulating tape, *Am* friction tape

chat-tigre [ʃatigr] (*pl* **chats-tigres**) **NM** *Zool* tiger cat

CHAUD, -E [ʃo, ʃod] **ADJ 1** *(dont la température est → douce)* warm; *(→ élevée)* hot; **climat/temps/vent c.** *(tempéré)* warm climate/weather/wind; *(tropical)* hot climate/weather/wind; **un bain c.** a hot bath; **une boisson chaude** a hot drink; **un repas c.** a hot meal; *Culin* **mettre à four c.** cook in a hot oven; **un petit pain tout c.** a hot bun; **ton thé est à peine c.** your tea is barely warm; **son front est tout c.** his/her forehead is hot; **les nuits deviennent plus chaudes en juin** the nights become warmer in June; **au (moment le) plus c. de la journée** in the heat of the day; **marrons chauds** roasted chestnuts; **c. comme une caille** snug as a bug in a rug; **c. devant!** *(au restaurant)* excuse me! *(said by waiters carrying plates to clear the way)*

2 *(veste, couverture)* warm

3 *(qui n'a pas refroidi)* warm; **le lit est encore c.** the bed is still warm; *Fig* **la place du directeur est encore chaude** the manager's shoes are still warm

4 *(ardent → ambiance)* warm; *(→ partisan)* keen, ardent; *(→ défenseur)* ardent; **avoir une chaude discussion sur qch** to debate sth heatedly; *Fam* **je ne suis pas très c. pour le faire** I'm not really keen to do it; **son accueil n'a pas été très c.** he/she didn't welcome us too warmly; **avoir un tempérament c.** to be hot-tempered

5 *(agité, dangereux)* hot; **les quartiers chauds** the dangerous areas; **les points chauds du monde** the world's hot spots *or* flash points; **le mois de septembre sera c.** there will be (political) unrest in September; **l'alerte a été chaude** it was a near *or* close thing

6 *Fam (récent)* hot (off the press); **une nouvelle toute chaude** an up-to-the-minute piece of news

7 *très Fam (sexuellement)* hot, horny; **c. lapin** randy devil

8 *(couleur, voix)* warm

9 *Can Fam (ivre)* wasted, *Br* pissed

NM 1 *(chaleur)* **le c.** the heat *or* hot weather **2** *Méd* **un c. et froid** a chill

ADV hot; **servir c.** serve hot; **j'aime manger c.** I like my food hot; **bois-le c.** drink it (while it's) hot; **avoir c.** *(douce chaleur)* to be warm; *(forte chaleur)* to be hot; **il fait c.** *(douce chaleur)* it's warm; *(forte chaleur)* it's hot; *Fam* **on a eu c. (aux fesses)!** that was a close *or* near thing!; **il fera c. le jour où tu l'entendras dire merci!** that'll be the day when you hear him/her say thank you!; **ça ne me fait ni c. ni froid** I couldn't care less

▫ **chaude NF 1** *Métal* heat, melt; **chaude blanche/rouge** white/red heat **2** *Vulg* horny babe

▫ **à chaud ADV 1** *(sans préparation)* **l'opération s'est faite à c.** it was emergency surgery; **sonder à c.** to do a spot poll; **ne lui pose pas la question à c.** don't just spring the question on him/her

2 *Métal* **souder à c.** to hot-weld; **étirer un métal à c.** to draw metal under heat; **travailler un métal à c.** to hot-work a metal

▫ **au chaud ADV restez bien au c.** *(au lit)* stay

nice and cosy or warm in your bed; *(sans sortir)* don't go out in the cold; **mettre** *ou* **garder des assiettes au c.** to keep plates warm

chaudasse [ʃodas] *Vulg* **ADJ** hot, horny
 NF horny bitch

chaudeau, -x [ʃodo] **NM** *Fam* egg flip, eggnog

chaudement [ʃodmã] **ADV 1** *(contre le froid)* warmly; **se vêtir c.** to put on warm clothes **2** *(chaleureusement → gén)* warmly, warmheartedly; *(→ recommander)* heartily; *(→ féliciter)* with all one's heart

chaude-pisse [ʃodpis] *(pl* **chaudes-pisses)** **NF** *Vulg* clap

chaud-froid [ʃofrwa] *(pl* **chauds-froids)** **NM** *Culin* chaudfroid

chaudière [ʃodjɛr] **NF 1** *(de chauffage)* boiler; **c. à bois/charbon** wood-/coal-fired boiler; **c. accumulatrice de chaleur** heat storage vessel; **c. à eau chaude** hot water boiler; **c. à vapeur** steam boiler; **c. nucléaire** nuclear-powered boiler **2** *Arch (chaudron)* copper **3** *Can (seau)* bucket; **c. à sucre** = bucket for collecting maple sap

chaudron [ʃodrɔ̃] **NM 1** *(récipient → en fonte)* cauldron; *(→ en cuivre)* copper kettle *or* boiler **2** *Can (marmite)* cooking pot

chaudronnerie [ʃodrɔnri] **NF 1** *(profession)* boilermaking, boilerwork **2** *(marchandises → de grande taille)* boilers; *(→ de petite taille)* hollowware **3** *(usine)* boilerworks

chaudronnier, -ère [ʃodrɔnje, -ɛr] **NM,F** *(gén)* boilermaker; *(sur du cuivre)* coppersmith
 ADJ industrie chaudronnière boilermaking

chauffage [ʃofaʒ] **NM 1** *(d'un lieu)* heating; **le c. coûte cher** heating costs a lot; **système de c.** heating system
  2 *(installation, système)* heating (system); *(dans une voiture)* heater; **installer le c.** to put heating in; **mettre le c.** to put *or* turn the heating on; **baisser/monter le c.** *(dans une maison)* to turn the heating down/up; *(en voiture)* to turn the heater down/up; **c. central/urbain** central/district heating; **c. électrique/solaire** electric/solar heating; **c. au gaz/au mazout** gas-fired/oil-fired heating; **c. à air pulsé** warm-air heating; **c. par induction** induction heating; **c. par le sol** underfloor heating

chauffagiste [ʃofaʒist] **NM** heating engineer

chauffant, -e [ʃofã, -ãt] **ADJ** *(surface)* heating

chauffard [ʃofar] **NM** reckless driver; *(qui s'enfuit)* hit-and-run driver

chauffe [ʃof] **NF 1** *(opération)* stoking; **chef de c.** head stoker **2** *(temps)* heating time; **pendant la c.** *(d'une machine)* while the machine's warming up; *(d'une chaudière)* while the boiler's heating
 ❑ **de chauffe ADJ** boiler *(avant n)*

chauffe-assiettes [ʃofasjɛt] **NM INV** plate warmer, hostess tray

chauffe-bain [ʃofbɛ̃] *(pl* **chauffe-bains)** **NM** water heater

chauffe-biberon [ʃofbibrɔ̃] *(pl* **chauffe-biberons)** **NM** bottle warmer

chauffe-eau [ʃofo] **NM INV** water heater; **c. électrique** immersion heater

chauffe-lit [ʃofli] *(pl* **chauffe-lits)** **NM** bedwarmer, warming-pan

chauffe-moteur [ʃofmɔtœr] *(pl* **chauffe-moteurs)** **NM** *Aut* (engine) block heater

chauffe-pieds [ʃofpje] **NM INV** footwarmer

chauffe-plat [ʃofpla] *(pl* **chauffe-plats)** **NM** chafing dish

chauffer [3] [ʃofe] **VI 1** *(eau, plat, préparation)* to heat up; **mettre qch à c., faire c. qch** to heat sth up; **ça chauffe trop, baisse le gaz** it's overheating, turn the gas down
  2 *(dégager de la chaleur → radiateur)* to give out heat; **ce radiateur chauffe bien/mal** this radiator gives out/doesn't give out a lot of heat; **un pâle soleil d'hiver qui chauffe à peine** a pale wintry sun, hardly giving out any heat; **en avril, le soleil commence à c.** in April, the sun gets hotter
  3 *(surchauffer → moteur)* to overheat; **faire c. sa voiture** to warm up one's car; **ne laissez pas ch. l'élément** don't allow the element to overheat *or* to get too hot
  4 *Fam (être agité)* **ça commence à c.** things are getting heated; **ça va c.!** there's trouble

brewing!; **je te promets que ça va c. s'il est en retard!** I promise you there'll be trouble if he's late!; **ça chauffe** *(à un concert)* things are really cooking
  5 *(dans un jeu)* to get warm; **tu chauffes!** you're getting warmer!
  6 *Can Fam (conduire)* to drive▪
 VT 1 *(chambre, plat)* to warm *or* to heat up; **c. une maison à l'électricité** to have electric heating in a house; **la chambre n'est pas chauffée** there's no heating in the bedroom, the bedroom's not heated; **piscine chauffée** heated swimming pool
  2 *Métal* **c. un métal à blanc/au rouge** to make a metal white-hot/red-hot
  3 *(moteur)* to warm up; *(chaudière, locomotive)* to fire, to stoke
  4 *Fam (exciter)* **c. la salle** to warm up the audience; **il a chauffé la salle à blanc** *ou* **à bloc** he worked the audience up into a frenzy; **c. un étudiant pour un examen** to cram a student for an exam
  5 *Fam (locution)* **tu commences à me c. les oreilles** you're starting to get my goat, *Br* you're getting up my nose
 ▸**se chauffer VPR 1** *(se réchauffer)* to warm oneself (up); **viens te c. près du feu** come and warm yourself up *or* get warm by the fire
  2 *(dans un local)* **ils n'ont pas les moyens de se c.** they can't afford heating; **se c. à l'électricité** to have electric heating; **se c. au bois** to use a wood stove for heating
  3 *(s'échauffer)* to warm up

chaufferette [ʃofrɛt] **NF** *(bouillotte, boîte)* footwarmer

chaufferie [ʃofri] **NF 1** *(local)* boiler room **2** *Naut & Nucl* stokehold

chauffeur [ʃofœr] **NM 1** *(conducteur)* driver; **c. (routier), c. de camion** truck *or Br* lorry driver; **c. de taxi** taxi *or* cab driver; *Péj* **c. du dimanche** Sunday driver
  2 *(employé)* chauffeur; **location de voiture avec c.** chauffeur-driven *Br* hire cars *or Am* rental cars; *Fam* **j'ai fait le c. de ces dames toute la journée** I drove the ladies around all day long; **il est le c. du président** he chauffeurs for the chairman; **c. de maître** chauffeur
  3 *(d'une locomotive)* stoker
  4 *TV* **c. de salle** warm-up man

chauffeuse [ʃoføz] **NF** low armless chair

chaulage [ʃolaʒ] **NM 1** *Agr* liming **2** *Constr* whitewashing

chauler [3] [ʃole] **VT 1** *Agr* to lime **2** *Constr* to whitewash

chaumard [ʃomar] **NM** *Naut* fairlead

chaume [ʃom] **NM 1** *(sur un toit)* thatch; **recouvrir un toit de c.** to thatch a roof **2** *Agr (paille)* haulm; *(sur pied)* stubble **3** *Littéraire (champ)* stubble field

---

'Chaumes à Cordeville, Auvers-sur-l'Oise' Van Gogh 'Stubble Fields at Cordeville, Auvers-sur-l'Oise'

---

chaumer [3] [ʃome] *Agr* **VT** *(champs)* to clear stubble from, to clear of stubble
 VI to clear stubble

chaumière [ʃomjɛr] **NF** ≃ cottage; *(avec un toit de chaume)* thatched cottage; **faire causer** *ou* **jaser dans les chaumières** to give the neighbours something to talk about; **un roman à faire pleurer dans les chaumières** a tear-jerking novel

chaumine [ʃomin] **NF** *Vieilli* small (thatched) cottage

chaussant, -e [ʃosã, -ãt] **ADJ** *(botte, soulier)* well-fitting
 NM fitting qualities *(of a shoe or boot)*

chaussé [ʃose] **NM** *Hér* chaussé

chaussée [ʃose] **NF 1** *(d'une route)* roadway, *Am* pavement; **ne restez pas sur la c.** stay off the road *or* roadway; **c. déformée** *(sur panneau)* uneven road surface; **c. glissante** *(sur panneau)* slippery road, slippery when wet **2** *(talus)* dyke, embankment; *(voie surélevée)* causeway; **la c. des Géants** the Giant's Causeway **3** *(écueil)* reef, line of rocks

chausse-pied [ʃospje] *(pl* **chausse-pieds)** **NM** shoehorn

chausser [3] [ʃose] **VT 1** *(escarpins, skis, palmes)* to put on; *Sport* **c. les étriers** to put one's feet into the stirrups; **elle était chaussée de pantoufles de soie** she was wearing silk slippers
  2 *(enfant, personne)* **viens c. les enfants** come and put the children's shoes on for them
  3 *(fournir en chaussures)* to provide shoes for, to supply with shoes; **je suis difficile à c.** it's hard for me to find shoes that fit
  4 *(aller à)* to fit; **ce modèle te chausse mieux que l'autre** this style fits you better than the other one
  5 *(lunettes)* to put *or* to slip on
  6 *Aut* **la voiture est chaussée de pneus neige** the car has snow tyres on
  7 *Hort (arbre, plante)* to earth up
 VI voici un modèle qui devrait mieux c. this style of shoe should fit better; **ces chaussures chaussent petit** these shoes are small to size; **du combien chausses-tu?** what size shoes do you take?; **je chausse du 38** I take a size 38 shoe
 ▸**se chausser VPR 1** *(emploi réfléchi)* **chausse-toi, il fait froid** put something on your feet, it's cold; **se c. avec un chausse-pied** to use a shoehorn; **il se chausse tout seul maintenant** he can put his shoes on all by himself now
  2 *(se fournir)* **je me chausse chez Lebel** I buy my shoes at *or* I get my shoes from Lebel's

chausses [ʃos] **NFPL** *Arch* hose, chausses

chausse-trape, chausse-trappe [ʃostrap] *(pl* **chausse-trapes** *ou* **chausse-trappes)** **NF** *aussi Fig* trap

chaussette [ʃosɛt] **NF 1** *(pièce d'habillement)* sock; **une paire de chaussettes** a pair of socks; **en chaussettes** in one's stockinged feet; *Fam* **laisser tomber qn comme une vieille c.** to ditch sb; **chaussettes de contention** support socks **2** *Fam Vieilli* **c. à clous** (policeman's) boot▪

chausseur [ʃosœr] **NM 1** *(fabricant)* shoemaker **2** *(vendeur)* shoemaker, footwear specialist; *(magasin)* shoe shop

chausson¹ [ʃosɔ̃] **NM 1** *(d'intérieur)* slipper; *(de bébé)* bootee **2** *(de danseuse)* ballet shoe, pump; *(de gymnastique)* soft shoe; *(dans la chaussure de ski)* inner shoe **3** *Culin* turnover; **c. aux pommes** apple turnover; *Can Ironique* **et un c. avec ça?** does His Lordship/Her Ladyship require anything else? **4** *Can Vieilli (chausette)* (thick) sock, boot sock **5** *Couture* **point de c.** blind hem stitch

chausson², -onne [ʃosɔ̃, -ɔn] **NM,F** *Can Fam* twit, idiot

chaussure [ʃosyr] **NF 1** *(gén)* shoe; **acheter des chaussures** to buy shoes; **une paire de chaussures** a pair of shoes; **chaussures basses** shoes; **chaussures à lacets** lace-ups; **chaussures montantes** ankle boots; **chaussures plates** flat shoes, flats; **chaussures à semelles compensées** platform shoes; **chaussures à talons** (shoes with) heels; **chaussures de ville** town shoes; *Fig* **trouver c. à son pied** to find a suitable match; **elle a trouvé c. à son pied** she found the right person
  2 *Sport* **chaussures de marche** *ou* **de montagne** walking *or* hiking boots; **chaussures de ski** ski boots; **chaussures de sport** sports shoes, *Br* trainers, *Am* sneakers
  3 *Com* shoe *or* footwear trade; *(industrie)* shoe *or* footwear industry

chaut *voir* **chaloir**

chauve [ʃov] **ADJ** *(crâne, tête)* bald; *(personne)* bald, baldheaded; *(montagne, pic)* bare; **c. comme un œuf** *ou* **une bille** *ou* **un genou** as bald *Br* as a coot *or Am* as an egg; **il devient c.** he's balding *or* going bald
 NMF bald person, bald man, *f* woman

chauve-souris [ʃovsuri] *(pl* **chauves-souris)** **NF** *Zool* bat; **c. frugivore** fruit bat

chauvin, -e [ʃovɛ̃, -in] **ADJ** chauvinistic, jingoist, jingoistic
 NM,F chauvinist, jingoist

chauvinisme [ʃovinism] **NM** chauvinism, jingoism

chaux [ʃo] **NF** lime; **mur passé** *ou* **blanchi à la c.** whitewashed wall; **enduire un arbre de c.** to lime a tree; **c. éteinte** slaked lime; **c. vive** quicklime; **bâtir à c. et à sable** to build firmly *or* solidly; **être bâti à c. et à sable** *(personne)* to have an iron constitution

chavée [ʃave] = **cavée**

chavirement [ʃavirmɑ̃] NM **1** *Littéraire (d'un navire)* capsizing, keeling over, overturning **2** *Fig (effondrement)* collapse

chavirer [3] [ʃavire] VI **1** *Naut* to capsize, to keel over, to turn turtle; **faire c.** to capsize; **arrête, tu vas faire c. la barque!** stop it, you'll tip the boat over!

2 *(se renverser)* to keel over, to overturn; **tout chavire autour de moi** everything around me is spinning

3 *(tourner → yeux)* to roll; **avoir le cœur qui chavire** *(de dégoût)* to feel nauseated; *(de chagrin)* to be heartbroken

VT **1** *(basculer)* to capsize, to overturn

2 *(émouvoir)* to overwhelm, to shatter; **il a l'air tout chaviré** he looks devastated

3 *Can (en acadien) (renverser)* to spill, to tip over

4 *Can (en acadien) (devenir fou)* to go crazy, to lose one's mind

chayote, chayotte [ʃajɔt] NF *Hort* chayote

cheap [tʃip] ADJ *Fam (peu cher)* cheap■; *(de mauvaise qualité, de mauvais goût)* tacky

chebec, chebek [ʃebɛk] NM *Naut* xebec, zebec(k)

chébran [ʃebrɑ̃] ADJ INV *Fam (verlan de* **branché***)* hip, trendy

chèche [ʃɛʃ] NM North African scarf

checker [3] [tʃɛke] VT *Can Joual* to check

chéchia [ʃeʃja] NF tarboosh, fez

check-list [tʃɛklist] *(pl* **check-lists***)* NF *Aviat* checklist

check-up [tʃɛkœp] NM INV *Méd* check-up; **faire un c. à qn** to give sb a check-up; **le médecin me conseille de faire un c.** the doctor is advising me to have a check-up

chédail [ʃɛdaj] NM *Suisse* farm machinery

cheddar [ʃedar, tʃedar] NM cheddar

cheddite [ʃedit] NF *Tech* cheddite

cheeseburger [tʃizbœrgœr] NM cheeseburger

chef [ʃɛf] NM **1** *(responsable → gén)* head; *(→ d'une entreprise)* manager, boss; *(→ d'un parti politique)* leader; *(→ d'une tribu)* chief, chieftain; *Fam (patron)* boss; *Com* **c. des achats** purchasing manager; **c. d'antenne** programme supervisor; **c. d'atelier** shop foreman; **c. de bureau** head clerk; **c. de cabinet** *Br* minister's *or Am* secretary of state's principal private secretary; **c. de chantier** site foreman; **c. chasseur** head porter, *Am* bell captain; **c. de clinique** senior registrar; **c. comptable, c. de la comptabilité** *Br* chief accountant, *Am* chief financial officer; **c. de la diplomatie** foreign minister, *Br* ≃ Foreign Secretary, *Am* ≃ Secretary of State; **c. de l'Église** Head of the Church; **c. d'entreprise** company manager; **c. d'équipe** foreman; *Scol* **c. d'établissement** *Br* headmaster, *f* headmistress, *Am* principal; **c. de l'État** Head of the State; **chefs d'État** heads of state; **c. de fabrication** production manager, manufacturing manager; **c. de famille** head of the family; **c. de file** *Mktg (produit)* leader; *Banque & Bourse* lead manager; **c. du gouvernement** head of government; **c. de magasin** store manager; *Mktg* **c. de marque** brand manager; *TV & Cin* **c. opérateur** cinematographer; **c. du personnel** personnel manager, head of personnel; *TV* **c. de plateau** stage manager, floor boss; *Com* **c. de produit** product manager; **c. de projet** project manager; *Com* **c. de (la) publicité** publicity manager; **c. de rang** head waiter; **c. de rayon** *(dans un magasin)* department manager; *Com* **c. de service** *(dans une société)* department manager; *Ordinat* **c. des traitements** data processing manager; *Com* **c. des ventes** sales manager; *Com* **c. de zone** area manager

2 *Mil* **c. de bataillon** ≃ major; **c. d'état-major** chief of staff; **c. d'État-major de l'armée de l'air** *Br* ≃ Marshal of the Royal Air Force, *Am* ≃ General of the Air Force; **c. de patrouille** patrol leader; **c. de pièce** gun captain; **c. de section** platoon commander; *Aviat* flight commander

3 *Rail* **c. de gare** station master; **c. mécanicien** chief mechanic; **c. de train** guard, *Am* conductor

4 *Culin* **c. (cuisinier** *ou* **de cuisine)** (head) chef, chef de cuisine; **la spécialité du c. aujourd'hui** the chef's special today; **c. pâtissier** chef patissier, pastry chef

5 *Mus* **c. de pupitre** head of section; **c. des chœurs** choirmaster

6 *(en aviron)* **c. de nage** stroke; **être c. de nage** to row stroke

7 *(leader)* leader; **elle a toutes les qualités d'un c.** she has all the qualities of a leader; *Hum* **bravo, c'est toi le c.!** well done, boss!; *Hum* **c. de bande** gang leader; **c. de file** leader; *Péj* **petit c.** *(dans une famille)* domestic tyrant; *(au bureau, à l'usine)* slave driver; **une mentalité de petit c.** a petty-minded attitude to one's subordinates; *Fam* **elle s'est débrouillée comme un c.!** she did really well!

8 *(comme adj)* head *(avant n)*, chief *(avant n)*; **infirmière c.** head nurse; **ingénieur c.** chief engineer

9 *Littéraire & Hum (tête)* head; **opiner du c.** to nod

10 *Jur* **c. d'accusation** charge *or* count (of indictment)

11 *Hér* chief

12 *Belg Univ* **c. de travaux** *Br* ≃ (senior) lecturer, *Am* ≃ assistant professor

NF *Fam (responsable)* **la c.** the boss

▫ **au premier chef** ADV above all, first and foremost; **leur décision me concerne au premier c.** their decision has immediate implications for me

▫ **de mon/son/***etc* **(propre) chef** ADV on my/ their/*etc* own authority *or* initiative; **j'ai agi de mon propre c.** I acted on my own initiative

▫ **en chef** ADJ **commandant en c.** commander-in-chief; **ingénieur en c.** chief engineer ADV **commander en c.** to be commander-in-chief

▫ **chef d'orchestre** NM **1** *Mus* conductor

2 *Fig* organizer, orchestrator

chefaillon [ʃɛfajɔ̃] NM *Fam* little Hitler

chef-d'œuvre [ʃɛdœvr] *(pl* **chefs-d'œuvre***)* NM masterpiece; **un c. de la littérature** a literary masterpiece; **Chefs-d'œuvre en péril** = organization which renovates historic buildings

chefferie [ʃɛfri] NF **1** *(organisation politique)* chiefdom, chieftaincy **2** *Can Pol* party leadership

chef-garde [ʃɛfgard] *(pl* **chefs-gardes***)* NM *Belg Rail* ticket inspector

chef-lieu [ʃɛfljø] *(pl* **chefs-lieux***)* NM *Admin* = in France, administrative centre of a "département", "arrondissement" or "canton"

cheftaine [ʃɛftɛn] NF *(de louveteaux) Br* cubmistress, *Am* den mother; *(chez les jeannettes) Br* Brown Owl, *Am* den mother; *(chez les éclaireuses)* captain

cheik, cheikh [ʃɛk] NM sheik, sheikh

chéilite [keilit] NF *Méd* cheilitis

cheire [ʃɛr] NF *Géol (en Auvergne)* = rough-surfaced solidified lava flow

chéiroptère [keirɔptɛr] *Zool* NM chiropteran

▫ **chéiroptères** NMPL Chiroptera

chélate [kelat] NM **1** *Zool* chela **2** *Chim* chelate

chélateur [kelatœr] *Chim* ADJ M chelated; **agent c.** chelating agent

NM chelating agent

chelem [ʃlɛm] NM *Sport & Cartes* slam; **grand c.** grand slam; **petit c.** small *or* little slam

chéleutoptère [kelɔtɔptɛr] NM *Entom* phasmid, stick *or* leaf insect

chélicérate [keliserat] NM *Zool* chelicerate

chélicère [kelisɛr] NM *Zool* chelicera

chélidoine [kelidwan] NF *Bot* tetterwort, devil's milk, *Spéc* chelidonium; **(grande) c.** greater celandine; **petite c.** lesser celandine, pilewort, figwort

chéloïde [kelɔid] NF *Méd* cheloid, keloid, cheloma

chélonien [kelɔnjɛ̃] *Zool* NM chelonian

▫ **chéloniens** NMPL chelonians, Chelonia

chelou [ʃəlu] ADJ INV *Fam (verlan de* **louche***)* shady, seedy, *Br* dodgy

chemin [ʃəmɛ̃] NM **1** *(allée)* path, lane; **c. creux** sunken lane; **c. de halage** towpath; **c. de ronde** covered way; **c. de terre** rough *or* dirt track; **c. de traverse** path across the fields; *Fig* short cut; **c. vicinal** *ou* **départemental** minor road; **être toujours sur les (quatre) chemins** *ou* **par voies et par chemins** to be always on the move *or* road; *Prov* **tous les chemins mènent à Rome** all roads lead to Rome

2 *(parcours, trajet)* way; **faire** *ou* **abattre du c.** to go a long way; **le c. que nous avons fait** *ou* **abattu** the long way we've come *or* distance we've covered; *aussi Fig* **nous avons beaucoup de c. à faire** we've a long way to go; **nous avons fait la moitié du c. ensemble/à pied** we went half the way together/on foot; **nous avons déjà fait la moitié du c.** we're already halfway there; **il faut compter deux ou trois heures de c.** it takes two or three hours to get there; **on s'est retrouvés à mi-c.** *ou* **à moitié c.** we met halfway; **le c. de la gare** the way to the station; **suivre le c. de la balle** *(au tennis)* to follow the path of the ball; **demandons-lui notre c.** let's ask him/her the way *or* how to get there; **pas de problème, c'est sur mon c.** no problem, it's on my way; **c'est le c. le plus court/long** it's the shortest/ longest way; **le plus court c. d'un point à un autre** the shortest distance between two points; **le c. de la gloire/réussite** the road to glory/ success; **nous avons fait tout le c. à pied/en voiture** we walked/drove all the way; **se frayer** *ou* **s'ouvrir un c. dans la foule** to force one's way through the crowd; **barrer** *ou* **couper le c. à qn** to be in *or* to bar sb's way; *Vieilli* **passer son c.** to go on one's way; **passez votre c.!** on your way!; **prendre le c. de l'exil** to go into exile; *Fig* **prendre des chemins détournés pour faire qch** to use roundabout means in order to do sth; **par un c. détourné** by a roundabout route; *Fig* in a roundabout way; **prendre le c. des écoliers** to go the long way around; **je voudrais des petits-enfants mais ça n'en prend pas le c.** I'd like grandchildren but it doesn't seem to be on the agenda; *Littéraire* **le c. de velours** *ou* **de fleurs** *ou* **fleuri** the primrose path, the easy way

3 *(destinée, progression)* way; **barrer** *ou* **couper le c. à qn** to bar sb's way, to impede sb's progress; **ouvrir/montrer le c.** to open/to lead the way; **il va son c. sans se préoccuper des autres** he goes his own way without worrying about other people; **nos chemins se sont croisés autrefois** we met *or* our paths crossed a long time ago; **faire son c.** *(personne)* to make one's way in life; *(idée)* to gain ground, to catch on; **cet enfant fera du c., croyez-moi!** this child will go far *or* a long way, believe me!; **mettre un obstacle sur le c. de qn** to put an obstacle in sb's way; **se mettre sur le c. de qn** to stand in sb's way; **trouver qn sur son c.** *(ennemi)* to find sb standing in one's way; **que je ne te retrouve pas sur mon c.!** don't let me ever bump into you again!; *Bible* **le c. de Damas** the road to Damascus; *Fig* **trouver son c. de Damas** to see the light; **le bon c.** the right track; **leur affaire est en bon c.** their business is off to a good start; **ne t'arrête pas en si bon c.** don't give up now that you're doing so well; **le droit c.** the straight and narrow

4 *Rel* **c. de croix** Way of the Cross

5 *(napperon)* **c. de table** table runner

6 *Ordinat* path; **c. d'accès** path; **c. d'accès aux données** data path; **c. du courrier électronique** mail path

7 *(en sciences)* **c. critique** critical path

8 *Tech* **c. de roulement** ball race

▫ **chemin faisant** ADV while going along; **nous en avons parlé c. faisant** we talked about it on our way there

▫ **en chemin** ADV on one's way, on the way; **ne t'amuse pas en c.** don't mess around on the way; **se mettre en c.** to set out *or* off

chemin de fer [ʃəmɛ̃dfɛr] *(pl* **chemins de fer***)* NM **1** *Rail Br* railway, *Am* railroad; **voyager en c.** to travel by train; **employé des chemins de fer** *Br* railwayman, rail worker, *Am* railroad man

2 *Cartes* chemin de fer

3 *Typ* page plan

chemineau, -x [ʃəmino] NM *Vieilli* tramp, vagrant, *Am* hobo

cheminée [ʃəmine] NF **1** *(gén)* shaft; *(de maison)* chimney (stack); *(dans un mur)* chimney; *(d'usine)* chimney (stack), smokestack; *(de paquebot)* funnel; **c. d'aération** ventilation shaft

2 *(âtre)* fireplace; *(chambranle)* mantelpiece; **viens te réchauffer près de la c.** come and get warm by the fire *or* fireplace; **un feu dans la c.** a fire in the grate

3 *Géol (d'un volcan)* vent; *(d'un massif)* chimney; **c. des fées** devil's chimney

cheminement [ʃəminmɑ̃] NM **1** (parcours) movement; **le c. des eaux souterraines** the movement of underground water **2** Fig (développement) development, unfolding; **le c. de sa pensée** the development of his/her thought **3** Mil advance (under cover) **4** (en topographie) traverse

cheminer [3] [ʃəmine] VI **1** Littéraire (avancer → marcheur) to walk along; (→ eau, fleuve) to flow; **la caravane chemine dans le désert** the caravan makes its way through the desert; **ils cheminaient avec difficulté à travers bois** they struggled through the woods **2** Fig (progresser → régulièrement) to progress, to develop; (→ lentement) to make slow progress or headway **3** Mil to advance (under cover) **4** (en topographie) to traverse

cheminot [ʃəmino] NM Rail Br railwayman, rail worker, Am railroad man

chemisage [ʃəmizaʒ] NM Tech **1** (d'un projectile) jacketing **2** (d'un conduit, d'un moule) lining

chemise [ʃəmiz] NF **1** (vêtement) shirt; **c. à manches longues/courtes** long-/short-sleeved shirt; **c. américaine** undershirt; **c. de nuit** (de femme) nightgown, nightdress, (d'homme) nightshirt; **en** (bras ou manches de) **c.** in shirtsleeves; **il donnerait jusqu'à sa c.** he'd give the shirt off his back; Fig **ils ne lui ont laissé que sa c.** they took everything but what he stood up in; Fam **je m'en fiche** ou **soucie** or **moque comme de ma première c.** I couldn't care less about it; **perdre au jeu jusqu'à sa dernière c.** to gamble one's last Br penny or Am cent away **2** Hist **Chemises brunes** Brownshirts; **Chemises noires** Blackshirts; **Chemises rouges** Redshirts **3** (de carton) folder **4** Tech (enveloppe → intérieure) lining; (→ extérieure) jacket; (→ d'un mur) facing; Aut **c. flottante/humide/sèche** slip/wet/dry liner

chemiser [3] [ʃəmize] VT **1** Tech (intérieurement) to line; (extérieurement) to jacket **2** Culin to coat with aspic jelly

chemiserie [ʃəmizri] NF **1** (fabrique) shirt factory **2** (boutique) Br men's outfitter's, Am haberdasher's **3** (industrie) shirt trade

chemisette [ʃəmizɛt] NF (pour femme) short-sleeved blouse; (pour homme, pour enfant) short-sleeved shirt

chemisier, -ère [ʃəmizje, -ɛr] NM,F (fabricant) Br shirtmaker, Am haberdasher; (marchand) Br men's outfitter, Am haberdasher ▪ NM blouse

chémocepteur, -trice [kemosɛptœr, -tris], **chémorécepteur, -trice** [kemoreseptœr, -tris] Biol ADJ chemoreceptive ▪ NM chemoreceptor

chênaie [ʃɛnɛ] NF stand of oak trees

chenal, -aux [ʃənal, -o] NM **1** (canal → dans les terres) channel; (→ dans un port) fairway, channel **2** Géol (sous la mer) trench **3** (de moulin) millrace **4** Métal **c. de coulée** runner

chenapan [ʃənapɑ̃] NM Hum rascal, rogue, scoundrel

chenau, -x [ʃəno] NF Suisse gutter (on a roof)

chêne [ʃɛn] NM **1** Bot oak; **c. blanc** white oak; **c. chevelu, c. lombard** Turkey oak; **c. des marais** pin oak; **c. pédonculé** English or common oak; **c. pubescent** downy oak; **c. rouge (d'Amérique)** red oak; **c. rouvre, c. sessile** durmast; **c. vert** holm oak, ilex; **fort** ou **solide comme un c.** as strong as an ox **2** Menuis (bois) oak; **une table en c. massif** a solid oak table

chéneau, -x [ʃeno] NM gutter (on a roof)

chêne-liège [ʃɛnljɛʒ] (pl **chênes-lièges**) NM Bot cork oak

chenet [ʃənɛ] NM andiron, firedog

chènevière [ʃɛnvjɛr] NF hemp field

chènevis [ʃɛnvi] NM hempseed

Chengdu [ʃɛ̃du] NM Chengdu

cheni, chenil[1] [ʃəni] NM Suisse Fam **1** (balayures) sweepings▪; (débris, déchets) Br rubbish, Am garbage **2** (désordre) mess, shambles **3** (objets sans valeur) junk, stuff

chenil[2] [ʃənil, ʃəni] NM **1** (établissement → pour la reproduction) breeding kennels; (→ pour la garde) boarding kennels; (→ pour le dressage) training kennels **2** Fig (logement malpropre) hovel

chenille [ʃənij] NF **1** Entom caterpillar; **c. arpenteuse** looper, measuring worm; **c. du bombyx** silk worm; **c. processionnaire** processionary caterpillar **2** Tech caterpillar; **véhicule à chenilles** tracked vehicle **3** Tex chenille

chenillé, -e [ʃənije] ADJ (engin, véhicule) tracked

chenillette [ʃənijɛt] NF Mil small tracked vehicle; (pour neige) snowmobile

chenis, chenit [ʃni] = **cheni**

chénopode [kenopɔd] NM Bot goosefoot, Spéc chenopodium

chénopodiacée [kenopɔdjase] Bot NM goosefoot, Spéc chenopodium
　❑ **chénopodiacées** NMPL Chenopodiaceae

chénopodium [kenopɔdjɔm] = **chénopode**

chenu, -e [ʃəny] ADJ Littéraire **1** (vieillard) hoary **2** (arbre) bald or leafless (with age), Spéc glabrous

cheptel [ʃɛptɛl] NM **1** (bétail) stock, livestock; **avoir un c. de 1000 têtes** to have 1,000 head of cattle; **le c. ovin de la région** the sheep population of the region; **le c. bovin de la France** France's national herd **2** Jur **c. (vif)** livestock; **c. mort** farm equipment

chèque [ʃɛk] NM **1** Fin & Banque Br cheque, Am check; **faire** ou **remplir un c.** to write (out) or make out a cheque; **faire un c. de 100 euros à qn** to write sb a cheque for 100 euros; **tirer/toucher un c.** to draw/to cash a cheque; **établir** ou **libeller un c. à l'ordre de qn** to make a cheque out to sb; **faire opposition à un c.** to stop a cheque; **payer** ou **régler par c.** to pay by cheque; **refuser d'honorer un c.** to refer a cheque to drawer; **remettre** ou **déposer un c. à la banque** to pay a cheque into the bank; **c. bancaire** cheque; **c. de banque** banker's cheque, banker's draft, Am cashier's check; **c. barré** crossed cheque; **c. en blanc** blank cheque; Fig **donner un c. en blanc à qn** to give sb carte blanche; Fam **c. en bois** Br dud cheque, Am bad check; **c. certifié** certified cheque; **c. en circulation** outstanding cheque; **c. hors-place** = cheque drawn on a bank in a different "département" from the bank in which it is cashed; **c. non barré** uncrossed cheque; **c. à ordre** cheque to order; **c. ouvert** open cheque; **c. périmé** out-of-date cheque; **c. au porteur** bearer cheque, cheque made payable to bearer; **c. postal** = cheque drawn on the postal banking system, Br ≃ Giro (cheque); **c. postdaté** post-dated cheque; **c. sans provision** bad cheque; **il a fait un c. sans provision** his cheque bounced; **c. de voyage** traveller's cheque
　2 (bon, coupon) **un c. d'une valeur de 40 euros** a gift token to the value of 40 euros; **c. de caisse** credit voucher; **c. emploi-service** = special cheque used to pay casual workers such as part-time cleaners, babysitters etc

chèque-cadeau [ʃɛkkado] (pl **chèques-cadeaux**) NM Br gift token, gift voucher, Am gift certificate; **un c. d'une valeur de 40 euros** a gift Br token or voucher or Am certificate to the value of 40 euros

Chèque-Déjeuner® [ʃɛkdeʒœne] (pl **Chèques-Déjeuners**) NM Br ≃ luncheon voucher, Am ≃ meal ticket

chèque-dividende [ʃɛkdividɑ̃d] (pl **chèques-dividende**) NM Fin dividend warrant

chèque-essence [ʃɛkesɑ̃s] (pl **chèques-essence**) NM Br petrol or Am gas coupon or voucher

chèque-livre [ʃɛklivr] (pl **chèques-livre**) NM book token

chéquer [tʃɛke] = **checker**

chèque-repas [ʃɛkrəpa] (pl **chèques-repas**) NM Br ≃ luncheon voucher, Am ≃ meal ticket

Chèque-Restaurant® [ʃɛkrɛstorɑ̃] (pl **Chèques-Restaurants**) NM Br ≃ luncheon voucher, Am ≃ meal ticket

chèque-service [ʃɛksɛrvis] (pl **chèques-service**) NM = payment method using special cheques designed to simplify social security and tax arrangements for employers of home helps, whereby the employer's social security contribution is deducted automatically from their bank account

chéquier [ʃekje] NM Br chequebook, Am checkbook

Cher [ʃɛr] NM **le C.** Cher

[ʃɛr] ADJ **1** (aimé) dear; **elle m'est plus chère qu'une sœur** she's dearer to me than a sister; **ceux qui vous sont chers** your loved ones, the ones you love; **un être c.** a loved one
　2 (dans des formules de politesse) dear; **c. Monsieur, chère Madame** dear Sir, dear Madam; **bonjour, chère Madame** hello, my dear lady; **mon c. ami** my dear friend; **mes bien** ou **très chers amis** dearest friends; **bien chers tous** dearest friends; Hum ou Ironique **le c. homme n'a pas compris** the dear man didn't understand; **cette chère Marie!** dear old Marie!; Rel **mes bien** ou **très chers frères** dearly beloved brethren
　3 (précieux) dear, beloved; **il a retrouvé sa chère maison/son c. bureau** he's back in his beloved house/office; Hum **il est retourné à ses chères études** he's gone back to his ivory tower or to his beloved books; **la formule si chère aux hommes politiques** the phrase beloved of politicians, that favourite phrase of politicians; **mon souhait le plus c.** my dearest or most devout wish
　4 (onéreux) expensive, Br dear; **la vie est chère en ville** it's expensive living in town, the cost of living is high in town(s); **c'est plus c.** it's more expensive or Br dearer; **c'est moins c.** it's cheaper or less expensive; **un petit restaurant pas c.** an inexpensive little restaurant; **voilà un dîner pas c.!** now this is a cheap dinner!; **ne va pas chez Pablet, c'est trop c.** don't go to Pablet's, his prices are too high
　▪ NM,F **mon c.** my dear (fellow); **ma chère** my dear (girl); **ah ma chère! quel plaisir de vous voir!** how nice to see you, my dear!
　▪ ADV **1** Com **coûter c.** to cost a lot, to be expensive; **payer qch c./trop c.** to pay a high price/too much for sth; **est-ce que ça te revient c.?** does it cost you a lot?; **ça me revient trop c.** it's too expensive for me, I can't afford it; Fam **prendre c.** to charge a lot; **il te prend c.?** does he charge you a lot?; **il prend trop c.** he charges too much; **tu ne prends pas assez c.** you don't charge enough; **il vaut c.** (bijou de famille) it's valuable or worth a lot; (article en magasin) it's expensive; Fam **je l'ai eu pour pas c.** I didn't pay much for it▪, I got it cheap; Fam **elle vend c.** her prices are high; **ce n'est pas vendu assez c.** it's underpriced
　2 (locutions) **je donnerais c. pour le savoir** I'd give anything to know; **je ne donne pas c. de sa vie** I wouldn't give much for his/her chances of survival; **il ne vaut pas c.** he's a good-for-nothing; **et toi, tu ne vaux pas plus c.** and you're no better

chérant, -e [ʃerɑ̃, -ɑ̃t] ADJ Can pricey, expensive

cherche-midi [ʃɛrʃmidi] NM INV Entom pyrrhocoris

[3] [ʃɛrʃe]

> **VT** to look for **1, 3–5** ▪ to search for **1, 2, 4** ▪ to try to find **2** ▪ to fetch, to get, to pick up **6**
> **VPR** to look for each other **1** ▪ to find oneself **2**

VT 1 (dans l'espace) to look for, to search for; **que cherches-tu?** what are you looking for?; **je l'ai cherché partout** I searched or looked for it high and low, I hunted for it everywhere; **cherche les clefs dans tes poches** look in your pockets for the keys; **c. un mot dans un dictionnaire** to look up a word in a dictionary; **c. qn du regard** ou **des yeux** to look around for sb; **c. qn/qch à tâtons** to fumble or to grope for sb/sth; **il cherchait son enfant à tâtons dans le noir** he groped around in the dark trying to find his child; Fam **c. la petite bête** to split hairs; Fam **c. des poux dans la tête de qn** to try and pick a fight with sb; **cherchez la femme** cherchez la femme
　2 (mentalement) to try to find, to search for; **c. une solution** to try to find a solution; **je cherche son nom** I'm trying to think of or remember his/her name; **c. ses mots** to search for words; Fam **c. des crosses** ou **des histoires à qn** to try and cause trouble for sb; **c. chicane** ou **querelle à qn** to try and pick a quarrel with sb; Fam **c. midi à quatorze heures** to look for complications

che-che

(where there are none); **pas besoin de c. midi à quatorze heures pour expliquer son départ** no need to look too far to understand why he/she left

3 *(essayer de se procurer)* to look for, to hunt for; **je cherche cette édition rare depuis longtemps** I've been hunting for this rare edition for years; **c. du travail** to look for work, to be job-hunting; **c. une maison** to look for a house, to be house-hunting; **il faut vite c. du secours** you must get help quickly; **il est parti c. fortune à l'étranger** he went abroad to look for fame and fortune; **c. refuge auprès de qn** to seek refuge with sb; *Vieilli* **c. femme** to look for a wife

4 *(aspirer à → tranquillité, inspiration)* to look for, to search for, to seek (after); **il ne cherche que son intérêt** he thinks only of his own interests

5 *Fam (provoquer)* to look for; **tu l'as bien cherché!** you asked for it!; **tu me cherches, là?** do you want a fight?; **si tu me cherches, tu vas me trouver!** if you're looking for trouble, you've come to the right place!, if you're looking for a fight, you'll get one!; **toujours à c. la bagarre!** always looking *or* spoiling for a fight!

6 *(avec des verbes de mouvement)* **aller c. qn/qch** to fetch sb/sth; **aller c. les enfants à l'école** to pick the children up from school; **aller c. qn à l'aéroport** to go and pick sb up at the airport; **allez me c. le directeur** *(client mécontent)* I'd like to speak to the manager; **aller c. du secours** to go for help, to get help; **envoyer c. qn/qch** to send for sb/sth; **monte/descends c. la valise** go up/down and fetch the suitcase; **viens me c. à 17 heures** come for me at 5 o'clock; *Fig* **que vas-tu c. là?** what on earth are you going on about?; **mais qu'est-ce que tu vas encore c., je n'ai rien dit de mal** now what are you thinking of? I didn't mean anything bad; **où va-t-il donc c. tout ça?** where on earth does he get that from?; **où as-tu été c. que j'avais accepté?** what made you think I said yes?; *Fam* **ça va bien c. dans les 60 euros** it's worth at least 60 euros; *Fam* **ça peut aller c. jusqu'à dix ans de prison** it could get you up to ten years in prison; *Fam* **ça va c. loin, cette histoire** this is a bad business; *Fam* **injures à magistrat, ça peut aller c. loin!** insulting a magistrate can get you into serious trouble!

USAGE ABSOLU **tu donnes ta langue au chat? – attends, je cherche** give up? – wait, I'm still thinking *or* trying to think; **cherche!** *(à un chien)* fetch!; *Bible* **cherchez et vous trouverez** seek and ye shall find

◻ **chercher à** VT IND to try to, to attempt to, *Sout* to seek to; **je ne cherche qu'à t'aider** I'm only trying to help you; **c. à plaire** to aim to please; *Fam* **cherche pas à comprendre** don't even try to understand

◻ **chercher après** VT IND *Fam* to look for, to be *or* to chase after; **je cherche encore après ces maudites lunettes!** I'm still after those damn glasses!

▶**se chercher** VPR **1** *(emploi réciproque)* to look for each other; **ils se sont cherchés pendant longtemps** they spent a long time looking for each other

2 *(emploi réfléchi)* to find oneself; **il se cherche** he's trying to find himself

---

chercheur, -euse [ʃɛrʃœr, -øz] ADJ *(esprit, mentalité)* inquiring

NM,F **1** *Univ* researcher, research worker; **travailler comme c.** to be a researcher, to do research **2** *(aventurier)* **un c. de trésor** a treasure seeker; **c. d'or** gold digger

NM *Astron* **c. de comètes** finder; **c. de fuites** gas leak detector

chère[1] [ʃɛr] *voir* **cher**

chère[2] NF *Littéraire ou Hum* food, fare; **la c. y est excellente** the food there is superb; **faire bonne c.** to eat well; **aimer la bonne c.** to be a lover of good food

chèrement [ʃɛrmɑ̃] ADV **1** *(à un prix élevé)* dearly, at great cost; **la victoire fut c. payée** the victory was won at great cost; **il a payé c. sa liberté** his freedom cost him dearly, he paid a high price

for his freedom **2** *Littéraire (tendrement)* dearly, fondly; **aimer c. qn** to love sb dearly

chergui [ʃɛrgi] NM = east wind in Morocco

chéri, -e [ʃeri] ADJ darling, dear, *Sout* beloved; **mon gros bébé c.** my sweet darling baby; **à notre grand-mère chérie** *(au cimetière)* to our beloved grandmother

NM,F **1** *(en appellatif)* darling, honey; **qu'y a-t-il, c.?** what's the matter, darling?; **mon c., je te l'ai dit cent fois** darling, I've already told you a hundred times

2 *(personne préférée)* **il a toujours été le c. de ses parents** he was always the darling of the family; *Hum* **voilà le c. de ces dames** here comes the ladykiller

3 *Fam (amant)* boyfriend, *f* girlfriend; **sa chérie l'a larguée** his girlfriend ditched him

chérif [ʃerif] NM *(prince arabe)* sherif, sharif

chérifien, -enne [ʃerifjɛ̃, -ɛn] ADJ **1** *(d'un chérif)* sharifian **2** *(du Maroc)* Moroccan

chérimole [ʃerimɔl] NF *Bot Br* custard apple, *Am* cherimoya

chérimolier [ʃerimɔlje] NM *Bot Br* custard apple tree, *Am* cherimoya tree

chérir [32] [ʃerir] VT *Littéraire (aimer → personne)* to cherish, to love (dearly); *(→ démocratie, liberté)* to cherish; *(→ mémoire, souvenir)* to cherish, to treasure; **chéri des dieux** beloved of the gods

chérissable [ʃerisabl] ADJ cherishable

chermes, chermès [kɛrmɛs] NM *Entom* chermes, pine gall louse

chérot [ʃero] *Fam* ADJ INV pricey, on the pricey side

ADV **il vend plutôt c.!** his prices are on the stiff side!

cherra *etc voir* **choir**

cherry [ʃeri] *(pl* **cherrys** *ou* **cherries)** NM cherry brandy

cherté [ʃɛrte] NF **la c. des fraises** the high price of strawberries; **la c. de la vie** the high cost of living

Chérubin [ʃerybɛ̃] NPR Cherubino

chérubin [ʃerybɛ̃] NM **1** *Rel* cherub **2** *(enfant)* cherub

chester [ʃɛstɛr] NM Cheshire cheese

chétif, -ive [ʃetif, -iv] ADJ **1** *(peu robuste)* sickly, puny **2** *Bot* stunted **3** *Littéraire (peu riche → récolte)* meagre, poor; *(→ existence)* poor, wretched

chétognathe [ketɔɲat] *Zool* NM chaetognath
◻ **chétognathes** NMPL Chaetognatha

chétopode [ketopɔd] NM *Zool* bristleworm

chevaine [ʃəvɛn] NM *Ich* chub

cheval, -aux [ʃəval, -o] NM **1** *(animal)* horse; **c. d'attelage** carthorse, plough horse; **c. de bât** packhorse; *Fig* **c. de bataille** hobbyhorse, pet subject; **c. de chasse** hunter; **c. de cirque** circus horse; **c. de course** racehorse; **c. de labour** plough horse; **c. de manège** school horse; **c. marin** *(hippocampe)* sea horse; **c. de poste** *ou* **relais** posthorse; **c. de Przewalski** *ou* **Prjevalski** Przewalski's horse; **c. pur sang** thoroughbred *(horse)*; **c. de retour** *(récidiviste)* recidivist; **c. de selle** saddle horse; **c. de trait** draught horse; **changer** *ou* **échanger** *ou* **troquer son c. borgne pour un aveugle** to jump from the frying pan into the fire; **travailler comme un c.** to work like a dog *or* slave; *Prov* **à c. donné on ne regarde pas la bouche** don't look a gift horse in the mouth; *Fig* **monter sur ses grands chevaux** to get on one's high horse; **ce n'est pas un** *ou* **le mauvais c.** he's not a bad guy *or* sort; **ça ne se trouve pas sous le pas** *ou* **sabot d'un c.** it doesn't grow on trees

2 *Équitation* (horseback) riding; **elle aime beaucoup le c.** she loves riding; **faire du c.** to ride, to go riding

3 *(loisirs)* **c. à bascule** rocking horse; **c. de bois** wooden horse; **faire un tour sur les chevaux de bois** to go on the roundabout *or* carousel; **jouer aux petits chevaux** ≃ to play ludo

4 *Aut & Admin* **c. fiscal** horsepower *(for tax purposes)*; *Fam* **une voiture de 20 chevaux, une 20 chevaux** a 20 horsepower car

5 *Mil* **c. de frise** cheval-de-frise

6 *Antiq* **le c. de Troie** the Trojan horse

7 *(viande)* horsemeat

8 *Fam Péj (femme)* **grand c.** great horse of a woman

◻ **à cheval** ADV **1** *Équitation* on horseback; **aller à c.** to ride; **aller au village à c.** to ride to the village, to go to the village on horseback; **traverser une rivière à c.** to ride across a river; **se tenir bien/mal à c.** to have a good/poor seat, to sit a horse well/badly

2 *(à califourchon)* **être à c. sur une chaise** to be sitting astride a chair; **l'étang est à c. sur deux propriétés** the pond straddles two properties; **mon congé est à c. sur février et mars** my period of leave starts in February and ends in March

3 *Fam (pointilleux)* **être à c. sur** to be particular about; **il est très à c. sur les principes** he is a stickler for principles; **ils sont très à c. sur la tenue** they're very particular about dress ADJ **gendarme à c.** mounted policeman; **une promenade à c.** a ride; **faire une promenade à c.** to go for a ride, to go horseriding

◻ **de cheval** ADJ **1** *Culin* horse *(avant n)*, horse-meat *(avant n)*

2 *Fam (fort)* **fièvre de c.** raging fever; **remède de c.** drastic remedy

3 *Péj (dents)* horsey, horselike

cheval-d'arçons [ʃəvaldarsɔ̃] NM INV *Gym* vaulting horse

chevalement [ʃəvalmɑ̃] NM **1** *Constr* shoring **2** *Mines* (pit) head frame, gallows frame

chevaler [3] [ʃəvale] VT *Constr* to shore up

chevaleresque [ʃəvalrɛsk] ADJ **1** *(généreux)* chivalrous; **agir de façon c.** to behave like a gentleman **2** *(des chevaliers)* **l'honneur/le devoir c.** a knight's honour/duty

chevalerie [ʃəvalri] NF **1** *(ordre)* knighthood **2** *(institution)* chivalry; *Littérature* **roman de c.** romance of chivalry

chevalet [ʃəvalɛ] NM **1** *(d'un peintre)* easel **2** *(support)* stand, trestle; **c. de scieur** sawbench, sawhorse **3** *Mus* bridge **4** *Hist (de torture)* rack

chevalier [ʃəvalje] NM **1** *Hist* knight; **il a été fait c.** he was knighted; **c. errant** knight-errant; **c. d'industrie** wheeler-dealer; **c. servant** *(devoted)* escort; *Littérature* **le c. de la Triste Figure** the Knight of the Sorrowful Countenance; **les chevaliers de Colomb** the Knights of Columbus *(Roman Catholic organization)*; **les chevaliers de la Table ronde** the Knights of the Round Table

2 *(grade)* **c. de la Légion d'honneur** chevalier of the Legion of Honour

3 *Orn (Tringa hypoleucos)* sandpiper; *(Tringa nebularia)* greenshank; **c. combattant** ruff; **c. cul-blanc** green sandpiper; **c. gambette** redshank; **c. grivelé** spotted sandpiper; **c. guignette** common sandpiper; **c. sylvain** wood sandpiper

4 *Bourse* **c. blanc** white knight; **c. gris** grey knight; **c. noir** black knight

chevalière [ʃəvaljɛr] NF signet ring

chevalin, -e [ʃəvalɛ̃, -in] ADJ **1** *(race)* equine **2** *(air, allure, visage)* horsey, horselike

cheval-vapeur [ʃəvalvapœr] *(pl* **chevaux-vapeur** [ʃəvovapœr]) NM horsepower

chevauchant, -e [ʃəvoʃɑ̃, -ɑ̃t] ADJ overlapping

chevauchée [ʃəvoʃe] NF **1** *(course à cheval)* ride; **la c. des Valkyries** the ride of the Valkyries **2** *(personne)* cavalcade

'La Chevauchée fantastique' Ford 'Stagecoach'

chevauchement [ʃəvoʃmɑ̃] NM **1** *(superposition)* overlap, overlapping; **pour éviter tout c. dans l'emploi du temps des élèves** to avoid clashes between subjects in the students' timetable **2** *Constr* spanning **3** *Géol* thrust fault **4** *Typ* falling *or* dropping out of place

chevaucher [3] [ʃəvoʃe] VT **1** *(monter sur → cheval, moto, balai)* to sit astride; *(→ chaise)* to sit astride, to straddle; *(→ vague)* to ride **2** *(recouvrir en partie)* to overlap

VI **1** *(se recouvrir en partie)* to overlap **2** *Typ* to fall *or* drop out of place **3** *Littérature* to ride (a horse)

▶**se chevaucher** VPR **1** *(être superposé → dents)* to grow into each other; *(→ tuiles)* to overlap; **mon cours et le sien se chevauchent** my lesson

overlaps with his/hers **2** *Géol* to overthrust

chevaucheur [ʃəvoʃœr] **NM** *Littéraire* horseman, rider; **c. de ressac** surf-rider

chevau-léger [ʃəvoleʒe] *(pl* **chevau-légers***)* **NM** *Hist & Mil* **1** *(soldat)* light horseman, *Br* ≃ member of the Household Cavalry **2** *(corps)* **les chevau-légers** light horse, *Br* ≃ Household Cavalry

chevêche [ʃəvɛʃ] **NF** *Orn* little owl

chevêchette [ʃəvɛʃɛt] **NF** *Orn* pygmy owl

chevelu, -e [ʃəvly] **ADJ 1** *(ayant des cheveux)* hairy **2** *(à chevelure abondante)* long-haired **3** *Bot* comose, comate

NM,F *Péj (personne)* long-haired man, *f* woman

NM *Bot* root-hairs

chevelure [ʃəvlyr] **NF 1** *(cheveux)* hair; **son abondante c.** his/her thick hair; **une femme à la c. rousse/blonde** a red-haired/blonde woman **2** *Fig* **la c. des saules** the verdure of the willows **3** *Astron* tail

chevenne, chevesne [ʃəvɛn] = **chevaine**

chevet [ʃəvɛ] **NM 1** *(d'un lit)* bedhead **2** *Archit* chevet

❑ **au chevet de PRÉP** at the bedside of

❑ **de chevet ADJ** bedside *(avant n)*

'Notes de chevet' *Shōnagon, Greenaway* 'The Pillow Book'

chevêtre [ʃəvɛtr] **NM** *Constr* trimmer joist *or* beam

cheveu, -x [ʃəvø] **NM 1** *(poil)* hair; **ses cheveux** his/her hair; **avoir les cheveux noirs/longs/frisés** to have black/long/curly hair; **aux cheveux blonds/noirs/frisés** blond-/black-/curly-haired; **une fille aux cheveux courts** a girl with short hair, a short-haired girl; **avoir les cheveux raides** to have straight hair; **les cheveux en désordre** *ou* **bataille** with unkempt *or* tousled hair; **(les) cheveux au vent** with his/her/*etc* hair blowing freely in the wind; **un c. blanc** a grey hair; **avoir les cheveux blancs** to have grey hair; **avoir des cheveux blancs** to have some grey hairs; **avoir le c. rare** to be thinning (on top); **s'il touche à un seul c. de ma femme...** if he dares touch a hair on my wife's head...; *Vieilli* **en cheveux** bare-headed; **une histoire à faire dresser les cheveux sur la tête** a story that makes your hair stand on end; **le coup l'a manqué d'un c.** the blow missed him by a hair's breadth; **il s'en est fallu d'un c. qu'on y reste** we missed death by a hair's breadth; **il s'en est fallu d'un c. qu'il ne soit renversé par une voiture** he very nearly got run over; **avoir un c. sur la langue** to (have a) lisp; **se faire des cheveux (blancs)** to worry oneself sick; **venir** *ou* **arriver comme un c. sur la soupe** to come at the wrong time; **sa question est tombée comme un c. sur la soupe** his/her question couldn't have come at a worse time; **saisir une occasion aux cheveux** to seize an opportunity; **c'est un peu tiré par les cheveux** it's a bit far-fetched; **se prendre aux cheveux** to come to blows; *Fam* **avoir mal aux cheveux** to have a hangover

2 *(coiffure)* hairstyle; **tu aimes mes cheveux comme ça?** how do you like my haircut *or* hairstyle?

❑ **à cheveux ADJ** hair *(avant n)*

❑ **à un cheveu de PRÉP** within a hair's breadth of

❑ **à un cheveu près ADV** by a hair's breadth; **à un c. près, je ratais mon train** I caught my train by a hair's breadth

❑ **cheveux d'ange NMPL 1** *(guirlande)* tinsel garland

2 *Culin* vermicelli

cheveu-de-Vénus [ʃəvødəvenys] *(pl* **cheveux-de-Vénus***)* **NM** *Bot* maidenhair (fern)

chevillard [ʃəvijar] **NM** wholesale butcher

cheville [ʃəvij] **NF 1** *Anat* ankle; **ils avaient de la boue jusqu'aux chevilles, la boue leur arrivait aux chevilles** they were ankle-deep in mud, the mud came up to their ankles; *Fig* **son fils ne lui arrive pas à la c.** his/her son's hardly in the same league as him/her; **personne ne lui arrive à la c.** he's head and shoulders above everybody else; *Fam Péj* **tu as les chevilles qui enflent** you're getting too big for your boots *or Am* britches

2 *Menuis (pour visser)* plug; *(pour boucher)* dowel; **c. ouvrière** *(d'un véhicule)* kingpin; *Fig* **il est la c. ouvrière du mouvement** he's the mainspring *or* kingpin of the movement

3 *Mus* peg

4 *Littérature* cheville, expletive

5 *(de boucher)* hook; **vente à la c.** wholesale butchery trade

❑ **en cheville ADV être en c. avec qn** to be in cahoots with sb; **ils sont en c. tous les deux** they're in it together, they're in cahoots

cheviller [3] [ʃəvije] **VT 1** *Menuis* to peg; **l'armoire est chevillée** the wardrobe is pegged together; *Fig* **avoir l'âme chevillée au corps** to hang on grimly to life **2** *Littérature* **c. un vers** to pad *or* to tag a line of verse

chevillette [ʃəvijɛt] **NF** *Menuis (clé)* (wooden) peg

chevillier [ʃəvilje] **NM** *Mus* peg-box

chevillière [ʃəviljɛr] **NF** *Suisse* tape measure

cheviotte [ʃəvjɔt] **NF** *Tex* Cheviot wool

chèvre [ʃɛvr] **NF 1** *(animal → mâle)* goat, billy-goat; *(→ femelle)* goat, she-goat, nanny-goat; **c. aegagre** wild goat, bezoar goat; **c. des montagnes rocheuses** Rocky Mountain goat; **c. sauvage** wild goat; **fromage/lait de c.** goat's cheese/milk; *Fam* **devenir c.** to go up the wall *or* round the bend; *Fam* **rendre qn c.** to drive sb up the wall *or* round the bend; **la c. de M. Seguin** = the best known of Daudet's stories in 'Les Lettres de mon moulin' (1866), familiar to generations of schoolchildren **2** *(treuil)* hoist; *(chevalet)* trestle

NM goat's cheese

chevreau, -x [ʃəvro] **NM 1** *Zool* kid **2** *(peau)* kid; **des gants de c.** kid gloves

chèvrefeuille [ʃɛvrəfœj] **NM** *Bot* honeysuckle

chevrer [19] [ʃəvre] **VI** *Suisse Fam* **faire c. qn** to drive sb up the wall *or* round the bend

chevrette [ʃəvrɛt] **NF 1** *Zool (chèvre)* kid, young nanny-goat *or* she-goat; *(femelle du chevreuil)* doe; *(crevette)* shrimp **2** *(fourrure)* goatskin **3** *(trépied)* tripod

chevreuil [ʃəvrœj] **NM 1** *Zool* roe deer **2** *Culin* venison

chevrier, -ère [ʃəvrije, -ɛr] **NM,F** goatherd

NM chevrier bean

chevrillard [ʃəvrijar] **NM** *Chasse* male kid, roe-buck in its first year

chevron [ʃəvrɔ̃] **NM 1** *Constr* rafter **2** *Mil* chevron, V-shaped stripe **3** *(motif)* chevron; **veste à chevrons** *(petits)* herringbone jacket; *(grands)* chevron-patterned jacket **4** *Hér* chevron

chevronné, -e [ʃəvrɔne] **ADJ** seasoned, experienced, practised; **c'est un grimpeur c.** he's an old hand at climbing *or* a seasoned climber

chevrotage [ʃəvrɔtaʒ] **NM** *Zool* kidding

chevrotain [ʃəvrɔtɛ̃] **NM** *Zool* chevrotain, mouse deer; **c. aquatique** water chevrotain; **c. porte-musc** musk deer

chevrotant, -e [ʃəvrɔtɑ̃, -ɑ̃t] **ADJ** *(voix)* quavering

chevrotement [ʃəvrɔtmɑ̃] **NM** quavering; **avec des chevrotements dans la voix** with a quaver *or* a tremor in one's voice, in a quavering *or* trembling voice

chevroter [3] [ʃəvrɔte] **VI 1** *(voix)* to quaver; *(personne → en parlant)* to speak in a quavering voice, to quaver; *(→ en chantant)* to sing in a quavering voice, to quaver **2** *(chèvre)* to kid

chevrotin [ʃəvrɔtɛ̃] **NM 1** *Zool* fawn *(of roe deer)* **2** *Culin (fromage)* goat's cheese

chevrotine [ʃəvrɔtin] **NF** *Chasse* piece of buck-shot; **de la c., des chevrotines** buckshot

chewing-gum [ʃwingɔm] *(pl* **chewing-gums***)* **NM** gum, chewing-gum; **un c.** a piece of gum

Cheyenne [ʃejɛn] **NMF** Cheyenne; **les Cheyennes** the Cheyenne

cheyletiellose [ʃɛltjɛloz] **NF** *Vét* cheyletiellosis

CHEZ [ʃe] **PRÉP 1** *(dans la demeure de)* **je rentre c. moi** I'm going home; **c. soi** at home; **rentrer c. soi** to go home; **rester c. soi** to stay at home *or* in; **est-elle c. elle en ce moment?** is she at home *or* in at the moment?; **il habite c. moi en ce moment** he's living with me *or* he's staying at my place at the moment; **elle l'a raccompagné c. lui** *(à pied)* she walked him home; *(en voiture)* she gave him a lift home; **je vais c. ma sœur/Nadine** I'm going to my sister's (house)/Nadine's (house); **puis-je venir c. vous?** may I come over (to your place)?; **les amis c. qui j'étais ce week-end** the friends I stayed with this weekend; **c'est juste à côté de c. lui** it's just round the corner from his place; **derrière c. moi** behind my house (*or Br* flat *or Am* apartment/*etc*); **ça s'est passé pas loin de/devant c. nous** it happened not far from/right outside where we live; **elle arrive de c. lui** she's just come from his place; **on pourrait passer c. elle** we could drop by at her place *or* drop in on her; **c. M. Durand** *(dans une adresse)* care of Mr Durand; **il se sent partout c. lui** he's at home everywhere; **fais comme c. toi** make yourself at home; *Ironique* do make yourself at home, won't you; **c. nous** *(dans ma famille)* in my *or* our family; *(dans mon pays)* in my *or* our country; **c. nous, on ne fait pas de manières** we don't stand on ceremony in our family; **c. moi, ma mère disait toujours...** in my family *or* at home, my mother always used to say...; **chacun c. soi** everyone should look after his own affairs; **c'est une coutume/un accent bien de c. nous** it's a typical local custom/accent; **un bon vin bien de c. nous** one of our good local wines; *Hum* **une bonne tarte aux pommes bien de c. nous** a good old apple pie like mother used to make

2 *(dans un magasin, dans une société etc)* **aller c. le coiffeur/le médecin** to go to the hairdresser's/the doctor's; **il est c. le coiffeur/le médecin** he's at the hairdresser('s)/the doctor('s); **acheter qch c. l'épicier** to buy sth at the grocer's; **je l'ai acheté c. Denver & Smith** I bought it from Denver & Smith; **dîner c. Maxim's** to dine at Maxim's; **une robe de c. Dior** a Dior dress, a dress designed by Dior; **il a travaillé c. IBM** he worked at *or* for IBM; **il a fait ses études c. les jésuites** he studied with the Jesuits *or* at a Jesuit school

3 *(dans un pays, dans un groupe)* **c. les Russes** in Russia; **c'est une coutume c. les Suédois** it's a Swedish custom; **c. les Grecs** in Ancient Greece; **c. les Vikings** during the Viking period; **cette expression est courante c. les jeunes** this expression is widely used among young people; **c. l'homme/la femme** in men/women; **c'est fréquent c. les mammifères** it's often the case in *or* with mammals

4 *(d'une personne)* **ce qui me gêne c. lui, c'est...** the problem with him is...; **c'est quand même curieux, c. un homme de son âge** it is strange, for *or* in a man of his age; **c'est devenu une habitude c. elle** it's become a habit with her; **il y a quelque chose que j'apprécie particulièrement c. eux, c'est leur générosité** something I particularly like about them is their generosity

5 *(dans l'œuvre de)* in; **c. Molière/Giotto** in Molière's/Giotto's work; **c'est souvent le cas c. Marivaux** it's often the case with *or* in Marivaux

6 *Fam* **côté humour, ce film, c'est vraiment lourd de c. lourd** the humour in this movie *or Br* film is SO in your face; **son nouveau petit copain, c'est le style blaireau de c. blaireau** her new boyfriend is a complete and total jerk; **il est nul ton lecteur de CD, le son est carrément pourri de c. pourri!** your CD player's useless, the sound's as crap as you can get!

Allusion

Chez de chez

This very generative colloquial expression imitates the wording used in French perfume advertisements, which give the name of the perfume followed by the name of the perfume house, for example "Coco, de chez Chanel". It indicates that whatever is being talked about possesses the quality discussed to an utmost degree, as in **Son costume est ringard de chez ringard** ("His suit is really, really tacky").

chez-moi [ʃemwa] **NM INV** *Fam* home■ ; **mon petit c.** a home of my own

chez-soi [ʃeswa] **NM INV** *Fam* home■ ; **son petit c.** a home of one's own

chez-toi [ʃetwa] **NM INV** *Fam* home■ ; **ton petit c.** a home of your own

chiac [ʃjak] *Can (en acadien)* **NM** = traditional Acadian dialect

NMF = nickname for an Acadian

Culture

LE CHIAC

"Chiac" is a vernacular spoken in the south-east of the Canadian Province of New Brunswick, near the towns of Moncton and Shediac – the word "chiac" is in fact believed to be derived from "Shediac". Its base is Acadian French (see box at entry "Acadie") but as it developed in predominantly Anglophone areas it has incorporated a huge number of English words and turns of phrase. It has long been deprecated by French- and English-speakers alike as it is considered to be neither proper French nor proper English. However, "chiac" is now in the process of being reclaimed as an increasing number of Acadian writers and songwriters have started using it in their works.

chiadé, -e [ʃjade] ADJ *Fam* elaborate■; **c'est vachement c. comme bagnole!** this car's got the works!

chiader [3] [ʃjade] VT *très Fam* **1** *(perfectionner)* to polish up; **il l'a vachement chiadée, sa lettre de candidature** he really took pains over his application letter **2** *Scol* to cram for, *Br* to swot (up)

chiadeur, -euse [ʃjadœr, -øz] NM,F *très Fam Scol Br* swot, *Am* grind; *(au travail)* perfectionist■

chialer [3] [ʃjale] VI *très Fam* to blubber, to bawl; **c. un bon coup** to bawl one's head off

chiâler [3] [ʃjɑle] VI *Can Fam* to whine

chialeur, -euse [ʃjalœr, -øz] *très Fam* ADJ blubbering, bawling

NM,F blubbering *or* bawling brat

chiant, -e [ʃjɑ̃, -ɑ̃t] ADJ *très Fam* **1** *(assommant → personne, chose à faire, livre)* boring■; **ce qu'elle est chiante avec ses histoires!** she's so boring when she gets going with her stories!; **ce que c'est c. cette vérification!** having to check all this is a real drag!; **son dernier bouquin est d'un c.!** his/her latest book is really *Br* bloody *or Am* goddamn boring!; **c. comme la pluie** as boring as hell, dead boring

2 *(difficile → chose à faire)* **c'est c. à mettre en service, cette imprimante!** this printer is a real pain *or Br* a bugger to install!

3 *(contrariant → personne, événement)* annoying■; **t'es chiante de pas répondre quand on te parle!** why can't you answer me when I speak to you, it really pisses me off!; **c'est c., cette coupure de courant!** this power cut is a real pain in the *Br* arse *or Am* ass!

chianti [kjɑ̃ti] NM *(vin)* Chianti

chiaque [ʃjak] = **chiac**

chiard, -e [ʃjar, -ard] *Fam* ADJ *Suisse (peureux)* chicken, cowardly■

NM,F *Suisse (peureux)* chicken, coward■

NM *(enfant)* brat

chiasma [kjasma] NM *Méd & Opt* chiasm, chiasma

chiasmatique [kjasmatik] ADJ *Méd & Opt* chiasmal, chiasmatic

chiasme [kjasm] NM **1** *Littérature (figure de style)* chiasmus **2** *Anat & Beaux-Arts* chiasm, chiasma

chiasse [ʃjas] NF **1** *Vulg (diarrhée)* **avoir la c.** to have the trots *or* runs; **attraper la c.** to get the trots *or* runs **2** *très Fam (poisse)* **quelle c.!** what a pain in the *Br* arse *or Am* ass! **3** *très Fam (de mouche, d'oiseau)* shit

chiatique [ʃjatik] ADJ *très Fam* **t'es vraiment c.** you're a damn *or Br* bloody pain; **c'est vraiment c.!** it's a pain in the *Br* arse *or Am* ass!

chibouk, chibouque [ʃibuk] NM chibouk, chibouque

chibre [ʃibr] NM *Suisse Cartes* = popular Swiss card game

chic [ʃik] ADJ INV **1** *(élégant)* stylish, smart, classy; **pour faire c.** in order to look smart *or* classy; **c'est très c.!** very classy!

2 *(distingué)* smart; **il paraît que ça fait c. de...** it's considered smart (these days) to...; **les gens c.** the smart set

3 *(sympathique)* nice; **c'est un c. type!** he's a nice guy!; **c'est une c. fille!** she's really nice!; **être c. avec qn** to be nice to sb; **c'était (vraiment) c. de sa part** it was (really) nice of him/her; **sois c., donne-le-moi!** be an angel, give it to me!

NM **1** *(élégance → d'une allure, d'un vêtement)* style, stylishness, chic; **avoir du c.** to have style, to be chic; **une veste qui a du c.** a stylish jacket; **s'habiller avec c.** to dress smartly; *Fam* **bon c. bon genre** *Br* ≃ Sloaney, *Am* ≃ preppy

2 *Fam (locution)* **il a le c. pour dire ce qu'il ne faut pas** he has a gift for *or* a knack of saying the wrong thing; **tu as vraiment le c. pour trouver des petites robes chouettes** you've really got the knack of finding great little dresses

EXCLAM *Fam Vieilli* **c. (alors)!** great!, smashing!; **tu viens? c. alors!** you're coming? great!

❑ **de chic** ADV *Vieilli* off the cuff, impromptu

Chicago [ʃikago] NM Chicago

chicane [ʃikan] NF **1** *(dans un procès)* quibble, pettifogging *(UNCOUNT)*, chicanery *(UNCOUNT)* **2** *(querelle)* quarrel, squabble; **chercher c. à qn** to try to pick a quarrel with sb; *Can* **à la prochaine c.!** see you (soon)!, *Am* so long! **3** *Sport (de circuit)* chicane; *(de gymkhana)* zigzag **4** *Cartes* chicane **5** *Aut (de silencieux)* baffle

❑ **en chicane** ADJ zigzag *(avant n)*

chicaner [3] [ʃikane] VT to quibble with; **c. qn sur** to quibble with sb about; **on me chicane sur l'emploi de ce mot** they're quibbling about my use of this word

VI to quibble; **c. sur les frais** to haggle *or* to quibble over the expense

▸ **se chicaner** VPR to squabble

chicanerie [ʃikanri] NF quibbling *(UNCOUNT)*; **arrête tes chicaneries!** stop quibbling!

chicaneur, -euse [ʃikanœr, -øz], **chicanier, -ère** [ʃikanje, -ɛr] ADJ quibbling

NM,F **1** *(au tribunal)* pettifogger **2** *(ergoteur)* quibbler

chicano [ʃikano] *Fam* ADJ Chicano

❑ **Chicano** NMF Chicano

chiche [ʃiʃ] ADJ **1** *(avare)* mean; **il n'a pas été c. de son temps/de ses efforts** he didn't spare his time/efforts; **il n'a pas été c. de compliments** he was generous with his compliments

2 *(peu abondant → repas, dîner, récolte)* scanty, meagre

3 *Fam (capable)* **tu n'es pas c. de le faire!** I'll bet you couldn't do it!; **elle est c. de le faire!** she's quite capable of doing it!■; **c.! want to** bet?; **c.? – c.!** want to bet? – you're on!; **c. que je mange tout!** bet you I can eat it all!; **je vais lui dire ce que je pense! – allez, c.!** I'm going to give him/her a piece of my mind! – go on, I dare you!

chiche-kebab [ʃiʃkebab] *(pl* **chiches-kebabs***)* NM *Culin* kebab, shish kebab

chichement [ʃiʃmɑ̃] ADV **1** *(de façon mesquine)* meanly, stingily **2** *(pauvrement)* scantily; **vivre c.** to lead a meagre existence

chicheté [ʃiʃte] NF *Vieilli ou (aux Antilles)* miserliness, avarice

chichi [ʃiʃi] NM *Fam (simagrées)* airs (and graces); **faire des chichis** *(faire des simagrées)* to put on airs; *(faire des complications)* to make a fuss; **ne fais pas tant de chichis pour une simple piqûre!** don't make such a fuss about a little injection!; **ce sont des gens à chichis** these people give themselves airs; **un dîner sans chichis** an informal dinner■

chichiteux, -euse [ʃiʃitø, -øz] *Fam* ADJ affected■

NM,F show-off, poseur

chichon [ʃiʃɔ̃] NM *Fam Arg drogue* hash, dope, *Br* blow

chicle, chiclé [tʃikle, ʃikle] NM chicle gum

chicon [ʃikɔ̃] NM **1** *(pomme de laitue) Br* cos *or Am* romaine lettuce heart **2** *Belg (endive)* chicory

chicorée [ʃikɔre] NF **1** *(salade) Br* endive, *Am* chicory **2** *(à café)* chicory **3** *(fleur)* (wild) chicory

chicos [ʃikos] ADJ *Fam* classy, smart, chic

chicot [ʃiko] NM *(d'une dent)* stump; *(d'un arbre)* tree stump; *Can Fam* **maigre comme un c.** sickly thin

chicote [ʃikɔt] NF chicote

chicoter [3] [ʃikɔte] VI **1** *(souris)* to squeak **2** *Can (chipoter)* to quibble, to split hairs

VT *Can (tracasser)* to worry, to bother; **ça me chicote de voir qu'il n'est pas encore de retour** it worries me that he's not back yet

chicotin [ʃikɔtɛ̃] NM sap of aloes

chicotte [ʃikɔt] = chicote

chié, -e [ʃje] *très Fam* ADJ **1** *(réussi → soirée, livre)* shit-hot; **c'est un c. spectacle** it's a fantastic show; **oh, dis donc, c'est c. comme appareil photo!** wow, what a brilliant camera!

2 *(culotté)* **il est c., lui!** he's got a nerve!

3 *(drôle)* **il est c.** he's a scream; **il est c. quand il imite le directeur** he's a scream when he mimics the boss

4 *(difficile → tâche)* hard■; **alors là, c'est c. comme question!** well, that's a hell of a question!

❑ **chiée** NF *(grande quantité)* **une chiée de** a whole lot *or* loads of; **on a eu une chiée d'ennuis pendant le voyage** it was just one damn thing after another during the whole journey; **des chiées** loads; **des gens serviables, y en a pas des chiées!** helpful people don't exactly grow on trees!

chie-en-culotte [ʃiɑ̃kylɔt] NM INV *Can très Fam* coward■, wimp, wuss

chien, -enne [ʃjɛ̃, ʃjɛn] NM,F **1** *(animal)* dog, *f* bitch; **petit c.** puppy, pup; **c. d'appartement** lapdog; **c. d'arrêt** gun dog, pointing dog, pointer; **c. d'aveugle** *Br* guide dog, *Am* seeing eye dog; **c. de berger** sheepdog; **c. de brousse** brush dog; **c. de chasse** hound, gun dog, retriever; **c. couchant** setter; **faire le c. couchant** to fawn, to crawl; **c. courant** hound; **c. errant** stray dog; **c. de garde** guard dog; *Fig* watchdog; **c. de manchon** lapdog; **c. méchant** *(sur panneau)* beware of the dog; **c. de meute** hound; **c. policier** police dog; **c. de prairie** prairie dog; **c. de race** pedigree dog; **c. de rapport** retriever; **c. savant** *(dans un cirque)* performing dog; *Péj (enfant)* performing monkey; **c. sauvage** wild dog; **c. sauvage d'Asie** Indian *or* Asiatic wild dog, dhole; **c. sauveteur** rescue dog; **c. de traîneau** sled dog, husky; **c. viverrin** raccoon dog; **un air de c. battu** a hangdog expression; **bon à jeter aux chiens** fit for the *Br* bin *or Am* garbage; **(rubrique des) chiens écrasés** minor news items; **se regarder en chiens de faïence** to glare at one another; **il est comme le c. du jardinier** he's a dog in the manger; **ils sont comme c. et chat** they fight like cat and dog; **comme un c.** like a dog; **comme un jeune c.** excitedly; **arriver comme un c. dans un jeu de quilles** to turn up at just the wrong moment; **entre c. et loup** at dusk *or* twilight; *Péj* **ce n'est pas fait pour les chiens** it's there for a good reason; *Fam* **et ta fourchette, c'est pour les chiens?** what do you think your fork's for?; *Hum* **merci mon c.!** I never heard you say thank you!; *Fam* **je ne suis pas ton c.!** don't order me about!; **je lui réserve** *ou* **garde un c. de ma chienne** I've got something up my sleeve for him/her that he's/she's not going to like one bit; *Fam* **chienne de vie!** life's a bitch!; *Can Fam* **avoir la chienne** *(avoir peur)* to be scared stiff; *(être paresseux)* to be lazy■; *Prov* **un c. regarde bien un évêque** a cat may look at a king; *Prov* **bon c. chasse de race** good breeding always tells; *Prov* **il menace beaucoup, mais c. qui aboie ne mord pas** his bark is worse than his bite; *Prov* **les chiens aboient, la caravane passe** = let the world say what it will

2 *très Fam (terme d'insulte → homme)* bastard; *(→ femme)* bitch

NM **1** *Astron* **le Grand/Petit C.** the Great/Little Dog

2 *(d'une arme)* hammer, cock

3 *Ich* **c. de mer** dogfish

4 *Naut* **coup de c.** squall

5 *Cartes (au tarot)* stock, talon

6 *Fam (locution)* **elle a du c.** she's quite horny, there's something quite horny about her; *Can Fam* **avoir du c. (dans le corps)** to be full of beans

❑ **chienne** NF *Belg* (long) fringe

❑ **chiens** NMPL (long) fringe ADJ *Fam* **être c.** to be rotten *or* nasty■; *Can* **ce qu'il dit de ses concurrents, c'est pas mal c.** the stuff he says about his competitors is pretty nasty

❑ **à la chien** ADV *(coiffé)* with a long fringe

❑ **de chien** ADJ *Fam (caractère, temps)* lousy, rotten; **ça fait un mal de c.** it hurts like hell; **avoir un mal de c. à faire qch** to have a hard job doing sth

❑ **en chien** ADV *Fam (très)* very■, *Br* dead, *Am* real; **il court vite en c.** he runs *Br* dead *or Am* real fast; *Can* **ce film-là, c'est le fun en c.** that movie *or Br* film is a laugh a minute

❑ **en chien de fusil** ADV curled up

'Le Chien des Baskerville' *Conan Doyle* 'The Hound of the Baskervilles'

chien-assis [ʃjɛ̃asi] (*pl* **chiens-assis**) **NM** *Br* dormer window, *Am* dormer

chien-chien [ʃjɛ̃ʃjɛ̃] (*pl* **chiens-chiens**) **NM** doggy; **le c. à sa mémère** Mummy's little doggie-woggie

chiendent [ʃjɛ̃dɑ̃] **NM** *Bot* couch grass; **ça pousse comme du c.** it grows like weeds

chienlit [ʃjɑ̃li] **NF** *Fam* **1** *(désordre)* mess, shambles; **c'est la c.** it's a shambles! **2** *(masque)* mask■ **3** *(mascarade)* masquerade■

chien-loup [ʃjɛ̃lu] (*pl* **chiens-loups**) **NM** wolfhound

chienne [ʃjɛn] *voir* **chien**

chiennerie [ʃjɛnri] **NF** **1** *très Fam (saleté)* **cette c. de métier!** what a lousy job! **2** *Littéraire (comportement)* meanness

chier [9] [ʃje] **VI** **1** *Vulg (déféquer)* to (*Br* have *or Am* take a) shit

2 *très Fam (locutions)* **ça chie (des bulles)** *(ça fait du scandale)* it's a total scandal; *(entre deux personnes)* they're having a real go at each other; **si elle l'apprend, ça va c. (des bulles)!** the shit's really going to hit the fan *or* all hell's going to break loose if she ever finds out!; **c. dans les bottes de qn** *(l'ennuyer à l'excès)* to piss sb off; *(lui jouer un sale tour)* to play a dirty trick on sb; **c. dans la colle** to be *Br* bang *or Am* smack out of order; **en c. (des bulles** *ou* **des ronds de chapeau)** to have a hell of a time; **j'en ai chié pour le terminer à temps!** I've had a hell of a job getting this finished on time!; **envoyer c. qn** to tell sb to get stuffed; **faire c. qn** *(l'importuner, le contrarier)* to bug sb; *(l'ennuyer)* to bore the pants off sb; **fais pas c.!** give me a break!, don't be such a pain in the *Br* arse *or Am* ass!; **tu (me) fais c.** give me a break, will you?; **(ça) fait c., ce truc!** this thing's a real pain in the *Br* arse *or Am* ass!; **qu'est-ce qu'on s'est fait c. hier soir!** it was so damned boring last night!; **qu'est-ce que je me fais c. avec elle!** she bores me stiff!; **je vais pas me faire c. à tout recopier!** I'm not damned well writing it all out again!, I can't be bothered *or Br* arsed writing it all out again!; **il se fait pas c., lui!** he's got a damn *or Br* bloody nerve!; **y a pas à c., faut que j'aie fini ce soir!** I've damned *or Br* bloody well got to finish by tonight and that's that!

❑ **à chier** *très Fam* **ADJ** **1** *(très laid)* **son costard est à c.** his suit looks *Br* bloody awful *or Am* godawful

2 *(très mauvais)* crap; **ce film est à c.** this movie is (a load of) crap

3 *(insupportable)* **il est à c., ce prof!** that teacher is a pain in the *Br* arse *or Am* ass!

VT *très Fam* **tu vas pas nous c. une pendule!** don't make such a fuss *or Br* a bloody song and dance about it!

chierie [ʃiri] **NF** *très Fam* **quelle c.!** what a pain in the *Br* arse *or Am* ass!, *Br* what a bloody pain!

chieur, -euse [ʃjœr, -øz] **NM,F** *très Fam* **c'est un vrai c./une vraie chieuse** he's/she's a real pain in the *Br* arse *or Am* ass; **quel c., ce type!** God, that guy's a pain!

chiffe [ʃif] **NF** **1** *Fam* **c'est une vraie c. molle** he's got no guts, he's totally spineless; **je suis une vraie c. molle aujourd'hui** *(fatigué)* I feel like a wet rag today **2** *Vieilli* rag

chiffon [ʃifɔ̃] **NM** **1** *(torchon)* cloth; **c. à poussière** *Br* duster, *Am* dust cloth **2** *(vieux tissu)* rag **3** *Péj (texte)* **qui est l'auteur de ce c.?** who's responsible for this mess?

❑ **chiffons** **NMPL** *Vieilli (vêtements)* clothes; **parler chiffons** to talk clothes *or* fashion

❑ **en chiffon** **ADJ** crumpled up (in a heap); **toutes ses affaires sont en c.** his/her things are all crumpled up **ADV** **mettre ses vêtements en c.** to leave one's clothes in a heap

chiffonnade [ʃifɔnad] **NF** *Culin* chiffonnade

chiffonnage [ʃifɔnaʒ] **NM** *(de vêtement)* creasing, crumpling; *(de papier)* crumpling

chiffonne [ʃifɔn] **NF** *Hort* = slender branch of peach tree with flower-buds all along it

chiffonné, -e [ʃifɔne] **ADJ** **1** *(froissé → vêtements)* creased, crumpled; *(→ papier)* crumpled **2** *(fatigué → visage)* tired, worn **3** *(préoccupé → air)* bothered, worried

chiffonnement [ʃifɔnmɑ̃] **NM** **1** *(action → de vêtement)* creasing, crumpling; *(→ de papier)* crumpling **2** *Fig (ennui)* annoyance

chiffonner [3] [ʃifɔne] **VT** **1** *(vêtement)* to crease, to crumple; *(papier)* to crumple **2** *Fam (préoccuper)* to bother, to worry■ ; **ça n'a pas eu l'air de la c.** it didn't seem to bother her; **quelque chose me chiffonne** something's bothering me

VI to do a bit of sewing

►**se chiffonner** **VPR** to crease, to crumple; **ça se chiffonne facilement** it creases easily, it's easily creased

chiffonnier, -ère [ʃifɔnje, -ɛr] **NM,F** rag dealer, rag-and-bone man, *f* woman; **se battre** *ou* **se disputer comme des chiffonniers** to fight like cat and dog

NM *(meuble)* chiffonier, chiffonnier

chiffrable [ʃifrabl] **ADJ** quantifiable; **facilement/difficilement c.** easy/difficult to calculate

chiffrage [ʃifraʒ] **NM** **1** *(d'un code)* ciphering **2** *(évaluation)* (numerical) assessment **3** *Mus* figuring

chiffre [ʃifr] **NM** **1** *Math* figure, number; **nombre à deux/trois chiffres** two/three digit number; **inflation à deux chiffres** double digit inflation; **jusqu'à deux chiffres après la virgule** up to two decimal points; **arrondi au c. supérieur/inférieur** rounded up/down; **écrivez la somme en chiffres** write the amount out in figures; **en chiffres ronds** in round figures; **les chiffres du cadran de la montre** the figures on the watch-face; **aimer les chiffres** *(le calcul)* to like maths **c. arabe/romain** Arabic/Roman numeral

2 *(montant)* amount, sum; **le c. des dépenses s'élève à 500 euros** total expenditure amounts to 500 euros; **c. de diffusion** *(d'un magazine)* sales figures, circulation figures

3 *Écon (taux)* figures, rate; **les chiffres du chômage** the unemployment figures; **chiffres bruts** unweighted figures

4 *Com* **c. d'affaires** turnover; **faire un c. d'affaires de 2 millions d'euros** to have a turnover of 2 million euros; *Fam* **faire du c.** to run at a healthy profit■ ; **c. d'affaires annuel** annual turnover; **c. d'affaires consolidé** group turnover; **c. d'affaires critique** breakeven point; **c. d'affaires à l'exportation** total export sales; **c. d'affaires global** total sales; **c. d'affaires hors taxes** pre-tax turnover; **c. d'affaires prévisionnel** projected turnover, projected sales revenue; **c. de vente** sales figures; **ils ont augmenté leur c. de vente** they have increased their sales

5 *Ordinat* digit; **c. ASCII** ASCII number; **c. binaire** bit, binary digit; **c. de contrôle** check digit; **chiffres numériques** numerics

6 *Tél* code, ciphering; *(service)* cipher (office)

7 *Biol* code

8 *(d'une serrure)* combination

9 *(initiales)* initials; *(à l'ancienne)* monogram; **du papier à lettres à son c.** (his/her) personalized *or* monogrammed stationery; **brodé à leur c.** embroidered with their monogram

10 *Mus* figure

11 *Jur* **c. noir** dark figure *(difference between the number of crimes committed and those reported)*

chiffré, -e [ʃifre] **ADJ** **1** *(évalué)* assessed, numbered **2** *(codé)* coded, ciphered **3** *Mus* figured

chiffrement [ʃifrəmɑ̃] **NM** *(codage)* ciphering, (en)coding; *Ordinat* **c. de données** data encryption

chiffrer [3] [ʃifre] **VT** **1** *(évaluer)* to assess, to estimate; **c. des travaux** to draw up an estimate (of the cost of work); **il est trop tôt pour c. le montant des dégâts** it's too early to put a figure to the damage

2 *(numéroter)* to number; **c. les pages d'un document** to number the pages of *or Spéc* to paginate a document

3 *Admin & Mil* to cipher, to code; *Ordinat* to encode, to encrypt

4 *(linge, vêtement → marquer de ses initiales)* to mark *or* to inscribe with initials; *(→ marquer d'un monogramme)* to monogram

5 *Mus* to figure

VI *Fam* to cost a packet; **ça chiffre!** it mounts up!

►**se chiffrer** **VPR** **1 se c. à** *(se monter à)* to add up *or* to amount to

2 se c. en *ou* **par** to amount to, to be estimated at; **sa fortune se chiffre par milliards** his/her fortune amounts to billions; **les pertes se chiffrent en centaines de têtes** losses are estimated at several hundreds

chiffreur, -euse [ʃifrœr, -øz] **NM,F** *(du service du chiffre)* coder, ciphering clerk

NM *Ordinat* encoder, encrypter

chiffrier [ʃifrije], **chiffrier-balance** [ʃifrijebalɑ̃s] (*pl* **chiffriers-balance**) **NM** *Compta* counter cash-book

chignole [ʃiɲɔl] **NF** **1** *(outil → à main)* hand drill; *(→ électrique)* electric drill **2** *Fam Péj (voiture)* heap

chignon [ʃiɲɔ̃] **NM** **1** *(cheveux)* bun, chignon; **se faire un c.** to put one's hair in a bun; **défaire son c.** to take one's hair down; **porter un c.** to wear one's hair in a bun; **c. banane** French roll **2** *Can Fam (tête)* head■ , nut; **c. du cou** nape (of the neck)■

chihuahua [ʃiwawa] **NM** *Zool (chien)* chihuahua

chiisme [ʃiism] **NM** *Rel* Shiism; **c. duodécimaine** twelver Shi'ism

chiite [ʃiit] *Rel* **ADJ** Shiah, Shiite

❑ **Chiite** **NMF** Shiite

chikungunya [ʃikungunja] **NM** *Méd* chikungunya

Chili [ʃili] **NM** **le C.** Chile; **vivre au C.** to live in Chile; **aller au C.** to go to Chile

chili [tʃili, ʃili] (*pl* **chiles**) **NM** *Bot & Culin* chili (pepper), chilli (pepper); **c. con carne** chilli con carne

chilien, -enne [ʃiljɛ̃, -ɛn] **ADJ** Chilean

❑ **Chilien, -enne** **NM,F** Chilean

chilom [ʃilɔm] **NM** chillum

Chimborazo [ʃimbɔrazo] **NM** *Géog* **le C.** Chimborazo

Chimène [ʃimɛn] **NPR** = character from Corneille's 'le Cid', whose sense of duty takes precedence over her passion for Rodrigue

chimère [ʃimɛr] **NF** **1** *Myth* chimera **2** *(utopie)* dream, fantasy; **le pays des chimères** the land of fantasy *or* dreams; **se complaire dans des chimères** to live in a dream world; **je vous laisse à vos chimères** I'll leave you alone with your pipe dreams **3** *Ich* chimaera, rabbitfish **4** *Hist (en Haïti)* = member of President Aristide's armed militia when he was President of Haiti (1994-1996 and 2001-2004)

chimérique [ʃimerik] **ADJ** **1** *(illusoire)* fanciful; **des espoirs/projets chimériques** fanciful hopes/plans; **rêve c.** pipe dream **2** *(mythique → animal)* mythical, fabled

chimie [ʃimi] **NF** chemistry; **la c. de l'amour/des sentiments** the chemistry of love/emotions; **c. biologique** biochemistry; **c. industrielle** chemical engineering; **c. inorganique** *ou* **minérale** inorganic chemistry; **c. nucléaire** nuclear chemistry; **c. organique** organic chemistry

chimiluminescence [ʃimilyminɛsɑ̃s], **chimioluminescence** [ʃimjɔlyminɛsɑ̃s] **NF** *Chim* chemiluminescence

chimio [ʃimjo] **NF** *Fam Méd (abbr* **chimiothérapie***)* chemo; **faire une c.** to have chemo

chimioluminescence [ʃimjɔlyminɛsɑ̃s] = **chimiluminescence**

chimiorécepteur [ʃimjɔresɛptœr] **NM** *Biol* chemoreceptor

chimiorésistance [ʃimjɔrezistɑ̃s] **NF** *Méd* chemoresistance

chimiosynthèse [ʃimjɔsɛ̃tɛz] **NF** *Biol* chemosynthesis

chimiotactisme [ʃimjɔtaktism] **NM** *Biol* chemotaxis

chimiotaxie [ʃimjɔtaksi] **NF** *Biol* chemotaxis

chimiothèque [ʃimjɔtɛk] **NF** *Chim* combinatorial library

chimiothérapeute [ʃimjɔterapøt] **NMF** *Méd* chemotherapist

chimiothérapeutique [ʃimjɔterapøtik] **ADJ** *Méd* chemotherapeutic

chimiothérapie [ʃimjɔterapi] **NF** *Méd* chemotherapy; **faire une c.** to have chemotherapy

chimiothérapique [ʃimjɔterapik] **ADJ** *Méd (méthode)* chemotherapeutic; *(traitement)* drug-based, *Spéc* chemotherapeutic

chimique [ʃimik] **ADJ** **1** *(de la chimie)* chemical **2** *Fam (artificiel)* chemical, artificial; **tous ces trucs chimiques qu'on trouve dans la nourriture** all these additives you find in food

chimiquement [ʃimikmɑ̃] **ADV** chemically

chimiquier [ʃimikje] NM chemical tanker

chimiste [ʃimist] NMF chemist; **ingénieur c.** chemical engineer

chimiurgie [ʃimjyrʒi] NF *Chim & Ind* chemurgy

chimpanzé [ʃɛ̃pɑ̃ze] NM chimpanzee; **c. pygmée** pygmy chimpanzee

chinage¹ [ʃinaʒ] NM **1** *Tex* = dyeing or printing of the warp to obtain the chiné or shadow effect **2** *Typ* tinting

chinage² [ʃinaʒ] NM *Fam* ragging

chinchard [ʃɛ̃ʃard] NM *Ich* mackerel scad, horse mackerel

chinchilla [ʃɛ̃ʃila] NM **1** *(rongeur, fourrure)* chinchilla; **une veste en c.** a chinchilla jacket **2** *(chat)* chinchilla **3** *(lapin)* chinchilla

chinder [ʃɛ̃de] = **schinder**

Chine [ʃin] NF **la C.** China; **aller en C.** to go to China; **vivre en C.** to live in China; **C. communiste** Red *or* Communist China; **C. nationaliste** Nationalist China; **C. populaire, République populaire de C.** People's Republic of China; **la mer de C.** the China Sea

chine [ʃin] NM **1** *(porcelaine)* china **2** *(papier)* rice paper
  NF *(brocante)* second-hand goods trade
  □ **à la chine** ADJ **vente à la c.** hawking; **vendeur à la c.** hawker ADV **vendre qch à la c.** to hawk sth

chiné, -e [ʃine] ADJ *(tissu)* chiné, mottled; *(laine)* bicoloured wool

chiner [ʃine] VT **1** *Tex* to mottle **2** *Fam (taquiner)* to kid, to tease
  VI *(faire les boutiques)* to go round the second-hand shops

chinetoque [ʃintɔk] ADJ = racist term used to refer to a Chinese person, ≃ Chink, Chinky
  □ **Chinetoque** NMF = racist term used to refer to a Chinese person, ≃ Chink, Chinky

chineur, -euse [ʃinœr, -øz] NM,F **1** *(amateur de brocante)* bargain hunter **2** *Vieilli (taquin)* teaser

chinois, -e [ʃinwa, -az] ADJ **1** *(de Chine)* Chinese **2** *Fam (compliqué)* twisted
  NM **1** *(langue)* Chinese; **c. du Nord** Mandarin (Chinese); **c. du Sud** Cantonese; **pour moi, c'est du c.** it's all Greek to me **2** *Culin (passoire)* (conical) strainer, chinois; **passer qch au c.** to sieve sth **3** *(orange)* candied kumquat
  □ **Chinois, -e** NM,F Chinese; **les C.** the Chinese

chinoiser [ʃinwaze] VI to split hairs

chinoiserie [ʃinwazri] NF **1** *Fam (complication)* complication; **chinoiseries administratives** red tape **2** *Beaux-Arts* chinoiserie

chinook [ʃinuk] NM **1** *Météo (vent)* chinook **2** *Ich (poisson)* chinook

chintz [ʃints] NM *Tex* chintz; **des rideaux en c.** chintz curtains

chinure [ʃinyr] NF *Tex* mottled effect, shadowing

chionis [ʃjɔni] NM *Orn* sheathbill

chiot [ʃjo] NM puppy, pup

chiotte [ʃjɔt] *très Fam* NF **1** *(désagrément)* **quelle c.!** what a pain in the *Br* arse *or Am* ass!; **quel temps de c.!** what shitty weather! **2** *(voiture)* car, wheels; *Br* motor; *(moto)* bike, *Am* hog, ride; *(cyclomoteur)* (motor) scooter, moped
  □ **chiottes** NFPL *Br* bog, *Am* john; **aux chiottes l'arbitre!** the referee's a *Br* wanker *or Am* jerk!; **il a un goût de chiottes** he's got shit taste

chiourme [ʃjurm] NF *Hist* **1** *(rameurs)* **la c.** the slaves *(on a galley)* **2** *(forçats)* **la c.** the convicts *(in a penitentiary)*

chiper [ʃipe] VT *Fam* to pinch, to swipe; **elle me chipe tous mes pulls** she's always pinching my sweaters; **je me suis fait c. mon stylo** someone's pinched *or* swiped my pen

chipeur, -euse [ʃipœr, -øz] *Fam* ADJ thieving
  NM,F petty thief

chipie [ʃipi] NF minx

chipolata [ʃipolata] NF *Culin* chipolata

chipotage [ʃipotaʒ] NM *Fam* **1** *(en discutant)* quibbling, hairsplitting **2** *(en mangeant)* nibbling **3** *(marchandage)* haggling

chipoter [ʃipote] VI *Fam* **1** *(discuter)* to quibble, to split hairs; **ne chipotons pas!** let's not quibble!; **c. sur les prix** to haggle over prices **2** *(sur la nourriture)* to pick at one's food **3** *Belg (bricoler)* to fiddle about
  VT *Belg (tripoter)* to fiddle with

chipoteur, -euse [ʃipotœr, -øz] *Fam* ADJ **1** *(en discutant)* quibbling; **ils sont chipoteurs** they

quibble over everything **2** *(en mangeant)* fussy, finicky; **il est c.** he's a fussy eater, he's finicky
  NM,F **1** *(ergoteur)* fault-finder, quibbler **2** *(mangeur)* picky eater

Chippendale [ʃipɛndal] ADJ INV *Beaux-Arts* Chippendale

chips [ʃips] NFPL **(pommes) c.** (potato) *Br* crisps *or Am* chips

chique [ʃik] NF **1** *(tabac)* quid, chew (of tobacco); *Fam* **ça ne vaut pas une c.** it's not worth a bean *or Am* a red cent
  2 *Fam (enflure de la joue)* swollen cheek *(due to toothache)*
  3 *(cocon de soie)* = small, poor-quality silk cocoon
  4 *Entom (puce)* jigger
  5 *Belg* sweet
  6 *(locutions) Fam* **ça m'a coupé la c.** I was speechless *or Br* gobsmacked; *Belg* **mordre sur sa c.** to grit one's teeth; **bout de c.** *(enfant)* toddler; *(homme, femme)* small person

chiqué [ʃike] NM *Fam Péj* **c.!** *(dans un match)* that's cheating!; **il n'a pas mal, c'est du** *ou* **il fait du c.** he's not in pain at all, he's putting it on

chiquement [ʃikmɑ̃] ADV *Fam* **1** *(avec élégance)* smartly, stylishly **2** *(avec fair-play)* decently; **elle m'a c. invité** she was good *or* kind *or* decent enough to invite me

chiquenaude [ʃiknod] NF **1** *(pichenette)* flick; **donner une c. à qn** to flick sb with one's finger; **d'une c.** with a flick of the finger; **d'une c., il envoya la boulette de papier sur le bureau du prof** he flicked the pellet of paper onto the teacher's desk **2** *(impulsion)* push

chiquer [ʃike] VT to chew
  VI **1** *(mâcher du tabac)* to chew tobacco **2** *très Fam (locution)* **y a pas à c.** there's no doubt about it

chiqueur, -euse [ʃikœr, -øz] NM,F tobacco chewer

chiral, -e, -aux, -ales [kiral, -o] ADJ *Phys & Chim* chiral

chiralité [kiralite] NF *Chim* chirality

chiraquien, -enne [ʃirakjɛ̃, -jɛn] ADJ **1** *(de Jacques Chirac)* Chirac *(avant n)*; **le QG c.** the Chirac HQ **2** *(partisan de Jacques Chirac)* pro-Chirac
  NM,F Chirac supporter

chiro [kiro] NM,F *Can Fam* chiropractor

chirographaire [kirografɛr] *Jur* ADJ **1** *(créance, créancier)* unsecured; **obligation c.** simple contract **2** *(document)* bearing the autograph signature of the monarch
  NM unsecured creditor

chirographie [kirografi] NF palmistry, *Sout* chiromancy

chiromancie [kiromɑ̃si] NF palmistry, *Sout* chiromancy

chiromancien, -enne [kiromɑ̃sjɛ̃, -ɛn] NM,F palmist, *Sout* chiromancer

chironome [kironom] NM *Entom* midge, *Spéc* chironomid

chiropracteur, -trice [kiropraktœr, -tris] NM,F *Méd* chiropractor

chiropractie [kiroprakti] NF *Méd* chiropractic

chiropraticien, -enne [kiropratisjɛ̃, -ɛn] NM,F *Méd* chiropractor

chiropratique [kiropratik] NF *Can Méd* chiropractic

chiropractrice [kiropraktris] *voir* **chiropracteur**

chiropraxie [kiropraksi] NF *Méd* chiropractic

chiroptère [kiroptɛr] *Zool* NM chiropteran
  □ **chiroptères** NMPL Chiroptera

Chiroubles [ʃirubl] NM Chiroubles (wine)

chirurgical, -e, -aux, -ales [ʃiryrʒikal, -o] ADJ **1** *Méd* surgical **2** *(précis)* accurate

chirurgicalement [ʃiryrʒikalmɑ̃] ADV surgically

chirurgie [ʃiryrʒi] NF surgery; **petite/grande c.** minor/major surgery; **c. ambulatoire** day surgery; **c. cardiaque** cardiac *or* heart surgery; **c. à cœur ouvert** open-heart surgery; **c. de confort** elective surgery; **c. dentaire** dental surgery; **c. endoscopique** keyhole surgery; **c. esthétique** cosmetic surgery; **c. à invasion minimale** minimal invasive therapy; **c. plastique** *ou* **réparatrice** plastic surgery

chirurgien, -enne [ʃiryrʒjɛ̃, -ɛn] NM,F surgeon
  NM *Ich* surgeon fish

chirurgien-dentiste [ʃiryrʒjɛ̃dɑ̃tist] *(pl* **chirurgiens-dentistes**) NM dental surgeon

chirurgienne [ʃiryrʒjɛn] *voir* **chirurgien**

Chisinau [kiʃinao] NM Chisinau

chistera [ʃistera] NM *Sport (à la pelote basque)* chistera

chital, -als [ʃital] NM *Zool* chital (deer)

chitine [kitin] NF *Biol* chitin

chitineux, -euse [kitinø, -øz] ADJ *Biol* chitinous

chiton [kitɔ̃] NM **1** *Antiq* chiton **2** *Zool (mollusque)* chiton, coat-of-mail shell

chiure [ʃjyr] NF **c. de mouche** fly speck

ch-l *Admin (abrév écrite* **chef-lieu**) = in France, administrative centre of a "département", "arrondissement" or "canton"

chlamyde [klamid] NF *Antiq* chlamys

chlamydia [klamidja] *(pl* **chlamydiae** [-je]) NF *Méd* chlamydia

chlamydomonas [klamidɔmɔnas] NF *Bot* chlamydomonas

châlsse [ʃlas] ADJ *très Fam* **1** *(ivre)* wasted, *Br* ratarsed; **il était complètement c.** he was totally wasted *or Br* pissed out of his head **2** *(fatigué)* all in, *Br* knackered

chleuh, chleuhe [ʃlø] ADJ & NM,F *Fam Hist* = offensive term used to refer to German people; **les chleuhs** ≃ the Jerries, ≃ the Boche

chlinguer [ʃlɛ̃ge] VI *très Fam* to stink, *Br* to pong; **ça chlingue, par ici!** *Br* it's a bit whiffy *or Am* it sure stinks around here!

chloasma [klɔasma], **chloasme** [klɔasm] NM *Méd* chloasma

chlorage [klɔraʒ] NM *Ind* chloring, chlorination

chloral, -als [klɔral] NM *Chim* chloral, trichloroethanol; **c. hydraté, hydrate de c.** chloral (hydrate)

chloramphénicol [klɔrɑ̃fenikɔl] NM *Chim* chloramphenicol

chlorate [klɔrat] NM *Chim* chlorate

chloration [klɔrasjɔ̃] NF *Chim* chlorination

chlore [klɔr] NM **1** *Chim* chlorine **2** *(Javel)* bleach, bleaching agent

chloré, -e [klɔre] ADJ chlorinated

chlorelle [klɔrɛl] NF *Bot* chlorella

chlorer [klɔre] VT *Chim* to chlorinate; **eau chlorée** chlorinated water

chloreux [klɔrø] ADJ M chlorous

chlorhydrate [klɔridrat] NM *Chim* hydrochloride

chlorhydrique [klɔridrik] ADJ *Chim* hydrochloric

chlorique [klɔrik] ADJ *Chim* chloric

chlorite [klɔrit] NM *Chim* chlorite

chlorobutadiène [klɔrɔbytadjɛn] NF *Chim* chloroprene

chlorofibre [klɔrɔfibr] NF *Chim* polyvinyl

chlorofluorocarbone [klɔrɔflyɔrɔkarbɔn] NM *Chim* chlorofluorocarbon

chlorofluorocarbure [klɔrɔflyɔrɔkarbyr] NM *Chim* chlorofluorocarbon

chloroforme [klɔrɔfɔrm] NM *Chim & Méd* chloroform

chloroformer [klɔrɔfɔrme] VT **1** *Méd* to administer chloroform to **2** *(abrutir)* to stultify

chlorométrie [klɔrɔmetri] NF *Chim* chlorometry

chloro-organique [klɔrɔɔrganik] *(pl* **chloro-organiques**) ADJ *Biol & Chim* chloro-organic; **composé c.** chloro-organic compound

chlorophène [klɔrɔfɛn] NM *Méd* chlorophene

chlorophycée [klɔrɔfise] *Bot* NF green alga
  □ **chlorophycées** NFPL green algae, *Spéc* Chlorophyceae

chlorophylle [klɔrɔfil] NF **1** *Bot* chlorophyll **2** *(nature)* **les citadins avides de c.** city dwellers eager to breathe the fresh country air

chlorophyllien, -enne [klɔrɔfiljɛ̃, -ɛn] ADJ chlorophyll *(avant n)*

chlorophytum [klɔrɔfitɔm] NM *Bot* spider plant, *Spéc* chlorophytum

chloroplaste [klɔrɔplast] NM *Biol* chloroplast

chloroprène [klɔrɔprɛn] NM *Chim* chloroprene

chloroquine [klɔrɔkin] NF *Pharm* chloroquine

chlorose [klɔroz] NF **1** *Vieilli Méd* greensickness, *Spéc* chlorosis **2** *Bot* chlorosis, etiolation

chlorotique [klɔrɔtik] ADJ *Méd & Bot* chlorotic

chlorure [klɔryr] NM *Chim* chloride; **c. de chaux** chloride of lime, bleaching powder; **c. de calcium/sodium** calcium/sodium chloride

chloruré, -e [klɔryre] ADJ *Chim* chlorinated

chlorurer [klɔryre] VT *Chim* to chlorinate

chnoque [ʃnɔk] = **schnock**

chnouf [ʃnuf] = **schnouf**

choane [kɔan] NF *Anat* choana

choc [ʃɔk] NM **1** *(heurt)* collision; **c. de deux objets** collision of two objects; **à l'épreuve des ou résistant aux chocs** shock-proof, shock-resistant; **l'essieu a subi un c.** the axle sustained a shock; **projeté dans le fossé par la violence du c.** thrown into the ditch by the force of the collision; **la poutre a cassé sous le c.** the beam snapped under the impact; *Fam* **tenir le c.** to withstand the impact; **le verre n'a pas tenu le c.** the glass shattered with the impact

2 *Mil (affrontement)* clash

3 *(incompatibilité)* clash, conflict; **c. culturel** culture shock; **le c. des générations** the generation gap

4 *(émotion)* shock; **ça fait un c.!** it's a bit of a shock!; **ça m'a fait un sacré c. de les revoir** it was a great shock to meet them again

5 *Élec* shock; *Phys* collision; **par chocs** by collision; **c. moléculaire** molecule collision; *Météo* **c. en retour** return shock

6 *Méd & Psy* shock; **être sous le c.** *Méd* to be in shock; *(bouleversé)* to be in a daze *or* in shock; **c. allergique/anaphylactique/anesthésique** allergic/anaphylactic/anaesthesia shock; **c. émotif** emotional *or* psychic shock; **c. hypovolémique** hypovolaemic shock; **c. opératoire** post-operative trauma *or* shock; **c. thermique** thermal shock

7 *Mil* shock; **c. et stupeur** *(stratégie)* shock and awe

8 *Bourse* **c. boursier** market crisis; *Écon* **c. pétrolier** oil crisis

9 *(bruit → métallique)* clang; *(→ sourd)* thwack; *(→ cristallin)* clink, tinkle

10 *(comme adj; avec ou sans trait d'union)* **argument/discours c.** hard-hitting argument/ speech; **image-c.** shocking image; **mesures-chocs** hard-hitting measures; **des prix-chocs** rock-bottom prices

▫ **de choc** ADJ **1** *Méd, Psy & Mil* shock *(avant n)*; **état de c.** state of shock; **être en état de c.** to be in a state of shock

2 *Fam (efficace)* super-efficient; **un patron de c.** a go-getting *or* whizz-kid manager

3 *Fam (d'avant-garde)* ultra-modern; **une mamie de c.** a glamorous granny

chocard [ʃɔkar] NM *Orn* **c. à bec jaune, c. des Alpes** Alpine chough

chochotte [ʃɔʃɔt] NF *Fam Péj* **quelle c. tu fais!** *(mijaurée)* don't be so stuck-up!; *(effarouchée)* don't be so squeamish!; **elle n'aime pas ça, c.!** fancy that, her Ladyship doesn't like it!; **il ne supporte pas cette odeur, c.!** oh dear, his Lordship can't stand the smell!

ADJ *(douillet)* squeamish; *(efféminé)* camp, affected

chocolat [ʃɔkɔla] NM **1** *(produit)* chocolate; **c. blanc** white chocolate; **c. à croquer** *ou* **noir** *Br* dark *or* plain chocolate, *Am* bittersweet chocolate; **c. à cuire** cooking chocolate; **c. au lait** milk chocolate; **c. de ménage** cooking chocolate; **c. aux noisettes** hazelnut chocolate; **c. de régime** diet chocolate

2 *(friandise)* chocolate; **c. fourré à la fraise** chocolate filled with strawberry cream; **c. glacé** *Br* choc ice *or* *Am* chocolate ice cream bar

3 *(boisson)* hot chocolate, cocoa; **un c. chaud** a (cup of) hot chocolate; **boire du c.** to drink a cup of hot chocolate *or* cocoa

ADJ INV **1** *(couleur)* chocolate (brown)

2 *Fam (locution)* **on est c.!** *(dupés)* we've been had!; *(coincés)* we've blown it!; **me voilà c. une fois de plus!** and I'm the sucker, yet again!

▫ **au chocolat** ADJ chocolate *(avant n)*; **gâteau au c.** chocolate cake

▫ **en chocolat** ADJ chocolate *(avant n)*; **des œufs en c.** chocolate eggs

chocolaté, -e [ʃɔkɔlate] ADJ chocolate *(avant n)*, chocolate-flavoured

chocolaterie [ʃɔkɔlatri] NF **1** *(fabrique)* chocolate factory **2** *(magasin)* chocolate shop

'Charlie et la chocolaterie' Dahl, Burton 'Charlie and the Chocolate Factory'

chocolatier, -ère [ʃɔkɔlatje, -ɛr] NM,F **1** *(fabricant)*

chocolate-maker **2** *(marchand)* confectioner

ADJ chocolate *(avant n)*

▫ **chocolatière** NF hot chocolate pot

chocottes [ʃɔkɔt] NFPL *très Fam* **avoir les c.** to be scared witless *or* stiff; **ça m'a donné ou filé les c.** it scared me out of my wits; **foutre les c. à qn** to scare sb witless *or* stiff, to put the wind up sb

choéphore [kɔefɔr] NF *Antiq* libation-bearer

chœur [kœr] NM **1** *Mus (chorale)* choir, chorus; *(morceau)* chorus; **le c. des prisonniers de 'Fidelio'** the prisoners' chorus in 'Fidelio'; **les chœurs** *(d'un opéra, d'un spectacle)* the chorus **2** *Fig (ensemble)* body, group; **le c. des critiques n'a pas ménagé ses louanges** the critics were unanimous in their praise **3** *Antiq* chorus **4** *Archit* choir

▫ **en chœur** ADV **1** *Mus* **chanter en c.** to sing in chorus **2** *(ensemble)* (all) together; **tous en c.** all together!; **parler en c.** to speak in unison; **ils sont tous allés à la plage en c.** they all went to the beach together

choie *etc voir* **choyer**

choir [72] [ʃwar] VI to fall; **se laisser c. sur une chaise/dans un fauteuil** to flop onto a chair/down in an armchair; *Fig* **laisser c. qn** *(s'en séparer)* to drop sb; *(manquer à sa promesse)* to let sb down; *Fam* **tout laisser c.** to pack it all in, *Br* to jack it all in, *Am* to chuck everything

choisi, -e [ʃwazi] ADJ **1** *(raffiné)* **une assemblée choisie** a select audience; **en termes choisis** in a few choice phrases; **il parle un langage c.** he chooses his words carefully **2** *(sélectionné)* selected, picked; **bien c.** well-chosen, appropriate; **mal c.** inappropriate; **cocher les articles choisis** tick the selected items

choisir [32] [ʃwazir] VT **1** *(sélectionner)* to choose, to pick; **c. entre** *ou* **parmi** to choose from (among); **choisis ce que tu veux** take your pick; **à ta place, je choisirais celle-ci** if I were you, I'd choose this one; **voilà ce que/celui que j'ai choisi** this is/he's the one I've chosen; **j'ai choisi les pommes les plus mûres** I selected the ripest apples; *Ironique* **tu as choisi ton moment!** you really picked a good time!; **il a choisi la liberté** he chose freedom

2 *(décider)* to decide, to choose, *Sout* to elect; **ils ont choisi de rester** they decided *or* chose to stay; **à lui de c. quand il veut y aller** it's up to him to decide when he wants to go

USAGE ABSOLU **bien c.** to choose carefully, to be careful in one's choice; **je n'ai pas eu le temps de c.** I had no time to make my choice; **je n'ai pas choisi, c'est arrivé comme ça** it wasn't my decision, it just happened

choix [ʃwa] NM **1** *(liberté de choisir)* choice; **donner le c. à qn** to give sb a *or* the choice; **avoir un ou le c.** to have a choice; **je n'avais pas le c.** I had no choice, I didn't have any choice; **nous n'avons pas d'autre c. que de…** we have no option *or* choice but to…; **ils ne nous ont pas laissé le c.** they left us no alternative *or* other option; **je vous laisse le c.** you choose; **tu as le c. entre rester et partir** you may choose either to stay or go; **avoir le c. de qch** to be able to choose sth; **vous avez le c. des moyens** you may use whatever means you choose; *aussi Fig* **avoir le c. des armes** to have the choice of weapons

2 *(sélection)* choice; **faire un c.** to make a choice; **faire le bon c.** to make the right choice; **faites votre c.** take your pick; **arrêter** *ou* **fixer son c. sur** to decide on, to choose; **à c. multiples** *(question, questionnaire, enquête)* multiple-choice; **mon c. est fait** I've made up my mind; **ses c. sont toujours réfléchis** he's/she's always cautious in his/her choices; **précisez votre c. par téléphone** phone in your selection; **nous allons procéder au c. des couleurs** we are going to choose the colour scheme; **chacun peut y trouver un article de son c.** everybody can find something that appeals to them; **vous avez gagné un voyage aux Seychelles avec la personne de votre c.** you've won a holiday for two in the Seychelles; **la carrière de votre c.** your chosen career; *Com* **c. du marché** market choice

3 *(gamme)* **un c. de** a choice *or* range *or* selection of; **ils ont un bon/grand c. de robes** they have a good/large selection of dresses

4 *Com* **premier c.** top quality; **de premier c.**

top-quality; **viande** *ou* **morceaux de premier c.** prime cuts; **de second c.** *(fruits, légumes)* standard *(avant n)*, grade 2 *(avant n)*; *(viande)* standard *(avant n)*; **articles de second c.** seconds, rejects

5 *Psy* **c. d'objet** object choice

▫ **au choix** ADJ *(question)* optional ADV **être promu au c.** to be promoted by selection; **prenez deux cartes au c.** choose *or* select (any) two cards; **vous avez fromage ou dessert au c.** you have a choice of either cheese or a dessert; **viande** *ou* **poisson au c.** *(sur le menu)* choice of meat or fish; **répondre au c. à l'une des trois questions** answer any one of the three questions

▫ **de choix** ADJ **1** *(de qualité)* choice *(avant n)*, selected; **des vins/mets de c.** choice wines/ food

2 *(spécial)* special; **il gardera toujours une place de c. dans nos cœurs** he will always have a special place in our hearts

▫ **par choix** ADV out of choice

choke¹ [tʃok, tʃɔk] NM *Suisse Aut* choke

choke² [tʃɔk], **choke-bore** [tʃɔkbɔr] *(pl* **choke-bores)** NM *Chasse* chokebore, choke

cholagogue [kɔlagɔg] *Physiol* ADJ cholagogue, cholagogic

NM cholagogue

cholécalciférol [kɔlekalsiferɔl] NM *Biol* cholecalciferol

cholécystectomie [kɔlesistɛktɔmi] NF *Méd* cholecystectomy

cholécystite [kɔlesistit] NF *Méd* cholecystitis

cholécystographie [kɔlesistɔgrafi] NF *Méd* cholecystography

cholécystostomie [kɔlesistɔstɔmi] NF *Méd* cholecystostomy

cholédoque [kɔledɔk] *Physiol* ADJ M bile *(avant n)* NM **(canal) c.** bile duct

choléra [kɔlera] NM *Méd & Vét* cholera

cholérétique [kɔleretik] *Physiol* ADJ choleretic NM choleretic

cholériforme [kɔleriform] ADJ *Méd & Vét* choleriform

cholérique [kɔlerik] *Méd & Vét* ADJ choleraic NMF cholera sufferer

cholestérinémie [kɔlesterinemi] NF *Méd* cholesterol level (of the blood), *Spéc* cholesteraemia

cholestérol [kɔlɛsterɔl] NM *Méd* cholesterol; **avoir du c.** to have high cholesterol *or* a high cholesterol level

cholestérolémie [kɔlɛsterɔlemi] NF *Méd* cholesterol level (of the blood), *Spéc* cholesteraemia

choline [kɔlin] NF *Biol & Chim* choline

cholinergique [kɔlinɛrʒik] *Méd & Physiol* ADJ cholinergic NM cholinergic agent

cholinestérase [kɔlinɛsteraz] NF *Physiol* cholinesterase

chômable [ʃomabl] ADJ **jour c.** public holiday

chômage [ʃomaʒ] NM **1** *(inactivité)* unemployment; **la montée du c.** the rise in unemployment; **le c. des femmes/des jeunes** female/ youth unemployment, unemployment among women/young people; **mettre au c.** to lay off; **c. conjoncturel** cyclical unemployment; **c. déguisé** hidden unemployment; **c. frictionnel** frictional unemployment; **c. keynésien** Keynesian unemployment; **c. de longue durée** long-term unemployment; **c. partiel** short-time working; **être en c. partiel** to work short time; **c. récurrent** periodic *or* recurrent unemployment; **c. saisonnier** seasonal unemployment; **c. structurel** structural *or* long-term unemployment; **être mis au c. technique** to be laid off; **être en c. technique** to have been laid off

2 *Fam (allocation)* unemployment benefit, *Br* dole (money); **toucher le c.** to claim unemployment benefit, *Br* to be on the dole; **s'inscrire au c.** to register as unemployed, *Br* to sign on

▫ **au chômage** ADJ *(sans emploi)* unemployed, out of work; **être au c.** to be unemployed *or* out of work ADV **s'inscrire au c.** to register as unemployed, *Br* to sign on

chômé, -e [ʃome] ADJ **jour c.** public holiday

chômedu [ʃomdy] NM *Fam* unemployment▪, *Br* dole; **être au c.** to be unemployed▪ *or* out of work▪; **pointer au c.** to be *Br* on the dole *or Am* on welfare▪

chômer [3] [ʃome] VI **1** *(être sans emploi)* to be unemployed *or* out of work
2 *(être en arrêt d'activité → entreprise, machine)* to stand idle, to be at a standstill
3 *(faire le pont)* **c. entre Noël et le jour de l'An** to take time off between Christmas and New Year
4 *(avoir du loisir)* to be idle, to have time on one's hands; **elle n'a pas le temps de c.** she hasn't got time to sit around and twiddle her thumbs; **il ne chôme pas** he's never short of something to do; **eh bien, vous n'avez pas chômé!** well, you certainly haven't been idle!
5 *(être improductif)* **laisser c. une terre** to allow land to lie fallow; **laisser c. son argent** to let one's money lie idle
VT *(jour férié)* to take off, not to work on

chômeur, -euse [ʃomœr, -øz] NM,F *(sans emploi)* unemployed person; **il est c.** he's unemployed *or* out of work; **les chômeurs** the unemployed; **un million de chômeurs** a million unemployed; **le nombre des chômeurs est très élevé** the unemployment *or* jobless figures are high; **les chômeurs de longue durée** the long-term unemployed

chondre [kɔ̃dr] NM *Géol* chondrule

chondrichtyen [kɔ̃driktjɛ̃] NM *Ich* chondrichthian

chondriome [kɔ̃drijɔm] NM *Biol* chondriome, chondrioma

chondriosome [kɔ̃drijɔsɔm] NM *Biol* chondriosome

chondrite [kɔ̃drit] NF *Géol* chondrite

chondrocalcinose [kɔ̃drɔkalsinoz] NF *Méd* chondrocalcinosis

chondrodystrophie [kɔ̃drɔdistrɔfi] NF *Méd* chondrodystrophy

chondromatose [kɔ̃drɔmatoz] NF *Méd* synovial chondromatosis, osteochondromatosis

chondrome [kɔ̃drɔm, kɔ̃drom] NM *Méd* chondroma

chondro-sarcome, chondrosarcome [kɔ̃drɔsarkom] *(pl* **chondro-sarcomes***)* NM *Méd* chondrosarcoma

chondrostéen [kɔ̃drɔsteɛ̃] *Ich* NM chondrostean
❑ **chondrostéens** NMPL Chondrostei

chope [ʃɔp] NF *(récipient)* beer mug, tankard; *(contenu)* mugful

choper [3] [ʃɔpe] *Fam* VT **1** *(contracter)* to catch▪; **j'ai chopé la grippe** I've caught the flu; *Fig* **c. la grosse tête** *ou* **le melon** to get bigheaded
2 *(intercepter)* to catch▪, to get▪, to nab; **tâche de la c. à sa descente du train** try to get hold of her when she gets off the train; **je l'ai chopé en train de fouiller dans mes affaires** I caught him rummaging through my things; **se faire c.** to be nicked *or* nabbed
3 *(voler)* to swipe, to pinch; **elle s'est fait c. son porte-monnaie, on lui a chopé son porte-monnaie** she had her *Br* purse nicked *or Am* wallet snatched
VI *Sport* to chop▪, to slice▪

chopine [ʃɔpin] NF **1** *Fam (bouteille)* bottle▪ **2** *Fam (verre)* glass▪; **aller boire une c.** to go and have a drink *or Br* a jar **3** *Can (mesure)* pint

chopiner [3] [ʃɔpine] VI *Fam* to booze

chopinette [ʃɔpinɛt] NF *Fam* small bottle▪

chopper [ʃɔpœr] NM **1** *(outil préhistorique)* chopper tool **2** *(moto)* chopper **3** *Électron* chopper, vibrator

chopper [3] [ʃɔpe] VI *Vieilli ou Littéraire* **1** *(trébucher)* to trip, to stumble **2** *(se tromper)* to make a mistake, to be mistaken

chopping-tool [tʃɔpiŋtul] *(pl* **chopping-tools***)* NM *(outil préhistorique)* chopping tool

chop suey [ʃɔpsu, ʃɔpsyɛ] *(pl* **chop sueys***)* NM *Culin* chop suey

choquable [ʃɔkabl] ADJ easily shocked; **peu c.** not easily shocked

choquant, -e [ʃɔkɑ̃, -ɑ̃t] ADJ **1** *(déplaisant → attitude)* outrageous, shocking; **avec un mépris c. de la justice** with outrageous disregard for justice **2** *(déplacé → tenue)* offensive, shocking; **ça n'a rien de c.** it's not at all shocking; **tu trouves sa tenue choquante?** do you find the way she's dressed offensive?

choquard, choquart [ʃɔkar] NM *Orn* **c. à bec jaune, c. des Alpes** Alpine chough

choqué, -e [ʃɔke] ADJ shocked; **il les regardait d'un air profondément c.** he looked at them, visibly shocked; *Can* **être c. (contre qn)** to be angry (at sb), *Am* to be mad (at sb)

choquer [3] [ʃɔke] VT **1** *(heurter)* to hit, to knock, to bump; **nous avons choqué nos verres** we clinked glasses
2 *(scandaliser)* to shock, to offend; **ça te choque qu'elle pose nue?** do you find it shocking *or* offensive that she should pose in the nude?; **ça ne me choque pas du tout** I don't see anything wrong with that; **être choqué (de/par qch)** to be shocked (at/by sth)
3 *(aller contre)* to go against, to be contrary to; **c. le bon goût** to be *or* to run contrary to good taste; **ce raisonnement choque le bon sens** this line of argument is an insult to common sense
4 *(être désagréable à → l'oreille)* to grate on, to offend; **c. la vue** *(couleur, saleté)* to offend the eye; *(bâtiment)* to be an eyesore
5 *(traumatiser)* **ils ont été profondément choqués par sa mort** they were devastated by his/her death; **j'ai été choqué de le voir tellement changé** I was shocked *or* it gave me a shock to see such a change in him; **la vue du sang l'a choqué** the sight of blood has shaken him; *Méd* **être choqué** to be in shock
USAGE ABSOLU *(scandaliser)* **son intention était de c.** he intended to be offensive *or* to shock; **leur album a beaucoup choqué** their album caused great offence; **ce qui choque le plus, dans ces images, c'est...** the most shocking thing about these pictures is...
▸**se choquer** VPR **1** *(se heurter → véhicules)* to come into collision; *(→ verres)* to knock against each other
2 *(être scandalisé)* to be shocked; **il n'y a pas de quoi se c.** there's nothing to be shocked at

choral, -e, -als *ou* **-aux, -ales** [kɔral, -o] *Mus & Rel* ADJ choral; **chants chorals** choral songs
❑ **choral, -als** NM choral, chorale
❑ **chorale** NF choir, choral society

chorde [kɔrd] = **corde**[2]

chordé [kɔrde] = **cordé**[2]

chorée [kɔre] NF *Méd* Saint Vitus' dance, *Spéc* chorea; **c. de Huntington** Huntington's chorea; **c. rhumatismale, c. de Sydenham** Sydenham's chorea

chorège [kɔrɛʒ] NM *Antiq* choragus, choregus

chorégie [kɔreʒi] NF *Antiq* choregy
❑ **chorégies** NFPL choral festival

chorégraphe [kɔregraf] NMF choreographer

chorégraphie [kɔregrafi] NF choreography; **faire la c. de** to choreograph

chorégraphier [9] [kɔregrafje] VT to choreograph

chorégraphique [kɔregrafik] ADJ choreographic

choréique [kɔreik] *Méd* ADJ choreal, choreic
NMF chorea sufferer

choreute [kɔrøt] NM *Antiq* chorist *(in ancient Greek drama)*

chorio-épithéliome [kɔrjoepiteljɔm] *(pl* **chorio-épithéliomes***)* NM *Méd* chorionepithelioma

chorion [kɔrjɔ̃] NM **1** *Anat* corium **2** *Biol & Obst* chorion

choriste [kɔrist] NMF **1** *Rel* chorister **2** *(à l'opéra)* chorus singer; *(d'un chanteur de variétés)* backing singer; **les choristes** *(au cabaret)* the chorus line

'Les Choristes' *Barratier* 'The Chorus'

chorizo [ʃɔrizo, tʃɔrizo] NM chorizo

choroïde [kɔrɔid] NF *Anat* choroid (coat *or* membrane)

choroïdien, -enne [kɔrɔidjɛ̃, -ɛn] ADJ *Anat* choroidal

chorus [kɔrys] NM **faire c.** to (all) agree, to speak with one voice; **faire c. avec qn** to voice one's agreement with sb

CHOSE [ʃoz] NF **A.** *SENS CONCRET* **1** *(bien matériel, nourriture, vêtement)* thing; **un livre et une table sont des choses** tables and books are things *or* objects; **les belles choses** nice things; **il n'avait acheté que de bonnes choses** he had only bought good things to eat; **elle a eu trop de choses à Noël** she got too many things *or* presents for Christmas; **j'ai encore deux ou trois choses à acheter** I still have a couple of things to buy; **j'ai encore des choses à lui chez moi** I still have a few of his things *or* some of his belongings at home
2 *(objet ou produit indéterminé)* thing; **quelle est cette c. affreuse?** what is this hideous thing?; **tu sais faire marcher cette c.?** do you know how this thing works?
3 *Phil* thing; **la c. en soi** the thing in itself
B. *PERSONNE* creature, thing; **être la c. de qn** *(avoir été modelé par qn)* to be (like) putty in sb's hands; *(être la possession de qn)* to belong to sb; **elle me prend pour sa c.** she thinks she can do what she wants with me, she thinks she owns me
C. *SENS ABSTRAIT* **1** *(acte, fait)* **une c.** a thing, something; **les choses** things; **j'ai encore beaucoup de choses à faire** I've still got lots (of things) to do; **j'ai bien des choses à vous raconter** I've a lot (of things) to tell you; **elle fait beaucoup de choses pour les handicapés** she does a lot for handicapped people; **c'est une c. que je ne savais pas** that's something I didn't know; **il se passe des choses au ministère** there's something going on in the department; **ah, encore une c., je ne viendrai pas demain** oh, one more thing, I won't be coming tomorrow; **s'il y a bien une c. qui m'agace, c'est son manque de ponctualité** if there's one thing that annoys me (about him/her), it's that he's/she's never on time; **l'hypocrisie, c'est une c. que je ne supporte pas** hypocrisy is something I can't bear; **une c. est sûre, il perdra** one thing's (for) sure, he'll lose; *Littéraire* **y a-t-il une c.** *ou* **y a-t-il c. plus belle que l'amour?** is there anything more beautiful than love?; **c'est une bonne c. qu'elle soit restée** it's a good thing she stayed; **en avril, ce sera c. faite** *ou* **la c. sera faite** it will be done by April; **ce n'est pas la même c.** *(cela change tout)* it's a different matter; **je suis retourné à mon village, mais ce n'est plus la même c.** I went back to my village, but it's just not the same any more; **la fidélité est une c., l'amour en est une autre** faithfulness is one thing, love is quite another; **ce n'est pas la c. à dire/faire!** what a thing to say/do!; *Fam* **c'est pas des choses à dire/faire!** you just don't say/do that kind of thing!; **c'est la c. à ne pas faire** it's the wrong thing to do; **ce ne sont pas des choses à faire en société** that's just not done in polite circles; **c. extraordinaire/curieuse, il était à l'heure!** amazingly/strangely enough, he was on time!; **et, c. rare...** for once...; **ce n'est pas c. aisée que de...** it's no easy matter to...; **c. promise c. due** a promise is a promise; **je ne crois pas à toutes ces choses** I don't believe in all that; **ce sont des choses qui arrivent** it's just one of those things; **s'occuper de choses et d'autres** to potter about; **accomplir** *ou* **faire de grandes choses** to do great things; **faire bien les choses** *(savoir recevoir)* to do things in style; **il ne fait pas les choses à demi** *ou* **moitié** he doesn't do things by halves
2 *(parole)* thing; **il dit une c. et il en fait une autre** he says one thing and does another *or* something else; **la c. que je n'ai pas comprise** what *or* the thing I didn't understand; **je vais te dire une (bonne) c., ça ne marchera jamais** let me tell you something, it'll never work; **elle dit de ces choses parfois!** the things she comes out with sometimes!; **il est sorti de sa voiture et il m'a dit de ces choses!** he got out of his car and gave me a right mouthful!; **elle dit toujours des choses sur ses collègues** she's always saying things about the people she works with; **qu'a-t-il dit? – peu de choses en vérité** what did he say? – very little *or* nothing much, actually; **bavarder** *ou* **parler de choses et d'autres** to chat about this and that; **dites-lui bien des choses** give him/her my best regards
3 *(écrit)* thing; **elle a écrit de bonnes choses** she wrote some good things *or* stuff; **comment peut-on écrire des choses pareilles!** how can anyone write such things!
4 *(ce dont il est question)* **comment a-t-il pris la c.?** how did he take it?; **comment vois-tu la c.?** how do you see it *or* things *or* the matter?; **la c. est entendue** we're agreed on this; **la c. n'est pas faisable** it can't be done; **laisse-moi t'expliquer la c.** let me explain what it's all about; **la c. en question** the case in point; *Euph* **être porté sur la c.** to have a one-track mind
5 *Pol (affaires)* **la c. publique** the state

6 *Jur* **choses communes** common things (*which cannot be owned*); **choses consomptibles** consumables; **choses corporelles** tangible assets; **choses fongibles** fungible assets; **choses frugifères** profit-yielding objects; **choses hors du commerce** non-negotiable objects; **c. jugée** res judicata

NM *Fam* **1** (*pour désigner un objet*) thingy, whatsit; **passe-moi le…, le c. bleu sur la table** give me the…, the blue thing on the table

2 (*pour désigner une personne*) **C.** (*homme*) what's-his-name, thingy; (*femme*) what's-her-name, thingy; **c'est une pièce avec C., tu sais, le grand blond!** it's a play with what's-his-name, you know, the tall blond guy!; **Madame C., elle devrait savoir ça** what's-her-name *or* Mrs thingy should know that

ADJ *Fam* funny, peculiar; **être** *ou* **se sentir un peu c.** to feel a bit peculiar; **ton fils a l'air tout c. aujourd'hui** your son looks a bit peculiar today

❑ **choses** NFPL (*situation*) things; **les choses de la vie** the things that go to make up life; **les choses étant ce qu'elles sont** as things stand, things being as they are; **au point où en sont les choses** as things now stand; **voilà où en sont les choses** this is how things stand (at the moment); **en mettant les choses au mieux/pire** looking on the bright/dark side (of things); **prendre les choses comme elles viennent** to take life as it comes; **prendre les choses à cœur** to take things to heart

❑ **de deux choses l'une** ADV de deux choses l'une, tu es avec moi ou avec lui! either you're on my side *or* you're on his!; **de deux choses l'une, ou tu m'obéis ou tu vas te coucher!** either you do as I tell you *or* you go to bed, it's up to you!

'**Les Choses. Une histoire des années soixante'** *Perec* 'Things. A Story of the Sixties'

chosification [ʃozifikasjɔ̃] NF reification
chosifier [9] [ʃozifje] VT to reify, to consider as a thing
Chostakovitch [ʃostakovitʃ] NPR Shostakovich
chott [ʃɔt] NM *Géol* salt lake
chotte [ʃɔt] NF *Suisse* (*étable d'alpage*) cowshed; *Fig* **à la c.** under cover
chou¹, -x [ʃu] NM **1** *Bot* cabbage; **c. (cabus)** white cabbage; **c. de Bruxelles** Brussels sprout; **c. chinois** Chinese cabbage *or* leaves; **c. frisé** (curly) kale; **c. de palmier** palm heart; **c. pommé** round cabbage; **c. romanesco** Romanesco; **c. rouge** red cabbage

2 (*pâtisserie*) **(petit) c.** chou; **c. à la crème** cream puff

3 (*ornement*) round knot, rosette

4 *Fam* (*locutions*) **être dans les choux** to be in a mess; **c'est dans les choux!** that's torn it!, that's the end of that!; **avec cette pluie, son barbecue est dans les choux** it's curtains for his/her barbecue in this rain; **faire c. blanc** to draw a blank, to be out of luck; **faire ses choux gras de qch** to have a field day with sth; **rentrer dans le c. à qn** (*en voiture*) to slam into sb; (*agresser*) to go for sb; *Belg* **c'est c. vert et vert c.** it's six of one and half a dozen of the other, *Br* it's all much of a muchness
chou², choute [ʃu, ʃut] *Fam* NM,F **1** (*en appellatif*) honey, sugar, sweetheart; **mon pauvre c.!** you poor little thing!; **viens voir mamie, mon petit c.** come along with granny, sweetheart

2 (*personne aimable*) darling, love; **c'est un c.** he's such a darling *or* love

ADJ INV (*gentil*) nice■, kind■; (*mignon*) cute; **tu es c.** (*en demandant un service*) there's a dear; (*pour remercier*) you're so kind, you're an absolute darling; **il est vraiment c. sur cette photo** isn't he cute in this picture?
chouan [ʃwɑ̃] NM *Hist* Chouan (*member of a group of counter-revolutionary royalist insurgents, one of whose leaders was Jean Chouan, in the Vendée area of western France from 1793 to 1800*)
chouannerie [ʃwanri] NF *Hist* **la c.** the Chouan uprising
choucas [ʃuka] NM *Orn* jackdaw
chouchen [ʃuʃɛn] NM (*mot breton*) mead
chouchou, -oute [ʃuʃu, -ut] NM,F *Fam Péj* (*préféré*)

favourite■; **c'est le c. du prof** he's the teacher's pet; **le c. de sa grand-mère** his grandmother's blue-eyed boy

NM (*pour les cheveux*) scrunchie
chouchoutage [ʃuʃutaʒ] NM *Fam Péj* favouritism■
chouchouter [3] [ʃuʃute] VT *Fam* (*élève*) to give preferential treatment to■; (*enfant, ami*) to mollycoddle■, to pamper■; **j'adore être chouchouté quand je suis malade** I love being pampered when I'm ill; **ton mari, tu le chouchoutes trop!** you shouldn't mollycoddle your husband so much!; **se faire c.** to let oneself be spoiled
choucroute [ʃukrut] NF **1** *Culin* (*chou*) pickled cabbage; (*plat*) sauerkraut; **c. garnie** sauerkraut with meat **2** *Fam* (*coiffure*) beehive
Chou En-lai [ʃuɛnlaj] NPR Chou En-lai
chouette¹ [ʃwɛt] NF **1** *Orn* owl; **c. blanche** snowy owl; **c. des bois** brown owl, wood owl; **c. des clochers, c. effraie** barn owl; **c. épervière** hawk owl; **c. hulotte** tawny owl

2 *Fam Péj* (*femme*) **vieille c.** old bag
chouette² [ʃwɛt] *Fam* ADJ **1** (*agréable*) fantastic, lovely, terrific; **il me reste 20 euros, c'est c.!** fantastic, I've got 20 euros left!; **c. journée, non?** lovely day, isn't it?; **elle est c., ta sœur** your sister's really nice; **il a une c. petite bouille, ce gosse** that kid's got a cute face; *Ironique* **ben il est c. avec ce chapeau!** doesn't he look great with that hat on!

2 (*gentil*) kind■; (*coopératif*) helpful■; **il est vraiment c.** he's so good-natured; **il est très c. avec nous** he's very good to us; **elle est drôlement c. avec les enfants** she's really good with the kids; **sois c., prête-moi ta voiture** oh go on, lend me your car

EXCLAM c. (alors)! great!
chouettement [ʃwɛtmɑ̃] ADV *Fam Vieilli* **1** (*gentiment*) nicely■ **2** (*agréablement*) fantastically, terrifically
chou-fleur [ʃuflœr] (*pl* **choux-fleurs**) NM cauliflower; **oreille en c.** cauliflower ear
chouia [ʃuja] NM *Fam* **un c. (de)** a little *or* tiny bit (of); **encore un c. de crème** just a drop more cream; **un c. trop à gauche** a tiny bit too much to the left
chouille [ʃuj] NF *Fam* party■, bash
chouiller [3] [ʃuje] VI *Fam* to party
chouiner [3] [ʃwine] VI *Fam* to whine
chouleur [ʃulœr] NM *Tech* front-end loader
chou-navet [ʃunavɛ] (*pl* **choux-navets**) NM *Bot & Culin Br* swede, *Am* rutabaga
choune [ʃun] NF *Vulg* (*sexe de la femme*) pussy, snatch, *Br* fanny; **avoir de la c.** to be fucking lucky *or Br* jammy
chou-palmiste [ʃupalmist] (*pl* **choux-palmistes**) NM *Bot* palm-heart, palm-cabbage
chouquette [ʃukɛt] NF *Culin* = small choux bun coated with sugar
chou-rave [ʃurav] (*pl* **choux-raves**) NM *Bot & Culin* kohlrabi
chouraver [3] [ʃurave], **chourer** [3] [ʃure] VT *très Fam* to swipe, to pinch; **c. qch à qn** to pinch sth from sb; **on m'a chouravé mon vélo** I've had my bike pinched
chouriner [3] [ʃurine] VT *Fam Arg crime* (*blesser avec un couteau*) to knife■, to cut; (*tuer avec un couteau*) to stab to death■
choute [ʃut] *voir* **chou²** NM,F
chow-chow [ʃoʃo] (*pl* **chows-chows**) NM (*chien*) chow-chow, chow (dog)
choyer [13] [ʃwaje] VT to pamper, to make a fuss of; **se faire c.** to be pampered
CHR [seaɛr] NM (*abrév* **centre hospitalier régional**) = regional hospital

NMPL (*abrév* **cafés, hôtels et restaurants**) = hotels, cafés and restaurants (*collectively*)
chrême [krɛm] NM *Rel* chrism, consecrated oil
chrestomathie [krɛstomati, krɛstomasi] NF chrestomathy
chrétien, -enne [kretjɛ̃, -ɛn] ADJ Christian

NM,F Christian
chrétien-démocrate, chrétienne-démocrate [kretjɛ̃demokrat] (*mpl* **chrétiens-démocrates**, *fpl* **chrétiennes-démocrates**) *Pol* ADJ Christian Democrat

NM,F Christian Democrat
chrétienne [kretjɛn] *voir* **chrétien**

chrétiennement [kretjɛnmɑ̃] ADV **vivre c.** to live as a good Christian; **être enterré c.** to have a Christian burial
chrétienté [kretjɛte] NF Christendom
Chris-Craft® [kriskraft] NM INV *Naut* Chris-Craft
chrisme [krism] NM *Rel* chrisma, labarum
Christ [krist] NPR **le C.** Christ

❑ **christ** NM (*crucifix*) (Christ on the) cross, crucifix
christiania [kristjanja] NM *Ski* christie, christy
christianisation [kristjanizasjɔ̃] NF Christianization, conversion to Christianity; **le pays avant la c.** the country before the spread of Christianity
christianiser [3] [kristjanize] VT to Christianize, to convert to Christianity
christianisme [kristjanism] NM Christianity
christique [kristik] ADJ Christlike
christologie [kristɔlɔʒi] NF Christology
chromage [kromaʒ] NM *Tech* chromium plating
chromate [kromat] NM *Chim* chromate
chromatide [kromatid] NF *Biol* chromatid
chromatine [kromatin] NF *Biol* chromatin
chromatique [kromatik] ADJ **1** *Mus* chromatic **2** (*relatif aux couleurs*) chromatic **3** *Biol* chromosomal
chromatisme [kromatism] NM *Mus & Opt* chromaticism
chromatogramme [kromatogram] NM *Chim* chromatogram
chromatographie [kromatografi] NF *Chim* chromatography
chromatographique [kromatografik] ADJ *Chim* chromatographic
chromatophore [kromatofor] NM *Biol* chromatophore
chromatopsie [kromatopsi] NF *Physiol* (*perception des couleurs*) colour perception; *Méd* (*trouble de la vision*) chromatopsia
chrome [krom] NM *Chim & Métal* chromium

❑ **chromes** NMPL (*d'un véhicule*) chrome (UNCOUNT), chromium-plated parts; **faire les chromes d'une voiture/bicyclette** to polish up the chrome on a car/bicycle
chromer [3] [krome] VT *Métal* **1** (*métal*) to chromium-plate **2** (*acier*) to chrome; **acier chromé** chrome steel
chromeux, -euse [kromø, -øz] ADJ *Chim* chromous
chrominance [krominɑ̃s] NF *TV* **signal de c.** chrominance signal
chromique [kromik] ADJ *Chim* chromic
chromisation [kromizasjɔ̃] NF *Métal* chromizing
chromiser [3] [kromize] VT *Métal* to chromize
chromite [kromit, kromit] NF *Minér* chromite, chrome iron
chromo [kromo] NM *Péj* poor-quality colour print
chromodynamique [kromodinamik] NF *Phys* chromodynamics (*singulier*)
chromogène [kromoʒɛn] *Chim* ADJ chromogenic, colour-producing

NM chromogen
chromolithographie [kromolitografi] NF chromolithography, process offset
chromomère [kromomɛr] NM *Biol* chromomere
chromophore [kromofor] NM *Chim* chromophore
chromoprotéine [kromoprotein] NF *Biol* chromoprotein
chromosome [kromozom] NM *Biol* chromosome; **c. somatique** autosome; **c. X/Y** X/Y chromosome; **jeu de chromosomes** set of chromosomes
chromosomique [kromozomik] ADJ *Biol & Méd* (*gén*) chromosomal, chromosomic, chromosome (*avant n*); (*maladie*) chromosomal, genetic
chromosphère [kromosfɛr] NF *Astron* chromosphere
chroniciser [3] [kronisize] **se chroniciser** VPR *Méd* to become chronic
chronicité [kronisite] NF *Méd* chronicity
chronique [kronik] ADJ **1** *Méd* chronic **2** (*constant*) chronic; **chômage c.** chronic unemployment

NF 1 *Journ* (*rubrique*) column; **tenir la c. sportive** to write the sports column; **c. boursière** markets column; **c. financière** financial news; **c. judiciaire** court column; **c. littéraire** arts

page; **c. mondaine** gossip column; **c. des spectacles** (entertainments) listings; **c. des tribunaux** Law Reports **2** *Littérature* chronicle **3** *Bible* **les Chroniques** Chronicles

'Chronique d'une mort annoncée' *García Márquez* 'Chronicle of a Death Foretold'

chroniquement [kʀɔnikmɑ̃] ADV **1** *Méd* chronically **2** *(constamment)* chronically, perpetually

chroniquer [3] [kʀɔnike] VT **1** *(consacrer une rubrique de presse à)* to review **2** *(traiter sous forme de chronique)* to chronicle

chroniqueur, -euse [kʀɔnikœʀ, -øz] NM,F **1** *(journaliste)* commentator, columnist; **c. boursier** market commentator; **c. financier** financial columnist; **c. judiciaire** court reporter; **c. littéraire** book editor, book reviewer; **c. mondain** gossip columnist **2** *(historien)* chronicler

chrono [kʀɔno] *Fam* NM stopwatch ▪ ADV by the clock ▪; **250 c.** recorded speed 250 kph

chronobiologie [kʀɔnobjɔlɔʒi] NF *Biol* chronobiology

chronogramme [kʀɔnogram] NM time-series chart

chronographe [kʀɔnograf] NM *Astron* chronograph

chronologie [kʀɔnolɔʒi] NF chronology, time sequence; **c. des événements** calendar of events

chronologique [kʀɔnolɔʒik] ADJ chronological; **série c.** time series

chronologiquement [kʀɔnolɔʒikmɑ̃] ADV chronologically

chronométrage [kʀɔnometraʒ] NM timing

chronomètre [kʀɔnometʀ] NM *(pour le sport)* stopwatch; *(montre de précision)* chronometer

chronométrer [18] [kʀɔnometʀe] VT to time *(with a stopwatch)*

chronométreur, -euse [kʀɔnometʀœʀ, -øz] NM,F *(en sport)* timekeeper; *(dans l'industrie)* time and motion *(study)* expert

chronométrie [kʀɔnometʀi] NF chronometry

chronométrique [kʀɔnometʀik] ADJ chronometric

chronophotographie [kʀɔnofɔtɔɡʀafi] NF chronophotography

Chronopost® [kʀɔnopɔst] NM = express mail service

chronostratigraphie [kʀɔnostʀatiɡʀafi] NF *Archéol* chronostratigraphy

chronotachygraphe [kʀɔnotakiɡʀaf] NM *Transp* tachograph

Chrysale [kʀizal] NPR = the down-to-earth husband of the bluestocking Philaminte in Molière's 'Les Femmes savantes'

chrysalide [kʀizalid] NF *Entom* chrysalis; *Fig* **sortir de sa c.** to come out of one's shell

chrysanthème [kʀizɑ̃tɛm] NM *Bot* chrysanthemum; **inaugurer les chrysanthèmes** = General de Gaulle's description of the traditional function of the President of the Republic, to which he did not wish to be confined

Culture

CHRYSANTHÈME

Chrysanthemums are often associated with funerals in France, and so are never offered as gifts. They are traditionally used to decorate graves, especially on All Saints' Day.

chrysanthémique [kʀizɑ̃temik] ADJ *Bot* **acide c.** chrysanthemic acid

chryséléphantin, -e [kʀizelefɑ̃tɛ̃, -in] ADJ *Beaux-Arts* chryselephantine

chrysobéryl [kʀizoberil] NM *Minér* chrysoberyl, cymophane

chrysocale [kʀizokal] NF ormolu

chrysocolle [kʀizokɔl] NF *Minér* chrysocolla

chrysoïdine [kʀizoidin] NF *Chim* chrysoidine

chrysolite [kʀizolit] NF *Minér* chrysolite, chrysolith

chrysolithe [kʀizolit] NF *Minér* chrysolite, olivine

chrysomèle [kʀizomɛl] NF *Entom* leaf beetle

chrysomélidé [kʀizomelide] *Entom* NM leaf beetle, *Spéc* hrysomelid
▫ **chrysomélidés** NMPL Chrysomelidae

chrysophycée [kʀizofise] NF *Bot* chrysophyte

---

chrysoprase [kʀizopraz] NF *Minér* chrysoprase

CHS [seaʃɛs] NM *(abrév* **centre hospitalier spécialisé**) = psychiatric hospital

CHSCT [seaʃɛssete] NM *(abrév* **comité d'hygiène, de sécurité et des conditions de travail**) = health and safety committee

chtar [ʃtaʀ] NM *Fam* **1** *(cachot)* slammer, clink **2** *(coup)* clout, wallop

chtarbé, -e [ʃtaʀbe] ADJ *Fam* crazy, nuts, off one's rocker

ch'timi [ʃtimi] ADJ from the north of France ▪ NMF northerner *(in France)*

chtonien, -enne [ktɔnjɛ̃, -jɛn] ADJ *Myth* chthonian, chthonic

chtouille [ʃtuj] NF *très Fam* **la c.** the clap

CHU [seaʃy] NM **1** *(abrév* **centre hospitalo-universitaire**) teaching hospital **2** *(abrév* **centre d'hébergement d'urgence**) emergency refuge

chuchotage [ʃyʃɔtaʒ] NM whispering

chuchotement [ʃyʃɔtmɑ̃] NM whisper; **des chuchotements** whispering *(UNCOUNT)*

chuchoter [3] [ʃyʃɔte] VI to whisper ▪ VT *(mot d'amour, secret)* to whisper; **c. qch à qn** to whisper sth to sb; **il lui a chuchoté quelques mots à l'oreille** he whispered a few words in his/her ear

chuchoterie [ʃyʃɔtʀi] NF whispers, whispered conversation

chuchoteur, -euse [ʃyʃɔtœʀ, -øz] ADJ whispering ▪ NM,F whisperer

chuchotis [ʃyʃɔti] NM whisper; **des c.** whispering *(UNCOUNT)*

chuintant, -e [ʃɥɛ̃tɑ̃, -ɑ̃t] ADJ *(son)* hushing; *Ling* **consonne chuintante** palato-alveolar fricative
▫ **chuintante** NF *Ling* palato-alveolar fricative

chuintement [ʃɥɛ̃tmɑ̃] NM **1** *Ling* = use of palato-alveolar fricatives instead of sibilants (characteristic of certain French regional accents) **2** *(sifflement d'une bouilloire)* hiss, hissing

chuinter [3] [ʃɥɛ̃te] VI **1** *(d'une chouette)* to hoot **2** *(siffler)* to hiss **3** *Ling* to pronounce *or* articulate sibilants as fricatives

churinga [ʃyʀɛ̃ɡa] NM *(en anthropologie)* tjuringa, churinga

churrigueresque [ʃyʀiɡeʀɛsk] ADJ *Archit & Beaux-Arts* Churrigueresque

chut [ʃyt] EXCLAM hush!, sh!, shhh!

chute [ʃyt] NF **1** *(perte d'équilibre)* fall; **faire une c.** to fall, to take a tumble; **faire une c. de cheval** to fall off one's horse; **il a fait une c. de neuf mètres** he fell nine metres; **il m'a entraîné dans sa c.** he dragged *or* pulled me down with him; **attention, c. de pierres** *(sur panneau)* danger! falling rocks; **c. libre** free fall; **faire du saut en c. libre** to skydive; *Fig* **la livre est en c. libre** the pound's plummetting
2 *(perte)* fall; **la c. des cheveux** hair loss; **au moment de la c. des feuilles** when the leaves fall
3 *(baisse → des prix, des températures)* drop, fall (**de** in); *Com* **c. des ventes** fall-off in sales; **c. de tension** *Méd* drop in blood pressure; *Élec & Phys* voltage drop; **c. de pression** pressure drop
4 *(effondrement → d'un gouvernement, d'une institution)* collapse, fall; **entraîner qn dans sa c.** to drag sb down with one
5 *Mil* fall; **la c. de Metz** the fall of Metz
6 *Bible* **la C.** the Fall
7 *Météo* **chutes de neige** snowfall; **chutes de pluie** rainfall
8 *(chute d'eau)* **les chutes du Niagara** (the) Niagara Falls; **les chutes Victoria** (the) Victoria Falls; **les chutes d'Iguaçu** (the) Iguaçu Falls
9 *(fin → d'une histoire)* punchline; *(→ d'un roman, d'une pièce)* end; **j'ai été surpris par la c.** *(d'une situation)* I was surprised by the outcome; **j'attends la c. avec grand intérêt** I wonder how things will turn out; *Littéraire* **la c. du jour** nightfall, the day's end, eventide
10 *(inclinaison, pente)* **c. d'un toit** pitch of a roof; **c. d'une robe** hang of a dress; **c. de la voix** fall *or* cadence of the voice; *Littérature* **c. de la phrase** round-off of the sentence; *Anat* **c. des reins** small of the back
11 *(déchet → de tissu)* scrap; *(→ de bois, de métal)* offcut, trimming; **chutes de pellicule** film trims; **c'est une scène qui est restée parmi les chutes** that scene ended up on the

---

cutting-room floor; **une couverture faite avec des chutes (de tissu)** a blanket made of remnants (of fabric)
12 *Constr (d'un toit)* pitch, slope
13 *Cartes* **avoir deux levées de c.** to be two tricks down
▫ **chute d'eau** NF waterfall

'La Chute' *Camus* 'The Fall'

'La Chute' *Hirschbiegel* 'Downfall'

chuter [3] [ʃyte] VI **1** *Fam (tomber)* to fall ▪ **2** *(ne pas réussir)* to fail, to come to grief; **c. sur** to fail on; **le candidat a chuté sur la dernière question** the candidate failed on the final question **3** *(baisser)* to fall, to tumble; **faire c. les ventes** to bring sales (figures) tumbling down; **la crise a fait c. les ventes** the crisis sent sales plummetting **4** *Cartes* to go down

chuteur [ʃytœʀ] NM *Mil* **c. opérationnel** combat paratrooper

chutney [ʃœtnɛ] NM *Culin* chutney

chyle [ʃil] NM *Physiol* chyle

chylifère [ʃilifɛʀ] ADJ *Physiol* chyliferous

chylurie [ʃilyʀi] NF *Méd* chyluria

chyme [ʃim] NM *Physiol* chyme

chymotrypsine [ʃimotʀipsin] NF *Biol & Chim* chymotrypsin

Chypre [ʃipʀ] NF Cyprus; **aller à C.** to go to Cyprus; **vivre à C.** to live in Cyprus

chypriote [ʃipʀijɔt] = **cypriote**

CI [sei] NM *Fin (abrév* **certificat d'investissement**) investment certificate

Ci *Phys (abrév écrite* **curie**) Ci

ci [si] PRON DÉMONSTRATIF INV **ci et ça** this and that; **faire ci et ça** to do this and that

-ci [si] ADV **1** *(dans l'espace)* **ce livre-ci** this book; **celui-ci** this one; **celui-ci ou celui-là?** this one or that one?
2 *(dans le temps → présent)* **à cette heure-ci il n'y a plus personne** there's nobody there at this time of day; **ce mois-ci** this month; **cette semaine-ci** this week
3 *(dans le temps → futur)* **ils viennent dîner ce mercredi-ci** they're coming for dinner next Wednesday
4 *(dans le temps → passé)* **il n'a pas fait très beau ces jours-ci** the weather hasn't been too good just lately; **je ne l'ai pas beaucoup vu ces temps-ci** I haven't seen much of him lately
5 *(pour insister)* **je ne t'ai pas demandé ce livre-ci** THAT's not the book I asked for; **cette fois-ci j'ai compris!** NOW I've got it!; **c'est à cette heure-ci que tu rentres?** what time do you call this?

CIA [seia] NF *(abrév* **Central Intelligence Agency**) CIA

ciao [tʃao] EXCLAM *Fam* ciao!

ci-après [siapʀɛ] ADV *(gén)* below; *Jur* hereafter, hereinafter; **voir c.** see below; **c. dénommé l'acheteur** hereafter *or* hereinafter referred to as the Buyer

cibiche [sibiʃ] NF *Fam Vieilli* cig, ciggie

cibiste [sibist] NMF CB user

ciblage [siblaʒ] NM targeting; *Méd* **c. génique** gene targeting; **c. stratégique** strategic targeting

cible [sibl] NF **1** *Mil & Phys* target; **c. fixe/mobile** stationary/moving target; **c. d'amarrage** docking target; **c. panoramique** landscape target
2 *Fig (victime)* target; **prendre qn pour c.** to make sb the target of one's attacks; **c'est toujours lui qu'on prend pour c.** he's always the scapegoat; **servir de c. aux railleries de qn** to be the butt *or* the target for sb's jokes; **sa maladresse fait de lui une c. toute trouvée** his clumsiness makes him the obvious target for *or* the butt of everybody's jokes
3 *Com & Mktg* target; **c. commerciale/de communication** marketing/promotional target; **c. publicitaire** advertising target; **c. visée** intended target; **population c.** target population

ciblé, -e [sible] ADJ targeted

cibler [3] [sible] VT *(produit)* to define a target group for; *(public)* to target; **notre campagne publicitaire cible en priorité les jeunes** our

advertising campaign is targeted principally at young people

ciboire [sibwar] NM *Rel* ciborium
  EXCLAM *Can Fam* goddammit!

ciborium [sibɔrjɔm] NM *Rel* ciborium

ciboule [sibul] NF *Br* spring onion, *Am* scallion

ciboulette [sibulɛt] NF chives

ciboulot [sibulo] NM *Fam* head■, nut; **se creuser le c.** to rack one's brains; **il n'a rien dans le c.** he's a dope, he's got nothing between his ears; **elle en a dans le c.!** she's got a good head on her shoulders!; **travailler du c.** to be off one's rocker *or Br* trolley

CIC [seise] NF (*abrév* **Confédération internationale des cadres**) CIC, International Confederation of Executives and Managerial Staff

cicatrice [sikatris] NF **1** *Méd* scar, *Spéc* cicatrice **2** *Fig (marque)* mark, scar; **c. indélébile** permanent scar; **laisser des cicatrices** to leave scars; **cette séparation a laissé une c. profonde en lui** the separation scarred him deeply *or* left a deep scar on him **3** *Bot* scar (of attachment); **c. de feuille/de bourgeon** leaf/bud scar; **c. du haricot** hilum

cicatriciel, -elle [sikatrisjɛl] ADJ scar *(avant n)*, *Spéc* cicatricial

cicatricule [sikatrikyl] NF *Zool* germ, *Spéc* cicatricula

cicatrisable [sikatrizabl] ADJ that can be healed

cicatrisant, -e [sikatrizɑ̃, -ɑ̃t] ADJ healing
  NM healing agent, *Spéc* cicatrizant

cicatrisation [sikatrizasjɔ̃] NF **1** *Méd* scarring, *Spéc* cicatrization; **la c. se fait mal** the wound is not healing *or* closing up properly **2** *(apaisement)* healing

cicatriser [3] [sikatrize] VT **1** *Méd* to heal, *Spéc* to cicatrize; **cette pommade fera c. la plaie plus vite** this cream will help the wound heal up more quickly
  2 *(adoucir)* to heal; **le temps cicatrise toutes les blessures** time heals all wounds
  VI *(coupure)* to heal *or* to close up; *(tissus)* to form a scar
  ▶**se cicatriser** VPR *(coupure)* to heal *or* to close up; *(tissus)* to form a scar; *Fig* to heal

cicéro [sisero] NM *Typ* em

Cicéron [siserɔ̃] NPR Cicero

cicérone [siseron] NM *Littéraire* guide, mentor

cicéronien, -enne [siserɔnjɛ̃, -ɛn] ADJ Ciceronian

cichlidé [siʃlide] NM *Ich* cichlid

cicindèle [sisɛ̃dɛl] NF *Entom* cicindela, tiger-beetle

ciclée [sikle] NF *Suisse Fam* shriek■

cicler [3] [sikle] VI *Suisse Fam* to shriek■

ciclosporine [siklɔsporin] NF *Pharm* cyclosporin

ciconiidé [sikɔniide] *Orn* NM stork
  ❑ **ciconiidés** NMPL Ciconiidae

ciconiiforme [sikɔniiform] *Orn* NM ciconiiform
  ❑ **ciconiiformes** NMPL Ciconiiformes

ci-contre [sikɔ̃tr] ADV opposite; **illustré c.** as shown in the (picture) opposite; *Compta* **porté c.** as per contra

CICR [seisɛer] NM (*abrév* **Comité international de la Croix-Rouge**) IRCC

cicutine [sikytin] NF *Pharm* cicutoxin

Cid [sid] NPR **le C.** El Cid

ci-dessous [sidəsu] ADV below

ci-dessus [sidəsy] ADV above; **l'adresse c.** the above address

ci-devant [sidəvɑ̃] ADV *Vieilli* previously, formerly
  NMF INV *Hist* former aristocrat

-CIDE [sid] SUFF

● This suffix is found at the end of words such as **suicide**, **homicide**, **infanticide**, **génocide**, **ethnocide**, where it suggests the KILLING of human beings, but also in **herbicide**, **pesticide**, **fongicide** or **spermicide**, which are all products designed to kill undesirable micro-organisms.

● Note that both the murder and the murderer are referred to by the same word in the case of **infanticide** (infanticide/child-killer), **régicide** (regicide), **fratricide** (fratricide), **matricide** (matricide), **parricide** (parricidal).

● Note also that, where the French uses the same word for the adjective and the noun, the English has two different words: infantici**dal**/infantici**de**, homici**dal**/homici**de**, herbici**dal**/herbici**de**, etc.

● In recent years, the adjective **liberticide**, originally considered literary in register, has become very widespread in the media, as in the following examples:
  un projet de loi liberticide a bill that will destroy civil liberty; **un député liberticide** a member of parliament intent on destroying one's civil liberty

● Following the same pattern, adjectives like **démocraticide** (which threatens to destroy democracy) are being spontaneously coined, even if they don't appear in dictionaries.

CIDEX, Cidex [sidɛks] NM (*abrév* **courrier individuel à distribution exceptionnelle**) = system grouping letter boxes in country areas

CIDJ [seidɛʒi] NM (*abrév* **centre d'information et de documentation de la jeunesse**) = careers advisory service

cidre [sidr] NM *Br* cider, *Am* hard cider; **c. bouché** bottled cider *(with a seal)*; **c. brut** dry cider; **c. doux** sweet cider

cidrerie [sidrəri] NF cider-house

Cidunati [sidynati] NM (*abrév* **Comité interprofessionnel d'information et de défense de l'union nationale des travailleurs indépendants**) = union of self-employed craftsmen

Cie (*abrév écrite* **compagnie**) Co

ciel [sjɛl] (*pl sens 1, 3–5,* **cieux** [sjø], *pl sens 2, 6–8* **ciels**) NM **1** *(espace)* sky; **haut dans le c.** (high) up in the sky; **à c. ouvert** in the open air, out of doors; **entre c. et terre** in the air, in midair; **une explosion en plein c.** a midair explosion; **jusqu'au c.** (up) to the skies; **c. pommelé** mackerel sky; **lever les bras au c.** to throw up one's hands *(in exaspération, despair etc)*; **lever les yeux au c.** *(d'exaspération)* to roll one's eyes; **tomber du c.** *(arriver opportunément)* to be heaven-sent *or* a godsend; *(être stupéfait)* to be stunned
  2 *Météo* **c. clair/nuageux** clear/cloudy sky **3** *Astron* sky
  4 *Rel* Heaven; **Mamie est montée** *ou* **partie au c.** Grandma has gone up to Heaven; **le c. m'en est témoin** (as) Heaven is my witness
  5 *Littéraire (fatalité)* fate; *(providence)* **c'est le c. qui t'envoie** you're a godsend; **c'est le c. qui nous envoie cet argent** that money's a godsend; **le c. soit loué** thank heavens; **que le c. vous entende!** may heaven help you!
  6 *Mines* roof; **carrière/mine à c. ouvert** opencast quarry/mine
  7 *(plafond)* **c. de chambre** canopy; **c. de lit** canopy
  8 *Mil* **c. protecteur** overhead cover
  EXCLAM *Vieilli* **(juste) c.!** heavens above!, (good) heavens!
  ❑ **ciels** NMPL *Littéraire (temps)* **les ciels changeants de Bretagne** the changing skies of Brittany; *Beaux-Arts* **les ciels tourmentés de Van Gogh** Van Gogh's tortured skies
  ❑ **cieux** NMPL *Littéraire (région)* climes, climate; **sous des cieux plus cléments** in milder climes; **partir vers d'autres cieux** to be off to distant parts
  ❑ **à ciel ouvert** ADJ INV **1** *Mines Br* open-cast, *Am* open-cut
  2 *(piscine, stade)* open-air

Allusion
Ciel! mon mari!
This is the classic cry of the unfaithful wife whose husband returns home unexpectedly, famous from a thousand farces and vaudeville plays featuring a love triangle: "Heavens! my husband!" In modern idiom people say this in situations where they have been surprised, and have to rush.

CIEP [seiøpe] NM (*abrév* **Centre international d'études pédagogiques**) = French centre for educational research

cierge [sjɛrʒ] NM **1** *Rel (bougie)* altar candle; **brûler un c. à un saint** to burn a candle to a saint; **c. magique** sparkler **2** *Bot* cereus

cieux [sjø] *voir* **ciel**

CIG [seiʒe] NF (*abrév* **Conférence Intergouvernementale**) IGC

cigale [sigal] NF *Entom* cicada

cigare [sigar] NM **1** *(à fumer)* cigar **2** *Fam (tête)* head■, nut; **avoir mal au c.** to have a headache■; **mets-toi ça dans le c.** get that into

your thick skull **3** *Belg (réprimande)* talking-to

cigarette [sigarɛt] NF **1** *(à fumer)* cigarette; **fumer une c.** to smoke a cigarette, to have a smoke; **la c. ce n'est pas bon pour la santé** smoking is bad for you *or* for your health; **c. filtre** filter-tipped cigarette **2** *(à manger)* **c. (russe)** = shortcake biscuit shaped like a brandy snap

cigarettier, -ère [sigarətje, -ɛr] NM,F cigarette manufacturer

cigarier, -ère [sigarje, -ɛr] NM,F cigar-maker

cigarillo [sigarijo] NM cigarillo

ci-gît [siʒi] ADV here lies

cigogne [sigɔn] NF **1** *Orn* stork; **c. blanche** white stork; **c. noire** black stork **2** *Tech (levier)* crank lever

cigogneau, -x [sigɔno] NM *Orn* young *or* immature stork

ciguë [sigy] NF *Bot* **grande c.** hemlock; **petite c.** fool's-parsley; **c. vireuse** water hemlock

ci-inclus, -e [siɛ̃kly, -yz] *(mpl inv, fpl* **ci-incluses**) ADJ *(après le nom)* enclosed; **la copie ci-incluse** the enclosed copy
  ❑ **ci-inclus** ADV **(vous trouverez) c. vos quittances** please find bill enclosed; **c. une copie du testament et les instructions du notaire** enclosures: one copy of the will and the solicitor's instructions

CIJ [seiʒi] NF (*abrév* **Cour internationale de justice**) ICJ

ci-joint, -e [siʒwɛ̃, -ɛt] *(mpl* **ci-joints**, *fpl* **ci-jointes**) ADJ *(après le nom)* attached, enclosed; **après examen des pièces ci-jointes** on studying the enclosed documents
  ❑ **ci-joint** ADV *(avant le nom)* **c. photocopie** photocopy enclosed; **(veuillez trouver) c. la facture correspondante** please find enclosed *or* attached the invoice relating to your order

cil [sil] NM **1** *Anat* eyelash, lash, *Spéc* cilium **2** *Biol* **cils vibratiles** cilia

ciliaire [siljɛr] ADJ *Anat* ciliary

cilice [silis] NM hair shirt, *Spéc* cilice

cilié, -e [silje], **cilifère** [silifɛr] ADJ *Biol* ciliate, ciliated

cillement [sijmɑ̃] NM blinking, *Spéc* nictitation

ciller [3] [sije] VI **1** *(battre des cils)* to blink **2** *(réagir)* **il n'a pas cillé** he didn't bat an eyelid *or* turn a hair; **ils contemplaient le spectacle sans c.** they contemplated the sight with no visible sign of emotion

cimaise [simɛz] NF **1** *Beaux-Arts* picture rail; **pendre un tableau aux plus hautes cimaises** to sky a painting **2** *Archit* cymatium

cime [sim] NF **1** *Géog* peak, summit, top; *Littéraire* **les cimes** the mountain tops **2** *(d'un arbre, d'un mât)* crown, top; **les singes vivent dans les cimes** monkeys live in the canopy of the forest

ciment [simɑ̃] NM **1** *Constr* cement; **c. à prise lente/rapide** slow-setting/quick-setting cement; **c. armé** reinforced concrete; **c. dentaire** amalgam **2** *Fig (lien)* bond; **l'enfant fut le c. de leur amour** the child acted as a bond between them

cimentation [simɑ̃tasjɔ̃] NF *Constr & Fig* cementing

cimenter [3] [simɑ̃te] VT **1** *Constr* to cement **2** *Fig (renforcer)* to consolidate

cimenterie [simɑ̃tri] NF cement factory, cement works *(singulier)*

cimentier [simɑ̃tje] NM cement manufacturer

cimeterre [simtɛr] NM *(sabre)* scimitar

cimetière [simtjɛr] NM cemetery, graveyard; *(autour d'une église)* churchyard; **le c. des éléphants** elephants' graveyard; **c. de voitures** scrapyard *(for cars)*

'**Le Cimetière marin**' *Valéry* 'The Graveyard by the Sea'

cimicaire [simikɛr] NF *Bot* bugbane, bugwort, cimicifuga

cimier [simje] NM **1** *(d'un casque)* crest **2** *Hér* crest **3** *Culin (d'un cerf etc)* haunch; *(d'un bœuf)* rump

cinabre [sinabr] NM **1** *Miner* cinnabar **2** *Beaux-Arts* vermilion

cincle [sɛ̃kl] NM *Orn* **c. (plongeur)** dipper

cindynique [sɛ̃dinik] NF risk studies
  ❑ **cindyniques** NFPL risk studies

ciné [sine] NM *Fam* **1** *(spectacle)* **le c.** the cinema■, the movies■; **se faire un c.** to go and see a movie■ *or Br* film■ **2** *(édifice) Br* cinema■, *Am* movie theater■

cinéaste [sineast] NMF movie director, *Br* film director; **c. amateur** amateur movie-maker *or Br* film-maker; **c. indépendant** independent movie-maker *or Br* film-maker

ciné-club [sineklœb] *(pl* **ciné-clubs**) NM *Br* film society, *Am* movie club

cinéma [sinema] NM **1** *(édifice) Br* cinema, *Am* movie theater; **aller au c.** to go to the movies *or Br* cinema; **c. d'art et d'essai** arthouse; **c. à domicile** home cinema; **c. Imax** IMAX cinema; **c. multisalle** multiplex, multiscreen cinema; **c. permanent** continuous performance; **c. en plein air** *(dans les pays chauds)* open-air cinema; *(aux États-Unis)* drive-in (movie-theater); **un c. de quartier** a local cinema

2 *(spectacle, genre)* **le c.** the movies, the cinema; **des effets encore jamais vus au c.** effects never before seen on screen; **le c. de Pasolini** Pasolini's movies *or Br* films; **le c. d'animation** cartoons, animation; **le c. d'art et d'essai** arthouse movies *or Br* films; **c. d'auteur** independent film-making; **c. direct** direct cinema; **c. indépendant** independent cinema; **le c. muet** silent movies *or Br* films; **c. novo** Cinema Nôvo; **le c. parlant** talking pictures, talkies; **c. réaliste** realist cinema; **le c. en relief** three-dimensional *or* 3-D movies *or Br* films

3 *(métier)* **le c.** *Br* film-making, *Am* movie-making; **faire du c.** *(technicien)* to work in *Br* films *or Am* the movies; *(acteur)* to be a screen actor, *Br* to act in films; **étudiant en c.** student of *Br* film *or Am* movies; **école de c.** film school

4 *(industrie)* **le c.** the movie *or Br* film industry

5 *Fam (locutions)* **c'est du c.** it's (all) play acting; **alors c'était du c., ton voyage en Inde?** so your trip to India was all a sham?; **faire du** *ou* **tout un c. (pour)** to kick up a huge fuss (about); **le gosse a fait un c. pas possible pour y retourner** the kid made an awful fuss to go back there; **arrête (de faire) ton c.!** *(de faire des histoires)* stop making such a fuss!; *(de mentir)* stop winding us up!; *(de bluffer)* stop shooting your mouth off!; **se faire du c.** to fantasize **□ de cinéma** ADJ *(festival, revue, vedette)* movie *(avant n)*, *Br* film *(avant n)*

CinémaScope® [sinemaskɔp] NM *Cin* Cinemascope®

cinémathèque [sinematɛk] NF movie *or Br* film library; **la C. française** = the French film institute

cinématique [sinematik] NF kinematics *(singulier)*

cinématographe [sinematɔgraf] NM cinematograph

cinématographie [sinematɔgrafi] NF cinematography

cinématographique [sinematɔgrafik] ADJ cinematographic, movie *(avant n)*, *Br* film *(avant n)*; **les techniques cinématographiques** cinematic techniques; **une grande carrière c.** a great career in the cinema; **droits d'adaptation c.** film rights; **droits de reproduction c.** film printing rights

cinématographiquement [sinematɔgrafikmã] ADV cinematographically; **c. parlant** from a cinematic point of view

cinéma-vérité [sinemaverite] NM INV cinéma vérité

cinémographe [sinemɔgraf] NM tachograph

cinémomètre [sinemɔmɛtr] NM tachometer, speedometer

ciné-parc [sinepark] *(pl* **ciné-parcs**) NM *Can Br* drive-in cinema, *Am* drive-in (movie theater)

cinéphage [sinefaʒ] *Hum* NMF avid moviegoer *or Br* cinemagoer

ADJ **être c.** to enjoy going to the movies *or Br* cinema

cinéphile [sinefil] NMF movie buff, *Br* film buff

ADJ **être (très) c.** to be a movie buff *or Br* a film buff

cinéphilie [sinefili] NF love of movies *or Br* films

cinéphilique [sinefilik] ADJ movie-going, *Br* cinema-going

cinéraire [sinerɛr] ADJ cinerary; **urne c.** funeral urn

NF *Bot* cineraria

Cinérama® [sinerama] NM Cinerama®

cinérite [sinerit] NF *Géol* vitric tuff

cinéroman [sinerɔmã] NM cinenovel

cinèse [sinɛz] NF *Biol* kinesis

cinesthésie [sinɛstezi] NF kinaesthesia

cinesthésique [sinɛstezik] ADJ kinaesthetic

cinéthéodolite [sineteɔdɔlit] NM *Tech* kinetheodolite

cinétique [sinetik] *Phys* ADJ kinetic
NF kinetics *(singulier)*

cinétisme [sinetism] NM kinetic art

cinghalais, -e [sɛ̃galɛ, -ɛz] ADJ Singhalese, Sinhalese
NM *(langue)* Singhalese, Sinhalese
□ **Cinghalais, -e** NM,F Singhalese, Sinhalese; **les C.** the Singhalese *or* Sinhalese

cinglant, -e [sɛ̃glã, -ãt] ADJ **1** *(violent → pluie)* lashing; *(→ vent)* bitter, biting; *(→ gifle)* stinging **2** *(blessant → remarque, paroles)* biting, cutting, scathing; **d'un ton c.** scathingly; **des reproches cinglants** bitter *or* scathing criticism

cinglé, -e [sɛ̃gle] *Fam* ADJ crazy, nuts; **t'es pas un peu c.!** are you crazy?
NM,F *Br* nutter, *Am* screwball; **les cinglés du volant/jazz/cinéma** car/jazz/movie fanatics

cingler [3] [sɛ̃gle] VI **1** *Naut* **c. vers** to sail (at full sail) towards, to make for **2** *(tournure impersonnelle) Fam* **ça cingle** it's freezing *or Br* baltic
VT **1** *(fouetter)* to lash; **la pluie cingle les vitres** the rain is lashing the windowpanes **2** *(blesser)* to sting; **la grêle lui cinglait le visage** the hail was stinging his/her face

Cinna [sina] NPR 'Cinna', = play by Corneille

Allusion

Prends un siège, Cinna

Every French schoolchild has studied Corneille's play *Cinna* (1640) and is familiar with this phrase used by Auguste who wants to talk to Cinna. It means "Cinna, take a seat" and can be used jokingly today when inviting someone to sit down.

---

cinnamique [sinamik] ADJ *Chim* **acide c.** cinnamic acid

cinnamome [sinamɔm] NM *Bot* cinnamomum

cinoche [sinɔʃ] NM *Fam* **1** *(bâtiment) Br* cinema■, *Am* movie theater■; **aller au c.** to go to the movies■ *or Br* pictures; **je me ferais bien un petit c. ce soir** I quite fancy going to the movies■ *or Br* pictures tonight **2** *(art)* movies■, cinema■

cinoque [sinɔk] *Fam* ADJ crazy, loopy
NMF nutcase, *Br* nutter, *Am* screwball

cinq [sɛ̃k] ADJ **1** *(gén)* five; **c. livres de pommes** five pounds of apples; **c. cents/mille étoiles** five hundred/thousand stars; **c. pour cent** five per cent; **c. dixièmes** five tenths; **couper/partager qch en c.** to cut/divide sth into five; **c. par c.** five by five, in fives; **entrer (c.) par c.** to come in in fives *or* five at a time; **c. fois mieux** five times better; **elle a c. ans** *(fille)* she's five (years old *or* of age); *(voiture)* it's five years old; **une fille de c. ans** a five-year-old (girl); *Euph* **les c. lettres** ≃ a four-letter word; **dire les c. lettres à qn** to tell sb where to go; **bouteille c. étoiles** = inexpensive wine bottle (with five stars embossed on the neck) for which a deposit is payable; *Aut* **une c. portes** a five-door model; *Journ* **c. colonnes à la une** a banner headline

2 *(dans des séries)* fifth; **à la page c.** on page five; **au chapitre c.** in chapter five, in the fifth chapter; **il arrive le c. novembre** he's arriving on November (the) fifth *or* the fifth of November; **quel jour sommes-nous? – le c. novembre** what's the date today? – the fifth of November; **Louis V** Louis the Fifth

3 *(pour exprimer les minutes)* **trois heures c.** five past three; **trois heures moins c.** five to three; *Fam* **elle est arrivée à c.** she arrived at five past; **c. minutes** *(d'horloge)* five minutes; *(un moment)* a short while; **c. minutes plus tard, il a changé d'avis** a few minutes later he changed

his mind; **j'en ai pour c. minutes** it'll only take me a few minutes; **il doit s'absenter c. minutes pour changer sa voiture de place** he's got to go and move his car, it'll only take him a few minutes; **c'est à c. minutes (d'ici)** it's not very far from here

PRON five; **nous étions c. dans la pièce** there were five of us in the room; **j'en ai c.** I've got five; *Fam* **en serrer c. à qn** to shake hands with sb■

NM INV **1** *(gén)* five; **c. est la moitié de dix** five is half of ten; **c. et c. font dix** five and five are ten; **deux fois c.** two times five, twice five

2 *(numéro d'ordre)* number five; **c'est le c. qui a gagné** number five wins; **allez au c.** *(maison)* go to number five

3 *(chiffre écrit)* five; **dessiner un c.** to draw a five

4 *(dans un jeu)* five; *(quille)* kingpin; *Cartes* **le c. de carreau/pique** the five of diamonds/spades

5 *TV* **La C., La 5** = former French television channel

6 *Mus* **le groupe des C.** the Five

□ **cinq sur cinq** ADV *aussi Fig* **je te reçois c. sur c.** I'm reading *or* receiving you loud and clear; **t'as compris? – c. sur c.!** got it? – got it!

□ **en cinq sec** ADV *Fam* in no time at all, in two shakes; **en c. sec, c'était fait** it was done in no time

□ **cinq à sept** NM INV *Fam (réunion)* afternoon get-together; *(rendez-vous amoureux)* lovers' rendez-vous *(typically after work)*

cinquantaine [sɛ̃kãtɛn] NF **1** *(quantité)* **une c.** around *or* about fifty, fifty *or* so; **une c. de voitures** around *or* about fifty cars; **elle a une c. d'années** she's around *or* about fifty (years old) **2** *(âge)* **avoir la c.** to be around *or* about fifty; **quand on arrive à** *ou* **atteint la c.** when you hit fifty

cinquante [sɛ̃kãt] ADJ **1** *(gén)* fifty; **c. est la moitié de cent** fifty is half of one hundred; **c. et un** fifty-one; **c.-deux** fifty-two; **c. et unième** fifty-first; **mille habitants** fifty thousand inhabitants; *Fam* **deux billets de c.** two fifty-euro notes■ *or* fifties; **dans les années c.** in the fifties; **la mode des années c.** fifties' fashions; **c. pour cent des personnes interrogées pensent que...** fifty per cent of *or* half the people we asked think that...; **il est mort à c. ans** he died at *or* when he was fifty

2 *(dans des séries)* fiftieth; **page/numéro c.** page/number fifty

3 *Sport* **le c. mètres** the fifty metres

4 *Fam (locutions)* **des solutions, il n'y en a pas c.** there aren't that many ways to solve the problem; **je te l'ai dit c. fois!** if I've told you once, I've told you a hundred times!

PRON fifty

NM INV **1** *(gén)* fifty; **c. est la moitié de cent** fifty is half of one hundred; **c. et c. font cent** fifty and fifty are a hundred; **deux fois c.** two times fifty

2 *(numéro d'ordre)* number fifty; **c'est le c. qui a gagné** number fifty wins; **allez au c.** *(maison)* go to number fifty

3 *(chiffre écrit)* fifty; **le c. n'est pas lisible** the fifty is illegible

cinquantenaire [sɛ̃kãtnɛr] ADJ **1** *(qui dure cinquante ans)* fifty-year *(avant n)* **2** *(bâtiment)* over fifty years old

NM fiftieth anniversary, golden jubilee

cinquantième [sɛ̃kãtjɛm] ADJ fiftieth

NMF **1** *(personne)* fiftieth **2** *(objet)* fiftieth (one)

NM **1** *(partie)* fiftieth **2** *(étage) Br* fiftieth floor, *Am* fifty-first floor **3** *Naut* **les cinquantièmes hurlants** the Howling Fifties

NF *Théât* fiftieth performance; *voir aussi* **cinquième**

cinquantièmement [sɛ̃kãtjɛmmã] ADV in fiftieth place

cinquième [sɛ̃kjɛm] ADJ fifth; **le c. volume de la collection** the fifth volume in the series; **le c. de la somme globale** the fifth part of the total sum; **le vingt-c.** concurrent the twenty-fifth competitor; **la quarante-c. année** the forty-fifth year; **arriver c.** to come fifth; **c. colonne** fifth column; *Méd* **c. maladie** fifth disease; *Fig* **être la c. roue du carrosse** *ou* **de la charrette** to be a fifth wheel

NMF **1** *(personne)* fifth; **je suis c.** *(dans une file)* I'm fifth; *(dans un classement)* I came fifth

2 *(objet)* fifth (one); **le c. était cassé** the fifth (one) was broken
NM 1 *(partie)* fifth
2 *(étage) Br* floor, *Am* sixth floor
3 *(arrondissement de Paris)* fifth (arrondissement)
NF 1 *Scol Br* ≃ second year, *Am* ≃ seventh grade
2 *Aut* fifth gear; **en c.** in fifth (gear); **passer la c.** to go into fifth (gear)
3 *Mus* fifth
4 *(en danse)* fifth (position)

cinquièmement [sɛ̃kjɛmmɑ̃] **ADV** fifthly, in fifth place

cintrage [sɛ̃traʒ] **NM 1** *Métal* bending **2** *Archit* centering

cintre [sɛ̃tr] **NM 1** *(pour un habit)* (coat-)hanger **2** *Archit* arch **3** *Métal* bend, curve **4** *(d'un siège)* crest **5** *Théât* rigging loft; **les cintres** the flies

cintré, -e [sɛ̃tre] **ADJ 1** *Couture* close-fitting *(at the waist)*, waisted **2** *(fenêtre)* arched; *(poutre)* bent, curved **3** *Fam (fou)* crazy, nuts

cintrer [3] [sɛ̃tre] **VT 1** *Archit* to arch, to vault **2** *(courber)* to bend, to curve **3** *Couture* to take in *(at the waist)*

cintreuse [sɛ̃trøz] **NF** *Tech* bending machine, bender

CIO [seio] **NM 1** *(abrév* **Comité international olympique)** IOC **2** *(abrév* **centre d'information et d'orientation)** careers advisory centre

CIP¹ [seipe] *Com (abrév* **carriage and insurance paid to)** CIP

CIP² [seipe] **NM** *(abrév* **conseiller d'insertion et de probation)** probation officer

cipaille [sipaj] **NM** *Can* = type of meat pie made with hare, duck or partridge

cipaye [sipaj] **NM** *Mil* sepoy; *Hist* **la révolte des cipayes** the Indian Mutiny

cipolin [sipɔlɛ̃] **NM** *Géol* cipolin (marble), onion marble

cippe [sip] **NM** *Archéol* cippus

cipre [sipr] **NM** *Bot* bald cypress, swamp cypress

ciprière [siprijɛr] **NF** = swamp where bald cypresses grow

cirage [siraʒ] **NM** *(cire)* shoe polish; *(polissage)* polishing; *Fam* **être dans le c.** to be flying blind; *Fig* to be groggy

circadien, -enne [sirkadjɛ̃, -ɛn] **ADJ** *Biol* circadian

circaète [sirkaɛt] **NM** *Orn* circaetus

circassien, -enne [sirkasjɛ̃, -ɛn] **ADJ** Circassian **NM,F** Circassian

Circé [sirse] **NPR** *Myth* Circe

circée [sirse] **NF** *Bot* enchanter's nightshade

circompolaire [sirkɔ̃pɔlɛr] **ADJ** circumpolar

circoncire [101] [sirkɔ̃sir] **VT** to circumcise

circoncis [sirkɔ̃si] **ADJ** circumcised
NM *(garçon)* circumcised boy; *(homme)* circumcised man

circoncisait *etc voir* **circoncire**

circoncision [sirkɔ̃sizjɔ̃] **NF** circumcision

circonférence [sirkɔ̃ferɑ̃s] **NF 1** *Géom* circumference; **avoir dix centimètres de c.** to have a circumference of ten centimetres, to be ten centimetres in circumference **2** *(tour)* periphery

circonflexe [sirkɔ̃flɛks] **ADJ** *Ling* circumflex

circonlocution [sirkɔ̃lɔkysjɔ̃] **NF** *Péj* circumlocution; **que de circonlocutions!** what a roundabout way of putting it!; **parler par circonlocutions** to speak in a roundabout way; **après de longues circonlocutions…** after much beating about the bush…

circonscriptible [sirkɔ̃skriptibl] **ADJ** *Géom* circumscribable

circonscription [sirkɔ̃skripsjɔ̃] **NF 1** *Admin & Pol* area, district; **c. administrative** constituency; **c. électorale** *(aux municipales)* ward; *(aux législatives)* constituency; **c. consulaire** consular district **2** *Géom* circumscription, circumscribing

circonscrire [99] [sirkɔ̃skrir] **VT 1** *(limiter → extension, dégâts)* to limit, to control; **c. un incendie** to bring a fire under control, to contain a fire **2** *(préciser → sujet)* to define the limits or scope of **3** *Géom* to circumscribe

circonspect, -e [sirkɔ̃spɛ, -ɛkt] **ADJ** *(observateur, commentateur)* cautious, wary; *(approche)* cautious, *Sout* circumspect; **il était c. dans ses propos** he spoke cautiously

circonspection [sirkɔ̃spɛksjɔ̃] **NF** caution, cautiousness, wariness; **avec c.** cautiously, warily; **agir avec la plus extrême c.** to be extremely cautious

circonstance [sirkɔ̃stɑ̃s] **NF 1** *(situation)* circonstances circumstances; **quelles étaient les circonstances?** what were the circumstances?; **étant donné les circonstances** given the circumstances or situation; **en pareille c.** under such circumstances, in such a case
2 *(conjoncture)* circumstance, occasion; **profiter de la c.** to seize the opportunity
3 *Jur* **circonstances aggravantes/atténuantes** aggravating/extenuating circumstances
▫ **de circonstance ADJ 1** *(approprié)* appropriate, fitting; **vers de c.** occasional verse; **ce ne serait pas de c.** it would not be appropriate
2 *Gram* **complément de c.** adverbial phrase
▫ **pour la circonstance ADV** for the occasion

circonstancié, -e [sirkɔ̃stɑ̃sje] **ADJ** detailed; **je ne vous ferai pas un rapport c.** I won't go into great detail

circonstanciel, -elle [sirkɔ̃stɑ̃sjɛl] **ADJ 1** *Gram* adverbial **2** *Littéraire* circumstantial; **déclaration/mesure circonstancielle** declaration/measure dictated by the circumstances

circonvallation [sirkɔ̃valasjɔ̃] **NF** *Mil* circumvallation

circonvenir [40] [sirkɔ̃vnir] **VT** *(abuser → juge, témoin)* to circumvent; **c. l'électorat** to trick the voters

circonvoisin, -e [sirkɔ̃vwazɛ̃, -in] **ADJ** *Littéraire* neighbouring, surrounding

circonvolution [sirkɔ̃vɔlysjɔ̃] **NF 1** *(enroulement)* circumvolution **2** *Anat* convolution, gyrus; *Méd* **circonvolutions cérébrales** cerebral convolutions

circuit [sirkɥi] **NM 1** *Aut & Sport* circuit; **c. automobile** racing circuit
2 *(itinéraire)* tour, trip; **faire le c. des châteaux/vins** to do a tour of the chateaux/vineyards; **c. touristique** organized trip or tour
3 *(détour)* detour, circuitous route; **faire un long c. pour arriver quelque part** to make a long detour to get somewhere; *Fig* **par tout un c. de raisonnement** through a long and complicated thought process
4 *Élec & Électron* circuit; **couper le c.** to switch off; **mettre qch en c.** to connect sth, to switch sth on; **mettre qch hors c.** to disconnect sth; **c. basse tension** low-tension circuit; **c. haute tension** high-tension circuit; **c. d'induction** inductive circuit; **c. de retour à la masse** earth return circuit
5 *Ordinat* **c. de commande** command circuit; **c. ET** AND circuit; **c. imprimé** printed circuit; **c. intégré** integrated circuit; **c. de liaison** link circuit; **c. logique** logic circuit
6 *Tech & Aut* **c. d'allumage** ignition system; **c. d'allumage par bobine** coil-ignition system; **c. de carburant étanche** sealed fuel system; **c. de charge** *(de pile)* charging system; **c. de démarrage** starting circuit; **c. d'eau** water circuit; **c. de freinage** braking system; **c. de graissage** lubrication circuit; **c. hydraulique** hydraulic circuit; **c. d'injection d'essence** petrol injection system; **c. de lubrification** lubrication system; **c. oléopneumatique** air/hydraulic system; **c. de préchauffage** pre-heating system; **c. de refroidissement** cooling system
7 *(parcours)* progression, route
8 *Écon & Com* channel; **c. commercial** commercial channel; **c. de distribution** distribution network; **le c. de distribution du pain** the distribution channels for bread; **c. de commercialisation** marketing network, trade or marketing channel; **circuits de vente** commercial channels
9 *Cin* network; **le film est fait pour le c. commercial** it's a mainstream movie
10 *Rad* **c. de cryptage** scrambling circuit
11 *(pourtour d'une ville)* circumference
12 *(location)* **elle est encore dans le c.** she's still around; **quand je rentrerai dans le c.** when I'm back in circulation
▫ **en circuit fermé ADJ** *(télévision)* closed-circuit *(avant n)* **ADV 1** *Électron* in closed circuit **2** *(discuter, vivre)* without any outside contact

circulaire [sirkylɛr] **ADJ 1** *(rond)* circular, round **2** *(tournant → mouvement, regard)* circular **3**
Transp Br return *(avant n)*, *Am* round-trip *(avant n)* **4** *(définition, raisonnement)* circular
NF circular

circulairement [sirkylɛrmɑ̃] **ADV** *(marcher, rouler)* in a circle

circulant [sirkylɑ̃] **ADJ** *Fin (billets, devises)* in circulation; *(capitaux)* circulating

circulariser [3] [sirkylarise] **VT** to make circular, to circularize

circularité [sirkylarite] **NF 1** *(forme)* roundness **2** *(d'un raisonnement)* circularity

circulation [sirkylasjɔ̃] **NF 1** *Transp* traffic; **la c. des camions est interdite le dimanche** *Br* lorries or *Am* trucks are not allowed to run on Sundays; **la c. est très difficile** the traffic is very heavy; **il y a de la/peu de c. aujourd'hui** the traffic is heavy/there isn't much traffic today; **encore quelques petits problèmes de c. au nord de Lyon** still some congestion north of Lyons; **une route à grande c.** a trunk road; **c. aérienne/ferroviaire/routière** air/rail/road traffic
2 *(du sang, de l'air, d'un fluide)* circulation; **avoir une bonne/mauvaise c.** to have good/bad circulation; **des problèmes de c.** circulation or circulatory problems
3 *(déplacement)* movement, circulation; **la libre c. des personnes/des biens/des capitaux** the free movement of people/goods/capital; **c. monétaire** circulation of money, money in circulation
4 *(circuit)* **enlever** ou **retirer de la c.** *Com* to take off the market; *Fig* to take out of circulation; **être en c.** to be on the market; **mettre en c.** *(argent)* to put into circulation; *Com* to bring out, to put on the market

circulatoire [sirkylatwar] **ADJ** *(appareil, troubles)* circulatory

circuler [3] [sirkyle] **VI 1** *(se déplacer → personne)* to move; **circulez, il n'y a rien à voir** move along now, there's nothing to see; **je n'aime pas que les enfants circulent dans toute la maison** I don't like the children to have the run of the whole house
2 *Transp (conducteur)* to drive; *(flux de voitures)* to move; *(train, bus)* to run; **rien ne circule ce matin** the traffic's at a standstill this morning; **on circule très mal à ce moment de la journée** it's very difficult to get anywhere at this time of day; **en Angleterre on circule à gauche** they drive on the left in England; **le bus 21 circule de nuit** the number 21 bus runs at night
3 *(air, fluide)* to circulate
4 *(passer de main en main)* to be passed around or round; *Fin (billets, devises)* to be in circulation; *Fin (capitaux)* to be circulating; **le rapport circule** the report's being circulated; **faites c. la bouteille** pass the bottle round; **faire c. des faux billets** to put forged banknotes into circulation; **faire c. une pétition** to circulate a petition; *Fin* **faire c. des effets** to keep bills afloat
5 *(se propager)* to circulate; **faire c. des bruits** to spread rumours; **c'est une rumeur qui circule** it's a rumour that's going around; **l'information ne circule pas** information is not getting around

---

Allusion

Circulez, y'a rien à voir!

This was originally said by police when an accident or a disturbance in the crowd was making people slow down to stare: "Move along now, there's nothing to see." Comedians such as Francis Blanche and Coluche have used this phrase figuratively to mean "We won't dwell on that, will we?", particularly when there is an idea of cover-up, or information being swept under the carpet. In newspaper articles, the expression is used to suggest deliberate obfuscation on the part of the authorities, and means "They don't want us to know about this."

---

circumambulation [sirkɔ̃mɑ̃bylasjɔ̃] **NF** *Rel* circumambulation

circumduction [sirkɔ̃mdyksjɔ̃] **NF** *Physiol* circumduction

circumlunaire [sirkɔ̃mlynɛr] **ADJ** *Astron* circumlunar

cin–cir

circumnavigation [sirkɔmnavigasjɔ̃] NF circumnavigation

circumnaviguer [3] [sirkɔmnavige] VT to circumnavigate

circumpolaire [sirkɔmpɔlɛr] ADJ circumpolar

circumstellaire [sirkɔmstelɛr] ADJ circumstellar

circumterrestre [sirkɔmterɛstr] ADJ around-the-world (*avant n*)

cire [sir] NF **1** (*pour le bois*) (wax) polish
  2 (*plastique, dans une ruche*) wax; **un personnage en c.** a waxwork; **c. d'abeille** beeswax; **c. à cacheter** sealing wax
  3 (*dans l'oreille*) earwax
  4 *Pétr* mineral *or* earth wax
  5 (*locution*) **c'est une c. molle** he's/she's got no will of his/her own
  ❑ **à (la) cire perdue** ADJ lost-wax ADV using the lost-wax process
  ❑ **de cire** ADJ (*poupée, figurine*) wax (*avant n*); *Vieilli* **musée de c., cabinet de c.** waxworks

ciré, -e [sire] ADJ (*meuble, parquet*) waxed, polished; (*chaussures*) polished
  NM **1** (*vêtement* → *gén*) (oil) skin; (→ *de marin*) sou'wester **2** *Tex* oilskin

cirer [3] [sire] VT **1** (*faire briller* → *meuble, parquet*) to wax, to polish; (→ *chaussure*) to polish; *Fam Fig* **c. les pompes à qn** to lick sb's boots **2** *très Fam* (*locution*) **il en a rien à c. (de tes histoires)** he doesn't give a damn (abour your stories)

cireur, -euse[1] [sirœr, -øz] NM,F (*de rue*) shoeshiner; *Fam* **un c. de pompes** a bootlicker
  ❑ **cireuse** NF floor polisher

cireux, -euse[2] [sirø, -øz] ADJ **1** (*comme la cire*) waxy, wax-like, *Littéraire* waxen **2** (*jaunâtre*) wax-coloured, *Littéraire* waxen

cirier, -ère [sirje, -jɛr] ADJ wax-producing, wax (*avant n*)
  NM **1** (*marchand ou fabricant de cierges*) (wax) chandler; (*personne qui travaille la cire*) wax worker **2** *Hist* **C. de la grande chancellerie** chafewax, chaffwax **3** *Bot* wax-myrtle, candleberry tree, *Am* bayberry
  ❑ **cirière** NF **1** (*abeille*) wax-making bee **2** (*personne qui vend des cierges*) candle-seller (*in church*)

ciron [sirɔ̃] NM *Entom* cheese-mite

cirque [sirk] NM **1** (*chapiteau*) circus, big top; (*représentation*) circus; **aller au c.** to go to the circus; **c. forain** *ou* **ambulant** travelling circus; *Fig* **c. médiatique** media circus
  2 *Fam* (*agitation, désordre*) **c'est pas un peu fini ce c.?** will you stop fooling around?; **c'est un vrai c. ici!** it's chaos *or* pandemonium in here!
  3 *Fam* (*complications*) **quel c. pour obtenir ces renseignements!** what a performance *or* carry-on just to get this information!; **arrête un peu ton c.!** stop making a fuss!; **faire son c.** to make a fuss; **tous les matins, elle fait son c. pour s'habiller** every morning she makes an awful fuss about getting dressed
  4 *Géog* cirque, corrie; (*sur la Lune*) crater; **c. glaciaire** curm
  5 *Antiq* amphitheatre; **les jeux du c.** the circus games

'Le Cirque' Seurat 'The Circus'

cirre, cirrhe [sir] NM **1** *Bot* cirrus, tendril **2** *Zool* barbel, tentacle

cirrhose [siroz] NF *Méd* cirrhosis; **c. du foie** cirrhosis of the liver; **avoir une c. du foie** to have cirrhosis (of the liver)

cirrhotique [sirɔtik] *Méd* ADJ (*foie*) cirrhotic
  NMF cirrhotic, cirrhosis sufferer

cirripède [siripɛd] *Zool* NM (*crustacé*) cirripede
  ❑ **cirripèdes** NMPL Cirripedia

cirrocumulus [sirɔkymylys] NM INV *Météo* cirrocumulus

cirrostratus [sirɔstratys] NM INV *Météo* cirrostratus

cirrus [sirys] NM INV *Météo* cirrus

cirse [sirs] NM *Bot* plume thistle

cisaillage [sizajaʒ] NM **1** *Métal* shearing, cutting **2** (*du linge*) quilling, fluting

cisaille [sizaj] NF **1** *Tech* (*outil*) **c., cisailles** (pair of) shears; **c. à bordures** edging shears; **c. à haies** hedge clipper(s); **c. à lame** guillotine; **c.**

circulaire rotary shears **2** *Métal* (*rognures*) parings, cuttings

cisaillement [sizajmɑ̃] NM **1** *Métal* cutting **2** *Hort* pruning **3** *Tech* (*usure*) shearing, shear

cisailler [3] [sizaje] VT **1** (*barbelés, tôle*) to cut **2** (*branches*) to prune **3** (*couper grossièrement*) to hack (at)
  ▸**se cisailler** VPR **1** (*métal*) to shear off **2** (*se couper*) **il s'est cisaillé la joue** he cut *or* slashed his cheek

cisalpin, -e [sizalpɛ̃, -in] ADJ Cisalpine; **la Gaule cisalpine** Cisalpine Gaul

ciseau, -x [sizo] NM **1** *Tech* (*outil*) chisel; **sculpter une figure au c.** to chisel out a figure; **c. à froid** cold chisel **2** *Sport* (*prise de catch, de lutte*) scissors hold
  ❑ **ciseaux** NMPL **1** (*outil*) (**une paire de**) **ciseaux** (a pair of) scissors; (**une paire de**) **grands ciseaux** (a pair of) shears; **donner un coup de ciseaux dans un tissu** to cut a piece of material with scissors; **donner des coups de ciseaux dans un texte** to make cuts in a text; **ciseaux à bouts ronds** blunt- *or* round-ended scissors; **ciseaux de couturière** dressmaking scissors; **ciseaux à denteler** pinking shears; **ciseaux à ongles** nail scissors; *Littéraire* **les ciseaux de la Parque** the shears of Atropos
  2 *Sport* **saut en ciseaux** scissor jump; **sauter en ciseaux** to do a scissor jump
  3 *Gym* **faire des ciseaux** to do the scissors

ciselage [sizlaʒ], **cisèlement** [sizɛlmɑ̃] NM (*d'une grappe de raisin*) shearing; (*du métal*) engraving; (*du cuir*) embossing

ciseler [25] [sizle] VT **1** (*métal* → *en défonçant*) to engrave; (→ *en repoussant*) to emboss; (*pierre*) to chisel; **un bracelet en or ciselé** an engraved gold bracelet; *Fig* **son nez délicatement ciselé** his/her finely chiselled nose **2** *Littéraire* (*texte*) **un sonnet délicatement ciselé** a delicately crafted sonnet **3** (*ciboulette*) to snip **4** (*grappe de raisin*) to shear (off)

ciselet [sizlɛ] NM *Tech* small chisel

ciseleur [sizlœr] NM engraver

ciselure [sizlyr] NF **1** *Métal* (*en défoncé*) engraving; (*en repoussé*) embossing; (*sur un bijou*) (engraved) design **2** *Beaux-Arts & Menuis* chiselling **3** (*de reliure*) embossing

Cisjordanie [sisʒɔrdani] NF **la C.** the West Bank

cisjordanien, -enne [sisʒɔrdanjɛ̃, -ɛn] ADJ of/from the West Bank
  ❑ **Cisjordanien, -enne** NM,F = inhabitant of or person from the West Bank

CISL [seiɛsɛl] NF (*abrév* **Confédération internationale des syndicats libres**) ICFTU

ciste[1] [sist] NM *Bot* (*arbrisseau*) cistus, rockrose

ciste[2] [sist] NF *Antiq* **1** (*corbeille*) cist **2** (*tombe*) cist, kist

cistercien, -enne [sistɛrsjɛ̃, -ɛn] *Rel* ADJ Cistercian
  NM,F Cistercian; **les cisterciens** the Cistercians

cisticole [sistikɔl] NM *Orn* **c. des joncs** fan-tailed warbler

cistre [sistr] NM *Mus* cithern, cittern

cistron [sistrɔ̃] NM *Biol* cistron

cistude [sistyd] NF *Zool* European pond tortoise

citable [sitabl] ADJ quotable, citable

citadelle [sitadɛl] NF **1** *Constr* citadel; *Fig* **la ferme avait été transformée en c.** the farm had been made into a fortress **2** (*centre*) stronghold

citadin, -e [sitadɛ̃, -in] ADJ (*habitude, paysage*) city (*avant n*), town (*avant n*); (*population*) town-dwelling, city-dwelling
  NM,F (*habitant d'une grande ville*) city-dweller, town-dweller; **les citadins** the townsfolk, the townspeople; **moi, je suis un c., je ne pourrais pas vivre à la campagne** I'm a real city person, I could never live in the country

citateur, -trice [sitatœr, -tris] NM,F quoter, citer
  NM book of quotations

citation [sitasjɔ̃] NF **1** (*extrait*) quotation; **fin de c.** unquote **2** *Jur* summons; **c. à comparaître** (*pour un témoin*) subpoena; (*pour un accusé*) summons; **il a reçu une c. à comparaître** (*témoin*) he was subpoenaed; (*accusé*) he was summonsed; **c. directe** private prosecution **3** *Mil* **c. à l'ordre du jour** mention in dispatches

citatrice [sitatris] *voir* **citateur**

cité [site] NF **1** (*ville*) city; (*plus petite*) town; **c. linéaire** ribbon development
  2 (*dans des noms de lieux*) **la C. interdite** the Forbidden City; **la C. de la Musique** = cultural centre devoted to music in the Parc de la Villette in Paris; **la c. des Papes** Avignon; **la c. phocéenne** Marseille, Marseilles; **la C. des Sciences et de l'Industrie** = science and technology museum complex at La Villette in the north of Paris
  3 (*résidence*) (housing) *Br* estate *or* *Am* development; **les cités de banlieue** suburban housing estates (*in France, often evocative of poverty and delinquency*); **c. de transit** transit *or* temporary camp; **c. ouvrière** *Br* ≃ council estate, *Am* ≃ housing project; **c. universitaire, Fam c. U** *Br* hall of residence, halls of residence, *Am* dormitory
  4 *Antiq* city-state
  5 *Rel* **la c. céleste** the Heavenly City; **la c. sainte** the Holy City

'La Cité de Dieu' saint Augustin 'The City of God'

Cîteaux [sito] *voir* **abbaye**

cité-dortoir [sitedɔrtwar] (*pl* **cités-dortoirs**) NF commuter town

cité-État [siteeta] (*pl* **cités-États**) NF city state

cité-jardin [siteʒardɛ̃] (*pl* **cités-jardins**) NF garden city

citer [3] [site] VT **1** (*donner un extrait de*) to cite, to quote (from); **je vous ai cité dans mon article** I quoted you in my article; **il a dit, je cite:...** he said, and I quote:...
  2 (*mentionner*) to mention; **son ouvrage principal n'est même pas cité** his/her main work isn't even mentioned; **c. qn en exemple** to cite sb as an example
  3 (*énumérer*) to name, to quote, to list
  4 *Jur* (*témoin*) to subpoena; (*accusé*) to summons
  5 *Mil* to mention; **c. un soldat à l'ordre du jour** to mention a soldier in dispatches

citerne [sitɛrn] NF **1** (*cuve*) tank; (*pour l'eau*) water tank, cistern; **c. à mazout** oil tank **2** *Naut* tank **3** (*camion*) tanker **4** *Rail Br* tank wagon, *Am* tank car

CITES [sitɛs] NF (*abrév* **Convention on the International Trade of Endangered Species**) CITES

cithare [sitar] NF *Antiq* cithara; (*instrument moderne*) zither

citharède [sitarɛd] NMF *Antiq* citharist

cithariste [sitarist] NMF *Mus* cithara player

citizen band [sitizɛnbɑ̃d] (*pl* **citizen bands**) NF Citizens' Band, CB

citoyen, -enne [sitwajɛ̃, -ɛn] NM,F **1** *Hist & Pol* citizen; **les droits du c.** civic rights; **accomplir son devoir de c.** (*voter*) to do one's civic duty, to vote; **c. d'honneur** = freeman **2** *Fam* (*personnage*) **qu'est-ce que c'est que ce c.-là?** (*inquiétant*) he's a bit of *Br* a queer fish *or* *Am* an odd duck; (*amusant*) what an eccentric!
  ADJ (*relatif à la citoyenneté*) civic; **il s'est produit une sorte de rassemblement c. contre l'extrême-droite** there was a sort of citizens' movement against the far right; **il faut encourager l'engagement c. au niveau local pour renforcer le tissu social** civic engagement on a local level should be encouraged as a way of strengthening the fabric of society; **on attend de nos élus un véritable projet c., pas une simple gestion de l'économie** we expect those we elected to come up with a manifesto which truly benefits society, not one which simply manages the economy; **cette société rêve de troquer sa réputation de pollueuse contre celle d'entreprise citoyenne** this company wants to banish its reputation as a polluter and instead to be known for being socially responsible

citoyenneté [sitwajɛnte] NF citizenship; **prendre la c. française** to acquire French citizenship

citrate [sitrat] NM *Chim* citrate

citrin, -e [sitrɛ̃, -in] ADJ *Littéraire* lemon-yellow; *Pharm* **onguent c.** citrine ointment
  ❑ **citrine** NF **1** *Minér* citrine **2** *Chim* lemon oil

citrique [sitrik] ADJ *Chim* citric

citron [sitrɔ̃] NM **1** (*fruit*) lemon; **c. givré** lemon *Br* sorbet *or* *Am* sherbet (*served inside the skin of a whole lemon*); **c. pressé** freshly squeezed lemon juice; **c. vert** lime

2 *Fam (tête)* nut; **se presser** *ou* **se creuser le c.** to rack *or Am* cudgel one's brains
3 *Minér* brimstone
4 *Can Joual (voiture)* defective car, *Am* lemon
ADJ INV (jaune) c. lemon-yellow, lemon
❑ **au citron ADJ** *(lotion, savon)* lemon *(avant n)*; *(gâteau, sauce)* lemon *(avant n)*, lemon-flavoured; **parfumé au c.** lemon-scented

citronnade [sitrɔnad] **NF** *Br* lemon squash, *Am* lemonade

citronné, -e [sitrɔne] **ADJ** *(gâteau, sauce)* lemon-flavoured; *(pochette)* lemon-scented; *(eau de toilette, lotion)* lemon *(avant n)*

citronnelle [sitrɔnɛl] **NF 1** *(mélisse)* lemon balm **2** *(aromate tropical)* lemongrass **3** *(baume)* citronella oil **4** *(boisson)* citronella liqueur

citronner [3] [sitrɔne] **VT** *Culin* to squeeze lemon juice over

citronnier [sitrɔnje] **NM 1** *Bot* lemon tree **2** *Menuis* East Indian *or* Ceylon satinwood

citrouille [sitruj] **NF 1** *(fruit)* pumpkin; *Fam* **j'ai la tête comme une c.** my head is fit to burst **2** *Fam (tête)* nut

citrus [sitrys] **NM** *Bot* Citrus

çivaïsme [ʃivaism] = **shivaïsme**

çivaïte [ʃivait] = **shivaïte**

cive [siv] **NF** chives

civelle [sivɛl] **NF** elver

civet [sivɛ] **NM** civet, stew; **c. de lapin** rabbit stew; **c. de lièvre, lièvre en c.** civet of hare, ≃ jugged hare

civette [sivɛt] **NF 1** *Bot* chives **2** *(animal, parfum, fourrure)* civet; *Zool* **c. des palmiers** palm civet

civière [sivjɛr] **NF** *Méd* stretcher

civil, -e [sivil] **ADJ 1** *(non religieux)* civil; **mariage c.** civil marriage ceremony; **enterrement c.** non-religious burial
2 *(non militaire)* civilian; **porter des vêtements civils** to wear civilian clothes
3 *Admin* **jour c.** civil *or* calendar day
4 *(non pénal)* civil
5 *Littéraire (courtois)* courteous, civil
NM 1 *(non militaire)* civilian
2 *Jur* civil action; **porter une affaire au c.** to bring a case before the civil courts
❑ **dans le civil ADV** in civilian life
❑ **en civil ADJ être en c.** *(soldat)* to be wearing civilian clothes; **policier en c.** plain clothes policeman

civilement [sivilmɑ̃] **ADV 1** *Jur* **se marier c.** to have a civil wedding, *Br* ≃ to get married in a registry office; **être enterré c.** to be buried without religious ceremony; **être c. responsable** to be legally responsible; **poursuivre qn c.** to bring a civil action against sb **2** *(courtoisement)* courteously

civilisable [sivilizabl] **ADJ** civilizable

civilisateur, -trice [sivilizatœr, -tris] **ADJ** civilizing
NM,F civilizer

civilisation [sivilizasjɔ̃] **NF 1** *(culture)* civilization; **les grandes civilisations du passé** great civilizations of the past
2 *(action de civiliser)* civilization, civilizing
3 *(fait d'être civilisé)* civilization
4 *Hum (confort)* civilization; **nous sommes revenus à la c. après dix jours sous la tente** we got back to civilization after ten days under canvas
❑ **de civilisation ADJ langue de c.** language of culture; **maladie de c.** social disease

civilisatrice [sivilizatris] *voir* **civilisateur**

civilisé, -e [sivilize] **ADJ** *(nation, peuple)* civilized; *Fam* **on est chez des gens civilisés, ici!** we're not savages!
NM,F civilized person, member of a civilized society

civiliser [3] [sivilize] **VT** *(société, tribu)* to civilize, to bring civilization to; *Fig* **c. qn** to civilize sb, to have a civilizing influence on sb
▸**se civiliser VPR** to become civilized

civiliste [sivilist] **NMF** specialist in civil law

civilité [sivilite] **NF** *Littéraire (qualité)* politeness, polite behaviour, *Sout* civility; **la plus élémentaire c. voudrait que l'on fasse** *ou* **serait de...** it would be only polite to...
❑ **civilités NFPL** *Littéraire (paroles)* polite greetings; **présenter ses civilités à qn** to pay one's respects to sb; **rivalisant de civilités** making polite comments to one another

civique [sivik] **ADJ** *(gén)* civic; *(droits)* civil; **avoir l'esprit c.** to be public-spirited; *Anciennement Scol* **éducation** *ou* **instruction c.** civics *(singulier)*

civisme [sivism] **NM** sense of citizenship, public-spiritedness

CJAI [seʒiai] **NF** *UE (abrév* **Coopération concernant la justice et les affaires intérieures)** CJHA

CJE [seʒeə] **NM** *(abrév* **contrat jeune en entreprise)** = contract to help young unemployed people (aged 16–22) with few qualifications into the job market, under which employers must pay at least the minimum wage but receive government aid with employer contributions

cl *(abrév écrite* **centilitre)** cl

clabaud [klabo] **NM 1** *Chasse (chien)* babbler, mouthy hound **2** *Fam* ill-natured gossip, scandalmonger, *Vieilli* idle talker, chatterer

clabaudage [klabodaʒ] **NM** *Littéraire (médisance)* (spiteful) gossip, backbiting

clabauder [3] [klabode] **VI** *Littéraire* **1** *(chien de chasse)* to bark (a lot) **2** *Fig* **c. sur** *ou* **contre qn** to say nasty things about sb

clabauderie [klabodri] **NF** *Littéraire (médisance)* (spiteful) gossip, backbiting

clabaudeur, -euse [klabodœr, -øz] **ADJ 1** *(chien)* barking **2** *Fig* gossiping, backbiting
NM,F *Fig* gossip, scandalmonger

clabot [klabo] **NM** dog clutch

clabotage [klabɔtaʒ] **NM 1** *(d'une carrière d'ardoise)* first shaft (of a slate quarry) **2** *Tech* jaw clutching; *Aut* **c. du différentiel** four wheel drive system

claboter [3] [klabɔte] **VT** to connect with a dog clutch

clac [klak] **EXCLAM** *(bruit → de fouet)* crack!; *(→ d'une fenêtre)* slam!; **le c. c. c. des sabots des chevaux** the clip-clop of the horses' hooves

clacher [3] [klaʃe] **VT** *Belg* **1** *(peinturlurer)* to daub with paint **2** *(barbouiller lors d'un bizutage, d'une manifestation)* to throw paint at

clacos [klakos] **NM** *Fam* camembert■

clade [klad] **NM** *Biol* clade

cladisme [kladism] **NM** cladistics *(singulier)*

cladistique [kladistik] *Biol* **ADJ** cladistic
NF cladistics *(singulier)*

cladocère [kladɔsɛr] *Zool* **NM** *(crustacé)* cladoceran
❑ **cladocères NMPL** Cladocera

cladogramme [kladɔgram] **NM** *Biol* cladogram

cladonie [kladɔni] **NF** *Bot* reindeer moss

clafoutis [klafuti] **NM** clafoutis *(dessert made from cherries or other fruit cooked in batter)*

claie [klɛ] **NF 1** *(pour les fruits)* rack **2** *(barrière)* fence, hurdle **3** *(tamis)* riddle, screen

claim [klɛm] **NM 1** *(titre)* claim, mining concession **2** *(terrain)* claim

---

CLAIR, -E [klɛr]

> **ADJ** light **1, 4** ▪ clear **2, 5–8** ▪ thin **3** ▪ obvious **8**
> **NM** light colour **1**
> **ADV** light

ADJ 1 *(lumineux)* light; **la pièce est très claire le matin** the room gets a lot of light in the morning; **une nuit claire** a fine *or* cloudless night; **une claire journée de juin** a fine *or* bright day in June; **un ciel c.** a clear *or* cloudless sky; **par temps c.** in clear weather; **il a le regard c.** he's got bright eyes
2 *(limpide → eau)* clear, transparent; **teint c.** *(frais)* clear complexion; *(pâle)* fair complexion
3 *(peu épais → gén)* thin; *(→ soupe)* clear; *(rare)* sparse; **des bois clairs** sparsely wooded area
4 *(couleur)* light; **porter des vêtements clairs** to wear light *or* light-coloured clothes; **vert/rose c.** light green/pink; **une robe bleu c.** a pale blue dress
5 *(bien timbré)* clear; **d'une voix claire** in a clear voice
6 *(précis → compte-rendu)* clear; **un résumé c. de la situation** a clear *or* lucid account of the situation; **ce n'est pas très c., précisez** it's not very clear, be more precise; **il a été on ne peut plus c. (là-dessus)** he was perfectly clear (about it); **se faire une idée claire de** to form a clear *or* precise picture of; **vous pourriez être plus c.?** could you elucidate?
7 *(perspicace)* clear; **je n'ai plus les idées très claires** I can't see things clearly any more; **avoir l'esprit c.** to be clear-thinking
8 *(évident)* clear, obvious; **il est c. que nous irons** obviously we'll go; **c'est c. et net** it's obvious; **il n'a rien compris, c'est c. et net** he clearly hasn't understood a thing; **je veux une réponse claire et nette** I want a definite answer; **cette affaire n'est pas très claire** there's something fishy about all this; **c'est c. comme le jour** *ou* **comme de l'eau de roche** *ou* **comme deux et deux font quatre** it's crystal clear
NM 1 *(couleur)* light colour; *Beaux-Arts* **les clairs et les sombres** light and shade
2 *Astron* **c. de lune** moonlight; **il y a un beau c. de lune ce soir** it's a fine moonlit night tonight; **au c. de lune** in the moonlight; **c. de terre** earthlight
3 *(locution)* **le plus c. de** the best part of; **passer le plus c. de son temps à faire qch** to spend most *or* the best part of one's time doing sth
ADV il fait déjà c. dehors it's already light outside; **il fait plus c. dans cette pièce** this room is brighter, there's more light in this room; **il ne fait pas très c. ici** there isn't much light here; **parlons c.** let's not mince words!; **il ne voit pas très c.** he can't see too clearly *or* well; **on n'y voit plus très c. à cette heure-ci** the light's not really good enough at this time of the day; **y voir c.** *(dans une situation)* to see things clearly; **j'aimerais y voir c.** I'd like to understand; **y voir c. dans le jeu de qn** to see right through sb, to see through sb's little game
❑ **au clair ADJ** *voir* **sabre ADV tirer du vin au c.** to decant wine; **mettre** *ou* **tirer qch au c.** to clarify sth; **il faut tirer cette affaire au c.** this matter must be cleared up; **mettre ses idées au c.** to get one's ideas straight; **mettre qch au c. avec qn** to sort sth out with sb, to get sth straight with sb
❑ **en clair ADV 1** *(sans code)* **envoyer un message en c.** to send an unscrambled message; *TV* **diffuser en c.** to broadcast unscrambled programmes; *TV* **en c. jusqu'à 20 heures** can be watched by non-subscribers until 8 o'clock
2 *(bref)* in plain language
❑ **claire NF 1** *(bassin)* oyster bed
2 *(huître)* fattened oyster

---

clairance [klɛrɑ̃s] **NF** *Méd* clearance

clairement [klɛrmɑ̃] **ADV** clearly; **il a répondu très c.** his answer was quite clear; **on le voit c. sur le tableau** it's clearly visible on the board

clairet, -ette [klɛrɛ, -ɛt] **ADJ 1** *(léger → sauce, vin)* light, *Péj* thin **2** *(faible → voix)* thin, reedy
NM = light red wine
❑ **clairette NF** = light sparkling wine

claire-voie [klɛrvwa] *(pl* **claires-voies) NF 1** *(barrière)* lattice, open-worked fence **2** *Archit* clerestory, clearstory **3** *Naut* deadlight
❑ **à claire-voie ADJ** open-work

clairière [klɛrjɛr] **NF 1** *(dans une forêt)* clearing, glade **2** *Tex* thin place

clair-obscur [klɛrɔpskyr] *(pl* **clairs-obscurs) NM 1** *Beaux-Arts* chiaroscuro **2** *(pénombre)* twilight, half-light

clairon [klɛrɔ̃] **NM** *Mus (instrument)* bugle; *(joueur)* bugler; *(d'orgue)* clarion stop

claironnant, -e [klɛrɔnɑ̃, -ɑ̃t] **ADJ** *(voix)* resonant, *Littéraire* stentorian; **...dit-il d'une voix claironnante** ...he said, his words ringing out

claironner [3] [klɛrɔne] **VI 1** *(crier)* to shout **2** *(jouer du clairon)* to sound the bugle
VT to proclaim far and wide, to broadcast (to all and sundry)

clairsemé, -e [klɛrsəme] **ADJ** *(barbe, cheveux)* sparse, thin; *(arbres)* scattered; *(public, gazon)* sparse; *(population)* scattered, sparse; **il a eu quelques succès clairsemés au cours des 20 dernières années** he has had occasional successes over the last 20 years

clairsemer [19] [klɛrsəme] **se clairsemer VPR** to become scattered, to thin out; **la foule se clairsema** the crowd thinned out

Clairvaux [klɛrvo] *voir* **abbaye**

clairvoyance [klɛrvwajɑ̃s] **NF 1** *(lucidité)* clearsightedness; **faire preuve de c.** to be clearsighted; **il l'avait analysé avec c.** he had analysed it perceptively **2** *(de médium)* clairvoyance

clairvoyant, -e [klɛrvwajɑ̃, -ɑ̃t] **ADJ 1** *(lucide → personne)* clearsighted, perceptive; *(→ esprit)* perceptive **2** *(non aveugle)* sighted **3** *(médium)* clairvoyant

NM,F 1 *(non aveugle)* sighted person; **les clairvoyants** the sighted **2** *(médium)* clairvoyant

clam [klam] **NM** clam

clamecer [16] [klamse] = **clamser**

clamer [3] [klame] **VT 1** *(proclamer)* **c. son innocence** to protest one's innocence; **clamant leur mécontentement** making their dissatisfaction known **2** *(crier)* to clamour, to shout

clameur [klamœr] **NF** clamour *(UNCOUNT)*; **pousser des clameurs** to shout; **la c. du marché montait** *ou* **les clameurs du marché montaient jusqu'à nos fenêtres** the hubbub of the market could be heard from our windows

clamp [klɑ̃p] **NM** *Méd* clamp

clampage [klɑ̃paʒ] **NM** *Méd* clamping

clamper [3] [klɑ̃pe] **VT** *Méd* to clamp

clampin [klɑ̃pɛ̃] **NM** *Fam* guy, *Br* bloke; **il y avait juste deux trois clampins accoudés au bar** there were just a couple of random guys propping up the bar

clamser [3] [klamse] **VI** *très Fam* to kick the bucket, to croak

clan [klɑ̃] **NM 1** *(en sociologie)* clan; **chef de c.** clan chief **2** *Péj (coterie)* clan, coterie, clique

clandé [klɑ̃de] **NM** *très Fam* **1** *(maison de passe)* whorehouse **2** *(maison de jeux)* gambling den

clandestin, -e [klɑ̃dɛstɛ̃, -in] **ADJ 1** *(secret)* secret, underground, clandestine; **un mouvement c.** an underground movement **2** *(illégal)* illegal, *Sout* illicit

NM,F *(passager)* stowaway; *(immigré)* illegal immigrant; *(travailleur)* illegal worker

clandestinement [klɑ̃dɛstinmɑ̃] **ADV 1** *(secrètement)* secretly, in secret, clandestinely **2** *(illégalement)* illegally, *Sout* illicitly

clandestinité [klɑ̃dɛstinite] **NF** secrecy, clandestine nature

❑ **dans la clandestinité ADV** underground; **entrer dans la c.** to go underground; **des armes sont fabriquées dans la c.** weapons are made clandestinely

clanique [klanik] **ADJ 1** *(en sociologie)* clan *(avant n)* **2** *Péj (coterie)* clannish

clanisme [klanism] **NM 1** *(en sociologie)* clan system **2** *Péj (comportement)* clannishness

claouis [klawi] **NMPL** *très Fam* balls, nuts

clap [klap] **NM** *Cin* clapperboard; **c. de fin** tail slate

claper [3] [klape] **VI** *Fam* to eat▪

clapet [klapɛ] **NM 1** *Tech (soupape)* valve; **c. à charnière** poppet valve; **c. d'admission/ d'échappement** inlet/exhaust valve; **c. de dérivation** by-pass valve; **c. de limitation de pression** pressure limiting valve

2 *Tél* **téléphone à c.** flip-top phone

3 *Fam (bouche)* **elle a un de ces clapets!** she's a real chatterbox!, she can talk the hind legs off a donkey!; **ferme ton c.!** shut your mouth!

clapier [klapje] **NM 1** *(à lapins)* hutch **2** *Péj (appartement)* **c'est un vrai c. ici!** it's like living in a shoe box in this place! **3** *Géol* scree

clapir [32] [klapir] **VI** *(lapin)* to squeal

clapman [klapman] *(pl* **clapmans)** **NM** *Cin* clapper boy

clapotage [klapɔtaʒ] **NM** *(des vagues)* lapping

clapotant, -e [klapɔtɑ̃, -ɑ̃t] **ADJ** lapping

clapotement [klapɔtmɑ̃] **NM** *(de l'eau)* lapping

clapoter [3] [klapɔte] **VI** *(eau, vague)* to lap

clapoteux, -euse [klapɔtø, -øz] **ADJ** lapping

clapotis [klapɔti] **NM** *(de l'eau)* lapping

clappement [klapmɑ̃] **NM** *(de la langue)* clicking; **des clappements de langue** clicks of the tongue

clapper [3] [klape] **VI c. de la langue** to click one's tongue

claquage [klakaʒ] **NM 1** *Méd (muscle)* strained muscle; *(ligament)* strained ligament; **se faire** *ou* **avoir un c.** *(muscle)* to strain a muscle; **pour éviter les claquages** *(ligament)* to avoid strained ligaments *or* straining a ligament **2** *Élec* (electric) breakdown; **c. thermique** thermal breakdown

claquant, -e [klakɑ̃, -ɑ̃t] **ADJ** *Fam* killing, *Br* knackering

claque [klak] **NM 1** *(chapeau)* opera hat

2 *Can (chaussure)* galosh, *Am* rubber

3 *très Fam (maison de passe) Br* knocking-shop, *Am* cathouse

NF 1 *(coup)* smack, slap; *Fam* **donner** *ou* **mettre une c. à qn** to give sb a slap *or* smack; *Fam* **tu vas recevoir** *ou* **prendre une c.!** you'll get a smack!; *Fig* **se prendre une c.** to get a slap in the face; **les centristes se sont pris une c. aux dernières élections** the last elections were a slap in the face for the centre party; **une bonne c.** a stinger; *très Fam* **une c. dans la gueule** a smack in the *Br* gob *or Am* kisser; *Fig* a slap in the face

2 *Théât* claque

3 *(d'une chaussure)* upper

4 *Can (chaussure)* rubber overshoe

5 *Fam (locution)* **j'en ai ma c.** *(saturé)* I've had it up to here

claqué, -e [klake] **ADJ 1** *Fam (éreinté) Br* shattered, *Am* bushed **2** *Méd* strained

claquement [klakmɑ̃] **NM** *(bruit violent)* banging, slamming; **le c. sec du fouet** the sharp crack of the whip; **un c. de doigts** a snap of the fingers; *Fig* **sur un c. de doigts** in the twinkling of an eye; **un c. de langue** a clicking of the tongue; **entendre un c. de portière** to hear a car door slam

claque-merde [klakmɛrd] **NM INV** *Vulg (bouche)* trap, *Br* gob; **tu vas le fermer ton c., dis?** will you shut the fuck up?

claquemurer [3] [klakmyre] **VT** to shut in

▸**se claquemurer VPR** to shut oneself in *or* away

claquer [3] [klake] **VT 1** *(fermer)* to bang *or* to slam (shut); **c. la porte** to slam the door; *Fig* to storm out; **c. la porte au nez à qn** to slam the door in sb's face; *Fig* to send sb packing; *Fam* **c. le beignet à qn** to shut sb up

2 *(faire résonner)* **c. sa langue** to click one's tongue; **c. des talons** to click one's heels

3 *Fam (dépenser)* to spend▪, to blow; **ils ont claqué tout l'héritage** they blew their entire inheritance; **elle claque un fric fou en vêtements** she spends a fortune on clothes; **j'ai tout claqué** I blew the lot

4 *Fam (fatiguer)* to wear out; **ça m'a claqué** *Br* it was absolutely knackering, *Am* it wiped me out

5 *Fam (gifler)* to slap

VI 1 *(résonner → porte)* to bang, to slam; *(→ drapeau, linge)* to flap; **un coup de feu a claqué** a shot rang out; **faire c. ses doigts** to snap one's fingers; **faire c. une porte** to slam a door; **faire c. sa langue** to click one's tongue; **le cocher fit c. son fouet** the coachman cracked his whip

2 *Fam (mourir)* to peg out; *(tomber en panne)* to conk out; *(griller → ampoule électrique)* to go, to blow; **le frigo va c.** the fridge is on the way out *or Br* on its last legs; **elle lui a claqué dans les bras** she just died on him/her; **le projet lui a claqué dans les doigts** *(il a échoué)* his/her project fell through

3 *(céder avec bruit → sangle)* to snap; *(→ baudruche, chewing-gum)* to pop

❑ **claquer de VT IND il claque des dents** his teeth are chattering; **c. des doigts** to snap one's fingers; *Fam* **je claque du bec** I'm starving

▸**se claquer VPR 1** *Fam (se fatiguer)* to wear oneself out; **je me suis claqué pour rien** I worked myself into the ground for nothing

2 *(se blesser)* **se c. un muscle** to strain *or* to pull a muscle; **se c. un ligament** to strain *or* to pull a ligament

claqueter [27] [klakte] **VI** *(cigogne)* to clapper

claquette [klakɛt] **NF** *Cin* clapperboard

❑ **claquettes NFPL 1** *(danse)* tap-dancing; **faire des claquettes** to tap-dance **2** *(tongs)* flipflops

claquoir [klakwar] **NM** clapperboard

clarain [klarɛ̃] **NM** *Minér* clarain

clarificateur, -trice [klarifikatœr, -tris] **ADJ** clarifying

NM clarifier, clarifying substance

clarification [klarifikasjɔ̃] **NF 1** *(explication)* clarification **2** *(d'une suspension, d'une sauce, du beurre)* clarification; *(d'un vin)* settling

clarificatrice [klarifikatris] *voir* **clarificateur**

clarifier [9] [klarifje] **VT 1** *(expliquer)* to clarify, to make clear **2** *(rendre limpide → suspension, beurre, sauce)* to clarify; *(→ vin)* to settle

▸**se clarifier VPR 1** *(situation)* to become clearer **2** *(suspension, sauce)* to become clear **3** *Chim* to become clarified

clarine [klarin] **NF** cowbell

clarinette [klarinɛt] **NF** clarinet; **c. basse** bass clarinet

clarinettiste [klarinetist] **NMF** clarinettist, clarinet player

clarisse [klaris] **NF** Clarisse; **les clarisses** the Poor Clares

clarté [klarte] **NF 1** *(lumière)* light; *(luminosité)* brightness; **la c. du jour** daylight; **à la c. de la lune** by the light of the moon, by moonlight

2 *(transparence → gén)* clarity, limpidness, clearness; *(→ du teint)* clearness

3 *(intelligibilité)* clarity, clearness; **son raisonnement n'est pas d'une grande c.** his/her reasoning is not particularly clear; **manquer de c.** *(texte, devoir, argument)* to be unclear; **parler avec c.** to speak clearly; **voir avec c. que...** to see with great clarity *or* perfectly clearly that...

❑ **clartés NFPL** *Littéraire* knowledge; **avoir des clartés sur qch** to have some knowledge of sth

clash [klaʃ] *(pl* **clashs** *ou* **clashes)** **NM** *Fam* clash, conflict; **il y a eu un c. entre nous (à propos de)** we clashed (over)

classable [klasabl] **ADJ** classable; **cette musique est difficilement c.** it's hard to classify this kind of music

CLASSE [klas] **NF A.** *Scol* **1** *(salle)* classroom

2 *(groupe)* class; **sa c.** his/her class *or* classmates; **camarade de c.** classmate; **toute la c. riait** the whole class laughed; **c. de mer** = residential classes at the seaside for schoolchildren; **c. de nature** nature study trip; **c. de neige** = residential classes in the mountains for schoolchildren; **classes de niveau** *(groupes d'élèves)* classes segregated according to pupils' ability, *Br* streamed classes; *(pratique)* segregation of classes according to pupils' ability, *Br* streaming; **c. transplantée** = generic term referring to "classe de neige", "classe de mer" and "classe verte"; **c. unique** = class where pupils belonging to different years are taught together by one teacher; **c. verte** = residential classes in the countryside for urban schoolchildren

3 *(cours)* class, lesson; **c. de français** French class; **c. de perfectionnement** advanced class; **faire la c.** *(être enseignant)* to teach; *(donner un cours)* to teach *or* to take a class; **c'est moi qui leur fais la c.** I'm their teacher; **en sortant de c.** on coming out of school

4 *(niveau)* class, *Br* year, form, *Am* grade; **il y a plusieurs classes de sixième au collège** there are several *Br* first-year *or Am* sixth grade classes at high school; **dans les grandes/petites classes** in the upper/lower *Br* years *or* forms *or Am* grades; **passer dans la c. supérieure** to move up to the next *Br* year *or* form *or Am* grade; **refaire** *ou* **redoubler une c.** to repeat a year; **classes préparatoires** *(aux grandes écoles)* = preparatory classes for the entrance examinations for the "grandes écoles"

B. *DANS UNE HIÉRARCHIE* **1** *(espèce)* class, kind; *Math* class; *(dans des statistiques)* bracket, class, group; *Compta* group of accounts; **c. d'âge** age group; **c. de revenus** income bracket

2 *(rang)* class, rank; **former une c. à part** to be in a class *or* league of one's own

3 *Pol & (en sociologie)* class; **c. sociale** social class; **les classes dirigeantes** the ruling classes; **les classes moyennes** the middle classes; **la c. ouvrière** the working class; **les classes populaires** *ou* **laborieuses** the working classes; **l'ensemble de la c. politique** the whole of the political establishment *or* class; **la c. des petits commerçants** shopkeepers as a group; **une société sans c.** a classless society

4 *Transp* class; **première/deuxième c.** first/ second class; **billet de première/deuxième c.** first-/second-class ticket; **voyager en première c.** to travel first class; *Aviat* **c. affaires/économique** business/economy class; **c. club/touriste** club/tourist class; **voyager en c. affaires/ club** to travel business/club class

5 *(niveau)* quality, class; **de grande c.** top-quality; **de première c.** first-class; **un hôtel de c. internationale** a hotel of international standing; **un biologiste/sportif de c. internationale** a biologist/sportsman of international rank, a world-class biologist/sportsman

6 *(distinction)* class, style; **avec c.** smartly, with elegance; **avoir de la c.** to have class *or* style; *Fam* **la c.!** classy!

7 *Ling* class; **c. grammaticale** part of speech; **c. de mots** word class

C. *Mil* **1** *(de conscrits)* annual contingent; **la c. 70** the 1970 levy *or* draft

2 *(rang)* **(soldat de) deuxième c.** *(armée de terre)* private; *(armée de l'air)* *Br* aircraftman, *Am* airman basic; **(soldat de) première c.** *(armée de terre)* *Br* private, *Am* private first class; *(armée de l'air)* *Br* leading aircraftman, *Am* airman first class

ADJ INV *Fam (élégant)* classy

ADV *Fam* **s'habiller c.** to be a classy *or* stylish dresser

❑ **classes** NFPL **faire ses classes** *Mil* to go through training; *Fig* to learn the ropes

❑ **en classe** ADV **aller en c.** to go to school; **il a l'âge d'aller en c.** he's of school age; **être en c.** to be in *or* at school; **rentrer en c.** *(pour la première fois)* to start school; *(à la rentrée)* to go back to school, to start school again

'La Classe de danse' *Degas* 'The Dancing Class'

Culture

CLASSES PRÉPARATOIRES

This term refers to the two years of intensive preparation required for students who have passed their baccalauréat and wish to enter the "grandes écoles". These two years of study are extremely competitive and highly demanding. Students are completely immersed in their subject, which can be in humanities, economics or the sciences, and do little other than study for the "grandes écoles" exams. For students who are not successful in these exams, two years of "prépas" are considered equivalent to a **DEUG** (see box at this entry), and these students often go on to study at a university.

---

classé, -e [klase] ADJ **1** *(terminé)* closed, dismissed; **pour moi, c'est une affaire classée** all that's over and done with *or* the matter's closed as far as I'm concerned **2** *(protégé)* listed; **monument/château c.** listed *or* scheduled building/castle **3** *Sport* ranked, graded; *(au tennis)* seeded; **cheval non c.** also-ran

classement [klasmɑ̃] NM **1** *(tri → de documents)* classifying, ordering, sorting; *(→ d'objets)* sorting, grading; **faire un c. de livres** to sort out *or* to classify books; **c. alphabétique/chronologique** alphabetical/chronological order

2 *(rangement)* filing; **faire du c.** to do some filing; **faire une erreur de c.** to file something in the wrong place

3 *Chim* grading; **c. volumétrique** sizing

4 *(palmarès)* ranking, placing; **avoir un mauvais/bon c.** to do badly/well; **donner le c. d'un examen/d'une course** to give the results of an exam/of a race; **être troisième au c.** to be in third place; **c. général** overall classification; **c. des élèves** class list; **c. de sortie** pass list; **c. trimestriel** end of term results; **premier au c. général** first overall

5 *Ordinat* sequencing

6 *Admin* listing

7 *Jur (d'une affaire)* closing; **c. sans suite** discontinuing proceedings, dropping the case; **rendre une décision de c. sans suite** to discontinue proceedings, to drop the case

classer [3] [klase] VT **1** *(archiver → vieux papiers)* to file (away); *(→ affaire)* to close

2 *(agencer)* to arrange, to classify, to sort; **c. qch par ordre alphabétique** to put sth in alphabetical order; **ils sont classés par pays** they are classified according to country

3 *Ordinat* to sequence

4 *Admin (site)* to list, to schedule

5 *(définir)* **c. qn comme** to categorize *or* *Péj* to label sb as; **à sa réaction, je l'ai tout de suite classé** I could tell straight away what sort of person he was from his reaction; **ce chanteur, que l'on classe parmi les meilleurs ténors...** this singer, who is ranked among the best tenors...

▶**se classer** VPR **1** *(dans une compétition)* to finish, to rank; **se c. troisième** to rank third; **mon cheval s'est classé premier** my horse came in *or* finished first; **il n'a pas réussi à se c.** *(au tennis)* he failed to get into the rankings

2 *(prendre son rang)* **se c. parmi** to rank among

classeur [klasœr] NM **1** *(chemise)* binder, folder, *Am* jacket; **c. à anneaux** ring binder; **c. à feuilles mobiles** loose-leaf binder; **c. à levier** lever-arch file **2** *(tiroir)* filing drawer; *(meuble)* filing cabinet **3** *Ordinat* filer

classicisme [klasisism] NM **1** *Beaux-Arts & Littérature* classicism **2** *(conformisme)* traditionalism

classieux, -euse [klasjø, -øz] ADJ *Fam* classy

classificateur, -trice [klasifikatœr, -tris] ADJ classifying

NM,F classifier

NM **1** *Ordinat* classifier **2** *Chim* screen, sizer

classification [klasifikasjɔ̃] NF **1** *(répartition)* classification; **c. socio-économique** socio-economic grouping; **c. socio-professionnelle** socio-economic classification; **c. du bois** lumber grading

2 *(système)* classification system; **c. décimale universelle** Dewey decimal system; **c. périodique des éléments** periodic table

3 *Naut (mode d'identification)* class logo

4 *Biol* classification; **c. des animaux/végétaux** animal/plant classification

classificatoire [klasifikatwar] ADJ classifying, classificatory

classificatrice [klasifikatris] *voir* **classificateur**

classifier [9] [klasifje] VT **1** *(ordonner)* to classify **2** *(définir)* to label **3** *Méd (échantillon de sang)* to type **4** *Mil (documents)* to classify

classique [klasik] ADJ **1** *Univ* classical; **faire des études classiques** to study classics

2 *Ling & Littérature* classical; **les auteurs classiques** the classical *or* seventeenth- and eighteenth-century authors; **le français c.** seventeenth- and eighteenth-century French

3 *Mus & (en danse → traditionnel)* classical; *(→ du XVIIIème siècle)* classical, eighteenth-century

4 *Antiq* classical

5 *(conventionnel)* conventional; **matériel/armement c.** conventional equipment/weapons; **vêtement de coupe c.** classically cut garment

6 *(connu → sketch, plaisanterie, recette)* classic; **réaction c.** classic response; *Fam* **c'est le coup c.** *(ça arrive souvent)* that's typical!; *(une ruse connue)* that's a well-known trick!; **il m'a fait le coup c. de la panne** he gave me the old breakdown scenario

7 *Écon* classic

NM **1** *Littérature (auteur)* classical author; *(œuvre)* classic; **un c. du genre** a classic of its kind; **connaître ses classiques** to be well-read; **c'est un des grands classiques de la littérature russe** it's one of the great classics of Russian literature

2 *Mus (œuvre → gén)* classic; *(→ de jazz)* (jazz) standard; **le c.** *(genre)* classical music

3 *(style → d'habillement, de décoration)* classic style

4 *Équitation* classic

NF *Sport* classic

classiquement [klasikmɑ̃] ADV **1** *(avec classicisme)* classically **2** *(habituellement)* customarily; **méthode c. utilisée** customary *or* classic method

clastique [klastik] ADJ **1** *Psy* **crise c.** = unpredictable violent fit **2** *Géol* clastic

Claude [klod] NPR *(empereur romain)* Claudius

claudicant, -e [klodikɑ̃, -ɑ̃t] ADJ limping

claudication [klodikasjɔ̃] NF limp, *Spéc* claudication

claudiquer [3] [klodike] VI *Littéraire* to limp

Claudius [klodjys] NPR Claudius

clause [kloz] NF **1** *Jur* clause, stipulation; **c. abusive** unfair clause; **c. additionnelle** additional clause, rider; **c. d'administration conjointe** joint administration clause; **c. d'annulation** cancellation clause; **c. d'arbitrage** arbitration clause; **c. attributive de compétence** jurisdiction clause; **c. commerciale** = clause in a marriage contract allocating property to the surviving spouse subject to indemnity; **c. comminatoire** incitative clause; **c. compromissoire** arbitration clause; **c. conditionnelle** proviso; **c. de confidentialité** confidentiality clause; *Presse* **c. de conscience** conscience clause; **c. contractuelle** clause of a/the contract; **c. contraire** stipulation to the contrary; **c. dérogatoire** derogatory clause; **c. de droits acquis** grandfather clause; **c. échappatoire** escape clause; **c. d'échelle mobile** indexation clause; *Com* **c. d'exclusivité** exclusivity clause, exclusive rights clause; **c. d'exonération** exemption clause; **c. exorbitante du droit commun** = term to which the ordinary law does not apply; **c. de franchise** excess clause; *Compta* **c. d'indexation** escalation clause, indexation clause; **c. léonine** leonina societas; **c. limitative** limiting clause; *Bourse* **c. de lockup** lockup clause; **c. de mobilité** mobility clause; **c. de non-concurrence** non-competition clause; **c. de non-rétablissement** non-reestablishment clause; **c. or** gold clause; **c. de paiement anticipé** acceleration clause; **c. pénale** penalty clause; **c. au porteur** pay to bearer clause; **c. de rémanence** continuing-effect clause; *Fin* **c. de remboursement** refunding clause; **c. de remboursement par anticipation** prepayment clause; **c. de réserve de propriété** retention of title clause; **c. de résiliation** termination clause, cancellation clause; **c. résolutoire** resolutive clause; **c. de retour à meilleure fortune** repayment clause *(guaranteeing repayment when the borrower has the means)*; **c. de retrait** withdrawal clause; **c. de sauvegarde** safeguard *or* safety clause; **c. de style** standard *or* formal clause; *Fig* **ce n'est qu'une c. de style** it's only a manner of speaking; **c. type** boilerplate; **c. de variation** index clause

2 *Pol (d'un traité)* clause; **c. de la nation la plus favorisée** most-favoured-nation status

claustra [klostra] NM open-work partition *or* window

claustral, -e, -aux, -ales [klostral, -o] ADJ **1** *(d'un cloître)* claustral, cloistral **2** *(retiré)* cloistered

claustration [klostrasjɔ̃] NF confinement

claustrer [3] [klostre] VT to confine; **vivre claustré** to lead the life of a recluse

▶**se claustrer** VPR to shut oneself away; **se c. dans le silence** to retreat into silence

claustromanie [klostromani] NF claustromania

claustrophobe [klostrofɔb] ADJ claustrophobic

NMF claustrophobe, claustrophobic

claustrophobie [klostrofɔbi] NF claustrophobia

clausule [klozyl] NF clausule

clavaire [klavɛr] NF *Bot* coral fungus, *Spéc* clavaria

clavardage [klavardaʒ] NM *Can Ordinat (sur Internet)* chat; **site de c.** chat room

clavarder [3] [klavarde] VI *Can Ordinat* to chat (online)

clavé, -e [klave] ADJ *Bot* club-shaped, *Spéc* clavate

claveau, -x [klavo] NM **1** *(pierre taillée)* gauged stone **2** *(voussoir)* arch stone, voussoir **3** *Vét* sheep-pox

clavecin [klavsɛ̃] NM harpsichord

'Le Clavecin bien tempéré' *Bach* 'The Well-Tempered Clavier'

---

claveciniste [klavsinist] NMF harpsichordist, harpsichord player

clavelé, -e [klavle] ADJ *Vét (mouton)* which has sheep-pox

clavelée [klavle] NF *Vét* sheep-pox

claveleux, -euse [klavlø, -øz] ADJ *Vét (mouton)* which has sheep-pox

claver [3] [klave] VT *Typ & Ordinat* to keyboard, to type, to key (in)

clavetage [klavtaʒ] NM **1** *(au moyen d'une clavette)* keying, cottering **2** *Typ* keyboarding, keying

claveter [27] [klavte] VT to key, to cotter

clavette [klavɛt] NF key, pin, cotter; **c. de commande** actuating pin; **c. plate/creuse** flat/hollow key

clavicorde [klavikɔrd] NM clavichord

claviculaire [klavikylɛr] ADJ *Anat* clavicular

clavicule [klavikyl] NF collarbone, *Spéc* clavicle

clavier [klavje] NM 1 *(d'une machine)* keyboard; *(d'un téléphone)* keypad; **c. alphanumérique** alphanumeric keyboard; **c. azerty** azerty keyboard; **c. dactylographique** alphanumeric keyboard; **c. étendu** expanded keyboard, extended keyboard; **c. de fonctions** function keyboard; **c. multifonction** multifunctional keyboard; **c. numérique** numeric keypad; **c. qwerty** qwerty keyboard 2 *Mus (d'un piano)* keyboard; *(d'un orgue)* manual; **c. main gauche** *(d'un accordéon)* fingerboard; **c. de pédales** pedal board 3 *(registre)* range; **tout le c. des émotions** the whole spectrum of emotions □ **claviers** NMPL *Mus* keyboards

claviériste [klavjerist] NMF *(instrumentiste)* keyboard player

claviste [klavist] NMF *Typ* typesetter; *Ordinat* keyboard operator, keyboarder

clayère [klɛjɛr] NF oyster bed

clayette [klɛjɛt] NF 1 *(petite claie)* shelf, tray; **c. coulissante** *(d'un réfrigérateur)* slide-out shelf 2 *(cageot)* crate

claymore [klɛmɔr] NF *(épée)* claymore

clayon [klɛjɔ̃] NM 1 *(petite claie)* wire stand 2 *Can (barrière)* fence

clayonnage [klɛjɔnaʒ] NM *Tech* 1 *(clôture)* wattle fencing, wattling; *(d'un gabion)* waling 2 *(pour soutenir des terres)* mat, mattress *(of canal bank, river etc)*

clayonner [3] [klɛjɔne] VT *(talus d'une rivière)* to protect with wattle fencing, to mat; *(gabion)* to wale

clé [kle] = **clef**

clean [klin] ADJ *Fam (homme)* clean-cut■, wholesome-looking■; *(femme)* wholesome-looking■; **elle a un look c.** she's very wholesome-looking

clearance [klirɑ̃s] NF clearance

clearing [klirin] NM *Banque* clearing

clébard [klebar], **clebs** [klɛps] NM *très Fam* dog■, mutt

clédar [kledar] NM *Suisse* gate *(of field, garden etc)*

clef [kle] NF 1 *(de porte, d'horloge, de boîte de conserve)* key; *(d'un tuyau de poêle)* damper; **la c. est sur la porte** the key's in the lock *or* door; **mettre la c. sous la porte** *ou* **le paillasson** to shut up shop; *Fig* to disappear overnight; **prendre la c. des champs** to get away; **c. à pompe** pump-action key; **les clefs de saint Pierre** the papal authority; **fausse c.** picklock

2 *(outil) Br* spanner, *Am* wrench; **c. allen** Allen key, *Am* Allen wrench; **c. anglaise** monkey wrench, *Br* adjustable spanner; **c. à bougie** (spark)plug spanner; **c. BTR** Allen key, *Am* Allen wrench; **c. à douilles** socket wrench; **c. hexagonale** Allen key, *Am* Allen wrench; **c. à molette** monkey wrench, *Br* adjustable spanner; **c. à pipe** box spanner; **c. plate** (open) end wrench; **c. à six pans** Allen key, *Am* Allen wrench; **c. à tube** tube spanner; **c. universelle** monkey wrench, *Br* adjustable spanner

3 *Aut* **c. de contact** ignition key; **mes clefs de voiture** my car keys

4 *Élec* switch (key)

5 *Tél* **c. d'appel** call button; **c. d'écoute** audioswitch; **c. de réponse** reply key

6 *Ordinat (sous DOS)* switch; **c. d'accès** enter key; **c. de chiffrement** encryption key; **c. électronique** electronic key; **c. gigogne** dongle; **c. de protection** data protection; **c. USB** memory stick, flash drive

7 *Mus (signe)* clef, key; *(touche)* key; *(d'un instrument à cordes)* peg; **c. de sol** key of G, treble clef; **c. de fa** key of F, bass clef; **c. d'ut** key of C, C clef; **clefs de tension** screws

8 *(moyen)* **la c. de** the key to; **la c. de la réussite** the key to success; **la philosophie, c. de la connaissance** philosophy, the key to (all) knowledge

9 *(explication)* key; **une étude/l'histoire de son enfance nous livre quelques clés** a study/the story of his/her childhood gives us a few clues;

la c. de l'énigme the key to the puzzle; **la c. du mystère** the key to the mystery; **c. des songes** *(livre)* = how to interpret your dreams

10 *(influence déterminante)* **la c. de** the key to; **le parti écologiste détient la c. des élections** the green party holds the key to *or* is a key factor in the election results; **Gibraltar est la c. de la Méditerranée** he who holds Gibraltar holds the Mediterranean

11 *(introduction)* **clefs pour l'informatique/la philosophie** introduction to computer technology/philosophy

12 *(prise de lutte)* lock; **faire une c. au bras à qn** to have sb in an arm lock

13 *Archit* **c. d'arc** keystone; **c. de voûte** keystone, quoin; *Fig* linchpin, cornerstone

14 *Banque* **c. RIB** = two-digit security number allocated to account holders

15 *(comme adj; avec ou sans trait d'union)* *(essentiel)* key *(avant n)*; **mot/position c.** key word/post; **témoin c.** key witness □ **à clef** ADV **fermer une porte à c.** to lock a door □ **à clefs** ADJ **roman/film à clefs** novel/film based on real characters *(whose identity is disguised)* □ **à la clef** ADV 1 *Mus* in the key signature; **il y a un bémol/dièse à la c.** the key signature has a flat/sharp 2 *(au bout du compte)* **avec… à la c.** *(récompense)* with… as a bonus; *(punition)* with… into the bargain; **une promenade dans la campagne, avec visite des vignobles à la c.** a ride in the country with a tour of the vineyards thrown in; **il y a une forte somme d'argent à la c.** there is a large sum of money at stake *or* involved □ **clef(s) en main**, *Belg* **clef sur porte** ADJ 1 *Com* **prix c.** *ou* **clefs en main** *(d'un véhicule)* on-the-road price; *(d'une maison)* all-inclusive price 2 *Ind (usine)* turnkey *(avant n)* ADV 1 *Com* **acheter une maison c.** *ou* **clefs en main** to buy a house with vacant *or* immediate possession; **acheter une voiture c.** *ou* **clefs en main** to buy a car ready to drive away 2 *Ind* on a turnkey basis □ **sous clef** ADV 1 *(en prison)* behind bars; **mettre qn sous c.** to lock sb up, to put sb behind bars

2 *(à l'abri)* **garder qch sous c.** to lock sth away, to put sth under lock and key; **mettre qch sous c.** to lock sth away

clématite [klematit] NF *Bot* clematis; **c. des Alpes** Alpine clematis; **c. des haies, c. vigne blanche** traveller's joy, old man's beard

clémence [klemɑ̃s] NF 1 *Météo* mildness 2 *Littéraire (pardon)* leniency, mercy, clemency; **faire preuve de c. à l'égard de qn** to be lenient with sb; **s'en remettre à la c. de qn** to throw oneself on sb's mercy; **l'accusé s'en remet à la c. des juges** the defendant throws himself on the mercy of the Court

clément, -e [klemɑ̃, -ɑ̃t] ADJ 1 *Météo* mild; **temps c. sur toutes les régions** mild weather throughout the country; *Littéraire* **ciel c.** mild climate 2 *Littéraire (indulgent)* lenient, merciful, clement; **ils ont été cléments envers elle** they were lenient with her 3 *(favorable)* **à une époque moins clémente** in less happy times

clémentine [klemɑ̃tin] NF clementine

clémentinier [klemɑ̃tinje] NM clementine tree

clenche [klɑ̃ʃ] NF 1 *(loquet)* latch 2 *Belg (poignée)* doorhandle

clephte [klɛft] = **klephte**

'**Cléo de 5 à 7**' *Varda* 'Cleo from 5 to 7'

Cléopâtre [kleopatr] NPR Cleopatra

clepsydre [klɛpsidr] NF clepsydra

cleptomane [klɛptɔman] = **kleptomane**

cleptomanie [klɛptɔmani] = **kleptomanie**

clerc [klɛr] NM 1 *Rel* cleric 2 *(savant)* scholar; **il est grand c. en la matière** he's an expert on the subject; **point n'est besoin d'être grand c. pour deviner la fin de l'histoire** you don't need to be a genius to guess the end of the story 3 *(employé)* **c. d'huissier** ≃ bailiff; **c. de notaire** clerk; *Littéraire* **faire un pas de c.** to blunder

clergé [klɛrʒe] NM clergy; **c. régulier** regular clergy; **le bas c.** the lower clergy

clergyman [klɛrʒiman] *(pl* **clergymans** *ou* **clergymen** [-mɛn]) NM clergyman

clérical, -e, -aux, -ales [klerikal, -o] ADJ *(du clergé)* clerical

cléricalisme [klerikalism] NM clericalism

Clermont-Ferrand [klɛrmɔ̃ferɑ̃] NM Clermont-Ferrand

clermontois, -e [klɛrmɔ̃twa, -az] ADJ of/from Clermont-Ferrand □ **clermontois, -e** NM,F = inhabitant of or person from Clermont-Ferrand

clérouque [kleruk] NM *Antiq* cleruch

clérouquie [kleruki] NF *Antiq* cleruchy

CLES, Cles [klɛs] NM *(abrév* **contrat local emploi-solidarité)* = community work scheme for young unemployed people

clic [klik] NM *(gén)* & *Ordinat* click; **double c.** double click; **faire un c. (sur)** to click (on) EXCLAM click!

Clic-clac® [klikklak] NM INV *(canapé)* = spring-action sofa bed

clic-clac [klikklak] NM INV *(bruit → d'un appareil photo, d'une ceinture de sécurité)* click; *(→ des talons)* click-clack ADJ INV *voir* **canapé**

clichage [kliʃaʒ] NM 1 *Typ* stereotyping, electrotyping 2 *Mines* caging, setting (of hutches)

cliché [kliʃe] NM 1 *Phot (pellicule)* negative; *(photo)* photograph, shot; **il a pris quelques clichés de la cérémonie** he took some photographs of the ceremony 2 *Typ* stereotype; *(de caractères)* plate; *(d'illustration)* block; **c. au trait** line block 3 *Ordinat* format, layout; **c. mémoire** dump 4 *Littérature* cliché 5 *Péj (banalité)* cliché; **tous ses gags sont des clichés** his/her gags are all so corny

clicher [3] [kliʃe] VT *Typ* to plate, to stereotype

clicherie [kliʃri] NF *Typ (endroit)* stereotype room *(of newspaper)*

clicheton [kliʃtɔ̃] NM *Fam* cliché■; **l'histoire est d'une banalité affligeante: tous les clichetons sont au rendez-vous** the story is as banal as can be and completely cliché-ridden

clicheur [kliʃœr] NM 1 *Typ* stereotyper, electrotyper, blockmaker 2 *Mines* cager, setter of hutches 3 *Ordinat* screen dump program

click [klik] NM click (of the tongue)

client, -e [klijɑ̃, -ɑ̃t] NM,F 1 *(d'un magasin, d'un restaurant)* customer; *(d'une banque)* customer, client; *(d'un hôtel)* guest; *(d'un médecin)* patient; *(d'un taxi)* passenger; *Mktg* account; **je suis c. chez eux** I'm one of their regular customers; *Fig* **désolé, je ne suis pas c.** sorry, I'm not interested; **ici, le c. est roi** the customer is always right; **c. actuel** existing customer; **c. douteux** doubtful debt, possible bad debt; *Mktg* **c. éventuel** prospective customer, prospect; **c. habitué** regular customer; **c. imprévu** chance customer; *Mktg* **c. mystère** mystery shopper; **c. de passage** passing customer; **c. potentiel** potential customer; *Mktg* **c. de référence** reference customer; **c. régulier** regular customer; **c. sans réservation** *(dans un hôtel)* chance guest, walk-in 2 **les clients** *(la clientèle)* customers, the clientele; **les clients d'un médecin** a doctor's patients; **les clients d'un hôtel** hotel guests; **les clients de passage** passing trade 3 *Hist* client 4 *Fam Péj (individu)* **un drôle de c.** a dodgy customer; **qu'est-ce qu'ils veulent, ces clients-là?** what's this crew after?; **chez eux, c'est à la tête du c.** they charge you what they feel like NM *Ordinat* client; **c. de messagerie électronique** e-mail client, mail reader

clientèle [klijɑ̃tɛl] NF 1 *(clients → gén)* clientele, customers; *(d'un médecin)* patients; *(d'un avocat)* clients, clientele; **la c. est priée de se diriger à la sortie** customers are requested to make their way to the exit; **acheter une c. à un confrère** to buy a practice from a colleague; **perdre sa c.** to lose one's customers; **tirer la c.** to attract custom; **avoir une grosse c.** to have a large clientele *or* customer base; **c. de passage** passing trade 2 *(fait d'acheter)* custom; **obtenir la c. de qn** to obtain sb's custom *or* business; **accorder sa c. à** to give one's custom to, to patronize 3 *Pol* **c. électorale** electorate, voters 4 *Hist* patronage, protection

clientélisme [klijɑ̃telism] NM *Péj* clientelism

clientéliste [clijɑ̃telist] ADJ *Péj* clientelist; **pratiques clientélistes** vote-catching practices

client-serveur [klijɑ̃sɛrvœr] ADJ INV *Ordinat (architecture, base de données)* client-server

clignement [kliɲəmɑ̃] NM **c. d'œil** *ou* **d'yeux** *(involontaire)* blink; *(volontaire)* wink; **des clignements d'œil** *ou* **d'yeux** blinking

cligner [3] [kliɲe] VT *(fermer)* **c. les yeux** to blink
VI *(paupières, yeux)* to blink
▫ **cligner de** VT IND **1** *(fermer involontairement)* **c. de l'œil** to blink; **c. des yeux** to blink **2** *(faire signe avec)* **c. de l'œil (en direction de qn)** to wink (at sb)

clignotant, -e [kliɲɔtɑ̃, -ɑ̃t] ADJ *(signal)* flashing; *(lampe défectueuse)* flickering; *(étoile)* twinkling; *(guirlande)* twinkling, flashing
NM **1** *Aut (lampe) Br* indicator, *Am* turn signal; **mettre son c. (à droite/gauche)** *Br* to indicate (to the right/left), *Am* to put on one's turn signal (to turn right/left) **2** *(signal)* warning light; *Sport* sequenced starting lights **3** *Écon (indice)* (key) indicator

clignotement [kliɲɔtmɑ̃] NM **1** *(lumière → d'une guirlande, d'une étoile)* twinkling; *(→ d'un signal)* flashing; *(→ d'une lampe défectueuse)* flickering **2** *(mouvement → des paupières)* flickering; *(→ des yeux)* blinking

clignoter [3] [kliɲɔte] VI **1** *(éclairer → étoile, guirlande)* to twinkle; *(→ signal)* to flash (on and off); *(→ lampe défectueuse)* to flicker **2** *(automobiliste) Br* to indicate, *Am* to put on one's turn signal **3** *Ordinat (d'un marqueur etc)* to flash, to blink

clignoteur [kliɲɔtœr] NM *Belg* **1** *Aut (lampe) Br* indicator, *Am* turn signal; **mettre son c. (à droite/gauche)** *Br* to indicate (to the right/left), *Am* to put on one's turn signal (to turn right/left) **2** *(signal)* warning light

clim [klim] NF *Fam* air-conditioning▪, air-con

climacique [klimasik] ADJ *Écol* climax *(avant n)*

climat [klima] NM **1** *Géog* climate; **sous nos climats** in our country; **sous d'autres climats** in other countries; **partir vers des climats plus sereins** to travel to sunnier climes; **c. artificiel** artificial climate **2** *(ambiance)* climate, atmosphere; **un c. de méfiance** an atmosphere of suspicion; **le c. devient malsain!** things are turning nasty!; **c. économique** economic climate

climatérique [klimaterik] *Antiq* ADJ climacteric
NF **la grande c.** the grand climacteric

climatique [klimatik] ADJ **1** *Météo* weather *(avant n)*, climatic; *Écol* **changement c.** climate change **2 centre/station c.** health centre/resort

climatisation [klimatizasjɔ̃] NF **1** *(dans un immeuble)* air-conditioning **2** *(dans une voiture)* heating and ventilation

climatiser [3] [klimatize] VT to air-condition, to install air-conditioning in; **restaurant climatisé** air-conditioned restaurant

climatiseur [klimatizœr] NM *(gén)* air-conditioner, air-conditioning unit; *Aut* climate control system

climatisme [klimatism] NM climatism

climatologie [klimatɔlɔʒi] NF climatology

climatologique [klimatɔlɔʒik] ADJ climatological

climatologue [klimatɔlɔg] NMF climatologist

climax [klimaks] NM *Écol & Littérature* climax

clin [klɛ̃] **à clin** ADJ **un pont à c.** a clapboard bridge; *Naut* **bordé à c.** *ou* **clins** clinker built

clinamen [klinamɛn] NM clinamen

clin d'œil [klɛ̃dœj] *(pl* **clins d'œil**) NM **1** *(clignement)* wink; **faire un c. à qn** to wink at sb **2** *(allusion)* allusion, implied reference; **un c. à...** an allusion *or* an implied reference to...
▫ **en un clin d'œil** ADV in the twinkling of an eye, in less than no time, in a flash

cline [klin] NM *Biol* cline

clinfoc [klɛ̃fɔk] NM *Naut* flying jib

clinicat [klinika] NM ≃ registrarship *(in a teaching hospital)*

clinicien, -enne [klinisjɛ̃, -ɛn] NM,F **1** *Méd* clinician, clinical practitioner **2** *Psy* clinical psychologist

clinique [klinik] ADJ clinical; **conférence/médecine/psychologie c.** clinical lecture/medicine/psychology; **leçon c.** teaching at the bedside; **les signes cliniques de l'affection** the visible signs of the disease
NF **1** *(établissement)* (private) clinic; **c. d'accouchement** maternity hospital **2** *(service)* teaching department *(of a hospital)* **3** *(médecine)* clinical medicine

cliniquement [klinikmɑ̃] ADV clinically

clinker [klinkər] NM *Tech* clinker

clinomètre [klinɔmɛtr] NM **1** *(en topographie)* clinometer, gradient indicator **2** *Mil* inclinometer **3** *(en anthropologie)* clinometer; **c. à bulle** bead clinometer

clinquant, -e [klɛ̃kɑ̃, -ɑ̃t] ADJ **1** *(brillant)* glittering, *Péj* tinselly **2** *(superficiel → style)* flashy; **le monde c. du show-business** the razzmatazz of show business
NM **1** *(faux éclat)* **le c. de leurs conversations** the superficial sparkle of their conversations **2** *(paillettes)* tinsel

Clio [klijo] NPR *Myth* Clio

clip [klip] NM **1** *(broche)* clip, brooch **2** *(boucle d'oreille)* clip-on earring **3** *(attache)* clamp, clip; **c. de blocage** lock clip; **clips de fixation** holders **4** *(film)* video; **c. vidéo** video (clip)

clipart [klipart] NM *Ordinat* clip art

clipper[1] [klipœr] NM **1** *Aviat* transport aircraft **2** *Naut* clipper

clipper[2] [3] [klipe] VT *(fixer)* to clip (**à** to, onto)

clippeur [klipœr] NM *Fam* video director

cliquable [klikabl] ADJ *Ordinat* clickable; **une icône c.** a clickable icon

cliquart [klikar] NM **1** *Géol (dans le bassin parisien)* stratum of limestone *or* gypsum **2** *Cér* fine-grained sandstone **3** *Constr* building stone

clique [klik] NF **1** *Fam (coterie)* clique, gang; **et toute la c.** and the rest of the gang, and all the rest of them **2** *Mil (fanfare)* band
▫ **cliques** NFPL *Fam* **prendre ses cliques et ses claques** *(partir)* to up and leave; *(emporter ses affaires)* to pack one's bags (and go)

cliquer [3] [klike] VI *Ordinat* to click (**sur** on); **c. deux fois** to double-click; **c. avec le bouton gauche/droit de la souris** to left-click/right-click; **c. et glisser** to click and drag

cliquet [klikɛ] NM **1** *(mécanisme)* catch, dog, pawl; **c. de retenue** holding-dog; **c. d'entraînement** driving pawl **2** *(outil)* pawl; **à c.** pawl *(avant n)*

cliquetant, -e [kliktɑ̃, -ɑ̃t] ADJ *(clefs, bijoux)* jangling; *(chaînes)* rattling; *(épées, aiguilles à tricoter)* clicking; *(pièces de monnaie)* clinking, chinking; *(machine à écrire)* clacking; *(assiettes)* clattering; *(verres)* clinking; *(engrenage, moteur)* pinking, knocking

cliquètement [klikɛtmɑ̃] = **cliquetis**

cliqueter [27] [klikte] VI *(clefs, bijoux)* to jangle; *(chaînes)* to rattle; *(épées, aiguilles à tricoter)* to click; *(pièces de monnaie)* to clink, to chink; *(machine à écrire)* to clack; *(assiettes)* to clatter; *(verres)* to clink; *(engrenage, moteur)* to pink, to knock

cliquetis [klikti] NM *(de clefs, de bijoux)* jangling *(UNCOUNT)*; *(de chaînes)* rattling *(UNCOUNT)*; *(d'épées, d'aiguilles à tricoter)* clicking *(UNCOUNT)*; *(de pièces de monnaie)* clinking *(UNCOUNT)*, chinking *(UNCOUNT)*; *(d'une machine à écrire)* clacking *(UNCOUNT)*; *(d'assiettes)* clatter, clattering *(UNCOUNT)*; *(de verres)* clinking *(UNCOUNT)*; *(d'un engrenage, d'un moteur)* pinking, knocking

cliquette *etc voir* **cliqueter**

cliquettement [klikɛtmɑ̃] = **cliquetis**

clisse [klis] NF **1** *(pour fromages)* wicker tray **2** *(pour bouteilles)* wicker casing

clisser [3] [klise] VT to cover in a wicker casing; **bouteille clissée** bottle in a wicker casing

clitocybe [klitɔsib] NM *Bot* clitocybe

clitoridectomie [klitɔridɛktɔmi] NF *Méd* clitoridectomy

clitoridien, -enne [klitɔridjɛ̃, -ɛn] ADJ clitoral

clitoris [klitɔris] NM clitoris

clivable [klivabl] ADJ cleavable

clivage [klivaʒ] NM **1** *(de roche, de cristal)* cleavage, splitting; **plan de c.** cleavage plane **2** *(séparation)* divide, division; **c. idéologique** ideological divide; **clivages partisans** ideological divide, sectarianism; **dépasser les clivages partisans** to bridge the ideological divide; **c. social** social divide; **il y a un net c. entre les riches et les pauvres/la droite et la gauche** there's a sharp divide between rich and poor/right and left **3** *Chim (de molécule)* cleavage

cliver [3] [klive] *Minér & Chim* VT to cleave, to split
►**se cliver** VPR to cleave, to split

cloacal, -e, -aux, -ales [klɔakal, -o] ADJ *Anat* cloacal

cloaque [klɔak] NM **1** *(égout)* cesspool, open sewer; **le grand C.** the Cloaca Maxima **2** *Littéraire (lieu sale)* cesspool, cloaca; *(lieu de corruption)* cesspit, cesspool **3** *Zool* cloaca

clochard, -e [klɔʃar, -ard] NM,F tramp, *Am* hobo; **si tu continues comme ça, tu vas finir c.** if you carry on like that, you're going to end up destitute

clochardisation [klɔʃardizasjɔ̃] NF **on observe une c. croissante chez les jeunes sans emploi** more and more young unemployed people are turning into vagrants *or* down-and-outs

clochardiser [3] [klɔʃardize] VT to make destitute; *(sans domicile)* to make homeless
►**se clochardiser** VPR to become destitute; *(sans domicile)* to be made homeless

cloche [klɔʃ] ADJ *Fam (idiot)* stupid▪, *Br* daft; **c'est c., cette histoire** what a stupid story; **ce que tu peux être c.!** you can be such a dope!; **avoir l'air c.** to look stupid
NF **1** *(instrument, signal)* bell; **les enfants, c'est la c.!** *(à l'école)* children, the bell's ringing!; *Fam* **s'en mettre plein** *ou* **se taper la c.** to stuff one's face; *Fam* **déménager** *ou* **partir à la c. de bois** to leave without paying the rent▪, *Br* to do a moonlight flit; **les cloches de Pâques** Easter bells *(traditionally believed to fly to Rome at Easter)*
2 *Hort* cloche
3 *Culin* dome, dish-cover; **c. à fromage** cheese dish *(with cover)*, cheese-bell
4 *(chapeau)* **(chapeau) c.** cloche hat
5 *Naut* **c. de plongée** *ou* **à plongeur** diving-bell
6 *Chim* **c. à vide** vacuum bell-jar; **c. de verre** bell glass
7 *Aut* **c. d'embrayage** clutch bell housing
8 *Fam (personne)* jerk, *Br* prat, *Am* geek; **quelle c., ce type!** what an idiot!; **salut, vieille c.!** hello, old thing!; **ne reste pas là à me regarder comme une c.!** don't just stand there gawping at me!
9 *Fam (vagabondage)* **la c.** vagrancy▪; **être de la c.** to be of no fixed abode; **c'est la c. là-bas sous le pont** it's cardboard city over there under the bridge
10 *Belg Méd* blister
▫ **en cloche** ADJ bell-shaped; **courbe en c.** bell-shaped curve
▫ **sous cloche** ADV **mettre sous c.** *Hort* to put under glass, to cloche; *Fig* to mollycoddle

cloche-pied [klɔʃpje] **à cloche-pied** ADV **sauter à c.** to hop

clocher[1] [klɔʃe] NM **1** *(tour)* bell-tower, church tower **2** *(village)* **son c.** the place where he was born; **il n'a jamais quitté son c.** he knows nothing of the world
▫ **de clocher** ADJ **esprit de c.** parochialism, parish-pump mentality; **intérêts de c.** parochial interests; **querelles de c.** petty bickering

clocher[2] [3] [klɔʃe] VI **1** *Fam (ne pas aller)* to be wrong▪; **qu'est-ce qui cloche?** what's wrong *or* up?; **il y a quelque chose qui cloche** there's something wrong somewhere; **il y a quelque chose qui cloche dans son histoire** there's something not right about his/her story **2** *Arch (boiter)* to limp, to hobble
VT *Hort* to (put under a) cloche

clocheton [klɔʃtɔ̃] NM *(petit clocher)* (small) steeple; *(ornement)* pinnacle turret

clochette [klɔʃɛt] NF **1** *(petite cloche)* small bell; **c. à vache** cow-bell; **c. à mouton** sheep-bell **2** *Bot (campanule)* bell-flower

clodo [klodo] NMF *Fam* tramp, *Am* bum; **si tu continues comme ça, tu vas finir c.** if you carry on like that, you're going to end up on the streets

cloison [klwazɔ̃] NF **1** *Constr* partition; **mur de c.** dividing wall **2** *Aviat & Naut* bulkhead; **c. étanche** *Naut* watertight bulkhead; *Aviat* pressure bulkhead **3** *Anat & Bot* dissepiment, septum; **c. nasale** nasal septum **4** *Fig (sociale, raciale)* barrier

cloisonnage [klwazɔnaʒ] NM **1** *Archit* partitioning

2 *Naut* bulkheading 3 *(en joaillerie)* cloisonné work

cloisonné, -e [klwazɔne] ADJ 1 *(pièce)* partitioned (off) 2 *Fig (divisé)* compartmentalized 3 *Anat & Bot* septated 4 *(en joaillerie)* cloisonné

NM *(en joaillerie)* cloisonné

cloisonnement [klwazɔnmɑ̃] NM 1 *(d'une pièce)* partitioning (off) 2 *Fig (division)* division; **le c. des services dans une entreprise** the excessive compartmentalization of departments in a firm 3 *Archit* partitioning 4 *Naut* bulkheading 5 *(en joaillerie)* cloisonné work

cloisonner [3] [klwazɔne] VT 1 *(pièce)* to partition off 2 *Naut* to bulkhead 3 *(séparer)* to compartmentalize

cloisonnisme [klwazɔnism] NM *Beaux-Arts* Cloisonnism

cloître [klwatr] NM 1 *(couvent)* convent, monastery 2 *Archit (d'un couvent)* cloister; *(d'une cathédrale)* close

cloîtré, -e [klwatre] ADJ *(moine, religieuse)* cloistered, enclosed; *(ordre)* monastic

cloîtrer [3] [klwatre] VT 1 *Rel* **c. qn** to shut sb up in a convent 2 *(enfermer)* to shut up *or* away; **nous sommes cloîtrés toute la journée/dans notre atelier** we're shut up all day/in our workshop

▸**se cloîtrer** VPR to shut oneself away; **elle se cloître chez elle** she shuts herself away at home; **se c. dans le silence** to retreat into silence

clonage [klonaʒ] NM *Biol* cloning; **c. reproductif** reproductive cloning; **c. thérapeutique** therapeutic cloning

clone [klon] NM *Biol & Fig* clone

cloner [3] [klone] VT to clone

clonie [kloni] NF *Méd* muscle spasm

clonique [klonik] ADJ clonic

clonus [klɔnys] NM *Méd* clonus, clonic spasm

clope [klɔp] NM OU NF *Fam Br* fag, *Am* smoke; **la c. ce n'est pas bon pour la santé** smoking is bad for you *or* for your health▪

cloper [3] [klɔpe] VI *Fam* to smoke▪

clopet [klɔpe] NM *Suisse* nap

clopin-clopant [klɔpɛ̃klɔpɑ̃] ADV 1 *(en boitant)* **avancer c.** to hobble along; **traverser c.** to hobble across 2 *(irrégulièrement)* **ça va c.** it has its ups and downs

clopiner [3] [klɔpine] VI *Fam* to hobble along

clopinettes [klɔpinɛt] NFPL *Fam* **des c.** (next to) nothing▪; **gagner des c.** to earn peanuts; **des c.!** *(pas question)* nothing doing!, no way!

cloporte [klɔpɔrt] NM 1 *Zool* woodlouse 2 *Fam Vieilli (concierge)* door-keeper▪, concierge▪ 3 *Fam (individu répugnant)* creep

cloque [klɔk] NF 1 *Bot & Méd* blister 2 *(défaut)* raised spot, blister; **faire des cloques** to blister; **la peinture fait des cloques** the paint has blistered 3 *très Fam (locution)* **être en c.** to have a bun in the oven, to be knocked up, *Br* to be up the duff; **foutre qn en c.** to knock sb up

cloqué, -e [klɔke] ADJ 1 *(tissu)* seersucker *(avant n)* 2 *Bot* blistered

NM seersucker; **c. de soie** ripple silk

cloquer [3] [klɔke] VI 1 *(peinture, papier)* to blister 2 *Fam (peau)* to come up in a blister▪, to blister▪

clore [113] [klɔr] VT 1 *(fermer → porte, volet)* to close, to shut; *(entourer → parc)* to shut off 2 *Fin* **c. un compte** to close an account 3 *(conclure)* to conclude, to end, to finish; **c. les débats** *(s'arrêter)* to end the discussion, to bring the discussion to a close; *(reporter)* to adjourn (the discussion); **la scène qui clôt le film** the very last scene of the movie 4 *Ordinat* **c. une session** to log off, to log out

clos, -e [klo, kloz] ADJ 1 *(fermé)* closed, shut; **les yeux c.** with one's eyes shut; **garder** *ou* **rester la bouche close** to keep one's mouth shut; **trouver porte close** to find nobody at home 2 *(achevé)* finished, concluded; *Univ* **les inscriptions seront closes le lundi 15** the closing date for enrolment is Monday 15; *Compta* **exercice c. le 31 décembre 2007** year ended 31 December 2007; **l'incident est c.** the matter is closed 3 *(enceint → jardin)* walled 4 *Ling* closed

NM enclosure; **c. (de vigne)** vineyard

closeau, -x [klozo] NM enclosed garden

close-combat [klɔzkɔ̃ba] *(pl* **close-combats**) NM close combat

closent *etc voir* **clore**

closerie [klozri] NF enclosed garden

clostridion [klɔstridjɔ̃] NM *Biol* clostridium

clostridium [klɔstridjɔm] NM INV *Biol* clostridium

clôt *etc voir* **clore**

clôture [klotyr] NF 1 *(de bois)* fence; *(grille)* railings; **c. à claire-voie** split-rail fencing; **c. métallique** wire fence; *Can Fig* **regarder pardessus la c.** to take an interest in girls

2 *Rel* enclosure

3 *(fermeture → gén)* closing; *(→ d'un débat)* closure; **c. annuelle** *(d'un magasin)* closed for the season; **j'ai assisté à la c.** I attended the closing ceremony; *Univ* **c. des inscriptions le 20 décembre** the closing date for enrolment is 20 December; **la c. de la chasse** the close of the season

4 *Bourse* close; **à la c.** at the close

5 *Compta* **c. annuelle des livres** year-end closing of accounts; **c. de l'exercice** end of the financial year

6 *Ordinat* close; **c. de session** logging off

▫ **de clôture** ADJ *(gén) & Bourse & Com* closing

▫ **en clôture** ADV *Bourse* at closing; **combien valait l'euro en c.?** what was the closing price of the euro?

clôturer [3] [klotyre] VT 1 *(fermer)* to enclose, to fence (in) 2 *(terminer)* to close, to end; **c. les débats** to close the debate 3 *Fin (compte)* to close

VI *Bourse* to close; **le CAC 40 a clôturé en baisse/hausse de 9 points** the CAC 40 closed 9 points down/up; **la livre a clôturé à 1,76 dollars** the pound closed at 1.76 dollars

clou [klu] NM 1 *(pointe)* nail; **c. d'ameublement** (upholstery) tack; **c. cavalier** staple; **c. à crochet** hook; **c. doré** brass-headed nail, stud; **c. à souliers** shoe tack; **c. (de) tapissier** (carpet) tack; **c. sans tête** brad; *Prov* **un c. chasse l'autre** one nail drives out another

2 *(d'un spectacle)* star turn, chief attraction; **le c. de la soirée** the climax *or* highlight of the evening

3 *Culin* **c. de girofle** clove

4 *Fam (furoncle)* boil▪

5 *Fam Péj* **vieux c.** *(voiture)* old *Br* banger *or Am* crate; *(bicyclette)* old bike *or Br* boneshaker

6 *Fam (locutions)* **ça ne vaut pas un c.** it's not worth a bean; **il n'en fiche pas un c.** he doesn't do a stroke of work, he never lifts a finger; **il n'assure pas un c. avec les filles, il ne dit jamais ce qu'il faut** he hasn't got a clue when it comes to girls, he never says the right thing; **qu'est-ce qu'il a eu? – pas un c.!** what did he get? – *Br* not a sausage *or Am* zilch!; **des clous!** no way!, nothing doing!; **pour des clous** for nothing; *Belg* **je ne suis pas pendu à son c.** I'm not his/her slave!, I'm not there to do his/her bidding!; *Can* **cogner des clous** to keep nodding off

▫ **clous** NMPL *(passage piétons) Br* pedestrian *or* zebra crossing, *Am* crosswalk

▫ **à clous** ADJ *(chaussure)* hobnail *(avant n)*, hobnailed; *(pneu, ceinture)* studded

▫ **au clou** ADV *Fam* in the pawnshop▪; **mettre qch au c.** to pawn sth▪, to hock sth

clouage [kluaʒ] NM nailing; **c. droit/en biais** face/edge nailing

clouer [6] [klue] VT 1 *(fixer)* to nail (down) 2 *(fermer)* to nail shut; *Fam* **c. le bec à qn** to shut sb up 3 *(immobiliser)* **c. qn au sol** to pin sb down; **il est resté cloué au lit pendant trois jours** he was laid up in bed for three days; **la peur le clouait sur place** he was rooted to the spot with fear

cloutage [klutaʒ] NM *(décoration)* studding, studwork

clouté, -e [klute] ADJ 1 *(décoré)* studded 2 *(renforcé → chaussure, semelle)* hobnailed; *(→ pneu)* studded

clouter [3] [klute] VT to stud

clouterie [klutri] NF 1 *(fabrication)* nail-making 2 *(commerce)* the nail trade 3 *(fabrique)* nail works *or* factory, nailery

Clovis [klɔvis] NPR Clovis

clovisse [klɔvis] NF clam

clown [klun] NM clown; **faire le c.** to clown, to fool around; *Fig* **quel c., ce gosse!** that kid's a clown!; **c. blanc** white-faced clown

clownerie [klunri] NF 1 *(pitrerie)* **des clowneries** clown's antics, clowning 2 *Péj (bêtise)* (stupid) prank; **faire des clowneries** to clown *or* to fool around

clownesque [klunɛsk] ADJ clownish, clownlike

clownesse [klunɛs] NF *Littéraire* (female) clown

CLS [seɛlɛs] NM *(abrév* **contrat local de sécurité**) = list of measures to increase public safety within a town, involving all the official bodies who work together with the residents

CLT [seɛlte] NF *(abrév* **Compagnie luxembourgeoise de télévision**) = Luxembourg TV company

club [klœb] NM 1 *(groupe → de personnes)* club; *(→ de nations)* group; *Littérature* **le C. des cinq** the Famous Five; **c. d'investissement** investment club

2 *(association)* **c. de gym** health club, gym; **c. de rencontres** dating agency; **c. sportif** sports club; **c. de vacances** travel club

3 *Sport (équipe)* club, team

4 *Golf* club

5 *Com* **c. de gros** warehouse club

6 *Can* **c. de nuit** nightclub

clubbing [klœbiŋ] NM clubbing

clunisien, -enne [klynizjɛ̃, -jɛn] ADJ *Rel & Archit* Cluniac

NM *Rel* Cluniac

Cluny [klyni] NM 1 *(ville)* Cluny; **l'abbaye de C.** the Abbey of Cluny 2 *(à Paris)* **l'hôtel de C.** = fifteenth-century mansion adjoining the remains of some Roman baths, "les thermes de Cluny", and now housing the Cluny Museum; **le musée de C.** = national museum of the Middle Ages in the centre of Paris

clupéidé [klypeide] *Ich* NM clupeoid, clupeid

▫ **clupéidés** NMPL Clupeidae

cluse [klyz] NF cluse, transverse valley

clusiacée [klyzjase] *Bot* NF clusia

▫ **clusiacées** NFPL Clusiaceae

cluster [klystɛr, klœstœr] NM *Mus* tone cluster

clypéastéroïde [klipeasterɔid] NM *Zool* sand dollar

clystère [klistɛr] NM clyster

Clytemnestre [klitɛmnɛstr] NPR *Myth* Clytemnestra

CM [seɛm] NF *(abrév* **Chambre des métiers**) Guild Chamber

NM *(abrév* **cours moyen**) = two-year subdivision of primary-level education in France (ages 10 to 11); **CM1** = fourth year of primary school, *Br* ≃ year 5; **CM2** = fifth year of primary school, *Br* ≃ year 6

cm *(abrév écrite* **centimètre**) cm; **cm²** sq.cm., cm²; **cm³** cu.cm., cm³

CMF [seɛmɛf] NM *Bourse (abrév* **Conseil des Marchés Financiers**) = regulatory body of the French stock market

CMH [seɛmaʃ] NM *Méd (abrév* **complexe majeur d'histocompatibilité**) MHC

CMJN *Ordinat (abrév écrite* **cyan, magenta, jaune, noir**) CMYK

CMP [seɛmpe] NM *Fin (abrév* **coût moyen pondéré**) weighted average cost

CMT [seɛmte] NF *(abrév* **Confédération mondiale du travail**) WCL

CMU [seɛmy] NF *Admin (abrév* **couverture maladie universelle**) = law introduced to ensure free health care for people on low incomes who have no social security cover

CMV [seɛmve] NM *Méd (abrév* **cytomégalovirus**) CMV

CNA [seɛna] NM *Tech (abrév* **convertisseur numérique-analogique**) DAC

CNAC [knak] NM *(abrév* **Centre national d'art et de culture**) = official name of the Pompidou Centre

CNAM [knam] NM *(abrév* **Conservatoire national des arts et métiers**) = science and technology school in Paris

NF *Admin (abrév* **Caisse nationale d'assurance maladie**) = French goverment department dealing with health insurance and sickness benefit

CNAV [knav] NF *(abrév* **Caisse nationale d'assurance vieillesse**) = French government department dealing with benefit payments relating to old age

CNC [seɛnse] NM 1 *(abrév* **Conseil national de la**

consommation) = consumer protection organization **2** (*abrév* **Centre national de la cinématographie, Centre national du cinéma**) = national cinematographic organization

CNCE [seɛnseə] NM (*abrév* **Centre national du commerce extérieur**) = national export organization

CNCL [seɛnseɛl] NF (*abrév* **Commission nationale de la communication et des libertés**) = former French TV and radio supervisory body

CND [seɛnde] NM INV *Ind & Tech* (*abrév* **Contrôle non destructif**) non-destructive control

CNDP [seɛndepe] NM (*abrév* **Centre national de documentation pédagogique**) = national organization for educational resources

CNE [seɛnə] NF **1** *Banque* (*abrév* **Caisse nationale d'épargne**) ≃ National Savings Bank **2** (*abrév* **contrat nouvelles embouches**) = open-ended employment contract for companies of up to 20 employees, under which employment can be terminated without justification within the first two years

CNEC [knɛk] NM (*abrév* **Centre national de l'enseignement par correspondance**) = national educational body organizing correspondence courses

CNED [knɛd] NM (*abrév* **Centre national d'enseignement à distance**) = national educational body organizing correspondence courses

cnémide [knemid] NF *Antiq* greave

CNES, Cnes [knɛs] NM (*abrév* **Centre national d'études spatiales**) = French national space research centre

CNI [seɛni] NM (*abrév* **Congrès national irakien**) INC

cnidaire [knidɛr] *Zool* NM cnidarian
❏ **cnidaires** NMPL Cnidaria

cnidoblaste [knidɔblast] NM *Biol* cnidoblast

cnidocyste [knidɔsist] NM *Biol* cnidocyst, nematocyst

CNIL [knil] NF (*abrév* **Commission nationale de l'informatique et des libertés**) = board which enforces data protection legislation

CNIT, Cnit [knit] NM (*abrév* **Centre national des industries et des techniques**) = trade centre at la Défense in Paris

CNJA [seɛnʒia] NM (*abrév* **Centre national des jeunes agriculteurs**) = farmers' union

Cnossos [knɔsɔs] NF Knossos

CNPF [seɛnpeɛf] NM *Anciennement* (*abrév* **Conseil national du patronat français**) = national council of French employers, *Br* ≃ CBI

CNR [seɛnɛr] NM (*abrév* **Conseil national de la Résistance**) = central organization of the French Resistance founded in 1943

CNRS [seɛnɛrɛs] NM (*abrév* **Centre national de la recherche scientifique**) = French national organization for scientific research, *Br* ≃ SRC

Culture
CNRS

The CNRS is a multidisciplinary research organization, established by the government through laws passed in 1941 and 1948 and affiliated to the ministry of education. It receives state funding and its members, who are highly qualified specialists in their fields, are engaged in research in the areas of science, engineering, humanities and social sciences. Being a member of the CNRS is a prestigious, often lifelong position.

CNSF–FNCR [seɛnɛsɛfɛfɛnseɛr] NF (*abrév* **Confédération nationale des salariés de France–Fédération nationale des chauffeurs routiers**) = French trade union representing lorry drivers and workers from other sectors

CNTS [seɛntɛɛs] NM (*abrév* **Centre national de transfusion sanguine**) = national blood transfusion centre

CNUCED, Cnuced [knysɛd] NF (*abrév* **Conférence des Nations unies pour le commerce et l'industrie**) UNCTAD

CO- [ko] PRÉF

● The prefix **co-** is widely used in French to convey the idea of TOGETHERNESS or COMMUNITY OF INTERESTS. It is worth noting three relatively recent coinages or uses:

● **cohabitation**: although not a recent word in itself, **la cohabitation** has come to refer to three

episodes in French political life, between 1986 and 2002, when a Prime Minister from one side of the political spectrum has had to share power with a president from the other side (see cultural box at the entry **cohabitation**)

● **covoiturage**: this word was given particular prominence in 1995, when a national public transport strike forced commuters to resort to car-pooling

● **cododo**: this is the colloquial equivalent of *sommeil partagé* (from the baby talk word *dodo*, meaning sleep), a practice where parents share a bed, or at least a bedroom, with their offspring

---

coaccusé, -e [kɔakyze] NM,F codefendant

coacervat [kɔaсerva] NM *Chim* coacervate

coacervation [kɔaсervasjɔ̃] NF *Chim* coacervation

coach [kotʃ] (*pl* **coachs** *ou* **coaches**) NM **1** (*entraîneur*) coach; *Sport* trainer; **c. personnel** life coach **2** (*voiture*) two-door car

coaching [kotʃiŋ] NM coaching; *Sport* training; **c. personnel** life coaching

coacquéreur [kɔakerœr] NM joint purchaser

coacquisition [kɔakizisjɔ̃] NF joint purchase

coadjuteur [kɔadʒytœr] NM coadjutor

coadministrateur, -trice [kɔadministratœr, -tris] NM,F *Com* co-director; *Jur* co-trustee

coagulabilité [kɔagylabilite] NF coagulability

coagulable [kɔagylabl] ADJ coagulable, liable to coagulate

coagulant, -e [kɔagylɑ̃, -ɑ̃t] ADJ coagulating
NM coagulant

coagulation [kɔagylasjɔ̃] NF (*du sang*) coagulation, coagulating (UNCOUNT); (*du lait*) curdling (UNCOUNT)

coaguler [3] [kɔagyle] VT (*sang*) to coagulate; (*lait*) to curdle
VI (*sang*) to coagulate; (*lait*) to curdle
▶ **se coaguler** VPR (*sang*) to coagulate; (*lait*) to curdle

coagulum [kɔagylɔm] NM clot, *Spéc* coagulum

coalescence [kɔalɛsɑ̃s] NF coalescence, coalescing (UNCOUNT)

coalescent, -e [kɔalɛsɑ̃, -ɑ̃t] ADJ coalescent

coalescer [21] [kɔalɛse] VT *Métal* to blend, to mix

coalisé, -e [kɔalize] ADJ allied
NM,F allied nation, ally

coaliser [kɔalize] VT to make into a coalition
▶ **se coaliser** VPR to form a coalition; *Fig* **ils se sont tous coalisés contre moi** they all ganged up on me *or* joined forces against me

coalition [kɔalisjɔ̃] NF *Pol* coalition; *Péj* conspiracy; **former une c. contre qn/qch** to join forces against sb/sth; **gouvernement de c.** coalition government

coaltar [kɔltar] NM coal tar; *Fam Fig* **être dans le c.** to be in a daze

coaptation [kɔaptasjɔ̃] NF setting (*of bones*), *Spéc* coaptation

coapteur [kɔaptœr] NM *Méd* fixator (*for fractured bone*)

coarctation [kɔarktasjɔ̃] NF *Méd* coarctation

coassement [kɔasmɑ̃] NM (*de grenouille*) croaking (UNCOUNT)

coasser [3] [kɔase] VI **1** (*grenouille*) to croak **2** *Péj* (*commère*) to gossip

coassociation [kɔasɔsjasjɔ̃] NF copartnership

coassocié, -e [kɔasɔsje] NM,F copartner

coassurance [kɔasyrɑ̃s] NF coinsurance

coassurer [3] [kɔasyre] VT to co-insure

coati [kɔati] NM *Zool* coati

coauteur [kootœr] NM **1** *Littérature* coauthor, joint author; **mon c.** my coauthor **2** (*d'un crime*) accomplice

coaxial, -e, -aux, -ales [kɔaksjal, -o] ADJ coaxial

COB, Cob [kɔb] NF (*abrév* **Commission des opérations de Bourse**) = French Stock Exchange watchdog, *Br* ≃ SIB, *Am* ≃ SEC

cob [kɔb] NM (*cheval*) cob

cobæa [kɔbea] NF *Bot* Mexican ivy, *Spéc* cobaea

cobalt [kɔbalt] NM cobalt

cobalthérapie [kɔbalterapi] NF cobaltotherapy

cobaltine [kɔbaltin], **cobaltite** [kɔbaltit] NF *Minér* cobaltine

cobaltothérapie [kɔbaltɔterapi] NF cobaltotherapy

cobaye [kɔbaj] NM guinea pig; *Fig* **servir de c.** to be used as a guinea pig

cobe [kɔb] NM *Zool* kob; **c. de Buffon** Buffon's kob; **c. defassa** *ou* **onctueux** defassa waterbuck; **c. des roseaux** reedbuck

cobéa [kɔbea], **cobée** [kɔbe] = **cobæa**

cobelligérant, -e [kɔbeliʒerɑ̃, -ɑ̃t] ADJ cobelligerent
NM,F cobelligerent

Coblence [kɔblɑ̃s] NM Koblenz

cobol [kɔbɔl] NM *Ordinat* Cobol, COBOL

Cobra [kɔbra] NM *Beaux-Arts* (*abrév* **Copenhague, Bruxelles, Amsterdam**) Cobra, CoBrA; **le groupe C.** the Cobra group, the Cobra artists

cobra [kɔbra] NM cobra; **c. cracheur** spitting cobra; **c. indien** Indian cobra; **c. royal** king cobra

co-branding [kobrɑ̃diŋ] NM *Mktg* co-branding

coca [kɔka] NF **1** *Bot* coca **2** *Pharm* coca extract
❏ **Coca®** NM INV (*boisson*) Coke®

Coca-Cola® [kɔkakɔla] NM INV Coca-Cola®

cocagne [kɔkaɲ] **de cocagne** ADJ **époque de c.** years of plenty; **pays de c.** land of plenty

cocaïer [kɔkaje] NM *Bot* coca (shrub)

cocaïne [kɔkain] NF cocaine

cocaïnisme [kɔkainism] NM cocaine addiction

cocaïnomane [kɔkainɔman] NMF cocaine addict

cocaïnomanie [kɔkainɔmani] NF cocaine addiction

cocarcinogène [kɔkarsinɔʒen] ADJ cocarcinogenic
NM cocarcinogen

cocard [kɔkar] NM *Fam* black eye■, shiner

cocarde [kɔkard] NF **1** (*en tissu*) rosette; *Hist* cockade; **la c. tricolore** the revolutionary cockade **2** (*signe* → *militaire, sur un avion*) roundel; (→ *sur une voiture officielle*) official logo

cocardier, -ère [kɔkardje, -ɛr] ADJ *Péj* chauvinistic, jingoistic
NM,F chauvinist, jingoist

cocasse [kɔkas] ADJ comical

cocasserie [kɔkasri] NF (*d'une situation*) funniness; **c'était d'une c.!** it was a scream!

cocci [kɔksi] NMPL cocci

coccidie [kɔksidi] *Zool* NF coccid
❏ **coccidies** NFPL Coccidia

coccidiose [kɔksidjoz] NF coccidiosis

coccinelle [kɔksinɛl] NF **1** *Entom Br* ladybird, *Am* ladybug **2** (*voiture*) *Br* beetle, *Am* bug

coccobacille [kɔkɔbasil] NM coccobacillus

coccolite [kɔk(k)ɔlit] NF **1** *Minér* coccolite **2** *Géol* coccolith

coccolithophore [kɔkɔlitɔfɔr] *Bot* ADJ coccolithophorid
NF coccolithophorid, coccolithophore

coccygien, -enne [kɔksiʒjɛ̃, -jɛn] ADJ *Anat* coccygeal

coccyx [kɔksis] NM *Anat* coccyx

coche [kɔʃ] NF **1** (*encoche*) notch **2** (*symbole*) *Br* tick, *Am* check **3** (*truie*) sow **4** *Can Fam* (*locutions*) **il lui manque une c.** he's/she's got a screw loose; **péter une c.** to throw *or* have a fit
NM **1** (*voiture*) stagecoach; *Fig* **manquer** *ou* **rater** *ou* **louper le c.** to miss the boat **2** *Naut* **c. d'eau** (horse-pulled passenger) barge

cochenille [kɔʃnij] NF **1** (*insecte*) mealybug **2** (*teinture*) cochineal

cocher¹ [kɔʃe] NM coach driver; **c. de fiacre** cabman

cocher² [3] [kɔʃe] VT **1** (*marquer d'un trait*) *Br* to tick (off), *Am* to check (off) **2** *Vieilli* (*faire une entaille dans*) to nick, to notch

côcher [3] [kɔʃe] VT to tread

cochère [kɔʃɛr] ADJ F **porte c.** carriage entrance, porte cochère

cochet [kɔʃe] NM cockerel

cochette [kɔʃɛt] NF *Zool* gilt, young sow

cocheur [kɔʃœr] NM *Can Golf* **c. d'allée** pitching wedge; **c. de lisière** chipper; **c. de sable** sand wedge

cochevis [kɔʃvi] NM *Orn* crested lark

Cochinchine [kɔʃɛ̃ʃin] NF **la C.** Cochin China

cochléaire [kɔkleɛr] ADJ cochleate, spiral

cochlée [kɔkle] NF cochlea

cochon, -onne [kɔʃɔ̃, -ɔn] ADJ *Fam* **1** (*sale*) dirty■, filthy■, disgusting■; **tu ne vas pas rendre un devoir aussi c.?** are you really going to hand in such a messy piece of homework?; **ce n'est pas c.!** it's not bad!
2 (*obscène*) smutty, dirty, filthy

NM,F *Fam* **1** (*vicieux*) lecher; **un vieux c.** a dirty old man; **tu es une petite cochonne!** you've got a filthy mind *or* a mind like a sewer!

2 (*personne sale*) (filthy) pig; **oh, le petit c.!** (*à un enfant*) you dirty thing!

NM 1 *Zool* pig; **c. de lait** suckling pig; **c. d'eau** capybara; **c. de mer** porpoise; **faire le c. pendu** to hang by one's legs; **sale comme un c.** filthy dirty; **manger comme un c.** to eat like a pig; **tu écris comme un c.** your writing is appalling; **amis** *ou* **copains comme cochons** as thick as thieves; *Hum* **si les petits cochons ne te mangent pas** if the wolf doesn't get you

2 (*homme méprisable*) dirty dog; **c. qui s'en dédit!** you've got a deal!; *Fam* **ben mon c.!** well, I'll be damned!

3 *Can* (*tirelire*) piggybank

◻ **de cochon** ADJ **1** (*mauvais → temps*) foul, filthy; (→ *caractère*) foul

2 (*yeux*) piggy

◻ **cochon d'Inde** NM guinea pig

cochonceté [kɔʃɔ̃ste] NF *Fam* **1** (*saleté*) **faire des cochoncetés** to make a filthy mess **2** (*nourriture*) junk food (*UNCOUNT*) **3** (*obscénité*) piece of smut; **dire des cochoncetés** to say dirty things; **allez faire vos cochoncetés ailleurs!** go and do that sort of thing somewhere else!

cochonnaille [kɔʃɔnaj] NF *Fam* pork products■; **des cochonnailles pendaient au plafond** sausages and hams were hanging from the ceiling■

cochonne [kɔʃɔn] *voir* **cochon**

cochonner [3] [kɔʃɔne] VT (*dessin, chambre*) to make a mess of

VI (*truie*) to pig

cochonnerie [kɔʃɔnri] NF *Fam* **1** (*chose médiocre*) *Br* rubbish (*UNCOUNT*), *Am* trash (*UNCOUNT*); (*nourriture → mal préparée*) pigswill (*UNCOUNT*); (→ *de mauvaise qualité*) junk food (*UNCOUNT*); **on t'a vendu une c.** they sold you a piece of junk *or Br* rubbish; **il ne mange que des cochonneries** he only eats junk food

2 (*saleté*) mess (*UNCOUNT*); **faire des cochonneries** to make a mess

3 (*obscénité*) smut (*UNCOUNT*); **dire des cochonneries** to say filthy things

4 (*action déloyale*) dirty trick; **faire une c. à qn** to play a dirty trick on sb

5 (*dans des exclamations*) **c. de voiture/de brouillard!** damn this car/this fog!

cochonnet [kɔʃɔnɛ] NM **1** (*aux boules*) jack **2** (*porcelet*) piglet

cochylis [kɔkilis] NM *OU* NF *Entom* cochylis (moth)

cocker [kɔkɛr] NM cocker spaniel

cockney [kɔknɛ] ADJ & NMF cockney

cockpit [kɔkpit] NM cockpit

cocktail [kɔktɛl] NM **1** (*boisson*) cocktail; (*réception*) cocktail party **2** (*mélange*) mix, mixture; **c. de fruits** fruit cocktail **3** (*bombe*) **c. Molotov** Molotov cocktail

COCO [koko] NM **1** (*plante*) coconut; (*fibre*) coir

2 *Fam Vieilli ou Can* (*tête*) nut, head■; **il a rien dans le c.!** he's got nothing between his ears!

3 *Fam* (*estomac*) belly; **qu'est-ce qu'elle se met dans le c.!** she really puts it away!

4 *Fam* (*individu*) **un sacré c.** a bit of a lad; **un drôle de c.** a weirdo, an oddball; *Ironique* **c'est un joli c.!** what a charming individual!

5 *Fam* (*en appellatif affectueux → à un adulte*) sweetheart, honey; **toi mon c., je t'ai à l'œil** just watch it, *Br* mate *or* pal *or Am* buddy; **qu'est-ce qu'il y a, mon petit c.?** what's wrong, little man?

6 (*en langage enfantin → œuf*) egg

7 (*boisson*) = drink made from liquorice and water

NMF *Fam Péj* (*communiste*) commie

NF *Fam* (*cocaïne*) coke, snow

◻ **cocos** NMPL (*haricots*) = type of small white haricot bean

cocoler [3] [kɔkɔle] VT *Suisse* to cosset

cocon [kɔkɔ̃] NM cocoon; *Fig* **le c. familial** the family nest; *Fig* **vivre dans un c.** to live a cocooned *or* sheltered existence, to live in a cocoon; *Fig* **s'enfermer** *ou* **rester dans son c.** to stay in one's shell

coconisation [kɔkɔnizasjɔ̃] NF cocooning

cocontractant, -e [kɔkɔ̃traktɑ̃, -ɑ̃t] NM,F contracting partner

cocooning [kɔkuniŋ] NM cocooning; **on a fait du**

c. ce week-end we had a quiet time at home this weekend

cocorico [kɔkɔriko] ONOMAT cock-a-doodle-doo; **faire c.** to crow

EXCLAM three cheers for France!

NM 1 (*chant du coq*) cock-a-doodle-doo **2** *Fig* = expression of French national pride; **les cocoricos qui ont salué leur victoire dans la presse** the national pride which their victory generated in the press

cocoter [kɔkɔte] = **cocotter**

cocoteraie [kɔkɔtrɛ] NF coconut grove

cocotier [kɔkɔtje] NM coconut palm; *Fig* **secouer le c.** to get rid of the dead wood; *Fig* **tomber du c.** to be forced to retire

cocotte [kɔkɔt] NF **1** (*casserole*) casserole dish; **cuire à la c.** to casserole **2** (*en langage enfantin → poule*) hen; **c. en papier** paper bird **3** (*en appellatif*) **ma c.** darling, honey **4** *Péj* (*femme*) tart; **sentir ou puer la c.** to stink of cheap perfume **5** *Can* (*pomme de pin*) pine cone

◻ **cocottes** NFPL *Mus* high staccato notes

◻ **en cocotte** ADV **cuit en c.** casseroled; **(faire) cuire qch en c.** to casserole sth ADJ (*œuf*) coddled

Cocotte-Minute® [kɔkɔtminyt] NF pressure cooker ◻ **à la Cocotte-Minute** ADJ pressure-cooked ADV (*cuit*) in a pressure cooker

cocotter [3] [kɔkɔte] VI *Fam Péj* to stink; **ça cocotte!** it stinks!

cocréancier, -ère [kokreɑsje, -ɛr] NM,F *Fin* joint creditor

cocu, -e [kɔky] *Fam* ADJ **il est c.** his wife's cheated on him

NM,F 1 (*conjoint trompé*) cuckold■, deceived husband■, *f* wife■; **elle l'a fait c.** she cheated on him, she was unfaithful to him■ **2** (*en appellatif*) sucker; **va donc, eh c.!** get lost, you sucker!

cocuage [kɔkyaʒ] NM *Fam* cuckoldry■

cocufier [9] [kɔkyfje] VT *Fam* to cheat on, to be unfaithful to■, *Vieilli* to cuckold■

cocyclique [kɔsiklik] ADJ belonging to the same circle

COD, C.O.D. [seɔde] NM *Gram* (*abrév* **complément d'objet direct**) direct object

coda [kɔda] NF *Mus* coda

codage [kɔdaʒ] NM **1** (*chiffrement*) coding; **c. de données** data encryption **2** *Ling* encoding

code [kɔd] NM **1** (*ensemble de lois*) code; **c. administratif** Administrative Code; **le c. (civil)** the civil code; **c. de commerce** commercial law; **c. de déontologie** code of ethics; **c. général des impôts** general tax code; **c. maritime** navigation laws; **c. martial** articles of war; *Hist* **c. noir** = law passed in 1685 regulating the slave trade between France, Africa and the West Indies and ensuring the protection of the slaves; **c. pénal** penal code; **c. de procédure civile** Code of Civil Procedure; **c. de procédure pénale** Code of Criminal Procedure; **c. de la route** *Br* Highway Code, *Am* rules of the road; **passer le c.** to sit the written part of a driving test; **C. du travail** Labour Code

2 (*normes*) code; **c. moral** moral code; **c. de la politesse** code of good conduct

3 (*ensemble de conventions*) code; *Naut* **c. international de signaux** International Code; **c. télégraphique** telegraphic code; **c. des transmissions** signal *or* signalling code

4 (*groupe de symboles*) code; **science des codes** cryptography; **c. alphanumérique** alphanumeric code; **c. assujetti TVA** VAT registration number; **c. (à) barres** bar code; **c. binaire** binary code; **c. client** customer code, customer reference number; **c. confidentiel** (*d'une carte bancaire*) personal identification number, PIN (number); **c. contrainte** duress code; **c. couleur** colour code; **c. d'entrée** (*sur une porte*) door code; **c. guichet** bank branch code; **c. à lecture optique** machine readable code line; **c. personnel** (*pour carte bancaire*) personal identification number, PIN (number); *Banque* **c. porteur** personal identification number, PIN (number); **c. postal** *Br* post *or Am* zip code; **c. de routage** routing information; *Fin* **c. SICOVAM** = five-digit code allocated to French securities by the central securities depository

5 *Ordinat* code; **c. abrégé** shortcode; **c. d'accès** access code; **c. d'arrêt** stop code; **c. ASCII**

ASCII code; **c. d'autorisation d'accès** access authorization code; **c. de caractère** character code; **c. de commande** command code; **c. de contrôle** control code; **c. de départ** start code; **c. d'erreur** error code; **c. d'imprimante** printer code; **c. machine** machine code; **c. malicieux** malware; **c. natif** source code; **c. objet** object code; **c. source** source code

6 (*manuel*) code-book; **c. de chiffrement** cipher book; **c. de déchiffrement** code-book

7 *Ling* language

8 *Biol* code; **c. génétique** genetic code

◻ **codes** NMPL *Aut Br* dipped headlights, *Am* low beams

◻ **en code** ADV (*sous forme chiffrée*) in code; **mettre qch en c.** to cipher *or Am* to code sth

◻ **en codes** ADV *Aut* **se mettre en codes** *Br* to dip one's headlights, *Am* to put on the low beams; **rouler en codes** *Br* to drive with dipped headlights, *Am* to drive with one's headlights on low beam

═══════════════
🎬

'**Code Inconnu**' *Haneke* 'Code Unknown'

CODE POSTAL

In France, the first two numbers of a given post code correspond to the administrative code number of the relevant "département". Thus all postal codes for Paris begin with 75. This system also applies to vehicle registration numbers.

codé, -e [kɔde] ADJ encoded, coded; **caractère/programme c.** coded character/program; **générateur d'impulsions codées** pulse coder; **message c.** cryptogram; **question codée** encoded question; **langage c.** secret language

code-barres [kɔdbar] (*pl* **codes-barres**) NM bar code

codébiteur, -trice [kɔdebitœr, -tris] NM,F joint debtor

codécision [kɔdesizjɔ̃] NF *UE* codecision (procedure)

codéfendeur [kɔdefɑ̃dœr] NM co-respondent

codéine [kɔdein] NF codeine

codemandeur, -eresse [kɔdəmɑ̃dœr, -drɛs] NM,F joint plaintiff

codépendance [kɔdepɑ̃dɑ̃s] NF *Psy* codependency

codépendant, -e [kɔdepɑ̃dɑ̃, -ɑ̃t] ADJ *Psy* codependent

coder [3] [kɔde] VT **1** (*chiffrer*) to code, to encipher **2** *Ling* to encode

code-sharing [kɔdʃeriŋ] NM *Aviat* code-sharing

codétenteur, -trice [kɔdetɑ̃tœr, -tris] NM,F joint holder

codétenu, -e [kɔdetny] NM,F fellow prisoner

codeur, -euse [kɔdœr, -øz] NM,F coder

NM coding machine

codéveloppement [kɔdevlɔpmɑ̃] NM cooperative development

CODEVI, codevi, codévi [kɔdevi] NM *Banque* (*abrév* **compte pour le développement industriel**) = type of instant-access savings account, money from which is invested in industrial development

codex [kɔdɛks] NM codex; **c. pharmaceutique** pharmacopoeia

codicillaire [kɔdisilɛr] ADJ *Jur* codicillary

codicille [kɔdisil] NM *Jur* codicil

codificateur, -trice [kɔdifikatœr, -tris] ADJ codifying

NM,F codifier

codification [kɔdifikasjɔ̃] NF **1** (*d'une profession, d'un système*) codification **2** *Jur* (*de lois*) codification **3** *Ordinat* **c. binaire** binary code; **c. décimale** decimal coding

codificatrice [kɔdifikatris] *voir* **codificateur**

codifier [9] [kɔdifje] VT **1** (*pratique, profession*) to codify **2** *Jur* (*lois*) to codify

codirecteur, -trice [kɔdirɛktœr, -tris] NM,F joint manager

codirection [kɔdirɛksjɔ̃] NF joint management

codirectrice [kɔdirɛktris] *voir* **codirecteur**

codiriger [17] [kɔdiriʒe] VT **c. qch** to manage sth together *or* jointly

cododo [kɔdodo] NM *Fam* co-sleeping■

codominance [kɔdɔminɑ̃s] NF *Biol* codominance

codominant, -e [kɔdɔminɑ̃, -ɑ̃t] ADJ **1** *Biol* codominant **2** *(espèces)* codominant

codon [kɔdɔ̃] NM *Biol* codon

co-donataire [kɔdɔnatɛr] *Jur* ADJ **enfants co-donataires** = children who jointly benefit from a donation made by their parents

NMF co-donee, co-donatee

co-donateur, -trice [kɔdɔnatœr, -tris] *Jur* ADJ joint-donor *(avant n)*; **époux co-donateurs** married couple who make a joint donation

NM,F co-donor, joint donor

coéchangiste [kɔeʃɑ̃ʒist] NMF party to an exchange

coéditer [3] [kɔedite] VT to copublish

coéditeur, -trice [kɔeditœr, -tris] ADJ copublishing *(avant n)*

NM,F copublisher

coédition [kɔedisjɔ̃] NF *(procédé)* copublishing, coedition, joint publishing; *(livre)* joint publication

coéditrice [kɔeditris] *voir* **coéditeur**

coéducation [kɔedykasjɔ̃] NF coeducation

coefficient [kɔefisjɑ̃] NM **1** *Math & Phys* coefficient; *Écon* **c. de corrélation** correlation coefficient; *Tech* **c. de dilatation** coefficient of expansion; **c. d'élasticité** modulus of elasticity; **c. multiplicateur** multiplying factor; **c. numérique** numerical coefficient; *Aut* **c. de pénétration dans l'air** drag factor; *Math* **c. de pondération** weighting; **c. de rendement** coefficient of efficiency; **c. de rupture** modulus of rupture

2 *(proportion)* rating, ratio; *Fin* **c. d'activité** activity ratio; *Fin* **c. de capital** output ratio; *Fin* **c. de capitalisation des résultats** price-earnings ratio; *Fin* **c. d'exploitation** operating ratio, performance ratio; **c. d'erreur** *ou* **d'incertitude** margin of error; *Compta* **c. d'exploitation** performance *or* operating ratio; *Compta* **c. de liquidité** liquidity ratio; **c. d'occupation des sols** plot ratio; *Fin* **c. de perte** loss ratio; *Compta* **c. de rotation** stock turnover ratio; *Écon* **c. saisonnier** seasonal index; *Compta* **c. de solvabilité** risk asset ratio, solvency coefficient; *Fin* **c. de trésorerie** cash ratio

3 *(valeur)* weight, weighting; **affecter qch d'un c.** to weight sth; **l'anglais est affecté du c. 3** English will be weighted at a rate equal to 300 percent; **c. correcteur applicable aux salaires** weighting applicable to salaries; **c. statistique** statistical weight

> *Culture*
>
> **COEFFICIENT**
>
> In baccalauréat examinations, the grade for each subject is multiplied by a "coefficient" which is determined by the type of baccalauréat chosen. For a "bac S", which has a scientific bias, the "coefficient" for maths will be higher than the philosophy "coefficient", for example.

cœlacanthe [selakɑ̃t] NM *Ich* coelacanth

cœlentéré [selɑ̃tere] *Zool* NM coelenterate

❑ **cœlentérés** NMPL Coelenterata

cœliaque [seljak] ADJ *Méd* coeliac; **région c.** coeliac area; **maladie c.** coeliac disease; **tronc c.** abdominal aorta

cœliochirurgie [seljɔʃiryrʒi] NF *Méd* laparotomy

cœlioscopie [seljɔskɔpi] NF *Méd* caelioscopy, laparoscopy

cœlomate [selɔmat] NM coelomate, celomate

cœlome [selɔm] NM *Zool* coelom

cœlomique [selɔmik] ADJ *Zool* coelomic

cœnesthésie [senestezi] = **cénesthésie**

coentreprise [koɑ̃trəpriz] NF joint venture

cœnure [senyr] = **cénure**

coenzyme [kɔɑ̃zim] NM OU NF coenzyme

coépouse [kɔepuz] NF co-wife

coéquation [kɔekwasjɔ̃] NF proportional assessment

coéquipier, -ère [kɔekipje, -ɛr] NM,F team mate

coercible [kɔɛrsibl] ADJ coercible, which can be coerced

coercitif, -ive [kɔɛrsitif, -iv] ADJ coercive

coercition [kɔɛrsisjɔ̃] NF coercion

coercitive [kɔɛrsitiv] *voir* **coercitif**

Coëtquidan [kɔɛtkidɑ̃] NF = important army base in Brittany where the Saint-Cyr military college is situated

CŒUR [kœr] NM **A.** *ORGANE* **1** *Anat* heart; **une balle en plein c.** a bullet through the heart; **il est malade du c.** he's got a heart condition; **c. droit/gauche** right/left side of the heart; **greffe du c.** heart transplant; **ça m'a donné** *ou* **j'ai eu un coup au c.** it really made me jump; **beau** *ou* **joli** *ou* **mignon comme un c.** as pretty as a picture; **c. artificiel** artificial heart

2 *(poitrine)* heart, breast, *Littéraire* bosom; **serrer** *ou* **presser qn contre** *ou* **sur son c.** to hold sb close

3 *(estomac)* **avoir le c. au bord des lèvres** to feel queasy *or* sick; **ça va mieux, ton mal au** *ou* **de c.** do you still feel sick?; **avoir mal au c.** to feel sick; *Fig* **ça fait mal au c. de voir tout cet argent gaspillé** it makes you sick to see all that money wasted *or* go to waste; *Fam* **ça me ferait mal au c. de devoir le lui laisser!** I'd hate to have to leave it to him/her!; *Fam* **mettre le c. à l'envers à qn** *(le dégoûter)* to sicken sb▪, to turn sb's stomach; **lever** *ou* **soulever le c. à qn** to sicken sb, to turn sb's stomach; **un spectacle à vous lever** *ou* **soulever le c.** a nauseating *or* sickening sight; *Fam* **avoir le c. bien accroché** to have a strong stomach▪; **pour regarder cette émission il faut avoir le c. bien accroché** this programme is not for the squeamish

B. *SYMBOLE DE L'AFFECTIVITÉ* **1** *(pensées, for intérieur)* heart; **ouvrir son c. à qn** to open one's heart to sb; **vider son c.** to pour out one's heart; **je veux en avoir le c. net** I want to know *or* to find out the truth; **je vais lui demander franchement, comme cela j'en aurai le c. net** I'll ask him/her straight out, that way, I'll get to the bottom of the matter

2 *(énergie, courage)* courage; **le c. lui a manqué** his/her courage failed him/her; **avoir le c. de faire qch** to have the heart to do sth; **tu n'aurais pas le c. de la renvoyer!** you wouldn't have the heart to fire her!; **avoir** *ou* **mettre du c. à l'ouvrage** to put one's heart into one's work; **il n'avait pas le c. à l'ouvrage** his heart wasn't in it; **avoir du c. au ventre** to be courageous; **donner du c. au ventre à qn** to give sb courage; **elle adore son travail, elle y met du c.** she loves her work, she really puts her heart (and soul) into it; **allez, haut les c.!** come on, chin up!

3 *(humeur)* **il est parti le c. joyeux** *ou* **gai** he left in a cheerful mood; **avoir le c. léger/triste** to be cheerful/heavy-hearted; **d'un c. léger** light-heartedly; **d'un c. content** contentedly; **avoir le c. à faire qch** to be in the mood to do *or* to feel like doing sth; **je n'ai plus le c. à rire** I don't feel like laughing any more; **ne plus avoir le c. à rien** to have lost heart; **je n'ai pas le c. à l'ouvrage** I haven't got the heart for the work; **ils travaillent, mais le c. n'y est pas** they're working but their hearts aren't in it; **si le c. t'en dit** if you feel like it, if the fancy takes you

4 *(charité, bonté)* **avoir du c., avoir bon c.** to be kind *or* kind-hearted; **elle a du** *ou* **bon c.** her heart is in the right place; **tu n'as pas de c.!** you're heartless!, you have no heart!; **ton bon c. te perdra!** you're too kind-hearted for your own good!; **c'était un homme au grand c.** *ou* **de c.** he was a good man; *Fam* **il a un c. gros comme ça** he'd give you the shirt off his back; **avoir le c. sur la main** to be very generous; **avoir un c. d'or** to have a heart of gold; **avoir le c. dur** *ou* **sec, avoir un c. de pierre** *ou* **d'airain** to have a heart of stone, to be hard-hearted; **à vot' bon c. (M'sieurs-Dames)** can you spare *Br* a few pence *or Am* a dime?

5 *(siège des émotions, de l'amour)* heart; **son c. se remplit de joie** his/her heart filled with joy; **son c. a parlé** he/she spoke from the heart; **laisser parler son c.** to let one's feelings come through; **venir du c.** to come (straight) from the heart; **des mots venus du (fond du) c.** heartfelt words; **vos paroles me sont allées droit au c.** your words went straight to my heart; **je garderai son souvenir dans mon c.** I will always remember him/her very fondly; **son c. de mère ne pouvait s'y résigner** as a mother, her heart just couldn't accept it; **briser le c. à qn** *(par chagrin d'amour)* to break sb's heart; **cela me brise le c. de le voir dans cet état** it breaks my heart to see him in such a state; **c'était à vous briser** *ou* **fendre le c.** it was heartbreaking *or* heartrending; **cette fille lui a mis le c. à l'envers** he lost his heart to that girl; **cela chauffe** *ou* **réchauffe le c.** it warms the cockles of your heart, it's heartwarming; **avoir le c. serré** to have a lump in one's throat; **avoir le c. déchiré** *ou* **brisé** to be heartbroken; **avoir le c. lourd** to feel very sad, *Littéraire* to have a heavy heart; **avoir un c. sensible/pur** to be a sensitive/candid soul; **mon c. est libre** *ou* **à prendre** I'm fancy-free; **donner son c. à qn** to lose one's heart to sb; **comment trouver le chemin de** *ou* **gagner son c.?** how can I win his/her heart?; *Littéraire* **c'était un ami selon mon c.** he was a friend after my own heart; **ce sont des amis de c.** they're bosom friends; **une affaire de c.** a love affair, an affair of the heart; **ses problèmes de c.** the problems he/she has with his/her love life; **avoir le c. gros** to feel sad, to have a heavy heart; *Fam* **je ne le porte pas dans mon c.** I'm not particularly fond of him

C. *PERSONNE* **1** *(personne ayant telle qualité)* **c'est un c. d'or** he's got a heart of gold; **c'est un c. sensible** he's a sensitive soul; **c'est un c. dur** *ou* **sec** *ou* **de pierre** *ou* **d'airain** he has a heart of stone, he's heartless; **c'est un c. de lion** he's a real lionheart; *Prov* **à c. vaillant rien d'impossible** where there's a will there's a way

2 *(terme affectueux)* darling, sweetheart; **mon (petit) c.** my darling; **tu viens, mon c.?** coming, darling?

D. *CENTRE* **1** *(d'un chou, d'une salade, d'un fromage)* heart; *(d'un fruit, d'un réacteur nucléaire)* core; *(d'une ville)* heart, centre; **enlever le c. d'une pomme** to core an apple; **c. de laitue** lettuce heart; **c. de palmier** palm heart; **cœur d'artichaut** artichoke heart; *Fig* **c'est un vrai c. d'artichaut** he/she is always falling in love; *Mktg* **c. de cible** core market, core audience; **cette région est véritablement le c. de l'Allemagne industrielle** this region is really the heartland of industrial Germany

2 *(partie la plus importante → d'un débat)* central point; **le c. de mon argument est que…** the central point of my argument is that…; **le c. du problème** the heart of the matter; **la question de la sécurité est au c. des préoccupations de notre parti** the issue of security is at the heart of our party's concerns

3 *Menuis* **c. de merisier/peuplier** heart of cherry/poplar

E. *OBJET EN FORME DE CŒUR* **1** *(bijou)* heart-shaped jewel

2 *Culin* heart-shaped delicacy; **petits cœurs à la crème** hearts of fromage frais with cream

3 *Cartes* **du c.** hearts; **dame/dix de cœur** queen/ten of hearts; **jouer à** *ou* **du c.** to play hearts

❑ **à cœur** ADV **1** *(avec sérieux)* **prendre les choses à c.** to take things to heart; **elle prend vraiment son travail à c.** she really takes her job seriously; **ne prends pas ses critiques tant à c.** don't take his/her criticism so much to heart; **ce rôle me tient beaucoup à c.** the part means a lot to me; **avoir à c. de faire qch** to have one's heart set on doing sth **2** *Culin* **fromage fait à c.** fully ripe cheese; **café grillé à c.** high roast coffee; **avocat mûr à c.** fully ripe avocado

❑ **à cœur de** ADV *Can* **à c. de jour/année** all day/year long

❑ **à cœur joie** ADV to one's heart's content; **s'en donner à c. joie** to have tremendous fun *or* a tremendous time

❑ **à cœur ouvert** ADJ *(opération)* open-heart *(avant n)* ADV **parler à c. ouvert à qn** to have a heart-to-heart (talk) with sb

❑ **au cœur de** PRÉP **au c. de l'été** at the height of summer; **au c. de l'hiver** in the depths of winter; **au c. de la forêt** deep in the forest; **au c. de la nuit** in the *or* at dead of night; **au c. du Morvan** in the heart of the Morvan region; **au c. de la ville** in the centre of town, in the town centre; **le sujet fut au c. des débats** the subject was central to the debate

❑ **cœur à cœur** ADV *Littéraire* **parler c. à c. avec qn** to have a heart-to-heart (talk) with sb

❑ **de bon cœur** ADV **1** *(volontiers → donner)* willingly; *(→ parler)* readily; **ne me remerciez pas, c'est de bon c. (que je vous ai aidé)** no need to thank me, it was a pleasure (helping you) **2** *(énergiquement → rire)* heartily; **y aller de bon c.** to get down to it

cœ–coh

❏ **de tout cœur** ADV wholeheartedly; **être de tout c. avec qn** (*condoléances*) to sympathize wholeheartedly with sb; **je ne pourrai assister à votre mariage mais je serai de tout c. avec vous** I won't be able to attend your wedding but I'll be with you in spirit

❏ **de tout mon/son**/etc **cœur** ADV 1 (*sincèrement* → *aimer, remercier*) with all my/his/etc heart, wholeheartedly, from the bottom of my/his/etc heart; (→ *féliciter*) warmly, wholeheartedly; **je l'espère de tout mon c.** I sincerely hope so 2 *Fam* (*énergiquement*) **y aller de tout son c.** to go at it hammer and tongs, to give it all one's got; **rire de tout son c.** to laugh one's head off

❏ **en cœur** ADJ (*bouche, pendentif*) heart-shaped

❏ **par cœur** ADV 1 (*apprendre, connaître*) by heart; **connaître qn par c.** to know sb inside out; **je connais toutes tes excuses par c.** I know all your excuses by heart 2 (*locution*) **dîner par c.** to go without (one's) dinner NM **c'est du par c.** it's been learnt (off) by heart *or* parrot-fashion

❏ **sans cœur** ADJ heartless

❏ **sur le cœur** ADV **la mousse au chocolat m'est restée sur le c.** the chocolate mousse lay in the pit of my stomach; **ses critiques me sont restées** *ou* **me pèsent sur le c.** I still haven't got over the way she criticized me; **avoir qch sur le c.** to have sth on one's mind; **dis ce que tu as sur le c.** say what's (weighing) on your mind; **avoir un poids sur le c.** to have a heavy heart; *Fam* **en avoir gros sur le c.** to be really upset

---

'**Un Cœur simple**' *Flaubert* 'A Simple Heart'

Allusion

Le cœur a ses raisons (que la raison ne connaît point)

This celebrated saying from Blaise Pascal's *Pensées* (1658) is also well-known in English: "The heart has its reasons (of which reason knows nothing)." Pascal was pointing out that rational judgement was not always and invariably man's main motivating force. Today we say this when the logical motivation for behaviour, or for an attitude someone may hold, is not immediately clear to an outside observer.

Allusion

Tu me fends le cœur

This expression was a coded reference to the suit hearts in cards. It comes from Marcel Pagnol's play *Marius* (1929), later a film with the actor Raimu in the leading role. In one scene, four people are playing cards and Marius is forbidden to speak to his partner. With this line, delivered in a strong Provençal accent, he tries to convey the crucial message "hearts!". The comic delivery of the line stuck in the public imagination, and so **Tu me fends le cœur** ("You're breaking my heart") has a particular connotation.

Allusion

Rodrigue, as-tu du cœur?

In Corneille's play *Le Cid* (1636) Don Diego ("Don Diègue" in French) is counting on his son Rodrigo ("Rodrigue" in French) to avenge an insult he has received. He asks him, **Rodrigue, as-tu du cœur?**, i.e. "Do you have the courage to do it?" Today these words can be used teasingly to someone who has to do something that requires a modicum of courage. In that context it means "Do you think you're up to it?" People may also use the phrase humorously as a pun during card games, when asking another player if he or she has any hearts.

---

cœur-de-pigeon [kœrdəpiʒɔ̃] (*pl* **cœurs-de-pigeon**) NM = variety of red cherry

cœur-poumon [kœrpumɔ̃] NM INV *Méd* **c. artificiel** (artificial) heart-lung machine

coévolution [kɔevɔlysjɔ̃] NF coevolution

---

coexistence [kɔɛgzistɑ̃s] NF coexistence; **c. pacifique** peaceful coexistence

coexister [3] [kɔɛgziste] VI **c. (avec)** to coexist (with)

coextensif, -ive [kɔɛkstɑ̃sif, -iv] ADJ coextensive; **c. à** sharing the same area of application as

COFACE [kɔfas] NF (*abrév* **Compagnie française d'assurances pour le commerce extérieur**) = export insurance company, ≃ ECGD

cofacteur [kɔfaktœr] NM contributory factor; *Biol, Chim & Math* cofactor

coffrage [kɔfraʒ] NM 1 *Mines & (en travaux publics)* lagging, (plank) lining 2 *Constr (moule)* form, formwork, *Br* shuttering; *(pose de moule)* form *or* formwork preparation

coffre [kɔfr] NM 1 (*caisse*) box, chest; **c. à jouets** toybox; **c. à linge** linen chest; **c. à outils** tool box

2 *Naut* locker; **c. d'amarrage** mooring buoy, trunk buoy

3 *Aut Br* boot, *Am* trunk; **c. de rangement** (*d'un camion*) storage compartment; **c. à bagages** (*d'un autocar*) baggage *or* luggage compartment

4 (*coffre-fort*) safe, strongbox; (*à la banque*) safe-deposit box; **les coffres de l'État** the coffers of the State; **les coffres sont vides à la fin du mois** the coffers are empty by the end of the month; **c. de nuit** night safe

5 (*d'un piano*) case

6 *Aviat* **c. à parachute** parachute canister

7 *Ich* (*poisson-coffre*) boxfish, trunkfish, coffer fish

8 *Fam* (*poitrine*) chest ■; (*voix*) (big) voice ■; **avoir du c.** (*du souffle*) to have a good pair of lungs

coffre-fort [kɔfrfɔr] (*pl* **coffres-forts**) NM safe, strongbox

coffrer [3] [kɔfre] VT 1 *Fam (emprisonner)* to put behind bars; **se faire c.** to be sent down, to get put inside *or* away *or* behind bars 2 *Mines* to lag 3 *Constr* to form

coffret [kɔfrɛ] NM 1 (*petit coffre*) box, casket; **dans un c. cadeau** in a gift box; **un c. de cinq savons** a box of five soaps; **c. à bijoux** jewellery box 2 (*cabinet*) cabinet 3 *Ordinat* case

❏ **en coffret** ADV présenté *ou* vendu en c. sold in a presentation box; **la présentation en c. est ce qui fait le succès de ce produit** this item sells so well because it comes in a presentation box

coffreur [kɔfrœr] NM *Ind* formworker

cofidéjusseur [kɔfideʒysœr] NM *Jur* co-surety

cofinancement [kɔfinɑ̃smɑ̃] NM cofinancing

cofinancer [16] [kɔfinɑ̃se] VT to cofinance, to finance jointly

cofondateur, -trice [kɔfɔ̃datœr, -tris] NM,F co-founder

cogénération [kɔʒeneʁasjɔ̃] NF *Tech* cogeneration

cogérance [kɔʒeʁɑ̃s] NF joint management

cogérant, -e [kɔʒeʁɑ̃, -ɑ̃t] NM,F joint manager

cogérer [18] [kɔʒeʁe] VT to manage jointly

cogestion [kɔʒɛstjɔ̃] NF joint management *or* administration

cogitation [kɔʒitasjɔ̃] NF *Hum* cogitation (UNCOUNT), pondering (UNCOUNT); **je te laisse à tes cogitations** I'll leave you to think things over

cogiter [3] [kɔʒite] *Hum* VI to cogitate; **il faut que je cogite!** I must put my thinking cap on!; **c. sur qch** to ponder over sth
VT to think over, to ponder

cogito [kɔʒito] NM INV *Phil* cogito; **le c. de Descartes** the Cartesian cogito, Descartes' cogito

cognac [kɔɲak] NM (*gén*) brandy; (*de Cognac*) Cognac

cognassier [kɔɲasje] NM *Bot* quince tree; **c. du Japon** japonica

cognat [kɔɲa] NM cognate

cognation [kɔɲasjɔ̃] NF *Jur* cognation

cognatique [kɔɲatik] ADJ *Jur* cognatic

cogne [kɔɲ] NM *Fam Arg* crime **les cognes** the cops, *Br* the fuzz

cognée [kɔɲe] NF axe, hatchet

cognement [kɔɲmɑ̃] NM (*gén*) knock, thump; (*d'un moteur*) knock

cogner [3] [kɔɲe] VI 1 (*heurter*) to bang, to knock; **qu'est-ce qui cogne?** what's that banging?; **le moteur cogne** there's a knocking sound

---

coming from the engine; **son cœur cognait dans sa poitrine** his/her heart was thumping; **c. à la fenêtre** (*fort*) to knock on the window; (*légèrement*) to tap on the window; **sa tête a cogné contre le bureau** he/she banged his/her head on the desk; **c. du poing sur la table** to bang (one's fist) on the table

2 *Fam* (*user de violence*) **mon père cognait** my father was handy with his fists; **il cogne dur** he knows how to use his fists; **c. sur qn** to beat sb up; **ça va c.** things are going to get rough

3 *Fam* **ça cogne** (*le soleil chauffe*) it's scorching *or Br* roasting

4 *Fam* (*puer*) to stink (to high heaven), *Br* to pong

VT 1 (*entrer en collision avec*) to bang *or* to knock *or* to smash into; **c. qn en passant** to bump into sb (in passing)

2 *Fam* (*battre*) to knock about; **se faire c.** to get knocked about

▶ **se cogner** VPR 1 (*se faire mal*) **je me suis cogné** I banged into something; **se c. à** *ou* **contre qch** to bang into sth

2 (*heurter*) **se c. le coude** to hit *or* to bang one's elbow; *Fig* **se c. la tête contre les murs** to bang one's head against a brick wall

3 *Fam* **se c. qn/qch** (*corvée*) to get stuck *or Br* lumbered *or* landed with sb/sth

4 *très Fam* (*locution*) **il s'en cogne** he doesn't give a shit *or Br* a toss

cogneur [kɔɲœr] NM *Boxe & (gén)* hard hitter, bruiser

cogniticien, -enne [kɔgnitisjɛ̃, -ɛn] NM,F *Ordinat* knowledge engineer

cognitif, -ive [kɔgnitif, -iv] ADJ cognitive

cognition [kɔgnisjɔ̃] NF cognitive processes, cognition

cognitive [kɔgnitiv] *voir* **cognitif**

cognitivisme [kɔgnitivism] NM 1 *Psy* cognitive psychology, cognitivism 2 *Phil* cognitivism

cognitiviste [kɔgnitivist] ADJ cognitivist
NMF cognitivist

cohabitation [kɔabitasjɔ̃] NF 1 (*vie commune*) cohabitation, cohabiting, living together 2 *Pol* = coexistence of an elected head of state and an opposition parliamentary majority; **c. monétaire européenne** European monetary cohabitation

---

Culture

LA COHABITATION

Originally, this term refers to the period (1986–1988) during which the socialist President (François Mitterrand) had a right-wing Prime Minister (Jacques Chirac), following the victory of the RPR in the legislative elections and Mitterrand's decision not to resign as President. It has since been used to refer to the similar situation which arose following the 1993 elections (with Édouard Balladur as Prime Minister) and also after the 1997 elections (with the left-wing government of Lionel Jospin co-ruling with the President Jacques Chirac).

---

cohabitationniste [kɔabitasjɔnist] *Pol* ADJ relating to the coexistence of an elected head of state and an opposition parliamentary majority
NMF = advocate of a system where the elected head of state and an opposition party with a parliamentary majority coexist

cohabiter [3] [kɔabite] VI 1 (*partenaires*) to cohabit, to live together; (*amis*) to live together; **c. avec qn** to live with sb; **ici, plusieurs races cohabitent** people of several different races live together here 2 (*coexister*) to coexist; **faire c. deux théories** to reconcile two theories

cohérence [kɔeʁɑ̃s] NF 1 (*logique*) coherence; **manque de c.** incoherence 2 (*homogénéité*) consistency; **manque de c.** inconsistency 3 *Phys* coherence

cohérent, -e [kɔeʁɑ̃, -ɑ̃t] ADJ 1 (*logique*) coherent; **de façon cohérente** coherently 2 (*homogène*) consistent 3 (*fidèle à soi-même*) consistent; **être c.** to be true to oneself 4 *Phys* coherent

cohériter [3] [kɔeʁite] VI to inherit jointly

cohéritier, -ère [kɔeʁitje, -ɛr] NM,F co-heir, *f* heiress

cohésif, -ive [kɔezif, -iv] ADJ cohesive

cohésion [kɔezjɔ̃] NF 1 (*solidarité*) cohesion,

cohesiveness; **la c. du groupe** the way the members of the group stick together **2** *(d'un corps, de molécules)* cohesion

cohésive [kɔeziv] *voir* **cohésif**

cohorte [koɔrt] **NF 1** *Antiq* cohort **2** *Péj (foule)* **une c. de** hordes *or* droves of **3** *(en sociologie)* population **4** *Vieilli ou Littéraire* band of soldiers, cohort; **les célestes cohortes** the heavenly host

cohue [kɔy] **NF 1** *(foule)* crowd, throng **2** *(bousculade)* **dans la c.** amidst the general pushing and shoving, in the (general) melee

COI, C.O.I. [seoi] **NM** *Gram (abrév* **complément d'objet indirect)** indirect object

coi, coite [kwa, kwat] **ADJ** speechless; **en rester c.** to be speechless; **se tenir c.** to keep quiet

coiffage [kwafaʒ] **NM 1** *(de cheveux)* hairdressing; *(de ses cheveux)* doing one's hair **2** *(pour recouvrir)* covering **3** *Méd (d'une dent)* crowning

coiffant, -e [kwafɑ̃, -ɑ̃t] **ADJ 1** *(qui coiffe bien)* becoming; **un chapeau bien c.** *(seyant)* a very attractive hat; *(de la bonne taille)* a hat which fits very well **2 crème coiffante** *(qui sert à coiffer)* hair cream

NM way of wearing one's hat

coiffe [kwaf] **NF 1** *(de costume régional)* (traditional) headdress; *(de nonne)* (nun's) headdress; *(garniture de chapeau)* lining **2** *Tech & Bot* cap **3** *(d'un livre relié)* head cap **4** *Anat* caul

coiffé, -e [kwafe] **ADJ 1** *(portant coiffure)* wearing a hat; **une femme coiffée** a woman in a hat, a woman wearing a hat; **être c. de noir** to be wearing a black hat; **il était c. d'une casquette** he was wearing a cap

2 *(avec les cheveux bien mis)* **être c.** to have combed/brushed one's hair; **je ne suis pas encore coiffée** I haven't done my hair yet; **elle était bien coiffée** her hair looked nice; **tu es très mal c.** your hair's all over the place; **il est c. en brosse** he's got a brush cut

3 *(locutions)* **être né c.** *(chanceux)* to be born lucky *or* under a lucky star; *Vieilli* **être c. de qn** *(épris)* to be smitten with sb

coiffer [3] [kwafe] **VT 1** *(peigner → cheveux, frange)* to comb; *(→ enfant, poupée)* to comb the hair of; **cheveux faciles/difficiles à c.** manageable/unmanageable hair

2 *(réaliser la coiffure de)* to do *or* to style the hair of; **elle s'est fait c. par Paolo, c'est Paolo qui l'a coiffée** she had her hair done by Paolo; **qui vous coiffe d'habitude?** who normally does your hair?; **sur ces photos, les mannequins sont coiffés par Maniatis** in these photos the models' hair is by Maniatis; **coiffez-le court, s'il vous plaît** cut his hair short, please; **j'ai payé une fortune pour être mal coiffé!** I spent a fortune on a hairstyle I don't like!

3 *(chapeauter)* to cover the head of; **c. un enfant d'un bonnet** to put a bonnet on a child('s head); **il a coiffé la statue d'une casquette** he's put a cap on the statue

4 *(aller à)* **un rien la coiffe** she suits any hat; **cette toque te coiffe à ravir** you look wonderful in that fur hat

5 *(mettre sur sa tête)* to put on; **c. la couronne** to be crowned; **c. la mitre** to be ordained a bishop

6 *Littéraire (couvrir)* **la neige coiffait les sommets** the mountain-tops were capped with snow; **la tour était coiffée d'étendards** the tower was crowned with flags

7 *(diriger)* to be in charge of, to head up; **elle coiffe plusieurs services** she's in charge of several departments

8 *(locution)* **c. qn (au** *ou* **sur le poteau)** *Br* to pip sb at the post, *Am* to pass sb up; **se faire c. au poteau** to be pipped at the post

▸**se coiffer VPR 1** *(se peigner)* to comb one's hair; *(arranger ses cheveux)* to do one's hair

2 *(mettre un chapeau)* to put a hat on; **se c. d'une casquette** to put on a cap

3 *(acheter ses chapeaux)* **se c. chez les grands couturiers** to buy one's hats from the top designers

coiffeur, -euse [kwafœr, -øz] **NM,F** hairdresser, hairstylist; **aller chez le c.** to go to the hairdresser's; **c. pour hommes** gentlemen's hairdresser, barber; **c. pour dames** ladies' hairdresser

❑ **coiffeuse NF** dressing-table

coiffure [kwafyr] **NF 1** *(coupe)* hairdo, hairstyle; **se faire faire une nouvelle c.** to have one's hair styled *or* restyled; **c. à la garçonne** urchin cut, *Br* Eton crop; **c. à la Jeanne d'Arc** pageboy haircut **2** *(technique)* **la c.** hairdressing **3** *(chapeau)* headgear; *(de costume régional)* headdress

COIN [kwɛ̃]

> corner **1, 2** ■ place **3** ■ patch **4** ■ die, stamp **5** ■ wedge **6**

NM 1 *(angle)* corner; **se cogner au c. de la table** to bang into the corner of the table; **le c. de la rue** the corner of the street; **la maison qui fait le c.** the house on the corner, the corner house; **à un c. de rue** on a street-corner; *Rail* **un c. couloir/fenêtre** an aisle/a window seat; **à chaque c. de rue, à tous les coins de rue** on every street corner, everywhere; **une robe comme on en trouve à tous les coins de rue** a common-or-garden dress; **il n'y en a pas à tous les coins de rue** you don't see many of them about; **manger sur un c. de table** to eat a hasty meal; **travailler sur un c. de table** to bungle one's work; **ce n'est pas le genre de calcul qui peut se faire sur un c. de table** that's not the sort of calculation you can do on the back of an envelope; **au c. du feu** by the fireside; *Fig* **rester au c. du feu** to stay at home; **au c. d'un bois** somewhere in a wood; *Fig* in a lonely place; **on n'aimerait pas le rencontrer au c. d'un bois!** you wouldn't like to meet him on a dark night!

2 *(commissure → des lèvres, de l'œil)* corner; **du c. de l'œil** *(regarder, surveiller)* out of the corner of one's eye

3 *(endroit quelconque)* place, spot; **dans un c. de la maison** somewhere in the house; **j'ai dû laisser mon livre dans un c.** I must have left my book somewhere or other; **dans un c. de sa mémoire** in a corner of his/her memory; **il connaît les bons coins** he knows all the right places; **quel c. charmant!** what a lovely place!; **un petit c. tranquille à la campagne** a quiet spot in the country; **un c. perdu** *(isolé)* an isolated spot; *Péj (arriéré)* a godforsaken place; **trouver un petit c. pas cher (pour passer l'été)** to find somewhere not too expensive (for the summer); *Fam* **c'est vraiment un c. pourri!** what a dump!; *Com* **le c. des bricoleurs** the do-it-yourself department; **c. enfants** *(au restaurant)* children's area; **chercher dans tous les coins et les recoins** to look in every nook and cranny; **connaître qch dans les coins** to know sth like the back of one's hand; *Fam Euph* **le petit c.** the smallest room in the house; **c. cuisine** kitchen recess; **c. repas** *ou* **salle à manger** dining area; **c. salon** lounge area; **c. travail** workspace, work area

4 *(parcelle)* patch, plot; **un c. de terre** a plot *or* patch of land; **le c. des fleurs** the flower plot; **il reste un c. de ciel bleu** there's still a patch of blue sky

5 *Typ (forme)* die; *(poinçon)* stamp, hallmark; **idée marquée au c. du bon sens** idea full of common sense

6 *(cale)* wedge; **c. de centrage/serrage** centering/tightening wedge

❑ **au coin ADV** *(de la rue)* on *or* at the corner; **la boulangerie qui est au c.** the baker's on *or* at the corner; **mettre un enfant au c.** to make a child stand in the corner (as punishment)

❑ **dans le coin ADV** *(dans le quartier → ici)* locally, around here; *(→ là-bas)* locally, around there; **elle habite dans le c.** *(ici)* she lives (somewhere) around here; *(là-bas)* she lives somewhere around there; **et Victor? – il est dans le c.** where's Victor? – he's around somewhere; **je passais dans le c. et j'ai eu envie de venir te voir** I was in the area and I felt like dropping in (on you)

❑ **dans son coin ADV laisser qn dans son c.** to leave sb alone; **allons, ne laisse pas ton petit frère dans son c.** come on, make an effort to include your little brother; **rester dans son c.** to keep oneself to oneself; **elle reste toujours dans son c.** she doesn't mix

❑ **de coin ADJ** *(étagère)* corner *(avant n)*

❑ **du coin ADJ** *(du quartier → commerce)* local; **la boucherie du c.** the butcher's just round the corner, the local butcher's; **les gens du c.** *(ici)* people who live round here, the locals; *(là-bas)* people who live there, the locals; **être du c.** to live locally *or* in the area; **désolé, je ne suis pas du c.** sorry, I'm not from around here

❑ **en coin ADJ** *(regard)* sidelong; **un sourire en c.** a half-smile **ADV** *(regarder, observer)* sideways; **sourire en c.** to give a half-smile

coh–coi

coinçage [kwɛ̃saʒ] **NM** *Tech* keying, wedging

coincé, -e [kwɛ̃se] **ADJ** *Fam* **1** *Péj (inhibé)* uptight, hung-up **2** *(mal à l'aise)* tense, uneasy

coincement [kwɛ̃smɑ̃] **NM** jamming

coincer [16] [kwɛ̃se] **VT 1** *(immobiliser → volontairement)* to wedge; *(→ accidentellement)* to catch, to stick, to jam; **coince la roue avec une pierre** wedge the wheel with a stone; **mon manteau est coincé dans la portière** my coat's caught *or* stuck in the door; **j'ai coincé la fermeture de ma robe** I got the *Br* zip *or Am* zipper of my dress stuck; **il était coincé entre la voiture et le mur** he was jammed *or* trapped between the car and the wall; **la voiture est coincée entre deux camions** *(en stationnement)* the car is boxed in by two lorries

2 *Fam (attraper)* to corner, to nab, to collar; **se faire c.** to get nabbed; **je me suis fait c. dans le couloir par Darival** I got cornered by Darival in the corridor; **j'arriverai bien à le c. après le dîner** I'll corner him somehow after dinner

3 *Fam (retenir)* **je suis resté coincé dans un embouteillage** I got stuck in a traffic jam; **je suis coincé à Prague/dans l'ascenseur** I'm stuck in Prague/the *Br* lift *or Am* elevator; **il est coincé tout le week-end** he's tied up all weekend; **plus de trains? je suis coincé, maintenant!** the last train's gone? I'm stuck *or* I'm in a real fix now!; **je suis coincé par ce qu'il a dit à ma mère** because of what he said to my mother, my hands are tied *or* I'm stuck; **elle est coincée entre ses convictions et les exigences de la situation** she's torn between her convictions and the demands of the situation

4 *(mettre en difficulté → par une question)* to put on the spot, *Br* to catch out; **là, ils t'ont coincé!** they've got you there!

5 *Fam* **c. la bulle** to get some shut-eye *or* some *Br* zeds *or Am* zees

VI 1 *(être calé)* **c'est la chemise bleue qui coince au fond du tiroir** the blue shirt at the back is making the drawer jam

2 *(être entravé)* to stick; **les négociations coincent** the negotiations are deadlocked; *Fam* **ça coince (quelque part)** there's a hitch somewhere; **ça coince au niveau de mes parents!** my parents aren't too keen on the idea!

3 *très Fam (sentir mauvais)* to stink, *Br* to pong

▸**se coincer VPR 1** *(se bloquer → clef, fermeture)* to jam, to stick

2 se c. la main/le pied to get one's hand/foot caught; **l'enfant s'est coincé le doigt dans la serrure** the child got his finger stuck in the lock; **se c. le doigt dans la porte** to catch one's finger in the door; **je me suis coincé le dos** my back's seized up; **il s'est coincé une vertèbre** he's got a trapped nerve

coincetot [kwɛ̃sto] **NM** *Fam* corner■

coinceur [kwɛ̃sœr] **NM** *(en escalade)* cam, nut

coïncidence [kɔɛ̃sidɑ̃s] **NF 1** *(hasard)* chance; **quelle c. de vous voir ici!** what a coincidence seeing you here!; **c'est (une) pure c.** it's purely coincidental **2** *Math* coincidence **3** *Électron* **c. d'oscillations** surging

❑ **par coïncidence ADV** coincidentally, by coincidence; **par c., il était là aussi** by coincidence *or* chance, he was there as well; **par une étrange c.** by a strange coincidence

coïncident, -e [kɔɛ̃sidɑ̃, -ɑ̃t] **ADJ 1** *(dans l'espace)* coextensive, coincident **2** *(dans le temps)* concomitant, simultaneous

coïncider [3] [kɔɛ̃side] **VI 1** *(s'ajuster l'un sur l'autre)* to line up, to coincide, *Sout* to be coextensive; **faites c. les deux triangles** line up the two triangles (so that they coincide); **faire c. les gains et les pertes** to equate gains and losses

2 *(se produire ensemble)* to coincide; **nos anniversaires coïncident** our birthdays fall on the same day; **j'ai essayé de faire c. ma visite avec le début du festival** I tried to make my visit coincide with the beginning of the festival

3 *(concorder)* to coincide; **les deux témoignages coïncident** the two statements are consistent; **leurs intérêts coïncident** they have similar interests

coin-coin [kwɛ̃kwɛ̃] NM INV quacking; **des c.** quacks, quacking
▫ ONOMAT quack quack; **faire c.** to go quack quack

coïnculpé, -e [koɛ̃kylpe] NM,F co-defendant

coing [kwɛ̃] NM *Fam* **bourré comme un c.** plastered, *Br* legless

coinsteau, -x [kwɛ̃sto] NM *Fam* corner ▪

coir [kwar] NM *Bot* coir, coconut fibre

coït [kɔit] NM coitus; **c. interrompu** coitus interruptus

coite [kwat] *voir* **coi**

coïter [3] [kɔite] VI to copulate

coitron [kwatrɔ̃] NM *Suisse* small slug

coke [kɔk] NM coke
▫ NF *Fam (cocaïne)* coke

cokéfaction [kɔkefaksjɔ̃] NF coking

cokéfiable [kɔkefjabl], **cokéfiant, -e** [kɔkefjɑ̃, -ɑ̃t] ADJ coking

cokéfier [9] [kɔkefje] VT to coke

cokerie [kɔkri] NF coking plant

coking [kɔkiŋ] NM coking

co-koter [3], **cokoter** [3] [kɔkɔte] VI *Belg Fam* to share a room ▪

co-koteur, -euse, cokoteur, -euse [kɔkɔtœr, -øz], **cokotier, -ère** [kɔkɔtje, -ɛr] NM,F *Belg Fam* (student) roommate ▪, roomie

Col. *(abrév écrite* **Colonel**) Col

col [kɔl] NM **1** *Couture* collar; **c. Bardot** Bardot neckline; **c. blanc/bleu** white-collar/blue-collar worker; **c. boutonné** button-down collar; **c. camionneur** zipped rollneck; **c. cassé** wing collar; **c. châle** shawl collar; **c. cheminée** turtleneck; **c. chemisier** shirt collar; **c. Claudine** Peter Pan collar; **c. Mao** Mao collar; **c. marin** sailor's collar; **c. montant** turtleneck; **c. officier** mandarin collar; **c. rond** round neck; **c. roulé** polo-neck; **c. en V** V-neck; **faux c.** detachable collar; *(de la bière)* head; **un demi sans faux c.** a glass of beer with as little froth as possible; *Littéraire* **se pousser du** *ou* **se hausser du** *ou* **se hausser le c.** to blow one's own trumpet

2 *(d'une bouteille)* neck

3 *Anat* cervix, neck; **c. du fémur** neck of the femur; **c. de l'utérus** cervix, neck of the womb; **cancer du c. de l'utérus** cervical cancer

4 *Géog* pass, col; **le c. du Brenner** the Brenner Pass; **le c. du Saint-Bernard** the Saint Bernard Pass; **le c. du Saint-Gothard** the Saint Gotthard Pass

col. *(abrév écrite* **colonne**) col

cola [kɔla] = **kola**

colapte [kɔlapt] NM *Orn* **c. doré** yellowhammer

colback [kɔlbak] NM **1** *Hist* kalpak, (Napoleonic) busby **2** *Fam* **attraper/prendre qn par le c.** to catch/grab sb by the scruff of the neck

colbertisme [kɔlbɛrtism] NM = economic policy of state intervention and protectionism *(from Colbert, finance minister to Louis XIV)*

col-bleu [kɔlblø] *(pl* **cols-bleus**) NM *Fam Vieilli* sailor ▪, jack tar

colchicine [kɔlʃisin] NF *Pharm* colchicine

colchique [kɔlʃik] NM *Bot* colchicum; **c. d'automne** autumn crocus, meadow saffron

colcotar [kɔlkɔtar] NM *Chim* colcothar, red peroxide of iron, (jewellers') rouge

cold-cream [kɔldkrim] *(pl* **cold-creams**) NM cold cream

col-de-cygne [kɔldəsiɲ] *(pl* **cols-de-cygne**) NM swan neck

colectomie [kɔlɛktɔmi] NF *Méd* colectomy

colée [kɔle] NF *Hist* buffet

colégataire [kɔlegatɛr] NMF joint legatee

coléoptère [kɔleɔptɛr] NM *Entom* member of the Coleoptera
▫ **coléoptères** NMPL Coleoptera

colère [kɔlɛr] NF **1** *(mauvaise humeur)* anger, rage; **passer sa c. sur qn** to take out one's anger on sb; **avec c.** angrily, in anger; **il se retourna avec c.** he turned round angrily; **va-t'en, dit-il**

avec c. go away, he said angrily; **c. froide** cold fury; *Prov* **la c. est mauvaise conseillère** anger and haste hinder good counsel

2 *(crise)* fit of anger *or* rage; *(d'un enfant)* tantrum; **il avait des colères terribles** he was subject to terrible fits of anger; *Fam* **piquer** *ou* **faire une c.** *(adulte)* to fly into a temper; *(enfant)* to have *or* to throw a tantrum; **entrer dans une violente c.** to fly into a violent rage; **se mettre** *ou* **entrer dans une c. bleue** *ou* **noire** to fly into a towering rage

3 *Littéraire (des éléments, des dieux)* wrath; *Bible* **la c. de Dieu** the wrath of God
▫ ADJ *Vieilli* **être c.** to be bad-tempered *or* choleric
▫ **en colère** ADJ angry, livid, mad; **être en c. contre qn** to be angry *Br* with sb *or* *Am* at sb; **mettre qn en c.** to make sb angry; **se mettre en c.** to flare up, to lose one's temper; **je vais me mettre en c.!** I'm going to get angry!

━━━━━━━━━━━━━━━━

'Aguirre ou la colère de Dieu' *Herzog* 'Aguirre, the Wrath of God'

coléreux, -euse [kɔlerø, -øz], **colérique** [kɔlerik] ADJ *(personne)* irritable, quick-tempered; **il a un caractère très c.** he's got quite a temper

coléus [kɔleys] NM coleus

colibacille [kɔlibasil] NM *Biol* colibacillus, colon bacillus

colibacillose [kɔlibasiloz] NF *Méd* colibacillosis

colibri [kɔlibri] NM *Orn* hummingbird; **c. sasin** rufous hummingbird

colicitant, -e [kɔlisitɑ̃, -ɑ̃t] *Jur* ADJ co-vendor
NM,F co-vendor

colifichet [kɔlifiʃɛ] NM knick-knack, trinket; **vendre des colifichets** to sell fancy goods

colimaçon [kɔlimasɔ̃] NM snail
▫ **en colimaçon** ADJ **escalier en c.** spiral staircase

colin [kɔlɛ̃] NM **1** *(lieu noir)* *Br* coley, coalfish, *Am* pollock; *(lieu jaune)* pollack; *(merlan)* whiting; *(merlu)* hake **2** *Orn* **c. de Californie** Californian quail

colinéaire [kɔlineɛr] ADJ *Math* collinear

colinéarité [kɔlinearite] NF *Math* collinearity

colineau, -x [kɔlino] NM codling

colin-maillard [kɔlɛ̃majar] *(pl* **colin-maillards**) NM blind man's buff

colinot [kɔlino] = **colineau**

colin-tampon [kɔlɛ̃tɑ̃pɔ̃] *(pl* **colin-tampons**) NM drum beat; *Fam Vieilli* **il s'en moque** *ou* **il s'en soucie comme de c.** he doesn't give two hoots about it

coliou [kɔlju] NM *Orn* mousebird, colie

colique [kɔlik] NF **1** *Fam (diarrhée)* diarrhoea ▪, runs; **avoir la c.** to have the runs; *Fig* **ça me flanque la c.** it gives me the heebie-jeebies **2** *Méd (douleur)* colic (UNCOUNT), stomach ache; *(chez le nourrisson)* colic (UNCOUNT), gripes; **coliques hépatiques** biliary colic; **coliques néphrétiques** renal colic **3** *très Fam (contrariété)* hassle, drag; **quelle c.!** what a pain!
▫ ADJ *Anat* colic

colis [kɔli] NM package, packet, parcel; **c. exprès** special delivery parcel; **c. piégé** *Br* parcel *or* *Am* package bomb; **c. postal** postal packet; **par c. postal** by parcel post; **c. contre remboursement** *Br* cash on delivery parcel, *Am* collect on delivery parcel; *Fam* **un joli petit c.** a knockout, a babe, *Br* a cracker

Colisée [kɔlize] NM **le C.** the Coliseum, the Colosseum

colis-épargne [kɔliepárɲ] NM INV *Com* saving stamps scheme

Colissimo [kɔlisimo] NM = rapid parcel service run by the French Post Office

colistier, -ère [kɔlistje, -ɛr] NM,F fellow candidate *(on a list or platform)*

colite [kɔlit] NF *Méd* colitis

colitigant, -e [kɔlitigɑ̃, -ɑ̃t] NM *Jur* co-litigant

coll. 1 *(abrév écrite* **collection**) coll **2** *(abrév écrite* **collaborateurs**) et c. et al

collabo [kɔlabo] NMF *Péj Hist (abrév* **collaborateur**)

collaborateur, -trice [kɔlabɔratœr, -tris] NM,F **1** *(assistant)* assistant **2** *(collègue)* associate; *(à une revue, un journal)* contributor **3** *(membre*

du personnel) member of staff **4** *Hist* collaborator, collaborationist

collaboration [kɔlabɔrasjɔ̃] NF **1** *(aide)* collaboration, co-operation, help; **merci de votre c.** thank you for your co-operation; **en c. étroite avec** in close co-operation with **2** *Hist (politique)* collaborationist policy; *(période)* collaboration

collaborationniste [kɔlabɔrasjɔnist] *Hist* ADJ collaborationist
NMF collaborationist

collaboratrice [kɔlabɔratris] *voir* **collaborateur**

collaborer [3] [kɔlabɔre] VI **1** *(participer)* to participate; *(travailler ensemble)* to collaborate, to work together; **les deux services collaborent étroitement** the two departments work closely together; **ont aussi collaboré…** also taking part were…; **c. à** to take part *or* to participate in; *Journ* to write for, to contribute to, to be a contributor to **2** *Hist* to collaborate

collage [kɔlaʒ] NM **1** *(fixation)* gluing, sticking; **c. d'affiches** billposting, bill sticking; **c. du papier peint** paperhanging **2** *Beaux-Arts* collage **3** *Fam (concubinage)* affair **4** *(en œnologie)* fining **5** *Ind* sizing

collagène [kɔlaʒɛn] NM *Biol* collagen; **crème de beauté au c.** collagen(-based) cream

collagénose [kɔlaʒenoz] NF *Vieilli* collagen disease, connective tissue disease

collant, -e [kɔlɑ̃, -ɑ̃t] ADJ **1** *(adhésif)* adhesive, sticky; *(poisseux)* sticky; **j'ai les mains collantes** my hands are sticky **2** *(moulant)* tight-fitting, skintight; **un pull c.** a skintight sweater **3** *Fam Péj (importun)* limpet-like; **qu'il est c.!** *(importun)* he just won't leave you alone!; *(enfant)* he's so clingy!, he won't give you a minute's peace!
▫ NM **1** *(bas)* (pair of) tights, *Am* pantyhose (UNCOUNT); **c. de contention** support tights; **c. uni/fantaisie** self-coloured/patterned tights **2** *(de danse)* leotard **3** *Can* **c. à mouches** flypaper
▫ **collante** NF *Fam Arg scol (convocation)* = letter asking a student to present him- or herself for an exam

collapsus [kɔlapsys] NM *Méd* collapse; **c. cardio-vasculaire** circulatory collapse

collatéral, -e, -aux, -ales [kɔlateral, -o] ADJ **1** *(de chaque côté)* collateral; **les rues collatérales** *(les rues parallèles)* the streets that run parallel; *(les rues perpendiculaires)* the side streets **2** *Anat & Jur* collateral; **parents collatéraux** collaterals, collateral relatives **3** *Géog* **points collatéraux** intermediate points *(of the compass)* **4** *Mil* collateral; **dommages** *ou* **dégâts collatéraux** collateral damage
NM **1** *Archit* aisle **2** *Jur* collateral (relative)

collation [kɔlasjɔ̃] NF **1** *(repas)* light meal, snack **2** *Rel* collation, conferral, conferment **3** *(de textes)* collation

collationnement [kɔlasjɔnmɑ̃] NM checking, collation

collationner [3] [kɔlasjɔne] VT **1** *(texte)* to collate **2** *(en reliure)* to collate

collationnure [kɔlasjɔnyr] NF *(en reliure)* collation

colle [kɔl] **NF 1** *(glu)* glue, adhesive; *(pour papier peint)* (wallpaper) paste; **de la c. en pot/stick/tube** a pot/stick/tube of glue; **c. blanche** paste; **c. à bois** wood glue; **c. forte** glue; **c. de poisson** fish glue, isinglass; **c. végétale** vegetable glue

2 *Fam (énigme)* trick question, poser, teaser; **poser une c. à qn** to set sb a poser; **là, vous me posez une c.!** you've got me there!

3 *Fam Arg scol (examen)* oral▪; *(retenue)* detention▪; **avoir une c.** to get detention, to be kept in *or* behind (after school); **j'ai eu une c.** I got detention; **mettre une c. à qn** to keep sb behind (in detention); **une heure de c.** an hour's detention

❑ **à la colle ADV** *Fam* **ils sont à la c.** they've shacked up together

collé, -e [kɔle] **ADJ** *Can Fam* **en avoir de c.** to be loaded

collectage [kɔlɛktaʒ] **NM** collection, picking up

collecte [kɔlɛkt] **NF 1** *(ramassage)* collection; **faire la c. du lait** to collect milk *(from farms for transportation to the local creamery)*; **faire la c. des vieux journaux** to pick up (bundles of) old newspapers set aside for collection

2 *Ordinat* **c. des données** data collection *or* gathering

3 *(quête)* collection; **c. de fonds** fundraising; **c. d'informations** data collection; *Journ* news gathering; **faire une c.** to collect money, to make a collection; **je fais une c. pour lui acheter un cadeau de notre part à toutes** I've started a kitty to buy him/her a present from us all

4 *Rel (prière)* collect

collecter [4] [kɔlɛkte] **VT** *(argent)* to collect; *(lait, ordures)* to collect, to pick up

▸**se collecter VPR** *Méd* to gather

collecteur, -trice [kɔlɛktœr, -tris] **ADJ** *(gén)* collecting; *(égout)* main

NM,F *Admin* **c. d'impôts** tax collector

NM 1 *Élec (lames)* commutator; *Électron (d'un transistor)* collector

2 *Tech* manifold; *Aut* **c. d'admission** intake manifold; *Électron* **c. d'air** air-trap; **c. de dynamo** collector ring; *Aut* **c. d'échappement** exhaust manifold; *Rad* **c. d'ondes** aerial; *Naut* **c. de pont** deck manifold; **c. supérieur** upper header

3 *Culin* drip cup, juice collector cup

4 *(égout)* main sewer

collectif, -ive [kɔlɛktif, -iv] **ADJ 1** *(en commun)* collective, common; **une démarche collective serait plus efficace** collective representations would be more effective

2 *(de masse)* general, mass *(avant n)*, public; **suicide c.** mass suicide; **licenciements collectifs** mass redundancies; **terreur collective** general panic; **viol c.** gang rape

3 *Transp* group *(avant n)*

4 *Gram* collective

NM 1 *Gram* collective noun

2 *Fin* **c. budgétaire** interim budget, extra credits

3 *(équipe)* collective; **ouvrage rédigé par un c. sous la direction de Jean Dupont** by Jean Dupont et al

collection [kɔlɛksjɔ̃] **NF 1** *(collecte)* collecting; **il fait c. de timbres** he collects stamps

2 *(ensemble de pièces)* collection; **sa c. de timbres** his/her stamp collection; **c. privée** private collection; **aller voir les collections d'un musée** to visit the collections of a museum; *Hum* **une amende, je l'ajoute à ma c.!** another fine for my collection!; **j'en ai toute une c.** I've got a whole collection *or* set of them

3 *Fam Péj (clique)* **une c. de** a bunch *or* crew of

4 *Com (série → gén)* line, collection; *(→ de livres)* collection, series; **toute la c.** *(de revues)* the complete set, all the back issues; **dans la c. jeunesse** in the range of books for young readers; **la c. complète des œuvres de Victor Hugo** the collected works of Victor Hugo

5 *(de mode)* collection; **les collections** *(présentations)* fashion shows; **pendant les collections** during the fashion show season

6 *Méd* gathering

collectionner [3] [kɔlɛksjɔne] **VT 1** *(tableaux, timbres)* to collect **2** *Hum (avoir en quantité)* **il collectionne les contraventions** he's been collecting parking tickets; **les enfants collectionnent les virus!** children pick up every virus (that's) going!; **je collectionne les factures en ce moment!** I'm inundated with bills at the moment!

collectionneur, -euse [kɔlɛksjɔnœr, -øz] **NM,F** collector

collectionnisme [kɔlɛksjɔnism] **NM** = obsessive need to collect useless objects

collectionnite [kɔlɛksjɔnit] **NF** *Fam* love of collecting things▪

collective [kɔlɛktiv] *voir* **collectif**

collectivement [kɔlɛktivmɑ̃] **ADV** collectively; **ils sont c. responsables** they're collectively responsible; **ils se sont élevés c. contre la nouvelle loi** they protested as a group against the new law

collectivisation [kɔlɛktivizasjɔ̃] **NF** collectivization, collectivizing

collectiviser [3] [kɔlɛktivize] **VT** to collectivize

collectivisme [kɔlɛktivism] **NM** collectivism

collectiviste [kɔlɛktivist] **ADJ** collectivist

NMF collectivist

collectivité [kɔlɛktivite] **NF 1** *(société)* community; **au sein de la c.** within the community; **dans l'intérêt de la c.** in the public interest; **la c. nationale** the nation, the country; **la vie en c.** community life *or* living **2** *Admin* **les collectivités locales** *(dans un État)* the local authorities; *(dans une fédération)* the federal authorities; **c. d'outre-mer** = French overseas collectivity; **c. publique** government organization; **c. territoriale** = administrative division with a higher degree of autonomy than a "département" **3** *(propriété en commun)* common ownership

collector [kɔlɛktœr] **NM** collector's piece

collectrice [kɔlɛktris] *voir* **collecteur**

collège [kɔlɛʒ] **NM 1** *Scol* school *(for pupils aged 11–15)*; **c. privé/technique** private/technical school; *Anciennement* **c. d'enseignement secondaire** = secondary school; *Anciennement* **c. d'enseignement technique** = technical school; **le C. de France** the Collège de France **2** *Rel* private school *(run by a religious organization)*; **le Sacré C.** the College of Cardinals **3** *(corps constitué)* college **4** *Admin* body; **c. électoral** body of electors, constituency

> *Culture*
>
> **LE COLLÈGE DE FRANCE**
>
> This seat of learning near the Sorbonne in Paris holds public lectures given by prominent academics and specialists. It is not a university and does not confer degrees, although it is controlled by the Ministry of Education.

collégial, -e, -aux, -ales [kɔleʒjal, -o] **ADJ** collegial, collegiate; **exercer un pouvoir c.** to rule collegially

❑ **collégiale NF** *Rel* collegiate church

collégialement [kɔleʒjalmɑ̃] **ADV** collegially

collégialité [kɔleʒjalite] **NF** collegiality, collegial structure *or* authority

collégien, -enne [kɔleʒjɛ̃, -ɛn] **NM,F** schoolboy, *f* schoolgirl *(aged 11–15)*; **rougir comme un c.** to blush like a schoolboy; **se conduire comme un c.** to behave like a schoolkid; **prendre qn pour un c.** to take sb for a fool; **tu me prends pour un c.?** do you think I was born yesterday?; **je me suis fait avoir comme un c.** I fell for it like a fool, I should have known better

collègue [kɔlɛg] **NMF 1** *(employé)* colleague, *Am* coworker; **je l'ai prêté à un c. de bureau** I lent it to somebody at the office **2** *(homologue)* opposite number, counterpart **3** *Fam Hum (camarade)* **demande au c. de se pousser** ask our friend here to move over; **salut, c.** how's things?

collembole [kɔlɑ̃bɔl] *Entom* **NM** collembolan

❑ **collemboles NMPL** Collembola

collenchyme [kɔlɑ̃ʃim] **NM** *Bot* collenchyma, collenchyme

COLLER [3] [kɔle]

> **VT** to stick **1, 2, 7** ▪ to glue **1** ▪ to paste **1** ▪ to press **4** ▪ to follow closely **5** ▪ to put **7** ▪ to catch out **8**
>
> **VI** to stick **1, 2** ▪ to cling **3** ▪ to be OK, to be right **4**

VT 1 *(fixer → étiquette, timbre)* to stick (down); *(→ tissu, bois)* to glue (on); *(→ papier peint)* to paste (up); *(→ affiche)* to post, to stick up, to put up; *Ordinat* to paste; *TV & Cin (bande, film)* to splice; **il est resté collé à la télé toute la soirée** he was glued to the TV all evening

2 *(fermer → enveloppe)* to close up, to stick down; **elle avait les paupières collées** her eyelids were stuck together

3 *(emmêler)* to mat, to plaster; **le poil du chien est tout collé** the dog's coat is all matted; **les cheveux collés par la pluie** his/her hair plastered flat by the rain

4 *(appuyer)* to press; **c. son nez à la vitre** to press one's face to the window; **c. son oreille contre le mur** to press one's ear against the wall; **elle a toujours l'oreille collée aux portes** she's always listening at doors; **c. qn au mur** to put sb against a wall

5 *Fam (suivre)* to follow closely▪, to tag along behind; **il me colle!** he sticks to me like glue!; **ne me colle pas comme ça!** stop following me everywhere!, just let go of me, will you!; **la voiture nous colle de trop près** the car's tailgating us

6 *Fam (punir)* to keep in; *(refuser)* to fail▪, *Am* to flunk; **se faire c.** *(punir)* to get a detention; **se faire c. à un examen** to fail *or Am* flunk an exam

7 *Fam (mettre → chose)* to dump, to stick; *(→ personne)* to put, to stick; **colle ton sac là** stick *or* dump your bag over there; **ils l'ont collée en pension/en prison** they packed her off to boarding school/threw her in jail; **je vais lui c. mon poing sur la figure!** I'm going to thump him/her on the nose!; **si tu continues, je t'en colle une!** if you don't stop, I'm going to thump you one!; **je vous colle une contravention!** I'm booking you!; **c. une punition/une amende à qn** to give sb a punishment/fine; **ils m'ont collé le bébé pour la semaine** they've saddled *or Br* lumbered me with the baby for a week; **ils l'ont collé responsable de la rubrique sportive** they saddled him with the sports editorship

8 *(poser une question difficile à)* to catch out

9 *(en œnologie)* to fine

10 *Ind* to size

VI 1 *(adhérer → timbre)* to stick (**à** to); **ces vieilles étiquettes ne collent plus** these old labels don't stick any more; **les pâtes ont collé à la casserole** the pasta has stuck to the pan; **le caramel colle aux dents** toffee sticks to your teeth; *Fam* **c. aux basques** *ou* **aux semelles à qn** to stick to sb like glue; **c.** *Fam* **aux fesses** *ou très Fam* **au cul à qn** to stick to sb like a limpet; **ce rôle lui colle à la peau** he/she was made for that role, that role was tailor-made for him/her; **la peur qui lui collait à la peau** the fear that was ingrained in him/her; **la réputation qui lui colle à la peau** the reputation he/she carries around with him/her, the reputation he/she can't shake off

2 *(être poisseux)* to be sticky; **avoir les doigts qui collent** to have sticky fingers; **j'ai horreur de la confiture, ça colle** I hate jam, it's so sticky

3 *(vêtement)* to cling; **une robe qui colle au corps** a clingy dress

4 *Fam (aller bien)* **ça colle!** OK!, cool!; **ça ne colle pas** it doesn't work, something's wrong; **il y a quelque chose qui ne colle pas** there's something wrong somewhere; **ça ne colle pas pour demain soir** tomorrow night's off, it's no go for tomorrow night; **ça ne colle pas entre eux** they don't really see eye to eye; **les couleurs sont bien, c'est la taille qui ne colle pas** it's the right shade, but the size is no good; **c. avec** to match up to, to fit in with; **ça ne colle pas avec son caractère** it's just not like him; **leurs témoignages ne collent pas** their testimonies don't tally

5 *Fam* **toi, tu colles (et nous, on se cache)!** you count (up to ten and we hide)!

❑ **coller à VT IND** *(respecter)* to be faithful to; **c. à son sujet** to stick to one's subject; **vous collez trop à l'original** you're too close to the original text; **c. à la réalité** to be true to life; **une émission qui colle à l'actualité** a programme that keeps up with current events

▸**se coller VPR 1** *(se blottir)* **se c. à qn** to snuggle

up *or* to cling to sb, to hug sb; **les chatons se collaient les uns aux autres** the kittens were snuggling up to each other; **se c. à** *ou* **contre un mur pour ne pas être vu** to press oneself up *or* flatten oneself against a wall in order not to be seen

2 *Fam (s'installer)* **les enfants se sont collés devant la télé** the children plonked themselves down in front of theTV

3 *Fam (subir)* **se c. qch** to take sth on; **c'est moi qui me colle les gosses!** I'm the one who has to put up with the kids!; **il s'est collé tout Proust pour l'examen** he got through all of Proust for the exam

4 *(locutions) très Fam* **se c. ensemble** *(vivre ensemble)* to shack up together; *Fam* **s'y c.** *(s'atteler à un problème, une tâche)* to make an effort to do sth■, to set about doing sth■; **maintenant, il faut t'y c.** you must get down to work now; **je vais m'y c. sérieusement** I'm going to get down to it seriously

collerette [kɔlrɛt] NF **1** *Couture* collar, collarette; *Hist* frill, ruff; **c. de dentelle** lace collar **2** *Culin* (paper) frill **3** *(sur une bouteille)* neck-band label **4** *Tech* flange **5** *Bot* annulus

collet [kɔlɛ] NM **1** *(col)* collar; **mettre la main au c. à qn** to nab *or* to collar sb; **prendre qn au c.** to seize *or* to grab sb by the neck; *Fig* to nab sb in the act; **être c. monté** to be straight-laced

2 *Culin* neck; **c. de veau/bœuf** neck of veal/beef

3 *(cape)* short cape

4 *(d'une dent)* neck

5 *Bot* annulus, ring

6 *Tech* flange

7 *(piège)* noose, snare; **prendre un lapin au c.** to snare a rabbit

colleter [27] [kɔlte] VT to seize by the collar; **se faire c.** to be collared *or* nabbed

▶**se colleter** VPR **1** *(emploi réciproque)* to fight **2** **se c. avec** to struggle *or* to wrestle with

colleur, -euse[1] [kɔlœr, -øz] NM,F **1** **c. d'affiches** billsticker, bill poster **2** *Fam Scol* examiner■

□ **colleuse** NF *Cin & TV* splicer, splicing unit **2** *Typ* pasting machine **3** *Phot* mounting press

colleux, -euse[2] [kɔlø, -øz] ADJ *Can* cuddly

colley [kɔlɛ] NM collie

collier [kɔlje] NM **1** *(bijou)* necklace, necklet; **c. de perles** string of pearls; **c. ras du cou** choker

2 *(parure)* collar; **c. de fleurs** garland of flowers

3 *(courroie → pour chien, chat)* collar; **c. anti-puces** flea collar; **c. de cheval** horse-collar; **c. de misère** yoke of misery; *Fig* **donner un coup de c.** to make a special effort; **encore un petit coup de c.!** just one more try!; **reprendre le c.** to get back into harness *or Péj* on the treadmill

4 *Tech* clip, collar, ring; **c. d'arbre** shaft collar; **c. de blocage** clamping ring; **c. de câble** cable clamp; **c. de fixation** bracket, clip; **c. de serrage** clamp collar; **c. ressort** spring clip

5 *(de plumes, de poils)* collar, frill, ring; **pigeon à c.** ring-necked pigeon; **c. (de barbe)** short *or* clipped beard; **porter le c.** to be bearded, to have a beard

6 *Culin (de bœuf, mouton)* neck

colligatif, -ive [kɔligatif, -iv] ADJ *Biol & Chim* colligative

colliger [17] [kɔliʒe] VT *Littéraire* to collect and compare; **c. les livres rares** to collect rare books

collimateur [kɔlimatœr] NM *Astron & Opt* collimator; *(d'une arme à feu)* sight; **avoir qn dans le c.** *ou* **son c.** to have one's eye on sb; **il est dans le c. du patron** the boss has got his eye on him

collimation [kɔlimasjɔ̃] NF *Opt* collimation

colline [kɔlin] NF hill; **les collines** *(au pied d'un massif)* the foothills; **au sommet de la c.** up on the hilltop; **sur le versant de la c.** on the hillside

collision [kɔlizjɔ̃] NF **1** *(choc)* collision, impact; *Aut* crash; **entrer en c. avec** to collide with; **une c. entre les manifestants et la police** a clash between demonstrators and police; **c. en chaîne** *ou* **série** (multiple) pile-up; **c. frontale** head-on collision, frontal collision; **c. latérale** side-on collision, side impact **2** *(désaccord)* clash; **c. d'intérêts** clash of interests **3** *Géog & Phys* collision

collisionneur [kɔlizjɔnœr] NM *Phys* collider ring; **c. à électron-positron** electron-positron collider

collocation [kɔlɔkasjɔ̃] NF **1** *Jur* = classification of creditors in order of priority **2** *Ling* collocation

collodion [kɔlɔdjɔ̃] NM *Chim* collodion

colloïdal, -e, -aux, -ales [kɔlɔidal, -o] ADJ colloidal

colloïde [kɔlɔid] NM colloid

colloque [kɔlɔk] NM **1** *(conférence)* conference, seminar **2** *Hum (conversation)* confab

colloqué, -e [kɔlɔke] NM,F *Jur* = creditor whose payment date has been judicially determined

colloquer [3] [kɔlɔke] VT **c. des créanciers** = to list creditors in bankruptcy proceedings in the order in which they should be paid

collure [kɔlyr] NF **1** *(en reliure)* gluing **2** *Cin* splice

collusion [kɔlyzjɔ̃] NF collusion; **il y a c. entre eux** they're in collusion; **c. d'intérêts** merging of interests

collusoire [kɔlyzwar] ADJ collusive; *Com* **offre c.** collusive bidding

collutoire [kɔlytwar] NM antiseptic throat preparation; **c. en aérosol** throat spray

colluvion [kɔlyvjɔ̃] NF *Géol* colluvium

collyre [kɔlir] NM *Méd* eyewash, antiseptic eye lotion

colmatage [kɔlmataʒ] NM **1** *(réparation)* filling-up, plugging; **après le c. des brèches du barrage** after plugging the gaps in the dam **2** *Mil* consolidation **3** *Agr* warping **4** *(fait d'obstruer)* clogging, choking

colmater [3] [kɔlmate] VT **1** *(boucher)* to fill in, to plug, to repair; **c. un déficit** to plug a deficit; *aussi Fig* **c. les brèches** to close the gaps **2** *Agr* to warp **3** *Mil* to consolidate

colo [kɔlo] NF *Fam Br* (children's) holiday camp■, *Am* (summer) camp■

colobe [kɔlɔb] NM *Zool* colobus monkey

colocalisation [kɔlɔkalizasjɔ̃] NF *Ordinat & Tél* co-location

colocase [kɔlɔkaz] NF *Bot* cush-cush

colocataire [kɔlɔkatɛr] NMF *(dans un appartement) Br* flatmate, *Am* roommate; *(dans une maison) Br* housemate, *Am* roommate; *Admin* co-tenant

colocation [kɔlɔkasjɔ̃] NF joint tenancy, joint occupancy

cologarithme [kɔlɔgaritm] NM *Math* cologarithm

Cologne [kɔlɔɲ] NM Cologne

Colomb [kɔlɔ̃] NPR **Christophe C.** Christopher Columbus

colombage [kɔlɔ̃baʒ] NM frame wall, stud-work; *(pièce)* stud

□ **à colombages** ADJ half-timbered

colombe [kɔlɔ̃b] NF **1** *(oiseau)* dove; *Pol* **les colombes et les faucons** the doves and the hawks **2** *(en appellatif)* **ma c.** my (little) dove

Colombie [kɔlɔ̃bi] NF **la C.** Colombia; **vivre en C.** to live in Colombia; **aller en C.** to go to Colombia

Colombie-Britannique [kɔlɔ̃bibritanik] NF **la C.** British Columbia

colombien, -enne [kɔlɔ̃bjɛ̃, -ɛn] ADJ Colombian

□ **Colombien, -enne** NM,F Colombian

colombier [kɔlɔ̃bje] NM dovecot, dovecote, pigeon house

colombin, -e [kɔlɔ̃bɛ̃, -in] ADJ reddish-purple

NM **1** *Orn* stock dove **2** *Cér* coil *(of clay)* **3** *très Fam Vieilli (étron)* turd

□ **colombine** NF *Agr* guano

Colombine [kɔlɔ̃bin] NPR Columbine

colombium [kɔlɔ̃bjɔm] NM columbium

Colombo [kɔlɔ̃bo] NPR Colombo

colombo[1] [kɔlɔ̃bo] NM *(racine)* calumba

colombo[2] [kɔlɔ̃bo] NM **1** *(épices)* spice mixture *(used in Caribbean cuisine)* **2** *(ragoût)* = Caribbean stew flavoured with a mixture of spices

colombophile [kɔlɔ̃bɔfil] ADJ pigeon-fancying

NMF pigeon fancier

colombophilie [kɔlɔ̃bɔfili] NF pigeon fancying

colon [kɔlɔ̃] NM **1** *(pionnier)* colonist, settler **2** *(enfant)* boarder, camper *(at a "colonie de vacances")* **3** *Agr* farmer, smallholder **4** *Can Fam Péj (rustre)* peasant **5** *Fam Arg mil* colonel■; *Fam Hum* **ben mon c.!** goodness me!, *Br* blimey!, *Am* gee (whiz)!

côlon [kɔlɔ̃] NM *Anat* colon; *Méd* **cancer du c.**

colon cancer; **c. transverse** transverse colon

colonage [kɔlɔnaʒ], **colonat** [kɔlɔna] NM *Jur* **c. partiaire** *Br* tenant farming, *Am* sharecropping

colonel [kɔlɔnɛl] NM *(de l'armée → de terre)* colonel; *(→ de l'air) Br* ≃ group captain, *Am* ≃ colonel; **oui mon c.** yes Sir

colonelle [kɔlɔnɛl] NF *(épouse d'un colonel → de l'armée de terre)* colonel's wife; *(→ de l'armée de l'air) Br* ≃ group captain's wife, *Am* ≃ colonel's wife

colonial, -e, -aux, -ales [kɔlɔnjal, -o] ADJ colonial; **l'empire c.** the (colonial) Empire, the colonies; **style c. (américain)** colonial style, Early American

NM,F *(habitant)* colonial; **mon père était un c.** my father lived in the colonies

NM *Mil* soldier of the colonial troops

□ **coloniale** NF *Mil* **la coloniale** the colonial troops

colonialisme [kɔlɔnjalism] NM colonialism

colonialiste [kɔlɔnjalist] ADJ colonialistic

NMF colonialist

colonie [kɔlɔni] NF **1** *(population)* settlement

2 *Pol (pays)* colony; **vivre aux colonies** to live in the colonies

3 *(fondation)* **c. pénitentiaire** penal colony

4 *(communauté)* community, (little) group; **la c. indienne de Vancouver** the Indian colony in Vancouver; **la c. bretonne de Paris** the Breton community in Paris; **une c. de peintres** a little group of painters

5 *Zool* colony group; **une c. de fourmis** a colony of ants; **des colonies de touristes marchaient vers la plage** crowds of tourists were marching along to the beach

6 **c. (de vacances)** *Br* (children's) holiday camp, *Am* summer camp; **envoyer ses enfants en c.** to send one's children to camp; **faire une c. de vacances** *(moniteur)* to be a camp leader *or* counsellor

COLONIE DE VACANCES

The "colonie de vacances" or "colo" is an integral part of childhood for many French people. The children's parents do not stay with them at the "colonie", the group being supervised by "moniteurs" or "animateurs" (group leaders), who organize games and activities.

colonisable [kɔlɔnizabl] ADJ colonizable, fit for colonization

colonisateur, -trice [kɔlɔnizatœr, -tris] ADJ colonizing

NM,F colonizer

colonisation [kɔlɔnizasjɔ̃] NF **1** *(conquête)* colonization; **après la c. de l'Afrique** after the colonization of Africa **2** *(période)* **la c.** (the age of) colonization **3** *Péj (influence)* subjugation, colonization

colonisatrice [kɔlɔnizatris] *voir* **colonisateur**

colonisé, -e [kɔlɔnize] ADJ colonized

NM,F inhabitant of a colonized country; **les colonisés** colonized peoples

coloniser [3] [kɔlɔnize] VT **1** *Pol* to colonize **2** *Fam (envahir)* to take over■, to colonize■; **ne les laissez pas c. nos plages!** don't let them take over our beaches! **3** *Péj (influencer)* to subjugate, to influence; **les productions américaines ont-elles colonisé notre télévision?** have American programmes taken over our TV channels?

colonnade [kɔlɔnad] NF *Archit* colonnade

colonnage [kɔlɔnaʒ] NM *Presse & Typ* column space

colonnaire [kɔlɔnɛr] ADJ columnar

NM *Bot* columnar plant

colonne [kɔlɔn] NF **1** *Archit* column, pilaster, pillar; **lit à colonnes** four-poster bed; **c. dorique/ionique** Doric/Ionic column

2 *(monument)* column; *(colonnette)* pillar; **la C. de juillet** = the monumental column at the centre of the place de la Bastille in Paris; **c. Morris** = dark green ornate pillar used to advertise forthcoming attractions in Paris; **la c. Trajane** Trajan's Column

3 *Constr & (en travaux publics → poteau)* column, post, upright; *(→ conduite)* riser, pipe; **c. d'appui** support beam; **c. de levage** lifting

column; **c. de distribution** standpipe; **c. montante** rising main, riser; **c. sèche** dry riser

4 *Anat* **c. (vertébrale)** backbone, *Spéc* spinal column; **avoir mal à la c.** to have backache

5 *Tech* column; **c. de direction** steering column

6 (*masse cylindrique*) **c. de liquide/mercure** liquid/mercury column

7 (*forme verticale*) column, pillar; **c. d'eau** column of water, waterspout; **c. de feu/fumée** pillar of fire/smoke

8 (*file*) column, line; *Mil* **c. de tête/queue** front/rear column; **c. d'assaut** attacking column; **c. de blindés** column of armoured vehicles; **c. de ravitaillement** supply column; **c. de secours** relief column; **c. de véhicules** vehicle column; *Hist* **la c. infernale** = Republican soldiers fighting the people of Vendée in 1793

9 (*d'un formulaire, d'une table, d'un tableur*) column; **ne rien inscrire dans cette c.** do not write in this column; **les rangées et les colonnes d'un tableau** the rows and columns of a table; **c. des unités** unit column; *Compta* **c. créditrice/débitrice** credit/debit column

10 *Journ* column; **colonnes rédactionnelles** editorial columns; **écrire une c.** to write or have a column; **dans les colonnes de votre quotidien** in your daily paper; **comme je l'écrivais hier dans ces colonnes** as I wrote yesterday in these pages

▫ **en colonne** ADV **en c. par trois/quatre** in threes/fours; **les enfants étaient en c. par deux** the children formed a line two abreast

colonnette [kɔlɔnɛt] NF small column, colonnette
colonoscopie [kɔlɔnɔskɔpi] NF colonoscopy
colopathie [kɔlɔpati] NF colonopathy
colophane [kɔlɔfan] NF colophony, rosin
colophon [kɔlɔfɔ̃] NM *Typ* colophon
coloquinte [kɔlɔkɛ̃t] NF **1** *Bot* colocynth **2** *Fam* (*tête*) head■, nut
Colorado [kɔlɔrado] NM **1** (*État*) **le C.** Colorado; **au C.** in Colorado **2** (*fleuve*) **le C.** the Colorado (River)
colorant, -e [kɔlɔrɑ̃, -ɑ̃t] ADJ colouring
NM colorant, dye, pigment; **c. alimentaire** food colouring (UNCOUNT), edible dye; **sans colorants** (*sur emballage*) no artificial colouring
coloration [kɔlɔrasjɔ̃] NF **1** (*fait de colorer*) colouring **2** (*couleur*) pigmentation, colouring **3** (*chez le coiffeur*) hair tinting or colouring; **se faire faire une c.** to have one's hair tinted or coloured; **je vous fais une c.?** shall I give you a colour rinse? **4** (*de la voix, d'un instrument*) colour; **la tristesse donnait une c. inhabituelle à sa voix** his/her voice had changed, there was a note of sadness in it **5** (*tendance*) **c. politique** political colour or tendency **6** *Biol* **c. de Gram** Gram staining
coloratura [kɔlɔratyr] NF coloratura
coloré, -e [kɔlɔre] ADJ **1** (*teinté*) coloured; (*vif*) brightly coloured; (*bariolé*) multicoloured; **une eau colorée** (*à la teinture*) water with dye in it; (*avec du vin*) water with just a drop of wine in it **2** (*expressif*) colourful, vivid, picturesque; **leur langage c.** their colourful language
colorectal, -e, -aux, -ales [kɔlɔrɛktal, -o] ADJ *Méd* colorectal
colorer [3] [kɔlɔre] VT **1** (*teinter → dessin, objet*) to colour; (*→ ciel, visage*) to tinge, to colour; **c. qch en rouge/jaune** to colour sth red/yellow; **l'émotion lui colorait les joues** he/she was flushed with emotion; **l'aurore colore de rose les maisons des pêcheurs** dawn gives a pink tinge to the fishermen's cottages
2 (*teindre → tissu*) to dye; (*→ bois*) to stain, to colour
3 (*oignons, viande*) to brown lightly
4 (*rendre plus pittoresque → récit*) to lend colour to
▸ **se colorer** VPR **1** (*visage*) to blush, to redden; **les pêches commencent à se c.** the peaches are beginning to ripen; **son visage se colora sous l'effet de la confusion** his/her face reddened with embarrassment
2 *Fig* **se c. de** to be tinged with; **sa colère se colorait d'attendrissement** his anger was tinged with pity
coloriage [kɔlɔrjaʒ] NM **1** (*technique*) colouring; **faire du c.** *ou* **des coloriages** to colour (a drawing) **2** (*dessin*) coloured drawing

colorier [10] [kɔlɔrje] VT to colour in; **colorie le crocodile en vert** colour in the crocodile (in or with) green
colorimètre [kɔlɔrimɛtr] NM colorimeter, tintometer
colorimétrie [kɔlɔrimetri] NF colorimetry, colorimetrics (*singulier*)
coloris [kɔlɔri] NM (*couleur*) colour; (*nuance*) shade; **les c. pastel** pastel shades or colours; **nous avons cette jupe dans d'autres c.** we have the same skirt in other colours; **la subtilité du c.** (*dans un tableau*) the subtlety of the colours
colorisation [kɔlɔrizasjɔ̃] NF colourization
coloriser [3] [kɔlɔrize] VT to colourize
coloriste [kɔlɔrist] NMF **1** *Beaux-Arts* colourist **2** *Typ* colourer, colourist **3** (*coiffeur*) colourist
coloscopie [kɔlɔskɔpi] NF *Méd* colonoscopy
colossal, -e, -aux, -ales [kɔlɔsal, -o] ADJ huge, colossal
colossalement [kɔlɔsalmɑ̃] ADV hugely, colossally
colosse [kɔlɔs] NM **1** (*statue*) colossus; **le c. de Rhodes** the Colossus of Rhodes; **un c. aux pieds d'argile** an idol with feet of clay **2** (*homme de grande taille*) giant; *Fig* **un c. de l'automobile** a car manufacturing giant
colostomie [kɔlɔstɔmi] NF *Méd* colostomy; **subir une c.** to have a colostomy
colostomique [kɔlɔstɔmik] ADJ *Méd* colostomic; **poche c.** colostomy bag; **ceinture c.** colostomy belt
colostrum [kɔlɔstrɔm] NM colostrum
coloured [kɔlɔrd] NMF Cape Coloured
colpocèle [kɔlpɔsɛl] NF colpocele
colportage [kɔlpɔrtaʒ] NM **1** (*vente*) hawking, peddling **2** (*de nouvelles, de ragots*) spreading
colporter [3] [kɔlpɔrte] VT **1** (*vendre*) to hawk, to peddle **2** (*nouvelles, ragots*) to spread; **qui a colporté la nouvelle?** who spread the news?
colporteur, -euse [kɔlpɔrtœr, -øz] NM,F hawker, pedlar; **c. de mauvaises nouvelles** bringer of bad tidings; **c. de ragots** scandalmonger
colposcope [kɔlpɔskɔp] NM *Méd* colposcope
colposcopie [kɔlpɔskɔpi] NF *Méd* colposcopy
colt [kɔlt] NM (*revolver*) gun
coltinage [kɔltinaʒ] NM (*d'une charge sur le dos*) porterage, carrying
coltiner [3] [kɔltine] VT to carry; **c. de lourdes charges** to carry heavy loads
▸ **se coltiner** VPR *Fam* **1** (*porter*) **se c. une valise/boîte** to lug a suitcase/box around **2** (*supporter → corvée*) to take on, to put up with; (→ *personne indésirable*) to put up with; **celui-là, faut se le c.!** you need the patience of a saint to put up with him!
coltineur [kɔltinœr] NM porter (*who carries heavy loads*); **c. de charbon** coal heaver
colubridé [kɔlybride] *Zool* NM colubrid
▫ **colubridés** NMPL Colubridae
Coluche [kɔlyʃ] NPR = French comedian and champion of the underprivileged (1944–1986), who founded the "Restaurants du Cœur"
columbarium [kɔlɔ̃barjɔm] NM columbarium
columbidé [kɔlɔ̃bide] *Orn* NM pigeon, *Spéc* columbid
▫ **columbidés** NMPL Columbidae
columbiforme [kɔlɔ̃bifɔrm] *Orn* NM columbiform
▫ **columbiformes** NMPL Columbiformes
columelle [kɔlymɛl] NF **1** *Archéol* columel **2** *Anat & Biol* columella
colvert [kɔlvɛr] NM *Orn* mallard
colza [kɔlza] NM *Bot* colza, rape
COM [kɔm] NF (*abrév* **collectivité d'outre-mer**) = French overseas collectivity

COM
There are four COMs, or "collectivités d'outre-mer": French Polynesia, Mayotte (in the Indian Ocean), St Pierre and Miquelon (off Newfoundland) and Wallis and Futuna Islands (in the Pacific Ocean).

coma [kɔma] NM *Méd* **le c.** a coma; **être/tomber dans le c.** to be in/to go or to fall into a coma; **être dans un c. dépassé** to be brain dead
Comanche [kɔmɑ̃ʃ] NMF Comanche; **les Comanches** the Comanche
comandant [kɔmɑ̃dɑ̃] NM joint mandator

comandataire [kɔmɑ̃datɛr] NMF joint proxy
comarketing [komarkɛtiŋ] NM comarketing
comater [3] [kɔmate] VI *Fam* to veg (out); **j'ai passé la journée à c. devant la télé** I spent the day vegging (out) in front of the TV
comateux, -euse [kɔmatø, -øz] ADJ comatose
NM,F patient in a coma
combat [kɔ̃ba] *voir* **combattre**
NM **1** *Mil* battle, fight; **c. aérien** air battle; **c. naval** sea battle; *Belg* (*jeu*) battleships; *aussi Fig* **c. d'arrière-garde** rearguard action; **des combats de rue** street fighting; **quelques combats isolés dans les montagnes** some isolated skirmishes in the mountains; **les tanks ne sont jamais allés au c.** the tanks never went into battle; **il n'est jamais allé au c.** he never saw action
2 (*lutte physique*) fight; **c. corps à corps** hand-to-hand combat; **c. rapproché** close combat; **c. singulier** single combat; *Fig* **en c. singulier** on a one-to-one basis
3 *Sport* contest, fight; **c. de boxe** boxing match; **c. en cage** cage fighting; **c. de coqs** cockfight
4 (*lutte morale, politique*) struggle, fight; **continuons le c.!** the struggle goes on!; **même c.!** we're fighting for the same thing!; **le bon c.** the good fight; **mener le bon c.** to fight for a just cause; **le c. contre l'alcoolisme/la pauvreté** the fight against alcoholism/poverty; **son c. de tous les instants contre l'injustice** her relentless fight or battle against injustice; **son long c. contre le cancer** his/her long fight against cancer; **c. d'intérêts** clash of interests
▫ **de combat** ADJ **1** *Mil* (*zone*) combat (*avant n*); (*réserves*) battle (*avant n*), war (*avant n*); **avion de c.** warplane, fighter plane; **navire de c.** battleship; **tenue de c.** battledress
2 (*de choc*) militant

COMBAT DES REINES
These strange "cowfighting" competitions, in which the winning cow (**la reine**) is allowed to lead the herd up to higher summer pastures, have become a popular attraction in the Valais canton of Switzerland. The cows, which are all of the Hérens breed, are naturally aggressive and compete for dominance within the herd. In this organized event they are encouraged by their owners to shove each other around in order to be judged the most aggressive.

combatif, -ive [kɔ̃batif, -iv] ADJ (*animal*) aggressive; (*personne*) combative, aggressive, *Littéraire* pugnacious; **se montrer c.** to be ready for a fight; **être d'humeur combative** to be full of fight; **tu n'es pas d'humeur très combative aujourd'hui** you haven't got any fight in you today
combativité [kɔ̃bativite] NF combativeness, aggressiveness, *Littéraire* pugnacity
combattant, -e [kɔ̃batɑ̃, -ɑ̃t] ADJ fighting; **unité combattante** combatant or fighting unit
NM,F **1** *Mil* combatant, fighter, soldier **2** (*adversaire*) fighter **3** *Orn* ruff
combattre [83] [kɔ̃batr] VT **1** *Mil* to fight (against); **c. l'ennemi** to fight the enemy, *Sout* to give battle to the enemy
2 (*s'opposer à → inflation, racisme*) to combat, to fight, to struggle against; (→ *politique*) to oppose, to fight; **il est difficile de c. son instinct** it's difficult to go against one's instincts; **il a longtemps combattu la maladie** he fought or struggled against the disease for a long time
3 (*agir contre → incendie*) to fight; (→ *effets*) to combat; **une lotion qui combat l'acné** a lotion for acne; **pour c. l'effet nocif du soleil sur vos cheveux** to combat the harmful effects of the sun on your hair
VI **1** *Mil* to fight; **l'armée est prête à c.** the troops are ready to fight or for action; **c. aux côtés d'une nation** to fight alongside a nation
2 (*en politique, pour une cause*) to fight, to struggle; **les femmes ont combattu pour obtenir l'égalité des droits** women have fought or struggled for equal rights
combe [kɔ̃b] NF combe, valley
combi [kɔ̃bi] NM *Belg* police van

COMBIEN [kɔ̃bjɛ̃] ADV 1 *(pour interroger sur une somme)* how much; **c'est c.?, ça fait c.?** how much is it?; **c. coûte ce livre?** how much is this book?, how much does this book cost?; **c. je vous dois?** how much do I owe you?; **c. te faut-il?** how much (money) do you need?; **je ne sais même pas c. il gagne** I don't even know how much he earns; **à c. doit-on affranchir cette lettre?** how much postage does this letter need?; **à c. se montent vos frais?** how much are your expenses?; **à c. cela vous est-il revenu?** how much did you pay for that?; **l'indice a augmenté de c.?** how much has the rate gone up by?; **de c. est le déficit?** how large is the deficit?

2 *(pour interroger sur le nombre)* how many; **c. serons-nous ce soir?** how many of us will there be this evening?; **c. sont-ils?** how many of them are there?; **c. se souviendront de lui?** how many will remember him?; **je me demande c. ils sont** I wonder how many of them there are

3 *(pour interroger sur la distance, la durée, la mesure etc)* **c. tu pèses?** how much do you weigh?; **c. tu mesures?** how tall are you?; **c. y a-t-il de Londres à Paris?** how far is it from London to Paris?; **c. dure le film?** how long is the movie?, how long does the movie last?; **il a fait c. au saut à la perche?** how high did he jump in the pole vault, what was his height in the pole vault?; **il est arrivé c.?** where did he come?; *Fam* **c. ça lui fait maintenant?** how old is he/she now?■; **il y a c. entre lui et sa sœur?** what's the age difference between him and his sister?; **à c. sommes-nous de Paris?** how far are we from Paris?; **de c. votre frère est-il votre aîné?** how much older than you is your brother?; **elle est enceinte – de c.?** she's pregnant – how far gone is she?, how many months?

4 *(en emploi exclamatif)* how; **vous ne pouvez pas savoir c. il est distrait!** you wouldn't believe how absent-minded he is!; **j'ai pu constater c. tu avais changé** I could see how much you'd changed; **c. je regrette de ne pas vous voir plus souvent!** how I regret not seeing you more often!; **tu ne peux pas savoir c. je suis heureuse!** you can't imagine how happy I am!; **ces mesures étaient sévères mais c. efficaces** these measures were drastic but extremely effective; **c'est plus cher mais c. meilleur!** it's more expensive but all the better for it!; **c. plus crédible était sa première version des faits!** his first version of the facts was so much more believable!; *Littéraire* **c. rares sont les gens sans ambition!** how few are those without ambition!; *Littéraire ou Hum* **elle a souffert, ô c.!** she suffered, oh how she suffered!

NM INV **le c. sommes-nous?** what's today's date?; **le bus passe tous les c.?** how often does the bus come?; **tu chausses du c.?** what's your shoe size, what shoe size do you take?

▫ **combien de** DÉT 1 *(pour interroger → suivi d'un nom indénombrable)* how much; *(→ suivi d'un nom dénombrable)* how many; **c. d'argent avez-vous sur vous?** how much money have you got on *or* with you?; **c. de sucre reste-t-il?** how much sugar is there left?; **c. de paquets reste-t-il?** how many packets are left?; **c. de fois** how many times, how often; **c. de fois par semaine vas-tu au cinéma?** how many times a week do you go to the movies?; **c. de fois faut-il que je te le répète?** how often *or* how many times do I have to tell you?; **c. de temps** how long; **c. de temps resterez-vous?** how long will you be staying?; **depuis c. de temps habitent-ils ici?** how long have they been living here for?; **tu en as pour c. de temps?** how long will it take you?, how long will you be?; **c. y a-t-il de pays en Europe?** how many countries are there in Europe?; **c. veux-tu de lait dans ton thé?** how much milk do you want in your tea?; **c. de jours resterez-vous?** how many days *or* how long will you be staying?; **c. d'enfants ont-ils?** how many children have they got? 2 *(emploi exclamatif)* **c. d'ennuis il aurait pu s'éviter!** he could have saved himself so much trouble!; **c. de gens furent tués pendant cette guerre!** what a lot of people were killed in that war!

---

combientième [kɔ̃bjɛ̃tjɛm] ADJ INTERROGATIF **c'est ta c. tasse de thé aujourd'hui?** just how many cups of tea have you drunk today?; **c'est la c. fois que tu viens?** how often have you been now?; **c'est la c. fois que je te le dis?** how many times have I told you?, I must have told you umpteen times!, if I've told you once I've told you a hundred times!; **tu es c. dans la liste?** where are you on the list?, what position are you in the list?

NMF 1 *(personne)* **c'est la c. qui demande à être remboursée depuis ce matin?** how many does that make wanting their money back since this morning?; **elle est arrivée la c.?** where did she come in?

2 *(objet)* **prends le troisième – le c.?** have the third one – which one did you say?

3 *(rang)* **tu es le c. en math?** how high are you *or* where do you come in *Br* maths *or Am* math?

combinable [kɔ̃binabl] ADJ combinable

combinaison [kɔ̃binɛzɔ̃] NF 1 *Chim (action)* combining; *(résultat)* combination; *(composé)* compound

2 *(d'un cadenas, d'un coffre-fort)* combination; **la c. gagnante** *(au tiercé)* the winning combination (of numbers)

3 *Ordinat* **c. de code** password; **c. de touches** key combination

4 *Math* combination

5 *Pol* **c. ministérielle** composition of a cabinet

6 *(sous-vêtement)* slip; **c. anti-g** G suit; **c. de plongée** wetsuit; **c. de ski** ski suit; **c. spatiale** space suit; **c. de travail** overalls; **c. de vol** flying suit; **c. pantalons** jump suit

7 *(assemblage)* combination; **la c. des deux éléments est nécessaire** the two elements must be combined; **la c. de l'ancien avec le moderne est très réussie** the combination *or* mixture of ancient and modern is very successful; **une heureuse c. de couleurs** a pleasing combination of colours *or* colour scheme

▫ **combinaisons** NFPL 1 *Péj (manigances)* schemes, tricks

2 *Can (sous-vêtement)* all-in-one thermal underwear

combinard, -e [kɔ̃binar, -ard] *Fam Péj* ADJ scheming; **il est vraiment c.** he's a real schemer, he always knows some dodge or other

NM,F schemer; **c'est un c.** he's a real schemer, he always knows some dodge or other

combinat [kɔ̃bina] NM (industrial) combine

combinateur [kɔ̃binatœr] NM 1 *Aut* selector switch 2 *Rail* controller

combinatoire [kɔ̃binatwar] ADJ 1 *(capable d'agencer)* combinative 2 *Ling* combinatory 3 *Math* combinatorial

NF 1 *Ling* combinatorial rules 2 *Math* combinatorial mathematics *(singulier)*

combine [kɔ̃bin] NF *Fam* 1 *(astuce, truc)* scheme, trick; **il a toujours des combines, lui!** he always knows some trick or other; **j'ai une c. pour entrer sans payer** I know a way of getting in for free■; **il a trouvé la c. pour voyager gratuitement** he's found a way of travelling for free■; **c'est simple, il suffit de connaître la c.** it's easy when you know how■; **être dans la c.** to be in on it; **mettre qn dans la c.** to let sb in on it 2 *(sous-vêtement)* slip

▫ **combines** NFPL *Can (sous-vêtement)* all-in-one thermal underwear

combiné, -e [kɔ̃bine] ADJ joint, combined; **état-major c.** joint chief of staff

NM 1 *(sous-vêtement)* corselet, corselette 2 *Tél* receiver, handset 3 *Chim* compound 4 *Sport* athletics event; *Ski* combined competition; **c. alpin** alpine combined competition; **c. nordique** Nordic combined competition 5 *Hort* **c. d'arrosage** sprinkler (system)

combiner [3] [kɔ̃bine] VT 1 *(harmoniser → styles)* to combine, to match; *(→ couleurs)* to match, to harmonize, to mix; *(→ sons)* to harmonize, to mix; **on peut c. glaïeuls et marguerites** you can mix gladioli with daisies; **c. son travail et ses loisirs** to combine business with pleasure

2 *(comprendre)* to combine; **un sentiment qui combine la crainte et le désir** a feeling of both fear and desire; **un appareil qui combine deux/diverses fonctions** a two-function/multi-function apparatus

3 *(planifier)* to plan, to work out; **combine ton voyage de sorte que...** plan your trip so that...; **un itinéraire combiné à l'avance** an itinerary planned in advance; **bien combiné** well planned

4 *Fam Péj (manigancer)* to think up■; **on avait pourtant combiné de raconter la même chose!** but the idea was to give them the same story!; **elle combine un sale coup** she's plotting something nasty, she's planning a dirty trick

5 *Chim* to combine; **c. une base avec un acide** to combine a base with an acid

▸**se combiner** VPR 1 *(exister ensemble → éléments)* to be combined; **en lui se combinent la sensibilité et l'érudition** he combines sensitivity with erudition

2 *(s'harmoniser → couleurs)* to match, to harmonize, to mix; *(→ sons)* to harmonize, to mix

3 *Chim* **se c. avec** to combine with

4 *Fam (se passer)* **ça se combine** *ou* **les choses se combinent bien** it's *or* things are working out very well; **ça s'est mal combiné** it didn't work out

combi-short [kɔ̃biʃɔrt] *(pl* **combi-shorts***)* NM unitard

comblanchien [kɔ̃blɑ̃ʃjɛ̃] NM = type of limestone from eastern France

comble [kɔ̃bl] ADJ packed, crammed

NM 1 *(summum)* **le c. de** the height *or* epitome of; **le c. du chic** the ultimate in chic; **le c. du snobisme est de...** the last word in snobbery is to...; **du champagne et, c. du luxe, du caviar** champagne and, luxury of luxuries, caviare; **c'est un** *ou* **le c.!** that beats everything!, that takes *Br* the biscuit *or Am* the cake!; **le c., c'est que...** to crown *or* to cap it all...; **le c., c'est qu'il est parti sans payer** and to crown it all *or* to add insult to injury, he left without paying; **les objectifs ne sont pas atteints, un c. pour une usine-pilote!** they haven't met their targets, which is just not on for a model factory!

2 *(charpente → en bois)* roof timbers *or* gable; *(→ en métal)* roof structure; **c. brisé** curb roof; **c. mansardé** mansard roof; **faux c.** mansard roof deck; **les combles** the attic; **elle loge sous les combles** she lives in the attic; **combles aménageables** attic suitable for conversion

▫ **à son comble** ADV at its height; **la panique était à son c.** the panic was at its height

▫ **au comble de** PRÉP at the height of, in a paroxysm of; **au c. du bonheur** deliriously happy; **au c. de la douleur** prostrate with *or* in a paroxysm of grief

▫ **pour comble de** PRÉP **et pour c. de malchance, la voiture est tombée en panne** and then, to cap it all, the car broke down; **pour c. d'hypocrisie, ils envoient leur fille chez les sœurs** then, to compound the hypocrisy, they send their daughter to a convent

comblé, -e [kɔ̃ble] ADJ *(personne)* happy, contented, satisfied; **il est c.** he has everything he could wish for

comblement [kɔ̃bləmɑ̃] NM filling in

combler [3] [kɔ̃ble] VT 1 *(boucher → cavité, creux)* to fill in; **c. un trou avec de la terre** to fill in a hole with earth

2 *(supprimer → lacune, vide)* to fill; *(→ silence)* to break; *(→ perte, déficit)* to make up for; *(→ découvert bancaire)* to pay off; **c. son retard** to make up for lost time

3 *(satisfaire → personne)* to satisfy; *(→ désir, vœu, besoin)* to satisfy, to fulfil; **vous me comblez!** you are too kind, I'm overwhelmed!

4 *Fig (couvrir, emplir)* **c. un enfant de cadeaux** to shower a child with gifts; **c. qn de joie** to fill sb with joy

▸**se combler** VPR *(trou)* to get filled in, to fill up

combo [kɔ̃bo] NM combo

comburant, -e [kɔ̃byrɑ̃, -ɑ̃t] ADJ comburent

NM oxidizer, oxidant

combustibilité [kɔ̃bystibilite] NF combustibility

combustible [kɔ̃bystibl] ADJ combustible

NM fuel; **c. fossile** fossil fuel; **c. liquide** liquid fuel; **c. MOX** MOX fuel; **c. nucléaire** nuclear fuel

combustion [kɔ̃bystjɔ̃] NF combustion; **à c. externe** external-combustion *(avant n)*; **à c. interne** internal-combustion *(avant n)*; **à c. lente** slow-combustion *(avant n)*; **à c. rapide** fast-combustion *(avant n)*; **mettre qch en c.** to set sth on fire

Côme [kom] NM Como; **le lac de C.** Lake Como

come-back [kɔmbak] NM INV comeback; **faire son** *ou* **un c.** to make *or* to stage a comeback

COMECON, Comecon [kɔmekɔn] **NM** *Anciennement Écon* (*abrév* **Council for Mutual Economic Assistance**) COMECON

comédie [kɔmedi] **NF 1** (*art dramatique*) theatre; **jouer la c.** to act, to be an actor

2 (*pièce comique*) comedy; **c. de caractères** character comedy; **c. dramatique** comedy drama; **c. de mœurs** comedy of manners; **c. musicale** musical; **c. de situation** situation comedy

3 (*genre*) comedy; **acteur spécialisé dans la c.** comic actor

4 (*nom de certains théâtres*) **la C. du Nord** the Comédie du Nord

5 *Péj* (*hypocrisie*) act; **cette réception, quelle c.!** what a farce that party was!; **jouer la c.** to put on an act; **il n'est pas vraiment malade, c'est de la c.** *ou* **il nous joue la c.** he's only play-acting *or* it's only an act, he's not really ill

6 *Fam* (*caprice, colère*) tantrum; **c'est une vraie c. quand il faut aller à l'école** it's a real fuss when it's time to go to school; **faire une c.** to throw a tantrum, to make a fuss; **il m'a fait toute une c. pour que je lui achète le jouet** he kicked up a huge fuss to get me to buy the toy

7 *Fam* (*histoire*) **c'est toute une c. pour lui faire avaler sa soupe** you have to go through a whole rigmarole to get him/her to eat his/her soup; **pour avoir un rendez-vous, quelle c.!** what a palaver to get an appointment!

8 *Arch* (*pièce de théâtre*) play

❑ **de comédie ADJ** comic, comedy (*avant n*); **personnage de c.** comedy character; *Fig* clown, buffoon

═══════╗🕮╔═══════

'La Comédie humaine' *Balzac* 'The Human Comedy'

Comédie-Française [kɔmedifrɑ̃sɛz] **NF la C.** = French national theatre company

╔══════════════════════╗
║ *Culture* ║
║ **LA COMÉDIE-FRANÇAISE** ║
This state-subsidized company dates back to the seventeenth century; the theatre itself, officially called "le Théâtre-Français" or "le Français", is situated in the rue Richelieu in Paris. Its repertoire consists mainly of classical works, although modern plays are sometimes staged. Actors who perform in the Comédie-Française fall into two categories: the "**sociétaires**", who are fully-fledged members of the company, and the "**pensionnaires**", who work with the company on a fixed salary but are not shareholders in it.
╚══════════════════════╝

comédien, -enne [kɔmedjɛ̃, -ɛn] **ADJ 1** (*acteur*) **être plus c. que tragédien** to be more of a comic than a tragic actor **2** (*qui exagère*) melodramatic; **elle est comédienne** she's a drama queen
NM,F 1 (*acteur → gén*) actor, *f* actress; (*→ comique*) comic actor, *f* actress, comedian, *f* comedienne; **comédiens ambulants** strolling players **2** (*personne qui exagère*) **c'est une comédienne** she's a drama queen; **quel c.!** he can really overdo it!

comédogène [kɔmedɔʒɛn] **ADJ** *Méd* comedogenic

comédon [kɔmedɔ̃] **NM** *Méd* blackhead, *Spéc* comedo

COMES, Comes [kɔmɛs] **NM** (*abrév* **Commissariat à l'énergie solaire**) = solar energy commission

COMESA [kɔmesa] **NM** (*abrév* **Common Market for Eastern and Southern Africa**) COMESA

comestibilité [kɔmɛstibilite] **NF** edibility

comestible [kɔmɛstibl] **ADJ** edible; **denrées comestibles** food, foodstuffs; **non c.** inedible
❑ **comestibles NMPL** food, foodstuffs

cométaire [kɔmetɛr] **ADJ** *Astron* cometary, cometic

comète [kɔmɛt] **NF 1** *Astron* comet **2** (*tranchefile*) headband

cométique [kɔmetik] **NM** *Can* dog sled
comice[1] [kɔmis] **NF** (*poire*) comice pear
comice[2] [kɔmis] **NM c. agricole** agricultural association
NM 1 *Antiq* comitia; *Hist* (*pendant la Révolution*) electoral meeting **2** (*foire*) **comices agricoles** agricultural fair

comics [kɔmiks] **NMPL** comic strips, cartoon strips, *esp Am Fam* funnies

comique [kɔmik] **ADJ 1** *Littérature & Théât* comic, comedy (*avant n*); (*acteur, auteur, rôle*) comic; **le genre c.** comedy

2 (*amusant*) comical, funny; **avec une expression c. sur le visage** with a comical look on his face
NMF 1 (*artiste*) comic, comedian, *f* comedienne; **c'est un grand c.** he's a great comic actor
2 (*boute-en-train*) comic, comedian
3 (*auteur*) comic author, writer of comedies *or* comedy
NM 1 (*genre*) comedy; **le c. de caractères/situation** character/situation comedy; **le c. de répétition** comedy based on repetition; **le c. troupier** barrack-room comedy
2 (*ce qui fait rire*) **c'était du plus haut c.!** it was hysterically funny!; **le c. de l'histoire, c'est que…** the funny part of it is that…

comiquement [kɔmikmɑ̃] **ADV** comically, funnily

comité [kɔmite] **NM** committee, board; **faire partie d'un c.** to sit on a committee; **se constituer en c.** to form a committee; **c. d'action** action committee; **C. d'aide au développement** Development Aid Committee; **c. central** central committee; **le c. Colbert** = association of top luxury goods manufacturers; **c. de conciliation** arbitration committee; **c. consultatif** advisory board; **c. de défense** defence committee; **c. directeur** steering committee; *Pol* **c. électoral** electoral committee; **c. d'enquête** board of enquiry; **c. d'entreprise** works council; **c. des établissements de crédit et des entreprises d'investissement** = French public authority empowered to authorize suppliers of investment services; **C. européen de normalisation** European Standards Commission; *Pol* **c. exécutif** executive committee *or* board; **c. de gestion** management board, managerial board; **c. d'hygiène et de sécurité** health and safety committee; **le C. international olympique** the International Olympic Committee; *Littérature & Théât* **c. de lecture** reading panel *or* committee; **c. de locataires** tenants' association; **le c. des parents** = representative body made up of parents of primary school children; *Jur* **c. de probation** probation committee; *Pol* **c. de quartier** local committee; **le C. de salut public** the Committee of Public Safety; *Mktg* **c. synectique** ideas committee
❑ **en comité secret ADV** secretly
❑ **en petit comité, en comité restreint ADV** as a select group; **on a dîné en petit c.** the dinner was just for a select group; **pour leur anniversaire ils seront en petit c.** they'll celebrate their anniversary with just a few friends (and relations)

╔══════════════════════╗
║ *Culture* ║
║ **COMITÉ D'ENTREPRISE** ║
The "CE" looks after the general welfare of company employees and organizes subsidized leisure activities, outings, holidays etc. It also deals with industrial problems.
╚══════════════════════╝

comitial, -e, -aux, -ales [kɔmisjal, -o] **ADJ** *Méd* comitial; **mal c.** epilepsy
comitialité [kɔmisjalite] **NF** *Méd* epilepsy
comma [kɔma] **NM** *Mus* comma
command [kɔmɑ̃] **NM** principal (*in purchase*)
commandant [kɔmɑ̃dɑ̃] **NM 1** *Mil* (*de l'armée de terre*) ≃ major; **c. d'armes** garrison commander; **c. en chef** commander-in-chief; *Suisse* **c. de corps** ≃ lieutenant-general
2 *Mil* (*de l'armée de l'air*) *Br* ≃ squadron leader, *Am* ≃ major
3 *Mil* (*de la marine*) ≃ commanding officer
4 (*de la marine marchande*) captain
5 *Aviat* **c. (de bord)** captain; **le c. Durcot vous souhaite…** Captain Durcot wishes you…; **c. en second** second in command
6 (*de camp, base*) commandant

commande [kɔmɑ̃d] **NF 1** *Com* order; (*marchandises*) order, goods ordered; **faire** *ou* **passer une c. (à qn/de qch)** to put in *or* place an order (with sb/for sth); **passer c. de 10 véhicules** to order 10 vehicles; **annuler une c.** to cancel an order; **exécuter/livrer une c.** to fill/deliver an order; **payable à la c.** payment with order, cash

with order; **le garçon a pris la c.** the waiter took the order; **notre c. vient d'être livrée** our order has just been delivered; **j'ai été obligé de renvoyer toute la c.** I had to return all the goods (I had) ordered; **conformément à votre c.** as per (your) order; **c. d'essai** trial order; **c. export** export order; **c. ferme** firm order; **c. par ordinateur** teleorder; **c. par quantité** bulk order; **c. renouvelée** repeat order; **c. téléphonique, c. par téléphone** telephone order

2 *Tech* (*action*) control, operation; (*dispositif*) control mechanism; **la c. des essuie-glaces** the wiper mechanism; **une machine à c. électrique** an electrically-operated machine; **c. d'allumage** ignition control; **c. à distance** remote control; *Aut* **c. électronique du moteur** engine management system; **c. manuelle** hand *or* manual control; **à c. manuelle** manually controlled; **c. tactile** one-touch operation; *Aut* **c. de vitesse de croisière** cruise control

3 *Ordinat* command; **c. d'annulation** undo command; **c. à bascule** toggle switch; **c. binaire** bit command; **c. de copie** copy command; **c. du DOS** DOS command; **c. d'effacement** delete command; **c. erronée** (*message d'erreur*) bad command; **c. d'insertion** insert command; **c. numérique** digital control; **à c. numérique** digitally controlled *or* operated; **c. de recherche** search *or* find command; **c. système d'exploitation** operating system command; **à c. vocale** voice-activated
❑ **commandes NFPL** (*dispositif de guidage*) controls; **être aux commandes** to be at the controls; *Fig* to be in charge; **prendre les** *ou* **se mettre aux commandes** to take over at the controls; *Fig* to take charge
❑ **à la commande ADV** payer à la c. to pay while ordering; **payable à la c.** payment with order; **travailler à la c.** to work to order
❑ **de commande ADJ 1** *Tech* control (*avant n*)
2 *Péj* (*factice → enthousiasme, humour*) forced, unnatural
3 *Littéraire* (*indispensable*) **la plus grande circonspection/générosité est de c.** prudence/generosity is of the essence
❑ **sur commande ADV** *Com & Fig* to order; **fait sur c.** made to order

commandement [kɔmɑ̃dmɑ̃] **NM 1** (*ordre*) command, order; **donner un c.** to give an order; **obéir aux commandements de qn** to obey sb's orders; **à mon c., prêts, partez!** on my command, ready, go!
2 (*fait de diriger*) command; **prendre le c. d'une section** to take over command of a platoon; **avoir le c. de** (*armée, pays*) to be in command of, to lead
3 (*état-major*) command; **le c. allié** allied command; **c. en chef** command-in-chief; **commandements territoriaux** territorial commands; **le haut c.** the High Command
4 *Jur* court order to pay
5 *Bible* commandment; **les Dix Commandements** the Ten Commandments

commander [3] [kɔmɑ̃de] **VT 1** (*diriger → armée, expédition, soldats, équipe*) to command; (*→ navire*) to be in command of; **il commande 200 hommes** he has 200 men under his command; **sans vous c., est-ce que vous pourriez fermer la fenêtre?** I wonder if you'd mind closing the window?
2 (*ordonner*) **c. la retraite aux troupes** to order the troops back *or* to retreat; **c. à qn de faire** *ou* **qu'il fasse qch** to order sb to do sth; **il a commandé de se taire** *ou* **que l'on se taise** he demanded silence
3 *Tech* to control; **l'ouverture des portes est commandée par une manette** the doors open by means of a lever; **la porte qui commande l'accès à la cave** the door to the cellar; **la télévision est commandée à distance** the television is remote-controlled
4 *Com* (*tableau, ouvrage*) to commission; (*objet manufacturé, repas*) to order; **c. qch chez qn** to order sth from sb; **c. qch par téléphone** to order sth by telephone; **c. qch en ligne** to order sth online; **on m'a commandé une affiche pour le festival** I was commissioned to do a poster for the festival; **peux-tu me c. un sandwich?** could you order me a sandwich?; **c. une robe sur catalogue** to order a dress from a catalogue; **je**

com–com

vais c. le menu I'll take the fixed-price menu

5 *(requérir)* to demand; **la prudence commande le silence absolu** prudence demands total discretion, total discretion is required for the sake of prudence; **l'intérêt général commande que l'on soit modéré** for the sake of the general interest, moderation is required

6 *(susciter)* to command; **c. le respect/l'attention** to command respect/attention

7 *Littéraire (maîtriser)* to control; **il ne commande plus ses nerfs** he is no longer in control of his emotions

8 *(dominer → vallée, plaine)* to dominate, to command

9 *Ordinat* to drive; **commandé par menu** menu-driven; **commandé à la voix** voice-activated

USAGE ABSOLU *Com* **c'est fait, j'ai déjà commandé** I've already ordered; **vous avez commandé?** has somebody taken your order?

VI 1 *(primer)* **le devoir commande!** duty calls!; **le travail commande!** back to work!

2 *(diriger)* **tu dois lui obéir, c'est lui qui commande** you must obey him, he's in charge; **c'est moi qui commande ici!** I'm the one who gives the orders around here!

❑ **commander à VT IND 1** *(donner des ordres à → armée)* to command

2 *Littéraire (maîtriser)* to control, to be in control *or* command of; **on ne commande pas à ses désirs** desire cannot be controlled

▸**se commander VPR 1** *Fam (être imposé)* **je n'aime pas ces gens, ça ne se commande pas** I don't like those people, I can't help it; **l'amour ne se commande pas** you can't make love happen

2 *(être relié → pièces)* to be connected *or* interconnected, to connect, to interconnect; **toutes les pièces se commandent** all the rooms are interconnected

commanderie [kɔmɑ̃dri] **NF** commandery

commandeur [kɔmɑ̃dœr] **NM 1** *Rel* commander **2** *(dans un ordre civil)* commander; **grand c.** Grand Commander

commanditaire [kɔmɑ̃ditɛr] **NM 1** *(d'une entreprise commerciale) Br* sleeping *or Am* silent partner; *(d'un tournoi, d'un spectacle)* backer, sponsor **2** *(d'un crime)* **nous ne savons pas qui sont les commanditaires de l'attentat** we don't know who is behind the attack **3** *(comme adj)* **associé c.** *Br* sleeping *or Am* silent partner

commandite [kɔmɑ̃dit] **NF** *Com* **1** *(fonds)* capital invested by *Br* sleeping *or Am* silent partner(s) **2 (société en) c. simple** limited partnership, mixed liability company; **(société en) c. par actions** partnership limited by shares

commandité, -e [kɔmɑ̃dite] *Com* **ADJ** *(entreprise commerciale)* financed *(as a limited partner)*; *(tournoi, spectacle)* sponsored

NM,F (associé) c. active partner

commanditer [3] [kɔmɑ̃dite] **VT 1** *Com (entreprise commerciale)* to finance *(as a limited partner)*; *(tournoi, spectacle)* to sponsor **2** *(meurtre, attentat)* to be behind

commando [kɔmɑ̃do] **NM** commando

COMME [kɔm]

> **CONJ** as **1, 2, 4, 7, 8** ▪ like **1, 3** ▪ since **7** ▪ when **8**
> **ADV** how

CONJ 1 *(introduisant une comparaison)* as, like; **c'est un jour c. les autres** it's a day like any other; **ce n'est pas un homme c. les autres** he's not like other men; **une maison pas c. les autres** a very unusual house; **il fut c. un second père pour moi** he was like a second father to me; **ce fut c. une révélation** it was like a revelation; **il fait beau c. en plein été** it's like a beautiful summer's day; **nous nagerons c. quand nous étions en Sicile** we'll swim like when we were in Sicily; **c'est c. ta sœur, elle ne téléphone jamais** your sister's the same, she never phones; **je suis c. toi, j'ai horreur de ça** I'm like you, I hate that kind of thing; **fais c. moi, ne lui réponds pas** do as I do, don't answer him/her; **qu'est-ce que tu veux? – choisis c. pour toi** what do you want? – get me the same as you; **blanc c. neige** white as snow; **il parle c. un livre** he talks like a book; **je l'ai vu c. je vous vois** I saw it as sure as I'm standing here; **il reviendra – je ne dis pas c. toi** he'll be back – I wouldn't be too sure; **il sera dentiste, tout c. sa mère** he'll be a dentist, just like his mother; **la voiture fait c. un bruit** the car's making a funny noise; **elle a eu c. une hésitation avant de répondre** she seemed to hesitate before answering; **j'ai c. l'impression qu'on s'est perdus!** I've got a feeling we're lost!; *Fam* **il y a c. un défaut!** something seems to be wrong!; **c'est tout c.** as good as; **il ne m'a pas injurié, mais c'était tout c.** he didn't actually insult me, but it was close *or* as good as; **elle n'a pas encore le rôle, mais c'est tout c.** she hasn't got the part yet, but it's as good as *or* as near as makes no difference

2 *(exprimant la manière)* as; **fais c. il te plaira** do as you like *or* please; **fais c. je t'ai appris** do it the way I taught you; **tout s'est passé c. je l'ai dit** everything happened as I said (it would); **il est venu, c. je l'espérais** he came, as I hoped he would; **si, c. je le crois, il n'est pas trop tard** if, as I believe, it's not too late; **c. on pouvait s'y attendre, nos actions ont baissé** as could be expected, our shares have gone down; **c. je l'ai fait remarquer...** as I pointed out...; **ça s'écrit c. ça se prononce** it's written as it's pronounced; **la connaissant c. je la connais** knowing her as well as *or* like I do; **si, c. le dit Aristote...** if, as Aristotle says...; **je passerai vous prendre à 9 heures c. convenu** I'll pick you up at 9 as (we) agreed *or* planned; *Fam* **c. dirait l'autre, c. dit l'autre** as the saying goes, to coin a phrase, as they say; **c. on dit** as they say; **c. il se doit** as is fitting, in a fitting manner; **on le recevra c. il se doit** we'll receive him in a fitting manner; **c. il se doit en pareilles circonstances** as befits the circumstances, as is fitting in such circumstances; *Fam* **c. qui dirait** so to speak; **c'était c. qui dirait un gémissement** it was a sort of moan; **c. bon vous semble** as you think best; **fais c. bon te semble** do whatever you wish *or* like; **vous pouvez amener quelqu'un ou non, c. bon vous semblera** you can bring someone or not, whichever you like; *Fam* **c. ci c. ça** so-so; **comment ça va? – c. ci c. ça** how are you? – so-so; **tu t'entends bien avec lui? – c. ci c. ça** do you get on with him? – sort of *or* so-so

3 *(tel que)* like, such as; **une femme c. elle mérite mieux** a woman like her deserves better; **une grande fille c. toi ne pleure pas** a big girl like you doesn't cry; **des montres c. on n'en fait plus maintenant** the kind of watches they don't make anymore; **mince c. elle est, elle peut porter n'importe quoi** being as slim as she is everything suits her, she is so slim that everything suits her; **bête c. il est, il serait capable de lui dire** he's so stupid, he'd probably tell him/her; **les arbres c. le marronnier...** trees like *or* such as the chestnut...; **les grands mammifères, c. l'éléphant...** large mammals, such as *or* like elephants...

4 *(en tant que)* as; **il vaut mieux l'avoir c. ami que c. ennemi** I'd sooner have him as a friend than as an enemy; **je l'ai eu c. élève** he was one of my students; **je l'ai eue c. professeur** I had her as my *or* a teacher; **elle a réussi c. actrice** she's a success as an actress; **ils se sont présentés à l'élection c. libéraux** they ran in the election as liberals; **qu'est-ce que vous avez c. vin?** what (kind of) wine do you have?; **qu'y a-t-il c. dessert?** what's for dessert?; **c'est plutôt faible c. excuse!** it's a pretty feeble excuse!; *Fam* **c'est pas mal c. clip** it's not a bad video; *Fam* **c. gaffeur, tu te poses là!** you really know how to put your foot in it!; **c'est tout ce que j'ai eu c. remerciements** that's all the thanks I got; **il n'y a qu'une table et deux chaises c. meubles** the only furniture is a table and two chairs

5 *(pour ainsi dire)* **il restait sur le seuil, c. paralysé** he was standing on the doorstep, (as if he was) rooted to the spot; **ta robe est c. neuve!** your dress is as good as new!; **le village était c. mort** the village was dead; **il était c. fou** he was like a madman

6 *(et)* **l'un c. l'autre aiment beaucoup voyager** they both love travelling; **lui c. moi adorons les longues promenades** we both love long walks; **cette robe peut se porter avec c. sans ceinture** you can wear this dress with or without a belt; **le règlement s'applique à tous, à vous c. aux autres** the rules apply to everybody, you included; **un spectacle que les parents, c. les enfants, apprécieront** a show which will delight parents and children alike; **elle sort tous les jours, été c. hiver** she goes out every day, summer and winter alike; **à la ville c. à la scène** in real life as well as on stage; **tout le monde s'y est mis, les jeunes c. les vieux** everybody, young and old, got down to work; **la solidarité a joué son rôle en France c. à l'étranger** solidarity played its part in France as well as abroad

7 *(indiquant la cause)* since, as; **c. elle arrive demain, je prépare sa chambre** since *or* as she's arriving tomorrow, I'll get her room ready; **c. j'ai bon cœur, je le lui ai donné** since *or* as I'm generous, I gave it to him/her; **c. il était en retard, on a raté le film** because he was late, we missed the film

8 *(au moment où)* as, when; *(pendant que)* while; **le pot de fleurs est tombé juste c. je passais** the flowerpot fell just as *or* when I was walking past; **c. le soir tombait, il se mit à neiger** as evening approached, it began to snow; **c. le rôti cuisait, je préparais les légumes** while the joint was cooking, I prepared the vegetables

ADV 1 *(emploi exclamatif)* how; **c. c'est triste!** how sad (it is)!, it's so sad!; **c. tu es grande!** what a big girl you are now!, how tall you've grown!; **c. je regrette de l'avoir fait!** I'm so sorry I did it!, how I regret having done it!; **c. il court vite!** he runs so fast!; **c. tu as de beaux cheveux!** what beautiful hair you have!; **c. je te comprends!** I know exactly how you feel!

2 *(indiquant la manière)* **tu sais c. il est** you know what he's like *or* how he is; **tu as vu c. elle m'a traité!** you saw how *or* the way she treated me!

❑ **comme ça ADJ 1** *(ainsi)* like that; **je suis c. ça** I'm like that; **va lui dire – je ne suis pas c. ça, moi!** go and tell him/her – I'm not like that!; **il est c. ça, on ne le changera pas!** that's the way he is, you won't change him!; **c'est c. ça et pas autrement** that's the way it is and that's all there is to it; **c'est c. ça, que ça te plaise ou non!** that's how *or* the way it is, whether you like it or not!; **puisque** *ou* **si c'est c. ça** if that's how *or* the way it is; **je ne te dirai jamais plus rien, puisque c'est c. ça** I'll never tell you anything ever again, if that's the way *or* how it is; **j'ai fait pousser une citrouille c. ça!** I grew a pumpkin THAT big!; **une petite femme haute c. ça** a little woman no taller than that *or* only so high **2** *(admirable)* great; **c'est une fille c. ça!** she's a great girl!; **il a un vin blanc c. ça!** he's got a fantastic white wine!; **et l'expo? – c'était c. ça!** what about the exhibition? – it was great! **ADV 1** *(de cette manière)* like this *or* that; **je ne peux pas sortir c. ça** I can't go out (dressed) like this *or* that; **qu'as-tu à me regarder c. ça?** why are you looking at me like that?; *Fam* **il m'a répondu c. ça qu'il était majeur** I'm old enough, he says to me; **depuis quand tousses-tu c. ça?** how long have you been coughing like that?; **ne crie pas c. ça!** don't shout like that! **2** *(en intensif)* **alors c. ça, tu te maries?** (oh,) so you're getting married?; **où vas-tu c. ça?** where are you off to? **3** *(de telle manière que)* that way, so that; **je te laisse la clef, c. ça tu pourras entrer** I'll leave you the key, so that you can let yourself in

❑ **comme il faut ADJ** respectable, proper; **une jeune fille c. il faut** a very well-bred girl; **des gens très c. il faut** very respectable people **ADV 1** *(correctement)* properly; **fais ton travail c. il faut** do your work properly; **tu ne t'y prends pas c. il faut** you're doing it the wrong way, you're not doing it properly; **tu n'as pas refermé la boîte c. il faut** you didn't close the box properly; **elle est un peu maigre – et pourtant elle mange c. il faut!** she's a bit skinny – she eats well though *or* and yet she eats properly! **2** *Fam (emploi exclamatif)* **il s'est fait battre, et c.**

il faut (encore)! he got well and truly thrashed!

❑ **comme quoi** CONJ **1** *(ce qui prouve que)* which shows *or* (just) goes to show that; **c. quoi, on ne peut pas tout prévoir** which (just) goes to show that you can't foresee everything; **c. quoi tu aurais mieux fait de te taire!** which just goes to show that you should have kept quiet!

2 *Fam (selon quoi)* **j'ai reçu des ordres c. quoi personne ne devait avoir accès au dossier** I've been instructed not to allow anybody access to the file; **c'est une lettre c. quoi je dois me présenter à leur bureau** it's a letter telling me to go to their office

❑ **comme si** CONJ **1** *(exprimant la comparaison)* as if *or* though; **il se conduit c. s'il était encore étudiant** he behaves as if he was still a student; **c. si de rien n'était** as though nothing was wrong *or* amiss; **elle faisait c. si de rien n'était** she pretended (that) there was nothing wrong, she pretended (that) nothing had happened; **mais je n'y connais rien – fais c. si!** but I don't know anything about it – just pretend!

2 *(emploi exclamatif)* as if, as though; **c'est c. si c'était fait!** it's as good as done!; **c. s'il ne savait pas ce qu'il faisait!** as if *or* as though he didn't know what he was doing!

❑ **comme tout** ADV really, extremely, terribly; **tu es jolie c. tout!** you really are pretty!, aren't you pretty!; **il est malin c. tout** he's extremely cunning *or* as cunning as they come; **j'ai été malade c. tout sur le bateau** I was (as) sick as a dog on the boat

---

'Comme il vous plaira' *Shakespeare* 'As You Like It'

---

commedia dell'arte [kɔmedjadɛlarte] NF commedia dell'arte

commémoraison [kɔmemɔrɛzɔ̃] NF *Rel* commemoration

commémoratif, -ive [kɔmemɔratif, -iv] ADJ memorial *(avant n)*, *Sout* commemorative; **un monument c.** a memorial; **une plaque commémorative** a commemorative plaque

commémoration [kɔmemɔrasjɔ̃] NF commemoration; **en c. de** in commemoration of, in memory of

commémorative [kɔmemɔrativ] *voir* **commémoratif**

commémorer [3] [kɔmemɔre] VT to commemorate, to celebrate the memory of

commençant, -e [kɔmɑ̃sɑ̃, -ɑ̃t] NM,F beginner

commencement [kɔmɑ̃smɑ̃] NM **1** *(première partie → de la vie, d'un processus)* beginning, start, early stages; **du c. jusqu'à la fin** from start to finish, from beginning to end; **commencements** *(période)* beginnings, early *or* initial stages; **les commencements ont été durs** the early days were tough, things were pretty hard at the beginning; *Hum* **c'est le c. de la fin** it's the beginning of the end; **il y a un c. à tout** you have to start somewhere

2 *(essai)* beginning, start, attempt; **il y a eu un c. d'émeute, vite réprimé** a riot started, but was soon brought under control; **son texte ne comporte pas même le c. d'une idée** there isn't even a vestige of an idea in his text

3 *Jur* **c. d'exécution** = initial steps in the commission of a crime; **c. de preuve par écrit** prima facie evidence

❑ **au commencement** ADV in *or* at the beginning; *Bible* **au c. était le Verbe** in the beginning was the Word

❑ **au commencement de** PRÉP at the beginning *or* start of; *Jur* **au c. de la période** when the period commences

COMMENCER [16] [kɔmɑ̃se] VT **1** *(entreprendre → ouvrage, jeu, apprentissage)* to start, to begin; **as-tu commencé le livre que je t'ai prêté?** have you started *or* begun (reading) the book I lent you?; **il a commencé le repas** he's started eating; **allez, commence la vaisselle!** come on, get going on the dishes!; **vous commencez le travail demain** you start (work) tomorrow; **j'ai commencé des chaussons pour le bébé** I've started (knitting) some bootees for the baby; **c. le piano/la compétition très jeune** to start playing the piano/taking part in tournaments very young; **nous allons c. notre descente vers Milan** we are beginning our descent towards Milan

2 *(passer au début de → journée, soirée)* to start, to begin; **nous commencerons cette heure par un exposé** we will begin this class with a presentation; **j'ai bien/mal commencé l'année** I've made a good/bad start to the year

3 *(être au début de)* to begin; **la maille qui commence le rang** the first stitch in the row; **le mot qui commence la phrase** the word which starts the sentence *or* with which the sentence begins; **c'est son numéro qui commence le spectacle** his/her routine begins the show, the show begins with his/her routine

4 *Vieilli* **c. un élève en chimie** to give a pupil a grounding in chemistry

USAGE ABSOLU **à quelle heure tu commences?** *(au lycée)* what time do you start school?; *(au travail)* what time do you start work?

VI **1** *(débuter)* to start; **tu ne vas pas c.!, ne commence pas!** don't start!; **ce n'est pas moi, c'est lui qui a commencé!** it wasn't me, HE started it!; *aussi Ironique* **ça commence bien!** that's a great start!; **c. à faire qch** to start *or* to begin doing sth; **elle a commencé à repeindre la cuisine** she started redecorating the kitchen; **je commençais à m'inquiéter** I was beginning to worry; **tu commences à m'énerver!** you're beginning to annoy me!, you're getting on my nerves!; **je commence à en avoir assez!** I've had just about enough!, I'm getting fed up with all this!; *Fam* **ça commence à bien faire!** enough is enough!, things have gone quite far enough!; *Littéraire* **nous commencions de déjeuner** we had started luncheon; **la pièce commence par un dialogue** the play starts *or* opens with a dialogue; **la dispute a commencé par** *ou* **sur un malentendu** the argument started with a misunderstanding; **commençons par le commencement** let's begin at the beginning, first things first; **commence par enlever les couvertures** first, take the blankets off; **tu veux une moto? commence par réussir ton examen** if you want a motorbike, start by passing your exam; **je vais c. par l'appeler** the first thing I'm going to do is call him/her; **ça commence par un g** it begins with (a) g; **je ne sais par où c.** I don't know where to start; **il commence à pleuvoir/neiger** it's started to rain/to snow; *Fam* **il commence à se faire tard** it's getting late■

2 *(avoir tel moment comme point de départ)* to start, to begin; **quand commence le trimestre?** when does term start?; **la séance commence à 20 heures** the session starts *or* begins at 8 pm; *Fam* **à quelle heure ça commence?** *(cours, spectacle, match)* what time does it start?■; **le spectacle est commencé depuis un quart d'heure** the show started a quarter of an hour ago; **les vendanges ont commencé tard cette année** the grape harvest started *or* is late this year; **les ennuis ont commencé quand il s'est installé au-dessous de chez moi** the trouble started *or* began when he moved in downstairs; **on fait généralement c. la crise après le premier choc pétrolier** the recession is generally said to have started after the first oil crisis

3 *(se mettre à travailler)* **c. dans la vie** to start off in life; **c. sur la scène/au cinéma** to make one's stage/screen debut; **j'ai commencé en 78 avec deux ouvrières** I set up *or* started (up) in '78 with two workers

4 *(dans un barème de prix)* to start; **les pantalons commencent à/vers 40 euros** trousers start at/at around 40 euros

❑ **à commencer par** PRÉP starting *or* beginning with; **que tout le monde contribue, à c. par toi!** everyone can give something, starting with you!

❑ **pour commencer** ADV **1** *(dans un programme, un repas)* first, to start with; **pour c., du saumon** to start the meal *or* as a first course, salmon

2 *(comme premier argument)* for a start, in the first place; **pour c., tu es trop jeune, et ensuite c'est trop cher!** for a start you're too young, and anyway, it's too expensive!

commendataire [kɔmɑ̃datɛr] ADJ commendatory

commende [kɔmɑ̃d] NF *Rel & Hist* commendam; **abbaye en c.** abbey (held) in commendam

commensal, -e, -aux, -ales [kɔmɑ̃sal, -o] NM,F **1** *Littéraire (compagnon de table)* table companion; *(hôte)* guest **2** *Biol* commensal

commensalisme [kɔmɑ̃salism] NM *Biol* commensalism

commensalité [kɔmɑ̃salite] NF *Littéraire* commensality

commensurable [kɔmɑ̃syrabl] ADJ commensurable, measurable

comment [kɔmɑ̃] ADV **1** *(de quelle manière)* how; **c. lui dire que…?** how am I/are we/*etc* going to tell him/her that…?; **c. t'appelles-tu?** what's your name?; **c. est-il, ce garçon?** what's this young man like?; **c. se fait-il qu'il n'ait pas appelé?** how come he hasn't called?; **c. est-ce possible?** how is it possible?; **c. faire?** what shall we do?; **je me demande c. tout cela va finir** I wonder how it's all going to end; *Fam* **c. tu parles!** what kind of language is that!; **il faut voir c. elle lui parle** you should see *or* hear the way *or* how she speaks to him/her; **c. allez-vous?** how are you?; *Fam* **c. va?** how's things?; **et les enfants, c. ça va?** and how are the children?

2 *(pour faire répéter)* **c.?** sorry?, what (was that)?; **je pars – c.? – j'ai dit, je pars** I'm leaving – what (did you say)? – I said, I'm leaving

3 *(exprimant l'indignation, l'étonnement)* **c., c'est tout ce que tu trouves à dire?** what! is that all you can say?; **c., tu n'as pas compris?** what? you didn't understand? *or* you mean you didn't understand?; **c. oses-tu me parler ainsi!** how dare you talk to me like this!; **c., ce n'est pas encore prêt?** you mean it's still not ready?; *Fam* **c. ça, tu pars?** what do you mean, you're leaving?; **c., mais c'est scandaleux!** what! but that's scandalous!; **le concert t'a plu? – et c.!** did you like the concert? – I certainly did!; **il l'a bien eu – et c.!** he really took him in – and how! *or* he certainly did!; **mais c. donc!** of course!, by all means!; **pouvons-nous entrer? – mais c. donc!** can we come in? – of course! *or* by all means!; *Ironique* **mais c. donc! ne vous gênez surtout pas!** don't mind me!

NM **le c.** the how

commentaire [kɔmɑ̃tɛr] NM **1** *(remarque)* comment, remark, observation; **avez-vous des commentaires?** any comments *or* remarks?; **faire un c.** to make a remark *or* a comment; **il n'a pas fait de commentaires dans la marge** he didn't write any remarks in the margin; **puis-je me permettre (de faire) un c.?** may I say something?; **je te dispense** *ou* **je me passe de tes commentaires** I can do without your remarks; *Fam* **c'est comme ça, et pas de c.!** that's how it is, and don't argue (with me)!; **cela se passe de c.** *ou* **commentaires** it speaks for itself; **sans c.!** no comment! **commentaires de presse** press comments

2 *Péj (critique)* comment; **son mariage a suscité bien des commentaires** his/her marriage caused a great deal of comment *or* gossip; **les commentaires vont bon train** comment is rife; **les commentaires des voisins ne vont pas manquer** the neighbours will have a few things to say; **j'aurais des commentaires à faire sur ton attitude d'hier soir** I'd like to say something about your attitude last night

3 *Rad & TV* commentary; **c. de notre envoyé permanent à Bonn** the commentary is by our correspondent in Bonn; **c. de la rencontre, Pierre Pastriot** with live commentary from the stadium, Pierre Pastriot; **c. en direct** live commentary; **c. sur image** voice-over, voice-over narration; **c. sportif** sports commmentary; **c. en voix off** off-screen narration

4 *Scol & Univ* **un texte avec c.** an annotated text; **un c. de la Bible** a biblical commentary, *Sout* a biblical exegesis; **faire un c. de texte** to comment on a text; **un c. composé** a written commentary

5 *Ordinat* comment

6 *Ling* comment, theme

commentateur, -trice [kɔmɑ̃tatœr, -tris] NM,F **1** *(auteur → d'un commentaire)* commentator, reviewer, critic **2** *(d'une cérémonie, d'un match)* commentator; *(d'un documentaire)* presenter; **c. du journal télévisé** newscaster, anchorman, *f* anchorwoman; **c. sportif** sports commentator **3**

(observateur) observer, commentator; **pour certains commentateurs, il s'agit là d'une victoire** some observers see this as a victory

commenter [3] [kɔmɑ̃te] **VT 1** *(expliquer → œuvre)* to explain, to interpret; **veuillez c. ce dernier vers du poème** please write a commentary on the last line of the poem; **la façon dont Sartre a commenté Flaubert** the way in which Sartre interpreted Flaubert; **on leur fait c. Dante dès la troisième année d'italien** they start doing literary criticism of Dante after studying Italian for three years; **le directeur va maintenant c. notre programme de fabrication** the manager will now explain our manufacturing schedule

2 *(donner son avis sur)* to comment on; **c. l'actualité** to comment on current events; **voulez-vous c. les récentes critiques de l'opposition?** would you care to respond to recent objections by the Opposition?

3 *Rad & TV (cérémonie, match)* to cover, to do the commentary of *or* for

commérage [kɔmeraʒ] **NM** piece of gossip; **commérages** gossip; **être friand de commérages** to be fond of gossip; **faire des commérages** to gossip; **ce ne sont que des commérages** it's only gossip *or* hearsay

commerçant, -e [kɔmɛrsɑ̃, -ɑ̃t] **ADJ 1** *(peuple, port, pays)* trading *(avant n)*; *(rue, quartier)* shopping *(avant n)*; **un quartier très c.** a good shopping area **2** *(qui a le sens du commerce)* **il a l'esprit c.** he's a born salesman, he could sell you anything; **il n'est pas très c.** he's not got much business sense; *Péj* **un sourire c.** a mercenary smile

NM,F *(négociant)* trader, merchant; *(qui tient un magasin) Br* shopkeeper, *Am* storekeeper; **tous les commerçants étaient fermés** all the *Br* shops *or Am* stores were closed; **c. de** *ou* **en détail** retail trader, retailer; **c. en gros** wholesale; **les petits commerçants** small *or* retail traders

commerce [kɔmɛrs] **NM 1** *(activité)* **le c.** trade; **être dans le c.** to be in trade, to run a business; **faire du c. avec qn/un pays** to trade with sb/a country; **faire le c. de qch** to trade in sth; **c. bilatéral** bilateral trade; **c. de demi-gros** cash and carry; **c. de détail** retail trade; **c. dirigé** managed trade; *Ordinat* **c. électronique** electronic commerce, e-commerce; **c. équitable** *ou* **éthique** fair trade; **c. extérieur** foreign trade; **c. d'exportation** export trade; **c. frontalier** border trade; **c. en gros** wholesale trade; **c. d'importation** import trade; **c. intérieur** domestic trade, home trade; **c. intermédiaire** middleman's business; **c. international** international trade; **c. mobile** m-commerce; **c. réciproque** reciprocal trade *or* trading; **c. de réexportation** re-export trade; **c. de services** invisible trade; **c. transfrontalier** cross-border trade; **c. triangulaire** triangular trade; *Euph* **faire c. de ses charmes** to sell one's body

2 *(affaires)* business; **cela fait marcher le c.** it's good for business; **le c. marche mal** business is slow; **le monde du c.** the business world; **le c. français** business in France; **le c. dominical** Sunday trading; **c. intégré** corporate *or* combined chain

3 *(commerçants)* **le petit c.** small *or* retail traders

4 *(circuit de distribution)* **on ne trouve pas encore ce produit dans le c.** this item is not yet available in the *Br* shops *or Am* stores; **cela ne se trouve plus dans le c.** this item is not on the market any more

5 *(magasin) Br* shop, *Am* store; **ouvrir** *ou* **monter un c.** to open *or* to start a business; **tenir un c.** to run a business; **c. de proximité** local *Br* shop *or Am* store

6 *Littéraire (relation, fréquentation)* company; **entretenir un c. d'amitié avec qn** to keep company with sb; **renoncer au c. des hommes** to renounce the company of one's fellow men; **être d'un c. agréable** to be easy to get on with *or* pleasant to deal with

❑ **de commerce ADJ 1** *(opération)* commercial, business *(avant n)*; *(acte)* trade *(avant n)*; *(code, tribunal)* commercial; *(école)* business *(avant n)*

2 *Naut (marine, navire, port)* trading, merchant *(avant n)*

commercer [16] [kɔmɛrse] **VI** to trade, to deal; **c. avec un pays** to trade with a country

commercial, -e, -aux, -ales [kɔmɛrsjal, -o] **ADJ 1** *(activité, attaché)* commercial; *(délégué, direction, service)* sales *(avant n)*; *(relation, embargo, tribunal)* trade *(avant n)*; **adressez-vous à notre service** *ou* **secteur c.** please apply to our sales department; **avoir des contacts commerciaux avec** to have trading *or* trade links with; **pour des raisons commerciales** for commercial reasons; **droit c.** commercial law; **l'anglais c.** business English; **un gros succès c.** *(film, pièce)* a big box-office success; *(livre)* a best-selling book, a best-seller

2 *TV* commercial; **les chaînes commerciales** commercial channels

3 *Péj (sourire)* ingratiating; **vos anciens fans trouvent que vous êtes devenu c.** your old fans think you've sold out; **c'est une chanson très commerciale** it's a very commercial song

NM,F sales person

❑ **commerciale NF** *Fam* commercial vehicle■

commercialement [kɔmɛrsjalmɑ̃] **ADV** commercially; **c. parlant** from a business point of view

commercialisable [kɔmɛrsjalizabl] **ADJ** marketable

commercialisation [kɔmɛrsjalizasjɔ̃] **NF** marketing

commercialiser [3] [kɔmɛrsjalize] **VT 1** *Com* to market, to commercialize; **le modèle sera commercialisé en janvier** the model will be coming onto the market in January **2** *Jur (dette, lettre de change)* to market **3** *Fin (effet)* to negotiate

commère [kɔmɛr] **NF 1** *(médisante)* gossip **2** *(bavarde)* chatterbox **3** *Littérature* **ma c. la tortue** Mrs Tortoise

commérer [18] [kɔmere] **VI** *Fam Vieilli* to gossip

commets *etc voir* **commettre**

commettage [kɔmɛtaʒ] **NM** *Naut* **1** *(action)* laying, stranding *(of rope)* **2** *(cordage)* lay of rope

commettant [kɔmetɑ̃] **NM** principal

commettre [84] [kɔmɛtr] **VT 1** *(perpétrer → erreur)* to make; *(→ injustice)* to perpetrate; *(→ meurtre)* to commit; **quand le crime a-t-il été commis?** when did the crime take place?; **c. une maladresse** to make a blunder, to make a gaffe; **c. une imprudence** to take an unwise step; **l'impatience lui a fait c. une faute impardonnable** his impatience led him to make an inexcusable mistake

2 *Jur (nommer → arbitre, avocat, huissier)* to appoint; **c. un avocat (à la défense)** to appoint *or* to name a lawyer (for the defence); **commis d'office** appointed by the court

3 *Naut* to lay up

4 *Hum Péj (produire → livre, émission)* to perpetrate; **il avait commis quelques articles dans les années 80** he had penned a few articles back in the eighties

5 *Vieilli (confier)* **c. qn à qn** to entrust sb to sb's care; **c. qch à qn** to entrust sth to sb *or* to sb's care, to entrust sb with sth

▸**se commettre VPR** *Littéraire* to compromise oneself; **se c. avec qn** to associate *or* consort with sb

comminatoire [kɔminatwar] **ADJ 1** *Littéraire (menaçant)* threatening **2** *Jur* = involving a penalty for non-compliance

comminutif, -ive [kɔminytif, -iv] **ADJ** comminuted

commis, -e [kɔmi, -iz] **PP** *voir* **commettre**

NM 1 *Jur* agent

2 *(employé → de magasin) Br* sales assistant, *Am* sales clerk; *(→ de banque)* runner, junior clerk; *(→ de ferme)* lad, boy, farm hand; *Bourse* floor trader; **c. boucher** *ou* **de boucherie** butcher's boy; **c. aux comptes** government auditor; **c. de cuisine** commis chef; **c. aux écritures** accounting clerk; **c. greffier** assistant to the court clerk; **c. principal** senior clerk; *Vieilli* **c. voyageur** travelling salesman

3 *Admin* **grand c. de l'État** senior *or* higher civil servant

4 *Mil & Naut* **c. aux vivres** steward

commisération [kɔmizerasjɔ̃] **NF** commiseration; **témoigner de la c. à qn** to show sb sympathy; **sans c.** ruthlessly, pitilessly

commissaire [kɔmisɛr] **NM 1** *(membre d'une commission)* commissioner; **c. européen** European commissioner

2 *Sport* steward; **c. d'une course** race steward

3 *Admin* **c. divisionnaire** *Br* chief superintendent, *Am* police chief; **c. enquêteur** investigating commissioner; **c. du gouvernement** government commissioner; **c. de police** *Br* (police) superintendent, *Am* (police) captain, precinct captain; **bonjour, Monsieur le c.** good morning, *Br* Superintendent *or Am* Captain; **c. principal** *Br* chief superintendent, *Am* chief of police; **c. de la Marine/de l'Air** chief administrator in the Navy/the Air Force; **c. de la République** commissioner of the Republic

4 *Fin* **c. aux comptes** auditor

5 *(d'une exposition)* organizer

6 *Naut* **c. de** *ou* **du bord** purser

7 *Hist (en URSS)* commissar

commissaire-priseur [kɔmisɛrprisœr] *(pl* **commissaires-priseurs)** **NM** auctioneer; **c. judiciaire** auctioneer

commissariat [kɔmisarja] **NM 1** *(fonction)* commissionership; *Naut* **c. de** *ou* **du bord** pursership **2** *Admin* **c. de l'Air** Air Force staff; **C. à l'énergie atomique** = French atomic energy commission, *Br* ≃ AEA, *Am* ≃ AEC; **c. de la Marine** *Br* Admiralty Board, *Am* Naval Command **3** *Fin* **c. aux comptes** auditorship **4** *(local)* **c. (de police)** police station *or Am* precinct

commission [kɔmisjɔ̃] **NF 1** *(groupe)* commission, committee; **C. d'admission des pourvois en cassation** Appeal Committee; **c. de l'application des peines** sentence board; **c. d'arbitrage** arbitration committee; **C. d'accès aux documents administratifs** Commission for Access to Administrative Documents; **c. du budget** budget committee; **C. des communautés européennes** European Communities Commission; **c. de conciliation** arbitration committee; **c. de contrôle** supervisory committee; **C. du droit international** International Law Commission; **c. d'enquête** board *or* commission of enquiry; **la C. européenne** the European Commission; **C. européenne des droits de l'homme** European Human Rights Commission; **c. d'examen** examination board; **c. d'examen des pratiques commerciales** commercial practice commission; **c. d'indemnisation des victimes d'infractions** commission for the compensation of victims of crime; **c. mixte paritaire** mixed joint commission; **c. de normalisation** standards commission; **c. d'office** ex-officio appointment of counsel; **C. des opérations de Bourse** = French Stock Exchange watchdog, *Br* ≃ SIB, *Am* ≃ SEC; **c. paritaire** joint commission; **c. parlementaire** parliamentary committee *or* commission; **c. permanente** standing committee; **C. permanente** *(au Conseil d'État)* Standing Committee; **être en c.** to be in committee; **renvoyer un projet de loi en c.** to commit a bill

2 *Jur (pouvoir)* commission; **c. rogatoire** letters rogatory

3 *Mil* **c. d'armistice** armistice council; **c. militaire** army exemption tribunal

4 *Fin (pourcentage)* commission, percentage; *(frais de courtage)* brokerage; **3 pour cent de c.** 3 percent commission; **il reçoit** *ou* **touche une c. de 5 pour cent sur chaque vente** he gets a commission of 5 percent on each sale; **travailler à la c.** to work on a commission basis *or* for a percentage; *Banque* **c. d'acceptation** acceptance fee; **c. d'affacturage** factoring charges; **c. de change** exchange commission; **c. de chef de file** management fee; *Banque* **c. de compte** account fee; **c. de désintéressement** drop dead fee; **c. d'endos** endorsement fee; **c. d'engagement** commitment fee; **c. de garantie** underwriting fee; **c. de gestion** agency fee; **c. immédiate** flat fee; **c. de montage** loan origination fee; **c. de placement** underwriting fee; *Bourse* **c. de rachat** redemption fee; *Bourse* **c. de souscription** front load; **c. de tenue de compte** account handling fee; **c. de vente** sales commission

5 *(course)* errand; **faire une c.** to run an errand; **j'ai envoyé mon fils faire des commissions** I've sent my son off on some errands; **n'oublie pas de lui faire la c.** *(de lui donner le message)* don't forget to give him/her the message

6 *Fam Euph* **la petite/grosse c.** a number one/

two; **faire la petite/grosse c.** to do a number one/two

7 *(perpétration)* **la c. d'un crime** the commission of a crime

❑ **commissions** NFPL *(achats)* shopping; **faire les commissions** to do the shopping; **sors les commissions de la voiture** get the shopping out of the car

commissionnaire [kɔmisjɔnɛr] NMF **1** *Fin (intermédiaire)* commission agent, broker, agent; **c. d'achat** buyer; **c. en banque** outside broker; **c. en douane** customs agent *or* broker; **c. expéditeur** forwarding agent, carrier; **c. à l'export, c. exportateur** export agent; **c. en gros** factor; **c. à l'import, c. importateur** import agent; **c. de transport** forwarding agent **2** *(coursier)* commissionaire

commissionnement [kɔmisjɔnmɑ̃] NM commissioning

commissionner [3] [kɔmisjɔne] VT to commission

commissoire [kɔmiswar] ADJ **clause c.** commissoria lex

commissural, -e, -aux, -ales [kɔmisyral, -o] ADJ commissural

commissure [kɔmisyr] NF **1** *(dans le cerveau)* commissure **2** *(de la bouche)* corner

commissurotomie [kɔmisyrɔtɔmi] NF commissurotomy

commodat [kɔmɔda] NM *Jur* = free loan of something to be returned in unimpaired condition

commode¹ [kɔmɔd] ADJ **1** *(pratique → moyen de transport)* useful, convenient; *(→ outil)* useful, handy; **c'est bien c. d'avoir un marché dans le quartier** it's very handy *or* convenient having a market in the area; **les talons aiguilles ne sont pas très commodes pour marcher** high heels aren't very practical for walking (in) **2** *(facile)* easy; **ce n'est pas c. à analyser** it's not easy to analyse; **ce n'est pas c. de concilier deux activités** combining two different jobs is not easy *or* a simple task; **c'est** *ou* **ce serait trop c.!** that would be too easy! **3** *(aimable)* **elle n'est pas c. (à vivre)** she's not easy to live with; **son patron n'est pas c.** his/her boss isn't an easy person to get along with; **il est peu c.** he's awkward *or* difficult **4** *Vieilli (indulgent → morale)* liberal, easy-going

commode² [kɔmɔd] NF chest of drawers

commodément [kɔmɔdemɑ̃] ADV **1** *(confortablement)* comfortably **2** *Vieilli (aisément)* easily

commodité [kɔmɔdite] NF **1** *(facilité)* convenience; **pour plus de c.** for greater convenience, to make things more convenient **2** *(aspect pratique)* **la c. d'une maison** the comfort *or* convenience of a house; **j'habite à côté de mon bureau, c'est d'une grande c.** I live next door to my office, it's extremely convenient ❑ **commodités** NFPL **1** *(agréments)* conveniences; **les commodités de la vie moderne** the comforts *or* conveniences of modern life **2** *Vieilli (toilettes)* toilet, toilets

commodore [kɔmɔdɔr] NM *Can Mil Br* ≃ commodore, *Am* ≃ rear-admiral (lower half)

common law [kɔmɔnlo] NF *Jur* common law

Commonwealth [kɔmɔnwɛls] NM *Pol* **le C.** the Commonwealth

commotion [kɔmɔsjɔ̃] NF **1** *(choc)* shock; **être sous le coup de la c.** to be dazed by the shock **2** *Méd* **c. cérébrale** concussion **3** *(perturbation)* upheaval, agitation; **les commotions sociales/politiques dans l'Allemagne de 1933** the social/political upheavals in the Germany of 1933

commotionner [3] [kɔmɔsjɔne] VT **1** *(choquer)* to shake (up); **la terrible nouvelle l'a commotionné** the appalling news gave him a shock **2** *Méd* to concuss; **il a été fortement commotionné** he was severely concussed, he had severe concussion

commuabilité [kɔmɥabilite] NF *Jur* commutability

commuable [kɔmɥabl] ADJ commutable

commuer [7] [kɔmɥe] VT to commute; **c. une peine de prison en amende** to commute a prison sentence to a fine

commun, -e¹ [kɔmœ̃, -yn] ADJ **1** *(non exclusif → jardin, local)* shared, common; *(→ ami)* mutual; **salle commune** common room; **hôtel avec salle de télévision commune** hotel with public TV lounge; **une langue commune à cinq millions de personnes** a language shared by five

million people; **le court de tennis est c. à tous les propriétaires** the tennis court is the common property of all the residents

2 *(fait ensemble → travail, politique)* shared, common; *(→ décision)* joint; **nous avons pris la décision commune de...** we took a joint decision to...; **la vie commune** *(conjugale)* conjugal life, the life of a couple; **ils vont reprendre la vie commune** they're going to live together again

3 *(identique → caractère, passion, intérêts)* similar; *(→ habitude)* common, shared, identical; **nous avons des problèmes communs** we share the same problems, we have similar problems; **il n'y a rien de c. entre eux** they've (got) nothing in common; **il n'y a pas de commune mesure entre...** there's no similarity whatsoever between...; **c'est sans commune mesure avec...** there's no comparison with...

4 *(courant → espèce, usage, faute)* common, ordinary, run-of-the-mill; **une plante commune dans cette région** a plant that is common in this region; **il est d'un courage peu c.** he's uncommonly *or* exceptionally brave; **un nom peu c.** a very unusual name

5 *Péj (banal)* common, coarse; **il la trouvait commune** he thought she was common

6 *Ling* common

7 *Math* **le plus grand dénominateur c.** the highest common denominator

NM *Vieilli* **l'homme du c.** the common man; **un homme hors du c.** an exceptional *or* unusual man; **cela sort du c.** this is very unusual; **le c. des mortels** the common run of people; **le c. des mortels ne pourra sans doute pas comprendre** the man in the street won't be able to understand; **le c. des lecteurs** the average reader ❑ **communs** NMPL outbuildings, outhouses

❑ **d'un commun accord** ADV by mutual agreement, by common consent; **tous d'un c. accord ont décidé que...** they decided unanimously that...

❑ **en commun** ADV **avoir qch en c. (avec)** to have sth in common (with); **mettre qch en c.** to pool sth; **nous mettons tout en c.** we share everything; **on s'est mis en c. pour lui acheter un cadeau** we all clubbed together to buy him/her a present; **travailler en c.** to work together; **vivre en c.** to live communally

communal, -e, -aux, -ales [kɔmynal, -o] ADJ **1** *Admin (en ville)* ≃ of the urban district; *(à la campagne)* ≃ of the rural district **2** *(du village → fête)* local, village *(avant n)* **3** *Belg* **conseil c.** town council; **maison communale** town hall

❑ **communale** NF *Fam Br* primary school■, *Am* grade school■

❑ **communaux** NMPL *Belg (terres)* common land

communalement [kɔmynalmɑ̃] ADV communally

communaliser [3] [kɔmynalize] VT ≃ to put under the jurisdiction of the local authority

communard, -e [kɔmynar, -ard] ADJ *Hist* of the (Paris) Commune

NM,F *Hist* Communard, member of the (Paris) Commune

NM = red wine mixed with crème de cassis liqueur

communautaire [kɔmynotɛr] ADJ **1** *(vie, esprit)* communal, community *(avant n)* **2** *(du Marché commun)* Community *(avant n)*; **droit c.** (European) Community law **3** *(lié à une communauté de personnes)* **des conflits communautaires** conflicts between different communities; **on assiste à un repli c. au sein des quartiers sensibles** we're seeing ethnic communities withdrawing into themselves in sensitive areas; **reflexe c.** = tendency to see oneself as part of a particular community rather than part of society at large

communautarisation [kɔmynotarizasjɔ̃] NF = joint exploitation of oceanic or maritime resources

communautariser [3] [kɔmynotarize] VT **1** *UE* **c. la santé/la défense/le droit des travailleurs** to handle the issue of health/defence/workers' rights at EU level **2** *Belg Pol* = to devolve a political power to the French-, Flemish- and German-speaking Communities in Belgium

communautarisme [kɔmynotarism] NM **1** *(tendance du multiculturalisme américain)* =

emphasis on issues relating to minorities and ethnic communities within society **2** *(conception qui place la communauté avant l'individu)* communitarianism **3** *(dans le contexte des sociétés multiculturelles)* = tendency to withdraw into one's ethnic or religious community rather than seeing oneself as part of society at large

communautariste [kɔmynotarist] ADJ **1** *(relatif à une certaine tendance du multiculturalisme américain → démarche, politique)* = that takes into account issues relating to minorities and ethnic communities within society **2** *(relatif à la conception qui place la communauté avant l'individu)* communitarianist

communauté [kɔmynote] NF **1** *(similitude → de vues, de pensées)* likeness, closeness; *(→ d'intérêts)* community; *(→ de sentiments)* commonness

2 *(groupe)* community; *(de hippies)* commune; **la c. des fidèles** *(d'une paroisse)* the congregation; **c. financière** financial community; **c. internationale** international community; **c. linguistique** linguistic community; **c. religieuse** religious community; **la c. scientifique** the scientific community; *Psy* **c. thérapeutique** therapeutic community; **la c. universitaire** the academic community; **c. urbaine** = syndicate made up of a large town and surrounding "communes" responsible for the infrastructure of the area; **la C. (économique) européenne** the (European) Economic Community; **la C. des États indépendants** the Commonwealth of Independent States; **la C. européenne du charbon et de l'acier** the European Coal and Steel Community; **la C. européenne de l'énergie atomique** the European Atomic Energy Community; **les Communautés européennes** the European Community

3 *(public)* **la c.** the general public

4 *Jur* joint estate; **mariés sons le régime de la c.** married with a communal estate settlement; **c. des biens** community (of) property; **c. entre époux** community (of) property regime; **c. réduite aux acquêts** = marriage settlement whereby only goods acquired since the marriage are deemed to be held in common; **c. de vie** marital obligation to live together

❑ **en communauté** ADV *(vivre)* communally, as a community

commune² [kɔmyn] ADJ *voir* **commun**

NF **1** *(agglomération)* commune; **une jolie petite c. rurale** a nice little country village; **la c. et ses alentours** *(en ville)* the urban district; *(à la campagne)* the rural district

2 *(habitants)* **la c.** *(en ville)* people who live within the urban district; *(à la campagne)* people who live within the rural district

3 *(administrateurs)* **c'est la c. qui paie** the local authority *or Br* the council is paying

4 *Hist (ville autonome)* free town; **la C. (de Paris)** the (Paris) Commune

5 *(en Grande-Bretagne)* **les Communes** the House of Commons

6 *Belg* **c. à facilités**, *Offic* **c. de la frontière linguistique** = village or town where the local authorities are required to make provision for the linguistic needs of a section of the community speaking a minority language

---

Culture

COMMUNE

There are over 36,000 "communes" or administrative districts in France, some with fewer than 25 inhabitants. Each "commune" has an elected mayor and a town council.

Culture

LA COMMUNE

When the Prussian siege of Paris was lifted in 1871, a socialist uprising in the city, massively supported by the workers, resulted in the setting up of a revolutionary government, in defiance of the official regime. This government, which lasted from 18 March to 28 May 1871, was brutally put down by soldiers sent in by Thiers' pro-monarchist government in Versailles. The "Commune de Paris" is an important landmark in the history of European socialism.

communément [kɔmynemɑ̃] ADV commonly, usually; **il n'arrive pas c. que les femmes soient plus nombreuses** it is unusual for there to be more women; **la torture est encore c. pratiquée là-bas** torture is still routinely practised there; **la renoncule terrestre, c. appelée bouton d'or** ranunculus, commonly known as or usually called the buttercup

communiant, -e [kɔmynjɑ̃, -ɑ̃t] NM,F Rel communicant; **premier c., première communiante** first communicant

communicable [kɔmynikabl] ADJ 1 (exprimable) communicable; **c'est une impression difficilement c.** it's a feeling difficult to put into words 2 (transmissible → données, informations) communicable; **ces données ne sont pas communicables** this data is classified 3 Méd (maladie) communicable, contagious

communicant, -e [kɔmynikɑ̃, -ɑ̃t] ADJ communicating; **deux chambres communicantes** two Br connecting or Am adjoining rooms

communicateur, -trice [kɔmynikatœr, -tris] ADJ (fil etc) connecting
NM,F communicator

communicatif, -ive [kɔmynikatif, -iv] ADJ 1 (qui se répand → rire, bonne humeur) infectious 2 (bavard) communicative, talkative; **peu c.** not very communicative, quiet

communication [kɔmynikasjɔ̃] NF 1 (annonce) announcement, communication; **j'ai une c. importante à vous faire** I have an important announcement to make; **donner c. de qch** to communicate sth
2 (exposé → fait à la presse) statement; (→ fait à des universitaires, des scientifiques) paper; **les communications des intervenants seront publiées** all papers read at the conference will be published; **faire une c. sur l'atome** to deliver a lecture or give a paper on the atom
3 (transmission) communicating, passing on, transmission; **pour éviter la c. de ces maladies** to stop the spread of these diseases; **avoir c. d'un dossier** to get hold of a file, to have a file passed on to one; **je n'ai pas eu c. de sa nouvelle adresse** his/her new address hasn't been passed on to me; **demander c. d'un dossier** to ask for a file (to be handed on to one); **donner c. d'un dossier (à qn)** to pass on a file (to sb); **arrêt des communications à 16 heures** (dans une bibliothèque) no book deliveries after 4 pm; Jur **c. au ministère public** = court order submitting a case to the public prosecutor; Jur **c. du dossier** discovery of documents; **c. de pièces** production of documents; **donner c. de pièces** to produce documents
4 (contact) communication, contact; **être en c. avec qn** to be in contact or touch with sb; **vous devriez vous mettre en c. avec elle** you should get in touch with her; **mettre deux personnes en c.** to put two people in touch or in contact with each other; **cela rend désormais possible la c. entre gens malentendants** this has made it possible for the hard of hearing to communicate with each other; **depuis l'explosion, nous n'avons plus de c. avec l'extérieur** we haven't been able to communicate with the outside world since the blast
5 (échange entre personnes) communication; **il a des problèmes de c. (avec les autres)** he has problems communicating with or relating to people; **il n'y a pas de c. possible avec elle** it's impossible to relate to her
6 (diffusion d'informations) **les techniques de la c.** media techniques; **études de c.** media studies; **la c. de masse** the mass media; **c. commerciale** business correspondence; **c. interne** (dans une entreprise) interdepartmental communication
7 Mktg (dans la publicité) promotion; **c. événementielle** event promotion; **c. institutionnelle** corporate promotion; **c. sur le lieu de vente** point-of-sale promotion; **c. produit** product promotion
8 (moyen de liaison) (means of) communication; **toutes les communications entre les deux pays ont été interrompues** all communication between the two countries has been stopped
9 Tél **c. téléphonique** (phone) call; **je vous passe la c.** I'll put you through; **je prends la c.** I'll take the call; **vous avez la c.** you're through;

pour obtenir la c., faites le 12 dial 12 (in order) to get through; **mettez-moi en c. avec M. Martin** put me through to Mr Martin; **il est en c. avec...** he's speaking to..., he's on the phone to...; **la c. a été coupée** we were cut off; **la c. est mauvaise** the line is bad; **le prix de la c. a augmenté** the cost of a phone call has gone up; **c. internationale** international call; **c. interurbaine** inter-city or long-distance call; **c. locale** local call; **c. longue distance** long-distance call; **c. en PCV** Br reverse-charge call, Am collect call
10 Ordinat **c. de données** data communications, datacomms; **c. homme-machine** man-machine dialogue; **c. en ligne** on-line communication; **c. télématique** datacommunications, datacomms
▫ **de communication** ADJ 1 (porte, couloir) connecting
2 (réseau, satellite) communications (avant n); **moyens de c.** means of communication
3 (agence) publicity (avant n)

communicationnel, -elle [kɔmynikasjɔnɛl] ADJ communicational

communicative [kɔmynikativ] voir **communicatif**

communicatrice [kɔmynikatris] voir **communicateur**

communier [9] [kɔmynje] VI 1 Rel to communicate, to receive Communion 2 Littéraire (s'unir spirituellement) **c. dans un même idéal** to be united in or to share the same ideals; **c. avec qn** to share the same feelings as sb; **c. avec la nature** to be at one or to commune with nature

communion [kɔmynjɔ̃] NF 1 Rel communion; **c.** (partie de la messe) (Holy) Communion; **donner la c. à qn** to give Communion to sb; **recevoir la c.** to receive or take Communion; **première c.** First Communion; **c. solennelle** Solemn Communion; **C. des saints** communion of saints
2 Littéraire (accord) **nous nous sommes découvert une c. d'idées et de sentiments** we found that we shared the same ideas and feelings; **être en c. avec qn** to be at one or to commune with sb; **être en c. d'idées ou d'esprit avec qn** to share sb's ideas; **être en c. avec la nature** to commune with nature

communiqué [kɔmynike] NM communiqué; **un c. officiel** an official communiqué or announcement; **un c. de presse** a press release

communiquer [3] [kɔmynike] VT 1 (transmettre → information) to communicate, to give; (→ demande) to transmit; (→ dossier, message) to pass on; (→ savoir, savoir-faire) to pass on, to hand down; **c. le goût de la lecture à ses enfants** to pass on one's love of reading to one's children; **il s'est fait c. le dossier** he asked for the file to be passed on to him; **c. qch par écrit à qn** to communicate or convey sth in writing to sb
2 Phys (chaleur, lumière) to transmit; (mouvement, impulsion) to impart; **c. de l'énergie à un corps** to transmit energy to a body
3 (donner par contamination) to transmit; **il leur a communiqué son fou rire/enthousiasme** passed on his giggles/enthusiasm to them
4 (annoncer) to announce, to impart, to communicate; **j'ai une chose importante à vous c.** I have something important to say to you; **rien ne nous a été communiqué** we have heard nothing; **selon une nouvelle qu'on nous communique à l'instant** according to news just in
VI 1 (avoir des relations) to communicate; **c. par téléphone/lettre** to communicate by phone/letter; **les dauphins communiquent entre eux** dolphins communicate with each other; **leur problème est qu'ils n'arrivent pas à c. avec leurs parents** their problem is that they can't communicate with their parents; **dans une famille, il faut apprendre à c.** members of a family must learn to communicate with each other; **j'ai besoin de c.** I need to express my feelings (to others)
2 (être relié) to interconnect; **la chambre communique avec la salle de bains** there's a connecting door between the bathroom and the bedroom; **toutes les chambres communiquent** all the bedrooms are interconnecting; **une chambre avec salle de bains qui communique** a bedroom with en suite bathroom
▶ **se communiquer** VPR 1 (être transmis → don,

savoir, savoir-faire) to be passed on, to be handed down; **le vrai talent ne se communique pas** you can't teach people how to be talented
2 (se propager → incendie) to spread; (→ maladie) to spread, to be passed on; **se c. à** to spread to; **sa peur risque de se c. à tout son entourage** he's likely to make everyone else as frightened as he is

communisant, -e [kɔmynizɑ̃, -ɑ̃t] ADJ Communistic; **un journal c.** a paper with Communist sympathies
NM,F Communist sympathizer, fellow traveller

communisme [kɔmynism] NM Communism

communiste [kɔmynist] ADJ Communist
NMF Communist

Culture

LE PARTI COMMUNISTE
Founded in 1920 on Leninist principles, the French Communist party holds an important position in French political life. It played a key role in the Resistance movement of World War II, and later in the creation of the social security system. The party's popularity has declined since the early 1980s.

---

commutable [kɔmytabl] ADJ commutable

commutateur [kɔmytatœr] NM Élec & Électron (de circuits) changeover switch, commutator; (interrupteur) switch; **actionner un c.** (pour allumer) to switch on; (pour éteindre) to switch off; Ordinat **c. de données** data switch; **c. téléphonique** exchange

commutatif, -ive [kɔmytatif, -iv] ADJ 1 Math commutative 2 Ling commutable 3 Jur commutative

commutation [kɔmytasjɔ̃] NF 1 (substitution) commutation, substitution; Ling & Math commutation
2 Jur **c. de peine** commutation of a sentence 3 Élec & Électron commutation, switching; **une c. permet de passer automatiquement sur piles** it switches itself on to battery
4 Ordinat & Tél switch-over, switching; **c. de bande/circuits** tape/circuit switching; **c. de message/de paquets** message/packet switching; **c. temporelle asynchrone** asynchronous transfer mode

commutative [kɔmytativ] voir **commutatif**

commutativité [kɔmytativite] NF 1 Math commutativity 2 Ling commutability

commutatrice [kɔmytatris] NF rotary converter

commuté, -e [kɔmyte] ADJ (réseau) switched

commuter [3] [kɔmyte] VT 1 (gén) to substitute 2 Ling & Math to commute; **c. A et B** to commute A and or with B 3 Élec & Électron to commutate
VI 1 Math to commute 2 Ling to substitute, to commute

Comores [kɔmɔr] NFPL **les C.** the Comoro Islands, the Comoros; **aller aux C.** to go to the Comoro Islands; **vivre aux C.** to live in the Comoro Islands

comorien, -enne [kɔmɔrjɛ̃, -ɛn] ADJ Comoran, Comorian
▫ **Comorien, -enne** NM,F Comoran, Comorian

comourants [kɔmurɑ̃] NMPL Jur commorientes

compacité [kɔ̃pasite] NF compactness

compact, -e [kɔ̃pakt] ADJ 1 (dense → matière) solid, dense; (→ foule) dense, packed; (→ poudre) pressed, compacted 2 Fig (majorité) large, solid 3 Ski short 4 Aut, Phot & (disque) compact 5 Math compact
NM 1 Ski short ski 2 Vieilli (poudre) pressed powder 3 (disque) compact disc, CD; **disponible en c.** available on CD 4 (appareil photo) compact (camera)

compactage [kɔ̃paktaʒ] NM 1 (technique) compacting (UNCOUNT) 2 (résultat) compaction

Compact Disc® [kɔ̃paktdisk] (pl **Compact Discs**) NM compact disc, CD

compacter [3] [kɔ̃pakte] VT to compact; Ordinat (base de données) to pack

compacteur [kɔ̃paktœr] NM 1 (engin) road roller, steamroller 2 Ordinat **c. d'exécutables** execute file compressor; **c. de données** data compressor

compagne [kɔ̃paɲ] NF 1 (camarade) (female) companion; **c. de classe/jeux** (female) classmate/playmate; **mes compagnes de captivité**

my fellow captives; **elle a été ma c. d'infortune** she suffered with me, she was my companion in misery; *Littéraire* **l'envie, c. de l'ambition** envy, the attendant upon ambition **2** *(épouse)* wife; *(concubine)* partner **3** *(animal domestique)* companion; **sa chatte est une fidèle c.** her cat is a faithful companion

compagnie [kɔ̃paɲi] NF **1** *(présence)* company; **sa c. m'est insupportable** I can't stand him/her company *or* being with him/her; **elle avait un chien pour toute c.** her dog was her only companion; **être d'une c. agréable/sinistre** to be a pleasant/gloomy companion; **être de bonne/mauvaise c.** to be good/bad company; *Vieilli* **aller de c. avec qn** to accompany sb; **être en bonne/mauvaise c.** to be in good/bad company; **je te laisse en bonne c.** I leave you in good hands; **je l'ai trouvé en joyeuse/galante c.** I found him in cheerful company/in the company of a lady; **tenir c. à qn** to keep sb company; **il te faudrait de la c.** you need some company; **tu sais, je me passerais bien de c.!** I could do with being left alone, you know!; **il n'aime pas la c.** he doesn't enjoy company *or* being with people

2 *(groupe)* party, company, gang; **une joyeuse c.** a lively company *or* group *or* gang; **toute la c. était là** the whole gang was there

3 *Com & Ind* company; **c. aérienne** airline (company); **c. d'assurances** insurance company; **c. d'assurance captive** captive insurer; **c. maritime** shipping company *or* line; **c. pétrolière** oil company; **c. de transports** carrier; **Michel Darot et c.** Michel Darot and Company; *Fam Fig* **tout ça, c'est mensonge/arnaque et c.** that's nothing but a pack of lies/a swindle

4 *Théât* **c. (théâtrale)** (theatre) group *or* company *or* troupe

5 *Zool (de sangliers)* herd, sounder; *(de perdreaux)* covey, flock

6 *Mil* company; **c. de chars** tank brigade; **c. de discipline** = company consisting of convicted soldiers; **c. d'éclairage et d'appui** lighting and support company

7 *(dans des noms d'organisations)* **C. des agents de change** Institute of stockbrokers; **C. de Jésus** Society of Jesus; **Compagnies républicaines de sécurité** state security police, *Br* ≃ riot police, *Am* ≃ state troopers

❑ **de compagnie** ADJ *(animal)* domestic ADV *(voyager)* together

❑ **en compagnie de** PRÉP accompanied by, (in company) with

compagnon [kɔ̃paɲɔ̃] NM **1** *(camarade)* companion; **c. d'armes** brother *or* comrade in arms; **c. de bord** shipmate; **c. de captivité** companion in captivity; **c. de cellule** cellmate; **c. d'exil** fellow exile; **c. d'infortune** companion in misfortune; **c. de jeux** playmate; **c. de route** *ou* **voyage** travelling companion; *Pol* **c. de route** fellow traveller; **c. de table** table companion

2 *(époux)* husband, companion; *(ami, concubin)* partner

3 *(animal)* friend; **il a un chien pour tout c.** his only friend is a dog

4 *(franc-maçon)* Fellow of The Craft

5 *(artisan)* journeyman; *(membre d'un compagnonnage)* member of a trade guild; **C. du Tour de France** journeyman *(who has completed his apprenticeship and rounds off his training with different employers in various parts of France)*

6 *Hist* **C. de la Libération** (French) Resistance fighter

7 *Ind* = workman who has finished his initial apprenticeship and is learning further skills from his employer

8 *Bot* **c. rouge/blanc** red/white campion

compagnonnage [kɔ̃paɲɔnaʒ] NM *Hist* **1** *(chez un maître)* ≃ apprenticeship **2** *(association)* guild

compagnonnique [kɔ̃paɲɔnik] ADJ guild *(avant n)*

comparabilité [kɔ̃parabilite] NF comparability

comparable [kɔ̃parabl] ADJ comparable, similar; **on aboutit à des résultats comparables** we arrive at similar results; **comparons ce qui est c.** let's compare like with like; **ce n'est pas c.** there's no comparison; **je n'ai jamais rien goûté de c.** I've never tasted anything like it; **une fonction c. à celle de comptable** a function

comparable with *or* similar to that of an accountant

comparais *etc voir* **comparaître**

comparaison [kɔ̃parɛzɔ̃] NF **1** *(gén)* comparison; **faire la** *ou* **une c. entre deux qualités** to compare two qualities; **il n'y a pas de c. possible** there's no possible comparison; **c'est sans c. avec le mien** it cannot possibly be compared with mine; **elle est, sans c., la plus grande chanteuse du moment** she's by far our best contemporary singer; **aucune c.!** there's no comparison!; **point de c.** point of comparison; **comment décider sans avoir un point de c.?** how can you possibly make up your mind without some means of comparison?; **supporter** *ou* **soutenir la c. avec qch** to bear *or* to stand comparison with sth; *Prov* **c. n'est pas raison** comparisons are odious; *Mktg* **c. par paire** paired comparison

2 *(figure de style)* comparison, simile; **adverbe de c.** comparative adverb

❑ **en comparaison de, en comparaison avec** PRÉP in comparison *or* as compared with, compared to

❑ **par comparaison avec, par comparaison à** PRÉP compared with *ou* to

comparaître [91] [kɔ̃parɛtr] VI *Jur* to appear; **c. en justice** to appear before a court; **c. en personne** to appear in person; **c. par avoué** to be represented by counsel; **appelé** *ou* **cité à c.** summoned to appear; **faire c. qn devant un tribunal** to bring sb before a court

comparant, -e [kɔ̃parɑ̃, -ɑ̃t] *Jur* ADJ appearing before the court

NM,F = person appearing before the court

comparateur [kɔ̃paratœr] NM comparator

comparatif, -ive [kɔ̃paratif, -iv] ADJ comparative; **étude comparative** comparative study

NM comparative; **c. de supériorité/d'infériorité** comparative of greater/lesser degree; **adjectif au c.** comparative adjective

comparatisme [kɔ̃paratism] NM **1** *Ling* comparative linguistics **2** *Littérature* comparative literature

comparatiste [kɔ̃paratist] NMF **1** *Ling* specialist in comparative linguistics **2** *Littérature* specialist in comparative literature

comparative [kɔ̃parativ] *voir* **comparatif**

comparativement [kɔ̃parativmɑ̃] ADV comparatively, by *or* in comparison; **c. à** compared with *or* to

comparé, -e [kɔ̃pare] ADJ *(littérature, anatomie, grammaire)* comparative

comparer [3] [kɔ̃pare] VT **1** *(confronter)* to compare; **c. deux tableaux** to compare two pictures; **c. un livre à** *ou* **avec un autre** to compare a book to *or* with another; **comparez (les prix) avant d'acheter** compare prices before you buy; **il faut c. ce qui est comparable** you must compare like with like

2 *(assimiler)* **c. qn/qch à** to compare sb/sth to; **il compare les étoiles filantes à des cheveux** he compares *or* likens shooting stars to strands of hair; **comme artiste, il ne peut être comparé à Braque** as an artist, he cannot compare with Braque; **je le compare toujours à Groucho Marx** he always reminds me of Groucho Marx

▶ **se comparer** VPR **1** *(emploi passif)* **ce sont deux choses qui ne se comparent pas** there can be no comparison between these two things

2 *(soi-même)* **se c. à** to compare oneself with

❑ **comparé à** PRÉP compared to *or* with, in comparison to *or* with

comparse [kɔ̃pars] NMF **1** *Théât* extra, walk-on; **un rôle de c.** a walk-on part **2** *Péj (d'un brigand, d'un camelot)* stooge

compartiment [kɔ̃partimɑ̃] NM **1** *Rail* compartment; **c. de première classe** first-class compartment **2** *(case → d'une boîte)* compartment; *(→ d'un sac)* pocket; **c. à bagages** *(d'autocar)* luggage compartment; **c. à glace** freezer compartment **3** *(carreau)* square **4** *Naut* tank **5** *Ordinat* **c. protégé** hold area

❑ **à compartiments** ADJ *(tiroir, classeur)* divided into compartments

compartimentage [kɔ̃partimɑ̃taʒ] NM *(d'une caisse, d'une armoire)* partitioning; *(d'une administration, des connaissances)* compartmentalization, fragmenting

compartimentation [kɔ̃partimɑ̃tasjɔ̃] NF = **compartimentage**

compartimenter [3] [kɔ̃partimɑ̃te] VT *(caisse, armoire)* to partition, to divide into compartments; *(administration, connaissances)* to compartmentalize, to split into small units

comparu, -e [kɔ̃pary] PP *voir* **comparaître**

comparution [kɔ̃parysjɔ̃] NF *Jur* appearance; **c. immédiate** immediate hearing; **c. en conseil de discipline** appearance before a disciplinary committee; **c. en justice** court appearance; **c. personnelle** personal appearance; **c. volontaire** voluntary appearance

compas [kɔ̃pa] NM **1** *Aviat & Naut* compass; **c. gyroscopique** gyrocompass; **c. de route** steering compass **2** *Géom* (pair of) compasses; **c. d'épaisseur** spring-adjusting callipers; **c. à pointes sèches** dividers; **c. quart de cercle** wing compasses; **c. de réduction** proportional compasses; **avoir le c. dans l'œil** to be a good judge of distances/measurements/*etc*; **le placard tient juste, tu as eu le c. dans l'œil!** the cupboard just fits, you judged that well!

❑ **au compas** ADV **1** *Naut* by the compass **2** *(avec précision)* with military precision

compassé, -e [kɔ̃pase] ADJ stiff, strait-laced

compasser [3] [kɔ̃pase] VT **1** *(distances sur la carte etc)* to measure with compasses; *Naut (carte)* to prick **2** *Littéraire (ses actes etc)* to control, to regulate

compassion [kɔ̃pasjɔ̃] NF compassion, sympathy; **avec c.** compassionately

compassionnel, -elle [kɔ̃pasjɔnɛl] ADJ **1** *(donné par compassion)* compassionate **2** *(suscitant la compassion)* that arouses sympathy *or* compassion

compatibilité [kɔ̃patibilite] NF *(gén)* & *Ordinat* compatibility; **c. sanguine** blood-group compatibility *or* matching

compatible [kɔ̃patibl] ADJ compatible; **leurs modes de vie ne sont pas compatibles** their lifestyles are totally incompatible; **cela n'est pas c. avec mon emploi du temps** this won't fit into my schedule; *Ordinat* **ces deux applications ne sont pas compatibles** these two applications are incompatible *or* not compatible; *Ordinat* **c. vers le haut/vers le bas** upward/downward compatible; *Ordinat* **c. avec les versions antérieures** backward compatible; *Ordinat* **c. IBM** IBM-compatible; *Ordinat* **c. Mac** Mac-compatible

NM *Ordinat* compatible

compatir [32] [kɔ̃patir]

❑ **compatir à** VT IND **je compatis à votre douleur** I sympathize with you in your grief, I share in your grief

USAGE ABSOLU **je compatis!** I sympathize!; *Ironique* my heart bleeds!

compatissant, -e [kɔ̃patisɑ̃, -ɑ̃t] ADJ sympathetic, compassionate

compatriote [kɔ̃patrijɔt] NMF compatriot, fellow countryman, *f* countrywoman

compendieuse [kɔ̃pɑ̃djøz] *voir* **compendieux**

compendieusement [kɔ̃pɑ̃djøzmɑ̃] ADV *Vieilli* compendiously, concisely

compendieux, -euse [kɔ̃pɑ̃djø, -øz] ADJ *Vieilli* compendious, concise

compendium [kɔ̃pɛ̃djɔm] NM compendium

compensable [kɔ̃pɑ̃sabl] ADJ **1** *(perte)* that can be compensated, *Am* compensable **2** *(chèque)* clearable; **être c. à Paris** to be cleared at Paris, to be domiciled in Paris

compensateur, -trice [kɔ̃pɑ̃satœr, -tris] ADJ **1** *(indemnité)* compensating, compensatory **2** *(pendule)* compensation *(avant n)*

NM **1** *(appareil)* compensator; *Électron* equalizer; *Aut* **c. de frein** brake compensator **2** *Aviat* (trim) tab

compensation [kɔ̃pɑ̃sasjɔ̃] NF **1** *(dédommagement)* compensation; **je travaille dur mais il y a des compensations** I work hard but there are compensations **2** *Fin (de dette)* offsetting; *(de chèque)* clearing **3** *Jur* **c. des dépens** sharing of the costs *(among different parties)* **4** *Méd & Psy* compensation; **elle mange par c.** she eats for comfort, she comfort eats **5** *Naut* correction, adjustment **6** *Aviat* tabbing **7** *Tech & Phys* balancing; *(de son)* equalization

com–com

❑ **en compensation** ADV as a *or* by way of (a) compensation
❑ **en compensation de** PRÉP by way of compensation *or* as compensation *or* to compensate for
compensatoire [kɔ̃pɑ̃satwar] ADJ **1** *(qui équilibre)* compensatory, compensating **2** *Fin* compensatory
compensatrice [kɔ̃pɑ̃satris] *voir* **compensateur**
compensé, -e [kɔ̃pɑ̃se] ADJ **1** *Méd* compensated **2** *(semelle)* **chaussures à semelles compensées** platform shoes **3** *Com* **publicité compensée** prestige advertising
compenser [3] [kɔ̃pɑ̃se] VT **1** *(perte, défaut)* to make up for, to compensate for; **rien ne compense la perte d'un ami** nothing makes up for the loss of a friend; **son efficacité compense son mauvais caractère** his/her efficiency compensates for *or* makes up for his/her bad temper
2 *Jur* **c. les dépens** to order each party to pay its own costs
3 *Méd* to compensate, to counterbalance; *Psy* to compensate
4 *Tech & Phys* to balance
5 *Naut* to adjust, to correct
6 *Fin (dette, pertes financières)* to offset; *(chèque)* to clear
USAGE ABSOLU **1** *(racheter)* **pour c., je l'ai emmenée au théâtre** to make up for it, I took her to the theatre; **au moins, le dîner était bon, cela compense** at least the meal was good, that makes up for it
2 *Psy* **elle mange pour c.** she eats for comfort, she comfort eats
►**se compenser** VPR to make up for one another
compérage [kɔ̃peraʒ] NM *Littéraire* **1** *(lien spirituel)* compaternity, = spiritual relationship between godparents and godchild or his/her parents **2** *(entente)* = conspiracy between instigators of a swindle
compère [kɔ̃pɛr] NM **1** *(complice → d'un camelot)* accomplice; *(→ d'un artiste)* stooge **2** *Fam Vieilli (camarade)* comrade, crony; **un bon c.** a pleasant companion **3** *Littérature* **mon c. le lapin** Mister Rabbit
compère-loriot [kɔ̃pɛrlɔrjo] *(pl* **compères-loriots)** NM **1** *Orn* golden oriole **2** *Méd (sur la paupière)* sty, stye
compète [kɔ̃pɛt] NF *Fam* competition■ ; **faire de la c.** to enter competitions
compétence [kɔ̃petɑ̃s] NF **1** *(qualification, capacité)* competence; **faire qch avec beaucoup de c.** to do sth very competently; **j'ai des compétences en informatique** I am computer literate; **ses compétences en traduction** his/her skills as a translator; **avoir recours aux compétences d'un expert** to refer to an expert; **cela n'entre pas dans mes compétences, ce n'est pas de ma c.** *(cela n'est pas dans mes attributions)* this doesn't come within my remit; *(cela me dépasse)* that's beyond my competence; **compétences techniques** technical skills; **compétences transférables** transferable skills
2 *Jur* jurisdiction; **c. d'attribution** subject matter jurisdiction *(in civil law)*; **c. civile** civil jurisdiction; **c. commerciale** commercial jurisdiction; **c. discrétionnaire** discretionary powers; **c. de droit commun** ordinary jurisdiction; **c. exclusive** exclusive jurisdiction; **c. générale** omnicompetence; **c. internationale** international jurisdiction; **c. matérielle** subject matter jurisdiction *(in criminal law)*; **c. nationale** national jurisdiction; **c. personnelle** = jurisdiction based on the identity of the defendant; **c. subsidiaire** ancillary jurisdiction; **c. territoriale** jurisdiction
3 *Ling & Méd* competence
4 *(personne)* top expert
compétent, -e [kɔ̃petɑ̃, -ɑ̃t] ADJ **1** *(qualifié)* competent, skilful, skilled; *Jur* who has jurisdiction; **en cuisine, je suis assez compétente** I'm quite a good cook; **un ouvrier c.** a competent worker; **les gens compétents en la matière** *(qui savent)* people who know about *or Sout* are conversant with this topic; **seul le maire est c. en la matière** *(habilité)* only the mayor is competent to act *or* has jurisdiction in this matter **2** *(approprié → service)* relevant; **les services compétents** the relevant departments, the departments concerned
compétiteur, -trice [kɔ̃petitœr, -tris] NM,F **1** *(rival)* rival **2** *Com & Sport* competitor
compétitif, -ive [kɔ̃petitif, -iv] ADJ competitive; **leurs produits sont très compétitifs** their products are highly competitive *or* very competitively priced; **des prix très compétitifs** very good *or* competitive prices; **leurs chaînes hi-fi sont à des prix compétitifs** their hi-fi equipment is competitively priced
compétition [kɔ̃petisjɔ̃] NF **1** *(rivalité)* competition, competing; **j'ai horreur de la c.** I hate having to compete (with others)
2 *(niveau d'activité sportive)* competition; **faire de la c.** *(athlétisme)* to take part in competitive events; *Aut & Naut* to race; **j'arrête la c.** I'm giving up competing
3 *(comme adj inv)* **elle a le niveau c. en aviron** she's a top-level oarswoman; *Ski* **le cours c.** the advanced (ski) class
4 *(concours → en athlétisme, en natation)* competition, event; *(→ au tennis)* tournament; *Aut & Naut* competition, race; **c. sportive** sports competition, sporting event
❑ **de compétition** ADJ **des skis de c.** *(de descente)* racing skis; *(de fond)* eventing skis; **sport de c.** competitive sport
❑ **en compétition** ADJ competing, in competition
❑ **en compétition avec** PRÉP competing *or* in competition with
compétitive [kɔ̃petitiv] *voir* **compétitif**
compétitivité [kɔ̃petitivite] NF competitiveness
compétitrice [kɔ̃petitris] *voir* **compétiteur**
compil [kɔ̃pil] NF *Fam* compilation album■
compilateur, -trice [kɔ̃pilatœr, -tris] NM,F **1** *(auteur)* compiler **2** *Péj (plagiaire)* plagiarist
NM *Ordinat* compiler; **c. croisé** cross-compiler
compilation [kɔ̃pilasjɔ̃] NF **1** *(fait de réunir des textes)* compiling; *(ensemble de textes, de morceaux de musique)* compilation **2** *Péj (plagiat)* plagiarizing, synthesizing; *(ouvrage)* (mere) compilation *or* synthesis **3** *Ordinat* compilation
compilatrice [kɔ̃pilatris] *voir* **compilateur**
compiler [3] [kɔ̃pile] VT **1** *(réunir)* to compile **2** *Péj (sujet: plagiaire)* to borrow from **3** *Ordinat* to compile
compisser [3] [kɔ̃pise] VT *Vieilli ou Hum* to urinate on
complainte [kɔ̃plɛ̃t] NF **1** *Mus, Littérature & Littéraire* lament, plaint **2** *Jur* complaint
complaire [110] [kɔ̃plɛr] **complaire à** VT IND *Littéraire* to please
►**se complaire** VPR **1 se c. dans qch** to revel *or* to delight *or* to take pleasure in sth; **il se complaît dans son malheur** he wallows in his own misery **2 se c. à dire/faire qch** to take great pleasure in saying/doing sth
complaisamment [kɔ̃plɛzamɑ̃] ADV **1** *(avec amabilité)* kindly, obligingly **2** *Péj (avec vanité)* smugly, complacently, with self-satisfaction
complaisance [kɔ̃plɛzɑ̃s] NF **1** *(amabilité)* kindness, obligingness; **auriez-vous la c. de le faire?** would you be so good *or* so kind as to do it?, would you oblige me by doing it?; **avec c.** kindly, obligingly
2 *(vanité)* complacency, smugness, self-satisfaction; **avec c.** smugly, complacently; **il s'écoute avec c.** he likes the sound of his own voice; **un ton plein de c.** a self-satisfied *or* smug tone
3 *(indulgence → des parents)* laxity, indulgence; *(→ d'un tribunal, d'un juge)* leniency, indulgence; *(→ d'un mari)* connivance
❑ **complaisances** NFPL favours
❑ **de complaisance** ADJ **sourire de c.** polite smile; **certificat** *ou* **attestation de c.** phoney certificate *(given to please the person concerned)*; *Com* **billet de c.** accommodation bill
❑ **par complaisance** ADV out of kindness
complaisant, -e [kɔ̃plɛzɑ̃, -ɑ̃t] ADJ **1** *(aimable)* kind; *(serviable)* obliging, complaisant **2** *(vaniteux)* smug, self-satisfied, complacent; **prêter une oreille complaisante aux éloges** to lap up praise **3** *(indulgent → parents)* lax, indulgent; *(→ juge, tribunal)* indulgent, lenient; **elle a un mari c.** her husband turns a blind eye to her infidelities
complaisons *etc voir* **complaire**
complanter [3] [kɔ̃plɑ̃te] VT to plant with trees
complément [kɔ̃plemɑ̃] NM **1** *(supplément)* **un c. d'information est nécessaire** further *or* additional information is required; **demander un c. d'enquête** to order a more extensive inquiry
2 *(reste)* rest, remainder; **voici 70 euros, vous aurez le c. ce soir** here's 70 euros, you'll get the remainder tonight; **si on manque de crème brûlée, on fera le c. avec des yaourts** if we don't have enough crème brûlée to go round, we'll give the rest of them yoghurts
3 *Méd* complement; **fixation** *ou* **déviation du c.** complement fixation; **c. inactivé** complementoid
4 *Math* complement
5 *Gram* complement; **c. (d'objet) direct/indirect** direct/indirect object; **c. d'agent** agent; **c. de comparaison** comparative expansion; **c. circonstanciel** adverbial phrase; **c. circonstanciel de temps** adverbial phrase of time
6 *Admin* **c. familial** means-tested family allowance *(for parents with three children above the age of three)*; **c. (de) retraite** supplementary pension
complémentaire [kɔ̃plemɑ̃tɛr] ADJ **1** *(supplémentaire → information)* additional, further **2** *(industries, couleurs)* complementary **3** *Ling & Math* complementary **4** *Écon* complementary **5** *Scol* **cours c.** ≃ secondary modern school **6** *Compta (écriture)* supplementary
NM *Math* complementary
complémentarité [kɔ̃plemɑ̃tarite] NF **1** *(fait de se compléter)* complementarity; **la c. du jaune et du violet** the complementary qualities of yellow and purple **2** *Écon* complementarity
complémentation [kɔ̃plemɑ̃tasjɔ̃] NF *Math* complementation

COMPLET, -ÈTE [kɔ̃plɛ, -ɛt]

ADJ complete **1, 5, 6, 9** ■ full **1–4** ■ thorough **2** ■ total **6** ■ wholemeal **8**
NM suit

ADJ **1** *(qui a tous ses éléments → série, collection, parure)* complete, full; *(→ œuvre)* complete; **la panoplie n'est pas complète** there's something missing from the set; *Com* **café/thé c.** continental breakfast with coffee/tea; **change c.** disposable *Br* nappy *orAm* diaper
2 *(approfondi → compte-rendu, description)* full, comprehensive; *(→ analyse, examen)* thorough, full; **une lecture complète du manuscrit** a thorough *or* an in-depth reading of the manuscript
3 *(entier)* full; **nous resterons un mois c.** we'll stay a full month; **le ticket est valable pour la journée complète** the ticket is valid for the whole day
4 *(bondé → bus, métro, stade)* full; **c.** *(sur panneau) (→ hôtel)* no vacancies; *(→ parking)* full; **nous sommes complets** *(salle de concert, théâtre, restaurant)* we're (fully) booked
5 *(parfait → homme, artiste)* all-round *(avant n)*, complete; **un sportif c.** an all-round athlete
6 *(total, absolu → silence)* total, absolute; *(→ repos)* complete; *(→ échec)* total; **ils vivent dans la pauvreté la plus complète** they live in utter *or* absolute *or* abject poverty; **un fiasco c.** a complete (and utter) disaster; **un abruti c.** a complete *or* total *or* absolute moron; **c'est c.!** that's all we needed!, that's the last straw!, that caps it all!
7 *(fournissant tout le nécessaire)* **la natation est un sport c.** swimming is an all-round sport; **le lait est un aliment c.** milk is a complete food, milk contains all the necessary nutrients
8 *Culin (pain, farine, spaghettis)* wholemeal; *(riz)* brown
9 *Bot* complete
NM *(vêtement)* (man's) suit
❑ **au (grand) complet** ADJ **(toute) l'équipe au c.** the whole team; **mes amis étaient là au c.** all my friends showed up; **j'attends que l'assistance soit au c. pour commencer** I'm waiting for everyone to arrive before I begin; **tous les documents au c.** the complete set of documents; **les couverts ne sont pas au c.** there are some knives and forks missing

complètement [kɔ̃plɛtmɑ̃] ADV 1 *(totalement)* completely, totally; **une maison c. refaite** a completely renovated house; **c'est c. faux** it's totally *or* completely wrong; **c. nu** stark naked; **il n'est pas c. responsable** he's not wholly to blame; **sa thèse est c. terminée** her thesis is completely finished; **le jeu les a c. ruinés** gambling left them totally penniless

2 *(vraiment)* absolutely; **elle est c. folle** she's stark raving mad; **je suis c. d'accord** I absolutely *or* totally agree; **il est c. fou d'elle** he's absolutely mad about her

compléter [18] [kɔ̃plete] VT 1 *(ajouter ce qui manque à → collection, dossier)* to complete; *(→ somme, remboursement)* to make up; **il a complété sa collection par un Van Gogh** he completed his collection with a painting by Van Gogh; **c. une gamme de produits** to add to a range of products

2 *(approfondir → analyse, notes, formation)* to complete; *(→ enquête)* to finish, to complete **3** *(constituer le dernier élément de)* to complete, to finish *or* to round off; **un index complète le guide** the guide is completed by an index; **pour c. le tout** to cap *or* to crown it all

4 *(remplir → formulaire)* to complete, to fill in *or* out

▶**se compléter** VPR 1 *(emploi passif)* **ma collection se complète peu à peu** my collection will soon be complete

2 *(personnes, caractères)* to complement (one another); **le vin et le fromage se complètent parfaitement** wine complements cheese perfectly

complétif, -ive [kɔ̃pletif, -iv] ADJ **proposition complétive** noun clause
□ **complétive** NF noun clause

complétion [kɔ̃plesjɔ̃] NF completion

complétive *voir* **complétif**

complétude [kɔ̃pletyd] NF *(fait d'être complet)* completeness

complet-veston [kɔ̃plevɛstɔ̃] *(pl* **complets-vestons)** NM (man's) suit

complexe [kɔ̃plɛks] ADJ 1 *(compliqué → processus, trajet)* complicated; *(→ caractère, personne)* complex, complicated; **pour des raisons complexes** for complex reasons

2 *Ling & Math* complex

NM 1 *(gêne)* hang-up; *Psy* complex; **avoir des complexes** to have a lot of hang-ups; **ça me donne des complexes** it's giving me a complex; **c. d'infériorité/de supériorité/d'Œdipe** inferiority/superiority/Oedipus complex

2 *Constr & Écon* complex; **c. hospitalier/industriel** medical/industrial complex; **un grand c. hôtelier** a large hotel complex; *Cin* **c. multisalles** multiplex (*Br* cinema *or Am* movie theater), multiscreen *Br* cinema *or Am* movie theater; **un c. sportif** a sports centre *or* complex; **un c. touristique** a *Br* holiday *or Am* vacation resort

3 *Chim & Math* complex
□ **sans complexe(s)** ADJ 1 *(simple)* natural 2 *Péj (sans honte)* uninhibited; **elle est sans c., celle-là!** she's so brazen! ADV 1 *(sans manières)* quite naturally *or* simply, uninhibitedly **2** *Péj (avec sans-gêne)* uninhibitedly; **elle s'est ruée sur le buffet sans c.** she went straight for the buffet quite unashamedly

complexé, -e [kɔ̃plɛkse] ADJ hung up; **il est très c.** he's got a lot of hang-ups; **elle est complexée par son poids** she has a complex about her weight

NM,F **c'est un c.** he has a lot of hang-ups

complexer [4] [kɔ̃plɛkse] VT 1 *(personne)* **arrête, tu vas le c.** stop, you'll give him a complex **2** *Chim* to unite into a complex

complexification [kɔ̃plɛksifikasjɔ̃] NF increasing complexity

complexifier [9] [kɔ̃plɛksifje] VT to complicate, to make more complex

▶**se complexifier** VPR to become more complex

complexion [kɔ̃plɛksjɔ̃] NF 1 *Littéraire (constitution)* constitution; **être de c. robuste/délicate** to have a healthy/delicate constitution **2** *Vieilli (caractère)* temperament, disposition **3** *Vieilli (teint)* complexion

complexité [kɔ̃plɛksite] NF complexity

complication [kɔ̃plikasjɔ̃] NF 1 *(problème)* complication; **oui mais attendez, il y a une c.** yes but wait, it's more complicated than you think; **elle aime les complications** she likes things to be complicated; **tu cherches des complications là où il n'y en a pas** you're reading more into it than there is; **pourquoi faire des complications?** why make things more complicated than they need be? **2** *(complexité)* complicatedness, complexity
□ **complications** NFPL *Méd* complications; **s'il n'y a pas de complications, il s'en sortira** if no complications set in *or* arise, he'll pull through

complice [kɔ̃plis] ADJ *(regard, sourire, silence)* knowing; **être c. de qch** to be (a) party to sth

NMF 1 *(malfrat)* accomplice; **c'est un de leurs complices** he's in league with them **2** *(ami, confident)* partner, friend; **sa femme et c. de tous les instants** his wife and constant companion **3** *(dans un spectacle, un canular)* partner **4** *Jur* **c. de l'adultère** *(dans un procès de divorce)* co-respondent

complicité [kɔ̃plisite] NF 1 *Jur* complicity; **il a été accusé de c. de meurtre** he was accused of being an accessory to murder; **avec la c. de qn** with the complicity of sb, with sb as an accomplice **2** *(entente, amitié)* complicity; **elle lui adressa un sourire de c.** she smiled at him knowingly, she gave him a knowing smile; **on sent une grande c. entre eux** there is clearly a deep bond between them; **nous avons retrouvé ce très vieux film avec la c. du réalisateur** we've unearthed this very old footage, with the kind help of the director
□ **en complicité avec** PRÉP in collusion with

complies [kɔ̃pli] NFPL complin, compline

compliment [kɔ̃plimɑ̃] NM 1 *(éloge)* compliment; **faire un c. à qn** to pay sb a compliment, to pay a compliment to sb; **on m'a fait des compliments sur mon soufflé** I was complimented on my soufflé; *Vieilli* **on lui a fait c. de sa jolie robe** she was complimented on her pretty dress

2 *(félicitations)* congratulations; **adresser des compliments au vainqueur** to congratulate the winner; *Ironique* **(je vous fais) mes compliments!** congratulations!, well done!

3 *(dans des formules de politesse)* compliment; **mes compliments à votre épouse** my regards to your wife; **avec les compliments de l'auteur** with the author's compliments; *aussi Hum* **(mes) compliments au chef!** my compliments to the chef!

4 *(discours)* congratulatory speech

complimenter [3] [kɔ̃plimɑ̃te] VT 1 *(féliciter)* to congratulate; **c. qn sur son succès** to congratulate sb on *or* for having succeeded **2** *(faire des éloges à)* to compliment; **Julie m'a complimentée sur** *ou* **pour ma robe** Julie complimented me on my dress; **c. qn pour son courage** to congratulate sb on his/her courage

complimenteur, -euse [kɔ̃plimɑ̃tœr, -øz] *Littéraire* ADJ obsequious
NM,F flatterer

compliqué, -e [kɔ̃plike] ADJ 1 *(difficile à comprendre → affaire, exercice, phrase)* complicated; *(→ jeu, langue, livre, problème)* difficult; *(→ plan)* intricate; **elle avait un nom c.** she had a real tongue-twister of a name; **c'est trop c. à expliquer** it's too hard to explain; **c'est d'un c.!** it's so complicated!; **regarde, ce n'est pourtant pas c.!** look, it's not so difficult to understand!; *Fam* **ce n'est pas c., si tu ne viens pas je n'y vais pas non plus** it's quite simple, if you don't come I'm not going either

2 *(ayant de nombreux éléments → appareil, mécanisme)* complicated, complex, intricate

3 *(qui manque de naturel → personne)* complicated; *(→ esprit)* tortuous; **que les rapports entre les gens sont compliqués!** relationships (between people) are complicated!

4 *Méd* **fracture compliquée** compound fracture
NM,F *Fam* **ta sœur, c'est une compliquée!** your sister certainly likes to make life difficult for herself!

compliquer [3] [kɔ̃plike] VT to complicate, to make (more) difficult *or* complicated; **la pluie a compliqué la tâche des sauveteurs** the rain made things harder for the rescuers; **ça risque**

de c. les choses that may *or* might well complicate matters; **il me complique la vie** he makes things *or* life difficult for me

▶**se compliquer** VPR 1 *(devenir embrouillé → gén)* to become (more) complicated; *(→ intrigue d'une pièce, d'un film)* to thicken; **ça se complique!** things are getting complicated!, *Hum* the plot thickens!; **la situation se complique** the situation is becoming more and more involved

2 *Méd* to be followed by complications; **un rhume mal soigné peut se c.** a cold left untreated can lead to complications

3 **se c. la vie** *ou* **l'existence** make life difficult for oneself; **ne te complique donc pas la vie!** don't make life difficult for yourself!

complot [kɔ̃plo] NM 1 *Pol* plot; *Hist* **le c. des poudres** the Gunpowder Plot **2** *(menées)* plot, scheme; **mettre qn dans le c.** to let sb in on the plot

comploter [3] [kɔ̃plote] VT to plot; **qu'est-ce que vous complotez tous les deux?** what are you two plotting?, what are you two up to?

VI to be part of a plot; **punis pour avoir comploté** punished for their part in the plot; **c. de faire qch** to conspire to do sth; **c. de tuer qn** to conspire to kill sb, to plot sb's murder

comploteur, -euse [kɔ̃plotœr, -øz] NM,F plotter

complu, -e [kɔ̃ply] PP *voir* **complaire**

compluvium [kɔ̃plyvjɔm] NM *Antiq* compluvium

compo [kɔ̃po] NF 1 *Fam Scol (abrév* **composition)** *(dissertation)* essay ■ ; *(examen)* test ■ ; *(plus important)* exam ■ **2** *Typ (abrév* **composition)** typesetting department; **partir en c.** to go to be typeset

componction [kɔ̃pɔ̃ksjɔ̃] NF 1 *(gravité affectée)* gravity, solemnity; **avec c.** with solemnity **2** *Rel* compunction, contrition

componé, -e, componné, -e [kɔ̃pone] ADJ *Hér* compony, componé; **bordure componée** compony bordure; **pièces componées** compony ordinary

comporte [kɔ̃pɔrt] NF *(en Provence)* wooden vat *(used to transport grapes at harvest time)*

comportement [kɔ̃pɔrtmɑ̃] NM 1 *(attitude)* behaviour; **elle a un c. très bizarre avec les enfants** her behaviour towards children is very strange, she behaves very strangely towards children

2 *Aut & Phys (d'un véhicule)* performance, behaviour; *(de pneus)* performance; *(d'une molécule)* behaviour; *Aut* **c. en courbe** *ou* **en virage** cornering (ability)

3 *Psy* behaviour; **c. passif-agressif** passive aggression, passive aggressivity

4 *Mktg* **c. d'achat** buying *or* purchasing behaviour; **c. d'achat habituel** habitual buying *or* purchasing behaviour; **c. de l'acheteur** buyer *or* purchaser behaviour; **c. du consommateur** consumer behaviour; **c. post-achat** post-purchase behaviour

5 *Bourse & Fin (du marché, des cours, des actions)* performance

comportemental, -e, -aux, -ales [kɔ̃pɔrtəmɑ̃tal, -o] ADJ 1 *(relatif à la façon d'être)* behaviour *(avant n)* **2** *Psy* behaviourist

comportementalisme [kɔ̃pɔrtəmɑ̃talism] NM behaviourism

comporter [3] [kɔ̃pɔrte] VT 1 *(être muni de)* to have, to include; **l'immeuble ne comporte pas d'escalier de secours** the building doesn't have a fire escape

2 *(être constitué de)* to be made up *or* to consist of; **la maison comporte trois étages** it's a three-storey house

3 *(contenir)* to contain; **le reportage comporte des interviews inédites** the report contains original interviews

4 *(entraîner)* to entail, to imply; **c'est un voyage qui comporte des risques** it's a risky trip; **tout métier comporte des inconvénients** every profession has its disadvantages; **elle a choisi l'aventure, avec tout ce que cela comporte de dangers** she chose to lead a life of adventure with all the risks it entailed

5 *(permettre, admettre)* to allow, to admit; **la règle comporte quelques exceptions** there are one or two exceptions to this rule

▶**se comporter** VPR 1 *(réagir → personne)* to act,

com-com

to behave; **tâche de bien te c.** try to behave (yourself *or* well); **il s'est très mal comporté** he behaved very badly; **se c. en enfant/en adulte** to act childishly/like an adult; **comment se comporte-t-elle en classe?** how does she behave in class?

2 *(fonctionner → voiture, pneus)* to behave, to perform; *(→ molécule)* to behave; **la voiture se comporte très bien sur verglas** the car handles very well on ice; *Bourse & Fin* **ses actions se sont bien comportées** his/her shares have performed well

composant, -e [kɔ̃pozɑ̃, -ɑ̃t] **ADJ 1** *(qui constitue)* constitutive **2** *Ling* compound *(avant n)*

NM 1 *(élément)* component, constituent **2** *Constr, Ind & Ling* component; **c. de base** base component

❑ **composante** NF *(gén)* & *Math & Phys* component

composé, -e [kɔ̃poze] **ADJ 1** *(formé d'un mélange → bouquet, salade)* mixed

2 *(affecté → attitude)* studied; **un visage c.** a studied look

3 *Bot (feuille)* compound; *(inflorescence)* composite; **fleur composée** composite (flower)

4 *Archit* composite

5 *Ling (temps)* compound *(avant n)*; **mot c.** compound (word)

6 *Chim, Écon & Math* compound *(avant n)*; *Chim* **corps c.** compound

NM 1 *(ensemble)* **c. de** mixture *or* blend *or* combination of

2 *Chim & Math* compound

3 *Ling* compound (word)

❑ **composée** NF composite (flower)

❑ **composées** NFPL *Bot* Compositae

composer [3] [kɔ̃poze] **VT 1** *(rassembler pour faire un tout → équipe, cabinet)* to form, to select (the members of); *(→ menu)* to prepare, to put together; *(→ bouquet)* to make up; **c. un plateau de fromages** to prepare a selection of cheeses

2 *(écrire → roman, discours)* to write; *(→ poème, symphonie)* to compose; *(→ programme)* to draw up, to prepare; **une chanson que j'ai composée en cinq minutes/une nuit** a song I dashed off in five minutes/composed in one night

3 *(faire partie de)* to (go to) make up; **les personnes qui composent le gouvernement** the politicians who make up the government; **être composé de** to be made up of, to consist of

4 *Chim (combiner)* to compound

5 *Littéraire (apprêter, étudier)* **c. son visage** to compose one's features; **c. son personnage** to create an image for oneself

6 *(numéro de téléphone)* to dial; *(code)* to key (in)

7 *Typ* to set

VI 1 *(transiger)* to compromise; **entre époux, il faut c.** there must be a certain amount of give and take between husband and wife; **tu ne sais pas c.** you're (too) uncompromising; **c. avec qn/sa conscience** to come to a compromise with sb/one's conscience

2 *Scol* to take an exam; **c. en histoire** to take a history test *or* exam

3 *Mus* **il ne compose plus depuis des années** he hasn't composed *or* written anything for years; **il compose** he writes music

▶**se composer** VPR **1 se c. un visage de circonstance** to assume an appropriate expression

2 se c. de to be made up *or* composed of; **l'équipe se compose de onze joueurs** the team is made up of *or* comprises eleven players; **le noyau se compose d'un proton et d'un neutron** the nucleus is made up of *or* is composed of a proton and a neutron

composeur [kɔ̃pozœr] NM *Tél* **c. de numéros** dialler

composeuse [kɔ̃pozøz] NF typesetter *(machine)*

composite [kɔ̃pozit] **ADJ 1** *(mobilier, population)* heterogeneous, mixed, composite; *(foule, assemblée)* mixed; **matériau c.** composite (material) **2** *Archit & Tech* composite

NM *Archit* composite order

compositeur, -trice [kɔ̃pozitœr, -tris] NM,F **1** *Mus* composer **2** *Typ* compositor, typesetter

composition [kɔ̃pozisjɔ̃] NF **1** *(fabrication, assemblage → d'un produit, d'un plat, d'un menu)* making up, putting together; *(→ d'un bouquet)* making up, arranging; *(→ d'une équipe, d'une assemblée, d'un gouvernement)* forming, formation, setting up; *(→ d'un portefeuille d'actions)* building up **c.**

2 *(écriture → d'une symphonie)* composition; *(→ d'un poème, d'une lettre)* writing; *(→ d'un programme)* drawing up

3 *(éléments → d'une assemblée, d'un plat, d'un corps chimique)* composition; *(→ d'un programme)* elements; **quelle sera la c. du jury?** who will the members of the jury be?, who will make up the jury?; **la c. des équipes n'est pas encore connue** the teams haven't been announced yet; **des conservateurs entrent dans la c. du produit** this product contains preservatives; **c.: eau, sucre, fraises** ingredients: water, sugar, strawberries

4 *Beaux-Arts & Phot (technique, résultat)* composition; **avoir le sens de la c.** to have a good eye for composition; **la c. est déséquilibrée** the composition is unbalanced

5 *Typ* typesetting, composition; **c. automatique** *ou* **programmée** *ou* **par ordinateur** automatic typesetting

6 *Chim* composition

7 *Ling* compounding

8 *Scol (dissertation)* essay, composition; *(examen)* test, exam, paper; **c. française** French paper

9 *Jur* **c. pénale** criminal mediation

❑ **à composition** ADV **amener qn à c.** to lead sb to a compromise; **arriver** *ou* **venir à c.** to come to a compromise

❑ **de bonne composition** ADJ accommodating, good-natured, easy-going

❑ **de composition** ADJ *(rôle)* character *(avant n)*

❑ **de ma/sa/**etc **composition** ADJ **il a chanté une petite chanson de sa c.** he sang a little song he'd written; **je vais servir une ratatouille de ma c.** I'm going to serve my own version of ratatouille

❑ **de mauvaise composition** ADJ difficult

compositrice [kɔ̃pozitris] *voir* **compositeur**

compost [kɔ̃pɔst] NM compost

compostage [kɔ̃pɔstaʒ] NM **1** *(pour dater)* date-stamping **2** *(pour valider)* punching **3** *Agr* composting

composter [3] [kɔ̃pɔste] **VT 1** *(pour dater)* to date stamp **2** *(pour valider)* to punch **3** *Agr* to compost

---

Culture

COMPOSTER

Rail passengers in France are required to insert their ticket into a special punching machine ("composteur") on the platform before beginning their journey. The words "à composter" printed across the ticket mean that the passenger must do this before boarding the train.

---

composteur [kɔ̃pɔstœr] NM **1** *(dateur)* datestamp **2** *(pour valider)* ticket-punching machine **3** *Typ* composing stick **4** *Ordinat* **c. de données** data cartridge

compote [kɔ̃pɔt] NF *Culin* **c. (de fruits)** stewed fruit, compote; **c. de pommes** stewed apples, apple compote, *Am* applesauce

❑ **en compote** ADJ **1** *(fruits)* stewed; **elle ne mange que des fruits en c.** all she ever eats is stewed fruit **2** *Fam (meurtri, détruit)* smashed up; **j'ai les pieds en c.** my feet are killing me; **il a la figure en c.** his face has been beaten to a pulp

compotée [kɔ̃pɔte] NF *Culin* **c. d'oignons** stewed onions; **c. de chou** stewed cabbage

compotier [kɔ̃pɔtje] NM fruit bowl

compound [kɔ̃pund] ADJ INV compound *(avant n)*

comprador [kɔ̃pradɔr] *(pl* **compradors** *ou* **compradores)** ADJ comprador *(avant n)*

NM comprador

compréhensibilité [kɔ̃preɑ̃sibilite] NF intelligibility, comprehensibility

compréhensible [kɔ̃preɑ̃sibl] **ADJ 1** *(intelligible)* intelligible, comprehensible; **c. de** *ou* **par tous** easy for anyone to understand, comprehensible to everyone **2** *(excusable, concevable)* understandable; **c'est tout à fait c. de sa part** it's altogether understandable on his/her part

compréhensif, -ive [kɔ̃preɑ̃sif, -iv] ADJ **1** *(disposé à comprendre)* understanding **2** *Phil* comprehensive

compréhension [kɔ̃preɑ̃sjɔ̃] NF **1** *(fait de comprendre)* comprehension, understanding; **des notes nécessaires à la c. du texte** notes that are necessary to understand *or* for a proper understanding of the text; **nous testons leur rapidité de c.** we try to see how quickly they understand **2** *(bienveillance)* sympathy, understanding; **être plein de c.** to be very understanding **3** *Ling & Math* comprehension

compréhensive [kɔ̃preɑ̃siv] *voir* **compréhensif**

COMPRENDRE [79] [kɔ̃prɑ̃dr]

VT to understand **A** ■ to see **A5** ■ to comprise **B1** ■ to include **B2, 3** ■ to see **5**

USAGE ABSOLU to see

VPR to be understandable **1** ■ to understand one another **2**

VT A. 1 *(saisir par un raisonnement)* to understand, *Sout* to comprehend; **je ne comprends pas ce que vous voulez dire** I don't understand what you mean; **ce que je n'arrive pas à c. c'est…** what I can't work out is…; **elle n'a pas compris la plaisanterie** she didn't get the joke; **vous m'avez mal compris** you've misunderstood me; **on ne te comprend pas** *(tu ne parles pas clairement)* nobody can understand *or* make out what you say; **c'est simple, qu'y a-t-il à c.?** it's very obvious, what is there to understand?; **ne cherche pas, il n'y a rien à c.** don't even try to understand; **va y c. quelque chose!** YOU try to make head or tail of it!, *Am* go figure!; **dois-je c. que…?** am I to understand *or* do you mean to say that…?; **je n'y comprends rien** I can't make head nor tail of it, it makes no sense to me; **c'est à n'y rien c.** it's just baffling; **il ne comprend rien à rien** he hasn't a clue about anything; **(c'est) compris?** *(vous avez suivi?)* is it clear?, do you understand?; *(c'est un ordre)* do you hear me!; **(c'est) compris!** all right!, OK!; **faire c. qch à qn** *(le lui prouver)* to get sb to understand sth; *(l'en informer)* to give sb to understand sth; **je lui ai bien fait c. que tout était fini** I gave him to understand that it was all over; **est-ce que je me fais bien c.?** *(mon exposé est-il clair?)* is my explanation clear enough?; *(ton menaçant)* do I make myself clear?

2 *(saisir grâce à ses connaissances → théorie, langue)* to understand; **elle comprend parfaitement le russe** she understands Russian perfectly; **je n'arrive pas à c. cette phrase** I can't make sense of this sentence; **se faire c.** to make oneself understood; **je n'arrive pas à me faire c. en allemand** I can't make myself understood in German

3 *(saisir par une intuition)* to understand, to realize; **il a compris qu'il était condamné** he understood *or* realized he was doomed; **c. la portée d'un acte** to realize *or* understand the consequences of an action; **comprends-tu l'importance d'une telle décision?** do you realize how important a decision it is?; **je commence à c. où il veut en venir** I'm beginning to realize what he's after; *Fig* **il a vite compris son malheur** *ou* **sa douleur!** it didn't take him long to understand that he was in trouble!; **quand j'ai vu la pile de dossiers, j'ai compris mon malheur** *ou* **ma douleur!** when I saw that great pile of files, I realized what I had let myself in for!

4 *(admettre)* to understand; **je comprends qu'on s'énerve dans les bouchons** it's quite understandable that people get irritable when caught in traffic jams; **je ne comprends pas qu'elle ne m'ait pas appelé** I don't understand why she didn't call me; **je n'arrive toujours pas à c. ce qui lui a pris** I still can't figure out what got into him/her; **je ne comprends pas pourquoi il a fait ça** I don't understand why he did it

5 *(concevoir)* to understand, to see; **voilà comment je comprends la vie!** now this is what I call living!; **c'est ainsi que je comprends le rôle** this is how I understand *or* see the part; **comment c. ce poème?** what is one to make of this poem?

6 *(avoir les mêmes sentiments que)* to understand, to sympathize with; **je ne le comprendrai jamais** I'll never understand him; **elle comprend les jeunes** she understands young people; **il faut la c.** you have to see things from her point of view, you have to put yourself in her shoes; **je vous comprends, cela a dû être terrible** I know how you feel, it must have been awful; **je la comprends, avec un mari pareil!** I don't blame her with the sort of husband she's got!

7 *(apprécier)* to have a feeling for, to understand; **un public qui comprend l'art abstrait** an audience that understands abstract art; **il ne comprend pas la plaisanterie** he can't take a joke

B. 1 *(être composé entièrement de)* to be composed *or* made up of, to comprise, to consist of; **la maison comprend cinq pièces** the house consists of five rooms; **l'examen comprend trois parties** the exam comprises *or* contains *or* is made up of three (different) sections

2 *(être composé en partie de)* to include, to contain; **l'équipe comprend trois joueurs étrangers** there are three foreign players in the team

3 *(englober → frais, taxe)* to include; **si l'on comprend les cousins et cousines** if you include the cousins (as well); **le prix comprend tous les frais d'hébergement** the price is fully inclusive of accommodation

4 *(au passif)* *(se situer)* **l'inflation sera comprise entre 5 pour cent et 8 pour cent** inflation will be (somewhere) between 5 percent and 8 percent; **la partie comprise entre la table et le mur** the section between the table and the wall

USAGE ABSOLU **ah! je comprends!** oh! I see!; **elle a fini par c.** she finally got the message; **elle comprend vite** she's quick on the uptake, she catches on quickly; *Hum* **il comprend vite mais il faut lui expliquer longtemps!** he's a bit slow on the uptake!; **ai-je bien compris?** have I understood correctly?; **ça va, j'ai compris, tu préfères que je m'en aille!** OK, I get the message, you want me to go!; **je l'ai fait sans trop c.** I did it without really knowing what I was doing; **elle n'a pas osé, il faut c. (aussi)!** she didn't dare, you have to put yourself in her shoes!; **tu comprends?, comprends-tu?** you see?, you know?; **tu comprends, ce qui me plaît c'est de vivre à la campagne** you see, what I like is living in the country; *Fam* **elle est belle, hein? – je comprends!** she's lovely, isn't she? – you bet! *or* and how!

►**se comprendre** VPR **1** *(être compréhensible)* to be understandable; **c'est une réaction/un motif qui se comprend** it's an understandable response/motive; **cela se comprend, ça se comprend** that's quite understandable; **elle ne veut plus le voir, cela se comprend** understandably enough, she won't see him any more

2 *(l'un l'autre)* to understand one another; **nous nous sommes mal compris** we failed to understand *or* we misunderstood each other

3 *Fam* **je me comprends!** I know what I'm getting at *or* trying to say (even if nobody else does)!

Allusion

Je vous ai compris

In 1958 General de Gaulle visited Algiers, when Algeria was in the throes of the War of Independence. He opened his speech with these words: **Je vous ai compris. Je sais ce qui s'est passé ici. Je vois ce que vous avez voulu faire** ("I understand. I know what has happened here. I can see what you have been trying to do."). People sometimes use the phrase in connection with de Gaulle, parodying his stately delivery. When you want to convey the message that you have all the information you require and that no further explanation is necessary, you can say this, and it implies "Say no more."

---

comprenette [kɔ̃prənɛt] NF *Fam* **il n'a pas la c. facile, il a la c. dure** he's a bit slow (on the uptake)

comprenne *etc voir* **comprendre**

comprenure [kɔ̃prənyr] NF *Belg & Can Fam* **être dur de c.** to be slow (on the uptake)

compresse [kɔ̃prɛs] NF compress, pack

compresser [4] [kɔ̃prese] VT to pack (tightly) in, to pack in tight; *Ordinat (données)* to compress; *(fichier)* to compact, to compress, to zip

compresseur [kɔ̃prescer] NM **1** *Tech (d'un réfrigérateur)* compressor; *(d'un moteur)* supercharger; *Aut* **c. centrifuge** centrifugal compressor; *Aut* **c. à palettes** palette compressor; *Aut* **c. Roots** Roots blower; *Aut* **c. sur vilebrequin** crankshaft compressor **2** *(en travaux publics)* **(rouleau) c.** steamroller **3** *Ordinat* **c. de données** data compressor

compressibilité [kɔ̃presibilite] NF **1** *Tech & Phys* compressibility **2** *Fig (flexibilité)* **cela dépend de la c. des dépenses** it depends on how much expenditure can be cut down *or* reduced

compressible [kɔ̃presibl] ADJ **1** *Tech & Phys* compressible **2** *Fig (réductible)* reducible; **commençons par les dépenses compressibles** let's begin with expenses that can be cut down *or* reduced

compressif, -ive [kɔ̃presif, -iv] ADJ *(bandage, appareil)* compressive

compression [kɔ̃presjɔ̃] NF **1** *Tech & Phys* compression; **temps de c.** compression stroke **2** *(des dépenses, du personnel)* reduction, cutting down; **procéder à une c. des effectifs** to cut down the workforce; **des compressions budgétaires** cuts *or* reductions in the budget **3** *Méd* compression **4** *Ordinat (de données)* compression; *(d'un fichier)* compacting, compression, zipping; **c. des caractères** digit compression

□ **à compression (de vapeur)** ADJ compression *(avant n)*

□ **de compression** ADJ *Tech (pompe)* compression *(avant n)*

compressive [kɔ̃presiv] *voir* **compressif**

comprimable [kɔ̃primabl] ADJ compressible

comprimé, -e [kɔ̃prime] ADJ compressed
  NM tablet, pill

comprimer [3] [kɔ̃prime] VT **1** *(serrer → air, vapeur, gaz)* to compress; *(→ objets)* to pack (in) tightly; *(→ foin, paille)* to compact, to press tight; **cette robe me comprime la taille** this dress is much too tight for me around the waist; **les voyageurs étaient comprimés dans le train** the travellers were jammed *or* packed tight in the train **2** *(diminuer → dépenses)* to curtail, to trim, to cut down; *(→ effectifs)* to trim *or* to cut down **3** *(contenir → colère, joie, rire)* to hold back, to suppress, to repress; *(→ larmes)* to hold back **4** *Ordinat* to compress **5** *Méd* to compress

compris, -e [kɔ̃pri, -iz] PP *voir* **comprendre**
  ADJ **1** *(inclus → service, boisson)* included; *(→ dans les dates)* inclusive; **450 euros de loyer, charges comprises** 450 euros rent, all maintenance charges included; **ils vivent à cinq, l'oncle c.** the five of them live together, the uncle included; **non c.** not included; **service non c.** service not included, not inclusive of the service charge; **y c.** included, including; **trente-deux personnes y c. l'équipage** thirty-two people including the crew *or* the crew included; **je travaille tous les jours y c. le dimanche** I work every day including Sundays *or* Sundays included; **je serai parti du premier au 15 c.** I'll be away from the first to the 15th inclusive **2** *(pensé)* **bien c.** well thought-out
  EXCLAM *Aviat & Tél* OK!
□ **tout compris** ADV net, all inclusive, *Br* all in; **on a payé 600 euros tout c.** we paid 600 euros all inclusive *or* all in

compromets *etc voir* **compromettre**

compromettant, -e [kɔ̃prɔmɛtɑ̃, -ɑ̃t] ADJ *(document, action)* incriminating; *(situation)* compromising; **évitez toute relation compromettante** avoid associating with anybody who might compromise you

compromettre [84] [kɔ̃prɔmɛtr] VT **1** *(nuire à la réputation de)* to compromise; **ils ont tenté de la c.** they tried to compromise her; **compromis par une cassette** compromised *or* incriminated because of a tape; **il est compromis dans l'affaire** he's implicated *or* involved in the affair

2 *(mettre en danger → fortune, avenir, santé)* to put in jeopardy, to jeopardize; **s'il pleut, notre sortie est compromise** if it rains, our outing is unlikely to go ahead
  VI *Jur* to compromise

►**se compromettre** VPR *(risquer sa réputation)* to compromise oneself, to jeopardize one's reputation; *(s'impliquer)* to commit oneself; **il s'est compromis dans une affaire de fausses factures** he became implicated in a scandal involving falsified invoices; **le mouvement s'est compromis avec le nazisme** the movement became involved with Nazism

compromis, -e [kɔ̃prɔmi, -iz] PP *voir* **compromettre**
  NM **1** *(concession)* compromise; *(moyen terme)* compromise (solution); **faire des c.** to make compromises; **trouver un c., parvenir à un c.** to reach *or* to come to a compromise; **cette robe est un c. entre élégance et décontraction** this dress is neither too elegant nor too casual **2** *Jur* **mettre une affaire en c.** to submit a case for arbitration; **c. de vente** provisional sale agreement **3** *Assur* **c. d'avarie** average bond

compromission [kɔ̃prɔmisjɔ̃] NF base action, (piece of) dishonourable behaviour; **elle est prête à n'importe quelle c. pour réussir** she will stoop to anything in order to succeed

compromissoire [kɔ̃prɔmiswar] ADJ arbitration *(avant n)*

compta [kɔ̃ta] NF *Fam* accounting■, accounts■

comptabilisation [kɔ̃tabilizasjɔ̃] NF **1** *Compta* posting, entering in the accounts; **faire la c. de qch** to enter sth in the accounts; **c. de la survaleur** goodwill accounting **2** *(dénombrement)* counting

comptabiliser [3] [kɔ̃tabilize] VT **1** *Compta* to post, to enter in the accounts **2** *(compter)* to count; **je n'ai pas comptabilisé ses allées et venues** I didn't keep a record of his/her comings and goings; **c. les appels** to list *or* to itemize phone calls

comptabilité [kɔ̃tabilite] NF **1** *(profession)* accountancy, accounting; **faire de la c.** to work as an accountant **2** *(comptes)* accounts, books; **passer qch en c.** to put sth through the books *or* the accounts; **tenir la c.** to keep the books *or* the accounts; **faire sa c.** to do one's books *or* bookkeeping; **faire la c. de qn** to do sb's books *or* bookkeeping; **ma c. est à jour** my books are *or* my bookkeeping is up-to-date **3** *(technique)* accounting, book-keeping; **c. analytique** cost accounting; **c. analytique d'exploitation** operational cost accounting; **c. budgétaire** budgeting; **c. de caisse** cash basis accounting; **c. commerciale** business accounting; **c. en coûts actuels** current cost accounting; **c. par coûts historiques** historical cost accounting; **c. des coûts variables** direct cost accounting; **c. de la dépréciation** depreciation accounting; **c. d'engagements** accrual accounting; **c. d'exploitation** cost accounting; **c. financière** financial accounting; **c. générale** general accounts; **c. de gestion** management accounting; **c. informatisée** computerized accounts; **c. en partie double** double-entry bookkeeping; **c. en partie simple** single-entry bookkeeping; **c. de prix de revient** cost accounting; **c. uniforme** uniform accounting **4** *(service, bureau)* accounts (department); **adressez-vous à la c.** apply to the accounts department **5** *Écon & Fin* **c. nationale** national auditing; **c. publique** public finance

comptable [kɔ̃tabl] ADJ **1** *Fin* accounting *(avant n)*, book-keeping *(avant n)* **2** *Ling* count *(avant n)*, countable **3** *(responsable)* **être c. (à qn) de qch** to be accountable *or* answerable (to sb) for sth
  NMF accountant; *Can* **c. agréé** *Br* chartered accountant, *Am* certified public accountant; **c. du Trésor public** Treasury official

comptage [kɔ̃taʒ] NM counting; **faire le c. de** to count

comptant [kɔ̃tɑ̃] ADJ M **je lui ai versé 100 euros comptants** I paid him/her 100 euros in cash
  ADV cash; **payer c.** to pay (in) cash; **payer 50**

euros c. to pay 50 euros in cash; **acheter/vendre (qch) c.** to buy/to sell (sth) for cash □ NM cash; **c. contre documents** cash against documents, CAD □ **au comptant** ADV cash; **acheter/vendre (qch) au c.** to buy/to sell (sth) for cash; **payable au c.** *(lors d'un achat)* Br cash *or* Am collect on delivery; *(sur présentation de titre, de connaissement)* payable on presentation

COMPTE [kɔ̃t]

> NM counting, count **A1** ▪ total **A2** ▪ account **B1, 3** ▪ bill, check **B2**
> NMPL accounts, accounting

NM **A.** *CALCUL, SOMME CALCULÉE* **1** *(opération)* counting; *Boxe* count; **faire le c. (de)** *(personnes)* to count (up); *(dépenses)* to add up; **ils ont fait le c. des absents** they counted (up) the number of people absent; **faites le c. vous-même** work it out (for) yourself; **quand on fait le c....** when you add it all up...; **le c., les comptes** calculation; *aussi Fig* **c. à rebours** countdown; *aussi Fig* **commencer le c. à rebours** to start the countdown

2 *(résultat)* (sum) total; **j'ai le c.** I've got the right money; **je vous remercie, monsieur, le c. est bon** *ou* **y est!** thank you sir, that's right!; **il n'y a pas le c.** *(personnes)* they're not all here *or* there, some are missing; *(dépenses)* it doesn't add up; **ça ne fait pas le c.** it doesn't come to the right amount, it doesn't add up; **cela fait un c. rond** that makes it a (nice) round sum *or* figure; **cela ne fait pas un c. rond** it comes to an odd figure; **faire bon c.** to be generous (when serving), to give generous helpings; **comment fais-tu ton c. pour te tromper à chaque fois/pour que tout le monde soit mécontent?** how do you manage to get it wrong every time/manage it so (that) nobody's satisfied?; **mais comment il a fait son c.?** but how did he make such a mess of it?; **vous êtes loin du c.** you're wide of the mark

3 *(avantage)* **j'y trouve mon c.** I do well out of it, it works out well for me; **il n'y trouvait pas son c., alors il est parti** *(il ne gagnait pas assez d'argent)* he wasn't doing well enough out of it, so he left; *(dans une relation)* he wasn't getting what he wanted out of it, so he left

4 *(dû)* **demander son c.** to ask for one's wages; **donner son c. à qn** to give sb (his/her) notice; **avoir son c. (de)** to have more than one's fair share *or* more than enough (of); **je n'ai pas mon c. de sommeil** I don't get all the sleep I need *or* enough sleep; **avoir eu son c. d'ennuis** to have had one's fair share of trouble; *Fam* **il a déjà son c.** *(il a beaucoup bu)* he's had quite enough to drink already▪; **recevoir son c.** to get one's (final) wages; *Fam Fig* to get one's marching orders *or* Br the sack; **régler son c. à qn** to pay sb off; *Fam Fig* to give sb a piece of one's mind; **je vais lui régler son c.!** I'm going to give him/her a piece of my mind!; **régler ses comptes** *(mettre en ordre ses affaires)* to put one's affairs in order; **régler ses comptes avec qn** *(le payer)* to settle up with sb; *(se venger)* to settle one's *or* old scores with sb; *Fam* **son c. est bon** he's had it, he's done for

B. *DANS LE DOMAINE FINANCIER ET COMMERCIAL* **1** *(de dépôt, de crédit)* account; **avoir un c. chez qn** to have an account with sb; **ouvrir un c. chez qn** to open an account with sb; **déposer un montant sur son c.** to pay a sum into one's account; **régler un c.** to settle an account; **c. d'abonnement** budget account; *Ordinat* **c. d'accès par ligne commutée** dial-up account; **c. bancaire** *ou* **en banque** Br bank *or* Am banking account; **c. de caisse d'épargne** savings account; **c. chèques** Br current *or* Am checking account; **c. chèque postal** = account held at the Post Office, Br ≃ giro account; **c. commercial** office *or* business account; **c. de compensation** clearing account; **c. conjoint** joint account; **c. de contrepartie** contra account; **c. courant** Br current *or* Am checking account; *Ordinat* **c. de courrier électronique** e-mail account; **c. crédit** budget account; **c. à**

découvert overdrawn account; **c. de dépôt** deposit account; **c. de dépôt à vue** drawing account; **c. des dépenses et recettes** income and expenditure account; **c. d'épargne** savings account; **c. d'épargne en actions** share savings account, savings and investment account; **c. épargne logement** savings account *(for purchasing a property)*; **c. épargne temps** *(dans le cadre de la réduction du temps de travail)* = scheme which allows employees to save up the hours of overtime they accumulate under the "RTT" system for up to five years, eventually being compensated either financially or with additional holidays; **c. étranger** foreign account; **c. inactif** dead account; **c. individuel** personal account; **c. d'intermédiaire** nominee account; *Ordinat* **c. Internet** Internet account; **c. d'investissement** investment account; **c. joint** joint account; **c. (sur) livret** savings account; *Can* **c. de non-résident** foreign account; **c. numéroté** numbered account; **c. ouvert** open account; **c. permanent** Br credit account, Am charge account; **c. de prêt** loan account; **c. prête-nom** nominee account; **c. professionnel** business account; *Bourse* **c. propre** personal account; **c. rémunéré** interest-bearing account; **c. de réserve** reserve account; *Bourse* **c. à terme** forward account; **c. des ventes** sales account

2 *(facture)* bill, *Am* check; **faites-moi** *ou* **préparez-moi le c.** may I have the bill, please?; **mettre** *ou* **inscrire qch sur le c. de qn** to enter sth to sb's account; **mettez-le** *ou* **inscrivez-le à mon c.** charge it to my account; **régler un c.** *(payer)* to settle a bill; *(mettre au net une situation)* to clear the air; *(se venger)* to settle a score *or* an old score; **pour règlement de tout c.** *(sur facture)* in full settlement

3 *(bilan)* account; **c. accréditif** charge account; **c. d'achats** purchase account; **c. d'agence** agency account; **c. bloqué** frozen account, *Am* escrow account; **c. de caisse** cash account; **c. de capital** capital account; **c. centralisateur** central account; **c. de charges** expense account; **c. client** customer account; **c. créditeur** account in credit, credit balance; **c. débiteur** account in debit, debit balance; **c. définitif** final accounts; **c. d'exploitation** profit and loss form, P&L; **c. des flux financiers** flow of funds account; **comptes fournisseurs** book debts; **c. de pertes et profits, c. de résultat** profit and loss account; **c. de produits** income account; **c. des recettes et des dépenses** revenue account; **c. de régularisation** *(de l'actif)* prepayments and accrued income; *(du passif)* accruals and deferred income; **c. de résultat prévisionnel** interim profit and loss account, *Am* interim income statement; **c. de stock** inventory account

C. *LOCUTIONS* **reprendre à son c.** *(magasin)* to take over in one's own name; *(idée, écrit)* to adopt; **il a pris le repas à son c.** he paid for the meal; **être** *ou* **travailler à son c.** to be self-employed; **il est à son c. maintenant** he's his own boss now, he's set up on his own now; **se mettre** *ou* **s'installer à son c.** to set up in business on one's own (account); **à c. d'auteur** at the author's own expense; **passer** *ou* **porter une somme en c.** *(recette)* to credit a sum; *(dépense)* to debit a sum; **je suis en c. avec ton frère** I've got some business to settle with your brother; **nous sommes en c., vous me réglerez tout à la fin** as we're doing business together, you may pay me in full at the end; **demander c. de qch à qn** to ask sb for an explanation of sth, to ask sb to account for sth; **demander des comptes à qn** to ask sb for an explanation, to call sb to account; **rendre des comptes (à qn)** to give *or* to offer (sb) an explanation; **je n'ai de comptes à rendre à personne** I don't owe anybody any explanations, I don't have to justify my actions to anybody; **je n'ai pas de comptes à vous rendre** I don't have to justify myself to you; **rendre c. de qch à qn** *(s'en expliquer)* to justify sth to sb; *(faire un rapport)* to give an account of sth to sb; **si vous rencontrez des difficultés, rendez-en c. au chef d'équipe** if you have any difficulties, report to the team leader; **il est venu nous**

rendre c. de l'accident he came to give us an account of the accident; **devoir des comptes à qn** to be responsible *or* accountable to sb; **je ne dois de comptes à personne** I don't have to account for *or* to justify my actions to anybody; **il ne te doit pas de comptes** he doesn't owe you any explanations; **prendre qch en c.** *(prendre en considération)* to take sth into account *or* consideration; **se rendre c. de qch/que** to realize sth/that; **je ne me rendais pas c. de l'effort que cela lui avait coûté** I hadn't realized *or* appreciated the effort he'd/she'd put into it; **te rends-tu c. de ce que tu fais?** do you realize *or* really understand what you're doing?; **on lui a collé une étiquette dans le dos mais il ne s'en est pas rendu c.** somebody stuck a label on his back but he didn't notice; **non mais, tu te rends c.!** *(indignation)* can you believe it?; **te-nir c. de qch** to take account of sth, to take sth into account; **ne tenir aucun c. de qch** to take no notice of sth, to disregard sth; **elle n'a pas tenu c. de mes conseils** she took no notice of *or* ignored my advice; **si vous avez réglé récemment, ne tenez pas c. du présent rappel** if you have settled the account in the last few days, please ignore this reminder; **c. tenu de** in view of, bearing in mind, taking into account; **c. non tenu de** leaving out, excluding

□ **comptes** NMPL accounts, accounting; **faire/tenir les comptes** to do/to keep the accounts; **elle tient bien ses comptes** she keeps her accounts in good order; **faire ses comptes** to make up *or* do one's accounts; **j'ai mal fait mes comptes** I've made a mistake in my accounts; **faire des comptes d'apothicaire** to work things out to the last penny *or* Am cent; *Prov* **les bons comptes font les bons amis** = pay your debts and you'll keep your friends; **comptes analytiques d'exploitation** operational cost accounts; **comptes annuels** annual accounts; **comptes approuvés** certified accounts; **comptes clients** accounts receivable, *Am* receivables; **comptes consolidés** consolidated accounts; **comptes de gestion** management accounts; **comptes intégrés** consolidated accounts; **comptes de résultats courants** above-the-line accounts; **comptes de résultats exceptionnels** below-the-line accounts; **comptes semestriels** interim accounts; **comptes sociaux** company accounts; **comptes trimestriels** interim accounts; **comptes de valeur** real accounts

□ **à bon compte** ADV *(acheter)* cheap, cheaply; **s'en tirer à bon c.** *(sans frais)* to manage to avoid paying a fortune; *(sans conséquences graves)* to get off lightly

□ **à ce compte, à ce compte-là** ADV *(selon ce raisonnement)* looking at it *or* taking it that way

□ **de compte à demi** ADV *(en partageant → les frais)* sharing the expenses *or* costs; *(→ les bénéfices)* sharing the profits, with a half-share of the profits

□ **pour compte** ADV **laisser des marchandises pour c.** to leave goods on a merchant's hands

□ **pour le compte** ADV for the count; **il est resté à terre pour le c.** he was out for the count

□ **pour le compte de** PRÉP for; **elle travaille pour le c. d'une grande société** she works for a large company

□ **pour mon/son/etc compte** ADV for my/his/etc part, as for me/him/etc; **pour son c., il la trouvait antipathique** as for him, he thought she was unpleasant

□ **sur le compte de** PRÉP **1** *(à propos de)* on, about, concerning; **on a dit bien des bêtises sur son c.** people talked a lot of nonsense about him/her

2 *(locution)* **mettre qch sur le c. de qn** to attribute *or* ascribe sth to sb; **mettre qch sur le c. de qch** to put sth down to sth; **je mets ses excentricités sur le c. de sa jeunesse** I put his/her eccentric behaviour down to his/her youth

□ **tout compte fait, tous comptes faits** ADV **1** *(en résumé)* all in all, on balance, all things considered

2 *(après tout)* thinking about it, on second thoughts

'Tout compte fait' *de Beauvoir* 'All Said and Done'

Le compte est bon

This is a catchphrase from the very popular TV game show *Des chiffres et des lettres*, the French equivalent of the British show *Countdown*. In the "numbers" part of the show, when a contestant manages to get the right number, he or she has to say **Le compte est bon**, meaning here "It's the right number". One often hears this expression when buying something, as the seller counts out the small change; the meaning is simply "That's right, thank you."

compte-chèques, compte chèques [kɔ̃tʃɛk] (*pl* **comptes-chèques** *ou* **comptes chèques**) NM *Br* current *or Am* checking account; **c. postal** = account held at the Post Office, *Br* ≃ giro account; **les comptes-chèques postaux** = the banking service of the French Post Office, *Br* ≃ the Giro Bank

compte-clé [kɔ̃tkle] (*pl* **comptes-clés**) NM key account

compte-fils [kɔ̃tfil] NM INV *Tex* thread counter, linen tester, linen counter

compte-gouttes [kɔ̃tgut] NM INV dropper
▫ **au compte-gouttes** ADV very sparingly; **payer qn au c.** to pay sb off in dribs and drabs; **distribuer qch au c.** to dole sth out; **ils les prêtent au c., leurs vidéos!** they don't like lending out too many videos at a time!

COMPTER [3] [kɔ̃te]

> VT to count **1, 2, 5** ■ to charge **3** ■ to pay **4** ■ to include **5** ■ to take into account **7** ■ to have **8** ■ to expect **9** ■ to intend **10** ■ to allow **11**
> VI to count **1, 3** ■ to add up **1** ■ to matter **3**
> VPR to be counted **1** ■ to count oneself **2**

VT **1** (*dénombrer → objets, argent, personnes*) to count; **avez-vous compté l'argent de la caisse/les absents?** have you counted the money in the till/the people who are absent?; **il s'est mis à c. les billets** he started to count the notes; *Péj* **on peut c.** *ou* **on a vite compté les cadeaux qu'elle a faits!** you can count the presents she's given on the fingers of one hand!; **on ne compte plus ses bévues** we've lost count of his/her mistakes; **on ne compte plus ses crimes** he/she has committed countless *or* innumerable crimes; **as-tu compté combien de jours elle a été absente?** have you counted the number of days she was missing *or* absent?; **j'ai compté qu'il restait 100 euros dans la caisse** according to my reckoning, there are 100 euros left in the till; **c. les heures/jours** (*d'impatience*) to be counting the hours/days; **on peut lui c. les côtes** he's/she's as thin as a rake; *Fam* **il m'a compté absent/présent** he marked me (down as) absent/present; *Fig* **c. les moutons** to count sheep; *aussi Fig* **c. les points** to keep score; **on peut les c. sur les doigts de la main** you can count them on the fingers of one hand; **il y a de cela 20 ans bien comptés** a good 20 years have passed since then

2 (*limiter*) to count (out); **le temps lui est compté, ses jours sont comptés** his/her days are numbered; **il ne comptait pas sa peine/ ses efforts** he spared no pains/effort; **tu es toujours à c. tes sous!** you're always counting your pennies!; *Fig* **il lui compte chaque sou** *ou* **son argent** he grudges him/her every penny *or Am* cent

3 (*faire payer*) to charge for; **c. qch à qn** to charge sb for sth; **j'ai compté trois heures de ménage** I've charged for three hours' housework; **nous ne vous compterons pas la pièce détachée** we won't charge you *or* there'll be no charge for the spare part; **le serveur nous a compté trois euros de trop** the waiter has overcharged us by three euros, the waiter has charged us three euros too much

4 (*payer, verser*) to pay; **il m'a compté deux**

jours à 60 euros he paid me (for) two days at 60 euros

5 (*inclure*) to count (in), to include; **dans le total nous n'avons pas compté le vin** wine has not been included in the overall figure; **tu as compté les boissons aussi?** did you count the drinks as well?

6 (*classer → dans une catégorie*) **c. qn/qch parmi** to count sb/sth among, to number sb/sth among; **je compte ce livre parmi mes préférés** I count this book among my favourites

7 (*prendre en considération*) to take into account, to take account of; **on vous comptera vos années d'ancienneté** your length of service will be taken into account; **et je ne compte pas la fatigue!** and that's without mentioning the effort!; **nous devons c. sa contribution pour quelque chose** we must take some account of her contribution

8 (*avoir → membres, habitants*) to have; **notre musée compte quelques tableaux rares** our museum has *or* boasts several rare paintings; **la capitale compte deux millions d'habitants** the capital has two million inhabitants; **l'association compte maintenant 67 adhérents** the association now has *or* numbers 67 members; **nous sommes heureux de vous c. parmi nous ce soir** we're happy to have *or* to welcome you among us tonight; **il compte beaucoup d'artistes au nombre de** *ou* **parmi ses amis** he can count many artists among his friends; **elle compte déjà cinq victoires dans des grands tournois** she's already won five major tournaments; **quand on compte 20 années de service** when you've been 20 years with the same company

9 (*s'attendre à*) to expect; **je compte recevoir les résultats cette semaine** I'm expecting the results this week

10 (*avoir l'intention de*) to intend; **c. faire qch** to intend to do sth, to mean to do sth, to plan to do sth; **que comptes-tu faire ce soir?** what are your plans for *or* what are you planning to do tonight?; **ils m'ont renvoyé – que comptes-tu faire maintenant?** I've been fired – what do you intend to do now?; **dis-lui ce que tu comptes faire** tell him what your intentions are *or* what you have in mind; **nous comptions aller en Grèce cet été** we'd planned to go to Greece this summer

11 (*prévoir*) to allow; **nous comptons une demi-bouteille de vin par personne** we allow half a bottle of wine per person; **il faut c. entre 15 et 20 euros pour un repas** you have to allow between 15 and 20 euros for a meal; **je compte qu'il y a un bon quart d'heure de marche/une journée de travail** I reckon there's a good quarter of an hour's walk/a day's work

12 *Sport* (*boxeur*) to count out

13 *Can* (*but*) to score

USAGE ABSOLU (*prévoir*) **c. juste** to skimp; **c. large** to be generous; **deux canards pour 10 personnes? c'est c. un peu juste!** two ducks between 10 people? that's cutting it a bit fine!; **il faudra deux heures pour y aller, en comptant large** it will take two hours at the most to get there

VI **1** (*calculer*) to count, to add up; **apprendre à c.** to learn to count; **ça fait 37 – je sais c.!** it's 37 – I do know how to count(, thank you)!; **ne me dérange pas quand je compte** don't disturb me when I'm counting; **c. jusqu'à 10** to count (up) to 10; **c. de tête/sur ses doigts** to count in one's head/on one's fingers; **c. avec une calculette** to add up with a calculator; **c. vite** to add up quickly; **si je compte bien, tu me dois 85 euros** if I've counted right *or* according to my calculations, you owe me 85 euros; **tu as dû mal c.** you must have got your calculations wrong, you must have miscalculated *or* miscounted

2 (*limiter ses dépenses*) to be careful (with money); **ils sont obligés de c. maintenant** they have to be careful with money now; **c'est quelqu'un qui n'a jamais compté** he has never been one to worry about money; **savoir c.** to be good at looking after one's money

3 (*importer*) to count, to matter; **ce qui compte, c'est ta santé/le résultat** the important thing is your health/the end result; **40 ans d'ancienneté, ça compte!** 40 years' service DOES count for something!; **une des personnes qui ont le plus compté dans ma vie** one of the most important people in my life; **tu comptes beaucoup pour moi** you mean a lot to me; **le médecin est un personnage qui compte dans le village** the doctor is a highly respected figure in the village; **je prendrai ma décision seule! – alors moi, je ne compte pas?** I'll make my own decision! – so I don't count *or* matter, then?; **tu as triché, ça ne compte pas** you cheated, it doesn't count; **à l'examen, la philosophie ne compte presque pas** philosophy is a very minor subject in the exam; **c. double/triple** to count double/triple; **c. pour** to count for; **c. pour quelque chose/ rien** to count for something/nothing; **et moi, je ne compte pour rien?** what about me then? don't I count *or* mean anything?; **quand il est invité à dîner, il compte pour trois!** when he's invited to dinner he eats enough for three!; *Fam* **c. pour du beurre** to count for nothing; **et moi, dans tout ça, je compte pour du beurre?** so I don't count, then?

4 (*figurer*) **c. parmi** to rank among, to be numbered among; **elle compte parmi les plus grands pianistes de sa génération** she is one of the greatest pianists of her generation

▫ **compter avec** VT IND to reckon with; **désormais, il faudra c. avec l'opposition** from now on, the opposition will have to be reckoned with; **dans une course, il faut toujours c. avec le vent** in a race, you always have to allow for the wind

▫ **compter sans** VT IND to fail to take into account, to fail to allow for; **il avait compté sans la rapidité de Jones** he had failed to take Jones' speed into account

▫ **compter sur** VT IND (*faire confiance à*) to count on, to rely on, to depend on; (*espérer → venue, collaboration, événement*) to count on; **on ne peut pas c. sur lui** he can't be relied on, you can't count *or* rely *or* depend on him; **c'est quelqu'un sur qui tu peux c.** he's/she's a reliable person; **je compte sur son aide** I'm counting on his/her help; **ne compte pas trop sur la chance** don't count *or* rely too much on luck; **je vous le rendrai – j'y compte bien!** I'll give it back to you – I should hope so!; **je peux sortir demain soir? – n'y compte pas!** can I go out tomorrow night? – don't count *or* bank on it!; **compte sur lui pour aller tout répéter au patron!** you can rely on him to go and tell the boss everything!; **si c'est pour lui jouer un mauvais tour, ne comptez pas sur moi!** if you want to play a dirty trick on him/her, you can count me out!; **ne compte pas sur moi pour que j'arrange les choses!** don't count on me to patch things up!; *Fam Ironique* **compte là-dessus (et bois de l'eau fraîche)!** you should be so lucky!, dream on!; **tu me prêteras ta moto? – c'est ça, compte là-dessus (et bois de l'eau fraîche)!** will you lend me your motorbike? – you must be joking!

▫ **à compter de** PRÉP as from, as of; **à c. du 7 mai** as from *or* of 7 May; **à c. de ce jour, nous ne nous sommes plus revus** from that day on, we never saw each other again

▫ **à tout compter** ADV all things considered, all in all

▫ **en comptant** PRÉP including; **il faut deux mètres de tissu en comptant l'ourlet** you need two metres of material including *or* if you include the hem

▫ **sans compter** ADV (*généreusement*) **donner sans c.** to give generously *or* without counting the cost; **dépenser sans c.** to spend money freely *or* like water; **se dépenser sans c.** to spare no effort PRÉP (*sans inclure*) not counting; (*sans parler de*) to say nothing of, not to mention; **il y aura beaucoup de monde, sans c. ceux qui viennent sans prévenir** there'll be a lot of people, even without counting *or* not to mention the ones who'll come without letting us know beforehand

❑ **sans compter que** CONJ quite apart from the fact that; **il est trop tôt pour aller dormir, sans c. que je n'ai pas du tout sommeil** it's too early to go to bed, quite apart from the fact that I'm not at all sleepy

❑ **tout bien compté** ADV all things considered, all in all

▸**se compter** VPR **1** (*être compté*) to be counted; **les détournements de fonds se comptent par dizaines** there have been dozens of cases of embezzlement; **ses succès ne se comptent plus** his/her successes are innumerable *or* are past counting

2 (*se considérer*) to count *or* to consider oneself; (*s'inclure dans un calcul*) to count *or* to include oneself; **je ne me compte pas parmi les plus malheureux** I count myself as one of the luckier ones; **non, nous sommes six – ah oui, j'avais oublié de me c.** no, there are six of us – oh yes, I forgot to count *or* to include myself

compte rendu, compte-rendu [kɔ̃trɑ̃dy] (*pl* **comptes rendus** *ou* **comptes-rendus**) NM (*d'une conversation*) account, report; (*d'une séance, d'un match, d'une visite professionnelle*) report; (*d'un livre, d'un spectacle*) review; (*d'une réunion*) minutes; **faire le c. d'un livre** to review a book; **faire le c. de la réunion** to take the minutes of the meeting; *Jur* **c. d'audience** court session record

compte-titres [kɔ̃ttitr] (*pl* **comptes-titres**) NM *Bourse* share account

compte-tours [kɔ̃ttur] NM INV rev counter, *Spéc* tachometer

compteur [kɔ̃tœr] NM **1** (*appareil*) meter; (*affichage*) counter; **relever le c.** to read the meter; **mettre le c. à zéro** to set the counter on zero; **remettre le c. à zéro** to reset the counter; *Fig* **remettre les compteurs à zéro** to start from scratch, to go back to square one; **la voiture a 1000 kilomètres au c.** the car has 1,000 kilometres on the clock; **le c. marquait 16 euros** there was 16 euros on the meter; **c. à gaz/d'eau/d'électricité** gas/water/electricity meter; **c. Geiger** Geiger counter; *Cin* **c. d'images** frame counter; **c. kilométrique** *Br* milometer, mileometer, *Am* odometer; *Fam* **c. bloqué** (*conduire, rouler*) with one's foot to the floor, like a maniac; **c. de vitesse** speedometer; **c. volumétrique** volumeter

2 *Ordinat* counter

comptine [kɔ̃tin] NF (*chanson*) nursery rhyme; (*formule*) counting-out rhyme

comptoir [kɔ̃twar] NM **1** (*bar*) bar; **j'ai pris un café au c.** I had a coffee at the bar *or* counter

2 *Com* (*table*) counter, desk; **c. d'enregistrement** check-in desk; **c. d'information** information desk; **c. de réception** reception desk; **c. de vente** sales counter

3 *Hist* trading post; **les anciens comptoirs de l'Inde** = trading posts which were the last enclaves of the French colonial presence in India

4 *Écon* trading syndicate

5 *Banque* bank branch; **c. d'escompte** discount house; **c. national d'escompte** national discount house

6 *Suisse* (*foire*) fair (*where items are exhibited and sold*)

7 *Can* **c. de cuisine** *Br* worktop, *Am* kitchen counter

comptoir-caisse [kɔ̃twarkɛs] (*pl* **comptoirs-caisses**) NM cash desk

compulser [3] [kɔ̃pylse] VT to consult, to refer to

compulsif, -ive [kɔ̃pylsif, -iv] ADJ *Psy* compulsive

compulsion [kɔ̃pylsjɔ̃] NF *Psy* compulsion

compulsionnel, -elle [kɔ̃pylsjɔnɛl] ADJ *Psy* compulsive

compulsive [kɔ̃pylsiv] *voir* **compulsif**

comput [kɔ̃pyt] NM *Rel* (*du calendrier*) computation

computation [kɔ̃pytasjɔ̃] NF computation (of time)

computer [kɔ̃pjutœr], **computeur** [kɔ̃pytœr] NM computer

comtal, -e, -aux, -ales [kɔ̃tal, -o] ADJ of a count, *Br* of an earl

comtat [kɔ̃ta] NM (*en Provence*) county

comte [kɔ̃t] NM count; (*en Grande-Bretagne*) earl; *Hist* **c. palatin** Count Palatine; **le C. de Paris**

= title of the present claimant to the French throne

📖

'Le Comte de Monte-Cristo' *Dumas* 'The Count of Monte Cristo'

comté [kɔ̃te] NM **1** (*territoire d'un comte*) earldom **2** (*division géographique*) county **3** (*fromage*) Comté (cheese) **4** *Can Pol* riding

comtesse [kɔ̃tɛs] NF countess

comtois, -e [kɔ̃twa, -az] ADJ of/from Franche-Comté

❑ **Comtois, -e** NM,F = inhabitant of or person from Franche-Comté

❑ **comtoise** NF grandfather *or* longcase clock

con, -onne [kɔ̃, kɔn] ADJ *très Fam* **1** (*stupide*) *Br* bloody *or Am* goddamn stupid; (*irritant*) *Br* bloody *or Am* goddamn infuriating; **ce que c'est c.!** it's so *Br* bloody *or Am* goddamn stupid!; **il est pas c.!** he's no fool!; **c'est pas c.!** that's pretty clever!ᵉ; **qu'est-ce qu'elle est c.** *ou* **conne!** what's so *Br* bloody *or Am* goddamn stupid!; **c. comme un balai** *ou* **la lune** *ou* **un manche** *Br* daft as a brush, *Am* dumb as they come; **se retrouver tout c.** to look an idiot, to end up looking stupid; **quand sa perruque s'est envolée, il s'est retrouvé tout c.** he looked a total idiot when his wig blew off

2 (*regrettable*) silly, stupid; **c'est vraiment c. que t'aies pas pu le prévenir!** it's really stupid that you weren't able to let him know in time!

NM,F *très Fam* (*imbécile*) *Br* arsehole, *Am* asshole; **pauvre c.!** you complete *Br* arsehole *or Am* asshole!; **pauvre conne!** silly cow!; **bande de cons!** what a bunch of *Br* arseholes *or Am* assholes!; **quel c. ce mec!** what a stupid bastard that guy is!; **le roi des cons** a complete and utter jerk; **jouer au c., faire le c.** *Br* to arse around, *Am* to screw around; (*faire semblant de ne pas comprendre*) to act dumb; **fais pas le c., ça va s'arranger** don't do anything stupid, it'll sort itself out; **fais pas le c. avec ce rasoir!** put that *Br* bloody *or Am* goddamn razor down!

NM *Vulg* (*sexe*) cunt

❑ **à la con** ADJ *très Fam* **1** (*stupide*) *Br* bloody *or Am* goddamn stupid; **c'est une histoire à la c.** it's a *Br* bloody *or Am* goddamn stupid story

2 (*de mauvaise qualité*) crappy, lousy; **j'en ai ras le bol de cette bagnole à la c.!** I'm fed up with this *Br* bloody *or Am* goddamn car!

Conakry [kɔnakri] NM Conakry, Konakri

conard [kɔnar] = **connard**

conasse [kɔnas] = **connasse**

conatus [kɔnatys] NM *Phil* conatus

concassage [kɔ̃kasaʒ] NM (*de la pierre, du sucre*) crushing, pounding; (*du poivre*) grinding

concassé, -e [kɔ̃kase] ADJ (*poivre, blé*) coarse-ground

concasser [3] [kɔ̃kase] VT (*pierre, sucre*) to crush, to pound; (*poivre*) to grind

concasseur [kɔ̃kasœr] ADJ M crushing; **cylindre c.** crushing cylinder

NM crusher

concaténation [kɔ̃katenasjɔ̃] NF concatenation

concaténer [18] [kɔ̃katene] VT *Ordinat* to concatenate

concave [kɔ̃kav] ADJ concave

concavité [kɔ̃kavite] NF **1** (*fait d'être concave*) concavity **2** (*creux*) hollow, cavity

concédant [kɔ̃sedɑ̃] NM *Fin* grantor

concéder [18] [kɔ̃sede] VT **1** (*donner → droit, territoire*) to concede, to grant; **on leur a concédé des terres** they were granted some land

2 (*admettre*) to admit, to grant; **je concède que j'ai tort** I admit that I'm wrong; **je te concède ce point** I grant you that point; **elle parle bien, ça je te le concède** I must admit that she's a good speaker, she's a good speaker, I grant you

3 *Sport* (*point, corner*) to concede, to give away; **il n'a pas concédé un seul set en dix matches** he hasn't given away *or* conceded a single set in his last ten matches

concélébration [kɔ̃selebrasjɔ̃] NF concelebration

concélébrer [18] [kɔ̃selebre] VT to concelebrate

concentrateur [kɔ̃sɑ̃tratœr] NM *Ordinat* concentrator

concentration [kɔ̃sɑ̃trasjɔ̃] NF **1** (*attention*) **c.**

(*d'esprit*) concentration; **l'exercice nécessite une grande c.** the exercise requires great concentration; **faire un effort de c.** to try to concentrate; **elle fait des erreurs par manque de c.** she makes mistakes because she doesn't concentrate enough

2 (*rassemblement*) concentration; **pour éviter la c. de tous les pouvoirs chez un seul homme** to make sure that all power isn't concentrated in the hands of one man; **la c. de l'industrie textile dans le Nord** the concentration of the textile industry in the North; **une zone à haute c. de population** a high-density area; *Mil* **c. du feu** *ou* **tir** concentration of fire; *Mil* **c. de troupes** troop concentration; **c. urbaine** conurbation

3 *Chim, Culin & Pharm* concentration; **augmenter la c. en sucre d'un sirop** to increase the sugar content of a syrup

4 *Écon* concentration; **c. horizontale/verticale** horizontal/vertical concentration

concentrationnaire [kɔ̃sɑ̃trasjɔnɛr] ADJ **1** *Hist* **l'univers c.** life in the (concentration) camps; **l'horreur c.** the horror of the (concentration) camps **2** (*rappelant les camps*) concentration camp-like

concentré, -e [kɔ̃sɑ̃tre] ADJ **1** (*attentif*) **je n'étais pas assez c.** I wasn't concentrating hard enough

2 *Chim, Culin & Pharm* concentrated

3 (*concis → style*) compact, taut; **dans une lettre très concentrée** in a letter that was very much to the point

NM **1** (*de jus de fruit*) concentrate; **c. de tomate** tomato purée

2 (*de parfum*) extract

3 (*résumé*) summary, *Péj* boiled-down version; **on leur fait apprendre un c. d'histoire de France** they're made to learn a boiled-down *or* potted version of French history

concentrer [3] [kɔ̃sɑ̃tre] VT **1** (*rassembler → troupes, foule, élèves*) to concentrate, to mass; **c'est là que l'on a concentré les malades** this is where all the sick people have been gathered together

2 (*intérêt, efforts*) to concentrate, to focus; **c. (toute) son attention sur** to concentrate (all) one's attention on

3 *Chim, Culin & Pharm* to concentrate

4 *Opt* to focus

5 *Vieilli & Littéraire* (*retenir*) to hold back, to repress; **je n'ai pu c. ma fureur** I could not contain my fury, my fury knew no bounds

▸**se concentrer** VPR (*être attentif*) to concentrate; **la radio m'empêche de me c.** the radio is preventing me from concentrating *or* is ruining my concentration; **se c. sur qch** to concentrate *or* to focus on sth; **je vais me c. sur l'anglais pour l'examen** I'm going to concentrate on English for the exam

2 (*se réunir → foule*) to gather, to cluster, to concentrate; **la population se concentre de plus en plus dans les grandes villes** the population is concentrating more and more in the big cities; **la foule s'était concentrée sur le parvis** the crowd had converged on the square

3 (*se canaliser*) to be concentrated *or* focused; **se c. sur un seul problème** to concentrate on a single issue

concentrique [kɔ̃sɑ̃trik] ADJ concentric

concentriquement [kɔ̃sɑ̃trikmɑ̃] ADV concentrically

concept [kɔ̃sɛpt] NM concept, notion; **c. de marketing** marketing concept; **c. de marque** brand concept; **c. publicitaire** advertising concept

conceptacle [kɔ̃sɛptakl] NM *Bot* conceptacle

concept-car [kɔ̃sɛpkar] (*pl* **concept-cars**) NM concept car

concepteur, -trice [kɔ̃sɛptœr, -tris] NM,F designer; **c'est plutôt un c. qu'un gestionnaire** he's more of an ideas man than a manager; **c. graphiste** graphic designer; **c. multimédia** multimedia designer; **c.-rédacteur** copywriter; *Ordinat* **c. de sites Web** web designer

conception [kɔ̃sɛpsjɔ̃] NF **1** (*notion*) idea, concept, notion; **sa c. du socialisme** his/her idea of socialism; **nous avons la même c. des choses** we see things the same way; **elle a une c. originale de la vie** she has a unique way of looking at life

2 *Littéraire (compréhension)* understanding **3** *Biol* conception

4 *(élaboration → gén)* design; **produit de c. française** French-designed product; **un ventilateur d'une c. toute nouvelle** a fan with an entirely new design; **c. graphique** graphic design; **c. du produit** product design

5 *Ordinat* **c. assistée par ordinateur** computer-aided *or* computer-assisted design; **c. et fabrication assistées par ordinateur** computer-aided *or* computer-assisted manufacturing

conceptisme [kɔ̃sɛptism] NM *Littérature* conceptism

conceptrice [kɔ̃sɛptris] *voir* **concepteur**

conceptualisation [kɔ̃sɛptɥalizasjɔ̃] NF conceptualization

conceptrice [kɔ̃sɛptris] *voir* **concepteur**

conceptualiser [3] [kɔ̃sɛptɥalize] VT to conceptualize

conceptualisme [kɔ̃sɛptɥalism] NM conceptualism

conceptuel, -elle [kɔ̃sɛptɥɛl] ADJ conceptual

concernant [kɔ̃sɛrnɑ̃] PRÉP **1** *(relatif à)* concerning, regarding; **pour toutes questions c. nos nouveaux produits** for all questions concerning *or* regarding *or* relating to our new products **2** *(à propos de)* regarding, with regard to; **c. la réduction des impôts, voilà ce qu'il a dit** regarding *or* with regard to taxes, this is what he said

concerner [3] [kɔ̃sɛrne] VT to concern; **écoute un peu, cette discussion te concerne** listen, this discussion has implications for you *or* concerns you; **cette histoire ne nous concerne pas** this business doesn't concern us *or* is of no concern to us *or* is no concern of ours; **les salariés concernés par cette mesure** the employees concerned *or* affected by this measure; **veuillez passer me voir pour affaire vous concernant** please come and see me to discuss a matter which concerns *or* involves you; **se sentir concerné** to feel involved; **il ne se sent pas concerné** he's indifferent

❏ **en ce qui concerne** PRÉP concerning, as regards; **en ce qui me/le concerne** as far as I'm/he's concerned, from my/his point of view, as for me/him

concert [kɔ̃sɛr] NM **1** *Mus* concert; **c. rock/de musique classique** rock/classical (music) concert; **c. de musique de chambre** chamber concert; **c. de musique sacrée** concert of sacred music; **aller au c.** to go to a concert; **je vais peu au c.** I don't go to concerts very often, I'm not much of a concert-goer; **il faut les voir en c.** you have to see them in concert *or* on stage; **Béhel en c.** *(sur une affiche, un disque)* Béhel live *or* in concert

2 *Fig (ensemble)* chorus; **c. de louanges/protestations** chorus of praises/protests; **un c. de sifflets/marteaux-piqueurs** a chorus of whistles/pneumatic drills

3 *(entente)* entente; **le c. des nations africaines** the entente between African nations

❏ **de concert** ADV together, jointly; **nous avons décidé de c. que...** together we have decided that...; **agir de c. avec qn** to act jointly *or* in conjunction with sb

concertant, -e [kɔ̃sɛrtɑ̃, -ɑ̃t] ADJ concertante

concertation [kɔ̃sɛrtasjɔ̃] NF **1** *(dialogue)* dialogue; **une plus grande c. entre les pays industrialisés serait désirable** a greater dialogue between the industrialized countries would be welcome **2** *(consultation)* consultation; **sans c. préalable avec les syndicats** without consulting the unions

concerté, -e [kɔ̃sɛrte] ADJ **1** *(commun → plan, action)* concerted, joint **2** *Écon* **fixation concertée des prix** common pricing, common price fixing

concerter [3] [kɔ̃sɛrte] VT to plan *or* to devise jointly

▸ **se concerter** VPR to consult each other, to confer; **ils se concertèrent sur les moyens d'action** they consulted each other as to how to act

concertina [kɔ̃sɛrtina] NM *Mus* concertina

concertino [kɔ̃sɛrtino] NM *(groupe, morceau)* concertino

concertiste [kɔ̃sɛrtist] NMF **1** *(gén)* concert performer *or* artist **2** *(soliste)* soloist *(in a concerto)*

concerto [kɔ̃sɛrto] NM concerto; **c. grosso** concerto grosso

'Les Concertos brandebourgeois' *Bach* 'The Brandenburg Concertos'

'Concerto pour la main gauche' *Ravel* 'Piano Concerto for the Left Hand'

concert-promenade [kɔ̃sɛrprɔmnad] *(pl* **concerts-promenades**) NM promenade concert

concessible [kɔ̃sesibl] ADJ concessible

concessif, -ive [kɔ̃sesif, -iv] *Gram* ADJ concessive

❏ **concessive** NF concessive clause

concession [kɔ̃sesjɔ̃] NF **1** *(compromis)* concession; **faire des concessions** to make concessions; **je l'ai fait, mais au prix de nombreuses concessions** I did it but I had to concede a lot (of ground); **c'est un homme sans c.** he's an uncompromising man

2 *Jur (d'un privilège, d'un droit)* concession; **faire la c. d'un terrain à** to grant a piece of land to; **accorder une c. à** to grant a concession to; **retirer une c. à** to withdraw a concession from; **c. exclusive** tied outlet; **c. de franchise** grant of franchise; **c. immobilière** = concession of land for a minimum of 20 years; **c. de licence** licensing; **c. de voirie** = contract permitting the private occupation of part of a public road

3 *Com (dans l'automobile)* dealership

4 *(terrain)* concession; **c. minière/pétrolière** mining/oil concession; **c. funéraire** burial plot; **c. à perpétuité** plot held in perpetuity

❏ **de concession** ADJ *Gram* concessive

concessionnaire [kɔ̃sesjɔnɛr] ADJ concessionary NMF **1** *Jur (détenteur → d'une licence)* licensee; *(→ d'une franchise)* franchisee **2** *Com* agent, dealer; **renseignez-vous auprès de votre c. (automobile)** see your (car) dealer; **c. agréé** approved dealer, authorized dealer; **c. exclusif** sole agent, sole dealer; **c. export** export agent

concessive [kɔ̃sesiv] *voir* **concessif**

concetti [kɔ̃tʃetti] NMPL *Littéraire* conceits, concetti

concevable [kɔ̃svabl] ADJ conceivable; **c'est difficilement c.** it's hardly conceivable; **il n'est pas c. que...** it's inconceivable that...

concevoir [52] [kɔ̃səvwar] VT **1** *(avoir une notion de)* to conceive of, to form a notion of; **c. l'infini** to form a notion of infinity

2 *(imaginer)* to imagine, to conceive of; **c. la maison idéale** to imagine the ideal home; **je ne conçois pas de repas sans vin** I can't imagine a meal without wine; **je ne conçois pas de ne jamais le revoir** I can't accept that I'll never see him again

3 *(comprendre)* to understand, to see; **c'est ainsi que je conçois l'amour** this is my idea of love *or* how I see love; **cela vous est difficile, je le conçois** I can (well) understand that it's difficult for you; **c. qch comme** to conceive *or* to see sth as

4 *Littéraire (ressentir → haine, amitié)* to conceive, to develop; **il en conçut une vive amertume** he felt very bitter about it

5 *(créer → meuble, décor, ouvrage)* to design; *(→ plan, programme)* to conceive, to devise, to think up; **parc bien/mal conçu** well-/poorly-designed garden

6 *(rédiger → message, réponse)* to compose, to couch; **une lettre conçue en ces termes** a letter written as follows *or* couched in the following terms

7 *Biol* to conceive

USAGE ABSOLU **1** **la faculté de c.** the ability to think; **ce que l'on conçoit bien s'énonce clairement** what is clearly understood can be clearly expressed

2 *(avoir des enfants)* to conceive; **les femmes qui ne peuvent pas c.** women who cannot have children *or* conceive

▸ **se concevoir** VPR to be imagined; **une telle politique se conçoit en temps de guerre** such a policy is understandable in wartime; **cela se conçoit facilement** that is easy to understand *or* easily understood

conche [kɔ̃ʃ] NF **1** *Vieilli (coquillage)* conch, marine shell **2** *(dans le Sud-Ouest de la France)* creek, cove

conchier [9] [kɔ̃ʃje] VT *Vulg Littéraire* to soil (with excrement)▪; **conchié de mouches** fly-blown▪

conchoïdal, -e, -aux, -ales [kɔ̃kɔidal, -o] ADJ conchoidal

conchoïde [kɔ̃kɔid] NF conchoid

conchyliculteur, -trice [kɔ̃kilikyltœr, -tris] NM,F shellfish breeder

conchyliculture [kɔ̃kilikyltyr] NF shellfish breeding

conchyliologie [kɔ̃kiljɔlɔʒi] NF conchology

conchylis [kɔ̃kilis] NM OU NF *Entom* cochylis (moth)

concierge [kɔ̃sjɛrʒ] NMF **1** *(gardien → d'immeuble)* caretaker, *Am* janitor; *(→ en France)* concierge; *(→ d'hôtel)* doorman; *(→ d'une école)* caretaker, *Am & Scot* janitor **2** *Fam Péj (bavard)* gossip, blabbermouth; **c'est une vraie c.** she's a terrible gossip

<Culture>

CONCIERGE

In French apartment buildings, the "concierge" traditionally does general cleaning jobs, sees to it that no unwelcome visitors enter the building and often also delivers mail to the occupants of the building. The "concierge" usually lives in a small flat ("la loge") just inside the front entrance. "Concierges" are traditionally portrayed as nosy and interfering. Nowadays, however, there are fewer and fewer of them as most apartment buildings are equipped with entryphone systems, and where a caretaker is employed he or she is usually referred to as "le gardien" or "la gardienne". For the past 30 years or so the Portuguese have been overrepresented in the profession as a result of the influx of unskilled labour from Portugal. In fact, the vast majority of women still working as "concierges" in France today are Portuguese.

conciergerie [kɔ̃sjɛrʒəri] NF **1** *(loge)* caretaker's office, *Am* janitor's lodge **2** *Hist* **la C.** the Conciergerie prison *(in Paris)*

concile [kɔ̃sil] NM council; **c. œcuménique** ecumenical council; **le c. de Trente** the Council of Trent

conciliable [kɔ̃siljabl] ADJ reconcilable, compatible; **les études sont-elles conciliables avec le métier de chanteur?** is studying compatible with a singing career?; **des principes difficilement conciliables** principles difficult to reconcile

conciliabule [kɔ̃siljabyl] NM **1** *(conversation)* confab; **les enfants étaient en grand c.** the children were having a big confab **2** *Arch (réunion)* secret meeting, secret assembly

conciliaire [kɔ̃siljɛr] ADJ conciliar

conciliant, -e [kɔ̃siljɑ̃, -ɑ̃t] ADJ *(personne)* conciliatory, accommodating; *(paroles, ton)* conciliatory, placatory

conciliateur, -trice [kɔ̃siljatœr, -tris] ADJ conciliatory, placatory NM,F conciliator, arbitrator; *Jur* **c. en justice** civil magistrate

conciliation [kɔ̃siljasjɔ̃] NF **1** *(médiation)* conciliation; **esprit de c.** spirit of conciliation; **geste de c.** conciliatory gesture **2** *Jur* conciliation, arbitration; **comité de c.** arbitration committee **3** *Littéraire (entre deux personnes, deux partis)* reconciliation

conciliatoire [kɔ̃siljatwar] ADJ conciliatory

conciliatrice [kɔ̃siljatris] *voir* **conciliateur**

concilier [9] [kɔ̃silje] VT **1** *(accorder → opinions, exigences)* to reconcile; **c. travail et plaisir** to manage to combine work with pleasure **2** *(gagner → faveurs, sympathie)* to gain, to win; **sa droiture lui a concilié l'admiration de tous les employés** his/her uprightness won *or* gained him/her the admiration of all the employees; **sa gentillesse lui a concilié la sympathie de tous** his/her kindness made him/her popular with everybody

▸ **se concilier** VPR **1** *(être compatible)* to go together **2 se c. l'amitié de qn** to gain *or* to win sb's friendship; **se c. les électeurs** to win the voters over

concis, -e [kɔ̃si, -iz] **ADJ** (style) concise, tight; (écrivain) concise; **de manière concise** concisely; **soyez plus c.** come to the point

concision [kɔ̃sizjɔ̃] **NF** concision, conciseness, tightness; **avec c.** concisely; **style d'une extrême c.** extremely concise or tight style

concitoyen, -enne [kɔ̃sitwajɛ̃, -ɛn] **NM,F** fellow citizen

conclave [kɔ̃klav] **NM** conclave

concluant, -e [kɔ̃klyɑ̃, -ɑ̃t] **ADJ** (essai, démonstration) conclusive; **peu c.** inconclusive

conclure [96] [kɔ̃klyr] **VT 1** (terminer → discussion, travail) to end, to conclude, to bring to a close or conclusion; (→ repas) to finish or to round off
2 (déduire) to conclude; **que peut-on c. de cette expérience?** what conclusion can be drawn from this experience?; **n'ayant pas eu de réponse, j'en conclus que…** not having had an answer I conclude that…
3 (accord) to conclude; (contrat) to enter into, Br to conclude; (traité) to sign, to conclude; (vente) to close, to complete; **c. un marché** to strike or make a deal; **c. un cessez-le-feu** ou **un accord de cessez-le-feu** to sign a ceasefire agreement; **marché conclu!** it's a deal!
USAGE ABSOLU 1 (terminer) **c. par** to end or to conclude with; **elle a conclu par un appel à l'unité** she ended with a call for unity; **maintenant, vous devez c.** now you must come to a conclusion; **il faut savoir c.** you've got to know when to stop
2 Fam (en matière amoureuse) to get a result, to close the deal; **ce soir, je sens que je vais c.!** I'm going to close the deal tonight, I can feel it!
VI Jur **les témoignages concluent contre lui/en sa faveur** the evidence goes against him/in his favour
❏ **conclure à VT IND** ils ont dû c. au meurtre they had to conclude that it was murder; **le jury a conclu au suicide** the jury returned a verdict of suicide
❏ **pour conclure ADV** as a or in conclusion, to conclude

conclusif, -ive [kɔ̃klyzif, -iv] **ADJ** (paragraphe) closing, final

conclusion [kɔ̃klyzjɔ̃] **NF 1** (fin) conclusion
2 (déduction) conclusion; **nous en sommes arrivés à la c. suivante** we came to or reached the following conclusion; **gardons-nous des conclusions hâtives** let's not jump to conclusions; **tirer une c. de qch** to draw a conclusion from sth; Fam **c., la voiture est fichue** the upshot is that the car's a write-off
3 (d'un accord) conclusion; (d'un contrat) entering into, Br to conclude; (d'un traité) signing, conclusion; (d'un cessez-le-feu) agreement; (d'une vente) closing, completion; (d'un marché) agreement; **la c. d'un accord de cessez-le-feu** the signing of a ceasefire agreement
❏ **conclusions NFPL** (d'un rapport, d'une enquête) findings; Jur submissions; **déposer** ou **signifier des conclusions** to file submissions with a court; **conclusions qualificatives** pleadings; **conclusions récapitulatives** final submissions, summation; **conclusions subsidiaires** accessory claims
❏ **en conclusion ADV** as a or in conclusion, to conclude

conclusive [kɔ̃klyziv] voir **conclusif**

concocter [3] [kɔ̃kɔkte] **VT** to concoct

concoction [kɔ̃kɔksjɔ̃] **NF** digestion

conçois etc voir **concevoir**

conçoivent etc voir **concevoir**

concombre [kɔ̃kɔ̃br] **NM 1** Bot cucumber **2** Can Fam Péj idiot, twit **3** Ich **c. de mer** sea cucumber

concomitamment [kɔ̃kɔmitamɑ̃] **ADV** concomitantly

concomitance [kɔ̃kɔmitɑ̃s] **NF** concomitance

concomitant, -e [kɔ̃kɔmitɑ̃, -ɑ̃t] **ADJ** concomitant, attendant

concordance [kɔ̃kɔrdɑ̃s] **NF 1** (conformité) agreement, similarity; **la c. des empreintes/dates** the similarity between the fingerprints/dates **2** Gram **c. des temps** sequence of tenses **3** Géol conformability **4** (index) concordance
❏ **en concordance avec PRÉP** in agreement or keeping or accordance with

concordant, -e [kɔ̃kɔrdɑ̃, -ɑ̃t] **ADJ 1** (correspondant) **les versions sont concordantes** the stories agree or match **2** Géol conformable

concordat [kɔ̃kɔrda] **NM 1** Rel concordat **2** Jur scheme of composition, scheme of arrangement; **c. préventif** composition (in bankruptcy)

concordataire [kɔ̃kɔrdatɛr] **ADJ 1** Rel concordat (avant n) **2** Jur **failli c.** certified bankrupt

concorde [kɔ̃kɔrd] **NF** Littéraire concord, harmony

concorder [3] [kɔ̃kɔrde] **VI** (versions, chiffres) to agree, to tally; (groupes sanguins, empreintes) to match; **faire c. qch et** ou **avec qch** to make sth and sth agree

concourant, -e [kɔ̃kurɑ̃, -ɑ̃t] **ADJ 1** Géom **droites concourantes** concurrent or convergent lines **2** (actions, volontés) joint, concerted, united

concourir [45] [kɔ̃kurir] **VI 1** (être en compétition) to compete; **elle a refusé de c. cette année** she has refused to enter competitions or to compete this year; **il est trop jeune pour que je le fasse c.** he's too young for me to enter him in competitions; **c. avec qn** to compete with or against sb
2 Géom to converge
3 Jur to have concurrent claims
❏ **concourir à VT IND** to contribute to; **beaucoup de facteurs ont concouru à sa réussite** a number of factors contributed to his/her success; **tout concourt à me faire croire qu'il ment** everything leads me to believe that he's lying

concours [kɔ̃kur] **NM 1** (aide) aid, help, support; **prêter son c. à** to lend one's support to; **grâce au c. du maire** thanks to the mayor's help or support; **c. bancaire** bank lending; **c. financier** financial aid
2 (combinaison) **un heureux/un fâcheux c. de circonstances** a lucky/an unfortunate coincidence
3 (épreuve) competition, contest; **c. de beauté/de chant** beauty/singing contest; **c. agricole/hippique** agricultural/horse show; **le c. de l'Eurovision** the Eurovision song contest; **le c. Lépine** = annual exhibition of the "Association des inventeurs et des fabricants français", where many ingenious new gadgets are displayed and demonstrated
4 Scol & Univ competitive (entrance) exam; **le c. d'entrée à l'ENA** the entrance exam for the "ENA"; **c. interne/externe** in-house or internal/open competition; **c. administratifs** = examinations for entry into administrative posts in the government or civil service; **c. de la fonction publique** = examinations for entry into government or civil service jobs, including teaching; **le c. général** = competition in which the best pupils in the two upper forms at French "lycées" compete for prizes in a variety of subjects
5 Arch & Littéraire (de personnes) concourse, gathering; **grand c. de curieux** great concourse of sightseers
❏ **avec le concours de PRÉP** with the participation of, in association with
❏ **par concours, sur concours ADV** (recruter, entrer) on the results of a competitive entrance exam

concouru [kɔ̃kury] **PP** voir **concourir**

concrescible [kɔ̃krɛsibl] **ADJ** concrescible, coagulable, congealable

concret, -ète [kɔ̃krɛ, -ɛt] **ADJ 1** (palpable) concrete; **un objet c.** a thing, a concrete object **2** (non théorique) concrete, practical; **faire des propositions concrètes** to make concrete or practical proposals; **je veux des résultats concrets** I want concrete or tangible results; **cas c.** actual case, concrete example **3** (s'appuyant sur l'expérience) concrete, empirical, experiential; **un esprit c.** a practical mind **4** Ling & Mus concrete
NM le c. that which is concrete, the concrete; **ce qu'il nous faut, c'est du c.** we need something we can get our teeth into

concrètement [kɔ̃krɛtmɑ̃] **ADV** concretely, in concrete terms; **je ne vois pas c. ce que ça peut donner** I can't visualize what it would be like; **c., qu'est-ce que cela va entraîner pour les usagers?** in real terms, what will that mean for the users?

concrétion [kɔ̃kresjɔ̃] **NF** Chim, Géol & Méd concretion; Méd **concrétions calcaires** chalk stones

concrétisation [kɔ̃kretizasjɔ̃] **NF** concretization, materialization; **la c. d'un rêve** a dream come true

concrétiser [3] [kɔ̃kretize] **VT** (rêve) to realize; (idée, proposition) to make concrete; **ils n'ont pas réussi à c. leur domination** (équipe) they were the stronger side but they didn't capitalize on it or they didn't manage to push their advantage home
▶**se concrétiser VPR** (rêve) to come true, to materialize; (proposition, idée) to be realized, to take concrete form or shape

conçu, -e [kɔ̃sy] **PP** voir **concevoir**

concubin, -e [kɔ̃kybɛ̃, -in] **NM,F 1** (amant) concubine, partner **2** Jur partner, cohabitee

concubinage [kɔ̃kybinaʒ] **NM 1** (vie de couple) **vivre en c.** to live together or as man and wife, to cohabit **2** Jur cohabitation, cohabiting; **c. notoire** common-law marriage

concupiscence [kɔ̃kypisɑ̃s] **NF** (envers les biens) greed; (envers le sexe) lust, Littéraire concupiscence

concupiscent, -e [kɔ̃kypisɑ̃, -ɑ̃t] **ADJ** (envers les biens) greedy; (envers le sexe) lustful, Littéraire concupiscent

concurremment [kɔ̃kyramɑ̃] **ADV** (ensemble) jointly, in conjunction or Sout concert; (en même temps) at the same time, concurrently
❏ **concurremment avec PRÉP 1** (de concert avec) in conjunction or Sout concert with **2** (en même temps que) concurrently with

concurrence [kɔ̃kyrɑ̃s] **NF 1** (rivalité) competition; **faire (de la) c. à** to be in competition or to compete with; **faire jouer la c.** to allow market forces to operate; **les Japonais nous livrent une c. acharnée** we're engaged in a cut-throat competition with the Japanese; **la libre c.** free or open competition; **c. déloyale** unfair competition or trading; **c. directe** direct competition; **c. étrangère** foreign competition; **c. imparfaite** imperfect competition; **c. parfaite** perfect competition; **c. pure** pure competition
2 (rivaux) **la c.** the competition; **nos prix défient toute c.** our prices are unbeatable
❏ **en concurrence ADV** in competition; **être en c. avec qn** to be in competition with sb; **entrer en c. avec qn** to compete with sb; **il est en c. avec son frère** he's in competition with or he's competing with his brother
❏ **à concurrence de, jusqu'à concurrence de PRÉP** up to, to the limit of; **vous pouvez être à découvert jusqu'à c. de 1000 euros** your overdraft limit is 1,000 euros

concurrencer [16] [kɔ̃kyrɑ̃se] **VT** to compete with; **leur nouvelle gamme ne peut c. la nôtre** their new line can't compete with ours; **ils nous concurrencent dangereusement** they're very dangerous competitors

concurrent, -e [kɔ̃kyrɑ̃, -ɑ̃t] **ADJ 1** (entreprises, produits) competing, rival (avant n) **2** Arch (actions, efforts) joint, concerted, united
NM,F 1 Com & Sport competitor, rival; Com **c. principal** major competitor; Mktg **c. tardif** late entrant **2** (à une épreuve, un poste) candidate

concurrentiel, -elle [kɔ̃kyrɑ̃sjɛl] **ADJ** competitive; **ces marchandises sont vendues à des prix concurrentiels** these goods are competitively priced

concussion [kɔ̃kysjɔ̃] **NF** embezzlement, misappropriation of public funds

concussionnaire [kɔ̃kysjɔnɛr] ADJ embezzling
NMF embezzler

conçut *etc voir* **concevoir**

condamnable [kɔ̃danabl] ADJ blameworthy, reprehensible

condamnation [kɔ̃danasjɔ̃] NF **1** *Jur (action)* sentencing, convicting; *(peine)* sentence; **il a fait l'objet de trois condamnations pour vol** he's had three convictions for theft, he's been convicted three times for theft; **il a déjà quatre condamnations à son actif** he already has four convictions; **c. différée** deferred sentence; **c. à mort** death sentence; **c. à la réclusion à perpétuité** life sentence, sentence of life imprisonment; **c. aux travaux forcés** sentence of hard labour; **c. par défaut/par contumace** decree by default/in absentia
2 *(blâme)* condemnation, blame; **c'est une c. sans appel de sa politique extérieure** it's an out-and-out condemnation of his/her foreign policy
3 *(fin → d'un projet, d'une tentative)* end; **ce projet est la c. de l'enseignement privé** this project spells the end of private education
4 *Aut (blocage)* locking; *(système)* locking device; **c. automatique des portes** automatic door locking; **c. centralisée des portes** central locking

condamnatoire [kɔ̃danatwar] ADJ *Jur* condemnatory

condamné, -e [kɔ̃dane] NM,F *Jur* sentenced *or* convicted person; **l'aile des condamnés à mort** Death Row; **c. à mort** prisoner under sentence of death; **c. à la réclusion perpétuelle** life prisoner, lifer; **la cigarette du c.** the condemned man's last cigarette

'Un Condamné à mort s'est échappé' *Bresson* 'A Man Escaped'

condamner [3] [kɔ̃dane] VT **1** *Jur (accusé)* to sentence; **c. qn à mort/aux travaux forcés** to sentence sb to death/to hard labour; **condamné à trois mois de prison pour...** sentenced to three months' imprisonment for...; **c. qn à 2000 euros d'amende** to fine sb 2,000 euros; **condamné aux dépens** ordered to pay costs; **condamné pour meurtre** convicted of murder; **c. qn par défaut/par contumace** to sentence sb by default/in absentia; **faire c. qn** to get *or* to have sb convicted
2 *(interdire → magazine)* to forbid publication of; *(→ pratique)* to forbid, to condemn; **la société condamne la bigamie** society forbids *or* condemns bigamy; **la loi condamne l'usage de stupéfiants** the use of narcotics is forbidden by law
3 *(désapprouver → attentat, propos)* to express disapproval of; *(→ personne)* to condemn, to blame; **c. qn pour avoir fait** *ou* **d'avoir fait qch** to blame sb for having done sth; **nous condamnons cet acte avec indignation** we fiercely condemn what has been done here; **l'expression est condamnée par les puristes** the use of the phrase is condemned *or* is disapproved of by purists
4 *(accuser)* to condemn; **son silence la condamne** her silence condemns her
5 *(sujet: maladie incurable)* to condemn, to doom; **les médecins disent qu'il est condamné** the doctors say that there is no hope for him; **les malades condamnés sont renvoyés chez eux** terminally-ill patients are sent back home; *Fig* **ce projet est condamné par manque d'argent** the project is doomed through lack of money
6 *(murer → porte, fenêtre)* to block up, to seal off; *(→ pièce)* to close up; **la troisième chambre avait été condamnée** the third bedroom had been closed up; **c. toutes les fenêtres d'une maison** to board up the windows in a house; *Fig* **c. sa porte** to bar one's door
7 *(obliger)* **il était condamné à vivre dans la misère** he was condemned to live in poverty; **je suis condamnée à rester alitée pendant dix jours** I'm confined to bed for ten days; **je suis condamnée à l'attendre** I have to wait for him/her; **être condamné à la solitude** to be condemned to loneliness

condé [kɔ̃de] NM *Fam Arg crime (policier)* cop; **les condés** the cops, *Br* the fuzz

condensable [kɔ̃dɑ̃sabl] ADJ condensable

condensat [kɔ̃dɑ̃sa] NM *Phys* condensate; **c. de Bose-Einstein** Bose-Einstein condensate

condensateur [kɔ̃dɑ̃satœr] NM **1** *Élec* condenser, capacitor **2** *Opt* **c. optique** condenser

condensation [kɔ̃dɑ̃sasjɔ̃] NF **1** *Chim & Phys* condensation **2** *(buée)* condensation; **une pièce où il y a beaucoup de c.** a very damp room **3** *(d'un texte)* condensing, cutting down

condensé [kɔ̃dɑ̃se] NM digest, summary, abstract

condenser [3] [kɔ̃dɑ̃se] VT **1** *Chim & Phys* to condense **2** *(raccourcir → récit)* to condense, to cut down; **style condensé** terse style **3** *Ordinat (base de données)* to pack
▸**se condenser** VPR to condense

condenseur [kɔ̃dɑ̃sœr] NM condenser; **c. à mélange** jet *or* injection condenser; **c. à surface** surface condenser

condescendance [kɔ̃desɑ̃dɑ̃s] NF condescension; **avec c.** condescendingly; **traiter qn avec c.** to patronize sb; **faire preuve de c. à l'égard de qn** to patronize sb

condescendant, -e [kɔ̃desɑ̃dɑ̃, -ɑ̃t] ADJ *(hautain → regard, parole)* condescending, patronizing; **d'un air c.** patronizingly

condescendre [73] [kɔ̃desɑ̃dr] **condescendre à** VT IND to condescend to; *aussi Hum* **elle a condescendu à me recevoir** she condescended *or* deigned to see me

condiment [kɔ̃dimɑ̃] NM *(épices)* condiment; *(moutarde)* (mild) mustard

condisciple [kɔ̃disipl] NMF *Scol* classmate, schoolmate; *Univ* fellow student

condition [kɔ̃disjɔ̃] NF **1** *(préalable)* condition; **une des conditions du progrès** one of the conditions of *or* requirements for progress; **c'est la c. de votre réussite** that's what will determine your success; **les conditions n'étaient pas réunies** the conditions weren't quite right; **il met une c. à son accord** there's a condition to his agreement; **il veut bien signer le contrat, mais il y met une c.** he's happy to sign the contract, but on one condition; **j'accepte mais à une c.** I accept but on one condition; **c. nécessaire/suffisante** necessary/sufficient condition; **c. préalable** prerequisite; **c. requise** requirement; **une c. sine qua non pour** an absolute prerequisite for
2 *(état → de quelqu'un)* condition, shape; *(→ de quelque chose)* condition; **c. physique/psychologique** physical/psychological shape; **être en bonne c. physique** to be in condition, to be fit; **en grande** *ou* **excellente c. physique** in excellent shape; **être en mauvaise c. physique** to be in poor physical shape, to be unfit; **les marchandises nous sont parvenues en bonne c.** the goods arrived in good condition
3 *(position sociale)* rank, station; **des gens de toutes conditions** people from all walks of life; **une femme de c. modeste** a woman from a modest background; *Arch* **personne de c.** person of rank; **épouser qn de sa c.** to marry sb of one's own station *or* social background; **épouser qn au-dessous de sa c.** to marry beneath one's station; **la c. paysanne au XIXème siècle** the situation of peasants in the 19th century; **pour améliorer leur c.** in order to improve their lot; **la c. féminine** the lives of women, women's status; **la c. ouvrière** the condition of the working-class
4 *(destinée)* **la c. humaine** the human condition
5 *Jur* condition; **c. casuelle** fortuitous condition; **c. des étrangers** status of aliens; **c. mixte** mixed condition; **c. potestative** potestative condition; **c. résolutoire** condition subsequent; **c. simplement potestative** potestative and fortuitous condition; **c. suspensive** condition precedent
❑ **conditions** NFPL **1** *(environnement)* conditions; **conditions climatiques/économiques** weather/economic conditions; **dans des conditions normales de température** at normal temperatures; **voyager dans les meilleures conditions** to travel under the most favourable conditions; **conditions de vie/travail** living/working conditions; **conditions du marché** market conditions; **conditions météo** weather conditions
2 *(termes)* terms; **les conditions d'un accord** the terms of an agreement; **aux conditions les plus avantageuses** on the most favourable terms; **vos conditions seront les miennes** I'll go along with whatever conditions you wish to lay down; **quelles sont ses conditions?** what terms is he/she offering?; **conditions d'achat** terms of purchase; **conditions d'admission** admission requirements; **conditions générales de vente** general (terms and) conditions of sale; **conditions de livraison** terms of delivery; **conditions de paiement** terms of payment; **conditions particulières** *(d'un billet etc)* restrictions; **conditions de remboursement** terms of repayment; **conditions de vente** terms of sale
❑ **à condition** ADV **envoyer des marchandises à c.** to send goods on approval
❑ **à condition de** PRÉP on condition that, provided (that); **tu peux y aller à c. de ne pas rentrer tard** you may go on condition that *or* provided (that) you don't come back late
❑ **à (la) condition que** CONJ on condition that, provided (that); **je ne dirai rien à c. que tu en fasses autant** I won't say anything on condition that *or* provided (that) you do the same
❑ **dans ces conditions** ADV under these conditions; **dans ces conditions, j'accepte** under these conditions, I accept; **dans ces conditions, pourquoi se donner tant de mal?** if that's the case, why go to so much trouble?
❑ **en condition** ADJ *(en forme)* in shape ADV **1** *(en forme)* in shape; **mettre en c.** *(athlète, candidat)* to get into condition *or* form; **se mettre en c.** to get (oneself) fit *or* into condition *or* into shape **2** *(dans un état favorable)* **mettre le public en c.** to condition the public **3** *Arch (dans la domesticité)* **entrer en c. chez qn** to enter sb's service
❑ **sans condition(s)** ADV unconditionally ADJ unconditional; **reddition sans conditions** unconditional surrender
❑ **sous condition** ADV conditionally; **acheter qch sous c.** to buy sth on approval

'La Condition humaine' *Malraux* 'Man's Estate' (UK), 'Man's Fate' (US)

conditionnalité [kɔ̃disjɔnalite] NF *Écon* conditionality

conditionné, -e [kɔ̃disjɔne] ADJ **1** *Psy* conditioned **2** *(climatisé → bureau, autocar)* air-conditioned **3** *Com (emballé → marchandise)* prepacked, prepackaged

conditionnel, -elle [kɔ̃disjɔnɛl] ADJ **1** *(soumis à condition)* conditional, tentative; **notre soutien est c. et dépend de...** our support is conditional on... **2** *Psy* conditioned **3** *Gram* conditional
NM *Gram* conditional (mood); **c. présent/passé** present/perfect conditional tense
❑ **conditionnelle** NF *Gram* conditional clause
❑ **au conditionnel** ADV **1** *Gram* in the conditional **2** *(comme une hypothèse)* **la nouvelle est à prendre au c.** the news has yet to be confirmed *or* checked; **il faut l'annoncer au c.** it's not yet certain

conditionnellement [kɔ̃disjɔnɛlmɑ̃] ADV conditionally, tentatively

conditionnement [kɔ̃disjɔnmɑ̃] NM **1** *(fait d'emballer, emballage)* packaging **2** *Tex* conditioning **3** *Ind* processing **4** *Psy* conditioning; **c. classique** classical conditioning; **c. instrumental** *ou* **opérant** instrumental learning

conditionner [3] [kɔ̃disjɔne] VT **1** *(emballer → marchandise, aliments)* to package **2** *Tex* to condition **3** *Ind* to process **4** *Psy (influencer)* to condition, to influence; **la publicité conditionne nos choix** advertising conditions *or* influences our choices; **on l'a conditionné pour réagir de la sorte** he's been conditioned to react this way; **notre départ est conditionné par son état de santé** our going away depends on *or* is conditional on his/her state of health **5** *(climatiser)* to air-condition

conditionneur, -euse [kɔ̃disjɔnœr, -øz] NM,F food-processing specialist
NM **1** *(climatiseur)* air conditioner **2** *Ind* packer

condo [kɔ̃do] NM *Can (abrév* **condominium***)* condo

condoléances [kɔ̃dɔleɑ̃s] NFPL condolences; **lettre de c.** letter of condolence; **présenter**

ses c. (à qn) to offer one's condolences (to sb); **veuillez accepter mes plus sincères c.** please accept my deepest sympathy *or* my most sincere condolences; **toutes mes c., Paul** with deepest sympathy *or* heartfelt condolences, Paul

condom [kɔ̃dɔm] **NM** condom, sheath

condominium [kɔ̃dɔminjɔm] **NM** condominium

condor [kɔ̃dɔr] **NM** *Orn* condor; **c. papa** king vulture

condottiere [kɔ̃dɔtjɛr] (*pl* **condottieri** [-ri]) **NM** condottiere

conductance [kɔ̃dyktɑ̃s] **NF** conductance

conducteur, -trice [kɔ̃dyktœr, -tris] **ADJ 1** *Élec* conductive **2** *Fig (principal → principe, fil)* guiding

NM,F 1 *Transp* driver; **c. d'autobus** bus driver; **c. de camions** truck *or Br* lorry driver **2** *Ind* operator; **c. de travaux** foreman, *f* forewoman, clerk of works

NM *Phys* conductor

conductibilité [kɔ̃dyktibilite] **NF** conductivity

conductible [kɔ̃dyktibl] **ADJ** conductive

conduction [kɔ̃dyksjɔ̃] **NF** conduction; **c. électrolytique** electrolysis

conductivité [kɔ̃dyktivite] **NF** conductivity

conductrice [kɔ̃dyktris] *voir* **conducteur**

CONDUIRE [9] [kɔ̃dɥir]

> **VT** to take **1** ▪ to drive **1, 4** ▪ to lead **2, 3, 5** ▪ to run **5** ▪ to conduct **5, 7, 9** ▪ to carry **8**
> **USAGE ABSOLU** to lead **1** ▪ to drive **2**
> **VPR** to drive, to be driven **1** ▪ to behave **2**

VT 1 *(emmener → gén)* to take; *(→ en voiture)* to drive, to take; **c. les enfants à l'école** to take *or* to drive the children to school; **je vais t'y c., si tu veux** I'll drive *or* take you there, if you like; **j'ai dû le c. chez le dentiste de toute urgence** I had to rush him to the dentist; **c. qn jusqu'à la porte** to see sb to the door, to show sb the way out; **on la conduisit à sa chambre** she was shown *or* taken to her room; **c. le troupeau à l'alpage** to drive the cattle to the high pastures; **le policier l'a conduit au poste** the policeman took him down to the station; **il est obligé de se faire c. au bureau par sa femme** he has to get his wife to drive him to work

2 *(guider)* to lead; **c. un cheval par la bride** to lead a horse by the bridle; **c. un aveugle dans la rue** to lead a blind man along the street; **c. ses hommes au combat** to lead one's men into battle; **les empreintes m'ont conduit jusqu'au hangar** the footprints led me to the shed

3 *(mener)* **c. qn à** to lead sb to; **c. qn au désespoir** to drive sb to desperation; **cela va nous c. à la catastrophe/ruine** it's going to lead us to disaster/ruin; **cela me conduit à penser que...** this leads me to believe that..., I am led to believe that...; **ce qui nous conduit à la conclusion suivante** which leads *or* brings us to the following conclusion; **c. qn à la victoire** *(entraîneur, entraînement)* to lead sb (on) to victory

4 *Transp (véhicule)* to drive; *(hors-bord)* to steer

5 *(diriger → État)* to run, to lead; *(→ affaires, opérations)* to run, to conduct, to manage; *(→ travaux)* to supervise; *(→ recherches, enquête)* to conduct, to lead; *(→ délégation, révolte)* to head, to lead

6 *(être en tête de)* **c. le deuil** to be at the head of the funeral procession, to be a chief mourner

7 *Mus (orchestre, symphonie)* to conduct

8 *(faire passer → eau)* to carry, to bring; **l'oléoduc qui conduit le pétrole à travers le désert** the pipeline which carries the oil across the desert

9 *Phys (chaleur, électricité)* to conduct, to be a conductor of; **un corps qui conduit bien l'électricité** a good conductor of electricity

USAGE ABSOLU 1 *(mener)* **c. à** to lead to, to open out onto; **cet escalier ne conduit nulle part** this staircase doesn't lead anywhere; **cette filière conduit au bac technique** this stream allows you to go on to *or* this stream leads to a vocational school-leaving qualification; **la jalousie conduit aux pires excès** jealousy leads to *or* can cause extremes of bad behaviour

2 *(diriger un véhicule)* **qui conduisait?** who was driving?, who was behind the wheel?; **ils conduisent trop longtemps sans s'arrêter** they spend too much time behind the wheel without a break; **c. à droite/gauche** to drive on the right-/left-hand side of the road; **c. bien/mal/vite** to be a good/bad/fast driver

▸**se conduire VPR 1** *(être piloté)* to be driven, to drive; **une voiture qui se conduit facilement** a car that's easy to drive

2 *(se comporter)* to behave, to conduct oneself; **ce n'est pas une façon de se c. avec une dame** that's no way to behave to a lady; **se c. bien** to behave (oneself) well; **tâche de bien te c.** try to behave (yourself); **se c. mal** to behave badly, to misbehave; **nos joueurs se sont conduits comme des sauvages** our players behaved like brutes

---

conduit, -e [kɔ̃dɥi, -it] **PP** *voir* **conduire**

NM 1 *Tech* conduit, pipe; **c. d'aération** air duct; *Aut* **c. d'aspiration** suction pipe; *Aut* **c. de carburant** fuel pipe; *Naut* **c. de chaîne** hawse hole; *Aut* **conduits d'échappement** exhaust manifold; **c. de fumée** flue; **c. de ventilation** ventilation shaft

2 *Anat* canal, duct; **c. auditif** auditory canal; **c. lacrymal** tear *or Spéc* lachrymal duct; **c. urinaire** urinary canal

▫ **conduite NF 1** *(pilotage → d'un véhicule)* driving; *(→ d'un hors-bord)* steering; **conduite tout terrain** cross-country driving; **la conduite à droite/gauche** driving on the right-/left-hand side of the road; **avec conduite à droite** right-hand drive *(avant n)*; **avec conduite à gauche** left-hand drive *(avant n)*; **prendre des leçons de conduite** to take driving lessons; **conduite accompagnée** = driving practice accompanied by a qualified driver for learners who have passed their theory test; **conduite en état d'ivresse** drink driving, drinking and driving; **conduite imprudente** careless driving; **faire un bout** *ou* **brin de conduite à qn (jusqu'à)** to walk sb part of the way (to)

2 *(comportement)* conduct, behaviour; **je ne sais vraiment plus quelle conduite adopter avec elle** I really don't know what line to take with her *or* how to handle her any more; **avoir une conduite étrange** to behave oddly; **pour bonne conduite** *(libéré, gracié)* for good behaviour; **mauvaise conduite** misbehaviour, misconduct; *Psy* **conduite d'échec** defeatist behaviour

3 *(direction → des affaires)* management, conduct, handling; *(→ de la guerre)* conduct; *(→ d'une armée, d'une flotte)* command; *(→ d'un pays)* running; *(→ des travaux)* supervision; **sous la conduite de qn** under sb's leadership

4 *(voiture)* **conduite intérieure** *Br* saloon (car), *Am* sedan

5 *Tech* pipe; *(canalisation principale)* main; **conduite d'eau/de gaz** water/gas pipe; *Aut* **conduite d'arrivée du combustible** supply pipe; **conduite forcée** pressure pipeline; **conduite montante** flow pipe, rising main; **conduite souple** hose, flexible pipe

condyle [kɔ̃dil] **NM** condyle

condylien, -enne [kɔ̃diljɛ̃, -ɛn] **ADJ** condylar

condylome [kɔ̃dilɔm] **NM** *Méd* condyloma

cône [kon] **NM 1** *Géom* cone; **en forme de c.** conical, cone-shaped

2 *Bot* **c. de pin** pine cone

3 *Géol* **c. de déjection** alluvial cone; **c. volcanique** volcanic cone

4 *Anat* **c. rétinien** retinal cone

5 *Zool* cone shell

6 *(glace)* cone, cornet

7 *Aut* **c. d'embrayage** clutch cone; **c. de friction** friction cone; **c. de synchronisation** synchromesh cone, baulking cone

8 *Astron* **c. d'ombre** umbra

conf. *(abrév écrite* **confort)** **tt c.** *Br* all mod cons, *Am* modern conveniences

confabulation [kɔ̃fabylasjɔ̃] **NF** *Psy* confabulation

confection [kɔ̃fɛksjɔ̃] **NF 1** *Culin* preparation, making; **elle nous a offert des gâteaux de sa c.** she offered us some of her home-made cakes **2** *Couture (d'une robe)* making; *(d'un veston)* tailoring; *Ind* **la c.** the clothing industry *or* business; **je ne trouve pas ma taille en c.** I can't find my size in ready-to-wear clothes *or* in the shops

▫ **de confection ADJ** ready-to-wear, ready-made, *Br* off-the-peg

confectionner [3] [kɔ̃fɛksjɔne] **VT 1** *(préparer → plat, sauce)* to prepare, to make **2** *Couture (robe)* to make, to sew; *(veston)* to tailor; **c'est sa mère qui confectionne les costumes des enfants** her mother runs up the children's costumes

confectionneur, -euse [kɔ̃fɛksjɔnœr, -øz] **NM,F** clothes manufacturer

confédéral, -e, -aux, -ales [kɔ̃federal, -o] **ADJ** confederal

confédération [kɔ̃federasjɔ̃] **NF 1** *(nation)* confederation, confederacy; **la C. helvétique** the Swiss Confederation **2** *Pol* **c. générale du travail** = major association of French trade unions (affiliated to the Communist Party); **C. européenne des syndicats** European Trade Union Confederation; **C. paysanne** = militant French association that defends the rights of farmers and campaigns on rural and environmental issues

confédéré, -e [kɔ̃federe] **ADJ** confederate

NM,F *Suisse* = person from another canton

▫ **confédérés NMPL** *Hist* **les confédérés** the Confederates

confédérer [18] [kɔ̃federe] **VT** to confederate

confer [kɔ̃fɛr] **VT** *(à l'infinitif seulement)* **c. page 36** see page 36

conférence [kɔ̃ferɑ̃s] **NF 1** *(réunion)* conference; **c. intergouvernementale** intergovernmental conference; **c. internationale sur la paix** international peace conference; **donner** *ou* **tenir une c.** to hold a meeting *or* conference; **ils sont en c.** they are in a meeting; **c. ministérielle** ministerial conference; **C. des Nations unies pour le commerce et le développement** United Nations Conference on Trade and Development; **c. de presse** press conference; *Journ* **c. de rédaction** (editors') conference; *UE* **C. sur la sécurité et la coopération en Europe** Council for Security and Cooperation in Europe; **c. au sommet** summit conference

2 *(cours)* lecture; **il a fait une c. sur Milton** he gave *or* he delivered a lecture on Milton, he lectured on Milton

3 *Bot (poire)* conference pear

conférencier, -ère [kɔ̃ferɑ̃sje, -ɛr] **NM,F** speaker

conférer [18] [kɔ̃fere] **VT 1** *(décerner → titre, droit)* to confer, to bestow; **c. une médaille à qn** to confer a medal on *or* upon sb; **ils lui ont conféré les pleins pouvoirs** they invested him/her with *or* granted him/her full authority **2** *Fig (donner → importance, prestance)* to impart

VI *(discuter)* to talk, to hold talks

confesse [kɔ̃fɛs] **NF** *(confession)* **aller à/revenir de c.** to go to/to come back from confession; *Hum* **chacun son tour, comme à c.** one at a time

confesser [4] [kɔ̃fese] **VT 1** *Rel (péché)* to confess (to); *(foi)* to confess; *(personne)* to hear the confession of, to be the confessor of **2** *Fam (faire parler)* **c. qn** to make sb talk▪ **3** *Littéraire (foi, convictions)* to proclaim **4** *(reconnaître, admettre)* to admit, to confess; **je confesse mon ignorance** I confess *or* admit my ignorance; **j'ai eu tort, je le confesse** I admit *or* confess I was wrong

USAGE ABSOLU *Rel* **le Père Guérin ne confessera pas aujourd'hui** Father Guérin is not hearing confessions today

▸**se confesser VPR 1** *Rel* to confess, to make one's confession; **se c. à un prêtre** to confess to a priest; **c. de qch** to confess sth **2 se c. à qn** *(se confier)* to confide in sb, to tell sb; **se c. de qch** to confess (to) sth

confesseur [kɔ̃fesœr] **NM 1** *Rel* confessor **2** *(confident)* confidant, *f* confidante

confession [kɔ̃fesjɔ̃] **NF 1** *Rel (aveu, rite)* confession; **entendre qn en c.** to hear sb's confession; *aussi Fig* **faire une c.** to make a confession, to confess; **je vais vous faire une c.** I've got a confession to make to you **2** *(appartenance)* faith, denomination; **des élèves de toutes confessions** pupils of all denominations; **être de c. luthérienne/anglicane** to belong to the Lutheran/Anglican faith **3** *Littéraire (proclamation)* proclaiming

'Confessions' *Rousseau* 'Confessions'

confessionnal, -aux [kɔ̃fesjɔnal, -o] NM confessional

confessionnalisme [kɔ̃fesjɔnalism] NM *Pol* confessionalism

confessionnel, -elle [kɔ̃fesjɔnɛl] ADJ denominational

confetti [kɔ̃feti] NM (piece of) confetti; **des confettis** confetti; **ils ont quitté le bal masqué sous une pluie de confettis** they were showered with confetti as they left the masked ball; *Fam* **tu peux en faire des confettis!** *Br* you can chuck it out!, you can throw it in the bin!, *Am* you can throw it in the garbage!

confiance [kɔ̃fjɑ̃s] NF **1** *(foi → en quelqu'un, quelque chose)* trust, confidence; **avec c.** confidently; **envisager son avenir avec c.** to feel confident about one's future; **un climat de c. économique** a climate of economic confidence; **c. excessive** overconfidence; **avoir c. en qn/qch** to trust sb/sth, to have confidence in sb/sth; **faire c. à qn** to trust sb; **peut-on lui faire c.?** can he/she be trusted?, is he/she trustworthy *or* reliable?; **faites-moi c.** *(croyez-moi)* believe me; **elle va être en retard, tu peux lui faire c.!** she is absolutely guaranteed to be late!, you can rely on her to be late!; **elle a mon entière c.** I have complete confidence in her; **placer sa c. en qn** to put one's trust *or* to place one's confidence in sb; **j'ai c. en l'avenir de mon pays** I have faith in the future of my country

2 *Pol* **voter la c. au gouvernement** to pass a vote of confidence in the government; **vote de c.** vote of confidence

3 *(aplomb)* **c. en soi** confidence, self-confidence, self-assurance; **manquer de c. en soi** to lack self-confidence; **reprendre c. en soi** to regain one's self-confidence

❑ **de confiance** ADJ **poste de c.** position of trust; **personne de c.** reliable *or* trustworthy person; **les hommes de c. du président** the President's advisers

❑ **en confiance** ADV **mettre qn en c.** to win sb's trust; **se sentir** *ou* **être en c. (avec qn)** to feel safe (with sb)

❑ **en toute confiance** ADV with complete confidence; **tu peux l'acheter en toute c.** you can buy it with complete confidence, you needn't have any doubts or misgivings about buying it; **tu peux y aller en toute c.** you needn't have any qualms *or* misgivings about going there; **je vous parle en toute c.** I know this will go no further than ourselves, I know I can trust you (with what I have to say)

confiant, -e [kɔ̃fjɑ̃, -ɑ̃t] ADJ **1** *(qui fait confiance)* trusting, trustful **2** *(qui exprime la confiance)* trusting, confident **3** *(qui a confiance)* **être c. dans** *ou* **en** to have confidence in; **je suis c. dans la réussite de notre programme** I have confidence in the success of our programme, I'm confident that our programme will be a success; **il est c. (en lui-même)** he's self-assured *or* self-confident

confidence [kɔ̃fidɑ̃s] NF confidence; **faire une c. à qn** to confide something to sb, to trust sb with a secret; **faire des confidences à qn** to confide in sb; **mettre qn dans la c.** to take sb into one's confidence, to let sb into the secret; **être dans la c.** to be in on the *or* a secret; **se faire des confidences** to confide in each other; *Hum* **confidences sur l'oreiller** pillow talk; **c. pour c., je ne l'aime pas non plus** between ourselves, I don't like him/her either

❑ **en confidence** ADV in (strict) confidence

confident, -e [kɔ̃fidɑ̃, -ɑ̃t] NM,F confidant, *f* confidante

confidentialité [kɔ̃fidɑ̃sjalite] NF confidentiality; *Ordinat* **c. des données** data privacy

confidentiel, -elle [kɔ̃fidɑ̃sjɛl] ADJ **1** *(secret → information)* confidential; *(→ entretien)* private; *(sur document)* private and confidential; **à titre c.** in confidence, confidentially **2** *(limité)* **un tirage c.** a small print-run; **un livre un peu c.** a book that only appeals to a limited readership

confidentiellement [kɔ̃fidɑ̃sjɛlmɑ̃] ADV confidentially, in (strict) confidence

confier [9] [kɔ̃fje] VT **1** *(dire → craintes, intentions)* to confide, to entrust; **c. un secret à qn** to confide *or* to entrust a secret to sb, to share a secret with sb; **est-ce que je peux te c. un secret?** can I tell you a secret?, can I share a secret (with you)?; **il m'a confié qu'il voulait divorcer** he confided to me that he wanted to get a divorce

2 *(donner)* to entrust; **c. ses clefs à un ami** to entrust one's keys to a friend; **c. une mission à qn** to entrust a mission to sb, to entrust sb with a mission; **la garde de Marie a été confiée à sa mère** Marie has been put in her mother's care; **c. qch aux soins de qn** to entrust sth to sb's care

3 *Littéraire (livrer)* to consign

▶**se confier** VPR **1** *(s'épancher)* to confide; **se c. à qn** to confide in sb; **je n'ai personne à qui me c.** I have nobody to confide in; **elle ne se confie pas facilement** she doesn't confide in people easily

2 se c. à *(s'en remettre à)* to trust to; **se c. à sa bonne étoile** to trust to one's lucky star

configurable [kɔ̃figyrabl] ADJ *Ordinat* configurable

configuration [kɔ̃figyrasjɔ̃] NF **1** *(aspect général)* configuration, general shape; **la c. des lieux** the layout of the place; **la c. du terrain** the lie of the land **2** *Chim & Ordinat* configuration; **c. par défaut** default setting; **c. matérielle** hardware configuration

configurer [3] [kɔ̃figyre] VT *Ordinat & (gén)* to configure

confiné, -e [kɔ̃fine] ADJ *(air)* stale; *(atmosphère)* stuffy; **vivre c. chez soi** to live shut up indoors

confinement [kɔ̃finmɑ̃] NM **1** *(enfermement)* confinement **2** *Phys* **c. d'un plasma** confinement, containment **3** *(d'une espèce animale)* concentration *(in a particular area)*

confiner [3] [kɔ̃fine] VT **1** *(reléguer)* to confine; **on le confine dans des rôles comiques** he's confined to comic parts **2** *(enfermer)* to confine, to shut away

❑ **confiner à** VT IND **1** *(être voisin de → pays, maison)* to border on **2** *Fig (être semblable à)* to border *or* to verge on; **passion qui confine à la folie** passion bordering *or* verging on madness

▶**se confiner** VPR **1** *(s'enfermer)* **se c. dans son bureau** to confine oneself to one's study, to shut oneself away in one's study **2 se c. à** *(se limiter à)* to confine oneself *or* to limit oneself *or* to keep to; **je préfère ne pas me c. aux auteurs que je connais bien** I'd rather not confine myself to *or* keep to those writers I'm familiar with

confins [kɔ̃fɛ̃] NMPL *(limites → d'un pays)* borders; *(→ d'un savoir, de l'intelligence)* confines, bounds; **les c. de l'Europe et de l'Asie** the borders of Europe and Asia

❑ **aux confins de** PRÉP on the borders of; *Fig* **aux c. du conscient et de l'inconscient** on the borders of the conscious and the unconscious

confiote [kɔ̃fjɔt] NF *Fam (confiture)* jam▪

confire [101] [kɔ̃fir] VT *(dans du sucre)* to preserve, to candy; *(dans du vinaigre)* to pickle; *(dans de la graisse)* to preserve

▶**se confire** VPR *Littéraire* **se c. en dévotion** to be excessively pious

confirmand, -e [kɔ̃firmɑ̃, -ɑ̃d] NM,F confirmand

confirmatif, -ive [kɔ̃firmatif, -iv] ADJ confirmative

confirmation [kɔ̃firmasjɔ̃] NF **1** *(attestation)* confirmation; **obtenir c. d'un résultat** to receive confirmation of a result, to have a result confirmed; **donnez-nous c. de votre rendez-vous** please give us confirmation of *or* please confirm your appointment; **il m'en a donné c. lui-même** he confirmed it to *or* for me himself; **c'est la c. de ce que je pensais** that (just) confirms what I thought; **en c. de** as a *or* in confirmation of, confirming

2 *Rel* confirmation; **recevoir la c.** to be confirmed; **donner la c. (à qn)** to confirm (sb)

3 *Jur* upholding

confirmative [kɔ̃firmativ] *voir* **confirmatif**

confirmé, -e [kɔ̃firme] ADJ *(professionnel)* experienced

confirmer [3] [kɔ̃firme] VT **1** *(rendre définitif → réservation, nouvelle)* to confirm; **c. par écrit** to confirm by letter *or* in writing; **cela reste à c.** it remains to be confirmed, it is as yet unconfirmed

2 *(renforcer → témoignage, diagnostic, impression)* to confirm, to bear out; **ceci confirme mes** *ou* **me confirme dans mes soupçons** this bears out *or* confirms my suspicions; **les derniers chiffres confirment cette tendance** the latest figures confirm this trend

3 *(affermir → position, supériorité)* to reinforce; **c. qn dans ses fonctions** to confirm sb in office

4 *Rel* to confirm; **se faire c.** to be confirmed

▶**se confirmer** VPR **1** *(s'avérer → rumeur)* to be confirmed; **son départ se confirme** it's been confirmed that he's leaving; **il se confirme que...** it has now been confirmed that...

2 *(être renforcé → tendance, hausse)* to become stronger

confisait *etc voir* **confire**

confiscable [kɔ̃fiskabl] ADJ liable to seizure *or* to being seized, confiscable

confiscation [kɔ̃fiskasjɔ̃] NF **1** *(saisie)* confiscation, seizure, seizing **2** *Jur* forfeiture

confiscatoire [kɔ̃fiskatwar] ADJ confiscatory, forfeitary

confiserie [kɔ̃fizri] NF **1** *(produit) Br* sweet, *Am* candy; **acheter des confiseries** to buy *Br* sweets *or Am* candy **2** *(industrie)* confectionery (business *or* trade) **3** *(magasin)* confectioner's, *Br* sweet shop, *Am* candy store

confiseur, -euse [kɔ̃fizœr, -øz] NM,F confectioner

confisquer [3] [kɔ̃fiske] VT **1** *(retirer → marchandises, drogue)* to confiscate, to seize; *(→ sifflet, livre)* to take away, to confiscate; **c. qch à qn** to take sth away from *or* to confiscate sth from sb; **se faire c. qch par qn** to have sth confiscated by sb **2** *(supprimer)* to take away, to suppress; **le pouvoir a confisqué nos libertés** the authorities have taken away *or* suppressed our civil rights **3** *Jur* to seize, to confiscate

confit, -e [kɔ̃fi, -it] PP *voir* **confire**

ADJ **1** *(fruits)* candied, crystallized; *(cornichons)* pickled; **ailes de canards confites** confit of duck wings **2** *Littéraire* **être c. en dévotion** to be steeped in piety

NM conserve; **c. d'oie** goose confit *(goose cooked in its own fat to preserve it)*

confiteor [kɔ̃fiteɔr] NM INV Confiteor

confiture [kɔ̃fityr] NF jam, preserve; **c. de fraises/mûres** strawberry/blackberry jam; **c. d'oranges** (orange) marmalade; **tartine de c.** slice of bread with jam; **faire des confitures** to make jam; **donner de la c. aux cochons** to cast pearls before swine

❑ **en confiture** ADV **mettre qch en c.** to reduce sth to a pulp

confiturerie [kɔ̃fityrri] NF **1** *(fabrication)* jam manufacture **2** *(fabrique)* jam factory

confiturier, -ère [kɔ̃fityrje, -ɛr] ADJ jam *(avant n)*

NM,F jam *or* preserve manufacturer

NM jam dish

conflagration [kɔ̃flagrasjɔ̃] NF **1** *(conflit)* conflagration, conflict **2** *(bouleversement)* major upheaval

conflictuel, -elle [kɔ̃fliktɥɛl] ADJ *(pulsions, désirs)* conflicting, clashing; **situation/relation conflictuelle** antagonistic situation/relationship

conflit [kɔ̃fli] NM **1** *Mil* conflict, war; **le c. irano-irakien** the Iran-Iraq war; **c. armé** armed conflict *or* struggle; **c. limité** limited conflict

2 *(heurt → d'intérêts)* conflict, clash; **entrer en c. avec** to conflict with, to come into conflict with; **être en c. avec qn** to be in conflict with sb; **il y a beaucoup de conflits internes** there's a lot of infighting; **le c. des générations** the clash between generations

3 *Jur* conflict; **c. d'attribution** conflict of authority; **c. de décisions** conflicting decisions; **c. de juridictions** conflict of jurisdiction; **c. de lois dans le temps** legal transition; **c. négatif (d'attributions)** negative conflict; **c. international** conflict of laws; **c. de jugements** conflicting judgments; **c. de lois** conflict of laws; **c. de nationalités** = situation where a person can invoke two nationalities; **c. positif (d'attributions)** positive conflict; **c. social** *ou* **du travail** labour *or* industrial *or* employment dispute; **c. salarial** wage dispute

confluence [kɔ̃flyɑ̃s] NF **1** *Géog* confluence **2** *(rencontre)* confluence, convergence; **à la c.**

de at the junction of; **à la c. du marxisme et de la psychanalyse** where Marxism and psychoanalysis meet

confluent [kɔ̃flyɑ̃] NM **1** *Géog* confluence; **au c. du Rhône et de la Saône** at the confluence of the Saône and the Rhône **2** *(point de rencontre)* junction **3** *Anat* confluence

confluer [7] [kɔ̃flye] VI **1** *Géog* to meet, to merge; **l'Oise conflue avec la Seine** the Oise flows into the Seine **2** *Littéraire (être réunis)* to converge

confondant, -e [kɔ̃fɔ̃dɑ̃, -ɑ̃t] ADJ astonishing, astounding

confondre [75] [kɔ̃fɔ̃dr] VT **1** *(prendre pour un autre → films, auteurs, dates)* to confuse, to mix up; **il a confondu la clef du garage et celle de la porte** he mistook the garage key for the door key, he mixed up the garage key and the door key; **j'ai confondu leurs voix** I got their voices mixed up; **c. qn/qch avec** to mistake sb/sth for; **on me confond avec ma cousine** I'm mistaken for *or* people mix me up with my cousin

2 *(réunir)* to merge, to mingle, to intermingle; **tous âges confondus** irrespective of age

3 *(démasquer → menteur, meurtrier)* to unmask, to expose; **le misérable était enfin confondu!** at last the rogue was unmasked!

4 *(étonner)* to astound, to astonish; **une telle naïveté a de quoi vous c.** such naivety is truly astounding; **être** *ou* **rester confondu devant** to be speechless in the face of *or* astounded by

USAGE ABSOLU *(faire une confusion)* **on ne se connaît pas, vous devez c.** we've never met, you must be making a mistake *or* be mistaken; **attention, ce n'est pas ce que j'ai dit, ne pas c.** *ou* **ne confondons pas!** hey, let's get one thing straight, that's not what I said!

▸**se confondre** VPR **1** *(se mêler → fleuves)* to flow together, to merge; *(→ formes, couleurs)* to merge; *(→ intérêts, aspirations)* to merge, to be identical; **dans mon rêve, Marie et Sophie se confondaient en une seule personne** in my dream, Marie and Sophie merged into one person *or* were one and the same (person)

2 *(être embrouillé)* to be mixed up *or* confused; **les dates se confondaient dans mon esprit** the dates became confused *or* were all mixed up in my mind

3 se c. en excuses to be effusive in one's apologies, to apologize profusely; **elle se confondit en remerciements** she thanked him/her/*etc* profusely

conformateur [kɔ̃fɔrmatœr] NM *Tech* conformator; *Électron* **c. d'impulsions** pulse shaper, pulse-shaping network

conformation [kɔ̃fɔrmasjɔ̃] NF **1** *(aspect physique)* build; **sa c. anatomique** its anatomical structure; **avoir une c. normale** to be of normal build; **un enfant qui a une mauvaise c.** a child with poor bone structure **2** *Chim* conformation, configuration

conformationnel, -elle [kɔ̃fɔrmasjɔnɛl] ADJ *Biol & Chim* conformational

conforme [kɔ̃fɔrm] ADJ **1** *(qui répond à une règle)* standard; **on ne peut pas brancher l'appareil, la fiche n'est pas c.** the machine can't be plugged in, the plug isn't standard; **ce n'est pas c. à la loi** this is not in accordance with the law; *Ordinat* **c. à l'an 2000** year 2000 compliant

2 *(conventionnel → pensée, idée)* conventional, orthodox; **non c.** unconventional, unorthodox

3 *(semblable)* identical; *Com* **c. à la demande** as per order; *Com* **c. à la description** as represented; **c. à l'original** true to the original; **ce n'est pas c. à l'esquisse** it bears little resemblance to *or* doesn't match the sketch; **la réalisation des travaux n'est pas c. à ce qui avait été prévu** the work is not being carried out in accordance with what was agreed

conformé, -e [kɔ̃fɔrme] ADJ **bien c.** *(fœtus)* well-formed; *(enfant)* well-built; **mal c.** *(fœtus)* malformed; **un enfant mal c.** a child with poor bone structure

conformément [kɔ̃fɔrmemɑ̃] **conformément à** PRÉP in accordance with, according to; **c. à la législation en vigueur** in accordance with (the) current legislation; **c. au souhait que vous avez exprimé** in accordance with your wish; **vivre c. à ses principes** to live in accordance *or* conformity with one's principles; **tout s'est déroulé c. au plan** everything went according to plan; **c. à l'article 26** in accordance with clause 26

conformer [3] [kɔ̃fɔrme] VT **1** *Com (standardiser)* to make standard, to produce according to the standards **2** *(adapter)* **c. qch à** to adapt *or* to match sth to; **c. ses envies à ses possibilités financières** to tailor *or* to match one's desires to one's financial means; **ils ont conformé leur tactique à la nôtre** they modelled their tactics on ours

▸**se conformer** VPR **se c. à** *(se plier à → usage)* to conform to; *(→ ordre, décision)* to comply with, to abide by; **se c. aux habitudes de qn** to conform to sb's habits

conformisme [kɔ̃fɔrmism] NM **1** *(traditionalisme)* conventionality, conformism **2** *Rel* conformism, conformity

conformiste [kɔ̃fɔrmist] ADJ **1** *(traditionaliste)* conformist, conventional **2** *Rel* conformist

NMF **1** *(traditionaliste)* conformist, conventionalist **2** *Rel* conformist

conformité [kɔ̃fɔrmite] NF **1** *(ressemblance)* similarity; **étonné par la c. des deux statuettes** surprised by the similarity of the two figurines; **c. de goûts/d'intérêts** similarity of tastes/of interests; **être en c. de goûts avec qn** to have similar tastes to sb **2** *(obéissance)* **la c. à** *(gén)* conformity to; *(aux normes)* compliance with; **la c. aux usages sociaux** conformity to social customs **3** *(conventionnalisme)* conventionality

▫ **en conformité avec** PRÉP in accordance with, according to; **être en c. avec** to conform to

confort [kɔ̃fɔr] NM **1** *(commodités)* **le c.** *(d'un appartement, d'un hôtel)* modern conveniences; *(d'un aéroport)* modern facilities; **un cinq-pièces tout c.** a five-room apartment with all *Br* mod cons *or Am* modern conveniences

2 *(aise physique)* **le c.** comfort; **j'aime (avoir) mon c.** I like my (creature) comforts; **son petit c.** his/her creature comforts; **pour votre c., nous avons prévu des serviettes parfumées** scented tissues are available for your convenience; **améliorer le c. d'écoute** to improve sound quality; **c. d'emploi** *(d'un ordinateur)* user-friendliness

3 *(tranquillité)* **le c. intellectuel** self-assurance

confortable [kɔ̃fɔrtabl] ADJ **1** *(douillet → lit, maison)* comfortable, cosy, snug; **la chaise n'est pas très c.** the chair's rather uncomfortable **2** *(tranquillisant → situation, routine)* comfortable; *aussi Fig* **être dans une position peu c.** to be in an awkward position **3** *(aisé → vie, situation)* comfortable **4** *(important → retraite, bénéfice, majorité)* comfortable

NM *Can (édredon) Br* quilt, *Am* comforter

confortablement [kɔ̃fɔrtabləmɑ̃] ADV comfortably; **être c. assis** to be comfortably seated; **installe-toi c.** make yourself comfortable; **vivre c.** *(dans l'aisance)* to lead a comfortable existence, to be comfortably off; **être c. rémunéré** to be on a good salary, to be well paid

conforter [3] [kɔ̃fɔrte] VT *(renforcer → position, avance)* to reinforce, to strengthen; **ce que tu dis conforte mon interprétation** what you say bears out *or* confirms my interpretation; **cela la conforte dans la mauvaise opinion qu'elle a de moi** it confirms her poor opinion of me; **l'euro a conforté sa position** the euro has strengthened its position

confraternel, -elle [kɔ̃fratɛrnɛl] ADJ fraternal

confraternité [kɔ̃fratɛrnite] NF fraternity *or* brotherhood between colleagues

confrère [kɔ̃frɛr] NM *(professionnellement)* colleague, *Am* coworker; *(dans une société)* fellow member; **un c. de la BBC** a BBC colleague *or Am* coworker; **un de mes confrères du journal** one of my colleagues *or Am* coworkers on the paper, one of my fellow journalists; **un de mes confrères qui est spécialiste des maladies vasculaires** one of my colleagues *or Am* coworkers who specializes in vascular diseases; **à cette heure-là, nos confrères de France 3 diffusaient un match** at that time our colleagues *or Am* coworkers at France 3 were showing a match

confrérie [kɔ̃freri] NF **1** *(groupe professionnel)* fraternity; **la c. des journalistes sportifs** the fraternity of sports writers; **c. gastronomique** = association for the promotion of good food **2** *Rel* confraternity, brotherhood

confrérique [kɔ̃frerik] ADJ *Rel* confraternal

confrontant, -e [kɔ̃frɔ̃tɑ̃, -ɑ̃t] ADJ *Can* **1** *(personne)* confrontational; **il est toujours c. quand on discute** he's always so confrontational when we discuss anything **2** *(expérience, changement)* challenging, difficult

confrontation [kɔ̃frɔ̃tasjɔ̃] NF **1** *(face-à-face)* confrontation; **la c. du violeur avec la victime** *ou* **entre le violeur et la victime est-elle une bonne chose?** is it a good idea to confront the rapist with his victim? **2** *Jur* confrontation **3** *(comparaison)* comparison **4** *(conflit)* confrontation; **c. armée** armed confrontation *or* conflict; **il cherche toujours à éviter les confrontations** *ou* **la c.** he always tries to avoid confrontation

confronter [3] [kɔ̃frɔ̃te] VT **1** *(mettre face à face → accusés, témoins)* to confront; **être confronté à** *ou* **avec qn** to be confronted with sb; *Fig* **être confronté à une difficulté** to be faced *or* confronted with a difficulty; **c. qn avec les conséquences de ses actes** to confront sb with the consequences of his/her actions; **il n'est pas toujours facile d'être confronté à la réalité** it's not always easy to face up to reality

2 *(comparer → textes, points de vue)* to compare; **c. un vers avec un autre** *ou* **un vers et un autre** *ou* **deux vers** to compare one line with another *or* one line to another *or* two lines (together)

confucéen, -enne [kɔ̃fyseɛ̃, -ɛn] ADJ Confucian

NM,F Confucian

confucianisme [kɔ̃fysjanism] NM Confucianism

confucianiste [kɔ̃fysjanist] ADJ Confucian

NM,F Confucian

Confucius [kɔ̃fysjys] NPR Confucius

confus, -e [kɔ̃fy, -yz] ADJ **1** *(imprécis → souvenir, impression)* unclear, confused, vague; *(→ idées)* muddled; *(→ situation, histoire)* confused, involved; *(→ explication)* muddled, confused; *(→ style, texte)* obscure, unclear; **c'est un esprit c.** he/she is muddleheaded

2 *(désordonné → murmures, cris)* confused; *(→ amas)* confused, disorderly; **des voix confuses** a confused babble of voices; **un enchevêtrement c. de fils multicolores** a confused tangle of many-coloured threads

3 *(embarrassé)* **c'est un cadeau magnifique, je suis c.** it's a wonderful present, I'm quite overwhelmed *or* I really don't know what to say; **je l'ai tellement regardé qu'il en est resté tout c.** I stared at him so much he didn't know what to do with himself; **c. de** ashamed at, embarrassed by; **être c. de sa propre ignorance** to be ashamed of one's (own) ignorance; **je suis c. de t'avoir fait attendre** I'm awfully *or* dreadfully sorry to have kept you waiting

confusément [kɔ̃fyzemɑ̃] ADV **1** *(vaguement)* confusedly, vaguely; **sentir c. que** to have a vague feeling that; **j'entrevoyais c. la solution du problème** I was slowly beginning to see a solution to the problem **2** *(indistinctement)* unintelligibly, inaudibly

confusion [kɔ̃fyzjɔ̃] NF **1** *(méprise)* mix-up, confusion; **la c. entre les deux notions est fréquente** the two notions are often mixed up *or* confused; **il y a eu c. entre deux personnes** they got two people mixed up *or* confused

2 *(désordre)* confusion, disarray, chaos; **la fête s'est terminée dans la c. générale** the party ended in total confusion; **semer** *ou* **répandre la c. dans une assemblée** to throw a meeting into confusion; **il régnait une c. indescriptible dans la gare** the station was in a state of indescribable confusion *or* chaos; **jeter la c. dans l'esprit de qn** to sow confusion in sb's mind, to throw sb into confusion

3 *Psy* **c. mentale** mental confusion

4 *(gêne)* embarrassment, confusion; **rougir de c.** to blush (with shame); **à ma grande c.** to my great embarrassment

5 *Jur* **c. de dette** confusion; **c. des peines** concurrent sentences; **avec c. des peines** the sentences to run concurrently

6 *Pol* **c. des pouvoirs** non-separation of legislative, executive and judiciary powers

confusionnel, -elle [kɔ̃fyzjɔnɛl] ADJ confusional

confusionnisme [kɔ̃fyzjɔnism] NM disinformation

conga [kɔ̃ga] NM **1** *(danse)* conga **2** *(tambour)* conga drum

congaï, congaye [kɔ̃gaj] NF (young) Vietnamese woman, congaie

conge [kɔ̃ʒ] NM **1** *Antiq* congius **2** *Mines* ore basket

congé [kɔ̃ʒe] NM **1** *(vacances) Br* holiday, *Am* vacation; *Admin & Mil* leave; **trois semaines de c.** three weeks off, three weeks' leave; **j'ai pris tous mes congés** I've used up all my holiday (entitlement); **vous avez c. le 11 novembre?** do you have the 11th of November off?; **les écoles ont c. le 30** the schools are out *or* break up on the 30th; **j'ai c. le lundi** I have Mondays off, I'm off on Mondays, Monday is my day off; **c. d'adoption** = unpaid leave for an adopting parent; **c. annuel** *Br* annual leave *or* holiday, *Am* vacation leave; **c. pour convenance personnelle** compassionate leave; **c. d'enseignement et de recherche** = unpaid leave enabling an employee to study or carry out research; **c. d'examen** = paid leave enabling an employee to take an examination relating to a training course; **c. formation** = leave of absence to enable an employee to follow a training course; **c. de longue durée** extended leave; **c. de maladie** sick leave; **c. (de) maternité** maternity leave; **c. de naissance** (three-day) paternity leave; **c. parental (d'éducation)** = parent's right to take time off without pay (after a birth or an adoption); **c. de paternité** paternity leave; **congés payés** = annual paid leave (at least 30 days per year in France); **c. sabbatique** sabbatical (leave); **congés scolaires** school *Br* holidays *or Am* vacation; **c. sans solde** time off without pay, unpaid leave; **jour de c.** day off. **2** *(avis de départ)* notice; **donner son c. à son patron** to hand in one's notice to one's boss; **donner son c. à son propriétaire** to give notice to one's landlord; **donner (son) c. à un employé** to give notice to *or* to dismiss an employee; **demander son c.** *(serviteur)* to ask to leave; **c. pour vente** notice to quit *(issued to tenants when the landlord wants to sell the property)* **3** *(adieu)* **donner c. à qn** to dismiss sb; **prendre c.** to (take one's) leave, to depart; **prendre c. de qn** to take one's leave of sb **4** *(autorisation)* authorization, permit; *(de vin en douane)* release; *Naut* **c. de navigation** clearance certificate

□ **en congé** ADV **être en c.** *(soldat)* to be on leave; *(écolier, salarié)* to be on *Br* holiday *or Am* vacation; **je suis en c. demain jusqu'à lundi** I'm off (from) tomorrow till Monday

congéable [kɔ̃ʒeabl] ADJ that may be terminated *(at landlord's request)*

congédiable [kɔ̃ʒedjabl] ADJ liable to be dismissed *(at any time)*

congédiement [kɔ̃ʒedimɑ̃] NM **1** *(licenciement)* dismissal **2** *(d'un bail)* termination

congédier [9] [kɔ̃ʒedje] VT *(employé)* to dismiss, to discharge; *(locataire)* to give notice to; *(importun)* to send away; **se faire c.** to be dismissed

congelable [kɔ̃ʒlabl] ADJ freezable, suitable for freezing

congélateur [kɔ̃ʒelatœr] NM deep freeze, freezer

congélation [kɔ̃ʒelasjɔ̃] NF **1** *(technique)* freezing; *(durée)* freezing time; **supporte bien la c.** *(sur emballage)* suitable for (home) freezing; **ne supporte pas la c.** *(sur emballage)* unsuitable for (home) freezing; **sac de c.** freezer bag **2** *(solidification → de l'eau)* freezing, turning to ice; *(→ de l'huile)* congealing; **point de c.** freezing point

congeler [25] [kɔ̃ʒle] VT to freeze; **tarte/viande congelée** frozen pie/meat

▸ **se congeler** VPR **1** *(emploi passif) (dans un congélateur)* to freeze; **la mayonnaise ne se congèle pas** you can't freeze mayonnaise (successfully), mayonnaise doesn't freeze well **2** *(eau)* to freeze

congélo [kɔ̃ʒelo] NM *Fam* freezer

congénère [kɔ̃ʒenɛr] ADJ *Biol* congeneric; *Anat (muscle)* congenerous; **c. à** congeneric with

NMF **1** *(animal)* congener **2** *Péj (personne)* **toi et tes congénères** you and your sort; **sans ses congénères, il se comporte correctement** away from his peers, he behaves well

congénital, -e, -aux, -ales [kɔ̃ʒenital, -o] ADJ congenital; *Hum* **il est bête, c'est c.!** he was born stupid!; **une maladie congénitale** a congenital illness

congénitalement [kɔ̃ʒenitalmɑ̃] ADV congenitally

congère [kɔ̃ʒɛr] NF snowdrift

congestif, -ive [kɔ̃ʒɛstif, -iv] ADJ congestive

congestion [kɔ̃ʒɛstjɔ̃] NF *Méd* congestion; **il a eu une c.** he has had a stroke; **c. cérébrale** stroke; **c. pulmonaire** congestion of the lungs

congestionné, -e [kɔ̃ʒɛstjɔne] ADJ **1** *(visage)* flushed; *(route)* congested **2** *Méd (organe)* congested

congestionner [3] [kɔ̃ʒɛstjɔne] VT **1** *Méd (partie du corps)* to congest; *(visage)* to flush **2** *(encombrer → réseaux routiers)* to congest, to clog up

▸ **se congestionner** VPR **1** *Méd (partie du corps)* to congest, to become congested; *(visage)* to become flushed **2** *(être encombré)* to become clogged up *or* congested

congestive [kɔ̃ʒɛstiv] *voir* **congestif**

congiaire [kɔ̃ʒjɛr] NM *Antiq* congiary

congloméral, -e, -aux, -ales [kɔ̃glɔmeral, -o] ADJ *Écon & Géol* conglomerate

conglomérat [kɔ̃glɔmera] NM *Écon & Géol* conglomerate

conglomération [kɔ̃glɔmerasjɔ̃] NF conglomeration

conglomérer [18] [kɔ̃glɔmere] VT to conglomerate

conglutiner [3] [kɔ̃glytine] VT to conglutinate

Congo [kɔ̃go] NM **le C.** *(pays)* the Congo; **vivre au C.** to live in the Congo; **aller au C.** to go to the Congo; **le C.** *(fleuve)* the Congo River, the River Congo; **le C. Belge** the Belgian Congo

Congo-Kinshasa [kɔ̃gokinʃasa] NM = former name of the Republic of Zaïre

congolais, -e [kɔ̃gɔlɛ, -ɛz] ADJ Congolese
   NM *Culin* coconut cake
   □ **Congolais, -e** NM,F Congolese; **les C.** the Congolese

congratulations [kɔ̃gratylasjɔ̃] NFPL *Littéraire* felicitations

congratuler [3] [kɔ̃gratyle] *Littéraire* VT to congratulate

▸ **se congratuler** VPR to congratulate each other

congre [kɔ̃gr] NM *Ich* conger (eel)

congréer [15] [kɔ̃gree] VT *Naut* to worm

congréganiste [kɔ̃greganist] *Rel* ADJ congregational
   NMF congregant

congrégation [kɔ̃gregasjɔ̃] NF *Rel* **1** *(ordre)* congregation, order **2** *(assemblée de prélats)* congregation

congrégationalisme [kɔ̃gregasjɔnalism] NM *Rel* Congregationalism

congrégationaliste [kɔ̃gregasjɔnalist] *Rel* ADJ Congregational, Congregationalist
   NMF Congregationalist

congrès [kɔ̃grɛ] NM congress; **c. médical/scientifique** medical/scientific conference *or* congress; **le C. (américain)** Congress; **membre du C.** member of Congress, Congressman, *f* Congresswoman; **le c. d'Épinay** = the unification congress (1971) where the French Socialist Party adopted the title "Parti socialiste", developed new policies and elected François Mitterrand as its first secretary; **C. national africain** African National Congress; **C. national irakien** Iraqi National Congress; **C. du parti** party conference; **le c. de Tours** = the Socialist party congress (1920) which marked the split between the Second International and the Third; *Hist* **le c. de Vienne** the Congress of Vienna

congressiste [kɔ̃gresist] NMF participant at a congress

congru, -e [kɔ̃gry] ADJ **1** *Math* congruent **2** *Arch (adéquat)* sufficient, adequate

congruence [kɔ̃gryɑ̃s] NF congruence

congruent, -e [kɔ̃gryɑ̃, -ɑ̃t] ADJ congruent

congrûment [kɔ̃grymɑ̃] ADV *Littéraire (de façon convenable)* congruously, appropriately, pertinently; *(de façon adéquate)* adequately

conicine [kɔnisin] NF *Chim* conicine, coniine, conine

conicité [kɔnisite] NF conic shape

conidie [kɔnidi] NF *Bot* conidium

conifère [kɔnifɛr] ADJ coniferous
   NM conifer

conique [kɔnik] ADJ **1** *(pointu)* conical, cone-shaped **2** *Math* conic **3** *Tech (tige, goupille)* coned, tapering; **engrenage c.** bevel gearing

conjectural, -e, -aux, -ales [kɔ̃ʒɛktyral, -o] ADJ conjectural

conjecturalement [kɔ̃ʒɛktyralmɑ̃] ADV conjecturally

conjecture [kɔ̃ʒɛktyr] NF conjecture, surmise; **se perdre en conjectures** to be perplexed; **nous en sommes réduits aux conjectures** we can only guess

conjecturer [3] [kɔ̃ʒɛktyre] VT to speculate about *or Sout* to conjecture; **c. l'évolution d'une situation politique** to speculate about how a political situation will develop; **je ne conjecture rien de bon de la situation** I can't see anything good coming out of the situation; **c. que** to surmise that

USAGE ABSOLU **que s'est-il passé? – on ne peut que c.** what happened? – one can but guess; **c. sur** to make guesses about

conjoint, -e [kɔ̃ʒwɛ̃, -ɛ̃t] ADJ **1** *(commun → démarche)* joint **2** *(lié → cas, problème)* linked, related **3** *(qui accompagne)* **note conjointe** attached note **4** *Mus* conjoint, conjunct
   NM,F *Admin* spouse; **il faut l'accord des deux conjoints** the agreement of both husband and wife is necessary; **les conjoints n'ont pas été invités** partners weren't invited; **les futurs conjoints** the bride and groom, the future couple; *Jur* **c. successible** spouse entitled to inherit; *Jur* **c. survivant** surviving spouse

conjointement [kɔ̃ʒwɛ̃tmɑ̃] ADV jointly; **c. avec mon associé** together with my associate; **vous recevrez c. la facture et le catalogue** you'll find the invoice enclosed with the catalogue; *Jur* **c. et solidairement** jointly and severally

conjoncteur [kɔ̃ʒɔ̃ktœr] NM **1** *Élec* circuit breaker, cut-out **2** *Tél* telephone socket

conjoncteur-disjoncteur [kɔ̃ʒɔ̃ktœrdisʒɔ̃ktœr] *(pl* **conjoncteurs-disjoncteurs**) NM *Élec* circuit breaker, cut-out

conjonctif, -ive [kɔ̃ʒɔ̃ktif, -iv] ADJ **1** *Gram* conjunctive **2** *Anat* connective
   □ **conjonctive** NF **1** *Gram* conjunctive clause **2** *Anat* conjunctiva

conjonction [kɔ̃ʒɔ̃ksjɔ̃] NF **1** *(union)* union, conjunction; **dû à la c. de deux facteurs** due to the conjunction of two factors **2** *Gram* conjunction; **c. de coordination/de subordination** coordinating/subordinating conjunction **3** *Astron* conjunction
   □ **en conjonction avec** PRÉP in conjunction with

conjonctival, -e, -aux, -ales [kɔ̃ʒɔ̃ktival, -o] ADJ conjunctival

conjonctive [kɔ̃ʒɔ̃ktiv] *voir* **conjonctif**

conjonctivite [kɔ̃ʒɔ̃ktivit] NF *Méd* conjunctivitis; **faire** *ou* **avoir de la c.** to have conjunctivitis; **c. aiguë** contagious conjunctivitis

conjoncture [kɔ̃ʒɔ̃ktyr] NF **1** *(contexte)* situation, conditions; **la c. internationale actuelle** the current international context *or* situation; **dans la c. actuelle** under the present circumstances, at this juncture; **c. boursière** market trend **2** *Écon* **c. (économique)** economic situation, economic conditions; **attendre une amélioration de la c.** to wait for economic conditions to improve; **on assiste à une dégradation de la c. économique** the economic situation is deteriorating; **de c.** conjunctural; **crise de c.** economic crisis; **étude de c.** study of the (overall) economic climate

conjoncturel, -elle [kɔ̃ʒɔ̃ktyrɛl] ADJ *(chômage)* cyclical; **crise conjoncturelle** economic crisis *(due to cyclical and not structural factors)*; **prévisions conjoncturelles** economic forecasts; **test c.** economic test

conjoncturiste [kɔ̃ʒɔ̃ktyrist] NMF economic planner

conjugable [kɔ̃ʒygabl] ADJ which can be conjugated

conjugaison [kɔ̃ʒygɛzɔ̃] NF **1** *Biol, Chim & Gram* conjugation **2** *(union)* union, conjunction; **grâce à la c. de leurs efforts** thanks to their joint efforts

conjugal, -e, -aux, -ales [kɔ̃ʒygal, -o] ADJ *(devoir)* conjugal; **bonheur c.** wedded *or* married bliss; **vie conjugale** married life

conjugalement [kɔ̃ʒygalmɑ̃] ADV conjugally; **vivre c.** to live as a married couple *or* as husband and wife

conjugalité [kɔ̃ʒygalite] NF conjugality

conjugateur [kɔ̃ʒygatœr] NM *Ordinat* conjugator

conjugué, -e[1] [kɔ̃ʒyge] ADJ **1** *(uni → efforts)* joint, combined **2** *Chim, Math, Bot & Opt* conjugate **3** *Tech* paired, twin
❑ **conjugués** NMPL *Math* conjugate complex numbers

conjuguée[2] [kɔ̃ʒyge] *Bot* NF = member of the Conjugatae class
❑ **conjuguées** NFPL Conjugatae

conjuguer [3] [kɔ̃ʒyge] VT **1** *(verbe)* to conjugate; **c. au futur** to conjugate in the future tense **2** *(unir → efforts, volontés)* to join, to combine
▸**se conjuguer** VPR **1** *Gram* to conjugate, to be conjugated **2** *(s'unir)* to work together, to combine

conjurateur, -trice [kɔ̃ʒyratœr, -tris] NM,F conjuror, sorcerer

conjuration [kɔ̃ʒyrasjɔ̃] NF **1** *(complot)* conspiracy **2** *(incantation)* conjuration

conjuratoire [kɔ̃ʒyratwar] ADJ *(mot, pouvoir)* magical; **formule c.** spell; *Fig* **ce fut un procès c.** the trial laid ghosts to rest *or* exorcised the demons of the past

conjuratrice [kɔ̃ʒyratris] *voir* **conjurateur**

conjuré, -e [kɔ̃ʒyre] NM,F conspirator, plotter

conjurer [3] [kɔ̃ʒyre] VT **1** *Littéraire (supplier)* to beg, to beseech; **il la conjura de ne pas le dénoncer** he begged *or* besought her not to give him away; **ne le bats pas, je t'en conjure** don't hit him, I beseech you *or* I beg (of) you
2 *(écarter → mauvais sort, danger, crise)* to ward off, to keep at bay
3 *Littéraire (manigancer)* to plot; **c. la perte de qn** to plot sb's downfall
▸**se conjurer** VPR *Littéraire* to conspire; **se c. contre** to plot *or* to conspire against

Connacht [kɔnakt] NM **le C.** Connaught

connais *etc voir* **connaître**

connaissable [kɔnɛsabl] ADJ knowable

connaissait *etc voir* **connaître**

connaissance [kɔnɛsɑ̃s] NF **1** *(maîtrise dans un domaine)* knowledge; **avoir une c. intuitive/empirique de** to have an intuitive/empirical knowledge of; **une c. approfondie de l'espagnol** a thorough knowledge *or* good command of Spanish; **la c. de soi** self-knowledge
2 *Phil* **la c.** knowledge; **toutes les branches de la c.** all areas of (human) knowledge
3 *(fait d'être informé)* **avoir c. de qch** to know *or* to learn about sth, to be aware of sth; **il n'en a jamais eu c.** he never learnt about it, he was never notified of it; **prendre c. des faits** to learn about *or* to hear of the facts; **prendre c. d'un dossier** to study *or* examine a case, to familiarize oneself with a case; **il est venu à notre c. que...** it has come to our attention that...; **porter qch à la c. de qn** to bring sth to sb's knowledge *or* attention; *Mktg* **c. de la marque** brand awareness
4 *(conscience)* consciousness; **avoir toute sa c.** to be fully conscious; **il gisait là/il est tombé, sans c.** he was lying there/he fell unconscious; **perdre c.** to lose consciousness; **reprendre c.** to come to, to regain consciousness; **faire reprendre c. à qn** to bring sb to *or* round
5 faire la c. de qn, faire c. avec qn to make sb's acquaintance, to meet sb; **on a fait c. à Berne** we met in Berne; **lier c. avec qn** to strike up an acquaintance with sb; **une fois que vous aurez mieux fait c.** once you've got to know each other better; **prendre c. d'un texte** to read *or* to peruse a text; **faire c. avec qch** *(aborder qch)* to discover sth, to get to know sth
6 *(ami)* acquaintance; **c'est une simple c.** he's/she's a mere *or* nodding acquaintance; **c'est une vieille c.** I've known him/her for ages, he's/she's an old acquaintance; **faire de nouvelles connaissances** to make new acquaintances, to meet new people; **agrandir le cercle de ses connaissances** to widen one's circle of acquaintances
7 *Jur* cognizance
❑ **connaissances** NFPL knowledge; **l'acquisition des connaissances** the acquisition of knowledge, the learning process; **avoir des connaissances** to be knowledgeable; **avoir de solides connaissances en** to have a thorough knowledge of *or* a good grounding in; **avoir des connaissances sommaires en** to have a basic knowledge of, to know the rudiments of; **connaissances informatiques** computer literacy; **avoir des connaissances en informatique** to be computer literate; **connaissances livresques** book-learning; **mes connaissances en chimie sont tout ce qu'il y a de rudimentaire** my knowledge of chemistry is extremely rudimentary
❑ **à ma/sa/***etc* **connaissance** ADV to (the best of) my/his/*etc* knowledge, as far as I know/he knows/*etc*; **pas à ma c.** not to my knowledge, not as far as I know, not that I know of; **il n'y avait pas, à sa c., de cas semblable dans la famille** there was, as far as he/she knew, no similar case in the family
❑ **de connaissance** ADJ **un visage de c.** a familiar face; **être entre gens de c.** to be among familiar faces; **nous sommes entre gens de c. ici** we all know each other here; **être en pays de c.** *(dans un domaine)* to be on familiar ground; *(dans un milieu)* to be among familiar faces
❑ **de ma/sa/***etc* **connaissance** ADJ **une personne de ma c.** an acquaintance of mine, somebody I know
❑ **en connaissance de cause** ADV **faire qch en c. de cause** to do sth with full knowledge of the facts; **je souhaite que vous preniez la décision en toute c. de cause** I hope you're making an informed decision; **et j'en parle en c. de cause** and I know what I'm talking about

connaissement [kɔnɛsmɑ̃] NM *Com* bill of lading, waybill; **c. aérien** air waybill; **c. clausé** dirty bill of lading; **c. direct** through bill; **c. net** clean bill of lading

connaisseur, -euse [kɔnɛsœr, -øz] ADJ *(regard, air)* expert *(avant n)*, knowledgeable; **je ne suis pas du tout c.** I'm by no means an expert
NM,F connoisseur; **un public de connaisseurs** a knowledgeable audience, an audience of experts; **parler de qch en c.** to speak knowledgeably about sth; **être c. en pierres précieuses** to be a connoisseur of *or* knowledgeable about gems

CONNAÎTRE [91] [kɔnɛtr]

> **VT** to know **A1–4** ■ **B1** ■ **C1** ■ **D1, 2** ■ to recognize **A4** ■ to meet **B2** ■ to feel **C1** ■ to experience **C1–3** ■ to have **D1**
> **VPR** to know **1** ■ to be acquainted, to have met **2** ■ to meet **3**

VT **A.** *AVOIR UNE IDÉE DE* **1** *(avoir mémorisé → code postal, itinéraire, mot de passe)* to know; **connais-tu le chemin pour y aller?** do you know how to get there *or* the way there?; **la cachette était connue d'elle seule** she was the only one who knew where the hiding place was; **je connais des bars espagnols à Paris** I know some Spanish bars in Paris; **c. les bonnes adresses** to know (all) the best places to go
2 *(être informé de → information, nouvelle)* to know; **je suis impatient de c. les résultats** I'm anxious to know *or* to hear the results; **connaissez-vous la nouvelle?** have you heard the news?; *Fam* **tu connais celle du cheval qui ne voulait pas boire?** do you know *or* have you heard the one about the horse who wouldn't drink?; **tu ne connais pas ta chance** you don't know how lucky you are, you don't know your luck; **faire c.** *(avis, sentiment)* to make known; *(décision, jugement)* to make known, to announce; **je vous ferai c. ma décision plus tard** I'll inform you of my decision *or* I'll let you know what I've decided later; **je vous ferai c. mes intentions** I'll let you know what I intend to do; **les patrouilleurs nous font c. la position des canons ennemis** scout planes let us know the position of enemy fire *or* give us intelligence about the position of enemy fire; **je ne te connaissais pas ce manteau** I didn't know you had this coat, I've never seen you wearing this coat (before); **je ne lui connais aucun défaut** I'm not aware of him/her having any faults; **on ne lui connaissait aucun ennemi** he/she had no known enemies
3 *(avoir des connaissances sur → langue, ville, appareil, œuvre)* to know, to be familiar with; *(→ technique)* to know, to be acquainted with; *(→ sujet)* to know (about); **je ne connais pas l'italien** I don't know *or* cannot speak Italian; **je connais un peu l'informatique** I have some basic knowledge of computing; **apprenez à c. votre corps** learn to know your body; **je ne conduirai pas, je ne connais pas ta voiture** I won't drive, I'm not familiar with *or* I don't know your car; *aussi Ironique* **elle connaît tout sur tout** she knows everything there is to know; **il connaît bien les Alpes** he knows the Alps well; **je connais mal les dauphins** my knowledge of dolphins is patchy, I don't know much about dolphins; **connais-tu Flaubert?** do you know (the work of) *or* have you read Flaubert?; **faire c. un produit** to publicize a product; **son dernier film l'a fait c. dans le monde entier** his/her latest movie has brought him/her worldwide fame; **sa traduction a fait c. son œuvre en France** his/her translation has brought his/her work to French audiences; **cette émission est destinée à faire c. des artistes étrangers** this programme is aimed at introducing foreign artists; *Fam* **les bons vins, ça le connaît!** he knows a thing or two about *or* he's an expert on good wine!; **la mécanique, ça le connaît!** he's a whizz *or Br* a dab hand at mechanics!; **c. qch comme sa poche** to know sth inside out *or* like the back of one's hand; *Fam* **à cet âge-là, la propreté, connaît pas** at that age they don't know the meaning of the word cleanliness; **y c. quelque chose en** to have some idea *or* to know something about; **tu y connais quelque chose en informatique?** do you know anything about computers?; **je n'y connais rien en biologie** I don't know a thing about biology; **je ne mange pas de cette horreur! – tu n'y connais rien!** I won't eat that horrible stuff! – you don't know what's good for you!; **c. son affaire** *ou* **métier** to know one's job; *Fam* **en c. un bout** *ou* **rayon sur** to know a thing or two about; *Fam* **c. la chanson** *ou* **musique** to have heard it all before; **il te remboursera – ouais, je connais la musique!** he'll pay you back – yeah, I've heard that one before!
4 *Littéraire (reconnaître)* to recognize, to know; **c. qn à qch** to recognize sb because of sth
B. *IDENTIFIER, ÊTRE EN RELATION AVEC* **1** *(par l'identité)* to know; **c. qn de vue/nom/réputation** to know sb by sight/name/reputation; **on la connaissait sous le nom de Louise Michel** she was known as Louise Michel; **se faire c.** *(révéler son identité)* to make oneself known; *(devenir une personne publique)* to make oneself *or* to become known; **notre auditeur n'a pas voulu se faire c.** our listener didn't want his name to be known *or* wished to remain anonymous; **la police ne le connaît que trop bien!** the police know him only too well!; **je suis patient, tu me connais** I'm patient, you know me; **la connaissant, ça ne me surprend pas** knowing her, I'm not surprised; **tu me connais mal!** you don't know me (at all)!; **elle a bien connu ton oncle** she knew your uncle well; **je ne le connais qu'un peu** he's only an acquaintance of mine; **je la connais depuis toujours** I've always known her; **je t'ai connu plus enjoué** I've known you to be chirpier; **je l'ai connu enfant** I knew him when he was a child; **si tu fais ça, je ne te connais plus!** if you do that, I'll have nothing more to do with you!; *Fam* **je te connais comme si je t'avais fait!** I know you as if you were my own *or* like the back of my hand!; *Fam* **j'en connais un qui ne va pas être content!** I know at least one person who's not going to be happy!
2 *(rencontrer)* to meet; **j'aimerais le c.** I'd like to meet him; **ah, si je t'avais connu plus tôt!** if only I'd met you earlier!; **je l'ai connu au cours du tournage** I got to know him while we were shooting the picture; **j'aimerais vous faire c. mon frère** I would like to introduce you to my brother

3 *Bible (sexuellement)* to have carnal knowledge of, to know

C. *ÉPROUVER* **1** *(peur, amour)* to feel, to know, to experience; **dans ses bras, j'ai connu l'amour** in his/her arms, I understood what love was; **une famille où il pourra enfin c. la tendresse** a family where he will at last experience affection

2 *(faire l'expérience de)* to experience; **tu n'as pas connu les petits bars de Saint-Germain!** you never knew *or* experienced the little bars in Saint-Germain!; **il n'a jamais connu l'amour** he has never known *or* experienced love; **elle n'a jamais connu la faim** she's never known hunger *or* what hunger means; **la tour avait connu des jours meilleurs** the tower had seen better days; **ah, l'insouciance de la jeunesse, j'ai connu ça!** I was young and carefree once!; *Fam* **ses promesses, je connais!** don't talk to me about his/her promises!; **faire c. qch à qn** to introduce sb to sth

3 *(obtenir → succès, gloire)* to have, to experience; **enfin, elle connut la consécration** she finally received the highest accolade; **ma douleur ne connaîtra jamais aucun soulagement** there will never be any relief from my pain

4 *(subir → crise)* to go *or* to live through, to experience; *(→ épreuve, humiliation, guerre)* to live through, to suffer, to undergo; **il a connu bien des déboires** he has had *or* suffered plenty of setbacks; **il a connu un destin tragique** his was a tragic fate; **puis Rome connut la décadence** then Rome went through a period of *or* fell into decline; **sa carrière a connu des hauts et des bas** his/her career has had its ups and downs; **cette région connaît actuellement une famine** this region is now experiencing a famine; **le corps de l'enfant connaît ensuite une période d'intenses bouleversements** profound changes then take place in the child's body

D. *ADMETTRE* **1** *(sujet: chose)* to have; *(au négatif)* to know; **son ambition ne connaît pas de bornes** *ou* **limites** his/her ambition is boundless *or* knows no bounds

2 *(sujet: personne) Littéraire* **il ne connaît pas de maître** he knows no master; **Rex ne connaît que son maître** Rex only responds to *or* knows his master; **il ne connaît que le travail** work is the only thing he's interested in *or* he knows; *Fam* **les voitures, tu ne connais que ça!** cars, that's all you're interested in!; **il ne connaît que le mensonge** he is incapable of telling the truth; **ils ne connaissent que le règlement!** they always stick to the rules *or* do things by the book!; **contre les rhumes, je ne connais qu'un bon grog** there's nothing like a good old rum toddy to cure a cold

USAGE ABSOLU **tu sais comment ça marche? – oui, je connais** do you know how it works? – yes, I do

❏ **connaître de** VT IND *Jur* **ce tribunal ne connaît pas des fraudes fiscales** this court is not empowered to deal with tax fraud

▶ **se connaître** VPR **1** *(soi-même)* to know oneself, to be self-aware; **je n'oserai jamais, je me connais** I'd never dare, I know what I'm like; **le yoga vous aide à mieux vous c.** yoga helps you to get to know yourself better *or* is the way to greater self-knowledge; **connais-toi toi-même** know thyself; *Vieilli* **ne plus se c.** *(de colère)* to be beside oneself

2 *(l'un l'autre)* to be acquainted, to have met (before); **vous vous connaissez?** have you met (before)?; **tout le monde se connaît?** has everybody met everybody else?; **ils se connaissent bien** they know each other well

3 *(se rencontrer)* to meet; **ils se sont connus en 1970** they met in 1970

4 **s'y c. en architecture** to know a lot about architecture; **je ne m'y connais pas en antiquités** I don't know anything about antiques; **je m'y connais peu en informatique** I don't know much about computers; *Fam* **ah ça, pour râler, il s'y connaît!** he's very good at grumbling!; *Fam* **pour les gaffes, tu t'y connais!** when it comes to putting your foot in it, you take some beating!;

c'est un escroc, ou je ne m'y connais pas! I know a crook when I see one!; **ça c'est un diamant bleu ou je ne m'y connais pas!** that's a blue diamond, if I'm not very much mistaken!

connard, -asse [kɔnar, -as] NM,F *très Fam* **1** *(homme stupide)* stupid bastard, prick; *(femme stupide)* stupid bitch **2** *(homme déplaisant)* bastard; *(femme déplaisante)* bitch

Connaught [kɔnɔkt] = **Connacht**

conne [kɔn] *voir* **con**

conneau, -x [kɔno] NM *très Fam* stupid bastard, prick

connectable [kɔnɛktabl] ADJ connectable

connecter [4] [kɔnɛkte] VT to connect; *Ordinat* **connecté** on line; *Ordinat* **connecté en anneau/bus/étoile** in a ring/bus/star configuration; *Ordinat* **connecté en série** series-connected; *Ordinat* **c. en boucle** to daisy-chain
▶ **se connecter à** VPR *Ordinat (système)* to log on to; *(l'Internet)* to connect to

connecteur [kɔnɛktœr] NM *Ordinat* connector

Connecticut [kɔnɛktikœt] NM **le C.** Connecticut; **dans le C.** in Connecticut

connectif, -ive [kɔnɛktif, -iv] ADJ *Anat & Ling* connective
NM *Bot* connective

connectique [kɔnɛktik] NF (electrical) connections

connective [kɔnɛktiv] *voir* **connectif**

connectivite [kɔnɛktivit] NF *Méd* collagenosis

connectivité [kɔnɛktivite] NF *Ordinat* connectivity

connement [kɔnmɑ̃] ADV *très Fam* stupidly■; **il s'est fait c. piquer sa caisse** the stupid idiot got his car pinched; **et c. j'ai accepté** and like the idiot that I am, I said yes

connerie [kɔnri] NF *très Fam* **1** *(stupidité)* stupidity■; **sa c. se lit sur sa figure** you can tell he's/she's a *Br* prat *or Am* schmuck just by looking at him/her **2** *(acte, remarque)* stupid thing■; **raconter des conneries** to talk crap; **arrête de me raconter des conneries!** don't talk crap!; **c'est incroyable ce qu'il peut raconter comme conneries** it's incredible what crap he comes out with sometimes; **depuis qu'elle est arrivée, elle ne fait que des conneries** she's been an absolute *Br* bloody *or Am* goddamn liability since the day she arrived; **j'ai peur qu'il fasse une c.** *(un acte inconsidéré)* I'm afraid he might do something stupid■

connétable [kɔnetabl] NM *Hist* constable

connexe [kɔnɛks] ADJ *(idées, problèmes)* closely related

connexion [kɔnɛksjɔ̃] NF connection

connexité [kɔnɛksite] NF relatedness

connivence [kɔnivɑ̃s] NF connivance, complicity; **avec la c. du gardien** with the warden's connivance; **être de c. avec qn** to connive with sb; **ils sont de c.** they're in league with each other; **un regard de c.** a conniving look

connivent, -e [kɔnivɑ̃, -ɑ̃t] ADJ connivent

conniver [3] [kɔnive] VI *Vieilli & Littéraire* to connive (**à** at); **c. avec qn** to be in collusion with sb

connotation [kɔnɔtasjɔ̃] NF **1** *Ling* connotation **2** *(nuance)* overtone

connoter [3] [kɔnɔte] VT **1** *Ling* to connote **2** *Physiol* to connote, to imply, to have overtones of

connu, -e [kɔny] PP *voir* **connaître**
ADJ **1** *(découvert → univers)* known
2 *(répandu → idée, tactique)* well-known, widely known; **c'est bien c.!** that's a well-known fact!, everyone knows that!
3 *(célèbre → personnalité, chanteur)* famous, well-known; **peu c.** *(personne, œuvre)* little-known; *(lieu)* out-of-the-way; **un de ses tableaux les moins connus** one of his/her least-known paintings; *Fam* **une blague connue** an old joke; **il est c. comme le loup blanc** everybody knows him
NM **le c. et l'inconnu** the known and the unknown

conoïde [kɔnɔid] *Géom* ADJ conoid
NM conoid

conopée [kɔnɔpe] NM *Rel (d'un tabernacle)* canopy

conque [kɔk] NF **1** *Zool* conch **2** *Anat* external ear, *Spéc* concha

conquérant, -e [kɔkerɑ̃, -ɑ̃t] ADJ **1** *Mil & Pol* conquering **2** *(hautain → sourire)* domineering; *(→ démarche)* swaggering; **il entra d'un air c.** he swaggered in
NM,F conqueror

conquérir [39] [kɔkerir] VT **1** *Mil & Pol* to conquer **2** *(acquérir → espace, pouvoir)* to gain control over, to capture, to conquer; *(→ marché, part de marché)* to conquer; **c. de nouveaux marchés** to conquer new markets; **se comporter comme en pays conquis** to act as if one owns the place **3** *(séduire → cœur, public)* to win (over), to conquer; *(→ estime, respect)* to win, to gain; **c. un homme/une femme** to win a man's/a woman's heart; **être conquis** to be entirely won over
▶ **se conquérir** VPR to be (hard) won *or* earned; **l'amitié ça se conquiert** friendship is something you have to work at

conquête [kɔkɛt] NF **1** *(action)* conquest; **partir à la c. de l'Amérique** to set out to conquer America; **faire la c. d'un pays** to conquer a country; **il a fait la c. de ma cousine** he's made a conquest of my cousin, he's won my cousin's heart; **se lancer à la c. du pouvoir** to make a bid for power; **la c. de nouveaux marchés en Asie est une des priorités de l'entreprise** conquering new Asian markets is one of the company's priorities
2 *(chose gagnée)* conquest, conquered territory; **les conquêtes des premiers jours de la révolution** the conquests of the early days of the revolution
3 *(personne)* conquest; **sa dernière c. s'appelle Peter** her latest conquest is called Peter

conquiert *etc voir* **conquérir**

conquis, -e [kɔki, -iz] PP *voir* **conquérir**

conquistador [kɔkistador] NM conquistador

consacrant [kɔsakrɑ̃] ADJ M consecrating
NM consecrating priest, consecrator

consacré, -e [kɔsakre] ADJ **1** *Rel (hostie)* consecrated; *(terre)* hallowed **2** *(accepté → rite, terme)* accepted, established; **c'est l'expression consacrée** it's the accepted way of saying it; **selon la formule consacrée** as the saying goes; **c. par l'usage** sanctioned by usage **3** *(célèbre → artiste, cinéaste)* established, recognized

consacrer [3] [kɔsakre] VT **1 c. qch à** *(réserver qch à)* to devote *or* to dedicate sth to; **les week-ends sont consacrés aux enfants/au sport** weekends are devoted to the children/to sport; **combien de temps consacrez-vous à la lecture?** how much time do you devote to *or* spend reading?; **as-tu dix minutes à me c.?** can you spare me ten minutes?; **consacrons-lui notre couverture cette semaine** let's devote our front page to him/her this week
2 *Rel (pain, église, évêque)* to consecrate; *(prêtre)* to ordain; **c. un temple à Jupiter** to consecrate *or* to dedicate a temple to Jupiter; *Littéraire* **le sang de nos fils a consacré ce lieu** the blood of our sons has hallowed this place
3 *(entériner → pratique, injustice)* to sanction, to hallow; **expression consacrée par l'usage** expression that has become established by usage; **tradition consacrée par le temps** time-honoured tradition
4 *(couronner → artiste, acteur)* to crown, to turn into a star; **le jury l'a consacré meilleur acteur de l'année** the jury voted him best actor of the year
▶ **se consacrer** VPR **se c. à** to devote *or* to dedicate oneself to; **je ne peux me c. à mon fils que le soir** I can only find time for my son in the evenings; **se c. à Dieu** to consecrate one's life to the service of *or* to devote oneself to God

consanguin, -e [kɔsɑ̃gɛ̃, -in] ADJ **sœur consanguine** half-sister *(on the father's side)*; **mariage c.** intermarriage, marriage between blood relations *or* relatives
NM,F half-brother, *f* half-sister *(on the father's side)*; **les consanguins** blood relations *or* relatives

consanguinité [kɔsɑ̃ginite] NF **1** *(parenté)* consanguinity **2** *(mariages consanguins)* intermarriage

consciemment [kɔ̃sjamɑ̃] ADV consciously, knowingly

conscience [kɔ̃sjɑ̃s] NF **1** *(connaissance)* consciousness, awareness; **avoir c. de qch/d'avoir fait qch** to be conscious *or* aware of sth/of having done sth; **j'ai c. de mes capacités** I'm aware of my abilities; **prendre c. de qch** to become aware of *or* to realize sth; **ça m'a fait prendre c. de la précarité du bonheur** it made me realize *or* aware (of) how precarious happiness is; **c. de classe** class consciousness; **c. collective/politique** collective/political consciousness; **c. de soi** self-awareness

2 *(sens de la morale)* conscience; **agir selon sa c.** to do as one thinks right; **libérer** *ou* **soulager sa c.** to relieve one's conscience; **avoir qch sur la c.** to have sth on one's conscience; **elle a un poids sur la c.** there is a heavy weight on her conscience; *Fam* **il a la c. large** *ou* **élastique** he has a very flexible sense of right and wrong; **sa c. ne le laissera pas tranquille** *ou* **en paix** his conscience will give him no rest; **avoir la c. tranquille** to have an easy conscience; **pour avoir la c. tranquille je vais vérifier que tout est bien fermé** to set my mind at rest, I'll just make sure everything's locked up; **je n'ai pas la c. tranquille de l'avoir laissé seul** I have an uneasy conscience *or* I feel bad about having left him alone; **avoir bonne c.** to have a clear conscience; **tu dis ça pour te donner bonne c.** you're saying this to appease your conscience; **le monde occidental se donne bonne c.** the Western world is appeasing its conscience; **avoir mauvaise c.** to have a guilty *or* bad conscience; **c'est une affaire** *ou* **un cas de c.** it's a matter of conscience; **crise de c.** crisis of conscience; **j'ai ma c. pour moi** my conscience is clear; **acheter les consciences** to buy off people's consciences

3 *(lucidité)* consciousness; **perdre c.** to lose consciousness; **reprendre c.** to regain consciousness, to come to

4 *(application)* **c. professionnelle** conscientiousness; **faire son travail avec beaucoup de c. professionnelle** to do one's job very conscientiously, to be conscientious in one's work

❑ **en (toute) conscience** ADV in all conscience; **je ne peux, en c., te laisser partir seul** I can't in all conscience let you go on your own

consciencieuse [kɔ̃sjɑ̃sjøz] *voir* **consciencieux**

consciencieusement [kɔ̃sjɑ̃sjøzmɑ̃] ADV conscientiously

consciencieux, -euse [kɔ̃sjɑ̃sjø, -øz] ADJ *(élève)* conscientious, meticulous; *(travail)* meticulous

conscient, -e [kɔ̃sjɑ̃, -ɑ̃t] ADJ **1** *(délibéré* → *geste, désir, haine)* conscious; **c'est un choix tout à fait c.** it's an entirely conscious choice

2 *Phil* (self-)conscious

3 *(averti)* aware; **être c. du danger** to be aware *or* conscious of the danger; **es-tu c. que tu as failli tous nous tuer?** are you aware *or* do you realize that you nearly killed us all?

4 *(lucide* → *blessé)* conscious

NM **le c.** the conscious (mind)

conscientiser [3] [kɔ̃sjɑ̃tise] VT **c. qn (sur qch)** to raise sb's awareness (of sth)

conscription [kɔ̃skripsjɔ̃] NF *Br* conscription, *Am* draft

conscrit [kɔ̃skri] NM *(qui a l'âge d'être inscrit)* person liable to conscription; *(qui fait son service) Br* conscript, *Am* draftee; **armée de conscrits** *Br* conscript *or Am* draft army; *Fam* **se faire avoir comme un c.** to be completely taken in

consécrateur [kɔ̃sekratœr] ADJ M consecrating

NM consecrating priest, consecrator

consécration [kɔ̃sekrasjɔ̃] NF **1** *Rel (du pain, d'une église, d'un évêque)* consecration; *(d'un prêtre)* ordination **2** *(confirmation* → *d'une coutume)* establishment, sanctioning; *(*→ *d'une injustice)* sanctioning **3** *(d'une carrière)* apotheosis, crowning point; **exposer dans cette galerie sera pour lui une c.** having an exhibition in that gallery will set the seal on his reputation *or* will establish his reputation once and for all

consécutif, -ive [kɔ̃sekytif, -iv] ADJ **1** *(successif)* consecutive; **dormir douze heures consécutives** to sleep for twelve consecutive hours *or* for twelve hours solid; **c'est la cinquième fois consécutive qu'il remet le rendez-vous** this is the fifth time running *or* in a row that he's postponed the meeting; **les dégâts consécutifs à l'incendie** the damage brought about *or* caused by the fire; **l'infarctus est souvent c. au surmenage** heart attacks are often the result of stress **2** *Gram & Math* consecutive

consécution [kɔ̃sekysjɔ̃] NF *(gén) & Ling* consecution

consécutive [kɔ̃sekytiv] *voir* **consécutif**

consécutivement [kɔ̃sekytivmɑ̃] ADV consecutively; **notre équipe a subi c. quatre défaites** our team has suffered four consecutive defeats *or* four defeats in a row; **les accidents se sont produits c.** the accidents happened one after another *or* the other

❑ **consécutivement à** PRÉP after, as a result of, following; **c. à un incident technique** as a result of *or* following a technical hitch

conseil [kɔ̃sɛj] NM **1** *(avis)* piece of advice, *Sout* counsel; *(en marketing, finance etc)* consultancy; **un dernier petit c.** one last word *or* piece of advice; **un c. d'ami** a friendly piece of advice; **des conseils** *(d'ami)* advice; *(trucs)* tips, hints; **j'ai besoin de tes conseils** *ou* **ton c.** I need your advice; **conseils aux bricoleurs/jardiniers** hints for handymen/gardeners; **agir sur/suivre le c. de qn** to act on/to take sb's advice; **écouter le c. de qn** to listen to *or* to take sb's advice; **demander c. à qn** to ask sb's advice, to ask sb for advice; **donner un c. à qn** to advise sb; **si j'avais un c. à te donner** if I had one piece of advice to give you; **prendre c. auprès de qn** to take advice from sb; **suivre les conseils de qn** to follow *or Sout* heed sb's advice; **c. conjugal** marriage guidance *or* counselling

2 *(conseiller)* adviser, consultant; **c. en communication** media consultant, PR consultant; **c. financier** financial consultant *or* adviser; **c. en gestion** management consultant; **c. judiciaire** guardian, trustee; **c. juridique** legal adviser; **c. en marketing** marketing consultant; **c. en organisation** organizational consultant; **c. en promotion, c. en publicité** advertising consultant; **c. en recrutement** recruitment consultant; **ingénieur c.** consultant engineer

3 *(assemblée* → *gén)* council, committee; *(*→ *d'une entreprise)* board; *(réunion)* meeting; **tenir c.** to hold a meeting; **c. d'administration** *(d'une société)* board of directors; *(d'une organisation internationale)* governing body; **c. d'arbitrage** conciliation *or* arbitration board; **c. d'arrondissement** district council; **C. des Bourses de Valeurs** = regulatory body of the Paris Stock Exchange; **c. de cabinet** cabinet council, council of ministers; **le C. constitutionnel** = French government body ensuring that laws, elections and referenda are constitutional; **c. Ecofin** ECOFIN; **c. économique** economic council; **le C. économique et social** = consultative body advising the government on economic and social matters; **c. d'entreprise** works committee; **le C. d'État** the (French) Council of State; **le C. de l'Europe** the Council of Europe; *Can* **C. exécutif** ≃ Cabinet; **c. de famille** board of guardians; *Hum* family gathering; **c. général** ≃ county council; **c. de guerre** *(réunion)* council of war, ≃ War Cabinet; *(tribunal)* court-martial; **passer en c. de guerre** to be court-martialled; **faire passer qn en c. de guerre** to court-martial sb; **c. interministériel** interministerial council; **le C. des ministres** ≃ the Cabinet; **c. municipal** *(en ville)* ≃ town council, ≃ local (urban) council; *(à la campagne)* ≃ local (rural) council, *Br* ≃ parish council; *Jur* **c. national de l'aide juridique** = French legal aid review board; **C. national des autochtones du Canada** Native Council of Canada; *Jur* **c. national des barreaux** national Bar council; **C. national du crédit** National Credit Council; *Jur* **c. national des greffiers des tribunaux de commerce** = professional body for commercial registrars; *Hist* **C. national de la Résistance** = central organization of the French Resistance founded in 1943; *Jur* **c. de l'ordre** = council of a professional body; **c. de prud'hommes** industrial arbitration court, *Br* ≃ ACAS; **c. régional** regional council; *Mil* **c. de révision** recruiting board, *Am* draft board; **le C. de sécurité** the Security Council; **C. supérieur de l'Éducation nationale** = consultative body dealing with educational matters; **le C. supérieur de la magistrature** = French state body that appoints members of the judiciary; *Jur* **c. supérieur de la prud'homie** = industrial arbitration review board; **c. de surveillance** supervisory board

4 *Scol & Univ* **c. de classe** staff meeting *(concerning a class)*; **c. de discipline** disciplinary committee; **passer en c. de discipline** to appear before the disciplinary committee; **c. d'école** = committee responsible for internal organization of a primary school; **c. d'établissement** *Br* ≃ board of governors, *Am* ≃ board of education; **c. des maîtres** = teachers' committee at a primary school; **c. des professeurs** = meeting which takes place each term where teachers discuss progress made by individual pupils; **c. d'UFR** departmental (management) committee; **C. d'Université** *Br* ≃ university Senate, *Am* ≃ Board of Trustees

5 *Arch (résolution)* (firm) resolution; **ne savoir quel c. prendre** not to know what decision to make

❑ **de bon conseil** ADJ **un homme de bon c.** a man of sound advice, a wise counsellor; **demande-lui, elle est de bon c.** ask her, she's good at giving advice

Culture

CONSEILS

The "Conseil constitutionnel" has nine members appointed for a nine-year period, and also includes the surviving former Presidents of France. The President of the Republic and any member of parliament can refer laws to the Conseil constitutionnel for scrutiny. The "Conseil d'État" has 200 members. It acts both as the highest court to which the legal affairs of the state can be referred, and as a consultative body to which bills and rulings are submitted by the government prior to examination by the "Conseil des ministres". The "Conseil général", the "Conseil régional", the "Conseil municipal" and the "Conseil d'arrondissement" operate at the "département", the regional, the "commune" and the "arrondissement" levels respectively. The "Conseil supérieur de la Magistrature" has ten members: the Minister of Justice and nine others appointed by the President of the Republic. It advises on the appointment of members of the "magistrature", and on specific points of law concerning the judiciary. It is also consulted when the President wishes to exercise his official pardon.

Culture

CONSEIL DE CLASSE

The French school year is divided into three terms. In secondary schools, a "conseil de classe", or staff meeting, is held at the end of each term to discuss the progress made by pupils in a given class. A report containing the marks obtained during the term with teachers' comments is filled in for each pupil. The "conseil de classe" is initially held behind closed doors, attended by the teachers of a given class and the head teacher, and then with two elected class representatives present. During the last "conseil de classe" of the year, decisions are taken such as which pupils repeat a year and which should change courses.

conseiller[1] [4] [kɔ̃seje] VT **1** *(recommander* → *livre, dentiste)* to recommend; **c. qn/qch à qn** to recommend sb/sth to sb

2 *(donner son avis à* → *ami, enfant)* to advise, to give advice to; **elle conseille le président sur les questions économiques** she advises *or* counsels the President on economic matters; **on m'a bien/mal conseillé** I was given good/bad advice; **c. à qn de faire qch** to advise sb to do sth; **je vous conseille de réserver** I would advise you to make a reservation; **je ne vous le conseille pas** I wouldn't recommend it; **il n'est pas conseillé de conduire par ce temps** it's not advisable to drive in this weather; **beaucoup**

d'étudiants souhaitent se faire c. dans le choix d'une filière many students want to be advised about choosing a field of study; **il se fait c. par un cabinet spécialisé** he has a group of experts to advise him

conseiller[2], -ère [kɔ̃seje, -ɛr] **NM,F 1** *(guide)* adviser, counsellor; *(spécialiste)* adviser, consultant; **c'est un très bon c.** he gives very good advice; **c. de clientèle** consumer adviser; **c. commercial** marketing *or* sales consultant; **c. conjugal** marriage guidance counsellor; **c. économique** economic adviser; **c. financier** financial adviser *or* consultant; **c. financier indépendant** independent financial adviser; **c. fiscal** tax consultant; **c. en gestion (d'entreprise)** management consultant; **c. d'insertion et de probation** probation officer; **c. juridique** legal adviser; **c. en marketing** marketing consultant; **c. matrimonial** marriage guidance counsellor; *Fin* **c. en placements** investment adviser; **c. technique** technical adviser

2 *Scol* **c. d'éducation** = non-teaching staff member in charge of general discipline; **c. d'orientation** *Br* careers adviser, *Am* guidance counselor; **c. pédagogique** educational adviser

3 *(membre d'un conseil)* council member, councillor; *Admin* **c. d'État** member of the Conseil d'État; *Admin* **c. général** regional councillor; *Admin* **c. municipal** *(en ville)* ≃ local *or* town councillor; *(à la campagne)* ≃ local councillor

conseilleur, -euse [kɔ̃sejœr, -øz] **NM,F** *Péj* giver of advice; *Prov* **les conseilleurs ne sont pas les payeurs** = it's very easy to give advice when you're not going to suffer the consequences

consens *etc voir* **consentir**

consensualisme [kɔ̃sɑ̃sɥalism] **NM** mutual agreement

consensuel, -elle [kɔ̃sɑ̃sɥɛl] **ADJ 1** *(contrat)* consensus *(avant n)*, consensual; **une politique consensuelle** a strategy of seeking the middle ground, consensus politics **2** *Anat* consensual

consensus [kɔ̃sɛ̃sys] **NM** consensus (of opinion); **il n'y a pas de c. là-dessus** there's no consensus of *or* generally agreed opinion on this; *Écon & Bourse* **c. de place** market consensus

consentant, -e [kɔ̃sɑ̃tɑ̃, -ɑ̃t] **ADJ 1** *(victime)* willing **2** *Jur* **les trois parties sont consentantes** the three parties are in agreement *or* are agreeable; **adultes consentants** consenting adults

consentement [kɔ̃sɑ̃tmɑ̃] **NM** consent; **donner son c. à** to (give one's) consent to; **avec/sans le c. de la famille** with/without the family's consent; *Jur* **c. exprès/tacite** formal/tacit consent; **c. éclairé** informed consent; **divorce par c. mutuel** divorce by mutual consent

consentir [37] [kɔ̃sɑ̃tir] **VT** *(délai, réduction)* to grant; **c. qch à qn** to grant *or* to allow sb sth; **on m'a consenti une remise de 10 pour cent/un délai supplémentaire de quinze jours** I was allowed a 10 percent discount/another two weeks

USAGE ABSOLU to consent

▫ **consentir à VT IND** to consent *or* to agree to; **c. à une hausse des salaires** to consent *or* to agree to a wage increase; **elle n'a pas consenti à m'accompagner** *(n'a pas été d'accord pour le faire)* she didn't agree to come with me; *(n'a pas daigné le faire)* she didn't deign to *or* stoop so low as to accompany me; **consentiront-ils à ce que tu épouses un étranger?** will they consent to your marrying a foreigner?; **j'y ai consenti à contrecœur** I agreed to it *or* allowed it reluctantly

conséquemment [kɔ̃sekamɑ̃] **ADV** consequently; **c. à** as a result of, following (on *or* upon)

conséquence [kɔ̃sekɑ̃s] **NF 1** *(résultat)* consequence, repercussion; **lourd de conséquences** with serious consequences; **ma gaffe a eu pour c. de les brouiller** my blunder resulted in their falling out (with each other); **les conséquences de ce choix sur ma vie** the effects this choice would have on my life; **cela ne tirera pas à c.** this won't have any repercussions *or* will be of no consequence; **une déclaration sans c.** *(sans importance)* a statement of no *or* little consequence; *(sans suite)* an inconsequential statement; **ton acte sera sans c. sur ton avenir** your action will have no effect on your future

2 *(conclusion)* inference, conclusion

▫ **de conséquence ADJ personne de c.** person of consequence *or* importance; **une affaire de c.** a matter of (some) consequence

▫ **en conséquence ADV 1** *(par conséquent)* consequently, therefore

2 *(comme il convient)* accordingly

▫ **en conséquence de PRÉP 1 en c. de quoi** as a result of which

2 *(conformément à)* according to

conséquent, -e [kɔ̃sekɑ̃, -ɑ̃t] **ADJ 1** *(cohérent)* consistent; **être c. avec soi-même** to be consistent; **être c. dans ses engagements** to be consistent in one's commitments **2** *Littéraire (conforme)* **c. à** in keeping *or* conformity *or* agreement with **3** *Fam (important → moyens, magasin)* sizeable; *(→ somme)* tidy

4 *Géog* consequent **NM 1** *Phil & Gram* consequent **2** *Mus* answer

▫ **par conséquent ADV** consequently, as a result

conservable [kɔ̃sɛrvabl] **ADJ être c.** to keep

conservateur, -trice [kɔ̃sɛrvatœr, -tris] **ADJ 1** *(prudent → placement, gestion)* conservative; **avoir un esprit c.** to be conservative-minded

2 *Pol (gén)* conservative; **le parti c.** *(en Grande-Bretagne)* the Conservative *or* Tory Party; *(au Canada)* the Progressive Conservative Party

NM,F 1 *Pol (gén)* conservative; *(en Grande-Bretagne)* Conservative, Tory

2 *(responsable → de musée)* curator; *(→ de bibliothèque)* librarian; **c. des Eaux et Forêts** *Br* ≃ Forestry Commissioner, *Am* ≃ member of the Forest Service; **c. des hypothèques** ≃ mortgage registrar; *Bourse* **c. de titres** custodian

NM *(additif)* preservative; **sans c.** preservative-free, free of preservatives

conservation [kɔ̃sɛrvasjɔ̃] **NF 1** *(dans l'agro-alimentaire)* preserving; **c. par le froid** cold storage; *(congélation)* freezing

2 *(maintien en bon état)* keeping, preserving, safeguarding; **pour ce qui est de la c. des archives** as far as keeping the archives is concerned

3 *Biol & Phys* **c. de l'énergie** conservation of energy

4 *(état)* state of preservation; **des originaux dont la c. est remarquable/lamentable** originals in a remarkable/appalling state of preservation; **des bâtiments en bon état de c.** well-preserved buildings

5 *Admin* **c. des Eaux et Forêts** *Br* ≃ Forestry Commission, *Am* ≃ Forest Service; **C. des hypothèques** ≃ Land Registry

6 *Bourse* custody; **c. internationale** *(d'actions)* global custody; **c. nationale** *(d'actions)* local custody, subcustody

conservatisme [kɔ̃sɛrvatism] **NM 1** *(prudence)* conservatism **2** *Pol (gén)* conservatism; *(en Grande-Bretagne)* Conservatism

conservatoire [kɔ̃sɛrvatwar] **ADJ** protective

NM *(école)* school, academy; **c. de musique** conservatoire; **le C. (national supérieur d'art dramatique)** = national drama school in Paris; **le C. (national supérieur de musique)** the Conservatoire *(in Paris and Lyons)*; **c. national de région** = regional advanced music college; **le C. national des arts et métiers** = science and technology school in Paris

conservatrice [kɔ̃sɛrvatris] *voir* **conservateur**

conserve [kɔ̃sɛrv] **NF** *(en boîte)* item of canned *or Br* tinned food; *(en bocal)* bottled preserve; **les conserves** canned *or Br* tinned food; **c. de viande** canned *or Br* tinned meat; **conserves de fruits** conserves; **se nourrir de conserves** to live on *or* out of cans *or Br* tins; **aliments en c.** canned *or Br* tinned food; **mettre en c.** to can, *Br* to tin; *Hum* **on ne va pas en faire des conserves!** we're not going to hang on to it forever!

▫ **de conserve ADV naviguer de c.** to sail in convoy; *Fig Littéraire* **aller de c.** to go (all) together; *Littéraire* **agir de c.** to act in concert

conservé, -e [kɔ̃sɛrve] **ADJ bien c.** well-preserved

conserver [3] [kɔ̃sɛrve] **VT 1** *(aliment → dans le vinaigre)* to pickle; *(→ dans le sel, par séchage, en congelant)* to preserve; *(→ dans le sucre)* to preserve, to conserve; *(→ dans des boîtes)* to preserve, to can, *Br* to tin, *(→ en bocal)* to bottle

2 *(édifice, énergie)* to preserve

3 *(stocker)* to keep, to store, to stock; **c. à l'abri de l'humidité** *(sur mode d'emploi)* keep *or* store in a dry place; **c. hors de la portée des enfants** *(sur mode d'emploi)* keep out of the reach of children

4 *(avoir en sa possession → photos, relations)* to keep, to hang on to; **j'ai toujours conservé mes amis** I've always kept (up with) my friends; **c. qch précieusement** to treasure sth; **c. la partie B de ce formulaire** keep *or* retain part B of this form

5 *(garder → charme, force, illusion, calme)* to keep, to retain; **c. (toute) sa tête** *(rester calme)* to keep one's head *or* self-control; *(être lucide)* to have all one's wits about one; **une idée qui conserve toute son actualité** an idea which is still very topical; **elle a conservé sa beauté** she's kept *or* retained her looks; **cette crème conserve à votre peau toute sa jeunesse** this cream will help your skin retain its youthfulness; *Fam* **le sport, ça conserve** sport keeps you young; **c. son amitié à qn** to stay friendly with sb

6 *(à la suite d'une expérience)* **c. des séquelles d'une maladie** to suffer the after-effects of a disease; **j'en ai conservé un excellent souvenir** I've retained very good memories of it; **j'en ai conservé la peur du noir** it left me with a fear of the dark; **je veux en c. le souvenir** I want to hold on to the memory of it

7 *Naut* **c. sa position** to hold one's position

8 *Mil* **c. ses positions** to hold fast

▸**se conserver VPR 1** *(être stocké)* to be kept; **les pommes doivent se c. sur des clayettes** apples must be stored on racks

2 *(durer → aliment)* to keep; *(→ poterie, parchemin)* to survive; **les truffes au chocolat ne se conservent pas longtemps** (chocolate) truffles don't keep long; **les seuls documents qui se soient conservés** the only documents which survived

conserverie [kɔ̃sɛrvəri] **NF 1** *(industrie)* canning industry **2** *(technique)* canning **3** *(usine)* canning factory

conserveur [kɔ̃sɛrvœr] **NM** manufacturer of canned *or Br* tinned food

considérable [kɔ̃siderabl] **ADJ 1** *(important → somme)* considerable, sizeable; *(→ changement)* significant; **cela représente un travail c.** that represents a considerable *or* significant amount of work; **un problème d'une importance c.** a major *or* serious problem

2 *(éminent → personne)* prominent; **une personnalité c. dans le monde des lettres** a prominent figure in the world of literature

considérablement [kɔ̃siderabləmɑ̃] **ADV** considerably; **elle nous a c. influencés** she had a considerable influence on us

considérant [kɔ̃siderɑ̃] **NM** *Jur* preamble

considération [kɔ̃siderasjɔ̃] **NF 1** *(examen)* consideration, scrutiny; **la question mérite c.** the question is worth considering

2 *(préoccupation)* consideration, factor; **ce ne sont pas les seules considérations** these are not the only considerations; **ce sont des considérations bassement matérielles** these are very mundane preoccupations; **les considérations de temps** the time factor; **se perdre en considérations techniques** to get lost in technical considerations; **si l'on s'arrête à ce genre de considérations** if we pay too much attention to this kind of detail

3 *(respect)* regard, esteem; **par c. pour** out of respect *or* regard for; **jouir d'une grande c.** to be highly considered *or* regarded, to be held in great esteem; **quel manque de c.!** how inconsiderate!; **veuillez agréer l'assurance de ma c. distinguée** *(à quelqu'un dont on connaît le nom) Br* yours sincerely, *Am* sincerely (yours); *(à quelqu'un dont on ne connaît pas le nom) Br* yours faithfully, *Am* sincerely (yours)

▫ **considérations NFPL** *(remarques)* observations, reflections, thoughts; **se perdre en considérations inutiles** to get bogged down in idle considerations, to waste time on irrelevancies

▫ **en considération ADV faire entrer qch en c.** to bring sth into play *or* consideration; **prendre**

qch en c. to take sth into account *or* consideration; **toutes les candidatures seront prises en c.** all applications will be given careful consideration; **omettre de prendre en c.** to leave out of consideration

□ **en considération de** PRÉP **en c. de votre état de santé** because of *or* given *or* considering your (state of) health; **en c. de vos services** in (full) recognition of your services

□ **sans considération de** PRÉP **sans c. de personne** without taking individual cases into consideration *or* account; **sans c. du coût** regardless *or* heedless of *or* without considering (the) cost

considérer [18] [kɔ̃sidere] VT **1** *(regarder)* to gaze *or* to stare at; **c. qn avec hostilité** to stare at sb in a hostile manner; **considérons la droite AB** consider the line AB

2 *(prendre en compte → offre, problème)* to consider, to take into consideration, to weigh up; **c. le pour et le contre** to weigh up the pros and cons; **nous devons c. l'intérêt de tous** we have to take everybody's interests into account *or* consideration; **il faut c. que l'accusé est mineur** it must be taken into account *or* be borne in mind that the defendant is underage

3 *(croire)* to consider, *Sout* to deem; **je la considère qualifiée pour ce travail** I consider her (to be) qualified for this job; **je considère ne pas en avoir le droit** *ou* **que je n'en ai pas le droit** I consider that I don't have any right to do so

4 *(juger)* **c. bien/mal** to hold in high/low esteem; **c. qn/qch comme** to regard *or* to consider sb/sth as; **elle me considère comme sa meilleure amie** she regards me as *or* looks upon me as *or* considers me to be her best friend; **je considère ta réponse comme un refus** I regard your answer as a refusal

5 *(respecter)* to respect, to hold in high esteem *or* regard; **on considérait beaucoup votre père dans les milieux financiers** your father was highly respected *or* was held in high regard in financial circles; **un spécialiste hautement considéré** a highly-regarded *or* highly-respected expert

▶**se considérer** VPR **se c. comme responsable** to consider *or* hold oneself responsible; **il se considère comme un très grand artiste** he considers himself (as) a great artist

□ **à tout bien considérer, tout bien considéré** ADV **1** *(en résumé)* all things considered, taking everything into consideration, considering; **elle s'est bien débrouillée, tout bien considéré** she managed rather well, considering

2 *(pour changer d'avis)* on second thoughts *or* further consideration; **tout bien considéré, je ne me présente plus** having thought (further) about it *or* on further consideration, I'm not standing after all

consignataire [kɔ̃siɲatɛr] NMF **1** *Com* consignee **2** *Naut* consignee, forwarding agent **3** *Jur* depositary

consignateur, -trice [kɔ̃siɲatœr, -tris] NM,F *Com* consigner, consignor

consignation [kɔ̃siɲasjɔ̃] NF **1** *Com* consignment; **en c.** on consignment; **envoyer qch à qn en c.** to consign sth to sb, to send sth to sb on consignment **2** *Jur* deposit **3** *(d'un emballage)* charging a deposit on; **la c. est de 10 centimes** there's a 10-cent refund on return

consignatrice [kɔsiɲatris] *voir* **consignateur**

consigne [kɔ̃siɲ] NF **1** *(instruction)* orders, instructions; **c'est la c.** those are the orders; **observer la c.** to obey orders; **ils ont reçu pour c. de ne pas tirer** they've been given orders not to shoot; **je n'ai pas (reçu) de consignes** I have received no instructions; **elle avait pour c. de surveiller sa sœur** she'd been told to keep an eye on her sister; **consignes en cas d'incendie** fire notice, fire regulations

2 *(punition) Mil* confinement to barracks; *Scol* detention; *Fam* **on m'a filé deux heures de c.** I got two hours' detention

3 *Rail Br* left-luggage office, *Am* checkroom; **c. automatique** (*Br* left-luggage) lockers; **mettre qch à la c.** *(automatique)* to put sth in a (*Br* left-luggage) locker; *(manuelle)* to check sth in at the *Br* left-luggage office *or Am* checkroom

4 *(pour emballage)* deposit; **il y a 20 centimes de c. sur la bouteille** there's a 20-cent deposit on the bottle, you get 20 cents back on the bottle

consigné, -e [kɔ̃siɲe] ADJ *(bouteille)* returnable; **non c.** non returnable

consigner [3] [kɔ̃siɲe] VT **1** *(déposer → valise)* to put in the *Br* left-luggage office *or Am* checkroom

2 *Fin (somme)* to deposit

3 *(emballage)* to put *or* to charge a deposit on; **la bouteille est consignée 20 centimes** there's a 20-cent deposit on the bottle, you get 20 cents back on the bottle

4 *Com (marchandises etc)* to consign

5 *(noter)* to record, to put down; **c. ses pensées dans un journal** to put *or* to write down one's thoughts in a diary; **c. qch par écrit** to put sth down in writing *or* on paper; **c. les déclarations des témoins** to take down statements

6 *Mil* to confine to barracks; *Scol* to keep in (detention)

7 *(interdire)* **c. sa porte à qn** to bar one's door to sb, to refuse sb admittance; **c. une salle de jeux** to bar entrance to a gaming room; **être consigné à la troupe** to be out of bounds to troops

8 *Naut* to consign

consistance [kɔ̃sistɑ̃s] NF **1** *(état)* consistency; **c. crémeuse/dure** creamy/firm consistency; **donner de la c. à une sauce** to thicken a sauce; *Fig* **donner de la c. à un personnage** to flesh out *or* give substance to a character; **prendre c.** *(sauce)* to thicken; *Fig* **le projet prend c.** the project is taking shape; *Fig* **sans c.** *(rumeur)* groundless, ill-founded; *(personne)* spineless; *(discours, raisonnement)* woolly

2 *(cohérence)* consistency

consistant, -e [kɔ̃sistɑ̃, -ɑ̃t] ADJ **1** *(épais → sauce, peinture)* thick **2** *(substantiel → plat, repas)* substantial **3** *(bien établi → argument, rumeur)* well-founded, well-grounded

consister [3] [kɔ̃siste] **consister à** VT IND **c. à faire qch** to consist in doing sth; **son rôle consistait à claquer une porte** his part consisted in slamming a door

□ **consister dans, consister en** VT IND to consist of; **en quoi consiste votre mission?** what does your mission consist of?, what is your mission all about?; **l'exposition consiste en sculptures et tableaux** the exhibition consists of *or* is made up of sculptures and paintings; **l'intérêt de la pièce consiste dans les effets scéniques** the interest of the play lies in *or* lies with its stage effects

consistoire [kɔ̃sistwar] NM *Rel* consistory

consistorial, -e, -aux, -ales [kɔ̃sistɔrjal, -o] *Rel* ADJ consistorial

NM member of a consistory

conso [kɔ̃so] NF *Fam (consommation)* drink■

consœur [kɔ̃sœr] NF **1** *(collègue)* (female) colleague; *(dans une société)* fellow member **2** *Rel* sister nun

consol [kɔ̃sɔl] NM *Fin* consol

consolable [kɔ̃sɔlabl] ADJ consolable

consolant, -e [kɔ̃sɔlɑ̃, -ɑ̃t] ADJ consoling, comforting; **ce qui est c., c'est que...** the comforting thing (about it) is that...

consolateur, -trice [kɔ̃sɔlatœr, -tris] ADJ comforting, consolatory

NM,F comforter

consolation [kɔ̃sɔlasjɔ̃] NF **1** *(soulagement)* consolation, comfort, *Littéraire* solace; **la compagnie de ses amis était une maigre c.** his/her friends were of little comfort to him/her; **chercher une c. dans qch** to seek consolation *or* solace *or* comfort in sth **2** *(personne ou chose qui réconforte)* consolation; **sa fille est sa seule c.** his/her daughter is his/her sole consolation

□ **de consolation** ADJ *(épreuve, tournoi)* runners-up *(avant n)*; *(lot, prix)* consolation *(avant n)*; **des paroles de c.** words of comfort, comforting *or* consoling words

consolatrice [kɔ̃sɔlatris] *voir* **consolateur**

console [kɔ̃sɔl] NF **1** *(table)* console table **2** *Constr* cantilever, bracket **3** *Archit* console **4** *Mus (d'un orgue)* console; *(d'une harpe)* neck **5** *Ordinat* console; **c. de visualisation** (visual) display unit; **c. de jeux** games console **6** *(en audiovisuel)* **c. de mixage** sound mixer, mixing desk

consoler [3] [kɔ̃sɔle] VT to console, to comfort; **rien ne pouvait le c.** *(enfant)* nothing could cheer him up *or* console him; **c. qn de sa peine** to comfort *or* console sb in his/her grief; **si cela peut te c.** if it's any consolation; **ça me console de voir que ça t'est déjà arrivé** it consoles me *or* is a consolation that it's happened to you too; **il avait besoin de se faire c.** he was in need of consolation

▶**se consoler** VPR **1** *(emploi réfléchi)* to console oneself; **se c. dans l'alcool** to find solace in drink; **je me console en pensant que...** I console myself with the thought that...; *Littéraire* **consolez-vous** be comforted

2 *(emploi passif)* to console oneself, to be consoled; **il ne s'est jamais consolé de la mort de sa femme** he never got over losing his wife; **on dirait qu'elle s'est vite consolée!** it looks like she got over it fast!

3 *(emploi réciproque)* to console *or* comfort each other

consolidation [kɔ̃sɔlidasjɔ̃] NF **1** *(d'un édifice, d'un meuble)* strengthening, reinforcement; *(d'un mur)* bracing, buttressing, reinforcement

2 *Couture (d'un bouton, d'un talon)* reinforcement

3 *(renforcement → d'une amitié, d'une position, d'un pouvoir)* consolidation, strengthening; **on assiste à la c. de la dictature** the dictatorship is consolidating its power

4 *Méd* setting

5 *Jur* consolidation

6 *Fin (d'une dette)* funding, financing; *(des bénéfices, des fonds, d'un bilan)* consolidation; *Mktg* **c. de ligne** line filling

7 *Géol & (en travaux publics)* bracing, strengthening

consolidé, -e [kɔ̃sɔlide] *Fin* ADJ *(bénéfices, fonds, bilan)* consolidated; *(dette)* funded, financed

□ **consolidés** NMPL consols

consolider [3] [kɔ̃sɔlide] VT **1** *(renforcer → édifice, meuble)* to strengthen; *(→ mur, bouton, talon)* to reinforce

2 *(affermir → position, majorité, amitié)* to consolidate, to strengthen

3 *Méd* to set

4 *Jur* to consolidate

5 *Fin (dette)* to fund, to finance; *(bénéfices, fonds, bilan)* to consolidate; **l'euro a consolidé son avance à la Bourse** the euro has strengthened its lead on the Stock Exchange

▶**se consolider** VPR **1** *(s'affermir → position, majorité, régime)* to be consolidated *or* strengthened; *(amitié)* to be strengthened

2 *Méd* to set

consommable [kɔ̃sɔmabl] ADJ **1** *(nourriture)* edible; *(boisson)* drinkable; **ce produit n'est c. que cru/cuit** this product can only be eaten raw/must be cooked before eating **2** *Chim* consumable

□ **consommables** NMPL *Ordinat* consumables

consommateur, -trice [kɔ̃sɔmatœr, -tris] ADJ **système c. d'électricité** system that runs on electricity; **pays c.** consumer nation; **les pays fortement consommateurs de pétrole** the countries that consume large quantities of crude oil

NM,F **1** *(par opposition à producteur)* consumer; **mes collègues sont de grands consommateurs de café** my colleagues are great coffee drinkers; *Mktg* **c. cible** target consumer; *Mktg* **c. final** end-user **2** *(client → d'un service)* customer, user

consommation [kɔ̃sɔmasjɔ̃] NF **1** *(absorption → de nourriture, de boisson)* consumption; **viande impropre à la c.** meat unfit for (human) consumption

2 *(utilisation → de gaz, d'électricité)* consumption; **elle fait une grande c. de parfum/papier** she gets through a lot of perfume/paper; **pour ma c. personnelle** for my own *or* personal use

3 *Écon* consumption; **c. de capital** capital consumption; **c. à crédit** credit-based consumption; **la c. des ménages** household consumption; **c. intérieure** home consumption; **c. de masse** mass consumption; **biens/société de c.** consumer goods/society; **c. par tête** per capita consumption

4 *Aut* **c. (d'essence)** (*Br* petrol *or Am* gas) consumption; **une c. de 4 litres aux 100 (km)** a

consumption of 4 litres per 100 km; **la c. en ville** urban fuel consumption; **c. d'huile** oil consumption; **c. spécifique** specific fuel consumption

5 *(au café)* drink; **prendre une c.** *(boire)* to have a drink; *Fam* **la serveuse a déjà pris les consommations** the waitress has already taken the (drinks) order

6 *Compta* **consommations de l'exercice** total annual expenses

7 *Littéraire (accomplissement → d'un crime)* perpetration; *(→ d'un mariage)* consummation; **jusqu'à la c. des siècles** until the end of time

consommatique [kɔsɔmatik] NF consumer research

consommatisme [kɔsɔmatizm] NM consumerism

consommatrice [kɔsɔmatris] *voir* **consommateur**

consommé, -e [kɔsɔme] ADJ consummate
  NM clear soup, consommé; **c. de poulet** chicken consommé

consommer [3] [kɔsɔme] VT **1** *(absorber → nourriture)* to eat, *Sout* to consume; *(→ boisson)* to drink, *Sout* to consume; **les Français consomment beaucoup de pain** French people eat a lot of bread; **le pays où l'on consomme le plus de vin** the country with the highest wine consumption; **à c. frais** *(sur mode d'emploi)* serve chilled; **à c. avant (fin)...** *(sur emballage)* best before (end)...; *Fam* **je consommais des montagnes de BD** I used to devour loads of comics

2 *(utiliser → combustible)* to use (up), to consume, to go through; **une voiture qui consomme beaucoup/peu (d'essence)** a car that uses a lot of/that doesn't use much petrol; **les industries qui consomment de l'aluminium** industries that use aluminium

3 *Jur (mariage)* to consummate

4 *Littéraire (accomplir → crime)* to perpetrate; *(→ ruine)* to bring about the completion of; **la rupture est consommée** they have broken up for good

USAGE ABSOLU **toute personne attablée doit c.** anyone occupying a table must order a drink; **les gens qui ne consomment pas** non-drinking customers; **c. sur place** *(dans un fast-food)* to eat in
  ▸ **se consommer** VPR **ça se consomme froid** it's eaten cold, you eat it cold

consomptible [kɔsɔptibl] ADJ consumable; **produits consomptibles** consumables

consomptif, -ive [kɔsɔptif, -iv] ADJ *Vieilli Méd* wasting *(avant n)*; *(tuberculeux)* consumptive

consomption [kɔsɔpsjɔ] NF *Vieilli Méd (amaigrissement)* wasting; *(tuberculose)* consumption

consomptive [kɔsɔptiv] *voir* **consomptif**

consonance [kɔsɔnɑs] NF **1** *Littérature & Mus* consonance **2** *(sonorité)* sound; **je n'aime pas la c. de ce mot** I don't like the sound of that word; **de c. anglaise, aux consonances anglaises** English-sounding

consonant, -e [kɔsɔnɑ, -ɑt] ADJ *Littérature & Mus* consonant

consonantique [kɔsɔnɑtik] ADJ **1** *Ling (des consonnes)* consonantal, consonant *(avant n)*; **le système c.** the consonant system **2** *(en acoustique)* consonant, resonant

consonantisme [kɔsɔnɑtism] NM *Ling* consonant system *(of a language)*

consonne [kɔsɔn] NF consonant; **c. occlusive** occlusive or plosive or stop consonant; **c. labiale/dentale** labial/dental (consonant)

consort [kɔsɔr] ADJ M consort
  NM consort
  ❑ **consorts** NMPL **1** *Jur* jointly interested parties **2** *Péj* **Paul et consorts** *(et sa bande)* Paul and company, Paul and his gang; *(et ceux de son espèce)* Paul and his kind, Paul and those like him

consortage [kɔsɔrtaʒ] NM *Suisse (dans le Valais)* = farmers' association

consortial, -e, -aux, -ales [kɔsɔrsjal, -o] ADJ = relating to a consortium or a syndicate

consortium [kɔsɔrsjɔm] NM consortium, syndicate; **constituer un c.** to form a consortium; **les chaînes ont constitué un c.** the channels have become syndicated; **c. de banques** banking consortium

consoude [kɔsud] NF *Bot* comfrey, consound; **c. royale** field larkspur

conspirateur, -trice [kɔspiratœr, -tris] NM,F conspirator, plotter, conspirer; **ils se donnaient des airs de conspirateurs** they had a conspiratorial air about them
  ADJ conspiratorial

conspiration [kɔspirasjɔ] NF conspiracy, plot; *Hist* **la C. des poudres** the Gunpowder Plot

conspiratrice [kɔspiratris] *voir* **conspirateur**

conspirer [3] [kɔspire] VI to conspire, to plot, to scheme; **c. contre qn** to conspire or to plot or to scheme against sb
  VT *Littéraire* to plot, to scheme
  ❑ **conspirer à** VT IND to conspire to; **tout conspire à la réussite de ce projet** everything conspires or combines to make this project a success

conspuer [7] [kɔspɥe] VT to shout down; **se faire c.** *(orateur)* to be shouted down; *(comédien)* to be booed off the stage

constable [kɔstabl] NM (police) constable

constamment [kɔstamɑ] ADV **1** *(sans interruption)* continuously, continually **2** *(très fréquemment)* constantly

Constance [kɔstɑs] *voir* **lac**

constance [kɔstɑs] NF **1** *(persévérance)* constancy, steadfastness; **vous avez de la c.!** you don't give up easily!; **travailler avec c.** to work steadily **2** *Littéraire (fidélité)* constancy, fidelity, faithfulness; **manquer de c.** to be fickle; **faire preuve d'une grande c. en amitié** to be unswerving in one's friendships **3** *(de la température, d'un phénomène)* constancy, invariability **4** *Psy* invariability, constancy

constant, -e [kɔstɑ, -ɑt] ADJ **1** *(invariable)* unchanging, constant; **c. dans ses amitiés** faithful to one's friends or in friendship; **être c. dans ses goûts** to be unchanging in one's tastes **2** *(ininterrompu)* continual, continuous, unceasing **3** *Math* constant **4** *Fin* constant; **en euros constants** in constant euros
  ❑ **constante** NF **1** *Math & Phys* constant; **c. calorifique** calorific constant **2** *Élec* **constante diélectrique** (dielectric) permittivity, dielectric constant **3** *Météo* **constante solaire** solar constant **4** *(caractéristique)* stable or permanent trait **5** *Ordinat* constant; **constante complexe/double précision/réelle** complex/double precision/real constant

constantan [kɔstɑtɑ] NM *Métal* constantan

Constantin [kɔstɑtɛ] NPR *(empereur)* Constantine

Constantine [kɔstɑtin] NF Constantine

constantinien, -enne [kɔstɑtinjɛ, -ɛn] ADJ Constantinian, Constantian

Constantinople [kɔstɑtinɔpl] NM Constantinople

constat [kɔsta] NM **1** *(acte)* certified statement or report; **c. d'accident** accident statement; **faisons le c.** *(après un accident)* let's fill in the necessary papers (for the insurance); **c. d'adultère** adultery report; **c. (à l')amiable** = report of road accident agreed by the parties involved; **le c. de Grenelle** = the agreement between government and unions on working hours and wages concluded in 1968; **c. d'huissier** = affidavit drawn up by a bailiff

2 *(bilan)* review; **faire un c. d'échec** to acknowledge or to admit a failure

constatable [kɔstatabl] ADJ observable; **cette tendance est c. chez les jeunes** this tendency can be observed in young people

constatation [kɔstatasjɔ] NF **1** *(observation)* noting, noticing; **la c. d'une fuite a entraîné une vérification de l'ensemble du système** the discovery of a leak led to a check-up of the entire system

2 *(remarque)* remark, comment, observation; **faites-moi part de vos constatations** let me have your comments; **ce n'est pas un reproche, c'est une simple c.** this isn't a criticism, it's just an observation or I'm just stating a fact; **première c., le liquide vire au bleu** the first thing to note is that the liquid turns blue

3 *Compta* **c. de stock** stock take
  ❑ **constatations** NFPL **1** *(d'une enquête)* findings; **procéder aux constatations** to establish the facts **2** *Assur* **c. des dommages** assessment of damages

constaté [kɔstate] ADJ *Fin (valeur)* registered; **c. d'avance** *(charge)* prepaid

constater [3] [kɔstate] VT **1** *(remarquer → gén)* to note, to observe, to notice; *(→ erreur)* to discover, to find; **on constate une régression de la criminalité** a decline in criminality can be observed; **je constate que tu fumes toujours autant** I notice you still smoke just as much; **j'ai constaté une légère amélioration de son état de santé** I've noticed a slight improvement in his/her health; **je suis forcé de c. que je ne peux te faire confiance** I am forced to the conclusion that I can't trust you; **vous pouvez c. vous-même qu'elle est partie** you can see for yourself that she's gone

2 *(enregistrer → décès)* to certify; *(→ faits)* to record, to list; **l'expert est venu c. les dégâts** the expert came to assess the damage

USAGE ABSOLU **constatez par vous-même!** just see for yourself!; **je ne critique pas, je ne fais que c.** I'm not criticizing, I'm just stating the facts

constellation [kɔstelasjɔ] NF **1** *Astron* constellation **2** *(ensemble → de savants, de célébrités)* constellation, galaxy; **une c. de taches** stains all over

consteller [4] [kɔstele] VT to spangle, to stud; **de nombreuses décorations constellent son uniforme** his/her uniform is adorned with medals; **un ciel constellé d'étoiles** a star-studded sky; **une robe constellée de taches** a dress spattered with stains; **un visage constellé de taches de rousseur** a face covered in freckles
  ▸ **se consteller** VPR **le ciel se constella d'étoiles** the stars came out in the sky

consternant, -e [kɔstɛrnɑ, -ɑt] ADJ distressing; **d'une bêtise consternante** appallingly stupid; **la pièce est consternante** the play's dire or appallingly bad

consternation [kɔstɛrnasjɔ] NF consternation, dismay; **jeter la c. dans un groupe** to fill a group with consternation or dismay; **la c. était générale** everybody was appalled; **à la c. générale** to everyone's consternation or dismay

consterner [3] [kɔstɛrne] VT to appal, to fill with consternation; **consterné par une nouvelle** appalled or dismayed by a piece of news; **regarder qch d'un air consterné** to look aghast or with consternation upon sth

constipant, -e [kɔstipɑ, -ɑt] ADJ constipating

constipation [kɔstipasjɔ] NF constipation

constipé, -e [kɔstipe] ADJ **1** *Méd* constipated **2** *Fam (guindé)* **être** ou **avoir l'air c.** to look ill-at-ease or uncomfortable; **un style c.** a constipated style
  NM,F **1** *Méd* constipated person **2** *Fam (personne guindée)* uptight or stuffy person; **quel c.!** he's so uptight!

constiper [3] [kɔstipe] VT to constipate
  USAGE ABSOLU **les œufs constipent** eggs cause constipation

constituant, -e [kɔstitɥɑ, -ɑt] ADJ **1** *(élément)* constituent **2** *Jur & Pol* constituent; **pouvoir c.** constituent power
  NM **1** *Jur & Pol* constituent; *Hist* = member of the 1789 Constituent Assembly **2** *Chim* component **3** *Ling* constituent; **c. immédiat** immediate constituent
  ❑ **Constituante** NF *Hist* **la Constituante** the Constituent Assembly

constitué, -e [kɔstitɥe] ADJ **1** *(personne)* **un homme normalement c.** a (physically) normal man; **un enfant mal c.** a child of poor constitution; **un individu solidement c.** a sturdily-built individual; **bien c.** hardy **2** *Pol (autorité)* constituted; *(corps)* constituent

constituer [7] [kɔstitɥe] VT **1** *(créer → collection)* to build up, to put together; *(→ bibliothèque)* to build or to set up; *(→ société anonyme, association, gouvernement)* to form, to set up; *(→ équipe, cabinet)* to form, to select (the members of); *(→ dossier)* to prepare; **c. des réserves/des stocks de qch** to stock up on sth; *Jur* **c. une dot/une rente à qn** to settle a dowry/a pension on sb; **son père voulait lui c. un patrimoine** his/her father wanted to set him/her up with an estate

2 *(faire partie de)* to form, to constitute, to (go to) make up; **ces cinq pages constituent l'introduction** these five pages form the introduction; **les timbres qui constituent sa collection**

the stamps that make up his/her collection; **être constitué de** to be made up of, to consist of; **l'eau est constituée de…** water consists or is composed of…; **un appartement constitué de six pièces** a six-roomed flat

3 (*être*) to be, to represent; **ce mobilier constitue tout mon bien** this furniture represents all my worldly goods, this furniture is all I own; **le vol constitue un délit** theft is or constitutes an offence; **sa présence constitue un danger** his presence spells danger

4 *Jur* (*nommer*) to name, to appoint; **c. qn président** to appoint sb as or to make sb chairman; **c. qn son légataire** to name or to appoint sb one's legatee

▸**se constituer** VPR **1 se c. de** (*être composé de*) to be made up of

2 (*se mettre en position de*) **se c. prisonnier** to give oneself up; *Jur* **se c. partie civile** to file a civil action in a criminal proceeding

3 (*se former*) to form, to be formed; **un nouveau comité s'est constitué** a new committee has formed or has been formed or has been created; **se c. en** to form; **ils se sont constitués en association** they formed a society

4 se c. qch to build sth up or to amass sth (for oneself); **se c. une vidéothèque** to build up a video library; **se c. un patrimoine** to amass an estate

constitutif, -ive [kɔ̃stitytif, -iv] ADJ **1** (*qui compose*) constituent, component; **les éléments constitutifs de l'eau** the elements which make up or the constituent elements of water **2** (*typique* → *propriété*) constitutive **3** *Jur* constitutive

constitution [kɔ̃stitysjɔ̃] NF **1** (*création* → *d'une collection*) building up, putting together; (→ *d'une bibliothèque*) building up, setting up; (→ *d'une société anonyme, d'une association, d'un gouvernement*) forming, formation, setting up; (→ *d'une équipe, d'un cabinet*) selection; (→ *d'un dossier*) preparation, putting together

2 (*composition* → *d'un groupe*) composition; (→ *d'une substance*) make-up, composition

3 *Pol* (*lois*) constitution; **c. républicaine** (*régime*) republic; **c. monarchique** monarchy

4 (*santé*) constitution, physique; **une bonne/ solide c.** a sound/sturdy constitution; **être de c. fragile** (*souvent malade*) to be susceptible to disease

5 *Pharm* (*en homéopathie*) composition

6 *Jur* (*d'une dot, d'une rente*) settling, settlement; (*d'un avocat*) *Br* briefing, *Am* hiring; **c. de partie civile** filing of a civil action in a criminal proceeding

constitutionnaliser [3] [kɔ̃stitysjɔnalize] VT to constitutionalize, to make constitutional

constitutionnalisme [kɔ̃stitysjɔnalism] NM *Pol* constitutionalism

constitutionnaliste [kɔ̃stitysjɔnalist] NMF *Jur* constitutional lawyer

constitutionnalité [kɔ̃stitysjɔnalite] NF constitutionality

constitutionnel, -elle [kɔ̃stitysjɔnɛl] ADJ constitutional

constitutionnellement [kɔ̃stitysjɔnɛlmã] ADV constitutionally

constitutive [kɔ̃stitytiv] *voir* constitutif

constricteur [kɔ̃striktœr] ADJ M *Anat & Zool* constrictor

NM **1** *Anat* constrictor **2** *Zool* boa constrictor

constrictif, -ive [kɔ̃striktif, -iv] ADJ *Méd* constrictive

❑ **constrictive** NF *Ling* constrictive

constriction [kɔ̃striksjɔ̃] NF constriction

constrictive [kɔ̃striktiv] *voir* constrictif

constrictor [kɔ̃striktɔr] ADJ M *Anat & Zool* constrictor

NM *Zool* boa constrictor

constringent, -e [kɔ̃strɛ̃ʒã, -ãt] ADJ constringent

constructeur, -trice [kɔ̃stryktœr, -tris] ADJ **1** (*d'édifices, de bateaux*) building (*avant n*); (*d'appareils, d'engins*) manufacturing (*avant n*) **2** *Zool* **animaux constructeurs** home-building animals

NM **1** (*d'édifices*) builder **2** (*d'appareils, d'engins*) manufacturer; **c. automobile** car manufacturer; **c. naval** shipbuilder **3** *Ordinat* handler, builder **4** *Littéraire* **c. d'empire** empire builder

constructible [kɔ̃stryktibl] ADJ constructible; **terrain** ou **parcelle c.** plot suitable for building on, building land

constructif, -ive [kɔ̃stryktif, -iv] ADJ **1** (*qui fait progresser*) constructive, positive **2** *Constr* constructional, building (*avant n*)

construction [kɔ̃stryksjɔ̃] NF **1** (*édification*) building, construction; **la c. de la tour a duré un an** it took a year to build or to erect the tower; **c'était de la bonne c. à l'époque** building standards were high in those days; *Fig* **la c. européenne** European integration

2 (*édifice*) building, construction; **des constructions récentes** new buildings, recent constructions

3 (*fabrication*) building, manufacturing; **la c. aéronautique** aircraft manufacturing; **la c. automobile** car manufacturing; **la c. mécanique** (mechanical) engineering; **appareil de c. française** French-built machine

4 (*entreprise*) **constructions navales** ship-building (industry); **constructions aéronautiques** aircraft industry

5 (*structure* → *d'une œuvre*) structure; (→ *d'une phrase*) construction, structure; **ce n'est qu'une c. de l'esprit** it's purely hypothetical

6 *Gram* construction; **ce verbe a une c. passive** this verb is construed passively or has a passive construction

7 *Math* figure, construction

❑ **de construction** ADJ **1** (*matériau*) building (*avant n*), construction (*avant n*)

2 jeu de c. set of building blocks

❑ **en construction** ADV under construction; **la maison est encore en c.** the house is still being built or still under construction

constructive [kɔ̃stryktiv] *voir* constructif

constructivisme [kɔ̃stryktivism] NM *Beaux-Arts & Phil* constructivism

constructiviste [kɔ̃stryktivist] *Beaux-Arts & Phil* ADJ constructivist

NMF constructivist

constructrice [kɔ̃stryktris] *voir* constructeur

construire [98] [kɔ̃strɥir] VT **1** (*route, barrage*) to build, to construct; (*maison*) to build; **une maison récemment construite** a newly-built house; **se faire c. une maison** to have a house built; *Fig* **c. une nouvelle Europe** to build a new Europe

2 *Ind* (*fabriquer*) to build, to manufacture

3 (*structurer* → *pièce, roman*) to structure, to construct; (→ *théorie, raisonnement*) to build, to develop; (→ *figure de géométrie*) to draw, to construct; **c. correctement une phrase** to construct a sentence properly

4 *Gram* to construe; **on construit "vouloir" avec le subjonctif** "vouloir" takes the subjunctive or is construed with the subjunctive

USAGE ABSOLU **leur rêve, c'est de pouvoir faire c.** they dream of having their own house built

▸**se construire** VPR **1** (*être édifié*) to be built; **il s'est construit beaucoup de maisons** a lot of houses have been built; *Fam* **ça se construit par ici!** a lot of stuff's going up or a lot of building's going on around here!; **la campagne environnante s'est construite** the surrounding countryside has become a built-up area

2 *Gram* **se c. avec** to take, to be construed with

consubstantialité [kɔ̃sypstãsjalite] NF *Rel* consubstantiality

consubstantiation [kɔ̃sypstãsjasjɔ̃] NF *Rel* consubstantiation

consubstantiel, -elle [kɔ̃sypstãsjɛl] ADJ *Rel* consubstantial

consul [kɔ̃syl] NM

Note that it is no longer considered a mistake to feminize this word and to say **une consule** (with a final **e**) for sense 1 but some French speakers nonetheless regard this form as unacceptable, especially in France. See also the entry **féminisation**.

1 (*diplomate*) consul; **le c. de France** the French Consul; **c. général** consul general

2 *Hist* Consul (*in France from 1799 to 1804*)

3 *Antiq* consul

consulaire [kɔ̃sylɛr] ADJ consular

consulat [kɔ̃syla] NM **1** (*résidence, bureaux*) consulate **2** (*fonction diplomatique*) consulship

3 *Hist* **le C.** the Consulate (*in France from 1799 to 1804*) **4** *Antiq* consulship

consultable [kɔ̃syltabl] ADJ (*ouvrage, fichier*) which may be consulted, available for reference or consultation

consultant, -e [kɔ̃syltã, -ãt] ADJ *voir* avocat² , médecin

NM,F consultant; **c. en gestion** management consultant

consultatif, -ive [kɔ̃syltatif, -iv] ADJ (*gén*) advisory; (*assemblée*) consultative; **à titre c.** in an advisory capacity

consultation [kɔ̃syltasjɔ̃] NF **1** (*d'un plan, d'un règlement*) consulting, checking; **la c. d'un dictionnaire** looking words up in a dictionary; **un livre d'une c. facile** a book that is easy to consult or use; **après c. de mon emploi du temps** after checking my timetable

2 *Pol* **c. électorale** election; **c. populaire** consultation of the people

3 (*chez un professionnel*) consultation; **donner des consultations** (*gén*) to hold consultations; (*médecin*) to have one's *Br* surgery or *Am* office hours; **il est en c.** (*médecin*) he's with a patient; **horaires de c.** (*chez un médecin*) *Br* surgery or *Am* office hours; **il demande 80 euros pour la c.** he charges 80 euros for (his) professional services; **c. externe** out-patients' department

4 *Ordinat* **c. de table** table lookup; **c. de fichier** file browsing or browse

consultative [kɔ̃syltativ] *voir* consultatif

consulte [kɔ̃sylt] NF **1** *Jur* = Corsican consultative assembly **2** *Hist* **c. d'État** consulta; **c. sacrée** judiciary court (*at Rome*)

consulter [3] [kɔ̃sylte] VT **1** (*médecin*) to visit, to consult; (*avocat, professeur*) to consult, to seek advice from; (*voyante*) to visit; **il ne m'a même pas consulté** he didn't even ask for my opinion; **c. qn du regard** to look questioningly at sb

2 (*livre, dictionnaire*) to refer to, to consult; (*plan, montre, baromètre, horaire*) to look at, to check; (*horoscope*) to read; **quand je consulte le miroir** when I look at myself in the mirror; **c. ses notes** to go over one's notes

3 (*au négatif*) (*prendre en compte*) **il ne consulte que son intérêt** he's guided only by self-interest

4 *Ordinat* to search

USAGE ABSOLU **se décider à c.** to decide to go to the doctor's; **lorsqu'il est venu c., j'ai prescrit des antibiotiques** when he came to see me, I prescribed some antibiotics

VI (*docteur*) to hold surgery, to see patients

▸**se consulter** VPR (*discuter*) to confer; **ils se sont consultés avant de m'annoncer la nouvelle** they conferred before giving me the news; **se c. du regard** to look questioningly at one another

consulteur, -trice [kɔ̃syltœr, -tris] NM *Rel* adviser

consumable [kɔ̃symabl] ADJ **cette matière est c.** this substance will burn

consumer [3] [kɔ̃syme] VT **1** (*brûler*) to burn, to consume; **le feu a consumé tous les livres** the fire destroyed all the books; **les bûches consumées dans la cheminée** the charred logs in the fireplace

2 *Littéraire* (*tourmenter*) **la jalousie la consume** she's consumed with jealousy; **il est consumé de chagrin** ou **par le chagrin** he is racked with grief

3 *Littéraire* (*fortune, énergie*) to waste

▸**se consumer** VPR **1** (*brûler*) to burn; **laisser une cigarette se c.** to let a cigarette burn (out)

2 *Littéraire* **se c. de qch** (*être tourmenté*) to be consumed with sth; **il se consume de désespoir** he's consumed with despair; **se c. d'amour pour qn** to pine for sb; **se c. en efforts inutiles** to wear oneself out in useless efforts

consumérisme [kɔ̃symerism] NM **le c.** consumerism

consumériste [kɔ̃symerist] ADJ consumerist

consumer magazine [kɔ̃symœrmagazin] NM *Mktg* = free leaflet advertising the products of a shop or other company, usually promoting particular products and/or special offers

contact [kɔ̃takt] NM **1** (*toucher*) touch, contact; **je n'aime pas le c. du marbre** I don't like the feel

of marble; **maladies transmises par c.** diseases transmitted by (direct) contact

2 *Aut, Élec & Rad* contact, switch; **le c. ne se fait pas** there's no contact; **il y a un mauvais c.** there's a loose connection somewhere; **mettre/couper le c.** *Élec* to switch on/off; *Aut* to turn the ignition on/off; **nous avons perdu le c. radio avec eux** we're no longer in radio contact with them

3 *(lien)* contact; **avoir des contacts avec** to have contact with; **j'ai su qu'il m'était hostile dès le premier c.** I knew that he was hostile towards me from the moment we met; **il a perdu tout c. avec le réel** he's lost all contact with reality; **prendre des contacts** to establish some contacts; **prendre c. avec qn** to contact sb, to get in touch with sb; **j'ai gardé le c. avec mes vieux amis** I'm still in touch with my old friends; **il est d'un c. facile** he's easy to get on with; **avec ma belle-famille, il n'y a pas tellement de c.** my in-laws aren't very close (to us)

4 *(personne → dans les affaires, l'espionnage)* contact, connection

5 *Géom* **(point de) c. de deux plans** intersection *or* meeting point of two planes

6 *Phot* contact (print)

7 *Équitation* contact

8 *Ordinat* **c. de page** *(sur l'Internet)* hit

❏ **au contact de** PRÉP **au c. de l'air** in contact with *or* when exposed to the air; **elle sursauta au c. de ma main sur son épaule** she jumped at the touch of my hand on her shoulder; **ne pas mettre au c. de l'œil** *(sur mode d'emploi)* avoid contact with the eyes; **il a changé à mon c.** he's changed since he met me

❏ **de contact** ADJ **1** *Aut* ignition *(avant n)*
2 *Rail* *(fil, ligne)* contact *(avant n)*
3 *Opt* contact *(avant n)*

❏ **en contact** ADJ **1** *(reliés → personnes)* in touch; **être en c. avec qn** to be in touch with sb; **rester en c. avec qn** to keep *or* to stay *or* to remain in touch with sb **2** *(adjacents → objets, substances)* in contact **3** *Élec* connected ADV **entrer en c. avec** *(toucher)* come into contact with; *(joindre)* to contact, to get in touch with; *Aviat & Mil* to make contact with; **mettre en c.** *(personnes)* to put in touch (with each other); *(objets, substances)* to bring into contact; *Aviat & Mil* to establish contact between

contacter [3] [kɔ̃takte] VT to contact, to get in touch with; **on peut me c. par téléphone au bureau** you can reach me by phone at the office; **veuillez c. ma secrétaire** please get in touch with my secretary

contacteur [kɔ̃taktœr] NM *Élec* contactor; *(du système d'allumage)* switch; **c. d'interdiction** inhibitor switch; **c. de coupure à inertie** inertia cut-off switch; **c. à solénoïde** solenoid switch

contactologie [kɔ̃taktɔlɔʒi] NF = branch of ophthalmology concerned with contact lenses

contactologue [kɔ̃taktɔlɔg] NMF contact lens specialist

contage [kɔ̃taʒ] NM *Méd* virus of contagion, contagium

contagieux, -euse [kɔ̃taʒjø, -øz] ADJ *(personne)* contagious; *(maladie, rire)* infectious, contagious; *(virus, enthousiasme)* catching
NM,F contagious patient; **les c. ne sont pas acceptés à la crèche** children with contagious diseases will not be admitted to the nursery

contagion [kɔ̃taʒjɔ̃] NF **1** *Méd* contagion; **pour éviter tout risque de c.** to avoid any risk of infection *or* contagion **2** *(d'un rire, d'une peur)* contagiousness, infectiousness

contagiosité [kɔ̃taʒjozite] NF contagiousness; **à haute** *ou* **forte c.** highly contagious

container [kɔ̃tɛnɛr] NM **1** *Ind & Com* container; **c. à gaz** gas tank; **mise en c.** containerization **2** *Hort* *(large)* plant holder

containérisation [kɔ̃tɛnerizasjɔ̃] NF *Ind & Com* containerization

containériser [3] [kɔ̃tɛnerize] VT *Ind & Com* to containerize

contaminateur, -trice [kɔ̃taminatœr, -tris] ADJ infectious
NM,F infectious carrier; **chercher le c. de qn** to look for the contact who infected sb

contamination [kɔ̃taminasjɔ̃] NF **1** *Méd* contamination, infection; **pour éviter la c.** to avoid

contamination **2** *(de l'environnement, des aliments)* contamination; **c. radioactive** radioactive contamination **3** *Ling* contamination **4** *Littéraire (corruption)* (moral) pollution

contaminatrice [kɔ̃taminatris] *voir* **contaminateur**

contaminer [3] [kɔ̃tamine] VT **1** *Méd* to infect, to contaminate **2** *(environnement, aliments)* to infect, to contaminate **3** *Littéraire (corrompre → personne)* to corrupt

conte [kɔ̃t] NM **1** *(histoire)* story, tale; **contes de Bretagne** Breton stories *or* tales *or* legends; **c. de bonnes femmes** old wives' tale; *aussi Fig* **c. de fées** fairy tale; **elle vit un c. de fées** her life is a fairy tale **2** *Vieilli (histoire invraisemblable)* (tall) story, yarn; **c. à dormir debout** cock-and-bull story

---

'**Contes du chat perché**' *Aymé* 'The Wonderful Farm'

'**Les Contes de ma mère l'Oie**' *Perrault* 'Mother Goose Tales'

contemplateur, -trice [kɔ̃tɑ̃platœr, -tris] NM,F contemplator

contemplatif, -ive [kɔ̃tɑ̃platif, -iv] ADJ **1** *(pensif)* thoughtful, contemplative, meditative **2** *Rel* contemplative
NM,F contemplative; **c'est un c.** he likes to muse

contemplation [kɔ̃tɑ̃plasjɔ̃] NF **1** *(admiration)* admiration; **elle est restée en c. devant le tableau** she stood gazing at the picture in admiration
2 *(méditation)* contemplation, reflection; **plongé dans la c. (de qch)** lost in contemplation (of sth)
3 *Rel* contemplation

contemplative [kɔ̃tɑ̃plativ] *voir* **contemplatif**

contemplatrice [kɔ̃tɑ̃platris] *voir* **contemplateur**

contempler [3] [kɔ̃tɑ̃ple] VT **1** *(admirer)* to admire; *(regarder)* to gaze at; **d'ici, vous pouvez c. le superbe paysage** you can admire the superb view from here; **c. qn avec amour** to gaze lovingly at sb
▸ **se contempler** VPR to gaze at oneself

contemporain, -e [kɔ̃tɑ̃pɔrɛ̃, -ɛn] ADJ **1** *(de la même époque)* contemporary; **être c. de** to be contemporary with; **elle est contemporaine de Colette** she's a contemporary of Colette's **2** *(moderne)* contemporary, modern, present-day
NM,F contemporary; **mon/son c.** my/his/her contemporary; *Suisse* **contemporains** = people born in the same year who get together, often in a club, for various activities

contemporanéité [kɔ̃tɑ̃pɔraneite] NF contemporaneity, contemporaneousness

contempteur, -trice [kɔ̃tɑ̃ptœr, -tris] NM,F *Littéraire* denigrator, despiser; **ses contempteurs** those who derided him/her

contenable [kɔ̃tnabl] ADJ controllable

contenance [kɔ̃tnɑ̃s] NF **1** *(attitude)* attitude, bearing; **il essayait de prendre** *ou* **se donner une c.** he was trying to put on a brave face; **faire qch pour se donner une c.** to do sth to give oneself an air of assurance; **faire bonne c.** to put up a bold *or* good front; **perdre c.** to lose one's composure
2 *(capacité → d'un tonneau, d'un réservoir)* capacity; *(→ d'un navire)* (carrying *or* holding) capacity; **d'une c. de 10 litres** capable of holding 10 litres, with a capacity of 10 litres

contenant [kɔ̃tnɑ̃] NM container

conteneur [kɔ̃tnœr] = **container**

conteneurisation [kɔ̃tnœrizasjɔ̃] = **containérisation**

conteneuriser [3] [kɔ̃tnœrize] = **containériser**

contenir [40] [kɔ̃tnir] VT **1** *(renfermer)* to contain, to hold; **chaque boîte contient dix cigares** each box contains *or* holds ten cigars; **l'enveloppe contenait le reçu** the receipt was enclosed in the envelope; **que contient ce colis?** what's in this parcel?; **votre article contient beaucoup de paradoxes** your article is full of *or* contains many contradictions
2 *(être constitué de)* to contain; **boissons qui**

contiennent de l'alcool drinks containing alcohol

3 *(avoir telle capacité)* to hold; **véhicule pouvant c. 35 personnes assises/debout** vehicle seating 35/with standing room for 35 people; **le théâtre peut c. mille spectateurs** the theatre holds *or* seats a thousand

4 *(réprimer → foule, larmes, sanglots)* to hold back; *(→ poussée, invasion, ennemi)* to contain; *(→ rire, colère)* to suppress; **une colère mal contenue** barely suppressed anger
▸ **se contenir** VPR to control oneself; **ils ne pouvaient plus se c.** *(ils pleuraient)* they couldn't hold back their tears any longer; *(ils riaient)* they couldn't disguise their mirth any longer

content, -e [kɔ̃tɑ̃, -ɑ̃t] ADJ **1** *(heureux)* happy, glad, pleased; **ils avaient l'air très contents** they looked very happy *or* pleased; **je suis très c. de vous voir** I'm very pleased to see you; **je suis c. que tu aies pu venir** I'm glad that you could make it; **je ne suis pas c. du tout** I'm not at all pleased *or* happy; *Fam* **s'il n'est pas c., c'est pareil!** he can like it or lump it!
2 *(satisfait)* **être c. de qch** to be pleased with sth; **vous êtes contents de vos vacances?** are you enjoying your holiday?; **elle a l'air contente de sa nouvelle voiture** she seems pleased *or* happy with her new car; **je suis très c. de moi** I'm very pleased with myself; **tu peux être c. de toi, tu as vu ce que tu as fait!** I hope you're pleased with yourself *or* happy, just look what you've done!; **non c. de** not content with; **non c. d'être riche, il veut aussi être célèbre** not content with being rich or not satisfied with being rich, he wants to be famous as well
NM **avoir (tout) son c. de qch** to have (had) one's fill of sth; **manger tout son c.** to eat one's fill; **laisse-les s'amuser tout leur c.** let them play as much as they like

contentement [kɔ̃tɑ̃tmɑ̃] NM satisfaction, contentment; **avec c.** contentedly; **un sourire de c.** a satisfied *or* contented smile; **c. de soi** self-satisfaction

contenter [3] [kɔ̃tɑ̃te] VT **1** *(faire plaisir à)* to please, to satisfy; **voilà qui devrait c. tout le monde** this should satisfy *or* please everybody
2 *(satisfaire → curiosité, envie)* to satisfy
▸ **se contenter** VPR **se c. de qch/de faire qch** to be content *or* to content oneself with sth/doing sth, to make do with sth/doing sth; **elle s'est contentée d'une modeste chambre** she contented herself *or* was satisfied with a modest room; **pour tout repas, elle s'est contentée de sandwiches** by way of a meal, she made do with sandwiches; **il se contente de peu** he's easily satisfied; **en guise de réponse, elle s'est contentée de sourire** she merely smiled in reply; **je me contenterai de faire remarquer que...** I will merely point out that...

contentieuse [kɔ̃tɑ̃sjøz] *voir* **contentieux**

contentieusement [kɔ̃tɑ̃sjøzmɑ̃] ADV contentiously

contentieux, -euse [kɔ̃tɑ̃sjø, -øz] ADJ contentious
NM **1** *(conflit)* dispute, disagreement; **avoir un c. avec qn** to be in dispute with sb; **il y a un c. entre eux** they're in dispute
2 *Jur (service)* legal department *or* bureau
3 *Jur (affaire)* litigation; **c. administratif** procedure in contentious administrative matters; **c. fiscal** tax litigation; **c. électoral** procedure in contentious electoral matters; **c. territorial** territorial dispute

contention [kɔ̃tɑ̃sjɔ̃] NF **1** *Littéraire* exertion, application; **c. d'esprit** concentration **2** *Méd (d'un os)* setting, reduction; *(d'un malade)* restraint; **moyen de c.** splint **3** *Psy (d'une personne)* restraint

contenu, -e [kɔ̃tny] PP *voir* **contenir**
NM **1** *(d'un récipient, d'un paquet)* content, contents **2** *(teneur → d'un document)* content, text; **quel est le c. du texte?** what does the text say?; *Journ* **c. rédactionnel** editorial content **3** *Ling* (linguistic) content **4** *Psy* **c. latent/manifeste** latent/manifest content

conter [3] [kɔ̃te] VT *Can ou Littéraire* to relate, to tell; **je vais vous c. l'histoire de Barbe-Bleue** I'll tell you the story of Bluebeard; **que me contez-vous là?** what are you talking about?;

c. fleurette à qn to murmur sweet nothings to sb; **c. des balivernes** to talk nonsense; **on m'en a conté de belles sur toi!** I've heard some fine things about you!; **elle ne s'en laisse pas c.** she's not easily taken in; *Can* **c. des peurs** to tell tall tales

contestabilité [kɔ̃tɛstabilite] **NF** *Littéraire* contestableness

contestable [kɔ̃tɛstabl] **ADJ** debatable, questionable; **de manière c.** dubiously

contestant, -e [kɔ̃tɛstɑ̃, -ɑ̃t] *Jur, Pol & Littéraire* **ADJ** contending

NM,F contending party

contestataire [kɔ̃tɛstatɛr] **ADJ** protesting *or* revolting *(against established values)*; **un journal c.** an anti-establishment newspaper

NMF anti-establishment protester; **c'est un c.** he's always calling things into question

contestateur, -trice [kɔ̃tɛstatœr, -tris] **ADJ** contentious

contestation [kɔ̃tɛstasjɔ̃] **NF 1** *(d'une loi, d'un testament, d'un document)* contesting, opposing; *(d'un récit, d'un droit)* contesting, questioning; *(d'une compétence)* questioning, challenging, doubting; **élever une c. sur qch** to raise an objection to sth; **il y a matière** *ou* **sujet à c.** there are grounds for dispute; **sans c. (possible)** beyond (all possible) dispute *or* question

2 *(litige)* dispute, controversy, debate

3 *Pol* **la c.** protests, protesting, the protest movement

contestatrice [kɔ̃tɛstatris] *voir* **contestateur**

conteste [kɔ̃tɛst] **sans conteste ADV** indisputably, unquestionably

contester [3] [kɔ̃tɛste] **VT 1** *(testament)* to contest; *(récit, document, véracité)* to contest, to dispute, to question; *(compétence)* to question, to dispute, to throw into doubt; **je ne conteste pas que votre tâche ait été difficile** I don't dispute *or* doubt the fact that you had a difficult task; **je ne lui conteste pas le droit de…** I don't challenge *or* question his/her right to…; **être contesté** *(théorie)* to be a subject of controversy; **une personnalité très contestée** a very controversial personality **2** *Pol* to protest *or* to rebel against

VI 1 *(discuter)* **obéir aux ordres sans c.** to obey orders blindly *or* without raising any objections **2** *Pol* to protest

conteur, -euse [kɔ̃tœr, -øz] **NM,F 1** *(narrateur)* narrator, storyteller **2** *(écrivain)* storyteller

contexte [kɔ̃tɛkst] **NM 1** *(situation)* context; **il faut remettre cet événement dans son c.** we must put this event in its context; **dans le c. de l'économie européenne** (with)in the context of the European economy; **dans le c. actuel** under the present circumstances, in the context of the present situation **2** *Ordinat* environment **3** *Ling* context; **hors c.** out of context; **c. linguistique/de situation** linguistic/situational context

▫ **en contexte ADV** in context; **mettre qch en c.** to put sth into context, to contextualize sth

contextualisation [kɔ̃tɛkstɥalizasjɔ̃] **NF** contextualization

contextualiser [3] [kɔ̃tɛkstɥalize] **VT** to contextualize

contextuel, -elle [kɔ̃tɛkstɥɛl] **ADJ** contextual

contexture [kɔ̃tɛkstyr] **NF 1** *(d'un tissu, d'un matériel)* texture **2** *(d'une œuvre)* structure

contient *etc voir* **contenir**

contigu, -ë [kɔ̃tigy] **ADJ 1** *(bâtiments, terrains, objets)* adjacent, adjoining, *Sout* contiguous; **les maisons contiguës à la nôtre** *(accolées)* the houses joining on to ours **2** *(époques, sujets, domaines)* close, *Sout* contiguous

contiguïté [kɔ̃tigɥite] **NF 1** *(proximité → de bâtiments, de terrains, d'objets)* adjacency, proximity, *Sout* contiguity **2** *(d'époques, de sujets, de domaines)* closeness, *Sout* contiguousness, contiguity **3** *Ordinat* adjacency

continence [kɔ̃tinɑ̃s] **NF 1** *(abstinence)* continence, (self-imposed) chastity **2** *(sobriété, discrétion)* restraint **3** *Méd* continence

continent[1] [kɔ̃tinɑ̃] **NM 1** *Géog* continent; **l'Ancien/le Nouveau C.** the Old/the New World **2** *(par opposition à une île)* **le c.** the mainland

continent[2], **-e** [kɔ̃tinɑ̃, -ɑ̃t] **ADJ 1** *(chaste)* continent, chaste; *(discret)* discreet, restrained, reserved **2** *Méd* continent

continental, -e, -aux, -ales [kɔ̃tinɑ̃tal, -o] **ADJ 1** *(par opposition à insulaire)* mainland *(avant n)* **2** *Géog (climat, température)* continental

NM,F person who lives on the mainland; **les continentaux** people from the mainland

continentalité [kɔ̃tinɑ̃talite] **NF** continental climatic characteristics

contingence [kɔ̃tɛ̃ʒɑ̃s] **NF** *Math & Phil* contingency

▫ **contingences NFPL** contingencies, eventualities; **les contingences de la vie quotidienne** everyday happenings *or* events; **prévoir toutes les contingences** to take unforeseen circumstances into consideration

contingent[1] [kɔ̃tɛ̃ʒɑ̃] **NM 1** *(quantité)* (allotted) share **2** *(quota)* quota; **contingents d'importation/d'exportation** import/export quotas **3** *(troupe)* contingent; *(ensemble des recrues) Br* call-up, *Am* draft; **le c., les soldats du c.** those conscripted, the conscripts, *Am* the draft

contingent[2], **-e** [kɔ̃tɛ̃ʒɑ̃, -ɑ̃t] **ADJ 1** *Phil* contingent **2** *Littéraire (sans importance)* incidental

contingentement [kɔ̃tɛ̃ʒɑ̃tmɑ̃] **NM 1** *Écon* fixing of quotas, restriction; **le c. des importations** the fixing of import quotas **2** *Com* quota system, apportioning by quota

contingenter [3] [kɔ̃tɛ̃ʒɑ̃te] **VT 1** *Écon (importations)* to limit, to fix a quota on; *(produits de distribution)* to restrict the distribution of; **des produits contingentés** fixed quota products **2** *Com* to distribute *or* to allocate according to a quota

contint *etc voir* **contenir**

continu, -e [kɔ̃tiny] **ADJ 1** *(ininterrompu → effort, douleur, bruit)* continuous, unremitting, relentless; *(→ soins, attention)* constant; *(→ ligne, trait)* continuous, unbroken; *(→ sommeil)* unbroken

2 *Élec (courant)* direct

3 *Math* continuous

4 *Tex (métier)* throstle (frame)

NM *Math & Phil* continuum

▫ **continue NF** *Ling* continuant

▫ **en continu ADV 1** *(sans interruption)* continuously, uninterruptedly; **la nouvelle chaîne diffuse des informations en c.** the new channel gives non-stop *or* round-the-clock news coverage

2 *Typ* continuously

3 *Ordinat* **papier en c.** continuous paper

continuateur, -trice [kɔ̃tinɥatœr, -tris] **NM,F** *(de personne)* heir; *(de tradition)* continuator

continuation [kɔ̃tinɥasjɔ̃] **NF 1** *(suite)* continuation, extension; **notre politique doit être la c. de la vôtre** our policy must be a continuation of yours **2** *(fait de durer)* continuing, *Sout* continuance **3** *Fam (locution)* **bonne c.!** all the best!

continuatrice [kɔ̃tinɥatris] *voir* **continuateur**

continuel, -elle [kɔ̃tinɥɛl] **ADJ 1** *(ininterrompu)* continual **2** *(qui se répète)* constant, perpetual; **des pannes continuelles** constant breakdowns

continuellement [kɔ̃tinɥɛlmɑ̃] **ADV 1** *(de façon ininterrompue)* continually **2** *(de façon répétitive)* constantly, perpetually

continuer [7] [kɔ̃tinɥe] **VT 1** *(faire durer → exposé)* to carry on; *(→ conversation)* to carry on, to maintain, to keep up; *(→ études)* to continue, to keep up, to go on with; **continuez le repas sans moi** go on with the meal without me; **je veux c. le chant** I want to keep up my singing

2 *(dans l'espace)* to continue, to extend; **continue le trait jusqu'au bout** continue the line to the end; **nous voulons c. la cuisine en démolissant la resserre** we want to extend the kitchen by pulling down the pantry; **c. son chemin** *(sujet: voyageur)* to keep going; *(sujet: idée)* to keep gaining momentum

VI 1 *(dans le temps)* to go *or* to carry on; **la vente continue pendant les travaux** *(sur panneau ou vitrine)* business as usual during alterations; **son histoire a continué pendant tout le repas** his/her story went on throughout the meal; **si tu continues, ça va mal aller!** if you keep this up, you'll be sorry!; **"tu vois", continua-t-elle** "you see," she went on; **une telle situation ne peut c.** this situation cannot be allowed to continue; **c. à** *ou* **de faire qch** to continue to do *or* to keep on doing sth; **il continue de** *ou* **à pleuvoir** it keeps on raining; **malgré cela, il continue à fumer** in spite of this, he continues to smoke *or* carries on smoking; **je continue à me demander si…** I keep wondering if…; **ma plante continue de grandir** my plant keeps getting bigger

2 *(dans l'espace)* to continue, to carry on, to go on; **la route continue jusqu'au village** the road runs straight on to the village; **arrête-toi ici, moi je continue** you can stop right here, I'm going on; **continue!** *(à avancer)* keep going!; **continue tout droit jusqu'au carrefour** keep straight on to the crossroads

3 *Ordinat (dans boîte de dialogue)* to proceed

►**se continuer VPR 1** *(dans le temps)* to carry on, to be carried on; **la fête se continua tard dans la nuit** the party went on late into the night

2 *(dans l'espace)* to extend

continuité [kɔ̃tinɥite] **NF 1** *(d'un effort, d'une tradition)* continuity; *(d'une douleur)* persistence; **assurer la c. d'une tradition** to carry on *or* to perpetuate a tradition; **la c. dans l'action** continuity of action **2** *Math* continuity **3** *Fin* **c. d'exploitation** going-concern status

continûment [kɔ̃tinymɑ̃] **ADV** *Littéraire* continually

continuo [kɔ̃tinɥo] **NM** *Mus* continuo

continuum [kɔ̃tinɥɔm] **NM** continuum; **c. espace-temps** space-time continuum

contondant, -e [kɔ̃tɔ̃dɑ̃, -ɑ̃t] **ADJ** blunt

contorsion [kɔ̃tɔrsjɔ̃] **NF** *(d'acrobate)* contortion, acrobatic feat *(involving twisting the body)*; **il a fait toutes sortes de contorsions pour atteindre la boîte** he had to twist right round to reach the box

contorsionner [3] [kɔ̃tɔrsjɔne] **se contorsionner VPR** to twist one's body, to contort oneself; **se c. comme un ver** to squirm *or* to wriggle about like a worm

contorsionniste [kɔ̃tɔrsjɔnist] **NMF** contortionist

contour [kɔ̃tur] **NM 1** *(d'un objet, d'une silhouette)* contour, outline, shape; **la nuit estompait les contours du vieux moulin** darkness blurred the outlines of the old mill; *Ordinat* **c. d'un caractère** character outline **2** *(arrondi → d'un visage)* curve; *(→ d'une rivière, d'un chemin)* winding part *or* section; **contours** *(méandres)* twists and turns **3** *Suisse (virage)* bend

contourné, -e [kɔ̃turne] **ADJ 1** *(avec des courbes)* **la balustrade contournée d'un balcon** the curved railing of a balcony **2** *(peu naturel)* overelaborate; **style c.** convoluted style **3** *Hér* **animal c.** animal regardant

contournement [kɔ̃turnəmɑ̃] **NM 1** *(d'un obstacle → à pied)* bypassing, walking round *or* around; *(→ en voiture)* driving round *or* around **2** *(d'une difficulté)* bypassing, circumventing; *(d'une loi)* circumventing

contourner [3] [kɔ̃turne] **VT 1** *(faire le tour de → souche, flaque)* to walk around; *(→ ville)* to bypass, to skirt; *Mil (→ position)* to skirt; **ayant contourné la forêt** *(à pied)* having walked round the forest; *(en voiture)* having driven round the forest **2** *(éluder → loi, difficulté)* to circumvent, to get round **3** *Littéraire (modeler → vase, piédestal)* to fashion *or* to shape (into complex curves)

contra [kɔ̃tra] **NM** *(au Nicaragua)* Contra

contraceptif, -ive [kɔ̃trasɛptif, -iv] **ADJ** contraceptive

NM contraceptive, method of contraception; **c. local/oral** barrier/oral contraceptive

contraception [kɔ̃trasɛpsjɔ̃] **NF** contraception; **moyen de c.** method of contraception; **c. d'urgence** emergency contraception

contraceptive [kɔ̃trasɛptiv] *voir* **contraceptif**

contractant, -e [kɔ̃traktɑ̃, -ɑ̃t] *Jur* **ADJ** contracting

NM,F les contractants the contracting parties

contracte [kɔ̃trakt] **ADJ** *Gram* contracted

contracté, -e [kɔ̃trakte] **ADJ 1** *Anat (muscle, voix)* taut, tense; **il avait les mâchoires contractées** his jaw was stiff **2** *(nerveux → personne)* tense; **avant la représentation, elle est toujours très contractée** before the performance, she's always very tense **3** *Ling* contracted

contracter [3] [kɔ̃trakte] **VT 1** *(se charger de → dette)* to incur, to run up; *(→ assurance)* to take

out; (→ *obligation, engagement*) to take on; **c. un emprunt** to take out a loan; *Fig* **c. une dette de reconnaissance** to be beholden to sb; **c. une alliance** to enter into an alliance; **c. mariage avec qn** to contract a marriage with sb

2 (*acquérir* → *manie, habitude*) to develop, to acquire; (→ *maladie*) to catch, *Sout* to contract **3** (*réduire* → *liquide, corps*) to contract **4** (*raidir* → *muscle*) to contract, to tighten (up), to tauten; (→ *visage, traits*) to tense (up), to tighten (up); **le visage contracté par la peur** his/her face taut with fear

5 (*rendre anxieux*) to make tense

6 *Ling* to contract

▸**se contracter** VPR **1** (*être réduit* → *liquide, corps*) to contract, to reduce; (→ *fibre*) to shrink **2** (*se raidir* → *visage, traits*) to tense (up), to become taut; (→ *muscle*) to contract, to tighten up; (→ *cœur*) to contract; **ne vous contractez pas** don't tense up

3 *Ling* (*mot*) to contract, to be contracted

contractile [kɔ̃traktil] ADJ contractile

contractilité [kɔ̃traktilite] NF contractility

contraction [kɔ̃traksjɔ̃] NF **1** (*raidissement* → *d'un muscle*) contracting, tensing; (→ *du visage, des traits, de l'estomac*) tensing, tightening (up); (→ *des mâchoires*) clamping; (*raideur* → *d'un muscle*) tenseness, tautness; (→ *de l'estomac*) tightness; (→ *des mâchoires*) stiffness

2 *Méd* **c. (utérine)** contraction; **c. antipéristaltique** antiperistalsis

3 *Ling* contraction

4 *Scol* **c. de texte** summary; **faire une c. de texte** to summarize a text

5 *Phys* contraction; **c. des longueurs** *ou* **de Lorentz** Lorentz *or* Lorentz-Fitzgerald contraction

6 *Écon* (*de l'activité, du crédit*) reduction (**de** in); **la c. de la demande** the fall in demand

contractualisation [kɔ̃traktɥalizasjɔ̃] NF **1** (*d'un problème*) contract-based solution **2** (*d'un agent*) appointment as a public servant

contractualiser [3] [kɔ̃traktɥalize] VT **1** (*problème*) to solve by a contract **2** (*employé*) to hire as a public servant

contractuel, -elle [kɔ̃traktɥɛl] ADJ (*gén*) contractual, contract (*avant n*); (*employé*) contract (*avant n*); (*droits*) granted by contract

NM *Admin* contract public servant; (*agent de police*) *Br* (male) traffic warden, *Am* traffic policeman

❑ **contractuelle** NF *Admin* contract public servant; (*agent de police*) *Br* (female) traffic warden, *Am* traffic policewoman

contractuellement [kɔ̃traktɥɛlmɑ̃] ADV contractually

contracture [kɔ̃traktyr] NF **1** *Méd* contraction, cramp **2** *Archit* contracture

contracturer [3] [kɔ̃traktyre] VT to contract

contradicteur [kɔ̃tradiktœr] NM contradictor; **il y avait de bruyants contradicteurs dans l'auditoire** there were some noisy hecklers in the audience

contradiction [kɔ̃tradiksjɔ̃] NF **1** (*contestation*) contradiction; **elle ne supporte pas la c.** she can't stand contradiction *or* being contradicted; **porter la c. dans une discussion** to be a dissenter in a discussion; **désolé de devoir porter la c. mais...** I'm sorry to have to differ but...

2 (*inconséquence*) contradiction, inconsistency; **il y a trop de contradictions dans son témoignage** there are too many contradictions *or* inconsistencies in his/her testimony; **il est plein de contradictions** he's full of contradictions; **"soleil" et "noir", il y a une c. entre ces deux mots** "soleil noir" is a contradiction in terms

3 *Ling* contradiction

4 *Jur* allegation

❑ **en contradiction avec** PRÉP in contradiction with; **c'est en c. avec sa façon de vivre** it goes against his lifestyle; **être en c. avec soi-même** to be inconsistent

contradictoire [kɔ̃tradiktwar] ADJ **1** (*opposé* → *théories, idées*) contradictory, clashing; (→ *témoignages*) conflicting; **débat/réunion c.** open debate/meeting; **c. à** in contradiction to, at variance with; **c'est c. à** *ou* **avec ce que tu viens**

de dire this contradicts what you've just said

2 *Ling* contradictory

3 *Jur* **jugement c.** = judgment rendered in the presence of the parties involved

contradictoirement [kɔ̃tradiktwarmɑ̃] ADV **1** (*de façon opposée*) contradictorily **2** *Jur* = in the presence of the parties involved

contragestif, -ive [kɔ̃traʒɛstif, -iv] ADJ anti-pregnancy, abortifacient; **la pilule contragestive** the morning-after pill

NM anti-pregnancy drug, abortifacient

contraignable [kɔ̃trɛɲabl] ADJ that can be constrained

contraignait *etc voir* **contraindre**

contraignant, -e [kɔ̃trɛɲɑ̃, -ɑ̃t] ADJ (*occupation*) restricting; (*contrat*) restrictive; (*horaire*) restricting, limiting

contraindre [80] [kɔ̃trɛ̃dr] VT **1** (*obliger*) **la situation nous contraint à la prudence** the situation forces us to be careful; **les grèves nous ont contraints à annuler notre voyage** the strikes forced us to cancel our trip; **être contraint de** to be obliged to; **je suis contraint de rester à Paris** I'm obliged *or* forced to stay in Paris

2 *Littéraire* (*réprimer* → *désir, passion*) to constrain, to restrain, to keep a check on

3 *Littéraire* (*réprimer*) **c. une personne dans ses choix** to restrict sb's choice

4 *Jur* to constrain

▸**se contraindre** VPR **1** (*s'obliger*) **se c. à faire qch** to force oneself to do sth

2 *Littéraire* (*se retenir*) to restrain oneself

contraint, -e [kɔ̃trɛ̃, -ɛ̃t] ADJ **1** (*emprunté* → *sourire*) constrained, forced, unnatural; (→ *politesse*) unnatural

2 (*obligé*) **c. et forcé** under duress; **elle est venue contrainte et forcée** she came under duress *or* because she had no choice

❑ **contrainte** NF **1** (*obligation*) constraint, imposition; **les contraintes sociales** social constraints

2 (*force*) constraint; **obtenir qch par la contrainte** to get sth by force; **faire qch par contrainte** to be forced to do sth; **céder sous la contrainte** to give in under pressure

3 (*gêne*) constraint, embarrassment; **parler sans contrainte** to speak uninhibitedly

4 *Jur* **contrainte par corps** imprisonment for non-payment of debts

5 *Phys* stress; **contrainte de cisaillement** shearing stress; **contrainte en compression** compressive stress; **contrainte en flambage** bending stress; **contrainte de torsion** torsional stress; **contrainte de traction** tensile stress

contraire [kɔ̃trɛr] ADJ **1** (*point de vue, attitude*) opposite; **ils ont des avis contraires** they hold opposite opinions; **face à cela, on peut avoir deux attitudes contraires** in the face of this, two radically opposed attitudes are possible; **sauf avis c.** unless otherwise informed

2 (*inverse* → *direction, sens*) **fais le tour dans le sens c.** go the opposite way round; **dans le sens c. des aiguilles d'une montre** *Br* anti-clockwise, *Am* counterclockwise

3 (*défavorable, nuisible*) unfavourable, *Sout* contrary

4 *Ling* contrary

5 *Mus* contrary

NM **1** (*inverse*) le c. the opposite; **j'avais raison, ne me dis pas le c.** I was right, don't deny it; **le c. de** the opposite of; **elle timide? c'est tout le c.!** her, shy? quite the opposite *or* contrary!; **il est le c. de son père** he's the opposite of his father; **elle dit toujours le c. de ce que disent les autres** she always says the opposite of what everyone else says; **on peut comprendre par là une chose et son c.** you can interpret this statement either one way or the other; **dire tout et son c.** to contradict oneself

2 *Ling* opposite, antonym

❑ **au contraire, bien au contraire, tout au contraire,** *Belg* **que du contraire** ADV quite the reverse *or* opposite

❑ **au contraire de** PRÉP unlike

❑ **contraire à** PRÉP **c. à la règle** *ou* **aux règlements** against the rules, contrary to the rules; **c'est c. à mes principes** it's against my principles; **des pratiques contraires à l'hygiène** unhygienic practices; *Littéraire* **le sort était c. à leur amour** fate stood in the way of their love

contrairement [kɔ̃trɛrmɑ̃] ❑ **contrairement à** PRÉP **c. à ce qu'il m'a dit/aux prévisions** contrary to what he told me/to all expectations; **c. à son frère** unlike his/her brother

contralto [kɔ̃tralto] NM contralto

contrapointiste [kɔ̃trapwɛ̃tist], **contrapontiste** [kɔ̃trapɔ̃tist] NMF *Mus* contrapuntist

contrapuntique [kɔ̃trapɔ̃tik] ADJ *Mus* contrapuntal

contrapuntiste [kɔ̃trapɔ̃tist] = **contrapointiste**

contrariant, -e [kɔ̃trarjɑ̃, -ɑ̃t] ADJ (*personne*) contrary; (*nouvelle*) annoying; **il n'est pas c.** he's really easy-going

contrarié, -e [kɔ̃trarje] ADJ (*amour*) frustrated, thwarted; (*projet*) disrupted; **tu as l'air c.** you look annoyed; **un gaucher c.** = a left-handed person forced to write with his/her right hand

contrarier [10] [kɔ̃trarje] VT **1** (*ennuyer* → *personne*) to annoy; **je ne voulais pas te c.** I didn't mean to annoy you; **ça la contrarie de devoir arrêter de travailler** she's annoyed at having to stop work; **ça me contrarie qu'elle ne veuille pas rester** I'm annoyed *or* rather put-out that she doesn't want to stay; **si cela ne te contrarie pas** if you don't mind

2 (*contrecarrer* → *ambitions, amour*) to thwart; (→ *projets*) to disrupt; (→ *mouvement, action*) to impede, to bar; **c. un gaucher** = to force a left-handed person to use his/her right hand

3 (*contraster*) **c. des couleurs** to use contrasting shades

▸**se contrarier** VPR **1** (*aller à l'encontre de* → *forces*) to oppose one another

2 (*être en conflit* → *personnes*) to clash

3 (*s'opposer* → *formes, couleurs*) to contrast

contrariété [kɔ̃trarjete] NF **1** (*mécontentement*) annoyance, vexation; **éprouver une c.** to be annoyed *or* upset; **elle doit avoir une grosse c.** something must have upset her a lot; **elle a dû avoir une petite c.** she must have had some minor setback **2** (*opposition*) clash; **c. d'humeur** clash of personalities **3** *Jur* **c. de décisions** conflicting decisions; **c. de jugements** conflicting judgments

contrarotatif, -ive [kɔ̃trarɔtatif, -iv] ADJ *Tech* contrarotating; **hélice contrarotative** contra-rotating propeller

contrastant, -e [kɔ̃trastɑ̃, -ɑ̃t] ADJ contrasting

contraste [kɔ̃trast] NM contrast; **faire c. avec qch** to contrast with sth; **deux couleurs qui font c.** two contrasting shades; *TV* **réglage du c.** contrast control *or* adjustment; *Opt* **c. simultané** simultaneous contrast

❑ **de contraste** ADJ (*substance*) contrast (*avant n*); (*effet*) contrasting

❑ **en contraste** ADV **mettre deux choses en c.** to contrast two things

❑ **en contraste avec** PRÉP **1** (*par opposition à*) by contrast to *or* with, in contrast to *or* with **2** **mettre qch en c. avec** to contrast sth with

❑ **par contraste** ADV in contrast

❑ **par contraste avec** PRÉP by contrast to *or* with, in contrast to *or* with

contrasté, -e [kɔ̃traste] ADJ **1** (*couleurs, situations*) contrasting **2** (*photo, image*) with strong contrast, *Spéc* contrasty **3** *Ordinat* highlighted **4** (*nuancé* → *bilan, résultats*) uneven, mixed

contraster [3] [kɔ̃traste] VT (*caractères, situations, couleurs*) to contrast; (*photo*) to give contrast to

VI to contrast; **des couleurs qui contrastent** contrasting colours; **c. avec qch** to contrast with sth

contrat [kɔ̃tra] NM **1** (*acte, convention*) contract; **passer un c. avec qn** to enter into a contract with sb; **un c. de deux ans** a two-year contract; **un c. de plusieurs milliards de dollars** a contract worth several billion dollars; **remplir son c.** *Jur* to fulfil the terms of one's contract; *Fig* (*s'exécuter*) to keep one's promise; **c. d'adhésion** membership agreement; **c. administratif** public service contract; **c. d'agence** agency contract; **c. aléatoire** aleatory contract; **c. d'apprentissage** training contract; **c. d'assurance** insurance policy; **c. d'avenir** = short-term contract subsidized by the government to help people on benefits get back into part-time work; **c. de bail** lease contract; **c. bilatéral** bilateral contract; **c. collectif** group contract; **c. commutatif** commutative contract; **c. de**

concession licence agreement; **c. consensuel** consensual contract; **c. à durée déterminée/indéterminée** fixed-term/permanent contract; **c. d'embauche** *Br* employment contract, contract of employment, *Am* labor contract; **c. emploi-solidarité** = short-term contract subsidized by the government; **c. d'entreprise** service contract; **c. exclusif** sole contract; **c. innomé** innominate contract; **c. intuitu pecuniae** contract signed in consideration of the money; **c. intuitu personae** contract signed in consideration of the person; **contrat jeune en entreprise** = contract to help young unemployed people (aged 16–24) with few qualifications into the job market, under which employers must pay at least the minimum wage but receive government aid with employer contributions; **c. judiciaire** settlement; **c. de licence** licensing agreement; **c. local de sécurité** = list of measures to increase public safety within a town, involving all the official bodies who work together with the residents; **c. de location-vente** hire purchase agreement; **c. de louage** rental contract; **c. de mariage** marriage contract; **il n'y a pas eu de c. de mariage** there was no marriage contract drawn up; **c. de mission d'intérim** temporary contract; **c. nommé** nominate contract; **c. notarié** notarized contract; **contrat nouvelles embauches** = open-ended employment contract for companies of up to 20 employees, under which employment can be terminated without justification within the first two years; **c. pignoratif** pignorative contract; **c. première embauche** = employment contract for people under 26 which could be terminated without justification in the first two years, proposed by the French government but abandoned under public pressure; **c. de prestation de service** service contract; **c. de prêt** loan agreement; **c. de promotion immobilière** property development contract; **c. de qualification** training contract; **c. réel** real contract; **c. de représentation exclusive** sole agency contract; **c. de service** service contract; **c. solennel** formal contract; **c. de sponsoring** sponsorship deal; **c. synallagmatique** bilateral contract, synallagmatic contract; **c. temporaire** temporary contract; **c. à temps partiel** part-time contract; **c. à temps plein** full-time contract; *Bourse* **c. à terme** forward contract, futures contract; **c. à terme d'instruments financiers** financial futures contract; **c. à terme sous option** underlying futures contract; **c. à titre onéreux** contract for valuable consideration; **c. de transport** contract of carriage; **c. de travail** *Br* employment contract, contract of employment, *Am* labor contract; **c. unilatéral** unilateral contract; **c. de vente** bill of sale, sales contract; **c. verbal** verbal contract *or* undertaking

2 *(entente)* agreement, deal; **un c. tacite** an unspoken agreement

3 *Phil* **c. social** social contract

4 *Fam Arg crime (de tueur)* contract■

5 *Cartes* contract; **réaliser son c.** to make one's contract

---

'Du Contrat social' *Rousseau* 'The Social Contract'

---

contrat-type [kɔ̃tratip] (*pl* **contrats-types**) **NM** skeleton contract

contravention [kɔ̃travɑ̃sjɔ̃] **NF 1** *(amende)* (parking) fine; *(avis)* (parking) ticket; **donner une c. à qn** to book sb, to give sb a (parking) ticket **2** *(infraction)* contravention, infringement; **être en c., se mettre en état de c.** to be in breach of the law; **c. au stationnement** parking offence

contravis [kɔ̃travi] **NM** *(opinion contraire)* counter-advice, contrary opinion; *(contrordre)* notification to the contrary, countermand; **sauf c.** unless I hear to the contrary

CONTRE [kɔ̃tr]

> **PREP** against **1–3, 5, 6** ■ on **1** ■ for **4**
> **ADV** against **2**

PRÉP 1 *(indiquant la proximité)* against, on; **s'appuyer c. un arbre/une palissade** to lean against a tree/a fence; **l'échelle était dressée c. le mur** the ladder was against the wall; **se frotter c. qch** to rub (oneself) against *or* on sth; **se blottir c. qn** to cuddle up to sb; **serrer qn c. son cœur** to hug sb, to clasp sb to one's breast; **elle s'est endormie c. moi** she fell asleep on me *or* against me; **joue c. joue** cheek to cheek; **pare-chocs c. pare-chocs** bumper to bumper; **tenir qn tout c. soi** to hold sb close; **allongé tout c. elle** lying right next to *or* beside her; **sa maison est tout c. la mienne** his house is right next to mine *or* adjoins mine; **un coup c. la vitre** a knock on *or* at the window; **je me suis cogné la tête c. le radiateur** I hit my head on the radiator; **les vagues se brisaient c. la jetée** the waves were breaking against *or* on the jetty; **lancer une balle c. le mur** to throw a ball against *or* at the wall; **jeter des cailloux c. un carreau** to throw pebbles at a window; **gare ta voiture c. la mienne** park your car next to mine; **mettez-vous c. le mur** stand (right) by the wall

2 *(indiquant l'opposition)* against; **nager c. le courant** to swim upstream *or* against the current; **notre équipe aura le vent c. elle** our team will play into the wind; **une attaque c. qn** an attack against *or* on sb; **agir c. qn** to act against sb; **être en colère c. qn** to be angry at *or* with sb; **nous avons des preuves c. lui** we have (some) evidence against him; **je suis c. l'intervention** I'm opposed to *or* against (the idea of) intervention; **trop de gens sont c. cette réforme** there are too many people against this reform; **qui se présente c. le candidat sortant?** who's running against the outgoing candidate?; **voter c. qn/qch** to vote against sb/sth; *Jur* **Durier c. Chardin** Durier versus Chardin; **le match c. le Brésil** the Brazil match, the match against *or* with Brazil; **l'Angleterre c. l'Irlande** England against *or* versus Ireland; **jouer c. qn** to play against sb; **c'est c. mes principes** that goes *or* it's against my principles; **c'est c. ma religion** it's against my religion; **avoir quelque chose c. qn** to have something against sb; **je n'ai rien c. toi personnellement** it's nothing personal, I've nothing personal against you; **tout le monde est c. moi** everyone is against me; **je l'ai fait c. ma volonté** I did it against my will; **agir c. les ordres/son devoir** to act against orders/counter to one's duty; **pour une fois, j'irai c. mon habitude** for once, I'll break my habit; **ce serait aller c. sa nature** it would go *or* be against his/her nature; **vous allez c. l'usage/le règlement** you're going against accepted custom/the regulations

3 *(pour protéger de)* against; **pastilles c. la toux** cough lozenges; **bombe c. les acariens** spray against acarids; **la loi c. l'avortement** the anti-abortion law; **lutter c. l'alcoolisme** to fight (against) alcoholism; **que faire c. l'inflation?** what can be done about *or* against *or* to combat inflation?; **c'est le seul recours c. cette décision** it's the only appeal against this decision; **s'assurer c. le vol** to take out insurance against theft

4 *(en échange de)* for, in exchange *or* return for; **j'ai échangé mon livre c. le sien** I swapped my book for his/hers; **elle est revenue sur sa décision c. une promesse d'augmentation** she reconsidered her decision after being promised a rise; **il leur demande de l'argent c. son silence** he's asking them for money in return *or* exchange for his silence; **livraison c. remboursement** cash on delivery

5 *(indiquant une proportion, un rapport)* against, to; **parier à 10 c. 1** to bet at 10 to 1; **10 c. 1 qu'ils vont gagner!** 10 to 1 they'll win!; **156 voix c. 34** 156 votes to 34; **ils nous sont tombés dessus à trois c. un** there were three of them for every one of us, they were three to one against us; **la livre s'échange à 1,46 euros c. 1,62 hier** the pound is trading at 1.46 euros compared to *or* (as) against 1.62 yesterday

6 *(contrairement à)* **c. toute apparence** contrary to *or* despite all appearances; **c. toute attente** contrary to *or* against all expectations; **c. toute logique** against all logic; **c. toute prévision** against all the odds

ADV 1 *(indiquant la proximité)* **le radiateur est allumé, mets-toi tout c.** the heater is on, stand right next to it; **approche-toi du mur, et appuie-toi c.** go up to the wall and lean against it; **il n'a pas vu le poteau, et sa tête a heurté c.** he didn't see the post, and he banged his head against *or* on it

2 *(indiquant l'opposition)* against; **cette réforme ne passera pas, trop de gens sont c.** this reform won't get through, too many people are against it; **ah non, moi je suis c.!** I'm against it!; **on partage? – je n'ai rien c., je ne suis pas c.** shall we share? – I've nothing against it *or* it's OK by me; **c'est l'instinct, tu ne pourras pas aller c.** it's instinctive, you won't be able to fight it; **c.? levez la main** *Br* hands up those against, *Am* all against, hands up

NM 1 *(argument opposé)* **le pour et le c.** the pros and cons; **il y a toujours du pour et du c.** there are two sides to everything

2 *Sport (au volley, au basket)* block; *(en escrime)* counter; *(au billard)* kiss; *(au bridge)* double; **faire un c.** to intercept the ball; *Ftbl* **marquer sur un c.** to score on a counter-attack

❑ **par contre ADV** on the other hand; **il est très compétent, par c. il n'est pas toujours très aimable** he's very competent, but on the other hand he's not always very pleasant; **il parle espagnol, par c. son anglais laisse encore à désirer** his Spanish is good, but his English isn't all it might be *or* leaves a bit to be desired

---

contre-acculturation [kɔ̃trakyltyrasjɔ̃] (*pl* **contre-acculturations**) **NF** counteracculturation

contre-accusation [kɔ̃trakyzasjɔ̃] (*pl* **contre-accusations**) **NF** *Jur* counter-charge

contre-alizé [kɔ̃tralize] (*pl* **contre-alizés**) **NM** *Météo* anti-trade (wind)

contre-allée [kɔ̃trale] (*pl* **contre-allées**) **NF** *(d'une avenue) Br* service *or Am* frontage road; *(d'une promenade)* side track *or* path

contre-amiral [kɔ̃tramiral] (*pl* **contre-amiraux** [-o]) **NM** *Mil Br* ≃ commodore, *Am* ≃ rear-admiral (lower half); *Can (grade) Br* ≃ rear-admiral, *Am* ≃ rear-admiral (upper half)

contre-analyse [kɔ̃tranaliz] (*pl* **contre-analyses**) **NF** second analysis, reanalysis

contre-appel [kɔ̃trapɛl] (*pl* **contre-appels**) **NM** *Mil* second roll call

contre-arc [kɔ̃trark] (*pl* **inv** *ou* **contre-arcs**) **NM** *Archit* sag, sagging; **avoir du c.** to sag

contre-argument [kɔ̃trargymɑ̃] (*pl* **contre-arguments**) **NM** counterargument

contre-assurance [kɔ̃trasyrɑ̃s] (*pl* **contre-assurances**) **NF** reinsurance

contre-attaque [kɔ̃tratak] (*pl* **contre-attaques**) **NF 1** *Mil (gén)* counterattack; *(à l'explosif)* counter-blast **2** *(dans une polémique)* counter-attack, counter-blast

contre-attaquer [3] [kɔ̃tratake] **VT** to counter-attack, to strike back

contre-autopsie [kɔ̃trotɔpsi] (*pl* **contre-autopsies**) **NF** *Méd* control autopsy, second autopsy

contrebalancer [16] [kɔ̃trəbalɑ̃se] **VT 1** *(poids)* to counterbalance

2 *(compenser → inconvénients, efforts)* to offset, to make up for, to compensate; **les bénéfices ne contrebalancent plus les pertes** profits are no longer balancing losses

►**se contrebalancer VPR 1** *(raisons, hypothèses)* to counterbalance each other; *(dépenses)* to cancel each other out

2 *Fam* **se c. de qch** *(se moquer)* not to give a damn about sth; **je m'en contrebalance** I couldn't give a damn; **je me contrebalance de perdre mon boulot** I don't give a damn about losing my job

contrebande [kɔ̃trəbɑ̃d] **NF 1** *(trafic)* smuggling, contraband; **faire de la c.** to smuggle (in) goods **2** *(marchandises)* contraband, smuggled goods; *(alcool)* bootleg; **c. de guerre** wartime smuggling

❑ **de contrebande ADJ** *(marchandises)* smuggled, contraband *(avant n)*; *(alcool)* bootleg

❑ **en contrebande ADV faire entrer/sortir qch en c.** to smuggle sth in/out

contrebandier, -ère [kɔ̃trəbɑ̃dje, -ɛr] **NM,F** smuggler

contrebas [kɔ̃trəba] ❑ **en contrebas ADV** lower down, below

❑ **en contrebas de** PRÉP below; **le café est en c. de la rue** the café is below street level

contrebasse [kɔ̃trəbas] NF **1** (*instrument*) (double) bass, contrabass **2** (*musicien*) (double) bass player, double bassist

contrebassiste [kɔ̃trəbasist] NMF (double) bass player, double bassist

contrebasson [kɔ̃trəbasɔ̃] NM contrabassoon, double bassoon

contrebatterie [kɔ̃trəbatri] NF Mil counterbattery

contre-braconnage [kɔ̃trəbrakɔnaʒ] NM poaching control

contre-braquage [kɔ̃trəbrakaʒ] (*pl* **contre-braquages**) NM Aut opposite lock

contre-braquer [3] [kɔ̃trəbrake] VI Aut to drive into a skid

contrebutement [kɔ̃trəbytmɑ̃] NM Constr (*action*) buttressing, shoring-up; (*dispositif*) buttress

contrebuter [3] [kɔ̃trəbyte] VT Constr to buttress, to prop up, to shore up

contrecarrer [3] [kɔ̃trəkare] VT (*personne*) to thwart; (*projet, initiative*) to thwart, to block

contrechamp [kɔ̃trəʃɑ̃] NM Cin reverse shot

contre-chant [kɔ̃trəʃɑ̃] (*pl* **contre-chants**) NM counterpoint

contrechâssis [kɔ̃trəʃasi] NM INV double (window) frame

contre-choc [kɔ̃trəʃɔk] (*pl* **contre-chocs**) NM backlash

contrecœur¹ [kɔ̃trəkœr] NM **1** (*d'un foyer*) fireback **2** Rail guardrail, Br checkrail

contrecœur² [kɔ̃trəkœr] ❑ **à contrecœur** ADV reluctantly, unwillingly, grudgingly

contrecollé, -e [kɔ̃trəkɔle] ADJ **bois c.** thick plywood

contrecoup [kɔ̃trəku] NM **1** (*répercussion*) repercussion, aftereffect; **subir le c. de qch** to suffer the aftershock or aftereffects of sth **2** (*ricochet*) rebound

contre-courant [kɔ̃trəkurɑ̃] (*pl* **contre-courants**) NM countercurrent

❑ **à contre-courant** ADV **1** (*d'un cours d'eau*) against the current, upstream **2** (*à rebours*) **aller à c.** to go against the grain

❑ **à contre-courant de** PRÉP **aller à c. de la mode** to go against the trend; **cela va à c. de ce que je voulais faire** that is the (exact) opposite of what I wanted to do

contre-courbe [kɔ̃trəkurb] (*pl* **contre-courbes**) NF countercurve

contre-culture [kɔ̃trəkyltyr] (*pl* **contre-cultures**) NF counterculture

contredanse [kɔ̃trədɑ̃s] NF **1** (*danse*) contredanse, contradanse **2** Fam (*contravention*) ticket▪; **avoir une c.** to get a ticket, to get booked▪

contre-dénonciation [kɔ̃trədenɔ̃sjasjɔ̃] (*pl* **contre-dénonciations**) NF Jur writ of garnishment

contre-digue [kɔ̃trədig] (*pl* **contre-digues**) NF Constr strengthening dike

contredire [103] [kɔ̃trədir] VT (*personne, propos*) to contradict; **sa version contredit la tienne** his/her version is at variance with or contradicts yours; **les faits contredisent cette hypothèse** the facts contradict or go against this assumption

▸ **se contredire** VPR **1** (*personnes*) **ils se contredisent (l'un l'autre)** they contradict each other **2** (*témoignages, faits*) to be in contradiction (with each other), to contradict each other **3** (*emploi réfléchi*) **il se contredit** he contradicts himself

contredit [kɔ̃trədi] **sans contredit** ADV unquestionably, undoubtedly

contrée [kɔ̃tre] NF Littéraire (*pays*) country, land; (*région*) region, area; **dans une c. lointaine** in a faraway land

contre-écriture [kɔ̃trekrityr] (*pl* **contre-écritures**) NF Compta contra-entry

contre-écrou [kɔ̃trekru] (*pl* **contre-écrous**) NM locknut

contre-électromoteur, -trice [kɔ̃trelɛktrəmɔtœr, -tris] (*mpl* **contre-électromoteurs**, *fpl* **contre-électromotrices**) ADJ Élec **force contre-électromotrice** back or counter electromotive force

contre-emploi [kɔ̃trɑ̃plwa] (*pl* **contre-emplois**) NM miscasting; **utiliser qn à c.** to miscast sb

contre-empreinte [kɔ̃trɑ̃prɛ̃t] (*pl* **contre-empreintes**) NF fossil imprint

contre-enquête [kɔ̃trɑ̃kɛt] (*pl* **contre-enquêtes**) NF counterinquiry

contre-épreuve [kɔ̃treprœv] (*pl* **contre-épreuves**) NF **1** Typ counterproof **2** (*contre-essai*) repetition or second test, countercheck

contre-espalier [kɔ̃trespalje] (*pl* **contre-espaliers**) NM counter-espalier

contre-espionnage [kɔ̃trespjɔnaʒ] (*pl* **contre-espionnages**) NM counterespionage

contre-essai [kɔ̃trese] (*pl* **contre-essais**) NM repetition or second test, countercheck

contre-exemple [kɔ̃trɛgzɑ̃pl] (*pl* **contre-exemples**) NM (*illustration*) counterexample; **choisir un c.** to choose an example that goes against the rule; **il a donné un c.** he gave evidence to the contrary

contre-expertise [kɔ̃trɛkspɛrtiz] (*pl* **contre-expertises**) NF second expert evaluation or opinion

contre-extension [kɔ̃trɛkstɑ̃sjɔ̃] (*pl* **contre-extensions**) NF Méd counterextension

contrefaçon [kɔ̃trəfasɔ̃] NF **1** (*action d'imiter* → *une signature, une écriture, une monnaie*) counterfeiting, forging; (→ *un brevet*) infringement **2** (*copie* → *d'un produit, d'un vêtement*) imitation, fake; (→ *d'une signature, d'une écriture, de monnaie*) counterfeit, forgery; **méfiez-vous des contrefaçons** beware of imitations

contrefacteur, -trice [kɔ̃trəfaktœr, -tris] NM,F (*de produits*) copier, imitator, faker; (*de billets, d'une signature, d'une marque*) counterfeiter, forger

contrefaire [109] [kɔ̃trəfɛr] VT **1** (*parodier*) to mimic, to take off **2** (*signature, écriture, argent*) to counterfeit, to forge; (*brevet*) to infringe; (*vidéo, enregistrement*) to pirate **3** (*déformer* → *visage*) to distort; (→ *voix*) to alter, to change, to distort **4** Vieilli (*feindre*) to feign

contrefait, -e [kɔ̃trəfɛ, -ɛt] ADJ **1** (*déformé*) deformed, misshapen **2** (*falsifié* → *signature, écriture, argent*) counterfeit, forged

contrefaites voir **contrefaire**

contre-fenêtre [kɔ̃trəfənɛtr] (*pl* **contre-fenêtres**) NF double window sash

contre-fer [kɔ̃trəfɛr] (*pl* **contre-fers**) NM Menuis back iron

contrefera etc voir **contrefaire**

contre-feu [kɔ̃trəfø] (*pl* **contre-feux**) NM **1** (*plaque*) fireback **2** (*incendie*) backfire

contrefiche [kɔ̃trəfiʃ] NF **1** (*étai*) oblique prop or stay **2** Archit (*jambe de force*) brace, strut

contreficher [3] [kɔ̃trəfiʃe] **se contreficher** VPR Fam **se c. de** not to care less about; **je me contrefiche de ses problèmes** I couldn't care less about his/her problems; **je m'en contrefiche** I couldn't care less

contre-fil [kɔ̃trəfil] (*pl* **contre-fils**) NM opposite direction

❑ **à contre-fil** ADV against the grain

contre-filet [kɔ̃trəfilɛ] (*pl* **contre-filets**) NM sirloin (steak)

contrefit etc voir **contrefaire**

contrefort [kɔ̃trəfɔr] NM **1** Archit buttress, abutment **2** (*d'une chaussure*) stiffener **3** Bot & Géog spur

❑ **contreforts** NMPL Géog foothills

contrefoutre [116] [kɔ̃trəfutr] **se contrefoutre** VPR très Fam **se c. de qch** not to give a damn or Br a toss about sth; **je m'en contrefous** I don't give a damn or Br a toss (about it)

contre-fracture [kɔ̃trəfraktyr] (*pl* **contre-fractures**) NF Méd counter fracture

contre-fugue [kɔ̃trəfyg] (*pl* **contre-fugues**) NF Mus counter-fugue

contre-haut [kɔ̃trəo] ❑ **en contre-haut** ADV (up) above

❑ **en contre-haut de** PRÉP (up) above

contre-hermine [kɔ̃trɛrmin] (*pl* **contre-hermines**) NF Hér counter-ermine, ermines

contre-indication [kɔ̃trɛ̃dikasjɔ̃] (*pl* **contre-indications**) NF **1** Méd contra-indication **2** (*argument*) counter-argument; **je ne vois pas de c. à ce que nous construisions sur ce terrain** I see no reason why we shouldn't build on this piece of land

contre-indiqué, -e [kɔ̃trɛ̃dike] (*mpl* **contre-indiqués**, *fpl* **contre-indiquées**) ADJ **1** Méd contra-indicated **2** (*déconseillé*) inadvisable

contre-indiquer [3] [kɔ̃trɛ̃dike] VT Méd to contra-indicate

contre-interrogatoire [kɔ̃trɛ̃terɔgatwar] (*pl* **contre-interrogatoires**) NM cross-examination

contre-jour [kɔ̃trəʒur] (*pl* **contre-jours**) NM **1** (*éclairage*) backlighting; **un effet de c.** a backlit or Spéc contre-jour effect

2 (*photo*) backlit shot, Spéc contre-jour shot

❑ **à contre-jour, en contre-jour** ADV (*être placé* → *personne*) with one's back to the light; (→ *objet*) against the light or sunlight; **prendre une photo à c.** to take a photograph against the light; **une photo prise à c.** a backlit or Spéc contre-jour shot

contre-la-montre [kɔ̃trəlamɔ̃tr] NM INV time trial

contre-lettre [kɔ̃trəlɛtr] (*pl* **contre-lettres**) NF Jur counter-letter, counter-deed

contremaître [kɔ̃trəmɛtr] NM **1** (*dans un atelier*) foreman, supervisor **2** Naut petty officer

contremaîtresse [kɔ̃trəmɛtrɛs] NF forewoman, supervisor

contre-manifestant, -e [kɔ̃trəmanifɛstɑ̃, -ɑ̃t] (*mpl* **contre-manifestants**, *fpl* **contre-manifestantes**) NM,F counterdemonstrator

contre-manifestation [kɔ̃trəmanifɛstasjɔ̃] (*pl* **contre-manifestations**) NF counterdemonstration

contre-manifester [3] [kɔ̃trəmanifɛste] VI to hold a counterdemonstration

contremarche [kɔ̃trəmarʃ] NF **1** (*d'escalier*) riser **2** Mil countermarch

contre-marché [kɔ̃trəmarʃe] (*pl* **contre-marchés**) NM countermove

contremarketing [kɔ̃trəmarketiŋ] NM countermarketing

contremarque [kɔ̃trəmark] NF **1** (*billet* → *au spectacle*) voucher (*exchanged for ticket at the entrance*); (→ *de transport*) extra portion (of ticket) **2** Équitation bishopping (*of horse's teeth*) **3** Com & Hér countermark

contremarquer [3] [kɔ̃trəmarke] VT Com & Hér to countermark

contre-mesure [kɔ̃trəməzyr] (*pl* **contre-mesures**) NF **1** (*gén*) & Mil countermeasure; **c. électronique** jamming device **2** Mus **jouer à c.** to play against the beat or out of time

contre-mine [kɔ̃trəmin] (*pl* **contre-mines**) NF Mil countermine

contre-miner [3] [kɔ̃trəmine] VT Mil to countermine

contre-nature [kɔ̃trənatyr] ADJ INV unnatural, contrary to nature

contre-offensive [kɔ̃trɔfɑ̃siv] (*pl* **contre-offensives**) NF **1** Mil counteroffensive **2** (*réplique*) counteroffensive, counterblast **3** Fin counteroffer

contre-offre [kɔ̃trɔfr] (*pl* **contre-offres**) NF counter-offer

contre-OPA [kɔ̃trɔpea] NF INV Fin counterbid

contrepartie [kɔ̃trəparti] NF **1** (*compensation*) compensation; **ce travail est pénible, mais il y a des contreparties** this job is difficult but there are compensations; **c. financière** financial compensation; **vous aurez la c. financière de la perte subie** you will be financially compensated for the loss incurred

2 Compta (*registre comptable*) duplicate register; (*entrée*) counterpart; **en c.** per contra

3 (*dans une transaction*) other party or side

4 Bourse market making, hedging; **faire (de) la c.** to operate against one's client

5 (*d'une opinion*) opposite view; (*d'un argument*) corollary, obverse, converse

❑ **en contrepartie** ADV **1** (*en compensation*) in or by way of compensation

2 (*en revanche*) on the other hand

3 (*en retour*) in return

❑ **en contrepartie de** PRÉP (as a or in compensation) for; **service en c. duquel vous devrez payer la somme de…** for which services you will pay the sum of…

contre-passation [kɔ̃trəpasasjɔ̃] (*pl* **contre-passations**) NF **1** Compta journal entry, contra-entry; (*d'un article, d'une entrée*) reversing, transferring **2** Fin (*d'un effet*) re-endorsement

contrepassement [kɔ̃trəpasmɑ̃] NM **1** Compta journal entry, contra-entry; (*d'un article, d'une entrée*) reversing, transferring **2** Fin (*d'un effet*) re-endorsement

contre-passer [3] [kɔ̃trəpase] VT **1** Compta (*article, entrée*) to reverse, to contra, to transfer **2** Fin (*effet*) to endorse back, to re-endorse

contre-pente [kɔ̃trəpɑ̃t] (*pl* **contre-pentes**) NF reverse slope

contre-performance [kɔ̃trəpɛrfɔrmɑ̃s] (*pl* **contre-performances**) NF bad result, performance below expectation; **elle a eu** *ou* **fait une série de contre-performances** she's had a run of bad results

contre-peser [19] [kɔ̃trəpəze] VT *Vieilli & Littéraire* to counterbalance, to counterpoise

contrepet [kɔ̃trəpɛ] NM (*art d'inventer les contrepèteries*) = art of inventing spoonerisms; (*art de résoudre les contrepèteries*) = art of deciphering spoonerisms

contrepèterie [kɔ̃trəpɛtri] NF spoonerism

contre-pied [kɔ̃trəpje] (*pl* **contre-pieds**) NM 1 (*d'une opinion*) opposite (view); (*d'un argument*) converse, obverse; **prendre le c. d'une hypothèse** to oppose a hypothesis; **prenons le c. de sa position** let's take the (exact) opposite position to his/hers; **il prend toujours le c. de ce qu'on lui dit** (*en paroles*) he always says the opposite of what people say; (*en actions*) he always does the opposite of what he's told 2 *Sport* **prendre un adversaire à c.** to catch an opponent off balance, to wrong-foot an opponent 3 *Chasse* backscent; **aller à c., prendre le c.** (*chien*) to run heel, to hunt counter; *Fig* to take the opposite view

contreplacage [kɔ̃trəplakaʒ] NM 1 (*procédé*) plywood construction 2 (*feuille*) plywood panel

contreplaqué [kɔ̃trəplake] NM plywood

contreplaquer [3] [kɔ̃trəplake] VT to laminate into plywood

contre-plongée [kɔ̃trəplɔ̃ʒe] (*pl* **contre-plongées**) *Cin & Phot* NF low-angle shot ◻ **en contre-plongée** ADV from below; **prends-la en c.** get a low-angle shot of her, shoot her from below

contrepoids [kɔ̃trəpwa] NM (*gén*) counterbalance, counterweight; (*d'une horloge*) balance weight; (*d'un funambule*) balancing pole; *aussi Fig* **faire c. (à qch)** to provide a counterweight (to sth)

contre-poil [kɔ̃trəpwal] ◻ **à contre-poil** ADV the wrong way; *Fam* **prendre qn à c.** to rub sb up the wrong way

contrepoint [kɔ̃trəpwɛ̃] NM *Littérature & Mus* counterpoint ◻ **en contrepoint** ADV *Littérature & Mus* contrapuntally 2 *Littéraire* (*en même temps*) at the same time, concurrently ◻ **en contrepoint de** PRÉP 1 *Littérature & Mus* as counterpoint to 2 (*avec*) as an accompaniment to

contre-pointe [kɔ̃trəpwɛ̃t] (*pl* **contre-pointes**) NF 1 (*d'une épée*) back edge of sword 2 *Tech* tailstock

contrepointiste [kɔ̃trəpwɛ̃tist] = **contrapointiste**

contrepoison [kɔ̃trəpwazɔ̃] NM antidote

contre-porte [kɔ̃trəpɔrt] (*pl* **contre-portes**) NF (*d'isolation*) inner door; (*de protection*) screen door

contre-pouvoir [kɔ̃trəpuvwar] (*pl* **contre-pouvoirs**) NM = challenge to established authority

contre-préparation [kɔ̃trəpreparasjɔ̃] (*pl* **contre-préparations**) NF counterpreparation

contre-pression [kɔ̃trəprɛsjɔ̃] (*pl* **contre-pressions**) NF *Aut* back-pressure

contre-prestation [kɔ̃trəprɛstasjɔ̃] (*pl* **contre-prestations**) NF bartered commodity; **un système de contre-prestations** a barter system

contre-productif, -ive [kɔ̃trəprɔdyktif, -iv] (*mpl* **contre-productifs**, *fpl* **contre-productives**) ADJ counterproductive

contre-programmation [kɔ̃trəprɔgramasjɔ̃] (*pl* **contre-programmations**) NF *Cin & TV* counter-programming

contre-projet [kɔ̃trəprɔʒɛ] (*pl* **contre-projets**) NM counterplan, counterproject; **y a-t-il des contre-projets?** are there any (other) projects to rival this one?

contre-propagande [kɔ̃trəprɔpagɑ̃d] (*pl* **contre-propagandes**) NF counterpropaganda

contre-proposition [kɔ̃trəprɔpozisjɔ̃] (*pl* **contre-propositions**) NF counterproposal

contre-publicité [kɔ̃trəpyblisite] (*pl* **contre-publicités**) NF (*qui concurrence*) knocking copy;

(*qui manque son objectif*) adverse publicity; **cet article fait de la c. à son auteur** this article is a poor advertisement for its author

contrer [3] [kɔ̃tre] VT 1 (*s'opposer à →personne*) to block, to counter; (*→argument*) to counter, to refute; (*→attaque, initiative, interlocuteur*) to counter; **elle me contre systématiquement** she tries to block everything I do; **des mesures drastiques s'imposent pour c. la maladie** drastic measures must be taken to combat disease; **se faire c.** to come a cropper 2 *Cartes* to double 3 *Sport* (*au volley →smash*) to block; (*au rugby →coup de pied*) to block; (*à la boxe*) to counter

contre-rail [kɔ̃trəraj] (*pl* **contre-rails**) NM check-rail, *Br* guardrail

Contre-Réforme [kɔ̃trəreform] NF *Hist* Counter-Reformation

contre-rejet [kɔ̃trərəʒɛ] (*pl* **contre-rejets**) NM *Littérature* contre-rejet (*word or phrase that begins towards the end of a line and runs onto the next line*)

contre-révolution [kɔ̃trərevɔlysjɔ̃] (*pl* **contre-révolutions**) NF counter-revolution

contre-révolutionnaire [kɔ̃trərevɔlysjɔnɛr] (*pl* **contre-révolutionnaires**) ADJ counter-revolutionary NMF counter-revolutionary

contrescarpe [kɔ̃trɛskarp] NF counterscarp

contreseing [kɔ̃trəsɛ̃] NM counter-signature; **c. ministériel** = ministerial counter-signature to a presidential decree

contresens [kɔ̃trəsɑ̃s] NM 1 (*mauvaise interprétation*) misinterpretation; (*mauvaise traduction*) mistranslation; **faire un c.** = to mistranslate a word or a phrase etc 2 (*aberration*) utter nonsense; **la politique pétrolière de ce pays est un c.** this country's oil policy is an absurdity 3 *Tex* wrong way (*of fabric*) ◻ **à contresens** ADV 1 (*traduire, comprendre, marcher*) the wrong way; **prendre une rue à c.** to go the wrong way down a street 2 *Tex* against the grain

contresignataire [kɔ̃trəsiɲatɛr] NMF counter-signer

contresigner [3] [kɔ̃trəsiɲe] VT to countersign

contre-société [kɔ̃trəsɔsjete] (*pl* **contre-sociétés**) NF alternative society

contre-sujet [kɔ̃trəsyʒɛ] (*pl* **contre-sujets**) NM *Mus* countersubject

contre-taille [kɔ̃trətaj] (*pl* **contre-tailles**) NF 1 (*gravure*) cross-hatch 2 *Com* counter-tally

contretemps [kɔ̃trətɑ̃] NM 1 (*empêchement*) hitch, mishap, setback; **à moins d'un c.** unless there's a hitch, unless something unexpected crops up; **voilà un c. bien fâcheux!** what an awful nuisance! 2 *Mus* offbeat ◻ **à contretemps** ADV 1 (*inopportunément*) at the wrong time *or* moment 2 *Mus* off the beat

contre-terrorisme [kɔ̃trətɛrɔrism] (*pl* **contre-terrorismes**) NM counterterrorism

contre-terroriste [kɔ̃trətɛrɔrist] (*pl* **contre-terroristes**) ADJ counterterrorist NMF counterterrorist

contre-timbre [kɔ̃trətɛ̃br] (*pl* **contre-timbres**) NM *Jur* counterstamp

contre-torpilleur [kɔ̃trətɔrpijœr] (*pl* **contre-torpilleurs**) NM destroyer

contre-transfert [kɔ̃trətrɑ̃sfɛr] (*pl* **contre-transferts**) NM *Psy* countertransfer, counter-transference

contretypage [kɔ̃trətipaʒ] NM *TV etc* duping

contretype [kɔ̃trətip] NM *TV etc* duplicate

contretyper [3] [kɔ̃trətipe] VT *TV etc* to duplicate

contre-ut [kɔ̃tryt] NM INV *Mus* top C, high C

contre-vair [kɔ̃trəvɛr] (*pl* **contre-vairs**) NM *Hér* counter-vair

contre-valeur [kɔ̃trəvalœr] (*pl* **contre-valeurs**) NF exchange value; **pour la c. de 20 euros** in exchange for 20 euros

contrevallation [kɔ̃trəvalasjɔ̃] NF *Mil* contravallation, countervallation

contrevenant, -e [kɔ̃trəvnɑ̃, -ɑ̃t] NM,F offender

contrevenir [40] [kɔ̃trəvnir] **contrevenir à** VT IND to contravene, to infringe

contrevent [kɔ̃trəvɑ̃] NM 1 (*volet*) shutter 2 *Métal* back-draught 3 *Constr* strut, brace

contreventement [kɔ̃trəvɑ̃tmɑ̃] NM *Constr* wind-bracing; **entretoise de c.** wind-brace

contreventer [3] [kɔ̃trəvɑ̃te] VT *Constr* to wind-brace

contrevenu, -e [kɔ̃trəvny] PP *voir* **contrevenir**

contrevérité [kɔ̃treverite] NF falsehood, untruth

contrevient *etc voir* **contrevenir**

contre-visite [kɔ̃trəvizit] (*pl* **contre-visites**) NF further consultation (*for a second medical opinion*)

contre-voie [kɔ̃trəvwa] (*pl* **contre-voies**) NF parallel track (*going in the opposite direction*) ◻ **à contre-voie** ADV monter/descendre **à c.** to get on/off on the wrong side of the train

contribuable [kɔ̃tribyabl] NMF taxpayer; **petits contribuables** basic-rate taxpayers; **gros contribuables** people in high tax brackets

contribuer [7] [kɔ̃tribɥe] VI (*financièrement*) to contribute (money), to pay a share ◻ **contribuer à** VT IND **c. à qch** to have a part in *or* to contribute to sth; **c. à l'achat d'un cadeau** to contribute to (buying) a present; **c. au succès de** to contribute to *or* to have a part in the success of; **il a beaucoup contribué à...** he has made a great contribution to..., he has played a great part in...; **elle n'a pas contribué à la discussion** she took no part in the discussion; **la forêt contribue à l'agrément de la région** the forest is one of the things that helps to make the area so pleasant; **c. à faire qch** to go towards doing sth; **cela contribue pour beaucoup à la rendre heureuse** that goes a long way towards making her happy

contributeur, -trice [kɔ̃tribytœr, -tris] NM,F contributor NM *UE* **c. net** net contributor

contributif, -ive [kɔ̃tribytif, -iv] ADJ contributory

contribution [kɔ̃tribysjɔ̃] NF 1 (*argent apporté*) contribution, sum contributed; **ma c. a été de 10 euros** I contributed 10 euros 2 (*aide*) contribution, help; **sa c. au spectacle se limite à la rédaction du programme** his/her only contribution to the show is the writing of the programme 3 (*impôt*) tax; **contributions** (*à l'État*) taxes; (*à la collectivité locale*) *Br* ≃ council tax, *Am* ≃ local taxes; **contributions directes** direct taxation; **c. foncière** land tax; **contributions indirectes** indirect taxation; **c. au remboursement de la dette sociale** = income-based tax deducted at source as a contribution to paying off the French social security budget deficit; **les contributions sociales** social security contributions; **c. sociale généralisée** = income-based tax deducted at source as a contribution to paying off the French social security budget deficit ◻ **Contributions** NFPL tax office, *Br* ≃ Inland Revenue, *Am* ≃ Internal Revenue Service ◻ **à contribution** ADV **mettre qn à c.** to get sb involved; **mets-le à c.** ask him to help

contributive [kɔ̃tribytiv] *voir* **contributif**

contributrice [kɔ̃tribytris] *voir* **contributeur**

contrister [3] [kɔ̃triste] VT *Littéraire* to grieve, to sadden

contrit, -e [kɔ̃tri, -it] ADJ contrite, chastened

contrition [kɔ̃trisjɔ̃] NF 1 *Littéraire* (*repentir*) contrition, remorse 2 *Rel* **acte de c.** act of contrition; **faire** *ou* **réciter un acte de c.** to make an act of contrition

contrôlabilité [kɔ̃trolabilite] NF controllability

contrôlable [kɔ̃trolabl] ADJ 1 (*maîtrisable*) that can be controlled, controllable; **des éléments difficilement contrôlables** elements that are hard to control 2 (*vérifiable*) that can be checked *or* verified, checkable, verifiable

contrôle [kɔ̃trol] NM 1 (*maîtrise*) control; **garder/perdre le c. de sa voiture** to keep/to lose control of one's car; **avoir le c. de** (*d'un secteur, de compagnies*) to have (owning) control of; (*d'un pays, d'un territoire, d'un match*) to be in control of; **prendre le c. d'une entreprise** to take over a company; **c. des naissances** birth control; **c. de soi(-même)** self-control 2 (*surveillance →de personnes, de travail*) supervision, control; **exercer un c. sévère sur qn** to maintain strict control over sb, to keep sb under strict supervision; *Méd* **visite** *ou* **examen de c.** check-up; **c. aérien** flight control; *Sport* **c. antidopage** dope test; *Écon* **c. budgétaire** budgetary control; **c. des changes** exchange

control; *Mktg* **c. continu** monitoring; **c. économique** *ou* **des prix** price control; **c. d'efficacité marketing** marketing efficiency study; *Écon* **c. de gestion** management control; **c. monétaire** monetary control; **c. monopolistique** monopoly control; **c. de (la) qualité** quality control; **c. de la qualité totale** total quality control; **c. des stocks** *Br* stock control, *Am* inventory control; *Aut* **c. de vitesse** speed trap

3 *(inspection → d'actes, de documents)* control, check, checking; *(→ des marchandises)* inspection; *(→ d'un magasin)* audit; **c. bancaire** banking controls; *Compta* **c. du bilan** audit; **c. de la comptabilité** accounting control; **c. des comptes** *ou* **fiscal** audit; **il a un c. fiscal** ≃ the *Br* Inland Revenue *or* Am IRS is checking his returns; **c. de douane** customs control; **c. formel** = in-depth tax inspection to rectify any errors or anomalies on a tax return; **c. d'identité** *ou* **de police** identification papers control *or* check; **contrôles à l'importation** import controls; **c. sur pièces** = in-depth tax inspection to rectify any errors or anomalies on a tax return; **c. des points de vente** store audit; **c. de routine** routine check-up; **c. par sondage(s)** random check; *Aut* **c. technique** *Br* MOT (test), *Am* inspection

4 *(bureau)* check point

5 *Sport (de la balle)* control

6 *Scol* test; **avoir un c. en chimie** to have a chemistry test; **c. continu (des connaissances)** continuous assessment

7 *(poinçon)* hallmark; *(bureau)* hallmark centre

8 *Mil (liste)* list, roll; **rayer qn des contrôles de l'armée** to remove sb from the army list

9 *Ordinat* **touche c.** control key; **c. d'accès** access control; **c. croisé** cross-check; **c. de la coupure de mot** hyphenation control; **c. du curseur** cursor control; **c. de parité** odd-even check

10 *Tél* monitoring

11 *Jur* **c. de constitutionnalité** review of constitutionality; **c. judiciaire** ≃ probation; **placé sous c. judiciaire** ≃ put on probation; **c. juridictionnel** judicial review; **c. de légalité** judicial review

contrôler [3] [kɔ̃tʀole] VT **1** *(maîtriser → émotions, sentiments)* to control, to master, to curb; *(→ respiration, prix, naissances, personne)* to control; *(→ discussion, match)* to control, to master; *(→ véhicule)* to control, to be in control of; **contrôle tes nerfs!** get a grip (on yourself)!; **nous ne contrôlons plus la situation** the situation is out of our control

2 *(surveiller → personnes, travail)* to supervise; **nous sommes contrôlés toutes les semaines** a supervisor checks our work every week

3 *(vérifier → renseignement, exactitude)* to check, to verify; *(→ billet, papiers)* to check, to inspect; *(→ marchandises)* to inspect; *(→ magasin)* to audit; *(→ qualité)* to control; *(→ bon fonctionnement)* to check, to monitor; *(→ traduction)* to check; *Compta (comptes)* to check, to audit; **c. les livres** to check the books; **je vais c. ce que tu m'as dit/si tu m'as dit la vérité** I'll check what you told me/whether you told me the truth; **se faire c.** *(dans un bus, un train)* to have one's ticket checked; *(par un agent de police)* to have one's ID checked

4 *(avoir sous son autorité → affaires, secteur)* to be in control of, to control; *(→ territoire, zone)* to control, to be in command of

5 *Sport (ballon)* to have control of

6 *(argent, or)* to hallmark

7 *Tél* to monitor

8 *Fin (prix)* to control; *(dépenses, comptes)* to audit

9 *Ordinat* **contrôlé par le logiciel** software-controlled; **contrôlé par menu** menu-driven, menu-controlled; **contrôlé par ordinateur** computer-controlled

►**se contrôler** VPR to control oneself, to be in control of oneself; **il ne se contrôlait plus** he'd lost his grip on himself, he was (totally) out of control

contrôleur, -euse [kɔ̃tʀolœʀ, -øz] NM,F **1** *Rail* ticket inspector

2 *Aviat* **c. aérien** air traffic controller

3 *Admin & Fin* **c. du crédit** credit controller; **c.**

(des impôts *ou* **contributions)** (tax) inspector *or* assessor; **c. des douanes** customs inspector; **c. financier** financial controller; **c. de gestion** management controller; **c. aux liquidations** controller in bankruptcy

NM **1** *Ind* regulator

2 *(horloge)* time clock

3 *Ordinat* controller; **c. d'affichage** display *or* screen controller; **c. de bus** bus controller; **c. de disques** disk controller; **c. de transmission** transmission controller

contrordre [kɔ̃tʀɔʀdʀ] NM countermand, counter-order; **il y a c., vous ne partez plus** orders have been countermanded *or* changed, you're not leaving; **à moins d'un** *ou* **sauf c.** unless otherwise informed; **sauf c., je te retrouve à six heures à la gare** unless you hear from me, I'll meet you at six at the station

controuvé, -e [kɔ̃tʀuve] ADJ *Littéraire* false, fabricated, concocted

controversable [kɔ̃tʀɔvɛʀsabl] ADJ debatable, disputable

controverse [kɔ̃tʀɔvɛʀs] NF *(débat)* controversy; **donner lieu à c.** to be controversial

controversé, -e [kɔ̃tʀɔvɛʀse] ADJ *(décision, théorie, personne)* controversial; **une question controversée** a controversial *or* much debated question

controverser [3] [kɔ̃tʀɔvɛʀse] VT to discuss, debate

USAGE ABSOLU *(discussion)* to have or to hold; *(opinion)* to controvert

controversiste [kɔ̃tʀɔvɛʀsist] NMF *Rel* controversialist, disputant

contumace [kɔ̃tymas], **contumax** [kɔ̃tymaks] ADJ contumacious, defaulting

NF refusal to appear in court, contempt of court, *Sout* contumacy

❏ **par contumace** ADV in absentia

contus, -e [kɔ̃ty, -yz] ADJ *Méd (contusionné)* bruised; **plaie contuse** contusive injury

contusion [kɔ̃tyzjɔ̃] NF *Méd* bruise, *Spéc* contusion

contusionné, -e [kɔ̃tyzjɔne] ADJ *Méd* bruised, *Spéc* contused

contusionner [3] [kɔ̃tyzjɔne] VT *Méd* to bruise, *Spéc* to contuse

conurbation [kɔnyʀbasjɔ̃] NF conurbation

convainc *etc voir* **convaincre**

convaincant, -e [kɔ̃vɛ̃kɑ̃, -ɑ̃t] ADJ convincing, persuasive; **de façon convaincante** convincingly; **peu c.** unconvincing; **un argument peu c.** a rather thin argument; **faites-vous c.** try to be persuasive

convaincre [114] [kɔ̃vɛ̃kʀ] VT **1** *(persuader)* to convince, to persuade; **je n'ai pas su le c.** I couldn't convince him; **c. qn de faire qch** to persuade sb to do sth, to talk sb into doing sth; **essaie de la c. de venir** try to persuade her to come; **se laisser c.** to let oneself be persuaded *or* convinced *or* won over; **votre dernier argument m'a convaincu** your last argument has won me over; **j'en suis convaincu** I'm convinced of it

2 *(prouver coupable)* **c. qn de mensonge** to force sb to admit he/she lied; **c. qn de vol** to convict sb of theft, to find sb guilty of theft

►**se convaincre** VPR to realize, to accept; **il faut te c. que tout est fini** you must realize *or* understand *or* accept that it's all over; **il est difficile de s'en c.** it's difficult to accept it

convaincu, -e [kɔ̃vɛ̃ky] ADJ convinced; **être c. de qch** to be convinced of sth; **un partisan c. du socialisme** a firm believer in socialism; **un végétarien c.** a committed vegetarian; **parler d'un ton c.** to talk with conviction

NM,F firm *or* great *or* strong believer *(in an idea)*

convainquait *etc voir* **convaincre**

convalescence [kɔ̃valesɑ̃s] NF **1** *Méd* convalescence; **être en c.** to be convalescing **2** *Mil* = army convalescence leave

convalescent, -e [kɔ̃valesɑ̃, -ɑ̃t] ADJ convalescent

NM,F convalescent

convalo [kɔ̃valo] *Fam Mil* NM convalescent■

NF sick leave■

convecteur [kɔ̃vɛktœʀ] NM convector

convection [kɔ̃vɛksjɔ̃] NF convection

convenable [kɔ̃vnabl] ADJ **1** *(approprié → moment, lieu)* suitable, appropriate; **au moment c.** at the right *or* appropriate moment

2 *(décent → tenue)* decent, respectable; *(→ comportement)* seemly, correct; **peu c.** improper; **de manière peu c.** inappropriately; **mets une robe plus c.** put a more decent dress on; **une famille très c.** a very respectable *or* decent *or* upstanding family; **ce n'est pas très c. de parler fort** it's not very polite to talk loudly

3 *(acceptable → devoir)* passable, adequate; *(→ logement, rémunération)* decent, adequate

convenablement [kɔ̃vnabləmɑ̃] ADV **1** *(de façon appropriée)* suitably, appropriately

2 *(décemment)* decently, properly; **habille-toi c.** dress decently *or* respectably; **se tenir c.** to behave properly

3 *(de façon acceptable)* **gagner c. sa vie** to earn a decent wage; **il s'exprime très c. en italien** he has a fairly good knowledge of Italian; **une pièce c. éclairée** a fairly well-lit room; **il travaille c. à l'école** his schoolwork is fairly good; **on y mange c.** the food is quite adequate there

convenance [kɔ̃vnɑ̃s] NF *Littéraire (adéquation)* appropriateness, suitability; **la c. d'humeur** *ou* **de goût entre deux personnes** affinity of taste between two people; **mariage de c.** marriage of convenience

❏ **convenances** NFPL propriety, decorum, accepted (standards of) behaviour; **respecter les convenances** to respect *or* to observe the proprieties; **contraire aux convenances** unseemly, improper

❏ **à ma/sa/**etc **convenance** ADV as suits me/him/etc (best); **je choisirai une couleur à ma c.** I'll choose a shade to suit me; **il n'a pas trouvé l'hôtel à sa c.** he didn't find the hotel to his liking *or* suitable

❏ **pour convenance(s) personnelle(s)** ADV for personal reasons

convenir [40] [kɔ̃vniʀ] VT **c'est convenu ainsi** it's been agreed this way; **comme (cela a été) convenu** as agreed; **c. que** to agree *or* to accept *or* to admit that; **tu dois bien c. qu'elle a raison** you must admit she's right

USAGE ABSOLU *(être approprié)* **dire les mots qui conviennent** to say the right words; **trouver le ton qui convient** to find the right *or* suitable tone

❏ **convenir à** VT IND **1** *(être approprié à)* to suit; **une robe qui convient à la circonstance** a dress that suits the occasion, a dress suitable for *or* befitting the occasion; **cette table conviendra parfaitement à ma cuisine** this table's perfect for my kitchen

2 *(plaire à)* to suit; **lundi matin me conviendrait assez** Monday morning would suit me fine; **dix heures, cela vous convient-il?** does ten o'clock suit you?; **ce travail ne lui convient pas du tout** this job's not right for him/her at all; **une mode qui convient à toutes les femmes** a style that looks good on *or* suits all women; **la vie que je mène me convient parfaitement** the life I lead suits me perfectly; **cette chaleur ne me convient pas du tout** this heat doesn't agree with me at all

❏ **convenir de** VT IND **1** *(se mettre d'accord sur)* to agree upon; **nous avions convenu de nous retrouver à midi** we had agreed to meet at noon; **c. d'un endroit** to agree upon a place; **il est convenu avec la direction de…** it's agreed with the management to…; **somme convenue** agreed sum; **comme convenu** as agreed

2 *(reconnaître)* **c. de qch** to admit sth; **c. de ses erreurs** to admit *or* to acknowledge one's errors; **je conviens d'avoir dit cela** I admit to having said that; **j'en conviens volontiers** I don't mind admitting it

❏ **il convient de** V IMPERSONNEL **1** *(il est souhaitable de)* it is advisable *or* a good idea to; **il convient de fermer cette porte à clé** it is advisable to lock this door; **il voudrait savoir ce qu'il convient de faire** he would like to know the right thing to do

2 *(il est de bon ton de)* it is proper *or* the done thing to; **il convient d'apporter des fleurs à la maîtresse de maison** it is the done thing to bring flowers for one's hostess

❑ **il convient que** v IMPERSONNEL **il convient que vous y alliez** you should or ought to go
▶**se convenir** VPR to suit one another
convent [kɔ̃vã] NM Masonic assembly
convention [kɔ̃vãsjɔ̃] NF 1 *(norme)* convention; **les conventions orthographiques** spelling conventions; **un système de conventions** an agreed system
  2 *(règle de bienséance)* (social) convention; **respecter les conventions** to conform to accepted social behaviour or established conventions
  3 *(accord → tacite)* agreement, understanding; *(→ officiel)* agreement; *(→ diplomatique)* convention; *(clause)* article, clause; **c. écrite** written agreement; **C. européenne des droits de l'homme** European Convention on Human Rights; **C. européenne de sauvegarde des droits de l'homme et des libertés fondamentales** European Convention for the Protection of Human Rights and Fundamental Freedoms; **c. collective (du travail)** collective agreement; **c. de crédit** credit agreement; **c. internationale** international convention or treaty; **c. monétaire** monetary agreement; **c. salariale** wage agreement; **c. signée entre le patronat et les syndicats** union or union–management agreement; **c. verbale** simple contract, verbal agreement
  4 *Pol (assemblée → aux États-Unis)* convention; *(→ en France)* assembly
  5 *Hist* **la C.** the French National Convention *(1792–1795)*
  ❑ **de convention** ADJ *(gén)* conformist, conventional; *(amabilité, sourire)* superficial
  ❑ **par convention** ADV **par c., nous appellerons cet ensemble N** let us call this set N; **par c., on symbolise l'heure par un h** "hour" is usually symbolised by an "h", the generally-accepted abbreviation for "hour" is "h"
convention-cadre [kɔ̃vãsjɔ̃kadr] *(pl* **conventions-cadres)** NF framework convention; **la C. des Nations Unies sur les changements climatiques** the United Nations Framework Convention on Climate Change
conventionnalisme [kɔ̃vãsjɔnalism] NM conventionalism, conformism
conventionnalité [kɔ̃vãsjɔnalite] NF conformity to a convention
conventionné, -e [kɔ̃vãsjɔne] ADJ 1 *(médecin, clinique)* subsidized, designated by the health system, *Br* ≃ National Health; **non c.** private 2 *(honoraires, prix)* set; **prêt c.** low-interest (subsidized) loan
conventionnel, -elle [kɔ̃vãsjɔnɛl] ADJ 1 *(conformiste)* conventional, conformist; **formules conventionnelles** clichés, platitudes
  2 *(arbitraire → signe, valeur)* conventionally agreed; *(→ langage)* conventional
  3 *Pol* **accords conventionnels** agreements resulting from collective bargaining; **politique conventionnelle** policies relating to union–management agreements
  4 *Jur* contractual
  5 *(classique → armement)* conventional
  NM,F *(membre)* member *(of a convention)*
  ❑ **Conventionnel** NM *Hist* member of the French National Convention *(1792–1795)*
conventionnellement [kɔ̃vãsjɔnɛlmã] ADV 1 *(sans originalité)* conventionally, *Péj* unoriginally 2 *Jur* by agreement
conventionnement [kɔ̃vãsjɔnmã] NM *Méd* medical care, *Br* ≃ National Health Service contract; **le c. d'une clinique** a clinic's adherence to a (public) medical care system
conventionner [3] [kɔ̃vãsjɔne] VT = to register with the state health system
  ▶**se conventionner** VPR = to register as a doctor within the state health system
conventuel, -elle [kɔ̃vãtɥɛl] *Rel* ADJ *(maison)* conventual; *(vie)* monastic
  NM Friar Minor Conventual
conventum [kɔ̃vãtɔm] NM *(colloque)* colloquium 2 *Can (réunion d'anciens élèves)* school reunion
convenu, -e [kɔ̃vny] PP *voir* **convenir**
  ADJ 1 *(décidé → prix, somme)* agreed, stipulated; *(→ date, moment)* agreed, appointed 2 *(sans originalité → style)* conventional;

l'intrigue est très convenue the plot is very obvious
convergence [kɔ̃vɛrʒãs] NF 1 *(confluence → de chemins, de lignes)* convergence, confluence; **point de c.** focal point 2 *(concordance)* **la c. de nos efforts** the convergence of our efforts (on a common goal); **la c. de nos conclusions** the fact that our conclusions lead to a single result; *UE* **c. économique** economic convergence 3 *Math & Opt* convergence
convergent, -e [kɔ̃vɛrʒã, -ãt] ADJ convergent
converger [17] [kɔ̃vɛrʒe] VI 1 *(confluer)* to converge, to meet at a point; **tous les chemins convergent vers la clairière** all paths converge on the clearing; **nos efforts convergent vers le même but** all our efforts are focused on the same objective 2 *(aboutir au même point)* **nos conclusions convergent** we tend toward the same conclusions 3 *Math & Opt* to converge
convers, -e [kɔ̃vɛr, -ɛrs] ADJ 1 *Rel* lay *(avant n)* 2 *Ling* converse
conversation [kɔ̃vɛrsasjɔ̃] NF 1 *(discussion)* discussion, conversation, talk; **une c. animée** a heated discussion; **être en grande c.** to be deep in conversation; **elle est en grande c. avec son mari** she's deep in conversation with her husband; **engager la c. (avec qn)** to start up a conversation (with sb); **faire la c. (à qn)** to make conversation (with sb); **suite à ma c. téléphonique avec votre secrétaire** following my phone conversation with your secretary; **interrompre sa c.** to break off in mid-conversation; **interrompre une c.** to interrupt a conversation; **détourner la c.** to change the subject; **amener la c. sur qch** to steer the conversation towards sth, to bring sth up in the conversation; **il écrit dans le style de la c.** he writes in a conversational style, his style of writing is colloquial; **il a une c. ennuyeuse** he's boring to talk to; **avoir de la c.** to be a good conversationalist; **il n'a aucune c.** he's a poor conversationalist
  2 *Ling* **dans la c. courante** in everyday or ordinary speech
  3 *(pourparlers)* **conversations diplomatiques** diplomatic talks or negotiations; **des conversations entre les syndicats et le patronat** talks between unions and management
conversationnel, -elle [kɔ̃vɛrsasjɔnɛl] ADJ interactive; **en mode c.** in interactive or conversational mode
converser [3] [kɔ̃vɛrse] VI to converse, to talk
conversion [kɔ̃vɛrsjɔ̃] NF 1 *(de chiffres, de mesures)* conversion, converting; **c. des miles en kilomètres** converting of miles to kilometres; *Ordinat* **c. de fichier** file conversion
  2 *Rel* conversion; **à cause de sa c. au judaïsme** because of his/her conversion or because he/she converted to Judaism
  3 *(ralliement)* conversion
  4 *Fin (d'argent, de devises étrangères, de titres, d'un emprunt)* conversion
  5 *Naut* turning around
  6 *Ski* kick turn
  7 *Jur & Phys* conversion
  8 *(changement d'activité → d'un employé)* retraining; *(→ d'une entreprise)* change in the line of business
  9 *Biol & Méd* **c. génique** gene conversion
converti, -e [kɔ̃vɛrti] ADJ converted
  NM,F convert
convertibilité [kɔ̃vɛrtibilite] NF convertibility
convertible [kɔ̃vɛrtibl] ADJ 1 *(transformable)* convertible (**en** into); **avion c.** convertiplane, convertoplane; **canapé c.** sofa bed, *Br* bed-settee, *Am* convertible sofa; **fauteuil c.** convertible armchair 2 *Fin* convertible
  NM 1 *(canapé)* sofa bed, *Br* bed-settee, *Am* convertible sofa 2 *Aviat* convertiplane, convertoplane
  NF 1 *Fin* convertible bond 2 *Can Joual (voiture)* convertible
convertir [32] [kɔ̃vɛrtir] VT 1 *(convaincre)* to convert; **c. qn à** *(religion)* to convert sb to; *(opinion, mouvement)* to win sb over or to convert sb to
  2 *Fin & Math (mesure, grandeur, argent)* to convert; **c. des euros en dollars** to convert euros into dollars; **c. des rentes** to convert stock

  3 *Ordinat (données)* to convert; **c. en numérique** to digitize
  4 *(en logique)* to convert, to transpose
  5 *(transformer)* to convert (**en** into); **ils ont converti la vieille gare en musée** they converted or transformed the old railway station into a museum
  ▶**se convertir** VPR 1 *(athée)* to become a believer; *(croyant)* to change religion
  2 *(entreprise)* to change its line of business; *(employé)* to retrain
  3 **se c. à** *(religion, mouvement)* to be converted to, to convert to
convertissage [kɔ̃vɛrtisaʒ] NM *Métal* conversion
convertissement [kɔ̃vɛrtismã] NM *Fin (de valeurs en espèces)* conversion (**en** into)
convertisseur, -euse [kɔ̃vɛrtisœr, -øz] NM,F *Rel* converter
  NM 1 *Métal* converter; **c. Bessemer** Bessemer converter
  2 *Élec* converter, convertor
  3 *TV* converter; **c. d'images** image converter; **c. numérique de graphiques** graphics digitizer
  4 *Tech* **c. catalytique à oxydation** oxidization catalytic converter; **c. de couple** torque converter; **c. de couple hydraulique** hydraulic torque converter
  5 *Ordinat* **c. analogique numérique** digitizer; **c. série-parallèle** staticizer; **c. de signal** converter; **c. tournant** motor generator (set)
  6 **c. de monnaie** currency converter
convexe [kɔ̃vɛks] ADJ convex
convexion [kɔ̃vɛksjɔ̃] = **convection**
convexité [kɔ̃vɛksite] NF convexity
conviction [kɔ̃viksjɔ̃] NF *(certitude)* conviction, belief; **j'ai la c. que...** it's my belief that..., I'm convinced that...; **avec/sans c.** with/without conviction; **sans grande c.** without much conviction; **manquer de c.** to lack conviction
  ❑ **convictions** NFPL *(credo)* fundamental beliefs; **avoir des convictions politiques** to have political convictions
convient etc *voir* **convenir**
convier [9] [kɔ̃vje] VT *Littéraire* 1 *(faire venir)* to invite; **c. qn à une soirée/un repas** to invite sb to a party/a meal 2 *(inciter)* **c. qn à faire qch** to invite or to urge sb to do sth
convint etc *voir* **convenir**
convive [kɔ̃viv] NMF guest *(at a meal)*; **combien y aura-t-il de convives?** how many guests will there be?
convivial, -e, -aux, -ales [kɔ̃vivjal, -o] ADJ 1 *(ambiance, fête)* convivial 2 *Ordinat* user-friendly
convivialité [kɔ̃vivjalite] NF 1 *(d'une société)* conviviality 2 *Ordinat* user-friendliness
convocable [kɔ̃vɔkabl] ADJ summonable
convocation [kɔ̃vɔkasjɔ̃] NF 1 *(d'une assemblée, de ministres)* calling together, convening; *(de témoins, d'un employé)* summoning 2 *(avis écrit)* notification; *Jur* summons *(singulier)*; **c. à un examen** notification of an examination; **vous recevrez bientôt votre c.** you'll be notified shortly
convoi [kɔ̃vwa] NM 1 *Aut & Naut* convoy; **c. d'ambulances/de péniches** string of ambulances/of barges; **c. exceptionnel** *(sur panneau)* wide or dangerous load
  2 *Rail* train; **c. de marchandises** goods or freight train; **c. postal** *Br* postal or *Am* mail train
  3 *(cortège)* convoy; **un c. de prisonniers** a convoy of prisoners; **un c. de troupes** a convoy of troops; **c. funèbre** funeral procession
  ❑ **en convoi** ADV in convoy
convoie etc *voir* **convoyer**
convoiement [kɔ̃vwamã] NM *(gén)* escorting, convoying; *Aviat* = shuttling of new planes to operational zones
convoiter [3] [kɔ̃vwate] VT 1 *(vouloir → argent, héritage, poste)* to covet, to be after; **j'avais enfin le rôle tant convoité** at last, I had the role I had longed for 2 *Littéraire (par concupiscence)* to lust after
convoitise [kɔ̃vwatiz] NF 1 *(désir → d'un objet)* desire, covetousness; *(→ d'argent)* greed, *Sout* cupidity; **agir par c.** to act out of greed; **regarder qch avec c.** to stare at sth greedily; **exciter** ou **exaspérer les convoitises** to arouse envy or

greed **2** *Littéraire* *(concupiscence)* **c. (de la chair)** lust

convoler [3] [kɔ̃vɔle] **VI** *Arch ou Hum* **c. en secondes noces** to re-marry; **c. en justes noces** to be wed

convoluté, -e [kɔ̃vɔlyte] **ADJ** convolute *(avant n)*, coiled

convolvulacée [kɔ̃vɔlvylase] **NF** *Bot* convolvulus

convoquer [3] [kɔ̃vɔke] **VT** *(assemblée, concile)* to convene; *(ministres, membres)* to convene, to call together; *(actionnaires)* to call to a meeting; *(témoin)* to summon to a hearing; *(employé, postulant)* to call in; *(journalistes, presse)* to invite; **c. une assemblée générale** to call a general meeting; **ils m'ont convoqué pour passer un entretien** they've called or invited me for an interview; **elle est convoquée chez le proviseur** she's been summoned to the *Br* head's or *Am* principal's office; **c. qn à un examen** to notify sb of an examination; **je suis convoqué à neuf heures au centre d'examens** I have to be at the examination centre at nine o'clock

convoyage [kɔ̃vwajaʒ] = **convoiement**

convoyer [13] [kɔ̃vwaje] **VT** *(accompagner → gén)* to escort; *(→ fonds)* to transport by armed guard; *Mil* to convoy

convoyeur, -euse [kɔ̃vwajœr, -øz] **ADJ** escort *(avant n)*
   NM,F escort
   NM 1 *(transporteur)* **c. de fonds** *(entreprise)* security firm *(transporting money)*; *(homme)* security guard **2** *Naut* convoy (ship) **3** *(tapis roulant)* conveyor belt; *Agr* grain elevator

convulser [3] [kɔ̃vylse] **VT** to convulse; **la peur convulsait son visage** his/her face was convulsed or contorted or distorted with fear
   ▸**se convulser VPR** *(personne)* to be convulsed; *(visage)* to become contorted or convulsed; **il se convulsait de douleur** he was convulsed with pain

convulsif, -ive [kɔ̃vylsif, -iv] **ADJ 1** *Méd* convulsive **2** *(brusque)* **un mouvement c.** a sudden or uncontrolled movement

convulsion [kɔ̃vylsjɔ̃] **NF 1** *Méd* convulsion; **avoir des convulsions** to have convulsions; **il fut soudain pris de convulsions** he suddenly went into convulsion or convulsions; **c. tonique** tonic spasm **2** *(agitation)* convulsion, upheaval, disturbance

convulsionnaire [kɔ̃vylsjɔnɛr] **NMF** convulsionary mystic

convulsionner [3] [kɔ̃vylsjɔne] **VT** *Méd (visage)* to convulse, to distort; *(patient)* to send into convulsion or convulsions

convulsivant, -e [kɔ̃vylsivɑ̃, -ɑ̃t] *Méd* **ADJ** *(médicament)* convulsant
   NM convulsant

convulsive [kɔ̃vylsiv] *voir* **convulsif**

convulsivement [kɔ̃vylsivmɑ̃] **ADV** *Méd* convulsively

convulsiothérapie [kɔ̃vylsjɔterapi] **NF** *Psy (gén)* shock therapy; *(par électrochoc)* electroconvulsive therapy, ECT

coobligé, -e [kɔɔbliʒe] **NM,F** *Jur* joint debtor

cooccupant, -e [kɔɔkypɑ̃, -ɑ̃t] **NM,F** co-occupier

cooccurrence [kɔɔkyrɑ̃s] **NF** co-occurrence

Cook [kuk] *voir* **détroit**

cookie [kuki] **NM 1** *(gâteau) Br* biscuit, *Am* cookie **2** *Ordinat* cookie

cool [kul] *Fam* **ADJ INV 1** *(détendu)* cool, laid-back; **ils sont c., ses parents** his/her parents are cool or laid-back; **c., mon vieux!** chill (out)!, take it easy! **2** *(bien, beau)* cool; **il est c. son nouveau portable** his/her new *Br* mobile's or *Am* cell's really cool
   NM INV *Mus* cool jazz ▪

coolie [kuli] **NM** coolie

coolitude [kulityd] **NF** *Fam* coolness, hipness

coolos [kulos] **ADJ INV** *Fam* **1** *(détendu)* laid-back, cool **2** *(bien)* cool

coopé [kɔpe] **NF** *Fam (coopération → aide aux PVD)* aid to developing countries; *Ancienne-ment (→ service militaire)* = voluntary work overseas carried out as an alternative to national service

coopérant, -e [kɔɔperɑ̃, -ɑ̃t] **ADJ** cooperative
   NM,F aid worker
   NM *Anciennement (soldat)* = conscript doing

voluntary work overseas as an alternative to national service

coopérateur, -trice [kɔɔperatœr, -tris] **ADJ** cooperative
   NM,F *(collaborateur)* cooperator, collaborator; *(adhérent)* member of a cooperative

coopératif, -ive [kɔɔperatif, -iv] **ADJ** cooperative, helpful; **se montrer c.** to cooperate, to be cooperative
   ❑ **coopérative NF 1** *Écon (association)* cooperative, co-op; *(magasin)* cooperative store, co-op; **coopérative agricole** agricultural cooperative; **coopérative ouvrière** workers' cooperative; **coopérative de production** production cooperative **2** *Scol* **coopérative scolaire** fund-raising group *(of pupils under the supervision of a teacher)*

coopération [kɔɔperasjɔ̃] **NF 1** *(collaboration)* cooperation; **il nous a offert sa c.** he offered to cooperate (with us)
   2 *Écon & Pol* economic cooperation
   3 *Admin & Mil (aide aux PVD)* aid to developing countries; *Anciennement (à la place du service militaire)* = voluntary work overseas carried out as an alternative to national service; **le minis-tère de la C. et du Développement** *Br* ≃ the Overseas Development Administration; **partir en c. en Afrique** *Br* ≃ to go off to do VSO in Africa, *Am* ≃ to go to Africa with the Peace Corps
   4 *Écon* cooperation, cooperative action
   ❑ **en coopération avec PRÉP** in collaboration with

coopératisme [kɔɔperatism] **NM** = doctrine encouraging the cooperative movement

coopérative [kɔɔperativ] *voir* **coopératif**

coopératrice [kɔɔperatris] *voir* **coopérateur**

coopérer [18] [kɔɔpere] **VI** to cooperate; **il a coopéré à la création de l'association** he collaborated in setting up the organization

coopétition [kɔɔpetisjɔ̃] **NF** *Com* coopetition

cooptation [kɔɔptasjɔ̃] **NF** co-option; **élu par c.** elected by co-option

coopter [3] [kɔɔpte] **VT** to co-opt

coordinateur, -trice [kɔɔrdinatœr, -tris] **ADJ** co-ordinating
   NM,F coordinator

coordination [kɔɔrdinasjɔ̃] **NF 1** *(d'une opération)* coordination **2** *(comité)* representative committee; **c. étudiante** student committee **3** *(des mouvements)* coordination; **il n'a aucune c.** he is totally uncoordinated

coordinatrice [kɔɔrdinatris] *voir* **coordinateur**

coordinence [kɔɔrdinɑ̃s] **NF** *Chim* coordination number

coordonnant [kɔɔrdɔnɑ̃] **NM** *Gram (adverbe)* co-ordinating adverb; *(conjonction)* coordinating conjunction; *(expression)* coordinating expression

coordonnateur, -trice [kɔɔrdɔnatœr, -tris] **ADJ** coordinating
   NM,F coordinator

coordonné, -e [kɔɔrdɔne] **ADJ 1** *(harmonieux → mouvements)* coordinated
   2 *Ling* **propositions coordonnées** coordinate clauses
   3 *(assorti)* matching; **veste et jupe coordon-nées** matching or coordinating jacket and skirt
   ❑ **coordonnés NMPL** *(vêtements)* coordinates, *(matching)* separates; *(linge)* matched set
   ❑ **coordonnées NFPL 1** *Géog & Math* coordinates **2** *(adresse)* contact) details; **laissez-moi vos coordonnées** leave me your address and phone number, leave me your details; **je n'ai même pas ses coordonnées!** I don't even know where to reach him/her!

coordonner [3] [kɔɔrdɔne] **VT 1** *(organiser)* to coordinate, to integrate; **il est là pour c. les secours** his job is to act as coordinator for the emergency services **2** *(assortir)* to match (**à ou avec** with); **c. des accessoires** to match or to coordinate accessories **3** *Ling* to coordinate

Copacabana [kɔpakabana] **NM** Copacabana

copahier [kɔpaje] **NM** *Bot* copaiba, copaiba tree

copahu [kɔpay] **NM** *Bot & Pharm* copaiba; **baume de c.** copaiba balsam

copaïer [kɔpaje] = **copahier**

copain, copine [kɔpɛ̃, kɔpin] *Fam* **NM,F** *(ami)* friend ▪, *Br* pal, *Am* buddy; **Anne, c'est vraiment**

une super copine Anne's a really good friend; **un c. d'école/de bureau** a school/an office friend, a friend from school/the office; **être/rester bons copains** to be/to remain good friends; **salut les copains!** *(en arrivant)* hi guys!; *(en partant)* see you guys later!; **fais-en profiter les copains!** let everybody share it!; **il retrou-vera vite du boulot grâce aux copains** he'll soon find another job through his connections; **(petit) c.** boyfriend; **(petite) copine** girlfriend; **soirée entre copines** *(à la maison)* girls' night in; *(en ville)* girls' night out
   ADJ **être très copains** to be great friends or *Br* pals or *Am* buddies; **il est très c. avec Marc** he's a great friend of Marc's; **être très c.-copain** to be very pally; **être copains comme cochons** to be as thick as thieves

copal, -als [kɔpal] **NM** copal-resin; **c. tendre** gum-elemi

copale [kɔpal] **NF** copal-resin; **c. tendre** gum-elemi

coparent [kɔparɑ̃] **NM** coparent

coparental, -e, -aux, -ales [kɔparɑ̃tal, -o] **ADJ** coparental

coparentalité [kɔparɑ̃talite] **NF** coparenthood

copartage [kɔpartaʒ] **NM** coparcenary

copartageant, -e [kɔpartaʒɑ̃, -ɑ̃t] **NM,F** *Jur* coparcener, parcener

copartager [17] [kɔpartaʒe] **VT** *Jur* **c. qch** to be coparcener or coparceners in sth

coparticipant, -e [kɔpartisipɑ̃, -ɑ̃t] *Jur* **ADJ** in copartnership
   NM,F copartner

coparticipation [kɔpartisipasjɔ̃] **NF** copartner-ship

copaternité [kɔpatɛrnite] **NF** joint responsibility *(for invention)*

copayer [kɔpaje] = **copahier**

copeau, -x [kɔpo] **NM** *(de métal)* chip; *(de bois)* shaving; **des copeaux** *(de métal)* chips, filings; *(pour l'emballage)* woodwool; **des copeaux de chocolat** chocolate shavings; **le sol était jonché de copeaux de bois** the ground was littered with wood shavings

Copenhague [kɔpənag] **NM** Copenhagen

copépode [kɔpepɔd] *Zool* **NM** *(crustacé)* copepod
   ❑ **copépodes NMPL** Copepoda

copermuter [3] [kɔpɛrmyte] **VT** *Rel* to exchange

Copernic [kɔpɛrnik] **NPR** Copernicus

copernicien, -enne [kɔpɛrnisjɛ̃, -ɛn] **ADJ** Copernican

copiage [kɔpjaʒ] **NM** *Péj (plagiat)* copying; *Scol* cribbing

copie [kɔpi] **NF 1** *(reproduction légitime → d'un document)* copy, duplicate; *(→ d'une lettre)* copy; **je vais en faire une c.** I'll go and make a copy (of it); **c'est la c. exacte de son père** he's/she's the (spitting) image of his/her father; **c. carbone** carbon copy, cc; **c. certifiée conforme (à l'original)** certified copy; **c. papier** paper copy
   2 *(reproduction → d'un tableau, d'une cassette, d'un produit)* copy, imitation, reproduction; **ce n'était pas un vrai Pollock mais une c.** it wasn't a real Pollock but a copy or fake; **ce n'est qu'une pâle c. de l'original** it's only a pale imitation of the original
   3 *(feuille)* sheet; **des copies simples/doubles** = single-/double-width sheets of squared paper used for schoolwork
   4 *Scol (devoir)* paper; **il m'a rendu une très bonne c.** he did a very good paper or piece of work for me; **rendre c. blanche** to hand in a blank paper; *Fig* to fail to come up with the solution *(for a problem)*; **le ministre va devoir revoir sa c.** the minister will need to have a rethink
   5 *Cin & TV* print, copy; **c. antenne** broadcast-ing copy or print; **c. d'exploitation** release print; **c. de film** print; **c. de montage** first answer print, cutting copy, workprint; **c. positive** positive print; **c. standard** composite or combined print
   6 *Journ* la **c.** copy; **être en mal de c.** to be short of copy; **des journalistes en mal de c.** journa-lists short of copy or desperate for something to write about
   7 *Ordinat* copy; **c. archivée** archive (copy); **c. de bloc** copy block; **c. en clair** hard copy; **c. de disquette** *(commande DOS)* disk copy; **c. libre**

blind copy; **c. sur papier** hard copy, printout; **c. prête pour la reproduction** CRC, camera-ready copy; **c. de sauvegarde** *ou* **de secours** backup (copy), security copy

8 *Jur* **c. exécutoire** execution copy *(of a judgment)*; **c. exécutoire à ordre** execution copy *(of a notarial instrument, transferable by endorsement)*

▫ **pour copie conforme** ADV certified accurate

copier [9] [kɔpje] VT **1** *(modèle)* to reproduce, to copy; **j'ai copié cette robe sur un modèle de couturier** I copied this dress from a designer model

2 *(bijou, tableau)* to fake, to copy

3 *(transcrire → document, texte)* to copy (out), to make a copy of; *(punition)* to copy out; **c. un rapport au propre** to make a fair copy of a report; **vous me copierez dix fois cette phrase** write out this sentence ten times

4 *Ordinat* to copy; **c. qch sur le disque dur** to copy sth onto hard disk; **c. qch sur disquette** to copy sth to disk

5 *Scol (pour tricher)* to copy; **il a copié (l'exercice) sur moi/son livre** he copied (the exercise) from me/his book

6 *(attitude, personne)* to copy, to imitate; **ils copient les Américains** they imitate the Americans; **elle me copie en tout** she copies everything I do, she copies me in everything

7 *Fam (locution)* **tu me la copieras!, vous me la copierez!** that's something that's going to stick with me for a while!

copier-coller [3] [kɔpjekɔle] *Ordinat* VT to copy and paste
  VI to copy and paste
  NM INV copy-and-paste; **faire un c. (sur qch)** to copy and paste (sth)

copieur, -euse[1] [kɔpjœr, -øz] NM,F *(plagiaire)* plagiarist; *Scol & Univ* cribber
  NM *(photocopieuse)* copier

copieusement [kɔpjøzmɑ̃] ADV *(manger)* heartily; *(annoter)* copiously; *(servir)* generously; **il s'est servi c.** he took a generous helping; **après un repas c. arrosé** after a meal washed down with copious *or* generous amounts of wine; *Hum* **il s'est fait c. insulter par sa femme** he got quite a mouthful from his wife

copieux, -euse[2] [kɔpjø, -øz] ADJ *(repas)* copious, hearty, lavish; *(ration)* lavish, big, giant; *(pourboire)* generous; *(notes)* copious

copilote [kɔpilɔt] NMF co-pilot

copinage [kɔpinaʒ] NM *Fam Péj* cronyism; **par c.** through cronyism *or* one's connections

copine [kɔpin] *voir* **copain**

copiner [3] [kɔpine] ▫ **copiner avec** VT IND *Fam* to to be *Br* pals *or Am* buddies with

copinerie [kɔpinri] NF *Fam* chumminess

coping [kɔpiŋ] NM *Psy* coping mechanism(s)

copion [kɔpjɔ̃] NM *Belg Fam Arg scol (antisèche)* *Br* crib, *Am* cheat sheet

copiste [kɔpist] NMF **1** *(scribe)* copyist, transcriber **2** *Typ* platemaker

copla [kɔpla] NF *Mus* copla

coplanaire [kɔplanɛr] ADJ *Géom* coplanar

copolymère [kɔpɔlimɛr] NM *Chim* copolymer

copolymérisation [kɔpɔlimerizasjɔ̃] NF *Chim* copolymerization

coporteur [kɔpɔrtœr] NM *Fin* joint holder

coposséder [18] [kɔpɔsede] VT *Jur* to own jointly, to have joint ownership of

copossesseur [kɔpɔsesœr] NM *Jur* joint owner

copossession [kɔpɔsesjɔ̃] NF *Jur* joint ownership

coppa [kɔpa] NF *culin* coppa (ham)

copra, coprah [kɔpra] NM copra

copreneur, -euse [kɔprənœr, -øz] NM,F *Jur* co-lessee, co-tenant

coprésentateur, -trice [kɔprezɑ̃tatœr, -tris] NM,F co-presenter

coprésenter [3] [kɔprezɑ̃te] VT to co-present

coprésidence [kɔprezidɑ̃s] NF co-chairmanship, co-presidency

coprésident, -e [kɔprezidɑ̃, -ɑ̃t] NM,F co-chairman, co-president

coprin [kɔprɛ̃] NM *Bot* ink cap

coprocesseur [kɔprɔsesœr] NM *Ordinat* co-processor; **c. arithmétique** maths co-processor

coproculture [kɔprɔkyltyr] NF *Méd* coproculture

coproducteur [kɔprɔdyktœr] NM co-producer

coproduction [kɔprɔdyksjɔ̃] NF coproduction; **ce**

---

film est une c. des télévisions française et italienne this film has been coproduced by French and Italian television

coproduire [80] [kɔprɔdɥir] VT to coproduce, to produce jointly

coprolalie [kɔprɔlali] NF *Psy* coprolalia

coprolite, coprolithe [kɔprɔlit] NM **1** *Géol* coprolite **2** *Méd* coprolith

coprologie [kɔprɔlɔʒi] NF *Méd & Zool* coprology, scatology **2** *Biol* scatology

coprologique [kɔprɔlɔʒik] ADJ **1** *Méd & Zool* coprological, scatological **2** *Biol* scatological

coprophage [kɔprɔfaʒ] ADJ *Zool & Psy* coprophagous
  NMF *Psy* coprophagist
  ▫ **coprophages** NMPL *Zool* Coprophagi

coprophagie [kɔprɔfaʒi] NF *Psy* coprophagy

coprophile [kɔprɔfil] ADJ **1** *Zool* coprophilous **2** *Psy* coprophiliac
  NM **1** *Zool* coprophilous organism **2** *Psy* coprophiliac

coprophilie [kɔprɔfili] NF *Psy* coprophilia

copropriétaire [kɔprɔprijetɛr] NMF co-owner, joint owner, coproprietor

copropriété [kɔprɔprijete] NF joint ownership, co-ownership
  ▫ **en copropriété** ADJ jointly owned ADV *(acheter, posséder)* jointly

cops [kɔps] NM *(enroulement)* cop; *(tube)* spindle

copte [kɔpt] ADJ Coptic
  ▫ **Copte** NMF Copt NM *(langue)* Coptic

copulateur, -trice [kɔpylatœr, -tris] ADJ *Zool* copulatory, copulative

copulatif, -ive [kɔpylatif, -iv] ADJ *Ling* copulative

copulation [kɔpylasjɔ̃] NF copulation

copulative [kɔpylativ] *voir* **copulatif**

copulatrice [kɔpylatris] *voir* **copulateur**

copule [kɔpyl] NF *Ling* copula

copuler [3] [kɔpyle] VI to copulate

copy [kɔpi] NF *Mktg* **c. stratégie** copy strategy; **c. stratégie créative** creative copy strategy

copy art [kɔpiart] NM *Beaux-Arts* copy art

copyright [kɔpirajt] NM copyright

copyrighter [3] [kɔpirajte] VT to copyright

coq [kɔk] NM **1** *Orn (mâle → de la poule)* *Br* cock, *Am* rooster; *(→ des gallinacés)* cock, cockbird; **jeune c.** cockerel; **c. des bouleaux** black grouse; **c. de bruyère** capercaillie; **c. de combat** gamecock; **c. d'été** hoopoe; **c. faisan** cock pheasant; **c. d'Inde** turkey-cock; **c. de perdrix** partridge; **c. de roche** cock-of-the-rock; **c. sauvage** jungle fowl; **être comme un c. en pâte** to be in clover; **avoir des mollets de c.** to be spindly-legged, to have legs like matchsticks; **passer** *ou* **sauter du c. à l'âne** to jump from one subject to another

2 *(figure, symbole)* **c. de clocher** weathercock, weather vane; **c. gaulois** = French national symbol (a cockerel)

3 *Culin* chicken; **c. au vin** coq au vin

4 *Fam (fanfaron, séducteur)* lady-killer; **le c. de** *ou* **du village** the local Casanova

5 *Naut* (ship's) cook
  ADJ *Sport (catégorie, poids)* bantam *(avant n)*

Culture

LE COQ GAULOIS
The cockerel is the symbol of France. Its cry, "co-corico!", is sometimes used to express national pride: "trois médailles d'or pour la France – co-corico!"

coq-à-l'âne [kɔkalan] NM INV **1** *(dans la conversation)* sudden change of subject; **faire un c.** to go on to something completely different **2** *Littérature* skit, satirical farce

coq-l'œil [kɔklœj] *Can Fam* ADJ INV cross-eyed ▪
  NMF INV cross-eyed person ▪

coquard, coquart [kɔkar] NM *Fam* shiner, black eye ▪

coque [kɔk] NF **1** *(mollusque)* cockle **2** *(de noix, de noisette, d'amande)* shell **3** *(boucle → de ruban)* loop, bow; *(→ de cheveux)* curl, lock **4** *(châssis) & Naut* hull; *Aviat* hull, fuselage; *Aut* shell, body **5** *(de chaussure de ski)* shell **6** *Tél (de téléphone portable)* cover, fascia **7** *Biol (bactérie)* coccus **8** *Fam (embarcation)* **c. (de noix)** skiff
  ▫ **à coque** ADJ *(chaussures)* steel-capped
  ▫ **à la coque** ADJ *(œuf)* soft-boiled

---

coquecigrue [kɔksigry] NF **1** *Littéraire* legendary bird, chimaera; *(acte)* act of coquetry *or* flirtatiousness never **2** *Bot* smoke-bush, smoke-plant
  ▫ **coquecigrues** NFPL *Arch* twaddle, balderdash

coquelet [kɔklɛ] NM young cockerel

coqueleux [kɔklø] NM *Belg & (dans le Nord de la France)* breeder of gamecocks

coquelicot [kɔkliko] NM poppy

▭

'**Les Coquelicots à Argenteuil**' *Monet* 'Poppies, Argenteuil'

coqueluche [kɔklyʃ] NF **1** *Méd* whooping-cough, *Spéc* pertussis; **avoir la c.** to have whooping-cough **2** *Fam Fig* **être la c. de l'école** to be the school heart-throb; **être la c. des adolescents** to be a teenage idol; **il est devenu la c. de ces dames** he has become a heart-throb

coquelucheux, -euse [kɔklyʃø, -øz] ADJ *(personne)* suffering from whooping-cough; **toux coquelucheuse** whooping-cough
  NM,F whooping-cough sufferer

coquerelle[1] [kɔkrɛl] NF *Hér* bunch of three hazelnuts

coquerelle[2] [kɔkrɛl] NF *Can* cockroach

coqueret [kɔkrɛ] NM *Bot* winter-cherry, strawberry tomato; **c. du Pérou** Cape gooseberry

coquerie [kɔkri] NF *Naut (cuisine d'un bateau)* galley

coqueron [kɔkrɔ̃] NM **1** *Naut* peak; **c. avant** forepeak; **c. arrière** after-peak **2** *Can Péj (logement)* tumbledown house; *(pièce)* pokey room

coquet, -ette [kɔkɛ, -ɛt] ADJ **1** *(soucieux de son apparence)* concerned about one's appearance
  2 *(élégant → maison, mobilier)* pretty, charming; *(jardin)* trim
  3 *Vieilli (qui cherche à séduire)* coquettish, flirtatious
  4 *Fam (important → somme, indemnité)* tidy, nice (little)
  ▫ **coquette** NF **1** *(femme)* coquette, flirt
  2 *Théât* stage coquette; **jouer les grandes coquettes** to specialize in stage coquette parts; *Fig* to be a coquette

coquetel [kɔktɛl] NM *Can (boisson)* cocktail; *(réception)* cocktail party

coqueter [27] [kɔkte] VI *(coq)* to mate; *Vieilli (personne)* to play the coquette; **c. avec qn** to flirt with sb; **c. avec une idée** to toy with an idea

coquetier [kɔktje] NM **1** *(godet)* eggcup **2** *(pêcheur)* cockle gatherer **3** *Fam (locution)* **gagner** *ou* **décrocher le c.** to hit the jackpot

coquetière [kɔktjɛr] NF egg boiler

coquette [kɔkɛt] *voir* **coquet**

coquettement [kɔkɛtmɑ̃] ADV *(décorer, meubler)* prettily, charmingly; *(s'habiller)* smartly, stylishly

coquetterie [kɔkɛtri] NF **1** *(goût de la toilette)* concern about one's appearance; **avec c.** *(décorer, meubler)* prettily, charmingly; *(s'habiller)* smartly, stylishly
  2 *(fausse modestie)* affectation; **je vous le dis sans c. aucune** I'm saying that without any false modesty
  3 *Littéraire (désir de plaire)* coquetry, flirtatiousness; *(acte)* act of coquetry *or* flirtatiousness; **faire des coquetteries à qn** to flirt with sb; **être en c. avec qn** to be flirtatious with sb
  4 *Fam (locution)* **avoir une c. dans l'œil** to have a cast in one's eye *or* a slight squint

coquillage [kɔkijaʒ] NM **1** *(mollusque)* shellfish **2** *Culin* **manger des coquillages** to eat shellfish *or* seafood **3** *(coquille)* shell; **collectionner des coquillages** to collect seashells

coquillard [kɔkijar] NM *Fam (œil)* eye ▪; **coquillards** peepers

coquillart [kɔkijar] NM *Minér & Constr* = shell-based building material

coquille [kɔkij] NF **1** *(de mollusque, d'œuf, de noix)* shell; *Fig* **rentrer dans sa c.** to withdraw *or* to retire into one's shell; *Fig* **rester dans sa c.** to be introverted ▪; *Fig* **sortir de sa c.** to come out of one's shell, to open up; **c. Saint-Jacques** *(mollusque)* scallop; *(enveloppe)* scallop shell
  2 *(récipient)* shell, scallop, scallop-shaped dish

3 *Culin* **c. de beurre** butter curl; **c. de poisson** fish served in a shell
4 *(d'épée)* hand guard *or* shell
5 *Archit* shell
6 *Fam (bateau)* **c. de noix** cockleshell
7 *Sport* box
8 *Méd* spinal bed
9 *Typ (erreur → en composition)* misprint; *(→ d'une seule lettre)* literal; *(→ en dactylographie)* typo
10 *Typ (format)* demy
11 *Com & Fin* shell company *(exempt from taxes)*
□ **coquille d'œuf** ADJ INV eggshell

coquillettes [kɔkijɛt] NFPL pasta shells

coquillier, -ère [kɔkije, -ɛr] ADJ *Minér* shell *(avant n)*

coquin, -e [kɔkɛ̃, -in] ADJ **1** *(espiègle)* mischievous; **comme elle est coquine, cette petite!** what a little rascal *or* devil she is! **2** *(suggestif → histoire)* risqué, naughty; *(→ sous-vêtement)* sexy, naughty; **une œillade coquine** a provocative glance **3** *Vieilli* **c. de sort!** I'll be darned!
NM,F *(enfant)* (little) rascal *or* devil
NM **1** *Arch (voyou)* rogue, scoundrel
2 *Géol* nodule of phosphate of lime
□ **coquine** NF *Arch* strumpet

coquinement [kɔkinmɑ̃] ADV *(d'une manière espiègle)* mischievously; *(coquettement)* coquettishly, flirtatiously; **avec un petit bibi c. posé sur l'oreille** with a little hat worn coquettishly over one ear

coquinerie [kɔkinri] NF *Littéraire* **1** *(caractère malicieux)* mischievousness, roguishness **2** *(acte malicieux)* trick, prank; *(acte malfaisant)* dirty *or* mean trick; *(escroquerie)* swindle; **faire une c. à qn** *(farce)* to play a trick on sb

coquinet, -ette [kɔkinɛ, -ɛt] NM,F *Fam* little rogue, little rascal

cor [kɔr] NM **1** *Mus* horn; **c. (de chasse)** hunting horn; **c. des Alpes** Alpen horn; **c. anglais** cor anglais, English horn; **c. de basset** basset horn; **c. d'harmonie** French horn; **c. à piston** valve horn **2** *(au pied)* corn **3** *(d'un andouiller)* tine
□ **à cor et à cri** ADV réclamer qn/qch **à c. et à cri** to clamour for sb/sth

coraciiforme [kɔrasiiform] NM *Orn* coraciiform

coracoïde [kɔrakɔid] *Anat* ADJ coracoid
NF coracoid

corail, -aux [kɔraj, -o] NM **1** *Zool & (en bijouterie)* coral **2** *Culin* coral, red part
□ **corail** ADJ INV coral-red
□ **de corail** ADJ *(rouge)* coral-red, coral, coral-coloured

corailleur, -euse [kɔrajœr, -øz] NM,F *(pêcheur)* coral gatherer; *(artisan)* coral worker

corallien, -enne [kɔraljɛ̃, -ɛn] ADJ *(gén)* coralloid, coralline; *(île, récif)* coral *(avant n)*

corallifère [kɔralifɛr] ADJ coralliferous

coralline [kɔralin] NF coralline

Coran [kɔrɑ̃] NM **le C.** the Koran

coranique [kɔranik] ADJ *(texte, école)* Koranic

corb [kɔrb] NM *Ich* brown meagre

corbeau, -x [kɔrbo] NM **1** *Orn* crow; **c. corneille** crow; **c. freux** rook; **grand c.** raven **2** *Fam Péj (auteur anonyme)* = writer of poison-pen letters; **la police savait qui était le c.** the police knew who'd written the poison-pen letter **3** *Vieilli (escroc)* shark **4** *Vieilli Fam (prêtre)* priest▪ **5** *Archit* corbel, bracket

corbeille [kɔrbɛj] NF **1** *(contenant, contenu)* basket; **une c. de fruits** a fruit basket; **c. à courrier** desk tray; **c. à linge** laundry basket; **c. de mariage** *(des invités)* wedding presents; *(du marié)* groom's wedding presents *(to the bride)*; **mon père avait mis la voiture dans ma c. de mariage** the car was a wedding present from my father; **c. à ouvrage** workbasket; **c. à pain** breadbasket; **c. à papier** wastepaper basket *or* bin
2 *(massif de fleurs)* (round *or* oval) flower-bed
3 *Théât* dress circle
4 *Archit* bell
5 *Bourse (à Paris)* trading floor; **à la c.** *(en style journalistique)* on the (Paris) Stock Exchange; **c. des obligations** bond-trading ring
6 *Ordinat (de Mac) Br* wastebasket, *Am* trash; *(dans Windows®)* recycle bin; **c. d'arrivée**

(pour courrier électronique) in box; **c. de départ** *(pour courrier électronique)* out box

corbeille-d'argent [kɔrbɛjdarʒɑ̃] *(pl* **corbeilles-d'argent)** NF *Bot* alyssum

corbillard [kɔrbijar] NM hearse

corbillon [kɔrbijɔ̃] NM **1** *(corbeille)* small basket **2** *(jeu)* ≃ crambo

corbleu [kɔrblø] EXCLAM *Arch* by Jove!

Corcyre [kɔrsir] NF *Géog* Corcyra

cordage [kɔrdaʒ] NM **1** *(lien)* rope; **les cordages** ropes and cables **2** *(mesure)* measuring by the cord **3** *(d'une raquette → cordes)* strings; *(→ action de corder)* stringing; **faire refaire le c. de sa raquette** to have one's racket re-strung
□ **cordages** NMPL *Naut* rigging

corde [kɔrd] NF **1** *(lien)* rope; **attaché au poteau par une c.** roped to the post; *Fam* **tirer (un peu trop) sur la c.** *(profiter d'autrui)* to push one's luck, to go a bit too far; *(abuser de sa santé, ses forces)* to push oneself to the limits, to overdo it; *Fam* **il tombe** *ou* **pleut des cordes** it's raining cats and dogs, it's bucketing down
2 *(câble tendu)* **c. à linge** clothes-line; *Can Fam* **coucher sur la c. à linge** to have a wild night of it; **c. raide** high wire, tightrope; **être sur la c. raide** to be on *or* to walk the tightrope; *Fig* to walk a tightrope, to do a (difficult) balancing act
3 *(pour pendre)* rope; **la c.** *(supplice)* the rope; **il mérite la c.!** he deserves to be hanged *or* to hang!; **passer la c. au cou à qn** to send sb to the gallows; *Fig* **se mettre** *ou* **se passer la c. au cou** *(se mettre à la merci de quelqu'un)* to put one's head in a noose; *(se marier)* to get hitched; *Prov* **il ne faut pas parler de c. dans la maison d'un pendu** talk not of ropes in a hanged man's house; *Fig* **toucher la c. du pendu** to touch wood; **il ne vaut pas la c. pour le pendre** hanging's too good for him
4 *(matériau)* cord, rope
5 *Mus* string; **instruments à cordes** stringed instruments; **toucher** *ou* **faire vibrer la c. sensible** to touch an emotional chord, to tug at the heartstrings
6 *Sport & (jeux)* rope; **c. lisse** climbing rope; **c. à nœuds** knotted climbing rope; **c. à sauter** *Br* skipping rope, *Am* jump rope; **sauter à la c.** *Br* to skip, *Am* to jump rope
7 *(d'une arbalète, d'une raquette)* string; *Fig* **avoir plus d'une c.** *ou* **plusieurs cordes à son arc** to have more than one string to one's bow
8 *Sport (intérieur d'une piste de course à pied)* inside lane; *Équitation* rails; **tenir la c.** *(coureur)* to keep to the inside; **monter à la c.** *(coureur)* to move to the inside lane
9 *Anat* cord; **c. dorsale** dorsal cord, notochord; **c. du jarret** hamstring; **c. du tympan** chorda tympani; **cordes vocales** vocal cords; **c'est dans ses cordes** it's right up his/her street, it's his/her line; **quelque chose qui soit dans vos cordes** something in your line
10 *Tex* thread; **il avait des manches qui montraient la c.** his sleeves were threadbare
11 *(mesure)* cord; *Can* **c. de bois** cord of wood *(128 cubic feet)*
12 *Math* chord
□ **cordes** NFPL *(instruments)* strings, stringed instruments
□ **à la corde** ADV *Aut & Équitation* **être à la c.** to be on the inside, to be on the rails; **prendre un virage à la c.** to hug a bend
□ **dans les cordes** ADV *Boxe* on the ropes; *aussi Fig* **aller dans les cordes** to be on the ropes
□ **de corde, en corde** ADJ *(semelle)* cord *(avant n)*; *(revêtement)* whipcord *(avant n)*; *(échelle)* rope *(avant n)*

cordé[1], -e[1] [kɔrde] ADJ *(en forme de cœur)* heart-shaped, cordate

cordé[2] [kɔrde] *Zool* NM = member of the Cordata
□ **cordés** NMPL Cordata

cordeau, -x [kɔrdo] NM **1** *(fil)* string, line; *aussi Fig* **tiré au c.** perfectly straight, straight as a die **2** *(mèche)* fuse; **c. Bickford** Bickford fuse; **c. détonant** detonator fuse **3** *(pour pêcher)* paternoster *(line)*
□ **cordeaux** NMPL *Can (rênes)* reins; *Fig* **tenir les cordeaux** to wear the trousers

cordée[2] [kɔrde] NF *(alpinistes)* roped party

cordelette [kɔrdəlɛt] NF cord

cordelier, -ère [kɔrdəlje, -ɛr] NM,F **1** *Rel* Franciscan friar, Cordelier, *f* Franciscan nun **2** *Hist* **le Club des Cordeliers** = a left-wing club of the Revolutionary period
□ **cordelière** NF *(de robe de chambre etc)* cord; *Archit* cable moulding

corder [3] [kɔrde] VT **1** *(lier → valise, malle)* to rope up **2** *(tordre)* to twist (into ropes *or* a rope) **3** *(raquette)* to string **4** *(mesurer → bois)* to cord
▶ **se corder** VPR *(légume)* to become *or* to go stringy

corderie [kɔrdəri] NF **1** *(industrie)* ropemaking trade *or* industry **2** *(usine)* rope factory

corderoy [kɔrdərwa] NM *Can* corduroy

cordial, -e, -aux, -ales [kɔrdjal, -o] ADJ warm, cordial, friendly; **une haine/aversion cordiale pour...** a heartfelt hatred of/disgust for...
NM *(boisson)* tonic, pick-me-up

cordialement [kɔrdjalmɑ̃] ADV **1** *(saluer)* warmly, cordially; **ils se détestent c.** they heartily detest each other **2** *(dans la correspondance)* **c. vôtre** (best) regards; **(bien) c.** best wishes

cordialité [kɔrdjalite] NF warmth, cordiality

cordier [kɔrdje] NM **1** *Ind* ropemaker **2** *Mus (d'un violon etc)* tailpiece

cordiérite [kɔrdjerit] NF *Minér* cordierite

cordiforme [kɔrdiform] ADJ cordate, cordiform

cordillère [kɔrdijɛr] NF mountain range, *Spéc* cordillera; **la c. des Andes** the Andes (cordillera); **la C. australienne** the Great Dividing Range;

cordite [kɔrdit] NF cordite

cordoba [kɔrdoba] NM *(monnaie)* cordoba

cordon [kɔrdɔ̃] NM **1** *(de rideaux)* cord; *(d'un bonnet, d'un sac)* string; *(de soulier)* lace; **c. de sonnette** bellpull; **tenir les cordons de la bourse** to hold the purse strings
2 *(ligne → de policiers)* row, cordon; *(→ de peupliers)* row, line; **c. sanitaire** *Méd* cordon sanitaire; *Mil* cordon sanitaire, buffer zone
3 *Anat* **c. médullaire** spinal cord; **c. ombilical** umbilical cord; *Fig* **couper le c.** to cut the umbilical cord; **c. spermatique** spermatic cord; **c. testiculaire** testicular cord
4 *Géol* **c. littoral** offshore bar
5 *(insigne → écharpe)* sash; *(→ ruban)* ribbon; **avoir** *ou* **recevoir le grand c.** to be awarded the Grand Cross of the "Légion d'honneur"
6 *Archit* cordon
7 *(d'une pièce de monnaie)* milled edge

cordon-bleu [kɔrdɔ̃blø] *(pl* **cordons-bleus)** NM cordon bleu (cook), gourmet cook

cordonner [3] [kɔrdone] VT **1** *(soie, cheveux)* to twist **2** *(pièce de monnaie)* to mark, to mill **3** *Archit* to decorate with a cordon

cordonnerie [kɔrdɔnri] NF **1** *(boutique → moderne)* heel bar, shoe repair *Br* shop *or Am* store; *(→ artisanale)* cobbler's **2** *(activité → de réparation)* shoe repairing, cobbling; *(→ de fabrication)* shoemaking

cordonnet [kɔrdonɛ] NM **1** *(pour lier)* (piece of) cord **2** *(pour orner)* (piece of) braid

cordonnier, -ère [kɔrdonje, -ɛr] NM,F *(qui répare)* shoe repairer, cobbler; *(qui fabrique)* shoemaker; *Prov* **les cordonniers sont toujours les plus mal chaussés** the shoemaker's children are always the worst shod

cordouan, -e [kɔrdwɑ̃, -an] ADJ of/from Cordoba
NM *(de chèvre, de cheval)* cordovan
□ **Cordouan, -e** NM,F = inhabitant of or person from Cordoba

Cordoue [kɔrdu] NM Cordoba

coré [kɔre] = korê

Corée [kɔre] NF Korea; **la C. du Nord/Sud** North/South Korea; **vivre en C.** to live in Korea; **aller en C.** to go to Korea

coréen, -enne [kɔreɛ̃, -ɛn] ADJ Korean
NM *(langue)* Korean
□ **Coréen, -enne** NM,F Korean

corégone [koregon] *Ich* NM whitefish, *Spéc* Coregonus
□ **corégones** NMPL Coregonidae

coreligionnaire [kɔreliʒjɔnɛr] NMF coreligionist; **vos coreligionnaires** those who share your religious denomination

coréopsis [kɔreopsis] NM *Bot* coreopsis

coresponsable [kɔrɛspɔ̃sabl] ADJ jointly responsible

NMF person sharing responsibility; **les co-responsables** those jointly responsible

Corfou [kɔrfu] NM Corfu; **à C.** in Corfu

coriace [kɔrjas] ADJ **1** *(dur → viande)* tough, chewy **2** *(problème, personne)* tough; **des taches coriaces** tough stains, stains that won't come out; **c'est c.!** *(situation)* it's a tough one!; **elle est c.!** she's a tough one!; **être c. en affaires** to be hard-headed in business

coriandre [kɔrjɑ̃dr] NF *(plante)* coriander; *(graines)* coriander seeds

coricide [kɔrisid] NM corn remover

corindon [kɔrɛ̃dɔ̃] NM corundum

Corinthe [kɔrɛ̃t] NM Corinth

corinthien, -enne [kɔrɛ̃tjɛ̃, -ɛn] ADJ Corinthian

❑ **Corinthien, -enne** NM,F Corinthian

Coriolan [kɔrjɔlɑ̃] NPR Coriolanus

corme [kɔrm] NF whitebeam berry

cormier [kɔrmje] NM *(en Europe)* (true) service tree; *(en Amérique du Nord)* (American) mountain ash

cormophyte [kɔrmɔfit] *Bot* NM cormophyte

❑ **cormophytes** NMPL Cormophyta

cormoran [kɔrmɔrɑ̃] NM *Orn* cormorant; **grand c.** great cormorant; **c. africain** long-tailed cormorant; **c. huppé** shag

cornac [kɔrnak] NM elephant keeper, mahout

cornacée [kɔrnase] *Bot* NF cornel

❑ **cornacées** NFPL Cornaceae

cornage [kɔrnaʒ] NM **1** *Zool* horns **2** *Vét* wheezing, whistling, roaring; *(cheval)* wind-sucking **3** *Méd* wheezing

cornaline [kɔrnalin] NF *Minér* cornelian

cornaquer [3] [kɔrnake] VT *Fam* to lead▪, to guide▪, to act as a guide to▪

cornard [kɔrnar] NM *Fam Vieilli* cuckold

corne [kɔrn] NF **1** *(d'un animal, d'un diable)* horn; **faire les cornes à qn** to mock sb *(by making a gesture with one's fingers shaped like horns)*; *Fam* **hou les cornes!** shame on you!; *Fam* **avoir** *ou* **porter des cornes** to be a cuckold; *Fam* **faire porter des cornes à qn** to cuckold sb

2 *(matériau)* horn; **bouton de c.** horn button; **lunettes à monture de c.** horn-rimmed glasses *or* spectacles

3 *(outil)* **c. à chaussures** shoehorn

4 *Mus* horn; **c. de brume** fog horn

5 *(récipient)* horn; **c. d'abondance** *(ornement)* horn of plenty, cornucopia; *Bot* horn of plenty

6 *(callosité)* **avoir de la c.** to have calluses

7 *(coin de page)* dog-ear; **faire une c. à** to turn down the corner of

8 *(forme → d'un mont)* peak; *(→ d'un bois)* (horn-shaped) corner; *(→ de la lune, d'un champ, d'une terre)* horn; *(→ d'un croissant)* end, tip; **la C. de l'Afrique** the Horn of Africa

9 *Culin* **c. de gazelle** = crescent-shaped cake, a North African speciality

❑ **à cornes** ADJ **1** *(bête)* horned

2 *(chapeau)* cocked

corné, -e[1] [kɔrne] ADJ *(qui a l'apparence de la corne)* corneous, horned

corned-beef [kɔrnbif] NM INV corned beef

cornée[2] [kɔrne] NF *Anat* cornea

cornéen, -enne [kɔrneɛ̃, -ɛn] ADJ corneal

corneille [kɔrnɛj] NF **1** *Orn* crow; **c. américaine** American crow; **c. mantelée** hooded crow; **c. noire** carrion crow **2** *Can très Fam (religieuse)* nun▪, penguin

cornélien, -enne [kɔrneljɛ̃, -ɛn] ADJ *(héros, vers)* Cornelian, of Corneille; **choix** *ou* **dilemme c.** conflict of love and duty

cornemuse [kɔrnəmyz] NF (set of) bagpipes; **joueur de c.** bagpiper, piper

cornemuseur [kɔrnəmyzœr], **cornemuseux** [kɔrnəmyzø] NM bagpiper, piper

corner[1] [kɔrnɛr] NM *Ftbl* corner kick; **tirer un c.** to take a corner

corner[2] [3] [kɔrne] VT **1** *(plier → par négligence)* to dog-ear; *(→ volontairement)* to turn down the corner *or* corners of **2** *(clamer → nouvelle)* to blare out

USAGE ABSOLU *(hurler)* **c. aux oreilles** *ou* **dans les oreilles de qn** to deafen sb

VI **1** *Chasse* to sound a horn **2** *Arch Aut* to hoot, to sound one's horn; **corne!** sound your horn! **3** *Vét* to wheeze **4** *(locution)* **les oreilles ont dû lui/te c.** his/her/your ears must have been burning

cornet [kɔrnɛ] NM **1** *(papier)* cornet; *(contenu)* cornet, cornetful; **un c. de frites** a bag of *Br* chips *or Am* (French) fries; **mettre sa main en c.** to cup one's hand to one's ear

2 *Suisse (sac en papier)* paper bag; *(sac en plastique)* plastic bag

3 *Culin* **c. à la crème** cream horn; **c. de glace** *(gaufrette)* cone; *(gaufrette et glace)* ice cream cone, *Br* cornet; **c. de jambon** stuffed slice of ham *(rolled in the shape of a horn)*

4 *(gobelet)* **c. à dés** dice cup

5 *Mus (d'un orgue)* cornet stop; **c. (à pistons)** *(instrument)* cornet

6 *Anat* **c. de nez** turbinate body

7 *(en acoustique)* **c. acoustique** ear trumpet

8 *Fam (locution)* **se mettre qch dans le c.** to get sth inside one; **qu'est-ce qu'on s'est mis dans le c.!** we really stuffed ourselves *or* our faces!

cornette [kɔrnɛt] NF **1** *(de religieuse)* cornet **2** *(salade)* endive **3** *Arch Mil (étendard)* pennant, standard

NM *Arch Mil (officier)* cornet, ensign

❑ **cornettes** NFPL *Suisse* (elbow) macaroni

cornettiste [kɔrnetist] NMF cornet player

corn flakes [kɔrnflɛks] NMPL cornflakes

corniaud [kɔrnjo] NM **1** *(chien)* mongrel, cur (dog) **2** *Fam (imbécile)* twit, nincompoop

corniche [kɔrniʃ] NF **1** *Géog (roche)* ledge; *(neige)* cornice **2** *(route)* corniche (road) **3** *Archit* cornice **4** *Fam Arg scol* = class preparing for admission to Saint-Cyr

cornichon [kɔrniʃɔ̃] NM **1** *(légume)* gherkin; *(condiment)* (pickled) gherkin, *Am* pickle **2** *Fam (imbécile)* nitwit, twit, nincompoop **3** *Fam Arg scol* = student preparing for the entrance examination to Saint-Cyr

cornier, -ère [kɔrnje, -ɛr] ADJ (at the) corner, angle; *Constr* **poteau c.** corner *or* angle post

❑ **cornière** NF **1** *Constr (sous les combles)* valley **2** *(pièce en équerre)* angle (iron *or* bar)

corniot [kɔrnjo] = **corniaud**

cornique [kɔrnik] *Ling* ADJ Cornish

NM Cornish

corniste [kɔrnist] NMF horn player

cornouaillais, -e [kɔrnwajɛ, -ɛz] ADJ **1** *(de la Cornouaille)* of/from Cornouaille **2** *(de la Cornouailles)* Cornish

NM *(langue)* Cornish

❑ **Cornouaillais, -e** NM,F **1** *(de la Cornouaille)* = inhabitant of or person from Cornouaille **2** *(de la Cornouailles)* Cornishman, *f* Cornishwoman; **les C.** the Cornish

Cornouaille [kɔrnwaj] NF **la C.** Cornouaille *(region in north-west France)*

Cornouailles [kɔrnwaj] NF **la C.** Cornwall

cornouille [kɔrnuj] NF cornelian cherry

cornouiller [kɔrnuje] NM dogwood (tree), *Spéc* cornus; *(rouge)* redwood

corn-picker [kɔrnpikœr] (*pl* **corn-pickers**) NM corn picker

corn-sheller [kɔrnʃɛlœr] (*pl* **corn-shellers**) NM *Br* maize sheller, *Am* corn sheller

cornu, -e [kɔrny] ADJ horned

❑ **cornue** NF **1** *Chim* retort **2** *Métal* steel converter

Corogne [kɔrɔɲ] NF **La C.** Corunna

corollaire [kɔrɔlɛr] NM *(conséquence)* consequence; *Ling & Math* corollary; **le c. obligé de la hausse des prix** the inevitable consequence of the rise in prices; **cela a pour c. une inflation endémique** a consequence of this is endemic inflation, this results in endemic inflation

corolle [kɔrɔl] NF corolla

Coromandel [kɔrɔmɑ̃dɛl] NF **la côte de C.** Coromandel Coast

coron [kɔrɔ̃] NM *(quartier)* mining village; *(maison)* miner's cottage

coronaire [kɔrɔnɛr] *Anat* ADJ coronary

NF coronary artery

coronal, -e, -aux, -ales [kɔrɔnal, -o] ADJ **1** *Astron* of the solar corona **2** *Anat* coronal

coronarien, -enne [kɔrɔnarjɛ̃, -ɛn] ADJ *Anat* coronary

coronarite [kɔrɔnarit] NF *Méd* coronaritis

coronarographie [kɔrɔnarɔgrafi] NF *Méd* radiography of the coronary arteries

coronaropathie [kɔrɔnarɔpati] NF *Méd* coronary disease

coronavirus [kɔrɔnavirys] NM *Biol* coronavirus

coronelle [kɔrɔnɛl] NF *Zool* coronella

coroner [kɔrɔnœr] NM coroner

coronille [kɔrɔnij] NF *Bot* coronilla; *Fam* **c. des jardins** scorpion-senna

coronographe [kɔrɔnɔgraf] NM *Astron* coronagraph, coronograph

coronographie [kɔrɔnɔgrafi] NF *Méd* radiography of the coronary arteries

corossol [kɔrɔsɔl] NM *Bot (arbre, fruit)* custard-apple; **c. hérissé** sour-sop; **c. écailleux** sweet-sop

corossolier [kɔrɔsɔlje] NM *Bot* custard-apple-tree

corozo [kɔrɔzo, korozo] NM **1** *Bot* corozo-nut, ivory-nut **2** *Com* vegetable ivory

corporal, -aux [kɔrpɔral, -o] NM *Rel* corporal(-cloth)

corporatif, -ive [kɔrpɔratif, -iv] ADJ *(institution, système)* corporative; *(image, esprit)* corporate *(avant n)*

corporation [kɔrpɔrasjɔ̃] NF **1** *(groupe professionnel)* corporate body; **dans notre c.** in our profession; **c. de droit public** public body **2** *Hist* (trade) guild

corporatisme [kɔrpɔratism] NM **1** *Pol* corporatism **2** *Péj (esprit de caste)* professional protectionism

corporatiste [kɔrpɔratist] ADJ corporatist

NMF corporatist

corporative [kɔrpɔrativ] *voir* **corporatif**

corporel, -elle [kɔrpɔrɛl] ADJ **1** *(douleur)* physical; *(fonction)* bodily; *(châtiment)* corporal; *(hygiène)* personal; **soins corporels** care of *or* caring for one's body **2** *Phil* endowed with a (physical) body

corporellement [kɔrpɔrɛlmɑ̃] ADV corporeally, corporally, bodily

CORPS [kɔr] NM **1** *Physiol* body; **tremblant de tout son c.** trembling all over; *Fig Hum* **nationaliser? il faudra me passer sur le c.!** nationalize? (it'll be) over my dead body!; *Fig* **elle te passerait sur le c. pour obtenir le poste** she'd trample you underfoot to get the job; **faire c. avec** to be at *or* as one with

2 *(cadavre)* body; **porter un c. en terre** to lay a body to rest

3 *(élément, substance)* body; **c. céleste** celestial *or* heavenly body; **c. composé** compound body; **c. conducteur** conductor; **c. dissous** solute; **c. étranger** foreign body; **c. gras** fatty substance; **c. noir** black body; **c. simple** simple body

4 *(groupe, communauté)* **grand c. de l'État** = senior civil servants recruited through the "École nationale d'administration"; **le c. de ballet** the corps de ballet; **c. constitué** constituent body; **le c. diplomatique** the diplomatic corps; **le c. électoral** the electorate, the body of voters; **le c. enseignant** the teaching profession; **c. d'état** building trade; **le c. exécutif** the executive; **c. législatif** legislative body; **c. de la magistrature** magistrature; **le c. médical** the medical profession; **c. de métier** building trade; **c. politique** body politic; **le c. professoral** the teaching profession *(excluding primary school teachers)*; **le c. professoral de l'université** the teaching staff of the university

5 *Mil* **c. d'armée** army corps; **c. de cavalerie** cavalry brigade; **c. expéditionnaire** task force; **c. franc** commando; **c. de garde** *(soldats)* guards; *(local)* guardroom; **chansons de c. de garde** ≃ rugby songs; **plaisanteries de c. de garde** barrack-room *or Am* locker-room jokes; **c. de troupes** unit of troops

6 *(partie principale → d'un document)* body; *(→ d'une machine)* main part; *(→ d'un cylindre)* barrel; *(→ d'une robe)* body, bodice; *(majorité)* bulk, greater part; **c. de bâtiment** main (part of a) building; **c. de logis** main (part of a) building

7 *(ensemble → de lois, de textes)* body, corpus; *(→ de preuves)* body; *Jur* **le c. du délit** corpus delicti

8 *(consistance → d'un tissu, d'un arôme)* body; **un vin qui a du c.** a full-bodied wine; **donner c. à une idée/un plan** to give substance to an idea/a scheme; **prendre c.** *(sauce)* to thicken; *(projet)* to take shape

9 *Typ & Ordinat (de police de caractères)* point size, type size

10 *Anat* **c. jaune** yellow body; **c. caverneux**

erectile tissue (of the penis); **c. vitré** vitreous body

11 Rel **le c. mystique du Christ** the Body of Christ

❑ **à corps perdu** ADV with all one's might; **se jeter** ou **se lancer à c. perdu dans une aventure/entreprise** to throw oneself headlong into an affair/a task; **il se jeta** ou **lança à c. perdu dans son travail** he immersed himself in his work

❑ **à mon/son/etc corps défendant** ADV reluctantly

❑ **corps et âme** ADV body and soul

❑ **corps et biens** ADV Naut **perdu c. et biens** lost with all hands; Fig **il s'est perdu c. et biens** he's disappeared without trace

corps à corps [kɔrakɔr] NM INV hand-to-hand combat or fight; Fig hard struggle
   ADV (lutter) hand to hand

corps-mort [kɔrmɔr] (pl **corps-morts**) NM moorings, (mooring) buoys

corpulence [kɔrpylãs] NF **1** (volume corporel) build; **de forte c.** stoutly built, of stout build; **de faible c.** slightly built **2** (obésité) stoutness, corpulence; **avoir de la c.** to be stout or corpulent; Euph **un monsieur d'une certaine c.** a rather portly gentleman, a gentleman of ample girth

corpulent, -e [kɔrpylã, -ãt] ADJ stout, corpulent, portly

corpus [kɔrpys] NM **1** (recueil) corpus, collection **2** Ling corpus

corpusculaire [kɔrpyskylɛr] ADJ Anat & Phys corpuscular

corpuscule [kɔrpyskyl] NM Anat & Phys corpuscle

corral, -als [kɔral] NM corral

corrasion [kɔrazjõ] NF Géol corrasion

correct, -e [kɔrɛkt] ADJ **1** (sans fautes → calcul, description) correct, accurate; (→ déroulement) correct, proper

2 (tenue) proper, correct, decent

3 (courtois) courteous, polite; **un monsieur tout à fait c.** a well-bred gentleman, a gentleman with (good) manners; **tu n'as pas été très c. en partant sans prévenir** it was rather ill-mannered or impolite of you to leave without warning; **elle a été correcte avec moi** she behaved correctly towards me

4 (honnête → somme, offre) acceptable, fair; **200 euros, c'est c.** 200 euros, that's fair enough or acceptable; **500 euros pour trois jours de travail, c'est plutôt c.** 500 euros for three days' work, that's fair enough; **il est c. en affaires** he's an honest businessman

5 (peu remarquable → repas, soirée) decent, OK; **le concert était c., sans plus** the concert was all right but nothing special

6 Can **c'est c.!** (c'est d'accord) OK!, right!; **vous devez finir le travail jeudi – c.!** you must finish the work on Thursday – OK!

correctement [kɔrɛktəmã] ADV **1** (sans fautes) correctly, accurately **2** (selon la décence, la courtoisie) properly, decently **3** (de façon peu remarquable) reasonably well; **on a mangé c.** we had a reasonable meal; **elle gagne c. sa vie** she makes a decent or reasonable living

correcteur, -trice [kɔrɛktœr, -tris] ADJ corrective
   NM,F Scol & Univ examiner **2** Typ proofreader; Journ copy reader; **c. d'épreuves** proofreader
   NM 1 (dispositif) corrector; Ordinat **c. grammatical** grammar checker; **c. d'images** image enhancer; **c. de mise en page** stone sub; Ordinat **c. orthographique** ou **d'orthographe** spell-checker **2** (liquide) **c. liquide** correction fluid **3** (maquillage) **c. de teint** concealer **4** Rad **c. automatique de fréquence** automatic frequency control

correctif, -ive [kɔrɛktif, -iv] ADJ corrective
   NM 1 (rectification) qualifying statement, corrective; **je voudrais apporter un c. à ce qu'a dit mon collègue** I'd like to qualify what my colleague said **2** (atténuation) toning down; **apporter un c. à des mesures** to soften measures

correction [kɔrɛksjõ] NF **1** (rectificatif) correction; (action de rectifier) correction, correcting; **apporter une c. à une déclaration** (mise au point) to qualify a statement; (atténuation) to tone down a statement; **la c. des troubles de la vue** correcting eye defects

2 Scol Br marking, Am grading; **elle fait ses corrections** she's doing her Br marking or Am grading

3 Typ **la c.** (lieu) the proofreading department; (personnel) the proofreaders, the proofreading department; **c. d'auteur** author's corrections or emendations; **c. d'épreuves** proofreading

4 (punition) beating, thrashing; **tu vas recevoir une bonne c.!** you're going to get a good beating or thrashing!

5 (conformité) accuracy; **la c. d'une traduction** the accuracy of a translation

6 (comportement) correctness, propriety; **apprenez-leur la c.** teach them manners or how to behave (properly); **il a agi avec c.** he showed good manners; **il a été d'une parfaite c. avec moi** he behaved very correctly towards me; **c'est la plus élémentaire des corrections** it's basic good manners; **j'ai accepté par c.** I accepted out of politeness

7 Aut **c. d'avance** (à l'allumage) ignition advance adjustment; Aviat & Naut **c. de compas** compass adjustment; Écon **c. des variations saisonnières** seasonal adjustment

correctionnalisation [kɔrɛksjɔnalizasjõ] NF Jur = downgrading of a serious crime to a lesser offence, for trial in the "Tribunal correctionnel"

correctionnaliser [3] [kɔrɛksjɔnalize] VT Jur = to downgrade to a lesser offence, for trial in the "Tribunal correctionnel"

correctionnel, -elle [kɔrɛksjɔnɛl] Jur ADJ **peine correctionnelle** = penalty of more than five days' (but less than five years') imprisonment; **tribunal c.** Br ≃ magistrate's court, Am ≃ criminal court
   ❑ **correctionnelle** NF **la correctionnelle** Br ≃ magistrate's court, Am criminal court; **passer en correctionnelle** to go before a judge or Br magistrate

corrective [kɔrɛktiv] voir **correctif**

correctrice [kɔrɛktris] voir **correcteur**

Corrège [kɔrɛʒ] NPR **le C.** Correggio; **un tableau du C.** a painting by Correggio

corregidor [kɔreʒidɔr] NM Anciennement corregidor

corrélat [kɔrela] NM correlate

corrélatif, -ive [kɔrelatif, -iv] Ling ADJ correlative
   NM correlative

corrélation [kɔrelasjõ] NF **1** (rapport) correlation; **il y a (une) c. entre A et B** A and B are correlated; **il n'y a aucune c. entre les deux** the two are unrelated; **mettre en c.** to correlate; **être en c. étroite** to be closely connected or related **2** Math correlation

corrélationnel, -elle [kɔrelasjɔnɛl] ADJ correlational

corrélative [kɔrelativ] voir **corrélatif**

corrélativement [kɔrelativmã] ADV correlatively

corrélé, -e [kɔrele] ADJ correlated

corréler [18] [kɔrele] VT to correlate

correspondance [kɔrɛspõdãs] NF **1** (lettres) letters, Sout correspondence; (échange de lettres) correspondence; **c. commerciale** business correspondence; **être en c. avec** (par lettre) to correspond with; **cours par c.** correspondence courses; **elle étudie l'anglais par c.** she's learning English through a correspondence course; **faire des études supérieures par c.** to take a degree through a correspondence course, Br ≃ to do an Open University course

2 Journ correspondence

3 Transp connection; (train, bus) connection; (vol) connecting flight; **j'attends la c.** I'm waiting for my connection; **la c. est au bout du quai** change trains at the end of the platform; **la c. est assurée entre les aérogares** a shuttle service is provided between the air terminals

4 (similitude) conformity; (rapport) correspondence; **la c. de leurs ambitions** the uniformity of their ambitions

5 Math correspondence

correspondancier, -ère [kɔrɛspõdãsje, -ɛr] NM,F Admin & Com correspondence clerk

correspondant, -e [kɔrɛspõdã, -ãt] ADJ **1** (qui s'y rapporte) corresponding, relevant, Sout correspondent; **une commande et la facture correspondante** an order and the corresponding

invoice or the invoice that goes with it; **il n'y a pas de terme grec c.** there's no equivalent or corresponding term in Greek

2 (qui écrit) corresponding; **membre c. de la société** corresponding member of the society
   NM,F 1 Tél = person one is speaking to; **votre c. est en ligne** you're through; **nous recherchons votre c.** we're trying to connect you

2 (épistolaire) correspondent; **le c. de mon fils** my son's pen-friend; **tous mes correspondants me disent que…** all the people who write to me tell me that…

3 (avec qui l'on traite) correspondent; **mon c. était Butier** Butier was the person I was dealing with

4 Journ **c. (de presse)** (press) correspondent; **notre c. à Moscou** our Moscow correspondent; **c. à l'étranger** foreign correspondent; **c. financier** business correspondent; **c. de guerre** war correspondent; **c. permanent** permanent or resident correspondent

5 Scol guardian (of a boarder)

correspondre [75] [kɔrɛspõdr] VI **1** (par lettre) to write (letters to one another), Sout to correspond; (par téléphone) to be in touch by telephone; **c. avec qn** (par lettre) to write to sb, Sout to correspond with sb; (par téléphone) to stay in touch with sb; **l'entreprise correspond avec l'Allemagne** the firm has contacts in Germany

2 (communiquer → pièces) to communicate, to connect
   ❑ **correspondre à** VT IND **1** (équivaloir à) to be equivalent to; **mon rôle correspond à celui d'un de vos "tutors"** my function is equivalent or may be compared to that of what you call a tutor

2 (être conforme à → désir) to correspond to; (→ vérité) to correspond to, to tally with; (→ besoin) to meet; **son attitude correspond à ce qu'on m'en avait dit** his/her attitude fits in with or corresponds to what I was told

3 (être lié à) to correspond to

USAGE ABSOLU (être conforme) **j'ai les vis, mais pas les écrous qui correspondent** I have the screws but I don't have the nuts that go with them or the corresponding nuts
   ▸**se correspondre** VPR **1** (communiquer → salles) to communicate, to connect

2 (être en relation → idées, mots) to correspond; **leurs goûts se correspondent** they have similar or the same tastes

Corrèze [kɔrɛz] NF **(la) C.** the Corrèze

corrézien, -enne [kɔrezjɛ̃, -ɛn] ADJ of/from the Corrèze
   ❑ **Corrézien, -enne** NM,F = inhabitant of or person from the Corrèze

corrida [kɔrida] NF **1** (de taureaux) bullfight **2** Fam (agitation) to-do, Br carry-on; **les gosses font la c. dans leur chambre** the kids are racing or tearing round their bedroom; **cette c. pour la faire s'habiller!** what a performance trying to get her dressed!; **quelle c. hier soir, pour rentrer chez moi!** what a hassle or Br carry-on I had getting home last night! **3 c. pédestre** road race

corridor [kɔridɔr] NM **1** (d'un bâtiment) corridor, passage **2** (territoire) corridor **3 c. humanitaire** (voie de communication) humanitarian corridor

corrigé [kɔriʒe] NM correct version; **faire un c. de qch** to give the correct version of sth; **un c. du problème de physique** a model answer to the physics problem; Com & Écon **c. des variations saisonnières** seasonally adjusted

corriger [17] [kɔriʒe] VT **1** Scol (copie) Br to mark, Am to grade; (en cours) to correct, to give the correct version of

2 (vérifier → texte) to correct, to amend; (→ faute) to correct; Typ to proofread; Journ (article) to sub-edit, to sub

3 (punir) to give a beating or a thrashing to; **cet enfant mérite qu'on le corrige** that child deserves a good hiding; **se faire c.** to get a beating or a thrashing

4 (modifier → vice) to cure; (→ mauvaise habitude) to break; (→ posture, myopie) to correct; (→ comportement) to improve; **c. qch à la hausse/à la baisse** (chiffre) to round sth up/ down; **en données corrigées des variations saisonnières** seasonally-adjusted

cor–cos

5 (*débarrasser*) **c. qn de** (*vice, mauvaise posture*) to cure sb of; (*mauvaise habitude*) to rid sb of

6 (*adoucir → agressivité*) to mitigate; (→ *parole dure*) to soften; **l'ajout de miel corrige l'acidité du fruit** adding honey softens the acid taste of the fruit

7 c. le tir to adjust the firing; *Fig* **corrigeons le tir, je l'accuse non de malveillance mais de négligence** my words are in danger of being distorted, I didn't say he's/she's been malicious, just careless

▸**se corriger VPR 1** (*élève, auteur*) to correct one's (own) work; (*orateur, présentateur*) to correct oneself

2 (*devenir → plus sage*) to improve (one's behaviour); (→ *moins immoral*) to mend one's ways

3 (*se guérir*) **se c. de** (*avarice, paranoïa*) to cure oneself of; (*mauvaise habitude*) to rid oneself of

4 (*être rectifié*) to be put right; **la myopie se corrige avec une bonne paire de lunettes** short-sightedness can be corrected with a good pair of glasses

corrigible [kɔriʒibl] **ADJ** rectifiable
corroboration [kɔrɔbɔrasjɔ̃] **NF** corroboration
corroborer [3] [kɔrɔbɔre] **VT** to corroborate, to confirm
corrodable [kɔrɔdabl] **ADJ** corrodible, corrosible
corrodant, -e [kɔrɔdɑ̃, -ɑ̃t] **ADJ** corrosive
corroder [3] [kɔrɔde] **VT** (*métal*) to corrode, to eat into; (*amitié, bonheur*) to corrode
▸**se corroder VPR** to corrode
corroierie [kɔrwari] **NF 1** (*industrie*) currying **2** (*atelier*) curriery
corrompre [78] [kɔrɔ̃pr] **VT 1** (*vicier → denrée*) to taint, to spoil; (→ *sang*) to taint, to rot; (→ *air*) to taint, to pollute **2** (*pervertir → innocent, enfant*) to corrupt **3** (*soudoyer → fonctionnaire*) to bribe **4** *Littéraire* (*faire dévier → langue, sens*) to distort, to debase **5** *Littéraire* (*troubler → joie, bonheur*) to mar, to taint, to spoil
corrompu, -e [kɔrɔ̃py] **ADJ 1** *Vieilli* (*en décomposition*) rotting **2** (*vil*) corrupt; **des juges corrompus** corrupt judges
corrosif, -ive [kɔrozif, -iv] **ADJ 1** (*satire, auteur*) corrosive, biting, caustic **2** (*acide*) corrosive ▪ **NM** corrosive
corrosion [kɔrozjɔ̃] **NF** *Chim, Géol & Métal* corrosion
corrosive [kɔrosiv] *voir* **corrosif**
corroyage [kɔrwajaʒ] **NM** (*du cuir*) currying; (*du métal*) welding; (*du bois*) rough-planing, trimming
corroyer [13] [kɔrwaje] **VT 1** (*cuir*) to curry **2** (*métal*) to weld **3** (*bois*) to rough-plane, to trim
corroyeur [kɔrwajœr] **NM** currier
corrupteur, -trice [kɔryptœr, -tris] **ADJ** corrupting ▪ **NM,F 1** (*qui soudoie*) briber **2** *Littéraire* (*qui débauche*) corrupter
corruptible [kɔryptibl] **ADJ** corruptible
corruption [kɔrypsjɔ̃] **NF 1** (*vénalité*) corruption; (*fait de soudoyer*) corruption, bribing; **il a tout utilisé, même la c.** he used every available means, including corruption; *Jur* **c. de fonctionnaire** bribery and corruption (*of a civil servant*)

2 (*avilissement → de la jeunesse, d'un innocent*) corruption

3 (*putréfaction → d'un cadavre, d'une substance*) corruption, decomposition, putrefaction

4 *Littéraire* (*déviation → d'une langue, de termes*) distortion, corruption, debasement; **la c. du goût** corruption of taste; **la c. du jugement** distortion of judgement
corruptrice [kɔryptris] *voir* **corrupteur**
corsac [kɔrsak] **NM** *Zool* corsac, Afghan fox
corsage [kɔrsaʒ] **NM** (*blouse*) blouse; (*d'une robe*) bodice
corsaire [kɔrsɛr] **NM 1** (*pirate*) pirate, corsair; **du temps des corsaires** when pirates used to roam the high seas **2** (**pantalon**) **c.** (pair of) pedal pushers
Corse [kɔrs] **NF la C.** Corsica; **vivre en C.** to live in Corsica; **aller en C.** to go to Corsica

---

LA CORSE
Since the 1970s, the Corsican independence movement has become more radical and the FLNC (the Corsican Liberation Movement) is still engaged in a sometimes violent struggle against the French government. In 1982, as part of the law on decentralization, Corsica was attributed a "statut spécial" (special statute) allowing for the election of its own assembly, and became a "collectivité locale" in 1991. However, in 1998 tension between the French authorities and the pro-independence movement reached new heights following the assassination of the prefect of Corsica. In 2003, Corsicans rejected offers of greater autonomy in a referendum, so the problem of the island's status is no nearer to a resolution.

---

corse [kɔrs] **ADJ** Corsican ▪ **NM** (*langue*) Corsican ▫ **Corse NMF** Corsican
corsé, -e [kɔrse] **ADJ 1** (*café*) full-flavoured; (*vin*) full-bodied; (*mets*) spicy; **la sauce est trop corsée** the sauce is too spicy; **l'addition était plutôt corsée!** the bill was a bit steep! **2** (*scabreux*) racy, spicy **3** (*difficile*) **il était c., cet examen!** that exam was a real stinker!
Corse-du-Sud [kɔrsdysyd] **NF la C.** Corse-du-Sud
corselet [kɔrsəlɛ] **NM 1** (*d'une armure*) corselet, corslet **2** *Zool & (vêtement)* corselet
corser [3] [kɔrse] **VT 1** (*compliquer → problème*) to aggravate, to make harder to solve; (→ *exercice*) to complicate

2 (*rendre → plus intéressant*) to liven up; (→ *plus osé*) to make racier; **elle corsait ses récits de détails savoureux** she livened up her stories with spicy details

3 *Culin* to make spicier; (*boisson*) to spike; (*vin*) to strengthen

▸**se corser VPR 1** (*se compliquer*) to get complicated; **c'est là que l'histoire se corse** at this point the story gets really complicated; **l'affaire se corse, ça se corse** the plot thickens

2 (*devenir osé*) to become spicy

3 (*devenir plus intéressant*) to liven up; **vers minuit, au club, les choses se corsaient** the club used to liven up *or* to come to life around midnight
corset [kɔrsɛ] **NM 1** (*sous-vêtement*) corset **2** *Méd* **c. orthopédique** (orthopedic) corset **3** (*d'un arbre*) protective fence **4** *Fig* (*contrainte*) straightjacket
corseter [28] [kɔrsəte] **VT 1** (*institution, jeunesse*) to constrict; **corseté de principes** hemmed in by principles **2** (*personne*) to fit with a corset
corsetier, -ère [kɔrsətje, -ɛr] **NM,F** corsetiere
corso [kɔrso] **NM** procession of floats; **c. fleuri** procession of flowered floats
cortège [kɔrtɛʒ] **NM 1** (*accompagnateurs*) cortege; (*d'un roi*) retinue

2 (*série*) series, succession; **un c. d'échecs** a series of failures; **tout le c. des maladies infantiles** the full complement of childhood diseases; **la guerre et son c. de malheurs** the war and its attendant tragedies

3 (*défilé*) procession; **un long c. de fourmis** a long trail of ants; **c. (de voitures)** motorcade; **un c. de manifestants** a march (of protesters); **le c. allait de la Bastille à la République** the demonstration stretched from the Bastille to the Place de la République; **défiler en c.** to go past in a procession, to process past; **c. funèbre** funeral cortege *or* procession; **c. nuptial** bridal procession
Cortes [kɔrtɛs] **NFPL** Cortes
cortex [kɔrtɛks] **NM** cortex; **c. cérébral** cerebral cortex
cortical, -e, -aux, -ales [kɔrtikal, -o] **ADJ** cortical ▫ **corticale NF** cortex
corticoïde [kɔrtikɔid], **corticostéroïde** [kɔrtikɔsteroid] *Méd* **ADJ** corticoid, corticosteroid ▪ **NM** corticoid, corticosteriod
corticostimuline [kɔrtikɔstimylin] **NF** *Physiol* corticotrop(h)in, adrenocorticotropic hormone
corticosurrénal, -e, -aux, -ales [kɔrtikɔsyrenal, -o] *Anat* **ADJ** adrenocortical ▫ **corticosurrénale NF** adrenal cortex

corticothérapie [kɔrtikɔterapi] **NF** *Méd* corticotherapy
cortinaire [kɔrtinɛr] **NM** *Bot* cortinarius
cortine [kɔrtin] **NF 1** *Bot* cortina **2** *Physiol* cortin
cortisol [kɔrtisɔl] **NM** *Biol & Chim* hydrocortisone, cortisol
cortisone [kɔrtizon] **NF** *Biol & Chim* cortisone
cortisonique [kɔrtizonik] **ADJ** *Biol & Chim* **1** (*relatif à la cortisone*) cortisone (*avant n*) **2** (*dérivé*) cortisone-based
corton [kɔrtɔ̃] **NM** (*vin*) Corton (*variety of red Burgundy wine*)
coruscant, -e [kɔryskɑ̃, -ɑ̃t] **ADJ** *Littéraire* coruscating, glittering; **dames en toilettes coruscantes** ladies in dazzling finery
corvéable [kɔrveabl] *Hist* **ADJ** liable to the corvée ▪ **NMF** vassal who is liable to the corvée
corvée [kɔrve] **NF 1** (*activité pénible*) chore; **les corvées ménagères** the household chores; **repasser, quelle c.!** ironing's such a chore *or* a drag!

2 (*service*) duty; *Mil* fatigue; **être de c.** (*soldat*) to be on fatigue duty; **être de c.** *Fam* **de pluches/** *très Fam* **de chiottes** to be on spud-peeling/on latrine duty; *Hum* **c'est toujours la mère qui est de c.** it's always the mother who has to do everything; **on est de c. de vaisselle** we're on dishwashing duty

3 *Suisse* (*travaux d'intérêt public*) voluntary community work

4 *Hist* corvée
corvette [kɔrvɛt] **NF** corvette
corvidé [kɔrvide] **NM** member of the crow family *or Spéc* Corvidae
corybante [kɔribɑ̃t] **NM** *Antiq* Corybant
corymbe [kɔrɛ̃b] **NM** *Bot* corymb
coryphée [kɔrife] **NM 1** *Antiq* coryphaeus **2** *Mus* choirmaster **3** (*en danse*) coryphee
coryphène [kɔrifɛn] **NF** *Ich* dolphin (fish)
coryza [kɔriza] **NM** head cold, *Spéc* coryza
COS [seɔɛs] **NM 1** *Gram* (*abrév* **complément d'objet second**) prepositional complement **2** *Constr* (*abrév* **coefficient d'occupation des sols**) plot ratio
Cos [kɔs] **NM** Kos
cosaque [kɔzak] **NM** Cossack
coscénariste [kosenarist] **NMF** *Cin* co-scriptwriter
cosécante [kosekɑ̃t] **NF** *Math* cosecant
Cosette [kozɛt] **NPR** = the persecuted girl in Hugo's 'les Misérables' who is saved by Jean Valjean, a symbol of innocence and vulnerability
cosignataire [kosiɲatɛr] **NMF** cosignatory
cosigner [3] [kosiɲe] **VT** to cosign
cosinus [kosinys] **NM** *Math* cosine
cosmétique [kɔsmetik] **ADJ** cosmetic ▪ **NM** cosmetic
cosmétologie [kɔsmetolɔʒi] **NF** cosmetology
cosmétologue [kɔsmetɔlɔg] **NMF** cosmetologist
cosmique [kɔsmik] **ADJ** *Astron* cosmic
cosmodrome [kɔsmodrom] **NM** cosmodrome
cosmogonie [kɔsmogoni] **NF** cosmogony
cosmogonique [kɔsmogonik] **ADJ** cosmogonic, cosmogonical
cosmographe [kɔsmograf] **NMF** cosmographer
cosmographie [kɔsmografi] **NF** cosmography
cosmographique [kɔsmografik] **ADJ** cosmographic, cosmographical
cosmologie [kɔsmolɔʒi] **NF** cosmology
cosmologique [kɔsmolɔʒik] **ADJ** cosmologic, cosmological
cosmologiste [kɔsmolɔʒist], **cosmologue** [kɔsmolog] **NM** cosmologist
cosmonaute [kɔsmonot] **NMF** cosmonaut
cosmopolite [kɔsmopolit] **ADJ 1** (*ville, foule*) cosmopolitan, multi-ethnic **2** (*personne*) cosmopolitan, international **3** *Bot & Zool* ubiquitous ▪ **NMF** cosmopolitan person
cosmopolitisme [kɔsmopolitism] **NM 1** (*d'une personne*) cosmopolitanism, internationalism **2** (*d'un lieu*) cosmopolitan air
cosmos [kɔsmos] **NM** (*univers*) cosmos; (*espace*) space, outer space
cossard, -e [kɔsar, -ard] *très Fam* **ADJ** lazy ▪ **NM,F** lazybones
cosse [kɔs] **NF 1** *Bot* pod, husk; (*de pois*) shell **2** *Élec* cable terminal **3** *Naut* eye **4** *très Fam* (*locution*) **avoir la c.** to feel lazy

cosser [3] [kɔse] **VI** *(béliers)* to butt; **c. contre qch** to ram one's head against sth
cossette [kɔsɛt] **NF c. (de betterave)** cossette
cossins [kɔsɛ̃] **NMPL** *Can (effets)* things, stuff, gear
cossu, -e [kɔsy] **ADJ** *(famille)* affluent, well-off, wealthy; *(quartier)* affluent, moneyed; *(maison, pièce)* luxurious
cossus [kɔsys] **NM** *Entom* cossus
Costa Brava [kɔstabrava] **NF la C.** the Costa Brava; **sur la C.** on the Costa Brava
Costa del Sol [kɔstadɛlsɔl] **NF la C.** the Costa del Sol; **sur la C.** on the Costa del Sol
costal, -e, -aux, -ales [kɔstal, -o] **ADJ** rib *(avant n)*, *Spéc* costal
costard [kɔstar] **NM** *Fam* suit▪; *Hum* **c. de sapin** wooden overcoat
costard-cravate [kɔstarkravat] *(pl* **costards-cravates)** **NM** *Fam (costume)* suit▪; *(personne)* **un (homme en) c.** a man in a suit▪, a suit
costarde [kɔstard] **NF** *Can* confectioner's custard
Costa Rica [kɔstarika] **NM le C.** Costa Rica; **vivre au C.** to live in Costa Rica; **aller au C.** to go to Costa Rica
costaricain, -e [kɔstarikɛ̃, -ɛn] **ADJ** Costa Rican
❑ **Costaricain, -e NM,F** Costa Rican
costaricien, -enne [kɔstarisjɛ̃, -ɛn] **ADJ** Costa Rican
❑ **Costaricien, -enne NM,F** Costa Rican
costaud, -e [kɔsto, -od] *Fam* **ADJ 1** *(personne)* hefty, beefy; **elle est c.** *ou* **costaude** she's pretty hefty; **un type c.** a great hulk of a *Br* bloke *or Am* guy
2 *(meuble, arbre, tissu)* strong, tough, resilient
3 *(problème)* tough; **c'est c., comme bouquin!** it's pretty solid stuff, that book!
4 *(alcool)* strong, robust; *(café)* strong; *(plat)* hot, spicy; *(épices)* hot
NM,F big guy, *f* girl
NM c'est du c. it's solid stuff
costière [kɔstjɛr] **NF 1** *Métal* tuyère-sides, twyer-sides, side hearthstones **2** *Théât* cut *(in stage flooring)*
costume [kɔstym] **NM 1** *(complet)* suit; **c. trois-pièces** three-piece suit **2** *(tenue)* costume; **en c. de cérémonie** in ceremonial costume *or* dress; **c. régional/national** regional/national dress; **en c. d'Adam/d'Ève** in his/her birthday suit; *Vieilli & Can & Suisse* **c. de bain** *(de femme) Br* swimsuit, swimming costume, *Am* bathing suit; *(d'homme) Br* swimming trunks, *Am* swim shorts; *Fam Hum* **un c. en sapin** a wooden overcoat **3** *Hist & Théât* costume; **l'histoire du c.** the history of costume
costumé, -e [kɔstyme] **ADJ des enfants costumés** children in fancy dress; **bal c.** fancy-dress ball
costume-cravate [kɔstymkravat] *(pl* **costumes-cravates)** **NM** *Fam* **un (homme en) c.** a man in a suit▪, a suit
costumer [3] [kɔstyme] **VT c. qn en Pierrot** to dress sb up as a Pierrot
▶**se costumer VPR** to wear fancy dress; **se c. en diable** to dress up as a devil
costumier, -ère [kɔstymje, -ɛr] **NM,F 1** *(vendeur, loueur)* costumier, costumer **2** *Théât* wardrobe master, *f* mistress; *Cin* costume supervisor
cosy [kɔzi] **ADJ INV** cosy
NM *Vieilli* = bed with built-in shelves running along the headboard and down one side
cosy(-corner) [kɔzi(-kɔrnɛr)] *(pl* **cosy-corners)** **NM** = corner divan-bed surrounded by right-angle book-shelves and cupboards
cotable [kɔtabl] **ADJ** *Bourse* quotable
cotangente [kɔtɑ̃ʒɑ̃t] **NF** *Math* cotangent
cotation [kɔtasjɔ̃] **NF 1** *Bourse* quotation, listing; **c. assistée en continu** automated quotation; **c. en continu** continuous trading; **c. à la corbeille** floor trading; **c. au cours du marché** market quotation; **c. à la criée** open-outcry trading; **c. de l'or** gold fixing; **c. par téléphone** telephone dealing; **c. à vue** spot quotation
2 *Archit & Constr* **c. fonctionnelle** = illustration of the most important dimensions of machine parts in a drawing
cote [kɔt] **NF 1** *Bourse (valeur)* quotation; *(liste)* share (price) index; **inscrit à la c.** *(valeurs)* listed; **retirer de la c.** *(société, action)* to delist; **hors c.** *(actions)* unlisted; *(marché) Br* unofficial, *Am* over-the-counter; **c. de clôture** closing price; **c. officielle** official list; **c. des prix** official list, official share list
2 *Com* quoted value
3 *Courses de chevaux* odds
4 *(estime)* **c. d'amour** *ou* **de popularité** *(d'un homme politique)* standing with the electorate, (popular) rating, popularity; *(d'un film, d'une idée)* (popular) rating; *Fam* **avoir la c. (avec)** to be popular (with)
5 *Archit, Constr & (en travaux publics)* measurement
6 *Géog* height; **c. d'alerte** flood *or* danger level; *Fig* crisis *or* flash point; **la c. d'alerte est atteinte** we're at flash point
7 *(taille)* (indication of) dimensions
8 *(dans une bibliothèque → sur un livre)* shelf mark, *Am* call number; *(→ sur un périodique)* serial mark
9 *Admin* assessment; **c. mobilière** property assessment *or* rate; **c. mal taillée** awkward compromise
10 *Belg (note scolaire) Br* mark, *Am* grade
coté, -e [kɔte] **ADJ** *(prisé → quartier)* sought-after; *(→ produit)* highly rated; **un architecte/gynécologue c.** an architect/a gynaecologist who's (much) in demand; **être bien/mal c.** to have a good/bad reputation; **elle est bien cotée** she's highly thought of; **il est mal c.** he has a very poor reputation
côte [kot] **NF 1** *(hauteur)* slope, incline; *(à monter, à descendre)* hill; **monter la c.** to go uphill; **descendre la c.** to go downhill; **en haut de la c.** on the top of the hill
2 *(rivage)* coast; *(vu d'avion, sur une carte)* coastline; **ils vivent sur la c.** they live on the coast; **on a fait toute la c.** we went all around the coast; **la C.** the (French) Riviera; **la C. d'Amour** = the Atlantic coast near La Baule; **la C. d'Argent** = the Atlantic coast between the Gironde and Bidassoa estuaries; **la C. d'Azur** the French Riviera; **aller sur la C. d'Azur** to go to the south of France *or* the French Riviera; **la C. de Coromandel** the Coromandel Coast; **la C. d'Émeraude** = part of the northern French coast, near Saint-Malo; **la C. de Malabar** the Malabar Coast; **la C. d'Opale** = the coast between Calais and Dieppe; **la C. Vermeille** = part of the Mediterranean coast, between Collioure and Cerbère
3 *Anat* rib; **vraie/fausse c.** true/false rib; **c. flottante** floating rib; **on lui voit les côtes** he's/she's nothing but skin and bone; *Fam* **se tenir les côtes (de rire)** to be in stitches; *Fam* **caresser** *ou* **chatouiller les côtes à qn** to give sb a good hiding; *Fam* **avoir les côtes en long** to be bone idle
4 *(de porc, d'agneau, de veau)* chop; *(de bœuf)* rib; **côtes découvertes** middle neck; **c. première** *(de veau)* shoulder chop; *(d'agneau) Br* lamb chop, *Am* loin chop; **c. seconde** *(d'agneau) Br* neck cutlet, *Am* rib chop
5 *Archit, Bot & Tex* rib; **c. de bette** rib of beet *or* chard; **point de côtes** ribbing stitch; **un pull à côtes** a ribbed sweater
6 *Naut* **aller à la c.** to hug the coast; **faire c.** to beach, to run aground; **c. moins/plus 500** 500 below/above sea level; **la c. 304** hill 304
❑ **côte-à-côte ADV** *(marcher, s'asseoir)* side by side; *(travailler, lutter)* side by side, shoulder to shoulder

CÔTÉ [kote] **NM 1** *(d'un tissu, d'une médaille)* side; **le c. humide du mur** the damp side of the wall; **une feuille de papier écrite des deux côtés** a sheet of paper written on on both sides
2 *(d'un jardin, d'une pièce, d'une rue, d'un rectangle)* side; **ton c. du lit** your side of the bed; **le c. sud de la ville** the south side *or* part of town; **il y a un arbre de chaque c.** there's a tree (on) each side; **de quel c.?** *(direction)* in which direction?, which way?; *(position)* which side?; **allons de ce c.-ci** let's go this way; **on voit mieux de ce c.-là** you can see better from that side; **la tour penche d'un c.** the tower leans to one side *or* leans sideways; **ta jupe est plus longue d'un c. que de l'autre** your skirt is longer on one side than (on) the other; *aussi Fig* **de ce/de l'autre c. de la barrière** on this side/on the other side of the fence; *Théât* **c. cour** stage left, *Br* prompt side; *Théât* **c. jardin** stage right, *Br* opposite prompt side; **appartement c. jardin** *Br* flat *or Am* apartment overlooking the garden; *Rugby* **c. ouvert** open side; **c. piste** *(d'un aéroport)* air side; *Naut* **c. sous le vent** leeward side; *Naut* **c. du vent** windward side; *Fig* **voir de quel c. vient le vent** to see which way the wind blows; **tomber du c. où ça penche** to follow one's inclinations
3 *(du corps)* side; **il a le c. gauche entièrement paralysé** his left side is completely paralysed; **dormir sur le c.** to sleep on one's side; **recevoir un coup au c.** to be hit in the side; **une douleur au c.** a pain in the side; **aux côtés de qn** at *or* by sb's side
4 *(parti)* side; **il s'est mis de mon c.** he sided with me; **se ranger du c. du plus fort** to side with the strongest; **il a toujours été du c. des opprimés** he's always been on the side of *or* sided with the oppressed; **je suis de ton c.** I'm on your side; **être aux côtés de qn** to be by sb's side
5 *(aspect)* side; **le c. publicité** the advertising side (of things); **de ce c. il n'y a rien à craindre** there's nothing to worry about on that score; *Fam* **c. travail** on the work front, workwise; **c. repos, ça aurait pu être mieux** on the relaxation side *or* front, it could have been better
6 *(facette → d'une personnalité)* side, facet; *(→ d'une situation)* side, aspect; **elle a un c. naïf** there's a naive side to her; **il a un c. méchant** there's a mean streak in him, there's a nasty side to him; **c'est son c. paternel qui ressort** it's the paternal streak in him *or* his paternal side coming out; **chaque emploi a ses bons et ses mauvais côtés** every job has its good and bad sides *or* points; **prendre qch du bon/mauvais c.** to take sth in good/bad part; **les bons côtés de la vie** the good things in life; **voir le bon c. des choses** to look on the bright side; **d'un c.** in a way, in some respects; **d'un c...., d'un autre c....** on the one hand..., on the other hand...
7 *(dans la famille)* side; **sa tante du c. maternel** his/her aunt on his/her mother's side; *Vieilli* **être né du c. gauche** to be born out of wedlock
❑ **à côté ADV 1** *(tout près)* next door; *(pas très loin)* nearby; **les voisins d'à c.** the next-door neighbours; **si vous voulez bien passer à c.** if you'd like to go that way
2 *(mal)* **passer** *ou* **tomber à c.** to miss; **elle a répondu à c.** *(exprès)* she avoided the question; *(involontairement)* her answer was not to the point
❑ **à côté de PRÉP 1** *(pas loin)* next to; **le salon est à c. de la cuisine** the living room is next to the kitchen; **à c. l'un de l'autre** side by side; **à c. de la cible** off target; **passer à c. de** *(chemin, difficulté, porte)* to miss; *(occasion)* to miss out on; **il est passé à c. du sujet** he missed the point; **il est passé à c. du bonheur** he missed out on happiness; **à c. de ça** on the other hand; *Fam* **être à c. de la plaque** to have got (hold of) the wrong end of the stick
2 *(par rapport à)* by *or* in comparison with; **il fait plutôt avare à c. de son frère** he seems rather mean compared to his brother
❑ **de côté ADJ** *(regard)* sidelong **ADV 1** *(regarder)* sideways; *(sauter, tomber)* aside, to one side; **la casquette posée de c.** the cap worn to *or* on one side; **avoir une raie de c.** to have a side *Br* parting *or Am* part **2** *(en réserve)* aside, to one side; **mettre qch de c.** to put sth aside *or* by; **j'ai 5000 euros de c.** I've got 5,000 euros put by; **laisser qch de c.** to put sth to one side; **laisser qn de c.** to leave sb out
❑ **de mon/son/***etc* **côté ADV 1** *(séparément)* **ils s'en allèrent chacun de son c.** they went their separate ways; **vivre chacun de son c.** to live separately
2 *(en ce qui concerne)* for my/his/*etc* part
3 *(de la famille)* on my/his/*etc* side of the family
❑ **de tous côtés ADV 1** *(partout → courir)* everywhere, all over the place; *(→ chercher)* everywhere, high and low; *(→ être cerné)* on all sides
2 *(de partout)* from all sides *or* directions
❑ **du côté de PRÉP 1** *(dans l'espace)* **elle est partie du c. du village** she went towards the village; **du c. de chez toi** around where you live; **il habitait du c. de la rivière** he lived near the river; **la maison est située du c. sud de la baie**

the house is on the south side of the bay; **le vent vient du c. de la mer** the wind's blowing from the sea

2 *(parmi)* **cherchons du c. des auteurs classiques** let's look among classical authors

❑ **d'un côté à l'autre** ADV from side to side

❑ **d'un côté et de l'autre** ADV here and there

'Du Côté de chez Swann' *Proust* 'Swann's Way'

---

coteau, -x [kɔto] NM **1** *(versant)* hillside, slope **2** *(colline)* hill

❑ **coteaux** NMPL vineyards *(on a hillside)*

Côte-de-l'Or [kotdəlɔr] NF **la C.** the Gold Coast

Côte-d'Ivoire [kotdivwar] NF **la C.** Côte-d'Ivoire, the Ivory Coast; **vivre en C.** to live in Côte-d'Ivoire *or* in the Ivory Coast; **aller en C.** to go to Côte-d'Ivoire *or* the Ivory Coast

Côte-d'Or [kotdɔr] NF **(la) C.** the Côte-d'Or

côtelé, -e [kotle] ADJ ribbed

côtelette [kotlɛt] NF **1** *(de viande)* **c. d'agneau** lamb chop; **côtelettes découvertes** *(d'agneau)* ≃ middle of neck; **côtelettes premières** *(d'agneau)* ≃ best end of neck **2** *Fam (d'une personne)* rib▪; **en plein dans les côtelettes** slap bang in the ribcage

coter [3] [kɔte] VT **1** *Bourse* to list (on the share index); **coté en Bourse** ≃ listed on the Stock Exchange; **des valeurs qui seront cotées en Bourse demain** ≃ shares which will go on the Stock Exchange tomorrow; **être coté à 25 euros** to be trading at 25 euros

2 *Com* to price, to give a list price for; **ma voiture n'est plus cotée à l'argus** my car's not listed in the car buyer's guide any more

3 *(évaluer → œuvre d'art)* to rate

4 *(dans une bibliothèque → livre)* to assign a class *or* shelf mark to; *(→ périodique)* to assign a serial mark to

5 *Géog* to write in the heights on

6 *Archit, Constr & (en travaux publics → dessin)* to mark the dimensions on; *(→ carte)* to put references on; **un croquis coté** a dimensioned sketch

VI **les actions Rivetti cotaient autour de 22 euros** Rivetti shares were listed at around 22 euros

coterie [kɔtri] NF *Péj* set, clique

Côtes-d'Armor [kotdarmɔr] NFPL **les C.** the Côtes-d'Armor

Côtes-du-Nord [kotdynɔr] NFPL = former name for Côtes-d'Armor

côtes-du-Rhône [kotdyron] NM INV *(vin)* Côtes-du-Rhône

coteur [kɔtœr] NM *Bourse* jobber

cothurne [kɔtyrn] NM buskin, cothurnus; *Littéraire* **chausser le c.** *(écrire)* to write tragedies; *(jouer)* to act in tragedy; *(simuler)* to affect a tragic manner

cotice [kɔtis] NF *Hér* cotise, cottise

cotidal, -e, -aux, -ales [kɔtidal, -o] ADJ co-tidal

côtier, -ère [kotje, -ɛr] ADJ *(région, navigation)* coastal; *(pêche)* inshore; *(chemin)* coast *(avant n)*; **un fleuve c.** a coastal river

cotignac [kɔtiɲak] NM quince preserve

cotillon [kɔtijɔ̃] NM **1** *Arch ou Hum (jupon)* petticoat **2** *(farandole)* cotillion, cotillon

❑ **cotillons** NMPL party novelties

cotinga [kɔtɛ̃ga] NM *Orn* cotinga

cotir [32] [kɔtir] VT *(fruit)* to bruise

cotisant, -e [kɔtizɑ̃, -ɑ̃t] ADJ contributing

NM,F *(à une association)* subscriber; *(à une assurance, à une fête)* contributor

cotisation [kɔtizasjɔ̃] NF *(pour une fête)* contribution; *(à une association)* subscription, dues; *(pour la protection sociale)* contribution; **c. chômage** unemployment contribution; **cotisations maladie** health insurance contributions; **c. ouvrière** employee's contribution; **c. patronale** employer's contribution; **c. à la Sécurité sociale** ≃ National Insurance contribution; **cotisations sociales** ≃ National Insurance and National Health contributions; **c. syndicale** union dues; **c. vieillesse** pension contribution

cotiser [3] [kɔtize] VI *(à une association)* to subscribe; *(à la Sécurité sociale)* to pay one's contributions; **c. à une caisse de retraite** to contribute to a pension fund

▸**se cotiser** VPR to club together; **le groupe s'est cotisé** everyone in the group contributed

cotitulaire [kotitylɛr] ADJ **être c. d'un droit** to be jointly entitled to a right

NMF **les cotitulaires d'un droit** the persons jointly entitled to a right

côtoie *etc voir* **côtoyer**

côtoiement [kotwamɑ̃] NM contact; **le c. du danger** contact with danger

coton [kɔtɔ̃] NM **1** *Bot (fibre, culture)* cotton; *(plante)* cotton plant

2 *Tex (tissu)* cotton; *(fil)* (cotton) thread, piece of cotton; **de c.** *(vêtements)* cotton; *(fil)* sewing; **c. à broder** embroidery thread; **c. égyptien** Egyptian cotton; **c. à repriser** darning thread *or* cotton; *Can Fam Fig* **être au c.** to be at one's wits' end, to be at the end of one's rope

3 *(ouate)* **c. (hydrophile)** *Br* cotton wool, *Am* (absorbent) cotton; *Fam* **avoir du c. dans les oreilles** to be cloth-eared

4 *(tampon de ouate)* *Br* cotton wool pad, *Am* cotton pad

ADJ *Fam* tough, tricky; **c'est (plutôt) c.!** it's (rather) tough *or* tricky!

cotonéaster [kɔtɔneastɛr] NM *Bot* cotoneaster

cotonnade [kɔtɔnad] NF cotton fabric, cottonade

cotonner [3] [kɔtɔne] **se cotonner** VPR *(tissu)* to fluff (up); *(fruit)* to go like cotton-wool

cotonnerie [kɔtɔnri] NF **1** *(culture)* cotton-growing **2** *(terrain)* cotton plantation **3** *(fabrique)* cotton mill

cotonneux, -euse [kɔtɔnø, -øz] ADJ **1** *Bot* downy **2** *Littéraire (vaporeux → nuages)* fleecy; **un ciel c.** a cotton-wool sky **3** *(sourd → bruit)* muffled **4** *(texture → fruit)* mushy

cotonnier, -ère [kɔtɔnje, -ɛr] ADJ cotton *(avant n)*

NM,F cotton spinner

NM cotton (plant)

coton-poudre [kɔtɔ̃pudr] *(pl* **cotons-poudres***)* NM *Br* guncotton, *Am* nitrocotton

Coton-Tige® [kɔtɔ̃tiʒ] *(pl* **Cotons-Tiges***)* NM *Br* cotton bud, *Am* Q-tip®

Cotopaxi [kɔtopaksi] N *Géog* **le C.** Cotopaxi

côtoyer [13] [kotwaje] VT **1** *(fréquenter)* to mix with

2 *(être confronté à)* to deal with; **elle côtoie le danger tous les jours** she faces danger every day; **ce travail me fait c. des gens intéressants** I meet some interesting people in this job; **cette expérience lui a fait c. la misère** this experience brought him/her face to face with poverty

3 *(sujet: chemin)* to skirt *or* to run alongside; *(sujet: fleuve)* to flow *or* to run alongside

4 *(friser)* **cela côtoie le ridicule** it's verging *or* bordering on the ridiculous

▸**se côtoyer** VPR *(personnes)* to rub shoulders; **on se côtoie constamment au travail** we see each other all the time at work

cotre [kɔtr] NM *Naut* cutter

cotriade [kɔtrijad] NF *Culin* fish soup

cottage [kɔtaʒ] NM (country) cottage

cotte[1] [kɔt] NF **1** *Hist* **c. d'armes** coat of arms; **c. de mailles** coat of mail **2** *(bleu de travail)* *Br* overalls, *Am* coveralls; *(sans manches)* *Br* dungarees, *Am* overalls **3** *Arch (jupon)* petticoat

cotte[2] [kɔt] NM *Ich* miller's-thumb, bull-head, *Spéc* cottus

cotutelle [kotytɛl] NF *Jur* joint guardianship

cotuteur, -trice [kotytœr, -tris] NM,F *Jur* joint guardian

cotyle [kɔtil] NF **1** *Antiq* cotyle **2** *Anat* cotyle, cotyla, acetabulum

cotylédon [kɔtiledɔ̃] NM *Anat & Bot* cotyledon

cotyloïde [kɔtilɔid] ADJ *Anat* cotyloid

cou [ku] NM **1** *Anat* neck; **un pendentif autour du c.** a pendant round her neck; **sauter** *ou* **se jeter au c. de qn** to throw one's arms around sb's neck; **se casser** *ou* **se rompre le c.** to break one's neck; *Fig* to take a tumble, *Br* to come a cropper; **il y est jusqu'au c.** he's up to his neck in it; **endetté jusqu'au c.** up to one's eyes in debt **2** *Zool* neck **3** *(d'un vêtement)* neck **4** *(d'une bouteille, d'un vase)* neck

couac [kwak] NM *(note)* false note; *Fig* discordant note; **faire un c.** *(chanteur)* to hit the wrong note; *(musicien)* to play the wrong note

ONOMAT arrk, quack

couard, -e [kwar, -ard] *Littéraire* ADJ cowardly

NM,F coward, poltroon

couardise [kwardiz] NF *Littéraire* cowardice

couchage [kuʃaʒ] NM *(lit)* bed; *(préparatifs)* sleeping arrangements; **matériel de c.** bedding

couchailler [3] [kuʃaje] VI *Fam Péj* to sleep around

couchant, -e [kuʃɑ̃, -ɑ̃t] ADJ *voir* **chien, soleil**

NM *(coucher de soleil)* sunset; *Littéraire (occident)* west

couche [kuʃ] NF **1** *(épaisseur → de peinture)* coat; *(→ de maquillage)* layer; *(→ de glace)* sheet; **passer une c. de peinture sur qch** to give sth a coat of paint; **étaler qch en couches épaisses/fines** to spread sth thickly/thinly; **c. d'apprêt** priming coat; **c. de fond** undercoat; *Fam* **avoir** *ou* **en tenir une c.** *Br* to be (as) thick as a brick *or* as two short planks, *Am* to be as dumb as they come

2 *Astron & Géol* layer, stratum; **c. d'ozone** ozone layer; **préserve la c. d'ozone** *(sur emballage)* ozone-friendly

3 *(en sociologie)* **c. sociale** level, social stratum

4 *Hort* hotbed

5 *(de bébé)* *Br* nappy, *Am* diaper; **c. jetable** disposable *Br* nappy *or Am* diaper

6 *Littéraire (lit)* bed

❑ **couches** NFPL *Vieilli (accouchement)* confinement; **être en couches** to be in labour; **elle est morte en couches** she died in childbirth

couché, -e [kuʃe] ADJ **1** *(allongé)* lying down; *(au lit)* in bed; **c.!** *(à un chien)* (lie) down! **2** *(écriture)* slanting, sloping **3** *(pli)* recumbent

couche-culotte [kuʃkylɔt] *(pl* **couches-culottes***)* NF disposable *Br* nappy *or Am* diaper

coucher[1] [kuʃe] NM **1** *(action)* going to bed; **le c. est à onze heures** bedtime is at eleven o'clock; **le c. du roi** the king's going-to-bed ceremony; **le c. d'un enfant** a child's bedtime routine

2 *(moment)* bedtime; **deux cachets au c.** *(sur mode d'emploi)* two tablets to be taken at bedtime *or* before bed; *Littéraire* **la lune à son c.** the setting moon; **c. de soleil** sunset; **au c. du soleil** at sunset, *Am* at sundown

3 *(gîte)* accommodation; **le c. et la nourriture** board and lodging

coucher[2] [3] [kuʃe] VT **1** *(mettre au lit)* to put to bed; *(allonger)* to lay down; *Fam* **c. qn sur le carreau** to knock sb down, to lay sb out

2 *(héberger)* to put up, to accommodate; **on peut c. toute la famille** we can accommodate the entire family; **la caravane peut c. cinq personnes** the camping-car can accommodate *or* sleep five; **je ne peux pas vous c.** I can't put you up

3 *(poser → par terre)* to lay down; **c. une bouteille/moto** to lay a bottle/motorbike on its side; **la pluie a couché les herbes** the rain flattened the grasses; **l'orage a couché les arbres** the storm brought the trees down; **des poteaux couchés en travers de la route** poles lying across the road; **le vent coucha le bateau** the wind made the boat keel over *or* keeled the boat over; **c. un fusil en joue** to aim a gun; **c. qn en joue** to (take) aim at sb

4 *(écrire)* to set down (in writing); **c. ses pensées sur le papier** to write down one's thoughts, *Sout* to commit one's thoughts to writing; **c. qn sur son testament** to name sb in one's will; **c. qn sur une liste** to include sb's name in a list

VI **1** *(aller dormir)* to go to bed; **cela va te faire c. tard** that will keep you up late

2 *(dormir)* to sleep; **on couchera à l'hôtel** *(une nuit)* we'll spend the night *or* we'll sleep in a hotel; *(plusieurs nuits)* we'll stay in a hotel; **les deux enfants couchent au grenier** the two children sleep in the attic; **tu restes c.?** are you staying overnight *or* the night?; **c. à la belle étoile** to sleep out in the open; **c. sous les ponts** to sleep rough; **la voiture couche dehors** the car stays in the street at night

3 *très Fam (sexuellement)* to sleep around; **ils couchent ensemble** they're sleeping together

❑ **coucher avec** VT IND *Fam* to go to bed with, to sleep with

▸**se coucher** VPR **1** *(dans un lit)* to go to bed; **je vous empêche de vous c.?** am I keeping you up?; **je ne veux pas vous faire c. tard** I don't want to keep you up; *Fam* **va te c.!** get lost *or Br* stuffed!; *Fam* **se c. comme** *ou* **avec les poules** to go to bed early▪

2 *(s'allonger)* to lie down; **se c. en chien de fusil** to lie curled up *or* in the foetal position; **se c. à plat ventre** to lie face down *or* flat on one's stomach; **il se couchait sur sa copie pour que je ne puisse pas la lire** he was leaning over his work so I couldn't read it; **se c. sur son guidon** to lean hard against one's handlebars

3 *(soleil, lune)* to set, to go down

4 *Naut* to keel over

coucherie [kuʃri] **NF** *Fam* sleeping around, casual sex■; **qui s'intéresse à leurs coucheries?** who's interested in their sexual goings-on *or* in who they go to bed with?

couche-tard [kuʃtar] **NMF INV** night owl; **c'est un c.** he's always late to bed, he's a night owl

couche-tôt [kuʃto] **NMF INV c'est un c.** he always goes to bed early

couchette [kuʃɛt] **NF** *(d'un train)* couchette; *(d'un bateau)* bunk; *Can Fam* **être fort sur la c.** to bed-hop

coucheur, -euse [kuʃœr, -øz] **NM,F** *Fam* **c'est un c.** he sleeps around; **mauvais c.** awkward customer

couchis [kuʃi] **NM** *Constr (d'un revêtement de sol)* sand bed; *(d'un plancher)* floor grid; *(d'une voûte)* lagging

couchitique [kuʃitik] *Ling* **ADJ** Cushitic, Kushitic
NM Cushite, Kushite

couchoir [kuʃwar] **NM** = cone-shaped tool made of ebony used to twist the strands together in rope-making

couci-couça [kusikusa] **ADV** *Fam* so-so

coucou [kuku] **NM 1** *Orn* cuckoo; **c. terrestre de Californie** roadrunner **2 (pendule à) c.** cuckoo clock **3** *Bot* cowslip **4** *Fam (avion)* crate, heap
EXCLAM 1 *(bonjour)* hi! **2** *(en langage enfantin)* peekaboo!, coo-ee!

coucoumelle [kukumɛl] **NF** *Bot* grisette

coude [kud] **NM 1** *Anat* elbow; **coudes au corps** elbows in; **jusqu'au c.** up to one's elbow; **faire du c. à qn** to nudge sb; **jouer des coudes** to push and shove, to jostle; *Fig* to manoeuvre; **les gens jouaient des coudes pour atteindre le guichet** people were pushing and shoving to get to the kiosk; **j'ai dû jouer des coudes pour parvenir au bar** I had to elbow my way to the bar; **c. à c.** *(marcher, travailler)* shoulder to shoulder, side by side; **garder** *ou* **mettre** *ou* **tenir qch sous le c.** to keep sth shelved indefinitely, to keep sth on the back burner; *Fam* **lever le c.** to booze; **se serrer** *ou* **se tenir les coudes** to stick together

2 *(d'un vêtement)* elbow; *(pièce en cuir, en tissu)* elbow patch

3 *(d'un tuyau)* bend, elbow; *(d'une route)* bend; **le couloir fait un c.** there's a sharp bend in the passage

coudé, -e [kude] **ADJ** bent, angled
❑ **coudée NF 1** *Arch (mesure)* cubit **2** *(locutions)* **avoir les coudées franches** to have elbow room; **être à cent coudées au-dessus de qn** to be head and shoulders above sb

coude-à-coude [kudakud] ❑ **au coude-à-coude ADV** neck and neck

cou-de-pied [kudpje] *(pl* **cous-de-pied***)* **NM** *Anat* instep

couder [3] [kude] **VT** to bend (at an angle)

coudière [kudjɛr] **NF** elbow pad

coudoie *etc voir* **coudoyer**

coudoiement [kudwamɑ̃] **NM** *Sout (fréquentation)* rubbing shoulders; **le c. des stars lui a donné des idées** rubbing shoulders with the stars has given him/her ideas

coudou [kudu] **NM** *Zool* kudu

coudoyer [13] [kudwaje] **VT 1** *(fréquenter)* to rub shoulders *or* to mix with; *Fig (sujet: idée, image)* to stand side by side with **2** *(frôler)* to brush past

coudraie [kudrɛ] **NF** hazel grove

coudre [86] [kudr] **VT 1** *(ourlet)* to sew, to stitch; *(robe)* to make up; *(morceaux)* to sew *or* to stitch together; *(bouton)* to sew on; *(semelle)* to sew *or* to stitch on; **cousu (à la) machine** machined, machine-stitched; **cousu (à la) main** hand-stitched

2 *(volaille)* to sew up

3 *(plaie)* to stitch up, to sew up

4 *(livre)* to stitch (together)

USAGE ABSOLU j'aime c. I enjoy sewing; **c. à la main/machine** to sew by hand/machine; *Fam* **du cousu main** top-quality stuff; **cousu (à la) main** hand-stitched; *Fig* **être (tout) cousu d'or** to be extremely wealthy; *Fig* **c'est cousu de fil blanc** it's plain for all to see; **mensonge cousu de fil blanc** transparent lie
❑ **à coudre ADJ** sewing

coudrier [kudrije] **NM** hazel tree

Coué [kwe] **NPR méthode C.** autosuggestion, Couéism; *Fig* self-persuasion

couenne NF 1 [kwan] *(de porc)* rind **2** [kwen] *Suisse (de fromage)* rind **3** [kwan] *Méd* buffy coat **4** [kwan] *Fam (peau)* skin■; *Can* **avoir la c. épaisse** to be thick-skinned

couenneux, -euse [kwanø, -øz] **ADJ 1** *(semblable à la couenne)* rind-like **2** *Méd* buffy

couette [kwɛt] **NF 1** *(de cheveux)* **des couettes** bunches; **elle avait des couettes** she wore her hair in bunches; **se faire des couettes** to put *or* gather one's hair in bunches **2** *(édredon)* duvet, (continental) quilt **3** *Tech* bearing **4** *Naut* **couettes courantes** bilge ways

couffin [kufɛ̃] **NM 1** *(pour bébé) Br* Moses basket, *Am* bassinet **2** *(cabas)* (straw) basket

coufique [kufik] *Ling* **ADJ** Kufic
NM Kufic

cougouar [kugwar], **couguar** [kug(w)ar] **NM** cougar, puma, mountain lion

couic [kwik] **ONOMAT** eek
❑ **que couic ADV** *très Fam* zilch, *Br* sod all

couille [kuj] **NF** *Vulg* **1** *(testicule)* nut, ball, *Br* bollock; **un coup de pied dans les couilles** a kick in the balls; **avoir des couilles (au cul)** to have balls; **il n'a pas de couilles** he's got no balls; **casser** *ou* **peler les couilles à qn** *Br* to get on sb's tits, *Am* to break sb's balls; **se faire des couilles en or** to make a bundle *or Br* a packet

2 *(échec, erreur) Br* cock-up, balls-up, *Am* ball-up; **il m'est arrivé une c.** there's been a bit of a *Br* cock-up *or* balls-up *or Am* ball-up; **partir en c.** to go down the tubes, *Br* to go tits-up

3 *(personne)* **une c. molle** a wimp

couillon [kujɔ̃] **NM 1** *très Fam (imbécile)* airhead, *Br* wally; *(dupe)* mug **2** *Fam (dans le Midi)* **salut, c.!** *Br* hi, mate!, *Am* hi, buddy!
ADJ *très Fam* damned stupid

couillonnade [kujɔnad] **NF** *très Fam (histoire)* damn stupid thing to say; *(action)* damn stupid thing to do; *(objet)* piece of junk; **dire des couillonnades** to talk crap *or* bull; **fais pas de couillonnades** don't do anything daft; **après on te donne une médaille ou une c. de ce genre** afterwards they give you a medal or some shit like that; **c'est de la c.** *(discours)* it's a load of crap *or* bull; **l'entraînement le samedi, c'est de la c.** you'd have to be a complete idiot to train on Saturdays

couillonner [3] [kujɔne] **VT** *très Fam* to screw, to rip off; **te laisse pas c.** don't let yourself be screwed *or* ripped off; **se faire c.** to get screwed *or* ripped off

couillu, -e [kujy] **ADJ** *très Fam* ballsy

couinement [kwinmɑ̃] **NM 1** *(d'une souris)* squeak, squeaking; *(d'un lièvre, d'un porc)* squeal, squealing **2** *(d'un enfant)* whine, whining **3** *(d'un frein)* squeal, squealing

couiner [3] [kwine] **VI 1** *(souris)* to squeak; *(lièvre, porc)* to squeal **2** *(enfant)* to whine **3** *(frein)* to squeal

coulabilité [kulabilite] **NF** *Métal* flowability

coulage [kulaʒ] **NM 1** *(d'une statue)* casting; *(d'un métal, de la cire, du verre)* pouring **2** *(gaspillage)* waste; *(chapardage)* shrinkage

coulant, -e [kulɑ̃, -ɑ̃t] **ADJ 1** *Fam (personne)* easy-going■, *Péj* lax; **ils sont coulants avec les passeurs** they close their eyes to smuggling; **elle est plus coulante avec toi** she lets you get away with more

2 *(léger → vin)* smooth; **il est c.** it slips down easily

3 *(style, prose)* free, free-flowing

4 *(fromage)* runny

NM 1 *(anneau)* sliding ring; *(d'une ceinture)* loop

2 *(d'une plante)* runner

3 *Fam (fromage)* = very ripe cheese, particularly Camembert

coule[1] [kul] **NF** *Fam* **être à la c.** to know the tricks of the trade, to know the ropes, to know what's what

coule[2] [kul] **NF** *(de religieux)* cowl

coulé, -e[1] [kule] **ADJ** *(mouvement)* smooth
NM 1 *Mus* slur **2** *(pas de danse)* glide **3** *(au billard)* follow-through

coulée[2] [kule] **NF 1** *(de sang, de peinture)* streak **2** *(chute)* **c. de boue** mudslide; **c. de lave** lava flow; **c. de neige** snowslide **3** *Métal* casting **4** *Chasse (d'un animal)* run, pass, path **5** *Can* (maple) sap flow

coulemelle [kulmɛl] **NF** parasol mushroom

COULER [3] [kule]

> **VI** to flow **1, 2** ▪ to run **1, 4** ▪ to leak **3** ▪ to go under **5** ▪ to sink
> **VT** to sink **1** ▪ to pour **3** ▪ to cast **3, 4**
> **VPR** to slip into **1**

VI 1 *(fleuve, eau)* to run, to flow; *(larmes)* to run down, to flow; **la sueur coulait sur son visage** *(abondamment)* sweat was pouring down his/her face; *(goutte à goutte)* sweat was trickling down his/her face; **le vin coulait à flots** wine flowed freely; **le sable/l'argent coule entre ses doigts** sand/money trickles through his/her fingers; **le sang a coulé** there was bloodshed; **fais c. l'eau** turn on the water; **faire c. un bain** to run a bath; **il faisait c. du sable entre ses doigts** he was letting the sand run *or* trickle through his fingers; **fais c. un peu d'eau dessus** pour a little water over it; **avoir le nez qui coule** to have a runny nose; **il a les yeux qui coulent** he has watery eyes; **laisser c. son sang** to let oneself bleed; *Fig* **faire c. de la salive** to cause some tongue-wagging, to set the tongues wagging; *Fig* **faire c. beaucoup d'encre** to cause a lot of ink to flow; **il coulera de l'eau sous les ponts avant que...** there'll be a lot of water under the bridge before...

2 *(progresser facilement)* to flow; *Littéraire* **le temps coule** time slips by; **depuis, sa vie a coulé, calme et tranquille** since then, he/she has enjoyed a calm and peaceful life; **c. de source** to follow (on naturally); **cela coule de source** *(c'est évident)* it's obvious; *(c'est une conséquence naturelle)* it follows naturally; *Fam* **laisse c.!** don't bother!, just drop it!

3 *(avoir une fuite → robinet)* to leak, to drip; *(→ stylo)* to leak

4 *(se liquéfier → fromage, bougie)* to run

5 *(sombrer → nageur)* to go under; *(→ bateau)* to go down, to sink; *Fig (→ entreprise)* to go under; **c. à pic** to sink straight to the bottom, to sink like a stone; **c. pavillon haut** to lose gracefully

VT 1 *(faire sombrer → bateau)* to sink; *Fig (→ entreprise, concurrent)* to sink, to bring down

2 *Littéraire (passer)* **c. des jours heureux** to spend some happy days

3 *(ciment)* to pour; *(métal)* to cast; **c. l'eau d'une chaudière** to run *or* to draw water out of a boiler; **c. du plomb dans un joint** to run lead into a joint

4 *(fabriquer → statue)* to cast

5 *(glisser)* **c. un sourire/regard à qn** to steal a smile/look at sb; **c. un mot à l'oreille de qn** to drop *or* whisper a word in sb's ear

6 *Aut* **c. une bielle** to run a rod

▸**se couler VPR 1** *(se glisser)* **se c. dans** *(lit, foule)* to slip into; **elle se coula dans son lit et s'endormit aussitôt** she slipped into her bed and went straight to sleep; *Fig* **il s'est coulé dans le moule** he slipped into the mould; **se c. le long de** to slide alongside; **se c. le long des murs** to hug the walls

2 *Fam* **se la c. douce** to have an easy time (of it)

couleur [kulœr] **NF 1** *(impression visuelle)* colour; **le vert est une c.** green is a colour; **de c. vive** brightly-coloured; **une jolie c. verte** a pretty shade of green; **de quelle c. est sa voiture?** what colour is his/her car?; *Fig* **je n'ai jamais vu la c. de son argent** I've never seen the colour of his/her money; **couleurs complémentaires** complementary colours; **c. de muraille** stone grey; **couleurs primaires** *ou* **fondamentales** primary colours; **couleurs spectrales** colours of the spectrum; *Fam* **en faire voir à qn de toutes les couleurs** to give sb a hard time; *Fam* **il nous en a fait voir de toutes les couleurs** he gave us a

hard time; *Fam* **on en a vu de toutes les couleurs** we've been through some hard times

2 *(pour les cheveux)* tint, colour; **se faire faire une c.** to have one's hair tinted, to have a colour put through *or* in one's hair

3 *Cartes* suit

4 *(vivacité)* colour; **le texte a beaucoup de c.** the text has a good deal of colour *or* is very colourful; **c. locale** local colour; **un restaurant très c. locale** a restaurant with plenty of local colour; **pour faire c. locale** to add a bit of local colour

5 *(aspect)* light, colour; **voir la situation sous de nouvelles couleurs** to see the situation in a new light; **l'avenir m'apparaissait sous les couleurs les plus sombres/sous de belles couleurs** the future presented itself (to me) in an unfavourable/favourable light; **quelle sera la c. politique de votre nouveau journal?** what will be the political colour of your new newspaper?; **la c. du temps** the spirit of the times

6 *(d'une personne)* shade, colour; **changer de c.** to change colour; **passer par toutes les couleurs de l'arc-en-ciel** to go through all the colours of the rainbow; **la c. de la peau** skin colour

7 *Hér & Mus* colour

8 *(dans l'imprimerie)* **c. chromatique** chromatic colour; **c. de fond** tint; **c. saturée** saturated colour; **c. soustractive** subtractive colour

▫ **couleurs** NFPL **1** *(linge)* coloureds

2 *(peintures)* coloured paints; **couleurs à l'huile** oil paints; **couleurs à l'eau** watercolours; **boîte de couleurs** box of paints, paintbox

3 *(bonne mine)* (healthy) glow, colour; **avoir des couleurs** to look well; **perdre ses couleurs** to lose one's colour, to become pale; **prendre des couleurs** to get a bit of colour in one's cheeks, to catch the sun; **tu as repris des couleurs** you're getting your colour back, you're getting some colour (back) in your cheeks

4 *Sport (d'une équipe)* colours; *(d'un jockey, d'un cheval)* livery, colours; **elle a défendu les couleurs de la France** she defended the French flag

5 *(drapeau)* colours; *Mil* **envoyer** *ou* **hisser les couleurs** to hoist the colours *or* the flag

6 *Hér* colour

▫ **aux couleurs de** PRÉP **aux couleurs du parti** in party colours; **aux couleurs du propriétaire** *(yacht)* flying the owner's flag; *(cheval)* in the owner's colours

▫ **de couleur** ADJ coloured; **une personne de c.** a coloured person, a non-white

▫ **en couleur** ADV *(gén)* in colour; *(photo, télévision)* colour *(avant n)*; **tout en c.** in full colour; **haut en c.** very lively *or* colourful *or* picturesque

▫ **sous couleur de** CONJ under the pretext *or* guise of; **sous c. de me rendre service** under the pretext *or* guise of doing me a service

couleuvre [kulœvr] NF *Zool* garter snake, colubrid snake; **c. à collier** grass snake; **c. lisse** smooth snake; **c. vipérine** viperine grass snake

couleuvreau, -x [kulœvro] NM *Zool* young garter snake

couleuvrine [kulœvrin] NF culverin

coulis [kuli] NM **1** *Culin (des légumes, de la viande, du poisson)* purée; *(de fruits)* coulis **2** *(mortier)* grout; *(métal)* molten metal

ADJ M *voir* **vent**

coulissant, -e [kulisɑ̃, -ɑ̃t] ADJ sliding

coulisse [kulis] NF **1** *Théât* **la c., les coulisses** the wings; **les coulisses du pouvoir** the corridors of power; **dans les coulisses, en c.** *Théât* in the wings; *Fig* behind the scenes; **on murmure en c. que...** *Théât* there's an off-stage rumour that...; *Fig* they say behind the scenes that... **2** *(glissière)* runner **3** *Couture* hem *(through which to pass tape)* **4** *Bourse* outside market, kerb market

▫ **à coulisse** ADJ sliding

▫ **en coulisse** ADJ *(regard)* sidelong

coulisseau, -x [kuliso] NM sliding block; *(de pièce de machine)* slide; *(de tiroir)* runner; *Aut* slider; *Aut* **c. de sélection** selector rod

coulissement [kulismɑ̃] NM sliding motion

coulisser [3] [kulise] VI to slide

VT **1** *(porte, tiroir)* to provide with runners **2** *Couture* to hem *(in order to run a tape through)*; **pantalon coulissé** trousers with a drawstring waist

coulissier [kulisje] NM *Bourse* outside broker, kerb broker

couloir [kulwar] NM **1** *(d'un bâtiment)* corridor, passage; *(d'un wagon)* corridor; **les couloirs du métro** the corridors of the *Br* tube *or Am* subway; **intrigues de c.** backstage manoeuvring; **bruits de couloirs** rumours

2 *Transp* **c. (de circulation)** lane; **c. aérien** air traffic lane; **c. d'autobus** bus lane; **c. de navigation** sea lane; **c. à vélos** cycle lane

3 *(entre des régions, des pays)* corridor; **c. humanitaire** humanitarian corridor

4 *Géog* gully, *Spéc* couloir; **le c. rhodanien** the Rhône Corridor; **c. d'avalanche** avalanche corridor

5 *(d'un appareil de projection)* track

6 *(en athlétisme)* lane; *(au tennis) Br* tramlines, *Am* alley

couloiriste [kulwarist] NM *Journ* lobby correspondent

coulomb [kulɔ̃] NM *Élec* coulomb

coulommiers [kulɔmje] NM Coulommiers cheese

coulon [kulɔ̃] NM *Belg* pigeon

coulpe [kulp] NF *Littéraire* **battre sa c.** to beat one's breast

coulure [kulyr] NF **1** *(traînée)* streak **2** *Métal* runout **3** *Bot* = washing-away of pollen by spring rains, causing crop failure

coumarine [kumarin] NF *Chim* coumarin, cumarin

country [kuntri] NF INV *Mus* country (and western) music; **c. alternative** alt-country

COUP [ku]

blow **A1–3** ▪ punch **A1, 3** ▪ kick **A1** ▪ shock **A2** ▪ shot **A4, B3** ▪ knock **A5** ▪ stroke **A6, B3** ▪ used with body part, or instrument **B1, 2** ▪ knack **B4** ▪ drink **B7** ▪ throw **B8** ▪ move **B9** ▪ go **B9, 1D** ▪ trick **C1** ▪ job **C2** ▪ coup **C5**

NM **A.** *HEURT, DÉFLAGRATION* **1** *(gén)* blow, knock; *(avec le poing)* punch, blow; *(avec le pied)* kick; **un c. violent** a hard knock; **un c. brutal** a nasty blow; **elle a failli mourir sous ses coups** he thrashed her to within an inch of her life, he nearly battered her to death; **frapper à coups redoublés** to hit twice as hard; **donner un petit c. à** *ou* **sur qch** to tap sth lightly; **donner un c. sec sur qch** to give sth a (hard *or* smart) tap; **il frappait sur la porte à grands coups/à petits coups** he banged on the door/knocked gently at the door; **un c. dans les tibias** a kick in the shins; **donner un c. sur la table** *(avec le poing)* to thump the table, to bang one's fist (down) on the table; **se donner un c. contre qch** to knock against sth; **en arriver** *ou* **en venir aux coups** to come to blows; **j'ai pris un c. sur la tête** I got a knock *or* a bang on the head; **prendre des coups** to get knocked about; **recevoir un c.** to get hit; **il a reçu un c. sur la tête** he was hit on the head; **j'en ai reçu des coups quand j'étais petit!** I was constantly knocked about when I was little!; *aussi Fig* **rendre c. pour c.** to hit back, to give as good as one gets; *Jur* **coups et blessures** grievous bodily harm; *Jur* **inculpé de coups et blessures** charged with inflicting grievous bodily harm; *aussi Fig* **porter un c. à qn** to deal sb a blow; **porter un c. mortel à qn** to strike sb a fatal blow; *Fig* **les grandes surfaces ont porté un (rude) c. au petit commerce** small traders have been dealt a (severe) blow by large retail chains; *aussi Fig* **le c. a porté** the blow struck home

2 *(attaque, choc)* blow, shock; **ça m'a fait un c.** *(émotion)* it gave me a shock; *(déception)* it was a blow; **les mauvais coups de la vie** the nasty blows that life deals you; *Fam* **sale c. (pour la fanfare)!** that's a bit of a blow *or* downer!; *Fam* **le buffet en a pris un c. pendant le déménagement** the dresser got a bit bashed in the move; **trois échecs d'affilée, son moral en a pris un c.** with three successive failures, his/her morale has taken a bit of a battering; **avec le krach boursier, l'économie en a pris un c.** the economy has suffered a great deal from the crash; **j'ai trop de travail, je ne sais pas si je tiendrai le c.** I've got too much work, I don't know if I'll be able to cope; **il faut que tu tiennes le c. jusqu'à la fin de la semaine** you'll have to keep going until the end of the week

3 *Boxe* punch, blow; *aussi Fig* **c. bas** blow *or* punch below the belt; **il m'a fait un c. bas** he played a lousy trick on me; *aussi Fig* **tous les coups sont permis** (there are) no holds barred; *aussi Fig* **compter les coups** to keep score

4 *(d'une arme à feu)* shot, blast; **un c. de revolver** a shot, a gunshot; **le c. est parti** *(revolver)* the gun went off; *(fusil)* the rifle went off; **tirer un c. de canon** to fire *or* to blast a cannon; **le c. est passé très près** the bullet just whistled past; **(revolver à) six coups** six-shot gun; **faire c. double** *Chasse* to kill two animals with one shot; *Fig* to kill two birds with one stone

5 *(bruit→ gén)* knock; *(→ sec)* rap; *(→ craquement)* snap; **des coups au carreau** knocking *or* knocks on the window; **un c. de gong** a bang on a gong

6 *(heure sonnée)* stroke; **c. de cloche** stroke of the bell; **l'horloge sonna trois coups** the clock struck three; **le dernier c. de trois heures** the last stroke of three; **les douze coups de minuit** the twelve strokes of midnight

7 *Vulg (éjaculation)* **tirer un** *ou* **son c.** to shoot one's load

B. *GESTE, ACTION* **1** *(mouvement d'une partie du corps)* **un c. de corne** a butt with the horn; **donner un c. de corne à qn** to butt sb; **un c. de langue** a lick; **elle nettoyait ses chatons à (grands) coups de langue** she was licking her kittens clean; **un c. de bec** a peck; *Fig* a cutting remark; **un c. de dent** a bite; *Fig* a cutting remark; **d'un grand c. de dent** with one snap of the jaws; **à petits coups de dents** in little nibbles; **c. de griffe** *ou* **patte** swipe of the paw; *Fig* cutting remark

2 *(emploi d'un instrument)* **donner un (petit) c. de brosse/chiffon à qch** to give sth a (quick) brush/wipe; **passe un c. d'aspirateur au salon** give the living room a quick vacuum; **passe un c. d'éponge sur la table** give the table a wipe (with the sponge); **il a reçu un c. de gourdin sur la tête** he was clubbed on the head; **un c. de marteau** a blow with a hammer; **il s'est donné un c. de marteau sur le doigt** he hit his finger with a hammer; **il a reçu un c. de marteau sur la tête** he was hit on the head with a hammer; **en deux coups de rame nous pouvons traverser la rivière** we can cross the river in a couple of strokes; *Fam* **passe un c. dans la salle de bains** give the bathroom a going-over; *Fam* **en donner** *ou* **ficher** *ou* **mettre un c.** to get down to business; **il va falloir qu'on en mette** *ou* **en mettre un c.** we'll have to get down to it *or* to get a move on; **mets-en un bon c.!** give it everything you've got!, go for it!; **il a fallu qu'ils en mettent un sacré c.** they really had to pull out all the stops

3 *Golf & (au billard)* stroke; *(au tennis)* shot, stroke; **c. droit** forehand stroke; **c. droit croisé** cross court forehand (stroke); **elle a retourné le service en c. droit** she returned the serve with her forehand

4 *Fam (savoir-faire)* knack; **pour la pâtisserie, il a le c.** he's *Br* a dab hand *or Am* a champ at baking cakes; **elle a le c. pour tailler dans le tissu sans patron** she's got the knack of cutting material without a pattern; **ah, tu as le c. pour mettre la pagaille!** you really have a gift *or* a knack for creating havoc, don't you!; **une fois que tu auras pris le c., ça ira tout seul!** you'll find it's very easy once you get used to it *or* once you've got the knack!

5 *Météo* **c. de roulis/tangage** sudden roll/dip; **il y a eu un petit c. de roulis/tangage** the boat started rolling/pitching a bit; **c. de chaleur** heatwave; **c. de mer** heavy swell; **c. de vent** gust of wind

6 *(effet soudain)* **j'ai un c. de cafard** I feel down all of a sudden; **j'ai eu un c. de fatigue** suddenly a wave of tiredness came over me; **il a eu un c. de folie et a acheté une Rolls** he had a moment of madness and bought himself a Rolls-Royce; **avoir un c. de chaleur** to get heatstroke

7 *Fam (boisson)* drink; **j'ai le hoquet – bois un c.** I've got (the) hiccups – drink something *or* have a drink; **tu me sers un c. (à boire)?** could you pour me a drink?; **tu boiras** *ou* **prendras bien un c. avant de partir?** you'll have a drink before you go *or* you'll have one for the road, won't you?; **boire un c. de trop** to have one too many; **avoir un c. dans le nez** to have had one too many; **un c. de rouge** a glass of red wine; **un c. de gnôle** a nip of brandy

8 *(lancer)* throw; *(aux dés)* throw (of the dice); **elle a renversé toutes les boîtes de conserve en un seul c.** she knocked down all the cans in one throw; **on joue la tournée en trois coups** let's have three goes with the dice to see who'll pay for the round

9 *(action)* move; *Cartes* go; **la partie se joue dans les premiers coups** the game is won or lost in the opening moves; **c'est un c. pour rien** *(essai)* it's a trial run; *(échec)* it's a failure

C. *ACTE OU SITUATION EXCEPTIONNELS* **1** *Fam (mauvais tour)* trick; **il prépare un c.** he's up to something *or* some trick; **(faire) un mauvais** *ou* **sale c. (à qn)** (to play) a dirty trick (on sb); **je parie que c'est un c. de Julie!** I bet Julie's behind this!; **c'est encore un c. de ton ami** it's another of your friend's tricks; **c. en traître** blow below the belt, stab in the back; **monter un c. contre qn** to set sb up, to frame sb; **il nous a encore fait le c.** he's pulled the same (old) trick on us again; **il a essayé de me faire le c. de la panne** he tried to pull the old running-out-of-petrol trick on me; **il m'a fait le c. du charme et j'ai craqué** he turned on the charm and I fell for it; **on ne me refera pas le c. de la vaisselle!** I won't get conned into doing the dishes again!; **ne me fais pas le c. de ne pas venir!** now don't stand me up, will you!; **c. monté** put-up job, frame-up; **l'accusé affirmait être victime d'un c. monté** the accused claimed it was a put-up job *or* claimed that he'd been framed; **elle a fait un c. en douce** she's cooked up something behind everybody's back; **il fait toujours ses coups en douce** he's always going behind people's backs

2 *Fam (vol, escroquerie)* job; **ils sont sur un gros c. avec le Balafré** they're on to a big job *or* number with Scarface; **il était sur le c. du supermarché** he was in on the supermarket job

3 *Fam (affaire)* **je suis sur un c.** I'm on to something; *Journ* I have a lead; **je veux l'acheter mais on est plusieurs sur le c.** I want to buy it but there are several people interested; **expliquer le c. à qn** to explain the situation *or* set-up to sb; **être dans tous les coups** to have a finger in every pie; **rattraper le c.** to sort things out; **il a manqué** *ou* **raté son c.** he didn't pull it off; **elle a réussi son c.** she pulled it off; **tu as vu le c. de la marée noire, ç'a été vite étouffé!** did you see that business about the oil spill, they hushed that one up quickly!; **c'est un c. à avoir un accident, ça!** that's the sort of thing that causes accidents!; **combien crois-tu que ça va coûter? – oh, c'est un c. de 200 euros** how much do you think it will cost? – oh, about 200 euros

4 *Vulg (personne → sexuellement)* **c'est un bon c.** he/she's a good lay

5 *(action remarquable, risquée)* coup; **faire un beau** *ou* **joli c.** to pull a (real) coup; **elle a décroché le contrat, quel joli c.!** she landed the contract, what a coup!; **tenter le c.** to have a go, to give it a try; **c'est un c. à faire** *ou* **tenter** it's worth trying *or* a try

6 *(circonstance marquante)* **marquer le c.** to mark the occasion; **un c. du ciel** *ou* **de la providence** a twist of fate; *Fam* **un c. de chance** *ou* **de pot** *ou* **de bol** a stroke of luck, a lucky break; **t'as vraiment eu un c. de chance** *ou* **pot** *ou* **bol!** you were a lucky dog *or Br* a jammy beggar!, you certainly got a lucky break there!

D. *FOIS* time, go; **du premier c.** first time, at the first attempt; **j'ai eu mon permis au second c.** I passed my driving test at the second attempt; **au prochain c., tu vas y arriver** you'll do it next time *or* at your next go; **tu as encore droit à un c.** you've still got another go; **essaie encore un c.** have another go; **ce c.-ci, on s'en va** this time, we're off; **ce c.-là, je crois qu'elle a compris** I think she got the message that time; *Fam* **pour un c.** just for once; *Fam* **c'est ça, pleure un bon c.** that's it, have a good cry; **dites-le lui un bon c., qu'on n'en parle plus!** tell him once and for all, and let's not talk about it any more!; **vous devriez vous expliquer un bon c.!** you should have it out once and for all!; *Fam* **souffle un grand c.!** *(en se mouchant, sur des bougies)* blow!; **respire un grand c.** take a deep breath

□ **coup d'aile** NM **d'un puissant c. d'aile, le rapace gagne les hauteurs** the bird of prey gains height on its powerful wings; **la cane a donné un petit c. d'aile** the duck flapped its wings; **tous les moineaux se sont envolés d'un c. d'aile** all the sparrows took wing suddenly; *Fig* **Paris-Bruxelles en un c. d'aile** Paris-Brussels in one short hop; **on peut aller n'importe où dans le monde d'un c. d'aile** you can fly anywhere in the world in no time at all

□ **coup de balai** NM **la cuisine a besoin d'un bon c. de balai** the kitchen needs a good sweep; **donner un c. de balai** to sweep (out) a room; *Fig* **le comité aurait besoin d'un bon c. de balai** the committee could do with a shake-up; *Fig* **donner un bon c. de balai dans les traditions/la direction** to revamp the traditions/management

□ **coup de barre** NM *Fam* sudden feeling of exhaustion■; **j'ai le c. de barre** I feel *Br* shattered *or Am* beat all of a sudden

□ **coup de chapeau** NM praise; **donner un c. de chapeau à qn** to praise sb; **son livre mérite un c. de chapeau** his/her book deserves some recognition

□ **coup de chien** NM **1** *Naut* sudden squall

2 *Fig* bolt from the blue

□ **coup de cœur** NM **avoir un** *ou* **le c. de cœur pour qch** to fall in love with sth, to be really taken with *or* by sth; **voici nos coups de cœur dans la collection de printemps** here are our favourite spring outfits; **des prix c. de cœur** special offers

□ **coup de coude** NM **donner un c. de coude à qn** *(en signe)* to nudge sb; *(agressivement)* to dig one's elbow into sb

□ **coup d'éclat** NM feat; **faire un c. d'éclat** to pull off a coup

□ **coup d'État** NM *(putsch)* coup (d'état); *Fig* coup

□ **coup de feu** NM **1** *(tir)* **tirer un c. de feu** to fire a shot, to shoot; **on a entendu des coups de feu** we heard shots being fired *or* gunfire

2 *Fig (dans un restaurant)* **c'est le c. de feu** there's a sudden rush on

□ **coup de fil = coup de téléphone**

□ **coup de filet** NM *(poissons)* draught, haul; *(suspects)* haul

□ **coup de force** NM takeover by force

□ **coup de foudre** NM **1** *Météo* flash of lightning

2 *Fig* love at first sight; **entre eux deux, ç'a été le c. de foudre** it was love at first sight between (the two of) them

□ **coup de fouet** NM **donner un c. de fouet à qn** to lash *or* to whip sb; *Fig* to give sb a boost; **le cocher a donné un c. de fouet aux chevaux** the coachman cracked his whip at the horses; *Fig* **ces vitamines te donneront un c. de fouet** these vitamins will give you a boost *or* a lift

□ **coup fourré** NM **1** *Escrime* double hit

2 *Fig* low trick

□ **coup franc** NM *Ftbl* free kick

□ **coup de fusil** NM **1** *(acte)* shot; *(bruit)* shot, gunshot; **donner un c. de fusil à qn** to shoot sb (with a rifle); **on entendait des coups de fusil** you could hear shots being fired *or* gunfire; **un c. de fusil a déchiré le silence** the silence was shattered by the sound of a shot; **recevoir un c. de fusil** to get shot; **il fut tué d'un c. de fusil** he was shot dead

2 *Fig* **on y mange bien, mais après c'est le c. de fusil!** it's a good restaurant, but the bill is a bit of a shock!

□ **coup de grâce** NM *aussi Fig* coup de grâce, deathblow

□ **coup du lapin** NM *(coup)* rabbit punch; *(dans un accident de voiture)* whiplash (injury) *(UNCOUNT)*

□ **coup de main** NM **1** *(raid)* smash-and-grab (attack); *Mil* coup de main

2 *(aide)* **donner un c. de main à qn** to give *or* to lend sb a hand

3 *(savoir-faire)* **avoir le c. de main** to have the knack *or* the touch; **avoir le c. de main pour faire qch** to have the knack of doing sth

□ **coup d'œil** NM **1** *(regard)* look, glance; **elle s'en rendit compte au premier c. d'œil** she noticed straight away *or* immediately *or* at a glance; **donner** *ou* **jeter un petit c. d'œil à** to have a quick look *or* glance at; **d'un c. d'œil, il embrassa le tableau** he took in the situation at a glance; **avoir le c. d'œil** to have a good eye; **pour les coquilles, elle a le c. d'œil** she has a keen eye for misprints; **valoir le c. d'œil** to be (well) worth seeing

2 *(panorama)* view; **de là-haut, le c. d'œil est unique** the view up there is unique

□ **coup de pied** NM *(d'une personne, d'un cheval)* kick; *Fig* **le c. de pied de l'âne** the parting shot; **donner un c. de pied à qn** to kick sb; **donner un c. de pied dans qch** to kick sth; **il a donné un c. de pied dans le flipper** he gave the pinball machine a kick

□ **coup de poing** NM punch; **les coups de poing pleuvaient** it was raining blows *or* punches; **donner un c. de poing à qn** to give sb a punch, to punch sb; **il a reçu un c. de poing** he was punched; **faire le c. de poing** to brawl, to fight ADJ INV **opération c. de poing** *(sur vitrine)* prices slashed

□ **coup de poker** NM (bit of a) gamble; **on peut tenter la chose, mais c'est un c. de poker** we can try it but it's a bit risky

□ **coup de pompe** NM *Fam* sudden feeling of exhaustion■; **j'ai un c. de pompe** I suddenly feel completely *Br* shattered *or Am* beat

□ **coup de pouce** NM bit of help; **donner un c. de pouce à qn** to pull (a few) strings for sb; **donner un c. de pouce à qch** to give sth a bit of a boost; **il nous faudrait de la publicité pour donner un c. de pouce à nos ventes** we need some advertising to give our sales a bit of a boost

□ **coup de sang** NM **1** *Méd* stroke

2 *Fig* angry outburst; **elle a eu un c. de sang** she exploded (with rage)

□ **coup de soleil** NM sunburn *(UNCOUNT)*; **prendre** *ou* **attraper un c. de soleil** to get sunburnt

□ **coup du sort** NM *(favorable)* stroke of luck; *(défavorable)* stroke of bad luck

□ **coup de téléphone** NM (phone) call; **donner** *ou* **passer un c. de téléphone** to make a call; **donner** *ou* **passer un c. de téléphone à qn** to phone *or* to call *or Br* to ring sb; **recevoir un c. de téléphone** to receive *or* to get a phone call; **j'ai eu un c. de téléphone de Jean** I had a call from Jean

□ **coup de tête** NM **1** *(dans une bagarre)* headbutt; **donner un c. de tête à qn** to headbutt sb

2 *Sport* header

3 *Fig* (sudden) impulse; **sur un c. de tête** on (a sudden) impulse

□ **coup de théâtre** NM *Théât* coup de théâtre, sudden twist in the action; *Fig* sudden turn of events; **et alors, c. de théâtre, on lui demande de démissionner** and then, out of the blue, he/she was asked to resign

□ **coup de torchon** NM *Fam (bagarre)* fist-fight; *(nettoyage)* clean-up, *Br* clear-out

□ **coup de vent** NM **1** *(rafale)* gust (of wind)

2 *(locution)* **en c. de vent** in a flash *or* a whirl; **entrer/partir en c. de vent** to rush in/off; **elle est passée par Lausanne en c. de vent** she paid a flying visit to Lausanne; **je passe en c. de vent pour te dire...** I've just dropped in to tell you...; **manger en c. de vent** to grab something to eat

□ **à coups de** PRÉP **démoli à coups de marteau** smashed to pieces with a hammer; **ils se battaient à coups d'oreillers** they were having a pillow-fight; **il ne discute qu'à coups de statistiques** the only thing he puts forward is statistics; **faire une traduction à coups de dictionnaire** to do a translation using a dictionary; **la productivité a été augmentée à**

coups de primes spéciales productivity was increased through *or* by dint of special bonuses
▫ **à coup sûr** ADV definitely, certainly, for sure; **tu vas à c. sûr rater ton train!** one thing's (for) sure, you'll miss your train!; **à c. sûr, tu ne t'attendais pas à ça!** you certainly never expected that!; **elle ne s'engage qu'à c. sûr** she only commits herself when she's certain of the outcome
▫ **après coup** ADV afterwards, later on; **ce n'est qu'après c. que j'ai compris ce qu'il voulait dire** it was only afterwards *or* later on that it dawned on me what he meant
▫ **à tous les coups** ADV *Fam* **1** *(chaque fois)* every time■; **ça marche à tous les coups** it never fails■; **à tous les coups l'on gagne** you win every time■
2 *(sans aucun doute)* **à tous les coups, il a oublié** he's bound to have forgotten■
▫ **au coup par coup** ADV *Fam* bit by bit; **négocier au c. par c.** to have piecemeal negotiations■; **les avantages sociaux ont été obtenus au c. par c.** welfare benefits were won bit by bit
▫ **coup sur coup** ADV one after the other, in quick succession; **deux angines c. sur c.** two attacks of tonsillitis in quick succession
▫ **dans le coup** *Fam* ADJ **les gens dans le c.** hip *or* trendy people; **elle est dans le c.** *(complice)* she's in on it *or* involved in it■; *(à la mode)* she's hip *or* with it; **moi, je ne suis pas dans le c.** *(dans l'affaire)* it's nothing to do with me■, it doesn't involve me■; **moi, je ne suis plus dans le c.** *(dans l'affaire)* count me out *or* leave me out of it; *(au courant)* I'm a bit out of touch *or* out of it; **pour la pop, je ne suis plus dans le c.** I've not kept up with *or* I'm rather out of touch with the pop scene■ ADV **mettre qn dans le c.** *(faire participer qn)* to let sb in on the act; *(expliquer les choses à qn)* to put sb in the picture; **c'est Ramon qui m'a mis dans le c.** Ramon got me involved in it *or* in on it
▫ **du coup** ADV so, as a result; **alors, du c., tu ne pars plus!** so that means you're not going any more!; **elle ne pouvait pas venir, du c. j'ai reporté le dîner** as she couldn't come, I put the dinner off, she couldn't come so I put the dinner off
▫ **d'un (seul) coup** ADV **1** *(en une seule fois)* in one (go), all at once; **tu peux mettre toute la farine d'un seul c.** you can add the flour all at once; **avale-les d'un c.** swallow them down in one (go); **il a tout bu d'un c.** he drank the whole lot in one go; *Fam* **d'un seul c., je fais sortir le lapin du chapeau!** and hey presto, with one wave of my hand, I pull the rabbit out of the hat!
2 *(soudainement)* all of a sudden; *Fam* **j'ai eu envie de pleurer/de le gifler, ça m'a pris d'un c.** I got a sudden urge to cry/to slap him
▫ **pour le coup** ADV **pour le c., je ne savais plus quoi faire** at that point, I didn't know what to do next; *Fam* **j'ai aussi failli renverser le lait, c'est pour le c. qu'il aurait été en colère!** I nearly spilt the milk as well, he really would have been furious then!
▫ **sous le coup de** PRÉP **sous le c. de la colère, on dit des choses qu'on regrette après** when you're in a temper, you say things which you regret later; **sous le c. de l'excitation, il a trop promis** in the heat of the moment, he made promises he couldn't keep; **il est encore sous le c. de l'émotion** he still hasn't got over the shock; **être sous le c. d'une condamnation** to have a current conviction; **tomber sous le c. de qch** to come within the scope of sth; **tomber sous le c. de la loi** to be punishable by law; **si vous ne payez pas, vous tombez sous le c. d'une expulsion** if you don't pay, you become liable to eviction
▫ **sur le coup** ADV **1** *(mourir)* instantly
2 *(à ce moment-là)* straight away, there and then; **je n'ai pas compris sur le c.** I didn't understand immediately *or* straight away; **sur le c., j'ai accepté, mais je le regrette aujourd'hui** I accepted straight away, but now I regret it
▫ **sur le coup de** PRÉP **sur le c. de six heures/de midi** roundabout six o'clock/midday

---

'Coup de foudre' *Kurys* 'At First Sight'

'Coup de torchon' *Tavernier* 'Clean Slate'

---

coupable [kupabl] ADJ **1** *(fautif)* guilty; **se sentir c.** to feel guilty; **prendre un air c.** to look sheepish *or* guilty
2 *(responsable)* guilty, *Sout* culpable; *Jur* guilty; **c. de vol** guilty of theft
3 *Littéraire (amour, rêve, pensée)* sinful, reprehensible; *(action)* culpable
NMF **1** *(élément responsable)* culprit; **le vrai c., c'est l'amour** the real culprit is love
2 *Jur* guilty party

coupage [kupaʒ] NM *(mélange)* blending; *(avec de l'eau)* diluting, dilution, watering down

coupailler [3] [kupaje] VT *Péj* to hack away at

coupant, -e [kupɑ̃, -ɑ̃t] ADJ **1** *(tranchant → ciseaux)* sharp; **herbe coupante** grass you can cut yourself on **2** *(caustique → ton, remarque)* cutting, biting
NM cutting edge

coup-de-poing [kudpwɛ̃] *(pl* **coups-de-poing***)* NM **1 c. américain** knuckleduster **2** *(silex taillé)* hand axe
ADJ *(argument, chanson)* hard-hitting; *(politique)* tough and uncompromising

coupe [kup] NF **1** *(action)* cutting (out); *(coiffure)* **c. (de cheveux)** cut, haircut; **changer de c.** to have one's hair restyled; **c. au carré** (square) bob
2 *Couture (forme)* cut; *(action)* cutting; *(tissu)* length; **un ensemble à la c. impeccable** an impeccably cut suit
3 *(dessin)* section; **c. longitudinale** longitudinal section; **c. transversale** cross-section; **la machine vue en c.** a section of the machine
4 *(au microscope)* section
5 *Cartes (séparation)* cut, cutting
6 *(sciage)* cutting (down); *(étendue)* felling area; *(entaille)* section; **c. sombre** thinning out; *Fig* drastic cut; **faire des coupes sombres dans un budget** to drastically cut a budget; **c. réglée** periodic felling; **mettre en c. réglée** to fell on a regular basis; *Fig* to bleed *or* to drain systematically; **coupes budgétaires** budget cuts
7 *Ling & Littérature* break, caesura; **c. syllabique** syllable break
8 *Cin* **c. sèche** jump cut
9 *Sport* cup; **la c. de l'America** the America's Cup; **la c. du monde** the World Cup; **la c. africaine des nations** the African Cup of Nations; **la c. Davis** the Davis Cup
10 *(verre, contenu → à boire)* glass; *(→ à entremets)* dish; *(compotier)* dish, bowl; **c. de glace/fruits** *(dessert)* ice cream/fruit *(presented in a dish)*; **je t'offre une c.** *(de champagne)* let me buy you a glass of champagne; **c. à glace** sundae dish; **la c. est pleine** the cup is full
▫ **à la coupe** ADJ **fromage/jambon à la c.** cheese cut/ham sliced at the request of the customer
▫ **sous la coupe de** PRÉP **1** *(soumis à)* **être sous la c. de qn** to be under sb's thumb; **tomber sous la c. de qn** to fall into sb's clutches
2 *Cartes* **jouer sous la c. de qn** to lead after sb has cut

coupé [kupe] NM *Aut & (en danse)* coupé; **c. sport** sports coupé

coupe-choux [kupʃu] NM INV *Fam* **1** *(sabre)* sabre **2** *Hum* (cut-throat) razor

coupe-cigares [kupsigar] NM INV cigar cutter

coupe-circuit [kupsirkɥi] *(pl* **inv** *ou* **coupe-circuits***)* NM *Élec* cutout, circuit breaker

coupe-coupe [kupkup] NM INV machete

coupée [kupe] NF gangway

coupe-faim [kupfɛ̃] NM INV **1** *(gén)* snack **2** *Méd* appetite suppressant

coupe-feu [kupfø] NM INV **1** *(espace)* firebreak, fire line **2** *(construction)* fireguard
ADJ INV **porte c.** fire door

coupe-file [kupfil] *(pl* **coupe-files***)* NM pass

coupe-gorge [kupgɔrʒ] NM INV *(quartier)* dangerous area; *(bâtiment)* death trap

coupe-jambon [kupʒɑ̃bɔ̃] NM INV bacon slicer

coupe-jarret [kupʒarɛ] *(pl* **coupe-jarrets***)* NM *Littéraire* cut-throat

coupe-légumes [kuplegym] NM INV vegetable cutter, vegetable slicer

coupellation [kupɛlasjɔ̃] NF *Métal* cupellation, assaying

coupelle [kupɛl] NF **1** *(petite coupe)* (small) dish **2** *Chim* cupel

coupe-œufs [kupø] NM INV egg slicer

coupe-ongles [kupɔ̃gl] NM INV nail clippers

coupe-papier [kuppapje] *(pl* **inv** *ou* **coupe-papiers***)* NM paper knife

---

COUPER [3] [kupe]

> **VT** to cut **1, 3–7, 10, 13, 15** ■ to cut off **2, 4, 9, 11** ■ to cut up **3** ■ to cut down **4** ■ to cut out **5, 6** ■ to interrupt **8** ■ to intersect **10** ■ to water down **12** ■ to trump **15** ■ to slice **16**
> **VI** to cut **1** ■ to cut in **3**

VT **1** *(entailler → légèrement)* to cut; *(→ gravement)* to slash; *Fig* **le vent qui lui coupait le visage** the wind stinging his/her face; **c. la gorge à qn** to slit *or* cut sb's throat; **c. le souffle** *ou* **la respiration à qn** to take sb's breath away; **beau à c. le souffle** breathtakingly beautiful; **le brouillard était à c. au couteau** the fog was so thick you couldn't see your hand in front of your face; **un accent à c. au couteau** a very strong accent; **un silence à c. au couteau** a silence you could cut with a knife
2 *(membre)* to cut off; *(tête)* to cut off, to chop (off); **il a fallu lui c. un doigt** he/she had to have a finger cut off *or* amputated; **c. la tête** *ou* **le cou à un canard** to chop a duck's head off; **c. la tête** *ou* **le cou à qn** to cut off sb's head; *Fig* **c. bras et jambes à qn** *(surprise)* to stun sb; *Fig* **ça lui a coupé les jambes** *(de fatigue)* that's really tired him/her out
3 *(mettre en morceaux → ficelle)* to cut; *(→ gâteau)* to cut up; *(→ saucisson)* to cut up, to slice (up); *(→ bois)* to chop (up); **elle est obligée de lui c. sa viande** she has to cut up his/her meat (for him/her); **c. de la viande en morceaux** to cut up meat (into pieces); **c. une tomate en quartiers** to cut a tomato into quarters, to quarter a tomato; **c. en tranches** to cut up, to cut into slices, to slice; **c. qch en tranches fines/épaisses** to slice sth thinly/thickly, to cut sth into thick/thin slices; **elle se ferait c. en morceaux plutôt que de...** she'd rather die than...; *Fig* **c. la poire en deux** to meet halfway, to come to a compromise; **c. les ponts avec qn** to break all ties *or* to break off relations with sb; *Fig* **c. les cheveux en quatre** to split hairs
4 *(tailler → fleurs)* to cut; *(→ bordure)* to cut off; *(→ arbre)* to cut down, to chop down, to fell; **c. les cheveux à qn** to cut sb's hair; **se faire c. les cheveux** to have one's hair cut; **c. qn de qch** to cut sb off from sth; **c. le mal à la racine** to strike at the root of the evil; **c. la queue à un cheval** to dock a horse *or* a horse's tail
5 *Couture (robe)* to cut out; *(tissu)* to cut
6 *(écourter → film, texte)* to cut; *(ôter → remarque, séquence)* to cut (out), to edit out; **garde l'introduction mais coupe les citations latines** keep the introduction but edit *or* cut *or* take out the Latin quotations
7 *(arrêter → crédit)* to cut; **c. l'eau** *(par accident)* to cut off the water; *(volontairement)* to turn *or* to switch off the water; **c. le courant** *ou* **l'électricité** to switch off the current; *(sujet: compagnie d'électricité)* to cut off the power; **son père va lui c. les vivres** his/her father will stop supporting him/her *or* will cut off his/her means of subsistence
8 *(interrompre → fièvre)* to bring down; *(→ appétit)* to spoil, to ruin; *(→ relations diplomatiques, conversation)* to break off; **c. la parole à qn** to cut sb short; **ne coupe pas la parole comme ça!** don't cut in like that!; **la joie lui coupait la parole** joy rendered him/her speechless; *Fam* **c. qn** to interrupt sb■; **vous me coupez tout le temps!** you're always cutting in (when I'm speaking) *or* interrupting (me)!; **je vais à la gym à midi, ça (me) coupe la journée** I go to the gym at lunchtime, it helps to break up the day; **ces chaussettes sont trop serrées, elles me coupent la circulation** these socks are too

tight, they're cutting off my circulation; *Fam* **c. la chique** *ou* **le sifflet à qn** to shut sb up; *Fam* **ça te la coupe, hein?** you weren't expecting that one, were you!, that shut you up, didn't it!; **c. ses effets à qn** to take the wind out of sb's sails; **c. le souffle à qn** to take sb's breath away; *(coup de poing)* to wind sb

9 *(barrer → route)* to cut off; *(→ retraite)* to block off, to cut off; **l'arbre nous coupait la route** the tree blocked our path; **la voiture nous a coupé la route** the car cut across in front of us

10 *(diviser → surface)* to cut; *(→ ligne)* to cut, to intersect; *(→ voie)* to cross, to cut across; **le mur coupe la ville en deux** the wall cuts the town in two *or* bisects the town; **où le chemin de fer coupe la route** where the railway line cuts across *or* crosses the road; **la droite AB coupe le plan** the straight line AB cuts the plane; **la proue du navire coupait les vagues** the bow of the ship cut through the waves; *Fig* **depuis, la famille est coupée en deux** since then, the family has been split in two; **sur la question de l'euro, le Danemark est coupé en deux** Denmark is divided *or* split down the middle on the issue of the euro

11 *(séparer)* to cut off; **c. l'ennemi de ses bases** to cut off the enemy from its base; **je me sens coupé de tout** I feel cut off from everything *or* totally isolated

12 *(diluer → lait)* to add water to, to thin down, to water down; **coupé d'eau** diluted, watered down; **c. du vin** *(à l'eau)* to water wine down; *(avec d'autres vins)* to blend wine

13 *Cin* **coupez!** cut!

14 *Tél* to cut off

15 *Cartes (partager)* to cut; *(jouer l'atout)* to trump; **c'est à vous de c.** it's your turn to cut; **c. à carreau/à cœur** to trump with a diamond/heart

16 *Sport (balle)* to slice

17 *Vét (castrer)* to neuter, to castrate; **il a fait c. son chat** he had his cat neutered

VI 1 *(être tranchant)* to cut, to be sharp; **le couteau coupe bien** the knife cuts well; **attention, ça coupe!** careful, it's sharp!

2 *(prendre un raccourci)* **c. à travers champs** to cut across fields *or* country; **c. par une petite route** to cut through by a minor road; **coupons par le moulin** let's take a shortcut via the mill; **c. au plus court** to take the quickest way; **il nous a fait c. à travers champs** he showed us a shortcut across the fields

3 *(interrompre)* to cut in, to interrupt; **"faux", coupa-t-elle** "not true," she cut in; *Tél* **ne coupez pas!** hold the line!

❑ **couper à VT IND c. court à qch** *(mettre fin à)* to cut sth short, to curtail sth; **c. à qch** *(se dérober)* to get out of sth; **tu ne couperas pas à la vaisselle!** you won't get out of doing the dishes!; **on n'y a pas coupé, à son sermon!** sure enough we got a lecture from him!; **tu dois y aller, tu ne peux pas y c.!** you've got to go, there's no way you can get out of it!

▶**se couper VPR 1** to cut oneself; **se c. les ongles** to cut *or* to trim one's nails; **se c. le** *ou* **au front** to cut one's forehead; **se c. les veines** to slit *or* to slash one's wrists; **se c. en quatre pour qn** *(une fois)* to bend over backwards to help sb; *(continuellement)* to devote oneself utterly to sb

2 *(lignes, routes)* to cut across one another, to intersect

3 *(se contredire)* to contradict oneself

4 se c. de qn *(interrompre le contact)* to cut oneself off from sb, to sever links with sb

---

coupe-racines [kuprasin] **NM INV** *Agr* root-slicer, rootcutter

couper-coller [3] [kupekɔle] *Ordinat* **VT & VI** to cut and paste

NM INV cut-and-paste; **faire un c. (sur qch)** to cut and paste (sth)

couperet [kuprɛ] **NM 1** *(d'une guillotine)* blade, knife **2** *(à viande)* cleaver, chopper

couperose [kuproz] **NF** red blotches (on the face), *Spéc* rosacea

couperosé, -e [kuproze] **ADJ** blotchy and red, *Spéc* affected by rosacea

Coupéspace® [kupespas] **NM** *Aut* Coupéspace®

coupeur, -euse [kupœr, -øz] **NM,F 1** *Couture* cutter **2** *(locution)* **un c. de cheveux en quatre** a nitpicker

coupe-vent [kupvɑ̃] **NM INV 1** *Br* windcheater, *Am* Windbreaker® **2** *Transp* V-shaped deflector

couplage [kuplaʒ] **NM** *Élec & Tech* coupling

couple [kupl] **NM 1** *(d'amoureux, de danseurs)* couple; *(de patineurs)* pair; *(d'animaux)* pair; **leur c. ne marche pas très fort** their relationship isn't going too well; **ils ont des problèmes de c.** they're having relationship problems; **vivre en c.** to live together (as a couple); *Zool* **c. alpha** alpha pair; *Mktg* **c. produit/marché** product/market pair

2 *Tech & Phys* couple; *Aut* **c. de démarrage** starting *or* cranking torque; **c. moteur** engine torque; *Phys* **c. thermoélectrique** thermocouple

3 *Math* pair

4 *Naut* frame; **interdiction de se mettre à c.** *(sur panneau)* no double-mooring

NF 1 *Chasse (chiens)* couple; *(colliers)* brace

2 *Vieilli & Littéraire ou Can* **une c. de** a couple of

couplé [kuple] **NM** *(au tiercé)* double; **c. gagnant** forecast bet; **c. placé** each-way double

coupler [3] [kuple] **VT 1** *(mettre deux à deux)* to couple together, to pair up *or* off **2** *Élec & Tech* to couple **3** *Chasse* to leash together

couplet [kuplɛ] **NM 1** *(strophe)* verse; *(chanson)* song **2** *Péj (discours)* tirade; **il y est allé de son c. sur la jeunesse d'aujourd'hui** he gave his little set piece on the young people of today

coupleur [kuplœr] **NM 1** *Élec, Rail & Transp* coupler **2** *Aut* **c. hydraulique** fluid flywheel *or* coupling **3** *Ordinat* coupler; **c. acoustique** acoustic coupler; **c. synchrone** synchronous coupler

coupole [kupɔl] **NF 1** *Archit* dome; **petite c.** cupola; **la C.** *(Académie)* the "Académie française"; *(restaurant)* = restaurant in Paris famous as a former meeting place for artists; **être reçu sous la C.** to be made a member of the "Académie française" **2** *Mil* cupola

coupon [kupɔ̃] **NM 1** *Tex* remnant **2** *(de papier)* coupon, voucher **3** *Fin (droit attaché à un titre)* coupon; **c. d'action** coupon; **c. attaché** cum dividend *or* coupon; **c. détaché** *ou* **échu** ex dividend *or* coupon **4** *Transp* **c. annuel/mensuel** yearly/monthly pass; *Belg* rail *or* train ticket

couponing [kupɔ̃iŋ], **couponnage** [kupɔnaʒ] **NM** *Mktg* couponing

coupon-prime [kupɔ̃prim] *(pl* **coupons-prime**) **NM** gift voucher, gift token

coupon-réponse [kupɔ̃repɔ̃s] *(pl* **coupons-réponse**) **NM** reply coupon

coupure [kupyr] **NF 1** *(blessure)* cut; **se faire une c.** to cut oneself; **la c. est profonde** it's a deep cut, it's quite a gash; *Fam Arg crime* **il connaît la c.** he knows just the trick

2 *(trêve, repos)* break; **une bonne c. dans la semaine** a good break during the week

3 *(rupture)* break

4 *Élec* **c. (de courant)** power cut, blackout; **il y a une c. de gaz/d'eau** the gas/the water has been cut off

5 *(suppression → dans un texte)* deletion

6 *(article)* **c. de journal/presse** newspaper/press cutting

7 *Fin* note, *Am* bill; **grosses/petites coupures** large/small denominations; **2000 euros en petites coupures** 2,000 euros in small notes *or* denominations; **en coupures usagées** in used notes

8 *Typ* **c. automatique de fin de ligne** automatic line break *or* wrap; **c. de mots** word splits; **c. de page** page break

9 *Rad & TV* **c. publicitaire** commercial break

couque [kuk] **NF** *Belg* cake

cour [kur] **NF 1** *(d'immeuble)* courtyard; *(de ferme)* yard, farmyard; **avec vue sur (la) c.** looking onto the inside of the building *or* onto the courtyard; *Can* **c. à bois** *Br* timber yard, *Am* lumber yard; **c. d'honneur** main courtyard; **c. intérieure** inner courtyard; *Scol* **c. de récréation** *Br* playground, *Am* schoolyard; *Fig* **jouer dans la c. des grands** to be up there with the leaders; **la société a été admise dans la c. des grands** the company has now become a serious contender; *Hist* **c. des Miracles** = area in Paris where vagrants had the right of sanctuary; *Fig* **c'était la c. des Miracles dans la salle d'attente** the waiting room was full of sorry characters; *Fam* **n'en jetez plus, la c. est pleine!** please, no more!

2 *(d'un roi)* court; *Fig (admirateurs)* following, inner circle (of admirers); **vivre à la c.** to live at court; **être bien en c.** to be in favour; **être mal en c.** to be out of favour

3 *Jur (magistrats, tribunal)* court; **Messieurs, la C.!** all rise!, *Br* be upstanding in court!; **c. administrative d'appel** Administrative Court of Appeal; **c. d'appel** court of appeal, *Am* court of appeals; **c. d'assises** *Br* ≃ Crown Court, *Am* ≃ Circuit Court; **c. d'assises des mineurs** Juvenile Assize Court; **c. d'assises spéciale** special Assize Court; **C. de cassation** final Court of Appeal; **C. de discipline budgétaire et financière** Budget and Finance Disciplinary Court; **C. européenne des droits de l'homme** European Court of Human Rights; **C. internationale de justice** International Court of Justice; **c. de juridiction inférieure** inferior court; **C. de justice des Communautés européennes** Court of Justice of the European Communities; **C. de justice de la République** = ad hoc tribunal for trying government ministers for crimes committed in office; **c. martiale** court martial; **passer devant la c. martiale, passer en c. martiale** to be court-martialled; *Belg* **c. des mineurs** juvenile court; **c. pénale internationale** International Criminal Court; **c. permanente d'arbitrage** Permanent Court of Arbitration; **c. prévôtale** provostal court *(temporary criminal court without appeal)*, summary court; **c. de renvoi** = appellate court which can retry cases after a decision is quashed by the "Cour de Cassation"; *Can* **la C. suprême** the Supreme Court; **Haute c.** High Court *(for impeachment of president or ministers)*

4 *Admin* **C. des comptes** = the French audit office, *Br* ≃ controller and auditor general, *Am* ≃ General Accounting Office; *UE* **c. des comptes européenne** European Court of Auditors

5 *Belg* toilets; **aller à la c.** to go to the toilets

6 *(locution)* **faire la c. à qn** *(chercher à séduire)* to court sb, to woo sb; *(flatter)* to curry favour with sb

> *Culture*
>
> **COUR**
>
> The "cour d'assises", made up of a president, two assessors and a jury of laymen, is the court which hears criminal cases. Normally the court meets every three months in each "département". The "Cour de cassation" is the highest court of civil and criminal appeal in France. The court has the power to overturn the decisions of lower courts when they believe the law has been misinterpreted. They do not rehear cases but simply analyse their use of law. The "Cour des comptes" is a state body which supervises the financial affairs of public bodies and local authorities, and monitors the way public funds are used.

> *Allusion*
>
> **C'est la cour du roi Pétaud**
>
> This is an expression from the sixteenth century. King Pétaud was a mythical figure whose court was said to be in utter chaos, full of noisy and ill-disciplined retainers. So today if one complains that some gathering is **la cour du roi Pétaud**, this means "It's like a madhouse."

courage [kuraʒ] **NM 1** *(bravoure)* courage, bravery; **avec c.** courageously, bravely; **je n'ai pas eu le c. de le lui dire** *(mauvaise nouvelle)* I didn't have the heart to tell him/her; **le c. me manqua** my courage failed me; **avoir le c. de ses opinions** to have the courage of one's convictions; **prendre son c. à deux mains** to muster all one's courage

2 *(énergie)* will, spirit; **travailler avec c.** to work with a will; **bon c.!** good luck!, hope it goes well!; *Ironique* good luck!; **c., la journée est bientôt finie** chin up *or* hang in there, the day's nearly over; **allez, c., les choses vont bien finir par s'arranger** don't worry, everything will be alright in the end; **un whisky pour te donner**

du c. a whisky to buck you up; **prendre c.** to take heart; **perdre c.** to lose heart, to become discouraged; **je n'ai pas le c.** *ou* **je ne me sens pas le c. d'aller travailler/de le lui dire** I don't feel up to going to work/to telling him/her

courageuse [kuraʒøz] *voir* **courageux**

courageusement [kuraʒøzmɑ̃] ADV 1 *(se battre, parler)* courageously, bravely 2 *(travailler)* with a will

courageux, -euse [kuraʒø, -øz] ADJ courageous, brave; **c. mais pas téméraire** brave but not reckless *or* foolhardy; **je ne me sens pas très c. aujourd'hui** I don't feel up to much today

courailler [3] [kuraje] *Can Fam* VI to run around
 VT **c. la galipote** to chase after women

courailleur [kurajœr] NM *Can Fam* womanizer

couramment [kuramɑ̃] ADV 1 *(bien)* fluently; **elle parle danois c., elle parle c. le danois** she speaks Danish fluently *or* fluent Danish
 2 *(souvent)* commonly; **objet employé c.** object in general use; **l'expression s'emploie c.** the expression is in common usage; **ça se dit c.** it's a common *or* an everyday expression; **cela m'arrive c.** it happens to me frequently; **cela se fait c.** it's common practice

courant¹ [kurɑ̃] NM 1 *Élec* **c. (électrique)** (electric) current; **branché sur le c.** plugged into the mains; **couper le c.** to cut the power off; **mettre le c.** to switch the power on; **rétablir le c.** to put the power back on; *Fam* **prendre le c.** to get a shock *or* an electric shock; **c. alternatif/continu** alternating/direct current; **le c. passe bien entre nous** we're on the same wavelength; **le c. passe bien entre lui et le public** he has a good rapport with the public
 2 *(dans l'eau)* current, stream; **il y a trop de c.** the current is too strong; **suivre le c.** to go with the current; *Fig* to follow the crowd, to go with the tide; **nager contre** *ou* **remonter le c.** to swim against the current; *Fig* to go against the tide; **c. sous-marin** undercurrent, undertow
 3 *(dans l'air)* current; **c. (atmosphérique)** airstream, current; **c. d'air** draught; **il y a des courants d'air** it's draughty; *Hum* **se déguiser** *ou* **se transformer en c. d'air** to vanish into thin air
 4 *(tendance)* current, trend; **c. d'affaires** business trend; **le c. classique** the classical movement; **les courants de l'opinion** currents *or* trends in public opinion; **un c. d'optimisme** a wave of optimism; **c. de pensée** way of thinking; **les courants du PS** = the ideological tendencies which have traditionally existed within the Socialist party
 5 *(masse mouvante)* movement, shift; **les courants de population** shifts of population; **les courants commerciaux sont perturbés** commercial progress is disturbed
 6 *(ce qui est quotidien)* **le c.** everyday life
 ❑ **au courant** ADJ *(informé)* **personne/journal bien au c.** well-informed person/paper; **il est parti mais les gens au c. n'ont rien dit** he left but those who knew about it *or* who were in the know kept quiet; **je ne suis pas au c.** I don't know anything about it; **oui, je suis au c.** yes, I know; **tu veux dire que tu étais au c.?** you mean you knew all about it? ADV **se tenir au c.** to keep abreast of things *or* oneself informed; **allez, on se tient au c.** let's keep in touch; **tiens-moi au c.** let me know how things are going; **mettre qn au c. (de qch)** to let sb know (about sth), to fill sb in (on sth); **pour vous mettre au c.** so that you know, (in order) to fill you in; **tenir qn au c.** to keep sb up to date, to keep sb posted
 ❑ **au courant de** PRÉP 1 *(informé de)* **au c. des nouvelles méthodes** well up on new methods; **être très au c. de ce qui se passe** to be very well-informed about what's happening; **tu es au c. de la panne?** do you know about the breakdown?; **on ne me tient jamais au c. de rien!** nobody ever tells me anything!; **je n'en suis pas au c.** I don't know anything about it; **je suis au c. de rien, moi!** I'm completely in the dark!
 2 *Littéraire (au fil de)* **écrire qch au c. de la plume** *(rapidement)* to dash sth off; *(sans effort)* to pen sth with ease; **des mots qui viennent au c. de la plume** words that flow from the pen
 ❑ **dans le courant de** PRÉP in *or* during the course of

courant², -e [kurɑ̃, -ɑ̃t] ADJ 1 *(quotidien → vie, dépenses)* everyday; *(→ travail)* everyday, routine; **en anglais c.** in everyday *or* conversational English
 2 *(commun → problème, maladie)* common; *(→ incident)* everyday; **un mot d'usage c.** a word in current *or* common *or* general use, an everyday word
 3 *(normal → modèle, pointure)* standard
 4 *(actuel)* current; **le mois c.** the current month; **votre lettre du 17 c.** your letter of the 17th of this month; **fin c.** at the end of this month
 ❑ **courante** NF 1 *Fam (diarrhée)* **la courante** the runs
 2 *(danse)* courante

courant-jet [kurɑ̃ʒɛ] *(pl* **courants-jets)** NM *Météo* jet stream

courbatu, -e [kurbaty] ADJ aching (and stiff)

courbature [kurbatyr] NF ache; **plein de courbatures** aching (and stiff) all over

courbaturé, -e [kurbatyre] ADJ aching (and stiff); **je me sens tout c.** I'm stiff all over

courbaturer [3] [kurbatyre] VT *(personne)* to tire out; *(cheval)* to founder

courbe [kurb] ADJ curving, rounded, curved
 NF 1 *Géom* curve, curved *or* rounded line; **la route fait des courbes** the road curves; **c. plane** plane curve
 2 *(sur un graphique)* curve; *(graphique)* graph; **tracer la c. de** to plot the curve of, to graph; **la c. d'apprentissage** the learning curve; **c. de Bézier** Bézier curve; *Compta* **c. des coûts** cost curve; **c. de croissance** growth curve; *Mktg* **c. du cycle de vie** *(d'un produit)* life-cycle curve; **c. de la demande** demand curve; **c. de la demande globale** aggregate demand curve; **c. d'expérience** experience curve; **c. d'investissement** investment curve; **c. en J** J-Curve; **c. de l'offre** supply curve; **c. de l'offre globale** aggregate supply curve; **la c. des prix/des salaires** the price/salary curve; **c. des taux** yield curve; *Méd* **c. de température** temperature curve; **c. des ventes** sales chart
 3 *Géog* **c. de niveau** contour line

courbement [kurbəmɑ̃] NM curving

courber [3] [kurbe] VT 1 *(plier)* to bend; **arbre courbé par le poids des fruits** tree bending under *or* with the weight of the fruit
 2 *(partie du corps)* **c. la tête** to bow *or* to bend one's head; **c. le front sur qch** to bend over sth; **marcher le dos courbé** to walk with a stoop; **c. l'échine** *ou* **le dos devant qn** to give in *or* to submit to sb
 3 *Suisse Fam (cours)* to skip; **c. l'école** to skip school, *Br* to bunk off
 VI *Littéraire* **c. sous le poids** to bend beneath the weight; **il a courbé sous le poids des difficultés** he buckled under the strain
 ►**se courber** VPR 1 *(ployer → arbre, barre)* to bend
 2 *(personne → gén)* to bend down; *(→ de vieillesse)* to stoop; *(→ pour saluer)* to bow (down); **se c. en deux** to bend double; **se c. devant qch** *(par soumission)* to bow before sth, to submit to sth

courbette [kurbɛt] NF 1 *(salut)* low bow; *Péj* **faire des courbettes à qn** to kowtow to sb, to bow and scrape to sb 2 *(d'un cheval)* curvet

courbine [kurbin] NF *Ich* meagre

courbure [kurbyr] NF *(d'une ligne, d'une surface, du dos)* curvature; *(d'une poutre)* sagging

courcailler [3] [kurkaje] VI *(caille)* to call

courcaillet [kurkajɛ] NM 1 *(cri)* quail call 2 *(appeau)* quail pipe

courçon [kursɔ̃] = **courson**

courée [kure] NF communal backyard *(typical of some Northern French towns)*

courette [kurɛt] NF *(d'un immeuble)* small yard *or* courtyard, close; *(d'une ferme)* small yard *or* farmyard

coureur, -euse [kurœr, -øz] ADJ 1 *(cheval)* racing
 2 *Fam (séducteur)* **il est très c.** he's a womanizer *or* philanderer; **elle est très coureuse** she's always chasing men
 NM,F 1 *Sport* runner; *(sauteur de haies)* hurdler; **c. automobile** racing driver; **c. cycliste** (racing) cyclist; **c. de fond/demi-fond** long-distance/middle-distance runner; **c. motocycliste** motorcycle *or* motorbike racer
 2 *Fam (séducteur → homme)* womanizer; *(→ femme)* man-eater; **c. de dot** dowry-hunter; **c. de jupons** womanizer, philanderer
 3 *(amateur)* **un c. de fêtes/musées** inveterate party-goer/museum-goer
 4 *Can* **c. des bois** fur trader, trapper
 ❑ **coureurs** NMPL *Vieilli* running birds

courge [kurʒ] NF 1 *Culin Br* (vegetable) marrow, *Am* squash; *(plante, fruit)* gourd, squash 2 *Fam (imbécile)* idiot, dope, twit

courgette [kurʒɛt] NF *Br* courgette, *Am* zucchini

COURIR [45] [kurir]

VI to run 1–3, 5, 6 ▪ to race 1, 2 ▪ to rush 2, 3 ▪ to go round 4
VT to run 1, 4 ▪ to roam 2 ▪ to go round 3 ▪ to seek 4

VI 1 *(gén)* to run; *(sportif, lévrier)* to run, to race; **il courra chez Renault l'année prochaine** he'll be driving for Renault next year; **entrer/sortir/traverser en courant** to run in/out/across; **monter/descendre l'escalier en courant** to run up/down the stairs; **partir en courant** to run off; **il arriva vers moi en courant** he ran up to me; **j'ai couru à fond de train** *ou* **à toutes jambes** I ran as fast as my legs could carry me; **il partit en courant à toutes jambes** he raced off; **c. ventre à terre** to run flat out; **c. tête baissée (vers)** to rush headlong (towards); **elle a fait c. son cheval dans le Grand Prix** she entered her horse in the Grand Prix; **c. comme un lièvre** to run like a hare; **c. comme le vent** to run like the wind; **l'assassin court toujours** the murderer is still on the run
 2 *(se déplacer → nuée)* to race along *or* by; *(→ eau)* to rush, to run; **ses doigts couraient sur les touches** his/her fingers ran up and down the keyboard; **sa plume courait sur le papier** his/her pen was racing across the paper; **laisser c. sa plume** to let one's pen run freely; **des frissons glacés couraient le long de son dos** icy shivers were running down his/her spine
 3 *(se précipiter)* to rush, to run; **toujours en train de c. chez le médecin** always running to the doctor; **cours acheter du pain** run out *or Br* nip out and get some bread; **j'ai couru le prévenir** I ran to warn him; **j'y cours** I'll rush over; **et tes confitures? – j'y cours!** what about the jam you're making? – I'm just going to see to it now!; **la pièce qui fait c. tout Paris** the play all Paris is flocking to see; *Fig* **qu'est-ce qui le fait c.?** what drives him?; **faire qch en courant** to do sth in a hurry; **un mot écrit en courant** a rushed note, a note that's been dashed off; **j'ai couru partout pour les cadeaux** I ran around all over the place for presents; **j'ai couru toute la journée** I've been in a rush *or* I've been run off my feet all day
 4 *(se propager → rumeur, idée)* **un bruit qui court** a rumour that's going round; **faire c. des bruits sur qn** to spread rumours about sb; **le bruit court que…** rumour has it that…
 5 *(temps)* to run; **l'année qui court** the current year; **la location court jusqu'au 25** it's rented until the 25th; **le bail n'a plus qu'un an à c.** the lease has only one more year to run; **par les temps qui courent** nowadays
 6 *(s'étendre)* **c. le long de** *(rivière, voie ferrée)* to run *or* to stretch along; **le lierre court le long du mur** the ivy crawls *or* runs along the wall; **ses notes couraient en marge du texte** his/her notes ran in the margin (next to the text)
 7 *Fin (intérêt)* to accrue; **laisser c. des intérêts** to allow interest to accrue
 8 *Naut* to sail; **c. au large** to stand out to sea; **c. à terre** to stand in for the land
 9 *Fam (locutions)* **tu peux (toujours) c.!** no way!; **l'épouser? il peut toujours c.!** marry her? he doesn't have a hope in hell!; **laisse c.!** forget it!, drop it!; **c. sur le système** *ou* **le haricot à qn** *(l'énerver)* to get on sb's nerves *or Br* up sb's nose; **il commence à me c.!** he's beginning *Br* to get up my nose *or Am* to tick me off!
 VT 1 *Sport (course)* to compete in, to run
 2 *(sillonner → ville, mers)* to roam, to rove; **c. le monde/la campagne** to roam the world/the

countryside; *Littéraire* **chemins courant la campagne** paths darting through the countryside; *Fig* **c. les rues** to be run-of-the-mill *or* nothing unusual; **cela court les rues** *(idée, style)* it's run-of-the-mill; **quelqu'un comme ça, ça ne court pas les rues** people like that are hard to come by

3 *(fréquenter)* to go round; **elle court les musées** she's an inveterate museum-goer; **c. les fêtes** to go to all the parties; **c. les filles/les garçons** to chase girls/boys; **c. le jupon** *ou* **le cotillon** to flirt with women, to womanize; *Hum & Vieilli* **c. la gueuse** *ou* **le guilledou** *ou* **la prétentaine** to chase women, to go wenching, to philander

4 *(rechercher → honneurs, poste)* to seek; **acteur courant le cachet** actor desperate for work

5 *(encourir)* **c. un risque** to run a risk; **faire c. un risque** *ou* **danger à qn** to put sb at risk

6 *(tenter)* **c. sa chance** to try one's chance

7 *Chasse* to hunt; *Prov* **il ne faut pas c. deux lièvres à la fois** if you run after two hares you will catch neither

❑ **courir à** VT IND *(faillite, désastre)* to head for; **elle court à sa perte** she's heading for disaster, she's on the road to ruin

❑ **courir après** VT IND **1** *(pour rattraper)* to run after

2 *Fam (rechercher)* **c. après qn** to chase *or* run after sb; **il n'arrête pas de me c. après** he won't leave me alone, he's forever running after me; **c. après un poste** to be after a job; **c. après la célébrité** to strive for recognition; **il court toujours après le temps** he's always short of time; **elle ne court pas après l'argent** she's not after money; **il peut toujours c. après son argent!** he'll never see his money again!

V IMPERSONNEL **il court des bruits sur lui** there are rumours going round about him

❑ **courir sur** VT IND *(approcher de)* **c. sur ses 60 ans** to be approaching 60

▸**se courir** VPR **le tiercé se court à Enghien aujourd'hui** today's race is being run at Enghien

Allusion

Rien ne sert de courir, il faut partir à point

In La Fontaine's fable, taken from Aesop, *The Tortoise and the Hare*, the two animals take part in a race. The over-confident hare keeps stopping for a rest, while the tortoise plods onward to win. This expression means "It's no use running, you must leave on time", and people say it when making a disparaging allusion to someone who appears too self-confident.

courlan [kurlɑ̃] NM *Orn* limpkin

courlieu, -x [kurljø] NM *Orn* whimbrel

courlis [kurli] NM *Orn* curlew; **c. de terre** stone curlew

couronne [kurɔn] NF **1** *(coiffure → d'un souverain)* crown; *(→ d'un pair)* coronet; *aussi Fig* **porter la c.** to wear the crown; **c. d'épines** crown of thorns; **c. de fleurs d'oranger** crown *or* circlet of orange blossom; **c. de lauriers** crown of laurels, laurel wreath; **c. mortuaire** (funeral) wreath; **c. royale** royal crown

2 *Hist & Pol* **la C. d'Angleterre/de Belgique** the English/Belgian Crown; **prétendre à la C.** to lay claim to the throne; **il aspire à la C. de France** he wants to become King of France; **les joyaux de la C.** the Crown jewels; *Can* **société de la C.** Crown corporation

3 *(cercle)* crown, circle; **une c. de nuages entourait la montagne** the mountain was surrounded by a ring of clouds

4 *(périphérie)* **la grande c.** = the area around Paris which takes in the "départements" of Seine-et-Marne, Yvelines, Essonne and Val-d'Oise; **la petite c.** = the suburbs adjacent to Paris in the "départements" of Seine-Saint-Denis, Val-de-Marne and Hauts-de-Seine

5 *(en danse)* crown

6 *(pain)* ring, ring-shaped loaf

7 *(prothèse dentaire)* crown; **se faire poser une c.** to have *or* get a tooth crowned

8 *Aut* **c. dentée** crown wheel; **c. d'embrayage** clutch ring

9 *Archit, Astron & Bot* corona

10 *(monnaie)* crown; **c. danoise/norvégienne** krone; **c. suédoise** krona

11 *(d'un arbre)* crown

❑ **en couronne** ADJ **1** *(en rond)* **fleurs en c.** wreath of flowers; **nattes en c.** plaits (worn) in a crown

2 *Culin* in a ring

couronné, -e [kurɔne] ADJ *(souverain)* crowned

couronnement [kurɔnmɑ̃] NM **1** *(cérémonie)* coronation, crowning **2** *(réussite)* crowning achievement **3** *(récompense)* **cette année a vu le c. de ses efforts** this year his/her efforts were finally rewarded **4** *(de jetée)* capping; *(de bâtiment, de colonne)* top; *(de mur)* coping; *(de toit)* ridge

couronner [3] [kurɔne] VT **1** *(roi)* to crown; *Antiq & Hist (orateur, soldat)* to crown with a laurel wreath; **elle fut couronnée reine/impératrice** she was crowned queen/empress

2 *(entourer, couvrir)* **des pics couronnés de neige** snow-capped peaks

3 *(récompenser → poète, chercheur)* to award a prize to; *(→ œuvre, roman)* to award a prize for

4 *(conclure → carrière, recherches, vie)* to crown; **sa nomination vient c. sa carrière** his/her nomination is the crowning achievement of his/her career; *Fam* **et pour c. le tout** and to crown it all, and on top of all that

5 *(dent)* to crown

▸**se couronner** VPR *(cheval)* to break its knee; *Fam* **se c. les genoux** to graze one's knees

couros [kuros] = **kouros**

courrai *etc voir* **courir**

courre [kur] *voir* **chasse**

courriel [kuriɛl] NM *Ordinat (abrév* **courrier électronique***)* e-mail

courrier [kurje] NM **1** *(correspondance → reçue)* mail, letters, *Br* post; *(→ à envoyer)* letters (to be sent); **j'ai beaucoup de c. en retard** I've got a lot of letters to write; **faire son c.** to write one's letters; **il y a du c. pour moi aujourd'hui?** are there any letters for me *or* have I got any mail *or Br* is there any post for me today?; **elle reçoit beaucoup de c.** she receives a lot of mail; **le c. est-il arrivé?** has the *Br* postman *or Am* mailman been yet?; **avec la grève, il y a du retard dans le c.** with the strike, there are delays in mail deliveries; **faites partir ça avec le premier c.** *Br* send this first post today, *Am* send this by the first mail; **c. interne** internal mail

2 *(lettre)* **un c.** a letter

3 *Admin & Pol (messager)* courier

4 *(chronique)* column; **c. du cœur** problem page, *Br* agony column, *Am* advice column; **c. des lecteurs** letters (to the editor)

5 *Ordinat* **c. électronique** e-mail; **envoyer un c. électronique à qn** to e-mail sb; **envoyer qch par c. électronique** to send sth by e-mail; **contacter qn par c. électronique** to contact sb by e-mail; **c. escargot** snail mail

6 *Transp* mail; *Hist (homme)* messenger

7 *Presse* **le C. de l'Ouest** = daily newspaper published in Angers

courriériste [kurjerist] NMF columnist; **c. du cœur** *Br* agony aunt, *Am* advice columnist

courroie [kurwa] NF **1** *(gén)* belt strap **2** *Tech* belt; **c. de transmission** driving belt; *Aut* **c. de ventilateur** fan belt; *Aut* **c. d'arbre à cames** cam *or* timing belt; *Aut* **c. d'entraînement** *ou* **de commande** drive belt

courroucé, -e [kuruse] ADJ *Littéraire* wrathful

courroucer [16] [kuruse] *Littéraire* VT to anger, to infuriate

▸**se courroucer** VPR to become infuriated

courroux [kuru] NM *Littéraire* anger, ire, wrath; **les flots en c.** the raging sea

COURS [kur]

course **A1–3, C1, 2** ■ rate **B1, 2** ■ price **B2** ■ class **C1, 3** ■ lesson **C1** ■ coursebook **C2**

NM **A.** *ÉCOULEMENT, SUCCESSION* **1** *Géog (débit)* flow; *(parcours)* course; **avoir un c. lent** to be slow-flowing; **avoir un c. rapide** to be fast-flowing; **descendre le c. de la Tamise** to go down the Thames; **dévier le c. d'une rivière** to divert the course of a river; **c. d'eau** *(gén)* waterway; *(ruisseau)* stream; *(rivière)* river; **au long c.** *(voyage)* long-haul; *Naut* **navigation au long c.** deep-sea navigation

2 *(déroulement → des années, des saisons, de pensées)* course; *(→ d'événements)* course, run; *(→ de négociations, d'une maladie, de travaux)* course, progress; **donner** *ou* **laisser (libre) c. à** *(joie, indignation)* to give vent to; *(imagination, chagrin)* to give free rein to; **suivre le c. de ses idées** to follow one's train of thought; **suivre son c.** *(processus)* to continue; **ils ont voulu changer le c. de l'Histoire** they wanted to change the course of history; **la vie reprend son c.** life goes on; **en suivant/remontant le c. du temps** going forward/back in time

3 *Astron* course

4 *(dans des noms de rue)* avenue

5 *Constr* **c. d'assise** course *or* layer *(of bricks etc)*

B. *DANS LE DOMAINE FINANCIER* **1** *(de devises)* rate; **avoir c.** *(monnaie)* to be legal tender *or* legal currency; *(pratique)* to be common *or* current; **avoir c. légal** to be legal tender *or* legal currency; **ne plus avoir c.** *(monnaie)* to be out of circulation, to be no longer legal tender *or* legal currency; *(pratique, théorie)* to be obsolete; *(expression, terme)* to be obsolete *or* no longer in use; **c. du change** exchange rate; **c. des devises** foreign exchange rate; **c. étranger** foreign exchange; **c. forcé** forced currency; **c. de liquidation** settlement price

2 *Bourse (d'actions)* price, trading rate; **au c. du marché** at the market *or* trading price; **au c. (du jour)** at the today's rate, at the current daily price; **quel est le c. du sucre?** what is the price *or* quotation for sugar?; **dernier c.** closing price; **le c. d'ouverture/de clôture de ces actions était de 3 euros** these shares opened/closed at 3 euros; **c. acheteur** bid price; **c. des actions** share prices; **c. en Bourse** official price; **les cours de la Bourse** Stock Exchange prices; **c. de clôture** closing price; **c. de compensation** settlement price; **c. du dont** call price; **c. hors Bourse, c. hors cote** unofficial price; **c. légal** legal tender; **c. limite** limit price; **c. du marché** market price *or* rate; **c. officiel** official exchange rate; **c. d'ouverture** opening price; **c. pivot** central rate; **c. à terme** forward rate; **c. vendeur** offer price

C. *DANS LE DOMAINE SCOLAIRE ET UNIVERSITAIRE* **1** *(classe) Scol* class, lesson; *Univ* class, lecture; *(ensemble des leçons)* course; **des heures de c.** teaching hours; **aller en c.** *(à un cours)* to go to one's class; *(à l'école)* to go to school; *(à l'université)* to attend lectures; **être en c.** to be in class; **suivre des c.** to attend *or* take a course; **suivre un c.** *ou* **des c. d'espagnol** to go to *or* to attend a Spanish class; **prendre des c.** to take lessons *or* a course; **elle prend des c. au Conservatoire** she attends the Conservatoire; **j'ai c. tout à l'heure** *(élève, professeur)* I have a class later; **j'ai c. tous les jours** *(élève, professeur)* I have classes every day; **faire** *ou* **donner un c. d'histoire** to give a history lecture/lesson/course; **c'est moi qui vous ferai c. cette année** I'll be teaching you this year; **les professeurs ne font pas c. cet après-midi** there are no lessons this afternoon; **qui nous fera c. pendant votre absence?** who's going to take our class while you're away?; **tu ne vas pas me faire un c. sur la politesse?** are you going to give me a lecture on how to be polite?; **c. par correspondance** correspondence course; **c. magistral** lecture; **donner/prendre des c. particuliers** to give/to have private tuition; **je prends des c. particuliers de français** I get *or* have private tuition in French; **c. de perfectionnement** proficiency course; **c. du soir** evening class

2 *(manuel)* course, coursebook, textbook; *(notes)* notes

3 *(degré → dans l'enseignement primaire)* **c. préparatoire** *Br* ≃ first-year infants class, *Am* ≃ nursery school; **c. élémentaire** = two-year subdivision of primary-level education in France (ages 8 to 9); **c. élémentaire 1** = second year of primary school, *Br* ≃ year 3; **c. élémentaire 2** = third year of primary school, *Br* ≃ year 4; **c. moyen** = two-year subdivision of primary-level

education in France (ages 10 to 11); **c. moyen 1** = fourth year of primary school, *Br* ≃ year 5; **c. moyen 2** = fifth year of primary school, *Br* ≃ year 6

4 *(établissement)* school; **c. privé** private school

▫ **au cours de** PRÉP during, in *or* during the course of; **au c. du débat** in the course of *or* during the debate; **au c. des siècles** over the centuries; **au c. de notre dernier entretien** when we last spoke; **ça se décidera au c. des prochaines semaines** it'll be decided in the weeks to come

▫ **en cours** ADJ *(actuel)* **l'année/le tarif en c.** the current year/price; **affaire/travail en c.** business/work in hand; **examen en c.** examination in progress; **être en c.** *(débat, réunion, travaux)* to be under way, to be in progress; **une enquête est en c.** investigations are taking place

▫ **en cours de** PRÉP in the process of; **il nous a laissés en c. de partie** he left us in the middle of the game; **c'est en c. d'étude** it's being examined; **en c. de construction** under construction, in the process of being built; **en c. d'investigation** being investigated, under investigation; **en c. de production** in production; **en c. de réparation** in the process of being repaired, undergoing repairs; **en c. de route** on the way

course [kurs] NF **1** *Sport (compétition)* race; **il a dû arrêter en pleine c.** he had to stop in the middle of the race; **faire la c.** to race; **on fait la c. jusqu'à la cabane!** race you *or* last (one) to the hut!; **faire la c. avec qn** to race (with) sb; **les enfants, on ne fait pas la c.!** children, no running!; *Fig* **c'est toujours la c. au bureau** we're always run off our feet at the office; **c. attelée/handicap** harness/handicap race; **c. de fond** *ou* **d'endurance** long-distance race; **c. de** *ou* **en chars** chariot race; **c. automobile** motor *or* car race; **c. de chevaux** (horse) race; **c. à la cocarde** = traditional sport in Southern France in which rosettes are snatched from the horns of young cattle; **c. cycliste** cycle race; **c. de demi-fond** middle-distance race; *Équitation* **c. d'obstacles** steeplechase; **c. d'orientation** orienteering; **c. à pied** race; **c. de plat** flat race; **c. de relais** relay race; **c. en sac** sack race; **c. de taureaux** *(corrida)* bullfight; *(dans les rues)* bull-running; **c. de vaches landaises, c. de vachettes, c. landaise** = bullfight with young cows; **c. de vitesse** *Br* sprint, *Am* dash; **c. contre la montre** race against the clock, time-trial; *Fig* race against time; *Fam Fig* **être dans la c.** to be hip *or* with it; *Fam Fig* **rester dans la c.** to stay in *or* to be still in the race; **l'entreprise essaie de rester dans la c.** the company's trying to keep up with the competitors

2 *(activité, action)* **épuisé par sa c.** exhausted from his/her running; **c. d'élan** run-up; **la c.** *(à pied)* running; *(en voiture, à cheval)* racing; **je fais de la c. à pied tous les jours** I run every day; **la c. aux armements** the arms race; **la c. au pouvoir/à la présidence** the race for power/the presidency; *TV* **la c. à l'audimat** *ou* **à l'audience** the ratings war

3 *(randonnée)* **faire une c. en montagne** to go for a trek in the mountains

4 *(d'un taxi → voyage)* journey; *(→ prix)* fare; **payer (le prix de) la c.** to pay the fare

5 *(commission)* errand; **j'ai une c. à faire** I've got to buy something *or* to get something from the shops

6 *(trajectoire → d'un astre, d'un pendule)* course, trajectory; *(→ d'un missile)* flight; *(→ d'un piston)* stroke

7 *Suisse (trajet)* trip *(by train or boat)*; *(excursion)* excursion

8 *Hist (d'un navire corsaire)* privateering

▫ **courses** NFPL **1** *(commissions)* shopping; **faire les/des courses** to do the/some shopping; **il est parti faire quelques courses** he went out to do a bit of shopping; **la liste des courses** the shopping list

2 *(de chevaux)* races; **jouer aux courses** to bet on the races *or* on the horses; **il a gagné 3000 euros aux courses** he won 3,000 euros on the races

course-croisière [kurskrwazjɛr] *(pl* **courses-croisières***)* NF boat race

course-poursuite [kurspursɥit] *(pl* **courses-poursuites***)* NF **1** *Sport* track race **2** *(entre policiers et voleurs)* car chase

courser [3] [kurse] VT *Fam* to chase▪, to run after▪; **elle s'est fait c. par des voyous** she was chased by some thugs

VI *Joual (faire la course)* to race

coursier, -ère [kursje, -ɛr] NM,F errand boy, *f* girl; *(à moto)* dispatch rider

NM **1** *(transporteur)* **envoyer qch par c.** to send sth by courier; **c. international** courier company **2** *Littéraire (cheval)* steed

coursive [kursiv] NF **1** *Naut* gangway **2** *Constr* (raised) passageway

courson, -onne [kursõ, -ɔn] ADJ *Hort* spur bearing

NM **1** *Hort* spur bearer **2** *Mil* submerged stake

COURT, -E [kur, kurt]

> **ADJ** short **A1–3, B1, 2** ▪ small **C1** ▪ slender **C3**
> **ADV** short **1,2**
> **NM** court **3**

ADJ **A.** *DANS L'ESPACE* **1** *(en longueur → cheveux, ongles)* short; **il a les jambes courtes** he's got short legs; *Fam* **c. sur pattes** *(chien)* short-legged; *(personne)* short; **à manches courtes** short-sleeved, with short sleeves; **la jupe est trop courte de 3 centimètres** the skirt is 3 centimetres too short; **la ligne droite est le plus c. chemin d'un point à un autre** a straight line is the shortest distance between two points; **quel est le plus c. chemin de Sens à Troyes?** what's the shortest route between Sens and Troyes?, what's the quickest way to get from Sens to Troyes?; **il y a un chemin plus c.** there's a shorter *or* quicker way; **je l'ai suivi sur une courte distance** I followed him a short *or* little way

2 *Anat (os, muscle)* short

3 *Rad (ondes)* short

4 *Naut* **vague** *ou* **mer courte** choppy sea

B. *DANS LE TEMPS* **1** *(bref → discours, lettre, séjour, durée etc)* short, brief; *Fam* **son histoire était courte mais bonne** his/her story was short but sweet; **les jours sont de plus en plus courts** the days are getting shorter (and shorter) *or* are drawing in; **les années semblent bien courtes!** the years seem to fly by *or* to pass so quickly!; **pendant un c. instant** for a brief *or* fleeting moment; **mon séjour a été plus c. que prévu** my stay was shorter than planned

2 *(proche)* **à c. terme** short-term *(avant n)*; **dette/emprunt à c. terme** short-term debt/loan; **j'ai des projets à c. terme** I have some plans in *or* for the short term

C. *FAIBLE, INSUFFISANT* **1** *(faible → avance, avantage)* small; *(→ majorité)* small, slender; **après sa courte victoire sur son compatriote** after a narrow victory over his fellow countryman; **Zanoa a mené la course sur une courte distance** Zanoa led the race over a short distance; **au virage, il avait une courte avance sur le peloton** in the bend, he was leading the bunch by a short distance; *aussi Fig* **gagner d'une courte tête** to win by a short head

2 *(restreint)* **avoir la respiration courte** *ou* **le souffle c.** to be short of breath *or* wind

3 *Fam (insuffisant → connaissances)* slender▪, limited▪; *(→ quantité, mesure)* meagre▪, skimpy; **nos revenus sont un peu courts pour envisager un emprunt** we don't really earn enough to consider taking out a loan; **10 sur 20, c'est un peu c.** 10 out of 20, it's a bit borderline; **deux bouteilles pour six, c'est un peu c.** two bottles for six people, that's a bit on the stingy side; **1500 euros pour refaire le toit, l'estimation me semble courte** 1,500 euros to redo the roof, the estimate seems on the low side to me; **tu n'as que 3 mètres de tissu? c'est un peu c.** you've only got 3 metres of material? that's a bit skimpy; **l'avion décolle dans 30 minutes – c'est trop c. pour l'avoir** the plane takes off in 30 minutes – we won't make it in time▪; **plutôt c. comme excuse!** (it's) a bit of a pathetic excuse!; **sa rubrique est amusante mais les idées sont courtes** his/her column is entertaining but short on ideas; **à courtes vues** *(personne)* limited (in one's understanding); *(explication)* limited; *aussi Fig* **avoir la vue courte** to be *Br* short-sighted *or Am* near-sighted; **avoir la mémoire courte** to have a short memory

4 *(sans arguments)* **demeurer** *ou* **rester c.** to be at a loss

ADV **1** *(en dimension)* **je me suis fait couper les cheveux c.** I had my hair cut short; **des cheveux coupés** *ou* **taillés très c.** hair cut very short; **se coiffer c.** to keep one's hair short; **elle s'habille c.** she wears her skirts short; **cet été, on s'habillera c.** this summer, short dresses and skirts will be in fashion *or* hemlines will be high

2 *Fam (en durée)* **pour faire c.** to cut a long story short

3 *(brusquement)* **s'arrêter c.** to stop short; **tourner c.** *(discussion, projet)* to come to an abrupt end

NM **1** *(terrain)* **c. (de tennis)** tennis court; **sur le c.** on (the) court; **c. en bitume** hard court; **c. en gazon** grass court; **c. en terre battue** clay court

2 *Couture* **le c.** short fashions *or* hemlines *or* styles

3 *(locutions)* **aller au plus c.** to take the quickest course of action; **allons au plus c., qui a pris l'argent?** let's not beat about the bush, who took the money?; **prendre par le** *ou* **au plus c.** *(chemin, procédure)* to take a short cut

▫ **à court** ADV *Fam* short on cash, hard-up, a bit short

▫ **à court de** PRÉP **être à c. d'idées/de vivres** to have run out of ideas/food; **nous étions presque à c. d'eau** we were low on *or* running short of water; **être à c. d'argent** to be short of money; **à c. de personnel** short-staffed; **elle n'est jamais à c. d'arguments** she's never at a loss for an argument; *Belg* **être à c. d'haleine** to be out of breath

▫ **de court** ADV **prendre qn de c.** *(ne pas lui laisser de délai de réflexion)* to give sb (very) short notice; *(le surprendre)* to catch sb unawares *or* napping

▫ **tout court** ADV **Maximilien de la Fontanière, Maxime tout c. pour les amis** Maximilien de la Fontanière, or just Maxime to his friends; **appelez-moi Jeanne, tout c.** just call me Jeanne; **cela indigne les chrétiens démocrates et même les chrétiens tout c.** this is shocking to Christian Democrats and even to Christians *Br* full stop *or Am* period

> *Allusion*
> **C'est un peu court, jeune homme**
> Cyrano de Bergerac, the hero of Edmond Rostand's play of the same name (1897), has an enormous nose and commensurate sense of honour. In one scene, Cyrano is taken to task by a Viscount who makes a weak attempt at an insult by stammering "Your nose is – er – er – very – er... big", to which Cyrano makes this rejoinder, "It's rather short, young man", referring to the man's statement, before launching into a long comic description of the nose, one of the best-known speeches in all of French drama. This expression is used today of a feeble and disappointing verbal performance, as a reproof to the speaker.

courtage [kurtaʒ] NM *(profession)* brokerage; *(commission)* brokerage, commission; **faire le c.** to be a broker; **ces articles sont vendus par c.** these items are sold on commission; **vente par c.** selling on commission; **c. électronique** e-broking, on-line broking; **c. officiel** official brokerage

courtaud, -e [kurto, -od] ADJ **1** *(personne)* short-legged, squat, dumpy **2** *Vét* docked and crop-eared

NM,F **1** *(personne)* short-legged *or* squat *or* dumpy person **2** *(chien)* docked and crop-eared dog; *(cheval)* docked and crop-eared horse

courtauder [3] [kurtode] VT to dock the tail and crop the ears of

court-bouillon [kurbujõ] *(pl* **courts-bouillons***)* NM *Culin* court-bouillon; **faire cuire au** *ou* **dans un c.** to cook in a court-bouillon

court-circuit [kursirkɥi] (*pl* **courts-circuits**) NM *Élec* short circuit; **faire c.** to short-circuit

court-circuitage [kursirkɥitaʒ] (*pl* **courts-circuitages**) NM *Élec* short-circuiting

court-circuiter [3] [kursirkɥite] VT **1** *Élec* to short, to short-circuit **2** *Fam (assemblée, personnel)* to bypass; *(procédure)* to bypass, to short-circuit; **court-circuite-le avant qu'il ne signe** grab him before he signs

court-courrier [kurkurje] (*pl* **court-courriers**) NM short-haul plane

courtepointe [kurtəpwɛ̃t] NF (quilted) bedspread, counterpane

courtier, -ère [kurtje, -ɛr] NM,F **1** *Bourse* broker; **c. de Bourse** stockbroker; **c. de change** exchange broker; **c. électronique** e-broker, on-line broker; **c. intermédiaire** inter-dealer broker; **c. en matières premières** commodity broker, commodity dealer; **c. en valeurs mobilières** stockbroker

2 *Com* **c. en assurances** insurance broker; **c. de commerce** general broker; **c. à la commission** commission agent; **c. libre** outside broker; **c. de marchandises** commercial broker; **c. maritime** ship *or* shipping broker; **c. marron** outside broker; **c. en valeurs mobilières** stockbroker; **c. en vins** wine broker

courtilière [kurtiljɛr] NF *Entom* mole cricket

courtine [kurtin] NF curtain

courtisan [kurtizɑ̃] NM **1** *Hist* courtier **2** *(flatteur)* flatterer, sycophant

courtisane [kurtizan] NF *Littéraire* courtesan

courtisanerie [kurtizanri] NF *Littéraire* flattery, sycophancy

courtiser [3] [kurtize] VT **1** *(femme)* to court, to woo, to pay court to **2** *(pays, puissants)* to woo; **c. le pouvoir/la gloire** to woo power/fame; **il le courtisait servilement** he fawned on him obsequiously

court-jointé, -e [kurʒwɛ̃te] (*mpl* **court-jointés,** *fpl* **court-jointées**) ADJ *Zool* short-pasterned, short in the pastern

court-jus [kurʒy] (*pl* **courts-jus**) NM *Fam Élec* short

court-métrage [kurmetraʒ] (*pl* **courts-métrages**) NM short film, short

courtois, -e [kurtwa, -az] ADJ **1** *(poli → personne, manières)* civil, courteous; **de manière courtoise** politely; **un homme c.** a courteous man; **d'un ton c.** civilly, courteously; **être c. envers qn** to be courteous *or* civil towards sb **2** *Hist & Littérature (roman, poésie, littérature)* about courtly love; **amour c.** courtly love

courtoisement [kurtwazmɑ̃] ADV courteously

courtoisie [kurtwazi] NF courtesy, courteousness; **avec c.** courteously

court-vêtu, -e [kurvety] (*mpl* **court-vêtus,** *fpl* **court-vêtues**) ADJ **des femmes court-vêtues** women in short skirts

couru, -e [kury] PP *voir* **courir**

ADJ **1** *(populaire)* fashionable, popular; *(spectacle)* popular; **les bars les plus courus** the most fashionable bars **2** *Fam (certain)* **c'est c. (d'avance)!** it's a sure thing!, *Br* it's a (dead) cert!; **c'était c.!** it was bound to happen!, it was a foregone conclusion!

courvite [kurvit] NM *Orn* courser; **c. gaulois** *ou* **isabelle** cream-coloured courser

cousait *etc voir* **coudre**

couscous [kuskus] NM **1** *Culin* couscous **2** *Zool* cuscus

couscoussier [kuskusje] NM couscous steamer, couscoussier, couscoussière

cousette [kuzɛt] NF **1** *(étui)* sewing kit **2** *Fam Vieilli* dressmaker's apprentice

couseur, -euse [kuzœr, -øz] NM,F *(sur une machine à coudre)* machinist; *(dans la reliure)* stitcher

▫ **couseuse** NF **1** *Typ* stitcher **2** *(machine à coudre)* industrial sewing-machine

cousin, -e [kuzɛ̃, -in] NM,F cousin; **c. germain** first *or* full cousin; **petit c., c. au second degré** second cousin; *Hum* **c. éloigné** *ou* **à la mode de Bretagne** distant relation

NM *Entom* (big) mosquito

'La Cousine Bette' *Balzac* 'Cousin Bette'

cousinage [kuzinaʒ] NM *Vieilli* **1** *(parenté)* cousinhood **2** *(cousins)* **son c.** his/her kith and kin, his/her kinsfolk *or Am* kinfolk

cousine [kuzin] *voir* **cousin**

cousiner [3] [kuzine] VI **c. (avec qn)** to be on friendly terms (with sb)

coussin [kusɛ̃] NM **1** *(de siège, de meuble)* cushion; *Belg & Suisse (oreiller)* pillow; **un c. de feuilles/mousse** a cushion of leaves/moss **2** *Tech* **c. d'air** air cushion; **c. gonflable** Airbag® **3** *(au base-ball)* base

coussinet [kusinɛ] NM **1** *(petit coussin)* small cushion **2** *Zool* pad **3** *Tech* bearing; *Rail* chair; **c. de bielle** big end bearing; **c. de palier** bearing bush **4** *Archit* coussinet, cushion

cousu, -e [kuzy] PP *voir* **coudre**

coût [ku] NM **1** *(prix)* cost, price; **c. d'achat** purchase cost; *(sur bilan)* cost of goods purchased; **c. d'acquisition** acquisition cost; **coûts administratifs** administrative costs; **c. assurance fret** cost insurance freight; *Compta* **coûts attribuables** relevant costs; **coûts cachés** hidden costs; **c. du capital** capital cost; **c. ciblé** target cost; **coûts constants** fixed costs *or* expenses; **c. du crédit** credit charges *or* cost; **c. complet unitaire** total unit cost; **coûts cumulés** cumulative costs; **coûts de détention** holding costs; **coûts de développement** development costs; **coûts discrétionnaires** discretionary costs; **c. (total) de distribution** (total) distribution cost; **c. économique** economic cost; **c. de l'élaboration du produit** product development cost; *Compta* **coûts engagés** committed costs; **c. d'entretien** maintenance cost; **coûts évitables** avoidable costs; **coûts d'exploitation** operational costs; **c. fixe (total)** (total) fixed cost; **coûts fixes communs** common fixed costs; **coûts fonciers** landed costs; **c. de fonctionnement** operating *or* running cost; **c. de fret** freight cost; **c. et fret** cost and freight; *Mktg* **coûts hors-média** below-the-line costs; **coûts indirects** indirect costs; **coûts induits** unavoidable costs; **coûts irrécupérables** sunk costs; **c. de la main-d'œuvre** labour costs; **c. marginal** marginal cost; **c. par mille** cost per thousand; **c. moyen pondéré** weighted average cost; **c. moyen unitaire** average unit cost; **coûts opérationnels** operational costs; **coûts opératoires** operating costs; **c. d'opportunité** opportunity cost; **coûts prévisionnels** estimated costs; **c. de production** production cost; **coûts de promotion** promotional costs; **c. réel** real cost; **c. de remplacement** replacement cost; **c. de revient** cost price; **c. salarial** labour cost; **c. social** social cost; **c. de transaction** transaction cost; **c. unitaire (de travail)** unit (labour) cost; **c. unitaire moyen** average cost per unit; **c. variable** variable cost; **le c. de la vie** the cost of living

2 *Fig* cost; **le c. social de la privatisation** the social cost of privatization; **le c. de ses imprudences** the cost *or* consequences of his foolishness

coûtant [kutɑ̃] ADJ M cost *(avant n)*; **au** *ou* **à prix c.** at cost price

couteau, -x [kuto] NM **1** *(à main)* knife; *(d'une machine, d'un mixer)* blade; **il a ouvert le paquet avec un c.** he cut the parcel open with a knife; **il joue facilement du** *ou* **manie facilement le c.** he's quick with the knife; **comme si on lui enfonçait un c. dans le cœur** as if he'd/she'd been stabbed in the heart; **coup de c.** stab (with a knife); **donner un coup de c. à qn** to stab sb (with a knife); *Fam* **prendre** *ou* **recevoir un coup de c.** to be knifed, to get stabbed; **ils l'ont tué à coups de c.** they stabbed *or* knifed him to death; *Fig* **enfoncer le c. dans la plaie** to dig the knife in; *Fig* **remuer** *ou* **retourner le c. dans la plaie** to twist the knife in the wound; *Fig* **mettre le c. sous** *ou* **sur la gorge à qn** to hold a gun to sb's head, to point a gun at sb's head; *Fig* **avoir le c. sous la gorge** to have a gun pointed at one's head; **jouer les seconds couteaux (dans une affaire)** to play a secondary role in a business, to play second fiddle; **être à couteaux tirés avec qn** to be at daggers drawn with sb; **c. à beurre/pain** butter/bread knife; **c. de chasse** hunting knife; **c. à cran d'arrêt** *Br* flick knife, *Am* switchblade; **c. de cuisine/de table** kitchen/table knife; **c. à découper** carving knife; **c. à désosser** boning knife; **c. économe** *ou* **éplucheur** *ou* **à éplucher** potato peeler; **c. électrique** electric carving knife; **c. à filets de sole** filleting knife; **c. à fromage** cheese knife; **c. à mastiquer** *ou* **mastic** putty knife; **c. pliant** *ou* **de poche** pocket knife; **c. suisse** Swiss army knife; **c. à viande** carving knife

2 *(d'une balance)* knife edge

3 *Beaux-Arts* palette knife; **peinture au c.** knife painting

4 *Zool (mollusque)* razor *Br* shell *or Am* clam

couteau-scie [kutosi] (*pl* **couteaux-scies**) NM serrated-edge knife

coutelas [kutla] NM **1** *(de cuisine)* large kitchen knife **2** *(sabre)* cutlass

coutelier, -ère [kutəlje, -ɛr] NM,F cutler, cutlery specialist

coutellerie [kutɛlri] NF **1** *(ustensiles)* cutlery **2** *(lieu de fabrication)* cutlery works **3** *(lieu de vente)* kitchenware *Br* shop *or Am* store *(specializing in cutlery)* **4** *(industrie)* cutlery industry

coûter [3] [kute] VT **1** *(somme)* to cost; *Fam* **combien ça coûte?** how much is it?, how much does it cost?; **cela coûte 100 euros** it costs 100 euros; **cela m'a coûté 20 euros** it cost me 20 euros; **je veux cette maison, ça coûtera ce que ça coûtera** I want that house no matter how much it costs; *Fam* **c. la peau des fesses** *ou* **une fortune** *ou* **les yeux de la tête** *ou Can* **un bras** to cost a fortune *or* the earth *or* an arm and a leg; **c. cher** *(produit, service)* to be expensive, to cost a lot of money; *Fig* **ça va lui c. cher!** he/she's going to pay for this!; **cela ne coûte pas cher** it's cheap *or* inexpensive

2 *(exiger → efforts)* to cost; **ça ne coûte rien d'essayer** there's no harm in trying; **ça ne coûte rien d'être aimable!** it doesn't cost anything to be kind!; **ça te coûterait beaucoup d'être poli/de me répondre?** would it be asking too much for you to be polite/to answer me?; **cette démarche lui a beaucoup coûté** it was a very difficult *or* painful step for him/her to take; **ça me coûte de te quitter** it pains me to leave you; **ça ne m'a pas beaucoup coûté de ne pas y aller** it was no great hardship for me not to go; **tu peux bien l'aider, pour ce que ça te coûte!** it wouldn't be any trouble for you to help him/her!; **il m'en coûte de le dire** it pains me to have to say this

3 *(provoquer → larmes)* to cost, to cause; **les nuits blanches que son roman lui a coûtées** the sleepless nights his/her novel cost him/her

4 *(entraîner la perte de → carrière, membre, vote)* to cost; **ça a failli lui c. la vie** it nearly cost him/her his/her life; **un accident qui a coûté la vie à dix personnes** an accident which claimed the lives of ten people

USAGE ABSOLU *Fam* **une voiture, ça coûte!** a car is an expensive thing!

▫ **coûte que coûte** ADV at all costs, whatever the cost, no matter what

coûteuse [kutøz] *voir* **coûteux**

coûteusement [kutøzmɑ̃] ADV expensively

coûteux, -euse [kutø, -øz] ADJ **1** *(onéreux)* expensive, costly; **peu c.** cheap; **c'est d'un entretien c.** it's expensive to maintain; **une guerre coûteuse en vies humaines** a war costing many human lives *or* with a high cost in human lives **2** *(lourd de conséquences)* costly; **il a pris une décision coûteuse pour son avenir** he made a decision which was to cost him dear

coutil [kuti] NM *(toile → gén)* drill; *(→ pour literie)* ticking

coutre [kutr] NM *(de charrue)* coulter

coutume [kutym] NF **1** *(tradition)* custom; **c'est une c. bretonne** it's a Breton custom; **je t'embrasse, c'est la c.** I'll give you a kiss, it's the custom; **comme c'est la c. en Alsace** as is the custom *or* is customary in Alsace; **d'après** *ou* **selon la c.** as custom dictates; **selon une c. ancienne** according to an age-old tradition

2 *(habitude, manie)* habit, custom; **selon** *ou* **comme c'était ma c.** as was my habit *or Littéraire* wont; **avoir (pour) c. de faire** to be in the habit of *or* accustomed to doing; **elle n'a pas c. de partir sans prévenir** she doesn't usually leave without warning; **comme de c.** as usual; **il pleuvait, comme de c.** as usual, it was raining; **elle a porté un toast de bienvenue, comme de c.** she made a welcoming toast, as was her custom; **moins que de c.** less than usual, not as much as

usual; **plus que de c.** more than usual; **plus aimable que de c.** nicer than usual

3 *Jur* customary

coutumier, -ère [kutymje, -ɛr] **ADJ 1** *(habituel)* customary, usual **2** *(habitué à)* **il ne m'a pas rendu toute ma monnaie – il est c. du fait!** he short-changed me – that wouldn't be the first time *or* that's one of his usual tricks!; **j'ai oublié et pourtant je ne suis pas c. du fait** I forgot, and yet it's not something I usually do; **boire est une chose dont elle n'est pas coutumière** she doesn't usually drink

NM customary

couture [kutyr] **NF 1** *(action de coudre, passe-temps, produit)* **la c.** sewing; **j'ai de la c. à faire** I've got some sewing to do; **elle fait de la c. dans le jardin** she's sewing in the garden; **ne touche pas à ma c.** leave my sewing alone; **la c. (artisanale)** *(confection)* dressmaking; **la haute c.** (haute) couture, fashion design

2 *(suite de points)* seam; **sans c.** seamless; **faire une c. à qch** to seam sth; **c. anglaise** French seam; **c. apparente** *ou* **sellier** top stitching, overstitching; **c. plate** *ou* **rabattue** flat seam

3 *Littéraire (cicatrice)* scar; *(points de suture)* stitches

4 *(d'un moulage, d'une sculpture)* seam

ADJ INV designer *(avant n)*

▫ **à coutures ADJ** *(bas, collant)* seamed, with seams

▫ **à plate couture, à plates coutures ADV** *voir* **battre**

▫ **sans coutures ADJ** *(bas, collant)* seamless

▫ **sous toutes les coutures ADV** from every angle, very closely, under a microscope

couturé, -e [kutyre] **ADJ** scarred; **tout c. de cicatrices/rides** criss-crossed with scars/wrinkles

couturier, -ère [kutyrje, -ɛr] **NM,F** *(fabricant → de complets)* tailor; *(→ de chemises)* shirtmaker; *(→ de robes)* dressmaker; **j'ai besoin d'une couturière pour mes ravaudages** I need somebody to do some sewing (and mending) for me

NM 1 *(de haute couture)* **(grand) c.** fashion designer **2** *Anat* **grand c.** tailor's muscle *or Spéc* sartorius

▫ **couturière NF** *Théât* = rehearsal preceding the final dress rehearsal, enabling last-minute alterations to costumes

couvade [kuvad] **NF** couvade

couvain [kuvɛ̃] **NM** *(amas)* nest of insect eggs; *(rayon)* brood comb

couvaison [kuvɛzɔ̃] **NF 1** *(période)* incubation **2** *(action)* brooding

couvée [kuve] **NF 1** *(œufs)* clutch **2** *(oisillons)* brood, clutch; *Fig* **la nouvelle c. de jeunes cinéastes** the new generation *or* breed of young film-makers **3** *Fam (famille)* **sa c.** his/her brood

couvent [kuvɑ̃] **NM 1** *(de religieuses)* convent; *(de religieux)* monastery; **entrer au c.** to enter a convent **2** *(pensionnat)* convent school

couventine [kuvɑ̃tin] **NF** *(religieuse)* conventual; *(pensionnaire)* convent schoolgirl

couver [3] [kuve] **VT 1** *(sujet: oiseau)* to sit on; *(sujet: incubateur)* to hatch, to incubate

2 *(protéger → enfant)* to overprotect; **c. des yeux** *ou* **du regard** *(personne aimée)* to gaze fondly at; *(friandise, bijou)* to look longingly at

3 *(maladie)* to be coming down with; **je crois que je couve quelque chose** I think I'm coming down with something

4 *Littéraire (vengeance, revanche)* to plot

USAGE ABSOLU *(oiseau)* to brood, to sit on its eggs

VI 1 *(feu)* to smoulder

2 *(rébellion)* to be brewing (up); *(sentiment)* to smoulder; **la haine qui couvait en elle** the hatred that was smouldering inside her; **la révolte couvait chez les paysans** a peasant revolt was brewing (up); **c. sous la cendre** to be brewing (up), to bubble under the surface

couvercle [kuvɛrkl] **NM 1** *(qui se pose, s'enfonce)* lid, cover; *(qui se visse)* top, screw-top, cap **2** *Aut (de piston)* cover

couvert[1] [kuvɛr] **NM 1** *(cuillère, fourchette, couteau)* knife, fork and spoon; *(avec assiette et verre)* place setting; **des couverts en argent** silver cutlery; **couverts à salade** salad servers; **mettre le c.** to lay *or* to set the table; **j'ai mis trois couverts** I've laid three places *or* the table for three; **mets deux couverts de plus** lay *or* set two extra places; **elle a son c. chez Triot** she has her meals *or* she's a regular at Triot's; **tu auras toujours ton c. chez moi** there'll always be a place for you at my table; *Fam Fig* **remettre le c.** *(faire quelque chose à nouveau)* to do it again; *(faire l'amour à nouveau)* to be at it again

2 *(prix d'une place au restaurant)* cover charge

couvert[2], **-e**[1] [kuvɛr, -ɛrt] **PP** *voir* **couvrir**

ADJ 1 *(abrité → allée, halle, marché)* covered; *(→ piscine, terrain de sports)* indoor *(avant n)*

2 *(vêtu → chaudement)* warmly dressed, (well) wrapped-up *or* muffled-up; *(→ décemment)* covered (up); **j'aime avoir les jambes couvertes** I like my legs to be covered up; **rester c.** *(garder son chapeau)* to keep one's hat on

3 *Météo (temps)* dull, overcast; *(ciel)* overcast, clouded-over; **attendez-vous à un après-midi c.** expect a cloudy afternoon

▫ **couvert NM** *Littéraire* leafy canopy

▫ **à couvert ADV être à c.** *(de projectiles)* to be under cover; *(de critiques, de soupçons)* to be safe; **se mettre à c.** *(de projectiles)* to get under *or* to take cover; *(de critiques, de soupçons)* to cover *or* to safeguard oneself; *Fin* **être à c.** *(pour un crédit)* to be covered; *Bourse* **vendre à c.** to hedge, to sell for futures

▫ **à couvert de PRÉP** protected against; **se mettre à c. de la pluie** to shelter from the rain; **ici, nous serons à c. de la pluie** here, we'll be sheltered from the rain

▫ **sous couvert de PRÉP** in the guise of; **sous c. de sollicitude, elle me suit partout** under the pretext of being concerned for me, she follows me around everywhere

▫ **sous le couvert de PRÉP 1** *(sous l'apparence de)* in the guise of

2 *(sous la responsabilité de)* **il l'a fait sous le c. de son chef/frère** he did it using his boss/brother as a shield

3 *Littéraire (à l'abri de)* **sous le c. d'un bois** in the shelter of a wood

couverte[2] [kuvɛrt] **NF 1** *Cér* glaze; **peinture sous c.** underglaze painting **2** *Can (couverture)* blanket **3** *(dans la fabrication du papier)* deckle

couverture [kuvɛrtyr] **NF 1** *(morceau de tissu)* blanket, cover; **sous les couvertures** under the blankets *or* covers; **c. chauffante** electric blanket; **c. de survie** space *or* survival blanket; **amener** *ou* **tirer la c. à soi** *(après un succès)* to take all the credit; *(dans une transaction)* to get the best of the deal

2 *Constr (activité)* roofing; *(ouvrage)* (type of) roof

3 *Journ (activité)* coverage; *(page)* cover, front page; **assurer** *ou* **faire la c. d'un événement** to give coverage of *or* to cover an event; **c. maximum** saturation coverage; **c. médiatique** media coverage, media exposure; **c. presse** press coverage; **mettre un sujet en c.** to put a story on the front page, to make a story front-page news

4 *(d'un livre)* cover; **première de c.** front cover; **deuxième de c.** inside front cover; **troisième de c.** inside back cover; **quatrième de c.** back cover; **c. cartonnée** case

5 *Com* coverage, exposure; **c. du marché** sales coverage

6 *(d'un besoin)* covering, catering for; **la c. des besoins en électricité n'est pas assurée** the electricity needed is not being provided; **c. sociale** Social Security cover; **avoir une c. sociale** to belong to a benefit scheme

7 *(prétexte)* disguise, façade; **le financier/la société qui leur servait de c.** the financier/the company they used as a front

8 *Mil* cover; **c. aérienne** air cover

9 *(d'une police d'assurance)* cover; **c. maladie universelle** = free health care for people on low incomes who have no Social Security cover; **c. santé** health cover

10 *Fin* cover; *Bourse* margin, hedge; **une commande sans c.** an order without security *or* cover; **exiger une c. de 20 pour cent en espèces** to claim a margin of 20 percent in cash; **opérer avec c.** to hedge; **c. courte** short hedge; **c. longue** long hedge; **c. (boursière) obligatoire** margin requirement

11 *Météo* **c. neigeuse** snow cover

▫ **de couverture ADJ** *Mil & Journ* cover *(avant n)*

couveuse [kuvøz] **NF 1** *(oiseau)* brooder, sitter **2** *(machine)* **c. (artificielle)** incubator; **il a été mis en c.** he was put in an incubator

couvi [kuvi] **ADJ M** *Vieilli (œuf)* addled

couvoir [kuvwar] **NM** *(local)* hatchery

couvrant, -e [kuvrɑ̃, -ɑ̃t] **ADJ** *(peinture, vernis)* that covers well

▫ **couvrante NF** *Fam* blanket, cover

couvre-chef [kuvrəʃɛf] *(pl* **couvre-chefs**) **NM** *Hum* hat, headgear

couvre-feu [kuvrəfø] *(pl* **couvre-feux**) **NM** curfew

couvre-joint [kuvrəʒwɛ̃] *(pl* **couvre-joints**) **NM** *Constr* bead, batten

couvre-lit [kuvrəli] *(pl* **couvre-lits**) **NM** bedspread

couvre-livre [kuvrəlivr] *(pl* **couvre-livres**) **NM** dust jacket

couvre-nuque [kuvrənyk] *(pl* **couvre-nuques**) **NM 1** *(de casquette)* flap *(to protect back of neck from sun)* **2** *(de casque)* neck protector

couvre-objectif [kuvrɔbʒɛktif] *(pl* **couvre-objectifs**) **NM** *Phot* lens cap

couvre-objet [kuvrɔbʒɛ] *(pl* **couvre-objets**) **NM** cover glass

couvre-pied, couvre-pieds [kuvrəpje] *(pl* **couvre-pieds**) **NM** quilt

couvre-plat [kuvrəpla] *(pl* **couvre-plats**) **NM** dish cover

couvreur [kuvrœr] **NM** roofer

COUVRIR [34] [kuvrir] **VT 1** *(d'une protection, d'une couche → meuble)* to cover; *(→ livre, cahier)* to cover, to put a dust cover on; *(d'un couvercle → poêle)* to cover, to put a lid on; **c. avec** *ou* **de** *(protéger)* to cover with; **c. le feu** to bank up the fire; **c. un mur de peinture** to paint a wall; **c. un toit d'ardoises/de tuiles/de chaume** to slate/to tile/to thatch a roof; **toit couvert de chaume** thatched roof; **il avait couvert le mur de graffitis/posters** he'd covered the wall with graffiti/posters; **couvrez les fraisiers avec de la paille** cover *or* protect your strawberry plants with straw; **c. qn de son corps** to shield sb with one's body; **être couvert de poussière** to be covered with *or* in dust; **c. qn de cadeaux/d'injures/de louanges/de reproches** to shower sb with gifts/insults/praise/criticism; **c. qn de caresses/baisers** to stroke/to kiss sb all over; **c. qn de honte** to make sb feel ashamed; **c. qn d'or** to shower sb with gifts

2 *(vêtir)* to wrap up, to cover up, to muffle up; *(envelopper)* to cover; **il faut c. cet enfant** that child needs to be covered up *or* wrapped up; **couvre bien ta gorge!** make sure your throat is covered up!; **une mantille lui couvrait la tête** her head was covered with a mantilla, a mantilla covered her head; **la jupe couvre tout juste le genou** the skirt barely covers the knee

3 *(dissimuler → erreur)* to cover up; *(protéger → complice)* to cover up for; **ils le couvrent** *(pour une erreur)* they're covering up for him; **il avance l'argent, mais en cas de difficulté, c'est moi qui le couvre** he puts up the money but if there's a problem, I step in

4 *(voix)* to drown (out); **les basses couvrent trop les ténors** the basses drown out the tenors

5 *(assurer → dégâts, frais, personne)* to cover, to insure; *(→ risques)* to insure against; **l'assurance me couvre contre l'incendie** the insurance policy covers me against fire

6 *(inclure)* to cover, to include; **le prix couvre la livraison et l'entretien** the price covers *or* includes delivery and maintenance

7 *(compenser)* to cover; **les recettes ne couvrent plus les dépenses** income no longer covers expenses; **nous couvrons nos frais maintenant** we're paying our way now

8 *Mil (retraite, soldat)* to cover, to give cover to; **on te couvre** we've got you covered; **c. ses arrières** to cover one's rear

9 *(parcourir)* to cover; **elle a couvert les 15 kilomètres en 52 minutes** she covered *or* ran the 15 kilometres in 52 minutes

10 *(englober → dans l'espace)* to cover; *(→ dans le temps)* to span; **leur propriété couvre dix hectares** their estate covers *or* occupies ten hectares; **le réseau couvre toute la région** the network covers the whole area; **ses recherches couvrent près de 30 ans** his research spans nearly 30 years

11 *(sujet: émetteur, représentant)* to cover

12 *Journ* to cover, to give coverage to; **c. entièrement un procès** to give full coverage to a trial

13 *Fin (emprunt)* to underwrite; **c. l'enchère de qn** to outbid sb, to bid higher than sb; **prière de nous c. par chèque** kindly remit by cheque

14 *Vét* to cover

15 *Cartes* to cover

VI **cette peinture couvre bien** this paint covers well

▸**se couvrir** VPR **1** *(se vêtir → pour sortir)* to dress warmly, to wrap up (well); *(→ pour cacher sa nudité)* to cover oneself up; **couvre-toi bien, il fait très froid dehors** wrap up well, it's very cold out

2 *(mettre un chapeau)* to put on one's hat

3 *Sport* to cover oneself

4 *(se garantir)* to cover oneself; *Bourse* **se c. en achetant à long terme** to hedge by buying long; *Bourse* **se c. en rachetant** to cover oneself by buying back

5 *(ciel)* to become overcast, to cloud over; **le temps se couvre, ça se couvre** it's *or* the sky is clouding over

6 **se c. de qch** *(honte, gloire)* to cover oneself with sth; **se c. de fleurs/bourgeons/feuilles** to come into bloom/bud/leaf; **le champ s'est couvert de coquelicots** poppies have come up all over the field; **se c. de boutons** to come out *or* to become covered in spots; **la place s'est couverte de monde** the square became crowded *or* swamped with people; **se c. de ridicule** to make oneself look ridiculous

couvrure [kuvʀyʀ] NF covering

covalence [kɔvalɑ̃s] NF *Chim* covalence, covalency

covalent, -e [kɔvalɑ̃, -ɑ̃t] ADJ *Chim* covalent

covariance [kɔvaʀjɑ̃s] NF covariance

covendeur, -euse [kɔvɑ̃dœʀ, -øz] NM,F co-vendor, joint vendor

cover-girl [kɔvœʀɡœʀl] *(pl* **cover-girls)** NF cover girl

covoiturage [kɔvwatyʀaʒ] NM car-pooling, *Br* lift-sharing

cow-boy [kɔbɔj] *(pl* **cow-boys)** NM cowboy; **jouer aux cow-boys et aux Indiens** to play (at) cow-boys and Indians

cowper [kopœʀ] NM cowper

cow-pox [kopɔks, kaupɔks] NM *Vét* cowpox

coxal, -e, -aux, -ales [kɔksal, -o] ADJ *Anat* coxal; **os c.** hip bone

coxalgie [kɔksalʒi] NF coxalgia

coxarthrose [kɔksaʀtʀoz] NF arthritis of the hip

coxo-fémoral, -e, -aux, -ales [kɔksofemɔʀal, -o] *Anat* ADJ coxo-femoral

❑ **coxo-fémorale** NF coxo-femoral joint

coyote [kɔjɔt] NM coyote

CP [sepe] NM *(abrév* **cours préparatoire)** *Br* ≃ first-year infants class, *Am* ≃ nursery school

CPAM [sepeaɛm] NF *Admin (abrév* **caisse primaire d'assurance maladie)** = French Social Security department in charge of medical insurance

CPAS [sepeaɛs] NM *Belg (abrév* **centre public d'aide sociale)** welfare office *or* centre

CPE [sepeœ] NM *(abrév* **contrat première embauche)** = employment contract for people under 26 which could be terminated without justification in the first two years, proposed by the French government but abandoned under public pressure

CPGE [sepeʒeœ] NF *(abrév* **classe préparatoire aux grandes écoles)** = preparatory class for the entrance examinations for the "grandes écoles"

cpl *Typ (abrév écrite* **caractères par ligne)** cpl

CPM [sepeɛm] NM *Com (abrév* **coût par mille)** cost per thousand

CPNT [sepeɛnte] NF *Pol (abrév* **Chasse, Pêche, Nature et Traditions)** = French political movement that promotes rural life, hunting, fishing and environmental protection

cpp *Ordinat (abrév écrite* **caractères par pouce)** cpi

cps *Ordinat (abrév écrite* **caractères par seconde)** cps

CPT [sepete] *(abrév* **carriage paid to)** CPT

cpt *(abrév écrite* **comptant)** cpt

CQFD [sekyɛfde] NM *(abrév* **ce qu'il fallait démontrer)** QED; **et voilà, C.!** and there you have it!

CR *(abrév écrite* **compte-rendu)** *(d'une réunion)* minutes

crabe [kʀab] NM **1** *Zool* crab; **c. appelant** fiddler crab; **c. à carapace molle** soft-shell crab; **c. des cocotiers** purse crab, palm crab, robber crab; **c. dormeur** Dungeness crab, edible crab; **c. enragé** *ou* **vert** shore crab, green crab; **c. des Moluques** horseshoe crab, king crab; **c. nageur** swimming crab; **c. terrestre** land crab; **c. tourteau** common crab, edible crab; **c. violoniste** fiddler crab; **c. voleur** robber crab

2 *Fam Péj (personne)* rat, foul creature

❑ **en crabe** ADV **marcher/se déplacer en c.** to walk/to move sideways; *Aviat* **voler en c.** to drift

crabot [kʀabo] NM dog clutch

crabotage [kʀabotaʒ] NM **1** *(d'une carrière d'ardoise)* first shaft *(of a slate quarry)* **2** *Tech* jaw clutching; *Aut* **c. du différentiel** four-wheel drive system

craboter [3] [kʀabote] VT *Tech* to connect with a dog clutch

crac [kʀak] ONOMAT *(de bois, d'os)* crack, snap; *(biscuit)* snap; *(tissu)* rip

EXCLAM *Fam (locution)* **et c.!** hey presto!

❑ **Crac** NM **le baron du C.** = archetypal big talker and teller of tall stories

crac-crac [kʀakkʀak] NM *Fam* **faire c.** *(faire l'amour)* to do it

crachat [kʀaʃa] NM **1** *(salive)* spit, *Méd* sputum; **un c.** a gob of spit; **des crachats** spit, spittle **2** *Fam (médaille)* medal, *Br* gong

crache [kʀaʃ] NF *Fam* spit ▪

craché [kʀaʃe] ADJ INV *Fam* **c'est son père tout c.!** he's the spitting image of his dad!; **ça, c'est du Maud tout c.!** that's just like Maud!, that's Maud all over!

crachement [kʀaʃmɑ̃] NM **1** *(fait de cracher)* spitting; *(crachat)* mucus, *Spéc* sputum; **avoir des crachements de sang** to spit blood **2** *(projection → de flammes, de vapeur)* burst, shower; *(→ de scories, d'étincelles)* shower **3** *(bruit → d'un haut-parleur)* crackle, crackling

cracher [3] [kʀaʃe] VI **1** *(personne)* to spit; **c. par terre** to spit on the ground; **c. sur qn** to spit at sb; *Fig* to spit on sb; *aussi Fig* **c. à la figure de qn** to spit in sb's face; *Fam* **c'est comme si on crachait en l'air!** it's like whistling in the wind!; **il ne faut pas c. dans la soupe** don't bite the hand that feeds you; *Fam* **il ne crache pas sur le champagne** he doesn't turn his nose up at champagne; **je ne cracherais pas sur 2000 euros!** I wouldn't turn my nose up at *or* say no to 2,000 euros!; **ce système a du bon, ne crache pas dessus!** there are things to be said for this system, don't knock it!; **c. au bassinet** to cough up

2 *(chat, marmotte)* to spit, to hiss

3 *(fuir → stylo)* to splutter; *(→ robinet)* to splutter, to splash

4 *(nasiller → haut-parleur, radio)* to crackle

VT 1 *(rejeter → sang)* to spit; *(→ aliment)* to spit out; *Fam* **c. ses poumons** to cough up one's lungs

2 *(sujet: volcan, canon)* to belch (forth) *or* out; *(sujet: fusil)* to shoot a burst of, to spit; *(sujet: robinet)* to spit *or* to splutter out; **c. des flammes** *ou* **du feu** *(sujet: dragon)* to breathe fire; *Fam Hum* **il est fort ton calvados, je vais c. des flammes!** your Calvados is pretty strong, I'll be breathing fire!

3 *(énoncer → insultes)* to spit out, to hiss; **"racaille!" cracha-t-elle en sortant** "scum!" she hissed on her way out

4 *Fam (donner → argent)* to cough up, to fork out; **grand-père ne les crache pas facilement!** grandpa's a real old skinflint!

USAGE ABSOLU **si tu veux sa marchandise, il faut c.** if you want the stuff, you've got to cough up

cracheur, -euse [kʀaʃœʀ, -øz] ADJ *Zool* spitting *(avant n)*

NM,F spitter; **c. de feu** fire-eater

crachin [kʀaʃɛ̃] NM *(fine)* drizzle

crachiner [3] [kʀaʃine] V IMPERSONNEL **il crachine** it's drizzling

crachoir [kʀaʃwaʀ] NM spittoon; *Fam* **tenir le c.** to go on and on, to monopolize the conversation;

je n'ai pas envie de lui tenir le c.! I don't feel like listening to him/her rambling on for hours!

crachotant, -e [kʀaʃɔtɑ̃, -ɑ̃t] ADJ *(radio, téléphone)* crackling; *(personne, robinet)* spluttering

crachotement [kʀaʃɔtmɑ̃] NM *(d'une radio, d'un téléphone)* crackle, crackling; *(d'une personne, d'un robinet)* splutter, spluttering

crachoter [3] [kʀaʃɔte] VI *(radio, téléphone)* to crackle; *(personne, robinet)* to splutter

crachouiller [3] [kʀaʃuje] VI *Fam (radio, téléphone)* to crackle ▪; *(personne, robinet)* to splutter ▪

crack [kʀak] NM **1** *Équitation* crack **2** *Fam (personne → gén)* wizard; *(→ en sport)* ace; **c'est un c. en ski** he's/she's an ace skier; **c'est un c. en latin** he's/she's brilliant at Latin **3** *(drogue)* crack

cracker [kʀakœʀ] NM **1** *Culin* cracker **2** *Ordinat (pirate informatique)* cracker

cracking [kʀakiŋ] NM *Pétr* cracking

Cracovie [kʀakɔvi] NM Cracow, Krakow

cracovienne [kʀakɔvjɛn] NF **1** *(danse)* krakowiak, cracovienne **2** *(morceau de musique)* = piece of instrumental music with fast tempo

cracra [kʀakʀa] ADJ INV *Fam (personne, objet)* filthy ▪; *(endroit) Br* grotty, *Am* lousy

crade [kʀad] = **crado**

cradingue [kʀadɛ̃g] ADJ très *Fam (personne, objet)* filthy ▪; *(endroit) Br* grotty, *Am* lousy

crado [kʀado] ADJ INV *Fam (personne, objet)* filthy ▪; *(endroit) Br* grotty, *Am* lousy

craie [kʀɛ] NF chalk, limestone; **falaise de c.** chalk cliff; **une c.** a stick of chalk; **dessiner qch à la c.** to chalk sth out; **écrire qch à la c.** to chalk sth, to write sth with chalk; **il y avait des croix à la c. sur leurs portes** crosses had been chalked on their doors; **c. de tailleur** French chalk

craignait *etc voir* **craindre**

craignant-Dieu [kʀɛɲɑ̃djø] NMF INV *Can* believer, God-fearing person

craignos [kʀɛɲos] ADJ INV *Fam* **c'est c.** *(louche)* it's shady *or Br* dodgy; *(ennuyeux)* it's a real pain; *(laid)* it's hideous; *(mauvais)* it's crap, it's the pits

crailler [3] [kʀaje] VI to caw

craindre [80] [kʀɛ̃dʀ] VT **1** *(redouter → personne)* to fear, to be frightened *or* afraid of; *(→ événement)* to fear, to be afraid *or* scared of; **c. Dieu** to go in fear of *or* to fear God; **il est très craint** he is greatly feared; **je ne crains personne!** nobody can frighten me!, I'm not afraid of anyone!; **sa grosse voix le faisait c. de tous ses élèves** his booming voice made all his pupils afraid of him; **elle sait se faire c. de ses subordonnés** she knows how to intimidate her subordinates; **qui ne craint pas la mort?** who isn't afraid of death *or* dying?; **je ne crains pas les piqûres** I'm not afraid *or* scared of injections; **c. le pire** to fear the worst; **ne crains rien** *(n'aie pas peur)* have no fear, never fear, don't be afraid; *(ne t'inquiète pas)* don't worry; **il n'y a rien à c.** there's nothing to fear, *Sout* there's no cause for alarm; **il y a tout à c. d'une intervention militaire** one can expect the worst from a military intervention; **c. de prendre l'avion** to be afraid of flying; **elle craignait toujours d'être en retard** she was always afraid of being late; **si je ne craignais pas de vous choquer** if I wasn't afraid of shocking you; **craignant de la réveiller, il retira ses chaussures** he took off his shoes, for fear of waking her up

2 *(tenir pour probable)* to fear; **alors, je suis renvoyé? – je le crains** so, I'm fired? – I'm afraid so; **elle pourrait nous dénoncer – c'est à c.** she might give us away – unfortunately, (I think) it's likely; **il est à c. que** *ou* **il y a lieu de c. que le colis se soit égaré** I fear the parcel has gone astray; **il n'y a pas à c. qu'il revienne** there is no fear of his coming back; **je crains de l'avoir blessée** I'm afraid I've hurt her; **je crains qu'il (n')ait oublié** I'm afraid that he might have forgotten; **on craint un peu partout que les mesures prises ne soient pas suffisantes** there are widespread fears that the measures taken are inadequate; **je crains fort qu'il (ne) soit déjà trop tard** I fear *or* I'm very much afraid it's already too late; **je crains que oui/non** I'm afraid so/not

3 *(être sensible à)* **ça craint le froid** *(plante)* it's sensitive to cold, it doesn't like the cold; **je crains le froid** I can't stand *or* bear the cold; **c'est un bois qui craint les chocs** it's a fairly fragile kind of wood; **craint l'humidité** *(sur emballage)* keep *or* store in a dry place; **c'est une étoffe qui ne craint rien** it's a material that'll stand up to anything

VI *Fam (locution)* **ça craint** *(c'est louche)* it's shady *or Br* dodgy; *(c'est ennuyeux)* it's a real pain; *(c'est laid)* it's hideous; *(c'est mauvais)* it's crap, it's the pits; **elle craint** she's really awful

❑ **craindre pour VT IND c. pour qn/qch** to fear for sb/sth; **je crains pour sa santé** I fear for his/her health; **c. pour sa vie** to fear for *or* to go in fear of one's life

craint, -e [krɛ̃, -ɛ̃t] **PP** *voir* **craindre**

❑ **crainte NF** *(anxiété)* fear; **la crainte de l'échec** fear of failure *or* failing; **il vivait dans la crainte d'être reconnu** he lived *or* went in fear of being recognized; **n'aie (aucune) crainte** *ou* **sois sans crainte, tout se passera bien** don't worry *or* never fear, everything will be all right; **éveiller** *ou* **susciter les craintes de qn** to alarm sb; **avoir des craintes au sujet de qch** to have some fears *or* worries about sth; **je n'ai aucune crainte quant à l'issue de ce projet** I've no fears *or* worries about how this project will turn out

❑ **de crainte de PRÉP** *(suivi de l'infinitif)* for fear of; **de crainte de la blesser** for fear of hurting her

❑ **de crainte que CONJ** *(suivi du subjonctif)* for fear of, fearing that; **de crainte qu'on (ne) l'accuse** for fear of being accused, fearing that she might be accused; **il faut agir vite, de crainte que la situation (n')empire** we must act quickly, lest *or* in case the situation should get worse

❑ **par crainte de PRÉP** for fear of

craintif, -ive [krɛ̃tif, -iv] **ADJ 1** *(facilement effarouché → personne)* timid, shy; *(→ animal)* timid **2** *(qui reflète la peur → regard, geste)* timorous, fearful

NM,F 1 *(timide)* timid *or* shy person **2** *(timoré)* faint-hearted *or* timorous person

craintivement [krɛ̃tivmɑ̃] **ADV 1** *(timidement)* timidly, shyly **2** *(avec peur)* timorously, fearfully

crambe[1] [krɑ̃b] **NM** *Bot* crambe; **c. maritime** seakale

crambe[2] [krɑ̃b] **NM** *Entom* grass moth

crambé [krɑ̃be] = **crambe**[1]

cramcram [kramkram] **NM** *(en Afrique francophone → plante)* cram-cram, (long-spined) sandbur; *(→ graine)* cram-cram, sand-bur

cramé, -e [krame] *Fam* **ADJ 1** *(brûlé → rôti)* burnt■, charred■; *(→ tissu)* burnt■, scorched■; **la tarte est complètement cramée** the tart is burnt to a cinder **2** *(ivre)* blitzed, *Br* off one's face, *Am* stewed (to the gills)

NM ça sent le c. there's a smell of burning■; **ne mange pas le c.** don't eat the burnt bits■

cramer [3] [krame] *Fam* **VI** *(rôti, tissu, immeuble)* to burn■; *(circuit électrique, prise)* to burn out■; **tout a cramé** everything got burnt■; **il y a quelque chose qui crame dans la cuisine** there's something burning in the kitchen■; **faire c. qch** to burn sth■

VT *(rôti)* to burn (to a cinder), to let burn■; *(vêtement)* to burn■, to scorch■

▶**se cramer VPR se c. les doigts** to burn one's fingers■

cramine [kramin] **NF** *Suisse Fam* (intense) cold■

cramique [kramik] **NM** *Belg* = brioche with raisins

cramoisi, -e [kramwazi] **ADJ** *(velours)* crimson; *(visage)* flushed, crimson; **il est devenu c.** *(de honte, de timidité)* he flushed crimson *or* blushed; *(de colère)* his face turned crimson; **rouge c.** crimson red

NM crimson

cramouille [kramuj] **NF** *Vulg* pussy, *Br* fanny

crampant, -e [krɑ̃pɑ̃, -ɑ̃t] **ADJ** *Can Fam (amusant)* hysterical; **le film était c.!** the film was hysterical!, *Br* the film cracked me up!

crampe [krɑ̃p] **NF 1** *Méd* cramp; **j'ai une c. au pied** I've got *Br* cramp *or Am* a cramp in my foot; **c. d'estomac** *(gén)* stomach cramp; *(de faim)* hunger pang; **la c. de l'écrivain** writer's cramp **2** *(pièce de serrage)* cramp **3** *Vulg* **tirer sa c.** *(coïter)* to screw, *Br* to have a shag; *(s'enfuir)* to beat it, *Br* to piss off, *Am* to book it

crampillon [krɑ̃pijɔ̃] **NM** staple *(for wire)*

crampon [krɑ̃pɔ̃] **NM 1** *(de chaussures → de sport)* stud; *(→ de montagne)* crampon; *(de fer à cheval)* calk

2 *Bot (de plante grimpante)* tendril; *(d'algue)* sucker

3 *(crochet)* cramp

4 *(comme adj)* **un enfant un peu c.** a clingy child; **laisse-moi, ce que tu peux être c.!** give me some space, will you!

NMF INV *Fam Péj (personne)* leech; **j'espère qu'elle viendra sans son c. de mari!** I hope she won't bring along her husband, he's so clingy!

❑ **crampons NMPL** *(semelle)* crampons

cramponnement [krɑ̃pɔnmɑ̃] **NM** clutching, clinging

cramponner [3] [krɑ̃pɔne] **VT 1** *(s'accrocher à)* to cling to; **ne cramponne pas tout le temps ton père!** just leave your father alone will you!, give your father a break!

2 *Fam (importuner)* to pester; **tu me cramponnes avec tes questions!** stop pestering me with your questions!

3 *Tech (pièces)* to cramp together

▶**se cramponner VPR 1** *(s'agripper)* to hold on, to hang on; **cramponne-toi bien, on démarre!** hold on tight, here we go!; **se c. à** *(branche, barre)* to cling (on) *or* to hold on to; *(personne)* to cling (on) to

2 *Fam (s'acharner → malade)* to cling *or* to hang on; *(→ étudiant)* to stick with it; **il est distancé mais il se cramponne** he's lagging behind, but he's hanging on in there; **se c. à la vie** to cling to life; **il se cramponne à cet espoir** he's clinging to this hope

cran [krɑ̃] **NM 1** *(entaille → d'une étagère, d'une crémaillère)* notch; *(trou → d'une ceinture)* hole, notch; **il resserra/desserra sa ceinture d'un c.** he tightened/loosened his belt one notch; **baisser/monter d'un c.** *(dans une hiérarchie)* to come down/to move up a peg; *(voix)* to fall/to rise slightly

2 *Couture (sur un ourlet)* notch; *(point de repère)* nick

3 *(mèche)* wave

4 *Tech* catch; **c. de sûreté** *ou* **sécurité** safety catch; **c. de l'armé** full-cock notch; **c. d'arrêt** *(couteau) Br* flick knife, *Am* switchblade

5 *Fam (courage)* **allons, un peu de c.!** *(sois courageux)* come on, be brave!; *(ne te laisse pas aller)* come on, pull yourself together!; **avoir du c.** to have guts; **il a du c.** he's got guts

❑ **à cran ADJ** *Fam (personne)* uptight, edgy, on edge; **être à c., avoir les nerfs à c.** to be edgy *or* uptight

crâne [kran] **NM 1** *Anat* skull, *Spéc* cranium

2 *Fam (tête)* **avoir mal au c.** to have a headache; **mets-toi bien ça dans le c.!** get that into your head!; **tu as le c. dur!** *(têtu)* you're so pigheaded!; *(lent à comprendre)* you're so thick-skulled! **alors, c. d'œuf!** hey, baldy!

3 *Fam Arg crime* **faire un c.** *(policier)* to make an arrest■, to get a result

ADJ 1 *Littéraire (courageux)* bold, gallant; **très c., il entra dans la pièce** he swaggered into the room

2 *(bien portant)* **il n'est pas encore bien c.** he hasn't quite recovered yet

crânement [kranmɑ̃] **ADV** *Littéraire (fièrement)* gallantly

crâner [3] [krane] **VI** *Fam* to show off, *Br* to swank; **tu crânes moins maintenant!** you aren't so sure of yourself now, are you!

crânerie [kranri] **NF 1** *Littéraire (bravoure)* gallantry **2** *(vanité)* conceit

crâneur, -euse [kranœr, -øz] *Fam* **ADJ être c.** to be a bit of a show-off

NM,F show-off, *Am* hotshot; **faire le c.** to show off, *Br* to swank

crânien, -enne [kranjɛ̃, -ɛn] **ADJ** cranial

craniologie [kranjɔlɔʒi] **NF** *Méd* craniology

craniopharyngiome [kranjɔfarɛ̃ʒjom] **NM** *Méd* craniopharyngioma

craniosténose [kranjɔstenoz] **NF** *Méd* craniostenosis

craniotomie [kranjɔtɔmi] **NF** *Méd* craniotomy

cranson [krɑ̃sɔ̃] **NM** *Bot* horseradish

cranté, -e [krɑ̃te] **ADJ** *(ourlet)* notched; *(lame de ciseaux)* serrated; *(cheveux)* wavy

cranter [3] [krɑ̃te] **VT** *(ourlet)* to notch; *(roue)* to put notches on; *(cheveux)* to wave

crapahuter [3] [krapayte] **VI 1** *Fam (marcher)* to schlep *or* traipse about **2** *Fam Arg mil* to yomp

crapaud [krapo] **NM 1** *Zool* toad; **c. accoucheur** midwife toad; **c. commun** (Eurasian) common toad; **c. cornu** horned toad; **c. géant** agua (toad), cane toad; *Ich* **c. de mer** angler-fish; **c. des roseaux** natterjack (toad); **c. vert** green toad, variable toad **2** *Minér* flaw **3** *Mus* **(piano) c.** baby grand piano **4 (fauteuil) c.** squat armchair **5** *Fam (gamin)* kid, *Br* sprog

crapaud-buffle [krapɔbyfl] *(pl* **crapauds-buffles)** **NM** agua (toad), cane toad

crapaudine [krapɔdin] **NF 1** *(de gouttière)* strainer; *(de baignoire)* pop-up waste hole **2** *Constr* gudgeon **3** *Tech* pivot bearing *or* box *or* hole; *(de gond)* socket, gudgeon **4** *Minér* toadstone

❑ **à la crapaudine ADJ** *Culin* spatchcock *(avant n)*

crapette [krapɛt] **NF** = card game (played by two people)

craponne [krapɔn] **NF** watchmaker's file

crapoter [3] [krapɔte] **VI** *Fam* = to smoke without inhaling

crapoteux, -euse [krapɔtø, -øz] **ADJ** *Fam* filthy

crapouille [krapuj] **NF** *Can* crook, vilain

crapouillot [krapujo] **NM** *Mil* trench mortar

crapule [krapyl] **NF 1** *(individu)* crook, villain; **petite c.!** you little rat! **2** *Littéraire (pègre)* **la c.** the riff-raff

ADJ roguish; **une expression/un air c.** a roguish phrase/look

crapulerie [krapylri] **NF 1** *(débauche)* debauchery, dissoluteness **2** *(acte)* foul trick

crapuleuse [krapyløz] *voir* **crapuleux**

crapuleusement [krapyløzmɑ̃] **ADV** crookedly, dishonestly

crapuleux, -euse [krapylø, -øz] **ADJ 1** *(malhonnête)* crooked, villainous **2** *Littéraire (débauché)* dissolute; **fêtes crapuleuses** dissolute festivities

craquage [krakaʒ] **NM** *Chim* cracking

craquant, -e [krakɑ̃, -ɑ̃t] **ADJ 1** *(croustillant → laitue)* crisp; *(→ céréales)* crunchy **2** *Fam (personne)* irresistible

craque [krak] **NF 1** *Fam (mensonge)* fib, whopper, *Br* porky (pie); **et me raconte pas de craques!** and no fibbing! **2** *Can Fam (fissure)* crack■; *Fig* **avoir une c.** to be off one's rocker

craquée [krake] **NF** *Suisse Fam* **une c. de** a load of

craquelage [kraklaʒ] **NM 1** *(effet)* **le c. d'un vernis** the cracks in a varnish **2** *(fabrication, art)* crackled china manufacture

craquelé, -e [krakle] **ADJ 1** *(fissuré)* cracked; **j'ai la peau des mains toute craquelée** my hands are badly chapped **2** *(décoré de craquelures)* crackled

NM le c. *(procédé)* crackling; *(verre)* crackleware

craquèlement [krakɛlmɑ̃] **NM** cracks, cracking

craqueler [24] [krakle] **VT** *(fendiller)* to crack; *(poterie)* to crackle

▶**se craqueler VPR** *(peinture, peau)* to crack; *(poterie)* to crackle

craquelin [kraklɛ̃] **NM** *Belg* = brioche with crystallized sugar

craquelure [kraklyr] **NF 1** *(accidentelle)* crack; *Beaux-Arts* **les craquelures du tableau** the craquelure on *or* cracks in the painting **2** *(artificielle)* crackle

craquement [krakmɑ̃] **NM** *(de bois qui casse)* snap, crack; *(d'un plancher)* creak; *(d'herbes sèches)* crackle; *(de chaussures)* squeak, creak

craquer [3] [krake] **VI 1** *(bois qui casse)* to snap, to crack; *(plancher)* to creak; *(herbes sèches)* to crackle; *(chaussures)* to squeak, to creak; **faire c. ses doigts** to crack one's knuckles; **faire c. une allumette** to strike a match; **les branches du chêne craquaient dans la bourrasque** the oak branches were creaking in the gale

2 *(se déchirer, se fendre → couture, tissu)* to split; *(→ sac)* to split open; *(→ fil, lacets)* to break, to snap off; *(→ banquise)* to crack, to split (up); *(→ collant)* to rip; **le pull a craqué aux emmanchures** the sweater split at the armholes

3 *Fam (psychologiquement)* to break down■, to

crack up; **ses nerfs ont craqué** she had a nervous breakdown■, she cracked up; **ils ont essayé de me faire c. en fumant devant moi** they tried to make me crack by smoking in front of me

4 *Fam (être séduit)* to go wild; **je craque** I can't resist it/them/*etc*; **il me fait c.** I'm crazy about him; **j'ai craqué pour cette robe** I really fell for that dress

5 *Fam (s'effondrer → institution, projet)* to founder, to be falling apart, to be on the verge of collapse

6 *Can Fam* **riche à c.** really rich■; *Fam* **fou à c.** totally mad

VT 1 *(couture)* to split, to tear

2 *(allumette)* to strike

3 *Fam (dépenser)* to blow; **elle a craqué tout son argent au jeu** she blew all her money at the gambling tables

4 *Pétr* to crack

5 *Can (fissurer)* to crack

craquètement [krakɛtmɑ̃] = **craquettement**

craqueter [27] [krakte] **VI 1** *(brindille)* to crackle; *(sachet en plastique)* to rustle **2** *(cigogne, grue)* to screech; *(cigale)* to chirp

craquette [krakɛt] **NF** *Vulg* pussy

craquettement [krakɛtmɑ̃] **NM 1** *(de brindilles)* crackling; *(de sachet en plastique)* rustling **2** *(d'une cigogne, d'une grue)* screeching; *(d'une cigale)* chirping

craqueur, -euse [krakœr, -øz] **NM,F** fibber

crase [krɑz] **NF 1** *Ling* crasis **2** *Méd* = study of the coagulative properties of blood

crash [kraʃ] **NM 1** *(accident)* crash **2** *(atterrissage forcé)* crash-landing; **faire un c.** to crash-land

crasher [3] [kraʃe] **se crasher VPR** *Fam* **1** *Aviat (s'écraser)* to crash■; *(atterrir accidentellement)* to crash-land■ **2** *(conducteur, véhicule)* to crash■; **il s'est crashé contre un arbre** he smashed *or* crashed into a tree; **il s'est crashé en voiture** he crashed his car

craspec [kraspɛk] **ADJ** *Fam* filthy

crassane [krasan] **NF** *Bot* = kind of pear

crasse [kras] **NF 1** *(saleté)* filth; **couvert de c.** filthy, covered in filth; **il vit dans la c.** he lives in squalor

2 *Fam (mauvais tour)* dirty *or* nasty trick; **faire une c. à qn** to play a dirty *or* nasty trick on sb

3 *Tech* **la c., les crasses** *(scories)* scum, dross, slag; *(résidus)* scale

4 *Méd* **c. sénile** senile keratosis; *Vét* **c. des porcelets** keratosis of pigs

5 *Can (personne malhonnête)* crook

ADJ *Fam (stupidité)* crass; **d'une ignorance c.** abysmally ignorant, pig-ignorant

crasseux, -euse [krasø, -øz] **ADJ** *(mains, vêtements)* filthy, grubby; *(maison)* filthy, squalid; *(personne)* filthy; **une cuisinière toute crasseuse** a cooker caked with dirt

NM *Fam* comb■

crassier [krasje] **NM** slag heap

crassulacée [krasylase] *Bot* **NF** Crassula

❑ **crassulacées NFPL** Crassulaceae

cratère [kratɛr] **NM** *Antiq & Géog* crater

craterelle [kratrɛl] **NF** *Bot* craterellus

cratériforme [krateriform] **ADJ** crater-shaped

cratérisé, -e [kraterize] **ADJ** covered with craters

craton [kratɔ̃] **NM** *Géol* craton

cravache [kravaʃ] **NF** riding-crop, horsewhip

❑ **à la cravache ADV** ruthlessly, with an iron hand

cravacher [3] [kravaʃe] **VT** *(cheval)* to use the whip on; *(personne)* to horsewhip

VI *Fam* **1** *(en voiture)* to belt along, to go at full tilt *or* speed **2** *(travailler dur)* *Br* to slog away, *Am* to plug away

cravate [kravat] **NF 1** *(d'homme)* tie, *Am* necktie; **en costume (et) c.** wearing a suit and tie; *Fam* **c. de chanvre** hangman's noose; *Fam* **s'en envoyer** *ou* **s'en jeter un derrière la c.** to knock back a drink

2 *(d'un drapeau)* bow and tassels

3 *(décoration)* insignia, ribbon

4 *(prise de lutte)* headlock

5 *Naut* sling

6 *Fam* **c'est de la c.** it's a load of baloney *or* bull

cravater [3] [kravate] **VT 1** *(homme)* to put a tie on **2** *(attraper par le cou)* to grab by the neck; *Sport* to get in a headlock, to put a headlock on **3** *Fam* *Arg crime (arrêter)* **se faire c.** to get nabbed **4** *Fam (voler)* to pinch, to swipe; **je me suis fait c. mes papiers** someone's pinched *or* swiped my papers

►**se cravater VPR** to put on a tie

crave [krav] **NM** *Orn* chough

craw-craw [krokro] **NM INV** craw-craw

crawl [krol] **NM** crawl; **faire du** *ou* **nager le c.** to do *or* to swim the crawl

crawlé [krole] *voir* **dos**

crawler [3] [krole] **VI** to do *or* to swim the crawl

crawleur, -euse [krolœr, -øz] **NM,F** crawl specialist *(swimmer)*

crayeux, -euse [krɛjø, -øz] **ADJ 1** *Géol* chalky **2** *(teint)* chalk-like; **d'un blanc c.** chalky-white

crayon [krɛjɔ̃] **NM 1** *(pour écrire, dessiner)* pencil; *(stylo)* pen; **c. gras** *ou* **à mine grasse** soft lead pencil; **c. à** *ou* **de papier** lead pencil; **c. sec** *ou* **à mine sèche** dry lead pencil; **c. de couleur** coloured pencil, crayon; **c. à dessin** drawing pencil; **c. à lèvres** lip-liner, lip pencil; **c. noir** *(à papier)* (lead) pencil; **c. pour les yeux** eye *or* eyeliner pencil; **c. à sourcils** eyebrow pencil; **coup de c.** *(rature)* pencil stroke; *(d'un artiste)* drawing style; **avoir un bon coup de c.** to be good at drawing

2 *Beaux-Arts (œuvre)* pencil drawing, crayon-sketch; **c. lithographique** litho crayon, *Am* grease pencil

3 *Littéraire (ébauche)* **le premier c. de son projet** the first rough outline *or* draft of his/her project

4 *Nucl* **c. (combustible)** fuel rod *or* pin

5 *Opt* **c. optique** *ou* **lumineux** electronic *or* light pen

6 *Pharm* **c. (médicamenteux)** pencil; **c. au nitrate d'argent** silver-nitrate *or* caustic pencil; **c. hémostatique** styptic pencil

❑ **crayons NMPL** *Fam (cheveux)* **se faire tailler les crayons** to get a haircut

❑ **au crayon ADJ** *(ajout, trait)* pencilled; *(dessin)* pencil *(avant n)* **ADV** *(dessiner, écrire)* in pencil; **écrire/dessiner qch au c.** to write/to draw sth in pencil; **écris-le au c. dans ton cahier** pencil it in your notebook; **dessiner qch au c. de couleur** to crayon sth; **faire ses yeux au c.** to outline one's eyes with eye pencil

crayon-feutre [krɛjɔ̃føtr] *(pl* **crayons-feutres)** **NM** felt-tip (pen)

crayon-lecteur [krɛjɔ̃lɛktœr] *(pl* **crayons-lecteurs)** **NM** electronic *or* light pen

crayonnage [krɛjɔnaʒ] **NM 1** *(action → d'écrire)* scribbling; *(→ de dessiner)* sketching **2** *(esquisse)* pencil sketch *or* drawing

crayonné [krɛjɔne] **NM** *Typ (avant-projet, maquette)* rough, rough layout

crayonner [3] [krɛjɔne] **VT 1** *(dessiner rapidement)* to sketch (in pencil); **il crayonna son visage sur la nappe** he made a quick pencil sketch of his/her face on the tablecloth **2** *(gribouiller → feuille, mur)* to scribble on **3** *(écrire → au crayon)* to pencil; *(→ rapidement)* to jot down

USAGE ABSOLU *(gribouiller)* **c. sur un bloc-notes** to doodle on a notepad

crayonneur [krɛjɔnœr] **NM** sketch artist, cartoonist

Crazy Horse [kreziɔrs] **NM le C.** = nightclub and cabaret in Paris

CRDP [seɛrdepe] **NM** *(abrév* **centre régional de documentation pédagogique)** = local centre for educational resources

CRDS [seɛrdeɛs] **NF** *(abrév* **contribution au remboursement de la dette sociale)** = income-based tax deducted at source as a contribution to paying off the French social security budget deficit

créance [kreɑ̃s] **NF 1** *Fin (dette)* debt; *(titre)* letter of credit; *Jur* claim; **mauvaise c.** bad debt; **c. alimentaire** claim for *Br* maintenance *or Am* alimony; **c. chirographaire** unsecured debt; **c. douteuse** doubtful debt; **c. exigible** debt due; **c. garantie** secured debt; **créances gelées** frozen credits; **c. hypothécaire** debt secured by a mortgage; **c. irrécouvrable** bad debt; **c. litigieuse** contested debt; **c. privilégiée** preferential *or* preferred debt

2 *Littéraire (foi)* credence; **donner c. à** *(ajouter foi à)* to give *or* to attach credence to; *(rendre vraisemblable)* to lend credibility to

créancier, -ère [kreɑ̃sje, -ɛr] **NM,F** creditor; **c. chirographaire** unsecured creditor; **c. entièrement nanti** fully-secured creditor; **c. d'exploitation** trade creditor; **c. hypothécaire** mortgagee; **c. nanti** secured creditor; **c. privilégié** preferential *or* preferred creditor

créateur, -trice [kreatœr, -tris] **ADJ** creative; **imagination créatrice** creativity; **industrie créatrice d'emplois** job-creating industry

NM,F creator; *(de mode, d'un produit)* designer; **c. d'entreprise** *ou* **d'entreprises** entrepreneur

❑ **Créateur NM le C.** the Creator, our Maker

créatif, -ive [kreatif, -iv] **ADJ** *(esprit)* creative, imaginative, inventive; **une atmosphère créative** a creative atmosphere

NM,F creative person; *(de publicité)* designer, creative

créatine [kreatin] **NF** *Biol & Chim* creatin, creatine

créatinine [kreatinin] **NF** *Biol & Chim* creatinine

création [kreasjɔ̃] **NF 1** *(œuvre originale → bijou, parfum, vêtement)* creation; *Com & Ind* new product; **nos nouvelles créations** our new range; **une des plus belles créations humaines** one of the finest works of man

2 *Théât (d'un rôle)* creation; *(d'une pièce)* first production, creation; **il y aura de nombreuses créations au festival** a lot of new plays will be performed at the festival

3 *(fait de créer → une mode, un style)* creation; *(→ un vêtement, un produit)* designing, creating; *(→ une entreprise)* setting up, founding; *(→ une association)* founding, creating; *(→ des emplois)* creating, creation; **je connais cette société depuis sa c.** I have known this firm since it was founded *or* set up; **c. d'emplois** job creation; **il y a eu 3000 créations d'emplois en mai** 3,000 new jobs were created in May; **il s'agit d'une c. de poste** it's a newly created post; *Ordinat* **c. de pages Web** web authoring; **c. télévisuelle** television production

4 *(département, service)* **la c.** creative; **le département c.** creative, the creative department

5 *Rel* **la C.** the Creation; **les merveilles de la C.** the wonders of nature

créationnisme [kreasjɔnism] **NM** *Rel* creationism

créationniste [kreasjɔnist] **ADJ** creationist

NM creationist

créative [kreativ] *voir* **créatif**

créativité [kreativite] **NF 1** *(qualité)* creativity, creativeness, creative spirit **2** *Ling* creativity

créatrice [kreatris] *voir* **créateur**

créature [kreatyr] **NF 1** *(personne ou bête créée)* creature; **les créatures de Dieu** God's creatures; **c. humaine** human being **2** *(femme)* **c. de rêve** gorgeous creature **3** *Can Fam (fille)* *Br* bird, *Am* chick **4** *Vieilli Péj (femme dissolue)* trollop **5** *(personne soumise)* slave, tool

crécelle [kresɛl] **NF** rattle; **jouer de la c.** to play the rattle

❑ **de crécelle ADJ bruit de c.** grating sound; **une voix de c.** a grating *or* rasping voice

crécerelle [kresrɛl] **NF** *Orn* kestrel

crèche [krɛʃ] **NF 1** *(établissement préscolaire)* *Br* crèche, *esp Br* day nursery, *Am* child-care center; *(dans un centre sportif, un magasin)* *Br* crèche, *Am* day-care center; **notre université est pourvue d'une c.** there are *Br* crèche *or Am* day-care facilities in our university **2** *(de la Nativité)* **c. (de Noël)** (Christ Child's) crib; **c. vivante** = nativity play **3** *Littéraire (mangeoire)* manger, crib **4** *Fam (chambre, maison)* pad

> *Culture*
>
> **CRÈCHE**
>
> State-subsidized care for children under three years of age of working families is well established in France, although this is subject to the availability of places.

crécher [18] [kreʃe] **VI** *Fam* **1** *(habiter)* to live■ **2** *(loger temporairement)* to crash, *Br* to doss (down); **il faut qu'on trouve un endroit où c.** we need to find somewhere to crash *or Br* to doss (down); **je peux c. chez toi ce soir?** can I crash *or Br* doss (down) at your place tonight?

crédence [kredɑ̃s] **NF 1** *(desserte d'église)* credence (table), credenza **2** *(buffet)* credenza

crédibiliser [3] [kredibilize] **VT** to give credibility to

crédibilité [kredibilite] NF credibility; **perdre sa c.** to lose one's credibility; **il a perdu presque toute c.** his credibility (rating) is very low

crédible [kredibl] ADJ credible, believable; **son histoire n'est pas c.** his/her story is unconvincing *or* is hardly credible

CRÉDIF, Crédif [kredif] NM *(abrév* **Centre de recherche et d'étude pour la diffusion du français**) = official body promoting use of the French language

crédirentier, -ère [kredirɑ̃tje, -ɛr] ADJ = recipient of an allowance

crédit [kredi] NM **1** *Banque (actif)* credit; *(en comptabilité)* credit, credit side; **porter 100 euros au c. de qn** to credit sb *or* sb's account with 100 euros, to credit 100 euros to sb *or* sb's account; **j'ai 156 euros euros à mon c.** I am 156 euros in credit

2 *Com (paiement différé, délai)* credit; *(somme allouée)* credit; **c. sur six mois** six months' credit; **faire c. à qn** to give sb credit; **il n'a pas voulu me faire c. pour la table** he wouldn't let me have the table on credit; **la maison ne fait** *ou* **nous ne faisons pas c.** *(sur panneau)* no credit given; **accorder/obtenir un c.** to grant/to obtain credit; **ouvrir un c. à qn** to open a credit account in sb's favour *or* in sb's name; **ouvrir un c. chez qn** to open a credit account with sb; **j'ai pris un c. sur 25 ans pour la maison** I've got a 25-year mortgage on the house; **la banque pratique des crédits** *(sur un compte courant)* the bank grants overdrafts; *(prêts)* the bank grants loans; **c. acheteur** buyer credit; **c. back to back** back-to-back credit; **c. bancaire, c. en banque** bank credit; **c. en blanc** blank credit, loan without security, unsecured loan; **c. bloqué** frozen credit; **c. commercial** trade credit; **c. à la consommation, c. au consommateur** consumer credit; **c. consortial** syndicated credit; **c. (à) court terme** short-term credit; *Bourse* **c. croisé** cross-currency swap; **c. à découvert** open credit; **c. documentaire** documentary credit; **c. dos à dos** back-to-back credit; **c. de droits** = delay in payment of indirect taxes; **c. évaluatif** = budget allocation for a variable expense; **c. fournisseur** supplier's credit, trade credit; **c. gratuit** interest-free credit; **c. immobilier** mortgage, home loan; **c. d'impôt** *(abattement)* tax rebate; *(report)* tax credit; **c. interentreprises** supplier's credit, trade credit; **c. irrévocable** irrevocable letter of credit; **c. (à) long terme** long-term credit; **c. (à) moyen terme** medium-term credit; **c. permanent** *Br* revolving *or Am* revolver credit; **c. personnalisé** individual *or* personal credit arrangement; **c. ponctuel (à court terme)** spot credit; **c. public** public loan; **c. relais** *Br* bridging loan, *Am* bridge loan; **c. renouvelable** *Br* revolving *or Am* revolver credit; **c. de restructuration** new money; **c. révocable** revocable letter of credit; **c. revolving** *Br* revolving *or Am* revolver credit; **c. de sécurité** swing line; **c. à taux réduit** low-interest loan; **c. à taux révisable** rollover credit; **c. à terme** term loan; **c. transférable** transferable credit; **crédits de trésorerie** (short term) credit facilities; **c. de TVA** VAT credit

3 *(établissement)* **c. foncier** = government-controlled *Br* building society *or Am* savings and loan association; **c. municipal** pawnbroker

4 *(confiance, estime)* credibility, esteem; **jouir d'un grand c. auprès de qn** to be high in sb's esteem; **connaître un grand c.** *(idée, théorie)* to be widely accepted *or* held; **il n'a plus aucun c.** he's lost all credibility; **elle comptait sur son c. pour faire accepter l'idée** she was relying on her influence to get her idea accepted; **donner du c. aux propos de qn** to give credence to what sb says; **faire c. à qn/qch** to trust sb/sth; **trouver c. auprès de qn** *(personne)* to win sb's confidence; *(histoire)* to find credence with *or* to be believed by sb

5 *Can Univ* credit

❑ **crédits** NMPL **1** *(fonds)* funds; **l'enseignement a besoin de plus de crédits** education needs more funding; **on s'attend à une réduction des crédits pour les bibliothèques** a reduction in funding for libraries is to be expected; **accorder des crédits** to grant *or* to allocate funds; **crédits de développement** development loans; **crédits d'équipement** equipment financing; **crédits à l'exportation** export credit; **crédits à l'importation** import credit

2 *(autorisation de dépenses)* **voter des crédits** to vote supplies; **crédits budgétaires** supplies

3 crédits de carbone carbon credits

❑ **à crédit** ADJ *voir* **achat, vente** ADV **acheter/vendre qch à c.** to buy/to sell sth on credit *or* on hire purchase *or Am* on the installment plan

❑ **à mon/son/***etc* **crédit** ADV to my/his/her/*etc* credit; **c'est à mettre** *ou* **porter à son c.** one must credit him/her with it; **il faut dire à son c. qu'il a respecté les délais** it must be said to his credit that he met the deadlines

❑ **de crédit** ADJ *(agence, établissement)* credit *(avant n)*

crédit-acheteur [krediaʃtœr] *(pl* **crédits-acheteurs**) NM buyer credit

crédit-bail [kredibaj] *(pl* **crédits-bails**) NM leasing

crédit-bailleur [kredibajœr] *(pl* **crédits-bailleurs**) NM lessor

créditer [3] [kredite] VT **1** *Banque (somme)* to credit; **mon compte a été crédité** *ou* **j'ai été crédité de 500 euros** 500 euros were credited to my account; **les intérêts seront crédités sur votre compte à la fin de chaque mois** the interest will be credited to your account at the end of every month

2 *Sport* to credit with; **on a crédité le coureur de dix secondes** the runner has been credited with ten seconds

3 *Fig* **c. qn de qch** to give sb credit for sth, to credit sb with sth; **c'est lui qui en sera crédité** he'll get (all) the credit for it

créditeur, -trice [kreditœr, -tris] ADJ *(solde)* credit *(avant n)*; **avoir un compte c.** to have an account in credit

NM,F customer in credit

crédit-fournisseur [kredifurnisœr] *(pl* **crédits-fournisseurs**) NM supplier credit

crédit-preneur [kredipranœr] *(pl* **crédits-preneurs**) NM lessee

crédit-relais [kredirəlɛ] *(pl* **crédits-relais**) NM *Br* bridging loan, *Am* bridge loan

créditrice [kreditris] *voir* **créditeur**

crédit-scoring [krediskɔriŋ] NM *Fin* credit scoring

credo [kredo] NM INV **1** *(principe)* credo, creed; **c. politique** political creed *or* credo; **c'est mon c.** it's the thing I most fervently believe in **2** *Rel* **le C.** the (Apostles') Creed

Credoc [kredɔk] NM *Mktg* *(abrév* **Centre de recherche pour l'étude et l'observation des conditions de vie**) = large state-funded market research company in Paris

crédule [kredyl] ADJ gullible, credulous; **qu'est-ce que tu peux être c.!** you'll believe anything!, you're so gullible!

crédulité [kredylite] NF gullibility, credulity

creek [krik] NM *(en Nouvelle-Calédonie)* river

créer [15] [kree] VT **1** *(inventer → personnage, style)* to create; *(→ machine)* to invent; *(→ vêtement, produit)* to create, to design; *(→ mot)* to invent, to coin; **c'est lui qui a créé la formule** he coined the phrase *or* expression; **écharpe/bague créée par Mélodie** scarf/ring created by Mélodie

2 *Théât (rôle)* to create, to play for the first time; *(pièce)* to produce for the first time

3 *(occasionner, engendrer → emploi, différences, difficultés)* to create; *(→ poste)* to create, to establish; *(→ atmosphère)* to create, to bring about; *(→ tension)* to give rise to; *(→ précédent)* to set; **c. des ennuis** *ou* **difficultés à qn** to create problems for *or* to cause trouble to sb; **il ne nous a créé que des ennuis** he's given us nothing but trouble; **cela crée des jalousies** it causes jealousy; **elle a créé la surprise en remportant le match** she caused a sensation by winning the match

4 *(fonder → association, mouvement)* to create, to found; *(→ entreprise)* to set up; *(→ État)* to establish, to create

▶**se créer** VPR **1** *(être établi)* to be set up *or* created; **des associations se créent un peu partout** societies are being founded *or* set up almost everywhere

2 *(pour soi-même)* **se c. une image** to create an image for oneself; **il s'est créé un monde à lui** he's created a world of his own; **se c. une excuse** to invent an excuse for oneself; **se c. des problèmes** to create problems for oneself; **se c. une clientèle** to build up a clientele

crémage [kremaʒ] NM **1** *(du lait)* creaming **2** *Tex* tinting, dying

crémaillère [kremajɛr] NF **1** *(de cheminée)* trammel (hook) **2** *Tech, Aut & Rail* rack; *Aut* **c. de direction** steering rack **3** *(fête)* **(pendaison de) c.** housewarming (party); **pendre la c.** to have a housewarming (party)

❑ **à crémaillère** ADJ **engrenage/direction à c.** rack (and pinion) gearing/steering; **chemin de fer à c.** cog railway

crémant [kremɑ̃] ADJ M slightly sparkling

NM Crémant wine

crémation [kremasjɔ̃] NF cremation

crématiste [krematist] ADJ cremationist, pro-cremation

NM cremationist, advocate of cremation

crématoire [krematwar] ADJ crematory

NM *Br* cremator, *Am* cinerator

crématorium [krematɔrjɔm] NM *Br* crematorium, *Am* crematory

crème [krɛm] NF **1** *Culin (préparation)* cream; *(entremets)* cream (dessert); *(peau du lait)* skin; **c'est la c. des maris** he's the perfect husband; **c. anglaise** custard; **c. au beurre** buttercream; **c. brûlée** crème brûlée; **c. (au) caramel** crème caramel; **c. Chantilly** sweetened chilled whipped cream, Chantilly cream; **c. au chocolat/citron** chocolate/lemon cream; **c. épaisse** ≃ *Br* double *or Am* heavy cream; **c. fleurette** ≃ *Br* single *or Am* light cream; **c. fouettée** whipped cream; **c. fraîche** crème fraîche; **c. glacée,** *Can* **c. à la glace** ice cream; **c. du lait** top of the milk; **c. liquide** *Br* single *or Am* light cream; **c. de marrons** chestnut purée; **c. pâtissière** confectioner's custard; **c. renversée** ≃ crème caramel

2 *(potage)* **c. de brocoli** cream of broccoli soup; **c. de poireaux** cream of leek soup

3 *(boisson)* **c. de cassis** crème de cassis; **c. de cacao/menthe** crème de cacao/menthe

4 *(cosmétique)* cream; **c. antirides** anti-wrinkle cream; **c. de beauté** skin cream; **c. décolorante** bleaching cream; **c. dépilatoire** hair removing cream; **c. hydratante** moisturizing cream, moisturizer; **c. de jour** day cream; **c. médicinale** treatment cream; **c. de nuit** night cream; **c. à raser** shaving cream; **c. (de soins) pour les mains/le visage** hand/face cream

5 *(produit d'entretien)* **c. pour chaussures** shoe cream *or* polish

ADJ INV cream, cream-coloured

NM **1** *(couleur)* cream

2 *Fam (café)* coffee with milk *or* cream, *Br* white coffee; **un grand/petit c.** a large/small cup of white coffee

❑ **à la crème** ADJ *(gâteau)* cream *(avant n)*; **framboises à la c.** raspberries and cream; **escalopes à la c.** escalopes with cream sauce

crémé, -e [kreme] ADJ *(sauce)* cream *(avant n)*

crémer[1] [18] [kreme] VT *(incinérer)* to cremate

crémer[2] [18] [kreme] VT **1** *(sauce)* to add cream to **2** *(vêtement)* to dye cream

VI *(lait)* to cream

crémerie [krɛmri] NF **1** *(boutique)* = shop selling cheese and other dairy products **2** *Vieilli (café, restaurant)* café **3** *Fam Fig* **changer de c.** to go somewhere else, to move on

crémeux, -euse [kremø, -øz] ADJ **1** *(onctueux)* creamy, unctuous, smooth **2** *(gras → fromage)* soft

crémier, -ère [kremje, -ɛr] NM,F dairyman, *f* dairywoman

Crémone [kremɔn] NM *Géog* Cremona

crémone [kremɔn] NF **1** *(espagnolette)* bolt on casement window, espagnolette **2** *Can (cache-nez)* scarf

crénage [krenaʒ] NM *Ordinat* kerning

créneau, -x [kreno] NM **1** *Archit (creux)* crenel (embrasure), crenelle; *(bloc de pierre)* crenellation; **les créneaux** the crenellations *or* battlements; **à créneaux** crenellated

2 *(meurtrière)* slit, loophole; **c. de visée** aiming slit; *Fam* **monter au c.** to step into the breach

3 *Aut (espace)* gap, (parking) space; **faire un c.** to parallel park; **elle a raté son c.** she's parked badly *or* made a mess of parking the car

4 *(dans un emploi du temps)* slot, gap; *Rad & TV*

(temps d'antenne) slot; **c. horaire/publicitaire** time/advertising slot; **l'émission occupera le c. 20–22 heures** the programme will take the 8 to 10 p.m. slot

5 *Écon* (market) niche, gap in the market; **trouver un bon c.** to find a niche in the market; **exploiter un nouveau c.** to fill a new gap *or* niche in the market; **c. porteur** potentially lucrative market

crénelage [krɛnlaʒ] NM **1** *(fait d'entailler)* milling *(UNCOUNT)* **2** *(entailles)* milled edge **3** *Ordinat (en PAO)* aliasing

crénelé, -e [krɛnle] ADJ **1** *Archit* crenellated **2** *Bot* crenate, scalloped **3** *Métal* notched; *(pièce de monnaie)* milled

créneler [24] [krɛnle] VT **1** *Archit* to crenellate **2** *Métal* to notch; *(pièce de monnaie)* to mill

crénelure [krɛnlyr] NF **1** *Archit* crenellation **2** *Métal* notch **3** *Bot* crenelling

créner [18] [krene] VT *Typ* to kern

crénom [krenɔ̃] EXCLAM *Fam Vieilli* **c. (de nom** *ou* **de Dieu)!** *(d'impatience)* for God's *or* Pete's sake!; *(de colère)* damn it!; *(de surprise) Br* blimey!, *Am* holy cow!

crénothérapie [krenɔterapi] NF *Méd* crenotherapy

créodonte [kreodɔ̃t] *Zool* NM creodont

❑ **créodontes** NMPL creodonts

créole [kreɔl] ADJ creole

NM *(langue)* Creole

❑ **Créole** NMF Creole

❑ **créoles** NFPL hoop earrings

créolisation [kreɔlizasjɔ̃] NF creolization

créoliser [3] [kreɔlize] VT to creolize

▸**se créoliser** VPR to become creolized

créolisme [kreɔlism] NM creole expression

créolophone [kreɔlɔfɔn] ADJ Creole-speaking

NMF Creole speaker

Créon [kreɔ̃] NPR Creon

créosotage [kreɔzɔtaʒ] NM creosoting

créosote [kreɔzɔt] NF creosote

créosoter [3] [kreɔzɔte] VT to creosote

crêpage [krɛpaʒ] NM **1** *(de tissu)* crimping; *(de papier)* cockling *or* crinkling (up) **2** *(des cheveux)* backcombing; **c. de chignon** *(coups)* catfight; **attention au c. de chignon!** be careful the women don't come to blows!

crêpe[1] [krɛp] NM **1** *Tex* crepe, crêpe; **c. de Chine** crepe de Chine; **c. de deuil** *ou* **noir** black mourning crepe; **porter un c.** *(brassard)* to wear a black armband; *(au revers de la veste)* to wear a black ribbon; *(sur le chapeau)* to wear a black hatband **2** *(caoutchouc)* crepe rubber

❑ **de crêpe** ADJ **1** *(funéraire)* mourning; **voile de c.** mourning veil **2** *(chaussures, semelle)* rubber *(avant n)*

crêpe[2] [krɛp] NF *Culin* pancake, crepe; **c. au beurre/sucre** crepe with butter/sugar; **c. au jambon et aux champignons** crepe filled with ham and mushrooms; **c. dentelle** = very thin crepe; **c. Suzette** crepe suzette

crêpelé, -e [krɛple] ADJ *(ondulé)* frizzy; *(à l'africaine)* afro

crêpelure [krɛplyr] NF *(ondulations)* frizziness; *(à l'africaine)* Afro hairstyle

crêper [4] [krepe] VT **1** *(cheveux)* to backcomb **2** *Tex* to crimp, to crisp **3** *(papier)* to cockle *or* to crinkle (up)

▸**se crêper** VPR **se c. les cheveux** to backcomb one's hair; *Fam* **se c. le chignon** to have a catfight

crêperie [krɛpri] NF *(restaurant)* pancake restaurant, creperie; *(stand)* pancake *or* crepe stall

crépi, -e [krepi] ADJ roughcast *(avant n)*

NM roughcast

crêpier, -ère [krepje, -ɛr] NM,F *(d'un restaurant)* pancake restaurant *or* creperie owner; *(d'un stand)* pancake *or* crepe maker *or* seller

❑ **crêpière** NF *(poêle)* pancake *or* crepe pan; *(plaque)* griddle

crépine [krepin] NF **1** *Zool & Culin* caul **2** *Tech* strainer **3** *(de passementerie)* fringe

crépinette [krepinɛt] NF *Culin* flat sausage *(in a caul)*

crépir [32] [krepir] VT to roughcast

crépissage [krepisaʒ] NM roughcasting

crépitation [krepitasjɔ̃] NF *Méd* **c. osseuse** crepitation, crepitus; **c. pulmonaire** lung crepitation

❑ **crépitations** NFPL *(d'un feu)* crackle, crackling

crépitement [krepitmɑ̃] NM *(d'un feu)* crackle, crackling; *(d'une fusillade)* rattle; *(d'une friture)* splutter; *(de la pluie)* pitter-patter; **les crépitements de la grêle sur les feuilles** the pattering of hail on the leaves

crépiter [3] [krepite] VI **1** *(feu, coups de feu)* to crackle; *(pluie)* to patter; *(friture)* to splutter; **les applaudissements crépitèrent** there was a ripple of applause **2** *Méd* to crepitate

crépon [krepɔ̃] NM **1** *(papier)* crepe paper **2** *Tex* crepon, seersucker

CREPS, Creps [krɛps] NM *(abrév* **centre régional d'éducation physique et sportive**) = regional sports centre

crépu, -e [krepy] ADJ *(cheveux)* frizzy

crépure [krepyr] NF **1** *(des cheveux)* frizzing, crimping **2** *(crêpe)* crimped appearance

crépusculaire [krepyskylɛr] ADJ **1** *Littéraire (lueur, moment)* twilight *(avant n)*; **lumière c.** twilight, half-light; *Fig* **une beauté c.** a fading beauty **2** *Zool* crepuscular

crépuscule [krepyskyl] NM **1** *(fin du jour)* twilight, dusk **2** *Astron (lumière → du soir)* twilight; *(→ du matin)* dawn light

❑ **au crépuscule de** PRÉP *Littéraire* **au c. de sa vie** in the twilight of his/her life; **au c. du siècle** in the closing years of the century

'Le Crépuscule des dieux' *Wagner* 'Götterdämmerung' *or* 'Twilight of the Gods'

crescendo [kreʃɛndo, kreʃɛ̃do] NM **1** *Mus* crescendo; **faire un c.** to go crescendo; **ça se joue en c.** it must be played crescendo

2 *(montée)* escalation; **pour enrayer le c. de la violence** to stop the rising tide *or* the escalation of violence

ADV crescendo; **aller c.** *(notes)* to go crescendo; *(bruits, voix)* to grow louder and louder; *(violence, mécontentement)* to rise, to escalate

crésol [krezɔl] NM *Chim* cresol

cresson [kresɔ̃] NM cress; **c. (d'eau** *ou* **de fontaine)** watercress; **c. alénois** garden cress; **c. de cheval** brooklime; **c. des prés** lady's smock; **c. de terre** land cress

cressonnette [kresɔnɛt] NF *Bot* lady's smock

cressonnière [kresɔnjɛr] NF *Bot* watercress bed

Crésus [krezys] NPR Croesus

crésus [krezys] NM Croesus, rich man

Crésyl® [krezil] NM disinfectant *(containing cresol)*

crêt [krɛ] NM hogsback

crétacé, -e [kretase] ADJ Cretaceous

NM Cretaceous (period)

Crète [krɛt] NF **la C.** Crete

crête [krɛt] NF **1** *(d'oiseau, de lézard)* crest; *(de volaille)* comb **2** *Mil (d'un casque)* crest **3** *(d'une montagne, d'un toit)* crest, ridge; *(d'un mur)* crest, top; *(d'une vague)* crest; *Géog* **c. de plage** *ou* **prélittorale** watershed **4** *Anat* **c. du tibia** *ou* **iliaque** edge *or* crest of the shin **5** *Élec & Électron* peak

crêté, -e [krete] ADJ *Littéraire (oiseau, casque)* crested

crête-de-coq [krɛtdəkɔk] *(pl* **crêtes-de-coq)** NF **1** *Bot* cockscomb **2** *Méd* venereal papilloma

crételle [kretɛl] NF *Bot* dog's-tail grass; **c. des prés** crested dog's-tail

crétin, -e [kretɛ̃, -in] ADJ *Fam* moronic; **vous êtes encore plus c. que lui** you're even more of a cretin *or* a moron *or* an idiot than he is

NM,F **1** *Fam (imbécile)* moron, cretin **2** *Méd & Vieilli* cretin

crétinerie [kretinri] NF **1** *(caractère)* stupidity, idiocy **2** *(acte)* idiotic thing (to do); *(propos)* idiotic thing (to say)

crétinisant, -e [kretinizɑ̃, -ɑ̃t] ADJ *(abêtissant)* mind-numbing

crétinisation [kretinizasjɔ̃] NF becoming or making stupid; **on assiste à une lente c. des esprits** people are becoming more and more stupid

crétiniser [3] [kretinize] VT *(public)* to turn into morons; *(personne)* to turn into a moron

crétinisme [kretinism] NM **1** *(caractère)* stupidity, idiocy **2** *Méd & Vieilli* cretinism

crétois, -e [kretwa, -az] ADJ Cretan

❑ **Crétois, -e** NM,F Cretan

cretonne [krətɔn] NF *Tex* cretonne

cretons [krətɔ̃] NMPL *Can Culin* cretons, = type of pork pâté

Creuse [krøz] NF **la C.** the Creuse

creuse[1] [krøz] NF *(portugaise)* Portuguese oyster; *(Pacifique)* Pacific oyster

creuse[2] [krøz] *voir* **creux**

creusé, -e [krøze] ADJ *(joue)* hollow

creusement [krøzmɑ̃] NM **1** *(d'un trou)* digging; *(d'un canal)* digging, cutting; *(d'un puits)* digging, sinking **2** *Fig (augmentation)* deepening; **le c. des inégalités dans la société** the deepening inequalities in society

creuser [5] [krøze] VT **1** *(excaver → puits, mine)* to dig, to sink; *(→ canal)* to dig, to cut; *(→ tranchée)* to dig, to excavate; *(→ sillon)* to plough; *(→ passage souterrain, tunnel)* to bore, to dig; **c. un trou** *(à la pelle)* to dig a hole; *(en grattant)* to scratch a hole; **c. un terrier** to burrow; **la taupe creuse des chemins sous terre** moles make tunnels underground; **ils ont creusé une piscine dans leur jardin** they've made *or* built a swimming pool in their garden; **les marches ont été creusées à même la roche** the steps have been carved out of the rock; **la carrière a été creusée à ciel ouvert** it's an opencast quarry; **la rivière a creusé son lit** the river has hollowed out its bed; *Fig* **c. sa propre tombe** to dig one's own grave; *Fig* **c. sa tombe avec ses dents** to eat oneself into an early grave; **ça a creusé un abîme** *ou* **fossé entre eux** this has opened up a gulf between them; **c. l'écart entre soi et le reste du peloton/de ses concurrents** to widen the gap between oneself and the rest of the bunch/and one's competitors

2 *(faire un trou dans → gén)* to hollow (out); *(→ avec une cuillère)* to scoop (out); **c. la terre** to dig (a hole in the earth)

3 *(ployer)* **c. les reins** *ou* **le dos** to arch one's back; **c. la taille** to exaggerate one's waist

4 *(marquer → traits du visage)* **la maladie lui avait creusé les joues** illness had hollowed his/her cheeks; **joues creusées par la souffrance** cheeks sunken with pain; **il avait le visage creusé par la fatigue** his face was hollow with fatigue; **il avait le front creusé de rides** his forehead was furrowed with wrinkles

5 *Fam (ouvrir l'appétit de)* to make hungry▪; **la marche m'a creusé (l'estomac)** the walk gave me an appetite▪

6 *(approfondir → idée)* to look *or* to go into; *(→ problème, question)* to look *or* to delve into; **tu n'as pas assez creusé l'aspect sociologique du problème** you didn't go into enough detail about the sociological aspect of the problem

7 *Couture (décolleté)* to make deeper *or* lower; *(emmanchure)* to make bigger

USAGE ABSOLU *Hum* **toutes ces émotions, ça creuse!** all this excitement gives you an appetite!; *Hum* **il paraît intelligent, mais il vaut mieux ne pas c. (trop loin)** he seems intelligent, but it might be better not to scratch too far beneath the surface

▸**se creuser** VPR **1** *Fam (réfléchir)* **tu ne t'es pas beaucoup creusé pour écrire ce texte!** you didn't overtax yourself when you wrote this text!; **se c. la tête** *ou* **la cervelle** to rack one's brains

2 *(yeux, visage)* to grow hollow; *(joues)* to grow gaunt *or* hollow; *(fossettes, rides)* to appear

3 *(augmenter → écart)* to grow bigger; **le fossé entre eux se creuse** the gap between them is widening

creuset [krøzɛ] NM **1** *Pharm & Tech* crucible, melting pot; *(d'un haut-fourneau)* crucible, hearth **2** *(rassemblement)* melting pot, mixture; **un c. de cultures** a melting pot of cultures **3** *Littéraire (épreuve de purification)* crucible

creux, -euse [krø, krøz] ADJ **1** *(évidé → dent, tronc)* hollow; *Fig* **j'ai le ventre c.** my stomach feels hollow, I'm hungry; **je ne peux pas travailler quand j'ai le ventre** *ou* **l'estomac c.** I can't work on an empty stomach

2 *(concave → joues)* hollow, gaunt; *(→ visage)* gaunt; *(→ yeux)* sunken, hollow; **aux joues creuses** hollow-cheeked; **aux yeux c.** hollow-eyed; **un chemin c.** a sunken lane

3 *(qui résonne → voix)* cavernous, hollow; *(→ son)* hollow

4 *Péj (inconsistant → discours, phrases)* empty, meaningless; *(→ argumentation)* weak
5 *(sans activité)* **périodes creuses** *(au travail)* slack periods; *(dans une tarification)* off-peak periods; **pendant la saison creuse** *(pour le commerce)* during the slack season; *(pour les vacanciers)* during the off-peak season; **la communication/le trajet aux heures creuses ne vous coûtera que six euros** the phone call/journey will cost you only six euros off-peak
6 *Can (profond)* deep
7 *Can Fam (grave)* heavy, bad; **c'est un truc pas mal c., elle est allée jusqu'à poursuivre ses parents** it's pretty heavy stuff, she even took her parents to court
8 *Couture* **pli c.** box pleat, inverted pleat
NM 1 *(trou → dans un roc)* hole, cavity; *(→ d'une dent, d'un tronc)* hollow (part), hole, cavity; **une succession de c. et de bosses** a succession *or* series of bumps and hollows; **la route est pleine de c. et de bosses** the road is bumpy *or* is full of potholes; *Fam* **avoir un c. (à l'estomac)** to feel a bit hungry■ *or Br* peckish; **j'ai un petit c.** I'm a bit hungry■ *or Br* peckish
2 *(concavité → de la main, de l'épaule)* hollow; *(→ de l'estomac)* pit; **tenir qch dans le c. de la main** to hold sth cupped in one's hand; **il a bu dans le c. de ma main** it drank out of my hand; **c'est si petit que ça tient dans le c. de la main** it's so small you can hold it in the palm of your hand; **j'ai mal dans le c. du dos** *ou* **des reins** I've a pain in the small of my back; **le c. de l'aisselle** the armpit
3 *(dépression → d'une courbe, d'une vague)* trough; **il y avait des c. de dix mètres** *(sur la mer)* there were waves ten metres high
4 *(inactivité)* **une période de c., un c.** a slack period; **il y a un c. des ventes en janvier** business slows down *or* slackens off in January; **j'ai un c. dans mon emploi du temps entre deux et quatre** I've got a gap in my timetable between two and four
5 *Can (profondeur)* hole; **avoir 30 mètres de c.** to be 30 metres deep
6 *Beaux-Arts* mould
7 *Naut (d'une voile)* belly
ADV sonner c. to give *or* to have a hollow sound; *Fig* to ring hollow
❑ **au creux de PRÉP au c. de ses bras** (nestled) in his/her arms; **au c. de la vague** in the trough of the wave; *Fig* **être au c. de la vague** *(entreprise, personne)* to be at a low ebb, to be going through a bad patch
❑ **en creux ADJ 1** *Beaux-Arts* **gravure en c.** intaglio engraving
2 *Fig (sous-jacent)* indirect; **ce film est un portrait en c. de l'écrivain** this film is an indirect portrait of the writer

crevaison [krəvɛzɔ̃] **NF** *Br* puncture, *Am* flat; **avoir une c.** *Br* to have a puncture *or* a flat tyre, *Am* to have a flat

crevant, -e [krəvɑ̃, -ɑ̃t] **ADJ** *Fam* **1** *(fatigant → travail, enfant)* exhausting **2** *(drôle → personne, histoire, spectacle)* hilarious, priceless; **elle est crevante, leur gamine** their kid's a scream *or* a hoot

crevard, -e [krəvar, -ard] **NM,F** *Fam* **1** *(personne famélique)* half-starved wretch■ **2** *(personne affamée)* pig, *Br* gannet, *Am* hog

crevasse [krəvas] **NF 1** *Géog (dans le sol)* crevice, fissure, split; *(sur un roc)* crack, crevice, fissure; *(d'un glacier)* crevasse **2** *(sur les lèvres, sur les mains)* crack, split; **j'ai des crevasses aux doigts** my fingers are badly chapped

crevassé, -e [krəvase] **ADJ 1** *(sol)* cracked, fissured **2** *(peau)* chapped

crevasser [3] [krəvase] **VT 1** *(sol)* to cause cracks *or* fissures in **2** *(peau)* to chap
►**se crevasser VPR 1** *(sol)* to become cracked **2** *(peau)* to become chapped

crevé, -e [krəve] **ADJ 1** *(pneu)* flat, punctured; *(tympan)* pierced; *(yeux)* gouged-out; *(ballon)* burst; **j'ai un pneu c.** I've got a *Br* puncture *or Am* flat **2** *(mort → animal)* dead **3** *Fam (fatigué) Br* shattered, *Am* bushed
NM *Couture* slash
❑ **à crevés ADJ** *(chaussure, manche)* slashed

crève [krɛv] **NF** *Fam (rhume)* stinking cold; **j'ai la c.** I've got a stinking cold; **attraper** *ou* **choper la c.** to catch one's death

crève-cœur [krɛvkœr] **NM INV c'est un c. de les voir comme ça** it's a heartbreaking *or* heart-rending sight to see them like that; **c'est un c. d'entendre cela** it's heartbreaking *or* heart-rending to hear this

crevée [krəve] **NF** *Suisse Fam* blunder

crève-la-faim [krɛvlafɛ̃] **NM INV** *Fam* half-starved wretch■

crever [19] [krəve] **VT 1** *(faire éclater → abcès)* to burst (open); *(→ bulle, ballon, sac)* to burst; *(→ pneu)* to puncture, to burst; *(→ tympan)* to puncture, to pierce; **un cri vint c. le silence** a cry pierced *or* rent the silence; **la pierre a crevé le pare-brise** the stone put a hole in the windscreen; **c. un œil à qn** *(agression)* to gouge *or* to put out sb's eye; *(accident)* to blind sb in one eye; **cela crève le cœur** it's heartbreaking *or* heart-rending; **ça me crève le cœur de devoir abandonner cette maison** I'm heartbroken about *or* it's heart-breaking having to leave this house; **tu me crèves le cœur!** you're breaking my heart!; *Fam* **ça crève les yeux** *(c'est évident)* it's as plain as the nose on your face, it sticks out a mile; *(c'est visible)* it's staring you in the face, it's plain for all to see; **c. le plafond** *(prix)* to go through the roof; **c. l'écran** *(acteur)* to have great screen presence
2 *Fam (fatiguer)* to wear out■, *Br* to knacker; **ce boulot/gosse me crève** this job/kid is killing me; **c'est ce rhume qui m'a crevé** that cold took it out of me; **ça vous crève, les transports en commun!** using public transport wears you out■ *or Br* is knackering!; **c. sa monture** to ride one's horse to death■; **c. ses bœufs** to work one's oxen to death■
3 *Fam (locution)* **c. la faim** *(par pauvreté)* to be starving
VI 1 *(éclater → pneu)* to puncture; *(→ ballon, bulle, nuage, abcès)* to burst; *Fam* **on a crevé sur la rocade** we had *Br* a puncture *or Am* a flat on the bypass; *Culin* **faire c. du riz** to burst rice
2 *Fam (mourir)* to kick the bucket, *Br* to snuff it; **qu'il crève!** to hell with him!; **s'il veut que je l'aide, il peut toujours c. (la gueule ouverte)!** he can go to hell if he thinks I'm going to help him!; **ils me laisseraient c. comme un chien** they'd just let me die like a dog; **on monte jusqu'au sommet – tu veux me faire c.?** let's go up to the top – do you want to kill me?■; **il fait une chaleur à c.** it's stifling *or* boiling; **plutôt c.!** I'd rather die!, I'll die first!
3 *(mourir → animal, végétal)* to die (off); **faire c. qch** to kill sth (off); **les moutons crevaient tous** the sheep were all dying
4 *Suisse Fam (voiture)* to stall■
❑ **crever de VT IND 1** *(éprouver)* **c. de faim** *(par pauvreté)* to be starving; *(être en appétit)* to be starving *or* famished; **c. de soif** to be parched; **je crève de chaud!** I'm baking *or* boiling!; **on crève de froid ici** it's freezing cold *or* you could freeze to death here; **faire c. qn de faim** to starve sb to death; **faire c. qn de soif/froid** to make sb die of thirst/cold; **c. d'ennui** to be bored to death; **c'est à c. de rire** it's a hoot *or* scream *or* riot; **c. de peur/d'inquiétude** to be scared/worried to death
2 *(être plein de)* **c. de jalousie** to be eaten up with jealousy; **c. d'orgueil** to be puffed up *or* bloated with pride; **c. de suffisance** to be puffed up *or* bloated with self-importance; **je crève d'impatience de le voir** I can't wait to see him; **c. d'envie de faire qch** to be dying to do sth; **je ne veux pas y aller – mais si, tu en crèves d'envie** I don't want to go – oh yes you do, you're dying to go
►**se crever VPR se c. au boulot** *ou* **à la tâche** to work oneself to death; **je ne me suis pas crevé à faire des études pour gagner si peu!** I didn't kill myself studying to earn such a small salary!; *très Fam* **se c. le cul** *Br* to bust a gut, *Am* to bust one's ass

crevette [krəvɛt] **NF** prawn, *Am* shrimp; **c. d'eau douce** freshwater shrimp; **c. grise** shrimp; **c. nordique** deep-water *or* northern prawn; **c. rose** (common) prawn

crevettier [krəvɛtje] **NM** *Pêche* **1** *(filet)* shrimping net **2** *(bateau)* shrimper, shrimp boat

crevoter [3] [krəvɔte] **VI** *Suisse Fam (entreprise)* to decline■; *(plante)* to wilt■, to wither■

Creys-Malville [krɛsmalvil] **NF** = nuclear power station in the Isère, site of the controversial fast-breeder reactor Superphénix

CRF [seɛrɛf] **NF** *(abrév* **Croix-Rouge française***)* **la C.** the French Red Cross

cri¹ [kri] *Can* **NM** *(langue)* Cree
❑ **Cri NMF** Cree; **les Cris** the Cree

cri² [kri] **NM 1** *(éclat de voix → gén)* cry; *(→ puissant)* shout, yell; *(→ perçant)* shriek, scream; **un petit c. aigu** a squeak; **un c. perçant** a shriek; **un c. rauque** a squawk; **les cris des rues** street cries; **des cris me parvenaient du jardin** I could hear somebody shouting in *or* cries coming from the garden; **qu'est-ce que c'est que tous ces cris?** what is all this shouting *or* noise about?; **c. de douleur** cry *or* scream of pain; **c. de guerre** battle cry; **c. de joie** cry *or* shout of joy; **c. d'indignation** cry *or* scream of indignation; **c. d'horreur** shriek *or* scream of horror; **c. primal** primal scream; **jeter** *ou* **pousser un c.** to cry out; **pousser un c. de joie/douleur** to cry out with joy/in pain; **pousser des cris** to cry out, to shout; *Fig* to make loud protests; *Fig* **jeter** *ou* **pousser des hauts cris** to raise the roof, to raise a hue and cry, to kick up a fuss; **pousser des cris d'orfraie** *ou* **de paon** *(hurler)* to screech like a thing possessed; *(protester)* to raise the roof
2 *Zool (d'un oiseau)* call; *(d'un petit oiseau)* chirp; *(d'une chouette, d'un paon, d'un singe)* screech; *(d'une mouette)* cry; *(d'un dindon)* gobble; *(d'un perroquet)* squawk; *(d'un canard)* quack; *(d'une oie)* honk; *(d'une souris)* squeak; *(d'un porc)* squeal; **quel est le c. de la chouette?** what noise does the owl make?
3 *(parole)* cry; **c. d'amour** cry of love; **c. d'avertissement** warning cry; **c. de détresse** cry of distress; **jeter** *ou* **lancer un c. d'alarme** to warn against the danger; **défiler au c. de "des subventions!"** to march chanting "subsidies!"; **c. du cœur** cry from the heart, *Littéraire* cri de coeur; **sa réaction a été un c. du cœur** his/her reaction was straight from the heart
❑ **à grands cris ADV appeler qn à grands cris** to shout for sb; **demander** *ou* **réclamer qch à grands cris** to cry out *or* to clamour for sth
❑ **dernier cri ADJ** *(machine, vidéo)* state-of-the-art; **il s'est acheté un portable dernier c.** he bought the latest thing in *Br* mobiles *or Am* cellphones **NM INV c'est le dernier c.** *(vêtement)* it's the (very) latest fashion *or* thing; *(machine, vidéo)* it's state-of-the-art

'Le Cri' *Munch* 'The Scream'

'Cris et chuchotements' *Bergman* 'Cries and Whispers'

criaillement [kriajmɑ̃] **NM** *Orn (d'une oie)* honk; *(d'un paon)* screech; *(d'un faisan)* cry
❑ **criaillements NMPL** *(de dispute)* screeching, shrieking

criailler [3] [kriaje] **VI 1** *(crier sans cesse)* to screech, to shriek; **c. après qn** to shriek at sb **2** *(se plaindre)* to whine, to complain **3** *Orn (faisan)* to cry; *(oie)* to honk; *(paon)* to squawk, to screech

criailleries [kriajri] **NFPL 1** *(cris)* screeching, shrieking **2** *(récriminations)* whining, complaining

criailleur, -euse [kriajœr, -øz] **ADJ 1** *(qui crie)* screeching, shrieking **2** *(qui se plaint)* whining, complaining

criant, -e [krijɑ̃, -ɑ̃t] **ADJ** *(erreur)* glaring; *(mauvaise foi, mensonge)* blatant, glaring, rank; *(parti pris)* blatant; *(différence, vérité)* obvious, striking; *(injustice)* flagrant, blatant, rank; *(preuve)* striking, glaring; *(contraste)* striking; **être c. de vérité** *(témoignage, reportage)* to be obviously *or* patently true, to ring true; *(personnage, image)* to be extremely true to life; *(acteur)* to be extremely convincing

criard, -e [krijar, -ard] **ADJ 1** *(voix)* shrill, piercing; **un enfant c.** a noisy child **2** *(couleur)* loud, garish; *(tenue)* garish, gaudy; **meublé avec un luxe c.** furnished ostentatiously **3** *(urgent → dettes)* pressing

crib [krib] **NM** *Agr* crib

criblage [kriblaʒ] **NM 1** *(tamisage → de sable, de*

grains) riddling, sifting; *(→ de charbon)* riddling, screening, sifting; *(→ d'un minerai)* screening, jigging **2** *(calibrage → de fruits, d'œufs, d'huîtres)* grading

crible [kribl] NM *(pour du sable, des grains)* riddle, sift; *(pour un charbon, un minerai)* screen; **passer au c.** *(charbon)* to riddle, to screen, to sift; *(sable, grains)* to riddle, to sift; *(fruits, œufs, huîtres)* to grade; *(région)* to go over with a fine-tooth comb, to comb; *(preuves)* to sift *or* to examine closely; *(document)* to examine closely, to go over with a fine-tooth comb; *(candidat)* to screen (for a job)

cribler [3] [krible] VT **1** *(tamiser → sable, grains)* to riddle, to sift; *(→ minerai)* to screen, to jig; *(→ charbon)* to riddle, to screen

2 *(calibrer → fruits, œufs, huîtres)* to grade

3 c. de *(trouer de)* **c. qch de trous** to riddle sth with holes; **un tronc criblé de flèches** a trunk riddled with arrows; **la façade est criblée d'impacts de balles** the facade is riddled with bullet holes

4 c. de *(assaillir de)* **c. qn de coups** to rain blows on sb; **c. qn de questions** to bombard sb with questions, to fire questions at sb; **c. qn de reproches** to heap reproaches on sb

5 être criblé de *(accablé, couvert de)* to be covered in; **être criblé de dettes** to be crippled with debt, to be up to one's eyes in debt; **elle a le visage criblé de taches de rousseur** her face is covered with freckles

cribleur [kriblœr] NM **1** *(personne)* screener, sifter **2** *(machine)* sifter, sifting machine

cribleuse [kribløz] NF *(machine)* sifter, sifting machine

cric[1] [krik] ONOMAT *(bruit de déchirement)* rip, crack; **c. (crac)!** *(tour de clé)* click!

cric[2] [krik] NM *Aut* (car) jack; **mettre une voiture sur** *ou* **élever une voiture avec un c.** to jack a car up; **c. hydraulique/à vis** hydraulic/screw jack

cricket [krikɛt] NM *Sport* cricket; **jouer au c.** to play cricket

cricoïde [krikɔid] *Anat* ADJ cricoid

NM cricoid cartilage

cricri [krikri] NM **1** *Fam (grillon)* cricket **2** *(cri du grillon)* chirp, chirp-chirp

criée [krije] NF **1** *(lieu de vente)* fish market *(where auctions take place)* **2** *(vente)* auction; *(salle)* auction room **3** *Bourse* open outcry **4** *Can (annonce)* = announcement made outside a church after Mass; *(vente)* = auction held to raise money for funerals

❑ **à la criée** ADJ *voir* **vente** ADV by auction; **vendre du thon à la c.** to auction off tuna

crier [10] [krije] VI **1** *(gén)* to cry (out); *(d'une voix forte)* to shout, to yell; *(d'une voix perçante)* to scream, to screech, to shriek; **il n'a même pas crié quand on lui a fait la piqûre** he didn't even cry out when he got the injection; **ne crie pas, je ne suis pas sourd!** there's no need to shout *or* yell, I'm not deaf!; **ne fais pas c. ta mère!** don't get your mother angry!; *Fam* **ça crie, ta radio, baisse-la donc!** your radio's blaring, turn it down!; **c. de douleur** to scream with *or* to cry out in pain; **c. de joie** to shout for joy; **c. de plaisir** to cry out with pleasure; *Fam* **c. comme un sourd** to shout one's head off; *Fam* **c. comme un damné** *ou* **putois** *ou* **veau** *ou* **un cochon qu'on égorge** *(fort)* to shout *or* to yell at the top of one's voice; *(avec des sons aigus)* to squeal like a stuck pig; *(protester)* to scream blue murder; **c. à l'assassin** to cry blue murder; **c. à l'injustice** to call it an injustice; **c. au génocide** to call it a genocide, to brandish the word genocide; **c. au loup** to cry wolf; **ils ont crié au miracle** they hailed it a miracle; **c. au scandale** to call it a scandal, to cry shame; **c. au voleur** to cry (stop) thief; **c. à l'aide** *ou* **au secours** to shout *or* to cry for help

2 *Zool (oiseau)* to call; *(souris)* to squeak; *(porc)* to squeal; *(chouette, singe)* to call, to screech; *(perroquet)* to squawk; *(paon)* to screech; *(oie)* to honk

3 *(freins, pneu)* to squeak, to screech; *(cuir, craie)* to squeak; *(charnière)* to creak

VT **1** *(dire d'une voix forte → avertissement)* to shout *or* to cry (out); *(→ insultes, ordres)* to bawl *or* to yell out; **il criait "arrêtez-le, arrêtez-le"** "stop him, stop him," he shouted; **elle nous cria de partir** she shouted at us to go; **quelqu'un criait "au feu!"** someone was shouting "fire!"; **sans c. gare** *(arriver)* without warning; *(partir)* without so much as a by-your-leave

2 *(faire savoir)* to proclaim; **c. son innocence** to proclaim *or* to protest one's innocence; **c. son dégoût/horreur** to proclaim one's disgust/indignation; **c. casse-cou** to point out the danger; **c. famine** to complain of hunger; **c. misère** *(se plaindre)* to complain of hardship; **ce taudis criait misère** the slum reeked of poverty; **c. victoire** to crow (over one's victory); **c. contre qch** to complain *or* to shout about sth; **ils crient contre la TVA** they're shouting about VAT; **c. qch sur les toits** *(le rendre public)* to shout *or* to proclaim sth from the rooftops; *(s'en vanter)* to let everyone know about sth; **ne va pas le c. sur les toits!** there's no need to publicize it!

3 *(demander)* **c. vengeance** to call for revenge; **c. grâce** to beg for mercy; *Fig* to cry for mercy

4 *(vendre)* to put up for auction, to auction

❑ **crier après** VT IND *Fam* **1** *(s'adresser à)* to shout *or* to yell at ■

2 *(réprimander)* to bawl out

crieur, -euse [krijœr, -øz] NM,F **1** *(vendeur)* **c. (de journaux)** newspaper seller *or* vendor **2** *(dans une criée)* auctioneer **3** *Hist* **c. (public)** town crier

crignasse [kriɲas] NF *Can Fam Péj* mane (of hair) ■, thatch

Crillon [krijɔ̃] NM **le C.** = luxury hotel overlooking the place de la Concorde in Paris

crime [krim] NM **1** *Jur (infraction pénale)* crime, (criminal) offence; **commettre un c.** to commit a crime; **un c. contre l'État** (high) treason *or* a crime against the state; **c. contre l'humanité** crime against humanity; **c. informatique** electronic crime; **c. contre la paix** crime against peace; **c. de guerre** war crime; **c. de lèse-majesté** act *or* crime of lèse-majesté; *Fig Hum* **il n'a pas salué le patron, c. de lèse-majesté!** he didn't say hello to the boss, what a heinous crime!; **c. politique** political offence

2 *(meurtre)* murder; **c'est le c. parfait** it's the perfect crime; **l'heure du c.** the time of the murder; **le motif du c.** the motive for the murder; **commettre un c.** to commit a murder; **c. crapuleux** heinous crime; **c. (à motif) sexuel** sex crime *or* murder; **c. passionnel** crime passionnel, crime of passion; **l'arme du c.** the murder weapon

3 *(acte immoral)* crime, act; **c'est un c. de démolir ces églises** it's a crime *or* it's criminal to knock down these churches; **son seul c. est d'avoir dit tout haut ce que chacun pensait** his/her only crime *or* fault was to say aloud what everybody was thinking; **ce n'est pas un c.!** it's not a crime!; *Littéraire* **faire à qn un c. de qch** to reproach sb with sth; **c. contre nature** act *or* crime against nature

4 *(criminalité)* **le c.** crime; **la lutte contre le c.** the fight against crime; **le c. organisé** organized crime; *Prov* **le c. ne paie pas** crime doesn't pay

EXCLAM *Can Joual Br* bloody hell!, *Am* goddammit!

❑ **en crime** ADV *Can Joual* **1** *(beaucoup)* a lot, very much; **c'est bon en c.** *(plat, gâteau)* it's to die for; *(jeu, film)* it's fantastic, *Br* it's wicked

2 être en c. (contre qn) to be fuming mad (with sb)

'Crime et châtiment' *Dostoïevski* 'Crime and Punishment'

'Le Crime était presque parfait' *Hitchcock* 'Dial M for Murder'

Crimée [krime] NF **la C.** the Crimea

criminalisation [kriminalizasjɔ̃] NF criminalization

criminaliser [3] [kriminalize] VT to criminalize

▸**se criminaliser** VPR to become criminalized

criminaliste [kriminalist] NMF specialist in criminal law

criminalistique [kriminalistik] NF crime-detection techniques

criminalité [kriminalite] NF **1** *(ensemble des actes criminels)* crime; **lutter contre la c.** to fight crime; **la grande/petite c.** serious/petty crime; **c. en col blanc** white-collar crime; **c. informatique** computer crime; **c. organisée** organized crime, racketeering **2** *(caractère criminel)* criminality, criminal nature

criminel, -elle [kriminɛl] ADJ **1** *(répréhensible → action, motif)* criminal; **acte c.** criminal offence, crime; **une organisation criminelle** a criminal organization, a crime syndicate

2 *(relatif aux crimes → droit, enquête)* criminal; *(→ brigade)* crime *(avant n)*

3 *(condamnable → acte)* criminal, reprehensible; **c'est c. de...** it's criminal to..., it's a crime to...; **avoir des pensées criminelles** to think wicked thoughts

NM,F *(gén)* criminal; *(meurtrier)* murderer; **c. de guerre** war criminal

NM *Jur (juridiction criminelle)* **le c.** criminal law; **avocat au c.** criminal lawyer; **poursuivre qn au c.** to institute criminal proceedings against sb

criminellement [kriminɛlmɑ̃] ADV **1** *(répréhensiblement)* criminally **2** *Jur* **poursuivre qn c.** to institute criminal proceedings against sb

criminogène [kriminɔʒɛn] ADJ **des attitudes criminogènes** attitudes liable to encourage crime

criminologie [kriminɔlɔʒi] NF criminology

criminologiste [kriminɔlɔʒist], **criminologue** [kriminɔlɔg] NMF criminologist

crin [krɛ̃] NM **1** *(de cheval)* hair **2** *(rembourrage)* horsehair **3** *Bot* **c. végétal** vegetable (horse)-hair

❑ **à tout crin, à tous crins** ADJ out-and-out, diehard; **les conservateurs à tout c.** the diehard *or* dyed-in-the-wool conservatives

❑ **de crin, en crin** ADJ horsehair *(avant n)*

crincrin [krɛ̃krɛ̃] NM *Fam* (squeaky) fiddle; **il a joué un air sur son c.** he scraped out a tune on his fiddle

crinière [krinjɛr] NF **1** *Zool* mane **2** *Fam (chevelure)* mane, *Péj ou Hum* mop **3** *(d'un casque)* plume

crinoïde [krinɔid] *Zool* ADJ crinoid, crinoidal

NM sea lily, *Spéc* crinoid

❑ **crinoïdes** NMPL Crinoidea

crinoline [krinɔlin] NF **1** *Tex* crinoline **2** *(de jupe, de robe)* crinoline petticoat

❑ **à crinoline** ADJ *(de robe)* crinoline *(avant n)*

crinqué, -e [krɛ̃ke] ADJ *Can Joual* seething

crinquer [3] [krɛ̃ke] VT *Can Joual* to wind up ■, to crank up

criocère [kriɔsɛr] NM *Entom* crioceris; **c. de l'asperge** asparagus beetle

crique [krik] NF **1** *Géog* creek, inlet, (small) rocky beach **2** *Métal* tear, split

criquet [krikɛ] NM locust; **c. pèlerin** *ou* **migrateur** migratory locust

crise [kriz] NF **1** *Psy (période, situation difficile)* crisis; **traverser une c.** to go through a crisis *or* a critical time; **c. d'adolescence** adolescent *or* teenage crisis; **il est en pleine c. d'adolescence** he's right in the middle of an adolescent *or* a teenage crisis; **c. d'angoisse** anxiety attack; **c. de confiance** crisis of confidence; **c. de conscience** crisis of conscience; **c. d'identité** identity crisis; **la c. de la quarantaine** a mid-life crisis

2 *Écon & Pol* crisis; **c. du logement/papier** housing/paper shortage; **c. boursière** *(grave)* crisis *or* panic on the Stock Exchange; *(passagère)* blip on the Stock Exchange; **c. conjoncturelle** economic crisis *(due to cyclical and not structural factors)*; **c. diplomatique** diplomatic crisis; **c. économique** economic crisis *or* slump, recession; **c. politique** political crisis; **c. pétrolière** oil crisis; **la c. de 1929** the 1929 slump

3 *(accès)* outburst, fit; **c. de colère** fit of temper; **c. de désespoir** fit of despair; **c. de jalousie** fit of jealousy; **c. de larmes** crying fit; **c. de rage** angry outburst; *Fam* **quelle** *ou* **la c. (de rire)!** what a scream *or* hoot!; *Fam* **piquer une c.** to throw *or* to have a fit; *Fam* **pas besoin de nous faire une c. pour ça!** there's no need to kick up such a fuss!; **il a été pris d'une c. de rangement** he had the sudden urge to tidy up

4 *Méd* **c. d'apoplexie** apoplectic fit; **c. d'appendicite/d'arthrose** attack of appendicitis/arthritis; **c. cardiaque** heart attack; **c. épileptique**

ou **d'épilepsie** epileptic fit, seizure; **c. de foie** indigestion; **elle a été prise d'une c. d'appendicite** she was struck down with appendicitis, she went down with appendicitis; *Fam* **tu vas attraper une c. de foie à manger tous ces chocolats** you'll make yourself sick if you eat all these chocolates; **c. de nerfs** fit of hysterics, attack of nerves; **elle a fait une c. de nerfs** she went into hysterics

❑ **en crise** ADJ **être en c.** to undergo a crisis

Culture

LA CRISE D'OCTOBRE

This is the term given to the crisis that shook Quebec in October 1970. Members of the FLQ (Front de Libération du Québec) first kidnapped a British diplomat, and then kidnapped and executed the Quebec employment minister. The War Measures Act (Loi des mesures de guerre) was introduced as emergency legislation and the Canadian army took control of Quebec, arresting over 450 suspects.

criser [3] [krize] VI *Fam* to lose it, *Br* to go off one's head

crispant, -e [krispɑ̃, -ɑ̃t] ADJ *(attente)* nerve-racking; *(stupidité, personne)* exasperating, irritating, infuriating; *(bruit)* irritating; **arrête de me dire comment jouer, c'est c. à la fin!** stop telling me how to play, it's getting on my nerves!; **ce que tu peux être c.!** you are SO infuriating!

crispation [krispasjɔ̃] NF **1** *(du visage)* tension; *(des membres)* contraction; *(de douleur)* wince **2** *(tic)* twitch; **le médicament peut provoquer des crispations au niveau des mains** the drug can cause the hands to twitch **3** *(anxiété)* nervous tension **4** *(du cuir)* shrivelling; *(du papier)* cockling

crispé, -e [krispe] ADJ **1** *(contracté → sourire, rire)* strained, tense; *(→ personne, visage, doigts)* tense; **le visage c. par la douleur** his/her face contorted *or* screwed up with pain; **les deux mains crispées sur la serviette** clutching the briefcase with both hands **2** *Fam (irrité)* irritated▪, exasperated▪

crisper [3] [krispe] VT **1** *(traits du visage)* to contort, to tense; *(poings)* to clench; **ne crispez pas vos doigts sur le volant** don't grip the wheel too tightly; **le visage crispé par la souffrance** his/her face contorted *or* tense with pain

2 *Fam (irriter)* **c. qn** to get on sb's nerves; **ce bruit me crispe** this noise grates on my nerves

3 *(rider → cuir)* to shrivel up; *(papier)* to cockle up

▸**se crisper** VPR **1** *(se contracter → visage)* to tense (up); *(→ personne)* to become tense; *(→ doigts)* to contract; *(→ sourire)* to become strained *or* tense; *(→ poings)* to clench; **ses mains se crispèrent sur les barreaux** his/her hands tightened on the bars; **je me crispe dès que je suis sur des skis** I get all tensed up as soon as I put on skis; *Fig* **les rapports entre les deux parties se sont crispés** tension has mounted between the two parties

2 *Fam (s'irriter)* to get irritated *or* exasperated▪

crispin [krispɛ̃] NM *(de gant)* gauntlet; **gants à c.** *(d'escrimeur, de motocycliste)* gauntlets

criss [kris] = **kriss**

crisse [kris] *Can Joual* NMF jerk; **mon (petit) c.** *(enfant)* you (little) jerk *or Br* bugger

EXCLAM for Christ's sake!, shit!

❑ **en crisse** ADV hopping mad, fuming

crissement [krismɑ̃] NM *(de pneus, de freins)* squealing, screeching; *(de cuir)* squeaking; *(de neige, de gravillons)* crunching; *(d'étoffe, de papier)* rustling; *(d'une craie, d'une scie)* grating; **j'ai entendu le c. des pneus sur le gravier** I heard the crunch of tyres on the gravel

crisser [3] [krise] VI *(pneus, freins)* to squeal, to screech; *(cuir)* to squeak; *(neige, gravillons)* to crunch; *(étoffe, papier)* to rustle; *(craie, scie)* to grate; **la craie crissait sur le tableau** the chalk squeaked on the blackboard

cristal, -aux [kristal, -o] NM **1** *Minér* crystal; **c. de roche** rock crystal

2 *Phys* **cristaux de givre** ice crystals; **cristaux liquides** liquid crystals; **cristaux de neige** ice crystals; **cristaux de sel** salt crystals; **cristaux de sucre** sugar granules *or* crystals; **cristaux de soude** washing soda

3 *(objet)* piece of crystalware *or* of fine glassware; **des cristaux** crystalware, fine glassware; *(d'un lustre)* crystal droplets

4 *Littéraire* **la nappe de c. de la cascade** the crystal sheet of the waterfall; **le c. d'un rire d'enfant** the crystalline sound of children's laughter

❑ **de cristal** ADJ **1** *(vase)* crystal *(avant n)*

2 *(pur → eau)* crystal-like, crystalline; *(→ voix)* crystal-clear, crystalline

cristallerie [kristalri] NF **1** *(fabrication)* crystal-making **2** *(usine)* (crystal) glassworks **3** *(objets)* **de la c.** crystalware, fine glassware

cristallin, -e [kristalɛ̃, -in] ADJ **1** *Littéraire (voix)* crystal-clear, crystalline; *(son, note)* ringing; *(eau)* crystal-like, crystalline **2** *Chim & Minér (massif, rocher)* crystalline **3** *Phys* **réseau c.** crystal lattice

NM *Anat* crystalline lens

cristallinien, -enne [kristalinjɛ̃, -ɛn] ADJ crystalline lens *(avant n)*

cristallisable [kristalizabl] ADJ *Chim* crystallizable

cristallisant, -e [kristalizɑ̃, -ɑ̃t] ADJ *Chim* crystallizing

cristallisation [kristalizasjɔ̃] NF *Chim* crystallization, crystallizing

cristallisé, -e [kristalize] ADJ *Chim* crystallized

cristalliser [3] [kristalize] *Chim* VT to crystallize

VI to crystallize

▸**se cristalliser** VPR to crystallize

cristallisoir [kristalizwar] NM *Chim* crystallizer, crystallizing dish *or* pan

cristallite [kristalit] NF *Chim* crystallite

cristallochimie [kristalɔʃimi] NF *Chim* crystallochemistry

cristallochimique [kristalɔʃimik] ADJ *Chim* crystallochemical

cristallogenèse [kristalɔʒənɛz] NF *Chim* crystallogenesis

cristallographe [kristalɔgraf] NMF *Chim* crystallographer

cristallographie [kristalɔgrafi] NF *Chim* crystallography

cristallographique [kristalɔgrafik] ADJ *Chim* crystallographic

cristalloïde [kristalɔid] *Chim* ADJ crystalloid

NM crystalloid

cristallomancie [kristalɔmɑ̃si] NF crystal-gazing

cristallophyllien, -enne [kristalɔfiljɛ̃, -ɛn] ADJ crystalliferous

cristaux [kristo] *pl de* **cristal**

criste-marine [kristmarin] *(pl* **cristes-marines***)* NF *Bot* (rock) samphire

cristophine [kristɔfin] NF *Bot* christophene; *Culin* **gratin de cristophines** gratin of cristophenes

critère [kritɛr] NM **1** *(principe)* criterion; **c. moral/religieux** moral/religious criterion; **nos produits doivent remplir certains critères** our products must meet certain standards *or* comply with certain criteria; *UE* **critères d'adhésion** membership criteria; *UE* **critères de convergence** convergence criteria; *UE* **critères d'élargissement** enlargement criteria; **critères de sélection** selection criteria; **nous n'avons pas les mêmes critères de sélection** we don't select according to the same criteria; **quels sont les critères de segmentation les plus importants?** what are the most important criteria for segmentation?; *Ordinat* **c. de tri** sort criterion

2 *(référence)* reference (point), standard; **les résultats de l'année précédente nous servent de c.** we use the results of the previous year as a reference point *or* a benchmark; **ce n'est pas un c.** *(on ne peut rien en conclure)* that's nothing to go by, that doesn't mean anything

critérium [kriterjɔm] NM criterium; *Cyclisme & Natation* gala; *Équitation* **le grand c., le c. des deux ans** maiden race for two-year-olds

criticailler [3] [kritikaje] VT *Fam Péj (personne)* to niggle at; *(ouvrage, idée)* to niggle about

criticisme [kritisism] NM *Phil* critical philosophy, Kantianism, Kantism

critiquable [kritikabl] ADJ which lends itself to criticism; **une décision peu c.** an uncontentious decision

critique [kritik] ADJ **1** *(qui condamne → article, personne)* critical; *Péj (personne)* fault-finding; **se montrer très c. envers** *ou* **à l'égard de** to be very critical towards; **elle est très c.** she's always finding fault, she's hypercritical; **examiner qch d'un œil c.** to examine sth critically *or* with a critical eye

2 *(plein de discernement → analyse, œuvre, personne)* critical; **je souhaite que tu portes un regard c. sur mon texte** I'd like you to have a critical look at my text; **avoir l'esprit** *ou* **le sens c.** to have good judgement, to be discerning; **il n'a aucun esprit** *ou* **sens c.** he lacks discernment

3 *(crucial → étape, période)* critical, crucial; *(→ opération, seuil)* critical; **à un moment c.** at a critical moment

4 *(inquiétant → état de santé, situation)* critical; **atteindre un stade c.** to reach a critical stage; **l'heure est c.** we are faced with a crisis, we have a crisis on our hands

5 *(en science)* critical

NMF *(commentateur)* critic, reviewer; **c. d'art** art critic; **c. de cinéma** movie *or Br* film critic *or* reviewer; **c. gastronomique** food and wine critic; **c. littéraire** book reviewer, literary critic; **c. musical** music critic; **c. de théâtre** theatre critic

NF **1** *Journ* review; *Univ* critique, appreciation; **je ne lis jamais les critiques** I never read reviews *or* what the critics write; **c. cinématographique** movie *or Br* film review; **c. littéraire** literary *or* book review; **c. musicale/théâtrale** music/theatre review

2 *(activité)* **la c.** criticism; **faire la c. de** *Journ* to review; *Univ* to write an appreciation *or* a critique of; **la c. gastronomique** food writing; **c. génétique** = branch of literary criticism which focuses on the genesis of a text through its various manuscript forms; **la c. littéraire** literary criticism; **la c. théâtrale** theatre *or* drama criticism

3 *(personnes)* **la c.** the critics; **très bien/mal accueilli par la c.** acclaimed/panned by the critics; **l'approbation/le mépris de la c.** critical acclaim/scorn

4 *(blâme)* criticism; **adresser** *ou* **faire une c. à un auteur** to level criticism at an author; **ce n'est pas une c., mais...** don't take this as a criticism, but...

5 *(fait de critiquer)* **la c.** criticism, criticizing; **faire la c. de qch** to criticize sth; **la c. est aisée** *ou* **facile (mais l'art est difficile)** it's easy to be a critic (but hard to be an artist)

'Critique de la raison pure' *Kant* 'Critique of Pure Reason'

critiquer [3] [kritike] VT **1** *(blâmer → initiative, mesure, personne)* to criticize, to be critical of; **tu es toujours à me c.!** you're always criticizing me!, you find fault with everything I do!; **ce n'est pas pour te c., mais...** don't take this as a criticism, but..., I don't mean to criticize (you), but...; **c. qn pour qch/pour ne pas avoir fait qch** to criticize sb for sth/for not doing sth; **il s'est déjà fait c. pour sa négligence** he has already been criticized for his negligence

2 *(analyser) Journ* to review; *Univ* to write an appreciation *or* a critique of

USAGE ABSOLU **arrête de c.!** stop criticizing!

critiqueur, -euse [kritikœr, -øz] NM,F *Péj* fault-finder; **les critiqueurs** those who carp *or* who find fault

croassement [krɔasmɑ̃] NM *(de corneille)* cawing; *(de corbeau)* croaking

croasser [3] [krɔase] VI *(corneille)* to caw; *(corbeau)* to croak

croate [krɔat] ADJ Croat, Croatian

NM *(langue)* Croat, Croatian

❑ **Croate** NMF Croat, Croatian

Croatie [krɔasi] NF **la C.** Croatia; **vivre en C.** to live in Croatia; **aller en C.** to go to Croatia

crobard, crobar [krɔbar] NM *Fam* sketch▪

croc [kro] NM **1** *(de chien)* tooth, fang; *(d'ours, de loup)* fang; **montrer les crocs** *(animal)* to bare its teeth *or* fangs; *Fig* **la Prusse montrait les crocs** Prussia was showing its teeth **2** *Fam (dent)* (long) tooth; **j'ai les crocs** I could eat a horse **3** *(crochet → de boucher)* butcher's *or* meat-hook; *(→ de marinier)* hook, boat-hook;

c. à fumier muck rake; **moustache en crocs** handlebar moustache

croc-en-jambe [krɔkɑ̃ʒɑ̃b] (*pl* **crocs-en-jambe**) **NM faire un c. à qn** to trip sb up; *Fig* to set sb up

croche [krɔʃ] **NF** *Mus Br* quaver, *Am* eighth note; **double c.** *Br* semiquaver, *Am* sixteenth note; **triple c.** *Br* demisemiquaver, *Am* thirty-second note; **quadruple c.** *Br* hemidemisemiquaver, *Am* sixty-fourth note

NMF *Can Fam (personne malhonnête)* crook

ADJ *Can Fam* **1** *(malhonnête)* crooked **2** *(courbé)* curved ■; *(pas droit)* crooked ■

croche-patte [krɔʃpat] (*pl* **croche-pattes**), **croche-pied** [krɔʃpje] (*pl* **croche-pieds**) **NM faire un c. à qn** to trip sb up; *Fig* to set sb up

crocher [3] [krɔʃe] **VT 1** *Naut* to hook **2** *Suisse (accrocher)* to hang (**à** on)

crochet [krɔʃɛ] **NM 1** *(attache, instrument)* hook; *(pour volets)* catch; **c. d'arrêt** pawl, catch; **c. d'attelage** coupling hook; **c. à bottes** boot-hook; **c. de boucher** *ou* **boucherie** meat-hook, butcher's hook; **c. à boutons** buttonhook; **c. de bureau** spike file

2 *(de serrurier)* picklock, lockpick

3 *Couture (instrument)* crochet hook; *(technique)* crochet; *(ouvrage)* crochetwork; **faire du c.** to crochet

4 *Méd (instrument)* tenaculum

5 *Sport* hook; **il l'a envoyé à terre d'un c. à la tête** he knocked him down with a hook to the head; **c. du droit/gauche** right/left hook

6 *(détour)* detour, roundabout way; **faire un c.** to make a detour, to go a roundabout way

7 *(virage brusque* → *d'une voie)* sudden *or* sharp turn; *(*→ *d'une voiture)* sudden swerve; **faire un c.** *(rue)* to bend sharply; *(conducteur)* to swerve suddenly

8 *(concours)* **c. radiophonique** talent contest

9 *Typ* square bracket; **entre crochets** in square brackets

10 *Zool (d'un serpent)* fang; *(d'un chamois)* horn

❑ **crochets NMPL** *Vieilli (châssis)* frame; **vivres aux crochets de qn** to live off sb

❑ **au crochet ADJ** *(nappe, châle)* crocheted **ADV faire un vêtement au c.** to crochet a garment; **terminer un vêtement au c.** to finish a garment with a crocheted trim

crochetable [krɔʃtabl] **ADJ** *(serrure)* that can be picked, pickable

crochetage [krɔʃtaʒ] **NM** *(d'une serrure)* picking

crocheter [28] [krɔʃte] **VT 1** *(serrure)* to pick; *(porte)* to pick the lock on **2** *Couture* to crochet

crocheteur [krɔʃtœr] **NM** picklock

crocheur, -euse [krɔʃœr, -øz] *Suisse* **ADJ** *(tenace, travailleur)* dedicated and hard-working

NM,F *(personne tenace et travailleuse)* dedicated and hard-working person

crochu, -e [krɔʃy] **ADJ** *(nez)* hooked, hook *(avant n)*; *(doigts, mains)* claw-like; *Fig* **avoir les doigts crochus** *ou* **les mains crochues** to be tight-fisted *or Am* a tightwad

croco [krɔko] *Fam (abrév* **crocodile***)* **NM** crocodile ■, crocodile skin ■

❑ **en croco ADJ** crocodile ■ *(avant n)*, crocodile skin ■

crocodile [krɔkɔdil] **NM 1** *(animal)* crocodile; **c. marin** saltwater *or* estuarine crocodile; **c. du Nil** Nile crocodile **2** *(peau)* crocodile, crocodile skin **3** *Rail* alarm contact

❑ **en crocodile ADJ** crocodile *(avant n)*, crocodile skin

crocodilien [krɔkɔdiljɛ̃] *Zool* **NM** crocodilian

❑ **crocodiliens NMPL** Crocodilia

crocus [krɔkys] **NM** crocus

CROIRE [107] [krwar] **VT 1** *(fait, histoire, personne)* to believe; **tu crois son histoire?** do you believe what he/she says?; **je te crois sur parole** I'll take your word for it; **je te crois!** *(et comment)* you can say that again!; *Ironique* I believe you!, is that so?; **crois-moi, on n'a pas fini d'en entendre parler!** believe me, we haven't heard the last of this!; **je te prie de c. qu'il va entendre parler de nous!** believe me, we haven't finished with him!; **cela, je ne peux pas le c.** I can't believe that, I find that hard to believe; **je ne peux pas c. pareille méchanceté de ta part** I can't believe (that) you could be so nasty; **je n'en crois pas un mot** I don't believe a word of it; **tu ne me feras pas c. que...** I refuse to believe that...; **on lui a fait c. que la réunion était annulée** they told him/her that the meeting had been cancelled; **croyez-en ceux qui ont l'expérience** take it from those who know; **à l'en c.** if he is to be believed; **si j'en crois cette lettre** if I go by what this letter says; **si vous m'en croyez** if you ask me *or* want my opinion; **n'en croyez rien!** don't believe (a word of) it!; **je n'en crois pas mes yeux/oreilles** I can't believe my eyes/ears; *Fam* **c. dur comme fer que...** to be firmly convinced that... ■; **ne va pas c. ça!** don't you believe it!; **ne va pas c. qu'il a toujours raison** don't think he's always right

2 *(penser)* to believe, to think; **je croyais pouvoir venir plus tôt** I thought *or* assumed I could come earlier; **j'ai cru bien faire** I thought *or* believed I was doing the right thing; **j'ai cru devoir le prévenir** I thought I ought to warn him; **j'ai cru nécessaire de...** I thought it necessary to...; **je ne crois pas que cela suffise** I don't think that will be enough; **je crois que oui** I believe *or* think so; **il croit que non** he doesn't think so; **vous croyez?** do you really think so?; **à la voir on croirait sa sœur** to look at her, you'd think she was her sister; **on croirait qu'il dort** he looks as if he's asleep; **on croit rêver!** it's unbelievable!; **tu ne crois pas si bien dire** you don't know how right you are; **je vous croyais anglais/riche** I thought you were English/rich; **on l'a crue enceinte** she was believed *or* thought to be pregnant; **je n'aurais pas cru cela de lui** I wouldn't have *or* would never have believed *or* thought it of him; **je veux c. qu'il finira par accepter la vérité** I want to believe he'll accept the truth in the end; **elle en sait plus long que tu ne crois** she knows more than you think; **je ne suis pas celle que vous croyez** I'm not that kind of person; **il est à** *ou* **il faut c. que tout lui réussit** seemingly, everything comes right for him/her; **il faut c. que tu avais tort** it looks like you were wrong; *Fam* **il faut c., faut c.** (it) looks like it ■, it would seem so ■; *Fam* **elle est intelligente, faut pas c.!** she may not look smart, but believe me, she is!

VI 1 *(sans analyser)* to believe; **on leur apprend à réfléchir et non à c.** they're taught to think and not simply to believe what they're told

2 *Rel* to believe; **il croit** he's a believer; **je ne crois plus** I've lost my faith

❑ **croire à VT IND 1** *(avoir confiance en)* to believe in; **c. à la paix** to believe in peace; **il faut c. à l'avenir** one must have faith in the future; **je ne crois pas à ses promesses** I don't believe *or* I have no faith in his/her promises

2 *(accepter comme réel)* to believe in; **c. aux fantômes** to believe in ghosts; **tu crois encore au Père Noël!** you're so naive!; **c'est à n'y pas c.!** you just wouldn't believe *or* credit it!; **franchement, je n'y crois pas** quite frankly, I don't believe it; **le médecin crut à une rougeole** the doctor thought it was measles; **elle voulait faire c. à un accident** she wanted it to look like an accident

3 *Rel* to believe in; **c. à la vie éternelle** to believe in eternal life; **il ne croit ni à Dieu ni au diable** he's a complete heathen

4 *(dans la correspondance)* **je vous prie de c. à mes sentiments les meilleurs** *(à quelqu' un dont on connaît le nom) Br* yours sincerely, *Am* sincerely (yours); *(à quelqu'un dont on ne connaît pas le nom) Br* yours faithfully, *Am* sincerely (yours); **croyez à mon amitié toute dévouée** yours ever

❑ **croire en VT IND 1** *(avoir confiance en)* to believe in; **j'ai vraiment cru en lui** I really believed in him

2 *Rel* **c. en Dieu** to believe in God

►**se croire VPR 1** *(penser avoir)* **il se croit tous les droits** *ou* **tout permis** he thinks he can get away with anything; **il se croit du génie** he thinks he's a genius; *Fam* **qu'est-ce qu'il se croit?** who does he think he is?

2 *(se juger)* **il se croit beau/intelligent** he thinks he's handsome/intelligent; **tu te crois malin?** think you're clever, do you?; **elle se croit quelqu'un** she thinks she's something special; **où te crois-tu?** where do you think you are?; **on se serait cru en octobre** it felt like October

3 *Fam (locutions)* **se c. sorti de la cuisse de Jupiter** to think one is God's gift (to mankind); **il s'y croit!** he really thinks a lot of himself!; **et ton nom en grosses lettres sur l'affiche, mais tu t'y crois déjà!** and your name in huge letters on the poster, you're letting your imagination run away with you!

croîs *etc voir* **croître**

croisade [krwazad] **NF 1** *Hist* crusade; **les croisades** the (Holy) Crusades; **partir en c.** to go on a crusade; **la C. des aveugles** = association for the blind **2** *Fig (campagne)* campaign, crusade; **partir en c. contre l'injustice** to go on a crusade *or* to mount a campaign against injustice

croisé, -e [krwaze] **ADJ 1** *(bras)* folded; *(jambes)* crossed; **il était debout, les bras croisés** he was standing with his arms folded; **ne reste pas là les bras croisés!** don't just stand there!; **assis les jambes croisées** sitting cross-legged

2 *Littérature (rimes)* alternate

3 *(hybride* → *animal, plante)* crossbred

4 *(veste, veston)* double-breasted

5 *Écon* **détention** *ou* **participation croisée** crossholding

NM 1 *Tex* twill

2 *Hist* crusader

❑ **croisée NF 1** *(intersection)* crossing; **être à la croisée des chemins** to be standing at the crossroads; *Fig* to be at the parting of the ways

2 *Archit* **croisée d'ogives** intersecting ribs; **croisée de** *ou* **du transept** transept crossing

3 *(châssis de fenêtre)* casement; *(fenêtre)* casement window

croisement [krwazmɑ̃] **NM 1** *(intersection)* crossroads, junction; **au c. de la rue et de l'avenue** at the intersection of the street and the avenue

2 *(hybridation)* crossbreeding, crossing; **faire des croisements (de races)** to crossbreed *or* to interbreed (animals); **c'est un c. entre un épagneul et un setter** it's a cross between a spaniel and a setter, it's a spaniel-setter crossbreed; **c. consanguin** interbreeding

3 *(rencontre)* **le c. de deux voitures/navires** two cars/boats passing each other

croiser [3] [krwaze] **VT 1** *(mettre en croix* → *baguettes, fils)* to cross; **c. les jambes** to cross one's legs; **c. les bras** to cross *or* to fold one's arms; **je croise les doigts pour que tu réussisses** I've got my fingers crossed for you; *aussi Fig* **c. le fer** *ou* **l'épée avec qn** to cross swords with sb

2 *(traverser)* to cross, to intersect, to meet; **là où la route croise la voie ferrée** where the road and the railway cross, at the junction of the road and the railway; *Fig* **c. la route** *ou* **le chemin de qn** to come across sb; **il a croisé ma route il y a longtemps** our paths crossed a long time ago

3 *(rencontrer)* to pass, to meet; **je l'ai croisé dans la rue** I passed him in the street; **je l'ai croisée en sortant de chez toi** I met her as I was leaving your place; **son regard a croisé le mien** her eyes met mine

4 *(hybrider)* to cross, to crossbreed, to interbreed

VI 1 *(vêtement)* to cross over; **ce manteau ne croise pas assez** this coat doesn't cross over enough

2 *Naut* to cruise

►**se croiser VPR 1** *(se rencontrer)* to come across *or* to meet *or* to pass each other; **nous nous sommes croisés chez ton frère** we saw each other briefly *or* met (each other) at your brother's; **leurs regards se sont croisés** their eyes met

2 *(aller en sens opposé* → *trains)* to pass (each other); *(*→ *lettres)* to cross; *(*→ *routes)* to cross, to intersect; **nos chemins se sont croisés, nos routes se sont croisées** our paths met

3 se c. les bras to fold one's arms; *Fig (être oisif)* to twiddle one's thumbs

4 *Hist* to go off to the Crusades

Croisette [krwazɛt] **NF (le boulevard de) la C.** = famous boulevard running along the seafront in Cannes

croisette [krwazɛt] **NF 1** *Vieilli (croix)* small cross **2** *Bot* crosswort

croiseur [krwazœr] **NM** *Mil* cruiser

croisière [krwazjɛr] **NF** cruise; **faire une c. aux Bahamas** to go on a cruise to the Bahamas; **ils sont en c.** they're on a cruise

cro–cro

croisiériste [krwazjerist] NMF tourist on a cruise

croisillon [krwazijɔ̃] NM **1** *(d'une fenêtre)* cross bar; *(au dos d'un meuble)* strengthener; **fenêtre à croisillons** lattice window **2** *Archit* transept
▫ **croisillons** NMPL *(sur une tarte, d'une fenêtre, d'un meuble)* lattice pattern

croissait *etc voir* **croître**

croissance [krwasɑ̃s] NF **1** *Physiol* growth; **elle est en pleine c.** she's growing fast
2 *(développement → d'une plante)* growth; *(→ d'un pays)* development, growth; *(→ d'une entreprise)* growth, expansion; **facteur de c.** growth factor; **notre entreprise est en pleine c.** our company is growing rapidly; **c. démographique** demographic growth, population growth; **c. déséquilibrée** imbalanced *or* unbalanced growth; **c. économique** economic growth *or* development; **c. économique nulle** zero growth; **c. équilibrée** balanced growth; **c. externe** external growth; **c. par intégration** integrative growth; **c. interne** internal growth; **c. du marché** market growth; **c. réelle** real growth; **c. par tête** per capita growth; **la c. zéro** zero growth

croissant¹ [krwasɑ̃] NM **1** *Culin* croissant; **c. aux amandes** almond croissant; **c. au beurre** all-butter croissant; **c. au fromage** cheese-filled croissant; **c. ordinaire** croissant made without butter
2 *(forme incurvée)* crescent; **des boucles d'oreille en c.** crescent-shaped earrings
3 *Astron* **c. de lune** crescent moon
4 *Hist & Géog* **le C. fertile** the Fertile Crescent

croissant²,-e [krwasɑ̃, -ɑ̃t] ADJ **1** *(→ grandissant → gén)* growing, increasing; *(→ ordre)* ascending; **tension croissante dans le sud du pays** increasing tension in the south of the country; **les jeunes diplômés arrivent en nombre c.** there's an increasing number of young graduates
2 *Math (nombre, fonction)* monotonic

croissanterie [krwasɑ̃tri] NF croissant *Br* shop *or Am* store

Croissant-Rouge [krwasɑ̃ruʒ] NM **le C.** the Red Crescent

croît [krwa] NM *Agr* **1** *(augmentation du nombre de têtes)* natural increase in stock *(by breeding)* **2** *(augmentation de poids)* = increase in weight of fat stock

croître [93] [krwatr] VI **1** *(augmenter)* to increase, to grow; *(→ rivière)* to swell; *(→ lune)* to wax; *(→ vent)* to rise; **les jours ne cessent de c.** the days are growing longer; **elle sentait c. en elle une violente colère** she could feel a violent rage growing within her; **ça ne fait que c. et embellir** it's getting better and better; *Ironique* it's getting worse and worse; **c. en volume/nombre** to increase in volume/number; **c. en beauté et en sagesse** to grow wiser and more beautiful; **aller croissant** to be on the increase; **le bruit allait croissant** the noise kept growing; *Bible* **croissez et multipliez** go forth and multiply
2 *(grandir, pousser)* to grow; **quelques fleurs croissent sur la berge** there are a few flowers growing on the bank

croix [krwa] NF **1** *(gibet)* cross; **mettre qn sur la c. ou en c.** to crucify sb; **il est mort sur la c.** he died on the cross; *Rel* **la (Sainte) C.** the (Holy) Cross; *Fig* **porter sa c.** to have one's cross to bear
2 *(objet cruciforme)* cross; **une petite c. autour du cou** a small cross round his/her neck; **les (deux) poutres font une c.** the beams form a cross; **c'est la c. et la bannière pour le faire manger** it's an uphill struggle to get him to eat; **c. de bois, c. de fer, si je mens, je vais en enfer** cross my heart (and hope to die)
3 *(emblème)* cross; **c. de Malte/St André** Maltese/St Andrew's cross; **c. latine/grecque** Latin/Greek cross; **c. en tau** *ou* **de St-Antoine** tau *or* St Anthony's cross; **c. ansée** ankh cross; **c. gammée** swastika; **la c. de Lorraine** the cross of Lorraine *(cross with two horizontal bars, the symbol of the Gaullist movement)*
4 *(récompense)* cross, medal; *(de la Légion d'honneur)* Cross of the Legion of Honour; **la c. de guerre** the Military Cross
5 *(signe écrit)* cross; **signer d'une c.** to sign with a cross; **marquer qch d'une c.** to put a cross

on sth; **mettre une c. dans une case** to put a cross in a box; **c'est un jour à marquer d'une c. blanche** it's a red-letter day; **faire** *ou* **mettre une c. sur qch** to forget *or* to kiss goodbye to sth; **les vacances, j'ai fait** *ou* **mis une c. dessus** I've decided I might as well forget about going on holiday; **tu peux faire une c. là-dessus** you might as well kiss it goodbye *or* forget it
6 *Couture* **point de c.** cross-stitch
7 *Astron* **C. du Sud** Southern Cross
▫ **en croix** ADJ **les bras en c.** with one's arms stretched out to the sides; **les skis en c.** with skis crossed ADV **placer** *ou* **mettre deux choses en c.** to lay two things crosswise *or* across each other; **mettre les bras en c.** to stretch one's arms out to the sides

━━━━📖━━━━

'**Les Croix de bois**' *Dorgelès* 'The Wooden Crosses'

Croix-Rouge [krwaruʒ] NF **la C.** the Red Cross; **la C. française** the French Red Cross

crolle [krɔl] NF *Belg Fam* curl▪

crollé,-e [krɔle] ADJ *Belg Fam* curly▪

croller [3] [krɔle] VT *Belg Fam* to curl▪ VI to curl▪

Cromalin® [krɔmalɛ̃] NM *Typ* Cromalin

cromlech [krɔmlɛk] NM cromlech

cromorne [krɔmɔrn] NM *Mus* **1** *(instrument de musique)* krumm horn, cromorne **2** *(d'orgue)* stop

crooner [krunœr] NM crooner

croquant¹ [krɔkɑ̃] NM **1** *Hist* = name given to a peasant revolutionary during the reigns of Henry IV and Louis XIII **2** *Péj (paysan)* (country) bumpkin, yokel

croquant²,-e [krɔkɑ̃, -ɑ̃t] ADJ crisp, crunchy NM *Fam* **le c.** the crunchy part▪

croque-au-sel [krɔkosɛl] **à la croque-au-sel** ADV *(raw)* with salt; **manger des artichauts à la c.** to eat raw artichokes dipped in salt

croque-madame [krɔkmadam] NM INV = toasted cheese and ham sandwich with a fried egg on top

croquembouche [krɔkɑ̃buʃ] NM = larged tiered cake made from profiteroles covered in caramelized sugar

croquemitaine, croque-mitaine [krɔkmitɛn] *(pl* **croque-mitaines**) NM bogeyman

croque-monsieur [krɔkmɔsjø] NM INV = toasted cheese and ham sandwich

croque-mort [krɔkmɔr] *(pl* **croque-morts**) NM undertaker's assistant; **il a vraiment une allure de c.** he has a really funereal look about him

croquenot [krɔkno] NM *Fam* clodhopper, beetle-crusher

croquer [3] [krɔke] VT **1** *(pomme, radis etc)* to crunch; *Fam Fig* **il est (joli)** *ou* **mignon à c.** he looks good enough to eat
2 *Fam (dépenser → héritage)* to squander▪; **elle va c. ta fortune** she'll squander all your money
3 *(esquisser)* to sketch; *(décrire)* to outline
4 *Fam* **c. le marmot** *(attendre)* to cool *or* kick one's heels
VI to be crunchy; **des radis qui croquent (sous la dent)** crunchy radishes
▫ **croquer dans** VT IND to bite into

croquet [krɔkɛ] NM **1** *(jeu)* croquet; **faire une partie de c.** to have a game of croquet **2** *Couture* braid **3** *Culin* almond *Br* biscuit *or Am* cookie

croquette [krɔkɛt] NF *Culin* croquette; **c. de poisson** fishcake
▫ **croquettes** NFPL *(pour animal)* dry food

croqueur,-euse [krɔkœr, -øz] ADJ crisp, crunchy NM,F *Fam* devourer; *Fam* **croqueuse de diamants** gold-digger; *Fam* **croqueuse d'hommes** man-eater

croquignole [krɔkiɲɔl] NF = small crisp biscuit

croquignolet,-ette [krɔkiɲɔlɛ, -ɛt] ADJ *Fam Ironique* cutesy

croquis [krɔki] NM sketch; **faire un c. de qch** to sketch sth; **elle est partie faire des c. dans la vieille ville** she went to do some sketches in the old town; **c. coté** dimensional sketch

croskill [krɔskil] NM *Agr* toothed roller

crosne [kron] NM Chinese artichoke

cross [krɔs] NM INV **1** *(sport → à pied)* cross-country running; *(→ à vélo)* mountain-biking;

(→ à moto) motocross; *(→ à cheval)* cross-country riding; **faire du c.** *(à pied)* to go cross-country running; *(à vélo)* to go mountain-biking; *(à moto)* to do motocross; *(à cheval)* to go cross-country riding
2 *(épreuve → à pied)* cross-country run *or* race; *(→ à vélo)* mountain-bike race; *(→ à moto)* motocross event; *(→ à cheval)* cross-country horse ride

cross-country [krɔskuntri] *(pl* **cross-countrys** *ou* **cross-countries**) NM = **cross**

crosse [krɔs] NF **1** *Rel* crosier, crozier
2 *Sport (canne → de hockey)* stick; *(→ de golf)* club; *(→ du jeu de crosse)* crosse
3 *Can (jeu)* lacrosse
4 *(extrémité → d'une canne)* crook; *(→ d'un violon)* scroll
5 *(partie → d'un revolver)* grip, butt; *(→ d'un fusil)* (butt) stock; *(→ d'un canon)* trail; **ils l'ont tué à coups de c.** they beat him to death with their rifle butts; **lever** *ou* **mettre la c. en l'air** *(se révolter)* to refuse to fight; *(se rendre)* to surrender; **c. anglaise** straight stock
6 *Bot (d'une fougère)* crosier
7 *Anat (de l'aorte)* arch
8 *Culin* **c. de bœuf** knuckle of beef
9 *Fam* **chercher des crosses à qn** to try to pick a fight with sb

crossé [krɔse] ADJ M *Rel* crosiered

crosser [3] [krɔse] *Can* VT *Fam* **se faire c.** to be conned *or* had
▶ **se crosser** VPR *Vulg* to jerk off

crosseur,-euse [krɔsœr, -øz] *Can Fam* ADJ crooked; **c'est c.** it's a con; **c'est une politicienne crosseuse** she's a crooked politician NM,F con artist

crossing-over [krɔsiɲovœr] NM INV *Biol* crossing-over

crossman [krɔsman] *(pl* **crossmen** [-men]) NM cross-country runner

crossoptérygien [krɔsɔpteriʒjɛ̃] *Ich* NM Crossopterygian
▫ **crossoptérygiens** NMPL Crossopterygia

cross-trainer [krɔstrɛjnœr] *(pl* **cross-trainers**) NM *Sport (machine)* cross-trainer

cross-training [krɔstrɛjniŋ] NM *Sport* cross-training

crosswoman [krɔswuman] *(pl* **crosswomen** [-wimen]) NF *(female)* cross-country runner

crotale [krɔtal] NM *Zool (serpent à sonnette)* rattlesnake; *(famille)* pit viper; **c. cornu** sidewinder

croton [krɔtɔ̃] NM *Bot* croton

crotte [krɔt] NF **1** *(d'un animal)* dropping; *(d'un bébé)* poo; *Fam·*ton **chien pourrait aller faire sa c. ailleurs!** your dog could do its business somewhere else!; *Fam* **c. (de bique)!** oh, poo!, *Am* shoot!
2 *Fam Péj (chose ou personne méprisée)* **c'est de la c. (de bique)** it's a load of poo *or Br* rubbish *or Am* garbage; *Fam* **c'est pas de la c.!** it's none of your (cheap) *Br* rubbish *or Am* garbage!; **il se prend pas pour de la c.!** he thinks he's God's gift!, *Br* he really fancies himself!
3 *Arch (boue)* mud
4 *Culin* **c. en chocolat** chocolate
5 *(morve)* **c. de nez** *Br* bogey, *Am* booger
6 *Fam (par affection)* **ma petite c.!** you little sweetie you!

crotté,-e [krɔte] ADJ muddy, mucky; **c. comme un barbet** covered in mud

crotter [3] [krɔte] VT *(chaussures, voiture)* to dirty, to muddy
VI *Fam (chien)* to do its business
▶ **se crotter** VPR to get dirty, to get covered in *or* with mud

crottin [krɔtɛ̃] NM **1** *(de cheval)* dung, manure **2** *Culin* crottin, = small round goat's milk cheese

crouille [kruj] NF *Suisse* **1** *(vaurien)* crook **2** *(farceur)* rascal
ADJ *Suisse* **1** *(de mauvaise qualité)* miserable **2** *(farceur)* playful
NM *très Fam* = racist term used to refer to a North African Arab

croulant,-e [krulɑ̃, -ɑ̃t] ADJ crumbling, tumbledown; **une vieille maison croulante** a tumbledown old house
NM,F *Fam Péj* **(vieux) c.** old fogey, old codger, *Br* wrinkly

croulants NMPL *Fam (parents) Br* old dears, *Am* rents

croule [krul] NF *Chasse* roding; (**chasse à la**) **c.** woodcock shooting

crouler [3] [krule] VI 1 (*tomber → édifice*) to collapse, to crumble, to topple; **le mur menace de c.** the wall is about to collapse; **l'étagère croule sous le poids des livres** the shelf is sagging under the weight of the books; **un arbre croulant sous les fruits** a tree laden with fruit; **un baudet qui croulait sous son chargement** a donkey weighed down with its load; *Fig* **c. sous le poids des ans/soucis** to be weighed down by age/worry; *Fig* **la salle croula sous les applaudissements** the auditorium thundered with applause; *Fig* **il croule sous le travail depuis deux mois** he's been buckling under his workload for the last two months

   2 (*se désintégrer → empire, société*) to be on the verge of collapse, to be crumbling; **le krach boursier a fait c. certaines entreprises** some firms collapsed *or* went under as a result of the Stock Market crash

   3 *Chasse (crier → bécasse)* to croak

croup [krup] NM *Méd* croup; **faux c.** false croup

croupade [krupad] NF *Équitation* curvet

croupe [krup] NF 1 *Zool* croup, rump; **prendre qn en c.** to have sb ride pillion; **monter en c.** to ride pillion 2 *Fam (fesses)* behind 3 (*sommet → d'une colline*) hilltop; (*→ d'une montagne*) mountain top 4 *Archit (de toit)* hip

croupetons [kruptɔ̃] **à croupetons** ADV **être à c.** to crouch, to squat; **se mettre à c.** to squat down, to crouch (down)

croupi, -e [krupi] ADJ *(eau)* stagnant, foul

croupier [krupje] NM *(au jeu)* croupier

croupière [krupjɛr] NF *Équitation* crupper

croupion [krupjɔ̃] NM 1 *Orn* rump 2 *Culin Br* parson's *or Am* pope's nose 3 *Fam (fesses) Br* bum, *Am* butt 4 (*comme adj; avec ou sans trait d'union*) *Pol* **parti c.** rump of a party

croupir [32] [krupir] VI 1 *(eau)* to stagnate, to grow foul 2 *Fig (s'encroûter, moisir)* **c. dans un cachot** to rot in jail; **je ne vais pas c. ici toute ma vie** I'm not going to rot here all my life; **c. dans l'ignorance** to wallow in one's ignorance

croupissant, -e [krupisã, -ãt] ADJ *(eau, mare)* putrid, foul

croupissement [krupismã] NM *Littéraire* **le c. des eaux** the fouling of the waters

croupon [krupɔ̃] NM *(en tannerie)* butt

CROUS, Crous [krus] NM *(abrév* **Centre régional des œuvres universitaires et scolaires**) = student representative body dealing with accommodation, catering etc

crousille [kruzij] NF *Suisse* piggybank

croustade [krustad] NF *Culin* croustade

croustillant, -e [krustijã, -ãt] ADJ 1 *Culin (biscuit, gratin)* crisp, crunchy; *(baguette, pain)* crusty 2 *(osé)* saucy

croustiller [3] [krustije] VI *(biscuit, gratin)* to be crisp *or* crunchy; *(baguette, pain)* to be crusty

croustilles [krustij] NFPL *Can* (potato) *Br* crisps *or Am* chips

croustillon [krustijɔ̃] NM *Belg (beignet sphérique)* = type of doughnut

croûte [krut] NF 1 *(partie → du pain)* crust; (*→ du fromage*) rind; **une c. de pain** a crust; *Fam* **casser la c.** to have a bite to eat; *Péj* **il ne reste que quelques croûtes** there are only a few (old) crusts left; *Suisse* **c. dorée** French toast

   2 *(préparation)* pastry shell; **c. de vol-au-vent** vol-au-vent case

   3 *Fam (nourriture)* grub; **t'as préparé la c.?** is the food ready?■; **apporter sa c.** to bring one's own grub

   4 *(dépôt)* layer; **c. de rouille/saleté** layer of rust/dirt

   5 *Géol* **la c. terrestre** the earth's crust

   6 *Can (de neige)* crust

   7 *Méd* scab; **croûtes de lait** cradle cap

   8 *Fam Péj (tableau)* (bad) painting■, daub

   9 *(de cuir)* hide

   10 *Fam Péj (personne)* **quelle c.!** *(routinier)* what a stick-in-the-mud!; *(idiot)* what a dope!

croûter [3] [krute] VI *Fam* to have a bite (to eat); **tout le monde a besoin de c.** everybody has to eat■

croûteux, -euse [krutø, -øz] ADJ scabby

croûton [krutɔ̃] NM 1 *Culin (frit)* crouton; *(quignon)* (crusty) end, crust 2 *Fam Péj (personne)* **vieux c.** old fossil

crowbar [krobar] NF *Can Joual* crowbar■

crow-crow [krokro] NM INV craw-craw

crown [kraun] NM crown glass

croyable [krwajabl] ADJ believable, credible; **c'est à peine c.** it's hardly credible; **son histoire n'est pas c.** his/her story is incredible *or* unbelievable

croyait etc voir **croire**

croyance [krwajãs] NF 1 *(pensée)* belief; **les croyances populaires** popular beliefs, conventional wisdom 2 *(fait de croire)* faith; **la c. en Dieu** faith *or* belief in God; **la c. à** *ou* **en la démocratie** belief in democracy 3 *(religion)* faith, religion

croyant, -e [krwajã, -ãt] ADJ **il est/n'est pas c.** he's a believer/non-believer, he believes/he doesn't believe in God

   NM,F believer; **les croyants** *(de l'Islam)* the Faithful

CRS [seɛrɛs] NM *(abrév* **compagnie républicaine de sécurité)** *(policier)* state security policeman, *Br* ≃ riot policeman, *Am* state trooper; **les C. ont chargé les manifestants** the security police charged the demonstrators; **les C. responsables de la surveillance des plages** the security police responsible for keeping watch over the beaches

---

Culture

CRS

The CRS is the Minister of the Interior's police force, whose primary responsibility is to ensure public order at demonstrations and riots. They have been criticized for certain strong-arm tactics.

---

cru¹ [kry] NM *(en œnologie → terroir)* vineyard; *(→ vin)* vintage, wine; **les grands crus de Bourgogne** the great wines of Burgundy

   de mon/son etc **cru** ADJ **une histoire de son c.** a story of his/her own invention

   du cru ADJ **un vin du c.** a local wine; **les gens du c.** the locals

cru², -e¹ [kry] ADJ 1 *(non cuit → denrée)* raw, uncooked; *(→ céramique)* unfired

   2 *(non pasteurisé → beurre, lait)* unpasteurized

   3 *(sans préparation → soie)* raw; *(→ minerai)* crude; *(→ bois)* untreated

   4 *(aveuglant → couleur)* crude, harsh, glaring; *(→ éclairage)* harsh, blinding, glaring

   5 *(net)* blunt, uncompromising; **c'est la vérité toute crue** it's the pure, unadorned truth

   6 *(osé)* coarse, crude

   7 *Belg, Can & Suisse (temps, bâtiment)* damp and cold

   NM *Culin* **le c. et le cuit** the raw and the cooked

   ADV 1 *(sans cuisson)* **manger qch c.** to eat sth raw; **avaler** *ou* **manger qn tout c.** to make mincemeat out of or to wipe the floor with sb; **je ne vais pas t'avaler tout c.!** I'm not going to eat you!, I don't bite!

   2 *(brutalement)* **parler c.** to speak bluntly; **je vous le dis tout c.** I'm telling you it like it is

   à cru ADV 1 *Équitation* bareback

   2 *Archit* without foundations

cru³, -e² [kry] PP voir **croire**

crû, -ue³ [kry] PP voir **croître**

cruauté [kryote] NF 1 *(dureté)* cruelty; **avec c.** cruelly; **c. mentale** mental cruelty 2 *(acte)* cruel act, act of cruelty 3 *Littéraire (rudesse)* harshness, *(extreme)* severity, cruelty; **la c. de l'hiver** the severity of the winter

cruche [kryʃ] NF 1 *(récipient)* jug, pitcher 2 *(contenu)* jugful 3 *Fam Péj (personne)* dope, *Br* plonker, *Am* goof 4 *Suisse (bouillotte)* hot-water bottle

   ADJ *Fam Péj Br* thick, *Am* dumb; **ce que tu peux être c.!** you can be so *Br* thick *or Am* dumb; **avoir l'air c.** to look *Br* thick *or Am* dumb

cruchée [kryʃe] NF jugful, pitcherful

cruchon [kryʃɔ̃] NM 1 *(récipient)* small jug 2 *(contenu)* small jugful

crucial, -e, -aux, -ales [krysjal, -o] ADJ 1 *(capital)* crucial, vital 2 *(en croix)* cross-shaped

crucifère [krysifɛr] *Bot* ADJ cruciferous

   NF crucifer

   crucifères NFPL Cruciferea

crucifié, -e [krysifje] ADJ crucified

   NM,F 1 *(victime)* crucified person 2 *Rel* **le C.** Jesus Christ

crucifiement [krysifimã] NM crucifixion

crucifier [9] [krysifje] VT 1 *(mettre en croix)* to crucify 2 *Littéraire (humilier)* to crucify

crucifix [krysifi] NM crucifix

crucifixion [krysifiksjɔ̃] NF crucifixion

cruciforme [krysiform] ADJ shaped like a cross, *Sout* cruciform

cruciverbiste [krysivɛrbist] NMF crossword (puzzle) enthusiast, *Spéc* cruciverbalist

crudité [krydite] NF 1 *(d'une couleur, de la lumière)* harshness 2 *(brutalité → d'une réponse)* bluntness 3 *(vulgarité)* coarseness, crudeness

   crudités NFPL *Culin* (assorted) raw vegetables, crudités

crue⁴ [kry] NF 1 *(élévation de niveau)* rise in the water level; **la rivière en c. a inondé la ville** the river burst its banks and flooded the town 2 *(inondation)* **la c. des rivières au printemps** the swelling of the rivers in the spring; **en période de c.** when there are floods

cruel, -elle [kryɛl] ADJ 1 *(méchant → personne)* cruel; *(dur → propos)* cruel, harsh 2 *(pénible → destin)* cruel, harsh, bitter; *(→ dilemme, choix)* cruel, painful; *(→ perte)* cruel; **être dans un c. embarras** to be in a painfully difficult situation; **être dans une cruelle incertitude** to be horribly uncertain

   NM,F *Littéraire* cruel man, f woman

cruellement [kryɛlmã] ADV 1 *(méchamment)* cruelly; **traiter qn c.** to be cruel to sb 2 *(péniblement)* sorely; **j'ai c. ressenti son absence** I missed him/her dreadfully; **être c. déçu** to be sorely *or* bitterly disappointed; **faire c. défaut** to be sorely lacking

cruenté, -e [kryãte] ADJ *(plaie, blessure)* raw, bleeding

cruiser¹ [kruzœr] NM cruiser

cruiser² [3] [kruze] *Can Fam* VT to come on to, *Br* to chat up, *Am* to hit on, to cruise; **il ne pense qu'à c. les filles** all he thinks about is picking up *or Br* pulling women

   VI to be *Br* on the pull *or Am* cruising

crumble [krœmbœl] NM *Culin* crumble

crûment [krymã] ADV 1 *(brutalement)* bluntly; **laissez-moi vous dire c. ce que j'en pense** let me tell you quite frankly what I think about it; **pour parler c.** to put it bluntly 2 *(grossièrement)* coarsely; **il ne faut pas s'exprimer c. devant les enfants** you mustn't use coarse language in front of the children 3 *(vivement → éclairé)* garishly

crural, -e, -aux, -ales [kryral, -o] ADJ *(de la cuisse)* crural; **arcade crurale** inguinal ligament; **nerf c.** femoral nerve

Crusoé [kryzoe] NPR **Robinson C.** Robinson Crusoe

crustacé, -e [krystase] *Zool* ADJ crustacean, crustaceous

   NM crustacean; *Culin* **des crustacés** shellfish

   crustacés NMPL Crustacea, Crustaceans

crut etc voir **croire**

crût etc voir **croître**

cryochimie [krijoʃimi] NF cryochemistry

cryochirurgie [krijoʃiryrʒi] NF cryosurgery

cryoclastie [krioklasti] NF *Géol* disintegration caused by ice

cryoconducteur, -trice [krijokɔ̃dyktœr, -tris] *Phys* ADJ cryoconductive

   NM cryoconductor

cryoconservation [krijokɔ̃sɛrvasjɔ̃] NF *Phys* cryoconservation

cryodessication [krijodesikasjɔ̃] NF *Phys* cryodessication

cryofracture [krijofraktyr] NF *Phys* cryofracture

cryogène [krijoʒɛn] ADJ *Phys* cryogenic; **mélange c.** freezing mixture

cryogénie [krijoʒeni] NF *Phys* cryogenics *(singulier)*

cryogénique [krioʒenik] ADJ *Phys* cryogenic

cryogénisation [krioʒenizasjɔ̃] NF *Biol* cryonics *(singulier)*

cryohydrate [kriohidrat] NM *Chim* cryohydrate

cryolithe [krijolit] NF *Minér* cryolite, Greenland spar

cryologie [krijɔlɔʒi] NF *Phys* cryology

cryoluminescence [krijɔlyminɛsɑ̃s] NF *Phys* cryoluminescence

cryométrie [krijɔmetri] NF *Phys* low-temperature thermometry, cryometry

cryophysique [krijɔfisik] NF *Phys* cryophysics

cryoscopie [krijɔskɔpi] NF *Phys* cryoscopy

cryostat [krijɔsta] NM *Phys* cryostat

cryotechnique [krijɔtɛknik] NF *Phys* cryotechnics *(singulier)*

cryotempérature [krijɔtɑ̃peratyr] NF *Phys* cryotemperature

cryothérapie [krijɔterapi] NF *Méd* cryotherapy

cryoturbation [krijɔtyrbasjɔ̃] NF *Géol* cryoturbation

cryptage [kriptaʒ] NM **1** *(d'un message)* coding **2** *(d'une émission de télévision)* coding, scrambling

crypte [kript] NF *Archit & Anat* crypt

crypté, -e [kripte] ADJ **1** *(message)* coded **2** *(émission de télévision)* scrambled *(for non-subscribers)*, encrypted

crypter [3] [kripte] VT **1** *(message)* to encode **2** *(émission de télévision)* to scramble, to encrypt

cryptique [kriptik] ADJ **1** *Anat* cryptal **2** *(personne)* living in a crypt *or* a catacomb, troglodytic **3** *(caché, secret)* cryptic

cryptococcose [kriptɔkɔkɔz] NF *Méd* cryptococcosis

cryptocommuniste [kriptɔkɔmynist] ADJ cryptocommunist
  NMF cryptocommunist

cryptogame [kriptɔgam] *Bot* ADJ cryptogamic, cryptogamous
  NM OU NF cryptogam

cryptogamie [kriptɔgami] NF *Bot* cryptogamy

cryptogamique [kriptɔgamik] ADJ *Bot* cryptogamic, cryptogamous

cryptogénétique [kriptɔʒenetik] ADJ *Méd* cryptogenetic, cryptogenic

cryptogramme [kriptɔgram] NM cryptogram

cryptographe [kriptɔgraf] NM ciphering machine, cryptograph
  NMF cryptographer, cryptographist

cryptographie [kriptɔgrafi] NF cryptography

cryptographique [kriptɔgrafik] ADJ cryptographic

cryptologie [kriptɔlɔʒi] NF cryptography

cryptomeria [kriptɔmerja] NM *Bot* **c. (du Japon)** Japanese cedar, *Spéc* cryptomeria

cryptophyte [kriptɔfit] *Bot* ADJ cryptophytic
  NF cryptophyte

cryptorchidie [kriptɔrkidi] NF *Méd* cryptorchidism

cryptosporidiose [kriptɔspɔridjoz] NF *Méd* cryptosporidiosis

cryptosporidium [kriptɔspɔridjɔm] NF *Biol* cryptosporidium

cs *(abrév écrite* **cuillère à soupe)** tbs, tbsp

CSA [seɛsa] NM *(abrév* **Conseil supérieur de l'audiovisuel)** = French broadcasting supervisory body

csardas [gzardas, tsardas] NF *(danse)* csardas, czardas

CSCE [seɛseə] NF *(abrév* **Conférence sur la sécurité et la coopération en Europe)** CSCE

CSEN [seɛsaɛn] NF *(abrév* **Confédération des syndicats de l'éducation nationale)** = confederation of teachers' unions

CSG [seɛsʒe] NF *Fin (abrév* **contribution sociale généralisée)** = income-based tax deducted at source as a contribution to paying off the French social security budget deficit

CSM [seɛsɛm] NM *(abrév* **Conseil supérieur de la magistrature)** = French state body that appoints members of the judiciary

CSP [seɛspe] NF *(abrév* **catégorie socio-professionnelle)** socio-professional group

CT [sete] NF *(abrév* **collectivité territoriale)** = administrative division with a higher degree of autonomy than a "département"

Cte *(abrév écrite* **comte)** Count

cténaire [ktenɛr] *Zool* NM ctenophore, ctenophoran
  ❑ **cténaires** NMPL Ctenophora

cténize [kteniz] NM *Entom* trapdoor spider

cténophore [ktenɔfɔr] *Zool* NM ctenophore, ctenophoran
  ❑ **cténophores** NMPL Ctenophora

Ctesse *(abrév écrite* **comtesse)** Countess

CTI [setei] NF *(abrév* **Confédération des travailleurs intellectuels de France)** = French trade union representing non-manual workers

cuadro [kwadro] NM cuadro *(flamenco group)*

CUB [kyb] NF *Anciennement (abrév* **Communauté urbaine de Bordeaux)** = syndicate of local authorities in the Bordeaux area

Cuba [kyba] NF Cuba; **vivre à C.** to live in Cuba; **aller à C.** to go to Cuba

cubage [kybaʒ] NM **1** *(évaluation)* calculating the cubic volume **2** *(volume)* cubic volume, cubature, cubage

cubain, -e [kybɛ̃, -ɛn] ADJ Cuban
  ❑ **Cubain, -e** NM,F Cuban

cubature [kybatyr] NF *Tech* cubature

cube [kyb] ADJ cubic; **centimètre c.** cubic centimetre
  NM **1** *Géom & Math* cube; **quel est le c. de 4?** what's 4 cubed *or* the cube of 4?; **élever un nombre au c.** to cube a number
  2 *(objet cubique)* cube; **couper de la viande en cubes** to cut meat into cubes; **la bâtisse ressemble à un gros c. de béton** the building's like a big concrete box
  3 *(jeu)* (building) block
  4 *Fam (cylindrée)* **un gros/petit c.** *(moto)* a big/small bike
  5 *Fam Arg scol (en classe préparatoire)* = student repeating the second year of "classes préparatoires"

cubèbe [kybɛb] NM *Bot & Pharm* cubeb

cuber [3] [kybe] VT to determine the cubic volume of
  VI **1** *(contenir)* **le réservoir cube 100 litres** the tank has a cubic capacity of 100 litres **2** *Fam (être cher)* **tout ça finit par c.** it all adds up **3** *Fam Arg scol (redoubler → en classe préparatoire)* = to repeat the second year of "classes préparatoires"

cubilot [kybilo] NM cupola furnace

cubique [kybik] ADJ **1** *(en forme de cube)* cube-shaped, cubic **2** *Math & Minér* cubic
  NF *Math* cubic

cubisme [kybism] NM *Beaux-Arts* Cubism

cubiste [kybist] *Beaux-Arts* ADJ Cubist, Cubistic
  NMF Cubist

Cubitainer® [kybitenɛr] NM = large cubic plastic container for bulk purchase of wine etc

cubital, -e, -aux, -ales [kybital, -o] ADJ *Anat* ulnar

cubitière [kybitjɛr] NF cubitière, couter

cubitus [kybitys] NM *Anat* ulna

cuboïde [kybɔid] ADJ cuboid

cuboméduse [kybɔmedyz] *Zool* NF box jellyfish, *Spéc* cubomedusa
  ❑ **cuboméduses** NFPL Cubomedusa

cuchaule [kyʃol] NF *Suisse* brioche

cucul [kyky] ADJ INV *Fam* **c. (la praline)** *(personne, air)* cutesy, *Br* twee; *(film, livre)* corny

cucurbitacée [kykyrbitase] *Bot* NF cucurbit
  ❑ **cucurbitacées** NFPL Cucurbitaceae

cucurbitain [kykyrbitɛ̃] NM *Zool (formé par un ténia)* terminal segment

cucurbite [kykyrbit] NF *Tech* boiler, cucurbit *(of distilling apparatus)*

CUE [seya] NM *(abrév* **Conseil de l'Union européenne)** CEU

cueillage [kœjaʒ] NM gathering

cueillaison [kœjɛzɔ̃] NF **1** *Littéraire (récolte)* gathering, harvesting **2** *(saison)* fruit-picking season **3** *(du verre)* gathering

cueillera *etc voir* **cueillir**

cueillette [kœjɛt] NF **1** *(ramassage → de fruits)* gathering, picking; *(→ de fleurs)* picking **2** *(récolte)* crop, harvest; **as-tu fait bonne c.?** did you get a good crop *or* collect a lot? **3** *(en sociologie)* gathering; **une tribu qui vit de la c.** a tribe of gatherers

cueilleur, -euse [kœjœr, -øz] NM,F *(de fruits)* picker, gatherer; *(de fleurs)* picker

cueillir [41] [kœjir] VT **1** *(récolter → fruits)* to gather, to pick; *(→ fleurs)* to pick; *Fig* **c. des lauriers** to win laurels; *Littéraire* **cueillez le jour** seize the day
  2 *(trouver)* to pick up, to collect; **il est venu me c. chez moi** he came to pick me up at my place; **où es-tu allé c. pareille idée?** where on earth did you get that idea?
  3 *Fam (surprendre)* to catch, to grab; **si tu veux**

---

sa permission, cueille-la à son arrivée if you want to get her permission, (make sure you) catch her as she comes in; **être cueilli à froid** to be caught off guard
  4 *Fam (arrêter)* to nab, to collar
  5 *(saisir au passage)* to snatch, to grab; **c. un baiser** to snatch a kiss; **la serveuse cueillit un menu au passage** the waitress grabbed a menu as she walked past

cueilloir [kœjwar] NM *(instrument)* fruit picker; *(corbeille)* fruit basket

Cuenca [kwɛŋka] NM Cuenca

cuesta [kwɛsta] NF cuesta

cueva [kweva] NF cueva *(flamenco entertainment held in cellar bar)*

cui-cui [kɥikɥi] NM INV tweet-tweet, twittering; **faire c.** to tweet, to go tweet-tweet

cuillère, cuiller [kɥijɛr] NF **1** *(instrument)* spoon; **c. à café** *ou* **à moka** teaspoon; *(plus petite)* coffee spoon; **c. en bois** wooden spoon; *Sport* **la c. de bois** the wooden spoon; **c. à dessert** dessert spoon; **c. parisienne** melon baller; **c. à soupe**, *Can* **c. à table** soup spoon; *(pour mesurer)* tablespoon; **petite c.**, *Can* **c. à thé** teaspoon; *Fam* **en deux** *ou* **trois coups de c. à pot** in a jiffy, in no time at all
  2 *(contenu)* spoonful; **une c. à café de sucre** a teaspoonful of sugar; **deux cuillères à soupe de farine** two tablespoonfuls of flour; **une c., pour papa, une c., pour maman** *(à un enfant)* one (spoonful) for Daddy, one (spoonful) for Mummy
  3 *Pêche* spoon, spoonbait
  4 *(pièce d'amorçage d'une grenade)* safety catch
  5 *très Fam (main)* mitt, paw
  ❑ **à la cuillère** ADJ *pêche* à la c. spinning, trolling ADV **1** *(en mangeant)* **nourrir** *ou* **faire manger qn à la c.** to spoon-feed sb; **mange ton yaourt à la c.** eat your yoghurt with a spoon; **mange le reste de ta sauce à la c.** spoon up the rest of your gravy **2** *Pêche* **pêcher la truite à la c.** to spin *or* to troll for trout

cuillerée [kɥijere] NF spoonful; **une c. à café de sucre** a teaspoonful of sugar; **une c. à dessert** a dessertspoonful; **une c. à soupe de farine** a tablespoonful of flour; **une c. pour papa, une c. pour maman!** *(à un enfant)* one (spoonful) for Daddy, one (spoonful) for Mummy!

cuilleron [kɥijrɔ̃] NM **1** *(d'une cuillère)* bowl; **en c.** *(feuille)* spoon-shaped **2** *Entom* alula, alulet, winglet

cuir [kɥir] NM **1** *(peau → traitée)* leather; *(→ brute)* hide; **le c.** *(vêtements en cuir)* leather clothes; *(objets en cuir)* leather goods; *Fam* **un c.** a leather jacket; **c. brut** *ou* **cru** *ou* **vert** rawhide; **c. bouilli** cuir-bouilli; **c. de Russie** Russia leather
  2 *(peau humaine)* skin; **c. chevelu** scalp; **entre c. et chair** under the skin; *Fam* **tomber sur** *ou* **tanner le c. à qn** to tan sb's hide
  3 *(lanière)* **c. à rasoir** strop
  4 *Fam (faute de liaison)* incorrect liaison *(introducing an unwanted consonant between two words)*
  ❑ **de cuir, en cuir** ADJ leather *(avant n)*

cuirasse [kɥiras] NF **1** *Hist (armure)* breastplate, cuirass, corselet **2** *Fig* protective shell; **une c. de froideur** an air of aloofness **3** *Mil (d'un char, d'un navire de guerre)* armour **4** *(carapace)* cuirass

cuirassé, -e [kɥirase] ADJ *(char, navire)* armoured, armour-plated
  NM battleship

'Le Cuirassé Potemkine' Eisenstein 'The Battleship Potemkin'

---

cuirassement [kɥirasmɑ̃] NM **1** *(équiper d'une cuirasse)* armouring **2** *(cuirasse)* armour, armour-plating

cuirasser [3] [kɥirase] VT **1** *Mil* to armour, to armour-plate **2** *(endurcir)* to harden; **son enfance difficile l'a cuirassé contre tout** his difficult childhood has made him very thick-skinned
  ▶**se cuirasser** VPR **1** *Hist* to put on a breastplate **2** *(s'endurcir)* to harden oneself; **se c. contre qch** to harden oneself to sth

cuirassier [kɥirasje] NM *Hist* cuirassier

cuire [98] [kɥir] VT **1** *Culin (gén)* to cook; *(pain, gâteau, tarte)* to bake; **c. à l'eau** to boil; **c. à la vapeur** to steam; **c. au four** to cook in the oven; *(pain, gâteau, tarte)* to bake; **pain cuit au feu de bois** bread baked in a wood-burning oven

2 *(brûler → peau)* to burn; **la canicule a cuit les prés** the fields are parched as a result of the heatwave

3 *Suisse (eau, lait)* to boil; *(vêtements, linge)* to boil-wash

VI **1** *Culin (aliment)* to cook; **c. à feu doux** *ou* **petit feu** to simmer; **c. à gros bouillons** to boil hard; **il faut le temps que ça cuise!** give it time to cook!; **poulet prêt à c.** oven-ready chicken; **faire c. qch** to cook sth; **faire c. qch à feu doux** to simmer sth; **faire c. qch à feu vif** to cook sth over a high flame; **faire c. qch au four** to bake sth; **faire trop c. qch** to overcook sth; **j'ai trop fait c. les légumes** I've overcooked the vegetables; **tu n'as pas fait assez c. la viande** you've undercooked the meat; *Fam* **laisser qn c. dans son jus** to let sb stew in his/her own juice; *Fam* **va te faire c. un œuf!** go and take a running jump!, go and jump in a lake!; *Fam* **je l'ai envoyé se faire c. un œuf** I sent him packing

2 *Fam (souffrir de la chaleur)* **je cuis!** I'm roasting!; **on cuit dans cette voiture!** it's boiling (hot) in this car!

3 *(brûler)* to burn, to sting; **les yeux me cuisent** my eyes are burning *or* stinging

4 il vous en cuira you'll regret it; **il pourrait t'en c.** you might regret it

❑ **à cuire** ADJ **chocolat à c.** cooking chocolate; **pommes à c.** cooking apples

cuirette [kɥirɛt] NF *Can (similicuir)* imitation leather, leatherette

cuisant, -e [kɥizɑ̃, -ɑ̃t] ADJ **1** *(douleur, sensation)* burning, stinging; **il ressentit une douleur cuisante à la jambe** he felt a burning pain in his leg **2** *(affront, injure)* stinging, bitter; *(défaite)* stinging; **c'était pour lui un échec c.** he was smarting at this failure

cuiseur [kɥizœr] NM large cooking pot

cuisine [kɥizin] NF **1** *(lieu)* kitchen; **c. roulante** field kitchen

2 *(activité)* cooking, *Br* cookery; **faire la c.** to cook; **elle fait très bien la c.** she's an excellent cook; **sais-tu faire la c.?** can you cook?; **j'aime faire la c.** I enjoy cooking; **c'est lui qui fait la c.** he does the cooking; **la c. au beurre/à l'huile** cooking with butter/oil; **c. bourgeoise** good plain home cooking

3 *(ensemble de mets)* cuisine, food, dishes; **c. fine et soignée** carefully prepared dishes *or* food; **j'apprécie la c. chinoise** I enjoy Chinese food; **c. allégée, c. minceur** cuisine minceur, lean cuisine; **nouvelle c.** nouvelle cuisine

4 *(cuisiniers)* **la c.** *(dans un château, dans un restaurant)* the kitchen staff; *(à la cantine)* the catering *or* kitchen staff

5 *(meubles)* kitchen (furniture); **c. américaine** = kitchen with a bar separating the cooking and eating areas; **c. intégrée,** *Suisse* **c. agencée** fitted kitchen; **c. en kit** kitchen units in kit form

6 *Fam Péj (malversations)* wheeling and dealing; **la c. électorale/parlementaire** electoral/parliamentary wheeling and dealing, electoral/parliamentary dirty tricks

❑ **cuisines** NFPL *(au restaurant)* kitchen; *Naut* galley

❑ **de cuisine** ADJ *(table, couteau)* kitchen *(avant n)*

cuisiné, -e [kɥizine] ADJ *voir* **plat**[1]

cuisine-cave [kɥizinkav] *(pl* **cuisines-caves***)* NF *Belg* basement kitchen

cuisiner [3] [kɥizine] VT **1** *(plat, dîner)* to cook; **spécialités cuisinées au vin rouge** specialities cooked in red wine; **qu'est-ce que tu nous as cuisiné pour ce soir?** what have you cooked for us tonight?

2 *Fam (interroger → accusé, suspect)* to grill; **il s'est fait c. par la police** he was grilled by the police

3 *Fam (préparer → promotion, élection)* to prepare carefully

VI to cook; **j'aime c.** I like cooking; **elle cuisine bien** she's a good cook

cuisinette [kɥizinɛt] NF *Offic & Can & Suisse* kitchenette

cuisinier, -ère [kɥizinje, -ɛr] NM,F cook

❑ **cuisinière** NF stove, *Br* cooker; **cuisinière électrique** electric stove *or Br* cooker; **cuisinière à gaz** gas stove *or Br* cooker; **cuisinière mixte** combined gas and electric stove *or Br* cooker

cuisons *etc voir* **cuire**

cuissage [kɥisaʒ] *voir* **droit**[3]

cuissard [kɥisar] NM **1** *(d'un cycliste)* cycling shorts **2** *(d'une armure)* cuisse, cuish

cuissardes [kɥisard] NFPL **1** *(de femme)* thigh boots **2** *(de pêcheur)* waders

cuisse [kɥis] NF **1** *(partie du corps)* thigh; *Fam Hum* **avoir la c. légère** to put it about; *très Fam* **il y a de la c.!** check out the babes *or Br* talent! **2** *Zool* leg **3** *Culin* leg; **cuisses de grenouille** frogs' legs; **c. de poulet** chicken leg

cuisseau, -x [kɥiso] NM *(de veau)* haunch

cuisse-de-nymphe [kɥisdənɛ̃f] *(pl* **cuisses-de-nymphe***)* ADJ INV *Littéraire (ému)* flesh pink

NF *Hort* = white rose with pink tints

cuissettes [kɥisɛt] NFPL *Suisse* (sports) shorts

cuisson [kɥisɔ̃] NF **1** *(fait de cuire → gén)* cooking; *(→ pain, gâteau)* baking; *(→ rôti)* roasting, cooking; **c. au grill** grilling; **c. à la vapeur** steaming; **temps de c.** cooking time; **quelle c.?** *(viande)* how would you like your meat cooked? **2** *(des briques, de la porcelaine)* burning, firing **3** *(brûlure)* burning, smarting

cuisson-extrusion [kɥisɔ̃ɛkstryzjɔ̃] *(pl* **cuissons-extrusions***)* NF extrusion-cooking

cuissot [kɥiso] NM **1** *(de gibier)* haunch **2** *(d'une armure)* cuisse, cuish

cuistance [kɥistɑ̃s] NF *Fam* grub; **faire la c.** to make the grub

cuistax [kɥistaks] NM *Belg* = pedal-operated vehicle used in seaside resorts

cuistot [kɥisto] NM *Fam* cook■, chef■

cuistre [kɥistr] NM *(pédant)* pedant, prig

ADJ pedantic, priggish

cuistrerie [kɥistrəri] NF **1** *(pédanterie)* pedantry, priggishness **2** *(grossièreté)* boorishness

cuit, -e [kɥi, kɥit] ADJ **1** *(aliment)* cooked; **viande bien cuite** well-done meat; **viande cuite à point** medium-rare meat; **mal c., pas assez c.** undercooked; **trop c.** overcooked; **jambon c.** cooked ham; **attendre que ça tombe tout c. (dans le bec)** to wait for things to fall into one's lap

2 *(brûlé → peau)* burnt, sunburnt; *(→ jardin, champ)* parched

3 *Fam (usé)* worn out, threadbare; **elles sont cuites, mes bottes!** my boots have had it!; **mon embrayage est c.** my clutch has had it

4 *Fam (perdu)* **je suis c.!** I'm done for!, I've had it!; **notre sortie de dimanche, c'est c.!** we can kiss our Sunday outing goodbye!

5 *très Fam (ivre)* wasted, plastered

NM **1** *Culin* **le c.** the cooked

2 *(locution)* **c'est du tout c.** it's as good as done (already); **ça n'a pas été du tout c.** it was no walkover

❑ **cuite** NF **1** *très Fam (beuverie)* **(se) prendre une cuite** to get loaded *or* plastered; **il tenait une de ces cuites!** he was totally wasted *or* plastered!

2 *(de céramiques)* baking, firing

cuiter [3] [kɥite] **se cuiter** VPR *très Fam* to get wasted *or* plastered

cuivrage [kɥivraʒ] NM copperplating

cuivre [kɥivr] NM **1** *Métal* copper; **mine de c.** copper mine; **c. jaune** brass; **c. rouge** copper **2** *Beaux-Arts (planche)* copperplate

❑ **cuivres** NMPL **1** *(objets)* copperware; *(en cuivre jaune)* brasses; *(casseroles)* copper (pots and) pans; **faire (briller) les cuivres** to polish the brassware, to do the brasses **2** *Mus* brass instruments

❑ **de cuivre, en cuivre** ADJ copper *(avant n)*

cuivré, -e [kɥivre] ADJ **1** *Beaux-Arts & Métal* copperplated **2** *(rouge)* copper-coloured; **avoir le teint c.** *ou* **la peau cuivrée** *(par le soleil)* to be tanned; *(naturellement)* to have a ruddy complexion; **des cheveux aux reflets cuivrés** auburn hair **3** *(son, voix)* resonant

cuivrer [3] [kɥivre] VT **1** *Beaux-Arts & Métal* to copperplate **2** *(donner une teinte rougeâtre à)* to bronze, to tan

cuivreux, -euse [kɥivrø, -øz] ADJ cupreous, cuprous

cuivrique [kɥivrik] ADJ cupric

cul [ky] NM **1** *très Fam (postérieur) Br* arse, *Am* ass; **un coup de pied au c.** a kick up the pants *or Br* backside; **être** *ou* **aller (le) c. nu** to go around *Br* bare-arsed or *Am* bare-assed; **en avoir plein le c. (de)** *(en avoir assez)* to be *Br* pissed off (with) *or Am* pissed (with); **en avoir plein le c.** *(être fatigué)* to be *Br* knackered *or Am* bushed; **plein le c., de leurs conneries!** I've had it up to here with their stupid tricks!; **avoir** *ou* **être le c. entre deux chaises** to have a foot in each camp; *Vulg* **l'avoir dans le c.** to have been shafted *or* screwed; *Vulg* **tu peux te le mettre au c.!** shove it up your *Br* arse *or Am* ass!; **avoir qn au c.** to have sb on one's tail; **on va lui foutre les flics au c.** let's get the cops on his/her tail *or Am* ass; **pousser qn au c.** to be on sb's back; **tomber sur le c.** to fall on one's *Br* arse *or Am* ass; **en tomber** *ou* **en rester sur le c.** to be flabbergasted *or Br* gobsmacked; **ça m'a mis le c. par terre** I was flabbergasted *or Br* gobsmacked; **je suis sur le c.!** *(fatigué) Br* I'm knackered!, *Am* I'm bushed!; *(surpris)* I can't believe it!, *Br* I'm gobsmacked!; **tirer au c.** *Br* to do sod all, *Am* to goldbrick; **faire la bouche en c. de poule** to purse one's lips, to pout; **avoir le c. bordé de nouilles** to be a lucky bastard; **et mon c., c'est du poulet?** *Br* you're taking the piss, aren't you!, *Am* gimme a break!; *Vulg* **parle à mon c., ma tête est malade** *(personne ne m'écoute)* I might as well talk to the fucking wall; *(laisse-moi tranquille)* fuck off!; *Vulg* **mon c.!** no fucking way!, my *Br* arse *or Am* ass!; **être comme c. et chemise** to be as thick as thieves; **il y a des coups de pied au c. qui se perdent** a kick in the *Br* arse *or Am* ass is too good for some people; *Can* **n'avoir rien que le c. et les dents** to be at rock bottom; **c. par-dessus tête** head over heels■, *Br* arse over tit

2 *très Fam (sexe)* screwing, *Br* shagging; **leurs histoires de c. ne m'intéressent pas** what they get up to in the sack is of no interest to me; **un film de c.** a porn *or* porno movie, *Am* a skin flick; **un magazine de c.** a porn *or* porno *or* girlie mag, *Am* a skin mag; **il s'intéresse qu'au c.** all he thinks about is screwing, *Br* he's got shagging on the brain

3 *très Fam (chance)* **avoir du c.** to be a lucky bastard

4 *très Fam Péj* **c. béni** Jesus freak

5 *très Fam (camion)* **un gros c.** *Br* a juggernaut, *Am* a semi, an eighteen-wheeler

6 *(fond d'une bouteille)* **un c. de bouteille** the bottom of a bottle; **faire c. sec** to down one's drink in one; **c. sec!** down in one!, *Br* bottoms up!

culasse [kylas] NF **1** *(d'une arme à feu)* breech; **c. mobile** *(de carabine)* bolt **2** *Tech* cylinder head

culard [kylar] *Agr* ADJ double-muscled

NM *(bovin)* double-muscled cow; *(porcin)* double-muscled pig

cul-blanc [kyblɑ̃] *(pl* **culs-blancs***)* NM *(traquet motteux)* wheatear

culbutage [kylbytaʒ] NM knocking over, tumbling

culbute [kylbyt] NF **1** *(galipette)* somersault; **faire des culbutes** to do somersaults; **c. à l'envers** backflip **2** *(chute)* fall, tumble; **il a fait la c. dans l'escalier** he fell head over heels down the stairs **3** *Fam Fin* collapse■; **faire la c.** *(faire faillite)* to go bust *or* under; *(en revendant quelque chose)* to double one's money■, to sell for double the cost price■ **4** *Fam (être déchu)* to fall■, to collapse■; **le gouvernement a fait la c.** the government fell *or* collapsed

culbutement [kylbytmɑ̃] NM **1** *(galipette)* turning a somersault **2** *(fait de faire tomber)* knocking over, upsetting; *(d'une charrette)* tipping; *(d'un minerai)* dumping **3** *Astron* abnormal rotation

culbuter [3] [kylbyte] VI *(à la renverse)* to tumble, to fall (over backwards); *(en avant)* to fall *or* to tumble (headfirst)

VT **1** *(faire tomber → personne)* to knock over **2** *(venir à bout de → régime)* to topple, to overthrow **3** *Mil* **c. l'ennemi** to overwhelm the enemy **4** *très Fam (femme)* to screw, to lay, *Br* to shag

culbuteur [kylbytœr] NM **1** *(jouet)* tumbler **2** *Mines* tippler, tipper **3** *Aut* rocker arm

cul-de-basse-fosse [kydbasfos] *(pl* **culs-de-basse-fosse***)* NM dungeon

cul-de-four [kydfur] *(pl* **culs-de-four***)* NM *Archit* *(d'une abside)* half dome; *(d'une niche)* cul-de-four

cul-de-jatte [kydʒat] *(pl* **culs-de-jatte***)* **NMF** person with no legs

cul-de-lampe [kydlɑ̃p] *(pl* **culs-de-lampe***)* **NM 1** *Typ* tailpiece **2** *Archit (dans une église)* cul-de-lampe, pendant; *(dans une maison)* bracket, corbel

cul-de-porc [kydpɔr] *(pl* **culs-de-porc***)* **NM** *(nœud)* stopper knot

cul-de-poulin [kydpulɛ̃] *(pl* **culs-de-poulin***)* **NM** *Belg Culin* = prime rump cut of meat

cul-de-poule [kydpul] **en cul-de-poule ADJ une bouche en c.** a pouting little mouth; **faire la bouche en c.** to purse one's lips

cul-de-sac [kydsak] *(pl* **culs-de-sac***)* **NM 1** *(rue)* dead end, cul-de-sac **2** *(situation)* blind alley, impasse, no-win situation **3** *Anat* cul-de-sac

culée [kyle] **NF** abutment pier

culer [3] [kyle] **VI** *Naut* to drop astern

culeron [kylrɔ̃] **NM** *Équitation* crupper-loop, dock-piece

culinaire [kylinɛr] **ADJ** culinary; **mes talents culinaires** my culinary skills; **les délices culinaires de la Bourgogne** the gastronomic delights of Burgundy

culminant, -e [kylminɑ̃, -ɑ̃t] *voir* **point**[2]

culmination [kylminasjɔ̃] **NF** *Astron* culmination

culminer [3] [kylmine] **VI 1** *Géog* **les plus hauts sommets culminent à plus de 8000 mètres** the highest peaks are more than 8,000 metres high; **l'Everest culmine à 8848 mètres** Everest is 8,848 metres at its highest point

2 *(être à son maximum → gén)* to reach its peak, to peak; *(→ carrière)* to reach its height *or* peak; **la fréquentation culmine en juillet–août** the number of visitors peaks in July–August

3 *Astron* to culminate

culot [kylo] **NM 1** *Fam (aplomb)* nerve, *Br* cheek; **tu as un sacré c.!** you've got a nerve *or* a cheek!; **il ne manque pas de c.** he's a cool customer; **tu parles d'un c.!** talk about nerve!

2 *(partie inférieure → d'une lampe)* base, bottom; *(→ d'une cartouche)* base, cap; *(→ d'une ampoule)* base; *Aut (→ d'une bougie)* body

3 *Métal (résidu)* residue, cinder, slag

4 *(d'une pipe)* dottle

❑ **au culot ADV** *Fam* **faire qch au c.** to bluff one's way through sth; **il faut y aller au c.** you've got to bluff it out *or* brazen it out

culottage [kylɔtaʒ] **NM 1** *(d'une pipe)* seasoning **2** *(dépôt)* sooty layer

culotte [kylɔt] **NF 1** *(sous-vêtement) Br* pants, knickers, *Am* panties; **petite c.** panties; *Fam* **faire dans sa c.** to dirty one's pants; *(avoir peur)* to be scared stiff; *Fam* **on a ri à en faire dans nos culottes** we wet *or* pissed ourselves laughing; *Fam* **poser c.** to *Br* have *or Am* take a dump *or* a crap

2 *(pantalon) Br* trousers, *Am* pants; *Hist* breeches; **culottes courtes** shorts; *Fig* **tu étais encore en c. courte** *ou* **culottes courtes** you were still in short *Br* trousers *or Am* pants; **des peintres/explorateurs en c. courte** *ou* **culottes courtes** young painters/explorers; **pour nos gastronomes en c. courte** *ou* **culottes courtes** for our young gourmets; *Fam* **je m'en moque** *ou* **m'en fiche comme de ma première c.** I don't give a damn; **porter la c.** to wear *Br* the trousers *or Am* pants; *Can Fam* **se faire prendre les culottes à terre** to be caught with one's pants down; **c. de cheval** riding breeches, jodhpurs; *Fig* jodhpur thighs; **c. de golf** plus-fours; **(vieille) c. de peau** (old) military type, *Br* Colonel Blimp

3 *(pièce de viande)* rump

4 *très Fam Sport & (à un jeu)* **prendre** *ou* **ramasser une c.** to get trounced

culotté, -e [kylɔte] **ADJ** *Fam (effronté) Br* cheeky, *Am* sassy; **il est drôlement c. en affaires!** he's a businessman who takes risks!

culotter [3] [kylɔte] **VT 1** *(vêtir)* to put *Br* trousers *or Am* pants on **2** *(pipe)* to season; *(théière)* to blacken; **culotté par la suie** sooty, covered in soot; **culotté par l'âge** blackened with age

culottier, -ère [kylɔtje, -ɛr] **NM,F** tailor *(who specializes in making trousers)*

culpa [kylpa] **NF** *Jur* **c. in contrahendo** culpa in contrahendo, pre-contractual liability; **c. lata** lata culpa, gross negligence; **c. lessivima** levissima culpa, slight negligence; **c. levis** levis culpa, ordinary negligence

culpabilisant, -e [kylpabilizɑ̃, -ɑ̃t] **ADJ** guilt-provoking

culpabilisation [kylpabilizasjɔ̃] **NF 1** *(action)* **la c. des victimes** making the victims feel guilty, putting the burden of guilt on the victims **2** *(sentiment)* (feeling of) guilt

culpabiliser [3] [kylpabilize] **VT c. qn** to make sb feel guilty

VI to feel guilty, to blame oneself; *Fam* **je culpabilise à fond** I'm on a real guilt-trip

▸**se culpabiliser VPR** to feel guilty, to blame oneself

culpabilité [kylpabilite] **NF 1** *(sentiment)* guilt, guilty feeling; **je ressens un certain sentiment de c. à son égard** I feel rather guilty about him/her **2** *Jur* guilt; **nier sa c.** to deny that one is guilty

culpeu, -x [kylpø] **NM** *Zool* culpeo

culte [kylt] **NM 1** *(religion)* religion, faith; *(cérémonie)* service

2 *(dans le protestantisme)* **aller au c.** to go to church; **assister au c.** to attend church; **célébrer le c.** to worship

3 *(adoration)* cult, worship; **c. du soleil** sun worship; **le c. de la personnalité** personality cult; **elle a le c. du passé** she worships the past; **vouer un c. à qn** to worship sb; **il voue à son maître un véritable c.** he worships his master

4 *(comme adj)* cult; **film c.** cult movie *or Br* film

cultéranisme [kylteranism] **NM** *Littérature* cultism, Gongorism

cul-terreux [kytɛrø] *(pl* **culs-terreux***)* **NM** *Fam Péj* country bumpkin, yokel, *Am* hick

cultipacker [kyltipakœr] **NM** *Agr* Cultipacker

cultisme [kyltism] **NM** *Littérature* cultism, Gongorism

cultiste [kyltist] **NM** *Littérature* cultist, Gongorist

cultivable [kyltivabl] **ADJ** *(région, terre)* arable, farmable

cultivar [kyltivar] **NM** cultivar

cultivateur, -trice [kyltivatœr, -tris] **NM,F** farmer; **les petits cultivateurs** small farmers, smallholders

NM *(machine)* cultivator

cultivé, -e [kyltive] **ADJ 1** *Agr* cultivated; **passer dans les terres cultivées** to walk across ploughed fields **2** *(éduqué)* cultured, educated, well-educated; **les gens cultivés** educated people

cultiver [3] [kyltive] **VT 1** *Agr (champ, terres)* to cultivate, to farm; *(plantes)* to grow

2 *Biol (virus, tissu)* to cultivate

3 *(conserver → accent, image)* to cultivate; **elle cultive le paradoxe** she cultivates a paradoxical way of thinking

4 *(entretenir → relations, savoir)* to keep up; **cultive ton russe** keep up your Russian; **c. sa mémoire** to work on one's memory; **cultivez l'ambassadeur** make sure you're in with the Ambassador

5 *(protéger)* to protect, to safeguard; **elle cultive son indépendance** she protects her independence

▸**se cultiver VPR 1** *(accroître ses connaissances)* to educate oneself; **elle s'est cultivée par elle-même** she's self-taught

2 se c. l'esprit to cultivate the mind

> *Allusion*
>
> **Il faut cultiver notre jardin**
>
> This expression comes from the very end of Voltaire's *Candide, ou l'optimisme* (1759). The innocent young Candide has witnessed and experienced every sort of horror in his quest for Princess Cunégonde. Finally forced to abandon the philosophy of Optimism, he and his companions, settled at last in one place, wonder how to carry on. Candide concludes "I know one thing, we must cultivate our garden." Much ink has been spilt over the interpretation of this celebrated expression; essentially it means "We must get on with the nearest practical task to hand, and do something useful." At the same time, however, it means "We must concentrate on things close to home, since we cannot make sense of the human condition." Today the expression is sometimes used in connection with retirement from public life, perhaps to a quieter existence.

cultuel, -elle [kyltɥɛl] **ADJ** *(association, liberté)* religious; **édifice c.** place of worship

cultural, -e, -aux, -ales [kyltyral, -o] **ADJ** *(activité, méthode)* farming *(avant n)*

culturalisme [kyltyralism] **NM** culturalism

culturaliste [kyltyralist] **ADJ** culturalist

NMF culturalist

culture [kyltyr] **NF 1** *(production → de blé, de maïs)* farming; *(→ d'arbres, de fleurs)* growing; **faire de la c. commerciale** *ou* **de rapport** to specialize in cash crops; **c. associée** companion crop; **c. biologique** organic farming; **légumes de c. biologique** organically grown vegetables; **c. intensive/extensive** intensive/extensive farming; **c. maraîchère** *Br* market gardening, *Am* truck farming; **c. sèche** dry farming

2 *(terrain)* **cultures** fields *or* lands (under cultivation); **ne passe pas à travers les cultures** don't walk across fields with crops; **l'étendue des cultures renseigne sur la richesse d'un pays** the size of the fields under cultivation indicates the wealth of a country; **de grande/moyenne c.** *(pays, région)* with a high percentage of large/middle-sized farms

3 *(espèce)* crop; **introduire une nouvelle c.** to introduce a new crop

4 *(connaissance)* **la c.** culture; **parfaire sa c.** to improve one's mind; **un homme d'une grande c.** a highly cultured man; **c. générale** general knowledge; **avoir une bonne c. générale** *(candidat)* to have good general knowledge; *(étudiant)* to have had a broadly based education; **et maintenant, une question de c. générale** and now, a general knowledge question; **c. de masse** mass culture; **c. scientifique** scientific knowledge; *Fam* **la c., c'est comme la confiture, moins on en a, plus on l'étale** empty vessels make most noise

5 *(civilisation)* culture, civilization; **c. d'entreprise** corporate culture

6 *Biol* culture; **faire une c. de cellules** to grow *or* cultivate cells; **c. microbienne** bacterial culture; **c. repiqué** *ou* **secondaire** subculture; **c. de tissus** tissue culture

7 *Vieilli* **c. physique** physical education, *Br* PE, *Am* Phys. Ed.; **elle fait de la c. physique tous les matins** she does exercises every morning

❑ **de culture ADJ** *Agr* farming *(avant n)*

❑ **en culture ADV** under cultivation; **combien avez-vous d'hectares en c.?** how many hectares do you farm *or* do you have under cultivation?

culturel, -elle [kyltyrɛl] **ADJ** cultural

culturellement [kyltyrɛlmɑ̃] **ADV** culturally

culturisme [kyltyrism] **NM** bodybuilding

culturiste [kyltyrist] **NMF** bodybuilder

culturologie [kyltyrɔlɔʒi] **NF** cultural anthropology

cumin [kymɛ̃] **NM** cumin; **c. des prés** caraway; **du pain au c.** caraway seed bread

cumul [kymyl] **NM 1** *(de plusieurs activités)* multiple responsibilities *or* functions; *(de plusieurs salaires)* concurrent drawing; *Fam* **faire du c.** *(directeur)* to wear several hats; *(artisan)* to moonlight; *Pol* **le c. des fonctions** *ou* **mandats** plurality of offices

2 *Jur* plurality, combination; **c. d'actions** plurality of actions; **c. d'infractions** combination of offences; **c. des peines** cumulative sentence

cumulable [kymylabl] **ADJ** *(fonctions)* which may be held concurrently; *(retraites, salaires)* which may be drawn concurrently; **ces deux réductions ne sont pas cumulables** the two discounts may not be claimed at the same time

cumulard, -e [kymylar, -ard] **NM,F** *Fam Péj* **1** *Pol* = politician with several mandates **2** *(directeur)* = person making money as the head of several companies **3** *(employé)* holder of several jobs

cumulatif, -ive [kymylatif, -iv] **ADJ** cumulative

cumulativement [kymylativmɑ̃] **ADV** cumulatively

cumulé, -e [kymyle] **ADJ** *Fin (intérêt)* accrued

cumuler [3] [kymyle] **VT 1** *(réunir → fonctions)* to hold concurrently; *(→ retraites, salaires)* to draw concurrently; **il cumule plusieurs emplois** he has several jobs **2** *(accumuler)* to pile up; **il cumule les erreurs depuis son arrivée** he's done nothing but make mistakes since he

arrived **3** *Fin* to accrue; **intérêts cumulés** accrued interest

cumulet [kymylɛ] NM *Belg* somersault

cumulo-nimbus [kymylɔnɛ̃bys] NM INV *Météo* cumulonimbus

cumulus [kymylys] NM **1** *Météo* cumulus **2** *(citerne)* hot-water tank

cunéiforme [kyneifɔrm] ADJ cuneiform, wedge-shaped
□ NM cuneiform

cuniculiculture [kynikylikyltyr], **cuniculture** [kynikyltyr] NF rabbit breeding

cunnilingus [kynilɛ̃gys], **cunnilinctus** [kynilɛ̃ktys] NM cunnilingus

cupesse [kypɛs] NF *Suisse Fam* **1** *(culbute)* tumble▪; **faire la c.** to fall head over heels **2** *(faillite)* collapse▪; **faire la c.** to go bust *or* under; **être en c.** to have gone bust **3** *(désordre)* shambles; **être en c.** to be a shambles

cupesser [4] [kypɛse] VI *Suisse Fam* **1** *(culbuter)* to fall head over heels **2** *(faire faillite)* to collapse▪

cupide [kypid] ADJ *Littéraire* grasping, greedy; **il regardait l'argent d'un air c.** he was looking greedily at the money; **il est vraiment c.** he's a money grabber

cupidement [kypidmɑ̃] ADV *Littéraire* greedily

cupidité [kypidite] NF *Littéraire* greed

Cupidon [kypidɔ̃] NPR *Myth* Cupid

cupidon [kypidɔ̃] NM *Myth (ange)* cupid

cupressacée [kypresase] *Bot* NF member of the cypress tree family
□ **cupressacées** NFPL Cupressaceae

cuprifère [kyprifɛr] ADJ cupriferous

cuprique [kyprik] ADJ cupric, cupreous

cuprite [kyprit] NF *Minér* cuprite, red copper

cuproalliage [kyprɔaljaʒ] NM copper alloy

cuproaluminium [kyprɔalyminjɔm] *(pl* **cuproaluminiums***)* NM cupro-aluminium, aluminium bronze

cuproammoniaque [kyprɔamɔnjak] NF cuprammonium

cupronickel [kyprɔnikɛl] NM cupro-nickel

cuproplomb [kyprɔplɔ̃] NM copper-lead

cupule [kypyl] NF *Bot* cupule

cupulifère [kypylifɛr] *Bot* ADJ cupuliferous, cupule-bearing
□ **cupulifères** NFPL Cupuliferae

curabilité [kyrabilite] NF curableness, curability

curable [kyrabl] ADJ curable, which can be cured; **la lèpre est c.** leprosy can be cured, leprosy is curable

curaçao [kyraso] NM curaçao

curage [kyraʒ] NM *(d'un égout, d'un fossé)* cleaning out

curaillon [kyrajɔ̃] NM *Fam Péj* priest▪

curare [kyrar] NM *Bot* curare, curari

curarisant, -e [kyrarizɑ̃, -ɑ̃t] ADJ curarizing
□ NM curarizing substance

curarisation [kyrarizasjɔ̃] NF curarization

curatélaire [kyratelɛr] NMF *Jur* ward

curatelle [kyratɛl] NF *Jur* guardianship, trusteeship

curateur, -trice [kyratœr, -tris] NM,F *Jur* guardian, trustee

curatif, -ive [kyratif, -iv] ADJ healing

curatrice [kyratris] *voir* **curateur**

curculionidé [kyrkyljɔnide] *Entom* NM Curculio
□ **curculionidés** NMPL Curculionidae

curcuma [kyrkyma] NM *(plante)* curcuma; *(épice)* turmeric

cure [kyr] NF **1** *Méd (technique, période)* treatment; **c. d'amaigrissement** weight-loss *or Br* slimming course; **c. de désintoxication** detoxification programme; **faire une c. de désintoxication** to undergo treatment for alcoholism/drug addiction; **c. de repos** rest cure; **faire une c. de repos** to go on a rest cure; **c. de sommeil** sleep therapy; **faire une c. de sommeil** to have sleep therapy; **c. thermale** treatment at a spa
2 *Psy* **la c.** the talking cure
3 *Fig* **faire une c. de romans policiers** to go through a phase of reading nothing but detective stories; **faire une c. de fruits** to eat a lot of fruit
4 *Rel (fonction)* cure; *(paroisse)* parish; *(presbytère)* vicarage
5 *Littéraire (locution)* **n'avoir c. de** to care nothing about

curé [kyre] NM (Catholic) priest; **monsieur le c.** Father; **aller à l'école chez les curés** to be educated by priests; *Fam* **elle est toujours fourrée chez les curés** she's very churchy

cure-dent, cure-dents [kyrdɑ̃] *(pl* **cure-dents***)* NM toothpick

curée [kyre] NF **1** *Chasse* quarry, reward; *Fig* **il a provoqué les médias, et ç'a été la c.** he provoked the media and they were soon baying for his blood; *Fig* **ce fut la c. entre les héritiers** the heirs started to fight over the spoils; **c. chaude/froide** hot/cold quarry **2** *(ruée)* (mad) scramble, rush; **à son départ ça a été la c. pour prendre sa place** people trampled all over each other to get his/her job after he/she left

cure-ongle, cure-ongles [kyrɔ̃gl] *(pl* **cure-ongles***)* NM nail-cleaner

cure-oreille [kyrɔrɛj] *(pl* **cure-oreilles***)* NM ear-pick

cure-pipe, cure-pipes [kyrpip] *(pl* **cure-pipes***)* NM pipe-cleaner

curer [3] [kyre] VT to scrape clean
▸**se curer** VPR **se c. les ongles** to clean one's nails; **se c. les dents** to pick one's teeth (clean); **se c. les oreilles** to clean (out) one's ears

curetage [kyrtaʒ] NM **1** *Méd* curettage **2** *Constr* renovation *(of a historical part of a town)*

cureter [27] [kyrte] VT to curette

cureton [kyrtɔ̃] NM *Fam Péj* priest▪

curette [kyrɛt] NF *Tech* scraper; *Méd* curette, curet

Curiace [kyrjas] NPR **les Curiaces** the Curiatii

curial, -e, -aux, -ales [kyrjal, -o] ADJ curial; **maison curiale** presbytery

Curia regis [kyrjaregis] NF *Hist* Curia regis

curie¹ [kyri] NF **1** *Antiq* curia **2** *Rel* curia, Curia

curie² [kyri] NM *Phys (unité)* curie

curiethérapie [kyriterapi] NF *Méd* radiotherapy

curieuse [kyrjøz] *voir* **curieux**

curieusement [kyrjøzmɑ̃] ADV **1** *(avec curiosité → regarder)* curiously **2** *(étrangement → s'habiller)* oddly, strangely; **c., il n'a rien voulu dire** strangely *or* funnily enough, he wouldn't say anything; **c., les valises avaient disparu** oddly enough, the suitcases had disappeared

curieux, -euse [kyrjø, -øz] ADJ **1** *(indiscret)* curious, inquisitive
2 *(étrange)* curious, odd, strange; **c'est un c. personnage** he's a strange character; **il m'a répondu d'une manière curieuse** he gave me a strange answer
3 *(intéressé)* inquiring, inquisitive; **avoir un esprit c.** to have an inquiring mind; **il est c. d'entomologie** he has a keen interest in entomology; **soyez c. de tout** let your interests be wide-ranging; **je serais c. de voir cela** I'd be interested in seeing that
4 *Vieilli ou Littéraire* careful (**de** of); **éviter un soin trop c.** to avoid being over-meticulous; **être c. de ses livres** to take care of one's books
□ NM,F **1** *(badaud)* bystander, onlooker; *Péj* **autour d'un accident, il y a toujours des c.** people always gather round when there's been an accident
2 *(indiscret)* inquisitive person
□ NM **1** *(ce qui est étrange)* **c'est là le plus c. de l'affaire** that's what's so strange
2 *Fam Arg crime* examining magistrate▪, *Br* beak
□ **en curieux** ADV **je suis venu en c.** I just came to have a look

curiosité [kyrjozite] NF **1** *(indiscrétion)* curiosity, inquisitiveness; **puni sa c.** punished for being over-inquisitive; **mû par une c. malsaine** out of morbid curiosity; **par (pure) c.** out of (sheer) curiosity, just for curiosity's sake; *Prov* **la c. est un vilain défaut** curiosity killed the cat
2 *(intérêt)* curiosity; **c. intellectuelle** intellectual curiosity; **regarder qn avec c.** to look at sb curiously *or* enquiringly; **il faut éveiller la c. des enfants** it's a good thing to arouse children's curiosity; **vous avez de drôles de curiosités!** you're interested in some very strange things!
3 *(caractéristique)* oddity, idiosyncrasy; **c'est une des curiosités de son caractère** it's one of the odd things about him/her
4 *(objet)* curio, curiosity, oddity; **boutique** *ou* **magasin de curiosités** bric-à-brac *or Vieilli* curiosity shop

□ **curiosités** NFPL **les curiosités de Nemours** interesting and unusual things to see in Nemours

curiste [kyrist] NMF = person taking the waters at a spa; **les curistes viennent ici pour des problèmes vasculaires** people come to this spa to help vascular problems

curium [kyrjɔm] NM *Chim* curium

curling [kœrliŋ] NM *Sport* curling

curriculum vitae [kyrikylɔmvite] NM INV *Br* curriculum vitae, CV, *Am* résumé

curry [kyri] NM **1** *(épice)* curry powder **2** *(plat)* curry
□ **au curry** ADJ **poulet au c.** chicken curry, curried chicken

curseur [kyrsœr] NM cursor

cursif, -ive [kyrsif, -iv] ADJ *(écriture)* cursive; *(lecture, style)* cursory
□ **cursive** NF cursive

cursus [kyrsys] NM degree course; **c. universitaire** degree course

curule [kyryl] ADJ *Antiq* curule chair

curviligne [kyrvilin] ADJ curvilinear, curvilineal

curvimètre [kyrvimɛtr] NM curvometer

CUS [kys] NF *(abrév* **Communauté urbaine de Strasbourg***)* = syndicate of local authorities in the Strasbourg area

cuscute [kyskyt] NF *Bot* dodder; **c. du lin** flax dodder

custode [kystɔd] NF **1** *Aut* rear side panel **2** *Rel (pour hostie)* custodial

custom [kœstɔm] NM *(voiture)* customized car; *(moto)* customized motorbike

customiser [3] [kœstɔmize] VT to customize

cut [kœt] NM *Cin* cut

cutané, -e [kytane] ADJ skin *(avant n)*, *Spéc* cutaneous; **maladie cutanée** skin disease

cut-back [kœtbak] *(pl* **cut-backs***)* NM cutback

cute [kjut] ADJ *Can Fam (mignon)* cute

cuti [kyti] NF *Fam* skin test▪

cuticule [kytikyl] NF *Anat, Bot & Zool* cuticle

cuticuleux, -euse [kytikylø, -øz] ADJ skin-like, *Spéc* cuticular

cutine [kytin] NF *Bot* cutin

cuti-réaction [kytireaksjɔ̃] *(pl* **cuti-réactions***)* NF *Méd* skin test *(for detecting TB or allergies)*

cutter [kœtœr, kytɛr] NM Stanley® knife

cuvage [kyvaʒ] NM *(en œnologie)* fermentation in vats

cuvaison [kyvɛzɔ̃] NF = cuvage

cuve [kyv] NF **1** *(réservoir → gén)* tank, cistern; *(→ de machine à laver)* tub; *Phot* **c. à laver/à développement** washing/developing tank **2** *(pour le blanchissage, la teinture)* vat **3** *(en œnologie)* vat, tank; **c. close** pressure tank

cuvée [kyve] NF **1** *(contenu)* tankful, vatful **2** *(en œnologie)* vintage; **la c. du patron** the house wine; **la c. 1995 sera excellente** the 1995 vintage will be excellent; **vin de première c.** wine of the first growth *or* vintage; *Hum* **la dernière c. de Polytechnique/du festival de Cannes** the latest batch of graduates from the "École Polytechnique"/batch of movies *or Br* films from the Cannes film festival

cuvelage [kyvlaʒ] NM tubbing

cuveler [24] [kyvle] VT to tub

cuver [3] [kyve] VI *(vin)* to ferment
□ VT *Fam* **c. son vin** to sleep off the booze; **c. sa colère** to simmer down
□ USAGE ABSOLU *Fam* **laisse-le c. en paix** leave him to sleep it off

cuvette [kyvɛt] NF **1** *(récipient → gén)* basin, bowl, washbowl; *(→ des W-C)* pan; *(→ d'un lavabo)* basin **2** *(d'un thermomètre)* bulb **3** *Géog* basin **4** *Phot* **c. de fixage** fixing bath

cuvier [kyvje] NM tub *(for washing, winemaking etc)*

CV¹ [seve] NM *(abrév* **curriculum vitae***)* *Br* CV, *Am* résumé; **ça fera bien dans ton CV** it'll look good on your *Br* CV *or Am* résumé

CV² *Aut (abrév écrite* **cheval-vapeur***)* hp

CVG [seveʒe] NM *Bourse (abrév* **certificat de valeur garantie***)* CVR

CVS [sevees] ADJ *Com & Écon (abrév* **corrigé des variations saisonnières***)* seasonally adjusted

CX [seiks] NM INV *(coefficient de pénétration dans l'air)* drag coefficient

cyan [sjan] ADJ INV cyan
□ NM cyan

cyanamide [sjanamid] **NM OU NF** *Chim* cyanamide

cyanée [sjane] **NF** Cyaneid

cyanelle [sjanɛl] **NF** *Biol* cyanelle

cyanhydrique [sjanidrik] **ADJ** *Chim* hydrocyanic

cyanoacrylate [sjanɔakrilat] **NM** cyanoacrylate

cyanobactérie [sjanɔbakteri] **NF** *Biol* cyanobacterium

cyanocobalamine [sjanɔkɔbalamin] **NF** *Méd* vitamin B

cyanogène [sjanɔʒɛn] **NM** *Chim* cyanogen

cyanogénèse [sjanɔʒenɛz] **NF** *Chim* cyanogenesis

cyanophycée [sjanɔfise], **cyanophyte** [sjanɔfit] *Bot* **NF** blue-green alga, *Spéc* cyanobacterium
  ❏ **cyanophycées** **NFPL** blue-green algae, *Spéc* cyanobacteria

cyanose [sjanoz] **NF** *Méd* cyanosis

cyanosé, -e [sjanoze] **ADJ** *Méd* cyanotic; **enfant c.** blue baby

cyanoser [3] [sjanoze] **VT** *Méd* to cause cyanosis in

cyanuration [sjanyrasjɔ̃] **NF** *Chim* cyanidation, cyanization

cyanure [sjanyr] **NM** *Chim* cyanide

cyanurer [3] [sjanyre] **VT** *Chim* to cyanide, to cyanize

Cybèle [sibɛl] **NPR** *Myth* Cybele

cyber- [sibɛr] **PRÉF** cyber-

cyberbanque [sibɛrbɑ̃k] **NF** *Ordinat* Internet bank, online bank; *(activité)* online banking

cybercafé [sibɛrkafe] **NM** *Ordinat* cybercafé

cybercasino [sibɛrkazino] **NM** online casino

cybercommerce [sibɛrkɔmɛrs] **NM** *Ordinat* e-commerce

cybercrime [sibɛrkrim] **NM**, **cybercriminalité** [sibɛrkriminalite] **NF** *Ordinat* cybercrime

cyberculture [sibɛrkyltyr] **NF** *Ordinat* cyberculture

cyberespace [sibɛrɛspas] **NM** *Ordinat* cyberspace; **dans le c.** in cyberspace

cyberguerre [sibɛrgɛr] **NF** cyberwar

cyberharcèlement [sibɛrarsɛlmɑ̃] **NM** *Ordinat* cyberstalking

cyberjargon [sibɛrʒargɔ̃] **NM** *Ordinat* netspeak

cyberlibraire [sibɛrlibrɛr] **NM** Internet bookshop

cyberlibrairie [sibɛrlibrɛri] **NF** Internet bookshop

cybermonde [sibɛrmɔ̃d] **NM** *Ordinat* cyberspace; **dans le c.** in cyberspace

cybernaute [sibɛrnot] **NM** *Ordinat* Internet surfer, cybernaut

cybernéticien, -enne [sibɛrnetisjɛ̃, -ɛn] *Ordinat & Biol* **ADJ** cybernetic
  NM,F cybernetician, cyberneticist

cybernétique [sibɛrnetik] *Ordinat & Biol* **ADJ** cybernetic
  NF cybernetics *(singulier)*

cyberparesse [sibɛrparɛs] **NF** *Ordinat* cyberslacking

cyberpunk [sibɛrpœ̃k] **NM** *Littérature* cyberpunk

cybersexe [sibɛrsɛks] **NM** *Ordinat* cybersex

cybersquatter [sibɛrskwatɛr] **NM** *Ordinat* cybersquatter

cybersquatting [sibɛrskwatiŋ] **NM** *Ordinat* cybersquatting

cyberterrorisme [sibɛrtɛrɔrism] **NM** *Ordinat* cyberterrorism

cyberterroriste [sibɛrtɛrɔrist] **NM** *Ordinat* cyberterrorist

cybertraque [sibɛrtrak] **NF** *Ordinat* cyberstalking

cycadale [sikadal] *Bot* **NF** cycad
  ❏ **cycadales** **NFPL** Cycadales

cycas [sikas] **NM** *Bot* cycas, cycad

cyclable [siklabl] **ADJ** cycle *(avant n)*

Cyclades [siklad] **NFPL** **les C.** the Cyclades

cycladique [sikladik] **ADJ** Cycladic

cyclamate [siklamat] **NM** *Chim* cyclamate

cyclamen [siklamɛn] **NM** *Bot* cyclamen

cyclane [siklan] **NM** *Chim* cycloalkane, cyclo-paraffin

cycle [sikl] **NM 1** *(série → gén)* cycle; *(→ de conférences)* series; **le c. des saisons** the cycle of the seasons; *Astron* **c. lunaire/solaire** lunar/solar cycle
  2 *(évolution)* cycle; **le c. d'un produit** the cycle of a product *(from manufacture to consumption)*; **c. des affaires** business cycle; **c. commande-livraison-facturation** order-to-remittance cycle; **c. de commercialisation** trade cycle; **c. conjoncturel** business or economic cycle; **c.**

de la distribution distribution cycle; **c. économique** business *or* economic cycle; **c. d'exploitation** operating cycle; **c. d'opération** operating cycle; *Mktg* **c. de vie** lifecycle; *Mktg* **c. de vie familial** family lifecycle; *Mktg* **c. de vie de la marque** brand lifecycle; *Mktg* **c. de vie du produit** product lifecycle, PLC

  3 *Scol & Univ* cycle; **il suit un c. court/long** ≃ he'll leave school at sixteen/go on to higher education; **c. élémentaire** = term referring to the years spent at primary school between the ages of 7 and 9; **c. moyen** = term referring to the years spent at primary school between the ages of 9 and 11; **c. d'observation** = first two years at a "collège"; **c. d'orientation** = final two years at a "collège"; **c. préparatoire** = first stage of primary school education (from the age of 6); **premier c.** *Scol Br* ≃ lower secondary school years, *Am* ≃ junior high school; *Univ Br* ≃ first and second years, *Am* ≃ freshman and sophomore years; **second c.** *Scol Br* ≃ upper school, *Am* ≃ high school; *Univ* ≃ last two years of a degree course; **troisième c.** postgraduate studies; **être en troisième c.** to be a postgraduate student; **un étudiant de troisième c.** a postgraduate

  4 *Littérature* cycle; **le c. d'Arthur** the Arthurian cycle

  5 *Aut* **c. d'allumage** ignition cycle; **c. à deux temps** *Br* two-stroke cycle, *Am* two-cycle; **c. à quatre temps** *Br* four-stroke cycle, *Am* four-cycle; **c. urbain** urban cycle

  6 *(véhicule)* cycle; *Ind* **le c.** the bicycle industry; **magasin/fabricant de cycles** cycle shop/manufacturer

  7 *Physiol* **c. Krebs** Krebs cycle; **c. menstruel** menstrual cycle; **c. œstral** oestrous cycle

  8 *Chim* **le c. de l'azote** nitrogen cycle; **le c. du carbone** carbon cycle

  9 *Biol & Météo* **c. de l'eau** water cycle

  10 *Ordinat* **c. d'exécution** execute cycle

  11 *Cin (de films)* season; **un c. Truffaut** a Truffaut season

---

Culture

CYCLES
The French education system is split into "cycles". The "cycle primaire" corresponds to the first five years of schooling (from age 6 to age 10). The "cycle secondaire" comprises the years spent both at "collège" (from age 11 to age 14) and at "lycée" (from age 15 to age 18). "Collège" education is split into three "cycles": "cycle d'adaptation" (the first year), "cycle central" (the next two years) and "cycle d'orientation" (the final year). "Second cycle des lycées" corresponds to the three years spent at the "lycée". French higher education comprises three "cycles": "premier cycle" corresponds to the first two years, up to "DEUG" level, and "deuxième cycle" to the third and fourth years, up to "licence" and "maîtrise"; "troisième cycle" corresponds to postgraduate study leading to a "doctorat".

---

cyclique [siklik] **ADJ** cyclic, cyclical

cycliquement [siklikmɑ̃] **ADV** cyclically

cyclisation [siklizasjɔ̃] **NF** cyclization

cycliser [3] [siklize] **VT** to cyclize

cyclisme [siklism] **NM** cycling; **il fait du c. tous les dimanches** he goes cycling every Sunday; **c. sur piste** track cycling; **c. sur route** road racing

cycliste [siklist] **ADJ** **coureur c.** *Br* racing cyclist, *Am* cycler; **course c.** cycle race
  NMF *Br* cyclist, *Am* cycler
  NM *(short)* (pair of) cycling shorts

cycloalcane [siklɔalkan] **NM** *Chim* cycloalkane

cycloalcène [siklɔalsɛn] **NM** *Chim* cycloalkene

cyclo-cross [siklɔkrɔs] **NM INV** cyclo-cross

cyclohexane [siklɔɛksan] **NM** *Chim* cyclohexane

cycloïdal, -e, -aux, -ales [siklɔidal, -o] **ADJ** *Géom* cycloidal

cycloïde [siklɔid] **NF** *Géom* cycloid

cyclomoteur [siklɔmœtœr] **NM** moped, scooter

cyclomotoriste [siklɔmɔtɔrist] **NMF** scooter rider

cyclonal, -e, -aux, -ales [siklɔnal, -o] **ADJ** cyclonic, cyclonical, cyclonal

cyclone [siklon] **NM** *(dépression)* cyclone; *(typhon)*

cyclone, hurricane; *Fig* **elle est entrée comme un c.** she came in like a whirlwind

cyclonique [siklɔnik] **ADJ** cyclonic

cyclope [siklɔp] **NM** *Zool (crustacé)* cyclops
  ❏ **Cyclope** **NM** *Myth* Cyclops

cyclopéen, -enne [siklɔpeɛ̃, -ɛn] **ADJ 1** *Archéol* Pelasgian, Pelasgic **2** *Littéraire (gigantesque)* Cyclopean, titanic, colossal

cyclopentane [siklɔpɛ̃tan] **NM** *Chim* cyclopentane

cycloplégie [siklɔpleʒi] **NF** *Méd* cycloplegia

cyclo-pousse [siklɔpus] **NM INV** (pedal-powered) rickshaw, cyclo

cyclopropane [siklɔprɔpan] **NM** *Chim* cyclopropane

cyclorama [siklɔrama] **NM** *Cin & Théât* cyclorama

cyclorameur [siklɔramœr] **NM** go-kart

cyclosporine-A [siklɔsporina] **NF** *Pharm* cyclosporin-A

cyclostome [siklɔstɔm] **NM** *Ich* cyclostome

cyclothymie [siklɔtimi] **NF** *Psy* cyclothymia

cyclothymique [siklɔtimik] *Psy* **ADJ** cyclothymic, cyclothymiac
  NMF cyclothymic, cyclothymiac

cyclotourisme [siklɔturism] **NM** cycle touring; **faire du c.** to go on a cycling *Br* holiday *or Am* vacation

cyclotron [siklɔtrɔ̃] **NM** *Phys* cyclotron

cygne [siɲ] **NM** *Orn* swan; **c. mâle** cob; **c. femelle** pen; **jeune c.** cygnet; **c. chanteur** *ou* **sauvage** whooper swan; **c. muet** *ou* **tuberculé** mute swan; **c. nain** *ou* **de Bewick** Bewick's swan
  ❏ **Cygne** **NM** *Astron* **le C.** Cygnus, the Swan

cylindrage [silɛ̃draʒ] **NM 1** *(en travaux publics)* rolling **2** *Tex* mangling

cylindre [silɛ̃dr] **NM 1** *Aut & Géom* cylinder; **un moteur à quatre/six cylindres** a four-/six-cylinder engine; **une six cylindres** a six-cylinder car **2** *Tech* roller **3** *Typ* **c. blanchet** blanket cylinder

cylindrée [silɛ̃dre] **NF** *Br* cubic capacity, *Am* capacity displacement; **une petite c.** a small *or* small-engined car; **grosse c.** a big *or* big-engined car

cylindrer [3] [silɛ̃dre] **VT 1** *(en travaux publics)* to roll **2** *Tex* to mangle

cylindre-sceau [silɛ̃drəso] *(pl* **cylindres-sceaux***)* **NM** cylinder seal

cylindreur, -euse [silɛ̃drœr, -øz] **NM,F 1** *Tech* man in charge of roller, roller-man **2** *Tex* calender-man, mangler

cylindrique [silɛ̃drik] **ADJ** cylindric, cylindrical

cylindroïde [silɛ̃drɔid] **ADJ** cylindroid

cymaise [simɛz] = **cimaise**

cymbalaire [sɛ̃balɛr] **NF** *Bot* ivy-leaved toadflax

cymbale [sɛ̃bal] **NF** cymbal; **coup de cymbales** crash of cymbals

cymbalier, -ère [sɛ̃balje, -ɛr] **NM,F** cymbalist

cymbaliste [sɛ̃balist] **NMF** cymbalist

cymbalum [sɛ̃balɔm] **NM** cymbalo, dulcimer

cyme [sim] **NF** *Bot* cyme

cynégétique [sineʒetik] **ADJ** hunting *(avant n)*; **gestion c.** game management
  NF hunting

cynhyène [sinjɛn] **NM** *Zool* wild dog

cynipidé [sinipide] *Entom* **NM** Cynipid
  ❏ **cynipidés** **NMPL** Cynipidae

cynips [sinips] **NM** *Entom* gall wasp, *Spéc* cynips

cynique [sinik] **ADJ 1** *(gén)* cynical **2** *Phil* Cynic
  NMF 1 *(gén)* cynic **2** *Phil* Cynic

cyniquement [sinikmɑ̃] **ADV** cynically

cynisme [sinism] **NM 1** *(attitude)* cynicism **2** *Phil* Cynicism

cynocéphale [sinɔsefal] **NM** *Zool* dog-faced baboon

cynodrome [sinɔdrom] **NM** greyhound track

cynoglosse [sinɔglɔs] **NF** *Bot* hound's-tongue

cynologie [sinɔlɔʒi] **NF** the study of dogs

cynophile [sinɔfil] **ADJ** *Mil* **unité** *ou* **équipe c.** dog-training *or* dog-handling unit; **brigade c.** dog-training *or* dog-handling unit
  NMF dog lover

cynorhodon, cynorrhodon [sinɔrɔdɔ̃] **NM** *(fruit)* rosehip; **confiture/tisane de c.** rosehip jam/tea

cypéracée [siperase] *Bot* **NF** Cyperus
  ❏ **cypéracées** **NFPL** Cyperaceae

cyphoscoliose [sifoskɔljoz] **NF** *Méd* kyphoscoliosis

cyphose [sifoz] **NF** *Méd* kyphosis

cyphotique [sifɔtik] *Méd* **ADJ** kyphotic
  NMF kyphosis sufferer
cyprès [siprɛ] **NM** *Bot* cypress; **c. de l'Arizona**
  Arizona cypress; **c. chauve** bald cypress; **c. de**
  Lambert Monterey cypress; **c. de la Louisiane**
  bald cypress; **c. de Monterey** Monterey cypress;
  c. toujours vert Italian cypress
cyprière [sipriɛr] **NF** cypress plantation *or* grove
cyprin [siprɛ̃] **NM** *Ich* crucian
cyprinidé [siprinide] *Ich* **NM** cyprinid
  ◻ **cyprinidés NMPL** Cyprinidae
cypriote [siprijɔt] **ADJ** *(paysan, village)* Cypriot,
  Cypriote; *(paysage)* Cypriot, Cyprus *(avant n)*
  ◻ **Cypriote NMF** Cypriot, Cypriote
Cypris [sipris] **NM** *Zool* Cypris, water-flea
Cyrénaïque [sirenaik] **ADJ 1** *(de Cyrène)* Cyrenian
  2 *Phil* Cyrenaic
    NMF 1 *(habitant de Cyrène)* Cyrenian **2** *Phil*
  Cyrenaic
    NF *Géog* Cyrenaica
cyrillique [sirilik] **ADJ** Cyrillic
Cyrus [sirys] **NPR** Cyrus
cystalgie [sistalʒi] **NF** *Méd* cystalgia
cystectomie [sistɛktɔmi] **NF** *Méd* cystectomy

cystéine [sistein] **NF** *Biol & Chim* cysteine
cysticerque [sistisɛrk] **NM** *Zool* bladder worm,
  Spéc cysticercus
cystine [sistin] **NF** *Chim* cystine
cystinose [sistinoz] **NF** *Méd* cystinosis
cystique [sistik] **ADJ** *Méd* cystic
cystite [sistit] **NF** *Méd* cystitis
cystogramme [sistɔgram] **NF** *Méd* cystogram
cystographie [sistɔgrafi] **NF** *Méd* cystography
cystoscope [sistɔskɔp] **NM** *Méd* cystoscope
cystoscopie [sistɔskɔpi] **NF** *Méd* cystoscopy
cystostomie [sistɔstɔmi] **NF** *Méd* cystostomy
cytaphérèse [sitaferɛz] **NF** *Méd* cytapheresis
Cythère [sitɛr] **NF** Cythera
cytise [sitiz] **NM** *Bot* laburnum, golden rain
cytobiologie [sitɔbjɔlɔʒi] **NF** cytobiology
cytochrome [sitɔkrom] **NM** *Biol* cytochrome
cytodiagnostic [sitɔdjagnɔstik] **NM** *Méd* cytodi-
  agnosis
cytogénéticien, -enne [sitɔʒenetisjɛ̃, -ɛn] **NM,F**
  Biol cytogeneticist
cytogénétique [sitɔʒenetik] *Biol* **ADJ** cytogenetic
  NF cytogenetics *(singulier)*

cytokine [sitɔkin] **NF** *Biol* cytokinin
cytokinèse [sitɔkinɛz] **NF** *Biol* cytokinesis
cytologie [sitɔlɔʒi] **NF** *Biol* cytology
cytologique [sitɔlɔʒik] **ADJ** *Biol* cytologic, cyto-
  logical
cytologiste [sitɔlɔʒist] **NMF** *Biol* cytologist
cytolyse [sitɔliz] **NF** *Biol* cytolysis
cytolytique [sitɔlitik] **ADJ** *Biol* cytolytic
cytomégalovirus [sitɔmegalɔvirys] **NM** *Méd* cyto-
  megalovirus, CMV
cytoplasme [sitɔplasm] **NM** *Biol* cytoplasm
cytoplasmique [sitɔplasmik] **ADJ** *Biol* cytoplas-
  mic
cytosine [sitɔzin] **NF** *Biol & Chim* cytosine
cytosol [sitɔsɔl] **NM** *Biol* cytosol
cytosquelette [sitɔskɔlɛt] **NM** *Biol* cytoskeleton
cytotoxine [sitɔtɔksin] **NF** *Biol* cytotoxin
cytotoxique [sitɔtɔksik] **ADJ** *Biol* cytotoxic
CZ [sezɛd] **NM** *Aviat* lift
czar [tsar] = **tsar**
czardas [tzardas] = **csardas**
czimbalum [sɛ̃balɔm] **NM** *Mus* cimbalom, cym-
  balom

cyp-czi

D¹, d¹ [de] **NM INV 1** *(lettre)* D, d; **D comme Désiré** ≃ D for dog **2** *Mus (note)* D

D² [de] **NF 1** *(abrév* **route départementale***)* = designation of secondary road **2** *Ftbl (abrév* **division***)* Div; **D1/2/3** Div 1/2/3

D³ *Météo (abrév écrite* **dépression***)* cyclone, barometric depression, low

d² *(abrév écrite* **déci***)* = decilitre of wine

d' [d] *voir* **de**

DA *(abrév écrite* **dinar algérien***)* DA

da *(abrév écrite* **déca-***)* da

DAB [dab] **NM** *(abrév* **distributeur automatique de billets***)* Br cashpoint, Am ATM

dab [dab] **NM** *Fam (père)* old man; **les dabs** *(parents)* folks, Br old dears, Am rents

daba [daba] **NF** *(en Afrique francophone)* = short-handled hoe

dabe [dab] = **dab**

d'abord [dabɔr] *voir* **abord**

d'ac [dak] **ADV** *Fam* OK; **on y va, d.?** we're going, OK?; **être d. (avec qn)** to agree▪ (with sb)

da capo [dakapo] **ADV** *Mus* da capo

Dacca [daka] **NM** *(jusqu'en 1982)* Dacca; *(depuis 1982)* Dhaka

d'accord [dakɔr] *voir* **accord**

dace [das] *Antiq* **ADJ** Dacian
   NMF Dacian

Dachau [daʃo] **N** Dachau

d'acodac [dakodak] **ADV** *Fam* OK; **on y va? – d.!** are we going? – OK!

dacquois, -e [dakwa, -az] **ADJ** of/from Dax
   ▫ **Dacquois, -e NM,F** = inhabitant of or person from Dax

Dacron® [dakrɔ̃] **NM** *Br* Terylene®, *Am* Dacron®

dacryadénite [dakriadenit] **NF** *Méd* dacryadenitis

dacryocystite [dakriɔsistit] **NF** *Méd* dacryocystitis

dactyle [daktil] **NM 1** *Littérature* dactyl, dactylic **2** *Bot* cocksfoot

dactylique [daktilik] **ADJ** dactylic

dactylo [daktilo] **NMF** *(personne)* typist
   NF *(technique)* typing; **prendre des cours de d.** to learn how to type
   NM *Can Vieilli (machine à écrire)* typewriter

dactylogramme [daktilɔgram] **NM** dactylogram, fingerprint

dactylographe [daktilɔgraf] **NMF** typist

dactylographie [daktilɔgrafi] **NF** typing, typewriting; **prendre des cours de d.** to learn how to type

dactylographier [9] [daktilɔgrafje] **VT** to type (up)

dactylographique [daktilɔgrafik] **ADJ** typing

dactylologie [daktilɔlɔʒi] **NF** dactylology

dactyloscopie [daktilɔskɔpi] **NF** fingerprinting, fingerprint identification

dada [dada] **ADJ** *Beaux-Arts & Littérature* Dadaist, Dadaistic; **le mouvement d.** Dada, Dadaism
   NM 1 *Beaux-Arts & Littérature* Dada, Dadaism
   2 *(en langage enfantin) (cheval)* horsey, *Br* gee-gee; **à d.** on horseback
   3 *Fam (passe-temps)* hobby▪; *(idée)* hobbyhorse▪; **le voilà reparti sur** *ou* **il a enfourché son d.** he's off on his hobby-horse again; **c'est son nouveau d.** it's his latest obsession▪

dadais [dadɛ] **NM** oaf; **grand d.** clumsy oaf

dadaïsme [dadaism] **NM** *Beaux-Arts & Littérature* Dada, Dadaism

dadaïste [dadaist] *Beaux-Arts & Littérature* **ADJ** Dadaist, Dadaistic
   NMF Dadaist

DADS [deadɛs] **NF** *Admin (abrév* **déclaration annuelle des données sociales***)* ≃ PAYE and NIC return

DAF [deaɛf] **ADJ** *Com (abrév* **delivered at frontier***)* DAF

dague [dag] **NF 1** *(poignard)* dagger; **d. de chasse** large hunting knife **2** *Zool (du cerf)* spike

daguerréotype [dagerɛɔtip] **NM** daguerreotype

daguerréotypie [dagerɛɔtipi] **NF** daguerreotypy

daguet [dagɛ] **NM** *Zool* young male deer, brocket

dahabieh [daabje] **NF** *Naut* dahabiyah, dahabiyeh, dahabieh

dahlia [dalja] **NM** dahlia

Dahomey [daɔmɛ] **NM** *Anciennement* **le D.** Dahomey; **aller au D.** to go to Dahomey; **vivre au D.** to live in Dahomey

dahu [day] **NM** imaginary animal *(featuring in stories told to the gullible)*

daïdzéine [daidzein] **NF** *Biol & Chim* daidzein

daigner [4] [deɲe] **VT d. faire qch** to deign to do sth

daim [dɛ̃] **NM 1** *Zool (fallow)* deer; **d. mâle** buck **2** *(cuir suédé)* suede; **de d., en d.** suede *(avant n)*

daïmio, daimyo [daimjo] **NM INV** *Hist* daimio

daine [dɛn] **NF** *Zool* doe *(female fallow deer)*

daiquiri [dajkiri] **NM** daiquiri

dais [dɛ] **NM** canopy

Dakar [dakar] **NM** Dakar

dakin [dakɛ̃] **NM** *Chim* Dakin's solution

Dakota [dakɔta] **NM le D.** Dakota; **au D.** in Dakota; **le D. du Nord/Sud** North/South Dakota; **dans le D. du Nord/Sud** in North/South Dakota

dal¹ *(abrév écrite* **décalitre***)* dal

dal² [dal] **que dal** *voir* **dalle**

dalaï-lama [dalailama] *(pl* **dalaï-lamas***)* **NM** Dalai Lama

daleau, -x [dalo] **NM 1** *Naut* scupper **2** *Constr* culvert

Dalila [dalila] **NPR** *Bible* Delilah

dallage [dalaʒ] **NM** *(action)* paving; *(surface)* pavement

dalle [dal] **NF 1** *(plaque → de pierre)* flagstone; *(→ de moquette, de lino)* tile; **d. de marbre/pierre** marble/stone slab; **recouvrir une allée de dalles** to surface a driveway with stone slabs; **d. funéraire** tombstone
   2 *Constr* slab; **d. de béton** concrete slab; **d. pleine** reinforced concrete slab; **d. de recouvrement** cover slab
   3 *Can Vieilli (gouttière)* gutter; *(tuyau de descente)* drainpipe; *(dans une étable)* = channel for collecting manure
   4 *Fam (faim)* **avoir** *ou* **crever la d.** to be starving *or* famished; **je crève la d.** I could eat a horse
   5 *Fam (locution)* **avoir la d. en pente** to be a boozer, to be fond of the bottle
   ▫ **que dalle ADV** *Fam* zilch, *Br* sweet FA; **j'y comprends que d.** I don't understand a damn *or Br* bloody thing

daller [3] [dale] **VT** to pave

dalleur [dalœr] **NM** paviour

Dalloz [daloz] **NM INV les D.** = series of law reference books

dalmate [dalmat] **ADJ** Dalmatian
   ▫ **Dalmate NMF** Dalmatian

Dalmatie [dalmasi] **NF la D.** Dalmatia

dalmatien [dalmasjɛ̃] **NM** Dalmatian (dog)

dalmatique [dalmatik] **NF** dalmatic

dalot [dalo] **NM 1** *Naut* scupper **2** *Constr* culvert

dalton [daltɔn] **NM** *Chim* dalton

daltonien, -enne [daltɔnjɛ̃, -ɛn] **ADJ** colour-blind, *Spéc* daltonic
   NM,F colour-blind person

daltonisme [daltɔnism] **NM** colour blindness, *Spéc* daltonism

dam¹ *(abrév écrite* **décamètre***)* dam

dam² [dam] **NM** *Rel* **peine du d.** eternal damnation
   ▫ **au grand dam de PRÉP** *Littéraire (à son préjudice)* to the detriment of; *(à son mécontentement)* to the great displeasure of

damage [damaʒ] **NM** *(de la terre)* packing (down), ramming down; *(de la neige)* packing down; *(d'une piste)* grooming

damalisque [damalisk] **NM** *Zool* topi

daman [damɑ̃] **NM** *Zool* hyrax, dassie

Damas [damas] **NM** Damascus

damas [dama(s)] **NM 1** *Tex* damask **2** *Bot* damson **3** *Métal* damask steel

damasquinage [damaskinaʒ] **NM** *Métal* damascening

damasquiner [3] [damaskine] **VT** *Métal* to damascene

damassé, -e [damase] **ADJ** damask *(avant n)*
   NM damask

damasser [3] [damase] **VT** to damask

damassine [damasin] **NF** *Suisse (fruit)* plum; *(eau de vie)* plum brandy

damassure [damasyr] **NF** *Tex* damask design

dame [dam] **NF 1** *(femme)* lady; **nous parlions avec ces dames** we were talking to these ladies; **que prendront ces dames?** what will you have, ladies?; *Jur* **la d. Simon** Mrs Simon; **D. Nature** Mother Nature; *Fam* **ah, ma bonne** *ou* **pauvre d., les temps ont bien changé!** ah, my dear, times have changed!; *Fam* **qu'est-ce que je vous sers, ma petite d.?** what would you like, miss *or Br* love?; **d. de charité** Lady Bountiful; **d. de compagnie** lady's companion; **la D. de fer** the Iron Lady; **d. patronnesse** Lady Bountiful; *Fam* **d. pipi** toilet attendant▪
   2 *Fam (épouse)* **votre d.** your old lady
   3 *(femme noble)* lady; **une grande d.** a (noble) lady; **les dames de France** the royal princesses of France; **la première d. de France** France's First Lady; **d. d'honneur** lady-in-waiting; *Péj* **faire** *ou* **jouer les grandes dames** to put on airs; **sa d., la d. de ses pensées** his ladylove
   4 *(aux dames)* king; *Cartes & Échecs* queen; **aller à la** *ou* **mener un pion à d.** *(aux dames)* to crown a king; *Échecs* to queen a pawn; *Cartes* **la d. de cœur** the queen of hearts
   5 *Naut* **d. de nage** rowlock, oarlock, swivel
   6 *Constr (mur)* **d. de remblai** dam
   7 *(outil de pavage)* beetle, rammer
   EXCLAM *Vieilli* of course!; **d. oui!** yes, indeed!
   ▫ **dames NFPL (jeu de) dames** *Br* draughts, *Am* checkers
   ▫ **de dames, pour dames ADJ** *(bicyclette)* ladies'

═══════════════

'La Dame aux camélias' *Dumas* 'The Lady of the Camellias'

──────────

dame-d'onze-heures [damdɔ̃zœr] *(pl* **dames-d'onze-heures***)* **NF** *Bot* star-of-Bethlehem, starflower

dame-jeanne [damʒan] *(pl* **dames-jeannes***)* **NF** demijohn

damer [3] [dame] **VT 1** *(tasser → terre)* to ram down, to pack down; *(→ neige)* to pack down; *(→ piste)* to groom **2** *(pion → aux dames)* to crown; *(→ aux échecs)* to queen; *Fig* **d. le pion à qn** to outwit sb

dameuse [damøz] **NF** *Ski* piste basher

damiana [damjana] **NM** *Bot* damiana

damier [damje] **NM** *Br* draughtboard, *Am* checkerboard; **un tissu à** *ou* **en d.** *Br* checked *or Am* checkered material

damnable [danabl] **ADJ** *Littéraire (qui mérite la damnation)* damnable; *(répréhensible)* to be condemned

damnation [danasjɔ̃] **NF** *Rel* damnation
   EXCLAM *Arch* damnation!

'La Damnation de Faust' *Berlioz* 'The Damnation of Faust'

damné, -e [dane] **ADJ 1** *Fam Péj (maudit)* cursed, damn, damned **2** *Rel* damned
NM,F *Rel* damned person *or* soul; **les damnés** the damned

'Les Damnés de la terre' *Fanon* 'The Wretched of the Earth'

damner [3] [dane] **VT** *Rel* to damn; *Littéraire* **dieu me damne!** damn!; *Fam Fig* **faire d. qn** to drive sb crazy *or Br* round the bend
▸**se damner VPR** to damn oneself; **je me damnerais pour un chocolat** I'd give anything for a chocolate

Damoclès [damɔklɛs] **NPR** *Myth* Damocles; **l'épée de D.** the sword of Damocles

damoiseau, -x [damwazo] **NM 1** *Hist (gentilhomme)* (young) squire **2** *Hum (jeune empressé)* (dashing) young blade

damoiselle [damwazɛl] **NF** *Hist* **1** *(fille noble)* damsel *(title given to an unmarried noblewoman)* **2** *(femme de damoiseau)* (young) squire's wife

damper [dampœr] **NM** *Aut* damper

dan [dan] **NM** dan; **premier/deuxième d.** first/second dan

danaïde [danaid] **NF** *Entom* monarch butterfly

Danaïdes [danaid] **NPR** *Myth* **les D.** Danaides

dancing [dɑ̃siŋ] **NM** dance hall

dandin [dɑ̃dɛ̃] **NM** *Fam Vieilli* simpleton, ninny

dandinement [dɑ̃dinmɑ̃] **NM** *(d'un canard, d'une personne)* waddling; **son d. a fait rire tout le monde** everybody was laughing at the way he/she waddled about

dandiner [3] [dɑ̃dine] **se dandiner VPR** *(canard, personne)* to waddle; **il est entré/sorti en se dandinant** he waddled in/out; **se d. d'un pied sur l'autre** to shift from foot to foot

dandinette [dɑ̃dinɛt] **NF 1** *(technique)* dapping **2** *(appât)* dap

dandy [dɑ̃di] **NM** dandy

dandysme [dɑ̃dism] **NM** dandyism

Danemark [danmark] **NM le D.** Denmark; **aller au D.** to go to Denmark; **vivre au D.** to live in Denmark

danger [dɑ̃ʒe] **NM** danger; **attention d.!** danger!; **les dangers de la route** the hazards of the road; **en grand d. de** in great danger of; **en d. de mort** in danger of one's life; **il y a un d. d'inondation** there is a danger of flooding; *Fam* **il n'y a pas de d. qu'il dise oui** it's not likely he'll say yes; *Fam* **moi, t'accompagner? pas de d.!** you mean I'd have to go with you? no way! *or Br* no danger!; *Fam* **d. public** public menace
❑ **en danger ADJ être en d.** *(personne)* to be in danger; *(paix, honneur)* to be jeopardized; **la patrie est en d.** the nation is under threat; **ses jours sont en d.** there are fears for his/her life; **ses jours ne sont plus en d.** his/her condition is now stable; **mettre qn en d.** to put sb's life at risk; **mettre un projet en d.** to jeopardize a project
❑ **sans danger ADJ** *(médicament)* safe; **c'est sans d., ouvre-le** it's safe, open it **ADV** safely; **tu peux y aller sans d.** it's quite safe (to go there)

dangereuse [dɑ̃ʒrøz] *voir* **dangereux**

dangereusement [dɑ̃ʒrøzmɑ̃] **ADV** dangerously, perilously

dangereux, -euse [dɑ̃ʒrø, -øz] **ADJ 1** *(risqué)* dangerous, perilous, hazardous; **zone dangereuse** danger area *or* zone; **baignade/escalade dangereuse** *(sur panneau)* danger, no swimming/no climbing **2** *(nuisible)* dangerous, harmful; **les couleuvres ne sont pas dangereuses** grass snakes are harmless; **c'est d. pour la santé** it's bad for *or* harmful to your health

dangerosité [dɑ̃ʒrozite] **NF** *Littéraire* dangerousness

danien, -enne [danjɛ̃, -ɛn] *Géol* **ADJ** Danian
NM Danian

danois, -e [danwa, -az] **ADJ** Danish
NM 1 *(langue)* Danish **2** *(chien)* Great Dane
❑ **Danois, -e NM,F** Dane; **les D.** the Danish

DANS [dɑ̃]

> in **1, 4–6** ▪ within **1, 4** ▪ into **1** ▪ out of **2** ▪ through **3** ▪ during **4** ▪ around, about **7**

PRÉP 1 *(dans l'espace → gén)* in; *(→ avec des limites)* within; *(→ avec mouvement)* into; **ils ont cherché partout d. la maison** they looked through the whole house, they looked everywhere in the house; **il pleut d. tout le pays** it's raining all over the country; **d. la rue** in the street; **d. le métro** *(wagon)* on the underground; *(couloirs)* in the underground; **d. le train/l'avion** on the train/the plane; **monte d. la voiture** get in *or* into the car; **partout d. le monde** all over the world, the world over; **d. le quartier** in the neighbourhood; **habiter d. Paris** to live in (central) Paris; **d. l'espace** in space; **je suis bien d. ces chaussures** I feel comfortable in these shoes, these shoes are comfortable; **avoir mal d. le dos** to have backache; **ils se sont couchés d. l'herbe** they lay down in *or* on the grass; **elle avait des reflets d'or d. les cheveux** she had golden highlights in her hair; **j'aime être d. tes bras** I love being in your arms; **prenant sa tête d. ses mains** holding his/her head in his/her hands; **d. ces murs** within these walls; **le triangle est inscrit d. le cercle** the triangle is circumscribed within the circle; **d. un rayon de 15 km** within a 15 km radius; **restez d. les limites du parc** stay within the boundaries of the estate; **entrer d. une pièce** to go into a room; **passez d. la salle d'attente** go into the waiting room; **plonger d. une piscine** to dive into a swimming-pool; **tomber d. l'escalier** to fall down the stairs; **mettre qch d. une boîte** to put sth in(to) a box; **jette-le d. le vide-ordures** throw it down the chute; **prendre qn d. ses bras** to take sb in one's arms; **d. la brume/pénombre** in the mist/dark; **je n'arrivais pas à l'entendre d. ce vacarme** I couldn't hear him/her in all that noise; **elle a une profonde tristesse d. le regard** there is a great deal of sadness in her eyes; **d. Descartes** in (the works of) Descartes; **d. son dernier film** in his/her last movie *or Br* film; **c'est d. le journal** it's in the paper

2 *(à partir de → prendre, boire, manger)* out of, from; **j'ai pris l'argent d. le tiroir** I took the money out of *or* from the drawer; **boire d. un verre** to drink out of *or* from a glass; **copier qch d. un livre** to copy sth out of *or* from a book; **la phrase a été prise d. mon discours** the quote was lifted from my speech; *Culin* **un morceau d. la poitrine** a cut off the breast

3 *(à travers)* through; **passe le doigt d. l'anneau** put your finger through the ring; **ils progressaient lentement d. la neige** they were making slow progress through the snow; **un murmure a couru d. la foule** a murmur ran through the crowd

4 *(dans le temps → gén)* in; *(→ insistant sur la durée)* during; *(→ indiquant un délai)* within; **d. l'Antiquité** in Antiquity; **d. son enfance** in *or* during his/her childhood, when he/she was a child; **c'était à la mode d. les années 50** it was fashionable in *or* during the 50s; **être d. sa vingt-cinquième année** to be in one's twenty-fifth year; **d. un déménagement, on casse toujours quelque chose** when you move house, something always gets broken; **les gaz qui se dégagent d. une réaction chimique** gases given off in a chemical reaction; **je n'ai qu'un jour de libre d. la semaine** I only have one day off during the week; **l'avion atterrit d. 25 minutes** the plane will be landing in 25 minutes *or* 25 minutes' time; **d. dix ans, on ne parlera plus de son livre** in ten years *or* years' time, his book will be forgotten; **d. quelques minutes, la suite de notre programme** normal service will be resumed as soon as possible; **vous serez livré d. la semaine** you'll get the delivery within the week *or* some time this week; **je passerai d. l'après-midi** I'll call by in *or* during the afternoon; **à consommer d. les cinq jours** eat within five days of purchase; **arriver d. l'heure qui suit** to arrive within the next hour

5 *(indiquant l'appartenance à un groupe)* **d. l'enseignement** in *or* within the teaching profession; **il est d. le commerce** he's in business; **quelqu'un d. l'assistance** someone in the audience; **être d. l'Union européenne** to be in *or* a member of the European Union; **il est d. mon équipe** he's on *or* in my team; **d. nos rangs** within our ranks; **nous sommes d. le même club** we're in *or* we belong to the same club; **ministre de la Santé d. le dernier gouvernement** Minister of Health in the last government

6 *(indiquant la manière, l'état)* **d. son sommeil** in his/her sleep; **mettre qn d. l'embarras** to put sb in an awkward situation; **mourir d. la misère** to die in poverty; **tomber d. l'oubli** to sink into oblivion; **je ne suis pas d. le secret** I haven't been let in on *or* I'm not in on the secret; **d. sa hâte, elle a perdu une chaussure** in her haste, she lost a shoe; **d. l'effervescence des préparatifs** in the excitement of the preparations; **il la voyait d. son délire** in his delirium he thought he could see her; **je ne peux pas travailler d. le bruit** I can't work when it's noisy; **je l'ai fait d. ce but** I did it with this aim in mind; **d. le but de** in order to, with the aim of; **d. l'espoir de** in the hope of; **je l'aime bien d. ce rôle** I like him/her in this role; **une maison bâtie d. le style Régence** a house built in Regency style; **un contrat rédigé d. les formes légales** a contract drawn out *or* up in legal terms; **prendre un mot d. son sens littéral** to take a word in its literal sense *or* literally; **c'est quelqu'un d. ton genre** it's somebody like you

7 *(indiquant une approximation)* **d. les** around, about; **ça coûtera d. les 200 euros** it'll cost around 200 euros; **il était d. les cinq heures du soir** it was around five p.m.; **il doit avoir d. les 50 ans** he must be about 50

dansable [dɑ̃sabl] **ADJ la musique que les jeunes écoutent maintenant n'est pas d.** you can't dance to the music that young people listen to nowadays

dansant, -e [dɑ̃sɑ̃, -ɑ̃t] **ADJ 1** *(qui danse)* dancing; *Fig (reflet)* shimmering, dancing; *(lueur)* flickering **2** *(qui invite à danser)* **un rythme d.** a rhythm which makes you want to (get up and) dance **3** *(où l'on danse)* **soirée dansante** dance; **thé d.** tea dance

danse [dɑ̃s] **NF 1** *(activité)* dancing; **il aime la d.** he likes dancing; **entrer dans la d.** to join in the dance; *Fig* to join in; **conduire** *ou* **mener la d.** to lead the dance; *Fig* to call the tune; *Can* **d. callée** = folk dance led by a caller; *Can* **d. carrée** square dance; **d. classique** ballet (dancing), classical dancing; **d. folklorique** folk dancing; **d. sur glace** ice-dancing; **d. paysanne** country dancing; **d. de salon** ballroom dancing; **d. aux tables** table dancing; **d. du ventre** belly dancing

2 *(suite de pas → dans un ballet, au bal)* dance; **jouer une d.** to play a dance (tune); **la d. des reflets sur le lac** reflections dancing on the surface of the lake; **la d. des hirondelles dans les airs** swallows swooping back and forth in the sky; **d. folklorique** folk dance; **d. de salon** ballroom dance

3 *(agitation)* **c'est la d. des valeurs ce mois-ci à la Bourse** share values are fluctuating this month on the Stock Exchange

4 *Méd* **d. de Saint-Guy** St Vitus' dance; *Fam* **tu as la d. de Saint-Guy, ou quoi?** can't you stop fidgeting?

5 *très Fam (correction)* hiding, thrashing, belting; **flanquer une d. à qn** to beat the living daylights out of sb

6 *Beaux-Arts* **d. macabre** dance of death, danse macabre

danser [3] [dɑ̃se] **VI 1** *(évoluer)* to dance; **vous dansez?** would you like to dance?; **on danse?** shall we (have a) dance?; *Fig* **d. sur une corde raide** to walk a tightrope; **faire d. qn** *(sujet: cavalier)* to (have a) dance with sb; *(sujet: musicien)* to play dance tunes for sb; *Fam* **chez nous, on dansait devant le buffet** at home, the cupboard was always bare

2 *(bouger → reflet, bouchon)* to move, to bob up and down; *(→ mots, lignes)* to swim; **tout dansait devant ses yeux** everything was swimming before his/her eyes; **le vent faisait d. la flamme** the flame flickered in the wind

VT to dance; **d. une valse/un tango** to (dance a) waltz/tango; **d. 'Casse-Noisette'** to dance *or* to perform the 'Nutcracker Suite'
▸**se danser VPR un ballet qui se danse en costumes modernes** a ballet performed in contemporary dress; **le twist ne se danse plus** nobody dances the twist any more

danseur, -euse [dɑ̃sœr, -øz] **NM,F 1** *(gén)* dancer; *(de ballet)* ballet dancer; **danseuse de cabaret** cabaret dancer; **d. de claquettes** tap-dancer; **d. de corde** tightrope walker; **d. étoile** principal dancer; **danseuse étoile** prima ballerina; **danseuse orientale** belly dancer; *Fig* **entretenir une danseuse** *(avoir une maîtresse)* to keep a mistress; *(avoir un passe-temps coûteux)* to indulge in an expensive hobby
2 *(cavalier)* **mon d.** my partner
NM d. mondain (male) escort
▫ **danseuse ADJ F** flexible, yielding
▫ **en danseuse ADV se mettre en danseuse** to stand up on the pedals; **monter la colline en danseuse** to cycle up the hill standing on the pedals

'Danseuses dans les coulisses' *Degas* 'Dancers in the Wings'

dansoter, dansotter [3] [dɑ̃sɔte] **VI** *Fam* to dance around▪
Dante [dɑ̃t] **NPR** Dante
dantesque [dɑ̃tɛsk] **ADJ** *Littéraire* Dantean, Dantesque
Danube [danyb] **NM le D.** the (River) Danube
danubien, -enne [danybjɛ̃, -ɛn] **ADJ** Danubian
DAO [deao] **NM** *(abrév* **dessin assisté par ordinateur***)* CAD
dao [dao] **NM** Tao
daphné [dafne] **NM** *Bot* daphne
daphnie [dafni] **NF** *Entom* water flea, *Spéc* daphnia
daraise [darɛz] **NF** *(d'un étang)* outlet
darbouka [darbuka] **NF** *(instrument de percussion)* darbouka
darbysme [darbism] **NM** *Rel* Darbyism
darbyste [darbist] *Rel* **ADJ** of the Plymouth Brethren
NMF member of the Plymouth Brethren; **les darbystes** the Plymouth Brethren
DARC [dark] **NF** *(abrév* **data radio channel***)* DARC
darce [dars] **NF** *(en Méditerranée)* harbour basin
dard [dar] **NM 1** *(d'une abeille, d'une guêpe)* sting; *(d'un serpent)* forked tongue **2** *Hist* javelin **3** *Pêche* spear, harpoon **4** *Vulg* dick, prick, cock
Dardanelles [dardanɛl] **NFPL** *voir* **détroit**
darder [3] [darde] **VT 1** *(lancer)* to shoot; **le soleil du matin dardait ses rayons sur la plage** shafts of morning sunlight fell on the beach; **d. un regard furieux sur qn** to shoot sb an angry look **2** *(dresser)* to point; **une rose qui darde ses épines** a rose pointing its thorns
dare-dare [dardar] **ADV** *Fam* double-quick, on the double; **va chercher la boîte, et d.!** go and get the box, and be quick about it!
Dar es-Salaam [darɛssalam] **NM** *Géog* Dar es-Salaam
Darfour [darfur] **NM** *Géog* Darfur
dari[1] [dari] **NM** *Agr* Indian millet, durra
dari[2] [dari] **NM** *Ling* dari
dariole [darjɔl] **NF** *Culin (dessert)* = type of light custard tart; *(moule)* dariole
Darios [darjos], **Darius** [darjys] **NPR** *Hist* Darius
Darjeeling [darʒiliŋ] **NM 1** *(ville)* Darjeeling **2** *(thé)* Darjeeling (tea)
Darling [darliŋ] **N** *Géog* Darling
darne [darn] **NF** steak, thick slice *(cut across the fish)*; **d. de saumon** salmon steak
daron [darɔ̃] **NM** *Fam (père)* old man
daronne [darɔn] **NF** *Fam (mère)* old lady
darsana [darʃana] = **darshana**
darse [dars] = **darce**
darshana [darʃana] **NM 1** *Phil* darshana **2** *Rel* darshana
dartois [dartwa] **NM** *Culin* dartois pastry *(two puff pastry rectangles forming a sweet or savoury sandwich when filled)*
dartre [dartr] **NF** *Méd* dartre; **avoir des dartres** to have dry patches on one's skin
dartreux, -euse [dartrø, -øz] **ADJ** *Méd* dartrous
dartrose [dartroz] **NF** *Bot* dartrose
Darwin [darwin] **NPR** Darwin
NM *Géog* Darwin
darwinien, -enne [darwinjɛ̃, -ɛn] **ADJ** Darwinian
darwinisme [darwinism] **NM** Darwinism
darwiniste [darwinist] **ADJ** Darwinist, Darwinistic
NMF Darwinist
DAS [deaɛs] **NM** *Com & Mktg (abrév* **domaine d'activité stratégique***)* SBU
dasein [dazajn] **NM** *Phil* Dasein
dasyure [dazjyr] **NM** *Zool* Australian native cat, *Spéc* dasyure
DAT [deate] **NM INV** *(abrév* **digital audio tape***)* DAT
datable [databl] **ADJ** datable, dateable; **ces rochers sont facilement/difficilement datables** these rocks are easy to date/are not easily dated
datage [dataʒ] **NM le d. de qch** assigning a date to *or* dating sth
DATAR, Datar [datar] **NF** *(abrév* **Délégation à l'aménagement du territoire et à l'action régionale***)* = regional land development agency
data room [datarum] **NF** *Com* data room
datation [datasjɔ̃] **NF** dating; **il y a eu une erreur de d. du fossile** the fossil was incorrectly dated; **d. au carbone 14** carbon dating; *Chim* **d. au potassium-argon** potassium-argon dating
datcha [datʃa] **NF** dacha
date [dat] **NF 1** *(moment précis)* date; **je n'arrive pas à lire la d.** I can't read the date; **une lettre sans d.** an undated letter; **la lettre porte la d. du 5 mai** the letter is dated 5 May; **nous avons fixé la d. de la conférence au 13 juin** we have decided to hold the conference on 13 June; **à quelle d. arrivent-ils?** what date are they arriving on?; **se retrouver chaque année à d. fixe** to meet on the same day every year; *Com & Fin* **à 30 jours de d.** 30 days after date; **prenons d.** let's decide on a date; **d. d'achèvement** completion date, date of completion; **d. de base** base date; **d. butoir** deadline, cut-off date; **d. de clôture** closing date; **d. de départ** date of departure; *Fin* **d. d'échéance** *(de dû)* maturity date, due date; *(de terme)* expiry date; **d. d'émission** date of issue; **d. d'exécution** completion date; **d. d'exigibilité** due date; **d. d'expiration** expiry date; **d. de facturation** invoice date; *Banque & Fin* **d. de jouissance** date from which interest begins to run; **d. limite** *(pour un projet)* deadline; **d. limite de consommation** best-before date; **d. limite de paiement** deadline for payment; **d. limite de vente** sell-by date; **d. de livraison** delivery date; **d. de naissance** date of birth; *Fin* **d. d'ouverture de l'exercice** first day of the *Br* financial *or Am* fiscal year; **d. de péremption** *(d'un document)* expiry date; *(d'un aliment)* use-by date; **d. de remise** remittance date; *Banque* **d. de valeur** value date; **d. de validité** expiry date
2 *(période)* date; **à la d. dont tu me parles, j'étais encore aux États-Unis** at the time you're telling me about, I was still in the United States; **à cette d. j'étais déjà parti** I'd already left by then; **les grandes dates de notre histoire** the most important dates in our history; **c'est une réalisation qui fera d. (dans l'histoire)** it's an achievement which will stand out (in history); **de longue d.** long-standing; **une amitié de longue d.** a long-standing friendship; **ils se connaissent de longue d.** they've known each other for a long time; **c'est une amitié de fraîche d.** they haven't been friends for very long
▫ **en date ADV qui est sa dernière conquête en d.?** who is his latest conquest?
▫ **en date du PRÉP lettre en d. du 28 juin** letter dated 28 June
dater [3] [date] **VT 1** *(inscrire la date)* to date, to put a date on; **carte datée de mardi/du 20** postcard dated Tuesday/the 20th
2 *(déterminer l'âge de → fossile, manuscrit, édifice)* to date
VI 1 *(compter)* to stand out, to be a milestone; **cet événement datera dans sa vie** this event will stand out in his/her life
2 *(être désuet → tenue)* to look dated *or* old-fashioned; *(→ expression)* to sound old-fashioned; *(→ film)* to show its age, to have aged, to be dated
▫ **dater de VT IND** to date from, to go back to; **un livre qui date du XVIIème siècle** a book dating back to the 17th century; **de quand date votre dernière visite?** when was your last visit?; **notre amitié ne date pas d'hier** we go *or* our friendship goes back a long way; **voilà une idée qui ne date pas d'hier** this idea's been around for quite some time; **ça date d'avant notre rencontre** it happened before we met
▫ **à dater de PRÉP à d. de ce jour** *(d'aujourd'hui)* from today; *(de ce jour-là)* from that day; **à d. du 1er mars, vous ne faites plus partie du service** as of *or* effective from 1 March, you are no longer on the staff
dateur [datœr] **ADJ M** *voir* **timbre**[1]
NM date stamp; **d. automatique de billets** ticket-dating machine
datif, -ive [datif, -iv] **ADJ** *Jur* **tuteur d.** guardian appointed by a court; **tutelle dative** trusteeship *or* guardianship ordered by a court
NM *Ling* dative; **au d.** in the dative
dation [dasjɔ̃] **NF** *(action de donner)* giving, conferring; **d. en paiement** accord and satisfaction
dative [dativ] *voir* **datif**
datte [dat] **NF** date *(fruit)*; **il n'en** *Fam* **fiche** *ou très Fam* **fout pas une d.** he doesn't do a damn thing, *Br* he does bugger all
dattier [datje] **NM** date palm
datura [datyra] **NM** *Bot* datura, *Am* stinkweed, jimsonweed; **d. stramonium** thorn-apple
daube [dob] **NF 1** *Culin* stew; **bœuf en d.** beef braised in red wine **2** *Suisse Fam* idiot **3** *Fam* **c'est de la d.** it's (a load of) *Br* rubbish *or Am* garbage
dauber [3] [dobe] **VT** *Littéraire* to mock
VI 1 *Littéraire (se moquer)* to jeer, to scoff **2** *Fam (sentir mauvais)* to stink, *Br* to pong
daubeur, -euse [dobœr, -øz] **ADJ** *Littéraire* mocking
NM,F *Littéraire* scoffer, mocker
NM *Métal* smith's hammerman
daubière [dobjɛr] **NF** *Culin* = earthenware pot for braising
dauffer [3] [dofe] **VT** *Vulg* **d. qn** to bugger sb, to fuck sb up the *Br* arse *or Am* ass
dauphin[1] [dofɛ̃] **NM 1** *Zool* dolphin; **grand d.** bottlenosed dolphin; **d. blanc** beluga (whale); **d. à gros nez** bottlenosed dolphin; **d. souffleur** bottlenosed dolphin **2** *(tuyau)* shoe
dauphin[2]**, -e** [dofɛ̃, -fin] **NM,F 1** *Hist* **le d.** the dauphin; **la dauphine** the dauphine **2** *(successeur)* heir apparent, successor; **qui est votre d.?** who's in line for your job?
Dauphiné [dofine] **NM** *Géog* **le D.** the Dauphiné (region); *Presse* **le D. libéré** = daily newspaper published in Grenoble
dauphinelle [dofinɛl] **NF** *Bot* delphinium; **d. consoude** forking larkspur
dauphinois, -e [dofinwa, -az] **ADJ** of/from the Dauphiné
▫ **Dauphinois, -e NM,F** = inhabitant of or person from the Dauphiné
daurade [dɔrad] **NF** *Ich* sea bream; **d. grise** black bream; **d. rose** red sea bream; **d. (royale)** gilthead (sea bream)
davantage [davɑ̃taʒ] **ADV 1** *(plus)* more; **donne-m'en d.** give me some more; **tu devrais lire d.** you should read more; **vous êtes riche, mais il l'est bien d.** you're rich, but he's much richer; **je ne t'en dirai pas d.** I won't tell you any more; **je ne l'interrogerai pas d.** I won't question him/her any further; **le droit l'intéresse d. que l'économie** law interests him/her more than economics; **je ne lui ferai pas d. de reproches** I won't reproach him/her any more; **je voudrais d. de cerises** I'd like (some) more cherries; **il a eu d. de chance que les autres** he was luckier than the others
2 *(de plus en plus)* **chaque jour qui passe nous rapproche d.** each day that goes by brings us closer together; **je t'aime chaque jour d.** I love you more and more every day
3 *(plus longtemps)* **je n'attendrai pas d.** I won't wait any longer
David [david] **NPR** *Bible* David
davidien, -enne [davidjɛ̃, -ɛn] *Beaux-Arts* **ADJ** = relating to the artist Jacques-Louis David
NMF = follower of the artist Jacques-Louis David or of his style
davier [davje] **NM 1** *Menuis* cramp **2** *(de dentiste)* forceps

Davis [devis] *voir* **coupe**

dawa(h) [dawa] NM *Fam* havoc; **ils arrêtent pas de foutre le d. en classe** they're always creating havoc in class

Dawha [dɔa] NM (**al-)D.** Doha

day time [dɛtajm] *Rad & TV* ADJ daytime; **l'audience d.** the daytime audience
  NM daytime programming; **transmettre une émission en d.** to broadcast a programme as part of the daytime schedule

dazibao [dazibao] NM = news sheets pasted on the wall in public places

DB [debe] NF *Mil* (*abrév* **division blindée**) armoured division

dB (*abrév écrite* **décibel**) dB

DBO [debeo] NF *Écol* (*abrév* **demande biologique** *ou* **biochimique en oxygène**) BOD

DBS [debeɛs] NM (*abrév* **direct broadcasting satellite**) DBS

DC [dese] NM *Fam* (*abrév* **directeur de la création**) creative director ▪

DCA [deseɑ] NF *Mil* (*abrév* **défense contre les aéronefs**) AA, anti-aircraft

DCC [desese] NM (*abrév* **digital compact cassette**) DCC

Dchesse (*abrév écrite* **duchesse**) Duchess

DCO [deseo] NF *Écol* (*abrév* **demande chimique en oxygène**) COD

DCT [desete] NM *Méd* (*abrév* **diphtérie, coqueluche, tétanos**) DPT

DD [dede] *Ordinat* ADJ (*abrév* **double densité**) DD
  NM (*abrév* **disque dur**) HD

DDA [dedeɑ] NF (*abrév* **Direction départementale de l'agriculture**) = local offices of the Ministry of Agriculture

DDASS, Ddass [das] NF *Admin* (*abrév* **Direction départementale d'action sanitaire et sociale**) = Department of Health and Social Security; **un enfant de la D.** a state orphan

DDD *Électron* (*abrév écrite* **digital digital digital**) DDD

DDE [dedeə] NF (*abrév* **Direction départementale de l'équipement**) = local offices of the Ministry of the Environment
  NM *Ordinat* (*abrév* **dynamic data exchange**) DDE

DDP [dedepe] *Com* (*abrév* **delivered duty paid**) DDP

DDT [dedete] NM *Chim* (*abrév* **dichloro-diphényl-trichloréthane**) DDT

DDU [dedey] *Com* (*abbr* **delivered duty unpaid**) DDU

DE [deə] NM (*abrév* **diplôme d'État**) = recognized qualification

---

DE [də]

> PRÉP from **A1, 2, B1** ▪ by **A3, D** ▪ during **B2** ▪ with **C, D** ▪ for **C** ▪ of **G, H2, 3, I1–3, 6, 7** ▪ in **G**
> ART PARTITIF some **1** ▪ any **3**
> ART INDÉFINI some **1** ▪ any **2**

de becomes **d'** before vowel and h mute; **de + le** is contracted to **du**, and **de + les** to **des**.

PRÉP A. *INDIQUANT L'ORIGINE, LE POINT DE DÉPART* **1** (*indiquant la provenance*) from; **il n'est pas d'ici** he's not from (around) here; **il vient de Paris** he comes from Paris; **la voiture venait de la gauche** the car was coming from the left; **l'express d'Aberdeen** the Aberdeen express; **un vin d'Alsace** an Alsace wine; **une boule s'est décrochée du sapin** a bauble fell off the Christmas tree; **vue de l'intérieur** seen from (the) inside; **il a sorti un lapin de son chapeau** he produced *or* pulled a rabbit out of his hat; **sortir de table** to leave the table; **c'est un cadeau de mon oncle** it's a present from my uncle; **l'idée est de vous** the idea is yours *or* comes from you; **je l'ai oublié? c'est bien de moi** did I forget it? that's just like me

2 (*à partir de*) **de quelques fleurs des champs, elle a fait un bouquet** she made a posy out of *or* from a few wild flowers; **faire un drame de rien** to make a fuss over nothing

3 (*indiquant l'auteur*) by; **un roman de Mishima** a novel by Mishima; **'Amarcord' de Fellini** 'Amarcord' by Fellini, Fellini's 'Amarcord'; **une aria de Bach** a Bach aria; **la statue est de Rodin** the statue is by Rodin

4 (*particule*) **Madame de Sévigné** Madame de Sévigné; *Fam* **épouser un/une de quelque chose** ≃ to marry a man/woman with an aristocratic-sounding name

B. *DANS LE TEMPS* **1** (*à partir de*) from; **notre amitié date de cette époque** our friendship dates from that period; **de ce jour** from that day; **de pauvre, il devint riche** he went from rags to riches

2 (*indiquant le moment*) **de jour** during the *or* by day; **de nuit** during the *or* by night; **travailler de nuit** to work nights; **se lever de bonne heure** to get up early; **je ne l'ai pas vu de la soirée** I haven't seen him all evening; **je ne le vois pas de la semaine** I don't see him at all during the week; **le train de 9 heures 30** the 9.30 train; **le journal d'hier** yesterday's paper; **de longtemps, on n'avait vu cela** such a thing hadn't been seen for a long time

C. *INDIQUANT LA CAUSE* **rougir de plaisir** to blush with pleasure; **mourir de peur/de faim** to die of fright/of hunger; **trembler de froid** to shiver with cold; **pleurer/sauter de joie** to cry/jump for joy; **souffrir de rhumatismes** to suffer from rheumatism; **se tordre de douleur/de rire** to be doubled up in pain/with laughter; **puni de sa gourmandise** punished for his greed

D. *INDIQUANT L'AGENT, LE MOYEN, L'INSTRUMENT* **accompagné de ses amis** accompanied by his friends; **il est détesté de tous** everybody hates him; **faire signe de la main** to wave; **effleurer du doigt** to brush with one's finger; **d'un coup de fouet** with a crack of the whip; **il voit mal de l'œil gauche** he can't see properly with his left eye; **se nourrir de fruits** to eat fruit; **ce champ est entouré d'une palissade** this field is surrounded by a fence; **il a été tué d'une balle** he was killed by a bullet *or* shot dead; **armé de pierres** armed with stones; **poussez la porte du pied** push the door (open) with your foot

E. *INDIQUANT LA MANIÈRE* **manger de bon appétit** to eat heartily; **de toutes ses forces** with all his/her strength; **d'un air coupable** looking guilty, with a guilty look on his/her/*etc* face; **d'un pas décidé** with a purposeful stride

F. *AVEC DES NOMBRES, DES MESURES* **1** (*emploi distributif*) **30 euros de l'heure** 30 euros per *or* an hour; **cinq euros du kilomètre** five euros per *or* a kilometre

2 (*introduisant une mesure*) **un appartement de 60m²** a 60m² *Br* flat *or* *Am* apartment; **un homme d'1 m 80** a man who is 1 m 80 tall; **une hausse de 10 pour cent** a 10 percent increase; **une femme de 30 ans** a 30-year-old woman; **un moteur de 15 chevaux** a 15 h.p. engine; **un cadeau de 200 euros** a gift worth 200 euros; **une pièce de 20 centimes** a 20-cent piece; **un chèque de 100 euros** a cheque for 100 euros; **il a été condamné à deux ans de prison** he was sentenced to two years' imprisonment; **une équipe de 15 personnes** a team of 15

3 (*indiquant une différence dans le temps, l'espace, la quantité*) **distant de cinq kilomètres** five kilometres away; **ma montre retarde de dix minutes** my watch is ten minutes slow; **ce colis est trop lourd de 100 grammes** this parcel is 100 grammes too heavy; **il est plus grand que moi d'une tête** he's a head taller than I am

G. *INDIQUANT L'APPARTENANCE* of; **la maison de mes parents/Marie** my parents'/Marie's house; **le frère de Pierre** Pierre's brother; **la porte du salon** the living-room door; **le toit de la maison** the roof of the house; **les rues de Paris** the streets of Paris; **la chambre du second** the room on the *Br* second *or* *Am* third floor; **les clefs de la voiture** the car keys; **les pays de l'UE** the countries in the EU, the EU countries; **pour les membres du club** for members of the club *or* club members; **pour les joueurs du club** for the players belonging to the club; **les élèves de sa classe** the pupils in his/her class

H. *MARQUANT LA DÉTERMINATION* **1** (*indiquant la matière, la qualité, le genre etc*) **un buffet de chêne** an oak dresser; **un bonhomme de neige** a snowman; **une robe de mariée** a wedding dress; **une équipe de spécialistes** a team of specialists; **une réaction d'horreur** a horrified reaction; **un problème d'algèbre** an algebra problem; **une pause de publicité** a commercial break; **la bataille de Culloden** the battle of Culloden; **la conférence de Berlin** the Berlin conference; **un hôtel de la rive gauche** a hotel on the left bank; **un livre d'un grand intérêt** a book of great interest; **des vêtements d'un goût contestable** clothes of questionable taste; **elle est d'un snob!** she is SO snobbish!, she's such a snob!

2 (*indiquant le contenu, le contenant*) **l'eau de la citerne** the water in the tank; **un verre d'eau** a glass of water; **un pot de fleurs** (*récipient*) a flowerpot; (*fleurs*) a pot of flowers; **une bouteille de whisky** a bottle of whisky; (*récipient*) a whisky bottle

3 (*dans un ensemble*) **la plupart de ses amis** most of his/her friends; **le plus jeune de la classe** the youngest pupil in the class; **le plus jeune des deux** the younger of the two

4 (*avec une valeur emphatique*) **l'as des as** the champ; **le fin du fin** the very latest thing

I. *SERVANT DE LIEN SYNTAXIQUE* **1** (*après un verbe*) **parler de qch** to speak about *or* of sth; **douter de qch** to doubt *or* to have doubts about sth; **se séparer de qn** (*conjoint*) to leave sb, to split up with sb; **cessez de faire qch** to stop doing sth; **se libérer du passé** to free oneself from the past; **se souvenir de qch** to remember sth; **instruire qn de ses intentions** to notify sb of one's plans; **traiter qn de menteur** to call sb a liar

2 (*après un substantif*) **l'amour de qch** the love of sth; **l'acquisition du langage** language acquisition; **troubles de l'audition** hearing problems; **sur présentation de votre carte** on presentation of your card; **la volonté de vaincre** the will to win

3 (*après un adjectif*) **sûr de soi** sure of oneself; **fier de son succès** proud of one's success; **il est facile de critiquer** it's easy to criticize

4 (*après un pronom*) **rien de nouveau** nothing new; **personne d'absent?** nobody missing?; **qui d'autre l'aurait fait?** who else would have done it?; **quoi de plus beau que la mer?** what is more beautiful than the sea?; **y a-t-il quelqu'un de blessé?** is anybody hurt?; **quelque chose de bon** something good

5 (*devant un adjectif, participe ou adverbe*) **c'est une heure de perdue** that's an hour lost; **encore un verre de cassé!** another glass broken!, another broken glass!; **il y a eu trois hommes de tués** three men were killed; **j'ai quelques heures de libres** I have a few hours free; **restez une semaine de plus** stay (for) another *or* an extra week

6 (*introduisant un nom en apposition*) **la ville de Paris** the city of Paris; **le mois de janvier** the month of January; **au mois de janvier** in January; **cet imbécile de Pierre** that idiot Pierre

7 (*indiquant le sujet d'un ouvrage, d'un chapitre*) **De l'Art d'être mère** The Art of Being a Mother; **des dangers du remords** (on) the dangers of remorse

8 (*introduisant un infinitif*) *Littéraire* **de lire me fatigue** reading tires me; *Littéraire* **et tous de rire** they all burst into laughter; **j'aime mieux attendre que de me faire mouiller** I would rather wait than get wet

ART PARTITIF **1** (*dans une affirmation*) **j'ai acheté de la viande** I bought (some) meat; **il me faudra du courage** I'll need (some) courage; **respirer de l'air frais** to breathe fresh air; **c'est de la provocation/de l'entêtement!** it's sheer provocation/pig-headedness!; **j'ai bu de ce vin** I drank some of that wine; **manger de tous les plats** to have some of everything; **écouter de la musique** to listen to music; **manger de la viande** to eat meat; **je ne porte que du coton** I only (ever) wear cotton, I wear nothing but cotton; **je préfère ne boire que de l'eau** I prefer to drink only water *or* nothing but water; **lire du Proust** to read something by Proust *or* some Proust; **chanter du Fauré** to sing some Fauré *or* a piece by Fauré; **c'est du Bach, n'est-ce pas?** it's Bach, isn't it?

de-deb

2 *(dans une interrogation)* **prends-tu du sucre dans ton café?** do you take sugar in your coffee?

3 *(dans une négation)* **il n'y a pas de place** there's no room, there isn't any room; **ils ne vendent pas de viande** they don't sell meat; **n'as-tu pas de lavande dans ton jardin?** haven't you got any lavender in your garden?

4 *(exprimant une comparaison)* **il y a du prophète chez lui** he's a bit like a prophet; **ça c'est du Julien tout craché** *ou* **du pur Julien** that's Julien all over, that's typical of Julien

ART INDÉFINI **1** *(dans une affirmation)* **il a de bonnes idées** he has *or* he's got (some) good ideas; **cela pose de grands problèmes** this poses (some) serious problems; **de grands artistes se trouvaient là** there were some distinguished artists there

2 *(dans une négation)* **je n'ai pas de bouteilles à la cave** I have no *or* I haven't got any bottles in the cellar; **nous ne faisons pas de projets pour cet été** we are not making any plans for this summer; **sans faire de fautes** without making any mistakes; **je ne veux pas qu'on lui mette de collier** I won't have a collar put on him/her

◻ **de... à** PRÉP **1** *(dans l'espace)* from... to; **de Paris à Marseille** from Paris to Marseilles; **du Nord au Midi** from (the) North to (the) South

2 *(dans le temps)* from... to; **du 15 au 20 mars** from 15 to 20 March; **de Noël à Pâques** from Christmas to Easter; **ouvert du lundi au vendredi** open (from) Monday to Friday, *Am* open Monday through Friday; **d'un instant à l'autre** *(bientôt)* any minute *or* time now; **d'ici à demain** by tomorrow

3 *(dans une évolution)* from... to; **passer de la tristesse à la joie** to go from sadness to joy

4 *(dans une énumération)* from... to; **on y trouve tout, des chaussettes aux fours à micro-ondes** they've got everything from socks to microwave ovens

5 *(dans une évaluation)* **ça vaut de 50 à 60 euros** it's worth between 50 and 60 euros; **il y a de 4000 à 5000 emplois en jeu** there are between 4,000 and 5,000 jobs at stake; **des sommes allant de 1500 à 3000 euros** sums between 1,500 and 3,000 euros

6 de vous à moi... between ourselves...

◻ **de... en** PRÉP **1** *(dans l'espace)* from... to; **aller de ville en ville** to go from town to town

2 *(dans le temps)* **de jour en jour** from day to day; **l'espoir s'amenuisait d'heure en heure** hope dwindled as the hours went by; **le nombre d'étudiants augmente d'année en année** the number of students is getting bigger by the year *or* every year *or* from one year to the next

3 *(dans une évolution)* **aller de mal en pis** to go from bad to worse; **de déduction en déduction, il avait trouvé le coupable** he'd deduced who the culprit was; **aller de déception en déception** to go from one disappointment to the next; **un musée où vous irez de surprise en surprise** a museum where surprise after surprise awaits you

dé [de] NM **1** *(pour jouer)* die, dice; **des dés** dice; **jouer aux dés** to play dice; **jeter les dés** to cast the dice; **coup de dé** *ou* **dés** throw of the dice; **jouer qch sur un coup de dés** to gamble sth away; **les dés (en) sont jetés** the die is cast **2** *Culin* cube; **couper du lard en dés** to dice bacon, to cut bacon into dice **3** *Couture* **dé (à coudre)** thimble; **je prendrai un dé à coudre de cognac** I'll have a thimbleful of cognac **4** *Archit (de piédestal)* dado, die

DÉ-/DES-/DÉS- [de, dɛz, dez] PRÉF

• The prefix **dé-** (or its alternative forms **des-** and **dés-**) has three main functions: it can suggest DISTANCE, LOSS or an OPPOSITE EFFECT to that of the word – often a verb – it is added to, eg:

déplacer to move, to displace; **dévier** to swerve, to deviate, to divert; **détourner** to divert, to hijack; **désespoir** dispair; **décapiter** to decapitate; **débrancher** to disconnect, to unplug; **désinstaller** to uninstall; **dépourvu de** devoid of

Note that there are several equivalent English prefixes that can translate **dé-**: *dis-, de-* and *un-*.

• French slang is an area where **dé-** is often used, sometimes to amusing effect:

se défroquer (originally a term meaning "to leave the priesthood") to take one's trousers off; **se décalcifier** (a pun on the word *calcif* – slang for underpants – and the verb meaning "to become decalcified") to take one's trousers off; **ça te défrise?** (literally, "is it straightening your hair out?") do you have a problem with that?

DEA [deɔa] NM *(abrév* **diplôme d'études approfondies***)* = postgraduate qualification which is a prerequisite for PhD candidates

Culture

DEA/DESS

The DEA and DESS are one-year degree courses taken at "troisième cycle", or postgraduate, university level. Obtaining a DEA involves submitting several pieces of written and oral work on the themes of the compulsory seminars attended throughout the year, and completing a dissertation (which is generally expanded to produce a thesis, should further study be undertaken). The DESS, which was introduced in 1974, is a vocational diploma combining theoretical instruction with a period of work experience in the appropriate area of study (finance, publishing etc).

dead-heat [dɛdit] *(pl* **dead-heats***)* NM dead heat

deadline [dɛdlajn] NM deadline

deal [dil] NM **1** *(accord)* deal **2** *Fam Arg drogue* (drug) deal■; **il a fait de la taule pour d. d'héro** he did a stretch for dealing smack

dealer[1] [dilœr] NM *Fam Arg drogue* dealer■

dealer[2] [3] [dile] *Fam Arg drogue* VT to deal■ VI to deal■

déambulateur [deɑ̃bylatœr] NM walking frame, *Br* Zimmer® frame

déambulation [deɑ̃bylasjɔ̃] NF *Littéraire* strolling, ambling (along)

déambulatoire [deɑ̃bylatwar] NM ambulatory

déambuler [3] [deɑ̃byle] VI to stroll, to amble (along)

deb [dɛb] *Fam* NMF deb, debutante■ ADJ *Br* daft, *Am* dumb

débâcher [3] [debaʃe] VT *(camion, toit)* to take the canvas sheet *or* the tarpaulin off

débâcle [debakl] NF **1** *(d'une rivière)* breaking up (of ice); **nous sommes arrivés au moment de la d.** we arrived when the ice was starting to break up **2** *Mil* rout **3** *(faillite → d'une institution, d'un système)* collapse; **après la d. des actions Unilor** after the Unilor share collapse; **c'est la d.!** it's absolute chaos!

débâcler [3] [debakle] VI *(glace)* to break up VT **1** *(port)* to clear **2** *(porte, fenêtre)* to unfasten, to unbar

débagouler [3] [debagule] VT *Fam* to throw up; **d. un torrent d'injures** to spew out a torrent of abuse

débâillonner [3] [debajɔne] VT **d. qn** to remove sb's gag; **d. la presse** to end press censorship

déballage [debalaʒ] NM **1** *(des bagages, de marchandises)* unpacking; **le d. de nos affaires nous a pris plusieurs heures** it took us several hours to unpack our things **2** *(exposition)* display; **je l'ai acheté au d. du marché Saint-Pierre** I bought it on display at the Marché St Pierre **3** *Fam (sentiments)* outpouring; **un d. de sentiments** an outpouring of feeling

déballastage [debalastaʒ] NM ballast dumping

déballer [3] [debale] VT **1** *(bagages, marchandises)* to unpack; **aide-moi à d. les livres** help me (to) unpack the books **2** *(exposer → produits)* to display **3** *Fam (sentiments)* to unload, to pour out■; *(vérité)* to admit■; **il est venu me d. ses histoires** he came and poured out his problems to me

USAGE ABSOLU **il déballe le dimanche aux Puces** he has a stall on Sundays at the flea market

déballonner [3] [debalɔne] **se déballonner** VPR *Fam* to chicken out

débandade [debɑ̃dad] NF **1** *(déroute)* rout **2** *(panique)* panic, rush; **ce fut la d. générale** there was a mad rush

◻ **à la débandade** ADV **les enfants sortent de l'école à la d.** children are piling out of school

débander [3] [debɑ̃de] VT **1** *Méd (plaie)* to remove the bandages from, to take the bandages off; **d. les yeux d'un prisonnier** to remove the blindfold from a prisoner's eyes

2 *Tech (arc)* to unbend; *(ressort)* to slacken, to loosen

VI **1** *Vulg (ne plus avoir une érection)* to lose one's hard-on

2 *Fam (location)* **sans d.** without letting up

▶**se débander** VPR **1** *(s'éparpiller)* to scatter, to disperse

2 *(ressort)* to recoil; *(arc)* to unbend

débaptiser [3] [debatize] VT *(place, rue)* to change the name of, to give another name to

débarbouillage [debarbujaʒ] NM *(du visage)* wash; **j'ai dû me contenter d'un rapide d.** I had to make do with giving my face a quick wash

débarbouiller [3] [debarbuje] VT *(visage)* to wash; **d. qn** to wash sb's face

▶**se débarbouiller** VPR *Fam* to wash one's face■; **débarbouille-toi avant de venir dîner** wash your face before dinner

débarbouillette [debarbujɛt] NF *Can Br* face flannel, facecloth, *Am* washcloth

débarcadère [debarkader] NM *(de passagers)* landing stage; *(de marchandises)* wharf

débardage [debardaʒ] NM *(de marchandises)* unloading; *(de bois)* hauling

débarder [3] [debarde] VT *(marchandises)* to unload; *(bois)* to haul

débardeur [debardœr] NM **1** *(ouvrier)* *Br* docker, *Am* longshoreman **2** *(tricot)* tank top; *(tee-shirt)* singlet, *Br* vest; *(pour hommes)* vest top

débarqué, -e [debarke] ADJ *(passager)* disembarked

NM,F disembarked passenger; *Fig* **un nouveau d.** a new arrival

débarquement [debarkəmɑ̃] NM **1** *(déchargement → de marchandises)* unloading; *(→ de passagers)* landing; **le d. des marchandises prendra plusieurs jours** it will take several days to unload the goods

2 *Mil* landing; *Hist* **le (jour du) d.** D-day, the Normandy landings; **troupes de d.** landing force; *Fig* **dès juillet c'est le d., toute la famille arrive** the invasion begins in July when the whole family arrives

◻ **de débarquement** ADJ *(quai)* arrival *(avant n)*; *(navire, troupe, fiche)* landing *(avant n)*

débarquer [3] [debarke] VT **1** *(d'un bateau → marchandises)* to unload; *(→ voyageurs)* to land

2 *Fam (limoger)* to fire, *Br* to sack, *Am* to can; **il s'est fait d.** he got the boot *or Br* sack

3 *Can Fam (faire descendre)* to knock off■ VI **1** *(d'un bateau)* to disembark, to land; *(d'un avion)* to disembark; *(d'un train, d'un bus)* to get off, to alight

2 *Mil* to land

3 *Fam (arriver)* to turn up■, to show up■; **il a débarqué chez moi à minuit** he turned up at my place at midnight; **toute la famille débarque le week-end prochain** the whole family's descending on me/us next weekend

4 *Fam (être ignorant)* **tu débarques ou quoi?** where have you been?, what planet have you been on?; **mets-moi au courant, je débarque** give me an update, I haven't a clue what's going on

5 *Can Fam (descendre)* to get down■

6 *Can Fam (de l'école, d'un parti politique)* to drop out

débarras [debara] NM **1** *(dépôt)* storage room **2** *Fam (location)* **bon d.!** good riddance!

débarrasser [3] [debarase] VT **1** *(nettoyer → table)* to clear; *(enlever → assiette)* to clear (away); **ne débarrasse pas les verres** leave the glasses on the table; *Fam* **d. le plancher** to clear *or* to buzz off; **je serai ravi quand ils auront débarrassé le plancher** I'll be delighted to see the back of them

2 *(désencombrer)* **je vais te d. de ta valise** I'll take your case; **il m'a demandé de le d. de sa vieille table** he asked me to take his old table off his hands; **d. la ville de ses voyous** to rid the city of its hooligans, to flush the hooligans out of the city; **l'arrivée du livreur m'a débarrassé de cette bavarde** the arrival of the deliveryman

gave me the opportunity to get rid of that chatterbox; **d. la cave de vieilles bouteilles** to clear old bottles out of the cellar; **je fais le nettoyage maintenant pour en être débarrassé (plus tard)** I'll do the cleaning now to get it out of the way; **d. qn de ses mauvaises habitudes** to cure sb of his/her bad habits

▸**se débarrasser** VPR **1 se d. de** *(se défaire de)* to get rid of; **je me suis débarrassé de mes vieux livres** I got rid of my old books; **je n'arrive pas à me d. de mon rhume** I can't get rid of this cold

2 se d. de *(éloigner → importun)* to get rid of; *(→ serviteur)* to get rid of, to dismiss

3 *Euph* **se d. de** *(tuer)* to get rid of

4 se d. de *(veste, gants)* to take off, to remove; *(sac à main, éventail)* to put down

USAGE ABSOLU **débarrasse-toi, tu vas avoir trop chaud** take your coat *or* jacket off, you'll be too hot

débarrer [3] [debare] VT **1** *(porte, fenêtre)* to unbar **2** *Can & (régional) (déverrouiller)* to unlock

débat [deba] NM **1** *(controverse)* debate, discussion; **trancher un d.** to conclude a discussion; **d. avec l'auteur** discussion with the author; **d. télévisé** discussion programme; *(politique)* televised debate **2** *(conflit intérieur)* inner turmoil; **d. de conscience** moral dilemma

❑ **débats** NMPL *Pol & Jur* proceedings; **débats à huis clos** hearing in camera

debater [debatœr] = **débatteur**

débâter [3] [debɑte] VT to take the pack-saddle off, to unsaddle

débâtir [32] [debatir] VT *Couture* to unpick the basting from

débattement [debatmɑ̃] NM *Aut & Tech* clearance; **d. de roue** wheel deflection

débatteur [debatœr] NM debater

débattre [83] [debatr] VT *(discuter → thème, question)* to discuss, to thrash out; **ils ont longtemps débattu le prix** they haggled at length over the price

❑ **débattre de, débattre sur** VT IND to debate, to discuss; **il faudra d. de ces problèmes** these problems will have to be discussed

❑ **à débattre** ADJ **prix à d.** *(dans une annonce)* open to offers, negotiable; **300 euros à d.** *(dans une annonce)* 300 euros or nearest offer; **conditions à d.** conditions to be negotiated

▸**se débattre** VPR **1** *(s'agiter → victime)* to struggle; *(→ poisson)* to thrash about; **se d. contre un voleur** to struggle with a thief; **se d. comme un forcené** *ou* **comme un beau diable** to struggle like a madman

2 *(lutter)* **se d. dans les problèmes financiers** to struggle against financial difficulties; **se d. contre l'angoisse** to wrestle *or* to grapple with anxiety

débattue [debaty] NF *Suisse* **j'ai la d.** my fingers are numb with cold

débauchage [deboʃaʒ] NM **1** *(renvoi)* laying off, *Br* making redundant **2** *(d'employés d'autres entreprises)* poaching

débauche [deboʃ] NF **1** *(dévergondage)* debauchery; **inciter qn à la d.** to debauch sb; **vivre dans la d.** to live a life of debauchery; **lieu de d.** den of vice **2** *(profusion)* **une d. de mets rares** an abundance of rare delicacies; **une d. d'imagination** unbridled imagination; **une d. de couleurs** a riot of colours

❑ **de débauche** ADJ *(passé, vie)* dissolute

débauché, -e [deboʃe] ADJ *(personne)* debauched; *(vie)* dissolute

NM,F debauched person, libertine

débaucher [3] [deboʃe] VT **1** *(renvoyer)* to lay off, *Br* to make redundant

2 *(employés d'autres entreprises)* to poach; **d. les meilleurs cerveaux** to lure away *or* to poach the best brains

3 *(corrompre)* to corrupt

4 *Fam (détourner)* to lure *or* to tempt away; *Hum* **allez, je vous débauche!** I've come to drag you away!

5 *(inciter → à la grève)* to incite to strike

USAGE ABSOLU *(licencier)* **on débauche dans le textile** there are lay-offs *or Br* redundancies in the textile industry

débecter [4] [debɛkte] VT *très Fam* **ça me débecte** it turns my stomach, it makes me feel sick; **t'es pas débecté!** you're a brave man, I wouldn't touch that with *Br* a bargepole *or Am* a ten-foot pole!

débenture [debɑ̃tyr] NF *Can Fin* debenture bond

débenzolage [debɛ̃zɔlaʒ] NM *Chim* debenzolization

débenzoler [3] [debɛ̃zɔle] VT *Chim* to debenzolize

débéqueter [27] [debɛkte] = **débecter**

débet [debɛ] NM *Fin* balance due

débile [debil] ADJ **1** *Fam (inepte → livre, film, décision) Br* daft, *Am* dumb; **il est complètement d.** he's a complete idiot; **c'est d., comment peux-tu dire ça?** how can you talk such nonsense? **2** *Littéraire (faible → corps)* frail, weak, feeble; *(→ intelligence)* deficient

NMF **1** *Fam (idiot)* dope, *Br* divvy, *Am* dork **2** *Psy* **d. léger/moyen/profond** mildly/moderately/severely retarded person; *Vieilli* **d. mental** retarded person

débilement [debilmɑ̃] ADV weakly, feebly

débilisation [debilizasjɔ̃] NF (increasing) mental retardation

débilitant, -e [debilitɑ̃, -ɑ̃t] ADJ **1** *(affaiblissant)* debilitating, enervating **2** *(démoralisant)* demoralizing, discouraging **3** *Fam (abrutissant)* mind-numbing, soul-destroying; **complètement d., ce boulot!** this job's completely soul-destroying!

débilité [debilite] NF **1** *Fam (caractère stupide)* stupidity; **les films que tu regardes sont d'une d.!** you watch such *Br* daft *or Am* dumb movies *or Br* films! **2** *Psy* **d. (mentale)** (mental) retardation **3** *Littéraire (faiblesse)* debility

débiliter [3] [debilite] VT **1** *(affaiblir)* to debilitate, to enervate, to weaken **2** *(déprimer)* to drag down, to dishearten, to demoralize

débillarder [3] [debijarde] VT to cut in a curved shape

débilos [debilos] *Fam* ADJ daft, lame, *Am* dumb

NMF dope, *Br* divvy, *Am* dork

débine [debin] NF *Fam* poverty■; **être dans la d.** to be hard up *or* broke *or Br* strapped; **c'est la d.!** times are hard!

débiner [3] [debine] *Fam* VT *Br* to bitch about, to slag off, *Am* to bad-mouth

▸**se débiner** VPR **1** *(s'enfuir)* to take off, to make oneself scarce; **te débine pas, j'ai à te parler** stick around, I want to talk to you; *Fig* **n'essaie pas de te d., je veux une réponse** don't try to wriggle out of it, I want an answer **2** *(s'écrouler)* to come *or* to fall apart■; **un vieux fauteuil qui se débine de partout** an old armchair falling apart at the seams

débineur, -euse [debinœr, -øz] NM,F *Fam* backbiter

débirentier, -ère [debirɑ̃tje, -ɛr] NM,F *Fin* payer of an allowance

débit [debi] NM **1** *(d'eau, de passagers)* flow; *(de vapeur)* capacity; *(de gaz)* output; *(de marchandises, de clients)* turnover; *(d'une machine)* output; *Géog* flow

2 *(élocution)* (speed of) delivery; *Fam* **il a un sacré d.** he talks nineteen to the dozen

3 *Ordinat & Tél* rate; **d. en bauds** baud rate; **d. binaire** bit rate; **d. de traitement** *ou* **de données** data throughput *or* speed; **d. de transmission** transmission rate; **haut d.** broadband

4 *Élec* output; **d. capacitif** charging capacity; **d. de courant** power output, delivery rate

5 *Com (ventes)* (retail) sale; **il n'y a pas beaucoup de d. dans ce magasin** this *Br* shop *or Am* store doesn't have a large turnover; **d. de boissons** bar; **d. de tabac** *Br* tobacconist, *Am* tobacco store

6 *Méd* output, rate; **d. cardiaque** cardiac output; **d. expiratoire de pointe** peak flow; **d. sanguin** circulation rate

7 *Fin & Compta* debit; *(sur un relevé)* debit side; **inscrire** *ou* **porter un article au d.** to debit an entry; **d. de caisse** cash debit; **d. cumulé** cumulative debit; **d. différé** deferred debit; **d. immédiat** immediate debit

8 *Com* bill; **je n'ai pas encore fait le d. (à la caisse)** I haven't rung it up yet

9 *(de bois)* cutting up

❑ **au débit de** PRÉP **inscrire une somme au d. d'un compte** to charge an amount of money to sb's account; **porter une somme au d. de qn** to debit sb *or* sb's account with an amount; **porter une somme au d. d'un compte** to debit an account; **520 euros à votre d.** 520 euros on the debit side (of your account)

débitable [debitabl] ADJ **1** *(bois)* good *or* ready for cutting up **2** *Banque* **compte d.** account one may draw money from, account with open access

débitage [debitaʒ] NM cutting up; **d. de bois** conversion of timber

débitant, -e [debitɑ̃, -ɑ̃t] NM,F **d. de boissons** *Br* publican, *Am* bar owner; **d. de tabac** *Br* tobacconist, *Am* tobacco dealer

débiter [3] [debite] VT **1** *(couper → matériau, tissu, bœuf)* to cut up; *(→ bois)* to cut *or* to saw up; **d. qch en tranches** to slice sth

2 *Com* to retail, to sell (retail); **d. du vin** to retail wine, to be in the wine retail trade

3 *Ind (sujet: machine, usine)* to turn out, to produce; *Fam* **je ne veux pas d. du roman de gare** I don't want to churn out trashy novels

4 *(déverser → pompe)* to discharge, to yield; *(→ fleuve)* to have a flow rate of

5 *Péj (texte)* to reel off; *(sermon)* to deliver; *(banalité)* to trot out; **d. des mensonges** to come out with a lot of lies; **d. des idioties** to talk *Br* rubbish *or Am* garbage; **d. ses leçons par cœur** to recite one's homework parrot-fashion

6 *Fin & Compta* to debit; **d. qn d'une somme** to debit sb with an amount; **d. une somme d'un compte** to debit an account with an amount, to debit an amount to an account; **votre compte sera débité (de 40 euros) à la fin du mois** your account will be debited (by 40 euros) at the end of the month

USAGE ABSOLU *Fam Ind* **pas de temps à perdre, il faut que ça débite!** there's no time to waste, we have to just churn the stuff out!

débiteur, -trice [debitœr, -tris] ADJ *(colonne, compte, solde)* debit *(avant n)*; *(personne, société)* debtor *(avant n)*; **mon compte est d. de plusieurs milliers d'euros** my account is several thousand euros overdrawn

NM,F **1** *Fin & Compta* debtor; **d. défaillant** defaulting debtor; **d. hypothécaire** mortgagor **2** *(obligé)* **être d. de qn** to be indebted to sb *or* in sb's debt

débitmètre [debimɛtr] NM flow meter; *Méd* **d. de pointe** peak flow meter

déblai [deblɛ] NM *(dégagement)* digging *or* cutting (out)

❑ **déblais** NMPL *(gravats)* debris, excavated material, rubble; *(terre)* (dug *or* excavated) earth

❑ **en déblai** ADJ sunken; **route en d.** sunken road

déblaie *etc voir* **déblayer**

déblaiement [deblɛmɑ̃] NM **1** *(d'un terrain, d'une ruine)* clearing (out); **ils ont procédé au d. de la forêt après l'accident aérien** they cleared the forest of wreckage after the plane crash **2** *Mines* removing the overburden, stripping

déblatérer [18] [deblatere] **déblatérer contre** VT IND *Péj* to rant (and rave) about, to sound off about

déblayage [deblɛjaʒ] = **déblaiement**

déblayer [11] [debleje] VT **1** *(dégager → neige, terre)* to clear away; *(→ lieu)* to clear out; **d. la neige autour de la maison** to clear the snow from around the house; **d. un chantier des gravats** to clear rubble from a building site

2 *(en travaux publics)* to cut, to excavate, to dig

3 *Fig (travail)* to do the groundwork *or* spadework on; **d. le terrain** *(se débarrasser des détails)* to do the groundwork; *Fam* **allez, déblaie le terrain!** *(va-t'en)* go on, get out of here *or* get lost!

déblocage, débloquage [deblɔkaʒ] NM **1** *Tech (d'un écrou, d'un dispositif)* unblocking, releasing; *(de freins)* freeing; *Tél (de portable)* unlocking

2 *(réouverture → d'un tuyau)* clearing, freeing, unblocking; *(→ d'une route)* clearing

3 *Écon (des salaires, des prix, de crédits)* unfreezing; *(de fonds)* releasing, making available; *Banque (d'un compte)* freeing; *Com (de stock)* release, releasing

4 *Mines* haulage

5 *Psy* getting rid of inhibitions

débloquer [3] [deblɔke] VT **1** *Tech (écrou, dispositif)* to unblock, to release; *(freins)* to free

2 *(rouvrir → tuyau)* to clear, to free, to unblock; *(→ route)* to clear (of obstructions); *Fig* **d. les**

deb–deb

discussions to get the negotiations back on course; **d. la situation** *(après un conflit)* to break the stalemate; *(la sortir de l'enlisement)* to get things moving again

3 *Écon (salaires, prix, crédits)* to unfreeze; *(fonds)* to release, to make available; *Banque (compte)* to free, to unfreeze; *Com (stock)* to release

4 *Tél (portable)* to unlock

5 *Fam (décontracter)* **ça m'a débloqué** it got rid of some of my inhibitions

VI *Fam* **1** *(en parlant)* to talk nonsense *or Br* rubbish

2 *(être déraisonnable)* to be off one's rocker; **tu débloques!** you're out of your mind!; **son grand-père est vieux, il commence à d.** his/her grandfather is old and not all there

3 *(ne pas fonctionner correctement)* to be on the blink, *Am* to be on the fritz

débobiner [3] [debɔbine] VT to unwind, to unreel, to uncoil

débogage [debɔgaʒ] NM *Ordinat* debugging

déboguer [3] [debɔge] VT *Ordinat* to debug

débogueur [debɔgœr] NM **(programme) d.** debugger

déboires [debwar] NMPL disappointments, setbacks, (trials and) tribulations; **s'épargner** *ou* **s'éviter des d.** to spare oneself a lot of trouble; **elle a essuyé bien des d.** she suffered many disappointments *or* setbacks

déboisage [debwazaʒ] NM *Mines* prop-drawing

déboisement [debwazmɑ̃] NM deforestation, clearing (of trees)

déboiser [3] [debwaze] VT **1** *(couper les arbres de)* to deforest, to clear of trees; **il faudra d. le terrain avant de construire** we'll have to clear the area of trees before we can start building **2** *Mines* to draw the timbers of, to clear

▸**se déboiser** VPR *(terrain, région)* to lose its trees, to be deforested

déboîtement [debwatmɑ̃] NM **1** *(luxation → de l'épaule, de la hanche)* dislocation; *(→ de la rotule)* slipping **2** *(en voiture)* pulling out

déboîter [3] [debwate] VT **1** *(démonter → tuyau)* to disconnect; *(→ objet)* to unfasten, to release, to uncouple; *(→ porte, fenêtre)* to take off its hinges **2** *Méd* to dislocate, to put out

VI *(véhicule)* to pull out

▸**se déboîter** VPR **1** *(partie du corps)* **mon genou s'est déboîté** I've dislocated my knee **2** *(personne)* **se d. l'épaule** to dislocate one's shoulder

débonder [3] [debɔ̃de] VT to unplug

▸**se débonder** VPR **1** *(tonneau)* to overflow **2** *(personne)* to pour out one's troubles, to open up

débonnaire [debɔnɛr] ADJ *(air)* kindly; *(personne)* good-natured, easy-going; **répondre d'un ton d.** to answer good-naturedly

débonnairement [debɔnɛrmɑ̃] ADV *Littéraire* good-naturedly

débonnaireté [debɔnɛrte] NF *Littéraire* good humour, good nature

débord [debɔr] NM *Com* excess

débordant, -e [debɔrdɑ̃, -ɑ̃t] ADJ *(extrême → affection)* overflowing; *(→ activité)* tireless; *(→ imagination)* wild, vivid; **d'un enthousiasme d.** bubbling with enthusiasm; **ressentir une joie débordante** to be bursting with joy; **être d. de** to be full of; **d. d'éloges/d'énergie** full of praise/of energy; **d. de santé/de vie** bursting with health/with vitality; **il est d. de tendresse envers elle** he is full of tenderness for her

débordé, -e [debɔrde] ADJ **1** *(occupé)* snowed under **2** *(dépassé)* overwhelmed

débordement [debɔrdəmɑ̃] NM **1** *(écoulement → d'une rivière)* overflowing; *(→ d'un liquide)* running over, overflowing

2 *(profusion → de paroles)* rush, torrent; *(→ d'injures)* outburst, volley; *(→ de joie)* outburst, explosion; **des débordements d'émotion** emotional outbursts

3 *(manœuvre)* outflanking; **il y a eu d. des syndicats par la base** the rank and file have gone further than the union intended

4 *Ordinat* overflow

5 *Mktg (d'une annonce)* overlap

▫ **débordements** NMPL *(agitation)* wild *or* uncontrolled *or* extreme behaviour; *Littéraire (débauche)* excesses

déborder [3] [debɔrde] VI **1** *(rivière)* to overflow; *(bouillon, lait)* to boil over; **le fleuve a débordé de son lit** the river has burst its banks; **l'eau a débordé du lavabo** the sink has overflowed; **les papiers débordent de la corbeille** the papers are spilling out of the wastepaper basket; **j'ai fait d. le lait** I let the milk boil over; **les pluies ont fait d. la rivière** the rain made the river burst its banks; **son chagrin/sa joie débordait** he/she could no longer contain his/her grief/delight; *Fig* **d. de qch** to overflow *or* to be bursting with sth; **d. d'énergie** to be overflowing with energy; **d. d'imagination** to have a wild *or* vivid imagination; **d. de joie** to be bursting with joy; **son cœur déborde de reconnaissance** his/her heart is brimming over with gratitude

2 *(récipient)* to overflow, to run over; *(tiroir, sac)* to be crammed, to spill over; **la casserole est pleine à d.** the saucepan's full to the brim *or* to overflowing; **laisser d. la baignoire** to let the bath overflow; **le train débordait de voyageurs** the train was crammed *or* overflowing with passengers; **le sac débordait de vêtements** the bag was overflowing with clothes

3 *(faire saillie)* to stick *or* to jut out, to project; **la pile de gravats débordait sur l'allée** the heap of rubble had spilled out into the lane; **d. en coloriant un dessin** to go over the edges while colouring in a picture

4 *Naut* to shove off

VT **1** *(dépasser)* to stick *or* to jut out from; **la pierre déborde le mur d'un centimètre** the stone juts out one centimetre from the wall

2 *(s'écarter de)* **vous débordez le sujet** you've gone beyond the scope of the topic; **cela déborde le cadre de mes responsabilités/de notre débat** that exceeds my responsibilities/the limits of our discussion

3 *(submerger → troupe, parti, équipe)* to outflank; **le syndicat est débordé par la base** the rank and file are going further than the union intended; **être débordé de travail** to be up to one's eyes in *or* snowed under with work; **être débordé par les événements** to let things get on top of one; **je suis débordé par toutes ces nouvelles modes** I can't keep up with all these new fashions

4 *(tirer)* **d. les draps** to untuck the sheets

5 *(enlever les bords de)* to remove the edging from; *Tech* **d. une tôle** to trim the edges of an iron plate

USAGE ABSOLU **nous débordons un peu, il est midi et deux minutes** we're going slightly over time, it's two minutes past twelve

▸**se déborder** VPR **se d. en dormant** to throw off one's covers in one's sleep

débossage [debɔsaʒ] NM *Can* **1** *(réparation de carrosserie)* car body repair, *Am* auto body repair **2** *(fait d'enlever une bosse)* dent removal

débosseler [24] [debɔsle] VT *Tech* to remove the dents from

débosser [3] [debɔse] VT *Can Tech* to remove the dents from

débosseur [debɔsœr] NM *Can* car body repairman, *Am* auto body repairman

débotté, débotter[1] [debɔte] **au débotté** ADV *Littéraire* **prendre qn au d.** to pounce on sb, to take sb unawares; **répondre au d.** to answer off the cuff

débotter[2] [3] [debɔte] VT to remove the boots of

▸**se débotter** VPR to take one's boots off

débouchage [debuʃaʒ] NM **1** *(d'un tuyau)* unblocking **2** *(d'une bouteille)* uncorking

débouché [debuʃe] NM **1** *(possibilité d'emploi)* career prospect; **cette formation n'offre aucun d.** this training does not lead to any career openings

2 *(perspective de vente)* outlet, opening; *(marché)* market; **créer de nouveaux débouchés pour un produit** to create new outlets for a product

3 *(issue → d'un passage)* opening; *(→ d'une vallée)* mouth; **avoir un d. sur la mer** to have an outlet to the sea

▫ **au débouché de** PRÉP at the end of; **au d. du défilé dans la vallée** where the pass opens out into the valley

déboucher [3] [debuʃe] VT **1** *(ouvrir → bouteille de bière, tube)* to uncap, to take the top off, to open; *(→ bouteille de vin)* to uncork, to open; *(→ flacon)* to unstop, to remove the stopper from; **on débouche une bouteille pour fêter ça!** let's crack open a bottle to celebrate!

2 *(débloquer → pipe, trou, gicleur)* to clear, to clean out; *(→ lavabo)* to unblock, to unstop, to clear; *(→ tuyau, conduit)* to clear, to unclog; *(→ nez)* to unblock; *(→ oreille)* to clean out

VI **1** *(aboutir)* **d. de** to emerge from, to come out of; **d. sur** to open into, to lead to; **la rue débouche sur l'avenue** the street leads to the avenue

2 *Fig* **d. sur** to lead to; **des études qui ne débouchent sur rien** a course that doesn't lead anywhere; **d. sur des résultats** to have positive results

▸**se déboucher** VPR **1** *(lavabo, tuyau)* to unblock; *(nez, oreilles)* to clear

2 se d. le nez to clear one's nose

déboucheur [debuʃœr] NM **1** *(produit)* drain clearing liquid **2** *(dispositif)* **d. à ventouse** plunger, *Am* plumber's friend; **d. flexible** flexible cable *(for clearing pipes)*

déboucler [3] [debukle] VT **1** *(détacher → ceinture)* to unbuckle, to undo, to unfasten **2** *(cheveux)* **la pluie avait débouclé ses cheveux** the rain had straightened his/her curly hair

débouillir [48] [debujir] VI *Tex* **1** *(pour éprouver la teinture)* to boil for testing dye **2** *(pour blanchir)* to bleach; **cuve à d.** kier

débouillissage [debujisaʒ] NM *Tex* **1** *(pour éprouver la teinture)* testing dye by boiling **2** *(pour blanchir)* boiling off

déboulé [debule] NM **1** *(en danse)* déboulé **2** *Sport* burst of speed **3** *Chasse* breaking of cover

▫ **au déboulé** ADV *Chasse* **tirer un animal au d.** to shoot an animal as it breaks cover

débouler [3] [debule] VI **1** *Fam (surgir)* to shoot out, to burst out; *(arriver brusquement)* to show up, to turn up; **l'enfant a déboulé de derrière une voiture** the child shot out *or* emerged suddenly from behind a parked car; **elle a déboulé du coin de la rue** she came hurtling round the corner; **ils ont déboulé chez moi sans prévenir** they showed up at my place without any warning; **les flics ont déboulé dans le café** the cops burst into the bar **2** *Chasse* to start, to bolt **3** *(tomber)* to tumble down

VT **d. les escaliers** *(en courant)* to race *or* to hurtle down the stairs; *(après être tombé)* to tumble down the stairs

déboulis [debuli] NM *Can* landslide, landslip

déboulonnage [debulɔnaʒ], **déboulonnement** [debulɔnmɑ̃] NM **1** *Tech* unbolting, removal of bolts **2** *Fam (fait de discréditer)* trashing; *(renvoi)* firing, *Br* sacking

déboulonner [3] [debulɔne] VT **1** *Tech* to unbolt, to remove the bolts (from); **d. une statue** to take down a statue **2** *Fam (discréditer)* to trash; *(renvoyer)* to fire, *Br* to sack; **se faire d.** to get fired, *Br* to get the sack

débouquement [debukmɑ̃] NM *Naut* **1** *(fait de quitter un détroit)* disemboguing, disemboguement **2** *(extrémité)* passage, strait

débouquer [3] [debuke] VI *Naut* to disembogue

débourbage [deburbaʒ] NM *(lavage)* washing, clearing (from mud)

débourber [3] [deburbe] VT **1** *(nettoyer → minerai, charbon)* to wash, to clean, to clear (from mud); *(→ rivière)* to dredge **2** *(sortir de la boue)* to pull *or* to drag *or* to haul out of the mud

débourbeur [deburbœr] NM clearing *or* washing drum, trommel washer

débourrage [deburaʒ] NM **1** *(vidage)* clearing **2** *Tex* fluffing, shredding

débourrement [deburmɑ̃] NM bud burst

débourrer [3] [debure] VT **1** *(trou)* to clear **2** *(cheval)* to break in **3** *(pipe)* to scrape out **4** *Tex* to fettle, to strip **5** *Vulg (déféquer)* to *Br* have *or Am* take a dump *or* a crap

débours [debur] NM expenditure, outlay

déboursement [debursəmɑ̃] NM spending, laying out

débourser [3] [deburse] VT to spend, to lay out; **je ne débourserai pas un centime** I won't pay a penny; **sans rien d.** without spending *or* paying a penny; **impossible de lui faire d. le moindre centime** he/she just refuses to part with any money

déboussoler [3] [debusɔle] VT to confuse, to disorientate, to bewilder; **il est déboussolé depuis le départ de sa mère** his mother's departure has unsettled him

debout [dəbu] ADV 1 *(en parlant des personnes → en station verticale)* standing up; **manger d.** to eat standing up; **d.!** get *or* stand up!; **il était d. sur la table** he was standing on the table; **elle est d. toute la journée** she's on her feet all day; **ils l'ont mis d.** they helped him to his feet *or* helped him up; **se mettre d.** to stand (up), to rise; **je préfère rester d.** I'd rather stand; **je suis resté d. toute la journée** I was on my feet all day; **ne restez pas d.** (please) sit down; **ça glisse, on ne peut pas rester d.** it's so slippery it's difficult to stop falling over; **tenez-le d.** keep him upright *or* in a standing position; **depuis l'opération elle a du mal à se tenir d.** she's been very unsteady on her feet since the operation; **bébé se tient d.** baby can stand up; **on peut se tenir d. dans sa camionnette** his van is big enough to stand up in; **il ne tient plus d.** *(fatigué)* he's dead on his feet; *(ivre)* he can hardly stand

2 *(en parlant d'animaux)* **le poulain se tient déjà d.** the foal is already up on its feet; **le vieux chien s'est mis d.** the old dog got up *or* to its feet

3 *(en parlant d'objets)* upright, vertical; **mettre une échelle d. contre un mur** to stand a ladder against a wall; **mettre une chaise d.** to stand a chair up; **mettre un cercueil d.** to upend a coffin, to stand a coffin on end; *Fig* **mettre un projet d.** to set up a project; **ça ne tient pas d.** it doesn't make sense; **le raisonnement ne tient pas d.** the argument doesn't hold water *or* hold up; **votre idée tient d.** your idea really makes sense

4 *(éveillé)* up; **d.!** get up!; **d. là-dedans!** get up, you lot!; **être d. à 5 heures** to be up at 5 o'clock; **il n'est pas encore d.** he's not up *or* out of bed yet; **je reste d. très tard** I stay up very late; **nous sommes restés d. toute la nuit à jouer aux cartes** we sat *or* stayed up all night playing cards

5 *(en bon état)* standing; **les murs sont encore d.** the walls are still standing; **la maison de mon enfance est encore d.** the house where I lived as a child is still there; **la république ne restera pas longtemps d.** the republic won't hold out for long

6 *(guéri)* up on one's feet (again), up and about; *(sorti de chez soi, de l'hôpital)* out and about

7 *Littéraire (dignement)* uprightly, honourably; **mourir (tout) d.** to die with one's boots on

débouté, -e [debute] *Jur* NM,F severed plaintiff
NM *Br* nonsuit, *Am* dismissal

déboutement [debutmɑ̃] NM *Jur Br* nonsuiting, *Am* dismissal

débouter [3] [debute] VT *Jur Br* to nonsuit, *Am* to dismiss; **être débouté de sa plainte** *Br* to be nonsuited, *Am* to have one's case dismissed

déboutonnage [debutɔnaʒ] NM unbuttoning

déboutonner [3] [debutɔne] VT to unbutton
▸ **se déboutonner** VPR 1 *(pour se déshabiller)* to unbutton (oneself) 2 *(parler franchement)* to open up 3 *(vêtement)* to unbutton 4 *Can Fam (se montrer généreux)* to splash out

débraie *etc voir* **débrayer**

débraillé, -e [debraje] ADJ *(allure, vêtements, personne)* slovenly, sloppy, scruffy; *(manières)* slovenly; *(conversation)* unrestrained
NM slovenliness; **être en d.** to be scruffy; **traîner en d.** to slop around

débrailler [3] [debrɑje] **se débrailler** VPR *Fam* to loosen one's clothing▪; *Fig* **la conversation se débraille** the conversation is getting a bit out of hand

débranchement [debrɑ̃ʃmɑ̃] NM 1 *(déconnexion → d'un tuyau)* disconnecting; *(→ d'un appareil électrique)* unplugging 2 *Rail* splitting up; **d. en palier** flat shunting, shunting on level-tracks

débrancher [3] [debrɑ̃ʃe] VT 1 *(déconnecter → tuyau)* to disconnect; *(→ appareil électrique)* to unplug; *Fam Hum* **débranchez-le!** shut him up, will you!; *Fam* **d. un malade** to turn off a patient's life support machine▪ 2 *Rail (train)* to split up

débrasage [debrazaʒ] NM *Tech* unsoldering

débraser [3] [debraze] VT *Tech* to unsolder

débrayage [debrɛjaʒ] NM 1 *Aut* disengaging of the clutch, *Br* declutching 2 *(grève)* stoppage, walkout

débrayer [11] [debreje] VT 1 *Aut* to disengage the clutch of, *Br* to declutch 2 *(machine)* to throw out of gear, to put out of operation
VI 1 *Aut* to disengage the clutch, *Br* to declutch; **débrayez!** take your foot off the clutch! 2 *(faire grève)* to stop work, to come out *or* to go on strike

débridé, -e [debride] ADJ unbridled, unrestrained, unfettered

débridement [debridmɑ̃] NM 1 *(d'un cheval)* unbridling 2 *Littéraire (déchaînement)* unbridling, unleashing 3 *Méd (d'un abcès, d'une blessure)* incision, *Spéc* debridement

débrider [3] [debride] VT 1 *(cheval)* to unbridle 2 *Méd (abcès, blessure)* to incise, *Spéc* to debride 3 *Culin (volaille)* to untruss
❑ **sans débrider** ADV nonstop, without stopping, at a stretch

débriefer [3] [debrife] VT to debrief

débriefing [debrifiŋ] NM *Mktg* debriefing

débris [debri] NM 1 *(surtout au pl) (fragment → de verre)* piece, splinter, shard; *(→ de vaisselle)* (broken) piece *or* fragment; *(→ de roche)* crumb, debris *(singulier)*; *(→ de métal)* scrap; *(→ d'un avion, d'une voiture)* remains, debris *(singulier)*, wreckage; *(→ de végétal)* piece *or* crumb of vegetable matter, debris *(singulier)*

2 *(surtout au pl) (nourriture)* scraps, crumbs; *(détritus)* litter, *Br* rubbish; *Littéraire (restes → d'une fortune, d'un royaume)* last shreds, remnants

3 *très Fam (vieillard)* **(vieux) d.** old codger, *Am* geezer

débrochage [debrɔʃaʒ] NM *(d'un livre)* stripping, unstitching

débrocher [3] [debrɔʃe] VT 1 *Culin* to remove from the spit, to unspit 2 *(livre)* to strip, to unstitch
▸ **se débrocher** VPR *(livre)* to become unstitched

débrouillage [debrujaʒ] NM 1 *(de fils)* disentangling, untangling, unravelling 2 *(d'une énigme)* puzzling out, unravelling, untangling

débrouillard, -e [debrujar, -ard] ADJ resourceful
NM,F resourceful person

débrouillardise [debrujardiz] NF resourcefulness; **faire preuve de d.** to be resourceful

débrouille [debruj] NF *Fam* **s'en sortir par la d.** to improvize one's way out of trouble; **l'art de la d.** the art of making do (with what's at hand)

débrouillement [debrujmɑ̃] NM 1 *(de fils)* disentangling, untangling, unravelling 2 *(d'une énigme)* puzzling out, unravelling, untangling

débrouiller [3] [debruje] VT 1 *(démêler → fils)* to unravel, to untangle, to disentangle; *(→ énigme)* to puzzle out, to untangle, to unravel; **d. les affaires de qn** to sort out sb's business affairs

2 *Fam (enseigner les bases à)* to teach the basics to▪; **d. qn en gestion** to give sb a grounding in management▪

▸ **se débrouiller** VPR 1 *(faire face aux difficultés)* to manage; **débrouille-toi** you'll have to manage by yourself; **comment vas-tu te d. maintenant qu'elle est partie?** how will you cope now that she's gone?; **elle se débrouille très bien dans Berlin** she really knows her way around Berlin; **tu parles espagnol? – je me débrouille** do you speak Spanish? – I get by; **se d. en anglais** to have a working knowledge of English; **j'ai dû me d. avec le peu que j'avais** I had to make do *or* manage with what little I had; **je me suis débrouillé pour avoir des places** I managed to wangle some seats; **se d. pour se faire inviter par qn** to wangle an invitation out of sb; *Fam* **donne cette casserole, tu te débrouilles comme un pied** give me that pan, you're all thumbs

2 *(subsister financièrement)* to make ends meet, to manage; **j'étais seule dans la vie, j'ai dû me d.** I was on my own, I had to fend for myself; **on se débrouille** we get by *or* manage

débroussaillage [debrusajaʒ] NM 1 *(nettoyage)* clearing; **le d. d'un sous-bois** clearing of the undergrowth 2 *Fig (étude)* groundwork, spadework (**de** on)

débroussaillant, -e [debrusajɑ̃, -ɑ̃t] ADJ clearing *(avant n)*
NM chemical clearing agent

débroussaillement [debrusajmɑ̃] NM 1 *(nettoyage)* clearing; **le d. d'un sous-bois** clearing of the undergrowth 2 *Fig (étude)* groundwork, spadework (**de** on)

débroussailler [3] [debrusaje] VT 1 *(terrain)* to clear 2 *Fig (travail, problème)* to do the groundwork *or* spadework on

débroussailleuse [debrusajøz] NF *Hort* slash cutter

débrousser [3] [debruse] VT *(en Afrique francophone)* to prepare for cultivation

débuché, débucher[1] [debyʃe] NM *Chasse* breaking cover

débucher[2] [3] [debyʃe] *Chasse* VT to start, to drive from cover
VI to break cover

débudgétisation [debydʒetizasjɔ̃] NF removing from the budget, debudgeting

débudgétiser [3] [debydʒetize] VT to remove from the budget, to debudget

débureaucratiser [3] [debyrokratize] VT to make less bureaucratic

débusquement [debyskəmɑ̃] NM dislodgement

débusquer [3] [debyske] VT 1 *Chasse* to start, to flush 2 *(découvrir)* to hunt out; **le logiciel débusque la moindre faute d'orthographe** the software can track down the slightest spelling mistake

début [deby] NM 1 *(commencement)* beginning, start; **le d. de la semaine** the beginning *or* start of the week; **le d. de notre amitié** the beginning *or* start of our friendship; **le d. d'une maladie** the beginning *or* onset of an illness; **le d. d'un livre** the beginning *or* opening of a book; **salaire de d.** starting salary; **être en d. de carrière** to be at the start of one's career; **ce n'est pas mal pour un d.** it's quite good for a first try *or* attempt; **ce n'est qu'un d.** that's just the start *or* beginning; **il y a un d. à tout** you have to start sometime; **ressentir un d. de fatigue** to start feeling tired; **un d. de grippe** the first signs of flu

2 *(dans l'expression des dates)* **d. mars** at the beginning of *or* in early March

3 *Ordinat* home; **aller au d.** *(commande)* go top

❑ **débuts** NMPL 1 *(dans une carrière)* start; *(dans le spectacle, en société)* debut; **il a eu des débuts difficiles** it wasn't easy for him at the start; **mes débuts dans le journalisme** my first steps *or* my early days as a journalist; **en être à ses débuts** *(projet)* to be in its early stages; *(personne)* to have just started (out); **faire ses débuts** to make one's debut

2 *(première période)* beginnings; **les débuts de l'aviation** the beginnings of aviation; **le rock à ses débuts** early rock music

❑ **au début** ADV at first, to begin with; **au d. il voulait un vélo, maintenant il veut une voiture** he started out wanting a bike, now he wants a car

❑ **au début de** PRÉP **au d. du printemps/de l'année** at the beginning of spring/of the year; **j'en suis encore au d. du livre** I've only just started the book; **il m'a aidé au d. de ma carrière** he started me (off) in my career

❑ **au tout début, tout au début** ADV at the very beginning, right at the beginning

❑ **dès le début** ADV from the outset *or* very start *or* very beginning; **je le savais depuis le d.** I knew all along *or* from the start

❑ **du début à la fin** ADV *(d'un livre, d'une histoire)* from beginning to end; *(d'une course, d'un événement)* from start to finish

débutant, -e [debytɑ̃, -ɑ̃t] ADJ *(dans un apprentissage)* novice *(avant n)*; *(dans une carrière)* young; **un professeur d.** a young teacher; **un conducteur d.** a newly qualified driver
NM,F *(dans un apprentissage)* beginner, novice; *(dans une carrière)* beginner; **espagnol pour les débutants** beginner's Spanish; **grand d.** absolute beginner; *Fam* **se faire avoir comme un d.** to be taken in like a real greenhorn

❑ **débutante** NF *(dans la haute société)* debutante

débuter [3] [debyte] VI 1 *(commencer)* to start, to begin; **mal/bien d. dans la vie** to get off to a

deb-dec

bad/good start in life; **d. par** to start (off) with; **l'histoire débute par un mariage** the story starts (off) *or* begins with a wedding

  2 *(être inexpérimenté)* to be a beginner, to begin; **elle débute dans le métier** she's new to the job **3** *(commencer à travailler)* to start (out), to begin; **il a débuté comme serveur dans un restaurant** he started out as a waiter in a restaurant

  4 *(artiste)* to make one's debut; **il a débuté dans le rôle de Faust** he made his debut *or* first appearance as Faust

  5 *(en société)* **d. (dans le monde)** to make one's debut, to come out

  vt *Fam* **c'est nous qui débutons le concert** we're on first■, we're opening the show■

debye [dəbaj] **NM** *Élec* Debye unit

dec [dek] *(abrév* **déconner)** **sans dec** **ADV** *Fam* **sans d.!** *(je t'assure)* no kidding!, *Br* straight up!; **sans d.?** *(est-ce vrai?)* no kidding?, yeah?, *Br* straight up?

deçà [dəsa] **ADV** *Littéraire* **d. (et) delà** hither and thither

  ❏ **en deçà** **ADV** on this side; **ne franchissez pas la rivière, restez en d.** don't cross the river, stay on this side

  ❏ **en deçà de PRÉP 1** *(de ce côté-ci de)* (on) this side of; **en d. de la frontière** on this side of the border; **en d. des Alpes** this side of the Alps **2** *Fig* **en d. d'un certain seuil** below a certain level; **rester en d. de la vérité** to be short of the truth; **ce travail est en d. de ses possibilités** this job doesn't exploit his potential to the full

déca [deka] **NM** *Fam* decaf

déca- [deka] **PRÉF** deca-

décabosser [3] [dekabose] **vt** *(gén)* to straighten out; *(en martelant)* to beat *or* to hammer out; *(en tirant)* to pull back into shape; *(en poussant)* to push back into shape

décabriste [dekabrist] **NM** *Hist* Decembrist

décachetage [dekaʃtaʒ] **NM** *(en déchirant)* opening; *(en rompant le cachet)* unsealing

décacheter [27] [dekaʃte] **vt** *(ouvrir → en déchirant)* to open, to tear open; *(→ en rompant le cachet)* to unseal, to break open

décadaire [dekadɛr] **ADJ** *Hist* = relating to a ten-day period in the Republican calendar

décade [dekad] **NF 1** *(série de dix)* decade **2** *(dix jours)* period of ten days **3** *(dix ans)* decade

décadenasser [3] [dekadnase] **vt** to remove the padlock from, to take the padlock off

décadence [dekadɑ̃s] **NF 1** *(état)* decadence; *(évolution)* decline, decay; **la d. romaine** Roman decadence; **la d. de l'Empire romain** the decline *or* fall of the Roman Empire **2** *Beaux-Arts & Littérature* decadence, decadent period

  ❏ **en décadence ADJ** declining, decaying, decadent **ADV** **tomber** *ou* **entrer en d.** to become decadent, to start to decline

décadent, -e [dekadɑ̃, -ɑ̃t] **ADJ 1** *(en déclin)* decadent, declining, decaying **2** *Beaux-Arts & Littérature* decadent

  NM,F decadent

  ❏ **décadents NMPL** *Littérature* **les décadents** the Decadents

décadentisme [dekadɑ̃tism] **NM** *Beaux-Arts & Littérature* decadentism

décadi [dekadi] **NM** *Hist* = tenth day of a ten-day period in the Republican calendar

décadrage [dekadraʒ] **NM 1** *Cin* off-centring **2** *Ordinat* off-registration

décadré, -e [dekadre] **ADJ** *Cin* off-centre

décadrer [3] [dekadre] **vt 1** *Mines* to draw the timbers of, to remove the timbering of **2** *(décentrer) Ordinat* **être décadré** *(perforation)* to be off-punch; *Cin* to be off-centre

décaèdre [dekaɛdr] **ADJ** decahedral

  NM decahedron

décaféiné, -e [dekafeine] **ADJ** decaffeinated

  NM decaffeinated coffee

décagonal, -e, -aux, -ales [dekagɔnal, -o] **ADJ** decagonal

décagone [dekagɔn] **NM** decagon

décaissement [dekɛsmɑ̃] **NM 1** *Banque (retrait)* cash withdrawal; *(somme)* sum withdrawn; **faire un d.** to make a withdrawal **2** *(déballage)* unpacking **3** *Bot* planting out

  ❏ **décaissements NMPL** *Compta* outgoings

décaisser [4] [dekese] **vt 1** *Banque (retirer)* to withdraw **2** *(déballer)* to unpack, to take out of its container **3** *Bot* to plant out

décalage [dekalaʒ] **NM 1** *(dans l'espace)* space, interval, gap

  2 *(dans le temps)* interval, time-lag, lag; **d. horaire** time difference; **souffrir du d. horaire** to have jet lag

  3 *(manque de concordance)* discrepancy, gap; **il y a un d. entre la théorie et la pratique** there's a discrepancy between theory and practice

  4 *(en audiovisuel)* shift, displacement; **d. de fréquence** frequency shift; **d. de l'image** image displacement; **d. son-image** pull-up sound advance, sound to image stagger

  5 *Astron* **d. spectral** spectral shift

  6 *Ordinat* shift; **introduire qch par d.** to shift sth in; **d. arithmétique/logique/de la virgule** arithmetic/logical/point shift

  ❏ **en décalage ADV 1** *(dans le temps)* **nous sommes en d. par rapport à Bangkok** there's a time difference between here and Bangkok

  2 *(sans harmonie)* **être en d. par rapport à qn** to be on a different wavelength from sb; **on est en complet d.** we're on completely different wavelengths

décalaminage [dekalaminaʒ] **NM 1** *(d'un moteur)* decarbonization, decoking, decarburization **2** *Métal* descaling

décalaminer [3] [dekalamine] **vt 1** *(moteur)* to decarbonize, to decoke, to decarburize **2** *Métal* to descale

décalcifiant, -e [dekalsifjɑ̃, -ɑ̃t] **ADJ** decalcifying

décalcification [dekalsifikasjɔ̃] **NF** decalcification, decalcifying

décalcifier [9] [dekalsifje] **vt** to decalcify

  ▶ **se décalcifier VPR** to become decalcified

décalcomanie [dekalkɔmani] **NF 1** *(image)* transfer, *Am* decal, *Spéc* decalcomania; **faire des décalcomanies** to do transfers *or* *Am* decals **2** *(procédé)* transfer process, *Am* decal, *Spéc* decalcomania

décalé, -e [dekale] **ADJ** *(original)* offbeat, quirky

décaler [3] [dekale] **vt 1** *(dans l'espace)* to pull *or* to shift (out of line); **d. qch vers l'avant/l'arrière/la gauche** to shift sth forward/back/to the left; **les sièges sont décalés** the seats are staggered; **cette façade est légèrement décalée par rapport aux autres** this house is slightly out of line with the others

  2 *(dans le temps → horaire)* to shift; **l'horaire a été décalé d'une heure** *(avancé)* the schedule was brought forward an hour; *(reculé)* the schedule was brought *or* moved one hour back; **essaie de faire d. l'heure de ton départ** see if you can get your departure time changed

  3 *(désorienter)* **être décalé par rapport à la réalité** to be out of phase with reality

  4 *(ôter les cales de)* to unwedge

  ▶ **se décaler VPR** to move (out of line); **décalez-vous à droite** move to the right; **décalez-vous d'un rang en avant/arrière** move forward/back a row

décalitre [dekalitr] **NM** decalitre

décalogue [dekalɔg] **NM** Decalogue

'Le Décalogue' *Kieslowski* 'The Ten Commandments'

décalotter [3] [dekalɔte] **vt 1** *Méd* **d. le gland** to pull back the foreskin **2** *Fam* **d. une bouteille** to crack open a bottle

décalquage [dekalkaʒ] **NM** tracing, transferring

décalque [dekalk] **NM 1** *(reproduction)* tracing **2** *Fig (imitation)* copy

décalquer [3] [dekalke] **vt** to trace, to transfer

décalvant, -e [dekalvɑ̃] **ADJ** *Méd* decalvant

Décaméron [dekamerɔ̃] **NM**

'Décaméron' *Boccace* 'The Decameron'

décamètre [dekamɛtr] **NM** decametre

décamétrique [dekametrik] **ADJ** ten-metre *(avant n)*

décamper [3] [dekɑ̃pe] **vi** *Fam* to make oneself scarce, to take off; **décampe!** beat it!; **faire d. qn** to chase *or* to drive sb out

décan [dekɑ̃] **NM** decan

décanal, -e, -aux, -ales [dekanal, -o] **ADJ** decanal

décanat [dekana] **NM 1** *(fonction)* deanship **2** *(locaux)* deanery

décaniller [3] [dekanije] **vi** *Fam* to clear off, to scram; **il n'y a pas moyen de les faire d.** there's no budging them

décantage [dekɑ̃taʒ] **NM** *(d'un liquide)* settling, clarification; *(de l'argile)* washing; *(des eaux usées)* clarification; *(du vin)* decantation, settling; *(d'un produit chimique)* decantation

décantation [dekɑ̃tasjɔ̃] **NF** *(d'un liquide)* settling, clarification; *(de l'argile)* washing; *(des eaux usées)* clarification; *(du vin)* decantation, settling; *(d'un produit chimique)* decantation

décanter [3] [dekɑ̃te] **vt 1** *(purifier → liquide)* to allow to settle, to clarify; *(→ argile)* to wash; *(→ eaux usées)* to clarify; *(→ vin)* to decant, to allow to settle; *(→ produit chimique)* to decant **2** *(éclaircir)* to clarify; **d. ses idées** to think things over

  ▶ **se décanter VPR 1** *(liquide)* to settle **2** *(situation)* to settle down; **il faut laisser les choses se d.** one must allow things to sort themselves out *or* to settle down

décanteur [dekɑ̃tœr] **NM 1** *Chim* decantation *or* decanting glass **2** *Pétr* settler **3** *(pour les eaux usées)* tank; **d. primaire** detritus pit

décantonnement [dekɑ̃tɔnmɑ̃] **NM** *Chasse* driving animals from their territory

décantonner [dekɑ̃tɔne] *Chasse* **vt** *(animal)* to drive from its territory

  ▶ **se décantonner VPR** *(animal)* to change territory

décapage [dekapaʒ] **NM** *(nettoyage → en grattant)* scraping, scouring; *(→ par un produit chimique)* stripping, pickling; *(→ par la chaleur)* burning off; *(→ au papier de verre)* sanding (down); *(→ à la sableuse)* sandblasting

décapant, -e [dekapɑ̃, -ɑ̃t] **ADJ 1** *(nettoyant)* **agent** *ou* **produit d.** stripper **2** *(incisif → remarque)* caustic, vitriolic; *(→ roman, article)* corrosive; **elle avait un humour d.** she had a caustic sense of humour

  NM stripper *(product)*

décapeler [24] [dekaple] **vt** *Naut* to unrig, to strip; **d. le double d'une amarre** to take off the bight of a rope

décaper [3] [dekape] **vt 1** *(nettoyer→ gén)* to clean off; *(→ en grattant)* to scrape clean; *(→ avec un produit chimique)* to strip; *(→ à la chaleur)* to burn off; *(→ au papier de verre)* to sand (down); *(→ à la sableuse)* to sandblast; **d. la peinture d'une porte** to strip the paint off a door; **d. une façade** to sandblast the outside of a building **2** *Fam (racler)* to burn through■, to scour■; **ça décape la gorge** it burns your throat **3** *Géol* to clear of surface soil

décapeuse [dekapøz] **NF** scraper

décapitaliser [3] [dekapitalize] **vt** *Fin* to decapitalize

décapitation [dekapitasjɔ̃] **NF** beheading, decapitation

décapiter [3] [dekapite] **vt 1** *(personne)* **d. qn** *(le supplicier)* to behead sb, to cut sb's head off, to decapitate sb; *(accidentellement)* to cut sb's head off, to decapitate sb **2** *(arbre, fleur)* to top, to cut the top off **3** *(entreprise, gouvernement)* to decapitate, to deprive of leaders

décapode [dekapɔd] *Zool* **NM** decapod

  ❏ **décapodes NMPL** Decapoda

décapotable [dekapɔtabl] **ADJ** convertible; **sa voiture est d.** his/her car has a folding top *or* is a convertible

  NF convertible

décapoter [3] [dekapɔte] **vt 1** *(replier le toit de) Br* to fold back the roof of, *Am* to lower the top of **2** *(enlever le toit de)* to remove the *Br* roof *or* *Am* top of **3** *Can (ôter)* to take off

  ▶ **se décapoter VPR** *Can* to take off one's outdoor clothes

décapsulage [dekapsylaʒ] **NM** opening

décapsulation [dekapsylasjɔ̃] **NF** *Méd* decortication, decapsulation

décapsuler [3] [dekapsyle] **vt** to uncap, to take the top off

décapsuleur [dekapsylœr] **NM** bottle opener

décapuchonner [3] [dekapyʃɔne] **vt** to take the cap off

décarbonatation [dekarbɔnatasjɔ̃] NF *Chim* decarbonation

décarbonater [3] [dekarbɔnate] VT *Chim* to decarbonate

décarboxylation [dekarbɔksilasjɔ̃] NF *Chim* decarboxylation

décarburation [dekarbyrasjɔ̃] NF *Chim* decarburization

décarburer [3] [dekarbyre] VT *Chim* to decarburize

décarcasser [3] [dekarkase] **se décarcasser** VPR *Fam* to sweat blood, to bust a gut (**pour qch** over sth; **pour faire qch** to do sth); **se d. pour faire qch** to sweat blood *or* bust a gut to do sth

décarreler [24] [dekarle] VT *(sol, mur)* to take the tiles off

décarrer [3] [dekare] VI *Fam* **1** *(partir)* to make tracks, to hit the road **2** *(s'enfuir)* to beat it, to clear off, *Am* to book it

décartellisation [dekartelizasjɔ̃] NF decartelization

décasyllabe [dekasilab], **décasyllabique** [dekasilabik] ADJ decasyllabic
   NM decasyllable

décathlon [dekatlɔ̃] NM decathlon

décathlonien, -enne [dekatlɔnjɛ̃, -ɛn] NM,F decathlete

décati, -e [dekati] ADJ *Fam (personne)* decrepit; *(corps)* decrepit, wasted; **un vieux tout d.** an old man gone all to seed *or* to pot

décatir [32] [dekatir] VT to hot-press, *Br* to decatize, *Am* to decate
   ▶**se décatir** VPR *Fam* to become decrepit ■

décatissage [dekatisaʒ] NM hot-pressing, *Br* decatizing, *Am* decating

décauser [3] [dekoze] VT *Belg* to malign

décauville [dɔkovil] NM narrow-gauge railway

décavaillonner [3] [dekavajɔne] VT *Agr* to plough between the rows of vine

décavaillonneuse [dekãvajɔnøz] NF *Agr* French plough

décavé, -e [dekave] *Fam* ADJ *(qui a perdu au jeu)* cleaned out; *(ruiné)* flat broke, *Br* skint
   NM,F ruined gambler ■

décaver [3] [dekave] VT *Cartes* **d. qn** to clean sb out

decca [deka] NM Decca

Deccan [dekã] NM Deccan

décédé, -e [desede] ADJ deceased

décéder [18] [desede] VI to die, *Euph* to pass away; **il est décédé dans la nuit** he passed away during the night; **il est décédé depuis longtemps** he died a long time ago; **personne décédée** deceased person; **s'il vient à d.** in the event of his death

décelable [deslabl] ADJ **1** *(par analyse)* detectable **2** *(par observation)* discernible, detectable, perceivable

déceler [25] [desle] VT **1** *(repérer → erreur)* to detect, to spot, to discover; *(percevoir)* to detect, to discern, to perceive; **d. une fuite** to detect *or* to find *or* to trace a leak; **d. un don pour la musique chez qn** to detect *or* to notice an aptitude for music in sb; **je n'ai rien décelé d'anormal** I've found nothing wrong **2** *(révéler)* to reveal, to betray, to give away; **sa voix décelait son émotion** his/her voice betrayed his/her emotion

décélération [deselerasjɔ̃] NF deceleration, slowing down; **d. économique** economic slowdown

décélérer [18] [deselere] VI to decelerate, to slow down

décembre [desãbr] NM December; *voir aussi* **mars**

décembriste [desãbrist] NM *Hist* Decembrist

décemment [desamã] ADV **1** *(comme il se doit)* decently, properly; **se tenir d.** to behave properly; **j'espère que tu te nourris d.** I hope you're feeding yourself properly
   2 *(passablement)* reasonably, decently; **elle parle anglais d.** her English is reasonable *or* quite good, she speaks quite decent English; **je gagne d. ma vie** I make a reasonable *or* decent living
   3 *(raisonnablement)* decently; **on ne peut pas d. lui raconter ça** we can't very well *or* we can hardly tell him/her that

décemvir [desɛmvir] NM *Hist* decemvir

décemviral, -e, -aux, -ales, [desɛmviral, -o] ADJ *Hist* decemviral

décemvirat [desɛmvira] NM *Hist* decemvirate

décence [desãs] NF decency; **avoir la d. de faire qch** to have the (common) decency to do sth

décennal, -e, -aux, -ales [desenal, -o] ADJ decennial

décennat [desena] NM decade *(of leadership)*

décennie [deseni] NF decade, *Spéc* decennium, decennary

décent, -e [desã, -ãt] ADJ **1** *(convenable)* decent; **être en tenue décente** to be appropriately dressed; **il serait plus d. de ne rien lui dire** it would be more appropriate *or* proper not to tell him/her anything **2** *(passable)* decent, reasonable; **avoir un salaire d.** to earn a decent salary; **faire qch d'une manière décente** to do sth reasonably well; **un prix d.** a reasonable *or* fair price; **un repas d.** a decent meal

décentrage [desãtraʒ] NM off-centring

décentralisateur, -trice [desãtralizatœr, -tris] ADJ decentralization *(avant n)*, decentralist
   NM,F decentralist, supporter of decentralization

décentralisation [desãtralizasjɔ̃] NF *(de l'administration)* decentralization, decentralizing; *(des entreprises, des écoles)* moving away from the capital

Culture
LA DÉCENTRALISATION
This term is used to describe the shifting of a degree of administrative power from Paris to regional bodies, accompanied by the relocation of certain economic and business activities from the capital to the provinces. It has been a key aspect of French domestic policy since the early 1980s. This policy was adopted in an attempt to counteract the highly centralized nature of the French state.

décentralisatrice [desãtralizatris] *voir* **décentralisateur**

décentraliser [3] [desãtralize] VT *(administration)* to decentralize; *(entreprise, école)* to move away from the capital

décentré, -e [desãtre] ADJ **1** **être d.** to be off-centre **2** *Suisse (quartier, endroit)* outlying, away from the town centre

décentrement [desãtrəmã] NM *Phot* **d. vertical/horizontal** vertical/horizontal movement of the lens

décentrer [3] [desãtre] VT to bring out of centre; **être décentré** to be off-centre
   ▶**se décentrer** VPR to come *or* move off centre

déception [desɛpsjɔ̃] NF disappointment; **la grande d. de sa vie** the great disappointment of his/her life; **quelle d.!** what a disappointment!; **d. sentimentale** disappointment in love

décercler [3] [desɛrkle] VT to unhoop

décérébration [deserebrasjɔ̃] NF *Physiol* decerebration, pithing

décérébré, -e [deserebre] *Physiol* ADJ decerebrated
   NM,F decerebrate

décérébrer [18] [deserebre] VT *Physiol* to decerebrate, to pith

décerner [3] [desɛrne] VT **1** *(prix, médaille)* to award; *(titre, distinction)* to confer on; **se voir d. un prix** to be awarded a prize **2** *Jur* to issue

décervelage [desɛrvəlaʒ] NM braining

décerveler [24] [desɛrvəle] VT to brain

décès [desɛ] NM *Sout ou Jur* death

décevant, -e [desəvã, -ãt] ADJ disappointing

décevoir [52] [desəvwar] VT to disappoint; **elle attendait beaucoup mais elle a été très déçue** she was expecting a lot but she was very disappointed; **elle l'a beaucoup déçu** he was quite disappointed in *or* with her; **tu me déçois** I'm disappointed in you; **d. l'attente de qn** to disappoint sb, not to live up to sb's expectations; *Ironique* **il ne va pas être déçu (du voyage)!** he's going to get a shock!; *Ironique* **je croyais rencontrer l'homme idéal, je n'ai pas été déçue (du voyage)!** I thought I was meeting the ideal man, what a let-down!; *Suisse* **d. qn en bien** to give sb a pleasant surprise

déchaîné, -e [deʃene] ADJ *(tempête, mer, vent)* raging, wild; *(passions)* unbridled, raging; *(personne)* wild; *(public)* raving, delirious; *(opinion publique)* outraged; *(foule)* riotous, uncontrollable; *Fam* **tu es d., ce soir!** you're on top form tonight!

déchaînement [deʃɛnmã] NM *(des éléments, de la tempête)* raging, fury; *(de colère, de rage)* outburst; **rien ne justifie un tel d.** this outburst is totally unjustified

déchaîner [4] [deʃene] VT **1** *(déclencher → violence, colère)* to unleash, to arouse; *(→ enthousiasme)* to arouse; *(→ rires)* to trigger off; **d. l'hilarité générale** to cause general hilarity; **Greta Garbo a déchaîné les passions** Greta Garbo inspired many great passions; **son article a déchaîné les passions** his/her article caused an outcry *or* aroused strong passions
   2 *(mettre en colère)* **c'est ce que j'ai dit qui l'a déchaîné** it was what I said that sent him wild; **il est déchaîné contre vous** he's ranting and raving about you
   ▶**se déchaîner** VPR **1** *(tempête, mer, vent)* to rage
   2 *(hilarité, applaudissements)* to break *or* to burst out; *(instincts)* to be unleashed; **se d. contre qn** to rant at sb; **la presse s'est déchaînée contre le gouvernement** the press railed at the government; **elle s'est déchaînée contre son frère** she lashed out *or* let fly at her brother; **sa colère s'est déchaînée contre nous** he/she unleashed his/her anger on us

déchant [deʃã] NM *Mus* descant, discant

déchanter [3] [deʃãte] VI to be disillusioned, to become disenchanted; **il croyait avoir trouvé l'amour mais il a déchanté** he thought he'd found love but his illusions were shattered

déchaperonner [3] [deʃaprɔne] VT **1** *Chasse* to unhood **2** *Constr* to remove the coping from

décharge [deʃarʒ] NF **1** *(tir)* shot; **il y a eu trois décharges** there were three shots; **prendre** *ou* **recevoir une d. en pleine poitrine** to get shot in the chest
   2 *Élec* discharge; **d. électrique** electric *or* field discharge; *Fam* **prendre une d.** to get a shock *or* an electric shock
   3 *(écrit)* discharge paper; *(reçu)* receipt; **je veux qu'on me signe une d.** I want a signed piece of paper saying I'm not responsible
   4 *(dépotoir)* **d. (publique)** dump, *Br* rubbish tip, *Am* garbage dump; **d. interdite** *(sur panneau)* no dumping
   5 *Fin* (tax) rebate; **porter une somme en d.** to mark a sum as paid
   6 *Typ* set-off sheet, offset sheet
   7 *Physiol* rush; **d. d'adrénaline** rush of adrenaline
   8 *Can (trop-plein → d'un lac)* overflow channel, runoff
   ❏ **à la décharge de** PRÉP **à sa d.,** il faut dire que... in his/her defence, it has to be said that...
   ❏ **de décharge** ADJ **1** *Géog* **courant de d.** discharge *or* discharging current
   2 *Constr (arc)* relieving

déchargement [deʃarʒəmã] NM **1** *(d'une arme, d'un véhicule, d'une cargaison)* unloading **2** *Électron* dump

décharger [17] [deʃarʒe] VT **1** *(débarrasser de sa charge → véhicule, animal)* to unload; *(→ personne)* to unburden; **je vais te d. (à un voyageur)** let me take your luggage; *(au retour des magasins)* let me take your parcels for you
   2 *(enlever → marchandises)* to unload, to take off; *(→ gravier d'un camion)* to tip, to dump; *(→ passagers)* to set down; **d. la cargaison/des caisses d'un navire** to unload the cargo/crates off a ship; **d. le sable d'un camion** to dump the sand from a truck; **le train déchargeait ses passagers** the train was setting down its passengers
   3 *(soulager)* to relieve, to unburden; **d. sa conscience** to relieve *or* to unburden one's conscience; *Littéraire* **d. son cœur** to unburden one's heart; **d. qn de qch** to relieve sb of sth; *(dette)* to discharge sb from sth; *(impôt)* to exempt sb from sth; **j'aimerais être déchargé de la comptabilité** I would like to be relieved of the accounting; **être déchargé de ses fonctions** to be discharged *or* dismissed
   4 *(disculper)* to clear, to exonerate
   5 *Constr* to relieve, to discharge

6 *(tirer avec)* to fire, to discharge; **d. son arme sur qn** to fire one's gun at sb; *(ôter la charge de)* to unload

7 *Élec* to discharge

8 *Électron* to dump

9 *(laisser libre cours à)* to vent, to give vent to; **d. sa bile** to vent one's spleen; **d. sa colère** to give vent to one's anger; **d. sa mauvaise humeur sur qn** to vent one's temper on sb

VI 1 *(déteindre → étoffe)* to run

2 *Vulg (éjaculer)* to shoot one's load

▶**se décharger** VPR 1 *Élec (batterie)* to run down, to go flat; *(accumulateur)* to run down, to lose its charge

2 *(se débarrasser)* **je vais essayer de me d. de cette corvée sur quelqu'un** I'll try to hand over the chore to somebody else; **tu te décharges toujours sur les autres** you're always shifting responsibility onto other people

déchargeur [deʃarʒœr] NM 1 *(appareil)* unloader 2 *Vieilli (personne → dans un port)* stevedore, *Br* docker, *Am* longshoreman; *(→ aux halles)* labourer

décharné, -e [deʃarne] ADJ 1 *(maigre → personne)* emaciated, gaunt, wasted; *(→ visage)* emaciated, gaunt, haggard; *(→ main)* bony 2 *Fig (aride → paysage, vallée)* bare, bald; *(→ style)* bald

décharner [3] [deʃarne] VT *(personne)* to emaciate; *(os)* to strip the flesh off

déchaumage [deʃomaʒ] NM stubble ploughing

déchaumer [3] [deʃome] VT to plough up the stubble of

déchaumeuse [deʃomøz] NF disc tiller

déchaussage [deʃosaʒ] NM baring of the roots *(by frost)*

déchaussé, -e [deʃose] ADJ 1 *(sans chaussures → pied)* bare, shoeless; *(→ personne)* barefoot 2 *(branlant → dent)* loose; *(→ mur)* laid bare; **avoir les dents déchaussées** to have receding gums 3 *(moine, nonne)* discalced

déchaussement [deʃosmɑ̃] NM *(d'une dent)* loosening, *Spéc* agomphiasis; *(d'un mur)* laying bare

déchausser [3] [deʃose] VT 1 *(personne)* **d. qn** to take off sb's shoes 2 *(retirer → skis)* to take off 3 *Hort* to bare the roots of 4 *Constr (mur)* to lay bare

USAGE ABSOLU *Ski* to lose one's skis

▶**se déchausser** VPR 1 *(personne)* to take off one's shoes 2 *(dent)* to come loose; **avoir les dents qui se déchaussent** to have receding gums

déchausseuse [deʃosøz] NF *Agr* vineyard plough

déchaux [deʃo] ADJ M **moine d.** barefoot friar

dèche [dɛʃ] NF *Fam* dire poverty▪; **je ne peux pas l'acheter, c'est la d.!** I can't afford it, I'm broke *or Br* skint *or* strapped; **être dans la d.** to be broke *or Br* skint *or* strapped

'Dans la dèche à Paris et à Londres' *Orwell* 'Down and Out in Paris and London'

déchéance [deʃeɑ̃s] NF 1 *(dégradation → morale)* (moral) degradation, (moral) decline; *(→ physique)* deterioration, decline; **tomber dans la d.** to go into (moral) decline

2 *(déclin social)* lowering of social standing

3 *Rel* fall

4 *Jur (d'un droit, d'un titre, d'un brevet)* forfeiture; *Assur (d'une police d'assurance)* expiry; **d. de l'autorité parentale** loss of parental authority

5 *Pol (d'un monarque)* deposition, deposing; *(d'un président)* removal *(after impeachment)*

6 *Compta* **tomber en d.** to lapse; *Fin* **d. du terme** event of default

déchet [deʃɛ] NM 1 *(portion inutilisable)* **il y avait du d. parmi les fruits** some of the fruit was ruined; **dans un ananas il y a beaucoup de d.** there's a lot of waste in a pineapple

2 *Péj (personne)* (miserable) wretch

3 *Com* **d. de route** losses in transit

▫ **déchets** NMPL 1 *(résidus)* waste; **déchets de fabrication** *ou* **production** waste products; **des déchets de tissu** offcuts; **des déchets de viande** meat scraps; **des déchets de nourriture** food scraps; **déchets radioactifs/toxiques** radioactive/toxic waste

2 *Physiol* waste matter

déchetterie® [deʃɛtri] NF waste collection centre *(for sorting and recycling)*

déchiffonner [3] [deʃifɔne] VT to uncrumple, to smooth out, to smooth the creases out of

déchiffrable [deʃifrabl] ADJ decipherable; *(écriture)* legible

déchiffrage [deʃifraʒ] NM 1 *(d'un texte codé, de hiéroglyphes)* deciphering 2 *(d'un morceau de musique)* sight-reading

déchiffrement [deʃifrəmɑ̃] NM deciphering; *Ordinat* decryption; **d. de données** data decryption

déchiffrer [3] [deʃifre] VT 1 *(comprendre → inscription, manuscrit)* to decipher; *(→ langage codé)* to decipher, to decode; *Ordinat* to decrypt; **je déchiffre à peine son écriture** I can barely make out his/her handwriting 2 *(lire)* to spell out 3 *(morceau de musique)* to sight-read 4 *(élucider → énigme)* to puzzle out, to make sense of; *(→ sentiments, personnalité)* to fathom, to make out

USAGE ABSOLU *(lire)* **apprendre à d.** to start spelling out words

déchiffreur, -euse [deʃifrœr, -øz] NM,F *(gén)* decipherer; *(de messages codés)* decoder

déchiquetage [deʃiktaʒ] NM shredding, tearing

déchiqueté, -e [deʃikte] ADJ 1 *(irrégulier → feuille)* jagged; *(→ montagne, littoral)* jagged, ragged 2 *(tailladé)* torn to bits, hacked about 3 *Fam (ivre)* wasted, trashed; *(drogué)* stoned

déchiqueter [27] [deʃikte] VT *(papier, tissu)* to rip (to shreds), to tear (to bits); *(viande, proie)* to tear to pieces; **le chien a déchiqueté la couverture** the dog chewed the blanket to pieces *or* bits; **les corps ont été déchiquetés par l'explosion** the bodies were torn to pieces by the explosion

déchiqueteur [deʃiktœr] NM chipper, chopper

déchiqueture [deʃiktyr] NF 1 *(partie déchiquetée)* shred 2 *(entaille)* tear, rip 3 *(bord irrégulier)* jagged edge

déchirant, -e [deʃirɑ̃, -ɑ̃t] ADJ *(spectacle, adieux)* heartbreaking, heartrending; *(cri)* agonizing, harrowing; *(séparation)* unbearably painful

déchiré, -e [deʃire] ADJ *Fam (ivre)* wasted, trashed; *(drogué)* stoned

déchirement [deʃirmɑ̃] NM 1 *(arrachement)* tearing, ripping, rending 2 *(souffrance)* wrench; **le d. des adieux** the wrench of separation 3 *(désunion)* rift; **un pays en proie à des déchirements politiques** a country torn apart by internal strife

déchirer [3] [deʃire] VT 1 *(lacérer)* to tear, to rip; **attention, tu vas d. ton collant** be careful, you're going to rip your tights

2 *(mettre en deux morceaux)* to tear; *(mettre en morceaux)* to tear up *or* to pieces; **d. une page en deux** to tear a page into two; *Fig* **il s'est fait d. par la critique** he was torn apart *or* torn to shreds by the critics

3 *(arracher)* to tear off; **d. un ticket d'un carnet** to tear a ticket out from a book; *Fig* **d. le voile** to unmask the truth

4 *(ouvrir)* **d. une enveloppe** to tear open *or* to rip open an envelope

5 *(blesser)* to tear (the skin *or* flesh of), to gash; **le barbelé m'avait déchiré la jambe** I'd gashed my leg on the *Br* barbed wire *or Am* barbwire; **un bruit qui déchire les tympans** an earpiercing *or* earsplitting noise; **une douleur qui déchire la poitrine** a stabbing pain in the chest; *Littéraire* **d. qn** *ou* **le cœur de qn** to break sb's heart, to make sb's heart bleed; **être déchiré par la douleur** to be racked with pain

6 *Littéraire (interrompre → nuit, silence)* to rend, to pierce; **un cri déchira la nuit** a scream pierced the night; **un éclair déchira le ciel** a flash of lightning rent the sky

7 *(diviser)* to tear apart; **le pays est déchiré par la guerre depuis dix ans** the country has been torn apart by war for ten years; **des familles déchirées par la guerre** war-torn families; **je suis déchiré entre eux deux** I'm torn between the two of them

▶**se déchirer** VPR 1 *(emploi réciproque) (se faire souffrir)* to tear each other apart

2 *(emploi passif)* to tear; **ce tissu se déchire facilement** this material tears easily

3 *(vêtement, tissu, papier)* to tear, to rip; *(membrane)* to break; **mon gant s'est déchiré** my glove got torn; *Littéraire* **les brumes matinales se déchirent au premier soleil** the morning mists dissolve as the sun comes out; **mon cœur s'est déchiré** I was heartbroken

4 *Méd* **se d. un muscle/tendon/ligament** to tear a muscle/tendon/ligament

déchirure [deʃiryr] NF 1 *(accroc)* tear, rip, split 2 *Littéraire (souffrance)* wrench 3 *Méd* tear; **d. musculaire** torn muscle 4 *(trouée)* crack, opening

déchlorurer [3] [deklɔryre] VT to dechloridize

déchoir [71] [deʃwar] VI 1 *(aux être)* **il est déchu de son rang** he has lost *or* forfeited his social standing 2 *(aux avoir) Littéraire (s'abaisser)* to demean oneself; **il croira d. en acceptant cela** he'll think he's demeaning himself if he agrees to this; **ce ne serait pas d. que de...** it wouldn't be demeaning to... 3 *Littéraire (diminuer → fortune, prestige)* to wane

VT *(priver)* **d. qn d'un droit** to deprive sb of a right

déchristianisation [dekristjanizasjɔ̃] NF dechristianization, dechristianizing

déchristianiser [3] [dekristjanize] VT to dechristianize

déchu, -e [deʃy] PP *voir* **déchoir**

ADJ *(prince, roi)* deposed, dethroned; *(président)* deposed; *(ange, humanité)* fallen

déci [desi] NM *Suisse* = decilitre of wine

décibel [desibɛl] NM decibel; *Fam* **les décibels du festival de musique** the deafening noise coming from the music festival

décidabilité [desidabilite] NF decidability

décidable [desidabl] ADJ decidable

décidé, -e [deside] ADJ 1 *(résolu)* resolute, determined, decided; **elle est entrée d'un pas d.** she strode resolutely into the room; **d'un ton d.** in a decisive tone, decisively 2 *(réglé)* settled 3 *(déterminé)* **être d. à faire qch** to be determined *or* resolved to do sth

décidément [desidemɑ̃] ADV **d., ça ne marchera jamais** obviously it'll never work out; **d., c'est une manie** you're really making a habit of it, aren't you?; **d., tu exagères!** honestly, you are the limit!; **j'ai encore cassé un verre – d.!** I've broken another glass – it's not your day, is it!

décider [3] [deside] VT 1 *(choisir)* to decide (on); **ils ont décidé la guerre** they've decided to go to war; **d. de faire** to decide *or* to resolve to do; **ils ont décidé d'accepter/de ne pas accepter la proposition** they've decided in favour of/against the proposal; **ils décidèrent de se rendre plutôt que de mourir** they decided to surrender rather than die; **il a décidé que nous irions demain** he's decided that we'll go tomorrow; **il a décidé qu'il ne prendrait pas l'avion** he's decided not to *or* that he won't fly; **il fut décidé qu'on attendrait sa réponse** it was decided to wait for his/her reply, it was decided *or* settled that we/they/*etc* should wait for his/her reply; **d. combien/quoi/comment/si** to decide how much/what/how/whether; **c'est décidé** it's settled; **c'est décidé, je reste** I'm staying, that's settled

2 *(entraîner)* **d. qn à faire qch** to convince *or* to persuade sb to do sth; **ce n'est pas cela qui m'a décidé à partir** that's not what convinced *or* persuaded me to go; **décide-la à rester** persuade her to stay; **la pluie m'a décidé à ne pas sortir** I decided to stay in because of the rain

3 *(régler → ordre du jour)* to decide, to set; *(→ point de droit)* to resolve, to give a ruling on, to decide on

USAGE ABSOLU **c'est toi qui décides** it's your decision, it's up to you; **c'est moi qui décide ici** I'm the one who makes the decisions *or* who decides here; **je déciderai pour toi** I'll decide for you; **c'est le temps qui décidera** it will depend on the weather; **en cas de guerre, c'est la force de frappe qui décidera** if there's a war, the outcome will be decided solely by firepower; *Jur* **d. en faveur de qn** to give a ruling in favour of sb, to find for sb

▫ **décider de** VT IND 1 *(influencer)* to determine; **leur intervention a décidé de la victoire** their intervention brought about the victory; **le résultat de l'enquête décidera de la poursuite de ce projet** the results of the survey will determine whether (or not) we carry on with the project

2 *(choisir → lieu, date)* to choose, to determine, to decide on

3 *(juger)* **c'est le patron qui doit d. de son renvoi** it's the boss who'll have to decide (on) whether or not to sack him/her; **ta mère en a décidé ainsi!** your mother's decision is final!; **le sort en décida autrement** fate decreed otherwise

►**se décider** VPR **1** *(être déterminé)* to be decided (on); **les choses se sont décidées très vite** things were decided very quickly; **la couleur des tissus se décide au printemps** fabric shades are decided on *or* decisions are made about fabric shades in the spring

2 *(faire son choix)* to make up one's mind; **décide-toi** make up your mind; **je n'arrive pas à me d.** I can't make up my mind; **se d. pour** to decide on; **elle s'est décidée pour un chat siamois** she decided on a Siamese cat; **je me suis décidé à l'acheter** I decided *or* resolved to buy it; **elle s'est décidée à déménager** she's made up her mind to move house; **je ne me décide pas** *ou* **je ne peux pas me d. à le jeter** I can't bring myself to throw it out; **la voiture s'est enfin décidée à démarrer** the car finally decided to start; **il se décide à faire beau** it looks like the weather's trying to improve

décideur, -euse [desidœr, -øz] NM,F decision-maker

décidu, -e [desidy] ADJ *Bot* deciduous

déciduale [desidɥal] ADJ F **1** *Obst* **membrane d.** decidua **2** *Anat* **dent d.** deciduous tooth

décigrade [desigrad] NM one-tenth of a grade

décigramme [desigram] NM decigramme, decigram

décilage [desilaʒ] NM division into deciles

décile [desil] NM decile

décilitre [desilitr] NM decilitre

décimal, -e, -aux, -ales [desimal, -o] ADJ decimal; **fraction décimale** decimal, decimal fraction

▫ **décimale** NF decimal place; **nombre à trois décimales** number given to three decimal places

décimalisation [desimalizasjɔ̃] NF decimalization

décimaliser [3] [desimalize] VT to decimalize

décimateur [desimatœr] NM *Rel* tithe-owner

décimation [desimasjɔ̃] NF decimation, decimating

décime [desim] NM **1** *Admin* ten percent increase *(in tax)* **2** *Hist (dix centimes)* tenth part of a franc, ten centimes

décimer [3] [desime] VT to decimate

décimètre [desimɛtr] NM decimetre

décimétrique [desimetrik] ADJ decimetric

décintrage [desɛ̃traʒ], **décintrement** [desɛ̃trəmɑ̃] NM **1** *Constr* striking down of the centre, taking down of the centre **2** *Couture* letting out

décintrer [3] [desɛ̃tre] VT **1** *Constr* to strike down *or* to take down the centre **2** *Couture* to let out

décisif, -ive [desizif, -iv] ADJ *(déterminant → influence, intervention)* decisive; *(→ preuve)* conclusive; *(→ élément, facteur, coup)* decisive, deciding; **il n'y a encore rien de d.** there's nothing conclusive *or* definite yet; **il a eu un argument d.** what he said clinched the argument; **ça, c'est la question décisive!** that's the decider!; **à un moment d. de ma vie** at a decisive moment *or* at a watershed in my life; **de façon** *ou* **manière décisive** decisively, conclusively

décision [desizjɔ̃] NF **1** *(résolution)* decision; **arriver à une d.** to come to *or* to reach a decision; **prendre une d.** to make a decision; **prendre la d. de faire qch** to decide to do sth; **je n'ai pas pris de d. là-dessus** I haven't made up my mind about it; **qui a pris cette d.?** whose decision was it?; **la d. t'appartient** the decision is yours, it's for you to decide; **soumettre qch à la d. d'un comité** to ask a committee to make a decision on sth; *Mktg* **d. d'achat** buying decision, purchasing decision

2 *Jur* **d. arbitrale** arbitration ruling; **d. autonome** autonomous decision; **d. collective** *ou* **commune** joint decision; **d. d'espèce** = ruling on the facts of the case; **d. exécutoire** enforceable judgment; **d. gracieuse** = decision in a non-contentious matter; **d. implicite d'acceptation** tacit approval; **d. implicite de rejet** tacit rejection; **d. judiciaire** court ruling; **par d. judiciaire** by order of the court; **d. provisoire** provisional decision; **d. rectificative** = decision rectifying a clerical error or an omission affecting a judgment

3 *(fermeté)* decisiveness, resolution; **agir avec d.** to be decisive, to act decisively; **avoir de la d.** to be decisive; **manquer de d.** to be hesitant *or* undecisive; **montrer de la d.** to show resolution *or* decisiveness

4 *Ordinat* decision

▫ **de décision** ADJ *(organe, centre)* decision-making

décisionnaire [desizjɔnɛr] NMF decision-maker

décisionnel, -elle [desizjɔnɛl] ADJ decision-making *(avant n)*; **avoir un poste d.** to have a job with decision-making responsibilities

décisive [desiziv] *voir* **décisif**

décisoire [desizwar] ADJ **serment d.** decisive oath

décitex [desitɛks] NM *Tex* decitex

déclamateur, -trice [deklamatœr, -tris] *Péj* ADJ bombastic

NM,F declaimer

déclamation [deklamasjɔ̃] NF **1** *(art de réciter)* declamation **2** *(emphase)* declamation, ranting

déclamatoire [deklamatwar] ADJ **1** *(art)* declamatory **2** *Péj (style)* declamatory, bombastic

déclamatrice [deklamatris] *voir* **déclamateur**

déclamer [3] [deklame] VT to declaim

VI *Littéraire* **d. contre qn** to rail against sb

déclarant, -e [deklarɑ̃, -ɑ̃t] ADJ declaratory

NM,F declarant; **d. de TVA** VAT-registered person

déclaratif, -ive [deklaratif, -iv] ADJ **1** *Jur* declaratory **2** *Gram* declarative

déclaration [deklarasjɔ̃] NF **1** *(communication)* declaration, statement; **faire une d. à la presse** to issue a statement to the press; **j'ai une importante d. à faire** I have an important announcement to make; **je ne ferai aucune d.!** no comment!; **je ne peux pas faire de d.** I can't comment

2 *(témoignage)* declaration, statement; **faire une d. aux gendarmes** to make a statement to the police; **selon les déclarations du témoin** according to the witness's statement

3 *Admin* declaration; **faire une d. à la douane** to declare something at customs; **faire une d. à son assurance** to file a claim with one's insurance company; **d. d'accident** accident claim; **d. d'avarie** (ship's) protest; **d. de changement de domicile** notification of change of address; **d. de décès** = official registration of death *(submitted to the Mairie)*; **d. d'entrée** declaration *or* clearance inwards; **d. d'exportation** export declaration; **d. d'importation** import declaration; **d. d'impôts** tax return; **remplir sa d. d'impôts** to *Br* make *or Am* file one's tax return; **d. d'incendie** fire claim; **d. d'intention** statement of intent; **d. de naissance** = official birth registration *(submitted to the Mairie)*; **d. de patrimoine** = official statement of net personal assets made by French politicians on being elected to office; **faire une d. de perte de passeport à la police** to report the loss of one's passport to the police; **d. de sinistre** damage claim; **d. sous serment** statement under oath; **d. de solvabilité** declaration of solvency; **d. de sortie** declaration *or* clearance outwards; **d. de succession** = official document naming the beneficiaries of a will; **d. de transit** transit entry; **d. de vol** report of theft; **faire une d. de vol** to report something stolen

4 *Compta* return; **d. annuelle de résultats** annual statement of results; **d. de cessation de paiement** declaration of bankruptcy; **d. de faillite** declaration of bankruptcy; **d. fiscale** income tax return; **d. d'insolvabilité** declaration of insolvency; **d. de résultats** statement of results, financial statement; **d. de revenu** income tax return; **d. de solvabilité** declaration of solvency; **d. de TVA** VAT return

5 *Bourse* **d. de dividende** dividend announcement, declaration of dividend; **d. de valeur** declaration of value

6 *(aveu)* declaration; **faire une d. d'amour** *ou* **sa d. (à qn)** to declare one's love (to sb)

7 *(proclamation)* declaration, proclamation; **d. d'appel** statement of appeal; **d. de commande** = declaration of the true buyer by a third party; **d. des créances** declaration of debts; **d. au greffe** = declaration before the clerk of the court; **d. de guerre/d'indépendance** declaration of war/of independence; **D. des Droits de l'Homme et du Citoyen** Declaration of Human and Civic Rights *(of 1789)*; **d. de politique générale** = French Prime Minister's address to the "Assemblée Nationale" outlining his legislative programme; **d. de principe** declaration of principle; **d. solonnelle** formal affirmation; **d. universelle des droits de l'homme** Universal Declaration of Human Rights; **d. d'urgence** = declaration by the government that a bill is urgent in order to speed up parliamentary procedure; *Admin* **d. d'utilité publique** = government decision that a large public works project is vital and should therefore go ahead despite public protest

8 *Ordinat* **d. de champ** field definition

Culture

DÉCLARATION D'IMPÔTS

People in France are required to declare their taxable earnings at the beginning of the year. Thrice-yearly tax payments ("tiers provisionnels") are based on one third of the previous year's total, the final payment being adjusted according to the actual tax owed. It is also possible to pay tax on a monthly basis. This is known as "mensualisation".

Culture

LA DÉCLARATION DES DROITS DE L'HOMME ET DU CITOYEN

Adopted by the National Assembly in August 1789, the Declaration proclaimed the inalienable natural right of all men to freedom, condemned the privileged class of the Ancien Régime and declared all citizens equal before the law. In 1793, the preface to the Constitution of year 1 added the right to education, work and freedom of assembly to the text of 1789.

déclarative [deklarativ] *voir* **déclaratif**

déclaratoire [deklaratwar] ADJ declaratory

déclaré, -e [deklare] ADJ **1** *(ennemi)* declared, sworn; *(intention, opinion)* declared; **une animosité déclarée** a declared animosity; **un fasciste d.** a professed *or* self-confessed fascist; **un opposant d.** an avowed opponent **2** *Admin* **d. d'utilité publique** *(entreprise)* declared vital by the government despite public protest

déclarer [3] [deklare] VT **1** *(proclamer)* to declare, to announce, to assert; **le gouvernement a déclaré que...** the government announced *or* declared that...; **d. une séance ouverte** to declare a meeting open; **d. forfait** *Sport* to withdraw; *Fig* to throw in the towel; *aussi Fig* **d. la guerre à** to declare war on

2 *(juger)* **d. qn coupable** to find sb guilty; **on l'a déclaré incapable de gérer sa fortune** he was pronounced incapable of managing his estate

3 *(affirmer)* to profess, to claim; **elle déclare agir pour le bien de tous** she professes to work for the good of everyone; **il déclare être innocent** he claims to be innocent *or* protests his innocence; **il déclare être resté chez lui** he claims he stayed at home

4 *(révéler → intention)* to state, to declare; *Littéraire* **d. son amour** *ou* **sa flamme à qn** to declare one's love to sb

5 *(dire officiellement)* to declare; **d. ses employés** to declare one's employees; **d. ses revenus au fisc** to *Br* make *or Am* file one's tax return; **d. un enfant à la mairie** to register the birth of a child; **d. un vol** to report a theft; **rien à d.** nothing to declare; **si vous avez quelque chose à d. à la douane** if you have anything to declare at customs

6 *Ordinat (valeur)* to define

►**se déclarer** VPR **1** *(se manifester → incendie, épidémie)* to break out; *(→ fièvre, maladie)* to set in

2 *(se prononcer)* to take a stand; **se d. sur une question/un point** to take a stand on a question/a point; **elle ne veut pas se d. sur cette question** she refuses to state her opinion on the matter; **se d. pour/contre l'avortement** to come

dec-dec

out in favour of/against abortion, **to declare for/against abortion**

3 *(se dire)* to say; **il s'est déclaré coupable** he said he was guilty; **il s'est déclaré ravi** he said how pleased he was; **elle s'est déclarée satisfaite de l'accord passé** she declared herself satisfied with the agreement that was reached

4 *Bourse* **se d. acheteur** to call the shares; **se d. vendeur** to put the shares

5 *Littéraire (dire son amour)* to declare one's love

déclassé, -e [deklase] ADJ **1** *(personne)* déclassé **2** *(hôtel)* downgraded; *(joueur, équipe)* relegated **3** *Bourse (valeurs)* displaced
▶ NM,F **c'est un d.** he has lost his social status *or* come down in the world

déclassement [deklasmɑ̃] NM **1** *(dans la société)* fall *or* drop in social standing **2** *(d'un hôtel)* downgrading; *(d'un joueur, d'une équipe)* relegation **3** *(mise en désordre)* putting out of order **4** *Bourse (de valeurs)* displacement **5** *Rail* change to a lower class **6** *Mil, Naut & Nucl* decommissioning

déclasser [3] [deklase] VT **1** *(déranger)* to put out of order
2 *(rétrograder → hôtel)* to downgrade; *(→ joueur, équipe)* to relegate
3 *(déprécier)* to demean; **ce travail le déclassait** he was lowering *or* demeaning himself in that job
4 *Rail* to change to a lower class
5 *Mil, Naut & Nucl* to decommission
▶ **se déclasser** VPR **1** *(dans l'échelle sociale)* to move one step down the social scale
2 *(dans un train)* to change to a lower-class compartment; *(dans un navire)* to change to lower-class accommodation

déclassifier [9] [deklasifje] VT *Mil* to declassify

déclaveter [27] [deklavte] VT *Tech* to unkey

déclenchement [deklɑ̃ʃmɑ̃] NM **1** *(début → d'un événement)* starting point, start, trigger; *(→ d'une attaque)* launching **2** *(d'un mécanisme, d'une minuterie)* triggering, activation; *(d'une sonnerie, d'une alarme)* setting off; *Tech (d'une pièce)* release; *Obst (de l'accouchement)* induction, inducing

déclencher [3] [deklɑ̃ʃe] VT **1** *(provoquer → attaque)* to launch; *(→ révolte, conflit)* to trigger (off), to bring about; *(→ grève, émeute, rires)* to trigger *or* to spark off
2 *(mettre en marche → mécanisme, minuterie)* to trigger, to activate; *(→ sonnerie, alarme)* to set off; *Tech (→ pièce)* to release; *Obst (accouchement)* to induce
▶ **se déclencher** VPR **1** *(commencer → douleur, incendie)* to start
2 *(se mettre en marche → sirène, sonnerie, bombe)* to go off; *(→ mécanisme)* to be triggered off *or* released

déclencheur [deklɑ̃ʃœr] NM **1** *Élec* release, circuit breaker **2** *Phot* shutter release; **d. automatique** time release, self-timer **3** *Tech* release, tripping device

déclic [deklik] NM **1** *(mécanisme)* trigger, releasing mechanism
2 *(bruit)* click; **se fermer avec un d.** to click shut; **s'enclencher avec un d.** to click into place
3 *(prise de conscience)* **il s'est produit un d. et elle a trouvé la solution** things suddenly fell into place *or* clicked and she found the answer; **pour moi, la lecture de ce livre a été le d.** things finally fell into place for me when I read this book; **pour moi, cette aventure a été le d.** what happened made me come to my senses

déclin [deklɛ̃] NM **1** *(diminution)* decline, waning; **le d. de la popularité d'un acteur** the decline of an actor's popularity; **le d. de l'influence de Rome** the waning influence of Rome; **le soleil à son d.** the setting sun
2 *Littéraire (fin)* close; **le d. du jour** nightfall, dusk; **le d. de la vie** the twilight years
▢ **en déclin** ADJ on the decline; **les adhésions sont en d.** membership is declining *or* falling off *or* on the decline; **un hebdomadaire en d.** a weekly paper with falling readership figures
▢ **sur le déclin** ADJ *(prestige, puissance)* declining, on the wane; *(malade)* declining; **votre pauvre mère est sur le d.** your poor mother is

getting worse; **un acteur sur le d.** an actor who's seen better days

'**Le Déclin de l'empire américain**' *Arcand* 'The Decline of the American Empire'

déclinable [deklinabl] ADJ declinable; **une gamme d'ordinateurs d. en plusieurs configurations** a range of computers enabling several different configurations

déclinaison [deklinɛzõ] NF **1** *Gram* declension **2** *Astron & Phys* declination; **d. magnétique** magnetic declination **3** *Mktg* **d. de gamme** range extension

déclinant, -e [deklinɑ̃, -ɑ̃t] ADJ *(force)* declining, deteriorating; *(influence, grandeur)* declining, waning, fading; *(société)* declining, decaying

déclinatoire [deklinatwar] NM **1** *(boussole)* surveyor's compass **2** *Jur* declinatory; **élever un d.** to except the jurisdiction of the court; **d. de compétence** objection to jurisdiction

décliner [3] [dekline] VT **1** *Gram* to decline; *Fig* **l'amour est décliné dans toutes les chansons** love is an ever-recurrent theme in songs; **un imprimé décliné dans plusieurs tons** a pattern available in several shades
2 *(énoncer → identité)* to give, to state
3 *(refuser → responsabilité, invitation)* to decline, to refuse; *(→ offre)* to decline, to refuse, to reject; **d. toute responsabilité** to refuse all responsibility; *(dans un contexte commercial)* to accept no liability; *Jur* **d. la compétence d'une juridiction** to refuse to acknowledge a jurisdiction
4 *Mktg* **d. une gamme** to extend a range
▶ VI *(soleil)* to set; *(vieillard, jour)* to decline; *(malade)* to decline, to fade; *(santé, vue)* to deteriorate; *(prestige)* to wane, to decline
▶ **se décliner** VPR **1** *Gram* to be declined
2 *Com* **une robe qui se décline dans différentes couleurs** a dress available in different colours

déclinologie [deklinɔlɔʒi] NF = typically French preoccupation with the state of one's country

déclinologue [deklinɔlɔg] NMF = person preoccupied with the decline of his/her country

décliquetage [dekliktaʒ] NM *Tech* release, disengaging

décliqueter [27] [deklikte] VT *Tech* to release, to disengage

déclive [dekliv] ADJ downward sloping, *Spéc* declivitous
▶ NF **en d.** sloping

déclivité [deklivite] NF **1** *(descente)* downward slope, incline, *Spéc* declivity **2** *(inclinaison → d'une route, d'un chemin de fer)* gradient

décloisonnement [deklwazɔnmɑ̃] NM decompartmentalization, decompartmentalizing

décloisonner [3] [deklwazɔne] VT to decompartmentalize

déclore [113] [deklɔr] VT *(terrain)* to open up

déclouer [6] [deklue] VT *(planche)* to remove *or* to pull the nails out of; *(couvercle)* *Br* to prise *or* *Am* to pry open
▶ **se déclouer** VPR to fall *or* to come apart

déco [deko] ADJ PL *(abrév* **décoratifs)** **arts d.** art deco
▶ NF *(abrév* **décoration)** decor, decoration; *(métier)* (interior) decorating, interior design; **j'aime beaucoup faire de la d.** I love decorating

décochage [dekɔʃaʒ] NM *Métal* shaking out

décocher [3] [dekɔʃe] VT **1** *(flèche)* to shoot, to fire; *(coup)* to throw; **il m'a décoché un coup de pied** he kicked me; **le cheval lui a décoché une ruade** the horse lashed out *or* kicked at him/her **2** *(regard)* to shoot; *(sourire)* to flash; *(plaisanterie, méchanceté)* to fire, to shoot; **il lui a décoché un regard assassin** he shot him/her a murderous look; **elle lui a décoché une remarque acerbe** she bit his/her head off

décocté [dekɔkte] NM *Pharm* decoction

décoction [dekɔksjõ] NF *Pharm* decoction

décodage [dekɔdaʒ] NM **1** *(d'un texte)* decoding, deciphering **2** *Ordinat & TV* decoding, unscrambling

décoder [3] [dekɔde] VT **1** *(texte)* to decode **2** *Ordinat & TV* to decode, to unscramble

décodeur [dekɔdœr] ADJ M decoding
▶ NM decoder; **d. numérique** set-top box, digibox

décoffrage [dekɔfraʒ] NM striking of formwork, *Br* dismantling of shuttering

décoffrer [3] [dekɔfre] VT to strike the formwork of, *Br* to dismantle the shuttering of

décoiffant, -e [dekwafɑ̃, -ɑ̃t] ADJ *Fam* exciting ▪

décoiffer [3] [dekwafe] VT **1** *(déranger la coiffure de)* **d. qn** to mess up *or* *Am* to muss up sb's hair; **elle est toute décoiffée** her hair's a mess
2 *(ôter le chapeau de)* **d. qn** to remove sb's hat
3 *Fam (location)* **ça décoiffe** it's mindblowing, it takes your breath away
▶ **se décoiffer** VPR **1** *(déranger sa coiffure)* to mess up *or* *Am* to muss up one's hair
2 *(ôter son chapeau)* to remove one's hat

décoincement [dekwɛ̃smɑ̃], **décoinçage** [dekwɛ̃saʒ] NM *(déblocage → d'un objet)* unjamming, freeing, loosening; *(→ d'une vertèbre, d'une articulation)* loosening up

décoincer [16] [dekwɛ̃se] VT **1** *(débloquer → objet)* to unjam, to free; *(→ vertèbre, articulation)* to loosen up **2** *Fam (personne)* to loosen up
▶ **se décoincer** VPR **1** *(objet)* to unjam, to work loose **2** *Fam (personne)* to relax ▪, to let one's hair down

déçoit *etc voir* **décevoir**

décolérer [18] [dekɔlere] VI **il ne décolérait pas** he was still fuming; **il n'a pas décoléré de la journée** he's been furious *or* fuming all day; **elle ne décolère jamais** she's permanently in a temper

décollage [dekɔlaʒ] NM **1** *Aviat* takeoff; *Astron* lift-off, blast-off; **au d.** *Aviat* at *or* on takeoff; *Astron* at *or* on lift-off **2** *(d'une enveloppe, d'un papier)* unsticking **3** *Écon & (en sociologie)* takeoff

décollation [dekɔlasjõ] NF *Arch* decollation

décollé, -e [dekɔle] ADJ **avoir les oreilles décollées** to have ears that stick out

décollectivisation [dekɔlɛktivizasjõ] NF decollectivization

décollectiviser [3] [dekɔlɛktivize] VT to decollectivize

décollement [dekɔlmɑ̃] NM **1** *(d'un papier)* unsticking **2** *Méd* **d. de la rétine** detachment *or* separation of the retina; **d. épiphysaire** epiphysial fracture

décoller [3] [dekɔle] VI **1** *Aviat* to take off; *Astron & Naut* to take *or* to lift *or* to blast off
2 *(quitter le sol → skieur, motocycliste)* to take off
3 *Fam (partir)* to leave ▪, **elle ne décolle pas de la bibliothèque** she never moves from *or* leaves the library; **j'ai eu du mal à le faire d. d'ici** I had trouble getting rid of him
4 *(progresser → exportation, pays)* to take off; **au troisième trimestre, il a fini par d.** his work finally took off in the third term; **ces mesures n'ont pas réussi à faire d. l'économie** these measures failed to restart the economy
5 *(s'échapper)* to escape; **d. du réel** *ou* **de la réalité** to be in another world; **d. du peloton** *(coureur cycliste)* to peel away from the pack
6 *Fam (être distancé → sportif, élève)* to fall *or* to drop behind
7 *Fam (maigrir)* to lose weight ▪
▶ VT **1** *(détacher → papier)* to unstick, to unglue, to peel off; **d. à la vapeur** to steam off; **d. dans l'eau** to soak off; **d. une enveloppe** *(en tirant)* to open an envelope; *(à la vapeur)* to steam open an envelope
2 *Fam (faire partir)* to tear *or* to prise away; **on ne peut pas le d. de la télévision** there's no prising him away from the TV
3 *Fam (quitter)* **il ne nous a pas décollés de la journée** he stuck to us like glue all day long
4 *(au billard)* to nudge away from the cushion
▶ **se décoller** VPR **1** *(emploi passif)* to come off; **ça se décolle simplement en tirant dessus** just pull it and it comes off
2 *(se détacher)* to come *or* to peel off; **du papier peint qui se décolle** peeling wallpaper
3 *Méd* to become detached

décolletage [dekɔltaʒ] NM **1** *(action)* cutting out of the neck; *(décolleté)* low-cut neckline, décolletage **2** *Agr* topping **3** *Tech* cutting off

décolleté, -e [dekɔlte] ADJ **1** *(échancré)* low-cut, décolleté; **robe décolletée dans le dos** dress

cut low in the back; **tu ne trouves pas que c'est trop d.?** you don't think it's too low?

2 *(femme)* décolleté, wearing a low-cut dress

3 *Vieilli ou Littéraire* **propos décolletés** loose or licentious talk

NM 1 *(échancrure)* low neckline; **d. bateau** boat neck; **d. carré** square neck; **d. en pointe ou en V** V neck; **un d. plongeant** a plunging neckline; **en grand d.** *(en robe de soirée)* in full evening dress

2 *(d'une femme)* cleavage

décolleter [27] [dekɔlte] **VT 1** *(robe)* to give a low neckline to; *(personne)* to reveal the neck and shoulders of; **cette robe te décollette trop** this dress is too low(-cut) **2** *Agr* to top **3** *Tech* to cut off, to crop

décolleteur, -euse [dekɔltœr, -øz] **NM,F** lathe operator

❑ **décolleteuse NF 1** *Agr* (beet) topper **2** *Tech* automatic lathe, autolathe

décolleuse [dekɔløz] **NF** stripper *(for walls, floors)*

décolonisation [dekɔlɔnizasjɔ̃] **NF** decolonization

LA DÉCOLONISATION

In a French context, the word refers specifically to the period in the 40s and 50s when colonies progressively became independent of French colonial rule. The decolonization process in France was characterized by some negotiated withdrawals from former colonies, but it also involved two protracted wars, the Indochina war (1945–54) and the Algerian War (1954–62).

décoloniser [3] [dekɔlɔnize] **VT** to decolonize

décolorant, -e [dekɔlɔrɑ̃, -ɑ̃t] **ADJ 1** *(gén)* decolorant, decolouring **2** *(pour cheveux)* decolorizing *(avant n)*, decolorant, bleaching *(avant n)*

NM 1 *(gén)* decolorant **2** *(pour cheveux)* bleaching agent, bleach

décoloration [dekɔlɔrasjɔ̃] **NF 1** *(atténuation de la couleur)* fading, discolouration **2** *(disparition de la couleur)* bleaching, discolouring; **d. d'une plante** bleaching of a plant **3** *(des cheveux)* bleach treatment; **faire une d. à qn** to bleach someone's hair; **se faire faire une d.** to have one's hair bleached

décoloré, -e [dekɔlɔre] **ADJ 1** *(fané)* faded **2** *(blondi)* bleached; **une femme décolorée** a peroxide or bleached blonde **3** *(livide → visage, joue)* ashen, pale

décolorer [3] [dekɔlɔre] **VT 1** *(affaiblir la couleur de)* to fade

2 *(éclaircir → cheveux)* to bleach; **cheveux décolorés par le soleil** hair lightened or bleached by the sun; **elle se fait d. (les cheveux)** she has her hair lightened or bleached

▶**se décolorer VPR 1** *(emploi réfléchi)* *(personne)* to bleach one's hair

2 *(tissu, papier)* to fade, to lose its colour

3 *(liquide)* to lose its colour

décombres [dekɔ̃br] **NMPL 1** *(d'un bâtiment)* debris *(singulier)*, rubble, wreckage **2** *Littéraire (d'une civilisation)* ruins

décommander [3] [dekɔmɑ̃de] **VT** *(marchandise)* to cancel; *(invitation, rendez-vous)* to cancel, to call off; *(invité)* to put off

▶**se décommander VPR** *(à un rendez-vous)* to cancel (one's appointment); *(à un dîner, une soirée)* to cancel

décompacter [3] [dekɔ̃pakte] **VT** *Ordinat (données)* to unpack

décompartimentaliser [3] [dekɔ̃partimɑ̃talize] **VT** to decompartmentalize

décompensation [dekɔ̃pɑ̃sasjɔ̃] **NF** decompensation

décompensé, -e [dekɔ̃pɑ̃se] **ADJ** decompensated

décomplexer [4] [dekɔ̃plɛkse] **VT** to encourage, to reassure; **ça m'a décomplexé** it made me feel more confident or less inadequate

décomposable [dekɔ̃pozabl] **ADJ 1** *(corps chimique, matière)* decomposable **2** *(texte, idée)* analysable, that can be broken down **3** *Math (équation)* that can be factorized; *(polynôme)* that can be broken up **4** *Phys* resoluble

décomposer [dekɔ̃poze] **VT 1** *Chim* to decompose, to break down

2 *Phys (force)* to resolve; *(lumière)* to disperse

3 *Math* to factorize; **d. en facteurs premiers** to resolve into prime factors

4 *(analyser → texte, idée)* to break down, to analyse; *(→ mouvement, processus)* to decompose, to break up; *(→ exercice, mélodie)* to go through (step by step); *Gram (→ phrase)* to parse; *(→ pas de danse)* to go through

5 *Compta (compte, résultats)* to analyse, to break down; *(dépenses)* to break down

6 *(pourrir → terre, feuilles)* to decompose, to rot

7 *(altérer)* **l'horreur qui décomposait ses traits** the horror reflected in his/her contorted features; **un visage décomposé par la peur** a face distorted with fear; **être décomposé** to look stricken

▶**se décomposer VPR 1** *(emploi passif)* *Gram (phrase)* to be parsed; *Math* to be factorized; **se d. en** to break down into; **le texte se décompose en trois parties** the text can be broken down or divided into three parts

2 *(pourrir)* to decompose, to decay, to rot

3 *(s'altérer → visage)* to become distorted; **soudain son visage s'est décomposé** his/her face suddenly fell

décomposeur [dekɔ̃pozœr] **NM** decomposer

décomposition [dekɔ̃pozisjɔ̃] **NF 1** *Chim* decomposition, breaking down

2 *Phys (de la lumière)* dispersion; *(d'une force)* resolution

3 *Math* factorization; **d. en facteurs premiers** prime factorization; **d. en éléments simples** expansion into partial fractions

4 *(analyse)* analysis, breaking down; *Gram* parsing; **faire la d. d'un planning/d'une tâche** to break down a schedule/a task; **faire la d. d'une phrase** to parse a sentence

5 *Compta (d'un compte, de résultats)* analysis, breakdown; *(des dépenses)* breakdown

6 *Ordinat* breakdown

7 *(pourrissement → de la matière organique)* decomposition, decay, rot; *(→ de la société)* decline, decay, decadence; **en (état de) d.** *(cadavre)* decomposing, decaying, rotting; *(société)* declining, decaying; **en état de d. avancé** in an advanced state of decay

8 *(altération → des traits)* contortion

décompresser [4] [dekɔ̃prese] **VT 1** *Tech* to decompress **2** *Ordinat* to decompress

VI 1 *(plongeur)* to undergo decompression **2** *Fam (se détendre)* to relax■, to unwind

décompresseur [dekɔ̃presœr] **NM 1** *Phys* decompression device **2** *Aut & Tech* decompressor

décompression [dekɔ̃presjɔ̃] **NF 1** *Méd & Tech* decompression; **avoir un accident de d.** *(plongeur)* to get the bends **2** *Fam (détente)* unwinding, relaxing **3** *Aut & Tech* decompression; **robinet de d.** *(dans un moteur)* compression tap; *(dans une machine à vapeur)* petcock **4** *Ordinat* decompression, unbundling

décomprimer [3] [dekɔ̃prime] **VT** to decompress

décompte [dekɔ̃t] **NM 1** *(calcul)* working out, reckoning, calculation; **faire le d. des intérêts** to work out or to calculate the interest; **faire le d. des voix** to count the votes; **faire le d. des points** to add up or to reckon up the score

2 *(déduction)* deduction; **je vous fais le d. des deux fromages** I'll take the two cheeses off (your bill)

3 *(relevé)* detailed account, breakdown

4 *(solde)* balance; **payer le d.** to pay the balance due *(on an account)*

décompter [3] [dekɔ̃te] **VT 1** *(déduire)* to deduct **2** *(dénombrer)* to count

VI to strike the wrong time

déconcentration [dekɔ̃sɑ̃trasjɔ̃] **NF 1** *Admin* devolution **2** *Écon (décentralisation)* decentralization, dispersion **3** *(dilution)* dilution **4** *(manque d'attention)* lack of concentration

déconcentrer [3] [dekɔ̃sɑ̃tre] **VT 1** *(transférer → pouvoir)* to devolve; *(→ bureaux, entreprises)* to disperse **2** *(distraire)* **d. qn** to distract sb's attention; **le bruit l'a déconcentré** the noise distracted his attention **3** *Chim (diluer)* **d. une solution** to dilute a solution

▶**se déconcentrer VPR** to lose (one's) concentration

déconcertant, -e [dekɔ̃sɛrtɑ̃, -ɑ̃t] **ADJ** disconcerting, off-putting

déconcerter [3] [dekɔ̃sɛrte] **VT** to disconcert; **il ne**

faut pas te laisser d. par ses questions you mustn't let yourself be disconcerted by his/her questions

déconditionnement [dekɔ̃disjɔnmɑ̃] **NM** deconditioning

déconditionner [3] [dekɔ̃disjɔne] **VT** to decondition

déconfit, -e [dekɔ̃fi, -it] **ADJ** crestfallen

déconfiture [dekɔ̃fityr] **NF 1** *(échec)* collapse, defeat, rout; *(d'une société)* collapse, failure, downfall, ruin; **tomber en d.** to collapse **2** *Jur* insolvency

déconforté, -e [dekɔ̃fɔrte] **ADJ** *Can Vieilli ou Littéraire* distressed

décongélation [dekɔ̃ʒelasjɔ̃] **NF** defrosting, thawing

décongeler [25] [dekɔ̃ʒle] **VT** to defrost, to thaw

décongestif, -ive [dekɔ̃ʒɛstif, -iv] **ADJ** decongestant

NM decongestant

décongestion [dekɔ̃ʒɛstjɔ̃] **NF** decongestion

décongestionnement [dekɔ̃ʒɛstjɔnmɑ̃] **NM 1** *(dégagement → d'une route, d'un centre urbain)* relief of congestion **(de** in) **2** *Méd* decongestion

décongestionner [3] [dekɔ̃ʒɛstjɔne] **VT 1** *(dégager → route, centre urbain)* to relieve congestion in, to ease the traffic load in; *(aéroport, université)* to relieve congestion at **2** *Méd* to decongest, to relieve congestion in or the congestion of

décongestive [dekɔ̃ʒɛstiv] *voir* **décongestif**

déconnade [dekɔnad] **NF** *très Fam* **quelle d.!** what a hoot!, what a laugh!

déconnecté, -e [dekɔnɛkte] **ADJ** *Ordinat (imprimante)* off-line

déconnecter [4] [dekɔnɛkte] **VT 1** *(débrancher → tuyau, fil électrique)* to disconnect **2** *Fam Fig* to disconnect■, to cut off■; **il est totalement déconnecté de la réalité** he's totally cut off from reality

▶**se déconnecter VPR** *Ordinat* to go off-line

déconner [3] [dekɔne] **VI** *très Fam* **1** *(dire des bêtises)* to talk crap or *Br* bollocks; **arrête de d.** don't talk crap; **sans d.!** *(je t'assure)* no kidding!, *Br* straight up!; **sans d.?** *(est-ce vrai)* no kidding?, yeah?, *Br* straight up?

2 *(s'amuser)* to horse or to fool around

3 *(faire des bêtises)* to mess around; **déconne pas!** stop messing about!

4 *(mal fonctionner)* to be on the blink, *Am* to be on the fritz

5 *(ne plus avoir toute sa tête)* to be off one's rocker, to be not all there

6 *(ne pas être raisonnable)* **allez, déconne pas, viens avec nous!** come on, don't be like that, come with us!

déconneur, -euse [dekɔnœr, -øz] *très Fam* **ADJ** **être d.** to be a clown or a joker

NM,F clown, joker

déconnexion [dekɔnɛksjɔ̃] **NF** disconnection

déconseiller [4] [dekɔ̃seje] **VT** to advise against; **d. à qn de faire qch** to advise sb against doing sth; **un livre à d. aux jeunes** an unsuitable book for young people; **c'est déconseillé** it's not (to be) recommended, it's to be avoided; **baignade déconseillée** *(sur panneau)* bathing not recommended

déconsidération [dekɔ̃siderasjɔ̃] **NF** *Littéraire* discredit; **tomber dans la d.** to fall into disrepute

déconsidérer [18] [dekɔ̃sidere] **VT** to discredit; **ces révélations l'ont déconsidéré** these revelations have cast a slur on or have discredited him; **il est complètement déconsidéré** he is utterly discredited, he has lost all credibility

▶**se déconsidérer VPR** to discredit oneself, to bring discredit upon oneself, to lose one's credibility

déconsigner [3] [dekɔ̃siɲe] **VT 1** *(bagage)* to collect from the *Br* left-luggage office or *Am* checkroom **2** *(bouteille, emballage)* to return the deposit on **3** *Mil* to release from confinement to barracks

déconstruction [dekɔ̃stryksjɔ̃] **NF** deconstruction

déconstruire [98] [dekɔ̃strɥir] **VT** *Littérature & Phil* to deconstruct

décontamination [dekɔ̃taminasjɔ̃] **NF** decontamination; **d. d'un site nucléaire** decontaminating a nuclear site

dec-dec

décontaminer [3] [dekɔ̃tamine] VT to decontaminate

décontenancer [16] [dekɔ̃tnɑ̃se] VT to disconcert, *Sout* to discountenance

▸**se décontenancer** VPR to lose one's composure

décontract [dekɔ̃trakt] ADJ INV *Fam* = **décontracté**

décontractant, -e [dekɔ̃traktɑ̃, -ɑ̃t] ADJ relaxing

décontracté, -e [dekɔ̃trakte] ADJ **1** *(détendu → muscle, corps, ambiance)* relaxed; *(→ caractère)* easy-going, relaxed; *(→ attitude)* relaxed, composed, unworried; *(→ style, vêtements)* casual; **en tenue décontractée** in casual dress, casually dressed **2** *Péj (désinvolte)* casual, offhand

ADV *(s'habiller)* casually

décontracter [3] [dekɔ̃trakte] VT *(muscle)* to relax, to unclench; **elle sait d. les nouveaux venus** she knows how to put newcomers at ease

▸**se décontracter** VPR to relax

décontraction [dekɔ̃traksjɔ̃] NF **1** *(relâchement, détente)* relaxation, relaxing; **sa d. me sidère!** I'm amazed at how relaxed he/she is *or* laid back he/she is! **2** *(aisance)* coolness, collectedness

déconventionner [3] [dekɔ̃vɑ̃sjɔne] VT to allow to opt out *(of the National Health system)*

déconvenue [dekɔ̃vny] NF disappointment; **quelle ne fut pas ma d. lorsque...** I was so disappointed when...

décor [dekɔr] NM **1** *(décoration → d'un lieu)* interior decoration, decor; *(→ d'un objet)* pattern, design

2 *(environs)* setting; **la maison était située dans un d. magnifique** the house stood in magnificent scenery *or* surroundings

3 *Cin, Théât & TV* set, scenery, setting; *(toile peinte)* backdrop, backcloth; **d. de cinéma** *Br* film *or Am* movie set; **d. en extérieur** outdoor set; **d. de théâtre** stage set; **tourné en décors naturels** shot on location; *Fig* **le d. est planté, le roman peut commencer** the scene is set, the novel can start

4 *(apparence)* façade, pretence; **tout ceci n'est qu'un d.** this is all a façade

□ **dans le(s) décor(s)** ADV *Fam* **aller** *ou* **entrer ou valser dans le d.** *(voiture, automobiliste)* to go off the road■; **envoyer dans le d.** *(voiture, automobiliste)* to force off the road■; **d'un coup de poing, elle l'a envoyé dans le d.** she sent him flying against the wall with a punch

décorateur, -trice [dekɔratœr, -tris] NM,F **1** *(d'appartement)* interior decorator *or* designer; **d. (de vitrines)** shopfitter **2** *Théât (créateur)* set designer *or* decorator; *(peintre)* set painter

décoratif, -ive [dekɔratif, -iv] ADJ *(gén)* decorative, ornamental; *(plante, arbre)* ornamental; *Fig* **n'avoir qu'un rôle d.** to have a purely decorative role

décoration [dekɔrasjɔ̃] NF **1** *(ornement)* decoration; **décorations de Noël** Christmas decorations **2** *(technique)* decoration, decorating; *Théât* set design, stage design; **faire de la d. (d'intérieur)** to do interior decorating **3** *(médaille)* medal, decoration

décorative [dekɔrativ] *voir* **décoratif**

décoratrice [dekɔratris] *voir* **décorateur**

décorder [3] [dekɔrde] VT **1** *(détortiller)* to untwist, to unravel **2** *(enlever la corde de)* to untie, to take the string off

▸**se décorder** VPR to unrope

décoré, -e [dekɔre] ADJ *(qui a reçu une distinction)* decorated; *(qui porte des insignes)* wearing one's medals

NM,F = person who has been awarded a decoration

décorer [3] [dekɔre] VT **1** *(orner → intérieur, vase, assiette)* to decorate; *(→ table, arbre)* to decorate, to adorn; **une table décorée de fleurs** a table adorned with flowers; **une tente décorée de drapeaux** a marquee decked out with flags **2** *(personne)* to decorate; **être décoré de la Légion d'honneur** to be awarded the Legion of Honour; **il mérite d'être décoré** he deserves a medal

décorner [3] [dekɔrne] VT **1** *(animal)* to dehorn **2** *(page)* to smooth out

décorticage [dekɔrtikaʒ] NM **1** *(d'une crevette)* peeling, shelling; *(du grain)* hulling, husking; *(d'une noix, d'une amande)* shelling **2** *(analyse)* dissection, thorough analysis

décortication [dekɔrtikasjɔ̃] NF **1** *Hort* decortication, barking **2** *Méd* decortication

décortiqué, -e [dekɔrtike] ADJ *Méd* decorticated

décortiquer [3] [dekɔrtike] VT **1** *(éplucher → crevette)* to peel, to shell; *(→ grain)* to hull, to husk; *(→ noix, amande)* to shell; **riz non décortiqué** rice in the husk **2** *Hort (arbre)* to decorticate, to bark **3** *(analyser)* to dissect, to analyse; **apprendre à d. un texte** to learn to take a text to pieces *or* to dissect a text **4** *Méd* to decorticate

décorum [dekɔrɔm] NM **1** *(bienséance)* decorum, propriety; **observer le d.** to observe the proprieties **2** *(protocole)* etiquette, ceremonial

décote [dekɔt] NF **1** *(réduction d'impôt)* tax relief **2** *Bourse* below par rating; **d. en Bourse** *(d'une action)* discount; **société qui souffre d'une d.** undervalued company **3** *(baisse)* depreciation, loss in value

décoté, -e [dekɔte] ADJ *Bourse (société, valeur)* undervalued

découcher [3] [dekuʃe] VI to stay out all night; **elle a découché** she stayed out all night, she didn't come home last night

découdre [86] [dekudr] VT *(vêtement, couture)* to undo, to unpick; *(point)* to take out; *(bouton)* to take *or* to cut off; **mon bouton est décousu** my button has come off

VI **en d.** to fight; **vouloir en d.** to be spoiling for a fight; **en d. avec qn** to cross swords with sb

▸**se découdre** VPR *(vêtement)* to come unstitched; *(bouton)* to come off

découler [3] [dekule] **découler de** VT IND to stem from; **et tous les avantages qui en découlent** and all the ensuing benefits; **il découle de cette idée que...** it follows from this idea that...; **il n'en découle pas forcément que vous ayez raison** it doesn't necessarily follow that you are right

découpage [dekupaʒ] NM **1** *(partage → d'un tissu, d'un gâteau)* cutting (up); *(→ d'une volaille, d'une viande)* carving; *(→ en tranches)* slicing (up)

2 *(image → à découper)* figure *(for cutting out)*; *(→ découpée)* cut-out (picture); **faire des découpages dans un illustré** to cut things out of a comic

3 *Cin* shooting script

4 *Ordinat (d'un fichier, d'une image)* splitting; **d. du temps** time slicing

5 *Pol* **d. électoral** division into electoral districts, *Am* apportionment; **refaire le d. électoral** *Br* to review constituency boundaries, *Am* to redistrict

6 *Tech* blanking, cutting

découpe [dekup] NF **1** *Couture* piece of appliqué work **2** *(de la viande)* (type of) cut **3** *(tronçonnage)* cutting (up); **faire la d.** to cut to length **4** *Belg (article)* **d. de journal/presse** newspaper/press cutting

découpé, -e [dekupe] ADJ **1** *(irrégulier → côte)* indented, ragged; *(→ montagne)* rugged, craggy, jagged; *(→ feuille d'arbre)* incised, serrate **2** *(en morceaux)* cut

découper [3] [dekupe] VT **1** *(détacher → image)* to cut out; **d. des articles dans le journal** to take cuttings out of the newspaper

2 *(partager → gâteau, papier, tissu)* to cut up; *(→ viande, volaille)* to carve; **il a découpé le gâteau en parts égales** he cut the cake into equal pieces; **couteau à d.** carving knife

3 *Tech* to blank, to cut

4 *Ordinat (fichier, image)* to split; *(disque dur)* to partition

5 *(disséquer → texte, film)* to dissect; *(→ phrase)* to parse

6 *(échancrer)* **le temps a découpé la côte** over the years, the coast has become deeply indented

▸**se découper** VPR **1** *(emploi passif)* **ce poulet se découpe tout seul** this chicken practically carves itself

2 se d. sur to be outlined against

découpeur, -euse [dekupœr, -øz] NM,F *(ouvrier)* cutting machine operator; *Cin* cutter

□ **découpeuse** NF cutting machine

découplage [dekuplaʒ] NM **1** *Électron* decoupling **2** *Élec* uncoupling

découplé, -e [dekuple] ADJ **bien d.** well-built, strapping

découpler [3] [dekuple] VT **1** *Chasse & Élec* to uncouple **2** *Électron* to decouple

découpoir [dekupwar] NM punch, cutting press

découpure [dekupyr] NF **1** *(bord → d'une dentelle, d'une guirlande)* edge; *(→ d'une côte)* indentations **2** *Can (d'un journal)* cutting, clipping

□ **découpures** NFPL *(de papier)* clippings, shavings, shreds; *(de tissu)* cuttings, offcuts

décourageant, -e [dekuraʒɑ̃, -ɑ̃t] ADJ **1** *(nouvelle, situation)* discouraging, disheartening, depressing **2** *(personne)* hopeless

découragement [dekuraʒmɑ̃] NM discouragement, despondency, despondence; **le d. m'a envahi** I felt utterly discouraged *or* dispirited

décourager [17] [dekuraʒe] VT **1** *(abattre)* to discourage, to dishearten; **avoir l'air découragé** to look discouraged *or* dispirited; **ne te laisse pas d.** don't be discouraged

2 *(dissuader → personne, familiarité)* to discourage; **d. qn de faire qch** to discourage sb from doing sth

▸**se décourager** VPR to get discouraged, to lose heart; **ne te décourage pas** don't give up; **il se décourage tout de suite** he gives up easily

découronnement [dekurɔnmɑ̃] NM dethronement, deposal

découronner [3] [dekurɔne] VT **1** *(roi)* to dethrone, to depose; *Fig (héros)* to debunk **2** *Littéraire (ôter le sommet de)* to cut the top off

décours [dekur] NM **1** *Astron* wane; **lune en d.** moon on the wane **2** *Méd* regression

décousait *etc voir* **découdre**

décousu, -e [dekuzy] PP *voir* **découdre**

ADJ **1** *Couture (défait → vêtement)* undone, unstitched; *(→ ourlet)* undone **2** *(incohérent → discours)* incoherent, disjointed; *(→ conversation)* desultory, disjointed; *(→ style)* disjointed, rambling; *(→ idées)* disjointed, disconnected, random; *(→ travail)* unmethodical; **de manière décousue** disjointedly

décousure [dekuzyr] NF **1** *Couture* seam-rent, place that has come unsewn **2** *Chasse* gash, rip *(caused by horns or tusks of animal)*

découvert, -e[1] [dekuvɛr, -ɛrt] PP *voir* **découvrir**

ADJ *(terrain, allée, voiture)* open; *(tête, partie du corps)* bare, uncovered; **dormir d.** to sleep without any covers; **la tête découverte** bareheaded

NM **1** *Compta* deficit; **d. de la balance commerciale** trade gap

2 *Banque* overdraft; **avoir un d. de** to be overdrawn by; **demander une autorisation de d.** to apply for an overdraft; **accorder un d. à qn** to allow sb an overdraft; **d. en blanc** unsecured overdraft

3 *Bourse* short (account)

□ **à découvert** ADJ **1** *Fin (sans garantie)* uncovered, unsecured

2 *Bourse* without cover; **acheter à d.** to buy on margin; **vendre à d.** to go a bear, to sell short; **vente à d.** short sale

3 *Banque* overdrawn; **être à d.** to be overdrawn, to have an overdraft; **votre compte est à d. de 200 euros** your account is overdrawn by 200 euros ADV **1** *(sans dissimuler)* openly; **agir à d.** to act openly

2 *(sans protection)* without cover; **cuire à d.** to cook without a lid; **sortir à d.** to break cover; **la marée laisse ces rochers à d.** the tide leaves these rocks exposed

découverte[2] [dekuvɛrt] NF **1** *(détection)* discovery, discovering; **faire la d. d'un gisement de pétrole** to strike oil; **faire la d. d'un vieux livre au grenier** to unearth an old book in the attic

2 *(chose détectée → gén)* discovery, find; *(→ scientifique)* discovery; **faire une d. macabre** to make a macabre discovery; *Hum* **ce n'est pas une d.!** that's nothing new!

3 *(prise de conscience)* discovery, discovering; **la d. du monde extérieur par le petit enfant** a small child's discovery of the world

4 *(personne de talent)* discovery, find; **ce jeune auteur est la d. de l'année** this young writer is the year's big discovery

5 *Théât & TV* backcloth

6 *Mines* cutting

□ **à la découverte** ADV **aller** *ou* **partir à la d.** to explore, to go exploring

◻ **à la découverte de** PRÉP **1** *(en explorant)* on a tour of; **allez à la d. du Londres de Sherlock Holmes** discover London in the footsteps of Sherlock Holmes; **ils sont partis à la d. de la forêt amazonienne** they went exploring in the Amazon rainforest

2 *(à la recherche de)* in search of; **aller à la d. d'un trésor** to go in search of treasure

découverture [dekuvɛrtyr] **NF** unroofing, stripping (of the roof)

découvreur, -euse [dekuvrœr, -øz] **NM,F** discoverer

découvrir [34] [dekuvrir] **VT 1** *(dénicher)* to discover, to find; **d. qch au fond d'un coffre** to find sth in the bottom of a trunk; **d. des armes dans une cache** to unearth a cache of weapons; **on a découvert l'arme du crime** the murder weapon has been found; **d. du pétrole/de l'or** to strike oil/gold; **j'ai découvert les lettres par accident** I came across the letters by accident; **d. l'Amérique** to discover America; **d. des qualités insoupçonnées chez qn** to discover unsuspected qualities in sb

2 *(apprendre à connaître)* to discover; **il découvrit l'amour/la musique baroque sur le tard** he discovered love/baroque music late in life; **il m'a fait d. beaucoup de choses** he showed me so many things; **elle m'a fait d. la région** she took me around the area

3 *(solution → en réfléchissant)* to discover, to work out; *(→ subitement)* to hit on *or* upon; *(virus, vaccin)* to discover; **soudain j'ai découvert la signification de son silence** suddenly I discovered why he/she had been keeping silent; **il ne parvint pas à d. qui elle était** he couldn't find out who she was

4 *(détecter)* to discover, to detect; **on lui a découvert une tumeur** they found he/she had a tumour

5 *(surprendre → voleur, intrus)* to discover; *(→ secret, complot)* to discover, to uncover; **et si l'on vous découvrait?** what if you were found out?; **on a découvert un passager clandestin** a stowaway has been found; **j'ai découvert que c'était faux** I found out (that) it wasn't true; *Fig* **d. le pot aux roses** to discover the truth; *Fig* **c'est par hasard que j'ai découvert le pot aux roses** it was by chance that I found out what was going on

6 *(faire connaître)* to uncover, to disclose, to reveal; **d. ses projets à qn** to reveal *or* to disclose one's plans to sb; **d. son jeu** to show one's hand; *Littéraire* **d. son cœur à qn** to open one's heart to sb, to bare one's soul to sb

7 *(apercevoir)* to see; **du balcon on découvre la mer** from the balcony one has a view of the sea; **le rideau levé, on découvrit une scène obscure** the raised curtain revealed a darkened stage; **d. un ami dans la foule** to catch sight of *or* to spot a friend in a crowd; **d. des phoques sur les rochers** to sight *or* to spot seals on the rocks

8 *(ôter ce qui couvre → fauteuil)* to uncover; *(→ statue)* to uncover, to unveil; *(→ casserole)* to uncover, to take the lid off; **il fait chaud dans la chambre, va d. le bébé** it's hot in the bedroom, take the covers off the baby

9 *(exposer → flanc, frontière)* to expose

10 *(mettre à nu → épaule, cuisse)* to uncover, to bare, to expose; *(→ mur, pierre)* to uncover, to expose; **il découvrit son bras** he bared *or* exposed his arm; **sa robe lui découvrait le dos** her dress revealed her back; **un décolleté qui découvre les épaules** a neckline that leaves the shoulders bare; **d. ses dents** to bare *or* show one's teeth; **la mer a découvert des kilomètres de sable blanc en se retirant** the ebbing tide uncovered *or* exposed miles of white sand

VI *(récif)* to uncover (at low tide)

▶**se découvrir VPR 1** *(se déshabiller)* to take some layers off, to take off some clothes; *(au lit)* to throw off one's bedclothes

2 *(ôter son chapeau)* to take off one's hat

3 *(se connaître)* to (come to) understand oneself; **on se découvre avec l'âge** one comes to know oneself with age

4 *(s'exposer)* to expose oneself to attack; **un boxeur ne doit pas se d.** a boxer mustn't lower his guard

5 *(être révélé)* to emerge, to be discovered; **des scandales, il s'en découvre tous les jours** scandals come to light *or* are discovered every day; **la vérité se découvre toujours** truth will out

6 *(l'un l'autre)* to discover each other

7 se d. qch to discover sth; **je me suis découvert une grosseur à l'aine** I discovered I had a lump in my groin; **elle s'est découvert des amis partout** she discovered she had friends everywhere; **il s'est découvert un don pour la cuisine/une passion pour le jardinage** he discovered (that) he had a gift for cooking/a passion for gardening

8 *Météo* **ça se découvre** it's clearing up; **les cimes se découvrent** the mist is lifting off the mountain tops

9 *Littéraire (se confier)* **se d. à** to confide in, to open up to; **il ne se découvre à personne** he doesn't confide in anyone

décrassage [dekrasaʒ], **décrassement** [dekrasmɑ̃] **NM 1** *Aut & Ind* scrubbing, cleaning out, cleanup; **faire le d. du carburateur** to clean out *or* to decoke the carburettor; **faire le d. d'une tête de lecture** to clean a tape head **2** *(du corps)* scrubbing; *(de l'esprit)* training, sharpening up

décrasser [3] [dekrase] **VT 1** *(nettoyer → peigne, tête de lecture)* to clean; *(→ poêle, casserole)* to scour, to clean out; *(→ linge)* to scrub; *(→ enfant)* to scrub (down), to clean up

2 *Fam (dégrossir)* **d. qn** to give sb a basic grounding▪, to teach sb the basics▪

3 *Aut & Ind* to clean out, to decoke

4 *Fam (remettre en forme)* to get back into shape, to tone up; **un peu d'exercice vous décrassera** a bit of exercise will get you back into shape

▶**se décrasser VPR 1** *(se laver)* to clean up, to give oneself a good scrub; **décrasse-toi les mains** give your hands a scrub

2 *(se dérouiller)* to get a bit of exercise

décrédibiliser [3] [dekredibilize] **VT** to discredit, to deprive of credibility, to take away the credibility of

décréditer [3] [dekredite] *Littéraire* **VT d. qn** to bring sb into discredit *or* disrepute

▶**se décréditer VPR** to fall into discredit *or* disrepute (**auprès de qn** in sb's eyes)

décrément [dekremɑ̃] **NM** *Ordinat* decrement

décrêpage [dekrɛpaʒ] **NM** straightening

décrêper [4] [dekrepe] **VT** to straighten (out)

décrépir [32] [dekrepir] **VT** to strip the roughcast off

▶**se décrépir VPR la façade se décrépit** the roughcast is coming off the front of the house

décrépissage [dekrepisaʒ] **NM** stripping of roughcast

décrépit, -e [dekrepi, -it] **ADJ** decrepit

décrépiter [3] [dekrepite] **VI** *Phys* to decrepitate

décrépitude [dekrepityd] **NF 1** *(décadence)* decay; **tomber en d.** *(civilisation)* to decline, to decay; *(institution)* to become obsolete **2** *(mauvais état)* decrepitude, decrepit state

decrescendo [dekreʃɛndo] **NM INV** decrescendo

ADV jouer d. to decrescendo; *Fig* **aller d.** to be waning

décret [dekrɛ] **NM 1** *Jur* decree, edict; **promulguer un d.** to issue a decree; **d. d'application** implementing decree *(presidential decree affecting the application of a law)*; **d. autonome** autonomous decree *(decree enacted under the Constitution's regulatory power)*; **d. en Conseil d'État** = decree after consultation of the "Conseil d'État"; **d. en Conseil des ministres** decree in Cabinet; **d. ministériel** = order to carry out legislation given by the Prime Minister; **d. présidentiel** *Br* ≃ Order in Council, *Am* ≃ executive order; **d. de promulgation** promulgation decree; **d. simple** ordinary decree

2 *Rel* decree

◻ **décrets NMPL** *Littéraire* **les décrets du destin/de la Providence** what fate/Providence has decreed; **les décrets de la mode** the dictates of fashion

◻ **par décret ADV gouverner par d.** to rule by decree

décrétale [dekretal] **NF** *Rel & Jur* decretal

décréter [18] [dekrete] **VT 1** *(ordonner → nomination, mobilisation)* to order; *(→ mesure)* to decree, to enact

2 *(décider)* **d. que** to decree that; **le patron a décrété qu'on ne changerait rien** the boss decreed *or* ordained that nothing would change; **elle a décrété qu'elle n'irait pas se coucher** she said categorically that she wasn't going to bed; **elle a décrété qu'elle n'aimait pas les glaces** she claims not to like ice-cream; **quand il a décrété quelque chose, il ne change pas d'avis** when he's made up his mind about something, he doesn't change it

décret-loi [dekrelwa] *(pl* **décrets-lois)** **NM** *Hist* = Order in Council

décreusage [dekrøzaʒ] **NM 1** *(dans la fabrication du papier)* boiling **2** *Tex (de la soie)* degumming, discharging; *(du coton)* discharging

décreuser [5] [dekrøze] **VT 1** *(dans la fabrication du papier)* to boil; **non décreusé** unboiled **2** *Tex (soie)* to degum, to discharge; *(coton)* to discharge

décri [dekri] **NM** *Vieilli ou Littéraire* **1** *(critique)* disparagement, running down; **tomber dans le d.** to fall into disrepute, into discredit **2** *(perte de valeur)* fall in value **3** *(d'une monnaie)* crying down, depreciation by proclamation

décrier [10] [dekrije] **VT 1** *(collègues, entourage)* to disparage; *(livre, œuvre, théorie)* to criticize, to censure, *Sout* to decry; **ce genre de pratique est assez décrié** this kind of thing is generally frowned upon **2** *(monnaie)* to cry down, to depreciate by proclamation

décriminalisation [dekriminalizasjɔ̃] **NF** decriminalization

décriminaliser [3] [dekriminalize] **VT** to decriminalize

décrire [99] [dekrir] **VT 1** *(représenter)* to describe, to portray; **elle a très bien décrit son amie** she portrayed *or* described her friend very accurately; **l'histoire décrit une passion** the story depicts *or* describes a passion; **son exposé décrit bien la situation** his/her account gives a good picture of the situation

2 *(former → cercle, ellipse)* to describe, to draw; *(→ trajectoire)* to follow, to describe; **d. des cercles dans le ciel** to fly in circles; **d. des cercles dans l'eau** *(nageur)* to swim in circles; *(bateau)* to go in circles; **d. des méandres** to follow a winding course, to meander (along); **la route décrit une courbe** the road curves *or* bends

décrispation [dekrispasjɔ̃] **NF** thaw, thawing; **la d. entre les deux pays** the easing of tension between the two countries

décrisper [3] [dekrispe] **VT 1** *(muscle)* to relax, to untense **2** *(relations)* to thaw; *(ambiance)* to ease; **pour d. la situation** to ease the situation; **la plaisanterie l'a décrispé** the joke made him relax *or* calmed him down

▶**se décrisper VPR** to relax, to unwind

décrit, -e [dekri, -it] **PP** *voir* **décrire**

décrivait *etc voir* **décrire**

décrochage [dekrɔʃaʒ] **NM 1** *(enlèvement → d'un rideau, d'un tableau)* unhooking, taking down; *(→ d'un wagon)* uncoupling

2 *Élec* pulling out of synchronism

3 *Mil* disengagement

4 *Aviat* stall

5 *Astron* leaving orbit

6 *Rad* break in transmission; **le d. a lieu à 19 heures** regional programming begins at 7 p.m.; **émettre en d.** to broadcast its own programmes

7 *Fam (désengagement)* **le d. par rapport à la réalité** being out of touch with reality

décrochement [dekrɔʃmɑ̃] **NM 1** *(fait de se décrocher)* slipping **2** *Archit (retrait)* recess; **faire un d.** *(bâtiment)* to form an angle; *(mur)* to form *or* to have a recess **3** *Géol* thrust fault **4** *Méd* **d. de la mâchoire** dislocation of the jaw

décrocher [3] [dekrɔʃe] **VT 1** *(dépendre)* to unhook, to take down; **d. un peignoir** to take a bathrobe off the hook *or* peg; *Fig* **il a décroché ses gants de boxe** he went back to boxing *or* into the ring again; **d. la lune** to do the impossible; **ne me demande pas de (te) d. la lune** don't ask me to do the impossible; *Fam* **d. la timbale** *ou* **le cocotier** *ou* **le pompon** to hit the jackpot

2 *(enlever → chaîne, laisse)* to take off; *(→ wagon)* to uncouple; **d. le fermoir d'un collier** to undo (the clasp of) a necklace

3 *Tél* **d. le téléphone** *(le couper)* to take the

dec–dec

phone off the hook; *(pour répondre)* to pick up the phone; **le téléphone est décroché** the phone's off the hook

4 *Fam (obtenir)* to land, to get; **d. une grosse commande** to land a big order; **elle a décroché le boulot du siècle** she got *or* landed herself a plum job

5 *Fin* **d. le dollar de l'or** to take the dollar off the gold standard

USAGE ABSOLU **elle a décroché au bout de dix sonneries** she picked up the receiver *or* telephone after ten rings; **tu décroches?** could you answer it *or* get it?

VI **1** *Mil* to beat a retreat, to withdraw

2 *Fam (abandonner)* to opt out; **les étudiants qui décrochent** students who drop out

3 *Fam (se déconcentrer)* to switch off; **j'ai complètement décroché** *(cessé de comprendre)* I was completely lost; *(cessé d'écouter)* I stopped paying any attention■, I switched off completely

4 *(être distancé)* to drop *or* to fall behind; **j'ai décroché du reste du groupe** I fell behind *or* I couldn't keep up with the rest of the group

5 *Fam (se désintoxiquer)* to kick the habit; **ça fait trois mois qu'il a décroché** he's been clean for three months

6 *Can Fam (abandonner l'école)* to drop out (of school)

7 *Aviat* to stall

8 *Fin* **l'euro a décroché du dollar** the euro has lost against the dollar

►**se décrocher** VPR **1** *(tableau)* to come unhooked; *(médaille)* to come unpinned

2 se d. qch to dislocate sth; **il s'est décroché la mâchoire** he dislocated his jaw

décrocheur, -euse [dekrɔʃœr, -øz] NM,F *Can* (high school) dropout

décrochez-moi-ça [dekrɔʃemwasa] NM INV *Fam Vieilli* secondhand clothes *Br* shop■ *or Am* store■

décrois *etc voir* **décroître**

décroisement [dekrwazmɑ̃] NM *(de fibres)* uncrossing

décroiser [3] [dekrwaze] VT **d. les jambes/les bras** to uncross one's legs/one's arms

décroissait *etc voir* **décroître**

décroissance [dekrwasɑ̃s] NF **1** *(diminution)* decrease, fall, decline; **une d. rapide de la natalité** a sharp decline in the birth rate **2** *Nucl* **d. radioactive** radioactive decay

décroissant, -e [dekrwasɑ̃, -ɑ̃t] ADJ **1** *Math* decreasing **2** *Ling* falling **3** *Astron* waning, decreasing, decrescent

décroissement [dekrwasmɑ̃] NM *Littéraire (diminution)* decrease, decline; *(de la lune)* waning

décroît [dekrwa] NM **la lune est sur** *ou* **dans son d.** the moon is in its last quarter

décroître [94] [dekrwatr] VI **1** *(diminuer → nombre, intensité, force)* to decrease, to diminish; *(→ eaux)* to subside, to go down; *(→ fièvre)* to abate, to subside, to decrease; *(→ bruit)* to die down, to lessen, to decrease; *(→ son)* to fade, to die down; *(→ vent)* to let up, to die down; *(→ intérêt, productivité)* to decline, to drop off; *(→ vitesse)* to slacken off, to drop; *(→ taux d'écoute)* to drop; *(→ lumière)* to grow fainter, to grow dimmer, to fade; *(→ influence)* to decline, to wane; **le nombre des divorces a décru** the number of divorces has decreased; **les jours décroissent** the days are drawing in *or* getting shorter; **il voyait leurs silhouettes d. à l'horizon** he could see their silhouettes getting smaller and smaller on the horizon; **aller en décroissant** to be on the decrease; **le son va en décroissant** the sound is gradually fading

2 *Astron* to wane

décrottage [dekrɔtaʒ] NM scraping the mud off

décrotter [3] [dekrɔte] VT **1** *(nettoyer)* to scrape the mud off **2** *Fam (dégrossir)* to refine■, to take the rough edges off; **elle n'arrivera jamais à le d.** she'll never get him to change■

décrotteur [dekrɔtœr] NM *Agr* beet cleaning machine

décrottoir [dekrɔtwar] NM *(pour chaussures)* (boot) scraper

décru, -e [dekry] PP *voir* **décroître**

▫ **décrue** NF **1** *(d'une rivière)* decrease *or* dropping of the water level; **attendre la décrue** *(lors d'une inondation)* to wait for the flood to subside; *(lors d'une crue)* to wait for the water level to go down *or* to drop *or* to fall **2** *(diminution)* decrease, decline, fall

décruage [dekryaʒ], **décrusage** [dekryzaʒ] NM *Tex (de la soie)* degumming, discharging; *(du coton)* discharging

décruser [3] [dekryze] VT *Tex (soie)* to degum, to discharge; *(coton)* to discharge; **non décrusé** unboiled

décryptage [dekriptaʒ], **décryptement** [dekriptəmɑ̃] NM **1** *(décodage)* deciphering, decipherment, decoding **2** *(éclaircissement)* elucidation, working out

décrypter [3] [dekripte] VT **1** *(décoder → message, texte ancien)* to decode, to decipher **2** *(éclaircir)* to elucidate, to work out

DECS [deəseɛs] NM *(abrév* **diplôme d'études comptables supérieures***)* = postgraduate qualification in accounting

DECT [deəsete] NF *Tél (abrév* **digital enhanced cordless telecommunications***)* DECT

déçu, -e [desy] PP *voir* **décevoir**

ADJ **1** *(personne)* disappointed; *Suisse* **d. en bien** pleasantly surprised **2** *(amour)* disappointed, thwarted; *(espoir)* disappointed

décubitus [dekybitys] NM *Méd* decubitus

décuiter [3] [dekɥite] VI *Fam* to sober up■

décuivrer [3] [dekɥivre] VT to remove copper plating from

de cujus [dekyʒys] NM *Jur* **le d.** *(qui a fait un testament)* the testator; *(sans testament)* the deceased

déculasser [3] [dekylase] VT to debreech

déculottée [dekylɔte] NF *très Fam* thrashing, clobbering, hammering; **prendre une d.** to get thrashed *or* clobbered *or* hammered

déculotter [3] [dekylɔte] VT **d. qn** *(lui enlever sa culotte)* to take sb's underpants *or Br* pants off; *(lui enlever son pantalon)* to take sb's *Br* trousers *or Am* pants off

►**se déculotter** VPR **1** *(emploi réfléchi) (enlever → sa culotte)* to take one's underpants *or Br* pants down; *(→ son pantalon)* to drop one's *Br* trousers *or Am* pants

2 *Fam (se montrer lâche)* to lose one's nerve *or Br* bottle

3 *très Fam (avouer)* to squeal

déculpabilisation [dekylpabilizasjɔ̃] NF **la d. de la sexualité** removing the guilt attached to sexuality

déculpabiliser [3] [dekylpabilize] VT **d. qn** to stop sb feeling guilty; **je suis déculpabilisée** I no longer feel guilty; **d. la sexualité** to remove the guilt attached to sexuality

►**se déculpabiliser** VPR *(emploi réfléchi)* to get rid of one's guilt

déculturation [dekyltyrasjɔ̃] NF loss of cultural identity

décuple [dekyp] NM **le d. de trois** ten times three; **le d. de ton salaire** ten times your salary

▫ **au décuple** ADV tenfold

décuplement [dekypləmɑ̃] NM **1** *(d'une somme, d'un chiffre)* tenfold increase **2** *(augmentation)* **ceci permettra le d. de nos chances de succès** this will greatly increase our chances of success

décupler [3] [dekyple] VT **1** *(rendre dix fois plus grand)* to increase tenfold **2** *(augmenter)* to increase greatly; **la rage décuple les forces** rage greatly increases one's strength

VI to increase tenfold

décurie [dekyri] NF *Antiq* decury, decuria

décurion [dekyrjɔ̃] NM *Antiq* decurion

décurrent, -e [dekyrɑ̃] ADJ *Bot* decurrent

décuscuteuse [dekyskytøz] NF *Agr* = instrument for removing dodder

décussé, -e [dekyse] ADJ *Bot* decussate

déçut *etc voir* **décevoir**

décuvage [dekyvaʒ] NM racking

décuvaison [dekyvɛzɔ̃] NF racking

décuver [3] [dekyve] VT to rack

dédaignable [dedɛɲabl] ADJ **ce n'est pas d.** it's not to be sniffed at

dédaigner [4] [dedeɲe] VT **1** *(mépriser → personne)* to look down on, to despise, to scorn; *(→ compliment, richesse)* to despise, to disdain

2 *(refuser → honneurs, argent)* to despise, to disdain, to spurn; **une augmentation, ce n'est pas à d.** a salary increase is not to be sniffed at; **ne dédaignant pas la bonne chère** not being averse to good food

3 *(ignorer → injure, difficulté)* to ignore, to disregard

▫ **dédaigner de** VT IND *Littéraire* **elle a dédaigné de parler** she didn't deign to speak; **il n'a pas dédaigné de goûter à ma cuisine** he was not averse to tasting my cooking; **dédaignant de visiter le château** not deigning to visit the castle

dédaigneuse [dedɛɲøz] *voir* **dédaigneux**

dédaigneusement [dedɛɲøzmɑ̃] ADV contemptuously, disdainfully

dédaigneux, -euse [dedɛɲø, -øz] ADJ **1** *(méprisant → sourire, moue, remarque)* contemptuous, disdainful; **d'un ton d.** disdainfully **2 d. de** *(indifférent à)* disdainful *or* contemptuous of; **je n'ai jamais été d. de l'argent** I've never been one to spurn *or* to despise money

NM,F disdainful *or* scornful *or* contemptuous person; **les d.** those who scoff

dédain [dedɛ̃] NM **1** *(gén)* scorn, contempt, disdain; **avec d.** disdainfully **2** *Can (dégoût)* **avoir d. de qch** to loathe sth

▫ **de dédain** ADJ disdainful, scornful, contemptuous

Dédale [dedal] NPR *Myth* Daedalus

dédale [dedal] NM maze; **un vrai d., ces greniers!** these attics are like a rabbit warren!; **dans le d. des rues** in the maze of streets; **dans le d. des lois** in the maze of the law

dédaléen, -enne [dedaleɛ̃, -eɛn], **dédalien, -enne** [dedaljɛ̃, -ɛn], **dédalique** [dedalik] ADJ intricate, involved, *Spéc* daedalian

DEDANS [dədɑ̃] ADV *(reprenant "dans" + substantif)* inside, in it/them/*etc*; *(par opposition à "dehors")* inside, indoors; *(à partir de → prendre, boire, manger)* out of, from; **tu m'attendras dehors ou d.?** will you wait for me outside or inside *or* indoors?; **rentrons, il fait meilleur d.** let's go in, it's warmer inside; **de d., on ne voit rien** you can't see anything from inside; **une cabane, allons nous cacher d.** there's a hut, let's go and hide inside *or* in it; **prends les draps dans l'armoire, ils sont sûrement d.** take the sheets from the cupboard, I'm sure they're in there; **donne-moi mon sac, la lettre est d.** give me my bag, the letter is inside *or* in it; **il y a de l'anis d.** there's aniseed in it; **quand j'achète des chaussures, je veux me sentir bien d.** when I buy shoes, I want to feel comfortable in them; **quelle belle eau, cela donne envie de plonger d.** what lovely water, it makes you feel like diving into it *or* in; **c'est un bon film mais il y a trop de violence d.** it's a good film but there's too much violence in it; **le tiroir était ouvert, j'ai pris l'argent d.** the drawer was open, I took the money out of *or* from it; **ce verre est sale, ne bois pas d.** this glass is dirty, don't drink out of *or* from it; **il faut élargir l'ourlet et passer l'élastique d.** you must widen the hem and run the elastic through it; **on n'apprécie pas le luxe quand on vit d.** you don't appreciate luxury when you've got it; *Fam* **ne me parle pas de comptes, je suis en plein d.** don't talk to me about the accounts, I'm right in the middle of them *or* up to my eyeballs in them; **tu veux du mystère? on est en plein d.** you want mystery? we're surrounded by it; *Fam* **mettre** *ou* **ficher qn d.** *(le tromper)* to confuse *or* to muddle sb■; *(en prison)* to put sb inside; *Fam* **je me suis fichu d.** I got it wrong■; **tomber en plein d.** to fall right into it; **le piège, il est tombé en plein d.** he fell right into the trap

NM inside; **agir du d.** to act on the *or* from inside

▫ **en dedans** ADV **c'est creux en d.** it's hollow inside; **marcher les pieds en d.** to be pigeon-toed; **en d. il n'était pas si calme** inwardly, he was not so calm

▫ **en dedans de** PRÉP within; **en d. d'elle-même, elle regrette son geste** deep down *or* inwardly, she regrets what she did

dédicace [dedikas] NF **1** *(formule manuscrite → d'un ami)* (signed) dedication; *(→ d'une personnalité)* autograph, (signed) dedication **2** *(formule imprimée)* dedication **3** *Rad* dedication **4** *Rel (consécration)* dedication, consecration; *(fête)* = celebration of the consecration of a place of worship

dédicacer [16] [dedikase] VT **1** *(signer)* **d. un livre/une photo à qn** to autograph *or* to sign a book/photo for sb; **la valeur des livres dédicacés** the value of books signed by the author **2** *Rad* to dedicate

dedicataire [dedikatɛr] NMF dedicatee

dédicatoire [dedikatwar] ADJ dedicatory, dedicative; **formule** *ou* **inscription d.** dedication

dédié, -e [dedje] ADJ *Ordinat* dedicated; **ordinateur d.** dedicated computer

dédier [9] [dedje] VT **1** *(livre, symphonie)* to dedicate **2** *(église)* to dedicate, to consecrate **3** *Littéraire (vouer)* **dédiant toutes ses pensées à son art** dedicating *or* devoting all his/her thoughts to his/her art; **sans jamais lui d. une pensée** with never (so much as) a thought for him/her

dédifférenciation [dediferɑ̃sjasjɔ̃] NF **1** *(dans un processus)* dedifferentiation **2** *Biol* dedifferentiation

dédifférencier [9] [dediferɑ̃sje] **se dédifférencier** VPR to undergo dedifferentiation

dédire [103] [dedir] **se dédire** VPR **1** *(se rétracter → délibérément)* to recant, to retract **2** *(manquer → à sa promesse)* to go back on *or* to fail to keep one's word; *(→ à son engagement)* to fail to honour one's commitment **3 se d. de** *(promesse)* to go back on, to fail to keep; *(engagement)* to fail to honour

dédit [dedi] NM **1** *(rétractation)* retraction; *(désengagement)* failure to keep one's word; **un engagement qui ne tolère aucun d.** a binding commitment, a commitment which must be honoured **2** *Jur (modalité)* default; *(somme)* forfeit, penalty

dédite [dedit] NF *Suisse* = **dédit**

dédommagement [dedɔmaʒmɑ̃] NM compensation; **5000 euros de d.** 5,000 euros' compensation; **demander** *ou* **réclamer un d.** to claim compensation; **voilà un piètre d. de mes efforts** it's not much reward for all the effort I put in

❑ **en dédommagement** ADV as compensation; **il nous a offert une bouteille de champagne en d.** he gave us a bottle of champagne by way of *or* as compensation

❑ **en dédommagement de** PRÉP as a *or* in compensation for, to make up for; **tenez, en d. de votre dérangement** please take this for your trouble

❑ **à titre de dédommagement** ADV by way of *or* as compensation

dédommager [17] [dedɔmaʒe] VT **1** *(pour une perte)* to compensate, to give compensation to; **les paysans n'ont pas été dédommagés** the peasants have received no compensation; **d. qn d'une perte** to compensate sb for a loss, to make good sb's loss; **fais-toi d. pour le dérangement** claim compensation for the inconvenience; **j'ai réussi à me faire d.** *(en argent)* I managed to get reimbursed

2 *(pour un désagrément)* to compensate; **cela te dédommagera d'avoir attendu** this'll make up for your having had to wait; **le succès l'a dédommagé de tous ses efforts** success compensated *or* made up for all his/her effort

dédorage [dedɔraʒ] NM ungilding, removing the gilt from

dédorer [3] [dedɔre] VT to remove the gilt from; **cadre dédoré** tarnished frame; *Fig* **aristocratie dédorée** faded aristocracy

dédouanage [dedwanaʒ], **dédouanement** [dedwanmɑ̃] NM *Admin (action)* clearing through customs; *(résultat)* customs clearance

dédouaner [3] [dedwane] VT **1** *Admin (marchandise)* to clear through customs **2** *(personne)* to clear (the name of)

▸**se dédouaner** VPR to make up for one's past misdeeds; **ne crois pas te d. en me signant des chèques** don't think you can get round me by signing cheques

dédoublage [dedublaʒ] NM **1** *(d'alcool)* diluting **2** *(d'un vêtement)* removing the lining

dédoublement [dedubləmɑ̃] NM **1** *(d'un groupe, d'une image)* splitting *or* dividing in two **2** *Psy* **d. de la personnalité** split *ou* dual personality **3** *Transp* **d. d'un train** putting on an extra train

dédoubler [3] [deduble] VT **1** *(diviser → groupe, image)* to split *or* to divide in two; *(→ brin de laine)* to separate into strands

2 *Transp* **d. un train** to put on *or* to run an extra train

3 *Couture* to remove the lining of

4 *(en joaillerie)* to split lengthwise

▸**se dédoubler** VPR **1** *Psy* **sa personnalité se dédouble, il se dédouble** he suffers from a split *or* dual personality; *Hum* **je cuisine, viens ici, je ne peux pas me d.!** I'm cooking, come here, I can't be in two places at once!

2 *(se diviser → convoi, image)* to be split *or* divided in two; *(→ ongle)* to split

dédramatiser [3] [dedramatize] VT *(situation)* to make less dramatic

déductibilité [dedyktibilite] NF **1** *(d'une hypothèse)* deductibility **2** *Math* deductibility

déductible [dedyktibl] ADJ deductible; **non d.** non-deductible; **frais déductibles des revenus** expenditure deductible against tax; **d. de l'impôt** tax-deductible

déductif, -ive [dedyktif, -iv] ADJ deductive

déduction [dedyksjɔ̃] NF **1** *(d'une somme)* deduction; **entrer en d. de qch** to be deductible from sth; **d. faite de** after deduction of, after deducting; **sous d. de 10 pour cent** less 10 percent; **sans d.** terms net cash; **d. fiscale** tax allowance; **d. forfaitaire** *(d'impôts)* standard allowance; **d. pour dons** deduction for donations

2 *(conclusion)* conclusion, inference; **tirer des déductions de** to draw conclusions from

3 *(enchaînement d'idées)* deduction; **faire une d.** to go through a process of deduction; **avoir une grande puissance de d.** to have great powers of deduction

❑ **par déduction** ADV by deduction, through a process of deduction

déductive [dedyktiv] *voir* **déductif**

déduire [98] [dedɥir] VT **1** *(frais, paiement)* to deduct, to take off; **tous frais déduits** after deduction of expenses **2** *(conclure)* to deduce, to infer

déduit [dedɥi] NM *Vieilli (ébats amoureux)* lovemaking

déesse [deɛs] NF **1** *Myth & Rel* goddess; *Littéraire* **la d. aux cent bouches** *ou* **voix** Fame **2** *(femme)* goddess

❑ **de déesse** ADJ *(allure, port)* majestic

DEFA, Defa [defa] NM *(abrév* **diplôme d'État relatif aux fonctions d'animation***)* = diploma for senior youth leaders

de facto [defakto] ADV de facto

défaillance [defajɑ̃s] NF **1** *(évanouissement)* blackout; *(malaise)* feeling of faintness; **avoir une d.** *(s'évanouir)* to faint, to have a blackout; *(être proche de l'évanouissement)* to feel faint; **des défaillances dues à la chaleur** weak spells caused by the heat

2 *(faiblesse morale)* weakness; **avouer dans un moment de d.** to confess in a moment of weakness

3 *(lacune)* lapse, slip; **une d. de mémoire** a memory lapse; **une seule d. et vous êtes renvoyé** one single mistake and you're fired; **j'ai eu une d. à l'oral** I didn't do myself justice at the oral; **cet enfant a de sérieuses défaillances en lecture** the child has serious reading difficulties; **les défaillances du syndicat** the union's failings; **les défaillances du rapport** the weak spots in the report

4 *(mauvais fonctionnement)* failure, fault; **en cas de d. du système** in case of a failure in the system; **le moteur a régulièrement des défaillances** the engine is always breaking down; **d. mécanique** mechanical failure

5 *Méd* **d. cardiaque/rénale** heart/kidney failure

6 *Jur* default

7 *(faillite)* **d. d'entreprise** business failure

❑ **sans défaillance** ADJ *(mémoire)* faultless; *(attention, vigilance)* unflinching

défaillant, -e [defajɑ̃, -ɑ̃t] ADJ **1** *(près de s'évanouir)* **des spectateurs défaillants** spectators about to faint *or* on the verge of fainting

2 *(faible → santé)* declining, failing; *(→ cœur, poumon)* weak, failing; *(→ force, mémoire)* failing; *(→ détermination)* weakening, faltering; *(→ voix)* faltering; **il avançait d'un pas d.** he walked with a faltering step

3 *(qui ne remplit pas son rôle → appareil)* malfunctioning; **une télévision défaillante** a malfunctioning TV set; **dû à l'organisation défaillante du concert** due to the poor organization of the concert

4 *Jur* defaulting; **témoin d. au tribunal** witness who fails to appear in court

défaillir [47] [defajir] VI *Littéraire* **1** *(s'évanouir)* to faint; **en entendant ce nom, elle manqua d.** on hearing this name she nearly fainted *or* swooned **2** *(s'amollir)* **d. de** to swoon *or* to go weak at the knees with; **d. de plaisir** to swoon with pleasure **3** *(forces, mémoire)* to fail; *(détermination)* to weaken, to falter, to flinch; **j'accomplirai le travail sans d.** I'll do the job without flinching

défaire [109] [defɛr] VT **1** *(détacher → nœud)* to untie, to unfasten; *(→ fermeture)* to undo, to unfasten; *(→ cravate)* to undo, to untie; **d. les lacets d'une botte** to unlace a boot; **d. ses cheveux** to let one's hair down; **avec les cheveux défaits** *(pas encore arrangés)* with his/her hair undone, with tousled hair; *(que l'on a dérangés)* with his/her hair messed up

2 *(découdre → ourlet)* to undo, to unpick; **d. le bâti d'un ourlet** to unpick a hem

3 *(démonter → décor de théâtre)* to take down, to dismantle; *(→ maquette, puzzle)* to take apart, to disassemble; *(→ tente)* to take down

4 *(déballer → paquet)* to open, to unwrap; **d. ses valises** to unpack

5 *(mettre en désordre)* **d. le lit** *(pour changer les draps)* to strip the bed; *(en jouant)* to rumple the bedclothes; **le lit défait** *(pas encore fait)* the unmade bed; **le lit n'a pas été défait** the bed hasn't been slept in

6 *Ordinat (opération)* to undo

7 *(détruire)* **faire et d. des gouvernements** to make and break governments

8 *Littéraire (délivrer)* **d. qn de** to rid sb of; **défaites-nous de ces sots!** deliver *or* save us from these fools!

9 *Littéraire (armée)* to defeat

▸**se défaire** VPR **1** *(se détacher, se disloquer → nœud)* to come loose *or* undone; *(→ coiffure, paquet)* to come undone; *(→ tricot)* to fray, to come undone, to unravel; *(→ viande à la cuisson)* to fall apart

2 *(être détruit → gouvernement, amitié)* to break

3 *(se décomposer)* **son visage se défit** *(de chagrin)* he/she looked distraught; *(de déception)* his/her face fell

4 se d. de *(employé, dettes, meuble)* to get rid of, *Sout* to rid oneself of; *(idée)* to put out of one's mind; *(habitude)* to break; **il ne veut pas se d. de son vieux chien** he won't get rid of his old dog

défait, -e[1] [defɛ, -ɛt] ADJ **1** *(accablé)* **être d.** to be broken **2** *(décomposé)* **il est arrivé à l'hôpital, complètement d.** he arrived at the hospital in total distress; **il se tenait là, le visage d.** he stood there, looking distraught

défaite[2] [defɛt] NF *Mil, Pol & Sport* defeat

défaites *voir* **défaire**

défaitisme [defetism] NM **1** *Mil* defeatism **2** *(pessimisme)* defeatism, negative attitude

défaitiste [defetist] ADJ defeatist

NMF **1** *Mil* defeatist **2** *(pessimiste)* defeatist

défalcation [defalkasjɔ̃] NF deduction; *(d'une mauvaise créance)* writing off; **d. faite des frais** after deduction of expenses

défalquer [3] [defalke] VT to deduct; *(mauvaise créance)* to write off

défanant [defanɑ̃] NM *Agr* haulm killer

défasse *etc voir* **défaire**

défatigant, -e [defatigɑ̃, -ɑ̃t] ADJ relaxing, soothing

NM muscle relaxant

défatiguer [3] [defatige] VT to refresh, to relax

défaufiler [3] [defofile] VT to remove the tacking from

défausse [defos] NF *Cartes* discarding an unwanted card

défausser [3] [defose] VT to straighten out again

▸**se défausser** VPR *Cartes* to discard an unwanted card; **se d. à cœur** to discard one's hearts; **se d. d'un valet** to discard a jack

défaut [defo] NM **1** *(imperfection → d'un visage, de la peau)* blemish, imperfection; *(→ d'un tissu, d'un appareil)* defect, flaw; *(→ d'un diamant, d'une porcelaine)* flaw; *(→ d'une explication, d'une théorie)* flaw (**de** in); *(→ d'un projet)*

ded–def

def-def

drawback, snag; **avoir un d.** *(machine)* to be defective; **cette école n'a qu'un d.: elle est trop loin** the school has only one drawback: it's too far away; **il y a un d. de fonctionnement** it doesn't work *or* work properly; *Fam* **le d. de** *ou* **avec ton attitude, c'est que...** the trouble with your attitude is that...; **ce roman/jardin a le grand d. de manquer de couleur** the big problem with this novel/garden is (that) it lacks colour; *Fam Hum* **il y a comme un d.!** there's something wrong somewhere!; *Com* **d. apparent** visible defect; *Com* **d. caché** hidden defect; **d. de conception** design fault; **d. d'élocution** *ou* **de prononciation** speech defect *or* impediment; **d. de fabrication** manufacturing defect

2 *(tache morale)* fault, failing; **son plus gros d., c'est qu'il est égoïste** his biggest fault is that he's selfish; **chacun a ses défauts** we all have our faults

3 *(manque)* **d. de** lack *or* want of; **d. de mémoire** memory lapse; **d. d'attention** lapse in concentration; **d. de sagesse** lack *or* want of wisdom; **chèque refusé pour cause de d. de provision** cheque refused by the bank because of insufficient funds; **d. de provision** *(tampon sur chèque)* ≃ refer to drawer; **faire d.** to be lacking; **les provisions font d.** there is a shortage of supplies, supplies are short; **l'argent faisant d.** *(il y a peu d'argent)* money being short; **(il n'y a pas d'argent)** there being no money; **ses forces lui ont fait d.** his/her strength failed him/her; **le temps me fait d.** I don't have the time; **l'imagination est loin de lui faire d.** he/she is far from lacking (in) imagination; **le bon sens lui fait cruellement d.** he/she is sadly lacking in common sense; **si ma mémoire ne me fait pas d.** if I'm not mistaken, if my memory serves me right; **notre fournisseur nous a fait d.** our supplier let us down

4 *(bord, lisière)* **au d. des côtes** under the ribcage; **le d. de la cuirasse** *ou* **de l'armure** the chink in one's *or* the armour

5 *Jur* default; **faire d.** to default; **d. de base légale** lack of legal basis; **d. de comparution** failure to appear; **d. de motif** lack of motive; **d. de paiement** default in payment, non-payment

6 *Phys* **d. de masse** mass defect

7 *Ordinat* default setting

8 *Chasse* **relever le d.** to recover the scent

□ **à défaut** ADV if not, failing that; **des roses ou, à d., des tulipes** roses or, failing that, tulips

□ **à défaut de** PRÉP for lack *or* for want of; **à d. d'un bon salaire, elle a au moins l'avantage de travailler près de chez elle** she might not have a very good salary but at least she works close to home; **un voyage reposant à d. d'être intéressant** a restful if not interesting trip

□ **en défaut** ADV **1** **être en d.** *(se tromper)* to be wrong; *(en faute)* to be at fault; **son pouvoir de réflexion est en d.** his/her ability to think is at fault; **prendre qn en d.** to catch sb out, to fault sb; **on ne le prend pas en d.** you can't fault him

2 *Chasse* **mettre les chiens en d.** to set the hounds on the wrong scent, to put the hounds off the scent; **tomber en d.** *(chien)* to check, to be at fault

□ **par défaut** ADJ *Ordinat* default *(avant n)*; **lecteur/clavier par d.** default drive/keyboard ADV **1** *(sans agir)* by default; **avoir un poste par d.** to get a job by default; *Rel* **pécher par d.** to sin by omission, to commit a sin of omission

2 *Math* **total approché par d.** total rounded down **3** *Jur* by default **4** *Ordinat* by default; **sélectionner qch par d.** to default to sth

□ **sans défaut** ADJ flawless

défaut-congé [defokɔ̃ʒe] *(pl* **défauts-congés)** NM = unjustified non-appearance by the claimant

défaveur [defavœr] NF discredit, disfavour; **s'attirer la d. de qn** to incur the disfavour of sb; **être en d. auprès de qn** to be in disfavour with sb; **c'est tombé en d.** it's gone out of favour *or* fashion; **cela a tourné à ma d.** it worked against me in the end

défavorable [defavɔrabl] ADJ unfavourable; **voir qch d'un œil d.** to view sth unfavourably; **en cas d'avis d. du jury** should the jury return an unfavourable verdict; **être d. à qn/qch** to be against sb/sth; **le taux de change nous est d.** the exchange rate is unfavourable

défavorablement [defavɔrabləmɑ̃] ADV unfavourably

défavorisé, -e [defavɔrize] ADJ **régions défavorisées** depressed areas; **classes défavorisées** underprivileged social classes

défavoriser [3] [defavɔrize] VT *(dans un partage)* to treat unfairly; *(dans un examen, une compétition)* to put at a disadvantage; **il est défavorisé par sa timidité** his shyness puts him at a disadvantage

défécation [defekasjɔ̃] NF **1** *Physiol* defecation **2** *Chim* defecation, purification

défectif, -ive [defɛktif, -iv] ADJ *Gram* defective

défection [defɛksjɔ̃] NF **1** *(fait de quitter)* abandonment, abandoning; **après la d. de son père** after his/her father walked out

2 *(désistement → d'un allié, d'un partisan)* withdrawal of support; *(→ d'un espion)* defection; *(→ d'un soldat)* defection, desertion; *(→ d'un touriste, d'un client, d'un invité)* failure to appear; **cet été, nous avons eu beaucoup de défections** many tourists stayed away this summer; **faire d.** *(allié, partisan)* to withdraw support; *(espion)* to defect; *(soldat)* to defect, to desert; *(touriste, client, invité)* to fail to appear

défective [defɛktiv] *voir* **défectif**

défectueuse [defɛktɥøz] *voir* **défectueux**

défectueusement [defɛktɥøzmɑ̃] ADV in a faulty manner

défectueux, -euse [defɛktɥø, -øz] ADJ *(appareil, produit)* faulty, defective, substandard; *(loi)* defective

défectuosité [defɛktɥozite] NF **1** *(mauvaise qualité)* substandard quality, defectiveness **2** *(malfaçon)* imperfection, defect, fault

défendable [defɑ̃dabl] ADJ **1** *Mil* defensible **2** *(justifiable → position)* defensible; *(→ comportement)* justifiable; *(→ idée)* tenable, defensible; **des théories qui ne sont pas défendables** indefensible theories

défendeur, -eresse [defɑ̃dœr, -drɛs] NM,F defendant

défendre [73] [defɑ̃dr] VT **1** *(interdire)* to forbid; **d. l'accès au jardin** to forbid access to the garden; **son père lui a défendu l'entrée de sa maison** his/her father has forbidden him/her to set foot over the doorstep; **il défend qu'on passe par là** he forbids anyone to go that way; **d. à qn de faire qch** to forbid sb to do sth; **son père lui défend de sortir le soir** his/her father does not allow him/her to go out at night; **je te défends d'approcher/de parler** I forbid you to come nearer/to speak; **elle lui défend les bonbons** she doesn't allow him/her to eat sweets; **l'alcool lui est défendu** he's/she's not allowed to drink alcohol; **ce médicament est défendu aux enfants** this medicine must not be given to children; **c'est défendu** it's not allowed, it's forbidden; **il est défendu de fumer dans les classes** smoking is prohibited in the classrooms; **il est défendu de parler au chauffeur** *(dans autobus)* please do not speak to the driver; **il m'est défendu de fumer** I'm not allowed to smoke

2 *(protéger → pays, population)* to defend; *(→ forteresse)* to defend, to hold; **ville mal défendue** badly defended town; **d. chèrement sa vie** to fight for dear life; **la propriété est défendue par deux chiens** the estate is guarded by two dogs; *Ftbl* **Durant défendra les buts de l'équipe d'Aix** Durant will be the goalkeeper for Aix

3 *(donner son appui à → ami)* to defend, to stand up for; *(→ idée, cause)* to defend, to champion, to support; *(→ droit, opinion)* to defend, to uphold; *(→ intérêts)* to protect; **d. son honneur** to defend one's honour; **d. ses couleurs/son titre** to defend *or* to fight for one's colours/title; **d. l'intérêt national** to defend *or* to safeguard the national interest; **je défends mon point de vue** I'm defending *or* standing up for my point of view

4 *(préserver)* **d. qn contre** *ou* **de qch** to protect sb from *or* against sth; **de lourdes tentures défendaient la pièce contre les regards indiscrets** heavy curtains shielded the room from prying eyes; **les fourrures défendent les esquimaux du froid** fur clothing protects the Eskimos from the cold

5 *Jur* to defend

6 *Sport (service)* to defend

►**se défendre** VPR **1** *(en luttant → physiquement)* to defend oneself **(contre** against); *(→ verbalement)* to stand up for *or* to defend oneself **(contre** against); **se d. jusqu'au bout** to fight to the last

2 *(se protéger)* **se d. de** *ou* **contre** to protect oneself from *or* against; **se d. des microbes** to protect oneself against germs; **se d. des tentations** to steer clear of temptation; **se d. des agressions** to defend oneself against attack; **se d. de la pluie** to shelter from the rain

3 *(être plausible)* to make sense; **c'est une idée qui se défend** there is something to be said for the idea; **cela se défend** that makes sense; **il dit que c'est trop long et cela se défend** he says it's too long and he has a point *or* it's a fair point

4 *Fam (être compétent)* to get by; **elle n'est pas la meilleure mais elle se défend** she's not the best but she gets by; **il se défend bien en maths** he's quite good at maths*; **il ne se défend pas trop bien avec les femmes** he doesn't have much success with women*; **pour un débutant il ne se défend pas mal!** he's not bad for a beginner!

5 **se d. de faire qch** *(s'interdire de)* to refuse to do sth; *(s'empêcher de)* to refrain from doing sth; **se défendant de penser du mal d'elle** refusing to think ill of her; **on ne peut se d. de l'aimer** you can't help liking him/her

6 **se d. de qch** *(nier)* to deny sth; **se d. de toute compromission** to deny being compromised; **se défendant d'avoir dit cela** denying having said that; **il se défend de vouloir la quitter** he won't admit that he wants to leave her

défends [defɑ̃] = **défens**

défendu, -e [defɑ̃dy] PP *voir* **défendre**

défenestration [defənɛstrasjɔ̃] NF defenestration

défenestrer [3] [defənɛstre] VT to defenestrate, to throw out of the window

►**se défenestrer** VPR to jump out of the window

défens [defɑ̃] **en défens** ADJ = to which access is forbidden to grazing animals

défense [defɑ̃s] NF **1** *(interdiction)* prohibition; **malgré la d. de sa mère** despite his/her mother having forbidden it; **mais d. expresse d'en parler!** but you're strictly forbidden to talk about it!; *Vieilli* **faire d. à qn de faire qch** to forbid sb to do sth; **d. d'entrer** *(sur panneau)* no admittance *or* entry; **danger, d. d'entrer** *(sur panneau)* danger, keep out; **d. d'afficher** *(sur panneau)* stick no bills; **d. de fumer** *(sur panneau)* no smoking; **d. de déposer des ordures** *(sur panneau)* no dumping

2 *(protection, moyen de protection)* defence; **la d. de la langue française** the defence of the French language; **association de d. du consommateur** *ou* **des consommateurs** consumer (protection) group; **pour la d. des institutions** in order to defend *or* to safeguard the institutions; **ne pas avoir de d.** to be unable to defend oneself; **sans d. contre le désespoir** defenceless in the face of despair; *Mktg* **d. contre-offensive** counteroffensive defence; *Mktg* **d. mobile** mobile defence; *Mktg* **d. préventive** pre-emptive defence

3 *(dans un débat)* defence; **prendre la d. de qn/ qch** to stand up for *or* to defend sb/sth

4 *Mil* defence; **d. contre avions** anti-aircraft defence; **la D. nationale** national defence; **un problème concernant la D. nationale** a problem of national defence; **d. opérationnelle du territoire** home defence; **d. passive** civil defence; **un secret D.** a military secret

5 *Physiol & Psy* defence; **les défenses de l'organisme** the body's defences; **défenses immunitaires** immune defences; **impossible de discuter, il est toujours en position de d.** there's no talking to him, he's always on the defensive

6 *Jur* defence; **assurer la d. de qn** to defend sb; **présenter la d.** to put the case for the defence; **d. au fond** defence on the merits

7 *Sport* **la d.** the defence; **jouer la d.** to play a defensive game

8 *Zool* tusk

9 *Naut* fender

□ **défenses** NFPL *Mil* defences

□ **de défense** ADJ **1** *Mil voir* **ligne**

2 *Psy* defence *(avant n)*

□ **pour ma/sa/***etc* **défense** ADV in my/his/*etc*

defence; **je dirai pour ma d. que...** I will say in my (own) defence that...
❑ **sans défense** ADJ **1** *(animal, bébé)* defenceless, helpless
2 *Mil* undefended
❑ **Défense** NF **la D.** = ultra-modern business district in western Paris
défenseur [defɑ̃sœr] NM **1** *(partisan → de la foi)* defender; *(→ d'une cause)* supporter, advocate; **les défenseurs de ces idées** advocates *or* supporters of these ideas; **d. de l'art pour l'art** believer in art for art's sake; **jouer les défenseurs de la veuve et de l'orphelin** *ou* **des faibles et des opprimés** to play the champion of the poor and needy
2 *Jur Br* counsel for the defence, *Am* defense attorney; **l'accusé et son d.** the accused and his counsel; **d. des enfants** = independent authority charged with the defence and promotion of children's rights
3 *Sport* defender; **d. droit/gauche** *(au hockey)* right/left defence
défensif, -ive [defɑ̃sif, -iv] ADJ *(armes, mesures)* defensive
❑ **défensive** NF **la défensive** the defensive; **être** *ou* **se tenir sur la défensive** to be (on the) defensive; **ne sois pas toujours sur la défensive** don't be so defensive
défensivement [defɑ̃sivmɑ̃] ADV defensively
déféquer [18] [defeke] VI to defecate
défera *etc voir* **défaire**
déféré, -e [defere] *Jur* ADJ referred
NM *(d'un prévenu)* referral to trial
déférence [deferɑ̃s] NF respect, deference; **avec d.** deferentially; **par d. pour...** in *or* out of deference to...
déférent, -e [deferɑ̃, -ɑ̃t] ADJ **1** *(employé, attitude, discours)* deferential, respectful **2** *Anat* **canal d.** vas deferens
NM *Anat* vas deferens
déférer [18] [defere] VT *(affaire)* to refer to a court; *(accusé)* to bring before a court; **d. qn à la justice** to hand sb over to the law; **d. un officier en conseil de guerre** to bring an officer before a court-martial; **il a été déféré au Parquet** he was sent to appear before the public prosecutor
❑ **déférer à** VT IND to defer to
déferlage [defɛrlaʒ] NM *Naut (d'une voile)* unfurling; *(d'un drapeau)* breaking
déferlant, -e [defɛrlɑ̃, -ɑ̃t] ADJ *(vague)* breaking
❑ **déferlante** NF **1** *(vague)* breaker **2** *(invasion)* tidal wave; **la grande déferlante du tourisme estival** the tidal wave of summer tourists
déferlement [defɛrləmɑ̃] NM **1** *(de vagues)* breaking **2** *(invasion)* **d. de** *(soudain)* flood of; *(continu)* stream of; **on s'attend à un d. de visiteurs** crowds of visitors are expected **3** *(accès)* wave; **un d. d'émotion** a surge *or* wave of emotion; **un d. de colère dans le parti** a wave of anger sweeping the party
déferler [3] [defɛrle] VI **1** *(vague)* to break; *Fig* **une vague de violence/racisme déferla sur le pays** a wave of violence/racism spread through the country
2 *(se répandre)* to rush; **déferlant dans le parc** streaming into the park; **ils déferlaient dans la rue** they flooded into the streets; **les vacanciers déferlent sur les routes** holiday-makers are taking to the roads in droves; **la famille déferlait chez elle** her whole family turned up at her door
3 *(fuser → émotion, applaudissements)* to erupt
VT *Naut (voile)* to unfurl; *(drapeau)* to break
déferrage [defɛraʒ] NM *(d'un cheval)* unshoeing
déferrement [defɛrmɑ̃] NM *(d'un cheval)* unshoeing; *(d'un coffre)* removing the iron plates
déferrer [4] [defere] VT *(cheval)* to unshoe; *(coffre)* to remove the iron plates from
déferrure [defɛryr] NF unshoeing
défervescence [defɛrvesɑ̃s] NF abatement of fever, defervescence
défet [defɛ] NM *Typ* waste sheets
défeuillaison [defœjɛzɔ̃] NF defoliation, falling of leaves; **à la d.** when the leaves fall, when the trees lose their leaves
défeuiller [5] [defœje] VT *Littéraire* to strip of leaves; **paysage défeuillé** leafless scenery
►**se défeuiller** VPR *Littéraire* to shed its leaves, to defoliate
défeutrer [5] [defœtre] VT *Tex* to defelt

défi [defi] NM **1** *(appel provocateur)* challenge; **jeter** *ou* **lancer un d. à qn** to throw down the gauntlet to sb, to challenge sb; **relever un d.** to take up the gauntlet *or* a challenge
2 *(attitude provocatrice)* defiance; **refuser par d.** to refuse out of defiance
3 *(remise en question)* **un d. à** a challenge to; **c'est un d. à ma position de chef de famille** it's a challenge to my position as head of the family; **c'est un d. au bon sens** it defies common sense
❑ **au défi** ADV **mettre qn au d. (de faire)** to challenge sb (to do); **je mets quiconque au d. de comprendre leur formulaire** I challenge anybody to understand their form
❑ **de défi** ADJ *(attitude, air)* defiant
défiance [defjɑ̃s] NF **1** *(méfiance)* mistrust, distrust; **inspirer** *ou* **éveiller la d.** to arouse suspicion; **avec d.** mistrustfully, distrustfully; **mettre qn en d.** to make sb wary; **enfant sans d.** unsuspecting child; **parler sans d.** to speak unsuspectingly **2** *(désapprobation)* **vote de d.** vote of no confidence
défiant, -e [defjɑ̃, -ɑ̃t] ADJ *(enfant, air)* mistrustful, distrustful
défibrage [defibraʒ] NM **1** *(de canne à sucre)* grinding **2** *(du bois)* pulping, defibration
défibrer [3] [defibre] VT **1** *(canne à sucre)* to grind
2 *(bois)* to pulp, to defibrate
défibreur [defibrœr] NM **1** *(dans la fabrication du papier)* wood-grinder, stuff-grinder; **d. en continu** caterpillar grinder **2** *(de canne à sucre)* cane-shredder **3** *Tex* disintegrator
défibrillateur [defibrijatœr] NM *Méd* defibrillator
défibrillation [defibrijasjɔ̃] NF *Méd* defibrillation
déficeler [24] [defisle] VT *(paquet)* to untie, to take the string off; *(rôti)* to remove the string from, to take the string off
►**se déficeler** VPR to come untied *or* undone
déficience [defisjɑ̃s] NF **1** *Méd* deficiency; **d. musculaire** muscle deficiency; **d. immunitaire** immune deficiency; **d. en vitamine B** vitamin B deficiency **2** *Psy* **d. mentale** *ou* **intellectuelle** mental retardation
déficient, -e [defisjɑ̃, -ɑ̃t] ADJ **1** *Méd* deficient **2** *(insuffisant → théorie)* weak, feeble
NM,F **d. moteur** person with motor deficiency; **d. mental** person who is mentally deficient
déficit [defisit] NM **1** *Écon & Fin* deficit; **être en d.** to be in deficit; **accuser un d.** to show a deficit; **combler un d.** to make up a deficit; **société en d.** company in deficit; **d. de la balance commerciale** trade deficit; **d. budgétaire** budget deficit; **d. de caisse** cash deficit; **d. commercial** trade deficit *or* gap; **d. démocratique** democratic deficit; **d. d'exploitation** operating deficit; **d. extérieur** external deficit, balance of payments deficit; **d. de financement** financing gap; **d. fiscal remboursable** negative income tax; **d. fiscal reportable** tax loss; **d. public** government deficit; *Compta* **d. reportable** loss carry forward; **d. du secteur public** public sector deficit; **d. social** public spending deficit; **d. de trésorerie** cash deficit
2 *Méd* **d. immunitaire** immunodeficiency; *Psy* **d. intellectuel** mental retardation
3 *(manque)* gap, lack
déficitaire [defisitɛr] ADJ **1** *Écon & Fin (entreprise)* loss-making; *(compte)* in debit; *(budget)* in deficit, adverse; *(bilan)* showing a loss; **être d.** to be in deficit **2** *(insuffisant → production, récolte)* poor
défier [9] [defje] VT **1** *(dans un duel, un jeu)* to challenge; **d. qn du regard** to give sb a challenging look; **je te défie de trouver moins cher** I defy you to find a better price; **il m'a défié au tennis** he challenged me to a game of tennis
2 *(résister à → danger)* to defy, to brave; **il ne craint pas de d. l'autorité paternelle** he's not afraid to stand up to his father; **d. l'imagination/les lois de l'équilibre** to defy the imagination/the laws of gravity; **prix/qualité défiant toute concurrence** absolutely unbeatable prices/quality
►**se défier** VPR *Littéraire* **se d. de** to mistrust, to distrust; **elle se défie d'elle-même** she doesn't trust herself
défigurer [3] [defigyre] VT **1** *(personne)* to disfigure; **l'accident/la maladie l'a défiguré** the accident/illness has disfigured him; **défiguré par les larmes/la colère** his face disfigured by tears/distorted with anger
2 *(ville, environnement)* to blight, to ruin; **la tour défigure la place** the tower block ruins the square
3 *(caricaturer → vérité, faits)* to distort; **défigurant les intentions de l'auteur** distorting the author's intentions
défilage [defilaʒ] NM **1** *Tex* shredding **2** *(dans la fabrication du papier)* breaking in
défilé [defile] NM **1** *(procession → pour une fête)* procession; *(→ de militaires)* march, parade; *(→ de manifestants)* march; **d. aérien** flypast; **un d. de mode** a fashion show **2** *(multitude → d'invités, de pensées)* stream, procession; *(→ de souvenirs)* string, procession **3** *Géog* defile, narrow pass
défilement [defilmɑ̃] NM *(d'un film, d'une bande)* unwinding; *Ordinat (d'un texte sur écran)* scrolling
défiler [3] [defile] VI **1** *(marcher en file)* to file (along); *(pour être vu)* to march, to parade; *(pour manifester)* to march; **les élèves défilent devant la statue** the pupils file past the statue; **d. dans la rue** to march through the streets; **les mannequins défilaient** the models were parading up and down the *Br* catwalk *or Am* runway
2 *(être nombreux)* **des centaines de voitures défilent vers la côte** hundreds of cars are streaming towards the coast; **les journalistes ont défilé au ministère toute la journée** the journalists were in and out of the ministry all day; **ses amis ont défilé à son chevet** his/her friends came to his/her bedside one after the other; **les petites amies défilent** he has one girlfriend after another
3 *(se dérouler → bande magnétique)* to unwind; *(→ texte informatique)* to scroll; *(→ souvenirs, publicité)* to stream past; **faire d.** *(bande, bobine)* to run; *(données sur écran)* to scroll; *Ordinat* **faire d. un document** to scroll through a document; *Ordinat* **d. vers le bas/haut** to scroll down/up; **les pâturages défilaient sans fin** the fields rolled past endlessly; *(rapidement)* the fields flashed by; **toute ma vie a défilé dans ma tête** my whole life flashed before my eyes
VT **1** *(perles)* to unthread; *(collier)* to unstring
2 *Mil* to put under cover, to defilade
3 *Tex* to shred
4 *(dans la fabrication du papier)* to break in
►**se défiler** VPR *Fam* **1** *(fuir)* to slip away
2 *(esquiver une responsabilité)* **n'essaie pas de te d.** don't try to get *or* wriggle out of it; **il s'est défilé** he got *or* wriggled out of it
défini, -e [defini] ADJ **1** *(qui a une définition)* defined; *(précis)* precise; **une utilisation bien définie** a well-defined usage; **mal d.** ill-defined **2** *Gram* **article d.** definite article; **passé d.** preterite **3** *Ordinat* **d. par l'utilisateur** user-defined
NM **le d.** that which is defined
définir [32] [definir] VT **1** *(donner la définition de)* to define; **on définit le dauphin comme un mammifère** the dolphin is defined as a mammal
2 *(décrire → sensation)* to define, to describe; *(→ personne)* to describe, to portray
3 *(circonscrire → objectif, politique, condition)* to define; **notre mode de travail reste à d.** our method of working has still to be defined; **je définirais mon rôle comme étant celui d'un négociateur** I'd define *or* describe my role as that of a negotiator
►**se définir** VPR **1** *(concept)* **se d. comme** to be defined as
2 *(soi-même)* to describe oneself; **comment vous définissez-vous?** how would you describe yourself?
définissable [definisabl] ADJ definable; *Ordinat* **d. par l'utilisateur** user-definable
définiteur [definitœr] NM *Rel* definitor
définitif, -ive [definitif, -iv] ADJ **1** *(irrévocable → décision)* final; *(→ acceptation)* definitive; **à titre d.** permanently; **leur séparation est définitive** they're splitting up for good; **soldes avant fermeture définitive** *(sur vitrine d'un magasin)* closing-down sale; **c'est non et c'est d.!** it's no and that's that!; **rien de d.** nothing definite
2 *(qui fait autorité → œuvre)* definitive; *(→ argument)* conclusive; **il a écrit un article d.**

sur le matérialisme he's written the definitive article on materialism

NM **le d.** that which is definitive; **à ce stade de ma vie, je veux du d.** at my time of life I want something more definite

❑ **en définitive** ADV **1** *(somme toute)* finally, when all's said and done, in the final analysis; **elle n'est pas malheureuse, en définitive** when all is said and done, she's not unhappy

2 *(après tout)* after all; **en définitive, je ne crois pas que je le lui dirai** I don't think I'll tell him/her after all

définition [definisjɔ̃] NF **1** *(d'une idée, d'un mot)* definition; **d. de poste** job description **2** *Ling* definition **3** *(de mots croisés)* clue **4** *Phot & Tél* definition

❑ **par définition** ADV by definition; **pour elle les hommes sont égoïstes, par d.** as far as she is concerned men are, by definition, selfish

définitionnel, -elle [definisjɔnɛl] ADJ *(relatif à une définition)* definitional; *(qui est une définition)* definitional

définitive [definitiv] *voir* **définitif**

définitivement [definitivmɑ̃] ADV *(partir, s'installer)* for good; *(décider)* definitely; *(nommé)* permanently

définitoire [definitwar] ADJ definitional

défiscalisation [defiskalizasjɔ̃] NF tax exemption

défiscalisé, -e [defiskalize] ADJ tax free

défiscaliser [3] [defiskalize] VT to exempt from tax

défit *etc voir* **défaire**

déflagrant, -e [deflagrɑ̃, -ɑ̃t] ADJ deflagrating

déflagration [deflagrasjɔ̃] NF **1** *(explosion)* explosion; *(combustion)* deflagration **2** *(conflit)* clash; **une d. mondiale** a worldwide conflict

déflagrer [3] [deflagre] VI to deflagrate

déflation [deflasjɔ̃] NF *Fin & Géol* deflation

déflationniste [deflasjɔnist] ADJ *(principe)* deflationist; *(mesure)* deflationary

NMF deflationist

défléchir [32] [defleʃir] VT to deflect; *Bot* **rameau défléchi** deflected branch

VI to deflect

déflecteur [deflɛktœr] NM **1** *Aut Br* quarter light, *Am* vent **2** *Naut & Phys* deflector

défleurir [32] [deflœrir] *Littéraire* VT *(rose)* to deadhead, to take the heads off, to top; *(arbre)* to remove the blossom from; *(paysage)* to remove the flowers from

VI *(arbre)* to shed its blossom; *(paysage)* to lose its flowers

déflexion [deflɛksjɔ̃] NF **1** *Physiol* deflection; *Obst* disengagement, extension **2** *Phys* deflection **3** *Aviat (vers le haut)* upwash; *(vers le bas)* downwash

déflocage [deflɔkaʒ] NM *Constr* removal of asbestos

défloquer [3] [deflɔke] VT *Constr* to remove asbestos from

défloraison [deflɔrɛzɔ̃] NF *Littéraire* falling of blossoms

défloration [deflɔrasjɔ̃] NF defloration

déflorer [3] [deflɔre] VT **1** *(fille)* to deflower **2** *Littéraire (sujet)* to corrupt, to spoil

défluent [deflyɑ̃] NM distributary

défoliant [defɔljɑ̃] NM defoliant

défoliation [defɔljasjɔ̃] NF defoliation

défolier [9] [defɔlje] VT to defoliate

défonçage [defɔ̃saʒ] NM **1** *(destruction → d'une porte)* breaking down; *(→ d'un mur)* smashing down; *(→ d'un tonneau, d'une caisse)* smashing open **2** *Agr* deep ploughing

défonce [defɔ̃s] NF *Fam* getting stoned; **son seul plaisir, c'est la d.** his/her only pleasure in life is getting stoned; **d. aux solvants** solvent abuse; **d. à l'acide** dropping acid; **d. aux amphétamines** taking speed, speeding

défoncé, -e [defɔ̃se] ADJ **1** *(cabossé → lit, sofa)* battered; *(→ chemin)* rutted; **un matelas d.** a mattress with all the stuffing hanging out **2** *Fam (drogué)* stoned; **ils étaient complètement défoncés** they were stoned out of their minds **3** *Can Fam (affamé)* starving

NM,F *Can Fam* **manger comme un d.** to eat like a horse

défoncement [defɔ̃smɑ̃] NM **1** *(destruction → d'une porte)* breaking down; *(→ d'un mur)* smashing down; *(→ d'un tonneau, d'une caisse)* smashing open **2** *Agr* deep ploughing

défoncer [16] [defɔ̃se] VT **1** *(démolir → porte)* to smash in, to knock down; *(→ mur)* to smash down, to knock down, to demolish; *(→ lit)* to break (up), to smash (up); *(→ chaussée)* to break up; *(→ caisse, tonneau)* to smash in, to stave in; **d. qch à coups de pied** to kick sth in; **le choc lui a défoncé trois côtes** the impact cracked three of his/her ribs; **les chars ont défoncé la route** the tanks have broken up the road surface; **il a eu le crâne défoncé** his skull was smashed; *Fam* **d. la gueule à qn** to smash sb's face in, *Br* to punch sb's lights out, *Am* to punch sb out

2 *Fam (sujet: drogue)* **d. qn** to get sb high; *Hum* **moi, c'est le café qui me défonce** I get my kicks from coffee

3 *Agr* to deep-plough

▸**se défoncer** VPR *Fam* **1** *(se démener → au travail)* to work flat out, to sweat blood; *(→ en se distrayant)* to have a wild time; **je me suis défoncé pour finir le manuscrit** I worked flat out to get the manuscript finished; **il s'est défoncé sur scène hier soir** he gave it all he had on stage last night

2 *(se droguer)* to get stoned; **elle se défonce tous les soirs** she gets stoned every night; **il se défonce à l'héroïne/à la colle** he does heroin/sniffs glue; *Hum* **moi je me défonce au café** I'm hooked on coffee

défonceuse [defɔ̃søz] NF **1** *Agr* breaker plough **2** *(en travaux publics)* ripper, rooter

défont *voir* **défaire**

déforcer [16] [defɔrse] VT *Belg* to weaken, to make weaker

déforestation [defɔrɛstasjɔ̃] NF deforestation; **faire de la d.** to deforest

déformable [defɔrmabl] ADJ that can be distorted; *Métal* ductile

déformant, -e [defɔrmɑ̃, -ɑ̃t] ADJ distorting

déformation [defɔrmasjɔ̃] NF **1** *(changement de forme → gén)* putting out of shape; *(→ par torsion)* bending out of shape; *(→ en frappant)* knocking out of shape; *(→ par la chaleur)* warping

2 *Méd* deformation; **avoir une d. du pied** to have a deformed foot; **il fume tellement qu'il souffre d'une d. du goût** he smokes so much that he's lost all sense of taste; **d. en boutonnière** Boutonnière deformity

3 *(travestissement → d'une pensée, de la réalité)* distortion, misrepresentation; *(→ d'une image)* distortion, warping; **elle pose toujours des questions, c'est une d. professionnelle** she's always asking questions because she's used to doing it in her job; *Hum* **ne fais pas attention, c'est de la d. professionnelle!** don't worry, it's just my job!

déformer [3] [defɔrme] VT **1** *(changer la forme de → planche)* to warp; *(→ barre)* to bend (out of shape); *(→ pare-chocs)* to knock out of shape, to buckle; *(→ chaussure, pantalon)* to put out of shape, to ruin the shape of; **chapeau déformé** hat that's gone out of shape *or* lost its shape

2 *(transformer → corps)* to deform; *(→ visage, voix)* to distort; **les mains déformées par les rhumatismes** hands deformed by rheumatism; **traits déformés par la haine** features contorted with hatred

3 *(changer le comportement de)* **déformé par dix ans de journalisme** marked by ten years as a journalist; **l'enseignement l'a déformé** he's taken on all the mannerisms of the typical teacher

4 *(fausser → réalité, pensée)* to distort, to misrepresent; *(→ image)* to distort; *(→ goût)* to warp; *(→ paroles)* to misquote; **vous déformez la réalité/vérité** you're twisting the facts/truth

▸**se déformer** VPR *(vêtement)* to become shapeless, to go out of shape, to lose its shape; *(planche)* to become warped; *(barre)* to become bent; **le pull ne s'est pas déformé** the sweater kept its shape

défoulement [defulmɑ̃] NM release; **danser est un bon d.** dancing is a good way of unwinding; **crier par d.** to shout to release one's pent-up emotions

défouler [3] [defule] VT to liberate; **ça défoule** it helps you let off steam

▸**se défouler** VPR to let off steam, to unwind; **rien de tel que le sport pour se d.** there's nothing like sport for letting off steam; **se d. sur qn** to take it out on sb

défouloir [defulwar] NM *Fam* escape valve, way of letting off steam; **danser me sert de d.** dancing is my way of letting off steam

défournage [defurnaʒ], **défournement** [defurnəmɑ̃] NM *(du pain)* drawing from the oven; *(de la poterie)* drawing from the kiln; *(de la coke)* discharging from the oven; **aire de défournement** coking wharf

défourner [3] [defurne] VT *(pain)* to take out (of the oven); *(poterie)* to take out (of the kiln); *(coke)* to discharge (from the oven)

défragmentation [defragmɑ̃tasjɔ̃] NF *Ordinat (de fichiers)* defragmentation

défragmenter [3] [defragmɑ̃te] VT *Ordinat* to defragment

défraîchi, -e [defreʃi] ADJ *Com (articles)* shopsoiled; *(usé → vêtement)* shabby, past its best; **les fleurs sont défraîchies** the flowers are past their best; *Fig* **des idées un peu défraîchies** rather stale ideas

défraîchir [32] [defreʃir] VT *(rideau)* to give a worn look to; *(couleur)* to fade

▸**se défraîchir** VPR *(rideau, couleur)* to fade; *(vêtement)* to become shabby

défrayer [11] [defreje] VT **1** *(indemniser)* **d. qn** to meet or pay sb's expenses; **d. qn de qch** to reimburse sb for sth **2** *(locutions)* **d. la chronique** to be the talk of the town; **d. la conversation** to be the main topic of conversation

défrichage [defriʃaʒ] NM **1** *(d'un terrain)* clearing **2** *(approche)* **le d. d'un texte du programme** a first look at a book on the syllabus

défriche [defriʃ] NF clearing, clear patch

défrichement [defriʃmɑ̃] NM **1** *(d'un terrain)* clearing **2** *(approche)* **le d. d'un texte du programme** a first look at a book on the syllabus

défricher [3] [defriʃe] VT **1** *(nettoyer → terrain)* to clear; *Fig* **d. le terrain avant de négocier** to clear the way for negotiations **2** *(dégrossir → texte)* to have a first look at; *(→ domaine)* to pioneer; **mon assistant a défriché votre dossier** my assistant did some preliminary work on your file

défricheur, -euse [defriʃœr, -øz] NM,F **1** *(agriculteur)* **les premiers défricheurs** the people *or* settlers who first cleared the land **2** *Fig (d'un nouveau domaine)* pioneer

défriper [3] [defripe] VT to smooth out, to take the creases out of

défriser [3] [defrize] VT **1** *(cheveux, moustache)* to straighten out; **se faire d. (les cheveux)** to have one's hair straightened **2** *Fam (contrarier)* to bug; **ça me défrise, ce genre d'attitude!** that sort of attitude really bugs me *or* gets to me!; **et alors, ça te défrise?** have you got a problem with that?

défroisser [3] [defrwase] VT to smooth out, to take the creases out of

▸**se défroisser** VPR to lose its creases

défroncer [16] [defrɔ̃se] VT **1** *Couture* to take the gathers from **2** *(détendre)* **d. les sourcils** to stop frowning

défroque [defrɔk] NF **1** *(vêtement)* (old) rag; **on lui passait les défroques de son frère** he used to get his brother's cast-offs **2** *(d'un religieux)* effects

défroqué, -e [defrɔke] ADJ defrocked, unfrocked

NM *(prêtre)* defrocked priest; *(moine)* defrocked monk

défroquer [3] [defrɔke] VI *(prêtre)* to leave the priesthood; *(moine)* to leave the order

▸**se défroquer** VPR **1** *(prêtre)* to leave the priesthood; *(moine)* to leave the order **2** *Fam (enlever son pantalon)* to take one's *Br* trousers *or Am* pants off[▪], *Br* to get one's keks off

défruiter [3] [defrɥite] VT *(huile d'olive)* to remove the fruity flavour from

défunt, -e [defœ̃, -œ̃t] *Littéraire* ADJ **1** *(décédé → parent, mari)* late; **son d. cousin** her late cousin **2** *(terminé → royauté)* defunct; *(→ espoir, amour)* lost, extinguished

NM,F deceased person; **le d.** the deceased; **prière pour les défunts** prayer for the dead

dégagé, -e [degaʒe] ADJ **1** *(vue)* open; *(pièce, passage)* cleared; **une allée dégagée** a treeless drive

2 *(épaules)* bare; **bien d. sur les oreilles, s'il vous plaît** *(chez le coiffeur)* nice and short over the ears, please; **je la préfère avec le front d.** I prefer her with her hair back

3 *(désinvolte → air, ton)* casual; *(→ mouvements, démarche)* swinging, free; **dit-elle d'un air d.** she said casually *or* trying to look casual

4 *Météo* clear, cloudless

NM *(en danse)* dégagé

dégagement [degaʒmɑ̃] **NM 1** *(émanation → d'odeur)* emanation; *(→ de chaleur)* release, emission, emanation; **un d. de gaz** *(accidentel)* a gas leak; *(volontaire)* a release of gas

2 *(espace → dans une maison)* passage, hall; *(→ dans une ville)* open space; *(→ dans un bois)* clearing; **un d. d'un mètre entre le pont et le véhicule** one metre headroom between the bridge and the vehicle

3 *(déblaiement)* opening out, digging out; **le d. du temple par les archéologues** the excavation of the temple by the archaeologists

4 *Mil & Pol* disengagement

5 *(au mont-de-piété)* redeeming *(from pawn)*

6 *Sport (d'un ballon)* clearance; **d. interdit** *(en hockey sur glace)* icing

7 *Escrime* disengagement

8 *Méd (à l'accouchement)* crowning

9 *Fin (de fonds, de crédits)* release

dégager [17] [degaʒe] **VT 1** *(sortir)* to free; **il a essayé de d. sa main de la mienne** he tried to pull his hand away *or* to free his hand from mine; **il a fallu deux heures pour le d. de la voiture** it took two hours to free him from the car; **ils l'ont dégagée au chalumeau** they cut her loose (from the wreckage) with a blowtorch; **d. les blessés des décombres** to pull *or* dig the injured out from the rubble; **d. un prisonnier de ses chaînes** to unshackle *or* to unfetter a prisoner

2 *(enlever → arbres tombés, ordures)* to remove, to clear; **d. les branches de la route** to clear the branches off the road, to clear the road of branches; *Fam* **tu vas me d. toutes ces bricoles de tes étagères** I want you to clear all these odds and ends off your shelves

3 *(désencombrer → couloir, table, salle)* to clear (out); *(→ sinus)* to clear, to unblock; *(→ poitrine, gorge)* to clear; *(→ chemin, pont)* to clear; **ils ont dégagé une ouverture dans la haie** they made an opening in the hedge; **une coupe qui dégage la nuque** a hairstyle cut very short at the back; **la robe dégage les épaules** the dress leaves the shoulders bare; *Fam Fig* **dégagez la piste!** (get) out of the way!

4 *Fin (fonds, crédits)* to release; *(bénéfices, excédent)* to show

5 *(annuler)* **d. sa parole** to go back on one's word; **d. sa responsabilité** to deny responsibility; **d. qn de sa promesse** to release *or* to free sb from their promise; **d. qn de ses dettes** to cancel sb's debt; **il est dégagé des obligations militaires** he has completed his military service

6 *(émettre → odeur)* to give off, to emit; *(→ gaz)* to release, to emit; *(→ chaleur)* to emit, to give out

7 *(manifester → quiétude)* to radiate; **la bibliothèque dégageait une impression de sérénité** the library had an atmosphere of great calm

8 *(extraire → règle, principe)* to draw; *(→ vérité)* to draw, to bring out, to extract; **d. l'idée principale d'un texte** to identify the main idea of a text

9 *(du mont-de-piété)* to redeem *(from pawn)*

10 *Escrime* to disengage

11 *Sport (ballon)* to clear; **d. le ballon en touche** to kick the ball into touch

USAGE ABSOLU 1 *(en danse)* to perform a dégagé **2** *Fam* **dégage!** clear off!, get lost! **3** *Sport* **d. en touche** to put the ball into touch

VI 1 *très Fam (sentir mauvais)* to stink, *Br* to pong, to hum

2 *Fam (produire un effet puissant → musique)* to be mind-blowing, to kick ass; *(→ plat, épice)* to blow the top of one's head off, to pack a punch

▶**se dégager VPR 1** *(conclusion)* to be drawn; *(vérité)* to emerge, to come out; **il se dégage du rapport que les torts sont partagés** it appears from the report that both sides are to blame

2 *(s'extraire → d'une voiture accidentée, d'un piège)* to free oneself (**de** from); **se d. d'une étreinte** to extricate oneself from an embrace; **le chien s'est dégagé de sa laisse** the dog's slipped its lead; **se d. du peloton** to leave the pack behind

3 *(se libérer → d'un engagement)* **j'étais invité mais je vais me d.** I was invited but I'll get out of it; **il s'est dégagé en prétextant une indisposition** he cried off on the grounds of being unwell; **se d. d'une affaire/d'une association** to drop out of a deal/an association; **se d. d'une dette** to discharge *or* pay off a debt; **se d. d'une obligation** to free oneself from an obligation; **se d. de sa promesse** to go back on one's promise

4 *(se vider → route, ciel)* to clear; *(→ nez, sinus)* to become unblocked, to clear

5 *(émaner → odeur, gaz, fumée)* to emanate, to be given off; *(se manifester → quiétude)* to emanate, to radiate; **la tendresse qui se dégageait de sa lettre m'émut** the love which permeated his/her letter moved me; **le magnétisme qui se dégage d'elle** the magnetism she radiates

dégaine [degɛn] **NF 1** *Fam (démarche)* (peculiar) gait■; *(aspect ridicule)* strange appearance■; **tu parles d'une d.!** just look at that!; **il a vraiment une d. pas possible** he looks like something from another planet! **2** *(en alpinisme)* quickdraw

dégainer [4] [degene] **VT 1** *(épée)* to unsheathe, to draw; *(revolver)* to draw **2** *Tech* to unsheathe

USAGE ABSOLU avant que le gangster ait pu d. before the gangster could draw his gun

déganter [3] [degɑ̃te] **se déganter VPR** to take off *or* to remove one's glove/gloves

dégarni, -e [degarni] **ADJ 1** *(arbre, rayon, mur)* bare; **le placard est bien d.** the cupboard's rather empty *or* bare; **mon portefeuille est plutôt d.** I'm rather low on funds **2** *(personne, crâne)* balding; **il a le front d.** he has a receding hairline

dégarnir [32] [degarnir] **VT 1** *(ôter les objets de → salon, salle)* to empty; *(→ collection)* to deplete; **j'ai complètement dégarni le mur** I've taken everything off the wall; **les devantures sont dégarnies de leurs mannequins** the dummies have been removed from the window displays; **l'autel est dégarni de ses bougies** the altar has been stripped of its candles

2 *(ôter l'argent de → portefeuille)* to empty, to deplete; *(→ compte en banque)* to drain, to draw heavily on

3 *(ôter les cheveux de → crâne)* to cause to go bald; **un peu dégarni par les années** balding slightly with age

4 *(ôter les feuilles de)* to strip of its leaves; **l'hiver a dégarni les arbres** winter has stripped the trees of their leaves; **la rose, dégarnie de ses piquants** the rose, stripped of its thorns; **le parc, dégarni de ses cyprès** the park, stripped of its cypresses

▶**se dégarnir VPR 1** *(se vider → boîte, collection, rayonnage)* to become depleted; *(→ salle)* to empty; *(→ groupe)* to become depleted, to thin out

2 *(devenir chauve)* to go bald, to start losing one's hair; **il commence à se d. sur le dessus (du crâne)** he's going thin on top; **son front se dégarnit** his hairline is receding; **son crâne se dégarnit** he's losing hair, he's thinning on top

3 *(arbre)* to lose its leaves; *(forêt)* to become depleted *or* thinner

dégarnissage [degarnisaʒ] **NM 1** *Constr* raking out of the jointing **2** *Rail* clearing away of ballast, stripping off **3** *Mil* **d. du front/des arrières** thinning out of the front line/of the rear

dégasolinage [degazɔlinaʒ] **NM** *(d'un gaz)* recovery of crude oil

dégasoliner [3] [degazɔline] **VT** *(gaz)* to recover crude oil from

dégât [dega] **NM** damage *(UNCOUNT)*; **il y a du d.** *ou* **des dégâts** there's some damage; *Fam* **il n'y a pas de dégâts?** *(après un accident)* no harm done?; *Fam* **si tu le perds, il va y avoir du d.** if you lose it, there'll be trouble; **faire des dégâts** to cause damage; **les chenilles ont fait des dégâts/de gros dégâts dans le verger** the caterpillars have caused some damage/wreaked havoc in the orchard; **dégâts des eaux** water damage; **assuré contre les dégâts des eaux** insured against water damage; **dégâts matériels** structural damage

dégauchir [32] [degoʃir] **VT 1** *(redresser)* to straighten out **2** *(aplanir → planche)* to plane; *(→ pierre)* to trim

dégauchissage [degoʃisaʒ], **dégauchissement** [degoʃismɑ̃] **NM 1** *(redressement)* straightening **2** *(fait d'aplanir → une planche)* planing; *(→ une pierre)* trimming

dégauchisseuse [degoʃisøz] **NF** surfacing machine, surfacer

dégazage [degazaʒ] **NM 1** *Métal* (gas) extraction **2** *(d'un pétrolier, d'une mine de charbon)* degassing

dégazer [3] [degaze] **VT** *Métal* to extract gas from

VI *(pétrolier)* to degas

▶**se dégazer VPR** to degas

dégazolinage [degazɔlinaʒ] = **dégasolinage**

dégazoliner [3] [degazɔline] = **dégasoliner**

dégazonnage [degazɔnaʒ], **dégazonnement** [degazɔnmɑ̃] **NM** turf-cutting, paring

dégazonner [3] [degazɔne] **VT** to unturf, to take the turf up from

dégel [deʒɛl] **NM 1** *Météo* thaw; **au d.** when the thaw comes **2** *(après un conflit)* thaw; *Pol* **une période de d.** a period of détente

dégelée [deʒle] **NF** *Fam* thrashing, hiding; **foutre une d. à qn** to give sb a thrashing *or* a hiding; **prendre une d.** to get a thrashing *or* a hiding

dégeler [25] [deʒle] **VT 1** *(décongeler)* to defrost

2 *(réchauffer → sol, étang)* to thaw (out); *(→ tuyau)* to unfreeze

3 *Fam (mettre à l'aise)* to thaw (out), to relax■; **je n'arrive pas à d. mon collègue** I can't get my colleague to loosen up; **elle sait d. un auditoire** she knows how to warm up an audience

4 *(améliorer → relations diplomatiques)* to thaw; **d. l'atmosphère** to make the atmosphere less chilly

5 *Fin (crédits)* to unfreeze

VI 1 *(se réchauffer → banquise, étang)* to thaw

2 *(décongeler)* to defrost

V IMPERSONNEL il dégèle it's thawing

▶**se dégeler VPR 1** *(se décongeler)* to defrost

2 *(se réchauffer → sol, étang)* to thaw (out)

3 *Fam (être moins timide)* to thaw (out), to relax■; **dégèle-toi un peu!** come on, relax *or* let your hair down!

4 *(s'améliorer → relations)* to improve; **les relations entre les deux pays se dégèlent** there is a thaw in relations between the two countries

dégénératif, -ive [deʒeneratif, -iv] **ADJ** degenerative

dégénéré, -e [deʒenere] **ADJ** degenerate

NM,F degenerate

dégénérer [18] [deʒenere] **VI 1** *(perdre ses qualités → race, plante)* to degenerate; **ses gags ont beaucoup dégénéré** his jokes have really gone downhill

2 *(s'aggraver → situation)* to worsen, to deteriorate; *(→ discussion)* to get out of hand; **à chaque fois qu'on se voit, ça finit toujours par d.** every time we see each other it ends up getting out of hand

3 *Méd (tumeur)* to become malignant; *(infection)* to become severe

4 *(se changer)* **d. en** to degenerate into; **sa bronchite a dégénéré en pneumonie** his/her bronchitis developed into pneumonia

dégénérescence [deʒeneresɑ̃s] **NF 1** *Biol* degeneration; *Méd* **d. graisseuse** fatty degeneration **2** *Littéraire (déclin)* degeneration, becoming degenerate; **d. morale** degeneration of moral standards

dégermer [3] [deʒɛrme] **VT** to remove the germ from, to degerm

dégingandé, -e [deʒɛ̃gɑ̃de] **ADJ** gangling, lanky

dégivrage [deʒivraʒ] **NM 1** *(processus → d'un réfrigérateur)* defrosting; *(→ d'une surface, d'un avion)* de-icing; **le d. des vitres d'une voiture** de-icing the windows of a car **2** *(dispositif → d'un réfrigérateur)* defroster; *(→ d'une voiture)* de-icer; **d. arrière** rear windscreen de-icer

dégivrer [3] [deʒivre] **VT** *(réfrigérateur)* to defrost; *(surface)* to de-ice; **d. les vitres d'une voiture** to de-ice the windows of a car

dégivreur [deʒivrœr] **NM** *(d'un réfrigérateur)* defroster; *Aviat & Aut* de-icer

déglaçage [deglasaʒ] **NM 1** *Culin* deglazing **2**

(d'un bassin) melting of the ice, thawing **3** *(du papier)* removal of gloss

déglacement [deglasmɑ̃] NM melting of the ice, thawing

déglacer [16] [deglase] VT **1** *Culin (poêle)* to deglaze; **déglacez au vin blanc** deglaze the pan with white wine **2** *(papier)* to remove the gloss from **3** *(étang)* to remove the ice from, to melt the ice on

déglaciation [deglasjasjɔ̃] NF retreating of glaciers, deglaciation

déglingue [deglɛ̃g] NF *Fam* **1** *Vieilli (physique, morale)* decline■ **2** *(d'un milieu)* decline■, deterioration■

déglinguer [3] [deglɛ̃ge] *Fam* VT **1** *(mécanisme)* to break■, to bust; **un vélo tout déglingué** a bike which is coming apart *or* falling to pieces

2 *(santé)* to wreck; **la fugue de son fils l'a déglingué** his son running away from home just broke him

▶**se déglinguer** VPR **1** *(ne plus fonctionner)* to be bust; *(mal fonctionner)* to go on the blink; *(se détacher)* to come *or* to work loose

2 *(santé)* to get worse; *(poumons, reins)* to go to pieces; *Hum* **je me déglingue** I'm falling to pieces

dégluer [7] [deglye] VT to unglue, to deglutinate

déglutination [deglytinasjɔ̃] NF *Ling* aphesis

déglutir [32] [deglytir] VI to swallow, to gulp

déglutition [deglytisjɔ̃] NF **1** *(de salive)* swallowing, *Spéc* deglutition **2** *(d'aliments)* swallowing, *Spéc* deglutition

dégobiller [3] [degobije] *Fam* VT to throw up, to puke up

VI to throw up, to puke

dégoiser [3] [degwaze] *Fam Péj* VT to spout, to come out with; **qu'est-ce que tu dégoises?** what are you going *or* banging on about?

VI to bang on, to go on and on; **d. sur qn** *Br* to bitch about sb, to slag sb off, *Am* to bad-mouth sb

dégommage [degomaʒ] NM **1** *(d'un timbre)* removing the gum (**de** from) **2** *Fam (renvoi)* firing, *Br* sacking; *(destitution)* unseating

dégommer [3] [degome] VT **1** *(timbre)* to remove the gum off *or* from **2** *Fam (tuer)* to blow away, to gun down■ **3** *Fam (tirer sur)* to shoot at■ **4** *Fam (évincer)* to kick out, to boot out

dégonflage [degɔ̃flaʒ] NM **1** *(d'un ballon, d'une bouée, d'un pneu)* letting air out of; **ajuster la pression par d.** to adjust the pressure by letting air out **2** *Fam (lâcheté)* chickening *or Br* bottling out; **dès qu'il a vu le patron, ç'a été le d. total** as soon as he saw the boss he totally chickened out

dégonflard, -e [degɔ̃flar, -ard] NM,F *Fam* chicken *(person)*

dégonflé, -e [degɔ̃fle] ADJ **1** *(ballon)* deflated; *(pneu)* flat **2** *Fam (lâche)* chicken

NM,F *Fam* chicken *(person)*

dégonflement [degɔ̃fləmɑ̃] NM **1** *(d'un pneu, d'une bouée, d'un ballon)* deflation; **pour compenser le d. du pneu** in order to compensate for the amount of air that's been let out of the tyre **2** *Méd* **d. d'un doigt/pied** reduction of the swelling in a finger/foot **3** *(des dépenses)* cutback (**de** in)

dégonfler [3] [degɔ̃fle] VT **1** *(ballon, bouée, pneu)* to deflate, to let air out of

2 *Méd (jambes, doigt)* to bring down *or* to reduce the swelling in

3 *(prix)* to bring down

4 *(démystifier → prétention, mythe)* to deflate, to debunk

VI *(jambes, doigt)* to become less swollen; **ma cheville dégonfle** the swelling in my ankle's going down

▶**se dégonfler** VPR **1** *(ballon)* to go down, to deflate; *(pneu)* to go flat

2 *Méd (jambes, doigt)* to become less swollen; **ma cheville se dégonfle** the swelling in my ankle's going down

3 *Fam (perdre courage)* to chicken out, *Br* to bottle out, to lose one's bottle

dégorgement [degɔrʒəmɑ̃] NM **1** *(fait de déverser)* disgorging **2** *(fait de déboucher → conduit, évier)* unblocking **3** *(décharge → d'égout)* discharging, overflow **4** *(en œnologie)* = removing of the sediment from a champagne bottle

dégorgeoir [degɔrʒwar] NM **1** *(d'un tuyau)* overflow pipe *or* duct **2** *(à huîtres)* disgorger **3** *(d'un forgeron)* fuller, creaser **4** *Pêche* disgorger

dégorger [17] [degɔrʒe] VT **1** *(déverser)* to disgorge; *Fig* **la rue a dégorgé un flot de gens** a crowd of people surged from the street

2 *(débloquer → conduit, évier)* to unblock

3 *Pêche* to disgorge

4 *Tex* to clean, to cleanse

5 *(en œnologie)* to remove the sediment from

6 *(vomir)* to vomit

VI **1** *(se déverser)* to empty

2 *Tex* to bleed

3 *Culin (ris de veau, cervelle)* to soak *(in cold water)*; *(concombre)* to drain *(having been sprinkled with salt)*; **faire d.** *(ris de veau, cervelle)* to (leave to) soak; *(concombre)* to drain of water *(by sprinkling with salt)*; *(escargot)* to clean *(by salting and starvation)*

▶**se dégorger** VPR *(se déverser)* to empty

dégoter, dégotter [3] [degɔte] VT *Fam (objet rare)* to unearth; *(idée originale)* to hit on; **où tu l'as dégoté, ce type?** where on earth did you find this guy?

dégoudronner [3] [degudrɔne] VT to remove the tar from

dégoulinade [degulinad] NF *(coulée)* trickle, drip

dégoulinant, -e [degulinɑ̃, -ɑ̃t] ADJ dripping; **les mains toutes dégoulinantes** with dripping wet hands; **être d.** *(après la pluie)* to be dripping wet

dégoulinement [degulinmɑ̃] NM *(en traînées)* trickling; *(goutte à goutte)* dripping

dégouliner [3] [deguline] VI *(peinture, sauce)* to drip; *(larmes, sang)* to trickle down; *(maquillage)* to run; **ça dégouline partout sur la moquette** it's dripping all over the carpet; **la pluie me dégoulinait dans le cou** the rain was trickling down my neck; **je dégouline** I'm dripping, I'm soaking wet

dégoupiller [3] [degupije] VT *(grenade)* to take the pin out of

dégourdi, -e [degurdi] *Fam* ADJ **être d.** to be smart *or* on the ball; **il n'est pas très d.** he's a bit slow on the uptake

NM,F **c'est un petit d.!** there are no flies on him!

dégourdir [32] [degurdir] VT **1** *(ranimer → membres)* to bring the circulation back to

2 *(réchauffer → liquide)* to warm up

3 *Fam (rendre moins timide)* **d. qn** to teach sb a thing or two, to wise sb up

▶**se dégourdir** VPR **1** *(remuer)* **se d. les jambes** to stretch one's legs; **se d. les doigts avant de jouer du piano** to warm up before playing the piano

2 *(en marchant)* to stretch one's legs

3 *Fam (devenir moins timide)* to learn a thing or two, to wise up

dégourdissement [degurdismɑ̃] NM *(d'un membre → ankylosé)* bringing the circulation back (**de** to); *(→ gelé)* warming up (**de** of)

dégoût [degu] NM **1** *(aversion)* disgust, distaste; **éprouver** *ou* **avoir du d. pour qn/qch** to have an aversion to sb/sth; **prendre qch en d.** to take a dislike to sth **2** *(lassitude)* weariness; **par d. de la vie** through world-weariness

dégoûtamment [degutamɑ̃] ADV disgustingly

dégoûtant, -e [degutɑ̃, -ɑ̃t] ADJ *(sale)* disgusting, disgustingly dirty; *(salace → film, remarque)* disgusting, dirty; *(condamnable)* disgusting; **c'est d.!** *(injuste)* it's disgusting *or* awful!

NM,F **1** *(personne sale)* **petit d.!** you little pig!

2 *(vicieux)* **vieux d.!** you dirty old man!

3 *Fam (personne injuste)* **quelle dégoûtante!** that wretched woman!; **quel d.!** the swine!

dégoûtation [degutasjɔ̃] NF *Fam* **1** *(dégoût)* disgust■ **2 quelle d.!** *(chose)* how disgusting!■; *(situation)* what a disgusting state of affairs!■

dégoûté, -e [degute] ADJ **1** *(écœuré)* repulsed, disgusted; **prendre des airs dégoûtés** to put on a look of disgust, to wrinkle one's nose; **elle m'a regardé d'un air d.** she gave me a look of utter disgust; *Hum* **il n'est pas d.!** he's not very fussy!

2 *(indigné)* outraged, revolted, disgusted

3 *Fam (découragé)* bummed (out), *Br* gutted

4 *(las)* **d. de** weary of; **d. de la vie** weary of life

NM,F **faire le d.** to be fussy, to make a fuss; **ne fais pas trop la dégoûtée, tu n'as pas d'autres propositions** you've had no other offers, so don't turn your nose up at it

dégoûter [3] [degute] VT **1** *(écœurer)* to disgust, to repel, to be repugnant to; **son contact le dégoûta** his/her touch repulsed him, he found his/her touch repulsive

2 *(indigner)* to disgust, to outrage, to be (morally) repugnant to; **les égoïstes comme toi me dégoûtent** selfish people like you disgust me; **tu me dégoûtes avec ton cynisme!** you're so cynical you make me sick!

3 *(lasser)* to put off; **il gagne toujours, c'est à vous d.!** he always wins, it's enough to make you sick!; **la vie le dégoûtait** he was weary of life *or* sick of living; **d. qn de qch** to put sb off sth; **cela m'a dégoûté de la viande** that put me off meat; **c'est à vous d. d'être serviable** it's enough to put you (right) off being helpful

▶**se dégoûter** VPR **1** *(emploi réfléchi)* **je me dégoûte!** I disgust myself!

2 se d. de qn/qch to get sick of sb/sth; **tu vas te d. des gâteaux** you're going to put yourself right off cakes

dégouttant, -e [degutɑ̃, -ɑ̃t] ADJ dripping; **toute dégouttante de pluie** dripping wet; **les mains dégouttantes de sang** hands dripping with blood

dégoutter [3] [degute] VI to drip; **son front dégoutte de sueur** his/her forehead is dripping with sweat, sweat is dripping off his/her forehead; **la pluie dégoutte de son chapeau** the rain is dripping from his/her hat

dégradabilité [degradabilite] NF *Écol* degradability

dégradable [degradabl] ADJ *Écol* degradable

dégradant, -e [degradɑ̃, -ɑ̃t] ADJ degrading

dégradation [degradasjɔ̃] NF **1** *(destruction naturelle → d'un objet, d'un bâtiment)* wear and tear, deterioration; **les meubles en osier subissent la d. du temps** wicker furniture suffers wear and tear with time

2 *(destruction volontaire → d'un monument)* defacement; *(→ de matériel scolaire, de l'environnement)* damage (**de** to)

3 *(détérioration → de rapports, d'une situation)* deterioration, worsening; *(→ de l'environnement)* degradation

4 *(avilissement)* degradation; **d. morale** moral degradation

5 *Chim* degradation

6 *Phys* **d. de l'énergie** dissipation of energy

7 *Ordinat* **d. de données** corruption of data

8 *(d'une couleur)* toning down, gradation; *(de la lumière)* gradation

9 *(d'un officier)* ≃ dishonourable discharge; **d. civique** loss of civil rights

dégradé [degrade] NM **1** *(technique)* shading off; *(résultat)* gradation; **un d. de verts** greens shading off into each other; *Ordinat* **d. de couleur** colour scale **2** *(d'une coiffure)* layered style; **se faire faire un d.** to have one's hair layered

❑ **en dégradé** ADV **tons en d.** colours shading off (into one another); **coupe en d.** layered cut

dégrader [3] [degrade] VT **1** *(abîmer → gén)* to damage; *(→ monument)* to deface; **quartier dégradé** run-down district

2 *(envenimer → rapports humains)* to damage, to cause to deteriorate

3 *(avilir)* to degrade

4 *(couleurs)* to shade (into one another); *(lumières)* to reduce gradually

5 *(cheveux)* to layer

6 *Mil* **d. un officier** to strip an officer of his rank

7 *Ordinat (données)* to corrupt

▶**se dégrader** VPR **1** *(se détériorer → meuble, bâtiment, rapports)* to deteriorate; *(→ santé)* to decline; *(→ langage)* to deteriorate, to become debased; *(→ temps)* to get worse

2 *(s'avilir)* to degrade oneself

3 *Phys (énergie)* to dissipate

dégrafer [3] [degrafe] VT *(papiers)* to unstaple; *(col, robe)* to undo, to unfasten; *(ceinture)* to undo; *(bracelet)* to unclasp, to unhook; *Fam* **tu veux que je te dégrafe?** shall I undo your dress for you?

▶**se dégrafer** VPR **1** *(emploi passif)* *(robe)* to undo

2 *(emploi réfléchi)* *(ôter sa robe)* to undo *or* to unfasten one's dress; *(ôter son corset)* to undo *or* to unfasten one's corset

3 *(jupe)* to come undone; *(papiers)* to come unstapled; *(collier)* to come unhooked

dégraffitage [degrafitaʒ] **NM** graffiti removal

dégraissage [degrɛsaʒ] **NM 1** *(nettoyage)* removal of grease marks **2** *Fam (diminution du personnel)* downsizing■ **3** *Fam (élimination du surplus)* trimming■; **faire du d. sur un manuscrit** to trim a manuscript down **4** *Culin (d'un bouillon)* skimming off the fat; *(d'une viande)* trimming off the fat

dégraissant, -e [degrɛsɑ̃, -ɑ̃t] **ADJ** *(détachant)* grease-removing

NM *(détachant)* grease remover

dégraisser [4] [degrese] **VT 1** *(ôter les taches de)* to remove grease marks from **2** *Fam (entreprise)* to downsize■, to streamline■; *(personnel)* to cut back■, to shed■ **3** *Fam (dissertation, manuscrit)* to cut down■, to trim down■ **4** *Culin (sauce)* to skim the fat off; *(viande)* to cut *or* to trim the fat off

USAGE ABSOLU *Fam* **il va falloir d.** we'll have to downsize■

dégraisseur, -euse [degrɛsœr, -øz] **NM,F** *Tex (de vêtements)* dry-cleaner; *(de laine)* scourer

NM 1 *Ind* grease remover **2** *Tech* **d. de vapeur** oil separator

❑ **dégraisseuse NF 1** *Tex* scouring machine **2** *(pour le cuir)* grease extractor

dégras [degrɑ] **NM** degras, dubbin, dubbing

dégravoiement [degravwamɑ̃] **NM 1** *Constr* = undermining by action of running water **2** *(nettoyage)* washing away of gravel

dégravoyer [13] [degravwaje] **VT 1** *Constr* = to undermine *or* to lay bare by running water **2** *(nettoyer)* to wash away the gravel from

degré [dəgre] **NM 1** *(échelon → d'une hiérarchie)* degree, grade; *(→ d'un développement)* stage; **d'accord, il faut sévir, mais il y a des degrés** of course, you should be strict but there are degrees of strictness; **à un d. avancé de** at an advanced stage of; **cancéreux au dernier d.** in the last stages of cancer; *Scol* **le premier/second d.** primary/secondary education; **prendre une plaisanterie au premier d.** to take a joke seriously; **tu prends tout au premier d.** you take everything literally; **une remarque à prendre au second d.** a remark not to be taken literally; **c'est de l'humour au second d.** it's tongue-in-cheek humour

2 *(point)* degree; **un tel d. de dévouement** such a degree of devotion; **compréhensif jusqu'à un certain d.** understanding up to a point *or* to a degree; **intelligent au plus haut d.** of the highest intelligence; **courageux au plus haut d.** most courageous

3 *(unité)* degree; **du gin à 47,5 degrés** 83° proof gin, 47.5 degree gin *(on the Gay-Lussac scale)*; **d. alcoolique** *ou* **d'alcool** alcohol content; **d. Baumé/Celsius/Fahrenheit** degree Baumé/Celsius/Fahrenheit

4 *Astron, Géom & Math* degree; **un angle de 45 degrés** a 45-degree angle; **équation du premier/second d.** equation of the first/second degree; **d. zéro** degree zero; **son bouquin, c'est le d. zéro de la littérature** his book hardly deserves to be classed as literature

5 *Gram* degree

6 *Mus* degree; **d. conjoint** conjoint *or* conjunct degree; **d. disjoint** disjunct degree

7 *(de parenté)* degree; **cousin au premier d.** first cousin; **d. de parenté** degree of kinship

8 *Fin* **d. de liquidité** degree of liquidity, liquidity ratio; **d. de solvabilité** credit rating

9 *Jur* **d. de juridiction** degree of jurisdiction

10 *(surtout au pl) (d'un escalier)* step; *(d'une échelle)* rung; *Fig* **les degrés de l'échelle sociale** the rungs of the social ladder

❑ **par degrés ADV** by *or* in degrees, gradually

> *Allusion*
>
> **Le degré zéro de...**
>
> This expression comes from the title of an essay by Roland Barthes, *Le degré zéro de l'écriture* (1953), and is used today to describe a total lack of whatever it might be. For example, one might speak of **Le degré zéro des droits des femmes dans certains pays** ("Women's rights being absolutely zero in some countries") or of **Le degré zéro de l'intelligence** ("Unadulterated silliness") when talking about a particularly inane TV game show.

dégréer [15] [degree] **VT** *Naut* to unrig

dégressif, -ive [degresif, -iv] **ADJ** *(impôt, amortissement)* graded, graduated; *(tarif, taux)* tapering

NM discount; **d. sur le volume** bulk discount

dégressivité [degresivite] **NF** degression

dégrèvement [degrɛvmɑ̃] **NM** *Fin* **d. fiscal** *(d'une entreprise)* tax relief; *(d'un produit)* reduction of tax *or* duty

dégrever [19] [degrəve] **VT** *Fin & Jur (produit)* to reduce tax on; *(contribuable)* to grant tax relief to; *(industrie)* to derate; *(édifice)* to reduce the assessment on

dégreyer [11] [degreje] **se dégreyer VPR** *Can* to take one's outdoor clothes off

dégriffé, -e [degrife] **ADJ** reduced *(and with the designer label removed)*

NM reduced (and unlabelled) designer item

dégrillage [degrijaʒ] **NM** *Tech* screening

dégringolade [degrɛ̃gɔlad] **NF** *Fam* **1** *(chute)* tumbling (down)■ **2** *(baisse → des prix)* slump■ (**de** in); *(→ des cours)* collapse■; *(→ d'une réputation)* plunge■; **l'industrie est en pleine d.** the industry is in the middle of a slump; **il était si admiré, quelle d.!** he was so admired, what a comedown!

dégringoler [3] [degrɛ̃gɔle] *Fam* **VI 1** *(chuter)* to tumble down■; *(bruyamment)* to crash down■; **j'ai tout fait d.** I brought the whole lot down

2 *(baisser → prix)* to slump■, to tumble■; *(→ réputation)* to plunge■; **ça a fait d. les prix** it sent prices plummeting■

3 *(pleuvoir)* **ça dégringole!** it's tipping it down!

VT d. l'escalier *(courir)* to run *or* to race down the stairs■; *(tomber)* to tumble down the stairs■

dégrippant [degripɑ̃] **NM** penetrating grease

dégripper [3] [degripe] **VT** to release *(parts which are stuck)*

dégrisement [degrizmɑ̃] **NM** *(désillusion)* sobering up, coming back down to earth; *(après l'ivresse)* sobering up

dégriser [3] [degrize] **VT** *(désillusionner)* to bring back down to earth, to sober up; *(après l'ivresse)* to sober up; **le lendemain, dégrisé, il réfléchit** the next day, having sobered up, he started to think

▸**se dégriser VPR** to sober up

dégrosser [3] [degrose] **VT** *Métal* to draw down

dégrossir [32] [degrosir] **VT 1** *(apprenti, débutant)* to polish, to smooth the rough edges of; **des jeunes gens mal dégrossis** uncouth young men; **son séjour la dégrossira un peu** her stay will smooth off some of her rough edges **2** *(théorie, question)* to do the groundwork on; *(texte du programme)* to have a first look at **3** *(bloc de pierre)* to rough-hew; *(bloc de bois)* to trim

dégrossissage [degrosisaʒ], **dégrossissement** [degrosismɑ̃] **NM 1** *(d'une personne)* polishing, smoothing the rough edges **2** *(d'une théorie, d'une question)* sorting out (**de** of), doing the spadework (**de** on); **faire le d. d'un projet** to do a first rough sketch for a project **3** *(d'un bloc de pierre)* rough-hewing; *(d'un bloc de bois)* trimming

dégrossisseur [degrosisœr] **NM** *Métal* roughing roll

dégrouiller [3] [degruje] **se dégrouiller VPR** *Fam* to get a move on, to hurry up■; **dégrouillez-vous!** hurry up!, get a move on!

dégroupage [degrupaʒ] **NM** *Tél* unbundling

dégroupement [degrupmɑ̃] **NM** *(d'une classe)* dividing *or* splitting (up); *(d'objets)* splitting (up); **il va falloir procéder à un d. de la classe** the class will have to be divided up *or* split into groups

dégrouper [3] [degrupe] **VT** *(classe)* to divide (up), to split (up); *(objets)* to split (up)

déguenillé, -e [degənije] **ADJ** ragged, tattered; **tout d.** in rags, in tatters

NM,F ragamuffin

déguerpir [32] [degɛrpir] **VI** to run away, to decamp; **faire d. un intrus** to drive away an intruder

dégueu [degø] **ADJ INV** *très Fam (sale)* disgusting■, gross; *(mauvais)* lousy, crappy, *Br* poxy; **c'est pas d.!** it's pretty good!; **trois millions, pas d.!** three million, not bad!

dégueulasse [degœlas] *très Fam* **ADJ 1** *(sale)* disgusting■, filthy■, yucky **2** *(injuste)* disgusting■, lousy **3** *(vicieux)* disgusting■, filthy **4** *(sans valeur)* lousy, crappy, *Br* poxy; **c'est pas d. comme cadeau** it's a pretty nice present, it's not a bad present

NMF 1 *(personne sale)* filthy pig **2** *(pervers)* **un gros d.** a filthy lech **3** *(personne immorale)* *Br* swine, *Am* stinker

dégueulasser [3] [degœlase] **VT** *très Fam* to mess up

dégueulasserie [degœlasri] **NF** *très Fam* **1** *(crasse)* filth■; *(chose sale)* filthy thing■ **2** *(injustice)* **c'est de la d.** it's rotten *or* disgusting!■; **ils l'ont exécuté, une d. de plus!** they've executed him, yet another atrocity!■

dégueuler [5] [degœle] *très Fam* **VI** to throw up, to puke

VT to throw up, to puke up

dégueulis [degœli] **NM** *très Fam* puke

déguiller [3] [degije] *Suisse* **VT** *(objet dressé)* to knock over; *(pommes, noix, cerises)* to get down; *(arbre)* to cut down

VI to tumble down

déguisé, -e [degize] **ADJ 1** *(pour une fête)* in fancy dress; *(pour duper)* in disguise, disguised **2** *Péj (mal habillé)* ridiculously dressed **3** *(changé → voix)* disguised **4** *(caché → intention)* disguised, masked, veiled; *(impôt, chômage)* hidden; *(→ agressivité)* veiled; **avec une joie non déguisée** with unconcealed delight

déguisement [degizmɑ̃] **NM** *(pour une fête)* fancy dress, costume; *(pour duper)* disguise

❑ **sans déguisement ADV** *Littéraire* plainly, openly

déguiser [3] [degize] **VT 1** *(pour une fête)* to dress up; *(pour duper)* to disguise; **déguisé en pirate** dressed (up) as a pirate, wearing a pirate costume

2 *(mal habiller)* to dress ridiculously; **ne lui mets pas tous ces rubans, tu la déguises** don't put all those ribbons on her, you'll make her look ridiculous

3 *(changer → voix)* to disguise

4 *(cacher → intention, vérité)* to disguise, to mask, to veil; *(→ honte)* to conceal; **parler sans d. sa pensée** to speak plainly *or* openly

▸**se déguiser VPR** *(pour une fête)* to dress up; *(pour duper)* to put on a disguise, to disguise oneself; **se d. en pompier** to dress up as a fireman; *Fam* **se d. en courant d'air** to vanish into thin air, to do a disappearing act

dégurgiter [3] [degyrʒite] **VT 1** *(aliment)* to bring (back) up **2** *(leçon)* to regurgitate, to repeat parrot fashion

dégustateur, -trice [degystatœr, -tris] **NM,F** taster

dégustation [degystasjɔ̃] **NF 1** *(par un convive)* tasting *(UNCOUNT)*; *(par un dégustateur)* tasting, sampling **2** *(dans une cave)* (free) tasting; **d. (de vins)** wine-tasting **3** *(à un étalage, dans un restaurant)* tasting; **d. de fruits de mer à toute heure** seafood served all day

dégustatrice [degystatris] *voir* **dégustateur**

déguster [3] [degyste] **VT 1** *(goûter → sujet: convive)* to taste; *(→ sujet: dégustateur professionnel)* to taste, to sample; **venez d. nos spécialités** come and taste *or* try our specialities

2 *(savourer → aliment, boisson, spectacle, musique)* to savour, to enjoy

VI *Fam (recevoir des coups)* to *Br* get *or Am* take a pasting; *(se faire réprimander)* to get a roasting; *(être éprouvé)* to have a rough time of it; **ils dégustent, les parents d'adolescents!** parents of teenagers go through hell!; **attends qu'il rentre, tu vas d.!** just wait till he gets home, you're really going to catch it!

déhaler [3] [deale] *Naut* **VT** to haul out

▸**se déhaler VPR** to haul itself out

déhanché, -e [deɑ̃ʃe] **ADJ 1** *(balancé)* swaying **2** *(boiteux)* lop-sided

déhanchement [deɑ̃ʃmɑ̃] **NM 1** *(démarche → séduisante)* swaying walk; *(→ claudicante)* lop-sided walk **2** *(posture)* = standing with one's weight on one leg

déhancher [3] [deɑ̃ʃe] **se déhancher VPR 1** *(en marchant)* to sway (one's hips) **2** *(sans bouger)* to stand with one's weight on one leg

déharnacher [3] [dearnaʃe] **VT** to unharness

déhiscence [deisɑ̃s] **NF** *Bot* dehiscence

déhiscent, -e [deisɑ̃, -ɑ̃t] **ADJ** *Bot* dehiscent

DEHORS [dəɔr] **NM 1** *(surface extérieure d'une boîte, d'un bâtiment)* outside

2 *(plein air)* outside; **odeur venue du d.** smell coming from outside; **les bruits du d.** the noises from outside

3 *(étranger)* **menace venue du d.** threat from abroad

4 *Sport (en patinage)* outside edge; **faire un d.** to go on one's outside edge

NMPL *(apparences)* appearances; **sous des d. égoïstes** beneath a selfish exterior

ADV *(à l'extérieur)* outside; *(en plein air)* outside, outdoors, out of doors; *(hors de chez soi)* out; **manger d.** to eat outside; **dormir d.** to sleep outdoors or in the open; **il est bronzé parce qu'il passe son temps d.** he's brown because he spends all his time outside or outdoors or out of doors; **on ne voit rien de d.** you can't see anything from the outside; **passe par d. pour aller dans la cuisine** go round the outside to get to the kitchen; **elle est toujours d.** she's always out (and about); **j'étais d. toute la matinée** I was out all morning; **mettre qch d.** to put sth out; *Fam* **mettre qn d.** to kick sb out; *(renvoyer)* to sack sb; *très Fam* **si tu recommences je te fous d.** do it again and you're out (on your ear)

❑ **en dehors ADV 1** *(à l'extérieur)* outside

2 *(vers l'extérieur)* **avoir** ou **marcher les pieds en d.** to walk with one's feet turned out

❑ **en dehors de PRÉP 1** *(à l'extérieur de)* outside

2 *(excepté)* apart from; **en d. de toi** apart from you; **en d. de ce que j'ai vu** apart from what I have seen

3 *(à l'écart de)* **une petite auberge en d. des grands axes** a small inn off the beaten track; **il se tient toujours en d. des discussions** he always keeps out of discussions; **reste en d. de leur dispute** don't get involved in or stay out of their quarrel

4 *(au-delà de)* outside (of), beyond; **c'est en d. de ses capacités** it's beyond his capabilities

déhouiller [3] [deuje] **VT** to extract coal from

déhoussable [deusabl] **ADJ** with loose or removable covers, with a loose or removable cover

déicide [deisid] **ADJ** deicidal

NMF *(meurtrier)* deicide

NM *(meurtre)* deicide

déictique [deiktik] **ADJ** deictic

NM deictic

déification [deifikasjɔ̃] **NF** deification

déifier [9] [deifje] **VT** to, to turn into a god

déionisation [deionizasjɔ̃] **NF** *Chim* deionization

déioniser [3] [deionize] **VT** *Chim* to deionize

déisme [deism] **NM** deism

déiste [deist] **ADJ** deistic, deistical

NMF deist

déité [deite] **NF** deity, god

déj [deʒ] **NM** *Fam* **petit d.** breakfast▪, *Br* brekkie, brekky

DÉJÀ [deʒa]

already **1, 2** ▪ yet **1** ▪ ever **2** ▪ as it is **3** ▪ again **4**

ADV 1 *(dès maintenant, dès lors)* already; **d. là!** here already!; **j'ai fini - d.!** I've finished – already!; **cela fait trois ans d.** it's been three years already; **est−ce qu'il est d. parti?** has he left yet?; *(exprimant la surprise)* has he left already?; **il doit être d. loin** he must be far away by now; **il savait d. lire à l'âge de quatre ans** he already knew how to read at the age of four; **enfant, il aimait d. les fleurs** even as a child he liked flowers; **d. en 1900** as early as 1900; **quand nous rentrerons, il fera d. nuit** when we get back it will already be dark; **on serait d. riches!** we would be rich by now!

2 *(précédemment)* already; **je vous l'ai d. dit** I've told you already; **tu lui en as d. parlé?** have you already spoken to him/her about it?; **vous êtes d. allé au Canada?** have you ever been to Canada?; **tu l'as d. vu sur scène?** have you ever seen him on stage?; **il l'a d. vue quelque part** he's seen her somewhere before

3 *(emploi expressif)* **j'aurais dû le faire il y a d. trois jours** I should have done it three days ago as it is; **il est d'accord sur le principe, c'est d.**

beaucoup he's agreed on the principle, that's something; **d. qu'il est en mauvaise santé** he's in poor health as it is; **elle est d. assez riche** she's rich enough as it is; **ce n'est d. pas si mal** you could do worse; **c'est d. quelque chose** it's better than nothing; **donne dix euros, ce sera d. ça** give ten euros, that'll be a start; **on a perdu une valise, mais ni l'argent ni les passeports, c'est d. ça!** we lost a case, but not our money or passports, which is something at least!; **il faut d. qu'il ait son examen** he needs to pass his exam first, before he does anything else he has to pass his exam; **mange d. ta soupe** eat your soup first or for a start

4 *Fam (pour réitérer une question)* again ▪; **tu as payé combien, d.?** how much did you pay again?; **elle s'appelle comment, d.?** what did you say her name was?, what's she called again?; **le sucre est où, d.?** where's the sugar again?

5 *Suisse (fort probablement)* most likely; **il veut d. pleuvoir** it's bound to rain

6 *Suisse (bien)* definitely; **je le ferai d.** I'll definitely do it

déjanté, -e [deʒɑ̃te] *Fam* **ADJ** wacko, *Br* mental, *Am* gonzo; **complètement d., le mec** that guy's off his trolley

NM,F headcase, *Br* headbanger

déjanter [3] [deʒɑ̃te] **VT** *(pneu)* to remove from its rim, to take the rim off

VI *Fam* to flip one's lid, to lose it, *Br* to lose the plot

déjauger [17] [deʒɔʒe] **VI** *(navire, hydravion)* to hydroplane

déjà-vu [deʒavy] **NM INV 1** *(banalité)* commonplace; **c'est du d. comme idée** that idea's a bit banal **2** *(sensation)* **(sensation** ou **impression de) d.** (feeling of) déjà vu

déjection [deʒɛksjɔ̃] **NF 1** *Physiol (action)* evacuation **2** *Géol (d'un volcan)* **déjections** ejecta

❑ **déjections NFPL** *Physiol* faeces, *Spéc* dejecta

déjeté, -e [deʒte] **ADJ 1** *Fam (diminué physiquement)* worn, worn-down; *Hum* **elle n'est pas déjetée!** she's pretty well preserved! **2** *(dévié →* mur, corps) lop-sided, crooked; *(→* colonne vertébrale*)* twisted **3** *Belg Fam (en désordre)* messy; *(déformé)* deformed ▪

déjeter [27] [deʒte] **VT** to cause to become lop-sided

déjeuner¹ [5] [deʒœne] **VI 1** *(le midi)* to (have) lunch; **invite-le à d.** invite him for or to lunch; **nous avons les Dupont à d. dimanche** the Duponts are coming for lunch on Sunday; **j'ai déjeuné d'une salade** I had a salad for lunch; **j'ai fait d. les enfants plus tôt** I gave the children an early lunch

2 *Belg, Can & Suisse & (régional en France) (le matin)* to have breakfast

déjeuner² [deʒœne] **NM 1** *(repas de la mi-journée)* lunch, *Sout* luncheon; **prendre son d.** to have lunch; **un d. d'affaires** a business lunch; **d. sur l'herbe** picnic (lunch); **qu'est-ce qu'il y a pour le d.?** what's for lunch?

2 *Belg, Can & Suisse & (régional en France) (repas du matin)* breakfast

3 *(tasse et soucoupe)* (large) breakfast cup and saucer

4 *(locution)* **d. de soleil** *(sentiment)* short-lived feeling, flash in the pan

'Le Déjeuner sur l'herbe' *Manet* 'Picnic on the Lawn'

déjouer [6] [deʒwe] **VT** *(vigilance)* to evade, to elude; *(complot, machination)* to thwart, to foil; *(plan)* to thwart, to frustrate; *(feinte)* to outsmart

déjucher [3] [deʒyʃe] **VI** *(volaille)* to come off the roost; *(personne)* to get out of bed; **faire d. qn** to make sb come down from his/her perch

VT *(volaille)* to unroost; **d. qn** to make sb come down from his/her perch

déjuger [17] [deʒyʒe] **se déjuger VPR** *(changer d'avis)* to go back on or to reverse one's decision

de jure [deʒyre] **ADV** de jure

DEL [deɛl] **NF** *Électron (abrév* diode électroluminescente*)* LED

delà [dəla] *voir* **deçà, au-delà, par-delà**

délabré, -e [delabre] **ADJ 1** *(en ruine →* maison, mur*)* dilapidated, crumbling **2** *(qui n'est plus florissant →* santé, réputation*)* ruined

délabrement [delabrəmɑ̃] **NM 1** *(d'un bâtiment)* disrepair, ruin, dilapidation **2** *(d'un esprit, d'un corps)* deterioration; **les patients étaient dans un état de d. total** the patients were in a state of total neglect **3** *(d'une réputation)* ruin; *(d'une fortune)* depletion

délabrer [3] [delabre] **VT 1** *(bâtiment, meuble)* to ruin **2** *(santé)* to ruin; *(organe)* to damage **3** *(réputation)* to ruin

▶ **se délabrer VPR 1** *(bâtiment)* to go to ruins; *(meuble)* to become rickety, to fall apart **2** *(entreprise)* to collapse; *(santé)* to deteriorate

délacer [16] [delase] **VT** *(soulier, botte)* to undo (the laces of); *(corset)* to unlace

▶ **se délacer VPR** *(emploi réfléchi) (ôter ses souliers)* to undo or to unlace one's shoes; *(ôter ses bottes)* to undo or to unlace one's boots; *(ôter son corset)* to unlace one's corset; *(ôter sa robe)* to unlace one's dress **2** *(soulier)* to become undone; *(corset)* to become unlaced

delacroix [dəlakrwa] **NM** *Anciennement Fam* one-hundred franc note ▪

délai [delɛ] **NM 1** *(répit)* extension (of time); **demande un d. pour trouver l'argent** ask for more time to find the money; **donner** ou **accorder un d. (supplémentaire) à qn** to grant sb an extension; **laissez-moi un d. de réflexion** give me time to think

2 *(temps fixé)* time limit; **dans le d. prescrit** ou **fixé** within the required or allotted time, on time; **quel est le d. à respecter?** what is the deadline?; **tu donnes des délais trop longs aux sous-traitants** you give the sub-contractors too much delivery time; **d. d'attente** waiting period; **d. de carence** waiting period; **d. de chargement** loading time; **d. de commercialisation** *(d'un produit)* launching period; **d. de crédit** credit period; **d. d'embarquement** loading time; **d. d'exécution** deadline; *(de livraison, de production)* lead time; **un d. franc de cinq jours** five clear days' grace; **d. de garantie** guarantee period, term of guarantee; **d. garanti de livraison** guaranteed delivery period; **d. de livraison** delivery time; **d. de paiement** *(fixé par contrat)* term of payment; **demander un d. de paiement** to request a postponement of payment; **d. de préavis** term of notice; **d. de production** production lead time; **d. de réachat** repurchase period; **d. de recouvrement** break-even period; **d. de récupération du capital investi** payback period; **d. de réflexion** cooling-off period; **d. de règlement** settlement period; **d. de remboursement** payback period; **d. de rigueur** strict deadline; **avant le 20 février, d. de rigueur** by 20 February at the very latest; **d. de validité** period of validity

3 *(période d'attente)* waiting period; **il faut un d. de trois jours avant que votre compte soit crédité** the cheque will be credited to your account after a period of three working days

4 *Jur* **d. de carence** = period during which benefit is not paid; **d. de congé** term of notice; **d. de grâce** period of grace; **un d. de grâce de dix jours** ten days' grace; **d. préfix** allotted time; **d. de préscription** prescription period; **d. de prévenance** advance notice; **d. probatoire** probation; **d. de procédure** procedural time limit; **d. raisonnable** reasonable time; **d. de souffrance** days of grace; **d. de viduité** = time a widow or divorced woman must wait before remarrying in order to avoid paternity conflicts

❑ **à bref délai ADV** shortly, soon

❑ **dans les délais ADV** within the required or allotted time, on time

❑ **dans les meilleurs délais, dans les plus brefs délais ADV** in the shortest possible time, as soon as possible; **j'y serai dans les plus brefs délais** I'll be there very shortly

❑ **dans un délai de PRÉP** within (a period of); **livrable dans un d. de 30 jours** allow 30 days for delivery

❑ **sans délai ADV** without delay, immediately, forthwith

délai-congé [delɛkɔ̃ʒe] *(pl* **délais-congés)** **NM** *Jur* term of notice

délaie *etc voir* **délayer**

délainage [delɛnaʒ] NM fellmongering, fellmongery

délainer [4] [delene] VT to remove wool from

délaissé, -e [delese] ADJ 1 *(époux)* deserted; *(ami)* forsaken, neglected; *(parc)* neglected 2 *Bourse (valeurs)* neglected

délaissement [delɛsmɑ̃] NM 1 *(abandon → par un époux)* desertion; *(→ par un ami)* neglecting 2 *(solitude)* loneliness 3 *(désengagement → d'une activité)* neglecting, dropping 4 *Jur (d'un bien)* relinquishment; *(d'un droit)* relinquishment, renunciation 5 *Assur* abandonment

délaisser [4] [delese] VT 1 *(quitter → époux)* to desert; *(→ ami)* to neglect 2 *(ne plus exercer → temporairement)* to neglect; *(→ définitivement)* to give up 3 *Jur (droit, succession)* to relinquish, to forego 4 *Assur (à l'assureur)* to abandon

délaitage [delɛtaʒ], **délaitement** [delɛtmɑ̃] NM *(du beurre)* working, drying

délaiter [3] [delɛte] VT *(beurre)* to work, to dry

délarder [3] [delarde] VT 1 *Culin (cochon)* to remove the fat from; *(viande)* to unlard 2 *(bois)* to thin down, to pare 3 *Constr* to chamfer, to bevel

délassant, -e [delasɑ̃, -ɑ̃t] ADJ *(bain, lotion)* relaxing, refreshing, soothing; *(film)* relaxing, entertaining; *(lecture)* light, entertaining

délassement [delasmɑ̃] NM 1 *(passe-temps)* way of relaxing 2 *(état)* relaxation, rest; **avoir besoin de d.** to need to relax

délasser [3] [delase] VT *(physiquement)* to relax, to refresh, to soothe; *(mentalement)* to relax, to soothe

►**se délasser** VPR to relax

délateur, -trice [delatœr, -tris] NM,F *Péj* informer

délation [delasjɔ̃] NF 1 denouncing, informing; **mais ce serait de la d.!** but that would be tantamount to denunciation! 2 *Jur* **d. de serment** decisive oath

délatrice [delatris] *voir* **délateur**

délavage [delavaʒ] NM 1 *(d'un tissu)* fading; *(d'une aquarelle)* toning down 2 *(de terres)* soaking, waterlogging

délavé, -e [delave] ADJ *(tissu)* faded; *(jean → volontairement)* faded, stone-washed; *(aquarelle)* toned down; *(terres)* waterlogged

délaver [3] [delave] VT 1 *(tissu)* to fade 2 *(terre)* to soak (with water)

Delaware [dəlawar] NM **le D.** Delaware; **dans le D.** in Delaware

délayage [delɛjaʒ] NM 1 *(mélange → de farine, de poudre)* mixing; *(→ de peinture)* thinning out 2 *Fig Péj (d'un discours)* padding out; *(d'une idee, d'un exposé)* watering down; **faire du d.** *Br* to waffle, *Am* to spout off; **elle fait du d. en attendant la liaison avec Moscou** she's filling in time while she waits for the Moscow link-up

délayer [11] [deleje] VT 1 *(mélanger→ farine, poudre)* to mix; *(→ peinture)* to thin 2 *Fig Péj (discours)* to pad *or* to spin out; *(idée, exposé)* to water down

Delco® [dɛlko] NM *Aut* distributor

déléatur [deleatyr] NM INV *Typ* delete (mark), dele

délébile [delebil] ADJ deletable

délectable [delɛktabl] ADJ *Littéraire* delectable, delightful

délectation [delɛktasjɔ̃] NF *Littéraire* delight, delectation

délecter [4] [delɛkte] **se délecter** VPR *Littéraire* **se d. à qch/à faire qch** to take great delight in sth/in doing sth; **je me délecte à la regarder** I find her delightful to watch

délégalisation [delegalizasjɔ̃] NF *Jur* criminalization

délégaliser [3] [delegalize] VT *Jur* to criminalize

délégant, -e [delegɑ̃, -ɑ̃t] NM,F *Jur* delegant

délégataire [delegatɛr] NMF delegatee

délégateur, -trice [delegatœr, -tris] NM,F delegator

délégation [delegasjɔ̃] NF 1 *(groupe envoyé)* delegation; **envoyé en d. (auprès de qn)** sent as a delegation (to sb); **les élèves sont allés trouver le directeur en d.** a delegation of pupils went to see the head teacher

2 *(commission)* commission

3 *(fait de mandater)* delegation; **agir par d. pour qn** to act on the authority of *or* as a proxy for sb; **d. de l'autorité parentale** delegation of parental authority; **d. judiciaire** = delegation of powers to the "commissaire de police" by the Public Prosecutor's Department; **d. de pouvoirs** delegation of powers; **d. de service public** = contracting out of a public service; **d. de signature** power of attorney; **d. de vote** proxy voting

4 *(dans des noms d'organismes)* delegation

5 *Jur (de dette)* assignment, transfer; **d. imparfaite** addition of debtor; **d. parfaite** substitution of debtor

6 *Rel* **d. apostolique** apostolic delegation

délégatrice [delegatris] *voir* **délégateur**

délégitimer [3] [deleʒitime] VT to make illegitimate

délégué, -e [delege] NM,F delegate, representative; **d. apostolique** apostolic delegate; **d. de classe** = pupil elected to represent his or her class at "conseils de classe", ≃ class rep; **d. commercial** sales representative; **d. des parents** parents' representative; **d. du personnel** staff representative; **d. syndical** union representative, shop steward

déléguer [18] [delege] VT 1 *(envoyer → groupe, personne)* to delegate; **j'ai délégué mon oncle pour voter à ma place** I have asked my uncle to cast my vote 2 *(transmettre → pouvoir)* to delegate 3 *Jur (créance)* to assign, to transfer

USAGE ABSOLU **il faut savoir d.** you must learn to delegate

délestage [delɛstaʒ] NM 1 *Aviat & Naut* unballasting 2 *Transp* relief; **itinéraire de d.** relief route; **opération de d.** scheme for relieving congestion 3 *Élec* selective power cut

délester [3] [delɛste] VT 1 *Fam Hum (voler)* **d. qn de qch** to relieve sb of sth 2 *(décharger)* **d. qn d'une valise/d'une obligation** to relieve sb of a suitcase/of an obligation 3 *Aviat & Naut* to unballast 4 *Transp* to relieve traffic congestion on 5 *Élec (secteur)* to cut off power from, to black out

►**se délester** VPR **se d. de** to get rid of

délétère [deletɛr] ADJ 1 *(gaz)* noxious, *Sout* deleterious 2 *(doctrine, pouvoir)* obnoxious, *Sout* deleterious

délétion [delesjɔ̃] NF *Biol* deletion

Delhi [deli] NM Delhi

délibérant, -e [deliberɑ̃, -ɑ̃t] ADJ *(assemblée)* deliberative

délibératif, -ive [deliberatif, -iv] ADJ *(fonction)* deliberative; **avoir voix délibérative** to be entitled to speak and vote

délibération [deliberasjɔ̃] NF 1 *(discussion)* deliberation; **le projet sera mis en d.** the project will be debated; **après d. du jury** after due deliberation by the jury 2 *(réflexion)* deliberation, thinking; **après (mûre) d.** after careful consideration

▫ **délibérations** NFPL *(décisions)* resolutions, decisions

délibérative [deliberativ] *voir* **délibératif**

délibératoire [deliberatwar] ADJ deliberative

délibéré, -e [delibere] ADJ 1 *(intentionné)* deliberate, wilful 2 *(décidé)* resolute, determined, thought-out

NM deliberation of the court; **mettre en d.** to adjourn for further deliberation

délibérément [deliberemɑ̃] ADV 1 *(intentionnellement)* deliberately, intentionally, wilfully 2 *(après réflexion)* after thinking it over (long and hard), after due consideration

délibérer [18] [delibere] VI 1 *(discuter)* to deliberate; **le jury ayant délibéré** after due deliberation by the jury; **d. de** to deliberate 2 *Littéraire (réfléchir)* to ponder, to deliberate

délicat, -e [delika, -at] ADJ 1 *(fragile → tissu)* delicate; *(→ peau)* sensitive; *(→ santé)* delicate, frail; *(→ intestin, estomac)* sensitive, delicate; *(→ enfant, plante)* fragile

2 *(sensible → palais)* discerning, delicate

3 *(subtil → dentelle, aquarelle, nuance, travail)* delicate, fine; *(→ doigts, traits)* delicate, dainty; *(→ mets, saveur)* refined; *(→ odeur)* delicate; **il posa le vase d'un geste d.** he put the vase down delicately *or* gently; **le d. doigté du pianiste** the pianist's delicate *or* light touch

4 *(difficile → situation)* delicate, awkward, tricky; *(→ opération chirurgicale, problème)* difficult, tricky; *(→ question)* delicate, sensitive; **c'est d., je n'aurais pas voulu que cela se sache** it's tricky, I'd have preferred it to have remained a secret

5 *(courtois)* thoughtful, considerate; **c'est un geste d. que de téléphoner avant d'y aller** it's a considerate gesture to phone before going; **peu d. avec ses parents** not very considerate towards his/her parents; **quelle délicate attention!** how thoughtful!, how considerate!

6 *(difficile à contenter)* fussy, particular; **être d. sur un point d'honneur** to be particular about a point of honour; **être d. sur la nourriture** to be fussy about one's food *or* a fussy eater

7 *(scrupuleux → conscience, procédé)* scrupulous; **elle est peu délicate en affaires** she's rather unscrupulous when it comes to business

NM,F **faire le d.** *(devant un mets)* to be fussy; *(devant le sang, la malhonnêteté)* to be squeamish; **ne fais pas le d., tu en as entendu bien d'autres!** don't act so shocked, you've heard worse than that in your life!; **quel petit d.!** what a sensitive soul!

délicatement [delikatmɑ̃] ADV 1 *(sans brusquerie → poser, toucher)* delicately, gently; *(→ travailler, orner)* delicately, daintily 2 *(agréablement et subtilement → peindre, écrire)* delicately, finely; *(→ parfumer)* delicately, subtly 3 *(avec tact)* delicately, tactfully

délicatesse [delikatɛs] NF 1 *(subtilité → d'une saveur, d'un coloris)* delicacy, subtlety; *(→ d'une dentelle, d'un visage)* delicacy, fineness, daintiness; *(→ d'un travail artisanal)* delicacy; *(→ d'une mélodie)* subtlety; **elle posa les verres sur la table avec d.** she put the glasses down gently on the table; **avoir une grande d. de goût** to have very refined tastes

2 *(fragilité → d'un tissu)* delicate texture, fragility; *(→ de la peau)* sensitivity; *(→ de la santé)* delicacy; *(→ de l'intestin, de l'estomac)* sensitivity, delicacy; *(→ d'un enfant, d'une plante)* fragility

3 *(honnêteté)* scrupulousness, punctiliousness; **agir en affaires avec une grande d.** to be scrupulously honest in business

4 *(tact)* delicacy, tact, tactfulness; **il n'en a rien dit, par d.** he kept quiet out of tact, he tactfully said nothing; **quelle d.!** how tactful!

5 *(difficulté → d'une situation, d'une opération)* delicacy, sensitiveness, trickiness

▫ **délicatesses** NFPL *Littéraire (gestes aimables)* kind attentions; **elle a eu des délicatesses à notre égard** she showed consideration towards us

▫ **en délicatesse** PRÉP **être en d. avec qn** to be on bad terms with sb; **nous sommes en d.** relations are a bit strained between us at the moment

délice [delis] NM 1 *(source de plaisir)* delight; **c'est un d.** *(mets, odeur)* it's delicious; *(d'être au soleil, de nager)* it's sheer delight

2 *(ravissement)* delight, (great) pleasure; **ses paroles la remplissaient de d.** his/her words filled her with delight

▫ **délices** NFPL 1 *(plaisirs)* delights, pleasures; **les délices de la campagne** the delights of the countryside; **faire les délices de qn** to delight sb, to give sb great pleasure; **faire ses délices de qch** to take delight in sth, to enjoy sth greatly

2 *Culin* **délices de brebis** prairie oyster

▫ **avec délice(s)** ADV with great pleasure, with delight

délicieuse [delisjøz] *voir* **délicieux**

délicieusement [delisjøzmɑ̃] ADV 1 *(agréablement)* deliciously, delightfully, exquisitely; **elle était d. parfumée** her perfume was delightful *or* divine 2 *(en intensif)* **son repas était d. bon** his/her meal was absolutely delicious; **elle était d. bien dans ses bras** she was wonderfully happy in his arms; **il peint d. bien** he paints delightfully well

délicieux, -euse [delisjø, -øz] ADJ 1 *(qui procure du plaisir → repas, parfum, sensation)* delicious; *(→ lieu, promenade, chapeau)* lovely, delightful 2 *(qui charme → femme, geste)* lovely, delightful; **votre sœur est délicieuse!** your sister's a delight (to be with)!

délictuel, -elle [deliktɥɛl] ADJ *Jur (nature)* criminal

délictueux, -euse [deliktɥø, -øz] ADJ *Jur (fait, activité)* criminal

délié, -e [delje] ADJ 1 *(sans épaisseur → écriture)*

fine; (→ *cou*) slender; **avoir la silhouette déliée** to be slender **2** *(agile* → *esprit)* sharp; (→ *doigts)* nimble, agile; **avoir la langue déliée** to be chatty

NM upstroke

délièment [delimɑ̃] **NM 1** *(des jambes, des doigts)* loosening **2** *Rel* absolution

délier [9] [delje] **VT 1** *(dénouer* → *ruban, mains)* to untie; (→ *gerbe, bouquet)* to undo

2 *(rendre agile)* **un exercice pour d. les jambes/les doigts** an exercise to warm up the leg muscles/the fingers; **pour lui d. la langue** to make him/her talk; **le vin lui a délié la langue** the wine loosened his/her tongue

3 *(délivrer* → *prisonnier)* to untie; **d. qn de** *(promesse, engagement)* to free *or* to release sb from

4 *Rel* to absolve

▸**se délier VPR 1** *(se défaire)* to come undone *or* untied, to come loose

2 *(langue)* to loosen; **après quelques verres, les langues se délient** a few drinks help to loosen people's tongues

3 *(s'exercer)* **se d. les jambes/les doigts** to warm up one's leg muscles/one's fingers

4 se d. de to release oneself from; **se d. d'une obligation** to free oneself from an obligation

délignage [deliɲaʒ] **NM** *(du bois)* edging

délimitation [delimitasjɔ̃] **NF 1** *(fait de circonscrire* → *un terrain)* demarcation, delimitation; (→ *un sujet, un rôle)* defining, delineating, delimitation **2** *(limites)* delimitation

délimiter [3] [delimite] **VT** *(espace, frontière)* to demarcate, to delimit, to circumscribe; *(sujet, rôle)* to define, to delineate

délimiteur [delimitœr] **NM** *Ordinat* delimiter; **d. de bloc** block delimiter, block marker; **d. de champ** field delimiter

délinéament [delineamɑ̃] **NM** outline, shape, contour

délinéateur [delineatœr] **NM** reflective marker post

délinéer [15] [delinee] **VT** to outline

délinquance [delɛ̃kɑ̃s] **NF la d.** criminality; **la d. juvénile** juvenile delinquency; **la petite d.** petty crime

délinquant, -e [delɛ̃kɑ̃, -ɑ̃t] **ADJ** delinquent

NM,F offender; **jeune d., d. juvénile** juvenile delinquent; **d. mineur** juvenile offender; **d. primaire** first offender; **d. sexuel** sex offender

déliquescence [delikesɑ̃s] **NF 1** *Chim* deliquescence **2** *(déclin)* gradual decay, creeping rot

❑ **en déliquescence ADJ** declining, decaying **ADV tomber en d.** to be on the decline, to fall into decline

déliquescent, -e [delikesɑ̃, -ɑ̃t] **ADJ 1** *Chim* deliquescent **2** *(déclinant)* declining, decaying, decrepit

délirant, -e [delirɑ̃, -ɑ̃t] **ADJ 1** *(malade)* delirious; **fièvre délirante** delirious fever **2** *Fam (insensé* → *accueil, foule)* frenzied, tumultuous; (→ *joie)* frenzied; (→ *imagination)* frenzied, wild; (→ *luxe, prix)* unbelievable, incredible; **une atmosphère complètement délirante** an atmosphere of total delirium; **c'est d. de travailler dans de telles conditions** working in such conditions is sheer madness *or* lunacy

délire [delir] **NM 1** *Méd* delirium, delirious state; **avoir le d.** to be delirious *or* raving; **d. alcoolique** alcoholic dementia; *Psy* **d. de grandeur** delusions of grandeur; **d. hallucinatoire** hallucination; **d. de persécution** persecution mania

2 *(incohérences)* **un d. d'ivrogne** a drunkard's ravings

3 *Fam (moment amusant)* **le d.!** it was wicked *or Br* mental *or Am* awesome!; **on s'est tapé un super d.!** we had a wicked *or Br* mental *or Am* awesome time!

4 *Fam (locution)* **partout où il se produit, c'est le** *ou* **du d.** wherever he performs, audiences go wild *or* crazy; **sa nouvelle collection, c'est du d. total** his/her new collection is out of this world; **demander aux gens de payer 50 pour cent en plus, c'est du d.!** asking people to pay 50 percent over the odds is completely insane!; **ce n'est plus de la mise en scène, c'est du d.!** it's no longer stage production, it's sheer madness!

❑ **en délire ADJ** delirious, ecstatic; **des supporters en d.** delirious *or* frenzied supporters

délirer [3] [delire] **VI 1** *(malade)* to be delirious, to rave; **d. de joie** to be delirious, to be mad with joy; *Fig* **tu délires!** you're out of your mind! **2** *Fam (s'amuser)* to have a great time, *Am* to have a blast

delirium tremens [delirjɔmtremɛ̃s] **NM INV** delirium tremens; **avoir une crise de d.** to have an attack of delirium tremens

délissage [delisaʒ] **NM** *(dans la fabrication du papier)* shredding

délisser [3] [delise] **VT** *(dans la fabrication du papier)* to shred

délit [deli] **NM 1** *Jur (infraction) Br* (nonindictable) offence, *Am* misdemeanor; **d. par abstention** non-feasance; **d. d'adultère** adultery; **d. d'audience** contempt of court; **d. civil** tort; **d. formel** conduct crime; **d. de fuite** = failure to stop after causing a road accident; **d. d'imprudence** negligence; **être incarcéré pour d. d'opinion** to be put in prison because of one's beliefs; **d. intentionnel** = offence committed intentionally; **d. non-intentionnel** = offence committed unintentionally; **d. matériel** result crime; **d. pénal** criminal offence; **d. politique** political offence; **d. de presse** press offence; **d. sans victime** victimless crime; *Fam* **ils l'ont arrêté pour d. de sale gueule** they arrested him because they didn't like the look of him

2 *Com* **d. d'initié** insider trading *or* dealing

délitage [delitaʒ] **NM** *Géol* splitting

délitement [delitmɑ̃] **NM** *Géol* splitting

déliter [3] [delite] **VT** *Géol* to split

▸**se déliter VPR 1** *Géol* to exfoliate **2** *Littéraire (se désagréger)* to crumble

délitescence [delitesɑ̃s] **NF** *Méd* delitescence

délitescent, -e [delitesɑ̃, -ɑ̃t] **ADJ** efflorescent

délivrance [delivrɑ̃s] **NF 1** *Littéraire (libération* → *d'une ville)* liberation, deliverance; (→ *d'un captif)* release

2 *(soulagement)* relief; **son départ fut une vraie d.** it was a real relief when he/she left; *Euph* **attendre la d.** to await death as a release from pain

3 *(d'un visa, d'un certificat, d'un brevet)* issue

4 *Méd (accouchement)* delivery; *(expulsion du placenta)* delivery of the afterbirth

délivre [delivr] **NM** *Vieilli Vét* placenta

délivrer [3] [delivre] **VT 1** *(libérer* → *prisonnier)* to release, to (set) free; **d. le peuple** to set the people free; **d. qn de ses liens** to free sb from his/her bonds

2 *(soulager)* to relieve; **se sentir délivré** to feel relieved; **ainsi délivré de ses incertitudes, il décida de…** thus freed from doubt, he decided to…; *Littéraire* **rien ne pouvait la d. de la jalousie** nothing could release her from jealousy; **tu me délivres d'un grand poids** you've taken a weight off my shoulders; *Bible* **délivre-nous du mal** deliver us from evil

3 *(visa, certificat, brevet)* to issue; *(ordonnance, autorisation)* to give, to issue

4 *(faire parvenir* → *paquet, courrier)* to deliver; (→ *signal)* to put out

▸**se délivrer VPR 1** *(se libérer)* to free oneself

2 *Fig* **se d. de** to get rid of

délivreur, -euse [delivrœr, -øz] **ADJ** *Tex* **cylindre d.** doffing cylinder, delivery roll

NM,F *(libérateur)* liberator

NM *Tex* doffing cylinder, delivery roll

délocalisation [delɔkalizasjɔ̃] **NF 1** *(dans le cadre de la décentralisation)* relocation **2** *Écon (d'entreprises vers l'étranger)* offshoring; **la d. des capitaux** the expatriation of capital

délocaliser [3] [delɔkalize] **VT 1** *(dans le cadre de la décentralisation)* to relocate **2** *Écon (des entreprises vers l'étranger)* to offshore; **d. des capitaux** to expatriate capital

▸**se délocaliser VPR** to relocate

déloger [17] [delɔʒe] **VT 1** *(congédier* → *locataire)* to throw *or* to turn out, to oust; **après trois ans, comment d. les locataires?** after three years, how do you get the tenants out?

2 *(débusquer* → *lapin)* to start

3 *(objet coincé)* to dislodge (**de** from)

VI 1 *(décamper)* to move out (hurriedly); *Fam* **allez, déloge!** *(pousse-toi)* come on, move (out of the way)!; **il finira bien par d.** he'll clear off eventually; **faire d. qn** to throw sb out, to get sb to move

2 *Belg (découcher)* to sleep out; **il a délogé hier** he didn't come home last night

déloquer [3] [delɔke] **VT** to undress ■

▸**se déloquer VPR** to get undressed ■

Délos [delos] **NF** Delos; **à D.** on Delos

délot [delo] **NM** fingerstall

déloyal, -e, -aux, -ales [delwajal, -o] **ADJ 1** *(infidèle* → *ami)* disloyal, unfaithful, *Littéraire* untrue **2** *(malhonnête* → *concurrence)* unfair; (→ *méthode)* dishonest, underhand; *Sport* **un coup d.** a foul

déloyalement [delwajalmɑ̃] **ADV** disloyally, unfairly, in an underhand manner

déloyauté [delwajote] **NF 1** *(caractère perfide)* disloyalty, treacherousness **2** *(action)* disloyal act, betrayal; **commettre une d. envers qn** to play sb false, to be disloyal to sb; **les petites déloyautés finissent par tuer l'amour** petty betrayals eventually spell the death of love

Delphes [dɛlf] **NM** Delphi

delphinarium [dɛlfinarjɔm] **NM** dolphin tank

delphinidé [dɛlfinide] *Zool* **NM** member of the Delphinidae family

❑ **delphinidés NMPL** Delphinidae

delphinium [dɛlfinjɔm] **NM** delphinium

delphinologie [dɛlfinɔlɔʒi] **NF** (scientific) study of dolphins

delta [dɛlta] **NM INV** *(lettre)* delta; **en d.** delta-shaped

NM *Géog* **d. (littoral)** delta; **le d. du Mississippi** the Mississippi Delta; **le d. du Nil** the Nile Delta

deltaïque [dɛltaik] **ADJ** delta *(avant n)*, *Sout* deltaic

deltaplane, delta-plane [dɛltaplan] *(pl* **deltaplanes** *ou* **delta-planes)** **NM 1** *(véhicule)* hang-glider **2** *(activité)* hang-gliding; **faire du d.** to go hang-gliding

deltiste [dɛltist] **NMF** hang-glider *(person)*

deltoïde [dɛltɔid] *Anat* **ADJ** deltoid

NM deltoid

deltoïdien, -enne [deltɔidjɛ̃, -ɛn] **ADJ** *Anat* deltoid

déluge [delyʒ] **NM 1** *(averse)* downpour, deluge

2 *Bible* **le D.** the Flood; *Fam* **ça remonte au d.** it's ancient history; **ne remonte pas au d.** *(en racontant une histoire)* give us the short version!

3 *(abondance* → *de paroles, de larmes, de plaintes)* flood, deluge; (→ *d'injures)* torrent; (→ *de coups)* shower; **je reçois un d. de publicités par la poste** I'm inundated with junk mail; **le standard est submergé par un d. d'appels** the switchboard is jammed with calls

> *Allusion*
>
> **Après moi, le déluge**
>
> This is a phrase expressing sublime indifference to the future. It is attributed to Madame de Pompadour, and means literally "After me, the Flood". Its true meaning is "what happens when I'm gone is none of my concern!"; in other words, the entire world could go to rack and ruin for all the speaker cares.

déluré, -e [delyre] **ADJ 1** *(malin* → *enfant, air)* quick, sharp, resourceful **2** *Péj (effronté* → *fille)* forward, brazen

NM,F un petit d. a smart kid; **une petite délurée** a brazen little thing

délurer [3] [delyre] **VT 1** *Littéraire (éveiller)* to awaken to the world around **2** *(dévergonder)* **d. qn** to open sb's eyes

▸**se délurer VPR 1** *(devenir éveillé)* to wake up; *Fig* to become aware **2** *(se dévergonder)* to become streetwise; **vers 14 ans, ils se délurent** when they're about 14 they start to become streetwise

délustrage [delystraʒ] **NM** *Tex* taking the lustre *or* gloss off

délustrer [3] [delystre] **VT** *Tex* to take the lustre *or* gloss off

délutage [delytaʒ] **NM 1** *Cér* unluting **2** *(des cornues à gaz)* opening

déluter [3] [delyte] **VT 1** *Cér* to unlute **2** *(cornues à gaz)* to open

démagnétisation [demaɲetizasjɔ̃] **NF 1** *(d'une bande, d'une carte)* demagnetization **2** *Naut* degaussing

démagnétiser [3] [demaɲetize] **VT 1** *(bande, carte)* to demagnetize **2** *Naut* to degauss

▸**se démagnétiser VPR** to become demagnetized

démago [demago] *Fam* **ADJ** demagogic ▪
  NMF demagogue ▪

démagogie [demagɔʒi] **NF** demagogy, demagoguery

démagogique [demagɔʒik] **ADJ** demagogic, demagogical

démagogue [demagɔg] **ADJ** rabble-rousing, *Sout* demagogic; **ils sont très démagogues** they're real rabble-rousers
  NMF demagogue

démaigrir [32] [demɛgrir] **VT** *Tech* to thin down

démaigrissement [demɛgrismɑ̃] **NM** *Tech* thinning down

démaillage [demajaʒ] **NM 1** *(d'un tricot)* undoing, unravelling **2** *Naut* unlinking

démailler [3] [demaje] **VT 1** *(défaire → tricot)* to undo, to unravel; *(→ bas, collant) Br* to ladder, *Am* to run; *(→ chaîne)* to unlink **2** *Pêche* to take out of the net
  ► **se démailler VPR** *(tricot)* to unravel, to fray, to come undone; *(bas, collant)* to run, *Br* to ladder

démailloter [3] [demajɔte] **VT** *(doigt blessé)* to take the bandage off; *(momie)* to unwrap; **d. un bébé** to take off a baby's *Br* nappy *or Am* diaper

demain [dəmɛ̃] **ADV 1** *(le jour après aujourd'hui)* tomorrow; **d. matin/après-midi** tomorrow morning/afternoon; **d. soir** tomorrow evening *or* night; **à partir de d.** as from tomorrow, from tomorrow on, starting tomorrow; **pendant la journée de d.** tomorrow; **les journaux de d.** tomorrow's papers; **c'est d. le grand jour** tomorrow's the big day; **d. en huit** a week tomorrow, *Br* tomorrow week; **d. en quinze** two weeks tomorrow, *Br* a fortnight tomorrow; **salut, à d.!** bye, see you tomorrow!; *Fam* **avance, sinon on y sera encore d.!** come on, let's not stay here all night!; **d. il fera jour** tomorrow is another day; *Hum* **d. on rase** *ou* **rasera gratis** tomorrow never comes; **ce n'est pas d. la veille** it's not going to happen overnight *or* in a hurry; **ce n'est pas d. la veille que le système changera** the system's not going to change overnight; **l'égalité des salaires n'est pas pour d.** equal pay isn't just around the corner
  2 *(à l'avenir)* in the future; **et si d. ils nous déclaraient la guerre?** what if in the future *or* at some future point they were to declare war on us?
  NM tomorrow; **tu as tout d. pour y réfléchir** you've got all tomorrow to think about it
  ❑ **de demain ADJ** *(futur)* **les architectes/écoles de d.** the architects/schools of tomorrow

---
Allusion

À demain, si vous le voulez bien
This was the signing-off formula used by radio game show host Lucien Jeunesse in his famous *Jeu des 1000 francs* (now known as *Le Jeu des 1000 euros*). It passed into everyday language to such an extent that if one friend says **À demain** ("See you tomorrow") the other may reply **Si vous le voulez bien** ("If that suits you").

---

démanché, -e [demɑ̃ʃe] **ADJ 1** *(membre)* dislocated **2** *(outil)* handleless, with no handle
  NM *Mus* shift

démanchement [demɑ̃ʃmɑ̃] **NM 1** *(d'un membre)* dislocation **2** *(d'un outil)* removal of the handle

démancher [3] [demɑ̃ʃe] **VT** *(couteau, marteau)* to remove the handle of; *(lame)* to work out of its handle
  VI *Mus* to shift
  ► **se démancher VPR 1** *(balai)* to lose its handle, to work loose in the handle **2** *Fam (se démener)* **se d. pour obtenir qch** to move heaven and earth *or* to bust a gut to get sth **3** *(se déboîter)* **se d. l'épaule/le bras** to put one's shoulder/arm out, to dislocate one's shoulder/arm

demande [dəmɑ̃d] **NF 1** *(requête)* request; **d. d'argent** request for money; **adresser toute d. de renseignements à...** send all inquiries to...; **accéder à/refuser une d.** to grant/to turn down a request; **d. (en mariage)** (marriage) proposal; **faire sa d. en mariage (auprès de qn)** to propose (to sb); **d. de rançon** ransom demand
  2 *Admin & Com* application; **faire une d. de bourse/visa** to apply for a scholarship/visa; **d. d'indemnité** claim for compensation; **d. de dommages-intérêts** claim for damages; **remplir une d.** to fill in an application (form); **d.**

d'emploi *(candidature)* job application; *(petite annonce)* job wanted advertisement; **demandes d'emploi** *(dans un journal)* situations wanted
  3 *Écon* demand; **l'offre et la d.** supply and demand; **répondre à la d.** to meet demand; **la d. est en hausse/en baisse** demand is up/down; **la d. croissante de portables** the increasing demand for *Br* mobile phones *or Am* cellphones; **il y a une forte d. de traducteurs** translators are in great demand, translators are very much sought after; **d. des consommateurs** consumer demand; **d. excédentaire** overdemand; **d. du marché** market demand; **d. prévisionnelle** projected demand; **d. primaire** primary demand; **d. soutenue** full demand
  4 *Jur* **d. accessoire** related claim; **d. additionnelle** additional claim; **d. incidente** petition; **d. indéterminée** unspecified claim; **d. initiale** originating application; **d. en intervention** = request for third-party intervention; **d. introductive d'instance** complaint; **d. en justice** petition; **d. principale** main claim; **d. reconventionnelle** counterclaim; **d. de renvoi** application for removal of action; **d. en renvoi** request for transfer of a case (to another court); **d. subsidiaire** subsidiary claim
  5 *Fin* **d. d'éclaircissement** = request from the tax authorities for further information when anomalies are found on a tax return
  6 *(expression d'un besoin)* need; **la d. doit venir du patient lui-même** the patient must express a need; **donne-leur de la tendresse, car il y a une d. de leur part** be loving to them, they're in need of it
  7 *Écol* **d. biochimique/biologique en oxygène** biochemical/biological oxygen demand; **d. chimique en oxygène** chemical oxygen demand
  8 *Vieilli (question)* question, inquiry, enquiry
  9 *Cartes* bid
  ❑ **à la demande ADJ** on demand **ADV** on demand
  ❑ **à la demande de, sur la demande de PRÉP** at the request of; **faire qch à** *ou* **sur la d. de qn** to do sth at sb's request
  ❑ **à la demande générale ADV** by popular request

demandé, -e [dəmɑ̃de] **ADJ** sought-after, in demand; **le modèle B est très d.** model B is in great demand, demand for model B is high

---
DEMANDER [3] [dəmɑ̃de]

| **VT** to ask **4** ▪ to ask for **1–3** ▪ to apply for **1** ▪ to claim **2** ▪ to demand **2** ▪ to want **3, 6** ▪ to send for **5** ▪ to require **6, 7** ▪ to need **7** |
| **USAGE ABSOLU** to ask |
| **VPR** to ask **1** ▪ to wonder **2** |

VT 1 *(solliciter → rendez-vous, conseil, addition)* to ask for, *Sout* to request; *(→ emploi, visa)* to apply for; **d. un congé** to ask for leave; **le cuisinier a demandé son samedi** the cook has asked to have Saturday off; **qu'as-tu demandé pour Noël?** what did you ask for for Christmas?; **d. l'aumône** *ou* **la charité** to ask for charity, to beg for alms; *Fig* **je ne demande pas la charité** I'm not asking for any favours; **d. le divorce** to file *or* petition for divorce; **d. la main de qn** to ask for sb's hand (in marriage); **d. qn en mariage** to propose to sb; **d. grâce** to ask *or* to beg for mercy; **d. pardon** to apologize; **je te demande pardon** I'm sorry; **il m'a demandé pardon de sa conduite** he apologized to me for his behaviour; **je vous demande pardon, mais c'est ma place** I beg your pardon, but this is my seat; **je vous demande pardon?** (I beg your) pardon?; **d. qch à qn** to ask sb for sth; **on nous a demandé nos passeports** we were asked for our passports; **d. une faveur** *ou* **un service à qn** to ask sb a favour; **d. son avis à qn** to ask sb's opinion; **d. un délai à son éditeur** to ask one's publisher for more time; **d. audience à qn** to request an audience with sb; **je ne t'ai jamais demandé quoi que ce soit** I never asked you for anything; **d. à qn de faire qch** to ask sb to do sth; **il m'a demandé de lui prêter ma voiture** he asked me to lend him my car; **ne me demande pas de m'en réjouir** don't ask *or* expect me to be pleased about it
  2 *(exiger → indemnité, dommages)* to claim, to

demand; *(→ rançon)* to demand, to ask for; **nous demandons de meilleures conditions de travail** we want *or* we're asking for better working conditions; **d. l'ouverture d'une enquête** to call for an inquiry; **il demande qu'on lui rende justice** he wants justice; **il a demandé qu'on le laisse en paix** he asked to be left alone; **d. l'impossible** to ask (for) the impossible; **d. justice** to demand justice *or* fair treatment; **d. qch à qn** to ask sth of sb; **je ne peux pas faire ce que vous me demandez** I can't do what you're asking of me; **que demande un citoyen à l'État?** what does a citizen ask of the State?; **il ne demandait pas beaucoup à la vie** he didn't ask much of life; **combien demandez-vous de l'heure?** how much do you charge an hour?; **il en demande 50 euros** he wants *or* he's asking 50 euros for it; **il ne faut pas trop m'en d./leur en d.** you mustn't ask too much of me/them, you shouldn't expect too much of me/them; **c'est trop me d.** it's too much to ask of me, it's asking too much; **tout ce que je demande** *ou* **je ne demande qu'une chose, c'est qu'on me laisse seul** all I want *or* ask is to be left alone; **qui ne demande rien n'a rien** if you don't ask, you don't get; **je ne demande que ça** *ou* **pas mieux!** I'd be only too pleased!; **elle ne demande pas mieux que de t'héberger** she'll be only too pleased to put you up; *Fam* **ils ont tous les avantages possibles, que demande le peuple?** they've got all kinds of perks, what more could they want?; **partir sans d. son compte** *ou* **son reste** to leave without further ado *or* without so much as a by-your-leave
  3 *(réclamer la présence de → gén)* to want; *(→ médecin, prêtre)* to ask for; **on te demande au téléphone** there's a call for you, you're wanted on the telephone; **on te demande aux urgences** you're wanted in *Br* casualty *or Am* the ER; **il y a une demoiselle qui vous demande** there's a young lady wanting to see you; **M. Dubois est demandé au téléphone** *(annonce)* telephone for Mr Dubois; **un conseiller en peinture est demandé à la caisse no. 3** paint consultant to checkout 3 please; **qui demandez-vous?** *(au téléphone)* who would you like to speak to?; **demandez-moi le siège à Paris/M. Blanc** get me the head office in Paris/Mr Blanc
  4 *(chercher à savoir)* to ask; **je n'ai pas compris ce qu'il m'a demandé** I didn't understand what he asked me; **d. l'heure à qn** to ask sb the time; **d. son chemin à qn** to ask sb for directions; **je lui ai demandé la raison de son départ** I asked him/her why he/she (had) left; **il y a des choses qu'il vaut mieux ne pas d.** some things are better left unasked, there are some things one had better not ask; **d. des nouvelles de qn** to ask after sb; **j'ai demandé de tes nouvelles à Marie** I asked for news of you from Marie, I asked Marie about you; **demande-lui comment il s'appelle et d'où il vient** ask him what his name is and where he comes from; **je lui demanderai s'il peut t'aider** I'll ask him whether he can help you; **on ne t'a rien demandé (à toi)!** nobody asked YOU!, nobody asked for YOUR opinion!; *Fam* **je ne te demande pas l'heure qu'il est, est-ce que je t'ai demandé si ta grand-mère fait du vélo?** mind your own business!, who asked your opinion?; *Fam* **à quoi sert la police, je vous le demande** *ou* **je vous demande un peu!** what are the police for, I ask you?; *Fam* **il avait tout peint en noir, je te demande un peu!** he'd painted everything black, I ask you *or* can you believe it!
  5 *(faire venir → ambulance, taxi)* to send for, to call (for)
  6 *(chercher à recruter → vendeur, ingénieur)* to want, to require; **on demande un livreur** *(petite annonce)* delivery boy wanted *or* required; **on demande beaucoup de secrétaires** there's a great demand for secretaries, secretaries are in great demand
  7 *(nécessiter)* to require, to call for, to need; **cela demande une patience que je n'ai pas** this requires *or* needs the kind of patience I don't have; **cela demande une explication** this calls for an explanation; **ça demande de gros sacrifices**

dem–dem

great sacrifices are called for; **ça demande ré-flexion** it needs thinking about, it needs some thought; **cette plante demande un arrosage quotidien** this plant needs to be watered every day; **une manipulation qui demande une grande précision** an experiment that calls for the utmost precision; **ce travail demande toute votre attention** the work demands all your attention; **ce livre a demandé beaucoup de re-cherches** the writing of this book required much research

USAGE ABSOLU il suffisait de d. you only had to *or* all you had to do was ask; **il n'y a qu'à d.** you/he/*etc* only have/has to ask; **demandez à votre agent de voyages** ask your travel agent

▫ **demander à** VT IND to ask to; **je n'ai pas de-mandé à naître** I never asked to be born; **il de-mande à voir le chef de rayon** he wants to see the department supervisor; **je demande à par-ler** may I speak, please let me speak; **d. à man-ger/boire** to ask for something to eat/drink; **il demande à ce qu'on lui rende son argent** he's asking for *or* he wants his money back; *Fam* **de-mande à ce qu'on vienne te chercher** ask someone to come and collect you ■; **ce vin de-mande à être bu frais** this wine should be drunk chilled; *Fam* **je demande à voir!** I'll be-lieve it when I see it!; **je ne demande qu'à vous embaucher/aider** I'm more than willing to hire/help you; **ce pauvre petit ne demande qu'à vivre** this poor little mite's only asking for a chance to live

▫ **demander après** VT IND **ils ont demandé après toi** *(ils t'ont réclamé)* they asked for you; *(pour avoir de tes nouvelles)* they asked how you were, they asked after you

►**se demander** VPR **1** *(être demandé)* **des cho-ses comme ça, ça ne se demande pas!** you don't ask that sort of question!; **cela ne se de-mande pas!** *(c'est évident)* need you ask!

2 *(s'interroger sur)* to wonder, to ask oneself; **c'est ce que je me demande** that's what I'm wondering, that's what I'd like to know; **je me demande où j'ai bien pu le mettre** I wonder where I can have possibly put it; **je me de-mande bien pourquoi/ce que/où…** I wonder why/what/where…, I really can't think why/what/where…; **on est en droit de se d. pour-quoi/comment/si…** one may rightfully ask oneself why/how/whether…; **c'est à se d. s'il n'est pas fou** one may well wonder if he isn't mad

demandeur[1], **-eresse** [dəmɑ̃dœr, -ərɛs] NM,F *Jur* plaintiff, claimant; **d. en appel** appellant

demandeur[2], **-euse** [dəmɑ̃dœr, -øz] NM,F **1 d. d'asile** asylum-seeker; **d. d'emploi** job seeker; **je suis d. d'emploi** I'm looking for a job; **me-sures pour les demandeurs d'emploi** measures for those seeking work *or* employment

2 *Tél* caller; **d., parlez** you're through, caller

ADJ **les Français sont très demandeurs de ce produit** there is an enormous demand for this product in France

démangeaison [demɑ̃ʒɛzɔ̃] NF **1** *(irritation)* itch; **j'ai des démangeaisons partout** I'm itching all over; **donner des démangeaisons à qn** to make sb itch; **où ressentez-vous cette d.?** where does it *or* do you itch? **2** *Fam (envie)* itch

démanger [17] [demɑ̃ʒe] VT **ce pull le démange** that jumper makes him itch; *Fam* **ça le déman-geait de dire la vérité** he was itching *or* dying to tell the truth

VI to itch; **ce pull lui démange** that jumper makes him/her itch; *Fam Fig* **la langue lui dé-mangeait** he/she was itching *or* dying to say something

démantèlement [demɑ̃tɛlmɑ̃] NM **1** *(démolition)* demolition, pulling *or* taking to pieces **2** *(d'un réseau, d'une secte)* breaking up, dismantling **3** *Com* **d. d'entreprise** asset stripping

démanteler [25] [demɑ̃tle] VT **1** *(démolir → rem-part)* to demolish, to tear down **2** *(désorganiser → réseau, secte)* to break up; *(→ entreprise, ser-vice)* to dismantle

démantibuler [3] [demɑ̃tibyle] VT to demolish, to take to bits *or* pieces

►**se démantibuler** VPR *Fam (se rompre)* to fall apart ■, to come to pieces ■

démaquillage [demakijaʒ] NM make-up removal; **le d. dure deux heures** it takes two hours to remove *or* to take off the make-up; **gel/lotion pour le d. des yeux** eye make-up removing gel/lotion

démaquillant, -e [demakijɑ̃, -ɑ̃t] ADJ **crème/lotion démaquillante** cleansing cream/lotion

NM cleanser, make-up remover; **d. pour les yeux** eye make-up remover

démaquiller [3] [demakije] VT *(yeux, visage)* to remove the make-up from; **d. qn** to remove sb's make-up

►**se démaquiller** VPR to remove *or* to take off one's make-up; **se d. les yeux** to remove one's eye make-up

démarcage [demarkaʒ] = **démarquage**

démarcatif, -ive [demarkatif, -iv] ADJ demarca-ting

démarcation [demarkasjɔ̃] NF **1** *(limite)* demarca-tion, dividing line; **c'est sur ce problème que la d. entre les deux partis est la plus claire** it is on this problem that the dividing line between the two parties is most evident **2** *(fait de démarquer)* boundary-defining, demarcating

démarcative [demarkativ] *voir* **démarcatif**

démarchage [demarʃaʒ] NM *Com (porte-à-porte)* door-to-door selling; *(prospection)* canvassing; **faire du d. (à domicile)** to do door-to-door selling, to sell door-to-door; **d. à distance** tele-phone canvassing; **d. téléphonique** telephone prospecting; **d. interdit** *(sur panneau)* no haw-kers; *Pol* **d. électoral** canvassing

démarche [demarʃ] NF **1** *(allure)* gait, walk; **avoir une d. gracieuse** to have a graceful gait, to walk gracefully

2 *(initiative)* step, move; **faire toutes les dé-marches nécessaires** to take all the necessary steps; **faire une d. auprès d'un organisme** to approach an organization; **démarches admi-nistratives/juridiques** administrative/legal pro-cedures

3 *(approche → d'un problème)* approach; **d. intellectuelle/philosophique** intellectual/philosophical approach; **trois démarches différentes à partir d'un même sujet** three dif-ferent ways of approaching *or* tackling the sa-me subject; **d. marketing** marketing approach

démarcher [3] [demarʃe] VT *(client, entreprise)* to visit

VI *(faire du porte-à-porte)* to do door-to-door selling, to sell door-to-door

démarcheur, -euse [demarʃœr, -øz] NM,F *Com (représentant)* door-to-door salesman, *f* sales-woman; **d. en assurances** insurance agent **2** *(prospecteur)* canvasser; **d. en publicité** adver-tisement canvasser

démariage [demarjaʒ] NM *Agr* thinning out

démarier [10] [demarje] VT **1** *Vieilli Jur* to sever the marriage tie of, to unmarry **2** *Agr* to thin out

démarketing [demarketiŋ] NM demarketing; **une politique de d. doit être mise en œuvre pour encourager le public à consommer moins d'al-cool** a policy of demarketing must be imple-mented to encourage the public to reduce their consumption of alcohol

démarquage [demarkaʒ] NM **1** *Com* markdown, marking down **2** *(fait d'ôter la marque)* **le d. des vêtements** *(pour les vendre moins cher)* remov-ing the designer labels from clothes **3** *(plagiat)* copying, plagiarizing; **la pièce n'est qu'un ha-bile d.** the play is nothing but a clever copy **4** *Sport* **le d. d'un joueur** escaping from a marker

démarque [demark] NF **1** *Com* marking down, markdown; **d. inconnue** shrinkage *(losses through shoplifting and pilfering)* **2** *Sport* freeing

démarquer [3] [demarke] VT **1** *(enlever la marque de)* **d. des vêtements** to remove the designer labels from clothes **2** *Com* to mark down **3** *Sport* to free **4** *(plagier)* to copy, to plagiarize

VI *(cheval)* to lose mark of mouth

►**se démarquer** VPR **1** *Sport* to shake off one's marker **2 se d. de** to distinguish oneself *or* to be different from

démarqueur, -euse [demarkœr, -øz] NM,F pla-giarist

démarrage [demaraʒ] NM **1** *Aut & Tech (mouve-ment)* moving off; **faire un d. en trombe** to shoot off

2 *(mise en marche)* starting; **le d. de la voiture** starting the car; **d. en côte** hill-start; *Ordinat* **d. automatique** autostart; *Ordinat* **d. à chaud/froid** warm/cold start

3 *(commencement)* start; **le d. d'une campagne publicitaire** the start of an advertising campaign

4 *Sport* spurt

5 *Naut* casting off, unmooring

démarrer [3] [demare] VT to start; *Ordinat* to boot (up), to start up; **on a démarré cette affaire avec très peu d'argent** we started this business with very little money

VI **1** *Aut & Tech (se mettre à fonctionner)* to start (up); *(s'éloigner → voiture)* to move off; *(→ conducteur)* to drive away *or* off; **je n'arrive pas à faire d. la voiture** I can't get the car started

2 *(débuter)* to start; **le feuilleton démarre le 18 mars** the series starts on 18 March; **faire d. un projet** to get a project off the ground

3 *(dans une progression → économie)* to take off, to get off the ground; **les ventes ont bien démarré** sales have got off to a good start; **l'association a mis du temps à d.** the associ-ation got off to a slow start

4 *Sport (coureur)* to put a spurt on

5 *Naut* to cast off, to unmoor

6 *Fam (s'en aller)* to budge, *Br* to shift; **je ne démarrerai pas d'ici tant que tu ne m'auras pas dit la vérité** I'm not moving *or* budging from here until you've told me the truth

démarreur [demarœr] NM *Aut & Tech* starter; **d. automatique** self-starter

démasclage [demasklaʒ] NM = stripping of the outer layer of cork

démascler [3] [demaskle] VT *(chêne-liège)* to strip the outer cork from

démasquer [3] [demaske] VT **1** *(ôter le masque de)* to unmask **2** *(confondre → traître, menteur)* to unmask, to expose; **se faire d.** to be unmasked **3** *(dévoiler → hypocrisie)* to unmask, to reveal; *(→ complot, mensonge)* to expose **4** *(locution)* **d. ses batteries** to unmask one's guns; *Fig* to show one's hand

►**se démasquer** VPR **1** *(ôter son masque)* to take off one's mask, to unmask oneself **2** *Fig* to throw off *or* to drop one's mask

démassification [demasifikasjɔ̃] NF *(des médias)* demassification

démassifier [9] [demasifje] VT *(médias)* to demas-sify

►**se démassifier** VPR to demassify

démastiquer [3] [demastike] VT to remove the putty from

démâtage [demataʒ] NM dismasting

démâter [3] [demate] VT to dismast

VI to lose its mast/masts, to be dismasted

dématérialisation [dematerjalizasjɔ̃] NF dema-terialization

dématérialiser [3] [dematerjalize] VT to dema-terialize

démazouter [3] [demazute] VT to remove fuel oil from

dème [dɛm] NM **1** *Biol* deme **2** *Antiq* deme

démédicalisation [demedikalizasjɔ̃] NF *(d'une profession, d'un hôpital, des soins)* demedicali-zation

démédicaliser [3] [demedikalize] VT *(une profes-sion, un hôpital des soins)* to demedicalize

démêlage [demɛlaʒ] NM *(des cheveux)* detang-ling, untangling

démêlant, -e [demɛlɑ̃, -ɑ̃t] ADJ *(baume)* condi-tioning

NM *(pour les cheveux)* conditioner, detangler

démêlé [demele] NM *(querelle)* quarrel; **démêlés** problems, trouble; **avoir des démêlés avec qn** to have a bit of trouble *or* a few problems with sb; **elle a eu des démêlés avec l'administration** she's had some trouble *or* problems with the authorities

démêlement [demɛlmɑ̃] NM *(des cheveux)* disen-tangling, untangling

démêler [4] [demele] VT **1** *(cheveux)* to untangle, to detangle, to comb out; *(nœud, filet)* to disen-tangle, to untangle

2 *(éclaircir → mystère, affaire)* to clear up, to disentangle, to see through); **d. les intentions de qn** to fathom (out) sb's intentions; **d. la vérité du mensonge** *ou* **le vrai du faux** to disentangle truth from falsehood, to sift out the truth from the lies

3 *Littéraire (locution)* **avoir quelque chose à d. avec qn** to have a bone to pick with sb

▸**se démêler** VPR **1** *(cheveux)* to comb out, to be disentangled; **ses cheveux se démêlent tout seuls** his/her hair combs out beautifully

2 *Vieilli* **se d. de** to extricate oneself from; **se d. de ses affaires de famille** to extricate oneself from one's family problems

démêloir [demɛlwar] NM large-toothed comb

démêlures [demelyr] NFPL combings

démembrement [demɑ̃brəmɑ̃] NM *(d'un empire)* breaking up; *(d'une propriété agricole)* division

démembrer [3] [demɑ̃bre] VT *(empire)* to break up; *(propriété agricole)* to divide

déménagement [demenaʒmɑ̃] NM **1** *(changement de domicile)* move; **c'est mon quatrième d.** it's my fourth move, it's the fourth time I've moved (*Br* house); **on les a aidés à faire leur d.** we helped them to move *or Br* move house; **camion de d.** *Br* removal *or Am* moving van; **entreprise de d.** *Br* removal company *or* firm, *Am* mover

2 *(déplacement des meubles)* **le d. du salon est fini** we've finished moving the furniture out of the living room

3 *(mobilier)* furniture; **le d. est arrivé** the furniture has arrived

déménager [17] [demenaʒe] VT *(salon)* to move the furniture out of, to empty of its furniture; *(piano, meubles)* to move; **j'ai tout déménagé dans ma chambre** I moved everything into my bedroom; *Fam* **qui est-ce qui vous déménage?** who's moving you?, which *Br* removal company *or Am* mover are you using?▪

VI **1** *(changer de maison)* to move (*Br* house); **il déménage, tu veux reprendre son appartement?** he's moving out, do you want to rent his flat?; **où déménage-t-il?** where's he moving to?

2 *(changer de lieu)* to move

3 *Fam (partir)* to clear off; **il est dans mon bureau? je vais le faire d. vite fait!** in my office, is he? I'll have him out of there in no time!

4 *très Fam (déraisonner)* to be off one's nut *or* rocker, to have lost it

5 *très Fam (faire de l'effet → musique)* to be mind-blowing; *(→ plat, épice)* to blow the top of one's head off, to pack a punch; **t'as vu la blonde? elle déménage!** did you see that blonde? she's a knockout!

déménageur [demenaʒœr] NM **1** *(ouvrier) Br* removal man, *Am* (furniture) mover; *(entrepreneur) Br* furniture remover, *Am* mover **2** *Fam (homme)* great hulk (of a man); **ses gardes du corps, c'est des vrais déménageurs!** his bodyguards are built like barn doors!

déménageuse [demenaʒøz] NF *Suisse Br* removal van, *Am* moving van

démence [demɑ̃s] NF **1** *(gén)* insanity, madness **2** *Méd* dementia; **d. précoce** dementia praecox; **d. présénile** presenile dementia **3** *Fam (conduite déraisonnable)* **c'est de la d.!** it's madness!

démener [19] [demne] **se démener** VPR **1** *(s'agiter)* to thrash about, to struggle; **se d. comme un beau diable** to thrash about, to struggle violently

2 *(faire des efforts)* **se d. pour** to exert oneself *or* to go out of one's way (in order) to; **il faut se d. pour trouver un emploi** you have to put yourself out if you want to find a job; **je me suis démenée pour le retrouver** I went to great lengths to find him

démens *etc voir* **démentir**

dément, -e [demɑ̃, -ɑ̃t] ADJ **1** *(gén)* mad, insane **2** *Méd* demented **3** *Fam (remarquable)* fantastic, wicked **4** *Fam Péj (inacceptable)* incredible, unbelievable; **c'est d., tout ce qu'on lui demande de faire!** it's unbelievable, the amount he's/she's being asked to do

NM,F *Méd* dementia sufferer, demented person

démenti [demɑ̃ti] NM denial; *Journ* disclaimer; **publier un d.** to issue a denial; *Journ* to publish a disclaimer; **opposer un d. formel à une rumeur** to deny a rumour categorically; **le témoignage reste sans d.** the testimony remains uncontradicted

démentiel, -elle [demɑ̃sjɛl] ADJ **1** *Psy* insane **2** *Méd* dementia *(avant n)* **3** *Fig (excessif, extravagant)* insane

démentir [37] [demɑ̃tir] VT **1** *(contredire → témoin)* to contradict

2 *(nier → nouvelle, rumeur)* to deny, to refute; **les autorités démentent avoir envoyé des troupes** the authorities deny having sent troops; **son regard démentait ses paroles** the look in his/her eyes belied his/her words; *Littéraire* **il a démenti nos espérances** he has not come up to our expectations, he has disappointed us

▸**se démentir** VPR **son amitié pour moi ne s'est jamais démentie** his/her friendship has been unfailing; **des méthodes dont l'efficacité ne s'est jamais démentie** methods that have proved consistently efficient

démerdard, -e [demɛrdar, -ard] *très Fam* ADJ resourceful▪; **toi qui es d., trouve-nous des places pour demain soir** you always seem to be able to wangle this kind of thing, find us some seats for tomorrow night; **il est d., il s'en sortira** he's always got some trick up his sleeve, he'll make it; **il n'est pas d. pour deux sous** he hasn't got a clue

NM,F **c'est un sacré d.** *(il est ingénieux)* he knows a trick or two; *(il sait se tirer d'un mauvais pas)* he can always wriggle his way out of a tricky situation

démerde [demɛrd] NF *très Fam* **dans ce pays, tout marche à la d.** you have to use your wits to get anything done in this country

démerder [3] [demɛrde] **se démerder** VPR *très Fam* **1** *(se débrouiller)* to get by, to manage▪; **il se démerde pas mal pour un débutant** he's not bad for a beginner; **t'inquiète pas, je me démerderai** don't worry, I'll manage somehow; **tu devras te d. sans moi** you'll have to get along without me; **et moi, comment je vais me d.?** and how the hell am I supposed to cope?; **elle se démerde pas mal en cuisine/tennis** she's not a bad cook/tennis player; **elle se démerde pas mal en anglais** she gets by quite well in English; **tu ne voulais pas que je t'aide, maintenant démerde-toi!** you didn't want me to help you, so you can manage on your own now!; **je sais pas comment il se démerde, il casse tout ce qu'il touche** I don't know how he does it, he breaks everything he gets his hands on

2 *(se dépêcher)* to get a move on, *Am* to get it in gear

démérite [demerit] NM *Littéraire* fault, flaw, demerit; **il n'y a aucun d. à avoir agi ainsi** there's nothing wrong in having acted this way

démériter [3] [demerite] VI *(s'abaisser)* **d. aux yeux de qn** to come down in sb's esteem; **il n'a jamais démérité** he has never proved unworthy of the trust placed in him; **il n'a démérité en rien** he has incurred no blame, he has in no way demeaned himself

démeshuy [deməzɥi] ADV *Can (en acadien)* from now on

démesure [deməzyr] NF *(d'un personnage)* excessiveness, immoderation; *(d'une passion, d'une idée)* outrageousness; **donner dans la d.** to (tend to) be excessive; **la d. absurde de ses projets** the absurdity of his grandiose projects

démesuré, -e [deməzyre] ADJ **1** *(énorme → empire)* vast, enormous; **d'une longueur démesurée** interminable **2** *(exagéré → orgueil)* inflated, inordinate; *(→ ambition)* excessive, enormous; *(→ appétit)* huge, enormous; **cette affaire a pris une importance démesurée** this affair has been blown up out of all proportion

démesurément [deməzyremɑ̃] ADV excessively, immoderately, inordinately; **la plante avait poussé d.** the plant had grown inordinately tall; **des yeux d. ouverts** eyes as round as saucers

démet *etc voir* **démettre**

Déméter [demetɛr] NPR *Myth* Demeter

Démétrios [demetrijos] NPR Demetrius

démettre [84] [demɛtr] VT **1** *Méd (os, bras)* to dislocate, to put out of joint

2 *(destituer)* to dismiss; **d. qn de ses fonctions** to dismiss sb from his/her duties

3 *Jur (débouter)* **d. qn de son appel** to dismiss sb's appeal

▸**se démettre** VPR **1** *Méd* **se d. le poignet** to dislocate one's wrist, to put one's wrist out of joint

2 *(démissionner)* to resign, to hand in one's resignation; **se d. de ses fonctions** *(directeur)* to resign one's post *or* from one's job; *(député, président)* to resign from office

démeubler [5] [demœble] VT to remove the furniture from; **la pièce est un peu démeublée** the room looks rather bare

demeurant [dəmœrɑ̃] **au demeurant** ADV *(du reste)* for all that, notwithstanding; **photographe de talent et très joli garçon au d.** a talented photographer and very good-looking with it

demeure [dəmœr] NF **1** *(maison)* residence **2** *(domicile)* dwelling-place, abode **3** *Jur* delay; **mettre qn en d. de payer** to give sb notice to pay; **mettre qn en d. de témoigner/de s'exécuter** to order sb to testify/to comply

▫ **à demeure** ADV **il s'est installé chez elle à d.** he moved in with her permanently *or* for good

demeuré, -e [dəmœre] ADJ *Vieilli* mentally retarded; *Fam Péj* halfwitted; **il est complètement d. ce mec** the guy's a complete halfwit

NM,F *Vieilli* mentally retarded person; *Fam Péj* halfwit

demeurer [5] [dəmœre] VI **1** *(aux être) (rester → dans tel état)* to remain; **d. silencieux/inconnu** to remain silent/unknown; **l'affaire en est demeurée là** the matter rested there; **il vaut mieux en d. là pour aujourd'hui** we'd better leave it at that for today

2 *(aux être) (subsister)* to remain, to be left; **peu de traces demeurent** there are few traces left; **d. à qn** *(rester sa propriété)* to be left to sb; **cette épée nous est demeurée de notre père** this sword was left to us by our father

3 *(aux avoir) Sout (habiter)* to live, to stay; **où demeuriez-vous alors?** where were you living then?; **il demeure toujours à la même adresse** he's still living at the same address

demi, -e [dəmi] ADJ INV *(devant le nom, avec trait d'union)* **1** *(moitié de)* half; **une d.-pomme** half an apple; **plusieurs d.-pommes** several halves of apple; **une d.-livre de pommes** a half-pound of *or* half a pound of apples

2 *(incomplet)* **cela n'a été qu'un d.-succès** it wasn't a complete *or* it was only a partial success

NM,F *(moitié)* half; **j'achète un pain? – non, un d.** shall I buy a loaf? – no, just half of one

NM **1** *(bière)* **un d. (de bière)** a beer, *Br* ≃ a half, a half-pint; **prends deux demis** get two beers

2 *Sport* **d. droite** *(au football)* right half *or* half-back; **d. de mêlée** *(au rugby)* scrum half; **d. d'ouverture** *(au rugby)* fly *or* stand-off half

3 *Suisse (vin)* = half a litre of wine

▫ **demie** NF **la demie** half past; **on va attendre la demie** we'll wait till half past; **je te rappelle à la demie** I'll call you back at half past; **à la demie de chaque heure** every hour on the half hour, at half past every hour; **à la demie de 4 heures** at half past 4

▫ **à demi** ADV **1** *(avec un adjectif)* **à d. mort** half-dead; **être à d. convaincu** to be half-convinced; **bûche à d. consumée** half-burnt log

2 *(avec un verbe)* **ouvrir la porte à d.** to half-open the door; **faire les choses à d.** to do things by halves; **ne croire qn qu'à d.** to only half-believe sb

▫ **et demi, et demie** ADJ **1** *(dans une mesure)* and a half; **quinze mètres et d.** fifteen and a half metres; **ça dure deux heures et demie** it lasts two and a half hours; **boire une bouteille et demie** to drink a bottle and a half

2 *(en annonçant l'heure)* **à trois heures et demie** at three thirty, at half past three

demiard [dəmjar] NM *Can* half-pint, = 0.284 litres

demi-bas [dəmiba] NM INV knee-length sock; *(pour femmes)* knee-high, popsock

demi-botte [dəmibɔt] (*pl* **demi-bottes**) NF half-boot

demi-bouteille [dəmibutɛj] (*pl* **demi-bouteilles**) NF half-bottle, half a bottle

demi-brigade [dəmibrigad] (*pl* **demi-brigades**) NF *(bataillons)* = group of two or three battalions led by a colonel

demi-canton [dəmikɑ̃tɔ̃] (*pl* **demi-cantons**) NM *Suisse* = state of the Swiss confederation which is one half of a divided canton

demi-centre [dəmisɑ̃tr] (*pl* **demi-centres**) NM *Sport* centre-half

demi-cercle [dəmisɛrkl] (*pl* **demi-cercles**) NM half-circle, semicircle
▫ **en demi-cercle** ADV in a semicircle

demi-circulaire [dəmisirkylɛr] (*pl* **demi-circulaires**) ADJ (*canal*) semicircular

demi-clef [dəmikle] (*pl* **demi-clefs**) NF half hitch

demi-colonne [dəmikɔlɔn] (*pl* **demi-colonnes**) NF demi-column, semi-column

demi-deuil [dəmidœj] (*pl* **demi-deuils**) NM (*tenue*) half-mourning
▫ **à la demi-deuil** ADJ *Culin* = coated in a white sauce and garnished with truffles

demi-dieu [dəmidjø] (*pl* **demi-dieux**) NM demigod

demi-douzaine [dəmiduzɛn] (*pl* **demi-douzaines**) NF 1 (*six*) half-dozen, half-a-dozen; **deux demi-douzaines** two half-dozens; **une d. de tomates** a half-dozen tomatoes, half-a-dozen tomatoes 2 *Fam* (*environ six*) **une d. de gens attendaient** half-a-dozen people were waiting

demi-droite [dəmidrwat] (*pl* **demi-droites**) NF half-line, half-ray

demi-écrémé [dəmiekreme] ADJ *Br* semi-skimmed, *Am* part-skim

démieller [26] [demjɛle] VT to remove the honey from; *Fam Fig* to get out of a mess *or* a jam

demi-figure [dəmifigyr] (*pl* **demi-figures**) NF half-length (portrait)

demi-fin, -e [dəmifɛ̃, -in] (*mpl* **demi-fins**, *fpl* **demi-fines**) ADJ *Com* **petits pois demi-fins** garden peas; **haricots demi-fins** green beans

demi-finale [dəmifinal] (*pl* **demi-finales**) NF semi-final; **les demi-finales femmes/hommes** the women's/men's semi-finals

demi-finaliste [dəmifinalist] (*pl* **demi-finalistes**) NMF semi-finalist

demi-fond [dəmifɔ̃] NM INV 1 (*activité*) middle-distance running; **faire du d.** to do middle-distance running 2 (*course*) middle-distance race

demi-frère [dəmifrɛr] (*pl* **demi-frères**) NM half-brother

demi-gras, -grasse [dəmigra, -gras] ADJ semi-bold
NM INV semi-bold (type)

demi-gros [dəmigro] NM INV wholesale (dealing in retail quantities)

demi-heure [dəmijœr] (*pl* **demi-heures**) NF half-hour; **une d.** half an hour; **il y en a un toutes les demi-heures** there's one every half-hour; **laisser mijoter une d.** allow to simmer for half an hour

demi-jour [dəmiʒur] (*pl* **demi-jours**) NM (*clarté*) half-light; (*crépuscule*) twilight, dusk

demi-journée [dəmiʒurne] (*pl* **demi-journées**) NF half-day, half a day; **une d. de travail** half a day's work, a half-day's work; **travailler trois demi-journées par semaine** to work three half-days a week; **je lui dois sa d.** I owe him/her half-a-day's pay *or* for half-a-day's work

démilitarisation [demilitarizasjɔ̃] NF demilitarization

démilitariser [3] [demilitarize] VT to demilitarize

demi-litre [dəmilitr] (*pl* **demi-litres**) NM half-litre, half a litre; **un d. de lait, s'il vous plaît** half a litre of milk, please

demi-longueur [dəmilɔ̃gœr] (*pl* **demi-longueurs**) NF half-length, half a length; **une d. d'avance** a half-length's lead; **gagner d'une d.** to win by half a length

demi-lune [dəmilyn] (*pl* **demi-lunes**) NF 1 (*ouvrage fortifié*) demi-lune, half-moon 2 (*place urbaine*) crescent
ADJ INV half-moon (avant n), half-moon-shaped
▫ **en demi-lune** ADJ half-moon (avant n), half-moon-shaped

demi-mal [dəmimal] (*pl* **demi-maux** [-mo]) NM **il n'y a que d.** there's no great harm done

demi-mesure [dəmiməzyr] (*pl* **demi-mesures**) NF 1 (*compromis*) half measure; **elle ne connaît pas les demi-mesures** *ou* **elle ne fait pas de demi-mesures** she doesn't do things by halves 2 *Couture* semi-finished tailoring 3 (*moitié d'une mesure*) half measure

demi-mondaine [dəmimɔ̃dɛn] (*pl* **demi-mondaines**) NF *Arch* demi-mondaine

demi-monde [dəmimɔ̃d] (*pl* **demi-mondes**) NM demi-monde

demi-mot [dəmimo] **à demi-mot** ADV **il comprend**

à d. he doesn't need to have things spelled out for him; **j'ai compris à d.** I took the hint; **on se comprend à d.** we know how each other's mind works

déminage [demina3] NM (*sur la terre*) mine clearance; (*en mer*) mine sweeping

déminer [3] [demine] VT to clear of mines

déminéralisation [demineralizasjɔ̃] NF 1 (*de l'eau*) demineralization 2 *Physiol* mineral deficiency

déminéraliser [3] [demineralize] VT 1 (*eau*) to demineralize 2 *Physiol* to deprive of minerals
▸ **se déminéraliser** VPR (*malade*) to become deficient in essential minerals

démineur [deminœr] ADJ M bomb-disposal (avant n)
NM bomb-disposal expert, member of a bomb-disposal unit

demi-pause [dəmipoz] (*pl* **demi-pauses**) NF *Br* minim *or Am* half-note rest

demi-pension [dəmipɑ̃sjɔ̃] (*pl* **demi-pensions**) NF (*à l'hôtel*) half-board; **sept jours en d.** seven days' half-board; *Scol* **être en d.** to have school lunches *or* dinners

demi-pensionnaire [dəmipɑ̃sjɔnɛr] (*pl* **demi-pensionnaires**) NMF = pupil who has school dinners

demi-pièce [dəmipjɛs] (*pl* **demi-pièces**) NF (110 litre) wine keg

demi-place [dəmiplas] (*pl* **demi-places**) NF 1 (*au spectacle*) half-price ticket *or* seat 2 *Transp* half-fare

demi-pointe [dəmipwɛt] (*pl* **demi-pointes**) NF (*position*) demi-point; **(chausson de) d.** demi-point shoe

demi-portion [dəmipɔrsjɔ̃] (*pl* **demi-portions**) NF 1 (*moitié de portion*) half-portion 2 *Fam Hum* (*personne*) weed, squirt

demi-produit [dəmiprɔdɥi] (*pl* **demi-produits**) NM *Écon* semi-finished product

demi-queue [dəmikø] (*pl* **demi-queues**) ADJ **un piano d.** a baby grand (piano)
NM baby grand (piano)

demi-relief [dəmirəljɛf] (*pl* **demi-reliefs**) NM mezzo-relievo

demi-reliure [dəmirəljyr] (*pl* **demi-reliures**) NF quarter-binding; **d. à (petits) coins** half-binding

demi-ronde [dəmirɔ̃d] (*pl* **demi-rondes**) *Tech* ADJ F **lime d.** half-round file
NF (lime) half-round file

démis, -e [demi, -iz] PP *voir* **démettre**

demi-saison [dəmisɛzɔ̃] (*pl* **demi-saisons**) NF (*printemps*) spring; (*automne*) autumn, *Am* fall; **un temps de d.** the sort of mild weather you get in spring or autumn; **vêtements (de) d.** spring or autumn clothes

demi-salaire [dəmisalɛr] (*pl* **demi-salaires**) NM half-pay

demi-sang [dəmisɑ̃] NM INV half-breed (horse)

demi-sel [dəmisɛl] ADJ INV slightly salted
NM INV 1 (*beurre*) slightly salted butter 2 (*fromage*) = slightly salted cream cheese 3 *Fam Arg crime* (*souteneur*) small-time pimp; (*voyou*) small-time gangster

demi-siècle [dəmisjɛkl] (*pl* **demi-siècles**) NM half-century

demi-sœur [dəmisœr] (*pl* **demi-sœurs**) NF half-sister

demi-solde [dəmisɔld] (*pl* **demi-soldes**) *Mil* NF half-pay
NM INV half-pay officer

demi-sommeil [dəmisɔmɛj] (*pl* **demi-sommeils**) NM half-sleep, doze; **dans mon d., j'ai entendu...** while I was half asleep, I heard...; *Méd & Obst* **d. provoqué** twilight sleep
▫ **en demi-sommeil** ADJ half-asleep; **entreprise/marché en d.** sluggish business/market

demi-soupir [dəmisupir] (*pl* **demi-soupirs**) NM *Br* quaver *or Am* eighth note rest

démission [demisjɔ̃] NF 1 (*départ*) resignation; **donner sa d.** to resign, to hand in *or Sout* to tender one's resignation 2 (*irresponsabilité*) abdication of responsibility; **la d. face au terrorisme** the abdication of responsibility in the face of terrorism; **à cause de la d. des parents** because of the refusal of parents to shoulder their responsibilities

démissionnaire [demisjɔnɛr] ADJ 1 (*qui quitte son poste*) resigning, outgoing 2 (*irresponsable*) who has abdicated his/her responsibilities
NMF person resigning; **les démissionnaires** those who have resigned

démissionner [3] [demisjɔne] VI 1 (*quitter son emploi*) to resign, to hand in one's resignation *or* notice; **qu'est-ce qui t'a fait d.?** what made you resign?; **d. de son poste de directeur** to resign (one's position) as manager
2 (*refuser les responsabilités*) to fail to shoulder one's responsibilities; **d. devant qn** to give in to sb; **d. devant qch** to give in when faced with sth; **c'est trop difficile, je démissionne** it's too hard, I give up
VT *Fam* (*renvoyer*) **d. qn** to talk sb into resigning ▪; **ils l'ont démissionné?** did he resign or was he fired?

demi-tarif [dəmitarif] (*pl* **demi-tarifs**) NM (*billet*) half-price ticket; (*carte*) half-price card; (*abonnement*) half-price subscription; **abonnement à d.** half-price subscription; **voyager à d.** to travel at half-fare; **enfants d.** (*billet*) children half-price

demi-teinte [dəmitɛ̃t] (*pl* **demi-teintes**) NF half-tone
▫ **en demi-teinte** ADJ 1 *Phot* half-tone 2 (*subtil*) subtle, delicate; **sa musique/personnalité en d.** his/her subtle music/personality

demi-tendineux [dəmitɑ̃dinø] *Anat* ADJ M INV semitendinosus
NM INV semitendinosus

démit *etc voir* **démettre**

demi-tige [dəmiti3] (*pl* **demi-tiges**) NF *Hort* half standard

demi-ton [dəmitɔ̃] (*pl* **demi-tons**) NM *Br* semitone, *Am* half-step; **d. diatonique/chromatique** diatonic/chromatic *Br* semitone *or Am* half-step

demi-tour [dəmitur] (*pl* **demi-tours**) NM 1 (*pivotement*) about-face, about-turn; **faire un d.** (*gén*) & *Mil* to about-face, to about-turn; *Mil* **d., droite!** (right) about face! 2 *Aut* U-turn; **faire un d.** to do *or* to pull a U-turn; **faire d.** (*piéton*) to retrace one's steps; (*conducteur*) to turn back

démiurge [demjyr3] NM demiurge, creator

demi-vérité [dəmiverite] (*pl* **demi-vérités**) NF half-truth

demi-vie [dəmivi] (*pl* **demi-vies**) NF *Biol & Phys* half-life

demi-vierge [dəmivjɛr3] (*pl* **demi-vierges**) NF *Vieilli & Littéraire* demi-vierge

demi-volée [dəmivɔle] (*pl* **demi-volées**) NF half-volley

demi-volte [dəmivɔlt] (*pl* **demi-voltes**) NF *Équitation* demi-volte

démixtion [demikstjɔ̃] NF *Chim* immiscibility

démo [demo] NF *Fam* (*d'un appareil, d'un objet*) demo

démobilisable [demɔbilizabl] ADJ eligible for demobilization

démobilisateur, -trice [demɔbilizatœr, -tris] ADJ (*démotivant*) demobilizing

démobilisation [demɔbilizasjɔ̃] NF 1 *Mil* demobilization; **à la d.** when demobilization time comes/came 2 (*démotivation*) growing apathy; **on constate une d. de l'opinion publique sur ces questions** public opinion has become apathetic about or has turned away from these issues

démobilisatrice [demɔbilizatris] *voir* **démobilisateur**

démobiliser [3] [demɔbilize] VT 1 *Mil* to demobilize 2 (*démotiver*) to cause to lose interest, to discourage
▸ **se démobiliser** VPR to lose interest, to become discouraged

démocrate [demɔkrat] ADJ 1 (*gén*) democratic 2 (*dans des noms de partis*) Democratic
NMF 1 (*gén*) democrat 2 (*aux États-Unis*) Democrat

démocrate-chrétien, -enne [demɔkratkretjɛ̃, -ɛn] (*mpl* **démocrates-chrétiens**, *fpl* **démocrates-chrétiennes**) ADJ Christian Democrat
NM,F Christian Democrat

démocratie [demɔkrasi] NF 1 (*système*) democracy; **d. directe/représentative** direct/representative democracy; **d. participative** participatory democracy; **d. populaire** people's democracy 2 (*pays*) democracy, democratic country; **vivre en d.** to live in a democracy;

Fam **on est en d., non?** this is a free country, as far as I know! **3** *Pol* **d. chrétienne** Christian Democracy; *Anciennement* **D. Libérale** = right-of-centre French political party

démocratique [demɔkratik] **ADJ** **1** *Pol* democratic **2** *(respectueux des désirs de tous)* democratic; **tu as pris une décision pas très d.** your decision was biased; **notre groupe est très d.** in our group, everyone gets a chance to have their say

démocratiquement [demɔkratikmã] **ADV** democratically

démocratisation [demɔkratizasjɔ̃] **NF 1** *Pol* democratization **2** *(mise à la portée de tous)* **la d. du ski** putting skiing holidays within everyone's reach

démocratiser [3] [demɔkratize] **VT 1** *Pol* to democratize, to make more democratic **2** *(rendre accessible)* to bring within everyone's reach; **d. les voyages à l'étranger** to put foreign travel within everyone's reach
▸**se démocratiser VPR 1** *Pol* to become more democratic **2** *(devenir accessible)* to become available to anyone

Démocrite [demɔkrit] **NPR** Democritus

démodé, -e [demode] **ADJ** *(style, technique, idée, théorie)* old-fashioned, out-of-date; *(parents)* old-fashioned

démoder [3] [demode] **se démoder VPR** to go out of fashion *or* vogue, to become old-fashioned; **le long ne se démode pas** long skirts will never go out of fashion

démodex [demɔdɛks] **NM INV** *Entom, Méd & Vét* follicle mite, *Spéc* demodex (mite)

démodulateur [demɔdylatœr] **NM** demodulator

démodulation [demɔdylasjɔ̃] **NF** demodulation

démoduler [3] [demɔdyle] **VT** to demodulate

démographe [demɔgraf] **NMF** demographer, demographist

démographie [demɔgrafi] **NF** *(science)* demography; *(croissance de la population)* population growth

démographique [demɔgrafik] **ADJ** demographic, population *(avant n)*; **poussée/explosion d.** population increase/explosion

demoiselle [dəmwazɛl] **NF 1** *(jeune femme)* young lady; **d. d'honneur** *(d'une mariée)* bridesmaid; *(d'une souveraine)* lady-in-waiting; **d. de compagnie** lady's companion
2 *Vieilli (célibataire)* maiden lady; **j'ai une tante qui est encore d.** I have an aunt who is still unmarried; **les demoiselles Dupin** the Misses Dupin
3 *(fille)* **votre d.** your daughter
4 *Entom (libellule)* dragonfly; **d. de Numidie** demoiselle (crane), Numidian crane
5 *Géol* **d. (coiffée)** chimney-rock
6 *(outil)* rammer

=======🗌========

'Les Demoiselles d'Avignon' *Picasso* 'Les Demoiselles d'Avignon' *or* 'The Young Ladies of Avignon'

=======🎬========

'Les Demoiselles de Rochefort' *Demy, Varda* 'The Young Girls of Rochefort'

démolir [32] [demɔlir] **VT 1** *(détruire → immeuble, mur)* to demolish, to pull *or* to tear down; *(→ jouet, voiture)* to wreck, to smash up; **d. une porte à coups de pied** to kick a door down
2 *(anéantir → argument, théorie)* to destroy, to demolish; *(→ projet)* to ruin, to play havoc with; *(→ réputation, autorité)* to shatter, to destroy; **l'alcool lui a démoli la santé** alcohol ruined *or* wrecked his/her health; *Fam* **la mort de son père l'a démolie** she was shattered by her father's death
3 *Fam (causer la ruine de → auteur, roman)* to pan; **la presse peut d. un homme politique** the press can break a politician
4 *Fam (battre)* to beat up; **il s'est fait d.** he got beaten up; **d. le portrait à qn** to beat *or* to smash sb's face in
5 *Fam (épuiser)* to wipe out, *Br* to shatter; **le déménagement m'a démoli** the move has left me wiped out *or Br* shattered
▸**se démolir VPR** **se d. la santé** to ruin one's

health; **se d. la santé à faire qch** to kill oneself doing sth; **te démolis pas la santé à les chercher** don't wear yourself out looking for them

démolissage [demɔlisaʒ] **NM** *Fam (critique)* panning

démolisseur [demɔlisœr] **NM 1** *(ouvrier)* demolition worker, *Am* wrecker **2** *(entrepreneur)* demolition contractor **3** *(détracteur)* destructive critic

démolition [demɔlisjɔ̃] **NF 1** *(d'un bâtiment)* demolition, pulling *or* tearing down
2 *Fig (d'une théorie)* destruction
❏ **de démolition ADJ** **chantier/entreprise de d.** demolition site/contractors; *Fig* **une campagne de d. systématique** a systematic campaign of destruction
❏ **démolitions NFPL** *(matériaux)* debris, rubble
❏ **en démolition ADJ** being demolished, under demolition

démon [demɔ̃] **NM 1** *Rel* **le d.** the Devil; **être possédé du d.** to be possessed by the Devil; **comme un d.** like a thing possessed
2 *Myth* daemon, daimon; *Fig* **son d. intérieur** *(mauvais)* the evil *or* demon within (him); *(bon)* the good spirit within (him)
3 *(tentation)* demon; **le d. de la curiosité/du jeu** the demon of curiosity/gambling; **le d. de midi** = lust affecting a man in mid-life
4 *(enfant turbulent)* **(petit) d.** (little) devil
5 *Can* **être en d.** to be furious

démone [demɔn] **NF 1** *Littéraire* demoness **2** *Can (femme méchante)* devil, troublemaker

démonétisation [demɔnetizasjɔ̃] **NF 1** *Fin* demonetization, demonetarization **2** *(discrédit)* discrediting

démonétiser [3] [demɔnetize] **VT 1** *Fin* to demonetize, to demonetarize **2** *(discréditer)* to discredit, to bring into disrepute

démoniaque [demɔnjak] **ADJ** *(ruse, rire)* diabolical, fiendish, *Sout* demonic
NMF person possessed by the devil

démonisme [demɔnism] **NM** belief in demons, *Sout* demonism

démonologie [demɔnɔlɔʒi] **NF** demonology

démonstrateur, -trice [demɔ̃stratœr, -tris] **NM,F** *Com* demonstrator, salesperson *(in charge of demonstrations)*

démonstratif, -ive [demɔ̃stratif, -iv] **ADJ 1** *(expressif)* demonstrative, expressive, effusive; **peu d.** reserved, undemonstrative **2** *(convaincant)* demonstrative, conclusive **3** *Gram* demonstrative
NM *(pronom)* demonstrative pronoun; *(adjectif)* demonstrative adjective

démonstration [demɔ̃strasjɔ̃] **NF 1** *Ling & Math (preuve)* demonstration, proof; *(ensemble de formules)* demonstration; **faire la d. de qch** to demonstrate *or* prove sth; *Fig* **la d. n'est plus à faire** it has been proved beyond all doubt; **d. par l'absurde** reductio ad absurdum
2 *Com (d'article)* demonstration; **faire la d. d'un aspirateur** to demonstrate a vacuum cleaner; **je ne peux pas vous vendre cet appareil, il est en d.** I can't sell you this appliance, it's a demonstration model; **d. sur le lieu de vente** in-store demonstration
3 *(prestation)* display, demonstration; **d. aérienne** air display; **faire une d. aérienne** to put on an air display; **faire une d. de karaté** to give a karate demonstration; **d. de force** display *or* show of force
4 *(fait de manifester)* demonstration, show; **faire une d. de force** to display one's strength; **faire la d. de son talent** to show one's talent; **voici la d. de sa duplicité** this shows his/her duplicity
❏ **démonstrations NFPL** *(effusions)* (great) show of feeling, gushing; *(crises)* outbursts; **démonstrations de tendresse/joie/colère** show of tenderness/joy/anger; **faire de grandes démonstrations d'amitié à qn** to put on a great show of friendship for sb; **toutes ces démonstrations ne te mèneront nulle part** these outbursts will get you nowhere

démonstrative [demɔ̃strativ] *voir* **démonstratif**

démonstrativement [demɔ̃strativmã] **ADV** demonstratively, conclusively

démonstratrice [demɔ̃stratris] *voir* **démonstrateur**

démontable [demɔ̃tabl] **ADJ** which can be dismantled *or* taken to pieces

démontage [demɔ̃taʒ] **NM** dismantling; **pour faciliter le d.** to make it easier to dismantle

démonté, -e [demɔ̃te] **ADJ 1** *(mer)* raging, stormy; **par une mer démontée** in heavy seas **2** *Chasse (oiseau)* winged

démonte-pneu [demɔ̃tpnø] *(pl* **démonte-pneus)** **NM** *Br* tyre lever, *Am* tire iron

démonter [3] [demɔ̃te] **VT 1** *(désassembler → bibliothèque, machine, tente)* to dismantle, to take down; *(→ moteur)* to strip down, to dismantle; *(→ fusil, pendule)* to dismantle, to take to pieces, to take apart; *(→ manche de vêtement, pièce rapportée)* to take off
2 *(détacher → pneu, store, persienne)* to remove, to take off; *(→ rideau)* to take down
3 *(décontenancer)* to take aback; **ma question l'a démonté** she was taken aback *or* flummoxed by my question; **ne te laisse pas d. par son ironie** don't be flustered by his/her ironic remarks
4 *Équitation* to unseat, to unhorse
5 *Can (décourager)* to discourage
▸**se démonter VPR 1** *(emploi passif)* to be taken to pieces, to be dismantled; **ça se démonte facilement** it can be easily dismantled
2 *(se troubler)* to lose countenance, to get flustered

démontrabilité [demɔ̃trabilite] **NF** demonstrability

démontrable [demɔ̃trabl] **ADJ** demonstrable, provable; **c'est facilement d.** it's easy to prove

démontrer [3] [demɔ̃tre] **VT 1** *Math* to prove; **démontrez que c'est une bijection** prove *or* demonstrate that it's a bijection; **d. qch par A plus B** to prove sth conclusively; **je ne peux pas te le d. par A plus B** I can't quote you chapter and verse
2 *(montrer par raisonnement)* to prove, to demonstrate; **d. son erreur à qn** to prove to sb that he's/she's wrong, to prove sb wrong
3 *(révéler)* to show, to reveal, to indicate; **un geste qui démontre notre bonne volonté** a gesture that shows *or* demonstrates our goodwill

démoralisant, -e [demɔralizã, -ãt] **ADJ** *(remarque, nouvelle)* demoralizing, disheartening, depressing; **elle est démoralisante!** she's depressing!

démoralisateur, -trice [demɔralizatœr, -tris] **ADJ** demoralizing

démoralisation [demɔralizasjɔ̃] **NF** demoralization; **ne nous laissons pas gagner par la d.!** let's not become disheartened *or* demoralized!

démoralisatrice [demɔralisatris] *voir* **démoralisateur**

démoralisé, -e [demɔralize] **ADJ** **il était complètement d.** he was completely demoralized *or* downcast

démoraliser [3] [demɔralize] **VT** to demoralize, to dishearten; **il ne faut pas te laisser d.** you mustn't let it get you down
▸**se démoraliser VPR** to become demoralized, to lose heart

démordre [76] [demɔrdr] **démordre de VT IND** **ne pas d. de** to stick to, to stand by; **il ne démord pas de son idée** he won't budge from his position; **rien ne m'en fera d.** I'll stick to my guns come what may; **elle n'en démord pas, elle ne veut pas en d.** she won't have it any other way

Démosthène [demɔstɛn] **NPR** Demosthenes

démotique [demɔtik] **ADJ 1** *(écriture)* demotic **2** *(grec)* modern

démotivant, -e [demɔtivã, -ãt] **ADJ** demotivating, disheartening, dispiriting; **c'est plutôt d.!** it's not exactly encouraging!

démotivation [demɔtivasjɔ̃] **NF** demotivation, loss of motivation; **il ne faut pas laisser s'installer la d. au sein de l'équipe** we mustn't let the team become demotivated

démotiver [3] [demɔtive] **VT** to demotivate, to discourage; **les salaires les ont démotivés** the salary levels have discouraged *or* demotivated them

démoucheter [27] [demuʃte] *Escrime* **VT** *(fleuret)* to remove the button from
▸**se démoucheter VPR** to lose its button

démoulage [demulaʒ] **NM** *(d'une statuette)* removal from the mould; *(d'un gâteau)* turning out; *Métal* **d. à chaud** hot stripping

dem–den

démouler [3] [demule] **VT** *(statuette)* to remove from the mould; *(gâteau)* to turn out; *(tarte)* to remove from its tin

démouleur [demulœr] **NM** *Métal* strip mill

démousquetonner [3] [demuskətɔne] **VT** *(en alpinisme)* to unclip from a karabiner

démoustication [demustikasjɔ̃] **NF** clearing of mosquitoes

démoustiquer [3] [demustike] **VT** to rid of mosquitoes

démultiplexage [demyltiplɛksaʒ] **NM** *Tél* demultiplexing

démultiplexer [3] [demyltiplɛkse] **VT** *Tél* to demultiplex

démultiplicateur [demyltiplikatœr] **ADJ** *(dispositif)* reducing, reduction *(avant n)* **NM** reduction system

démultiplication [demyltiplikasjɔ̃] **NF** *(action)* gearing down, (gear) reduction; **(rapport de) d.** reduction ratio

démultiplier [9] [demyltiplije] **VT 1** *Tech* to reduce, to gear down **2** *(multiplier)* to increase; **d. les pouvoirs de décision** to reinforce the executive through increased powers

démuni, -e [demyni] **ADJ 1** *(pauvre)* destitute; **des mesures d'aide aux plus démunis** an aid package to help those who need it most **2** *(sans défense)* powerless, resourceless

démunir [32] [demynir] **VT** to deprive; **d. qn de qch** to deprive or to divest sb of sth

▸ **se démunir** **VPR** **se d. de** to part with, to give up

démuseler [24] [demyzle] **VT** *(animal)* to unmuzzle, to remove the muzzle from; **d. la presse** to lift restrictions on the freedom of the press

démutisation [demytizasjɔ̃] **NF** *Psy* first phase in the teaching of deaf-mutes

démystifiant, -e [demistifjɑ̃, -ɑ̃t] **ADJ 1** *(qui détrompe)* eye-opening **2** *(qui rend moins mystérieux)* demystifying

démystificateur, -trice [demistifikatœr, -tris] **ADJ 1** *(qui détrompe)* eye-opening **2** *(qui rend moins mystérieux)* demystifying **NM,F** demystifier

démystification [demistifikasjɔ̃] **NF 1 la d. de qn** opening sb's eyes **2** *(d'un mystère, d'un phénomène)* demystification

démystificatrice [demistifikatris] *voir* **démystificateur**

démystifier [9] [demistifje] **VT 1** *(détromper)* to open the eyes of **2** *(rendre plus clair)* to explain, to demystify

démythification [demitifikasjɔ̃] **NF** demythologization; **on assiste à la d. de l'ordinateur** computers are no longer regarded with awe or are losing their mystique

démythifier [9] [demitifje] **VT** to demythologize, to make less mythical or into less of a myth; **il faut d. l'internet** we must remove the mystique that surrounds the Internet

dénantir [32] [denɑ̃tir] **VT** *Jur* to deprive of securities

denar [dənar] **NM** *(monnaie)* dinar

dénasalisation [denazalizasjɔ̃] **NF** *Ling* denasalization

dénasaliser [3] [denazalize] **VT** to denasalize

dénatalité [denatalite] **NF** fall or drop in the birth rate

dénationalisation [denasjɔnalizasjɔ̃] **NF** denationalization, denationalizing

dénationaliser [3] [denasjɔnalize] **VT** to denationalize

dénatter [3] [denate] **VT** *(cheveux)* to unplait

dénaturalisation [denatyralizasjɔ̃] **NF** denaturalization

dénaturaliser [3] [denatyralize] **VT** to denaturalize

dénaturant, -e [denatyrɑ̃, -ɑ̃t] **ADJ** adulterating **NM** denaturant

dénaturation [denatyrasjɔ̃] **NF** denaturation

dénaturé, -e [denatyre] **ADJ 1** *(alcool)* denatured **2** *(pervers → goût)* unnatural, perverted; **quelle mère dénaturée je fais!** what a bad mother I am!

dénaturer [3] [denatyre] **VT 1** *(modifier → alcool)* to adulterate, to denature; *(→ saveur)* to alter, to adulterate **2** *(fausser → propos, faits, intention)* to distort, to misrepresent, to twist; **vous dénaturez mes propos!** you're twisting my words or

putting words into my mouth!; **c'est d. nos efforts!** it's making a mockery of our efforts!

dénazification [denazifikasjɔ̃] **NF** denazification

dénazifier [9] [denazifje] **VT** to denazify

dendrite [dɑ̃drit] **NF** *Anat & Géol* dendrite

dendritique [dɑ̃dritik] **ADJ** dendritic, dendritical

dendrochronologie [dɑ̃drɔkrɔnɔlɔʒi] **NF** dendrochronology

dendrocygne [dɑ̃drɔsiɲ] **NM** *Orn* tree duck, whistling duck

dendrolague [dɑ̃drɔlag] **NM** *Zool* tree kangaroo

dénébulation [denebylasjɔ̃] **NF** *Aviat* fog dispersal

dénébuler [3] [denebyle] **VT** to clear of fog, to dispel the fog over

dénébulisation [denebylizasjɔ̃] **NF** *Aviat* fog dispersal

dénébuliser [3] [denebylize] **VT** to clear of fog, to dispel the fog over

dénégation [denegasjɔ̃] **NF 1** *(contestation)* denial; **convaincu de son innocence par des dénégations énergiques** persuaded of his/her innocence by his/her energetic denials **2** *Psy* denial

□ **de dénégation** **ADJ** *(geste, attitude)* denying, of denial; **en signe de d.** as a sign of disagreement

déneigement [denɛʒmɑ̃] **NM** snow clearance; **le d. des cols** clearing the cols of snow

déneiger [23] [deneʒe] **VT** to clear of snow, to clear snow from

déneigeuse [deneʒøz] **NF** snowplough; *(pour souffler la neige)* snowblower; *(pour fondre la neige)* snow remover

dénervation [denɛrvasjɔ̃] **NF** *Méd* denervation

dengue [dɑ̃g] **NF** *Méd* dengue fever, breakbone fever

déni [deni] **NM 1** *Jur* denial; **d. de justice** denial of justice **2** *Psy* **d. de réalité** denial

déniaiser [4] [denjeze] **VT 1** *(dépuceler)* **d. qn** to take away sb's innocence; **j'ai été déniaisé à 15 ans** I lost my innocence when I was 15 **2** *(rendre moins naïf)* to open the eyes of

▸ **se déniaiser** **VPR** *(devenir moins naïf)* to learn the ways of the world

dénicher [3] [deniʃe] **VT 1** *Fam (trouver → collier, trésor)* to find, to unearth; *(→ informations)* to dig up or out; *(→ chanteur, cabaret)* to discover, to spot; **d. de jeunes acteurs** to scout for young actors; **j'ai déniché un chouette petit restaurant** I've found a great little restaurant; **elle a l'art de d. des antiquités intéressantes** she has a talent for hunting out interesting antiques

2 *(oiseau)* to remove from the nest **VI** *(oiseau)* to leave the nest, to fly away

dénicheur, -euse [deniʃœr, -øz] **NM,F 1** *(d'oiseaux)* bird's nester **2** *(découvreur)* **d. de bibelots rares** curio-hunter; **d. de talents, d. de vedettes** talent scout or spotter

dénicotinisation [denikɔtinizasjɔ̃] **NF** reduction of nicotine

dénicotiniser [3] [denikɔtinize] **VT** to denicotinize; **du tabac dénicotinisé** low-nicotine tobacco

dénicotiniseur [denikɔtinizœr] **NM** cigarette filter

denier [dənje] **NM 1** *Hist (monnaie → romaine)* denarius; *(→ française)* denier; **le d. du culte** the contribution to parish costs; **le d. de Saint-Pierre** = annual diocesan gift made to the Pope (since 1849)

2 *Tex* denier; **bas de 20 deniers** 20-denier stockings

□ **deniers** **NMPL** money, funds; **je l'ai payé de mes deniers** I paid for it out of my own pocket; **j'en suis de mes deniers** I had to pay with my own money; **les deniers publics** ou **de l'État** public money or funds

dénier [9] [denje] **VT 1** *(rejeter → responsabilité)* to deny, to disclaim **2** *(refuser)* to deny, to refuse; **d. qch à qn** to deny or to refuse sb sth

dénigrement [denigrəmɑ̃] **NM** denigration, disparagement; **le mot ne s'emploie que par d.** the word is only used disparagingly

□ **de dénigrement** **ADJ** **esprit/paroles de d.** disparaging spirit/remarks; **campagne de d.** smear campaign

dénigrer [3] [denigre] **VT** to disparage, to denigrate, to run down

▸ **se dénigrer** **VPR** to do oneself down

dénigreur, -euse [denigrœr, -øz] **NM,F** disparager;

les dénigreurs those who are always finding fault

denim [dənim] **NM** denim

dénitratation [denitratasjɔ̃] **NF** *Chim* denitration

dénitrer [3] [denitre] **VT** *Chim* to denitrate

dénitrification [denitrifikasjɔ̃] **NF** *Chim* denitrification

dénitrifier [9] [denitrifje] **VT** *Chim* to denitrify

dénivelé [denivle] **NM** difference in level or height

dénivelée [denivle] **NF** difference in level or height

déniveler [24] [denivle] **VT** to make uneven, to put out of level

dénivellation [denivɛlasjɔ̃] **NF 1** *(action)* making uneven, putting out of level **2** *(écart)* difference in level or height; **les dénivellations d'une route** the gradients or ups and downs of a road

dénivelle [denivɛl] = **dénivelée**

dénivellement [denivɛlmɑ̃] **NM** = **dénivellation**

dénombrable [denɔ̃brabl] **ADJ** countable; **non d.** uncountable

dénombrement [denɔ̃brəmɑ̃] **NM** counting (out), count; **le d. des animaux** counting the animals; **faire un d. de la population** to do a population count

dénombrer [3] [denɔ̃bre] **VT** to count (out); **on dénombre 130 morts à ce jour** at the latest count there were 130 dead; **d. les habitants d'une ville** to count the population of a town

dénominateur [denɔminatœr] **NM** *Math* denominator; **d. commun** common denominator; **plus grand d. commun** highest common denominator; **avoir comme** ou **en d. commun** to have as a common denominator; **avoir un d. commun** *(personnes)* to have something in common, to share (some) common ground

dénominatif [denɔminatif] **NM** *Gram* denominative

dénomination [denɔminasjɔ̃] **NF 1** *(fait de nommer)* naming, *Sout* denomination **2** *(nom)* designation, denomination, name; *Pharm* **d. commune** generic name; **d. sociale** company name

dénommé, -e [denɔme] **ADJ** **le d. Joubert** the man called Joubert; **une dénommée Madame Barda** a certain or one Mrs Barda

dénommer [3] [denɔme] **VT 1** *(donner un nom à)* to name, to call **2** *Jur* to name

dénoncer [16] [denɔ̃se] **VT 1** *(complice, fraudeur)* to denounce, to inform on; *(camarade de classe)* to tell on; **d. qn aux autorités** to denounce sb or to give sb away to the authorities

2 *(condamner → pratiques, dangers, abus)* to denounce, to condemn; **tous les jours, nous dénonçons ces atrocités** every day we condemn these atrocities

3 *(annuler → armistice, traité)* to denounce, to renege on; *(→ contrat)* to terminate

4 *(dénoter)* to indicate, to betray; **son silence dénonçait sa culpabilité** his/her silence betrayed his/her guilt

▸ **se dénoncer** **VPR** to give oneself up

dénonciateur, -trice [denɔ̃sjatœr, -tris] **ADJ** denunciatory; **lettre dénonciatrice** letter of denunciation

NM,F informer; **les dénonciateurs de ses méfaits** those who exposed his/her wrongdoings

dénonciation [denɔ̃sjasjɔ̃] **NF 1** *(accusation)* denunciation; **arrêté sur la d. de son frère** arrested on the strength of his brother's denunciation; **d. calomnieuse** false accusation; *Jur* **d. de nouvel œuvre** = action whereby a property owner brings an action against a neighbouring property owner for carrying out work on that property **2** *(révélation → d'une injustice)* exposure, denouncing, castigating **3** *(rupture → d'un traité)* denunciation; *(→ d'un contrat)* termination

dénonciatrice [denɔ̃sjatris] *voir* **dénonciateur**

dénotation [denɔtasjɔ̃] **NF** *Ling & Phil* denotation; **cela fait partie de la d. du terme** it's part of the core meaning or the denotation of the word

dénoter [3] [denɔte] **VT 1** *Ling & Phil* to denote **2** *(être signe de)* to denote, to indicate

dénouement [denumɑ̃] **NM** *(d'un film, d'une histoire, d'une pièce)* dénouement; *(d'une crise, d'une affaire)* outcome, conclusion; **un heureux d.** a happy ending, a favourable outcome

dénouer [6] [denwe] **VT 1** *(défaire → ficelle, lacet)*

den-dep

to undo, to untie, to unknot; (→ *cheveux*) to let down, to loosen **2** (*résoudre* → *intrigue*) to unravel, to untangle

▶**se dénouer VPR 1** (*cheveux*) to come loose *or* undone; (*lacet*) to come undone *or* untied **2** (*crise*) to end, to be resolved **3 se d. les cheveux** to let one's hair down

dénoyage [denwajaʒ] **NM** Mines unwatering

dénoyautage [denwajotaʒ] **NM 1** (*d'un fruit*) Br stoning, Am pitting **2** Fig (*d'une entreprise*) = removal of officials appointed for reasons of political influence

dénoyauter [3] [denwajote] **VT 1** (*fruit*) Br to stone, Am to pit **2** Fig **d. une entreprise** = to remove officials appointed by politicians from a company

dénoyauteur [denwajotœr] **NM** Br stoner, Am pitter

dénoyer [13] [denwaje] **VT** Mines to unwater

denrée [dɑ̃re] **NF** commodity; (*aliment*) foodstuff; **denrées alimentaires** food products, foodstuffs; **denrées de base, denrées témoin** basic commodities; **denrées coloniales** exotic produce; **denrées de consommation courante** basic consumer goods; **denrées du pays** domestic products; **denrées périssables** perishable goods, perishables; **denrées de première nécessité** staple foods, staples; **une d. rare** a scarce commodity; **c'est une d. rare que la générosité** generosity is hard to come by

dense [dɑ̃s] **ADJ 1** (*épais* → *brouillard, végétation*) thick, dense **2** (*serré* → *foule*) thick, tightly packed; (→ *circulation*) heavy; **population peu d.** sparse population **3** (*concis* → *style*) compact, condensed **4** Phys dense **5** Math dense

densément [dɑ̃semɑ̃] **ADV** (*cultivé*) thickly, densely; (*peuplé*) densely; (*écrit*) tightly, tautly

densification [dɑ̃sifikasjɔ̃] **NF** (*du brouillard, de la foule*) thickening; **la d. de la population sur le littoral** the increasing concentration of population along the coast

densifier [9] [dɑ̃sifje] **VT** to make denser, to increase the density of

densimètre [dɑ̃simɛtr] **NM** densimeter

densimétrie [dɑ̃simetri] **NF** densimetry

densimétrique [dɑ̃simetrik] **ADJ** densimetric

densité [dɑ̃site] **NF 1** Phys density; Élec **d. de charge/courant** charge/current density

2 (*du brouillard, de la foule*) denseness, thickness; **selon la d. de la circulation** depending on how heavy the traffic is; **d. de population** population density; **pays à faible/forte d. de population** sparsely/densely populated country

3 Math **d. de probabilité** probability density

4 Phot density; **d. par réflexion** specular density

5 Ordinat **d. d'enregistrement** packing *or* recording *or* data density; **à double d.** double-density; **haute d.** high density; **simple d.** single density

dent [dɑ̃] **NF 1** Anat tooth; **faire** *ou* **percer ses dents** to cut one's teeth, to teethe; **faire une d.** to cut a (new) tooth; **avoir les dents en avant** to have protruding teeth; **dents du bas/haut** lower/upper teeth; **dents de devant/du fond** front/back teeth; Fam Fig **avoir les dents du fond qui baignent** to have stuffed oneself *or* one's face, to have pigged out; **d. barrée** impacted tooth; **d. de lait** baby *or* Br milk tooth; **d. permanente** permanent *or* second tooth; **d. à pivot** post; **d. de sagesse** wisdom tooth; **fausses dents** false teeth; **avoir la d.** to be ravenous *or* starving; Fam **avoir** *ou* **garder une d. contre qn** to have a grudge against sb, to bear sb a grudge; **avoir la d. dure** to be scathing; **avoir les dents longues** to be extremely ambitious, to set one's sights high; Fam **être sur les dents** (*occupé*) to be frantically busy; (*anxieux*) to be stressed out; **la police est sur les dents** the police are on red alert; Fam **il n'y a pas de quoi remplir une d. creuse** this wouldn't keep a sparrow alive; *aussi* Fig **montrer les dents** to bare one's teeth; **parler entre ses dents** to mutter; **répondre entre ses dents** to mutter an answer; **se faire les dents** to cut one's teeth; **l'escalade du mont Blanc, c'était juste pour se faire les dents** climbing Mont Blanc was just for starters; **le jeune ténor s'est fait les dents sur**

'**la Bohème**' the young tenor cut his teeth on 'La Bohème'; **se mettre quelque chose sous la d.** to find something to eat; **on n'avait rien à se mettre sous la d.** we didn't have a thing to eat; **tout ce qui lui tombe sous la d.** anything he can get his teeth into; **sourire toutes dents dehors** to give a beaming smile

2 (*de roue, d'engrenage*) cog; (*de courroie*) tooth

3 (*pointe* → *d'une scie, d'un peigne*) tooth; (→ *d'une fourchette*) prong; (→ *d'une herse*) tine, prong, tooth; (→ *d'un timbre*) perforation; **à deux dents** two-pronged; **à trois dents** three-pronged

4 Bot serration

5 Géog (jagged) peak, jag

6 Électron **dents de scie** sawtooth waveform

❏ **à belles dents** ADV **déchirer qch à belles dents** to tear into sth; **mordre dans** *ou* **croquer** *ou* **manger qch à belles dents** to eat one's way through sth; Fig **mordre dans** *ou* **croquer la vie à belles dents** to live (one's) life to the full

❏ **en dents de scie** ADJ (*couteau*) serrated; **évolution en dents de scie** uneven development; **elle a eu une scolarité en dents de scie** her education was a very uneven business

🎬

'**Les Dents de la mer**' Spielberg 'Jaws'

dentaire [dɑ̃tɛr] **ADJ** (*hygiène*) oral, dental; (*cabinet, études, école*) dental

NF 1 Fam (*école*) dental school▪; **faire d.** to study dentistry▪ **2** Bot toothwort

dental, -e, -aux, -ales [dɑ̃tal, -o] **ADJ** Ling dental

❏ **dentale NF** Ling dental (consonant)

❏ **dentale NM** Zool dentalium

dent-de-lion [dɑ̃dəljɔ̃] (*pl* **dents-de-lion**) **NF** dandelion

denté, -e [dɑ̃te] **ADJ** (*courroie*) toothed; (*feuille*) serrate, dentate

NM Ich dentex

dentelaire [dɑ̃tlɛr] **NF** Bot plumbago, leadwort

dentelé, -e [dɑ̃tle] **ADJ** (*contour*) jagged, indented; (*feuille*) dentate, serrate; (*timbre*) perforated

denteler [24] [dɑ̃tle] **VT** (*gén*) to indent the edge of, to give a jagged outline to; (*timbre*) to perforate; **machine/ciseaux à d.** pinking machine/shears

dentelle [dɑ̃tɛl] **NF 1** (*tissu*) lace, lacework; **faire de la d.** to do lacework; **des gants de** *ou* **en d.** lace gloves; **d. à l'aiguille** *ou* **au point** lace, needlepoint; **d. de Chantilly** Chantilly lace; **d. au fuseau** *ou* **aux fuseaux** pillow lace; **d. de papier** lacy paper; **d. au point** point lace, needlepoint; Fam **il ne fait pas dans la d.** he's completely unsubtle *or* in-your-face **2** (*morceau de tissu*) piece of lacework

ADJ INV 1 bas d. lace stocking **2** Culin **crêpes d.** paper-thin pancakes

❏ **de dentelle, en dentelle** ADJ lace (*avant n*)

dentellier, -ère [dɑ̃təlje, -ɛr] **ADJ** (*industrie*) lace(making) (*avant n*)

NM,F lacemaker, laceworker

❏ **dentellière NF** (*machine*) lacemaking machine

📖🎬

'**La Dentellière**' Lainé, Goretta 'The Lacemaker'

dentelure [dɑ̃tlyr] **NF 1** (*d'un rivage*) indentation; (*d'une montagne*) jagged summit; (*d'une feuille*) serration **2** Archit denticulation **3** (*d'un timbre*) perforations

denticule [dɑ̃tikyl] **NM** Zool denticle

❏ **denticules NMPL** Archit row of dentils

denticulé, -e [dɑ̃tikyle] **ADJ** Archit & Bot denticulate

dentier [dɑ̃tje] **NM** dentures

dentifrice [dɑ̃tifris] **ADJ** **eau d.** mouthwash; **pâte d.** toothpaste; **poudre d.** tooth powder

NM toothpaste

dentine [dɑ̃tin] **NF** dentin, dentine

dentiste [dɑ̃tist] **NMF** dentist

dentisterie [dɑ̃tistəri] **NF** dentistry

dentition [dɑ̃tisjɔ̃] **NF 1** (*dents*) teeth, Spéc dentition; **avoir une bonne d.** to have good teeth; **d. adulte** *ou* **définitive** adult teeth, Spéc secondary dentition; **d. lactéale** *ou* **de lait** baby *or* Br milk

teeth, Spéc primary dentition **2** (*poussée*) tooth growth

denture [dɑ̃tyr] **NF 1** Anat & Zool set of teeth, Spéc dentition **2** Tech teeth, cogs

denturologie [dɑ̃tyrɔlɔʒi] Can denturism

denturologiste [dɑ̃tyrɔlɔʒist] **NMF** Can denturist

dénucléarisation [denyklearizasjɔ̃] **NF** denuclearization

dénucléariser [3] [denyklearize] **VT** (*région*) to denuclearize

dénudation [denydasjɔ̃] **NF 1** Méd stripping **2** Littéraire (*d'un arbre*) baring, laying bare

dénudé, -e [denyde] **ADJ** (*dos, corps*) bare, unclothed; (*crâne*) bald; (*terrain*) bare, bald; (*fil électrique*) bare

dénuder [3] [denyde] **VT** (*dos, épaules*) to leave bare; (*sol, câble, os, veine*) to strip

▶**se dénuder VPR 1** (*se déshabiller*) to strip (off) **2** (*se dégarnir* → *crâne*) to be balding; (→ *arbre, colline*) to become bare; (→ *fil électrique*) to show through

dénué, -e [denye] **ADJ d. de** lacking in, devoid of; **d. d'intérêt** utterly uninteresting, devoid of interest; **d. de bon sens** devoid of common sense; **d. d'humanité** inhuman, devoid of human feeling; **d. d'ambiguïté** unambiguous; **d. de sincérité** lacking in *or* devoid of sincerity; **une accusation dénuée de tout fondement** a completely unfounded accusation; **être d. de tout** to be destitute

dénuement [denymɑ̃] **NM** destitution; **être dans le d. le plus complet** to be utterly destitute

dénuer [7] [denye] **se dénuer VPR** Littéraire **se d. de** to deprive oneself of; **se d. de ses biens** to part with all one's possessions

dénutri, -e [denytri] **ADJ** malnourished

NM,F = person suffering from malnutrition

dénutrition [denytrisjɔ̃] **NF** malnutrition

déodorant [deɔdɔrɑ̃] **ADJ M** deodorant (*avant n*)

NM deodorant

déontique [deɔ̃tik] **ADJ** deontological; **logique d.** deontology

déontologie [deɔ̃tɔlɔʒi] **NF** professional code of ethics, deontology; **la d. médicale** the medical code of ethics; **code de d.** (*écrit*) code of practice; **d. professionnelle** business ethics

déontologique [deɔ̃tɔlɔʒik] **ADJ** ethical, deontological; **règles déontologiques** rules of ethics

dép. 1 (*abrév écrite* **départ**) dep **2** (*abrév écrite* **département**) dept

dépaillage [depajaʒ] **NM** removal of the straw seating

dépailler [3] [depaje] **VT** to remove the straw seating from

dépalisser [3] [depalise] **VT** Hort (*arbre*) to remove the espaliers from

dépannage [depanaʒ] **NM 1** (*réparation*) repair job; (*remorquage*) recovery; Ordinat troubleshooting; **SOS dépannages** emergency breakdown service; **faire un d.** to fix a breakdown

2 Fam (*aide*) helping out▪, bailing out; **merci pour le d.** thanks for helping (me) out

❏ **de dépannage** ADJ **voiture de d.** Br breakdown lorry, Am tow truck; **service de d.** breakdown service

❏ **en dépannage** ADV Fam **prête-moi 20 euros en d.** lend me 20 euros just to tide me over *or* bail me out; **j'ai pris une intérimaire en d.** I got a temp in to help us out

dépanner [3] [depane] **VT 1** (*réparer* → *voiture, mécanisme*) to repair, to fix; **d. qn sur le bord de la route** to help sb who's broken down on the side of the road; **il m'a dépanné** he fixed the problem for me

2 Fam (*aider* → *gén*) to help out; (→ *financièrement*) to tide over, to bail out; **elle m'a dépanné en me prêtant sa voiture** she helped me out by lending me her car; **est-ce que 50 euros pourraient te d.?** would 50 euros bail you out *or* tide you over?; **est-ce que tu peux me d. de cinq euros?** can you give me five euros to bail me out?

USAGE ABSOLU nous dépannons 24 heures sur 24 we have a 24-hour breakdown service

dépanneur, -euse [depanœr, -øz] **NM,F** (*d'appareils*) repairman, f repairwoman; (*de véhicules*) breakdown mechanic

NM 1 Can (*magasin*) Br ≃ corner shop, Am ≃ convenience store **2** Ordinat troubleshooter

❑ **dépanneuse** NF *Br* breakdown lorry, *Am* tow truck

dépaquetage [depaktaʒ] NM unpacking, unwrapping

dépaqueter [27] [depakte] VT to unpack, to unwrap

▸**se dépaqueter** VPR *Can Joual* to sober up▪

déparaffinage [deparafinaʒ] NM paraffin extraction

déparasiter [3] [deparazite] VT *Électron & Rad* **1** *(débarrasser des parasites)* to eliminate the interference in **2** *(munir d'un dispositif antiparasite)* to fit with a suppressor

dépareillé, -e [depareje] ADJ **1** *(mal assorti → serviettes, chaussettes)* odd; **mes draps sont tous dépareillés** none of my sheets match; *Com* **articles dépareillés** oddments **2** *(incomplet → service, collection)* incomplete **3** *(isolé)* **un volume d. d'une collection** a single volume (that used to be part) of a collection **4** *Can (sans pareil)* **c'est un mari d.** he's a husband in a million

dépareiller [4] [depareje] VT **1** *(désassortir)* **d. des draps** to put unmatched *or* non-matching sheets together **2** *(ôter des éléments à)* to leave gaps in; **en cassant cette assiette, tu as dépareillé mon service de table** my dinner service is incomplete now that you've broken that plate

déparer [3] [depare] VT *(paysage)* to disfigure, to spoil, to be a blight on; *(visage)* to disfigure; **les fenêtres déparent la façade** the windows detract from the beauty of *or* spoil the façade; **un compact qui ne dépare pas ma collection** a CD well worthy of my collection; **le petit chapeau ne dépare pas du tout l'ensemble** the little hat goes very nicely with the rest

déparier [10] [deparje] VT **1** *(gants, chaussettes, chaussures)* to split **2** *(animaux)* to uncouple

déparler [3] [deparle] VI *Vieilli (dire n'importe quoi)* to rattle on

dépars *etc voir* **départir**

départ [depar] NM **1** *Transp* departure; **le d. du train est à 7 heures** the train leaves at 7 a.m.; **le d. est dans une heure** we're leaving in an hour; **départs grandes lignes** *(dans une gare)* mainline departures; **départs banlieue** suburban *or* local departures; **hall des départs** *Rail* (departure) concourse; *Aviat & Naut* departure lounge

2 *(fait de quitter un lieu)* departure, leaving; **on en a parlé après son d.** we discussed it after he/she left; **le d. de la navette spatiale** the launch of the space shuttle; **le d. du courrier a été retardé** the post was collected late; **les grands départs** = the mass exodus of people from Paris and other major cities at the beginning of the holiday period, especially in August; **le grand d.** the big departure; *Fig (la mort)* the final journey; **être sur le d.** to be ready to go

3 *(d'une course)* start; **donner le d. d'une course** to start a race, to give the signal to start a race; **12 chevaux/voitures/coureurs ont pris le d. (de la course)** there were 12 starters; **d. arrêté/lancé/décalé** standing/flying/staggered start; *Fig* **prendre un bon/mauvais d.** to get off to a good/bad start; **prendre un nouveau d. dans la vie** to make a fresh start in life, to turn over a new leaf

4 *(de son travail)* departure; *(démission)* resignation; **au d. du directeur** when the manager left *or* quit (the firm); **d. en préretraite** early retirement; **d. volontaire** voluntary redundancy

5 *(origine)* start, beginning; **au d.** at first, to begin with; **au d., je ne voulais pas qu'il le sache** at first *or* to begin with, I didn't want him to know

6 *Com* **d. entrepôt** ex warehouse; **d. usine** ex works; **prix d. usine** factory price, ex works price

7 *(d'un compte)* opening date

8 *(distinction)* distinction, separation, differentiation; **faire le d. entre** to draw a distinction between, to distinguish between; **une thèse où le d. n'a pas été bien fait entre causes et conséquences** a thesis which makes no attempt to distinguish *or* to differentiate between causes and effects

❑ **au départ de** PRÉP **visites au d. des Tuileries** tours departing from the Tuileries; **au d. du Caire, tout allait encore bien entre eux** when they left Cairo, everything was still fine between them

❑ **de départ** ADJ **1** *(gare, quai, heure)* departure *(avant n)*

2 *(initial)* **l'idée de d.** the initial *or* original idea; **prix de d.** *(dans une enchère)* upset *or* asking price; **salaire de d.** initial *or* starting salary

départager [17] [departaʒe] VT **1** *(séparer → ex æquo)* to decide between; **d. l'un de l'autre** to decide between one and the other **2** *Admin & Pol* **d. les votes** to settle the voting, to give the casting vote

département [departəmɑ̃] NM **1** *(du territoire français)* département, department; **les départements d'outre-mer** French overseas departments

2 *(service → d'une société)* department, service, division; *(→ d'une université)* department; *(→ d'un musée)* section; **le d. du contentieux** the legal department

3 *(ministère)* department, ministry; **d. ministériel** ministry; **le D. d'État** the State Department, the Department of State

4 *Suisse* = administrative authority in a Swiss canton

> *Culture*
>
> **DÉPARTEMENT**
>
> A "département" is the chief administrative division of France. There are 95 "départements" in metropolitan France and 4 overseas (Guadeloupe, Martinique, Guiana and Réunion) and each is administered by a "conseil général" and a "préfet". The number of the "département" corresponds to the first two figures in a postcode and the last two figures on a car registration number.

départemental, -e, -aux, -ales [departəmɑ̃tal, -o] ADJ **1** *(des départements français)* of the département, departmental **2** *(dans une entreprise, une organisation)* departmental, sectional **3** *(ministériel)* ministerial

❑ **départementale** NF *(route)* secondary road, *Br* ≃ B-road

départementalisation [departəmɑ̃talizasjɔ̃] NF *Admin* **1** *(d'un territoire d'entre-mer)* making into a département **2** *(d'un budget, d'une responsabilité)* devolving to the départements

départementaliser [3] [departəmɑ̃talize] VT *Admin* **1** *(territoire d'outre-mer)* to confer the statute of département on, to make into a département **2** *(budget, responsabilité)* to devolve to the départements

départir [32] [departir] VT *Littéraire (tâches)* to assign, to apportion; *(faveurs)* to distribute, to dispense, to deal out

▸**se départir** VPR **se d. de** to depart from, to abandon, to lose; **sans se d. de sa bonne humeur** without losing his/her good humour; **elle ne se départit pas de son calme** she remained unruffled; **il s'est départi de ses sarcasmes habituels** he abandoned his usual sarcasm

départiteur [departitœr] NM *Jur* **(juge) d.** arbitrator

dépassant [depasɑ̃] NM *Couture* piece of edging

dépassé, -e [depase] ADJ *(mentalité, technique)* outdated, old-fashioned; **c'est d. tout ça!** all that's old hat!; **tu es d., mon pauvre!** you're behind the times, my friend!

dépassement [depasmɑ̃] NM **1** *Aut Br* overtaking, *Am* passing

2 *(excès)* exceeding, excess; *Fin* **d. budgétaire** *ou* **de budget** overspending; **être en d. budgétaire** to be over budget; *Ordinat* **d. de capacité** overflow; **d. de coûts** cost overrun; *Fin* **d. de crédit** overspending; **il y a un d. de crédit de plusieurs millions** the budget has been exceeded by several million; **un d. d'horaire de 15 minutes** an overrun of 15 minutes

3 *(surpassement)* **d. (de soi-même)** surpassing oneself, transcending one's own capabilities

4 *Admin* = charging, by a medical practitioner, of more than the standard fee recognized by the social services; **pratiquer le d. d'honoraires** to charge more than will be reimbursed by Social Security

dépasser [3] [depase] VT **1** *(doubler → voiture) Br* to overtake, *Am* to pass; *(→ coureur)* to outrun, to outdistance; **se faire d.** *(en voiture)* to be overtaken

2 *(aller au-delà de → hôtel, panneau)* to pass, to go *or* to get past; *(→ piste d'atterrissage)* to overshoot; **attention de ne pas d. le tournant!** be careful you don't miss the turn-off!

3 *(être plus grand que)* to stand *or* to be taller than; **d. qch en hauteur** to be higher than sth; **notre immeuble dépasse les autres** our building stands higher *or* is taller than the others; **elle me dépasse d'une tête** she's a head taller than me

4 *(déborder sur)* to go over *or* beyond; **ne dépasse pas la ligne tracée par la maîtresse** don't go over the line drawn by the teacher; **il a dépassé son temps de parole** he talked longer than had been agreed, he went over time; **d. la date limite** to miss the deadline; **votre renommée dépasse les frontières** your fame has spread abroad

5 *(excéder)* to exceed, to go beyond; **ne pas d. la dose prescrite** *(sur mode d'emploi)* do not exceed the stated dose; **d. la limite de vitesse** to exceed the speed limit; **montants dépassant 500 euros** amounts in excess of *or* exceeding 500 euros; **les socialistes nous dépassent en nombre** the socialists outnumber us, we're outnumbered by the socialists; **l'exposé ne doit pas d. 20 minutes** the talk must not last longer than *or* exceed 20 minutes; **les ventes ont dépassé le chiffre de l'an dernier** sales figures have overtaken last year's; **d. le budget de 15 millions** to go 15 million over budget; **l'addition dépasse rarement 40 euros** the bill is seldom more than *or* seldom goes over 40 euros; **je n'ai pas dépassé 60 km/h** I did not exceed *or* I stayed below 60 km/h; **elle a dépassé la trentaine** she's turned thirty, she's over thirty; **ça dépasse mes moyens** it's beyond my means, it's more than I can afford

6 *(surpasser → adversaire)* to surpass, to do better than, to be ahead of; **elle veut d. sa sœur aînée** she wants to do better than her elder sister; **d. l'attente** *ou* **les espérances de qn** to surpass *or* to exceed sb's expectations; **cela dépasse tout ce que j'avais pu espérer** this is beyond all my hopes *or* my wildest dreams; **d. qn/qch en drôlerie/stupidité** to be funnier/more stupid than sb/sth; **ça dépasse tout ce que j'ai vu en vulgarité** for sheer vulgarity, it beats everything I've ever seen; **elle nous dépassait tous en musique** she was a far better musician than any of us

7 *(outrepasser → ordres, droits)* to go beyond, to overstep; **cela dépasse l'entendement** it is beyond comprehension; **la beauté des lieux dépasse l'imagination** the scene is beautiful beyond all imagination; **la tâche dépasse mes forces** the task is beyond me; **les mots ont dépassé ma pensée** I got carried away and said something I didn't mean; *Fam* **d. les limites** *ou* **la mesure** *ou* **les bornes** to go too far, to overstep the mark; *Fam* **cette fois, ça dépasse la mesure** *ou* **les bornes** this time it's gone too far

8 *(dérouter)* **être dépassé par les événements** to be overtaken *or* swamped by events; **une telle ignorance me dépasse** such ignorance defeats me; **les échecs, ça me dépasse!** chess is (quite) beyond me!

9 *(surmonter)* **avoir dépassé un stade/une phase** to have gone beyond a stage/a phase

VI **1** *Aut Br* to overtake, *Am* to pass; **interdiction de d.** *(panneau sur la route) Br* no overtaking, *Am* no passing

2 *(étagère, balcon, corniche)* to jut out, to protrude; **notre perron dépasse par rapport aux autres** our front steps stick out further than the others

3 *(chemisier, doublure)* to be hanging out, to be untucked; **ta combinaison dépasse** your slip's showing; **d. de** to be sticking out *or* protruding from/under; **pas une mèche ne dépassait de son chignon** her chignon was impeccable *or* hadn't a hair out of place; **un revolver dépassait de son sac** a gun was sticking out of his/her bag; **la doublure dépasse de** *ou* **sous la robe** the lining shows below the dress

▸**se dépasser** VPR **1** *(l'un l'autre)* to pass one another; **les voitures cherchent toutes à se d.** the cars are all jostling for position

2 *(se surpasser)* to surpass *or* to excel oneself

dépassionner [3] [depasjɔne] VT *(débat)* to take the heat out of, to calm *or* to cool down

dépatouiller [3] [depatuje] **se dépatouiller** VPR *Fam* to manage■, to get by■; **se d. d'une situation** to get out of *or* to wriggle one's way out of a situation; **qu'il se** *ou* **s'en dépatouille tout seul!** he can get out of this one by himself!

dépatrier [10] [depatrije] VT *Littéraire* to make stateless

dépavage [depavaʒ] NM **le d. des rues** removing the cobblestones from the streets

dépaver [3] [depave] VT to remove the cobblestones from

dépaysant, -e [depeizɑ̃, -ɑ̃t] ADJ **un voyage d.** a trip that gives you a complete change of scene

dépaysement [depeizmɑ̃] NM **1** *(changement de cadre)* change of scene *or* scenery; **un petit d. ne te ferait pas de mal** you could do with a change of scene; **à Moscou, on a une extraordinaire impression de d.** when you're in Moscow everything feels totally unfamiliar **2** *(malaise)* feeling of unfamiliarity; **les enfants n'aiment pas le d.** children don't like changes in environment

dépayser [3] [depeize] VT **1** *(changer de cadre)* to give a change of scenery *or* surroundings to; **mes vacances m'ont beaucoup dépaysé** my holiday provided a great change of scene; **laissez-vous d.** treat yourself to a change of scene *or* scenery

2 *(désorienter)* to disorientate; **se sentir dépaysé** to feel like a stranger; **on fait tout pour que le touriste ne soit pas dépaysé** we do everything possible to make the tourist feel at home

dépeçage [depəsaʒ], **dépècement** [depɛsmɑ̃] NM **1** *(de volaille)* cutting *or* carving up **2** *(d'un pays)* dismembering, carving up

dépecer [29] [depəse] VT **1** *(démembrer → proie)* to tear limb from limb; *(→ volaille)* to cut up **2** *(détruire → pays)* to dismember, to carve up

dépeceur, -euse [depəsœr, -øz] NM,F cutter-up; **d. (de baleines)** flenser; *Com* **d. d'entreprise** asset-stripper; **d. de gants** glove-cutter; **d. de vaisseaux** ship-breaker

dépêche [depɛʃ] NF **1** *Admin* dispatch; **d. diplomatique** diplomatic dispatch

2 *Tél* **d. (télégraphique)** telegram, wire; **envoyer une d. à qn** to wire *or* to telegraph sb

3 *(nouvelle)* news item *(sent through an agency)*; **une d. vient de nous arriver** a news item *or* some news has just reached us; **d. d'agence** agency copy

4 *Presse* **la D. du Midi** = daily newspaper published in Toulouse

dépêcher [4] [depeʃe] VT **1** *(enquêteur)* to send, to dispatch

2 *Arch ou Littéraire* **d. qn d'un coup d'épée** to dispatch sb *or* to put sb to death with the sword

▸**se dépêcher** VPR to hurry (up); **pas besoin de se d.** there's no (need to) hurry; **mais dépêche-toi donc!** come on, hurry up!; **se d. de faire qch** to hurry to do sth; **dépêche-toi de finir cette lettre** hurry up and finish that letter; **on s'est dépêchés de rentrer** we hurried home, we went back home in a hurry

dépeignait *etc* **1** *voir* **dépeindre 2** *voir* **dépeigner**

dépeigner [4] [depeɲe] VT **d. qn** to mess up *or* to muss *or* to ruffle sb's hair; **elle est toujours dépeignée** her hair's always untidy *or* dishevelled

dépeindre [81] [depɛ̃dr] VT to depict, to portray

dépenaillé, -e [depənaje] ADJ scruffy; **un mendiant tout d.** a beggar in rags

dépénalisation [depenalizasjɔ̃] NF decriminalization

dépénaliser [3] [depenalize] VT to decriminalize

dépendance [depɑ̃dɑ̃s] NF **1** *(rapport)* dependence

2 *(subordination)* dependence; **être dans** *ou* **sous la d. de qn** to be subordinate to sb; **vivre dans la d.** to be dependent, to lead a dependent life; **nous devrions diminuer notre d. économique/énergétique par rapport au nucléaire** we should reduce our dependence on the nuclear industry for our economic/energy needs

3 *(d'un drogué)* addiction

4 *(annexe)* outhouse, outbuilding

5 *(territoire)* dependency

6 *Ling* dependence

dépendant, -e [depɑ̃dɑ̃, -ɑ̃t] ADJ **1** *(lié, subordonné)* dependent; **être d. de qn/qch** to be dependent on sb/sth **2** *(drogué)* dependent (**de** on)

NM,F *Can Joual* dependent■

dépendeur [depɑ̃dœr] NM *Fam (locution)* **un (grand) d. d'andouilles** a lazy good-for-nothing

dépendre [73] [depɑ̃dr] VT *(décrocher → tableau, tapisserie)* to take down

▫ **dépendre de** VT IND **1** *(sujet: employé, service)* to be answerable to; **il dépend du chef de service** he's answerable *or* he reports to the departmental head; **nous dépendons du Ministère** we're answerable to the Ministry

2 *(sujet: propriété, domaine, territoire)* to be a dependency of, to belong to; **le parc dépend du château** the park is part of the castle property

3 *(financièrement)* to depend on *or* upon, to be dependent on; **d. (financièrement) de qn** to be financially dependent on *or* upon sb; **je ne dépends que de moi-même** I'm my own boss; **d. d'un pays pour le pétrole** to be dependent on a country for one's oil supply

4 *(sujet: décision, choix, résultat)* to depend on; **ça dépend de la couleur que tu veux** it depends on what shade you want; **notre avenir en dépend** our future depends *or* rests on it; **notre mariage dépend de sa décision** our marriage depends *or* hangs on his/her decision; **ça ne dépend pas que de moi** it's not entirely up to me; **ces événements ne dépendent pas de nous** such events are beyond our control; **ça dépend des fois** it depends

5 *(tournure impersonnelle)* **il dépend de toi que ce projet aboutisse** whether this project succeeds depends on *or* is up to you; **il dépend de toi de rester ou de partir** it's up to you whether you stay or not

USAGE ABSOLU **ça dépend!** it (all) depends!

dépens [depɑ̃] NMPL *Jur* costs; **être condamné aux d.** to be ordered to pay costs

▫ **aux dépens de** PRÉP at the expense of; **rire aux d. de qn** to laugh at sb's expense; **s'amuser aux d. de sa santé** to have a good time at the expense of one's health; **je l'ai appris à mes d.** I learnt it to my cost

dépense [depɑ̃s] NF **1** *(frais)* expense, expenditure; **occasionner de grosses dépenses** to entail a lot of expense; **c'est une grosse d.** it's a lot of money; **je ne peux pas me permettre cette d.** I can't afford to spend so much money; **faire des dépenses** to incur expenses; **faire trop de dépenses** to overspend; *Compta* **dépenses de caisse** cash expenditure; **dépenses en capital** capital expenditure *or* outlay; **dépenses de consommation** consumer spending; **dépenses courantes** current expenditure; **dépenses de création** above-the-line costs; **dépenses d'entretien** maintenance (costs); **dépenses d'équipement** capital expenditure; **dépenses de l'État** public spending, government spending; **dépenses d'exploitation** operating costs; **dépenses fiscales** tax expenditure; **dépenses de fonctionnement** operating costs; **dépenses globales** aggregate expenditure, aggregate spending; **dépenses d'infrastructure** social overhead capital; **dépenses d'investissement** capital expenditure; **dépenses des ménages** household expenditure; **dépenses publicitaires, dépenses de la publicité** publicity expenses; **dépenses publiques** public *or* government spending; **dépenses de santé** *(de l'État)* health expenditure; **dépenses sociales** welfare expenditure; *Écon & Fin* **dépenses et recettes** expenditure and income

2 *(fait de dépenser)* spending; **pousser qn à la d.** to push *or* to encourage sb to spend (money); **faire la d. de qch** to lay out *or* to spend money on sth; **regarder à la d.** to watch what one spends, to watch every penny; **ne regardez pas à la d.** spare no expense

3 *(consommation)* consumption; **d. physique** physical exertion; **d. de temps/d'énergie** expenditure of time/energy; **c'est une d. de temps inutile** it's a waste of time; **d. de carburant** fuel consumption

dépenser [3] [depɑ̃se] VT **1** *(argent)* to spend; **à quoi dépenses-tu ton argent?** what do you spend your money on?; **d. son salaire en cadeaux** to spend one's salary on gifts; **les enfants me font d. beaucoup d'argent** I spend a lot because of the children; **voilà de l'argent bien** *ou* **utilement dépensé** it's money well spent; **mal** *ou* **inutilement dépensé** wasted

2 *(consommer → mazout, essence)* to use

3 *(employer → temps)* to spend; *(→ énergie)* to expend; **d. toute son énergie/ses forces à faire qch** to use up all one's energy/one's strength in doing sth

USAGE ABSOLU **d. sans compter** to spend (money) lavishly *or* without counting the cost

▸**se dépenser** VPR **1** *(se défouler)* to let off steam; **il se dépense beaucoup physiquement** he uses up a lot of energy; **elle a besoin de se d.** she needs an outlet for her (pent-up) energy

2 *(se démener)* to expend a lot of energy, to work hard; **tu t'es beaucoup dépensé pour cette soirée** you've worked hard for (the success of) this party; **se d. en efforts inutiles** to waste one's energies in useless efforts; **se d. sans compter pour qch** to put all one's energies into sth, to give sth one's all

dépensier, -ère [depɑ̃sje, -ɛr] ADJ extravagant; **j'ai toujours été d.** I've always been a big spender, money has always slipped through my fingers

NM,F spendthrift; **un grand d.** a big spender

déperdition [depɛrdisjɔ̃] NF **1** *(de chaleur, de matière)* loss **2** *Littéraire (de volonté, d'enthousiasme)* fading, waning

dépérir [32] [deperir] VI *(malade)* to fade *or* to waste away; *(de tristesse)* to pine away; *(plante)* to wilt, to wither; *(industrie)* to decline

dépérissement [deperismɑ̃] NM **1** *(affaiblissement → d'un malade)* fading *or* wasting away; *(→ de tristesse)* pining away; *(→ d'une plante)* wilting, withering; *(déclin → d'une industrie)* decline **2** *Jur* **d. de preuves** loss of validity of evidence

déperlance [depɛrlɑ̃s] NF water-resistance

déperlant, -e [depɛrlɑ̃, -ɑ̃t] ADJ water-resistant

NM water-resistant material

dépersonnalisation [depɛrsɔnalizasjɔ̃] NF *(gén) & Psy* depersonalization

dépersonnaliser [3] [depɛrsɔnalize] VT *(gén) & Psy* to depersonalize

▸**se dépersonnaliser** VPR *(individu)* to become depersonalized, to lose one's personality; *(lieu, œuvre)* to become anonymous

dépêtrer [4] [depetre] VT **d. qn/qch de** to extricate sb/sth from; **d. qn d'une situation** to extricate sb from *or* to get sb out of a situation

▸**se dépêtrer** VPR **1 se d. de** *(de filets, de pièges)* to free oneself from; **le bouvreuil n'arrivait pas à se d. du filet** the bullfinch couldn't free itself from *or* find its way out of the net

2 se d. de *(d'un gêneur)* to shake off; *(d'une situation)* to get out of; **il nous a dit tant de mensonges qu'il ne peut plus s'en d.** he's told us so many lies that he can no longer extricate himself from them; **j'ai tant de dettes que je ne peux plus m'en d.** I have so many debts I don't even know how to start paying them off

dépeuplement [depœpləmɑ̃] NM **1** *(d'un pays, d'une région)* depopulation **2** *(désertion)* **le d. de la forêt** *(déboisement)* clearing *or* thinning (out) the forest; *(absence d'animaux)* the disappearance of animal life from the forest; **le d. des rivières** *(volontaire)* destocking the rivers; *(par la pollution)* the destruction of the fish stocks of the rivers

dépeupler [5] [depœple] VT **1** *(pays, région)* to depopulate

2 *(volontairement → étang)* to empty (of fish), to destock; *(→ forêt)* to clear (of trees), to thin out the trees of; *(involontairement → étang)* to kill off the fish stocks in; *(→ forêt)* to kill off the trees in

▸**se dépeupler** VPR **1** *(pays, région)* to become depopulated

2 *(rivière)* to lose its stock; *(forêt)* to thin out

3 *(salle, rues)* to empty

> *Allusion*
>
> **Un seul être vous manque et tout est dépeuplé**
>
> This immortal line is from Alphonse de Lamartine's poem *l'Isolement*, from *Méditations poétiques* of 1823, a chef-d'oeuvre of French Romantic poetry. It means "One single being is missing, and the world is empty." So very famous is this line that it lays itself open to infinite extension, and even parody. It can be used in any context, eg **Si vous êtes philatéliste, un seul timbre vous manque, et tout est dépeuplé** ("If you're a stamp collector, you only need to be short of one stamp for it to seem like the end of the world").

déphasage [defazaʒ] NM **1** *Élec* phase difference; **d. en avant** (phase) lead; **d. en arrière** lag **2** *(décalage)* difference; *Psy* loss of contact with reality, feeling of disconnectedness; **le d. entre le P-DG et le conseil d'administration est de plus en plus important** the chairman is getting increasingly out of touch with the board

déphasé, -e [defaze] ADJ **1** *Élec* out-of-phase; **d. en arrière** lagging; **d. en avant** leading **2** *(désorienté)* disorientated; **être d. par rapport à la réalité** to be out of touch with reality; **il est complètement d.** he is completely disorientated

déphaser [3] [defaze] VT **1** *Élec* to cause a phase difference in **2** *(désorienter)* **son séjour prolongé à l'hôpital l'a déphasé** his long stay in hospital made him lose touch with reality

déphaseur [defazœr] NM *Élec* phase splitter

déphosphatation [defɔsfatasjɔ̃] NF dephosphorization

déphosphater [3] [defɔsfate] VT to dephosphorize

déphosphoration [defɔsfɔrasjɔ̃] NF dephosphoration

déphosphorer [3] [defɔsfɔre] VT to dephosphorate

dépiauter [3] [depjote] VT *Fam* **1** *(enlever la peau de → lapin, poisson)* to skin, to take the skin off; *(→ fruit)* to peel **2** *(analyser)* **d. un texte** to dissect a text

dépicage [depikaʒ] = **dépiquage**

dépigeonnage [depiʒɔnaʒ] NM = control of the number of pigeons in urban areas

dépigmentation [depigmɑ̃tasjɔ̃] NF depigmentation, loss of pigmentation

dépilage[1] [depilaʒ] NM *(des peaux)* graining, depilation

dépilage[2] [depilaz] NM *Mines* removal of pit-props

dépilation [depilasjɔ̃] NF **1** *Méd* hair loss **2** *(épilation)* hair removal, removal of (unwanted) hair

dépilatoire [depilatwar] ADJ depilatory; *(crème)* hair-removing, depilatory

NM hair-removing *or* depilatory cream

dépiler [3] [depile] VT **1** *Méd* to cause hair loss to **2** *(cuirs, peaux)* to grain **3** *Mines* to remove pit-props from

dépiquage [depikaʒ] NM *Agr* threshing

dépiquer [3] [depike] VT **1** *(repiquer)* to transplant **2** *(égrener → blé)* to thresh; *(→ riz)* to hull **3** *Couture* to unstitch, to unpick

dépistage [depistaʒ] NM **1** *Méd* screening; **le d. du cancer** cancer screening; **le d. du sida** Aids testing; **d. précoce** early screening **2** *(recherche)* detection, unearthing; **l'auteur se livre à un travail de d. sur des documents historiques** the author is doing some detective work on historical documents **3** *Chasse* tracking down

dépister [3] [depiste] VT **1** *(criminel)* to track down; *(source, ruse)* to detect, to unearth **2** *Méd* to screen for; **des techniques pour d. le cancer** cancer screening techniques; **il a été dépisté séropositif** he tested HIV-positive **3** *Chasse (lièvre)* to track down; *(chien)* to put off the scent **4** *(perdre → poursuivant)* to throw off

dépit [depi] NM pique; **faire qch par d.** to do sth in a fit of pique *or* out of spite; **ressentir du d. contre qn** to be annoyed with sb; **j'en ai conçu un peu de d.** I was a little piqued *or* vexed at it; **j'en aurais pleuré de d.** I was so vexed I could have cried; **d. amoureux** heartache, unrequited love; **faire qch par d. amoureux** to do sth out of unrequited love; **se marier par d. amoureux** to marry on the rebound

▫ **en dépit de** PRÉP despite, in spite of; **faire qch en d. du bon sens** *(sans logique)* to do sth with no regard for common sense; *(n'importe comment)* to do sth any old how

dépité, -e [depite] ADJ (greatly) vexed, piqued

dépiter [3] [depite] VT to pique, to vex; **son refus m'a profondément dépité** I was greatly vexed *or* piqued at his/her refusal

▸**se dépiter** VPR *(concevoir du dépit)* to feel piqued

déplacé, -e [deplase] ADJ **1** *(malvenu → démarche, remarque, rire)* inappropriate; **sa présence était déplacée** his/her presence was uncalled-for **2** *(de mauvais goût → plaisanterie)* indelicate, shocking **3** *(personne)* displaced

déplacement [deplasmɑ̃] NM **1** *(mouvement)* moving, shifting; **le d. du piano n'a pas été facile** moving the piano wasn't easy; **le d. de l'aiguille sur le cadran** the movement of the hands around the clock face; **le d. à gauche de l'électorat** the swing to the left by the electorate; **d. d'air** displacement of air; *Ordinat* **d. du curseur** cursor movement; *Ordinat* **d. entre fichiers** movement between files

2 *(sortie)* moving about; *(voyage d'affaires)* (business) trip; **Josie me remplace pendant mes déplacements** Josie steps in for me when I'm away on business; **le docteur m'a interdit tout d.** the doctor said I mustn't move about; **merci d'avoir fait le d.** thanks for coming all this way; *Fam* **joli panorama, ça vaut le d.!** what a lovely view, it's definitely worth going out of your way to see it!; **la soirée ne valait pas le d.** the party wasn't worth going to

3 *(mutation → d'un employé)* transfer; **d. d'office** transfer

4 *Naut* displacement; **navire de 15 000 tonnes de d.** ship with a 15,000-ton displacement; **d. en charge** displacement loaded, load displacement

5 *Méd* displacement; **d. d'organe** organ displacement; **d. de vertèbre** slipped disc

6 *Psy* displacement

7 *Chim & Phys* displacement

8 *Biol* translocation

9 *Fin (de fonds)* movement

▫ **de déplacement** ADJ **1** *Transp* **moyen de d.** means *or* mode of transport

2 *Psy* displacement *(avant n)*

▫ **en déplacement** ADV away; *Sport* **Bordeaux est en d. à Marseille** Bordeaux are playing away against Marseilles; **la directrice est en d.** the manager's away (on business); **envoyer qn en d.** to send sb away on a business trip

déplacer [16] [deplase] VT **1** *(objet, pion, voiture)* to move, to shift; **déplace-le vers la droite** move *or* shift it to the right; *Fam Hum* **d. de l'air** *(en parlant)* to talk big *or* a lot of hot air; **la délégation déplaçait beaucoup d'air** the delegation looked as though it was taking itself very seriously indeed

2 *(élève, passager)* to move; *(population)* to displace

3 *(infléchir)* **d. la discussion** to shift the emphasis of the discussion; **ne déplacez pas le problème** *ou* **la question** don't change the question

4 *Méd (os)* to displace, to put out of joint; *(vertèbre)* to slip

5 *(muter → fonctionnaire)* to transfer; **d. qn par mesure disciplinaire** to transfer sb for disciplinary reasons

6 *(faire venir → médecin, dépanneur)* to send for; **ils ont déplacé l'ambulance pour cela?** did they really get the ambulance out for that?; **son concert a déplacé des foules** crowds flocked to his concert; **on avait déplacé des sommités** experts had been summoned

7 *(dans le temps → festival, rendez-vous)* to change, to shift, to move; **d. une date** *(l'avancer)* to move a date forward; *(la reculer)* to put back a date

8 *Chim & Phys* to displace

9 *Biol* to translocate

10 *Naut* to have a displacement of

11 *Mil* **d. le tir** to shift fire

12 *Pol* **d. des voix (en faveur de)** to shift votes (towards)

13 *Fin (fonds)* to move

▸**se déplacer** VPR **1** *(masse d'air, nuages)* to move, *Spéc* to be displaced; *(aiguille d'horloge)* to move

2 *(marcher)* to move about *or* around, to get about *or* around; **se d. à l'aide de béquilles** to get about on crutches; **ne pas se d. pendant le spectacle** do not move around during the show; **avec notre messagerie, faites vos courses sans vous d.** do your shopping from home with our Teletext service; *Fam* **cela ne vaut pas/vaut le coup de se d.** it's not worth/it's worth the trip

3 *(voyager)* to travel, to get about; **je me déplace beaucoup pour mon travail** I travel a lot in my job, my job involves a lot of travelling

4 se d. une vertèbre to slip a disc

déplafonnement [deplafɔnmɑ̃] NM **d. des cotisations** removal of the upper limit for contributions

déplafonner [3] [deplafɔne] VT to raise the ceiling on, to remove the upper limit for; *Fin* **d. un crédit** to raise the ceiling on a credit, to raise a credit limit

déplaire [110] [deplɛr] **déplaire à** VT IND **1** *(rebuter)* to put off; **son attitude m'a (souverainement) déplu** his/her attitude put me off (completely), I didn't like his/her attitude (at all); **il m'a tout de suite déplu** I took an instant dislike to him; **je lui déplais tant que ça?** does he/she dislike me as much as that?; **un café? voilà qui ne me déplairait pas** *ou* **ne serait pas pour me d.** a coffee? I wouldn't say no!; **il m'a parlé franchement, ce qui n'a pas été pour me d.** he was frank with me, which I liked; **il ne lui déplairait pas de vivre à la campagne** he/she wouldn't object to living in the country; *Littéraire* **il me déplaît d'avoir à vous dire ceci, mais…** I hate *or* I don't like having to tell you this but…

2 *(contrarier)* to annoy, to offend; **ce que je vais dire risque de vous d.** I'm afraid you may not like what I'm going to say; *Littéraire ou Hum* **ne vous (en) déplaise** whether you like it or not; **n'en déplaise à Votre Majesté** may it please your Majesty; **n'en déplaise aux libéraux** whatever the liberals may say

▸**se déplaire** VPR **1** *(ne pas se plaire l'un à l'autre)* to dislike each other *or* one another

2 *(être mal à l'aise)* to be unhappy *or* dissatisfied; **ils se sont déplu chez leur tante** they disliked staying with their aunt, they were unhappy at their aunt's; **je ne me suis pas déplu ici** I quite enjoyed *or* liked it here

déplaisant, -e [deplɛzɑ̃, -ɑ̃t] ADJ **1** *(goût, odeur, atmosphère)* unpleasant, nasty; **une déplaisante odeur de gaz** an unpleasant smell of gas **2** *(personne, comportement)* unpleasant, offensive; **une remarque déplaisante** an offensive *or* unpleasant remark; **cette surveillance est assez déplaisante** being watched like this is rather unpleasant

déplaisir [deplezir] NM **1** *Littéraire (tristesse)* unhappiness

2 *(mécontentement)* displeasure, disapproval; **elle me verrait sans d. accepter** she'd be quite pleased if I accepted; **je fais les corvées ménagères sans d.** I don't mind doing the housework; **ils constatèrent sa présence avec un vif d.** they were most displeased to see him/her; **à mon grand d.** much to my chagrin; **on ne lui a pas permis de donner son avis, à son grand d.** he/she was most put out that he/she wasn't allowed to give his/her opinion

déplaisons *etc voir* **déplaire**

de plano [deplano] ADV de plano, informally

déplantage [deplɑ̃taʒ] NM **le d. des arbustes** taking up *or* removing *or* uprooting the shrubs; **le d. de la forêt** clearing the forest

déplantation [deplɑ̃tasjɔ̃] NF **la d. des arbustes** taking up *or* removing *or* uprooting the shrubs; **la d. de la forêt** clearing the forest

déplanter [3] [deplɑ̃te] VT *(arbuste)* to uproot, to take up; *(forêt)* to clear; *(jardin)* to clear (of plants), to remove the plants from; *(piquet)* to dig out, to remove

déplantoir [deplɑ̃twar] NM hand-fork

déplâtrage [deplatraʒ] NM **1** *Constr* removal of the plaster; **le d. d'un mur** stripping the plaster off a wall **2** *Méd* removal of the plaster cast

déplâtrer [3] [deplatre] VT **1** *Constr* to strip of

plaster, to remove the plaster from **2** *Méd* to take out of a plaster cast; **on le déplâtre demain** his plaster cast comes off tomorrow

déplétion [deplesjɔ̃] NF *Chim & Physiol* depletion

dépliage [deplijaʒ] NM unfolding, spreading out

dépliant, -e [deplijɑ̃, -ɑ̃t] ADJ folding
NM **1** *(brochure)* brochure, leaflet; **d. publicitaire** advertising leaflet; **d. touristique** travel brochure **2** *Typ* foldout (page)

dépliement [deplimɑ̃] NM unfolding, spreading out

déplier [9] [deplije] VT **1** *(journal, lettre)* to open out *or* up, to unfold; *(mouchoir)* to unfold; **d. une pièce de tissu** to spread a cloth out; **dépliant ses dentelles devant les clientes** spreading his pieces of lace before the customers
2 *(bras, jambes)* to stretch; **d. bras et jambes avant de se lever** to stretch one's arms and legs before getting up; **les rangées étaient si serrées que je ne pouvais d. mes jambes** the rows of seats were so close (together) that I couldn't stretch my legs
3 *(mètre pliant, canapé)* to open out
▸**se déplier** VPR **1** *(document)* to unfold, to open out; **les cartes routières ne se déplient pas facilement** roadmaps aren't very easy to unfold
2 *(canapé, mètre pliant)* to open out; **un canapé qui se déplie** a foldaway sofa-bed

déplissage [deplisaʒ] NM **1** *(d'un tissu plissé)* unpleating **2** *(défroissage)* smoothing out

déplisser [3] [deplise] VT **1** *(vêtement plissé)* to unpleat; **d. une jupe** to take the pleats out of a skirt **2** *(défriper)* to smooth out; **d. une écharpe au fer** to iron the creases out of a scarf
▸**se déplisser** VPR *(vêtement plissé)* to come unpleated, to lose its pleats

déploguer [3] [deplɔge] *Can Joual* VT to unplug■
VI to take the plug out■

déploie *etc voir* **déployer**

déploiement [deplwamɑ̃] NM **1** *(des ailes d'un oiseau)* spreading out, unfolding; *(d'un drapeau, des voiles)* unfurling
2 *Mil* deployment; **un grand d.** *ou* **tout un d. de police** a large deployment of police; **d. en éventail** fan-shaped deployment; **d. en tirailleurs** deployment in extended order
3 *(manifestation)* **d. de** show *or* demonstration *or* display of; **un brillant d. d'érudition** a brilliant display *or* show of erudition; **un grand d. de force** a great show of strength; **un d. d'affection** a display of affection; *Péj* a gush of affection

déplombage [deplɔ̃baʒ] NM **1** *(d'une dent)* removing the filling (**de** from) **2** *(ouverture)* removal of the seal *or* seals; **la douane a procédé au d. des wagons** the customs officials proceeded to remove the seals from the trucks **3** *Ordinat* cracking

déplomber [3] [deplɔ̃be] VT **1** *(dent)* to remove the filling from **2** *(ouvrir)* to take the seals off, to remove the seals from **3** *Ordinat* to crack

déplorable [deplɔrabl] ADJ **1** *(regrettable)* deplorable, regrettable, lamentable **2** *(mauvais → résultat)* appalling; *(→ plaisanterie)* awful, terrible, appalling; **elle s'habille avec un goût d.** she dresses with appallingly bad taste

déplorablement [deplɔrabləmɑ̃] ADV deplorably, lamentably

déploration [deplɔrasjɔ̃] NF **1** *Mus* lament **2** *Beaux-Arts* **D. du Christ** Pietà **3** *Littéraire & Rel* lamentation, lament

déplorer [3] [deplɔre] VT **1** *(regretter)* to object to, to regret, to deplore; **nous déplorons cet incident** we regret this incident; **je déplore que vous n'ayez pas compris** I find it regrettable that you didn't understand; **on déplore que l'auteur n'ait pas eu plus souvent recours à l'autocensure** it is to be regretted that the author did not exercise self-censorship more often; **il est à d. que vous ayez eu cette conduite** your behaviour was regrettable
2 *(constater)* **nous n'avons eu que peu de dégâts à d.** fortunately, we suffered only slight damage; **on ne déplore que deux blessés légers** fortunately, only two people were slightly injured; **on déplore la mort d'une petite fille dans l'accident** sadly, a little girl was killed in the accident
3 *Littéraire (pleurer sur)* to lament *or* to mourn

for; **d. le départ de qn** to mourn sb's departure; **d. la mort d'un ami** to grieve over the death of a friend

déployer [13] [deplwaje] VT **1** *(déplier)* to spread out, to unfold, to unroll; *Naut* **d. les voiles** to unfurl *or* to extend the sails
2 *(faire montre de)* to display, to exhibit; **d. un luxe impressionnant** to indulge in a great display of luxury; **elle a déployé toute son éloquence** she brought all her eloquence to bear; **il m'a fallu d. des trésors de persuasion auprès d'elle** I had to work very hard at persuading her
3 *Mil* to deploy
▸**se déployer** VPR **1** *Naut* to unfurl
2 *(foule)* to extend, to stretch out
3 *Mil* to be deployed

déplu, -e [deply] PP *voir* **déplaire**

déplumé, -e [deplyme] ADJ **1** *(sans plumes)* moulting; **des tourterelles déplumées** turtledoves that have lost their feathers **2** *Fam (chauve)* bald■, balding■; **un nounours tout d.** a balding teddy-bear

déplumer [3] [deplyme] **se déplumer** VPR **1** *(perdre ses plumes)* to lose *or* to drop its feathers; **un vieux chapeau qui se déplume** an old hat that's losing its feathers **2** *Fam (devenir chauve)* **il** *ou* **son crâne se déplume** he's going bald *or* thinning on top■

déplut *etc voir* **déplaire**

dépoétiser [3] [depɔetize] VT to depoetize, to deprive of its poetic character

dépogner [3] [depɔɲe] **se dépogner** VPR *Can Fam* to chill out

dépointer [3] [depwɛ̃te] VT **1** *(arme)* to move *or* to point away from the target **2** *TV* to point away from its best reception position
▸**se dépointer** VPR **1** *(d'une arme)* to move away from the *or* off target **2** *TV* to move away from its best reception position

dépoitraillé, -e [depwatraje] ADJ *Fam Péj* barechested■; **tout d.** with his shirt open almost down to his navel

dépolarisant, -e [depɔlarizɑ̃, -ɑ̃t] ADJ depolarizing
NM depolarizer

dépolarisation [depɔlarizasjɔ̃] NF depolarization

dépolariser [3] [depɔlarize] VT to depolarize

dépoli, -e [depɔli] ADJ frosted, ground
NM **1** *(verre)* ground glass **2** *Phot* focusing screen

dépolir [32] [depɔlir] VT *(surface)* to dull, to tarnish; *(verre)* to frost, to grind
▸**se dépolir** VPR to lose its shine, to become tarnished

dépolissage [depɔlisaʒ], **dépolissement** [depɔlismɑ̃] NM *(du verre)* frosting, grinding

dépolitisation [depɔlitizasjɔ̃] NF *(d'une personne, d'un thème)* depoliticization

dépolitiser [3] [depɔlitize] VT to depoliticize; **faut-il d. le sport?** should politics be kept out of sport?

dépolluant, -e [depɔlɥɑ̃, -ɑ̃t] ADJ depolluting
NM depolluting agent

dépolluer [7] [depɔlɥe] VT to cleanse, to clean up; **d. les plages** to clean up the beaches

dépollution [depɔlysjɔ̃] NF cleaning up, decontamination; **d. de l'eau** water purification

dépolymérisation [depɔlimerizasjɔ̃] NF *Chim* depolymerization

dépolymériser [3] [depɔlimerize] VT *Chim* to depolymerize

dépondre [75] [depɔ̃dr] *Suisse* VT to separate
▸**se dépondre** VPR to come loose

déponent, -e [depɔnɑ̃, -ɑ̃t] *Gram* ADJ deponent
NM deponent verb

dépopulation [depɔpylasjɔ̃] NF depopulation

déport [depɔr] NM **1** *Tél* radar data, transmission **2** *Bourse & Fin* backwardation

déportation [depɔrtasjɔ̃] NF **1** *(exil)* transportation, deportation **2** *Hist (en camp de concentration)* deportation, internment; **pendant mes années de d.** during my years in a concentration camp; **mort en d.** *(sur plaque)* died in Nazi concentration camp **3** *Hist & Jur (peine)* deportation

déporté, -e [depɔrte] NM,F **1** *(prisonnier)* deportee, internee **2** *Hist (en camp de concentration)* concentration camp prisoner **3** *Hist & Jur* convict *(sentenced to deportation)*

déportement [depɔrtəmɑ̃] NM *(embardée)* swerve, swerving
❑ **déportements** NMPL *Littéraire* misbehaviour, misconduct

déporter [3] [depɔrte] VT **1** *(prisonnier)* to transport, to deport **2** *Hist (dans un camp de concentration)* to deport, to send to a concentration camp **3** *Hist & Jur* to deport **4** *(déplacer)* **la voiture a été déportée sur la gauche** the car swerved to the left
▸**se déporter** VPR *(doucement)* to move aside; *(brusquement)* to swerve; **se d. vers la droite/gauche** to veer (off) to the right/left

déposant, -e [depozɑ̃, -ɑ̃t] NM,F **1** *Banque* depositor **2** *Jur* deponent, witness **3** *(d'un brevet, d'une marque)* applicant

dépose [depoz] NF removal; **d. gratuite de vos anciens appareils** your old appliances removed free of charge

déposé, -e [depoze] ADJ *(marque, nom)* registered

déposer [3] [depoze] VT **1** *(poser → gén)* to lay *or* to put down; **d. un bébé dans un landau** to lay a baby down in a *Br* pram *or Am* baby carriage; **d. un bébé dans une poussette** to put *or* to sit a baby in a *Br* pushchair *or Am* stroller
2 *(laisser → gerbe)* to lay; *(→ objet livré)* to leave, to drop off; *(→ valise)* to leave; **quelqu'un a déposé une lettre pour vous** somebody left a letter for you
3 *(faire descendre d'un véhicule)* to drop (off); *(décharger → matériel)* to unload, to set down; **je te dépose?** can I drop you off?, can I give you a lift?; **le car a déposé le matériel près de la plage** the coach unloaded the equipment near the beach
4 *(argent, valeurs)* to deposit; **d. de l'argent en banque** to deposit money with a bank; **d. de l'argent sur son compte** to pay money into one's account; **d. des titres en garde** to deposit securities in safe custody; **d. une caution** to leave a deposit
5 *Admin* **d. son bilan** to file for bankruptcy, to go into (voluntary) liquidation; **d. un brevet** to file a patent application, to apply for a patent; **d. sa candidature** to apply; **d. une plainte (contre qn)** to lodge a complaint (against sb); **d. un projet de loi** to introduce *or* to table a bill
6 *(destituer → roi)* to depose
7 *Littéraire (donner)* **d. un baiser sur le front de qn** to kiss sb's forehead gently
8 *(démonter → radiateur, étagère)* to remove; *(tapis, moquette)* to lift, to take up
9 *(laisser s'accumuler → limon, sédiments)* to deposit
VI **1** *Jur* to give evidence, to testify
2 *Chim* to form a deposit, to scale
3 *(en œnologie)* to settle, to form a sediment
▸**se déposer** VPR to settle

dépositaire [depoziter] NMF **1** *Jur* depositary, trustee; **être le d. d'une lettre** to hold a letter in trust; **il n'est que le d. de la fortune de son frère** he is merely the trustee of his brother's fortune; **d. de valeurs** holder of securities on trust
2 *Com (de produits)* agent; **d. agréé** authorized agent; **d. exclusif** sole agent; **d. d'une marque** agent for a brand; **d. de journaux** newsagent
3 *Admin* **d. de l'autorité publique** = officer of the State; **d. public** = government official with responsibility for the management of public funds
4 *Littéraire (confident)* repository; **faire de qn le d. d'un secret** to entrust sb with a secret

déposition [depozisjɔ̃] NF **1** *(témoignage)* deposition, evidence, statement; **faire une d.** to testify; **recueillir une d.** to take a statement **2** *(destitution → d'un roi)* deposition **3** *Beaux-Arts* **D. (de Croix)** Deposition

dépositionner [3] [depozisjɔne] VT *Mktg* to deposition

déposséder [18] [deposede] VT to dispossess; **sa famille a été dépossédée** his/her family was stripped of all its possessions; **d. qn de** to deprive sb of

dépossession [deposesjɔ̃] NF deprivation, dispossessing; *Jur* **d. illicite** ouster

dépôt [depo] NM **1** *(remise → d'un rapport)* handing in, submission; *(→ d'un paquet, d'un télégramme)* handing in
2 *(pose → d'une gerbe)* laying

3 *Admin (inscription)* application, filing; *(enregistrement)* filing, registration; **d. d'une liste électorale** presentation of a list of candidates; **d. de bilan** petition in bankruptcy; **d. de brevet** patent registration; **d. légal** copyright deposit *(in France, copies of published or recorded documents have to be deposited at the Bibliothèque nationale)*; **numéro de d. légal** book number; **d. d'une marque** registration of a trademark; **d. d'une plainte** lodging of a complaint; **d. d'un projet de loi** introduction *or* tabling of a Bill

4 *Fin (démarche)* depositing; *(somme)* deposit; **faire un d.** to make a deposit; **d. bancaire** bank deposit; **d. en coffre-fort** safe-deposit; **d. à échéance fixe** fixed deposit; **d. d'espèces** cash deposit; **d. fiduciaire** escrow; *Bourse* **d. de garantie** margin deposit; **d. interbancaire** interbank deposit; **d. à terme** short-term deposit; **d. à terme fixe** fixed deposit; **d. à vue** demand *or* sight deposit

5 *Géol* deposit; **d. alluvial/de cendres/de carbone** alluvial/ash/carbon deposit; **d. glaciaire** glacial drift

6 *(couche)* layer; *(sédiment)* deposit, sediment; **d. calcaire** *ou* **de tartre** *(dans une bouilloire, un chauffe-eau)* layer of scale *or* fur; **d. marin** silt; **d. de poussière** layer of dust

7 *(en œnologie)* sediment

8 *Métal* depositing, deposition; **d. de cuivre** copperfoiling; **d. électrolytique** electrodeposition; **d. métallique** sputtering

9 *(entrepôt)* store, depot; **d. des machines** engine house; **d. de charbon** coal depot; **d. de distribution** distribution depot; **d. d'expédition** shipping depot; **d. de marchandises** goods depot, warehouse; **d. de matériel** storage yard; **d. mortuaire** mortuary; **d. d'ordures** *Br* rubbish dump *or* tip, *Am* garbage dump

10 *Mil* depot; **d. de munitions** ammunition dump; **d. de vivres** supply dump, *Am* commissary

11 *Transp* depot, *Am* station

12 *(boutique)* retail outlet; **d. de pain** ≃ bread shop; **l'épicier fait d. de pain** the grocer sells bread

13 *(prison)* (police) cells *(in Paris)*; **au d.** in the cells; **écroué au d.** committed to the cells

❑ **en dépôt** ADV *Fin* in trust, in safe custody; **confier qch en d. à qn** to entrust sb with sth; **avoir en d.** to have on bond; **mettre en d.** to bond

dépotage [depɔtaʒ], **dépotement** [depɔtmɑ̃] NM **1** *Hort* transplanting **2** *Chim* decanting **3** *(vidage)* discharging, dumping

dépoter [3] [depɔte] VT **1** *Hort* to plant out, to transplant **2** *Chim* to decant **3** *(vider)* to discharge, to dump

dépotoir [depɔtwar] NM **1** *(décharge)* dump; *(usine)* disposal plant, sewage works

2 *Péj (lieu sale)* pigsty; **ta chambre est un vrai d.** your bedroom's a complete pigsty; **il faut empêcher la Manche de devenir un d.** we must prevent the Channel becoming an open sewer

3 *Fam (débarras)* dumping ground; **l'enseignement technique ne doit pas devenir un d.** vocational schools must not be used as dumping grounds

dépôt-vente [depovɑ̃t] *(pl* **dépôts-ventes***)* NM = second-hand shop which gives the original owner a percentage of the profits on goods sold, *Am* consignment store; **mettre qch en d.** to put sth *Br* on sale or return *or Am* on consignment

dépouille [depuj] NF **1** *(cadavre)* **d. (mortelle)** (mortal) remains; **les dépouilles des victimes ont été rapatriées hier** the bodies of the victims were repatriated yesterday **2** *(peau → d'un mammifère)* hide, skin; *(→ d'un reptile)* slough **3** *Tech* clearance **4** *Métal* draft, draw

❑ **dépouilles** NFPL *(trophée)* booty, plunder, spoils

dépouillé, -e [depuje] ADJ **1** *(sans peau)* skinned; *(sans feuilles)* bare, leafless **2** *(sans ornement)* plain, simple, uncluttered; **un style d.** a concise *or* terse style **3** *(dénué)* **d. de** lacking in **4 vin d.** = wine that has lost its alcohol content

dépouillement [depujmɑ̃] NM **1** *(analyse)* breakdown, collection and analysis; **d. des données** data reduction; **d. du scrutin** tally *or* counting of the votes

2 *(ouverture → du courrier)* opening; *(→ d'appels d'offres)* checking

3 *(simplicité → d'un décor)* bareness, soberness

4 *(concision)* conciseness, terseness

5 *(dénuement)* dispossession, destitution; **ils ont choisi de vivre dans le d. le plus complet** they chose to live an ascetic life

dépouiller [3] [depuje] VT **1** *(lapin)* to skin

2 *(câble)* to strip; **la bise a dépouillé les arbres de leurs feuilles** the north wind has stripped the trees bare *or* of their leaves

3 *(voler)* to rob; **d. un héritier** to deprive *or* rob an heir of his inheritance; **d. qn de qch** *(terres, droits)* to deprive *or* dispossess sb of sth; **d. qn de ses droits** to strip sb of his/her rights; **ils m'ont dépouillé de tout ce que j'avais sur moi** they stripped me of *or* took everything I had on me; **il s'est fait d. de tout ce qu'il avait sur lui** he was robbed of everything he was carrying

4 *(priver)* **dans le film, le personnage est dépouillé de tout son charme** all the character's charm is lost in the *Br* film *or Am* movie

5 *(lire → journal, courrier, inventaire)* to go through; *(analyser → questionnaire, réponses)* to analyse, to study, to scrutinize; *(→ données)* to process; *(→ appels d'offres)* to check; *Pol* **d. le scrutin** to count the votes

6 *(quitter)* to cast aside, to strip off; **d. ses vêtements** to throw off *or* to strip off one's clothes; *Zool* **les reptiles dépouillent leur peau** reptiles slough off *or* shed their skin

▶**se dépouiller** VPR **1** *(arbre, végétation)* **les arbres se dépouillent peu à peu** the trees are gradually losing *or* shedding their leaves

2 *Zool* to slough off its skin

3 **se d. de** *(se défaire de)* to rid oneself of; **se d. de ses vêtements** to strip off; **se d. de tous ses biens** to give away all one's property

4 *Littéraire* **se d. de** *(se départir de)* to cast off; **il ne s'est pas dépouillé un seul instant de son arrogance** he didn't depart from his arrogant attitude for a single moment

dépourvu, -e [depurvy] ADJ **1** *(misérable)* destitute

2 *(manquant)* **d. de** devoid of, lacking in; **c'est d. de tout intérêt** it is of *or* holds no interest at all; **chambre dépourvue de confort** room lacking in comfort; **totalement d. de scrupules** totally unscrupulous; **sa remarque n'était pas entièrement dépourvue de bon sens** his/her remark was not entirely devoid of common sense; **un décor monotone d. d'arbres** a drab treeless landscape

❑ **au dépourvu** ADV **prendre qn au d.** to catch sb off guard *or* unawares; **ils ont été pris au d. par cette information** the news caught them unawares

dépoussiérage [depusjeraʒ] NM dusting

dépoussiérant, -e [depusjerɑ̃, -ɑ̃t] ADJ dust-removing; **filtre d.** dust filter

NM dust remover

dépoussiérer [18] [depusjere] VT **1** *(nettoyer)* to dust **2** *(rajeunir)* to rejuvenate, to give a new lease of life to

dépoussiéreur [depusjerœr] NM **d. électrostatique** electrostatic dust precipitator

dépravant, -e [depravɑ̃, -ɑ̃t] ADJ depraving

dépravation [depravasjɔ̃] NF depravity, perversion, perverseness

dépravé, -e [deprave] ADJ immoral, depraved, perverted

NM,F degenerate, pervert

dépraver [3] [deprave] VT **1** *(corrompre)* to deprave, to corrupt, to pervert **2** *Littéraire (altérer → goût, jugement)* to corrupt, to spoil

▶**se dépraver** VPR to become depraved *or* perverted

déprécation [deprekasjɔ̃] NF *Rel* **1** *(pour détourner un malheur)* prayer for the averting of *or* deliverance from evil *or* disaster, deprecation **2** *(pour demander pardon)* prayer for forgiveness, *Vieilli* deprecation

dépréciateur, -trice [depresjatœr, -tris] ADJ disparaging, deprecatory, depreciative

NM,F depreciator, disparager

dépréciatif, -ive [depresjatif, -iv] ADJ derogatory, disparaging

dépréciation [depresjasjɔ̃] NF depreciation, drop *or* fall in value; **la d. des propriétés foncières** the drop in property values; *Compta* **d. annuelle** annual depreciation; **d. de créances** write-down of accounts receivable; *Compta* **d. fonctionnelle** *(du matériel)* wear and tear

dépréciative [depresjativ] *voir* **dépréciatif**

dépréciatrice [depresjatris] *voir* **dépréciateur**

déprécié, -e [depresje] ADJ *(monnaie)* depreciated

déprécier [9] [depresje] VT **1** *Fin* to depreciate, to cause to drop in value **2** *(dénigrer)* to run down, to belittle, to disparage **3** *(mal évaluer)* to undervalue

▶**se déprécier** VPR **1** *(se déconsidérer)* to belittle *or* to disparage oneself, to run oneself down **2** *Fin* to depreciate, to fall in value

déprédateur, -trice [depredatœr, -tris] ADJ plundering, *Sout* depredatory

NM,F *(pilleur)* plunderer, *Sout* depredator; *(escroc)* swindler, embezzler

déprédation [depredasjɔ̃] NF **1** *(pillage)* pillaging; *(dégâts)* (wilful) damage; **commettre des déprédations sur qch** to cause wilful damage to sth **2** *(détournement)* **d. de biens** misappropriation of property; **d. des finances publiques** embezzlement of public funds

déprédatrice [depredatris] *voir* **déprédateur**

déprendre [79] [deprɑ̃dr] **se déprendre** VPR *Littéraire* **se d. de** to give up; **il lui a été difficile de se d. de sa façon de vivre** he/she found it difficult to give up his/her old way of life; **se d. de qn** to fall out of love with sb

dépresseur [depresœr] NM *Méd* depressant

dépressif, -ive [depresif, -iv] ADJ *(personne)* depressive, easily depressed; *(caractère)* depressive; **avoir des tendances dépressives** to be depressive

NM,F depressive

dépression [depresjɔ̃] NF **1** *Méd & Psy* depression; **d. nerveuse** nervous breakdown; **avoir** *ou* **faire une d. (nerveuse)** to have a nervous breakdown; **tu ne vas pas nous faire une d., au moins?** you're not going to get depressed, are you?; **d. hivernale** seasonal affective disorder, SAD

2 *Géog* depression

3 *(absence de pression)* vacuum; *(différence de pression)* suction

4 *Météo* cyclone, barometric depression, low

5 *Écon* depression, slump

dépressionnaire [depresjɔnɛr] ADJ **1** *Écon* slump *(avant n)*; **le marché a des tendances dépressionnaires** the market's sliding towards a slump **2** *Météo* low pressure *(avant n)*; **zone d.** area of low pressure

dépressive [depresiv] *voir* **dépressif**

dépressurisation [depresyrizasjɔ̃] NF depressurization

dépressuriser [3] [depresyrize] VT to depressurize

déprimant, -e [deprimɑ̃, -ɑ̃t] ADJ *(démoralisant)* depressing, disheartening, demoralizing

NM *Mines* wetting agent

déprime [deprim] NF **1** *Fam* **faire une d.** to be depressed; **tu ne vas pas nous faire une d. pour si peu?** you're not going to get depressed over such a small thing?; **avoir un (petit) coup de d.** to be (a bit) depressed; **il est en pleine d.** he's really down at the moment **2** *Écon* depression; **la d. des ménages** consumer depression; **la d. des agriculteurs** depression in the farming community

déprimé, -e [deprime] ADJ **1** *(abattu)* dejected, depressed; **je suis plutôt d. aujourd'hui** I feel rather down today **2** *(aplati)* depressed, flattened **3** *Bourse (marché)* depressed

déprimer [3] [deprime] VT **1** *(abattre)* to depress, to demoralize **2** *(enfoncer)* to push in, to press down; **le choc a déprimé l'aile avant** the front wing was dented in the crash

VI *Fam* to be depressed

déprise [depriz] NF *Littéraire (d'une habitude)* giving up; *(d'une personne)* falling out of love

dépriser [3] [deprize] VT *Vieilli & Littéraire* to undervalue, to underrate

De profundis [deprɔfundis] NM *Rel* de profundis

déprogrammation [deprɔgramasjɔ̃] NF *Rad & TV* withdrawal *or* removal from the schedule

déprogrammer [3] [deprɔgrame] VT **1** *Rad & TV* to withdraw *or* to remove from the schedule **2**

Ordinat to remove from a program **3** *Fam (déconditionner)* to debrief▪ **4** *(annuler → rendez-vous)* to cancel

DEPS [deəpɛs] **NM** *Com & Compta (abrév* **dernier entré premier sorti**) LIFO

dépucelage [depyslaʒ] **NM** *Fam (d'une fille)* defloration▪, deflowering▪; *(d'un garçon)* loss of virginity▪

dépuceler [24] [depysle] **VT** *Fam (fille)* to deflower▪, to take the virginity of▪; *(garçon)* to take the virginity of▪; **c'est elle qui l'a dépucelé** he lost his virginity to her▪; **se faire d.** to lose one's virginity▪

DEPUIS [dəpɥi]

> **PRÉP** since **1** ▪ for **2** ▪ from **3**
> **ADV** since

PRÉP 1 *(à partir d'une date ou d'un moment précis)* since; **il est là d. hier** he has been here since yesterday; **je ne suis pas sorti d. hier** I haven't been out since yesterday; **d. le 10 mars** since 10 March; **d. le début** from the very beginning, right from the beginning; **elle est handicapée d. l'âge de cinq ans** she has been handicapped since she was five *or* from the age of five; **je suis là d. le déjeuner** I've been here (ever) since lunch; **je ne l'ai/l'avais pas vu d. son mariage** I haven't/hadn't seen him since he got married; **ils ne se sont jamais reparlé d. leur dispute** they haven't spoken to each other again since their argument; **d. son accident, il boite** he's walked with a limp since his accident; **il nous suit d. Tours** he's been following us since (we left) Tours; **je ne fais du golf que d. cette année** I only started to play golf this year

2 *(exprimant une durée)* for; **d. dix ans** for ten years; **il est parti d. plus d'un mois** he's been gone now for over a month; **je ne l'avais pas vu d. un an quand je l'ai rencontré** I hadn't seen him for a year when I met him; **il n'est pas en forme d. quelques jours** he hasn't been on form for the last few days; **d. longtemps** for a long time; **d. quelque temps** of late; **il ne joue plus d. quelque temps** he hasn't been playing of late *or* lately, he hasn't played for some time; **d. peu** recently, not long ago; **la piscine n'est ouverte que d. peu** the pool opened only recently; **d. toujours** always; **les hommes font la guerre d. toujours** men have always waged war; **nous répétons la pièce d. trois mois** we've been rehearsing the play for three months; **d. combien de temps le connais-tu?** how long have you known him for?; **et tu ne sais toujours pas t'en servir d. le temps!** and you still don't know how to use it after all this time!; **comment vas-tu, d. le temps?** how have you been all this time?; **ça devait casser, d. le temps!** it had to break sometime!, it was bound to break sometime!; **il me l'a rendu hier – d. le temps!** he gave it back to me yesterday – it took him long enough *or* and not before time!

3 *(dans l'espace, un ordre, une hiérarchie)* from; **il lui a fait signe d. sa fenêtre** he waved to him/her from his window; **téléphoner d. chez soi** to ring from home; **concert retransmis d. Londres** concert broadcast from London; **un embouteillage d. La Rochelle** a traffic jam all the way from La Rochelle; **d. le sommet, le village paraissait si petit** from the top of the hill, the village seemed so small; **des matelas d. 60 euros** mattresses from 60 euros (upwards); **toutes les tailles d. le deux ans** all sizes from two years upwards

ADV je ne l'ai rencontré qu'une fois, je ne l'ai jamais revu d. I only met him once and I've not seen him again since (then); **trois lettres en janvier et rien d.** three letters in January and nothing since (then); **je l'ai connu d.** I made his acquaintance after that *or* later

▫ **depuis... jusqu'à 1** *(dans le temps)* from... to; **d. le début jusqu'à la fin** from the beginning to the end; **d. 12 heures jusqu'à 20 heures** from 12 to *or* till 8; **d. le matin jusqu'au soir** from morning till night

2 *(dans l'espace, un ordre, une hiérarchie)* from... to; **remonter un fleuve d. son embouchure jusqu'à sa source** to follow a river from its mouth to its source; **d. le premier jusqu'au dernier** from the first to the last; **ils vendent de tout, d. les parapluies jusqu'aux sandwiches** they sell everything, from umbrellas to sandwiches

▫ **depuis le temps que CONJ d. le temps que tu me le promets...** you've been promising me that for such a long time...; **d. le temps que tu le connais, tu pourrais lui demander** considering how long you've known him you could easily ask him; **d. le temps que tu voulais y aller!** you've been wanting to go there for ages now!

▫ **depuis lors ADV** since then; **il n'est pas retourné au village d. lors** he hasn't been back to the village since then; **d. lors, plus rien** since then, nothing more

▫ **depuis quand ADV 1** *(pour interroger sur la durée)* how long; **d. quand m'attends-tu?** how long have you been waiting for me?; **d. quand travaillait-il pour vous?** how long had he been working for you?

2 *(exprimant l'indignation, l'ironie)* since when; **d. quand est-ce que tu me donnes des ordres?** since when do you give me orders?; **j'ai arrêté de fumer – ah oui, d. quand?** I've stopped smoking – oh yes, since when?

▫ **depuis que CONJ** since; **je ne l'ai pas revu d. qu'il s'est marié** I haven't seen him since he got married; **je veux être danseuse d. que j'ai cinq ans** I've wanted to be a dancer (ever) since I was five; **d. qu'il sait qu'il va la voir, il ne tient plus en place** he hasn't been able to keep still since he found out he was going to see her; **d. que j'ai arrêté de fumer, je me sens mieux** I feel better since I stopped smoking

dépulper [3] [depylpe] **VT** *(fruit)* to remove the pulp of; *(bois)* to pulp

dépuratif, -ive [depyratif, -iv] **ADJ** cleansing, depurative

NM depurative

dépuration [depyrasjɔ̃] **NF** *Méd (du sang)* cleansing, depuration

dépurative [depyrativ] *voir* **dépuratif**

dépurer [3] [depyre] **VT 1** *Méd* to cleanse, to depurate **2** *Chim* to purify

députation [depytasjɔ̃] **NF 1** *(envoi)* deputation, mandating **2** *(groupe)* delegation, deputation **3** *Pol* office of Deputy, membership of the Assemblée Nationale; **se présenter à la d.** to stand for the position of Deputy

député [depyte] **NM**

> Note that it is no longer considered a mistake to feminize this word and to say **une députée** but some French speakers nonetheless regard this form as unacceptable, especially in France. See also the entry **féminisation**.

1 *(représentant)* delegate, representative **2** *Pol (en France)* deputy; *(en Grande-Bretagne)* member of Parliament; *(aux États-Unis)* Congressman, *f* Congresswoman; **un d. européen** a member of the European Parliament, an MEP, a Euro-MP; **femme d.** *(en Grande-Bretagne)* woman MP; *(aux États-Unis)* Congresswoman

député-maire [depytemɛr] *(pl* **députés-maires**) **NM**

> Note that it is no longer considered a mistake to feminize this word and to say **une députée-maire** (plural: **députées-maires**). Some French speakers nonetheless regard this form as unacceptable, especially in France. See also the entry **féminisation**.

= deputy who also holds the post of mayor

députer [3] [depyte] **VT** to send, to delegate; **d. qn auprès du ministre** to send sb (as delegate) *or* to delegate sb to speak to the Minister

déqualification [dekalifikasjɔ̃] **NF** *(liée à la technologie)* deskilling; **la d. (professionnelle) est de plus en plus fréquente** more and more people are overqualified for their jobs *or* for the work they do; **cette catégorie de travailleur subit une rapide d.** workers who fall into this category quickly lose the professional skills needed to compete on the job market

déqualifier [9] [dekalifje] **VT** *(emploi, employé → à cause de la technologie)* to deskill; **en élevant le niveau d'exigence par rapport aux postes offerts, on déqualifie les diplômes** the rising threshold of qualifications being required of job applicants means that degrees are being devalued; **le chômage de longue durée déqualifie les travailleurs** people lose their professional skills as a result of long-term unemployment

der [dɛr] **NM INV OU NF INV la d. des d.** the war to end all wars

déracinable [derasinabl] **ADJ** eradicable, easy to suppress *or* to uproot

déraciné, -e [derasine] **ADJ** *Bot & Fig* uprooted; **ils se sentent déracinés** they feel cut off from their roots

NM,F person without roots; **les déracinés** people without roots

déracinement [derasinmɑ̃] **NM 1** *Bot* uprooting **2** *(extirpation)* eradication, suppression; **le d. des préjugés** eradicating prejudice **3** *(exil)* uprooting (from one's environment); **ce fut pour eux un d. complet** it was a complete change of environment for them

déraciner [3] [derasine] **VT 1** *Bot* to uproot; *Fig* **d. qn** to uproot sb, to deprive sb of his/her roots **2** *(détruire → vice, racisme)* to root out; **ces habitudes sont difficiles à d.** these habits die hard

dérader [3] [derade] **VI** *Naut* to go to sea, to drive out to sea

dérager [17] [deraʒe] **VI** *Fam* **il ne dérageait pas** he was still fuming; **il n'a pas déragé de la journée** he's been furious *or* fuming all day; **elle ne dérage jamais** she's permanently in a temper

déraidir [32] [derɛdir] **VT** *(membre, tissu etc)* to take the stiffness out of; *Fig (caractère de quelqu'un)* to soften

▸**se déraidir VPR** *(membre, tissu etc)* to lose its stiffness; *(personne)* to unbend, to thaw

déraillement [derajmɑ̃] **NM 1** *Rail* derailment; **il y a eu un d. à Foissy** a train came off the track *or* was derailed at Foissy **2** *(d'un disque)* groove jumping

dérailler [3] [deraje] **VI 1** *Rail* to go off *or* to leave the rails; **faire d. un train** to derail a train **2** *Fam (fonctionner mal)* to be on the blink *or Am* on the fritz; **elle déraille, cette radio!** this radio's on the blink *or Am* on the fritz!; **faire d. les négociations** to derail the talks **3** *Fam (dire des sottises)* to talk nonsense; *(divaguer)* to rave; **tu dérailles complètement!** you're talking utter nonsense!

dérailleur [derajœr] **NM** derailleur (gear)

déraison [derɛzɔ̃] **NF** *Littéraire* foolishness, folly

déraisonnable [derɛzɔnabl] **ADJ** foolish, senseless; **une attente/attitude d.** irrational expectation/behaviour; **il serait d. de partir si tard** it wouldn't be wise to leave so late

déraisonnablement [derɛzɔnabləmɑ̃] **ADV** foolishly, senselessly, unwisely

déraisonner [3] [derɛzɔne] **VI 1** *(dire des sottises)* to talk nonsense **2** *(divaguer)* to rave

déramer[1] [3] [derame] **VT** *(feuilles de papier)* to aerate

déramer[2] [3] [derame] **VI** *Naut* to backwater

dérangé, -e [derɑ̃ʒe] **ADJ 1** *Fam (fou)* deranged; **t'es pas un peu d.?** have you gone out of your mind?; **il a l'esprit un peu d.** he's lost his marbles, *Br* he's lost the place *or* plot

2 *(malade)* upset; **il a l'estomac** *ou* **il est d.** he's got an upset stomach

3 *(en désordre → coiffure)* dishevelled, messed-up; *(→ tenue)* untidy; **en rentrant j'ai trouvé le salon/tiroir d.** when I got home I found the living room/drawer in a mess

dérangeant, -e [derɑ̃ʒɑ̃, -ɑ̃t] **ADJ 1** *(qui fait réfléchir)* thought-provoking **2** *(qui crée un malaise)* distressing, upsetting, worrying

dérangement [derɑ̃ʒmɑ̃] **NM 1** *(désordre)* disarrangement, disorder

2 *(gêne)* trouble, inconvenience; **je peux le recevoir sans grand d.** it won't be any trouble for me to put him up; **causer du d. à qn** to inconvenience sb, to put sb to trouble; **je ne veux surtout pas vous causer de d.** I don't want to inconvenience you *or* put you to any trouble

3 *Méd* disturbance, upset; **d. de l'esprit** insanity, mental derangement; **d. gastrique** *ou* **intestinal** *ou* **de l'intestin** stomach upset

4 *(déplacement)* trip; **cela m'épargnera le d.** it'll save me having to go; **cela ne vaut pas/vaut le d.** it isn't/it's worth the trip

5 *Hist* **Le Grand D.** = mass deportation of the Acadian people in 1755 from their Canadian homeland by the British army

□ **en dérangement ADJ** out of order, faulty; **le circuit est en d.** there's a fault in the circuit

déranger [17] [deʁɑ̃ʒe] **VT 1** *(mettre en désordre → objets)* to mix *or* to muddle up, to make a mess of; *(→ pièce)* to make untidy, to make a mess in; **ne dérange pas mes papiers!** don't get my papers mixed up *or* in a muddle!; **rien n'a été dérangé** nothing was touched; **d. la coiffure de qn** to mess up sb's hair

2 *(gêner)* to bother, to disturb; **ne pas d.** *(sur panneau)* do not disturb; **si cela ne vous dérange pas** if you don't mind; **est-ce que cela vous dérange si** *ou* **que…?** do you mind if…?; **ça ne te dérange pas de poster ma lettre?** would you mind posting my letter for me?; *Fam* **et alors, ça te dérange?** so, what's it to you?; *Ironique* **je ne te dérange pas trop, au moins?** am I in your way?; *Fam* **ça te dérangerait d'être poli?** would it be too much trouble for you to be polite?

3 *(interrompre)* to interrupt, to intrude upon; **allô, Marie, je te dérange?** hello Marie, is this a good time to call?; **désolé de vous d.** sorry to disturb you; **je ne peux pas travailler, je suis sans arrêt dérangé** I can't work with all these interruptions

4 *(perturber → projets)* to interfere with, to upset; **d. l'esprit de qn** to affect the balance of sb's mind

5 *(estomac)* to upset

VI ses livres dérangent his books are challenging

▸ **se déranger VPR 1** *(venir)* to come; *(aller)* to go out; **il a refusé de se d.** he wouldn't come (out); **je refuse de me d.** I refuse to go; **s'est-elle dérangée pour la réunion?** did she put in an appearance at the meeting?; **ce coup de fil m'a évité de me d.** that phone call saved me a useless journey; **grâce à l'ordinateur, faites vos courses sans vous d.** thanks to computers, you can shop without leaving the house; **se d. pour rien** to have a wasted journey

2 *(se pousser)* to move (aside); **ne te dérange pas, je passe très bien** stay where you are, I can get through

3 *(se donner du mal)* to put oneself out; **ne te dérange pas** (please) don't put yourself out; **ne vous dérangez pas, je reviendrai** please don't go to any trouble, I'll come back later

dérapage [deʁapaʒ] **NM 1** *Sport & Ski* side-slipping; *(en moto)* skidding; *Ski* **faire du d.** to side-slip

2 *Aviat & Aut* skid; **d. contrôlé** controlled skid

3 *(dérive)* (uncontrolled) drifting; **le d. des prix** the uncontrolled increase in prices; **le d. de l'économie** the downward spiral of the economy; **il y a déjà eu plusieurs dérapages dans cette émission** there have already been several inappropriate outbursts in the programme; **un d. verbal** a verbal faux pas, a gaffe

4 *(erreur)* mistake, slip-up

déraper [3] [deʁape] **VI 1** *(gén)* to skid

2 *Ski* to sideslip

3 *Aviat* to skid sideways

4 *Fig (prix)* to rise uncontrollably; *(situation)* to go wrong; **il faut éviter que les négociations ne dérapent** the talks must not go wrong; **dommage que son article dérape à deux pages de la fin** it's a pity his/her article starts to go off at a tangent two pages before the end; **la conversation a vite dérapé sur la politique** the conversation soon got round to politics

5 *Naut (ancre)* to drag

dérasement [deʁazmɑ̃] **NM** *Constr* levelling down

déraser [3] [deʁaze] **VT** *Constr* to level down

dératé, -e [deʁate] **NM,F courir comme un d.** to run like lightning

dératisation [deʁatizasjɔ̃] **NF** rodent control; **la d. de l'immeuble est prévue le 10 décembre** the building will be cleared of rodents on 10 December

dératiser [3] [deʁatize] **VT** to clear of rats *or* rodents

dérayage [deʁejaʒ] **NM 1** *Tex (de cuir)* skiving, shaving **2** *Cin & TV* polishing out

dérayer [11] [deʁeje] **VT 1** *Agr (champ)* to cut the last furrow of **2** *(roue)* to unscotch **3** *Tex (cuir)* to skive, to shave

VI *(rayons)* to work loose

dérayeuse [deʁejøz] **NF** *Tex* skiving machine

dérayure [deʁejyʁ] **NF** *Agr* dead furrow

derbouka [deʁbuka] **NF** *(instrument de percussion)* darbouka

derby [dɛʁbi] *(pl* **derbys** *ou* **derbies)* **NM 1** *Équitation* derby; **le d. d'Epsom** the Derby **2** *(match)* local derby **3** *(chaussure)* derby shoe

derche [dɛʁʃ] **NM** *très Fam* butt, *Br* bum, *Am* fanny; **se magner le d.** to move one's butt *or Br* bum; **un faux d.** a two-faced *Br* swine *or Am* stinker

déréalisation [deʁealizasjɔ̃] **NF** loss of the sense of reality

déréaliser [3] [deʁealize] **VT** to remove the sense of reality from

derechef [dəʁəʃɛf] **ADV** *Hum* once again, one more time

déréel, -elle [deʁeɛl, -ɛl] **ADJ** *Psy* dereistic

déréférencement [deʁefeʁɑ̃smɑ̃] **NM** *Mktg (d'un produit)* delisting

déréférencer [16] [deʁefeʁɑ̃se] **VT** *Mktg (produit)* to delist; **certains produits ont été déréférencés par le distributeur** some products have been delisted by the distributor

déréglage [deʁeglaʒ] **NM** *(gén)* malfunction; *Rad & TV* detuning

dérèglement [deʁɛglǝmɑ̃] **NM 1** *(d'une machine, d'une horloge)* malfunctioning **2** *(du temps)* unsettled state; *(du pouls)* irregularity; **d. de l'esprit** mental derangement; **d. hormonal** hormone disorder

□ **dérèglements NMPL** *(écarts)* dissoluteness, debauchery

déréglementation [deʁeglǝmɑ̃tasjɔ̃] **NF** deregulation

déréglementer [3] [deʁeglǝmɑ̃te] **VT** to deregulate

dérégler [18] [deʁegle] **VT 1** *Tech (mécanisme)* to disturb; *(carburateur)* to put *or* to throw out of tuning; **le compteur est déréglé** the meter's not working properly; **l'orage a déréglé la pendule électrique** the storm has sent the electric clock haywire

2 *(perturber)* to unsettle, to upset; **d. son sommeil** to disturb one's sleep pattern; **d. son appétit** to upset one's appetite

▸ **se dérégler VPR** *Tech* to go wrong, to start malfunctioning; **le carburateur s'est déréglé** the carburettor's out; **ma fixation s'est déréglée** my binding's come loose

dérégulation [deʁegylasjɔ̃] **NF** deregulation

déréguler [3] [deʁegyle] **VT** to deregulate

déréliction [deʁeliksjɔ̃] **NF** *Rel* dereliction *(of man by God)*

déremboursement [deʁɑ̃buʁsǝmɑ̃] **NM** *(fait de ne plus rembourser)* = fact of stopping refunding patients (for a particular type of medicine) in an attempt to reduce the deficit in the French Social Security budget

dérembourser [3] [deʁɑ̃buʁse] **VT** *(cesser de rembourser)* = to stop refunding patients (for a particular type of medicine) in an attempt to reduce the deficit in the French Social Security budget; **la Sécurité sociale envisage de d. ce type de médicaments** the Health Service plans to stop refunding patients for this type of drug

déresponsabiliser [3] [deʁɛspɔ̃sabilize] **VT d. qn** *(le priver de responsabilité)* to deprive sb of responsibility; *(dans une entreprise)* to give sb a less responsible job

déridage [deʁidaʒ] **NM** *Méd* facelift

dérider [3] [deʁide] **VT 1** *(détendre)* to cheer up; **je n'ai pas réussi à le d.** I couldn't get a smile out of him; **ça l'a déridé** that brought a smile to his face, that cheered him up a bit **2** *(déplisser)* to unwrinkle

▸ **se dérider VPR** to brighten, to cheer up

dérision [deʁizjɔ̃] **NF 1** *(moquerie)* derision, mockery; **avec d.** mockingly, derisively; **dire qch par d.** to say sth derisively *or* mockingly; **un geste de d.** a derisive gesture; **tourner qn/qch en d.** to scoff at sb/sth; **ne tourne pas sa tentative en d.** don't mock his/her effort; **sur le ton de la d.** mockingly **2** *(ironie)* irony; **quelle d.!** how ironic!

dérisoire [deʁizwaʁ] **ADJ 1** *(risible)* ridiculous,

laughable **2** *(piètre → salaire, prix)* derisory, ridiculous **3** *(sans effet)* inadequate, trifling, pathetic

dérisoirement [deʁizwaʁmɑ̃] **ADV** ridiculously, preposterously

dérivable [deʁivabl] **ADJ** *Math* derivable

dérivatif, -ive [deʁivatif, -iv] **ADJ 1** *(activité, occupation)* derivative **2** *Ling* derivative

NM distraction, escape; **le travail sert de d. à son chagrin** work is an outlet for his/her grief; **le sport est un excellent d.** sport is an excellent way of taking your mind off things

dérivation [deʁivasjɔ̃] **NF 1** *(d'un cours d'eau)* diversion **2** *Élec* shunt, branch circuit; **monté en d.** shunt connected **3** *Chim, Ling & Math* derivation; *Ling* **d. régressive** back formation **4** *Naut* drift **5** *Méd* diversion

□ **de dérivation ADJ 1** *(détourné)* **canal de d.** headrace; **conduite de d.** by-pass **2** *Élec* dividing

dérivative [deʁivativ] *voir* **dérivatif**

dérive [deʁiv] **NF 1** *(dérapage)* drifting, drift; **la d. de l'économie** the downward spiral of the economy; **sa d. vers l'alcoolisme** his/her drifting *or* slipping into alcoholism; **une d. totalitaire est à craindre dans ce pays** this country is in danger of drifting into totalitarianism; **aller à la d.** to drift, to go adrift; *Fig* to go downhill

2 *Naut (déplacement)* drift, drifting off course; *(quille)* centreboard, keel; **partir à la d.** to drift; **un navire en d.** a drifting vessel

3 *Aviat (trajectoire)* drift, drifting off course; *(empennage)* fin, stabilizer; **d. d'empennage** tailfin; **d. de queue** vertical fin; **d. ventrale** lower vertical fin

4 *(d'un cerf-volant)* keel

5 *(en artillerie)* deflection

6 *Géog* **d. des continents** continental drift; **d. des vents d'ouest** west wind drift; **d. latérale** leeway

□ **en pleine dérive ADJ** on the decline; **ayant eu son heure de gloire, le chanteur est en pleine d.** after a successful spell, the singer's popularity is fading fast

dérivé, -e [deʁive] **ADJ 1** *Ling & Math* derived **2** *Élec* diverted, shunt *(avant n)*; **circuit d.** branch circuit

NM 1 *Chim* derivative **2** *Ling* derivation **3** *(sous-produit)* by-product

□ **dérivée NF** *Math* derivative

dériver [3] [deʁive] **VI** *Naut* to drift, to be adrift

VT 1 *(détourner → rivière)* to divert (the course of) **2** *Élec* to shunt **3** *Chim, Ling & Math* to derive **4** *Tech* to unrivet

□ **dériver de VT IND 1** *(être issu de)* to derive *or* to come from **2** *Chim* to be produced from **3** *Ling* to derive from, to be derived from; **mots français qui dérivent du latin** French words derived from Latin

dériveter [27] [deʁivte] **VT** to unrivet, to drive out the rivets from

dériveur [deʁivœʁ] **NM** *(bateau)* sailing dinghy *(with a centreboard)*; *(voile)* storm sail

dermabrasion [dɛʁmabʁazjɔ̃] **NF** *Méd* dermabrasion

dermatite [dɛʁmatit] **NF** *Méd* dermitis, dermatitis

dermato [dɛʁmato] **NMF** *Fam (abrév* **dermatologiste)** dermatologist, skin specialist

dermatoglyphe [dɛʁmatɔglif] **NM** *Méd* dermatoglyph

dermatologie [dɛʁmatɔlɔʒi] **NF** *Méd* dermatology

dermatologique [dɛʁmatɔlɔʒik] **ADJ** *Méd* dermatological, skin *(avant n)*

dermatologiste [dɛʁmatɔlɔʒist], **dermatologue** [dɛʁmatɔlɔg] **NMF** *Méd* dermatologist, skin specialist

dermatomyosite [dɛʁmatɔmjɔzit] **NF** *Méd* dermatomyositis

dermatophyte [dɛʁmatɔfit] **NM** *Méd* dermatophyte

dermatoplastie [dɛʁmatɔplasti] **NF** *Méd* dermatoplasty

dermatose [dɛʁmatoz] **NF** *Méd* dermatosis, skin disease; **d. professionnelle** industrial dermatosis

derme [dɛʁm] **NM** *Anat* dermis

dermeste [dɛʁmɛst] **NM** *Entom* dermestes

dermique [dɛʁmik] **ADJ** dermic, dermal

dermite [dɛʁmit] **NF** *Méd* dermitis, dermatitis

dermographisme [dɛrmɔgrafism] NM dermatography

DERNIER, -ÈRE [dɛrnje, -ɛr]

ADJ last **A1, 3, 4, B3, C1, 2** ■ final **A1, 2** ■ previous **A3** ■ latest **A4** ■ bottom **B1, 2** ■ highest **C3** ■ utmost **D1**
NM,F last **1, 3–5** ■ final **1** ■ youngest **2** ■ latter **6**
NM top floor **1** ■ last **2**
NF final performance **1** ■ last edition **2**

ADJ **A.** *DANS LE TEMPS* **1** *(avant le nom) (qui vient après tous les autres → avion, bus, personne)* last; *(→ détail, préparatif)* final; **la dernière femme à être condamnée à mort** the last woman to be sentenced to death; **un d. mot/point!** one final word/point!; **le d. jour des soldes** the last day of the sales; **le d. lundi d'avril** the last Monday in April; **il vient de terminer ses derniers examens** *(en fin de cycle d'études)* he's just taken his final exams *or* finals; **le d. enchérisseur** the highest bidder; **un Warhol dernière période** a late Warhol; **les dernières années de sa vie** the last years of his/her life; **jusqu'à son d. jour** to his/her dying day, until the day he/she died; **ce furent ses dernières paroles** these were his/her dying *or* last words; **ses dernières pensées sont allées vers sa fille** his/her last thoughts were for his/her daughter; **ses dernières volontés** his/her last wishes; **d. arrivant** *ou* **arrivé** *ou* **venu** latecomer; **les derniers arrivés s'assoient au fond, s'il vous plaît!** latecomers, please sit at the back!; **je résume pour les derniers venus** *ou* **arrivés** *ou* **arrivants** I'll sum up for those of you who've just got here; **sa dernière demeure** his/her final resting place; **la dernière édition** the late edition; **la dernière séance** the last *or* late performance; **il faut toujours qu'il ait le d. mot** he always has to have the last word; **rendre les derniers devoirs** *ou* **honneurs** *ou* **un d. hommage à qn** to pay a final tribute *or* one's last respects to sb

2 *(avant le nom) (ultime)* final; **c'est mon d. prix** *(vendeur)* it's the lowest I'll go; *(acheteur)* that's my final offer; **c'est le d. avertissement!** it's your last *or* final warning!; **d. rappel** *(de facture)* final reminder; **faire un d. effort** to make a final *or* one last effort; **dans un d. sursaut de rage** in a final burst of rage; **les derniers mètres de l'ascension** the final metres of the climb; **en dernière analyse** in the final *or* last analysis, when all's said and done; *Bourse* **d. cours** closing price

3 *(précédent)* last, previous; **mon d. patron était anglais** my last boss was English; **la nuit dernière** last night; **lundi d.** last Monday; **l'été/le mois d.** last summer/month; **mon d. emploi** my last *or* previous job; **la dernière fois, la fois dernière** last time; **où ont eu lieu les derniers jeux Olympiques?** where did the previous *or* last Olympic Games take place?; **ces dix dernières années** these last ten years

4 *(avant le nom) (le plus récent)* last, latest; **achète-moi la dernière biographie de Proust** get me the latest biography of Proust; **les derniers développements d'une affaire** the latest developments of an affair; **le d. modèle** the latest model; **une décision prise à la dernière seconde** *ou* **minute** a last-minute decision; **je ferai mes valises au d. moment** I'll pack at the last minute *or* last possible moment; **on nous apprend/ils apprirent en dernière minute que...** we've just heard this minute/at the last minute they heard that...; **ces derniers temps** lately, of late; **les derniers temps de** the last stages *or* days of, the end of; **pendant les derniers temps de son mandat** towards the end of his/her mandate; **tu connais la dernière nouvelle?** have you heard the latest?; **aux dernières nouvelles, le mariage aurait été annulé** the last I heard, the wedding's off; **aux dernières nouvelles, elle était en Alaska** she was last heard of in Alaska; **de dernière heure** *(changement)* last-minute; **une information de dernière heure** *ou* **minute** a late newsflash; *Presse* **les Dernières Nouvelles d'Alsace** = daily newspaper published in Strasbourg

B. *DANS L'ESPACE* **1** *(du bas → étagère)* bottom; **les chaussettes sont dans le d. tiroir** the socks are in the bottom drawer; **la dernière marche de l'escalier** the bottom step of the stairs

2 *(du haut)* top; **au d. étage** on the top floor; **la dernière marche de l'escalier** the top step of the stairs

3 *(du bout)* last; **un siège au d. rang** a seat in the back (row); **sur la photo, c'est la dernière personne à droite** in the picture, he's/she's the last person on the right

C. *DANS UN CLASSEMENT, UNE HIÉRARCHIE* **1** *(dans une série)* last; **la dernière lettre de l'alphabet** the last letter of the alphabet; **suite à la dernière page** continued on the back page; **quelqu'un vient d'acheter le d. billet** someone's just bought the last ticket; **j'ai dépensé jusqu'à mon d. sou** I've spent my last penny; *Presse* **d. édition** last edition; *Typ* **dernières épreuves** press proofs

2 *(le plus mauvais)* last, bottom; **en dernière position** in last position, last; **en dernière position du championnat** (at the) bottom of the league (table); **le d. élève de la classe** the pupil at the bottom of the class; **je suis d. à l'examen** I came last *or Br* bottom in the exam; **arriver bon d.** to come in last

3 *(le meilleur)* top, highest; **le d. échelon** the highest level

D. *EN INTENSIF* **1** *(avant le nom) (extrême, sens positif)* **de la dernière importance** of paramount *or* of the utmost importance; **du d. chic** extremely smart; **se battre avec la dernière énergie** to fight with the utmost vigour; **nos fauteuils sont du d. confort** our armchairs are the ultimate in comfort; **atteindre le d. degré de la perfection** to attain the summit of perfection; **le d. degré de la bêtise** the height of stupidity; **être du d. bien avec qn** to be extremely friendly with sb, to be great friends with sb

2 *(avant le nom) (extrême, sens négatif)* **le d. degré de la misère** the depths of poverty; **être du d. égoïsme** to be extraordinarily selfish; **un acte de la dernière lâcheté** the most cowardly of acts; **traiter qn avec le d. mépris** to treat sb with the greatest contempt; **c'est de la dernière effronterie/impolitesse** it's extremely cheeky/rude; **du d. mauvais goût** in appalling bad taste; **c'est la dernière chose à faire** it's the last thing one should do; **il est la dernière personne à qui je penserais** he's the last person I'd have thought of!; **un couteau électrique! c'est bien le d. appareil que j'achèterais!** an electric knife! that's the last thing I'd buy!; **c'est le d. métier qu'on puisse imaginer** it's the lowest job you could imagine; **se livrer aux derniers excès** to indulge in the most abominable excesses; *Euph* **faire subir les derniers outrages à une femme** to violate a woman

NM,F **1** *(dans le temps)* last *or* final one; **je suis partie la dernière** I left last, I was the last one to leave; **je suis arrivé dans les derniers** I was among the last *or* final ones to arrive; **le d. à l'avoir vue en vie** the last person to see her alive; **il est toujours le d. à sortir** he's always last out; **le d./la dernière en date** the latest (one)

2 *(dans une famille)* youngest; **le d.** the youngest *or* last (boy); **la dernière** the youngest *or* last (girl); **ses deux derniers** his two youngest (children); **le petit d.** the youngest son; **la petite dernière** the youngest daughter

3 *(dans l'espace → celui du haut)* top one; *(→ celui du bas)* last *or* bottom one; *(→ celui du bout)* last one; **son dossier est le d. de la pile** her file is at the bottom of the pile; **où es-tu sur la photo? – je suis le d. sur la gauche** where are you in the picture? – I'm the last one on the left

4 *(dans une hiérarchie → le pire)* **j'étais toujours le d. en classe** I was always (at the) bottom of the class; **il est le d. de sa promotion** he is bottom of his year; **tu arrives le d. avec 34 points** you come last with 34 points; **dans les derniers** among the last; **les six derniers** the last six; **elle est la dernière à qui je le dirais** she's the last person I'd tell; *Fam* **le d. des derniers** the lowest of the low; *Fam* **tu es le d. des imbéciles** you're a complete idiot; *Fam* **le d. des lâches n'aurait pas fait ça** even the worst coward wouldn't have done that; *Fam* **je serais vraiment le d. des idiots!** I'd be a complete fool!; *Fam* **c'est le d. des maris** he's a terrible husband

5 *(dans une série)* last one; **allez, on en prend un d.!** *(verre)* let's have a last one (for the road)!; **ils les ont tués jusqu'au d.** every single one of them was killed

6 *(dans une narration)* **ce d., cette dernière** *(de deux)* the latter; *(de plusieurs)* this last, the last-mentioned; **il attendait la réponse de Luc, mais ce d. se taisait** he was waiting for Luc's answer but the latter kept quiet; **Myriam, Annie et Joëlle étaient parties et on avait retrouvé la voiture de cette dernière sur une plage** Myriam, Annie and Joëlle had left and Joëlle's car had been found on a beach

NM **1** *(étage)* top floor

2 *(dans une charade)* **mon d. est/a...** my last is/has...

❑ **dernière** NF **1** *Théât* last night, final performance

2 *Presse (édition)* last edition; *(page)* back page

3 *Fam (nouvelle)* **tu connais la dernière?** have you heard the latest?; **je te raconte la dernière de Fred** let me tell you the latest about Fred

❑ **au dernier degré, au dernier point** ADV extremely, to the highest *or* last degree; **j'étais excédé au d. point** I was utterly furious; **méticuleux au d. point** meticulous to the last degree; **c'est un alcoolique au d. degré** he's a complete alcoholic; **drogué au d. degré** drugged to the eyeballs

❑ **au dernier degré de** PRÉP **au d. degré de la misère** in the depths of poverty; **au d. degré du désespoir** in the depths of despair

❑ **dernier délai** ADV at the latest

❑ **en dernier** ADV last; **entrer en d.** to go in last, to be the last one to go in; **il sort toujours en d.** he's always last out; **son nom a été mentionné en d.** his/her name was mentioned last *or* was the last one to be mentioned; **en d., je mangerais bien une glace** I wouldn't mind an ice cream to finish; **ajoute le sel en d.** add the salt last *or* at the end

---

'Le Dernier métro' *Truffaut* 'The Last Metro'

'Le Dernier des Mohicans' *Cooper, Mann* 'The Last of the Mohicans'

'Le Dernier tango à Paris' *Bertolucci* 'Last Tango in Paris'

---

dernièrement [dɛrnjɛrmɑ̃] ADV lately, not long ago, (quite) recently

dernier-né, dernière-née [dɛrnjene, dɛrnjɛrne] *(mpl* **derniers-nés,** *fpl* **dernières-nées)** NM,F **1** *(benjamin)* last-born (child), youngest child **2** *Com* **le d. de notre gamme d'ordinateurs** the latest addition to our range of computers

derny [dɛrni] NM derny

dérobade [derɔbad] NF **1** *(fuite)* avoidance, evasion; **il a pris mon silence pour une d.** when I said nothing, he thought I was trying to avoid answering **2** *Équitation* jib, refusal

dérobé, -e [derɔbe] ADJ **1** *(caché)* hidden, concealed, secret; **couloir/escalier d.** secret corridor/staircase **2** *(volé)* stolen, *Littéraire* purloined

❑ **à la dérobée** ADV secretly, on the sly, furtively; **regarder qn à la dérobée** to steal a glance at sb; **il la surveillait à la dérobée** he was watching her furtively; **ils sont sortis à la dérobée** they stole out

dérober [3] [derɔbe] VT **1** *(voler)* to steal; **d. qch à qn** to steal sth from sb; **on lui a dérobé son argent** he/she has been robbed of his/her money; *Littéraire* **d. un baiser (à qn)** to steal a kiss (from sb)

2 *(cacher)* **d. qch à la vue** to hide *or* to conceal sth from view; **ce mur dérobe la vue** the wall hides the view

▸**se dérober** VPR **1** *(éluder la difficulté)* to shy away; **elle se dérobe toujours** she always shies away; **n'essaie pas de te d.** don't try to be evasive

2 *Équitation* to jib, to refuse; **se d. devant l'obstacle** to refuse at the jump

3 *(s'effondrer)* to collapse, to give way; **ses jambes se sont dérobées sous lui** his legs gave way under him; **le sol s'est dérobé brusquement** the ground suddenly caved in

4 se d. à to avoid, to evade; **se d. aux regards** to conceal oneself, to hide; **se d. à ses obligations** to evade *or* to shirk one's responsibilities

dérochage [derɔʃaʒ] NM *Tech (décapage)* pickling

dérochement [derɔʃmɑ̃] NM rock excavation

dérocher [3] [derɔʃe] VT **1** *Tech (décaper)* to pickle, to strip **2** *(en travaux publics)* to clear of rocks **3** *Belg (nettoyer → gén)* to clean off; *(→ en grattant)* to scrape clean; *(→ avec un produit chimique)* to strip; *(→ à la chaleur)* to burn off; *(→ au papier de verre)* to sand (down); *(→ à la sableuse)* to sandblast

VI *(alpiniste)* to fall (from a rock face)

déroctage [derɔktaʒ] NM rock excavation

déroder [3] [derɔde] VT *(forêt)* to clear *or* to remove the tree-stumps and dead wood from

dérogation [derɔgasjɔ̃] NF (special) dispensation *or* exemption; **consentir une d.** to grant an exemption; **d. aux usages** departure from custom; **par d. à la réglementation** notwithstanding the rules; **sauf d. explicite** unless otherwise specified

dérogatoire [derɔgatwar] ADJ dispensatory; *Jur* **clause d.** waiver, *Spéc* derogatory clause

dérogeance [derɔʒɑ̃s] NF *Hist* derogation, losing of caste

déroger [17] [derɔʒe] VI to demean oneself; **en se mêlant à nous, il croirait d.** he thinks it's beneath him to associate with people like us

▫ **déroger à** VT IND **1** *(manquer à)* to depart from; **d. à la loi/ses principes** to depart from the law/one's principles; **sans d. à ses habitudes** without departing from one's usual practices **2** *Hist* **d. à son rang** to lose caste *(after working at a demeaning occupation)*

dérougir [32] [deruʒir] VI **1** *Vieilli (perdre de sa rougeur)* to stop blushing **2** *Can Fam* **ne pas d.** *(travail)* not to let up; *(être bondé)* to be jam-packed; *(être en colère)* to be always fuming; *(être soûl)* to be permanently plastered

dérouillée [deruje] NF *très Fam* thrashing, hammering; **je vais lui mettre une d.!** I'll give him/her what for!; **prendre une d.** to get thrashed *or* hammered

dérouiller [3] [deruje] VT **1** *(enlever la rouille sur)* to remove the rust from

2 *(assouplir → doigts, esprit)* to loosen up; *(→ jambes)* to stretch

3 *Fam (battre)* to beat up

VI *Fam* **1** *(être battu)* to get it; **tu vas d.!** you're for it *or* going to get it!

2 *(souffrir)* to be in agony[■]; **qu'est-ce que j'ai dérouillé avec mon entorse!** when I sprained my ankle, it was total agony!

▸**se dérouiller** VPR **se d. les doigts** to loosen up one's fingers; **se d. les jambes** to stretch one's legs; **se d. l'esprit** to exercise one's mind

déroulage [derulaʒ] NM **1** *(déroulement)* unrolling, unwinding **2** *Menuis (procédé)* veneering-cutting; *(industrie)* veneer-making

déroulement [derulmɑ̃] NM **1** *(débobinage)* unreeling, unwinding **2** *(cours → d'une cérémonie, d'un discours)* course; **le d. des événements** the course *or* sequence of events; **il a surveillé tout le d. des opérations** he monitored operations from start to finish; **pendant tout le d. de la cérémonie** throughout the ceremony

dérouler [3] [derule] VT **1** *(débobiner → câble)* to unroll, to unwind, to uncoil; *(→ tapis, rouleau)* to unroll; *(→ store)* to let down; *Fig* **d. le tapis rouge pour qn** to roll out the red carpet for sb

2 *Menuis* to cut *or* to plane veneer from

3 *Ordinat (menu)* to pull down

▸**se dérouler** VPR **1** *(se déployer → câble, bande)* to unwind, to uncoil, to unroll; *(→ store)* to come down; *(→ serpent)* to uncoil; **le paysage se déroule sous nos yeux** the landscape unfolds before our eyes

2 *(avoir lieu)* to take place, to be going on; **les spectacles qui se déroulent en ce moment** the shows currently running; **les deux opérations se déroulent en même temps** the two operations are concurrent; **les épreuves se sont déroulées conformément au règlement** the exams were conducted in accordance with the rules

3 *(progresser)* to develop, to progress; **sa carrière se déroule exactement comme prévu** his/her career's going *or* progressing according to plan

dérouleur [derulœr] NM **1** *(de papier)* holder; *(de bande)* winder **2** *(de cuisine)* kitchen roll dispenser **3** *Ordinat* **d. de bande magnétique** tape unit, magnetic tape drive; **d. de film magnétique** magnetic film handler

dérouleuse [deruløz] NF **1** *(à bois)* unwinding machine **2** *Élec* cable-drum

déroutage [derutaʒ] NM rerouting

déroutant, -e [derutɑ̃, -ɑ̃t] ADJ perplexing, disconcerting, puzzling

déroute [derut] NF **1** *Mil* retreat, rout; **être en pleine d.** to be in full flight; **mettre qn en d.** to rout sb, to put sb to rout *or* flight; **le loup a mis le troupeau en d.** the wolf scattered the flock **2** *(débâcle)* ruin; **l'entreprise est en pleine d.** the company is heading for ruin

déroutement [derutmɑ̃] NM rerouting

dérouter [3] [derute] VT **1** *(changer l'itinéraire de)* to reroute **2** *(étonner)* to disconcert, to perplex; **la question l'a dérouté** the question threw him off balance **3** *Chasse* to throw off the track

derrick [derik] NM derrick

DERRIÈRE [dɛrjɛr]

PRÉP	behind **1, 2** ■ beneath **3** ■ under **3**
ADJ	behind **2, 4** ■ at the back **1, 3**
NM	back **1** ■ bottom, behind **2** ■ rump **3**

PRÉP **1** *(en arrière de)* behind, *Am* in back of; **ça s'est passé d. chez moi** it happened behind my house; **d. la colline, il y a une forêt** on the other side of the hill *or* beyond the hill there is a forest; **il s'est caché d. le rideau** he hid behind the curtain; **il y a un chien d. la grille** there's a dog (on) the other side of the gate; **reste au coin, les mains d. la tête** remain standing in the corner with your hands behind your head; **regarde d. toi!** look behind you!; *Fig* **il a l'impression que ses plus belles années sont d. lui** he feels his best years are behind him; **avec une telle expérience d. elle, elle n'aura pas de mal à retrouver un emploi** with that kind of experience behind her she'll have no trouble finding a job; **être d. qn** *(le soutenir)* to support sb; **il sait que le public est d. lui** he knows that the public supports him *or* is behind him; **ne sois pas toujours d. moi!** *(à me surveiller)* stop watching everything I do all the time!; **je sais bien ce qu'elle dit d. mon dos** I'm quite aware of what she says behind my back; **il faut toujours être d. lui** *ou* **d. son dos** he has to be watched all the time, you have to be at his back all the time

2 *(à la suite de)* behind; **un motard roulait d. le convoi** a policeman was riding behind the convoy; **passe d. moi, tu sentiras moins le vent** get behind me, you won't feel the wind so much; **l'un d. l'autre** one behind the other; **le Kenyan est en première place, avec loin d. lui le Jamaïcain** the Kenyan is in first place with the Jamaican a long way behind; **il a rapidement laissé ses camarades loin d. lui** he soon left his classmates far behind; **leur équipe est passée d. nous au classement** their team has dropped behind us in the league; **les Italiens sont d. nous en matière d'électronique** as far as electronics is concerned, the Italians are lagging behind us

3 *(sous)* beneath, under; **d. son indifférence apparente** beneath his/her apparent indifference; **d. un abord chaleureux** behind a cordial facade; **c'est lui qui est d. tout ça** he's the one behind all this; **qu'y a-t-il d. tout ça?** what's the key to all this?, what's behind all this?, what's all this really about?

ADV **1** *(en arrière)* behind; **tu vois le bureau de poste? la bibliothèque est juste d.** do you see the post office? the library's just behind it; **laisser qn d.** to leave sb behind; **regarde d. avant de tourner** look behind you before you turn; **passe d., tu verras mieux** come through, you'll get a better view; **restez d. et suivez notre voiture** stay behind and follow our car

2 *(du côté arrière)* at the back; *(sur la face arrière)* on the back; **ça se boutonne d.** it buttons up at the back; **tes cheveux sont trop longs d.** your hair's too long at the back; **écris le nom de l'expéditeur d.** write the sender's name on the back

3 *(dans le fond)* at the rear *or* back; **le jardin est d.** the garden is at the rear *or* back (of the house); **mettez les plus grands de la classe d.** put the tallest pupils at the rear *or* back; **installe-toi d.** *(dans une voiture)* sit *Br* in the back *or Am* in back; **hé, taisez-vous d.!** *(dans une voiture)* hey, be quiet there in the back!; *(dans une pièce)* hey, be quiet at the back!

4 *Fig* behind; **elle est loin d.** she's a long way behind

NM **1** *(d'un objet, d'un espace)* back

2 *Fam (fesses)* bottom, behind, butt; **pousse ton d.!** shift your backside!; **avoir le d. à l'air** to be bare-bottomed; **coup de pied au d.** kick up the backside *or Am* in the pants; **être** *ou* **rester** *ou* **tomber le d. par terre** to be stunned *or* flabbergasted

3 *Zool* rump, hindquarters; **le chien assis sur son d.** the dog sitting on its haunches

▫ **de derrière** ADJ *(dent, jardin, roue etc)* back *(avant n)*; **la porte de d.** the back door; **voici une vue de d.** here's a rear view; **pattes de d.** hind legs PRÉP *(par l'arrière de)* from behind; **il est arrivé de d. la maison** he arrived from behind the house

dérushage [derœʃaʒ] NM *Cin & TV* film editing

dérusher [3] [derœʃe] VT *Cin & TV* to edit

derviche [dɛrviʃ] NM dervish; **d. tourneur** whirling dervish

des [de] ADJ *voir* **un**

PRÉP *voir* **de**

des-, dés- *voir* **dé-**

dès [dɛ] PRÉP **1** *(dans le temps)* from; **d. son arrivée, j'ai compris que quelque chose n'allait pas** from the moment *or* as soon as he/she arrived, I realised that there was something wrong; **d. son retour, il faudra y penser** as soon as he/she comes back, we'll have to think about it; **d. le début** from the beginning; **d. la première fois** right from the start; **d. les premiers jours d'avril** from early April onwards; **prêt d. 8 heures** ready by 8 o'clock; **d. le quinzième siècle** as far back as the fifteenth century; **d. Noël** from Christmas onwards; **je vais le faire d. aujourd'hui** I'm going to do it this very day; **d. maintenant** from now on; **vous pouvez réserver vos places d. maintenant** booking is now open; **pouvez-vous commencer d. maintenant?** can you start straight away?; **il y pensait d. avant sa retraite** he was thinking of it even before he retired

2 *(dans un ordre, une hiérarchie)* **d. le troisième échelon, on paye plus d'impôts** when you get to grade three *or* from grade three upwards you pay more taxes; **d. la sixième, on apprend l'anglais** English is studied from the first year onwards; **d. la seconde année** from the second year onwards; **d. sa nomination** as soon as he/she was appointed; **d. l'entrée en vigueur de la loi** as soon as the law comes into force; **d. le deuxième verre, il ne savait plus ce qu'il disait** after his second glass he started talking nonsense

3 *(dans l'espace)* **d. le seuil** on reaching the doorstep; **d. la frontière** on reaching the border; **d. la sortie du village commence la forêt** the woods lie just beyond the village

▫ **dès lors** ADV **1** *(à partir de là)* from then on, since (then); **il a quitté la ville; d. lors, on n'a plus entendu parler de lui** he left the town and he's never been heard of since

2 *(en conséquence)* consequently, therefore;

tu es d'accord avec lui: **d. lors, je n'ai plus rien à dire** you agree with him: in which case *or* consequently I have nothing more to say

❏ **dès lors que** CONJ **1** *(étant donné que)* as, since; *(du moment où)* from the moment (that); **d. lors qu'il a renoncé à ce poste, il ne peut prétendre à une augmentation** given that *or* since *or* as he refused that job, he can't expect a rise; **d. lors qu'il a été déclaré coupable, rien ne saurait le sauver** from the moment he was found guilty, nothing could possibly save him

2 *(dès que)* as soon as; **d. lors que la loi entre en vigueur, il faut s'y conformer** as soon as the law comes into force, it must be respected

❏ **dès que** CONJ **1** *(aussitôt que)* as soon as; **d. que possible** as soon as possible; **d. que tu pourras** as soon as you can; **nous partirons d. que tout le monde sera prêt** we'll go once *or* (just) as soon as everybody's ready

2 *(chaque fois que)* whenever; **d. qu'il peut, il part en vacances** whenever he can, he goes off on holiday

désabonnement [dezabɔnmã] NM cancellation of subscription

désabonner [3] [dezabɔne] VT to cancel the subscription of

▸**se désabonner** VPR to stop subscribing, to cancel *or* to withdraw *or* to discontinue one's subscription; **se d. à une revue** to stop taking a magazine

désabrier [10] [dezabrije] VT *Can* to uncover

désabusé, -e [dezabyze] ADJ **1** *(déçu)* disillusioned, disenchanted **2** *(amer)* embittered

désabuser [3] [dezabyze] VT to disabuse; **je la croyais honnête mais l'enquête m'a désabusé** I thought she was honest but the inquiry opened my eyes

désacclimater [3] [dezaklimate] VT to disacclimatize

désaccord [dezakɔr] NM **1** *(litige)* conflict, disagreement, dissension *(UNCOUNT)*; **s'il y a d.** if there's any disagreement

2 *(contraste)* discrepancy, *Littéraire* disharmony ❏ **en désaccord** ADJ **les parties en d.** the dissenting parties; **ils sont en d. en ce qui concerne l'éducation de leurs enfants** they disagree about their children's education; **être en d. avec qn sur qch** to be in conflict with sb over sth; **sa conduite est en d. avec ses principes** his/her behaviour is not consistent with his/her principles

désaccorder [3] [dezakɔrde] *Mus* VT to detune; **le piano est désaccordé** the piano's out of tune

▸**se désaccorder** VPR to go out of tune

désaccoupler [3] [dezakuple] VT to uncouple

désaccoutumance [dezakutymãs] NF **1** *(perte d'une habitude)* loss of a habit **2** *Méd & Psy* end of a dependency; **la d. du tabac** breaking tobacco dependency; **la d. à la drogue demande un énorme effort de volonté** overcoming drug addiction requires a great deal of willpower

désaccoutumer [3] [dezakutyme] VT **1** *(déshabituer)* to disaccustom, to cause to lose a habit; **d. qn de faire qch** to get sb out of the habit of doing sth

2 *Méd & Psy* **d. qn** to end sb's dependency

▸**se désaccoutumer** VPR **1** *(se déshabituer)* **se d. de faire qch** to get out of the habit of doing sth **2** *Méd & Psy* **se d. de qch** to lose one's dependency on sth; **se d. du tabac** to kick the tobacco habit

désacralisation [desakralizasjɔ̃] NF deconsecration; *Fig* demythologization

désacraliser [3] [desakralize] VT to deconsecrate; *Fig* to demythologize

désactivation [dezaktivasjɔ̃] NF **1** *Chim* deactivation **2** *Nucl (d'un site)* decontamination, cleaning up **3** *Ordinat* deactivation

désactiver [3] [dezaktive] VT **1** *Chim* to deactivate, to make ineffective **2** *Nucl* to decontaminate, to clean up **3** *Ordinat* to deactivate, to disable **4** *Biol (gène)* to knock out

désadaptation [dezadaptasjɔ̃] NF loss of adaptability

désadapté, -e [dezadapte] ADJ **un malade d.** a patient who's lost the ability to adapt *or* to adjust (to normal life)

NM,F misfit; **les désadaptés** those who can't adapt *or* adjust (to normal life) any more

désadapter [3] [dezadapte] VT **d. qn de qch** to wean sb away from sth; **le risque de les d. à** *ou* **de leur vie quotidienne** the danger of creating a gulf between them and their everyday life

désaérer [18] [dezaere] VT to deaerate; **béton désaéré** vibrated concrete

désaffectation [dezafɛktasjɔ̃] NF **1** *Mil* transfer **2** *(d'une église)* deconsecration, secularization, secularizing; *(d'une gare)* closing down

désaffecté, -e [dezafɛkte] ADJ *(église)* deconsecrated, secularized; *(gare, entrepôt)* disused

désaffecter [4] [dezafɛkte] VT *(église)* to deconsecrate, to secularize; *(entrepôt)* to close down, to put out of use *or* commission; **il a désaffecté son garage pour en faire un atelier** he turned his garage into a workshop

désaffection [dezafɛksjɔ̃] NF disaffection, loss of interest; **manifester une certaine d. pour qch** to lose interest in *or* to turn one's back on sth; **expliquer la d. du public à l'égard de la religion** to explain why people turn their backs on religion

désafférenciation [dezaferãsjasjɔ̃] NF **1** *Méd* deafferentiation **2** *Psy* **d. sociale** = lack of stimulus in one's social environment

désaffilier [9] [dezafilje] VT to disaffiliate (**de** from)

désagréable [dezagreabl] ADJ **1** *(déplaisant)* disagreeable, unpleasant; **souvenirs désagréables** unpleasant memories; **caractère d.** disagreeableness; **d. à voir** unsightly; **une odeur d.** a nasty smell; **ce n'est pas d.** it's rather pleasant *or* nice; **ce petit vent n'est pas d.** this gentle breeze is (very) welcome

2 *(peu sociable)* bad-tempered, rude; **elle est d. avec tout le monde** she's rude to everybody

désagréablement [dezagreablemã] ADV unpleasantly, offensively; **un bruit qui résonne d. aux oreilles** a noise that grates on the ears

désagrégation [dezagregasjɔ̃] NF **1** *(d'un tissu, d'un béton)* disintegration **2** *Géol* weathering **3** *(d'une équipe)* break-up, breaking *or* splitting up, disbanding

désagréger [22] [dezagreʒe] VT **1** *(effriter)* to break up, to cause to disintegrate *or* to crumble; **la bombe a complètement désagrégé l'immeuble** the bomb completely destroyed the building

2 *(désunir → équipe)* to break up, to disband

▸**se désagréger** VPR **1** *(s'effriter)* to disintegrate, to break up; *Géol* to be weathered

2 *(groupe, équipe)* to break up, to disband; **le club s'est désagrégé** the club disbanded

désagrément [dezagremã] NM trouble *(UNCOUNT)*, inconvenience *(UNCOUNT)*; **causer du d.** *ou* **des désagréments à qn** to cause trouble for sb, to inconvenience sb; **les voyages impliquent parfois quelques désagréments** travelling sometimes involves inconvenience; **les désagréments du travail à domicile** the disadvantages of working from home

désaimantation [dezɛmãtasjɔ̃] NF demagnetization, demagnetizing

désaimanter [3] [dezɛmãte] VT to demagnetize

désaisonnalisé, -e [desezonalize] ADJ seasonally adjusted

désaisonnaliser [3] [desezonalize] VT to adjust seasonally

désajuster [3] [dezaʒyste] VT *(pièce)* to loosen, to undo; *(machine)* to upset the mechanism of

▸**se désajuster** VPR to work loose

désaliénation [dezaljenasjɔ̃] NF release from alienation

désaliéner [18] [dezaljene] VT to free from alienation

désalignement [dezaliɲmã] NM *(de bâtiments)* disalignment, irregular alignment

désaligner [3] [dezaliɲe] VT *(bâtiments)* to put out of line, to disalign

désalpe [dezalp] NF *Suisse* transhumance *(from the high pastures)*

désalper [3] [dezalpe] VI *Suisse* = to come down from the high pastures

désaltérant, -e [dezalterã, -ãt] ADJ refreshing, thirst-quenching

désaltérer [18] [dezaltere] VT *(apaiser la soif de)* to refresh, to quench the thirst of

USAGE ABSOLU **le thé désaltère mieux qu'une**

boisson glacée tea is more thirst-quenching than an ice-cold drink

▸**se désaltérer** VPR to quench one's thirst; **se d. de sang** to sate *or* to slake one's thirst for blood

désambiguïsation [dezãbigɥizasjɔ̃] NF clarification

désambiguïser [3] [dezãbigɥize] VT to disambiguate; **un mot est souvent désambiguïsé par un contexte** a word in context is rarely ambiguous

désâmer [3] [dezɑme] **se désâmer** VPR *Can* to work oneself to death

désamiantage [dezamjãtaʒ] NM removal of asbestos

désamianter [3] [dezamjãte] VT to remove asbestos from

désamidonner [3] [dezamidɔne] VT to remove the starch from

désamination [desaminasjɔ̃] NF *Biol & Chim* deamination

désamorçage [dezamɔrsaʒ] NM **1** *(d'une bombe)* defusing; *(d'une arme)* unpriming **2** *Élec* running down, de-energization **3** *Tech* air-binding **4** *(d'une situation)* defusing

désamorcer [16] [dezamɔrse] VT **1** *(bombe)* to defuse; *(arme)* to unprime **2** *Élec* to run down, to de-energize **3** *Tech* **d. une pompe** to draw off the water from a pump **4** *(contrecarrer)* to defuse, to forestall, to inhibit; **des mesures d'urgence pour d. la grève** emergency measures to defuse the strike

désamour [dezamur] NM **1** *(cessation de l'amour)* falling out of love **2** *(désillusion)* disenchantment, disillusionment

désaper [3] [dezape] **se désaper** VPR *Fam* to strip off

désapparier [10] [dezaparje] VT **1** *(animaux)* to uncouple **2** *Phys (électrons)* to split

désappointé, -e [dezapwɛte] ADJ disappointed, frustrated

désappointement [dezapwɛtmã] NM *Littéraire* disappointment, dissatisfaction

désappointer [3] [dezapwɛte] VT *Littéraire* to disappoint

désapprendre [79] [dezaprãdr] VT *(involontairement)* to forget; *(volontairement)* to unlearn; **il a désappris l'italien** he can't speak Italian any more; **ce n'est pas facile de d. à mentir** it's not easy to get out of the habit of lying; **l'enfant avait désappris à sourire** the child no longer knew how to smile; *Littéraire* **d. de faire qch** to lose the habit of doing sth

désapprobateur, -trice [dezaprɔbatœr, -tris] ADJ disapproving, *Sout* censorious; **d'un air d.** with a look of disapproval; **d'un ton d.** disapprovingly

désapprobation [dezaprɔbasjɔ̃] NF disapproval; **exprimer ouvertement sa d.** to disapprove openly; **un regard/murmure de d.** a look/murmur of disapproval

désapprobatrice [dezaprɔbatris] *voir* **désapprobateur**

désapprouver [3] [dezapruve] VT **1** *(condamner)* to disapprove of; **un mariage civil? sachez que je désapprouve!** a registry office wedding? let me say that I thoroughly disapprove *or* I do not approve!

2 *(s'opposer à → projet, idée)* to object to, to reject; **la commission désapprouvera cette solution** this solution will be unacceptable to the committee; **nous désapprouvons le concept de discrimination** we strongly oppose the notion of discrimination

désapprovisionné, -e [dezaprɔvizjɔne] ADJ *(compte)* overdrawn

désapprovisionnement [dezaprɔvizjɔnmã] NM **1** *(d'un magasin)* emptying of supplies (**de** in); *(d'un marché)* draining of stocks (**de** in); **la panique des consommateurs a conduit au d. des magasins** as a result of consumer panic the shops were emptied of their stocks **2** *Banque (d'un compte)* emptying **3** *(d'une arme)* unloading, emptying

désapprovisionner [3] [dezaprɔvizjɔne] VT **1** *(magasin, placard)* to empty of supplies; *(marché)* to drain of stocks **2** *Banque* **d. son compte** to withdraw all the funds from *or* to empty one's account **3** *(arme)* to unload, to empty

désarçonner [3] [dezarsɔne] VT **1** *Équitation* to

unseat, to unhorse; **il a été désarçonné plusieurs fois** he was unhorsed several times **2** *(déconcerter)* to throw, to put off one's stride; **son intervention a désarçonné l'orateur** his remark threw the speaker off balance

désarêter [4] [dezarete] **VT** to bone

désargenté, -e [dezarʒɑ̃te] **ADJ** *Fam* penniless; **une famille désargentée** a family fallen on hard times; **je suis plutôt d. ces jours-ci** I'm a bit short (of money) at the moment

désargenter [3] [dezarʒɑ̃te] **VT 1** *Mines* to desilver **2** *(bijou, couvert)* to wear off the silver plate of **3** *Fam (priver d'argent)* to leave penniless

▸**se désargenter VPR les couteaux se sont désargentés** the knives have lost their silver plating

désarmant, -e [dezarmɑ̃, -ɑ̃t] **ADJ 1** *(touchant)* disarming; **un sourire d.** a disarming smile; **de façon désarmante** disarmingly; **elle est désarmante de gentillesse** she is disarmingly sweet **2** *(confondant)* amazing, breathtaking; **une telle ignorance est désarmante** such ignorance is breathtaking

désarmé, -e [dezarme] **ADJ 1** *(personne → qui n'a plus d'arme)* disarmed; *(→ qui n'a jamais eu d'arme)* unarmed, defenceless **2** *(arme, mine)* uncocked **3** *Naut* laid up **4** *(surpris)* dumbfounded **5** *(privé de moyens)* **être d. devant la vie/les mauvaises influences** to be ill-equipped to cope with life/to deal with bad influences

désarmement [dezarməmɑ̃] **NM 1** *Mil & Pol* disarmament; **d. nucléaire** nuclear disarmament; **d. unilatéral** unilateral disarmament **2** *(d'une arme, d'une mine)* uncocking **3** *Naut* laying-up, release

désarmer [3] [dezarme] **VT 1** *Mil & Pol* to disarm **2** *(arme, mine)* to uncock

3 *(attendrir)* to disarm; **être désarmé par la bonne volonté de qn** to find sb's willingness disarming; **ce genre de remarque vous désarme** this kind of remark takes the wind out of your sails

4 *Naut* to lay up, to put out of commission

VI 1 *Mil* to disarm

2 *(locution)* **il ne désarme pas** he won't give in, he keeps battling on; **sa haine ne désarme pas** his/her hatred is unrelenting; **les journaux ne désarmeront pas** the press stories will go on and on

désarrimage [dezarimaʒ] **NM 1** *Naut* shifting, slipping *(of cargo)* **2** *(sur un véhicule)* **à cause du d. de la cargaison** *(accidentel)* because the load came off; *(volontaire)* because the load was unfastened

désarrimer [3] [dezarime] **VT 1** *Naut* to cause to move about **2** *(sur un véhicule)* to unfasten

▸**se désarrimer VPR 1** *Naut* to come loose **2** *(sur un véhicule)* to come off *or* loose

désarroi [dezarwa] **NM** confusion; **être dans le d. le plus profond** to be completely at a loss; **jeter qn dans le d.** to throw sb into utter confusion

désarticulation [dezartikylasjɔ̃] **NF 1** *(torsion)* disarticulation, dislocation, disjointing **2** *Écon* disarticulation

désarticulé, -e [dezartikyle] **ADJ** dislocated, out of joint

désarticuler [3] [dezartikyle] **VT** to disjoint, to dislocate

▸**se désarticuler VPR 1** *(se contorsionner)* to twist *or* to contort oneself **2** *(par accident)* **se d. un doigt/le genou** to put a finger/one's knee out of joint

désasphaltage [desasfaltaʒ] **NM** de-asphalting

désasphalter [3] [desasfalte] **VT** to de-asphalt

désassembler [3] [dezasɑ̃ble] **VT** to dismantle, to take apart, to take to pieces, to disassemble

désassimilation [dezasimilasjɔ̃] **NF** dissimilation, catabolism

désassimiler [3] [dezasimile] **VT** to catabolize

désassorti, -e [dezasɔrti] **ADJ 1** *(mal accordé)* ill-matched; **ils sont parfaitement désassortis** they're completely ill-matched **2** *(dépareillé)* odd; **je ne trouve que des gants désassortis** I can only find odd gloves; **le service à thé est d.** the tea set is incomplete

désassortiment [dezasɔrtimɑ̃] **NM 1** *(d'un magasin)* running down the stock **2** *(de gants, de chaussettes)* splitting up

désassortir [32] [dezasɔrtir] **VT 1** *(série, collection etc)* to spoil, to break up; **service de table désassorti** dinner service made up of odd pieces **2** *(magasin)* to clear (of stock)

désastre [dezastr] **NM 1** *(calamité)* calamity, catastrophe, disaster; **ils ne purent que constater l'ampleur du d.** they could only record the extent of the damage **2** *(échec)* disaster, failure; **le gâteau d'anniversaire fut un d.** the birthday cake was a complete disaster *or* failure; **sa coiffure est un vrai d.!** her hair's a disaster!; **courir au d.** to be heading for disaster

désastreuse [dezastrøz] *voir* **désastreux**

désastreusement [dezastrøzmɑ̃] **ADV** disastrously, catastrophically

désastreux, -euse [dezastrø, -øz] **ADJ 1** *(catastrophique)* calamitous, disastrous, catastrophic; **des conditions de vie désastreuses** wretched living conditions

2 *(résultat, effet)* disastrous, awful, terrible; **des résultats d. en physique** appalling results in physics; **cela a eu un effet d. sur la suite de sa carrière** it had a disastrous effect on his/her later career; **le spectacle/pique-nique a été d.** the show/picnic was a complete disaster

désatellisation [desatelizasjɔ̃] **NF 1** *(d'une station spatiale)* de-orbit **2** *(d'un pays)* making more autonomous

désatelliser [3] [desatelize] **VT 1** *(station spatiale)* to de-orbit **2** *(pays)* to make more autonomous

désaturer [3] [desatyre] **VT** to desaturate

désavantage [dezavɑ̃taʒ] **NM 1** *(inconvénient)* disadvantage, drawback; **avoir tous les désavantages de qch** to get the worst of sth, to bear the brunt of sth

2 *(infériorité)* disadvantage, handicap; **avoir un d. par rapport à qn** to be at a disadvantage compared with sb

▫ **au désavantage de PRÉP c'est à ton d.** it's not to your advantage; **se montrer à son d.** to show oneself in an unfavourable light; **tourner au d. de qn** to go against sb, to turn out to be a handicap for sb

désavantager [17] [dezavɑ̃taʒe] **VT** *(défavoriser)* to (put at a) disadvantage, to penalize; **d. un concurrent** to put a competitor at a disadvantage; **être désavantagé par rapport à qn** to be at a disadvantage compared with sb; **l'animal est désavantagé par son poids** the animal is handicapped by its weight; **il est désavantagé par son jeune âge** he is handicapped by his youth, his youth is against him; **elle est désavantagée simplement parce que c'est une femme** she's at a disadvantage simply because she is a woman

désavantageuse [dezavɑ̃taʒøz] *voir* **désavantageux**

désavantageusement [dezavɑ̃taʒøzmɑ̃] **ADV** disadvantageously

désavantageux, -euse [dezavɑ̃taʒø, -øz] **ADJ** detrimental, disadvantageous; **vendre à des conditions moins désavantageuses** to sell at a better price; **c'est d. pour les petites entreprises** this works against the interests of small businesses

désaveu, -x [dezavø] **NM 1** *(reniement)* disavowal, retraction; **contraindre qn au d.** to force sb to retract; **faire un d. public** to make a public retraction

2 *(condamnation)* repudiation; **encourir le d. de ses supérieurs** to incur the disapproval of one's superiors; **il n'a pas supporté ce d. public** he couldn't stand the idea of being condemned in public

3 *Jur* **d. d'avocat** = action against a legal representative for an ultra vires action; **d. de paternité** repudiation of paternity

4 *Psy* denial

désavouer [6] [dezavwe] **VT 1** *(renier → propos)* to disavow, to repudiate; *(→ dette)* to repudiate; **d. sa promesse** to go back on one's word, to break one's promise

2 *(refuser de reconnaître → représentant, candidat)* to challenge the authority *or* legitimacy of; **elle avait un si bon accent qu'un autochtone ne l'aurait pas désavouée** her accent was so good that she could have passed for a native

3 *(condamner → personne, comportement)* to disapprove of

4 *Jur* to disclaim, to repudiate

▸**se désavouer VPR** to retract

désaxé, -e [dezakse] **ADJ 1** *Tech* out of alignment; **cylindre d.** offset cylinder; **rotor d.** unbalanced rotor; **roue désaxée** dished wheel **2** *(dérangé)* mentally deranged, unbalanced, unhinged

NM,F (dangerous) lunatic, psychopath

désaxer [3] [dezakse] **VT 1** *Tech* to offset, to throw out of alignment **2** *(perturber)* to unhinge; **ils ont été désaxés par la guerre** the war unhinged them *or* left them psychologically disturbed

Descartes [dekart] **NPR** Descartes

descellement [desɛlmɑ̃] **NM à cause du d. des dalles** *(accidentel)* because the flagstones have worked loose; *(volontaire)* because the flagstones have been loosened

desceller [4] [desele] **VT 1** *(ouvrir)* to unseal, to take the seal off **2** *(détacher)* to loosen; **les briques sont descellées** the bricks have worked loose *or* are loose

▸**se desceller VPR** to work loose

descendance [desɑ̃dɑ̃s] **NF 1** *Jur* descent, lineage **2** *(progéniture)* descendants

descendant, -e [desɑ̃dɑ̃, -ɑ̃t] **ADJ** down *(avant n)*, downward, descending; **escalator d.** down escalator; **mouvement d.** downward movement

NM,F 1 *(dans une famille)* descendant **2** *(partisan)* follower; **un d. des pointillistes** a latter-day pointillist

NM *Astrol* descendant

descenderie [desɑ̃dri] **NF** *Mines* winze

descendeur, -euse [desɑ̃dœr, -øz] **NM,F** *(skieur)* downhill skier, downhiller; *(cycliste)* downhill racer; **d. en rappel** *(alpiniste)* abseiler

NM *(en alpinisme)* descender

DESCENDRE [73] [desɑ̃dr]

> **VI** to go down **A1–3, 7, B1, 2, C3** ▪ to come down **A1, 2, B1, C1** ▪ to climb down, to get down **A1** ▪ to get off **A1, 4** ▪ to stay **A6** ▪ to raid **A5** ▪ to drop, to fall **C1**
> **VT** to go down **1** ▪ to lower **2** ▪ to take down **3, 4** ▪ to bring down **3** ▪ to shoot down **5** ▪ to criticize **6** ▪ to knock back **7**

VI *(aux être)* **A. 1** *(personne, mécanisme, avion → vu d'en haut)* to go down; *(→ vu d'en bas)* to come down; *(oiseau)* to fly *or* to swoop down; **d. à la cave** to go down to the cellar; **tu peux d.? j'ai besoin de toi à la cuisine** can you come down(stairs)? I need you in the kitchen; **j'ai rencontré la concierge en descendant** I met the caretaker on my way down; **d. en courant** to run down; **aide-moi à d.** help me down; **ils descendront par la face nord** they'll climb down *or* make their descent via the North face; **je descends toujours par l'escalier** I always go down by the stairs *or* take the stairs down; **dès qu'ils ont 15 ans, ils descendent dans la mine** as soon as they're 15 they go down the mine; **les plongeurs descendent jusqu'à 60 mètres** the divers go down to *or* reach depths of 60 metres; **quand les saumons descendent vers la mer** when the salmon go *or* swim downriver to the sea; **notre équipe est descendue à la huitième place** our team moved down *or* dropped to eighth place; **d. en seconde division** to move down to the second division; **le premier coureur à d. au-dessous de dix secondes au 100 mètres** the first runner to break ten seconds for the 100 metres; **l'ascenseur ne descend pas plus bas** the *Br* lift *or Am* elevator doesn't go down any further; **la pièce de monnaie ne voulait pas d. (dans la fente)** the coin wouldn't go down (the slot); **le store ne veut pas d.** the blind won't come down; **le yo-yo monte et descend** the yo-yo's going up and down; **son chapeau lui descendait jusqu'aux yeux** his/her hat came down over his/her eyes; **mes chaussettes descendent** my socks are coming down *or* slipping down; **fais d. la malade** help the patient down; **ils ont fait d. les passagers sur les rails** they made the passengers get down onto the tracks; **qu'il soit prêt ou non, fais-le d.** get him to come down, whether he's ready or not; **cette défaite fait d. notre équipe à la septième place** this defeat means that our team will move down *or* drop to seventh place; **je vais faire d. l'ascenseur** I'll call the *Br* lift *or Am* elevator; **c'est ce mécanisme qui fait**

d. la plate-forme this mechanism brings the platform down *or* lowers the platform; **d. de** *(échafaudage, échelle)* to come *or* to climb down from, to get down from; *(arbre)* to climb *or* to come down out of; *(balançoire)* to get off; *(colline)* to come down; **les marins descendent de la mâture** the seamen climb down the rigging; **descends de cette échelle!** get down from that ladder!; **peux-tu faire d. les enfants de cet arbre?** can you get the children down out of *or* down from that tree?; **descends de là, tu vas tomber** get down from there or you'll fall; **descends de ton nuage!** come down to earth!; **d. dans la rue** to take to the streets; **d. en soi-même** to take a close look at oneself

2 *(air froid, brouillard)* to come down; *(soleil)* to go down; **la nuit** *ou* **le soir descend** night is closing in *or* falling; **on sent la fraîcheur du soir d.** you can feel the cool of the evening coming down; **le soleil descend sur l'horizon** the sun is sinking *or* going down below the horizon

3 *(se rendre → dans un lieu d'altitude inférieure, dans le Sud, à la campagne)* to go down; **je descends au marché** I'm going to the market; **d. en ville** to go into town, *Am* to go downtown; **je suis descendu à Bordeaux en voiture** I drove down to Bordeaux; **ils sont descendus en auto-stop** they hitched down; **les voiliers descendront le long de la côte atlantique** the yachts will sail south along the Atlantic coast; **les réfugiés continuent à d. vers le sud** the refugees are still travelling south; **samedi, je descends chez mes parents** I'll go down to my parents' on Saturday

4 *(poser pied à terre → d'un véhicule)* to get off, *Sout* to alight; **ne pas d. avant l'arrêt complet du train** please do not attempt to alight until the train has come to a complete standstill; **tout le monde descend!** *(au terminus)* all change!; **d. à terre** to go ashore; **d. de bateau** to get off a boat, to land; **d. de voiture** to get out of a car; **il descendait de l'avion** he was getting off *or* out of the plane; **d. de cheval** to get off one's horse, to dismount; **d. de vélo** to get off one's bike; **ils nous ont fait d. du train** they made us get off the train; **descends vite!** *(d'une voiture, d'un train)* get *or* jump out, quick!; **à quelle station descendez-vous?** where do you get off?; **aider une vieille dame à d.** to help an old lady off

5 *(faire irruption)* **la police est descendue chez elle/dans son bar** the police raided her place/her bar

6 *(se loger)* to stay; **d. à l'hôtel** to put up at *or* to stay at a hotel; **nous descendons toujours à l'Hôtel de la Gare** we always stay at the Hôtel de la Gare

7 *Fam (repas, boisson)* to go down, to slip down; **ton petit vin rouge descend bien** your red wine goes down very easily; **les saucisses ne descendent pas** the sausages won't go down; **bois un café pour faire d. tout ça** have a coffee to wash it all down; **qu'est-ce qu'il descend!** *(il boit)* he certainly knows how to knock it back!; *(il mange)* he certainly knows how to put it away!

8 *Théât & (en danse)* to go downstage

B. 1 d. à *ou* **jusqu'à** *(cheveux, vêtement)* to come down to; *(puits)* to go down to; **des robes qui descendent jusqu'au genou/jusqu'aux chevilles** knee-length/ankle-length dresses; **la jupe doit d. jusqu'au-dessous du genou** the skirt must cover the knee; **cet automne, les robes descendront jusqu'au genou** this autumn, hemlines are coming down to the knee; **le puits descend jusqu'à 150 mètres** the well is 150 metres deep *or* goes down to 150 metres

2 *(suivre une pente → rivière)* to flow down; *(→ route)* to go down *or* downwards; *(→ toit)* to slope down; **le sentier descendait parmi les oliviers** the path threaded its way down through the olive grove; **un chemin qui descend** a downward path, a path that slopes down; **le fleuve descend vers la mer** the river flows down to the sea; **le jardin descend en pente douce jusqu'à la plage** the garden slopes gently down to the beach; **d. en pente raide** *(route, terrain, toit)* to drop sharply; **la route descend brusquement** the road suddenly dips; **la route descend en lacets** the road winds down

C. 1 *(baisser → marée, mer)* to go out, to ebb; *(→ prix)* to come down, to fall; **les eaux sont enfin descendues** the floods have subsided at last; **le mercure descend dans le baromètre** the mercury's dropping in the barometer; **la température est descendue au-dessous de zéro** the temperature has dropped *or* fallen below zero; **les températures ne descendent jamais au-dessous de 10°** temperatures never go below 10°; *Fam* **le thermomètre descend** the weather's *or* it's getting colder; **ses notes n'arrêtent pas de d. depuis mars** his/her marks have been getting worse since March; **les taux d'intérêt sont descendus brusquement** interest rates fell sharply *or* dropped suddenly; **le pain est descendu à un euro** bread's gone down to one euro; **faire d.** *(cours, fièvre, notes)* to bring down; *(inflation, prix)* to bring *or* to push down; **j'ai essayé de lui faire d. son prix** I tried to get him/her to lower his/her price; **ça a fait d. les prix** it brought prices down

2 *(s'abaisser moralement)* to stoop; **je ne descendrai jamais jusqu'à la supplier** I'll never stoop to begging her; **d. dans l'estime de qn** to go down in sb's estimation

3 *Mus* to go down, to drop down; **d. d'une octave** to go down *or* to drop an octave; **les altos descendent très bas dans la deuxième mesure** the altos go down very low in the second bar

VT *(aux avoir)* **1** *(parcourir → escalier, montagne)* to go down; **d. une pente** to go down a hill; **d. un escalier quatre à quatre** to race downstairs; **elle a descendu toute la pente sur le dos** she went *or* slid all the way down the slope on her back; **d. le courant** *(détritus, arbre)* to float downstream; **d. un fleuve** *(en nageant)* to swim downstream; *(en bateau)* to sail down a river; **ils ont descendu le Mississippi en radeau** they went down the Mississippi on a raft; *Ftbl* **il a descendu tout le terrain balle au pied** he ran the length of the field with the ball

2 *(placer plus bas → tableau)* to lower; *(→ store)* to pull down, to lower; **il faudrait d. le cadre de deux centimètres** the frame should be taken down two centimetres

3 *(porter vers le bas)* to take down, to get down; *(porter vers soi)* to bring down; **d. la poubelle** to take the rubbish down; **aide-moi à d. la valise du filet** help me take *or* lift *or* get the suitcase (down) from the rack; **descendez les chaises en bas de la pelouse** carry the chairs down to the far end of the lawn; **tu pourrais me d. une veste, s'il te plaît?** could you bring me down a jacket, please?; **d'abord, il faut d. l'équipement dans le puits** first, the equipment has to be lowered into the shaft; **ils ont descendu le sauveteur au bout d'une corde** they lowered the rescuer on the end of a rope

4 *(amener en voiture)* to take down, to drive down

5 *Fam (abattre → gangster)* to gun down ▀, to shoot down ▀; *(→ avion)* to bring down ▀, to shoot down ▀; **se faire d.** to get shot; **tu aurais pu te faire d.!** you could have got shot!

6 *Fam (critiquer)* to slate, to pan; **il s'est fait d. par le jury** he was slated by the jury

7 *Fam (boire → bouteille)* to down, to knock back; **il a descendu quelques bières** he knocked back a few beers

8 *Mus* **d. la gamme** to go *or* run down the scale

❑ **descendre de VT IND** *(être issu de)* to be descended from; **l'homme descend du singe** man is descended from the apes; **le prince descendait des Habsbourg** the prince was descended from the Habsburgs

---

descente [desɑ̃t] **NF 1** *(pente)* slope, hill; **d. dangereuse** steep gradient; **courir/déraper dans la d.** to run/to skid down; **on ira vite, il n'y a que des descentes** we'll do it in no time, it's all downhill

2 *(chute)* drop, fall

3 *(sortie d'un véhicule)* getting off, alighting; *Rail* **station en courbe, attention à la d.** *(sur panneau)* mind the gap; **à sa d. d'avion** as he/she disembarked *or* got off the aircraft; **à sa d. du bateau** as he/she landed *or* disembarked; **accueillir qn à la d. du train** to meet sb off the train

4 *Naut* companionway; **échelle de d.** companion ladder; **écoutille de d.** hatchway

5 *Mines* **d. de mine** descending shaft

6 *Ski* downhill race; **être bon en d.** *(cycliste)* to be good downhill *or* on the downhill sections; **d. en rappel** *(en alpinisme)* abseiling, *Am* rappeling; **faire une d. en rappel** to abseil down, *Am* to rappel down

7 *Aviat* descent; **d. en piqué** dive; **d. en spirale** spinning dive, spiral descent; **d. en vol plané** glide, gliding fall

8 *Méd* **d. d'organe** *ou* **d'organes** prolapse

9 *Constr* **d. d'antenne** downlead; **d. de gouttière** rainwater pipe, downpipe; **d. de paratonnerre** down inductor; **puits de d.** snow chute

10 *(contrôle)* inspection; *(attaque)* raid; **d. sur les lieux** inspection (on site); **faire une d.** *Admin* to carry out a (surprise) inspection; *Mil* to mount a raid; *Fam Fig* to make an unexpected visit ▀; *Fig Hum* **faire une d. sur qch** to raid sth; **il a encore fait une d. sur le chocolat!** he's been raiding *or* he's been at the chocolate again!; *Jur* **d. sur les lieux** visit to the scene *(of a crime etc)*; **d. de police** police raid

11 *Beaux-Arts* **d. de Croix** deposition

12 *Fam (locution)* **il a une bonne d.** *(il boit beaucoup)* he can really put it away *or* knock it back

❑ **descente de lit NF 1** *(tapis)* bedside rug

2 *Fam Péj (personne)* toady

déscolarisation [deskɔlarizasjɔ̃] **NF** *(action)* removal from school; *(résultat)* lack of schooling *or* education; **les impératifs des travaux agricoles conduisent à la d. des enfants des milieux ruraux** children in rural areas are taken out of school because of the demands of farm work; **on assiste à une d. massive des jeunes gitans** the level of school attendance among young gipsies is falling drastically

déscolarisé, -e [deskɔlarize] **ADJ un enfant d.** a child that has been taken out of the school system

déscolariser [3] [deskɔlarize] **VT** to take out of the school system

descripteur, -trice [dɛskriptœr, -tris] **NM,F** describer

NM *Ordinat* descriptor

descriptible [dɛskriptibl] **ADJ** describable; **sa joie n'était pas d.** his/her joy was beyond description *or* words

descriptif, -ive [dɛskriptif, -iv] **ADJ 1** *(présentation, texte)* descriptive; **devis d.** specification **2** *Beaux-Arts, Ling & Littérature* descriptive **3** *Géom* solid

NM *(d'un appartement)* description; *(de travaux)* specification

description [dɛskripsjɔ̃] **NF 1** *(fait de décrire)* description, depiction; **d. de poste** job description; **d. de brevet** patent specification; **faire la d. de qch** to describe *or* to depict sth **2** *Littérature* description, descriptive passage **3** *Ling* descriptive analysis *or* study

descriptive [dɛskriptiv] *voir* **descriptif**

descriptrice [dɛskriptris] *voir* **descripteur**

déséchouer [6] [dezeʃwe] **VT** to set afloat, to float off

►**se déséchouer VPR** to get afloat

déséconomie [dezekɔnɔmi] **NF** *Écon* diseconomy; **d. d'échelle** diseconomy of scale; **d. externe** external diseconomy

désectorisation [desɛktɔrizasjɔ̃] **NF** freedom of choice *(by virtue of the fact that parents no longer need to send their children to the school designated for their area)*; **la d. de l'école primaire se fera plus vite que celle de l'école secondaire** freedom of choice will come about in primary schools sooner than in secondary schools

désectoriser [3] [desɛktɔrize] **VT d. le primaire/secondaire** = to allow parents to choose which primary/secondary school they send their children to, regardless of where they live

déségrégation [desegregasjɔ̃] **NF** desegregation

désembellir [32] [dezɑ̃bɛlir] *Vieilli ou Littéraire* **VT** to disfigure, to spoil the beauty of

VI to lose one's beauty

des–des

désembourber [3] [dezãburbe] **VT** to pull or to get out of the mud

désembourgeoiser [3] [dezãburʒwaze] **VT** (personne) to free from bourgeois habits; (quartier) to make less bourgeois

▶**se désembourgeoiser VPR** (personne) to lose one's bourgeois mentality; (quartier, profession) to become less bourgeois

désembouteiller [4] [dezãbuteje] **VT 1** Aut to unblock; **d. les grandes villes** to ease the traffic in the big cities **2** Tél **d. le standard** to remove the overload from or to unjam the exchange

désembrayer [11] [dezãbreje] **VT** Ordinat to disconnect

désembrouiller [3] [dezãbruje] **VT 1** (gén) to disentangle, to make less complicated **2** Ordinat to unscramble

désembuage [dezãbɥaʒ] **NM** (processus) demisting; (dispositif) demister; **d. arrière** rear demister

désembuer [7] [dezãbɥe] **VT** to demist

désemparé, -e [dezãpare] **ADJ 1** (perdu) **être tout d.** to be lost; **sans argent dans cette ville étrangère, il était complètement d.** in a foreign town with no money, he had no idea what to do **2** Aviat & Naut crippled

désemparer [3] [dezãpare] **VT** (navire, avion) to disable

VI sans d. without a pause or break; **lire des heures sans d.** to read for hours on end

désemplir [32] [dezãplir] **VI leur maison ne désemplit pas** their house is always full

▶**se désemplir VPR** to empty

désencadrement [dezãkadrəmã] **NM 1** (d'un tableau) removal from its frame **2** Écon (des crédits) unblocking

désencadrer [3] [dezãkadre] **VT 1** (tableau) to remove from its frame **2** Écon **d. les crédits** to unblock credit, to ease credit restrictions

désenchaîner [4] [dezãʃene] **VT** Littéraire to unchain, to take out of or to free from one's chains

désenchanté, -e [dezãʃãte] **ADJ** (personne) disenchanted, disillusioned; (sourire) wistful

NM,F disenchanted or disaffected person; **les désenchantés du socialisme** those who have become disenchanted with socialism

désenchantement [dezãʃãtmã] **NM 1** Littéraire (désensorcellement) removal of a spell **2** (déception) disillusionment, disenchantment, disillusion

désenchanter [3] [dezãʃãte] **VT 1** Littéraire (désensorceler) to release or to free from a spell **2** (décevoir) to disillusion, to disappoint

désenclavement [dezãklavmã] **NM** (d'une région, d'un quartier) opening up

désenclaver [3] [dezãklave] **VT** (région, quartier) to open up

désenclencher [3] [dezãklãʃe] **VT** (mécanisme) to disengage

désencombrement [dezãkɔ̃brəmã] **NM** clearing, unblocking

désencombrer [3] [dezãkɔ̃bre] **VT** to clear (**de** of), to unblock

désencrage [dezãkraʒ] **NM** de-inking

désencrasser [3] [dezãkrase] **VT** (ustensile, four) to clean out; (moteur) to decarbonize, to decoke

désencrer [3] [dezãkre] **VT** to de-ink

désendettement [dezãdɛtmã] **NM** clearing of debts, degearing; **le d. des pays de l'Est se fera progressivement** Eastern European countries will gradually be relieved of their debt burden

désendetter [4] [dezãdete] **VT d. qn** to free sb of or to release sb from debt

▶**se désendetter VPR** to get out of debt, to clear one's debts

désenfiler [3] [dezãfile] **VT** (aiguille) to unthread; (perles) to unstring

▶**se désenfiler VPR** (aiguille) to come unthreaded; (perles) to come unstrung

désenflammer [3] [dezãflame] **VT** to reduce the inflammation in

▶**se désenflammer VPR** to become less inflamed

désenfler [3] [dezãfle] **VT** to bring down or to reduce the swelling of

VI to become less swollen; **ma cheville désenfle** the swelling in my ankle's going down; **la pommade a fait d. ma cheville** the cream made my swollen ankle go down or eased the swelling in my ankle

désenfumage [dezãfymaʒ] **NM** clearing of smoke (**de** from)

désenfumer [3] [dezãfyme] **VT** to clear of smoke

désengagement [dezãgaʒmã] **NM** disengagement, backing out

désengager [17] [dezãgaʒe] **VT 1** (libérer d'un engagement) to free or to release from a commitment; **d. qn d'une obligation** to free or release sb from an obligation **2** Mil to withdraw, to pull out

▶**se désengager VPR 1** (se dépolitiser) to give up one's political commitment **2** (se décommander) to back out of a commitment; **se d. d'une obligation** to free oneself of an obligation; **je ne peux pas me d.** I can't get out of it **3** Mil to withdraw, to pull out

désengorger [17] [dezãgɔrʒe] **VT** (tuyau, rue) to unblock, to clear; Écon **d. le marché** to reduce the overload on the market

désengrener [19] [dezãgrəne] **VT** to disengage, to ungear

▶**se désengrener VPR** to become disengaged

désenivrer [3] [dezãnivre] **VT** to sober up

VI to sober up; **il ne désenivre pas** he's never sober

▶**se désenivrer VPR** to sober up

désennuyer [14] [dezãnɥije] **VT** to dispel the boredom of

▶**se désennuyer VPR** to dispel one's boredom

désenrayer [11] [dezãreje] **VT** to unjam

▶**se désenrayer VPR** to come unstuck

désensablement [dezãsabləmã] **NM** (d'un cours d'eau) dredging (of sand)

désensabler [3] [dezãsable] **VT 1** (extraire) to get out of or to extract from the sand **2** (nettoyer) to free or to clear of sand

▶**se désensabler VPR** (chenal) to become clear of sand

désensibilisation [desãsibilizasjɔ̃] **NF 1** Méd & Phot desensitizing, desensitization **2** (perte d'intérêt) loss of interest (**à** in) **3** (perte de la sensibilité) desensitization; **la d. est l'une des conséquences de l'exposition répétée à la violence télévisuelle** the viewer becomes inured to violence through repeated exposure to violent images on television

désensibiliser [3] [desãsibilize] **VT 1** Méd & Phot to desensitize **2** (désintéresser) **d. qn à qch** to make sb lose interest in sth **3** (rendre insensible) to desensitize; **la violence à l'écran tend à d. les téléspectateurs** viewers become inured to violence through seeing so much of it on television

▶**se désensibiliser VPR** (devenir insensible) to become desensitized (**à** to)

désensorceler [24] [dezãsɔrsəle] **VT** to free or to release from a spell

désentoilage [dezãtwalaʒ] **NM** (d'un cadre) removal of the canvas (**de** from); (des ailes d'un planeur) removal of the fabric (**de** from)

désentoiler [3] [dezãtwale] **VT** (cadre) to remove the canvas from; (ailes d'un planeur) to remove the fabric from

désentortiller [3] [dezãtɔrtije] **VT 1** (détordre) to untwist **2** (démêler) to disentangle, to sort out

désentraver [3] [dezãtrave] **VT** to unchain

désenvaser [3] [dezãvaze] **VT 1** (extraire) to get out of or to extract from the mud **2** (nettoyer) to clear (of mud)

désenvelopper [3] [dezãvlɔpe] **VT** to unwrap, to remove the wrappings from

désenvenimer [3] [dezãvnime] **VT 1** Méd to cleanse of venom, to take the venom out of **2** (apaiser → querelle, discussion) to take the sting out of; **elle est intervenue pour d. le débat** she broke in to pour oil on troubled waters

désenverguer [3] [dezãvɛrge] **VT** Naut (voile) to unbend

désenvoûtement [dezãvutmã] **NM** removal of a/the spell; **procéder au d. de qn** to remove a/the spell from sb

désenvoûter [3] [dezãvute] **VT** to remove a/the spell from

désépaissir [32] [dezepesir] **VT** (sauce) to thin (down); (cheveux) to thin (out)

désépargne [dezeparɲ] **NF** Écon dissaving

déséquilibre [dezekilibr] **NM 1** (inégalité) imbalance; **il y a un d. dans les programmes de la chaîne** the channel's schedule is unbalanced **2** Écon disequilibrium, imbalance; **d. de la balance commerciale** unfavourable trade balance; **d. financier** financial imbalance **3** (perte d'équilibre) loss of balance **4** Psy **d. mental** ou **psychique** derangement **5** Physiol imbalance

❑ **en déséquilibre ADJ** (mal posé) off balance; (branlant) unsteady, wobbly

déséquilibré, -e [dezekilibre] **ADJ** (personne, esprit) unbalanced, mentally disturbed

NM,F unbalanced or mentally disturbed person

déséquilibrer [3] [dezekilibre] **VT 1** (faire perdre l'équilibre à) to throw off balance; (faire tomber) to tip over; **le vent l'a déséquilibré** the wind blew him off balance **2** (déstabiliser → système, économie) to throw off balance, to destabilize **3** (faire déraisonner) **d. qn** to disturb the balance of sb's mind

déséquiper [3] [dezekipe] **VT 1** (navire) to lay up; (machine) to take down; (voilages) to unrig **2** Théât (scène) to dismantle the scenery of

désert, -e [dezɛr, -ɛrt] **ADJ** (abandonné) deserted, empty; (inhabité) desolate, uninhabited; **l'endroit était d.** the place was deserted, there was nobody around

NM 1 Géog desert; **d. de sable** sandy desert; **le d. d'Arabie** the Arabian Desert; **le d. d'Atacama** the Atacama Desert; **le d. de Gobi** the Gobi Desert; **le d. du Kalahari** the Kalahari Desert; **le d. de Libye** the Libyan Desert; **le d. Mohave** the Mojave or Mohave Desert; **le d. du Namib** the Namib Desert; **le d. de Nubie** the Nubian Desert; **le d. du Sahara** the Sahara Desert; **le d. de Syrie** the Syrian Desert

2 (lieu inhabité) desert, wilderness, wasteland; **c'est le d. ici!** it's deserted here!; **un d. de béton** a concrete desert; **il parle** ou **parle** ou **prêche dans le d.** his words fall on deaf ears

3 Littéraire (monotonie) vacuity; **le d. de ma vie** my vacuous or empty life

déserter [3] [dezɛrte] **VI** Mil to desert

VT 1 (quitter sans permission) to desert; **pour avoir déserté son poste** for having deserted his post **2** (abandonner → parti, cause) to abandon, to give up on **3** (sujet: touristes, clients) to desert; **un village déserté** a deserted or abandoned village **4** Littéraire (amant, ami) to abandon, to forsake

déserteur [dezɛrtœr] **NM** deserter

désertification [dezɛrtifikasjɔ̃] **NF** (transformation en désert) desertification; (dépeuplement) depopulation

désertifier [9] [dezɛrtifje] **se désertifier VPR** to turn into a desert

désertion [dezɛrsjɔ̃] **NF 1** Mil desertion **2** (fait de quitter) **la d. des campagnes** the rural exodus **3** (d'une cause, d'un parti) deserting, abandoning

désertique [dezɛrtik] **ADJ** (du désert) desert (avant n); (sans végétation) infertile

désertisation [dezɛrtizasjɔ̃] **NF** (transformation en désert) desertification; (dépeuplement) depopulation

désescalade [dezɛskalad] **NF 1** Mil de-escalation **2** (diminution progressive) decline; **le conflit semble désormais en phase de d.** the conflict now seems to be winding down

désespérance [dezɛsperãs] **NF** Littéraire despair

désespérant, -e [dezɛsperã, -ãt] **ADJ 1** (navrant) hopeless; **d'une paresse désespérante** hopelessly lazy; **il ne sait toujours pas compter, c'est d.!** he still can't count, it's hopeless!; **toujours pas de lettre, c'est d.!** still no letter, it's enough to drive you to despair! **2** (très mauvais → temps) appalling, dreadful; **ses menus sont désespérants!** his/her menus are dreadful! **3** (douloureux) appalling, distressing, terrible; **le spectacle d. des enfants affamés** the heart-breaking sight of starving children

désespéré, -e [dezɛspere] **ADJ 1** (au désespoir → personne) in despair, distressed **2** (qui exprime le désespoir → regard, cri) desperate **3** (extrême → tentative) desperate, reckless; (→ mesure, situation) desperate **4** (sans espoir) hopeless; **c'est un cas d.**

(incorrigible) it's a hopeless case; *(gravement malade)* the patient is critical; **être dans un état d.** *(malade)* to be in a critical condition
NM,F1 *(personne sans espoir)* desperate person **2** *(suicidé)* suicide

désespérément [dezɛsperemã] **ADV 1** *(avec désespoir, avec acharnement)* desperately; **on entendait appeler d. à l'aide** desperate cries for help could be heard **2** *(extrêmement)* hopelessly, desperately; **ce train est d. lent** this train is desperately slow; **je suis d. seul** I'm desperately *or* horribly lonely

désespérer [18] [dezɛspere] **VI** to despair, to give up hope; **il ne faut jamais d.!** you should never give up hope!, *Hum* never say die!
VT 1 *(exaspérer)* to drive to despair; **tu me désespères!** what am I going to do with you? **2** *(décourager)* to drive *or* to reduce to despair; **elle en a désespéré plus d'un** she's driven more than one (suitor) to despair
❏ **désespérer de VT IND d. de qch** to have lost faith in sth; **d. de qn** to despair of sb; **je désespère de ses capacités** I no longer believe he's/she's capable of anything; **d. de faire qch** to despair of doing sth; **ils désespéraient d'atteindre la côte** they despaired of reaching the shore; **je ne désespère pas d'obtenir le poste** I still think I may get *or* I haven't yet given up on the idea of getting the job
▸**se désespérer VPR**to (be in) despair

désespoir [dezɛspwar] **NM 1** *(détresse)* despair; **faire le d. de qn** to drive *or* to reduce sb to despair; **à mon grand d., il n'a pu venir** to my despair, he was unable to come; **avec d.** despairingly, in despair; **cette sauce est mon d.** I despair of ever being able to make this sauce
2 *Bot* **d. des peintres** London pride
❏ **au désespoir ADJ**être au d. *(être désespéré)* to be desperate, to have lost all hope; **je suis au d. de ne pouvoir vous aider** I'm deeply *or* desperately sorry that I am unable to help you **ADV mettre qn au d.** to drive *or* to reduce sb to despair; **tu me mets au d.** I despair of you
❏ **en désespoir de cause ADV** in desperation, as a last resort; **en d. de cause, elle essaya sa propre clef** as a last resort she tried her own key
❏ **en désespoir ADV** *Can Fam (beaucoup) Br* dead, *Am* real; **je suis fatigué en d.** I'm *Br* dead *or Am* real tired

désétablissement [dezetablismã] **NM** disestablishment
désétatisation [dezetatizasjɔ̃] **NF** denationalization
désétatiser [3] [dezetatize] **VT** to denationalize
désexcitation [dezɛksitasjɔ̃] **NF** *Élec* de-energization, de-energizing
désexciter [3] [dezɛksite] **VT** *Élec* to de-energize
désexualiser [3] [desɛksɥalize] **VT** to desex
déshabillage [dezabijaʒ] **NM 1** *(d'une personne)* undressing; **une cabine pour le** *ou* **de d.** a cubicle *(for undressing)* **2** *(dégarnissage → d'une pièce)* emptying *(of ornaments)*; *(→ d'un fauteuil)* stripping of upholstery **(de** from)
déshabillé [dezabije] **NM**négligé
déshabiller [3] [dezabije] **VT 1** *(dévêtir)* **d. qn** to undress sb, to take sb's clothes off; **d. qn du regard** to undress sb with one's eyes; **c'est d. saint Pierre pour habiller saint Paul** it's robbing Peter to pay Paul **2** *(vider → pièce)* to empty *(of ornaments)*; *(dégarnir → fauteuil)* to strip the upholstery from
▸**se déshabiller VPR1** *(se dénuder)* to strip (off), to take one's clothes off **2** *(ôter son manteau etc)* **déshabille-toi** take off your coat
déshabituer [7] [dezabitɥe] **VT d. qn du tabac/de l'alcool** to wean sb off cigarettes/alcohol; **d. qn de faire qch** to get sb out of the habit of doing sth
▸**se déshabituer VPR il s'est déshabitué du tabac/de l'alcool** he got out of the habit of smoking/drinking; **se d. de faire qch** to get oneself out of the habit of doing sth
désherbage [dezɛrbaʒ] **NM**weeding
désherbant, -e [dezɛrbã, -ãt] **ADJ** weed-killing *(avant n)*
NMweedkiller
désherber [3] [dezɛrbe] **VT**to weed

déshérence [dezerãs] **NF**escheat
❏ **en déshérence ADJ** *(succession)* escheated **ADV**tomber en d. to escheat
déshérité, -e [dezerite] **ADJ 1** *(pauvre)* underprivileged, deprived **2** *(région)* poor *(lacking natural advantages)* **3** *(privé d'héritage)* disinherited
NM,Fdeprived person; **les déshérités** the destitute
déshéritement [dezeritmã] **NM**disinheritance
déshériter [3] [dezerite] **VT 1** *(priver d'héritage)* to cut out of one's will, to disinherit; *Hum* **si tu continues, je te déshérite!** carry on like this and I'll cut you off without a penny! **2** *(défavoriser)* **il se croit déshérité** he feels hard done by
déshonnête [dezɔnɛt] **ADJ** *Littéraire* immodest, improper, indecent
déshonneur [dezɔnœr] **NM 1** *(perte de l'honneur)* disgrace, dishonour; **vivre dans le d.** to live in dishonour **2** *(honte)* disgrace; **il n'y a aucun d. à travailler de ses mains** there's no disgrace in working with one's hands; **c'est le d. de sa famille** he's a disgrace to his family
déshonorant, -e [dezɔnɔrã, -ãt] **ADJ1** *(qui prive de l'honneur)* dishonourable, disgraceful **2** *(humiliant)* degrading, shameful; **cela n'a rien de d.** there's nothing shameful about it
déshonorer [3] [dezɔnɔre] **VT 1** *(nuire à l'honneur de)* to dishonour, to bring shame upon, to bring into disrepute; **cette attitude déshonore la profession tout entière** such behaviour brings the whole profession into disrepute; **il a déshonoré le nom de ses ancêtres** he has dishonoured the family name
2 *Littéraire (abuser de → femme, jeune fille)* to ruin
3 *Littéraire (lieu, monument)* to spoil *or* to ruin the look of
▸**se déshonorer VPR** to bring disgrace upon oneself
déshuilage [dezɥilaʒ] **NM**de-oiling
déshuiler [3] [dezɥile] **VT**to de-oil, to remove oil from
déshuileur [dezɥilœr] **NM**oil-separator
déshumanisant, -e [dezymanizã, -ãt] **ADJ**dehumanizing
déshumanisation [dezymanizasjɔ̃] **NF** dehumanization
déshumanisé, -e [dezymanize] **ADJ 1** *(lieu)* impersonal; *(personne, ton)* coldhearted, unsympathetic **2** *(fabrication, travail)* automated
déshumaniser [3] [dezymanize] **VT** to dehumanize
▸**se déshumaniser VPR** to become dehumanized
déshumidificateur [dezymidifikatœr] **NM** dehumidifier
déshumidification [dezymidifikasjɔ̃] **NF**dehumidification
déshumidifier [9] [dezymidifje] **VT**to dehumidify
déshydratant, -e [dezidratã, -ãt] **ADJ** demoisturizing
NMdesiccant
déshydratation [dezidratasjɔ̃] **NF1** *Physiol* dehydration; *(de la peau)* loss of moisture, dehydration; **évitez la d.** avoid dehydration *or* becoming dehydrated; **être dans un état de d.** to be dehydrated **2** *Tech* dehydration, dewatering; **d. des boues** sludge dewatering **3** *Chim* dehydration
déshydraté, -e [dezidrate] **ADJ1** *Physiol* dehydrated **2** *(aliment)* desiccated, dehydrated
déshydrater [3] [dezidrate] **VT 1** *Physiol* to dehydrate; *(peau)* to dehydrate, to dry (out) **2** *Tech* to dehydrate, to dewater **3** *(aliment)* to dehydrate, to desiccate; **noix de coco déshydratée** desiccated coconut **4** *Chim* to dehydrate
▸**se déshydrater VPR** *(personne)* to get dehydrated; *(peau)* to lose moisture, to become dehydrated; **on se déshydrate beaucoup en avion** you get very dehydrated when you fly
déshydrogénase [dezidrɔʒenaz] **NF** *Chim* dehydrogenase
déshydrogénation [dezidrɔʒenasjɔ̃] **NF** *Chim* dehydrogenation, dehydrogenization
déshydrogéné, -e [dezidrɔʒene] **ADJ** *Chim* dehydrogenated
déshydrogéner [18] [dezidrɔʒene] **VT** *Chim* to dehydrogenate, to dehydrogenize

déshypothéquer [18] [dezipoteke] **VT**to free from mortgage
désidérabilité [deziderabilite] **NF** *Écon* desirability, use-value
desiderata [deziderata] **NMPL** requirements, wishes; **les d. du personnel** the wishes of the staff; *Hum* **le menu est-il conforme à tes d.?** does the menu meet with your requirements?
design [dizajn] **NM 1** *(création)* design; **d. industriel** industrial design **2** *(comme adj inv)* designer *(avant n)*; **mobilier d.** modern *or* contemporary furniture
désignation [deziɲasjɔ̃] **NF 1** *(appellation)* designation; *(de marchandises)* description **2** *(nomination)* appointment, nomination; **d. de nouveaux membres d'une commission** appointment of new members of a committee **3** *Jur* **d. du défendeur/requérant** name of the defendant/plaintiff
désigné, -e [deziɲe] **ADJc'est le porte-parole tout d. des élèves** he's the ideal spokesperson for the students; **être tout désigné pour faire qch** to be the right person to do sth; **elle est toute désignée pour succéder à son oncle** she's the most suitable choice as her uncle's successor
designer [dizajnœr] **NM**designer
désigner [3] [deziɲe] **VT1** *(montrer)* to indicate, to point at *or* to, to show; **d. qn du doigt** to point at sb
2 *(choisir)* to choose, to single out; **d. qn comme héritier** to name sb as one's heir
3 *(nommer → expert, président)* to appoint; *(→ représentant)* to nominate; *(élire)* to elect; **d. qn pour un poste** to appoint sb to a post; **le président de séance a été désigné à la majorité des voix** the chairperson was elected by a majority of votes
4 *(nommer, s'appliquer à)* to refer to; **d. qn par son nom** to refer to sb by name; **d. qn par un surnom** to call sb by a nickname; **le mot "félin" désigne de nombreux animaux** the word "feline" refers to many animals
5 *Admin (répertorier)* to list, to set out; **les conditions désignées à l'annexe ii** the specifications set out in Annex ii
6 *(destiner)* **sa compétence la désigne pour cet emploi** his/her ability makes him/her the right person for the job
7 *(exposer)* **un geste qui vous désignera à sa fureur** a gesture which will surely unleash his/her fury on you; **d. qch à l'attention de qn** to call *or* draw sb's attention to sth
▸**se désigner VPR1** *(se proposer)* to volunteer; **se d. pour une mission** to volunteer for a mission **2 se d. à l'attention générale** to draw attention to oneself
désiliciage [desilisjaʒ] **NM***Chim* desilication
désillusion [dezilyzjɔ̃] **NF** disappointment, disillusion, disillusion; **connaître des désillusions** to be disillusioned *or* disenchanted
désillusionnement [dezilyzjɔnmã] **NM** disillusionment
désillusionner [3] [dezilyzjɔne] **VT**to disillusion; **être désillusionné** to be disenchanted *or* disillusioned
désincarcération [dezɛ̃karserasjɔ̃] **NF**freeing; **sa d. a pris une heure** it took an hour to free him/her
désincarcérer [18] [dezɛ̃karsere] **VT** *(des débris, d'une voiture etc)* to free
désincarnation [dezɛ̃karnasjɔ̃] **NF** disembodiment
désincarné, -e [dezɛ̃karne] **ADJ 1** *(sans corps)* disembodied **2** *(irréel)* insubstantial, unreal
désincarner [3] [dezɛ̃karne] **se désincarner VPR** to become disembodied
désincrustant, -e [dezɛ̃krystã, -ãt] **ADJ1** *(pour la peau)* cleansing; **masque d.** face pack *or* mask **2** *(détartrant)* descaling
NM 1 *(pour la peau)* cleanser **2** *(détartrant)* scale solvent
désincrustation [dezɛ̃krystasjɔ̃] **NF1** *(de la peau)* cleansing **2** *(détartrage)* descaling
désincruster [3] [dezɛ̃kryste] **VT 1** *(peau)* to cleanse **2** *(détartrer)* to descale
désindexation [dezɛ̃dɛksasjɔ̃] **NF** removal of index-linking **(de** from), deindexing **(de** of)
désindexer [4] [dezɛ̃dɛkse] **VT** to stop index-linking, to de-index; **ces retraites ont été**

désindexées these retirement schemes are no longer index-linked

désindustrialisation [dezɛ̃dystrijalizasjɔ̃] **NF** deindustrialization

désindustrialiser [3] [dezɛ̃dystrijalize] **VT** to deindustrialize

désinence [dezinɑ̃s] **NF 1** *Gram* inflection, ending **2** *Bot* terminal growing

désinentiel, -elle [dezinɑ̃sjɛl] **ADJ** *Ling* desinential

désinfectant, -e [dezɛ̃fɛktɑ̃, -ɑ̃t] **ADJ** disinfecting *(avant n)*
   NM disinfectant

désinfecter [4] [dezɛ̃fɛkte] **VT** to disinfect

désinfection [dezɛ̃fɛksjɔ̃] **NF** disinfection, disinfecting

désinflation [dezɛ̃flasjɔ̃] **NF** deflation, disinflation

désinflationniste [dezɛ̃flasjɔnist] **ADJ** deflationary, deflationist

désinformateur, -trice [dezɛ̃fɔrmatœr, -tris] **ADJ** disinformative
   NM disinformer

désinformation [dezɛ̃fɔrmasjɔ̃] **NF** disinformation

désinformatrice [dezɛ̃fɔrmatris] *voir* **désinformateur**

désinformer [3] [dezɛ̃fɔrme] **VT** to disinform

désinhiber [3] [dezinibe] **VT d. qn** to rid sb of his/her inhibitions

désinscrire [99] [desɛ̃skrir] **se désinscrire VPR** *Ordinat* to unsubscribe

désinsectisation [dezɛ̃sɛktizasjɔ̃] **NF** insect control; **la d. de l'immeuble aura lieu demain** the building will be cleared of insects tomorrow

désinsectiser [3] [dezɛ̃sɛktize] **VT** to clear of insects

désinsertion [dezɛ̃sɛrsjɔ̃] **NF d. sociale** dropping out

désinstallateur [dezɛ̃stalatœr] **NM** *Ordinat* deinstaller

désinstallation [dezɛ̃stalasjɔ̃] **NF** *Ordinat* deinstallation

désinstaller [3] [dezɛ̃stale] **VT** *Ordinat* to deinstall

désintégration [dezɛ̃tegrasjɔ̃] **NF 1** *(d'un matériau, d'un groupe)* disintegration, breaking-up, splitting **2** *Nucl* disintegration; **d. radioactive** radioactive decay

désintégrer [18] [dezɛ̃tegre] **VT 1** *(matériau)* to crumble, to disintegrate; *(groupe, famille)* to break up, to split (up) **2** *Nucl* to disintegrate
   ▶**se désintégrer VPR 1** *(exploser)* to disintegrate **2** *(groupe, famille, théorie)* to disintegrate, to collapse **3** *Hum (disparaître)* to vanish into thin air

désintéressé, -e [dezɛ̃terese] **ADJ 1** *(impartial → conseil, jugement)* disinterested, objective, unprejudiced **2** *(généreux → personne)* selfless, unselfish

désintéressement [dezɛ̃terɛsmɑ̃] **NM 1** *(impartialité)* disinterestedness, impartiality, absence of bias **2** *(générosité)* selflessness **3** *(désintérêt)* **d. pour** lack of interest in, indifference to **4** *Fin (d'un créancier)* paying off; *(d'un actionnaire, de partenaire)* buying out

désintéresser [4] [dezɛ̃terese] **VT** *(créancier)* to pay off; *(actionnaire, partenaire)* to buy out
   ▶**se désintéresser VPR se d. de** *(ignorer)* to be uninterested in; *(perdre son intérêt pour)* to lose interest in

désintérêt [dezɛ̃terɛ] **NM** indifference, lack of interest; **manifester du d. pour** to show indifference to *or* no interest in

désintermédiation [dezɛ̃tɛrmedjasjɔ̃] **NF** *Écon* disintermediation

désintoxication [dezɛ̃tɔksikasjɔ̃] **NF** *Méd* detoxification; *Fig* **la d. idéologique d'un pays** ridding a country of pernicious ideological influences

désintoxiquer [3] [dezɛ̃tɔksike] **VT** *Méd* to detoxify; **se faire d.** *(drogué)* to be weaned off drugs; *(alcoolique)* to be weaned off alcohol; *Fig* **l'association s'efforce de d. les exadeptes de la secte** the association is trying to wean the ex-members away from the influence of the sect; *Fam* **c'est un drogué de la télé, il faut le d.!** he's a complete TV addict, we need to get him out of the habit!
   ▶**se désintoxiquer VPR** *(drogué)* to kick the

habit; *(alcoolique)* to dry out; *Fig (se remettre en forme)* to detox

désinvestir [32] [dezɛ̃vɛstir] **VT 1** *Écon* to disinvest in **2** *Mil* **d. une ville** to raise the blockade of a town
   VI to become less involved

désinvestissement [dezɛ̃vɛstismɑ̃] **NM 1** *Écon* disinvestment; **d. marginal** marginal disinvestment **2** *Psy* withdrawal of involvement

désinvolte [dezɛ̃vɔlt] **ADJ 1** *(sans embarras → personne)* casual, nonchalant; *(→ mouvements)* easy, free; **d'un ton d.** casually **2** *Péj (trop libre)* offhand

désinvolture [dezɛ̃vɔltyr] **NF 1** *(légèreté → d'une personne)* casualness, nonchalance; *(→ des mouvements)* ease **2** *Péj (négligence)* offhandedness; **avec d.** offhandedly; **elle le traite avec d.** she's rather offhand with him

désir [dezir] **NM 1** *(aspiration)* want, wish, desire; *(souhait exprimé)* wish; **il a le d. de plaire** he aims to please; **ses désirs ont été satisfaits** his/her wishes have been met; **j'ai toujours eu le d. d'écrire** I've always wanted to *or* had a desire to write; **tu prends tes désirs pour des réalités!** wishful thinking!; **selon le d. de qn** following sb's wishes; **il sera fait selon votre d.** it shall be done as you wish; **à l'encontre des désirs de qn** against sb's wishes; *Hum* **tes désirs sont des ordres** your wish is my command **2** *(motivation)* desire, drive; *Psy* urge; **d. d'enfant** wish to reproduce; **d. de mort** death wish **3** *(appétit sexuel)* desire; **rempli de d.** *(personne)* consumed with desire; *(regard)* lustful

désirabilité [dezirabilite] **NF** desirability

désirable [dezirabl] **ADJ 1** *(souhaitable)* desirable; **il a toutes les qualités désirables** he has all the qualities one could wish for; **peu d.** undesirable **2** *(séduisant)* desirable, (sexually) exciting

désirer [3] [dezire] **VT 1** *(aspirer à → paix, bonheur)* to wish for; **d. ardemment qch** to crave (for) sth, to long for sth; **je ne désire pas leur perte** I do not wish to ruin them; **je n'ai plus rien à d.** I have nothing left to wish for; **il a tout ce qu'il peut d.** he has everything he could wish for; **elle a toujours désiré posséder un piano** she's always wanted to own a piano; **je désirerais savoir si...** I would like to know if...; **d. vivement rencontrer qn** to be eager to meet sb; **ton père se fait d.!** where could your father have got to?; **fais-toi d.** let them wait for you; **cette bière se fait d.!** how long's that beer going to take?; **laisser à d.** to leave a lot to be desired, to fail to come up to expectations; **ça laisse à d.** it leaves a lot to be desired
   2 *(vouloir)* **d. faire** to want *or* to wish to do; **désirez-vous ouvrir un compte?** do you want *or* wish to open an account?; **je désire faire une déposition** I would like to make a statement; **les enfants désirent rester avec leur père** the children would prefer to stay with their father; **il ne désirait pas vous faire de la peine** he didn't mean to hurt you; **je désire que tu restes** I want *or* Sout wish you to stay
   3 *(dans un achat, une prestation de service)* **vous désirez?** can I help you?; **quelle couleur désirez-vous?** which colour would you like?
   4 *(sexuellement)* to desire; **désirez-vous toujours votre mari?** do you still find your husband (sexually) attractive?
   USAGE ABSOLU tu ne peux d. mieux you couldn't wish for anything better

désireux, -euse [deziʁø, -øz] **ADJ d. de faire** inclined *or* willing to do; **d. de plaire** anxious to please; **très d. de faire** eager to do; **assez peu d. de le suivre** reluctant to follow him; **il était apparemment peu d. de poursuivre la discussion** apparently, he was not willing to continue the discussion

désistement [dezistəmɑ̃] **NM 1** *Pol* withdrawal, standing down **2** *Jur (d'une poursuite)* withdrawal; *(d'une demande)* waiver; **d. volontaire** withdrawal *(before committing crime)*

désister [3] [deziste] **se désister VPR 1** *Pol* to stand down, to withdraw **2** *Jur* **se d. d'une poursuite** to withdraw a suit; **se d. d'une demande** to waive a claim

desk [dɛsk] **NM** *Journ* desk

deskman [dɛskman] **NM** *Journ* deskman

desman [dɛsmɑ̃] **NM** *Zool* desman; **d. musqué** muskrat

desmodromique [dɛsmɔdrɔmik] **ADJ** *Tech* positive

desmolase [dɛsmɔlaz] **NF** *Biol* desmolase

desmosome [dɛsmɔzɔm] **NM** *Biol* desmosome

desmotropie [dɛsmɔtrɔpi] **NF** *Chim* desmotropism, desmotropy

désobéir [32] [dezɔbeir] **VI 1** *(être désobéissant)* to be disobedient
   2 *(enfreindre un ordre)* to disobey; **d. à** to disobey, to fail to obey; **d. aux ordres/à ses parents** to disobey orders/one's parents; **tu m'as désobéi!** you disobeyed me!, you didn't do as you were told!; **d. aux lois** to break the law; **d. à un code** to disregard a code
   VT *(au passif uniquement)* **elle n'accepte pas d'être désobéie** she will not stand for disobedience

désobéissance [dezɔbeisɑ̃s] **NF** disobedience (**à qn** to sb); **d. à une règle** disregard for *or* breaking of a rule; **d. civile** civil disobedience

désobéissant, -e [dezɔbeisɑ̃, -ɑ̃t] **ADJ** *(enfant)* disobedient, rebellious; *(chien)* disobedient

désobligeamment [dezɔbliʒamɑ̃] **ADV** disagreeably, unpleasantly

désobligeance [dezɔbliʒɑ̃s] **NF** disagreeableness

désobligeant, -e [dezɔbliʒɑ̃, -ɑ̃t] **ADJ 1** *(personne → désagréable)* disagreeable, unkind; *(→ impoli)* rude; **d'un ton d.** sharply **2** *(propos → blessant)* invidious; *(→ méchant)* nasty

désobliger [17] [dezɔbliʒe] **VT** to offend, to hurt, to upset; **vous le désobligeriez en ne venant pas à son dîner** you'd offend him by not coming to his dinner party; **sans vouloir vous d.** no offence (meant)

désobstruction [dezɔpstryksjɔ̃] **NF 1** *(d'un tuyau)* clearing **2** *Méd* removal of obstructions (**de** from)

désobstruer [7] [dezɔpstrye] **VT 1** *(tuyau)* to clear **2** *Méd* to remove an obstruction from

désoccupation [dezɔkypasjɔ̃] **NF** *Littéraire* want of occupation, idleness

désoccupé, -e [dezɔkype] **ADJ** *Littéraire* unoccupied, idle

désocialisation [desɔsjalizasjɔ̃] **NF** isolation from society; **on assiste à un phénomène de d. parmi les travailleurs à domicile** people who work from home are becoming cut off *or* isolated from society

désocialisé, -e [desɔsjalize] **ADJ** isolated *or* cut off from society
   NM,F social misfit

désocialiser [3] [desɔsjalize] **VT** to isolate from society

désodé, -e [desɔde] **ADJ** sodium-free, salt-free

désodorisant, -e [dezɔdɔrizɑ̃, -ɑ̃t] **ADJ** deodorizing *(avant n)*
   NM air freshener

désodoriser [3] [dezɔdɔrize] **VT** to deodorize

désœuvré, -e [dezœvre] **ADJ** **être d.** to have nothing to do; **d., il errait dans le parc** having nothing (better) to do, he would roam about the park; **je ne supporte pas de rester d. plus de cinq minutes** I can't bear to be idle for more than five minutes
   NM,F idle person

désœuvrement [dezœvrəmɑ̃] **NM** idleness; **ils ne le font que par d.** they only do it because they have nothing better to do

désolant, -e [dezɔlɑ̃, -ɑ̃t] **ADJ 1** *(triste → spectacle)* wretched, pitiful, awful **2** *(contrariant)* annoying, irritating; **il n'a rien fait, c'est d.!** he didn't do anything, it's so annoying!

désolation [dezɔlasjɔ̃] **NF 1** *(chagrin)* desolation, grief; **être plongé dans la d.** to be disconsolate; **après son départ, ce fut la d.** when he'd/she'd gone, gloom descended **2** *(cause de chagrin)* **cet enfant est ma d.** I despair of this child **3** *Littéraire (d'un lieu, d'un paysage)* desolation, desolateness, bleakness

désolé, -e [dezɔle] **ADJ 1** *(contrit)* apologetic, contrite; **à sa mine désolée, j'ai compris qu'il l'avait cassé** when I saw him looking so apologetic, I gathered he'd broken it
   2 *(pour s'excuser)* sorry; **je suis vraiment d.** I am awfully or really sorry; **d. de vous déranger** sorry to disturb you; **il est d. de ne pas vous avoir vu** he's sorry he missed you; **d., je n'ai pas**

le temps sorry, I haven't got the time; *Ironique* **d., j'étais là avant vous!** excuse me *or* sorry, (but) I was here before you!; **ah, je suis d., ces deux notions ne sont pas identiques** excuse me *or* I'm sorry, but these two concepts are not the same
3 *Littéraire (triste)* disconsolate, sorrowful
4 *Littéraire (aride)* desolate, bleak
désoler [3] [dezɔle] VT 1 *(attrister)* to distress, to sadden; **l'état de la maison le désole** he's distressed about the state of the house 2 *(irriter)* **tu me désoles!** I despair (of you)!
▸**se désoler** VPR to be sorry; **ne te désole pas pour une petite tache** there's no need to be sorry about a little stain; **se d. de qch** to be disconsolate *or* in despair about *or* over sth; **ses parents se désolent de la voir si malheureuse** it grieves her parents to see her so unhappy
désolidariser [3] [desɔlidarize] VT 1 *(personnes)* to divide 2 *(objets, pièces d'un ensemble)* to separate
▸**se désolidariser** VPR **se d. de** to dissociate oneself from
désoperculer [3] [dezɔpɛrkyle] VT *(rayon de miel)* to uncap
désopilant, -e [dezɔpilɑ̃, -ɑ̃t] ADJ hilarious, hysterically funny
désopiler [3] [dezɔpile] VT *Littéraire ou Vieilli* **d. (la rate à) qn** to have sb in stitches; **c'était à d. la rate** it was side-splitting
désorbitation [dezɔrbitasjɔ̃] NF *Astron* de-orbiting
désordonné, -e [dezɔrdɔne] ADJ 1 *(désorganisé → dossier, esprit)* confused, untidy 2 *(personne)* untidy 3 *(lieu)* untidy, messy 4 *(irrégulier)* helter-skelter *(avant n)*; **courir de façon désordonnée** to run helter-skelter *or* pell-mell; **le chien faisait des bonds désordonnés** the dog was leaping about all over the place 5 *Littéraire (immoral)* disorderly, disordered
désordre [dezɔrdr] NM 1 *(fouillis)* mess; **quel d. là-dedans!** what a mess *or* it's chaos in there!; **mettre le d. dans une pièce** to mess up a room; **c'est un peu le d. dans ses papiers** his papers are not altogether in order; *Fig* **ça fait d.!** *(ça ne se fait pas)* it's just not done!; *(ce n'est pas sérieux)* that's a laugh!
2 *(manque d'organisation)* muddle, confusion, disarray; **d. des idées** confused ideas
3 *(agitation)* disorder, disturbance; **semer le d.** to cause a disturbance, to wreak havoc; **lorsque le chat sauta, ce fut un beau d. parmi les poules** when the cat jumped, the hens went into a panic; *Jur* **d. sur la voie publique** disorderly conduct
4 *Méd* disorder; **d. nerveux/fonctionnel/hormonal** nervous/functional/hormone disorder
5 *Littéraire (immoralité)* dissoluteness, dissipation; **vivre dans le d.** to live a dissolute life
6 *(au tiercé)* **gagner le tiercé dans le d.** to win a place bet in the wrong order
ADJ messy, untidy; **que tu es d.!** you're so untidy!
▫ **désordres** NMPL 1 *(émeutes)* riots; **des désordres ont éclaté** riots have *or* rioting has broken out
2 *Littéraire (débauche)* dissolute *or* disorderly behaviour; **se livrer à des désordres** to lead a disorderly life
▫ **en désordre** ADJ *(lieu)* messy, untidy; *(cheveux)* unkempt, dishevelled; **une chambre en d.** an untidy room; **mon bureau était tout en d.** my desk was in a terrible mess ADV **mettre qch en d.** to mess sth up; **il a mis mes dossiers en d.** he got my files all muddled up
désordré, -e [dezɔrdre] ADJ *Suisse (personne, armoire)* messy; *(pays, société)* chaotic
désorganisateur, -trice [dezɔrganizatœr, -tris] ADJ disorganizing, disruptive
NM,F disorganizer
désorganisation [dezɔrganizasjɔ̃] NF disorganization, disruption
désorganisatrice [dezɔrganizatris] *voir* **désorganisateur**
désorganisé, -e [dezɔrganize] ADJ disorganized
désorganiser [3] [dezɔrganize] VT *(service)* to disorganize, to disrupt; *(fiches)* to disrupt the order of; *(projets)* to upset
désorientation [dezɔrjɑ̃tasjɔ̃] NF 1 *(perplexité)* disorientation, confusion 2 *Psy* **d. spatiale/temporelle** spatial/temporal disorientation
désorienté, -e [dezɔrjɑ̃te] ADJ 1 *(perplexe)* confused, disorientated 2 *(égaré)* lost
désorienter [3] [dezɔrjɑ̃te] VT 1 *(faire s'égarer)* to disorientate 2 *(déconcerter)* to confuse, to throw into confusion *or* disarray, to disorientate 3 *Mil & Opt* to disorientate
désormais [dezɔrmɛ] ADV *(à partir de maintenant)* from now on, *Sout* henceforth; *(dans le passé)* from that moment on, from then on, from that time (on); **je ferai attention d.** I'll pay attention from now on; **d. nous étions amis** from then on we were friends
désorption [dezɔrpsjɔ̃] NF *Chim* desorption
désossé, -e [dezɔse] ADJ *(gigot, jambon)* off the bone; *Fig (personne)* supple
désossement [dezɔsmɑ̃] NM boning
désosser [3] [dezɔse] VT 1 *(viande)* to bone 2 *Fam (étudier)* to go over with a fine-tooth comb 3 *Fam (démonter)* to take to bits
▸**se désosser** VPR *(se désarticuler)* to contort oneself
désoufrage [desufraʒ] NM *Chim* desulphurization
désoufrer [3] [desufre] VT *Chim* to desulphurize
désoxydant [dezɔksidɑ̃] NM *Chim* deoxidizer
désoxydation [dezɔksidasjɔ̃] NF *Chim* deoxidation, deactivation
désoxyder [3] [dezɔkside] VT *Chim* to deoxidize, to deactivate; **acier désoxydé** killed steel
désoxygénation [dezɔksiʒenasjɔ̃] NF *Chim* deoxygenation
désoxygéner [18] [dezɔksiʒene] VT *Chim* to deoxygenate
désoxyribonucléase [dezɔksiribɔnykleaz] NF *Biol & Chim* deoxyribonuclease
désoxyribonucléique [dezɔksiribɔnykleik] ADJ *Biol & Chim* **acide d.** deoxyribonucleic acid
désoxyribonucléotide [dezɔksiribɔnykleotid] NF *Biol & Chim* deoxyribonucleotid
désoxyribose [dezɔksiriboz] NM *Biol & Chim* deoxyribose
déspécialisation [despesjalizasjɔ̃] NF *Jur* despecialization
desperado [dɛsperado] NM desperado
despote [dɛspɔt] NM 1 *Pol* despot, tyrant 2 *(personne autoritaire)* tyrant, bully
ADJ **mari/femme d.** despotic husband/wife
despotique [dɛspɔtik] ADJ 1 *Pol* despotic, tyrannical, dictatorial 2 *(autoritaire)* despotic, domineering, bullying
despotiquement [dɛspɔtikmɑ̃] ADV *Pol & Fig* despotically, tyrannically, dictatorially
despotisme [dɛspɔtism] NM 1 *Pol* despotism; *Hist* **d. éclairé** enlightened despotism 2 *(autorité)* tyranny, bullying
desquamation [dɛskwamasjɔ̃] NF 1 *(de la peau)* flaking, *Spéc* desquamation; *(des écailles)* scaling off 2 *Géol* **d. en écailles** exfoliation
desquamer [3] [dɛskwame] VI *(peau)* to flake off, *Spéc* to desquamate; *(écailles)* to scale off
▸**se desquamer** VPR *(peau)* to flake (off), *Spéc* to desquamate; *(écailles)* to scale off
desquels, desquelles [dekɛl] *voir* **lequel**
DESS [deəɛsɛs] NM *(abrév* **diplôme d'études supérieures spécialisées***)* = postgraduate diploma lasting one year; *voir aussi encadré sous* **DEA**
dessablage [desablaʒ], **dessablement** [desabləmɑ̃] NM *(d'une allée)* removal of sand (**de** from); *(de l'eau, d'un chenal)* removal of silt (**de** from)
dessabler [3] [desable] VT *(allée)* to remove sand from; *(eau, chenal)* to remove silt from
dessaisir [32] [desezir] VT *Jur* **d. qn de** to deny sb jurisdiction over; **d. un tribunal d'une affaire** to remove a case from a court
▸**se dessaisir** VPR 1 **se d. de** *(se départir de)* to part with, to relinquish 2 *Jur* **se d. d'une affaire** to decline (to exercise) jurisdiction over a case
dessaisissement [desezismɑ̃] NM 1 *Jur (d'un tribunal)* removal of a case from 2 *(renoncement)* relinquishment
dessalage [desalaʒ] NM 1 *Chim* desalination 2 *Culin* removal of salt (**de** from)
dessalaison [desalɛzɔ̃] NF 1 *Chim* desalination 2 *Culin* removal of salt (**de** from)
dessalement [desalmɑ̃] = **dessalage**
dessaler [3] [desale] VT 1 *Chim* to desalinate 2 *Culin* to remove the salt from; **d. du poisson** to freshen fish 3 *Fam (dégourdir)* **d. qn** to teach sb a thing or two; **elle est très dessalée** she knows a thing or two
VI *Naut* to overturn, to capsize
▸**se dessaler** VPR *Fam* to learn a thing or two, to wise up; **il s'est drôlement dessalé depuis qu'il travaille!** he's learnt a thing or two since he started working!
dessaleur [desalœr] NM *Pétr* desalter
dessalure [desalyr] NF freshening *(of sea-water)*
dessangler [3] [desɑ̃gle] VT *(cheval)* to ungirth
dessaouler [3] [desule] = **dessoûler**
desséchant, -e [deseʃɑ̃, -ɑ̃t] ADJ 1 *(asséchant)* drying, withering; **un vent d.** a searing wind 2 *(activité, études)* soul-destroying 3 *Chim* desiccating
desséché, -e [deseʃe] ADJ 1 *(peau, cheveux)* dry; *(pétale, feuille)* withered; *(bois)* seasoned, dried; *(gorge)* parched 2 *(décharné)* emaciated, wasted 3 *(cœur, personne)* hardened; **un vieux solitaire d.** a hardened old recluse
dessèchement [desɛʃmɑ̃] NM 1 *(de peau, de cheveux)* drying (up); *(de pétale, de feuille)* withering; *(de bois)* seasoning, drying 2 *(procédé)* desiccation, drying (out) 3 *(amaigrissement)* emaciation, wasting away 4 *(stérilité → du cœur)* hardening; *(→ de la créativité)* drying up
dessécher [18] [deseʃe] VT 1 *(peau, cheveux)* to dry out; *(pétale, feuille)* to wither; *(bois)* to season, to dry; **trop de soleil dessèche la peau** too much sun dries the skin; **la bouche desséchée par la peur** mouth dry *or* parched with fear
2 *(amaigrir)* to emaciate, to waste; **son corps desséché par la maladie** his/her body wasted by illness
3 *(endurcir)* **d. le cœur de qn** to harden sb's heart
▸**se dessécher** VPR 1 *(peau, cheveux)* to go dry; *(pétale, feuille)* to wither; *(bois)* to dry out
2 *(maigrir)* to waste away
3 *(s'endurcir → cœur)* to harden; *(→ personne)* to become hardened
dessein [desɛ̃] NM *Littéraire* intention, goal, purpose; **son d. est de prendre ma place** his/her intention is to *or* he/she has determined to take my place; **former le d. de faire qch** to determine to do sth; **avoir le d. de faire qch** to intend to do sth
▫ **à dessein** ADV deliberately, purposely; **c'est à d. que je n'ai pas répondu** I deliberately didn't answer
▫ **dans ce dessein** ADV with this intention, with this in mind
▫ **dans le dessein de** PRÉP in order *or* with a view to
desseller [4] [desele] VT to unsaddle
desserrage [deseraʒ], **desserrement** [desɛrmɑ̃] NM 1 *(processus)* loosening, slackening 2 *(résultat)* looseness
desserrer [4] [desere] VT 1 *(vis, cravate, ceinture)* to loosen 2 *(relâcher → étreinte, bras)* to relax; *(→ poings, dents)* to unclench; *Fig* **il n'a pas desserré les dents** *ou* **lèvres** he didn't utter a word, he never opened his mouth 3 *(frein)* to release
▸**se desserrer** VPR 1 *(vis, cravate, ceinture)* to come loose 2 *(se relâcher → étreinte)* to relax
dessers *etc voir* **desservir**
dessert [desɛr] NM dessert, *Br* pudding, sweet; **veux-tu un d.?** will you have some dessert?; **qu'est-ce qu'il y a comme** *ou* **au d.?** what's for dessert?; **au d.** at the end of the meal
desserte [desɛrt] NF 1 *(meuble)* sideboard; *(table roulante) Br* tea-trolley, *Am* tea wagon 2 *Transp* service; **d. aérienne** air service; **l'hiver, la d. est supprimée** the service doesn't run in winter; **la d. du village est très mal assurée** the village is poorly served by public transport 3 *Rel* ministry
dessertir [32] [desɛrtir] VT to unset
▸**se dessertir** VPR to come unset
dessertissage [desɛrtisaʒ] NM unsetting
desservant [desɛrvɑ̃] NM *Rel* incumbent
desservir [38] [desɛrvir] VT 1 *(débarrasser)* to clear (away)
2 *(désavantager)* to be detrimental *or* harmful to, to go against; **son intervention m'a desservi** he/she did me a disservice by intervening; **son**

perfectionnisme la dessert the fact that she's such a perfectionist goes against her

3 *Transp* to serve; **le village est mal desservi** public transport to the village is poor; **l'hôpital est desservi cinq fois par jour** there is a bus (service) to the hospital five times a day; **ce train dessert les gares suivantes** this train stops at the following stations

4 *Rel (paroisse)* to serve

5 *(donner accès à)* to lead to; **une allée dessert la maison** a drive leads up to the house; **un couloir dessert les chambres** a corridor leads off to the bedrooms

USAGE ABSOLU *(débarrasser)* **puis-je d.?** may I clear the table?

des–des

dessévage [desevaʒ] NM *(en sylviculture)* = removal of the sap from tree trunks after felling

dessication [desikasjɔ̃] = **dessiccation**

dessiccateur [desikatœr] NM desiccator

dessiccation [desikasjɔ̃] NF *(gén)* desiccation, drying; *(du bois)* drying

dessiller [3] [desije] *Littéraire* VT **d. les yeux de** *ou* **à qn** to cause the scales to fall from sb's eyes, to open sb's eyes

▸**se dessiller** VPR **mes yeux se dessillent** the scales have fallen from my eyes

dessin [desɛ̃] NM **1** *(croquis)* drawing; **les dessins de Michel-Ange** Michelangelo's drawings; **des dessins d'enfants** children's drawings; **d. humoristique** *ou* **de presse** cartoon *(in a newspaper)*; **d. animé** cartoon; **d. à main levée** free hand drawing; **d. à la plume** pen and ink drawing; **d. au trait** *ou* **linéaire** outline drawing; *Fam* **tu veux que je te fasse un d.?** do you want me to spell it out for you?; *Fam* **pas besoin d'un** *ou* **de faire un d., elle a compris!** you don't have to spell it out for her, she's got the message!

2 *(art)* **le d.** drawing; **apprendre le d.** to learn (how) to draw; **être bon en d.** to be good at drawing, to be a good drawer

3 *(technique)* **la vigueur de son d.** the firmness of his/her drawing technique

4 *Tech* **d. industriel** draughtsmanship, industrial design; **d. coté** dimensioned drawing; **d. assisté par ordinateur** computer-aided design; **d. par ordinateur** computer art

5 *(forme, ligne)* line, outline; **pour donner à vos sourcils un d. parfait** to give your eyebrows the perfect shape

6 *(ornement)* design, pattern; **un tissu à d.** a patterned fabric; **un tissu à dessins géométriques** a fabric with geometric patterns

❑ **de dessin** ADJ **cours/école de d.** art class/school

dessinateur, -trice [desinatœr, -tris] NM,F **1** *(technicien)* **d. (industriel)** draughtsman, *f* draughtswoman **2** *(concepteur)* designer; **d. de mode** fashion designer **3** *Beaux-Arts* **il est meilleur d. que peintre** he draws better than he paints; **d. de bande dessinée** cartoonist; **d. d'études** design draughtsman; **d. humoristique** cartoonist

dessinateur-cartographe [desinatœrkartɔgraf] *(pl* **dessinateurs-cartographes**) NM cartographer

dessinatrice [desinatris] *voir* **dessinateur**

dessiné, -e [desine] ADJ **bien d.** well-formed, well-defined

dessiner [3] [desine] VT **1** *Beaux-Arts* to draw; **d. qch sur le vif** to draw sth from life

2 *(former)* to delineate; **menton/visage bien dessiné** firmly delineated chin/face; **bouche finement dessinée** finely drawn *or* chiselled mouth

3 *(concevoir* → *meuble, robe, bâtiment)* to design; *(*→ *paysage, jardin)* to landscape

4 *(souligner)* to emphasize the shape of; **un vêtement qui dessine bien la taille** a garment that shows off the waist

USAGE ABSOLU **il dessine bien** he's good at drawing; **d. à la plume/au crayon/au fusain** to draw in pen and ink/in pencil/in charcoal

▸**se dessiner** VPR **1** *(devenir visible)* to stand out; **un sourire se dessina sur ses lèvres** a smile formed on his/her lips; **les douces collines du Perche se dessinent au lointain** the gentle slopes of the Perche hills stand out in the far distance

2 *(apparaître* → *solution)* to emerge; **certaines tendances se dessinent** certain tendencies are beginning to emerge

> *Allusion*
>
> **Dessine-moi un mouton**
>
> This is possibly the most famous line of the most famous French children's book of all time, Antoine de Saint-Exupéry's *Le Petit Prince*. A pilot crashes in a desert, where he meets the naïve and charming Little Prince, who says to him **Dessine-moi un mouton** ("Draw me a sheep"). This innocent request is recalled whenever a French child asks "draw me this, draw me that", and the phrase is like an emblem of childhood.

dessoler [3] [desɔle] VT *Agr* **d. un champ** to change the rotation of crops in a field

dessouchage [desuʃaʒ] NM *Agr (d'un terrain)* clearing of tree stumps (**de** from)

dessoucher [3] [desuʃe] VT *Agr (terrain)* to clear of tree stumps

dessouder [3] [desude] VT **1** *Tech* to unsolder **2** *Fam Arg crime (tuer)* to do in, to waste

▸**se dessouder** VPR *Tech* to become unsoldered

dessoudure [desudyr] NF *Tech* unsoldering

dessoufler [3] [desufle] VT *Can* to deflate, to let down

dessoûler [3] [desule] VT to sober up; **tu es dessoûlé maintenant?** have you sobered up?

VI to sober up; **il ne dessoûle pas de la journée** he's been drunk all day

dessous [dəsu] ADV underneath; **les prix sont marqués d.** the prices are marked underneath; **mets-toi d.** get under it; **il porte une chemise, et rien d.** he's wearing a shirt, with nothing underneath

NM *(d'un meuble, d'un objet)* bottom; *(d'une feuille)* underneath; **le d. de l'assiette est sale** the bottom of the plate is dirty; **les gens du d.** the people downstairs, the downstairs neighbours; **d. de verre** *ou* **bouteille** coaster; **les d. de la politique/de la finance** the hidden agenda in politics/in finance; **le d. des cartes** *ou* **du jeu** the hidden agenda; **avoir le d.** to come off worst, to get the worst of it; **être dans le trente-sixième d.** to be down in the dumps

NMPL *(sous-vêtements)* underwear; **des d. coquins** sexy underwear

❑ **de dessous** PRÉP from under, from underneath; **enlève ça de d. la table** pick that up from under *or* underneath the table

❑ **en dessous** ADV underneath; **la feuille est verte en d.** the leaf is green underneath; *Fam* **les gens qui habitent en d., les gens d'en d.** the people downstairs, the downstairs neighbours; **agir en d.** to act in an underhand way; **rire en d.** to laugh up one's sleeve

❑ **en dessous de** PRÉP below; **en d. de zéro** below zero; **vous êtes très en d. de la vérité** you're very far from the truth

❑ **par en dessous** ADV *(prendre, saisir)* from underneath; *Fig* **regarder qn par en d.** to steal a glance at sb

dessous-de-bouteille [dəsudbutɛj] NM INV coaster *(for a bottle)*

dessous-de-bras [dəsudbra] NM INV dress shield

dessous-de-plat [dəsudpla] NM INV table mat *(to protect the table from hot dishes)*, *Am* hot pad

dessous-de-table [dəsudtabl] NM INV *Péj* bribe

dessous-de-verre [dəsudvɛr] NM INV coaster

dessuintage [desɥɛ̃taʒ] NM *Tex* scouring

dessuinter [3] [desɥɛ̃te] VT *Tex* to scour

dessus [dəsy] ADV *(placer, monter)* on top; *(marcher, écrire)* on it/them; *(passer, sauter)* over it/them; **écrivez l'adresse d.** write the address on it; **monte d., tu verras mieux** get on top (of it), you'll get a better view; **assieds-toi d.** sit on it; **avec du chocolat d.** with chocolate on top; **ils lui ont tiré d.** they shot at him/her; **ils lui ont tapé d.** they hit him/her; **ne compte pas trop d.** don't count on it too much; **je suis d. depuis un moment** *(affaire, travail)* I've been (working) on it for a while; **ça nous est tombé d. à l'improviste** it was like a bolt out of the blue; **il a fallu que ça me tombe d.!** it had to be me!; **qu'est-ce qui va encore me tomber d.?** what next?

NM **1** *(d'un objet, de la tête, du pied)* top; *(de la main)* back; **prends la nappe du d., elle est repassée** take the tablecloth on the top, it's been ironed; **avoir/prendre le d.** to have/to get the upper hand; **après 15 minutes de jeu, l'équipe marseillaise a nettement pris le d. sur ses adversaires** after 15 minutes of play the Marseilles team gained a definite advantage over their opponents; **reprendre le d.** *(gagner)* to get back on top (of the situation), to regain the upper hand; **elle a bien repris le d.** *(après une maladie)* she was soon back on her feet again; *(après une dépression)* she got over it quite well; **le d. du panier** *(personnes)* the cream, the elite; *(choses)* the top of the pile *or* heap

2 *(étage supérieur)* **les voisins du d.** the people upstairs, the upstairs neighbours; **l'appartement du d.** the *Br* flat *or Am* apartment above

❑ **dessus** NMPL *Théât* flies

❑ **de dessus** PRÉP **enlève ça de d. la table!** take it off the table!; **elle ne leva pas les yeux de d. son ouvrage** she didn't look up from *or* take her eyes off her work

❑ **en dessus** ADV on top

dessus-de-cheminée [dəsydʃəmine] NM INV mantleshelf runner

dessus-de-lit [dəsydli] NM INV bedspread

dessus-de-porte [dəsydpɔrt] NM INV *Beaux-Arts* overdoor

dessus-de-table [dəsydtabl] NM INV table runner

déstabilisant, -e [destabilizɑ̃, -ɑ̃t], **déstabilisateur, -trice** [destabilizatœr, -tris] ADJ *(pour un pays, un régime)* destabilizing; *(pour une personne)* unsettling

déstabilisation [destabilizasjɔ̃] NF *(d'un pays, d'un régime)* destabilization; *(d'une personne)* unsettling

déstabilisatrice [destabilizatrice] *voir* **déstabilisant**

déstabiliser [3] [destabilize] VT *(pays, régime)* to destabilize; *(personne)* to unsettle

déstalinisation [destalinizasjɔ̃] NF destalinization

déstaliniser [3] [destalinize] VT to destalinize

destin [dɛstɛ̃] NM **1** *(sort)* fate, destiny; **le d. a voulu que…** fate decreed that…; **un coup du d.** a blow from fate

2 *(vie personnelle)* life, destiny, fate; **il a eu un d. tragique** his destiny was tragic; **maître de son d.** master of his (own) fate

3 *(évolution)* destiny, fate; **son roman a connu un d. imprévu** his/her novel had an unexpected fate; **leur union devait avoir un d. malheureux** their marriage was destined to be unhappy

destinataire [dɛstinatɛr] NMF **1** *(d'une lettre)* addressee; *(de produits)* consignee; *(d'un mandat postal)* payee; *Ordinat (d'un message électronique)* recipient **2** *Ling* listener

destinateur, -trice [dɛstinatœr, -tris] NM,F sender

destination [dɛstinasjɔ̃] NF **1** *(lieu)* destination; **arriver à d.** to reach one's destination **2** *(emploi)* purpose, use; **quelle d. lui donneras-tu?** what do you plan to use it for?; **détourné de sa d. primitive** diverted from its original purpose **3** *Jur* **d. du père de famille** easement of necessity

❑ **à destination de** PRÉP **avion/vol à d. de Nice** plane/flight to Nice; **les voyageurs à d. de Paris** passengers for Paris, passengers travelling to Paris; **le train de 15h30 à d. de Bordeaux** the 3.30 train to Bordeaux

destinatrice [dɛstinatris] *voir* **destinateur**

destinée [dɛstine] NF **1** *(sort)* **la d.** fate; **la d. de qn/qch** the fate in store for sb/sth

2 *(vie)* destiny; **il tient ma d. entre ses mains** he holds my destiny in his hands; *Littéraire* **unir sa d. à celle de qn** to unite one's destiny with sb's

❑ **destinées** NFPL **les dieux qui président à nos destinées** the gods who decide our fate (on earth); **promis à de hautes destinées** destined for great things; **de hautes destinées l'attendaient** he/she was destined to achieve great things

destiner [3] [dɛstine] VT **1** *(adresser)* **d. qch à qn** to intend sth for sb; **cette remarque ne t'est pas destinée** this remark isn't meant *or* intended for you; **voici le courrier qui lui est destiné** here is his/her mail *or* the mail for him/her; **festival destiné aux enfants** children's festival

2 *(promettre)* **d. qn à** to destine sb for; **rien ne/ tout me destinait au violon** nothing/everything led me to become a violinist; **nous étions destinés l'un à l'autre** we were meant for each other; **on la destine à quelque gros industriel** her family wants to marry her off to some rich industrialist; **il avait destiné son fils au barreau** he had intended his son for the bar; **il était destiné à mourir jeune** he was fated to die young; **il était destiné à régner** he was destined to reign; **son idée était destinée à l'échec dès le départ** his/her idea was bound to fail *or* doomed (to failure) from the very start

3 *(affecter)* **d. qch à** to set sth aside for; **d. des fonds à** to allocate funds to, to set aside *or* to earmark funds for; **marchandises destinées à l'exportation** goods intended for export; **cette somme a été destinée à l'achat d'un microscope** this sum has been set aside to buy a microscope; **cette salle est destinée aux répétitions** this room is for rehearsing in

▸**se destiner** VPR **se d. à qch** to want to take up sth; **se d. au journalisme** to want to become a journalist

destituable [dɛstitɥabl] ADJ *(fonctionnaire)* dismissible; *(roi)* deposable; **il n'est pas d.** *(fonctionnaire)* he cannot be dismissed (from his post); *(officier)* he cannot be stripped of his rank

destituer [7] [dɛstitɥe] VT *(fonctionnaire)* to relieve from duties, to dismiss; *(roi)* to depose; *(officier)* to demote; **d. un général de son commandement** to relieve a general of his command

destitution [dɛstitysjɔ̃] NF *(d'un fonctionnaire)* dismissal; *(d'un roi)* deposition, deposal; *(d'un officier)* demotion

déstockage [destɔkaʒ] NM destocking, reduction in stocks; *Compta* **d. de production** *(poste de bilan)* decrease in stocks

déstocker [3] [destɔke] VT to destock, to reduce stocks of
VI to reduce stocks

déstressant, -e [destrɛsɑ̃, -ɑ̃t] ADJ *(soin, expérience)* destressing

déstresser [destrɛse] VI to destress; **les massages sont un bon moyen de d.** a massage is a good way to destress
❑ **se déstresser** VPR to destress oneself

destrier [dɛstrije] NM *Arch* charger, steed

destroy [dɛstrɔj] ADJ *Fam* **1** *(personne)* wasted-looking■; *(jean)* ripped■; **il avait l'air complètement d.** he looked a complete wreck, he looked totally wasted **2** *(style, esthétisme)* subversive■; *(musique)* loud and aggressive■ **3** *(en mauvais état → voiture)* beat up, wrecked■, *Br* knackered

destroyer [dɛstrwaje, dɛstrɔjœr] NM *Mil* destroyer

destructeur, -trice [dɛstryktœr, -tris] ADJ destructive; **caractère d.** destructiveness
NM,F destroyer
NM **d. de documents** document shredder

destructible [dɛstryktibl] ADJ destructible; **facilement d.** easy to destroy; **difficilement d.** virtually indestructible

destructif, -ive [dɛstryktif, -iv] ADJ *(action, croyance)* destructive

destruction [dɛstryksjɔ̃] NF **1** *(fait d'anéantir → gén)* destroying, destruction; *(→ des rats, des insectes)* extermination; **la d. des récoltes** the destruction of the crops; **après la d. de la ville par le feu/les bombardements** after the town had been gutted by fire/destroyed by bombing **2** *(dégâts)* damage; **les destructions causées par la tornade** the damage caused by the tornado

destructive [dɛstryktiv] *voir* **destructif**

destructrice [dɛstryktris] *voir* **destructeur**

déstructuration [destryktyrasjɔ̃] NF deconstruction, taking apart

déstructuré, -e [destryktyre] ADJ *(vêtement)* unstructured

déstructurer [3] [destryktyre] VT to remove the structure from
▸**se déstructurer** VPR to lose (its) structure, to become destructured

désuet, -ète [dezɥɛ, -ɛt] ADJ *(mot, vêtement)* outdated, old-fashioned, out-of-date; *(technique)* outmoded, obsolete; **une chambre au charme d.** a room with old-fashioned charm

désuétude [dezɥetyd] NF obsolescence; **tomber en d.** *(mot)* to fall into disuse, to become obsolete; *(technique, pratique)* to become obsolete; *Jur (droit)* to lapse; *(loi)* to fall into abeyance; **d. calculée** planned *or* built-in obsolescence

désulfiter [3] [desylfite] VT *(moût, vin)* to desulphurize

désulfuration [desylfyrasjɔ̃] NF *Chim* desulphurization

désulfurer [3] [desylfyre] VT *Chim* to desulphurize

désuni, -e [dezyni] ADJ **1** *(brouillé → famille, ménage)* disunited, divided **2** *Équitation* off its stride

désunion [dezynjɔ̃] NF division, dissension *(UNCOUNT)*

désunir [32] [dezynir] VT **1** *(séparer)* **des amants que le temps a désunis** lovers who grew apart with the passage of time **2** *(brouiller → famille)* to split, to divide; **ils sont désunis** they don't get on with each other any more **3** *(disjoindre)* **d. les éléments d'un ensemble** to separate the elements of a set (from each other), to split up a set
▸**se désunir** VPR *(athlète)* to lose one's stride

désurchauffe [desyrʃof] NF desuperheating

désurchauffer [3] [desyrʃofe] VT to desuperheat

désutilité [dezytilite] NF *Écon* disutility

désynchronisation [desɛ̃krɔnizasjɔ̃] NF desynchronization

désynchroniser [3] [desɛ̃krɔnize] VT to put out of synchronization; **être désynchronisé** *(film)* to be out of synch

désyndicalisation [desɛ̃dikalizasjɔ̃] NF declining level of unionization **(de** among)

désyndicaliser [3] [desɛ̃dikalize] VT *(entreprise)* to de-unionize

DET [deɔt] NF *TV (abrév* **durée d'écoute par téléspectateur)** average viewing time

détachable [detaʃabl] ADJ *(feuillet, capuchon)* removable, detachable; **facilement d.** easily detachable

détachage [detaʃaʒ] NM *(nettoyage)* stain removal

détachant, -e [detaʃɑ̃, -ɑ̃t] ADJ *(produit)* stain-removing
NM stain remover

détaché, -e [detaʃe] ADJ **1** *(ruban, animal)* untied **2** *(air, mine)* detached, casual, offhand **3** *Admin* **fonctionnaire d.** civil servant *Br* on secondment *or Am* on a temporary assignment **4** *Mus* detached

détachement [detaʃmɑ̃] NM **1** *(désintéressement)* detachment; **prendre un air de d.** to look detached *or* casual; **il montrait un certain d. vis-à-vis des biens de ce monde** he was quite indifferent to earthly riches

2 *(troupe)* detachment; **d. précurseur** advance party

3 *Admin Br* secondment, *Am* temporary assignment
❑ **en détachement** ADV *Br* on secondment, *Am* on a temporary assignment; **en d. auprès de** *Br* seconded to, *Am* on a temporary assignment with

détacher [3] [detaʃe] VT **1** *(libérer)* to untie; **d. un animal** to untie an animal; **d. ses cheveux** to untie one's hair, to let one's hair down; **d. les mains d'un prisonnier** to untie a prisoner's hands; **d. une guirlande** to take down a garland; **d. une caravane** to unhitch *or* to unhook a caravan; **la barque a été détachée par des voyous** the boat was detached from its moorings by vandals

2 *(séparer)* **d. une photo d'une lettre** *(enlever le trombone)* to unclip a photo from a letter; *(enlever l'agrafe)* to unstaple a photo from a letter; **d. une recette d'un magazine/un timbre d'un carnet** to tear a recipe out of a magazine/a stamp out of a book; **d. les pétales d'une fleur** to pick *or* pluck the petals off a flower

3 *(défaire → ceinture)* to unfasten; *(→ col)* to unfasten, to loosen; *(→ chaîne)* to undo

4 *(détourner)* **d. ses yeux** *ou* **son regard de qn** to take one's eyes off sb; **d. son attention d'une lecture** to stop paying attention to one's reading; **d. qn de** *(affectivement)* to take sb away from; **être détaché de** to be detached from *or* indifferent to; **il est détaché des biens**

de ce monde he has renounced all worldly goods

5 *Admin* to send *Br* on secondment *or Am* on a temporary assignment; *Mil* to detach; **je vais être détaché auprès du ministre** I will be sent on secondment to the Ministry; **d. un officier auprès de qn** to detach an officer to serve with sb; **il faut d. quelqu'un de votre service pour m'aider** you must assign *or Br* second somebody from your department to help me; **il a été détaché à Paris** he's on *Br* secondment *or Am* temporary assignment in Paris

6 *(faire ressortir)* to separate (out); **détachez bien chaque mot/note** make sure every word/ note stands out (clearly)

7 *(nettoyer)* to clean; **j'ai donné ton costume à d.** I took your suit to the cleaner's
USAGE ABSOLU *(séparer)* **d. suivant le pointillé** tear (off) along the dotted line
❑ **à détacher** ADJ **fiche/recette à d.** tear-off card/ recipe

▸**se détacher** VPR **1** *(se libérer → personne)* to untie *or* to free oneself; *(→ animal)* to break loose; **les prisonniers ont réussi à se d.** the prisoners managed to untie themselves

2 *(sandale, lacet)* to come undone; *(étiquette)* to come off; *(page)* to come loose; **l'écorce se détache** the bark is peeling off, the bark is coming away from the tree

3 *Sport (se séparer → du peloton)* to break away **4** **se d. les cheveux** *(enlever ce qui les attache)* to let one's hair down

5 *(se profiler)* to stand out; **le mont Blanc se détache à l'horizon** Mont Blanc stands out against the horizon

6 **se d. de** *(se décrocher de)* to come off

7 **se d. de qn** *(en devenant adulte)* to break away from sb; *(par manque d'intérêt)* to grow apart from sb; **il a eu du mal à se d. d'elle** he found it hard to leave her behind; **puis je me suis détachée de ma famille/de l'art figuratif** later, I grew away from my family/from figurative art

détacheur [detaʃœr] NM stain remover

détail [detaj] NM **1** *(exposé précis)* breakdown, detailed account, itemization; **faire le d. de qch** *(dépenses, travaux)* to break sth down, to itemize sth; **faites-moi le d. de ce qui s'est passé** tell me in detail what happened; *Fam* **il n'a pas fait le d.!** he was a bit heavy-handed!; *Fam* **ici, on ne fait pas le d.!** we make no distinctions here!

2 *(élément → d'un récit, d'une information)* detail, particular; **les détails croustillants de l'histoire** the juicy bits of the story; **donner des détails sur qch** to enlarge on sth, to go into more detail about sth; **je te passe les détails** *(ennuyeux)* I won't bore you with the detail *or* details; *(horribles)* I'll spare you the (gory) details; **jusque dans les moindres détails** down to the smallest detail; **soigner les détails** to pay attention to detail; **pour plus de détails, écrivez à...** for further details, write to...

3 *(point sans importance)* detail, minor point; **je trouve l'article longuet mais ce n'est qu'un d.** I think the article's a bit long, but that's a mere detail; **c'est un d. de l'Histoire** it is a mere footnote of history; **ne nous arrêtons pas à ces détails** let's not worry about these minor details

4 *Beaux-Arts* detail; **Clemenceau, d. d'un portrait par Manet** Clemenceau, a detail from a portrait by Manet

5 *Com* retail

6 *(petite partie → d'un meuble, d'un édifice)* detail; **il a été vendu plus cher à cause du d. Art nouveau** it was sold for a higher price because of the Art nouveau detail
❑ **au détail** ADJ *(vente)* retail *(avant n)* ADV **vendre qch au d.** to sell sth retail, to retail sth; **vous vendez les œufs au d.?** do you sell eggs individually?
❑ **de détail** ADJ **1** *(mineur)* **faire quelques remarques de d.** to make a few minor comments **2** *Com* retail *(avant n)*; **commerce de d.** retailing
❑ **en détail** ADV in detail; **raconter une histoire en d.** to tell a story in detail

détaillant, -e [detajɑ̃, -ɑ̃t] NM,F retailer, shopkeeper; **d. indépendant** independent retailer; **d. spécialisé** specialist retailer

détaillé, -e [detajø] **ADJ** *(récit)* detailed; *(facture, relevé de compte)* itemized

détailler [3] [detaje] **VT 1** *Com* to retail, to sell retail; **nous détaillons cet ensemble pull, jupe et pantalon** we sell the sweater, skirt and trousers separately; **nous ne les détaillons pas** *(service à vaisselle)* we don't sell it separately; *(fromage, gâteau)* we only sell it whole **2** *(dévisager)* to scrutinize, to examine; **d. qn de la tête aux pieds** to look sb over from head to foot, to look sb up and down; **d. qn effrontément** to stare insolently at sb **3** *(énumérer → faits, facture)* to itemize, to detail

détaler [3] [detale] **VI** *(animal)* to bolt; *(personne)* to decamp, *Am* to cut and run; **les gamins ont détalé comme des lapins** the kids scattered like rabbits; **tu aurais vu comme il a détalé!** you couldn't see him for dust!

détalonnage [detalɔnaʒ] **NM** *Tech* backing off

détalonner [3] [detalɔne] **VT** *Tech* to back off

détartrage [detartraʒ] **NM** *(des dents)* scaling; *(d'une bouilloire, d'une chaudière)* se **faire faire un d. (des dents)** to have one's teeth cleaned

détartrant, -e [detartrɑ̃, -ɑ̃t] **ADJ** *(produit, substance)* descaling; **dentifrice d.** toothpaste for tartar removal
NM descaling agent

détartrer [3] [detartre] **VT** *(dents → sujet: dentiste)* to scale; *(→ sujet: dentifrice)* to remove the tartar from; *(bouilloire, chaudière)* to descale

détartreur [detartrœr] **NM** *(pour chaudière)* scaler

détaxation [detaksasjɔ̃] **NF** **la d. des livres** *(réduction)* the reduction of duty *or* tax on books; *(suppression)* the lifting of duty *or* tax on books

détaxe [detaks] **NF 1** *(levée)* **la d. des tabacs** *(réduction)* the reduction of duty *or* tax on tobacco; *(suppression)* the lifting of tax *or* duty on tobacco; **vendus en d.** duty-free; **la d. des marchandises à l'exportation** the lifting of duty on exports **2** *(remboursement)* refund; **cela m'a fait 200 euros de d.** I got 200 euros in duty refunded

détaxé, -e [detakse] **ADJ** *(produits, articles)* duty-free

détaxer [3] [detakse] **VT** *(supprimer)* to lift the tax *or* duty on; *(diminuer)* to reduce the tax *or* duty on

détectable [detɛktabl] **ADJ** detectable; **le signal est à peine d.** the signal is almost undetectable

détecter [4] [detɛkte] **VT** to detect, to spot

détecteur [detɛktœr] **NM** detector; *Aut* **d. d'anomalie** fault warning sensor; *Aut* **d. anti-pincement** anti-pinch sensor; *Aut* **d. de choc** crash sensor; *Aut* **d. de cognement** knock sensor; *Aut* **d. de collision** crash sensor; **d. de faux billets** forged banknote detector; **d. de fumée** smoke detector, smoke alarm; **d. de grisou** firedamp detector; **d. d'incendie** fire detector; **d. de mensonges** lie detector, polygraph; **d. de mines** mine detector; **d. d'ondes** wave detector; **d. de particules** particle detector; **d. de radar** radar detector; **d. transistorisé** solid-state sensor; *Ordinat* **d. de virus** virus detector

détection [detɛksjɔ̃] **NF** *(gén)* detection, detecting, spotting; **d. électromagnétique** radio location; *Ordinat* **d. d'erreurs** error detection; *Ordinat* **d. virale** virus detection

détective [detɛktiv] **NMF** detective; **jouer les détectives** to play detective; **d. privé** private detective *or* investigator

déteindre [81] [detɛ̃dr] **VI 1** *(se décolorer)* to fade; **d. au lavage** to run in the wash; **le noir va d. sur le rouge** the black will run into the red **2** *Fam (humeur, influence)* **on dirait que la mauvaise humeur, ça déteint!** bad temper is catching, it seems!; **d. sur qn** to rub off on sb, to influence sb; **sa gentillesse a déteint sur tout le monde** his/her kindness has rubbed off on everybody
VT *(linge)* to discolour; *(tenture, tapisserie)* to fade

dételage [detlaʒ] **NM** *(d'un cheval)* unharnessing, unhitching; *(d'un bœuf)* unyoking; *(d'une voiture)* unhitching; *(de wagons)* uncoupling

dételer [24] [detle] **VT 1** *(cheval)* to unharness, to unhitch; *(bœuf)* to unyoke; **d. les chevaux de la carriole** to unhitch the horses from the cart **2**

(caravane, voiture) to unhitch; *(wagon)* to uncouple
VI *Fam (s'arrêter)* to ease off▪; **on dételle!** time for a break!, let's call it a day!
❑ **sans dételer** **ADV** *Fam* without a break▪, non-stop▪

détendeur [detɑ̃dœr] **NM** *Tech* pressure-reducing valve

détendre [73] [detɑ̃dr] **VT 1** *(relâcher → corde)* to ease, to loosen, to slacken; *(→ ressort)* to release; *(→ arc)* to unbend **2** *(décontracter)* to relax; **la musique me détend** music relaxes me; **il a réussi à d. l'atmosphère avec quelques plaisanteries** he made things more relaxed by telling a few jokes **3** *(gaz)* to depressurize
►**se détendre** **VPR 1** *(corde, courroie)* to ease, to slacken; *(ressort)* to uncoil **2** *(se décontracter)* to relax; **détends-toi!** relax!; **j'ai besoin de me d. après une journée au bureau** I need to unwind *or* relax after a day at the office **3** *(s'améliorer → ambiance)* to become more relaxed **4** *(gaz)* to be reduced in pressure

détendu, -e [detɑ̃dy] **ADJ 1** *(calme)* relaxed **2** *(corde, courroie)* slack

détenir [40] [detnir] **VT 1** *(posséder → record)* to hold, to be the holder of; *(→ actions, pouvoir, secret)* to hold; *(→ document, bijou de famille)* to hold, to have (in one's possession); **d. un monopole** to have a monopoly; **société détenue à 50 pour cent** 50 percent-owned company; **ils détiennent 30 pour cent des parts de la société/des parts de marché** they have a 30 percent shareholding in the company/a 30 percent market share; **détenu par des intérêts privés** privately-held **2** *Jur (emprisonner)* to detain; **d. qn préventivement** to hold sb on remand

détente [detɑ̃t] **NF 1** *(relaxation)* relaxation; **j'ai besoin de d.** I need to relax; **une heure de d. après une journée d'école** an hour's relaxation *or* break after a day at school; **quelques moments de d.** a few moments' relaxation **2** *Pol* **la d.** détente **3** *(d'une horloge)* catch; *(d'un ressort)* release mechanism **4** *(d'une arme)* trigger; *Fam* **il est dur à la d.** *(il est pingre)* he's tight-fisted *or* stingy; *(il ne comprend pas vite)* he's slow on the uptake **5** *Sport* spring; **avoir de la d., avoir une belle d.** to have a powerful spring **6** *(d'un gaz)* expansion; *(dans un moteur)* explosion *or* power stroke **7** *Écon (des taux d'intérêt)* lowering, easing

détenteur, -trice [detɑ̃tœr, -tris] **NM,F** holder; **être le d. d'un record** to hold a record; **le d. du titre** the titleholder; **d. d'actions** *ou* **de titres** *Br* shareholder, *Am* stockholder

détention [detɑ̃sjɔ̃] **NF 1** *(emprisonnement)* detention; **être maintenu en d.** to be detained; **d. criminelle** imprisonment; **d. criminelle à perpétuité** life imprisonment; **d. criminelle à temps** imprisonment for a fixed term; **d. illégale** unlawful imprisonment; **d. préventive** *ou* **provisoire** remand; **en d. préventive** *ou* **provisoire** in detention awaiting trial, on remand; **mettre qn en d. préventive** *ou* **provisoire** to remand sb in custody **2** *(possession → gén)* possession; *(→ d'actions)* holding; **arrêté pour d. d'armes** arrested for illegal possession of arms **3** *Écon* **d. croisée** crossholding

détentrice [detɑ̃tris] *voir* **détenteur**

détenu, -e [detny] **PP** *voir* **détenir**
ADJ *(accusé, prisonnier)* imprisoned
NM,F prisoner; **les détenus manifestent** the prison inmates are demonstrating

détergence [detɛrʒɑ̃s] **NF** detergency

détergent, -e [detɛrʒɑ̃, -ɑ̃t] **ADJ** detergent
NM *(gén)* detergent; *(en poudre)* washing powder; *(liquide)* liquid detergent

déterger [17] [detɛrʒe] **VT** to clean

détérioration [deterjɔrasjɔ̃] **NF** *(de la santé, des relations)* worsening, deterioration; *(des locaux)* deterioration

détériorer [3] [deterjɔre] **VT** to cause to deteriorate, to damage, to harm

►**se détériorer** **VPR** *(temps, climat social)* to deteriorate, to worsen; *(denrée)* to go bad

déterminable [detɛrminabl] **ADJ** determinable; **c'est facilement/difficilement d.** it's easy/difficult to determine

déterminant, -e [detɛrminɑ̃, -ɑ̃t] **ADJ** deciding, determining; **le prix a été l'élément d.** the price was the deciding factor
NM 1 *Math* determinant **2** *Ling* determiner

déterminatif, -ive [detɛrminatif, -iv] **ADJ** determinative; *(proposition)* defining
NM determiner, determinative

détermination [detɛrminasjɔ̃] **NF 1** *(ténacité)* determination, resoluteness **2** *(résolution)* determination, decision; **agir avec d.** to act determinedly **3** *(de causes, de termes)* determining, establishing; **la d. des causes de l'accident sera difficile** it will be difficult to determine the cause of the accident **4** *(des prix)* fixing, setting **5** *Ling & Phil* determination **6** *Biol* determination, determining; **d. des sexes** sex determination; **d. du groupe sanguin** blood typing

déterminative [detɛrminativ] *voir* **déterminatif**

déterminé, -e [detɛrmine] **ADJ 1** *(défini)* determined, defined, circumscribed; **non encore d.** to be specified (later); **il n'a pas d'opinion déterminée à ce sujet** he doesn't really have a strong opinion on the matter; **dans un but bien d.** for a definite reason; **à un prix bien d.** at a set price **2** *(décidé)* determined, resolute; **avoir l'air d.** to look determined; **être d. à faire qch** to be determined to do sth **3** *Ling & Phil* determined
NM *Ling* determinatum, determinandum

déterminément [detɛrminemɑ̃] **ADV** *Littéraire* resolutely, with determination

déterminer [3] [detɛrmine] **VT 1** *(définir)* to ascertain, to determine; *(fixer → lieu, heure)* to fix, to decide on; *(→ prix)* to fix; **d. les causes d'un accident/les mobiles d'un crime** to determine the cause of an accident/the motives for a crime **2** *(inciter)* to incite, to encourage; **d. qn à faire qch** to encourage sb to do sth; **qu'est-ce qui vous a déterminé à partir?** what made you (decide to) leave?; **est-ce lui qui vous a déterminé à agir ainsi?** did you act in this way because of him? **3** *(causer)* to determine; **qu'est-ce qui détermine l'achat?** what determines whether somebody will buy or not? **4** *Ling & Phil* to determine **5** *Biol (sexe)* to determine; *(groupe sanguin)* to type
►**se déterminer** **VPR** to decide, to make a decision, to make up one's mind; **se d. à faire qch** to make up one's mind to do sth

déterminisme [detɛrminism] **NM** determinism

déterministe [detɛrminist] **ADJ** determinist, deterministic
NMF determinist

déterrage [detɛraʒ] **NM 1** *(exhumation)* digging up, unearthing **2** *Agr* lifting *(of a ploughshare)* **3** *Chasse* unearthing; **d. du blaireau** badger-baiting

déterré, -e [detere] **NM,F** **avoir l'air d'un d.** *ou* **une mine de d.** *ou* **une tête de d.** to look like death warmed up

déterrement [detɛrmɑ̃] **NM** *(exhumation)* digging up, disinterment

déterrer [4] [detere] **VT 1** *(os, trésor)* to dig up, to unearth; *(arbre)* to uproot **2** *(exhumer → cadavre)* to dig up, to disinter **3** *(dénicher → secret, texte)* to dig out, to unearth

déterreur [detɛrœr] **NM 1** *(personne qui déterre)* exhumer; **d. de cadavres** body-snatcher **2** *(de manuscrit, de trésor)* discoverer

détersif, -ive [detɛrsif, -iv] **ADJ** detergent
NM *(gén)* detergent; *(en poudre)* washing powder; *(liquide)* liquid detergent

détersion [detɛrsjɔ̃] **NF** *(nettoyage au détergent)* cleaning with a detergent; *Méd* cleansing

détersive [detɛrsiv] *voir* **détersif**

détestable [detɛstabl] **ADJ** dreadful, detestable, foul

détestablement [detɛstabləmɑ̃] ADV appallingly, dreadfully

détestation [detɛstasjɔ̃] NF detestation; **d. du péché** abhorrence of sin; *Littéraire* **avoir de la d. pour qn/qch** to have an abhorrence of sb/sth, to hold sb/sth in detestation

détester [3] [detɛste] VT to hate, to detest, to loathe; **il me déteste cordialement** he passionately dislikes me; **il va se faire d.** he's going to make himself really unpopular, people are really going to hate him; **il déteste devoir se lever tôt** he hates having to get up early; **je déteste qu'on me mente** I hate *or* I can't stand being lied to; **je ne déteste pas une soirée tranquille à la maison** I'm quite partial to a quiet evening at home; **il ne déteste pas les sucreries** he's rather fond of sweets; **je ne détesterais pas dîner au restaurant ce soir** I wouldn't mind eating out tonight; **il m'a fait d. les maths** he put me off maths completely

déthéiné, -e [deteine] ADJ decaffeinated

détient *etc voir* **détenir**

détint *etc voir* **détenir**

détirer [3] [detire] VT to stretch

▸**se détirer** VPR to stretch oneself

détonant, -e [detɔnɑ̃, -ɑ̃t] ADJ *(substance)* explosive; **explosif d.** high explosive

NM explosive

détonateur [detɔnatœr] NM **1** *(d'une bombe, d'une charge)* detonator **2** *Fig (déclencheur)* detonator, trigger; **servir de d. à qch** to trigger off sth

détonation [detɔnasjɔ̃] NF **1** *(bruit → d'explosion)* explosion; *(→ de coup de feu)* shot; *(→ d'un canon)* boom, roar **2** *Aut* backfiring

détoner [3] [detɔne] VI to detonate; **faire d. qch** to detonate sth

détonner [3] [detɔne] VI **1** *Mus (instrument, personne)* to be out of tune *or* off key **2** *(contraster → couleurs, styles)* to clash; *(→ personne)* to be out of place; **la remarque détonne dans ce texte** the remark jumps out in this text *or* looks really out of place in this text

détordre [76] [detɔrdr] VT *(câble, corde, linge)* to untwist

▸**se détordre** VPR to come untwisted, to untwist

détors, -e [detɔr, -ɔrs] ADJ *(fil)* untwisted; *(corde)* unlaid

détorsion [detɔrsjɔ̃] NF untwisting

détortiller [3] [detɔrtije] VT *(câble, corde, linge)* to untwist; *(cheveux)* to disentangle; *(bonbon)* to unwrap

détour [detur] NM **1** *(tournant)* bend, curve, turn; *(méandre)* wind, meander; **la route fait de nombreux détours jusqu'au bout/jusqu'en bas/jusqu'en haut de la vallée** the road winds all the way through/down/up the valley; **faire un brusque d.** to make a sharp turn

2 *(crochet)* detour, diversion; **faire un d. par un village** to make a detour through a village; **elle nous a fait faire un d. pour venir ici** she brought us a roundabout way; *Fig* **faisons un petit d. par la psychanalyse** let's go off at a tangent for a minute and talk about psychoanalysis; **valoir le d.** *(restaurant, paysage)* to be worth the detour; *Fam* **tu verrais son nouveau copain, il vaut le d.!** her new boyfriend is really something!

3 *(faux-fuyant)* roundabout way; **un discours plein de détours** a roundabout *or Sout* circumlocutory way of speaking

❑ **au détour de** PRÉP **1** *(en cheminant le long de)* **je l'ai aperçue au d. du chemin** I spotted her at the bend in the path

2 *(en consultant, en écoutant)* **au d. de votre livre/œuvre, on devine vos préoccupations** leafing through your book/glancing through your work, one gets an idea of your main concerns; **au d. de la conversation** in the course of the conversation

❑ **sans détour** ADV *(parler, répondre)* straightforwardly, without beating about the bush

détourage [deturaʒ] NM *Tech* routing

détouré [deture] NM *Phot & Typ* cut-out

détourer [3] [deture] VT **1** *Tech* to rout **2** *Phot & Typ* to cut out

détourné, -e [deturne] ADJ **1** *(route, voie)* roundabout *(avant n)*, *Sout* circuitous **2** *(façon, moyen)* indirect, roundabout *(avant n)*, *Sout* circuitous; **par des moyens détournés** in a roundabout way; **apprendre qch de façon détournée** to learn sth indirectly; **agir de façon détournée** to behave deviously

détournement [deturnəmɑ̃] NM **1** *(dérivation → de la circulation)* redirection, diversion, rerouting; *(→ d'une rivière)* diverting, diversion

2 *Aviat* **d. d'avion** hijacking; **faire un d. d'avion** to hijack a plane

3 *Fin* misappropriation; **d. d'actif** embezzlement of assets; **d. de fonds** misappropriation of funds, embezzlement

4 *Jur* **d. de mineur** corruption of a minor; **d. de pouvoir** abuse of power; **d. de procédure** = use of improper but more expedient procedure *(especially by a local government body)*

5 *Ordinat* **d. de modem** modem hijacking

détourner [3] [deturne] VT **1** *(circulation)* to redirect, to divert, to reroute; *(rivière)* to divert; **il a fallu d. le convoi par le village** the convoy had to be rerouted through the village

2 *(avion, autocar)* to hijack

3 *(éloigner → coup)* to parry; *(→ arme)* to turn aside *or* away; **d. les yeux** *ou* **le regard** to avert one's eyes, to look away; **d. la tête** to turn one's head away; **d. l'attention de qn** to divert sb's attention; **d. la conversation** to change the subject; **d. les soupçons** to divert suspicion (away from oneself); **d. les soupçons sur qn** to divert suspicion towards sb

4 *(déformer → paroles, texte)* to distort, to twist; **il sait comment d. le sens du contrat à son profit** he knows how to make the wording of the contract work to his advantage

5 *(écarter)* to take away; **d. qn de sa route** to take sb out of his/her way; **d. qn de son devoir** to divert sb from his/her duty; **d. qn du droit chemin** to lead sb astray

6 *(extorquer)* to misappropriate; **d. des fonds** to embezzle *or* to misappropriate funds

7 *Jur (mineur)* to corrupt

▸**se détourner** VPR **1** *(tourner la tête)* to turn (one's head), to look away

2 se d. de to turn away from; **se d. de Dieu** to turn away from God; **ne te détourne pas de moi** don't turn away from me; **se d. de ses études** to turn away from one's studies; **en grandissant, je me suis détourné de la natation** I got tired of swimming as I grew older

détoxication [detɔksikasjɔ̃] NF detoxication, detoxification

détoxiquer [3] [detɔksike] VT to detoxicate, to detoxify

détracter [3] [detrakte] VT *Littéraire* to denigrate, to disparage

détracteur, -trice [detraktœr, -tris] ADJ disparaging, detractory

NM,F disparager, detractor; **tous ses détracteurs** all his/her critics *or* those who have attacked him/her

détraction [detraksjɔ̃] NF *Vieilli & Littéraire* denigration, disparagement

détractrice [detraktris] *voir* **détracteur**

détraqué, -e [detrake] ADJ **1** *(cassé)* broken; **ma montre/la télé est détraquée** my watch/the TV isn't working properly

2 *Fam (dérangé)* **le temps est d.** the weather's gone haywire; **ma santé est détraquée** my health is wrecked; **elle a les nerfs complètement détraqués** she's a nervous wreck

3 *Fam (désaxé)* crazy, psychotic; **il est complètement d.** he's totally cracked; **il a le cerveau d.** his mind is unhinged

NM,F *Fam* maniac, psychopath; **d. sexuel** sex maniac

détraquement [detrakmɑ̃] NM **depuis le d. de ma montre** *(elle fonctionne mal)* since my watch started going wrong; *(elle est cassée)* since my watch stopped working

détraquer [3] [detrake] VT **1** *(appareil)* to damage; *(mécanisme)* to throw out of gear

2 *Fam (déranger)* **ça va te d. l'estomac** that'll upset your stomach; *Hum* **toutes ces études lui ont détraqué le cerveau** all that studying has addled his/her brain

▸**se détraquer** VPR **1** *(mal fonctionner)* to go wrong; *(cesser de fonctionner)* to break down

2 *Fam (temps)* to become unsettled■; *(l'estomac)* to be upset ■

3 *Fam* **se d. le foie/le système** to wreck one's liver/health

détrempe [detrɑ̃p] NF **1** *Métal* softening, annealing **2** *(produit → à base de lait, d'eau)* distemper; *(→ à base d'œuf)* tempera; *(œuvre)* distemper painting; **peindre un tableau à la** *ou* **en d.** to distemper a painting

détremper [3] [detrɑ̃pe] VT **1** *Métal* to soften, to anneal **2** *(cuir)* to soak, to soften **3** *(mouiller → chiffon, papier)* to soak (through); *(→ chaux)* to slake; *(→ mortier)* to mix with water; **détrempé** *(champ, terre)* sodden, waterlogged **4** *Beaux-Arts* to distemper

détresse [detrɛs] NF **1** *(désespoir)* distress, anxiety; **pousser un cri de d.** to cry out in distress **2** *(pauvreté)* distress; **les familles dans la d.** families in dire need *or* dire straits; **tomber dans une grande d.** to fall on hard times, to encounter hardship **3** *Méd* **d. respiratoire** respiratory distress

❑ **en détresse** ADJ *(navire, avion)* in distress

détricoter [3] [detrikɔte] VT to unknit, to unravel

détriment [detrimɑ̃] NM *Littéraire* detriment

❑ **au détriment de** PRÉP to the detriment of; **je l'ai appris à mon d.** I found out to my cost

détritique [detritik] ADJ *(sol, terrain)* detrital

détritivore [detritivɔr] ADJ *(insecte)* waste-eating, *Spéc* detritivorous

détritus [detrity(s)] NM piece of *Br* rubbish *or Am* garbage; **des d.** refuse, detritus

Detroit [detrwa] NM Detroit

détroit [detrwa] NM **1** *Géog* strait; **les Détroits** the Dardanelles and the Bosphorus; **le d. de Bass** the Bass Strait; **le d. de Béring** the Bering Strait; **le d. du Bosphore** the Bosphorus Strait; **le d. de Cook** the Cook Strait; **le d. du Danemark** *ou* **de Danemark** the Denmark Strait; **le d. des Dardanelles** the Dardanelles; **le d. de Davis** the Davis Strait; **le d. de Floride** the Straits of Florida; **le d. de Gibraltar** the Strait of Gibraltar; **le d. d'Hormuz** *ou* **d'Ormuz** the Strait of Hormuz *or* Ormuz; **le d. de Magellan** the Strait of Magellan; **le d. de Malacca** the Strait of Malacca; **le d. de Messine** the Strait of Messina; **le d. du Yucatá** the Yucatan Channel

2 *Anat* strait; **d. inférieur/supérieur du bassin** pelvic outlet/inlet

détromper [3] [detrɔ̃pe] VT to disabuse

▸**se détromper** VPR **détrompez-vous!** don't be so sure!; **si tu crois qu'il va venir, détrompe-toi!** if you think he's coming, you'd better think again!

détrôner [3] [detrone] VT *(roi)* to dethrone, to depose; *(champion)* to dethrone; *(rival, produit)* to oust, to push into second position; **les MP3 vont-ils d. les compacts?** will CDs be ousted by MP3s?; **se faire d.** to be dethroned; *Fig* to be ousted

détroquage [detrɔkaʒ] NM = detaching of oysters from the cultch before fattening

détroquer [3] [detrɔke] VT **d. des huîtres** to detach oysters from the cultch before fattening

détrousser [3] [detruse] VT *Littéraire* to rob

détrousseur [detrusœr] NM *Littéraire* **d. de grands chemins** highwayman

détruire [98] [detrɥir] VT **1** *(démolir, casser)* to destroy; **le village a été détruit** the village was destroyed *or* razed to the ground; **les deux véhicules sont détruits** both cars are write-offs; **détruisez cette lettre** destroy this letter; **l'enfant construit un château, puis le détruit** the child builds a castle, then demolishes it; **ma vie est détruite** my life is in ruins; **d. par le feu** *(maison)* to burn down; *(objet, documents)* to burn

2 *(éliminer → population, parasites)* to destroy, to wipe out; *(tuer → ennemi)* to kill; *(→ animal malade, chien errant)* to destroy

3 *(porter préjudice à → santé, carrière)* to ruin, to destroy, to wreck; **tu as détruit la confiance que j'avais en toi** you have destroyed the trust I had in you; **tous ses espoirs ont été détruits en un instant** all his/her hopes were shattered in an instant; **ils cherchent à d. la paix** they want to destroy peace

▸**se détruire** VPR *Vieilli* to do away with oneself

dette [dɛt] NF **1** *(d'argent)* debt; **avoir une d.** to have run up a debt; **avoir 1000 euros de dettes**

to be 1,000 euros in debt; **avoir des dettes** to be in debt; **avoir de plus en plus de dettes** to get deeper and deeper into debt; **avoir des dettes vis-à-vis de qn** to be in debt to sb; **être couvert** *ou* **criblé** *ou* **perdu de dettes** to be up to one's *Br* eyes *or Am* ears in debt; **faire des dettes** to get *or* to run into debt; **je n'ai plus de dettes** I've cleared my debts; *Compta* **dettes actives** accounts receivable, assets; **dettes bancaires** bank debts; **d. caduque** debt barred by the Statute of Limitations; **dettes compte** book debts; *Écon & Fin* **d. consolidée** consolidated *or* funded debt; **d. à court terme** short-term debt; *Compta* **dettes à court terme** current liabilities; **d. de l'État** national debt; **d. exigible** debt due for (re)payment; **dettes d'exploitation** trade debt; **d. extérieure** external *or* foreign debt; **d. flottante** floating debt; **d. foncière** property charge; **dettes fournisseurs** accounts payable; **d. d'honneur** debt of honour; (*hypothécaire*) mortgage debt; **d. inexigible** unrecoverable debt; **d. inscrite** consolidated debt; **d. de jeu** gambling debt; **d. liquide** liquid debt; *Compta* **dettes à long terme** long term liabilities; *Compta* **dettes à moyen terme** medium-term liabilities; *Fin* **d. négociable** assignable debt; *Compta* **dettes passives** (*en comptabilité*) accounts payable, liabilities; **d. privilégiée** preferred *or* privileged debt; **d. publique** national debt; **d. en souffrance** outstanding debt; **d. subordonnée** subordinated debt; **d. véreuse** bad debt; *Prov* **qui paie ses dettes s'enrichit** he who pays his debts will prosper

2 (*obligation morale*) debt; **régler sa d. envers la société** to pay one's debt to society; **être en d. envers qn** to be indebted to sb, to be under an obligation to sb; **avoir une d. de reconnaissance envers qn** to be in sb's debt, to owe sb a debt of gratitude

3 *Physiol* **d. d'oxygène** oxygen debt

détumescence [detymesɑ̃s] NF detumescence

deuche [dœʃ], **deudeuche** [dœdœʃ] NF *Fam* Citroën 2CV▪

DEUG [dœg] NM (*abrév* **diplôme d'études universitaires générales**) = university diploma taken after two years

deuil [dœj] NM **1** (*chagrin*) grief, mourning; *Fam* **j'en ai fait mon d.** I've resigned myself to not having it; **ta nouvelle voiture, tu peux en faire ton d.** you might as well kiss your new car goodbye

2 (*décès*) bereavement; **il y a eu un d. dans la famille** there was a bereavement *or* death in the family

3 (*tenue conventionnelle*) mourning; **porter/prendre le d. (de qn)** to be in/to go into mourning (for sb); *Fig* **elle porte le d. de sa jeunesse/de sa fortune** she is mourning the loss of her youth/fortune; **quitter le d.** to come out of mourning

4 (*période*) mourning; **son d. n'aura pas duré longtemps** he/she didn't mourn for very long; **il l'a rencontrée pendant son d.** he met her when he was still in mourning; **une journée de d. national** a day of national mourning

5 (*convoi*) funeral procession; **conduire** *ou* **mener le d.** to be the chief mourner

▫ **de deuil** ADJ (*vêtement*) mourning (*avant n*); **brassard de d.** black armband

▫ **en deuil** ADJ bereaved; **une femme en d.** a woman in mourning; *Fig* **la Bretagne est en d.** the whole of Brittany is in mourning

▫ **en deuil de** PRÉP **être en d. de qn** to mourn for sb

▫ **en grand deuil** ADJ in deep mourning

deus ex machina [deysɛksmakina] NM INV deus ex machina

deusio [døzjo] ADV *Fam* secondly▪, second▪

DEUST [døst] NM (*abrév* **diplôme d'études universitaires scientifiques et techniques**) = university diploma taken after two years of science courses; *voir aussi encadré sous* **DEUG**

deutérium [døterjɔm] NM *Chim* deuterium

deutérocanonique [døterɔkanɔnik] ADJ *Bible* **les livres deutérocanoniques** the Apocrypha

deutéron [døterɔ̃] NM *Chim* deuteron

Deutéronome [døterɔnɔm] NM *Bible* **le D.** Deuteronomy

deutérostomien [døterɔstɔmjɛ̃] *Zool* NM deuterostomian

▫ **deutérostomiens** NMPL Deuterostomata

deuton [døtɔ̃] NM *Chim* deuteron

DeutscheMark [døtʃmark] NM *Anciennement* Deutschmark

DEUX [dø] ADJ **1** (*gén*) two; **on a dû lui enlever les d. yeux** they had to remove both his/her eyes; **des d. côtés** on both sides; **d. fois** twice; **d. fois plus de livres** twice as many books; **d. fois moins de livres** half as many books; **j'ai d. mots à te dire** I want a word with you, I've a bone to pick with you; **je reviens dans d. minutes** I'll be back in a minute; **tu peux venir ? – d. secondes!** can you come here? – just a minute!; **d. ou trois** (*quelques*) a few, one or two; **écris-moi d. ou trois lignes de temps en temps** drop me a line from time to time; **ça s'écrit avec d. g** it's spelt with a double g *or* two g's; **une personne à d. visages** a two-faced individual; **à d. pas** close by, not far away; **à d. pas de** close by, not far away from; **à d. doigts de** close to, within an inch of; **à d. doigts de mourir** *ou* **de la mort** within an inch of death *or* dying; **j'ai été à d. doigts de le renvoyer** I came very close to *or* I was within inches of firing him; **je suis à d. doigts d'avoir terminé** I've very nearly finished; **entre d. âges** middle-aged; *Mil & Fig* **pris entre d. feux** caught in the crossfire; **nager entre d. eaux** to sit on the fence; **je l'ai vu entre d. portes** I only saw him briefly; **il n'a pas d. sous de jugeote** he hasn't got a scrap of common sense; *Fam* **en d. temps trois mouvements** in no time at all, in a jiffy; *très Fam* **de mes d.** *Br* bloody, *Am* goddamn; **t'as vu ce chauffard de mes d.!** did you see that *Br* bloody *or Am* goddamn idiot driving that car?; **avoir d. poids d. mesures** to apply double standards; **d. avis valent mieux qu'un** two heads are better than one; *Prov* **d. précautions valent mieux qu'une** better safe than sorry; **de d. maux, il faut choisir le moindre** one must choose the lesser of two evils

2 (*dans des séries*) second; **page/numéro/chapitre d.** page/number/chapter two; **Charles D.** Charles the Second

PRON two; **casser qch en d.** to break sth in two; **venez, tous les d.** come along, both of you; **eux/nous d.** both of them/us, the two of them/us; **à nous d.!** right, let's get on with it!; (*à un adversaire*) let's fight it out!; *Fam* **lui et le dessin, ça fait d.!** he can't draw to save his life!; **les maths/les ordinateurs et moi, ça fait d.** I just don't get on with maths/computers; **elle et la propreté, ça fait d.!** she doesn't know the meaning of the word "clean"!; *Fam* **comme pas d.** as anything; **les d. font la paire** they're two of a kind

NM INV **1** (*gén*) two; (*date*) second; **d. fois d. font quatre** two times two *or* twice two is four; **aujourd'hui nous sommes le d.** today is the second, it's the second today; **en moins de d.** in no time at all, in the twinkling of an eye; *Fam* **je n'ai fait ni une ni d.** I didn't think twice

2 (*numéro d'ordre*) number two

3 (*chiffre écrit*) two

4 *Cartes* two; **le d. de cœur** the two of hearts; *Can Fam* **un d. de pique** (*personne*) a loser

5 *Can Fam* (*billet*) two-dollar coin▪

6 (*en aviron*) pair; **d. de couple** double scull; **d. de pointe avec/sans barreur** coxed/coxless pair; *voir aussi* **cinq**

▫ **à deux** ADV (*vivre*) as a couple, together; (*travailler*) in pairs; **il faudra s'y mettre à d.** it'll take two of us

▫ **deux à deux** ADV in twos *or* pairs

▫ **deux par deux** ADV in twos *or* pairs; **les enfants, mettez-vous d. par d.** children, get into twos *or* pairs

2G [døʒe] ADJ *Ordinat & Tél* 2G

deuxième [døzjɛm] ADJ second; *Gram* **la d. personne du singulier/pluriel** the second person singular/plural; *Anciennement Pol* **le D. Bureau** the intelligence service; **de d. choix, de d. qualité** (*marchandises, articles*) inferior; *Cin & TV* **d. équipe** second unit

NMF **1** (*personne*) second

2 (*objet*) second (one); *Typ* **d. de couverture** inside front cover, IFC; *Typ* **d. épreuve** revise proof

NM **1** (*partie*) second

2 (*étage*) *Br* second floor, *Am* third floor

3 (*arrondissement de Paris*) second (arrondissement)

4 *Fin* **d. de change** second of exchange; *voir aussi* **cinquième**

deuxièmement [døzjɛmmã] ADV secondly, in second place

deux-mâts [døma] NM INV two-master

deux-pattes [døpat] NF INV *Fam* Citroën 2CV▪

deux-pièces [døpjɛs] NM INV **1** (*maillot de bain*) two-piece **2** (*costume*) two-piece **3** (*appartement*) two-room *Br* flat *or Am* apartment

deux-points [døpwɛ̃] NM INV colon

deux-ponts [døpɔ̃] NM INV double-decker

deux-quatre [døkatr] NM INV *Mus* two-four time

deux-roues [døru] NM INV two-wheeled vehicle

Deux-Sèvres [døsɛvr] NFPL **les D.** Deux-Sèvres

deux-temps [døtã] NM INV (*moteur*) two-stroke; **(mélange) d.** two-stroke mixture

2.5G [døvirgylsɛ̃kʒe] ADJ *Ordinat & Tél* 2.5G

deuz, deuze [døz] *Fam* (*abrév* **deuxième**) ADJ second▪; **je suis d.!** I'm second!

NMF second▪

deuzio [døzjo] = **deusio**

dévaler [3] [devale] VT (*en courant*) to run *or* to race *or* to hurtle down; (*en roulant*) to tumble down

VI **1** (*personne*) to hurry *or* to hurtle down; (*torrent*) to gush down; (*animal*) to run down **2** (*s'abaisser* → *terrain*) to fall *or* to slope away **3** (*rouler*) to tumble *or* to bump down; **le chariot a dévalé tout seul** the trolley ran off on its own

dévaliser [3] [devalize] VT **1** (*cambrioler* → *banque, diligence*) to rob; (→ *maison*) to burgle; (*dépouiller* → *personne*) to rob; **il s'est fait d.** he was robbed **2** *Fam* (*vider*) to raid; **ils ont dévalisé le garde-manger** they raided the larder; **tous les marchands de glaces ont été dévalisés** all the ice-cream sellers have sold out▪

dévaloir [devalwar] NM *Suisse* **1** (*à la montagne*)

= path through a mountain forest for transporting logs **2** *(vide-ordures)* Br rubbish or Am garbage chute

dévalorisant, -e [devalɔrizɑ̃, -ɑ̃t] ADJ **1** *Fin* depreciating **2** *(humiliant)* humbling, humiliating

dévalorisation [devalɔrizasjɔ̃] NF **1** *Fin (de la monnaie)* depreciation; *(de marchandises)* mark-down **2** *(perte de prestige)* devaluing, loss of prestige; **la d. d'une profession/d'un diplôme** the loss of prestige of a profession/of a qualification

dévaloriser [3] [devalɔrize] VT **1** *(discréditer → personne, talent)* to depreciate, to devalue **2** *Fin (monnaie)* to devalue; *(marchandises)* to mark down

  ▸**se dévaloriser** VPR **1** *(se discréditer)* to put oneself down; **se d. aux yeux de qn** to discredit oneself in the eyes of sb **2** *Fin (monnaie)* to become devalued; *(marchandises)* to lose value; **ce diplôme s'est dévalorisé** this degree has lost its prestige

dévaluation [devalɥasjɔ̃] NF *Écon & Fin* devaluation, devaluing; **d. compétitive** competitive devaluation

dévaluer [7] [devalɥe] VT **1** *Fin* to devalue **2** *(déprécier)* to devalue; **il l'a fait pour te d. à tes propres yeux** he did it to make you feel cheap

  ▸**se dévaluer** VPR to drop in value

devanagari [dəvanagari] NF Devanagari

devancement [dəvɑ̃smɑ̃] NM **1** *Mil* **d. d'appel** enlistment before call-up **2** *Fin (d'une échéance)* payment before the due date, prepayment

devancer [16] [dəvɑ̃se] VT **1** *(dans l'espace → coureur, peloton)* to get ahead of, to outdistance; **je la devançais de quelques mètres** I was a few metres ahead of her; *Fig* **sur ce marché, nous ne sommes plus devancés que par les Japonais** now only the Japanese are ahead of us in this market

  2 *(dans le temps → personne)* to arrive ahead of; *(→ demande, désirs)* to anticipate; **elle m'avait devancé de deux jours** she had arrived two days before me; **d. son siècle** *ou* **époque** to be ahead of one's time; **d. l'appel** *Mil* to enlist before call-up; *Fig* to jump the gun

  3 *(agir avant → personne)* **tu m'as devancé, c'est justement ce que je voulais leur offrir/leur dire** you beat me to it, that's just what I wanted to give them/to say to them; **il s'est fait d. par les autres** the others got there before him

  4 *Fin* **d. une échéance** to make a payment before it falls due

devancier, -ère [dəvɑ̃sje, -ɛr] NM,F **1** *(précurseur)* precursor, forerunner **2** *(qui précède)* predecessor

---

DEVANT [dəvɑ̃]

PRÉP in front of **1–3** ∎ past **1** ∎ ahead of **2** ∎ in the face of **4** ∎ given **4**

ADV in front **1, 2** ∎ ahead **3** ∎ before **4**

NM front

PRÉP **1** *(en face de)* in front of; *(avec mouvement)* past; **il s'est garé d. la maison** he parked in front of the house; **ça s'est passé juste d. chez moi** it happened just in front of my house; **il a déposé le paquet d. la porte** he left the parcel outside the door; **tricoter d. la télévision** to knit in front of the TV or while watching TV; **toujours d. la télé!** always glued to the TV!; **assis d. un verre de vin** sitting over a glass of wine; **il faut mettre un zéro d. le code** you have to put a zero in front of or before the code; **elle est passée d. moi sans me voir** she walked right past (me) without seeing me; **la voiture est passée/un lièvre a détalé d. moi** the car drove/a hare bolted past me

  2 *(en avant de)* in front of; *(en avance sur)* ahead of; **il marchait d. nous** he was walking in front of us; **nous passerons d. lui pour lui montrer le chemin** we'll go ahead of him to show him the way; **passe d. moi, tu verras mieux** go in front of me, you'll get a better view; **elle est passée d. moi dans la queue** she went in front of or ahead of me in the queue; **il est loin d. nous** he is a long way in front of or ahead of us; **l'ère de la**

communication est d. nous the age of communication lies ahead of or before us; **ils sont d. nous en matière d'électronique** their electronics industry's ahead of ours; **leur équipe est passée d. nous au classement** their team is now ahead of us in the league; **aller droit d. soi** to go straight on or ahead; *Fig* to carry on regardless; **regardez d. vous** look where you're going; **j'ai une heure d. moi** I have an hour to spare; **elle avait une belle carrière d. elle** she had a promising career ahead of her; **tu as la vie d. toi** you've got your whole life ahead of you; **avoir quelques économies d. soi** to have some savings put by

  3 *(en présence de)* in front of; **pleurer d. tout le monde** *(devant les gens présents)* to cry in front of everyone; *(en public)* to cry in public; **il vaudrait mieux ne pas en parler d. lui** it would be better not to mention it in front of him; **d. témoins** in front of or in the presence of witnesses; **ils comparaîtront d. le tribunal demain** they will appear in court tomorrow; **porter une affaire d. la justice** to bring a case before the courts or to court; **je jure d. Dieu…** I swear to God…

  4 *(face à)* in the face of, faced with; *(étant donné)* given; **nos troupes ont reculé d. leur puissance de feu** our troops withdrew in the face of their (superior) fire power; **d. l'hostilité croissante de l'opinion, ils ont renoncé** faced with mounting public opposition, they gave up; **je n'ai su que faire d. cette petite fille en pleurs** I didn't know what to do when faced or confronted with this little girl in tears; **son attitude d. le malheur** his/her attitude to or *Littéraire* in the face of disaster; **d. des preuves accablantes** in the face of overwhelming evidence; **d. son hésitation…** as he/she was or seeing that he/she was reluctant…, given his/her reluctance…; **d. la gravité de cette affaire** given the serious nature of this matter; **égaux d. la loi** equal in the eyes of the law or before the law

ADV **1** *(à l'avant)* **mettez les plus petits de la classe d.** put the shortest pupils at the or in front; **avoir des places d.** to have seats at the front; **installe-toi d.** *(en voiture)* sit Br in the front or Am in front; **ça se boutonne d.** it buttons up Br at the front or Am in front; **tes cheveux sont trop longs d.** your hair's too long at the front; **écris le nom du destinataire d.** write the addressee's name on the front; **faites passer la pétition d.** pass the petition forward; **vous pouvez passer des verres d.?** will you pass some glasses forward?; **d. derrière** back to front, the wrong way round; **tu as mis ton pull d. derrière** you've put your jumper on back to front or the wrong way round

  2 *(en face)* **tu es juste d.** it's right in front of you; **tu peux te garer d.** you can park (right) in front; **je suis passé d. sans faire attention** I went past without paying attention

  3 *(en tête)* **elle est loin d.** she's a long way ahead; **tu n'as pas vu Martin? – je crois qu'il est d.** have you seen Martin? – I think he's up ahead; **passe d., tu verras mieux** come or go through, you'll get a better view; **marche d.** walk in front; **pars d., je te rattraperai** go ahead, I'll catch you up

  4 *Vieilli & Littéraire* **il revint plus effaré que d.** he came back more scared than before; **comme d.** as before

NM *(gén)* front; *Naut* bow, bows, fore; **avec cuisine sur le d. (de l'immeuble)** with a kitchen at the front (of the building); **la figure B indique le d.** figure B shows the front; **la jupe est plus longue sur le d.** the skirt is longer at the front; *Fig* **sur le d. de la scène** in the limelight; **prendre les devants** to make the first move, to be the first to act; **d. de caisse** checkout display

  ❑ **de devant** ADJ *(dent, porte)* front; **pattes de d.** forelegs PRÉP **va-t-en de d. la fenêtre** move away from the window; **sors de d. la télé** don't stand in front of the TV

---

devanture [dəvɑ̃tyr] NF **1** *(vitrine)* Br shop window, Am store window **2** *(étalage)* (window) display **3** *(façade)* Br shopfront, Am storefront **4** *Can Fam (seins)* boobs, rack

---

❑ **en devanture** ADV in the window; **nous l'avons en d.** it's in the window

dévastateur, -trice [devastatœr, -tris] ADJ devastating; **de manière dévastatrice** devastatingly NM,F wrecker

dévastation [devastasjɔ̃] NF devastation, havoc

dévastatrice [devastatris] *voir* **dévastateur**

dévaster [3] [devaste] VT **1** *(pays, ville)* to devastate, to lay waste; *(récolte)* to ruin, to destroy; **des villages dévastés** destroyed villages **2** *Littéraire (cœur)* to ravage; **l'âme dévastée par ces morts successives** devastated by this succession of bereavements; **la souffrance a dévasté son visage** his/her looks have been ravaged by suffering

déveine [devɛn] NF bad luck; **avec ma d. habituelle** with my (usual) luck; **être dans la d.** to be down on one's luck; **quelle d.!** (what) hard luck!

développable [devlɔpabl] ADJ *Math* developable

développante [devlɔpɑ̃t] NF *Math* involute

développé [devlɔpe] NM **1** *(en danse)* développé **2** *Sport* press

développée [devlɔpe] NF *Math* evolute

développement [devlɔpmɑ̃] NM **1** *(fait de grandir)* development; *(fait de progresser)* development, growth; **le d. normal de l'enfant/du chêne** a child's/an oak's normal development; **pour aider au d. du sens des responsabilités chez les jeunes** in order to foster a sense of responsibility in the young; **d. du marché** market development; **d. des ventes** sales expansion

  2 *Écon* **le d.** development; **une région/entreprise en plein d.** a fast-developing area/business; **d. durable** sustained development; **d. outre-mer** overseas development

  3 *(exposé)* exposition; **faire un d. sur qch** to develop the theme of sth; **entrer dans des développements superflus** to go into unnecessary detail

  4 *(perfectionnement)* developing; **nous leur avons confié le d. du prototype** we asked them to develop the prototype for us; **payé 5000 euros pour le d. du scénario** paid 5,000 euros for script development

  5 *Phot (traitement complet)* processing, developing; *(étape du traitement)* developing; **une heure pour le d. des photos** one hour to process the pictures; **faire ressortir des contrastes au d.** to bring out contrasts during developing; **appareil photo à d. instantané** instant camera

  6 *Tech* gear; **bicyclette avec un d. de six mètres** bicycle with a six metre gear

  7 *Math* development

  8 *(déploiement → d'une banderole)* unrolling

  9 *Mus, Beaux-Arts & Littérature (d'un thème)* development

  ❑ **développements** NMPL *(prolongements → d'une affaire)* developments; **à la lumière des récents développements** in the light of recent developments

développer [3] [devlɔpe] VT **1** *(faire croître → faculté)* to develop; *(→ usine, secteur)* to develop, to expand; *(→ pays, économie)* to develop; **pour d. les muscles** for muscle development; **un jeu qui développe l'intelligence** a game which develops the player's intelligence

  2 *(exposer → argument, plan)* to develop, to enlarge on

  3 *(symptôme, complexe, maladie)* to develop

  4 *Phot (traiter)* to process; *(révéler)* to develop; **faire d. une pellicule** to have a film processed; **faire d. des photos** to have some photos developed

  5 *Math* to develop

  6 *Tech* **une bicyclette qui développe cinq mètres** a bicycle with a five-metre gear

  7 *(déballer → coupon)* to unfold, to open out; *(→ paquet)* to unwrap; *(→ banderole)* to unroll

  8 *Mus, Beaux-Arts & Littérature (thème)* to develop

  ▸**se développer** VPR **1** *(croître → enfant, plante)* to develop, to grow; *(→ usine, secteur)* to develop, to expand; *(→ pays, économie)* to develop, to become developed; **les usines Viaut cherchent à se d.** Viaut wish to expand; **une région qui se développe** a developing area; **ça**

se développe beaucoup dans la région the region is developing quickly; **il s'est beaucoup développé sur le plan physique** he has grown quite a lot; **elle n'est pas très développée pour son âge** she's physically underdeveloped for her age

2 *(apparaître → membrane, moisissure)* to form, to develop

3 *(se déployer → armée)* to be deployed; *(→ cortège)* to spread out; *(→ argument)* to develop, to unfold; *(→ récit)* to develop, to progress, to unfold; **la plaine se développe à perte de vue** the plain extends *or* stretches out as far as the eye can see

4 *(se diversifier → technique, science)* to improve, to develop

5 *(s'aggraver → maladie)* to develop

développeur [devlɔpœr] **NM** *Ordinat* software developer

devenir[1] [dəvnir] **NM** *Littéraire* **1** *(évolution)* evolution

2 *(avenir)* future; **quel est le d. de l'homme?** what is the future of mankind?

❏ **en devenir ADJ** *Littéraire (société, œuvre)* evolving, changing; **en perpétuel d.** constantly changing, ever-changing

devenir[2] [40] [dəvnir] **VI 1** *(acquérir telle qualité)* to become; **d. professeur** to become a teacher; **d. la femme de qn** to become sb's wife; **tu es devenue une femme** you're a woman now; **d. réalité** to become a reality; **d. vieux** to get *or* to grow old; **d. rouge/bleu** to go red/blue; **l'animal peut d. dangereux lorsqu'il est menacé** the animal can be dangerous when threatened; *Fam* **d. chèvre** *(s'énerver)* to blow one's top; *Fam* **à (vous faire) d. dingue, à (vous faire) d. fou, à (vous faire) d. chèvre** enough to drive you round the bend *or* to make you scream

2 *(avoir tel sort)* **que sont devenus tes amis de jeunesse?** what happened to your childhood friends?; **que sont devenues tes belles intentions?** what has become of your good intentions?; **et moi, qu'est-ce que je vais d.?** what's to become of me?; **et moi, qu'est-ce que je deviens dans tout ça?** and where do I fit into all this?; **je ne sais pas ce que je deviendrais sans toi** I don't know what I'd do without you; **qu'est-ce que tu es devenu, il y a une heure qu'on t'attend!** where have you been *or* what have you been doing, we've been waiting for you for an hour!

3 *Fam (pour demander des nouvelles)* **que devenez-vous?** how are you getting on?, what have you been up to?; **et lui, qu'est-ce qu'il devient?** what's he up to these days?

4 *(tournure impersonnelle)* **il devient difficile de...** it's getting difficult to...; **il devient inutile de...** it's now pointless to...

déverbal, -e, -aux, -ales [devɛrbal, -o], **déverbatif, -ive** [devɛrbatif, -iv] *Gram* **ADJ** deverbal, deverbative

NM deverbal, deverbative

dévergondage [devɛrgɔ̃daʒ] **NM 1** *(immoralité)* licentiousness, licentious *or* immoral behaviour **2** *(fantaisie → du style, de l'imagination)* extravagance

dévergondé, -e [devɛrgɔ̃de] **ADJ** licentious, shameless

NM,F shameless person; **quel d.!** he's a wild one!; **cette petite dévergondée** the little hussy

dévergonder [3] [devɛrgɔ̃de] **VT** to corrupt, to pervert, to lead astray; *Hum* **j'ai décidé de te d., tu ne vas pas travailler aujourd'hui** I've decided to lead you astray, you're staying off work today

▸**se dévergonder VPR** to go off the rails; *Hum* **dis donc, tu te dévergondes!** you're letting your hair down!

déverguer [3] [devɛrge] **VT** *Naut (voile)* to unbend

dévernir [32] [devɛrnir] **VT** to strip the enamel off

déverrouillage [devɛrujaʒ] **NM 1** *Ordinat & (d'une arme)* unlocking **2** *(d'une porte)* unbolting **3** *Aut* **d. du capot/du hayon par l'intérieur** internal bonnet/hatchback release

déverrouiller [3] [devɛruje] **VT 1** *Ordinat & (arme)* to unlock; *(majuscules)* to lock off; **d. un fichier en écriture** to unlock a file, to remove the read-only lock on a file **2** *(porte)* to unbolt

dévers [devɛr] **NM 1** *(en travaux publics)* banking **2** *(d'un mur)* inclination, slope **3** *Rail* bank, banking, camber

déversement [devɛrsəmɑ̃] **NM 1** *(écoulement)* flowing **2** *(déchargement → d'eaux usées)* pouring, discharging; *(→ de passagers)* offloading, discharging; *(→ d'ordures)* dumping, *Br* tipping

déverser [3] [devɛrse] **VT 1** *(répandre → liquide)* to pour, to discharge; **le canal déverse ses eaux dans un bassin** the canal discharges its water into a pool

2 *(décharger)* to discharge; **les paysans ont déversé des tonnes de fruits sur la chaussée** the farmers dumped tons of fruit on the road; *Fig* **le train déversa des centaines de vacanciers sur le quai** the train deposited hundreds of holiday-makers on the platform

3 *(exprimer → chagrin, rage, plainte)* to vent, to let *or* to pour out; **d. des flots de larmes** to be in floods of tears; **d. des flots d'injures** to come out with a stream of abuse; **d. sa colère sur qn** to take one's anger out on sb

▸**se déverser VPR 1** *(couler)* to flow; **se d. dans la mer** to flow into the sea

2 *(tomber)* **le chargement s'est déversé sur la route** the load tipped over *or* spilled onto the road

déversoir [devɛrswar] **NM 1** *(d'un barrage)* spillway, *Br* wasteweir **2** *Fig (exutoire)* outlet, safety valve

dévestiture [devɛstityr] **NF** *Suisse* access; **(chemin de) d.** access road

dévêtir [44] [devetir] **VT** to undress; **dévêts-le** take his clothes off, undress him

▸**se dévêtir VPR** to undress oneself, to get undressed, to take one's clothes off

déviance [devjɑ̃s] **NF** deviance, deviancy

déviant, -e [devjɑ̃, -ɑ̃t] **ADJ** deviant

NM,F deviant

déviateur [devjatœr] **NM 1** *Électron* deflector **2** *Aviat* **d. de jet** thrust spoiler

déviation [devjasjɔ̃] **NF 1** *Transp* detour, *Br* diversion; **d. à 500 mètres** diversion in 500 metres **2** *(écart)* swerving, deviating; **il ne se permet aucune d. par rapport à la ligne du parti** he will not deviate from *or* be deflected away from the party line **3** *Méd (de la colonne vertébrale)* curvature; *(de l'utérus)* displacement **4** *Électron* deflection **5** *Naut (d'un compas)* deviation **6** *Mines* deviation

déviationnisme [devjasjɔnism] **NM** deviationism

déviationniste [devjasjɔnist] **ADJ** deviationist

NMF deviationist

dévidage [devidaʒ] **NM 1** *(d'une bobine)* unwinding; *(d'un câble, d'une corde)* uncoiling **2** *(mise en écheveau)* reeling

dévider [3] [devide] **VT 1** *(mettre en écheveau)* to reel **2** *(dérouler → bobine)* to unwind; *(→ câble, corde)* to uncoil; **d. son rosaire** to say the rosary

dévideur [devidœr] **NM** *Ordinat* streamer

dévidoir [devidwar] **NM 1** *Tex* reel, spool **2** *(de tuyau d'incendie)* reel; *(pour câbles)* drum

devient *etc voir* **devenir**

dévier [9] [devje] **VI 1** *(s'écarter)* to swerve, to veer; **le bus a brusquement dévié sur la droite/gauche** the bus suddenly veered off to the right/left; **le vent a fait d. la voiture** the wind blew the car off course; **d. de** to move away from, to swerve from; **nous n'irons pas, cela nous ferait d. de notre chemin** we won't go, it would mean making a detour

2 *(être tordu → colonne vertébrale)* to be out of alignment, not to be straight

3 *(dans un débat, un projet)* to diverge, to deviate; **faire d. la conversation** to change the subject; **la conversation dévie** the conversation is getting out of hand; **l'association ne doit pas d. par rapport à son but premier** the association must not be diverted from its original purpose *or* must pursue its original goal unswervingly; **d. de** to move away from, to stray off

VT 1 *(balle, projectile)* to deflect, to turn away *or* aside; *(coup)* to parry; *(circulation)* to divert, to redirect, to reroute; **le planeur a été dévié par le vent** the glider was blown off course *or* deflected by the wind; **les appels sont déviés vers le standard** calls are diverted *or* rerouted to the switchboard

2 *Phys* to refract

3 *(distraire → attention)* to divert

dévierger [17] [devjɛrʒe] **VT** *Can très Fam* **d. qn** to take sb's virginity▪, to take sb's cherry

devin, devineresse [dəvɛ̃, dəvinrɛs] **NM,F** soothsayer; **il n'est pas d.!** he's not a mind-reader!; **(il n'y a) pas besoin d'être d. pour comprendre** you don't need to be a genius to understand

devinable [dəvinabl] **ADJ 1** *(énigme)* solvable; *(secret)* guessable **2** *(prévisible → avenir)* foreseeable

deviner [3] [dəvine] **VT 1** *(imaginer → gén)* to guess, to work out, to figure (out); *(→ la pensée de quelqu'un)* to read; **devine qui est là!** guess who's here!; **je n'ai fait que d.** it was sheer guesswork; **à toi de d. la suite** I'll leave it to you to figure out what happened next; **je ne pouvais pas d.!** how was I supposed to know!

2 *(découvrir → énigme, mystère)* **il a tout de suite deviné ses intentions** he saw through him/her right away; **il devine toujours ce que je pense** he can read me like a book; **tu ne devineras jamais ce qui m'est arrivé** you'll never guess what happened to me; **je n'arrive pas à d. où il veut en venir** I can't work out what he's driving at; **j'ai deviné qu'il y avait quelque chose de bizarre** I guessed there was something strange

3 *(prédire → avenir)* to foresee, to foretell

4 *(apercevoir)* **on devinait son soutien-gorge sous son chemisier** her bra showed through slightly under her blouse

5 *Littéraire (percer à jour)* **d. qn** to see through sb

▸**se deviner VPR 1** *(être aperçu)* **sa tête se devine derrière le rideau** you can just make out his/her head behind the curtain; **la propriété se devine derrière les hauts murs** the property can just be made out behind the high walls

2 *(transparaître → sentiment)* to show (through); **sa détresse se devine derrière son extérieur enjoué** his/her distress can be seen through his/her apparent jollity; **son attachement se devine à de petits détails** his/her love shows through in the little things he/she does

devineresse [dəvinrɛs] *voir* **devin**

devinette [dəvinɛt] **NF** riddle; **poser une d. (à qn)** to ask (sb) a riddle; **jouer aux devinettes** to play (at) riddles; *Fig* to speak in riddles

devint *etc voir* **devenir**

dévirer [3] [devire] **VT 1** *(vis)* to turn back **2** *Naut (rame)* to feather; *(cabestan)* to veer; *(voile)* to put about

▸**se dévirer VPR** *(cabestan, winch)* to get out of control

dévirginiser [3] [devirʒinize] **VT d. une femme** to take a woman's virginity, *Am* to devirginate a woman

dévirilisation [devirilizasjɔ̃] **NF** *(action)* emasculation

déviriliser [3] [devirilize] **VT** *(homme)* to emasculate

devis [dəvi] **NM** estimate, quotation; **faire** *ou* **établir un d.** to draw up an estimate; **il m'a fait un d. de 8000 euros** he quoted me 8,000 euros (in his estimate); **sur d.** on the basis of an estimate; **d. appréciatif** estimate, quotation; **d. descriptif** specification; **d. estimatif** estimate, quotation

dévisager [17] [devizaʒe] **VT** to stare (persistently) at; **on ne dévisage pas les gens** it's rude to stare

devise [dəviz] **NF 1** *Hér* device

2 *(maxime)* motto; **laisser faire les autres, c'est sa d.!** let the others do the work, that's his/her motto!; **la d. de notre maison** our company motto

3 *Fin* currency; **acheter des devises** to buy foreign currency; **d. contrôlée** managed currency; **d. convertible** convertible currency; **devises étrangères** foreign currency; **d. faible** soft currency; **d. flottante** floating currency; **d. forte** hard currency; **d. internationale** international currency; **d. non convertible** non-convertible currency; **d. solide** strong currency

deviser [3] [dəvize] **VI** *Littéraire* to converse, to talk

VT *Suisse (projet de construction)* to draw up an estimate *or* a quotation for; **travaux devisés à 100 000 euros** work estimated to cost 100,000 euros

devise-titre [dəviztitr] *(pl* **devises-titres***)* **NF** *Fin* foreign security, exchange currency

dévissage [devisaʒ] **NM 1** *(d'un écrou, d'une vis)* unscrewing **2** *(en montagne)* fall

dévisser [3] [devise] **VT 1** *(desserrer → écrou, vis)* to loosen; *(détacher)* to undo, to unscrew; **dévissez le bouchon** unscrew the top off the bottle

2 *(tordre → bras, cou)* to twist

VI *(en montagne)* to fall *or* to come off

▸**se dévisser VPR 1** *(être amovible)* to unscrew; **le bouchon se dévisse facilement** the top twists off the bottle easily

2 *(se détacher)* to come unscrewed

3 *Fig* **se d. le cou/la tête** to screw one's neck/one's head round

de visu [devizy] **ADV je l'ai constaté d.** I saw it for myself *or* with my own eyes

dévitalisation [devitalizasjɔ̃] **NF** root canal treatment (**de** on)

dévitaliser [3] [devitalize] **VT** to carry out root canal work *or* treatment on; **se faire d. une dent** to have root canal work *or* treatment done on a tooth

dévitaminé, -e [devitamine] **ADJ** lacking in vitamins

dévitrification [devitrifikasjɔ̃] **NF** devitrification

dévitrifier [9] [devitrifje] **VT** to devitrify

dévoie *etc voir* **dévoyer**

dévoiement [devwamɑ̃] **NM** *(d'un conduit etc)* canting, tilting

dévoilement [devwalmɑ̃] **NM 1** *(d'un visage, d'une statue)* unveiling **2** *(d'un secret, d'une intention, d'un sentiment)* disclosing, revealing; *(d'une conspiration)* unmasking; *(d'une fraude)* uncovering

dévoiler [3] [devwale] **VT 1** *(dénuder → visage, statue)* to unveil, to uncover, *Littéraire* to unshroud; *Euph* **d. ses charmes** to reveal all

2 *(révéler → secret, intention, sentiment)* to disclose, to reveal, to unveil; *(→ conspiration)* to unmask; *(→ fraude)* to uncover; **il a dévoilé ses pensées les plus secrètes** he laid bare his innermost thoughts; **d. ses batteries** to reveal one's true intentions

▸**se dévoiler VPR 1** *(ôter son voile)* to unveil one's face *or* oneself

2 *(se manifester)* to be disclosed *or* revealed, to show up, to come to light; **son hypocrisie se dévoile peu à peu** his/her hypocrisy is gradually coming to light

devoir[1] [dəvwar] **NM 1** *Scol (en classe → exercice)* exercise; *(épreuve)* test; *(à la maison)* homework; *(dissertation)* essay, paper; **j'ai un d. de maths à rendre pour lundi** I've got maths homework *or* a maths exercise to hand in by Monday; **faire ses devoirs** to do one's homework; **d. sur table** (written) class test; **devoirs de vacances** *Br* holiday *or Am* vacation homework

2 *(impératifs moraux)* duty; **le d. m'appelle** duty calls; **je ne l'ai prévenu que par d.** I warned him only because I thought it was my duty

3 *(tâche à accomplir)* duty, obligation; **les devoirs d'une mère** a mother's duties; **faire** *ou* **accomplir** *ou* **remplir son d.** to carry out *or* to do one's duty; **merci – je n'ai fait que mon d.** thank you – I only did my duty; **avoir le d. de** to have the duty to; **vous avez le d. de le signaler** it's your duty to *or* you must report it; **se faire un d. de faire qch** to make it one's duty to do sth; **se mettre en d. de faire qch** to set about (doing) sth; **je me suis mis en d. de l'éclairer** I set about enlightening him/her; **d. conjugal** conjugal duties; *Pol* **d. d'ingérence** duty to intervene; **d. de mémoire** duty to remember *(historical tragedies etc)*; **avoir un d. de réserve** to be bound by professional secrecy

❑ **devoirs NMPL rendre les derniers devoirs à qn** to pay sb a final homage *or* tribute; **rendre ses devoirs à qn** to pay one's respects to sb

❑ **de devoir ADJ homme/femme de d.** man/woman with a (strong) sense of duty

❑ **du devoir de PRÉP il est du d. de tout citoyen de voter** it is the duty of every citizen to vote; **j'ai cru de mon d. de l'aider** I felt duty-bound to help him/her; **je l'ai rendu, comme il était de mon d.** I gave it back, as it was my duty to do *or* as was my duty

❑ **en devoir ADJ** *Can Joual* on duty■

DEVOIR[2] [53] [dəvwar]

> **V AUX** to have to **1, 5** ■ must **1, 4** ■ ought **2** ■ should **2, 3** ■ to be supposed to **3**
> **VT** to owe
> **VPR** must **1, 2** ■ to have it as one's duty to **3**

V AUX 1 *(exprime l'obligation)* **il doit** he has to, he needs to, he must; **je dois partir à midi** I must leave at midday; **dois-je être plus clair?** do I need *or* have to be more explicit?; **je dois admettre que...** I must admit that...; **si vous deviez donner une définition du bonheur, quelle serait-elle?** if you had to give a definition of happiness, what would it be?; **il ne doit pas** he must not, he mustn't; **on ne doit pas fumer** smoking is forbidden *or* is not allowed; **tu ne dois pas le punir** you mustn't punish him

2 *(dans des conseils, des suggestions)* **il devrait** he ought to, he should; **tu ne devrais pas boire** you shouldn't drink

3 *(indique une prévision, une intention)* **il doit m'en donner demain** he's due to *or* he should give me some tomorrow; **c'est une pièce que l'on doit voir depuis un an!** it's a play we've supposedly been going to see *or* we've been planning to see for a year!; **il devait venir mais je ne l'ai pas vu** he was supposed to come *or* to have come but I didn't see him

4 *(exprime une probabilité)* **il/cela doit** he/it must, he's/it's got to; **il doit savoir** he's bound to *or* he must know; **mais si, tu dois connaître son frère, un petit gros** but you must know *or* I'm sure you know his/her brother, a short fat man; **il doit être fatigué** he must be tired, he's probably tired; **tu dois t'ennuyer tout seul!** you must get bored on your own!, don't you get bored on your own?; **si, les confitures doivent être sur l'étagère** yes, the pots of jam must be *or* have got to be on the shelf; **il n'y a qu'une explication, elle a dû garder les clefs** there's only one explanation, she must have kept the keys; **il ne devait pas beaucoup l'aimer pour écrire cela** he can't have really loved him/her to write this; **il doit y avoir** *ou* **cela doit faire un an que je ne l'ai pas vu** it must be a year since I (last) saw him; **une offre qui devrait les intéresser** an offer which should interest them

5 *(exprime l'inévitable)* **nous devons tous mourir un jour** we all have to die one day; **il devait mourir à 20 ans** he was to die aged 20; **la maison où elle devait écrire 'Claudine'** the house where she was to write 'Claudine'

6 *(exprime une norme)* **un bon chanteur doit savoir chanter en direct** a good singer should be able to sing live; **le four ne devrait pas faire ce bruit** the oven isn't supposed to *or* shouldn't make that noise

7 dût-il refuser even if he should have to refuse; **je l'aiderai, dussé-je aller en prison/y passer ma vie** I'll help him/her, even if it means going to prison/devoting my life to it

VT 1 *(avoir comme dette)* to owe; **d. qch à qn** to owe sb sth, to owe sth to sb; **tu me dois 60 euros** you owe me 60 euros; **d. de l'argent** to owe money, to have debts; **je te dois l'essence** I owe you for the *Br* petrol *or Am* gas; **j'ai perdu, je te dois le repas** I lost, I'll buy the meal for you; **combien vous dois-je?** how much do I owe you?; **je ne demande que ce qui m'est dû** I'm only asking for my due; **ainsi, je ne te dois plus rien** that way, I've cleared my debt with you *or* I don't owe you anything now

2 *(être moralement obligé de fournir)* **d. qch à qn** to owe sb sth; **je te dois des excuses/une explication** I owe you an apology/explanation; **je vous dois cet aveu** I've got this to confess to you, I owe you this confession; **je te dois bien ça** that's the least I can do for you; **traiter qn avec le respect qu'on lui doit** to treat sb with due respect; **selon les honneurs dus à sa fonction** with such pomp as befits his/her office

3 *(être redevable de)* **d. qch à qn** to owe sth to sb; **je lui dois tout/beaucoup** I owe him/her everything/a lot; **je vous dois la vie** I owe you my life; **c'est à Guimard que l'on doit cette découverte** we have Guimard to thank *or* we're indebted to Guimard for this discovery; **on lui doit un remarquable 'Christ en croix'** he's/she's the creator of a remarkable 'Christ on the Cross'; **c'est à lui que je dois d'avoir trouvé du travail** it's thanks to him that I found a job; **le son doit sa qualité à des enceintes très performantes** the good sound quality is due to excellent speakers; **sa victoire ne doit rien au hasard** his/her victory has nothing to do with luck

▸**se devoir VPR 1** *(avoir comme obligation mutuelle)* **les époux se doivent fidélité** spouses *or* husbands and wives must be faithful to each other

2 se d. à qn/qch to have to devote oneself to sb/sth; **il se doit aux siens** he must spend time with his family; **tu te dois à ta musique** you must dedicate yourself to your music; **je me dois à mon public** I must attend to my fans

3 se d. de to have it as one's duty to; **tu es grand, tu te dois de donner l'exemple** you're a big boy now, it's your duty to set a good example

---

dévoisé, -e [devwaze] **ADJ** *Ling* devoiced

dévoisement [devwazmɑ̃] **NM** *Ling* devoicing *(UNCOUNT)*

dévoltage [devɔltaʒ] **NM** *Élec* reduction of voltage

dévolter [3] [devɔlte] **VT** *Élec (courant)* to reduce the voltage of

dévolteur [devɔltœr] **NM** *Élec* booster, negative booster

dévolu, -e [devɔly] **ADJ** *(somme, responsabilités)* assigned (**à** to); **argent d. à cet usage** money assigned to that purpose; **voilà la tâche qui vous a été dévolue** that is the task which has been assigned to you; **part dévolue à la ligne paternelle** share that falls to the heirs on the father's side; **c'est le terrain qui lui a été d.** the land went to him/her

NM jeter son d. sur *(chose)* to go for, to choose; *(personne)* to set one's cap at

dévoluer [7] [devɔlɥe] **VT** to devolve

dévolutif, -ive [devɔlytif, -iv] **ADJ** devolutive

dévolution [devɔlysjɔ̃] **NF** devolution

dévolutive [devɔlytiv] *voir* **dévolutif**

devon [dəvɔ̃] **NM** *Pêche* minnow

dévonien, -enne [devɔnjɛ̃, -ɛn] *Géol* **ADJ** Devonian

NM le d. the Devonian

dévorant, -e [devɔrɑ̃, -ɑ̃t] **ADJ 1** *(faim)* gnawing; *(soif)* burning; **avoir une faim dévorante** to be ravenous; **avoir une soif dévorante** to be dying of thirst **2** *(amour, passion)* consuming, all-consuming, burning, powerful; **éprouver une jalousie dévorante** to be consumed *or* devoured by jealousy **3** *Littéraire (feu)* all-consuming

dévorateur, -trice [devɔratœr, -tris] **ADJ** devouring

NM,F devourer

dévorer [3] [devɔre] **VT 1** *(manger → sujet: animal, personne)* to devour; **d. son repas à belles dents** to eat heartily; **les sauterelles dévorent les récoltes** the locusts eat away at the crops; *Fig* **dévoré par les moustiques** eaten alive *or* bitten to death by mosquitoes; **une voiture qui dévore les kilomètres** a car which eats up the miles; **d. qn/qch des yeux** *ou* **du regard** to stare hungrily *or* to gaze greedily at sb/sth; **d. qn de baisers** to smother sb with kisses

2 *(lire)* to devour, to read avidly; **j'ai dévoré tout Tolstoï** I read my way avidly through *or* devoured (the whole of) Tolstoy; **depuis le scandale, il dévore les journaux** since the scandal he reads the papers avidly

3 *(consommer)* to use (up); **dans mon métier, je dévore du papier/de la pellicule** in my job I use (up) huge quantities of paper/of film; **mon salaire est en grande partie dévoré par les impôts** my salary is swallowed up to a large extent by tax; **ne te laisse pas d. par ton travail** don't let your work monopolize your time

4 *(consumer → sujet: flammes)* to devour

5 *(tenailler)* to devour; **l'ambition le dévore** he's eaten *or* devoured by ambition; **être dévoré par l'envie/la curiosité** to be eaten up with envy/curiosity; **être dévoré de remords** to be eaten up with remorse; **elle n'est pas dévorée**

par les **scrupules** she isn't hampered by scruples

   USAGE ABSOLU *(manger)* **il dévore!** he eats like a horse!

dévoreur, -euse [devɔrœr, -øz] NM,F *Fam* **c'est une dévoreuse de romans/de pellicule** she's an avid reader of novels/photographer■

dévot, -e [devo, -ɔt] ADJ devout

   NM,F **1** *(qui croit)* staunch believer **2** *Péj (bigot)* sanctimonious individual; **faux d.** pharisee

dévotement [devɔtmɑ̃] ADV devoutly, religiously

dévotion [devosjɔ̃] NF **1** *Rel* devoutness, religiousness, piety; *Péj* **fausse d.** false piety; **d. à la Sainte Vierge** devotion to the Blessed Virgin; **avec d.** devoutly **2** *Littéraire (attachement)* devotion; **il voue une véritable d. à sa mère** he worships his mother; **être à la d. de qn** to be devoted to sb; **avec d.** devotedly

   ❏ **dévotions** NFPL *(prières)* devotions; **faire ses dévotions** to perform one's devotions

dévoué, -e [devwe] ADJ **1** *(fidèle)* devoted, faithful; **être d. à ses amis** to be devoted to one's friends; **nous vous remercions de votre appui d.** we thank you for your staunch support **2** *(dans des formules de politesse)* **votre (tout) d.** *Br* yours sincerely, *Am* sincerely (yours); **votre d. serviteur** your humble servant; **je vous prie de croire à mes sentiments les plus dévoués** *Br* yours sincerely, *Am* sincerely (yours)

dévouement [devumɑ̃] NM **1** *(abnégation)* dedication, devotedness, devotion; **soigner qn avec d.** to look after sb devotedly; **avoir l'esprit de d.** to be self-sacrificing **2** *(loyauté)* devotion; **son d. à la cause** his/her devotion to the cause

dévouer [6] [devwe] VT *Littéraire* **d. qch à** to dedicate *or* to devote sth to; **d. sa vie à ses parents/à l'aide aux pays du tiers-monde** to dedicate one's life to one's parents/to assisting Third World countries

   ►**se dévouer** VPR **1** *(proposer ses services)* to volunteer; **qui va se d. pour faire le ménage?** who's going to volunteer to clean up?; **allez, dévoue-toi pour une fois!** come on, make a sacrifice for once!; *Hum* **vous voulez que je finisse la tarte? bon, je me dévoue!** you want me to finish up the tart? oh well, if I must! **2 se d. à** *(se consacrer à)* to dedicate oneself to

dévoyé, -e [devwaje] ADJ perverted, corrupted

   NM,F corrupt individual

dévoyer [13] [devwaje] VT *Littéraire* to lead astray

   ►**se dévoyer** VPR to go astray

dewar [diwar] NM dewar

dexamphétamine [dɛksamfetamin] NF *Pharm* dexamphetamine

Dexédrine® [dɛksedrin] NF *Pharm* Dexedrine®

dextérité [dɛksterite] NF dexterity, deftness; **avec d.** dexterously, deftly

dextralité [dɛkstralite] NF dextrality

dextran [dɛkstran] NF *Chim & Méd* Dexedrine®

dextre [dɛkstr] ADJ *Hér* dexter

   NF *Vieilli, Hum & Littéraire* right hand; **veux-tu t'asseoir à ma d.?** will you sit on my right?

dextrine [dɛkstrin] NF *Chim & Ind* dextrin

dextrocardie [dɛkstrɔkardi] NF *Anat & Méd* dextrocardia

dextrochère [dɛkstrɔkɛr] NM *Hér* **d. armé** right arm in armour

dextrogyre [dɛkstrɔʒir] ADJ *Chim* dextrogyre, dextrorotatory; **composé d.** dextro-compound

dextrorse [dɛkstrɔrs], **dextrorsum** [dɛkstrɔrsɔm] ADJ INV dextrorse

   ADV clockwise

dextrose [dɛkstroz] NM dextrose

dey [dɛ] NM *Hist (à Alger)* ruler, dey; *(à Tripoli, à Tunis)* governor, dey

dézinguer [3] [dezɛ̃ge] VT *Fam* **1** *(démolir)* to pull down■ **2** *(critiquer)* to pull to pieces, to slam **3** *(tuer)* to bump off

dézipper [3] [dezipe] VT *Ordinat (fichier)* to unzip

dézoner [3] [dezone] VT **1** *Ordinat (DVD)* to remove the region lock from **2** *Can (terrain)* to change the zoning of

dfc *(abrév écrite désire faire connaissance)* WLTM

DG [deʒe] NM *(abrév* **directeur général**) *Br* GM, *Am* CEO

   NF *(abrév* **direction générale**) general management, senior management

dg *(abrév écrite décigramme)* dg

DGA [deʒea] NF *(abrév* **Délégation générale pour**

---

l'armement) = section of the French armed forces responsible for building and testing armaments

   NM *(abrév* **directeur général adjoint**) *Br* deputy managing director, *Am* vice-president

DGE [deʒeə] NF *(abrév* **dotation globale d'équipement**) = state contribution to local government capital budget

DGF [deʒeɛf] NF *(abrév* **dotation globale de fonctionnement**) = state contribution to local government revenue budget

DGI [deʒei] NF *(abrév* **Direction générale des impôts**) = central tax office

DGSE [deʒeɛse] NF *(abrév* **Direction générale de la sécurité extérieure**) = arm of the Defence Ministry in charge of international intelligence, *Br* ≃ MI6, *Am* ≃ CIA

DH *(abrév écrite* **dirham**) DH

dharma [darma] NM *Rel* dharma

DHDO [deaʃdeo] NF *(abrév* **Dynamique Humaine et Développement de l'Organisation**) = postgraduate diploma in management

DHEA [deaʃəa] NF *(abrév* **déhydroépiandrostérone**) DHEA

dhole [dɔl] NM *Zool* dhole

DI [dei] NF *Mil (abrév* **division d'infanterie**) infantry division

dia¹ [dia] NF *Belg (diapositive)* slide

dia² [dja] EXCLAM = signal to a horse to turn left

diabète [djabɛt] NM diabetes; **avoir du d.** to have diabetes; **d. sucré** diabetes mellitus

diabétique [djabetik] ADJ diabetic

   NMF diabetic; **chocolat/confiture pour diabétiques** diabetic chocolate/jam

diabétologie [djabetɔlɔʒi] NF diabetes research; **un spécialiste en d.** a diabetes specialist

diabétologue [djabetɔlɔg] NMF diabetes specialist

diable [djabl] NM **1** *Rel* devil; **le d.** the Devil; **les Diables** = nickname of Belgian national football team; **aller au d.** to go to hell; **envoyer qn au d.** to send sb packing; **envoie-les au d.** tell them they can go to hell; **au d. l'avarice!** hang the expense!; **nous partons en vacances, au d. les soucis!** we're off on holiday, let's leave our worries behind us *or* at home!; **au d. les convenances!** to hell with propriety!; *Fam* **avoir le d. au corps** to be a real handful; **comme un beau d.** *(courir, sauter)* like the (very) devil, like a thing possessed; *(hurler)* like a stuck pig; **se démener** *ou* **s'agiter comme un beau d.** to thrash about, to struggle violently; **comme un d. dans un bénitier** like a cat on a hot tin roof; **comme s'il avait le d. à ses trousses** *(courir, partir)* like greased lightning, as if his life depended on it; **faire le d. à quatre** *(faire du bruit)* to make a din; *(se démener)* to raise hell and high water; **habiter au d. vauvert** *ou* **vert** to live miles away; **tirer le d. par la queue** to live from hand to mouth; **c'est le d. pour lui faire entendre raison** it's damned hard to make *or* it's the devil of a job making him/her see reason; **ce serait bien le d. s'il refusait!** I'd be very surprised if he refused!; **ce n'est pourtant pas le d.!** it's really not that difficult!; **c'est bien le d. si je ne récupère pas mon argent!** I'll be damned if I don't get my money back!; *Can* **le d. est aux vaches** there's internal strife; *Arch* **le d. soit de ces gens-là/tes principes** the devil take these people/your principles; **le d. m'emporte si j'y comprends quelque chose!** I'll be hanged *or* damned if I understand (it)!; *Arch* **ils sont venus me réclamer de l'argent, le d. les emporte!** they came to ask me for money, damn them!; *Prov* **c'est le d. qui bat sa femme et marie sa fille** = it's rainy and sunny at the same time **2** *(enfant)* (little) devil

   3 *(homme)* **un bon d.** a good sort; **un grand d.** a great tall fellow; **un mauvais d.** a bad sort; **un pauvre d.** a wretched man, a poor wretch; **un petit d.** *(enfant)* a little devil

   4 *(chariot)* trolley

   5 *(jouet)* jack-in-the-box

   6 *(casserole)* earthenware (cooking) pot

   7 *Zool* **d. (de Tasmanie)** Tasmanian devil; *Ich* **d. de mer** devil fish, manta (ray)

   ADJ **1** *(espiègle)* **que tu es d.!** stop being such a little devil!

   2 *Culin (sauce)* devilled

   ADV **qui/que/comment d.?** who/what/how the devil?, who/what/how on earth?; **pourquoi d. est-il allé si loin?** why the devil *or* on earth did he go so far?

   EXCLAM my goodness!, goodness me!; **d., voilà une histoire bien compliquée!** goodness me, what a complicated story!; **que d.!** for heaven's *or* goodness' sake!

   ❏ **à la diable** ADV **1** *(vite et mal)* **un repas préparé à la d.** a meal thrown together quickly; **elle est sortie coiffée à la d.** she went out, after hastily running a comb through her hair

   2 *Culin* **œufs à la d.** devilled eggs

   ❏ **diable de** ADJ **ce d. de rhumatisme!** this damned rheumatism!; **son d. de frère** his/her damned brother

   ❏ **du diable, de tous les diables** ADJ *Fam* **faire un boucan du d.** *ou* **de tous les diables** to kick up a hell of a racket; **il a eu un mal du d.** *ou* **de tous les diables pour finir à temps** he had a devil of a job to finish in time; **il fait un froid/une chaleur du d.** *ou* **de tous les diables** it's dreadfully cold/hot

   ❏ **en diable** ADV devilishly; **difficile en d.** devilishy *or* fiendishly difficult; **jolie en d.** pretty as a picture; **retors en d.** sly as a fox ADJ *Can Fam* **être en d.** to be fed up, *Br* to be cheesed off

'Le Diable au corps' *Radiguet, Autant-Lara* 'Devil in the Flesh'

diablement [djabləmɑ̃] ADV *Fam Vieilli* damned; **c'est d. bon!** it's damn *or* damned good!; **cette pièce est d. longue!** this play's interminable!; **il était d. intéressé** he was awfully keen

diablerie [djabləri] NF **1** *(farce)* piece of mischief, trick; **avec leurs petits cousins, ce ne sont que diableries** they get up to all sorts of mischief with their little cousins **2** *(sortilège)* piece of devilry **3** *Beaux-Arts & Théât* = scene featuring devils

diablesse [djablɛs] NF **1** *Rel* she-devil **2** *(femme méchante)* witch **3** *(fillette)* **petite d.!** you little devil!

diablotin [djablɔtɛ̃] NM **1** *Myth* small *or* little devil **2** *(enfant)* imp **3** *(pétard)* cracker

diabolique [djabɔlik] ADJ diabolic, diabolical, devilish; **il a agi de façon d.** he acted diabolically

'Les Diaboliques' *Clouzot* 'Diabolique' *or* 'The Fiends'

diaboliquement [djabɔlikmɑ̃] ADV diabolically, devilishly

diabolisation [djabɔlizasjɔ̃] NF demonization

diaboliser [3] [djabɔlize] VT to demonize

diabolo [djabɔlo] NM **1** *(jouet)* diabolo **2** *(boisson)* **d. menthe/fraise** mint/strawberry syrup and lemonade

'Diabolo menthe' *Kurys* 'Peppermint Soda'

diacétylmorphine [diasetilmɔrfin] NF *Chim* diacetylmorphine

diachromie [djakrɔmi] NF *Phot* screen-plate colour-photography

diachronie [djakrɔni] NF diachrony

diachronique [djakrɔnik] ADJ diachronic

diachylon [djaʃilɔ̃], **diachylum** [djaʃilɔm] NM *Pharm* diachylon, diachylum; **emplâtre d.** lead plaster, diachylon plaster

diacide [diasid] NM *Chim* diacid

diaclase [djaklaz] NF *Géol* diaclase, joint

diaconal, -e, -aux, -ales [djakɔnal, -o] ADJ diaconal

diaconat [djakɔna] NM diaconate

diaconesse [djakɔnɛs] NF deaconess

diacre [djakr] NM deacon

diacritique [djakritik] ADJ diacritic; **signe d.** diacritic

   NM diacritic

diadème [djadɛm] NM *(insigne de la royauté)* diadem; *(parure de femme)* tiara

diadoque [djadɔk] NM **1** *Hist* **les diadoques** the Diadochi *(of Alexander the Great)* **2** *(en Grèce)* Crown prince

Diafoirus [djafwarys] **NPR** = the name of two pedantic and ignorant doctors (father and son) in Molière's 'le Malade imaginaire'

diagenèse [djaʒɛnɛz] **NF** diagenesis

diagnose [djagnoz] **NF 1** *Méd* art of diagnosis **2** *Biol* diagnosis, assignment of species

diagnostic [djagnostik] **NM** diagnosis; **établir un d.** to make a diagnosis; **ce médecin a un d. très sûr** this doctor makes very reliable diagnoses; *Ordinat* **d. d'autotest** self-test diagnosis; **d. financier** financial healthcheck, diagnostic audit; *Obst* **d. prénatal** antenatal diagnosis

diagnostique [djagnostik] **ADJ** diagnostic

diagnostiquer [3] [djagnostike] **VT** to diagnose; **on lui a diagnostiqué un diabète** he's/she's been diagnosed as suffering from diabetes

diagonal, -e, -aux, -ales [djagonal, -o] **ADJ** diagonal

▫ **diagonale NF** diagonal (line)

▫ **en diagonale ADV 1** *(en biais)* diagonally **2** *(vite)* **lire** *ou* **parcourir un livre en diagonale** to skim through a book

diagonalement [djagonalmã] **ADV** diagonally

diagramme [djagram] **NM** diagram; *(graphique)* graph, chart; **d. à bâtons** *ou* **à barres** bar chart; **d. de circulation** flow chart; **d. polaire** polar diagram; **d. à secteurs** pie chart

diagraphie [djagrafi] **NF** *Pétr* logging

dialcool [dialkol] **NM** dihydric alcohol

dialectal, -e, -aux, -ales [djalɛktal, -o] **ADJ** dialectal

dialectalisme [djalɛktalizm] **NM** dialectal variation

dialecte [djalɛkt] **NM 1** *(gén)* dialect **2** *Suisse* Swiss German

dialecticien, -enne [djalɛktisjɛ̃, -ɛn] **NM,F** dialectician

dialectique [djalɛktik] **ADJ** dialectic, dialectical **NF** dialectic, dialectics *(singulier)*

dialectiquement [djalɛktikmã] **ADV** dialectically

dialectiser [3] [djalɛktize] **VT** to dialectalize

dialectologie [djalɛktɔlɔʒi] **NF** dialectology

dialectologue [djalɛktɔlɔg] **NMF** dialectologist

dialectophone [djalɛktɔfɔn] **ADJ** who speaks a dialect

NM = person who speaks a dialect

dialogique [djalɔʒik] **ADJ** dialogic, dialogical

dialogue [djalɔg] **NM 1** *(discussion)* dialogue, **le d. Est-Ouest** dialogue between East and West; **d. Nord-Sud** dialogue or talks between North and South; **entre eux, c'était un véritable d. de sourds** they were not on the same wavelength at all

2 *Cin & Théât* dialogue; **écrire les dialogues d'un film** to write the dialogue for a movie or Br film; **le d. est de Flore Thiais** dialogue by Flore Thiais; *Phil* **les dialogues de Platon** Plato's dialogues

3 *Ordinat* **d. homme-machine** interactive use (of a computer); **d. en direct** Internet Relay Chat, IRC; **d. d'établissement de liaison** handshaking

dialoguer [3] [djalɔge] **VI 1** *(converser)* to converse **2** *(négocier)* to have or to hold talks; **les syndicats vont de nouveau d. avec le ministre** the unions are to resume talks or their dialogue with the minister **3** *Ordinat* **d. avec un ordinateur** to interact with a computer

VT *Littérature (roman)* to write in dialogue form

dialoguiste [djalɔgist] **NMF** dialogue writer

dialypétale [dialipetal] *Bot* **ADJ** dialypetalous

▫ **dialypétales NFPL** Dialypetalae

dialyse [djaliz] **NF** dialysis; **se faire faire une d.** to undergo dialysis; **être sous d.** to be on dialysis

dialysé, -e [djalize] **NM,F** dialysis patient

dialysépale [djalizepal] **ADJ** *Bot* dialysepalous

dialyser [3] [djalize] **VT** to dialyse

dialyseur [djalizœr] **NM** dialyser

diam [djam] **NM** *Fam (diamant)* sparkler, rock; **diams** ice, sparklers

diamagnétique [djamaɲetik] **ADJ** diamagnetic

diamagnétisme [djamaɲetism] **NM** diamagnetism

diamant [djamã] **NM 1** *(gén)* diamond; **d. brut** rough diamond; **d. de vitrier** glass cutter, *Spéc* glazier's diamond, diamond point; *Pol* **diamants de la guerre** conflict diamonds **2** *Orn* **d. modeste** plum-capped finch

diamantaire [djamãtɛr] **ADJ** *(pierre)* diamond-like, sparkling

NMF 1 *(vendeur)* diamond merchant **2** *(tailleur)* diamond cutter

diamanté, -e [djamãte, -in] **ADJ 1** *(bijou)* set with diamonds **2 fleurs diamantées** frosted artificial flowers

diamanter [3] [djamãte] **VT d. qch** *(sertir)* to set sth with diamonds; *(faire briller)* to make sth shine like a diamond

diamantifère [djamãtifɛr] **ADJ** diamantiferous

diamantin, -e [djamãtɛ̃, -in] **ADJ** diamond-like, diamantine

diamétral, -e, -aux, -ales [djametral, -o] **ADJ** diametral, diametric, diametrical

diamétralement [diametralmã] **ADV** diametrically; **d. opposé** diametrically opposed

diamètre [djamɛtr] **NM** diameter; **le fût fait 30 cm de d.** the barrel is 30 cm across or in diameter; **couper le cercle dans son d.** cut the circle across; *Aut* **d. de braquage hors tout** overall turning circle

diamide [diamid] **NM** *Chim* diamide

diamine [diamin] **NF** *Chim* diamine

diamorphine [djamɔrfin] **NF** *Chim* diamorphine

Diane [djan] **NPR** *Myth* Diana

'**Diane chasseresse**' *Houdon* 'Diana the Huntress'

diane [djan] **NF** *Arch ou Littéraire* reveille; **battre** *ou* **sonner la d.** to sound reveille

diantre [djãtr] *Arch ou Littéraire* **EXCLAM** ye gods! **ADV qui d. a dit cela?** who the deuce or the devil said that?; **que d....!** what the devil...?; **décidez-vous, que d.!** make up your mind, for heaven's sake!

diantrement [djãtrəmã] **ADV** *Arch ou Littéraire* devilishly

diapason [djapazɔ̃] **NM 1** *(instrument → métallique)* tuning fork; *(→ à vent)* pitch pipe **2** *(ton)* pitch, diapason **3** *(registre)* range, diapason ▫ **au diapason ADV** in tune; *Fig* **il n'est plus au d.** he's out of touch; **se mettre au d. (de qn)** to fall or to step into line (with sb)

diapause [djapoz] **NF** *Entom* state of suspended animation, *Spéc* diapause

diapédèse [djapedɛz] **NF** diapedesis

diaphane [djafan] **ADJ** diaphanous

diaphanoscopie [djafanɔskɔpi] **NF** *Méd* diaphanoscopy

diaphonie [djafɔni] **NF** diaphony

diaphorèse [djafɔrɛz] **NF** *Méd* perspiration, *Spéc* diaphoresis

diaphorétique [djafɔretik] *Méd* **ADJ** inducing perspiration, *Spéc* diaphoretic

NF drug to induce perspiration, *Spéc* diaphoretic

diaphragmatique [djafragmatik] **ADJ** *(artère, veine)* diaphragmatic

diaphragme [djafragm] **NM 1** *Anat & Tech* diaphragm **2** *(contraceptif)* (Dutch) cap, *Spéc* diaphragm **3** *(d'un télescope)* diaphragm; *(d'un objectif photographique)* stop, diaphragm; **d. iris** iris diaphragm **4** *(d'une enceinte)* soundbox

diaphragmer [3] [djafragme] *Phot* **VT** to stop down **VI** to stop down; **diaphragmez à 11** stop down to 11, use stop number 11

diaphyse [djafiz] **NF** diaphysis

diapir [djapir] **NM** *Géol* diapiric fold

diapo [djapo] **NF** *Fam Phot* slide ▪

diaporama [djapɔrama] **NM** slide show

diapositive [djapozitiv] **NF** *Phot* slide

diapré, -e [djapre] **ADJ** *Littéraire* shimmering, iridescent

diaprer [3] [djapre] **VT** *Littéraire* to make shimmer, to make iridescent

diaprure [djapryr] **NF** *Littéraire* shimmering or iridescent colours; **la d. de ses ailes** the rainbow colours of its wings

diariste [djarist] **NMF** *Littérature* diarist

diarrhée [djare] **NF** diarrhoea; **avoir la d.** to have diarrhoea; *Fig* **d. verbale** verbal diarrhoea

diarrhéique [djareik] **ADJ** diarrhoeal, diarrhoeic **NMF** person subject to diarrhoea

diarthrose [djartroz] **NF** diarthrosis

diascope [djaskɔp] **NM** diascope

diascopie [djaskɔpi] **NF** diascopy

diaspora [djaspora] **NF** diaspora; **la d. arménienne** the Armenian diaspora, Armenian communities throughout the world; **la D.** the Diaspora

diastase [djastaz] **NF** diastase

diastème [djastɛm] **NF** *Anat* diastema

diastole [djastɔl] **NF** *Physiol* diastole

diastolique [djastɔlik] **ADJ** *Physiol* diastolic

diathermane [djatɛrman] **ADJ** *Phys* diathermic, diathermanous

diathermie [djatɛrmi] **NF** *Méd* diathermy

diathèse [djatɛz] **NF** *Méd* diathesis, predisposition

diatomée [djatɔme] **NF** diatom

diatomique [djatɔmik] **ADJ** *Chim* diatomic

diatomite [djatɔmit] **NF** *Minér* diatomite, diatom earth

diatonique [djatɔnik] **ADJ** diatonic

diatoniquement [djatɔnikmã] **ADV** diatonically

diatonisme [djatɔnism] **NM** diatonicism

diatribe [djatrib] **NF** (vicious) attack, *Sout* diatribe

diaule [diol] **NF** *Antiq* **1** *Mus* diaulos, double flute **2** *Sport* diaulos, double course

diazépam [djazepam] **NM** *Pharm* diazepam

diazocopie [djazɔkɔpi] **NF** *Typ* diazocopy

diazoïque [djazɔik] *Chim* **ADJ** diazo, diazoic **NM** diazo compound

diazote [djazɔt] **NM** *Chim* nitrogen gas

dibasique [dibazik] **ADJ** *Chim* dibasic, bibasic

dicarbonylé, -e [dikarbɔnile] *Chim* **ADJ** dicarbonyl **NM** dicarbonyl compound

dicaryon [dikarjɔ̃] **NM** *Bot* dikaryon, dicaryon

dicaryotique [dikarjɔtik] **ADJ** *Bot* dikaryotic, dicaryotic

dicastère [dikastɛr] **NM** *Suisse* = administrative division in the Swiss local government system

dicentra [disɛtra] **NF** dicentra

dicétone [disetɔn] **NF** diketone

dichlorure [diklɔryr] **NM** dichloride, bichloride; **d. d'acétylène** ethylene dichloride

dichotome [dikɔtɔm] **ADJ 1** *Astron (astre)* dichotomized **2** *Bot* dichotomous, dichotomal

dichotomie [dikɔtɔmi] **NF** dichotomy

dichotomique [dikɔtɔmik] **ADJ** dichotomous; *Psy* **test d.** yes/no test, true/false test

dichroïque [dikrɔik] **ADJ** *Phys (crystal)* dichroic

dichroïsme [dikrɔism] **NM** *Phys* dichroism

dichromatique [dikrɔmatik] **ADJ** *Méd* dichromatic

dichromie [dikrɔmi] **NF** *Typ* two-colour printing or processing; *Beaux-Arts & Phot* duochrome

dicline [diklin] **ADJ** *Bot* diclinous

dico [diko] **NM** *Fam* dictionary ▪

dicotylédone [dikɔtiledɔn] *Bot* **ADJ** dicotyledonous

NF dicotyledon

▫ **dicotylédones NFPL** Dicotyledonae

dicrote [dikrɔt] **ADJ** *Méd* dicrotic

dictame [diktam] **NM 1** *Bot* dittany of Crete, Cretan dittany; **d. blanc** white dittany; **d. bâtard** bastard dittany **2** *Littéraire* solace, comfort, balm

Dictaphone® [diktafɔn] **NM** Dictaphone®

dictateur [diktatœr] **NM** dictator

'**Le Dictateur**' *Chaplin* 'The Great Dictator'

dictatorial, -e, -aux, -ales [diktatɔrjal, -o] **ADJ** dictatorial

dictatorialement [diktatɔrjalmã] **ADV** dictatorially

dictature [diktatyr] **NF** dictatorship; **d. militaire** military dictatorship; **la d. du prolétariat** the dictatorship of the proletariat; **la d. de la mode** the edicts of fashion; **il fait de la d. intellectuelle** he tells people what to think

dictée [dikte] **NF 1** *Scol* dictation; **d. musicale** musical dictation **2** *(à une secrétaire, un assistant)* dictating; **j'ai écrit le rapport sous sa d.** he/she dictated the report to me; **la d. de son courrier lui a pris plus d'une heure** it took him/her over an hour to dictate his/her letters; *Fig* **agir sous la d. de son cœur/de sa conscience** to follow the dictates of one's heart/one's conscience

dicter [3] [dikte] **VT 1** *Scol* to read out as dictation **2** *(courrier, lettre, résumé)* to dictate **3** *(imposer → choix)* to dictate, to impose, to force; *(→ conditions)* to dictate; **on lui a dicté ses réponses** his/her replies had been dictated to him/her **4** *(conditionner)* to dictate; **ses actes sont dictés par la haine** his/her actions are driven *or* motivated by hatred; **ces mesures ont été dictées par la conjoncture économique** these measures were dictated by the economic situation

diction [diksjɔ̃] **NF** diction; **avoir une d. parfaite** to have perfect diction; **professeur de d.** elocutionist
▫ **de diction ADJ** speech *(avant n)*

dictionnaire [diksjɔnɛr] **NM 1** *(livre)* dictionary; **d. analogique** thesaurus; **d. bilingue** bilingual dictionary; **d. anglais-français** English-French dictionary; **d. de la musique/des beaux-arts** dictionary of music/of art; **d. encyclopédique/ de langue** encyclopedic/language dictionary; **d. électronique** electronic dictionary; **d. de synonymes** thesaurus; *Fam* **traduire un livre à coup de d.** to translate a book with a dictionary in one hand; **c'est un d. ambulant** he's/she's a walking encyclopedia **2** *Ordinat* dictionary

dictionnairique [diksjɔnɛrik] **ADJ** dictionary *(avant n)*

dicton [diktɔ̃] **NM** *(popular)* saying, *Sout* dictum; **comme dit le d.** as they say, as the saying goes

dictyoptère [diktjɔptɛr] *Entom* **NM** member of the Dictyoptera genus
▫ **dictyoptères NMPL** Dictyoptera

didacthèque [didaktɛk] **NF** *Ordinat* set of educational software *or Am* teachware

didacticiel [didaktisjɛl] **NM** *Ordinat* tutorial, courseware, *Am* teachware

didactique [didaktik] **ADJ 1** *(de l'enseignement)* didactic **2** *(instructif)* didactic, educational **3** *(spécialisé → mot, langage)* technical **4** *Psy* **analyse d.** training analysis
NF didactics *(singulier)*

didactiquement [didaktikmɑ̃] **ADV** didactically

didactisme [didaktism] **NM** didacticism

didactyle [didaktil] **ADJ** didactyl, didactylous

didascalie [didaskali] **NF 1** *Antiq* didascaly, didascalia **2** *Théât* stage direction

didgeridoo, didjeridoo [didʒeridu] **NM** *Mus* didgeridoo

Didon [didɔ̃] **NPR** Dido

'**Didon et Énée**' *Purcell* 'Dido and Aeneas'

didot [dido] **NM** *Typ* modern (face)

diduction [didyksjɔ̃] **NF** *Physiol* diduction

didyme [didim] **ADJ** *Bot* didymous
NM *Minér* didymium

dièdre [djɛdr] **ADJ** dihedral
NM 1 *Géom* dihedron **2** *(en montagne)* corner, dièdre

dieffenbachia [difɛnbakja] **NM** diffenbachia

diégèse [djeʒɛz] **NF** diegesis

diégétique [djeʒetik] **ADJ** diegetic

diélectrique [djelɛktrik] **ADJ** dielectric
NM dielectric

Diên Biên Phu [djɛnbjɛnfu] **NM** Dien Bien Phu

diencéphale [diɑ̃sefal] **NM** diencephalon

diencéphalique [diɑ̃sefalik] **ADJ** diencephalic

diène [djɛn] **NM** diene

diérèse [djerɛz] **NF** *Ling & Littérature* diaeresis, dieresis

diergol [djɛrgɔl] **NM** diergol

dies academicus [djɛsakademikys] **NM INV** *Suisse* = annual public ceremony in universities marking the start of the new academic year and the conferment of honorary doctorates

dièse [djɛz] **ADJ** *Mus* **la d.** A sharp
NM *Mus* sharp; *Typ & Ordinat* hash; **double d.** double sharp

diesel [djezɛl] **NM 1** *(moteur)* **d.** diesel engine *or* motor **2** *(véhicule, camion)* **c'est un d.** it's a diesel **3** *(combustible)* diesel (oil)
NF *(voiture)* **c'est une d.** it's a diesel

diesel-électrique [djezɛlelɛktrik] *(pl* **diesels-électriques)** **ADJ** diesel-electric
NM diesel-electric

diésélisation [diezelizasjɔ̃] **NF** *Rail & Aut* dieselization

diéséliser [3] [diezelize] **VT** *Rail & Aut* to dieselize

diéséliste [djezelist] **NM** *Tech* diesel fitter

diéser [18] [djeze] **VT** *Mus* to sharpen, to make sharp

dies irae [djɛsire] **NM INV** *Rel* Dies Irae

diésis [djezis] **NM** *Typ* double dagger

Diester® [djɛstɛr] **NM** *(carburant)* diester

diète [djɛt] **NF 1** *(régime)* diet **2** *(absence de nourriture)* fasting *(for health reasons)* **3** *Hist (assemblée)* diet
▫ **à la diète ADV 1** *(au régime)* on a diet **2** *(sans nourriture)* **mettre qn à la d.** to prescribe a fast for sb

diététicien, -enne [djetetisjɛ̃, -ɛn] **NM,F** dietician, dietitian, nutritionist

diététique [djetetik] **ADJ** *(aliment)* health *(avant n)*; *(magasin)* health food *(avant n)*
NF nutrition science, *Spéc* dietetics *(singulier)*; **conseils de d.** nutritional advice

diéthylénique [dietilenik] **ADJ** diethylenic, diethylene *(avant n)*

diéthylique [dietilik] **ADJ** *Chim (éther)* diethyl *(avant n)*

dieu, -x [djø] **NM 1** *(divinité)* god; **le d. de la Guerre/l'Amour** the god of war/love; **une vie sans d.** a godless life; **il y a un d. pour les ivrognes!** there must be a god who looks after drunks!; **comme un d.** divinely, like a god; **jurer ses grands dieux** to swear to God; **il a juré ses grands dieux qu'il n'en savait rien** he swore to God *or* to heaven that he didn't know about it; *Littéraire* **grands dieux!** good heavens *or* gracious!; *Hum* **vingt dieux!** strewth! **2** *(héros)* god, idol; **les dieux du stade** the gods *or* idols of sport **3** *(objet de vénération)* god; **l'argent/l'art est son d.** money/art is his god, he idolizes money/art; **le d. dollar** the (great) god dollar, the almighty dollar
▫ **Dieu NM 1** *(gén)* God; **le D. vivant** the living God; **D. le père** God the father; *Péj* **il se prend pour D. le père** he thinks he's God (Himself); **vivre en D.** to live with God; **le bon D.** the good Lord; **c'est le bon D. qui t'a puni** you got your just deserts (for being bad); **recevoir le bon D.** to receive the Holy Sacrament; **apporter le bon D. à un malade** to bring the Holy Sacrament to a sick person; **tous les jours** *ou* **chaque jour que (le bon) D. fait** every blessed day; **il n'y a pas de bon D.!** there's no justice!; **on lui donnerait le bon D. sans confession** he/she looks as if butter wouldn't melt in his/her mouth; **comme le bon D. l'a fait** in his birthday suit; **il vaut mieux s'adresser à D. qu'à ses saints** it's better to talk to the organ-grinder than the monkey; *Vieilli* **comme D. en France** *(vivre)* exceedingly well, comfortably; **si D. le veut** God willing; **si D. me prête vie** if I'm still alive (by then) **2** *(dans des exclamations) Littéraire* **D. me damne** *ou* **maudisse (si…)!** may God strike me dead (if…)!; *Littéraire* **D. m'est témoin** as God is my witness; *Littéraire* **D. me pardonne!** (may) God forgive me!; **D. nous protège** God *or* Lord protect us; *Littéraire* **D. veuille que tout se passe bien!** God willing, all will be well!; *Littéraire* **D. vous bénisse/entende!** may God bless/hear you!; *Littéraire* **D. vous garde** God be with you; *Fam* **c'est pas** *ou* **c'est-y D. possible!** it just can't be (true)!; **D. sait God** *or* (the) Lord knows; **D. sait combien il l'a aimée!** God knows he loved her!; **D. sait si je l'ai aidé!** God knows I helped him!; **D. sait où je l'ai mis!** God only knows where I put it!; **et il est parti à l'étranger, D. sait où, chercher du travail** he's gone abroad, God knows where, to look for work; **D. seul le sait!** God (only) knows!; *Littéraire* **à D. va** *ou* **vat!** it's in God's hands!, in God's hands be it!; *Littéraire* **à D. ne plaise!** God forbid!; *Fam* **bon D.!** for God's sake!, for Pete's sake!; *Fam* **bon D. de…** blasted…, blessed…; *Fam* **ce bon D. de cabot a encore réveillé le gosse!** that blasted dog's woken up the kid again!; **bon D. de bon D.!** for crying out loud!; *Littéraire* **D. ait son âme!** God rest his soul!; *Littéraire* **D. le veuille!** God willing!; *Littéraire* **D. merci!** thank God *or* the Lord!; *Littéraire* **grand D.!** good God *or* Lord!; **mon D.!** my God!, my goodness!, good Lord!; **mon D.** *(dans des prières)* Lord, God; **mon D., aidez-moi!** help me, Lord!
▫ **des dieux ADJ** *(festin)* sumptuous, princely; *(plaisir)* divine, exquisite

'**Les Dieux ont soif**' *France* 'The Gods will have Blood'

'**Et Dieu créa la femme**' *Vadim* 'And God Created Woman'

'**Le Dieu des petits riens**' *Roy* 'The God of Small Things'

DIF [deiɛf] **NM** *(abrév* **droit individuel à la formation)** = law under which all salaried employees have the right to 20 hours' training per year

diffa [difa] **NF** *(en Algérie)* diffa

diffamant, -e [difamɑ̃, -ɑ̃t] **ADJ** *(texte)* defamatory, libellous; *(geste, parole)* slanderous; **des propos diffamants** slander

diffamateur, -trice [difamatœr, -tris] **ADJ** *(texte)* defamatory, libellous; *(geste, parole)* slanderous
NM,F *(par écrit)* libeller; *(en paroles)* slanderer

diffamation [difamasjɔ̃] **NF 1** *(accusation → gén)* defamation; *(→ par un texte)* libelling; *(→ par des discours)* slandering **2** *(texte)* libel; *(gestes, paroles)* slander
▫ **de diffamation ADJ** *(campagne)* smear *(avant n)*
▫ **en diffamation ADJ** **intenter un procès en d. à qn** *(pour un texte injurieux)* to bring an action for libel against sb; *(pour des paroles injurieuses)* to bring an action for slander against sb

diffamatoire [difamatwar] **ADJ** *(texte)* defamatory, libellous; *(geste, parole)* slanderous; **parler/agir de façon d.** to speak/to act slanderously

diffamatrice [difamatris] *voir* **diffamateur**

diffamé, -e [difame] **ADJ** *Hér (animal, lion)* defamed, tailless

diffamer [3] [difame] **VT** *(par écrit)* to defame, to libel; *(oralement)* to slander

différé, -e [difere] **ADJ 1** *(paiement, rendez-vous, réponse)* deferred, postponed **2** *Rad & TV* prerecorded **3** *Phot & Tech* **à action différée** delayed-action
▫ **en différé ADJ** *Rad & TV* prerecorded; *Ordinat (traitement)* off-line

différemment [diferamɑ̃] **ADV** differently; **il agit d. des autres** he's not behaving like the others, he's behaving differently from the others

différence [diferɑ̃s] **NF 1** *(distinction)* difference, dissimilarity; **il y a une d. entre A et B** there's a difference between A and B, A and B are different, A is different from B; **faire la d. entre** to make the distinction between, to distinguish between; **les électeurs indécis feront la d.** the don't-knows will tip the balance; **je ne fais aucune d. entre eux deux** I make no distinction between the two of them; **c'est ce qui fait toute la d.!** that's what makes all the difference!; **intéressé ou désintéressé? il y a une d.!** uninterested or disinterested? it's not the same thing at all *or* there's quite a difference between the two!; *Fam* **ça fait une sacrée d.!** there's a big difference!; **il s'est excusé – cela ne fait aucune d.** he apologized – it doesn't make any *or* it makes no difference; **faire des différences entre ses enfants** to treat one's children differently from each other; **toute la d. est là** it makes all the difference **2** *(écart)* difference; **d. d'âge** age difference *or* gap; **d. de caractère** difference in characters; **d. de taille** difference in size; **il y a une grande d. de température entre le jour et la nuit** there's a big difference between night-time and daytime temperatures; **il y a deux ans de d. entre eux** there are two years between them **3** *(particularité → culturelle, sexuelle)* **revendiquer sa d.** to be proud to be different **4** *Math (d'une soustraction)* result; *(ensemble)* difference; **je paierai la d.** I'll make up *or* pay the difference **5** *Phil* difference

6 *Bourse (entre le cours offert et le cours demandé)* spread
◻ **à la différence de** PRÉP unlike
◻ **à cette différence (près) que, à la différence que** CONJ except that; **j'ai accepté son offre à cette d. près que, cette fois, je sais ce qui m'attend** I accepted his/her offer but this time I know what to expect

différenciateur, -trice [diferɑ̃sjatœr, -tris] ADJ differentiating
NM *Psy* **d. sémantique** semantic differentiator

différenciation [diferɑ̃sjasjɔ̃] NF **1** *(distinction)* differentiation; *Mktg* **d. de ligne** line differentiation; **d. du produit** product differentiation **2** *Biol* **d. des sexes** sex determination

différenciatrice [diferɑ̃sjatris] *voir* **différenciateur**

différencié, -e [diferɑ̃sje] ADJ differentiated

différencier [9] [diferɑ̃sje] VT **1** *(distinguer)* to distinguish, to differentiate; **d. A et B** to differentiate between A and B; **rien ne les différencie** it's impossible to tell them apart; **ce qui nous différencie des animaux** that which sets us apart from animals
2 *Biol & Math* to differentiate
▸**se différencier** VPR **1** *(se distinguer)* to be different, to differ (**de** from); **ils se différencient (l'un de l'autre) par leur manière de parler** they're different from one another in the way they speak; **pour se d. de ses camarades, elle porte un blouson en cuir** to be different from her classmates, she wears a leather jacket
2 *Biol* to differentiate

différend [diferɑ̃] NM disagreement, dispute; *Jur* dispute; **avoir un d. avec qn (sur qch)** to be in dispute with sb (over sth), to have a difference of opinion with sb (over sth)

différent, -e [diferɑ̃, -ɑ̃t] ADJ **1** *(distinct)* different; **d. de** unlike, different *Br* from *or Am* than; **très différente de sa sœur** very unlike her sister; **ils sont très différents** they're very unlike each other *or* different; **il n'est pas désagréable, il est timide, c'est d.** he isn't unpleasant, he's shy, there's a difference
2 *(original)* different; **un week-end un peu d.** a weekend with a difference; **nous avons voulu faire un film d.** we wanted to make a different kind of *Br* film *or Am* movie
ADJ INDÉFINI *(devant un nom au pluriel)* different, various; **différentes personnes ont protesté** various people complained; **elle a écrit sous différents noms** she wrote under various names; **elle est venue à différentes reprises** she came on several different occasions; **les différents sujets que nous avons débattus** the various subjects we discussed

différentiable [diferɑ̃sjabl] ADJ *Math* differentiable

différentiateur [diferɑ̃sjatœr] NM differentiator

différentiation [diferɑ̃sjasjɔ̃] NF *Math* differentiation

différentiel, -elle [diferɑ̃sjɛl] ADJ differential
NM **1** *(pourcentage)* differential; **d. d'inflation** inflation differential; **d. de prix** price differential; **d. de taux (d'intérêt)** interest rate differential **2** *Aut* differential (gear)
◻ **différentielle** NF *Math* differential

différentier [9] [diferɑ̃sje] VT *Math* to differentiate

différer [18] [difere] VT *(repousser → rendez-vous, réponse, réunion)* to defer, to postpone; *(→ départ)* to postpone, to put off; **d. le paiement d'une dette** to put off *or* to delay paying a debt; *Littéraire* **d. de faire qch** to defer doing sth
VI **1** *(se différencier → personnes, choses)* to differ, to vary; **d. de** to differ from; **nous différons en tout** we differ on everything; **les coutumes diffèrent d'un endroit à un autre** customs vary from one place to another; **les traitements diffèrent du tout au tout** treatments vary quite drastically; **ils diffèrent par la taille** they differ in height, they are of different heights
2 *(s'opposer → dans un débat)* to differ, to be at variance; **ils diffèrent sur ce point** they differ on this point

difficile [difisil] ADJ **1** *(route, montée)* difficult, hard, tough; **la noire est la piste la plus d.** the toughest *or* most difficult ski run is the black one
2 *(tâche)* difficult, hard; **ce sera un livre d. à vendre** this book will be hard to sell; **rien n'est plus d. à faire** there's nothing more difficult to do; **ce n'est pourtant pas d.!** it's not that difficult!; **ce n'est pas d., je ne lui confierai plus rien!** it's quite simple, I won't confide in him/her again!; **il est d. de dire si...** it's hard to say whether...; **il s'en sortira? – d. à dire** will he manage? – it's hard to say
3 *(douloureux)* difficult, hard, tough; **il traverse une période d.** he's going through a bad *or* tough time; **il m'est d. de lui parler de son père** it's difficult *or* hard for me to talk to him/her about his/her father
4 *(personne → d'un tempérament pénible)* difficult, demanding; *(→ pointilleuse)* particular, awkward, fussy; **un enfant d.** a demanding child; **être d. (sur la nourriture)** to be fussy about one's food, to be a fussy eater; **elle est très d. sur le choix de ses amis** she's very particular about her friends; **il est si d. à satisfaire!** he's so hard to please!; **elle est d. à vivre** she is difficult to get on with
5 *(moralement)* difficult, tricky; *(financièrement)* difficult, tough; **la génétique pose des questions difficiles** genetics raises difficult *or* tricky questions; **connaître des années/moments difficiles** *(financièrement)* to go through years/a time of penury
6 *(impénétrable → œuvre, auteur)* difficult, abstruse
NMF *Br* fusspot, *Am* fussbudget; **ne fais pas le d.!** don't be so awkward *or* fussy!
NM **le d. dans cette affaire est de plaire à tous** the difficult part of this business is knowing how to please everyone; **le plus d. est fait** the hardest *or* most difficult part is over
ADV *Belg* **avoir d. à** *ou* **de faire qch** to have problems *or* difficulty doing sth

difficilement [difisilmɑ̃] ADV with difficulty; **il s'endort d.** he has a hard time getting to sleep; **je peux d. accepter** I can't possibly accept

difficulté [difikylte] NF **1** *(caractère ardu)* difficulty; **nous ne nous cachons pas la d. de l'entreprise** we're aware of the difficulty of the task; **exercices d'une d. croissante** increasingly difficult exercises; **aimer la d.** to enjoy a challenge; **chercher la d.** to look for problems
2 *(gêne)* difficulty; **avoir de la d. à faire qch** to find it difficult to do sth; **avoir de la d. à marcher** to have difficulty walking, to walk with difficulty
3 *(problème)* problem, difficulty; **il abandonne dès qu'il rencontre une d.** he gives up as soon as he comes up against a problem; **il a des difficultés en maths** he has problems with maths; **faire des difficultés** to create problems, to make a fuss; **il a fait toutes sortes de difficultés** he put up all sorts of arguments (against it); **je ne ferai pas de difficultés** I won't stand in the way; **avoir des difficultés à faire qch** to have problems *or* difficulty doing sth; **avoir des difficultés avec qn** to have difficulties *or* problems with sb; **avoir des difficultés financières** to be in financial difficulties *or* straits
4 *(point difficile)* difficulty; **les difficultés du français** the difficulties of the French language; **les difficultés de ce requiem** the difficult passages in this requiem; **cela ne présente aucune d.** that doesn't present any difficulty
5 *(impénétrabilité → d'une œuvre, d'un auteur)* difficult *or* abstruse nature
6 *Jur* **d. d'exécution** legal obstacle
◻ **en difficulté** ADJ *(nageur)* in difficulties; *(navire, avion)* in distress; *(entreprise, économie, secteur)* in difficulties *or* trouble; **un enfant en d.** *(scolairement)* a child with learning difficulties; *(psychologiquement)* a child with behavioural problems; **un couple en d.** *(sur le plan affectif)* a couple who are having problems; *(financièrement)* a couple with money problems; **mettre qn en d.** to put sb in a difficult *or* an awkward situation; **la crise a mis plusieurs banques en d.** the crisis put several banks in a difficult position
◻ **sans difficulté** ADV easily, with no difficulty

difficultueux, -euse [difikyltɥø, -øz] ADJ *Littéraire* difficult

diffluence [diflyɑ̃s] NF fork *(of a river)*

diffluent, -e [diflyɑ̃] ADJ diffluent

difforme [difɔrm] ADJ deformed, misshapen

difformité [difɔrmite] NF deformity

diffracter [3] [difrakte] VT to diffract

diffraction [difraksjɔ̃] NF diffraction

diffus, -e [dify, -yz] ADJ *(gén) & Bot* diffuse; *(souvenir)* vague; *(style)* loose; **il ressentait une douleur diffuse dans la poitrine** he felt a dull pain in his chest; **une sensation diffuse de bien-être** a general *or* overall feeling of well-being

diffusable [difyzabl] ADJ diffusible

diffusant, -e [difyzɑ̃] ADJ diffusing
NM diffuser

diffusément [difyzemɑ̃] ADV diffusely

diffuser [3] [difyze] VT **1** *(répandre → chaleur, lumière)* to spread, to diffuse, *Sout* to disseminate; **la lumière diffusée par une petite lampe de chevet** the (soft) light coming from a small bedside lamp
2 *Rad & TV* to broadcast; **émission diffusée en direct/différé** live/prerecorded broadcast; **de l'accordéon diffusé par haut-parleur** accordion music broadcast over a loudspeaker
3 *(propager → nouvelle, rumeur)* to spread
4 *(distribuer → tracts)* to hand out; *(→ produits)* to distribute; *(→ rapport)* to circulate; *(dans l'édition)* to distribute, to sell; **des affiches antitabac ont été diffusées dans les cabinets médicaux** anti-smoking posters have been distributed *or* circulated to doctors' *Br* surgeries *or Am* offices; **leurs produits sont diffusés sur une grande échelle** their products are widely available
▸**se diffuser** VPR *(information, racontars, chaleur, lumière)* to spread

diffuseur [difyzœr] NM **1** *Com* distributing agent, distributor; *Rad & TV* broadcaster; **d. hertzien** terrestrial broadcaster; **d. public** public broadcaster **2** *Élec, Tech & (en acoustique)* diffuser **3** *(de parfum)* diffuser **4** *(conduit)* diffuser

diffusible [difyzibl] ADJ diffusible

diffusion [difyzjɔ̃] NF **1** *(en acoustique)* diffusion, diffusivity
2 *Phys (d'une particule)* diffusion
3 *Opt* diffusion
4 *Méd* spreading
5 *Rad & TV* broadcasting; **d. audionumérique** digital audio broadcasting; **d. directe par satellite** direct satellite broadcasting, DSB; **d. hertzienne** terrestrial broadcasting; **d. numérique** digital broadcasting; **d. satellite** satellite broadcasting; **d. simultanée** simulcasting; **d. terrestre** terrestrial broadcasting
6 *(propagation → du savoir, d'une théorie)* spreading
7 *(distribution → de tracts)* distribution, distributing; *(→ de livres)* distribution, selling; **d. de masse** *(d'un journal)* mass circulation
8 *(exemplaires vendus)* number of copies sold, circulation
◻ **en deuxième diffusion, en seconde diffusion** ADJ *TV* repeated, repeat *(avant n)*

diffusionnisme [difyzjɔnism] NM diffusionism

diffusionniste [difyzjɔnist] ADJ diffusionist
NM diffusionist

digamma [digama] NM INV digamma

digastrique [digastrik] ADJ digastric

digérable [diʒerabl] ADJ digestible

digérer [18] [diʒere] VT **1** *Physiol* to digest; **je ne digère pas le lait** milk doesn't agree with me, I can't digest milk
2 *(assimiler → connaissances, lecture)* to digest, to assimilate; **des notions de psychologie mal digérées** half-understood ideas on psychology
3 *Fam (supporter)* to stomach, to take; **je n'ai pas digéré le coup qu'il m'a fait** I'm not about to forgive him for what he did to me; **je n'ai jamais pu d. le mensonge** I've never been able to stomach lies; **des vérités dures à d.** unpalatable truths
USAGE ABSOLU *Physiol* **je digère mal** my digestion isn't very good, I have poor digestion; **prendre qch pour d.** to take sth to help one's digestion; **bois une tisane, ça te fera d.** have some herbal tea, it'll help your food go down

digest [diʒɛst, daidʒɛst] NM digest

digeste [diʒɛst] ADJ **un aliment d.** an easily digested foodstuff; *Fig* **ce livre est vraiment peu d.** this book is indigestible

dig-dim

digesteur [diʒɛstœr] NM *Chim & Tech* digester

digestibilité [diʒɛstibilite] NF digestibility

digestible [diʒɛstibl] ADJ digestible

digestif, -ive [diʒɛstif, -iv] ADJ *(de la digestion)* digestive; *(substance, pastille)* which aids digestion
  NM after-dinner drink; *(liqueur)* liqueur *(taken after dinner)*; *(cognac, eau-de-vie etc)* brandy *(taken after dinner)*

digestion [diʒɛstjɔ̃] NF digestion; **avoir une d. lente** to digest one's food slowly; **ne te baigne pas pendant la d.** don't go swimming right after a meal

digestive [dizɛstiv] *voir* **digestif**

digicode® [diʒikɔd] NM door code *(for entrance to a building)*

digipuncture [diʒipɔ̃ktyr] NF acupressure

digit [diʒit] NM *(chiffre)* digit; *(caractère)* character

digital, -e[1], -aux, -ales [diʒital, -o] ADJ 1 *Anat* digital 2 *(numérique)* digital

digitale[2] [diʒital] NF *Bot* digitalis; **d. pourprée** foxglove

digitaline [diʒitalin] NF *Chim* digitalin

digitalique [diʒitalik] *Méd & Pharm* ADJ **traitement d.** treatment with digoxin, digoxin treatment; **glucosides digitaliques** digitalis glucosides
  NM digoxin

digitalisation [diʒitalizasjɔ̃] NF digitization

digitaliser [3] [diʒitalize] VT to digitalize, to digitize

digitaliseur [diʒitalizœr] NM digitizer

digité, -e [diʒite] ADJ digitate, digitated

digitiforme [diʒitifɔrm] ADJ finger-like, *Spéc* digitiform

digitigrade [diʒitigrad] ADJ digitigrade
  NM digitigrade

digitoplastie [diʒitɔplasti] NF finger graft

digitopuncture [diʒitɔpɔ̃ktyr] NF acupressure

digitoxine [diʒitɔksin] NF *Pharm* digitoxin

diglossie [diglɔsi] NF *Ling* diglossia

digne [diɲ] ADJ 1 *(noble)* dignified; **d'un air très d.** in a dignified manner; **rester d. dans la douleur** to carry one's grief with dignity
  2 **d. de** *(qui mérite)* worthy *or* deserving of; **un détail d. de votre attention** a detail worthy of your attention; **elle est d. du premier prix** she deserves first prize; **je ne suis pas d. de toi** I am not worthy of you, you're too good for me; **toute amie d. de ce nom aurait accepté** a true friend would have accepted; **je n'ai pas eu de vacances dignes de ce nom depuis une éternité** I haven't had any holidays as such for ages; **d. de confiance** trustworthy; **d. de foi** credible; **d. d'être mentionné** worth mentioning; **une pièce d. d'être vue** a play worth seeing; **il n'est pas d. d'être notre représentant** he does not deserve *or* he is not fit to be our representative
  3 **d. de** *(en conformité avec)* worthy of; **ce n'est pas d. de toi** it's unworthy of you; **il me faut une tenue d. de cette occasion** I need an outfit worthy of this occasion; *aussi Hum* **il est le d. fils de son père** like father like son

dignement [diɲmɑ̃] ADV 1 *(noblement)* with dignity, in a dignified manner; **il s'en est allé d.** he left with dignity 2 *Littéraire (justement)* **d. récompensé** justly rewarded

dignitaire [diɲitɛr] NM dignitary

dignité [diɲite] NF 1 *(noblesse)* dignity; *(maintien)* poise; **manquer de d.** to lack dignity, to be undignified 2 *(respect)* dignity; **la d. de la personne humaine** human dignity; **une atteinte à la d. de la personne humaine** an affront to human dignity 3 *(amour-propre)* pride, self-respect; **ah non, j'ai ma d.!** no, I have my pride! 4 *(fonction)* dignity 5 *(honneur)* honour

digon [digɔ̃] NM 1 *Naut* flagstaff 2 *Pêche* fishgig

digramme [digram] NM *Ling* digraph

digraphie [digrafi] NF *Compta* double-entry bookkeeping

digresser [3] [digrɛse] VI to digress, to wander from the subject

digression [digrɛsjɔ̃] NF digression; **faire une d.** to digress; **tomber** *ou* **se perdre dans des digressions** to digress (endlessly)

digue [dig] NF 1 *(mur)* dyke, seawall; *(talus)* embankment; **d. de retenue** flood barrier 2 *Fig (protection)* safety valve, barrier 3 *Can (de billes de bois)* logjam; *(de glace)* ice jam

diholoside [diɔlɔzid] NM *Chim* disaccharide

dihydrogène [diidrɔʒɛn] NM *Chim* dihydrogen

dik-dik [dikdik] NM INV *Zool* dik-dik

diktat [diktat] NM diktat

dilacération [dilaserasjɔ̃] NF dilaceration

dilacérer [18] [dilasere] VT to break *or* to tear in pieces, to dilacerate

dilapidateur, -trice [dilapidatœr, -tris] ADJ spendthrift, wasteful
  NM,F squanderer, spendthrift; **d. de fonds publics** embezzler of public funds

dilapidation [dilapidasjɔ̃] NF wasting, frittering away, squandering; **d. de fonds publics** embezzlement of public funds

dilapidatrice [dilapidatris] *voir* **dilapidateur**

dilapider [3] [dilapide] VT *(gén)* to waste, to fritter away, to squander; *(fonds publics)* to embezzle

dilatabilité [dilatabilite] NF dilatability

dilatable [dilatabl] ADJ dilatable

dilatant, -e [dilatɑ̃, -ɑ̃t] ADJ dilative

dilatateur, -trice [dilatatœr, -tris] ADJ dilatator *(avant n)*, dilator *(avant n)*
  NM dilatator, dilator

dilatation [dilatasjɔ̃] NF 1 *Phys* expansion 2 *(des narines, des pupilles)* dilation; *(de l'estomac)* distension; *(du col de l'utérus)* dilation, opening; *Méd* **d. et curetage** dilatation and curettage, D and C 3 *Littéraire (du cœur, de l'âme)* filling

dilatatrice [dilatatris] *voir* **dilatateur**

dilater [3] [dilate] VT 1 *Phys* to cause to expand
  2 *(remplir d'air → tuyau, pneu)* to inflate, to blow up
  3 *(élargir → narine, pupille, veine)* to dilate; *(→ estomac)* to distend; *(→ col de l'utérus)* to dilate, to open; *(→ poumons)* to expand; **il a les pupilles dilatées** his pupils are dilated; *Fam* **d. la rate à qn** to have sb in stitches
  ▶ **se dilater** VPR 1 *Phys* to expand
  2 *(être gonflé → tuyau, pneu)* to blow up, to inflate
  3 *(être élargi → narine, pupille, veine)* to dilate; *(→ estomac)* to become distended; *(→ col de l'utérus)* to dilate, to open; *(→ poumons)* to expand
  4 **se d. les poumons** to fill one's lungs; *Fam* **se d. la rate** to kill oneself laughing

dilatoire [dilatwar] ADJ delaying, *Sout* dilatory, procrastinating; *Jur* dilatory; **user de moyens dilatoires** to play for time; **donner une réponse d.** to answer evasively *(so as to play for time)*

dilatomètre [dilatɔmɛtr] NM dilatometer

dilection [dilɛksjɔ̃] NF *Littéraire* (tender) love

dilemme [dilɛm] NM 1 *(situation)* dilemma; **être devant un d.** to face a dilemma; **être aux prises avec un d.** to be (caught) on the horns of a dilemma; **d. du prisonnier** prisoner's dilemma 2 *Mktg (produit)* problem child

dilettante [diletɑ̃t] ADJ dilettantish, amateurish
  NMF dilettante, dabbler
  □ **en dilettante** ADV **il fait de la peinture en d.** he dabbles in painting

dilettantisme [diletɑ̃tism] NM 1 *(attitude dilettante)* dilettantism 2 *(amateurisme)* amateurishness

diligemment [diliʒamɑ̃] ADV *Littéraire* 1 *(soigneusement)* diligently, conscientiously 2 *(rapidement)* hastily, promptly, with dispatch

diligence [diliʒɑ̃s] NF 1 *(véhicule)* stagecoach 2 *Littéraire (rapidité)* haste, dispatch; **avec d.** hastily, promptly, with dispatch; **faire d.** to make haste 3 *(soin)* diligence, conscientiousness; *Jur* **d. normale** due care; *Jur* **d. raisonnable** reasonable care
  □ **à la diligence de** PRÉP *Jur* at the request *or* behest of

diligent, -e [diliʒɑ̃, -ɑ̃t] ADJ *Littéraire* 1 *(actif)* prompt, speedy, active 2 *(assidu → soins)* constant, assiduous; *(→ élève)* diligent; *(→ employé)* conscientious, scrupulous

diligenter [3] [diliʒɑ̃te] VT 1 *Littéraire (hâter)* to hasten, to expedite 2 *Jur (poursuites)* to bring

dilogie [dilɔʒi] NF 1 *Phil* dilogy 2 *Théât* play with a double plot

diluant [dilɥɑ̃] NM thinner, *Spéc* diluent

diluer [7] [dilɥe] VT 1 *(allonger → d'eau)* to dilute, to water down; *(→ d'un liquide)* to dilute
  2 *(délayer)* to thin down
  3 *Péj (discours, exposé)* to pad *or* to stretch out; *(idée, argument)* to dilute
  4 *Fin & Bourse (capital, actions)* to dilute; **d. le**

bénéfice par action to dilute equity; **d. entièrement des actions** to fully dilute shares
  ▶ **se diluer** VPR 1 *(se mélanger)* to become diluted; *(sel, sucre)* to dissolve
  2 *Fig (se disperser)* to become attenuated; **la responsabilité de l'échec se dilue au sein de la direction** there has been no clear admission of responsibility for the failure among the management

dilutif, -ive [dilytif, -iv] ADJ *Fin & Bourse* dilutive

dilution [dilysjɔ̃] NF 1 *(mélange de liquides)* dilution, diluting; *(ajout d'eau)* dilution, watering down 2 *(désépaississement)* thinning down 3 *(dissolution → d'un comprimé)* dissolving 4 *Péj (d'un discours)* padding *or* stretching out 5 *Fin (du capital, des actions)* dilution; **d. du bénéfice par action** dilution of equity

dilutive [dilytiv] *voir* **dilutif**

diluvien, -enne [dilyvjɛ̃, -ɛn] ADJ 1 *Bible* diluvial, diluvian 2 *(pluie)* torrential

dimanche [dimɑ̃ʃ] NM Sunday; **le d. de Pâques** Easter Sunday; **le d. des Rameaux** Palm Sunday □ **du dimanche** ADJ 1 *(journal, promenade)* Sunday *(avant n)* 2 *Fam Péj (amateur)* **chauffeur du d.** Sunday driver; **un peintre du d.** a weekend painter; *voir aussi* **mardi**

'Un dimanche après-midi à la Grande Jatte' *Seurat* 'Sunday Afternoon on the Island of La Grande Jatte'

'Un Dimanche à la campagne' *Tavernier* 'A Sunday in the Country'

'Un long dimanche de fiançailles' *Jeunet* 'A Very Long Engagement'

dîme [dim] NF tithe; **payer une d.** to (pay a) tithe; **prélever une d. (sur qch)** to levy a tithe (on sth); *Fig* to take one's cut (of sth)

dimension [dimɑ̃sjɔ̃] NF 1 *(mesure)* dimension, measurement; **quelles sont les dimensions de la pièce?** what are the measurements *or* dimensions of the room?; **coupé dans sa plus grande/plus petite d.** cut lengthways/crossways; **prendre les dimensions de qch** to measure sth (up); **prendre les dimensions d'un événement** to get the measure of an event
  2 *(taille)* size, dimension; **une pièce de petite/grande d.** a small-size(d)/large-size(d) room
  3 *(importance)* dimension; **cela donne une nouvelle d. au problème** this gives a new dimension to the problem; **une erreur de cette d.** an error of this magnitude; **lorsque l'information prend les dimensions d'une tragédie** when news assumes tragic proportions
  4 *(aspect)* dimension, feature; **le suspens est une d. prépondérante de son œuvre** suspense is a significant feature of his/her work; **à la lumière des récents événements, les manifestations anti-américaines prennent une nouvelle d.** the anti-American demonstrations have taken on a whole new dimension *or* significance in the light of recent events
  5 *Math & Phys* dimension
  □ **à deux dimensions** ADJ two-dimensional
  □ **à la dimension de** PRÉP corresponding *or* proportionate to; **un salaire à la d. du travail requis** wages proportionate to *or Sout* commensurate with the work involved
  □ **à trois dimensions** ADJ three-dimensional

dimensionnel, -elle [dimɑ̃sjɔnɛl] ADJ dimensional

dimensionner [3] [dimɑ̃sjɔne] VT to size; **un appartement bien dimensionné** a well laid-out apartment

dimère [dimɛr] ADJ 1 *Bot & Zool* dimerous 2 *Chim* dimeric
  NM *Chim* dimer

diméthyle [dimetil] NM *Chim* dimethyl

diminué, -e [diminɥe] ADJ 1 *(affaibli)* **il est très d.** *(physiquement)* his health is failing; *(mentalement)* he's losing his faculties 2 *Mus* diminished 3 *Archit* tapering 4 *(rang de tricot)* decreased

diminuendo [diminɥɛndo, diminɥ̃do] *Mus* ADV diminuendo
  NM diminuendo

diminuer[7] [diminɥe] **VT 1** (*réduire → prix, impôts, frais, ration*) to reduce, to cut; (→ *longueur*) to shorten; (→ *taille, effectifs, volume, vitesse, consommation*) to reduce; (→ *autorité, pouvoir, crédibilité*) to lessen, to diminish; **d. le chauffage** (*pour qu'il fasse moins chaud*) to turn down the heating; (*pour économiser l'énergie*) to cut down on the heating; **d. les impôts de 5 pour cent** to reduce tax by 5 percent; **montant net diminué du prix de vente** net amount less purchase price; **cela ne diminue en rien votre mérite** this doesn't detract from or lessen your merit at all
2 (*atténuer → douleurs, souffrance*) to alleviate, to lessen
3 (*personne → affaiblir*) to affect; (→ *humilier*) to belittle, to cut down to size; **la maladie l'a beaucoup diminué** his illness has affected him very badly; **sortir diminué d'une attaque** to suffer from the aftereffects of an attack; **elle sort diminuée de cette affaire** her reputation has been badly damaged by this business
4 (*en tricot*) to decrease
5 *Mus* to diminish
VI 1 (*pression*) to fall, to drop; (*volume*) to decrease; (*prix*) to fall, to come down; (*profits, ventes, recettes*) to fall (off), to drop; (*chômage, accidents, criminalité*) to fall, decrease; **le prix des ordinateurs a diminué de 20 pour cent** the price of computers has fallen by 20 percent; **le chiffre d'affaires a diminué de 10 pour cent par rapport à l'année dernière** turnover is 10 percent down on last year's figure; **d. de valeur** to drop in value
2 (*s'affaiblir → forces*) to ebb away, to wane; (→ *peur, douleur*) to lessen; (→ *fièvre*) to abate; (→ *intérêt, attention*) to drop, to lessen, to dwindle; **son appétit a diminué** he's/she's lost some of his/her appetite
3 (*raccourcir*) **les jours diminuent** the days are getting shorter or drawing in
▶**se diminuer VPR** (*se rabaisser*) to lower or demean oneself

diminutif, -ive [diminytif, -iv] **ADJ** *Ling* diminutive
NM 1 (*nom*) diminutive; **Greg est le d. de Gregory** Greg is short for Gregory **2** *Ling* diminutive

diminution [diminysjɔ̃] **NF 1** (*réduction → de prix, d'impôts, des frais, des rations*) reduction (**de** in); (→ *de longueur*) shortening (**de** of); (→ *de taille*) reduction (**de** in); (→ *de volume*) decrease (**de** in); (→ *de pression*) fall (**de** in); (→ *de vitesse, de consommation*) reduction (**de** in); (→ *du chômage, de la violence*) drop, decrease (**de** in); **une d. des effectifs** a reduction in the number of staff; **être en d.** (*effectifs*) to be dwindling or decreasing; (*naissances, ventes*) to be falling
2 (*affaiblissement → d'une douleur*) alleviation; (→ *des forces*) waning, lessening; (→ *de la fièvre*) abatement; (→ *de l'intérêt, de l'attention*) drop, lessening; (→ *de l'appétit*) decrease
3 *Mus* diminution
4 *Archit* taper
5 (*en tricot*) decrease; **faire une d.** to decrease; **faites trois diminutions** decrease three stitches

diminutive [diminytiv] *voir* **diminutif**

dimorphe [dimɔrf] **ADJ** dimorphic, dimorphous
dimorphisme [dimɔrfism] **NM** dimorphism

DIN, Din [din] **ADJ** *Élec & Phot* (*abrév* **Deutsche Industrie Normen**) DIN

dinanderie [dinɑ̃dri] **NF 1** (*technique*) sheet metal craft **2** (*objets*) objects made from sheet metal
dinandier [dinɑ̃dje] **NM** = person who makes or sells "dinanderie"
dinar [dinar] **NM** dinar
dînatoire [dinatwar] **ADJ buffet d.** buffet-dinner; **goûter d.** early supper, *Br* (high) tea
dinde [dɛ̃d] **NF 1** *Orn* turkey (hen) **2** *Culin* turkey **3** (*sotte*) **quelle petite d.!** what a silly little goose!
dindon [dɛ̃dɔ̃] **NM 1** *Orn* turkey (cock) **2** (*sot*) fool; **être le d. de la farce** (*dupe*) to be taken for a ride; (*victime de railleries*) to end up a laughing stock
dindonneau, -x [dɛ̃dɔno] **NM** *Orn* poult, young turkey
dindonner [3] [dɛ̃dɔne] **VT** *Fam Vieilli* to fool, to hoodwink

dîner¹ [dine] **NM 1** (*repas du soir*) dinner; (*réception*) dinner party; **d. dansant** dinner dance; **d.-débat** dinner-debate; **d.-concert** dinner-concert
2 *Belg, Can & Suisse* & (*régional en France & en Afrique francophone*) (*déjeuner*) lunch
dîner² [3] [dine] **VI 1** (*faire le repas du soir*) to dine, to have dinner; **dînons au restaurant** let's eat out, let's go out for dinner; **avoir des amis à d.** to have friends to dinner or round for dinner; **il est resté à d.** he stayed for dinner; **nous avons dîné d'un simple potage** we just had soup for dinner; **j'ai fait d. les enfants plus tôt** I gave the children an early dinner
2 *Belg, Can & Suisse* & (*régional en France & en Afrique francophone*) (*déjeuner*) to have lunch

'Le Dîner de cons' *Veber* 'The Dinner Game'

dîner-spectacle [dinespɛktakl] (*pl* **dîners-spectacles**) **NM** cabaret dinner; **aller au d.** to dine at a cabaret
dînette [dinɛt] **NF 1** (*jouet*) toy or doll's tea set; **jouer à la d.** to play (at) tea-parties **2** *Fam* (*repas*) light or quick meal ; **faire la d.** to have a bite to eat
dîneur, -euse [dinœr, -øz] **NM,F** diner
ding [diŋ] **ONOMAT** ding; **d. dong!** ding-dong!
dinghy [diŋgi] (*pl* **dinghys** *ou* **dinghies**) **NM** dinghy
dingo [dɛ̃go] **ADJ** *Fam* nuts, crazy; **il est complètement d.** he's completely nuts, he's got a screw loose
NMF *Fam* nutcase, loony, *Am* wacko
NM (*chien*) dingo
dingue [dɛ̃g] *Fam* **ADJ 1** (*fou*) nuts, crazy; **elle est vraiment d. de rouler aussi vite** she's got to be nuts to drive so fast; **il a signé, faut être d.!** he signed, how crazy can you get!
2 (*incroyable → prix, histoire*) crazy, mad; (*extravagant → vêtements, soirée*) great, terrific; **c'est d. ce qu'il peut faire chaud ici** it's hot as hell here; **en ce moment j'ai un boulot d.!** the amount of work I have at the moment is unreal or crazy!
NMF nutcase, *Am* wacko; **il conduit comme un vrai d.** he drives like a complete maniac; **c'est une maison de dingues!** this place is a real loony bin!; **envoyer qn chez les dingues** to send sb to the loony bin or funny farm; **c'est un d. de motos** he's a motorbike freak
dinguer [3] [dɛ̃ge] **VI** *Fam Vieilli* **les assiettes dinguaient dans la cuisine!** plates were flying all over the kitchen!; **il m'a attrapé, j'ai dingué** he grabbed me and I went flying; **sa voiture est allée d. contre un mur** his/her car went crashing or flying into a wall; **envoyer d. qn** (*l'éconduire*) to tell sb where to go, *Br* to send sb packing
dinguerie [dɛ̃gri] **NF** *Fam* stupidity; **ce livre est d'une d.!** this is an incredibly stupid book!; **voilà sa dernière d.: s'acheter une moto!** you know what his/her latest mad or crazy idea is? to buy a motorbike!; **ils ne savent faire que les dingueries** they get up to all sorts of nonsense; **il est capable des pires dingueries** he's capable of doing the most idiotic things
dinitrotoluène [dinitrotolɥen] **NM** *Chim* dinitrotoluene
dinoflagellé [dinoflaʒele] **NM** *Biol* dinoflagellate
dinornis [dinornis] **NM** *Orn* dinornis
dinosaure [dinozɔr] **NM** *Zool & Fig* dinosaur
dinosauriens [dinosɔrjɛ̃] **NMPL** Dinosauria
dinotherium [dinotɛrjɔm] **NM** dinotherium
dinucléotide [dinykleotid] **NM** *Biol & Chim* dinucleotide
diocésain, -e [djosezɛ̃, -ɛn] **ADJ** diocesan
NM,F diocesan
diocèse [djosɛz] **NM** diocese
diode [djod] **NF** diode; **d. électroluminescente** light-emitting diode
diodon [djodɔ̃] **NM** *Ich* puffer, globe-fish
Diogène [djoʒɛn] **NPR** Diogenes
dioïque [djoik] **ADJ** *Bot* dioecious
dioléfine [djolefin] **NF** *Chim* diene
dionée [djone] **NF** *Bot* catch-fly, Venus fly-trap, *Spéc* dionaea

dionysiaque [djonizjak] **ADJ** Dionysiac, Dionysian
❑ **dionysiaques NFPL** *Antiq* Dionysia
dionysien, -enne [djonizjɛ̃, -ɛn] **ADJ** of/from Saint Denis
❑ **Dionysien, -enne NM,F** = inhabitant of or person from Saint Denis
dionysies [djonizi] **NFPL** *Antiq* Dionysia
Dionysos [djonizos] **NPR** *Myth* Dionysus, Dionysos
diopside [djopsid] **NM** diopside
dioptase [djoptaz] **NF** dioptase
dioptre [djoptr] **NM** dioptre (*surface*)
dioptrie [djoptri] **NF** dioptre (*unit*)
dioptrique [djoptrik] **ADJ** dioptric
NF dioptrics (*singulier*)
diorama [djorama] **NM** diorama
diorite [djorit] **NF** *Géol* diorite
dioscoréacée [djoskorease] *Bot* **NF** Dioscorea
❑ **dioscoréacées NFPL** Dioscoreaceae
dioula [djula] **NM** (*dans l'ouest de l'Afrique francophone*) travelling salesman
dioxine [djoksin] **NF** *Chim* dioxin
dioxyde [djoksid] **NM** *Chim* dioxide; **d. de carbone** carbon dioxide
dioxygène [djoksiʒɛn] **NM** dioxygen
dipétale [dipetal] **ADJ** *Bot* dipetalous
diphasé, -e [difaze] **ADJ** diphase, diphasic, two-phase (*avant n*)
diphénol [difenol] **NM** *Chim* diphenol
diphényle [difenil] **NM** *Chim* diphenyl, biphenyl
diphtérie [difteri] **NF** diphtheria; **avoir la d.** to have diphtheria
diphtérique [difterik] **ADJ** diphtherial, diphtheric, diphtheritic
NMF diphtheria sufferer
diphtongaison [diftɔ̃gɛzɔ̃] **NF** *Ling* diphthongization
diphtongue [diftɔ̃g] **NF** *Ling* diphthong
diphtonguer [3] [diftɔ̃ge] **VT** to diphthongize, to make into a diphthong
diploblastique [diploblastik] **ADJ** *Biol* diploblastic
diplocoque [diplokɔk] **NM** *Biol* diplococcus
diplodocus [diplodokys] **NM** *Zool* diplodocus
diploïde [diploid] **ADJ** *Biol* diploid
diplomate [diplomat] **ADJ** diplomatic
NMF *Pol & Fig* diplomat
NM *Culin* = dessert made of sponge cake pieces covered with custard and glacé fruits, ≃ trifle
diplomatie [diplomasi] **NF 1** *Pol* (*relations, représentation*) diplomacy; **la d.** (*corps*) the diplomatic corps or service; **d. du dollar** dollar diplomacy **2** (*tact*) diplomacy, tact; **avec d.** diplomatically, tactfully
diplomatique [diplomatik] **ADJ 1** *Pol* diplomatic **2** (*adroit*) diplomatic, tactful, courteous; **faire un mensonge d.** to tell a white lie; **avoir une maladie d.** to pretend to be indisposed
NF diplomatics (*singulier*)
diplomatiquement [diplomatikmɑ̃] **ADV 1** *Pol* diplomatically **2** (*adroitement*) diplomatically, courteously, tactfully
diplôme [diplom] **NM 1** (*titre*) diploma, qualification; **un d. d'ingénieur** an engineering diploma; **elle a des diplômes** she's highly qualified; **d. d'État** recognized qualification; **d. d'études approfondies** = postgraduate qualification which is a prerequisite for PhD candidates; **d. d'études supérieures spécialisées** = postgraduate diploma lasting one year; **d. d'études universitaires générales** = university diploma taken after two years; **d. d'études universitaires scientifiques et techniques** = university diploma taken after two years of science courses; **d. universitaire d'études littéraires** = university diploma gained after two years of arts courses, still existing in some French-speaking countries but replaced in France in 1973; **d. universitaire d'études scientifiques** = university diploma gained after two years of science courses, still existing in some French-speaking countries but replaced in France in 1973; **d. universitaire de technologie** = diploma taken after two years at an institute of technology
2 (*examen*) exam; **il a raté son d. de programmeur** he failed his computer programming exam
3 *Hist* diploma

dim-dip

diplômé, -e [diplome] ADJ *(gén)* qualified; *(de l'université ou équivalent)* graduate; **un ingénieur d. de l'École Polytechnique** an engineering graduate of the "École Polytechnique"
NM,F *(gén)* holder of a qualification; *(de l'université ou équivalent)* graduate; **les hauts diplômés** highly qualified people; **embaucher des diplômés** to take on people with qualifications

diplômer [3] [diplome] VT to award a diploma to, to confer a diploma (up)on

diplopie [diplɔpi] NF *Méd* double vision, *Spéc* diplopia

dipneumone [dipnømɔn] ADJ *Zool* dipneumonous

dipneuste [dipnøst] *Ich* NM lungfish
❑ **dipneustes** NMPL Dipneusti

dipolaire [dipɔlɛr] ADJ dipolar, dipole

dipôle [dipol] NM dipole

dipsacacée [dipsakase], **dipsacée** [dipsase] *Bot* NF Dipsacus
❑ **dipsacacées** NFPL Dipsacaceae

dipsomane [dipsɔman], **dipsomaniaque** [dipsɔmanjak] ADJ dipsomaniac
NMF dipsomaniac

dipsomanie [dipsɔmani] NF dipsomania

diptère [diptɛr] ADJ **1** *Archit* dipteral **2** *Entom* dipteran, dipterous
NM *Entom* dipteran, dipteron
❑ **diptères** NMPL Diptera

diptyque [diptik] NM **1** *Beaux-Arts* diptych **2** *(œuvre)* = literary or artistic work in two parts

dircom [dirkɔm] *Fam* NF *(service)* communications department■
NMF *(responsable)* head of communications■

dire[1] [dir] NM *Jur (mémoire)* statement
❑ **dires** NMPL statement; **je tiens à confirmer les dires de M. Leblanc** I can confirm what Mr Leblanc said; **d'après** *ou* **selon les dires de son père** according to his/her father *or* to what his/her father said; **selon les dires de son professeur, il était bon élève** according to his teacher, he was good at school
❑ **au dire de** PRÉP according to; **au d. de la mère, il a fallu trois hommes pour le tenir** according to the mother, it took three men to restrain him

DIRE[2] [102] [dir]

> **VT** to say **A1, 2, B1, 3, 8, 9, 12, D1, 2** ■ to recite **A2** ■ to express **B2** ■ to give **B4** ■ to tell **B1, 5–7** ■ to claim **B9** ■ to think **C1** ■ to look/smell/ etc like **C2** ■ to show **D1** ■ to tempt **D4** ■ to be in the mood for **D4**
> **USAGE ABSOLU** to say **3**
> **VPR** to tell each other **1** ■ to be in use **3** ■ to say **2, 4–6** ■ to think **4** ■ to claim **5, 6**

VT **A.** *ARTICULER, PRONONCER* **1** *(énoncer)* to say; **dis "ah!"** say "ah!"; **dites "je le jure"** say "I swear by Almighty God"; **quel nom dis-tu? Castagnel?** what name did you say *or* what's the name again? Castagnel?; **il n'arrive pas à d. ce mot** he cannot pronounce that word; **une poupée qui dit "oui"** a doll which says "yes"; **"je t'attendais", dit-elle** "I was waiting for you," she said; **vous avez dit "démocratie"?** "democracy", did you say?; *Fam* **je te dis zut!** get lost!; *très Fam* **je te dis merde!** *(pour porter bonheur)* break a leg!; *(pour insulter)* get lost!; **comment dit-on "pain" en breton?** how do you say "bread" in Breton?, what's the Breton for "bread"?; **je ne dirais pas qu'il est distant, je dirais plutôt effarouché** I wouldn't say he's haughty, rather that he's been frightened off; **je n'ai pas dit "oublier", j'ai dit "pardonner"** I said "forgive", not "forget"; **une honte, que dis-je, une infamie!, une honte, pour ne pas d. une infamie!** a shame, not to say an infamy!; **en ce temps-là, qui disait vol disait galère** in those days, theft meant the gallows; **qui dit fatigue dit inattention et qui dit inattention dit accident** when you're tired you're less vigilant and therefore more likely to have an accident; **si (l')on peut d.** in a way, so to speak; **disons-le, disons le mot** let's not mince words; **c'est, disons le mot, une trahison** it's a betrayal, let's not mince words; **je me sens humilié, disons-le** I must admit *or* confess I feel humiliated, to be honest *or* frank (about it), I feel humiliated; **d. non** to say no, to refuse; **d. non au nucléaire** to say no to nuclear energy; **tu veux un gin? – je ne dis pas non** would you like a gin? – I wouldn't say no; **si on lui proposait le poste, il ne dirait pas non** if he was offered the job, he wouldn't say no *or* wouldn't refuse; **d. oui** *(gén)* to say yes; *(à une proposition)* to accept; *(au mariage)* to say I do; **l'impôt sur les grandes fortunes, moi je dis oui!** I'm all in favour of a supertax on the rich!; **d. bonjour de la main** to wave (hello); **d. oui de la tête** to nod; **d. non de la tête** to shake one's head; *Fam* **obéissant? il faut le d. vite** obedient? I'm not so sure about that; **malhonnêteté, c'est vite dit** dishonesty, that's a bit hasty; *Fam* **déménager, c'est vite dit!** move? that's easier said than done; *Fam* **menteur! – c'est celui qui (le) dit qui y est** *ou* **qui l'est!** liar! – it takes one to know one!

2 *(réciter → prière, table de multiplication)* to say; *(→ texte)* to say, to recite, to read; *(→ rôle)* to speak; **d. la/une messe** to say mass/a mass; **d. son chapelet** to say the rosary, to tell one's beads; **d. des vers** to recite verse, to give a recitation

B. *EXPRIMER* **1** *(oralement)* to say; **que dis-tu là?** what did you say?, what was that you said?; **tu ne sais pas ce que tu dis** you don't know what you're talking about; **elle dit tout ce qui lui passe par la tête** she says anything that comes into her head; **en physique, je ne comprends pas ce que dit le professeur** I can't understand what the physics teacher says *or* is talking about; **dis quelque chose!** say something!; **c'est juste pour d. quelque chose** it was just for the sake of saying something; **qu'est-ce que tu veux que je dise?** what do you expect me to say?; **j'ai l'habitude de d. ce que je pense** I always speak my mind *or* say what I think; **bon, bon, je n'ai rien dit!** OK, sorry I spoke!; **pourquoi ne m'as-tu rien dit de tout cela?** why didn't you speak to me *or* tell me about any of this?; **dis-moi où il est** tell me where he is; **ne me dis pas que c'est brûlé!** don't tell me it's burnt!; *Fam* **il me dit comme ça, "t'as pas le droit"** so he says to me, "you can't do that"; *Fam* **je suis un raté? tu sais ce qu'il te dit, le raté?** so I'm a loser, am I? well, do you want to hear what this loser's got to say to you?; **je te l'ai dit une fois, je ne te le redirai pas** *ou* **je ne te le dirai pas deux fois** I've told you before and I won't tell you again; **combien de fois faut-il que je te le dise?** how many times do I have to tell you?; **impossible de lui faire d. l'âge de sa sœur** he/she won't say *or* give his/her sister's age; **impossible de lui faire d. la vérité** he/she just refuses to tell the truth; **ne me fais pas d. ce que je n'ai pas dit!** don't put words into my mouth!; **laisser qn d. qch** to let sb say sth; **laissez-moi d. ceci** let me say this; **laissez-la d.!** let her speak!; **je peux d. que tu m'as fait peur!** you certainly frightened me!; **j'ai failli faire tout rater! – ça, tu peux le d.!** I nearly messed everything up – you can say that again!; **ce disant** with these words, so saying; **ce qui est dit est dit** there's no going back on what's been said (before); **c'est (te/vous) d. s'il est riche!** that gives you an idea how wealthy he is!; **c'est d. si je l'aimais!** so you see how much I loved him/her!; **il ne m'a même pas répondu, c'est tout d.** he never even answered me, that says it all; **pour tout d.** in fact, to be honest; **je ne te le fais pas d.** you said it, I couldn't have put it better myself; **de l'escroquerie, je ne vous le fais pas d.** a swindle, you said it! *or* as you so rightly say!; **il va sans d. que...** needless to say...; **ça va sans d.** it goes without saying; *Fam* **ça va sans d. mais ça va encore mieux en le disant** it doesn't hurt to overstate it; *Fam* **ce n'est pas pour d., mais à sa place j'aurais réussi** though I say it myself, if I'd been him/her I'd have succeeded; **ce n'est pas pour d. mais c'est bruyant** I don't mean to complain but it's noisy; **ce n'est pas pour d. mais elle se débrouille bien** she's doing well, you've got to give her that, give her her due, she's doing well; *Fam* **alors j'ai parlé de racisme, ce que j'avais pas dit là!** then I mentioned racism and that really set the cat among the pigeons!; **il en est incapable, enfin (moi), ce que j'en dis...** he's not capable of it, at least that's what I'd say...; *Fam* **je ne dis pas** may be; **je ne dis pas, mais...** that's as maybe but...; *Fam* **il a un petit manoir, je ne te dis que ça!** he owns a lovely little country house, what (more) can I say!; *Fam* **voici une confiture maison, je ne te dis que ça** here's some homemade jam that's out of this world; *Fam* **il y avait un monde, je te dis pas!** you wouldn't have believed the crowds!; *Fam* **je te dis pas la pagaille qu'il y avait!** you should've seen the chaos!

2 *(symboliquement)* to express, to tell of; **je voudrais d. mon espoir** I'd like to express my hope; **un journal où elle dit son dégoût de la vie** a diary in which she tells of her disgust for life; **comment d. mon amour?** how can I express my love?; **toute cette haine que je n'avais jamais dite** all my unexpressed hatred; **une lettre où il me disait sa surprise** a letter telling me how surprised he was; **un sculpteur qui n'a plus rien/qui a encore beaucoup à d.** a sculptor who has nothing left to say/who still has a lot left to say; **vouloir d.** *(signifier)* to mean; **un haussement d'épaules dans ce cas-là, ça dit bien ce que ça veut d.** in a situation like that, a shrug (of the shoulders) speaks volumes; **est-ce à d. que...?** does this mean that...?; *Arch* **vous partez, madame, qu'est-ce à d.?** Madam, what mean you by leaving?

3 *(écrire)* to say; **dans sa lettre, elle dit que...** in her letter she says that...

4 *(annoncer → nom, prix)* to give; **cela t'a coûté combien? – dis un prix!** how much did it cost you? – have a guess!; **dites un** *ou* **votre prix, je l'achète** name your price; **le général vous fait d. qu'il vous attend** the general has sent me to tell you he's waiting for you; **on m'a fait d. qu'elle était sortie** I was told she'd gone out; **faire d. à qn de venir** to send for sb; **je lui ai fait d. qu'on se passerait de lui** I let him know that we'd manage without him

5 *(prédire)* to foretell, to tell; **tu verras ce que je te dis!** you just wait and see if I'm right!; **qui aurait dit que je l'épouserais?** who would have said that I'd marry him/her?; **je te l'avais bien dit** I told you so; *Fam* **tu vas le regretter, moi je te le dis!** you'll be sorry for this, let me tell you *or* mark my words!

6 *(ordonner)* to tell; **il m'a dit d'arrêter** he told me to stop; **on ne me le dira pas** *ou* **je ne me le ferai pas d. deux fois** I don't need to be told twice; **il ne se l'est pas fait d. deux fois** he didn't have to be told twice

7 *(conseiller)* to tell; **tu me dis d'oublier, mais...** you tell me I must forget, but...

8 *(objecter)* to say, to object; **sa mère ne lui dit jamais rien** his/her mother never tells him/her off; **toi, on ne peut jamais rien te d.!** you can't take the slightest criticism!; **quand on lui a fait le vaccin, il n'a rien dit** when they gave him the injection he never said a word; **mais, me direz-vous, il n'est pas majeur** but, you will object *or* I hear you say, he's not of age; **as-tu quelque chose à d. sur la façon dont j'élève nos enfants?** have you got any objections to *or* anything to say about the way I bring up our children?; **j'aurais des choses à d. sur l'organisation du service** I have a few things to say *or* some comments to make about the organization of the department; **c'est tout ce que tu as trouvé à d.?** is that the best you could come up with?; **Pierre n'est pas d'accord – il n'a rien à d.** Pierre doesn't agree – he's in no position to make any objections; **il n'a rien trouvé à d. sur la qualité** he had no criticisms to make about the quality; *Fam* **elle est maligne, il n'y a pas à d.** *ou* **on ne peut pas d. (le contraire)** she's shrewd, there's no denying it *or* and no mistake

9 *(affirmer)* to say, to state; **le diriez-vous à la barre des témoins?** would you swear to it?; **si c'est vous qui le dites, si vous le dites, du moment que vous le dites** if you say so; **puisque je vous le dis!** I'm telling you!, you can take it from me!; **d. que** to say *or* to state that; **elle dit**

que ce n'est pas vrai she says it's not true; **moi je dis que c'est la seule solution** I say it's the only solution; **c'est le bon train? – je te dis que oui!** is it the right train? – yes it is! *or* I'm telling you it is!; **il va neiger – la météo a dit que non** it looks like it's going to snow – the weather forecast said it wouldn't; **je n'ai jamais dit que j'étais spécialiste!** I never claimed to be *or* said I was an expert!; **tu étais content, ne me dis pas le contraire!** you were pleased, don't deny it *or* don't tell me you weren't!; **on dit qu'il a un autre fils** rumour has it that *or* it's rumoured that *or* it's said that he has another son; **loin des yeux, loin du cœur, dit-on** out of sight, out of mind, so the saying goes *or* so they say; **je ne les laisserai pas d. que mon fils est un fainéant** I won't allow them to *or* let them say that my son's an idler; **on le disait lâche** he was said *or* alleged *or* reputed to be a coward; **qui (me) dit que tu n'es pas un espion?** how can I tell *or* who's to say (that) you're not a spy?; *Fam* **je m'en moque – on dit ça** I don't care – that's what you say *or* that's what they all say; *Fam* **ça ne coûtera pas grand-chose – que tu dis!** it won't cost much – that's what you think *or* say!; *Fam* **elle trouvera bien une place – qu'elle dit** she'll find a job, no problem – that's what she thinks!; **on dira ce qu'on voudra, mais l'amour ça passe avant tout** whatever people say, love comes before everything else; **on ne dira jamais assez l'importance d'un régime alimentaire équilibré** I cannot emphasize enough the importance of a balanced diet

10 *(prétendre)* to claim, to allege; **elle disait ne pas savoir qui le lui avait donné** she claimed *or* alleged that she didn't know who'd given it to her

11 *(dans des jeux d'enfants)* **on dirait qu'on serait des rois** let's pretend we're kings

12 *(admettre)* to say, to admit; **tu ne m'aimes plus, dis-le** you don't love me any more, say *or* admit it; **je dois d. qu'elle est jolie** I must say *or* admit she's pretty; **il a beaucoup travaillé, on doit le d.** it's got to be said that he's worked hard; **il faut bien d. qu'il n'est plus tout jeune** he's not young any more, let's face it; **il faut d. qu'elle a des excuses** (to) give her her due, there are mitigating circumstances; **disons que...** let's say (that)...

13 *(décider)* **il est dit que...** fate has decreed that...; **il ne sera pas dit que...** let it not be said that...; **rien n'est dit** *(décidé)* nothing's been decided yet; *(prévisible)* nothing's for certain (yet); **tout est dit** *(il n'y a plus à discuter)* the matter is closed; *(l'avenir est arrêté)* the die is cast; **tout n'est pas encore dit** nothing's final yet; **aussitôt dit, aussitôt fait** no sooner said than done

C. *PENSER, CROIRE* **1** *(penser)* to say, to think; **que disent les médecins?** what do the doctors say?; **que dis-tu de ma perruque?** what do you think of *or* how do you like my wig?; **que d. de ce geste?** what is one to make of this gesture?; **et comme dessert? – que dirais-tu d'une mousse au chocolat?** and to follow? – what would you say to *or* how about a chocolate mousse?; **d. que...** to think that...; **d. qu'elle était si jolie étant petite!** to think that she was so pretty as a child!

2 *(introduit une comparaison, une impression)* **si livide qu'on eût dit un fantôme** so pale he looked like a ghost; **quand il parle, on dirait son père** he sounds just like his father; **on dirait du thé** *(au goût)* it tastes like tea; *(à l'odeur)* it smells like tea; *(d'apparence)* it looks like tea; **on dirait de la laine** *(au toucher)* it feels like wool; **on dirait que je te fais peur** you behave as if *or* as though you were scared of me

3 *(pour exprimer une probabilité)* **on dirait sa fille, au premier rang** it looks like her daughter there in the front row; **on dirait qu'ils vont passer avec trois pour cent de marge** it looks like they'll get through with a three percent lead

D. *INDIQUER, DONNER DES SIGNES DE* **1** *(indiquer → sujet: instrument)* to say; *(→ sujet: attitude, regard)* to say, to show; **que dit le baromètre?** what does the barometer say?; **l'horloge de l'école disait 5 heures** it was five o'clock according to the *or* by the school clock; **ses yeux disaient sa détresse** you could see *or* read the distress in his/her eyes; **un geste qui disait sa peur** a gesture that betrayed his/her fear; **sa réponse te dira tout sur elle** her answer will tell you all you need to know about her; *Fam* **à la voir, quelque chose me dit qu'elle va nous laisser en plan** something about her tells me that she'll leave us in the lurch; **mon intuition** *ou* **quelque chose me dit qu'il reviendra** I have a feeling (that) he'll be back; *Fam* **que dit ton épaule?** how's your shoulder doing?; *Fam* **ça dit quoi, ce rosbif?** how's that joint of beef doing?

2 *(stipuler par écrit)* to say; **que dit la Bible/le dictionnaire à ce sujet?** what does the Bible/dictionary say about this?; **écoute ce que dit mon horoscope** listen to what my horoscope says; **la loi ne dit rien sur la vente de ces produits** the law says nothing about the sale of these products

3 *(faire penser à)* **son visage me dit quelque chose** I've seen his/her face before, his/her face seems familiar; **ce nom vous dit-il quelque chose?** have you come across *or* heard the name before?; **Lambert, cela ne vous dit rien?** Lambert, does that mean anything to you?; **cela ne me dit rien de bon** *ou* **qui vaille** I'm not sure I like (the look of) it

4 *(tenter)* **ta proposition me dit de plus en plus** your suggestion's growing on me; **tu viens? – ça ne me dit rien** are you coming? – I'm not in the mood *or* I don't feel like it; **la viande ne me dit rien du tout en ce moment** I'm off meat at the moment; **j'ai tellement attendu que maintenant ça ne me dit plus grand-chose** I waited so long that now I've lost interest in it; **ça te dirait d'aller à Bali?** (how) would you like a trip to Bali?; **ça te dirait d'aller jouer au tennis?** are you in the mood for a game of tennis?

USAGE ABSOLU **1** **nul n'a oublié à quel point elle disait juste** nobody can forget how accurate her rendering was

2 *Cartes* **à vous de d.!** your call!

3 **c'est idiot – dis toujours** it's silly – say it anyway; **j'ai une surprise – dis vite!** I have a surprise – let's hear it *or* do tell!; **comment d.** *ou* **dirais-je?** how shall I put it *or* say?; **bien dit!** well said!; **dites donc, pour demain, on y va en voiture?** by the way, are we driving there tomorrow?; **dites donc** *ou* **dites-moi Martin, vous n'étiez pas là à 9 heures!** by the way Martin, you weren't here at 9, were you?; *Fam* **dis donc** *ou* **dis-moi, faut pas se gêner!** hey, do you mind?; *Fam* **tu te fiches de moi, dis!** you're pulling my leg, aren't you?; *Fam* **tu me le sers, dis** *ou* **dis-moi, ce café?** am I getting that coffee or not?; *très Fam* **merde! – dis donc, sois poli!** shit! – hey, (mind your) language!; *Fam* **dis donc, t'as pas une gomme?** hey, have you got a rubber?; **je peux y aller, dis?** can I go, please?; **vous lui parlerez de moi, dites?** you will talk to him/her about me, won't you?; *Fam* **c'est beau – eh dis, j'y ai mis le prix!** that's beautiful – so it should be, I paid enough for it!; **tu es bien habillé, ce soir, dis donc!** my word, aren't you smart tonight!; *Fam* **il y a eu 60 morts – ben dites donc!** 60 people were killed – good God!; *Fam* **ah dis donc, la belle moto!** wow, get a load of that bike!; **il nous faut, disons, deux secrétaires** we need, (let's) say, two secretaries; **j'ai, disons, de bonnes raisons de ne pas te croire** let's say I've got good reasons not to believe you; **il a, disons, la cinquantaine bien sonnée** let's say he's on the wrong side of fifty; *Hum* **j'ai dit!** I have spoken!

▸**se dire** VPR **1** *(échanger → secrets, paroles)* to tell each other *or* one another; **nous n'avons plus rien à nous d.** we've got nothing left to say to each other; **ils se disaient des injures/des mots doux** they were exchanging insults/sweet nothings; **nous nous disions tout** we had no secrets from each other; *Arch* **qu'on se le dise** let this be known; *Hum* **je n'emmène personne au cirque si ce bruit continue, qu'on se le dise!** I'm not taking anyone to the circus if this noise doesn't stop, believe you me!

2 *(être formulé)* **comment se dit "bonsoir" en japonais?** how do you say "goodnight" in Japanese?, what's the Japanese for "goodnight"?; **il est vraiment hideux – peut-être, mais ça ne se dit pas** he's really hideous – maybe, but it's not the sort of thing you say; **cela ne se dit pas à table/devant les enfants** such things shouldn't be said at the table/in front of the children; **se dit de** *(pour définir un terme)* (is) said of, (is) used for, describes; **se dit d'une personne affaiblie par la maladie** said of a person weakened by ill-health

3 *(être en usage)* to be in use, to be accepted usage; **cela se dit encore par ici** it's still in use *or* they still say it around here; **cela ne se dit plus guère** it's not really accepted usage now *or* used any more

4 *(penser)* to think (to oneself), to say to oneself; **maintenant, je me dis que j'aurais dû accepter** now I think I should have accepted; *Fam* **il est malin, que je me dis** he's cunning, I thought to myself; **je me suis dit comme ça que je ne risquais rien en essayant** I thought *or* said to myself there was no harm in giving it a go; **dis-toi bien que tu n'auras rien!** you can be sure you won't get a thing!; **dis-toi bien que je ne serai pas toujours là pour t'aider** you must realize that *or* get it into your head that I won't always be here to help you

5 *(estimer être)* to say; **il se dit flatté de l'intérêt que je lui porte** he says he's *or* he claims to be flattered by my interest in him

6 *(se présenter comme)* to say, to claim; **elle se dit mannequin** she claims to be *or* she says she's a model; **ils se disent attachés à la démocratie** they claim to care *or* (that) they care about democracy

Allusion

Je dirais même plus!

Whenever someone says **Je dirais même plus** as a prelude to making virtually the same point as someone who has just spoken, they are making a reference to Dupond et Dupont, the bowler-hatted policemen in the Tintin cartoons (known in English as Thomson and Thompson), whose stupidity is legendary. It is simply a humorous way of saying that you agree with what has just been said. For instance, if someone says "Il fait froid aujourd'hui" (It's cold today), you could reply by saying "je dirai même plus: il ne fait pas chaud!" ("I'd even go as far as to say it's not warm"). In the English translations of Tintin, Thomson and Thompson use the phrase "to be precise", placed at the end of the sentence. For example, if one says "it's cold today", the other would reply "it's not warm, to be precise!"

direct, -e [dirɛkt] ADJ **1** *(sans détour → voie, route, chemin)* direct, straight

2 *Transp* direct, without a change; **c'est d. en métro jusqu'à Pigalle** the metro goes direct to Pigalle; **un vol d. Paris-New York** a direct *or* nonstop flight from Paris to New York; **c'est un train d. jusqu'à Genève** the train is nonstop to Geneva

3 *(franc → question)* direct; *(→ langage)* straightforward; *(→ personne)* frank, straightforward; **il y a fait une allusion directe** he made a direct reference to it, he referred to it directly

4 *(sans intermédiaire → cause, conséquence)* immediate; *(→ supérieur, descendant)* direct; **un rapport d. entre deux événements** a direct connection between two events; **mettez-vous en relation directe avec Bradel** get in touch with Bradel himself; **être en rapport d.** *ou* **contact d.** *ou* **relations directes avec qn** to be in direct contact with sb

5 *Astron, Gram & Tech* direct

6 *Ling* positive

7 *Math* direct

NM **1** *Sport* straight punch; **un d. du gauche** a straight left

2 *Rail* through *or* nonstop train

3 *TV* live; **il préfère le d. au playback** he prefers performing live to lipsynching

ADV *Fam ou Suisse* straight; **je pars d. vers Grenoble** I'm going to Grenoble direct; **s'il**

recommence, je vais d. chez le proviseur if he starts again, I'm going straight to the headmaster
▫ **directe** NF *(ascension)* direct route
▫ **en direct** ADJ live ADV live
▫ **en direct de** PRÉP live from

directement [dirɛktəmɑ̃] ADV **1** *(tout droit)* straight; **rentre d. à la maison** go straight home; **va d. au lit** go straight to bed; **la route mène d. à Deauville** the road goes straight to Deauville
2 *(franchement)* **entrer d. dans le sujet** to broach a subject immediately; **allez d. au fait** come straight to the point
3 *(inévitablement)* straight, inevitably; **cela vous mènera d. à la faillite** this will lead you inevitably to bankruptcy
4 *(sans intermédiaire)* direct; **adresse-toi d. au patron** go straight to the boss; **vendre d. au public** to sell direct to the public; **j'achète le lait d. à la ferme** I buy the milk direct from the farm; **d. du producteur au consommateur** direct *or* straight from the producer to the consumer; **il descend d. des du Mail** he's a direct descendant of the du Mail family
5 *(personnellement)* **adressez-moi d. votre courrier** address your correspondence directly to me; **cela ne vous concerne pas d.** this doesn't affect you personally *or* directly; **je me sens d. visé** I feel singled out *or* personally targeted

directeur, -trice [dirɛktœr, -tris] ADJ **1** *(principal → force)* controlling, driving; *(→ principe)* guiding; *(→ idée, ligne)* main, guiding
2 *Aut (roue)* front *(avant n)*
NM,F **1** *(d'un magasin, d'un service)* manager; *(qui fait partie du conseil d'administration)* director; **d. des achats** purchasing manager; **d. administratif** executive director; **d. administratif et financier** administrative and financial manager; **d. d'agence** *(dans une banque)* bank manager; **d. de banque** bank manager; **d. de la clientèle** customer relations manager; **d. commercial** sales director/manager; **d. de la communication** head of communications; **d. des comptes-clients** account director; **d. de la création** creative director; **d. du crédit** credit manager; **d. de division** *(au siège)* divisional director; **d. d'exploitation** operations director/manager; **d. export** export director/manager; **d. des exportations** export manager; **d. financier** financial manager; **d. général** *(d'une entreprise) Br* managing director, *Am* chief executive officer; *(d'une organisation internationale)* director general, general manager; **d. général adjoint** *Br* deputy managing director, *Am* vice-president; **d. gérant** executive director; **d. (de l')informatique** computer manager; **d. intérimaire** acting manager; **d. de marché** market manager; **d. du marketing** marketing director/manager; **d. de marque** brand manager; **d. du personnel** personnel manager; **d. de production** production manager; **d. de produit** product manager; **d. de projet** project director/manager; **d. de la publicité** advertising director/manager; **d. de recherche et développement** research and development director/manager; **d. de recherche marketing** marketing research director/manager; **d. régional** regional manager; **d. des relations publiques** public relations director/manager; **d. des ressources humaines** human resources manager; **d. de service** head of department; **d. des services techniques** technical director; **d. de succursale** branch manager; **d. technique** technical manager; **d. des ventes** sales director/manager; **d. de la vente-marketing** sales and marketing director/manager
2 *Admin & Pol* director; **d. de prison** prison *Br* governor *or Am* warden; **d. de cabinet** *Br* ≃ principal private secretary, *Am* ≃ chief of staff
3 *Scol Br* head teacher, *Am* principal
4 *Univ (d'un département)* head of department; **d. de recherche** supervisor; **d. de thèse** (thesis) supervisor
5 *Cin, Théât & TV* director; **d. d'antenne** station director; **d. artistique** artistic director; **d. de casting** casting director; **d. des effets spéciaux** special effects supervisor; **d. musical** musical director; **d. de la photographie** cinematographer, director of photography; **d. des programmes** director of programming, programme controller; **d. de scène** stage director; **d. du son** sound director
6 *Journ* **d. éditorial** publishing manager; **d. de la fabrication** production manager; **d. de la rédaction** managing editor
NM **1** *Hist* Director
2 *Rel* **d. spirituel** *ou* **de conscience** spiritual director
▫ **directrice** NF *Math* directrix

directif, -ive [dirɛktif, -iv] ADJ **1** *(entretien, méthode)* directive **2** *(antenne, micro)* directional
3 *(personne)* authoritarian; **elle est très directive** she's always giving orders
▫ **directive** NF *Admin, Mil & Pol* directive
▫ **directives** NFPL orders, instructions

direction [dirɛksjɔ̃] NF **1** *(fonction de chef → d'une entreprise)* management, managing; *(→ d'un parti)* leadership; *(→ d'un orchestre)* conducting, *Am* direction; *(→ d'un journal)* editorship; *(→ d'une équipe sportive)* captaincy; **prendre la d. de** *(société, usine)* to take over the running *or* management of; *(journal)* to take over the editorship of; **se voir confier la d. d'une société/d'un journal/d'un lycée** to be appointed manager of a firm/chief editor of a newspaper/head of a school; **avoir la d. d'une entreprise** to manage a company; **orchestre (placé) sous la d. de** orchestra conducted by; **d. commerciale** sales management; **d. des crédits** credit management; **d. des entreprises** business management; **d. export** export management; **d. financière** financial management; **d. générale** general management, senior management; **d. par objectifs** management by objectives; **d. de la production** production control; **d. des ventes** sales management
2 *(organisation → de travaux)* supervision; *(→ d'un débat)* chairing, conducting; *(→ de la circulation, des opérations)* directing; **c'est lui qui a pris la d. des opérations** he took charge of operations
3 *(maîtrise, cadres)* **la d.** the management; **la d. refuse toute discussion avec les syndicats** (the) management refuses to talk to the unions; *Admin* **d. centrale** = headquarters of a branch of the civil service
4 *(bureau)* manager's office
5 *(sens)* direction, way; **dans la même d.** the same way, in the same direction; **dans la d. opposée** in the opposite direction; **il est parti dans la d. de la gare** he went towards the station; **il a lancé la balle dans ma d.** he threw the ball towards me; **vous êtes dans la bonne d.** you're going the right way; **engagé dans une mauvaise d.** heading the wrong way; **vous allez dans quelle d.?** which way are you going?, where are you heading for?; **quelle d. ont-ils prise?** which way did they go?; **prenez la d. Nation** *(dans le métro)* take the Nation line; **toutes/autres directions** *(panneau sur la route)* all/other directions; **partir dans toutes les directions** *(coureurs, ballons)* to scatter; *(pétards)* to go off in all directions; *(conversation)* to wander; **la discussion a pris une tout autre d.** the discussion took a different turn *or* shifted to another subject
6 *Cin, Théât & TV* **d. (d'acteurs)** directing, direction
7 *Aut & Tech* steering; **la d. du vélo est faussée** the bicycle's handlebars are out of true; **d. assistée** power steering; **d. à crémaillère** rack and pinion steering; **d. mécanique** manual steering
8 *(service)* department; **d. du contentieux** legal department; **D. départementale de l'action sanitaire et sociale** = office administering health and social services at regional level; **D. départementale de l'équipement** = local government body responsible for public works; **d. de l'exploitation** operations department; **D. générale des Impôts** *Br* ≃ Inland Revenue, *Am* ≃ Internal Revenue; *Admin* **D. générale de la santé** = central administrative body for health and social services; **D. générale de la sécurité extérieure** = arm of the Defence Ministry in charge of international intelligence, *Br* ≃ MI6, *Am* ≃ CIA; *Admin* **D. des hôpitaux** = central government office for hospital administration; **d. marketing** marketing department; **d. du personnel** personnel department; **D. régionale de l'environnement** = local government body in charge of environmental issues; **D. de la surveillance du territoire** = internal state security department, *Br* ≃ MI5, *Am* ≃ CIA; **d. du trésor** finance department
9 *Ordinat* **d. systématisée** systems management
▫ **de direction** ADJ *(équipe)* managerial
▫ **en direction de** PRÉP in the direction of, towards; **embouteillages en d. de Paris** hold-ups for Paris-bound traffic; **les trains/avions/vols en d. de Marseille** trains/planes/flights to Marseilles; **jeter un regard en d. de qn** to cast a glance at *or* towards sb; **il a tiré en d. des policiers** he fired at the policemen

directionnel, -elle [dirɛksjɔnɛl] ADJ directional
directive [dirɛktiv] *voir* **directif**
directivisme [dirɛktivism] NM *Péj* authoritarianism
directivité [dirɛktivite] NF **1** *(d'une politique)* authoritative nature **2** *Électron* directivity
directo [dirɛkto] ADV *Fam* straight, right; **ça va d. à la poubelle** it's going straight in the bin
directoire [dirɛktwar] NM *Admin & Com* directorate, board of directors
▫ **Directoire** NM **le D.** the (French) Directory; **meuble D.** piece of Directoire furniture; **style D.** Directoire style
directorat [dirɛktɔra] NM **1** *Admin, Scol & Théât* directorate, directorship **2** *Com* managership
directorial, -e, -aux, -ales [dirɛktɔrjal, -o] ADJ **1** *(fonction, pouvoir)* managerial, executive, directorial; **le bureau d.** the executive suite *or* manager's office **2** *Hist* Directory *(avant n)*, of the Directory
directrice [dirɛktris] *voir* **directeur**
DiREN [dirɛn] NF *(abrév* **Direction régionale de l'environnement***)* = local government body in charge of environmental issues
dirham [diram] NM dirham
dirigé, -e [diriʒe] ADJ *(monnaie)* managed, controlled; *(économie)* controlled, planned
dirigeable [diriʒabl] ADJ dirigible
NM airship, dirigible
dirigeant, -e [diriʒɑ̃, -ɑ̃t] ADJ *(classes)* ruling; *(cadres)* managing
NM,F *Pol (d'un parti)* leader; *(d'un pays)* ruler, leader; *(d'une entreprise)* manager; **d. syndical** union leader; **les dirigeants d'une entreprise** the management of a company

DIRIGER [17] [diriʒe]

> VT to run **1** ▪ to manage **1, 2** ▪ to be in charge of **1** ▪ to supervise **2** ▪ to direct **1–4, 6, 7** ▪ to steer **4** ▪ to send **5** ▪ to aim **8**
> USAGE ABSOLU to be a good manager
> VPR to head for **1** ▪ to find one's way **2**

VT **1** *(être à la tête de → usine, entreprise)* to run, to manage; *(→ personnel, équipe)* to manage; *(→ service, département)* to be in charge of, to be head of; *(→ école)* to be head of; *(→ orchestre)* to conduct, *Am* to direct; *(→ journal)* to edit; *(→ pays)* to run; *(→ parti, mouvement)* to lead; **une firme bien dirigée** a well-managed *or* well-run firm; **mal d. une société** to mismanage a company
2 *(superviser → travaux)* to supervise, to manage, to oversee; *(→ débat)* to conduct; *(→ thèse, recherches)* to supervise, to oversee, to direct; *(→ circulation)* to direct; *(→ opérations)* to direct, to oversee; **ceux qui veulent d. les consciences** those who would influence other people's moral choices
3 *Cin, Théât & TV* to direct
4 *(piloter → voiture)* to steer; *(→ bateau)* to navigate, to steer; *(→ avion)* to fly, to pilot; *(→ cheval)* to drive; *(guider → aveugle)* to guide; *(→ dans une démarche)* to direct, to steer; **d. qn vers la sortie** to direct sb to the exit; **on vous a mal dirigé** you were misdirected; **d. les troupes vers le front** to move the troops up to the front; **un véhicule difficile à d. sur route verglacée** a vehicle which is hard to handle on an icy road; **d. un étranger dans le dédale administratif** to guide *or* to help a foreigner through the red tape; **elle a été mal dirigée dans son choix de carrière** she had poor career guidance; **d. un élève vers**

un cursus littéraire to guide *or* to steer a student towards an arts course; *Fig* **l'appât du gain dirige tous ses actes** the lure of gain motivates everything he does

5 (*acheminer → marchandises*) to send; (→ *investissements, fonds*) to channel (**vers** to); **d. des colis sur** *ou* **vers la Belgique** to send parcels to Belgium; **je fais d. mes appels sur mon autre numéro** I have my calls redirected *or* rerouted to my other number

6 (*orienter → pensée*) to direct; **d. son regard vers qn** to look in the direction of sb; **tous les yeux étaient dirigés sur elle** everyone was staring at her; **d. la conversation sur un autre sujet** to steer the conversation on to *or* to switch the conversation to a new subject; **d. ses espoirs vers qn** to pin one's hopes on *or* to vest one's hopes in sb; *aussi Fig* **d. ses pas vers** to head for

7 (*adresser hostilement*) to level, to direct; **d. des accusations contre qn** to level accusations at sb; **leurs moqueries étaient dirigées contre lui** he was the butt of their jokes

8 (*braquer → arme*) to aim; **il dirigea son télescope sur la lune** he trained his telescope on the moon; **une antenne dirigée vers la tour Eiffel** an aerial trained on the Eiffel tower; **lorsque la flèche est dirigée vers la droite** when the arrow points to the right; **d. un canon vers** *ou* **sur une cible** to aim *or* to level *or* to point a cannon at a target; **d. une arme sur qn** to aim a weapon at *or* to train a weapon on sb

USAGE ABSOLU **savoir d.** to be a good manager

▶**se diriger** VPR**1** (*aller*) **se d. sur** *ou* **vers** (*frontière*) to head *or* to make for; **se d. vers la sortie** to make one's way to the exit; **les voitures se dirigent vers la ligne d'arrivée** the cars are heading for the finish; *Fig* **les pourparlers se dirigent vers un compromis** the discussions are moving towards a compromise; *Fig* **nous nous dirigeons vers le conflit armé** we're headed for armed conflict

2 (*trouver son chemin*) to find one's way; **l'avion a réussi à se d. dans la tempête** the plane found its way through the storm; **un animal qui sait se d. dans le noir** an animal which can find its way in the dark; **savoir se d. dans une ville** to be able to find one's way round a city; **on apprend aux élèves à se d. dans leurs études** pupils are taught to take charge of their own studies

---

dirigisme [diriʒism] NM state control, state intervention

dirigiste [diriʒist] ADJ interventionist
     NMF partisan of state control

dirimant, -e [dirimɑ̃, -ɑ̃t] ADJ *Jur* diriment, nullifying; **cause dirimante de mariage** diriment impediment to marriage

dirlo [dirlo] NMF *Fam Arg scol Br* head ▪, *Am* principal ▪

disaccharide [disakarid] NM *Chim* disaccharide

disait *etc voir* **dire²**

discal, -e, -aux, -ales [diskal, -o] ADJ discal

discarthrose [diskartroz] NF *Méd* intervertebral disc arthrosis

discernable [disɛrnabl] ADJ discernible, perceptible

discernement [disɛrnəmɑ̃] NM **1** (*intelligence*) (good) judgement, *Sout* discernment; **il a agi avec d.** he showed (good) judgement in what he did **2** (*distinction*) distinguishing; **il est difficile de faire le d. entre ce qui est juste et ce qui ne l'est pas** it's difficult to distinguish between what is just and what is unjust

discerner [3] [disɛrne] VT **1** (*voir*) to discern, to distinguish, to make out; **on discernait à peine les contours** you could just make out the outline

2 (*deviner*) to discern, to perceive, to detect; **j'ai cru d. une certaine colère dans sa voix** I thought I could detect a hint of anger in his/her voice; **d. les motivations de qn** to see through sb

3 (*différencier*) **d. le bien du mal** to distinguish between right and wrong, to tell *or* distinguish right from wrong

disciple [disipl] NM **1** *Rel & Scol* disciple **2** (*partisan*) follower, disciple

---

disciplinable [disiplinabl] ADJ disciplinable, liable to be disciplined

disciplinaire [disiplinɛr] ADJ disciplinary

disciplinairement [disiplinɛrmɑ̃] ADV through the code of discipline

discipline [disiplin] NF **1** (*règlement*) discipline

2 (*obéissance*) discipline; **avoir de la d.** to be disciplined; **maintenir la d.** to maintain discipline; **il sait faire régner la d. dans sa classe** he maintains strict discipline in his classes; **faire grève par d. syndicale** to join an official strike; **d. alimentaire** observance of one's diet; **d. de vote** voting discipline

3 *Scol & Univ* (*matière*) subject, discipline

4 (*fouet*) discipline, whip, scourge

discipliné, -e [disipline] ADJ **1** (*personne*) obedient, disciplined **2** (*cheveux*) neat (and tidy), well-groomed

discipliner [3] [disipline] VT **1** (*faire obéir → élèves, classe*) to discipline, to (bring under) control **2** (*maîtriser → instincts*) to control, to master; (→ *pensée*) to discipline, to train **3** (*endiguer → rivière*) to control **4** (*coiffer → cheveux*) to groom

▶**se discipliner** VPR to discipline oneself

disc-jockey [diskʒɔkɛ] (*pl* **disc-jockeys**) NMF disc jockey

disco [disko] ADJ disco; **musique d.** disco (music) NM (*musique*) disco (music); (*danse, chanson*) disco number
     NF *Fam Vieilli* (*discothèque*) disco

discobole [diskɔbɔl] NM *Antiq* discobolus, discobolos

'**Le Discobole'** *Myron* 'Discobolus' *or* 'The Discus Thrower'

discographie [diskɔgrafi] NF discography; **avoir une importante d.** to have made many recordings, to have recorded many pieces

discographique [diskɔgrafik] ADJ (*rubrique, production*) record (*avant n*)

discoïde [diskɔid], **discoïdal, -e, -aux, -ales** [diskɔidal, -o] ADJ discoid, discoidal

discompte [diskɔ̃t] = **discount**

discompter [diskɔ̃te] = **discounter¹**

discompteur [diskɔ̃tœr] = **discounter²**

discomycète [diskɔmisɛt] *Bot* NM discomycete
     ▫ **discomycètes** NMPL Discomycetes

discontinu, -e [diskɔ̃tiny] ADJ **1** (*ligne*) broken; (*effort*) discontinuous, intermittent; **le bruit est d.** the noise occurs on and off **2** *Ling & Math* discontinuous
     NM **le d.** that which is discontinuous
     ▫ **discontinue** NF (*consonne*) stop (consonant)

discontinuer [7] [diskɔ̃tinɥe] VT *Littéraire* to stop, to cease
     VI *Littéraire* to stop, to cease
     ▫ **sans discontinuer** ADV nonstop, continuously; **il peut parler des heures sans d.** he can talk for hours nonstop *or* on end

discontinuité [diskɔ̃tinɥite] NF (*gén*) & *Math* discontinuity

disconvenance [diskɔ̃vnɑ̃s] NF *Littéraire* (*de climat, d'activité*) unsuitableness, unfitness; (*entre des personnes, des objets*) disparity, dissimilarity; **d. de mots** incongruity of terms, mixed metaphor; **d. de construction** (*d'une phrase*) faulty construction; **d. d'âge entre deux personnes** disproportion in age between two people

disconvenant, -e [diskɔ̃vnɑ̃, -ɑ̃t] ADJ *Littéraire* incongruous, disproportionate

disconvenir [40] [diskɔ̃vnir] **disconvenir de** VT IND **je ne disconviens pas de son utilité** I don't deny its being useful *or* its usefulness; **vous avez raison, je n'en disconviens pas** I don't deny that you're right

discopathie [diskɔpati] NF lesion of an intervertebral disc

discophile [diskɔfil] NMF record collector, *Spéc* discophile

discophilie [diskɔfili] NF record collecting

discord [diskɔr] *Vieilli* ADJ M *Mus* (*instrument*) out of tune; *Fig* **esprit d.** inconsequent mind
     NM *Vieilli ou Littéraire* discord, dispute

discordance [diskɔrdɑ̃s] NF **1** *Mus* discord, discordance, disharmony

2 (*disharmonie → de couleurs, de sentiments*)

---

lack of harmony, clash; (→ *entre des personnes, idées*) clash, conflict, disagreement

3 (*écart*) contradiction, inconsistency; **il existe certaines discordances entre les deux récits** the two stories contain several inconsistencies

4 *Géol* discordance, discordancy, unconformability

5 *Psy* dissociation

discordant, -e [diskɔrdɑ̃, -ɑ̃t] ADJ **1** (*son → faux*) discordant; (→ *criard*) harsh, grating **2** (*opposé → styles, couleurs, avis, diagnostics*) clashing; **ils ont présenté des témoignages discordants** their testimonies were at variance with each other **3** *Géol* discordant, unconformable

discorde [diskɔrd] NF discord, dissension, dissention

discorder [3] [diskɔrde] VI (*couleurs, témoignages*) to clash (**avec** with); **sa voix discorde dans l'orchestre** his/her voice clashes with the orchestra

discothécaire [diskɔtekɛr] NMF record librarian

discothèque [diskɔtɛk] NF **1** (*collection*) record collection **2** (*meuble*) record case *or* holder **3** (*établissement de prêt*) record *or* music library **4** (*boîte de nuit*) disco, discotheque, night club

discount [diskunt, diskaunt] NM **1** (*rabais*) discount; **un d. de 20 pour cent** 20 percent discount, 20 percent off **2** (*technique*) discount selling; **magasin de d.** discount *Br* shop *or* *Am* store
     ADJ INV discount (*avant n*); **des épiceries/prix d.** discount groceries/prices

discounter¹ [3] [diskunte, diskaunte] VT to sell at a discount
     VI to sell at a discount

discounter² [diskuntœr, diskauntɛr] NM (*commerçant*) discounter; **d. spécialisé** category killer

discoureur, -euse [diskurœr, -øz] NM,F *Péj* speechifier; **méfie-toi, c'est un grand d.** watch out, he loves the sound of his own voice

discourir [45] [diskurir] VI **1** *Littéraire* (*bavarder*) to talk **2** *Péj* (*disserter*) to speechify; **d. à perte de vue sur l'avenir** to talk endlessly about the future

discours [diskur] NM **1** (*allocution*) speech, address; **faire un d.** to make a speech; **d. de bienvenue** welcoming speech *or* address; **d. de clôture** closing speech; **d. d'inauguration** inaugural lecture *or* speech; **d.-programme** keynote speech; **d. de réception** acceptance speech; *Pol* **d. du trône** inaugural speech (*of a sovereign before a Parliamentary session*), *Br* ≃ King's/Queen's Speech; **le d. sur l'État de l'Union** the State of the Union Speech

2 *Péj* (*bavardage*) chatter; **se perdre en longs d.** to talk *or* to chatter endlessly; **tous ces (beaux) d. ne servent à rien** all this fine talk doesn't get us anywhere; **rien de concret, que des d.!** nothing concrete, just (a lot of) words!

3 *Ling* (*langage réalisé*) speech; (*unité supérieure à la phrase*) discourse; *Gram* **d. direct** direct speech; *Gram* **d. indirect** reported *or* indirect speech; **d. rapporté** reported speech

4 *Phil* discourse

5 (*expression d'une opinion*) discourse; **le d. des jeunes** the sorts of things young people say; **tenir un d. de droite** to talk like a right-winger

'**Discours de la méthode'** *Descartes* 'Discourse on Method'

discourtois, -e [diskurtwa, -az] ADJ discourteous, impolite

discourtoisement [diskurtwazmɑ̃] ADV discourteously, impolitely

discourtoisie [diskurtwazi] NF discourtesy

discouru, -e [diskury] PP *voir* **discourir**

discrédit [diskredi] NM discredit, disrepute; **le d. attaché à cette entreprise** this firm's discredited reputation; **être en d. auprès de qn** to be in disfavour with sb; **jeter le d. sur qn/qch** to discredit sb/sth; **tomber dans le d.** to fall into disrepute

discréditer [3] [diskredite] VT to discredit, to bring into disrepute

▶**se discréditer** VPR **1** (*personne*) to bring discredit upon oneself; **se d. auprès du public** to

lose one's good name **2** *(idée, pratique)* to become discredited (**auprès de** in the eyes of)

discret, -ète [diskrɛ, -ɛt] **ADJ 1** *(réservé → personne, attitude)* reserved, discreet; **de manière discrète** discreetly

2 *(délicat → personne)* tactful, discreet, diplomatic; *(→ allusion)* subtle

3 *(qui garde le secret)* discreet; **sois sans inquiétude, je serai d.** don't worry, I'll be discreet

4 *(effacé → personne, manières)* unobtrusive, unassuming

5 *(dissimulé)* **sous emballage d.** in a plain wrapper; **envoi d., sous pli d.** under plain cover

6 *(neutre → toilette, style)* plain, sober, understated; *(→ couleur)* subtle; *(→ lumière)* subdued, soft; *(→ parfum)* subtle; *(→ maquillage)* light, subtle

7 *(isolé → lieu)* quiet, secluded; **ils ont choisi une auberge discrète** they chose an inn where they could have some privacy

8 *Math* discrete

discrètement [diskrɛtmɑ̃] **ADV 1** *(sans être remarqué)* quietly, discreetly, unobtrusively; **entrer/sortir d.** to slip in/out (unobtrusively); **je lui en parlerai d.** I'll have a quiet word with him/her **2** *(se maquiller, se parfumer)* discreetly, lightly, subtly; *(s'habiller)* discreetly, quietly, soberly

discrétion [diskresjɔ̃] **NF 1** *(réserve)* discretion, tact, tactfulness; **manquer de d.** to be tactless

2 *(modestie)* unobtrusiveness, self-effacement

3 *(sobriété → d'un maquillage)* lightness, subtlety; *(→ d'une toilette)* soberness; **s'habiller avec d.** to dress soberly

4 *(silence)* discretion; **comptez sur ma d.** you can count on my discretion; **d. assurée** *(dans une petite annonce)* write in confidence

❑ **à discrétion ADV vous pouvez manger à d.** you can eat as much as you like; **champagne à d.** unlimited champagne

❑ **à la discrétion de PRÉP** at the discretion of; **pourboire à la d. du client** gratuities at the discretion of the customer

discrétionnaire [diskresjɔnɛr] **ADJ** discretionary

discrètos [diskrɛtɔs] **ADV** *Fam* on the quiet

discriminant, -e [diskriminɑ̃, -ɑ̃t] **ADJ** distinguishing, discriminating

NM discriminant

discrimination [diskriminasjɔ̃] **NF 1** *(ségrégation)* **d. fondée sur le sexe** gender discrimination; **d. positive** *Br* positive discrimination, *Am* affirmative action; **d. raciale/sexuelle** racial/sexual discrimination; **d. à rebours** reverse discrimination; **sans d. de race ni de sexe** regardless of race or sex, without discrimination on the grounds of race or sex

2 *Littéraire (distinction)* discrimination, distinction; **opérer la d. entre deux choses** to distinguish between two things

discriminatoire [diskriminatwar] **ADJ** discriminatory

discriminer [3] [diskrimine] **VT** *Littéraire* to distinguish between

disculpation [diskylpasjɔ̃] **NF** exoneration; **sa d. n'a pas été facile à obtenir** it was not easy to clear him/her *or* to prove him/her innocent

disculper [3] [diskylpe] **VT** to exonerate (**de** from)

▸**se disculper VPR pour se d. il invoqua l'ignorance** to vindicate *or* to exonerate himself, he pleaded ignorance; **se d. de qch** to exonerate oneself from sth

discursif, -ive [diskyrsif, -iv] **ADJ 1** *(raisonné)* discursive **2** *Ling* discourse *(avant n)*

discussion [diskysjɔ̃] **NF 1** *(négociation)* talk, discussion; **avec lui la d. est impossible** he's incapable of compromise

2 *(querelle)* quarrel, argument; **pas de d.!** no arguing!, don't argue!; **il s'exécuta sans d.** he complied without arguing

3 *(débat)* debate, discussion; **ils sont en pleine d.** they're in the middle of a debate; **la question de l'avortement donne matière** *ou* **est sujet à d.** the issue of abortion lends itself to debate; **le projet de budget est en d.** the budget proposal is under discussion

4 *(conversation)* discussion, conversation; **dans la d., il m'a dit que...** during our conversation, he told me that...

discutable [diskytabl] **ADJ** *(fait, théorie, décision)* debatable, questionable; *(sincérité, authenticité)* questionable, doubtful; *(goût)* dubious

discutailler [3] [diskytaje] **VI** *Fam Péj* to quibble

discutailleur, -euse [diskytajœr, -øz] **ADJ** *Fam Péj* **il est très d.** he's a real quibbler

discuté, -e [diskyte] **ADJ 1** *(débattu)* debated, discussed; **très d.** hotly debated **2** *(contesté → nomination)* controversial, disputed; **une œuvre à l'authenticité discutée** a work of art whose authenticity is the subject of controversy *or* is disputed

discuter [3] [diskyte] **VT 1** *(débattre → projet de loi)* to debate, to discuss; *(→ sujet, question)* to discuss, to argue, to consider; *Fam* **d. le coup** to have a chat

2 *(contester → ordres)* to question, to dispute; *(→ véracité)* to debate, to question; *(→ prix)* to haggle over; **un penalty qu'on discute encore** a penalty which they're still arguing about

USAGE ABSOLU cesse de d., avance! don't argue *or* no arguing, move on!; **suis-moi sans d.** follow me without any arguments, follow me and don't argue; **tu discutes?** *Br* no ifs and buts!, *Am* no ifs, ands or buts!; **inutile de d., je ne céderai pas** it's no use arguing, I'm not going to give in

VI 1 *(parler)* to talk, to have a discussion; **on ne peut pas d. avec toi** it's impossible to have a discussion with you; **d. de** *ou* **sur** to talk about, to discuss; **nous en avons longuement discuté** we've had a long discussion about it; **d. de choses et d'autres** to talk about this and that; **d. du sexe des anges** to discuss futilities

2 *(négocier)* to negotiate

▸**se discuter VPR 1** *(sujet, question)* to be debated; **le projet de loi se discute actuellement à l'Assemblée** the bill is being debated *or* is under discussion in the Assembly

2 *(point de vue)* **ça se discute** that's debatable

discuteur, -euse [diskytœr, -øz] **NM,F** arguer

dise *etc voir* **dire**[2]

disert, -e [dizɛr, -ɛrt] **ADJ** *Littéraire* articulate, eloquent, fluent

disertement [dizɛrtəmɑ̃] **ADV** *Littéraire* articulately, eloquently, fluently

disette [dizɛt] **NF 1** *(pénurie → gén)* shortage, dearth; *(→ de nourriture)* scarcity of food, food shortage **2** *Littéraire (manque)* **d. d'argent** want *or* lack of money; **d. d'eau** drought

disetteux, -euse [dizɛtø, -øz] *Vieilli* **ADJ** *(indigent)* destitute; *(qui manque de nourriture)* hungry

NM,F *(indigent)* destitute person; *(qui manque de nourriture)* hungry person

diseur, -euse [dizœr, -øz] **NM,F d. de bons mots** wit; **fin d.** fine talker; *Prov* **les grands diseurs ne sont pas les grands faiseurs** = those who talk most aren't necessarily those who get things done

❑ **diseuse NF diseuse de bonne aventure** fortune-teller

disgrâce [disgras] **NF 1** *(défaveur)* disgrace, disfavour; **la d. d'un homme politique** a politician's disgrace; *Littéraire* **encourir la d. de qn** to incur sb's displeasure; **tomber en d.** to fall into disfavour, to fall from grace **2** *Littéraire (manque de grâce)* inelegance, awkwardness

disgracié, -e [disgrasje] **ADJ 1** *(laid)* ungraceful, ugly **2** *(en disgrâce)* disgraced

disgracier [9] [disgrasje] **VT** *Littéraire* to disgrace

disgracieux, -euse [disgrasjø, -øz] **ADJ 1** *(laid → visage)* ugly, unattractive; *(→ geste)* awkward, ungainly; *(→ comportement)* uncouth; *(→ personne)* unattractive, unappealing; *(→ objet)* unsightly **2** *Littéraire (discourtois)* ungracious, discourteous

disharmonie [dizarmɔni] **NF 1** *(manque d'harmonie)* disharmony **2** *Géol* disharmonic structure

disjoindre [82] [disʒwɛ̃dr] **VT 1** *(planches)* to break up; **d. les pierres d'un mur** to break up a stone wall **2** *(causes, problèmes)* to separate, to consider separately; **il faudrait d. ces deux questions** these two questions should be considered separately

▸**se disjoindre VPR** to come apart

disjoint, -e [disʒwɛ̃, -ɛ̃t] **ADJ 1** *(planches)* disjointed **2** *(causes, problèmes)* unconnected, separate **3** *Math* disjoint **4** *Mus* disjunct

disjoncter [3] [disʒɔ̃kte] **VT** *(circuit)* to break

VI to short-circuit; **ça a fait d. tout le circuit** it blew the whole circuit; *Fam* **il disjoncte complètement** he's cracking up, he's losing it

disjoncteur [disʒɔ̃ktœr] **NM** circuit breaker, cutout (switch), trip switch

disjonctif, -ive [disʒɔ̃ktif, -iv] **ADJ** disjunctive

NM disjunctive

disjonction [disʒɔ̃ksjɔ̃] **NF 1** *Biol* disjunction **2** *Jur* **d. d'instance** disjoinder of proceedings

disjonctive [disʒɔ̃ktiv] *voir* **disjonctif**

dislocation [dislɔkasjɔ̃] **NF 1** *(d'une caisse)* breaking up; *(d'un empire)* dismantling; *(d'un parti)* breaking up, disintegration; *(d'une manifestation)* breaking up, dispersal **2** *Méd & Phys* dislocation **3** *(contorsion)* contorsion **4** *Géol* fault

disloquer [3] [dislɔke] **VT 1** *(caisse)* to take to pieces, to break up; *(poupée)* to pull apart; *(corps)* to mangle

2 *(faire éclater → empire)* to dismantle; *(→ parti)* to break up

3 *Méd* to dislocate

▸**se disloquer VPR 1** *(meuble)* to come *or* to fall apart, to fall to pieces

2 *(fédération)* to disintegrate, to break up; *(empire)* to break up

3 *(se disperser → manifestation)* to disperse, to break up

4 *Méd (articulation)* to be dislocated; **se d. l'épaule** to dislocate one's shoulder

5 *(se contorsionner)* to contort oneself

disneylandisation [disnɛlɑ̃dizasjɔ̃] **NF** *(d'un lieu, de l'histoire, de la culture)* Disneyfication

disneylandiser [3] [disnɛlɑ̃dize] **VT** *(lieu, histoire, culture)* to Disneyfy

disparaître [91] [disparɛtr] **VI 1** *(se dissiper → peur, joie)* to evaporate, to fade, to disappear; *(→ douleur, problème, odeur)* to disappear; *(→ bruit)* to stop, to subside; *(→ brouillard)* to clear, to vanish; **faire d. qch** *(gén)* to remove sth; *(supprimer)* to get rid of sth; **ce médicament a fait d. ma migraine** the medicine got rid of my migraine; **fais-moi d. cette horreur!** get that revolting thing out of my sight!; **il a fait d. tous mes doutes** he dispelled all my doubts; *Com* **tout doit d.** everything must go

2 *(devenir invisible → soleil, lune)* to disappear; *(→ côte, bateau)* to vanish, to disappear; **les rues ont disparu sous la neige** the roads have disappeared under the snow; **le soleil disparut à l'horizon** the sun disappeared below the horizon; **elle a disparu dans la foule** she vanished into the crowd; *Fam* **disparais, je t'ai assez vu** clear off, I've had enough of you

3 *(être inexplicablement absent)* to disappear, to vanish; **le temps que j'arrive, la clef/ma sœur avait disparu** by the time I got there, the key/my sister had disappeared; **la petite fille a disparu il y a une semaine** the little girl disappeared *or* went missing a week ago; **son mari a disparu (sans laisser d'adresse)** her husband has absconded; **d. sans laisser de traces** to disappear *or* vanish without trace; **faire d. qn/qch** to conceal sb/sth; *Hum* **où est-ce que tu as encore fait d. les clés?** where have you hidden the keys now?; *Fam* **d. de la circulation** *ou* **dans la nature** to vanish into thin air

4 *(ne plus exister → espèce, race)* to die out, to become extinct; *(→ langue, coutume)* to die out, to disappear; *(mourir)* to pass away, to die; *Euph* **faire d. qn** to eliminate sb, to have sb removed; **d. en mer** to be lost at sea

disparate [disparat] **ADJ 1** *(hétérogène → objets, éléments)* disparate, dissimilar **2** *(mal accordé → mobilier)* ill-assorted, non-matching; *(→ couleurs)* clashing; *(→ couple)* ill-assorted, ill-matched; **deux chaises disparates** two chairs that don't match

NF *Littéraire & Vieilli* **la d.** the ill-assorted character *or* nature

disparation [disparasjɔ̃] **NF** *Opt* **d. rétinienne** disparation

disparité [disparite] **NF** disparity; **une d. entre deux éléments** a disparity between two elements; **d. de** *(sommes d'argent)* disparity in

disparition [disparisjɔ̃] **NF 1** *(du brouillard)* lifting, clearing; *(du soleil)* sinking, setting; *(d'une côte, d'un bateau)* vanishing; *(de la peur, du bruit)* fading away; *(du doute)* disappearance; **frotter jusqu'à d. des taches** rub until the stains disappear; **à prendre jusqu'à d. de la douleur**

to be taken until the pain disappears *or* stops

2 *(absence → d'une personne, d'un porte-monnaie)* disappearance; **depuis la d. du bébé** since the baby went missing *or* disappeared; **j'ai remarqué la d. de ma carte de crédit deux jours plus tard** I first missed my credit card two days later

3 *(extinction → d'une espèce)* extinction; *(→ d'une langue, d'une culture)* dying out, disappearance

4 *(mort)* death, disappearance; **après sa d.** after his/her death

5 *Cin & TV* **d. en fondu** fade; **d. graduelle** fade-away, fade-out

'La Disparition' *Perec* 'A Void'

disparu, -e [dispary] **PP** *voir* **disparaître**

ADJ 1 *(mort)* dead; **porté d.** *(soldat)* missing (in action); *(marin)* lost at sea; *(passager, victime)* missing believed dead

2 *(espèce)* extinct; *(langue)* dead; *(coutume, culture)* vanished, dead; *(ère, époque)* bygone

NM,F 1 *(défunt)* dead person; **les disparus** the dead; **les disparus en mer** *(marins)* men lost at sea; **nos chers disparus** our dear departed

2 *(personne introuvable)* missing person; **cent vingt morts et plus de cinquante disparus** a hundred and twenty dead and more than fifty unaccounted for *or* missing

dispatcher[1] [dispatʃœr] **NM** dispatcher

dispatcher[2] [3] [dispatʃe] **VT** *(produits)* to distribute; *(personnes)* to spread out

dispatching [dispatʃiŋ] **NM** *(du courrier)* routing

dispendieuse [dispɑ̃djøz] *voir* **dispendieux**

dispendieusement [dispɑ̃djøzmɑ̃] **ADV** *Littéraire* extravagantly, expensively

dispendieux, -euse [dispɑ̃djø, -øz] **ADJ** *Littéraire* expensive, costly

dispensable [dispɑ̃sabl] **ADJ** *Jur* liable to be exempted

dispensaire [dispɑ̃sɛr] **NM** clinic

dispensateur, -trice [dispɑ̃satœr, -tris] **NM,F** dispenser

dispense [dispɑ̃s] **NF 1** *(exemption)* exemption; **d. d'oral/du service militaire** exemption from an oral exam/from military service **2** *(certificat)* exemption certificate **3** *(autorisation spéciale)* **d. d'âge** = special permission for people under or over the age limit **4** *Jur* **d. de peine** dismissal of charges **5** *Rel* dispensation

dispenser [3] [dispɑ̃se] **VT 1** *(exempter)* **d. qn de qch/de faire qch** to exempt sb from sth/from doing sth; **il est dispensé de service militaire** he is exempt *or* exempted from military service; **se faire d. de gymnastique** to be excused (from) gym; **je vous dispense de me rendre un rapport cette fois** I'll excuse you from writing me a report this time; **cela ne te dispense pas de payer** this doesn't exempt you from paying; **je te dispense de tes sarcasmes** spare me your sarcasm; **je vous dispense de vos commentaires** you can keep your remarks to yourself

2 *Rel* **d. qn de qch** to release sb from sth

3 *(donner → charité)* to dispense, to administer; *(→ parole)* to utter; **d. des soins aux malades** to provide patients with medical care

▸**se dispenser VPR se d. de** *(obligation)* to get out of; **je me dispenserais bien de cette corvée!** I could do without this chore!; **peut-on se d. de venir à la répétition?** is it possible to skip the rehearsal?; **un élève qui peut se d. de travailler en français** a pupil who can afford not to work at his French

dispersal, -als [dispɛrsal] **NM** *Aviat* apron

dispersant, -e [dispɛrsɑ̃, -ɑ̃t] **ADJ** dispersive

NM dispersant

dispersé, -e [dispɛrse] **ADJ 1** *(famille, peuple)* scattered; *(habitations)* scattered, spread out **2** *Fig* **élève trop d.** *(sur bulletin de notes)* should pay more attention in class; **dans mon ancien poste j'étais trop d.** in my old job, I had too many different things to do **3** *Phys* disperse *(avant n)*

dispersement [dispɛrsəmɑ̃] **NM** dispersal

disperser [3] [dispɛrse] **VT 1** *(répandre → cendres, graines)* to scatter

2 *(brume, brouillard)* to disperse, to lift

3 *(efforts)* to dissipate; *(attention)* to divide

4 *(foule, manifestants)* to disperse, to break up, to scatter; *(collection)* to break up, to scatter

5 *(troupes)* to spread out

▸**se disperser VPR 1** *(brume, brouillard)* to lift, to disperse; *(nuages)* to disperse, to break up

2 *(manifestation, foule)* to disperse, to break up

3 *(dans son travail)* to tackle too many things at once; **la production s'est (trop) dispersée** the firm has overdiversified

dispersif, -ive [dispɛrsif, -iv] **ADJ** dispersive

dispersion [dispɛrsjɔ̃] **NF 1** *(de cendres, de débris)* scattering

2 *(de la brume)* dispersal, lifting

3 *(de troupes, de policiers)* spreading out

4 *(d'une foule, de manifestants)* dispersal

5 *(des forces, de l'énergie)* waste; *(de l'attention)* dividing; **une trop grande d. de la production** overdiversification in manufacturing

6 *Chim & Phys* dispersion

7 *Élec* **d. magnétique** magnetic leak *or* leakage

8 *(en artillerie)* **d. du tir** dispersion

9 *(en statistiques)* dispersion

10 *Pol* **d. des voix** dispersion of votes

11 *Suisse (peinture)* emulsion (paint)

dispersive [dispɛrsiv] *voir* **dispersif**

disponibilité [dispɔnibilite] **NF 1** *(d'une fourniture, d'un service)* availability; **j'aimerais réserver, quelles sont les disponibilités en juin?** I'd like to book, what's availability like in June?

2 *(liberté)* availability *(for an occupation)*; **pour élever des enfants, il faut avoir une grande d.** to bring up children you need to have a lot of time to devote to them; **d. d'esprit** open-mindedness, receptiveness; **avoir une grande d. d'esprit** to be very open-minded

3 *Admin* **mise en d.** (extended) leave; **professeur en d.** teacher on (extended) leave; **se mettre en d.** to take leave of absence

4 *Mil* **la d.** the reserve; **mettre qn en d.** to release sb temporarily from duty

5 *Jur* **d. des biens** (owner's) free disposal of property

❑ **disponibilités NFPL** *Fin* available funds, liquid assets; **disponibilités en caisse** cash in hand; **disponibilités monétaires** money supply; **disponibilités du stock** items available in stock

disponible [dispɔnibl] **ADJ 1** *(utilisable → article, service)* available; **il n'y avait plus un siège (de) d.** there weren't any seats left, no seats were available; **ces articles sont disponibles en magasin** these items can be supplied from stock; *Ordinat* **d. pour Mac/PC** available for the Mac/PC; **revenu d.** disposable income; **non d.** unavailable

2 *(libre → personne)* free, available; **êtes-vous d. ce soir?** are you free tonight?

3 *(ouvert → personne)* receptive, open-minded; **mon père a toujours été quelqu'un de d.** my father has always been ready to listen

4 *Admin* on leave of absence; *Mil* **officier d.** unattached officer, half-pay officer

5 *Fin* available

NMF *Admin* civil servant on (extended) leave of absence; *Mil* reservist

NM *Com* stock items; *Fin* liquid *or* available assets

dispos, -e [dispo, -oz] **ADJ** *(personne)* in good form *or* shape; *(esprit)* alert

disposant, -e [dispozɑ̃, -ɑ̃t] **NM,F** benefactor, *f* benefactress

disposé, -e [dispoze] **ADJ 1** *(arrangé)* **bien/mal d.** well/poorly laid out **2** *(personne)* **bien/mal d.** in a good/bad mood; **être bien/mal d. à l'égard de** *ou* **envers qn** to be well-disposed/ill-disposed towards sb

disposer [3] [dispoze] **VT 1** *(arranger → verres, assiettes)* to lay, to set; *(→ fleurs)* to arrange; *(→ meubles)* to place, to arrange; **d. des convives autour d'une table** to seat guests at a table; **d. des sentinelles autour du camp** to position sentries around the camp; **j'ai disposé la chambre autrement** I've changed the layout of the bedroom

2 *(inciter)* **d. qn à** to incline sb to *or* towards; **l'isolement me disposait à l'écriture** being on my own induced me to write; **l'heure ne dispose pas aux confidences** this is not a suitable time for sharing secrets

3 *(préparer)* **d. qn à** to prepare sb for; **ses études ne le disposent pas à la recherche** his course of studies does not prepare him for research *or* to do research; **être disposé à faire qch** to feel disposed *or* to be willing to do sth; **être peu disposé à faire qch** to be disinclined to do sth; **j'étais en retard, ce qui l'a tout de suite mal disposé à mon égard** I was late, which put him off me straightaway

VI *(partir)* **vous pouvez d.** you may leave *or* go

❑ **disposer de VT IND 1** *(avoir)* to have (at one's disposal *or* available); **nous disposons de 30 hommes pour cette mission** we have 30 men (available *or* at our disposal) for this mission; **je ne dispose que de très peu d'argent liquide** I don't have much cash (available); **les renseignements dont je dispose** the information at my disposal; **le directeur va vous recevoir, mais sachez qu'il ne dispose que de trente minutes** the manager can see you now, but he only has half an hour

2 *(utiliser)* to use; **puis-je d. de votre téléphone?** may I use your phone?; **disposez de moi comme il vous plaira** I am at your service; **croyez-vous pouvoir d. de moi?** do you think you can just use me?

3 *Jur* **d. de ses biens** to dispose of one's property

▸**se disposer VPR se d. à faire qch** to prepare to do sth; **je me disposais à partir** I was preparing to leave

dispositif [dispozitif] **NM 1** *(appareil, mécanisme)* machine, device; **d. d'alarme/de sûreté** alarm/safety device; *Ordinat* **d. d'alimentation** *(électrique)* power unit; *(pour papier)* sheet feed; **d. d'alimentation feuille à feuille** *(d'une imprimante)* cut sheet feed, stacker; **d. d'alimentation papier** *(d'une imprimante)* sheet *or* paper feed; *Aut* **d. antidémarrage** engine immobilizer; *Rad* **d. antiparasite** suppressor; *Aut* **d. d'avance centrifuge** centrifugal advance mechanism; *Électron* **d. de balayage** scanning device; **d. de commande/de manœuvre** operating/controlling gear *or* mechanism; **d. de coupure** cut-out (device); **d. d'entraînement à traction** *(d'une imprimante)* tractor feed; *Ordinat* **d. externe** external device; *Aut* **d. de préchauffage** preheater; *Tél* **d. de renvoi automatique d'appels** call-forwarding device; *Ordinat* **d. de sortie** output device; *Ordinat* **d. de stockage** storage device; *Aut* **d. de verrouillage 'sécurité enfant'** child lock; *Ordinat* **d. de visualisation** display unit

2 *(mesures)* plan, measure; **il s'agit d'un d. gouvernemental pour favoriser l'emploi des jeunes** it's a government plan to stimulate youth employment; **un important d. policier sera mis en place** there will be a large police presence

3 *Mil* plan; **d. d'attaque** plan of attack; **d. de défense** defence system

4 *Cin, Théât & TV* **d. scénique** set

5 *Jur (jugement)* sentence; *(acte, traité)* purview

disposition [dispozisjɔ̃] **NF 1** *(arrangement → de couverts)* layout; *(→ de fleurs, de livres, de meubles)* arrangement; **la d. du terrain** the lie of the land; **la d. des pièces dans notre maison** the layout of the rooms in our house; **la d. de la vitrine** the window display; *Ordinat* **d. de texte/de clavier** text/keyboard layout

2 *(fait d'arranger → des couverts)* laying out, setting; *(→ des meubles)* placing, arranging; *(→ des fleurs)* arranging

3 *(tendance → d'une personne)* tendency; **avoir une d. à la négligence/à grossir** to have a tendency to carelessness/to put on weight

4 *Jur (clause)* clause, stipulation; **les dispositions testamentaires de...** the last will and testament of...; **d. fiscale** tax provision

5 *Jur (jouissance)* disposal; **d. à titre gratuit** provision free of charge; **avoir la d. de ses biens** to be free to dispose of one's property

6 *Admin* **mise à la d.** *Br* secondment, *Am* temporary transfer

❑ **dispositions NFPL 1** *(humeur)* mood; **être dans de bonnes/mauvaises dispositions** to be in a good/bad mood; **attends qu'il soit dans** *ou* **revenu à de meilleures dispositions** wait until he's in a better mood; **être dans de bonnes dispositions pour faire qch** to be in the right mood to do *or* for doing sth; **être dans de**

bonnes/mauvaises dispositions à l'égard de qn to be well-disposed/ill-disposed towards sb

2 *(mesures)* measures; **prendre des dispositions** *(précautions, arrangements)* to make arrangements, to take steps; *(préparatifs)* to make preparations; **prends tes dispositions pour être libre ce jour-là** make arrangements *or* arrange to be free that day

3 *(aptitude)* aptitude, ability, talent; **avoir des dispositions pour** to have a talent for

❑ **à la disposition de,** *Suisse* **à disposition de** PRÉP at the disposal of; **avoir qch à sa d.** to have sth at one's disposal; **mettre** *ou* **tenir qch à la d. de qn** to place sth at sb's disposal, to make sth available to sb; **se tenir à la d. de** to make oneself available for; **je suis à votre d.** I am at your service; **je suis** *ou* **me tiens à votre entière d. pour tout autre renseignement** should you require further information, please feel free to contact me

❑ **à disposition** ADJ *Suisse* available

disproportion [disprɔpɔrsjɔ̃] NF disproportion; **d. de salaire entre deux personnes** discrepancy between two people's salaries

disproportionné, -e [disprɔpɔrsjɔne] ADJ **1** *(inégal)* disproportionate; **d.** à out of (all) proportion to; **un prix d. avec** *ou* **à la qualité** a price out of (all) proportion to the quality; **tu utilises des moyens disproportionnés au but recherché** the means you're using are out of all proportion to the end

2 *(démesuré → cou, jambes)* long; *(→ mains, yeux)* large; **avoir des jambes disproportionnées** to have disproportionately *or* abnormally long legs

dispute [dispyt] NF quarrel, argument

disputé [dispyte] ADJ **une question très disputée** a very controversial *or* hotly disputed matter; **un match très d.** a very hard-fought match; **ce poste sera très d.** there will be a lot of competition for the position; **c'est un héritage d. par tous les membres de la famille** the entire family is quarrelling over the inheritance

disputer [3] [dispyte] VT **1** *(participer à → match, tournoi)* to play; *(→ course)* to run; *(→ combat)* to fight; **d. le terrain** *Mil* to dispute every inch of ground; *Fig* to fight tooth and nail

2 *(tenter de prendre)* **d. qch à qn** to fight with sb over sth; **d. la première place à qn** to contend *or* to vie with sb for first place

3 *Fam (réprimander)* to scold, to tell off; **tu vas te faire d.!** you're in for it!

4 *Littéraire (contester)* to deny; **je ne vous dispute pas le succès de votre opération** I don't deny the success of your operation

5 *Littéraire (locution)* **nul ne le lui disputait en courage** nobody could rival his/her courage

VI *Arch (se quereller)* to quarrel, to argue, to fight

❑ **disputer de** VT IND *Littéraire* to debate, to discuss

►**se disputer** VPR **1** *(avoir lieu)* to take place; **le tournoi se disputera demain** the tournament will take place *or* will be played tomorrow

2 *(se quereller)* to quarrel, to argue, to fight; **arrêtez de vous d.!** stop fighting *or* arguing!

3 se d. qch to fight over sth; **ils se disputent le même poste** they are fighting over the same job

4 se d. avec to have an argument *or* a row with; **je me suis disputé avec Anne pour une question d'argent** I had an argument *or* a row with Anne about money

disputeur, -euse [dispytœr, -øz] *Vieilli ou Littéraire* ADJ contentious, quarrelsome

NM,F quarreller, arguer

disquaire [diskɛr] NMF **1** *(commerçant)* record dealer; **tu trouveras ça chez un d.** you'll find this in a record shop **2** *(vendeur)* record salesman, *f* saleswoman

disqualification [diskalifikasjɔ̃] NF disqualification; **risquer la d.** to risk being disqualified

disqualifier [9] [diskalifje] VT **1** *Sport* to disqualify; **l'équipe s'est fait d.** the team was disqualified **2** *(discréditer)* to discredit, to bring discredit on

►**se disqualifier** VPR to lose credibility

disque [disk] NM **1** *(cercle plat)* disc; **d. de stationnement** parking disc

2 *Anat, Astron & Math* disc; **le d. de la lune** the disc of the moon; **d. intervertébral** intervertebral disc

3 *Sport* discus

4 *Aut* **d. d'embrayage** clutch plate

5 *(enregistrement)* record, disc; **mettre un d.** to play a record; **d. audionumérique** compact disc; **d. compact** compact disc; **d. compact interactif** interactive CD, CD-I; **d. compact vidéo** video compact disc; **d. laser** laser disc; **d. vidéo** videodisc; **d. vidéo numérique** digital video disk

6 *Ordinat* disk; **d. amovible** removable disk; **d. analyseur** scanner disk; **d. cible** target disk; **d. de démarrage** boot disk; **d. de destination** destination disk; **d. dur** hard disk; **d. fixe** fixed disk; **d. magnétique** magnetic disk; **d. maître** master disk; **d. optique** optical disk; **d. optique compact** CD-ROM; **d. optique numérique** digital optical disk; **d. souple, mini d.** floppy disk; **d. source** source disk; **d. système** system disk

7 *Rail* disc signal

disquette [diskɛt] NF floppy (disk), diskette; **sur d.** on diskette, on floppy; **d. cible** target disk; **d. de copie** copy disk; **d. de démarrage** boot disk, start-up disk; **d. de démonstration,** *Fam* **d. démo** demo disk; **d. de destination** destination disk; **d. de diagnostic** diagnostic disk; **d. (à) double densité** double density disk; **d. haute densité** high-density disk; **d. d'installation** installation disk, installer; **d. magnétique** magnetic disk; **d. optique** optical disk, floptical disk; **d. programme** program disk; **d. (à) simple densité** single density disk; **d. source** source disk; **d. système** system disk; **d. vierge** blank unformatted disk

disruptif, -ive [disryptif, -iv] ADJ *Élec* disruptive

disruption [disrypsjɔ̃] NF *Élec* disruption

disruptive [disryptiv] *voir* **disruptif**

dissection [disɛksjɔ̃] NF **1** *Méd* dissection **2** *(analyse)* (close *or* minute) analysis, dissection; **une d. du texte permet de voir que...** close analysis of the text allows one to see that...

dissemblable [disɑ̃blabl] ADJ different, dissimilar

dissemblance [disɑ̃blɑ̃s] NF dissimilarity, difference

dissémination [diseminasjɔ̃] NF *(de graines)* scattering; *(de troupes)* scattering, spreading, dispersion; *(de maisons, des habitants)* scattering; *(d'idées)* spread, dissemination

disséminer [3] [disemine] VT *(graines)* to scatter; *(idées)* to spread, to disseminate; **quelques maisons disséminées** a few scattered houses; **les écoles sont très disséminées** the schools are very thin on the ground; **sa famille est disséminée dans le monde** his/her family is scattered all over the world

►**se disséminer** VPR *(graines)* to scatter; *(personnes)* to spread (out)

dissension [disɑ̃sjɔ̃] NF disagreement, difference of opinion; **il y a des dissensions** opinions differ

dissentiment [disɑ̃timɑ̃] NM *Littéraire* disagreement

disséquer [18] [diseke] VT **1** *Méd* to dissect **2** *(analyser)* to dissect, to carry out a close *or* minute analysis of

dissert [disɛrt] NF *Fam Scol & Univ (abrév* **dissertation)** essay▪

dissertation [disɛrtasjɔ̃] NF **1** *Scol & Univ* essay **2** *Péj (discours)* (long and boring) speech; **on a eu droit à une d. sur la politesse** we were treated to a lecture on politeness

disserter [3] [disɛrte] VI **1 d. sur** *(à l'écrit)* to write an essay on; *(à l'oral)* to discourse on **2** *Fig Péj* to hold forth on *or* about

dissidence [disidɑ̃s] NF **1** *(rébellion)* dissidence; **un mouvement de d.** a rebel movement **2** *(dissidents)* dissidents, rebels **3** *(scission)* scission

dissident, -e [disidɑ̃, -ɑ̃t] ADJ **1** *(rebelle)* dissident *(avant n)*, rebel *(avant n)*; **un groupe d.** a splinter *or* breakaway group **2** *Rel* dissenting

NM,F **1** *(rebelle)* dissident, rebel **2** *Rel* dissenter, nonconformist

dissimilation [disimilasjɔ̃] NF *Ling* dissimilation

dissimilitude [disimilityd] NF dissimilarity

dissimulateur, -trice [disimylatœr, -tris] ADJ dissembling

NM,F dissembler

dissimulation [disimylasjɔ̃] NF **1** *(fait de cacher)* concealment **2** *(hypocrisie)* deceit, dissimulation, hypocrisy; *(sournoiserie)* dissembling, secretiveness; **agir avec d.** to act in an underhand way **3** *Jur* **d. d'actif** (fraudulent) concealment of assets

dissimulatrice [disimylatris] *voir* **dissimulateur**

dissimulé, -e [disimyle] ADJ **1** *(invisible → haine, jalousie)* concealed; **avec un plaisir non d.** with unconcealed delight **2** *Péj (fourbe)* deceitful, hypocritical

dissimuler [3] [disimyle] VT **1** *(cacher à la vue)* to hide (from sight); **des arbres dissimulaient la maison** the house was hidden by trees

2 *(ne pas révéler → identité)* to conceal; *(→ sentiments, difficultés)* to hide, to conceal, to cover up; *(→ faute)* to cover up; **n'essaie pas de me d. les faits** don't try to conceal the facts from me; **d. le fait que...** to hide the fact that...; **je ne vous dissimulerai pas que...** I won't hide from you (the fact) that...

3 *Jur (revenus, bénéfices)* to conceal

►**se dissimuler** VPR **1** *(se cacher)* to hide *or* to conceal oneself; **se d. derrière un rideau** to hide (oneself) behind a curtain

2 se d. qch to hide sth from oneself; **ne nous dissimulons pas la difficulté de l'entreprise** let us not delude ourselves as to the difficulties involved in the venture

dissipateur, -trice [disipatœr, -tris] *Littéraire* ADJ wasteful, spendthrift

NM,F squanderer, spendthrift

dissipatif, -ive [disipatif, -iv] ADJ *Phys* dissipative

dissipation [disipasjɔ̃] NF **1** *(de nuages)* dispersal, clearing; *(du brouillard)* lifting; *(de craintes, de soupçons)* dispelling; *(d'un malentendu)* clearing up; **après d. des brouillards matinaux** after the morning mist lifts *or* clears **2** *(d'un héritage)* wasting, squandering **3** *Littéraire (débauche)* dissipation **4** *(indiscipline)* lack of discipline, misbehaviour **5** *Phys (de l'énergie)* dissipation

dissipative [disipativ] *voir* **dissipatif**

dissipatrice [disipatris] *voir* **dissipateur**

dissipé, -e [disipe] ADJ **1** *(indiscipliné → classe)* unruly, rowdy, undisciplined; **élève d.** *(sur bulletin de notes)* this pupil doesn't pay enough attention in class **2** *(débauché)* dissolute

dissiper [3] [disipe] VT **1** *(brouillard, fumée)* to disperse, to clear away; *(nuages)* to break up, to disperse; *(malentendu)* to clear up; *(crainte, soupçons)* to dispel

2 *(dilapider → héritage, patrimoine)* to dissipate, to squander

3 *(distraire)* to distract, to divert; **il se laisse facilement d.** he is easily distracted

►**se dissiper** VPR **1** *(orage)* to blow over; *(nuages)* to break up, to disperse; *(brouillard)* to lift, to clear; *(fumée)* to clear

2 *(craintes, soupçons, malentendu)* to disappear, to vanish; *(migraine, douleurs)* to go, to disappear

3 *(s'agiter → enfant)* to misbehave, to be undisciplined *or* unruly; **se dissipe en classe** *(sur bulletin de notes)* pays little attention in class; **il se dissipe vite** his attention soon wanders

dissociabilité [disɔsjabilite] NF **1** *(de questions, de chapitres)* separableness, separability **2** *Chim* dissociability

dissociable [disɔsjabl] ADJ **1** *(questions, chapitres)* separable **2** *Chim* dissociable

dissociatif, -ive [disɔsjatif, -iv] ADJ dissociative

dissociation [disɔsjasjɔ̃] NF **1** *(de questions, de chapitres, d'une famille)* separation **2** *Chim* dissociation

dissociative [disɔsjativ] *voir* **dissociatif**

dissocier [9] [disɔsje] VT **1** *(questions, chapitres)* to separate; *(famille)* to break up; **il doit apprendre à d. ses désirs de ses besoins** he must learn to distinguish between his desires and his needs **2** *Chim* to dissociate

►**se dissocier** VPR **1** *(personnes)* to break up **2 se d. de** to dissociate oneself from

dissolu, -e [disɔly] ADJ *Littéraire* dissolute

dissolubilité [disɔlybilite] NF **1** *(d'une substance)* dissolubility, solubility **2** *(d'une assemblée)* dissolubility

dissoluble [disɔlybl] ADJ **1** *(substance)* dissoluble, soluble **2** *(assemblée)* which can be dissolved, dissoluble

dissolution [disɔlysjɔ̃] NF **1** *(d'un produit, d'un comprimé)* dissolving; **remuer jusqu'à d. du sucre** stir until the sugar has dissolved
2 *(d'une société)* winding-up, dissolution; *(d'un groupe)* splitting up, breaking up
3 *Jur & Pol (d'un mariage, d'une association, d'un parlement)* dissolution; *(d'un contrat)* dissolution, termination
4 *(pour pneus)* rubber solution
5 *Littéraire (débauche)* dissoluteness, debauchery
dissolvait *etc voir* **dissoudre**
dissolvant, -e [disɔlvɑ̃, -ɑ̃t] ADJ **1** *(substance)* solvent, dissolvent **2** *Littéraire (climat)* enervating; *(doctrine)* corrupt
NM **1** *(détachant)* solvent **2** *(de vernis à ongles)* **d. (gras)** nail polish remover
dissonance [disɔnɑ̃s] NF **1** *(cacophonie)* dissonance, discord **2** *Littéraire (de couleurs, d'idées)* discord, clash, mismatch **3** *Psy & Mktg* **d. cognitive** cognitive dissonance **4** *Mus* dissonance
dissonant, -e [disɔnɑ̃, -ɑ̃t] ADJ **1** *(sons, cris)* dissonant, discordant, jarring; *Littéraire (couleurs)* discordant, clashing **2** *Mus* discordant
dissoner [3] [disɔne] VI *Littéraire* to be discordant, to clash
dissoudre [87] [disudr] VT **1** *(diluer → sel, sucre, comprimé)* to dissolve; **faites d. le comprimé** dissolve the tablet **2** *(désunir → assemblée, mariage)* to dissolve; *(→ contrat)* to dissolve, to terminate; *(→ parti)* to break up, to dissolve; *(→ association)* to dissolve, to break up, to bring to an end; *(→ entreprise)* to wind up, to dissolve
►**se dissoudre** VPR **1** *(sel, sucre, comprimé)* to dissolve **2** *(groupement)* to break up, to come to an end
dissuader [3] [disɥade] VT **d. qn de faire qch** to dissuade sb from doing sth; **je l'ai dissuadé d'acheter une voiture** I dissuaded him from *or* talked him out of buying a car
dissuasif, -ive [disɥazif, -iv] ADJ **1** *(qui décourage)* dissuasive, discouraging, *Br* off-putting **2** *Mil* deterrent
dissuasion [disɥazjɔ̃] NF dissuasion; **d. nucléaire** nuclear deterrent
❑ **de dissuasion** ADJ *(puissance)* dissuasive
dissuasive [disɥaziv] *voir* **dissuasif**
dissyllabe [disilab] ADJ disyllabic
NM disyllable
dissyllabique [disilabik] ADJ disyllabic
dissymétrie [disimetri] NF dissymmetry
dissymétrique [disimetrik] ADJ dissymmetrical
distal, -e, -aux, -ales [distal, -o] ADJ distal, terminal
distance [distɑ̃s] NF **1** *(intervalle → dans l'espace)* distance; **la d. est grande entre Moscou et Londres** Moscow is a long way from London; **la d. entre Pau et Tarbes** *ou* **de Pau à Tarbes** the distance between Pau and Tarbes *or* from Pau to Tarbes; **on ne voyait rien à cette d.** you couldn't see anything at that distance; **on les entend à une d. de 100 mètres** you can hear them (from) 100 metres away *or* at a distance of 100 metres; **à quelle d. sommes-nous de l'hôtel?** how far are we from the hotel?; **nous habitons à une grande/courte d. de la ville** we live far (away)/a short distance (away) from the city; *Hum* **il a mis une d. respectueuse entre lui et le fisc** he made sure he stayed well out of reach of the taxman; **garder ses distances** to stay aloof, to remain distant; **prendre ses distances** *Sport* to space out; *Mil* to spread out in *or* to form open order; **prendre ses distances envers** *ou* **à l'égard de qn** to hold oneself aloof *or* to keep one's distance from sb; *Aut* **d. d'arrêt/de freinage** stopping/braking distance
2 *(parcours)* distance; **la jument est excellente sur cette d.** the mare is particularly suited to that distance; *aussi Fig* **tenir la d.** to go the distance, to stay the course
3 *(intervalle → dans le temps)* **ils sont nés à deux mois de d.** they were born within two months of each other; **il l'a revue à deux mois de d.** he saw her again two months later
4 *(écart, différence)* gap, gulf, great difference; **ce malentendu a mis une certaine d. entre nous** we've become rather distant from each other since that misunderstanding; **la d. qui existe entre la théorie et la pratique** the gulf between theory and practice
5 *(recul)* **prendre de la d. (par rapport à un événement)** to stand back (in order to assess an event)
6 *Géom* distance
7 *Opt* **d. focale** focal length
❑ **à distance** ADV **1** *(dans l'espace)* at a distance, from a distance; **cette chaîne peut se commander à d.** this stereo has a remote control; **tenir qn à d.** to keep sb at a distance *or* at arm's length; **se tenir à d. (de)** to keep one's distance (from)
2 *Ordinat* **à d.** remote
3 *(dans le temps)* with time
❑ **de distance, en distance** ADV at intervals, in places
distancement [distɑ̃smɑ̃] NM *(de cheval)* disqualification
distancer [16] [distɑ̃se] VT **1** *Sport* to outdistance; **se laisser d.** to drop away, to fall *or* lag behind **2** *(surclasser)* to outdistance, to outstrip; **le parti socialiste distance la droite de deux points** the socialists are two points ahead of the conservatives; **se laisser d.** to fall behind; **se faire d. économiquement** to lag behind economically
3 *Courses de chevaux* to disqualify
distanciation [distɑ̃sjasjɔ̃] NF **1** *(gén)* detachment
2 *Théât* **l'effet de d.** the alienation effect
distancier [9] [distɑ̃sje] **se distancier** VPR **se d. de qn/qch** to distance oneself from sb/sth
distant, -e [distɑ̃, -ɑ̃t] ADJ **1** *(dans l'espace)* far away, distant; **être d. de qch** to be far *or* some distance from sth; **les deux écoles sont distantes de cinq kilomètres** the (two) schools are five kilometres away from each other
2 *(dans le temps)* distant; **ces événements sont distants de plusieurs années** these events took place several years apart
3 *(personne)* aloof, distant; *(air, sourire)* remote, distant; *(rapports)* distant, cool; **elle est très distante avec moi** she's being very distant towards me
distendre [73] [distɑ̃dr] VT **1** *(étirer → ressort)* to stretch, to overstretch; *(→ peau)* to stretch, to distend; *(→ muscle)* to strain; *(→ estomac)* to distend **2** *(rendre moins intime → liens)* to loosen
►**se distendre** VPR **1** *(s'étirer → ressort)* to stretch; *(→ peau, estomac)* to stretch, to become distended **2** *(devenir moins intime → liens)* to loosen
distension [distɑ̃sjɔ̃] NF *(étirage → de l'intestin, de l'estomac)* distension; *(→ de la peau)* stretching; *(→ d'un muscle)* straining; *(→ d'un ressort)* slackening (off)
disthène [distɛn] NM *Minér* disthene, cyanite
distillat [distila] NM *Chim* distillate
distillateur [distilatœr] NM *(personne)* distiller
distillation [distilasjɔ̃] NF distillation, distilling; *Pétr* **d. fractionnée** fractional distillation
distiller [3] [distile] VT **1** *(alcool, pétrole, eau)* to distil **2** *Littéraire (suc, venin)* to secrete **3** *Littéraire (ennui, tristesse)* to exude **4** *Littéraire (philosophie)* to distill
VI *Chim* to distil
distillerie [distilri] NF **1** *(usine, atelier)* distillery **2** *(activité)* distilling
distilleuse [distiløz] NF *Suisse (alambic)* still
distinct, -e [distɛ̃, -ɛ̃kt] ADJ **1** *(clair, net)* distinct, clear **2** *(différent)* distinct, different; **un résultat d. du précédent** a result different from the previous one
distinctement [distɛ̃ktəmɑ̃] ADV distinctly, clearly
distinctif, -ive [distɛ̃ktif, -iv] ADJ **1** *(qui sépare)* distinctive, distinguishing **2** *Ling* distinctive
distinction [distɛ̃ksjɔ̃] NF **1** *(différence)* distinction; **faire une d. entre deux choses** to make *or* to draw a distinction between two things
2 *(élégance, raffinement)* refinement, distinction; **avoir de la d.** to be distinguished
3 *(honneur)* honour; *(décoration)* decoration
4 *Belg Univ (examen) Br* ≃ lower second-class honours, *Am* ≃ C grade; *(thèse)* = first level of distinction for a PhD; **grande d.** *(examen) Br* ≃ upper second-class honours, *Am* ≃ pass with honors; *(thèse)* = second level of distinction for a PhD; **plus grande d.** *(examen) Br* ≃ first-class honours, *Am* ≃ pass with high honors; *(thèse)* = highest level of distinction for a PhD
❑ **sans distinction** ADV indiscriminately, without exception; **il a renvoyé tout le monde sans d.** he fired everybody without exception
❑ **sans distinction de** PRÉP irrespective of
distinctive [distɛ̃ktiv] *voir* **distinctif**
distinguable [distɛ̃gabl] ADJ distinguishable
distingué, -e [distɛ̃ge] ADJ **1** *(élégant → personne)* distinguished; *(→ manières, air)* refined, elegant, distinguished; **ça ne fait pas très d.** it's not very elegant **2** *(brillant, éminent)* distinguished, eminent **3** *(dans une lettre)* **veuillez croire en l'assurance de mes sentiments distingués** *(à quelqu'un dont on connaît le nom) Br* yours sincerely, *Am* sincerely yours; *(à quelqu'un dont on ne connaît pas le nom) Br* yours faithfully, *Am* sincerely yours
distinguer [3] [distɛ̃ge] VT **1** *(voir)* to distinguish, to make out; **on distingue à peine leur contour** you can hardly distinguish their outline
2 *(entendre)* to hear, to distinguish, to make out; **je ne distingue pas les aigus** I can't make out *or* hear high notes
3 *(percevoir)* **je commence à d. ses mobiles** I'm beginning to understand his/her motives; **j'ai cru d. une certaine colère dans sa voix** I thought I detected a note of anger in his voice
4 *(différencier)* to distinguish; **d. le vrai du faux** to distinguish truth from falsehood; **d. des jumeaux** to tell twins apart; **il est facile à d. de son jumeau** he and his twin brother are easy to tell apart; **je n'arrive pas à les d.** I can't tell which is which, I can't tell them apart; **je n'arrive pas à d. ces deux arbres** I can't tell the difference between these two trees; **comment d. le diamant du zircon?** how can you tell the difference between diamond and zircon?; **la parole distingue l'homme de l'animal** speech distinguishes man from other animals; **sa voix la distingue des autres choristes** her voice distinguishes her *or* marks her out from the other choristers
5 *(honorer)* to single out (for reward), to honour
USAGE ABSOLU *(voir)* **on distingue mal dans le noir** it's hard to see in the dark
►**se distinguer** VPR **1** *(être vu)* to be seen *or* distinguished
2 se d. de qn/qch (par) *(se différencier)* to be distinguishable from sb/sth (by); **le safran se distingue du curcuma par l'odeur** you can tell the difference between saffron and turmeric by their smell; **ces vins se distinguent par leur robe** you can tell these wines are different because of their colour
3 *(se faire remarquer)* to distinguish oneself; **son fils s'est distingué en musique** his son has distinguished himself *or* done particularly well in music; **tu t'es particulièrement distinguée pour le repas de Noël** your Christmas dinner was particularly good
4 *(devenir célèbre)* to become famous; **elle devait se d. sur la scène de l'opéra** she was to become a famous opera singer
5 se d. de *(être supérieur à)* to stand out from; **il se distingue de tous les autres poètes** he stands out from all other poets
distinguo [distɛ̃go] NM distinction
distique [distik] NM *Littérature* distich
distomatose [distɔmatoz] NF *Méd* distomiasis
distome [distɔm] NM *Biol* distome
distordre [76] [distɔrdr] VT to twist
►**se distordre** VPR to twist, to distort
distorsion [distɔrsjɔ̃] NF **1** *(déformation)* distortion; *Électron* **d. de fréquence** frequency distortion; *TV* **d. géométrique** geometric distortion; *Rad & Électron* **d. harmonique** harmonic distortion; *TV* **d. de l'image** *ou* **d'image** image *or* picture distortion; *Rad & Électron* **d. de phase** phase distortion; *Mktg* **d. sélective** selective distortion
2 *(déséquilibre)* imbalance
distractif, -ive [distraktif, -iv] ADJ recreational
distraction [distraksjɔ̃] NF **1** *(caractère étourdi)* absent-mindedness; *(acte)* lapse in concentration; **par d.** inadvertently; **excusez ma d.** forgive me, I wasn't concentrating
2 *(détente)* **il te faut de la d.** you need to have your mind taken off things

3 *(activité)* source of entertainment; **ma principale d. est la musique** my main source of entertainment is music; **il n'y a pas assez de distractions le soir** there's not enough to do at night

4 *Jur* appropriation; **d. des dépens** award of costs

distraire [112] [distrɛr] **VT 1** *(déranger)* to distract; **il cherche à d. ses camarades** he's trying to distract his classmates; **tu te laisses trop facilement d.** you're too easily distracted; **d. qn de ses travaux** to distract sb from his work

2 *(amuser)* to entertain, to divert; **j'aime bien que tu viennes me voir, ça me distrait** I like you to visit me, it gives me something else to think about

3 *(détourner)* **d. un ami de ses soucis** to take a friend's mind off his worries

▶**se distraire VPR 1** *(s'amuser)* to have fun, to enjoy oneself

2 *(se détendre)* to relax, to take a break

3 se d. de qch to take one's mind off sth; **elle ne parvient pas à se d. de son malheur** she can't take her mind off her grief

distrait, -e [distrɛ, -ɛt] **ADJ** *(gén)* absent-minded; *(élève)* inattentive; **avoir l'air d.** to look preoccupied; **d'un air d.** absent-mindedly; **excusez-moi, j'étais d.** sorry, I wasn't paying attention

NM,F absent-minded person; **j'ai oublié ma montre, quel d.!** I forgot my watch, how absent-minded of me!

distraitement [distrɛtmã] **ADV** absent-mindedly

distrayait *etc voir* **distraire**

distrayant, -e [distrɛjã, -ãt] **ADJ** amusing, entertaining

distribanque [distribãk] **NM** *Br* cashpoint, *Am* ATM

distribuable [distribɥabl] **ADJ** distributable

distribué, -e [distribɥe] **ADJ 1** *(appartement)* **bien/mal d.** well/poorly laid-out **2** *(données, information)* distributed

distribuer [7] [distribɥe] **VT 1** *(donner → feuilles, cadeaux, bonbons)* to distribute, to give *or* to hand out; *(→ cartes)* to deal; *(→ secours)* to dispense, to distribute; *(→ courrier)* to deliver; *(→ vivres)* to dispense, to share out, to distribute; *(→ argent)* to apportion, to distribute, to share out; *Fin (→ dividendes)* to pay; *(→ actions, bénéfices)* to distribute; *Fam* **mon père n'hésitait pas à d. les coups** my father had no misgivings about handing out punishment; **d. des sourires à tout le monde** to bestow smiles on everybody

2 *(attribuer → rôles)* to allocate, to assign; *(→ tâches, travail)* to allot, to assign

3 *(répartir)* to divide (out); **d. les joueurs sur le terrain** to position the players on the field; **la richesse est mal distribuée à travers le monde** wealth is unevenly distributed throughout the world

4 *(approvisionner)* to supply; **un réseau qui distribue le courant** a network that supplies *or* provides power; **l'eau est distribuée dans tous les villages** water is supplied *or* carried to all the villages

5 *Cin & Théât (rôle)* to cast; *Cin (film)* to distribute

6 *Com & Typ* to distribute

distributaire [distribytɛr] **ADJ** distributional
NMF distributee

distributeur, -trice [distribytœr, -tris] **NM,F** distributor, dispenser

NM 1 *(machine non payante)* dispenser; **d. de savon/gobelets** soap/cup dispenser; **d. automatique de billets** *Br* cashpoint, *Am* ATM; **d. de monnaie** change machine

2 *(machine payante)* **d. (automatique)** vending *or* slot machine; **d. de cigarettes/de timbres** cigarette/stamp machine

3 *Aut & Élec* distributor; **d. de vapeur** steam distributor *or* regulator, steam valve

4 *Agr* **d. d'engrais** muckspreader

5 *Com (vendeur)* distributor, dealer; *(grande surface)* retailer; *(de films)* (film) distributor; **d. agréé** authorized distributor *or* dealer; **d. en détail** retailer; **d. en gros** wholesaler

distributif, -ive [distribytif, -iv] **ADJ** distributive

distribution [distribysjõ] **NF 1** *(remise → de feuilles, de cadeaux, de bonbons)* distribution,

---

giving *or* handing out; *(→ de cartes)* dealing; *(→ de secours)* dispensing, distributing; *(→ de tâches, du travail)* allotment, assignment; *(→ du courrier)* delivery; *Fin (→ de dividendes)* payment; *(de produits, de mailings)* distribution; **assurer la d. du courrier** to deliver the mail; *Scol* **la d. des prix** prize-giving day; *Mktg* **d. à domicile** door drop; *Mktg* **d. d'échantillons** sampling

2 *(répartition dans l'espace → de pièces)* layout; *(→ de joueurs)* positioning

3 *(approvisionnement)* supply; **d. d'eau/de gaz** water/gas supply

4 *Bot & (en sociologie → classement)* distribution

5 *Cin, Théât & TV (des rôles → choix)* casting; *(→ liste)* cast; **une brillante d.** an all-star cast; **c'est elle qui s'occupe de la d.** she's in charge of casting; **d. par ordre d'apparition** characters in order of appearance

6 *Com* distribution; *(par des grandes surfaces)* retail; **la grande d.** mass distribution; **d. exclusive** exclusive distribution; **d. à flux tendus** just-in-time distribution; **d. en gros** wholesale distribution; **d. de masse** mass distribution; *Cin* **d. massive** saturation release; **d. juste à temps** just-in-time distribution; **d. numérique** numerical distribution; **d. physique** physical distribution

7 *Écon, Jur & Math* distribution; **d. des richesses** distribution of wealth; **d. sélective** selective distribution; **d. valeur** weighted distribution; *Rad* **d. des fréquences** frequency distribution

8 *Aut* timing

9 *Ling* (distributional) context

distributionnalisme [distribysjɔnalism] **NM** *Ling* distributiveness

distributionnel, -elle [distribysjɔnɛl] **ADJ** distributional

distributive [distribytiv] *voir* **distributif**

distributivité [distribytivite] **NF** distributiveness

distributrice [distribytris] *voir* **distributeur**

district NM 1 [distrikt] *(région)* district, region **2** [distrikt] *(d'une ville)* district **3** [distri] *Suisse* = administrative subdivision of a canton **4** [distrikt] **le d. fédéral de Columbia** the District of Columbia; **dans le d. fédéral de Columbia** in the District of Columbia

distyle [distil] **ADJ 1** *Archit* distyle **2** *Bot* distylous
NM *Archit* distyle

disulfure [disylfyr] **NM** *Chim* disulphide

DIT [deite] **NF** *(abrév* **division internationale du travail**) international division of labour

dit, -e [di, dit] **PP** *voir* **dire²**
ADJ 1 *(surnommé → personne)* (also) known as; **Louis XIV, d. le Roi-Soleil** Louis XIV, (also) known as the Sun King; **Jeanne Dollé, dite la Chatte** Jeanne Dollé, alias the Cat; **la zone dite tempérée** the temperate zone, as it is called

2 *(fixé)* appointed, indicated; **à l'heure dite** at the appointed time, at the time indicated; **le jour d.** on the agreed *or* appointed day
NM 1 *Psy* **le d. et le non-d.** the spoken and the unspoken

2 *Littérature* traditional story *(usually in verse)*

dites *voir* **dire²**

dithyrambe [ditirãb] **NM 1** *Antiq* dithyramb **2** *(panégyrique)* panegyric, eulogy

dithyrambique [ditirãbik] **ADJ 1** *Antiq* dithyrambic **2** *(paroles)* eulogistic, laudatory; **un article d. sur son exposition** an article praising his/her exhibition to the skies

dito [dito] **ADV** ditto

diurèse [djyrɛz] **NF** *Méd* diuresis

diurétique [djyretik] *Méd* **ADJ** diuretic
NM diuretic

diurnal, -aux [djyrnal, -o] **NM** *Rel* diurnal

diurne [djyrn] **ADJ** diurnal

diva [diva] **NF 1** diva, (female) opera singer **2** *(célébrité)* star

divagation [divagasjõ] **NF** *(d'une rivière)* shifting from its course

☐ **divagations NFPL** *(propos)* ramblings, meanderings

divaguer [3] [divage] **VI 1** *(malade)* to ramble, to be delirious; **la soif le fait d.** he's delirious with thirst **2** *Fam Péj (déraisonner)* to talk nonsense **3** *(rivière)* to shift its course

---

divalent, -e [divalã, -ãt] **ADJ** divalent

divan [divã] **NM 1** *(meuble)* divan, couch **2** *Hist* **le d.** the divan **3** *Littérature* divan

dive [div] **ADJ F** *Vieilli* divine; *Littéraire* **la d. bouteille** wine, the bottle; **être adorateur de la d. bouteille** to be fond of the bottle

---
Allusion
La dive bouteille

In Rabelais' *Cinquième Livre* of 1564, Panurge and his companions go to Chinon to consult an oracle named "l'oracle de la dive bouteille" ("the oracle of the divine bottle", ie of drink). During an initiation rite, the oracle makes its pronouncement: "trinch" ("drink!"). Today **la dive bouteille** simply means the pleasures of drinking.
---

divergence [divɛrʒãs] **NF 1** *(différence)* **d. (d'idées ou de vues)** difference of opinion **2** *Opt & Phys* divergence

divergent, -e [divɛrʒã, -ãt] **ADJ 1** *(opinions, interprétations, intérêts)* divergent, differing **2** *Opt & Phys* divergent

diverger [17] [divɛrʒe] **VI 1** *(intérêts, opinions)* to differ, to diverge **(de** from) **2** *Opt & Phys* to diverge **(de** from)

divers, -e [divɛr, -ɛrs] **ADJ 1** *(variés → éléments, musiques, activités)* diverse, varied; **nous avons abordé les sujets les plus d.** we talked about a wide range of topics; **les candidats viennent des horizons les plus d.** the candidates come from a wide variety of backgrounds; **à usages d.** multipurpose *(avant n)*; **classique, jazz, d.** *(chez un disquaire)* classical, jazz, miscellaneous; **j'ai enregistré d. morceaux de jazz sur cette cassette** I put a mixture of jazz music on this cassette; *Com* **articles d.** miscellaneous items

2 *(dissemblables → formes, goûts, motifs)* different, various

3 *(multiple → sujet)* complex; *(→ paysage)* varied, changing; **l'homme est d.** man is a multifaceted being

ADJ INDÉFINI *(plusieurs)* various, several; **en diverses occasions** on several *or* various occasions; **pour diverses raisons** for a variety of reasons

diversement [divɛrsəmã] **ADV 1** *(différemment)* in different ways; **les participants ont d. compris la question** the contestants understood the question in different ways **2** *(de façon variée)* in diverse *or* various ways; **mes élèves ont d. réussi l'examen** my pupils had varying degrees of success in the exam

diversification [divɛrsifikasjõ] **NF** diversification; **l'entreprise a adopté une stratégie de d.** the company has adopted a policy of diversification; **une trop grande d.** overdiversification; **d. industrielle** diversification, lateral integration of industry; *Bourse* **d. de portefeuille** portfolio diversification; **d. des produits** product diversification

diversifier [9] [divɛrsifje] **VT 1** *(production, tâches)* to diversify **2** *(varier)* to make more varied; **dans sa deuxième période, l'artiste diversifie sa palette** in his second period, the artist uses a greater variety of colours

▶**se diversifier VPR** *(entreprise, économie, centres d'intérêt)* to diversify; *(produits)* to become diversified

diversion [divɛrsjõ] **NF 1** *(dérivatif)* diversion, distraction; **faire d.** to create a distraction; **pour faire d. à l'ennui** to alleviate boredom; **faire d. à la douleur de qn** to take sb's mind off his/her suffering **2** *Mil* diversion

diversité [divɛrsite] **NF 1** *(richesse)* diversity, variety; **un paysage étonnant dans sa d.** an amazingly varied landscape **2** *(pluralité → de formes, d'opinions, de goûts)* diversity

diverticule [divɛrtikyl] **NM** *Anat* diverticulum

diverticulite [divɛrtikylit] **NF** *Méd* diverticulitis

diverticulose [divɛrtikyloz] **NF** *Méd* diverticulosis

divertimento [divɛrtimɛnto] **NM** *Mus* divertimento, divertissement

divertir [32] [divɛrtir] **VT 1** *(amuser → sujet: clown, spectacle, lecture)* to entertain, to amuse; **le jeu divertit en instruisant** the game is entertaining as well as educational

2 *Jur* to divert, to misappropriate

div-dja

3 *Littéraire (éloigner)* **d. qn de qch** to turn sb away *or* to distract sb from sth
▸**se divertir** VPR **1** *(se distraire)* to amuse *or* to entertain oneself; **que faire pour se d. ici?** what do you do for entertainment around here?
2 *(s'amuser)* to enjoy oneself, to have fun; **nous nous sommes beaucoup divertis à 'Cyrano'** we enjoyed 'Cyrano' very much
3 se d. de qn/qch to make fun of sb/sth; **elle semblait se d. de mon embarras** she seemed to find my confusion amusing

divertissant, -e [divɛrtisɑ̃, -ɑ̃t] ADJ amusing, entertaining

divertissement [divɛrtismɑ̃] NM **1** *(jeu, passe-temps)* distraction; *(spectacle)* entertainment; *(type d'émission de télévision)* light entertainment show **2** *(amusement)* entertaining, distraction; **pour le d. de la Cour** to amuse *or* to entertain the Court **3** *Mus (intermède)* divertissement; *(divertimento)* divertimento **4** *(en danse)* divertissement **5** *Jur (de fonds)* misappropriation

dividende [dividɑ̃d] NM *Fin & Math* dividend; **toucher** *ou* **recevoir un d.** to draw a dividend; **avec d.** cum div(idend), *Am* dividend on; **sans d.** ex div(idend), *Am* dividend off; **dividendes accrus** accrued dividends; **d. par action** dividend per share; **d. d'action, d. en actions** share *or* stock dividend, dividend on shares; **d. anticipé** advance dividend; **d. brut** gross dividend; **d. cumulatif** cumulative dividend; **d. définitif** final dividend; **d. en espèces** cash dividend; **d. final** final dividend; **d. intérimaire, d. par intérim** interim dividend; **d. majoré** grossed-up dividend; **d. net** net dividend; **d. prioritaire, d. de priorité** preference dividend; **d. prioritaire cumulatif** preference cumulative dividend; **d. privilégié** preference dividend

divin, -e [divɛ̃, -in] ADJ **1** *Rel* divine; *Antiq* **le d. Auguste** the Divine Augustus; **le d. enfant** the Holy Child; **le d. Sauveur** the Holy *or* Heavenly Saviour **2** *(parfait → beauté, corps, repas, voix)* divine, heavenly, exquisite; **des fraises au champagne, c'est d.** strawberries with champagne are simply divine
▪ NM **le d.** the divine

'**La Divine Comédie**' *Dante* 'The Divine Comedy'

divinateur, -trice [divinatœr, -tris] ADJ divining, clairvoyant; **puissance divinatrice** power of divination; **science divinatrice** divination
▪ NM,F diviner

divination [divinasjɔ̃] NF divination, divining
divinatoire [divinatwar] ADJ divinatory
divinatrice [divinatris] *voir* **divinateur**
divinement [divinmɑ̃] ADV divinely, exquisitely
divinisation [divinizasjɔ̃] NF deification, deifying
diviniser [3] [divinize] VT to deify
divinité [divinite] NF **1** *(dieu)* deity, divinity **2** *(qualité)* divinity, divine nature
divis [divi] *Jur* ADJ divided
▪ ADV **par d. et indivis** jointly and severally
▪ NM INV divided ownership of property, severalty

divisé, -e [divize] ADJ **1** *(en désaccord → opinion, juges, parti)* divided; **être d. sur** to be divided on (the question of) **2** *(fragmenté)* divided
diviser [3] [divize] VT **1** *(fragmenter → territoire)* to divide up, to partition; *(→ somme, travail)* to divide up; *(→ cellule, molécule)* to divide, to split; **d. un domaine entre des héritiers** to divide up an estate between heirs; **les bénéfices ont été divisés en huit** the profits were divided into eight parts; **la classe est divisée en trois groupes** the class is divided up into three groups
2 *Math* to divide; **d. 9 par 3** to divide 9 by 3; **9 divisé par 3 égale 3** 9 divided by 3 makes *or* is 3
3 *(opposer)* to divide, to set against each other; **les dissensions qui nous divisent** the disagreements that divide us; **l'association est divisée en deux sur le problème de l'intégration** the association is split down the middle on the problem of integration; **c'est d. pour (mieux) régner** it's (a case of) divide and rule
4 *Fin & Bourse (actions)* to split
▸**se diviser** VPR **1** *Math* to be divisible

2 *(cellule)* to divide *or* to split (up); *(branche, voie)* to divide, to fork; **se d. en** to be divided into; **le texte se divise en cinq parties** the text is divided into five parts; **l'équipe s'est divisée en deux** the team divided itself *or* split up into two groups
3 *(opposition, parti)* to split

diviseur [divizœr] NM **1** *Math* divisor; **plus grand commun d.** highest common factor **2** *Tech* divider

divisibilité [divizibilite] NF divisibility; *(d'une créance, d'une dette)* divisibility, severability
divisible [divizibl] ADJ divisible; **8 n'est pas d. par 3** 8 cannot be divided *or* is not divisible by 3
division [divizjɔ̃] NF **1** *Math* division; **faire une d.** to do a division; **j'ai des divisions à faire** I've got some division to do; **d. à un chiffre** simple division; **d. à plusieurs chiffres** long division
2 *(fragmentation → d'un territoire)* splitting, division, partition; *Phys* splitting; *Écon* **d. internationale du travail** international division of labour; *Écon* **la d. du travail** the division of labour; *Biol* **d. cellulaire** cell division; *Écon* **d. du marché** market division
3 *(désaccord)* division, rift; **le problème de la défense nationale crée des divisions au sein du parti** the party is divided over the defence issue; **semer la d. au sein d'une famille** to create a rift in a family
4 *Ftbl* division; **la première d. du championnat** the first league division; **un club de première/deuxième/troisième d.** a first-/second-/third-division club; **d. d'honneur** ≃ fourth division; **en deuxième d., X bat Y** in league division two, X beat Y
5 *(en base-ball)* league; **première/deuxième d.** major/minor league
6 *Mil & Naut* division; **d. blindée** armoured division
7 *Bourse (des actions)* splitting
8 *(service → dans l'administration, dans une société)* division
9 *(graduation)* gradation

divisionnaire [divizjɔner] ADJ *Admin (service)* divisional
▪ NM **1** *Mil* major general **2** *(commissaire)* *Br* ≃ chief superintendent, *Am* ≃ police chief
divisionnisme [divizjɔnism] NM *Beaux-Arts* divisionism
divisionniste [divizjɔnist] *Beaux-Arts* ADJ divisionist
▪ NM divisionist
divorçants [divɔrsɑ̃] NMPL = couple engaged in divorce proceedings
divorce [divɔrs] NM **1** *Jur* divorce; **demander le d.** to ask for *or* to petition for a divorce; **obtenir le d. d'avec qn** to get a divorce from sb; **d. à l'amiable** *ou* **par consentement mutuel** divorce by mutual consent, *Am* no-fault divorce **2** *(divergence)* gulf
divorcé, -e [divɔrse] ADJ divorced
▪ NM,F divorcee
divorcer [16] [divɔrse] VI *Jur* to get a divorce, to get divorced; **elle a déjà divorcé une fois** she has already been divorced (once) before; **il veut d.** he wants a divorce; **d. de qn** *ou* **d'avec qn** to get divorced from *or* to divorce sb
divortialité [divɔrsjalite] NF **taux de d.** divorce rate
divulgateur, -trice [divylgatœr, -tris] NM,F divulger
divulgation [divylgasjɔ̃] NF divulgation, disclosure
divulgatrice [divylgatris] *voir* **divulgateur**
divulguer [3] [divylge] VT to divulge, to disclose, to reveal
divulsion [divylsjɔ̃] NF *Méd* divulsion
DIVX [deiveiks] NM *(abrév* **digital video express)** DIVX
dix [dis] ADJ **1** *(gén)* ten; **il ne sait rien faire de ses d. doigts** he can't do anything with his hands; *Bible* **les d. commandements** the Ten Commandments **2** *(dans des séries)* tenth; **page/numéro d.** page/number ten
▪ PRON ten
▪ NM INV **1** *(gén)* ten **2** *(numéro d'ordre)* number ten **3** *(chiffre écrit)* ten **4** *Cartes* ten; *voir aussi* **cinq**

'**Les Dix Commandements**' *De Mille* 'The Ten Commandments'

dix-cors [dikɔr] NM INV *Zool* ten-pointer, stag of ten, hart; **grand d.** royal (stag *or* hart)
dix-heures [dizœr] NM INV *Belg* = snack taken at around ten o'clock in the morning
▪ NMPL *Suisse* = snack taken at around ten o'clock in the morning
dix-huit [dizɥit] ADJ **1** *(gén)* eighteen **2** *(dans des séries)* eighteenth; **page/numéro d.** page/number eighteen
▪ PRON eighteen
▪ NM INV **1** *(gén)* eighteen **2** *(numéro d'ordre)* number eighteen **3** *(chiffre écrit)* eighteen; *voir aussi* **cinq**
dix-huitième [dizɥitjɛm] *(pl* **dix-huitièmes)** ADJ eighteenth
▪ NMF **1** *(personne)* eighteenth **2** *(objet)* eighteenth (one)
▪ NM **1** *(partie)* eighteenth **2** *(étage)* *Br* eighteenth floor, *Am* nineteenth floor **3** *(arrondissement de Paris)* eighteenth (arrondissement)
▪ NF *Mus* eighteenth; *voir aussi* **cinquième**
dix-huitièmement [dizɥitjɛmmɑ̃] ADV in eighteenth place
dixie(land) [diksi(lɑ̃d)] NM dixie, trad jazz
dixième [dizjɛm] ADJ tenth
▪ NMF **1** *(personne)* tenth **2** *(objet)* tenth (one)
▪ NM **1** *(partie)* tenth **2** *(étage)* *Br* tenth floor, *Am* eleventh floor **3** *(arrondissement de Paris)* tenth (arrondissement)
▪ NF **1** *Ancienne ment Scol* *Br* = second year of primary school, *Am* ≃ second grade **2** *Mus* tenth; *voir aussi* **cinquième**
dixièmement [dizjɛmmɑ̃] ADV tenthly, in tenth place
dixit [diksit] **il faudra tout ranger après, d. Papa** we must tidy everything up afterwards (so) Dad says
dix-neuf [diznœf] ADJ **1** *(gén)* nineteen **2** *(dans des séries)* nineteenth; **page/numéro d.** page/number nineteen
▪ PRON nineteen
▪ NM INV **1** *(gén)* nineteen **2** *(numéro d'ordre)* number nineteen **3** *(chiffre écrit)* nineteen; *voir aussi* **cinq**
dix-neuvième [diznœvjɛm] *(pl* **dix-neuvièmes)** ADJ nineteenth
▪ NMF **1** *(personne)* nineteenth **2** *(objet)* nineteenth (one)
▪ NM **1** *(partie)* nineteenth **2** *(étage)* *Br* nineteenth floor, *Am* twentieth floor **3** *(arrondissement de Paris)* nineteenth (arrondissement)
▪ NF *Mus* nineteenth; *voir aussi* **cinquième**
dix-neuvièmement [diznœvjɛmmɑ̃] ADV in nineteenth place
dix-sept [disɛt] ADJ **1** *(gén)* seventeen **2** *(dans des séries)* seventeenth; **page/numéro d.** page/number seventeen
▪ PRON seventeen
▪ NM INV **1** *(gén)* seventeen **2** *(numéro d'ordre)* number seventeen **3** *(chiffre écrit)* seventeen; *voir aussi* **cinq**
dix-septième [disɛtjɛm] *(pl* **dix-septièmes)** ADJ seventeenth
▪ NMF **1** *(personne)* seventeenth **2** *(objet)* seventeenth (one)
▪ NM **1** *(partie)* seventeenth **2** *(étage)* *Br* seventeenth floor, *Am* eighteenth floor **3** *(arrondissement de Paris)* seventeenth (arrondissement)
▪ NF *Mus* seventeenth; *voir aussi* **cinquième**
dix-septièmement [disɛtjɛmmɑ̃] ADV in seventeenth place
dizain [dizɛ̃] NM *Littérature* ten-line poem
dizaine [dizɛn] NF **une d.** around *or* about ten, ten or so; **une d. de voitures** around *or* about ten cars; **elle a une d. d'années** she's around *or* about ten (years old); **il y a une d. d'années** around *or* about ten years ago, ten or so years ago
dizygote [dizigɔt] *Biol* ADJ fraternal, *Spéc* dizygotic
▪ NM,F fraternal twin, *Spéc* dizygotic twin
DJ [didʒi, didʒe] NM *(abrév* **disc-jockey)** DJ
djaïn, -e [dʒain] *Rel* ADJ Jain, Jaina
▪ NM Jain, Jaina
djaïnisme [dʒainism] NM *Rel* Jainism
Djakarta [dʒakarta] NM Djakarta, Jakarta
djamaa [dʒama] = **djemaa**

djebel [dʒebɛl] **NM** *(en Afrique du Nord)* jebel mountain

Djedda [dʒɛda] **NM** Jedda, Jidda

djellaba [dʒɛlaba] **NF** djellaba

djemaa [dʒema] **NF INV** = gathering of local notables in certain regions of North Africa

djembé [dʒɛmbe] **NM** *Mus* djembe drum

Djerba [dʒɛrba] **NF** Djerba

djeune [dʒœn] *Fam Ironique* **ADJ** young and hip ▪ **NMF** hip young person

Djibouti [dʒibuti] **NM 1** *(république)* Djibouti; **à D.** in Djibouti **2** *(ville)* Djibouti City

djiboutien, -enne [dʒibusjɛ̃, -ɛn] **ADJ** Djiboutian ▫ **Djiboutien, -enne NM,F** Djiboutian

djihad [dʒiad] **NM** jihad

djinn [dʒin] **NM** jinn

djobeur [dʒɔbœr] **NM** *(aux Antilles)* odd-job man

djos [dʒo] **NMPL** *Can très Fam* tits, jugs

DL [deɛl] **NF** *Anciennement Pol (abrév* **Démocratie Libérale)** = right-of-centre French political party

DLC [deɛlse] **NF** *(abrév* **date limite de consommation)** best-before date

DM *Anciennement (abrév écrite* **Deutsche Mark)** DM

dm *(abrév écrite* **décimètre)** dm

DN [deɛn] **NF** *(abrév* **distribution numérique)** numerical distribution

Dniepr [dnjɛpr] **NM** **le D.** the (River) Dnieper

DNS [deɛnɛs] **NM** *Ordinat (abrév* **Domain Name System)** DNS

do¹ [do] **NM INV** C; *(chanté)* doh

do² *(abrév écrite* **dito)** do

doberman [dɔbɛrman] **NM** Doberman (pinscher)

DOC [dɔk] **NM** *Ordinat (abrév* **disque optique compact)** CD-ROM

doc [dɔk] **NF** *Fam (abrév* **documentation)** literature ▪, info; **est-ce que tu as de la d. sur les ordinateurs?** do you have any literature *or* info about computers?

doc. *(abrév écrite* **document)** doc

docétisme [dɔsetizm] **NM** *Rel* Docetism

docile [dɔsil] **ADJ** *(animal)* docile; *(enfant, nature)* docile, obedient; *(cheveux)* manageable

docilement [dɔsilmɑ̃] **ADV** docilely, obediently

docilité [dɔsilite] **NF** *(d'un animal, d'une personne)* docility; **avec d.** docilely

docimasie [dɔsimazi] **NF** *Antiq & Méd* docimasy

docimologie [dɔsimɔlɔʒi] **NF** docimology

dock [dɔk] **NM 1** *(bassin)* dock; **d. de carénage/ flottant** dry/floating dock **2** *(bâtiments, chantier)* **les docks** the docks, the dockyard; **entrer aux docks** *(bateau)* to dock; **les docks de Londres** London's Docklands **3** *(entrepôt)* warehouse; **d. frigorifique** cold storage dock

docker [dɔkɛr] **NM** docker

docte [dɔkt] **ADJ** *Littéraire* learned, erudite

doctement [dɔktəmɑ̃] **ADV** *Littéraire* knowledgeably

docteur [dɔktœr] **NM**

Note that it is no longer considered a mistake to feminize this word and to say **une docteur** or even **une docteure** (with a final **e**) in senses 1 and 2. Some French speakers nonetheless regard these forms as unacceptable, especially in France. See also the entry **féminisation**.

1 *(médecin)* **le d. Jacqueline R.** Dr Jacqueline R.; **faites venir le d.** send for the doctor; **dites-moi, d., est-ce que c'est sérieux?** tell me, Doctor, is it serious?; **d. en médecine** doctor (of medicine) **2** *Univ* Doctor; **quand je serai d.** when I get my doctorate *or* PhD; **d. en histoire/physique** doctorate *or* PhD in history/physics; **Paul Vuibert, d. ès lettres** Paul Vuibert, PhD **3** *Rel* **d. de l'Église** Doctor of the Church; **d. de la loi** Doctor of the Law

'Docteur Folamour' *Kubrick* 'Doctor Strangelove'

'Docteur Jekyll et M. Hyde' *Stevenson* 'Dr. Jekyll and Mr. Hyde'

'Le Docteur Jivago' *Pasternak, Lean* 'Doctor Zhivago'

doctoral, -e, -aux, -ales [dɔktɔral, -o] **ADJ 1** *(pédant)* pedantic **2** *Univ* doctoral

doctoralement [dɔktɔralmɑ̃] **ADV** pedantically

doctorant, -e [dɔktɔrɑ̃, -ɑ̃t] **NM,F** PhD student, doctoral student

doctorat [dɔktɔra] **NM** doctorate, PhD; **d. en droit/ chimie** doctorate *or* PhD in law/chemistry; **d. d'État** doctorate *(leading to high-level research)*; **d. de troisième cycle** doctorate, PhD *(awarded by a specific university)*

doctoresse [dɔktɔrɛs] **NF** *Vieilli* (woman) doctor

doctrinaire [dɔktrinɛr] **ADJ** doctrinaire, dogmatic ▪ **NMF** doctrinaire

doctrinal, -e, -aux, -ales [dɔktrinal, -o] **ADJ** doctrinal

doctrine [dɔktrin] **NF** doctrine

docu [dɔky] **NM** *Fam Cin & TV* documentary

docudrame [dɔkydram] **NM** *TV* docudrama, dramatized documentary

docu-fiction [dɔkyfiksjɔ̃] *(pl* **docu-fictions)** **NM OU NF** docufiction, fictional documentary

document [dɔkymɑ̃] **NM 1** *Jur & Com* document; **d. administratif unique** unique data folder; **documents contre acceptation** documents against acceptance; **documents contre paiement** documents against payment; **d. d'embarquement** shipping document; **d. d'expédition** shipping document; **d. interne à l'entreprise** internal company document; **d. maître** master document; **documents maritimes** shipping documents; **d. d'offre** tender document; **d. de politique générale** general policy document; *Mktg* **d. de publicité directe** direct mail; **d. source** source document; *Pol* **D. stratégique de réduction de la pauvreté** Poverty Reduction Strategy Paper; *Compta* **d. de synthèse** financial statement; **d. de tendre** tender document; **d. transmissible** transferable document; **documents de transport** transport documents; **d. de transport combiné** combined transport document; **d. de travail** working document; **d. type** standard document; **documents de voyage** travel documents

2 *Ordinat* document; **d. de base, d. source** source document; **d. transmissible** transferable document; **d. type** standard document

3 *(d'un service de documentation)* document

4 *(de travail)* document, paper; **des documents sont tombés de sa valise** documents *or* papers fell out of her case

5 *(témoignage)* document; **d. sonore** piece of sound archive

documentaire [dɔkymɑ̃tɛr] **ADJ 1** *(de témoignage → livre, intérêt)* documentary **2** *(de documentation)* document *(avant n)*; **ce rapport vous est fourni à titre d.** this report is supplied for information only ▪ **NM** *Cin & TV* documentary

documentaliste [dɔkymɑ̃talist] **NMF 1** *(gén)* archivist; **d. iconographique** picture researcher **2** *Admin* information officer **3** *Scol* (school) librarian

documentariste [dɔkymɑ̃tarist] **NMF** documentary maker

documentation [dɔkymɑ̃tasjɔ̃] **NF 1** *(publicités)* literature, information, documentation; *(instructions)* instructions, specifications; **voulez-vous recevoir notre d.?** would you like us to send you our literature?; **se référer à la d.** please refer to the instructions

2 *(informations)* (written) evidence; **réunir une d. sur qch** to gather evidence on sth

3 *(technique)* documentation (technique); **d. iconographique** picture research; **système de d. automatique** automated information service

4 *(service)* **la d.** the research department

5 *Journ* **d. de presse** press kit

documenté, -e [dɔkymɑ̃te] **ADJ** **bien** *ou* **très d.** *(reportage, thèse)* well-documented; *(personne)* well-informed

documenter [3] [dɔkymɑ̃te] **VT** *(thèse)* to document; *(avocat)* to supply *or* to provide with documents, to document

▸ **se documenter VPR** to inform oneself; **se d. sur qn/qch** to gather information *or* material about sb/sth; **mais tu sais tout! – je me suis documenté!** how come you know everything? – I've done my homework!

docusoap [dɔkysop] **NM** *TV* docusoap

dodécaèdre [dɔdekaɛdr] **NM** dodecahedron

dodécagonal, -e, -aux, -ales [dɔdekagonal, -o] **ADJ** twelve-sided, dodecagonal

dodécagone [dɔdekagon] **NM** dodecagon

Dodécanèse [dɔdekanɛz] **NM** **le D.** the Dodecanese

dodécaphonique [dɔdekafɔnik] **ADJ** dodecaphonic

dodécaphonisme [dɔdekafɔnism] **NM** dodecaphonism

dodécaphoniste [dɔdekafɔnist] **NMF** dodecaphonist

dodécastyle [dɔdekastil] **ADJ** *Archit* dodecastyle

dodécasyllabe [dɔdekasilab] **NM** dodecasyllable

dodelinement [dɔdəlinmɑ̃] **NM** nodding

dodeliner [3] [dɔdəline] **dodeliner de VT IND d. de la tête** to nod gently

dodine [dɔdin] **NF** *Culin* **1** *(filet de canard)* = dish consisting of fillets of roast duck and mushrooms served with wine sauce **2** *(ballottine)* meat roll *(made with poultry)*

dodo [dodo] **NM 1** *(en langage enfantin → sommeil)* beddy-byes; *(→ lit)* bed; **faire d.** to sleep; **c'est l'heure d'aller au d.!** time to go to beddy-byes! **2** *(oiseau)* dodo

Dodoma [dodoma] **NM** *Géog* Dodoma

dodu, -e [dɔdy] **ADJ** *(oie)* plump; *(personne, visage)* plump, fleshy, chubby; *(bébé)* chubby

dogaresse [dɔgarɛs] **NF** *Hist* doge's wife, dogaressa

dog-cart [dɔgkart] *(pl* **dog-carts)** **NM** dog-cart

doge [dɔʒ] **NM** doge

dogger [dɔgɛr] **NM** *Géol* dogger

dogging [dɔgiŋ] **NM** *Fam* dogging

dogmatique [dɔgmatik] **ADJ** dogmatic ▪ **NMF** dogmatic person ▪ **NF** dogmatics *(singulier)*

dogmatiquement [dɔgmatikmɑ̃] **ADV** dogmatically

dogmatiser [3] [dɔgmatize] **VI** to pontificate, to dogmatize

dogmatisme [dɔgmatism] **NM** dogmatism

dogmatiste [dɔgmatist] **NM** dogmatist

dogme [dɔgm] **NM** dogma; **le libéralisme, c'est bien, mais n'en faisons pas un d.** liberalism is a good thing but let's not stick to it too rigidly

dogue [dɔg] **NM** mastiff; **d. allemand/anglais** German/English mastiff

Doha [dɔa] **NM** **(al-) D.** Doha

doigt [dwa] **NM 1** *(partie du corps)* finger, *Spéc* digit; **des doigts fins/boudinés** slender/podgy fingers; **faire courir ses doigts sur un clavier** to run one's fingers up and down a keyboard; **le d. sur la bouche** with one's finger on one's lips; **lever le d.** to put one's hand up; **manger avec ses doigts** to eat with one's fingers; **mettre ses doigts dans** *ou* **se mettre les doigts dans le nez** to pick one's nose; **mettre son d. dans l'œil de qn** to poke sb in the eye; *Belg* **d. blanc** whitlow; **le d. de Dieu** the hand of God; **d. de pied** toe; *Fam* **les doigts de pied en éventail** with one's feet up; **une couturière aux doigts de fée** a seamstress with skilful hands; **les doigts de fée qui ont réalisé cette figurine** the delicate fingers which created this figurine; **les doigts de fée qui ont pansé ma blessure** the gentle hands which dressed my wound; **petit d.** little finger, *Am & Scot* pinkie; **ils sont comme les (deux) doigts de la main** they're like brothers, they're as thick as thieves; **glisser** *ou* **filer entre les doigts de qn** to slip through sb's fingers; **mettre le d. dans l'engrenage** to get involved; **une fois le d. dans l'engrenage, comment refuser?** once you've got involved, how can you say no?; *Fam* **se fourrer** *ou* *très Fam* **se foutre le d. dans l'œil (jusqu'au coude)** to be barking up the wrong tree; **mener** *ou* **faire marcher qn au d. et à l'œil** to have sb toe the line, to rule sb with a rod of iron; **il lui obéit au d. et à l'œil** he/she rules him with a rod of iron; *Fam* **tu pourrais le faire? – les doigts dans le nez!** could you do it? – standing on my head!; *Fam* **gagner les doigts dans le nez** to win hands down; **mettre le d. sur qch, toucher qch du d.** to identify sth precisely; **tu as mis le d. dessus!** that's precisely it!, you've put your finger on it!; **là, nous touchons du d. le problème principal** now we're getting to the crux of the problem; **il faut lui faire toucher le problème du d.** he/she has to have the problem

spelt out for him/her; **mettre le d. sur la plaie** to put one's finger on the source of the trouble; **c'est mon petit d. qui me l'a dit** a little bird told me; **il ne bougera** *ou* **lèvera pas le petit d. pour faire...** he won't lift a finger to do...; **le petit d. sur la couture du pantalon** standing to attention; *Fam* **faire un d. d'honneur à qn** *Br* to give sb the finger, *Am* to flip sb the bird

2 *(mesure)* little bit; **raccourcir une jupe de deux doigts** to take a skirt up a little bit; **servez-m'en un d.** just pour me out a drop; **deux doigts de whisky** two fingers of whisky

❑ **à un doigt de, à deux doigts de** PRÉP within an inch *or* a hair's breadth of

doigté [dwate] NM **1** *Mus (annotation, position)* fingering; *(technique)* fingering technique; **exercices de d.** five-finger exercises **2** *(adresse)* dexterity; **pour ouvrir un coffre-fort il faut beaucoup de d.** to open a safe you need a very fine touch **3** *(tact)* tact, diplomacy; **avoir du d.** to be tactful; **manquer de d.** to be tactless

doigter [3] [dwate] VT *Mus* to finger

doigtier [dwatje] NM fingerstall

doit[1] *voir* **devoir**

doit[2] [dwa] NM *Fin* debit, liability; *(d'un compte)* debit side; **d. et avoir** debits and credits; *(personnes)* debtors and creditors

doive *etc voir* **devoir**

dojo [doʒo] NM dojo

dol [dɔl] NM *Jur* fraud; **d. incident** = deception concerning a secondary element of a contract

Dolby® [dɔlbi] NM Dolby®; **en D. stéréo** in Dolby® stereo

dolce [dɔltʃe] ADV *Mus* dolce, softly

dolce vita [dɔltʃevita] NF INV dolce vita

dolcissimo [dɔltʃisimo] ADV *Mus* dolcissimo

doldrums [dɔldrœmz] NMPL *Météo* doldrums

dôle [dol] NF *Suisse* = red wine from the Valais canton

doléance [dɔleɑ̃s] NF complaint, grievance; **faire** *ou* **présenter ses doléances** to air one's grievances

dolence [dɔlɑ̃s] NF *Vieilli & Littéraire* dolefulness, plaintiveness

dolent, -e [dɔlɑ̃, -ɑ̃t] ADJ **1** *Littéraire (plaintif → personne)* doleful, mournful; *(→ voix)* plaintive, mournful **2** *Péj (sans énergie → personne)* sluggish, lethargic **3** *Vieilli ou Littéraire (douloureux → corps)* painful, sore

doler [3] [dɔle] VT *Vieilli Tech (bois)* to adze, to pare, to shave; *(peaux)* to skive, to pare, to whiten; *(moulage)* to sleek, to slick

dolic [dɔlik] NM *Bot* dolichos; **d. asperge** asparagus bean

dolichocéphale [dɔlikɔsefal] ADJ dolicephalous, dolicephalic

dolichocôlon [dɔlikɔkolɔ̃] NM *Méd* dolichocolon

doline [dɔlin] NF doline, dolina

dolique [dɔlik] = **dolic**

dollar [dɔlar] NM **1** *(en Amérique du Nord)* dollar; **d. américain** US dollar **2** *UE* **d. vert** green dollar

dollarisation [dɔlarizasjɔ̃] NF dollarization

dollariser [3] [dɔlarize] VT to dollarize

dolman [dɔlmɑ̃] NM dolman

dolmen [dɔlmɛn] NM dolmen

doloire [dɔlwar] NF *(de charpentier)* broad axe; *(de tonnelier)* adze; *(de maçon)* (mason's) larry; *Hist* **d. de guerre** battle-axe; *Bot* **feuille en d.** dolabriform leaf

dolomie [dɔlɔmi], **dolomite** [dɔlɔmit] NF dolomite

Dolomites [dɔlɔmit] NFPL **les D.** the Dolomites

dolomitique [dɔlɔmitik] ADJ dolomitic

dolorisme [dɔlɔrism] NM cult of redemptive suffering

dolosif, -ive [dɔlɔzif, -iv] ADJ *Jur* fraudulent

dolus [dɔlys] NM dolus, deceit; **d. bonus** dolus bonus, justifiable deceit; **d. malus** dolus malus, unjustifiable deceit

DOM [dɔm] NM *Anciennement (abrév* **département d'outre-mer**) = French overseas "département"; *voir aussi encadré à* **DOM-TOM**

dom [dɔm] NM **1** *Rel* Dom **2** *(au Portugal)* Dom

domaine [dɔmɛn] NM **1** *(propriété)* estate, (piece of) property; **entretenir les arbres du d.** to look after the trees on the estate; **vous êtes ici sur mon d.** you're on my land *or* property; **mis en bouteille au d.** *(dans le Bordelais)* chateau-bottled; **le d. forestier** the national forests; **le d. royal** ≃ Crown lands *or* property; *Hist (en France)* the property of the Kings of France; **d. skiable** area developed for skiing *(within a commune or across several communes)*; **d. vinicole** domaine

2 *(lieu préféré)* domain; **étant enfant, le grenier était mon d.** when I was a child, the attic was my domain *or* kingdom

3 *Jur* **le D.** State property; **d. privé** private ownership; **d. public** public ownership (of rights); **être dans le d. public** to be out of copyright; **tomber dans le d. public** to come into the public domain

4 *(secteur d'activité)* field, domain, area; **le d. musical/scientifique** the musical/scientific field; **dans le d. de la prévention, il y a encore beaucoup à faire** as far as preventive action is concerned, there's still a lot to do; **dans tous les domaines** in every field *or* domain; **dans tous les domaines de la recherche** in all research areas; *Com* **d. d'activité stratégique** strategic business unit; *Mktg* **d. concurrentiel** competitive scope

5 *(compétence, spécialité)* field; **c'est du d. du service commercial** that's for the marketing department to deal with; **ce n'est pas de mon d.** that's not my field *or* my line; **l'art oriental, c'est son d.** she's a specialist in oriental art; **l'électricité, c'est mon d.** I know quite a bit about electricity

6 *(d'un dictionnaire)* field; *(indication)* field label

7 *Math & Ordinat* domain

❑ **Domaines** NMPL *Admin* **cet étang appartient aux Domaines** this pond is State property

domanial, -e, -aux, -ales [dɔmanjal, -o] ADJ *Jur* **1** *(de l'État)* national, state *(avant n)* **2** *(privé)* belonging to a private estate

domanialité [dɔmanjalite] NF *Jur* = fact of belonging to the state

dôme [dom] NM **1** *(en Italie → cathédrale)* cathedral; *(→ église)* church **2** *Archit* dome, *Spéc* cupola **3** *Littéraire (voûte)* vault, canopy **4** *Géol* dome

domesticable [dɔmɛstikabl] ADJ domesticable

domestication [dɔmɛstikasjɔ̃] NF *(d'un animal, d'une plante)* domestication; *(d'une énergie)* harnessing

domesticité [dɔmɛstisite] NF **la d.** *(dans une maison)* the (domestic *or* household) staff; **avoir une nombreuse d.** to have a large staff *or* many servants

domestique [dɔmɛstik] ADJ **1** *(familial → problème, vie, querelle)* family *(avant n)*; *(→ dieu)* household *(avant n)* **2** *(du ménage → affaires, devoirs, tâches)* household *(avant n)*, domestic; **les travaux domestiques** household work, domestic chores; **personnel d.** domestic staff, (domestic) servants **3** *Écon (consommation, marché)* domestic, home *(avant n)* **4** *(animal)* domesticated; **les animaux domestiques** pets

NMF domestic, servant; **les domestiques** the servants, the domestic staff; **il nous prend pour ses domestiques** he thinks we're his servants

domestiquer [3] [dɔmɛstike] VT *(animal)* to domesticate; *(plante)* to turn into a cultivated variety; *(personne)* to subjugate, to bring to a state of subjection; *(énergie)* to harness

domicile [dɔmisil] NM **1** *(lieu de résidence)* home, *Sout* place of residence; *Admin & Jur* domicile; *(adresse)* (home) address; **dernier d. connu** last known address; **le chéquier sera renvoyé à votre d.** the chequebook will be sent to your home address; **nos représentants se rendent à votre d.** our representatives make house calls; **un(e) sans d. fixe** a homeless person; **être sans d. fixe** to be homeless; *Admin & Jur* to be of no fixed abode; **d. conjugal** marital home; *Jur* **d. élu** address for service; **d. fiscal** tax domicile; **d. légal** address for legal purposes; **d. permanent** permanent place of residence

2 *(d'une entreprise)* registered address

❑ **à domicile** ADJ **soins à d.** domiciliary care, home care; **vente à d.** door-to-door selling; *Sport* **match à d.** home game *or Br* match ADV *(chez soi)* at home; **travailler à d.** to work from home; **nous livrons à d.** we deliver to your home; *Sport* **jouer à d.** to play *or* be at home; **le P.S.G. joue à d. contre Lille** PSG are at home to Lille

domiciliaire [dɔmisiljɛr] ADJ *(visite)* home *(avant n)*, *Sout* domiciliary

domiciliataire [dɔmisiljatɛr] NMF *Banque* paying agent

domiciliation [dɔmisiljasjɔ̃] NF *(d'une société)* domiciliation; **d. (bancaire)** payment (by banker's order)

domicilié, -e [dɔmisilje] ADJ *(salaire)* paid directly into one's bank account; **être fiscalement d. dans un pays** to be liable to pay tax in a country; **d. à Tokyo/en Suède** resident *or Sout* domiciled in Tokyo/in Sweden

domicilier [9] [dɔmisilje] VT **1** *Admin* to domicile; **je me suis fait d. chez mon frère** I gave my brother's place as an accommodation address **2** *Banque & Com* to domicile

domien, -enne [dɔmjɛ̃, -ɛn] ADJ of/from the French overseas "départements"

❑ **Domien, -enne** NM,F = inhabitant of or person from the French overseas "départements"

dominance [dɔminɑ̃s] NF **1** *Biol & Physiol* dominance, dominant nature **2** *Zool* dominance, dominant behaviour

dominant, -e [dɔminɑ̃, -ɑ̃t] ADJ **1** *(principal → facteur, thème, trait de caractère)* dominant, main; *(→ espèce)* dominant; *(→ couleur)* dominant, main, predominant; *(→ intérêt)* main, chief; *(→ idéologie)* prevailing; *(→ position)* commanding

2 *Biol (caractère, gène)* dominant

3 *Météo (vent)* dominant, prevailing

❑ **dominante** NF **1** *(aspect prépondérant)* dominant *or* chief *or* main characteristic

2 *(teinte)* predominant colour; **la dominante bleue des vitraux** the predominant blue colour of the stained-glass windows; **j'ai choisi une tapisserie à dominante jaune** I chose wallpaper that is mainly yellow

3 *Mus* dominant; **cinquième/septième de dominante** dominant fifth/seventh

4 *Univ Br* main subject, *Am* major; **un cursus à dominante linguistique** a course with linguistics as the main subject; **suivre une licence à dominante sociologique** to take a degree specializing in sociology, *Am* to major in sociology

dominateur, -trice [dɔminatœr, -tris] ADJ **1** *(puissant → esprit, force, nation)* dominating; *(→ passion)* ruling **2** *(autoritaire → personne)* domineering, overbearing; *(→ ton)* imperious **3** *Zool* dominant

NM,F **1** *Pol* ruler **2** *(personne autoritaire)* tyrant, despot

domination [dɔminasjɔ̃] NF **1** *(politique, militaire)* domination (**sur** of), dominion, rule (**sur** over); **maintenir une île sous sa d.** to have control over an island; **territoires sous d. allemande** territories under German domination *or* rule

2 *(prépondérance → d'un facteur)* preponderance, domination

3 *(ascendant personnel, influence)* domination, influence; **il exerçait sur eux une étrange d.** he had a strange hold over them; **subir la d. de qn, être sous la d. de qn** to be dominated by sb

4 *(contrôle → de sentiments)* control; **d. de soi-même** self-control

❑ **dominations** NFPL *Rel* domination

dominatrice [dɔminatris] *voir* **dominateur**

dominer [3] [dɔmine] VT **1** *Pol (nation, peuple)* to dominate, to rule

2 *(contrôler → marché)* to control, to dominate; **ils ont dominé le match** they controlled *or* dominated the match

3 *(influencer → personne)* to dominate; **il la domine** he dominates her; **se laisser d. par qn** to let oneself be dominated by sb

4 *(surclasser)* to outclass; **il s'est fait d. pendant les premiers rounds** his opponent had the upper hand during the early rounds; **ils se sont fait d. en mêlée** they were weaker in the scrums; **elle domine toutes les autres danseuses** she outclasses the other dancers

5 *(colère)* to control; *(complexe, dégoût, échec, timidité)* to overcome; *(passion)* to master, to control; *(matière, question)* to master; **elle domine son sujet** she has a thorough knowledge *or* grasp of her subject; **d. la situation** to be in control of the situation

6 *(prédominer dans → œuvre, style, débat)* to

predominate in, to dominate; **sa voix dominait le brouhaha de la salle** his voice rose above the noise of the room; **le thème qui domine la campagne électorale** the main theme in *or* the theme which dominates the electoral campaign

7 *(surplomber)* to overlook, to dominate; **de la tour, on domine tout le village** from the tower you have a view over the whole valley; **d. qn de la tête et des épaules** to be taller than sb by a head; *Fig* to tower above sb, to be head and shoulders above sb

VI 1 *(être prédominant → couleur, intérêt)* to predominate, to be predominant; *(→ caractéristique)* to dominate, to be dominant; *(→ idéologie, opinion)* to prevail; **chez lui, c'est l'égoïsme/la gentillesse qui domine** selfishness/kindness is his dominant characteristic; **les femmes dominent dans l'enseignement** women outnumber men in teaching

2 *(l'emporter)* to dominate; **notre équipe a dominé tout le long du match** our team dominated the entire match *or* was in control throughout the match; **notre entreprise domine largement dans ce secteur** our company has the biggest share of the market *or* is the market leader in this sector

▶**se dominer VPR** to control oneself; **fou de rage, il ne se dominait plus** he was so angry, he could no longer control himself; **ne pas savoir se d.** to have no self-control

dominicain¹, -e¹ [dɔminikɛ̃, -ɛn] **ADJ** *Rel* Dominican

NM,F Dominican

dominicain², -e² [dɔminikɛ̃, -ɛn] **ADJ** *(de Saint-Domingue)* Dominican

◻ **Dominicain, -e NM,F** Dominican

dominical, -e, -aux, -ales [dɔminikal, -o] **ADJ** Sunday *(avant n)*, *Sout* dominical

dominion [dɔminjɔ̃] **NM** dominion

Dominique [dɔminik] **NF** la **D.** Dominica; **à la D.** in Dominica

domino [dɔmino] **NM 1** *(jeu)* domino; **jouer aux dominos** to play dominoes **2** *Élec* connecting block **3** *(vêtement)* domino

dominoterie [dɔminɔtri] **NF** *Vieilli* **1** *(fabrication)* = manufacture of decorative coloured paper for use in parlour games **2** *(papiers)* = decorative coloured paper for use in parlour games

Domitien [dɔmisjɛ̃] **NPR** Domitian

Dom Juan [dɔ̃ʒɥɑ̃] **NPR** Don Juan

dommage [dɔmaʒ] **NM 1** *Jur (préjudice)* harm, injury; **causer un d. à qn** to cause *or* to do sb harm; **il s'en est tiré sans d.** he came out of it unscathed; **d. corporel** physical injury; **dommages de guerre** war damage; **dommages indirects** consequential damages; **dommages et intérêts, dommages-intérêts** damages; **poursuivre qn en dommages-intérêts** to sue sb for damages, to bring an action for damages against sb; **verser/obtenir des dommages-intérêts** to pay/to be awarded damages; **dommages punitifs** punitive damages; **d. moral** non-pecuniary loss; **d. par ricochet** third-party damage

2 *(gén pl) (dégât matériel)* **d. matériel, dommages matériels** (material) damage; **le d. n'était pas bien grand** there wasn't much harm done; **causer des dommages à** to cause damage to; **en cas de dommages sur le véhicule** in case of damage to the vehicle; *Mil* **dommages collatéraux** collateral damage

3 *(expression d'un regret)* **(quel) d.!** what a shame *or* pity!; **c'est bien d.** it's a great shame *or* pity; **c'est vraiment d. de devoir abattre ce chêne** it's a real shame to cut down this oak; **ça ne m'intéresse pas! – d.!** I'm not interested! – pity!; **d. que tu n'aies pas pu venir!** what a pity *or* shame you couldn't come!; *Fam* **je ne peux pas venir – d. pour toi!** I can't come – too bad (for you)!; *Fam* **le plus d., c'est que...** the worst of it is that...

◻ **beau dommage EXCLAM** *Can* of course!, you bet!

dommageable [dɔmaʒabl] **ADJ** detrimental, damaging (**à** to)

domotique [dɔmɔtik] **NF** home automation

domper [3] [dɔ̃pe] **VT** *Can Joual (déposer, plaquer)* to dump

---

domptable [dɔ̃tabl] **ADJ** tameable; **facilement/difficilement d.** easy/difficult to tame

domptage [dɔ̃taʒ] **NM** *(apprivoisement)* taming; *(dressage → de cheval)* breaking in

dompter [3] [dɔ̃te] **VT 1** *(apprivoiser)* to tame; *(dresser → cheval)* to break in **2** *Littéraire (révoltés)* to quash; *(peuple)* to subjugate **3** *(énergie, vent, torrent)* to master; *(rébellion)* to break, to put down; *(sentiments, passions)* to subdue, to overcome

dompteur, -euse [dɔ̃tœr, -øz] **NM,F** *(d'animaux sauvages)* tamer; **d. de chevaux** horse-breaker

dompte-venin [dɔ̃tvənɛ̃] **NM INV** tame-poison

DOM-TOM [dɔmtɔm] **NMPL** *Anciennement (abrév* **départements et territoires d'outre-mer***)* = French overseas "départements" and territories

DOM-TOM

The acronym DOM-TOM officially ceased to exist in 2003, although it is still widely used outside official documents. It has been replaced by DROM and COM (see these entries). The term DOM-TOM referred to French overseas territorial possessions. These included the DOM (Départements d'Outre-Mer) – Guadeloupe, Martinique, Guiana and La Réunion, all of which still have "département" status – and the TOM (Territoires d'Outre-Mer), which included Wallis-and-Fortuna, French Polynesia, New Caledonia and French territories in the Antarctic. New Caledonia now has an autonomous status of its own.

DON [dɔn] **NM** *Ordinat (abrév* **disque optique numérique***)* digital optical disk

Don [dɔ̃] **NM** le **D.** the (River) Don

don [dɔ̃] **NM 1** *(aptitude naturelle)* talent, gift; **dons artistiques** artistic gifts *or* talents; **c'est un d. chez elle** it's a talent *or* a gift she has; **avoir le d. de voyance** to be clairvoyant; **avoir le d. des langues** to have the gift of tongues; **il a le d. de guérir les brûlures** he has the gift of healing burns; **elle a un d. pour la danse** she has a talent for dancing, she's a gifted dancer; **elle a le d. de trouver des vêtements pas chers** she has a flair for finding cheap clothes; **mes initiatives ont le d. de la contrarier** I seem to have a knack for upsetting her; **tu as le d. d'envenimer les situations!** you have a knack for stirring up trouble!

2 *(cadeau)* gift, donation; **faire d. de qch** to give sth as a present *or* gift; *Littéraire* **faire d. de son cœur/sa main à qn** to give one's heart/hand to sb; **la collection dont elle m'a fait d.** the collection she gave me as a present; **ceux qui ont fait d. de leur vie pour leur pays** those who have laid down *or* sacrificed their lives for their country; *Fig* **les dons de la terre** the fruits of the earth; *Fig* **d. du ciel** godsend; **le d. de soi** *ou* **de sa personne** self-denial, self-sacrifice; **d. en espèces** cash donation; **d. en nature** donation in kind

3 *Jur* donation; **faire d. d'un bien à qn** to donate a piece of property to sb; **d. de...** *(dans un musée)* gift of..., donated by...; **d. manuel** manual gift

4 *Méd* donation, donating; **faire d. d'un organe** to donate an organ; **encourager les dons d'organes** to promote organ donation; **d. du sang/ de sperme** blood/sperm donation

5 *(en Espagne)* Don

donacie [dɔnasi] **NF** *Entom* leaf beetle

Donald [dɔnald] **NPR** *(personnage)* Donald Duck

donataire [dɔnatɛr] **NMF** donee, recipient

donateur, -trice [dɔnatœr, -tris] **NM,F** donor

donation [dɔnasjɔ̃] **NF** *(gén)* donation, disposition; *(d'argent)* donation; **faire une d. à un musée** to make a donation to a museum; *Jur* **d. entre vifs** donation inter vivos; **d. de biens présents** donation of existing property; **d. de biens à venir** donation of future property; **d. déguisée** disguised donation; **d. entre époux** donation between spouses; **d. indirecte** indirect donation; **d. mutuelle** mutual donation; *Jur* **donations parents-enfants** donations from parents to children; **d. "propter nuptias"** = donation in consideration of marriage

---

donation-partage [dɔnasjɔ̃partaʒ] *(pl* **donations-partages***)* **NF** *Jur* = distribution of estate during one's lifetime to avoid inheritance tax

donatisme [dɔnatism] **NM** *Rel* donatism

donatiste [dɔnatist] **NM** *Rel* donatist

donatrice [dɔnatris] *voir* **donateur**

donax [dɔnaks] **NM** *Zool (mollusque)* donax

donc [dɔ̃k] **CONJ 1** *(par conséquent)* so; **je n'en sais rien, inutile d. de me le demander** I don't know anything about it, so there's no use asking me; **elle est tombée malade et elle a d. annulé son voyage** she fell ill, so she cancelled her trip; **nous devrions d. aboutir à un accord** we should therefore reach an agreement; **il faudra d. envisager une autre solution** we should therefore think of another solution

2 *(indiquant une transition)* so; **nous disions d. que...** so, we were saying that...; **d., vous n'avez rien entendu?** so, you didn't hear anything?

3 *(indiquant la surprise)* so; **c'était d. toi!** so it was you!; **c'est d. pour ça!** so that's why!; **voilà d. pourquoi il n'est pas venu!** so that's why he didn't come!

4 *(renforçant une interrogation, une assertion, une injonction)* **mais qu'y a-t-il d.?** what's the matter, then?; **mais pourquoi ris-tu d.?** what are you laughing at *or* about?; **que voulez-vous d.?** what do you want, then?; **fermez d. la porte!** shut the door, will you!; **viens d. avec nous!** come on, come with us!; **tais-toi d.!** just shut up, will you?; **range d. tes affaires!** why don't you put your things away?; **allons d., vous vous trompez** come on (now), you're mistaken; **allons d., je ne te crois pas!** come off it, I don't believe you!; **comment d. est-ce possible?** how can that be possible?; **eh ben dis d.!** well, really!; **essaie d.!** go on, try it!; *Ironique* **essaie d. pour voir!** just (you) try it!, go on then!; **tiens d.!** well, well, well!!; **ben, voyons d.!** *(évidemment)* naturally!, what else!; *(ne vous gênez pas)* don't mind me!; **dites d., pour qui vous vous prenez?** hold on, who do you think you are?; **dis d., à propos, tu l'as vue hier soir?** oh, by the way, did you see her yesterday evening?

Je pense donc je suis

This is the French translation of "Cogito, ergo sum", "I think, therefore I am", René Descartes' celebrated premise from the *Méditations métaphysiques* of 1640. In modern French, either half of the expression can be varied; for example **Je pense, donc je vote** ("I think, therefore I vote") or **Je mange, donc je suis** ("I eat, therefore I am"), or to quote Albert Camus, **Je me révolte, donc je suis** ("I rebel, therefore I am").

dondaine [dɔ̃dɛn] **NF 1** *Mus* bagpipes *(used in imitation of the drone in refrains of old songs)*, fol-de-rol **2** *Hist (d'un arc)* bolt, quarrel; *(machine)* engine of war

dondon [dɔ̃dɔ̃] **NF** *Fam Péj* **une grosse d.** a big fat lump

donf [dɔf] **à donf ADV** *Fam (verlan de* **à fond***) (vite) Br* like the clappers, *Am* like sixty; *(très fort)* at full blast; *(beaucoup)* really, like crazy; **je la kiffe à d., cette nana** she really gives me the horn

dông [dɔ̃g] **NM** dong

donjon [dɔ̃ʒɔ̃] **NM** keep, donjon

don Juan [dɔ̃ʒɥɑ̃] *(pl* **dons Juans***)* **NM** *(séducteur)* Don Juan, lady's man

♪♫𝄞🎶

'Don Juan' *Mozart, Byron, Pouchkine* 'Don Giovanni' (opera), 'Don Juan' (poem), 'The Stone Guest' (play)

donjuanesque [dɔ̃ʒɥanɛsk] **ADJ** *(attitude, manières)* of a Don Juan

donjuanisme [dɔ̃ʒɥanism] **NM** donjuanism, philandering

donne [dɔn] **NF** *Cartes* deal; **faire la d.** to deal; **c'est à moi la d.** it's my (turn to) deal; **il y a eu fausse** *ou* **mauvaise d.** there was a misdeal; *Fig* **nouvelle d.** *(situation)* new state of affairs; *(réorganisation)* new deal

donné, -e [dɔne] **ADJ 1** *(heure, lieu)* fixed, given; **sur un parcours d.** on a given *or* certain route; **à**

une distance donnée at a certain distance; **il doit improviser sur un thème d.** he must improvise on a given theme

2 *(particulier, spécifique)* **sur ce point d.** on this particular point; **à cet instant d.** at this (very) moment; **à un moment d.** *(dans le passé)* at one point; *(dans l'avenir)* at some point

3 *(bon marché)* **c'est d.!** it's dirt cheap!; **ce n'est pas d.!** it's hardly what you'd call cheap!

NM *Phil* given

❑ **donnée NF 1** *Ordinat & Math* piece of data, *Sout* datum; **données** data; **fichier/saisie/transmission de données** data file/capture/transmission; *Écon* **en données corrigées des variations saisonnières** with adjustments for seasonal variations, seasonally adjusted; *Ordinat* **données numériques** digital data

2 *(information)* piece of information; **données** facts, information; **je ne connais pas toutes les données du problème** I don't have all the information about this question; **données brutes** raw data; **données démographiques** demographic data; **données primaires** primary data; **données secondaires** secondary data; **données de style de vie** lifestyle data

---

DONNER [3] [dɔne]

> **VT** to give A1–3, 5–13, ◼ B1, 3, C, D1–3, 5 ◼ to give away A1, D4 ◼ to give out A1 ◼ to leave A2, 5 ◼ to donate A2 ◼ to hand out A3 ◼ to pass A12 ◼ to produce C1, 2 ◼ to cause C2 ◼ to yield C1, 4 ◼ to show D3
> **VI** to yield 1 ◼ to deal 2 ◼ to charge 3

VT A. *CÉDER, ACCORDER* **1** *(offrir)* to give; *(se débarrasser de)* to give away; *(distribuer)* to give out; **d. qch à qn** to give sth to sb, to give sb sth; **d. sa vie/son sang pour la patrie** to give (up) one's life/to shed blood for one's country; **d. qch à qn pour son anniversaire** to give sb sth (as a present) for his/her birthday; **d. qch en cadeau à qn** to make sb a present of sth; **d. qch en souvenir à qn** to give sb sth as a souvenir; **il est joli, ce tableau! – je te le donne** what a lovely picture! – please have it; **à ce prix-là, ma petite dame, je vous le donne!** at that price, dear, I'm giving it away!; **d. sa place à qn dans le train** to give up one's seat to sb on the train; **d. des timbres contre des disques** to swap stamps for records; **d. à boire à un enfant** to give a child a drink or something to drink; **d. à manger aux enfants/chevaux** to feed the children/horses; *Fam* **c'était donné, l'examen, cette année!** the exam was a piece of cake this year!; *Hum* **dis donc, on te l'a donné, ton permis de conduire!** how on earth did you pass your driving test!

2 *Jur (léguer)* to leave; *(faire don public de → argent, œuvre d'art, organe)* to donate, to give; **d. une collection à la ville** to donate a collection to the town

3 *(accorder → subvention)* to give, to hand out; *(→ faveur, interview, liberté)* to give, to grant; *(→ prix)* to give, to award; *(→ récompense)* to give; **d. sa fille en mariage à qn** to marry one's daughter to sb; **d. la permission à qn de faire qch** to allow sb to do sth, to give sb permission to do sth; **d. rendez-vous à qn** *Admin* to make an appointment with sb; *(ami, amant)* to make a date with sb; **d. à qn l'occasion de faire qch** to give sb the opportunity to do sth or of doing sth; **d. son soutien à qn** to give one's support to sb, to support sb; **d. son accord à qn** to give sb one's consent

4 *(tournure impersonnelle)* **il m'a été donné de voir l'original** I was privileged to see the original; **il n'est pas donné à tout le monde de partir en vacances** not everybody is fortunate enough to be able to go on *Br* holiday or *Am* vacation

5 *(laisser → délai)* to give, to leave; **ça me donne cinq jours pour le finir** that gives or leaves me five days to finish it; **il m'a donné trois heures/jusqu'en janvier pour le faire** he gave me three hours/until January to do it

6 *(confier)* to give **donne-moi ta lettre, je vais la poster** let me have or give me your letter, I'll

post it; **d. une tâche à qn** to entrust sb with a job; **d. son manteau au teinturier** to take one's coat to the dry cleaner's; **elle m'a donné sa valise à porter** she gave me her suitcase to carry; **d. qch à faire** *(à un professionnel)* to have sth done; **d. ses enfants à garder** to have one's children looked after; **d. son manteau à nettoyer** to have one's coat cleaned

7 *(remettre → gén)* to give; *(→ devoir)* to give, to hand in; **donne la balle, Rex, donne!** come on Rex, let go (of the ball)!; **donnez vos papiers** hand over your papers

8 *(vendre → sujet: commerçant)* to give; **donnez-moi un beau rôti** I'd like a nice joint; *Fam* **des pêches, combien je vous en donne?** how many peaches would you like?

9 *(payer)* to give; **je lui donne 15 euros de l'heure** I give or pay her 15 euros an hour; **et la table, combien m'en donnez-vous?** how much or what will you give me for the table?; **combien t'en a-t-on donné?** how much did you get for it?; **je vous en donne 25 euros** I'll give you 25 euros for it; **je donnerais cher pour le savoir** I'd give a lot to know that; **je donnerais n'importe quoi pour le retrouver** I'd give anything to find it again

10 *(administrer → médicament, sacrement)* to give, *Sout* to administer; *(→ bain)* to give; **d. 15 ans de prison à qn** to give sb a 15-year prison sentence; **d. une punition à qn** to punish sb; **ne pas d. aux enfants de moins de trois ans** *(sur mode d'emploi)* not suitable for or not to be given to children under three

11 *(appliquer → coup, baiser)* to give; **d. une claque à qn** to give sb a slap; **d. une fessée à qn** to smack sb's bottom, to spank sb; **d. un coup à qn** to hit sb; **d. un coup de pied/poing à qn** to kick/to punch sb; **d. un coup de rabot/râteau/pinceau à qch** to go over sth with a plane/rake/paintbrush

12 *(passer, transmettre)* to give, to pass on; **donnez-moi le sel** pass or hand me the salt; **d. son rhume à qn** to give sb one's cold, to pass one's cold on to sb; **son père lui a donné le goût du théâtre** he/she got his/her love of the theatre from his/her father

13 *(organiser → dîner, bal)* to give, to throw; **l'association donnera un goûter** the association will give a small party

14 *Fam (locution)* **je vous le donne en cent** ou **mille** you'll never guess in a month of Sundays or in a million years

B. *CONFÉRER* **1** *(assigner)* to give; **d. un nom à qn** to give sb a name, to name sb; **d. un titre à qn** to confer a title on sb; **je donne peu d'importance à ces choses** I attach little importance to these things; **on donne au verbe la valeur d'un substantif** the verb is given noun status

2 *(attribuer)* **on ne lui donnerait pas son âge** he/she doesn't look his/her age; **on lui donne facilement son âge** he/she looks his/her age; **quel âge me donnez-vous?** how old would you say I am or was?

3 *(prédire)* to give; **je ne lui donne pas trois mois** *(à vivre)* I give him/her less than three months to live; *(avant d'échouer)* I'll give it three months at the most

C. *GÉNÉRER* **1** *(sujet: champ)* to yield; *(sujet: arbre fruitier)* to give, to produce; **la graine donne une nouvelle plante** the seed produces a new plant; **le vieux noyer donne encore des kilos de noix** the old walnut tree still gives or produces masses of nuts; **les sources d'énergie qui donnent de l'électricité** the energy sources which produce electricity

2 *(susciter, provoquer → courage, énergie, espoir)* to give; *(→ migraine)* to give, to cause; *(→ sensation)* to give, to create; *(→ impression)* to give, to produce; **d. des forces à qn** to give sb strength; **cela m'a donné une belle frayeur** it gave me a real fright; **d. du souci à qn** to worry sb; **les enfants donnent du travail** children are a lot of work; **la promenade m'a donné de l'appétit** the walk has given me an appetite; **d. des boutons à qn** to make sb come out in spots; *Fig* **faire la vaisselle me donne des boutons** I'm allergic to washing up; **la maladie peut d. des**

complications the illness may have complications; **ça donne la diarrhée** it gives you or causes diarrhoea; **le poisson, ça donne de la mémoire** fish is good for your memory; **les tilleuls donnent de l'ombre** the lime trees give shade; **d. chaud/froid/faim/soif à qn** to make sb hot/cold/hungry/thirsty; **d. mal au cœur à qn** to make sb (feel) sick or nauseous

3 *(conférer → prestige)* to confer, to give; *(→ aspect, charme)* to give, to lend; **le procédé donne au tissu l'aspect du velours** this process gives the material a velvety look; **le grand air t'a donné des couleurs** the fresh air has brought colour to your cheeks; **ton maquillage te donne bonne mine** your make-up makes you look well; **d. de l'ampleur à une veste** to let a jacket out; **pour d. meilleur goût à la sauce** to improve the taste of the sauce; **pour d. de la vitalité à vos cheveux** to give bounce to your hair; **pour d. plus de mystère à l'histoire** to make the story more mysterious

4 *(aboutir à → résultats)* to give, to yield; *(→ effet)* to result in; **en ajoutant les impôts, cela donne la somme suivante** when you add (in or on) the tax, it comes to the following amount; **j'espère que vos efforts donneront des résultats** I hope your efforts will give or yield results; **le deuxième tour a donné la majorité aux écologistes** the second ballot resulted in a majority for the green party; **la combinaison de l'acide et du gaz donne un polymère** a polymer is obtained from combining the acid with the gas; **et ta candidature, ça donne quelque chose?** have you heard anything about your application?; **les recherches n'ont rien donné** the search was fruitless; **la robe ne donne pas grand-chose comme cela, essaie avec une ceinture** the dress doesn't look much like that, try it with a belt; **j'ai ajouté du vin à la sauce – qu'est-ce que ça donne?** I've added some wine to the sauce – what's it like now?; **et la fac, qu'est-ce que ça donne?** how's university going?; **et ton épaule, qu'est-ce que ça donne?** how's your shoulder doing?

D. *EXPRIMER, COMMUNIQUER* **1** *(présenter, fournir → garantie, preuve, précision)* to give, to provide; *(→ explication)* to give; *(→ argument)* to put forward; *(→ ordre, consigne)* to give; **d. un conseil à qn** to give sb a piece of advice, to advise sb; **d. une réponse** to give or to provide an answer; **d. son avis** to give one's opinion; **ceux qui ont donné la combinaison gagnante** those who had the winning numbers; **d. ses sources** to quote one's sources; **d. une certaine image de son pays** to show one's country in a particular light; **d. à entendre** ou **comprendre que...** to let it be understood that...; **ces faits nous ont été donnés comme vrais** we were led to believe that these facts were true; **d. qch pour certain** to give sth as a certainty; **on le donnait pour riche** he was said or thought to be rich; **dans le village, on la donnait pour une sorcière** in the village, she was rumoured to be a witch

2 *(dire)* to give; **d. son nom** to give one's name; **donnez la date de la bataille de Crécy** give the date of the battle of Crécy; **qui peut me d. la racine carrée de 196?** who can give or tell me the square root of 196?, who can tell me what the square root of 196 is?; **d. des nouvelles à qn** to give sb news; **d. des nouvelles de qn** to give news of sb; **donnez-moi de ses nouvelles** tell me how he/she is; *Fam* **je te le donne pour ce que ça vaut** that's what I was told, for what it's worth

3 *(indiquer → sujet: instrument)* to give, to indicate, to show; **l'altimètre donne l'altitude** an altimeter gives or shows the altitude

4 *Fam (dénoncer)* to give away, to rat on, *Br* to shop

5 *(rendre public → causerie, cours)* to give; *(→ œuvre, spectacle)* to put on; **l'année où j'ai donné 'Giselle'** *(dit par le metteur en scène)* the year I put on 'Giselle'; *(dit par le danseur)* the year I performed 'Giselle'; **elle donnera au printemps une édition critique de Proust** she has a critical edition of Proust coming out in the

don-dor

spring; **qu'est-ce qu'on donne au Rex?** what's on at the Rex?; **ce soir, on donne 'Médée' sur la deuxième chaîne** 'Medea' is on channel two tonight

USAGE ABSOLU to give; **tu as donné à la quête?** did you give anything to the collection?; **d. aux pauvres** to give to the poor; **d. de son temps** to give up one's time; **d. de sa personne** to give of oneself; *Fam* **j'ai déjà donné!** I've been there *or* through that already!

VI 1 *(produire → arbre)* to bear fruit, to yield; *(→ potager, verger, terre)* to yield; **le cerisier ne donnera pas avant deux ans** the cherry tree won't bear *or* have any fruit for a couple of years; **la vigne a bien/mal donné cette année** the vineyard had a good/bad yield this year; *Fam* **ça donne!** it's something else!, it's wicked *or Br* mental!; *Fam* **dis donc, elle donne, ta chaîne hi-fi!** that's a mean sound system you've got there!; **d. à plein** *(radio)* to be on full blast, to be blaring (out); *(campagne de publicité, soirée)* to be in full swing; **le soleil donne à plein** the sun is beating down

2 *Cartes* to deal; **à toi de d.** your deal

3 *(attaquer)* to charge; **la police va d.** the police are about to charge; **faire d. la garde/troupe** to send in the guards/troops

◻ **donner dans VT IND 1** *(tomber dans)* **d. dans une embuscade** to be ambushed; **sans d. dans le mélodrame** without becoming too melodramatic; **votre essai donne trop souvent dans le lyrisme** your essay lapses too frequently into lyricism; **on peut s'en réjouir, mais ne donnons pas dans l'excès d'optimisme** we may feel pleased about it, but let's not be over-optimistic

2 *(se cogner contre)* **l'enfant est allé d. dans la fenêtre** the child crashed into the window

3 *(déboucher sur)* to give out onto; **la porte donnait dans un couloir** the door opened *or* gave out onto a corridor; **l'escalier donne dans une petite cour** the staircase gives out onto *or* leads to *or* leads into a small courtyard

◻ **donner de VT IND 1** *(cogner avec)* **d. du coude/ de la tête contre une porte** to bump one's elbow/one's head against a door

2 *(utiliser)* **d. du cor** to sound the horn; **d. de l'éperon à son cheval** to spur one's horse; **d. de la voix** to raise one's voice **d. de la tête** *(animal)* to shake its head; *Fig* **ne plus savoir où d. de la tête** to be run off one's feet

3 *Naut* **d. de la bande** to list

4 *(locution)* **elle lui donne du "monsieur"** she calls him "Sir"

◻ **donner sur VT IND 1** *(se cogner contre)* **la barque alla d. sur le rocher** the boat crashed into the rock; **d. sur les écueils** to strike the rocks

2 *(être orienté vers)* **la chambre donne sur le jardin/la mer** the room overlooks the garden/ the sea; **chambre donnant sur la mer** room with a sea view

◻ **donnant donnant ADV** that's fair, fair's fair; **je te prête mon costume si tu me passes ta voiture, c'est donnant donnant** I'll lend you my suit if you lend me your car, you can't say fairer than that; **d'accord, mais c'est donnant donnant** OK, but I want something in return

▶ **se donner VPR 1** *(film, pièce)* to be on; **sa pièce se donne à l'Odéon** his play is being staged *or* is on at the Odéon

2 *(employer son énergie)* **monte sur scène et donne-toi à fond** get on the stage and give it all you've got; **se d. à une cause** to devote oneself *or* one's life to a cause; **elle s'est donnée à fond** *ou* **complètement dans son entreprise** she put all her effort into her business

3 *(sexuellement)* **se d. à qn** to give oneself to sb

4 *(donner à soi-même)* **se d. un coup de marteau sur les doigts** to hit one's fingers with a hammer; **se d. les moyens de faire qch** to give oneself the means to do sth; **se d. du bon temps** *(gén)* to have fun; *Euph* to give oneself a good time

5 *(s'accorder → délai)* to give *or* to allow oneself; **je me suis donné six mois pour finir ma thèse** I've given *or* allowed myself six months

to finish my thesis; **donne-toi un peu de repos** allow yourself to rest for a while

6 *(échanger)* to give one another *or* each other; **se d. un baiser** to give each other a kiss, to kiss; **se d. des coups** to exchange blows; **ils se sont donné leurs impressions** they swapped views

7 *(se doter de)* to give oneself; **se d. un chef** to give oneself a leader; **la capitale vient de se d. un second opéra** the capital has been given a second opera house

8 *(prétendre avoir)* **il se donne 30 ans** he claims to be 30

9 *Fam* **se la d.** to show off, to pose

10 **se d. pour** to pass oneself off as, to claim to be; **elle se donne pour l'amie du ministre** she claims to be the minister's friend

11 *(locutions)* **les enfants s'en sont donné au square** the children had the time of their lives in the park; **avec les crêpes, ils s'en sont donné à cœur joie** they really tucked into their pancakes

donneur, -euse [dɔnœr, -øz] **NM,F 1** *Méd* donor; **d. d'organes** organ donor; **d. de sang** blood donor; **d. universel** universal blood donor

2 *Cartes* dealer

3 je ne veux pas me transformer en d. de leçons, mais… I don't want to lecture you, but…; **c'est un d. de leçons** he likes lecturing *or* sermonizing people

4 *Fam* *(délateur)* squealer, informer

NM 1 *Écon & Fin* **d. d'aval** backer, referee; **d. de caution** guarantor; **d. d'ordre** principal

2 *Chim* donor

3 *Méd* **d. de sperme** sperm donor

don Quichotte [dɔ̃kiʃɔt] *(pl* **dons Quichottes**) **NM** *(redresseur de torts)* **se poser en d.** to adopt a quixotic stance

NPR Don Quixote

'Don Quichotte de la Manche' *Cervantès* 'Don Quixote'

donquichottisme [dɔ̃kiʃɔtism] **NM** quixotism

DONT [dɔ̃] **PRON RELATIF 1** *(exprimant le complément du nom → personne)* whose; *(→ chose)* whose, *Sout* of which; **le club d. je suis membre** the club I belong to, the club to which I belong *or Sout* of which I'm a member; **un projet d. vous pouvez voir les grandes lignes** a plan whose general outline you can see, *Sout* a plan, the general outline of which you can see; **un buffet d. le bois est vermoulu** a sideboard with woodworm; **cette femme, d. le charme les avait captivés** this woman whose charm had captivated them; **l'hôtel d. nous avons apprécié la tranquillité** the hotel whose quietness we appreciated, *Sout* the hotel of which we appreciated the quietness

2 *(exprimant la partie d'un tout → personnes)* of whom; *(→ choses)* of which; **il y a 95 candidats, d. 33 Canadiens** there are 95 candidates, of whom 33 *or* 33 of whom are Canadians; **des livres d. la plupart ne valent rien** books, most of which are worthless; **deux personnes ont téléphoné, d. ton frère** two people phoned, including your brother; **les invités étaient arrivés, d. nos amis marseillais** the guests had arrived, amongst whom were *or* including our friends from Marseilles

3 *(exprimant le complément de l'adjectif)* **le service d. vous êtes responsable** the service for which you are responsible; **c'est la seule photo d. je sois fier** it's the only photograph I'm proud of *or Sout* of which I'm proud

4 *(exprimant l'objet indirect)* **celui d. je vous ai parlé** the one I spoke to you about; **ce d. nous avons discuté** what we talked about; **explique-moi ce d. il s'agit** tell me what it's about; **une corvée d. je me passerais bien** a chore (which) I could well do without; **il n'y a rien là d. on puisse se féliciter** there's nothing to congratulate ourselves about; **une affaire d. il s'occupe** a matter which he is dealing with; **les vacances d. tu rêves** the holidays which you dream of *or* about

5 *(exprimant le complément du verbe → indiquant la provenance, l'agent, la manière etc)* **le**

mal d. il souffre the illness which he suffers from; **une personne d. on ne sait rien** a person nobody knows anything about; **cette femme d. je sais qu'elle n'a pas d'enfants** that woman who I know doesn't have any children; **la famille d. je viens** the family (which) I come from; **le nectar d. les abeilles tirent le miel** the nectar from which bees make honey, the nectar which bees make honey from; **les amis d. il est entouré** the friends he is surrounded by; **les cadeaux d. il a été comblé** the many presents (which) he received; **la façon d. elle s'y prend** the way (in which) she goes about it; **la manière d. il joue** the way (in which) he plays, his way of playing

donzelle [dɔ̃zɛl] **NF** *Fam Hum* little madam

doña [dɔɲa] **NF** Doña

dopage [dɔpaʒ] **NM 1** *(des sportifs)* drug use *(in competitive sport)* **2** *(de l'économie, des ventes)* boosting, artificial stimulation

dopamine [dɔpamin] **NF** *Biol & Chim* dopamine

dopaminergique [dɔpaminɛrʒik] **ADJ** *Biol & Chim* dopaminergic

dopant, -e [dɔpɑ̃, -ɑ̃t] **ADJ produit d.** drug **NM** drug *(used as stimulant in competitive sport)*

dope [dɔp] **NF** *très Fam Arg* drogue dope, stuff, *Br* gear

doper [3] [dɔpe] **VT 1** *(droguer)* to dope *(in competitive sport)* **2** *(économie, ventes)* to boost; **d. l'économie** to boost the economy, to stimulate the economy artificially; **la dépréciation du dollar a dopé les ventes à l'étranger** the depreciation in the value of the dollar has boosted export sales **3** *Chim* to dope

▶ **se doper VPR** to take drugs *(in competitive sport)*

dope sheet [dɔpʃit] **NM** *Cin & TV* dope sheet

doping [dɔpiŋ] **NM** drug use *(in competitive sport)*

Doppler [dɔpler] **NPR** *Phys* **effet D.** Doppler effect

doppler [dɔpler] **NM** *Méd* = use of Doppler's method to determine speed at which the blood is circulating

dorade [dɔrad] = **daurade**

dorage [dɔraʒ] **NM 1** *(d'un objet)* gilding **2** *Culin (d'un gâteau)* glazing; *(de la viande, du poisson)* browning

Dordogne [dɔrdɔɲ] **NF la D.** *(département)* (the) Dordogne; *(rivière)* the Dordogne (River)

doré, -e [dɔre] **ADJ 1** *(bouton, robinetterie)* gilt, gilded; **d. à la feuille** gilded with gold leaf; **d. sur tranche** *(livre)* gilt-edged, with gilded edges

2 *(chevelure, lumière, blés)* golden; *(peau)* golden brown; *(gâteau, viande)* golden brown; **ses cheveux étaient d'un blond d.** he had golden hair

3 *(idéal → jours, rêves)* golden

4 *(dans des noms d'animaux)* golden

NM 1 *(dorure)* gilt

2 *Can Ich* yellow *or* wall-eyed pike

◻ **dorée NF** *Ich* John Dory, dory

dorénavant [dɔrenavɑ̃] **ADV** *(à partir de maintenant)* from now on, *Sout* henceforth, henceforward; *(dans le passé)* from then on; **d., j'essaierai d'être moins distrait** from now on I'll try to be less absent-minded; **il décida que d. elle serait son assistante** he decided that from then on she would be his assistant

dorer [3] [dɔre] **VT 1** *(couvrir d'or)* to gild; **d. un cadre à la feuille** to gild a frame with gold leaf; **faire d. qch** to have sth gilded; *Fam* **d. la pilule à qn** to sugar the pill for sb

2 *(brunir → peau)* to give a golden colour to, to tan; *(→ blés, poires)* to turn golden; *(→ paysage)* to shed a golden light on; **le couchant dorait les roseaux** the setting sun tipped the reeds with gold

3 *Culin* **d. une pâte à l'œuf/au lait** to glaze pastry with egg yolk/with milk

VI 1 *Culin* to turn golden; **faire d. la viande** to brown the meat; **faites d. les oignons** cook *or* fry the onions until golden; **faites d. la tarte** bake the pie until golden; **faites d. les pommes de terre au four** put the potatoes in the oven to brown

2 **se faire d. au soleil** to sunbathe

▶ **se dorer VPR** to sunbathe; **se d. les jambes au soleil** to tan one's legs in the sun; *Fam* **se d. la pilule** *(bronzer)* to sunbathe ▪, to lie in the sun ▪; *(ne rien faire)* to do *Br* sweet FA *or Am* zilch

doreur, -euse [dɔrœr, -øz] **NM,F** gilder

dorien, -enne [dɔrjɛ̃, -ɛn] **ADJ 1** *Hist & Mus* Dorian **2** *Ling* Doric

NM *(dialecte)* Doric

❑ **Dorien, -enne NM,F** Dorian

dorin [dɔrɛ̃] **NM** *Suisse* = white wine produced in the Vaud canton

dorique [dɔrik] **ADJ** *(ordre)* Doric; **une colonne d'ordre d.** a Doric column

NM le d. the Doric order

doris[1] [dɔris] **NF** *Ich* Doris

doris[2] [dɔris] **NM** *Naut* dory

dorlotement [dɔrlɔtmɑ̃] **NM** coddling, pampering

dorloter [3] [dɔrlɔte] **VT** to pamper, to cosset; **il adore se faire d.** he loves being looked after

►**se dorloter VPR** to pamper oneself

dormance [dɔrmɑ̃s] **NF** dormancy

dormant, -e [dɔrmɑ̃, -ɑ̃t] **ADJ 1** *(eau)* still **2** *Littéraire (passion, sensualité)* dormant **3** *Biol* dormant, latent **4** *Constr (bâti, chassis)* fixed **5** *Fin (compte)* dormant; *(marché, capital)* unproductive, lying idle

NM 1 *Constr (bâti)* fixed frame, casing; *(vitre)* fixed pane **2** *Naut* standing end **3** *Can Rail Br* sleeper, *Am* tie

dormeur, -euse [dɔrmœr, -øz] **ADJ** *(poupée, poupon)* sleeping

NM,F sleeper; **c'est un grand** *ou* **gros d.** he likes his sleep

NM *(crabe)* (common *or* edible) crab

❑ **dormeuse NF** *(boucle d'oreille)* stud earring

dormir [36] [dɔrmir] **VI 1** *(gén)* to sleep; *(à un moment précis)* to be asleep, to be sleeping; **tu as bien dormi?** did you sleep well?; **dors bien!** sleep well!; **j'ai dormi tout l'après-midi** I was asleep *or* I slept all afternoon; **il dort tard le dimanche** he sleeps late on Sundays; **on dort mal dans ce lit** you can't get a good night's sleep in this bed; **tu as pu d. dans le train?** did you manage to get some sleep on the train?; **parler en dormant** to talk in one's sleep; **je n'ai pas dormi de la nuit** I didn't sleep a wink all night; **la situation m'inquiète, je n'en dors pas** *ou* **plus (la nuit)** the situation worries me, I'm losing sleep over it; **prends ce comprimé, ça te fera d.** take this, it'll help you sleep; **le thé m'empêche de d.** tea keeps me awake; **ma jambe m'empêche de d.** my leg keeps me awake, I can't sleep because of my leg; **ce n'est pas cette histoire de pots-de-vin qui va m'empêcher de d.!** I don't intend to lose any sleep over that corruption business!; **avoir envie de d.** to feel sleepy; **d. d'un sommeil léger** *(habituellement)* to be a light sleeper; *(à tel moment)* to be dozing; **d. d'un sommeil profond** *ou* **lourd** *ou* **de plomb** *(habituellement)* to be a heavy sleeper; *(à tel moment)* to be fast asleep, to be sound asleep, to be in a deep sleep; **d. à poings fermés** to be fast asleep, to be sleeping like a baby; **d. comme un ange** *(bébé)* to be sound asleep; *(adulte)* to sleep like a baby; **d. comme une bûche** *ou* **un loir** *ou* **une marmotte** *ou* **une souche** *ou* **un sabot** to sleep like a log; **il est là-haut, et dort comme une marmotte** he's upstairs, sound asleep *or* dead to the world; **tu dors debout** you can't (even) keep awake, you're dead on your feet; **elle a raconté au juge une histoire à d. debout** she told the judge a pack of lies; **d. du sommeil du juste** to sleep the sleep of the just; **tu peux d. sur tes deux oreilles** there's no reason for you to worry, you can sleep soundly in your bed at night; **je ne dors que d'un œil** *(je dors mal)* I can hardly sleep, I hardly get a wink of sleep; *(je reste vigilant)* I sleep with one eye open; *Prov* **qui dort dîne** he who sleeps forgets his hunger

2 *(être sans activité → secteur)* to be dormant *or* asleep; *(→ volcan)* to be dormant; *(→ économies personnelles)* to lie idle; *(→ économie nationale)* to be stagnant; **ils ont laissé d. le projet** they left the project on the back burner

3 *(être inattentif)* **dépêche-toi, tu dors!** come on, wake up!; **ce n'est pas le moment de d.!** now's the time for action!

VT *Littéraire* **d. un bon sommeil** to sleep peacefully

dormitif, -ive [dɔrmitif, -iv] **ADJ 1** *Arch (qui fait dormir)* sleep-inducing, soporific **2** *Hum (ennuyeux)* soporific

dormition [dɔrmisjɔ̃] **NF** *Rel* dormition

doronic [dɔrɔnik] **NM** *Bot* leopard's bane

dorsal, -e, -aux, -ales [dɔrsal, -o] **ADJ 1** *Anat & Zool* dorsal, back *(avant n)*; **la face dorsale de la main** the back of the hand **2** *Ling* dorsal

NM *Anat* **grand d., long d.** latissimus dorsi

❑ **dorsale NF 1** *Ling* dorsal consonant **2** *Zool* dorsal fin **3** *Géol (élévation)* ridge; *(montagne)* mountain range **4** *Météo* **dorsale barométrique** ridge of high pressure

dorsalgie [dɔrsalʒi] **NF** back pain

dort *etc voir* **dormir**

dort-en-chiant [dɔrɑ̃ʃjɑ̃] **NM INV** *Fam Br* slowcoach, *Am* slowpoke

dortoir [dɔrtwar] **NM** dormitory; **les dortoirs de la caserne** the sleeping quarters of the barracks

dorure [dɔryr] **NF 1** *(couche → d'or)* gilt; *(→ artificielle)* gold-effect finish; **bureau couvert de dorures** desk covered in gilding; **uniforme couvert de dorures** gold-braided uniform **2** *(processus)* gilding; **d. à la feuille** gold leaf gilding; **d. industrielle** foil blocking, gold blocking; **d. à la poudre** powder gilding; **d. sur tranches** *(reliure)* edge-gilding

doryphore [dɔrifɔr] **NM** *Entom* Colorado *or* potato beetle

DOS, Dos [dɔs] **NM** *Ordinat (abrév* **Disk Operating System**) DOS

DOS [do] **NM 1** *(partie du corps)* back; **le bas de son d.** the small of his/her back; **avoir le d. rond** to be hunched up *or* round-shouldered; **avoir le d. voûté** to have a stoop; **j'ai mal au d.** my back hurts, I've got backache; **j'avais le soleil dans le d.** the sun was behind me *or* on my back; **quand vous aurez l'église dans le d., tournez à droite** when you've passed the church, turn right; **être sur le d.** to be (lying) on one's back; **mets-toi sur le d.** lie on your back; **tourner le d. à qn** *(assis)* to sit with one's back to sb; *(debout)* to stand with one's back to sb; *(l'éviter)* to turn one's back on sb; **je ne l'ai vu que de d.** I only saw him from behind *or* the back; **j'étais d. à la fenêtre** I had my back to the window; **où est la gare? – vous lui tournez le d.** where is the station? – you're going away from it; **dès que j'ai le d. tourné, il fait des bêtises** as soon as my back is turned, he gets up to mischief; **partir sac au d.** to set off with one's rucksack on one's back *or* with one's backpack; **comme d'habitude, j'ai bon d.!** as usual, I get the blame!; *Ironique* **il a bon d., le mauvais temps!** (why not) blame the bad weather!; **j'ai le d. large mais il ne faut pas exagérer!** I can take a lot *or* I may be resilient, but there are limits!; *Fam* **ce gosse n'a rien sur le d.!** that kid's not dressed warmly enough!; *Fam* **elle a pas mal de dettes sur le d.** she's up to her ears *or* eyes in debt; *Fam* **c'est moi qui ai tous les préparatifs sur le d.** I've been saddled with all the preparations; **il est toujours derrière mon d.** he's always breathing down my neck; **faire qch dans** *ou* **derrière le d. de qn** to do sth behind sb's back; *Fam* **elle lui a fait un enfant dans le d.** she deliberately got pregnant■; *Fam* **être tombé sur le d. et se casser le nez** to be damned unlucky, to have rotten luck; *Fam* **tu es toujours sur le d. de ce gosse, laisse-le un peu!** you're always nagging the kid, leave him alone!; *Fam* **vous aurez les syndicats sur le d.** the unions will be breathing down your necks; **faire le gros d.** *(chat)* to arch its back; *Fig* to lie low; *Fam* **ils ont bâti leur empire sur le d. des indigènes** they built their empire at the expense of the natives; *Fam* **il l'a dans le d.!** he's been had *or* done!; *Fam* **fais gaffe, tu vas l'avoir dans le d.!** watch out or you'll get done!; **se mettre qn à d.** to put sb's back up; **je ne veux pas l'avoir** *ou* **me le mettre à d.** I don't want him to turn against me *or* to get his back up; **il les avait tous à d.** they were all after him; *Fam* **mettre qch sur le d. de qn** *(crime, erreur)* to pin sth on sb; **ils lui ont tout mis sur le d.!** they blamed *or* pinned everything on him/her; **c'est les flics qui m'ont mis ça sur le d.** I was set up by the cops!; **je n'ai rien/pas grand-chose à me mettre sur le d.** I've got nothing/virtually nothing to wear; **il s'est mis toute la responsabilité sur le d.** he shouldered the responsibility for the whole business; *Fig* **tirer dans le d. de qn** to shoot *or* to stab sb in the back; *Fam* **si le fisc lui tombe sur le d., ça va lui coûter cher!** if the *Br* Inland Revenue *or Am* IRS gets hold of *or* catches him/her, it'll cost him/her!; *Fig* **avoir le d. au mur** to have one's back to the wall

2 *(d'une fourchette, d'un habit)* back; *(d'un couteau)* blunt edge; *(d'un livre)* spine; **corsage décolleté dans le d.** low-backed blouse; *Fam* **il n'y est pas allé avec le d. de la cuillère!** *(dans une action)* he didn't go in for half-measures!; *(dans une discussion)* he didn't mince his words!

3 *Natation* **d. crawlé** backstroke; **on va jusqu'à la bouée en d. crawlé?** let's do the backstroke all the way to the buoy

❑ **à dos de PRÉP** on the back of; **aller à d. d'âne/d'éléphant** to ride (on) a donkey/an elephant; **le matériel est transporté à d. de lamas/d'hommes** the equipment is carried by llamas/men

❑ **au dos ADV** *(d'une feuille)* on the other side *or* the back, overleaf; **voir au d.** see over *or* overleaf

❑ **au dos de PRÉP** *(feuille)* on the back of; **signer au d. d'un chèque** to endorse a cheque, to sign the back of a cheque

❑ **dos à dos ADV** with their backs to one another; **mettez-vous d. à d.** stand back to back *or* with your backs to one another; *Fig* **mettre** *ou* **renvoyer deux personnes d. à d.** to refuse to get involved in an argument between two people

dosable [dozabl] **ADJ** which can be measured (out)

dosage [dozaʒ] **NM 1** *(détermination)* measurement, measuring; **faire un d.** to determine a quantity; **les dosages d'albumine montrent que...** the measured quantities of albumin show that...

2 *(dose précise de médicaments)* (prescribed) dose

3 *(proportions)* proportions; **le d. de ce cocktail est...** the (correct) proportions for this cocktail are...

4 *(équilibre)* balance; **il y a dans ses meubles un savant d. d'esthétisme et de fonctionnel** his furniture successfully combines aestheticism and functionality

5 *Méd* **d. hormonal** test to determine hormone levels; **d. immunologique** immunoassay; **d. radio-immunologique** radioimmunoassay

6 *(en œnologie)* sweetening *or* dosing (of champagne)

dos-d'âne [dodan] **NM INV** speed bump, *Br* sleeping policeman; **pont en d.** humpback bridge

dose [doz] **NF 1** *Pharm* dose; *Méd* dose, dosage; **une forte d. de ce médicament peut être mortelle** in large doses, this drug can be fatal; **prendre une forte d.** *ou* **une d. massive de sédatifs** to take an overdose of sedatives; **ne pas dépasser la d. prescrite** *(sur mode d'emploi)* do not exceed the prescribed dose

2 *Com (quantité prédéterminée → gén)* dose, measure; *(→ en sachet)* sachet; **mesurez trois doses de lait en poudre** take three measures of powdered milk; **une d. de désherbant pour dix doses d'eau** one part weedkiller to ten parts water; **réduisez la d. de lessive si votre eau n'est pas calcaire** reduce the amount of washing powder if the water in your area is soft

3 *(quantité → d'un aliment, d'un composant)* amount, quantity; **je ne connais pas les doses pour la vinaigrette** I don't know the right proportions *or* quantities to use when making vinaigrette; **ses documentaires ont tous une petite d. d'humour** there's a touch of humour in all his/her documentaries; **il a une d. de paresse peu commune** he's uncommonly lazy; **avec une petite d. de bon sens/volonté** with a modicum of common sense/willpower; **il faut une sacrée d. de bêtise/naïveté pour le croire** you have to be pretty stupid/naive to believe him; **du moment qu'il a sa d. journalière de télévision, il est content** as long as he gets his daily dose of television, he's happy

4 *Nucl* **d. absorbée** dose, dosage

5 *Fam (locutions)* **il a sa d.** *(lassé, ivre)* he's had a bellyful *or* as much as he can stand; **j'ai eu ma d. de problèmes!** I've had my (fair) share of problems!; **sa mère, j'en ai eu ma d.!** I've seen quite enough of his/her mother!; **les problèmes, j'en ai ma d.!** don't talk to me about problems!; **il tient sa** *ou* **en a une bonne d.** *Br* he's

as thick as two short planks, *Am* he's as dumb as they come; **ce type, la d. qu'il se trimballe!** he's an absolute moron, that guy!

❑ **à faible dose** ADV in small doses *or* quantities

❑ **à forte dose** ADV in large quantities *or* amounts

❑ **à haute dose** ADV in large doses *or* quantities; *Fam* **travailler à haute d.** to work like a dog; **être irradié à haute d.** to have received a large level of radiation

❑ **à petite dose, à petites doses** ADV in small doses *or* quantities; **j'aime bien le sport/ma sœur, mais à petites doses** I like sport/my sister, but (only) in small doses

doser [3] [doze] VT **1** *(médicament)* to measure a dose of; *(composant, ingrédient)* to measure out **2** *(équilibrer → cocktail, vinaigrette)* to use the correct proportions for; **comment doses-tu ta vinaigrette?** what proportions do you use for your vinaigrette? **3** *(utiliser avec mesure)* **d. ses forces** *ou* **son effort** to pace oneself; **il faut savoir d. ses critiques** you have to know how far you can go in your criticism **4** *Méd (albumine)* to determine the quantity of

doseur [dozœr] NM **1** *(appareil)* measure **2** *(comme adj)* **bouchon/gobelet d.** measuring cap/cup

dosimètre [dozimɛtr] NM *Nucl* dosimeter

dosimétrie [dozimetri] NF *Nucl* dosimetry

dossard [dosar] NM *Sport* number *(worn by player or competitor)*; **portant le d. numéro 3** wearing number 3

dosse [dos] NF flitch, slab of timber

dosseret [dosrɛ] NM **1** *Archit* pier; **d. de porte** door-jamb **2** *(outil)* back; *(d'une scie)* backing; **scie à d.** backed saw **3** *(d'un lit)* headboard

dossier [dosje] NM **1** *(d'une chaise, d'un canapé)* back; **chaise à d. droit** straight-backed chair

2 *(documents)* file; **avoir un d. sur qn** to keep a file on sb, to keep sb on file; **constituer** *ou* **établir un d. sur qn/qch** to build up a file on sb/sth; **il faudrait constituer** *ou* **établir un d. sur les mammifères** we should put together a file on mammals; **les élèves doivent faire un d. sur un sujet de leur choix** the pupils must do a project on the subject of their choice; **il connaît** *ou* **possède son d.** he knows what he's talking about; **d. d'appel d'offres** tender documents; **d. de candidature** application; **d. client** client file; **d. crédit** credit file; **d. de demande d'introduction en Bourse** listing agreement; **d. de demande de prêt** loan application form; **d. de domiciliation** domiciliation papers, domiciliation file; **d. de douane** customs papers *or* file; *Univ* **d. d'inscription** registration forms; **d. de lancement** *(d'un produit)* product launch file; **d. médical** medical file *or* records; *Scol* **d. scolaire** *Br* school record, *Am* student file

3 *Jur (d'un prévenu)* record; *(d'une affaire)* case; *Admin (d'un cas social)* case file; **ouvrir/fermer un d.** to open/to close a case file

4 *Journ, Rad & TV* **numéro spécial avec un d. sur le Brésil** special issue with an extended report on Brazil; **d. de presse** press pack

5 *(sujet)* question, matter; **c'est lui qui est chargé du d. environnement** he's in charge of environmental matters, he has special responsibility for the environment; **c'est un d. brûlant** it's a highly sensitive *or* topical issue

6 *(chemise cartonnée)* folder, file; **d. suspendu** suspension file

7 *Ordinat (répertoire)* folder; *(fichier)* file; **d. actif** active file; **d. archivé** archive file; **d. clos** closed file; **d. ouvert** open file; **d. sauvegardé** saved file; **d. système** system file

dossière [dosjɛr] NF *(d'un brancard, d'un limon)* back-strap, ridge-strap, back-band; *(d'une cuirasse)* back-plate; *(d'une scie)* backing; **scie à d.** backed saw

dossiste [dɔsist] NMF backstroker

Dostoïevski [dɔstɔjɛfski] NPR Dostoevski, Dostoyevsky

dot [dɔt] NF *(d'une mariée)* dowry; *(d'une religieuse)* (spiritual) dowry

❑ **en dot** ADV as a dowry; **apporter qch en d.** to bring sth as one's dowry, to bring a dowry of sth; **il lui avait laissé une ferme en d.** he'd left her a farmhouse as part of her dowry

dotal, -e, -aux, -ales [dɔtal, -o] ADJ dotal; *Arch Jur* **régime d.** (marriage) settlement in trust

dotation [dɔtasjɔ̃] NF **1** *(fonds versés → à un particulier, à une collectivité)* endowment; *(→ à un service public)* grant, funds

2 *(revenus → du président)* (personal) allowance, emolument; *(→ d'un souverain)* civil list

3 *(attribution → de matériel)* equipment; **la somme est réservée pour la d. du service en ordinateurs** the sum has been earmarked for providing *or* equipping the department with computers; *Can* **d. en personnel** staffing

4 *Compta* provision; **d. aux amortissements** depreciation provision, allowance for depreciation; **d. en capital** capital contribution; **d. aux provisions** charge to provisions

doter [3] [dɔte] VT **1** *(équiper)* **d. qch de qch** to provide *or* to equip sth with sth; **cette machine est dotée de mémoire** this machine is equipped with a memory

2 *(gratifier)* **la nature l'avait dotée d'une beauté/d'une volonté exceptionnelle** nature had endowed her with exceptional beauty/ with an exceptionally strong will; **un pays doté d'une puissante industrie** a country with a strong industrial base; **quand on est doté d'une bonne santé** when you enjoy good health

3 *(donner une dot à)* to give a dowry to; **ses filles sont richement dotées** his daughters have large dowries

4 *(financer → particulier, collectivité)* to endow; *(→ service public)* to fund

▶**se doter** VPR **se d. de** to acquire

douaire [dwɛr] NM dower

douairière [dwɛrjɛr] NF **1** *(veuve)* dowager (lady) **2** *Péj (femme)* rich old woman

Douala [dwala] NM Douala

douane [dwan] NF **1** *(à la frontière)* **(poste de) d.** customs; **passer à la d.** to go through customs; **il a été arrêté à la d.** he was stopped by customs officers *or* when going through customs; **d. volante** mobile customs and excise unit

2 *(administration)* **la d., les douanes, le service des douanes** *(gén)* the Customs (service); *(en Grande-Bretagne)* Customs and Excise (department); **entreposer qch en d.** to put sth in *or* into bond; **zone sous d.** area subject to customs authority

3 *(taxe)* **(droits de) d.** customs duty; **exempté de d.** duty-free, non-dutiable; **s'acquitter des droits de d.** to clear customs

douanier, -ère [dwanje, -ɛr] ADJ *(tarif, visite)* customs *(avant n)*

NM,F customs officer

douar [dwar] NM douar

doublage [dublaʒ] NM **1** *Cin (d'un film, d'une voix)* dubbing; *(par une doublure)* doubling; **il n'y a pas de d. pour les cascades** there's no body double for the stunts **2** *(habillage d'un coffre)* lining **3** *Couture* lining

doublant, -e [dublɑ̃, -ɑ̃t] NM,F **1** *Théât* understudy **2** *Cin* stand-in, body double **3** *Scol* = pupil who is repeating or has repeated a year at school

double [dubl] ADJ **1** *(deux fois plus grand → mesure, production)* double; **les profits seront doubles cette année** profits will be double *or* will have doubled this year; **un d. whisky** a double whisky; **chambre/lit d.** double room/ bed; *Ordinat* **disquette d. densité/d. face** double-density/double-sided disk; **d. imposition** double taxation; **d. menton** double chin

2 *(à deux éléments identiques)* double; **contrat en d. exemplaire** contract in duplicate; **d. deux/ cinq** *(à un jeu)* double two/five; **d. allumage** dual ignition; **en d. aveugle** double-blind; **d. commande** dual controls; **à d. commande** dual-control; **faire un d. débrayage** *Br* to double-declutch, *Am* to double-clutch; *Sport* **d. faute** *(au tennis)* double fault; **faire une d. faute** to serve a double fault, to double-fault; **stationner en d. file** to double-park; **je suis en d. file** I'm double-parked; **à d. fond** *(mallette)* double-bottomed, false-bottomed; **d. liaison** double bond; **d. nœud** double knot; **d. page** double-page spread; **à d. revenu** *(foyer, ménage)* two-income; **d. vitrage** double glazing; **faire poser un d. vitrage à une fenêtre** to double-glaze a window; **faire d. emploi** to be redundant; **faire d. emploi avec qch** to replicate sth

3 *(à éléments différents → avantage, objectif)* double, twofold; *(→ fonction, personnalité, tarification)* dual; **le préjudice est d.** the damage is of two kinds *or* is twofold; **avoir la d. nationalité** to have dual nationality; **mener une d. vie** to lead a double life; **à d. emploi** *ou* **usage** dual-purpose; **d. contrainte** double bind; *Com* **d. affichage des prix** dual pricing; *Fin* **d. circulation** *(de monnaies)* dual circulation; **à d. effet** double acting; *Fig* **d. jeu** double-dealing; *Bourse* **d. marché des changes** dual exchange market; *Bourse* **d. option** double option, put and call option; **jouer** *ou* **mener (un) d. jeu** to play a double game; **faire coup d.** *Chasse* to kill two animals with one shot; *Fig* to kill two birds with one stone

4 *Bot* double; **lilas d.** double lilac

5 *Jur* **d. degré de juridiction** double degree of jurisdiction; **avoir le droit à un d. degré de juridiction** to have the right to appeal; **d. peine** double punishment *(consisting of a prison sentence followed by expulsion from the country)*

NM **1** *(en quantité)* **six est le d. de trois** six is twice three *or* two times three; **coûter le d. de qch** to cost twice as much as sth; **j'ai payé le d.** I paid double that price *or* twice as much; **je croyais que ça coûtait 40 euros – c'est plus du d.** I thought it was 40 euros – it's more than twice that *or* double that price; *Fam* **les huîtres à 20 euros, ça les met au d. par rapport à l'an dernier!** oysters at 20 euros, they've doubled (in price) since last year!

2 *(exemplaire → d'un document)* copy; *(→ d'un timbre de collection)* duplicate, double; **tu as un d. de la clé?** have you got a spare *or* duplicate key?; **je garde des doubles de toute ma correspondance** I keep copies of all the letters I send; **faites un d.** *(d'un document)* make a copy; **j'ai fait faire un d. de la clé** I had a duplicate key made; **d. original** double original

3 *(sosie)* double, doppelgänger

4 *Sport* **jouer un d.** to play doubles *or* a doubles match; **c'est un bon joueur de d.** he's a good doubles player; **d. messieurs/dames/mixte** men's/women's/mixed doubles

ADV *(compter)* twice as much, double; *(voir)* double

❑ **à double sens** ADJ **un mot à d. sens** a double-entendre; **une phrase à d. sens** a double-entendre ADV **on peut prendre la remarque à d. sens** you can interpret *or* take that remark two ways

❑ **à double tranchant** ADJ *(couteau, action)* double-edged, two-edged; **c'est un argument à d. tranchant** the argument cuts both ways

❑ **à double tour** ADV **fermer à d. tour** to double lock; **enfermer qn à d. tour** to lock sb up

❑ **en double** ADV **les draps sont pliés en d.** the sheets are folded double *or* doubled over; **mettre qch en d.** *(corde)* to double sth over; *(couverture)* to double sth over, to fold sth double; **j'ai une photo en d.** I've got two of the same photograph; *Sport* **jouer en d.** to play (a) doubles (match)

'La Double vie de Véronique' *Kieslowski* 'The Double Life of Véronique'

doublé, -e [duble] ADJ **1** *Couture* lined (**de** with); **non d.** unlined **2** *Cin* dubbed

NM **1** *Chasse* right and left; **faire un d.** to shoot a right and left **2** *(succès)* double; **vainqueur du 100 et du 200 m, c'est un beau d.** he's won both the 100 and 200 m races, that's a nice double **3** *Mus* turn **4** *(en joaillerie)* **d. (or)** rolled gold; **d. argent** silver plate

doubleau, -x [dublo] NM **1** *Constr* ceiling-beam **2** *Archit* transverse rib

double-clic [dubləklik] *(pl* **doubles-clics***)* NM *Ordinat* double-click; **faire un d. (sur)** to double-click (on)

double-cliquer [3] [dubləklike] VI *Ordinat* to double-click

double-crème [dubləkrɛm] *(pl* **doubles-crèmes***)* NM ≃ cream cheese

double-croche [dubləkrɔʃ] *(pl* **doubles-croches***)* NF *Br* semi-quaver, *Am* sixteenth note

double-décimètre [dubləedesimɛtr] (*pl* **doubles-décimètres**) NM ruler

double-fenêtre [dubləfənɛtr] (*pl* **doubles-fenêtres**) NF double window

doublement[1] [dubləmã] NM **1** (*augmentation → des bénéfices, du personnel, d'une quantité, d'un prix, d'une production*) doubling (UNCOUNT), twofold increase; **ils demandent le d. de leur prime** they want their bonus to be doubled **2** (*d'un coureur, d'un véhicule*) passing, *Br* overtaking **3** (*d'une couverture, d'un papier, d'un tissu*) doubling, folding; (*d'une corde, d'un fil*) doubling (*d'une consonne*) doubling

doublement[2] [dubləmã] ADV doubly; **c'est d. ironique** there's a double irony there; **je suis d. déçu/surpris** I'm doubly disappointed/surprised

doubler [3] [duble] VT **1** (*dépasser → coureur, véhicule*) to pass, *Br* to overtake; **je me suis fait d. par un cycliste** a cyclist passed me, I was overtaken by a cyclist; **défense de d.** (*sur panneau*) no overtaking, no passing

2 (*porter au double → bénéfices, personnel, quantité, prix, production*) to double; **d. l'allure** *ou* **le pas** to quicken one's pace; **d. la mise** (*à un jeu*) to double the stake; *Fig* to raise the stakes

3 (*garnir d'une doublure → coffret, jupe, tenture*) to line (**de** with)

4 *Cin* (*film, voix*) to dub; (*acteur*) to stand in for, to double; **il se fait d. pour les cascades** he's got a stand-in *or* a double for his stunts

5 (*mettre en double → corde, fil*) to double; (→ *couverture, papier, tissu*) to fold (in half), to double (over); **les enfants, doublez les rangs** children, walk in twos; **ils ont doublé la route de Ligny à Verseil** they built a road parallel to the Ligny-Verseil road

6 *Fam* **d. qn** (*trahir*) to pull a fast one on sb, to double-cross sb; (*devancer*) *Br* to pip sb at the post, *Am* to beat sb out

7 *Chasse* **d. ses voies** to double back

8 *Mus* (*parties*) to split; **là, Verdi a doublé les altos** at that point, Verdi split the alto (into two semi-choruses)

9 *Naut* (*cap*) to double, to round; *Fig* **d. le cap de la trentaine** to turn thirty; *Fig* **l'inflation a doublé le cap des 5 pour cent** inflation has broken the 5 percent barrier

10 *Vieilli ou Belg, Can & Suisse Scol* to repeat; **il a doublé sa troisième** he had to do his fourth year again

VI **1** (*bénéfices, poids, quantité*) to double, to increase twofold

2 (*au tennis*) to double bounce

3 *Vieilli ou Belg, Can & Suisse Scol* to repeat a year

►**se doubler** VPR **se d. de** to be coupled with; **une mauvaise foi qui se double d'agressivité** insincerity coupled with aggressiveness

double-rideau [dublərido] (*pl* **doubles-rideaux**) NM double curtains

double-scull [dubləskœl] (*pl* **doubles-sculls**) NM double scull

doublet [dublɛ] NM **1** *Ling, Phys &* (*en joaillerie*) doublet **2** *Opt* doublet (lens)

doubleur[1], **-euse** [dublœr, -øz] NM,F *Belg* = pupil repeating a year; **c'est un d.** he's been put back a year

doubleur[2] [dublœr] NM *Ordinat* **d. de fréquence** clock speed doubler

doublier [dublije] NM **1** *Agr* double sheep rack **2** (*nappe*) large tablecloth (*folded double*) **3** (*vase*) large vase **4** (*plat*) large dish

ADJ *Hist* **haubert d.** hauberk of double mail; **heaume d.** tilting helm, heaume

doublière [dublijɛr] NF *Vét* = ewe or nanny-goat carrying twins

doublon [dublõ] NM **1** (*pièce*) doubloon **2** *Typ* doublet

doublonner [3] [dublɔne] **doublonner avec** VT IND to duplicate

doublure [dublyr] NF **1** (*garniture*) lining **2** *Cin* stand-in, body double; *Théât* understudy **3** *Métal* flaw, defect, scaling

Doubs [du] NM **le D.** Doubs

douçain [dusɛ̃] = **doucin**

douce [dus] *voir* **doux**

douce-amère [dusamɛr] (*pl* **douces-amères**) NF *Bot* woody nightshade, bittersweet

douceâtre [dusatr] ADJ (*odeur, goût, saveur*) sweetish; (*sourire, ton, voix*) sugary

doucement [dusmã] ADV **1** (*avec délicatesse, sans brusquerie → caresser, poser, prendre*) gently; (→ *manier*) gently, with care; (→ *démarrer*) smoothly; **d.** gently!, careful!; **d. avec les verres!** careful *or* go gently with the glasses!; **d. avec le champagne/poivre!** (go) easy on the champagne/pepper!; **il m'a poussé, et pas d. encore!** he gave me a real push!; **vas-y d., il est encore petit** go easy on *or* with him, he's only little

2 (*lentement → marcher, progresser, rouler*) slowly

3 (*graduellement → augmenter, s'élever*) gently, gradually; **le champ descend d. jusqu'à la rivière** the field slopes gently down to the river

4 (*sans bruit → chantonner*) softly; **parle plus d., il dort** lower your voice *or* keep your voice down, he's sleeping; **mets la radio, mais d.** put the radio on, but quietly

5 *Fam* (*discrètement*) **ça me fait d. rigoler, son projet de créer une entreprise** his idea of setting up a company is a bit of a joke

6 (*pour calmer, contrôler*) **d., d., vous n'allez pas vous battre, tout de même!** calm down, you don't want to fight, do you?; **d., je n'ai jamais dit ça!** hold on, I never said that!; *Fam* **d. les basses!** hey, hold on!

7 *Fam* (*moyennement*) so-so; **comment va ton commerce? – d.** how's your business doing? – so-so *or* it's just about keeping afloat

doucereusement [dusrøzmã] ADV in a sugary manner

doucereux, -euse [dusrø, -øz] ADJ (*goût, liqueur*) sweetish; *Péj* sickly sweet; (*voix, ton, paroles*) sugary, honeyed; (*manières, personne*) suave, smooth

doucet, -ette [dusɛ, -ɛt] ADJ *Arch* meek, mild
  ◻ **doucette** NF corn salad, lamb's lettuce

doucettement [dusɛtmã] ADV *Fam* (*marcher, progresser*) slowly■; **ton grand-oncle va bien? – tout d.** how is your great-uncle? – a bit frail but he's fine

douceur [dusœr] NF **1** (*toucher → d'une étoffe, d'une brosse*) softness; (→ *des cheveux, de la peau*) softness, smoothness; **vos mains conserveront ainsi toute leur d.** your hands will remain smooth *or* soft

2 (*goût → d'un vin, du miel*) sweetness; (→ *d'un fromage*) mildness

3 (*délicatesse → de caresses, de mouvements, de manières*) gentleness; (→ *d'une voix*) softness; **manipuler qch avec d.** to handle sth gently; **parler avec d.** to speak softly; **prendre qn par la d.** to use the soft approach with sb; **la d. de vivre** the gentle pleasures of life

4 (*bonté → d'une personne*) sweetness, gentleness; (→ *d'un regard, d'un sourire*) gentleness

5 (*d'un relief*) softness; **la d. de ses traits** his/her soft features

6 *Tech* (*de l'eau*) softness

7 (*du temps, du climat*) mildness; **j'étais surpris par la d. du soir** I was surprised by how mild an evening it was

8 (*friandise*) sweet

◻ **douceurs** NFPL **1** (*agréments*) pleasures; **les douceurs de la vie** the pleasures of life, the pleasant things in life

2 (*propos agréables*) sweet words; *Ironique* **les deux conducteurs échangeaient des douceurs** the two drivers were swapping insults

◻ **en douceur** ADJ (*décollage, démarrage*) smooth ADV (*sans brusquerie → gén*) gently; (→ *démarrer, atterrir*) smoothly; **réveille-moi en d. la prochaine fois** next time, wake me up gently; **allez-y en d.!** gently does it!, easy does it!

Douchanbe [duʃãbe] NM *Géog* Dushanbe

douche [duʃ] NF **1** (*jet d'eau*) shower; **prendre une d.** to have *or* to take a shower; **il est sous la d.** he's in the shower; **d. écossaise** hot and cold shower (*taken successively*); **ce mélangeur ne marche pas, c'est la d. écossaise!** that mixer tap's not working, you get scalded one minute and frozen the next!; **c'est la d. écossaise avec lui!** he blows hot and cold!

2 (*bac, cabine*) shower (unit); **les douches** the showers

3 *Fam* (*averse*) **recevoir** *ou* **prendre une bonne d.** to get drenched■ *or* soaked■

4 *Fam* (*choc, surprise*) shock■; (*déception*) letdown, anticlimax■; **ça m'a fait l'effet d'une d. (froide)** it came as a shock to me; **lui qui croyait être nommé directeur, quelle d.!** he thought he was going to be appointed manager, what a letdown for him!

5 *Fam* (*reproches*) telling-off, dressing-down

doucher [3] [duʃe] VT **1** (*laver*) to shower, to give a shower to; *Méd* to douche; *Fam* **je me suis fait d.** (*par la pluie*) I got drenched *or* soaked **2** *Fam* (*décevoir → personne*) to deflate **3** *Fam* (*réprimander*) **d. qn** to tell sb off, to give sb a good telling-off

►**se doucher** VPR to have *or* to take a shower

douchette [duʃɛt] NF shower rose

doucheur, -euse [duʃœr, -øz] NM,F bath attendant

douchière [duʃjɛr] NF (*en Afrique francophone*) bathroom

douci, -e [dusi] ADJ (*verre*) fine ground

doucin [dusɛ̃] NM *Hort* = wild apple tree for graft stock

doucine [dusin] NF **1** *Archit* cyma recta, doucine **2** (*outil*) ogee plane, ogee

douci-poli [dusipɔli] NM grinding and polishing

doucir [32] [dusir] VT (*verre*) to grind down; (*outil*) to set on the oil-stone

doucissage [dusisaʒ] NM (*du verre*) grinding down, fine grinding; (*d'un outil*) setting

doudou[1] [dudu] NF (*aux Antilles*) (*en appellatif*) honey, babe

doudou[2] [dudu] NM *Fam* (*tissu*) security blanket; (*objet fétiche*) = any object carried round by small children to make them feel secure

doudoune [dudun] NF (thick) quilted jacket *or* anorak

doué, -e [dwe] ADJ (*acteur, musicien*) gifted, talented; **être d. en dessin/pour les langues** to have a gift for *or* to be good at drawing/languages; **il est d. dans tous les sports** he's an all-round sportsman; **être d. pour tout** to be an all-rounder; **tu es vraiment d. pour envenimer les situations!** you've got a real knack for stirring things up!; *Fam* **je n'arrive pas à brancher le tuyau – tu n'es pas d.!** I can't connect the hose – you're hopeless!

douelle [dwɛl] NF (*en tonnellerie*) stave; *Archit* soffit; **d. extérieure** extrados; **d. intérieure** intrados

douer [6] [dwe] VT **d. qn de qch** to endow sb with sth; **la nature l'a doué d'une mémoire étonnante** nature has endowed *or* blessed him with an exceptional memory; **être doué de** (*intelligence, raison*) to be endowed with; (*mémoire*) to be gifted *or* blessed *or* endowed with

douille [duj] NF **1** (*de cuisine*) piping nozzle **2** (*d'une cartouche*) (cartridge) case **3** (*d'une ampoule*) (lamp) socket **4** (*de cylindre*) casing

douiller [3] [duje] VI *Fam* **1** (*payer*) to cough up, to fork out; **la bouffe est super, mais ça douille!** the food is great but it costs a packet *or* an arm and a leg! **2** (*avoir mal*) to be in agony■; **j'ai douillé pendant deux mois après mon opération** I was in agony for two months after my operation

douilles [duj] NMPL *Fam* (*cheveux*) hair■

douillet, -ette [dujɛ, -ɛt] ADJ **1** (*très sensible à la douleur*) oversensitive; (*qui a peur de la douleur*) afraid of getting hurt; *Péj* **que tu es d.!** don't be so soft! **2** (*confortable → vêtement, lit, appartement*) (nice and) cosy, snug

◻ **douillette** NF **1** (*robe de chambre*) quilted dressing gown **2** (*de prêtre*) quilted overcoat **3** *Can* (*couvre-lit*) *Br* quilted bedspread, *Am* comforter

douillettement [dujɛtmã] ADV cosily, snugly; **vous êtes d. installé ici!** you're nice and cosy here!; **il a été élevé trop d.** he was coddled too much as a child

douleur [dulœr] NF **1** (*physique → gén*) pain; (→ *diffuse*) ache; **je ne supporte pas la d.** I can't stand pain; **vous ne ressentirez aucune d.** you won't feel any pain; **une d. fulgurante/sourde** a searing/dull pain; **douleurs abdominales** stomach ache *or* pains; **douleurs rhumatismales** rheumatic pains; **j'ai une d. à la cuisse** my thigh hurts, my thigh's sore, I've got a pain in

my thigh; **quand mes vieilles douleurs se ré-veillent** when my old pains or aches and pains come back

2 (psychologique) grief, sorrow, pain; **à notre grande d., il s'est éteint hier** to our great sorrow, he passed away yesterday; **j'ai eu la grande d. de perdre ma femme il y a deux ans** I suffered the grief of losing my wife two years ago; **nous avons la d. de vous faire part du décès de…** it is with great or deep sorrow (and regret) that we have to announce the death of…; **nous avons eu la d. d'apprendre que…** it was with great sorrow that we learned that…; **les grandes douleurs sont muettes** great sorrow is often silent; Fam **si je le chope, il va comprendre sa d.** if I catch him, he'll get what's coming to him or his worst nightmares will come true

douloureuse [dulurøz] voir **douloureux**

douloureusement [dulurøzmɑ̃] ADV **1** (physiquement) painfully **2** (moralement) painfully, grievously; **la disparition de sa sœur l'a d. frappée** her sister's death was a great blow to her; **d. éprouvé par le départ de sa femme** wounded or deeply hurt by his wife's leaving him

douloureux, -euse [dulurø, -øz] ADJ **1** (brûlure, coup, coupure) painful; (articulation, membre) painful, sore; **mes jambes sont très douloureuses le soir** my legs are very sore or hurt a lot at night

2 (humiliation, souvenirs) painful; (circonstances, sujet, période) painful, distressing; (nouvelle) grievous, painful, distressing; (poème, regard) sorrowful

❑ **douloureuse** NF Fam Hum (au restaurant) Br bill▪, Am check▪; (facture) bill▪; **on va bientôt recevoir la douloureuse** we'll soon get the bad news

doum [dum] NM Bot doum palm, doom palm

douma [duma] NF Hist Duma

dourine [durin] NF Vét dourine

Douro [duro] NM Géog **le D.** the Douro

douro [duro] NM duro

douroucouli [durukuli] NM Zool night or owl monkey

doute [dut] NM **1** (soupçon) doubt; **avoir des doutes sur** ou **quant à** ou **au sujet de qch** to have (one's) doubts or misgivings about sth; **je n'ai pas le moindre d. là-dessus** I haven't the slightest doubt about it; **il n'y a aucun d. (possible), c'est lui** it's him, (there's) no doubt about it; **sa responsabilité ne fait pratiquement aucun d.** there's little doubt (about the fact) that he's/she's responsible; **il n'y a aucun d. que c'est lui le coupable** there's no doubt that he is the culprit; **sa victoire ne faisait aucun d.** there was no doubt about him/her being the winner, his/her victory was certain; **il aura l'oscar, ça ne fait aucun d.** he'll get the Oscar, there's no doubt about that; **de gros doutes pèsent sur lui** heavy suspicion hangs over him; **il y a des doutes quant à l'identité du peintre** there is some doubt as to the identity of the painter

2 (perplexité, incertitude) doubt, uncertainty; Phil doubt; **il ne connaît pas le d.** he never has any doubts; **le d. persiste sur ses motifs** there's still some doubt about his/her motives; **jeter le d. sur qch** to cast or to throw doubt on sth; **tu as semé** ou **mis le d. dans mon esprit** you've made me doubtful; **d. de soi** self-doubt

❑ **dans le doute** ADV **être dans le d.** to be doubtful or uncertain; **je suis toujours dans le d. quant à sa sincérité** I'm still in doubt or doubtful or uncertain about his/her honesty; **laisser qn dans le d.** (sujet: personne, circonstances) to leave sb in a state of uncertainty

❑ **en doute** ADV **mettre en d.** (sujet: personne) to question, to challenge; (sujet: circonstances, témoignage) to cast doubt on; **je ne mets pas votre sincérité en d.** I don't question your sincerity; **mettez-vous ma parole en d.?** do you doubt my word?

❑ **sans doute** ADV **1** (probablement) no doubt; **sans d. vous êtes-vous déjà rencontrés** you've no doubt met before; **comme elle te l'a sans d. appris** as she has no doubt told you; **sans d. aurait-il préféré cela** no doubt he would have preferred that

2 (assurément) **sans aucun** ou **nul d.** without (a) doubt, undoubtedly, Sout indubitably

3 (certes) **tu me l'avais promis – sans d., mais…** you'd promised me – that's true or I know, but…

douter [3] [dute] VT **je doute qu'il soit assez fort** I doubt whether he is strong enough; **je n'ai jamais douté que tu viennes** I never doubted that you would come; **je ne doute pas qu'il (ne) vous vienne en aide** I am confident that he will help you

❑ **douter de** VT IND **1** (ne pas croire à → succès, victoire) to be doubtful of; (→ fait, éventualité) to doubt; **d. de l'existence/la véracité de qch** to doubt the existence/truth of sth; **je n'ai jamais douté de ton talent** I never doubted your talent; **on peut d. de la sécurité du système** the safety of the system is open to doubt; **tu viendras? – j'en doute fort** will you come? – I very much doubt it; **elle ne doute de rien** she has no doubts about anything

2 (traiter avec défiance → ami, motivation) to have doubts about; **elle semble d. de mes sentiments** she seems to doubt my feelings; **d. de la parole de qn** to doubt sb's word; **d. de soi** (habituellement) to have doubts about or to lack confidence in oneself; (à un moment) to have doubts about oneself; **tu doutes trop de toi** you don't have enough confidence in yourself; **ça m'a fait d. de moi** it made me wonder if I was right

3 Rel to have doubts about

USAGE ABSOLU **j'étais prête à me marier, mais maintenant je doute** I was going to get married, but now I've got doubts about it

▸ **se douter** VPR **1** **se d. de** (s'attendre à) to know, to suspect; **j'aurais dû m'en d.** I should have known; **je me doutais un peu de sa réaction** I half expected him/her to react the way he/she did, his/her reaction didn't surprise me; **je me doutais un peu de son état d'esprit** I'd suspected or guessed the state of mind he/she was in; **comme tu t'en doutes sûrement** as you've probably guessed; **il a eu très peur – je m'en doute** he got quite a fright – I can (well) imagine that; **il faudra que tu viennes me chercher – je m'en doute!** (avec irritation) you'll have to come and fetch me – well, yes, I expected that!; **j'ai raté le train – vu l'heure, on s'en serait douté!** I missed my train – given the time, that's pretty obvious!

2 **se d. de** (soupçonner) to suspect; **son mari ne s'est douté de rien pendant des années** her husband suspected nothing for years; **je ne me serais jamais douté que c'était possible** I'd never have thought it (was) possible; **je lui ai proposé de travailler pour moi, tout en me doutant bien qu'il refuserait** I suggested he work for me, but I knew he wouldn't accept; **j'étais loin de me d. que…** little did I know that…; **tu te doutes bien que je te l'aurais dit si je l'avais su!** you know very well that I would have told you if I'd known!

douteur, -euse [dutœr, -øz] ADJ doubting; **siècle d.** age of doubt

NM,F doubter

douteusement [dutøzmɑ̃] ADV doubtfully

douteux, -euse [dutø, -øz] ADJ **1** (non certain, non assuré → authenticité, fait) doubtful, uncertain, questionable; (→ avenir, issue, origine etc) doubtful, uncertain; (→ signature) doubtful; **il est d. qu'il vienne** it's doubtful whether he will come; **il n'est pas d. que…** there's no doubt that…

2 Péj (inspirant la méfiance → individu) dubious-looking; (→ comportement, manœuvres, passé etc) dubious, questionable; **d'une manière douteuse** dubiously; **nature douteuse** dubiousness; **le portrait/ta plaisanterie était d'un goût d.** the portrait/your joke was in dubious taste

3 (sale, dangereux) dubious; **du linge d.** ou **d'une propreté douteuse** clothes that are none too clean; **jetez toujours une viande douteuse** always throw away any meat you're not sure of; **l'installation électrique est douteuse** the wiring's none too safe; **il s'est présenté sous un jour d.** he showed himself in a dubious or uncertain light

douvain [duvɛ̃] NM (en tonnellerie) = wood used for staving

douve [duv] NF **1** Équitation water jump **2** (fossé → dans les champs) trench, ditch; (→ d'un château) moat **3** (d'un fût) stave **4** Entom (fluke; **d. du foie** liver fluke **5** Bot spearwort

douvelle [duvɛl] NF (en tonnellerie) small stave

Douvres [duvr] NM Dover

doux, douce [du, dus] ADJ **1** (au toucher → cheveux, peau) soft, smooth; (→ brosse à dents) soft; **le d. contact de la soie** the soft touch of silk

2 (au goût → vin) sweet; (→ fromage) mild

3 (détergent, savon, shampooing) mild; (énergie, technique) alternative; (drogue) soft; **médecines douces** alternative medicine

4 (sans brusquerie → geste, caresse, personne) gentle; (→ pression) soft, gentle; (→ balancement, pente) gentle; (→ accélération) smooth; (→ véhicule) smooth-running; **il a eu une mort douce** he died peacefully

5 (bon, gentil → personne, sourire, tempérament) gentle; **d. comme un agneau** meek as a lamb

6 (modéré → châtiment) mild; (→ reproche) mild, gentle; (→ éclairage, teinte) soft, subdued; (→ chaleur, campagne, forme) gentle

7 Météo (air, climat) mild; (chaleur, vent) gentle

8 (harmonieux → intonation, mélodie, voix) soft, sweet, gentle; **quel d. prénom!** what a sweet-sounding name!

9 (plaisant → rêves, souvenir) sweet, pleasant; (→ paix, succès) sweet; Littéraire **ton amour m'était alors si d.** how sweet it was, being loved by you then; **que ces mots sont d. à entendre!** how sweet it is to hear these words!

10 Ling soft

NM,F (par affection) **ma douce** my sweet

ADV **1** (tiède) **il fait d.** it's mild out

2 (locution) **tout d.!** (sans brusquerie) gently (now)!; (pour calmer) calm down!, easy now!; **vas-y tout d. avec elle** be careful with her

❑ **Doux** NM Can Fam **mon D.!** my goodness!

❑ **douce** NF Vieilli **sa douce** (sa fiancée) his beloved

❑ **en douce** ADV Fam (dire, donner, partir etc) on the quiet, sneakily

'**Doux Oiseau de jeunesse**' Williams, Brooks 'Sweet Bird of Youth'

doux-amer, douce-amère [duzamɛr, dusamɛr] (mpl **doux-amers**, fpl **douces-amères**) ADJ bittersweet

doux-temps [dutɑ̃] NM INV Can milder spell of weather (during winter)

douzain [duzɛ̃] NM Littérature twelve-line poem

douzaine [duzɛn] NF **1** (douze) dozen; **une d. d'escargots/d'œufs** a dozen snails/eggs

2 (environ douze) **une d. de** a dozen or so, about twelve; **une d. de pages** about or roughly twelve pages, a dozen or so pages; **il y a une d. d'années** about twelve years ago, a dozen or so years ago

❑ **à la douzaine** ADV (acheter, vendre) by the dozen; **il y en a à la d.** Br they're ten a penny, Am they're a dime a dozen; Fam **des chanteurs comme lui, il y en a à la d.!** you'll find dozens of singers like him!

douze [duz] ADJ **1** (gén) twelve **2** (dans des séries) twelfth; **page/numéro d.** page/number twelve

PRON twelve

NM INV **1** (gén) twelve **2** (numéro d'ordre) number twelve **3** (chiffre écrit) twelve; voir aussi **cinq**

douze-huit [duzɥit] NM INV Mus twelve-eight time; (morceau) = piece in twelve-eight time

douzième [duzjɛm] ADJ twelfth

NMF **1** (personne) twelfth **2** (objet) twelfth (one)

NM **1** (partie) twelfth **2** (étage) Br twelfth floor, Am thirteenth floor **3** (arrondissement de Paris) twelfth (arrondissement)

NF Mus twelfth; voir aussi **cinquième**

douzièmement [duzjɛmmɑ̃] ADV in twelfth place

Dow Jones [doʒɔns] NM Bourse **(indice) D.** Dow Jones (index)

doxologie [dɔksɔlɔʒi] NF doxology

doyen, -enne [dwajɛ̃, -ɛn] NM,F **1** (d'un club, d'une communauté) most senior member; (d'un pays) eldest or oldest citizen; (d'une profession)

doyen, *f* doyenne; **d. (d'âge)** oldest person **2** *Univ* dean

NM *Rel* dean

doyenné [dwajene] **NM 1** *(district, demeure)* deanery **2** *(fonction)* deanship

NF d. (du comice) comice (pear)

doyenneté [dwajɛnte] **NF** *Vieilli* seniority in age

DP [depe] **NM** *(abrév* **délégué du personnel***)* staff representative

DPE [depeø] **NF** *(abrév* **direction par exceptions***)* management by exception

DPI [depei] **NM** *Méd (abrév* **diagnostic préimplantatoire***)* PGD

dpi [depei] *(abrév* **dots per inch***)* dpi

DPLG [depeɛlʒe] **ADJ** *(abrév* **diplômé par le gouvernement***)* = certificate for architects, engineers etc

DPO [depeo] **NF** *(abrév* **direction par objectifs***)* MBO

DQ *(abrév écrite* **dernier quartier de lune***)* = last quarter

DR *Anciennement (abrév écrite* **drachme***)* Dr

Dr *(abrév écrite* **Docteur***)* Dr

dr *(abrév écrite* **droite***)* R, r

dracena, dracæna [drasena] **NM** dracaena

drache [draʃ] **NF** *Belg (averse)* shower

dracher [3] [draʃe] **V IMPERSONNEL** *Belg* to pour with rain

drachme [drakm] **NF 1** *Anciennement* drachma **2** *Pharm* dram, drachm

draconien, -enne [drakɔnjɛ̃, -ɛn] **ADJ** *(mesure)* drastic, draconian, stringent; *(règlement)* harsh, draconian; *(régime)* strict

drag [drag] **NM 1** *Chasse* drag, draghunt **2** *Hist (véhicule)* drag

dragage [dragaʒ] **NM 1** *(pour prélèvement)* dragging, dredging; *(pour nettoyage)* dredging; **d. de mines** minesweeping

dragée [draʒe] **NF 1** *(confiserie)* sugared almond; *Pharm* (sugar-coated) pill; **tenir la d. haute à qn** *(dans une discussion, un match)* to hold out on sb **2** *(balle)* lead shot **3** *Agr* dredge

---

Culture

DRAGÉE

A paper cone filled with sugared almonds ("un cornet de dragées") is a traditional gift given to guests at christenings and weddings in France.

---

dragéifié, -e [draʒeifje] **ADJ** sugared, sugar-coated

dragéifier [9] [draʒeifje] **VT** *Pharm (pilule)* to coat with sugar, to sugar; **comprimé dragéifié** sugar-coated pill

drageoir [draʒwar] **NM 1** *(coupe)* dish for holding sweetmeats **2** *(boîte)* box for holding sweetmeats

dragéon [draʒɔ̃] **NM** *Bot* sucker

drageonnage [draʒɔnaʒ], **drageonnement** [draʒɔnmɑ̃] **NM** *Hort* throwing out of suckers, suckering

drageonner [3] [draʒɔne] **VI** *Hort* to throw out suckers, to sucker

dragline [draglin] **NM** dragline, dragline excavator

dragon [dragɔ̃] **NM 1** *Myth* dragon **2** *(gardien)* dragon; *Hum* **c'est un d. de vertu** she claims to be such a paragon of virtue **3** *Vieilli (mégère)* dragon **4** *Hist & Mil* dragoon **5** *Zool* **d. de Komodo** Komodo dragon *or* lizard; **d. volant** flying lizard

dragonnade [dragɔnad] **NF** dragonnade *(raid on Protestants under Louis XIV)*

dragonne [dragɔn] **NF** *(de bâton de ski, de piolet, de parapluie)* wrist-loop; *(d'épée)* sword-knot

dragonnet [dragɔnɛ] **NM** *Ich* dragonet

dragonnier [dragɔnje] **NM** *Bot* dracena, dragon tree

dragster [dragstɛr] **NM** dragster

drague [drag] **NF 1** *(en travaux publics)* dredge; **d. flottante** *ou* **hydrographique** dredger; **d. à godets** bucket dredger; **d. suceuse** pump dredger **2** *Pêche* dragnet

3 *Fam (flirt)* **pour la d., il est doué!** he's always *Br* on the pull *or Am* on the make; **la d. par Minitel®** picking people up via Minitel®, ≃ cruising the chatlines; **ce mec-là, c'est un pro de la d.** he's a bit of a pro at *Br* chatting up *or Am* hitting on women, that guy; **c'est un lieu de d.**

idéal it's an ideal place for *Br* chatting people up *or Am* hitting on people; **lieu de d. homo** gay cruising area

draguer [3] [drage] **VT 1** *(nettoyer → fleuve, canal, port)* to dredge; *(en cherchant)* to drag

2 *(retirer → mine)* to sweep; *(→ ancre)* to drag (anchor)

3 *(pêcher → coquillages)* to dredge for

4 *Fam (fille, garçon)* to come on to, *Br* to chat up, *Am* to hit on; *(en voiture)* to cruise; **je me suis fait d. par le serveur** I got *Br* chatted up *or Am* hit on by the waiter; **elle n'arrête pas de d. les mecs** she's always chasing after guys

VI *Fam* to be *Br* on the pull *or Am* on the make; **d. en voiture** to cruise

dragueur, -euse [dragœr, -øz] **ADJ** **il n'a jamais été très d.** he's never been one for *Br* chatting up *or Am* hitting on women

NM,F *Fam* **c'est un d.** he's always *Br* on the pull *or Am* on the make; **sa sœur est une sacrée dragueuse** his/her sister's always chasing after men

NM 1 *(navire)* dredger; **d. de mines** minesweeper **2** *(matelot)* dredgerman **3** *Pêche* dragnet fisherman

draille [draj] **NF** *(en Provence)* wide path *(for cattle on the move)*

drain [drɛ̃] **NM** *Méd & Tech* drain

drainage [drɛnaʒ] **NM 1** *(d'une plaie, d'un sol)* drainage **2** *(de capital, de ressources)* tapping **3** *(massage)* **d. lymphatique** lymph *or* lymphatic drainage

draine [drɛn] **NF** *Orn* mistle thrush

drainer [4] [drene] **VT 1** *(assécher)* to drain **2** *(rassembler → capital, ressources)* to tap; **d. des auditeurs/des téléspectateurs** to draw listeners/viewers **3** *(canaliser → foule)* to channel; **d. la circulation vers une voie de dégagement** to channel the traffic towards a relief road **4** *Géog* **la Seine draine les eaux de toute cette région** the waterways throughout the area flow towards *or* drain into the Seine

draineur, -euse [drɛnœr, -øz] **ADJ** *(plante, aliment)* that helps to eliminate toxins (from the body)

NM cet aliment est un excellent d. hépatique this food is very good at eliminating toxins from the liver

draineuse NF *(machine)* trenching machine *(with drain-laying apparatus)*

draisienne [drezjɛn] **NF** dandy horse

draisine [drezin] **NF** *Rail Br* track motorcar, *Am* gangcar, handcar

drakkar [drakar] **NM** *Naut & Hist* drakkar

Dralon® [dralɔ̃] **NM** Dralon®

DRAM [dram] **NF** *Ordinat (abrév* **dynamic random access memory***)* DRAM

dramatique [dramatik] **ADJ 1** *Théât (musique, œuvre)* dramatic **2** *(grave → conséquences, issue, période, situation)* horrendous, appalling; **elle ne comprend rien aux équations, c'est d.!** she hasn't got a clue about equations, it's appalling!; **j'ai raté mon permis de conduire – ce n'est pas d.!** I've failed my driving test – it's not the end of the world! **3** *(tragique → dénouement, événement)* tragic

NF *TV* television play *or* drama; *Rad* radio play *or* drama

dramatiquement [dramatikmɑ̃] **ADV** tragically; **encore une soirée qui se termine d.** yet another party with a tragic ending

dramatisant, -e [dramatizɑ̃, -ɑ̃t] **ADJ** over-dramatic

dramatisation [dramatizasjɔ̃] **NF** over-dramatization

dramatiser [3] [dramatize] **VT 1** *(exagérer → histoire)* to over-dramatize **2** *Théât (œuvre)* to dramatize, to turn into a play

USAGE ABSOLU ne dramatise pas! don't be so melodramatic!

dramaturge [dramatyrʒ] **NM** playwright, dramatist

dramaturgie [dramatyrʒi] **NF 1** *(art)* dramatic art, drama **2** *(traité)* treatise on dramatic art

drame [dram] **NM 1** *Théât (œuvre)* drama; *Arch (pièce)* play; *(genre)* drama; **d. bourgeois** bourgeois drama; **d. lyrique** opera

2 *Rad & TV* drama, play; **d. judiciaire** courtroom drama; **d. télévisé** television drama

3 *(événement)* drama; **il a raté son examen, mais ce n'est pas un d.** he failed his exam, but it's not the end of the world; **faire un d. de qch** to make a drama out of sth; **j'étais en retard, il en a fait tout un d.** I was late and he made such a fuss about it; **le d., c'est que personne ne le croit** the sad thing is that nobody believes him; **je lui ai emprunté son appareil photo, le d.!** I borrowed his/her camera and he/she made such a fuss!; **l'excursion a tourné** *ou* **viré au d.** the trip ended tragically; **d. de la jalousie hier à Lyon** *(titre de journal)* jealousy causes tragedy yesterday in Lyons

drap [dra] **NM 1** *(pour lit)* **d. (de lit)** (bed) sheet; **des draps** sheets, bedlinen; **d. de dessus/dessous** top/bottom sheet; **se mettre dans** *ou* **entre les draps** to get between the sheets; **se retrouver** *ou* **se trouver dans de beaux draps** to find oneself up the creek (without a paddle); **nous voilà dans de beaux** *ou* **vilains draps!** we're in a fine mess!; **tu m'as mis dans de beaux draps!** you've landed me in a fine mess!

2 *(serviette)* **d. de bain** bath sheet; **d. de plage** beach towel

3 *Belg* towel; **d. de maison** tablecloth

4 *Tex* woollen cloth; **d. fin** broadcloth; **gros d.** coarse woollen cloth; **d. d'or/de soie** gold/silk brocade

drapé [drape] **NM** *(plis, tombé)* **la jupe a un beau d.** the skirt hangs beautifully

drapeau, -x [drapo] **NM 1** *(pièce d'étoffe)* flag; *Mil* flag, colours; **saluer le d.** to salute the colours; **le d. blanc** the white flag, the flag of truce; **le d. britannique** the British flag, the Union Jack; **le d. noir** the black flag; **le d. rouge** the red flag; **le d. tricolore** the French flag, the tricolour (flag); **combattre/se ranger sous le d. de qn** to fight under/to rally round sb's flag; *Fig* **mettre son d. dans sa poche** to hide one's political opinions **2** *aussi Hum (patrie)* **pour le d.** *ou* **l'honneur du d.** *Br* ≃ for King/Queen and country, *Am* ≃ for the red, white and blue

3 *Aviat* **mettre en d.** *(hélice)* to feather

4 *Ordinat (flag)* marker

5 *Golf* flag, pin

□ sous les drapeaux ADV être sous les drapeaux *(au service militaire)* to be doing one's military service; *(en service actif)* to serve in one's country's armed forces

drapement [drapmɑ̃] **NM** draping

draper [3] [drape] **VT 1** *(couvrir → meuble)* to drape, to cover with a sheet **2** *(arranger → châle, rideaux)* to drape **3** *Tex (laine)* to process

▶ se draper VPR se d. dans qch to drape oneself in sth; **se d. dans un châle** to drape *or* to wrap oneself in a shawl; **se d. dans sa dignité** to stand on one's dignity; **se d. dans sa vertu** to cloak oneself in virtue

draperie [drapri] **NF 1** *(tissu disposé en grands plis)* drapery, hanging **2** *(industrie)* cloth trade; *(fabrique)* cloth manufacture **3** *Beaux-Arts* drapery

drap-housse [draus] *(pl* **draps-housses***)* **NM** fitted sheet

drapier, -ère [drapje, -ɛr] **ADJ** **marchand d.** *Br* draper, *Am* clothier; **ouvrier d.** cloth worker

NM,F *(fabricant)* cloth manufacturer; *(vendeur)* *Br* draper, *Am* clothier

DRASS [dras] **NF** *Admin (abrév* **Direction Régionale des Affaires Sanitaires et Sociales***)* = office administering health and social services at regional level

drastique [drastik] **ADJ 1** *(mesure)* harsh, drastic; *(règlement)* strict **2** *Pharm* drastic

NM *Méd* drastic purgative

drave [drav] **NF 1** *Can (flottage)* transport *(of floating logs)* **2** *Bot* whitlow grass; **d. printanière** common whitlow grass

draver [3] [drave] **VT** *Can* to float

draveur [dravœr] **NM** *Can* driver

dravidien, -enne [dravidjɛ̃, -ɛn] **ADJ** Dravidian

NM Dravidian

drawback [drɔbak] **NM** *Com* drawback

drayage [drɛjaʒ] **NM** *Vieilli* **1** *Tex* skiving, shaving **2** *Cin & Typ* polishing (out)

drayer [11] [drɛje] **VT 1** *Agr (champ)* to cut the boundary-furrow *or* the last furrow of **2** *(roue)* to unscotch **3** *Vieilli Tex (cuir)* to skive, to shave

VI *(rayons)* to work loose

dreadlocks [drɛdlɔks] NFPL dreadlocks

dreadnought [drɛdnɔt] NM *Naut* dreadnought

drèche, drêche [drɛʃ] NF draff, *Can* crude cod-liver oil

drège¹ [drɛʒ] NF *Tex* rippling comb, ripple

drège², **dreige** [drɛʒ] NF *Pêche* dragnet

drelin [drǝlɛ̃] EXCLAM *Fam Vieilli* ting-a-ling!

drenne [drɛn] NF *Orn* mistle thrush

drépanocytose [drepanɔsitɔz] NF *Méd* sickle-cell anaemia

Dresde [drɛzd] NM Dresden

dressage [drɛsaʒ] NM 1 *(d'un fauve)* taming *(UNCOUNT)*; *(d'un cheval sauvage)* training *(UNCOUNT)*; *(d'un cheval de cirque, d'un chien de garde)* training *(UNCOUNT)*; *(d'un cheval de parade)* dressage 2 *(d'un mât, d'un monument, d'un échafaudage)* erection, raising; *(d'une tente)* pitching

dressant [drɛsɑ̃] NM *Mines* edge seam, edge coal

dressé, -e [drese] ADJ 1 *(oreille, queue)* (standing) erect 2 *(chien)* trained

dresser [4] [drese] VT 1 *(ériger → mât, pilier)* to put up, to raise, to erect; *(→ statue)* to put up, to erect; *(→ tente, auvent)* to pitch, to put up; **d. une échelle contre un mur** to put up *or* to set up a ladder against a wall

2 *(construire → barricade, échafaudage)* to put up, to erect; *(→ muret)* to erect, to build; **d. des obstacles devant qn** to put obstacles in sb's way, to raise difficulties for sb

3 *(installer → autel)* to set up; **d. un camp** to set up camp; **d. le couvert** *ou* **la table** to lay *or* to set the table; **d. un buffet** to set out a buffet; *Fig* **d. ses batteries** to lay one's plans

4 *(lever → bâton)* to raise, to lift; *(→ menton)* to stick out; *(→ tête)* to raise, to lift; **d. les oreilles** *(chien)* to prick up *or* to cock its ears; **d. l'oreille** *(personne)* to prick up one's ears

5 *(dompter → fauve)* to tame; *(→ cheval sauvage)* to break in; *(→ cheval de cirque, chien de garde)* to train; **d. un chien à attaquer** to train a dog to attack

6 *Fam (mater → soldat)* to drill, to lick into shape; **ce gamin aurait besoin d'être dressé!** that kid needs to be taught his place!; **je vais te d., moi!** I'll make him toe the line!

7 *(établir → liste, inventaire)* to draw up, to make out; *(→ bilan)* to draw up, to prepare; **d. le bilan d'une situation** to take stock of a situation; **d. (une) contravention** to give a ticket *(for a driving offence)*

8 *(opposer)* **d. qn contre qn/qch** to set sb against sb/sth

9 *Menuis* to dress

►**se dresser** VPR 1 *(se mettre debout)* to stand up, to rise; **se d. sur la pointe des pieds** to stand on tiptoe; **l'ours se dressa sur ses pattes de derrière** the bear rose *or* reared *or* stood up on its hind legs; **se d. sur son séant** to sit up straight

2 *(oreille de chien)* to prick up; **à ce nom, ses oreilles se sont dressées** *(chien)* when he/she heard that name, he/she pricked up his/her ears; **un film à faire se d. les cheveux sur la tête** *ou* **à vous faire d. les cheveux sur la tête** a hair-raising movie *or Br* film; **c'est à vous faire d. les cheveux sur la tête!** it makes your hair stand on end!

3 *(être vertical → montagne, tour)* to stand, to rise; *(dominer)* to tower; **avec son clocher se dressant fièrement** with its belltower standing proudly; **un paravent se dresse entre le salon et la chambre** a screen stands between the lounge and the bedroom

4 *(surgir → obstacles)* to rise, to stand; *(→ objet)* to loom; **on vit soudain se d. les miradors** the watchtowers loomed up suddenly

5 *(manifester son opposition)* **se d. contre** to rise up *or* to rebel against

dresseur, -euse [drɛsœr, -øz] NM,F *(de fauves)* tamer; *(de chiens de cirque, de garde)* trainer; *(de chevaux sauvages)* horsebreaker

dressing [drɛsiŋ], **dressing-room** [drɛsiŋrum] *(pl dressing-rooms)* NM dressing room *(near a bedroom)*

dressoir [drɛswar] NM sideboard

drève [drɛv] NF *Belg* tree-lined avenue

Dreyfus [drɛfys] NPR **l'affaire D.** the Dreyfus Affair

Culture

L'AFFAIRE DREYFUS

Captain Alfred Dreyfus was wrongly convicted of passing military secrets to the Germans in 1894. His innocence was gradually established, notably by Zola's letter "J'accuse" published in *l'Aurore*. The affair, exacerbated by the fact that Dreyfus was Jewish, crystallized the opposition between the left and right wing, dividing the nation between "dreyfusards", calling for justice and favouring reformist and socialist trends, and the antisemitic "anti-dreyfusards".

---

dreyfusard, -e [drɛfyzar, -ard] NM,F supporter of Dreyfus

DRH [deɛraʃ] NF *(abrév direction des ressources humaines)* human resources department

NM *(abrév directeur des ressources humaines)* human resources manager

dribble [dribl] NM *Sport* dribble; **faire un d.** to dribble

dribbler [3] [drible] *Sport* VT *(ballon)* to dribble; *(joueur)* to dribble round

VT to dribble

dribbleur, -euse [driblœr, -øz] NM,F *Sport* dribbler

drift [drift] NM 1 *Géol (glacial)* drift 2 *Électron* drift transistor

drifter [drifter] NM *Pêche* herring drifter

drill [dril] NM *(singe)* drill

drille¹ [drij] NM *voir* **joyeux**

drille² [drij] NF *Tech* hand drill

driller [3] [drije] VT *Tech* to drill, to bore

dring [driŋ] EXCLAM ding!, ding-a-ling!

dringuelle [drɛ̃gɛl] NF *Belg Fam (pourboire)* tip ■

drink [driŋk] NM *Fam* drink ■

drisse [dris] NF halyard

drive [drajv] NM *Ordinat & Sport* drive

drive-in [drajvin] *(pl drive-ins)* NM *(restauration rapide)* drive-through; *(cinéma)* drive-in

driver¹ [drajvœr] NM *Équitation & Golf* driver

driver² [3] [drajve] *Sport* VT to drive

VT to drive

DRM [deɛrɛm] NM *(abrév digital rights management)* DRM

drogman [drɔgmɑ̃] NM *Hist* dragoman

drogue [drɔg] NF 1 *(narcotique)* drug; **le jeu était devenu une d. pour lui** gambling had become a drug for him; *Fam* **le travail est ma d.** I'm married to my job, I'm a workaholic; *Fam* **moi, ma d., c'est le chocolat** I'm addicted to chocolate, I'm a chocaholic; **la télévision est une d. pour eux** they're television addicts; **d. douce/ dure** soft/hard drug; **d. de synthèse** synthetic drug

2 *(usage)* **la d.** drug-taking, drugs; **la d. est un fléau** drugs are a scourge of society

3 *Vieilli (médicament)* drug; *Péj* nostrum, quack remedy

drogué, -e [drɔge] NM,F drug addict; *Fam* **c'est une droguée du café** she's addicted to coffee; *Fam* **les drogués du travail** workaholics; *Fam* **les drogués de l'information** information addicts

droguer [3] [drɔge] VT 1 *(prisonnier)* to drug; *(chien, cheval)* to dope

2 *(malade)* to dose with drugs; **on m'a complètement drogué pendant deux semaines** I was given massive doses of drugs for two weeks

3 *(boisson)* to drug, to lace with a drug; *(repas)* to put a drug in

►**se droguer** VPR 1 *(prendre des stupéfiants)* to take drugs, to be on drugs; **je ne me drogue pas** I don't take drugs; **se d. à l'héroïne** to be on heroin

2 *(prendre des médicaments)* to take drugs

droguerie [drɔgri] NF 1 *(boutique)* hardware *Br* shop *or Am* store 2 *(activité)* hardware trade

droguet [drɔgɛ] NM *Vieilli Tex* drugget

droguiste [drɔgist] NMF keeper of a hardware *Br* shop *or Am* store

droit¹, -e¹ [drwa, drwat] ADJ *(ailier, jambe, œil)* right; **le côté d.** the right-hand side

NM right; **crochet du d.** right hook; **direct du d.** straight right

❑ **à droite** NF 1 *(côté droit)* **la droite** the right (side), the right-hand side; **à ma droite, le château** to *or* on my right is the castle; **à la droite de Dieu** *ou* **du Père** on God's right hand; **sur la droite** on the right; *Aut* **tenir sa droite** to

---

keep to the right; **de droite et de gauche** from all quarters *or* sides

2 *Pol* **la droite** the right (wing); **droite dure** hard right; **droite modérée** soft right

❑ **à droite** ADV 1 *(du côté droit)* **conduire à droite** to drive on the right-hand side; **tourne à droite** turn right; **le poster est trop à droite** the poster's too far to the right; *Fig* **à droite et à gauche** here and there, all over the place

2 *Mil* **à droite, droite!** right wheel!; **à droite, alignement!** right, dress!

3 *Pol* **être à droite** to be right-wing *or* on the right; **être très à droite** to be very right-wing *or* on the far right; **voter à droite** to vote for the right

❑ **à droite de** PRÉP to *or* on the right of

❑ **de droite** ADJ 1 *(du côté droit)* **la porte de droite** the door on the right, the right-hand door

2 *Pol* right-wing; **les gens de droite** right-wingers, people on the right; **l'électorat de droite** right-wing electorate; **être de droite** to be right-wing

droit², -e² [drwa, drwat] ADJ 1 *(rectiligne → allée, bâton, nez)* straight; **après le village, la route redevient droite** after the village, the road straightens out again; **ta raie n'est pas droite** your parting isn't straight *or* is crooked; *Fig* **le d. chemin** the straight and narrow; **rentrer dans le d. chemin** to mend one's ways; **rester dans le d. chemin** to keep to the straight and narrow

2 *(vertical, non penché → mur)* upright, straight, *Spéc* plumb; *(→ dossier, poteau)* upright, straight; **restez le dos bien d.** keep your back straight; **être** *ou* **se tenir d.** *(assis)* to sit up straight; *(debout)* to stand up straight; **d. comme un cierge** *ou* **un i** *ou* **un piquet** (as) stiff as a poker *or* a ramrod *or* a post

3 *(d'aplomb)* straight; **tiens le plat d.** hold the dish straight *or* level *or* flat; **mettre d.** *(casquette, cadre)* to set straight, to put straight, to straighten

4 *(loyal → personne)* upright, honest

5 *(sensé → raisonnement)* sound, sane

6 **manteau/veston d.** single-breasted coat/jacket; **col d.** stand-up collar; **jupe droite** straight skirt

7 *Anat* **muscle d.** musculus rectus

ADV 1 *(écrire)* in a straight line; *(couper, rouler)* straight; **après le carrefour, c'est toujours tout d.** after the crossroads, keep going straight on *or* ahead; **il s'est dirigé d. vers moi** he walked straight towards me; **j'irai d. au but** I'll come straight to the point, I won't beat about the bush; **il est allé d. à l'essentiel** *ou* **au fait** he went straight to the point; **aller d. à la catastrophe/l'échec** to be heading straight for disaster/a failure; **aller d. à la ruine** to be on the road to ruin; **ça m'est allé d. au cœur** it went straight to my heart

2 *Suisse (exactement)* exactly; *(tout à fait)* completely, absolutely; *(tout juste)* just; **c'est d. son père** he's the spitting image of his father; **elle est d. arrivée** she's just arrived

❑ **droite** NF *Géom* straight line

DROIT³ [drwa]

| law 1 | ■ right 2, 3 | ■ tax 4 | ■ duty 4 | ■ fee 5 |

NM 1 *Jur* **le d.** *(lois, discipline)* law; **faire son d.** to study law; **étudiant en d.** law student; **en d., ça s'appelle "contrefaçon"** the legal term for that is "infringement"; **avoir le d. pour soi** to have right *or* the law on one's side; **d. administratif** administrative law; **d. des affaires** corporate law; **d. bancaire** banking law; **d. de brevet** patent law; **d. cambiaire** law of negotiable instruments; **d. civil** civil law; **d. commercial** business law; **d. commun** common law; **d. communautaire** Community law; **d. de la concurrence** competition law, *Am* antitrust law; **d. constitutionnel** constitutional law; **d. coutumier** customary law; **d. des contrats** contract law; **d. douanier** customs legislation; **d. écrit** statute law; **d. de l'environnement** environmental law; **d. fiscal** tax law; **d. international** international law; **d. judiciaire** (law of) procedure; **d. maritime** maritime law; **d. des obligations** law of contract; **d. pénal** criminal law; **d. positif** statute law; **d. privé** private law; **d. de procédure**

(law of) procedure; **d. public** public law; **d. social** employment law; **d. des sociétés** corporate law; **d. du travail** labour law

2 *(prérogative)* right; **connaître/défendre ses droits** to know/to defend one's rights; **nos droits en tant que consommateurs** our rights as consumers; **avoir des droits sur qch** to have rights to sth; **tu n'as aucun d. sur moi** you have no power over me; **avoir d. de vie et de mort sur qn** to have the power of life and death over sb; **d. d'accès aux documents administratifs** = right of access to government documents; **d. d'aînesse** primogeniture; **d. d'asile** right of asylum; **d. d'association** right of (free) association; **d. de chasse** hunting rights; **droits civiques** civil rights; **d. à la couronne** entitlement to the crown; *Hist* **d. de cuissage** droit de seigneur; *Fig* **le patron exerçait un d. de cuissage sur les jeunes employées** the boss forced the young female employees to have sex with him; **d. divin** divine right; **droits extrapatrimoniaux** non-pecuniary rights; **d. de grâce** right of reprieve; **d. de grève** right to strike; **les droits de l'homme** human rights; **d. incorporel** intangible right; **d. individuel à la formation** = law under which all salaried employees have the right to 20 hours' training per year; **d. de licenciement** right to dismiss; **d. de passage** right of *Br* way *or Am* easement; **d. patrimonial** pecuniary right; **le d. des peuples à disposer d'eux-mêmes** the right of peoples to self-determination; **d. de préemption** right of first refusal; **d. de préférence** pre-emptive right; **d. préférentiel de souscription** pre-emptive right; *Fin* **d. de rachat** repurchase right, buyback right; **d. de reprise** right of recovery; **d. de retention** tax lien; *Bourse* **d. de souscription (d'actions)** subscription right; *Fin* **droits de tirage** drawing rights; *Fin* **droits de tirage spéciaux** special drawing rights; **d. d'usage** right of user; **droits de visite** *Br* access rights, *Am* visitation rights; **d. de voirie** = tax paid by businesses who wish to place displays, signs etc on the public highway; **le d. de vote** the franchise, the right to vote; **avoir d. de cité** *(idéologie)* to be established, to have currency; *Fam* **ce gosse a tous les droits dans la maison** that kid lords it over the whole household; **ils se croient tous les droits, ces gens-là!** these people think they can do what they like!

3 *(autorisation sociale ou morale)* right; **j'ai ouvert ton courrier – de quel d.?** I opened your mail – who gave you permission?; **de quel d. l'a-t-il lue?** what gave him the right to read it?, what right had he to read it?; **le billet donne d. à une consommation gratuite** the ticket entitles you to a free drink; **son rang lui donne d. à des privilèges particuliers** his/her rank entitles him/her to certain privileges; **donner le d. à qn de faire qch** to give sb the right to *or* to entitle sb to do sth; **être en d. de faire qch** to be entitled *or* to have the right to do sth; **je suis en d. d'obtenir des explications** I'm entitled to an explanation; **faire d. à une demande** to comply with *or Sout* accede to a request; **reprendre ses droits** *(idée, habitude, nature)* to reassert itself; **après Noël, la politique reprend ses droits** after the Christmas break, politics returns to centre stage; **avoir d. à** *(explications)* to have a right to; *(bourse, indemnité)* to be entitled to, to be eligible for; *(reconnaissance, respect)* to deserve; **je n'ai pas d. à une retraite** I'm not entitled to a pension; **et moi, je n'y ai pas d., au gâteau?** don't I get any cake then?; **on a encore eu d. à ses souvenirs de guerre!** we were regaled with his war memories as usual!; *Fam* **on va avoir d. à une bonne saucée!** we'll get well and truly soaked!; *Fam* **ils parlent de licencier 300 personnes, je sens que je vais y avoir d.** they're talking about laying off 300 people and I think that's going to include me; **avoir d. de regard sur** *(comptabilité, dossier)* to have the right to examine *or* to inspect; *(activités)* to have the right to control; **avoir le d. de faire qch** *(gén)* to be allowed *or* to have the right to do sth; *(officiellement)* to have the right *or* to be entitled to do sth; **tu n'as pas le d. de parler ainsi!** you've no right to talk like that!; *Hum* **tu as le d. de te taire** you can shut up; **j'ai bien le d. de me reposer!** I'm entitled to some rest, aren't I?; **tu n'as pas le d.! – je le prends!** you can't do that! – who says I can't!; **le d. à la différence** the right to be different; **d. de réponse** right of reply

4 *(imposition)* duty; *(taxe)* tax; **payer des droits sur les alcools** to pay duty on alcohol; **exempt de droits** duty-free; **soumis à des droits** dutiable; **d. au bail** = tax on rented accommodation (usually included in the rent); **droits de douane** customs duties; **d. d'entrée** import duty; **d. d'exportation** export duty; **d. d'importation** import duty; **droits de port** harbour dues; **d. de sortie** export duty; **droits de succession** death duties, inheritance tax; **d. de timbre** stamp duty; *Bourse* **d. de transfert** transfer duty

5 *(frais)* fee; **droits à la charge du vendeur/de l'acheteur** duty to be paid by the seller/purchaser; **d. de courtage** brokerage (fee); **d. d'enregistrement** registration fee *(for legal documents)*; **d. d'entrée** entrance fee; **d. fixe** fixed fee; *Banque* **droits de garde** custody account charges; **droits d'inscription** registration fee *or* fees

6 *(locutions)* **à bon d.** quite rightly, with good reason; **à qui de d.** *(sur un document)* to whom it may concern; **s'adresser à qui de d.** to apply to the proper quarter *or* to an authorized person; **être dans son (bon) d.** to be within one's rights; **de (plein) d.** by rights, as a right; **c'est de plein d. qu'il l'a repris** he had every right to take it back; **membre de plein d.** ex officio member

❑ **droits** NMPL **droits (d'auteur)** *(prérogative)* rights, copyright; *(somme)* royalties; **avoir les droits exclusifs pour qch** to have (the) sole rights for sth; **tous droits (de reproduction) réservés** copyright *or* all rights reserved; **tous droits réservés pour le Canada** all rights reserved for Canada; **droits d'achat** purchasing rights; **droits de distribution, droits de diffusion** distribution rights; **droits étrangers** foreign rights; **droits exclusifs, droits d'exclusivité** sole rights, exclusive rights; **droits d'exclusivité** exclusive rights; **droits statutaires** statutory rights; **droits de traduction** translation copyright; **droits de vente exclusifs** exclusive selling rights; *Bourse* **droits de vote** *(des actionnaires)* voting rights

droit-de-l'hommisme [drwadlɔmism] NM *Péj* woolly liberalism

droit-de-l'hommiste [drwadlɔmist] NMF *Péj* woolly liberal

droitement [drwatmɑ̃] ADV uprightly, honestly

droit-fil [drwafil] *(pl* **droits-fils**) NM 1 *Couture* straight grain 2 *Fig* **dans le d. de** in line *or* keeping with; **sa déclaration était dans le d. de sa campagne** his/her statement was in keeping *or* in line with the drift of his/her campaign

droitier, -ère [drwatje, -ɛr] ADJ 1 *(qui utilise la main droite)* right-handed 2 *Pol* right-wing
NM,F right-handed person, right-hander

droitisme [drwatism] NM *Pol* rightism, right-wingness

droitiste [drwatist] *Pol* ADJ right-wing
NMF right-winger

droiture [drwatyr] NF *(d'une personne)* uprightness, honesty; *(d'intentions, de motifs)* uprightness

drolatique [drɔlatik] ADJ funny

drôle [drol] ADJ 1 *(amusant → personne, film, situation etc)* funny, amusing; **sa sœur est très d.** his/her sister's very funny *or* good fun; **tu te crois d.!** you think you're funny!; **le plus d. c'est que…** the funny thing is that…; *Ironique* **très d.!** very funny *or* droll *or* amusing!; **ça n'a rien de d.** it's not funny; **ce n'est pas d.!** *(pas amusant)* it's not funny!, I don't find that funny *or* amusing!; *(pénible)* it's no joke!; **ce n'est pas toujours d. au bureau!** life at the office isn't always a barrel of laughs!; **la grand-mère n'est pas toujours d.** grandma isn't always easy!; *Fam* **tu aurais dû le laisser faire – tu es d., il se serait fait mal!** you should have let him – are you kidding? he'd have hurt himself!

2 *(étrange)* strange, funny, peculiar; **je l'ai trouvé d. hier** he was behaving rather oddly *or* strangely yesterday; **c'est d., il était ici il y a un instant** that's strange *or* funny *or* peculiar, he was here a minute ago; *Fam* **ça me fait (tout) d. de revenir ici** it feels really strange *or* funny to be back; **se sentir (tout) d.** to feel (really) funny *or* weird; **en voilà une d. d'idée!** what a strange *or* funny *or* weird idea!; **il a une d. de façon d'exprimer sa gratitude!** he's got a funny way of showing his gratitude!; **ça fait un d. de bruit** it makes a strange *or* funny noise; **drôles de gens!** what peculiar *or* strange people!; **tu en fais une d. de tête!** you look as if something's wrong!; **avoir un d. d'air** to look strange *or* funny; *Hist* **la d. de guerre** the phoney war

3 *Fam (en intensif)* **il a de drôles de problèmes en ce moment** he's got some real problems at the moment; **il faut un d. de courage pour faire ça!** you need a hell of a lot of courage to do that!; **j'ai eu une d. de grippe!** I had a really bad case of flu; **ça a de drôles d'avantages!** it's got terrific *or* fantastic advantages!

NM 1 *Littéraire (voyou)* rascal, rogue; *(enfant déluré)* little rascal *or* rogue

2 *Arch (enfant)* child

❑ **drôles** NFPL *Fam (histoires)* **il en a entendu/raconté de drôles!** he heard/told some very weird stories!■; **en faire voir de drôles à qn** to give sb a terrible time of it

drôlement [drolmɑ̃] ADV 1 *Fam (vraiment)* **d. ennuyeux** deadly boring; **ça sent d. bon** it smells really great; **les prix ont d. augmenté** prices have gone up an awful lot■; **il fait d. chaud ici!** it's really hot in here!■; **j'ai d. eu peur** I got a real fright■; **je m'étais d. trompée sur son compte** I was really mistaken about him■; **tu l'as d. abîmée, la voiture** you've done the car a lot of damage■; **je me suis d. fait mal** I really hurt myself■

2 *(bizarrement → regarder, parler)* in a strange *or* funny *or* peculiar way■

3 *(de façon amusante)* amusingly■

drôlerie [drolri] NF 1 *(d'une personne, d'un spectacle, d'une remarque)* drollness, funniness 2 *(acte)* funny *or* amusing thing (to do); *(remarque)* funny *or* amusing thing (to say)

drôlesse [drolɛs] NF 1 *Vieilli (femme)* (brazen) hussy 2 *Arch (fille)* lass

drôlet, -ette [drolɛ, -ɛt], **drôlichon, -onne** [drolifɔ̃, -ɔn] ADJ *Fam* odd■, funny■

DROM [drom] NM *(abrév* **Département et Région d'outre-mer**) = French overseas department and region

> *Culture*
> **DROM**
> The acronym DROM replaced the acronym DOM in 2003 (see also entries DOM-TOM and COM). The "départements et régions d'outre-mer" are Guadeloupe, Martinique, Guiana and La Réunion.

dromadaire [drɔmadɛr] NM *Zool* dromedary

Drôme [drom] NF **la D.** Drôme

drome [drom] NM 1 *Naut* spare gear 2 *Orn* **d. (ardéole)** crab plover

dromon [drɔmɔ̃] NM *Naut* dromon, dromond

drone [drɔn] NM *Mil* drone; **d. d'attaque** attack drone; **d. de combat** combat drone; **d. de reconnaissance** reconnaissance drone

drongo [drɔ̃go] NM *Orn* drongo

dronte [drɔ̃t] NM *Orn* dodo

drop [drɔp] NM *Sport (au rugby)* drop goal

droper[1] [3] [drɔpe] VI *Fam* to clear off, to beat it

droper[2] [3] [drɔpe] VT 1 *Mil (parachuter)* to drop 2 *Fam (accompagner)* to drop (off)■ 3 *Fam (abandonner → personne)* to drop■; *(→ études, activité)* to drop■, to pack in 4 *Golf* **d. une balle** to take a drop

drop-goal [drɔpgɔl] *(pl* **drop-goals**) NM *Sport (au rubgy)* drop goal

droppage [drɔpaʒ] NM *Aviat* (parachute) drop; **zone de d.** drop zone

dropper[1] [3] [drɔpe] VI = **droper**[1]

dropper[2] [3] [drɔpe] VT = **droper**[2]

drosera [drɔzera], **drosère** [drɔzɛr] NF *Bot* sundew

drosophile [drozɔfil] *Entom* NF fruit fly, *Spéc* drosophila

❑ **drosophiles** NFPL fruit flies, *Spéc* Drosophilae

drosse [drɔs] NF *Naut* **drosses de gouvernail** wheel-ropes, tiller-ropes, rudder chains; **d. de vergue** truss

drosser [3] [drɔse] VT *Naut* to drive

Drouot [druo] *voir* **hôtel**

dru, -e [dry] ADJ *(cheveux)* thick; *(végétation)* dense, thick; *(barbe)* bushy, thick; *(pluie)* heavy
> ADV *(croître, pousser)* densely, thickly; *(pleuvoir)* heavily; **les mauvaises herbes ont poussé d.** there has been a thick growth of weeds; **la pluie tombe d.** it's raining heavily; *Fig* **les coups pleuvaient d.** blows rained down (on all sides)

drugstore [drœgstɔr] NM small shopping *Br* centre *or Am* mall

druide, -esse [drɥid, -ɛs] NM,F druid, *f* druidess

druidique [drɥidik] ADJ druidic, druidical

druidisme [drɥidism] NM druidism

drumlin [drœmlin] NM drumlin

drummer [drœmœr] NM *(batteur)* drummer

drums [drœmz] NMPL *(batterie)* drums

drupacé, -e [drypase] ADJ *Bot* drupaceous

drupe [dryp] NF *Bot* drupe

druze [dryz] ADJ Druzean, Druzian, Druze
> □ **Druze** NMF Druze; **les Druzes** the Druze

dry [draj] ADJ INV *(apéritif, champagne)* dry; *(whisky)* neat, straight
> NM INV dry Martini

dryade [drijad] NF **1** *Myth* dryad **2** *Bot* dryas, mountain avens

dry-farming [drajfarmiŋ] *(pl* **dry-farmings)** NM *Agr* dry farming

dryopithèque [drijopitɛk] NM dryopithocine

DS [deɛs] NF *(voiture)* = now legendary futuristic car produced by Citroën in the 1950s

DSL [deɛsɛl] NM *Ordinat (abrév* **Digital Subscriber Line)** DSL

DSRP [deɛsɛrpe] NM *(abrév* **Document stratégique de réduction de la pauvreté)** PRSP

DST [deɛste] NF *(abrév* **Direction de la surveillance du territoire)** = internal state security department, *Br* ≃ MI5, *Am* ≃ CIA

DT [dete] NM *Méd (abrév* **diphtérie, tétanos)** = vaccine against diphtheria and tetanus

D.T.Coq. [detekɔk] NM *Méd (abrév* **diphtérie, tétanos, coqueluche)** = vaccine against diphtheria, tetanus and whooping cough

DTP [detepe] NM, **DT-Polio** [detepoljo] NM *Méd (abrév* **diphtérie, tétanos, polio)** = vaccine against diphtheria, tetanus and polio

DTS [deteɛs] NMPL *Fin (abrév* **droits de tirage spéciaux)** SDRs

DTTAB [deteteɑbe] NM *Méd (abrév* **diphtérie, tétanos, tiphoïde A et B)** = vaccine against diphtheria, tetanus and typhoid

DTU *(abrév écrite* **dinar tunisien)** D

du [dy] *voir* **de**

dû, due [dy] PP *voir* **devoir**
> ADJ **1** *(à payer)* owed; **quelle est la somme due?** what's the sum owed *or* due?
> **2 dû à** *(causé par)* due to; **sa maladresse est due à sa timidité** his/her clumsiness is caused by *or* is due to his/her shyness; **son licenciement est dû aux difficultés économiques de l'entreprise** he/she was made redundant because of *or* due to the company's economic difficulties
> NM due; **je ne fais que lui réclamer mon dû** I'm only asking for what he/she owes me
> □ **en bonne et due forme** ADV *Jur* in due form
> □ **jusqu'à due concurrence de** PRÉP up to (a limit of); **jusqu'à due concurrence de 2000 euros** up to 2,000 euros

dual, -e, -aux, -ales [dɥal, -o] ADJ dual

dualiser [3] [dɥalize] **se dualiser** VPR to split into two

dualisme [dɥalism] NM dualism

dualiste [dɥalist] ADJ dualistic
> NMF dualist

dualité [dɥalite] NF duality; *Jur* **d. de juridictions** = French dual court system of administrative and judicial courts

Dubayy [dybaj] NF Dubai

dubitatif, -ive [dybitatif, -iv] ADJ dubious, sceptical

dubitativement [dybitativmɑ̃] ADV dubiously, sceptically

Dublin [dyblɛ̃] NM Dublin

dublinois, -e [dyblinwa, -az] ADJ of/from Dublin
> □ **Dublinois, -e** NM,F Dubliner

dubnium [dybnjɔm] NM *Chim* dubnium

duc [dyk] NM **1** *(titre)* duke **2** *Orn* horned owl

ducal, -e, -aux, -ales [dykal, -o] ADJ ducal; **un titre d.** a duke's title

ducasse [dykas] NF *(dans le nord de la France)* fair

ducat [dyka] NM ducat

ducaton [dykatɔ̃] NM ducatoon

duc-d'albe [dykdalb] *(pl* **ducs-d'albe)** NM *Naut* mooring post

Duce [dutʃe] NM *Hist* **le D.** the *or* il Duce

duce [dys] NM = system of secret signs used by cardsharpers or illusionists; *Fam* **balancer le d.** to give the sign

duché [dyʃe] NM duchy, dukedom

duché-pairie [dyʃeperi] *(pl* **duchés-pairies)** NF **1** *(titre)* ≃ dukedom **2** *(terre)* ≃ duchy

duchesse [dyʃɛs] NF **1** *(titre)* duchess; *Péj* **faire la d.** to play the fine lady **2** *(fruit)* **(poire) d.** duchess pear **3** *(meuble)* duchesse

Duchnoque [dyʃnɔk] NM *Fam Br* pal, matey, *Am* bud, buddy

Ducon [dykɔ̃] NM, **Ducon-la-joie** [dykɔ̃laʒwa] NM *très Fam* shit-for-brains, *Br* dick features

ducroire [dykrwar] NM *Com* del credere; *(agent)* del credere agent

ductile [dyktil] ADJ ductile

ductilité [dyktilite] NF ductility

dudgeon [dydʒɔ̃] NM *Tech* tube expander

dudgeonner [3] [dydʒone] VT *Tech (tube)* to expand; *(tubes)* to secure by flanging over; *(bouts)* to bead

dudit [dydi] *(pl* **desdits** [dedi]) *voir* **ledit**

Duduche [dydyʃ] NPR **le grand D.** = cartoon character created by Cabu representing an awkward adolescent

duègne [dɥɛɲ] NF duenna

DUEL, Duel [dɥɛl] NM *(abrév* **diplôme universitaire d'études littéraires)** = university diploma gained after two years of arts courses, still existing in some French-speaking countries but replaced in France in 1973

duel [dɥɛl] NM **1** *(entre deux personnes)* duel; **se battre en d. avec qn** to fight a duel *or* to duel with sb; **provoquer qn en d.** to challenge sb to a duel; **pistolet de d.** duelling pistol **2** *(conflit → entre États, organisations)* battle; **un d. entre la droite et la gauche** a battle between right and left; **d. d'artillerie** artillery battle **3** *(compétition)* **d. oratoire** verbal battle **4** *Ling* dual

duelliste [dɥelist] NMF duellist

DUES, Dues [dɥes] NM *(abrév* **diplôme universitaire d'études scientifiques)** = university diploma gained after two years of science courses, still existing in some French-speaking countries but replaced in France in 1973

duettiste [dɥetist] NMF duettist

duetto [dɥeto] NM *Mus* duet

duffle-coat [dœfœlkot] *(pl* **duffle-coats)**, **duffel-coat** *(pl* **duffel-coats)** [dœfœlkot] NM duffel coat

dugong [dygɔ̃(g)] NM *Zool* dugong

duit [dɥi] NM **1** *Pêche* = small dam across tidal river to act as a barrier to fish **2** *Constr (chemin)* cross-dyke *(in river)*

duite [dɥit] NF *Tex* pick; **d. d'envers** undershot pick; **d. d'endroit** overshot pick

dulçaquicole [dylsakwikɔl], **dulcicole** [dylsikɔl] ADJ *Biol & Bot* freshwater *(avant n)*

dulcification [dylsifikasjɔ̃] NF *Métal* blast roasting

dulcifier [9] [dylsifje] VT *Métal* to blast roast

Dulcinée [dylsine] NPR Dulcinea

dulcinée [dylsine] NF *Hum* ladylove, dulcinea

dulcite [dylsit] NF *Chim* dulcite

dulcitol [dylsitɔl] NM *Chim* dulcitol

dulie [dyli] NF *Rel* **culte de d.** worship of the saints, dulia

dum-dum [dumdum] *voir* **balle**

dûment [dymɑ̃] ADV duly; **d. expédié/reçu** duly dispatched/received; **d. accrédité** *(représentant)* duly authorized; **d. chapitré** told off in no uncertain terms

dumper [dœmpœr] NM dumper

dumping [dœmpiŋ] NM *Écon* dumping; **faire du d.** to dump (goods); **d. de change** currency dumping; **d. commercial** dumping; **d. fiscal** fiscal dumping; **d. social** social dumping

dundee [dœndi] NM *Naut* ketch

dune [dyn] NF dune

dunette [dynɛt] NF *Naut* poop

Dunkerque [dœ̃kɛrk] NM Dunkirk

duo [dyo, dɥo] NM **1** *(spectacle → chanté)* duet; *(→ instrumental)* duet, duo; **chanter en d.** to sing a duet; **un d. comique** a (comic) double-act **2** *(dialogue)* exchange **3** *Métal* two-high rolling mill

duodécimain, -e [dɥodesimɛ̃, -ɛn] ADJ *Rel* twelver

duodécimal, -e, -aux, -ales [dɥodesimal, -o] ADJ duodecimal

duodénal, -e, -aux, -ales [dɥodenal, -o] ADJ *Anat* duodenal

duodénite [dɥodenit] NF *Méd* duodenitis

duodénum [dɥodenɔm] NM *Anat* duodenum

duodi [dɥodi] NM *Hist* = second day of a ten-day period in the Republican calendar

duopole [dɥopɔl] NM duopoly

duopoliste [dɥopɔlist] ADJ *Écon* duopolistic

duopolistique [dɥopɔlistik] ADJ *Écon* duopolistic

duopsone [dɥopsɔn] NM *Écon* duopsony

dupe [dyp] NF dupe; **prendre qn pour d.** to dupe sb, to take sb for a ride; **jeu de dupes** fool's game
> ADJ **elle a été d. de ses promesses** she was fooled by his promises; **elle ment, mais je ne suis pas d.** she's lying but it doesn't fool me

duper [3] [dype] VT *Littéraire* to dupe, to fool
> ► **se duper** VPR to fool oneself

duperie [dypri] NF dupery

dupeur, -euse [dypœr, -øz] NM,F *Littéraire* duper

duplessisme [dyplesism] NM *Can* = authoritarian political policy of Maurice Duplessis

> *Culture*
>
> ## LE DUPLESSISME
> Maurice Duplessis (Premier of Quebec, 1936–39 and 1944–59) led the Quebec National Assembly in an authoritarian manner, dictating policies aimed primarily at preserving French-Canadian religious and traditional values, a policy which became known as "duplessisme". While defending the interest of Quebec against Ottawa, Duplessis promoted agriculture as the divine mission of Quebeckers, at a time of industrial expansion and urbanization in North America. Intellectual, political and artistic expression was stifled during his leadership. The death of "le Chef", as Duplessis was known, in 1959 heralded the end of "duplessisme" and the beginning of Quebec's "Révolution tranquille" (see box at this entry).

duplex [dyplɛks] NM **1** *(appartement en)* **d.** *Br* maisonnette *(on two floors)*, *Am* duplex **2** *Tél* duplex; **(émission en) d.** linkup; **d. bidirectionnel** duplex, diplex

duplexage [dyplɛksaʒ] NM *Tél* setting up a linkup

duplexer [4] [dyplɛkse] VT *Tél* to set up a linkup to

duplicata [dyplikata] NM duplicate

duplicate [dyplikat] *Cartes* ADJ duplicate
> NM duplicate

duplicateur [dyplikatœr] NM duplicator; **d. à alcool** spirit duplicator

duplication [dyplikasjɔ̃] NF **1** *(fait de copier)* duplication, duplicating; **d. de logiciel** software copying *(UNCOUNT)* **2** *(d'un enregistrement sonore)* linking up **3** *Biol* doubling **4** *Mktg* **d. d'audience** audience duplication

duplicité [dyplisite] NF duplicity, falseness, hypocrisy

duplique [dyplik] NF rejoinder

dupliquer [3] [dyplike] VT *(document)* to duplicate
> ► **se dupliquer** VPR *Biol* to be replicated; *Ordinat (virus informatique)* to spread

duquel [dykɛl] *voir* **lequel**

DUR, -E [dyr]

ADJ	hard **1–4, 6–9** ▪ tough **1, 6** ▪ difficult **2** ▪ harsh **3, 5**
NM,F	tough cookie **1** ▪ tough guy **2** ▪ hardliner **3**
NM	train
ADV	hard **1**

ADJ **1** *(ferme → viande)* tough; *(→ muscle)* firm,

hard; (→ *lit, mine de crayon*) hard; **bois d.** hardwood; **d. comme du bois** *ou* **le marbre** *ou* **le roc** rock-hard

2 *(difficile)* hard, difficult; **la route est dure à monter** it's a hard road to climb; *Fam* **c'est plutôt d. à digérer, ton histoire!** your story's rather hard to take!; **il est parfois d. d'accepter la vérité** accepting the truth can be hard *or* difficult; **le plus d. dans l'histoire, c'est de comprendre ce qui s'est passé** the hardest part of the whole business is understanding what really happened

3 *(pénible à supporter* → *climat)* harsh; **les conditions de vie sont de plus en plus dures** life gets harder and harder; **nous avons eu de durs moments** we've been through some hard times; **le plus d. est passé maintenant** the worst is over now; **les temps sont durs** these are hard times; **plus dure sera la chute** the higher they come the harder they fall; *Fam* **pas de congé?/plus de café? d. d.!** no time off?/no coffee left? bad luck!

4 *(cruel)* **il m'est d. de t'entendre parler ainsi** it's hard for me to hear you talk like this; **dis donc, tu es dure!** don't be so hard-hearted!; **ne sois pas d. avec lui** don't be nasty to *or* tough on him

5 *(rude, froid)* harsh; **d'une voix dure** in a harsh voice; **des couleurs dures** harsh colours; **des yeux d'un bleu très d.** steely blue eyes

6 *(endurci)* tough; **elle est dure, elle ne se plaint jamais** she's tough, she never complains; **il est d. à la douleur** he's tough, he can bear a lot of pain; **il est d. au travail** *ou* **à l'ouvrage** he's a hard worker; **avoir le cœur d.** to have a heart of stone, to be hard-hearted; *Fam* **il est d. à cuire** he's a hard nut to crack; *Fam* **d. à la détente** *(avare)* tight-fisted; *(peu vif)* slow on the uptake; *Fam* **être d. d'oreille** *ou* **de la feuille** to be hard of hearing■

7 *(intransigeant)* hard; **la droite/gauche dure** the hard right/left

8 *Ling* hard

9 *Phys* hard

10 *Métal* **fer d.** chilled iron

11 *Can Fam* **faire d.** to look awful■

NM,F *Fam* **1** *(personne sans faiblesse)* toughie, tough cookie *or Br* nut; **un d. en affaires** a hard-nosed businessman; **c'est un d. à cuire** he's a hard nut to crack

2 *(voyou)* tough guy, toughie; **un d. de d.** a real tough guy *or Br* tough nut

3 *Pol* hardliner, hawk; **les durs du parti** the hard core in the party

NM *Fam (train)* train■

ADV 1 *(avec force)* hard; **il a tapé** *ou* **frappé d.** he hit hard; **il travaille d. sur son nouveau projet** he's working hard *or* he's hard at work on his new project; **croire** *ou* **penser d. comme fer que...** to be firm in the belief that...; **il croit d. comme fer qu'elle va revenir** he believes doggedly *or* he's adamant that she'll come back

2 *(avec intensité)* **le soleil tape d. aujourd'hui** the sun is beating down today

❑ **dures NFPL** *Fam (histoires, moments)* **il lui en a fait voir de dures** he gave him/her a hard time; **il nous en a dit de dures** he told us some really nasty things

❑ **à la dure ADV élever ses enfants à la dure** to bring up one's children the hard way; **ils ont toujours vécu à la dure** they always had a tough life

❑ **en dur ADJ construction/maison en d.** building/house built with non-temporary materials

❑ **sur la dure ADV coucher sur la dure** *(sur le plancher)* to sleep on the floor; *(dehors)* to sleep on the ground

durabilité [dyrabilite] **NF** *(qualité)* durableness, durability

durable [dyrabl] **ADJ 1** *(permanent)* enduring, lasting, long-lasting; **caractère d.** durability; **faire œuvre d.** to create a work of lasting significance **2** *Écon* **biens durables** durable goods, durables

durablement [dyrabləmɑ̃] **ADV** durably, enduringly, for a long time; **le beau temps devrait persister d. dans notre pays** fine weather should persist over the country

duraille [dyraj] **ADJ** *Fam* hard■; **il était d., le problème de maths** the maths question was a real pig; **se faire piquer son mec par sa meilleure copine, c'est plutôt d.** it's a bit of a bummer *or* downer when your best friend steals your man

durain [dyrɛ̃] **NM** *Minér* durain

dural, -e, -aux, -ales [dyral, -o] **ADJ** dural, dure-matral

Duralumin® [dyralymɛ̃] **NM** Duralumin®

duramen [dyramɛn] **NM** *Bot* duramen

durant [dyrɑ̃] **PRÉP 1** *(avant le nom) (au cours de)* during, in the course of; **il est né d. la nuit** he was born during *or* in the middle of the night; **fermé d. les travaux** *(sur panneau ou vitrine)* closed for alterations

2 *(avant le nom) (exprime la durée)* for; **d. quelques instants, j'ai cru qu'il allait la frapper** for a few moments I thought he was going to hit her

3 *(après le nom) (pour insister)* for; **il peut parler des heures d.** he can speak for hours (on end); **toute sa vie d.** his/her whole life through, throughout his/her whole life

durassien, -enne [dyrasjɛ̃, -ɛn] **ADJ** *(œuvre, étude, poétique)* of Marguerite Duras

duratif, -ive [dyratif, -iv] *Ling* **ADJ** durative
NM durative

Durban [dœrban] **NM** Durban

dur-bec [dyrbɛk] *(pl* **durs-becs***)* **NM** *Orn* grosbeak; **d. des sapins** pine grosbeak

durcir [32] [dyrsir] **VT** *(rendre plus dur)* to harden, to make firmer; *Fig* to harden, to toughen; **cette coupe de cheveux lui durcit le visage** that haircut makes him/her look severe; **la colère durcissait son regard** his/her eyes were set in anger; **d. ses positions** to take a tougher stand; **d. les conditions du crédit au consommateur** to make it harder for consumers to obtain credit
VI *(sol, plâtre, pain)* to harden, to go hard
▸**se durcir VPR** *(personne)* to harden oneself; *(traits)* to harden; *(cœur)* to become hard; *(opposition)* to take a tougher stance

durcissement [dyrsismɑ̃] **NM 1** *(raffermissement* → *du sol, du plâtre)* hardening **2** *(renforcement)* **le d. de l'opposition** the tougher stance taken by the opposition; **le d. de la résistance ennemie** the stiffening of enemy resistance

durcisseur [dyrsisœr] **NM** hardener; **d. pour ongles** nail hardener

dure [dyr] **à la dure, sur la dure** *voir* **dur**

durée [dyre] **NF 1** *(période)* duration, length; *Fin (de crédit)* term; *(d'un prêt)* life; **quelle est la d. de votre congé?** how long is your leave?, how long does your leave last?; **pendant la d. de** during, for the duration of; **vente promotionnelle pour une d. limitée** special sale for a limited period; **la d. hebdomadaire du travail est de 39 heures** the statutory working week is 39 hours; **disque longue d.** long-playing record; *Compta* **d. d'amortissement** depreciation period; **d. de conservation** best-before date; **d. d'écoute** *Rad* listening time; *TV* viewing time; **d. de vie** *(d'une personne)* lifespan; *(d'une pile)* life; *(d'une machine)* useful life; **d. (utile) de vie** *(d'un produit)* life expectancy, shelf-life; **d. de vol** flight time

2 *(persistance)* lasting quality

3 *Mus, Ling & Littérature* length

4 *Psy* perceived (passage of) time; **vivre un traumatisme dans la d.** to experience a trauma through time

5 *Ordinat* **d. de connexion** on-line time

❑ **de courte durée ADJ** short-lived

❑ **de longue durée ADJ** *(chômeur, chômage)* long-term

durement [dyrmɑ̃] **ADV 1** *(violemment* → *frapper)* hard; **je suis tombé d.** I had a hard fall, I fell really hard

2 *(avec sévérité)* harshly, severely; **elle a élevé ses enfants d.** she brought up her children strictly

3 *(douloureusement)* deeply; **d. éprouvé par la mort de** deeply distressed by the death of; **son absence est d. ressentie** he's/she's sorely missed

4 *(méchamment* → *répondre)* harshly

dure-mère [dyrmɛr] *(pl* **dures-mères***)* **NF** dura mater

Durendal [dyrɑ̃dal] **NPR** = the holy and unbreakable sword of Roland in the medieval epic 'la Chanson de Roland'

durer [3] [dyre] **VI 1** *(événement, tremblement de terre)* to last, to go *or* to carry on; **la situation n'a que trop duré** the situation has gone on far too long; **ça ne peut plus d.!** it can't go on like this!; **ça fait longtemps/trois ans que ça dure** it's been going on for a long time/for three years; **ça va encore d. longtemps cette histoire?** this has gone on long enough!; **il pleure quand sa mère le quitte mais cela ne dure pas** he cries when his mother leaves him but it doesn't last *or* he doesn't carry on for long; **ça a duré toute la journée** it lasted all day; *Fam* **ça durera ce que ça durera!** it might last and then it might not!; **il a essayé de faire d. la réunion** he tried to make the meeting last *or* draw the meeting out

2 *(rester, persister)* to last; **ce soleil ne va pas d.** this sunshine won't last long; **cela ne durera pas** it can't *or* won't last; **faire d. les provisions** to stretch supplies, to make supplies last; **faire d. le plaisir** to spin things out

3 *(moteur, appareil)* to last; *(œuvre)* to last, *Sout* to endure; *Fam* **mon manteau m'a duré dix ans** my coat lasted me ten years, I got ten years' wear out of my coat; **voici une nouvelle montre, essaie de la faire d., celle-là** here's a new watch, try to make this one last

4 *(peser)* **le temps me dure** time is lying heavy (on my hands) *or* hangs heavily on me

5 *(vivre)* to last; **il ne durera plus longtemps** he won't last *or* live much longer

6 *(en Afrique francophone* → *rester)* to stay; (→ *habiter)* to live

Dürer [dyrɛr] **NPR Albrecht** *ou* **Albert D.** Albrecht Dürer

dureté [dyrte] **NF 1** *(du sol, du plâtre)* hardness, firmness **2** *(du climat, de conditions)* harshness **3** *(d'un maître, d'une règle)* severity, harshness; *(d'une grève)* bitterness, harshness; **traiter qn avec d.** to be harsh to *or* tough on sb **4** *(d'une teinte, d'une voix, d'une lumière)* harshness **5** *Chim (de l'eau)* hardness **6** *Phys* hardness

durham [dyram] *Agr* **ADJ** shorthorn, Durham
NMF shorthorn, Durham

durillon [dyrijɔ̃] **NM** callus

Durit® [dyrit] **NF** flexible pipe; **D. de radiateur** radiator hose; *Fam* **péter une D.** *(se mettre en colère)* to hit the *Br* roof *or Am* ceiling

Düsseldorf [dysɛldɔrf] **NM** Düsseldorf

DUT [deyte] **NM** *(abrév* **diplôme universitaire de technologie***)* = diploma taken after two years at an institute of technology

dut *etc voir* **devoir**

duumvir [dyɔmvir] **NM** *Antiq* duumvir; **les duumvirs** the duumvirs, the duumviri

duumvirat [dyɔmvira] **NM** *Antiq* duumvirate

duvet [dyvɛ] **NM 1** *(poils)* down, downy hairs; *(d'un animal)* underfur **2** *(plumes)* down; **un oreiller en d.** a down pillow **3** *(sac de couchage)* sleeping bag **4** *Belg & Suisse* duvet, (continental) quilt

duveté, -e [dyvte] **ADJ** downy

duveter [28] [dyvte] **se duveter VPR** to go *or* to become downy, to get covered in down

duveteux, -euse [dyvtø, -øz] **ADJ** downy

duxelles [dyksɛl] **NF** duxelles

DV [deve] **NF** *(abrév* **distribution valeur***)* weighted distribution

DVB [devebe] **NF** *(abrév* **Digital Video Broadcasting***)* DVB

DVD [devede] **NM** *(abrév* **Digital Versatile Disk, Digital Video Disk***)* DVD; **D. réenregistrable** re-recordable DVD

DVD-R [devedeɛr] **NM** *(abrév* **Digital Versatile Disk-recordable***)* DVD-R

DVD-ROM, DVD-Rom [devederɔm] **NM INV** *(abrév* **Digital Versatile Disk read-only memory***)* DVD-ROM

DVD-RW [devedeɛrdubləve] **NM** *(abrév* **Digital Versatile Disk-rewritable***)* DVD-RW

dyade [djad] **NF** *Biol* dyad, diad

dyadique [djadik] **ADJ** dyadic

dyarchie [djarʃi] **NF** dyarchy, diarchy

dyke [dik] **NM** *Géol* dyke

dynamique [dinamik] **ADJ 1** *(énergique)* dynamic, energetic **2** *(non statique)* dynamic
NF 1 *Mus & Tech* dynamics *(singulier)* **2** *(mouvement)* dynamics *(singulier)*, dynamic; **la d. du**

marché market dynamics; *Biol & Écol* **la d. des populations** population dynamics; **la d. révolutionnaire** the revolutionary dynamic **3** *Psy* **d. de groupe** group dynamics

dynamiquement [dinamikmã] **ADV** dynamically

dynamisant, -e [dinamizã, -ãt] **ADJ** motivating, stimulating

dynamisation [dinamizasjõ] **NF** *(excitation)* **responsable de la d. de l'équipe** responsible for making the team more dynamic

dynamiser [3] [dinamize] **VT** *(équipe)* to dynamize, to make more dynamic

dynamisme [dinamism] **NM 1** *(entrain)* energy, enthusiasm **2** *Phil* dynamism

dynamiste [dinamist] *Phil* **ADJ** dynamistic **NM,F** dynamist

dynamitage [dinamitaʒ] **NM** blowing up *or* blasting *(with dynamite)*

dynamite [dinamit] **NF** dynamite; *Fam Fig* **c'est de la d.!** it's dynamite!

dynamiter [3] [dinamite] **VT 1** *(détruire à l'explosif)* to blow up *or* to blast with dynamite **2** *(abolir → préjugé)* to do away with, to sweep away

dynamiterie [dinamitri] **NF** dynamite factory

dynamiteur, -euse [dinamitœr, -øz] **NM,F 1** *(à l'explosif)* dynamiter, dynamite expert **2** *(démystificateur)* destroyer of received ideas

dynamo [dinamo] **NF** dynamo, generator

dynamoélectrique [dinamoelɛktrik] **ADJ** dynamoelectric, dynamoelectrical

dynamogène [dinamoʒɛn], **dynamogénique** [dinamoʒenik] **ADJ** dynamogenic

dynamographe [dinamograf] **NM** dynamograph

dynamomètre [dinamomɛtr] **NM** dynamometer

dynamométrique [dinamometrik] **ADJ** dynamometric, dynamometrical

dynaste [dinast] **NM 1** *Antiq* dynast **2** *Entom* dynastes

dynastie [dinasti] **NF 1** *(de rois)* dynasty **2** *(famille)* **la d. des Rothschild** the Rothschild dynasty

dynastique [dinastik] **ADJ** dynastic, dynastical

dyne [din] **NF** dyne

dysarthrie [dizartri] **NF** *Méd* dysarthria

dysautonomie [dizotonomi] **NF** *Méd* **d. familial** familial dysautonomia

dyscalculie [diskalkyli] **NF** *Psy* dyscalculia

dyschondroplasie [diskõdroplazi] **NF** *Méd* enchondromatosis

dyschromatopsie [diskromatopsi] **NF** *Méd* dyschromatopsia

dyschromie [diskromi] **NF** *Méd* dyschromia

dyscinésie [disinezi] **NF** *Méd* dyskinesia

dyscrasie [diskrazi] **NF** *Méd* dyscrasia

dysembryome [dizãbrijom] **NM** *Méd* dysembryoma

dysembryoplasie [dizɛbrijoplazi] **NF** *Méd* dysembryoplasia

dysenterie [disãtri] **NF** dysentery

dysentérique [disãterik] **ADJ** dysenteric **NMF** dysentery sufferer

dysferline [disferlin] **NF** *Physiol* dysferlin

dysfonction [disfõksjõ] **NF** *Méd* *(d'un organe)* dysfunction, malfunction

dysfonctionnement [disfõksjonmã] **NM** *Méd* *(d'un organe)* dysfunction, malfunction; *(d'une institution, d'un service)* malfunctioning

dysgénésie [disʒenezi] **NF** *Méd* dysgenesia

dysgraphie [disgrafi] **NF** *Psy* dysgraphia

dysharmonie [dizarmoni] **NF** disharmony, discord

dyshidrose, dyshydrose, dysidrose [disidroz] **NF** *Méd* dyshidrosis, dysidrosis

dyskératose [diskeratoz] **NF** *Méd* dyskeratosis

dyskinésie [diskinezi] **NF** *Méd* dyskinesia

dyslalie [dislali] **NF** *Psy* dyslalia

dyslexie [dislɛksi] **NF** dyslexia

dyslexique [dislɛksik] **ADJ** dyslexic **NMF** dyslexic

dyslogie [disloʒi] **NF** *Méd* dyslogia

dysmature [dismatyr] **ADJ** *Méd* dysmature

dysménorrhée [dismenore] **NF** *Méd* dysmenorrhoea

dysmnésie [dismnezi] **NF** *Méd* dysmnesia

dysmorphie [dismorfi], **NF** *Méd* dysmorphia, deformity

dysmorphophobie [dismorfofobi] **NF** *Psy* body dysmorphic disorder

dysmorphose [dismorfoz] = **dysmorphie**

dysorexie [dizorɛksi] **NF** *Méd* dysorexia

dysorthographie [dizortografi] **NF** difficulty in spelling

dyspareunie [disparøni] **NF** *Méd* dyspareunia

dyspepsie [dispɛpsi] **NF** *Méd* dyspepsia

dyspepsique [dispɛpsik], **dyspeptique** [dispɛptik] *Méd* **ADJ** dyspeptic **NMF** dyspeptic

dysphagie [disfaʒi] **NF** *Méd* dysphagia

dysphagique [disfaʒik] **ADJ** *Méd* dysphagic

dysphasie [disfazi] **NF** *Méd* dysphasia

dysphasique [disfazik] **ADJ** *Méd* dysphasic

dysphonie [disfoni] **NF** *Méd* dysphonia

dysphonique [disfonik] **ADJ** *Méd* dysphonic

dysphorie [disfori] **NF** *Psy* dysphoria

dysphorique [disforik] **ADJ** *Psy* dysphoric

dysplasie [displazi] **NF** *Méd* dysplasia

dysplasique [displazik] **ADJ** *Méd* dysplasic

dyspnée [dispne] **NF** *Méd* dyspnoea

dyspnéique [dispneik] *Méd* **ADJ** dyspnoeal, dyspnoeic **NMF** = person suffering from dyspnoea

dyspraxie [dispraksi] **NF** *Méd* dyspraxia

dyspraxique [dispraksik] **ADJ** *Méd* dyspraxic

dysprosium [disprozjom] **NM** *Chim* dysprosium

dyssocial, -e, -aux, -ales [disosjal, -o] **ADJ** antisocial

dysthymie [distimi] **NF** *Psy* dysthymia

dystocie [distosi] **NF** *Obst* dystocia, dystokia

dystocique [distosik] **ADJ** *Obst* dystoical

dystonie [distoni] **NF** *Méd* **1** *(contraction)* dystonia **2 d. neurovégétative** neurovegetative dystonia

dystrophie [dystrofi] **NF** *Méd* dystrophy; **d. musculaire progressive** muscular dystrophy

dystrophine [distrofin] **NF** *Biol* dystrophin

dystrophique [distrofik] **ADJ** *Méd* dystrophic

dystrophisation [distrofizasjõ] **NF** *Méd* dystrophication

dysurie [dizyri] **NF** *Méd* dysuria, dysury

dysurique [dizyrik] *Méd* **ADJ** dysuric **NMF** = person suffering from dysuria

dzêta [dzeta] **NM** zeta

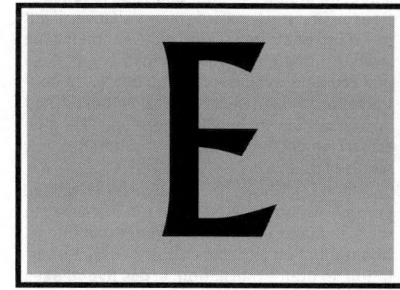

E¹, e [ə] NM INV **1** (*lettre*) E, e; **E comme Eugène** ≃ E for Eric; **e dans l'o** o and e joined together, œ ligature; **e dans l'a** a and e joined together, æ ligature **2** *Mus* (*note*) E **3** *Math & Phys* e

E² (*abrév écrite* **est**) E

EAO [əao] NM (*abrév* **enseignement assisté par ordinateur**) CAL

EARL [əaɛʁl] NF *Écon* (*abrév* **Exploitation agricole à responsabilité limitée**) = farm registered as a limited company

EAU (*abrév écrite* **Émirats arabes unis**) UAE

eau, -x [o] NF **1** (*liquide incolore*) water; **les fougères ont besoin d'e.** ferns need water; **des légumes/melons pleins d'e.** watery vegetables/melons; **cloque** *ou* **ampoule pleine d'e.** water blister; **prendre l'e.** (*chaussure, tente*) to leak, to let in water; **mettre un navire à l'e.** to launch a ship; **se mettre à l'e.** (*pour se baigner*) to go in the water (for a swim); **tomber à l'e.** to fall into the water; **passer qch à l'e.** to rinse sth; **il est tombé beaucoup d'e.** a lot of rain fell; **dans l'e. de votre bain** in your bathwater; **dans l'e. savonneuse** in soapy water; *Rel* **e. bénite** holy water; **e. calcaire** hard water; **e. courante** running water; **avoir l'e. courante** to have running water; **e. déminéralisée** demineralized water; **e. distillée** distilled water; **e. douce** (*non salée*) fresh water; (*sans calcaire*) soft water; **d'e. douce** freshwater, river (*avant n*); **e. dure** hard water; **eaux d'égout** waste water; **e. de jouvence** waters of youth; **e. de mer** seawater; **e. de pluie** rainwater; **e. de refroidissement** cooling water; **e. de roche** spring water; **eaux de ruissellement** runoff; **e. de source** spring water; **e. de vaisselle** dishwater; **e. de la ville** main(s) water; **e. vive** (*fresh*) running water; **sports d'e. vive** whitewater sports; **descente en e. vive** whitewater rafting; **jeu d'e.** *ou* **d'eaux** fountains; *Fig* **pêcher en e. trouble** to fish in troubled waters; *Fig* **nager** *ou* **naviguer en e. trouble** to sail close to the wind; *Fig* **nager entre deux eaux** (*ne pas s'engager*) to keep a foot in both camps; (*hésiter*) to hum and haw; *Fig* **être** *ou* **naviguer dans les eaux de qn** (*rallier ses opinions*) to take the same line as sb; **il navigue dans les eaux de plusieurs peintres en vue** he hangs around several well-known painters; **comme l'e. et le feu** as different *Br* as chalk and cheese *or Am* as night and day; *Fam* **ça doit valoir 3000 euros, enfin, c'est dans ces eaux-là!** it costs 3,000 euros or thereabouts; **cela amène de l'e. à son moulin** it's (all) grist to his/her mill; **tu apportes de l'e. à mon moulin** you're adding weight to my argument; **il est passé/il passera beaucoup d'e. sous les ponts** a lot of water has gone/will flow under the bridge; *Fam* **il y a de l'e. dans le gaz** there's trouble brewing; **porter de l'e. à la rivière** *ou* **à la mer** to take *or* to carry coals to Newcastle; **il ne trouverait pas d'e. à la rivière** *ou* **au lac** *ou* **à la mer** he can't find anything even if it's staring him in the face; **j'en ai l'e. à la bouche** my mouth is watering; **ça me donne** *ou* **me met l'e. à la bouche** it makes my mouth water; *Can Joual* **être dans l'e. chaude** to be in hot water

2 (*boisson*) water; **e. gazeuse** soda *or* fizzy water; **e. minérale** mineral water; **e. plate** still water; **e. du robinet** tap water; **e. rougie** = water with a drop of wine in it; **e. de Seltz** soda water, *Am* (Seltzer) water, club soda; **e. de source** spring water; **point d'e.** (*pour les animaux*) watering hole; (*dans un village*) standpipe; **mettre de l'e. dans son vin** to water down one's wine; *Fig* to climb down, to back off

3 *Culin* water; (*d'un melon*) juice; **les concombres rendent beaucoup d'e.** cucumbers give out a lot of water; **conservez l'e. des légumes** keep the cooking water from the vegetables; **e. de cuisson** cooking water; **e. de fleur d'oranger** orange flower water; **e. sucrée** sugar water; *Fam* **finir** *ou* **partir** *ou* **tourner** *ou* **s'en aller en e. de boudin** (*mal se terminer*) to end in tears; (*échouer*) to go down the tubes

4 (*parfum*) & *Pharm* **e. de Cologne** (eau de) Cologne; **e. dentifrice** mouthwash; **e. de lavande** lavender water; **e. de mélisse** = liqueur made from lemon balm; **e. de parfum** perfume; **e. de rose** rose water; **e. de toilette** toilet water

5 *Chim* **e. écarlate** stain-remover; **e. de Javel** bleach, *Am* Clorox®; **nettoyer une tache à l'e. de Javel** to bleach a stain out; **e. lourde** heavy water, *Spéc* deuterium oxide; **e. oxygénée** hydrogen peroxide

6 (*limpidité → d'un diamant*) water; *aussi Fig* **de la plus belle e.** of the first water; *Littéraire* **dans l'e. claire de ses yeux** *ou* **de son regard** in his/her limpid eyes, in the pools of his/her eyes

7 *Naut* **faire de l'e.** (*s'approvisionner*) to take on water; **faire e.** (*avoir une fuite*) to take on water; *Fig* **faire e. de toutes parts** to go under

❑ **eaux** NFPL **1** (*masse*) water; **les eaux se retirent** (*mer*) the tide's going out; (*inondation*) the (flood) water's subsiding; **eaux de fonte** meltwater; *Écol* **eaux grasses** swill; (*pour les porcs*) slops; **eaux ménagères** waste water; **eaux usées** sewage; *Géog* **hautes/basses eaux** high/low water; **les grandes eaux de Versailles** the fountains of Versailles; **dimanche: grandes eaux à Versailles** the fountains will play at Versailles on Sunday; *Fam Fig* **on a eu droit aux grandes eaux (de Versailles)** he/she turned on the waterworks

2 *Naut* (*zone*) waters; **eaux internationales/territoriales** international/territorial waters; **eaux côtières** inshore waters; **dans les eaux de** in the wake of

3 *Obst* (*d'une accouchée*) waters; **elle a perdu les eaux** her waters have broken; **poche des eaux** amniotic sac

4 (*thermes*) **eaux thermales** thermal *or* hot springs; **les eaux de Brouckke sont bonnes pour le foie** the waters at Brouckke are good for liver ailments; **prendre les eaux** to take the waters, to stay at a spa (*for one's health*)

5 *Admin* **les Eaux et Forêts** *Br* ≃ the Forestry Commission, *Am* ≃ the Forest Service

❑ **à grande eau** ADV **laver à grande e.** (*au jet*) to hose down; (*dans un évier, une bassine*) to wash in a lot of water; **rincer à grande e.** to rinse (out) thoroughly *or* in a lot of water

❑ **à l'eau** ADJ **1** *Culin* boiled

2 (*perdu*) **mon week-end est à l'e.** bang goes my weekend ADV **1** *Culin* **cuire à l'e.** (*légumes*) to boil; (*fruits*) to poach

2 (*locutions*) **se jeter** *ou* **se lancer à l'e.** to take the plunge; **tomber à l'e.** to fall through, to come to nothing; *Can* **s'en aller à l'e.** to be going bankrupt

❑ **à l'eau de rose** ADJ *Péj* sentimental; **des histoires à l'e. de rose** sentimental stories

❑ **de la même eau** ADV *Péj* of the same ilk; **ces deux-là sont de la même e.** they're two of a kind, they're tarred with the same brush

❑ **en eau** ADJ sweating profusely; **ils étaient en e.** the sweat was pouring off them, they were dripping with sweat

❑ **en eau profonde** ADV *Naut* in deep (sea) waters

eau-de-vie [odvi] (*pl* **eaux-de-vie**) NF eau de vie

eau-forte [ofɔʁt] (*pl* **eaux-fortes**) NF **1** *Chim* aqua fortis, nitric acid **2** *Beaux-Arts* etching

eaux-vannes [ovan] NFPL effluent, sewage (water)

ébahi, -e [ebai] ADJ astounded, dumbfounded, stunned; **regard é.** a look of blank astonishment; **prendre un air é.** to look astounded *or* dumbfounded *or* stunned

ébahir [32] [ebaiʁ] VT to astound, to dumbfound, to stun

▸ **s'ébahir** VPR to be dumbfounded; **s'é. de** *ou* **devant** (*s'étonner de*) to be dumbfounded at; **il s'ébahit d'un rien** it doesn't take much to impress him, he's easily impressed

ébahissement [ebaismɑ̃] NM amazement, astonishment

ébarbage [ebaʁbaʒ] NM **1** *Métal* (*d'une surface métallique*) deburring **2** (*d'un livre*) trimming the pages; (*d'une feuille de papier*) trimming **3** *Agr* clipping, trimming; (*d'une haie, d'une pelouse*) clipping **4** *Culin* (*du poisson*) trimming

ébarber [3] [ebaʁbe] VT **1** *Métal* (*surface métallique*) to deburr **2** (*livre*) to trim the pages of; (*feuilles de papier*) to trim **3** *Agr* to clip, to trim; (*haie, pelouse*) to clip **4** *Culin* (*poisson*) to trim

ébarbeur [ebaʁbœʁ] NM trimming machine

ébarbeuse [ebaʁbøz] NF trimming machine

ébarboir [ebaʁbwaʁ] NM *Métal* scraper, chipping chisel, burr-cutter

ébarbure [ebaʁbyʁ] NF *Ind* (*de métal*) burr, paring; (*de papier*) trimming

ébat *etc voir* **ébattre**

ébats [eba] NMPL frolics, frolicking; **é. amoureux** lovemaking

ébattre [83] [ebatʁ] **s'ébattre** VPR to frolic; (*animaux*) to gambol

ébaubi, -e [ebobi] ADJ *Vieilli* dumbfounded, stunned

ébauchage [eboʃaʒ] NM **1** (*façonnement → gén*) outlining; (→ *d'un tableau*) roughing out, sketching out; (→ *d'un roman etc*) outlining **2** *Métal* roughing out

ébauche [eboʃ] NF **1** (*première forme → d'un dessin*) rough sketch *or* draft; (→ *d'une lettre, d'une traduction*) draft; (→ *d'un plan*) outline; **projet à l'état d'é.** project in its early stages; **faire l'é. de** (*tableau*) to make a rough sketch of, to sketch out; (*roman, lettre, traduction*) to draft; (*projet*) to outline; **çà et là, des ébauches de barricades se dressaient** there were makeshift barricades here and there

2 (*fait de préparer → un dessin*) roughing *or* sketching out; (→ *un plan*) outlining; **j'ai travaillé trois mois à l'é. de mon scénario** I spent three months on the drafting of my scenario

3 (*début*) **l'é. d'un sourire** the beginning of a

smile, an incipient smile; **une é. de réconciliation** the first steps towards reconciliation; **il eut l'é. d'un geste vers elle puis se ravisa** he started moving towards her then stopped; **je n'ai réussi à avoir avec lui qu'une é. de conversation** I managed only a rather stilted conversation with him; **il a marmonné l'é. d'un remerciement** he grudgingly muttered a few words of thanks

ébaucher [3] [eboʃe] **VT 1** *(esquisser → dessin, portrait)* to rough *or* to sketch out; *(→ lettre)* to draft, to make a draft of; *(→ plan)* to outline; **é. une traduction** to make a draft *or* rough translation, to draft a translation; **é. des hypothèses** to put forward tentative hypotheses; **c'est un portrait qu'il a juste ébauché** it's a portrait he's just begun working on; **des formes vagues à peine ébauchées** a few indistinct shapes

2 *(commencer)* to begin, to start; **é. des négociations/une réconciliation** to start the process of negotiation/reconciliation; **les négociations de paix étaient à peine ébauchées et déjà...** peace talks had barely been mooted before...; **elle ébaucha un vague sourire** she made as if to smile; **elle ébaucha un geste de bienvenue** she made a vague gesture of welcome; **é. un salut** *(de la tête)* to nod vaguely; *(de la main)* to wave vaguely

3 *(en joaillerie)* to begin to cut

4 *Constr & Ind* to rough-hew

►**s'ébaucher VPR** to (take) form, to start up; **la relation qui s'ébauche entre eux** their fledgling relationship

ébaucheur [eboʃœr] **NM** *Métal* rougher

ébauchoir [eboʃwar] **NM 1** *Métal* roughing chisel **2** *(de charron, de potier)* chisel; *Menuis* cutting chisel

ébaudir [32] [ebodir] *Vieilli ou Littéraire* **VT** to amuse

►**s'ébaudir VPR** to rejoice

ébavurage [ebavyraʒ] **NM** *Métal* fettling

ébavurer [3] [ebavyre] **VT** *Métal* to fettle

ébénacée [ebenase] *Bot* **NF** member of the Ebenaceae

►**ébénacées NFPL** Ebenaceae

ébène [ebɛn] **NF** *Bot* ebony; **une table en é.** an ebony table; **(d'un) noir d'é., d'é.** ebony black; *Hist* **(bois d')é.** slaves; **marchand d'é.** slave-trader

ébénier [ebenje] **NM** *Bot* ebony (tree); **faux é.** laburnum

ébéniste [ebenist] **NM** *Menuis* cabinetmaker

ébénisterie [ebenistəri] **NF** *Menuis* **1** *(métier)* cabinetmaking **2** *(placage)* veneer; **une table en é.** a veneered table **3** *(meuble)* cabinet work

éberlué, -e [ebɛrlɥe] **ADJ** *Fam* dumbfounded, flabbergasted

éberluer [7] [ebɛrlɥe] **VT** *Fam* to dumbfound, to flabbergast

Eberth [ebɛrt] **NPR** *Méd* **bacille d'E.** Eberth's bacillus

ébionite [ebjɔnit] **NM** *Rel* Ebionite

ébiseler [24] [ebizle] **VT** *Tech* to chamfer, to bevel

EBIT [ebit] **NM** *Fin (abrév* **earnings before interest and tax***)* EBIT

EBITDA [ebitta] **NM** *Fin (abrév* **earnings before interest, tax, depreciation and amortization***)* EBITDA

éblouir [32] [ebluir] **VT 1** *(aveugler)* to dazzle; **les phares de la voiture m'ont ébloui** I was dazzled by the (glare of the) car's headlights **2** *(impressionner)* to dazzle, to stun; **elle l'a ébloui dès leur première rencontre** she dazzled him right from their first meeting; **nous avons été éblouis par son talent** we were dazzled by his/her talent

éblouissant, -e [ebluisɑ̃, -ɑ̃t] **ADJ 1** *(aveuglant → lumière)* dazzling, blinding; *(→ couleur)* dazzling **2** *(impressionnant → femme, performance)* dazzling, stunning; **d'une beauté éblouissante** dazzlingly *or* stunningly beautiful; **un violoniste é. de talent** a stunningly talented violinist; **mise en scène éblouissante d'ingéniosité** stunningly ingenious staging

éblouissement [ebluismɑ̃] **NM 1** *(fait d'être aveuglé)* being dazzled

2 *(vertige)* dizziness; **être pris d'éblouissements** to feel dizzy *or* faint; **avoir un é.** to have a dizzy spell; **il a eu un é. et s'est écroulé** he fell in a faint

3 *(enchantement)* dazzlement, bedazzlement; **quand on arrive chez eux, c'est un véritable é.** their place is dazzling; **l'é. qu'il ressentit lorsqu'il la vit** his sense of dazzlement when he saw her

Ébola [ebɔla] **NPR** *Méd* **virus É.** Ebola virus; **fièvre hémorragique É.** *ou* **d'É.** Ebola hemorrhagic fever

ébonite [ebɔnit] **NF** *Chim* ebonite, vulcanite

e-book [ibuk] **NM** e-book

éborgnage [ebɔrɲaʒ] **NM** *Hort* disbudding

éborgnement [ebɔrɲəmɑ̃] **NM** blinding (in one eye)

éborgner [3] [ebɔrɲe] **VT 1 é. qn** to blind sb in one eye, to put sb's eye out; **j'ai failli m'é.** I nearly put my eye out; **attention, tu vas m'é.!** hey, watch my eyes! **2** *Hort (arbre fruitier)* to disbud

►**s'éborgner VPR** to put one's eye out

éboueur [ebwœr] **NM** *Br* dustman, *Am* garbage collector

ébouillantage [ebujɑ̃taʒ] **NM** *Culin* scalding

ébouillanter [3] [ebujɑ̃te] **VT** *Culin* to scald

►**s'ébouillanter VPR** to scald oneself; **s'é. la main/le pied** to scald one's hand/foot

éboulement [ebulmɑ̃] **NM 1** *(chute)* crumbling, subsiding, collapsing; **un é. de terrain** a landslide; **l'é. de la falaise/carrière a fait deux morts** two people were killed when the cliff collapsed/the quarry fell in; **il y a eu un é. dans la mine** there has been a cave-in at the mine; **si vous allez vers la carrière, méfiez-vous des éboulements** if you're going in the direction of the quarry, watch out for falling rocks

2 *(éboulis → de terre)* mass of fallen earth; *(→ de rochers)* mass of fallen rocks, rock slide; *(→ en montagne)* scree

ébouler [3] [ebule] **VT** to break *or* to bring down; **la mer a éboulé les digues** the sea has broken down the dykes; **un vieux mur éboulé** a crumbling old wall

►**s'ébouler VPR** *(falaise, côte → petit à petit)* to crumble; *(→ brutalement)* to collapse; *(mine)* to cave in; **le talus s'est éboulé** there has been a landslide

éboulis [ebuli] **NM** *(de terre)* mass of fallen earth; *(de rochers)* mass of fallen rocks, rock slide; *(en montagne)* scree

ébourgeonnement [eburʒɔnmɑ̃], **ébourgeonnage** [eburʒɔnaʒ] **NM** *Hort* disbudding

ébourgeonner [3] [eburʒɔne] **VT** *Hort* to disbud

ébouriffage [eburifaʒ] **NM** ruffling, tousling

ébouriffant, -e [eburifɑ̃, -ɑ̃t] **ADJ** *Fam* amazing, stunning

ébouriffé, -e [eburife] **ADJ 1** *(décoiffé)* tousled, dishevelled; **je suis tout é.** my hair is all tousled *or* dishevelled **2** *Fam (ébahi)* amazed, stunned

ébouriffer [3] [eburife] **VT 1** *(décoiffer)* **é. qn** to ruffle *or* tousle sb's hair; **tu m'as tout ébouriffé** you've made my hair all tousled **2** *Fam (ébahir)* to amaze, to stun

ébourrer [3] [ebure] **VT** *(peau)* to unhair

ébouter [3] [ebute] **VT** *Tech* to take the end off

ébranchage [ebrɑ̃ʃaʒ], **ébranchement** [ebrɑ̃ʃmɑ̃] **NM** *Hort (d'un arbre)* lopping the branches off

ébrancher [3] [ebrɑ̃ʃe] **VT** *Hort (arbre)* to lop the branches off

ébranchoir [ebrɑ̃ʃwar] **NM** *Hort* billhook

ébranlement [ebrɑ̃lmɑ̃] **NM 1** *(départ, mise en route → d'un train, d'une procession, d'un convoi)* departure, setting off

2 *(tremblement → d'une vitre)* shaking; **l'é. de l'immeuble causé par l'explosion** the vibrations of the building caused by the explosion; **l'é. fut si violent que les murs se sont lézardés** the walls shook so violently that they cracked; *Fig* **causer l'é. du gouvernement** to shake *or* rock the government

3 *(choc)* shock

ébranler [3] [ebrɑ̃le] **VT 1** *(faire trembler)* to shake, to rattle; *(édifice, mur)* to shake, to rock; *(vitres)* to shake

2 *(affaiblir)* to shake, to weaken; **le scandale a ébranlé le gouvernement** the government was shaken by the scandal; **é. la résolution de qn** to shake sb's resolve; **é. la confiance de qn** to shake *or* to undermine sb's confidence; **é. la foi de qn** to shake sb's faith; **é. les nerfs de qn** to make sb very nervous; **é. la raison de qn** to unhinge sb; **é. la santé de qn** to undermine sb's health

3 *(atteindre moralement)* to shake; **ta gentillesse a fini par l'é.** your kindness finally touched him/her; **il ne faut pas te laisser é. par ses critiques** don't let his/her criticism get to you; **très ébranlé par la mort de son fils** shattered by the death of his son; **il a été très é. par l'annonce de cet accident** he was very shaken *or* upset by the news of the accident; **la nouvelle a ébranlé le pays tout entier** the entire country was rocked by the news

►**s'ébranler VPR** *(cortège)* to move *or* to set off; *(train)* to pull away, to start, to move off

ébrasement [ebrazmɑ̃] **NM** *Archit (d'une embrasure, d'un portail)* splay, splaying

ébraser [3] [ebraze] **VT** *Archit* to splay

ébrasure [ebrazyr] **NF** *Archit (d'une embrasure, d'un portail)* splay, splaying

Èbre [ɛbr] **NM l'È.** the Ebro

ébréché, -e [ebreʃe] **ADJ** chipped; **une assiette ébréchée** a chipped plate

ébrèchement [ebrɛʃmɑ̃] **NM 1** *(d'une assiette)* chipping; *(d'un couteau)* nicking, notching **2** *(d'une fortune)* depleting

ébrécher [18] [ebreʃe] **VT 1** *(assiette, vase)* to chip; *(couteau, lame)* to nick, to notch **2** *(fortune, héritage)* to make a hole in, to deplete; *Fig (réputation)* to damage; *Fig* **é. la confiance de qn** to dent sb's confidence

►**s'ébrécher VPR** to chip

ébréchure [ebreʃyr] **NF** *(sur un plat)* chip; *(sur une lame)* nick, notch

ébriété [ebrijete] **NF** *Jur* intoxication; **être en état d'é.** to be under the influence (of drink); **arrêté pour conduite en état d'é.** arrested for *Br* drink-driving *or Am* drunk-driving

ébroïcien, -enne [ebrɔisjɛ̃, -ɛn] **ADJ** of/from Évreux

▫ **Ébroïcien, -enne NM,F** = inhabitant of or person from Évreux

ébrouement [ebrumɑ̃] **NM 1** *(d'un cheval)* snort, snorting *(UNCOUNT)*; *(dans l'eau)* splashing about **2** *(d'ailes)* flap, flapping

ébrouer [6] [ebrue] **s'ébrouer VPR 1** *(cheval)* to snort; *(dans l'eau)* to splash about **2** *(personne, chien)* to shake oneself **3** *(ailes)* to flap

ébruitement [ebrɥitmɑ̃] **NM** disclosing, spreading

ébruiter [3] [ebrɥite] **VT** to disclose, to spread; *(nouvelle)* to spread; *(secret)* to give away; *(accord, pourparlers)* to leak

►**s'ébruiter VPR** to spread

EBS [əbeɛs] **NF** *Vét (abrév* **encéphalopathie bovine spongiforme***)* BSE

ébulliomètre [ebyljɔmɛtr] **NM** *Phys* ebulliometer

ébulliométrie [ebyljɔmetri] **NF** *Phys* ebulliometry

ébullioscope [ebyljɔskɔp] **NM** *Phys* ebullioscope

ébullioscopie [ebyljɔskɔpi] **NF** *Phys* ebullioscopy

ébullition [ebylisjɔ̃] **NF** *Phys* boiling; **pendant l'é.** while the liquid is boiling; **point d'é.** boiling point; **la température d'é. de l'eau est de 100°C** the boiling point of water is 100°C, water boils at 100°C

▫ **à ébullition ADV porter de l'eau/du lait à é.** to bring water/milk to the boil; **arriver à é.** to come to the boil

▫ **en ébullition ADJ** *(liquide)* boiling; *Fig* in turmoil; **maintenir en é. pendant cinq minutes** boil for five minutes; *Fam* **il a le cerveau en é.** he's bubbling over with excitement; **tout le pays est en é. depuis qu'ils l'ont arrêté** the whole country has been in turmoil since they arrested him

éburnation [ebyrnasjɔ̃] **NF** *Méd* eburnation

éburné, -e [ebyrne], **éburnéen, -enne** [ebyrneɛ̃, -ɛn] **ADJ** eburnean, eburneous; *Méd* **substance éburnée** dentine

EBV [əbeve] **NM** *Méd (abrév* **Epstein-Barr virus***)* EBV

écaillage [ekajaʒ] **NM 1** *(du poisson)* scaling; *(des huîtres)* opening, shucking **2** *(d'une peinture)* flaking *or* peeling *or* scaling off; *(d'un vernis)* chipping off; *(d'émail)* scaling off, chipping

écaille [ekaj] **NF 1** *Zool (de poisson, de serpent)* scale; *(de tortue)* shell; *(matière)* tortoiseshell; **lunettes à monture d'é.** tortoiseshell-rimmed spectacles; *Fig Littéraire* **les écailles lui tombèrent des yeux** the scales fell from his/her eyes

2 *(fragment → gén)* chip; *(→ de peinture)* flake; *(→ d'émail)* chip
3 *Bot* scale
4 *Constr* scalloped moulding
5 *Entom* tiger moth
❑ **en écaille** ADJ tortoiseshell *(avant n)*

écaillé, -e [ekaje] ADJ *(plâtre, vernis)* chipped, flaking off; *(peinture)* peeling

écailler[1] [3] [ekaje] VT **1** *Culin (poisson)* to scale; *(huître)* to open, to shuck **2** *(plâtre, vernis)* to cause to flake off *or* to chip **3** *(chaudière)* to scale **4** *Constr (couvrir d'écailles)* to scallop; **é. un dôme** to cover a dome with scalloped moulding
▸**s'écailler** VPR *(vernis, plâtre)* to flake off; *(peinture)* to peel off

écailler[2], **-ère** [ekaje, -ɛr] NM,F *(vendeur)* oyster seller; *(dans un restaurant)* = restaurant employee who opens oysters and prepares seafood platters
❑ **écaillère** NF *(instrument)* oyster knife

écailleur [ekajœr] NM fish scaler

écailleux, -euse [ekajø, -øz] ADJ **1** *Ich (poisson)* scaly **2** *Géol (ardoise, schiste)* flaky

écaillure [ekajyr] NF **1** *(d'un mur)* chipped patch **2** *(d'un poisson, d'un reptile)* scales

écale [ekal] NF **1** *Bot (d'une noix)* hull, husk; *(d'une châtaigne)* shuck **2** *Can (d'un poisson, d'un reptile)* scale

écaler [3] [ekale] VT **1** *Bot (noix)* to hull, to husk; *(châtaignes)* to shuck; *(œuf dur)* to shell **2** *(poisson)* to scale; *(huître)* to open, to shuck

écalure [ekalyr] NF *Bot* hard skin, husk; **écalures de café** husks of coffee beans

écang [ekɑ̃] NM *Tex* scutching blade, scutcher

écanguer [3] [ekɑ̃ge] VT *Tex* to scutch

écarlate [ekarlat] ADJ scarlet; **devenir é.** to blush, to go *or* turn scarlet
NF scarlet

écarquiller [3] [ekarkije] VT **é. les yeux** to open one's eyes wide, to stare (wide-eyed); **les yeux écarquillés par la peur** eyes wide with fear

ÉCART [ekar]

> difference **1** ■ gap **2, 8** ■ swerving **3** ■ margin **8**

NM **1** *(variation)* difference, discrepancy (**de** in); **on constate de grands écarts dans ses résultats** his/her results are very uneven; **il y a des écarts de niveau trop importants dans cette classe** ability differs *or* varies too much in the class; *Mktg* **é. de performance** gap level; *Com* **é. de poids/température** difference in weight/temperature; **é. d'opinions/de points de vue** difference of opinions/points of view; **é. de prix** price differential; **é. salarial** *ou* **de salaires** wage differential; **é. technologique** technology gap; *Com* **é. entre le prix de vente et le coût** margin between cost and selling price; *Tech* **é. admissible** tolerance, permissible deviation

2 *(intervalle)* gap, distance; **un é. de huit ans les sépare, il y a huit ans d'é. entre eux** there's an eight-year gap between them; **réduire** *ou* **resserrer l'é. entre** to close *or* to narrow the gap between; **l'é. entre les deux équipes s'est beaucoup réduit** the gap between the two teams has narrowed considerably; **l'é. entre chaque soldat doit être de...** there must be (a distance of)... between each soldier, soldiers must be... apart

3 *(déviation)* swerving; *Tech (de l'aiguille d'une boussole)* deflection; **é. par rapport à la norme** deviation from the norm; **faire un é.** *(cheval)* to shy; *(voiture, vélo)* to swerve; *(piéton)* to step aside, to swerve; **il a fait un é. pour éviter d'être aspergé de boue** he jumped aside to avoid being splashed with mud

4 *(excès)* **é. de conduite** misdemeanour, misbehaviour *(UNCOUNT)*; **ses écarts de conduite ont fini par lasser sa femme** his wife finally got tired of his behaviour; **écarts de langage** bad language; **faire des écarts de langage** to use bad language; **écarts de jeunesse** youthful indiscretions; **j'ai fait un petit é. aujourd'hui: j'ai mangé deux gâteaux** I broke my diet today: I ate two cakes; **il ne fait jamais d'écarts de régime** he never breaks his diet, he always keeps to his diet

5 *(hameau)* hamlet

6 *Cartes (action)* discarding; *(carte)* discard

7 *(en danse, en gymnastique)* **faire le grand é.** to do the splits

8 *Compta* margin; *(en statistique)* deviation; *Bourse* spread; *Mktg* gap; *(stratégie d'attaque)* bypass attack; **il y a un é. de cent euros entre les deux comptes** there is a discrepancy of a hundred euros between the two accounts; *Bourse* **l'é. entre le prix d'achat et le prix de vente** the spread between bid and asked prices; *Bourse* **é. d'acquisition** goodwill; **é. budgétaire** budgetary variance; *Compta* **é. de caisse** cash shortage; *Fin* **écarts de conversion** exchange adjustments; *Bourse* **écarts de cours** price spreads; **é. des coûts** cost variance; *Écon* **é. déflationniste** deflationary gap; **é. horizontal** horizontal spread; *Écon* **é. inflationniste** inflationary gap; *Compta* **é. net** net variance; **é. de prime** option spread; *Compta* **écarts de réévaluation** revaluation reserve; *Bourse* **é. vertical** vertical spread

❑ **à l'écart** ADV **1** *(de côté)* aside; **j'ai mis mes verres en cristal à l'é.** I've put my crystal glasses out of the way; **je mets mes sentiments personnels à l'é. dans cette histoire** I'm setting my personal feelings aside in this matter; **mettre qn à l'é.** to put sb on the sidelines; **les autres enfants le mettent** *ou* **tiennent à l'é.** the other children don't let him join in; **prendre qn à l'é.** to draw sb aside; **tenir qn à l'é.** to keep sb out of things; **rester** *ou* **se tenir à l'é.** *(dans une réunion, dans la société)* to remain an outsider, to stay in the background; *(du monde, de la foule etc)* to keep oneself apart, to hold oneself aloof; **se sentir à l'é.** to feel isolated *or* out of things

2 *(loin des habitations)* **vivre à l'é.** to live in a remote spot

❑ **à l'écart de** PRÉP **un terrain à l'é. de la ville** a piece of land outside the town; **nous sommes un peu à l'é. du village** we live a little way away from the village; **tenir qn à l'é. de qch** to keep sb away from sth; **il essaie de la tenir à l'é. de tous ses problèmes** he's trying to keep her away from all his problems; **se tenir à l'é. de la vie politique** to keep out of politics; **se tenir à l'é. du monde** to live apart from society

écartant, -e [ekartɑ̃, -ɑ̃t] ADJ *Can* disorienting

écarté, -e [ekarte] ADJ **1** *(isolé)* isolated, remote **2** *(loin l'un de l'autre)* **mettez-vous debout les jambes écartées** stand up with your legs wide apart; **gardez les bras écartés** keep your arms outspread; **avoir les dents écartées** to be gap-toothed; **avoir les yeux écartés** to have widely-spaced eyes **3** *Can (personne)* lost
NM *(jeu)* écarté

écartelé, -e [ekartəle] ADJ *Hér* quartered, quarterly

écartèlement [ekartɛlmɑ̃] NM *(torture)* quartering

écarteler [25] [ekartəle] VT **1** *(torturer)* to quarter **2** *(partager)* to tear apart; **écartelé entre le devoir et l'amour** torn between duty and love **3** *Hér* to quarter

écartelure [ekartəlyr] NF *Hér* quartering, quarter

écartement [ekartəmɑ̃] NM **1** *(distance → entre des barres etc)* space, gap, clearance; *Rail* **é. (des rails** *ou* **de voie)** gauge; *Aut* **é. des électrodes** spark *or* plug *or* electrode gap; *Aut* **é. des essieux** wheelbase; *Aut* **é. des roues** tracking
2 *(fait d'ouvrir)* spreading (open), opening; *Tech* **pièce d'é.** spacer
3 *(évincement → d'un directeur)* dismissing, removing; *(→ d'un obstacle)* setting aside; **depuis l'é. des gêneurs, la société va beaucoup mieux** things have been much better in the company since it got rid of the troublemakers

écarter [3] [ekarte] VT **1** *(séparer → objets)* to move apart; *(→ branches)* to part; *(→ personnes)* to separate; **é. les pinces d'un crabe** to prise open a crab's pincers; **é. les rideaux** *(le matin)* to open the curtains; *(pour observer)* to move the curtain aside; **ils écartèrent la foule pour passer** they pushed their way through the crowd; **é. les bras** to open *or* to spread one's arms; **é. les jambes/doigts/orteils** to spread one's legs/fingers/toes; **é. les coudes** to square one's elbows; *Fig* **le temps nous écarte l'un de l'autre** as time goes on we're drifting apart

2 *(éloigner)* to move away *or* aside, to pull away *or* aside; *(obstacle)* to move out of the way; *(danger)* to ward off, to divert; **é. les soupçons** to divert suspicion; **é. le danger** to ward off *or* avert danger; **é. les obstacles de son chemin** to brush aside the obstacles in one's path; **écarte les enfants au cas où ils se brûleraient** pull the children away in case they burn themselves; **écarte plus la table du mur** move the table further away from the wall

3 *(détourner)* to divert; **cette route vous écarte un peu** that road takes you a little bit out of your way; **ses interventions nous ont écartés de notre sujet** his/her interruptions caused us to stray *or* wander from the subject *or* to digress

4 *(refuser → idée)* to dismiss, to set aside, to rule out; *(→ candidat, proposition)* to turn down; **j'ai écarté ta solution** I ruled out your solution; **il écarte systématiquement toute idée de compromis** he refuses to countenance any suggestion of compromise

5 *(tenir à distance)* **é. qn de qch** *(succession, conseil d'administration)* to keep sb out of sth; **é. qn du pouvoir** *(aspirant)* to cut sb off from the road to power; *(homme d'État)* to manoeuvre sb out of power; **être écarté du processus de décision** to be kept away from the decision-making

6 *Cartes* to discard

▸**s'écarter** VPR **1** *(se séparer → personnes)* to move apart; *(→ routes)* to diverge; **plus on avance vers le nord, plus les maisons s'écartent les unes des autres** the further north you go, the further apart the houses become; **la foule s'est écartée sur le passage des pompiers** the crowd parted *or* drew aside to let the firemen through

2 *(s'éloigner)* to move away *or* out of the way, to step *or* to draw aside; *(de piéton)* to move *or* step aside; *(de voiture, de vélo)* to swerve; *(dévier)* to deviate, to stray (**de** from); **écarte-toi!** move *or* get out of the way!; **s'é. de sa trajectoire** *(fusée)* to deviate from its trajectory; *(pilote)* to deviate from one's course; **s'é. du droit chemin** to go off the straight and narrow (path); **s'é. du sujet** to stray *or* to wander from the subject; **ils se sont beaucoup écartés de l'idée initiale** they've strayed a long way away from the initial idea; **ne vous écartez pas de la route** keep to the road

3 *Can (s'égarer)* to get lost, to go astray

écarteur [ekartœr] NM *Méd* retractor; *Aut* **é. de mâchoire** shoe expander

écart-type [ekartip] *(pl* **écarts-types***)* NM *Math* average *or* standard deviation

e-cash [ikaʃ] NM *Ordinat* e-cash

ecballium [ɛkbaljɔm] NM *Bot* ecballium, squirting cucumber

ecce homo [etʃeɔmo, ɛkseɔmo] NM INV *Beaux-Arts* ecce homo

eccéité [ɛkseite] NF *Phil (en scolastique)* haecceity; *(chez Heidegger)* thisness

ecchymose [ekimoz] NF *Méd* bruise, *Spéc* ecchymosis

ecchymotique [ekimɔtik] ADJ *Méd* ecchymotic

ecclésia [eklezja] NF *Antiq* ecclesia

ecclésial, -e, -aux, -ales [eklezjal, -o] ADJ *Rel* ecclesial; **biens ecclésiaux** church property

Ecclésiaste [eklezjast] NM *Bible* **(le livre de) l'E.** Ecclesiastes

ecclésiastique [eklezjastik] *Rel* ADJ *(devoir)* ecclesiastic, ecclesiastical; *(habitude)* priestly, priestlike
NM ecclesiastic, clergyman

ecclésiologie [eklezjɔlɔʒi] NF *Rel* ecclesiology

ecdysone [ɛkdizɔn] NF *Physiol* ecdysone

écervelé, -e [esɛrvəle] ADJ scatterbrained
NM,F scatterbrain

ECG [əseʒe] NM *Méd (abrév* **électrocardiogramme***)* *Br* ECG, *Am* EKG

ecgonine [ɛkgɔnin] NF *Chim* ecgonine

échafaud [eʃafo] NM **1** *(lieu d'exécution)* scaffold; **cela l'a mené à l'é.** this brought him to the scaffold; **monter sur** *ou* **à l'é.** to be executed;

finir sur l'é. to die on the scaffold **2** *Vieilli (estrade)* stand, platform

échafaudage [eʃafodaʒ] **NM 1** *Constr* scaffolding; **matériel d'é.** scaffolding; **é. pour caméra** (camera) tower **2** *(pile)* heap, pile, stack; **un é. de livres** a pile *or* stack of books **3** *(élaboration → de systèmes)* elaboration, construction; *Fig (assemblage, structure)* structure, fabric

échafauder [3] [eʃafode] **VT 1** *(entasser)* to stack *or* to heap *or* to pile (up) **2** *(construire → systèmes, théories)* to devise, to construct; *(→ argumentation)* to put together, to construct; **é. des projets** to make plans

VI *Constr* to put up scaffolding, to scaffold

échalas [eʃala] **NM 1** *(perche)* pole, stake; **être droit** *ou* **raide** *ou* **sec comme un é.** to be as stiff as a poker *or* ramrod **2** *Fam (personne)* beanpole; **c'est un grand é.** he's a real beanpole

échalasser [3] [eʃalase] **VT** *Hort (haricot, vigne)* to stake (up)

échalier [eʃalje] **NM 1** *(clôture)* gate **2** *(échelle)* stile

échalote [eʃalɔt] **NF** *Bot* shallot

échancré, -e [eʃɑ̃kre] **ADJ 1** *Couture* low-necked; **une robe échancrée dans le dos** a dress cut low in the back, a dress with a low back; **une robe très échancrée sur le devant** a dress with a plunging neckline **2** *Bot* serrated **3** *Géog (côte, littoral)* indented, jagged

échancrer [3] [eʃɑ̃kre] **VT 1** *Couture* to cut a low neckline in **2** *(entailler)* to indent; *(planche)* to notch

échancrure [eʃɑ̃kryr] **NF 1** *Couture* low neckline; *(découpe de veste)* vent, slit; **é. en pointe** *ou* **en V dans le dos** V neckline in the back **2** *Bot* serration **3** *Géog* indentation **4** *(d'une planche)* notch

échange [eʃɑ̃ʒ] **NM 1** *(troc)* swap, exchange; **faire un é.** to swap, to do a swap; *(dans un magasin)* to exchange; **ils ont fait l'é. de leurs bicyclettes** they swapped bicycles; **on fait (l')é.?** do you want to swap?, do you want to do a swap?; **é. de prisonniers** exchange of prisoners; **é. standard** replacement *(of a spare part)*; *Pol* **é. de voix** vote-trading

2 *(aller et retour)* exchange; **avoir un é. de vues** to exchange opinions; **un long é. de correspondance** a long exchange of letters; **échanges culturels** cultural exchanges; **il y a eu un bref é. d'insultes/de coups entre les deux hommes** there was a brief exchange of insults/blows between the two men; **il y a eu plusieurs échanges de coups de feu** there were exchanges of gunfire; **de violents échanges entre la police et les manifestants** *(physique)* violent clashes between the police and demonstrators; *(verbal)* violent exchanges between the police and demonstrators; **c'est un é. de bons procédés** one good turn deserves another; **nous faisons des échanges de bons procédés** we do favours for each other, we help each other out

3 *(visite)* **é. (linguistique)** (language) exchange

4 *Échecs* **faire (un) é.** to exchange pieces

5 *Sport* **é. de balles** *(avant un match)* knocking up; *(pendant le match)* rally; **on va faire quelques échanges?** shall we knock a few balls about?; **quel bel é.!** what a beautiful rally!

6 *Biol* **échanges gazeux** gaseous interchange

7 *Jur* exchange

8 *Ordinat* **é. de données** data exchange *or* swap; **é. de données dynamique** dynamic data exchange; **é. de données informatisé** electronic data interchange; **É. Électronique de Données** Electronic Data Interchange

9 *Bourse* **é. d'actions** share swap; **é. cambiste** treasury swap; *Fin* **é. de créances** debt swap; *Fin* **é. de créances contre actifs** debt equity swap; *Fin* **é. de dette** debt swap; **é. de devises** currency swap; *Fin* **é. financier** swap; *Fin* **é. d'intérêts et de monnaies** currency interest-rate swap; **é. de taux d'intérêt** interest-rate swap; **é. à terme** forward swap; **é. en valeurs** turnover *(on a securities trading account)*

10 *Méd* **é. plasmatique** plasmapheresis

❑ **échanges NMPL** *Fin* exchange; *Écon* trade; **les échanges entre la France et l'Allemagne** trade between France and Germany; **le volume des échanges entre deux pays** the volume of trade between two countries; **échanges commerciaux** trade; **échanges industriels** industrial trade; **échanges internationaux** international trade; **échanges intracommunautaires** intra-Community trade

❑ **en échange ADV** in exchange, in return; **recevoir/donner qch en é.** to receive/give sth in exchange *or* in return

❑ **en échange de PRÉP** in exchange *or* return for; **recevoir/donner qch en é. de qch** to receive/give sth in exchange *or* in return for sth

échangeabilité [eʃɑ̃ʒabilite] **NF** exchangeability

échangeable [eʃɑ̃ʒabl] **ADJ** exchangeable; **nos articles sont échangeables sur présentation d'un ticket de caisse** articles may be exchanged on production of a receipt

échanger [17] [eʃɑ̃ʒe] **VT 1** *(troquer)* to exchange, to swap, *Vieilli* to barter (**contre** for); **é. un stylo contre** *ou* **pour un briquet** to exchange *or* to swap a pen for a lighter; **les articles soldés ne sont ni repris ni échangés** sales goods may not be returned or exchanged

2 *(se donner mutuellement)* to exchange; **ils ont échangé des lettres** there was an exchange of letters between them; **é. un regard/sourire** to exchange glances/smiles; **é. des impressions** to exchange *or* compare impressions; **é. des coups/des injures/des idées avec qn** to exchange blows/insults/ideas with sb; **é. quelques mots avec qn** to exchange a few words with sb

3 *Sport* **é. des balles** *(avant le match)* to knock up

▶ **s'échanger VPR 1** *(emploi passif) (être troqué)* to be swapped; *Bourse* to trade; **le dollar s'échange aujourd'hui à 1,12 euros** today the dollar is trading at 1.12 euros

2 *(emploi réciproque)* **s'é. des disques** to swap records with each other

échangeur [eʃɑ̃ʒœr] **NM 1** *Transp (sur une autoroute)* interchange; *(donnant accès à l'autoroute)* feeder; **un é. à niveaux multiples** a multiple interchange **2** *Phys* **é. (de chaleur)** heat exchanger **3** *Chim* **é. d'ions** ion exchanger **4** *Aut* **é. air/air** air-to-air exchanger

échangisme [eʃɑ̃ʒism] **NM** *(sexuel)* partner-swapping, swinging

échangiste [eʃɑ̃ʒist] **ADJ** partner-swapping, swinging

NMF 1 *Jur* exchanger **2** *(sexuellement)* swinger

échanson [eʃɑ̃sɔ̃] **NM** *Hist* cupbearer; *Hum* wine waiter

échantignole [eʃɑ̃tiɲɔl] **NF** *Constr* purlin-cleat, bracket

échantillon [eʃɑ̃tijɔ̃] **NM 1** *Com & Mktg (petite quantité)* sample; **é. de tissu/d'étoffe** swatch; **é. gratuit** free sample; **é. gratuit, ne peut être vendu** free sample, not for resale; **catalogue d'échantillons** *(gén)* sample *or* pattern book; *(d'étoffe)* swatch book; **non conforme à l'é.** not up to sample; **pareil** *ou* **conforme à l'é.** up to sample; **é. modèle** standard sample; **é. promotionnel** promotional sample; **é. publicitaire** free sample

2 *Méd (prélèvement)* sample, specimen; **prélever** *ou* **prendre des échantillons de qch** to take samples of sth, to sample sth

3 *Fig (cas typique)* example, sample; **voici un é. de son œuvre** here is an example of his/her work; **un é. de la poésie française du XVIème siècle** a typical example of 16th-century French poetry

4 *(de population)* cross-section; *(pour un sondage)* sample; **é. aléatoire** random sample; **é. aréolaire** cluster sample; **é. de convenance** convenience sample; **é. discrétionnaire** judgement sample; **é. empirique** purposive sample, non-random sample; **é. normal** average sample; **é. probabiliste/non-probabiliste** probability/non-probability sample; **é. par quotas** quota sample; **é. représentatif** cross-section, *Spéc* true sample; **é. stratifié** stratified sample; **é. type** representative sample

5 *Ordinat, Mus & Tel* sample

6 *Vieilli* **brique/tuile d'é.** standard brick/tile

échantillonnage [eʃɑ̃tijɔnaʒ] **NM 1** *Com & Mktg (action)* sampling; **l'é. se fait sur un produit sur cent** one product in a hundred is sampled *or* tested; **un é. est effectué systématiquement** sampling is done systematically; **é. aléatoire** random sampling; **é. aréolaire** cluster sampling; **é. empirique** purposive *or* non-random sampling; **é. probabiliste/non-probabiliste** probability/non-probability sampling; **é. par quotas** quota sampling; **é. stratifié** stratified sampling; **é. par zone** area sampling

2 *(personnes)* sample

3 *(série d'échantillons)* range of samples; *(de parfum)* selection; *(de papier peint, de moquette)* swatch *or* sample book; *Fig* **un é. de ce que je sais faire/de mes capacités** a sample of what I can do/of my ability

4 *Naut (dimensions)* scantling

5 *Ordinat, Mus & Tél* sampling

6 *Tex (de peaux)* trimming

échantillonner [3] [eʃɑ̃tijɔne] **VT 1** *Com* to sample; *(préparer des échantillons de)* to prepare samples of; *(tissus)* to take a sample of **2** *(population)* to take a cross-section of, to take a sample of **3** *(vin)* to sample, to taste **4** *Tex (peaux)* to trim **5** *Vieilli (étalonner → articles)* to make according to sample

échantillonneur, -euse [eʃɑ̃tijɔnœr, -øz] **NM,F** *Com (personne)* tester, sampler

NM *Mus* sampler

échappatoire [eʃapatwar] **NF** loophole, way out; **ne cherche pas d'é., réponds-moi!** don't avoid the issue, answer me!; **je n'ai pas d'é. possible** I can't get out of it; **le sommeil est mon é.** sleep is my escape mechanism; **é. comptabilité** accounting loophole; **é. fiscale** tax loophole

ADJ clause é. escape clause

échappé, -e [eʃape] **NM,F 1** *Sport (sportif)* = competitor who has broken away; **les échappés du peloton** the breakaway group

2 *Vieilli (évadé)* escaped prisoner, escapee; *Hum* **un é. de l'asile** *(fou)* a lunatic

❑ **échappée NF 1** *Sport* breakaway; **être dans l'échappée** to be part of the breakaway group

2 *(espace ouvert à la vue)* vista, view; **échappée (de vue) (sur)** vista (over); **échappée de lumière** shaft of light; **échappée de ciel** patch of sky

3 *(dans un escalier)* headroom

4 *(passage)* space, gap; *(pour véhicules)* turning space; **l'échappée d'un garage** a garage entrance

5 *(instant)* **une brève échappée de soleil** a brief sunny spell

❑ **par échappées ADV** every now and then, in fits and starts

échappement [eʃapmɑ̃] **NM 1** *Aut & Tech* exhaust; *(tuyau)* exhaust (pipe) **2** *Tech (d'horloge)* escapement; **montre à é.** lever watch **3** *(d'un escalier)* headroom **4** *Ordinat* escape

échapper [3] [eʃape] **VT 1** *Can (laisser échapper)* to let go; **le pêcheur a échappé le poisson** the fisherman let the fish go

2 *Can (laisser tomber)* to drop

3 *(locutions)* **nous l'avons échappé belle** we had a narrow escape; **ouf, on l'a échappé belle!** phew, that was close!

VI 1 *(s'enfuir)* **faire é.** *(animal)* to let out; *(détenu)* to help to escape; **laisser é.** *(personne, animal)* to let escape; *(de l'air d'un ballon)* to let out; *(vapeur)* to let off; **il a laissé é. le chien** he let the dog loose

2 *(sortir)* **pas un mot n'échappa de ses lèvres** *ou* **sa bouche** he/she didn't utter a single word; **laisser é. qch** *(secret)* to let sth slip, to let sth out; *(soupir, cri, grossièreté)* to let sth out; *(larme)* to let sth fall

3 *(glisser)* to slip; **le vase lui a échappé des mains** the vase slipped out of his/her hands

4 *(erreur, occasion)* **j'ai pu laisser é. quelques fautes** I may have overlooked a few mistakes; **laisser é. une occasion** to miss an opportunity, to let an opportunity go by

❑ **échapper à VT IND 1** *(se soustraire à)* to avoid, to evade; **é. de justesse à une amende** to narrowly avoid being fined *or* having to pay a fine; **é. à ses obligations** to evade one's duties; **é. aux recherches** *(criminel, animal)* to evade capture; **é. à la règle** to be an exception to the rule; **tu n'échappes pas à la règle** you're no exception to the rule; **é. à tout contrôle** to be out of control; **cet enfant/ce chien échappe à notre contrôle** this child/dog has got out of

hand *or* is beyond our control; **é. à toute définition** to defy definition; **je n'échapperai pas à une leçon de morale** I'm in for a sermon; **il va être difficile d'é. à ses calembours** it will be difficult to get away from his/her puns; **il n'y a pas moyen d'y é.** there is no escaping it *or* getting away from it

2 *(éviter)* to escape from, to get away from; *(grippe, punition)* to escape; *(corvées)* to get out of, to dodge; **il n'a pas pu é. à ses ennemis** he couldn't escape from his enemies; **le prisonnier nous a échappé** the prisoner got away from us *or* escaped; **elle sent que sa fille lui échappe** she can feel (that) her daughter's drifting away from her; **peux-tu é. quelques heures à ton patron?** can you get away from work for a few hours?; **é. à la mort** to escape death

3 *(être dispensé de)* **é. à l'impôt** *(officiellement)* to be exempt from taxation; *(en trichant)* to evade income tax

4 *(être oublié par)* **rien ne lui échappe** he/she doesn't miss a thing; **rien n'échappe à son regard** he/she sees everything; **leurs baisers n'ont pas échappé à mes regards** it did not escape my notice that they were kissing; **l'enfant a échappé à la vue de sa mère cinq minutes seulement** the child was out of his/her mother's sight for only five minutes; **ce fait a échappé à mon attention, ce fait m'a échappé** this fact escaped *or* slipped my attention, this fact escaped me; **ce détail m'a échappé** that detail escaped me; **quelques erreurs ont pu m'é.** I may have overlooked a few mistakes; **son nom m'échappe** his/her name escapes me *or* has slipped my mind; **je me souviens de l'air mais les paroles m'échappent** I remember the tune but I forget the lyrics; **il ne m'a pas échappé qu'il avait l'air ravi** it was obvious to me that he looked delighted; **il ne vous aura pas échappé que...** it will not have escaped your attention that...

5 *(être enlevé à)* **la victoire lui a échappé** victory eluded him/her; **la fortune de leur tante leur a échappé** they couldn't get their hands on their aunt's money

6 *(être prononcé par)* **si des paroles désagréables m'ont échappé, je te prie de m'excuser** if I let slip an unpleasant remark, I apologize; **la phrase lui aura échappé** the remark must have slipped out; **je n'aurais pas dû le dire mais ça m'a échappé** I shouldn't have said it but it just slipped out; **un sanglot/une injure lui échappa** he/she let out a sob/an oath

►**s'échapper** VPR **1** *(s'enfuir)* to escape, to get away (**de** from); **s'é. de prison** to escape from prison, to break out of prison; **s'é. d'un camp** to escape from a camp; **le chat s'est échappé** the cat ran away *or* escaped

2 *(se rendre disponible)* to get away; **quand les enfants étaient petits, nous ne pouvions pas nous é. facilement** when the children were small it was difficult for us to get away; **je ne pourrai pas m'é. avant midi** I won't be able to get away *or* escape before noon; **je n'arriverai jamais à m'é. de cette réunion de famille** I'll never manage to get out of this family reunion; **il faut que je m'échappe pendant quelques minutes** I've got to go somewhere (else) for a few minutes, I must be off

3 *(jaillir)* to escape, to leak; **le gaz s'échappe** the gas is leaking; **la lave s'échappe du volcan** lava is coming out of the volcano; **un cri s'échappa de ses lèvres** a cry burst from his/her lips; **de hautes flammes s'échappaient de tous côtés** great flames were shooting from every side; **des mèches s'échappaient de son foulard** wisps of hair poked out from underneath her scarf

4 *(disparaître)* to disappear, to vanish; **sa dernière chance s'est échappée** his/her last chance slipped away *or* disappeared

5 *Sport (coureur)* to break *or* to draw away

écharde [eʃard] NF splinter

échardonner [3] [eʃardɔne] VT to clear of thistles

écharnage [eʃarnaʒ], **écharnement** [eʃarnəmɑ̃] NM *(en tannerie)* fleshing

écharner [3] [eʃarne] VT *(en tannerie)* to flesh

écharneuse [eʃarnøz] NF *(en tannerie)* fleshing machine

écharnoir [eʃarnwar] NM *(en tannerie)* fleshing knife

écharpe [eʃarp] NF **1** *(vêtement)* scarf; *(d'un député, d'un maire)* sash; **l'é. tricolore** = sash worn by French mayors at civic functions **2** *(pansement)* sling

❑ **en écharpe** ADV **1 avoir le bras en é.** to have one's arm in a sling **2** *(locution)* **prendre qch en é.** to hit sth sideways on

écharper [3] [eʃarpe] VT to tear to pieces; **il s'est fait é. par sa femme quand il est rentré** his wife really laid into him when he got home; **vous allez vous faire é.!** you'll get torn to pieces!

échasse [eʃas] NF **1** *(bâton)* stilt; **marcher** *ou* **être monté sur des échasses** to walk *or* be on stilts; *Fam (avoir de longues jambes)* to have long legs■ **2** *Orn* stilt; **é. blanche** black-winged stilt

échassier [eʃasje] NM *Orn* wader, wading bird

échauboulure [eʃobulyr] NF *Vét* urticaria

échaudage [eʃodaʒ] NM **1** *(brûlure)* scalding **2** *Agr* shrivelling, withering

échaudé, -e [eʃode] ADJ *Agr (blé)* shrivelled by the sun

NM *Culin* canary-bread

échaudement [eʃodəmɑ̃] NM *Agr (de blé)* shrivelling

échauder [3] [eʃode] VT **1** *(ébouillanter → volaille)* to scald; *(→ vaisselle)* to run boiling water over; *(→ théière)* to warm **2** *(décevoir)* **l'expérience de l'année dernière m'a échaudé** my experience last year taught me a lesson; **il a déjà été échaudé une fois** he's had his fingers burned once already

échaudoir [eʃodwar] NM *(d'un abattoir → local)* scalding room; *(→ cuve)* scalding tub

échauffant, -e [eʃofɑ̃, -ɑ̃t] ADJ *Arch* constipating

échauffement [eʃofmɑ̃] NM **1** *(réchauffement → du sol, d'une planète)* warming (up) **2** *Sport (processus)* warming-up; *(exercices, période)* warm-up **3** *(excitation)* over-excitement; **dans l'é. de la discussion** in the heat of the argument **4** *Tech (d'une pièce, d'un moteur)* overheating; *(d'une corde)* chafing **5** *Fin (de l'économie)* overheating **6** *Agr* fermenting **7** *Arch (constipation)* constipation

échauffer [3] [eʃofe] VT **1** *(chauffer)* to heat (up), to warm up

2 *(exciter)* to heat, to fire, to stimulate; **discussion qui échauffe les esprits** discussion that gets people worked up; **les esprits sont échauffés** feelings are running high; *Fam* **il m'échauffe la bile** *ou* **les oreilles** *ou* **les sangs** he really gets my goat *or* on my nerves

3 *Tech* to overheat

4 *Agr (céréales, foin)* to cause fermentation in

5 *Sport* to warm up

►**s'échauffer** VPR **1** *Sport* to warm up

2 *(s'exciter)* to become heated; **laisser son imagination s'é.** to let one's imagination run wild *or* riot; **il s'échauffe pour un rien** he blows up *or* flares up at the slightest provocation; **ne vous échauffez pas** don't get excited

3 *(moteur, machine)* to become *or* get overheated, *Tech* to run hot

4 *Agr (de céréales, du foin)* to ferment

échauffourée [eʃofure] NF clash, skirmish

échauguette [eʃogɛt] NF *Hist* watchtower

èche [ɛʃ] NF *Pêche* bait

échéance [eʃeɑ̃s] NF **1** *Fin (date → de paiement)* date of payment; *(→ de maturité)* date of maturity; *(→ de péremption)* expiry date; **avant é.** *(paiement, règlement)* before the due date; **venir à é.** to fall due; **payable à l'é.** payable at maturity; **payable à quinze jours d'é.** payable in two weeks' time; **l'intérêt n'a pas été payé à l'é.** the interest is overdue; **é. à court terme** short-term maturity; **é. emprunt** loan maturity; **é. fixe** fixed maturity; **é. à long terme** long-term maturity; **é. moyenne** average due date; **é. à moyen terme** medium-term maturity; *Bourse* **é. proche** short maturity, near month; **é. à vue** sight bill *or* maturity

2 *Fin (somme d'argent)* financial commitment; **faire face à ses échéances** to meet one's financial commitments; **avoir de lourdes échéances** to have a lot of bills to pay each month, to have a lot of monthly payments to make; **é. commune** equation of payment; *Compta* **échéances de fin de mois** end-of-month payments

3 *(moment)* term; **l'é. électorale** election day, the elections; **nous sommes à trois mois de l'é. électorale** there are three months to go before the date set for the election; **un mois avant l'é. de l'examen** one month before the exam (is due to take place)

❑ **à brève échéance, à courte échéance** ADJ short-term; **billet à courte é.** short-dated bill ADV in the short term; **emprunter à courte é.** to borrow short; **prêter à courte é.** to lend short

❑ **à longue échéance** *Banque & Fin* ADJ long-term; **billet à longue é.** long-dated bill ADV in the long run; **emprunter à longue é.** to borrow long; **prêter à longue é.** to lend long

échéancier [eʃeɑ̃sje] NM **1** *(livre)* bill book, *Am* tickler; *Compta* due date file, aged debtor schedule; *Com* **é. de paiement** payment schedule **2** *(délais)* schedule of repayments

échéant, -e [eʃeɑ̃, -ɑ̃t] ADJ **1** *Fin* falling due **2** *voir* **cas**

échec [eʃɛk] NM **1** *(revers)* failure; **l'é. des discussions** the failure *or* breakdown of the negotiations; **après l'é. de la conférence au sommet** after the failure of the summit conference; **subir un é.** to suffer a setback; **reconnaître son é.** to admit defeat *or* failure; **cela va se solder par un é.** it will end in failure; **la réunion s'est soldée par un é.** nothing came out of the meeting; **faire é. à qn** to foil sb, to frustrate sb; **faire é. à qch** *(projet)* to foil sth, to prevent sth; *(activités, agissements)* to put a stop to sth; **faire é. à un coup d'État** to foil *or* to defeat a coup; **l'é. scolaire** academic failure, poor performance at school; **les problèmes familiaux sont très souvent à l'origine de l'é. scolaire** family problems are often the reason why children do badly at school; *Jur* **é. à l'exécution de la loi** failure to implement the law

2 *(défaite)* defeat; **son é. au championnat** his/her defeat in the championship

3 *Échecs* **é. (au roi)!** check!; **é. et mat!** checkmate!; **faire é.** to check; **faire é. au roi** to check the king; **faire é. et mat** to checkmate

❑ **échecs** NMPL *Échecs* chess; **jouer aux échecs** to play chess; **une partie d'échecs** a game of chess; **joueur d'échecs** chess player

❑ **en échec** ADV **mettre/tenir qn en é.** to put/to hold sb in check; **il a tenu toutes les polices d'Europe en é.** he thwarted the entire European police network; *Can* **mettre en é.** *(au hockey)* to (body) check

échelette [eʃlɛt] NF **1** *(de bât)* small ladder **2** *(de charrette)* rack, rail **3** *Orn* wall creeper

échelier [eʃəlje] NM peg ladder

échelle [eʃɛl] NF **1** *(outil)* ladder; **é. de corde** rope ladder; **é. coulissante** extension ladder; **é. double** (high) stepladder; **é. d'incendie** *ou* **de pompiers** fireman's ladder; **é. de marée** tide gauge; **é. de meunier** straight wooden staircase; **é. à poissons** fish ladder; **é. à saumons** fish ladder; **é. de sauvetage** fire (escape) ladder; *Fig* **l'é. sociale** the social ladder; **faire la courte é. à qn** to give sb a leg up *or Am* a boost; *Fig* to give sb a leg up, to help sb better his/her prospects; *Fig* **monter dans l'é. sociale** to climb the social ladder; *Fig* **être en haut** *ou* **au sommet de l'é.** to be at the top of the tree *or* the ladder; *Fam* **il n'y a plus qu'à tirer l'é.** we might as well just give up; **après lui, il n'y a plus qu'à tirer l'é.** he leaves all the rest standing; *Fam* **monter à l'é.** to be taken in; **vous voulez me faire monter à l'é.** you're having *or Am* putting me on

2 *(mesure)* scale; **une carte à l'é. 1/10 000** a map on a scale of 1/10,000; **ton train électrique est à quelle é.?** what scale is your electric train?; **réduire l'é. d'un dessin** to scale a drawing down

3 *Géol* scale; **l'é. de Richter** the Richter scale; **sur l'é. de Richter** on the Richter scale; **l'é. de Mercalli** the Mercalli scale; **l'é. de Mohs** the Mohs scale

4 *Météo* **l'é. de Beaufort** the Beaufort scale

5 *Ordinat* **é. des gris** levels of grey

6 *(dimension)* scale; **des évènements à l'é. mondiale** great world events; **à l'é. nationale** nationwide; **des villes à l'é. humaine** cities (built) on a human scale; *Fig* **faire les choses sur une grande é.** to do things in a big way *or* on a large scale

7 *Jur & Admin (hiérarchie)* scale; *Écon* **é. mobile** *(des prix, des salaires)* sliding scale; **é. (mobile) des salaires** *ou* **traitements** (sliding) salary scale; **é. des valeurs** scale of values; **é. des êtres** evolutionary ladder; **dans l'é. des êtres** on the evolutionary ladder; *Mktg* **é. d'attitude** attitude scale; *Mktg* **é. de classement** rating scale; *Mktg* **é. d'importance** scale of importance; *Écon* **é. minimale d'efficience** minimum efficient scale; **é. des prix** price scale

8 *Mus* **é. diatonique/chromatique/harmonique** diatonic/chromatic/harmonic scale; **é. des sons** scale

9 *Beaux-Arts* **é. des couleurs** range of colours

10 *Naut* **é. de commandement** *ou* **d'honneur** companion ladder; **é. de coupée** accommodation ladder; **é. de revers** Jacob's ladder; **é. de tirant d'eau** water *or* draught marks, *Am* immersion scale

11 *Hist* **les Échelles du Levant** the Ports of the Levant; **les échelles de Barbarie** the Barbary ports

12 *Rel* **é. de Jacob** Jacob's ladder

13 *Suisse (ridelle)* side *(of a farm trailer)*

14 **é. animale** evolutionary ladder

15 *(dans un collant) Br* ladder, *Am* run; **j'ai fait une é. à mon collant** *Br* I've laddered my tights, *Am* I have a run in my pantihose

16 *(dans les cheveux)* **elle me fait des échelles** she cuts my hair in steps; **dommage qu'il y ait toutes ces échelles** it's a pity that it's all so uneven *or* all so up and down

❑ **à grande échelle** ADJ **1** *(dessin)* large-scale **2** *(projet)* ambitious **3** *Ordinat* **intégration à grande é.** large-scale integration ADV on a big scale

❑ **à l'échelle** ADV **1** *Tech* **la façade n'est pas à l'é.** the façade isn't (drawn) to scale; **dessiner une carte à l'é.** to scale a map **2** *(suivi d'un adjectif)* **à l'é. régionale/internationale** on a regional/an international level

❑ **à l'échelle de** PRÉP at the level *or* on a scale of; **à l'é. de la région/planète** on a regional/world scale *or* level; **à l'é. de l'homme** on a human scale; **à l'é. de temps humain** on a human time scale

❑ **à petite échelle** ADJ **1** *(dessin, modèle)* small-scale **2** *Ordinat* **intégration à petite é.** small-scale integration

échelon [eʃlɔ̃] NM **1** *(barreau)* rung **2** *Admin* grade; **le dernier/premier é.** the bottom/top grade *or* step; **j'en suis au dernier é.** I'm at *or* I've reached the top of my grade; **changer d'é.** to change grade; **grimper d'un é.** to go up one step *or* grade; **grimper les échelons (de la hiérarchie)** to make one's way up the ladder; **il a gravi rapidement tous les échelons** he climbed the ladder rapidly; **monter par échelons** to rise by degrees *or* by successive stages **3** *(niveau)* level; **à l'é. local** at local level; **à l'é. régional/national** on a regional/national level; **à tous les échelons** at all levels, at every level **4** *Mil* echelon **5** *Bourse* **é. de cotation** tick size

❑ **à l'échelon de** PRÉP at the level of; **à l'é. du ministère** at Ministry level

échelonnement [eʃlɔnmɑ̃] NM **1** *(dans l'espace)* spreading out, placing at regular intervals **2** *(dans le temps → d'un paiement)* spreading (out); *(→ de congés)* staggering; **l'é. des travaux se fera sur plusieurs mois** the work will be spread out over several months; **le cours suit un é. bien précis** the course timetable is laid out very precisely **3** *(graduation → de difficultés)* grading

échelonner [3] [eʃlɔne] VT **1** *(dans l'espace → arbres, poteaux)* to space out, to place at regular intervals **2** *(dans le temps → livraisons, remboursements, publication)* to spread (out), to stagger, to schedule at regular intervals; *(→ congés, vacances)* to stagger; **paiements échelonnés** payments in instalments, staggered payments; **faire é. une dette** to arrange to pay back a debt in instalments; **les versements sont échelonnés sur dix ans** the instalments are spread (out) over ten years

3 *(graduer → difficultés, problèmes)* to grade, to place on a sliding scale **4** *Mil* to echelon

▸ **s'échelonner** VPR **1** **s'é. sur** *(dans le temps → sujet: projet, travaux)* to be spread out over; *(→ sujet: vacances, congés)* to be staggered over; **le remboursement de la dette s'échelonnera sur dix ans** the repayment of the debt will be spread out over a ten-year period **2** **s'é. sur** *(dans l'espace)* to be spaced out; **les arbres s'échelonnent sur plusieurs kilomètres** the trees stretch for several kilometres; **le cours s'échelonne sur dix niveaux** there are ten levels of difficulty in the course

échenillage [eʃnijaʒ] NM **1** *Hort* getting rid of caterpillars, worming **2** *Fig (d'une histoire, d'un récit)* trimming

écheniller [3] [eʃnije] VT **1** *Hort* to rid of caterpillars, to worm **2** *Fig (histoire, récit)* to trim

échenilloir [eʃnijwar] NM *Hort* pruning hook, billhook

écher [18] [eʃe] = **aicher**

écheveau, -x [eʃvo] NM **1** *Tex* hank, skein **2** *(labyrinthe de rues)* maze **3** *(embrouillamini)* tangle; **l'é. d'une intrigue** the intricacies *or* complexities of a plot; **démêler l'é. d'une intrigue** to untangle a plot

échevelé, -e [eʃəvle] ADJ **1** *(ébouriffé)* dishevelled, tousled **2** *(effréné)* frantic, wild, unbridled; **une danse échevelée** a wild dance **3** *Littéraire (arbre)* windswept

écheveler [24] [eʃəvle] VT *Littéraire* to tousle the hair of

échevette [eʃvɛt] NF *Tex* rap, lea

échevin [eʃvɛ̃] NM **1** *Hist* municipal magistrate *(under the Ancien Régime)*, ≃ alderman **2** *Belg* deputy burgmaster *or* burgomaster **3** *Can Hist* city councillor

échevinage [eʃvinaʒ] NM *Hist (fonction)* = office or rank of a municipal magistrate *(under the Ancien Régime)*, ≃ aldermanship; *(corps des échevins)* body of municipal magistrates *(under the Ancien Régime)*, ≃ aldermancy; *(territoire)* territory administered by municipal magistrates *(under the Ancien Régime)* **2** *Belg (corps des échevins)* deputy burgmasters *or* burgomasters; *(fonction)* = office or rank of a deputy burgmaster

échevinal, -e, -aux, -ales [eʃəvinal, -o] ADJ **1** *Hist* relating to a muncipal magistrate *(under the Ancien Régime)* **2** *Belg* **collège é.** = college made up of the burgmaster and deputy burgmasters of a town

échevinat [eʃəvina] NM *Belg* = office or rank of the deputy burgmaster

échidné [ekidne] NM *Zool* spiny anteater, *Spéc* echidna

échiffer [3] [eʃife] VT *Can Vieilli* to tear, to fray

échiffre [eʃifr] NM *Archit* **mur d'é.** *ou* **é.** string wall

échine [eʃin] NF **1** *Anat & Zool* backbone, spine; **courber** *ou* **plier l'é. devant qn** to submit to sb; **avoir l'é. souple** to be obsequious *or* subservient **2** *Culin* chine, loin; **une côte de porc dans l'é.** a pork loin chop **3** *Archit* echinus

échiné, -e [eʃine] ADJ *Can* tired out, exhausted

échiner [3] [eʃine] **s'échiner** VPR **s'é. à faire qch** *(se fatiguer)* to wear *or* tire oneself out doing sth; *(se donner du mal)* to go to great lengths *or* make a great effort to do sth

échinocactus [ekinokaktys] NM *Bot* hedgehog cactus, *Spéc* echinocactus

échinococcose [ekinokɔkoz] NF *Méd & Vet* echinococcosis

échinocoque [ekinokɔk] NM *Zool* echinococcus

échinoderme [ekinodɛrm] *Zool* NM echinoderm

❑ **échinodermes** NMPL Échinodermata

échiquéen, -enne [eʃikeɛ̃, -ɛn] ADJ *Échecs* chess *(avant n)*

échiqueté, -e [eʃikte] ADJ *Hér* checky, chequy

échiquier [eʃikje] NM **1** *Échecs* chessboard; *Fig* **le rôle que nous jouons sur l'é. européen/mondial** the part we play on the European/world scene **2** *Pol* **l'É.** the (British) Exchequer

❑ **en échiquier** ADV in a *Br* check *or* *Am* checkered pattern

échiurien [ekjyrjɛ̃] *Zool* NM echiuran

❑ **échiuriens** NMPL echiurans, *Spéc* Echiura

écho [eko] NM **1** *(acoustique)* echo; **faire é.** to echo (back); **il y a de l'é.** there is an echo; **é.**

multiple reverberations; **é. simple** echo; **échos parasites** clutter; *Électron* **éliminateur** *ou* **suppresseur d'é.** echo suppressor

2 *Fig* **j'en ai eu des échos** I heard something about it; **j'en ai eu de bons échos** I've had positive feedback about it; **trouver un é.** to get a response; **sa proposition n'a pas trouvé d'é., sa proposition est restée sans é.** his/her offer wasn't considered; **un é. des préoccupations de l'époque** one of the (major) preoccupations of the age; **se faire l'é. d'une information** to spread a piece of news; **se faire l'é. des opinions de qn** to echo *or* repeat sb's opinions; **aucun journal ne s'en est fait l'é.** the story was not picked up by any newspaper

3 *TV* ghosting; **à cause des arbres, nous avons de l'é.** we get ghosting because of the trees

4 *(rubrique de journal)* **échos** news in brief; **échos mondains** gossip column

5 *Presse* **les Échos** = French daily financial newspaper

6 *Ordinat* echo

❑ **à tous les échos** ADV in all directions

échocardiogramme [ekokardjɔgram] NM *Méd* echocardiogram

échocardiographie [ekokardjografi] NF *Méd* echocardiography

échoencéphalogramme [ekoɑ̃sefalɔgram] NM *Méd* echoencephalogram

échographe [ekograf] NF *Méd* (ultrasound) scanner

échographie [ekografi] NF *Méd* (ultrasound) scan; **se faire faire une é., passer une é.** to have a scan *or* an ultrasound scan

échographier [9] [ekografje] VT *Méd* to scan *(with an ultrasound scan)*

échographique [ekografik] ADJ *Méd* ultrasound *(avant n)*, ultrasonic

échographiste [ekografist] NMF *Méd* ultrasonographer, echocardiographer

échoir [70] [eʃwar] VI *Fin (dette)* to fall due; *(investissement)* to mature; **intérêts à é.** accruing interest, interest falling due; **abonnement échu** expired subscription; **billets échus** bills (over)due; **intérêts échus** outstanding interest, interest due; **la banque a fait é. le terme du remboursement plus tôt que prévu** the bank called in the loan earlier than had been expected; **le terme échoit le 20 de ce mois** the date for payment is the 20th of this month; **le délai est échu** the deadline has expired

❑ **échoir à** VT IND **é. à qn** to fall to sb; **le devoir m'échut de lui apprendre la nouvelle** it fell to me to break the news to him/her; **le sort qui lui est échu n'est guère enviable** one can hardly envy his/her lot; **c'est à moi qu'il échoit d'annoncer la mauvaise nouvelle** it falls to me to announce the bad news

écholalie [ekolali] NF *Méd* echolalia

écholocalisation [ekolɔkalizasjɔ̃], **écholocation** [ekolɔkasjɔ̃] NF *Zool* echolocation

échoppe [eʃɔp] NF **1** *Tech (outil)* burin **2** *(magasin)* booth, stall; *(de cordonnier)* small workshop

échopper [3] [eʃɔpe] VT *Tech* to grave, to gouge; *(bois)* to cut away; **machine à é.** routing machine

échopraxie [ekopraksi] NF *Méd* echopraxia

échosondage [ekosɔ̃daʒ] NM *Tech* echo sounding

échosondeur [ekosɔ̃dœr] NM *Tech* echo sounder

échotier, -ère [ekɔtje, -ɛr] NM,F *Journ (journaliste)* gossip columnist

échotomographie [ekotɔmografi] NF *Méd* (ultrasound) scan

échouage [eʃwaʒ], **échouement** [eʃumɑ̃] NM *Naut (d'un navire)* grounding, running aground; *(sur la plage)* beaching

échouer [6] [eʃwe] VI **1** *(rater → projet, tentative)* to fail, to fall through; *(→ personne)* to fail; **ils ont échoué dans leur tentative de coup d'État** their attempted coup failed; **é. à un examen** to fail an exam; **faire é.** *(projet)* to thwart, to frustrate; *(complot)* to foil

2 *Fam (finir)* to end *or* to wind up; **un tableau de valeur échoué dans un grenier** a valuable painting that has ended up in an attic; **ils ont échoué dans un bar vers minuit** they ended *or* wound up in a bar around midnight

3 *Naut* to ground, to run aground; *(baleine)* to beach

VT *Naut (accidentellement)* to ground, to run aground; *(volontairement)* to beach; **navire échoué** ship aground, stranded vessel *or* ship; **échoué à sec** high and dry; **quelques caisses échouées sur la plage** a few boxes washed up on the beach

▶**s'échouer VPR** *Naut* to run aground; *(baleine)* to beach

échu, -e [eʃy] **PP** *voir* **échoir**

ADJ *Fin* **payer un loyer à terme é.** to pay at the end of the rental term

écidie [esidi] **NF** *Bot* aecidium

écimage [esimaʒ] **NM** *Hort* pollarding

écimer [3] [esime] **VT** *Hort* to pollard

éclaboussement [eklabusmɑ̃] **NM** splashing, spattering

éclabousser [3] [eklabuse] **VT** 1 *(asperger)* to splash, to spatter; **éclaboussé de boue** mud-spattered; **les cheveux éclaboussés de peinture** hair spattered with paint

2 *(nuire à la réputation de)* **é. qn** to malign sb, to tarnish sb's reputation; **le scandale a éclaboussé certains de ses collègues** the scandal tarnished *or* sullied the reputation of some of his/her colleagues

3 *Littéraire (impressionner)* **é. qn de son luxe/sa richesse** to flaunt one's luxurious lifestyle/one's wealth at sb

éclaboussure [eklabusyr] **NF** 1 *(tache → de boue, de peinture)* splash, spatter; **des éclaboussures de sang** bloodstains 2 *(retombée)* smear; **atteint par les éclaboussures d'un scandale financier** implicated in a financial scandal

éclair [eklɛr] **NM** 1 *Météo* flash of lightning; **éclairs** lightning; **éclairs de chaleur** heat lightning; **éclairs en zigzag** forked lightning; **entrer/sortir/traverser comme un é.** to dart in/out/across; **le peloton est passé comme un é.** the pack of cyclists flashed past; **cette pensée traversa mon esprit comme un é.** the thought flashed through my mind; **prompt** *ou* **rapide** *ou* **vif comme l'é.** (as) quick as a flash; **avec la rapidité** *ou* **vitesse de l'é.** (as) quick as a flash

2 *(lueur → d'un coup de feu, d'un flash)* flash; **jeter** *ou* **lancer des éclairs** *(diamant, yeux etc)* to flash; **la lame jetait des éclairs dans la pénombre** the blade flashed *or* glinted in the shadows; **un é. de colère passa dans ses yeux** anger flashed *or* blazed in his/her eyes

3 *(bref instant)* **un é. de** a flash *or* spark of; **dans un é. de lucidité** in a flash of lucidity; **un é. de génie** a flash of inspiration

4 *Culin* éclair; **é. au chocolat** chocolate éclair

5 *(comme adj)* lightning *(avant n)*; **grève é.** lightning strike; **guerre é.** blitzkrieg; **visite é.** lightning *or* flying visit; **il a fait un passage é. au sein de la rédaction** he had a very brief spell on the editorial team

❑ **en un éclair ADV** in a flash *or* an instant; **tout lui est revenu à la mémoire en un é.** everything came back to him/her in a flash

éclairage [eklɛraʒ] **NM** 1 *(illumination artificielle)* lighting; **à l'époque, l'é. était assuré par des torches** in those days people used torches for lighting; **é. d'ambiance** background light; **é. d'appoint** fill light; **é. en contre-jour** backlighting; **é. direct** direct lighting; **é. doux** soft lighting; **é. à l'électricité** electric lighting; **é. de faible intensité** low-key lighting; **é. frisant** rimming; **é. au gaz** gas lighting; **é. indirect** indirect *or* concealed lighting; **é. public** street lighting **é. en trois points** three-point lighting; **é. rasant** rim light

2 *(intensité de lumière)* light; **l'é. est faible au premier étage** the first floor is badly lit

3 *(installation)* **l'é., les éclairages** the lighting; **les éclairages sont de Y. Dumais** lighting effects by Y. Dumais; **é. sur batterie** sungun; **é. de cyclorama** cyclorama light; *Aut* **é. intérieur automatique** courtesy light; *Cin & TV* **é. de plateau** stage lighting; **é. aux projecteurs** floodlighting; *Aut* **é. de route** full-beam headlights; **é. de sécurité** emergency lighting; *Aut* **é. de ville** dipped headlights

4 *Beaux-Arts* use of light; *Phot* light; **é. clair-obscur** Rembrandt *or* chiaroscuro lighting; **é. à la Rembrandt** Rembrandt lighting

5 *(aspect)* light, perspective; **sans cet é. historique, le problème ne peut pas être analysé** without this historical perspective the problem cannot be analysed; **vu sous cet é.** seen in this light; **apporter à qch un é. nouveau** to throw new light on sth

6 *Mil* scouting expedition

éclairagisme [eklɛraʒism] **NM** lighting engineering

éclairagiste [eklɛraʒist] **NMF** 1 *Cin, Théât & TV* lighting engineer 2 *Com* dealer in lights and lamps

éclairant, -e [eklɛrɑ̃, -ɑ̃t] **ADJ** 1 *(lumineux)* lighting 2 *(édifiant → commentaire, conclusion)* enlightening

éclaircie [eklɛrsi] **NF** 1 *Météo* sunny spell, bright interval 2 *(amélioration)* improvement 3 *(de forêt)* clearing

éclaircir [32] [eklɛrsir] **VT** 1 *(rendre moins sombre)* to make lighter; **ce papier éclaircit la pièce** this wallpaper brightens up the room *or* makes the room feel lighter; **é. ses cheveux** to lighten one's hair; *(par mèches)* to put highlights in one's hair; **é. le teint** to clear the complexion

2 *(rendre plus audible)* **des pastilles pour é. la voix** *ou* **gorge** lozenges to clear the throat

3 *Culin (sauce, soupe)* to thin (down)

4 *(forêt)* to thin; *(jeunes plantes)* to thin out

5 *(élucider → affaire, mystère)* to clear up; *(→ situation)* to clarify; **é. sa pensée** to make one's thoughts more intelligible, to explain what one has on one's mind

▶**s'éclaircir VPR** 1 *Météo* to clear (up), to brighten up; *(brouillard)* to clear (up); *(teint, voix)* to clear, to become clear(er); **le ciel s'est éclairci** the sky's cleared (up) *or* brightened up; *Fig* **l'avenir semble s'é.** the future seems to be getting brighter; *Fam* **ça s'éclaircit** it's brightening up; **son visage s'éclaircit** his/her face brightened up *or* lit up

2 *(pâlir → cheveux)* to go lighter *or* paler *or* blonder; **s'é. les cheveux** to lighten one's hair

3 *(se raréfier)* to thin (out); *(cheveux)* to grow thin, to be thinning; **ses cheveux s'éclaircissent** his hair's getting thinner, he's going bald

4 *(être clarifié → mystère)* to be solved; *(→ situation)* to become clearer

5 **s'é. la voix** *ou* **gorge** to clear one's throat

éclaircissage [eklɛrsisaʒ] **NM** 1 *Vieilli (du verre)* polishing 2 *(de forêt)* thinning; *Hort (de plantes)* thinning out

éclaircissant, -e [eklɛrsisɑ̃, -ɑ̃t] **ADJ** *(lotion, shampooing)* lightening, highlighting

éclaircissement [eklɛrsismɑ̃] **NM** 1 *(d'une peinture)* lightening

2 *(de cheveux)* lightening; **je me suis fait faire un é.** I had my hair lightened

3 *(élucidation)* clarification, *Sout* elucidation; **l'é. de ce mystère a pris des mois** it was months before the mystery was cleared up

4 *(explication)* explanation; **demander des éclaircissements** to ask for further information *or* an explanation; **je voudrais des éclaircissements sur ce point** I would like some further clarification on this point

éclaire [eklɛr] **NF** 1 *Bot* greater celandine 2 *Naut* hatchway

éclairé, -e [eklere] **ADJ** 1 *(lumineux)* **une pièce bien/mal éclairée** a well-/badly-lit room 2 *(intelligent)* enlightened

éclairement [eklɛrmɑ̃] **NM** 1 *Littéraire* lighting, brightening 2 *Phys* illumination

éclairer [4] [eklere] **VT** 1 *(chemin, lieu)* to light (up); **les phares éclairent la route** the road is lit by beacons; **une bougie éclairait la pièce** the room was lit by a candle; **é. une cuisine au néon** to use fluorescent lighting in a kitchen; **cafés éclairés au néon** cafés with neon lights, neon-lit cafés; **é. un stade avec des projecteurs** to floodlight a stadium; **marchez derrière moi, je vais vous é.** walk behind me, I'll light the way for you

2 *(égayer)* to brighten up, to light up, to illuminate; **ses derniers instants ont été éclairés par la présence de ses enfants** his/her last moments were brightened up by the presence of his/her children; **un sourire éclairait son visage** a smile lit up his/her face; **un foulard rose éclairait sa robe sombre** a pink scarf brightened up her dark dress

3 *(rendre compréhensible)* to clarify, to throw light on; **é. qch d'un jour nouveau** to shed *or* throw new light on sth; **ces notes éclairent la pensée de l'auteur** these notes throw some light on the author's ideas

4 *(informer)* to enlighten; **j'ai besoin qu'on m'éclaire sur ce point** I need someone to explain this point to me *or* to enlighten me on this point; *Fam* **é. la lanterne de qn** to put sb in the picture

5 *Mil* to scout out; **é. le terrain** *ou* **la marche** to reconnoitre the ground, to scout

VI 1 *(diffuser de la lumière)* **la lampe n'éclaire plus** the lamp's gone out; **cette ampoule éclaire bien/mal** this bulb throws out a lot of/doesn't throw out much light

2 *Can (lors d'un orage)* to flash (lightning)

▶**s'éclairer VPR** 1 *(emploi réfléchi)* **s'é. au gaz** to have gaslight; **s'é. à l'électricité** to have electric lighting; **s'é. à la bougie** to use candlelight; *(pour se diriger)* to light one's way with a candle; **il s'éclaire toujours au pétrole** he still has *or* uses oil lamps; **tiens, prends ma lampe électrique pour t'é.** here, take my *Br* torch *or Am* flashlight to let you see where you're going

2 *(s'allumer)* to be lit; **les fenêtres s'éclairent une à une** the windows light up one by one

3 *(visage, regard)* to brighten up, to light up

4 *(se résoudre)* to get clearer; **enfin, tout s'éclaire!** it's all clear (to me) now!

éclaireur, -euse [eklɛrœr, -øz] **NM,F** *(scout)* boy scout, *f* girl scout, *Br* girl guide; **les Éclaireurs de France** the (French) Scout Association; **chef é.** scoutmaster, *f* guide captain

NM 1 *Mil* scout; *Naut* scouting vessel, scout; *Aviat* **avion é.** reconnaissance aircraft

2 *Aut* **é. de coffre** *Br* boot *or Am* trunk light

❑ **en éclaireur ADV envoyer qn en é.** to send sb scouting; *aussi Fig* **partir en é.** to go (off) and scout around; *Fig* **parti en é. chercher un restaurant** scouting around for a restaurant; *Fig* **il part un mois avant, en é.** he's leaving a month in advance to check things out

éclampsie [eklɑ̃psi] **NF** *Obst* eclampsia

éclamptique [eklɑ̃ptik] *Obst* **ADJ** eclamptic

NF eclamptic

ÉCLAT [ekla]

splinter **1** ▪ burst **2** ▪ scandal **3** ▪ brightness **4, 5** ▪ glamour **6** ▪ luminosity **7**

NM 1 *(fragment → de métal)* splinter, shard; *(→ de bois)* splinter, sliver; *(→ de pierre)* chip; *(→ de mica)* flake; **un é. de verre** a fragment *or* splinter of glass; **éclats de verre** *(bris)* broken glass; *(projeté)* flying glass; **é. d'obus** piece of shrapnel; **des éclats d'obus** shrapnel

2 *(bruit)* burst; **é. de rire** burst *or* roar of laughter; **partir d'un grand é. de rire** to burst out laughing; **é. de colère** outburst of anger; **on entendait des éclats de voix** loud voices could be heard

3 *(scandale)* scandal; **faire un é. en public** to cause a public scandal *or* embarrassment; **j'espère qu'il n'y aura pas d'é. pendant la réunion** I hope the meeting passes off quietly, I hope nobody makes a fuss at the meeting; **il adore provoquer** *ou* **faire des éclats dans les soirées mondaines** he loves creating a commotion at society parties; **sans é.** quietly, without any fuss

4 *(de la lumière, du jour)* brightness; *(du soleil, de projecteur)* glare; **l'é. d'un diamant** the sparkle of a diamond; **le soleil d'hiver brillait d'un é. très doux** the winter sun shone with a pale light; **le soleil brille de son plus vif é.** the sun is (shining) at its brightest *or* most brilliant

5 *(du regard, d'un sourire)* brightness; *(d'une couleur)* vividness, brilliance; *(du teint)* radiance, bloom; *(d'un diamant)* glitter, lustre; **l'é. de ses yeux** the sparkle in his/her eyes; **sans é.** dull; **perdre son é.** *(peinture, couleur)* to dull; **elle a perdu tout son é.** *(vivacité)* she has lost all her sparkle; *(physiquement)* she has lost her bloom

6 *(splendeur)* glamour, glitter; *(de style etc)* brilliance; **l'é. de la conversation** the brilliant *or* scintillating conversation; **l'é. de la jeunesse**

the bloom *or* freshness of youth; **l'é. de son intelligence** his/her brilliant mind; **l'é. d'un festival** the glamour *or* glitter of a festival; **donner de l'é. à** to make glamorous; **aimer faire les choses avec é.** to like doing things in style

7 *Astron* **é. absolu/apparent** true/apparent luminosity

éclatant, -e [eklatɑ̃, -ɑ̃t] **ADJ 1** *(soleil, couleur)* dazzling, brilliant; *(miroir, surface)* sparkling; *(dents)* gleaming; **draps d'une blancheur éclatante** *ou* **éclatants de blancheur** dazzling white sheets; **aux couleurs éclatantes** *(tissus)* flamboyant; **écharpe d'un rouge é.** bright red scarf; **un sourire é.** a dazzling smile

2 *(excellent → santé, teint)* radiant, glowing; **être dans une forme éclatante** to be on brilliant *or* dazzling form; **éclatante de beauté** radiantly beautiful; **é. de santé** glowing *or* blooming with health

3 *(spectaculaire → revanche)* spectacular; *(→ triomphe, victoire)* resounding; **ce fut une victoire éclatante** it was a resounding victory

4 *(bruyant)* loud, resounding; **on entendait son rire é.** we could hear his/her booming laugh

éclate [eklat] **NF** *Fam* **c'est l'é.** it's a laugh *or* a hoot; **c'est pas l'é.** it's not exactly a barrel of laughs

éclaté, -e [eklate] **ADJ 1** *(groupe)* scattered, dispersed; *(programme, mesures)* fragmented, fragmentary; **paysage politique é.** fragmented political landscape; **avoir une vision éclatée des choses** to have a fragmented view of things

2 *Tech* **dessin é.** exploded drawing; **perspective éclatée** exploded perspective; **vue éclatée** exploded view

3 *Méd (rate)* ruptured

4 *Fam (épanoui)* **elle a l'air é.** *ou* **éclatée depuis qu'elle a changé de travail** she looks much happier since she's changed her job

5 *Fam (hilare)* **on était éclatés** we nearly died laughing

NM *Tech* exploded drawing

éclatement [eklatmɑ̃] **NM 1** *(déflagration → d'une bombe)* explosion; *(→ d'un pneu, d'un tuyau, d'un fruit)* bursting; *(→ d'un verre)* shattering; *(→ du foie, de la rate)* rupture; *Aut* **é. de l'étincelle** jump spark **2** *(rupture → d'un parti)* breakup; *(→ d'un convoi, d'un groupe)* dispersal

éclater [3] [eklate] **VI 1** *(exploser)* to explode, to blow up, to burst; *(obus)* to burst, to explode; *(arme)* to explode; *(mine)* to blow up; *(pneu, ballon)* to burst; *(verre)* to shatter; *Méd (rate)* to rupture; **faire é. qch** to burst/explode/shatter sth; **faire é. un pétard** to set off a firework; **le plat a éclaté lorsque je l'ai plongé dans l'eau bouillante** the dish shattered when I plunged it into the boiling water; **j'ai l'impression que ma tête/mon cœur/ma poitrine va é.** I feel as if my head/heart/chest is going to burst

2 *(se fractionner)* to split, to break up; **notre département a éclaté en plusieurs services** our department was broken up into several subdivisions

3 *(retentir)* **l'orage a enfin éclaté** the thunderstorm finally broke; **un coup de tonnerre a soudain éclaté** there was a sudden thunderclap; **des applaudissements éclatèrent** there was a burst of applause; **des coups de feu ont éclaté** shots rang out; **l'hymne national éclata dans la salle** the people in the room broke into the national anthem; **é. de rire** to burst out laughing; **é. en sanglots** to burst into tears, to burst out sobbing; **é. en applaudissements** to burst into applause; **é. en reproches** to let out a stream of reproaches

4 *(se déclencher → guerre, scandale)* to break out; *(→ scandale)* to break; *(→ colère)* to burst out; **quand la guerre éclata** at the outbreak of the war, when war broke out

5 *(apparaître)* to stand out; **son talent éclate à chaque page** his/her talent stands out on each page; **l'indignation éclatait dans ses yeux** his/her eyes were blazing with indignation

6 *(de colère)* to explode; **j'ai cru qu'il allait é.** I thought he was going to explode; **"mais enfin!", éclata-t-il** "for goodness sake!" he burst out *or* exploded; **é. de colère** to fly into a rage

7 *(être célèbre)* to be an instant success

VT *Fam (pneu)* to burst■; *très Fam Fig* **je vais l'é., je vais lui é. la tête** *ou* **la gueule** I'll smash his/her head in

►s'éclater VPR *Fam* to have a whale of a time, to have a ball; **s'é. comme une bête** to freak out; **il s'éclate en faisant de la photo** he gets his kicks from photography; **on s'est éclatés hier soir en boîte** we had a great time last night at the club

éclateur [eklatœr] **NM** *Tech* spark gap, spark discharger

éclectique [eklɛktik] **ADJ** *(distraction, goût, opinion)* eclectic, varied

NMF eclectic, person with eclectic tastes

éclectisme [eklɛktism] **NM** eclecticism

éclimètre [eklimɛtr] **NM** eclimeter

éclipse [eklips] **NF 1** *Astron* eclipse; **é. de Soleil/Lune** solar/lunar eclipse; **é. annulaire/totale/partielle** annular/total/partial eclipse

2 *(éloignement)* eclipse, decline; **revenir sur scène après une é. de plusieurs années** to return to the stage after an absence of several years; *Fig* **é. totale de la raison/mémoire** total loss of reason/memory

3 *Méd* blackout

□ à éclipses ADJ phare/feu à éclipses intermittent beacon/light; *Fig* **une carrière à éclipses** a career progressing in fits and starts

éclipser [3] [eklipse] **VT 1** *Astron* to eclipse **2** *Fig (surclasser → personne)* to eclipse, to overshadow, to outshine; *(→ événement, exploit etc)* to eclipse, to overshadow; **éclipsé sur le marché des ordinateurs par...** overshadowed *or* outclassed on the computer market by...

►s'éclipser VPR 1 *Fam (s'esquiver)* to slip away *or* out, to sneak off **2** *Astron* to be eclipsed; *(être voilé)* to be obscured

écliptique [ekliptik] *Astron* **ADJ** ecliptic

NM ecliptic

éclisse [eklis] **NF 1** *(plaque de bois)* (wooden) wedge **2** *(éclat)* piece of split wood **3** *Méd* splint **4** *Rail* fishplate **5** *Mus* rib **6** *(claie à fromages)* cheese tray

éclisser [3] [eklise] **VT** *Méd (membre)* to put in splints, to splint

éclogite [eklɔʒit] **NF** *Minér* eclogite

éclopé, -e [eklɔpe] **ADJ** lame, limping

NM,F person with a limp; *Mil* temporarily disabled soldier; **les éclopés avaient du mal à suivre le convoi** the walking wounded had difficulty keeping up with the convoy; *Hum* **les éclopés de l'amour** the victims of love

éclore [113] [eklɔr] **VI** *(aux être ou avoir)* **1** *(œuf, poussin)* to hatch (out); **faire é. un œuf** to hatch (out) an egg; **les œufs ont éclos ce matin** the eggs hatched (out) this morning

2 *Littéraire (fleur)* to open out; *Fig (talent)* to be born, to appear; **des roses fraîches écloses** newly-opened roses; **la chaleur fait é. les fleurs** the warm weather brings the flowers into bloom; *Fig* **faire é. un talent** to nurture *or* develop a talent

3 *Littéraire (apparaître → jour, amour)* to dawn; *(→ doute)* to be born; **le jour est près d'é.** dawn is near

écloserie [eklozri] **NF** hatchery

éclosion [eklozjɔ̃] **NF 1** *(d'un œuf)* hatching; **jusqu'à leur é.** until they hatch **2** *Littéraire (d'une fleur)* opening (out); *Fig (d'un talent)* birth **3** *Littéraire (d'un amour)* dawning

éclusage [eklyzaʒ] **NM** *(d'un bateau, d'une péniche)* locking, sluicing

écluse [eklyz] **NF 1** *(gén)* lock; **(porte d')é.** lock *or* sluice gate; **é. de moulin** mill dam; **lâcher** *ou* **ouvrir les écluses** to open the sluice gates; *Fig* to turn on the waterworks **2** *(d'un dock)* tide gate **3** *Ordinat* firewall

éclusée [eklyze] **NF** lockage water

écluser [3] [eklyze] **VT 1** *Naut (canal, voie d'eau)* to lock; *(bateau, péniche)* to lock, to sluice **2** *très Fam (boire)* to down, to knock back; **il avait déjà éclusé trois cognacs** he'd already downed three brandies

VI *très Fam* to booze, to knock back the booze; **qu'est-ce qu'il écluse!** he can certainly knock it back!

éclusier, -ère [eklyzje, -ɛr] **NM,F** lockkeeper

ecmnésie [ɛkmnezi] **NF** *Méd* ecmnesia

ÉCO- [eko] **PRÉF**

In recent years, growing interest and concern over the environment have given rise, in French as well as in English, to a string of new words including the prefix **éco-** (from the Greek *oikos* meaning "house"), with or without a hyphen:

écolabel ecolabel; **éco-recharge** eco-refill; **éco-produit** eco-friendly product; **éco-industrie** eco-friendly industry; **éco(-)certification** ecocertification

écobilan [ekɔbilɑ̃] **NM** *École & Écon* life cycle assessment *or* analysis

écobuage [ekɔbɥaʒ] **NM** *Agr* burn-beating

écobuer [7] [ekɔbɥe] **VT** *Agr* to burn-beat

écocide [ekɔsid] **NM** *École* ecocide

écodéveloppement [ekɔdevlɔpmɑ̃] **NM** *École* ecodevelopment

écœuramment [ekœramɑ̃] **ADV** *Can Joual* really■, *Am* real; **c'est é. bon** *(plat, gâteau)* it's absolutely delicious!, it's divine!; *(musique, film)* it's *Br* wicked *or Am* awesome!

écœurant, -e [ekœrɑ̃, -ɑ̃t] **ADJ 1** *(nauséeux → nourriture)* nauseating, sickly; *(→ personne)* disgusting, sickening; **la seule vue de ce gâteau est écœurante** just looking at that cake *or* the mere sight of that cake makes me feel sick; **il a une manière de manger vraiment écœurante** it's quite sickening *or* disgusting *or Fam* sick-making watching him eat, it really turns the stomach watching him eat

2 *(indigne)* disgusting; **j'ai trouvé son comportement é.** his/her behaviour sickened me, I found his/her behaviour disgusting

3 *Fam (démoralisant)* sickening, disheartening■; **elle réussit tout, c'est é.** she's good at everything, it's sickening *or* it makes you sick; **tu as une chance écœurante!** what disgusting luck!; **c'est é. ce que tu peux avoir de la chance** you're so lucky it makes me sick

4 *Can Joual* **c'est é. comme il fait chaud** it's absolutely boiling!, *Br* it's a scorcher!; **c'est é. comme c'est bon** *(plat, gâteau)* it's absolutely delicious!, it's divine; *(musique, film)* it's really good!, it's *Br* wicked *or Am* awesome!; **c'est é.!** it's really good!, it's *Br* wicked *or Am* awesome!

NM,F *Can Joual* pig *(unpleasant person)*; **espèce d'écœurante!** you pig!

écœuranterie [ekœrɑ̃tri] **NF** *Can Fam* **1** *(saleté)* filth■ **2** *(coup bas)* dirty trick; **elle m'a fait une é.** she played a dirty trick on me

écœurement [ekœrmɑ̃] **NM 1** *(nausée)* nausea; *(dégoût)* disgust, loathing; **manger des chocolats jusqu'à é.** to make oneself sick eating chocolates; *Fig* **j'ai jardiné jusqu'à é.** I've done so much gardening I'm sick (and tired) of it *or* I'm fed up **2** *(aversion)* disgust, aversion, distaste; **sa cruauté a provoqué l'é. général** everyone was disgusted *or* nauseated by his/her cruelty, his/her cruelty turned everyone's stomach; **on ne peut le regarder agir sans é.** it's impossible to watch him at work without feeling disgust **3** *Fam (découragement)* discouragement■; **quand les résultats ont été annoncés, ça a été l'é. général** everybody was pretty disheartened when they heard the results■; **ça a été l'é. dans toute la classe** the entire class lost heart■

écœurer [5] [ekœre] **VT 1** *(donner la nausée à)* **é. qn** to nauseate sb, to make sb feel sick *or Am* nauseous; *(dégoûter)* to disgust sb, to make sb feel sick; **la vue de ce gâteau m'écœure** looking at that cake makes me feel sick; **à vous é.** nauseating **2** *(inspirer le mépris à)* to disgust, to sicken; **sa mauvaise foi m'écœure** I'm disgusted by his/her dishonesty; **ça m'écœure que...** it sickens me *or* makes me sick that... **3** *Fam (décourager)* to dishearten■, to discourage■; **l'attitude de son patron l'écœure tellement que...** he/she finds his/her boss's attitude so disheartening *or* discouraging that... **4** *Can Fam (donner envie à)* **é. qn** to make sb green with envy

Ecofin [ekɔfin] **NM** *UE (abrév* **Economic Council of Finance Ministers***)* Ecofin

écoguerrier, -ère [ekɔgɛrje, -ɛr] **NM,F** *École* ecowarrior

écoinçon [ekwɛ̃sɔ̃] **NM 1** *Constr* corner piece *or* stone **2** *Archit* spandrel

écolabel [ekɔlabɛl] **NM** *Écol* eco-label

écolage [ekɔlaʒ] **NM 1** *Suisse (frais de scolarité)* school fees **2** *Belg (formation)* training

écolâtre [ekɔlatr] **NM** *Arch* = clergyman in charge of a school attached to a cathedral or abbey

école [ekɔl] **NF 1** *Scol (établissement)* school; **aller à l'é.** *(tous les matins)* to go to school; *(à six ans)* to start school, to reach school age; **reprendre l'é.** *(après les vacances)* to go back to school; **é. confessionnelle** = independent *or* private school; **é. communale** local primary school; *Vieilli ou Can* **é. élémentaire** primary school; **é. libre** private school; **é. maternelle,** *Fam* **petite é.,** *Suisse* **é. enfantine** nursery school, kindergarten; **é. primaire,** *Fam* **grande é.** primary school; **é. privée** private school; **é. publique** *Br* state school, *Am* public school; *Can & Suisse* **é. secondaire** *Br* secondary school, *Am* high school; **é. de filles/garçons** girls'/boys' school; **faire l'é. buissonnière** to play truant *or Am Fam* hooky; *Fig Hum* **tu peux retourner à l'é.** what did they teach you at school?

2 *(cours)* school; **faire l'é.** to teach; **l'é. recommencera le 9 septembre** school will reopen on 9 September; **l'é. est obligatoire jusqu'à 16 ans** schooling is compulsory up to the age of 16; **pas de chewing-gum pendant l'é.** chewing-gum must not be consumed during school hours; *Fam* **je n'ai pas é. aujourd'hui** I don't have any classes today; *Fig* **à l'é. de la vie** in the university of life

3 *(système)* **l'é. laïque** secular education; **l'é. obligatoire** compulsory schooling

4 *(collège supérieur)* **l'É. de l'Air** = training college for the French air force, at Salon-de-Provence; **É. des Arts et Métiers** = university-level engineering college; **é. des Beaux-Arts** art school; **É. (centrale) des arts et manufactures, É. centrale** = prestigious engineering school; **l'É. européenne des affaires** = prestigious business school in Paris; **É. du Louvre** = art school in Paris; **É. (nationale) des chartes** = "grande école" for archivists and librarians; **É. nationale d'administration** = prestigious university-level college preparing students for senior posts in the civil service and public management; **l'É. nationale d'ingénieurs** = one of five prestigious engineering schools throughout France; **É. nationale supérieure agronomique** = one of five competitive-entry agricultural engineering schools; **É. nationale supérieure des arts décoratifs** = "grande école" for applied arts; **É. nationale supérieure des beaux-arts** = leading art school in Paris; **É. nationale supérieure de l'enseignement technique** = "grande école" training science and technology teachers; **É. nationale supérieure d'ingénieurs** = university-level college for the continuing education of qualified engineers; **É. nationale de la magistrature** = "grande école" for the judiciary; **l'É. nationale vétérinaire** = one of four top veterinary colleges; **l'É. navale** = naval officer training college at Poulmic in Brittany; *Anciennement* **É. normale (d'instituteurs)** = primary school teachers' training college; **É. normale supérieure** = prestigious "grande école" for teachers and researchers; **É. supérieure des sciences économiques et commerciales** = "grande école" for management and business studies

5 *(lieu spécialisé)* school; **é. de l'air** flying school; **é. de commerce** business school; **é. de conduite** driving school; **é. de danse** ballet school; **é. de dessin** art school; **é. d'équitation** riding school; **é. d'escalade** artificial climbing wall; **é. hôtelière** hotel school; **é. de journalisme** school of journalism; **é. militaire** military academy; **é. de musique** music school; **é. navale** naval college; **é. de police** police college *or Am* academy; **é. de secrétariat** secretarial college; **é. de ski** skiing school; **é. de voile** sailing school

6 *(pédagogie)* **l'é. active** the active method of teaching

7 *(disciples)* school; **l'É. de Paris** the School of Paris *(bohemian group of international artists working in Paris in the early 20th century, producing various forms of modern art)*; **l'é. de Pythagore** the Pythagorean school; **l'é. française du Louvre** the French collections at the Louvre; **il est de la vieille é.** he's one of the old school; **faire é.** to attract a following; **une hypothèse qui fera é.** a hypothesis bound to gain wide currency

8 *Fig* **une é. de courage** a lesson in courage; **être à bonne é.** to be in good hands; **avec lui, j'ai été à bonne é.** he taught me a lot; **être à rude é.** to learn the hard way

9 *Équitation* **basse é.** basse école; **haute é.** haute école

10 *Mil (exercice)* drill, training; **é. du soldat** drill; **é. de tir** rifle drill, knotting and splicing; *Aviat* **appareil d'é.** training aircraft

'L'École des femmes' *Molière* 'The School for Wives'

> *Culture*
>
> **L'ÉCOLE LAÏQUE**
>
> The separation of Church and State, which reflects the Republican ideal and became law in 1905, is an important aspect of French culture. Since that date State education has been independent of the Church, and explicitly excludes religious instruction and religious ceremony.

E-coli [ekɔli] **NM** *Méd* E-coli

écolier, -ère [ekɔlje, -ɛr] **NM,F 1** *Scol* schoolboy, *f* schoolgirl **2** *(novice)* beginner

écolo [ekɔlo] *Fam* **ADJ** *(abrév* **écologique, écologiste***)* green

NMF *(abrév* **écologiste***)* environmentalist■

écologie [ekɔlɔʒi] **NF** *Écol* ecology; **é. radicale** deep ecology

écologique [ekɔlɔʒik] **ADJ** *Écol (gén)* ecological, environmental; *(politique)* green

écologiquement [ekɔlɔʒikmɑ̃] **ADV** *Écol* ecologically

écologisme [ekɔlɔʒism] **NM** *Écol* ecology

écologiste [ekɔlɔʒist] *Écol* **ADJ** *(parti)* green, ecology *(avant n)*; *(politique)* green, environmentalist

NMF 1 *(expert)* ecologist, environmentalist **2** *(partisan)* ecologist, green

écologue [ekɔlɔg] **NMF** *Écol (expert)* ecologist, environmentalist

e-commerce [ikɔmɛrs] **NM** e-commerce

écomusée [ekɔmyze] **NM** ecomuseum *(heritage centre in rural area)*

éconduire [98] [ekɔ̃dɥir] **VT 1** *(importun, vendeur)* to get rid of **2** *(refuser → soupirant)* to turn down, to reject; *(→ suppliant, requérant) (en personne)* to turn away; *(par lettre)* to turn down

éconocroques [ekɔnɔkrɔk] **NFPL** *Fam Vieilli* savings■

économat [ekɔnɔma] **NM 1** *(service → dans un collège, un hôpital)* bursarship; *(→ dans un club)* stewardship **2** *(bureau → dans un collège, un hôpital)* bursar's office; *(→ dans un club)* steward's office **3** *(coopérative)* staff co-op **4** *(fonction d'économe → dans une institution, un hôpital)* bursarship; *(→ dans un club, un collège)* stewardship

économe [ekɔnɔm] **ADJ 1** *(avec l'argent)* thrifty; **être é.** to be careful with money **2** *(parcimonieux)* **é. de** economical *or* sparing with; **être é. de ses paroles/gestes** to be sparing with one's words/gestures; **être é. de son temps** to give of one's time sparingly; **être é. de ses moyens** to use the means at one's disposal sparingly

NMF *(d'une institution, d'un hôpital)* bursar; *(d'un club, d'un collège)* steward

NM *(couteau)* (vegetable) peeler

économètre [ekɔnɔmɛtr] **NMF** *Écon* econometrist, econometrician

économétricien, -enne [ekɔnɔmetrisjɛ̃, -ɛn] **NM,F** *Écon* econometrist, econometrician

économétrie [ekɔnɔmetri] **NF** *Écon* econometrics *(singulier)*

économétrique [ekɔnɔmetrik] **ADJ** *Écon* econometric

économie [ekɔnɔmi] **NF 1** *Écon (système)* economy; **la nouvelle é.** the new economy; **é. du bien-être** welfare economy; **é. capitaliste** capitalist economy; **é. de champ** economy of scope; **é. classique** classical economics; **é. de la connaissance** knowledge economy; **é. de la demande** demand-side economics; **é. à deux vitesses** two-speed economy; **é. du développement** development economics; **é. dirigée** planned economy; **é. domestique** home economics; **é. duale** dual economy; **é. d'entreprise** *(études)* business management; **é. de l'environnement** environmental economics; **é. éthique** caring economy; **é. illégale** illegal economy; **é. immergée** underground economy; **é. industrielle** industrial organization; **é. informelle** informal economy; **é. keynésienne** Keynesian economics; **é. libérale** free-market economy; **é. de libre entreprise** free-enterprise economy; **é. de marché** market economy; **é. mixte** mixed economy; **é. mondiale** world economy; **é. néoclassique** neoclassical economics; **é. noire** black economy; **é. non monétaire** natural economy; **é. normative** normative economics; **é. numérique** Net economy; **é. de l'offre** supply-side economics; **é. ouverte** open economy; **é. parallèle** black economy, underground economy; **é. planifiée** planned economy; **é. politique** political economy; **é. de rente** rent economy; **e. rentière** rentier economy; **é. salariale** wage economy; **é. sociale** social economy; **é. socialiste** socialist economy; **é. solidaire** economy of solidarity, socially responsible economy; **é. de sous-emploi** underemployment economy; **é. souterraine** black economy, underground economy; **é. de subsistance** subsistence economy; **é. de transition** transition economy; **é. de troc** barter economy

2 *Écon (discipline)* economics *(singulier)*; **é. (politique)** economics; **é. d'entreprise** business *or* managerial economics

3 *(gain)* economy, saving; *(vertu)* economy, thrift; **avoir le sens de l'é.** to be thrifty, to be good with money; **elle n'a aucun sens de l'é.** she's no good at managing money, she's got no idea about money; **par é., je prendrai le train** I'll go by train to save money; **nous avons fait une é. de trois euros par livre** we saved three euros on each book; **nous avons réalisé une é. de deux euros par pièce produite** we made a saving of *or* we saved two euros on each item produced; **ce sera une é. de temps/d'argent/de vingt pour cent** it'll save time/money/twenty percent; **avec une grande é. de moyens** with very limited means; **faire l'é. de** to save; **je ferai l'é. d'un voyage** it'll save me a trip; **je vais faire l'é. d'un coup de fil** I'll save myself a phone call; *Fam* **une é. de bouts de chandelles** cheese-paring; **ce mariage a vraiment été fait à l'é.** the wedding was really done on the cheap

4 *(structure)* **nous n'approuvons pas l'é. générale du projet** we do not approve of the structure of the project

❑ **économies NFPL** savings; **faire des économies** to save money; **réaliser d'importantes économies** to save a lot of money, to make major savings; **prendre sur ses économies** to break into *or* draw on one's savings; **elle a quelques économies** she has some savings; **les économies d'énergie** energy conservation; **faire des économies d'énergie** to conserve *or* to save energy; **faire des économies de chauffage** to save money *or* economize on heating; **économies d'échelle** economies of scale; *Fam* **économies de bouts de chandelle** cheeseparing (economy); *Prov* **il n'y a pas de petites économies** take care of the pennies and the pounds will take care of themselves

économique [ekɔnɔmik] **ADJ 1** *Écon* economic **2** *(peu coûteux)* economical, cheap, inexpensive; **classe é.** economy class; **cycle é.** *(d'un lave-vaisselle etc)* economy cycle; **taille é.** economy size; **bouteille é.** economy (size) bottle; **voiture é.** economy car; **vitesse é.** *(d'une voiture etc)* economical speed

NM l'é. the economic situation

économiquement [ekɔnɔmikmɑ̃] **ADV 1** *Écon* economically, from an economic point of view; **é. viable** economically viable; **les é. faibles** the lower-income groups **2** *(à moindre frais)* inexpensively; *(frugalement)* frugally

économiser [3] [ekɔnɔmize] **VT 1** *(épargner → richesse, argent)* to economize, to save; *(→ temps)* to save; **économisez 10 euros** 10 euros off, save 10 euros

2 *(ménager → force)* to save; *(→ ressources)* to

eco–eco

husband; **é. ses paroles** to be sparing of one's words; **é. ses forces** to conserve one's strength; **é. sa salive** to save one's breath

3 *(énergie, électricité, denrée)* to save, to conserve

VI to save money, to economize; **je n'arrive pas à é.** I just can't manage to save any money; **é. sur l'électricité** to save on *or* economize on electricity; **é. sur l'habillement** to buy fewer clothes, to spend less on clothes

économiseur [ekɔnɔmizœr] **NM** *Aut* fuel-saving device; *Ordinat* **é. d'écran** screen saver

économisme [ekɔnɔmism] **NM** *Écon* economism

économiste [ekɔnɔmist] **NMF** *Écon* economist; **é. d'entreprise** business economist

eco–eco

écope [ekɔp] **NF** bailer

écoper [3] [ekɔpe] **VT** *(barque, bateau)* to bail out; **é. l'eau d'une embarcation** to bail out a boat *or* the water out of a boat

VI *Fam (recevoir une sanction, une réprimande)* to take the rap; **c'est lui qui a écopé** he was the one who took the rap; **j'en ai marre d'é. pour les autres** I'm sick of getting the blame for what other people do

❑ **écoper de VT IND** *Fam* to get, *Br* to cop; **il a écopé de cinq ans de prison** he got five years inside; **c'est encore moi qui ai écopé de la punition** it was me that caught it again

écoperche [ekɔpɛrʃ] **NF** *Constr* **1** *(d'échafaudage)* upright pole, standard **2** *(à poulie)* derrick

écophagie [ekɔfaʒi] **NF** *Écol* ecophagia; **é. globale** global ecophagia

écophase [ekɔfaz] **NF** *Écol* ecophase

écoproduit [ekɔprɔdɥi] **NM** *Écol* eco-friendly *or* environmentally-friendly product, eco-product

écorçage [ekɔrsaʒ] **NM** *(d'arbres)* barking; *(d'oranges)* peeling; *(de riz)* husking

écorce [ekɔrs] **NF 1** *Bot (d'un arbre)* bark; *(d'un fruit)* peel; *(d'une orange)* rind, peel; *(de riz)* husk; *(de châtaigne)* skin; **é. de cassia** cassia bark **2** *Bot* cortex **3** *Géog* **l'é. terrestre** the earth's crust **4** *Fig (extérieur)* exterior, outward appearance

écorcer [16] [ekɔrse] **VT** *(arbre)* to bark; *(fruit)* to peel; *(riz)* to husk

écorceur, -euse [ekɔrsœr, -øz] **NM,F** *(personne)* barker

❑ **écorceuse NF** *(machine)* barker

écorchage [ekɔrʃaʒ] **NM** *(d'un animal)* skinning

écorché, -e [ekɔrʃe] **NM,F c'est un é. vif/une écorchée vive** he's/she's hypersensitive; **une sensibilité d'é. vif** hypersensitivity

NM 1 *Beaux-Arts* écorché **2** *(dessin)* cutaway

écorchement [ekɔrʃəmɑ̃] **NM** *(d'un animal)* skinning

écorcher [3] [ekɔrʃe] **VT 1** *(animal)* to skin

2 *(torturer)* to flay; **é. vif** to flay alive; **il crie comme si on l'écorchait vif** he's squealing like a stuck pig; *Fig* **se faire é. vif** to be skinned alive

3 *(blesser)* to scratch, to graze; *(jambe, peau etc)* to graze, to scrape; *(la gorge → sujet: l'alcool, plat pimenté)* to burn; *(sujet: bonbon)* to scratch; **elle a eu les mains écorchées par les épines** her hands were scratched by the thorns; *très Fam* **ça t'écorcherait la bouche de dire merci/demander pardon?** it wouldn't actually hurt to say thank you/sorry, would it?; *Fig* **é. les oreilles à qn** to grate on sb's ears; **la musique lui écorchait les oreilles** the music grated on his/her ears; **ce langage lui écorchait les oreilles** he/she found these words offensive

4 *Fig (mal prononcer → mot)* to mispronounce; **il écorche toujours mon nom** he always mispronounces my name; **é. une langue** to murder *or* massacre a language

5 *Fam (escroquer)* to fleece, to swindle

▶ **s'écorcher VPR** to scrape *or* to scratch oneself; **s'é. le genou** to graze *or* scrape one's knee; **s'é. le tibia** to graze *or* bark one's shin

écorcheur [ekɔrʃœr] **NM 1** *(d'animaux)* flayer, skinner **2** *Fam (escroc)* swindler, crook; **ce sont de véritables écorcheurs** they rob you blind **3** *Orn* butcher bird

écorchure [ekɔrʃyr] **NF** scratch, graze; **se faire une é.** to scratch oneself

éco-recharge [ekɔrəʃarʒ] *(pl* **éco-recharges***)* **NF** eco-refill

écorner [3] [ekɔrne] **VT 1** *(endommager → cadre, meuble)* to chip a corner off; *(→ livre, page)* to fold down the corner of, to dog-ear; **un livre tout écorné** a dog-eared book **2** *(fortune, héritage)* to make a dent in **3** *Can (animal)* to dehorn; *Fig* **un vent à é. les bœufs** a fierce gale

écornifler [3] [ekɔrnifle] **VT** *Fam* **1** *Vieilli (grappiller)* to scrounge **2** *Can (être indiscret)* to snoop, to pry ▪

écornifleur, -euse [ekɔrniflœr, -øz] *Fam* **ADJ** *Can* snooping, prying ▪

NM,F 1 *Vieilli (profiteur)* scrounger **2** *Can (personne indiscrète)* snoop

écornure [ekɔrnyr] **NF** *(fragment)* chip; **la table est pleine d'écornures** the table is chipped all over

écosphère [ekɔsfɛr] **NF** *Écol* ecosphere

écossais, -e [ekɔsɛ, -ɛz] **ADJ 1** *Géog (coutume, lande)* Scottish; *(personne)* Scottish, Scots; **whisky é.** Scotch (whisky) **2** *Tex* tartan

NM 1 *Ling* Scots Gaelic **2** *Tex* tartan

❑ **Écossais, -e NM,F** Scot, Scotsman, *f* Scotswoman; **les É.** Scottish people, the Scots

Écosse [ekɔs] **NF l'É.** Scotland; **vivre en É.** to live in Scotland; **aller en É.** to go to Scotland

écosser [3] [ekɔse] **VT** *(petits pois)* to shell, to pod; *(fèves, haricots)* to shell

écosystème [ekɔsistɛm] **NM** *Écol* ecosystem

écot [eko] **NM** share; **payer chacun son é.** to pay one's share

écotaxe [ekɔtaks] **NF** ecotax

écoté, -e [ekɔte] **ADJ** *Hér* lopped

écotone [ekɔtɔn] **NF** *Écol* ecotone

écotourisme [ekɔturism] **NM** *Écol* ecotourism

écotoxicologie [ekɔtɔksikɔlɔʒi] **NF** *Écol* ecotoxicology

écotoxique [ekɔtɔksik] **ADJ** *Écol* ecotoxic

écotype [ekɔtip] **NM** *Écol* ecotype

écoulé, -e [ekule] **ADJ 1** *(du mois dernier)* of last month; **votre lettre du 25 é.** your letter of the 25th of last month; **payable fin é.** due at the end of last month **2** *(passé)* **l'exercice é.** the last financial year

écoulement [ekulmɑ̃] **NM 1** *(d'un liquide)* flow, outflow; *Constr (du toit etc)* run-off; **l'é. se fait mal** it's not flowing very well; **système d'é. des eaux** drainage system; **(tube d')é.** *(d'une baignoire)* waste pipe; *Aviat* **é. (des filets) d'air** air flow

2 *Méd* discharge; *(de l'urètre)* gleet

3 *(mouvement → de la foule, de la circulation)* flow; **l'é. de la foule dans le métro** the streams of people moving through the metro

4 *(passage → du temps)* passage, passing; **vous n'avez pas le droit de répondre après é. du temps** you must answer before the time is up

5 *(vente)* selling, sale; *(distribution)* distributing, distribution; **marchandises d'é. facile/difficile** fast-/slow-moving goods; **l'é. de ces vieux parapluies sera plus facile** it will be easier to sell *or* dispose of these old umbrellas

écouler [3] [ekule] **VT 1** *(vendre → marchandises, stocks)* to sell (off); **é. entièrement son stock** to clear one's stock; **é. qch à bas prix** to sell sth off cheaply; *Com* **é. qch à perte** to sell sth at a loss; **facile/difficile à é.** easy/difficult to sell

2 *(se débarrasser de)* to dispose *or* to get rid of; **é. des faux billets** to put forged notes into circulation

▶ **s'écouler VPR 1** *(se déverser → liquide)* to flow out (**de** of); *(→ foule, circulation)* to flow; **l'eau s'écoule peu à peu** the water trickles out; **le public s'écoulait sagement du théâtre** the audience was quietly leaving the theatre; **laisser s'é. l'eau du bain** to let the bathwater out; **faire s'é. l'eau** to run off *or* drain off the water

2 *(passer → année, temps)* to go by, to pass (by)

3 *(se vendre → marchandises, stocks)* to sell; **notre stock s'écoule rapidement** our stock is selling fast

écoumène [ekumɛn] **NM** *Géog* ecumene

écourgeon [ekurʒɔ̃] **NM** *Agr & Bot* winter barley

écourté, -e [ekurte] **ADJ** *(chien)* bobtailed

écourter [3] [ekurte] **VT 1** *(rendre plus court)* to shorten, to cut short; *(→ visite, discours)* to curtail, to cut short; *(→ barbe, moustache)* to trim **2** *Vét* to dock

écourtiché, -e [ekurtiʃe] **ADJ** *Can Fam (jupe, robe)* very short ▪; **elle est écourtichée** her skirt is very short

écoutant, -e [ekutɑ̃, -ɑ̃t] **NM,F** telephone counsellor

écoute [ekut] **NF 1** *Rad* listening; **dès la première é....** *(d'un disque, d'un morceau)* the first time you hear it...; **se mettre** *ou* **se porter à l'é., prendre l'é.** to listen in, to tune in; **heure** *ou* **période de grande é.** *Rad* peak listening time; *TV* peak viewing time, prime time; *Rad & TV* **aux heures de grande é.** in prime time; **émission programmée à une heure de grande é.** prime-time programme; **cette émission bénéficie d'une grande é.** the programme has a large audience *or* stands high in the ratings; **é. permanente** monitoring; *Tél & Rad* **é. de contrôle** monitoring

2 *(détection)* listening (in); **é. clandestine** wiretapping; **é. électronique** electronic listening; **é. sous-marine** sonar; **écoutes (téléphoniques)** phone tapping; **mettre** *ou* **placer qn sur é.** *ou* **écoutes** to tap sb's phone; **elle est sur é.** *ou* **écoutes** her phone's been tapped; **poste d'é.** listening post; **table d'é.** wiretapping set

3 *(attention)* ability to listen; **avoir une bonne é.** to be good at listening *or* a good listener

4 *Naut (d'une voile)* sheet; **nœud d'é.** sheet bend; **point d'é.** clew

5 *Zool (d'un sanglier)* **écoutes** ears

❑ **à l'écoute ADV 1** *Mil & Rad* **être à l'é. (de)** to be listening (to); *Rad* **restez à l'é. de nos programmes de nuit** stay tuned to our late-night programmes; **rester à l'é.** to stay tuned

2 *(attentif à)* **être à l'é. de** to be attentive to; *(électeurs, opinion publique)* to be in touch with; *(enfants)* to be attentive to the needs of; **il est toujours à l'é. (des autres)** he's always ready to lend a sympathetic ear *or* to listen (to others); **être à l'é. de l'actualité** to be well up on current affairs

❑ **aux écoutes ADV être** *ou* **se tenir aux écoutes** *Fam Vieilli* to listen ▪, to eavesdrop ▪; *Fig* to keep one's ears open; **être aux écoutes derrière la porte** to be listening at the door

écouter [3] [ekute] **VT 1** *(entendre → chanson, discours, émission)* to listen to; **c'est un des jeux les plus écoutés en France** it's one of the most popular radio game shows in France; **je vais te faire é. un truc génial** I'm going to play you something really great; *Rad* **vous écoutez France Inter** you are listening *or* tuned to France Inter; **é. la messe** to hear Mass; **é. qn jusqu'au bout** to hear sb out

2 *(être attentif à)* to listen to; **écoutez-moi avant de vous décider** listen to what I have to say before you make up your mind

3 *(obéir à)* to listen to; **il faut é. ses parents** you must do as your parents tell you; **tu vas finir par m'é., oui?** WILL you do as I say?; **n'écoutant que sa colère/sa douleur/son cœur** guided by his/her anger/pain/heart alone; **é. la voix de la sagesse** to listen to the voice of reason

4 *(suivre → personne, avis)* to listen to, to pay attention to; **é. sa conscience** to listen to *or* be guided by one's conscience; **il est très écouté au sein du gouvernement** the government listens closely to him *or* to what he has to say, he has the ear of the government; **ne les écoutez pas!** don't listen to them, don't pay them any attention!

5 *(à l'impératif, à valeur d'insistance)* **écoutez, nous n'allons pas nous disputer!** listen *or* look, let's not quarrel!; **écoute, ça suffit maintenant!** listen *or* look here, that's enough now!; **écoute, c'est simple, il suffit de lui demander** listen, it's very simple, all we have to do is ask him/her

USAGE ABSOLU je n'écoutais que d'une oreille I was only half listening; **é. de toutes ses oreilles** to be all ears; **é. aux portes** to eavesdrop; **il sait é.** he's a good listener; **il n'a même pas voulu é.** he wouldn't even listen

▶ **s'écouter VPR 1** *(emploi passif)* **c'est le genre de musique qui s'écoute dans le recueillement** this is the kind of music one should listen to with reverence

2 *(emploi réfléchi)* **il s'écoute trop** he's a bit of a hypochondriac; **si je m'écoutais, je le mettrais dehors** if I had any sense, I'd throw him out; **s'é. parler** to love the sound of one's own voice

écouteur [ekutœr] **NM 1** *Tél* earpiece; **prendre l'é.** to listen in **2** *(pour écouter de la musique)* earphone; *TV & Rad* **é. auriculaire** earpiece; **écouteurs** earphones, headphones

écoutille [ekutij] **NF** *Naut* hatch, hatchway
écouvillon [ekuvijɔ̃] **NM 1** *Méd & Mil* swab **2** *(goupillon)* bottlebrush
écouvillonner [3] [ekuvijɔne] **VT** *(bouteille)* to clean out; *Méd (cavité)* to swab
écrabouillage [ekrabujaʒ], **écrabouillement** [ekrabujmɑ̃] **NM** *Fam* crushing■, squashing■
écrabouiller [3] [ekrabuje] **VT** *Fam* to crush■, to squash■; **tu m'as écrabouillé le pied!** you've crushed my foot!; **le gâteau a été complètement écrabouillé** the cake was completely squashed; **se faire é.** to get squashed; **se faire é. par une voiture** to get flattened by a car
écran [ekrɑ̃] **NM 1** *(d'une console, d'un ordinateur)* screen; **à l'é.** on screen; **é. à affichage accéléré** accelerated display screen; **é. antireflets** antiglare screen; **é. basse radiation** low radiation screen; **é. couleur** colour screen *or* display; **é. à cristaux liquides** liquid crystal screen; **é. gris neutre** neutral density filter; **é. haute résolution** high resolution screen; **é. LCD** LCD screen; **é. à matrice active/passive** active/passive matrix screen; **é. monochrome** monochrome screen; **é. (à) plasma** (gas) plasma screen; **é. plat** flat screen; **é. protecteur** *ou* **de protection** shield; **é. rétro-éclairé** back-lit screen; **é. sans scintillement** flicker-free screen; **é. tactile** touch *or* touch-sensitive screen; **é. de visualisation** visual display unit, VDU
2 *Ordinat (page visualisée)* screen; **é. d'accueil** start-up screen; **é. d'aide** help screen; **é. de dialogue** dialog(ue) screen; **é. divisé** split screen; **é. à fenêtres** split screen; **é. pleine page** full-page display; **é. de saisie** input screen; **é. de travail** working *or* work screen
3 *Cin* screen; **é. de cinéma** cinema *or Am* movie screen; **porter un roman à l'é.** to adapt a novel for the screen; **à l'é.** *ou* **sur les écrans, cette semaine** what's on this week (at the *Br* cinema *or Am* movies); **Bourvil crève l'é. dans ce film** Bourvil gives a riveting performance in this movie *or Br* film; **le grand é.** the big screen; *Cin & Phot* **é. (de projection)** screen; **é. panoramique** wide screen; **é. de sûreté** *(de projecteur)* cut-off
4 *TV* screen; **é. de télévision** TV screen; **le petit é.** television; **les programmes du petit é. pour ce soir** what's on television tonight; *TV & Rad* **é. acoustique** acoustic screen; **é. cathodique** cathode ray tube screen; **é. de contrôle** control monitor; **é. de contrôle de l'image** picture monitor (screen); **é. de contrôle studio** studio monitor; **é. plat** flat-faced screen; **téléviseur à é. plat** flat-screen TV; **é. de prévisualisation** preview monitor; **é. de vision** review screen; **é. de visualisation** display screen
5 *(protection)* screen, shield; **il se fit un é. de sa main** he shielded his eyes with his hand; **il m'a fait é. de son corps pour me protéger** he shielded me with his body; **elle se cachait derrière l'é. de ses cheveux** she was using her hair as a screen to hide behind; **on ne peut pas voir le lac car les arbres font é.** you can't see the lake because it's screened by the trees; **les nombreuses citations font é. à la clarté de l'article** the numerous quotations make the article difficult to understand; *aussi Fig* **é. de fumée** smoke screen; **é. anti-bruit** noise barrier; **é. de cheminée** fire screen; **é. pare-fumée** smoke deflector; **é. de protection** shield; **é. solaire** sunscreen, sunblock; **crème é. total** total sunblock, total protection sun cream
6 *Beaux-Arts* silk screen
7 *Rad & TV* **é. publicitaire, é. de publicité,** *Fam* **é. de pub** commercial break
écran-mosaïque [ekrɑ̃mɔzaik] *(pl* **écrans-mosaïques)** **NM** multi-screen, multi-split screen
écran-témoin [ekrɑ̃temwɛ̃] *(pl* **écrans-témoins)** *nm* monitor
écrapoutir [32] [ekraputir] *Can Fam* **VT** to squish
❑ **s'écrapoutir VPR** *(personne)* to crouch■
écrasant, -e [ekrazɑ̃, -ɑ̃t] **ADJ 1** *(insupportable → gén)* crushing, overwhelming; *(→ chaleur)* unbearable; *(→ responsabilité)* weighty, burdensome; *(→ charge de travail)* overwhelming; *(→ travail)* backbreaking **2** *(manifeste → proportion, preuve, majorité, victoire)* overwhelming
écrasé, -e [ekraze] **ADJ** squashed; **nez é.** flat nose
écrasement [ekrazmɑ̃] **NM 1** *(de fruits, de graines, d'ail)* crushing; *(de pommes de terre)* mashing **2** *(d'un membre)* crushing **3** *(anéantissement → d'une révolte)* crushing; *(→ d'un peuple)* oppression; *(→ d'une armée, d'une équipe)* crushing defeat **4** *Aviat* **é. (au sol)** crash **5** *Ordinat (de données, d'un fichier)* overwriting
écrase-merdes [ekrɑzmɛrd] **NMPL** *Fam* clodhoppers, beetle-crushers
écraser [3] [ekraze] **VT 1** *(appuyer sur)* to crush; *(accidentellement)* to squash; *(boîte, membre, ail)* to crush; *(carton)* to flatten; *Fam* **é. l'accélérateur** *ou* **le champignon** to step on it, *Am* to step on the gas; **é. le frein** to slam on the brake
2 *(fruit, pomme de terre, œuf dur)* to mash; *(cafard)* to squash; *(mouche, moustique)* to swat; **é. une cigarette** to stub a cigarette out; *Fam Fig* **je compte sur toi pour é. le coup** I'm relying on you to keep your mouth shut
3 *(piéton, animal)* to run over; **il s'est fait é.** he was run over
4 *(faire mal à)* to crush, to squash; **tu m'écrases les pieds** you're treading on my feet
5 *(accabler)* to crush; **é. un pays d'impôts** to overburden a country with taxes; **écrasé d'impôts** crushed by taxation, staggering under the burden of taxation; **être écrasé de chaleur** to be dropping with the heat; **être écrasé de fatigue** to be overcome by fatigue; **écrasé de travail** overwhelmed with *or Fam* snowed under with work
6 *(rendre plus petit)* to dwarf; **le monument écrase les immeubles alentour** the monument dwarfs the surrounding buildings
7 *(anéantir → adversaire, troupes etc)* to crush; **se faire é. par l'équipe adverse** to get crushed by the opposing team; **il écrase tout le monde en latin** he is much better than everyone else at Latin
8 *(réduire considérablement)* **é. les prix** to slash prices
9 *(dominer)* to outdo; **essayer d'é. qn** to try and beat sb at his/her own game; **il écrase tout le monde de son luxe** he flaunts his luxurious lifestyle everywhere; *Fam* **é. le marché** to glut *or* flood the market■; *Fam* **é. la course** to dominate the race■
10 *Ordinat (fichier)* to overwrite
VI *très Fam* **1** *(se taire)* **écrase, tu veux bien!** shut up, will you!
2 *(locution)* **en é.** to sleep like a log
▸**s'écraser VPR 1** *(emploi passif)* to be crushed; **les tomates s'écrasent facilement** tomatoes are easily crushed
2 *(fruit, légume)* to get crushed *or* mashed *or* squashed; **les fraises se sont écrasées dans mon sac** the strawberries got squashed inside my bag; **la neige s'écrasait sous nos pieds** the snow crunched under our feet
3 *(se fracasser → aviateur, avion)* to crash; *(→ alpiniste)* to crash to the ground; **l'avion s'est écrasé au sol** the plane crashed; **s'é. contre un mur** to crash against a wall; **le ballon est allé s'é. contre le poteau** the ball whacked the post
4 *Fam (se presser)* to be *or* to get crushed■; **les gens s'écrasent pour entrer** there's a great crush to get in
5 *très Fam (se taire)* to shut up, to pipe down; **il vaut mieux s'é.** better keep quiet *or* mum; **toi, tu t'écrases!** just shut up, will you!
écraseur, -euse [ekrazœr, -øz] **NM,F** *Fam* road hog
écrémage [ekremaʒ] **NM 1** *Culin* skimming, creaming;
2 *Mktg* **é. du marché** market skimming
3 *Métal & Pétr* skimming
4 *Fig* **ce lycée n'aurait pas de si bons résultats sans un sévère é. des élèves** the school wouldn't get such good results if it didn't choose only the very best pupils *or* if it didn't pick and choose its pupils; **le recrutement de leurs élèves passe par un sacré é.** they only take the crème de la crème
écrémer [18] [ekreme] **VT 1** *Culin* to skim
2 *Mktg (marché)* to skim
3 *Métal & Pétr* to skim
4 *(sélectionner)* to cream off; **é. une collection** to cream off the best pieces from a collection
écrémeuse [ekremøz] **NF** *(mécanique)* skimmer; *(centrifugeuse)* cream separator
écrêtement [ekrɛtmɑ̃] **NM** *(nivelage)* levelling; **l'é. des salaires** the levelling out of salaries
écrêter [4] [ekrete] **VT 1** *(coq)* to remove the comb of **2** *Fig (revenus, prix)* to even out **3** *Tél* to clip
écrevisse [ekrəvis] **NF** *Zool* crayfish, *Am* crawfish; **avancer** *ou* **marcher comme une é.** to take one step forward and two steps back
écrier [10] [ekrije] **s'écrier VPR** to cry *or* to shout (out), to exclaim; **"j'arrive", s'écria-t-elle** "I'm coming," she cried
écrin [ekrɛ̃] **NM** *(gén)* box, case; *(à bijoux)* casket
écrire [99] [ekrir] **VT 1** *(tracer → caractère, mot)* to write; **é. un t à la place d'un d** to write a t instead of a d; **é. qch à** *ou* **avec de l'encre** to write sth in ink; *Ordinat* **é. qch sur un disque** to write sth to disk
2 *(rédiger → lettre, livre)* to write; *(→ chèque, ordonnance)* to write (out); **é. une lettre à la machine** to type a letter; **é. un mot à la hâte** to scribble a note; **é. un mot à qn** to drop sb a line; **je lui ai écrit de venir** I've written asking him/her to come; **je veux que cela soit écrit dans le contrat** I want it written into the agreement; *Fig* **c'est écrit noir sur blanc** *ou* **en toutes lettres** it's written (down) in black and white; **c'est écrit sur sa figure** you can tell from his/her face, it's written all over his/her face; **c'était écrit** it was bound to happen; **il était écrit qu'ils se retrouveraient** they were bound *or* fated to find each other again; **il est écrit que je n'irai jamais** I'm fated not to get there
3 *(noter)* to write down; **é. ses dépenses dans la marge** to write down one's expenses in the margin; **écris ce qu'il te dicte** write down what he dictates to you
4 *(épeler)* to spell; **tu écris ça comment?** how do you spell it?; **tu as mal écrit le mot "apéritif"** you spelled the word "apéritif" wrong
USAGE ABSOLU to write; **il écrit bien** his (hand)-writing is good, he has good handwriting; *(écrivain)* he's a good writer, he writes well; **ce stylo écrit très bien** this pen writes very well; **mon crayon écrit mal** my pencil doesn't write properly; **tu écris mal** *(illisiblement)* your handwriting is bad; **é. dans les journaux** to write for the papers; **é. à l'encre** to use ink; **les enfants écrivaient dans le sable avec un bâton** the children were writing in the sand with a stick; **é. comme un chat** to scrawl; **é. à qn** to write to sb; **é. pour demander des renseignements** to write in *or* off for information; **é. sous la dictée** to take a dictation; **elle a écrit sous ma dictée** she took down what I dictated
▸**s'écrire VPR 1** *(s'épeler)* to be spelled; **ça s'écrit comment?** how do you spell it?
2 *(échanger des lettres)* to write to each other
écrit, -e [ekri, -it] **ADJ** written; **bien é.** well-written; **mal é.** poorly written; **é. à la main** handwritten; **une feuille écrite des deux côtés** a piece of paper with writing on both sides; **épreuves écrites d'un examen** written part of an examination
NM 1 *(document)* document; **faire/signer un é.** to draw up/to sign a document; *Journ* **é. diffamatoire** libel
2 *(œuvre)* written work; **ses écrits le prouvent** the proof of it is in his/her written works
3 *Scol & Univ (examen)* written examination *or* papers; *(partie)* written part (of the examination); **échouer à l'é.** to fail in the written examination
❑ **par écrit ADV** in writing; **confirmez-le nous par é.** confirm it to us in writing, give us written confirmation; **mettre qch par é.** to put sth down in writing; **consigner** *ou* **coucher qch par é.** to put *or* set sth down in writing; **convention par é.** written agreement
écriteau, -x [ekrito] **NM** board, notice, sign
écritoire [ekritwar] **NF 1** *(coffret)* writing case **2** *(en Afrique)* writing implement
écriture [ekrityr] **NF 1** *(calligraphie)* writing; *(façon d'écrire)* (hand)writing; **faire une page d'é.** *(gén)* to do a one-page handwriting exercise; *(punition)* to do lines; **avoir une é. élégante** to have elegant handwriting, to write (in) an elegant hand
2 *(système)* writing; **é. abrégée** speedwriting; **é. chiffrée** coded writing; **é. idéographique** ideographic writing; **é. phonétique** phonetic script
3 *(type de caractère)* script; *Typ* **é. cursive** cursive; *Typ* **é. droite/en italique** upright/italic script; **é. grasse** bold typeface, bold face

4 *(création, style)* writing; **un roman d'une é. recherchée** a novel written in a mannered style; **il a trouvé son salut dans l'é.** he found his salvation in writing; *Littérature* **é. automatique** automatic writing; *TV & Cin* **é. de scénarios** scriptwriting, screenwriting

5 *Compta* entry; **passer une é.** to make an entry; **é. d'achats** purchase entry; **é. d'ajustement** corrected entry; **é. de clôture** closing entry; **é. complémentaire** supplementary entry; **é. comptable** accounting *or* journal entry; **é. conforme** corresponding entry; **é. d'inventaire** closing entry; **é. d'ouverture** opening entry; **é. rectificative** corrected entry; **é. de régularisation** adjusting entry; **é. regroupement** consolidated entry; **é. de virement** transfer entry

6 *Jur* written document

7 *Bible & Rel* **l'É. sainte, les (saintes) Écritures** the Scriptures, Holy Scripture

□ **écritures** NFPL *Compta* accounts; **tenir les écritures** to keep the accounts *or* the books; **arrêter les écritures** to close the accounts; **passer les écritures** to post (up) the books; **employé aux écritures** accounts *or* ledger clerk; **écritures en partie double** double-entry bookkeeping; **écritures en partie simple** single-entry bookkeeping

écrivailler [3] [ekrivaje] VI *Péj* to scribble

écrivailleur, -euse [ekrivajœr, -øz] NM,F *Péj (gén)* scribbler; *(journaliste)* hack

écrivaillon [ekrivajɔ̃] NM *Péj (gén)* scribbler; *(journaliste)* hack

écrivain [ekrivɛ̃] NM

> Note that it is no longer considered a mistake to feminize this word and to say **une écrivain** or even **une écrivaine** (with a final **e**). Some French speakers nonetheless regard these forms as unacceptable, especially in France. See also the entry **féminisation**.

writer; **elle est é.** she's a writer; **é. public** public letter writer; **femme é.** woman writer

écrivait *etc voir* **écrire**

écrivasser [3] [ekrivase] VI *Péj* to scribble

écrivassier, -ère [ekrivasje, -ɛr] NM,F *Péj* scribbler

écrou¹ [ekru] NM *Tech* nut; **é. à ailettes** *ou* **à oreilles** wing nut; **é. crénelé** *ou* **à créneaux** *ou* **à encoches** castellated nut; **é. de réglage** adjusting *or* adjuster nut

écrou² [ekru] NM *Jur* committal; **sous é.** detained, in detention

écrouelles [ekruɛl] NFPL *Arch* scrofula, king's evil

écrouer [6] [ekrue] VT to imprison, to jail

écrouir [32] [ekruir] VT *Métal* to work-harden, to strain-harden; *(en travaillant à froid)* to cold-work

écrouissage [ekruisaʒ] NM *Métal* work-hardening, strain-hardening; *(travail à froid)* cold-working

écroulement [ekrulmɑ̃] NM *(d'un édifice, d'une théorie, d'un empire)* collapse; *(de terre, roche)* fall

écrouler [3] [ekrule] **s'écrouler** VPR **1** *(tomber → mur)* to fall (down), to collapse; *(→ plafond, voûte)* to cave in; **le tremblement de terre a fait s'é. plusieurs immeubles** several buildings collapsed during the earthquake

2 *(être anéanti → empire, monnaie)* to collapse; **empire près de s'é.** empire on the verge of collapse; **tous ses espoirs se sont écroulés** all his/her hopes vanished

3 *(défaillir → personne)* to collapse; **le témoin s'est écroulé devant le juge** the witness broke down in front of the judge; **j'ai cru que j'allais m'é. quand on me l'a annoncé** I thought I was going to pass out when they told me; **s'é. de sommeil/fatigue** to be overcome by sleep/weariness; **s'é. sur une chaise** to drop *or* flop onto a chair; **écroulé dans un fauteuil** slumped in an armchair

4 *Fam (locution)* **s'é. (de rire)** to kill oneself laughing; **j'étais écroulé en l'écoutant** I nearly died laughing just listening to him/her; **ils étaient écroulés** they were killing themselves laughing, they were in stitches

écroûter [3] [ekrute] VT *Agr* to fallow

écru, -e [ekry] ADJ **1** *Tex* raw; **soie écrue** raw silk; **toile écrue** holland **2** *(couleur)* ecru

---

ecsta [eksta] NF *Fam Arg drogue* E

ecstasy [ekstazi] NM ecstasy *(drug)*; **e. liquide** liquid ecstasy

ecthyma [ektima] NM *Méd* ecthyma

ectoblaste [ektoblast] NM *Biol* ectoblast, ectoderm

ectoblastique [ektoblastik] ADJ *Biol* ectoblastic, ectodermal, ectodermic

ectocardie [ektokardi] NF *Méd* ectocardia

ectoderme [ektodɛrm] NM *Biol* ectoblast, ectoderm

ectodermique [ektodɛrmik] ADJ *Biol* ectoblastic, ectodermal, ectodermic

ectoparasite [ektoparazit] ADJ *Biol & Méd* ectoparasitic
  NM *Zool* ectoparasite

ectopie [ektopi] NF *Méd* ectopia, ectopy

ectoplasme [ektoplasm] NM **1** *(du corps du médium)* ectoplasm **2** *Péj (personne insignifiante)* lightweight **3** *Biol* ectoplasm

ectoplasmique [ektoplasmik] ADJ ectoplasmic

ectoprocte [ektoprɔkt] *Zool* NM ectoproct
  □ **ectoproctes** NMPL Ectoprocta

ectosome [ektosom] NM *Biol* ectosome

ectotherme [ektotɛrm] ADJ *Physiol* ectothermic

ectotrophe [ektotrɔf] ADJ *Biol* ectotrophic

ectropion [ektropjɔ̃] NM *Méd* ectropion

ÉCU, écu¹ [eky] NM *Anciennement UE (abrév* **European Currency Unit***)* ECU, ecu; **É. dur** hard ECU

écu² [eky] NM **1** *Hist (bouclier)* shield; *Hér* escutcheon, coat of arms **2** *(ancienne monnaie)* crown

écubier [ekybje] NM *Naut* hawsehole

écueil [ekœj] NM **1** *Naut* reef; **donner sur les écueils** *(bateau)* to strike the rocks **2** *Littéraire (difficulté)* pitfall, danger, hazard; *Fig* **se heurter à un é.** to hit a snag

écuelle [ekɥɛl] NF **1** *(assiette creuse)* bowl; **une é. de soupe** a bowlful of soup **2** *Bot* **é. d'eau** marsh pennywort

écuisser [3] [ekɥise] VT *(arbre)* to split the trunk of

éculé, -e [ekyle] ADJ **1** *(botte, chaussure)* down-at-heel, worn down at the heel **2** *(plaisanterie)* hackneyed, well-worn

écumage [ekymaʒ] NM **1** *Culin* skimming **2** *(pillage → gén)* scouring; *(→ d'une région)* plundering

écumant, -e [ekymɑ̃, -ɑ̃t] ADJ *Littéraire* foamy, frothy; **é. de rage** spitting with rage, foaming at the mouth (with rage)

écume [ekym] NF **1** *(de la bière, de la bouche)* foam, froth; *(de la mer)* foam, spume; *(sur la soupe, la confiture)* scum; **ôter l'é. des confitures** to remove the scum from jam; **ôter l'é. du bouillon** to skim broth; **il avait l'é. à la bouche** he was foaming at the mouth; **cheval couvert d'é.** foam-covered horse

2 *Minér* **é. de mer** meerschaum

3 *Littéraire (de la société)* scum, dross

4 *Métal* dross

'**L'Écume des jours**' Vian 'Froth on the Daydream'

écumer [3] [ekyme] VI *(vin, bouche etc)* to foam, to froth; *(mer)* to foam; *(soupe, confiture, métal fondu etc)* to form a scum; *(cheval)* to lather; **é. (de rage ou colère)** to be foaming at the mouth (with rage), to foam with anger
  VT **1** *Culin (confiture)* to remove the scum from; *(bouillon)* to skim
  2 *Métal* to scum
  3 *(piller)* to plunder; *Fig* to go through; **é. les mers** to scour the seas; **j'ai écumé tout le quartier pour trouver une boulangerie** I scoured the whole area to find a bakery; **en écumant les bibliothèques on devrait trouver cet ouvrage** if we go through the libraries systematically we should find this work

écumeur [ekymœr] NM *Hist* **é. des mers** pirate **2** *(escroc)* plunderer

écumeux, -euse [ekymø, -øz] ADJ *Littéraire* foamy, frothy, spumy; *(mer, vagues)* foaming; *(bière)* foamy, frothy; *(confiture etc)* scummy

écumoire [ekymwar] NF *Culin* skimmer, skimming ladle; **é. à friture** slotted spoon; *Fam* **transformer qn en é.** to pump sb full of lead

écurer [3] [ekyre] VT *Vieilli (pièce, écurie)* to clean (out); *(vaisselle, plancher)* to scrub

---

écureuil [ekyrœj] NM *Zool* squirrel; **é. gris/roux** grey/red squirrel; **é. volant** flying squirrel; **l'É.** = nickname for the "Caisse d'épargne" (whose logo is a squirrel)

écurie [ekyri] NF **1** *(local à chevaux, mulets, ânes)* stable; **é. (de courses)** *(de chevaux, voitures)* (racing) stable; **mettre à l'é.** to stable; *Myth* **les écuries d'Augias** the Augean stables; **sentir l'é.** to be in the home straight

2 *Fam (endroit sale)* pigsty

3 *(chevaux)* stable; *Sport* stable, team; **portant la casaque de l'é. Sarmantes** riding in the colours of the Sarmantes stable

4 *(dans une maison d'édition)* (writing) team

5 *Suisse & (français régional) (étable)* cowshed

écusson [ekysɔ̃] NM **1** *(écu)* badge; *Mil* tab, badge; (collar) patch **2** *Hist* escutcheon, coat of arms **3** *Hort* bud **4** *Entom (des insectes)* scutellum **5** *(de serrure)* key-plate, keyhole scutcheon

écussonnage [ekysonaʒ] NM *Hort* budding

écussonner [3] [ekysone] VT **1** *Hort* to bud **2** *Couture* to sew a badge onto

écussonnoir [ekysonwar] NM *Hort* budding knife

écuyer, -ère [ekɥije, -ɛr] NM,F **1** *(acrobate de cirque)* circus rider **2** *Équitation (cavalier)* rider; **bottes à l'écuyère** riding boots
  NM **1** *Hist (d'un chevalier)* squire; *(d'un souverain)* (royal) equerry; *Hist* **grand é.** Master of the Horse **2** *(professeur d'équitation)* riding teacher

eczéma [ɛgzema] NM *Méd* eczema; **avoir** *ou* **faire de l'e.** to have eczema

eczémateux, -euse [ɛgzematø, -øz] ADJ *Méd* eczema *(avant n)*, *Spéc* eczematous

éd. *(abrév écrite* **édition***)* ed., edit

édam [edam] NM *Culin* Edam (cheese)

édaphique [edafik] ADJ *Biol & Écol* edaphic, soil *(avant n)*

eddique [edik] ADJ *Littérature* Eddaic, Eddic

edelweiss [edelves] NM *Bot* edelweiss

éden [edɛn] NM **1** *Bible* **l'É., le jardin d'É.** (the Garden of) Eden **2** *Littéraire* **un é.** an earthly paradise

édénique [edenik] ADJ Edenic

édenté, -e [edɑ̃te] ADJ *(vieillard, peigne, sourire → totalement)* toothless; *(→ partiellement)* gaptoothed; *Biol* edentulous
  NM *Zool*
  □ **édentés** NMPL *Zool* Edentata

édenter [3] [edɑ̃te] VT *(peigne, scie, lame)* to break the teeth of

EDF [ədəɛf] NF *(abrév* **Électricité de France***)* = French national electricity company

EDI [ədi] NM *Ordinat (abrév* **échange de données informatisé***)* EDI

édicter [3] [edikte] VT *(loi)* to decree, to enact; *(peine)* to decree, to prescribe

édiction [ediksjɔ̃] NF *(d'une loi)* decree, enactment

édicule [edikyl] NM **1** *(petit édifice)* small edifice **2** *(toilettes)* public lavatory; *(abri)* shelter

édifiant, -e [edifjɑ̃, -ɑ̃t] ADJ **1** *(lecture)* instructive, improving, edifying **2** *Hum (révélateur)* edifying, instructive

édification [edifikasjɔ̃] NF **1** *(construction)* erection, construction; *Fig (d'un empire, d'une fortune)* building up **2** *(instruction)* edification, enlightenment; **pour l'é. des masses** for the edification of the masses; **pour votre é.** for your edification

édifice [edifis] NM **1** *Constr* edifice, building; **é. public** public building; *Fig* **apporter sa pierre à l'é.** to make a contribution, to do one's bit **2** *(structure)* structure, edifice, system; **l'é. des lois** the legal system, the structure of the law; **l'é. social** the social fabric **3** *(assemblage)* heap, mound, pile; **l'é. de sa chevelure** her elaborately piled-up hairstyle

édifier [9] [edifje] VT **1** *(construire → temple)* to build, to construct, to erect; **faire é. qch** to have sth built

2 *(rassembler → empire, fortune)* to build up, to accumulate; *(→ théorie)* to construct, to develop

3 *(instruire)* to edify, to enlighten; **vous voilà édifiés sur ses intentions** now you know what his/her (true) intentions are; *Ironique* **ces dernières révélations nous ont tous édifiés** these latest revelations were an education for us all;

c'est sans doute pour nous é. qu'il a tenu ce discours he probably made the speech for our edification

édile [edil] **NM 1** *Antiq* aedile, edile **2** *Hum (magistrat municipal)* town councillor, local worthy (on the town council)

édilité [edilite] **NF** *Antiq* aedileship

Édimbourg [edɛ̃bur] **NF** *Géog* Edinburgh

édimbourgeois, -e [edɛ̃burʒwa, -az] **ADJ** of/from Edinburgh

❑ **Édimbourgeois, -e NM,F** = inhabitant of or person from Edinburgh

édit [edi] **NM** edict, decree; **l'é. de Nantes** the Edict of Nantes

édit. *(abrév écrite* **éditeur***)* publ.

éditer [3] [edite] **VT 1** *Com (roman, poésie)* to publish; *(disque)* to produce, to release; *(meuble, robe)* to produce, to present **2** *(commenter → texte)* to edit **3** *Ordinat* to edit; **pouvant être édité** editable

éditeur, -trice [editœr, -tris] **ADJ** publishing; **société éditrice** publishing company

NM,F 1 *(maison d'édition)* publisher; *(personne, métier)* editor; **é. de disques** record producer; **é. de film** film releasing company; **é. de presse** newspaper publisher; **é. de vidéo** video publisher

2 *(commentateur)* editor

NM *Ordinat (de programme)* editor; **é. HTML** HTML editor; **é. d'icônes** icon editor; **é. de liens** linker, link editor; **é. de logiciels** software company; **é. orienté en lignes** line editor; **é. de texte** text editor

édition [edisjɔ̃] **NF 1** *(activité, profession)* publishing; **le monde de l'é.** the publishing world; **travailler dans l'é.** to be in publishing *or* in the publishing business; **é. électronique** electronic publishing; **é. musicale** music publishing

2 *(livre)* edition; **une é. critique de 'Hamlet'** a critical edition of 'Hamlet'; **é. augmentée** enlarged edition; **é. de luxe** *(d'un livre)* library edition; **é. originale** first edition; **é. pirate** pirate edition; **é. de poche** paperback edition, *Am* pocket book; **'Nana' dans l'é. de poche** the paperback edition *or* version of 'Nana'; **é. revue et corrigée** revised edition; **é. entièrement revue et corrigée** major new edition, **é. scolaire** school edition; **les Éditions de Minuit** = avant-garde publishing house which began as an underground operation during the Second World War and went on to sponsor the "nouveau roman"

3 *(disque → classique)* edition, release; *(→ de rock)* release; **é. de disques** record production

4 *(de journaux)* edition; **l'é. du matin/soir** the morning/evening edition; **é. exceptionelle** extra; **é. locale** local edition; **é. spéciale** *(de journal)* special edition; *(de revue)* special issue; *Journ* **dernière é.** final edition; *Fam Hum* **tu me l'as déjà dit, c'est la deuxième/troisième é.!** that's the second/third time you've told me that!▪

5 *TV* **é. du journal télévisé** (television) news bulletin; **dans la dernière é. de notre journal** in our late news bulletin; **é. spéciale en direct de Budapest** special report live from Budapest

6 *(action de commenter)* editing

7 *Ordinat* editing; **é. de liens** linking; **é. pleine page** full page editing

éditique [editik] **NF** *Ordinat* electronic publishing

édito [edito] **NM** *Fam Journ* editorial▪

éditorial, -e, -aux, -ales [editɔrjal, -o] **ADJ** editorial

NM *Journ (de journal)* editorial, *Br* leader

éditorialiste [editɔrjalist] **NMF** *Journ* editorial *or Br* leader writer

éditrice [editris] *voir* **éditeur**

Edmonton [ɛdmɔntɔn] **NM** Edmonton

Édouard [edwar] **NPR** *(roi)* Edward; **É. le Confesseur** Edward the Confessor

édouardien, -enne [edwardjɛ̃, -ɛn] **ADJ** Edwardian

EDR [ədeɛr] **NF** *(abbr* **empreinte digitale réduite***)* reduced fingerprint

édredon [edrədɔ̃] **NM** eiderdown, quilt

éduc [edyk] **NMF** *Fam (gén)* teacher▪; *(pour jeunes)* youth leader▪; **é. spé** special needs worker▪

éducable [edykabl] **ADJ** teachable

éducateur, -trice [edykatœr, -tris] **ADJ** educational, educative

NM,F *(gén)* teacher; *(pour jeunes)* youth leader; **é. spécialisé** special needs worker

éducatif, -ive [edykatif, -iv] **ADJ** educational; **le système é.** the education system

éducation [edykasjɔ̃] **NF 1** *Scol & Univ (instruction)* education; **faire l'é. de qn** to educate sb; **il n'a aucune é. musicale** *(technique)* he has no musical training; *(connaissances générales)* he has no musical education; **avoir reçu une bonne é.** to be well-educated; **je veux qu'elle reçoive une bonne é.** I want her to receive a good education; **é. du consommateur** consumer education; **é. manuelle et technique** handicraft classes; **l'É. nationale** *(ministère)* the (French) Ministry *or* Department of Education; *(system)* state education *(in France)*; **é. permanente** lifelong learning; **é. physique (et sportive)** physical education, PE; **é. professionnelle** vocational training; **é. religieuse** religious instruction; **é. sentimentale** initiation into love; **é. sexuelle** sex education; **é. spécialisée** special education; **é. surveillée** education in *Br* community homes *or Am* reform schools

2 *(d'un enfant)* upbringing; *(bonnes manières)* good manners; **avoir de l'é.** to be well-bred *or* well-mannered; **manquer d'é.** to be ill-bred *or* ill-mannered; **manque d'é.** bad manners; **quel manque d'é.!** what manners!; **sans é.** ill-bred, uncouth; **il faut lui refaire toute son é., à ce garçon** this boy needs to be taught good manners; *Hum* **comment, tu ne connais pas, c'est toute une é. à refaire!** what do you mean you've never heard of it, where on earth have you been?; **en rock, toute mon é. est à faire** I know absolutely nothing *or* I'm totally ignorant about rock music

3 *Fig (de la volonté, de l'esprit)* training

'L'Éducation sentimentale' *Flaubert* 'Sentimental Education'

éducationnel, -elle [edykasjɔnɛl] **ADJ** educational

éducative [edykativ] *voir* **éducatif**

éducatrice [edykatris] *voir* **éducateur**

édulcorant, -e [edylkɔrɑ̃, -ɑ̃t] **ADJ** sweetening

NM sweetener, sweetening agent; **é. de synthèse** artificial sweetener

édulcoration [edylkɔrasjɔ̃] **NF 1** *(sucrage)* sweetening **2** *Fig (modération)* toning down, watering down

édulcoré, -e [edylkɔre] **ADJ 1** *(sucré)* sweetened **2** *Fig (modéré)* toned-down, watered-down

édulcorer [3] [edylkɔre] **VT 1** *(sucrer)* to sweeten **2** *Fig (modérer → propos, texte, compte rendu)* to tone down, to water down

éduquer [3] [edyke] **VT 1** *Scol & Univ (instruire → élève, masses)* to teach, to educate **2** *(exercer → réflexe, volonté)* to train; **é. le goût de qn** to shape *or* to influence sb's taste; **é. l'œil/l'oreille de qn** to train sb's eye/ear **3** *(élever → enfant)* to bring up, to raise; **être bien éduqué** to be well brought up *or* well-bred *or* well-mannered; **être mal éduqué** to be badly brought up *or* ill-bred *or* ill-mannered

edutainment [edytɛjnmənt] **NM** edutainment

EED [əəde] **NM** *Ordinat (abrév* **Échange Électronique de Données***)* EDI

EEE [əəə] **NM** *Pol (abrév* **Espace économique européen***)* EEA

EEG [əəʒe] **NM** *Méd (abrév* **électro-encéphalogramme***)* EEG

éfaufiler [3] [efofile] **VT** to unravel

éfendi [efɛ̃di] = **effendi**

effaçable [efasabl] **ADJ 1** *(encre, crayon, inscription)* erasable **2** *Ordinat (mémoire)* erasable

efface [efas] **NF** *Can Fam* eraser▪, *Br* rubber▪

effacé, -e [efase] **ADJ 1** *(couleur)* faded, discoloured **2** *(personne)* self-effacing, retiring; *(rôle)* small, insignificant; **mener une vie très effacée** to live very quietly **3** *(épaules)* sloping; *(menton)* receding; *(poitrine)* flat

effacement [efasmɑ̃] **NM 1** *(annulation → d'une faute)* erasing; *(d'un mot → en gommant)* erasure; *Ordinat* deletion; *(d'une tache)* removal; *(par les éléments → d'une inscription)* wearing away **2** *(oubli → d'un cauchemar, d'un souvenir)* fading **3** *(modestie)* **e. (de soi)** self-effacement **4** *Ling* deletion **5** *(d'une bande magnétique)* erasing, wiping

effacer [16] [efase] **VT 1** *(ôter → graffiti)* to erase, to remove, to clean off; *(gommer → mot)* to erase, *Br* to rub out; *(nettoyer → ardoise, tableau noir)* to clean, to wipe; *Ordinat* to delete; **e. une tache** to remove a stain; *(en lavant)* to wash out a stain; *(avec un chiffon)* to wipe off a stain; **effacez avec un chiffon humide** wipe off with a damp cloth; **e. toutes traces de son passage** to remove *or* eliminate all traces of one's presence; *Ordinat* **e. l'écran** to clear the screen; **e. des imperfections** to smooth out imperfections; *Ordinat* **e. une page d'un écran** to clear a screen of a page, to wipe a page off a screen; **sculptures effacées par le temps** carvings worn away by time

2 *(cassette, disquette)* to erase, to wipe off; *(enregistrement, bande)* to wipe, to erase

3 *Fig (occulter → rêve, image)* to erase; *(→ bêtise)* to erase, to obliterate; **e. un mauvais souvenir** to erase *or* wipe out *or* blot out an unhappy memory; **e. qch de sa mémoire** to blot sth out of *or* erase sth from one's memory; **il a réussi à e. toutes mes craintes** he made my fears vanish; **on efface tout et on recommence** *(on se pardonne)* let bygones be bygones, let's wipe the slate clean; *(on reprend)* let's go back to square one, let's start afresh

4 *(éclipser → adversaire)* to eclipse, to outshine

5 e. le corps to stand side-on; **e. les épaules** to throw back one's shoulders

▸**s'effacer VPR 1** *(emploi passif)* **le crayon à papier s'efface très facilement** pencil rubs out easily *or* is easily erased; **cette encre ne s'efface pas bien** anything written in this ink doesn't rub out very well; **cela s'effacera à l'eau** it will wash off; **la tache ne s'est pas effacée au lavage** the stain didn't come out in the wash; *Fig* **avec le temps, tout s'efface** everything fades with time; *Fig* **ton chagrin s'effacera** you'll get over it

2 *(encre, lettres)* to fade, to wear away; *(couleur)* to fade

3 *(s'écarter)* to move *or* to step aside; **s'e. pour laisser passer qn** to step out of sb's way; **s'e. pour laisser entrer qn** to step aside (in order) to let sb in; *Fig* **il a dû s'e. au profit de son frère** he had to step aside in favour of his brother; *Fig* **depuis quelque temps il s'était effacé** for some time he had kept in the background; *Fig* **il a tendance à s'e. derrière elle** he tends to hide behind her

4 *(disparaître → souvenir, impression)* to fade, to be erased

effaceur [efasœr] **NM e. (d'encre)** ink eraser *or Br* rubber

effalé, -e [efale] **ADJ** *Can Fam* with one's shirt open (at the neck)▪

effaner [3] [efane] **VT** *Agr (pommes de terre, haricots, céréales)* to strip the haulm *or* stalks from; *(carottes)* to strip the leaves from, to top

effaneuse [efanøz] **NF** *Agr* potato haulm remover

effanure [efanyr] **NF** *Agr (gén)* = superfluous leaves stripped from plants; *(de pommes de terre)* haulm

effarant, -e [efarɑ̃, -ɑ̃t] **ADJ** frightening, alarming; *(cynisme, luxe)* outrageous, unbelievable; *(étourderie, maigreur)* unbelievable, stunning; **ils pratiquent des prix effarants** their prices are frightening *or* shocking; **il y avait un monde e. sur les plages** there were an awful lot of people on the beach; **d'une naïveté effarante** alarmingly *or* shockingly naive

effardocher [3] [efardɔʃe] **VT** *Can (terrain)* to clear *(of undergrowth etc)*; *(arbre)* to lop the branches off

effaré, -e [efare] **ADJ 1** *(effrayé)* alarmed **2** *(troublé)* bewildered, bemused; **elle le regarda d'un air e.** she looked at him in bewilderment

effarement [efarmɑ̃] **NM 1** *(peur)* alarm **2** *(trouble)* bewilderment, bemusement

effarer [3] [efare] **VT 1** *(effrayer)* to alarm **2** *(troubler)* to bewilder, to bemuse; **son hypocrisie m'effare!** his/her hypocrisy astounds me!; **je suis effaré par les prix!** the prices are frightening *or* shocking!, I'm astounded at the prices!

effares [efar] NMPL *Can (en acadien) (appât)* fish bait; *(engrais)* fish fertilizer

effarouchement [efaruʃmɑ̃] NM frightening off *or* away, scaring off *or* away

effaroucher [3] [efaruʃe] VT 1 *(effrayer)* to scare, to alarm; *(intimider)* to frighten away *or* off, to scare away *or* off; **il s'approcha doucement pour ne pas e. le cheval** he approached quietly so as not to frighten the horse

2 *(choquer)* to shock

▸**s'effaroucher** VPR 1 *(prendre peur)* to take fright; **s'e. de** to shy at, to take fright at; **elle s'effarouche pour un rien** she gets frightened at the least little thing, the least little thing frightens her; **il ne risque pas de s'e. pour si peu** he's unlikely to let a little thing like that frighten him

2 *(s'offusquer)* to be shocked (**de** by *or* at)

effarvatte [efarvat] NF *Orn* reed warbler

effecteur [efɛktœr] NM *Physiol* effector

effectif, -ive [efɛktif, -iv] ADJ 1 *Fin (coût, monnaie, taux)* effective; *(valeur, revenu)* real; *(circulation)* active; *(rendement)* actual

2 *(efficace → méthode, raisonnement)* effective

3 *(règlement, mesures)* in effect; **cette loi sera effective au 1er janvier** this law will come into effect on 1 January; **l'armistice est devenu e. ce matin** the armistice took effect *or* became effective this morning

NM *(employés)* manpower, (number of) employees, staff; *(d'un lycée)* size, (total) number of pupils; *(d'un parti)* size, strength; *(d'une armée)* strength; *Naut* complement; **réduction de l'e. des classes** reduction in the number of pupils per class; **réduire ses effectifs** to deman, to downsize; **à e. réduit** under *or* below strength; **l'e. est au complet, nos effectifs sont au complet** we are at full strength; **le parti a augmenté ses effectifs de 10 pour cent** the party has increased its membership by 10 percent; **70 pour cent de l'e. est féminin** women account for 70 percent of the workforce; **e. budgétaire** budgetary strength, *Am* authorized strength

▫ **effectifs** NMPL *Mil* numbers, strength; **crise d'effectifs** manpower crisis

effectivement [efɛktivmɑ̃] ADV 1 *(efficacement)* effectively, efficiently; **contribuer e. au processus de paix** to make a real contribution to the peace process

2 *(véritablement)* actually, really; **cela s'est e. produit** that actually *or* really happened; **c'est e. le cas** this is actually the case

3 *(en effet)* actually; **je suis e. sorti dans l'après-midi** I DID actually go out in the afternoon; **j'ai dit cela, e.** I did indeed say so; **on pourrait e. penser que...** one may actually *or* indeed think that...; **c'est pratique, hein? – e.!** it's practical, isn't it? – (yes) indeed! *or* indeed it is!; **e., on aurait pu prévoir un parapluie** we should have thought about bringing an umbrella, *Br* we should have brought an umbrella right enough

effectivité [efɛktivite] NF 1 *(efficacité)* effectiveness, efficiency, efficaciousness 2 *(d'une méthode, d'un raisonnement)* effectiveness

effectuer [7] [efektɥe] VT *(expérience, essai)* to carry out, to perform; *(trajet, traversée)* to make, to complete; *(voyage, calcul) & Mil (retraite)* to make; *(saut, pirouette)* to make, to execute; *(mouvement, geste)* to execute; *(service militaire)* to do; *(retouche, enquête)* to carry out; *(opération)* to execute, to carry out; *(réconciliation)* to bring about; *(paiement)* to make, *Sout* to effect; **e. des démarches** to take steps; **e. une réservation** to make a reservation; *Com* **e. une commande** to place an order

▸**s'effectuer** VPR 1 *(avoir lieu)* to take place; **l'aller-retour s'effectue en une journée** the *Br* return trip *or Am* round trip can be made in one day; **les inscriptions s'effectueront à 15 heures** registration will take place *or* will be at 3 p.m.

2 *(mouvement, opération)* to be executed; *(paiement, voyage)* to be made; *(réconciliation)* to be brought about

efféminé, -e [efemine] ADJ effeminate

NM *(garçon)* effeminate boy; *(homme)* effeminate man

efféminement [efeminmɑ̃] NM effeminacy

efféminer [3] [efemine] VT *Littéraire* to make effeminate

effendi [efɛ̃di] NM effendi

efférent, -e [eferɑ̃, -ɑ̃t] ADJ efferent

effervescence [efɛrvesɑ̃s] NF 1 *Chim* effervescence

2 *(agitation)* agitation, turmoil; *(excitation)* excitement

▫ **en effervescence** ADJ bubbling *or* buzzing with excitement; **les enfants étaient en e.** the children were terribly excited; **le pays était en e.** the country was in turmoil; **la victoire des Bleus a mis le pays en e.** France's victory threw the nation into a state of excitement; **il avait l'esprit en e.** his mind was in turmoil

effervescent, -e [efɛrvesɑ̃, -ɑ̃t] ADJ 1 *Chim (comprimé, aspirine)* effervescent 2 *(excité)* agitated

EFFET [efɛ]

effect **1, 3–5, 7** ▪ result **1** ▪ impression **2, 4** ▪ bill **6** ▪ spin **8**

NM 1 *(résultat)* effect, result, outcome; **c'est un e. de la pesanteur** it's a result of gravity; **c'est bien l'e. du hasard si...** it's really quite by chance that...; **les mesures du gouvernement n'ont eu aucun e.** the government's measures have had no effect; **cela n'a pas eu l'e. escompté** it didn't have the desired *or* intended effect; **sa fréquentation a un e. désastreux sur ma fille** going out with him has had a disastrous effect on my daughter; **ton insistance n'aura pour e. que de l'agacer** the only thing you'll achieve *or* do by insisting is (to) annoy him/her; **cela a eu pour e. de le mettre en colère** it had the effect of making him angry; **ce poison a pour e. de paralyser le système nerveux** this poison results in the paralysis of the nervous system; **le whisky lui fait toujours cet e.** whisky always has this effect on him/her; **attends que le médicament fasse son e.** wait for the medicine to take effect; **tes somnifères ne m'ont fait aucun e.** your sleeping pills didn't work on me *or* didn't have any effect on me; **faire de l'e.** to have an effect, to be effective; **faire de l'e. sur** to have an effect on; **faire e.** to take effect; **produire l'e. voulu** to produce the desired effect; **sans e.** ineffective, ineffectual; **le produit est sans e. sur les taches de fruit** the product does not work on fruit stains; **rester** *ou* **demeurer sans e.** to have no effect, to be ineffective; **mettre à e.** to bring into effect, to put into operation; **à quel e.?** to what end?; *Mktg* **e. d'expérience** experience effect; *Mktg* **e. de halo** halo effect; *Fin* **e. de levier** gearing, leverage; **e. pervers** undesired effect; *Méd* side effect; **e. placebo** placebo effect; **e. en retour** backlash; *Méd* **e. secondaire** side effect; **relation de cause à e.** cause and effect relationship

2 *(impression)* impression; **faire beaucoup d'e./peu d'e.** to be impressive/unimpressive; **la nouvelle fit peu d'e. sur les employés** the staff were not very impressed by the news, the news didn't make much of an impression on the staff; **les pleurs de sa femme ne lui firent aucun e.** his wife's tears had no effect on him; **sa réponse a fait l'e. d'une bombe** his/her answer came as *or* was a bombshell; **cela fait mauvais e. de le faire attendre** it looks bad to keep him waiting; **ça a fait bon e. que tu aies mis une jupe** your wearing a skirt made a good impression; **faire bon/mauvais e. à qn** to make a good/bad impression on sb; **son discours a fait (très) bon/mauvais e. sur l'auditoire** the audience was (most) favourably impressed/extremely unimpressed by his/her speech; **une jupe fera meilleur e. qu'un pantalon** a skirt will make a better impression than trousers; **ça m'a fait un drôle d'e.** it gave me a funny *or* strange feeling, it made me feel all funny *or* strange; **à chaque fois qu'il me parle, ça me fait un drôle d'e.** I feel all funny inside whenever he talks to me; **ça fait un drôle d'e. de penser que...** it's funny *or* strange to think that...; **il me fait l'e. d'un jeune homme sérieux** he strikes me as (being) a reliable young man; **elle me fait l'e. d'un personnage de bande dessinée** she reminds me of a cartoon character; **faire de l'e.** to make a show, to attract attention; **dès que je l'ai vu, il m'a fait de l'e.** I fancied him the minute I saw him; **eh bien! elle te fait de l'e.!** she's got quite an effect on you, I see!; *Fam* **ça m'a fait de l'e. de la voir si pâle** it gave me quite a turn to see her so pale; **son départ précipité a fait de l'e.** his/her hurried departure caused a stir; *Fam* **je t'assure que ça fera un e. bœuf** I bet you it will make a terrific impression; *Fam* **faire** *ou* **produire son petit e.** to cause a bit of a stir; **c'est l'e. que cela m'a fait** that's how it impressed *or* struck me; *Fam* **c'est tout l'e. que ça te fait?** is that all you've got to say?; **ça m'a fait un sale e.** it gave me a nasty turn; **ça m'a fait un drôle d'e. de le revoir** it felt strange seeing him again; **quel e. ça te fait qu'elle revienne?** how do you feel about her coming back?

3 *(procédé)* effect; **e. de contraste/d'optique** contrasting/visual effect; *Cin & TV* **effets optiques** camera effects; **e. (de) domino** domino effect; **e. de style** stylistic effect; **e. de perspective** 3-D *or* three-dimensional effect; **rechercher l'e.** to strive for effect; **manquer** *ou* **rater son e.** *(magicien)* to spoil one's effect; **créer un e. de surprise** to create a surprise, to cause a stir; **nous ne gagnerons cette bataille qu'en créant un e. de surprise** we won't win this battle unless we can take the enemy by surprise; *Théât* **e. de lumière** lighting effect; *Théât* **effets scéniques** stage effects; *Cin, Rad & TV* **effets sonores** sound effects; *Cin* **effets spéciaux** special effects; *Ordinat & TV* **e. de transition** melt; *TV* **effets vidéo** video effects; *Cin & TV* **effets visuels** visual effects

4 *(but recherché, force artistique)* **manquer son e.** *(discours)* not to have the desired effect; *(plaisanterie)* to misfire, to fall flat; **il voulait faire une entrée triomphale mais il a manqué son e.** he wanted to make a triumphant entry but it fell flat; **il fit une pause pour mieux juger de l'e. de ses paroles** he paused to see what effect his words were having; **il fit une pause, enchanté de son e.** he paused, delighted at the effect he was having; **soigner ses effets** to work hard to make the right impression; **rechercher les effets** to try to make an impression; **ménager ses effets** to have a sense of the dramatic; **faire des effets de jambes** to show off one's legs, to draw attention to one's legs; **faire des effets de manches** *(avocat)* to make dramatic gestures; **faire des effets de voix** to make dramatic use of one's voice; **ça m'a coupé tous mes effets** it stole my thunder; *Littéraire* **phrases à e.** words used for effect; *Beaux-Arts* **e. de lune** moonlight effect

5 *(application)* effect; **mettre un projet à e.** to put a plan into action *or* into effect; **prendre e. à partir de** to take effect *or* to come into operation as of; *Jur* **e. dévolutif des voies de recours** devolutive joinder of issue; *Jur* **e. direct** direct effect; *Jur* **e. immédiat de la loi** immediate effect; *Jur* **e. relatif des contrats** privity; *Jur* **e. rétroactif d'une loi/d'un accord** retroactive effect of a law/an agreement; **augmentation avec e. rétroactif au 1er avril** rise retroactive *or* backdated to 1 April

6 *Com & Fin* bill; **e. accepté** accepted bill; **e. balançoire** see-saw effect; **e. bancable** bankable bill, eligible paper; **e. bancaire** bill, draft; **e. de cavalerie** kite; **e. de commerce** bill of exchange; **e. de complaisance** accommodation bill; **e. à courte échéance** short *or* short-dated bill; **e. à date fixe** fixed-term bill; **e. domicilié** domiciled bill; **effets à encaisser** accounts receivable; **e. à l'encaissement** bill for collection; **e. endossé** endorsed bill; **e. escomptable** discountable bill; **e. escompté** discounted bill; **e. libre** clean bill; **e. à longue échéance** long *or* long-dated bill; **e. négociable** negotiable bill; *Bourse* **effets nominatifs** registered stock; **e. à ordre** promissory note; **e. payable à vue** sight bill; **effets à payer** bills payable; **e. au porteur** bill payable to bearer; **effets publics** government securities; **effets à recevoir** bills receivable; **e. en souffrance** overdue bill; **e. à taux flottant** floating rate note, FRN; **e. à terme**

period *or* term bill; **e. à usance** usance bill; **e. à vue** sight bill, demand bill *or* draft

7 *(en sciences)* effect; *Phys* **e. Doppler/Compton/Joule** Doppler/Compton/Joule effect; *Écol & Météo* **e. de serre** greenhouse effect; *Tech* **e. utile** efficiency; **à simple e.** single-action, single-acting; **à double e.** double-action, double-acting; **e. Edison** Edison effect; *Phys* **e. photoélectrique** photoelectric effect; *Phys* **e. tunnel** tunnel effect; *Aut* **e. de chasse** caster action

8 *Sport* spin; **donner de l'e. à une balle** to put spin on a ball; **mettre trop d'e.** to put on too much spin; **balle qui a de l'e.** ball that has spin; **e. de côté** *(au billard)* side (screw)

□ **effets** NMPL *(affaires)* things; *(vêtements)* clothes; *Jur* **effets mobiliers** chattels; **effets personnels** personal effects *or* belongings

□ **à cet effet** ADV to that effect *or* end *or* purpose; **cet appareil n'a pas été conçu à cet e.** the machine was not designed for that purpose *or* with that in mind

□ **en effet** ADV **1** *(effectivement)* actually, in (actual) fact; **en e., tu avais raison** you were right after all; **oui, je m'en souviens en e.** yes, I do remember; **c'est ce que je me suis en e. demandé** that's just what I wondered; **c'est en e. la meilleure solution** it's actually *or* in fact the best solution; **on peut en e. interpréter l'événement de cette façon** it is indeed possible to interpret what happened in that way

2 *(introduisant une explication)* **je ne pense pas qu'il vienne; en e. il est extrêmement pris ces derniers temps** I don't think he'll come, he's really very busy these days; **il n'a pas pu venir; en e., il était malade** he was unable to come since he was ill

3 *(dans une réponse)* **drôle d'idée! – en e.!** what a funny idea! – indeed *or* isn't it!; **y avez-vous songé? – en e.!** have you thought about it? – yes *or* indeed I have!; **mais c'est monstrueux! – en e.!** it's abominable! – isn't it just!

□ **sous l'effet de** PRÉP **être sous l'e. d'un calmant** to be under the effect of a tranquillizer; **être sous l'e. de l'alcool/la drogue** to be under the influence of alcohol/drugs; **j'ai dit des choses regrettables sous l'e. de la colère** anger made me say things which I later regretted; **il t'a injurié sous l'e. de la colère** he wouldn't have insulted you if he hadn't been angry; **je suis encore sous l'e. de la colère** I'm still angry, I still haven't calmed down; **les feuilles sont tombées sous l'e. de la chaleur** the leaves dropped off with the heat

effeuillage [efœjaʒ] NM **1** *Hort* leaf removal **2** *Fam (déshabillage)* striptease▪

effeuillaison [efœjɛzɔ̃] NF shedding of leaves

effeuillement [efœjmɑ̃] NM shedding of leaves

effeuilles [efœj] NFPL *Suisse (épamprage)* leaf removal

effeuiller [5] [efœje] VT *Hort (arbre)* to thin out (the leaves of); *(fleurs)* to pull the petals off; *(sujet: vent → arbre)* to blow off the leaves of; **e. la marguerite** *(fille)* to play "he loves me, he loves me not"; *(garçon)* to play "she loves me, she loves me not"

▸**s'effeuiller** VPR *(arbre)* to shed *or* to lose its leaves; *(fleur)* to shed *or* to lose its petals

effeuilleuse [efœjøz] NF *Fam* **1** *(strip-teaseuse)* stripper▪ **2** *Suisse (ouvrière)* = woman employed to strip vines of unwanted leaves

efficace [efikas] ADJ **1** *(politique, intervention)* effective; *(remède, prière)* effective, *Sout* efficacious; *(employé, machine)* efficient **2** *Élec* **watt e.** true watt

efficacement [efikasmɑ̃] ADV *(avec succès)* effectively; *(de façon productive)* efficiently

efficacité [efikasite] NF *(d'une politique, d'une intervention)* effectiveness; *(d'un remède, d'une prière)* effectiveness, *Sout* efficacy; *(d'un employé, d'une machine)* efficiency; **manque d'e.** inefficiency; **manquer d'e.** to be inefficient; *Écon* **e. du coût** cost-effectiveness; *Écon* **e. économique** economic efficiency; *Écon* **e.**

---

marginale du capital marginal efficiency of capital; *Écon* **e. parfaite** absolute efficiency; *Mktg* **e. promotionnelle** promotional effectiveness; *Mktg* **e. publicitaire** advertising effectiveness; *Mktg* **e. des ventes** sales effectiveness

efficience [efisjɑ̃s] NF efficiency

efficient, -e [efisjɑ̃, -ɑ̃t] ADJ efficient

effigie [efiʒi] NF effigy

□ **à l'effigie de** PRÉP bearing the effigy *or* image of

□ **en effigie** ADV in effigy

effilage [efilaʒ] NM **1** *Tex* fraying **2** *(des haricots)* stringing **3** *(des cheveux)* feathering

effilé, -e [efile] ADJ **1** *(mince → doigt)* slender, tapering; *(→ main)* slender; *(→ silhouette)* rangy; *(→ carrosserie)* streamlined; *(→ outil)* tapered, pointed; *(→ cheveux)* thinned; *Culin* **amandes effilées** flaked almonds **2** *(effiloché)* frayed; *(frange)* ragged **3** *Culin (poulet)* dressed, drawn

　NM *Couture* fringe

effilement [efilmɑ̃] NM **1** *(des doigts)* tapering **2** *Littéraire (de tissu)* fraying

effiler [3] [efile] VT **1** *(tissu)* to fray, to unravel **2** *(allonger → ligne, forme)* to streamline; **e. sa moustache** to trim one's moustache into a point **3** *(cheveux)* to thin out

▸**s'effiler** VPR **1** *(s'effilocher)* to fray, to unravel **2** *(s'allonger)* to taper (off)

effileur, -euse [efilœr, -øz] *Tex* NM,F *(ouvrier)* tearer

□ **effileuse** NF *(machine)* devil

effilochage [efilɔʃaʒ] NM fraying; *Tex (en peignant)* teasing out

effiloche [efilɔʃ] NF *Tex (de fils laissés libres)* fringe

effilocher [3] [efilɔʃe] VT to fray, to unravel; *(avec un peigne)* to tease out

▸**s'effilocher** VPR to fray, to unravel

effilocheuse [efilɔʃøz] NF *Tex* devil

effilochure [efilɔʃyr] NF *Tex* loose thread

effilopé, -e [efilɔpe] ADJ *Can (en acadien) (vêtement)* frayed, threadbare

effilure [efilyr] NF loose thread

efflanqué, -e [eflɑ̃ke] ADJ *(animal)* raw-boned; *(homme)* lanky, tall and skinny

effleurage [eflœraʒ] NM **1** *(du cuir)* buffing **2** *(massage)* gentle massage, *Spéc* effleurage

effleurement [eflœrmɑ̃] NM **1** *(contact)* light touch; *(de l'eau)* skimming **2** *(caresse)* light touch, gentle stroke *or* caress; *Ordinat* **touche/clavier à e.** touch-sensitive key/keyboard

effleurer [5] [eflœre] VT **1** *(frôler)* to touch lightly; *(accidentellement)* to brush (against); *(cime, eau)* to skim, to graze; **il m'a effleuré en passant** he brushed past me; **la balle n'a fait qu'e. sa joue** the bullet only grazed his/her cheek; **ses doigts effleuraient le clavier** his/her fingers ran lightly over the keyboard

2 *(égratigner → peau)* to graze

3 *(aborder → sujet)* to touch on *or* upon; **ça ne m'a même pas effleuré** it didn't even occur to me *or* cross my mind; **quelques soupçons l'avaient effleuré** some misgivings had crossed his mind

4 *(cuir)* to buff

effleurir [32] [eflœrir] VI *Chim* to effloresce

effloraison [eflɔrɛzɔ̃] NF *Bot* early flowering *or* blooming

efflorescence [eflɔresɑ̃s] NF **1** *Chim* efflorescence **2** *Littéraire (épanouissement)* blooming, flowering; **être en pleine e.** to be flourishing **3** *(sur les fruits)* bloom

efflorescent, -e [eflɔresɑ̃, -ɑ̃t] ADJ *Chim* efflorescent

effluent, -e [eflɥɑ̃, -ɑ̃t] ADJ effluent

　NM *(eaux → de ruissellement)* drainage water; *(→ usées)* (untreated) effluent; **e. radioactif** radioactive waste

effluve [eflyv] NM **1** *(émanation)* emanation; **effluves** *(bonnes odeurs)* fragrance, exhalations; *(mauvaises odeurs)* effluvia, miasma **2** *Phys* **e. électrique** discharge

effoiré, -e [efware] ADJ *Can Fam* **il passe sa vie e. devant la télévision** he's a real couch potato, he's forever slouched in front of the television

---

effoirer [3] [efware] **s'effoirer** VPR *Can Fam (tomber)* to fall flat on one's face; *(s'étendre paresseusement)* to slump, to lie slouched

effondrement [efɔ̃drəmɑ̃] NM **1** *(chute → d'un toit, d'un pont)* collapse, collapsing, falling down; *(→ d'un plafond, d'une voûte)* falling *or* caving in; *(→ d'une mine)* caving in; *Géol* subsidence; *Fig (→ d'un plan)* falling through **2** *(chute importante → d'une monnaie)* collapse, slump; *(→ des prix, du marché, de la demande)* slump *(de* in); *(→ d'un empire)* collapse **3** *(abattement)* dejection; **être dans un état d'e. complet** to be in a state of utter dejection

effondrer [3] [efɔ̃dre] VT **1** *Agr* to subsoil

2 *(briser → toit)* to bring down; *(→ mur)* to break down; *Fig* **après la mort de sa femme, il était effondré** he was prostrate with grief after his wife's death

▸**s'effondrer** VPR **1** *(tomber → mur, pont, bâtiment)* to fall (down), to collapse; *(→ plafond, voûte)* to collapse, to fall *or* to cave in; *(d'une mine)* to cave in

2 *(chuter → monnaie)* to collapse, to plummet, to slump; *(→ prix, marché, demande, cours, bénéfices)* to slump; *(→ empire)* to collapse, to crumble, to fall apart; *(→ rêve, projet)* to collapse, to fall through; *(→ raisonnement)* to collapse; **le marché s'est effondré** the bottom has fallen out of the market

3 *(défaillir)* to collapse, to slump; **s'e. en larmes** to break down and cry, to dissolve into tears; **s'e. dans un fauteuil** to slump *or* to sink into an armchair; **toute son histoire s'effondre** his/her whole story is collapsing *or* falling to pieces

efforcer [16] [efɔrse] **s'efforcer** VPR **s'e. de faire qch** to try hard *or* to endeavour to do sth; **s'e. de maigrir** to try hard *or* to do one's best to lose weight; **s'e. de sourire** to force oneself to smile; **s'e. à l'amabilité** to try one's best to be polite; **s'e. à la clarté** to try to be as clear as possible; **je m'y efforce** I'm doing my best *or* utmost

effort [efɔr] NM **1** *(dépense d'énergie)* effort; **e. physique/intellectuel** physical/intellectual effort; **e. de volonté** effort of (the) will; *Mktg* **e. de commercialisation** marketing effort; **e. financier** financial outlay; **e. de guerre** war effort; *Mktg* **e. de marketing** marketing effort; *Mktg* **e. de promotion** promotional campaign; *Mktg* **e. publicitaire** advertising campaign; **son médecin lui a interdit tout e.** his/her doctor has forbidden any exertion; **cela va te demander un certain e.** you'll need to exert yourself a bit; **après bien des efforts** after a great deal of effort; **avec e.** with an effort; **sans e.** effortlessly; **encore un (petit) e.!** one more try!; **fournir un gros e.** to make a great deal of effort; **il a fourni un gros e. au dernier trimestre** he worked very hard *or* he put in a great deal of work in the last term; **il est partisan du moindre e.** he doesn't do any more than he has to; **faire l'e. de faire qch** to make the effort to do sth; **tu aurais pu faire l'e. d'écrire/de comprendre** you could (at least) have tried to write/to understand; **faire un e.** to make an effort; **a progressé mais doit encore faire des efforts** has made progress but still needs to make an effort; **chacun doit faire un petit e.** everybody must do their share; **faire un e. sur soi-même** to exercise self-control; **faire un e. sur soi-même pour rester poli** to force oneself to remain polite; **faire un e. d'imagination** to try to use one's imagination; *Ironique* **cela demande un sacré e. d'imagination** it takes an awful lot of imagination, it puts quite a strain on the imagination; **faire un (gros) e. de mémoire** to try hard to remember; **faire un e. d'adaptation/de concentration** to try hard to adapt/to concentrate; **faire un e. pour faire qch** to make an effort to do sth; **faire un violent e. pour se lever** to make a great effort to get up; **faire tous ses efforts pour obtenir qch** to do one's utmost *or* all one can to obtain sth; **demander un e. trop important à son organisme** to over-strain oneself physically; *Fam* **après l'e., le réconfort** after all that hard work I/you/*etc* deserve this!

2 *Tech* stress, strain; **e. de cisaillement/torsion** shearing/torsional stress; **e. de rupture** breaking strain; **e. de tension** tensile stress; **e. de torsion** torque; **e. de traction** pull, tractive effort, tensile stress; *Aut* **efforts en virage** cornering force

3 *Fam Vieilli Méd* strain▪, rick▪; **se donner** *ou* **attraper un e.** to rick one's back▪

effraction [efraksjɔ̃] **NF** *Jur* breaking and entering, housebreaking; **entrer par e.** to break in; **entrer par e. dans une maison** to break into a house; **il n'y a pas eu e.** there was no sign of a burglary

effraie[1] *voir* **effrayer**

effraie[2] [efrɛ] **NF** *Orn* barn owl

effranger [17] [efrɑ̃ʒe] **VT** to fray into a fringe

▸**s'effranger VPR** to fray; **la veste s'effrange aux bords** the jacket is fraying at the edges

effrayant, -e [efrɛjɑ̃, -ɑ̃t] **ADJ 1** *(qui fait peur)* frightening, fearsome **2** *(extrême → chaleur, charge de travail)* frightful, appalling; *(→ prix, bêtise, laideur)* frightening; *Fam* **c'est e. ce qu'il peut être lent!** it's frightening how slow he can be!

effrayer [11] [efreje] **VT 1** *(faire peur à)* to frighten, to scare; *(inquiéter)* to alarm

2 *(décourager)* to put *or* to frighten off; **l'énormité de la tâche ne m'effrayait pas** the magnitude of the task didn't put me off; **sa petite phrase a effrayé les électeurs** his/her well-publicized remark frightened off the voters

▸**s'effrayer VPR 1** *(avoir peur)* to become frightened, to take fright; **s'e. de qch** to be frightened *or* scared *or* afraid of sth; **elle s'effraie pour un rien** the least little thing frightens her, she takes fright at the least little thing

2 *(s'alarmer)* to become alarmed; **je m'effraie de la lenteur avec laquelle elle travaille** I'm alarmed by how slowly she works

effréné, -e [efrene] **ADJ** *(poursuite, recherche)* wild, frantic; *(orgueil, curiosité, luxe)* unbridled, unrestrained; *(vie, rythme)* frantic, hectic; *(efforts)* frantic; *(galop)* frantic, mad

effritement [efritmɑ̃] **NM 1** *(désagrégation → d'une roche, de bas-relief)* crumbling away; *(→ du plâtre, d'un revêtement)* crumbling, disintegration **2** *(affaiblissement → d'une autorité, d'une majorité, de la popularité)* erosion **3** *Bourse (des valeurs, des cours)* crumbling; *Fin (de fonds)* erosion

effriter [3] [efrite] **VT** to cause to crumble

▸**s'effriter VPR 1** *(se désagréger → roche, bas-relief)* to crumble away; *(→ plâtre, revêtement)* to crumble, to disintegrate **2** *(s'affaiblir → autorité, majorité, popularité)* to erode **3** *Bourse (valeurs, cours)* to crumble; *Fin (fonds)* to erode

effroi [efrwa] **NM** *Littéraire* terror, dread; **regard plein d'e.** frightened look; **inspirer de l'e. à qn** to fill sb with terror; **un spectacle qui inspire l'e.** an awe-inspiring sight; **je fus saisi d'e.** I was seized by terror, I was terror-stricken

effronté, -e [efrɔ̃te] **ADJ** *(enfant, manières, réponse)* impudent, *Br* cheeky; *(menteur, mensonge)* shameless, barefaced, brazen

NM,F *(enfant)* impudent *or Br* cheeky child; *(homme)* impudent fellow; *(femme)* brazen hussy; **petite effrontée!** you *Br* cheeky *or Am* sassy little girl!

🎬 **'L'Effrontée'** *Miller* 'Impudent Girl'

effrontément [efrɔ̃temɑ̃] **ADV** impudently, *Br* cheekily; **mentir e.** to lie shamelessly *or* barefacedly *or* brazenly

effronterie [efrɔ̃tri] **NF** *(d'un enfant, d'une attitude)* insolence, impudence, *Br* cheek; *(d'un mensonge)* shamelessness, brazenness; **il a eu l'e. de me répondre** he had the nerve to *or* he was impudent enough to answer me back

effroyable [efrwajabl] **ADJ 1** *(épouvantable)* frightening, appalling, horrifying **2** *(extrême → maigreur, misère, erreur)* dreadful, frightful

effroyablement [efrwajabləmɑ̃] **ADV** awfully, terribly; **s'ennuyer e.** to be bored to death; **c'est e. compliqué** it's awfully *or* terribly complicated

effusif, -ive [efysif, -iv] **ADJ** *Géol* effusive

effusion [efyzjɔ̃] **NF 1 e. de sang** bloodshed; **sans e. de sang** without any bloodshed **2** *(de sentiments)* effusion, outpouring, outburst; *(exubérance)* effusiveness; **effusions de joie/tendresse** demonstrations of joy/affection; **remercier qn avec e.** to thank sb effusively; **leurs effusions m'étouffent** I find their effusiveness stifling

effusive [efyziv] *voir* **effusif**

éfourceau, -x [efurso] **NM** two-wheeled cart

éfrit [efri] **NM** *Myth* afreet, efreet

EGA [əʒea] **NM** *Ordinat (abrév* **enhanced graphics adaptor**) EGA

égagropile [egagrɔpil] **NM** *Vét* hair-ball

égaie *etc voir* **égayer**

égaiement [egɛmɑ̃] **NM** cheering up, enlivenment, brightening up

égailler [3] [egaje] **s'égailler VPR** to disperse, to scatter

égal, -e, -aux, -ales [egal, -o] **ADJ 1** *(identique → part, poids etc)* equal; **partager qch en parts égales** to divide sth up into equal parts; **deux mannequins de taille égale** two models of the same height; **ils sont de force/d'intelligence égale** they are equally strong/intelligent; **à travail é. salaire é.** equal pay for equal work; **à prix é., tu peux trouver mieux** for the same price, you can find something better; **à surface égale, je préfère mon appartement au sien** square foot for square foot, I prefer my flat to his/hers; **à expérience égale, ils préfèrent recruter un homme qu'une femme** if they have two candidates with identical experience, they prefer to hire a man rather than a woman; **des exercices d'égale difficulté** equally difficult exercises, exercises of equal difficulty; **à égale distance de A et de B** equidistant from A and B, an equal distance from A and B; **la partie n'est pas égale (entre les deux joueurs)** the players are unevenly matched; **toutes choses égales d'ailleurs** all (other) things being equal; **faire jeu é.** to have an equal score, to be evenly matched (in the game); *Fig* to be neck and neck; **être é. à** to be equal to, to equal; **être** *ou* **rester é. à soi-même** to remain true to form, to be still one's old self; **é. à lui-même, il n'a pas dit un mot** typically, he didn't say a word

2 *Math* **3 est é. à 2 plus 1** 3 is equal to 2 plus 1

3 *(régulier → terrain)* even, level; *(→ souffle)* even, regular; *(→ pas)* even, regular, steady; *(→ pouls)* steady, regular; *(→ allure)* steady; *(→ climat)* equable, unchanging; **être de caractère é.** *ou* **d'humeur égale** to be even-tempered

4 *(locutions)* **ça m'est (bien/complètement) é.** *(ça m'est indifférent)* I don't care either way, it's all the same *or* all one to me; *(ça ne m'intéresse pas)* I don't care at all, I couldn't care less; **tout lui est é.** he/she doesn't feel strongly about anything; **tout lui est é. désormais** he/she doesn't care about anything now; **en train ou en avion, ça m'est é.** I don't care whether we go by train or plane; **c'est é.** all the same; **c'est é., tu aurais pu téléphoner** all the same, you could have phoned

NM,F *(personne)* equal; **nos égaux** our equals; **la femme est l'égale de l'homme** woman is equal to man; **il n'a pas son é. pour animer une fête** he's second to none when it comes to livening up a party; **son arrogance n'a d'égale que sa sottise** his/her arrogance is only equalled by his/her foolishness; **traiter qn en é.** to treat sb as an equal

▫ **à l'égal de PRÉP** *Littéraire* **je l'aimais à l'é. d'un fils** I loved him like a son

▫ **d'égal à égal ADV** *(s'entretenir)* on equal terms; *(traiter)* as an equal; **nous avons eu une discussion d'é. à é.** we had a discussion as equals *or* on equal terms *or* on an equal footing

▫ **sans égal ADJ** matchless, unequalled, unrivalled; **elle est d'une malhonnêteté sans é.** she is incredibly dishonest

égalable [egalabl] **ADJ** which can be equalled *or* matched; **un exploit difficilement é.** a feat difficult to match

également [egalmɑ̃] **ADV 1** *(autant)* equally; **servir tout le monde é.** to give everyone an equal serving; **je crains é. le froid et la chaleur** I dislike the cold as much as the heat **2** *(aussi)* also, too, as well; **je l'ai vu é.** I saw him as well *or* too; **elle m'a é. dit que...** she also told me that...

égaler [3] [egale] **VT 1** *(avoir la même valeur que)* to equal, to match (**en** for); **é. le record mondial** to equal the world record; **la renommée de la fille égale celle de la mère** the daughter's renown equals *or* matches that of her mother; **rien n'égale sa beauté** her beauty is unequalled

2 *Math* **3 fois 2 égale 6** 3 times 2 equals 6; **deux et deux égalent quatre** two and two equal *or* make four; **si X égale Y** let X equal Y

3 *Arch (comparer)* to rank; *(rendre égal)* to make equal; **é. Milton à Shakespeare** to rank Milton with Shakespeare; **la douleur égale les hommes** grief makes all men equal

4 *(niveler)* to level (out), to make flat

égalisateur, -trice [egalizatœr, -tris] **ADJ** equalizing, levelling; *Sport* **but/point é.** *Br* equalizer, *Am* tying goal/point

égalisation [egalizasjɔ̃] **NF 1** *(nivellement → des salaires, d'un terrain)* levelling **2** *(équilibrage)* equalization, equalizing; *Math* **é. à zéro** equating to zero **3** *Sport* **le but/point de l'é.** *Br* the equalizer, *Am* the tying goal; **5 minutes après l'é.** five minutes after the *Br* equalizer *or Am* tying goal had been scored; **réussir l'é.** to score the *Br* equalizer *or Am* tying goal

égalisatrice [egalizatris] *voir* **égalisateur**

égaliser [3] [egalize] **VT** *(sentier)* to level (out); *(frange)* to trim; *(conditions, chances, salaire)* to make equal, to balance (out); **é. les cheveux de qn** to trim sb's hair; *Math* **é. une expression à zéro** to equate an expression to zero

VI *Sport* to tie, *Br* to equalize

▸**s'égaliser VPR** to become more equal, to balance out

égaliseur [egalizœr] **NM** *Tech* **é. graphique** graphic equalizer

égalitaire [egalitɛr] **ADJ** egalitarian

égalitarisme [egalitarism] **NM** egalitarianism

égalitariste [egalitarist] **ADJ** egalitarian

égalité [egalite] **NF 1** *(entre des quantités, des personnes)* equality; *Jur* **é. des armes** right to a fair trial; **é. des chances** equal opportunities; **é. devant les charges publiques** = principle by which any liability of the authorities is spread equally amongst all citizens; **é. devant l'impôt** equality of taxation; **é. des salaires/droits** equal pay/rights; **politique/principe d'é. des chances** equal opportunities policy/principle; **l'é. des citoyens devant la loi** the equality of citizens before the law; **être sur un pied d'é. avec qn** to be on an equal footing *or* on equal terms with sb

2 *Math* equality; **(signe d')é.** equal *or* equals sign

3 *Géom* **é. de deux triangles** isomorphism of two triangles

4 *Tennis* deuce; *Ftbl* draw, tie

5 *(uniformité → du pouls, de la respiration)* regularity, steadiness; *(→ d'une allure)* steadiness; *(→ du sol)* evenness, levelness; *(→ du tempérament)* evenness; **être d'une grande é. d'humeur** to be very even-tempered

▫ **à égalité ADV** *(au tennis)* at deuce; *(dans des jeux d'équipe)* drawn, in a draw *or* tie; *Golf* all square; *Sport* **être à é.** *(équipes)* to be level; **ils ont fini le match à é.** they tied; **ils sont à é. avec Riom** they're lying equal with Riom; *Fig* **maintenant, nous sommes à é.** now we're even; *Courses de chevaux* **parier à é. sur un cheval** to lay evens on a horse

égard [egar] **NM** *(point de vue)* **à bien des égards** in many respects; **à cet/aucun é.** in this/no respect; **n'ayez aucune crainte à cet é.** don't worry about that, don't have any worries on that score; **à certains égards** in some respects

▫ **égards NMPL** *(marques de respect)* consideration; **être plein d'égards** *ou* **avoir beaucoup d'égards pour qn** to show great consideration for *or* to be very considerate towards sb; **manquer d'égards envers qn** to show a lack of consideration for *or* to be inconsiderate towards sb; **être sans é.** *ou* **n'avoir aucun é. pour qn** to have no consideration for sb; **avoir des égards pour qn** to be considerate towards sb, to show sb consideration; **elle est toujours accueillie avec les égards dus à son rang** she is always greeted with the respect due to her rank; **il nous a reçus avec beaucoup d'égards** he received us very warmly

▫ **à l'égard de PRÉP 1** *(envers)* towards; **être**

dur/tendre à l'é. de qn to be hard on/gentle with sb; **être injuste à l'é. de qn** to be unjust to(wards) sb; **il a été très gentil à mon é.** he has been very kind to me; **ils ont fait une exception à mon é.** they made an exception for me *or* in my case

2 *(à l'encontre de)* against; **prendre des sanctions à l'é. de qn** to impose sanctions against *or* to apply sanctions to sb

3 *(quant à)* with regard to; **elle émet des résistances à l'é. de ce projet** she's putting up some resistance with regard to the project

❑ **à tous égards** ADV in all respects *or* every respect

❑ **eu égard à** PRÉP in view of, considering; **eu é. à son âge** in view of *or* given his/her age

❑ **par égard pour** PRÉP out of consideration *or* respect for

❑ **sans égard pour** PRÉP with no respect *or* consideration for, without regard for

égaré, -e [egare] ADJ **1** *(perdu → dossier, personne)* lost; *(→ animal)* lost, stray **2** *(affolé → esprit)* distracted; *(→ regard)* wild, distraught; *(→ yeux)* wild; **avoir l'air é.** to look distraught; **avoir le regard é.** to be wild-eyed; **il était é. par la colère** anger made him lose his head; **é. par tant de malheurs** distraught by so many misfortunes

égarement [egarmɑ̃] NM **1** *(folie)* distraction, distractedness; **dans son é., il a oublié de...** he was so distracted he forgot to...; **dans un moment d'é.** in a moment of panic *or* confusion

2 *(perte)* loss

❑ **égarements** NMPL *Littéraire (dérèglements de conduite)* wild behaviour, wildness; **les égarements de la passion** the follies of passion; **revenir de ses égarements** to see the error of one's ways

égarer [3] [egare] VT **1** *(perdre → bagage, stylo)* to lose, to mislay; *(en donnant de mauvaises indications → personne)* to mislead; **il jouait à é. les nouveaux arrivants** it amused him to get the newcomers lost; **é. les soupçons** to avert suspicion

2 *(tromper → opinion, lecteur)* to mislead, to deceive; *(→ jeunesse)* to lead astray; **un électorat égaré par des promesses fallacieuses** voters misled by fraudulent promises

3 *Littéraire (affoler)* to make distraught, to drive to distraction; **la douleur vous égare** you're distraught with pain

▸**s'égarer** VPR **1** *(se perdre → promeneur)* to lose one's way, to get lost; *(→ dossier, clef)* to get lost *or* mislaid; *(→ colis)* to get lost, to go stray; **s'é. dans des considérations secondaires** to get bogged down in minor considerations; **s'é. hors du droit chemin** to go off the straight and narrow

2 *(sortir du sujet)* to wander; **à partir de là, le débat/l'auteur s'égare** from then on, the discussion/author wanders off the point; **ne nous égarons pas!** let's not wander off the point!, let's stick to the subject!; **son esprit s'égare** his/her mind is wandering

3 *Littéraire (s'oublier)* to lose one's self-control, to forget oneself; **quelle grossièreté, vous vous égarez!** how coarse, you're forgetting yourself!

égayant, -e [egejɑ̃, -ɑ̃t] ADJ *Littéraire* cheerful, lively

égayement [egɛmɑ̃] = **égaiement**

égayer [11] [egeje] VT *(personne)* to cheer up; *(chambre, robe, vie)* to brighten up; *(ambiance, récit)* to brighten up, to liven up

▸**s'égayer** VPR *(s'amuser)* to have fun, to enjoy oneself; *(s'animer)* to cheer up; **s'é. aux dépens de qn** to have fun at sb's expense

Égée [eʒe] NPR *Myth* Aegeus

NF *Antiq & Géog* **la mer É.** the Aegean Sea

égéen, -enne [eʒeɛ̃, -ɛn] ADJ *Antiq & Géog* Aegean

e-génération [iʒenerasjɔ̃] NF e-generation

Égérie [eʒeri] NPR *Antiq & Myth* Egeria

❑ **égérie** NF *(inspiratrice)* muse; **elle est l'é. du groupe** she's the driving force of the group

égermer [3] [eʒɛrme] VT to degerm(inate)

égide [eʒid] NF *Myth* aegis

❑ **sous l'égide de** PRÉP *Littéraire* under the aegis of; **prendre qn sous son é.** to take sb under one's wing; **se mettre sous l'é. des lois** to take refuge in the law

Égine [eʒin] NF *Antiq & Géog* Aegina

églantier [eglɑ̃tje] NM *Bot* wild *or* dog rose (bush); **é. odorant** sweetbrier

églantine [eglɑ̃tin] NF *Bot* wild *or* dog rose

églefin [egləfɛ̃] NM *Ich* haddock

Église [egliz] NF *Rel* **l'É.** the Church; **l'É. anglicane** the Church of England, the Anglican Church; **l'É. catholique (romaine)** the (Roman) Catholic Church; **l'É. orthodoxe** the Orthodox Church; **l'É. protestante** the Protestant Church; **l'É. réformée** the Reformed Church; **l'É. réformée de France** = the largest Protestant church in France; **l'É. de scientologie** the Church of Scientology; **l'É. militante/triomphante** the Church militant/triumphant; **l'É. et l'État** Church and State

❑ **église** NF *Rel (édifice)* church; **aller à l'é.** *(pratiquer)* to go to church, to be a churchgoer; **se marier à l'é.** to be married in church, to have a church wedding; **on ne la voit pas souvent à l'é.** she doesn't often come to *or* attend church; **l'é. Saint-Pierre** St Peter's (church)

❑ **d'Église** ADJ **homme d'É.** clergyman; **gens d'É.** priests, clergymen

église-halle [eglizal] *(pl* **églises-halles**) NF *Archit* hall church *(type of medieval church in which the nave and the aisles are all of the same height)*

églogue [eglɔg] NF *Littérature* eclogue

ego [ego] NM *Psy* ego

égocentrique [egɔsɑ̃trik] ADJ egocentric, self-centred

NMF egocentric *or* self-centred person

égocentrisme [egɔsɑ̃trism] NM egocentricity, self-centredness; *Psy* egocentrism

égoïne [egɔin] NF handsaw

égoïsme [egɔism] NM selfishness

égoïste [egɔist] ADJ selfish

NMF selfish man, *f* woman

égoïstement [egɔistəmɑ̃] ADV selfishly

égorgement [egɔrʒəmɑ̃] NM cutting *or* slitting the throat

égorger [17] [egɔrʒe] VT **1** *(couper la gorge de)* to cut *or* to slit the throat of **2** *Fam Vieilli (ruiner)* to bleed white *or* dry

▸**s'égorger** VPR to butcher each other

égorgeur, -euse [egɔrʒœr, -øz] NM,F cut-throat

égosiller [3] [egozije] **s'égosiller** VPR **1** *(crier)* to shout oneself hoarse; **mais je m'égosille à vous le dire!** I've told you so till I'm blue in the face *or* I'm hoarse! **2** *(chanter fort)* to sing at the top of one's voice

ego-surfing [egɔsœrfiŋ] NM *Fam Ordinat* ego-surfing

égotisme [egɔtism] NM egotism

égotiste [egɔtist] ADJ egotistic, egotistical

NMF egotist

égout [egu] NM sewer; **les égouts** the sewers; **é. collecteur** main sewer; **eaux d'é.** sewage; **rat d'é.** sewer rat

égoutier [egutje] NM sewer worker

égouttage[1] [egutaʒ], **égouttement** [egutmɑ̃] NM *(du linge)* leaving to drip-dry; *(de légumes, de la vaisselle)* draining; **é. des légumes dans une passoire** straining vegetables in a sieve

égouttage[2] [egutaʒ] NM *Belg* **1** *(installation)* installation of a sewerage system (**de** in) **2** *(réseau d'égouts)* sewers, sewerage system

égoutter[1] [3] [egute] VT *(linge)* to leave to drip; *(vaisselle, fromage frais, pâtes)* to drain; **é. des légumes dans une passoire** to strain vegetables in a sieve

VI *(vaisselle)* to drain; *(linge)* to drip; **mettre les verres à é.** to put the glasses to drain *or* to drip; **laisser é. la vaisselle** to leave the dishes to drain; **faire é. les haricots** to strain the beans

▸**s'égoutter** VPR *(linge)* to drip; *(légumes, fromage frais, vaisselle)* to drain

égoutter[2] [3] [egute] VT *Belg* to install a sewerage system in

égouttoir [egutwar] NM **1** *(passoire)* strainer, colander; **panier é.** *(d'une friteuse)* basket **2** *(pour la vaisselle → élément de l'évier)* draining board; *(→ mobile)* drainer, draining rack

égoutture [egutyr] NF drop, dribble; **les égouttures du linge** the water dripping off the washing

égrainage [egrenaʒ] = **égrenage**

égrainer [4] [egrene] = **égrener**

égrappage [egrapaʒ] NM *Agr (de raisins, de baies)* destalking, stemming

égrapper [3] [egrape] VT *Agr (raisins, baies)* to destalk, to stem

égrappoir [egrapwar] NM *Agr (en viticulture)* destalking machine

égratigner [3] [egratiɲe] VT **1** *(jambe, carrosserie)* to scratch, to scrape; *(peau)* to graze

2 *Fam (critiquer)* to have a dig *or* a go at; **ils l'ont bien égratigné dans 'Le Monde'** they had a good go at him in the 'Le Monde'; **il s'est fait é. par la presse à propos de sa dernière déclaration** the papers had a real go at him about his latest statement

▸**s'égratigner** VPR **s'é. le genou** to scrape *or* to scratch *or* to skin one's knee

égratignure [egratiɲyr] NF **1** *(écorchure)* scratch, scrape, graze; *Fig (remarque)* dig, gibe; **il s'en est sorti sans une é.** he escaped without a scratch **2** *(rayure)* scratch; **faire une é. à un panneau peint** to scratch a painted panel; **une fine é. le long de l'aile avant** a thin scratch along the front wing

égrenage [egrənaʒ] NM *Agr (du blé, du maïs)* shelling; *(de pois)* shelling, podding; *(du coton)* ginning; *(des graines fourragères)* threshing; *(de raisins, de baies)* picking off

égrènement [egrɛnmɑ̃] NM *(de lumières, d'habitations)* string

égrener [19] [egrəne] VT **1** *Agr (blé, maïs)* to shell; *(pois)* to shell, to pod; *(coton)* to gin; *(graines fourragères)* to thresh; *(raisins, baies)* to pick off; **des groseilles égrenées** redcurrants off the stalk

2 *(faire défiler)* **é. son chapelet** *Br* to say one's rosary, *Am* to tell one's beads; **pendule qui égrène les heures** clock marking out the hours; **é. un chapelet d'injures** to let out a stream of abuse

3 *Can (pain)* to break into crumbs, to crumble

▸**s'égrener** VPR **1** *(grappe de raisin)* to drop off the stalk; *(blé)* to seed

2 *(se disperser → famille, foule)* to scatter *or* to disperse slowly, to trickle away

3 *Littéraire (heures)* to tick by; *(notes)* to be heard one by one; **des lumières s'égrenaient le long du quai** a string of lights stretched along the quay

égreneuse [egrənøz] NF *Agr (de blé)* threshing machine; *(de coton)* gin

égrillard, -e [egrijar, -ard] ADJ *(histoire)* bawdy, ribald; *(personne, ton)* ribald, lewd; **en société, il a des manières égrillardes** he tends to be bawdy in company

égrisage [egrizaʒ] NM *Minér* grinding

égrisé [egrize] NM *Minér* bort, boart, bortz

égrisée [egrize] NF *Minér* bort, boart, bortz

égriser [3] [egrize] VT *Minér* to grind

égrotant, -e [egrɔtɑ̃, -ɑ̃t] ADJ *Vieilli* sickly

égrugeage [egryʒaʒ] NM pounding, grinding

égrugeoir [egryʒwar] NM *(mortier)* mortar; *(moulin)* mill

égruger [17] [egryʒe] VT to pound, to grind

égueulé, -e [egœle] ADJ **1** *(bouteille)* cracked *or* broken at the neck; *(cruche)* cracked *or* broken at the lip **2** *Géol* breached

égueuler [5] [egœle] VT *(récipient)* to crack *or* break the mouth of; *(bouteille)* to crack *or* break the neck of; *(cruche)* to crack *or* break the lip of

Égypte [eʒipt] NF **l' É.** Egypt; **vivre en É.** to live in Egypt; **aller en É.** to go to Egypt; **la Basse-É.** Lower Egypt; **la Haute-É.** Upper Egypt

égyptien, -enne [eʒipsjɛ̃, -ɛn] ADJ Egyptian

NM *(langue)* Egyptian

❑ **Égyptien, -enne** NM,F Egyptian

❑ **égyptienne** NF *Typ* egyptian

égyptologie [eʒiptɔlɔʒi] NF *Antiq* Egyptology

égyptologue [eʒiptɔlɔg] NMF *Antiq* Egyptologist

eh [e] EXCLAM hey!; **eh vous, là-bas!** hey you, over there!; **eh là! attention!** hey, watch out!; **eh, eh! j'en connais un qui a fait une bêtise** who's done something silly then, eh?; **eh quoi, on n'a plus le droit de se reposer?** so can't we even have a rest any more?; **eh! que voulez-vous que j'y fasse?** well what do you want me to do about it?

❑ **eh bien** ADV **1** *(au début d'une histoire)* well, right

2 *(en interpellant)* hey; **eh bien, que faites-vous là-bas?** hey, what are you up to, over there?; **eh bien, comment ça va aujourd'hui?** so how are you today?

3 *(pour exprimer la surprise)* well, well; **eh bien, te voilà riche maintenant** well, well, you're a rich man/woman now; **eh bien, je ne sais pas** well I don't know; **eh bien, je vais m'en occuper** oh well, I'll deal with it

❑ **eh non** ADV well no; **eh non, je ne le lui ai jamais dit de son vivant** well no, I never told him/her when he/she was alive; **eh non, justement ce jour-là je ne peux pas** no, that's the one day I can't do it

❑ **eh oui** ADV well, (actually,) yes; **c'est fini? – eh oui!** is it over? – I'm afraid so!

éhonté, -e [eɔ̃te] ADJ *(menteur, tricheur)* barefaced, brazen, shameless; *(mensonge, hypocrisie)* brazen, shameless

eider [edɛr] NM *Orn* eider (duck)

eidétique [ɛjdetik] ADJ *Psy* eidetic

eidétisme [ɛjdetism] NM *Psy* eidetism

Eiffel [efɛl] NPR **la tour E.** the Eiffel Tower

Culture

LA TOUR EIFFEL

The Eiffel Tower is France's best known monument and has become a symbol for France itself. Standing 324 metres high, it was built in 1889 for the Universal Exhibition in Paris by engineer Gustave Eiffel (whose other achievements include designing the structural frame of the Statue of Liberty in 1886). At first the tower was supposed to be dismantled after the exhibition, but the decision was taken to keep it and it has since become the most distinctive feature of the Paris landscape. It remained the tallest building in the world for 40 years, until New York's Chrysler Building was built in 1930.

Eiger [ajgœr] NM **l'E.** the Eiger

Eilat [ejlat] NM Eilat, Elat

einsteinien, -enne [ɛnstɛnjɛ̃, -ɛn] ADJ Einsteinian

einsteinium [ɛnstɛnjɔm] NM *Chim* einsteinium

Eire [ɛr] NF *Géog* **l'E.** Eire

éjaculat [eʒakyla] NM *Physiol* ejaculate

éjaculateur, -trice [eʒakylatœr, -tris] ADJ ejaculatory

NM **é. précoce** man who suffers from premature ejaculation

éjaculation [eʒakylasjɔ̃] NF *Physiol* ejaculation; **é. nocturne** nocturnal emission, wet dream; **é. précoce** premature ejaculation

éjaculatoire [eʒakylatwar] ADJ *Physiol* ejaculatory

éjaculatrice [eʒakylatris] *voir* **éjaculateur**

éjaculer [3] [eʒakyle] *Physiol* VI to ejaculate

VT to ejaculate

éjectable [eʒɛktabl] *voir* **siège**

éjecter [4] [eʒɛkte] VT **1** *(sujet: arme)* to eject **2** *Aviat & Aut* to eject **3** *Fam (renvoyer)* to kick *or* to chuck *or* to boot out (**de** of); **elle s'est fait é.** she was *or* got thrown *or* kicked out; **il s'est fait é. de l'équipe** he was kicked out of the team; **se faire é. d'une boîte de nuit** to get kicked *or* chucked *or* booted out of a night club

▸**s'éjecter** VPR *Aviat* to eject

éjecteur [eʒɛktœr] NM **1** *Tech* ejector **2** *Ind (d'un réservoir)* outlet works

éjection [eʒɛksjɔ̃] NF **1** *Aviat & Aut* ejection; **éjections volcaniques** ejecta **2** *Fam (expulsion)* kicking *or* chucking *or* booting out

éjointer [3] [eʒwɛ̃te] VT to clip the wing of

Ektachrome® [ɛktakrɔm] NM *Phot* Ektachrome®

élaboration [elabɔrasjɔ̃] NF **1** *(d'une théorie, d'une idée)* working out; *(d'un plan, d'une stratégie)* development; *(d'une constitution, d'une loi, d'un budget etc)* drawing up; *Mktg* **é. de concept** concept development; *Mktg* **é. de produit** product development **2** *Physiol* elaboration **3** *Métal* processing **4** *Psy* **é. psychique** working out repressed emotions

élaboré, -e [elabɔre] ADJ **1** *(complexe → dessin)* elaborate, intricate, ornate; *(→ style littéraire)* studied; *(perfectionné → système)* elaborate, sophisticated; *(détaillé → carte, schéma)* elaborate, detailed; *(→ plan)* elaborate **2** *Bot (sève)* elaborated

élaborer [3] [elabɔre] VT **1** *(préparer → plan, système)* to develop, to design, to work out; *(→ constitution, loi, budget etc)* to draw up **2** *Physiol* to elaborate

▸**s'élaborer** VPR *(système, théorie)* to develop

élæis [eleis] NM *Bot* Elaeis, African oil palm

élagage [elagaʒ] NM *(d'un arbre) & Fig (d'un film, d'un roman etc)* pruning; *Mktg* **é. de la ligne** line pruning

élaguer [3] [elage] VT **1** *(arbre) & Fig (film, roman etc)* to prune **2** *(ôter → phrase, scène)* to edit out, to cut

élagueur [elagœr] NM *Hort* tree-trimmer

El-Alamein [ɛlalamejn] NM *Géog* El Alamein

élan¹ [elɑ̃] NM **1** *(dans une course)* run-up, impetus; **prendre son é.** to take a run-up; **saut avec/sans é.** running/standing jump; **mal calculer son é.** to misjudge one's run-up; **d'un seul é.** *(en sautant)* at one bound; *(en courant)* in one burst; *Fig* **elle courut chez sa mère d'un seul é.** she ran all the way to her mother's without stopping

2 *(énergie)* momentum; **prendre de l'é.** to gather speed *or* momentum; **prendre de l'é. avant de doubler un véhicule** to get up speed before passing *or Br* overtaking a vehicle; *aussi Fig* **être emporté par son (propre) é.** to be carried along by one's own momentum; **emportée par son é. la voiture alla au fossé** gathering momentum, the car went into the ditch; **emporté par son é., il a tout raconté à sa mère** he got carried away and told his mother everything; **le général Dupont brisa l'é. des forces ennemies en Libye** General Dupont broke the momentum of the enemy forces in Libya

3 *(impulsion)* impulse, impetus; **donner de l'é. à une campagne** to give an impetus to *or* to provide an impetus for a campaign; **donner de l'é. à l'industrie** to give a boost to industry

4 *(effusion)* outburst, surge, rush; **élans de tendresse** surges *or* rushes of affection; **é. de l'imagination** flight of fancy; **avoir des élans d'énergie** to have sudden fits *or* surges *or* bursts of activity; **é. de générosité** generous impulse; **avoir des élans** to have a surge of feeling; **contenir les élans du cœur** to check the impulses of one's heart; **l'é. créateur** creative drive; **l'é. patriotique/nationaliste** patriotic/nationalistic fervour; **avec é.** eagerly, keenly, enthusiastically; **dans un é. amoureux** in a surge of love; **il ne connaissait plus aucun des élans de sa jeunesse** he no longer felt the impulses of his youth; **rien n'a jamais pu briser l'é. qui me portait vers elle** nothing could ever break the force which drew me towards her

5 *(ferveur)* fervour; **parler avec é.** to speak with fervour *or* fervently

6 *(accent)* **sa voix avait des élans lyriques** his/her voice had a lyrical ring; **le violon avait des élans plaintifs** the violin had plaintive tones

7 *Golf* swing

8 *Phil* **l'é. vital** the life force

élan² [elɑ̃] NM *Zool* elk; **é. du Canada** moose

élancé, -e [elɑ̃se] ADJ *(silhouette, personne, arbre)* slim, slender; **à la taille élancée** slim-waisted; **à la silhouette élancée** willowy

élancement [elɑ̃smɑ̃] NM sharp *or* shooting *or* stabbing pain; **avoir des élancements dans la cuisse** to have a shooting *or* sharp pain in the thigh; **j'ai un é. au côté** I've got a sharp *or* shooting pain in my side

élancer [16] [elɑ̃se] VI **mon bras m'élance** I've got a shooting *or* sharp pain in my arm

VT **la cathédrale élance ses flèches vers le ciel** the cathedral's spires soar skywards

▸**s'élancer** VPR **1** *(courir)* to rush *or* to dash forward; **s'é. à la poursuite de qn** to dash after sb; **s'é. au secours de qn** to rush to sb's aid, to rush to help sb; **s'é. dans une course effrénée** to break into a mad dash; **s'é. dans la rue** to dash *or* to rush into the street; **s'é. vers qn** to dash *or* to rush towards sb; **s'é. sur qn** to rush *or* make a rush at sb; **le chat s'élança sur moi** the cat flew at me; **s'é. à l'assaut d'une forteresse** to launch an attack on a fortress; **s'é. à l'assaut des vagues** *(navire, surfeur)* to take to the water, *Littéraire* to brave the seas

2 *Sport* to take a run-up; **les coureurs s'élancent sur la piste** the athletes set off at a sprint

3 *Littéraire (se dresser → tour, flèche)* to soar upwards; **s'é. vers le ciel** to soar skywards; *Archit* **le vaisseau de la nef s'élance vers la voûte** the nave soars up to the vaulting

éland [elɑ̃] NM *Zool* eland; **é. du Cap** Cape eland; **é. de Derby** giant eland, Lord Derby's eland

élapidé [elapide] *Zool* NM elapid

❑ **élapidés** NMPL Elapidae

élargir [32] [elarʒir] VT **1** *(rendre moins étroit → veste, robe)* to let out; *(→ chaussure)* to stretch, to widen; *(→ route, rue)* to widen; *(→ tube)* to expand; *(→ trou)* to enlarge; *(→ propriété)* to enlarge, to extend, to add to; **le miroir élargit la pièce** the mirror makes the room look wider; **robe qui élargit les épaules** dress which makes the shoulders look broader

2 *(connaissance, débat)* to broaden, to widen; *(groupe, gamme de produits)* to expand; **é. le cercle de ses relations** to broaden *or* to widen the circle of one's acquaintances; **é. son horizon** to broaden *or* to widen one's outlook; **é. un marché** to broaden a market; **faut-il é. l'Union européenne à la Turquie?** should the EU be enlarged to include Turkey?

3 *(renforcer)* **le gouvernement cherche à é. sa majorité** the government is seeking to increase its majority

4 *Jur (libérer → détenu)* to free, to release

VI *Fam* to get broader ■, to get bigger *(across the shoulders)* ■

▸**s'élargir** VPR **1** *(être moins étroit → sentier, rivière, rue, route)* to widen, to get wider, to broaden (out); *(→ sourire)* to widen; *(→ hanches, épaules)* to broaden (out)

2 *(se relâcher → vêtement)* to stretch; **le col de l'utérus s'élargit** the neck of the womb opens *or* stretches

3 *(groupe)* to expand; *(horizon, débat)* to broaden out, to widen; **le cercle de mes amis s'est élargi** my circle of friends has broadened *or* grown wider; **ses idées se sont élargies au contact des jeunes** he/she became more broadminded through being in contact with young people

élargissement [elarʒismɑ̃] NM **1** *(agrandissement → d'une route, d'une rue)* widening; *(→ d'une robe)* letting out; *(→ de chaussures)* stretching; *(→ d'une propriété)* extension, enlargement

2 *(extension → d'un débat)* broadening, widening; *(→ d'un groupe, des connaissances, d'activités)* expansion; *UE* **l'é. de l'Union européenne** the enlargement *or* expansion of the EU; *Écon* **é. du capital** capital widening; *Mktg* **é. du marché** market expansion

3 *Jur (libération → d'un prisonnier)* freeing, release

élasthanne [elastan] NM *Tex* elastane

élasticimétrie [elastisimetri] NF *Tech* elastometry

élasticité [elastisite] NF **1** *(extensibilité)* stretchiness, stretch, elasticity; **la ceinture a perdu toute son é.** there's no stretch left in the waistband

2 *Anat (d'un corps, de la peau)* elasticity

3 *(souplesse → d'un geste)* suppleness; *(→ d'un pas)* springiness

4 *Fig Péj (laxisme → d'une conscience, d'un règlement)* accommodating nature ■

5 *(variabilité)* flexibility; *(du prix)* elasticity; **l'é. de l'offre/de la demande** the elasticity of supply/of demand; **quelle est l'é. de la demande par rapport au prix du produit?** how elastic is the demand in relation to the price?; **é. croisée de la demande** cross-elasticity of demand; **é. des prix** price elasticity

élastine [elastin] NF *Biol* elastin

élastique [elastik] ADJ **1** *(ceinture, cuir, tissu)* stretchy, elastic; *(badine)* supple; **gomme é.** india rubber; **balle é.** bouncy ball

2 *(agile → démarche)* springy, buoyant; **d'un pas é.** with a springy *or* buoyant step; **elle a un corps é.** she's got a supple body

3 *Fig Péj (peu rigoureux → conscience)* accommodating ■, elastic; *(règlement, principes)* flexible ■, elastic

4 *(variable → horaire)* flexible; *(→ demande, offre, prix)* elastic

5 *Anat (tissu)* elastic

NM **1** *Couture* elastic; **en é.** elastic; **de l'é.** elastic

2 *(de bureau)* rubber band, *Br* elastic band

3 *(jeu)* **jouer à l'é.** to play at elastics

élastiqué, -e [elastike] ADJ elasticated

Élastiss® [elastis] NM = elasticated material

élastomère [elastɔmɛr] *Chim* **ADJ** elastomeric
   NM elastomer

élatérides [elaterid], **élatéridés** [elateride] **NMPL**
Entom click beetles, *Spéc* Elateridae

élavé, -e [elave] **ADJ** washed out

Elbe [ɛlb] **NF 1** *(fleuve)* **l'E.** the (River) Elbe **2 l'île d'E.** Elba

elbeuf [ɛlbœf] **NM** *Tex* tweed *(made at Elbeuf)*

elbot [ɛlbo] **NM** *Belg Ich* halibut

Eldorado [ɛldɔrado] **NM l'E.** Eldorado

eldorado [ɛldɔrado] **NM** Eldorado; **il veut faire de son pays un véritable e. pour les investisseurs étrangers** he wants to turn his country into a land of opportunity for foreign investors

éléate [eleat] *Phil* **ADJ** Eleatic
   NMF Eleatic (philosopher); **les Éléates** the Eleatics

éléatique [eleatik] **ADJ** *Phil* Eleatic

électeur, -trice [elɛktœr, -tris] **NM,F 1** *Pol* voter; **les électeurs** the voters, the electorate; **mes électeurs** the people who voted for me; **les maires et leurs électeurs** the mayors and those who elected them; **grands électeurs** = body electing members of the (French) Senate; **é. flottant** *ou* **indécis** floating voter **2** *Hist* Elector; **Électrice** Electress; **le Grand É.** the Great Elector

électif, -ive [elɛktif, -iv] **ADJ 1** *Pol* elective **2** *(douleur, traitement)* specific

élection [elɛksjɔ̃] **NF 1** *Pol (procédure)* election, polls; **les élections ont lieu aujourd'hui** today is election *or* polling day; **procéder à une é.** to hold an election; **les résultats de l'é.** the results of the election *or* polling; **remporter les élections** to win the election; **annuler l'é. de qn** to unseat sb; **jour des élections** election *or* polling day; **se présenter aux élections** *Br* to stand *or* *Am* to run as a candidate; **élections cantonales** = elections held every three years to elect half the members of the ''Conseil général''; **élections européennes** European elections; **élections législatives** general elections *(held every five years)*; **élections municipales** = elections held every six years to elect members of the ''Conseil municipal''; **é. partielle** by-election; **é. présidentielle** presidential election; **élections prud'homales** industrial tribunal election; **élections régionales** = elections held every six years to elect members of the ''Conseil régional''; **élections sénatoriales** = elections held every three years to elect one third of the members of the ''Sénat''
   2 *(nomination)* election; **son é. à la présidence** his/her election as president *or* to the presidency
   3 *Littéraire (choix)* choice
   4 *Jur* **é. de domicile** address for service; **faire é. de domicile** to state an address for service
   ▫ **d'élection** **ADJ** *(choisi → patrie, famille)* of (one's own) choice *or* choosing, chosen

---

ÉLECTIONS
All French citizens of eighteen or over are entitled to vote in elections, which take place on a Sunday. Polling stations are often set up in local schools. Voters collect leaflets (each corresponding to the different political parties or candidates), go to a booth and put their chosen leaflet into the envelope provided, which is then placed in the ballot box (''l'urne'') supervised by an ''assesseur'', who then utters the words ''a voté!'' Unlike Britain with its first-past-the-post system, the French electoral system is based on a type of proportional representation. Since 2002 presidential elections take place every five years. General elections are also held every five years.

élective [elɛktiv] *voir* **électif**

électivement [elɛktivmɑ̃] **ADV** by choice

électivité [elɛktivite] **NF** electivity

électoral, -e, -aux, -ales [elɛktɔral, -o] **ADJ** *Pol (liste)* electoral; *(succès)* electoral, election *(avant n)*; *(campagne, promesses)* election *(avant n)*; **en période électorale** at election time; **nous avons le soutien é. des syndicats** we can rely on the union vote

électoralisme [elɛktɔralism] **NM** *Péj Pol* electioneering

électoraliste [elɛktɔralist] **ADJ** *Péj Pol (promesse, programme)* vote-catching

électorat [elɛktɔra] **NM 1** *Pol (électeurs)* electorate; **l'importance de l'é. féminin/noir** the importance of the women's/the black vote; **é. flottant** *ou* **indécis** floating voters **2** *Pol (droit de vote)* franchise **3** *Hist* electorate

Électre [elɛktr] **NPR** *Myth* Electra

électret [elɛktrɛ] **NM** *Phys* electret

électrice [elɛktris] *voir* **électeur**

électricien, -enne [elɛktrisjɛ̃, -ɛn] **NM,F 1** *(artisan)* electrician **2** *(commerçant)* electrical goods dealer

électricité [elɛktrisite] **NF 1** *(phénomène)* electricity; **é. atmosphérique** atmospherics; **é. statique** static (electricity)
   2 *(installation domestique)* wiring; **faire installer l'é. dans une maison** to have a house wired; **refaire l'é. dans une maison** to rewire a house; **nous n'avons pas l'é. dans notre maison de campagne** there's no electricity in our country cottage; **allumer l'é.** *(au compteur)* to switch on (at) the mains; **É. de France** = French national electricity company
   3 *(consommation)* electricity (bill); **payer son é.** to pay one's electricity bill; **combien dépenses-tu d'é.?** how much is your electricity bill?
   4 *Fam (tension)* tension, electricity; **il y a de l'é. dans l'air!** there's a storm brewing!

électrification [elɛktrifikasjɔ̃] **NF 1** *(d'une ligne de chemin de fer)* electrification, electrifying **2** *(d'une région)* **l'é. des campagnes reculées** bringing electricity to remote villages

électrifier [9] [elɛktrifje] **VT 1** *(ligne de chemin de fer)* to electrify **2** *(région, village)* to bring electricity to

électrique [elɛktrik] **ADJ** *Élec* **1** *Tech (moteur, radiateur, guitare, train, courant)* electric; *(appareil, équipement)* electric, electrical; *(système, énergie)* electrical; *Fig* **atmosphère é.** highly-charged atmosphere; **chaise é.** electric chair **2** *(par l'électricité statique)* static; *Fam* **elle a les cheveux électriques** her hair is full of static**=** **3** *(couleur)* **bleu é.** electric-blue

électriquement [elɛktrikmɑ̃] **ADV** electrically; **commandé é.** working off electricity

électrisable [elɛktrizabl] **ADJ** electrifiable, chargeable

électrisant, -e [elɛktrizɑ̃, -ɑ̃t] **ADJ 1** *Tech* electrifying **2** *(exaltant)* electrifying, exciting

électrisation [elɛktrizasjɔ̃] **NF** electrifying, charging; **à é. positive** positively charged, charged with positive electricity

électriser [3] [elɛktrize] **VT 1** *Tech* to electrify, to charge; *Élec* **fil électrisé** live wire **2** *Fig (stimuler)* to electrify, to rouse; **de voir cela, ça les a électrisés** this sight electrified them

électro- [elɛktro] **PRÉF** electro-

électro-acoustique, -enne [elɛktroakustiçjɛ̃, -ɛn] *(mpl* **électro-acousticiens**, *fpl* **électro-acousticiennes***)* *Élec* **ADJ** electroacoustics *(avant n)*
   NM,F electroacoustics expert

électroacoustique [elɛktroakustik] *Élec* **ADJ** electroacoustic, electroacoustical
   NF electroacoustics *(singulier)*

électroaffinité [elɛktroafinite] **NF** *Phys* electron affinity

électroaimant [elɛktroɛmɑ̃] **NM** *Élec* electromagnet

électrobiologie [elɛktrobjɔlɔʒi] **NF** *Élec & Biol* electrobiology

électrocapillarité [elɛktrokapilarite] **NF** *Élec & Phys* electrocapillarity

électrocardiogramme [elɛktrokardjɔgram] **NM** *Méd* electrocardiogram; **avoir un é. plat** to flatline

électrocardiographe [elɛktrokardjɔgraf] **NM** *Méd* electrocardiograph

électrocardiographie [elɛktrokardjɔgrafi] **NF** *Méd* electrocardiography

électrocardiographique [elɛktrokardjɔgrafik] **ADJ** electrocardiographic

électrocardioscope [elɛktrokardjɔskɔp] **NM** *Méd* electrocardioscope

électrocautère [elɛktrokotɛr] **NM** *Méd* electrocautery, galvanocautery

électrochimie [elɛktroʃimi] **NF** electrochemistry

électrochimique [elɛktroʃimik] **ADJ** electrochemical

électrochoc [elɛktroʃɔk] **NM** *Méd* electric shock *(for therapeutic purposes)*; **(traitement par) électrochocs** electroconvulsive *or* electroshock therapy; **faire des électrochocs à qn** to give sb electroconvulsive therapy

électrocinétique [elɛktrosinetik] **NF** *Phys* electrokinetics *(singulier)*

électrocoagulation [elɛktrokɔagylasjɔ̃] **NF** *Méd* electrocoagulation

électrocopie [elɛktrokɔpi] **NF** xerography

électrocuter [3] [elɛktrokyte] **VT** to electrocute; **se faire é.** to be electrocuted
   ▸**s'électrocuter** **VPR** to electrocute oneself, to be electrocuted; **attention, on peut s'é.** careful, you could get a fatal (electric) shock; **il a failli s'é.** he got a very bad electric shock

électrocution [elɛktrokysjɔ̃] **NF** electrocution; **vous risquez l'é.** you're at risk *or* in danger of being electrocuted

électrode [elɛktrɔd] **NF** *Élec & Chim* electrode; **é. de masse** earth electrode

électrodéposition [elɛktrodepozisjɔ̃] **NF** *Chim* electrodeposition

électrodiagnostic [elɛktrodjagnɔstik] **NM** *Méd* electrodiagnosis

électrodialyse [elɛktrodjaliz] **NF** *Chim* electrodialysis

électrodomestique [elɛktrodɔmɛstik] **ADJ** **appareils électrodomestiques** household electrical appliances, *Am* electricals
   NM **l'é.** *(appareils)* household electrical appliances *or Am* electricals; *(secteur)* electrical goods, *Am* electricals

électrodynamique [elɛktrodinamik] *Phys* **ADJ** electrodynamic
   NF electrodynamics *(singulier)*

électrodynamomètre [elɛktrodinamɔmɛtr] **NM** *Élec & Phys* electrodynamometer

électroencéphalogramme [elɛktroɑ̃sefalɔgram] **NM** *Méd* electroencephalogram

électroencéphalographe [elɛktroɑ̃sefalɔgraf] **NM** *Méd* electroencephalograph

électroencéphalographie [elɛktroɑ̃sefalɔgrafi] **NF** *Méd* electroencephalography

électrofaible [elɛktrofɛbl] **ADJ** *Phys* electroweak

électroformage [elɛktroformaʒ] **NM** *Métal* electroforming

électrogène [elɛktrɔʒɛn] **ADJ 1** *Ich* electric; **organe é.** *(d'un poisson)* electric organ **2** *Élec* electricity-generating

électrolocation [elɛktrolɔkasjɔ̃], **électrolocalisation** [elɛktrolɔkalizasjɔ̃] **NF** *Ich* electrolocation

électrologie [elɛktrolɔʒi] **NF** electrology

électroluminescence [elɛktrolyminesɑ̃s] **NF** *Phys* electroluminescence

électroluminescent, -e [elɛktrolyminesɑ̃, -ɑ̃t] *Phys* electroluminescent

électrolysable [elɛktrolizabl] **ADJ** *Chim* susceptible to electrolysis

électrolyse [elɛktroliz] **NF** *Chim & Méd* electrolysis

électrolyser [3] [elɛktrolize] **VT** *Chim* to electrolyse

électrolyseur [elɛktrolizœr] **NM** *Chim* electrolyser

électrolyte [elɛktrolit] **NM** *Chim* electrolyte

électrolytique [elɛktrolitik] **ADJ** *Chim* electrolytic

électromagnétique [elɛktromaɲetik] **ADJ** *Phys* electromagnetic

électromagnétisme [elɛktromaɲetism] **NM** *Phys* electromagnetism

électromécanicien, -enne [elɛktromekanisjɛ̃, -ɛn] **NM,F** electrical engineer

électromécanique [elɛktromekanik] *Élec* **ADJ** electromechanical
   NF electromechanical engineering

électroménager [elɛktromenaʒe] **ADJ** *(domestic or household)* electrical; **appareils électroménagers** domestic *or* household appliances, *Am* electricals
   NM **l'é.** *(appareils)* domestic *or* household electrical appliances; *(secteur)* the domestic *or* household electrical appliance industry; **le petit é.** small household appliances

électroménagiste [elɛktromenaʒist] **NMF** dealer in household *or* domestic electrical appliances

électrométallurgie [elɛktrometalyrʒi] **NF** *Métal* electrometallurgy

électrométallurgique [elɛktrometalyrʒik] **ADJ** *Métal* electrometallurgical

électromètre[elɛktrɔmɛtr] NM*Élec* electrometer

électrométrie[elɛktrɔmetri] NF*Élec* electrometry

électromoteur, -trice[elɛktrɔmɔtœr, -tris] *Élec & Tech* ADJelectromotive

  NMelectric motor

électromyogramme [elɛktrɔmjɔgram] NM *Méd* electromyogram

électromyographie [elɛktrɔmjɔgrafi] NF *Méd* electromyography

électron[elɛktrɔ̃] NM*Phys* electron; **é. célibataire** lone electron; **é. libre** free electron; *Fig* maverick; **é. lié** bound electron; **é. négatif** negatron; **é. positif** positron; **canon à électrons** electron tube

électronégatif, -ive[elɛktrɔnegatif, -iv] ADJ*Chim* electronegative

électronégativité [elɛktrɔnegativite] NF *Chim* electronegativity

électronicien, -enne[elɛktrɔnisjɛ̃, -ɛn] NM,F*Électron* electronics engineer; **ingénieur é.** electronics engineer

électronique [elɛktrɔnik] ADJ **1** *Électron (équipement)* electronic; *(microscope, télescope)* electron *(avant n)*; *(industrie)* electronics *(avant n)* **2** *(de l'électron → flux, faisceau)* electron *(avant n)* **3** *Mus* electronic **4** *(réservation, traitement de données, point de vente, argent)* electronic

  NF *Électron* electronics *(singulier)*; **l'é. grand public** the consumer electronics industry; **é. aérospatiale** avionics *(singulier)*

électroniquement [elɛktrɔnikmɑ̃] ADV electronically

électronucléaire [elɛktrɔnykleɛr] ADJ *(centrale, industrie)* nuclear *(avant n)*; **énergie é.** nuclear power

  NMnuclear energy production

électronvolt[elɛktrɔ̃vɔlt] NM*Phys* electronvolt

électro-osmose [elɛktroosmoz] *(pl* **électro-osmoses***)* NF *Chim* electro-osmosis, electroendosmosis

électrophile[elɛktrɔfil] ADJ*Chim* electrophilic

électrophone[elɛktrɔfɔn] NMrecord player

électrophorèse [elɛktrɔfɔrɛz] NF *Chim* electrophoresis

électrophysiologie [elɛktrɔfizjɔlɔʒi] NF *Physiol* electrophysiology

électrophysiologique [elɛktrɔfisjɔlɔʒik] ADJ*Physiol* electrophysiological

électrophysiologiste[elɛktrɔfisjɔlɔʒist] NMF*Physiol* electrophysiologist

électroponcture [elɛktrɔpɔ̃ktyr] NF*Méd* electropuncture

électroportatif, -ive[elɛktrɔpɔrtatif, -iv] ADJ**matériel é.** portable electrical equipment

électropositif, -ive [elɛktrɔpozitif, -iv] ADJ *Chim* electropositive

électropositivité [elɛktrɔpozitivite] NF electropositivity

électropuncture [elɛktrɔpɛ̃ktyr] = **électroponcture**

électroradiologie [elɛktrɔradjɔlɔʒi] NF*Méd* electroradiology

électroradiologiste [elɛktrɔradjɔlɔʒist] NMF *Méd* electroradiologist

électrorétinogramme [elɛktrɔretinɔgram] NM *Méd* electroretinogram

électroscope[elɛktrɔskɔp] NM*Élec* electroscope

électrosensible [elɛktrɔsɑ̃sibl] ADJ*Élec* electrosensitive

électrostatique [elɛktrɔstatik] *Phys* ADJ electrostatic

  NFelectrostatics *(singulier)*

électrostriction [elɛktrɔstriksjɔ̃] NF *Élec & Phys* electrostriction

électrotechnicien, -enne [elɛktrɔtɛknisjɛ̃, -ɛn] NM,F*Élec* electrotechnician

électrotechnique [elɛktrɔtɛknik] *Élec* ADJ electrotechnical

  NF electrotechnics *(singulier)*, electrical engineering

électrothérapeute[elɛktrɔterapøt] NMF*Méd* electrotherapeutist, electrotherapist

électrothérapeutique[elɛktrɔterapøtik] ADJ*Méd* electrotherapeutic

électrothérapie[elɛktrɔterapi] NF*Méd (pratique)* electrotherapy; *(étude)* electrotherapeutics *(singulier)*

électrothermie[elɛktrɔtɛrmi] NF *Élec, Métal & Phys* electrothermics *(singulier)*

électrothermique[elɛktrɔtɛrmik] ADJ*Élec, Métal & Phys* thermoelectrical, electrothermic

électrotropisme[elɛktrɔtrɔpism] NM *Élec* electrotropism

électrovalence [elɛktrɔvalɑ̃s] NF *Chim* electrovalence, electrovalency

électrovalent, -e[elɛktrɔvalɑ̃, -ɑ̃t] ADJ*Chim* electrovalent

électrovalve[elɛktrɔvalv] NF *Tech* electromagnetic valve; *Aut* solenoid; **é. de starter** starter solenoid

électrovanne[elɛktrɔvan] NF*Tech* electrical solenoid, solenoid valve

électrum[elɛktrɔm] NM*Minér* electrum

électuaire[elɛktɥɛr] NM*Pharm* electuary

élégamment [elegamɑ̃] ADV *(s'habiller)* elegantly, smartly; *(maquillée)* smartly; *(écrire, parler)* stylishly, elegantly; *(agir)* courteously; **coiffée é.** with an elegant *or* smart hairstyle

élégance [elegɑ̃s] NF **1** *(chic)* elegance, smartness; **s'habiller avec é.** to dress elegantly *or* smartly

  2 *(délicatesse → d'un geste, d'un procédé)* elegance; *(→ d'une méthode, d'une solution)* neatness; **savoir perdre avec é.** to be a good *or* graceful loser; **elle a eu l'é. de ne pas protester** she had the courtesy not to protest

  3 *(harmonie)* grace, elegance, harmoniousness; **d'une grande é. dans les proportions** very harmoniously proportioned; **l'é. du chat siamois** the elegance *or* grace of a Siamese cat

  4 *(d'un style littéraire)* elegance; *(tournure)* elegant *or* well-turned phrase; *Péj* **style plein d'élégances** over-ornate style

élégant, -e [elegɑ̃, -ɑ̃t] ADJ **1** *(chic → personne, mobilier, vêtement, restaurant, style)* elegant, smart, stylish; **se faire é.** to smarten oneself up

  2 *(courtois → procédé, excuse)* handsome, graceful; *(→ geste, comportement)* courteous; **c'était une façon élégante de me dire que...** it was a polite *or* diplomatic way of telling me that...; **il use de procédés peu élégants** he uses rather callous measures

  3 *(harmonieux → architecture, proportions)* elegant, harmonious, graceful; *(→ démonstration)* elegant, neat; *(→ méthode, solution)* neat; **une façon élégante de résoudre un problème mathématique** a neat solution to a mathematical problem

  NM,F *Vieilli (homme)* dandy; *(femme)* elegant *or* smart woman; **vouloir faire l'é.** to try to look fashionable

élégiaque [eleʒjak] ADJ **1** *Littérature* elegiac **2** *Littéraire (mélancolique)* melancholy

élégie[eleʒi] NF**1** *Antiq* elegy **2** *Littérature (poème, œuvre)* elegy, lament

éléis[eleis] NM*Bot* Elaeis, African oil palm

ÉLÉMENT [elemɑ̃]

| component **1** | ingredient **1** | element **1–5** |
| factor **2** | cell **5** | unit **6, 8** | item **9** |

NM**1** *(partie → d'un parfum, d'une œuvre)* component, ingredient, constituent; *(→ d'une structure, un problème)* element, component, constituent; *(→ d'un médicament)* ingredient; **les éléments d'un ensemble** the elements *or* parts of a whole; *Aut* **é. filtrant en papier** paper filtering element; *Ordinat* **é. de menu** menu item; *Tech* **é. mobile** working part; *Électron* **é. de calculateur** *ou* **de calculatrice** *ou* **électronique** computer unit; *Tech* **é. chauffant** heating unit *or* element

  2 *(donnée)* element, factor, fact; **éléments** data, information; **l'é. décisif** the deciding factor; **éléments d'information** facts, information; **le seul é. à prendre en considération** the only factor to be considered; **j'apporte un é. nouveau au dossier** I have new material to add to the file; **il n'y a aucun é. nouveau** there are no new developments; **aucun é. nouveau à signaler** nothing new to report; **d'après les premiers éléments de l'enquête** according to the initial findings of the inquiry; *Jur* **éléments constitutifs de l'infraction** elements of the offence

  3 *(personne)* element; **des éléments étrangers se sont infiltrés dans le mouvement** foreign elements have infiltrated the movement; **éléments indésirables** undesirable elements,

undesirables; **les éléments les plus conservateurs du parti** the party's most conservative elements; **l'é. féminin** the female element *or* contingent; **l'é. féminin est faiblement représenté dans cette société** there are few women in the company; **c'est un des meilleurs éléments de mon service** he's one of the best people in my department; **il y a de bons éléments dans ma classe** there are some good students in my class; **avec lui, nous avons perdu un très bon é.** we've lost a good man in him

  4 *Chim* element; **l'é. oxygène** the element oxygen; **é. radioactif** radioactive element; **é. de transition** transition element

  5 *Élec (de pile, d'accumulateur)* cell; *(de bouilloire, de radiateur)* element; **batterie de cinq éléments** five-cell battery

  6 *(de mobilier)* **é. (de cuisine)** kitchen unit; **acheter une cuisine par éléments** to buy kitchen units; **éléments préfabriqués** prefabricated *or* ready-made units; **éléments de rangement** storage units

  7 *(milieu)* element; **l'é. liquide** water; **les quatre éléments** the four elements; **lutter contre les éléments (naturels)** to struggle against the elements; **être dans son é.** to be in one's element; **je ne me sens pas dans mon é. ici** I don't feel at home *or* I feel like a fish out of water here

  8 *Mil* unit; **éléments blindés/motorisés** armoured/motorized units; *Mil* **é. de tir** piece of firing *or* range data

  9 *Compta (d'un compte)* item

  ▫ **éléments** NMPL**1** *(notions)* elements, basic principles; **j'en suis resté aux premiers éléments de latin** I've never had more than an elementary knowledge of Latin; **'Éléments de géométrie'** 'Elementary Geometry'

  2 *Biol* **éléments figurés du sang** formed elements of blood

élémentaire [elemɑ̃tɛr] ADJ **1** *(facile → exercice)* elementary; **c'est é.!** it's elementary!

  2 *(fondamental → notion, principe)* basic, elementary; *(→ habitation)* basic, rudimentary; **la plus é. politesse aurait dû l'empêcher de partir** basic good manners *or* common courtesy should have prevented him/her from leaving

  3 *Chim & Phys (relatif à un élément chimique)* elemental; *(relatif à une analyse chimique, à une particule d'atome)* elementary

  4 *Scol* primary

élémentarisme[elemɑ̃tarism] NM*Beaux-Arts* Elementarism

élémentariste [elemɑ̃tarist] *Beaux-Arts* ADJ Elementarist

  NMFElementarist

éléphant [elefɑ̃] NM **1** *Zool* elephant; **é. mâle/femelle** bull/cow elephant; **é. d'Asie/d'Afrique** Indian/African elephant; **é. de mer** sea elephant, elephant seal; **comme un é. dans un magasin de porcelaine** like a bull in a china shop; *Pol* **les Éléphants du parti** = the old guard of the Socialist party **2** *Fam (dans l'argot des marins)* landlubber

éléphanteau, -x[elefɑ̃to] NM*Zool* elephant calf; *(très jeune)* baby elephant

éléphantesque [elefɑ̃tɛsk] ADJ*Fam* elephantine, colossal, mammoth

éléphantiasique [elefɑ̃tjazik] ADJ*Méd* elephantiasic

éléphantiasis[elefɑ̃tjazis] NM*Méd* elephantiasis

éléphantin, -e[elefɑ̃tɛ̃, -in] ADJ*Littéraire* elephantine

élevage[ɛlvaʒ] NM*Agr & Écon* **1** *(activité)* animal husbandry, breeding *or* rearing *(of animals)*; **l'é.** stock breeding; **faire de l'é.** to breed animals; **é. de poulets/volaille** chicken/poultry farming; **é. des abeilles** beekeeping; **é. des animaux à fourrure** fur farming; **é. intensif/en batterie** intensive/battery farming; **é. des bovins** cattle-rearing; **é. des chevaux** horse-breeding; **é. des huîtres** oyster-farming; **é. industriel** factory farming; **é. des lapins** rabbit-breeding; **é. des moutons** sheep-farming

  2 *(entreprise)* farm, *Br* (stock) farm, *Am* ranch, *Austr* station; **un é. de vers à soie/de visons** a silkworm/mink farm; **un é. de porcs** a pig farm

3 *(en œnologie)* élevage *(stage in the wine-producing process between fermentation and bottling)*
❑ **d'élevage** ADJ 1 *(poulet)* battery-reared
2 *(région)* **pays d'é.** *(bovin)* cattle-rearing country; *(ovin)* sheep-farming country

élévateur, -trice [elevatœr, -tris] ADJ 1 *Anat* elevator *(avant n)*; **muscle é.** elevator 2 *Tech (appareil, matériel)* lifting
NM 1 *Anat* elevator 2 *(en manutention)* elevator, hoist; **é. (à fourche)** fork-lift truck; **é. à bascule** tip; **é. à augets** *ou* **à godets** bucket elevator 3 *Élec* **é. de tension** step-up transformer 4 *Can Joual (ascenseur) Br* lift■, *Am* elevator■; *Agr* **é. à grain** grain elevator■

élévation [elevasjɔ̃] NF 1 *(action d'élever → d'un mur, de la voix etc)* raising; *(→ de la température, des prix etc)* raising, increasing; *(→ d'une statue etc)* erection, setting up
2 *(augmentation)* rise; *(de la température, des prix etc)* rise, increase (**de** in); **é. du niveau de vie** rise in the standard of living; **é. du niveau des eaux** rise in water level; **é. du pouls** quickening of the pulse; **é. des températures** rise in temperatures
3 *Math* **é. d'un nombre au carré** squaring of a number; **é. d'un nombre à une puissance** raising a number to a power
4 *Archit (construction)* erection, putting up; *(plan, projection)* elevation; *(tertre)* rise (in the ground), mound
5 *(promotion)* raising; **l'é. à la dignité de...** being elevated to the rank of...
6 *(noblesse → de style)* elevation; *(→ des sentiments, du caractère)* nobility; **é. d'âme** *ou* **d'esprit** high-mindedness; **lire Platon contribue à l'é. de l'esprit** reading Plato improves the mind
7 *Mil* elevation; **donner à un canon 30° d'é.** to fire a gun at an elevation of 30°
8 *Rel* **l'É. (de l'hostie)** *(moment, geste)* the Elevation *(of the Host)*

élévatoire [elevatwar] ADJ lifting *(avant n)*, hoisting *(avant n)*, elevator *(avant n)*

élévatrice [elevatris] *voir* **élévateur**

élève [elɛv] NMF 1 *Scol (enfant)* pupil; *(adolescent)* student; **é. infirmière** student nurse; **é. pilote** trainee pilot; **é. professeur** student *or* trainee teacher 2 *(disciple)* disciple, pupil 3 *Mil* cadet; **é. officier** officer cadet *(in the Merchant Navy)*; **é. officier de réserve** military cadet 4 *Agr* young stock animal 5 *Hort* seedling

élevé, -e [elve] ADJ 1 *(fort → prix, niveau de vie)* high; **le nombre é. des victimes/guérisons** the high number of victims/of patients cured; **taux peu é.** low rate; **pouls é.** rapid pulse
2 *(étage)* high; *(arbre, montagne)* tall; **les branches les plus élevées** the highest *or* top branches; **de la position élevée où j'étais, je voyais trois comtés** from my lofty observation point I could see three counties
3 *(important → position)* high, high-ranking; *(→ rang, condition)* high, elevated; **de rang é.** high-ranking; **l'officier ayant le grade le plus é.** the senior *or* highest-ranking officer; **il occupe un rang é. dans ce parti** he ranks high in the party
4 *Littéraire (noble → inspiration, style)* elevated, noble, lofty; **un sens é. du devoir** a strong sense of duty; **avoir une âme élevée** to be high-minded
5 *(éduqué)* **bien é.** well-mannered, well-bred, well brought-up; **mal é.** bad-mannered, ill-mannered, rude; **c'est très mal é. de répondre** it's very rude *or* it's bad manners to answer back; **c'est un mal é., ce garçon** he has bad manners, that boy
6 *(grandi)* **avec des enfants élevés, je dispose de plus de liberté** now that my children are grown-up, I have more freedom

ÉLEVER [19] [elve]

> VT to bring up 1 ■ to raise 1–8, 10 ■ to breed 2 ■ to erect 4 ■ to elevate 8, 9
> VPR to rise 1, 4, 6 ■ to soar 3 ■ to arise 5 ■ to add up to 7

VT 1 *(éduquer → enfant)* to bring up, to raise; **nous avons été élevés ensemble** we were brought up *or* raised together; **j'ai été élevé dans le catholicisme** I was brought up a Catholic; **é. qn dans du coton** to overprotect sb, to mollycoddle sb; **bébé élevé au sein/au biberon** breast-/bottle-fed baby
2 *Agr (nourrir → bétail)* to breed, to raise; *(→ chevaux)* to rear, to breed; *(→ moutons, chiens, lapins)* to breed; *(→ abeilles, volaille)* to keep
3 *(hisser → fardeau)* to raise, to lift (up)
4 *(dresser → statue, monument, chapiteau)* to erect, to raise, to put up; *(→ les bras, le poing, les yeux)* to raise; *Fig* **é. des autels à qn** to praise sb to the skies
5 *(rehausser → immeuble, mur etc)* to raise, to make higher; *(→ plafond, plancher)* to raise; **é. un mur de 20 cm** to raise a wall by 20 cm, to make a wall 20 cm higher
6 *(augmenter → niveau, volume)* to raise; *(→ prix, température)* to increase, to raise; **é. la voix** *ou* **le ton** to raise one's voice
7 *(manifester → objection, protestation)* to raise; *(→ critique)* to make
8 *(promouvoir)* to elevate, to raise; *(porter à un rang supérieur)* to promote (**au rang de** to); **é. qn au grade d'officier** to promote *or* to raise sb to (the rank of) officer
9 *(ennoblir)* to elevate, to uplift; **une lecture qui élève l'esprit** an elevating *or* uplifting read; **é. le débat** to raise the tone of the debate
10 *Géom* **é. une perpendiculaire** to raise a perpendicular; *Math* **é. un nombre au carré/cube** to square/to cube a number; **é. un nombre à la puissance 3** to raise a number to the power of 3
▸**s'élever** VPR 1 *(augmenter → taux, niveau, prix)* to rise, to go up; **la température s'est élevée de 10 degrés** the temperature has risen by *or* has gone up 10 degrees
2 *(se manifester)* **on entend s'é. des voix** you can hear voices being raised; **un cri s'éleva** a shout went up; **s'é. contre** *(protester contre)* to rise up against; *(s'opposer à)* to oppose; **je m'élève contre la validité de ce testament** I contest the validity of this will
3 *(monter → oiseau)* to soar, to fly *or* to go up, to ascend; *(→ cerf-volant)* to go up, to soar; **l'hélicoptère s'élevait doucement dans les airs** the helicopter rose smoothly into the air
4 *(être dressé → falaise, tour)* to rise; *(→ mur, barricades)* to stand; **là où s'élève maintenant l'école** where the school now stands; **la maison s'élevait dans le soleil couchant** the house stood silhouetted against the setting sun
5 *(paraître → doutes, difficultés)* to arise
6 *Fig (moralement, socialement)* to rise; **s'é. à force de travail** to work one's way up; **s'é. socialement** to climb the social ladder; **s'é. au-dessus de** *(jalousies, passions, préjugés)* to rise above; **s'é. au-dessus de sa condition** to rise above one's condition; **s'é. dans l'échelle sociale** to work one's way up *or* to climb the social ladder; **s'é. à la force du poignet** to work one's way up unaided; **votre âme s'élèvera par des prières constantes** your soul will be elevated by constant prayer; **des lectures qui permettent à l'âme de s'é.** spiritually uplifting reading matter; **ses pensées ne s'élèvent jamais au-delà de sa petite personne** his/her thoughts never rise above himself/herself
7 **s'é. à** *(facture, bénéfices, pertes)* to add up to, to total, to amount to; **la note s'élève à 300 euros** the bill comes to *or* amounts to 300 euros; **le bilan s'élève à 10 morts et 12 blessés** the number of casualties is 10 dead and 12 injured

éleveur, -euse [elvœr, -øz] *Agr* NM,F stockbreeder; **é. de bétail** cattle breeder *or* farmer, *Am* cattle rancher; **é. de chevaux** horse breeder; **é. de chiens** dog breeder; **é. de moutons** sheep farmer; **é. de poulets/volaille** chicken/poultry farmer
❑ **éleveuse** NF **éleveuse à poussins** brooder

élevon [elvɔ̃] NM *Aviat* elevator aileron, elevon

elfe [ɛlf] NM elf, spirit of the air

élider [3] [elide] *Ling* VT to drop, *Spéc* to elide
▸**s'élider** VPR to be dropped, to disappear, *Spéc* to elide

Élie [eli] NPR *Bible* Elijah

éligibilité [eliʒibilite] NF *Pol* eligibility

éligible [eliʒibl] ADJ *Pol* eligible

élimé, -e [elime] ADJ worn, threadbare; **un pantalon é. aux genoux** trousers worn *or* threadbare at the knees

élimer [3] [elime] VT to wear thin
▸**s'élimer** VPR to wear thin, to become threadbare

éliminateur, -trice [eliminatœr, -tris] ADJ 1 *(qui exclut)* eliminative, eliminatory 2 *Physiol* eliminative

élimination [eliminasjɔ̃] NF 1 *Physiol* eliminating, voiding, expelling 2 *(exclusion)* elimination, eliminating, excluding; **procéder par é.** to use a process of elimination; **en procédant par é.** by a process of elimination; *Ind* **é. des déchets** waste disposal; *Rad* **é. des parasites** suppression of noise *or* interference

éliminatoire [eliminatwar] ADJ *(note, épreuve)* eliminatory; *(condition, vote)* disqualifying; **cinq est une note é.** five counts as a fail; **il a eu une note é.** he didn't get a *Br* pass mark *or Am* passing grade
NF *(souvent pl) Sport* preliminary heat

éliminatrice [eliminatris] *voir* **éliminateur**

éliminer [3] [elimine] VT 1 *(se débarrasser de)* to remove, to get rid of; *Physiol (déchets, urine)* to void, to expel; **é. les kilos en trop** to get rid of excess weight; **pour é. le tartre** to remove tartar
2 *Sport* to eliminate, to knock out; **ils ont tous été éliminés pour dopage** they were all disqualified for drug-taking
3 *(rejeter → hypothèse, théorie, possibilité)* to rule out, to eliminate; *(→ candidat, suspect)* to eliminate; **é. qch de** to exclude sth from; **é. un nom d'une liste** to strike *or* to cross a name off a list; **é. qn d'un comité** to throw sb off a committee; **se faire é.** to be eliminated; **être éliminé** *(candidat)* to be knocked out *or* eliminated
4 *(tuer)* to eliminate, to liquidate
5 *Math* to eliminate
USAGE ABSOLU *Physiol* to get rid of *or* eliminate body wastes; **il faut boire pour é.** you have to drink to clean out your system

élinde [elɛ̃d] NF dredging ladder

élingue [elɛ̃g] NF *Tech* sling *(of a crane)*

élinguer [3] [elɛ̃ge] VT *Tech* to sling

élire [106] [elir] VT 1 *Pol (candidat, représentant)* to elect; **é. un député** ≃ to elect *or* return a Member of Parliament; **être élu à une assemblée** to be elected to an assembly; **é. un nouveau président** to elect *or* to vote in a new president; **é. qn président** to elect sb president, to vote sb in as president; **ils l'ont élu membre de leur comité** they co-opted him onto their committee; **se faire é.** to be elected
2 *Littéraire (choisir)* to elect, to choose; **é. qn pour confident** to choose sb as one's confidant
3 *(locution)* **é. domicile à** to take up residence *or* to make one's home in; *Jur* to elect domicile in; **une souris a élu domicile dans notre grenier** a mouse has moved into *or* taken up residence in our attic

Élisabeth [elizabɛt] NPR **la reine É.** Queen Elizabeth

élisabéthain, -e [elizabetɛ̃, -ɛn] ADJ Elizabethan
❑ **Élisabéthain, -e** NM,F Elizabethan

élisait *etc voir* **élire**

Elisée [elize] NPR *Bible* Elisha

élision [elizjɔ̃] NF *Ling* elision; **il y a é. du "e"** the "e" elides

élitaire [elitɛr] ADJ elite *(avant n)*

élite [elit] NF 1 *(groupe)* elite; **une é.** an elite; **l'é. de** the elite *or* cream of; **l'é. de la haute couture** top fashion designers; **les élites** the élite 2 *Suisse Mil* = section of the Swiss army for reservists aged between 20 and 42 (before 1996, between 20 and 32)
❑ **d'élite** ADJ elite *(avant n)*, top *(avant n)*; **personnel d'é.** select *or* hand-picked personnel; *Mil* **régiment/tireur d'é.** crack regiment/shot

élitisme [elitism] NM elitism

élitiste [elitist] ADJ elitist
NMF elitist

élixir [eliksir] NM 1 *Myth & Pharm* elixir; **é. d'amour/de longue vie** elixir of love/life; **é. parégorique** paregoric (elixir) 2 *Arch (quintessence)* quintessence, substance

elle [ɛl] *(pl* **elles**) PRON 1 *(sujet d'un verbe → personne)* she; *(→ chose)* it; *(→ animal de compagnie, bébé, nation)* she, it; **elles** they; **e.**

ele–ell

chante she sings; **elles dansent** they dance; **Sophie est arrivée, e. déjeune avec nous** Sophie has just arrived, she's eating with us; **viendra-t-e.?** will she come?; **eh bien, ta cousine, e. n'est pas près de me revoir** well, your cousin isn't likely to see me again in a hurry; **e. arrivée, la fête a pu commencer** once she had arrived the party was able to start; **e., dégoûtée, a fait la grimace** she grimaced in disgust; **e., e. n'aurait même pas levé le petit doigt** she wouldn't have raised a finger; **e., se marier? tu ne la connais pas!** her get married? you don't know her!; **qui a fait ça? – c'est e.** who did that? – she did *or* her; **ah!, e. est bien bonne, celle-là!** that's a good one!

2 *(emphatique → dans une interrogation)* **ta mère est-e. rentrée?** has your mother come back?; **Sophie a-t-e. appelé?** has Sophie called?; **la télévision est-e. toujours en panne?** is the television still not working?

3 *(emphatique → avec "qui" et "que")* **c'est e. qui est partie la première** she left first; **c'est e. qui me l'a dit** she's the one who told me, it was she who told me; **ce sont elles qui ont voulu partir** they were the ones who wanted to leave, it was they who wanted to leave; **c'est e. que je ne supporte pas** she's the one I can't stand, it's her I can't stand; **son père est déjà là et e. qui n'arrive pas** her father's here already and she hasn't arrived yet; **c'est à e. qu'il veut avoir affaire** it's her he wants to talk to; **c'est à e. de dire si e. veut venir** it's up to her to say if she wants to come or not

4 *(complément → personne)* her; *(→ animal, chose)* it; *(→ animal de compagnie, bébé, nation)* her, it; **elles** them; **je suis content d'e./d'elles** I am pleased with her/them; **dites-le-lui à e.** tell it to her, tell her it; **ce n'est pas à moi, c'est à e.** it's not mine, it's hers; **e. possède une entreprise à e.** she has her own company; **je l'ai entendu dire par une relation à e.** I heard it from a relation of hers; **il n'aime qu'e.** he loves only her; **e. ne pense qu'à e.** she thinks only of herself; **un portrait d'e.** *(qu'elle a fait)* a portrait by her; *(où elle est représentée)* a portrait of her; **il aimait sa patrie et mourut pour e.** he loved his country and died for it; **et e., tu l'oublies?** and are you forgetting HER?; **tu la connais, e.?** do you know her?; **tu les imagines, e. et lui, sur des skis!** imagine the pair of them on skis!

5 *(dans les comparaisons)* **il est mieux qu'e.** he is better than she is *or* than her; **il boit plus qu'e.** he drinks more than she does *or* than her; **je fais mon travail aussi bien qu'e.** I work as well as she does, my work is as good as hers; **je fais comme e.** I do what she does

ellébore [elebɔr] = **hellébore**

elle-même [ɛlmɛm] **PRON** *(désignant une personne)* herself; *(désignant une chose)* itself; *(désignant un bébé, un animal, une nation)* itself, herself; **elles-mêmes** themselves; **mais e. n'est pas sans défauts** but she's no paragon herself; **c'est e. qui me l'a dit** she told me so herself, she herself told me so

elles [ɛl] *voir* **elle**

ellipse [elips] **NF 1** *Math* ellipse **2** *Ling* ellipsis; **parler par ellipses** *(allusivement)* to hint at things, to express oneself elliptically

ellipsoïdal, -e, -aux, -ales [elipsɔidal, -o] **ADJ** *Géom* ellipsoidal

ellipsoïde [elipsɔid] *Géom* **ADJ** ellipsoidal **NM** ellipsoid

elliptique [eliptik] **ADJ 1** *Math* elliptic, elliptical **2** *Ling* elliptical

elliptiquement [eliptikmɑ̃] **ADV** elliptically

élocution [elɔkysjɔ̃] **NF 1** *(débit)* delivery; *(diction)* diction, elocution; **avoir une é. claire** to have clear diction, to enunciate clearly; **avoir une é. trop rapide** to speak too quickly **2** *Belg Scol (exposé)* talk, presentation

élodée [elɔde] **NF** *Bot* water thyme, *Spéc* elodea

éloge [elɔʒ] **NM 1** *(compliment)* praise; **couvrir qn d'éloges** to shower sb with praise; **décerner un très bel é. à qn** to give sb an accolade; **digne d'éloges** praiseworthy; **faire l'é. de** to speak highly of *or* in praise of; **faire son propre é.** to sing one's own praises, to blow one's own *Br* trumpet *or Am* horn

2 *Littéraire (panégyrique)* eulogy; **faire l'é. d'un écrivain** to eulogize a writer; **é. funèbre** eulogy, funeral oration; **prononcer l'é. funèbre de qn** to deliver a eulogy *or* funeral oration in praise of sb

❑ **à l'éloge de PRÉP** (much) to the credit of; **elle a refusé, c'est tout à son é.** she said no, (much) to her credit; **il fait du bénévolat et c'est tout à son é.** to his credit, he does volunteer work; **c'est tout à votre é. d'avoir accepté** it's to your credit that you accepted

'Eloge de l'amour' *Godard* 'In Praise of Love'

élogieuse [elɔʒjøz] *voir* **élogieux**

élogieusement [elɔʒjøzmɑ̃] **ADV** highly, favourably; **il a décrit é. leur demeure** he was full of praise for their house

élogieux, -euse [elɔʒjø, -øz] **ADJ** laudatory, complimentary, eulogistic; **il a été très é. sur ton compte** he spoke very highly *or* most favourably of you; **parler en termes é. de** to speak very highly of, to be full of praise for

éloigné, -e [elwaɲe] **ADJ 1** *(loin de tout → province, village)* distant, remote, faraway

2 *(distant)* **la ville est très éloignée** the town is a long way away *or* off, the town is very far away; **la ville est éloignée de cinq kilomètres** the town is five kilometres away; **les deux villes sont éloignées de 50 kilomètres** the two towns are 50 kilometres apart; **maintenant que tout danger est é.** now that there is no further risk, now that the danger is past; **le point le plus é.** the furthest *or* furthermost point; **maison éloignée de la gare** house a long way from the station; **ce n'est pas très é. de l'aéroport** it's not very far (away) from the airport; **rien ne me tiendra é. de toi** nothing will keep me away from you; **se tenir é. du feu** to keep away from the fire; **se tenir é. de la politique** to keep away from *or* to steer clear of politics; **je n'étais pas é. de croire que l'affaire réussirait** I almost believed that the deal would come off; **je ne suis plus é. de croire que...** I'm coming round to believe that *or* to the belief that...

3 *(dans le temps)* distant, remote, far-off; **notre mariage est encore à une date éloignée** our wedding is still a long way off; **tout cela me semble si é. maintenant** all this seems so distant *or* far away now; **dans un passé/avenir pas si é. que ça** in the not-too-distant past/future; **la date en est trop éloignée pour que je puisse savoir si je serai libre** it's too far away for me to say whether I'll be free or not

4 *(par la parenté)* distant; **nous sommes parents éloignés** we're distantly related; **nous sommes cousins éloignés** we're distant cousins *or* cousins several times removed

5 *(différent)* **é. de** far removed *or* very different from; **rien n'est plus é. de ma pensée** nothing could be *or* nothing is further from my thoughts; **c'est assez é. de ce que j'ai fait jusqu'à maintenant** it's quite different from what I've been doing up to now

éloignement [elwaɲmɑ̃] **NM 1** *(distance dans l'espace)* distance, remoteness; *(dans le temps)* remoteness; **l'é. fait paraître la maison minuscule** distance makes the house look tiny; **l'é. du village ne facilite pas l'organisation des secours** the remoteness of the village makes rescue work more difficult; **l'é. de nos deux bureaux ne favorise pas la communication** the distance between our two offices does not help communication; **avec l'é. on arrive mieux à comprendre ce qui s'est passé** with the benefit of hindsight *or* the passage of time it is easier to understand what happened

2 *(fait d'être éloigné)* absence; **je ne supporte plus notre é.** I can't bear us to be apart any longer; **l'é. est difficile à vivre** it is difficult to be apart *or* separated; **l'é. de la vie politique m'a fait réfléchir** being away from politics made me do some thinking

3 *(mise à distance)* taking away, removing, removal; **le tribunal a ordonné l'é. de mes enfants** the court has ordered that my children be taken away from me; **l'é. de sa famille est nécessaire à sa guérison** his/her family must be kept away if he/she is to recover

éloigner [3] [elwaɲe] **VT 1** *(mettre loin → dans l'espace)* to move *or* to take away; **é. sa chaise de la table** to move one's chair away from the table; **é. qn du feu/de la voiture** to move sb away from the fire/car; **ils disent avoir éloigné l'enfant pour son propre bien** they say they took the child away for his/her own good; **ce trajet nous éloigne du centre ville** this route takes us away from the centre of town; **les verres concaves éloignent les objets** concave mirrors make objects look distant; **ça nous éloignerait du sujet** that would take us away from the point

2 *(dans le temps)* **chaque jour m'éloigne un peu plus de cette époque** that time recedes with each day that passes

3 *(séparer)* **é. qn de** to take sb away from; **mon travail m'a éloigné de ma famille** my work's kept me away from my family; **mon travail m'éloigne de toute vie sociale** my work makes it impossible to socialize; **elle a tout fait pour l'é. de moi** she tried everything to take him/her away from me; **tes parents cherchent à m'é. de toi** your parents are trying to keep me away from you; **é. qn du pouvoir** to keep sb out of power; **il a éloigné tous ses amis par son snobisme** his snobbish ways have alienated all his friends

4 *(repousser → insectes, bêtes féroces, mauvaises odeurs)* to keep off, to keep at bay

5 *(dissiper → idée, souvenir)* to banish, to dismiss; *(→ danger)* to ward off; **é. les soupçons de qn** to avert suspicion from sb; **é. une crainte/une pensée** to banish a fear/dismiss a thought

6 *(reporter → échéance)* to postpone, to put off

▸**s'éloigner VPR 1** *(partir → tempête, nuages, orage)* to pass, to go away; *(→ véhicule)* to move away (**de** from); *(→ personne)* to go away (**de** from); **les bruits de pas s'éloignèrent** the footsteps grew fainter; **s'é. à la hâte/à coups de rame** to hurry/to row away; **ne vous éloignez pas trop, les enfants** don't go too far (away), children; **éloignez-vous du bord de la falaise** move away *or* get back from the edge of the cliff; **éloignez-vous de cette ville quelque temps** leave this town for a while; **ne vous éloignez pas!** don't go too far away!; **j'ai fait s'é. les enfants de la fenêtre** I told the children to come away from the window; *Fig* **s'é. du sujet** to wander away from *or* off the point

2 *(s'estomper → souvenir, rêve)* to grow more distant *or* remote; *(→ crainte)* to go away; *(→ danger)* to pass

3 *(s'isoler)* to move *or* to grow away; **s'é. du monde des affaires** to move away from *or* to abandon one's involvement with the world of business; **s'é. de tout le monde** to distance oneself from everybody

4 *(se détourner)* **s'é. de la réalité** to lose touch with reality; **s'é. de la vérité** to stray *or* wander from the truth; **s'é. de son devoir** to neglect one's duty

5 *(affectivement)* **s'é. de qn** to grow away from sb; **il la sentait qui s'éloignait de lui** he could feel that she was growing away from him *or* becoming more and more distant; **il s'est lentement éloigné de nous** he slowly drifted away *or* grew away from us; **je sens bien que tu t'éloignes (de moi)** I feel you're growing away from me; **peu à peu ils se sont éloignés l'un de l'autre** they gradually drifted apart

6 *(dans le temps)* **plus on s'éloigne de cette période...** the more distant that period becomes...

éloise [elwaz] **NF** *Can (en acadien)* flash of lightning

élongation [elɔ̃gasjɔ̃] **NF 1** *Méd (d'un muscle)* strained *or* pulled muscle; *(d'un ligament)* pulled ligament; **se faire une é.** *(d'un muscle)* to strain *or* to pull a muscle; *(d'un ligament)* to pull a ligament; **je souffre d'une é. à la jambe** *(muscle)* I've strained *or* pulled a muscle in my leg **2** *Phys* displacement **3** *Astron* elongation

élonger [17] [elɔ̃ʒe] **VT** *Naut* to lay out, to run out

éloquemment [elɔkamɑ̃] **ADV 1** *(en parlant bien)* eloquently **2** *(avec expressivité)* eloquently, expressively **3** *(avec persuasion)* eloquently, persuasively

éloquence [elɔkɑ̃s] **NF 1** *(art de parler)* eloquence, fine oratory **2** *(expressivité)* eloquence, expressiveness; **avec é.** eloquently **3** *(persuasion)* persuasiveness, eloquence

éloquent, -e [elɔkã, -ãt] **ADJ 1** *(parlant bien)* eloquent; **il est très é.** he's a fine speaker

2 *(convaincant → paroles)* eloquent, persuasive; *(→ chiffres, réaction)* eloquent; **un discours é.** an eloquent speech

3 *(expressif)* eloquent, expressive; **le geste était très é.** the gesture said it all; **ces images sont éloquentes** these pictures speak volumes *or* for themselves; **52 à 0, le score est é.** 52 nil: the score speaks for itself; **son expression dégoûtée était éloquente** his/her expression of disgust said it all

Elseneur [ɛlsənœr] **NPR** Elsinore

ELSJ [ɔɛlɛsʒi] **NM** *UE (abrév* **Espace de liberté, de sécurité et de justice)** AFSJ

Eltsine [ɛltsin] **NPR Boris E.** Boris Yeltsin

élu, -e [ely] **PP** *voir* **élire**

    ADJ 1 *Rel* chosen **2** *Pol* elected; **président é.** president elect

    NM,F 1 *Pol (député)* elected representative; *(conseiller)* elected representative, councillor; **les élus locaux** local councillors **2** *Hum (bien-aimé)* **qui est l'heureux é.?** who's the lucky man?; **l'é. de mon/ton cœur** my/your beloved **3** *Rel* **les élus** the chosen ones, the elect

éluant [elyã] **NM** *Chim* eluant, eluent

élucidation [elysidasjõ] **NF** elucidation

élucider [3] [elyside] **VT** *(mystère)* to elucidate, to explain, to clear up; *(problème, texte)* to elucidate, to clarify

élucubrations [elykybrasjõ] **NFPL** *Péj Littéraire* ravings, rantings

élucubrer [3] [elykybre] **VT** *Péj Littéraire* to dream up

éluder [3] [elyde] **VT** to elude, to evade; **é. le paiement de l'impôt** to evade payment of tax

éluer [7] [elye] **VT** *Chim* to elute

élusif, -ive [elyzif, -iv] **ADJ** elusive

élut *etc voir* **élire**

élution [elysjõ] **NF** *Chim* elution

éluvial, -e, -aux, -ales [elyvjal, -o] **ADJ** *Géol* eluvial

éluvion [elyvjõ] **NF** *Géol* eluvium

Élysée [elize] **NM 1** *Myth* Elysium **2** *Pol* **(le palais de) l'É.** the Élysée Palace *(the official residence of the French President)*

Culture
L'ÉLYSÉE
This eighteenth-century palace near the Champs-Élysées in Paris is the official residence of the French President. The name is often used to refer to the presidency itself.

élyséen, -enne [elizeɛ̃, -ɛn] **ADJ 1** *Myth* Elysian **2** *Pol* of/from the Élysée Palace, presidential

élytre [elitr] **NM** *Entom* elytron, elytrum

elzévir [ɛlzevir] **NM** *Typ* elzevir

elzévirien, -enne [ɛlzevirjɛ̃, -ɛn] **ADJ** *Typ* elzevir, elzevirian

émaciation [emasjasjõ] **NF** emaciation

émacié, -e [emasje] **ADJ** emaciated, wasted

émaciement [emasimã] **NM** emaciation

émacier [9] [emasje] **VT** to emaciate

    ►**s'émacier** **VPR** to become emaciated *or* wasted

émail [emaj] *(pl sens* **1, 2 émaux** [emo], *pl sens* **3 émails)* **NM 1** *(matière) Cér (sur porcelaine)* glaze; *Littéraire* **l'é. des prés** the variegated colours of the meadows

2 *(objet)* piece of enamelware *or* enamelwork

3 *Anat* enamel

    ❑ **émaux** **NMPL** coloured enamels; **faire des émaux** to do enamel work

    ❑ **d'émail, en émail** **ADJ** enamel *(avant n)*, enamelled

e-mail [imɛl] *(pl* **e-mails)* **NM** *Ordinat* e-mail; **envoyer qch par e.** to send sth by e-mail; **envoyer un e. à qn** to e-mail sb

émaillage [emajaʒ] **NM 1** *(en décoration)* enamelling **2** *Cér* glazing

émailler [3] [emaje] **VT 1** *(en décoration)* to enamel; **émaillé au four** stove-enamelled

2 *Cér (porcelaine)* to glaze

3 *(parsemer)* to dot, to scatter, to speckle; **le pré est émaillé de coquelicots, les coquelicots émaillent le pré** the field is scattered *or* dotted *or* speckled with poppies; **é. un discours de citations** to pepper *or* to sprinkle a speech with

quotations; **texte émaillé de métaphores** text littered with *or* full of metaphors; **une lettre émaillée de fautes** a letter riddled with mistakes; **un ciel émaillé d'étoiles** a star-studded sky

émaillerie [emajri] **NF 1** *(art)* enamelling **2** *(produits)* enamelware, enamelwork

émailleur, -euse [emajœr, -øz] **NM,F** enamel worker

émaillure [emajyr] **NF** enamelling, enamel work

émanation [emanasjõ] **NF** *(expression)* expression; **l'é. de la volonté populaire** the expression of the people's will; **être l'é. de qch** to emanate from sth; **ce journal est une é. du pouvoir** this paper is a mouthpiece for the government

    ❑ **émanations** **NFPL** *(vapeurs)* smells, emanations; **des émanations de gaz** a smell of gas; **émanations pestilentielles** miasmas, foul emanations; **émanations volcaniques** volatiles; **émanations toxiques** toxic fumes

émanché, -e [emãʃe] *Hér* **ADJ** dancetty

    NM dancette

émancipateur, -trice [emãsipatœr, -tris] **ADJ** emancipatory, liberating

    NM,F emancipator, liberator

émancipation [emãsipasjõ] **NF 1** *(libération → gén)* emancipation; *(→ de la femme)* emancipation, liberation; *Fig (→ de l'esprit, de la pensée etc)* liberation, freeing **2** *Jur* emancipation

émancipatrice [emãsipatris] *voir* **émancipateur**

émancipé, -e [emãsipe] **ADJ** *(peuple)* emancipated; *(femme)* emancipated, liberated

    NM,F *(sans préjugés)* free spirit

émanciper [3] [emãsipe] **VT 1** *(libérer → gén)* to emancipate; *(→ femmes)* to emancipate, to liberate; **é. qn de** to liberate *or* to free sb from

2 *Jur* to emancipate

    ►**s'émanciper** **VPR 1** *(se libérer → gén)* to become emancipated; *(→ femme)* to become emancipated *or* liberated; **s'é. de** to become free from; **sa peinture s'est émancipée de tout académisme** his/her painting has freed itself from any hint of academicism; **elle n'a jamais réussi à s'é. de l'éducation stricte qu'elle a reçue** she never managed to break free from her strict upbringing

2 *Péj (devenir trop libre)* to become rather free in one's ways; **elle s'est drôlement émancipée** she's become very liberated

émaner [3] [emane] **émaner de** **VT IND** *(sujet: odeur, lumière, ordre)* to emanate from, to come from; *(sujet: demande, mandat)* to come from, to be issued by; *(sujet: autorité, pouvoir)* to issue from; **le doux parfum qui émane du chèvrefeuille** the sweet fragrance coming *or* emanating from the honeysuckle; **il émanait d'elle un charme mélancolique** she had an aura of melancholy charm

émargement [emarʒəmã] **NM 1** *Admin (fait de signer)* signing; **é. d'un contrat** initialling a contract; **feuille d'é.** *(de présence)* attendance sheet; *(de paie)* pay sheet **2** *Admin (signature)* signature **3** *(annotation)* marginal note **4** *Typ (de pages)* trimming

émarger [17] [emarʒe] **VT 1** *Admin (document, compte etc)* to initial (in the margin); *(signer)* to sign; *(courrier)* to sign for; *(annoter)* to annotate

2 *(réduire la marge de)* to trim

    ❑ **émarger à** **VT IND** to draw one's salary from; **é. au budget de l'État** to be paid out of state funds; **il émarge aux fonds secrets** he's paid out of the secret funds; **il émarge à cinquante mille par mois** his monthly salary is fifty thousand, he gets paid fifty thousand a month

e-marketer [imarketœr] **NM** *Ordinat* e-marketer

e-marketing [imarketiŋ] **NM** *Ordinat* e-marketing

émasculation [emaskylasjõ] **NF 1** *(castration)* emasculation, emasculating **2** *Littéraire (affaiblissement → gén)* emasculation, weakening; *(→ d'une œuvre)* weakening; **l'é. d'une politique** taking all the teeth out of a policy

émasculer [3] [emaskyle] **VT 1** *(castrer)* to emasculate **2** *Littéraire (affaiblir → politique, directive)* to weaken; *(→ œuvre)* to weaken

émaux [emo] *voir* **émail**

embâcle [ãbakl] **NM** *(obstruction dans un cours d'eau)* blockage; *(par un bloc de glace)* ice block *or* jam

emballage [ãbalaʒ] **NM 1** *Mktg & Tech (gén)* packaging; *(papier)* wrapper; *(matière)* wrapping *or* packing materials; **e. consigné** returnable packaging; **l'e. est consigné** there is a deposit on the packaging; **glaces en e. consigné** ice-cream sold in returnable containers; **e. compris** packaging included; **e. gratuit** packaging free of charge; **e. récupérable** recoverable packaging; **e. sous vide** vacuum-pack; **emballages vides** empty packaging; **e. bulle** blister pack; **e. factice** dummy pack; **e. géant** giant-sized pack; **e. d'origine** original packaging; **e. pelliculé** bubble pack; **e. perdu** non-returnable packaging; **e. de présentation, e. présentoir** display pack; **e. réutilisable** recyclable packaging; **e. transparent** blister pack

2 *Tech (processus → gén)* packing *or* wrapping (up), packaging; *(→ dans du papier)* wrapping (up)

3 *Vieilli Cyclisme* final sprint

    ❑ **d'emballage** **ADJ** *(papier)* wrapping; **toile d'e.** canvas wrapper

emballagiste [ãbalaʒist] **NM** *(créateur)* packaging designer; *(fabricant)* packaging manufacturer

emballant, -e [ãbalã, -ãt] **ADJ** *Fam* inspiring, thrilling, exciting; **une proposition emballante** an attractive *or* exciting proposition; **pas très e.** not very exciting

emballé, -e [ãbale] **ADJ** *Fam* (mad) keen, enthusiastic■; **il était complètement e. par l'idée** he was completely bowled over by the idea

emballement [ãbalmã] **NM 1** *(d'un cheval)* bolting; *(d'un moteur)* racing; **l'e. des cours à la Bourse** the Stock-Market boom; **cela aboutirait certainement à l'e. de l'économie** that would definitely lead to the economy spiralling out of control

2 *(enthousiasme)* sudden passion, flight *or* burst of enthusiasm; **son e. soudain pour le jazz** his/her sudden craze for jazz

3 *(emportement)* **il a des emballements** he gets worked up very easily; **dans un moment d'e.** without thinking; **pas d'e.** *(par enthousiasme)* let's not get carried away!; *(par colère)* let's not get worked up!

emballer [3] [ãbale] **VT 1** *Mktg & Tech (empaqueter → marchandises)* to pack (up); *(dans du papier → marchandises)* to package; *(→ cadeau)* to wrap (up); **emballé sous vide** vacuum-packed

2 *(moteur)* to race

3 *Fam (enthousiasmer → sujet: projet, livre)* to grab, to thrill (to bits); **ça l'a vraiment emballé** he was really taken with it; **ça n'a pas l'air de l'e.** he/she doesn't seem mad keen on the idea; **ça ne m'emballe pas vraiment de les voir** I'm not exactly thrilled about seeing them *or* mad keen to see them

4 *très Fam (arrêter → truand) Br* to nick, *Am* to bust

5 *très Fam (partir avec → partenaire sexuel) Br* to pull, to get off with, *Am* to pick up

6 *très Fam (embrasser)* to French kiss, *Br* to snog

    ►**s'emballer** **VPR 1** *(cheval)* to bolt; *(moteur)* to race; *(cours, taux)* to take off

2 *Fam (s'enthousiasmer)* to get carried away; **ne t'emballe pas trop vite!** don't get carried away!; **s'e. pour qch** to get excited about sth■

3 *(s'emporter)* to flare *or* to blow up

4 *Bourse (cours, monnaie)* to spiral out of control

emballeur, -euse [ãbalœr, -øz] **NM,F** packer

embarbouiller [3] [ãbarbuje] *Fam* **VT** to confuse■, to muddle■, to befuddle■

    ►**s'embarbouiller** **VPR** to get mixed *or* muddled up■

embarcadère [ãbarkadɛr] **NM** landing stage, pier

embarcation [ãbarkasjõ] **NF** (small) boat *or* craft

embardée [ãbarde] **NF** *(d'une voiture)* swerve, lurch; *(d'un bateau)* yaw, lurch; **faire une e.** *(voiture)* to swerve, to lurch; *(bateau)* to yaw, to lurch

embardoufler [3] [ãbardufle] *Suisse Fam* **VT** *(de peinture, de crème, de boue)* to cover■ (**de** in); **il a le visage embardouflé de confiture** his face is covered in jam

    ►**s'embardoufler** **VPR** to get dirty■

embargo [ãbargo] **NM 1** *Naut* embargo; **mettre l'e.**

sur un navire to lay *or* to put an embargo on a ship, to embargo a ship **2** *Écon* embargo; **mettre un e. sur** to enforce an embargo on, to embargo; **lever l'e. sur les ventes d'armes** to lift *or* to raise the embargo on arms sales; **e. commercial** trade embargo; **e. économique** economic embargo

embarqué, -e [ɑ̃barke] ADJ **1** *Aut & Aviat* on-board **2** *Journ (journaliste, reporter)* embedded

embarquement [ɑ̃barkəmɑ̃] NM **1** *(action d'embarquer* → *de marchandises)* loading; *(*→ *à bord d'un navire)* shipping; *Rail & Mil (*→ *de troupes)* entrainment; *Rail* **quai d'e.** departure platform; *(de chargement)* loading platform

2 *(action de s'embarquer* → *sur un navire)* embarkation, boarding; *(*→ *dans un avion, un train)* boarding; **le vol 123 est prêt pour l'e.** flight 123 is ready for boarding *or* is now boarding; **e. immédiat porte 16** now boarding at gate 16

'**L'Embarquement pour l'île de Cythère**' *Watteau* 'Embarkation for Cythera'

embarquer [3] [ɑ̃barke] VT **1** *Transp (matériel, troupeau)* to load; *(passagers)* to embark, to take on board; *(dans un navire* → *marchandises)* to ship; *Rail & Mil (troupes)* to entrain

2 *Naut* **e. de l'eau** to take in *or* to ship water

3 *Fam (emporter* → *voiture, chien)* to cart off *or* away; **m'embarque pas mon blouson!** don't walk *or* waltz off with my jacket!

4 *Fam (voler)* to pinch, *Br* to nick; **les voleurs avaient tout embarqué dans le salon** the burglars had walked off with everything there was in the living room

5 *Fam (arrêter* → *gang, manifestant)* to pull in; **se faire e. par les flics** to get pulled in by the police

6 *Fam (entraîner)* to drag off; **ils m'ont embarqué au match** they dragged me off to the match; **c'est eux qui l'ont embarqué dans cette affaire** they're the ones who got him involved *or* mixed up in this business ▪ **son divorce l'a embarqué dans un procès sans fin** his divorce got him involved *or* embroiled in an endless lawsuit ▪ **c'est un chemin non carrossable, où nous embarques-tu?** this is a dirt track, where are you taking us (off) to? ▪

7 *Fam (commencer)* **la réunion est bien/mal embarquée** the meeting's got off to a flying/lousy start

VI **1** *(aller à bord)* to board, to go aboard *or* on board; **e. (sur un navire)** to go on board *or* to board (a ship); **e. (dans un train/un autobus)** to get on *or* to board (a train/bus); **une personne supplémentaire peut e. dans ma voiture** there's room for one more in my car

2 *(partir en bateau)* to embark (**pour** for); **nous embarquons demain pour Rio** we're embarking *or* sailing for Rio tomorrow

3 *Naut* **l'eau embarquait dans les cales** the holds were taking in *or* shipping water

▸ **s'embarquer** VPR **1** *(aller à bord)* to embark, to go on board, to board; *(partir)* to embark (**pour** for); **s'e. pour une croisière** to embark on a cruise; **s'e. sur un navire** to go on board *or* to board a ship

2 *(s'engager)* **s'e. dans** to embark on *or* upon, to begin, to undertake; **s'e. dans une aventure financière** to embark on *or* to launch oneself into a business venture; **dans quelle histoire me suis-je embarqué!** what sort of a mess have I got myself into!; **je ne savais pas dans quoi je m'embarquais en acceptant** I didn't know what I was walking into *or* getting mixed up in when I said yes

embarras [ɑ̃bara] NM **1** *(malaise)* embarrassment, confusion; **à mon grand e., il m'a embrassé** to my great embarrassment, he kissed me; **répondre avec e.** to reply with embarrassment, to reply embarrassedly *or* in confusion; **plonger qn dans l'e.** to embarrass sb

2 *(souci)* **l'e., les e.** trouble; **tout l'e. que tu me causes** all the trouble you give me; **avoir des e. financiers** *ou* **d'argent** to be in financial difficulties, to have money problems; **être dans l'e.** *(dans la pauvreté)* to be short of money

3 *(cause de souci)* nuisance, cause of annoyance; **être un e. pour qn** to be a nuisance to sb

4 *(position délicate)* predicament, awkward position *or* situation; **être dans l'e.** *(mal à l'aise)* to be in a predicament *or* in an awkward position; *(face à un dilemme)* to be in a *or* caught on the horns of a dilemma; **ma question l'a mis dans l'e.** my question put him on the spot; **tirer un ami d'e.** to help a friend out of a predicament; **pour le tirer d'e., je suis allé sonner à la porte** to rescue him from an awkward situation *or* to get him out of his predicament, I went and rang the bell; **l'e. du choix** an embarrassment of riches; **on les a en dix teintes, vous avez** *ou* **vous n'avez que l'e. du choix** they come in ten different shades, you're spoilt for choice; **on n'a pas l'e. du choix, il faut accepter** we don't have much of a choice, we have to accept

5 *Péj (simagrées)* **faire des e.** to make a fuss

6 *Méd* **e. gastrique** upset stomach, stomach upset

7 *Vieilli* **les e. de la circulation** traffic congestion; **les e. de Paris** street congestion in Paris

embarrassant, -e [ɑ̃barasɑ̃, -ɑ̃t] ADJ **1** *(gênant* → *silence, situation)* embarrassing, awkward **2** *(difficile* → *problème, question)* awkward, thorny, tricky **3** *(encombrant* → *colis, vêtement)* cumbersome

embarrassé, -e [ɑ̃barase] ADJ **1** *(gêné* → *personne)* embarrassed; *(*→ *sourire, regard)* embarrassed, uneasy; *(*→ *gestes)* hampered; **avoir l'air e.** to look embarrassed *or* awkward; **dès qu'il met un costume, ses gestes sont embarrassés** he feels hampered in a suit; **me voilà bien e.** I'm in a really awkward situation, I'm really embarrassed

2 *(confus* → *explication)* confused, muddled; *(*→ *style)* awkward; **explications embarrassées** involved *or* confused explanations

3 *(encombré* → *table, pièce etc)* cluttered; **avoir les mains embarrassées** to have one's hands full

4 *(pauvre)* short (of money); **je me trouve plutôt e. en ce moment** I'm a bit short (of money) at the moment

5 *Méd* **avoir l'estomac e.** to have an upset stomach; **avoir la langue embarrassée** to have a coated *or* furred tongue

embarrasser [3] [ɑ̃barase] VT **1** *(mettre mal à l'aise)* to embarrass; **ça m'embarrasse de lui demander son âge** I'm embarrassed to ask him/her how old he/she is; **tu m'embarrasses beaucoup en me demandant ce service** you really embarrass me *or* put me in a very awkward situation by asking me this favour; **elle n'a dit cela que pour m'e.** she only said that to embarrass me *or* to make me feel ill at ease

2 *(rendre perplexe)* **ce qui m'embarrasse le plus c'est l'organisation du budget** what I find most awkward is how to organize the budget; **être embarrassé pour trouver le mot juste** to be at a loss for the right word; **je serais bien embarrassé de dire qui a raison** I'd be hard put *or* at a loss to decide who was right

3 *(encombrer* → *gén)* to clutter up, to obstruct; *(*→ *personne)* to hamper; *(*→ *table, pièce etc)* to clutter up (**de** with); **des colis embarrassaient le couloir** packages were cluttering up *or* obstructing the corridor; **laisse ta valise ici, elle va t'e.** leave your suitcase here, it'll get in your way; **cette valise t'embarrasse, laisse-moi la porter** that suitcase is cumbersome for you, let me carry it; **je peux poser mon manteau? il m'embarrasse** can I put my coat down? it's a bit of a nuisance; **si je t'embarrasse, dis-le moi** please tell me if I'm in your way

4 *Méd* **e. l'estomac** to cause a stomach upset

▸ **s'embarrasser** VPR **1** **s'e. dans qch** *(s'empêtrer dans)* to trip over sth, to get tangled up in sth; *Fig* **s'e. dans ses mensonges/explications** to get tangled up in one's lies/explanations

2 **s'e. de qn/qch** *(s'encombrer de)* to burden oneself with sb/sth

3 *(s'inquiéter de)* **pour réussir dans ce métier, il ne faut pas s'e. de scrupules** you mustn't trouble *or* burden yourself with scruples if you want to succeed in this job; **sans s'e. de présentations** without bothering with the (usual) introductions

embarrer [3] [ɑ̃bare] VI to place a lever underneath *(a heavy object, in order to lift it)*

▸ **s'embarrer** VPR *(cheval)* to get a leg over the pole

embarrure [ɑ̃baryr] NF *Méd* depressed skull fracture

embase [ɑ̃baz] NF *Menuis* base

embasement [ɑ̃bazmɑ̃] NM *Archit & Constr* foundations

embastillement [ɑ̃bastijmɑ̃] NM **1** *Hist* imprisonment in the Bastille **2** *(emprisonnement)* imprisonment, incarceration

embastiller [3] [ɑ̃bastije] VT **1** *Hist* to imprison in the Bastille **2** *(emprisonner)* to imprison, to incarcerate

embattage [ɑ̃bataʒ] NM *Tech (d'une roue avec un bandage de fer)* shoeing, tyring

embattre [83] [ɑ̃batr] VT *Tech (une roue avec un bandage de fer)* to shoe, to tyre

embauchage [ɑ̃boʃaʒ] NM hiring

embauche [ɑ̃boʃ] NF **1** *(action)* hiring **2** *(emploi)* employment; **il n'y a pas d'e. (chez eux)** they're not hiring anyone, there are no vacancies; **quelle est la situation de l'e.?** are companies taking on *or* hiring staff?

embaucher [3] [ɑ̃boʃe] VT *(recruter)* to take on, to hire; **e. qn pour le poste de** *ou* **comme** to engage *or* recruit sb as; *Fam* **je me suis encore fait e. pour faire la vaisselle** I got hired again to do the washing-up

USAGE ABSOLU to recruit, to hire people

embaucheur, -euse [ɑ̃boʃœr, -øz] NM,F employer; **les embaucheurs ne sont pas légion de nos jours** not many companies are recruiting people *or* taking people on these days

embauchoir [ɑ̃boʃwar] NM *Tech* shoetree

embaumement [ɑ̃bommɑ̃] NM embalming

embaumer [3] [ɑ̃bome] VT **1** *(parfumer* → *air)* to make fragrant; **l'encens embaume l'église** the scent of incense fills the church

2 *(dégager une odeur de* → *parfum)* to be fragrant with the scent of; *(*→ *aliment, épice etc)* to be fragrant with the aroma of; **air embaumé** fragrant *or* balmy air; **l'église embaume l'encens** the church is heavy with (the scent of) incense

3 *(momifier)* to embalm

VI *(femme)* to be fragrant; *(mets)* to fill the air with a pleasant smell *or* a delicious aroma; *(fleur, plante)* to fill the air with a lovely fragrance *or* a delicate scent

embaumeur, -euse [ɑ̃bomœr, -øz] NM,F embalmer

embecquer [3] [ɑ̃beke] VT **1** *(nourrir* → *oiseau)* to feed; *(*→ *volaille)* to cram **2** *(hameçon)* to bait

embéguiner [3] [ɑ̃begine] *Vieilli* VT to put a bonnet on

▸ **s'embéguiner** VPR **s'e. de qn** to become infatuated with sb

embellie [ɑ̃beli] NF **1** *Météo (de soleil)* bright interval; *(du vent)* lull; **courte e.** bright interval **2** *Fig (amélioration* → *de l'économie, d'une situation etc)* improvement; **une e. dans sa vie** a happier period in his/her life; **une e. dans leurs rapports** an improvement in their relationship

embellir [32] [ɑ̃belir] VT **1** *(enjoliver* → *rue, parc)* to make prettier; *(*→ *pièce)* to decorate, to adorn; *(*→ *personne)* to make look (more) beautiful, to improve the looks of; **la maturité l'a embellie** she's grown more beautiful with age; **la maternité l'embellit** pregnancy is making her look more beautiful

2 *(exagérer* → *histoire)* to embellish, to embroider on, to add frills to; **e. la réalité** to make things seem more attractive than they really are

VI to grow prettier *or* more beautiful

embellissement [ɑ̃belismɑ̃] NM **1** *(fait d'améliorer)* embellishment, embellishing **2** *(apport* → *à un décor)* embellishment, improvement; *(*→ *à une histoire)* embellishment, frill; **il faudra apporter des embellissements à l'appartement** the *Br* flat *or* *Am* apartment needs improving *or* needs a few embellishing touches; **il y a beaucoup d'embellissements dans son récit** there's a lot of poetic licence in his/her story

emberlificoter [3] [ɑ̃bɛrlifikɔte] *Fam* VT **1** *(tromper* → *personne)* to hoodwink; **se laisser e.** to let oneself be hoodwinked

2 *(compliquer)* to muddle up ▪ **quelle histoire**

emberlificotée! what a muddle *or* mix-up of a story!
3 (*empêtrer*) to tangle up ■
▸**s'emberlificoter** VPR **s'e. les pieds dans** to get (one's feet) tangled up in; **s'e. dans** (*tissu, câbles, récit, mensonges*) to get tangled up in

emberlificoteur, -euse [ãbɛrlifikɔtœr, -øz] *Fam* ADJ soft-soaping, sweet-talking
NM,F sweet-talker

embêtant, -e [ãbɛtã, -ãt] ADJ *Fam* **1** (*lassant → travail*) tiresome■, boring■ **2** (*importun → enfant*) annoying■; **tu es e. avec tes questions** you're a real pain with all these questions; **c'est drôlement e.!** it's really annoying!; **3** (*gênant*) tricky■, awkward■; **c'est e. d'inviter son ex-femme?** would it be awkward to invite his ex-wife *or* if we invited his ex-wife?

embêtement [ãbɛtmã] NM *Fam* problem■; **embêtements** hassle; **va les voir au commissariat, sinon tu peux avoir des embêtements** go and see them at the police station or you could get into trouble; **en ce moment, je n'ai que des embêtements** it's just one damn thing after another at the moment; **faire des embêtements à qn** to cause *or* make trouble for sb

embêter [4] [ãbɛte] *Fam* VT **1** (*importuner*) to annoy■, to bother■; **n'embête pas ce pauvre animal** stop tormenting *or* annoying that poor creature; **je leur renverrai le papier, rien que pour les e.** I'll send them back the form, just to annoy them!; **ça m'embête d'y aller** I wish I didn't have to go■; **se faire e. par qn** to be hassled by sb
2 (*lasser*) to bore■; **ça m'embête d'y aller** I can't be bothered going *or* to go
3 (*mettre mal à l'aise*) to bother■, to annoy■; **cela m'embête d'avoir oublié** it annoys *or* bothers me that I forgot; **ça m'embête d'arriver en retard** I don't like being late■; **je suis drôlement embêté avec ma fille** I'm having a lot of hassle with my daughter
▸**s'embêter** VPR **1** (*s'ennuyer*) to be bored■; **s'e. à mourir** to be bored to death *or* tears; **s'e. ferme** *ou* **à cent sous de l'heure** to be bored stiff *or* to tears
2 (*se donner la peine*) **s'e. à faire qch** to go to the trouble of doing sth; **je ne vais pas m'e. à les éplucher** I'm not going to bother peeling them; **et moi qui me suis embêtée à le refaire!** to think I went to (all) the trouble of doing it again!
3 (*locutions*) **il s'embête pas!** (*il est sans scrupules*) he's got a nerve!; (*il est riche*) he does pretty well for himself!; **s'e. avec** (*des histoires d'argent, des scrupules, sa belle-mère*) to bother oneself about *or* with

embiellage [ãbjɛlaʒ] NM *Tech* (*opération*) connecting rod assembly; **faire un e.** to assemble the connecting rods

emblavage [ãblavaʒ] NM *Agr* sowing with cereal crop

emblaver [3] [ãblave] VT *Agr* to sow (with cereal crop)

emblavure [ãblavyr] NF *Agr* field sown with cereal crop

emblée [ãble] **d'emblée** ADV straightaway, right away; (*réussir*) at the first attempt

emblématique [ãblematik] ADJ emblematic; *Fig* symbolic; **figure e.** (*légendaire*) legendary figure; (*marquant*) symbol

emblème [ãblɛm] NM **1** (*blason*) emblem **2** (*insigne*) emblem, symbol; **les emblèmes de la profession** the insignia of the trade; *Mktg* **e. de marque** brand mark

embobeliner [ãbɔbline] VT *Fam Vieilli* (*tromper*) to take in, to hoodwink; (*manipuler*) to get round; **il sait t'e.** he knows how to twist you round his little finger

embobiner [3] [ãbɔbine] VT **1** *Fam* (*tromper*) to take in; (*manipuler*) to get round; **ne vous laissez pas e.** don't let yourself be taken in; **je l'ai embobiné** I've got him where I want him; **tu ne m'embobineras pas avec toutes ces belles paroles** you won't get round me by sweet-talking me **2** *Tex* (*fil*) to wind round a bobbin

emboîtable [ãbwatabl] ADJ (*chaise*) stacking (*avant n*), stackable; **cubes/tuyaux emboîtables** cubes/pipes fitting into each other; **des tables emboîtables** a nest of tables

emboîtage [ãbwataʒ] NM **1** (*action d'empiler → de chaises, de boîtes, de tables*) stacking; *Constr* (→ de tuyaux, de poutres etc*) jointing **2** (*action d'envelopper → d'un livre*) casing **3** (*rangement en boîte*) packing (into boxes) **4** (*étui*) case, casing; (*d'un livre*) slipcase

emboîtement [ãbwatmã] NM **l'e. de deux tuyaux/os** the interlocking of two pipes/bones; **à l'e. des deux pièces** at the join between the two parts, where the two parts fit into each other

emboîter [3] [ãbwate] VT **1** (*empiler → chaises, boîtes, tables*) to stack; *Constr* (→ tuyaux, poutres etc*) to joint; (→ poupées russes*) to fit into each other **2** (*envelopper → livre*) to case **3** (*locution*) **e. le pas à qn** to follow close behind sb; *Fig* to follow sb, to follow sb's lead
▸**s'emboîter** VPR to fit together *or* into each other; (*chaises, boîtes, tables*) to stack; **des tables qui s'emboîtent les unes dans les autres** a nest of tables

emboîture [ãbwatyr] NF fit, joint

embole [ãbɔl] NM embolus

embolie [ãbɔli] NF *Méd* embolism; **e. gazeuse/pulmonaire** air/pulmonary embolism; **e. cérébrale** clot on the brain, *Spéc* cerebral embolism

embolique [ãbɔlik] ADJ *Méd* embolic

embolisation [ãbɔlizasjɔ̃] NF *Méd* embolization

embolus [ãbɔlys] NM *Méd* embolus

embonpoint [ãbɔ̃pwɛ̃] NM stoutness, portliness; **avoir de l'e.** to be stout *or* corpulent; **prendre de l'e.** to flesh out, to become stout, to put on weight

embossage [ãbɔsaʒ] NM **1** *Naut* mooring broadside on, mooring with a spring **2** (*sur une carte bancaire*) embossing

embosser [3] [ãbɔse] VT **1** *Naut* to moor broadside on, to moor with a spring **2** (*carte bancaire*) to emboss

embossure [ãbɔsyr] NF *Naut* spring

embouage [ãbwaʒ] NM *Mines* mudding off

embouche [ãbuʃ] NF *Agr* (*engraissement*) fattening up **2** (*pré*) grazing

embouché, -e [ãbuʃe] ADJ *Fam* **mal e.** (*grossier*) foul-mouthed; (*de mauvaise humeur*) in a foul mood

emboucher [3] [ãbuʃe] VT **1** *Mus* to put to one's mouth; *Fig* **e. la trompette** to wax lyrical; **il a allégrement embouché la trompette du libéralisme** he trumpeted *or* extolled the virtues of the free market **2** *Équitation* **e. un cheval** to put the bit in a horse's mouth

embouchoir [ãbuʃwar] NM *Mil* barrel clamp

embouchure [ãbuʃyr] NF **1** *Géog* mouth **2** *Mus* mouthpiece, embouchure **3** *Équitation* mouthpiece **4** (*d'un sac, d'un vase*) opening, mouth

embouer [6] [ãbwe] VT **1** (*mur etc*) to coat *or* to smear with mud/clay; *Mines* to mud off **2** *Vieilli* (*porter préjudice à*) to bespatter with mud; **e. la réputation de qn** to besmirch sb's reputation; *Prov* **qui se loue s'emboue** self-praise is no recommendation

embouquement [ãbukmã] NM *Naut* **1** (*engagement dans une passe, dans une rivière*) entering the mouth **2** (*entrée d'une passe, d'un canal*) entry of waterway

embouquer [3] [ãbuke] *Naut* VT to enter the mouth of
VI to enter a channel

embourber [3] [ãburbe] VT (*enliser*) to stick
▸**s'embourber** VPR (*dans la boue*) to get bogged down *or* stuck in the mud; **s'e. dans ses mensonges/contradictions** to get bogged down in one's lies/contradictions; **il s'est embourbé dans des explications compliquées** he got bogged down in complicated explanations

embourgeoisement [ãburʒwazmã] NM (*d'un groupe, d'un milieu, d'une profession*) becoming (more) bourgeois *or* middle-class; (*d'un quartier*) gentrification; **l'e. des vieux quartiers rénovés** the gentrification of renovated inner city areas

embourgeoiser [3] [ãburʒwaze] **s'embourgeoiser** VPR **1** (*quartier*) to become gentrified; (*parti politique*) to become (more) bourgeois *or* middle-class **2** *Péj* (*personne*) to become fonder and fonder of one's creature comforts

embourrer [3] [ãbure] VT **1** *Tex* to stuff, to pad **2** *Can* (*en acadien*) to wrap up

▸**s'embourrer** VPR *Can* (*en acadien*) to wrap oneself up

embourrure [ãburyr] NF **1** *Tex* ticking **2** *Can* (*bourre*) stuffing, filling

embout [ãbu] NM (*d'un parapluie*) tip, ferrule; (*d'un tuyau*) nozzle; (*d'une seringue*) adapter; (*d'un câble*) terminal; (*d'un tirant, d'un fil etc*) connector

embouteillage [ãbutɛjaʒ] NM **1** *Aut* traffic jam; (*à un carrefour*) gridlock; **il y a de gros embouteillages** traffic is (jammed) solid; **tomber dans les embouteillages** to get caught in traffic **2** *Fam* (*au téléphone*) logjam (of calls); **il y a un e. sur la ligne** the line is jammed with calls **3** *Naut* (*de navires*) bottling up

embouteiller [4] [ãbuteje] VT **1** *Aut* to jam (up); **les routes sont embouteillées** the roads are congested *or* jammed; **e. un carrefour** to gridlock a junction **2** (*mettre en bouteilles*) to bottle

emboutir [32] [ãbutir] VT **1** (*heurter*) to crash into; **je me suis fait e. par un bus** I was hit by a bus; **l'aile est toute emboutie** the wing's all dented; **tout l'arrière de ma voiture est embouti** the entire rear end of my car is bashed in **2** *Métal* to stamp; **châssis en tôle emboutie** pressed steel frame **3** (*arrondir*) to stamp, to emboss

emboutissage [ãbutisaʒ] NM **1** *Métal* stamping **2** (*fait d'arrondir*) stamping, embossing **3** *Aut* (*de voitures*) collision; **l'e. d'une voiture par un autobus** the collision between a bus and a car

emboutisseur, -euse [ãbutisœr, -øz] *Tech* NM,F (*personne*) stamper
❑ **emboutisseuse** NF (*machine*) stamper, stamping machine

emboutissoir [ãbutiswar] NM *Métal* stamping press, stamper

embraie *etc voir* **embrayer**

embranchement [ãbrãʃmã] NM **1** *Transp* (*carrefour → routier*) fork; (→ ferroviaire*) junction **2** *Transp* (*voie annexe → routière*) side road; *Rail* (→ ferroviaire*) branch line **3** (*d'égout*) junction **4** (*dans un arbre*) **un nid dans l'e.** a nest built where the trunk branches out **5** *Biol & Bot* subkingdom, *Spéc* phylum

embrancher [3] [ãbrãʃe] VT (*route, conduite etc*) to connect up, to join up (**à** to)
▸**s'embrancher** VPR **s'e. (sur)** to join (up with)

embraquer [3] [ãbrake] VT *Naut* (*cordage*) to tighten

embrasé, -e [ãbraze] ADJ *Littéraire* afire, aflame; **cœur e. d'amour** heart aflame with passion

embrasement [ãbrazmã] NM *Littéraire* **1** (*incendie*) blaze **2** (*rougeoiement*) **l'e. du couchant** the blaze of the setting sun **3** (*exaltation → de l'âme*) kindling; (→ de l'imagination*) firing; **il ne pouvait pas lutter contre l'e. de son cœur** he could not fight against the love that flared up in his heart

embraser [3] [ãbraze] VT *Littéraire* **1** (*incendier*) to set ablaze *or* on fire, to set fire to; *Fig* **la soif qui lui embrasait la gorge** the thirst burning his/her throat
2 (*illuminer*) to set ablaze *or* aglow; **le soleil levant embrasait le ciel** the rising sun set the sky aglow
3 (*rendre brûlant*) to make burning hot; **le soleil de midi embrasait la route** the road was burning hot under the midday sun
4 (*exalter → imagination*) to fire; (→ âme) to kindle, to set aflame; (→ foule) to fire, to set alight, *Péj* to inflame; **ces projets d'aventure l'embrasaient** this talk of adventure fired his/her imagination
▸**s'embraser** VPR *Littéraire* **1** (*prendre feu*) to catch fire, to blaze *or* to flare up
2 (*s'illuminer*) to be set ablaze; (*rougeoyer*) to glow
3 (*devenir brûlant*) to become burning hot
4 (*s'exalter → âme, imagination*) to be set on fire, to be kindled; (→ opprimés) to rise up; **dès que je l'ai vu, mon cœur s'est embrasé** the mere sight of him kindled a flame; **les esprits s'embrasaient** (*par enthousiasme*) imaginations were fired; (*par colère*) passions were running high

embrassade [ãbrasad] NF **une e.** a hug and a kiss; **des embrassades** hugging and kissing, hugs and kisses

embrasse [ãbras] NF (*de rideau*) tieback

embrassé, -e [ɑ̃brase] **ADJ 1** *Hér* embrassé **2** *Littérature* **rimes embrassées** introverted *or* enclosing rhymes

embrassement [ɑ̃brasmɑ̃] **NM** *Littéraire* embrace; **embrassements** embracing

embrasser [3] [ɑ̃brase] **VT 1** *(donner un baiser à)* to kiss; **l'embrassant sur le front** kissing him/her on the forehead, kissing his/her forehead; **e. qn sur la bouche/joue** to kiss sb on the lips/cheek; **embrasse Mamie, on s'en va!** kiss Granny goodbye!; **elle l'embrassait avant qu'il ne s'endorme** she used to kiss him goodnight; **vous embrasserez vos parents pour moi** (kind) regards to your parents; **embrasse Lucie pour moi!** give Lucie a big kiss *or* hug for me!; **je t'embrasse** *(dans une lettre)* with love; *(au téléphone)* take care

2 *Littéraire (serrer dans ses bras)* to embrace, to hug; *Prov* **qui trop embrasse, mal étreint** = one shouldn't spread oneself too thinly

3 *(adopter → idée, foi)* to embrace, to take up; *(→ carrière)* to take up; *(→ cause)* to embrace, to take up; **e. la carrière diplomatique** to enter the diplomatic service

4 *(saisir)* **e. du regard** to behold; **e. d'un seul coup d'œil** to take in at a single glance; **il embrassa toute sa famille d'un regard satisfait** he cast a satisfied eye over his family

5 *(comprendre)* to grasp; **e. les données complexes d'un problème** to grasp the complex elements of a problem

6 *(englober)* to encompass, to embrace
▶**s'embrasser VPR**to kiss (one another)

Embrassons-nous Folleville!
This is the title of a play by French playwright Eugène Labiche (1815–88). There is a passage in the play where a character called Folleville is about to challenge the father of the girl he wants to marry to a duel but changes his mind when the man benignly exclaims "Embrassons-nous Folleville!" ("Let me give you a hug, Folleville!"). The phrase is used allusively when speaking about the unexpected reconciliation of hitherto bitter enemies. For instance, when commenting on a meeting between two political enemies who have decided to work together, you could say **Cette rencontre a un air d'embrassons-nous Folleville**, suggesting that no-one could have predicted a rapprochement between the two apparently irreconcilable parties.

---

embrasseur, -euse [ɑ̃brasœr, -øz] **NM,F** obsessive kisser

embrasure [ɑ̃brazyr] **NF 1** *(cadre → de porte)* door-frame, door-jamb; *(→ de fenêtre)* window-frame; **dans l'e. de la porte/fenêtre** in the door/window recess; **se tenir dans l'e. d'une porte/fenêtre** to be framed in a doorway/window **2** *Archit* embrasure **3** *Mil* gun port

embrayage [ɑ̃brɛjaʒ] **NM 1** *(mécanisme) Aut* clutch; *Tech* coupling (gear); **e. à cônes** cone clutch; **e. à crabot** dog clutch; **e. à diaphragme** diaphragm spring *or* DS clutch; **e. électromagnétique** magnetic clutch; **e. à friction** friction clutch; **e. hydrodynamique** fluid clutch; **e. monodisque** single-plate *or* disc clutch; **e. multidisque** multi-disc clutch pack; **e. de prise directe** lock-up clutch

2 *Aut & Tech (pédale)* clutch (pedal); **pédale d'e.** clutch pedal

3 *(fait d'embrayer)* putting in the clutch; *Tech (de pièces de moteur)* coupling, engaging; **voiture à e. automatique** automatic car

embrayer [11] [ɑ̃breje] **VT** *Aut* to put in the clutch of; *Tech (pièces de moteur)* to couple, to engage

VI 1 *Aut* to put in *or* to engage the clutch; **embraye!** clutch in!

2 *Fam (commencer)* to get cracking, to go into action; **e. sur** to get straight into; **on pourrait peut-être e. sur un autre sujet** maybe we could change the subject ∎

3 *Can Fam (se dépêcher)* **embraye!** get a move on!

embrayeur[ɑ̃brɛjœr] **NM***Ling* shifter

embrèvement [ɑ̃brɛvmɑ̃] **NM** *Menuis* tongue-and-groove joint

---

embrever [19] [ɑ̃brəve] **VT** *Menuis* to join by tongue and groove, to match

embrigadement[ɑ̃brigadmɑ̃] **NM1** *Mil (dans une brigade)* brigading; *(enrôlement forcé)* dragooning (into the army) **2** *Fig Péj (adhésion forcée)* press-ganging

embrigader [3] [ɑ̃brigade] **VT 1** *Mil (dans une brigade)* to brigade; *(de force)* to dragoon into the army, to press into service **2** *Fig Péj (faire adhérer)* to press-gang; **je ne veux pas être embrigadé dans leur mouvement** I won't let myself be press-ganged into joining their movement

embringuer [3] [ɑ̃brɛ̃ge] *Fam* **VT e. qn dans** to drag sb into; **il ne veut pas se laisser e. dans cette histoire** he doesn't want to get mixed up in this affair
▶**s'embringuer VPR**to get mixed up (**dans** in)

embrocation[ɑ̃brɔkasjɔ̃] **NF**embrocation

embrochement [ɑ̃brɔʃmɑ̃] **NM** *Culin (d'un animal)* putting on a spit; *(en brochettes)* skewering

embrocher [3] [ɑ̃brɔʃe] **VT1** *Culin (un animal)* to spit, to spit-roast; *(en brochettes)* to skewer **2** *Fam (transpercer)* **e. qn avec qch** to run sth through sb ∎

embrouillage[ɑ̃bruja3] = **embrouillement**

embrouillamini[ɑ̃brujamini] **NM***Fam* (hopeless) muddle *or* mix-up; **sa vie sentimentale est un tel e. que...** his/her love life is so complicated *or* involved that... ∎, **comment veux-tu que je m'y retrouve dans cet e. de papiers?** how can I be expected to know what I'm doing when these papers are in such a muddle?

embrouille [ɑ̃bruj] **NF** *Fam* **1** *(situation confuse)* muddle; **il s'est foutu dans une e.** he got himself in a complete muddle

2 *(problème)* **tenez-vous tranquilles, je veux pas d'embrouilles!** keep quiet, I don't want any trouble *or* hassle!; **je vois venir les embrouilles** I can see trouble ahead

3 *(escroquerie)* swindle; **c'est encore une de ses embrouilles pour nous extorquer de l'argent** it's yet another of his/her tricks *or* schemes to extort money from us

embrouillé, -e[ɑ̃bruje] **ADJ1** *(fils, câbles)* tangled up, entangled, snarled up **2** *(situation)* muddled, confusing; *(style, affaire)* complicated, involved; **des idées embrouillées** confused ideas

embrouillement[ɑ̃brujmɑ̃] **NM1** *(de fils → action)* tangling; *(→ état)* tangle **2** *Fig (d'une situation, d'idées etc → action)* muddling, confusing; *(→ état)* muddle, confusion; **l'e. de la situation est tel que...** the situation is so confused that...; **tous ces incidents ont contribué à l'e. de la situation** all these incidents helped confuse the situation

embrouiller [3] [ɑ̃bruje] **VT1** *(emmêler)* to tangle up; **j'ai embrouillé les fils** I got the wires tangled up

2 *Fig* **e. qn** to muddle sb, to confuse sb; **il a réussi à m'e.** he managed to confuse me; *Fam* **ni vu ni connu je t'embrouille** hey presto; *Fam* **...alors qu'il était avec une autre: ni vu ni connu je t'embrouille** ...while all the time he was with another woman: talk about a con artist *or* about being conned!

3 *(compliquer)* to complicate; **e. la situation** *ou* **les choses** to confuse matters
▶**s'embrouiller VPR**to get muddled (up), to get confused; **je me suis embrouillé dans mes rendez-vous** I got my appointments muddled, I got into a muddle with my appointments

embroussaillé, -e [ɑ̃brusaje] **ADJ** *(jardin)* overgrown; *(sentier, jardin, dunes etc)* covered with *or* in bushes; *(cheveux)* bushy; *(barbe)* bushy, shaggy

embroussailler [3] [ɑ̃brusaje] **VT 1** *(terrain)* to cover with brushwood, with bushes **2** *(cheveux)* to tousle, to ruffle
▶**s'embroussailler VPR** *(jardin)* to become overgrown

embruiné, -e [ɑ̃brɥine] **ADJ** covered in (a fine) drizzle

embrumé, -e [ɑ̃bryme] **ADJ** *(temps)* misty; *(horizon)* hazy; *Fig (esprit → par l'alcool)* fuddled, fogged; **il avait l'esprit e. par toutes ces paroles** all that talking had left him feeling less than clear-headed

---

embrumer [3] [ɑ̃bryme] **VT 1** *Météo* to cover in mist; **la ligne embrumée des cimes** the misty mountain tops

2 *Fig Littéraire* to cloud; **le sommeil lui embrumait encore les yeux** his/her eyes were still heavy *or* blurred with sleep; **intelligence embrumée par la boisson** mind clouded with drink; **tous ces discours lui ont embrumé l'esprit** his/her mind is less than clear after all those speeches
▶**s'embrumer VPR1** *Météo* to mist over; *(ciel)* to become misty *or* hazy; *(paysage, ville, île)* to become covered with mist *or* haze

2 *(esprit, intelligence)* to become clouded

embruns [ɑ̃brœ̃] **NMPL les e.** the sea spray *or* spume

embryocardie [ɑ̃brijokardi] **NF** *Méd* embryocardia

embryogenèse [ɑ̃brijoʒɔnɛz] **NF** *Biol* embryogenesis

embryogénie[ɑ̃brijoʒeni] **NF***Biol* embryogeny

embryogénique [ɑ̃brijoʒenik] **ADJ** *Biol* embryogenic

embryologie[ɑ̃brijoloʒi] **NF***Biol* embryology

embryologique [ɑ̃brijoloʒik] **ADJ** *Biol* embryologic, embryological

embryologiste [ɑ̃brijoloʒist] **NMF***Biol* embryologist

embryon [ɑ̃brijɔ̃] **NM 1** *Biol & Bot* embryo **2** *Fig (commencement)* embryo, beginning; **un e. de projet** an embryonic project; **ne nous emballons pas, ce n'est encore qu'un e. de projet** let's not get carried away, it's still just a vague plan

embryonnaire [ɑ̃brijonɛr] **ADJ 1** *Biol & Bot* embryonic; **sac e.** embryo sac **2** *Fig (non développé)* embryonic, incipient; **idée encore à l'état e.** idea still at the embryonic stage; **le projet en est encore à un stade e.** the project is still at a very early stage *or* in its very early stages

embryopathie[ɑ̃brijopati] **NF***Méd* embryopathy

embryoscopie[ɑ̃brijoskopi] **NF***Méd* embryoscopy

embryotomie[ɑ̃brijotomi] **NF***Obst* embryotomy

embu, -e [ɑ̃by] *Beaux-Arts* **ADJ***(couleur, tableau)* flat, dull

NM*(d'une couleur)* flatness, dullness

embûche[ɑ̃byʃ] **NF1** *(difficulté)* pitfall, hazard **2** *(piège)* trap; **tendre** *ou* **dresser des embûches à qn** to set traps for sb; **sujet plein d'embûches** tricky subject; **examen semé d'embûches** exam paper full of trick questions; **la vie est semée d'embûches** life is full of pitfalls

embuer [7] [ɑ̃bɥe] **VT** to mist (up *or* over); **des lunettes embuées** misted-up spectacles; **les yeux embués de larmes** eyes misty with tears
▶**s'embuer VPR**to steam up

embuscade [ɑ̃byskad] **NF** ambush; **attirer qn dans une e.** to ambush sb; **se tenir en e.** to lie in ambush; *Fig* **tomber dans une e.** to be caught in an ambush; *Fig* **tendre une e. à qn** to set up an ambush for sb

embusqué, -e [ɑ̃byske] **NM,F1** *Péj & Mil* shirker, dodger; **les embusqués de l'arrière** the troops that keep behind the lines **2** *Sport* **les embusqués** the back row of forwards

embusquer [3] [ɑ̃byske] *Mil* **VT1** *(placer en embuscade)* to place in ambush **2** *(affecter loin du front)* to find a cushy posting for
▶**s'embusquer VPR 1** *(pour attaquer)* to lie in ambush **2***Péj (pendant la guerre)* to avoid active service

embuvage[ɑ̃byva3] **NM***Tex* contraction

éméché, -e[emeʃe] **ADJ***Fam* tipsy

émécher[18] [emeʃe] **VT***Fam* to make tipsy

émendation [emɑ̃dasjɔ̃] **NF***(d'un document, d'un arrêt)* amendment

émender [3] [emɑ̃de] **VT** *(document, arrêt)* to amend

émeraude[emrod] **NF***Minér* emerald
NM*(couleur)* emerald green
ADJ **inv**emerald *(avant n)*, emerald-green
◻ **Émeraude NF la côte d'É.** = part of the Northern Brittany coast, near Saint-Malo

émergé, -e[emɛrʒe] **ADJ** **les terres émergées** the land above water level; **la partie émergée de l'iceberg** the visible part of the iceberg

émergement[emɛrʒəmɑ̃] **NM**emergence

émergence [emɛrʒɑ̃s] **NF 1** *(apparition → d'une*

idée) (sudden) appearance *or* emergence; **on assiste à cette époque à l'é. de nouvelles théories politiques** at the time new political theories were emerging *or* were coming to the fore 2 *Géog (d'une source)* source; **c'est là que se trouve le point d'é. de la source** the spring emerges here 3 *Opt* **point d'é.** point of emergence

émergent, -e [emɛrʒɑ̃, -ɑ̃t] ADJ 1 *(idée)* emerging, developing; *(pays, économie, maladie)* emerging 2 *Opt* emergent

émerger [17] [emɛrʒe] VI 1 *(soleil)* to rise, to come up 2 *(dépasser)* **é. de** *(eau)* to float (up) to the top of, to emerge from; **une bonne copie/un bon élève qui émerge du lot** a paper/pupil standing out from the rest 3 *Fig (apparaître → vérité, fait)* to emerge, to come to light; *(→ nouvel écrivain)* to emerge 4 *Fam (d'une occupation, du sommeil)* to emerge; **il émerge à peine** he never surfaces before noon on Sundays

émeri [ɛmri] NM emery; **papier** *ou* **toile (d')é.** emery paper; **bouchon à l'é.** (ground glass) stopper

émerillon [emrijɔ̃] NM 1 *Orn* merlin 2 *Pêche* swivel

émerillonné, -e [emrijɔne] ADJ bright, gay

émeriser [3] [emrize] VT *Tech (recouvrir de poudre)* to coat with emery; *(gratter)* to grind with emery

émérat [emerita] NM *Belg Univ* emeritus professorship

émérite [emerit] ADJ 1 *(éminent)* (highly experienced and) skilled, expert *(avant n)* 2 *Belg Univ* **professeur é.** emeritus professor

émersion [emɛrsjɔ̃] NF 1 *(apparition)* emersion, surfacing 2 *Astron* emersion

émerveillement [emɛrvɛjmɑ̃] NM 1 *(émotion)* wonder, *Littéraire* wonderment; **il découvrait la mer avec é.** he discovered the sea with wonder 2 *(chose merveilleuse)* wonder; **le jardin ce matin, c'est un é.** the garden is a wonder to behold this morning; **c'était un é.** it was amazing *or* wonderful; **un é. perpétuel** a constant source of amazement

émerveiller [4] [emɛrveje] VT to fill with wonder *or Littéraire* wonderment; **être émerveillé par** to marvel at, to be filled with wonder by; **elle fixait la poupée d'un regard émerveillé** she gazed at the doll in wonder
▸**s'émerveiller** VPR to be filled with wonder, to marvel; **s'é. de** ou **devant** *(s'étonner de)* to be amazed by; *(s'enchanter de)* to marvel at; **il s'émerveillait d'un rien** he marvelled at the smallest thing

émet *etc voir* **émettre**

émétine [emetin] NF *Chim* emetin, emetine

émétique [emetik] *Med & Pharm* ADJ emetic
NM emetic

émétisant, -e [emetizɑ̃, -ɑ̃t] ADJ *Pharm* emetic

émetteur, -trice [emetœr, -tris] ADJ 1 *Rad* transmitting; **é. mono** mono transmitter; **poste é.** transmitter; **station émettrice** transmitting *or* broadcasting station 2 *Fin* issuing
NM,F 1 *Fin (de billets, d'actions, d'une carte)* issuer; *(d'un chèque)* drawer 2 *Ling* speaker
NM 1 *Rad (appareil)* transmitter; **é. monophonique**, *Fam* **é. mono** monoaural transmitter; *Fam* mono transmitter; **é. stéréo** stereo transmitter; **é. terrestre** ground transmitter 2 *(élément)* emitter

émetteur-récepteur [emetœrresɛptœr] *(pl* **émetteurs-récepteurs)** NM *Rad* transmitter-receiver, transceiver; **é. (portatif)** walkie-talkie; **é. additionnel** transverter

émettre [84] [emɛtr] VT 1 *(produire → rayon, son)* to emit, to give out; *(→ odeur)* to give off, to produce; *(→ chaleur)* to give out *or* off; *(→ lumière)* to give (out); **mon ordinateur émet un bruit bizarre** my computer is making a funny noise
2 *(exprimer → hypothèse, opinion)* to venture, to put forward, to volunteer; *(→ doute, réserve)* to express; *(→ objection)* to voice, to raise, to put forward
3 *Fin (billets, actions, chèque, timbres)* to issue; *(emprunt)* to float; *(lettre de crédit)* to open
4 *Rad & TV* to broadcast, to transmit; *(onde, signal)* to send out
5 *Jur (monnaie)* to utter

USAGE ABSOLU *Rad & TV* to transmit, to broadcast; **é. sur grandes ondes** to broadcast on long wave

émettrice [emetris] *voir* **émetteur**

émeu [emø] NM *Orn* emu

émeut *etc voir* **émouvoir**

émeute [emøt] NF riot; **il y a eu des émeutes** there has been rioting; **tourner à l'é.** to turn into a riot

émeutier, -ère [emøtje, -ɛr] NM,F rioter

émeuvent *etc voir* **émouvoir**

émiettement [emjɛtmɑ̃] NM 1 *(d'un gâteau)* crumbling 2 *(dispersion → des efforts)* frittering away, dissipating; *(→ du pouvoir)* fragmentation

émietter [4] [emjete] VT 1 *(mettre en miettes → gâteau)* to crumble, to break up (into crumbs) 2 *(morceler → propriété)* to break up 3 *Littéraire (gaspiller → efforts)* to fritter away, to disperse, to dissipate
▸**s'émietter** VPR *(gâteau)* to crumble; *(pouvoir)* to fragment; *(fortune)* to gradually disappear; *(domaine, empire)* to crumble away

émigrant, -e [emigrɑ̃, -ɑ̃t] NM,F emigrant

émigration [emigrasjɔ̃] NF 1 *(d'une personne, population)* emigration, emigrating; **pays à forte/faible é.** country with high/low emigration 2 *Zool* migration

émigré, -e [emigre] ADJ migrant; **travailleurs émigrés** migrant workers
NM,F emigrant; *Hist* emigré

émigrer [3] [emigre] VI 1 *(s'expatrier)* to emigrate 2 *Zool* to migrate

Émilie-Romagne [emiliromaɲ] NF *Géog* **l'É.** Emilia-Romagna

émincé [emɛ̃se] NM *Culin* 1 *(plat)* émincé; **é. de veau** émincé of veal, veal cut into slivers *(and served in a sauce)* 2 *(tranche)* thin slice *(of meat)*

émincer [16] [emɛ̃se] VT *Culin* to slice thinly, to cut into thin strips

éminemment [eminamɑ̃] ADV eminently

Éminence [eminɑ̃s] NF *Rel* 1 *(titre)* **son É. le cardinal Giobba** his Eminence Cardinal Giobba 2 *(cardinal)* cardinal, Eminence

éminence [eminɑ̃s] NF 1 *Géog* hill, hillock, knoll 2 *Anat* protuberance; **l'é. du pouce** the ball of the thumb 3 *Arch (excellence)* eminence 4 *(locutions)* **é. grise** éminence grise; **c'est l'é. grise du patron** he's/she's the power behind the throne

éminent, -e [eminɑ̃, -ɑ̃t] ADJ eminent, prominent, noted; **mon é. collègue** my learned colleague; **il nous a rendu d'éminents services** he rendered us outstanding service

éminentissime [eminɑ̃tisim] ADJ **é. seigneur** most eminent cardinal

émir [emir] NM emir, amir

émirat [emira] NM *Géog & Pol* emirate; **les Émirats arabes unis** the United Arab Emirates; **vivre aux Émirats arabes unis** to live in the United Arab Emirates; **aller aux Émirats arabes unis** to go to the United Arab Emirates

émis, -e [emi, -iz] PP *voir* **émettre**

émissaire¹ [emisɛr] NM *Pol (envoyé)* emissary, envoy

émissaire² [emisɛr] NM *Géog (d'un lac)* outlet, drainage channel

émissif, -ive [emisif, -iv] ADJ *Phys* emissive

émission [emisjɔ̃] NF 1 *Phys (de son, de lumière, de signaux, de gaz)* emission; **é. de particules** particle emission; **é. secondaire** secondary emission; **tuyau d'é.** discharge pipe
2 *Rad & TV (transmission de sons, d'images)* transmission, broadcasting; *(programme)* programme; **é. d'actualités** current affairs programme; **é. en différé** prerecorded broadcast; **é. en direct** live broadcast; **é. diffusée simultanément** simultaneous broadcast; **é. d'expression directe** live debate programme; **é. d'expression directe (de formation politique)** party political broadcast; **émissions pour enfants** children's television; **é. du matin** breakfast programme; **é. pilote** pilot; **é. en public** audience show; **é. de radio** radio programme; **é. radiotélévisée** simulcast; **é. relayée** relay; **émissions scolaires** schools broadcasting; **émissions à sensation** tabloid television, tabloid TV; **émissions de service public** public-service broadcasting; **é. spéciale** special programme; **é. de télévision** television programme, *Spéc* telecast; **é. de variétés** variety

show; **l'é. de nos programmes sera interrompue à 22 heures** transmission of our programmes will be interrupted at 10 p.m.; **poste d'é.** transmitter; **station d'é.** transmitting *or* broadcasting station
3 *Fin (de billets, d'actions, d'un chèque, de timbres)* issue; *(d'un emprunt)* flotation; *(d'une lettre de crédit)* opening; *Bourse* **é. boursière** ou **d'actions** share issue; *Bourse* **é. d'actions gratuites** scrip issue; *Bourse* **é. de conversion** conversion issue; *Banque* **é. fiduciaire** fiduciary *or* note issue; *Bourse* **é. obligataire** ou **d'obligations** bond issue; **é. premier jour** first day cover; *Bourse* **é. par séries** block shares; *Bourse* **é. des valeurs du Trésor** tap issue
4 *(de sons articulés)* **é. de voix** utterance
5 *Physiol* emission
6 *Électron* **é. électronique** electron emission
7 *Jur (d'une monnaie)* uttering

émissole [emisɔl] NF *Ich* smooth dogfish *or* hound

emmagasinage [ɑ̃magazinaʒ] NM 1 *Com (dans une arrière-boutique)* storage; *(dans un entrepôt)* warehousing; **frais d'e.** storage charges 2 *(d'électricité, de chaleur)* storing up, accumulation

emmagasiner [3] [ɑ̃magazine] VT 1 *Com (marchandises → dans une arrière-boutique)* to store; *(→ dans un entrepôt)* to warehouse 2 *(accumuler → connaissances)* to store up, to accumulate; *(→ provisions)* to stock up on, to stockpile; *(→ électricité, chaleur)* to store up, to accumulate

emmaillotement [ɑ̃majɔtmɑ̃] NM *(d'un bébé)* swaddling; *(d'un membre)* wrapping up

emmailloter [3] [ɑ̃majɔte] VT *(bébé)* to swaddle; *(membre)* to wrap up

emmanché, -e [ɑ̃mɑ̃ʃe] NM,F *Vulg* jerk, dickhead

emmanchement [ɑ̃mɑ̃ʃmɑ̃] NM 1 **l'e. d'un outil** fitting a handle on a tool 2 *(d'une pièce à une autre)* fitting; **cela rendait l'e. des deux pièces impossible** it made it impossible to fit the two parts together

emmancher [3] [ɑ̃mɑ̃ʃe] VT 1 *(ajuster → tête de râteau, lame)* to fit into a handle 2 *(tuyaux)* to fit together, to joint; *(pièce dans une autre)* to fit *(dans* to)
▸**s'emmancher** VPR 1 *(de deux pièces)* to fit together 2 *Fam* **s'e. bien/mal** *(commencer)* to be off to a good/bad start; **l'affaire était mal emmanchée** the business got off to a bad start

emmanchure [ɑ̃mɑ̃ʃyr] NF 1 *Couture (de vêtement)* armhole; **la veste me serre aux emmanchures** the jacket's too tight at the armpits 2 *Belg (combine)* scheme, trick

emmarchement [ɑ̃marʃɑ̃mɑ̃] NM *Constr (largeur d'un escalier)* width (of stair); *(disposition des marches)* stair configuration, configuration of steps; *(entaille)* step groove; *(escalier)* flight of steps

Emmaüs [emays] NM Emmaus; **E. International =** charitable organization that helps the poor and homeless

emmêlement [ɑ̃mɛlmɑ̃] NM *(de cheveux, de fils, de laine → action)* tangling; *(→ état)* tangle; *Fig (de faits, d'une histoire → action)* mixing up, muddling; *(→ état)* mix-up, muddle

emmêler [4] [ɑ̃mele] VT 1 *(mêler → cheveux, fils, laine)* to entangle, to tangle (up), to get into a tangle; **complètement emmêlé** all tangled up 2 *(rendre confus, confondre)* to mix up; **j'emmêle les dates** I'm getting the dates confused; **des explications emmêlées** confused *or* muddled explanations; **une situation emmêlée** a complicated situation
▸**s'emmêler** VPR 1 *(être mêlé)* to be tangled *or* knotted *or* snarled up 2 *(être confus → faits, dates)* to get mixed up 3 **s'e. les pieds dans** to get one's feet caught in; *Fam Fig* **s'e. les pieds** ou **pédales** ou **pinceaux** ou **crayons dans qch** to get sth all muddled up

emménagement [ɑ̃menaʒmɑ̃] NM moving in; **nous avons dû remettre notre e. à plus tard** we had to put off moving in *or* we had to put our move off to later; **comment s'est passé ton e.?** how did the move go?

emménager[17] [ɑ̃menaʒe] VI to move in; **e. dans** to move into

VT *(meubles, personne)* to move in; **e. qn/qch dans** to move sb/sth into

emménagogue [emenagɔg] *Méd* ADJ emmenagogue, emmenagogic

NM emmenagogue

emmener[19] [ɑ̃mne] VT **1** *(inviter à aller)* to take along; **je t'emmène en montagne** I'll take you (with me) to the mountains; **je vous emmène avec moi** I'm taking you with me; **je t'emmène passer le week-end à Florence** I'm taking you (off) to Florence for the weekend; **cette année nous emmenons les enfants** we're taking the children away this year; **e. qn dîner** to take sb out to dinner; **e. promener qn** to take sb for a walk

2 *(sujet: bateau, avion etc → passagers)* to take, to carry

3 *(forcer à aller)* to take away

4 *(accompagner)* **e. qn à la gare** to take sb to the station; *(en voiture)* to give sb a lift to *or* to drop sb off at the station; **il m'a emmené à l'aéroport en voiture** he drove me to the airport

5 *Fam (emporter)* to take (away) ▪; **emmène la fourchette à la cuisine** take the fork into the kitchen

6 *Sport & Mil (sprint, peloton, équipe, soldat)* to lead

emmenthal, emmental [emɛ̃tal] NM *Culin* Emmenthal, Emmental

emmerdant, -e [ɑ̃mɛrdɑ̃, -ɑ̃t] ADJ *très Fam* **1** *(importun)* **ce que tu peux être e.!** you can be a real pain (in the neck *or Am* butt)!; **il est e.** he's a pain (in the neck *or Am* butt)!; **il est pas e.** he's not too much of a pain

2 *(gênant)* damn *or Br* bloody awkward; **c'est e. d'avoir à laisser la porte ouverte** having to leave the door open is a real pain *or Br* a bloody nuisance

3 *(ennuyeux) Br* bloody *or Am* godawful boring; **je ne l'ai pas lu jusqu'au bout, c'était trop e.** I didn't read it to the end, it was too *Br* bloody boring *or Am* godawful boring

emmerde [ɑ̃mɛrd] NF *très Fam* hassle; **en ce moment j'ai que des emmerdes** it's just one frigging hassle after another at the moment; **faire des emmerdes à qn** to make trouble *or* to cause hassle for sb

emmerdement [ɑ̃mɛrdəmɑ̃] NM *très Fam* hassle; **en ce moment j'ai que des emmerdements** it's just one frigging hassle after another at the moment; **être dans les emmerdements jusqu'au cou** to be up the creek; **avoir des emmerdements** to have a hell of a lot of trouble; **j'ai encore eu un e. avec la bagnole** I had trouble with the car again

emmerder[3] [ɑ̃mɛrde] *très Fam* VT **1** *(gêner)* **e. qn** *(contrarier)* to get up sb's nose *or* on sb's nerves; *(ennuyer)* to bore sb stiff *or* silly *or* rigid; **elle va m'e. longtemps?** when is she going to stop hassling me?; **m'emmerde pas** stop bugging me; **plus j'y pense, plus ça m'emmerde** the more I think about it, the more it bugs me; **ça m'emmerde mais il va vraiment falloir que j'y aille** it's a real pain (in the neck *or Am* butt), but I'm going to have to go; **avoir l'air/être emmerdé** to look/be in a bit of a mess; **se faire e. par qn** to be hassled by sb

2 *(mépriser)* **je t'emmerde!** *Br* sod off!, *Am* screw you!; **je l'emmerde!** *Br* he can sod off!, *Am* screw him!; **dis-lui que je l'emmerde!** tell him/her from me he/she can (go and) get stuffed!

►**s'emmerder** VPR **1** *(s'ennuyer)* to be bored stiff *or* rigid; **on s'emmerde (à cent sous de l'heure) ici!** it's so damn boring here!

2 *(se donner la peine)* **je vais pas m'e. à les éplucher** I can't be bothered *or Br* arsed to peel them; **et moi qui me suis emmerdé à tout recopier!** to think I went to the trouble of copying the whole damn thing out!; **je ne me suis pas emmerdée à faire le ménage pour que...** I didn't go to all the bother *or* trouble of doing the housework just so that...

3 *(locution)* **il s'emmerde pas!** *(il est sans scrupules)* he's got a (damn) nerve!; *(il est riche)* he does pretty well for himself!

emmerdeur, -euse [ɑ̃mɛrdœr, -øz] NM,F *très Fam (qui contrarie)* damn *or Br* bloody pain; *(qui ennuie)* helluva *or Br* bloody bore

emmétrope [ɑ̃metrɔp] *Physiol* ADJ emmetropic

NMF emmetrope

émmétropie [emetrɔpi] NF *Physiol* emmetropia

emmieller[4] [ɑ̃mjele] VT *Fam Euph* to bother, to bug; **ça l'emmielle** he finds it a bit of a pain

emmitonner[3] [ɑ̃mitɔne] VT *Can Vieilli* to wrap up (well) (**dans** in)

emmitoufler[3] [ɑ̃mitufle] VT to wrap up (well) (**dans** in)

►**s'emmitoufler** VPR to wrap up well; **s'e. dans une cape** to wrap oneself up in a cape

emmoté, -e [emɔte] ADJ *Agr* balled

emmouscailler[3] [emuskaje] VT *Fam Vieilli* **e. qn** to get on sb's nerves

emmurer[3] [ɑ̃myre] VT **1** *(enfermer)* to wall up *or* in **2** *Fig Littéraire (isoler)* to immure

►**s'emmurer** VPR *Littéraire* **s'e. dans le silence** to retreat into silence

émoi [emwa] NM *Littéraire (émotion)* agitation; *(tumulte)* commotion; *(plaisir)* excitement; **elle était tout en é.** she was all in a fluster; **la population est en é.** there's great agitation among the population; **toute la ville était en é.** the whole town was in a commotion; **non sans é.** in some agitation

émollient, -e [emɔljɑ̃, -ɑ̃t] *Pharm* ADJ emollient

NM emollient

émolument [emɔlymɑ̃] *Jur* NM **1** *(part d'actif)* portion of inheritance **2** *(rémunération)* basic fee

❑ **émoluments** NMPL *(d'un employé)* salary, wages; *(d'un notaire)* fees; **percevoir des émoluments** to receive payment

émonctoire [emɔ̃ktwar] NM *Physiol* emunctory

émondage [emɔ̃daʒ] NM *Hort (d'arbuste, de buisson)* pruning; *(d'arbre)* trimming (the top of)

émonder[3] [emɔ̃de] VT *Hort (arbuste, buisson)* to prune; *(arbre)* to trim (the top of); *Fig (livre, texte)* to prune, to trim

émondes [emɔ̃d] NFPL *Hort* pruned branches, trimmings

émondeur, -euse [emɔ̃dœr, -øz] NM,F *Hort* pruner

émondoir [emɔ̃dwar] NM *Hort* pruning hook

émorfilage [emɔrfilaʒ] NM deburring

émorfiler[3] [emɔrfile] VT to deburr

émoticon [emotikɔ̃] NM *Ordinat* smiley, emoticon

émoticone [emotikon] NF = **émoticon**

émotif, -ive [emɔtif, -iv] ADJ *(personne)* emotional, sentimental; *(trouble, choc)* psychological

NM,F **c'est un grand é.** he's very emotional

émotion [emosjɔ̃] NF **1** *(sensation)* feeling; *Fam (inquiétude)* fright, shock; **une é. indicible** an indescribable feeling, a feeling that can't be put into words; **vive é.** strong emotion; *(exaltation)* excitement, thrill; **le meurtre de l'enfant a provoqué une vive é.** people were shocked by the child's murder; **l'atterrissage mouvementé a provoqué une vive é. parmi les passagers** the bumpy landing frightened the passengers; **ressentir une vive é.** *(attendrissement)* to be greatly moved; *(exaltation)* to be thrilled; **émotions fortes** strong feelings; **quelle é. de l'avoir revu!** seeing him again was quite a shock!; **ils se sont quittés avec é.** they had an emotional parting; **sans é.** without emotion

2 *(affectivité)* emotion, emotionality; **chargé d'é.** emotional, charged with emotion; **l'é. n'est pas bonne conseillère** do not be guided by emotion *or* your emotions; **se laisser gagner par l'é.** to become emotional; **parler avec é.** to speak emotionally

3 *(qualité → d'une œuvre)* emotion; **l'é. qui se dégage de ces lignes/cet oratorio** the emotion emanating from these lines/this oratorio

❑ **émotions** NFPL *Fam* **des émotions** a (nasty) fright; **j'ai eu des émotions** I got a fright; **donner des émotions à qn** to give sb a (nasty) turn *or* a fright

émotionnable [emosjɔnabl] ADJ emotional

émotionnant, -e [emosjɔnɑ̃, -ɑ̃t] ADJ *Fam* impressive ▪

émotionnel, -elle [emosjɔnel] ADJ *(réaction)* psychological

émotionner[3] [emosjɔne] *Fam* VT *(émouvoir)* to upset ▪, to shake up; **tout émotionné** very upset *or* shaken ▪

►**s'émotionner** VPR *(s'émouvoir)* **il s'émotionne pour un rien** he gets worked up about the slightest little thing

émotive [emɔtiv] *voir* **émotif**

émotivité [emɔtivite] NF emotionalism; **être d'une trop grande é.** to be too emotional

émottage [emɔtaʒ], **émottement** [emɔtmɑ̃] NM *Agr* breaking up into clods

émotter[3] [emɔte] VT *Agr (sol, terre)* to break up into clods

émotteur, -euse [emɔtœr, -øz] *Agr* ADJ **rouleau é.** clod-crusher roller

❑ **émotteuse** NF clod-crusher

émou [emu] NM *Zool* emu

émouchet [emuʃɛ] NM *Orn* = any of various types of small hawk, especially the kestrel

émouchette [emuʃɛt] NF *(pour cheval)* fly net

émoudre [85] [emudr] VT *Arch* to grind, to sharpen, to whet

émoulage [emulaʒ] NM *Arch* grinding, sharpening, whetting

émouleur [emulœr] NM *Arch (pour outil)* (tool-)grinder; *(pour couteau)* knife-grinder

émoulu, -e [emuly] *voir* **frais**[2]

émoussé, -e [emuse] ADJ blunt; *Fig (sentiment, qualité etc)* blunted, diminished; **une patience émoussée par le temps** patience diminished *or* worn thin by time; **il a l'appétit é. par la maladie** illness has blunted *or* taken the edge off his appetite

émousser[3] [emuse] VT **1** *(rasoir, épée)* to blunt, to take the edge off

2 *(affaiblir → appétit, goût, peine)* to dull, to take the edge off; *(→ curiosité)* to temper; *(→ sens, passions etc)* to dull, to blunt

►**s'émousser** VPR **1** *(couteau)* to become blunt, to lose its edge

2 *(faiblir → appétit, peine)* to dull; *(→ curiosité)* to become tempered; *(→ des sens, passions)* to become blunted *or* dulled; **mon appétit s'est émoussé depuis que je suis malade** I've not had much appetite *or* I haven't felt much like eating since I fell ill

émoustillant, -e [emustijɑ̃, -ɑ̃t] ADJ exhilarating; *(sexuellement)* titillating

émoustiller[3] [emustije] VT **1** *(animer)* to excite, to exhilarate; **le champagne les avait tous émoustillés** they'd all got merry on champagne **2** *(sexuellement)* to turn on

émouvant, -e [emuvɑ̃, -ɑ̃t] ADJ moving, touching; **de façon émouvante** movingly; **un moment é.** an emotional moment

émouvoir [55] [emuvwar] VT **1** *(attendrir)* to touch, to move; **é. qn (jusqu')aux larmes** to move sb to tears

2 *(perturber)* to disturb, to unsettle; **encore tout ému de la rencontre** still very upset by the meeting; **il est parti, cela ne semble pas t'é.** he's left, but you don't seem to be bothered (by it); **nullement ému par ces accusations** quite undisturbed *or* unperturbed by these accusations; **cela ne m'émeut pas le moins du monde** that doesn't upset me in the least; **ça n'a pas eu l'air de l'é.** he/she seemed quite unsympathetic; **se laisser é.** to let oneself be affected

3 *Littéraire (sexuellement)* to arouse, to excite

►**s'émouvoir** VPR **1** *(s'attendrir)* to be touched *or* moved; **s'é. à la vue de** to be affected by the sight of

2 *(être perturbé)* to be disturbed *or* perturbed; **ce qu'il me déclara sans s'é. le moins du monde** which he announced to me with perfect composure

3 *Littéraire (sexuellement)* to be aroused *or* excited

4 *Fig* **s'é. de** to pay attention to; **le gouvernement s'en est ému** it came to the notice *or* attention of the government; *Fam* **pas de quoi s'é.** it's nothing to get worked up about

empaffé [ɑ̃pafe] NM *Vulg* dickhead, prick, *Br* wanker

empagement [ɑ̃paʒmɑ̃] NM *Ordinat & Typ* text area, text block

empaillage [ɑ̃pajaʒ] NM **1** *(d'animaux)* taxidermy; **e. d'un animal** stuffing **2** *(d'une chaise)* bottoming with straw **3** *Hort* covering with straw

empaillé, -e [ɑ̃paje] **ADJ** *(animal)* stuffed; *Fam* **avoir l'air e.** to look self-conscious■ *or* awkward■
NM,F *Fam Péj* fat lump
empaillement [ɑ̃pajmɑ̃] **NM 1** *(d'une chaise)* bottoming with straw **2** *Hort* mulching **3** *(de produits)* packing in straw
empailler [3] [ɑ̃paje] **VT 1** *(animal)* to stuff; **ils ont fait e. leur chien** they had their dog stuffed **2** *(chaise)* to bottom with straw **3** *Hort* to mulch **4** *(produit)* to pack in straw
▸**s'empailler VPR** *Fam (se quereller)* to lay into each other
empailleur, -euse [ɑ̃pajœr, -øz] **NM,F 1** *(d'animaux)* taxidermist **2** *(de chaises)* chair caner
empalement [ɑ̃palmɑ̃] **NM** impalement
empaler [3] [ɑ̃pale] **VT 1** *(supplicier)* to impale **2** *(embrocher)* to put on a spit
▸**s'empaler VPR s'e. sur une fourche/un pieu** to impale oneself on a pitchfork/stake
empalmage [ɑ̃palmaʒ] **NM** palming
empalmer [3] [ɑ̃palme] **VT** to palm
empan [ɑ̃pɑ̃] **NM** (hand) span
empanacher [3] [ɑ̃panaʃe] **VT** to plume, to deck out *or* to decorate with plumes; **casque empanaché** plumed helmet
empannage [ɑ̃panaʒ] **NM** *Naut* gybing
empanner [3] [ɑ̃pane] **VT** *Naut* to gybe
empapaouté [ɑ̃papaute] **NM** *très Fam Br* arsehole, *Am* asshole
empapaouter [3] [ɑ̃papaute] **VT** *très Fam* to bugger, to take up the *Br* arse *or Am* ass; **va te faire e.!** go to hell!, *Br* bugger off!, sod off!
empaquetage [ɑ̃paktaʒ] **NM 1** *Com (action)* packing, packaging; *(emballage)* packaging **2** *(confection d'un paquet-cadeau)* wrapping up; *(enveloppe)* wrapping
empaqueter [27] [ɑ̃pakte] **VT 1** *Com* to pack, to package **2** *(envelopper)* to wrap up
empaqueteur, -euse [ɑ̃paktœr, -øz] **NM,F** packer
emparadiser [3] [ɑ̃paradize] **VT** *Littéraire* to imparadise
emparer [3] [ɑ̃pare] **s'emparer VPR 1 s'e. de** *(avec la main → gén)* to grab (hold of), to grasp, to seize; *(→ vivement)* to snatch
2 s'e. de *(prendre de force → territoire)* to take over, to seize; *(→ véhicule)* to commandeer; *(→ ville, otage, butin, pouvoir)* to seize; *Sport (→ ballon)* to take possession of, to get hold of; **la grande industrie s'est emparée des médias** big business has taken over the media; **s'e. de la conversation** to monopolize the conversation
3 s'e. de *(tirer parti de → prétexte, idée)* to seize (hold of); **la presse s'est emparée de cette histoire** the press got hold of the story
4 s'e. de *(envahir → sujet: doute, obsession, jalousie etc)* to take hold of; **la colère s'est emparée d'elle** anger swept over her; **l'émotion s'est emparée d'elle** she was seized by a strong emotion; **le doute s'est emparé de moi** *ou* **mon esprit** my mind was seized with doubt; **depuis que cette idée s'est emparée de mon esprit** since the idea took hold of me
empâté, -e [ɑ̃pate] **ADJ** *(voix)* slurred; *(langue)* coated; *(visage)* fleshy, bloated
empâtement [ɑ̃patmɑ̃] **NM 1** *Agr (de la volaille)* fattening (up) **2** *(obésité)* fattening out; *(épaississement → des traits)* coarsening; *(→ de la taille)* thickening **3** *Beaux-Arts* impasto
empâter [3] [ɑ̃pate] **VT 1** *Agr (engraisser → volaille)* to fatten (up)
2 *(bouffir)* to make podgier; *(visage)* to bloat, to coarsen; **l'âge ne l'a pas empâtée** she hasn't put on any weight as she's got older; **la vie à la campagne l'a empâtée** she has put on weight in the country; **les grossesses successives lui ont empâté la taille** she's grown fatter round the waist with each pregnancy
3 *(rendre pâteux → langue)* to coat, to fur up; **le vin lui a empâté la langue** his/her speech has become slurred from drinking wine
4 *Beaux-Arts* impaste
▸**s'empâter VPR** to put on weight; *(visage)* to coarsen; **sa taille/figure s'est empâtée** he's/she's grown fatter round the waist/fatter in the face
empathie [ɑ̃pati] **NF** empathy
empathique [ɑ̃patik] **ADJ** empathetic
empattement [ɑ̃patmɑ̃] **NM 1** *Constr (de planches)* tenoning; *(d'un mur)* footing; *(d'une grue)* base plate **2** *(d'un arbre, d'une branche)* (wide) base **3** *Aut* wheelbase **4** *Typ* serif
empatter [3] [ɑ̃pate] **VT** *Constr (mur)* to give footing to
empaumer [3] [ɑ̃pome] **VT 1** *(au jeu de paume → attraper)* to catch in the palm of the hand; *(→ frapper)* to strike with the palm of the hand **2** *Fam Vieilli (duper)* to con; **se laisser** *ou* **se faire e.** to be tricked *or* taken in **3** *(sujet: magicien etc → carte, pièce etc)* to palm
empaumure [ɑ̃pomyr] **NF 1** *(d'un gant)* palm piece **2** *Chasse (d'un cerf)* palm
empêché, -e [ɑ̃peʃe] **ADJ il a été e.** *(par un problème)* he hit a snag; *(il n'est pas venu)* he couldn't make it; *(il a été retenu)* he was held up
empêchement [ɑ̃pɛʃmɑ̃] **NM 1** *(obstacle)* snag, hitch; **je ne vois pas d'e. à ce que tu y ailles** I see no reason why you shouldn't go; **si tu as un e., téléphone** *(si tu as un problème)* if you hit a snag, phone; *(si tu ne viens pas)* if you can't make it, phone; *(si tu es retenu)* if you're held up, phone; **j'ai eu un e.** I got held up *or* detained, something came up at the last minute
2 *Jur* **e. à mariage** impediment to a marriage; **e. dirimant à mariage** diriment impediment to marriage; **e. prohibitif à mariage** prohibitive impediment to marriage
empêcher [4] [ɑ̃peʃe] **VT 1** *(ne pas laisser)* **e. qn de faire qch** to prevent sb (from) *or* to keep sb from *or* to stop sb (from) doing sth; **il m'a empêché de partir** he prevented me from leaving; **pousse-toi, tu m'empêches de voir!** move over, I can't see!; **il sera difficile de l'en e.** it will be difficult to stop *or* prevent him/her; **je ne vous empêche pas de partir/dîner, au moins?** I hope I'm not keeping you from leaving/your dinner?; **tu ne m'empêcheras pas de penser que j'ai raison** I still think I'm right, you won't convince me that I'm wrong; **un dispositif qui empêche l'eau de déborder** a device to stop the water overflowing; **e. qn d'entrer/de sortir/d'approcher** to keep sb out/in/away; **e. que qn/qch (ne) fasse** to stop sb/sth from doing, to prevent sb/sth from doing; **le café m'empêche de dormir** coffee keeps me awake; *Fig* **ce n'est pas ça qui va l'e. de dormir!** he's/she's not going to lose any sleep over that!
2 *(pour renforcer une suggestion)* to stop, to prevent; **cela ne t'empêche pas** *ou* **rien ne t'empêche de l'acheter à crédit** you could always buy it in instalments; **il n'y a rien qui t'empêche de lui téléphoner** there's nothing to stop you phoning him/her; **qu'est-ce qui nous empêche de le faire?** what's to prevent us (from) doing it?; **qu'est-ce qui vous empêche d'écrire à ses parents?** why don't you write to his/her parents?
3 *(prévenir → mariage, famine)* to prevent, to stop; *(→ action, événement etc)* to prevent; *(→ mouvement, progrès etc)* to obstruct, to impede; **pour e. l'hémorragie** to prevent a haemorrhage; **e. l'extension d'un conflit** to stop a conflict spreading; **cela n'empêche pas les sentiments!** you've got to have some feeling *or* heart!; *Fam* **ça n'empêche pas** *ou* **rien!** it makes no difference!
4 *(retenir)* **empêché de venir, il n'a pas pu voter** he couldn't vote, as he was (unavoidably) detained
V IMPERSONNEL il n'empêche que nevertheless; **il n'empêche que cela nous a coûté cher** all the same *or* nevertheless it has cost us dear; **il n'empêche qu'elle ne l'a jamais compris** the fact remains that she's never understood him; **il n'empêche que tu es encore en retard** maybe, but you're late again all the same
❑ **n'empêche ADV** *Fam* all the same■, though■; **il a été assez gentil, n'empêche!** he was kind, though!; **n'empêche, tu aurais pu (me) prévenir!** all the same *or* even so, you could have let me know!
❑ **n'empêche que CONJ** *Fam* **on ne m'a pas écouté, n'empêche que j'avais raison!** they didn't listen to me, even though I was right!
▸**s'empêcher VPR s'e. de faire** to refrain from *or* to stop oneself doing; **je ne pouvais pas m'e. de rire** I couldn't help laughing, I had to laugh; **je ne peux pas m'e. de penser qu'il a raison** I can't help thinking he's right; **il n'a pas pu s'e. de le dire** he just had to say it; **elle ne peut pas s'e. de se ronger les ongles** she can't stop (herself) biting her nails; **je ne peux pas m'en e.** I can't help it, I can't stop myself
empêcheur, -euse [ɑ̃pɛʃœr, -øz] **NM,F** *Fam* **un e. de danser** *ou* **tourner en rond** a spoilsport
Empédocle [ɑ̃pedɔkl] **NPR** Empedocles
empeigne [ɑ̃pɛɲ] **NF** *Tech* upper *(of a shoe)*; *Fam* **gueule d'e.** ugly mug
empennage [ɑ̃pɛnaʒ] **NM 1** *Aviat* empennage **2** *(d'un obus, d'une bombe)* tail fins; *(d'une arbalète, d'une flèche)* feathers; *(d'une torpille)* fins
empenne [ɑ̃pɛn] **NF** *(d'une arbalète, d'une flèche)* feathers
empenné, -e [ɑ̃pɛne] **ADJ** feathered
empenner [3] [ɑ̃pɛne] **VT** *(flèche)* to feather
empereur [ɑ̃prœr] **NM** emperor; *Hist* **l'E.** Napoleon (Bonaparte *or* the First)
emperler [3] [ɑ̃pɛrle] **VT 1** *Littéraire (couvrir)* **la sueur emperlait son front** his/her forehead glistened with beads of sweat; **pétales emperlés de rosée** petals covered with pearls of dew **2** *Couture* to bead
emperlousé, -e [ɑ̃pɛrluze] **ADJ** *très Fam* dripping with pearls
empesage [ɑ̃pəzaʒ] **NM** starching
empesé, -e [ɑ̃pəze] **ADJ 1** *(tissu)* starched **2** *(discours, style)* starchy
empeser [19] [ɑ̃pəze] **VT** to starch
empester [3] [ɑ̃pɛste] **VT 1** *(empuantir → pièce, réfrigérateur)* to make stink, *Br* to stink out; *(→ personne)* to stink out; **le fromage empeste le frigo** the cheese is making the fridge stink *or Br* is stinking out the fridge; **e. qn (avec sa fumée)** to stink sb out (with one's smoke) **2** *(dégager une forte odeur de)* to stink of; **e. l'alcool/le parfum** to reek *or* stink of alcohol/perfume; **le frigo empeste le fromage** the fridge stinks of cheese
VI *(sentir très mauvais)* to stink
empêtré, -e [ɑ̃petre] **ADJ** *(air)* awkward, self-conscious
empêtrer [4] [ɑ̃petre] **VT 1** *(entortiller → personne)* to trap, to entangle; *(→ jambes, chevilles)* to trap, to catch; **empêtrée dans sa grosse veste** hampered by her bulky jacket; **empêtré dans ses couvertures** all tangled up in his blankets
2 *(embarrasser)* to bog down; **être empêtré dans ses explications** to be bogged down *or* muddled up in one's explanations; **être empêtré dans ses mensonges** to be caught in the web of *or* trapped in one's own lies
▸**s'empêtrer VPR 1** *(s'entortiller)* to become tangled up *or* entangled; **elle s'est empêtrée dans la corde** she got tangled up in the rope; **s'e. les pieds dans les broussailles** to get one's feet caught in the undergrowth
2 *(s'enferrer)* **s'e. dans** *(mensonges, explications)* to get bogged down *or* tied up in; **s'e. dans une sale affaire** to get involved *or* mixed up in a bad business; **s'e. de qn** to land oneself with sb
emphase [ɑ̃faz] **NF 1** *Péj (grandiloquence)* pomposity, bombast; **un discours plein d'e.** a pompous speech; **avec e.** pompously, bombastically; **solennel mais sans e.** solemn but not pompous **2** *Ling* emphasis
emphatique [ɑ̃fatik] **ADJ 1** *Péj (grandiloquent)* pompous, bombastic **2** *Ling* emphatic
emphatiquement [ɑ̃fatikmɑ̃] **ADV** pompously, bombastically
emphysémateux, -euse [ɑ̃fizematø, -øz] *Méd* **ADJ** emphysematous
NM,F person suffering from emphysema
emphysème [ɑ̃fizɛm] **NM** *Méd* emphysema; **e. pulmonaire** pulmonary emphysema
emphytéose [ɑ̃fiteoz] **NF** *Jur* right to a long lease
emphytéote [ɑ̃fiteɔt] **NMF** *Jur* holder of a long lease
emphytéotique [ɑ̃fiteɔtik] **ADJ** *Jur* **bail e.** long lease
empiècement [ɑ̃pjɛsmɑ̃] **NM** *Tex* yoke
empierrement [ɑ̃pjɛrmɑ̃] **NM 1** *(couche de pierres)* gravel, *Br* road metal; *Rail* ballast **2** *(pour le drainage)* lining with stones **3** *(action → d'une route)* macadamization, *Br* metalling; *Rail* ballasting; **procéder à l'e. d'une route** to macadamize *or Br* to metal a road

empierrer [4] [ɑ̃pjere] **VT 1** *(route)* to macadamize, *Br* to metal; *Rail* to ballast **2** *(pour le drainage)* to line with stones

empiétement, empiètement [ɑ̃pjɛtmɑ̃] **NM** encroachment, encroaching *(UNCOUNT)* (**sur** on); **c'est un e. sur ma vie privée** it's an encroachment on my private life; **cette barrière est un e. sur mon terrain** that fence encroaches on my land; **e. sur les droits de qn** infringement of sb's rights

empiéter[18] [ɑ̃pjete] **empiéter sur VT IND1** *(dans l'espace, le temps)* to encroach on *or* upon, to overlap with; **cette affiche empiète sur l'autre** this poster overlaps the other

2 *(droit, liberté, pouvoir)* to encroach on *or* upon, to infringe; **mon travail empiète de plus en plus sur mes loisirs** my work encroaches more and more upon my leisure time; **son collègue essaie d'e. sur ses attributions** his/her colleague is trying to trespass on his/her territory; **e. sur les droits de qn** to infringe sb's rights; **empiétant peu à peu sur nos privilèges** gradually eating away at our privileges

empiffrer[3] [ɑ̃pifre] **s'empiffrer VPR** *Fam* to stuff oneself *or* one's face, to pig out; **s'e. de gâteaux** to stuff oneself with cakes

empilable[ɑ̃pilabl] **ADJ** stackable

empilage[ɑ̃pilaʒ] **NM1** *(action → de boîtes)* piling *or* stacking up; *(→ de chaises)* stacking up **2** *(pile)* pile, stack

empile[ɑ̃pil] **NF** *Pêche* trace, cast

empilement [ɑ̃pilmɑ̃] **NM** *(ordonné)* stack; *(désordonné)* heap, pile, mound

empiler[3] [ɑ̃pile] **VT1** *(mettre en tas)* to pile *or* to heap up; *(ranger en hauteur)* to stack (up)

2 *(thésauriser)* to amass (large quantities of)

3 *Fam (tromper)* to screw, to fleece; **se faire e. (par qn)** to get screwed *or* fleeced (by sb)

▸**s'empiler VPR1** *(emploi passif)* to be stacked up; **ces chaises s'empilent** the chairs are stackable

2 *(s'entasser)* to pile up; *(former une pile)* to be piled up; **s'e. dans** *(entrer nombreux dans)* to pile *or* to pack into

empileur, -euse [ɑ̃pilœr, -øz] **NM,F 1** *très Fam (escroc)* trickster, conman, crook **2** *(ouvrier)* stacker

Empire[ɑ̃pir] **NM l'E., le premier E.** the (Napoleonic) Empire; **sous l'E.** during the Napoleonic era; **noblesse d'E.** nobility created by Napoleon (Bonaparte); **le Second E.** the Second Empire; **meubles E.** Empire furniture, furniture in the French Empire style; **l'E. du Milieu** the Middle Kingdom, the Celestial Empire

empire[ɑ̃pir] **NM1** *Hist (régime, territoire)* empire; **je ne m'en séparerais pas pour (tout) un e.!** I wouldn't be without it for the world!; **l'e. d'Occident** the Western Empire; **l'e. d'Orient** *(romain)* the Eastern (Roman) Empire; *(byzantin)* the Byzantine Empire; **l'e. du Soleil Levant** the Land of the Rising Sun

2 *Myth & Rel* **l'e. céleste** the kingdom of heaven; **l'e. des ténèbres** hell; **l'e. des morts** the realm of the dead; **l'e. de Neptune** Neptune's empire

3 *(groupe d'états)* empire

4 *Com & Ind* empire

5 *Littéraire (domination)* **l'e. des mers** the control of the seas

6 *(influence)* influence; **avoir de l'e. sur qn** to have a hold on *or* over sb; **avoir de l'e. sur soi-même** to be self-controlled; **quand j'ai bu, je n'ai plus aucun e. sur moi-même** I lose all self-control when I drink; **prendre de l'e. sur qn** to gain influence over sb; **user de** *ou* **exercer son e. sur qn** to use one's power over sb

❑ **sous l'empire de PRÉP1** *(poussé par)* **sous l'e. de l'alcool** under the influence of alcohol; **sous l'e. de la jalousie** in the grip of jealousy; **sous l'e. du désir** possessed *or* consumed by desire; **faire qch sous l'e. de la colère** to do sth in a fit of anger; **elle s'est enfuie sous l'e. de la peur** she fled in fear

2 *(soumis à)* **sous l'e. d'un tyran** ruled by a tyrant, under the rule *or Littéraire* sway of a tyrant; **sous l'e. d'un mari brutal** under the sway of a brutal husband

empirer[3] [ɑ̃pire] **VI** *(santé)* to become worse, to worsen, to deteriorate; *(mauvais caractère)* to become worse; *(problème, situation)* to get worse

VT to make worse, to cause to deteriorate

empiriocriticisme [ɑ̃pirjɔkritisism] **NM** *Phil* empiriocriticism

empirique[ɑ̃pirik] **ADJ1** *Phil* empirical **2** *Péj (non rigoureux)* empirical, purely practical

empiriquement [ɑ̃pirikmɑ̃] **ADV 1** *Phil* empirically **2** *Péj (sans rigueur)* empirically, without a basis in theory

empirisme[ɑ̃pirism] **NM1** *Phil* empiricism **2** *Péj (pragmatisme)* empiricism, charlatanry

empiriste[ɑ̃pirist] *Phil* **ADJ** empiricist

NMF empiricist

emplacement [ɑ̃plasmɑ̃] **NM 1** *(pour véhicule)* (parking) space

2 *(position → d'un édifice, d'un monument, d'une tente)* site, location; *(→ d'une démarcation)* position, place; *(→ sur un marché)* space; **à l'e. d'un ancien tombeau** on the site of an old tomb; *Naut* **e. de chargement** loading berth

3 *Mktg (site)* site, location; *(dans un journal, à la télé)* space; **e. d'affichage** billboard site, *Br* hoarding site; **e. isolé** solus position, solus site; **e. publicitaire** advertising space

4 *Ordinat* slot; **e. pour carte** card slot; **e. pour carte d'extension** expansion slot; **e. d'évolutivité** upgrade slot; **e. (pour) périphériques** extension slot

emplafonner[3] [ɑ̃plafɔne] **VT** *Fam* to crash into; **elle s'est fait e. par mon voisin** my neighbour crashed into her

emplanture [ɑ̃plɑ̃tyr] **NF1** *Naut* step; **mettre un mât dans son e.** to step a mast **2** *Aviat* root, socket

emplâtre[ɑ̃platr] **NM1** *Pharm* plaster; *Fig* **c'est un e. sur une jambe de bois** it's like putting a plaster on a wooden leg **2** *Fam (aliment)* **un véritable e., leur purée!** their mashed potatoes go down like a lead weight! **3** *Fam (personne) Br* waster, *Am* klutz

emplette[ɑ̃plɛt] **NF1** *(fait d'acheter)* **faire ses/des emplettes** to do one's/some shopping; **faire l'e. de** to purchase **2** *(objet acheté)* purchase

emplir [32] [ɑ̃plir] **VT** *(récipient)* to fill (up) (**de** with); *(salle)* to fill (**de** with); **la foule emplissait les rues** the crowd filled the streets; **cette nouvelle m'emplit de joie** the news fills me with delight; **les enfants emplissaient la cour de leurs rires** the playground was filled with children's laughter

▸**s'emplir VPR** to fill up; **s'e. de** to fill up with; **s'e. d'air** to inflate, to fill with air

emplissage[ɑ̃plisaʒ] **NM** *Littéraire* filling

emploi [ɑ̃plwa] **NM 1** *(travail)* job; *(embauche)* employment; **être sans e.** to be out of work *or* out of a job, to be unemployed; **chercher un e.** to be looking for work *or* a job; **avoir un e.** to have a job, to be in work; **e. fictif** fictitious job; **emplois de proximité** = employment in the community *(as a way of reducing unemployment)*; **e. saisonnier** seasonal job; **e. à temps partiel** part-time job

2 *(fait d'employer)* employing; **l'e. de spécialistes coûte cher** employing experts is expensive

3 *Écon* **l'e.** employment; **la crise de l'e.** the employment crisis; **le marché de l'e.** the labour market; **le partage de l'e.** job-sharing; **la sécurité de l'e.** job security; **la situation de l'e.** the job *or* employment situation

4 *(au spectacle)* part; **limitée à des emplois de soubrette** restricted to playing chambermaids; **son e., c'est les ingénues** she's typecast as an ingénue, she (always) plays ingénue parts; **on le cantonne dans des emplois de grand amoureux** he is typecast as the great lover; **danser/jouer à contre-e.** to be miscast; *Fig* **cet e. de mari comblé te va mal** you're not playing the happy husband very convincingly; *Fam* **avoir le physique** *ou* **la tête** *ou* **la gueule de l'e.** to look the part

5 *(utilisation)* use; **il n'en a pas l'e.** he has no use for it; **d'un e. facile** easy to use; **faire bon/mauvais e. de qch** to make good/bad use of sth, to put sth to good/bad use; **faire mauvais e. de son argent** to misuse one's money; **faire double e.** to be redundant; **l'e. du béton est de plus en plus courant** concrete is being used increasingly; **quel e. vas-tu faire de tout cet argent/ce temps?** what are you going to do with all that money/time?; **prêt à l'e.** ready to use; *Écon* **e. optimum des ressources** optimum employment of resources

6 *Scol* **e. du temps** *(de l'année)* timetable; *(d'une journée, des vacances)* timetable, schedule; **un e. du temps chargé** a busy timetable *or* schedule; **quel est mon e. du temps aujourd'hui?** what's my schedule for today?

7 *(cas d'utilisation → d'un objet)* use; *(→ d'une expression)* use, usage; **les divers emplois d'un verbe** the different uses of a verb; **ce mot est d'un e. rare** the word is rarely used

8 *Compta* entry

emploie *etc voir* **employer**

emploi-jeunes [ɑ̃plwaʒœn] (*pl* **emplois-jeunes**) **NM** = job, usually in the public sector or in education, created for a young person as part of a programme to combat unemployment

employabilité[ɑ̃plwajabilite] **NF** employability

employable [ɑ̃plwajabl] **ADJ** *(personne)* employable; *(objet)* usable

employé, -e[ɑ̃plwaje] **NM,F** employee; **généreux avec leurs employés** generous to their staff *or* their employees; **e. de banque** bank clerk; **e. de bureau** office worker; **e. de chemin de fer** railway employee; **employés communaux** local authority employees; **e. aux écritures** accounts *or* ledger clerk; **j'attends un e. du gaz** I'm expecting someone from the gas *Br* board *or Am* company; **e. de maison** servant; **employés de maison** domestic staff; **être e. de maison** to do domestic work; **e. de mairie** town hall employee; **être e. de mairie** to work at the town hall; **e. occasionnel** casual worker; **e. des postes** postal worker; **être e. des postes** to work for the Post Office

employer [13] [ɑ̃plwaje] **VT 1** *(professionnellement)* to employ; **nous employons 200 personnes** we employ 200 people, we have 200 people on our staff, we employ a staff of 200; **la ganterie emploie 300 personnes dans la région** the glove trade provides jobs for *or* employs 300 local people; **e. qn à faire qch** *(l'assigner à une tâche)* to use sb to do sth; **e. qn comme secrétaire** to employ sb as secretary; **e. qn à des corvées/des petits travaux** to employ sb to do the chores/odd jobs; **employé à plein temps/à temps partiel** employed full-time/part-time

2 *(manier → instrument, machine)* to use

3 *(mettre en œuvre → méthode, ruse)* to employ, to use; **e. la force** to use force; **e. beaucoup d'énergie à faire qch** to expend a lot of energy doing sth; **e. son énergie à faire qch** to devote *or* to apply one's energy to doing sth; **e. toute son énergie à faire qch** to devote all one's energies to doing sth; **de l'argent bien employé** money well spent, money put to good use; **des fonds mal employés** misused funds; **elle ne sait pas e. son argent** she doesn't know what to do with her money; **à quoi vas-tu e. cette somme?** what are you going to spend the money on?; **tu vas y e. toutes tes réserves** you will use up all your reserves doing it

4 *(expression)* to use; **mal e. un mot** to misuse a word, to use a word incorrectly

5 *(temps, journée)* to spend; **bien e. son temps** to make good use of one's time; **mal e. son temps** to misuse one's time, to use one's time badly, to waste one's time; **e. son temps à nettoyer/étudier** to spend one's time cleaning/studying; **il ne sait à quoi e. son temps** he doesn't know what to do with his time

6 *Compta* to enter

▸**s'employer VPR1** *(mot)* to be used; **ce verbe ne s'emploie plus** that verb is no longer in common usage

2 *(outil, machine)* to be used

3 s'e. à *(se consacrer à)* to devote *or* to apply oneself to; **je m'y emploie** I'm working on it; *Vieilli* **s'e. pour** *ou* **en faveur de** *(s'activer)* to exert oneself on behalf of

employeur, -euse[ɑ̃plwajœr, -øz] **NM,F** employer

emplumer [3] [ɑ̃plyme] **VT** to decorate with feathers

empochage[ɑ̃pɔʃaʒ] **NM** pot *(in billiards)*

empocher[3] [ɑ̃pɔʃe] **VT1** *(mettre dans sa poche)* to pocket **2** *(s'approprier)* to snap up **3** *(au billard)* to pot

empoignade [ɑ̃pwaɲad] **NF** *Fam* **1** *(coups)* brawl, set-to **2** *(querelle)* row, set-to

empoigne [ɑ̃pwaɲ] *voir* **foire**

empoigner [3] [ɑ̃pwaɲe] **VT 1** *(avec les mains)* to grab, to grasp **2** *(émouvoir)* to grip

▸**s'empoigner VPR** to set to; **ils se sont tous empoignés** there was a general mêlée *or* a free-for-all

empointure [ɑ̃pwɛ̃tyr] **NF** *Naut (d'une voile)* earing, peak

empois [ɑ̃pwa] **NM** starch

empoise [ɑ̃pwaz] **NF** *Tech* chock

empoisonnant, -e [ɑ̃pwazɔnɑ̃, -ɑ̃t] **ADJ** *Fam* **1** *(exaspérant)* annoying■; **ce que tu peux être e.!** you can be such a pain sometimes! **2** *(ennuyeux)* tedious■, boring■

empoisonné, -e [ɑ̃pwazɔne] **ADJ** *(trait, paroles)* poisonous, vicious

empoisonnement [ɑ̃pwazɔnmɑ̃] **NM 1** *Physiol* poisoning; **e. par le plomb** lead poisoning **2** *Fam (souci, ennui)* problem■

empoisonner [3] [ɑ̃pwazɔne] **VT 1** *(tuer)* to poison; **il pensait qu'il s'était fait e.** he thought he'd been poisoned

2 *École* to contaminate, to poison

3 *(mettre du poison sur → flèche)* to poison

4 *(empester)* **des odeurs de cuisine empoisonnaient la pièce** the room was full of cooking smells

5 *(dégrader → rapports)* to poison, to taint, to blight; *(→ esprit)* to poison; **e. l'existence** *ou* **la vie à qn** to make sb's life a misery

6 *Fam (importuner)* to bug■; **tu m'empoisonnes avec tes questions!** you're being a real pain with your questions!

▸**s'empoisonner VPR 1** *(se tuer)* to poison oneself

2 *Physiol* to get food poisoning

3 *Fam (s'ennuyer)* to be bored stiff; **s'e. l'existence** *ou* **la vie** to make one's life a misery

4 s'e. à faire qch *(se donner du mal pour)* to go to the trouble to do sth; **je ne vais pas m'e. à coller toutes ces enveloppes!** I can't be bothered to seal all those envelopes!; **on va s'e. à peindre deux couches?** is it worth (going to) the trouble *or* bother of painting two coats?

empoisonneur, -euse [ɑ̃pwazɔnœr, -øz] **NM,F 1** *Fam (importun → qui lasse)* nuisance, bore; *(→ qui gêne)* nuisance, pain (in the neck) **2** *(assassin)* poisoner

empoissonnement [ɑ̃pwasɔnmɑ̃] **NM 1** *(action)* stocking with fish **2** *(état)* stock of fish

empoissonner [3] [ɑ̃pwasɔne] **VT** to stock with fish

emporium [ɑ̃pɔrjɔm] *(pl* **emporiums** *ou* **emporia** [-rja]) **NM** *Antiq* emporium

emport [ɑ̃pɔr] **NM** *Aviat* **capacité d'e.** maximum payload

emporté, -e [ɑ̃pɔrte] **ADJ** *(coléreux → personne)* quick-tempered; *(→ ton)* angry; **d'un ton e.** irascibly

NM,F quick-tempered person

emportement [ɑ̃pɔrtəmɑ̃] **NM 1** *(colère)* anger *(UNCOUNT)*; *(accès de colère)* fit of anger; **avec e.** angrily **2** *Littéraire ou Vieilli (passion)* transport; **aimer qn avec e.** to love sb passionately; **dans l'e. de la discussion** in the heat of the debate

emporte-pièce [ɑ̃pɔrtəpjɛs] **NM INV** *Tech* punch; *Culin Br* pastry cutter, *Am* cookie cutter; **découper qch à l'e.** to stamp *or* punch sth out; *Culin* to cut out (with a *Br* pastry cutter *or Am* cookie cutter)

❑ **à l'emporte-pièce ADJ** incisive **ADV** incisively; **répondre à l'e.** to reply incisively *or* trenchantly

emporter [3] [ɑ̃pɔrte] **VT 1** *(prendre avec soi)* to take; **n'oubliez pas d'e. vos pilules** don't forget to take your tablets (with you); **en randonnée, je n'emporte que le strict minimum** I only ever carry the lightest possible load on a hike; **ils ont emporté de quoi manger** they took some food with them; *Fig* **je n'emporterai que ta promesse** I will bring away *or* take with me nothing but your promise; **e. un secret dans la** *ou* **sa tombe** to take *or* to carry a secret to the grave; **il ne l'emportera pas au paradis!** he's not getting away with that!

2 *(transporter → stylo, parapluie, animal)* to take; *(→ bureau, piano, blessé)* to carry (off *or* away); **emporte tout ça au grenier/à la cave** take these things (up) to the attic/(down) to the cellar; **e. un malade sur un brancard** to carry off a sick person on a stretcher; **l'avion qui nous emporte vers le soleil** the plane taking *or* carrying us off to sunny climes; **le train qui m'emporte vers le nord** the train which is carrying *or* taking me northwards

3 *(retirer → livre, stylo)* to take (away), to remove; *(→ malle, piano)* to carry away, to remove; **qui a emporté la clef?** who removed the key?; **la mer emporte le varech** the wrack is carried away *or* swept away by the sea; **feuilles emportées par le vent** leaves carried away *or* swept along by the wind; **le vent emporta son chapeau** the wind blew his/her hat off *or* away; **autant en emporte le vent** promises are cheap, talk is easy

4 *(voler)* to take, to go off with; **ils ont tout emporté!** they took everything!

5 *(endommager)* to tear off; *(sujet: courant, lave)* to sweep *or* carry away; **l'ouragan a emporté les toits des maisons** the hurricane blew the roofs off the houses; **il a eu le bras emporté par l'explosion** he lost an arm in the explosion, the explosion blew his arm off; **il a eu une jambe emportée par un obus** a shell took *or* blew one of his legs off; **cette sauce emporte** *Fam* **la bouche** *ou très Fam* **la gueule** this sauce takes the roof of your mouth off

6 *(émouvoir → sujet: amour, haine)* to carry (along); *(→ sujet: élan)* to carry away; **se laisser e. par** *(la colère, l'enthousiasme, l'imagination, les sentiments)* to get *or* let oneself be carried away by; **il s'est laissé e. par son imagination** he let his imagination run away with him

7 *(tuer → sujet: maladie)* **il a été emporté par un cancer** he died of cancer

8 *(gagner → victoire)* to win, to carry off; *(→ fort, ville etc)* to take (by assault); *(→ marché)* to close; *(→ contrat)* to land; **e. la victoire (contre)** to be victorious (over), to be the victor (over); **e. la décision** to win *or* to carry the day; **e. l'adhésion de qn** to win sb's support; **e. tous les suffrages** *Pol* to get all the votes; *Fig* to win general approval; *Fam* **e. le morceau** to have the upper hand; **l'e.** *(argument)* to win *or* to carry the day; *(attitude, méthode)* to prevail; **la raison a fini par l'e.** reason finally triumphed *or* prevailed; **avec lui, c'est toujours l'amitié qui l'emporte** friendship is always the most important consideration *or* outweighs everything else as far as he's concerned; **le plus fort l'emportera** *(boxeurs)* the stronger man will win; *(concurrents)* the best competitor will come out on top *or* carry the day; **l'équipe nantaise l'a emporté par deux buts à zéro** the Nantes team won (by) two goals to nil; **Cendrillon l'emportait en beauté (sur les autres)** Cinderella's beauty far outshone the others; **l'e. sur** to win *or* to prevail over; **considérations qui l'emportent sur toutes les autres** considerations that override *or* outweigh all others; **ce dossier/ce candidat/ce prototype l'emporte sur tous les autres** this file/candidate/prototype stands head and shoulders above the others *or* is streets ahead of the others; **ici, la pluie l'emporte sur le soleil** there's much more rain than sunshine here; **ici, le rugby l'emporte sur le foot** rugby is more important *or* popular than football here

❑ **à emporter,** *Suisse* **à l'emporter ADJ** *Br* to take away, *Am* to go; **plats à e.** *Br* takeaway *or Am* takeout food; **nous faisons des plats à e.** we have a *Br* takeaway *or Am* takeout service

▸**s'emporter VPR 1** *(personne)* to lose one's temper, to fly into a rage (**contre qn** with sb)

2 *(cheval)* to bolt

emposieu, -x [ɑ̃pozjø] **NM** *Suisse* = funnel-shaped gully down which rainwater runs off from the high plains of the Jura mountains

empotage [ɑ̃pɔtaʒ] **NM** *Hort* potting

empoté, -e [ɑ̃pɔte] *Fam* **ADJ** clumsy■, awkward■

NM,F clumsy oaf, *Am* klutz

empotement [ɑ̃pɔtmɑ̃] **NM** *Hort* potting

empoter [3] [ɑ̃pɔte] **VT** *Hort* to pot

empourprer [3] [ɑ̃purpre] *Littéraire* **VT 1** *(horizon)* to (tinge with) crimson **2** *(de honte, de plaisir)* to make flush (bright crimson)

▸**s'empourprer VPR 1** *(horizon)* to turn crimson **2** *(joues, personne)* to flush (bright crimson)

empoussiérer [18] [ɑ̃pusjere] **VT** to cover with dust, to make dusty

empreindre [81] [ɑ̃prɛ̃dr] *Littéraire* **VT** *(dans la cire)* to impress, to imprint, to stamp; *(pensée)* to mark, to stamp; *(cœur, comportement)* to mark; **empreint d'un amour véritable** marked by true love; **d'un ton empreint de gravité** in a grave tone of voice; **article empreint d'un certain sérieux** article with serious overtones; **des histoires empreintes d'onirisme** stories with a dreamlike quality; **empreint de danger** fraught with danger

▸**s'empreindre VPR s'e. de qch** to be tinged with sth

empreint, -e [ɑ̃prɛ̃, -ɛ̃t] **PP** *voir* **empreindre**

❑ **empreinte NF 1** *(du pas humain)* footprint; *(du gibier)* track; **les loups ont laissé des empreintes dans la neige** the wolves left tracks *or* footprints in the snow; **empreinte de pas** footprint; **empreinte de doigt** fingermark; **empreintes (digitales)** fingerprints; **empreinte digitale réduite** reduced fingerprint; **les empreintes du cambrioleur** the burglar's fingerprints; **prendre** *ou* **relever les empreintes de qn** to take sb's fingerprints, to fingerprint sb; **relever les empreintes sur un revolver** to fingerprint a revolver

2 *(d'un sceau)* imprint; *(sur une médaille)* stamp; **(frappé) à l'empreinte du roi** stamped with the king's head

3 *(d'une serrure)* impression; **prendre l'empreinte de** to take the impression of; **empreinte en plâtre** plaster cast

4 *(influence)* mark, stamp; **marquer qn/qch de son empreinte** to put one's stamp *or* mark on sb/sth; **être marqué de l'empreinte de qn** to bear sb's stamp *or* mark

5 *Psy* imprint

6 *(en dentisterie)* **empreintes dentaires** dental impression

7 *Géol* imprint

8 *Biol* **empreinte génétique** genetic fingerprint; **e. génomique** genetic imprinting; **empreinte vocale** voiceprint

empressé, -e [ɑ̃prese] **ADJ 1** *(fiancé)* thoughtful, attentive; *(vendeur)* eager, willing; *(serveuse, garde-malade)* attentive; *Péj* overzealous; **des soins empressés** assiduous attention; **ils m'ont entouré de soins empressés** they gave me every care and consideration; **il lui fait une cour empressée** he is courting her assiduously **2** *Littéraire Vieilli (pressé)* **il est e. à vous revoir** he is eager to see you again

NM,F faire l'e. auprès de qn to fawn over sb

empressement [ɑ̃prɛsmɑ̃] **NM 1** *(zèle)* assiduousness, attentiveness; *(d'un vendeur)* eagerness, willingness (**à faire qch** to do sth); **montrer de l'e.** to be eager to please; **son e. auprès des femmes est presque gênant** he is almost embarrassingly attentive to women

2 *(hâte)* enthusiasm, eagerness, keenness; **avec e.** eagerly; **il est allé les chercher avec e./sans (aucun) e.** he went off to get them enthusiastically/(very) reluctantly; **son e. à se déclarer coupable éveilla les soupçons** suspicions were aroused by the fact that he/she was so eager to admit his/her guilt; **il montre peu d'e. à faire les travaux** he doesn't seem to be very eager *or* keen to do the work

empresser [4] [ɑ̃prese] **s'empresser VPR 1 s'e. autour** *ou* **auprès de qn** *(s'activer)* to bustle around sb; *(être très attentif)* to attend to sb's needs; **les hommes s'empressent autour d'elle** she always has men hovering around her, men are always dancing attendance on her; **s'e. autour d'un accidenté de la route** to be busy attending to the victim of a road accident

2 s'e. de faire qch to hasten to do sth; **il s'est empressé de mettre l'argent dans sa poche** he hastily put the money in his pocket; **il s'empressa de répondre à ma lettre** he lost no time in answering my letter

emprésurer [3] [ɑ̃prezyre] **VT** to add rennet to

emprise [ɑ̃priz] **NF 1** *(intellectuelle, morale)* hold; **l'e. du désir** the ascendancy of desire; **sous l'e. de la peur** in the grip of fear; **sous l'e. de mon amour pour elle** swayed by my love for her; **c'est sous l'e. de la colère qu'il l'a mise à la porte** he fired her in a fit of anger; **être sous l'e.**

de qn to be under sb's thumb; **avoir de l'e. sur qn** to have a hold over sb

2 *Admin & Jur* expropriation

emprisonnement [ɑ̃prizɔnmɑ̃] NM imprisonment; **peine d'e.** prison sentence; **condamné à cinq ans d'e.** *ou* **à une peine d'e. de cinq ans** sentenced to five years in prison, given a five-year sentence; **e. à perpétuité** life imprisonment

emprisonner[3] [ɑ̃prizɔne] VT 1 *Jur (incarcérer → malfaiteur)* to imprison, to put in jail, to put in prison

2 *(immobiliser)* to trap; *(esprit)* to imprison; **le cou emprisonné dans une minerve** his/her neck tightly held in *or* constricted by a surgical collar; **e. le buste dans un corset** to squeeze into a corset; **il ne supporte pas les cols roulés parce qu'il se sent emprisonné** he hates roll-necks because he feels constricted in them

3 *(psychologiquement)* **e. qn dans une morale** to put sb in a moral straitjacket; **emprisonné dans des habitudes dont il ne peut pas se défaire** trapped in habits he is unable to break

emprunt [ɑ̃prœ̃] NM 1 *Banque & Fin (procédé)* borrowing; *(argent)* loan; **faire un e.** to borrow money, to take out a loan; **faire un e. de 10 000 euros** to raise a loan of *or* to borrow 10,000 euros; **faire un e. à qn** to borrow (money) from sb; **faire un e. de plusieurs millions à la banque** to borrow several million from the bank, to take out a bank loan of several million; **e. à 11 pour cent** loan at 11 percent; **il faudra recourir à un e.** we'll have to borrow; **procéder à un nouvel e.** to make a new loan issue; **contracter un e.** to raise a loan; **couvrir un e.** to cover a loan; **rembourser un e.** to repay a loan; **souscrire un e.** to subscribe a loan; **émettre un e.** to float a loan; **e. consolidé** consolidated loan; **e. de conversion** conversion loan; **e. à court terme** short-term loan; **e. à découvert** unsecured loan; **e. en devises** currency loan; **e. d'État** government loan; *Bourse* **e. à fenêtre** put bond; **e. forcé** forced loan; **e. sur gage** loan against security; **e. garanti** secured loan; **e. indexé** indexed loan; **e. à long terme** long-term loan; **e. à lots** lottery loan; **e. obligataire** bond issue, loan stock; *(titre)* debenture bond; **e. obligataire convertible** convertible loan stock; **e. or** gold loan; **e. perpétuel** perpetual loan; **e. personnel** personal loan; **e. public** public loan; **e. public d'État** government loan; **e. remboursable sur demande** call loan, loan repayable on demand; **e. de remboursement** refunding loan; **e. à risques** non-accruing loan; **emprunts à taux fixe** fixed-rate borrowing; **e. à terme (fixe)** term loan; **e. sur titres** loan on securities *or* stock

2 *(d'un vélo, d'un outil)* borrowing; **ce n'est pas à moi, c'est un e.** it's not mine, it's borrowed

3 *Ling (processus)* borrowing (**à** from); *(mot)* loan (word)

4 *(fait d'imiter)* borrowing; *(élément imité)* borrowing

□ **d'emprunt** ADJ *(nom)* assumed

emprunté, -e[ɑ̃prœ̃te] ADJ 1 *(peu naturel → façon)* awkward; *(→ personne)* awkward, self-conscious; **il était tellement impressionné par elle qu'il en devenait e.** he was so impressed by her that it made him self-conscious; **dit-elle d'un ton e.** she said self-consciously *or* awkwardly 2 *Littéraire (factice → gloire)* usurped; *(→ sentiments)* feigned; **un air de bonté e.** a feigned air of goodness

emprunter [3] [ɑ̃prœ̃te] VT 1 *Banque & Fin* to borrow (**à** from)

2 *(outil, robe)* to borrow (**à** from); **est-ce que je peux t'e. ton fiancé pour cette danse?** can I borrow your fiancé for this dance?

3 *(nom)* to assume

4 *(imiter → élément de style)* to borrow, to take; **des coiffures empruntées aux punks** hairstyles borrowed from punk; **pour e. le style des publicitaires, nous dirons...** as they might say in the world of advertising,...

5 *(route)* to take; *(circuit)* to follow; **le cortège emprunta la rue de Rivoli** the procession took *or* went down the Rue de Rivoli; **vous êtes priés d'e. le souterrain** you are requested to use the underpass

6 *Ling* to borrow; **mot emprunté** loan (word); **un mot emprunté à l'anglais** a word borrowed from English, an English loan word

USAGE ABSOLU *Banque & Fin* to take out a loan, to borrow; **la société a dû e. pour s'acquitter de ses dettes** the company had to borrow to pay off its debts; **e. sur hypothèque** to borrow on mortgage; **e. sur titres** to borrow on securities; **e. à long/à court terme** to borrow long/short; **e. à intérêt** to borrow at interest

emprunteur, -euse [ɑ̃prœ̃tœr, -øz] ADJ borrowing

NM,F borrower

empuantir[32] [ɑ̃pɥɑ̃tir] VT *(salle)* to make stink, *Br* to stink out; *(air)* to fill with a foul smell

empuantissement [ɑ̃pɥɑ̃tismɑ̃] NM *(d'une salle, de l'air)* filling with a foul smell

empuse [ɑ̃pyz] NF 1 *Bot* empusa; **e. de la mouche** fly fungus 2 *Entom* empusa

empyème[ɑ̃pjɛm] NM *Méd* empyema, pyothorax

empyrée[ɑ̃pire] NM *Myth & Fig* empyrean

EMT[əemte] NF *Anciennement Scol (abrév* **éducation manuelle et technique**) = practical sciences

ému, -e[emy] PP *voir* **émouvoir**

ADJ *(de gratitude, de joie, par une musique, par la pitié)* moved; *(de tristesse)* affected; *(d'inquiétude)* agitated; *(d'amour)* excited; **é. (jusqu')aux larmes** moved to tears; **parler d'une voix émue** to speak with (a voice full of) emotion; **lis-le d'une façon plus émue** read it with more feeling; **trop é. pour parler** too overcome by emotion to be able to speak; **je garde d'elle un souvenir é.** I have fond memories of her; **j'en suis encore tout é.** I still haven't got over it

émulateur[emylatœr] NM emulator; *Ordinat* **é. de terminal** terminal emulator; **é. graphique** graphics emulator

émulation [emylasjɔ̃] NF 1 *(compétition)* emulation 2 *Ordinat* emulation; **é. de terminal** terminal emulation

émule [emyl] NMF emulator; **le dictateur et ses émules** the dictator and his followers; **j'ai fait des émules** people followed my lead *or* example

émuler[3] [emyle] VT *Ordinat* to emulate

émulseur[emylsœr] NM *Chim (appareil)* emulsifier

émulsif, -ive [emylsif, -iv] ADJ *Pharm* emulsive; *Chim* emulsifying

NM *Chim* emulsifier

émulsifiable[emylsifjabl] ADJ *Chim* emulsifiable

émulsifiant, -e [emylsifiɑ̃, -ɑ̃t] ADJ *Pharm* emulsive; *Chim* emulsifying

NM *Chim* emulsifier

émulsifier[9] [emylsifje] VT *Chim* to emulsify

émulsine[emylzin] NF *Chim* emulsin

émulsion [emylsjɔ̃] NF *Chim, Culin & Phot* emulsion

émulsionnable [emylsjɔnabl] ADJ *Chim & Phot* emulsible

émulsionnant, -e [emylsjɔnɑ̃, -ɑ̃t] ADJ *Pharm* emulsive; *Chim* emulsifying

NM *Chim* emulsifier, emulsifying agent

émulsionnement[emylsjɔnmɑ̃] NM *Chim* emulsification

émulsionner[3] [emylsjɔne] VT 1 *Chim (produit)* to emulsify 2 *Phot* to coat with emulsion

émulsive[emylsive] *voir* **émulsif**

ému *etc voir* **émouvoir**

EN[1][əen] NF *Anciennement Scol (abrév* **École normale**) = primary school teachers' training college

EN[2] *(abrév écrite* **Éducation Nationale**) *(ministère)* (French) Ministry *or* Department of Education; *(system)* state education *(in France)*

EN [ɑ̃]

> **PRÉP** in **A, B, C, E1, 2, G** ▪ during **A** ▪ to **B1** ▪ made of **D** ▪ into **E3** ▪ by **E4** ▪ + ing **F1–3** ▪ if **F4**
> **PRON** some/any **A3** ▪ about it **A5** ▪ of it/them **B, C**

PRÉP **A.** *DANS LE TEMPS (indiquant le moment)* in; *(indiquant la durée)* in, during; **en 1992** in 1992; **en été** in summer; **en avril** in April; **en soirée** in the evening; **je l'ai fait en dix minutes** I did it in ten minutes; **en deux heures c'était fini** it was over in two hours; **en quarante ans de carrière...** in my forty years in the job...; **il a plu une fois en trois mois** it rained once in three months; **je n'ai pas le temps en semaine** I have no time *or* I don't have the time during the week

B. *DANS L'ESPACE* 1 *(indiquant la situation)* in; *(indiquant la direction)* to; **habiter en montagne/en Turquie** to live in the mountains/in Turkey; **habiter en Arles/en Avignon** to live in Arles/in Avignon; **se promener en forêt/en ville** to walk in the forest/around the town; **faire une croisière en Méditerranée** to go on a cruise around the Mediterranean; **aller en Espagne** to go to Spain; **partir en mer** to go to sea; **partir en forêt** to go off into the forest

2 *Fig* **en moi-même, j'avais toujours cet espoir** deep down *or* in my heart of hearts, I still had that hope; **trouver en soi la force de faire qch** to find in oneself the strength to do sth; **en mon âme et conscience...** in all honesty...; **ce que j'apprécie en lui** what I like about him

C. *INDIQUANT LE DOMAINE* **bon en latin/physique** good at Latin/physics; **j'ai eu 18 sur 20 en chimie** I got 18 out of 20 in chemistry; **je ne m'y connais pas en peinture** I don't know much about painting; **il fait de la recherche en agronomie** he's doing research in agronomy; **en cela** *ou* **ce en quoi il n'a pas tort** and I have to say he's right *or* not wrong there; **elle est intraitable en affaires** she's very tough in business matters *or* when it comes to business; **malheureux en amour** unlucky in love; **je suis fidèle en amitié** I'm a faithful friend; **être expert en la matière** to be an expert on *or* in the subject

D. *INDIQUANT LA COMPOSITION* **chaise en bois/fer** wooden/iron chair; **table en marbre** marble table; **jupe en velours/coton** velvet/cotton skirt; *Fam* **c'est en quoi?** what's it made of? ▪

E. *INDIQUANT LA MANIÈRE, LE MOYEN* 1 *(marquant l'état, la forme, la manière)* **être en colère/en rage** to be angry/in a rage; **être en forme** to be on (good) form; **être en sueur** to be covered in *or* with sweat; **être en transe** to be in a trance; **le pays est en guerre** the country is at war; **les arbres sont en fleurs** the trees are in blossom; **se conduire en gentleman** to behave like a gentleman; **mourir en héros** to die like a hero; **en véritable ami, il m'a prévenu** good friend that he is *or* being a true friend, he warned me; **en gage de ma bonne foi** as a token of my goodwill; **je suis venu en ami** I came as a friend; **en mari fidèle** as a faithful husband; **je l'ai eu en cadeau** I was given it as a present; **il m'a envoyé ces fleurs en remerciement** he sent me these flowers to say thank you; **peint en bleu** painted blue; **je la préfère en vert** I prefer it in green; **un policier en uniforme** a policeman in uniform; **on ne te voit pas souvent en robe** you don't wear dresses very often, it's not often we see you in a dress; **il était en pyjama** he was in his pyjamas, he had his pyjamas on; **couper qch en deux** to cut sth in two *or* in half; **on nous a répartis en deux groupes** we were divided into two groups; **ils étaient disposés en cercle** they were in a circle; **en (forme de) losange** diamond-shaped; **il est en réunion** he's in a meeting; **j'ai passé Noël en famille** I spent Christmas with my family; **discuter qch en comité** to discuss sth in committee; **faire qch en cachette/en vitesse/en douceur** to do sth secretly/quickly/smoothly; **faire une photo en noir et blanc** to take a black-and-white picture *or* photo; **une video en super huit** a video in super-eight, a super-eight video; **c'est vendu en sachets** it's sold in sachets; **du sucre en morceaux** sugar cubes; **du lait en poudre** powdered milk; **un château en ruines** a ruined castle; **une rue en pente** a street on a slope *or* a hill

2 *(introduisant une mesure)* in; **je veux le résultat en dollars** I want the result in dollars; **je vous ai donné l'équivalent de 150 euros en livres** I've given you the equivalent of 150 euros in pounds; **un tissu en 140 de large** 140 cm wide material; **auriez-vous la même robe en 38?** do you have the same dress in a 38?; **la chanson est en sol** the song's in (the key of) G

3 *(indiquant une transformation)* into; **convertir des euros en yens** to convert euros into yen; **l'eau se change en glace** water turns into ice; **se déguiser en fille** to dress up as a girl; **la citrouille se transforma en carrosse** the pumpkin turned into a coach; **son chagrin s'est mué en amertume** his/her grief turned into bitterness

4 *(marquant le moyen)* **j'y vais en bateau** I'm going by boat; **ils ont fait le tour de l'île en voilier** they sailed round the island (in a yacht); **elle est venue en taxi** she came in a *or* by taxi; **en voiture/train** by car/train; **avoir peur en avion** to be scared of flying; **ils ont descendu le fleuve en canoë** they canoed down the river; **payer en liquide** to pay cash

F. *AVEC LE GÉRONDIF* **1** *(indiquant la simultanéité)* **il est tombé en courant** he fell while running; **il chantait tout en dansant** he was singing and dancing at the same time; **nous en parlerons en prenant un café** we'll talk about it over a cup of coffee; **en buvant et en mangeant, on a passé un bon moment** we had a good time, eating and drinking; **c'est en le voyant que j'ai compris** when I saw him I understood; **rien qu'en le voyant, elle se met en colère** she gets angry just seeing him, the mere sight of him makes her angry; **tout en marchant, elles tentaient de trouver une réponse** while walking *or* as they walked, they tried to find an answer

2 *(indiquant la concession, l'opposition)* **tout en se plaignant, il a fini par faire ce qu'on lui demandait** although he complained about it *or* for all his complaining, in the end he did what was asked of him; **tout en étant plus conciliant, il ne changeait toujours pas d'avis** whilst *or* although he was more conciliatory, he still wouldn't change his mind

3 *(indiquant la cause, le moyen, la manière)* **en ne voulant jamais la croire, tu l'as blessée** you hurt her by never believing her; **il marche en boitant** he walks with a limp; **il est parti en courant** he ran off; **retapez en changeant toutes les majuscules** type it out again and change all the capitals; **faites pénétrer la pommade en massant doucement** rub the cream in gently; **en s'entraînant tous les jours on fait des progrès** you can make progress by training every day; **ce n'est pas en criant que l'on résoudra le problème** shouting won't solve the problem; **vous y arriverez en persévérant** through perseverance you will succeed

4 *(introduisant une condition, une supposition)* if; **en travaillant avec plus de méthode, tu réussirais** if you worked more methodically, you would succeed; **en prenant un cas concret, on voit que...** if we take a concrete example, we can see that...; **en supposant que...** supposing that...; **bon, en admettant que vous ayiez raison...** OK, supposing you're right...

G. *INTRODUISANT LE COMPLÉMENT DU VERBE* in; **croire en Dieu** to believe in God; **croire en qn/qch** to believe in sb/sth; **espérer en qch** to put one's hope in sth

PRON A. *COMPLÉMENT DU VERBE* **1** *(indiquant le lieu)* **il faudra que tu ailles à la poste – j'en viens** you'll have to go to the post office – I've just got back from *or* just been there; **il partit à la guerre et n'en revint pas** he went off to war and never came back; **il est toujours là-bas, il n'en a pas bougé** he's still there, he hasn't moved

2 *(indiquant la cause, l'agent)* **on en meurt** you can die of *or* from it; **je n'en dors plus** it's keeping me awake at night; **il en a beaucoup souffert** he has suffered a lot because of it; **elle était tellement fatiguée qu'elle en pleurait** she was so tired (that) she was crying; **j'en suis étonné** that surprises me; **mes enfants la connaissent et elle en est très aimée** my children know her and love her very much *or* and she's very much loved by them

3 *(complément d'objet)* **voilà des fraises/du lait, donne-lui-en** here are some strawberries/ here's some milk, give him/her some; **passe-moi du sucre – il n'en reste plus** give me some

sugar – there's none left; **si tu n'aimes pas la viande/les olives, n'en mange pas** if you don't like meat/olives, don't eat any; **et du vin, tu n'en bois jamais?** what about wine? don't you ever drink any?; **tous les invités ne sont pas arrivés, il en manque deux** all the guests haven't arrived yet, two are missing; **j'ai ces deux cassettes – je voudrais en écouter une** I've got these two tapes – I'd like to listen to one of them; **j'en ai vu plusieurs/certaines** I saw several/some of them; **tu en as acheté beaucoup** you've bought a lot (of it/of them); **on en a trop entendu** *(des mensonges)* we've heard too many of them; *(d'un secret)* we've heard too much about it; **tu n'en as pas dit assez** you haven't said enough about it

4 *(avec une valeur emphatique)* **elle en a, de l'argent!** she's got plenty of money, she has!; **tu en as de la chance!** you really are lucky, you are!; **j'en ai chanté des chansons!** I've sung lots of songs, I have!

5 *(complément d'objet indirect)* about it; **parlez-m'en** tell me about it; **nous en reparlerons plus tard** we'll talk about it again later; **ne vous en souciez plus** don't worry about it any more; **j'en aviserai le directeur** I'll inform the manager about it

6 *(comme attribut)* **les volontaires? – j'en suis!** any volunteers? – me!; **c'en est** that's what it is; *Fam* **en être** *(être homosexuel)* to be one of them

B. *COMPLÉMENT DU NOM OU DU PRONOM* **j'en garde un bon souvenir** I have good memories of it; **j'aime beaucoup cette chanson – tu en connais les paroles?** I like this song a lot – do you know the lyrics *or* words?; **écoute ces voix et admires-en la beauté** listen to these voices and admire their beauty; **vous pouvez lui faire confiance, je m'en porte garant** you can trust him/her, take it from me *or* take my word for it; *Belg* **je n'en peux rien** I can't help it

C. *COMPLÉMENT DE L'ADJECTIF* **sa maison en est pleine** his/her house is full of it/them; **j'en suis très satisfait** I'm very satisfied with it/ them; **tu en es sûr?** are you sure (of that)?; **elle en est convaincue** she's convinced of it; **elle n'en est pas fière** she's not proud of it

D. *DANS DES LOCUTIONS VERBALES* **il en va de même pour lui** the same goes for him; **s'en prendre à qn** to blame *or* to attack sb; **s'en tenir à** to limit oneself to, to content oneself with; **si l'on en croit les journaux** if we are to believe the newspapers, if the newspapers are to be believed

ENA [ena] NF *Admin & Pol* *(abrév* **École nationale d'administration)** = prestigious university-level college in France preparing students for senior posts in the civil service and public management

enamouré, -e [ãnamure], **énamouré, -e** [enamure] ADJ *Vieilli ou Hum (regard, sourire)* amorous; **être e. de qn** to be enamoured of sb

enamourer [3] [ãnamure] **s'enamourer** VPR *Vieilli ou Hum* to become enamoured **(de** of)

énamourer [3] [enamure] = **enamourer**

énanthème [enãtɛm] NM *Méd* enanthem, enanthema

énantiomère [enãtjomɛr] NM *Biol & Chim* enantiomer

énantiomorphe [enãtjomɔrf] *Biol & Chim* ADJ enantiomorphous

NM enantiomorph

énantiotrope [enãtjotrop] ADJ *Chim* enantiotropic

énarchie [enarʃi] NF = network of graduates of the "ENA"

énarque [enark] NMF = student or former student of the "ENA"

énarthrose [enartroz] NF *Anat* ball-and-socket joint, *Spéc* enarthrosis

en-avant [ãnavã] NM INV *Sport (au rugby)* knock-on

en-but [ãbyt] NM INV *Sport (au rugby)* in-goal

encabanage [ãkabanaʒ] NM preparing of trays for rearing silkworms

encabaner [3] [ãkabane] VT *(vers à soie)* to put into trays

▸**s'encabaner** VPR *Can* to shut oneself up *or* away (at home)

encablure [ãkablyr] NF *Naut* cable, cable's length *(120 fathoms)*; *Fig* **à une e. de** a stone's throw away from; **à deux encablures de** not very far from

encadré, -e [ãkadre] ADJ *Typ* panelled-in, boxed NM *Typ* box; *(presse écrite)* boxed article; *Ordinat* **e. graphique** graphics box; *Ordinat* **e. texte** text box

encadrement [ãkadrəmã] NM **1** *(mise sous cadre)* framing; *(cadre)* frame

2 *(embrasure → d'une porte)* door frame; *(→ d'une fenêtre)* window frame; **il apparut dans l'e. de la porte** he appeared (framed) in the doorway; *Tech* **e. en caoutchouc** rubber seal

3 *(responsabilité → de formation)* training; *(→ de surveillance)* supervision; *(→ d'organisation)* backing; *Mil (→ d'une unité)* officering; **fonctions d'e.** executive functions

4 *(personnel → pour former)* training staff; *(→ pour surveiller)* supervisory staff; *Sport (→ pour entraîner)* coaching staff; *Mil* officers; **personnel d'e.** management, managerial staff

5 *Écon* **e. des prix** price controls; **e. du crédit** credit control; **diminuer l'e. du crédit** to reduce credit restrictions, to loosen the credit squeeze; **e. des loyers** rent control

encadrer [3] [ãkadre] VT **1** *(dans un cadre)* to (put into a) frame; **son frère, alors, il est à e.!** his brother's really priceless!

2 *(border)* to frame, to surround; **un dessin encadré de bleu** a drawing with a blue border; **le visage encadré de boucles** her face framed with curls

3 *(entourer → des mots, une phrase)* to circle; *(flanquer)* to flank; **encadré par deux gendarmes** flanked by two policemen; **encadré de ses gardes du corps/de jolies filles** surrounded by his/her bodyguards/by pretty girls; **deux potiches encadraient la cheminée** two large vases stood on either side of *or* flanked the fireplace

4 *(surveiller, organiser)* to lead, to organize, to supervise; *(personnel, équipe)* to manage; *(groupe d'enfants, de handicapés, d'étudiants)* to supervise; *Mil (unité)* to officer; **les guides qui encadrent l'expédition** the guides leading the expedition; **nous sommes bien encadrés** our management is good; **les scouts sont bien encadrés** the scout pack has responsible leaders

5 *Écon (prix, loyers, crédit)* to control

6 *Fam (percuter)* to smash *or* to slam into; **je me suis fait e. au carrefour** I had an accident at the crossroads▪

7 *Fam (supporter → personne)* **je ne peux pas l'e.** I can't stand (the sight of) him/her, *Br* I can't stick him/her

▸**s'encadrer** VPR **1** *Littéraire (apparaître)* to be framed **(dans** in)

2 *Fam (heurter)* to crash; **s'e. dans un arbre** to crash one's car into a tree

encadreur, -euse [ãkadrœr, -øz] NM,F picture framer

encagement [ãkaʒmã] NM **1** *(dans une cage)* caging; *(en prison)* caging **2** *Mil* **tir d'e.** box-barrage

encager [17] [ãkaʒe] VT *(mettre en cage)* to cage, to put in a cage; *(emprisonner)* to cage; **tenir qn encagé** *(en cage, en prison)* to keep sb caged up; **tenir un oiseau/un animal encagé** to keep a bird/an animal in a cage *or* caged up

encagoulé, -e [ãkagule] ADJ hooded, wearing a hood

encaissable [ãkɛsabl] ADJ *Fin (chèque)* cashable; *(argent, traite)* collectable, receivable; **ce chèque est e. à la banque** this cheque can be cashed at the bank

encaissage [ãkɛsaʒ] NM boxing, packing

encaissant, -e [ãkɛsã, -ãt] ADJ **1** *Géol (filon)* enveloping **2** *(rochers, terrain → en surplomb)* overhanging; **la rivière sillonnait entre des parois encaissantes** the river was hemmed in by steep rocks on either side

encaisse [ãkɛs] NF *Compta & Fin* cash in hand, cash balance; **e. de 100 euros** cash balance of 100 euros; **e. disponible** cash in hand; **e. métallique, e. or et argent** gold and silver reserves, bullion; *Banque* **pas d'e.** no funds

encaissé, -e [ãkese] ADJ *(vallée)* deep, steep-sided; *(rivière)* deeply embanked; *(route)* sunken

encaissement [ãkɛsmã] NM **1** *(d'une vallée)* steep-sidedness, depth; *(d'une rivière)* deep embankment; **dans l'e. de la route** in the deep cutting made by the road **2** *Fin (d'argent)* collection, receipt; *(d'un chèque)* cashing; *(d'une traite)* collection; **donner un chèque à l'e.** to cash a cheque; **encaissements et décaissements** cash inflows and outflows **3** *(de marchandises)* boxing, packing (in boxes) **4** *Hort* tubbing, planting in tubs

encaisser [4] [ãkese] VT **1** *Fin (argent)* to receive; *(chèque)* to cash; *(traite)* to collect; **e. de l'argent** *(sur son compte)* to pay in cash; *Bourse* **e. un premium** to receive a premium **2** *Fam (gifle, injure, échec, critiques)* to take ▪, *Sport* **e. un coup** to take a blow; **il n'a pas encaissé que tu lui mentes/ce que tu lui as dit** he just can't stomach the fact that you lied to him/what you told him **3** *Fam (tolérer)* **je ne peux pas l'e.** I can't stand him/her, *Br* I can't stick him/her **4** *(marchandises)* to box, to pack in boxes **5** *Bot (planter → arbuste)* to plant (out) in a box or tub **6** *(resserrer → sujet: collines)* to hem in; *Tech (rivière etc)* to embank
USAGE ABSOLU *Fam* **ne dis rien, encaisse!** take it, don't say anything! ▪, **il faut pouvoir e.** you have to be able to take a few hard knocks; **qu'est-ce qu'il a encaissé!** he took a lot of punishment; **elle a plutôt bien encaissé** she took it rather well ▪, **e. sans broncher** to grin and bear it
▸ **s'encaisser** VPR *(rivière, route etc)* to be hemmed in; **la route s'encaisse profondément entre les montagnes** mountains tower above the road on both sides

encaisseur, -euse [ãkɛsœr, -øz] *Fin* ADJ *(banque, établissement)* collecting
NM *(d'un chèque)* payee; *(de l'argent, d'une traite)* collector, receiver

encalminé, -e [ãkalmine] ADJ *Naut* becalmed

encan [ãkã] NM *Com* **vente à l'e.** auction; **vendre qch à l'e.** to sell sth by or at auction; *Fig Littéraire* **mettre qch à l'e.** to sell sth to the highest bidder; *Fig* **la loi semble mettre la justice à l'e.** the law seems to put a low price on justice

encanaillement [ãkanajmã] NM *(d'une personne)* mixing with the riff-raff, slumming it; *(du langage, d'un comportement)* increasing coarseness

encanailler [3] [ãkanaje] **s'encanailler** VPR to mix with the riff-raff, to slum it

encapsuler [3] [ãkapsyle] VT *Élec* to encapsulate

encapuchonner [3] [ãkapyʃɔne] VT **1** *(personne, tête)* to put a hood on; **la tête encapuchonnée** hooded; **enfants encapuchonnés** children with their hoods on **2** *(stylo)* to put the cap on
▸ **s'encapuchonner** VPR **1** *(personne)* to put on a/one's hood **2** *Équitation (cheval)* to curve or arch the neck

encaquement [ãkakmã] NM *(des harengs)* barrelling

encaquer [3] [ãkake] VT *(harengs)* to barrel; *Fig Vieilli (personnes)* to pack in like sardines

encart [ãkar] NM insert; *(mobile)* (loose) insert; *Journ* slip sheet; **e. dépliant** gatefold; **e. presse** press insert; **e. publicitaire** advertising insert; *TV & Rad* commercial break

encartage [ãkartaʒ] NM **1** *Typ* insetting **2** *(fixation sur un carton)* carding

encarté, -e [ãkarte] ADJ *(membre)* card-carrying; **il est e. au PC** he's a card-carrying or paid-up member of the communist party

encarter [3] [ãkarte] VT **1** *Typ* to insert, to inset **2** *(fixer sur un carton)* to card **3** *Tex* to card

encarteuse [ãkartøz] NF *Tex* carding machine

encartoucher [3] [ãkartuʃe] VT to put in a cartridge

en-cas, encas [ãka] NM INV snack; **j'ai un petit e. dans mon sac** I have something to eat in my bag

encaserner [3] [ãkazɛrne] VT to barrack; **être encaserné** to be barracked at

encasteler [25] [ãkastəle] **s'encasteler** VPR *Vét (cheval)* to have navicular disease

encastelure [ãkastəlyr] NF *Vét (d'un cheval)* navicular disease

encastrable [ãkastrabl] ADJ *(machine à laver, cuisinière)* that can be built in or fitted

encastré, -e [ãkastre] ADJ *(machine à laver, cuisinière)* built-in, fitted; *(four, baignoire)* built-in; *(interrupteur)* flush-fitting, set-in

encastrement [ãkastrəmã] NM **1** *(d'un placard → action)* building in, recessing; *(placard, étagères)* built-in fitting; *(d'une machine à laver, d'une cuisinière → action)* fitting, building in **2** *(d'un interrupteur → action)* flushing in; *(interrupteur)* flush fitting **3** *(espace prévu)* recess

encastrer [3] [ãkastre] VT **1** *(placard)* to build in, to slot in; *(machine à laver, cuisinière)* to build in, to fit; *(four, baignoire)* to build in; *(interrupteur)* to recess, to fit flush; *(coffre-fort)* to recess **2** *(dans un boîtier, un mécanisme)* to fit
▸ **s'encastrer** VPR *(deux éléments)* to fit together; **s'e. dans** *(machine à laver, cuisinière)* to fit into; **la voiture s'est encastrée sous un camion** the car embedded itself under a lorry

encaustiquage [ãkostikaʒ] NM *Beaux-Arts* polishing, waxing

encaustique [ãkostik] *Beaux-Arts* ADJ *(peinture)* encaustic
NF **1** *(cire)* polish, wax **2** *(technique)* encaustic (painting)

encaustiquer [3] [ãkostike] VT *Beaux-Arts* to polish, to wax

encavage [ãkavaʒ] NM *Suisse (du vin)* cellarage, cellaring; *(du fromage, de légumes, de fruits)* storage in a cellar

encavement [ãkavmã] NM *(du vin)* cellarage, cellaring

encaver [3] [ãkave] VT to store in a a cellar, to cellar

encaveur [ãkavœr] NM **1** *(ouvrier)* cellarman **2** *Suisse (négociant)* wine-maker, wine producer

enceindre [81] [ãsɛ̃dr] VT *Littéraire* **e. la ville de murs** to encircle or to surround the city with walls

enceinte¹ [ãsɛ̃t] NF **1** *(mur)* (surrounding) wall; *(palissade)* fence; **mur d'e.** surrounding wall **2** *(ceinture)* enclosure, fence; *Courses de chevaux* ring; **protégé par une e. de fossés** closed in by a circular moat **3** *Chasse (fourré)* cover; **battre l'e.** to beat the cover; **vider l'e.** *(animal)* to break cover **4** *(pour haut-parleur)* **e. (acoustique)** speaker ▫ **dans l'enceinte de** PRÉP within (the boundary of); **dans l'e. du parc** within or inside the park; **il est interdit de pénétrer en voiture dans l'e. du parc** cars may not enter the park, cars are not allowed into the park; **dans l'e. de l'école** on school premises; **en dehors de l'e. de l'école** outside school; **dans l'e. du tribunal** within the courtroom

enceinte² [ãsɛ̃t] ADJ F *Biol & Physiol (femme)* pregnant; **femme e.** pregnant woman, expectant mother; **e. de son premier enfant/d'une fille** expecting her first child/a little girl; **e. de trois mois** three months pregnant; **elle est e. de Paul** she's pregnant by Paul, she's expecting Paul's child; **elle est e. de ses œuvres** she's pregnant by him; **mettre qn e.** to make or get sb pregnant

enceinter [3] [ãsɛ̃te] VT *(en Afrique francophone)* to make or get pregnant

Encelade [ãsəlad] NPR *Myth* Enceladus

encens [ãsã] NM **1** *(résine)* incense; **bâtonnet d'e.** incense stick, joss stick **2** *Fig Littéraire* sycophancy, flattery

encensement [ãsãsmã] NM **1** *(d'un écrivain)* praising to the skies **2** *Rel* incensing

encenser [3] [ãsãse] VT **1** *(louer → mérites)* to praise to the skies; *(→ écrivain, œuvre)* to praise to the skies, to shower or heap praise upon **2** *Rel* to incense
VI *(cheval)* to toss its head up and down

encenseur, -euse [ãsãsœr, -øz] NM,F **1** *Rel* thurifer, censer bearer **2** *Vieilli (flatteur)* sycophant

encensoir [ãsãswar] NM **1** *Rel* censer **2** *Fam (locutions)* **un coup d'e.** a piece of flattery ▪, **manier l'e., donner des coups d'e.** to use flattery

encépagement [ãsepaʒmã] NM *Agr* stock of vines *(in a vineyard)*

encéphale [ãsefal] NM *Anat* encephalon

encéphaline [ãsefalin] NF *Chem & Physiol* enkephalin

encéphalique [ãsefalik] ADJ *Anat* encephalic

encéphalite [ãsefalit] NF *Méd* encephalitis; **e. léthargique** sleeping sickness; *Vét* **e. bovine spongiforme** bovine spongiform encephalopathy, BSE

encéphalogramme [ãsefalɔgram] NM *Méd* encephalogram

encéphalographe [ãsefalɔgraf] NM *Méd* encephalograph

encéphalographie [ãsefalɔgrafi] NF *Méd* encephalography

encéphalomyélite [ãsefalɔmjelit] NF *Méd* encephalomyelitis; **e. myalgique** myalgic encephalomyelitis, ME

encéphalopathie [ãsefalɔpati] NF *Méd* encephalopathy

encéphalopathique [ãsefalɔpatik] ADJ *Méd* encephalopathic

encerclement [ãsɛrkləmã] NM surrounding; **après l'e. de l'ennemi** after the enemy was surrounded or encircled

encercler [3] [ãsɛrkle] VT **1** *(marquer)* to ring, to draw a ring round, to encircle; **encerclé d'un trait rouge** circled in red **2** *(entourer)* to surround, to encircle, to form a circle around; **la barrière qui encercle la propriété** the fence encircling the property **3** *Mil (cerner)* to surround, to encircle, to hem in; **village encerclé par des soldats** village surrounded by troops

enchaîné [ãʃene] NM *TV & Cin* dissolve

enchaînement [ãʃɛnmã] NM **1** *(série)* sequence, series; **raconte-moi l'e. des événements** tell me what the sequence of events was; **un e. de circonstances favorables** a series of favourable circumstances **2** *(lien)* (logical) link; *TV & Cin (entre deux vues)* melt; **faire un e.** *(dans un raisonnement)* to link up two ideas; *(dans un exposé)* to link up two items **3** *(structure)* structure, logical sequence; **l'e. des paragraphes est très important** the way in which the paragraphs follow on from each other or the paragraphs are linked is very important; **les idées sont bonnes mais l'e. n'est pas assez apparent** the ideas are good but it's not apparent how they follow on from each other or how they are connected **4** *(en danse)* enchaînement, sequence of steps, linked-up steps **5** *Sport* linked-up movements; **un bel e. à la poutre** a fluid sequence of movements on the beam; **faire un e.** to perform a sequence **6** *Mus* **e. des accords** chord progression **7** *(dans un spectacle)* filler **8** *Ordinat* concatenation

enchaîner [4] [ãʃene] VT **1** *(lier → personne)* to put in chains, to chain; *(→ animal)* to chain up; **e. à** to chain (up) to; **chien enchaîné à un arbre** dog chained (up) to a tree **2** *(attacher ensemble → prisonniers)* to chain (up) together; *(→ maillons)* to link (up) **3** *(asservir → média)* to trammel, to shackle; *(→ personne)* to enslave; *(→ libertés)* to put in chains or shackles **4** *(relier → idées, mots, phrases)* to link (up), to link or to string together; **vos arguments ne sont pas bien enchaînés** your arguments aren't presented in logical sequence or don't follow on from each other; **ils enchaînaient les sujets très vite** they moved very quickly from one subject to another; **e. le tournage de plusieurs épisodes** to shoot several episodes one after the other; **pour la répétition de ce soir, on enchaîne toutes les scènes/chansons** at this evening's rehearsal we'll run through all the scenes/songs one after the other without a break **5** *(dans une conversation)* **"c'est faux", enchaîna-t-elle** "it's not true," she went on **6** *(en danse)* to link; *Sport (mouvements)* to run together or into each other, to link up (together); **la séquence est bien/mal enchaînée** the sequence flows naturally/feels jerky
VI **1** *(poursuivre)* to move or to follow on; **enchaîne avec les diapositives** follow on with the slides; **on enchaîne avec les nouvelles internationales** we'll move on to the international news; **elle a enchaîné sur les élections** she went on to talk about the election

2 *Rad & TV* to link up two items of news; **enchaînons** let's go on to the next item

3 *Cin* to fade; *Théât* to carry straight on; **e. sur une scène** to fade into a scene

▸**s'enchaîner** VPR *(idées)* to be connected, to follow on (from one another); *(images, épisodes)* to form a (logical) sequence; *(événements)* to be linked together; **tes paragraphes s'enchaînent mal** your paragraphs don't hang together well *or* are a bit disjointed; **on voit comme les choses s'enchaînent** you can see how things hang together *or* are linked together; **les événements se sont enchaînés très vite** things moved *or* happened very quickly

enchanté, -e [ɑ̃ʃɑ̃te] ADJ **1** *(magique)* enchanted

2 *(ravi)* delighted, pleased; **être e. de qch** to be enchanted by *or* delighted with sth; **e.!** pleased to meet you!; **je suis (vraiment) e. de vous rencontrer** I am (really) delighted *or* (very) pleased to meet you; **je serais e. de...** I'd be delighted *or* very pleased to...; **mon fils sera e. de vous raccompagner** my son will be delighted to *or* will gladly see you home; **e. de faire votre connaissance!** how do you do!, pleased to meet you!

enchantement [ɑ̃ʃɑ̃tmɑ̃] NM **1** *(en magie)* (magic) spell, enchantment; **c'est par e. qu'elle s'est transformée en princesse** she was magically turned into a princess; **comme par e.** as if by magic

2 *(merveille)* delight, enchantment; **la soirée fut un véritable e.** the evening was absolutely delightful *or* enchanting; **être dans l'e. (de)** to be enchanted *or* delighted (by)

enchanter [3] [ɑ̃ʃɑ̃te] VT **1** *(faire plaisir à)* to enchant, to charm, to delight; **elle nous a enchantés par son humour** we were charmed *or* delighted by her sense of humour; **cela ne l'enchante pas beaucoup** *ou* **guère** he's/she's none too pleased *or* happy (at having to do it); **cela ne m'enchante pas (beaucoup) de devoir y aller en voiture** I can't say I'm happy *or* thrilled at having to drive there **2** *(par la magie)* to bewitch, to cast a spell on

enchanteur, -eresse [ɑ̃ʃɑ̃tœr, -tərɛs] ADJ *(sourire)* enchanting, bewitching; *(discours, endroit)* enchanting, delightful

NM **1** *(magicien)* enchanter, sorcerer **2** *(séducteur)* charmer

▫ **enchanteresse** NF **1** *(magicienne)* enchantress, witch **2** *(séductrice)* charmer, enchantress

enchâssement [ɑ̃ʃasmɑ̃] NM *(en joaillerie)* setting

enchâsser [3] [ɑ̃ʃase] VT **1** *(en joaillerie)* to set **2** *(insérer* → *mot)* to insert **3** *Rel (relique)* to enshrine

▸**s'enchâsser** VPR to fit together exactly

enchâssure [ɑ̃ʃɑsyr] NF *(d'un bijou)* setting, mount

enchausser [3] [ɑ̃ʃose] VT *Agr* to earth (up)

enchemiser [3] [ɑ̃ʃmize] VT **1** *(projectile)* to jacket **2** *(tuyau)* to lag

enchère [ɑ̃ʃɛr] NF **1** *Com (vente)* auction; **vendre qch aux enchères** to sell sth by auction; **acheter qch aux enchères** to buy sth at an auction; **mettre qch aux enchères** to put sth up for auction; **enchères inversées** reverse auction; **enchères publiques** public auction; **enchères au rabais** Dutch auction

2 *Com (offre d'achat)* bid; **les enchères** the bidding; **faire une e.** to bid, to make a bid; **faire monter les enchères** to raise the bidding; *Fig* to raise the stakes; **couvrir une e.** to make a higher bid, to bid higher; **couvrir l'e. de qn** to bid higher than sb, to outbid sb; **commencer les enchères à 400 euros** to start the bidding at 400 euros

3 *Cartes* bid; **système des enchères** *(au bridge)* bidding system

enchérir [32] [ɑ̃ʃerir] VI **1** *Com (dépasser)* to make a higher bid; **e. de dix euros** to bid another ten euros **2** *Vieilli ou Littéraire (devenir cher)* to become dearer *or* more expensive, to go up in price

▫ **enchérir sur** VT IND **1** *Com (dans une enchère)* **e. sur une offre** to make a higher bid; **e. sur une somme** to go over and above an amount; **e. sur qn** to bid higher than sb; *Fig* to go one better than sb **2** *Littéraire (aller au-delà de)* to go (over and) beyond; **e. sur son devoir** to go above and beyond the call of duty

enchérissement [ɑ̃ʃerismɑ̃] NM *Littéraire* **l'e. de** the rise in the price of

enchérisseur, -euse [ɑ̃ʃerisœr, -øz] NM,F *Com* bidder; **au plus offrant et dernier e.** to the highest bidder

enchevaucher [3] [ɑ̃ʃəvoʃe] VT *Constr* to overlap

enchevauchure [ɑ̃ʃəvoʃyr] NF *Constr* overlapping

enchevêtré, -e [ɑ̃ʃəvetre] ADJ *(écheveau, fils)* tangled, in a tangle; *(style, idées)* confused; **un amas de branches enchevêtrées** a tangle of branches; **une intrigue enchevêtrée** a complicated *or* muddled plot

enchevêtrement [ɑ̃ʃəvɛtrəmɑ̃] NM **1** *(objets emmêlés)* tangle, tangled mass; **un e. de branches** tangled branches, a tangle of branches; **dans un e. de draps et de couvertures** in a tangle of sheets and blankets **2** *(confusion)* tangle, tangled state, confusion; **l'e. de ses idées est tel que...** he/she is so confused that...

enchevêtrer [4] [ɑ̃ʃəvɛtre] VT **1** *(mêler* → *fils, branchages)* to tangle (up), to entangle **2** *(embrouiller* → *histoire)* to confuse, to muddle

▸**s'enchevêtrer** VPR **1** *(être emmêlé* → *fils)* to become entangled, to get into a tangle; *(*→ *branchages)* to become entangled **2** *(être confus* → *idées, événements)* to become confused *or* muddled

enchevêtrure [ɑ̃ʃəvɛtryr] NF **1** *Vét* halter-cast **2** *Constr* trimming work

enchifrené, -e [ɑ̃ʃifrəne] ADJ *Vieilli (nez)* blocked; **une voix enchifrenée** a voice thick with catarrh

enclave [ɑ̃klav] NF **1** *(lieu)* enclave; **une e. de maisons isolées parmi les lotissements** an enclave of detached houses surrounded by housing developments **2** *(groupe, unité)* enclave; **notre petite e. culturelle perpétue les traditions de notre pays d'origine** within our little group of expatriates we uphold our native country's traditions **3** *Géol* inclusion, xenolith

enclavement [ɑ̃klavmɑ̃] NM **1** *(d'une région, d'un pays etc* → *action d'isoler)* cutting off, isolation; **la fermeture de stations de chemin de fer va accélérer encore plus l'e. des régions rurales** the closing down of train stations will make these country areas even more cut-off *or* isolated; **l'e. de ce pays a freiné son développement** the fact that this country is landlocked has hindered its development **2** *(d'un terrain, d'un jardin)* enclosing, hemming in **3** *(de deux éléments)* interlocking

enclaver [3] [ɑ̃klave] VT **1** *(région, pays etc)* to cut off, to isolate; **pays enclavé** *(sans accès maritime)* landlocked country **2** *(terrain, jardin etc)* to enclose, to hem in **3** *(deux éléments)* to fit into each other, to interlock

enclenche [ɑ̃klɑ̃ʃ] NF *Tech* gab

enclenchement [ɑ̃klɑ̃ʃmɑ̃] NM *Tech* **1** *(action)* engaging; *(résultat)* engagement; **avant l'e. du loquet** before the catch engages **2** *(dispositif)* interlock

enclencher [3] [ɑ̃klɑ̃ʃe] VT **1** *Tech* to engage; *(pièces)* to interlock **2** *(commencer* → *démarche, procédure)* to set in motion, to get under way, to set off

▸**s'enclencher** VPR **1** *Tech* to engage; *(pièces)* to interlock **2** *(démarche, procédure)* to get under way, to get started; **bien/mal s'e.** to get off to a good/bad start

enclin, -e [ɑ̃klɛ̃, -in] ADJ **e. à qch/à faire qch** inclined to sth/to do sth; **elle est encline à la paresse/à la panique** she is inclined *or* tends to be lazy/to panic; **il est e. à l'alcoolisme** he is inclined to drink, he has alcoholic tendencies; **peu e. au bavardage** not very talkative; **peu e. à partager ses secrets** reluctant to share his secrets

encliquetage [ɑ̃kliktaʒ] NM *Tech* ratchet mechanism

encliqueter [27] [ɑ̃klikte] VT *Tech* to ratchet

enclise [ɑ̃kliz] NF *Ling* enclisis

enclitique [ɑ̃klitik] NM *Ling* enclitic

enclore [113] [ɑ̃klɔr] VT to enclose; *(sujet: palissade)* to fence in; *(sujet: mur)* to wall in; **enclos d'une haie** hedged in; **enclos d'un mur** walled in

enclos [ɑ̃klo] NM **1** *Agr (terrain)* enclosed plot of land; *(à moutons)* pen, fold; *(à chevaux)* paddock **2** *(muret)* wall **3** *(grillage)* (wire) fence **4** *Hist (en Bretagne)* **e. paroissial** church precincts

enclosure [ɑ̃klozyr] NF *Hist (en Angleterre)* enclosure

enclosons *etc voir* **enclore**

enclôture [ɑ̃klotyr] NF *Agr* enclosure

enclouage [ɑ̃kluaʒ] NM *Méd (d'un os)* pinning

enclouer [6] [ɑ̃klue] VT **1** *Vét (cheval)* to prick *(a horse when shoeing)* **2** *Méd* to pin together

enclouure [ɑ̃kluyr] NF *Vét* prick *(given when shoeing a horse)*

enclume [ɑ̃klym] NF **1** *(du forgeron)* anvil; *(du couvreur)* (slater's) iron; *(du cordonnier)* last; *Fig* **entre l'e. et le marteau** between the devil and the deep blue sea **2** *Anat* anvil

encochage [ɑ̃kɔʃaʒ] NM notching

encoche [ɑ̃kɔʃ] NF **1** *(entaille)* notch **2** *(d'une flèche)* nock **3** *(d'un livre)* thumb index; **avec encoches** thumb-indexed, with a thumb index **4** *Ordinat* **e. de protection contre l'écriture** write-protect notch **5** *Élec* **armature à encoches** slotted armature

encochement [ɑ̃kɔʃmɑ̃] NM notching

encocher [3] [ɑ̃kɔʃe] VT **1** *(faire une entaille à)* to notch **2** *(flèche)* to nock **3** *(livre)* to thumb-index

encodage [ɑ̃kɔdaʒ] NM encoding

encoder [3] [ɑ̃kɔde] VT to encode

encodeur, -euse [ɑ̃kɔdœr, -øz] NM,F encoder

encoignure [ɑ̃kwaɲyr, ɑ̃kɔɲyr] NF **1** *(angle)* corner **2** *(table)* corner table; *(placard)* corner cupboard; *(siège)* corner chair

encollage [ɑ̃kɔlaʒ] NM *(à l'aide de colle* → *de papier)* pasting; *(*→ *de bois)* gluing; *(à l'aide d'apprêt* → *de papier, tissu, plâtre etc)* sizing; *Typ* perfect binding

encoller [3] [ɑ̃kɔle] VT *(papier)* to paste; *(bois etc)* to glue, to apply glue to; *(à l'aide d'apprêt* → *papier, tissu, plâtre etc)* to size

encolleur, -euse [ɑ̃kɔlœr, -øz] ADJ sizing

NM,F *(personne)* sizer

▫ **encolleuse** NF *(machine) Tech* sizing machine

encolure [ɑ̃kɔlyr] NF **1** *Anat* neck; *(tour de cou)* neck size; **homme de forte e.** thickset *or* stocky man **2** *Zool & Équitation* neck; **à une e. du vainqueur** a neck behind the winner; **gagner d'une e.** to win by a neck **3** *Couture (de vêtement)* neck; **e. carrée** square neck

encombrant, -e [ɑ̃kɔ̃brɑ̃, -ɑ̃t] ADJ **1** *(volumineux)* bulky, cumbersome; **j'ai dû m'en débarrasser, c'était trop e.** I had to get rid of it, it was taking up too much space *or* it was getting in the way

2 *(importun)* inhibiting, awkward; **le jeune couple trouvait la petite sœur encombrante** the young couple felt the little sister was in the way; **un témoin e.** an unwanted witness

NMPL *(régional)* **les encombrants passent demain** the bulk refuse disposal people are coming tomorrow; **mettre qch aux encombrants** to put sth out for collection; **j'ai trouvé cette table aux encombrants** I found this table in among rubbish put out for collection

encombre [ɑ̃kɔ̃br] **sans encombre** ADV safely, without mishap; **tu es rentré sans e.?** did you get home safely?; **s'ils parviennent à revenir sans e.** if nothing untoward happens to them on their way back

encombré, -e [ɑ̃kɔ̃bre] ADJ **1** *(route)* **l'autoroute est très encombrée** traffic on the motorway is very heavy, there is very heavy traffic on the motorway **2** *(plein d'objets)* **avoir les mains encombrées** to have one's hands full; **un salon e.** a cluttered living room **3** *(bronches)* congested **4** *(marché)* glutted, flooded

encombrement [ɑ̃kɔ̃brəmɑ̃] NM **1** *(embouteillage)* traffic jam

2 *(fait d'obstruer)* jamming, blocking; **par suite de l'e. des lignes téléphoniques/de l'espace aérien** because the telephone lines are overloaded/the air space is overcrowded

3 *(entassement)* clutter, cluttered state; **il y a un tel e. de livres dans son bureau** his/her office is so cluttered up with books

4 *(dimension)* size; **meuble de faible e.** small *or* compact piece of furniture

5 *Méd* **e. des voies respiratoires** congestion of the respiratory system

6 *Ordinat* footprint; **faible e. sur le disque dur** low use of hard disk space
7 *Com (de marchandises)* glut

encombrer [3] [ɑ̃kɔ̃bre] **VT 1** *(remplir)* to clutter (up), to fill *or* to clog up; **e. qch de** to clutter sth (up) with; **table encombrée de papiers** table littered with papers; **j'ai l'esprit encombré de souvenirs** my mind's cluttered up with memories
2 *(obstruer → couloir)* to block (up); *(→ route)* to block *or* to clog up; *(→ circulation)* to hold up; **une ville très encombrée** a congested city, a city choked with traffic; **sentier encombré de ronces** path overgrown with brambles
3 *(saturer → lignes téléphoniques)* to jam, to block; *(→ marché)* to glut, to flood; **les logiciels encombrent le marché** there's a glut or surplus of software packages on the market; **une profession encombrée** an overcrowded profession
4 *(charger → sujet: objet lourd)* to load (down), to encumber; **e. qn de** to load sb down with
5 *(sujet: objet gênant)* **tiens, je te donne ce vase, il m'encombre** here, have this vase, I don't know what to do with it; **que faire de ces sacs qui nous encombrent?** what shall we do with these bags that are in the way?
6 *(gêner)* to burden, to encumber; **son enfant l'encombre** his/her child's a burden to him/her; **je ne veux pas vous e. quand je serai vieux** I don't want to be a burden to you when I'm old; **encombré d'une famille nombreuse** encumbered *or* burdened with a large family
▸**s'encombrer VPR** *(avoir trop de bagages, de vêtements)* to be loaded *or* weighed down; **laisse ta valise là si tu ne veux pas t'e.** leave your case there if you don't want to be weighed down; **s'e. de** *(colis, équipement etc)* to load oneself down with; *Fig (obligations, enfants etc)* to burden oneself *or* saddle oneself with, to be overburdened with; **je ne m'encombre pas de biens matériels** I don't allow myself to become encumbered with material possessions; **il ne s'encombre pas de scrupules** he's not exactly overburdened with scruples; **ne nous encombrons pas de diplomatie** let's not be overly diplomatic; *Fig* **s'e. l'esprit de qch** to fill one's mind *or* to cram one's head with sth; **s'e. la mémoire de qch** to fill *or* to load one's memory with sth

encomienda [ɛnkɔmjɛnda] **NF** *Hist* encomienda

encontre [ɑ̃kɔ̃tr] **à l'encontre ADV** in opposition; **je n'ai rien à dire à l'e.** I have no objections
❑ **à l'encontre de PRÉP aller à l'e. de** to go against, to run counter to; **cette décision va à l'e. du but recherché** this decision is self-defeating *or* counterproductive; **ceci va à l'e. de toutes nos espérances** this goes against all our hopes; **cela va à l'e. de la loi** that's against the law; **cela va à l'e. de ce qu'il proposait la semaine dernière** that's the opposite of *or* contradicts what he was saying last week; **ces nouvelles méthodes vont à l'e. de tout ce qu'on m'a toujours appris** these new methods go against *or* are contrary to *or* run counter to everything I've been taught; **cela va à l'e. du bon sens** it goes against common sense

encoprésie [ɑ̃kɔprezi] **NF** *Méd* incontinence

encor [ɑ̃kɔr] *Littéraire* = **encore**

encorbellement [ɑ̃kɔrbɛlmɑ̃] **NM** corbelled construction; *(d'un mur etc)* corbelling; *(d'un étage supérieur)* overhang; **balcon en e.** corbelled balcony; **fenêtre en e.** oriel window

encorder [3] [ɑ̃kɔrde] *Sport* **VT** to rope up
▸**s'encorder VPR** to rope up (together)

ENCORE [ɑ̃kɔr]

still **1, 3** ■ only **2** ■ yet **3** ■ again **4** ■ more **5** ■ even **6**

ADV 1 *(toujours)* still; **il travaillait e. à minuit** he was still working at midnight; **la banque sera e. ouverte à 19 heures** the bank will still be open at 7 p.m.; **tu es e. là?** so you're still here?, are you still here?; **j'ai e. faim** I'm still hungry; **ils en sont e. à taper tout à la machine** they're still using typewriters; **je ne suis e. qu'étudiant** I'm still only a student, I'm only a student as yet
2 *(pas plus tard que)* only; **ce matin e., il était d'accord** only this morning he was in agreement; **hier e., je lui ai parlé** I spoke to him/her only yesterday
3 *(dans des phrases négatives)* **pas e.** not yet; **je n'ai pas e. fini** I haven't finished yet; **e. rien** still nothing, nothing yet; **je n'ai e. rien écrit** I haven't written anything (down) yet, I still haven't written anything (down); **vous n'avez e. rien vu!** you haven't seen anything yet!; **elle n'est e. jamais** *ou* **e. pas venue me voir** she hasn't come to see me yet, she still hasn't come to see me; **je n'avais e. jamais vu ça!** I'd never seen anything like it before!
4 *(de nouveau)* again; **il est e. venu la voir** he came to see her again; **voilà e. la pluie!** here's the rain again!; **tu manges e.!** you're not eating again, are you!; **e. toi!** (not) you again!; **je me suis coupé - e.!** I've cut myself – not again!; **e. une fois, c'est non!** the answer's still no!; **si tu fais ça e. une fois...** if you do that again *or* one more time or once more...; **nous l'avons e. vu hier** we saw him again yesterday; **e. de la glace?** some more *or* a little more ice-cream?; **je te sers e. un verre?** will you have another drink?; **e. une panne!** not another breakdown!; **il y a e. eu un meurtre d'enfant** another child has been murdered; **qui e.?** who else?; **quoi e.?** *(dans une énumération)* what else?; *Fam (ton irrité)* now what?; **et puis quoi e.?** *(dans une énumération)* what else?; *Ironique* will that be all?; *(marquant l'incrédulité)* whatever next?; **que faut-il que je prenne e.?** what else do I need to take?; **qu'est-ce qu'il y a e.?** what is it this time?; **qu'est-ce qu'il a e. fait?** now what's he done?, what's he done now *or* this time?; **elle est bien élevée, charmante, mais e.?** she's well brought-up and charming, and (apart from that)?; **il a dit qu'il avait bien aimé – mais e.?** he said he liked it – but what exactly did he say?; **elle est sympa – mais e.?** she's nice – yes, go on!; **e. un qui ne sait pas ce qu'il veut!** another one who doesn't know what he wants!
5 *(davantage)* more; **il va grandir e.** he's still got a bit more growing to do; **réduisez-le e.** reduce it even more; **il faudra e. travailler cette scène** that scene still needs more work on it; **e. un mot** (just) one word more; **en voulez-vous e.?** would you like some more?; **e. du vin, s'il vous plaît!** some more wine please!; **e. une tasse de café** another cup of coffee; **pendant trois mois e., pendant e. trois mois** for three months longer, for another three months; **réduire e. le prix** to reduce the price still *or* even further *or* more
6 *(devant un comparatif)* **il est e. plus gentil que je n'imaginais** he is even nicer than I'd imagined (he'd be); **ses affaires vont e. mieux que l'an dernier** his/her business is even more successful than it was last year, his/her business is going even better than it was last year; **elle travaille e. plus qu'avant** she works even harder than before; **il y a e. moins de relief que dans mon pays** it's even flatter than where I come from; **e. autant** as much again; **e. pire** even *or* still worse
7 *(introduisant une restriction)* **il ne suffit pas d'être beau, il faut e.** *ou* **e. faut-il être intelligent** it's not enough to be good-looking, you need to be intelligent too; **c'est bien beau d'avoir des projets, e. faut-il les réaliser** it's all very well having plans, but the important thing is to put them into practice; **si e. il** *ou* **e. s'il était franc, on lui pardonnerait** if only *or* if at least he was honest, you could forgive him; **si e. tu conduisais, on pourrait se relayer au volant** if only you could drive, we could take turns at the wheel; **je t'en donne 20 euros, et e.!** I'll give you 20 euros for it, if that!; **il aura peut-être une chance là-bas, et e.!** perhaps he'll have a chance over there, but only just *or* but not much of one!; **et e., on ne sait pas tout!** and even then we don't know the half of it!; **e. heureux!** thank goodness for that!; **e. une chance qu'il n'ait pas été là!** thank goodness *or* it's lucky he wasn't there!; **(mais) e. faudrait-il qu'elle accepte!** she has to agree first!; *Fam* **il faudrait e. que je trouve une voiture!** for a start *or* first I would have to find a car!
❑ **encore que CONJ** (al)though, even though; **j'aimerais y aller, e. qu'il soit tard** I'd like to go even though it's late; **e. qu'il ne me soit rien** (al)though he is nothing to me; **temps agréable e. qu'un peu froid** pleasant if *or* though rather cold weather; **on a assez d'argent, e. que, avec l'assurance à payer...** we've enough money, although with the insurance still to be paid...; **e. que...!** but then again...!

encorné, -e [ɑ̃kɔrne] **ADJ** *Littéraire (animal)* horned

encorner [3] [ɑ̃kɔrne] **VT** to gore; **se faire e.** to be gored

encornet [ɑ̃kɔrnɛ] **NM** *Zool (mollusque)* squid

encouble [ɑ̃kubl] **NF** *Suisse* obstacle

encoubler [3] [ɑ̃kuble] **s'encoubler VPR** *Suisse* to trip over

encourageant, -e [ɑ̃kuraʒɑ̃, -ɑ̃t] **ADJ** *(paroles, personne)* encouraging; *(succès, résultat)* encouraging, promising

encouragement [ɑ̃kuraʒmɑ̃] **NM** encouragement, support; **e. à la vertu/au crime** incentive to virtue/to crime; **quelques mots d'e.** a few encouraging words *or* words of encouragement; **recevoir peu d'encouragements à faire qch** to receive little encouragement *or* little inducement to do sth
❑ **encouragements NMPL** incentives; **encouragements à l'exportation** export incentives; **encouragements fiscaux** tax incentives

encourager [17] [ɑ̃kuraʒe] **VT 1** *(inciter)* to encourage; **e. qn du geste** to wave to sb in encouragement; **e. qn de la voix** to cheer sb (on); **elle l'a encouragé d'un sourire** she gave him an encouraging smile; **e. qn à faire qch** to encourage sb to do sth; **être encouragé par qn** to be encouraged by sb, to receive *or* get encouragement from sb; **encouragé par les premiers résultats** encouraged *or* heartened by the first results
2 *(favoriser)* to encourage, to promote; **l'oisiveté encourage le vice** idleness encourages *or* promotes vice; **un prix fondé pour e. l'initiative** an award set up to stimulate *or* to foster the spirit of enterprise
▸**s'encourager VPR 1** *(emploi réfléchi)* to spur oneself on
2 *(emploi réciproque)* to cheer each other on

encourir [45] [ɑ̃kurir] **VT** *(dédain, reproche, critique)* to incur, to bring upon oneself; **faire e. des risques à qn** to put sb at risk; **il sait qu'il encourt une lourde punition** he knows he risks being severely punished
▸**s'encourir VPR** *Vieilli ou Littéraire* to run, to hasten; **le pauvre homme s'encourut chez son voisin** *ou* **trouver son voisin** the poor man hastened round to his neighbour

encours, en-cours [ɑ̃kur] **NM INV 1** *Banque* loans outstanding; **l'e. de la dette** the outstanding debt; **e. de crédit** outstanding credits; **e. débiteur autorisé** authorized overdraft facility **2** *Compta* **e. de production de biens** work-in-progress **3 e. de fabrication** material undergoing processing; **e. de route** stock awaiting transfer *(to another department)*

encrage [ɑ̃kraʒ] **NM** *Typ* inking

encrassé, -e [ɑ̃krase] **ADJ** *(filtre)* clogged up; *(tuyau)* clogged (up), fouled (up); *(arme)* fouled (up); *Aut (bougie)* sooted-up; *(chaudière)* scaled-up

encrassement [ɑ̃krasmɑ̃] **NM** *(d'un filtre)* clogging (up); *(d'un tuyau)* clogging (up), fouling (up); *(d'une arme)* fouling (up); *Aut (d'une bougie)* fouling, sooting up

encrasser [3] [ɑ̃krase] **VT 1** *(obstruer → filtre)* to clog (up); *(→ tuyau)* to clog *or* to foul (up); *(→ arme)* to foul (up); *Aut (→ bougie)* to soot up **2** *(salir)* to dirty, to muck up
▸**s'encrasser VPR 1** *(s'obstruer → filtre)* to become clogged (up); *(→ tuyau)* to become clogged (up), to become fouled (up); *(→ arme)* to become fouled (up); *Aut (→ bougie)* to soot up **2** *(se salir)* to get dirty

encre [ɑ̃kr] **NF 1** *(pour écrire)* ink; **écrire à l'e.** to write in ink; **e. de Chine** Indian ink; **e. d'impression** *ou* **d'imprimerie** printing ink, printer's ink; **e. indélébile** indelible ink; **e. en poudre** toner; **e. sympathique** invisible ink; **doigts couverts**

d'e. inky fingers, fingers covered in ink; **noir comme de l'e.** inky black, black as ink; *Fig* **nuit d'e.** inky black night; **cela a fait couler beaucoup d'e.** a lot has been written about it

2 *(style)* **écrire de sa plus belle e.** to write in one's best style

3 *Zool* ink; *Culin* **calmars à l'e.** squid in its ink

encrer [3] [ɑ̃kre] VT *Typ* to ink

encreur [ɑ̃krœr] ADJ M inking; **ruban e.** (typewriter) ribbon; *Typ* **rouleau e.** inker

encrier [ɑ̃krije] NM *(pot)* inkpot; *(accessoire de bureau)* inkstand; *(récipient encastré)* inkwell

encrine [ɑ̃krin] NF *Zool* encrinite, encrinus, crinoid

encroué, -e [ɑ̃krue] ADJ *(arbre)* entangled, caught *(in the branches of other trees)*

encroûté, -e [ɑ̃krute] *Fam* ADJ **être e.** *(dans ses préjugés)* to be a fuddy-duddy *or* stick-in-the-mud; *(dans sa routine)* to be stuck in a rut; **vieux bonhomme e.** old fogey *or* stick-in-the-mud

NM,F 1 *(personne ayant des préjugés)* **un vieil e.** an old fuddy-duddy *or* stick-in-the-mud 2 *(personne routinière)* **mener une vie d'e.** to be in a rut

encroûtement [ɑ̃krutmɑ̃] NM 1 *Fam (d'une personne)* rut, mundane routine■; **sortir** *ou* **tirer qn de son e.** to get sb out of his/her rut 2 *(d'une paroi)* encrusting 3 *(d'une plaie)* scabbing

encroûter [3] [ɑ̃krute] VT 1 *(couvrir → de terre, de sang)* to encrust; *(→ de calcaire)* to fur up 2 *(rendre routinier)* to be (stuck) in a rut; **la retraite l'a encroûté** retirement has made him set in his ways *or* got him into a rut 3 *Fam (abêtir)* to turn into a vegetable

▸**s'encroûter** VPR 1 *(s'encrasser → vêtement)* to become encrusted; *(→ bouilloire)* to fur up 2 *Fam (devenir routinier)* to get into a rut; **il s'encroûte dans ses habitudes** he's got into a rut; **il s'encroûte dans son métier** he's really in a rut in that job

encrypter [3] [ɑ̃kripte] VT *Ordinat (données)* to encrypt

enculage [ɑ̃kylaʒ] NM *Vulg* 1 *(sodomisation)* buggery 2 **de l'e. de mouches** hair-splitting, nitpicking

enculé, -e [ɑ̃kyle] NM,F *Vulg* bastard, *Br* arsehole, *Am* asshole; **quelle bande d'enculés!** what a load of bastards!; **tous des enculés!** they're all bastards!

enculer [3] [ɑ̃kyle] VT *Vulg* 1 *(sodomiser)* to bugger, to fuck up the *Br* arse *or Am* ass; **va te faire e.!** fuck off!, go fuck yourself! 2 *(duper)* to screw, to shaft 3 **e. les mouches** to split hairs, to nit-pick

encuvage [ɑ̃kyvaʒ] NM *Tech* vatting

encuver [3] [ɑ̃kyve] VT *Tech* to vat

encyclique [ɑ̃siklik] *Rel* ADJ encyclical

NF encyclical

Encyclopédie [ɑ̃siklɔpedi] NF **l'E.** = groundbreaking 35-volume encyclopedia published in 1772, on which Diderot, Montesquieu, Voltaire and other key figures of the Enlightenment collaborated

encyclopédie [ɑ̃siklɔpedi] NF encyclopedia; *Fam* **une e. vivante** a walking encyclopedia

encyclopédique [ɑ̃siklɔpedik] ADJ 1 *(d'une encyclopédie)* encyclopedic 2 *(connaissances)* exhaustive, extensive, encyclopedic; **un esprit/une mémoire e.** a mind/memory that retains every detail

encyclopédisme [ɑ̃siklɔpedism] NM quest for all-round knowledge

encyclopédiste [ɑ̃siklɔpedist] NMF 1 *(auteur)* encyclopedist 2 *Hist* **les encyclopédistes** *ou* **Encyclopédistes** Diderot's Encyclopedists, the contributors to the "Encyclopédie"

endéans [ɑ̃deɑ̃] PRÉP *Belg* within

en-dehors [ɑ̃dəɔr] NM INV *(en danse)* turning out *(UNCOUNT)*

endémicité [ɑ̃demisite] NF *Méd* endemicity, endemic nature

endémie [ɑ̃demi] NF *Méd* endemic disease

endémique [ɑ̃demik] ADJ *(gén)* & *Écol* & *Méd* endemic; **e. en Malaisie/dans notre société** endemic to Malaysia/our society

endémisme [ɑ̃demism] NM *Écol* endemism

endenté, -e [ɑ̃dɑ̃te] ADJ 1 *(pourvu de dents)* having teeth; **les mâchoires fortes et vigoureusement endentées** with well-marked jaws and strong rows of teeth 2 *Hér* endented

endenter [3] [ɑ̃dɑ̃te] VT 1 *(roue)* to tooth, to cog 2 *(assembler → roues)* to mesh

endetté, -e [ɑ̃dete] ADJ *Fin* in debt; *Fig* in debt, indebted (**envers** to); **très e.** deep(ly) *or* heavily in debt

endettement [ɑ̃dɛtmɑ̃] NM 1 *Fin (état)* indebtedness, debt; *(action)* running *or* getting into debt; **e. des consommateurs** consumer debt; **e. extérieur** foreign debt; **e. intérieur** internal debt; **l'e. des pays du tiers-monde** the debt burden of Third World countries; **e. public** public debt; **cela a provoqué l'e. des pays de l'Est** this caused the Eastern countries to get into debt; **ratio d'e.** debt ratio; **facilité d'e.** borrowing capacity 2 *Compta* indebtedness, gearing

endetter [4] [ɑ̃dete] VT 1 *Fin* to get into debt; **il est lourdement endetté** he's heavily in debt; **l'acquisition de nouvelles machines a endetté la société** the purchase of new machinery has got the company into debt

2 *Fig* **être endetté envers qn** to be indebted to sb

▸**s'endetter** VPR *Fin* to get *or* to run into debt; **ne vous endettez pas davantage** don't get any further into debt; **je me suis endetté de 10 000 euros** I got 10,000 euros in debt; **s'e. trop lourdement** to take on too many debts

endeuiller [5] [ɑ̃dœje] VT 1 *(famille, personne)* to plunge into mourning; **maison endeuillée** house in mourning 2 *(réception, course)* to cast a tragic shadow over 3 *Littéraire (tableau, paysage)* to give a dismal aspect to

endêver [ɛdeve] VI *(à l'infinitif seulement) Fam Vieilli* **faire e. qn** to infuriate sb■

endiablé, -e [ɑ̃djable] ADJ 1 *(danse, musique, poursuite)* wild, frenzied; **se lancer dans une ronde endiablée** to begin to dance wildly *or* frenziedly in a circle 2 *(enfant)* boisterous, unruly

endiabler [3] [ɑ̃djɑble] VI *Vieilli* **faire e. qn** to torment sb

endigage [ɑ̃digaʒ], **endiguement** [ɑ̃digmɑ̃] NM 1 *(d'un cours d'eau)* dyking (up) 2 *(d'émotions, d'un développement)* holding back, checking; *(du chômage, de dettes)* curbing; **tenter l'e. de la violence/de la hausse des prix** to attempt to contain violence/price increases 3 *Bourse & Fin* hedging

endiguer [3] [ɑ̃dige] VT 1 *(cours d'eau)* to dyke (up) 2 *(émotion, développement)* to hold back, to check; *(chômage, excès)* to curb; *(violence)* to contain

endimanché, -e [ɑ̃dimɑ̃ʃe] ADJ in one's Sunday best; **avoir l'air e.** to be overdressed

endimancher [3] [ɑ̃dimɑ̃ʃe] **s'endimancher** VPR to put on one's Sunday best, to get all dressed up

endive [ɑ̃div] NF *Bot* chicory, French endive; *Fam* **pâle comme une e.** as white *or* pale as a sheet

endivisionner [3] [ɑ̃divizjɔne] VT *Mil* to form into a division

endoblaste [ɑ̃dɔblast] NM *Biol* endoblast, endoderm

endoblastique [ɑ̃dɔblastik] ADJ *Biol* endoblastic, endodermal

endocarde [ɑ̃dɔkard] NM *Anat* endocardium

endocardiaque [ɑ̃dɔkardjak] ADJ *Méd* endocardiac

endocardite [ɑ̃dɔkardit] NF *Méd* endocarditis

endocarpe [ɑ̃dɔkarp] NM *Bot* endocarp

endocrâne [ɑ̃dɔkran] NM *Anat* endocranium

endocrine [ɑ̃dɔkrin] ADJ *Physiol* endocrine

endocrinien, -enne [ɑ̃dɔkrinjɛ̃, -ɛn] ADJ *Physiol* endocrinal, endocrinous

endocrinologie [ɑ̃dɔkrinɔlɔʒi] NF *Méd* endocrinology

endocrinologue [ɑ̃dɔkrinɔlɔg], **endocrinologiste** [ɑ̃dɔkrinɔlɔʒist] NMF *Méd* endocrinologist

endoctrinement [ɑ̃dɔktrinmɑ̃] NM indoctrination

endoctriner [3] [ɑ̃dɔktrine] VT to indoctrinate

endoderme [ɑ̃dɔdɛrm] NM *Biol* endoblast, endoderm

endodermique [ɑ̃dɔdɛrmik] ADJ *Biol* endoblastic, endodermal

endodontie [ɛdodɔ̃ti] NF *Méd* endodontics *(singulier)*

endogame [ɑ̃dɔgam] ADJ endogamous

NMF endogamous man, *f* woman

endogamie [ɑ̃dɔgami] NF endogamy

endogamique [ɑ̃dɔgamik] ADJ endogamous

endogé, -e [ɑ̃dɔʒe] ADJ *Biol* **faune endogée** fauna living in the soil, soil-dwelling fauna

endogène [ɑ̃dɔʒɛn] ADJ 1 *Biol, Bot & Med* endogenetic, endogenous 2 *Géol* endogenetic

endolori, -e [ɑ̃dɔlɔri] ADJ painful, aching; **le corps tout e.** aching all over; **mon pied était e.** my foot hurt *or* was aching; **épaule e.** painful *or* aching shoulder

endolorir [32] [ɑ̃dɔlɔrir] VT to make painful

endolorissement [ɑ̃dɔlɔrismɑ̃] NM 1 *(action)* hurting 2 *(douleur)* ache, aching

endomètre [ɑ̃dɔmɛtr] NM *Anat* endometrium

endométriome [ɑ̃dɔmetriɔm] NM *Méd* endometrioma

endométriose [ɑ̃dɔmetrioz] NF *Méd* endometriosis

endométrite [ɑ̃dɔmetrit] NF *Méd* endometritis

endommagement [ɑ̃dɔmaʒmɑ̃] NM *(action)* damaging (**de** of); *(result)* damage (**de** to)

endommager [17] [ɑ̃dɔmaʒe] VT 1 *(bâtiment)* to damage; *(environnement, récolte)* to damage, to harm 2 *Ordinat* to corrupt; **fichier endommagé** damaged *or* corrupt file

endomorphe [ɑ̃dɔmɔrf] ADJ endomorphic

endomorphine [ɑ̃dɔmɔrfin] NF *Biol & Chim* endorphin

endomorphisme [ɑ̃dɔmɔrfism] NM *Géol & Math* endomorphism

endonucléase [ɑ̃dɔnykleaz] NF *Biol & Chim* endonuclease

endoparasite [ɑ̃dɔparazit] *Biol* ADJ endoparasitic

NM endoparasite

endoplasme [ɑ̃dɔplasm] NM *Biol* endoplasm

endoplasmique [ɛdɔplasmik] ADJ *Biol* endoplasmic

endoréique [ɑ̃dɔreik] ADJ *Géol* endorheic

endoréisme [ɑ̃dɔreism] NM *Géol* endorheism

endormant, -e [ɑ̃dɔrmɑ̃, -ɑ̃t] ADJ 1 *(professeur, film)* boring 2 *(massage, tisane)* sleep-inducing

endormeur, -euse [ɑ̃dɔrmœr, -øz] NM,F *Littéraire* beguiler, enticer; **les endormeurs** those who lull you into a false sense of false security

endormi, -e [ɑ̃dɔrmi] ADJ 1 *(sommeillant)* sleeping; **il est e.** he's asleep *or* sleeping; **à moitié e.** half asleep; **avoir l'air e.** to look sleepy

2 *(apathique)* sluggish, lethargic

3 *(calme → ville)* sleepy, drowsy

4 *(faible → désir)* dormant; *(→ vigilance)* lulled

5 *(ankylosé)* **une jambe endormie** a leg which has gone to sleep

NM,F *(personne apathique)* good-for-nothing, ne'er-do-well

endormir [36] [ɑ̃dɔrmir] VT 1 *(d'un sommeil naturel)* to put *or* to send to sleep; *(avec douceur)* to lull to sleep

2 *(anesthésier)* to put to sleep

3 *(ennuyer)* to send to sleep, to bore

4 *(tromper → électeurs, public)* to lull into a false sense of security

5 *(affaiblir → douleur)* to deaden; *(→ scrupules)* to allay; **e. les soupçons** to allay suspicion; **e. la vigilance de qn** to get sb to drop his/her guard

▸**s'endormir** VPR 1 *(d'un sommeil naturel)* to drop off *or* to go to sleep, to fall asleep

2 *(sous anesthésie)* to go to sleep

3 *(mourir)* to pass away *or* on

4 *(se relâcher)* to let up, to slacken off; **ne nous endormons pas, on joue dans deux jours!** this is no time to slacken off, we're playing in two days' time!; **s'e. sur ses lauriers** to rest on one's laurels

5 *(devenir calme → maisonnée, pays)* to grow calm

6 *(s'affaiblir → douleur)* to subside, to die down; *(→ scrupules)* to be allayed; *(→ vigilance)* to slacken

endormissement [ɑ̃dɔrmismɑ̃] NM 1 **au moment de l'e.** when falling asleep; **qui aide à l'e.** sleep-inducing 2 *Ordinat* hibernation, sleep mode

endorphine [ɑ̃dɔrfin] NF *Biol & Chim* endorphin

endort *etc voir* **endormir**

endos [ɑ̃do] NM *Banque & Fin* endorsement; **e. en blanc** blank endorsement

endoscope [ɑ̃dɔskɔp] NM *Méd* endoscope

endoscopie [ɑ̃dɔskɔpi] NF *Méd* endoscopy

endoscopique [ɑ̃dɔskɔpik] ADJ *Méd* endoscopic

endosmose [ɑ̃dɔsmoz] NF *Phys* endosmosis

enc–end

end-enf

endosperme[ɑ̃dɔspɛrm] NM*Bot* endosperm

endosquelette[ɑ̃dɔskəlɛt] NM*Zool* endoskeleton

endossable [ɑ̃dosabl] ADJ *Banque & Fin* endorsable

endossataire [ɑ̃dosatɛr] NMF *Banque & Fin* endorsee

endossement [ɑ̃dosmɑ̃] NM *Banque & Fin* endorsement; **e. en blanc** blank endorsement

endosser[3] [ɑ̃dose] VT1 (*revêtir*) to put or to slip on, to don

2 (*assumer*) to assume; **e. la responsabilité de qch** to shoulder or to assume the responsibility for sth; **e. les conséquences d'une erreur** to accept or to assume the consequences of a mistake; **il lui a fait e. la responsabilité de l'accident** he made him/her take responsibility for the accident

3 *Banque & Fin* to endorse; **e. en blanc** to blank endorse

4 (*livre*) to back

endosseur[ɑ̃dosœr] NM*Banque & Fin* endorser

endothélial, -e, -aux, -ales [ɑ̃dɔteljal, -o] ADJ *Physiol* endothelial

endothélium [ɑ̃dɔteljɔm] NM *Physiol* endothelium

endotherme[ɑ̃dɔtɛrm] ADJ*Physiol* endothermic

endothermique[ɑ̃dɔtɛrmik] ADJ*Phys* endothermic, endothermal

endotoxine[ɑ̃dɔtɔksin] NF*Biol* endotoxin

endroit[ɑ̃drwa] NM1 (*emplacement*) place; **à l'e. de sa chute** where he/she fell; **à quel e. tu l'as mis?** where or whereabouts did you put it?; **ce n'est pas au bon e.** it's not in the right place; **il est assis au même e. depuis une heure** he's been sitting in the same place or spot for the last hour; **j'ai besoin d'un e. pour ranger mes affaires** I need a place or space to store my things; **l'e. de la réunion** the place for or the venue of the meeting; **si tu ne peux pas le mettre à cet e., mets-le ailleurs** if you can't put it there, put it somewhere else; **rire au bon e.** to laugh in the right place

2 (*localité*) place, spot; **il y a de belles églises à cet e.** there are some beautiful churches in this area; **un e. tranquille** a quiet place or spot; **l'e.** the locality, the area; **les gens de l'e. sont très accueillants** the local people or the locals are very friendly

3 (*partie → du corps, d'un objet*) place; (*→ d'une œuvre, d'une histoire*) place, point; **cela fait mal à quel e.?** where does it hurt?; **en plusieurs endroits** in several places; **c'est l'e. le plus drôle du livre** it's the funniest part or passage in the book; **je me suis arrêté à cet e. du livre, j'ai arrêté ma lecture à cet e.** this is where I stopped reading, I stopped reading here; **on va reprendre au même e.** we'll start again at the same point; **tout le monde pleure au même e.** everybody cries at the same point; *Fig* **toucher à un e. sensible** to touch a sore spot or a nerve

4 (*d'un vêtement*) right side

5 *Euph* **petit e.** smallest room in the house; **aller au petit e.** to go and powder one's nose, *Br* to go and spend a penny

6 *Géog* south-facing slope

▫ **à l'endroit** ADV 1 (*le bon côté en haut*) right side up; (*le bon côté à l'extérieur*) right side out; (*le bon côté devant*) right side round; **ton pull n'est pas à l'e.** your sweater's on the wrong way round; (*les coutures ne sont pas à l'intérieur*) your sweater's on inside out; **remets la bouteille à l'e.** turn the bottle the right way up

2 *Couture* (*dans les explications*) **deux mailles à l'e.** two plain, knit two; **un rang à l'e.** knit one row

▫ **à l'endroit de** PRÉP *Littéraire* (*personne*) towards; (*événement, objet*) regarding, with regard to, in regard to

▫ **par endroits** ADVin places, here and there; **il y a de l'herbe par endroits** there's some grass here and there or in places

enduction[ɑ̃dyksjɔ̃] NF*Tex* coating

enduire [98] [ɑ̃dɥir] VT1 (*recouvrir*) **e. de** (*peinture, ciment, colle etc*) to coat or cover with; (*crème, boue etc*) to smear with; **e. de beurre le fond d'un plat** to grease the bottom of a dish with butter; **e. qch de colle** to apply glue to sth; **il enduisait ses jambes de crème solaire** he was smoothing or rubbing suntan cream on his legs;

enduit d'une substance collante smeared or coated with sticky matter

2 *Constr* **e. un mur** to plaster a wall over, to face a wall (*with finishing plaster*)

▸**s'enduire** VPRS**'e. de crème à solaire** to cover oneself with suntan cream

enduit[ɑ̃dɥi] NM1 *Constr* (*revêtement*) coat, coating; **e. au ciment** cement rendering **2** *Constr* (*plâtre*) plaster; **e. de lissage/de rebouchage** finishing/sealing plaster; **e. étanche** sealant; **e. imperméable** proofing **3** *Cér* glaze, glazing **4** *Méd* coating, fur (*on the tongue, the stomach*)

endurable[ɑ̃dyrabl] ADJendurable, bearable

endurance [ɑ̃dyrɑ̃s] NF1 (*d'une personne → physique*) endurance, stamina; (*→ morale*) endurance, powers of resistance; **il n'a pas eu l'e. nécessaire pour résister à la pression** he wasn't tough enough to stand up to the pressure; **e. à la chaleur** tolerance of heat; **e. à la douleur** pain threshold; **avoir une grande e. à la douleur** to have a high pain threshold; **e. à l'effort** staying power

2 (*d'une matière, d'une machine*) endurance, resilience; **e. à la flexion** bending endurance, stress fatigue limit

3 *Sport* (*discipline*) endurance; **épreuve/ course d'e.** endurance test/race

endurant, -e [ɑ̃dyrɑ̃, -ɑ̃t] ADJ 1 (*résistant*) resistant, tough **2** *Fam Vieilli* (*patient*) enduring ▪, long-suffering ▪

endurci, -e [ɑ̃dyrsi] ADJ 1 (*invétéré*) hardened, inveterate; **célibataire e.** confirmed bachelor **2** (*insensible → âme, caractère*) hardened; **des cœurs endurcis** hard-hearted people

endurcir [32] [ɑ̃dyrsir] VT 1 (*rendre résistant → corps, personne*) to harden, to toughen; **son séjour dans l'armée l'a endurci** his time in the army toughened him up; **être endurci à** to be hardened to, to be inured to

2 (*rendre insensible*) to harden; **être endurci à la fatigue** to be inured or hardened to fatigue

▸**s'endurcir** VPR1 (*devenir résistant*) to harden oneself, to become tougher; **je me suis endurci avec l'âge** age has made me tougher or has toughened me; **s'e.** à to become hardened or inured to

2 (*devenir insensible*) to harden one's heart; **il s'est beaucoup endurci** he has become very hard

endurcissement [ɑ̃dyrsismɑ̃] NM 1 (*endurance*) hardening, toughening **2** (*insensibilité*) **son e. au fil des années** his/her increasing hard-heartedness over the years; **l'e. du cœur** the hardening of the heart

endurer[3] [ɑ̃dyre] VTto endure, to bear, to stand; **comment peut-il e. qu'on lui parle ainsi?** how can he tolerate being spoken to in that way?; **il a dû e. beaucoup d'épreuves** he had to put up with or to suffer a lot of trials and tribulations; *Vieilli* **je n'endure plus vos critiques** I can't put up with or endure or tolerate you criticizing me any more; **le bourreau faisait e. à ses victimes des supplices épouvantables** the executioner subjected his victims to horrific torture; **je ne vois pas pourquoi je devrais e. cela** I can't see why I should put up with that; **je ne peux e. ses manières grossières** I can't stand or put up with his/her rude manners

enduro [ɑ̃dyro] NM *Sport* cross-country motorcycle race

endymion [ɑ̃dimjɔ̃] NM*Bot* bluebell

E-N-E(*abrév écrite* **Est-Nord-Est**) ENE

Énée[ene] NPR*Myth* Aeneas

Énéide[eneid] NF

'**L'Énéide**' *Virgile* 'The Aeneid'

énéolithique[eneɔlitik] *Hist* ADJAeneolithic
NMAeneolithic (period)

énergéticien, -enne [enɛrʒetisjɛ̃, -ɛn] NM,Fenergetics specialist

énergétique[enɛrʒetik] ADJ *Écol & Écon* energy (*avant n*) **2** (*boisson, aliment*) energy-giving; (*besoins, apport*) energy (*avant n*); **dépense é.** expenditure of energy
NFenergetics (*singulier*)

énergie[enɛrʒi] NF1 (*dynamisme*) energy; **parler avec é.** to speak vigorously; **se mettre au travail avec é.** to start work energetically; **avoir de l'é.**

to have a lot of energy; **je n'ai pas assez d'é. pour sortir ce soir** I haven't got the energy to go out this evening; **je ne me sens pas beaucoup d'é.** I'm not feeling very energetic; **donner de l'é. à qn** to invigorate or to energize sb; **être sans** ou **manquer d'é.** to lack energy, to be listless; **mettre toute son é. à** to devote or to apply all one's energies to

2 (*force*) energy, vigour, strength; **il faudrait dépenser trop d'é.** it would be too much of an effort; **avec l'é. du désespoir** with the strength born of desperation; **avec é.** energetically; (*refuser, répondre*) forcefully, vigorously; **il a fait face à la situation avec é.** he faced up to the situation with spirit

3 *Tech* energy, power; **la crise de l'é.** the energy crisis; **é. électrique/solaire** electrical/solar energy; **é. atomique** atomic power; **é. potentielle/cinétique** potential/kinetic energy; **é. des vagues/hydraulique** wave/water power; **é. éolienne** wind power; **é. nucléaire** nuclear power or energy; **les énergies nouvelles** new energy sources; **les énergies renouvelables** renewable energy sources; *Astron* **é. sombre** dark energy; **é. propre** clean energy; **é. thermique** thermal power

4 *Psy* **é. psychique** psychic energy

▫ **énergies** NFPLrassembler les énergies d'un **pays** to mobilize the people of a country; **nous aurons besoin de toutes les énergies** we'll need all the help we can get

énergique [enɛrʒik] ADJ 1 (*fort → mouvement, intervention*) energetic, vigorous; (*→ mesure*) energetic, drastic, extreme; (*→ paroles*) emphatic; (*→ traitement*) strong, powerful **2** (*dynamique → personne, caractère*) energetic, forceful, active; (*→ visage*) determined-looking; **une jeune femme é.** a young woman with plenty of spirit or drive

énergiquement [enɛrʒikmɑ̃] ADV (*bouger, agir, parler*) energetically; (*refuser*) emphatically; (*répondre, condamner*) vigorously

énergisant, -e [enɛrʒizɑ̃, -ɑ̃t] ADJ energizing, energy-giving
NMenergizer

énergivore [enɛrʒivɔr] ADJ (*véhicule, appareil, industrie*) energy-guzzling

énergumène[enɛrgymɛn] NMFwild-eyed fanatic or zealot, *Littéraire* energumen; **c'est un drôle d'é.** he's a queer fish

énervant, -e[enɛrvɑ̃, -ɑ̃t] ADJirritating, annoying, trying

énervation [enɛrvasjɔ̃] NF 1 *Méd* denervation **2** *Vieilli* (*affaiblissement*) enervation

énervé, -e [enɛrve] ADJ 1 (*irrité*) irritated, annoyed **2** (*tendu*) edgy; **il est souvent é.** he's often edgy or on edge **3** (*agité*) agitated, restless

énervement[enɛrvəmɑ̃] NM1 (*agacement*) irritation, annoyance; **notre départ s'est fait dans l'é. général** everyone was getting irritated with everyone else when we left **2** (*tension*) edginess **3** (*agitation*) restlessness

énerver [3] [enɛrve] VT 1 (*irriter*) to annoy, to irritate; **ça m'énerve quand il dit des idioties** it gets on my nerves when he says stupid things; **son attitude m'énerve** I find his/her behaviour annoying or irritating; **cette musique m'énerve** this music is getting on my nerves

2 (*agiter*) to make restless, to excite, to overexcite; **n'énerve pas le petit avant son coucher** don't excite the little one before he goes to bed **3** *Méd* to denervate

4 *Vieilli ou Littéraire* (*débiliter*) to enervate, to weaken

▸**s'énerver** VPR1 (*être irrité*) to get worked up or annoyed or irritated

2 (*être excité*) to get worked up or excited or overexcited; **il ne faut pas laisser les enfants s'é. avant de se coucher** the children mustn't get worked up or excited before going to bed

enfaîteau, -x[ɑ̃fɛto] NMConstr ridge tile

enfaîtement[ɑ̃fɛtmɑ̃] NMConstr ridge tiling

enfaîter[4] [ɑ̃fɛte] VTConstr to top with ridge tiles

enfance [ɑ̃fɑ̃s] NF 1 (*période de la vie → gén*) childhood; (*→ d'un garçon*) boyhood; (*→ d'une fille*) girlhood; **dans mon e.** in my childhood, when I was a child; **depuis mon e.** ever since I was a child; **dès sa plus tendre e.** from a very

tender age; **dès sa première e.** in his/her infancy; **dès son e.** from an early age; **retomber en e.** to regress; **il retombe en e.** he's in his second childhood; **la petite e.** infancy, babyhood, early childhood; **des souvenirs datant de la petite e.** memories of when one was very small, early childhood memories

2 *(enfants)* children; **l'e. délinquante/malheureuse** delinquent/unhappy children

3 *(commencement)* infancy, start, early stage; **l'e. d'une civilisation** the dawn *or* beginning of a civilization; **c'est l'e. de l'art** it's child's play

❑ **d'enfance** ADJ childhood *(avant n)*

'L'Enfance nue' *Pialat* 'Naked Childhood'

enfant [ɑ̃fɑ̃] ADJ **1** *(jeune)* **il était encore e. quand il comprit, tout e. encore, il comprit** he was still a child when he understood; **je l'ai connu e.** I have known him since he was a child

2 *(naïf)* childlike; **il est resté très e.** he's still a child at heart

NMF **1** *(jeune → gén)* child; *(→ garçon)* little boy; *(→ fille)* little girl; **c'est une belle e.** she's a beautiful child; **un e. à naître** an unborn child *or* baby; **e. en bas âge** infant; **faire l'e.** to act like a child; **ne fais pas l'e.!** act your age!, don't be such a baby!, grow up!; **il n'y a plus d'enfants!** children are so precocious these days!; **prendre qn pour un e.** to treat sb like a child; **elle me parle comme à un e.** she talks to me as if I was a child; *Méd* **e. bleu** blue baby; *Rel* **e. de chœur** altarboy; *Fig* **comme un e. de chœur** like an angel *or* a cherub; **ce n'est pas un e. de chœur** he's no angel; **prendre qn pour un e. de chœur** to think sb is still wet behind the ears; **e. gâté** spoilt child; *Rel* **l'e. Jésus** Baby Jesus; **e. légitime** legitimate child; **e. à naître** unborn child; **e. naturel, e. illégitime** illegitimate child; **e. prodige** child prodigy; **e. sauvage** *(vivant à l'état sauvage)* wolf child; **e. soldat** child soldier; **e. surdoué** exceptionally gifted child; **e. terrible** enfant terrible; **e. trouvé** foundling; **grand e.** overgrown child; **ce sont de grands enfants** they're very naive; **petit e.** infant, little child, small child; *Bible* **laissez venir à moi les petits enfants** suffer the little children to come unto me; **dormir comme un e.** to sleep like a baby; **comme l'e. qui vient de naître** (as) innocent as a new-born babe

2 *(descendant)* child; **faire un e.** to have a child; **faire un e. à une femme** to get a woman pregnant; **il lui a fait un e.** she had a child by him; **avoir de jeunes enfants/de grands enfants** to have a young family/grown-up children; **ils n'ont pas d'enfants** they're childless, they don't have children; **un couple sans enfants** a childless couple; **être en mal d'e.** to be broody; **mourir sans enfants** to die childless *or* *Jur* without issue; *Jur* **décédé sans enfants** having died without issue; **un e. de la crise/des années 80** a child of the depression/of the 80s; **la chorale, c'est son e.** the choir is his/her brainchild *or* baby; **e. de l'amour** love child; **je suis un e. de la balle** *(théâtre)* I was born into the theatre; *(cirque)* I was born under the big top; *Can très Fam* **être en e. de chienne** to be fuming, to be hopping mad; *Can très Fam* **cet e. de chienne m'a fait perdre mon boulot** I lost my job because of that son-of-a-bitch!; *Rel* **e. de Marie** child of Mary; *Fig* **ce n'est pas une e. de Marie** she's no saint; **un e. de Paris** a native of Paris; **e. du pays** *(homme)* son of the soil; *(femme)* daughter of the soil; **un e. du peuple** a child of the people; *Bible* **l'e. prodigue** the prodigal son; *Hist* **e. de troupe** = soldier's child who lives in barracks or in a special military school and whose education is paid for by the government; **les enfants d'Israël** the children of Israel

3 *(en appellatif)* child; **mon e.** my child; **belle e.** dear girl *or* child; *Fam* **alors, les enfants, encore un peu de champagne?** a bit more champagne, boys and girls *or* folks?; *Fam* **bon, les enfants, on y va?** come on you lot, let's go!; *Fam* **salut, les enfants!** *(à des adultes)* hello people!, hi guys *or* gang!; *Vulg* **e. de putain** *ou* **de salaud** son of a bitch

❑ **bon enfant** ADJ INV good-natured; **tenez, je suis bon e., je ne vous fais pas payer les intérêts** look, I'll be good to you, I won't charge you interest; **d'un ton bon e.** good-naturedly

❑ **d'enfant** ADJ **1** *(des enfants → dessin, imagination)* child's *(avant n)*

2 *Péj (puéril)* childlike, childish, babyish

'Les Enfants du paradis' *Carné* 'The Children of Paradise'

'Les Enfants terribles' *Melville, Cocteau* 'Les Enfants Terribles' (novel), 'The Strange Ones' (film)

'L'Enfant sauvage' *Truffaut* 'The Wild Child'

enfant-bulle [ɑ̃fɑ̃byl] (*pl* **enfants-bulles**) NM *Méd* = child who has to stay in a sterile tent

enfantement [ɑ̃fɑ̃tmɑ̃] NM *Littéraire* **1** *(création)* birth, bringing forth **2** *(accouchement)* childbirth

enfanter [3] [ɑ̃fɑ̃te] VT *Littéraire* **1** *(produire)* to give birth to, to create, to bring forth; **les héros que notre pays a enfantés** the heroes that our country has brought forth; **la discorde enfante le crime** discord begets crime **2** *(sujet: mère)* to give birth to; *Bible* **tu enfanteras dans la douleur** in sorrow thou shalt bring forth children

enfantillage [ɑ̃fɑ̃tijaʒ] NM **1** *(comportement)* infantile *or* childish behaviour; **arrête ces enfantillages!** don't be so childish!, do grow up! **2** *(chose sans importance)* trifle, trifling matter

enfantin, -e [ɑ̃fɑ̃tɛ̃, -in] ADJ **1** *(de l'enfance)* childlike; *(littérature)* children's *(avant n)*; **voix enfantine** child's *or* childlike voice; **avoir un sourire e.** *(homme)* to have a boyish smile; *(femme)* to have a girlish smile **2** *(simple)* easy; **c'est e.** there's nothing to it, it's child's play; **c'est d'une simplicité enfantine** it's childishly simple **3** *(puéril)* childish, infantile, puerile

enfarger [17] [ɑ̃farʒe] *Can Fam* VT to trip up[■]

▸**s'enfarger** VPR to trip up[■]; **s'e. dans les fleurs du tapis** to get bogged down in too much detail, to lose sight of the big picture

enfariné, -e [ɑ̃farine] ADJ *(visage, cheveux etc → de farine)* covered with flour; *(→ de poudre)* smothered in powder; *Fam* **il est arrivé à 4 heures, la gueule enfarinée** *ou* **le bec e.** he breezed in at 4 o'clock as if nothing was the matter; *Fam* **je suis arrivée, la gueule enfarinée, demander mon augmentation** I arrived in all innocence *or* quite unsuspecting to ask for my pay rise[■]; *Fam* **à chaque fois qu'il casse quelque chose, il vient la gueule enfarinée** whenever he breaks something he turns up looking all innocent[■] *or* as if butter wouldn't melt in his mouth

enfariner [3] [ɑ̃farine] VT *Culin* to cover with flour

enfer [ɑ̃fɛr] NM **1** *Rel* hell; *Fig* **aller en e.** to go to hell; *Hum* **e. et damnation!** (hell and) damnation!, heck!; *Prov* **l'e. est pavé de bonnes intentions** the road to hell is paved with good intentions; **l'E. de Dante** Dante's Inferno; **l'E. du Nord** = nickname for the Paris-Roubaix cycle race

2 *(lieu, situation désagréable)* hell; **sa vie est un véritable e.** his/her life is absolute hell; **il fait de ma vie un e.** he's making my life hell; **c'est vraiment l'e. à la maison** it's sheer hell at home; **quelque fois c'est l'e. pour se garer ici** it can be hell trying to park here; **l'e. de la drogue/de la prostitution/du chômage** the living hell of drug addiction/of prostitution/of unemployment; **l'e. de la guerre** the inferno of war; **descente en e.** descent into hell

3 *(d'une bibliothèque)* = section where books forbidden to the public are stored

❑ **enfers** NMPL *Myth* **les enfers** the underworld; **descendre aux enfers** to go down into the underworld; *Fig* **descente aux enfers** descent into hell

❑ **d'enfer** ADJ **1** *(très mauvais → vie)* hellish; *(→ bruit)* deafening; *(→ feu)* blazing, raging; **jouer un jeu d'e.** to play for high stakes; **une vision d'e.** a vision of hell; **aller un train d'e.** to go at top speed *or* *Fam* hell for leather

2 *Fam (très bien)* great, wicked; **il est d'e. ton blouson!** what a great jacket!

> *Allusion*
>
> **L'enfer, c'est les autres**
>
> This phrase, which has become famous in English too, as "Hell is other people", comes from Jean-Paul Sartre's *Huis Clos* (1944), a play in which three people are shut up together with no escape and find each other's presence unendurable. People use this expression today to complain about others, or about crowded conditions and lack of privacy.

enfermement [ɑ̃fɛrməmɑ̃] NM **1** *(action d'enfermer)* shutting *or* locking up **2** *(fait d'être enfermé)* seclusion

enfermer [3] [ɑ̃fɛrme] VT **1** *(mettre dans un lieu clos → personne, animal)* to shut up *or* in; **e. qn/qch (à clef)** to lock sb/sth up; **la nuit, on enferme le chien** at night we shut the dog up *or* in; **e. qn dans un placard** to lock sb in a cupboard; **e. qn dehors** to shut *or* lock sb out; **il s'est fait e.** *(chez lui)* he got locked in

2 *(emprisonner → criminel)* to lock up *or* away, to put under lock and key; *(→ fou)* to lock up; **e. qn dans une cellule** to shut sb up in a cell; **ce type-là, il faudrait l'e.!** *ou* **il est bon à e.!** *(dangereux)* that guy ought to be locked up!; *(fou)* that guy needs his head examined!; **faire e. qn** to have sb locked away; **il s'est fait e.** *(dans un asile)* he was put away

3 *(ranger)* to put *or* to shut away; *(en verrouillant)* to lock up *or* away

4 *(confiner)* to confine, to coop up; **enfermé dans une petite pièce toute la journée** cooped up in a small room all day; **je me sens enfermé** I feel cooped up; **ne restez pas enfermés, voilà le soleil!** don't stay indoors, the sun's come out!; **e. qn dans un dilemme** to put sb in a dilemma; *Fig* **e. qn dans un rôle** to typecast sb; **être enfermé dans ses contradictions** to remain trapped *or* bound by one's own contradictions

5 *(entourer)* to enclose; **les murailles enferment la ville** the walls enclose the town

6 *(contenir → allusion, menace)* to contain; **un triangle enfermé dans un cercle** a triangle circumscribed by *or* in a circle

7 *(maintenir → dans des règles)* to confine, to restrict; **e. la poésie dans des règles strictes** to confine poetry within strict rules

8 *Sport* to hem in

▸**s'enfermer** VPR **1** *(se cloîtrer → dans un couvent)* to shut oneself up *or* away

2 *(verrouiller sa porte)* to shut oneself up *or* in, to lock oneself in; **s'e. dehors** to lock *or* to shut oneself out

3 *(s'isoler)* to shut oneself away; **elle s'enferme à la bibliothèque toute la journée** she spends all day in the library; **s'e. dans le silence** to retreat into silence; **s'e. dans ses contradictions** to become caught up in one's own contradictions; **s'e. dans un rôle** to stick to a role; **depuis qu'il est prof, il s'est enfermé dans le rôle de M. je sais tout** he's turned into a real know-it-all since he became a teacher

enferrer [4] [ɑ̃fere] VT *(avec une lame)* to run through, to transfix

▸**s'enferrer** VPR **1** *(s'enfoncer)* to make matters worse; **s'e. dans ses explications** to get tangled up *or* muddled up in one's explanations; **s'e. dans ses mensonges** to be caught *or* trapped in the mesh of one's lies; **tais-toi, tu t'enferres** don't say any more, you're only making matters worse for yourself

2 *(s'embrocher)* to spike *or* to spear oneself

3 *Pêche (poisson)* to hook itself

enfeu [ɑ̃fø] NM *Archit* recess

enfichable [ɑ̃fiʃabl] ADJ *Élec* that can be plugged in; *Ordinat* slot-in

enficher [3] [ɑ̃fiʃe] VT *Élec* to plug in; *Ordinat* to slot in

enfiévré, -e [ɑ̃fjevre] ADJ *(front, imagination)* fevered; *(atmosphère)* feverish; *(foule)* in a fever (of excitement), at fever pitch

enfièvrement [ɑ̃fjɛvrəmɑ̃] NM fever (of excitement)

enfiévrer [18] [ɑ̃fjevre] VT **1** *(exalter)* to fire, to stir up; **e. les esprits** to stir people up; **e.**

l'imagination to fire the imagination **2** *Vieilli Méd* to make feverish

►**s'enfiévrer** VPRto get excited; **s'e. pour une idée nouvelle** to get very excited over a new idea

enfilade[ɑ̃filad] NF1 *(rangée)* row, line; **une e. de peupliers** a row of poplars; **je me suis perdu dans l'e. des couloirs** I got lost in the maze of corridors *or* the endless corridors

2 *Mil* enfilade; **tir d'e.** raking *or* enfilading fire

❏ **en enfilade** ADJ **des pièces en e.** a suite of adjoining rooms; **le salon et la salle à manger sont en e.** the living room opens into *or* adjoins the dining room; **la chambre et la salle de bains sont en e.** the bedroom has an en suite bathroom; **maisons en e.** *(toutes mitoyennes)* a row of *Br* terraced houses *or Am* townhouses, *Br* a terrace; *(mitoyennes deux à deux)* a row of semi-detached houses; *(isolées)* a row of houses

ADVMil prendre en e. to enfilade; **prendre les rues en e.** to follow along in a straight line from one street to the next

enfilage[ɑ̃filaʒ] NMCouture threading

enfiler[3] [ɑ̃file] VT1 *(faire passer)* **e. un élastique dans un ourlet** to thread a piece of elastic through a hem

2 *(disposer → sur un fil)* to thread *or* to string (on); *(→ sur une tige)* to slip on; **e. une aiguille** to thread a needle; **elle enfila ses bagues** she slipped her rings on; **e. des tomates sur une brochette** to slide tomatoes onto a skewer, to skewer tomatoes; *Fam Fig* **e. des perles** to waste one's time with trifles

3 *(mettre → vêtement)* to pull *or* to slip on, to slip into; **e. ses gants** to put *or* to pull one's gloves on; **e. son collant** to pull *or* to slip on one's *Br* tights *or Am* pantihose

4 *(suivre)* to take, to use; **e. un long couloir** *(à pied)* to walk down a long passage; *(à bicyclette)* to ride down a long passage; **la voiture a enfilé la rue jusqu'au carrefour** the car drove up the street to the crossroads

5 *Mil (troupes etc)* to enfilade, to rake

6 *Fam (débiter)* to string (together), to spout; **elle n'a fait qu'e. des banalités** she did nothing but spout one cliché after another

7 *Vulg (sexuellement)* to screw, *Br* to shag

►**s'enfiler** VPR1 *(gants, bottes)* to pull on, to go on; *(étui)* to slide on

2 s'e. dans to go into; **s'e. dans un couloir/une rue** to go along a corridor/street; **s'e. sous un porche** to disappear into a doorway

3 *Fam (avaler → boisson)* to knock back, to guzzle, to down; *(→ nourriture)* to guzzle, to gobble up, to put away; **s'e. un bon dîner** to have a slap-up meal; **je me suis enfilé un sandwich en vitesse** I grabbed a sandwich, I had a quick sandwich

4 *Fam (faire → corvée)* to get lumbered *or* landed with

enfileur, -euse [ɑ̃filœr, -øz] NM,F *(personne)* threader; **e. de perles** pearl stringer *or* threader NM(machine) threader, threading machine

❏ **enfileuse** NF *(machine)* threader, threading machine

enfin[ɑ̃fɛ̃] ADV1 *(finalement)* at last; **les voilà! – ah, e.!** here they are! – ah, at last!; **vous voilà e.** here *or* there you are at last!; **il est e. prêt!** he's ready at last!; **j'y suis e. arrivée** I finally managed, I managed it at last; **e.! depuis le temps!** and not before time!, and about time too!; **e. seuls!** alone at last!; **un accord a été e. conclu** an agreement has at last been reached; **e. bref...** *(à la fin d'une phrase)* anyway...; **e. bref, je n'ai pas envie d'y aller** well, basically, I don't want to go

2 *(en dernier lieu)* finally; **e., j'aimerais vous remercier de votre hospitalité** finally, I would like to thank you for your hospitality; **je vais en Suisse, en Allemagne et e. en Grèce** I'll go to Switzerland, Germany and finally to Greece

3 *(en un mot)* in short, in brief, in a word; **il est brutal, instable, e. c'est un homme dangereux** he's violent, unstable, in short *or* in a word (he's) a dangerous man

4 *(cependant)* still, however, after all; **ce sera difficile, e., on peut essayer** it'll be difficult, still we can try; **elle est triste, mais e. elle s'en remettra** she's sad, but still, she'll get over it;

oui mais e., c'est peut-être vrai after all it might well be true

5 *(avec une valeur restrictive)* well, at least; **blonde, e. châtain clair** blond, well, light brown; **elle est jolie, e., à mon avis** she's pretty, (or) at least I think she is; **elle n'est pas mal, e. pour son âge** she's not bad – for her age, that is; **c'est très joli, e. ce n'est pas mal** it's very pretty, well *or* at least, it's not bad; **il était malade, e. c'est ce qu'il dit** he was sick, at least that's what he says; **e., n'en parlons plus!** let's forget it; **mais e. bon, c'est son problème** oh well, that's HIS/HER problem!; **e.! ce qui est fait est fait** what's done is done; **e. je ne dis pas non, mais...** well, I'm not saying no, but...; **mais e., s'il acceptait!** but still, if he did accept!

6 *(emploi expressif)* **e.! c'est la vie!** oh well, such is life!; **ce n'est pas la même chose, e.!** oh come on, it's not the same thing at all!; **e., qu'est-ce qui t'a pris?** what on earth possessed you?; **e., reprends-toi!** come on, pull yourself together!; **e. qu'est-ce qu'il y a?** what on earth is the matter?; **c'est son droit, e.!** it's his/her right, after all!; **c'est un homme, e.!, il a sa dignité!** he's a man after all! he has his dignity!; **mais e., si elle est heureuse!** but as long as she's happy!; **tu ne peux pas faire ça, e.!** you can't DO that!; **e. quoi, tu n'as plus dix ans!** after all, you're not ten any more!; **on est en République e., quoi!** it's a free country after all!; **mais e. je te l'avais déjà dit!** I already TOLD you!; **mais e., c'est pas vrai!** I don't believe it!; **e., lâche-moi un peu!** give me some peace!, give it a rest!

enfirouâper [3] [ɑ̃firwape] VT Can Fam **1** *(tromper)* to fool ▪, to hoodwink; **se faire e.** *(se faire avoir)* to get taken for a ride, to be had; *(être enjôlé)* to be taken in; *(se faire mettre enceinte)* to get knocked up **2** *(nourriture)* to gulp down, to wolf down

enfirouâpette[ɑ̃firwapɛt] NFCan Fam **il a fait une belle e.!** he very cleverly managed to evade answering the question! ▪, **ce politicien est passé maître en enfirouâpettes!** that politician's a dab hand at wriggling out of journalists' questions!

enflammé, -e [ɑ̃flame] ADJ **1** *(allumette, torche)* lighted, burning; *(bûche)* burning **2** *Littéraire (visage)* burning; *(regard)* fiery; **elle est entrée, le visage tout e.** she came in, her face burning **3** *(passionné → discours, déclaration)* impassioned, fiery; *(→ nature)* fiery, hot-blooded **4** *Méd* inflamed

enflammer [3] [ɑ̃flame] VT **1** *(mettre le feu à → bois)* to light, to kindle, to ignite; *(→ branchages)* to ignite; *(→ allumette)* to light, to strike; *(→ papier)* to ignite, to set on fire, to set alight

2 *Littéraire (rougir)* to flush; **la fièvre enflammait ses joues** his/her cheeks were burning *or* flushed with fever; **la colère enflamme son regard** his/her eyes are blazing with anger

3 *(exalter → imagination, passion)* to kindle, to fire; *(→ foule)* to inflame

4 *Méd* to inflame

►**s'enflammer** VPR1 *(prendre feu → forêt)* to go up in flames, to catch fire, to ignite; *(→ bois)* to burst into flame, to light

2 *Littéraire (rougir → visage, ciel)* to flush; **le ciel s'enflammait au soleil levant** the rising sun set the sky ablaze; **son visage s'enflamma de colère** his/her face was flushed with anger

3 *(s'intensifier → passion)* to flare up

4 *(s'enthousiasmer)* to be fired with enthusiasm; **chaque jour, il s'enflamme pour une cause nouvelle/un auteur nouveau** he develops a passion for a new cause/a different author every day

enfle[ɑ̃flə] ADJSuisse *(cheville, joue)* swollen

enflé, -e[ɑ̃fle] ADJ *(cheville, joue)* swollen; *Fig (style)* bombastic, turgid, pompous; **des paupières enflées** swollen eyelids

NM,FTrès Fam fathead, jerk

enfléchure[ɑ̃fleʃyr] NFNaut ratline

enfler[3] [ɑ̃fle] VT1 *(gonfler → forme)* to cause to swell, to make swell; *(→ voix)* to make louder, to raise; **e. les joues** to puff out *or* blow out one's cheeks; **e. les voiles** *(vent)* to fill the sails

2 *(majorer → calcul, budget)* to inflate; *Fam* **e. le nombre/la dépense** to swell *or* add to the number/the expense

3 *Littéraire (exagérer → difficulté, prestige)* to overestimate; **e. son style** to inflate one's style VI(augmenter de volume → cheville) to swell (up); *(→ voix)* to boom (out)

►**s'enfler** VPR(voix) to boom (out); *(voile)* to billow *or* to swell *or* to fill out; *(rivière etc)* to swell, to rise; *(style)* to become inflated *or* turgid

enfleurage[ɑ̃flœraʒ] NMTech enfleurage

enfleurer[4] [ɑ̃flœre] VTTech to saturate with the perfume of flowers

enflure [ɑ̃flyr] NF **1** *(partie gonflée)* swelling **2** *(emphase)* bombast, turgidity, pompousness; **il donne dans l'e.** he tends to be pompous **3** *très Fam (personne détestable)* jerk

enfoiré, -e[ɑ̃fware] NM,Ftrès Fam bastard

enfoncé, -e[ɑ̃fɔ̃se] ADJ(yeux) sunken, deep-set; *(cavité, ravin etc)* sunken, deep

enfoncement[ɑ̃fɔ̃smɑ̃] NM1 *(destruction → d'un mur)* breaking down; *(→ d'une porte)* breaking down, bashing in **2** *(fait de faire pénétrer)* driving in **3** *(profondeur)* (penetration) depth **4** *(creux)* depression, hollow; *(dans un mur)* alcove, recess **5** *Méd* fracture; **e. de la boîte crânienne** skull fracture; **e. du thorax** flail chest **6** *Naut* difference of draught

enfoncer[16] [ɑ̃fɔ̃se] VT1 *(faire pénétrer → piquet, aiguille)* to push in; *(→ vis)* to drive *or* to screw in; *(→ clou)* to drive *or* to hammer in; *(→ épingle, punaise)* to push *or* to stick in; *(→ couteau)* to stick *or* to thrust in; **e. un clou dans une planche** to drive a nail into a plank; **e. un couteau dans** to thrust *or* plunge *or* stick a knife into; **e. la clef dans la serrure** to insert the key in the lock; **e. la main dans sa poche** to thrust one's hand into one's pocket; **e. au marteau** to hammer in; **il a enfoncé le pieu d'un seul coup** he drove *or* stuck the stake home in one; **elle lui a enfoncé un revolver dans le dos** she thrust *or* jabbed a gun into his/her back; *Fig* **il faut e. le clou** it's important to ram the point home

2 *(faire descendre)* to push *or* to ram (on); **il enfonça son chapeau jusqu'aux oreilles** he rammed his hat onto his head

3 *(briser → côte, carrosserie)* to stave in, to crush; *(→ porte)* to break down, to force open; *(→ barrière, mur)* to smash, to break down; *(voiture)* to smash in; **e. une porte à coups de pied** to kick a door in *or* down; **la voiture a enfoncé la barrière** the car crashed through the fence; **e. une porte ouverte** *ou* **des portes ouvertes** to labour the point

4 *(vaincre → armée, troupe)* to rout, to crush; **e. un front** to break through a frontline; *Fam* **e. un adversaire** to crush an opponent

5 *(condamner)* **son témoignage n'a fait que l'e.** he/she just dug himself/herself into a deeper hole with that statement

6 *Fam (humilier)* to humiliate ▪, **tu n'étais pas obligé de l'e. comme ça!** you didn't have to be so hard on him/her!

VIto sink; **e. dans la neige** to sink into the snow; **nous avons enfoncé jusqu'aux genoux** we sank into it up to our knees

►**s'enfoncer** VPR1 *(dans l'eau, la boue, la terre)* to sink (in); *(clou, couteau etc)* to sink *or* go in; **le navire s'enfonçait lentement** the boat was slowly going down *or* sinking; **s'e. dans un marécage** to sink *or* to be sucked into a bog; **s'e. jusqu'aux genoux** to sink up to one's knees; **ils s'enfoncèrent dans la neige jusqu'aux genoux** they sank knee-deep into the snow; **les vis s'enfoncent facilement dans le bois** screws go *or* bore easily through wood; **la balle s'enfonça dans le mur** the bullet embedded itself in the wall

2 *(se lover)* **s'e. dans** to sink into; **s'e. dans un fauteuil** to sink into an armchair; **s'e. sous une couette** to burrow *or* to snuggle under a quilt; *Péj* **s'e. dans son chagrin** to bury oneself in one's grief

3 *(s'engager)* **s'e. dans** to penetrate *or* to go into; **s'e. dans l'ombre/dans la nuit** to disappear into the darkness/night; **s'e. dans une rue/dans un bois** to go down a street/plunge into a wood; **le chemin s'enfonce dans la forêt** the path runs into the forest; **plus on s'enfonce dans la forêt plus le silence est profond** the further you go into the forest the quieter it becomes

4 *(s'affaisser→ plancher, terrain)* to give way, to cave in

5 *(aggraver son cas)* to get into deep *or* deeper waters, to make matters worse; **plus tu t'excuses, plus tu t'enfonces** you're only making matters worse (for yourself) by apologizing so much

6 *(se mettre)* **s'e. une épine dans le doigt** to get a thorn (stuck) in one's finger; *Fam* **s'e. une idée dans la tête** to get an idea into one's head; *Fam* **je ne reviendrai pas, enfonce-toi bien ça dans la tête!** and I won't be back, just get that into your thick head!

enfonceur, -euse [ɑ̃fɔ̃sœr, -øz] **NM,F c'est un e. de portes ouvertes** he's a great one for stating the obvious

enfonçure [ɑ̃fɔ̃syr] **NF** hollow *or* sunken part

enfouir [32] [ɑ̃fwir] **VT 1** *(mettre sous terre → os, trésor)* to bury (**dans/sous** in/beneath *or* under); *Agr (fumier)* to plough in

2 *(blottir)* to nestle; **les mains enfouies dans ses poches** with his/her hands buried in his/her pockets; **elle a enfoui sa tête dans l'oreiller** she buried her head in the pillow

3 *(cacher)* to stuff, to bury; **la lettre était enfouie sous une pile de dossiers** the letter was buried under a pile of files

►**s'enfouir VPR 1** *(s'enterrer)* to bury oneself; **s'e. dans le sable** to bury oneself in the sand

2 *(se blottir)* to burrow; **s'e. dans un terrier/sous les couvertures** to burrow in a hole/under the blankets

enfouissement [ɑ̃fwismɑ̃] **NM** burying

enfourchement [ɑ̃furʃəmɑ̃] **NM** *Menuis* forked mortise and tenon joint

enfourcher [3] [ɑ̃furʃe] **VT** *(bicyclette, cheval)* to mount, to get on; *(chaise)* to straddle; **e. son cheval de bataille** *ou* **son dada** to get on one's hobbyhorse

enfourchure [ɑ̃furʃyr] **NF** *Couture* crotch

enfournage [ɑ̃furnaʒ], **enfournement** [ɑ̃furnəmɑ̃] **NM 1** *Cér* setting **2** *(mise dans un four)* putting into the kiln

enfourner [3] [ɑ̃furne] **VT 1** *Culin* to put into the oven; *(briques, poteries)* to put into the kiln

2 *Fam (entasser)* to shove *or* to cram *or* to push (in); **e. du linge dans une machine à laver** to cram laundry into a washing machine

3 *Fam (manger)* to put away, to wolf down; **elle a enfourné une pizza entière** she put away a whole pizza

►**s'enfourner VPR** *Fam* **1 s'e. qch** *(le manger)* to wolf sth down; **s'e. qch dans la bouche** to cram *or* to stuff sth into one's mouth; **il se l'est enfourné dans le bec** he shoved it into his mouth

2 s'e. dans *(entrer dans)* to rush into, to pile into; **l'équipe s'enfourna dans le car** the team piled into the bus

enfourneur [ɑ̃furnœr] **NM** *(en boulangerie)* oven man; *Cér* kiln man

enfreindre [81] [ɑ̃frɛ̃dr] **VT** to infringe; *(ordres)* to disobey; *(vœu)* to break; **e. la loi** to break *or* to infringe the law; **e. le règlement** to fail to comply with *or* to break the rules; **e. les dispositions d'un traité** to violate a treaty; **e. un contrat** to violate a contract

enfuir [35] [ɑ̃fɥir] **s'enfuir VPR** *(se sauver)* to run away, to flee; *(s'échapper)* to run away, to escape; **ils se sont enfuis avec l'argent** they ran away *or* they ran off *or* they made off with the money; **s'e. avec qn** *(pour échapper à des sanctions)* to run away *or* off with sb; *(pour se marier)* to elope with sb; **s'e. de prison** to break out of *or* to escape from jail; **s'e. de chez soi** to run away from home; **s'e. d'un pays** to flee a country; **il s'est enfui en Suisse** he fled to Switzerland; **à mesure que les jours s'enfuyaient** as the days flew by; *Littéraire* **pleurer son bonheur enfui** to mourn one's lost happiness

enfumage [ɑ̃fymaʒ] **NM** *(d'un animal, d'un insecte)* smoking out

enfumé, -e [ɑ̃fyme] **ADJ** *(pièce)* smoky, smoke-filled; *(paroi)* sooty

enfumer [3] [ɑ̃fyme] **VT 1** *(abeille, renard)* to smoke out **2** *(pièce)* to fill with smoke; *(paroi)* to soot up

enfûtage [ɑ̃fytaʒ] **NM** barrelling, casking

enfutailler [3] [ɑ̃fytaje], **enfûter** [3] [ɑ̃fyte] **VT** to barrel, to cask

enfuyait *etc voir* **enfuir**

engagé, -e [ɑ̃gaʒe] **ADJ 1** *(artiste, littérature)* politically committed, engagé **2** *Archit* engaged **3** *(inscrit)* **les concurrents engagés dans la course** the competitors who are signed up to take part in the race

NM,F 1 *Mil* **e. (volontaire)** volunteer **2** *Courses de chevaux & Cyclisme* **la liste des engagés** the list of starters

engageable [ɑ̃gaʒabl] **ADJ** *Littéraire (objet)* that may be pawned; *(bien)* that may be pledged *or* mortgaged; *(argent)* that may be invested

engageant, -e [ɑ̃gaʒɑ̃, -ɑ̃t] **ADJ** *(manières, sourire)* engaging, winning; *(regard)* inviting; *(perspective)* attractive, inviting; **un restaurant bien peu e.** a less than inviting restaurant

engagement [ɑ̃gaʒmɑ̃] **NM 1** *(promesse)* commitment, undertaking, engagement; **contracter un e.** to enter into a commitment; **faire honneur à** *ou* **tenir** *ou* **respecter ses engagements** to honour *or* meet *or* fulfil one's commitments; **manquer à ses engagements** to fail to honour one's commitments; **passer un e. avec qn** to come to an agreement with sb; **prendre l'e. de** to undertake *or* to agree to; **respecter ses engagements envers qn** to fulfil one's commitments *or* obligations towards sb; **sans e. de date** date subject to change; **sans e. de votre part** with no obligation on your part; *(dans une publicité)* no obligation to buy; **faire face à ses engagements** to meet one's commitments; *Com* **e. d'achat** purchase agreement; **e. unilatéral de volonté** unilateral undertaking

2 *Fin (de capital, d'investissements)* tying up, locking up; *(de dépenses, de frais)* incurring; *(dette)* (financial) commitment, liability; **e. à court terme** short-term undertaking; **e. bancaire** (bank) commitment; **e. de dépenses** commitment of funds; **e. hors bilan** contingent liabilities

3 *(embauche)* appointment, hiring; *(d'un musicien etc)* booking; *Cin & Théât* job; **e. à l'essai** appointment for a trial period; **se trouver sans e.** to be out of work; *Théât* to be resting; **acteur sans e.** out-of-work actor

4 *(début)* beginning, start; **l'e. des travaux** the start *or* beginning of the work; **l'e. des négociations** the start *or* opening of the negotiations; **l'e. des négociations ne pourra se faire avant le mois prochain** negotiations cannot begin *or* start before next month

5 *(introduction → d'une clé)* fitting, inserting; *(→ d'un véhicule)* driving (**dans** into)

6 *Mil (combat)* engagement, action, clash; *(recrutement)* enlistment; **e. d'une troupe** *(mise en action)* committing troops to action

7 *(encouragement)* encouragement; **c'est un e. à poursuivre votre effort** it's an encouragement to continue your effort

8 *(prise de position)* commitment (**à** to); **c'est de cette époque que date son e.** he/she started getting involved politically from that point on, his/her political commitment dates from that time

9 *(mise en gage → au mont-de-piété)* pawning; *(→ auprès de créanciers)* pledging

10 *Obst* engagement; **l'e. de la tête** engagement of the head

11 *Sport (participation)* entry; *Ftbl* kick-off; *(au hockey)* bully-off; *Escrime* engagement; **son e. dans le tournoi** his/her entry into *or* entering the competition

ENGAGER [17] [ɑ̃gaʒe]

VT to insert **1** ■ to commit **2** ■ to invest **3** ■ to involve **4** ■ to advise **5** ■ to start **6** ■ to hire **7** ■ to commit to military action **8** ■ to enter **9** ■ to pawn **10** ■ to entangle **11** ■ to put in gear **12**
VPR to start **1** ■ to commit oneself **2, 6, 7** ■ to enlist **3** ■ to hire onself out **4** ■ to go into **8** ■ to fit **9** ■ to enter into **10** ■ to enter **11**

VT 1 *(insérer → clef, disquette)* to insert, to put *or* to slot in; **e. une vitesse** to put a car into gear; **e. le pied dans l'étrier** to put one's foot in the stirrup; **e. la clef dans la serrure** to fit *or* insert the key in the lock; **e. un véhicule dans une allée** to drive a vehicle into a lane; **e. une péniche dans une écluse** to move a barge into a lock

2 *(lier)* to bind, to commit; **cela vous engage à vie** it's a lifetime commitment; **voilà ce que je pense, mais ça n'engage que moi** that's how I see it, but it's my own view; **ce sont des conclusions qui n'engagent que vous/l'auteur** these are your own/the author's own conclusions; **cela ne t'engage à rien** it doesn't commit you to anything

3 *(mettre en jeu → énergie, ressources)* to invest, to commit; *(→ fonds)* to put in; *Fin (argent)* to lock up, to tie up; *(dépenses)* to incur; **e. sa parole** to give one's word (of honour); **e. sa responsabilité** to accept responsibility; **votre responsabilité est engagée dans cette affaire** you have certain responsibilities in this matter; **e. sa fortune/des capitaux dans une affaire** to lock up *or* tie up one's fortune/capital in a deal

4 *(entraîner)* to involve (**dans** in); **e. qn dans une querelle** to involve sb in *or* draw sb into a quarrel; **le gouvernement hésite à e. le pays dans le conflit** the government is hesitant about involving the country in the conflict

5 *(conseiller)* **e. qn à faire qch** to advise sb to do sth; **je vous engage à la prudence/modération** I advise you to be prudent/moderate

6 *(commencer)* to open, to start, to begin; **e. la conversation avec qn** to engage sb in conversation, to strike up a conversation with sb; **e. le débat** to start the discussion; **les négociations ont été engagées mardi** the talks got under way on Tuesday; **l'affaire est mal engagée** the whole thing is off to a bad start; **e. la partie** to begin the match *or* game; **la partie est maintenant bien engagée** the match is now well under way; **e. le match** *Ftbl* to kick off; *Sport* to begin

7 *(embaucher)* to take on, to hire; *(pianiste)* to book

8 *Mil (envoyer)* to commit to military action; *(recruter)* to enlist; *(mercenaire)* to hire; **e. le combat** to join battle, to engage; *aussi Fig* **e. les hostilités** to open hostilities

9 *Sport (inscrire sur liste des concurrents)* to enter; **cet entraîneur a deux chevaux engagés dans cette course** this trainer has two horses entered in the race

10 *(mettre en gage → au mont-de-piété)* to pawn; *(→ auprès de créanciers)* to pledge; *(→ propriété)* to mortgage

11 *(entraver → corde)* to catch, to foul, to entangle; *(→ machinerie)* to jam; *Naut* **e. une ancre** to foul an anchor; *Naut* **e. un aviron** to catch a crab; *Naut* **e. un vaisseau** to run a ship aground

12 *Tech (engrenage)* to engage, to put into gear; *Aut* **e. la première** to change into first (gear)

►**s'engager VPR 1** *(commencer → négociations, procédure, tournoi)* to start, to begin; **une conversation s'est engagée entre les voyageurs** the passengers struck up a conversation

2 *(prendre position)* to commit oneself; **elles n'ont pas peur de s'e.** they're not afraid of taking a stand; **s'e. contre la peine de mort** to campaign against *or* to take a stand against the death penalty

3 *Mil* to enlist; **s'e. avant l'appel** to volunteer before conscription

4 *(auprès d'un employeur)* to hire oneself out; **s'e. chez qn** to be *or* get taken on by sb; **s'e. comme jeune fille au pair** to get taken on as an au pair

5 *(corde, hélice)* to foul, to become fouled; *(machine)* to jam

6 s'e. à faire qch *(promettre)* to commit oneself to doing sth, to undertake to do sth; **sais-tu à quoi tu t'engages?** do you know what you're letting yourself in for?; **s'e. par traité à faire qch** to contract to do sth; **je m'engage à vous payer dans les 30 jours** I promise to pay you within 30 days; **je me suis trop engagé pour reculer** I have gone too far *or* I'm too far in to pull out now

7 s'e. vis-à-vis de qn to commit oneself to sb; **je ne veux pas m'e.** *(sentimentalement)* I don't want to get involved

8 s'e. dans *(avancer dans → sujet: véhicule,*

piéton) to go *or* to move into; **s'e. dans une rue/forêt** to turn into a street/enter a forest; **la voiture s'est engagée dans une rue étroite** the car drove *or* turned into a narrow street; **la voiture s'engagea dans le rond-point** the car pulled out onto the roundabout; **s'e. dans un carrefour** to pull out *or* to draw out into a crossroads

9 s'e. dans *(se loger)* to fit; **un tube s'engage dans l'ouverture** a pipe fits into the opening

10 s'e. dans *(entreprendre)* to enter into, to begin; **s'e. dans une aventure/un combat/une affaire** to get involved in an adventure/a fight/a deal; **s'e. dans des pourparlers difficiles** to embark on *or* to begin difficult negotiations; **le pays s'est engagé dans la lutte armée** the country has committed itself to *or* has entered into armed struggle

11 *Sport* **s'e. dans une course/compétition** to enter a race/an event

---

engainant, -e [ɑ̃gɛnɑ̃, -ɑ̃t] **ADJ** sheathing

engainer [4] [ɑ̃gene] **VT** to sheathe

engamer [3] [ɑ̃game] **VT** *Pêche (hameçon, appât)* to swallow

engane [ɑ̃gan] **NF** = salt-marsh grassland in the Camargue where horses and bulls roam

engazonnement [ɑ̃gazɔnmɑ̃] **NM** *(par plaques)* turfing; *(par semis)* grassing

engazonner [3] [ɑ̃gazɔne] **VT** *(par plaques)* to turf; *(par semis)* to grass

engeance [ɑ̃ʒɑ̃s] **NF** *Péj* scum, *Am* trash; **ils feraient n'importe quoi pour se procurer de l'argent, quelle (sale) e.!** they'd do anything for money, what scum!

engelure [ɑ̃ʒlyr] **NF** *Méd* chilblain

engendrement [ɑ̃ʒɑ̃drəmɑ̃] **NM 1** *(procreation)* fathering; *Bible* begetting **2** *(de chaleur)* generation; *(de maladie, pauvreté)* breeding

engendrer [3] [ɑ̃ʒɑ̃dre] **VT 1** *(procréer)* to father; *Bible* to beget; *(sujet: étalon etc)* to sire; **les fils qu'il a engendrés** the sons he fathered; **les fils qu'elle a engendrés** the sons she bore; **les fils qu'ils ont engendrés** the sons they brought into the world

2 *(provoquer → sentiment, situation)* to generate, to create, *Péj* to breed; *(→ maladie, pauvreté)* to breed; *(→ chaleur)* to generate, to develop; *Hum* **il n'engendre pas la mélancolie** he's great fun

3 *Ling & Math* to generate

engerbage [ɑ̃ʒɛrbaʒ] **NM** *Agr* sheaving

engerber [3] [ɑ̃ʒɛrbe] **VT** *Agr* to sheaf

engin [ɑ̃ʒɛ̃] **NM 1** *Tech (appareil)* machine, appliance; **e. agricole** piece of farm machinery; **engins de chasse** hunting equipment; **engins de levage** lifting gears; **e. de levage électrique** electric hoist; **e. de manutention** conveyor, handling equipment; **e. de nivelage** *Br* planer, *Am* leveler; **engins de pêche** fishing tackle; **e. prohibé** illegal hunting/fishing device; **e. de terrassement** earthmover; **attention: passage d'engins** *(sur panneau)* heavy plant crossing

2 *Astron* **e. spatial** spacecraft

3 *Mil* weaponry; **e. blindé** armoured vehicle; **e. blindé de reconnaissance** armoured car; **e. amphibie** amphibious craft *or* vehicle; **e. de mort** deadly weapon; **engins de guerre** engines of war

4 *Fam (chose)* contraption, thingamabob, thingamajig

5 *très Fam (pénis)* tool

engineering [ɛnʒiniriŋ] **NM** engineering

englacé, -e [ɑ̃glase] **ADJ** covered in ice

englober [3] [ɑ̃glɔbe] **VT 1** *(réunir)* to encompass; **son livre englobe tout ce qui est connu sur le sujet** his/her book encompasses *or* covers the whole range of knowledge on the subject **2** *(inclure)* to include (**dans** in); **e. un texte dans un recueil** to include a piece in an anthology **3** *(annexer)* to merge (**dans** into); **ces états furent englobés dans l'Empire** these states were merged into the Empire

engloutir [32] [ɑ̃glutir] **VT 1** *(faire disparaître)* to swallow up, to engulf; **une île engloutie par la mer** an island swallowed up by the sea

2 *(manger)* to gobble up, to gulp *or* to wolf down; **il engloutit des quantités incroyables de chocolat** he puts away an incredible amount of chocolate; **ils ont englouti le gâteau en un rien de temps** they demolished the cake in no time

3 *(dépenser)* to squander; **il a englouti son capital dans son agence** he sank all his capital into his agency; **ils ont englouti des sommes énormes dans la maison** they sank vast amounts of money into the house

4 *Fig* to swallow up; **les travaux ont englouti tout mon argent** the work swallowed up all my money

▶**s'engloutir VPR** *(vaisseau)* to be swallowed up *or* engulfed, to sink

engloutissement [ɑ̃glutismɑ̃] **NM 1** *(d'un navire, d'une ville)* swallowing up, engulfment **2** *(d'une fortune)* squandering

engluage [ɑ̃glyaʒ], **engluement** [ɑ̃glymɑ̃] **NM 1** *Chasse* liming, birdliming **2** *(enduit)* (bird)lime

engluer [7] [ɑ̃glye] **VT 1** *Chasse (oiseau, branche)* to lime, to birdlime **2** *(rendre collant)* to make sticky; **des doigts englués de colle** fingers sticky with glue

▶**s'engluer VPR 1** *(se couvrir de glu)* to become gluey **2 s'e. les doigts** to get sticky fingers **3** *Fig* **s'e. dans qch** to get bogged down in sth; **s'e. dans une vie médiocre** to become bogged down in a life of mediocrity

engobage [ɑ̃gɔbaʒ] **NM** *Cér* coating with slip

engobe [ɑ̃gɔb] **NM** *Cér* slip

engober [3] [ɑ̃gɔbe] **VT** *Cér* to coat with slip

engommage [ɑ̃gɔmaʒ] **NM 1** *(gén)* gumming **2** *Cér* glazing

engommer [3] [ɑ̃gɔme] **VT 1** *(gén)* to gum, to dress **2** *Cér* to glaze

engoncer [16] [ɑ̃gɔ̃se] **VT** to cramp, to restrict; **e. qn** *(vêtement)* to make sb look hunched up; **être engoncé dans ses vêtements** to be restricted by one's clothes; **tu as l'air (d'être) engoncé dans ce manteau** that coat looks too tight for you

engorgement [ɑ̃gɔrʒəmɑ̃] **NM 1** *(d'un tuyau)* flooding; *(d'un sol)* saturation; **l'e. des grandes villes** congestion in the big cities; **l'e. du marché automobile** saturation in the car industry, the glut of cars on the market **2** *Méd* **e. mammaire** engorgement

engorger [17] [ɑ̃gɔrʒe] **VT** *(canalisation)* to flood; *(route)* to congest, to jam; *(organe)* to engorge; *(sol)* to saturate; *(marché)* to saturate, to glut

▶**s'engorger VPR 1** *(tuyau etc)* to become choked (up) *or* blocked (up) *or* clogged **2** *Méd (organe)* to become engorged *or* congested **3** *(route, carrefour)* to become blocked up *or* congested

engouement [ɑ̃gumɑ̃] **NM 1** *(pour une activité, un type d'objet)* keen interest (**pour** in); **un e. pour le jazz** a keen interest in jazz; **d'où te vient cet e. soudain pour la politique?** how come you're so smitten with politics all of a sudden? **2** *(élan amoureux)* infatuation; **avoir un e. pour** to be infatuated with **3** *Méd (d'une hernie)* obstruction

engouer [6] [ɑ̃gwe] **VT** *Méd* to obstruct

▶**s'engouer VPR s'e. de, s'e. pour** *(activité, objet)* to have a craze *or* a sudden passion for; *(personne)* to become infatuated with

engouffrement [ɑ̃gufrəmɑ̃] **NM 1** *(consommation → de nourriture)* wolfing, cramming; *(→ d'argent)* sinking, squandering **2** *(entrée → du vent)* rushing *or* sweeping *or* blowing in; *(→ de la foule)* rushing in; *(→ de la mer)* surging *or* rushing in

engouffrer [3] [ɑ̃gufre] **VT 1** *(avaler)* to wolf *or* to shovel (down), to cram (in); *(bateau etc)* to engulf, to swallow up

2 *(entasser)* to cram *or* to stuff (in)

3 *(dépenser)* to swallow up; **ils ont engouffré des sommes énormes dans la maison** they sank vast amounts of money into the house

▶**s'engouffrer VPR** *(foule)* to rush, to crush; *(personne)* to rush, to dive; *(mer)* to surge, to rush; *(vent)* to blow, to sweep, to rush; *(bateau etc)* to be engulfed *or* swallowed up; **s'e. dans un taxi** *(seul)* to dive into a taxi; *(à plusieurs)* to pile into a taxi; **le vent s'engouffra par la porte** the wind swept in through the door

engoulevent [ɑ̃gulvɑ̃] **NM** *Orn* **e. (d'Europe)** nightjar; **e. (d'Amérique)** nighthawk; **e. de Californie** poor-will; **e. à collier roux** red-necked nightjar; **e. porte-étendards** standard-winged nightjar

engourdi, -e [ɑ̃gurdi] **ADJ 1** *(doigt, membre)* numb, numbed; **j'ai les doigts engourdis** my fingers have gone numb; **à force d'être resté dans cette position, j'ai la jambe engourdie** I've been sitting like this so long that my leg has gone to sleep **2** *(esprit, imagination)* slow, lethargic

engourdir [32] [ɑ̃gurdir] **VT 1** *(insensibiliser → doigt, membre)* to numb, to make numb; *(→ sens)* to deaden; **être engourdi par le froid** to be numb with cold; **la chaleur a engourdi les élèves** the heat made the pupils drowsy *or* sluggish; **mes gencives étaient engourdies par la piqûre** my gums had gone numb with the anaesthetic

2 *(ralentir → esprit, faculté)* to blunt, to dull; **la fatigue lui engourdissait l'esprit** he/she was so tired he/she couldn't think straight

▶**s'engourdir VPR 1** *(se rouiller)* to go numb; **mes doigts commençaient à s'e.** my fingers were starting to go numb

2 *Fig (l'esprit)* to become dull *or* sluggish

3 *(animal qui hiberne)* to become dormant

engourdissant, -e [ɑ̃gurdisɑ̃, -ɑ̃t] **ADJ** *(froid)* numbing; *(chaleur)* oppressive

engourdissement [ɑ̃gurdismɑ̃] **NM 1** *(insensibilité physique)* numbness **2** *(torpeur)* drowsiness, sleepiness **3** *(d'un animal qui hiberne)* torpor **4** *(action → d'un membre etc)* numbing; *(→ de l'esprit, des facultés)* blunting, dulling

engrais [ɑ̃grɛ] **NM 1** *Agr (fertilisant)* fertilizer; **e. (animal)** manure; **e. azotés** nitrate fertilizers, nitrates; **e. chimique** artificial fertilizer; **e. verts** *ou* **végétaux** green *or* vegetable manure **2** *(locution)* **mettre une bête à l'e.** to fatten (up) an animal

engraissage [ɑ̃grɛsaʒ], **engraissement** [ɑ̃grɛsmɑ̃] **NM** *Agr* fattening (up)

engraisser [4] [ɑ̃grese] **VT 1** *Agr (bétail)* to fatten (up); **e. une oie** to fatten a goose **2** *(personne)* to make fat **3** *(terre)* to feed

VI to grow fat *or* fatter, to put on weight; *Hum* **ta fille a besoin d'e. un peu** your daughter needs fattening up *or* feeding up a bit

▶**s'engraisser VPR** to get fat; *Fig* **il s'engraisse sur le dos de ses employés** he lines his pockets by underpaying his employees

engraisseur, -euse [ɑ̃grɛsœr, -øz] **NM,F** *Agr* fat stockman, *f* stockwoman

engramme [ɑ̃gram] **NM** *Psy* engram

engrangement [ɑ̃grɑ̃ʒmɑ̃] **NM 1** *Agr* gathering in, storing **2** *(de documents)* storing, collecting

engranger [17] [ɑ̃grɑ̃ʒe] **VT 1** *Agr* to gather in, to store **2** *(documents)* to store (up), to collect; *(connaissances)* to amass, to store (up)

engraver [3] [ɑ̃grave] **VT 1** *Littéraire (ensabler)* to ground, to run aground **2** *(couvrir de graviers)* to gravel (over) **3** *Constr* to notch *(a piece of roofing lead)*

engravure [ɑ̃gravyr] **NF** *Constr* roofing lead

engrêlé, -e [ɑ̃grɛle] **ADJ** *Hér* engrailed

engrêlure [ɑ̃grɛlyr] **NF** purl, edging, picot-edge

engrenage [ɑ̃grənaʒ] **NM 1** *Tech (roues dentées)* gears; *(disposition du système)* gearing; **les engrenages d'une machine** the wheelwork *or* train of gears *or* gearing of a machine; **système** *ou* **jeu d'engrenages** train *or* set of gears; **e. à chevrons** herringbone *or* double-helical gear; **e. conique** bevel gear pair; *Aut* **e. de démarrage** starter gear; **e. en prise constante** constant-mesh gear; **e. à train planétaire** planetary gearing; **e.** *ou* **engrenages de transmission** driving gear; **e. à variations progressives** gradually variable gear; **e. à vis sans fin** worm gears

2 *Fig* trap; **l'e. de la violence/de l'agressivité** the spiral of violence/aggression; **mettre le doigt dans l'e.** to get caught up in it; **être pris dans l'e.** to be caught in a trap; **être pris dans l'e. du jeu** to be trapped in the vicious circle of gambling

engrènement [ɑ̃grɛnmɑ̃] **NM 1** *Tech* meshing **2** *Agr (d'un moulin etc)* feeding with grain

engrener [19] [ɑ̃grəne] **VT 1** *Tech* to gear, to mesh; **e. dans** to engage into, to mesh with; *Fam* **e. une affaire** to set a thing going **2** *Agr* to feed with grain, to fill with grain

VI to gear, to mesh

▶**s'engrener VPR** to gear (**dans** into), to mesh (**dans** with)

engreneur [ãgrənœr] NM *Agr* mechanical feeder

engrenure [ãgrənyr] NF *Tech* gearing

engrois [ãgrwa] NM *Tech (d'un marteau)* wedge

engrosser [3] [ãgrose] VT *très Fam* to knock up; **se faire e. (par)** to get knocked up (by)

engueulade [ãgœlad] NF *très Fam* **1** *(réprimande)* bawling out; **lettre d'e.** angry letter■; **passer une e. à qn** to give sb a bawling out, to bawl sb out; **se prendre une e.** to get bawled out **2** *(querelle)* run-in, *Br* slanging match; **avoir une e. avec qn** to have a run-in *or Br* a slanging match with sb

engueuler [5] [ãgœle] *très Fam* VT **e. qn** to bawl sb out; **ce n'est pas la peine de m'e.** there's no need to have a go at me; **je vais l'e.** I'm going to give him/her what for; **se faire e.** to get bawled out
▸**s'engueuler** VPR to have a row *or Br* slanging match; **on ne va tout de même pas s'e. pour ça** we're not going to have a row over this, are we?; **s'e. avec qn** to have a row *or Br* slanging match with sb

enguichure [ãgiʃyr] NF *Hist* guige

enguirlander [3] [ãgirlãde] VT **1** *(décorer)* to garland, to deck with garlands; *Fig (discours)* to dress up **2** *Fam (réprimander) Br* to tick off, *Am* to chew out; **se faire e.** to get *Br* a ticking-off *or Am* a chewing-out

enhardir [32] [ãardir] VT to embolden, to make bolder, to encourage
▸**s'enhardir** VPR to become bold(er); **s'e. à faire qch** to pluck up the courage to do sth; **l'enfant s'enhardit et entra dans la pièce** the child plucked up courage and went into the room

enharmonie [ãnarmɔni] NF *Mus* enharmonic change

enharmonique [ãnarmɔnik] ADJ *Mus* enharmonic

enharnacher [3] [ãarnaʃe] VT *Équitation* to harness

enherber [3] [ãnɛrbe] VT *Agr* to grass (over)

ENI [eni] NF **1** *(abrév École normale d'instituteurs)* = former primary school teachers' training college **2** *(abrév École nationale d'ingénieurs)* = one of five prestigious engineering schools throughout France

énième [enjɛm] ADJ umpteenth, nth; **pour la é. fois** for the umpteenth time; **après une é. tentative** after countless attempts
NMF nth

énigmatique [enigmatik] ADJ enigmatic, mysterious, puzzling; **d'un air é.** enigmatically

énigmatiquement [enigmatikmã] ADV enigmatically

énigme [enigm] NF **1** *(mystère)* riddle, enigma, puzzle; **trouver le mot** *ou* **la clé de l'é.** to find the answer to the riddle, to guess *or* solve the riddle; **les enquêteurs tentent de résoudre l'é. de sa disparition** the police are trying to solve the riddle of his/her disappearance; **ce garçon est une é. pour moi** I can't make the boy out; **ça, c'est une é. pour moi** it's a mystery to me
2 *(devinette)* riddle; **le Sphinx parle par énigmes** the Sphinx talks in riddles

enivrant, -e [ãnivrã, -ãt] ADJ **1** *(qui rend ivre)* intoxicating **2** *(exaltant)* heady, exhilarating; **ce furent des moments enivrants** those were heady days

enivrement [ãnivrəmã] NM **1** *Vieilli (par l'alcool)* intoxication, inebriation **2** *Fig* elation, exhilaration; **dans l'e. de** intoxicated *or* exhilarated by

enivrer [3] [ãnivre] VT **1** *(soûler → sujet: vin)* to make drunk, to intoxicate **2** *Fig (exalter)* to intoxicate, to exhilarate, to elate; **le succès l'enivrait** he/she was intoxicated by his/her success
▸**s'enivrer** VPR to get drunk; *Fig* **s'e. de** to become intoxicated with

enjambée [ãʒãbe] NF stride; **avancer** *ou* **marcher à grandes enjambées** to stride along; **faire de grandes enjambées** to take long steps *or* strides; **il a franchi le ruisseau en une é.** he crossed the stream in one stride

enjambement [ãʒãbmã] NM **1** *Littérature* enjambment **2** *Biol* crossing-over

enjamber [3] [ãʒãbe] VT *(muret, rebord)* to step over; *(fossé)* to stride across *or* over; *(tronc*

d'arbre) to stride *or* to step over; **le pont enjambe le Gard** the bridge spans the river Gard

enjaveler [24] [ãʒavle] VT *Agr* to lay in swaths

enjeu, -x [ãʒø] NM **1** *(ce que l'on peut gagner ou perdre → dans un jeu)* stake, stakes; *Fig* **l'e. d'une guerre** the stakes of war; **quel est l'e. de cette élection?** what is at stake in this election?; **c'est un e. important** the stakes are high
2 *(sujet)* issue; *(défi)* challenge; **l'environnement est un e. primordial dans ces élections** the environment is a key issue in this election; **cela représente un e. économique majeur pour les entreprises** this represents a major economic challenge for companies; **c'est un secteur où les enjeux commerciaux sont de plus en plus importants** it's a sector that's becoming increasingly important on a commercial level; **l'énergie est un e. planétaire** energy is a worldwide concern

enjoindre [82] [ãʒwɛ̃dr] VT *Littéraire* **e. à qn de faire qch** to enjoin sb to do sth

enjôlement [ãʒolmã] NM wheedling, cajoling

enjôler [3] [ãʒole] VT to cajole, to wheedle; **il a réussi à m'e.** he managed to cajole me (into accepting); **se faire e.** to be taken in

enjôleur, -euse [ãʒolœr, -øz] ADJ cajoling, wheedling; **un sourire e.** a wheedling smile
NM,F cajoler, wheedler

enjolivement [ãʒolivmã] NM embellishment, embellishing

enjoliver [3] [ãʒolive] VT **1** *(décorer → vêtement)* to embellish, to adorn; **enjolivé de** adorned with **2** *(travestir → histoire, récit, vérité)* to embellish, to embroider; **e. les faits** to embroider the facts

enjoliveur, -euse [ãʒolivœr, -øz] NM,F **c'est un e.** he likes to embellish *or* embroider his stories
NM *Aut* hubcap; **e. de phare** headlamp rim

enjolivure [ãʒolivyr] NF embellishment, ornament

enjoué, -e [ãʒwe] ADJ *(personne, caractère)* cheerful, jolly, genial; *(remarque, ton)* playful, cheerful, jolly

enjouement [ãʒumã] NM cheerfulness, playfulness

enjouer [6] [ãʒwe] VT *Littéraire (conversation)* to give a pleasant *or* sprightly tone to

enjuguer [3] [ãʒyge] VT *Agr* to yoke

enképhaline [ãkefalin] NF *Chem & Physiol* enkephalin

enkysté, -e [ãkiste] ADJ *Méd* encysted

enkystement [ãkistəmã] NM *Méd* encystment, encystation

enkyster [3] [ãkiste] **s'enkyster** VPR *Méd* to encyst, to turn into a cyst

enlacement [ãlasmã] NM **1** *(entrecroisement)* intertwining, interlacing, entwinement **2** *(embrassement)* (lovers') embrace

enlacer [16] [ãlase] VT **1** *(étreindre)* to clasp; **e. qn** to embrace sb (tenderly); **ils étaient tendrement enlacés** they were locked in a tender embrace
2 *(mêler)* to interweave, to intertwine, to interlace; **e. des brins de laine** to weave *or* to braid yarns of wool; **initiales enlacées** interwoven initials; **les doigts enlacés** fingers entwined
▸**s'enlacer** VPR **1** *(amoureux)* to embrace, to hug; **amants enlacés** lovers (clasped) in an embrace
2 *(s'entrelacer)* to intertwine, to interlace

enlaçure [ãlasyr] NF *Menuis* **1** *(assemblage)* dowelled tenon-and-mortise joint **2** *(trou)* dowel-hole

enlaidir [32] [ãledir] VT *(personne)* to make ugly; *(paysage, ville etc)* to disfigure; **cette robe l'enlaidit** that dress makes her look ugly; **e. le paysage** to be a blot on the landscape *or* an eyesore; **une cicatrice lui enlaidissait le visage** a scar on his/her face spoilt his/her looks
VI to become ugly; **il a enlaidi avec l'âge** he's lost his (good) looks *or* become ugly with age
▸**s'enlaidir** VPR to make oneself (look) ugly

enlaidissement [ãledismã] NM *(de personne → par accident)* disfigurement; *(→ naturel)* growing ugly *or* plain, loss of good looks; *(de paysage, ville etc)* disfigurement; **les nouvelles constructions ont contribué à l'e. du quartier** the area has been disfigured partly by the new buildings

enlevage [ãlvaʒ] NM **1** *(en teinturerie)* bleaching,

decolorizing **2** *Sport (dans une course d'aviron)* spurt

enlevé, -e [ãlve] ADJ *(style, rythme)* lively, spirited; *(danse, sonate etc)* performed in a lively *or* spirited fashion; **ses dialogues sont enlevés** he/she writes quickfire dialogues; **une caricature enlevée** a rapidly drawn caricature

enlèvement [ãlɛvmã] NM **1** *(rapt)* abduction, kidnapping, *Littéraire* ravishment; *Jur* **e. de mineur** abduction of a minor; *Jur* **e. d'enfant** child abduction
2 *(fait d'ôter)* removal, taking away; **l'e. d'une tache/d'un organe** the removal of a stain/of an organ; *Com* **e. et livraison** collection and delivery
3 *Admin (ramassage)* **e. des ordures** *Br* rubbish collection, *Am* garbage disposal; **l'e. des ordures a lieu le mardi** *Br* rubbish *or Am* garbage is collected on Tuesdays
4 *Mil (d'une position)* taking, storming, carrying

'L'Enlèvement des Sabines' *Poussin* 'The Rape of the Sabine Women'

enlever [19] [ãlve] VT **1** *(ôter → couvercle, housse, vêtement)* to remove, to take off; *(→ étagère)* to remove, to take down; **enlève ton manteau, mets-toi à l'aise** take your coat off and make yourself comfortable; **e. les pépins** to take the pips out; **ne mets pas ta voiture là, elle va être enlevée** don't park your car here, it'll get towed away *or* removed; **ils ont enlevé le reste des meubles ce matin** they took away *or* collected what was left of the furniture this morning; **enlevez, c'est pesé!** that's it!
2 *(arracher)* to remove, to pull out; **e. les mauvaises herbes** to pull out the weeds; **e. les pissenlits d'une plate-bande** to weed the dandelions out of a flower bed; **e. un clou avec des tenailles** *Br* to prise *or Am* to pry a nail out with a pair of pliers; **une bombe lui a enlevé les jambes** a bomb took off *or* blew off his/her legs; *Littéraire* **enlevé par la mer** carried away *or* washed away by the sea
3 *(faire disparaître)* to remove; **e. une tache** *(gén)* to remove a stain; *(en lavant)* to wash out a stain; *(en frottant)* to rub out a stain; *(à l'eau de Javel)* to bleach out a stain; **e. les plis d'une chemise** to take the creases out of a shirt; **e. qch au burin** to chip *or* to chisel sth off; **e. un passage d'un texte** to remove a passage from *or* to cut a passage out of a text
4 *Méd* **se faire e. une dent** to have a tooth pulled out *or* extracted; **se faire e. un grain de beauté** to have a mole removed
5 *(soustraire)* **e. qch à qn** to take sth away from sb; **enlève-lui ces allumettes** take those matches off him/her; **cette erreur n'enlève rien à votre valeur** this mistake takes nothing away from *or* in no way detracts from your merit; **cela m'a enlevé tout mon courage/toute ma bonne humeur** it has drained me of all courage/of my good humour; **e. à qn la garde d'un enfant** to remove *or* take a child from sb's care *or* custody; **j'ai peur qu'on ne m'enlève la garde de mon enfant** I'm afraid they'll take my child away from me; **e. à qn le goût de qch** to take away sb's taste for sth; **ça lui a enlevé le goût des mathématiques** it put him/her off mathematics; **ça m'enlève mes scrupules** it dispels *or* allays my misgivings; **ne m'enlevez pas tous mes espoirs** don't deprive *or* rob me of all hope
6 *(obtenir → récompense)* to carry off, to win; *(→ course, victoire, prix)* to win; **il a enlevé la victoire** he ran away with the victory; **e. un marché/un contrat** to get *or* to secure a deal/a contract; **e. la décision** to win *or* carry the day, to win through; **e. les suffrages** *Pol* to win *or* capture votes; *Fig* to be liked by everyone, to be universally liked
7 *(soulever)* to lift; **e. 10 kilos sans effort** to lift 10 kilos easily; **le ballon les a enlevés haut dans les airs** the balloon took *or* lifted them high up into the air; **e. son cheval** *(le faire bondir)* to lift one's horse; *(le faire partir)* to set one's horse at full gallop
8 *Littéraire (faire mourir)* to carry off; **c'est un**

cancer qui nous l'a enlevé cancer took him from us

9 *Mil* to carry, to seize

10 *(morceau de musique)* to play brilliantly

11 *(kidnapper)* to abduct, to kidnap, to snatch; **il a été enlevé à son domicile** he was snatched from his home; **il l'a enlevée pour l'épouser** he ran off with her to get married; **se faire e.** to be kidnapped; **se faire e. par son amant** to elope (with one's lover)

▶**s'enlever** VPR **1** *(vêtement, étiquette)* to come off; *(écharde)* to come out; **le costume s'enlève par le haut** you slip the costume off over your head; **le costume s'enlève par le bas** you step out of the costume; **ça s'enlève en arrachant/décollant** it tears/peels off; **comment ça s'enlève?** how do you take it off?

2 *(s'effacer → tache)* to come out *or* off; **le vernis ne s'enlève pas** the varnish won't come off

3 *(marchandises)* to sell quickly, to be snapped up; **ça s'enlève comme des petits pains** it's selling like hot cakes

4 *(ballon etc)* to rise; *(cheval)* to take off

5 *Fam* **enlève-toi de là!** get out of there!

6 *(retirer)* **s'e. une écharde du doigt** to pull a splinter out of one's finger; *Fig* **s'e. une épine du pied** to get rid of a niggling problem

enliasser [3] [ɑ̃ljase] VT to bundle (up), to tie into a bundle

enlier [9] [ɑ̃lje] VT *Constr* to bond

enlisement [ɑ̃lizmɑ̃] NM **1** *(enfoncement)* sinking **2** *(stagnation)* stagnation; **le manque de coopération a entraîné l'e. des pourparlers** due to a lack of cooperation, the talks have reached a stalemate

enliser [3] [ɑ̃lize] VT *(voiture, roue etc → dans la boue, le sable etc)* to get stuck; **e. un bateau dans la vase** to get a boat stuck in the mud; **e. ses roues** to get one's wheels stuck

▶**s'enliser** VPR **1** *(s'embourber)* to get bogged down *or* stuck, to sink; **s'e. dans des sables mouvants** to sink *or* to get sucked (down) into quicksand

2 *Fig* to get bogged down; **s'e. dans la routine** to get *or* to be bogged down in routine

enluminer [3] [ɑ̃lymine] VT **1** *(manuscrit, livre)* to illuminate **2** *(colorer → gravure, carte etc)* to colour **3** *Fig* **visage enluminé** flushed *or* glowing face

enlumineur, -euse [ɑ̃lyminœr, -øz] NM,F illuminator

enluminure [ɑ̃lyminyr] NF **1** *(art, lettre)* illumination **2** *Fig (d'un visage)* colour

ENM [əenɛm] NF *(abrév* **École nationale de la magistrature**) = "grande école" for the judiciary

ennéade [enead] NF *Littéraire* ennead

ennéagonal, -e, -aux, -ales [ɛneagɔnal, -o] ADJ *Géom* enneagonal, nine-angled

ennéagone [ɛneagɔn] *Géom* ADJ enneagonal, nine-angled

NM enneagon, nonagon

enneigé, -e [ɑ̃neʒe] ADJ *(champ, paysage)* snow-covered; *(pic)* snow-capped; *(village etc)* snowbound, snowed up; **la campagne est enneigée** the countryside's covered in snow; **les routes sont enneigées** the roads are snowed up

enneigement [ɑ̃nɛʒmɑ̃] NM *Météo* snow cover; **l'e. annuel** yearly *or* annual snowfall; **il y a un bon e. cette année** there's a lot of snow this year; **bulletin d'e.** snow report

enneiger [23] [ɑ̃neʒe] VT to cover with *or* in snow

ennemi, -e [ɛnmi] ADJ **1** *Mil* enemy *(avant n)*, hostile; **l'armée ennemie** the hostile army, *Littéraire* the foe; **le camp e.** the enemy('s) camp; **en pays e.** in enemy country

2 *(inamical)* hostile, unfriendly

3 *(adverse)* **familles/nations ennemies** feuding families/nations

4 e. de *(opposé à)* opposed to; **être e. du changement** to be opposed *or* averse to change

NM,F **1** *Mil* enemy, *Littéraire* foe; **passer à l'e.** to go over to the enemy

2 *(individu hostile)* enemy; **on ne lui connaissait aucun e.** he/she had no known enemy; **se faire des ennemis** to make enemies; **se faire un e. de qn** to make an enemy of sb; **e. mortel** mortal enemy; **e. public (numéro un)** public enemy (number one)

3 *(antagoniste)* **le bien est l'e. du mal** good is the enemy of evil; **les ennemis de la liberté** the enemies of freedom

'Un Ennemi du peuple' *Ibsen* 'An Enemy of the People'

ennoblir [32] [ɑ̃nɔblir] VT **1** *(personne)* to ennoble; *(caractère, esprit)* to ennoble, to elevate; *(physique)* to lend dignity to **2** *Tex (tissu, fil)* to finish

ennoblissement [ɑ̃nɔblismɑ̃] NM **1** *(d'une personne)* ennoblement, ennobling **2** *Tex (d'un tissu, d'un fil)* finishing

ennoiement [ɑ̃nwamɑ̃], **ennoyage** [ɑ̃nwajaz] NM *Géog* submergence

ennoyer [13] [ɑ̃nwaje] VT *Géog* to submerge

ennuager [17] [ɑ̃nɥaʒe] *Littéraire* VT to cloud; **ciel ennuagé** cloudy sky

▶**s'ennuager** VPR to cloud over

ennui [ɑ̃nɥi] NM **1** *(problème)* problem, difficulty; **des ennuis** trouble, troubles, problems; **attirer des ennuis à qn** to get sb into trouble; **avoir des ennuis** *(soucis)* to be worried *or* anxious; *(problèmes)* to have problems; **avoir de gros ennuis** to be in serious trouble; **tu vas avoir des ennuis** you're going to get into trouble; **avoir des ennuis avec la police** to be in trouble with the police; **avoir des ennuis avec ses voisins** to have trouble *or* problems with one's neighbours; **avoir des ennuis d'argent/de santé** to have money/health problems; **avoir des ennuis de voiture** to have problems with one's car; **avoir des ennuis de moteur** to have engine trouble; **faire des ennuis à qn** to get sb into trouble; **c'est ça l'e.!** that's the trouble!; **l'e. c'est que...** the trouble is that...; **l'e., c'est qu'il ne peut pas venir** the problem *or* trouble is he can't come; *Prov* **un e. ne vient jamais seul** it never rains but it pours

2 *(lassitude)* boredom; **à mourir d'e.** deadly boring; **c'était à mourir d'e.** it was dreadfully *or* deadly boring; **ils me font mourir d'e.** they bore me to death *or* stiff; **sa conversation est d'un e.!** his/her conversation is so boring!

3 *Littéraire (mélancolie)* ennui

ennuyant, -e [ɑ̃nɥijɑ̃, -ɑ̃t] ADJ *Vieilli ou Belg & Can* **1** *(lassant → travail, conférencier, collègue)* boring, dull; **e. à mourir** *ou* **à périr** *ou* **comme la pluie** *ou* **comme la mort** (as) dull as *Br* ditchwater *or Am* dishwater, deadly boring

2 *(fâcheux)* annoying, tiresome; **c'est e. qu'il ne puisse pas venir** *(regrettable)* it's a pity (that) he can't come; *(contrariant)* it's annoying *or* a nuisance that he can't come; **comme c'est e.!** what a nuisance!

ennuyé, -e [ɑ̃nɥije] ADJ *(contrarié)* annoyed, bothered (**de** about); **je suis très e. de la savoir fâchée** it bothers *or* upsets me a lot to know that she is angry

ennuyer [14] [ɑ̃nɥije] VT **1** *(contrarier)* to worry, to bother; **ce contretemps m'ennuie beaucoup** this complication worries me a great deal; **avoir l'air ennuyé** to look bothered *or* worried; **ça m'ennuie de les laisser seuls** I am loath to *or* I don't like to leave them alone; **ça m'ennuie de te le dire mais...** I'm sorry to have to say this to you but...; **cela m'ennuierait d'être en retard** I'd hate to be late

2 *(déranger)* to bother, to annoy; **si cela ne vous ennuie pas** if you don't mind; **cela vous ennuierait-il d'attendre?** would you mind waiting?; **je ne voudrais pas vous e. mais...** I don't *or* wouldn't like to bother you but...; **sa sœur l'ennuie tout le temps** his/her sister keeps bothering him/her

3 *(agacer)* to annoy; **tu l'ennuies avec tes questions** you're annoying him/her with your questions; **qu'est-ce qu'elle m'ennuie avec ses chichis!** I'm really getting tired of the fuss she makes!

4 *(lasser)* to bore; **les jeux de cartes m'ennuient** I find card games boring; **il m'ennuie à mourir** he bores me to death

▶**s'ennuyer** VPR *(être lassé)* to be bored; **elle s'ennuie toute seule** she gets bored on her own; *Hum* **avec lui on ne s'ennuie pas!** he's great fun!, you're never bored with him!; *Hum* **au moins on ne s'ennuie pas ici!** at least you can't say it's boring here!; *Fam* **s'e. comme un rat mort** to be bored to death; **je m'ennuie à ne rien faire** *(maintenant)* I'm bored *or Fam* fed up with doing nothing; *(en général)* I get bored if I have nothing to do; **s'e. de qn/qch** to miss sb/sth

ennuyeux, -euse [ɑ̃nɥijø, -øz] ADJ **1** *(lassant → travail, conférencier, collègue)* boring, dull; **e. à mourir** *ou* **à périr** *ou* **comme la pluie** *ou* **comme la mort** (as) dull as *Br* ditchwater *or Am* dishwater, deadly boring

2 *(fâcheux)* annoying, tiresome; **c'est e. qu'il ne puisse pas venir** *(regrettable)* it's a pity (that) he can't come; *(contrariant)* it's annoying *or* a nuisance that he can't come; **comme c'est e.!** what a nuisance!

énol [enɔl] NM *Chim* enol

énolate [enɔlat] NM *Chim* enolate

énoncé [enɔ̃se] NM **1** *(libellé → d'un sujet de débat)* terms; *(→ d'une question d'examen, d'un problème d'arithmétique, d'un contrat, d'une loi)* wording **2** *(lecture)* reading, declaration; **é. des faits** statement of the facts; **à l'é. des faits** when the facts were stated; **é. du jugement** pronouncement of the verdict; **écouter l'é. du jugement** to listen to the verdict being read out **3** *Ling* utterance

énoncer [16] [enɔ̃se] VT *(formuler)* to formulate, to enunciate, to express; **cela peut être énoncé plus simplement** it can be formulated *or* expressed *or* put in simpler terms

▶**s'énoncer** VPR *(opinion)* to be stated; **énoncez-vous plus clairement** express yourself more clearly

énonciatif, -ive [enɔ̃sjatif, -iv] ADJ *Ling* enunciative

énonciation [enɔ̃sjasjɔ̃] NF **1** *(exposition)* statement, stating **2** *Ling* enunciation

énophtalmie [enɔftalmi] NF *Méd* enophthalmus

enorgueillir [32] [ɑ̃nɔrgœjir] *Littéraire* VT to make proud

▶**s'enorgueillir** VPR **s'e. de** to be proud of; **il s'enorgueillit du succès de son livre** he is proud of the success of his book

énorme [enɔrm] ADJ **1** *(gros)* enormous, huge

2 *(important)* huge, enormous, vast; **une somme é.** a huge *or* vast amount of money; **ça fait une différence é.** that makes all the difference; **20 euros, ce n'est pas é.** 20 euros isn't such a huge amount; **elle n'a pas dit non, c'est déjà é.!** she didn't say no, that's a great step forward!; **il n'est pas mort, c'est déjà é.** he's still alive, which is incredible

3 *(exagéré → mensonge)* outrageous; **raconter des choses énormes** to say outrageous things; **il a inventé une histoire é. pour expliquer son absence** he made up a (totally) outrageous story to account for his absence

énormément [enɔrmemɑ̃] ADV enormously, hugely; **le spectacle m'a é. plu** I liked the show very much indeed; **s'amuser é.** to enjoy oneself immensely *or* tremendously; **je le regrette é.** I'm extremely *or Fam* awfully sorry; **elle a é. changé** she has changed enormously *or* a great deal; **é. de** *(argent, bruit)* an enormous *or* a huge *or* a tremendous amount of; **il y avait é. de monde dans le train** the train was extremely crowded; **ils ont mis é. de temps à comprendre** it took them ages to understand

énormité [enɔrmite] NF **1** *(ampleur → d'une difficulté)* enormity; *(→ d'une tâche, d'une somme, d'une population)* enormity, size

2 *(taille démesurée → d'une personne, d'un édifice)* vastness, hugeness; **l'é. du gaspillage** the huge *or* enormous amount wasted

3 *(extravagance)* outrageousness, enormity; **l'é. de son crime** the enormity of his/her crime

4 *(propos)* piece of utter *or* outrageous nonsense; **dire des énormités** to say the most outrageous things; **vous dites des énormités** what you're saying is totally outrageous

énostose [enɔstoz] NF *Méd* enostosis

énouer [6] [enwe] VT *Tex* to burl

enquébécoiser [3] [ɑ̃kebekwaze] VT *Can Fam (texte, roman)* to put into Quebec French; *(personne)* to make into a Quebecker

enquérir [39] [ɑ̃kerir] **s'enquérir** VPR **s'e. de** to inquire about *or* after; **s'e. du prix** to ask the price; **s'e. de la santé de qn** to inquire *or* to ask after sb's health; **il s'est enquis de vous/de**

votre santé he inquired *or* asked after *or* about you/your health

enquerre [ɑ̃kɛr] **à enquerre** ADJ *Hér* à enquerre; **armes à e.** arms à enquerre, arms that violate the rules of tincture

enquête [ɑ̃kɛt] NF **1** *Jur (investigation)* investigation, inquiry; **faire** *ou* **mener sa petite e.** to make discreet inquiries; **il a fait l'objet d'une e.** he was the subject of an investigation; *Jur* **faire** *ou* **procéder à une e. sur qch** to hold *or* conduct an inquiry into sth; *(police)* to carry out *or* conduct an investigation into sth; **elle est chargée de l'e.** she's in charge of the investigation; **mener une e. sur un meurtre** to investigate a murder; **l'inspecteur mène l'e.** the inspector is leading the investigation(s) *or* inquiries; **ouvrir/conduire une e.** to open/to conduct an investigation; *Jur* **e. administrative** public inquiry; **e. de flagrance** = investigation into a flagrant offence; **e. de flagrant délit** expedited investigation *(for serious offences punishable by imprisonment)*; **e. judiciaire (suite à un décès)** inquest; **e. officielle** official *or* public inquiry; *Suisse* **e. parcellaire** division of properties *(in plots for compulsory purchase order)*; **e. de personnalité** = character report on an accused prepared by his/her welfare officer; **e. de police** police investigation; **e. préliminaire** preliminary investigation *or* inquiry; **e. publique** = stage in the obtaining of planning permission at which the applicant has to notify the public; **e. sociale** social inquiry report; **e. d'utilité publique** public inquiry

2 *(étude)* survey, investigation; *Mktg* survey; **faire une e.** to conduct a survey; **notre e. a porté sur l'alcoolisme** the topic of our survey was alcoholism; *Mktg* **e. d'attitude** attitude survey; **e. de conjoncture** business survey; **e. auprès des consommateurs** consumer survey; **e. fiscale** tax survey; **e. de marché** market survey; *Mktg* **e. omnibus** omnibus survey; **e. d'opinion** opinion poll; *Mktg* **e. pilote** pilot survey; **e. postale** postal survey; **e. sur les prix** price survey; **e. par questionnaire** questionnaire survey; **e. par sondage** opinion poll, sample survey; **e. par téléphone, e. téléphonique** telephone survey; **e. sur le terrain** field study

3 *Presse* (investigative) report, exposé

enquêté, -e [ɑ̃kete] NM,F interviewee

enquêter [4] [ɑ̃kete] VI to investigate; *Jur* to hold an inquiry; *(police)* to make investigations; *(faire un sondage)* to conduct a survey (**sur** into); **c'est elle qui enquête** she's in charge of the investigation; **e. sur un meurtre** to carry out an investigation into *or* to investigate a murder

enquêteur, -euse *ou* **-trice** [ɑ̃kɛtœr, -øz, -tris] ADJ *Jur* **commissaire e.** investigating commissioner

NM,F **1** *(de police)* officer in charge of investigations, investigator **2** *(de sondage) & Journ* interviewer **3** *(sociologue)* researcher

enquiert *etc voir* **enquérir**

enquiquinant, -e [ɑ̃kikinɑ̃, -ɑ̃t] ADJ *Fam (agaçant)* irritating■; *(lassant)* boring■; **des voisins enquiquinants** awkward neighbours■; **elle est enquiquinante à toujours se plaindre** the way she complains all the time is a real pain

enquiquinement [ɑ̃kikinmɑ̃] NM *Fam* **des enquiquinements** hassle; **je n'ai eu que des enquiquinements avec cette voiture** I've had nothing but hassle with this car

enquiquiner [3] [ɑ̃kikine] *Fam* VT **1** *(ennuyer)* to bore (stiff) **2** *(irriter)* to bug; **il m'enquiquine** he bugs me; **je les enquiquine!** to hell with them! **3** *(importuner)* **se faire e.** to be hassled

▶**s'enquiquiner** VPR *(s'ennuyer)* to be bored (stiff); **je ne vais pas m'e. à tout recopier** I can't be bothered *or* *Br* fagged to copy it out again

enquiquineur, -euse [ɑ̃kikinœr, -øz] NM,F *Fam* pain, drag, nuisance

enquis, -e [ɑ̃ki, -iz] PP *voir* **enquérir**

enraciné, -e [ɑ̃rasine] ADJ **bien e.** *(idée)* firmly implanted *or* entrenched; *(habitude)* deeply ingrained; *(croyance)* deep-seated, deep-rooted

enracinement [ɑ̃rasinmɑ̃] NM **1** *Bot* rooting **2** *Fig (d'une opinion, d'une coutume)* deep-rootedness

enraciner [3] [ɑ̃rasine] VT **1** *Bot* to root

2 *(fixer → dans un lieu, une culture)* to root; **se sentir profondément enraciné dans une culture** to feel deeply rooted in a culture

3 *(fixer dans l'esprit)* to fix, to implant

▶**s'enraciner** VPR **1** *Bot* to root, to take root

2 *Fig (personne)* to put down roots; *(sentiments, habitudes, coutume)* to take root, to become established *or* deeply rooted; **s'e. profondément dans une culture/l'esprit** to become deeply rooted in a culture/the mind

enragé, -e [ɑ̃raʒe] ADJ **1** *Méd* rabid **2** *(furieux)* enraged, livid **3** *Fam (passionné → partisan, supporter etc)* rabid, out-and-out

NM,F *Fam (passionné)* fanatic; **un e. de football/ski/musique** a football/skiing/music fanatic

❑ **enragés** NMPL *Hist* **les enragés** the Enragés *(faction of militant Parisian extremists during the French Revolution)*; *(en 1968)* leftist militants

enrageant, -e [ɑ̃raʒɑ̃, -ɑ̃t] ADJ *Fam* maddening, infuriating

enrager [17] [ɑ̃raʒe] VI *(être en colère)* to be furious *or* infuriated; **j'enrage de m'être laissé prendre** I'm enraged *or* furious at having been caught; **faire e. qn** *(l'irriter)* to annoy sb; *(le taquiner)* to tease sb mercilessly

enraie *etc voir* **enrayer**

enraiement [ɑ̃rɛmɑ̃] NM stopping, checking; **l'e. d'une épidémie** checking the progress of an epidemic

enrayage [ɑ̃rɛjaʒ] NM **1** *(blocage → d'une roue)* locking; *(→ d'un mécanisme, d'une arme)* jamming **2** *(montage des rayons → d'une roue)* spoking

enrayement [ɑ̃rɛjmɑ̃] = **enraiement**

enrayer [11] [ɑ̃reje] VT **1** *(bloquer → roue)* to lock; *(→ arme, mécanisme)* to jam

2 *Fig (empêcher la progression de)* to check, to stop, to call a halt to; **e. la crise** to halt the economic recession; **e. l'inflation** to check *or* to control *or* to curb inflation; **e. une maladie/un fléau** to arrest *or* check a disease/scourge; **l'épidémie est enrayée** the epidemic has been halted

3 *(équiper de rayons → roue)* to spoke

▶**s'enrayer** VPR **1** *(arme, mécanisme)* to jam

2 *Fig (épidémie)* to abate

enrayure[1] [ɑ̃rɛjyr] NF *Constr (pièces de bois)* = joists arranged radially about a centre

enrayure[2] [ɑ̃rɛjyr] NF *Agr* outside *or* first furrow

enrégimenter [3] [ɑ̃reʒimɑ̃te] VT **1** *Mil* to form into regiments **2** *(dans un parti, une organisation)* to press-gang; **je déteste être enrégimenté!** I hate being regimented!; **e. qn dans qch** to press-gang sb into sth

enregistrable [ɑ̃rəʒistrabl] ADJ **1** *Admin & Jur* receivable **2** *(sur une bande magnétique)* recordable

enregistrement [ɑ̃rəʒistrəmɑ̃] NM **1** *Jur (fait de déclarer)* registration, registering; *(entrée)* entry; **faire l'e. d'une société** to register a company; *Admin* **l'E.** the Registration department; **droit d'e.** stamp duty

2 *Com (fait d'inscrire)* booking; *(d'une commande)* booking, entering (up); *(entrée)* booking, entry; **e. comptable** accounting entry

3 *Transp (à l'aéroport)* check-in; *(à la gare)* registration; **procéder à l'e. de ses bagages** *(à l'aéroport)* to check one's luggage in; *(à la gare)* to register one's luggage; **e. anticipé** advanced check-in; **guichet d'e.** *(à l'aéroport)* check-in (desk)

4 *(de son)* recording; **e. magnétique** tape recording; **e. audio** audio recording; **e. sur bande/cassette** tape/cassette recording; **e. haute fidélité** hi-fi recording; **e. laser** *(procédé)* laser recording; *(disque)* laser disc; **e. sur magnétoscope** video recording; **e. numérique** digital recording; *TV & Rad* **e. son** *ou* **sonore** audio *or* sound recording; *TV* **camion d'e. (du son)** sound van; **e. vidéo** video recording; **e. vocal** voice recording

5 *Ordinat (article, informations)* record; *(action)* recording, logging

6 *(diagramme)* trace

❑ **d'enregistrement** ADJ **1** *Com* registration *(avant n)*

2 *Ordinat (clef, tête, structure)* format *(avant n)*; *(densité, support)* recording *(avant n)*; *(unité)* logging *(avant n)*

3 *(dans l'audiovisuel)* **tête d'e.** recording head

enregistrer [3] [ɑ̃rəʒistre] VT **1** *(inscrire → opération, transaction, acte)* to enter, to record; *(→ déclaration)* to register, to file; *(→ naissance, acte etc)* to register; *(→ note, mention)* to log; *(→ commande)* to enter up; **e. un jugement** to enter *or* enrol a judgement; **société enregistrée** registered company

2 *(constater)* to record, to note; **l'entreprise a enregistré un bénéfice de...** the company showed a profit of...; **les meilleures ventes enregistrées depuis des mois** the best recorded sales for months; **on enregistre une baisse du dollar** the dollar has fallen in value

3 *(réaliser une copie de → cassette audio, disque, émission)* to record, to tape; *(→ sur un magnétoscope)* to record, to video, to video-tape; *Ordinat (→ données)* to store; *(→ CD)* to write; **musique enregistrée** taped *or* recorded music; *Ordinat* **programme enregistré** stored programme

4 *(pour commercialiser → émission, dialogue)* to record; **e. un disque** to make a record

5 *(afficher)* to register, to record, to show; **l'appareil n'a rien enregistré** nothing registered on the apparatus, the apparatus did not register anything

6 *Fam (retenir)* to take in■; *(mémoriser)* to note■, to memorize■; **d'accord, c'est enregistré** all right, I've got that; **je n'ai rien enregistré de ce que j'ai lu** I haven't taken in any of what I read

7 *Transp (à l'aéroport)* to check in; *(à la gare)* to register; **les voyageurs sont priés de faire e. leurs bagages une heure avant le départ** passengers are requested to ensure that their luggage is checked in one hour before departure

USAGE ABSOLU **1 ils sont en train d'e.** they're doing *or* making a recording; **e. sur bande** to tape, to record on tape; **e. au magnétoscope** to video, to record on video

2 *Fam (retenir)* **je lui ai dit mais il n'a pas enregistré** I told him but it didn't register *or* he didn't take it in■; **je ne dis rien mais j'enregistre** I don't say anything but I take it all in■

enregistreur, -euse [ɑ̃rəʒistrœr, -øz] ADJ recording *(avant n)*

NM recorder, recording device; *Belg (magnétophone)* tape recorder; **e. à bande** (strip) chart recorder; *Belg* **e. à cassettes** cassette recorder; **e. de pression** pressure recorder; **e. de son** *ou* **sonore** sound recorder; **e. à tambour** drum recorder; *Ind* **e. de temps** time clock *or* recorder; **e. de vol** flight recorder

enrênement [ɑ̃rɛnmɑ̃] NM *Équitation* **1** *(courroies)* reins **2** *(action)* reining in

enrêner [4] [ɑ̃rɛne] VT *Équitation* to rein in

enrésinement [ɑ̃rezinmɑ̃] NM *Bot* planting with conifers

enrésiner [3] [ɑ̃rezine] VT *Bot* to plant with conifers

enrhumé, -e [ɑ̃ryme] ADJ **être e.** to have a cold

enrhumer [3] [ɑ̃ryme] VT **1 e. qn** to give sb a cold **2** *Fam* to overtake at top speed

▶**s'enrhumer** VPR to catch cold, to get a cold

enrichi, -e [ɑ̃riʃi] ADJ **1** *Péj (personne)* nouveau riche **2** *(amélioré)* enriched; **il est sorti e. de ses voyages** his travelling has enriched his mind; **céréales enrichies en vitamines** cereals with added vitamins, vitamin-enriched cereals **3** *Ordinat & Typ (texte)* enriched

enrichir [32] [ɑ̃riʃir] VT **1** *(en argent)* to enrich, to make rich *or* richer

2 *(améliorer → savon, minerai, culture) & Phys* to enrich; *(→ esprit)* to enrich, to improve; **e. la terre** to enrich the soil; **cette expérience m'a enrichi** I'm all the richer for that experience; **édition enrichie de nombreuses cartes** edition to which many new maps have been added

3 *Ordinat & Typ (texte)* to enrich

▶**s'enrichir** VPR **1** *(devenir riche)* to grow rich *or* richer, to become rich *or* richer

2 *(se développer → collection)* to increase, to develop; *(→ esprit)* to be enriched, to grow; *(→ langue)* to grow *or* become richer (**de/en** with/in); **s'e. à force de lectures/de voyages** to enrich one's mind through reading/travel; **s'e. l'esprit** to improve one's mind

enrichissant, -e [ɑ̃riʃisɑ̃, -ɑ̃t] ADJ enriching; *(travail)* rewarding

enrichissement [ɑ̃riʃismɑ̃] NM **1** *(en argent)* becoming rich *or* richer; *(d'une entreprise)* increase in capital; **l'e. personnel du dirigeant de l'association a fait scandale** the personal fortune *or* wealth accrued by the head of the organization caused a scandal; *Jur* **e. sans cause** unjust enrichment **2** *(développement → de l'esprit, d'une collection)* enriching, enrichment; *Fig* **l'ultime objectif est l'e. personnel** the ultimate objective is personal development **3** *(amélioration → d'un minerai, d'un sol)* improvement, improving **4** *Nucl* enrichment **5** *Ordinat & Typ (de texte)* enriching

enrobage [ɑ̃rɔbaʒ] NM *(action, enveloppe)* coating; **e. de sucre/chocolat** sugar/chocolate coating

enrobé, -e [ɑ̃rɔbe] ADJ *(personne)* plump, chubby
▪ NM *(revêtement)* surfacing
▫ **enrobés** NMPL coated materials; **enrobés à froid/chaud** cold/hot mix

enrobement [ɑ̃rɔbmɑ̃] NM *(action, enveloppe)* coating; **e. de sucre/chocolat** sugar/chocolate coating

enrober [3] [ɑ̃rɔbe] VT **1** *Culin (enduire)* to coat; **e. qch de** to coat sth with; **e. de chocolat** to coat with chocolate **2** *(adoucir)* to wrap *or* to dress up; **il a enrobé son reproche de mots affectueux** he wrapped his criticism in kind words

enrobeuse [ɑ̃rɔbøz] NF *Tech (en confiserie)* coating machine

enrochement [ɑ̃rɔʃmɑ̃] NM *(gén)* breakwater *(made of loose boulders)*; *(dans les travaux publics)* riprap

enrocher [3] [ɑ̃rɔʃe] VT *Constr* to riprap, to stonepack

enrôlé [ɑ̃role] NM enlisted private

enrôlement [ɑ̃rolmɑ̃] NM **1** *Mil* enlistment **2** *Admin & Jur* enrolment

enrôler [3] [ɑ̃role] VT **1** *Mil* to enrol, to enlist; *Hist* **e. de force** to press-gang, to impress; **il s'est fait e. dans l'armée à 16 ans** he was enlisted at the age of 16; *Fig* **je vois que tu t'es fait e. pour faire la vaisselle** I see you've been dragooned into doing the washing up; **e. qn dans un parti/groupe** to recruit sb into a party/group **2** *Admin & Jur* to enrol, to record
▸ **s'enrôler** VPR **1** *Mil* to enlist, to sign up **2** *(dans un groupe, dans un parti)* to enrol, to sign up

enrôleur [ɑ̃rolœr] NM *Hist & Mil* recruiting sergeant

enroué, -e [ɑ̃rwe] ADJ hoarse; **d'une voix enrouée** hoarsely

enrouement [ɑ̃rumɑ̃] NM hoarseness

enrouer [6] [ɑ̃rwe] VT *(voix, personne)* to make hoarse
▸ **s'enrouer** VPR *(de froid)* to get hoarse; *(en forçant sa voix)* to make oneself hoarse; **je me suis enroué à force de crier/chanter** I shouted/sang myself hoarse

enroulable [ɑ̃rulabl] ADJ windable; *Aut* **ceinture de sécurité e.** inertia-reel seat belt

enroulement [ɑ̃rulmɑ̃] NM **1** *(mise en rouleau → de carte, de tissu, de tapis etc)* rolling up; *(→ de câble, de ruban)* winding up; **pour assurer l'e. correct du papier** to ensure that the paper winds on properly **2** *(volute)* whorl, scroll **3** *Élec (bobinage)* winding; *(bobine)* coil; **e. du champ d'excitation** field winding; **e. en série** series winding

enrouler [3] [ɑ̃rule] VT **1** *(mettre en rouleau → carte, tissu, tapis etc)* to roll up; *(→ câble, ruban)* to wind up; *(→ ressort)* to coil; **lierre enroulé autour d'un arbre** ivy twined *or* wound round a tree **2** *(envelopper)* **e. dans** to roll *or* to wrap in; **e. un corps dans un drap** to wrap a body in a sheet
▸ **s'enrouler** VPR *(corde, fil)* to be wound *or* to wind (up); *(serpent)* to coil (itself); **s'e. dans une couverture** to wrap oneself up in a blanket; **le papier s'enroule autour de ce cylindre** the paper winds round this cylinder

enrouleur, -euse [ɑ̃rulœr, -øz] ADJ winding, coiling
▪ NM **1** *(tambour)* drum, reel **2** *(galet)* idle pulley,

idler, roller; *Aut* **e. de ceinture automatique** automatic seat belt winder, inertia reel
▫ **à enrouleur** ADJ self-winding; *Aut* **ceinture de sécurité à e.** inertia-reel seat belt

enrubannage [ɑ̃rybanaʒ] NM *Agr* baling

enrubanner [3] [ɑ̃rybane] VT **1** *(orner de rubans)* to decorate *or* to adorn with ribbons **2** *Agr* to bale

ENS [əɛnɛs] NF *Scol & Univ (abrév* **École normale supérieure**) = prestigious "grande école" for teachers and researchers

ENSA, Ensa [ɛnsa] NF *Univ (abrév* **École nationale supérieure agronomique**) = one of five competitive-entry agricultural engineering schools

ensablement [ɑ̃sabləmɑ̃] NM **1** *Naut (d'un bateau)* running aground; *(d'un tuyau)* choking (up) with sand; *(d'une route)* sanding over; *(d'un port)* silting up **2** *(dépôt → amené par l'eau)* sandbank, sand bar; *(→ amené par le vent)* sand dune

ensabler [3] [ɑ̃sable] VT **1** *(couvrir de sable)* **être ensablé** *(port, estuaire)* to be silted up; *(route, piste)* to be covered in sand (drifts) **2** *Naut (enliser → bateau)* to strand, to run aground; *(→ véhicule)* to get stuck in the sand; **une voiture ensablée** a car stuck in the sand
▸ **s'ensabler** VPR **1** *(chenal)* to silt up **2** *(véhicule)* to get stuck in the sand **3** *(poisson)* to bury itself in the sand

ensachage [ɑ̃saʃaʒ] NM *Ind* bagging (up), sacking

ensacher [3] [ɑ̃saʃe] VT *Ind* to bag (up), to sack

ensacheur [ɑ̃saʃœr] NM *Ind* bagger

ensacheuse [ɑ̃saʃøz] NF *(machine)* machine for bagging, bag-filling machine

ENSAD, Ensad [ɛnsad] NF *Scol & Univ (abrév* **École nationale supérieure des arts décoratifs**) = "grande école" for applied arts

ensaisinement [ɑ̃sɛzinəmɑ̃] NM *Arch Jur* enfeoffment

ensaisiner [3] [ɑ̃sɛzine] VT *Arch Jur* to enfeoff

ENSAM, Ensam [ɛnsam] NF *(abrév* **École nationale supérieure des arts et métiers**) = "grande école" for engineering

ensanglanter [3] [ɑ̃sɑ̃glɑ̃te] VT **1** *(tacher)* to bloody; **un mouchoir ensanglanté** a bloodstained handkerchief; **mains ensanglantées** bloodstained *or* bloody hands; **il entra, le visage ensanglanté** he came in with his face covered in blood **2** *(sujet: troubles, guerre, crime)* to bathe in blood; **les émeutes qui ont ensanglanté la capitale** the riots which have brought bloodshed to the streets of the capital; **un festival ensanglanté par un attentat** a festival marred by the bloody violence of an attempted murder

ENSBA *Scol & Univ (abrév écrite* **École nationale supérieure des Beaux-Arts**) = leading art school in Paris

enseignant, -e [ɑ̃sɛɲɑ̃, -ɑ̃t] ADJ *voir* **corps**
▪ NM,F *Scol & Univ* teacher

enseignant-chercheur [ɑ̃sɛɲɑ̃ʃɛrʃœr] *(pl* **enseignants-chercheurs**) NM *Univ* = university lecturer and researcher

enseigne [ɑ̃sɛɲ] NM **1** *Mil* **e. de vaisseau 1er classe** *Br* sub-lieutenant, *Am* lieutenant junior grade; **e. de vaisseau 2ème classe** *Br* midshipman, *Am* ensign **2** *Hist (porte-drapeau)* ensign
▪ NF **1** *(panneau)* sign; *Mktg* brand name; **lumineuse** *ou* **au néon** neon sign; **à l'e. du Lion d'or** at the (sign of the) Golden Lion; *Fam Fig* **nous sommes tous logés à la même e.** we're all in the same boat; *Prov* **à bon vin point d'e.** good wine needs no bush **2** *Littéraire (étendard)* ensign
▫ **à telle(s) enseigne(s) que** CONJ so much so that

enseignement [ɑ̃sɛɲmɑ̃] NM *Scol & Univ* **1** *(instruction)* education; **e. assisté par ordinateur** computer-assisted learning; **e. pour adultes** adult education; **e. par correspondance** correspondence courses **2** *(méthodes d'instruction)* teaching (methods); **méthode d'e.** teaching method; **son e. prend en compte la vie familiale de l'enfant** his/her teaching methods take the child's family background into account; **l'e. des langues est excellent dans mon collège**

languages are taught very well at my school **3** *(système scolaire)* **e. primaire/supérieur** primary/higher education; **e. privé** private education; **e. professionnel** vocational education; **e. programmé** programmed learning; **e. public** state education *or* schools; **l'e. du second degré** *ou* **secondaire** secondary education; **e. technique** technical education **4** *(profession)* **l'e.** teaching, the teaching profession; **entrer dans l'e.** to go into teaching; **travailler dans l'e.** to work in education *or* the teaching profession; **il est dans l'e.** he is a teacher, he teaches **5** *(leçon)* lesson, teaching; **tirer un e. de qch** to learn (a lesson) from sth; **quel e. en avez-vous tiré?** what did you learn from it?; **les enseignements d'un maître** the teachings of a master

enseigner [4] [ɑ̃sɛɲe] VT **1** *(apprendre)* to teach; **e. qch à qn** to teach sb sth *or* sth to sb; **e. à qn à faire qch** to teach sb (how) to do sth; **l'expérience nous enseigne que...** experience teaches *or* shows us that... **2** *Vieilli (indiquer)* to show, to point out; **e. à qn son devoir** to point out his/her duty to sb
USAGE ABSOLU **elle enseigne depuis trois ans** she's been teaching for three years

ensellé, -e [ɑ̃sɛle] ADJ saddle-backed, swaybacked

ensellement [ɑ̃sɛlmɑ̃] NM *Géol* saddle

ensellure [ɑ̃sɛlyr] NF *Méd* hollow-back, *Spéc* lordosis

ensemble [ɑ̃sɑ̃bl] ADV **1** *(l'un avec l'autre)* together; **ils y sont allés e.** they went together; **ne vous séparez pas, restez bien e.** don't separate, stay together; **mettre e.** to put together; **elles en sont convenues e.** they agreed (between themselves); **nous en avons parlé e.** we spoke *or* we had a talk about it; **on pourrait partir tous e.** we could all go together *or* in a group; **aller bien e.** *(vêtements, couleurs)* to go well together; *(personnes)* to be well-matched; **ils vont mal e.** *(vêtements)* they don't match; *(couple)* they're ill-matched; **être bien/mal e.** to be on good/bad terms; **ils sont e. depuis plusieurs mois** they've been together for several months **2** *(en même temps)* at once, at the same time; **ne parlez pas tous e.** don't all speak at once; **ils sont arrivés tous les deux e.** they both arrived at the same time
▪ NM **1** *(collection → d'objets)* set, collection; *(→ d'idées)* set, series; *(→ de données, d'informations, de textes)* set, body, collection; **la table et la chaise forment un e.** the table and chair are part of the same set; **un e. de conditions** a set of conditions; *Mktg* **e. de besoins** need set; *Mktg* **e. de considérations** consideration *or* product choice set; *Mktg* **e. évoqué** evoked set; *Aut* **e. moteur-boîte** power unit **2** *(totalité)* whole; **la question dans son e.** the question as a whole; **la classe, prise dans son e., a un bon niveau** the class, (taken) as a whole, is of a good standard; **il faudrait réunir ses écrits en un e. cohérent** we should collect his/her writings together in a coherent whole; **l'e. des joueurs** all the players; **l'e. du travail est bon** the work as a whole is good; **l'e. des réponses montre que...** the answers taken as a whole show that...; **il s'est adressé à l'e. des employés** he spoke to all the staff *or* the whole staff **3** *(simultanéité)* unity; **avec e.** all together, in unison, as one; **évoluer avec e.** to move simultaneously *or* in unison; **manquer d'e.** to lack unity; **ils ont protesté dans un e. parfait** they protested unanimously **4** *(groupe)* group; **e. de chanteurs** group of singers; **e. instrumental** (instrumental) ensemble; **e. vocal** vocal group **5** *(vêtement)* suit, outfit; **e. de plage** beach outfit; **e. pantalon** trouser suit **6** *(d'habitations)* block; **grand e.** residential estate **7** *Math* set; **e. fermé** closed set; **e. vide** empty set **8** *Ordinat (de caractères, d'informations)* set
▫ **dans l'ensemble** ADV on the whole, by and large, in the main; **dans l'e. tout va bien** on the whole *or* by and large *or* in the main everything's fine; **dans l'e. les prix montent** on the whole *or* overall, prices are rising

❑ **d'ensemble** ADJ **1** *(général)* overall, general; **mesures d'e.** comprehensive *or* global measures; **vue d'e.** overall *or* general view

2 *Mus* **faire de la musique d'e.** to play in an ensemble

ensemblier [ɑ̃sɑ̃blije] NM **1** *(décorateur)* interior designer **2** *Cin & TV* props assistant

ensembliste [ɑ̃sɑ̃blist] ADJ *Math* set *(avant n)*

ensemencement [ɑ̃səmɑ̃smɑ̃] NM **1** *Agr* seeding, sowing **2** *Pêche* stocking **3** *Biol* culturing

ensemencer [16] [ɑ̃səmɑ̃se] VT **1** *Agr* to sow, to seed; **champ ensemencé de tournesols** field seeded *or* sown with sunflowers **2** *Pêche* to stock **3** *Biol* to culture

enserrer [4] [ɑ̃sere] VT **1** *(agripper)* to clutch, to grasp, to grip; **e. qn dans ses bras** to clasp sb in one's arms, to embrace *or* hug sb **2** *(être autour de → sujet: col, bijou)* to fit tightly around; **un bracelet lui enserrait le bras** she wore a tightly-fitting bracelet around her arm; **des fortifications enserrent la vieille ville** fortified walls form a tight circle around the old town

ENSET, Enset [ɛnsɛt] NF *Scol & Univ (abrév* **École nationale supérieure de l'enseignement technique**) = "grande école" training science and technology teachers

ensevelir [32] [ɑ̃səvlir] VT **1** *Littéraire (dans un linceul)* to shroud, to enshroud; *(dans la tombe)* to entomb

2 *(enfouir)* to bury; **l'éruption a enseveli plusieurs villages** the eruption buried several villages; *Fig* **elle a enseveli l'image de cette tragédie au plus profond de sa mémoire** she buried the image of the tragedy deep in her memory

▸**s'ensevelir** VPR *aussi Fig* **s'e. dans** to bury oneself in

ensevelissement [ɑ̃səvlismɑ̃] NM **1** *Littéraire (mise → dans un linceul)* enshrouding; *(→ au tombeau)* entombment **2** *(disparition → d'une ruine, d'un souvenir)* burying

ENSI, Ensi [ɛnsi] NF *Scol & Univ (abrév* **École nationale supérieure d'ingénieurs**) = competitive-entry engineering institute

ensiforme [ɑ̃sifɔrm] ADJ ensiform, sword-shaped

ensilage [ɑ̃silaʒ] NM *Agr* **1** *(méthode)* ensilage, silaging **2** *(produit)* silage

ensiler [3] [ɑ̃sile] VT *Agr* to ensile, to silage

ensileuse [ɑ̃siløz] NF *Agr* silo filler

ensimage [ɑ̃simaʒ] NM *Tex* oiling, greasing

en-soi [ɑ̃swa] NM INV *Phil* **l'e.** the thing in itself

ensoleillé, -e [ɑ̃sɔleje] ADJ sunny, sunlit; **très e.** sundrenched

ensoleillement [ɑ̃sɔlɛjmɑ̃] NM (amount of) sunshine, *Spéc* insolation; **la pièce n'a pas un bon e.** the room doesn't get much sun *or* sunlight; **l'e. annuel** the number of days of sunshine per year; **cinq journées/heures d'e.** five days/hours of sun(shine)

ensoleiller [4] [ɑ̃sɔleje] VT **1** *(donner du soleil à)* to bathe in *or* to fill with sunlight **2** *Fig* to brighten (up); **cet enfant ensoleillait leur existence** that child was like a ray of sunshine in their lives

ensommeillé, -e [ɑ̃sɔmeje] ADJ sleepy, drowsy, dozy; *(yeux, visage)* sleepy; **les yeux tout ensommeillés** eyes heavy with sleep; **il était encore tout e.** he was still half-asleep

ensorcelant, -e [ɑ̃sɔrsəlɑ̃, -ɑ̃t] ADJ bewitching, entrancing, spellbinding

ensorcelé, -e [ɑ̃sɔrsəle] ADJ bewitched, under a spell

ensorceler [24] [ɑ̃sɔrsəle] VT **1** *(envoûter)* to bewitch, to cast a spell over; **elle m'a ensorcelé** I fell under her spell **2** *Fig (personne)* to bewitch, to captivate

ensorceleur, -euse [ɑ̃sɔrsəlœr, -øz] ADJ bewitching, entrancing, spellbinding

NM,F **1** *(sorcier)* enchanter, *f* enchantress, sorcerer, *f* sorceress **2** *(charmeur)* charmer

ensorcelle *etc voir* **ensorceler**

ensorcellement [ɑ̃sɔrsɛlmɑ̃] NM *(action)* bewitching; *(état)* bewitchment, enchantment; *Fig (charme)* charm, spell; **elle ne pouvait résister à l'e. de ce pays étrange** she fell irresistibly under the spell of that strange country

ensoufrer [3] [ɑ̃sufre] VT to sulphurate; *(allumettes)* to impregnate with sulphur

ensouple [ɑ̃supl] NF *Tex* beam, roller

ensuit *etc voir* **ensuivre**

ensuite [ɑ̃sɥit] ADV **1** *(dans le temps → puis)* then, next; *(→ plus tard)* later, after, afterwards; **qu'est-ce que vous prendrez e.?** what will you have to follow?; **et e., que s'est-il passé?** and what happened next?, and then what happened?; **d'abord, c'est très cher, et e. ça ne te va pas du tout** for one thing it's very expensive and for another it doesn't at all suit you; **ils ne sont arrivés qu'e.** they didn't arrive until later; **ils se sont disputés, e. de quoi on ne l'a jamais revu** they fell out, after which we didn't see him again

2 *(dans l'espace)* then, further on; **la porte d'entrée donnait sur le salon et e. venait la chambre** the front door opened into the living room and then came the bedroom; **les pompiers marchaient en tête, e. venait la musique** the firemen led the procession, next came the band

ensuivre [89] [ɑ̃sɥivr] **s'ensuivre** VPR **1** *(en résulter)* to follow, to ensue; **sa maladie et toutes les conséquences qui s'en sont suivies** his/her illness and all the ensuing consequences; **il s'ensuit que…** it follows that…; **il ne s'ensuit pas forcément que tu as raison** it doesn't necessarily follow that you are right; **il s'ensuit qu'il est sans emploi** the consequence is he's out of a job; **il s'en est suivi que…** it ensued that…; **jusqu'à ce que sa mort s'ensuive** *(battre quelqu'un etc)* to death

2 *Littéraire (venir après)* to follow (on); **les jours qui s'ensuivirent furent calmes** the following *or* subsequent days were quiet

3 *(locution)* **et tout ce qui s'ensuit** and so on (and so forth)

ensuqué, -e [ɑ̃syke] ADJ *Fam (dans le sud de la France)* dazed▪, in a daze▪

entablement [ɑ̃tabləmɑ̃] NM *Archit* entablature

entaché, -e [ɑ̃taʃe] ADJ **e. de nullité** *(contrat, texte)* voidable

entacher [3] [ɑ̃taʃe] VT **1** *(souiller)* to sully, to soil; **ce scandale a entaché son honneur** the scandal has sullied his/her reputation **2** *(marquer)* to mar; **une attitude entachée d'hypocrisie** an attitude marred by hypocrisy **3** *Jur (contrat, texte)* **entaché de nullité** null

entaillage [ɑ̃tajaʒ] NM notching

entaille [ɑ̃taj] NF **1** *(encoche)* notch, nick **2** *(blessure)* gash, slash, cut; **petite e.** nick; **se faire une e. au front** to gash one's forehead

entailler [3] [ɑ̃taje] VT **1** *(fendre)* to notch, to nick; **e. un rondin à coups de hache** to make notches in a log with an axe **2** *(blesser)* to gash, to slash, to cut; **la lame lui a entaillé l'arcade sourcilière** the blade slashed his/her face above the eye **3** *Can* to tap **e. un érable** to tap a maple tree

▸**s'entailler** VPR **s'e. le doigt** to cut one's finger

entame [ɑ̃tam] NF **1** *Culin (morceau → de viande)* first slice *or* cut; *(→ de pain)* crust **2** *Cartes (début)* opening; **dès l'e. de qch** from the start *or* beginning of sth

entamer [3] [ɑ̃tame] VT **1** *(jambon, fromage)* to start; *(bouteille, conserve)* to open; *(pot de confiture etc)* to start on, to open

2 *(durée, repas)* to start, to begin; *(négociation)* to launch, to start, to initiate; **e. une conversation** to strike up a conversation; **e. des démarches** to begin to take steps, to initiate steps; *Jur* **e. des poursuites (contre qn)** to initiate *or* institute proceedings (against sb); **nous avons entamé une longue procédure** we have started *or* launched a long procedure

3 *(réduire → fortune, économies)* to make a dent *or* hole in; *(→ capital, profits)* to eat into; *(→ résistance)* to lower, to deal a blow to; *(→ ligne ennemie)* to break through

4 *(ébranler)* to shake; **rien ne peut e. sa confiance en lui** nothing can shake *or* undermine his self-confidence

5 *(user)* to damage; **l'acide entame le fer** acid eats into *or* corrodes metal; **le coin a été entamé** the corner was damaged *or* chipped

6 *(écorcher → peau)* to graze

7 *Cartes* to open; **e. trèfle** to open clubs

entartage [ɑ̃tartaʒ], **entartement** [ɑ̃tartmɑ̃] NM pieing, pie throwing *(as an expression of protest)*

entarter [3] [ɑ̃tarte] VT to pie, to throw a pie at *(as an expression of protest)*

entartrage [ɑ̃tartraʒ] NM **1** *Tech (d'une chaudière, d'un tuyau)* scaling, *Br* furring (up) **2** *Méd (d'une dent → processus)* scaling; *(→ état)* scale, tartar deposit

entartré, -e [ɑ̃tartre] ADJ *Tech (chaudière, tuyau)* scaled, *Br* furred (up)

entartrer [3] [ɑ̃tartre] VT **1** *Tech (chaudière, tuyau)* to scale, *Br* to fur (up) **2** *Méd (dent)* to cover with tartar *or* scale

▸**s'entartrer** VPR **1** *Tech (chaudière, tuyau)* to scale, *Br* to fur (up) **2** *Méd (dent)* to become covered in tartar *or* scale

entassement [ɑ̃tasmɑ̃] NM **1** *(amas)* heap, pile, stack; *(mise en tas)* heaping *or* piling up, stacking **2** *(fait de s'agglutiner)* crowding; **l'e. des voyageurs dans le wagon** the crowding of passengers into the carriage

entasser [3] [ɑ̃tase] VT **1** *(mettre en tas)* to heap (up), to pile (up), to stack (up); **e. de la terre** to heap up *or* to bank up earth

2 *(accumuler → vieilleries, journaux)* to pile (up), to heap (up); **elle entasse toutes ses affaires dans cette pièce** she piles up *or* stores all her stuff in this room

3 *(thésauriser → fortune, argent)* to pile up, to heap up

4 *(serrer)* to cram (in), to pack (in); **ils vivent entassés à quatre dans une seule pièce** the four of them live in one cramped room

▸**s'entasser** VPR *(neige, terre)* to heap up, to pile up, to bank; *(vieilleries, journaux)* to heap up, to pile up; *(personnes)* to crowd (in) *or* together, to pile in; **s'e. dans une voiture** to pile into a car

ente [ɑ̃t] NF **1** *Agr (greffon)* scion; *(greffe)* graft **2** *(de pinceau)* handle

enté, -e [ɑ̃te] ADJ *Hér* **e. en pointe** enté en point

entéléchie [ɑ̃teleʃi] NF *Phil* entelechy

entelle [ɑ̃tɛl] NM *Zool* entellus monkey, langur

entendant, -e [ɑ̃tɑ̃dɑ̃, -ɑ̃t] NM,F hearing person

entendement [ɑ̃tɑ̃dmɑ̃] NM comprehension, understanding; **cela dépasse l'e.** it's beyond all comprehension *or* understanding

entendeur [ɑ̃tɑ̃dœr] NM *Prov* **à bon e. salut** a word to the wise is enough

ENTENDRE [73] [ɑ̃tɑ̃dr]

VT to hear **1, 2, 4, 5, 7** ▪ to listen to **2** ▪ to agree to **3** ▪ to understand **6** ▪ to mean **8** ▪ to intend **9**
USAGE ABSOLU to hear **1** ▪ to understand **2**
VPR to be heard **1, 2** ▪ to be understood **3** ▪ to hear each other **4** ▪ to agree, to reach an agreement **5** ▪ to get on **6** ▪ to hear oneself **7** ▪ to be good at **8**

VT **1** *(percevoir par l'ouïe)* to hear; **parlez plus fort, on n'entend rien (de ce que vous dites)** speak up, we can't hear a word (you're saying); **on l'entend à peine** you can hardly hear him/her/it, he/she/it is scarcely audible; **on n'entend que toi, ici! c'est lassant à la fin!** yours is the only voice we can hear, it's so annoying!; **silence, je ne veux pas vous e.!** quiet, I don't want to hear a sound from you!; **tu entends ce que je te dis?** do you hear me?; **tu entends ce que tu dis?** do you know what you're saying?; **elle a dû m'e. le lui dire** she must have overheard me telling him/her; **j'entends pleurer à côté** I can hear someone crying next door; **je l'entendis rire** I heard him/her laugh *or* laughing; **e. dire** to hear; **e. dire que…** to hear (it said) that…; **j'ai entendu dire qu'il était parti** I heard that he had left; **c'est la première fois que j'entends (dire) ça** that's the first I've heard of it; **je ne connais l'Islande que par ce que j'en ai entendu dire** I only know Iceland through what I've heard other people say about it; **on entend dire beaucoup de choses sur son compte** one hears many things about him/her; **e. qn dire qch** to hear sb say sth; **e. parler de** *(connaître l'existence de)* to hear of; *(être au courant de)* to hear about; **je ne veux pas en e. parler!** I don't want to hear (a word) about it!; **il ne veut pas e. parler d'informatique** he won't hear of computers; **j'ai entendu parler de leur maison** I've heard about their house; **je ne sais pas où il est, on n'entend plus parler de lui depuis un**

ens–ent

moment I don't know where he is, he's not been heard of for quite a while; **je ne veux plus e. parler de lui** I don't want to hear him mentioned again; **on entend beaucoup parler de lui ces temps-ci à la radio** we hear a lot about him on the radio at the moment; **on n'entend parler que de lui/de sa pièce** he's/his play's the talk of the town; **vous n'avez pas fini d'en e. parler!** you haven't heard the last of this!; **celui-là, il va e. parler de moi** *ou* **du pays!** he'll get a piece of my mind!; **je l'entends d'avance** *ou* **d'ici!** I can hear it already!; **on entendrait/on aurait entendu voler une mouche** you could hear/could have heard a pin drop; **j'aurai tout entendu!** whatever next?; *Fam* **j'en ai entendu de belles** *ou* **de bonnes** *ou* **des vertes et des pas mûres sur son compte** I've heard a thing or two about him/her; *Fam* **ce qu'il faut e.!, ce qu'il faut pas e.!** the things some people come out with!, the things you hear!; *Fam* **qu'entends-je, qu'ouïs-je, qu'acoustiqué-je?** *ou* **qu'entends-je, qu'ouïs-je, rêvé-je ou dors-je?** I can't believe my ears!

2 *(écouter)* to hear, to listen to; **aller e. un concert** to go to a concert; **essayer de se faire e.** to try to make oneself heard; **un bruit se fit e.** a noise was heard; **tout à coup, une fanfare se fit e. dans le village** suddenly, a fanfare sounded in the village; **il ne veut rien e.** he won't listen; **à les e. tout serait de ma faute** to hear them talk *or* according to them it's all my fault; **à vous e., il a eu tort** judging from *or* going by what you say, he was in the wrong; **e. raison** to see sense; **faire e. raison à qn** to make sb listen to reason, to bring sb to his/her senses; **il va m'e.!** I'll give him hell!; **si elle me pose encore un lapin, elle va m'e.!** if she stands me up once more, I'll give her a piece of my mind!

3 *(accepter → demande)* to agree to; *(→ vœu)* to grant; **nos prières ont été entendues** our prayers were answered

4 *Rel* **e. la messe** to attend *or* to hear mass; **e. une confession** to hear *or* to take a confession

5 *Jur (témoin)* to hear, to interview

6 *(comprendre)* to understand; **entend-il la plaisanterie?** can he take a joke?; **c'est comme ça que j'entends la vie!** this is the life!; **ce n'est pas ainsi qu'il l'entend** he doesn't see it that way *or* like that; **comment entendez-vous cette remarque?** how do you interpret this remark?; **il doit être bien entendu que…** it must be properly understood that…; **laisser e. qch** to insinuate *or* imply sth; **elle m'a laissé** *ou* **donné à e. que…** *(m'a fait croire)* she led me to believe that…; *(m'a fait comprendre)* she gave me to understand that…; **y entendez-vous quelque chose?** do you know anything about it?; *Vieilli* **je n'y entends rien** *ou* **goutte en politique** I don't understand a thing about politics; **il ne l'entend pas de cette oreille** he won't have any of it

7 *(apprendre)* to hear; **qu'est-ce que j'entends, tu n'as pas été sage?** what's this I hear *or* what did I hear, you didn't behave yourself?

8 *(vouloir dire)* to mean; **qu'entendez-vous par là?** what do you mean by that?; **un étranger, j'entends quelqu'un qui ne m'était pas connu** a stranger, I mean someone I didn't know; *Vieilli* **sans y e. malice** without meaning any harm (by it); *Vieilli* **elle n'y entendait pas malice** she never meant *or* intended any harm by it

9 *(vouloir)* to want, to intend; **e. faire qch** to intend *or* mean to do sth; **fais comme tu l'entends** do as you wish *or* please; **j'entends qu'on m'obéisse** I intend to *or* I mean to *or* I will be obeyed; **j'entends que vous veniez** I expect you to come; **je n'entends pas être exploité** I have no intention of being *or* I won't be exploited; **il entend bien partir demain** he's determined to go tomorrow; **elle voulait trouver du travail, mais lui ne l'entendait pas ainsi** she wanted to get a job, but he wouldn't hear of it

USAGE ABSOLU 1 *(percevoir par l'ouïe)* **est-ce qu'il entend?** can he hear properly?; **il entend mal** he is hard of hearing; **j'entends mal de l'oreille droite** my hearing's bad in the right ear; *Fam* **attends, j'ai mal entendu!** hold on, I don't think I heard you right!; **tu entends!** *(menace)* do you hear (me)!

2 *(comprendre)* **j'entends bien** I (do) understand; **certes, j'entends, mais…** certainly, I do understand, but…

▸**s'entendre VPR 1** *(être perçu)* to be heard; **cela s'entend de loin** you can hear it *or* it can be heard from far off

2 *(être utilisé → mot, expression)* to be heard; **cela s'entend encore dans la région** you can still hear it said *or* used around here

3 *(être compris)* to be understood; **ces chiffres s'entendent hors taxes** these figures do not include tax; **(cela) s'entend** *(c'est évident)* obviously, it's obvious, that much is clear; **après l'hiver, (cela) s'entend** when the winter is over, of course *or* it goes without saying

4 *(pouvoir s'écouter)* to hear each other *or* one another

5 *(s'accorder)* to agree; **s'e. avec** to reach an agreement with; **parvenir à s'e. avec qn sur qch** to come to an understanding *or* to reach an agreement with sb about sth; **s'e. directement avec qn** to come to a direct understanding with sb; **s'e. pour commettre un crime** to conspire to commit a crime; **s'e. sur un prix** to agree on a price; **entendons-nous bien** let's get this straight; **il faudrait vous e., il est venu ou il n'est pas venu?** get your story straight, did he come or not?

6 *(sympathiser)* to get on; **s'e. avec** to get on with; **ils ne s'entendent pas** they don't get on; **je crois que nous sommes faits pour nous e.** I think we were made to get on well together; **nous n'étions pas faits pour nous e.** we weren't suited to each other; **s'e. comme chien et chat** to fight like cat and dog; **s'e. comme larrons en foire** to be as thick as thieves

7 *(percevoir sa voix)* to hear oneself; **on ne s'entend plus tellement il y a de bruit** there's so much noise, you can't hear yourself think; **tu ne t'entends pas!** you should hear yourself (talking)!, if (only) you could hear yourself!

8 *(s'y connaître)* **il s'y entend en mécanique** he's good at *or* he knows (a lot) about mechanics; **s'y e. pour** to know how to; **s'y e. pour réparer un vélo** to know how to fix a bicycle; **elle s'y entend pour tout embrouiller!** she's a great one for getting into a mess!; **s'e. aux affaires** to have a good head for business

9 *(locution)* **quand je dis qu'il est grand, je m'entends, il est plus grand que moi** when I say he's tall I really mean he's taller than me

---

entendu, -e[ɑ̃tɑ̃dy] **ADJ 1** *(complice → air, sourire)* knowing; **hocher la tête d'un air e.** to nod knowingly **2** *(convenu)* agreed; **(c'est) e., je viendrai** all right *or* very well, I'll come; **c'est une affaire entendue** that's agreed *or* settled

enténébrer[18] [ɑ̃tenebre] *Littéraire* **VT** to darken, to fill with darkness

▸**s'enténébrer VPR** to grow dark *or* gloomy; **la plaine s'enténébrait** night was falling over the plain

entente [ɑ̃tɑ̃t] **NF 1** *(harmonie)* harmony; **entre eux c'est l'e. parfaite** they're in complete harmony (with each other); **il y a une bonne e. entre eux** they're on good terms (with each other); **la bonne/mauvaise e. qui règne dans la famille** the good/bad feeling that prevails in the family; **vivre en bonne e. avec** to live in harmony with

2 *Pol* agreement, understanding; **arriver à une e. sur** to come to an understanding *or* agreement over

3 *Écon* agreement, accord; **e. entre producteurs** agreement between producers; **e. industrielle** cartel, combine

4 *Hist* **l'E. cordiale** the Entente Cordiale

❑ **à double entente ADJ** ambiguous; **une expression à double e.** *(ambiguë)* an ambiguous expression; *(à connotation sexuelle)* a double entendre

enter[3] [ɑ̃te] **VT 1** *Constr* to scarf **2** *Hort* to graft

entéralgie[ɑ̃teralʒi] **NF** *Méd* enteralgia

entérectomie[ɑ̃terɛktɔmi] **NF** *Méd* enterectomy

entérinement[ɑ̃terinmɑ̃] **NM 1** *Jur* ratification **2** *(approbation → d'un usage)* adoption; *(→ d'un état de fait, d'une situation)* acceptance

entériner[3] [ɑ̃terine] **VT 1** *Jur* to ratify, to confirm **2** *(approuver → usage)* to adopt; *(→ état de fait, situation)* to go along with, to accept

entérique[ɑ̃terik] **ADJ** *Méd* enteric

entérite[ɑ̃terit] **NF** *Méd* enteritis

entérobactérie[ɑ̃terɔbakteri] **NF** *Biol* enterobacterium

entérocolite[ɑ̃terɔkɔlit] **NF** *Méd* enterocolitis

entérocoque [ɑ̃terɔkɔk] **NM** *Biol & Méd* enterococcus

entéroglucagon [ɑ̃terɔglykagɔ̃] **NM** *Biol* enteroglucagon

entérokinase[ɑ̃terɔkinaz] **NF** *Biol* enterokinase

entérolithe[ɑ̃terɔlit] **NM** *Méd* enterolith

entérorénal, -e, -aux, -ales [ɑ̃terɔrenal, -o] **ADJ** *Méd* enterorenal

entérotomie[ɑ̃terɔtɔmi] **NF** *Méd* enterotomy

entérovaccin [ɑ̃terɔvaksɛ̃] **NM** *Méd* enterovaccine

entérovirus[ɑ̃terovirys] **NM** *Méd* enterovirus

enterrage[ɑ̃tɛraʒ] **NM** *Métal* bedding

enterrement[ɑ̃tɛrmɑ̃] **NM 1** *(funérailles)* funeral; **cette soirée, c'était un e. de première classe** it was like watching paint dry, that party

2 *(ensevelissement)* burial

3 *(cortège)* funeral procession

4 *(abandon → d'une idée, d'une dispute)* burying; *(→ d'un projet)* shelving, laying aside; **e. de vie de garçon** *Br* stag night *or* party, *Am* bachelor party; **e. de vie de jeune fille** *Br* hen night *or* party, *Am* bachelorette party

❑ **d'enterrement ADJ** *(mine, tête)* gloomy, glum; **faire une tête d'e.** to wear a gloomy *or* long expression; **ne prends pas cette mine d'e.!** cheer up, it may never happen!

enterrer [4] [ɑ̃tere] **VT 1** *(ensevelir)* to bury; **être enterré vivant** to be buried alive

2 *(inhumer)* to bury, to inter; **vous nous enterrerez tous** you'll outlive us all; **e. sa vie de garçon** to have a *Br* stag night *or* party *or Am* bachelor party; **e. sa vie de jeune fille** to have a *Br* hen night *or* party *or Am* bachelorette party

3 *(oublier → scandale)* to bury, to hush up; *(→ souvenir, passé, querelle)* to bury, to forget (about); *(→ projet)* to shelve, to lay aside; **elle désire e. toute cette affaire** she wants the whole thing buried and forgotten

▸**s'enterrer VPR** to bury oneself; *Fig* to hide oneself away; **aller s'e. en province** to hide oneself away in the country

entêtant, -e[ɑ̃tɛtɑ̃, -ɑ̃t] **ADJ** heady

en-tête[ɑ̃tɛt] *(pl* **en-têtes)** **NM 1** *(sur du papier à lettres)* letterhead, heading

2 *Typ* head, header; **e. de facture** billhead; *Journ* **e. de colonne** column header

3 *Ordinat* header

❑ **à en-tête ADJ** *(papier, bristol)* headed; **papier à e. de la compagnie** company notepaper

❑ **en en-tête de PRÉP** at the head *or* top of; **mettez l'adresse en e. de la lettre** put the address at the top of the letter; **je veux le logo en e. de la feuille** I want the sheet headed with the logo

entêté, -e[ɑ̃tete] **ADJ** obstinate, stubborn

NM,F stubborn *or* obstinate person

entêtement [ɑ̃tɛtmɑ̃] **NM** stubbornness, obstinacy; **e. à faire qch** persistence in doing sth

entêter [4] [ɑ̃tete] **VT** to make dizzy; **ce parfum m'entête** I find this perfume quite intoxicating

▸**s'entêter VPR** to persist, to be persistent; **s'e. à faire qch** to persist in doing sth; **s'e. à écrire à qn** to persist in writing to sb; **elle s'entête à vouloir/à ne pas vouloir venir** she's set her mind on/against coming; **s'e. dans l'erreur/dans une opinion** to persist in one's error/in an opinion

enthalpie[ɑ̃talpi] **NF** *Phys* enthalpy

enthousiasmant, -e [ɑ̃tuzjasmɑ̃, -ɑ̃t] **ADJ** exciting, thrilling

enthousiasme[ɑ̃tuzjasm] **NM** enthusiasm, keenness; **être plein d'e., déborder d'e.** to be full of *or* to be bubbling with enthusiasm; **avec e.** enthusiastically; **parler de qch avec e.** to enthuse over sth; **faire qch sans e.** to do sth half-heartedly *or* without enthusiasm

enthousiasmer [3] [ɑ̃tuzjasme] **VT** to fill with enthusiasm; **cela n'avait pas l'air de l'e.** he/she

didn't seem very enthusiastic (about it); **il est revenu enthousiasmé** he came back full of *or* fired with enthusiasm

▶**s'enthousiasmer** VPR to be/become enthusiastic, to enthuse; **il s'enthousiasme facilement** he's easily carried away; **s'e. pour qn/ qch** to be enthusiastic about sb/sth

enthousiaste [ãtuzjast] ADJ enthusiastic, keen; **trop e.** overenthusiastic

NMF enthusiast; **c'est un grand e.** he's very keen!

enthymème [ãtimɛm] NM (*en logique*) enthymeme

entiché, -e [ãtiʃe] ADJ **être e. de** to be wild about

entichement [ãtiʃmã] NM *Littéraire* **1** (*amour*) infatuation; **mon e. pour lui n'a pas duré bien longtemps** my infatuation with him did not last very long **2** (*enthousiasme*) passion; **leur e. pour la Turquie** their passion for Turkey

enticher [3] [ãtiʃe] **s'enticher** VPR **s'e. de qn** (*s'amouracher de*) to become infatuated with sb; **s'e. de qch** (*s'enthousiasmer pour*) to become very keen on sth; **il s'est entiché de littérature espagnole** he's become very keen on Spanish literature

---

ENTIER, -ÈRE [ãtje, -ɛr]

ADJ whole **1, 5** ▪ entire **1, 6** ▪ absolute **2** ▪ complete **2** ▪ intact **3** ▪ intense **4**
NM integer

ADJ **1** (*complet*) whole, entire; **une semaine entière** a whole *or* an entire week; **la France entière** the whole of France; **pendant des journées/des heures entières** for days/hours on end; **manger un camembert e.** to eat a whole camembert; **dans le monde e.** in the whole world, throughout the world; **trois chapitres entiers lui sont consacrés** three whole chapters are devoted to him/her; **payer place entière** (*à un spectacle*) to pay the full price; (*en train ou en avion*) to pay full fare; **il a mangé le gâteau tout e.** he ate the whole (of the) cake; **je le voulais tout e. pour moi** I wanted him all to myself; **être tout e. à son travail** to be completely wrapped up *or* engrossed in one's work; **se donner tout e. à son travail** to devote oneself entirely to one's work

2 (*avant le nom*) (*en intensif*) absolute, complete; **il a mon entière confiance** I have complete confidence in him; **donner entière satisfaction à qn** to give sb complete satisfaction

3 (*après le verbe*) (*intact*) intact; **conserver sa réputation entière** to keep one's reputation intact; **le problème reste e.** the problem is no nearer solution *or* remains unsolved

4 (*absolu → personne*) intense; **c'est quelqu'un de très e.** he's/she's very intense

5 *Culin* (*lait*) whole, *Br* full-cream

6 *Vét* entire

NM *Math* (*nombre*) integer, whole number

◻ **dans son entier** ADV **as a whole; l'industrie automobile dans son e.** the car industry as a whole; **raconter une histoire dans son e.** to relate a story in its entirety

◻ **en entier** ADV **manger un gâteau en e.** to eat a whole *or* an entire cake; **je l'ai lu en e.** I read all of it, I read the whole of it, I read it right through; **il a fait ses devoirs en e.** he has done all (of) his homework

entiercement [ãtjɛrsəmã] NM *Jur* escrow

entiercer [16] [ãtjɛrse] VT *Jur* to place into escrow

entièrement [ãtjɛrmã] ADV entirely, completely; **le bureau a été e. refait** the office has been completely refitted; **la maison avait été construite e. en pierre de taille** the house had been made entirely of freestone; **je l'ai lu** I read all of it, I read the whole of it, I read it (all) through; **tu as e. raison** you're quite *or* absolutely right; **tu n'as pas e. tort** there's some truth in what you say; **ce n'est pas e. faux** it's not completely *or* entirely wrong, there's some truth in it; **il n'est pas e. mauvais** he's not all bad

entièreté [ãtjɛrte] NF entirety

entité [ãtite] NF **1** (*abstraction*) entity **2** *Méd* **e. morbide** morbid entity **3** *Jur* entity; **Largal est une e. juridique à part entière** Largal is a company in its own right **4** *Compta* item

entoilage [ãtwalaʒ] NM **1** (*technique → renforcement*) mounting on canvas; (*→ recouvrement*) covering with canvas; *Couture* stiffening with canvas **2** (*toile*) canvas cover

entoiler [3] [ãtwale] VT (*renforcer*) to mount on canvas; (*recouvrir*) to cover with canvas; *Couture* to stiffen with canvas; **carte entoilée** canvas-mounted map

entoir [ãtwar] NM *Hort* grafting-knife

entôlage [ãtolaʒ] NM *très Fam* fleecing (*of a prostitute's client*)

entôler [3] [ãtole] VT *très Fam* to fleece (*prostitute's client*)

entôleur, -euse [ãtolœr, -øz] NM,F *très Fam* (*gén*) swindler; (*prostitué(e)*) = prostitute who fleeces his/her client

entolome [ãtolom] NM *Bot* entoloma

entomologie [ãtomolɔʒi] NF *Entom* entomology

entomologique [ãtomolɔʒik] ADJ *Entom* entomologic, entomological

entomologiste [ãtomolɔʒist] NMF *Entom* entomologist

entomophage [ãtomofaʒ] ADJ *Entom, Zool & Bot* entomophagous

entomophile [ãtomofil] ADJ *Bot* entomophilous

entomostracé [ãtomostrase] NM *Entom* entomostracan

entonnage [ãtonaʒ] NM barrelling, casking

entonnaison [ãtonɛzõ] NF barrelling, casking

entonnement [ãtonmã] NM barrelling, casking

entonner [3] [ãtone] VT **1** (*hymne, air*) to strike up, to start singing; **e. les louanges de qn** to start singing sb's praises **2** (*vin*) to barrel, to cask

entonnoir [ãtonwar] NM **1** (*ustensile*) funnel **2** *Géog* sinkhole, swallow hole **3** (*trou d'obus*) shell-hole, crater **4** *Fam* (*locution*) **avoir un bon e.** to have hollow legs

entorse [ãtors] NF **1** *Méd* (*foulure*) sprain; **se faire une e. au poignet** to sprain one's wrist **2** (*exception*) infringement (**à** of); **faire une e. au règlement** to bend the rules; **faire une e. à la vérité** to twist *or* distort the truth; **ce serait une e. à mes principes** that would mean compromising my principles; **faire une e. à son régime** to break one's diet; **tu peux bien faire une petite e. à tes habitudes** you can surely make an exception

entortillement [ãtortijmã], **entortillage** [ãtortijaʒ] NM **1** (*action*) twisting, winding; (*d'un fil, du papier etc*) twisting, wrapping; (*d'un serpent, du lierre etc*) twisting, twining, coiling **2** (*état*) entwinement

entortiller [3] [ãtortije] VT **1** (*enrouler → ruban, papier*) to twist, to wrap (**autour de** round); (*→ bonbon etc*) to wrap (up) (**dans** in); **e. de la ficelle autour d'un bâton** to twist *or* to wrap a piece of string round a stick; **e. une mèche de cheveux autour de son doigt** to wind *or* to twist a strand of hair round one's finger

2 (*compliquer*) **être entortillé** to be convoluted; **e. une demande dans des explications fumeuses** to wrap up a request in woolly explanations

3 *Fam* (*tromper*) to hoodwink, to con; **il essaie de t'e.** he's trying to con you; **se faire e.** to be taken in

▶**s'entortiller** VPR **1** (*s'enrouler → lierre*) to twist, to wind (**autour de** round)

2 (*être empêtré*) to get caught *or* tangled up (**dans** in); **s'e. dans ses explications** to get tangled up in one's explanations

3 **il s'est entortillé les pieds dans le tapis** he got his feet entangled *or* tangled (up) in the carpet

entour [ãtur] NM *Vieilli* **à l'e. de** round (about); *Littéraire* **les entours de** the environs *or* surroundings of

entourage [ãturaʒ] NM **1** (*d'une personne*) circle; (*d'un roi, d'un président*) entourage; **e. familial** family circle; **on dit dans l'e. du Président que...** sources close to the President say that...; **il s'entend bien avec son e.** he gets on well with the people around him

2 (*bordure → d'une ouverture, d'un parterre de fleurs etc*) border; (*→ d'un bijou*) setting; **miniature avec un e. de perles** miniature set in pearls

entouré, -e [ãture] ADJ **1** (*populaire*) **une actrice**

très entourée an actress who is very popular *or* who is the centre of attraction **2** (*assisté*) **e. d'amis** surrounded by friends; **heureusement, elle est très entourée** fortunately, she has a lot of friends around her **3** (*enveloppé*) **e. de mystère** wrapped *or* shrouded in mystery

entourer [3] [ãture] VT **1** (*encercler → terrain, mets*) to surround; (*armée*) to encircle, to surround; **un châle entourait ses épaules** a shawl was wrapped around her shoulders; **e. un champ de barbelés** to surround a field with barbed wire, to put barbed wire around a field; **e. un mot de ou en rouge** to circle a word in red; **e. qn de ses bras** to put *or* to wrap one's arms around sb

2 (*être autour de*) to surround; **le monde qui nous entoure** the world around us *or* that surrounds us; **les gens qui vous entourent** the people around *or* about you; **un rang de perles entourait son cou** a string of pearls encircled her neck, she had a string of pearls round her neck

3 (*graviter autour de → sujet: foule, conseillers*) to surround, to be around

4 (*soutenir → malade, veuve*) to rally round; **au moment de son divorce, sa famille l'a beaucoup entouré** his family rallied round *or* supported him at the time of his divorce; **e. un ami de son affection** to surround a friend with affection; **e. qn de soins/respect** to lavish attention on sb/show respect to sb

▶**s'entourer** VPR **s'e. de** (*placer autour de soi*) to surround oneself with; **s'e. d'objets d'art/d'excellents musiciens** to surround oneself with works of art/with excellent musicians; **s'e. de mystère** to shroud oneself in mystery; **s'e. de beaucoup de précautions** to take elaborate precautions

USAGE ABSOLU **savoir s'e.** to know all the right people

entouroupe [ãturlup] NF *Fam* nasty *or* dirty trick; **faire une e. à qn** to play a dirty trick on sb, *Br* to do the dirty on sb, *Am* to do sb dirty

entourlouper [3] [ãturlupe] VT *Fam* **e. qn** to play a dirty trick on sb, *Br* to do the dirty on sb, *Am* to do sb dirty

entourloupette [ãturlupɛt] NF *Fam* nasty *or* dirty trick; **faire une e. à qn** to play a dirty trick on sb, *Br* to do the dirty on sb, *Am* to do sb dirty

entournure [ãturnyr] NF *Couture* armhole

ENTR-, ENTRE- [ãtr] PRÉF

This prefix, which has no equivalent in English, has several distinct uses.

● Added to a verb or a noun, it can convey the idea of RECIPROCITY. The verbal use is often translated by **each other** or **one another**, eg:
  ils s'entraident they help each other; **ils se sont presque entretués** they almost killed one another; **une entrevue** a meeting, an interview

● Added to a verb, **entr-** or **entre-** can mean HARDLY, SLIGHTLY or CURSORILY, eg:
  la porte était entrebâillée *ou* **entrouverte** the door was ajar, the door was half-open; **je l'ai entraperçue dans la rue** I caught a glimpse of her in the street

● Added to a noun, the prefix refers to something IN THE MIDDLE OF two things, eg:
  l'entrejambe the crotch; **une entrecôte** an entrecôte steak (from between the ribs); **à l'entresol** on the mezzanine floor (between the ground and first floors)

---

entracte [ãtrakt] NM **1** *Cin & Théât Br* interval, *Am* intermission; **à** *ou* **pendant l'e.** *Br* in the interval, *Am* during the intermission; **un e. de 15 minutes** a 15-minute *Br* interval *or Am* intermission **2** (*spectacle*) interlude, entr'acte **3** (*pause*) break, interlude

entraide [ãtrɛd] NF mutual aid; *Admin* **comité d'e.** support committee

entraider [4] [ãtrede] **s'entraider** VPR to help one another *or* each other

entrailles [ãtraj] NFPL **1** *Anat & Zool* entrails, guts; **être pris aux e.** (*être ému*) to be stirred to the depths of one's soul; **ne pas avoir d'e.** to be heartless **2** *Littéraire* (*ventre*) womb **3** (*profondeur → de la terre*) depths, bowels; (*→ d'un piano, d'un navire*) innards

entr'aimer [4] [ɑ̃treme] **s'entr'aimer** VPR *Littéraire* to love one another *or* each other

entrain [ɑ̃trɛ̃] NM **1** *(fougue)* spirit; **avoir beaucoup d'e., être plein d'e.** to be full of life *or* energy; **retrouver son e.** to cheer up *or* to brighten up again; **il faut y mettre un peu plus d'e.** you need to put a little more spirit into it

2 *(animation)* liveliness; **musique pleine d'e.** lively music; **la fête manquait d'e.** the party wasn't very lively

❑ **avec entrain** ADV with gusto, enthusiastically; **manger avec e.** to eat with gusto; **travailler avec e.** to work with a will

❑ **sans entrain** ADV half-heartedly, unenthusiastically

entraînable [ɑ̃trɛnabl] ADJ **facilement e.** easily influenced

entraînant, -e [ɑ̃trɛnɑ̃, -ɑ̃t] ADJ *(chanson)* catchy, swinging; *(rythme)* swinging, lively; *(style, éloquence)* rousing, stirring

entraînement [ɑ̃trɛnmɑ̃] NM **1** *Sport (d'un sportif)* training, coaching; *(d'un cheval)* training; **un e.** a training session, a work-out; **des centaines d'heures d'e.** hundreds of hours of training; **suivre un e.** to follow a training programme; **avoir de l'e.** to be well trained; **manquer d'e.** to be out of training; **se blesser à l'e.** to hurt oneself while training *or* during a training session; **il a marqué un but comme à l'e.** he scored a textbook goal

2 *(habitude)* practice; **il ne faut pas de technique spéciale, juste un peu d'e.** there's no need for any special skills, just some practice; **toi qui as de l'e., fais-le** you've had a lot of practice at this type of thing, you do it

3 *Tech* drive; **e. à chaîne/par courroie** chain/belt drive; **e. à friction** *(d'une imprimante)* friction feed; **e. du papier** *(d'une imprimante)* paper advance; **e. à picots** *ou* **à traction** *(d'une imprimante)* tractor drive *or* feed

4 *Littéraire (des passions)* force; **céder à des entraînements** to get carried away

❑ **d'entraînement** ADJ **1** *Équitation & Sport (séance, matériel)* training *(avant n)*; **match d'e.** practice game; **terrain d'e.** training *or* practice ground; **camp d'e. militaire** military training camp

2 *Tech* drive *(avant n)*; **arbre d'e.** drive shaft

entraîner [4] [ɑ̃trene] VT **1** *(emporter)* to carry along, to sweep along; *Fig* to carry away; **le torrent entraînait tout sur son passage** the torrent swept everything along with it; **entraînés par la foule** swept along by the crowd; **les nageurs se sont fait e. par le courant** the swimmers were carried away by the current; **se laisser e. par la musique** to let oneself be carried away by the music; **cette discussion nous entraînerait trop loin** that discussion would carry *or* take us too far

2 *(tirer → wagons)* to pull, to haul; *(actionner → bielle)* to drive; **poulie entraînée par une courroie** belt-driven pulley

3 *(conduire)* to drag (along); **e. qn quelque part** to drag *or* take sb off somewhere; **il m'a entraîné au fond de la salle** he dragged me (off) to the back of the room; **un étranger peut vous e. dans les bois** a stranger might entice you into the woods; **e. qn dans un piège** to lure sb into a trap; **c'est lui qui m'a entraîné dans cette affaire** he's the one who dragged me into this mess; **il s'est fait e. dans cette histoire par un sale type** he got dragged into the affair by a really nasty guy; **se laisser e.** to allow oneself to be led astray; **se laisser e. dans une polémique** to let oneself be dragged into a controversy; **il a entraîné son associé dans sa faillite** he dragged his partner down with him when he went bankrupt; **ce sont les grands qui les entraînent à faire des bêtises** it's the older children who encourage them to be naughty; **e. qn dans sa chute** to pull *or* to drag sb down in one's fall; *Fig* to pull sb down with one

4 *(occasionner)* to bring about, to lead to, to involve; **cela risque d'e. de gros frais** this is likely to involve heavy expenditure; **cela entraînera un retard** it will involve *or* lead to delay; **sa victoire entraînerait la fin de la démocratie** his/her victory would lead to *or* mean the end of democracy

5 *Équitation & Sport (équipe, boxeur, sportif)* to train, to coach; *(cheval)* to train; **e. qn à la natation** to coach sb in swimming; **e. qn à faire qch** to train sb to do sth

▸**s'entraîner** VPR *Sport* to train; **je m'entraîne tous les matins** I train every morning; **s'e. pour les** *ou* **en vue des jeux Olympiques** to be in training *or* to train for the Olympic Games; **s'e. au saut à la perche** to be in training *or* to train for the pole vault; **s'e. à faire qch** *(gén)* to teach oneself to do sth; *Sport* to train oneself to do sth

entraîneur, -euse [ɑ̃trɛnœr, -øz] NM,F **1** *(d'un cheval)* trainer; *(d'un sportif)* trainer, coach; *(d'une équipe de foot)* manager, coach; *Fig* **e. d'hommes** leader of men **2** *(d'un cycliste)* pacemaker

❑ **entraîneuse** NF **entraîneuse (de bar)** hostess *(in a bar)*

entrait [ɑ̃trɛ] NM *Constr* **1** *(d'une charpente en bois)* tie-beam, stringer, binder **2** *(d'une charpente en fer)* tie-rod

entrant, -e [ɑ̃trɑ̃, -ɑ̃t] ADJ incoming; *(fonctionnaire)* newly appointed; *(représentant parlementaire)* newly elected; **les élèves entrants** the new pupils

NM,F **1** *Sport* substitute **2** *(celui qui entre)* **les entrants et les sortants** those who go in and those who come out

entrapercevoir, entr'apercevoir [52] [ɑ̃trapɛrsəvwar] VT to catch a (fleeting) glimpse of

entrave [ɑ̃trav] NF **1** *(obstacle)* hindrance, obstacle; **e. à la circulation** hindrance to traffic; **e. à la liberté/à la bonne marche de la justice** interference with freedom/with the due process of the law; **cette mesure est une e. au libre-échange** this measure is an obstacle *or* a hindrance to free trade

2 *(chaîne → d'esclave)* chain, fetter, shackle; *(→ de cheval)* hobble, shackle, fetter; **mettre des entraves à un cheval** to fetter a horse

❑ **sans entraves** ADJ unfettered

entravé, -e [ɑ̃trave] ADJ **1** *Couture* hobble *(avant n)* **2** *Ling* checked

entraver [3] [ɑ̃trave] VT **1** *(gêner → circulation)* to hold up **2** *(contrecarrer → initiative, projet)* to hinder, to hamper, to get in the way of; **e. une négociation** to hamper negotiations **3** *(attacher → esclave)* to put in chains; *(→ cheval)* to hobble, to fetter, to shackle **4** *très Fam (comprendre)* to understand■, to get; **j'entrave que dalle** it beats me, I don't get it at all

ENTRE [ɑ̃tr] PRÉP **1** *(dans l'espace)* between; *(dans)* in; *(à travers)* through, between; **la distance e. la Terre et la Lune** the distance between the Earth and the Moon; **Lyon est à la cinquième place, e. Marseille et Bordeaux** Lyons is in fifth place, between Marseilles and Bordeaux; **e. de hautes murailles** between high walls; **e. ces murs** within these walls; **serrer qn e. ses bras** to clasp sb in one's arms, to hug sb; **tenir un enfant e. ses bras** to hold a child in one's arms; **tenir qch e. ses mains** to hold sth in one's hands; **tomber e. les mains de l'ennemi** to fall into the enemy's hands; **une phrase e. crochets** a sentence in square brackets; **ce sont deux moitiés de génoise avec du chocolat e.** it's two halves of sponge cake with chocolate in between; **il passa la main e. les barreaux** he put his hand through the bars; **le soleil passait e. les interstices des persiennes** the sun was filtering through the slats of the shutters; **l'aiguille glissa e. ses doigts** the needle slipped through his/her fingers

2 *(dans le temps)* between; **e. deux et trois (heures)** between two and three (o'clock); **e. 1830 et 1914** between 1830 and 1914; **il y a 15 ans de différence e. les deux frères** there is a 15-year age gap between the two brothers; **j'ai réussi à le voir e. deux réunions** I managed to see him between two meetings; **e. le travail et le transport, je n'ai plus de temps à moi** between work and travel, I haven't any time left

3 *(indiquant un état intermédiaire)* **une couleur e. le jaune et le vert** a colour between yellow and green; **elle était e. le rire et les larmes** she didn't know whether to laugh or cry; **pris e. le désir de le frapper et celui de l'embrasser** wanting both to hit him and kiss him; **le cidre est doux ou sec? – e. les deux** is the cider sweet or dry? – it's between the two *or* in between; *Fam* **c'était bien? – e. les deux** was it good? – so-so

4 *(exprimant une approximation)* between; **il y a e. 10 et 12 kilomètres** it's between 10 and 12 kilometres; **les températures oscilleront e. 10° et 15°** temperatures will range from 10° to 15°; **ils ont invité e. 15 et 20 personnes** they've invited 15 to 20 people

5 *(parmi)* among; **hésiter e. plusieurs solutions/routes/robes** to hesitate between several solutions/roads/dresses; **choisir une solution e. plusieurs autres** to choose one solution among *or* from several others; **partagez le gâteau e. les enfants** *(entre deux)* share the cake between the children; *(entre plusieurs)* share the cake among the children; **l'un d'e. vous** one of you; **plusieurs d'e. nous** several of us; **certains d'e. eux** some of them *or* among them; **ceux d'e. vous qui désireraient venir** those among you *or* of you who'd like to come; **lequel est le plus âgé d'e. vous?** who is the oldest amongst you?; **d'e. toutes ses sonates, c'est celle que je préfère** of all his sonatas, that's the one I like most; **tu as le choix e. trois réponses** you've got a choice of three answers; **choisir e. plusieurs candidats** to choose among *or* between several candidates; **un jour e. mille** a day in a thousand; **je me souvenais de ce jour e. tous** I remembered that day above all others; **je le reconnaîtrais e. tous** *(personne)* I'd know him anywhere; *(objet)* I couldn't fail to recognize it; **un homme dangereux e. tous** a most dangerous man; **brave e. les braves** bravest of the brave

6 *(dans un groupe)* **passer une soirée e. amis** to spend an evening among friends; **parle, nous sommes e. amis** you can talk, we're among friends *or* we're all friends here; **on se réunit e. anciens combattants** we've got together a gathering of veterans; **nous ferons une petite fête, juste e. nous** *(à deux)* we'll have a small party, just the two of us; *(à plusieurs)* we'll have a party, just among ourselves; **nous dînerons e. nous** we'll have dinner alone *or* by ourselves; **ils ont tendance à rester e. eux** they tend to keep themselves to themselves; **e. nous, il n'a pas tort** *(à deux)* between you and me, he's right; *(à plusieurs)* between us, he's right; **e. vous et moi** between you and me

7 *(indiquant une relation)* between; **le combat e. les deux adversaires a été sanglant** the fight between the two enemies was bloody; **les clans se battent e. eux** the clans fight (against) each other, there are fights between the clans; **ils se sont mis d'accord e. eux** they agreed among(st) themselves; **qu'y a-t-il e. vous?** what is there between you?; **mais qu'y a-t-il e. eux, exactement?** but what's (going on) between them exactly?; **il n'y a plus rien e. nous** there's nothing between us any more; **l'amitié e. ces deux hommes** the friendship between these two men; **la différence e. toi et moi** the difference between you and me; **qu'est-ce qu'il y a de semblable e. lui et moi?** what similarities are there between him and me?; **il y a une analogie e. ces deux situations** there's an analogy between these situations

❑ **entre autres** ADV among others; **sa fille, e. autres, n'est pas venue** his daughter, for one *or* among others, didn't come; **sont exposés, e. autres, des objets rares, des œuvres de jeunesse du peintre, etc** the exhibition includes, among other things, rare objects, examples of the artist's early work etc

❑ **entre quat'z'yeux** ADV *Fam* **il faut que je te parle e. quat'z'yeux** I've got to talk to you in private■

entre- *voir* **entr-**

entrebâillement [ɑ̃trəbajmɑ̃] NM **dans/par l'e. de la porte** in/through the half-open door

entrebâiller [3] [ɑ̃trəbaje] VT *(porte, fenêtre)* to half-open; **laisse la porte entrebâillée** leave the door half-open *or* ajar; **la porte était entrebâillée** the door was ajar *or* half-open

entrebâilleur [ɑ̃trəbajœr] NM door chain

entre-bande [ɑ̃trəbɑ̃d] *(pl* **entre-bandes***)* NF *Tex* coloured end-list, end-selvedge

entrechat [ɑ̃trəʃa] NM **1** *(en danse)* entrechat **2**

Hum (bond) leap, spring; **faire des entrechats** to leap about

entrechoquement [ɑ̃trəʃɔkmɑ̃] NM *(de verres)* clinking; *(d'épées)* clashing; *(des dents)* chattering

entrechoquer [3] [ɑ̃trəʃɔke] VT to knock or to bang together; **e. des verres** to chink glasses
  ▶**s'entrechoquer** VPR1 *(se heurter)* to knock or bang against one another; *(verres)* to clink (together); *(épées)* to clash (together); *(dents)* to chatter
  2 *(affluer → images, mots)* to jostle together; **elle parle tellement vite que les mots s'entrechoquent** the words come tumbling out when she speaks

entrecolonnement [ɑ̃trəkɔlɔnmɑ̃] NM *Archit* intercolumniation

entrecôte [ɑ̃trəkot] NF*Culin* entrecôte (steak); **e. minute** minute steak

entrecoupé, -e [ɑ̃trəkupe] ADJ *(voix)* broken; **d'une voix entrecoupée** with a catch in one's voice, in a broken voice

entrecouper [3] [ɑ̃trəkupe] VT **1** *(interrompre → discours, voyage, représentation etc)* to interrupt *(de* by *or* with); **la conversation a été entrecoupée de sonneries de téléphone** the phone kept interrupting the conversation; **une voix entrecoupée de sanglots** a voice broken by sobs **2** *(émailler)* **e. qch de** to intersperse or to pepper sth with
  ▶**s'entrecouper** VPRto intersect

entrecroisement [ɑ̃trəkrwazmɑ̃] NM *(de lignes)* intersecting, (criss)crossing; *(de fils)* intertwining, interlacing

entrecroiser [3] [ɑ̃trəkrwaze] VT*(lignes)* to intersect, to (criss)cross; *(fils)* to intertwine, to interlace
  ▶**s'entrecroiser** VPR *(de lignes, de routes)* to intersect, to (criss)cross; *(de fils)* to intertwine, to interlace

entrecuisse [ɑ̃trəkɥis] NMcrotch, *Br* crutch

entre-déchirer [3] [ɑ̃trədeʃire] **s'entre-déchirer** VPR*aussi Fig* to tear one another to pieces

entre-détruire [98] [ɑ̃trœdetrɥir] **s'entre-détruire** VPRto destroy one another

entre-deux [ɑ̃trədø] NM INV **1** *(dans l'espace)* space between, interspace **2** *(dans le temps)* intervening period, period in between **3** *Sport* jump ball **4** *Couture* **e. de dentelle** lace insert **5** *(meuble)* console table *(placed between two windows)*

entre-deux-guerres [ɑ̃trədøgɛr] NM INV OU NF INV *Hist* **l'e.** the interwar period; **la mode de l'e.** fashion of the interwar period

Entre-deux-Mers [ɑ̃trədømɛr] NM *Géog* **l'E.** the Entre-Deux-Mers area

entre-deux-mers [ɑ̃trədømɛr] NM INV*Culin (vin)* Entre-Deux-Mers

entre-dévorer [3] [ɑ̃trədevɔre] **s'entre-dévorer** VPR to devour one another; *Fig* to tear one another to pieces

ENTRÉE [ɑ̃tre]

entrance **1, 4, 5** ▪ entry **1–4, 8–10, 13, 14** ▪ admission **2, 3** ▪ hall **5** ▪ ticket **6** ▪ starter **7** ▪ input **8** ▪ cue **11**	

NF**1** *(arrivée)* entrance, entry; **l'e. au port du navire** the ship's entry into the port; **l'e. en gare du train** the entry of the train into the station; **à l'e. en Italie** when crossing into Italy; **à son e., tout le monde s'est levé** everybody stood up as he/ she walked in or entered; **faire une e. triomphale/discrète** to enter triumphantly/discreetly; **faire son e. dans une pièce** to make one's entrance into a room; **faire son e. dans le monde** *(demoiselle)* to come out into society, to make one's debut; **e. en action** coming into play; **dès son e. en fonction, il devra…** as soon as he takes up office, he will have to…; **l'e. en guerre de la France** France's entry into or France's joining the war; **depuis l'e. en guerre du pays** since the country entered the war; **il a marqué un but dès son e. en jeu** he scored a goal as soon as he entered the game; **e. en matière** *(d'un livre)* introduction; **e. en possession** taking of possession; **e. en scène** entrance; **au moment de mon e. en scène** as I made my entrance or as I walked

onto the stage; *Jur* **l'e. en vigueur d'une loi** the promulgation of a law; **date d'e. en vigueur** commencement
  2 *(adhésion)* entry, admission; **l'e. de la Finlande dans l'Union européenne** Finland's entry into the European Union; **au moment de l'e. à l'université** when students start university; **e. dans l'armée/le club/le parti** joining the army/ club/party; **depuis mon e. au parti** since I joined or became a member of the party; **son e. dans les ordres** his being ordained or taking holy orders
  3 *(accès)* entry, admission; **e. à l'hôpital** admission into hospital; **se voir refuser l'e. d'une discothèque** to be refused admission or entry to a nightclub; **l'e. est gratuite pour les enfants** there is no admission charge for children; **e.** *(sur panneau)* way in; **e. libre** *(dans un magasin)* no obligation to buy; *(dans un musée)* free admission; **e. interdite** *(dans un local)* no entry, keep out; *(pour empêcher le passage)* no way in, no access; *(dans un bois)* no trespassing; **e. interdite à tout véhicule** *(sur un panneau)* pedestrians only; **e. réservée au personnel** *(dans une entreprise)* staff only; **avoir ses entrées auprès de qn** to have (privileged) access to sb; **avoir ses entrées dans un club** to be a welcome visitor to a club
  4 *(voie d'accès → à un immeuble)* entrance (door) *(de* to); *(→ à un tunnel, une grotte)* entry, entrance, mouth; **e. des artistes** stage door; **e. des fournisseurs** tradesmen's entrance; **e. principale** main entrance; **e. de service** service or tradesmen's entrance
  5 *(vestibule → dans un lieu public)* entrance (hall), lobby; *(→ dans une maison)* hall, hallway
  6 *(billet)* ticket; *(spectateur)* spectator; *(visiteur)* visitor; **je te paie ton e.** I'll pay for you or buy your ticket; **nombre d'entrées par salle** number of tickets sold per auditorium; **le film a fait deux millions d'entrées** two million people have seen the film; **on n'a fait que 300 entrées** we sold only 300 tickets
  7 *Culin Br* starter, *Am* appetizer; *(dans un repas de gala)* **je prendrai une salade en e.** I'll have a salad to start with
  8 *Ordinat (processus)* input, entry; *(information)* entry; *(touche)* enter (key); *(de caractère etc)* entering; **e. des données** *(gén)* inputting of data, data input; *(par saisie)* keying in or keyboarding of data; **données d'e.** input (data); **e. (par le) clavier** keyboard input; **e. (à partir du) scanneur** scanned input; **e. de données à distance** remote data entry; **e. de gamme** entry level; **e. de papier** paper input; **e. opérateur** operator input
  9 *(inscription)* entry; *(dans un dictionnaire)* headword, *Am* entry word; **faire une e. dans un registre** to enter an item into a register
  10 *Com & Douanes* entry; *(de marchandises)* importation, import; **droit d'e.** import duty; **e. en douane** inward customs clearance; **e. en franchise** free import
  11 *(réplique)* cue; **ne rate pas ton e.** don't miss your cue
  12 *Tech (ouverture)* **e. d'air** air inlet; **e. de clef** keyhole; *Rad* **e. de poste** lead-in
  13 *Mus* entry
  14 *Compta (dans un livre de comptes)* entry
  □ **entrées** NFPL *Compta* takings, receipts; **entrées d'argent** cash inflow, cash received
  □ **à l'entrée de** PRÉP**1** *(dans l'espace)* at the entrance or on the threshold of; **à l'e. de la grotte** at the entrance or mouth of the cave
  2 *Littéraire (dans le temps)* at the beginning of; **à l'e. du printemps** at the beginning of spring; **à l'e. de la vie** at the dawn of life
  □ **d'entrée, d'entrée de jeu** ADVfrom the outset, right from the beginning

entrée-sortie, entrée/sortie [ɑ̃tresɔrti] *(pl* **entrées-sorties, entrées/sorties)** NF*Ordinat* input-output, input/output; **entrée/sortie parallèles** parallel input/output

entrefaites [ɑ̃trəfɛt] NFPL**sur ces e.** at that moment or juncture

entrefenêtre [ɑ̃trəfənɛtr] NM *(pan de mur)* pier *(between two windows)*

entrefer [ɑ̃trəfɛr] NM*Élec* air gap

entrefilet [ɑ̃trəfilɛ] NM *Journ* short piece, paragraph *(in a newspaper)*; **l'affaire a eu droit à un e.** there was a paragraph or there were a few lines in the newspaper about it

entregent [ɑ̃trəʒɑ̃] NMavoir de l'e. to know how to handle people

entr'égorger [17] [ɑ̃tregɔrʒe] **s'entr'égorger** VPR to cut one another's throats

entre-haïr [33] [sɑ̃trair] **s'entre-haïr** VPR *Littéraire* to hate one another

entre-heurter [3] [sɑ̃trœrte] **s'entre-heurter** VPR *Littéraire* to collide, to bump or to run into each other

entrejambe [ɑ̃trəʒɑ̃b] NMcrotch; **hauteur de l'e.** inside leg measurement

entrelacement [ɑ̃trəlasmɑ̃] NM intertwining, interlacing

entrelacer [16] [ɑ̃trəlase] VT to intertwine, to interlace; **initiales entrelacées** intertwined initials; **les mains entrelacées** with one's fingers entwined; *Ordinat* **écran entrelacé** interlaced screen
  ▶**s'entrelacer** VPRto intertwine, to interlace

entrelacs [ɑ̃trəla] NM*Archit* tracery

entrelardé, -e [ɑ̃trəlarde] ADJ*Culin (rôti)* larded; *(tranche de poitrine)* streaky

entrelarder [3] [ɑ̃trəlarde] VT **1** *Culin* to lard **2** *(entrecouper)* **e. qch de** to intersperse or to interlard sth with

entremêlement [ɑ̃trəmɛlmɑ̃] NM intermingling *(UNCOUNT)*, entanglement

entremêler [4] [ɑ̃trəmele] VT**1** *(mêler → rubans, fleurs)* to intermingle, to mix together **2** *(entrecouper)* **paroles entremêlées de sanglots** words broken with sobs
  ▶**s'entremêler** VPR *(fils, cheveux)* to become entangled; *(idées, intrigues)* to become intermingled

entremet*etc voir* **entremettre**

entremets [ɑ̃trəmɛ] NM*Culin* entremets

entremetteur, -euse [ɑ̃trəmɛtœr, -øz] NM,F **1** *Vieilli (intermédiaire)* mediator, go-between **2** *Péj (dans des affaires galantes)* procurer, f procuress

'Chez l'entremetteuse (La Courtisane)' *Vermeer* 'The Procuress (The Courtesan)'

entremettre [84] [ɑ̃trəmɛtr] **s'entremettre** VPR **1** *(à bon escient)* to intervene; **s'e. dans une querelle** to intervene in a quarrel; **s'e. entre deux délégations** to act as mediator or to mediate between two delegations **2** *(à mauvais escient)* to interfere

entremise [ɑ̃trəmiz] NFintervention, intervening *(UNCOUNT)*; **offrir son e.** to offer to act as mediator
  □ **par l'entremise de** PRÉPthrough

entremit*etc voir* **entremettre**

entre-nerf [ɑ̃trənɛr] *(pl* **entre-nerfs)** NMpanel

entre-nœud [ɑ̃trənø] *(pl* **entre-nœuds)** NM *Bot* internode

entre-nuire [97] [ɑ̃trənɥir] **s'entre-nuire** VPR*Littéraire* to harm each other, to do each other harm

entrepont [ɑ̃trəpɔ̃] NM*Naut* 'tweendecks; **voyager dans l'e.** to travel steerage or in steerage class

entreposage [ɑ̃trəpozaʒ] NM*(gén)* storing, storage, warehousing; *Douanes (douane)* bonding

entreposé, -e [ɑ̃trəpoze] ADJ**marchandises entreposées** *(en entrepôt)* warehoused goods; *Douanes (en douane)* bonded goods

entreposer [3] [ɑ̃trəpoze] VT**1** *(mettre en entrepôt)* to store, to put in a warehouse, to warehouse **2** *Douanes (en douane)* to bond, to put in bond **3** *(déposer)* to leave; **e. des livres chez un ami** to leave some books with a friend

entreposeur [ɑ̃trəpozœr] NM**1** *(qui tient un entrepôt)* warehouseman; *Douanes* officer in charge of a bonded store **2** *(commerçant)* = wholesaler selling goods under a government monopoly

entrepositaire [ɑ̃trəpozitɛr] NMF *(gén)* warehouse keeper; *Douanes (douane)* bonder

entrepôt [ɑ̃trəpo] NM **1** *(bâtiment)* warehouse; **marchandises en e.** warehoused goods, goods in storage; *Douanes* goods in bond; **mettre des marchandises en e.** to put goods into storage;

Douanes to bond goods; *Douanes* **e. de douane** bonded warehouse; **e. frigorifique** cold store; **e. de stockage** warehouse; **e. privé/public** private/public bonded warehouse

2 *(ville, port)* entrepôt, free port

entreprenait *etc voir* **entreprendre**

entreprenant, -e [ɑ̃trəprənɑ̃, -ɑ̃t] **ADJ 1** *(dynamique)* enterprising **2** *(hardi)* forward

entreprenaute [ɑ̃trəprənot] **NM** dot com entrepreneur

entreprendre [79] [ɑ̃trəprɑ̃dr] **VT 1** *(commencer → lecture, étude)* to begin, to start (on); *(→ croisière, carrière)* to set out on *or* upon; *(→ projet)* to undertake, to set about; **e. la rédaction d'une thèse** to begin *or* to start writing a thesis; **e. des études de droit** to begin studying law, to undertake law studies; **e. de faire qch** to undertake to do sth

2 *(séduire → femme)* to make (amorous) advances towards

3 *(interpeller → passant)* to buttonhole; **e. qn sur qch** to engage sb in conversation about sth

entrepreneur, -euse [ɑ̃trəprənœr, -øz] **NM,F 1** *Constr* contractor; **e. en bâtiment** *ou* **construction** (building) contractor, builder **2** *(chef d'entreprise)* entrepreneur; **petit e.** small businessman; **e. de roulage, e. de transport** haulage contractor, carrier; **e. de pompes funèbres** funeral director, undertaker

entrepreneurial, -e, -aux, -ales [ɑ̃trəprənœrjal, -o] **ADJ** entrepreneurial

entrepreneuriat [ɑ̃trəprənœrja] **NM** entrepreneurship

entreprennent *etc voir* **entreprendre**

entrepris, -e[1] [ɑ̃trəpri, -iz] **PP** *voir* **entreprendre**

entreprise[2] [ɑ̃trəpriz] **NF 1** *Com & Écon (société)* company, business, firm; **monter une e.** to set up a business; **e. agricole** farm; **e. commerciale** business concern; **e. commune** joint venture; *Mktg* **e. dauphin** runner-up company; *Mktg* **e. défendable** tenable firm; *Mktg* **e. dominante** dominant firm; **e. d'État** state-owned *or Br* public company; **e. exportatrice** export company; **e. familiale** family business *or* firm; **e. industrielle** industrial concern; *Mktg* **e. innovatrice** innovator, innovating company; **e. d'investissement** investment company; **e. marginale** firm with only a marginal profit; **e. de messageries** parcel delivery company; **e. multinationale** multinational company; **e. en participation** joint venture; **e. privée** private company; **e. publique** public corporation; **e. de pompes funèbres** funeral director's, undertaker's; **e. de services** service company; **e. sociale** social enterprise; *Mktg* **e. à la traîne** trailing firm; **e. de transports** transport company; **e. de travail intérimaire** temp agency; **e. de travaux publics** civil engineering firm; **e. unipersonnelle à responsabilité limitée** trader with limited liability; **e. d'utilité publique** public utility company; **e. de vente par correspondance** mail-order company; **junior e.** = company set up by students to gain experience in business; **petite/moyenne/grosse e.** small/medium-sized/large firm

2 *(monde des affaires)* **l'e.** business, the business world

3 *(régime économique)* enterprise; **l'e. publique/privée** public/private enterprise

4 *(initiative)* undertaking, initiative

5 *Jur (louage)* contracting; **travail à l'e.** contract work, work by *or* on contract; **mettre qch à l'e.** to put sth out to contract *or* tender

❑ **entreprises NFPL** *Hum (avances)* (amorous) advances

❑ **d'entreprise ADJ** *(matériel, véhicule)* company *(avant n)*

ENTRER [3] [ɑ̃tre]

VI to enter **A1, 3, 6, 7** ■ to go to **A2** ■ to fit **A4** ■ to sink in **A5** ■ to log in **A8** ■ to start **B**
VT to bring in **1** ■ to input **4**

VI *(aux être)* **A.** *PÉNÉTRER* **1** *(personne → gén)* to enter; *(→ vu de l'intérieur)* to come in; *(→ vu de l'extérieur)* to go in; *(→ à pied)* to walk in; *(→ à cheval, à bicyclette)* to ride in; *(véhicule)* to drive in; **toc, toc! – entrez!** knock, knock! – come in!; **entrez, entrez!** do come in!, come on in!; **la cuisine est à droite en entrant** the kitchen is on the right as you come/go in; **empêche-les d'e.** keep them out, don't let them in; **entrez sans frapper** go (straight) in; **il m'invita à e.** he invited me in; **il me fit signe d'e.** he beckoned me in; **les visiteurs sont contrôlés en entrant et en sortant** visitors are checked on the way in and out; **les voleurs sont entrés par la porte de derrière** the burglars got in by the back door; **je suis simplement entré en passant** I just popped in; **il n'a fait qu'e. et sortir** he just popped in for a moment; **e. en gare** to pull in (to the station); **e. au port** to come into *or* to enter harbour; **qui vous a permis d'e. chez moi?** who allowed you (to come) in?; **et voici les joueurs qui entrent sur le terrain/court** here are the players coming onto the field/court; **faire e. qn** to let sb in; **faites-la e.** *(en lui montrant le chemin)* show her in; *(en l'appelant)* call her in; **laisser e. qn** to let sb in; **le vent entrait par rafales** the wind was blowing in in gusts; **par où entre l'eau?** how does the water penetrate *or* get in?; **ce genre de fenêtre laisse e. plus de lumière** this kind of window lets more light in

2 *(adhérer)* **e. à l'université** to go to university; **elle entre à la maternelle/en troisième année** she's going to nursery school/moving up into the third year; **e. au barreau** to become a lawyer; **quand elle est entrée au ministère de l'Agriculture** when she was appointed to the Ministry of Agriculture; **e. au service de qn** to enter sb's service; **il a fait e. sa fille comme attachée de presse** he got a job for his daughter as a press attaché

3 *Écon (devises)* to enter; *(marchandises)* to enter, to be imported; **faire e. des marchandises** *(gén)* to get goods in; *(en fraude)* to smuggle goods in; **pour faire e. plus de devises étrangères** to attract more foreign currencies

4 *(tenir, trouver sa place)* **ton morceau de puzzle n'entre pas là** your piece doesn't fit in here *or* doesn't belong here; **je peux faire e. un autre sac sous le siège** *(gén)* I can fit another bag under the seat; *(en serrant)* I can squeeze another bag under the seat

5 *Fam (connaissances, explication)* to sink in; **la chimie n'entre pas du tout** I just can't get the hang of chemistry; **l'informatique, ça entre tout seul avec elle** learning about computers is very easy with her as a teacher

6 *Rel* **e. en religion** to enter the religious life; **e. au couvent** to enter a convent

7 *Théât* **la Reine entre** enter the Queen; **les sorcières entrent** enter the witches

8 *Ordinat* to log in *or* on

B. *DÉBUTER* **e. en pourparlers** to start *or* to enter negotiations; **e. en correspondance avec qn** to enter a *or* to start a correspondence with sb; **e. en conversation avec qn** to strike up a conversation with sb; **e. en concurrence** to enter into competition; **e. en ébullition** to reach boiling point, to begin to boil; **e. en guerre** to go to war

VT *(aux avoir)* **1** *(produits → gén)* to bring in; *(→ marchandises)* to import; *(→ en fraude)* to smuggle in

2 *(enfoncer)* to dig; **elle lui entrait les ongles dans le bras** *(volontairement)* she was digging her nails into his/her arm; *(involontairement)* her nails were digging into his/her arm

3 *(passer)* **entre la tête par ce trou-là** get your head through that hole

4 *Ordinat (données)* to enter, to input; *(au clavier)* to key in

❑ **entrer dans VT IND 1** *(pénétrer dans → lieu)* to enter *(venir)* to come into, *(aller)* to go into; *(à pied)* to walk into; **e. dans l'eau** to get into the water; **elle entra lentement dans son bain** she slowly lowered herself into the bath; **y a-t-il un autre moyen d'e. dans cette pièce?** is there another way into this room?; **comment entre-t-on dans ce parc?** where's the way into this park?; **le premier coureur à e. dans le stade** the first runner to enter the stadium; **ils nous ont fait e. dans une cellule** they got us into a cell; **il ne les laisse jamais e. dans la chambre noire** he never lets *or* allows them into the darkroom; **un rayon de soleil entra dans la chambre** a ray of sunlight entered the room

2 *(adhérer à → club, association, parti)* to join, to become a member of; *(→ entreprise)* to join; **e. dans l'Union européenne** to enter *or* to join *or* to become a member of the European Union; **e. dans le monde du travail** to start work; **e. dans la magistrature** to become a magistrate, to enter the magistracy; **e. dans un marché** to enter a market; **e. dans une famille** *(par mariage)* to marry into a family; **il l'a fait e. dans la société** he got him/her a job with the firm

3 *(heurter → pilier, mur)* to crash into, to hit; *(→ voiture)* to collide with

4 *(constituant)* **e. dans la composition de** to go into; **l'eau entre pour moitié dans cette boisson** water makes up 50 percent of this drink

5 *(se mêler de)* to enter into; **je ne veux pas e. dans vos histoires** I don't want to have anything to do with *or* to be involved in your little schemes

6 *(se lancer dans)* **sans e. dans les détails** without going into details; **elle est entrée dans des explications sans fin** she launched into endless explanations

7 *(être inclus dans)* **c'est entré dans les mœurs** it's become accepted; **e. dans l'usage** *(terme)* to come into common use, to become part of everyday language; **elle est entrée dans la légende de son vivant** she became a living legend; **la TVA n'entre pas dans le prix** *Br* VAT *or Am* sales tax isn't included in the price

8 *(s'enfoncer, pénétrer dans)* **les éperons entraient dans son poitrail** the spurs were digging into its breast; **l'écharde est entrée profondément dans sa cuisse** the splinter has gone deep into his/her thigh; **la balle/flèche est entrée dans son bras** the bullet/arrow lodged itself in his/her arm; **faire e. qch de force dans** to force sth into; **faire e. un clou dans une planche** *(avec un marteau)* to hammer a nail into a plank; **il s'évertuait à faire e. le bouchon dans le goulot** he was striving to get the cork into *or* to force the cork down the bottleneck; **faire e. une sonde dans l'estomac** to have a tube inserted into one's stomach

9 *(tenir dans)* to get in, to go in, to fit in; **tout n'entrera pas dans la valise** we won't get everything in the suitcase, everything won't fit in the suitcase; **ils ont réussi à e. à 15 dans une 2 CV** they managed to get 15 people in a 2 CV; **mais son pied n'entrait pas dans le soulier de verre** but the glass slipper didn't fit her; **la clé est trop grosse pour e. dans la serrure** the key is too big to get in the keyhole; **faire e. des vêtements dans une valise** *(en poussant)* to press clothes (down) in a suitcase

10 *(période)* to enter; **nous entrons dans une ère de changement** we're entering a time of change; **la phase de restructuration dans laquelle l'entreprise vient d'e.** the restructuring phase which the company has just entered; **elle entre dans sa 97ème année** she's entering her 97th year; **quand on entre dans l'âge adulte** when one becomes an adult

11 *(relever de → rubrique)* to fall into, to come into; *(→ responsabilités)* to be part of; **l'achat de votre société n'est jamais entré dans mes plans** buying your company has never been part of my plans; **cela n'entre pas dans mes attributions** this is not within my responsibilities; **nos réformes entrent dans le cadre d'un grand projet social** our reforms are part of a large social scheme; **j'espère ne pas e. dans cette catégorie de personnes** I hope I don't belong to that category of people

12 *Fam (connaissances, explication)* **faire e. qch dans la tête de qn** to put sth into sb's head; *(à force de répéter)* to drum *or* to hammer sth into sb's head; **elle lui fait e. de telles idées dans la tête!** she puts such wild ideas into his/her head!; **les professeurs leur en font e. dans la tête!** the teachers fill their heads with all sorts of ideas!; **comment veux-tu que je fasse e. toutes ces statistiques dans ma tête?** how do you expect me to get all these statistics into

my head?; **tu ne lui feras jamais e. dans la tête que c'est impossible** you'll never get it into his/her head or convince him/her that it's impossible

entre-rail [ãtrəraj] (pl **entre-rails**) NM Rail gauge
entresol [ãtrəsɔl] NM mezzanine, entresol; **à l'e.** on the mezzanine, at mezzanine level
entresolé, -e [ãtrəsɔle] ADJ **étage e.** mezzanine
entretailler [3] [ãtrətaje] **s'entretailler** VPR Vét to cut, to brush
entre-temps [ãtrətã] ADV meanwhile, in the meantime
 NM INV Arch **dans l'e.** in the meantime
entretenir [40] [ãtrətnir] VT 1 (tenir en bon état → locaux, château) to maintain, to look after, to see to the upkeep of; (→ argenterie, lainage) to look after; (→ matériel, voiture, route) to maintain; (→ santé, beauté) to look after, to maintain; **e. sa forme** ou **condition physique** to keep oneself fit or in shape; **e. sa santé/sa beauté** to look after or take care of one's health/beauty; **e. son français** to keep up one's French; **facile à e.** (maison, voiture) easy to maintain; (moquette, plante, jardin) easy to look after
 2 (maintenir → feu) to keep going or burning; (→ querelle, rancune) to foster, to feed; (→ enthousiasme) to foster, to keep alive; (→ espoirs, illusions) to cherish, to entertain; (→ fraîcheur, humidité) to maintain; **e. des soupçons/des craintes** to entertain or harbour suspicions/fears; **e. une correspondance avec qn** to keep up or to carry on a correspondence with sb; **e. de bonnes relations avec** (personne) to remain on good terms with; (pays) to maintain good relations with
 3 (encourager) **e. qn dans l'ignorance** to keep sb in ignorance; **c'est ce qui m'a entretenu dans l'erreur** that is what kept me from seeing the mistake; **e. qn dans l'idée que...** to keep sb believing that...
 4 (payer les dépenses de → enfants) to support; (→ maîtresse) to keep, to support; (→ troupes) to keep, to maintain; **entretenu à ne rien faire** paid to do nothing; **se faire e. par qn** to be kept by sb
 5 e. qn de (lui parler de) to converse with sb about; **e. qn d'un projet** to speak to sb about a project
 6 Compta (comptes) to keep in order
 ▶ **s'entretenir** VPR 1 (emploi réciproque) to have a discussion, to talk; **ils se sont longuement entretenus de...** they had a lengthy discussion about...
 2 (emploi passif) **le synthétique s'entretient facilement** man-made fabrics are easy to look after
 3 (emploi réfléchi) (se maintenir en forme) to keep fit
 4 (parler avec) **s'e. avec** to converse with, to speak to; **s'e. avec qn au téléphone** to speak to sb on the phone; **s'e. de qch avec qn** to have a discussion with sb about sth
entretenu, -e [ãtrətny] ADJ 1 (personne) kept 2 (lieu) **maison bien entretenue** (où le ménage est fait) well-kept house; (en bon état) house in good repair; **maison mal entretenue** (sale et mal rangée) badly kept house; (en mauvais état) house in bad repair; **jardin bien/mal e.** well-kept/neglected garden 3 Rad (oscillations) sustained; (ondes) undamped, continuous
entretien [ãtrətjɛ̃] NM 1 (maintenance) maintenance, upkeep; **facile/difficile d'e., d'e. facile/difficile** easy/difficult to maintain; **sans e.** (appareil) maintenance-free; **personnel d'e.** maintenance staff; **manuel d'e.** service manual
 2 (subsistance → d'une famille, armée etc) support, maintenance
 3 (discussion → entre employeur et candidat) interview; (colloque) discussion; **solliciter/accorder un e.** to request/to grant an interview; **j'ai réussi à décrocher un e.** (pour une embauche) I managed to get myself an interview; **avoir des entretiens avec le patronat** to hold talks or discussions with the employers; **e. d'embauche** job interview; **les entretiens de Bichat** = annual medical conference in Paris
 4 Rad & TV (questions) interview
 5 Mktg interview; **e. assisté par ordinateur** computer-assisted interview; **e. centré** structured interview; **e. directif** guided interview; **e.**

de groupe group interview; (activité) group interviewing; **e. libre** ou **non structuré** unstructured interview; **e. non directif** unguided interview; **e. organisé** arranged interview; **e. en profondeur** in-depth interview; **e. spontané** intercept interview; **e. structuré** structured interview; **e. par téléphone, e. téléphonique** telephone interview
entretient etc voir **entretenir**
entre-tisser [3] [ãtrətise] VT to weave together, to interweave
entretoile [ãtrətwal] NF Couture (lace) insertion
entretoise [ãtrətwaz] NF crosspiece, brace; Aut spacer; (étai) strut; **e. de réglage** distance piece
entretoisement [ãtrətwazmã] NM Constr 1 (action) bracing 2 (résultat) crosspiece, brace
entretoiser [3] [ãtrətwaze] VT Constr to brace
entre-tuer [7] [ãtrətɥe] **s'entre-tuer** VPR to kill one another
entreverra etc voir **entrevoir**
entrevit etc voir **entrevoir**
entrevoie [ãtrəvwa] NF Rail **l'e.** the space between the tracks
entrevoir [62] [ãtrəvwar] VT 1 (apercevoir) to catch sight or a glimpse of; **je n'ai fait que l'e.** I only caught a glimpse of him/her or saw him/her briefly 2 (pressentir → solution, vie meilleure) to glimpse; (→ difficultés, issue) to foresee, to anticipate; **il entrevoyait la vérité** he had an inkling of the truth; **le directeur lui a fait e. des possibilités de promotion** the director hinted at a possible promotion
entrevous [ãtrəvu] NM INV Constr case-bay, space between girders
entrevue [ãtrəvy] NF (réunion) meeting; (tête-à-tête) interview; **avoir/fixer une e. avec qn** to have/arrange a meeting/an interview with sb; **après son e. avec le pape** after his/her meeting or audience with the Pope
entrisme [ãtrism] NM Pol entryism, entrism
entriste [ãtrist] Pol ADJ entryist
 NMF entryist
entropie [ãtrɔpi] NF Phys entropy
entropion [ãtrɔpjɔ̃] NM Méd entropion, introversion of eyelid
entroque [ãtrɔk] NM Géol entrochite; **à entroques** (calcaire) entrochal
entrouvert, -e [ãtruvɛr, -ɛrt] ADJ (porte) half-open, ajar; **dormir la bouche entrouverte** to sleep with one's mouth slightly open; **laissez la porte entrouverte** leave the door ajar
entrouvrir [34] [ãtruvrir] VT to half-open
 ▶ **s'entrouvrir** VPR (porte) to half-open; (rideau) to draw back (slightly); (lèvres) to part
entuber [3] [ãtybe] VT Vulg to screw, to rip off; **se faire e.** to get screwed, to get ripped off
enturbanné, -e [ãtyrbane] ADJ turbaned
enture [ãtyr] NF 1 Hort incision, cut 2 (cheville) peg, pin 3 Menuis scarf-joint
énucléation [enykleasjɔ̃] NF 1 (d'un œil) enucleation 2 (d'un fruit) stoning, pitting
énucléer [15] [enyklee] VT 1 (œil) to enucleate 2 (fruit) to stone, to pit
énumérable [enymerabl] ADJ which can be enumerated
énumératif, -ive [enymeratif, -iv] ADJ enumerative
énumération [enymerasjɔ̃] NF 1 (énonciation) enumeration, enumerating 2 (liste) list, catalogue
énumérative [enymerativ] voir **énumératif**
énumérer [18] [enymere] VT to enumerate, to itemize, to list
énuquer [3] [enyke] **s'énuquer** VPR Suisse to break one's neck
énurésie [enyrezi] NF Méd bedwetting, Spéc enuresis
énurétique [enyretik] Méd ADJ bedwetting (avant n), Spéc enuretic
 NMF bedwetter, Spéc enuresis sufferer
env. (abrév écrite environ) approx.
envahir [32] [ãvair] VT 1 (occuper → pays, palais) to invade, to overrun
 2 (se répandre dans) to overrun; **les touristes envahissent les plages** the beaches are overrun with tourists; **grenier envahi par les souris** attic overrun with mice; **plate-bande envahie par les mauvaises herbes** border overrun with

weeds; **jardin envahi par la végétation** overgrown garden; **cette mode ne va pas tarder à e. la France** it won't be long before this fashion sweeps France; Com **e. le marché** to flood the market
 3 Fam (déranger) **e. qn** to intrude on sb ▪; **se laisser e. par les tâches quotidiennes** to let oneself be swamped by daily duties
 4 (sujet: sensation, crainte) to sweep over, to seize; **il a été envahi par le doute** he was seized with doubt
envahissant, -e [ãvaisã, -ãt] ADJ 1 (qui s'étend → végétation) overgrown, rampant; (→ ambition, passion) invasive; (→ odeur) overwhelming 2 (importun → voisin, ami) interfering, intrusive; **je commence à trouver ta famille un peu envahissante** I'm beginning to find your family a bit too intrusive
envahissement [ãvaismã] NM invasion
envahisseur [ãvaisœr] NM invader
envapé, -e [ãvape] ADJ Fam out of it, Br off one's face
envasement [ãvazmã] NM silting up
envaser [3] [ãvaze] VT to silt up
 ▶ **s'envaser** VPR (canal) to silt up; (barque) to get stuck in the mud
enveloppant, -e [ãvlɔpã, -ãt] ADJ 1 (couvrant) **regard e.** look that takes everything in; Aut **pare-chocs e.** wraparound bumper 2 (voix, paroles) enticing, seductive
enveloppe [ãvlɔp] NF 1 (pour lettre) envelope; **prière de joindre une e. affranchie** please enclose a stamped addressed envelope; **e. auto-adhésive** ou **autocollante** self-seal envelope; **e. à fenêtre** window envelope; **e. gommée** stick-down envelope; **e. de réexpédition** = special envelope used for forwarding several items at once; **e. matelassée** ou **rembourrée** padded envelope, Jiffy bag®; **e. premier jour** first-day cover; **e. timbrée** stamped envelope; **e. timbrée avec nom et adresse** stamped addressed envelope, SAE; **e. T** ≃ business reply or reply-paid envelope
 2 (d'un colis etc) wrapper, wrapping
 3 Biol (membrane) envelope, membrane; **e. nucléaire** nuclear envelope or membrane
 4 Bot (membrane) covering membrane; (cosse) husk
 5 Tech (revêtement → d'un pneu) cover, casing; (→ d'un tuyau) lagging (UNCOUNT), jacket; **e. calorifuge** lagging
 6 Fin (don) sum of money, gratuity; (don illégal) bribe; (crédits) budget; **l'e. (budgétaire) du ministère de la Culture** the Arts budget; **nous disposons d'une e. de 1000 euros pour la maintenance** we have a budget of or we've been allocated 1,000 euros for maintenance; **il a touché une e.** (pot-de-vin) he got a backhander; **e. budgétaire** budget (allocation); **e. fiscale** = savings scheme with tax advantages; **e. salariale** wages bill
 7 (aspect) exterior, outward appearance; **sous une e. de rudesse** beneath a rough exterior
 8 Littéraire (corps) **e. mortelle** ou **charnelle** earthly or mortal frame
 9 Géom envelope
 10 Jur **e. Soleau** = envelope for depositing designs etc at the patent office
 ❑ **sous enveloppe** ADV **mettre/envoyer sous e.** to put/to send in an envelope; **envoyer un magazine sous e.** (pour le dissimuler) to send a magazine under plain cover
enveloppé, -e [ãvlɔpe] ADJ Fam (personne) well-padded, plump ▪
enveloppement [ãvlɔpmã] NM 1 (emballage) wrapping, packing (UNCOUNT) 2 Mil encirclement, surrounding; **manœuvre d'e.** pincer movement, envelopment 3 Méd packing; **e. froid** cold pack
envelopper [3] [ãvlɔpe] VT 1 (empaqueter) to wrap (up); **e. qch dans un journal** to wrap sth up in a newspaper; **le papier qui enveloppait les réglisses** the paper in which the liquorice was wrapped; Hum **je vous l'enveloppe?** is that a deal?
 2 (emmailloter) to wrap (up); **e. un enfant dans une couverture** to wrap a child in a blanket or a blanket around a child; **enveloppé**

dans des bandages swathed in bandages; *Fig* **e. des remarques désagréables dans des phrases gentilles** to wrap up unpleasant remarks in kind words

3 *(entourer)* **e. qn de sa sollicitude** to lavish one's attention on sb; **e. qch du regard** to take sth in with one's gaze; **il enveloppa le paysage du regard** he took in the landscape; **e. qn du regard** to gaze at sb

4 *(voiler → sujet: brume, obscurité)* to shroud, to envelop; **la nuit nous enveloppa** darkness closed in on us; **enveloppé de mystère/brume** shrouded in mystery/in mist

5 *Mil* to encircle, to surround

▸**s'envelopper** VPR **s'e. dans** *(vêtement)* to wrap oneself in; *Fig* **s'e. dans son silence** to immure oneself in silence; *Fig* **s'e. dans sa dignité** to assume an air of dignity

enveloppe-réponse [ɑ̃vlɔprepɔ̃s] *(pl* **enveloppes-réponses)** NF *Com* reply-paid envelope

envenimation [ɑ̃vnimasjɔ̃] NF *Méd* poisoning *(from a snake or insect bite)*

envenimé, -e [ɑ̃vnime] ADJ *(plaie)* poisoned, septic; *Fig (discussion)* acrimonious

envenimement [ɑ̃vnimmɑ̃] NM worsening; *Fig (d'une querelle, d'une discussion)* embittering; *(d'une situation)* aggravation

envenimer [3] [ɑ̃vnime] VT 1 *Méd* to poison, to infect

2 *(aggraver → conflit)* to inflame, to fan the flames of; *(→ situation)* to aggravate; *(→ rapports)* to poison, to spoil; **tu n'as fait qu'e. les choses** you've only made things *or* matters worse

▸**s'envenimer** VPR 1 *Méd* to fester, to become septic

2 *(empirer → relation)* to grow more bitter *or* acrimonious; *(→ situation)* to get worse, to worsen; *(→ querelle, discussion)* to grow acrimonious

envergeure [ɑ̃vɛrʒyr] = **enverjure**

enverguer [3] [ɑ̃vɛrge] VT *Naut* to bend *(sail)*

envergure [ɑ̃vɛrgyr] NF 1 *(d'un oiseau, d'un avion)* wingspan, wingspread

2 *Naut* breadth

3 *(importance → d'une manifestation, d'une œuvre)* scale, scope; **de petite** *ou* **faible e.** small; **de grande e.** *(réforme, rapport, question)* far-reaching, wide-ranging; *(opération, firme)* large-scale; **son entreprise a pris de l'e.** his/her company has expanded

4 *(d'un savant, d'un président)* calibre; **homme d'e./de cette e.** man of calibre/of this calibre; **il manque d'e.** he doesn't have a strong personality

enverjure [ɑ̃vɛrʒyr] NF *Tex* shedding

enverra *etc voir* **envoyer**

envers [ɑ̃vɛr] PRÉP *(à l'égard de)* towards, to; **elle est loyale e. ses amis** she's loyal to her friends; **être cruel e. qn** to be cruel to *or* towards sb; **être juste e. qn** to be fair to *or* towards sb; **son attitude e. moi** his/her attitude towards me; **traître e. sa patrie** traitor to one's country; **leur devoir e. leur patrie** their duty to *or* towards their country; **ma dette e. vous** my indebtedness to you; **avoir une dette e. qn** to be indebted to sb; **e. et contre tout** *ou* **tous** in the face of *or* despite all opposition; **on a maintenu notre décision, e. et contre tout** we kept to our decision, despite all opposition *or* everything

NM 1 *(autre côté)* **l'e.** *(d'un papier)* the other side, the back; *(d'une feuille d'arbre)* the underside; *(d'une médaille, d'un tissu)* the reverse side; *(d'une peau)* the inside

2 *(mauvais côté)* wrong side; *Fig* **l'e. du décor** *ou* **tableau** the other side of the coin

3 *Géog* cold northern slope *(of valley)*

❑ **à l'envers** ADV 1 *(dans le mauvais sens)* **mettre à l'e.** *(chapeau)* to put on the wrong way round, to put on back to front; *(chaussettes)* to put on inside out; *(portrait)* to hang upside down *or* the wrong way up

2 *(mal, anormalement)* **tout va** *ou* **marche à l'e.** everything is upside down *or* topsy-turvy; **tu as tout compris à l'e.** you misunderstood the whole thing; **il a l'esprit** *ou* **la tête à l'e.** his mind is in a whirl, he doesn't know whether he's coming or going

3 *(dans l'ordre inverse)* backwards, in reverse; **faire les mouvements à l'e.** to do the movements backwards

---

'L'Envers et l'Endroit' *Camus* 'The Wrong Side and the Right Side'

---

envi [ɑ̃vi] **à l'envi** ADV *Littéraire* **ils se sont déchaînés contre moi à l'e.** they vied with one another in venting their rage on me; **trois sketches féroces à l'e.** three sketches, each more corrosive than the last

enviable [ɑ̃vjabl] ADJ enviable; **peu e.** unenviable

enviandé [ɑ̃vjɑ̃de] NM *Vulg* prick, *Br* arsehole, *Am* asshole; **c'est cet e. d'Alex qui m'a piqué ma mob** that prick Alex pinched my moped

enviander [3] [ɑ̃vjɑ̃de] VT *Vulg* to fuck up the *Br* arse *or Am* ass

envider [3] [ɑ̃vide] VT *Tex* to wind, to spool

envie [ɑ̃vi] NF 1 *(souhait, désir)* desire; **contenter** *ou* **passer son e.** to satisfy one's desire; **l'e. de qch/de faire qch** the desire for sth/to do sth; **avoir e. de qch** to want sth; **j'avais (très) e. de ce disque** I wanted that record (very much); **j'ai des envies de fraises** I have cravings for strawberries; *Fam* **j'ai une de ces envies de champagne!** I've got a real craving for champagne!, I could murder some champagne!; **avoir e. de faire qch** to want to do sth; **avoir e. de rire/pleurer** to feel like laughing/crying; **avoir e. de vomir** to feel sick; **j'avais e. de dormir/boire/manger** I felt sleepy/thirsty/hungry; **je n'ai pas e. de passer ma vie à ça** I don't want to spend the rest of my life doing that; **j'ai presque e. de ne pas y aller** I have half a mind not to go; **il avait moyennement e. de la revoir** he didn't really feel like seeing her again; **je le ferai quand j'en aurai e.** I'll do it when I feel like it; **avoir bien** *ou* **faire e. de faire qch** to really want to do sth; **brûler d'e. de faire qch** to be burning *or* dying to do sth; *Fam* **mourir** *ou* **crever d'e. de faire qch** to be dying to do sth; **ça m'a donné e. de les revoir** it made me want to see *or* feel like seeing them again; **elle n'a pas e. que tu restes** she doesn't want you to stay; **je n'ai pas e. que ça se sache** I don't want it to be known; **la robe beige me fait vraiment e.** I'm really tempted by the beige dress; **un voyage au Brésil, ça ne te fait pas e.?** aren't you tempted by a trip to Brazil?; **l'e. lui prend de** *ou* **il lui prend l'e. de faire...** he/she feels like *or* fancies doing...; **voilà qui lui ôtera l'e. de revenir** this'll make sure he's/she's not tempted to come back; **je vais lui ôter** *ou* **faire passer l'e. de s'amuser** I'll stop his/her messing around; **e. de femme enceinte** (pregnant woman's) craving

2 *(désir sexuel)* desire; **j'ai e. de toi** I want you

3 *(besoin)* urge; **être pris d'une terrible e. de rire** to have a terrible urge to laugh; **être pris d'une e. (pressante** *ou* **naturelle)** to feel the call of nature, *Br* to be caught short; *très Fam* **ça l'a pris comme une e. de pisser** he felt a sudden urge for it *or* to do it▪

4 *(jalousie)* envy; **regarder qch avec e.** to look enviously at sth; **sa réussite me fait e.** I envy his/her success, his/her success makes me jealous; **tant de luxe, ça (vous) fait e.** such luxury makes one *or* you envious; *Psy* **e. du pénis** penis envy

5 *Anat (tache)* birthmark; *(peau)* hangnail

envier [9] [ɑ̃vje] VT **e. qch à qn** to envy sb sth; **on lui envie sa fortune** people envy him/her his/her wealth; **crois-tu avoir quelque chose à lui e.?** do you feel he's/she's got something you haven't?; **vous n'avez rien à lui e.** you have no reason to be envious of him/her; **elle n'a rien à e. à personne** she has no cause to be envious of anyone; **e. qn d'avoir fait qch** to envy sb for having done sth; **je t'envie de ne jamais avoir faim!** I envy your never being hungry!

envieusement [ɑ̃vjøzmɑ̃] ADV enviously

envieux, -euse [ɑ̃vjø, -øz] ADJ envious; **être e. de** to be envious of, to envy

NM,F envious person; **faire des e.** to arouse *or* to excite envy

enviné, -e [ɑ̃vine] ADJ *(tonneau, fût)* which smells of wine

environ [ɑ̃virɔ̃] ADV about, around; **il y a e. six mois** about six months ago; **il était e. midi** it was around *or* about midday; **c'est à e. deux heures de vol** it's about two hours away by plane *or* a two-hour flight; **ça vaut e. 300 euros** it costs around *or* about 300 euros; **il habite à e. 100 m** *ou* **à 100 m e. d'ici** he lives about 100 m from here

environnant, -e [ɑ̃virɔnɑ̃, -ɑ̃t] ADJ surrounding; **la campagne environnante** the surrounding countryside, the country round about

environnement [ɑ̃virɔnmɑ̃] NM 1 *(lieux avoisinants)* environment, surroundings, surrounding area; **l'e. immédiat de l'école est agréable** the school's immediate surroundings are pleasant

2 *(milieu)* background; **l'e. culturel/familial** the cultural/family background; *Mktg* **e. d'achat** purchase environment; **e. commercial** business environment; **e. du marché** market environment; *Com* **e. institutionnel/marketing** corporate/marketing environment

3 *Écol* **l'e.** the environment; **un produit qui respecte l'e.** an environment-friendly product; **pollution/politique de l'e.** environmental pollution/policy

4 *Ordinat* environment; **e. partagé** shared environment

environnemental, -e, -aux, -ales [ɑ̃virɔnmɑ̃tal, -o] ADJ *Écol* environmental

environnementaliste [ɑ̃virɔnmɑ̃talist] NMF *Écol & Psy* environmentalist

environner [3] [ɑ̃virɔne] VT to surround, to encircle; **être environné de** to be surrounded with

▸**s'environner** VPR **s'e. de** to surround oneself with; **s'e. d'artistes** to surround oneself with artists

environs [ɑ̃virɔ̃] NMPL surroundings, surrounding area; **les e. sont assez pittoresques** the surroundings are *or* the surrounding area is quite picturesque; **les e. de Paris** the area around Paris

❑ **aux environs de** PRÉP 1 *(dans l'espace)* near, close to; **aux e. de Nantes** in the vicinity of *or* near Nantes

2 *(dans le temps)* around, round about; **aux e. de Noël** around *or* round about Christmas time, at Christmas or thereabouts; **aux e. de midi** around noon, at noon or thereabouts; **aux e. de 20 heures** around 8 p.m.

3 *(avec un chiffre)* **aux e. de cent euros** in the region *or* vicinity of a hundred euros, about *or* around a hundred euros

❑ **dans les environs** ADV in the local *or* surrounding area

❑ **dans les environs de** PRÉP in the vicinity of, near; **elle habite dans les e. d'Amiens** she lives near Amiens

envisageable [ɑ̃vizaʒabl] ADJ conceivable; **oui, c'est e.** yes, it's conceivable; **ce n'est guère e. à l'heure actuelle** it hardly seems possible at the present time, it's barely conceivable at present

envisager [17] [ɑ̃vizaʒe] VT 1 *(examiner)* to consider; **e. tous les aspects d'un problème** to consider all the aspects of a problem; **essayez d'e. le problème autrement** try to look at *or* consider the problem differently; **le cas que nous envisageons** the case under consideration; **il n'envisageait pas de partir** he wasn't thinking of leaving, he wasn't considering leaving

2 *(prévoir)* to envisage, to contemplate, to consider; **e. des licenciements/réparations** to consider lay-offs/repairs; **e. de faire qch** to consider *or* to contemplate doing sth; **j'envisage d'aller vivre là-bas** I'm contemplating going *or* I'm thinking of going to live there

envoi [ɑ̃vwa] NM 1 *(de marchandises, d'argent)* sending; **faire un e.** *(colis)* to send a parcel; *(lettre)* to send a letter; *(marchandises)* to send goods; **e. de fonds** remittance (of funds); **faire un e. de fonds à qn** to send *or* remit funds to sb; **contre e. de** on receipt of

2 *(d'un messager, de soldats)* sending in, dispatching, dispatch; **décider l'e. des troupes** to decide to send in (the) troops; **demander l'e. de troupes** to ask for troops to be dispatched; **l'e. d'un émissaire n'a pas réglé le problème** sending an emissary did not solve the problem

3 *(colis)* parcel, consignment; *(lettre)* letter; *(marchandises)* consignment (**de** of); **j'ai bien reçu votre e. du 10 octobre** I acknowledge

receipt of your consignment of 10 October; **e. postal** postal delivery; **e. exprès** express delivery; **e. franco de port** postage-paid consignment; **e. recommandé** (colis) registered parcel; (lettre) registered letter; **e. recommandé avec accusé de réception** (colis) Br recorded delivery parcel, Am registered package with return receipt; (lettre) Br recorded delivery letter, Am registered letter with return receipt; **e. contre paiement** cash with order; **e. contre remboursement** Br cash on delivery, Am collect on delivery; **e. à titre d'essai** sent on approval; **e. en valeur déclarée** registered letter; **e. en groupage, e. groupé** grouped consignment; **e. en nombre** mass mailing; **e. de l'auteur** presentation copy

4 Ordinat **e. multiple** crossposting; **faire un e. multiple de qch** to cross-post sth

5 Sport **coup d'e.** kick-off; **donner le coup d'e. d'un match** (arbitre) to give the sign for the match to start; (joueur) to kick off; Fig **donner le coup d'e. d'une campagne** to get a campaign off the ground

6 Littérature envoi

7 Jur **e. en possession** writ of possession

envoie etc voir **envoyer**

envoiler [3] [ɑ̃vwale] **s'envoiler** VPR Métal to bend, to warp

envol [ɑ̃vɔl] NM **1** (d'un oiseau) taking flight; **l'aigle prit son e.** the eagle took flight **2** Aviat taking off (UNCOUNT), takeoff

envolée [ɑ̃vɔle] NF **1** (élan) flight; **e. de l'imagination** flight of fancy; **e. lyrique** flight of lyricism; Hum **il s'est lancé dans une grande e. lyrique** he waxed lyrical **2** (augmentation) sudden rise; **l'e. de l'euro** the sudden rise of the euro

envoler [3] [ɑ̃vɔle] **s'envoler** VPR **1** (oiseau) to fly off or away; **faire s'e. des oiseaux** to put birds to flight

2 (avion) to take off; **je m'envole pour Tokyo demain** I'm flying (off) to Tokyo tomorrow; **mon avion s'envole** ou **je m'envole dans une heure** my plane takes off or my flight leaves in an hour

3 (passer → temps) to fly

4 (augmenter → cours, prix) to soar; **s'e. dans les sondages** to rise rapidly in the opinion polls

5 (être emporté → écharpe) to blow off or away; (→ chapeau) to blow off; (→ papiers) to blow away; **le vent a fait s'e. tous les papiers** the wind sent all the documents flying (everywhere)

6 (disparaître → voleur, stylo) to disappear, to vanish (into thin air); **il n'a pourtant pas pu s'e., ce livre!** the book can't just have vanished into thin air!

envoûtant, -e [ɑ̃vutɑ̃, -ɑ̃t] ADJ spellbinding, bewitching, entrancing

envoûtement [ɑ̃vutmɑ̃] NM aussi Fig bewitchment, spell; **cette région me fait l'effet d'un e.** this region has a bewitching or captivating effect on me

envoûter [3] [ɑ̃vute] VT aussi Fig to bewitch, to cast a spell on; Fig **être envoûté par une voix/femme** to be under the spell of a voice/woman; **elle était sûre de s'être fait e.** she was convinced that someone had cast or put a spell on her

envoûteur, -euse [ɑ̃vutœr, -øz] NM,F sorcerer, f sorceress

envoyé, -e [ɑ̃vwaje] ADJ aussi Fam Fig **bien e.** well-aimed; Fam Fig **c'est e.!** well said!

NM,F (gén) messenger; Pol envoy; Presse correspondent; **de notre e. spécial à Londres** from our special correspondent in London; **de notre e. permanent à New York** from our New York correspondent or permanent correspondent in New York

envoyer [30] [ɑ̃vwaje] VT **1** (expédier → gén) to send (off); (→ message radio) to send out; (→ lettre, colis) to send, to dispatch; (→ marchandises) to send, to consign; (→ invitation) to send (out); (→ vœux, condoléances) to send; (→ CV, candidature) to send (in); (→ argent, mandat) to send, to remit; **e. une lettre à qn** to send sb a letter, to send a letter to sb; **e. un (petit) mot à qn** to drop sb a line; **tu peux te faire e. la documentation** you can have the information

sent to you; **e. qch par courrier** ou **par la poste** to mail sth, Br to post sth; **e. qch par fax/télex** to fax/telex sth; **e. qch par bateau** to ship sth, to send sth by ship; **e. qch par chemin de fer** to send sth by rail; **e. des fleurs à qn** to send sb flowers; Fig to give sb a pat on the back; **Fred t'envoie ses amitiés** Fred sends you his regards

2 (personne) to send; **e. un homme dans** ou **sur la Lune** to send a man to the moon; **e. un enfant à l'école** to send a child (off) to school; **on les envoie à la mer/chez leur tante tous les étés** we send them (off) to the seaside/to their aunt's every summer; **on m'a envoyé aux nouvelles** I've been sent to find out whether there's any news; **e. un criminel en prison** to send a criminal to jail; Euph **e. qn dans l'autre monde** to send sb to meet his/her maker; **e. des soldats à la mort** to send soldiers to their deaths; **e. ses malades à un confrère** to send or to refer one's patients to a colleague; **e. chercher qn** to have sb picked up; **je l'ai envoyé la chercher à la gare** I sent him to the station to pick her up or to fetch her; **e. chercher un médecin** to send for a doctor; **j'ai envoyé (quelqu'un) prendre de ses nouvelles** I sent someone to ask after him/her; **elle ne le lui a pas envoyé dire** she told him/her straight or to his/her face; Fam **e. promener** ou **balader** ou **paître** ou **bouler qn, e. qn au diable, e. qn sur les roses** to send sb packing; **je l'ai envoyé promener** I told him where to get off; Fam **j'avais envie de tout e. promener** ou **valser** ou **dinguer** I felt like chucking the whole thing in; **j'ai envoyé promener la famille/ma thèse** I sent my family packing/packed in my thesis; **je me suis fait e. balader quand je leur ai demandé des explications** they sent me packing when I asked for an explanation; Fam **e. dinguer qn** (le repousser) to send sb sprawling; (l'éconduire) to send sb packing

3 (projeter) **e. qn par terre** to knock sb to the ground; **e. un adversaire à terre** ou **au tapis** to knock an opponent down or to the ground; Fam **e. qn dans le décor** to send sb flying; Fam **e. une voiture dans le décor** to send a car skidding off the road ▪

4 (lancer → projectile) to throw, to fling; (→ ballon) to throw; (→ balle de tennis) to send; **e. la balle hors du court** to send the ball out of court; **envoie-moi ma chemise** throw me my shirt; **e. sa fumée dans les yeux de qn** to blow smoke into sb's eyes; **e. des baisers à qn** to blow sb kisses

5 (donner → coup) Fam **e. des gifles** ou **baffes à qn** to slap sb (in the face) ▪, **e. des coups de pied/poing à qn** to kick/to punch sb; Fam **il le lui a envoyé dans les dents** he really let him/her have it

6 (hisser → pavillon) to hoist; Naut **e. les couleurs/une vergue** to hoist the colours/send up a yard; Naut **envoyez!** about ship!

7 Fam (locution) **ça envoie le** ou **du bois** it's the business

VI Fam **ce guitariste envoie grave** that guitarist really rocks; **elle envoie, ta moto** your motorbike goes like a bomb

▸**s'envoyer** VPR **1** (emploi réciproque) to send one another; **ils s'envoient des cartes postales régulièrement** they regularly send postcards to each other; **s'e. des lettres** to write to one another

2 Fam (subir → corvée) to get saddled with

3 Fam (consommer → bière, bouteille) to knock back, to down; (→ gâteau) to wolf down; très Fam **s'e. qn** (sexuellement) to screw sb, Br to have it off with sb

4 Fam (se donner) **je m'enverrais des gifles** ou **baffes!** I could kick myself!

5 très Fam (locution) **s'e. en l'air** to screw, Br to have it off

envoyeur, -euse [ɑ̃vwajœr, -øz] NM,F sender

enzootie [ɑ̃zɔɔti] NF Vét enzootic disease

enzymatique [ɑ̃zimatik] ADJ Biol & Chim enzymatic

enzyme [ɑ̃zim] NF OU NM Biol & Chim enzyme; **produit de lavage aux enzymes** cleaning product with biological action

enzymologie [ɑ̃zimɔlɔʒi] NF Biol & Chim enzymology

enzymopathie [ɑ̃zimɔpati] NF Méd enzyme deficiency

éocène [eɔsɛn] Géol ADJ eocene

NM Eocene (period)

Éole [eɔl] NPR Myth Aeolus

éolien, -enne [eɔljɛ̃, -ɛn] ADJ wind (avant n), Spéc aeolian; **moteur é.** wind-powered engine

❑ **éolienne** NF windmill, wind pump

Éoliennes [eɔljɛn] NFPL **les (îles) É.** the Aeolian or Lipari Islands

éolipile, éolipyle [eɔlipil] NM Phys aeolipile, aelopyle

éolithe [eɔlit] NM Géol eolith

éon [eɔ̃] NM Phil aeon

EONIA [eɔnja] NM Bourse (abrév Euro Overnight Index Average) EONIA

éonisme [eɔnism] NM Psy eonism

EOR [əɔɛr] NM Mil (abrév élève officier de réserve) military cadet

éosine [eɔzin] NF Chim eosin, eosine

éosinophile [eɔzinɔfil] Biol ADJ eosinophilic, eosinophilous

NM eosinophil, eosinophile

éosinophilie [eɔzinɔfili] NF Méd eosinophilia

épacte [epakt] NF epact

épagneul [epanœl] NM spaniel; **é. breton** Brittany spaniel

épair [epɛr] NM Tech look-through; **é. nuageux** wild look-through

épais, -aisse [epɛ, -ɛs] ADJ **1** (haut → livre, strate, tranche) thick; (→ couche de neige) thick, deep; **peu é.** thin; **une planche épaisse de 10 centimètres** a board 10 centimetres thick; Fig **avoir la langue épaisse** to have a coated tongue

2 (charnu → lèvres, cheville, taille) thick; (→ corps) thickset, stocky; **avoir la taille épaisse** to be thickset; Fam **il n'est pas (bien) é.** he's thin (as a rake)

3 (dense → fumée, sauce, foule, cheveux) thick; (→ sourcil) thick, bushy; (→ feuillage, brouillard) dense, thick

4 (profond → silence, sommeil) deep; (→ nuit) pitch-black

5 Péj (non affiné → esprit, intelligence) dull, coarse

6 Can Fam (stupide) Br thick, Am dumb

❑ **épais** NM **au plus é. de la foule** in the thick of the crowd; **au plus é. de la forêt** deep in the heart of the forest ADV (tartiner, semer, pousser) thick, thickly; Fam **il n'y en avait pas é., de la viande** there wasn't a ton of meat; Fam **il n'y en avait pas é., du bonhomme!** the man was as thin as a rake!; Fam **en avoir é. (sur le cœur)** to have a heavy heart ▪

épaisseur [epɛsœr] NF **1** (d'un mur, d'un tissu, d'une strate) thickness; **un mur de 30 centimètres d'é.** a wall 30 centimetres thick; **quelle en est l'é.?** how thick is it?

2 (couche) layer, thickness; **plusieurs épaisseurs de vêtements** several layers of clothes; **plier un papier en quatre/cinq épaisseurs** to fold a piece of paper in four/five; **le peu d'é. d'une planche** the thinness of a plank

3 (densité → du brouillard, d'une soupe, d'un feuillage) thickness

4 (intensité → du silence, du sommeil) depth; (→ de la nuit) darkness, depth

5 (substance) depth; **les personnages manquent d'é.** the characters lack depth

épaissir [32] [epesir] VT **1** (sauce, enduit) to thicken (up)

2 (grossir) to thicken; **le manque d'exercice lui a épaissi la taille** the lack of exercise has thickened his/her waistline; **les traits épaissis par l'alcool** his/her features bloated with alcohol

3 (ombre, mystère) to deepen

VI **1** (fumée, peinture, mayonnaise) to thicken, to get thicker; **faire é.** (sauce) to thicken

2 (grossir → taille) to get thicker or bigger; (→ traits du visage) to get coarser, to coarsen; **il a beaucoup épaissi** he's put on a lot of weight

▸**s'épaissir** VPR **1** (fumée, brouillard, crème) to thicken, to get thicker

2 (augmenter → couche de neige) to get thicker or deeper; (→ pile de feuilles) to get bigger

3 (grossir → traits) to get coarse or coarser; (→ taille) to get thicker or bigger; (→ personne) to grow stout or stouter

4 Fig (mystère, ténèbres) to deepen; **le mystère s'épaissit** (dans un fait divers) the mystery deepens; (dans un roman) the plot thickens

épaississant, -e [epesisã, -ãt] ADJ thickening *(avant n)* ◆ NM thickening agent

épaississement [epesismã] NM thickening

épaississeur [epesisœr] NM *Ind* thickener, thickening apparatus

épamprage [epãpraʒ], **épamprement** [epãprəmã] NM *Agr* thinning out of the leaves

épamprer [3] [epãpre] VT *Agr* to thin out the leaves of

épanalepse [epanalɛps] NF *Littérature* epanalepsis

épanchement [epãʃmã] NM **1** *(confidences)* outpouring **2** *Méd* extravasation; **é. de synovie** water on the knee **3** *Arch ou Littéraire (d'un liquide)* pouring out, discharge

épancher [3] [epãʃe] VT **1** *(tendresse, craintes)* to pour out; *(colère)* to vent, to give vent to; **é. sa bile sur qn** to vent one's spleen on sb; **é. son cœur** to open one's heart, to pour out one's feelings **2** *Méd* to extravasate **3** *Arch ou Littéraire (liquide)* to pour out, to discharge
▸**s'épancher** VPR **1** *(se confier)* **s'é. auprès d'un ami** to open one's heart to *or* to pour out one's feelings to a friend **2** *Arch ou Littéraire (couler)* to pour out

épandage [epãdaʒ] NM *Agr* muck spreading; **champ d'é.** sewage farm; **é. des eaux usées** wastewater spreading

épandeur [epãdœr] NM *Agr* muck spreader

épandeuse [epãdøz] NF gravel spreader

épandre [74] [epãdr] VT to spread
▸**s'épandre** VPR *Littéraire* to spread (**sur** over)

épanneler [24] [epanəle] VT *Archit & Beaux-Arts* to rough hew

épanner [3] [epane] VT *Constr (pierre meulière)* to flatten one side of

épanoui, -e [epanwi] ADJ *(rose, jeunesse)* blooming; *(sourire)* beaming, radiant; *(personne)* radiant; **son corps é.** his/her body in its prime; **le tableau représente une maternité épanouie** the painting depicts the fulfilment of motherhood

épanouir [32] [epanwir] VT **1** *Littéraire (fleur)* to open (up); *(voiles)* to spread **2** *(détendre → visage)* to light up; **un large sourire lui épanouit le visage** his/her face broadened into a grin
▸**s'épanouir** VPR **1** *(fleur)* to bloom, to open **2** *(visage)* to light up **3** *(personne)* to blossom; **une atmosphère où les enfants s'épanouissent** an atmosphere where children can blossom

épanouissant, -e [epanwisã, -ãt] ADJ fulfilling

épanouissement [epanwismã] NM **1** *(d'une plante)* blooming, opening up **2** *(d'un visage)* lighting up; *(d'un enfant, d'une personnalité)* fulfilment, self-fulfilment; **elle a trouvé son é. dans le mariage** she's found fulfilment in marriage, she's blossomed since she got married; **une civilisation en plein é.** a civilization in full bloom

épar [epar] NM *(d'une porte)* cross-bar; *Aut (d'un véhicule)* shaft-bar; *Naut* spar

éparchie [eparʃi] NF *Rel* eparchy

épargnant, -e [eparɲã, -ãt] NM,F *Banque, Écon & Fin* saver, investor; **petits épargnants** small investors

épargne [eparɲ] NF **1** *Banque, Écon & Fin (économies)* **l'é.** savings; **é. complément de retraite** pension fund savings; **é. des entreprises** company reserves; **é. forcée** forced saving; **é. institutionnelle** institutional savings; **é. investie** investments; **é. liquide** on-hand savings; **é. mobilière** fixed savings; **l'é. productive** re-invested savings; **é. salariale** save as you earn scheme, SAYE **2** *(fait d'économiser)* saving; **encourager l'é.** to encourage saving **3** *(épargnants)* **l'é. privée** private investors **4** *Fig (de temps, forces)* saving

épargne-logement [eparɲlɔʒmã] *(pl* **épargnes-logements)** NF *Banque, Écon & Fin* **plan d'é.** home savings plan, *Br* ≃ building society (savings) account, *Am* ≃ savings and loan association account; **prêt é.** home loan

épargner [3] [eparɲe] VT **1** *(économiser → argent, essence)* to save; *(→ beurre, sel etc)* to be sparing with; **é. ses forces** to save one's strength;

épargnez l'eau! save *or* don't waste water!; *Hum* **tu n'as pas épargné la chantilly!** you didn't skimp on the whipped cream!; **n'é. ni sa peine ni son temps** to spare neither time nor trouble **2** *(éviter)* **é. qch à qn** to spare sb sth; **tu m'as épargné un déplacement inutile** you spared *or* saved me a wasted journey; **je vous épargnerai les détails** I'll spare you the details; **é. à qn la honte/vue de qch** to spare sb the shame/sight of sth; **é. à qn la peine de faire qch** to save sb the trouble of doing sth; **épargne-moi tes commentaires!** spare me your comments! **3** *(ménager → vieillard, adversaire)* to spare; **personne ne sera épargné** nobody *or* no life will be spared; **l'incendie a épargné l'église** the church was spared by the fire; **elle a toujours tenté d'é. ses enfants** she has always tried to shield her children ◆ VI *Banque, Écon & Fin* to save (money), to put money aside; *Péj* **é. sur qch** to save on sth; **é. sur les loisirs** to save on leisure activities
▸**s'épargner** VPR **s'é. qch** to save oneself sth

épargne-retraite [eparɲrətrɛt] *(pl* **épargnes-retraites)** NF *Banque, Écon & Fin* pension fund, retirement fund

éparpillement [eparpijmã] NM **1** *(de papiers, de graines)* scattering; *(état)* scattered state **2** *(de la pensée, des efforts)* dissipation

éparpiller [3] [eparpije] VT **1** *(disperser → papiers, graines)* to scatter; *(→ troupes, famille)* to disperse; **éparpillés un peu partout dans le monde** scattered about the world **2** *(dissiper → attention, forces)* to dissipate
▸**s'éparpiller** VPR **1** *(se disperser → foule, élèves)* to scatter, to disperse **2** *(disperser son énergie)* to dissipate one's energies

éparque [epark] NM *Hist & Rel* eparch

épars, -e [epar, -ars] ADJ scattered; *(végétation, population, informations)* sparse

épart [epar] = **épar**

éparvin [eparvẽ] NM *Vét* spavin

épatamment [epatamã] ADV *Fam Vieilli* splendidly

épatant, -e [epatã, -ãt] ADJ *Fam Vieilli* splendid; **c'est un type é.!** he's a splendid fellow!

épate [epat] NF *Fam Péj* showing off; **faire de l'é.** to show off

épaté, -e [epate] ADJ **1** *Fam (étonné)* amazed ▪ **2** *(aplati → nez, forme)* flat, snub

épatement [epatmã] NM **1** *Fam (étonnement)* amazement ▪ **2** *(du nez)* flatness

épater [3] [epate] VT **1** *Fam (étonner)* to amaze ▪; **ça t'épate, hein?** how about that, then? **2** *Fam Péj (impressionner)* to impress ▪; **pour é. la galerie** in order to cause a sensation ▪; **pour é. le bourgeois** in order to shock ▪ *(middle-class values)* **3** *(rendre plat)* to flatten out the base of
▸**s'épater** VPR *(s'élargir)* to spread out

épaufrer [3] [epofre] **s'épaufrer** VPR *Tech* to spall

épaufrure [epofryr] NF *Tech* spall

épaulard [epolar] NM *Zool* killer whale

épaule [epol] NF **1** *Anat* shoulder; **être large d'épaules** to be broad-shouldered; *Fam* **avoir les épaules tombantes** *ou* **en accent circonflexe** to be round-shouldered ▪; **donner un coup d'é. à qn** to give sb a helping hand; **charger un fardeau sur é.** to shoulder a burden; *Mil* **l'arme sur l'é.** with rifle at the slope; **la réussite du projet repose sur ses épaules** the project's success rests on his/her shoulders **2** *Culin* shoulder; **é. d'agneau** shoulder of lamb

épaulée [epole] NF *Vieilli* **1** *(poussée)* = push with the shoulders **2** *(charge)* = load carried on the shoulders

épaulé-jeté [epoleʒəte] *(pl* **épaulés-jetés)** NM *Sport* clean-and-jerk

épaulement [epolmã] NM **1** *Constr* retaining wall **2** *(rempart)* breastwork **3** *Menuis* shouldering **4** *Géog* escarpment

épauler [3] [epole] VT **1** *(fusil)* to raise (to the shoulder) **2** *(aider)* to support, to back up; **il a besoin de se sentir épaulé** he needs to feel that people are supporting him *or* are behind him; **j'aurais besoin de me faire é. dans ce travail** I could do with some support *or* help in this job

3 *Couture* to put shoulder pads into; **veste très épaulée** jacket with big shoulder pads **4** *(mur)* to retain, to support ◆ USAGE ABSOLU *(viser)* to take aim ◆ VI *(en danse)* to shoulder
▸**s'épauler** VPR to help *or* to support one another

épaulette [epolɛt] NF **1** *Mil* epaulette **2** *Couture* shoulder pad **3** *(bretelle)* shoulder strap

épaulière [epoljɛr] NF *(d'une armure)* shoulderpiece, epauliere

épave [epav] NF **1** *(débris)* piece of flotsam (and jetsam); **épaves flottantes** flotsam; **épaves rejetées** jetsam **2** *(véhicule, bateau)* wreck **3** *Jur (objet perdu)* unclaimed object **4** *(personne)* (human) wreck

épaviste [epavist] NMF = person who salvages wrecked vehicles for a living

épeautre [epotr] NM *Agr & Bot* spelt

épée [epe] NF **1** *Mil* sword; *Escrime* épée; **coup d'é.** swordthrust; **l'é. de Damoclès** the sword of Damocles; **c'est un coup d'é. dans l'eau** it's a waste of time; **mettre l'é. dans les reins de qn** to chivy sb **2** *(escrimeur)* swordsman, *f* swordswoman

épeiche [epɛʃ] NF *Orn* great spotted woodpecker

épeichette [epɛʃɛt] NF *Orn* lesser spotted woodpecker

épeire [epɛr] NF *Entom* **é. diadème** garden spider

épéiste [epeist] NMF *Escrime* épéeist

épeler [24] [eple] VT **1** *(mot)* to spell (out); **mal é. qch** to misspell sth **2** *(lire avec difficulté → texte)* to spell out ◆ USAGE ABSOLU *(nommer les lettres)* to spell
▸**s'épeler** VPR **comment ça s'épelle?** how do you spell it?, how is it spelt?

épellation [epelasjõ] NF spelling out

ependyme [epãdim] NM *Anat* ependyma

épenthèse [epãtɛz] NF *Ling* epenthesis

épenthétique [epãtetik] ADJ *Ling* epenthetic

épépiner [3] [epepine] VT to seed, to de-seed; **tomates épépinées** de-seeded tomatoes

éperdu, -e [epɛrdy] ADJ **1** *(fou → regard, cri)* wild, distraught; **la quête éperdue de la vérité** the frantic quest for truth; **une fuite éperdue** a headlong flight; **é. de** overcome with; **é. de bonheur** overcome with happiness; **é. de joie** overcome with joy, overjoyed; **é. de douleur** frantic *or* distraught with grief **2** *(intense → gratitude)* boundless; *(→ besoin)* violent, intense; *(→ résistance)* desperate

éperdument [epɛrdymã] ADV **1** *(à la folie)* madly, passionately; **aimer qn é.** to love sb madly, to be madly in love with sb **2** *(en intensif) Fam* **je m'en moque** *ou* **fiche é.** I couldn't care less *or* give a damn

éperlan [epɛrlã] NM *Ich* smelt

éperon [eprõ] NM **1** *Équitation & Tech* spur; **donner de l'é. à son cheval, piquer de l'é.** to spur (on) one's horse; **gagner ses éperons** to win one's spurs **2** *(d'une fleur, d'une montagne, d'un coq)* spur; **é. rocheux** rocky spur **3** *Naut* cutwater **4** *Hist (d'un vaisseau de guerre)* ram

éperonner [3] [eprɔne] VT **1** *Équitation* to spur (on) **2** *(munir d'éperons)* to put spurs on **3** *(stimuler)* to spur on; **éperonné par la volonté de réussir** spurred on by the will to succeed **4** *Hist (vaisseau de guerre)* to ram

épervier [epɛrvje] NM **1** *Orn* sparrowhawk **2** *Pêche* cast *or* casting net

épervière [epɛrvjɛr] NF *Bot* hawkweed

épervin [epɛrvẽ] NM *Vét (d'un cheval)* spavin

e-pétition [ipetisjɔ̃] NF *Ordinat* e-petition

épeurant, -e [epœrã, -ãt] ADJ *Can* scary, frightening

épeuré, -e [epœre] ADJ *Littéraire* frightened, scared

épeurer [5] [epœre] VT *Littéraire* to frighten, to scare

éphèbe [efɛb] NM *Antiq* ephebe; *Fig Hum* **(jeune) é.** Adonis

éphébie [efebi] NF *Antiq* ephebia

éphédra [efedra] NM *Bot* ephedra, shrubby horsetail

éphédrine [efedrin] NF *Pharm* ephedrin, ephedrine

éphélide [efelid] NF *Méd* freckle

éphémère [efemɛr] ADJ *(gloire, sentiment)* short-lived, ephemeral, transient; *(mode)* short-lived; *(regret)* passing; **ce chanteur n'a connu**

qu'un succès é. this singer enjoyed only a short-lived *or* brief success

NM*Entom* mayfly, dayfly, *Spéc* ephemera

éphéméride [efemerid] NF *(calendrier)* tear-off calendar

□ **éphémérides** NFPL*Astron* ephemeris

Éphèse [efɛz] NF*Antiq* Ephesus

Éphésien, -enne [efezjɛ̃, -ɛn] NM,F*Ephesian; Bible* **(Épitre aux) Éphésiens** (Epistle to the) Ephesians

ephlet [eflɛ] NM *(abrév* **essai-pamphlet**) essay pamphlet

éphod [efɔd] NM*Antiq* ephod

éphorat [efɔra] NM*Antiq* ephoralty

éphore [efɔr] NM*Antiq* ephor

épi [epi] NM1 *Bot (de fleur)* spike; *(de céréale)* ear; **é. de maïs** corncob; *Culin* corn on the cob **2** *(de cheveux)* tuft; **il a un é.** *(toujours)* his hair sticks out; *(en ce moment)* his hair's sticking up **3** *(dans les travaux publics)* spur, groyne; *Archit* **é. de faîtage** finial

□ **en épi** ADV1 *Agr* **blés en é.** wheat in the ear **2 voitures stationnées en é.** cars parked at an angle to the kerb **3** *Constr* **appareil en é.** herringbone bond

épiage [epjaʒ] NM*Agr* earing, heading

épiaire [epjɛr] NM*Bot* (wood) betony

épiaison [epjɛzɔ̃] NF*Agr* earing, heading

épiblaste [epiblast] NM*Biol* epiblast

épicanthus [epikɑ̃tys] NM*Anat* epicanthic fold, epicanthus

épicarpe [epikarp] NM*Bot* epicarp

épice [epis] NF*spice*

épicé, -e [epise] ADJ1 *Culin* highly spiced, hot, spicy; **ce n'est pas très é.** it's quite mild, it's not very hot **2** *(grivois → histoire)* spicy, juicy

épicéa [episea] NM*Bot* spruce

épicène [episɛn] ADJ*Ling* epicene

épicentre [episɑ̃tr] NM*epicentre*

épicer [16] [epise] VT1 *Culin* to spice **2** *(corser → récit)* to add spice to

épicerie [episri] NF1 *(magasin)* grocery *Br* shop *or Am* store; **à l'é. du coin** at the local *Br* grocer's *or Am* grocery store, *Br* at the corner shop; **é. fine** delicatessen **2** *(profession)* grocery trade **3** *(aliments)* provisions, groceries **4** *Can Fig* **liste d'é.** *(de griefs etc)* shopping list

épichlorhydrine [epiklɔridrin] NF *Chim* epichlorhydrin

épicier, -ère [episje, -ɛr] NM,F*grocer*

□ **d'épicier** ADJ *Péj (idées, littérature etc)* common-or-garden; *(mentalité)* small-town, parochial

épiclèse [epiklɛz] NF*Rel* epiclesis, epiklesis

épicondyle [epikɔ̃dil] NM*Anat* epicondyl

épicondylite [epikɔ̃dilit] NF *Méd* tennis elbow, *Spéc* epicondylitis

épicontinental, -e, -aux, -ales [epikɔ̃tinãtal, -o] ADJ*Géog* epicontinental

épicrânien, -enne [epikranjɛ̃, -ɛn] ADJ*Anat* epicranial

épicrise [epikriz] NF*Méd* epicrisis

Épicure [epikyr] NPR*Epicurus*

épicurien, -enne [epikyrjɛ̃, -ɛn] ADJ 1 *Phil* Epicurean **2** *(hédoniste)* epicurean

NM,F1 *Phil* Epicurean **2** *(bon vivant)* epicure, bon viveur

épicurisme [epikyrism] NM1 *Phil* Epicureanism **2** *(hédonisme)* hedonism, epicureanism

épicycle [episikl] NM*Antiq* epicycle

épicycloïdal, -e, -aux, -ales [episiklɔidal, -o] ADJ *Géom* epicycloidal; *Tech (engrenage)* epicyclic

épicycloïde [episiklɔid] NF*Géom* epicycloid

Épidaure [epidɔr] NF*Antiq* Epidaurus

épidémicité [epidemisite] NF*Méd* epidemicity

épidémie [epidemi] NF*Méd* epidemic; **é. de typhus** epidemic of typhus, typhus epidemic; *aussi Fig* **c'est devenu une véritable é.** it has reached epidemic proportions

épidémiologie [epidemjɔlɔʒi] NF *Méd* epidemiology

épidémiologique [epidemjɔlɔʒik] ADJ *Méd* epidemiological

épidémiologiste [epidemjɔlɔʒist] NMF *Méd* epidemiologist

épidémique [epidemik] ADJ*Méd* epidemic; *Fig* contagious

épiderme [epidɛrm] NM*Anat* skin, *Spéc* epidermis;

avoir l'é. sensible to have a sensitive *or* a delicate skin; *Fig* to be thin-skinned *or* touchy

épidermique [epidɛrmik] ADJ1 *Anat* skin *(avant n)*, *Spéc* epidermic, epidermal; *(blessure)* surface *(avant n)*; *(greffe)* skin *(avant n)* **2** *(immédiat → sentiment, réaction)* instant; **je ne peux pas le sentir, c'est é.** I don't know why, I just can't stand him

épidermoïde [epidɛrmɔid] ADJ*Méd* epidermoid

épidermomycose [epidɛrmɔmikoz] NF*Méd* epidermomycosis

épidiascope [epidjaskɔp] NM*Opt* epidiascope

épididyme [epididim] NM*Anat* epididymis

épididymite [epididimit] NF*Méd* epididymitis

épidote [epidɔt] NF*Géol* epidote

épidural, -e, -aux, -ales [epidyral, -o] ADJ*Méd* epidural

épier [9] [epje] VT1 *(espionner)* to spy on **2** *(réaction, mouvement)* to watch closely; *(bruit)* to listen out for; *(signe, occasion)* to be on the look-out for, to watch (out) for

épierrage [epjɛraʒ], **épierrement** [epjɛrmɑ̃] NM *Agr* **l'é. d'un champ** removing stones from a field

épierrer [4] [epjere] VT*Agr* to clear of stones, to pick the stones out of

épierreur [epjerœr] NM*Agr* stone-removing machine

épierreuse [epjerøz] NF*Agr* stone-removing machine

épieu, -x [epjø] NM*Mil* pike; *Chasse* hunting spear

épieur, -euse [epjœr, -øz] NM,F*spy*

épigastre [epigastr] NM*Anat* epigastrium

épigastrique [epigastrik] ADJ*Anat* epigastric

épigé, -e [epiʒe] ADJ*Bot* epigeal, epigeous

épigenèse [epiʒənɛz] NF*Biol* epigenesis

épigénétique [epiʒenetik] ADJ*Biol* epigenetic

épigénie [epiʒeni] NF*Minér* epigenesis

épiglotte [epiglɔt] NF*Anat* epiglottis

épigone [epigon] NM*Littéraire* epigone

épigrammatique [epigramatik] ADJ *Littérature* epigrammatic

épigramme [epigram] NF*Littérature (poème)* epigram; *(mot)* witticism

NM*Culin* **épigrammes d'agneau** épigramme of lamb *(fried or grilled in breadcrumbs)*

épigraphe [epigraf] NF*epigraph*; **mettre une citation en é.** to use a quotation as an epigraph

épigraphie [epigrafi] NF*epigraphy*

épigraphique [epigrafik] ADJ*epigraphic, epigraphical*

épigraphiste [epigrafist] NMF*epigraphist, epigrapher*

épigyne [epiʒin] *Bot* ADJ*epigynous*

NF*epigyny*

épilateur [epilatœr] NM*hair remover, depilator*; **é. électrique** electric depilator; **é. à la cire** wax depilator

épilation [epilasjɔ̃] NF *hair removal*; **é. des jambes** removal of hair from the legs; **é. du visage** removal of facial hair; **é. des sourcils** plucking the eyebrows; **é. à la cire** waxing; **é. définitive** permanent hair removal; **é. au laser** laser hair removal; **e. au sucre** sugaring

épilatoire [epilatwar] ADJ*depilatory, hair-removing (avant n)*

épilepsie [epilɛpsi] NF*Méd* epilepsy

épileptiforme [epilɛptifɔrm] ADJ *Méd* epileptiform

épileptique [epilɛptik] *Méd* ADJ*epileptic*

NMF*epileptic*

épileptoïde [epilɛptɔid] ADJ*epileptoid*

NMF*Psy* epileptoid

épiler [3] [epile] VT*(aisselles, jambes)* to remove unwanted hair from; *(sourcils)* to pluck; **se faire é. les jambes à la cire** to have one's legs waxed

▸**s'épiler** VPR*to remove unwanted hair*; **s'é. les jambes à la cire** to wax one's legs

épileur, -euse [epilœr, -øz] NM,F*Antiq* depilator

épillet [epijɛ] NM*Bot* spikelet, spicule

épilobe [epilɔb] NM *Bot* willowherb; **é. en épis** rosebay willowherb

épilogue [epilɔg] NM 1 *Littérature & Théât* epilogue **2** *(issue)* conclusion, dénouement

épiloguer [3] [epiloge] VT*Arch* **1** *(récapituler)* to recapitulate **2** *(critiquer)* to pass censure on

VI**c'est fini, on ne va pas é.!** it's over and done with, there's no point going on about it!; **é. sur**

qch to hold forth about *or* to go over (and over) sth

épimaque [epimak] NM *Orn* long-tailed bird of paradise

épinaie [epinɛ] NF*brake, thicket*

Épinal [epinal] NF*Géog* Epinal

épinard [epinar] NM *Bot (plante)* spinach; *Culin* **épinards** spinach; **épinards en branches** leaf spinach

épinçage [epɛ̃saʒ] NM*Tex* burling

épincer [16] [epɛ̃se] VT1 *Tex* to burl **2** *Hort* to disbud

épinceter [27] [epɛ̃ste] VT*Tex* to burl

épine [epin] NF 1 *(de fleur)* thorn, prickle; *(de hérisson)* spine, prickle; **couvert d'épines** *(plante)* prickly; *(animal)* spiny; **tirer** *ou* **ôter une é. du pied à qn** *(tirer d'embarras)* to get sb out of a mess *or* a spot; *(soulager)* to relieve sb's mind; **tu m'a tiré une belle é. du pied!** you've saved my life!

2 *(buisson)* thorn bush; **é. blanche** hawthorn; **é. noire** blackthorn; **é. de rat** butcher's broom, knee holly

3 *Anat & Ordinat* **é. dorsale** backbone

épinette [epinɛt] NF1 *Mus* spinet **2** *Can Bot (épicéa)* spruce; **é. blanche** white spruce; **é. noire** black spruce; **é. rouge** tamarack, red spruce; **bière d'é.** spruce beer **3** *(cage)* hen coop

épinettière [epinɛtjɛr] NF *Can* spruce grove, spruce stand

épineurien, -enne [epinørjɛ̃, -ɛn] *Zool* ADJ*chordate*

NM*chordate, member of the Chordata*

épineux, -euse [epinø, -øz] ADJ1 *(fleur)* thorny, prickly; *(poisson)* spiny **2** *(délicat → problème, contexte)* thorny, tricky; *(→ situation)* tricky **3** *Vieilli (irritable)* prickly, touchy **4** *Anat (excroissance)* spinose, spinous

NM*Bot* thorn bush

épine-vinette [epinvinɛt] *(pl* **épines-vinettes**) NF *Bot* barberry

épinglage [epɛ̃glaʒ] NM*pinning*

épingle [epɛ̃gl] NF1 *Couture* pin; **é. anglaise** *ou* à **nourrice** *ou* **de sûreté** safety pin; **é. à chapeau** hatpin; **é. à cheveux** hairpin; **é. à linge** clothes *Br* peg *or Am* pin; **é. de cravate** tiepin; **monter qch en é.** to blow sth out of all proportion; **tirer** *ou* **retirer son é. du jeu** to pull out **2 é. de signalisation** *(d'une fiche)* marker tag

épinglé, -e [epɛ̃gle] ADJ*terry (avant n)*

NM*terry*

épingler [3] [epɛ̃gle] VT1 *(attacher → badge, papier)* to pin (on); **é. une robe** *(pour l'assembler)* to pin a dress together; *(pour l'ajuster)* to pin a dress up **2** *Fam (arrêter)* to nab; **se faire é.** to get nabbed

épinglerie [epɛ̃glɔri] NF1 *(entreprise)* pin factory **2** *(commerce)* pin trade

épinglette [epɛ̃glɛt] NF 1 *Can Vieilli (broche)* brooch **2** *Offic (pin's)* badge

épinglier [epɛ̃glije] NM*pin-tray, pin-box*

épinier [epinje] NM*Chasse* thicket

épinière [epinjɛr] *voir* **moelle**

épinoche [epinɔʃ] NF*Ich* stickleback

épinochette [epinɔʃɛt] NF*Ich* small stickleback

épipaléolithique [epipaleɔlitik] ADJ*Hist* post-paleolithic

épipélagique [epipelaʒik] ADJ*Géog* epipelagic

épiphane [epifan] ADJ*Antiq* Epiphanus

épiphanie [epifani] NF *Rel* **l'é.** *(du Christ)* the Epiphany

□ **Épiphanie** NF **l'É.** *(fête)* Twelfth Night, the Epiphany

épiphénomène [epifenɔmɛn] NM*Méd & Phil* epiphenomenon; *Fig* side-effect

épiphénoménisme [epifenɔmenism] NM*Phil* epiphenomenalism

épiphénoméniste [epifenɔmenist] *Phil* ADJ*epiphenomenalist*

NM*epiphenomenalist*

épiphonème [epifonɛm] NM *Ling & Littérature* epiphonema, epiphoneme

épiphylle [epifil] ADJ*Bot* epiphyllous

épiphyse [epifiz] NF*Anat (os)* epiphysis; *(glande)* epiphysis (cerebri), pineal gland

épiphysite [epifizit] NF*Méd* epiphysitis, physitis, physeal dysplasia

épiphyte [epifit] *Bot* ADJ*epiphytic, epiphytical*

NM*epiphyte*

épiphytie [epifiti] NF *Bot* epiphytic disease

épiploon [epiplɔɔ̃] NM *Anat* epiploon, omentum

épique [epik] ADJ **1** *Littérature* epic; **poème é.** epic (poem) **2** *(extraordinaire → discussion, scène)* epic; **pour retrouver sa trace, ça a été é.!** finding out where he/she was was quite a saga!

Épire [epir] NF *Géog* Epirus

épirogénèse [epirɔʒenɛz] NF *Géol* epirogenesis

épirogénique [epirɔʒenik] ADJ *Géol* epirogenic

épirote [epirɔt] *Géog* ADJ Epirotic
□ **Épirote** NMF Epirot, Epirote

épisclérite [episklerit] NF *Méd* episcleritis

épiscopal, -e, -aux, -ales [episkɔpal, -o] ADJ *Rel* episcopal

épiscopalien, -enne [episkɔpaljɛ̃, -ɛn] *Rel* ADJ episcopalian
NM,F episcopalian

épiscopalisme [episkɔpalism] NM *Rel* episcopalism, episcopalianism

épiscopat [episkɔpa] NM *Rel (fonction, évêques)* episcopate, episcopacy

épiscope [episkɔp] NM **1** *Opt Br* episcope, *Am* opaque projector **2** *Mil* periscope *(of a tank)*

épisiotomie [epizjɔtɔmi] NF *Méd* episiotomy

épisode [epizɔd] NM **1** *(partie)* episode, instalment; **feuilleton en six épisodes** six-part serial; *Fig Fam* **j'ai dû rater un é.** I must have missed something **2** *(circonstance)* episode; **un é. heureux de ma vie** a happy episode in my life **3** *Méd (trouble passager)* phase
□ **à épisodes** ADJ serialized; *Fig* **sa vie est un roman à épisodes** his/her life is a real saga

épisodique [epizɔdik] ADJ **1** *(ponctuel)* occasional; **de manière é.** occasionally; **le caractère é. de leur relation** the on-off nature of their relationship **2** *(secondaire)* minor, secondary

épisodiquement [epizɔdikmɑ̃] ADV occasionally

épisome [epizɔm] NM *Biol* episome

épispadias [epispadjas] NM *Méd* epispadias

épisser [3] [epise] VT *Élec & Naut* to splice

épissoir [episwar] NM *Élec & Naut* splicing fid

épissoire [episwar] NF *Élec & Naut* splicing fid

épissure [episyr] NF *Élec & Naut* splice

épistasie [epistazi] NF *Biol* epistasis

épistate [epistat] NM *Antiq* epistates

épistatique [epistatik] ADJ *Biol* epistatic

épistaxis [epistaksis] NF *Méd* nosebleed, *Spéc* epistaxis

épistémé [episteme] NF *Phil* epistemics *(singulier)*

épistémologie [epistemɔlɔʒi] NF *Phil* epistemology

épistémologique [epistemɔlɔʒik] ADJ *Phil* epistemological

épistémologiste [epistemɔlɔʒist], **épistémologue** [epistemɔlɔg] NMF *Phil* epistemologist

épistolaire [epistɔlɛr] ADJ *Littérature (roman)* epistolary; *(style)* letter-writing *(avant n)*; **être en relations épistolaires avec qn** to have a correspondence with sb; **nous n'avons que des relations épistolaires** our only contact is by letter

épistolier, -ère [epistɔlje, -ɛr] NM,F *Littérature* letter writer

épistyle [epistil] NM *Archit* epistyle, architrave

épitaphe [epitaf] NF epitaph

épitaxie [epitaksi] NF *Électron* epitaxy, epitaxis

épite [epit] NF *Naut* spile, treenail wedge

épithalame [epitalam] NM *Littérature* epithalamium

épithélial, -e, -aux, -ales [epiteljal, -o] ADJ *Biol & Bot* epithelial

épithélioma [epiteljɔma] NM *Méd* epithelioma

épithélioneurien [epiteljɔnœrjɛ̃] NM *Zool* = organism with an epithelial nervous system

épithélium [epiteljɔm] NM *Biol & Bot* epithelium; **é. pavimenteux** pavement epithelium; **é. simple** squamous epithelium

épithète [epitɛt] ADJ attributive; **adjectif é.** attributive adjective
NF **1** *Gram* attribute **2** *(qualificatif)* epithet; *Hum* **quelques épithètes malsonnantes** a few choice adjectives

épitoge [epitɔʒ] NF **1** *(écharpe)* sash **2** *Antiq* cloak *(worn over the toga)*

épitomé [epitɔme] NM epitome, abridgment

épître [epitr] NF **1** *Rel* epistle; *Bible* **l'É. aux Corinthiens** the Epistle to the Corinthians; **Épîtres des Apôtres** Epistles; **côté de l'é.** *(de l'autel)* Epistle side **2** *Littérature* epistle **3** *Antiq* epistle; *Hum* **quand j'ai reçu son é.** when I received his/her missive

épivarder [3] [epivarde] **s'épivarder** VPR *Can Vieilli* **1** *(faire sa toilette → gén)* to freshen up; *(→ en se levant)* to get washed and dressed; *(se pomponner)* to doll oneself up **2** *(prendre l'air frais)* to take the air **3** *(s'amuser follement)* to have a gay old time

épizootie [epizɔɔti] NF *Vét* epizootic disease

épizootique [epizɔɔtik] ADJ *Vét* epizootic

éploré, -e [eplɔre] ADJ *(parent, veuve)* tearful, weeping; *(voix)* tearful; *(visage)* bathed *or* covered in tears

éployer [13] [eplwaje] VT *Littéraire* to spread

épluchage [eplyʃaʒ] NM **1** *(de légumes, de fruits)* peeling; *(de poireaux)* stripping the outer leaves; *(d'une laitue)* picking out the best leaves; *(de crevettes)* peeling, shelling **2** *(examen)* dissection, critical examination

épluche-légumes [eplyʃlegym] NM INV potato *or* vegetable peeler

éplucher [3] [eplyʃe] VT **1** *(peler → légumes, fruits)* to peel; *(→ poireau)* to strip the outer leaves off; *(crevettes)* to peel, to shell; **é. une laitue** to pick the best leaves out of a lettuce **2** *(analyser → texte, comptes)* to dissect, to go over with a fine-tooth comb; *(→ liste, statistiques)* to go through; **ma mère épluche mon emploi du temps** my mother checks up on how I spend my time

épluchette [eplyʃɛt] NF *Can* **é. de blé d'Inde** = party at which corn is husked and eaten

éplucheur, -euse [eplyʃœr, -øz] NM,F peeler
NM *(couteau)* potato *or* vegetable peeler
□ **éplucheuse** NF *(appareil)* automatic potato *or* vegetable peeler

épluchure [eplyʃyr] NF piece of peeling; **épluchures** peelings; **épluchures de pommes de terre** potato peelings

EPO [əpeo] NF *Physiol (abrév* **érythropoïétine***)* EPO

épode [epɔd] NF *Littérature* **1** *(couplet)* epode **2** *(poème)* epode

époi [epwa] NM *Chasse (chez les vieux cerfs)* tine

époisses [epwas] NM *Culin* = type of cheese from Bourgogne

épointage [epwɛ̃taʒ], **épointement** [epwɛ̃tmɑ̃] NM *(en cassant → d'un crayon)* breaking the point; *(en usant → d'une aiguille, d'un crayon, d'un outil etc)* blunting

épointer [3] [epwɛ̃te] VT *(en cassant → crayon)* to break the point of; *(en usant → aiguille, crayon, outil etc)* to blunt

éponge [epɔ̃ʒ] NF **1** *Zool* sponge
2 *(pour nettoyer)* sponge; **é. métallique** scouring pad, scourer; **d'un coup d'é.** with a sponge; **effacer une tache d'un coup d'é.** to sponge a stain out *or* away; **jeter l'é.** to throw in the sponge *or* towel; **passer l'é.** to let bygones be bygones; **passer l'é. sur qch** to forget all about sth; **je passe l'é. pour cette fois** this time, I'll overlook it; **boire comme une é., avoir une é. dans le gosier** *ou* **l'estomac** to drink like a fish
3 *Bot* **é. végétale** loofah, vegetable sponge
4 *Fam (poumon)* lung■

épongeage [epɔ̃ʒaʒ] NM **1** *(d'un liquide)* sponging (up) **2** *(d'une surface)* wiping, sponging (down)

éponger [17] [epɔ̃ʒe] VT **1** *(absorber → liquide)* to soak *or* to sponge (up); **il épongea la sueur de son front** he wiped the sweat off his forehead **2** *(nettoyer → surface)* to wipe, to sponge (down); **é. le front à qn** to mop sb's brow **3** *(déficit)* to mop up, to absorb; **é. ses dettes** to pay off one's debts
▶**s'éponger** VPR **s'é. le front** to mop one's brow

éponte [epɔ̃t] NF *Mines* wall *(of lode)*

épontille [epɔ̃tij] NF *Naut (de pont)* shore, prop

éponyme [epɔnim] ADJ eponymous

éponymie [epɔnimi] NF *Antiq* **1** *(fonction)* = office of an eponymous magistrate **2** *(durée de cette fonction)* = year in office of an eponymous magistrate

épopée [epɔpe] NF *Littérature (poème)* epic (poem); *(récit)* epic (tale); *Fig (saga)* saga

époque [epɔk] NF **1** *(moment, date)* time; **il y a un an à pareille é.** this time last year; **à la même é.** at the same time, during the same period; **les savants de l'é.** the scientists of the time *or* day; **ça n'existait pas à l'é.** it didn't exist at the time *or* in those days; **à cette é.-là** at that time, in those days; **à l'é., elle était très connue** at the time she was very well known; **à l'é. où j'étais étudiant** when I was a student; **les jeunes de notre é.** the young people of today; **être de** *ou* **vivre avec son é.** to move with the times; **il n'est plus de son é.** he's out of step *or* tune with the times; **quelle é. (nous vivons)!** what times we live in!; **on vit une drôle d'é.** we live in strange times; **avec cette musique, c'est toute une é. qui lui revenait en mémoire** the music brought memories of an entire era flooding back to him/her
2 *(période historique)* age, era, epoch; **l'é. victorienne** the Victorian era *or* age; *Hist* **la Belle É.** the Belle Epoque; **faire é.** *(invention, déclaration etc)* to leave its mark on history; **découverte qui fait é.** epoch-making dis-covery
3 *(style)* period; **la Haute é.** *(Moyen Âge)* the Middle Ages; *(XVIème siècle)* the High Renaissance
4 *Géol* period
5 *Astron* epoch
□ **d'époque** ADJ period *(avant n)*; **meubles d'é.** period furniture, (genuine) antique furniture; **documents d'é.** archive documents; **la pendule est d'é.** it's a period clock

épouillage [epujaʒ] NM delousing

épouiller [3] [epuje] VT to delouse

époumoner [3] [epumɔne] **s'époumoner** VPR to shout oneself hoarse; **j'avais beau m'é., il n'entendait pas** even though I was yelling at the top of my voice, he still didn't hear me; **c'est ce que je m'époumone à te dire!** I've told you so until I'm hoarse

épousailles [epuzaj] NFPL *Arch* nuptials

épouse [epuz] NF wife, spouse; **voulez-vous prendre Maud Jolas pour é.?** do you take Maud Jolas to be your lawful wedded wife?

épousée [epuze] NF *Arch ou Littéraire* bride

épouser [3] [epuze] VT **1** *(se marier avec)* to marry; **veux-tu m'é.?** will you marry me?; **é. une grosse dot** *ou* **fortune** to marry into money *or* into a rich family; **elle cherche à se faire é.** she's looking for a husband
2 *(adopter → idées)* to espouse, to embrace; *(→ cause)* to take up
3 *(suivre)* **é. la forme de qch** to take on the exact shape of sth; **une robe qui épouse la forme du corps** a figure-hugging *or* close-fitting dress; **la route épouse la colline** the road follows the hill round
▶**s'épouser** VPR to marry, to get married

épouseur [epuzœr] NM *Arch ou Littéraire* suitor, gallant

époussetage [epustaʒ] NM dusting

épousseter [27] [epuste] VT **1** *(nettoyer)* to dust; *(vêtements)* to brush (the dust from) **2** *(enlever → poussière)* to dust *or* to flick off

époustouflant, -e [epustuflɑ̃, -ɑ̃t] ADJ *Fam* stunning, astounding, staggering

époustoufler [3] [epustufle] VT *Fam* to stun, to astound, to flabbergast

époutir [32] [eputir] VT *Tex* to burl

épouvantable [epuvɑ̃tabl] ADJ **1** *(très désagréable)* awful, horrible, terrible; **il fait un temps é.** the weather's abominable; **elle a un caractère é.** she has a foul temper **2** *(effrayant)* frightening, dreadful

épouvantablement [epuvɑ̃tabləmɑ̃] ADV **1** *(en intensif)* frightfully, terribly, dreadfully **2** *(de façon effrayante)* frighteningly, dreadfully

épouvantail [epuvɑ̃taj] NM **1** *(pour oiseaux)* scarecrow **2** *(menace)* bogey, bogeyman; **agiter l'é. de la drogue** to use the threat of drugs as a bogey **3** *Péj (personne → laide)* fright; *(→ mal habillée)* mess, sight; *(→ terrifiante)* bogey; **elle a l'air d'un é. habillée comme ça** she looks a real sight dressed like that

épouvante [epuvɑ̃t] NF horror, dread; **être glacé** *ou* **saisi d'é.** to be terror-struck *or* terror-stricken; **penser à qch avec é.** to think of sth with horror
□ **d'épouvante** ADJ *(film, roman)* horror *(avant n)*; *(cris)* terrified, terror-stricken

épouvanté, -e [epuvɑ̃te] ADJ horror-sticken, horrified; **regarder qn d'un air é.** to look at sb in horror; **prendre un air é.** to look horror-stricken *or* horrified

épouvantement [epuvɑ̃tmɑ̃] NM *Littéraire* deadly terror

épouvanter[3] [epuvɑ̃te] **VT** to terrify, to fill with terror

époux [epu] **NM** husband, spouse; **voulez-vous prendre Paul Hilbert pour é.?** do you take Paul Hilbert to be your lawful wedded husband?; **les é.** the married couple, the husband and wife; *Jur* **é. communs en biens** = married couple who have a community of property matrimonial regime; **les é. Bertier** Mr and Mrs Bertier; **les futurs é.** the engaged couple; **les jeunes é.** the newly-weds

époxy[epɔksi] **ADJ INV** *Chim* epoxy

époxyde[epɔksid] **NM** *Chim* epoxide

époxydique[epɔksidik] **ADJ** *Chim* epoxy

épreintes[eprɛ̃t] **NFPL** *Méd* tenesmus

éprendre [79] [eprɑ̃dr] **s'éprendre VPR** *Littéraire* **s'é. de qn** to fall for sb, to become enamoured of sb; *Littéraire* **s'é. d'une idée** to fall in love with *or* become passionate about an idea

épreuve[eprœv] **NF 1** *(test)* test; **l'é. du temps** the test of time; **é. de force** trial of strength; *Chim* **é. à la pierre de touche** acid test; **l'é. de vérité pour...** the critical test for...

2 *(obstacle)* ordeal, trial; **vie remplie d'épreuves** life of hardship

3 *Littéraire (adversité)* **l'é.** adversity, hardship; **rester digne dans l'é.** to retain one's dignity in the face of adversity

4 *Scol & Univ (examen)* test, examination; *(copie)* paper, script; **é. écrite** paper, written test; **é. orale** oral (test); **corriger des épreuves** to mark exam papers

5 *Sport* event; **épreuves d'athlétisme** track events; **é. éliminatoire** heat; **é. d'endurance** endurance trial; **é. contre la montre** time trial; **épreuves sur piste** track events; **les épreuves finales** the finals

6 *Typ* proof; **corriger** *ou* **revoir les épreuves d'un livre** to proofread a book; **dernière/première é.** final/galley *or* first proof; **é. bonne à filmer** camera-ready copy, CRC; **é. de calage** machine proof; **épreuves d'imprimerie** printer's proofs; **é. ozalide** ozalid; **é. de page** page proof; **é. en placard** galley (proof)

7 *Phot* print; **é. par contact** contact (print); **é. glacée** glossy print; **é. mate** matt print; **é. négative** negative print; **é. positive** positive print; *Cin* **épreuves de tournage** rushes

8 *Hist* ordeal; **épreuves judiciaires** trial by ordeal; **l'é. du feu** ordeal by fire

❑ **à l'épreuve ADV mettre qn/qch à l'é.** to put sb/sth to the test

❑ **à l'épreuve de PRÉP** proof against; **à l'é. des balles** bulletproof; **à l'é. du feu** fireproof; **à l'é. de l'eau** waterproof

❑ **à rude épreuve ADV mettre qch à rude é.** to put sth to the test; **mettre les nerfs de qn à rude é.** to put sb's nerves to the test; **être mis à rude é.** *(personne, patience, honneur etc)* to be severely tested; *(jouets etc)* to be roughly treated *or* handled; **les bateaux ont été mis à rude é. par la tempête** the boats took a battering from the storm

❑ **à toute épreuve ADJ** *(mécanisme)* foolproof; *(patience, bonne humeur, courage)* unfailing

épris, -e[epri, -iz] **PP** *voir* **éprendre**

ADJ *Littéraire* **j'étais très éprise à l'époque** I was very much in love at the time; **être é. de qn** to be in love with sb; **ils sont très é. (l'un de l'autre)** they're very much in love (with one another); **é. de qch** passionate about sth; **être é. de liberté** to be in love with freedom

eprom, EPROM [eprɔm] **NF INV** *Ordinat (abrév* **erasable programmable read-only memory)** EPROM

éprouvant, -e[epruvɑ̃, -ɑ̃t] **ADJ** trying, testing; **un climat é.** a difficult climate

éprouvé, -e[epruve] **ADJ 1** *(sûr → méthode, matériel)* well-tested, tried and tested, proven; *(→ compétence, courage)* proven; *(→ spécialiste)* proven, experienced; *(→ allié)* trusty, staunch **2** *(mis à rude épreuve → famille)* stricken; *(→ région)* hard-hit; **troupes très éprouvées** troops that have suffered a great deal

éprouver [3] [epruve] **VT 1** *(ressentir → douleur, haine)* to feel, to experience; **les sentiments qu'il éprouve pour moi** the feelings that he has for me; **je n'éprouve plus rien pour lui** I don't feel anything for him any more; **é. une grande honte/déception** to feel deeply ashamed/disappointed; **é. le besoin de** to feel the need to

2 *(tester → procédé)* to try *or* to test (out); *(→ courage, personne)* to test; **é. la résistance d'un matériau** to test (out) the resilience of a material; **é. la patience de qn** to try sb's patience, to put sb's patience to the test; **ils nous ont dit cela pour nous é.** they told us that to test us

3 *(subir → pertes)* to suffer, to sustain; *(→ difficultés)* to meet with

4 *(faire souffrir)* to try, to test; **son divorce l'a beaucoup éprouvée** her divorce was a very trying experience for her; **une région durement éprouvée par la crise** an area that has been hard hit by the recession; **le gel a durement** *ou* **fortement éprouvé les récoltes** the crops have suffered greatly *or* have sustained severe damage from the frost

éprouvette [epruvɛt] **NF** test tube; **é. graduée** burette

EPS[əpeɛs] **NF** *Scol (abrév* **éducation physique et sportive)** PE

NM *Ordinat (abrév* **encapsulated PostScript)** EPS

epsilon[ɛpsilɔn] **NM** epsilon

epsomite[ɛpsɔmit] **NF** epsomite, Epsom salts

épucer[16] [epyse] **VT** to rid of fleas

épuisable[epɥizabl] **ADJ** exhaustible

épuisant, -e[epɥizɑ̃, -ɑ̃t] **ADJ** exhausting

épuisé, -e [epɥize] **ADJ 1** *(fatigué)* exhausted, worn out, tired out; **être é. de fatigue** to be exhausted *or* worn out; **être é. nerveusement** to be emotionally drained

2 *(sol, mine)* exhausted, worked out; *Fig* **ma patience est épuisée** my patience has run out; *Élec* **pile épuisée** dead battery; *Nucl* **uranium é.** depleted *or* impoverished uranium

3 *Com (article)* sold out; *(marchandises)* sold out, out of stock; *(livre)* out of print; *(ressources, réserves, stocks)* exhausted, depleted

épuisement [epɥizmɑ̃] **NM 1** *(fatigue)* exhaustion; **mourir d'é.** to die of exhaustion; **être dans un état d'é. total** to be completely *or* utterly exhausted, to be in a state of complete *or* utter exhaustion; **danser/marcher jusqu'à l'é.** to dance/walk until one drops; **rouler/nager jusqu'à l'é.** to drive/swim until one is exhausted

2 *Com & Ind* exhaustion; *(de ressources)* depletion; *(de marchandises)* selling out; *(de stocks)* exhaustion, depletion; *(d'une citerne)* draining, emptying; **exploiter une mine jusqu'à é.** to exhaust a mine; **jusqu'à é. des stocks** while stocks last; **jusqu'à é. des provisions** until supplies run out

3 *Jur* **é. des voies de recours internes** exhaustion of local remedies

épuiser[3] [epɥize] **VT 1** *(fatiguer)* to exhaust, to wear *or* to tire out; *Fam* **tu m'épuises avec tes questions** you're wearing me out with your questions

2 *(exploiter → puits)* to work dry; *(→ gisement, veine)* to exhaust, to work out; *(→ sol, sujet)* to exhaust; *Fig* **é. la patience de qn** to exhaust *or* wear out sb's patience; **cette marche a épuisé toute mon énergie** that walking has used up all my energy

3 *(consommer → vivres, ressources)* to exhaust, to use up; *(→ stocks)* to exhaust; *(→ marchandises)* to sell out; *(→ citerne)* to drain, to empty

4 *(lettre de crédit)* to use up

▶**s'épuiser VPR 1** *(être très réduit → provisions, munitions)* to run out, to give out; *(→ source)* to dry up; *(→ filon)* to be worked out

2 *(se fatiguer → athlète)* to wear oneself out, to exhaust oneself; *(→ corps)* to wear itself out, to run out of steam; *Fam* **s'é. à faire qch** *(s'évertuer)* to wear oneself out doing sth; **je me suis épuisé à le lui faire comprendre** I wore myself out trying to make him/her understand; **mais oui, il viendra, puisque je m'épuise à te le répéter!** of course he'll come, I'm tired of telling you so! ▪*or* I've told you so until I'm blue in the face!

épuisette [epɥizɛt] **NF 1** *(filet)* landing net **2** *(pelle)* bailer

épulide[epylid], **épulie**[epyli] **NF** *Méd* epulis

épulis[epylis] **NM** *Méd* epulis

épulon[epylɔ̃] **NM** *Antiq* epulo

épulpeur[epylpœr] **NM** *Tech* pulp extractor

épurateur [epyratœr] **NM** *Tech* filter, purifier; **é. d'air** air filter; **é. d'eau** water filter; **é. de gaz** gas purifier, (gas) scrubber

épuratif, -ive[epyratif, -iv] **ADJ** purifying

épuration[epyrasjɔ̃] **NF 1** *(de l'eau)* purification, filtering; *(du gaz)* purification, scrubbing; *(du pétrole, d'un minerai)* refining; **é. biologique** biological treatment **2** *(du style)* refinement, refining **3** *Pol* purge; *Hist* **l'É.** = period after the Second World War during which collaborators were tried and punished; **é. ethnique** ethnic cleansing

épurative[epyrativ] *voir* **épuratif**

épuratoire[epyratwar] **ADJ** *Tech* purifying

épure[epyr] **NF 1** *Beaux-Arts (dessin fini)* working drawing **2** *(projections)* blueprint

épurement[epyrmɑ̃] **NM** *Littéraire* **1** *(pureté morale)* purification **2** *(style)* refinement

épurer[3] [epyre] **VT 1** *(liquide)* to filter; *(eau)* to purify; *(gaz)* to purify, to scrub; *(pétrole, minerai)* to refine **2** *(style, langue)* to refine, to make purer **3** *Pol (administration)* to purge

épurge[epyrʒ] **NF** *Bot* euphorbia

épyornis[epjɔrnis] **NM** aepyornis

équanimité[ekwanimite] **NF** *Littéraire* evenness of temper, equanimity

équarrir[32] [ekarir] **VT 1** *(bois, pierre)* to square (off) **2** *(animal)* to cut up

équarrissage [ekarisaʒ] **NM 1** *(du bois, de la pierre)* squaring (off) **2** *(d'un animal)* cutting up; **chantier d'é.** knacker's yard

équarrisseur[ekarisœr] **NM 1** *(de bois, de pierre)* squarer **2** *(aux abattoirs)* (meat) renderer

équarrissoir [ekariswar] **NM 1** *(couteau)* knacker's knife **2** *(abattoir)* knacker's yard

Équateur[ekwatœr] **NM** *Géog* **(la république de) l'É.** (the Republic of) Ecuador; **vivre en É.** to live in Ecuador; **aller en É.** to go to Ecuador

équateur[ekwatœr] **NM** *Géog* equator; **sous l'é.** at the equator; **é. magnétique** magnetic equator; *Astron* **é. céleste** celestial equator

équation [ekwasjɔ̃] **NF 1** *Math* equation; **é. du premier/second degré** simple/quadratic equation

2 *Astron* **é. du temps** equation of time

3 *Chim* **é. chimique** chemical equation

4 *Psy* **é. personnelle** personal equation

5 *Compta* **é. de bénéfice** profit equation; **é. de coût** cost equation

6 *Mktg* **é. de la demande** demand equation; **é. de réponse de marché** sales-response equation; **é. de vente** sales equation

équato-guinéen, -enne [ekwatɔgineɛ̃, -ɛn] **ADJ** Equatorial Guinean

❑ **Équato-Guinéen, -enne NM,F** Equatorial Guinean

équatorial, -e, -aux, -ales [ekwatɔrjal, -o] **ADJ 1** *Astron & Géog* equatorial **2** *Biol* **plaque équatoriale** equatorial plate

NM equatorial (telescope)

équatorien, -enne [ekwatɔrjɛ̃, -ɛn] **ADJ** Ecuadoran, Ecuadorian

❑ **Équatorien, -enne NM,F** Ecuadoran, Ecuadorian

équerrage[ekɛraʒ] **NM** *Menuis (mise à angle droit)* squaring

équerre[ekɛr] **NF 1** *(instrument)* **é. (à dessin)** set square; **é. d'arpenteur** cross-staff; **é. en T, double é.** T-square; **é. à coulisse** (sliding) calliper gauge; **é. à onglet** mitre square; **fausse é.** bevel square

2 *(pièce métallique)* corner plate

❑ **d'équerre ADJ** *(mur)* straight; *(pièce)* square; **mettre qch d'é.** to square sth

❑ **à l'équerre ADJ 1** *(mur)* straight; *(pièce)* square; **mettre qch à l'é.** to square sth

2 *Sport* with one's legs straight out *or* outstretched; **avoir les jambes à l'é.** to have one's legs straight out *or* outstretched

❑ **en équerre ADJ** *Sport* with one's legs straight out *or* outstretched; **avoir les jambes en é.** to have one's legs straight out *or* outstretched; **monter à la corde, les jambes en é.** to climb a rope with one's legs straight out *or* outstretched

équerrer[3] [ekere] **VT** *Menuis* to square

équestre [ekɛstr] **ADJ** *(statue, peinture)* equestrian; *(exercice, centre)* horseriding *(avant n)*; **le sport é.** (horse)riding

équeutage[ekøtaʒ] **NM** removing the stalk

équeuter [3] [ekøte] **VT** *(fruit)* to pull the stalk off, to remove the stalk from

équiangle [ekɥiɑ̃gl] **ADJ** *Math* equiangular

équidé [ekide] *Zool* **NM** member of the horse family *or Spéc* of the Equidae
❑ **équidés NMPL les équidés** the horse family, *Spéc* the Equidae

équidistance [ekɥidistɑ̃s] **NF** equidistance
❑ **à équidistance de PRÉP à é. de Moscou et de Prague** halfway between Moscow and Prague

équidistant, -e [ekɥidistɑ̃, -ɑ̃t] **ADJ** equidistant (**de** from)

équilatéral, -e, -aux, -ales [ekɥilateral, -o] **ADJ** *Math* equilateral; *Hum* **ça m'est é.!** I really couldn't care less!

équilatère [ekɥilatɛr] **ADJ** *Géom* **hyperbole é.** equilateral hyperbola

équilibrage [ekilibraʒ] **NM** *Aut* balancing, counterbalancing; **faire faire l'é. des roues** to have the wheels balanced

équilibrant, -e [ekilibrɑ̃, -ɑ̃t] **ADJ** balancing *(avant n)*; **lotion équilibrante** = cream that restores the skin's natural balance; **shampooing é.** = shampoo that restores the hair's natural balance; **poids é.** counterweight; *Psy* **c'est un facteur é. dans la vie d'un enfant** it's a stabilizing factor in a child's life

équilibration [ekilibrasjɔ̃] **NF** balancing, counterbalancing, *Spéc* equilibration

équilibre [ekilibr] **NM 1** *(stabilité du corps)* balance; *(d'un avion)* stability; *(en aviron)* set, balance; **avoir (le sens) de l'é.** to have a good sense of balance; **garder/perdre l'é.** to keep/to lose one's balance; **faire perdre l'é. à qn** to throw sb off balance; **cet acrobate fait de l'é.** *ou* **des tours d'é.** this acrobat does balancing tricks
2 *(rapport de force)* balance; **établir un é. entre** to strike a balance between; **rétablir l'é.** to restore the balance; **l'é. des forces** *ou* **du pouvoir** the balance of power; **é. instable** unstable equilibrium; **l'é. de la terreur** the balance of terror; **l'é. naturel** the balance of nature
3 *(des éléments d'un ensemble)* balance, harmony; *TV & Cin* **é. des couleurs** colour balance
4 *Écon & Fin* **é. budgétaire** balance in the budget; **é. économique** economic equilibrium; **é. fiscal** fiscal balance
5 *Psy* **é. (mental)** (mental) balance *or* equilibrium; **manquer d'é.** to be (mentally *or* emotionally) unbalanced
6 *Écol* **é. biologique/écologique** biological/ecological balance
7 *Chim & Phys* equilibrium; *Phys* **é. indifférent/stable** unstable/stable equilibrium
❑ **en équilibre ADJ** *(plateau, pile de livres)* stable; *(budget)* balanced; **la chaise est en é. instable** the chair is precariously balanced **ADV marcher en é. sur un fil** to balance on a tightrope; **mettre qch en é.** to balance sth; **le clown tenait un verre en é. sur son nez** the clown was balancing a glass on his nose

équilibré, -e [ekilibre] **ADJ 1** *Psy* balanced, stable **2** *(chargement, budget)* balanced; *(alimentation, repas, emploi du temps)* balanced, well-balanced; *(vie)* regular, stable; *(match, rencontre, mi-temps)* equal; **mal é.** unbalanced, unstable; **vie peu équilibrée** irregular *or* unstable life **3** *Méd (maladie)* controlled

équilibrer [3] [ekilibre] **VT 1** *(contrebalancer → poids, forces)* to counterbalance; *(→ roues)* to balance; **faire é. ses roues** to have the wheels balanced **2** *(rendre stable)* to balance; **é. ses comptes** to break even, to reach break-even point; **é. son alimentation** to eat a more balanced diet
▸**s'équilibrer VPR** to counterbalance each other *or* one another, to even out

équilibreur [ekilibrœr] **NM** *Aviat* stabilizer

équilibriste [ekilibrist] **NMF** *(acrobate)* acrobat; *(funambule)* tightrope walker

équille [ekij] **NF** *Ich* launce, sand eel *or* lance

équimolaire [ekɥimɔlɛr] **ADJ** *Chim* equimolar; **mélange é.** equimolar mixture

équimoléculaire [ekɥimɔlekylɛr] **ADJ** *Chim* equimolecular

équimultiple [ekɥimyltipl] *Math* **ADJ** equimultiple **NM** equimultiple

équin, -e [ekɛ̃, -in] **ADJ** *Méd* equine

équinisme [ekinism] **NM** *Méd* club foot

équinoxe [ekinɔks] **NM** *Géog* equinox; **é. de printemps/d'automne** spring/autumn equinox; **vent d'é.** equinoctial gale

équinoxial, -e, -aux, -ales [ekinɔksjal, -o] **ADJ** *Géog* equinoctial

équipage [ekipaʒ] **NM 1** *Aviat & Naut* crew; **membres de l'é.** members of the crew, crew members; **homme d'é.** crew member; *Naut* **maître d'é.** boatswain
2 *Arch (escorte → d'un prince)* retinue, suite; *Hum* **aller en** *ou* **mener grand é.** to live in grand style; **arriver en grand é.** to arrive in state
3 *(matériel) Mil* equipment; *Tech* equipment, gear; **é. de construction** builder's *or* building equipment *or* gear
4 *Hist (voiture, chevaux etc)* equipage
5 *Chasse* **l'é.** the hunt
6 *Vieilli (tenue)* attire
7 *Arch ou Littéraire (situation, état)* state; **le voilà en triste é.** he's in a sorry state

équipartition [ekɥipartisjɔ̃] **NF** equipartition

équipe [ekip] **NF 1** *(groupe → de travailleurs)* team; *(→ à l'usine)* shift; **travailler en é.** to work as a team; **travailler en** *ou* **par équipes** *(à l'usine)* to work in shifts; **ils forment une é. très soudée** they're a very close-knit team; **faire é. avec qn** to team up with sb; **vous deux, vous allez faire é.?** would you two like to work together?; **se mettre en** *ou* **par équipes** to get into *or* form teams; *Rail* **é. de conduite** *ou* **de locomotive** engine crew; *Mktg* **é. commando** venture team; **é. commerciale** marketing team; **é. de création** creative team; **é. dirigeante** management team; **é. gouvernementale** Government, *Br* ≃ Cabinet, *Am* ≃ Administration; **é. de jour/nuit** day/night shift; **é. ministérielle** ministerial team; *Méd* **é. de professionnels de (la) santé** healthcare team; **é. promotionnelle** promotion team; **é. de secours** *ou* **de sauveteurs** rescue team; **é. de vente** sales team
2 *Mil* working party
3 *Sport (gén)* team; *(sur un bateau)* crew; **jouer en** *ou* **par équipes** to play in teams; **l'é. de France de rugby/hockey** the French rugby/hockey team; **é. de cricket** cricket team *or* eleven; **é. d'amateurs/de professionnels** amateur/professional team; **é. de reserve** reserve team; *Presse* **l'É.** = French daily sports newspaper
4 *(bande)* crew, gang; **on formait une joyeuse é.** we were a happy lot
5 *Cin* **é. caméra** camera crew; *Journ* **é. d'investigation** investigative team; *Journ* **é. de nuit** back-bench; *TV & Cin* **é. de prise de vue** camera crew; *TV & Cin* **é. de production** production team; *Journ* **é. de soutien** back-bench; **é. de télévision** television crew
❑ **d'équipe ADJ 1** *(collectif)* **esprit d'é.** team *or* group spirit; **travail d'é.** teamwork
2 *(sport, jeu)* team *(avant n)*

équipée [ekipe] **NF 1** *(aventure)* escapade; **une folle é.** a mad escapade **2** *Hum (promenade)* jaunt

équipement [ekipmɑ̃] **NM 1** *(matériel → léger)* equipment, supplies; *(→ lourd)* equipment; **renouveler l'é. d'une usine** to refit a factory; **é. acoustique** audio equipment; **é. audiovisuel** audiovisual equipment; **é. de bureau** office supplies; **é. électrique** electrical supplies; **é. industriel** industrial plant; **é. informatique** computer equipment; *Aut* **é. intérieur** internal fittings; *Aut* **équipements spéciaux** *(pneus)* snow tyres; *(chaînes)* chains; *Ordinat* **é. terminal de traitement de données** data terminal equipment
2 *(panoplie)* kit, gear; **un é. de ski** a set of skiing equipment *or* gear; **un é. de pêche en rivière** fishing tackle *or* gear; **é. de survie** survival kit
3 *(infrastructure)* **équipements collectifs** public amenities; **équipements publics** public facilities; **équipements sportifs/scolaires** sports/educational facilities; **l'é. routier/ferroviaire du pays** the country's road/rail infrastructure; **(le service de) l'É.** = local government department responsible for road maintenance and issuing building permits
4 *(fait de pourvoir → atelier, cuisine)* equipping, equipment, fitting out (**de** with); **procéder à l'é. d'un régiment** to equip a regiment; **procéder à l'é. d'un terrain de jeu** to equip a playing field; **assurer l'é. en hommes et en matériel** to provide the workforce and material
5 *Aviat* **é. embarqué** *ou* **de bord** on-board equipment

équipementier [ekipmɑ̃tje] **NM** *Ind* manufacturer of components

équiper [3] [ekipe] **VT 1** *(pourvoir en matériel → armée, élève, skieur)* to kit out, to fit out (**de** *ou* **en** with); *(→ salle, atelier, cuisine)* to equip, to fit out (**de** with); *(→ usine)* to equip, to tool up (**de** *ou* **en** with); *(→ navire)* to equip, to fit out; *(pourvoir en hommes → navire)* to man; **cuisine tout** *ou* **entièrement équipée** fully-equipped kitchen; **é. une voiture pour la neige** to equip a car for the snow; **être bien équipé pour une expédition** to be all set up *or* kitted out for an expedition; **é. une maison d'un système d'alarme** to install a burglar alarm in a house; *Fam* **comme vous voilà équipé!** what a get-up!
2 *(pourvoir d'une infrastructure)* **é. une ville d'un réseau d'égouts** to equip a town with a sewage system; **é. une ville en terrains de sport** to provide a town with sports grounds; **é. industriellement une région** to bring industry to a region
▸**s'équiper VPR** to equip oneself, *Br* to kit oneself out; **un micro-ondes? eh bien, on s'équipe!** a microwave? we are getting organized, aren't we!; **sa société s'est équipée en ordinateurs** *ou* **d'ordinateurs** his/her company has equipped itself with computers

équipier, -ère [ekipje, -ɛr] **NM,F** *Sport* team member; *Naut* crew member; **son é.** his team mate *or* fellow team member; *Naut* **mené par 14 équipiers** manned by a crew of 14, with a 14-man crew

équipolé, équipollé [ekipɔle] **ADJ M** *Hér* **points équipollés** equipollent points

équipollence [ekipɔlɑ̃s] **NF** *Géom* equipollence

équipollent, -e [ekipɔlɑ̃, -ɑ̃t] **ADJ** *Géom* equipollent

équipotence [ekɥipɔtɑ̃s] **NF** *Math* equipotence

équipotent [ekɥipɔtɑ̃] **ADJ M** *Math* equipotent

équipotentiel, -elle [ekɥipɔtɑ̃sjɛl] **ADJ** *Math* equipotential

équiprobable [ekɥiprɔbabl] **ADJ** *Math* equiprobable

équisétales [ekɥisetal] **NFPL** *Bot* Equisetales

équisétinée [ekɥisetine] *Bot* **NF** equisetum, horsetail
❑ **équisétinées NFPL** equisetums, horsetails; **les équisétinées** equisetums, *Spéc* the Equiseta

équisétophyte [ekɥisetɔfit] **NM** *Bot* equisetophyte

équitable [ekitabl] **ADJ 1** *(verdict, répartition)* fair, equitable **2** *(personne)* fair, fair-minded, even-handed

équitablement [ekitabləmɑ̃] **ADV** fairly, equitably

équitant, -e [ekitɑ̃, -ɑ̃t] **ADJ** *Bot* equitant

équitation [ekitasjɔ̃] **NF** *Sport* horseriding, riding; **faire de l'é.** to go horseriding; **je n'ai jamais fait d'é.** I've never been horseriding, I've never ridden a horse
❑ **d'équitation ADJ** *(école, professeur)* riding *(avant n)*

équité [ekite] **NF** equity, fairness, fair-mindedness
❑ **en toute équité ADV** very equitably *or* fairly

équivalence [ekivalɑ̃s] **NF 1** *(gén) & Math* equivalence **2** *Univ* **faire une demande d'é., demander une é.** to request an equivalent rating of one's qualifications; **avoir une é.** to have an equivalent diploma; **quels sont les diplômes étrangers admis en é.?** which foreign diplomas are recognized? **3** *Jur* **é. des conditions** alternative causation

équivalent, -e [ekivalɑ̃, -ɑ̃t] **ADJ** *(gén) & Math* equivalent (**à** to); **le prix de vente est é. au prix de revient** the selling price is equivalent to the cost price
NM *(élément comparable)* equivalent; **sans é.** without equal, unequalled; **l'é. de 300 dollars en euros** the equivalent of 300 dollars in euros; **il n'y a pas d'é. anglais de ce mot** there is no English equivalent for this word; *Chim* **é. gramme** gram equivalent, equivalent weight; *Phys* **é. mécanique de la chaleur** mechanical equivalent of heat

équivaloir [60] [ekivalwar] **équivaloir à VT IND**

(être égal à) to be equal *or* equivalent to; *(revenir à)* to amount to; **le prix de cette voiture équivaut à un an de salaire** this car costs the equivalent of a year's salary; **ça équivaut à s'avouer vaincu** it amounts to admitting defeat; **cela équivaut à dire que...** that amounts to *or* is tantamount to *or* is equivalent to saying that...; **cela équivaut à un refus** that amounts to a refusal

▶ **s'équivaloir** VPRto be equivalent

équivoque [ekivɔk] ADJ **1** *(ambigu → terme, réponse, attitude)* equivocal, ambiguous; *(→ compliment)* double-edged, back-handed; **de manière é.** equivocally

2 *(suspect → fréquentation, comportement)* questionable, dubious; *(→ personnage)* shady

NF **1** *(caractère ambigu)* ambiguity; **sans é.** *(adj)* unequivocal; *(adv)* unequivocally; **un maître de l'é.** a master of equivocation

2 *(malentendu)* misunderstanding; **afin d'éviter toute é.** in order to avoid any possibility of misunderstanding; **cela pourrait prêter à é.** this could be misinterpreted *or* misconstrued

3 *(doute)* doubt; **pour lever** *ou* **dissiper l'é. sur mes intentions** so as to leave no doubt as to my intentions

équivoquer [3] [ekivɔke] VI*Littéraire* to equivocate

-ER[e] SUFF

● This very productive suffix is used in French to create verbs from nouns, verbs or adjectives, eg:
dégueulasser to mess up; **positiver** to think positive
Note that the final consonant of the adjective may change (positi*f* → positi*v*er).
● In recent years, this suffix has often been added to English nouns or verbs to create gallicized verbs, eg:
faxer to fax; **mailer** to e-mail; **zapper** to channel-hop; **tchater** to chat online (from *tchat*, a gallicized form of "chat", ie an online forum); **relooker quelqu'un** to give somebody a makeover

érable [erabl] NM *Bot* maple; **é. à sucre** *ou* **du Canada** sugar maple; **é. champêtre** field maple

érablière [erablijɛr] NF*Bot* maple grove, *Am* sugar bush

éradication [eradikasjɔ̃] NFeradication, rooting out

éradiquer [3] [eradike] VTto eradicate, to root out

éraflement [eraflǝmɑ̃] NMscratching

érafler [3] [erafle] VT**1** *(écorcher → peau, genou)* to scrape, to scratch, to graze **2** *(rayer → peinture, carrosserie)* to scrape, to scratch; *(→ bois, meuble)* to scratch

▶ **s'érafler** VPR **s'é. les mains** to graze one's hands

éraflure [eraflyr] NF scratch, scrape; *(au genou etc)* scratch, graze; *(sur cuir etc)* scuff (mark); *(sur bois, meuble)* scratch (mark); **se faire une é. au coude** to scrape *or* to graze one's elbow

éraillé, -e [eraje] ADJ**1** *(rauque)* rasping, hoarse; **avoir la voix éraillée** to be hoarse **2** *(rayé → surface)* scratched **3** *(tissu)* frayed; *(corde)* fretted **4** *(injecté)* **avoir l'œil é.** to have bloodshot eyes

éraillement [erajmɑ̃] NM **1** *(d'un tissu)* fraying; *(d'une corde)* fretting; *(d'une surface)* scratching **2** *(éraflure)* scratch **3** *(de voix)* hoarseness

érailler [3] [eraje] VT**1** *(tissu)* to fray; *(ourlet etc)* to unravel; *(corde)* to fret **2** *(peau, surface etc)* to scratch **3** *(voix)* to make hoarse

▶ **s'érailler** VPR**1** *(ourlet etc)* to unravel, to come unravelled; *(tissu)* to fray; *(corde)* to fret **2** *(voix)* to become hoarse; **s'é. la voix** to make oneself hoarse

éraillure [erajyr] NFscratch

Érasme [erasm] NPRErasmus

érathème [eratɛm] NM*Géol* erathem

erbine [ɛrbin] NFChim erbia, erbium oxide

erbium [ɛrbjɔm] NMChim erbium

ère [ɛr] NF**1** *Hist (époque)* era; **l'è. chrétienne** the Christian era; **è. de prospérité** period of prosperity; **une nouvelle è. commence** it's the beginning of a new era, a new era has begun; **270 ans avant notre è.** 270 BC; **en l'an 500 de notre è.** in the year 500 AD, in the year of our Lord 500 **2** *Géol* era

érecteur, -trice [erɛktœr, -tris] ADJ*Physiol* erector

érectile [erɛktil] ADJ*Physiol* erectile

érectilité [erɛktilite] NF*Physiol* erectility

érection [erɛksjɔ̃] NF**1** *Physiol* erection; **avoir une é.** to have an erection; **être en é.** *(personne)* to have an erection; *(organe)* to be erect **2** *Littéraire (édification → d'une statue, d'une église)* erection, raising **3** *Vieilli (établissement → d'un tribunal)* establishment, setting up

érectrice [erɛktris] *voir* **érecteur**

éreintage [erɛtaʒ] NM*Fam (critique)* panning, *Br* slating

éreintant, -e [erɛtɑ̃, -ɑ̃t] ADJ*Fam* gruelling, back-breaking

éreinté, -e [erɛte] ADJexhausted, worn out

éreintement [erɛtmɑ̃] NM **1** *Fam (d'un auteur)* panning, *Br* slating **2** *(fatigue)* exhaustion

éreinter [3] [erɛte] VT **1** *(épuiser)* to exhaust, to wear out **2** *Fam (critiquer → pièce, acteur)* to pan, *Br* to slate; **son spectacle s'est fait é. par tous les critiques** all the critics panned *or Br* slated his/her show

▶ **s'éreinter** VPRto wear oneself out; **s'é. à faire qch** to wear oneself out doing sth

éreinteur, -euse [erɛtœr, -øz] NM,F*(critique)* detractor

érémiste [eremist] NMF *Fam* = person receiving the "RMI" benefit

érémitique [eremitik] ADJ *Littéraire* eremitic, eremitical

érémitisme [eremitism] NM *Littéraire* hermit's way of life, eremitism

érésipèle [erezipɛl] NM*Méd* erysipelas, Saint Anthony's fire

éréthisme [eretism] NM **1** *Méd* erethism; **é. cardiaque** cardiac erethism **2** *Littéraire (exaltation)* (extreme) intensity; *(tension excessive)* nervous excitement

éreuthophobie, éreutophobie [erøtofɔbi] NF*Psy* ereuthrophobia, erythrophobia

Erevan [erevan] NM*Géog* Yerevan

erg¹ [ɛrg] NM*Phys (unité)* erg

erg² [ɛrg] NM*Géog (étendue désertique)* erg

ergastoplasme [ɛrgastɔplasm] NM *Biol* ergastoplasm, endoplasmic reticulum

ergastule [ɛrgastyl] NM*Antiq* ergastulum

ergatif [ɛrgatif] NM*Gram* ergative

ergocalciphérol [ɛrgokalsiferɔl] NM *Biol & Chim* ergocalciferol

ergographe [ɛrgograf] NM*Méd* ergograph

ergol [ɛrgɔl] NM*Astron* propellant

ergologie [ɛrgolɔʒi] NF*Tech* ergology

ergomètre [ɛrgomɛtr] NM*Tech* ergometer

ergométrie [ɛrgometri] NF*Tech* ergometry

ergométrique [ɛrgometrik] ADJ*Tech* ergometric

ergonome [ɛrgonɔm] NMF*Tech* ergonomist

ergonomie [ɛrgonɔmi] NF *Tech* ergonomics *(singulier)*; **ce téléphone portable est doté d'une excellente e.** this *Br* mobile phone *or Am* cellphone is very ergonomic; **il ont amélioré l'e. de leur nouveau modèle** their new model is more ergonomically designed

ergonomique [ɛrgonɔmik] ADJ*Tech* ergonomic

ergonomiste [ɛrgonomist] NMF*Tech* ergonomist

ergostérol [ɛrgosterɔl] NM*Biol & Chim* ergosterol

ergot [ɛrgo] NM **1** *Zool (de coq)* spur; *(de chien)* dewclaw; *Fig* **monter** *ou* **se dresser sur ses ergots** to get on one's high horse **2** *Bot* ergot **3** *Tech* lug; **e. d'arrêt** stop lug; **e. de tracteur** *(d'imprimante)* tractor pin

ergotage [ɛrgotaʒ] NMquibbling

ergotamine [ɛrgotamin] NF *Biol & Chim* ergotamine

ergoté, -e [ɛrgote] ADJ**1** *(oiseau)* spurred; *(chien)* dewclawed **2** *Agr (seigle, blé)* affected with ergot

ergoter [3] [ɛrgote] VIto quibble; **e. sur des détails** to quibble about details

ergoterie [ɛrgotri] NFquibbling

ergoteur, -euse [ɛrgotœr, -øz] ADJquibbling NM,Fquibbler

ergothérapeute [ɛrgoterapøt] NMF *Méd* occupational therapist

ergothérapie [ɛrgoterapi] NF *Méd* occupational therapy

ergotisme [ɛrgotism] NM*Méd* ergotism, Saint Anthony's fire

éricacée [erikase] *Bot* NF heather, *Spéc* ericaceous plant

❑ **éricacées** NFPLheathers, *Spéc* Ericaceae

-ERIE [ǝri] SUFF

This is a multifunctional suffix that is used to form feminine nouns.
● When added to an adjective, **-erie** can refer to a TRAIT OF CHARACTER and as such can often be translated by the English suffix *-ness*, eg:
étourderie carelessness; **sournoiserie** slyness; **galanterie** courteousness; **mesquinerie** meanness
● When added to a noun or a verb, the idea is that of an ACTION, often with derogatory undertones:
tromperie deception; **moquerie** jeering; **flatterie** flattery; **ânerie** stupid remark/stupid mistake; **faire des cochonneries** to make a mess
● At the end of a noun, the suffix **-erie** can refer to an ACTIVITY. When this activity is a trade, the French word can sometimes be translated by an English noun ending in *-ing*. As well as the activity, some of the words created by the addition of the suffix can also refer to the PLACE where it is practised – often a shop, hence the translation of some of the following items:
parfumerie perfume trade, perfume shop; **bijouterie** jewellery-making, jeweller's (shop); **ébénisterie** cabinet-making; **plomberie** plumbing; **boucherie** butcher's shop; **carterie** card shop; **sandwicherie** sandwich bar

Érié [erje] NM*Géog* **le lac É.** Lake Erie

ériger [17] [eriʒe] VT**1** *(édifier → statue, temple)* to erect, to raise

2 *(instituer → comité, tribunal)* to set up, to establish

3 *Fig* **é. qn en** to set sb up as, to elevate sb to the status of; **é. qch en** to elevate sth to the status of, to present sth as; **é. une église en cathédrale** to raise a church to (the dignity of) a cathedral; **le cynisme érigé en art** cynicism raised to the status of fine art

▶ **s'ériger** VPR **s'é. en moraliste/censeur** to set oneself up as a moralist/a censor

érigéron [eriʒerɔ̃] NM*Bot* erigeron, flea-bane; **é. du Canada** horse-weed

érigne [eriɲ] NF(surgeon's) tenaculum

Erik [erik] NPRE. **le Rouge** Eric the Red

Érin [erin] NF*Littéraire* Erin

érine [erin] NF*Vieilli* (surgeon's) tenaculum

Érinyes [erini] NFPL*Myth* **les É.** the Erinyes, the Erynies

érismature [erismatyr] NM *Orn* **é. roux** ruddy duck

éristale [eristal] NM*Entom* eristalis

éristique [eristik] NFeristic
ADJeristic

erlenmeyer [ɛrlɛnmɛjœr] NM *Chim* Erlenmeyer flask

erminette [ɛrminɛt] NFadze

ermitage [ɛrmitaʒ] NM**1** *(d'un ermite)* hermitage **2** *(retraite)* retreat

ermite [ɛrmit] NM**1** *Rel* hermit **2** *(reclus)* hermit, recluse; **vivre comme un e.** *ou* **en e.** to live like *or* as a hermit, to lead the life of a recluse

éroder [3] [erode] VT*(côte, rochers etc)* to erode, to wear away; *(métaux etc)* to corrode, to eat away

érogène [erɔʒɛn] ADJerogenous, erogenic

Éros [eros] NPR*Myth* Eros

éros [eros] NM*Psy* **l'é.** Eros

érosif, -ive [erozif, -iv] ADJerosive

érosion [erozjɔ̃] NM **1** *Géog & Méd* erosion; **é. côtière** coastal erosion; **é. dentaire** dental erosion **2** *(dégradation)* erosion; *Écon & Fin* **é. fiscale** fiscal drag; **é. monétaire** monetary erosion

érosive [eroziv] *voir* **erosif**

érotique [erotik] ADJerotic

érotiquement [erotikmɑ̃] ADVerotically

érotisant, -e [erotizɑ̃, -ɑ̃t] ADJerotic

érotisation [erotizasjɔ̃] NFeroticization, eroticizing

érotiser [3] [erotize] VTto eroticize

érotisme [erotism] NM**1** *(caractère érotique)* eroticism; **d'un é. torride** *(film)* steamy; *(situation)* sexy, *Am* hot **2** *(goût pour le plaisir sexuel)* erotism

érotogène [erotoʒɛn] ADJerogenous, erogenic

érotologie [erotolɔʒi] NFerotology

érotologique [erotolɔʒik] ADJerotological

érotologue [erotolog] NMFerotologist

érotomane [erɔtɔman] NMF *Psy* erotomaniac

érotomaniaque [erɔtɔmanjak] ADJ *Psy* erotomaniac

érotomanie [erɔtɔmani] NF *Psy* erotomania

erpétologie [ɛrpetɔlɔʒi] NF *Zool* herpetology

erpétologique [ɛrpetɔlɔʒik] ADJ *Zool* herpetologic, herpetological

erpétologiste [ɛrpetɔlɔʒist] NMF *Zool* herpetologist

errance [ɛrɑ̃s] NF *Littéraire* wandering, roaming

errant, -e [ɛrɑ̃, -ɑ̃t] ADJ wandering, roaming; **mener une vie errante** to lead the life of a wanderer

errata [erata] *voir* **erratum**

NM INV *(liste)* list of errata

erratique [eratik] ADJ **1** *Géol & Méd* erratic **2** *(variation)* erratic

erratum [eratɔm] (*pl* **errata** [-ta]) NM *Presse* erratum

erre [ɛr] NF *Naut* headway; *(lancée)* way; **e. pour gouverner** steerage way; **avoir de l'e.** to have way on; **perdre de l'e.** *ou* **son e.** to lose way

❑ **erres** NFPL *Chasse (traces)* track, trail; *Fig* **suivre les erres de qn** to follow in sb's footsteps

❑ **sur son erre** ADV **aller/continuer sur son e.** to coast (along), to freewheel

errement [ɛrmɑ̃] NM *Fin* **e. du marché** market fluctuation

❑ **errements** NMPL *Littéraire* erring ways, bad habits; **retomber dans** *ou* **revenir à ses errements passés** to fall back into one's bad old ways

errer [4] [ɛre] VI **1** *(marcher)* to roam, to wander; **e. par les rues** to wander about *or* roam the streets; **e. comme une âme en peine** to wander about like a lost soul **2** *(imagination, pensées)* to wander, to stray; *(regard)* to wander, to rove; **un sourire errait sur ses lèvres** a smile played on *or* over his/her lips **3** *Littéraire (se tromper)* to err

erreur [ɛrœr] NF **1** *(faute)* mistake, error; **il doit y avoir une e.** there must be a *or* some mistake; **il y a e. sur la personne** you've got the wrong person, it's a case of mistaken identity; **il n'y a pas d'e. (possible)** there's no doubt about it; **e.!** wrong!; **c'est lui, pas d'e.!** that's him all right!; **ce serait une e. (que) de penser cela** it would be wrong *or* a mistake to believe this; **être dans l'e.** to be wrong *or* mistaken; **faire** *ou* **commettre une e.** to make a mistake *or* an error; **faire e.** to be wrong *or* mistaken; **e. de calcul** miscalculation; **e. de jugement** error of judgement; **e. de plume** slip of the pen; **e. typographique** *ou* **d'impression** misprint, printer's error; **e. de traduction** mistake in translation, mistranslation; *Prov* **l'e. est humaine** to err is human

2 *(errement)* error; **des erreurs de jeunesse** youthful indiscretions; **racheter ses erreurs passées** to mend one's ways; **retomber dans les mêmes erreurs** to lapse back into the same old bad habits

3 *Jur* **e. de droit** error in law; **e. de fait** error of fact; **e. judiciaire** miscarriage of justice; **e. mutuelle** mutual mistake; **e. sur la personne** mistaken identity; **e. sur la substance** fundamental mistake

4 *Ordinat* error; **message d'e.** error message; **correction des erreurs** error correction; **e. aléatoire** random error; **e. d'analyse (syntaxique)** parse error; **e. de codage** coding error; **e. disque** disk error; **e. d'échantillonnage** sampling error; **e. d'écriture** write error; **e. de lecture** read error; **e. de logiciel** software *or* system error; **e. de programmation** programming error; **e. de saisie** keying error; **e. de syntaxe** syntax error; **e. système** system error

❑ **par erreur** ADV by mistake

❑ **sauf erreur** ADV **je crois, sauf e., qu'il est venu hier** I believe, if I'm not mistaken, that he came yesterday; **sauf e. de ma part, ce lundi-là est férié** unless I'm (very much) mistaken, that Monday is a public holiday

❑ **sauf erreur ou omission** ADV *Com & Jur* errors and omissions excepted

erroné, -e [ɛrɔne] ADJ erroneous, mistaken

érronément [eronemɑ̃] ADV erroneously

ers [ɛr] NM *Bot* vetch

ersatz [ɛrzats] NM ersatz, substitute; **un e. de café** ersatz coffee; **un e. d'aventure/d'amour** a substitute for adventure/for love

erse[1] [ɛrs] ADJ & NM *Ling* Erse

erse[2] [ɛrs] NF *Naut* grummet, grommet

erseau, -x [ɛrso] NM *Naut* grommet

érubescence [erybɛsɑ̃s] NF *Littéraire* erubescence, blushing

érubescent, -e [erybɛsɑ̃, -ɑ̃t] ADJ *Littéraire* erubescent, blushing

éruciforme [erysiform] ADJ *Entom* eruciform

érucique [erysik] ADJ *Chim* **acide é.** erucic acid

éructation [eryktasjɔ̃] NF belch, *Spéc* eructation

éructer [3] [erykte] VI to belch, *Spéc* to eructate

VT **é. des injures** to belch (forth) insults

érudit, -e [erydi, -it] ADJ erudite, learned, scholarly

NM,F scholar, erudite *or* learned person

érudition [erydisjɔ̃] NF erudition, scholarship

érugineux, -euse [eryʒinø, -øz] ADJ *Vieilli* eruginous

éruptif, -ive [eryptif, -iv] ADJ *Géol & Méd* eruptive

éruption [erypsjɔ̃] NF **1** *Astron & Géol* eruption; **entrer en é.** to erupt; **volcan en é.** erupting volcano **2** *Méd* outbreak; **é. de boutons** outbreak of spots; **é. cutanée** rash; **é. dentaire** *ou* **des dents** cutting of teeth **3** *Fig (crise)* outbreak; **é. de colère** fit of anger, angry outburst

eruptive [eryptiv] *voir* **eruptif**

érysipélateux, -euse [erizipelatø, -øz] ADJ *Méd* erysipelatous

érysipèle [erizipɛl] NM *Méd* erysipelas, Saint Anthony's fire

érythémateux, -euse [eritematø, -øz] ADJ *Méd* erythematous

érythème [eritɛm] NM *Méd* erythema; **é. fessier** *Br* nappy *or Am* diaper rash; **é. solaire** sunburn

érythrasma [eritrasma] NM *Méd* erythrasma

Érythrée [eritre] NF *Géog* **l'É.** Eritrea; **vivre en É.** to live in Eritrea; **aller en É.** to go to Eritrea

érythréen, -enne [eritreɛ̃, -ɛn] ADJ *Géog* Eritrean

❑ **Érythréen, -enne** NM,F *Géog* Eritrean

érythrémie [eritremi] NF *Méd* erythraemia

érythrine [eritrin] NF **1** *Chim* erythrin, erythric acid **2** *Bot* Erythrina

érythroblaste [eritrɔblast] NM *Biol* erythroblast

érythroblastose [eritrɔblastoz] NF *Méd* erythroblastosis

érythrocytaire [eritrɔsitɛr] ADJ *Biol* erythrocytic

érythrocyte [eritrɔsit] NM *Biol* red blood cell, *Spéc* erythrocyte

érythrocytose [eritrɔsitoz] NF *Méd* erythrocytosis

érythrodermie [eritrɔdɛrmi] NF *Méd* erythrodermia

érythromycine [eritrɔmisin] NF *Pharm* erythromycin

érythrophobie [eritrɔfɔbi] NF *Psy* ereuthrophobia, erythrophobia

érythropoïèse [eritrɔpɔjɛz] NF *Physiol* erythropoïesis

érythropoïétine [eritrɔpɔjetin] NF *Physiol* erythropoietin

érythrose [eritroz] NF *Méd* erythrosis; **é. faciale** facial erythrosis

érythrosine [eritrɔzin] NF *Chim* erythrosin, erythrosine

E/S *Ordinat* (*abrév écrite* **entrée/sortie**) I/O

es *voir* **être**[1]

ès [ɛs] PRÉP **licencié ès lettres** ≃ Bachelor of Arts, ≃ BA; **licencié ès sciences** ≃ Bachelor of Sciences, ≃ BSc; **docteur ès lettres** ≃ Doctor of Philosophy, ≃ PhD; *Admin & Jur* **ès qualités** ex officio

Ésaü [ezay] NPR *Bible* Esau

ESB [əɛsbe] NF *Vét* (*abrév* **encéphalopathie spongiforme bovine**) BSE

esbigner [3] [ɛzbiɲe] **s'esbigner** VPR *Fam Vieilli (s'enfuir)* to skedaddle, to make *or* to clear off

esbroufe [ɛzbruf] *Fam* NF showing off; **faire de l'e.** to show off

❑ **à l'esbroufe** ADJ **vol à l'e.** pickpocketing

ADV **il l'a fait à l'e.** he bluffed his way through it; **avoir qn à l'e.** to bluff sb

esbroufer [3] [ɛzbrufe] VT *Fam* to bluff

esbroufeur, -euse [ɛzbrufœr, -øz] NM,F *Fam* smooth talker, bluffer

escabeau, -x [ɛskabo] NM **1** *(tabouret)* stool **2** *(échelle)* stepladder

escabèche [ɛskabɛʃ] NF *Culin* escabèche *(marinated fish)*

escabelle [ɛskabɛl] NF *Belg* stepladder

escadre [ɛskadr] NF **1** *Naut* squadron; **chef d'e.** squadron commander **2** *Aviat* **e. aérienne** wing; **chef d'e.** wing commander

escadrille [ɛskadrij] NF **1** *Naut* flotilla **2** *Aviat* flight, squadron; **e. de chasse** fighter squadron

escadron [ɛskadrɔ̃] NM **1** *(dans la cavalerie, l'armée blindée)* squadron; *(dans la gendarmerie)* company; **e. de chars** armoured squadron; *Pol* **e. de la mort** death squad **2** *Aviat* squadron; **e. de chasse/bombardement** fighter/bomber squadron **3** *Fam Hum (groupe)* bunch, gang

escagasser [3] [ɛskagase] VT **1** *(dans le Sud) (objet)* to smash, to wreck **2** *(en Provence) (personne → éreinter)* to wear out; *(→ agacer)* to annoy, to pester

▸**s'escagasser** VPR to wear oneself out

escalade [ɛskalad] NF **1** *Sport (activité)* (rock) climbing; *(ascension)* climb; **faire de l'e.** to go (rock) climbing; **e. artificielle** artificial climbing; **e. libre** free climbing

2 *(d'un mur, d'une grille)* climbing, scaling; *Jur* illegal entry; **nous avons dû faire de l'e. pour arriver jusqu'à la maison** we had to scramble up to the house

3 *(parcours)* climb

4 *(aggravation)* escalation; **l'e. de la violence** the escalation of violence; **à cause de l'e. des prix/taux d'intérêt** because of escalating prices/interest rates; **les charges locatives n'ont pas cessé leur e.** service charges are still escalating

escalader [3] [ɛskalade] VT *(montagne)* to climb; *(portail)* to climb, to scale, to clamber up; *(grille)* to climb over; *(muret)* to scramble up; *Hist & Mil (forteresse)* to escalade

Escalator® [ɛskalatɔr] NM escalator, moving staircase

escale [ɛskal] NF **1** *(lieu) & Naut* port of call; *Aviat* stop **2** *(halte) & Naut* call; *Aviat* stop, stopover; **faire e.** *Naut* to put into port; *Aviat* to touch down; **faire e. à** *Naut* to call at, to put in at; *Aviat* to stop over at; **l'avion a fait une e. forcée à Rio** the plane was forced to stop over at Rio; **visiter une ville pendant l'e.** *Naut* to visit a town while the ship is in port; *Aviat* to visit a town during a stopover; **e. technique** refuelling stop

❑ **sans escale** ADJ nonstop, direct

escalier [ɛskalje] NM **1** *(marches)* (flight of) stairs; *(cage)* staircase; **les escaliers** the staircase *or* stairs; **en bas des escaliers** at the bottom of the stairs; **en haut des escaliers** at the top of the stairs; **être dans l'e.** *ou* **les escaliers** to be on the stairs; **rencontrer qn dans l'e.** *ou* **dans les escaliers** to meet sb on the stairs; *Ski* **monter en e.** to sidestep; *Fig* **avoir des escaliers dans les cheveux** to have unevenly cut hair; **e. en colimaçon** *ou* **en vrille** spiral staircase; **e. dérobé** hidden staircase; **e. d'honneur** main staircase; **e. mécanique** *ou* **roulant** escalator; *Can* **e. mobile** escalator; **e. de secours** fire escape; **e. de service** backstairs, service stairs; **e. à vis** spiral staircase

2 *Tech* step; **en e.** stepped

3 *Typ (de titres)* step effect; **une courbe en e.** a jaggy

❑ **escaliers** NMPL *Belg (marches)* steps

escalope [ɛskalɔp] NF *Culin* escalope; **e. de veau/de poulet** veal/chicken escalope; **e. milanaise** Milanese escalope; **e. panée** escalope in breadcrumbs

escaloper [3] [ɛskalɔpe] VT *Culin* to cut into thin slices

escamotable [ɛskamɔtabl] ADJ *Tech (antenne, train d'atterrissage, phares)* retractable; *(lit, table)* collapsible, foldaway

escamotage [ɛskamɔtaʒ] NM **1** *Aviat (d'un train d'atterrissage)* retraction **2** *(disparition)* conjuring *or* spiriting away; **tour d'e.** vanishing trick **3** *(vol)* filching **4** *(action d'éluder → de problèmes, questions)* dodging; *(→ de difficultés)* evading; *(→ de mot, note)* skipping

escamoter [3] [ɛskamɔte] VT **1** *(faire disparaître → mouchoir, carte)* to conjure *or* to spirit away; *(→ placard, lit)* to fold away **2** *(voler)* to filch **3** *Fig (éluder → difficultés)* to evade, to skirt round; *(→ mot, note)* to skip; *(→ problème, question)* to dodge **4** *Aviat (train d'atterrissage)* to retract

escamoteur, -euse [ɛskamɔtœr, -øz] NM,F *(prestidigitateur)* conjurer

escampette [ɛskɑ̃pɛt] *voir* **poudre**
escapade [ɛskapad] **NF 1** *(fugue)* running off *or* away; **faire une e.** to run off *or* away **2** *(séjour)* jaunt; **une e. de deux jours à Deauville** a two-day visit *or* jaunt to Deauville
escape [ɛskap] **NF** *Archit (fût d'une colonne)* scape; *(partie inférieure du fût)* apophyge
escarbille [ɛskarbij] **NF** piece of soot
escarbot [ɛskarbo] **NM** *Entom (coléoptère)* beetle; *Fam (bousier)* cockchafer, dung beetle; **e. doré** rose-chafer
escarboucle [ɛskarbukl] **NF 1** *(pierre)* carbuncle **2** *Hér* escarbuncle
escarcelle [ɛskarsɛl] **NF** *Arch* moneybag; **tomber** *ou* **rentrer dans l'e. de qn** *(argent, collection de tableaux etc)* to come sb's way; *Hum* **200 euros vont tomber** *ou* **rentrer dans mon e.** I'm about to have a little windfall of 200 euros
escargot [ɛskargo] **NM** *Zool* snail; **avancer comme un e.** *ou* **à une allure d'e.** to go at a snail's pace; **il marche comme un e.** he's walking at a snail's pace; **nous avancions à la vitesse d'un e.** we were moving at a snail's pace; **opération e.** slowing down of the traffic *(by protesting truck drivers)*
escargotière [ɛskargɔtjɛr] **NF 1** *(parc)* snailery, snail farm **2** *(plat)* snail dish
escarmouche [ɛskarmuʃ] **NF** skirmish
escarpe [ɛskarp] **NF** *(talus)* escarp
escarpé, -e [ɛskarpe] **ADJ** steep; *(falaise)* sheer
escarpement [ɛskarpəmɑ̃] **NM 1** *(pente)* steep slope **2** *Géog* escarpment; **e. de faille** fault scarp
escarpin [ɛskarpɛ̃] **NM** pump, *Br* court shoe; *(pour danser)* pump
escarpolette [ɛskarpɔlɛt] **NF** *Arch (balançoire)* swing
escarre[1] [ɛskar] **NF** *Méd* scab; *(due à l'alitement)* bedsore
escarre[2] [ɛskar] **NF** *Hér* = L-shaped border of quarter
escarrification [ɛskarifikasjɔ̃] **NF** *Méd* formation of a scab; *(due à l'alitement)* formation of a bedsore
escarrifier [9] [ɛskarifje] **s'escarrifier VPR** *Méd* to form a scab
Escaut [ɛsko] **NM** *Géog* **l'E.** the (River) Scheldt
escavèche [ɛskavɛʃ] **NF** *Belg Culin* escabèche *(marinated fish)*
eschare [ɛskar] **NF** *Méd* scab; *(due à l'alitement)* bedsore
eschatologie [ɛskatɔlɔʒi] **NF** *Rel* eschatology
eschatologique [ɛskatɔlɔʒik] **ADJ** *Rel* eschatological
esche [ɛʃ] = **aiche**
escher [3] [eʃe] **VT** *Pêche* to bait
Eschyle [eʃil] **NPR** Aeschylus
e-science [isjɑ̃s] **NF** e-science
escient [esjɑ̃] **NM à bon e.** advisedly, judiciously; **à mauvais e.** injudiciously, unwisely
esclaffer [3] [ɛsklafe] **s'esclaffer VPR** to burst out laughing, to guffaw
esclandre [ɛsklɑ̃dr] **NM** scene, scandal; **faire** *ou* **causer un e., faire de l'e.** to make a scene
esclavage [ɛsklavaʒ] **NM 1** *(pratique)* slavery; **réduire qn en e.** to reduce sb to slavery, to make a slave out of sb **2** *(contrainte)* slavery, *Littéraire* bondage; **c'est un véritable e.!** it's slave labour! **3** *(dépendance)* **vivre dans l'e. de** to be a slave to; **subir l'e. de la drogue** to be a slave to drugs
esclavagisme [ɛsklavaʒism] **NM 1** *(pratique)* slavery; *(doctrine)* pro-slavery **2** *Zool* helotism
esclavagiste [ɛsklavaʒist] **NMF** supporter of slavery; *Fig* slavedriver
ADJ État e. slave state
esclave [ɛsklav] **ADJ 1** *(en sociologie)* **un peuple e.** an enslaved people
2 *Fig (assujetti)* **être e. de ses habitudes** to be a slave to *or* the slave of one's habits; **ne sois pas e. de ses moindres désirs** don't give in to his/her every whim; **être e. de l'alcool/du tabac** to be a slave to drink/to tobacco; **je refuse d'être e. du ménage/de la cuisine!** I won't be a slave to housework/a kitchen slave!
NM 1 *(personne réduite en esclavage)* slave; **marchand d'esclaves** slave trader; **il fut vendu comme e.** he was sold into slavery
2 *Fig* slave; **elle en a fait son e.** she has made him/her (into) her slave, she has enslaved him/her; **elle est l'e. de sa famille** she is a slave to her family; **être l'e. de son travail/de ses passions** to be a slave to one's work/one's passions; **les esclaves de la mode** fashion victims
escobar [ɛskɔbar] **NM** *Vieilli Péj* hypocrite *(who uses casuistry)*
escogriffe [ɛskɔgrif] **NM un grand e.** a beanpole
escomptable [ɛskɔ̃tabl] **ADJ** *Compta* discountable
escompte [ɛskɔ̃t] **NM 1** *Com* discount; **accorder** *ou* **faire un e. à qn/sur qch** to allow *or* give a discount to sb/on sth; **à e.** at a discount; **e. sur les achats en gros** bulk discount, quantity discount; **e. de caisse** cash discount; **e. commercial** trade discount; **e. au comptant** cash discount; **e. à forfait** forfaiting; **e. professionnel** *(au détaillant)* trade discount; **e. d'usage** trade discount
2 *Fin* discount; **prendre à l'e. un effet de commerce** to discount a bill of exchange; **présenter une traite à l'e.** to have a bill discounted; **e. de banque** bank discount; **e. de créances** invoice discounting; **e. en dedans** true discount; **e. en dehors** bank discount; **e. officiel** *Br* bank discount rate, *Am* prime rate; **e. de règlement** discount for early payment; **e. de traites** invoice discounting
3 *Can (remise)* discount; **50 pour cent d'e. sur toute la marchandise** 50 percent discount on all goods
4 *Bourse (de valeurs)* call for delivery before settlement
escompter [3] [ɛskɔ̃te] **VT 1** *(espérer)* to expect, to anticipate (**que** that); **e. qch** to rely *or* to count *or* to bank on sth; **e. une hausse** to anticipate an increase; **il escompte une embauche définitive** he's relying on (getting) a permanent job; **c'est mieux que ce que j'escomptais** it's better than what I expected; **il m'a fait e. une augmentation de salaire dans les mois à venir** he told me I could count on a rise in the next few months; **e. faire qch** to expect to do sth; **obtenir le succès escompté** to be as successful as expected *or* anticipated
2 *Fin (traite)* to discount
3 *Bourse (valeurs)* to call for delivery of before settlement
escompteur [ɛskɔ̃tœr] **NM** *Com* discounter, discount broker
escopette [ɛskɔpɛt] **NF** *Arch* blunderbuss
escorte [ɛskɔrt] **NF 1** *Aviat, Mil & Naut* escort; **faire e. à qn** to escort sb **2** *(personne, groupe)* escort; **servir d'e. à qn** to escort sb; **il arriva avec toute son e. de photographes** he arrived escorted by a whole bunch of photographers
❑ **d'escorte ADJ** *(escadron, avion)* escort *(avant n)*
❑ **sous (bonne) escorte ADV être sous bonne e.** to be in safe hands; **conduire un prisonnier sous (bonne) e.** to escort a prisoner; **reconduit sous bonne e. jusqu'à la prison** brought back to prison under heavy escort; *Naut* **sous l'e. d'une corvette** convoyed *or* escorted by a corvette
escorter [3] [ɛskɔrte] **VT 1** *(ami, président, célébrité)* to escort; *(femme)* to escort, to be the escort of; **escortée de ses admirateurs** surrounded by her admirers **2** *Aviat, Mil & Naut* to escort
escorteur [ɛskɔrtœr] **NM** *Mil & Naut* escort ship
escouade [ɛskwad] **NF 1** *Mil* squad **2** *(équipe → de balayeurs, de contrôleurs)* squad, gang; *(de touristes, de jeunes gens etc)* group
escourgeon [ɛskurʒɔ̃] **NM** *Agr & Bot* winter barley
ESCP [əɛssepe] **NF** *Scol & Univ* (*abrév* **École supérieure de commerce de Paris**) = prestigious business and management school
escrime [ɛskrim] **NF** *Sport* fencing *(UNCOUNT)*; **faire de l'e.** to fence
escrimer [3] [ɛskrime] **s'escrimer VPR s'e. à faire qch** to strive to do sth; **il s'escrimait à faire démarrer la voiture** he was struggling to get the car started; *Fig* **s'e. sur qch** to plug away at sth; **ne t'escrime pas sur cet exercice** don't rack your brains over this exercise
escrimeur, -euse [ɛskrimœr, -øz] **NM,F** *Sport* fencer
escroc [ɛskro] **NM** swindler, crook
escroquer [3] [ɛskrɔke] **VT 1** *(voler → victime, client)* to swindle, to cheat; *(→ argent, milliard)* to swindle; **e. de l'argent à qn** to swindle money out of sb, to swindle sb out of (his/her) money; **se faire e. de qch** to be swindled out of sth **2** *(extorquer)* **e. une signature à qn** to worm a signature out of sb
escroquerie [ɛskrɔkri] **NF 1** *(pratique malhonnête)* swindle; *(action)* swindling; *Fam* **10 euros le kilo, c'est de l'e.!** 10 euros a kilo, it's *Br* daylight *or Am* highway robbery! **2** *Jur* fraud
escudo [ɛskydo] **NM** escudo
Esculape [ɛskylap] **NPR** Aesculapius
E-S-E (*abrév écrite* **Est-Sud-Est**) ESE
ésérine [ezerin] **NF** *Biol, Méd & Pharm* eserine, physostigmine
ESEU [ezø] **NM** *Anciennement* (*abrév* **examen spécial d'entrée à l'université**) = university entrance examination
esgourde [ɛsgurd] **NF** *Fam* ear■, *Br* lug, lughole
e-signature [isiɲatyr] **NF** *Ordinat* e-signature
eskimo [ɛskimo] = **esquimau**
Esméralda [ɛsmeralda] **NPR** = the heroine of Victor Hugo's 'Notre-Dame de Paris' (1831), a gipsy girl who is a victim of the jealousy of Archdeacon Claude Frollo
Ésope [ezɔp] **NPR** Aesop
ésopique [ezɔpik] **ADJ** Aesopic, Aesopian
ésotérique [ezɔterik] **ADJ** esoteric
ésotérisme [ezɔterism] **NM** esotericism
espace[1] [ɛspas] **NM 1** *(gén) & Astron* **l'e.** space; **voyager dans l'e.** to travel through space; **acquérir les notions de l'e. et du temps** to acquire notions of space and time
2 *(place, volume)* space, room; **as-tu assez d'e.?** do you have enough space *or* room?; **manquer d'e.** to be cramped; **la plante verte prend trop d'e.** the pot plant takes up too much space *or* room; *Fig* **ces réunions sont un e. de liberté** these meetings provide a forum for free expression; **e. vital** living space; *Pol* lebensraum; *Fig (d'une personne)* personal space
3 *(distance → physique)* space, gap; *(→ temporelle)* gap, interval, space; **il y a un petit e. entre la cuisinière et le placard** there's a small gap between the stove and the unit; **laisser de l'e.** to leave space *or* room; **laissez un e. d'un mètre entre les deux arbres** leave (a gap of) one metre between the two trees; **laisser un e. entre deux mots** to leave a space between two words; **l'e. parcouru** the distance covered; *Typ* **e. blanc** space; **l'e. d'un instant** just for a second; **il a relâché son attention l'e. d'un instant et il est rentré dans le véhicule de devant** he let his attention wander just for a second and crashed into the car in front
4 *(surface)* space, stretch; **e. désertique** desert area
5 *(lieu)* **e. de rangement** storage space; **un e. vert** a park; **des espaces verts** parkland; **e. chill-out** chill-out room; *Com* **e. cargo** cargo space
6 *Géom & Math* space; **e. euclidien** Euclidean space; **e. à trois/quatre dimensions** three-/four-dimensional space
7 *Psy* space; **e. auditif** range of hearing; **e. visuel** field of vision
8 *Aviat* **e. aérien** airspace; **dans l'e. aérien allemand** in German airspace
9 *UE* **e. économique européen** European economic area; **e. judiciaire européen** common European legal framework; **e. social européen** common European social legislation
10 *Ordinat* **e. disque** disk space; **e. insécable** hard space; **e. mémoire** memory space; **e. ressort** soft space; **e. de stockage** storage space; **e. Web** Web space
11 *Mktg* **e. d'exposition** display area; **e. de PLV** in-store advertising space; **e. publicitaire** advertising space; **e. de rayonnage** shelf space; **e. de vente** sales area
❑ **dans l'espace de, en l'espace de PRÉP** *(dans le temps)* within (the space of); **malade cinq fois en l'e. d'un mois** sick five times within (the space of) a month
espace[2] [ɛspas] **NF** *Typ* space; **e. fine/moyenne/forte** hair/middle/thick space
espacement [ɛspasmɑ̃] **NM 1** *(dans le temps → action)* spreading *or* spacing out; *(résultat)* spacing; **l'e. des paiements** staggering of payments; **l'e. de nos rencontres/tes visites** the

growing infrequency of our meetings/your visits

2 *(distance)* space; **l'e. entre les tables** the space between the tables

3 *Typ (entre deux lettres)* space; *(interligne)* space (between the lines), spacing; **e. des caractères/lignes** character/line spacing; **e. des colonnes** column spacing; **e. constant** monospace; **e. fixe/proportionnel** fixed/proportional spacing; *Ordinat* **e. arrière** backspace

espacer [16] [ɛspase] **VT 1** *(séparer → lignes, mots, arbustes)* to space out; **e. des choses d'un mètre** to space things out a metre apart

2 *(dans le temps)* to space out; **vous devriez e. vos rencontres** you should meet less often *or* less frequently; **j'ai espacé mes visites** my visits became less frequent

▶**s'espacer VPR 1** *(dans le temps → visites)* to become less frequent

2 *(s'écarter)* **espacez-vous** move further away from each other; **les caractères s'espacent sur l'écran et remplissent le cadre** the characters spread out to fill the frame

espace-temps [ɛspastɑ̃] *(pl* **espaces-temps***)* **NM** *Math & Phys* space-time (continuum)

espadon [ɛspadɔ̃] **NM** *Ich* swordfish

espadrille [ɛspadrij] **NF** espadrille; *Can Br* trainers, *Am* sneakers

Espagne [ɛspaɲ] **NF** *Géog* **l'E.** Spain; **vivre en E.** to live in Spain; **aller en E.** to go to Spain; **la guerre d'E.** the Spanish Civil War

espagnol, -e [ɛspaɲɔl] **ADJ** Spanish

NM *(langue)* Spanish

❑ **Espagnol, -e NM,F** Spaniard; **les Espagnols** the Spanish

espagnolette [ɛspaɲɔlɛt] **NF** window catch *(long vertical bar with pivoting central catch)*; **fermer une fenêtre à l'e.** to leave a window on the latch *or* ajar

espalier [ɛspalje] **NM 1** *Hort* espalier; **(mur d')e.** espalier wall; **(arbre en) e.** espalier **2** *Sport* gym ladder, wall bars

espar [ɛspar] **NM** *Mil & Naut* spar

esparcette [ɛsparsɛt] **NF** *Bot* sainfoin

espèce [ɛspɛs] **NF 1** *Biol, Bot & Zool* species *(singulier)*; **l'e. humaine** the human race, mankind; **des espèces animales/végétales** animal/plant species; **e. protégée** protected species; **e. en voie de disparition** endangered species

2 *(sorte)* sort, kind; **différentes espèces d'arbres** different sorts *or* kinds *or* species of trees; **il y a plusieurs espèces de café** there are various sorts of coffee; **rangez ensemble les livres de même e.** put books of the same kind together; **gens/livres de toute e.** people/books of all kinds *or* of every description; **de son e.** like him/her, of his/her kind; **des escrocs de ton/son e.** crooks like you/him/her; **des gens de leur e.** their sort, the likes of them; **les gens de cette e.** that sort, people like that *or* of that ilk; **de la pire e.** terrible, of the worst sort *or* kind; **un escroc/menteur/avare de la pire e.** a crook/liar/miser of the worst sort *or* kind, the worst sort *or* kind of crook/liar/miser; **ça n'a aucune e. d'importance!** that is of absolutely no importance!; *aussi Péj* **c'était une e. de ferme** it was a sort of farm *or* a farm of sorts; *Péj* **l'e. de malfrat barbu qui nous conduisait** the shady-looking character with a beard who was driving; *Péj* **l'e. de blonde qui lui sert de femme** that blonde he calls his wife; *Fam Péj* **e. d'idiot!** you idiot!; *Fam Péj* **e. de snob!** you're such a snob!

3 *Jur* particular *or* specific case; **cas d'e.** specific case

❑ **espèces NFPL 1** *Fin (argent)* cash; *Hist (monnaie métallique)* coin; **payer en espèces** to pay in cash; **espèces sonnantes et trébuchantes** hard cash; *Compta* **espèces en caisse** cash in hand

2 *Rel* species

❑ **en l'espèce ADV** in this particular case; **j'avais de bons rapports avec mes employés mais en l'e. l'affaire a fini au tribunal** I always had good relations with my employees but in this instance, the matter finished up in court; *Jur* **loi applicable en l'e.** law applicable to the case in point

❑ **sous les espèces de PRÉP** *Littéraire (sous la forme de)* in the form of

espérance [ɛsperɑ̃s] **NF 1** *(espoir)* hope, expectation; **dans l'e. de faire** in the hope of doing; **dans l'e. que...** in the hope that...; **au-delà de nos espérances** beyond our expectations, beyond expectation; **fonder son e.** *ou* **ses espérances sur qn/qch** to found one's hopes on sb/sth; **mettre ses espérances en qch** to pin one's hopes on sth; **répondre aux espérances de qn** to live up to sb's expectations

2 *(cause d'espoir)* hope; **vous êtes mon unique e.** you're my only hope

3 e. de vie *(d'une personne)* life expectancy; *(d'un produit)* life expectancy, shelf life

4 *Math* **e. mathématique** (mathematical) expected value

5 *Rel* hope

❑ **espérances NFPL 1** *(perspectives)* prospects; *(aspirations)* hopes; **avoir de magnifiques espérances** to have wonderful prospects; **donner des espérances** to be promising

2 *Euph (espoir d'hériter)* expectations, prospects of inheritance; **j'ai des espérances du côté maternel** I have great expectations on my mother's side

❑ **contre toute espérance ADV** contrary to (all) *or* against all expectations

espérantiste [ɛsperɑ̃tist] **ADJ & NMF** Esperantist

espéranto [ɛsperɑ̃to] **NM** Esperanto

espérer [18] [ɛspere] **VT 1** *(souhaiter)* to hope for; **e. le succès** to hope for success, to hope to succeed; **e. faire qch** to hope to do sth; **j'espère vous revoir bientôt** I hope to see you soon; **j'espère arriver à la convaincre** I hope (that) I will be able to sway her; **j'espère que vous viendrez** I hope (that) you will come; **je l'espère** I hope so; **j'espère que non** I hope not

2 *(escompter)* to expect; **n'espère pas qu'elle te rembourse** don't expect her to pay you back; **j'en espère de grandes choses** I expect great things to come of it; **je n'en espérais pas tant de lui** I didn't expect that much of him; **le médecin leur avait fait e. une guérison rapide** the doctor had led them to hope for a fast recovery; **c'est ce qu'il nous a laissé e.** that's what he led us to expect

3 *(attendre)* to expect, to wait for; **on ne vous espérait plus!** we'd given up on you!

4 *Can (en acadien)* **e. un enfant** to be expecting a child

USAGE ABSOLU *(souhaiter)* **j'espère (bien)!** I (do *or* certainly) hope so!; **espérons!** let's hope so!; **il est encore permis d'e.** there's still cause *or* room for hope

❑ **espérer de VT IND** *Arch ou Littéraire* **e. de faire qch** to hope to do something; **il aurait pu e. de vous convaincre** he might have had hopes of convincing you, he might have thought he would convince you

❑ **espérer en VT IND** to have faith in; **e. en Dieu** to have faith *or* to trust in God; **il faut e. en des temps meilleurs** we must live in hope of better times

esperluette [ɛspɛrlɥɛt] **NF** ampersand

espiègle [ɛspjɛgl] **ADJ** *(personne)* impish, mischievous; *(regard, réponse)* mischievous; **d'un air e.** mischievously

NMF (little) rascal, imp

espièglerie [ɛspjɛgləri] **NF 1** *(caractère)* impishness, mischievousness; **par pure e.** out of pure mischief **2** *(farce)* prank, trick, piece of mischief

espingole [ɛspɛ̃gɔl] **NF** *Hist* blunderbuss

espingouin, -e [ɛspɛ̃gwɛ̃, -in] *très Fam* **ADJ** dago, = offensive term used to refer to Spanish people or things

❑ **Espingouin, -e NM,F** dago, = offensive term used to refer to a Spanish person

espion, -onne [ɛspjɔ̃, -ɔn] **NM,F** spy

NM *(comme adj; avec ou sans trait d'union)* spy *(avant n)*; **avion e.** spy plane; **micro e.** bug; **satellite e.** spy satellite

espionite [ɛspjɔnit] = **espionnite**

espionnage [ɛspjɔnaʒ] **NM 1** *(action)* spying; **être accusé d'e.** to be accused of spying **2** *(activité)* espionage; **faire de l'e. (au profit de)** to spy (for); **e. industriel** industrial espionage

❑ **d'espionnage ADJ** *(film, roman)* spy *(avant n)*

espionner [3] [ɛspjɔne] **VT** to spy on; **faire e. qn** to have sb spied on *or* watched

USAGE ABSOLU to spy; **e. au profit de** *ou* **pour le compte de** to spy for; **elle est toujours là, à e.** she's always snooping (around)

espionnite [ɛspjɔnit] **NF** spymania

esplanade [ɛsplanad] **NF** esplanade

espoir [ɛspwar] **NM 1** *(espérance)* hope; **être plein d'e.** to be very hopeful; **avoir l'e. de faire qch** to have hopes of *or* to be hopeful of doing sth; **j'ai l'e. de le voir revenir** I'm hopeful that he'll return; **j'ai l'e. d'une récompense** I'm hoping for a reward; **avoir bon e.** to be full of hope; **nous avons encore bon e.** we remain confident; **j'ai bon e. qu'il va gagner** *ou* **de le voir gagner** I'm confident that he'll win; **reprendre e.** to be *or* become hopeful again; **mettre (tout) son e. en qn/qch** to put one's hopes in *or* to pin one's hopes on sb/sth; **nourrir l'e. de faire qch** to live in hope of doing sth; **il n'y a plus d'e.** there's no hope left, all hope is lost; **tous les espoirs sont permis** things look hopeful; *Prov* **l'e. fait vivre** hope springs eternal

2 *(cause d'espérance)* hope; **tu es mon dernier e.** you're my last hope; **c'est un des espoirs du tennis français/de la chanson française** he's one of France's most promising young tennis players/singers

❑ **dans l'espoir de PRÉP** in the hope of; **dans l'e. d'un succès immédiat** hoping for immediate success **CONJ** in the hope of + *gérondif*; **dans l'e. de vous voir bientôt** hoping to see you soon

❑ **sans espoir ADJ** hopeless

'L'Espoir' *Malraux* 'Days of Hope' (UK), 'Man's Hope' (US)

esponton [ɛspɔ̃tɔ̃] **NM** *Hist* spontoon

espressivo [ɛsprɛsivo] **ADV** *Mus* espressivo

ESPRIT [ɛspri]

mind **1, 2, 7** ▪ head **2** ▪ sense **3** ▪ spirit **4, 9, 10, 12** ▪ mood **5** ▪ wit **8**

NM 1 *(manière de penser)* mind; **les voyages ouvrent l'e.** travel broadens the mind; **avoir l'e. clair** to be clear-thinking; **avoir l'e. critique** to have a critical mind; **avoir l'e. étroit/large** to be narrow-minded/broad-minded; **avoir l'e. lent/vif** to be slow-witted/quick-witted; *Fam* **avoir l'e. mal tourné** to have a dirty mind; **avoir un e. positif** to have a positive outlook; **avoir l'e. scientifique/mathématique** to have a scientific/mathematical (turn of) mind; **avoir l'e. des affaires** to have a good head for business; **e. d'analyse** analytical mind; **avoir l'e. d'analyse** to have an analytical mind, to be analytical; **avoir l'e. d'aventure** to have a spirit of adventure; **avoir l'e. d'à-propos** to be quick off the mark; **avoir l'e. de contradiction** to be contrary *or* argumentative; **e. de suite** consistency; **sans e. de suite** inconsistently; **e. de système** methodical mind, systematic mind; **avoir l'e. de synthèse** to be good at drawing ideas together *or* at synthesizing information; **avoir l'e. de l'escalier** to be slow off the mark; **il a l'e. de l'escalier** he always thinks of the perfect retort too late; **un e. sain dans un corps sain** a healthy mind in a healthy body

2 *(facultés, cerveau)* mind, head; **avoir l'e. libre** to have a clear mind; **maintenant que j'ai fini le rapport, j'ai l'e. libre** now I've finished the report, I can relax; **avoir l'e. tranquille** to be easy in one's mind; **où avais-je l'e.?** what was I thinking of?; **elle avait l'e. ailleurs** her thoughts were *or* her mind was elsewhere, she was miles away; **il n'a pas l'e. à ce qu'il fait** his mind is elsewhere *or* is not on what he's doing; **qu'avez-vous à l'e.?** what are you thinking of?; **dites-moi ce que vous avez à l'e.** tell me what you have in mind; **ça m'a traversé l'e.** it occurred to me, it crossed my mind; **une idée me vient à l'e.** I've just thought of something; **une pareille idée ne me serait jamais venue à l'e.** such an idea would never have occurred to me *or* crossed my mind *or* entered my head; **ça m'est sorti de l'e.** it

slipped my mind, it went clean out of my head

3 *(idée)* sense; **il a eu le bon e. de ne pas téléphoner** he had the sense not to call

4 *(mentalité)* spirit; **l'e. dans lequel cela a été fait** the spirit in which it was done; **nous n'avons pas travaillé dans le même e.** we haven't worked in the same spirit; **l'e. du XVIIIème siècle** the spirit of the 18th century; **je déplore le mauvais e. qui règne ici** I hate the bad atmosphere that reigns here; **s'attacher à l'e. de la loi plutôt qu'à la lettre** to go by the spirit of the law rather than the letter; **j'ai horreur des déguisements mais il faut entrer dans l'e. de la fête** I hate dressing up, but you have to get into the party spirit; **avoir l'e. sportif** to be fond of sport; **e. de chapelle** *ou* **clan** *ou* **clocher** *ou* **parti** parochial attitude; **avoir l'e. de clocher** to be parochial; **e. de caste** class consciousness; **e. de compétition/d'équipe** competitive/team spirit; **(avoir l') e. de corps** (to have) esprit de corps; **avoir l'e. d'entreprise** to be enterprising; **avoir l'e. de famille** to be family-minded; **e. de révolte** rebelliousness; **e. de sacrifice** spirit of sacrifice; **c'est un mauvais e.** he's a troublemaker; **c'est du mauvais e.** he's/they're/*etc* just trying to make trouble; **faire preuve de mauvais e.** to be a troublemaker; **faire du mauvais e.** to be negative

5 *(humeur)* **je n'ai pas l'e. à rire** I'm not in the mood for laughing; **ce matin-là, elle n'avait pas l'e. à faire les comptes** that morning she was in no mood for doing any accounts

6 *(interprétation)* **dans son e., nous devrions voter** according to him/her we should vote; **dans mon e., la chambre était peinte en bleu** in my mind's eye, I saw the bedroom painted in blue; **dans mon e., les enfants partaient avant nous** what I had in mind was for the children to go before us; **dans mon e., ils arrivaient demain** I thought they were coming tomorrow

7 *(personne)* mind; **c'est un e. tatillon** he's far too fussy; **un des esprits marquants de ce siècle** one of the great minds *or* leading lights of this century; *Péj* **esprits chagrins** faultfinders; **un e. fort** a freethinker; **un e. libre** a freethinker; **un bel e.** a wit; *Hum* **les grands esprits se rencontrent** great minds think alike

8 *(humour)* wit; **une remarque pleine d'e.** a witty remark, a witticism; **une femme (pleine) d'e.** a witty woman; *Péj* **faire de l'e.** to try to be witty *or* funny; **avoir de l'e.** to be witty; **avoir de l'e. comme quatre** *ou* **jusqu'au bout des ongles** to be very intelligent; **l'e. court les rues** wits are *Br* two a penny *or* *Am* a dime a dozen

9 *Rel* spirit; **E.** *(ange)* Spirit; **Esprits célestes** Celestial *or* Heavenly Spirits; **l'E. malin, l'E. des ténèbres** the Evil Spirit, the Evil One; **E. Saint** Holy Spirit *or* Ghost; **l'e. est fort mais la chair est faible** the spirit is willing but the flesh is weak; *Hum* **je ne suis pas un pur e., il faut bien que je mange** I'm flesh and blood, I do have to eat; *Littéraire* **rendre l'e.** to give up the ghost

10 *(fantôme)* ghost, spirit; **e. frappeur** poltergeist; **croire aux esprits** to believe in ghosts *or* spirits; **y..., es-tu là?** is there anybody there?; *Arch* **e. follet** elfish spirit, sprite, (hob)goblin

11 *Ling* breathing; **e. doux/rude** smooth/rough breathing

12 *Chim (partie volatile)* spirit; **e. de bois** wood alcohol, wood spirit; **e. de parfum** esprit de parfum; **e. de sel** spirits of salt; **e. de vin** spirits of wine

13 *Arch Méd* **esprits animaux** animal spirits

◻ **esprits** NMPL senses; *Fam* **avoir les esprits chamboulés** to be nearly out of one's mind; **reprendre ses esprits** *(après un évanouissement)* to regain consciousness, to come to; *(se ressaisir)* to get a grip on oneself; **reprends tes esprits!** get a grip on yourself!

◻ **dans un esprit de** PRÉP **dans un e. de conciliation** in an attempt at conciliation; **dans un e. de justice** in a spirit of justice, in an effort to be fair

---

'De l'Esprit des lois' *Montesquieu* 'The Spirit of Laws'

Allusion

Les grands esprits se rencontrent

Voltaire used this expression, or to be exact **Les beaux esprits se rencontrent** ("Great minds think alike"), in a letter to Jean-Jacques Rousseau in 1760. The two did not always see eye-to-eye, but on this occasion at least, they did. The expression, which has become a proverb, is used in French exactly as in English.

esprit-de-bois [ɛspridəbwa] NM *Chim* wood alcohol, wood spirit

esprit-de-sel [ɛspridəsɛl] NM *Chim* spirits of salt

esprit-de-vin [ɛspridəvɛ̃] NM *Chim* spirits of wine

esprot [ɛspro] NM *Belg Ich* sprat

esquarre [ɛskar] NF *Hér* = L-shaped border of quarter

-ESQUE [ɛsk] SUFF

● This suffix is added to nouns or proper nouns to form adjectives with a notion of LIKENESS (hence the use of -*like* in some of the possible English translations). It is added to nouns as follows:

éléphantesque elephantine, colossal; **simiesque** (from the Latin word for *monkey*) monkey-like; **hippopotamesque** hippo-like; **clownesque** clownish, clownlike

As this is a suffix of Italian origin, some common adjectives ending in **-esque** are actually directly derived from an Italian word rather than based on a French word with suffix attached. This is the case of **gigantesque** (gigantic), **grotesque** (ridiculous, ludicrous), **romanesque** (novelistic/romantic) or **burlesque** (comical/burlesque).

● Some adjectives based on proper nouns are in common usage and appear in dictionaries, eg:

dantesque (from the XIIIth-century Italian writer Dante Alighieri) Dantean, Dantesque; **gargantuesque** (from Gargantua, a character in a novel by XVIth-century writer Rabelais) gargantuan; **donjuanesque** (from don Juan, a legendary Spanish seducer) of a Don Juan; **rocambolesque** (from Rocambole, a character in XVIIIth-century serialized novels) fantastic, incredible; **grand-guignolesque** (from the name of a XIXth-century theatre specialized in gruesome dramas) gruesome

But new adjectives are constantly being created using the suffix **-esque** at the end of a proper noun. They often refer to current public figures such as writers, artists or politicians, eg:

raffarinesque of Jean-Pierre Raffarin, former French Prime Minister 2002–2005; **talibanesque** of the Taliban; **dylanesque** of the American singer Bob Dylan; **woody allenesque** of the American film director Woody Allen

● Note that the use of the suffix can sometimes have a humorous effect, possibly because of the discrepancy between a rather formal ending and a proper noun taken from modern culture.

esquicher [3] [ɛskiʃe] VT *(dans le Midi)* to squeeze

esquif [ɛskif] NM *Littéraire* skiff; **frêle e.** frail barque *or* vessel

esquille [ɛskij] NF *(de bois)* splinter; *Méd (d'os)* bone splinter

Esquimau® [ɛskimo] NM *Culin Br* choc-ice on a stick, *Am* Eskimo

esquimau, -aude, -aux, -audes [ɛskimo, -od] ADJ Eskimo, *Can* Inuit; **chien e.** husky NM *(langue)* Eskimo

◻ **Esquimau, -aude, -aux, -audes** NM,F Eskimo, *Can* Inuit

esquimau-aléoute [ɛskimoaleut] *(pl* **esquimaux-aléoutes**) ADJ *Ling* Eskimo-Aleut

esquimautage [ɛskimotaʒ] NM *Sport* Eskimo roll

esquinancie [ɛskinɑ̃si] NF *Arch Méd* squinancy

esquintant, -e [ɛskɛ̃tɑ̃, -ɑ̃t] ADJ *Fam* killing, back-breaking

esquinté, -e [ɛskɛ̃te] ADJ *Fam (endommagé →* *chose)* wrecked; *(→ voiture)* smashed up

esquinter [3] [ɛskɛ̃te] *Fam* VT **1** *(endommager →*

---

chose) to wreck; *(→ voiture)* to smash up; *(→ santé)* to ruin; **la moto est complètement esquintée** the bike is a wreck; **tout l'avant est esquinté** the front is totally smashed up; **n'esquinte pas cette lampe!** don't break that lamp!; **sa voiture s'est fait e. par les manifestants** his/her car was smashed up by the demonstrators

2 *(amocher)* to do in; **il s'est drôlement fait e.** he got really badly smashed up

3 *(épuiser → personne)* to exhaust, to knock out; **toutes ces courses m'ont esquinté** all this shopping has knocked me out *or* done me in

4 *(dénigrer → livre, film)* to pan, to slam, *Br* to slate

▸ **s'esquinter** VPR **1** *(s'épuiser)* to kill oneself (**à faire** doing); **ne t'esquinte pas au travail** don't work yourself to death *or* into the ground

2 *(s'abîmer)* **s'e. la santé/la vue (à faire qch)** to ruin one's health/eyesight (doing sth); **tu vas t'e. les yeux avec cet écran** you'll strain your eyes with that screen

3 *(se blesser)* **elle s'est esquinté le dos** she's done her back in; **je me suis esquinté la jambe en tombant** I did my leg in when I fell

esquire [ɛskir] NM esquire

esquisse [ɛskis] NF **1** *Beaux-Arts* sketch **2** *Typ (de page)* rough layout **3** *(d'un projet, d'un discours, d'un roman)* draft, outline **4** *(d'un geste)* hint, shadow, ghost; *(d'un geste)* hint; **sans l'e. d'un regret** with no regrets at all, without the slightest regret

esquisser [3] [ɛskise] VT **1** *Beaux-Arts* to sketch **2** *(projet, histoire)* to outline, to draft **3** *Fig (geste, mouvement)* to give a hint of; **e. un geste de la main** to give a slight wave, to sketch a wave; **il esquissa un geste d'approbation** he gave a slight nod of approval; **e. un sourire** to give a faint *or* slight smile

▸ **s'esquisser** VPR *(sourire)* to appear, to flicker; *(solution, progrès)* to appear; **un sourire s'esquissa sur son visage** he/she gave a slight smile, he/she half-smiled; **un plan commençait à s'e. dans mon esprit** a plan started to take shape in my mind

esquive [ɛskiv] NF dodge, sidestep; *Fig (d'une question, d'un problème etc)* dodging, evasion; *Boxe* **e. de la tête** dodge

esquiver [3] [ɛskive] VT **1** *(éviter → coup)* to dodge **2** *(se soustraire à → question)* to evade, to avoid, to skirt; *(→ difficulté)* to skirt, to avoid, to sidestep; *(→ démarche, obligation)* to shirk, to evade VT. **(de la tête)** to dodge

▸ **s'esquiver** VPR to slip *or* to sneak out (unnoticed)

essai [ɛsɛ] NM **1** *(vérification → d'un produit, d'un appareil)* test, testing, trial; *(→ d'une voiture)* test, testing, test-driving; **e. nucléaire** nuclear test; *Aviat* **essais en vol** test flights; *Aut* **e. de chute** drop test; *Aut* **e. de collision frontale CE** EC frontal impact test; *Aut* **e. sur route** test drive; *Tech* **e. en endurance** endurance test; **e. à banc** benchtest; **essais comparatifs** comparative tests; **e. probatoire** feasibility test; **e. de produit** product test; **faire l'e. de qch** to test sth

2 *(tentative)* attempt, try; **au deuxième e.** at the second try; **nous avons fait plusieurs essais** we had several tries, we made several attempts; **après notre e. de vie commune** after our attempt at living together; **des essais de lancement** trial launches; **coup d'e.** first attempt *or* try

3 *(expérimentation)* **faire l'e. de qch** to try sth (out); **faites un e. avant de vous décider** try it out before you decide; **à titre d'e.** subject to approval; **e. gratuit** free trial

4 *Littérature* essay

5 *Chim & Pharm* assay; **e. biologique** bioassay

6 *Mines* assaying; **fourneau d'e.** assay furnace

7 *Sport (au rugby)* try; **marquer un e.** to score a try; **transformer un e. (en but)** to convert a try

8 *Ordinat* **e. approfondi** beta test; **e. de performance** benchmark; **e. préliminaire** alphatest

9 *Cin & TV* **e. (de) caméra** camera test; **e. image** test shot; *Rad & TV* **e. de voix** voice test

◻ **à l'essai** ADV **1** *(à l'épreuve)* **mettre qn/qch à l'e.** to put sb/sth to the test

2 *Com & Jur* on a trial basis; **engager** *ou* **prendre qn à l'e.** to appoint sb for a trial *or*

probationary period; **prendre/acheter qch à l'e.** to take/buy sth on approval

❑ **d'essai** ADJ **1** *Aviat* **pilote d'e.** test pilot

2 *(période)* trial *(avant n)*

3 *Cin* **bout d'e., e. de caméra** screen test

'Essais' *Montaigne* 'Essays'

essaie *etc voir* **essayer**

essaim [esɛ̃] NM **1** *Entom* swarm **2** *(foule)* **un e. de** *(supporters, admirateurs)* a throng *or* swarm of; *(adolescentes)* a bevy *or Péj* gaggle of

essaimage [esɛmaʒ] NM **1** *Entom* swarming; *(époque)* swarming time **2** *Littéraire (d'un peuple)* dispersion; *(d'une firme)* expansion

essaimer [4] [eseme] VI **1** *Entom* to swarm **2** *Littéraire (se disperser → groupe)* to spread, to disperse; *(→ firme)* to expand

VT *(sujet: firme → usines, filiales etc)* to spread

essanvage [ɛsɑ̃vaʒ] NM *Agr* destruction of wild mustard *or* charlock

essart [esar] NM *Vieilli* grubbed land

essartage [ɛsartaʒ], **essartement** [ɛsartəmɑ̃] NM **1** *Agr* grubbing *or* clearing of the ground **2** *Jur* assart

essarter [3] [esarte] VT to grub, to clear

essayage [esɛjaʒ] NM *Couture (séance)* fitting; *(action)* trying on

essayer [11] [eseje] VT **1** *(tenter)* **e. de faire** to try to do, to try and do; **n'essaie pas de patiner sur l'étang** don't try to *or* and skate on the pond; **as-tu essayé d'arrêter de fumer?** have you tried to stop smoking?; *Fam* **j'essaierai que la soirée soit réussie** I'll do my best to make the party a success

2 *(utiliser pour la première fois)* to try (out); *(vin, plat etc)* to try, to taste; **e. un (nouveau) restaurant** to try a new restaurant; **e. une (nouvelle) marque de lessive** to try out a new brand of washing powder

3 *(mettre → vêtement, chaussures)* to try on; **faire e. qch à qn** to give sb sth to try on

4 *(expérimenter)* to try (out), to test; **e. un nouveau médicament** to test a new drug; **e. un vaccin sur des animaux** to test a vaccine on animals; **e. une voiture** *(pilote, client)* to test-drive a car; **e. les agences matrimoniales** to try the marriage bureaux; **e. sa force** to test one's strength; **l'e. c'est l'adopter** = publicity slogan indicating that a product is sure to please (sometimes used ironically)

5 *Mines* to assay

USAGE ABSOLU to try; **d'accord, je vais e.** alright, I'll try; **laissez-moi e.** let me (have a) try; *Fam* **essaie un peu (pour voir)!** just you try!

▸**s'essayer** VPR **s'e. à qch/à faire qch** to try one's hand at sth/at doing sth

essayeur, -euse [esɛjœr, -øz] NM,F **1** *Couture* fitter **2** *Mines* assayer **3** *(d'une machine, d'un produit etc)* tester

essayiste [esejist] NMF *Littérature* essayist, essay writer

esse [ɛs] NF **1** *(crochet)* (s-shaped) hook; *(cheville)* linchpin **2** *(de violon)* (s-shaped) sound hole

-ESSE [ɛs] SUFF

• The use of the suffix **-esse** in WOMEN'S JOB TITLES is currently falling into disuse as it seems to have acquired over the years a pejorative connotation. (The same trend can be observed in English, where words such as *manageress* and *actress* have largely fallen out of favour.)

It is thus advisable to use **la maire** (the mayor) instead of **la mairesse**, **la poète** (the poet) instead of **la poétesse**, **la docteur(e)** (the doctor) instead of **la doctoresse**

• The suffix **-esse** is also added to adjectives to form feminine nouns expressing a QUALITY linked to that adjective, be it physical or moral. The English equivalent *-ness* can often be used in translation.

gentillesse kindness; **finesse** subtlety/fineness; **jeunesse** youth; **richesse** wealth/richness; **rudesse** roughness/harshness; **vieillesse** old age

ESSEC, Essec [esɛk] NF *Scol & Univ (abrév* **École supérieure des sciences économiques et commerciales**) = "grande école" for management and business studies

essence [esɑ̃s] NF **1** *Pétr Br* petrol, *Am* gas, gasoline; **à e.** petrol-powered; *Fam* **aller prendre** *ou* **faire de l'e.** to fill up; **e. ordinaire** *Br* two-star petrol, *Am* regular gas; **e. sans plomb** unleaded *Br* petrol *or Am* gasoline; **e. à faible indice d'octane** low-octane *Br* petrol *or Am* gas; **e. à indice d'octane élevé** high-octane *Br* petrol *or Am* gas

2 *Chim* spirit, spirits; **e. de térébenthine** spirit *or* spirits of turpentine, turps

3 *Culin* essence; **e. de café** coffee essence

4 *Pharm (cosmétique)* (essential) oil, essence; **e. de citron** lemon oil; **e. de roses** rose oil, essence of roses

5 *Bot* species; **essences résineuses** resinous trees, conifers; **le parc contient de nombreuses essences différentes** the park contains many different species of trees

6 *Phil* essence

7 *(contenu fondamental)* essence, gist

8 *Can (parfum)* flavour; **tu veux une sucette à quelle e.?** what flavour lollipop would you like?

❑ **par essence** ADV essentially, in essence

essencerie [esɑ̃sri] NF *(au Sénégal) Br* petrol *or Am* gas station

essénien, -enne [esenjɛ̃, -ɛn] *Hist & Rel* ADJ Essenian, Essenic

NM,F Essene

essentialisme [esɑ̃sjalizm] NM *Phil* essentialism

essentialiste [esɑ̃sjalist] ADJ *Phil* essentialist

essentiel, -elle [esɑ̃sjɛl] ADJ **1** *(indispensable)* essential (**à/pour** to/for); **e. à la vie** essential to life; **condition essentielle à la réussite du projet** condition which is essential for the success of the project; **il est e. d'avoir compris ce point** it is essential *or* necessary to have understood this point

2 *(principal)* main, essential; *(raison)* basic, main; **le point e. du débat** the main point of the debate

3 *Phil* essential

4 *Pharm* idiopathic

NM **1** *(l'indispensable)* **l'e.** the basic essentials; **n'apportez que l'e.** bring only the (bare) essentials *or* the basics

2 *(le plus important)* **vous avez la santé, c'est l'e.** you're healthy, that's the main *or* important thing; **l'e., c'est que tu comprennes** the most important *or* the main thing is that you should understand; **l'e. de l'article se résume en trois mots** the bulk of the article can be summed up in three words

3 *(la plus grande partie)* **l'e. de la conversation** most of the conversation; **elle passe l'e. de son temps au téléphone** she spends most of her time on the phone; **l'e. des effectifs est resté à la base** the greater part *or* most of the men stayed at base

essentiellement [esɑ̃sjɛlmɑ̃] ADV **1** *(par nature)* in essence, essentially **2** *(principalement)* mainly, essentially

esseulé, -e [esœle] ADJ *Littéraire* **1** *(délaissé)* forsaken **2** *(seul)* forlorn, lonely

essieu, -x [esjø] NM axle, axletree; **e. avant/arrière** front/rear axle; **e. fixe** dead axle

Essonne [esɔn] NF *Géog* **l'E.** Essonne

essor [esɔr] NM **1** *(d'un oiseau)* flight; **prendre son e.** to soar **2** *Fig (d'une entreprise, d'une industrie)* rise, rapid growth; **e. économique** (rapid) economic expansion, economic boom; **industrie en plein e.** booming *or* fast-growing industry; **la sidérurgie connaît un nouvel e.** the steel industry has taken on a new lease of life; **prendre son e.** *(adolescent)* to fend for oneself, to become self-sufficient; *(économie, entreprise)* to take off

essorage [esɔraʒ] NM *(à la machine)* spinning; *(à l'essoreuse à rouleaux)* mangling; *(à la main)* wringing; **pas d'e.** *(sur l'étiquette d'un vêtement)* do not spin; **au premier e., ajoutez l'assouplissant** at first cycle *or* spin-dry, add fabric softener; **l'e. de la salade** drying *or* spin-drying lettuce

essorer [3] [esɔre] VT **1** *(sécher)* **e. le linge** *(à la machine)* to spin-dry the laundry; *(à l'essoreuse à rouleaux)* to put the laundry through the mangle; *(à la main)* to wring the laundry; **e. la salade** to dry *or* to spin-dry the lettuce **2** *(terrain)* to drain, to dry

essoreuse [esɔrøz] NF **1** *(pour le linge)* **e. (à tambour)** spin-drier; **e. (à rouleaux)** mangle **2** *(pour la salade)* salad spinner **3** *(pour le sucre)* centrifugal separator

essoriller [3] [esɔrije] VT *(animal)* to crop the ears of

essouchage [esuʃaʒ], **essouchement** [esuʃmɑ̃] NM stubbing, grubbing out

essoucher [3] [esuʃe] VT to stub, to grub out

essoufflement [esufləmɑ̃] NM breathlessness; *Fig* **en raison de l'e. de l'économie** because the economy is running out of steam

essouffler [3] [esufle] VT to make breathless; **être (tout) essoufflé** to be breathless *or* out of breath; **ce sont les marches qui m'ont essoufflé** climbing the steps has left me breathless

▸**s'essouffler** VPR **1** *Physiol* to get breathless; *Fig* **s'e. à faire qch** to struggle to do sth **2** *(s'affaiblir → moteur)* to get weak; *(→ économie)* to run out of steam; *(→ production)* to lose momentum; *(→ inspiration, écrivain)* to dry up

essuie[1] *voir* **essuyer**

essuie[2] [esɥi] NM *Belg (essuie-mains)* hand towel; *(torchon)* cloth, dish towel, *Br* tea towel; *(serviette de bain)* bath towel

essuie-glace [esɥiglas] *(pl* **essuie-glaces**) NM *Aut Br* windscreen *or Am* windshield wiper; **e. arrière** back wiper; **e. deux vitesses** two-speed wiper; **e. intermittent à plusieurs vitesses** variable speed intermittent wiper

essuie-mains [esɥimɛ̃] NM INV hand towel

essuie-meubles [esɥimœbl] NM INV duster

essuie-pieds [esɥipje] NM INV doormat

essuie-tout [esɥitu] NM INV kitchen paper

essuie-verre, essuie-verres [esɥivɛr] NM INV glass cloth, tea towel

essuyage [esɥijaʒ] NM **1** *(séchage → de la vaisselle)* wiping, drying up; *(→ des mains, du sol, d'une surface)* wiping, drying; *(d'eau etc)* wiping up, mopping up **2** *(nettoyage → d'un meuble)* wiping (clean); *(époussetage)* dusting (down); *(→ d'un tableau noir)* wiping, cleaning; *(→ d'une planche farinée, d'un mur plâtreux)* wiping (down)

essuyer [14] [esɥije] VT **1** *(sécher → vaisselle)* to wipe, to dry (up); *(→ liquide, sueur)* to wipe, to mop up, to wipe (off); *(→ surface)* to wipe (down); *(→ sol)* to wipe, to dry; *(→ main)* to dry, to wipe; **essuie tes mains** wipe your hands; **e. une larme** to wipe away a tear; **e. les larmes de qn** to dry sb's tears; *Fam* **e. les plâtres** to have to endure initial problems; **les premiers acheteurs de cette voiture ont essuyé les plâtres** the first purchasers of this car had to put up with a few teething troubles

2 *(nettoyer → surface poussiéreuse)* to dust (down); *(→ tableau noir)* to wipe (clean), to clean; **tes mains sont pleines de farine, essuie-les** wipe your hands, they're covered in flour; **essuie tes pieds sur le paillasson** wipe your feet on the doormat

3 *(subir → reproches)* to endure; *(→ refus)* to meet with; *(→ défaite, échec, pertes)* to suffer; *(→ tempête)* to weather, to bear up against; **e. un coup de feu** to be shot at; **e. le feu de l'ennemi** to come under enemy fire

▸**s'essuyer** VPR *(se sécher)* to dry oneself; **s'e. les mains/pieds/yeux** to dry *or* to wipe one's hands/feet/eyes; **essuie-toi les mains** dry your hands

essuyeur, -euse [esɥijœr, -øz] NM,F wiper

NM *Typ* doctor blade, ductor blade

est[1] [ɛ] *voir* **être**[1]

est[2] [ɛst] NM INV **1** *(point cardinal)* east; **à l'e.** in the east; **où est l'e.?** which way is east?; **la partie la plus à l'e. de l'île** the easternmost part of the island; **le vent vient de l'e.** it's an east *or* easterly wind, the wind is coming from the east; **un vent d'e.** an easterly wind; **le vent d'e.** the east wind; **aller à** *ou* **vers l'e.** to go east *or* eastwards; **les trains qui vont vers l'e.** trains going east, eastbound trains; **rouler vers l'e.** to drive east *or* eastwards; **aller droit vers l'e.** to head due east; **la cuisine est plein e.** *ou* **exposée à l'e.** the kitchen faces due east; **le soleil se lève à l'e.** the sun rises in the east

2 *(partie d'un pays, d'un continent)* east, eastern area *or* regions; *(partie d'une ville)* east; **l'e. de l'Italie** eastern Italy, the east of Italy; **dans l'e. de l'Espagne** in eastern Spain, in the east of

Spain; **elle habite dans l'e.** she lives in the East; **il habite dans l'e. de Paris** he lives in the east of Paris; **elle est de l'e.** she's from the east; **les gens de l'e.** people who live in the east

ADJ INV east *(avant n)*, eastern; *(→ côte, face)* east; *(→ banlieue, partie, région)* eastern; **la façade e. d'un immeuble** the east-facing wall of a building; **la chambre est côté e.** the bedroom faces east; **dans la partie e. de la France** in the East of France, in eastern France; **la côte e. des États-Unis** the East coast *or* Eastern seaboard of the United States; **suivre la direction e.** to head *or* to go eastwards

❑ **Est** ADJ INV East NM 1 *Géog* **l'E.** the East

2 *Pol & Hist* **l'E.** Eastern Europe, Eastern European countries; **l'Europe de l'E.** Eastern Europe; **les pays de l'E.** the countries of Eastern Europe, Eastern European countries; *Hist* **le bloc de l'E.** the Eastern bloc

❑ **à l'est de** PRÉP (to the) east of; **il habite à l'e. de Paris** he lives to the east of Paris

'A l'Est d'Eden' *Kazan* 'East of Eden'

---

establishment [establiʃmɛnt] NM **l'e.** *(gén)* the dominant *or* influential group *or* body; *(en Grande-Bretagne)* the Establishment

estacade [ɛstakad] NF byre; *Naut (pieux)* stockade; *(jetée)* pier *(on piles)*

estafette [ɛstafɛt] NF 1 *Hist (courrier)* courier 2 *Mil (agent de liaison)* liaison officer 3 *Aut (camionnette)* van

estafier [ɛstafje] NM 1 *Hist* (armed) attendant 2 *Péj* bodyguard

estafilade [ɛstafilad] NF slash, gash

estagnon [ɛstaɲɔ̃] NM *(en Afrique francophone)* metal container *(for liquids)*

est-allemand, -e [ɛstalmɑ̃, -ɑ̃d] *Anciennement* ADJ East German

❑ **Est-Allemand, -e** NM,F East German

estaminet [ɛstaminɛ] NM *Vieilli* small café, bar; *Littéraire* estaminet

estampage [ɛstɑ̃paʒ] NM 1 *Tech (façonnage)* stamping; *(empreinte)* stamp 2 *Fam (action d'escroquer)* swindling, fleecing; *(résultat)* swindle

estampe [ɛstɑ̃p] NF 1 *(image)* engraving, print; *Hum* **et alors comme ça, il t'a invitée à aller voir ses estampes japonaises?** so he invited you up to see his etchings, did he? 2 *Tech (outil)* stamp

estamper [3] [ɛstɑ̃pe] VT 1 *Tech (façonner, marquer)* to stamp 2 *Fam (escroquer)* to swindle, to con; **e. qn de 20 euros** to con sb out of 20 euros

estampeur, -euse [ɛstɑ̃pœr, -øz] NM,F *Fam (escroc)* swindler, con-man

NM *Tech* stamper

estampillage [ɛstɑ̃pijaʒ] NM *(d'un document)* stamping; *(d'une marchandise)* marking

estampille [ɛstɑ̃pij] NF *(sur un document)* stamp; *(sur une marchandise)* mark, trademark; *Fam* **dans cette famille, ils sont tous marqués de la même e.** they're all tarred with the same brush in that family

estampiller [3] [ɛstɑ̃pije] VT *(document)* to stamp; *(marchandise)* to mark

estancia [ɛstɑ̃sja] NF estancia

estarie [ɛstari] NF *Naut* **(jours d')e.** lay days

est-ce que [ɛskə] ADV INTERROGATIF 1 *(suivi d'un verbe plein)* **e. je/tu/nous/vous...?** *(au présent)* do I/you/we/you...?; **est-ce qu'il/qu'elle...?** *(au présent)* does he/she...?; **e. vous aimez le thé?** do you like tea?; **e. vous avez acheté la maison?** did you buy the house?; **e. vous dormiez bien?** did you (use to) sleep well?; **e. tu iras?** will you go?

2 *(suivi d'un auxiliaire) (au présent)* **e. je suis...?** am I...?; **e. tu as une enveloppe?** do you have *or* have you got an envelope?; **e. je dois...?** must I...?; **e. tu peux...?** can you...?; *(au passé)* **e. tu y étais?** were you there?; **est-ce qu'il devait signer?** should he have signed?; *(au futur)* **e. tu seras là?** will you be there?; *(au futur proche)* **e. tu vas lui téléphoner?** are you going to *or* will you phone him/her?

3 *(avec un autre adverbe interrogatif)* **quand est-ce qu'il arrive?** when does he arrive?; **qui e. tu as vu?** who did you see?; **pourquoi e. tu ris?** why are you laughing?

este [ɛst] NM *(langue)* Estonian

ester[1] [ɛste] VI *(à l'infinitif seulement) Jur* **e. en justice** to go to court

ester[2] [ɛstɛr] NM *Chim* ester

estérase [ɛsteraz] NF *Chim* esterase

estérification [ɛsterifikasjɔ̃] NF *Chim* esterification

estérifier [9] [ɛsterifje] VT *Chim* to esterify

esterlin [ɛstɛrlɛ̃] NM *(ancienne monnaie)* sterling

Esther [ɛstɛr] NPR *Bible* Esther

esthésie [ɛstezi] NF *Physiol* aesthesia

esthésiogène [ɛstezjɔʒɛn] ADJ *Physiol* aesthesiogenic

esthète [ɛstɛt] NMF aesthete; **cela ne plaira sûrement pas aux esthètes** this will offend some people's aesthetic sense

esthéticien, -enne [ɛstetisjɛ̃, -ɛn] NM,F 1 *(en institut de beauté)* beautician 2 *Beaux-Arts & Phil* aesthetician 3 *Ind* **e. industriel** industrial designer

esthétique [ɛstetik] ADJ 1 *Beaux-Arts & Phil* aesthetic 2 *(joli)* beautiful, aesthetically pleasing; **ce chantier devant la maison n'est pas très e.** *ou* **n'a rien d'e.** this building site in front of the house is rather unsightly

NF 1 *Beaux-Arts & Phil (science)* **l'e.** aesthetics *(singulier)*; *(code)* aesthetic 2 *(harmonie)* beauty, harmony; *(beauté)* aesthetic quality, attractiveness; **ça ne sert à rien, c'est uniquement pour l'e.** it doesn't have any use, it's just there to look nice; **ça manque d'e.** it's not very attractive, it's not aesthetically pleasing 3 *Ind* **e. industrielle** industrial design

esthétiquement [ɛstetikmɑ̃] ADV 1 *Beaux-Arts & Phil* aesthetically 2 *(harmonieusement)* harmoniously, beautifully 3 *(du point de vue de la beauté)* aesthetically, from an aesthetic point of view; **e., ce n'est pas réussi** aesthetically, it's a failure

esthétisant, -e [ɛstetizɑ̃, -ɑ̃t] ADJ 1 *(présenté sous un jour séduisant)* glamorized 2 *(écrivain)* mannered

esthétiser [3] [ɛstetize] VT *(présenter sous un jour séduisant)* to glamorize; **e. la violence** to glamorize violence

VI *(privilégier l'esthétique)* to concentrate on the aesthetics; **certains designers esthétisent au détriment de la fonctionnalité** some designers concentrate on aesthetics at the expense of practicality

esthétisme [ɛstetism] NM aestheticism

estimable [ɛstimabl] ADJ 1 *(digne de respect → personne)* respectable 2 *(assez bon → ouvrage, film)* decent 3 *(calculable → frais, perte)* assessable

estimateur [ɛstimatœr] NM *Littéraire* estimator

estimatif, -ive [ɛstimatif, -iv] ADJ *(valeur, état)* estimated; **devis e.** estimate, quotation

estimation [ɛstimasjɔ̃] NF 1 *(évaluation → d'une marchandise, d'une œuvre d'art)* appraisal, valuation; *(→ de dégâts, de besoins, d'un poids)* estimation, assessment; *(→ d'une distance)* gauging; **faire une e.** to give an estimation/a valuation/an assessment; *Mktg* **e. des besoins** needs assessment

2 *(montant)* estimate, estimation; **d'après mon e.** according to my estimate *or* estimation; **nous sommes loin de l'e. de l'expert** we're not even close to the figure produced by the expert; *Compta* **e. des frais** estimate of costs

3 *(prévision)* projection; **le score réalisé par le candidat sortant dépasse toutes les estimations** the outgoing candidate's score surpasses all the pollsters' projections

estimative [ɛstimativ] *voir* **estimatif**

estimatoire [ɛstimatwar] ADJ estimatory

estime [ɛstim] NF esteem, respect; **avoir de l'e. pour qn/qch** to have a great deal of respect for sb/sth, to hold sb/sth in high esteem; **j'ai beaucoup d'e. pour lui/pour son travail** I have a great deal of respect for him/for his/her work; **baisser/monter dans l'e. de qn** to go down/up in sb's esteem; **il force l'e. par son intégrité** one cannot but respect his integrity; **tenir qn en grande** *ou* **haute e.** to hold sb in high esteem

❑ **à l'estime** ADV 1 *Naut* by dead reckoning; **navigation à l'e.** dead reckoning 2 *(approximativement)* roughly; **j'ai tracé les plans à l'e.** I drew the plans blind; **faire un budget à l'e.** to work out a budget roughly

estimé, -e [ɛstime] ADJ 1 *(respecté)* **notre e. collègue** our esteemed colleague; **une pneumologue très estimée** a highly regarded lung specialist 2 *Naut voir* **point**[2]

estimer [3] [ɛstime] VT 1 *(expertiser → valeur, prix)* to appraise, to evaluate, to assess; *(marchandises)* to value, to appraise; **faire e. un tableau** to have a painting valued; **ce tableau a été estimé à 2 millions d'euros** this painting has been estimated at 2 million euros

2 *(évaluer approximativement → quantité, poids)* to estimate; *(→ distance)* to gauge; *(dégâts, besoins)* to estimate, to assess; **on estime le taux d'abstention à 34%** the abstention rate has been estimated at 34%; **les dégâts ont été estimés à 500 euros** the damage was estimated at 500 euros; **les experts estiment que les pertes s'élèvent à plusieurs milliards** the experts estimate the losses at *or* that the losses total several hundred million; **pouvez-vous e. le nombre des victimes?** would you hazard a guess as to the number of casualties?; *Naut* **longitude estimée** longitude by dead reckoning

3 *(apprécier → ami, écrivain, collègue)* to regard with esteem, to esteem, to think highly of; **elle était estimée de tous** she was highly thought of *or* was esteemed by everyone; **je l'estime trop pour ça** I respect him/her too much for that; **e. qn à sa juste valeur** to judge sb correctly

4 *(juger)* to think, to consider, to believe (**que** that); **j'estime qu'il a eu tort** I think *or* believe (that) he was wrong; **si tu estimes que tu peux le faire** if you believe you can do it; **j'estime avoir mon mot à dire** I think I have the right to offer an opinion; **elle estime que l'argent n'a pas d'importance** she considers that money is of no importance; **j'estime qu'il est de mon devoir de parler** I consider *or* think it (is) my duty *or* that it is my duty to speak; **il n'a pas estimé nécessaire de me prévenir** he didn't consider *or* think it (was) necessary to warn me

5 *Naut* to reckon

▸**s'estimer** VPR *(suivi d'un adj)* **s'e. heureux** to count oneself lucky; **s'e. satisfait de/que** to be happy with/that

estivage [ɛstivaʒ] NM *Agr* mountain summering

estival, -e, -aux, -ales [ɛstival, -o] ADJ summer *(avant n)*; **station estivale** summer resort

estivant, -e [ɛstivɑ̃, -ɑ̃t] NM,F summer tourist, *Br* holidaymaker, *Am* vacationer

estivation [ɛstivasjɔ̃] NF *Bot & Zool* aestivation

estive [ɛstiv] NF *(pâturage)* mountain pasture

estiver [3] [ɛstive] VT *Agr* to summer on mountain pastures

Est-Nord-Est [ɛstnɔrɛst] NM INV & ADJ INV east-northeast

estoc [ɛstɔk] NM *Escrime* rapier; **coup d'e.** thrust; **frapper d'e. et de taille** to cut and thrust

estocade [ɛstɔkad] NF 1 *(lors d'une corrida)* final sword thrust, death-blow; **donner** *ou* **porter l'e. à un taureau** to deal the death-blow to a bull 2 *Littéraire (locutions)* **donner** *ou* **porter l'e. à qn** to deal the death-blow to sb

estomac [ɛstɔma] NM 1 *Anat* stomach; **j'ai mal à l'e.** I have a stomach ache; *Fam* **il a pris de l'e.** he's developed a paunch *or* potbelly; *Fam* **avoir l'e. bien accroché** to have a strong stomach; *Fam* **ça m'est resté sur l'e.** it weighed on my stomach; *Fig* it stuck in my craw; **avoir l'e. vide** *ou* **creux** to have an empty stomach; **avoir l'e. plein** *ou* **bien rempli** to be full (up); **avoir l'e. lourd** to feel bloated; *Fam* **avoir l'e. dans les talons** to be famished *or* ravenous; *Fam* **avoir un e. d'autruche** to have a cast-iron stomach; *Méd* **cancer de l'e.** stomach cancer

2 *Fam (hardiesse)* **avoir de l'e.** to have a nerve *or Br* a cheek; **manquer d'e.** to lack guts

❑ **à l'estomac** ADV *Fam* **ils y sont allés à l'e.** they bluffed their way through it; **quand on veut se faire accepter dans cette entreprise, il faut le faire à l'e.** you need a lot of nerve if you want to get on in this company; **avoir qn à l'e.** to intimidate sb

estomaquer [3] [ɛstɔmake] VT *Fam* to stagger, to flabbergast

estompage [ɛstɔ̃paʒ] NM *Beaux-Arts* stumping, shading off

estompe [ɛstɔ̃p] NF *Beaux-Arts* stump, tortillon; **(dessin à l')e.** stump drawing

estompé, -e [ɛstɔ̃pe] ADJ blurred; *Ordinat*

dimmed; **les contours estompés des immeubles** the dim outline of buildings

estompement [ɛstɔ̃pmɑ̃] **NM** fading

estomper [3] [ɛstɔ̃pe] **VT 1** *Beaux-Arts* to stump, to shade off **2** *(ride)* to smoothe over; *(silhouette, contours)* to dim, to blur; *(contraste)* to tone down **3** *(souvenir, sentiment)* to dim, to blur; **le temps estompera la douleur** time will ease the pain

▶**s'estomper VPR 1** *(disparaître → contours)* to become blurred; *(→ couleurs)* to fade; *(→ rides)* to be smoothed out **2** *(s'affaiblir → souvenir)* to fade away; *(→ douleur, rancune)* to diminish, to die down; *(→ peine)* to ease

Estonie [ɛstɔni] **NF** *Géog* **l'E.** Estonia; **vivre en E.** to live in Estonia; **aller en E.** to go to Estonia

estonien, -enne [ɛstɔnjɛ̃, -ɛn] **ADJ** Estonian

NM *(langue)* Estonian

❑ **Estonien, -enne NM,F** Estonian

estoppel [ɛstɔpɛl] **NM** *Jur* estoppel

estoquer [3] [ɛstɔke] **VT** *(taureau)* to deal the death blow to

estouffade [ɛstufad] **NF** *Culin* **e. de bœuf** ≃ beef stew

estourbir [32] [ɛsturbir] **VT** *Fam Vieilli* **1** *(assommer)* to knock out, to lay out **2** *(tuer)* to do in **3** *(étonner)* to astound, to knock sideways; **je suis encore tout estourbi de la chance que j'ai eue** I'm still quite astounded how lucky I was

estrade [ɛstrad] **NF 1** *(plancher surélevé)* platform **2** *Boxe* ring

estradiot [ɛstradjo] **NM** *Hist & Mil* Estradiot

estragon [ɛstragɔ̃] **NM** *Bot* tarragon

estramaçon [ɛstramasɔ̃] **NM** broadsword

estran [ɛstrɑ̃] **NM** *Géog* strand, foreshore

estrapade [ɛstrapad] **NF** *Hist (supplice)* strappado; *Naut* dipping from the yard arm

estrapasser [3] [ɛstrapase] **VT** *Équitation* to tire with prolonged exercise

Estrémadure [ɛstremadyr] **NF** Extremadura

estrien, -enne [ɛstrjɛ̃, -ɛn] *Can* **ADJ** = of/from the Eastern townships of Quebec

NM,F = inhabitant of or person from the Eastern townships of Quebec

estrogène [ɛstrɔʒɛn] = **œstrogène**

estrone [ɛstrɔn] = **œstrone**

estrope [ɛstrɔp] **NF** *Naut* strop, strap, grommet

estropié, -e [ɛstrɔpje] **ADJ** crippled, maimed; **il en restera e.** he'll be left a cripple

NM,F cripple, disabled *or* maimed person

estropier [9] [ɛstrɔpje] **VT 1** *(personne)* to cripple, to maim **2** *Fig (en prononçant)* to mispronounce; *(à l'écrit)* to misspell; *(texte)* to mutilate; *(morceau de musique)* to murder; **e. une citation** to misquote a text

Est-Sud-Est [ɛstsydɛst] **NM INV & ADJ INV** east-southeast

estuaire [ɛstɥɛr] **NM** *Géog* estuary

estuarien, -enne [ɛstɥarjɛ̃, -ɛn] **ADJ** estuarial, estuarine

estudiantin, -e [ɛstydjɑ̃tɛ̃, -in] **ADJ** *Littéraire* student *(avant n)*

esturgeon [ɛstyrʒɔ̃] **NM** *Ich* sturgeon

et [e] **CONJ 1** *(reliant des termes, des propositions)* and; **il est beau et intelligent** he is handsome and intelligent; **noir et blanc** black and white; **le père et le fils** the father and the son; **une belle et brillante jeune fille** a beautiful, clever girl; **ils jouent au tennis et au hand-ball** they play tennis and handball; **une robe courte et sans manches** a short sleeveless dress; **gentiment et avec le sourire** nicely and with a smile; **toi et moi, nous savons ce qu'il faut faire** you and I know what should be done; **2 et 2 font 4** two and two make four, two plus two makes four; **il y a mensonge et mensonge** there are lies, and then there are lies; **quand on a 20 ans et toute sa santé** when one is 20 and in excellent health; **peux-tu aller chercher le pain, et passer chez le photographe?** can you go and buy the bread and drop in at the photo shop?; **quand il pleut et qu'on s'ennuie** when it rains and you're feeling bored; **un livre ancien et qui n'est plus en librairie** an old book which is out of print; **il connaît l'anglais, et très bien** he speaks English, and very well at that

2 *(exprimant une relation de simultanéité, de succession ou de conséquence)* **il s'est levé et il a quitté la pièce** he got up and left the room; **tu viens de commencer et tu es déjà fatigué?** you've only just started and you're tired already?; **j'ai bien aimé ce film, et toi?** I really liked the film, how *or* what about you?; **ils ont donné un million et ils estiment que cela suffit!** they gave a million and they think that's enough!; **il travaille et ne réussit pas** he works but he's not successful; **c'est un jeune homme de grande énergie, et qui réussira dans la vie** he is a young man of great energy, who will succeed

3 *(reliant des propositions comparatives)* **plus ça va, et plus la situation s'aggrave** as time goes on, the situation just gets worse; **moins je le vois et mieux je me porte!** the less I see him the better I feel!; **moins il travaille et moins il a envie de travailler** the less he works the less he feels like working

4 *(avec une valeur emphatique)* **je ne peux pas et répondre au téléphone et ouvrir la porte** I can't answer the phone AND open the door; **et d'un, je n'ai pas faim, et de deux, je n'aime pas ça** for one thing I'm not hungry and for another I don't like it; **j'ai dû supporter et les enfants et les parents!** I had to put up with both the parents and the children *or* with the parents AND the children!; **et son frère et sa sœur** both his/her brother and his/her sister; **je l'ai dit et répété** I've said it over and over again, I've said it more than once; **c'est fini et bien fini!** that's the end of that!; **et moi alors?** (and) what about me?; **et les dix euros que je t'ai prêtés?** and (what about) the ten euros I lent you?; **et si on lui disait tout?** what if we told him/her everything?; **et les bagages?** what about the luggage?; **et pourquoi pas?** (and) why not?; **je n'ai pas envie d'y aller – et pourquoi?** I don't want to go – and why not?; **et pourtant...** and yet *or* still...; **et voilà!** there you are!, there you go!; **et moi je vous dis que je n'irai pas!** and I'm telling you that I won't go!; **et vous osez me proposer cela!** and you dare (to) suggest that!; **et voilà comment l'argent s'en va!** that's how money disappears!; **et tout à coup il se mit à courir** and suddenly he started running; **et c'est ainsi que se termine mon histoire...** and that is how my story ends...; **et on a ri!** how we laughed!; *Littéraire* **et le garçon de se sauver** at this the boy ran off; *Littéraire* **et chacun d'exprimer sa satisfaction** whereupon each expressed his satisfaction

5 *(dans les nombres composés, les horaires, les poids et les mesures)* **vingt et un** twenty one; **vingt et unième** twenty-first; **deux heures et demie** half past two; **cinq heures et quart** five fifteen, a quarter past five; **deux kilos et demi** two and a half kilos

NM 1 et commercial ampersand

2 *Ordinat* **ET** AND; **circuit ET** AND gate

ét. *(abrév écrite* **étage)** fl

-ET, -ETTE [ɛ, ɛt] **SUFF**

• When added to nouns, this suffix denotes SMALLNESS, eg:

un bâtonnet a small stick; **un jardinet** a small garden; **une maisonnette** a small house; **un garçonnet** a little boy; **une fillette** a little girl; **une gouttelette** a droplet; **un porcelet** a piglet

One interesting recent coinage is **la mesurette**, which is used to describe an inadequate or half-hearted measure taken by politicians.

• When added to adjectives, **-et** carries an idea of EXCESS and it is often (though not always) slightly derogatory, eg:

le roman est un peu longuet the novel is a bit on the long side; **il est un peu jeunet pour être nommé directeur** he's a bit young to be appointed director; **c'est un film gentillet, sans plus** it's a nice enough little film, nothing special; **elle est bien maigrelette** she's really skinny; **un petit jardin bien propret** a neat little garden

• As it denotes smallness, the suffix **-et** sometimes has positive connotations of ENDEARMENT (as in **mignonnet** pretty, **propret** neat and tidy, **mon biquet** my pet), but in other contexts it takes on DEROGATORY connotations associated with weakness (as in **une femmelette**, **une mauviette** a wimp).

Note that an **l** is frequently inserted when adding this suffix to words ending with a vowel, as in **gouttelette** and **maigrelet**.

ETA [əteɑ] **NF** *Pol (abrév* **Euskadi Ta Askatasuna)** ETA

êta [ɛta] **NM** eta

étable [etabl] **NF** cowshed

établer [3] [etable] **VT** to bring into the cowshed

établi[1] [etabli] **NM** workbench

établi[2]**, -e** [etabli] **ADJ** established; **bien é.** well-established; **avoir une réputation bien établie** to have a well established reputation; **contester les coutumes établies** to challenge convention; **l'ordre é.** the established order

établir [32] [etablir] **VT 1** *(duplex, liaison téléphonique)* to set up, to establish

2 *(implanter → usine, locaux, quartier général)* to establish, to set *or* put up; *(→ filiale, système de gouvernement)* to establish; *(→ camp)* to pitch; *(→ taxe, tribunal)* to institute, to create; **é. son domicile à Paris** to take up residence in Paris

3 *Vieilli (pourvoir d'une situation)* to set up in business; **j'attendrai d'avoir établi mes enfants** I'll wait until my children are settled in life; **il a établi son fils comme notaire** he set up his son as a solicitor; **elle est établie comme pharmacienne** she's set up as a chemist

4 *Vieilli (marier)* to marry off; **il lui reste une fille à é.** he still has a daughter at home

5 *(instaurer → règlement)* to introduce; *(→ usage)* to pass; *(→ pouvoir)* to install, to implement; *(→ ordre, relation, système de gouvernement)* to establish; *(→ principe)* to lay down; **une fois le silence établi** once everyone is quiet; **é. un précédent** to set a precedent; **é. des liens d'amitiés** to establish friendly relations

6 *(bâtir → réputation, autorité)* to establish; *(→ empire)* to build; **é. sa fortune sur** to establish *or* build up one's fortune on; **é. sa réputation sur des succès** to base one's reputation on (one's) success

7 *(prouver)* to establish, to prove; **é. l'innocence de qn** to establish sb's innocence, to vindicate sb; **é. l'identité de qn** to establish sb's identity; **é. la vérité** to establish the truth; **nous cherchons à é. qu'à 18 h notre client était chez lui avec son épouse** we are trying to establish that at 6 p.m., our client was at home with his wife

8 *(dresser → organigramme)* to set out; *(→ liste)* to draw up; *(→ devis)* to provide; *(→ chèque)* to make out; *(→ programme, prix)* to fix; *(→ plan, proposition, facture, bilan, budget)* to draw up; *(→ objectifs)* to determine; **é. une moyenne** to work out an average; **é. le prix d'un article** to price an item; **é. un parallèle entre** to establish *or* draw a parallel between

9 *Sport* **é. un record** to set a record

▶**s'établir VPR 1** *(vivre)* **ils ont préféré s'é. en banlieue** they chose to settle in the suburbs

2 *(professionnellement)* to set oneself up (in business); **s'é. épicier** to set (oneself) up as a grocer; **elle n'a pas assez d'argent pour s'é.** she doesn't have enough funds to start up on her own; **s'é. à son compte** to set oneself up in business, to become self-employed

3 *(être instauré → coutume, idée)* to become established; **enfin, le silence s'établit** silence was finally restored; **une atmosphère plus détendue finit par s'é.** the atmosphere eventually became more relaxed; **une relation stable s'est établie entre nous** a stable relation has developed between the two of us

établissement [etablismɑ̃] **NM 1** *(institution)* establishment, institution; *(école)* school; **é. d'enseignement primaire/secondaire** primary/secondary school; *(université)* university; **é. hospitalier** hospital; **é. pénitentiaire** prison, *Am* penitentiary; **é. privé hors contrat** = non-subsidized private school; **é. privé sous contrat** = state-subsidized private school; **é. religieux** *(monastère)* monastery; *(couvent)* convent; *(collège)* religious *or* denominational school; *(séminaire)* seminary; **é. scolaire** school; **é. thermal** hydropathic establishment, spa

2 *(institution commerciale)* business, firm; **les établissements Leroy** Leroy and Co; **les établissements Fourat et fils** Fourat and Sons; **é. bancaire** bank; **é. classé** = potentially dangerous industrial premises (having to conform to strict safety regulations); **é. commercial** commercial establishment *or* institution; *Fin* **é.**

de crédit credit institution; *Compta* **é. déclarant** company making the return; *Fin* **é. dépositaire** = financial institution holding securities on trust; *Fin* **é. financier** financial institution; **é. industriel** factory, manufacturing firm; *Fin* **é. payeur** paying bank; **é. d'utilité publique** public utility

3 *Admin* **é. public** state-owned company

4 *(construction → d'un barrage, d'une usine)* building, construction; *(→ d'un camp)* pitching

5 *(instauration → d'un empire)* setting up, establishing; *(→ d'un régime, d'une république)* installing; *(→ d'un usage)* establishing; *(→ d'un règlement)* prescribing, laying down; *(→ d'un principe)* laying down; *(→ d'objectifs)* determining; *(→ de la paix)* establishement; *(→ d'un prix)* fixing; *(→ d'une taxe, d'un tribunal)* institution, creation; *Tél* **é. d'appel** call connection; *Fin* **é. d'un compte** opening an account, setting up an account; *Com* **é. des prix** pricing; **é. des prix de revient** costing

6 *(préparation → d'un devis)* drawing up, preparation; *(→ d'une liste)* drawing up; *(→ d'un organigramme)* laying out, drawing up; *(→ d'un plan, d'une proposition)* drawing up

7 *(installation)* settling, fixing; *Hist* **établissements** *(colonies)* settlements, colonies; **l'é. des Français en Afrique** the settlement of the French in Africa

8 *Vieilli (dans une profession)* setting up; **son é. dans la profession médicale** his/her setting up in medical practice; **l'é. de ses enfants dans le commerce** *(il/elle les a établis)* his/her setting up his/her children in business; *(ils se sont établis)* his/her children setting (themselves) up in business; **l'é. de sa fille** *(par le mariage)* his/her marrying off his/her daughter

9 *(preuve → de la vérité)* establishment; **rien n'est possible sans l'é. de son identité** nothing can be done if his identity cannot be established

étage [etaʒ] NM **1** *(dans une maison)* floor, *Br* storey, *Am* story; *(dans un parking, un aéroport)* level; **au troisième é.** *(maison) Br* on the third floor; *Am* on the fourth floor; *(aéroport)* on level three; **habiter au premier é.** *Br* to live on the first floor, *Am* to live on the second floor; **au dernier é.** on the top floor; **elle est dans les étages** she's upstairs somewhere; **dévaler les étages** to race down the stairs; **à deux étages** *Br* two-storeyed, *Am* two-storied; **un immeuble de cinq étages** a *Br* five-storey *or Am* five-story building; *Archit* **l'é. noble** = second floor of a Parisian Haussmann apartment building, usually distinguished by a full-length balcony, where the most opulent apartment was traditionally located

2 *(division → d'une pièce montée)* tier; *(→ d'un buffet, d'une bibliothèque)* shelf; **dans le placard, sur l'é. du haut** in the cupboard on the top shelf

3 *Géol* stage, layer; *(d'un terrain)* level; *(d'un jardin)* terrace

4 *Bot* **é. de végétation** level of vegetation

5 *Aviat & Tech* stage; **é. de pression** pressure stage; **compression par étages** compression by stages; **fusée à trois étages** three-stage rocket

6 *Mines* level

7 *Can Sport* **le deuxième é.** the (club) management

8 *Arch & Littéraire* degree, rank; **étages de la société** strata *or* levels of society

❑ **étages** NMPL *(escaliers)* **grimper/monter les étages** to climb/to go upstairs; **monter les étages à pied/en courant** to walk/to run up the stairs; **monter les étages quatre à quatre** to take the stairs four at a time

❑ **à l'étage** ADV upstairs, on the floor above

❑ **de bas étage** ADJ *Péj* **1** *Vieilli (inférieur → personne)* low-born

2 *(vulgaire → cabaret)* sleazy; *(→ plaisanterie)* cheap

étagement [etaʒmɑ̃] NM *(de collines, de vignobles)* terracing

étager [17] [etaʒe] VT **1** *(mettre par étages)* to stack, to set out *or* to range in tiers; **jardin étagé** terraced garden; **vignes étagées** vines arranged in terraces; **poulie étagée** cone pulley **2** *Tech* **compression étagée** compression by stages, staged compression

▸**s'étager** VPR **les maisons s'étageaient le long de la pente** the houses rose up the slope in tiers

étagère [etaʒɛr] NF *(planche)* shelf; *(meuble)* (set of) shelves; **é. encastrée** built-in shelves *or* shelving

étagiste [etaʒist] NM *Ind* stage contractor

étai[1] [etɛ] NM *Naut (cordage)* stay; **voile d'é.** staysail

étai[2] [etɛ] NM *Constr* stay, prop, strut; *Mines* **é. de mine** pit prop

étaie *etc voir* **étayer**

étaiement [etɛmɑ̃] NM **1** *Constr (d'un mur)* propping-up, shoring-up **2** *(d'un raisonnement)* support, supporting, shoring-up

étain [etɛ̃] NM **1** *(métal blanc)* tin; **é. battu, é. en feuilles** thin sheet tin; **papier d'é.** tinfoil, silver paper **2** *(vaisselle)* piece of pewterware; **des étains** pewter (pieces), pewterware; **vaisselle d'é.** pewter (plate); **une très belle collection d'étains** a very fine collection of pewter (pieces) *or* pewterware

❑ **en étain** ADJ pewter *(avant n)*

était *etc voir* **être**[1]

et al [ɛtal] ADV et al

étal, -als [etal] NM **1** *(au marché)* (market) stall **2** *(de boucher)* block

étalage [etalaʒ] NM **1** *(des marchandises)* display; *(vitrine)* (display) window; *(stand)* stall; **il y a un bel é. de poisson le vendredi** there is a nice display of fish on Fridays; **faire un é.** *(vitrine)* to dress a window; *(stand)* to set up a stall; **mettre qch à l'é.** to display sth for sale; **é. publicitaire** display advertising

2 *Péj (démonstration)* display, show, parading; **un tel é. de luxe suscite des jalousies** such a display *or* show of wealth causes jealousy; **faire é. de ses bijoux/son savoir/sa richesse** to show off *or* parade one's jewels/knowledge/wealth; **faire é. de ses succès** to show off one's success; **faire é. de son argent** to flaunt one's wealth; **faire é. de ses qualifications** to make sure everyone knows about one's qualifications; **faire é. de sa force** to show one's strength; **elle fait é. de sa vie privée** she flaunts her private life

3 *(impôt)* tax paid by street trader

4 *Tex* roving (of flax)

❑ **étalages** NMPL *Métal* bosh

étalager [17] [etalaʒe] VT *Com* to display, to put on display

étalagiste [etalaʒist] NMF *Com* **1** *(dans un magasin)* window dresser **2** *(marchand)* street trader

étale [etal] ADJ **1** *Géog (mer, marée, fleuve)* slack; *(navire)* becalmed; *(vent)* steady **2** *(circulation)* slack

NM OU NF *Géog* **é. du flot** slack water

étalement [etalmɑ̃] NM **1** *(déploiement → de papiers, d'objets)* spreading (out); *(→ de marchandises)* displaying **2** *(des vacances, des horaires, des paiements)* staggering, spreading out (**sur** over); *(de travaux)* spreading (out) (**sur** over) **3** *(mise à plat)* spreading out **4** *(de connaissances)* showing off, flaunting

étaler [3] [etale] VT **1** *(exposer → marchandise)* to display, to lay out

2 *(exhiber → richesse, luxe)* to flaunt, to show off; **é. ses projets** to boast of one's plans; **é. ses malheurs** to parade one's misfortunes; **é. ses connaissances** to show off one's knowledge; **é. sa vie privée** to flaunt *or* parade one's private life; **é. une affaire au grand jour** to make a matter public

3 *(disposer à plat → tapis, tissu)* to spread (out); *(→ plan, carte, journal)* to open *or* to spread (out); *(→ papiers)* to spread out, to lay out; *(→ pâte à tarte)* to roll out; **é. ses cartes** *ou* **son jeu** to show one's hand

4 *(appliquer en couche → beurre, miel)* to spread; *(→ pommade, fond de teint)* to rub *or* to smooth on; *(→ enduit, peinture)* to apply (**sur** to); **une peinture facile à é.** paint which is easy to apply; *Hum* **la culture, c'est comme la confiture: moins on en a, plus on l'étale** = people who don't have much culture have to make the most of the little they have

5 *(échelonner → dates, rendez-vous)* to spread out; *(→ vacances, envoi du courrier)* to stagger (**sur** over); *(→ paiements)* to stagger, to spread out (**sur** over); *(→ travaux, cours, opération)* to spread (**sur** over); **les entreprises essaient d'é. les vacances de leurs employés** firms try to stagger their employees' holidays; **é. les remboursements (sur plusieurs exercices)** to spread (out) the repayments (over several financial years)

6 *Fam Arg scol* **se faire é. (à un examen)** to flunk an exam

7 *Naut (orage)* to weather out; *(courant, vent)* to stem

▸**s'étaler** VPR **1** *(s'appliquer)* to spread; **une peinture qui s'étale facilement** a paint which goes on easily

2 *(s'étendre → ville, plaine)* to stretch *or* to spread out; **arbre à cime étalée** large-crowned tree

3 *(être exhibé)* **son nom s'étale à la une de tous les journaux** his/her name is in *or* is splashed over all the papers

4 *Fam (s'affaler)* **s'é. dans un fauteuil/sur un canapé** to sprawl in an armchair/on a sofa

5 *Fam (tomber)* to take a tumble, to fall (down) ■

6 *Fam Péj (prendre trop de place)* to spread oneself out; **si tu t'étalais moins, j'aurais la place de m'asseoir** if you didn't take up so much room, I might be able to sit down

7 **s'é. sur** *(sujet: vacances, paiements)* to be spread over; **les vacances s'étalent sur trois mois** the holiday is spread over three months; **mon crédit s'étale sur cinq ans** my credit extends over five years; **ses rendez-vous s'étalent sur toute la semaine** he/she has appointments the whole week

étaleuse [etaløz] NF *Tex* spreader

étalier [etalje] ADJ M **garçon é.** butcher's assistant

NM butcher *(at a market)*

étalinguer [3] [etalɛ̃ge] VT *Naut* to clinch

étalingure [etalɛ̃gyr] NF *Naut* clinch

étalon[1] [etalɔ̃] NM *Zool (cheval)* stallion, stud; *(âne, taureau)* stud

étalon[2] [etalɔ̃] NM *(référence)* standard; *Fig (modèle)* standard, yardstick; **é. de change-or** gold exchange standard; **é. devise** currency standard; **é. monétaire** monetary standard

étalonnage [etalɔnaʒ], **étalonnement** [etalɔnmɑ̃] NM **1** *Tech (graduation)* calibration, calibrating **2** *(verification)* standardization, standardizing; *(d'un instrument)* gauging, testing **3** *Psy (d'un test)* standardization

étalonner [3] [etalɔne] VT **1** *Tech (graduer)* to calibrate **2** *(vérifier)* to standardize **3** *Psy (test)* to standardize, to set the standards for

étalonneur [etalɔnœr] NM *Cin & TV* grader

étalon-or [etalɔ̃ɔr] *(pl* **étalons-or***)* NM *Fin* gold standard; **é. lingot** gold bullion standard

étamage [etamaʒ] NM **1** *Métal (de cuivre)* tinning; *(d'une tôle de fer)* tinplating **2** *(d'une glace)* silvering

étambot [etɑ̃bo] NM *Naut* stern post

étambrai [etɑ̃brɛ] NM *Naut* partner

étamer [3] [etame] VT **1** *Métal (cuivre etc)* to tin; *(tôle de fer)* to tinplate **2** *(glace)* to silver

étameur [etamœr] NM **1** *Métal* tinsmith **2** *(en miroiterie)* silverer

étamine[1] [etamin] NF *Bot* stamen

étamine[2] [etamin] NF **1** *Tex* challis; *(pour drapeaux)* bunting; *(en tapisserie)* tammy **2** *Culin (pour filtrer)* cheese muslin *or* cloth, butter muslin; **passer qch à** *ou* **par l'é.** *(liquide)* to filter; *(farine)* to sift; *Fig Vieilli* to examine sth very closely

étampage [etɑ̃paʒ] NM *Métal* swaging

étampe [etɑ̃p] NF **1** *Métal* swage **2** *(pour fer à cheval)* punch

étamper [3] [etɑ̃pe] VT **1** *Métal* to swage **2** *(fer à cheval)* to punch

étamperche [etɑ̃pɛrʃ] NF *Constr* upright pole, standard

étampeur, -euse [etɑ̃pœr, -øz] NM,F stamper

étampure [etɑ̃pyr] NF **1** *(dans une plaque de métal)* mouth, splay **2** *(d'un fer à cheval)* nail hole

étamure [etamyr] NF *Métal* **1** *(couche)* coating of tin **2** *(matériau)* tinning metal

étanche [etɑ̃ʃ] ADJ *(chaussure, montre)* waterproof; *(réservoir, toit)* watertight; *(surface)* water-resistant, water-repellent; **é. à l'eau/à l'air/à la poussière** watertight/airtight/dustproof; **rendre é.** to waterproof

eta–eta

étanchéité [etɑ̃ʃeite] **NF** *(d'une montre, de chaussures)* waterproofness; *(d'un réservoir, d'un toit)* watertightness; *(d'un revêtement)* water-resistance; **é. à l'eau/à l'air** watertightness/airtightness; **vérifier l'é. (de)** to check for leaks (in)

étanchement [etɑ̃ʃmɑ̃] **NM** *Littéraire (du sang)* stemming, stanching, staunching; *(de la soif)* quenching, slaking; *(des larmes)* stanching, staunching; *(d'une voie d'eau)* stopping up

étancher [3] [etɑ̃ʃe] **VT 1** *(rendre étanche)* to make waterproof **2** *(arrêter → sang)* to stanch, to staunch, to stem; *(→ liquide)* to check the flow of; *(→ voie d'eau)* to stop up; *(→ larmes)* to dry; **é. sa soif** to quench *or* to slake one's thirst

étançon [etɑ̃sɔ̃] **NM** *Constr & Mines* stanchion, strut, post

étançonnement [etɑ̃sɔnmɑ̃] **NM** *Constr & Mines* shoring up

étançonner [3] [etɑ̃sɔne] **VT** *Constr & Mines* to shore *or* prop up, to strut, to stanchion

étang [etɑ̃] **NM** pond

étant[1] [etɑ̃] *voir* **être**[1]

étant[2] [etɑ̃] **NM** *Phil* being

étape [etap] **NF 1** *(arrêt)* stop, stopover; **arriver à l'é.** to reach the stopover point; **faire é. en chemin** to make a stop, to stop en route; **nous avons fait é. à Lille** we stopped off *or* over at Lille; **brûler une é.** *(train, autobus)* to go past *or* miss a stop, to fail to stop (at a scheduled stop); **comme nous étions pressés, nous avons brûlé l'é. de Strasbourg** since we were in a hurry, we missed out Strasbourg *or* we didn't stop in Strasbourg; *Fig* **brûler les étapes** *(dans son métier)* to move up the ladder very quickly; *(dans une tâche)* to cut corners

2 *(distance)* stage; **voyager par (petites) étapes** to travel in (easy) stages; **un voyage en deux étapes** a trip in two stages; **nous avons fait hier une é. de 500 kilomètres** we covered *or* did 500 kilometres yesterday

3 *Cyclisme* stage; **dans la prochaine é. du Tour de France** in the next stage of the Tour de France

4 *Fig (phase)* phase, stage, step; **les différentes étapes de la vie** the different stages *or* phases of life; **une réforme en plusieurs étapes** a reform in several stages; **une procédure en deux étapes** a two-stage *or* -step procedure; **par étapes** in stages; **nous allons procéder par étapes** we'll do it in stages *or* step by step; **é. par é.** stage by stage, step by step, one stage *or* step at a time

étarquer [3] [etarke] **VT** *Naut* to hoist home

État [eta] **NM 1** *Pol (nation)* state; **É. de droit** state governed by the rule of law; **É. fédéral** federal state; **l'É. français** the French state *or* nation; *Hist (le gouvernement de Vichy)* the French state, the Vichy regime; **l'É. d'Israël** (the state of) Israel; **l'É. de Washington** the State of Washington; **É. en balance** *(dans les élections américaines)* swing State; **les États membres** the member states; **É.-nation** nation-state; **É. de non-droit** = state in which law and order have broken down; **l'É. patron** the State as an employer; **les États pontificaux** the Papal States; **É. paria** rogue state; **É. policier** police state; **l'É. providence** the Welfare state; **É. tampon** buffer state; **É. voyou** rogue state; **un É. dans l'É.** a state within a state; *Can Fam* **les États** *(États-Unis)* the States; **l'É., c'est moi** = famous phrase attributed to Louis XIV, proclaiming the absolute nature of the monarchy

2 *Admin & Écon* state; **géré par l'É.** state-run, publicly run; **entreprise d'É.** state-owned *or* *Br* public company

ÉTAT [eta]

> state **A1–4, B** ▪ condition **A1, 2** ▪ profession **C1** ▪ social position **C1** ▪ account **D1** ▪ statement **D1, 2**

NM A. *MANIÈRE D'ÊTRE PHYSIQUE* **1** *(d'une personne → condition physique)* state, condition; *(→ apparence)* state; **le malade est dans un é. grave** the patient's condition is serious; **son é. empire/s'améliore** his/her condition is worsening/improving; **tu t'es mis dans un drôle d'é.!** look at the state of you!; **quand elle le vit dans cet é. pitoyable** when she saw him in such a pitiful state; **te voilà dans un triste é.!** you're in a sorry *or* sad state!; **être dans un é. second** *(drogué)* to be high; *(en transe)* to be in a trance; **être en é. d'ivresse** *ou* **d'ébriété** to be under the influence (of alcohol), to be inebriated; **être en é. de faire qch** to be fit to do sth; **être hors d'é. de, ne pas être en é. de** to be in no condition to *or* totally unfit to; **tu n'es pas en é. de conduire** you're in no condition to drive *or* not in a fit state to drive; **mettre qn hors d'é. de nuire** *(préventivement)* to make sb harmless; *(après coup)* to neutralize sb; **é. général** general state of health; **é. de santé** (state of) health, condition; *Méd* **é. végétatif chronique** persistent vegetative state; **é. de veille** waking state

2 *(d'un appartement, d'une route, d'une machine, d'un colis)* condition, state; **être en bon/mauvais é.** *(meuble, route, véhicule)* to be in good/poor condition; *(bâtiment)* to be in a good/bad state of repair; *(colis, marchandises)* to be undamaged/damaged; **le mauvais é. des pneus a pu causer l'accident** the bad condition of the tyres might have caused the accident; **vendu à l'é. neuf** *(dans petites annonces)* as new; **fauteuil en excellent é.** armchair in excellent condition; **voici l'é. du ciel pour demain** here is the weather forecast for tomorrow; **réduit à l'é. de cendres/poussière** reduced to ashes/a powder; **en é. de marche** in working order; *Fam Hum* **quand tu seras de nouveau en é. de marche** when you're back on your feet again *or* back in circulation; *Aut* **en é. de rouler** roadworthy; *Naut* **en é. de naviguer** seaworthy; *Aviat* **en é. de voler** airworthy; **être hors d'é. (de fonctionner)** to be out of order; **laisser une pièce en l'é.** to leave a room as it is; **remettre en é.** *(appartement)* to renovate, to refurbish; *(véhicule)* to repair; *(pièce de moteur)* to recondition; **maintenir qch en é.** *(bâtiment, bateau, voiture)* to keep sth in good repair

3 *(situation particulière → d'un développement, d'une technique)* state; **dans l'é. actuel des choses** as things stand at the moment, in the present state of affairs; **dans l'é. actuel de nos connaissances/de la science** in the present state of our knowledge/science; **l'é. de mes finances** my financial situation; **quand il est encore à l'é. larvaire** *ou* **de larve** when it's still a larva *or* in a larval state; **le chat était retourné à l'é. sauvage** the cat had gone back to its wild state; **(en) é. d'alerte/d'urgence** (in a) state of alarm/emergency; **être en é. d'arrestation** to be under arrest; **je me suis renseigné sur l'é. d'avancement des travaux** I enquired about the progress of the work; **é. de choses** state of things; **é. de fait** (established) fact; **é. de guerre** state of war; **é. de non-droit** = situation in which law and order have broken down; **être en é. de siège** to be under siege

4 *Chim & Phys* state; **é. gazeux/liquide/solide** gaseous/liquid/solid state; **é. amorphe/cristallin** amorphous/crystalline state; **é. ionisé/neutre** ionized/neutral state; **à l'é. brut** *(pétrole)* crude, unrefined, raw; **c'est de la bêtise à l'é. brut** it's plain stupidity; **à l'é. naturel** in its natural state; **à l'é. pur** *(gemme, métal)* pure; **c'est du racisme à l'é. pur** it's out-and-out racism

5 *Ling* **verbe d'é.** stative verb

B. *MANIÈRE D'ÊTRE MORALE, PSYCHOLOGIQUE* state; **être dans un é. de grande excitation** to be in a state of great excitement *or* very excited; **parfois, il tombait dans un é. de grand abattement** sometimes, he would fall into a state of utter dejection; **elle n'est pas dans son é. normal** she's not her normal *or* usual self; **qu'as-tu dit pour la mettre dans cet é.?** what did you say to put her in such a state?; **ne te mets pas dans cet é.!** *(à une personne inquiète, déprimée)* don't worry!; *(à une personne énervée)* don't get so worked up!; **é. de conscience** state of consciousness; **é. d'esprit** state *or* frame of mind; **é. limite** borderline state; *Fam* **être dans tous ses états** *(d'anxiété)* to be beside oneself with anxiety; *(de colère)* to be beside oneself (with anger); *Fam* **son fils n'est pas rentré de l'école, elle est dans tous ses états** her son hasn't returned from school, she's in a terrible state; *Fam* **se mettre dans tous ses états** *(en colère)* to go off the deep end, to go spare

C. *CONDITION SOCIALE* **1** *(profession)* trade, profession; *(statut social)* social position, standing, station; **l'é. militaire** the military profession; **il avait choisi l'é. ecclésiastique** he had chosen to become a clergyman; **il avait étudié pour sortir de son é.** he'd studied to climb the social ladder; **il est cordonnier de son é.** he's a shoemaker by trade

2 *Admin* **(bureau de l')é. civil** registry office; **é. civil** *(d'une personne)* (civil) status

3 *Hist* **les états généraux** the States *or* Estates General; *Fig* **organiser les états généraux de l'enseignement** to organize a conference *or* convention on education; **les états provinciaux** provincial assembly of the three orders

D. *DOCUMENT COMPTABLE OU LÉGAL* **1** *(compte rendu)* account, statement; *(inventaire)* inventory; *(rapport)* form; *(des paiements, des marchandises)* list; **l'é. des dépenses/des recettes** statement of expenses/takings; **é. appréciatif** evaluation, estimation; **é. comparatif/descriptif** comparative/descriptive account; **figurer sur les états d'une entreprise** to be on a company's payroll; **é. de frais** bill of costs; *Ordinat* **é. imprimé** printed output; **é. liquidatif** winding-up inventory; **états de service** *Mil* service record; *(professionnellement)* professional record; **é. des lieux** inventory (of fixtures); **dresser** *ou* **faire un é. des lieux** to draw up an inventory of fixtures; *Fig* to take stock of the situation; **é. parcellaire** list of properties *(in plots for compulsory purchase order)*

2 *Compta* statement; **é. de caisse** cash statement; **états comptables** accounting records; **états comptables et commerciaux** internal company records; **é. de compte** bank statement, statement of account; *Compta* statement of account; **é. détaillé** *(d'un compte)* breakdown; **é. financier** *(rapport)* financial statement; *(situation)* financial standing *or* situation; **é. de flux de trésorerie** source and application of funds statement; **é. de fortune** financial standing *or* situation; **é. néant** nil return; **é. de rapprochement** reconciliation statement; **é. récapitulatif** final assessment, adjustment account; **é. récapitulatif des redevances** royalty statement; **é. TVA** VAT statement

3 *(locution)* **faire é. de** *(sondage, témoignages, thèse)* to put forward; *(document)* to refer to; *(fait)* to mention; *(préoccupations)* to mention; **les premières estimations font é. de plusieurs centaines de victimes** according to the initial estimates, several hundred people have been killed; **s'il y a eu un témoin, le rapport de police devrait en faire é.** if there was a witness, the police report should mention *or* state this

▫ **état d'âme** **NM** mood; **elle ne me fait pas part de ses états d'âme** she doesn't confide in me; **j'en ai assez de leurs états d'âme!** I'm fed up with hearing about how THEY feel!; *Fam* **je me fiche de vos états d'âme!** I don't care whether you're happy about it or not!; **avoir des états d'âme** to suffer from angst; **faire qch sans états d'âme** to do sth without any qualms

▫ **état de grâce** **NM** *Rel* state of grace; *Pol* honeymoon period; **être en é. de grâce** to be in a state of grace; **le président est en é. de grâce** the President can do no wrong

'Harry dans tous ses états' *Allen* 'Deconstructing Harry'

Culture

LES ÉTATS GÉNÉRAUX

This term refers to the consultative assembly of representatives of the three estates: the clergy, the nobility and the Third Estate, or commoners. First convened in 1302 by Philippe le Bel, it had a turbulent relationship with the monarchy, which often tried to exploit it. It met for the last time in May 1789 in the "Jeu de Paume" in Versailles, where the Third Estate vowed not to disperse until they had established a constitution.

étatique [etatik] ADJ *Écon & Pol* under state control, state-controlled; **l'appareil é.** the machinery of state

étatisation [etatizasjɔ̃] NF *Écon & Pol* **1** *(gestion par l'État → de l'économie, d'un secteur d'activité)* establishment of state control (**de** of) **2** *(nationalisation → d'une industrie)* nationalization (**de** over) **3** *(dirigisme étatique)* state control

étatisé, -e [etatize] ADJ *Écon & Pol* state-controlled, state-run

étatiser [3] [etatize] VT *Écon & Pol* to bring under state control; **une firme étatisée** a state-owned company

étatisme [etatism] NM *Écon & Pol* state control

étatiste [etatist] ADJ state-control *(avant n)*; **système é.** system of state control

NMF supporter of state control

état-major [etamaʒɔr] *(pl* **états-majors**) NM **1** *Mil (officiers)* general staff; *(locaux)* headquarters; **officier d'é.** staff officer **2** *(direction → d'une entreprise)* management; *(→ d'un parti politique)* leadership; **le président et son é.** the president and his advisers

états-unien, -enne, étatsunien, -enne [etazynjɛ̃, -ɛn] ADJ (North) American

□ **États-Unien, -enne, Étatsunien, -enne** NM,F (North) American

États-Unis [etazyni] NMPL **les É. (d'Amérique)** the United States (of America); **vivre aux É.** to live in the United States; **aller aux É.** to go to the United States

étau, -x [eto] NM **1** *Tech* vice; **é. d'établi** bench vice

2 *Fig (restrictions)* stranglehold; **l'é. se resserre (sur les terroristes)** the noose is tightening around the terrorists; **les kidnappeurs sentaient l'é. se resserrer autour d'eux** the kidnappers could feel the net closing around them; **être pris** *ou* **enserré (comme) dans un é.** to be caught in a vice; **avoir le cœur dans un é.** *(avoir mal)* to feel as though one's chest is in a vice; *(être angoissé)* to feel pangs of anguish; *Fam* **avoir la tête comme dans un é.** to have a splitting headache; **la douleur relâcha son é.** the pain loosened its grip *or* hold

étau-limeur [etolimœr] *(pl* **étaux-limeurs**) NM *Tech* shaper

étayage [etɛjaʒ], **étayement** [etɛjmɑ̃] NM **1** *Constr (d'un mur)* propping-up, shoring-up **2** *(d'un raisonnement)* support, supporting, shoring-up

étayer [11] [eteje] VT **1** *Constr (mur)* to prop *or* to shore up **2** *(raisonnement, théorie)* to support, to back up; *(thèse, argument)* to support; *(argumentation)* to buttress; **pour é. ses allégations** in support of his allegations

▸**s'étayer** VPR **s'é. sur** *(s'appuyer sur)* to be based on

etc. *(abrév écrite* **et cetera, et cætera**) etc

et cætera, et cetera [ɛtsetera] ADV et cetera, and so on (and so forth)

été[1] [ete] PP *voir* **être**[1]

été[2] [ete] NM summer; **en é.** in (the) summer *or* summertime; **pendant l'é. 1989** in the summer of 1989; **l'é. prochain** next summer; **é. comme hiver, j'habite la campagne** I live in the country winter and summer alike; **l'é. est ma saison préférée** summer *or* summertime is my favourite season; **é. indien** *ou Can* **des Indiens** *ou Can* **des Sauvages** Indian summer; **l'é. de la Saint-Martin** Saint Martin's summer

□ **d'été** ADJ **robe d'é.** summer dress; **nuit/journée d'é.** summer's night/day; **temps d'é.** summer weather; **heure d'é.** summer time, *Am* daylight (saving) time

éteignait *etc voir* **éteindre**

éteignoir [etɛɲwar] NM **1** *(instrument)* extinguisher; **en é.** conical **2** *Fam (rabat-joie)* wet blanket, spoilsport, killjoy

éteindre [81] [etɛ̃dr] VT **1** *(arrêter la combustion de → cigarette, incendie)* to put out, to extinguish; *(→ bougie)* to put *or* to blow out; *(→ gaz, chauffage)* to turn off; *Ordinat* to power down, to shut down

2 *(phare, lampe, lumière)* to turn *or* to switch off; *(radio, télévision)* to turn off; *Fam* **va é. la chambre** switch off the light in the bedroom; **c'était éteint chez les voisins** the neighbours' lights were out

3 *Tech (chaux)* to slake, to slack; *(fer chauffé au rouge etc)* to quench

4 *(faire perdre son éclat à → couleur)* to fade, to soften; *Littéraire* **le chagrin avait éteint son regard** his/her eyes had been dulled by sorrow

5 *Compta & Fin (annuler → dette, rente)* to wipe out

6 *Littéraire (soif)* to quench, to slake; *(désirs, sentiments)* to kill; *(querelle)* to put an end to

USAGE ABSOLU to switch off (the lights) (**dans** in)

▸**s'éteindre** VPR **1** *(feu, gaz, chauffage)* to go out; *(bougie)* to blow out; *(cigarette)* to burn out; *(volcan)* to die down; **laisser s'é. le feu** to let the fire go out

2 *(lampe, lumière)* to go out; *(radio, télévision)* to go off; **la fenêtre s'éteignit** the light at the window went out

3 *Fig (s'affaiblir → couleur)* to fade; *(→ son, rires)* to die away, to subside; *(→ voix)* to die away; **le jour s'éteint** daylight is failing *or* fading

4 *Littéraire (se dissiper → ardeur, amour)* to fade away; *(→ colère)* to abate, to cool down

5 *Euph (mourir → personne)* to pass away

6 *(race)* to die out, to become extinct

éteint, -e [etɛ̃, -ɛ̃t] ADJ **1 être é.** *(incendie, cigarette, lampe)* to be out; *(électricité, radio)* to be off **2** *(race, famille, volcan)* extinct **3** *(sans éclat → regard)* dull, *Littéraire* lacklustre; *(→ visage, esprit)* dull; *(→ couleur)* faded; **d'une voix éteinte** faintly; **elle est plutôt éteinte ces temps-ci** she's lost her spark recently **4** *(chaux)* slaked

étemperche [etɑ̃pɛrʃ] NF *Constr (d'un échafaudage)* upright pole, standard

étendage [etɑ̃daʒ] NM **1** *(action)* hanging up *or* out **2** *(corde)* clothes line

étendard [etɑ̃dar] NM **1** *Mil* standard; *Fig* **lever l'é. de la révolte** to raise the standard of revolt; *Fig* **se ranger sous l'é. de qn** to join sb's camp **2** *Bot* standard, *Spéc* vexillum

étenderie [etɑ̃dri] NF *Tech* (glass) annealing lehr

étendoir [etɑ̃dwar] NM **1** *(corde)* clothes line; *(dispositif pliable)* clotheshorse **2** *(lieu)* drying shed

étendre [73] [etɑ̃dr] VT **1** *(beurre, miel)* to spread; *(pommade, fond de teint)* to rub *or* to smooth on

2 *(tapis, tissu)* to unroll; *(nappe)* to spread (out); *(plan, carte, journal)* to open *or* to spread (out); *(pâte à tarte)* to roll out; **é. le bras** to stretch out *or* reach out (one's arm); **é. les** *ou* **ses bras/jambes** to stretch (out) one's arms/legs

3 *(faire sécher)* **é. du linge** *(dehors)* to put the washing out to dry, to hang out the washing; *(à l'intérieur)* to hang up the washing

4 *(allonger → personne)* to stretch out; **é. un blessé sur une civière** to place an injured person on a stretcher; **il m'a fait é. sur le sol** he made me lie down on the ground; *Fam* **é. qn (par terre) d'un coup de poing** to knock sb down *or* flat, to deck sb

5 *(élargir → pouvoir, propriété)* to extend; *(→ recherches)* to broaden, to extend; *(→ cercle d'amis)* to extend, to widen; **é. la signification d'un mot** to extend the meaning of a word; **é. son vocabulaire** to increase *or* to extend one's vocabulary; **é. sa connaissance des langues étrangères au chinois et au japonais** to expand *or* extend one's knowledge of foreign languages to include Chinese and Japanese; **é. les termes d'une loi** to widen *or* broaden the terms of a law; **la société cherche à é. ses activités** the company is trying to branch out; **é. une grève au secteur privé** to extend a strike to the private sector; **j'étendrais cette définition à toutes les espèces animales** I'd extend this definition to all species of animal

6 *(diluer → peinture)* to dilute, to thin down; *(→ sauce)* to thin out *or* down, to water down; *(→ vin)* to water down; **é. d'eau une boisson** to water down a drink

7 *Fam (vaincre)* to thrash; **il a déjà étendu deux champions régionaux** he's already knocked out two regional champions; **se faire é.** *(à un match de boxe)* to get knocked *or* laid out; *(aux élections)* to be trounced; *(à un examen)* to be failed

8 *Ordinat (mémoire)* to upgrade

▸**s'étendre** VPR **1** *(dans l'espace)* to extend, to stretch; **la zone pluvieuse s'étendra du nord au sud** the rainy zone will stretch from North to South; **la ligne s'étend depuis Ivry jusqu'à Charenton** the line stretches *or* extends *or* runs from Ivry to Charenton; **les banlieues s'étendaient à l'infini** the suburbs stretched out endlessly; **notre parc s'étend sur plusieurs hectares** our grounds spread over several acres; **mes connaissances ne s'étendent pas jusque-là** my knowledge doesn't stretch that far; **son ambition s'étendait aux plus hautes sphères de la politique** his/her ambition extended to the highest echelons of politics; **une loi qui s'étend à toutes les circonscriptions** a law that covers all districts

2 *(dans le temps)* to extend; **la période qui s'étend du XVIIème au XIXème siècle** the period stretching from the 17th to the 19th century; **les vacances s'étendent sur trois mois** the *Br* holiday *or Am* vacation stretches over three months

3 *(se développer → épidémie, grève, incendie)* to spread; *(→ cercle d'amis)* to widen; *(→ pouvoir)* to widen, to increase, to expand; *(→ culture, vocabulaire)* to increase, to broaden; *(→ empire)* to expand, to grow larger; *(→ fortune, entreprise)* to expand, to grow larger; *(→ influence)* to spread, to widen, to increase

4 *(s'allonger → malade)* to stretch out, to lie down

5 s'é. sur *(évoquer en détail)* to enlarge on; **je ne m'étendrai pas davantage sur ce sujet** I won't discuss this subject at any greater length; **elle ne s'est pas étendue sur ses projets d'avenir** she didn't enlarge on her future plans; **il ne s'est pas étendu sur les raisons de son absence** he didn't enlarge *or* expand on the reasons for his absence

étendu, -e[1] [etɑ̃dy] ADJ **1** *(vaste → territoire)* big, wide, spread-out; *(→ banlieue)* sprawling; **un panorama é.** a vast panorama; **la ville/banlieue est très étendue** the town/suburb is very spread-out *or* covers a large area

2 *(considérable → pouvoir, connaissances)* extensive, wide-ranging; *(→ vocabulaire)* wide, extensive; *(→ influence)* far-reaching, widespread; *(→ dégâts)* extensive; **sa culture très étendue impressionne tous ses collègues** all of his/her colleagues are impressed by his/her vast erudition *or* by his/her breadth of culture

3 *(étiré)* **les bras étendus** with outstretched arms; **les jambes étendues** with legs stretched out; **les ailes étendues** with outstretched wings; **é. sur un divan** stretched out *or* lying on a couch; **é. sur le dos** lying (flat) on one's back

4 *(dilué → gén)* diluted (**de** with); *(→ vin, sauce)* watered-down; *(→ peinture, couleur)* thinned-down

étendue[2] [etɑ̃dy] NF **1** *(surface)* area, stretch; *(d'eau, de sable)* expanse, stretch; *(de terre)* expanse, tract; **la forêt occupe une grande** *ou* **vaste é. dans cette région** the forest covers a huge area in this region; **une é. désertique** a stretch of desert

2 *(dimension)* area; **un domaine d'une grande é.** a large estate; **quelle est l'é. de ce terrain?** how large is this piece of land?; **sur toute l'é. du pays** throughout the country; **sur toute l'é. du champ** over the entire field; **sur une grande é.** over a wide area

3 *(durée)* **l'é. d'un discours** the length of a speech; **sur une é. de dix ans** over a period of ten years

4 *(ampleur → gén)* extent; *(→ de connaissances, de vocabulaire, d'un pouvoir)* extent, scope; **pour évaluer** *ou* **mesurer l'é. du désastre** to assess the extent of the disaster; **ses propos révèlent l'é. de sa culture/de son ignorance** his/her remarks show the extent of his/her knowledge/of his/her ignorance; **te rends-tu compte de l'é. de ton erreur?** do you realize the extent *or* the magnitude of your error?

5 *Mus (d'une voix, d'un instrument)* range

6 *Phil* extension

Étéocle [eteɔkl] NPR Eteocles

éternel, -elle [etɛrnɛl] ADJ **1** *Phil & Rel* eternal; *(vie)* eternal, everlasting; *(jeunesse)* eternal; **neiges éternelles** eternal snow

2 *Fig (regrets)* eternal, endless; *(amour)* eternal, undying; **je lui voue une reconnaissance**

éternelle I'll be for ever *or* eternally grateful to him/her; **cette situation ne sera pas éternelle** this situation won't last for ever; **je ne suis pas é.** I won't live forever; *Fig Littéraire* **dans la nuit éternelle** in the endless night

3 *(avant le nom) (invariable)* **c'est un é. mécontent** he's perpetually discontented, he's never happy *or* satisfied; **leurs éternelles discussions politiques** their endless *or* interminable political discussions; **son é. cigare à la bouche** his inevitable cigar; **avec son éternelle petite robe noire** with her inevitable little black dress

NM l'é. féminin the eternal feminine

▫ **Éternel NM l'É.** the Eternal; *Fam* **grand voyageur/menteur devant l'É.** great *or* inveterate traveller/liar

éternellement [etɛrnɛlmɑ̃] **ADV 1** *Phil & Rel* eternally **2** *(durer, rester)* for ever; **je l'aimerai é.** I will always love him/her, I'll love him/her forever; **je ne l'attendrai pas é.** I'm not going to wait for him/her for ever; **avec ses cheveux é. ébouriffés** with his/her perpetually tousled hair; **je vous en serais é. reconnaissant** I would be eternally grateful (to you); **rester é. jeune** to stay young forever *or* forever young

éterniser [3] [etɛrnize] **VT 1** *Péj (prolonger → discussion, crise)* to drag *or* to draw out **2** *Littéraire (perpétuer)* **é. le nom/la mémoire de qn** to immortalize *or* to perpetuate sb's name/memory

►**s'éterniser VPR** *Péj* **1** *(durer → crise, discussion)* to drag on **2** *Fam (s'attarder)* **les invités se sont éternisés, j'ai cru qu'ils n'allaient jamais partir!** the guests overstayed their welcome, I thought they'd never leave!; **on ne va pas s'é. ici** we're not going to stay here for ever; **j'espère qu'elle ne va pas s'é. chez moi** I hope she's not going to hang around here too long

Éternit® [eternit] **NM** asbestos board *or* sheet

éternité [etɛrnite] **NF 1** *Phil & Rel* eternity **2** *(longue durée)* eternity; **il y avait une é. que je ne l'avais vu** I hadn't seen him for ages *or* an eternity; **l'attente chez le médecin m'a paru une é.** it seemed (like) an eternity before the doctor saw me; **j'ai attendu pendant une é.** I waited an eternity, I waited for ages; **la construction du stade va durer une é.** it will take forever to build the stadium

▫ **de toute éternité ADV** *Littéraire* from time immemorial

éternuement [etɛrnymɑ̃] **NM** sneeze; **être pris d'éternuements** to have a fit of sneezing

éternuer [7] [etɛrnɥe] **VI** to sneeze; **ça me fait é.** it makes me sneeze

êtes *voir* **être**[1]

étésien [etezjɛ̃] **ADJ M vents étésiens** Etesian winds

étêtage [etɛtaʒ], **étêtement** [etɛtmɑ̃] **NM** *Hort* pollarding

étêter [4] [etete] **VT** *Hort (arbre)* to pollard; *Culin (poisson)* to cut off the head of; *(clou, épingle)* to knock the head off

éteuf [etœf] **NM** *Hist* leather ball

éteule [etœl] **NF** *Agr* stubble

éthanal [etanal] **NM** *Chim* ethanal

éthane [etan] **NM** *Chim* ethane

éthanoïque [etanɔik] **ADJ** *Chim* **acide é.** ethanoic acid

éthanol [etanɔl] **NM** *Chim* ethanol

éther [etɛr] **NM** *Littéraire & Chim* ether

éthéré, -e [etere] **ADJ** *Littéraire & Chim* ethereal

éthérification [eterifikasjɔ̃] **NF** *Chim* etherification

éthérifier [9] [eterifje] **VT** *Chim* to etherify

éthériser [3] [eterize] **VT** *Méd* to etherise, to etherize

éthérisme [eterism] **NM** etherism

Ethernet® [etɛrnɛt] **NM** *Ordinat* Ethernet®

éthéromane [eterɔman] *Méd* **ADJ** addicted to ether

NMF ether addict

éthéromanie [eterɔmani] **NF** *Méd* addiction to ether

éthicien, -enne [etisjɛ̃, -ɛn] **NM,F** ethicist

éthionamide [etjɔnamid] **NF** *Méd* ethionamide

Éthiopie [etjɔpi] **NF** *Géog* **l'É.** Ethiopia; **vivre en É.** to live in Ethiopia; **aller en É.** to go to Ethiopia

éthiopien, -enne [etjɔpjɛ̃, -ɛn] **ADJ** Ethiopian

▫ **Éthiopien, -enne NM,F** Ethiopian

éthique [etik] **ADJ** ethic, ethical

NF 1 *Phil* ethics *(singulier)* **2** *(code moral)* ethic; **é. biomédicale** bioethics

ethmoïdal, -e, -aux, -ales [ɛtmɔidal, -o] **ADJ** *Anat* ethmoid, ethmoidal

ethmoïde [ɛtmɔid] *Anat* **ADJ M** ethmoid

NM ethmoid (bone)

ethnarchie [ɛtnarʃi] **NF** *Antiq* ethnarchy

ethnarque [ɛtnark] **NM** *Antiq* ethnarch

ethniciser [3] [ɛtnisize] **VT** *Pol* to ethnicize

ethnicité [ɛtnisite] **NF** *Pol* ethnicity

ethnie [ɛtni] **NF** ethnic group

ethnique [ɛtnik] **ADJ** ethnic

ethniquement [ɛtnikmɑ̃] **ADV** ethnically

ethno [ɛtno] **NF** ethnology

ethnobiologie [ɛtnɔbjɔlɔʒi] **NF** *Biol* ethnobiology

ethnocentrique [ɛtnɔsɑ̃trik] **ADJ** *Pol* ethnocentric

ethnocentrisme [ɛtnɔsɑ̃trism] **NM** *Pol* ethnocentrism

ethnocide [ɛtnɔsid] **NM** *Pol* ethnocide

ethnogenèse [ɛtnɔʒənɛz] **NF** *Hist* ethnogenesis

ethnographe [ɛtnɔgraf] **NMF** *Hist* ethnographer

ethnographie [ɛtnɔgrafi] **NF** *Hist* ethnography

ethnographique [ɛtnɔgrafik] **ADJ** *Hist* ethnographic, ethnographical

ethnolinguistique [ɛtnɔlɛ̃gɥistik] *Ling* **ADJ** ethnolinguistic

NF ethnolinguistics *(singulier)*

ethnologie [ɛtnɔlɔʒi] **NF** ethnology

ethnologique [ɛtnɔlɔʒik] **ADJ** ethnologic, ethnological

ethnologue [ɛtnɔlɔg] **NMF** ethnologist

ethnométhodologie [ɛtnɔmetɔdɔlɔʒi] **NF** *Hist* ethnomethodology

ethnomusicologie [ɛtnɔmyzikɔlɔʒi] **NF** *Mus* ethnomusicology

ethnonyme [ɛtnɔnim] **NM** *Ling* ethnonym

ethnopsychiatrie [ɛtnɔpsikjatri] **NF** *Psy* ethnopsychiatry

ethnopsychologie [ɛtnɔpsikɔlɔʒi] **NF** *Psy* ethnopsychology

éthogramme [etɔgram] **NM** *Zool* ethogram

éthologie [etɔlɔʒi] **NF** *Zool* ethology

éthologique [etɔlɔʒik] **ADJ** *Zool* ethological

éthologiste [etɔlɔʒist], **éthologue** [etɔlɔg] **NMF** ethologist

ethos [etɔs] **NM** *(en anthropologie)* ethos

éthuse [etyz] **NF** *Bot* fool's parsley, lesser hemlock, aethusa

éthylamine [etilamin] **NF** *Chim* ethylamine

éthyle [etil] **NM** *Chim* ethyl

éthylène [etilɛn] **NM** *Chim* ethylene

éthylénique [etilenik] **ADJ** *Chim* ethylenic

éthylique [etilik] *Chim* **ADJ** ethyl *(avant n)*, ethylic; **alcool é.** ethyl alcohol

NMF alcoholic

éthylisme [etilism] **NM** *Méd* alcoholism

éthylomètre [etilɔmɛtr], **éthylotest** [etilotɛst] **NM** *Br* breathalyser, *Am* Breathalyzer®

étiage [etjaʒ] **NM** *Géog* **1** *(niveau)* low water level *or* mark; **échelle d'é.** water gauge **2** *(abaissement)* low water

Étienne [etjɛn] **NPR le roi É.** King Stephen; *Fam (locution)* **à la tienne, É.!** cheers(, Big Ears)!

étier [etje] **NM** canal *(linking salt marshes with the sea, in Western France)*

étincelage [etɛ̃slaʒ] **NM 1** *Tech* spark erosion; **soudure par é.** flash welding **2** *Méd* fulguration, surgical diathermy

étincelant, -e [etɛ̃slɑ̃, -ɑ̃t] **ADJ 1** *(brillant → diamant, étoile)* sparkling, gleaming, twinkling; *(→ métal, lac)* sparkling, glittering; *(→ soleil)* brightly shining; *(bien lavé → vaisselle)* shining, sparkling, gleaming; **un diamant plus é. que celui-là** a diamond that sparkles more than that one; **la mer étincelante** the sparkling sea; **le lac était é. sous le soleil** the lake sparkled in the sunlight; **sapin de Noël é.** Christmas tree sparkling *or* gleaming with lights; **é. de propreté** gleaming

2 *(vif → regard, œil)* sparkling, twinkling; **les yeux étincelants de joie/de plaisir** eyes sparkling *or* twinkling with joy/pleasure; **les yeux étincelants de colère/de haine** eyes glinting with rage/with hate

3 *(plein de brio → conversation, esprit, style)* brilliant, sparkling; *(personne)* dazzling, brilliant

étinceler [24] [etɛ̃sle] **VI 1** *(diamant)* to sparkle, to glitter; *(étoile)* to sparkle, to gleam, to twinkle; *(mer, lac)* to sparkle, to glitter; *(soleil)* to shine brightly; *(vaisselle)* to shine, to sparkle, to gleam; *(métal, lame)* to gleam; **la mer étincelait** the sea was sparkling; **le sapin de Noël étincelait** the Christmas tree was glittering with lights; **é. de propreté** to be gleaming, to be sparkling clean; **é. de blancheur** to be gleaming white; **la lumière des spots faisait é. ses yeux** his/her eyes sparkled in the spotlights

2 *(regard, œil)* to sparkle, to glitter; **ses yeux étincelaient de colère/jalousie/passion** his/her eyes glittered with anger/jealousy/passion; **ses yeux étincelaient de bonheur/fierté** his/her eyes were sparkling with happiness/pride; **ses yeux étincelaient de convoitise** his/her eyes gleamed with envy

3 *(conversation, style)* to sparkle, to be brilliant

étincelle [etɛ̃sɛl] **NF 1** *(parcelle incandescente)* spark; **é. électrique** electric spark; **faire des étincelles** to throw off sparks; *Fig (avoir du succès)* to cause a huge sensation, to be a big success; *Hum* **on ne peut pas dire qu'il ait fait des étincelles pendant son mandat** he didn't exactly set the world on fire during his term of office; **c'est l'é. qui a mis le feu aux poudres** it was this which sparked everything off

2 *(lueur)* spark, sparkle; **jeter** *ou* **lancer des étincelles** to sparkle; **le casque poli jetait des étincelles** the highly polished helmet sparkled; **ses yeux jetaient des étincelles** *(de joie)* his/her eyes shone with joy; *(de colère)* his/her eyes flashed with rage

3 *(bref élan)* **é. d'intelligence** spark of intelligence; **l'é. du génie** the spark of genius; **il a eu une é. de génie** he had a stroke of genius, he had a brilliant idea

étincellement [etɛ̃sɛlmɑ̃] **NM** *(d'un diamant)* sparkle, glitter; *(d'une étoile)* sparkle, gleam, twinkle; *(d'un métal, d'une lame)* gleam; *(de la mer, d'un lac)* glittering *(UNCOUNT)*, sparkling *(UNCOUNT)*; *(des yeux → de joie)* sparkle, twinkle; *(→ de colère)* glint

étincellera *etc voir* **étinceler**

étiolement [etjɔlmɑ̃] **NM 1** *Agr & Bot* bleaching, blanching, *Spéc* etiolation; **pour empêcher l'é. de vos plantes** to stop your plants going leggy *or* straggly **2** *(affaiblissement → d'une personne)* decline, weakening; *(→ d'un esprit)* weakening

étioler [3] [etjɔle] **VT 1** *Agr & Bot (plante)* to make leggy; *Agr (intentionnellement)* to bleach, to blanch, *Spéc* to etiolate **2** *(personne)* to make weak *or* pale *or* sickly

►**s'étioler VPR 1** *Agr & Bot* to wilt, to blanch, *Spéc* to etiolate **2** *(s'affaiblir → personne)* to decline, to fade away, to become weak; *(→ esprit)* to become lacklustre *or* dull; *(→ mémoire)* to deteriorate

étiologie [etjɔlɔʒi] **NF** *Méd* aetiology

étiologique [etjɔlɔʒik] **ADJ** *Méd* aetiologic, aetiological

étiopathe [etjɔpat] **NMF** *Méd* aetiopath

étiopathie [etjɔpati] **NF** *Méd* aetiopathy

étique [etik] **ADJ** *Littéraire* skinny, emaciated, scrawny

étiquetage [etiktaʒ] **NM** *Com (d'une marchandise)* labelling; *(d'un colis, de bagages)* ticketing, labelling; **é. de l'apport nutritionnel** nutritional labelling; **é. de la composition** ingredient labelling; **é. des pourcentages** *(des principaux ingrédients)* percentage labelling; **é. préventif** precautionary labelling; **é. du prix** price marking *or* labelling

étiqueter [27] [etikte] **VT 1** *Com (marchandise)* to mark, to label; *(colis, bagages)* to ticket, to label **2** *Péj (cataloguer)* to label; **j'ai été étiqueté comme écologiste** I was labelled as a green

étiqueteur, -euse [etiktœr, -øz] **NM,F** labeller

▫ **étiqueteuse NF** *(machine)* labelling machine

étiquette [etikɛt] **NF 1** *(marque → de colis, de bagages)* label; *(→ portant le prix)* ticket; **coller une é. sur un paquet** to label a parcel, to stick a label on a parcel; **é. autocollante** *ou* **gommée** sticky label, sticker; *Com* **é. descriptive** descriptive label; *Com* **é. magnétique** security tag; *Com* **é. porte-prix** price label; **é. de prix** price ticket, price tag, price label; *Com* **é. d'un**

produit product label; *Com* **é. promotionnelle** promotional label; **é. de qualité** quality label

2 *(appartenance)* label; **mettre une é. à qn** to label sb; **on a collé cette é. socialiste à notre journal** our paper has been labelled as socialist; **é. politique** political affiliation; **sans é. politique** *(candidat, journal)* independent

3 *Ordinat* label

4 *(protocole)* **l'é.** etiquette; **é. de Cour** court etiquette

étirable [etirabl] ADJ stretchable

étirage [etiraʒ] NM **1** *Tech (du verre, du métal, du fil)* drawing; **é. à chaud/froid** hot/cold drawing; **é. du fil** wire drawing **2** *(du tissu, des peaux)* stretching

étirement [etirmɑ̃] NM *(des membres, du corps)* stretching; **faire des étirements** to do stretching exercises

étirer [3] [etire] VT **1** *(allonger → membres, cou)* to stretch; *(→ peloton, convoi)* to stretch out **2** *Tech (verre, métal)* to draw (out) **3** *Tex* to stretch

▸**s'étirer** VPR **1** *(personne, animal)* to stretch (out) **2** *(s'allonger → tissu, vêtement)* to stretch **3** *(s'éterniser → journée, récit)* to drag on (forever)

étireur, -euse [etirœr, -øz] *Métal* NM,F drawer, drawbench worker

❑ **étireuse** NF *(machine)* draw bench

Etna [ɛtna] NM *Géog* **l'E., le mont E.** (Mount) Etna

étoc [etɔk] NM rock *(exposed at low tide)*

étoffe [etɔf] NF **1** *Tex* material, fabric; **acheter de l'é.** to buy material; **des étoffes somptueuses** rich fabrics

2 *(calibre → d'un professionnel, d'un artiste)* calibre; **il est d'une autre/de la même é.** he's in a different/the same league; **manquer d'é.** *(personne)* to lack calibre; *(film, roman)* to lack substance, to be thin *or* insubstantial; **elle a de l'é.** she's got character, there's a lot to her; **avoir l'é. de** to have the makings of; **il a l'é. d'un héros** he has the makings of a hero, he's the stuff heroes are made of; **avoir l'é. d'un chef** to be leadership material

3 *Tech* base-metal alloy

❑ **étoffes** NFPL *Typ* mark-up *(on materials)*

étoffé, -e [etɔfe] ADJ **1** *(roman, récit)* full of substance, well-rounded; *(discours)* weighty **2** *(voix)* deep, sonorous **3** *(personne)* **il est é. maintenant** he has filled out

étoffer [3] [etɔfe] VT **1** *(faire grossir)* to put weight on; **son séjour à la campagne l'a étoffé** his spell in the country has made him fill out a bit **2** *(renforcer → effectifs, équipe)* to beef up **3** *(développer → roman, personnage)* to flesh *or* to fill out, to give substance to

▸**s'étoffer** VPR to fill out, to put on weight

étoile [etwal] NF **1** *Astron* star; **contempler** *ou* **observer les étoiles** to stargaze; **ciel parsemé** *ou* **semé d'étoiles** starry sky, sky studded with stars; **une nuit/un ciel sans étoiles** a starless night/sky; **à la clarté des étoiles** in the starlight; *Fam* **voir les étoiles en plein midi** to see stars; **é. géante/naine** giant/dwarf star; **é. du matin/soir** morning/evening star; **é. du berger** morning star; **é. double** double star; **é. filante** shooting star; **é. à neutrons** neutron star; **é. Polaire** pole star; **é. triple** triple star; **é. variable** variable star

2 *(insigne)* star; **hôtel trois/quatre étoiles** three-star/four-star hotel; **c'est un deux étoiles** it has a two-star rating; **congélateur à trois étoiles** three-star freezer; **général à quatre étoiles** four-star general; **é. à cinq branches** five-pointed star; **l'é. jaune/rouge** the yellow/red star; *Rel* **l'É. de David** the Star of David

3 *(destin)* stars, fate; **son é. blanchit** *ou* **pâlit** her fortunes are waning, her star is fading; **c'est sa bonne é.** it's his/her lucky star; **né sous une bonne/mauvaise é.** born under a lucky/an unlucky star; **croire** *ou* **avoir foi en son é.** *ou* **en sa bonne é.** to believe in *or* trust to luck

4 *Vieilli (célébrité)* star; **une é. du cinéma** a movie star; **c'est une é. montante** he's/she's a rising star; **elle est l'é. du spectacle** she's the star of the show

5 *(en danse)* prima ballerina

6 *Typ* star, asterisk

7 *(au ski)* badge (of achievement); **première/deuxième/troisième é.** beginners/intermediate/advanced badge of proficiency; **aujourd'hui l'école de ski fait passer les étoiles** the ski school is putting its pupils through the proficiency tests today

8 *Zool* **é. de mer** starfish

9 *Math* asterisk

10 *Aut* roundabout, *Am* traffic circle; **(la place de) l'É.** *(à Paris)* = junction of several main roads in Paris, where the Arc de Triomphe is situated

❑ **à la belle étoile** ADV *(coucher, dormir)* (out) in the open, outside

❑ **en étoile** ADV **disposé en é.** star-shaped; **carrefour en é.** multi-road junction; *Ordinat* **connecté en é.** in a star configuration

étoilé, -e [etwale] ADJ **1** *(ciel)* starry, star-studded; *(nuit)* starry **2** *(fêlé → pare-brise)* starred

étoile-d'argent [etwaldarʒɑ̃] *(pl* **étoiles-d'argent***)* NF *Bot* edelweiss

étoilement [etwalmɑ̃] NM **1** *(crevasse)* star-shaped crack **2** *Littéraire* **l'é. du ciel se faisait peu à peu** the sky gradually became filled with stars

étoiler [3] [etwale] VT **1** *Littéraire (parsemer d'étoiles)* to spangle with stars; **les vitres étoilées de givre** the window panes glittering with frost **2** *(fêler → vitre)* to craze, to crack

▸**s'étoiler** VPR **1** *Littéraire (ciel)* to become starry **2** *(vitre)* to crack

étole [etɔl] NF *(gén) & Rel* stole

étonnamment [etɔnamɑ̃] ADV surprisingly; *(plus fort)* amazingly, astonishingly

étonnant, -e [etɔnɑ̃, -ɑ̃t] ADJ **1** *(remarquable → personne, acteur, mémoire)* remarkable, astonishing; *(→ roman)* great, fantastic; *(→ voyage)* fabulous

2 *(surprenant)* surprising; *(plus fort)* amazing, astonishing; **c'est é. de sa part** it's quite amazing, coming from him/her; **ce n'est pas é. qu'il soit malade** it's not surprising *or* it's no wonder that he's ill; **rien d'é. à ce qu'il ait divorcé** no wonder he got divorced; **ça n'a rien d'é.** it's no wonder; **chose étonnante, il est arrivé à l'heure** astonishingly *or* amazingly *or* surprisingly (enough), he arrived on time

NM **l'é. est qu'il soit venu** the astonishing *or* amazing *or* surprising thing is that he came

étonné, -e [etɔne] ADJ surprised; *(plus fort)* astonished, amazed (**de qch** at sth; **de voir** to see); **prendre un air é., faire l'é.** to act surprised; **il avait l'air é.** he looked surprised; **un regard é.** a surprised look; *(plus fort)* a look of astonishment *or* amazement, an astonished look

étonnement [etɔnmɑ̃] NM surprise; *(plus fort)* astonishment, amazement; **je fus frappé d'é. en apprenant la nouvelle** I was astonished when I heard the news; **à mon grand é.** to my great surprise; **imaginez (quel a été) mon é. quand…** imagine my surprise *or* astonishment when…

étonner [3] [etɔne] VT to surprise; *(plus fort)* to amaze, to astonish; **je suis étonné de ses progrès** I'm amazed at the progress he's/she's made; **elle m'étonne par son courage** I'm astonished at her courage; **cet enfant m'étonne de plus en plus** this child never ceases to amaze me; **tu m'étonneras toujours!** you never cease to astonish me!; **ce que je vais vous dire va probablement vous é.** what I have to say may come as a surprise; **ça m'étonne qu'elle ne t'ait pas appelé** I'm surprised she didn't call you; **plus rien ne m'étonne** nothing surprises me anymore; **cela m'étonnerait** I'd be surprised; *Fam* **alors ça, ça m'étonnerait** that'll be the day; **cela ne m'étonnerait pas** it wouldn't surprise me, I wouldn't be the least bit surprised; **ça ne m'étonne pas du tout** it doesn't surprise me in the least, I'm not the least bit surprised; **ça ne m'étonne pas de toi!** you do surprise me!; *Ironique* **tu m'étonnes!** you DO surprise me!, you don't say!

▸**s'étonner** VPR to be surprised (**de** at); **je m'étonne de vous voir** I'm astonished *or* surprised to see you; **ne t'étonne pas si elle te quitte** don't be surprised if she leaves you; **je ne m'étonne plus de rien** nothing surprises me any more; **je m'étonne qu'il ne soit pas venu** I'm surprised he didn't show up; **comment s'é. qu'il ait refusé?** can you wonder *or* is it any wonder that he refused?

étouffade [etufad] NF *Culin* ≃ beef stew

étouffage [etufaʒ] NM *(des vers à soie, des abeilles)* stifling

étouffant, -e [etufɑ̃, -ɑ̃t] ADJ **1** *(oppressant → lieu, climat, ambiance)* stifling; *(→ temps)* oppressive, sultry; **une journée étouffante** a stifling hot day **2** *(indigeste → mets)* stodgy, heavy

étouffe-chrétien [etufkretjɛ̃] *Fam* ADJ heavy ▪, stodgy ▪; **c'est un peu é., sa quiche** his/her quiche is a bit stodgy

NM INV heavy *or* stodgy food ▪

étouffée [etufe] **à l'étouffée** ADJ steamed *(in a tightly shut saucepan)*

ADV **cuire à l'é.** to steam *(in a tightly shut saucepan)*

étouffement [etufmɑ̃] NM **1** *(asphyxie)* suffocation; **la victime a été tuée par é.** the victim was suffocated (to death); **mourir d'é.** to die of *or* from suffocation

2 *(respiration difficile)* breathlessness; *(crise)* fit of breathlessness; **avoir une sensation d'é.** to have a feeling of breathlessness *or* suffocation; **il a été pris d'étouffements pendant la nuit** he had a fit of breathlessness in the night

3 *(répression → d'une révolte)* quelling; *(→ d'une rumeur)* stifling; *(camouflage → d'un scandale)* hushing-up, covering-up

étouffer [3] [etufe] VT **1** *(asphyxier → personne, animal)* to suffocate, to smother; **é. qn de baisers** to smother sb with kisses; **le bébé a été étouffé** *(accident)* the baby suffocated to death; *(meurtre)* the baby was smothered; **mourir étouffé** to die of suffocation, to choke to death; **ne le serre pas si fort, tu l'étouffes!** don't hug him so hard, you'll smother him!; *Fam Hum* **ce n'est pas la politesse qui l'étouffe** politeness isn't exactly his/her strong point; *Fam Hum* **ce ne sont pas les scrupules qui l'étouffent** he's/she's not exactly over-scrupulous; *Fam* **ça t'étoufferait de dire bonjour?** would it kill you to say hello?

2 *(oppresser → sujet: famille, entourage)* to smother; *(→ sujet: ambiance)* to stifle; **le milieu familial l'étouffait** he/she found the family circle stifling; **cette chaleur m'étouffe** the heat is stifling (me)

3 *(émouvoir fortement)* **la colère/l'émotion l'étouffe** he's/she's choking with anger/emotion

4 *(arrêter, atténuer → feu)* to put out, to smother; *(→ bruit)* to muffle, to deaden; *(→ cris, pleurs, sentiment, rire)* to stifle, to hold back; *(→ bâillement)* to stifle, to smother, to suppress; *(→ sanglot)* to stifle, to choke back; *(→ voix)* to lower; *(→ révolte, rumeur)* to quash; *(→ scandale)* to hush *or* to cover up; *Mus* to damp; *Élec (étincelle)* to quench; **il a réussi à faire é. l'affaire** he managed to get the affair hushed up

VI **1** *(s'asphyxier)* to suffocate, to choke; **j'ai failli é. en avalant de travers** I almost choked on my food; **é. de colère/jalousie/rire** to choke with anger/jealousy/laughter; **é. d'indignation** to splutter with indignation

2 *(avoir chaud)* to suffocate, to be gasping for air

3 *(être oppressé)* to feel stifled; **j'étouffe dans ce milieu** this atmosphere stifles me

▸**s'étouffer** VPR to suffocate; *(en mangeant)* to choke; **une sardine et une demi-tomate, on ne risque pas de s'é.!** a sardine and half a tomato! there's no fear of us choking on that!; **arrête de la faire rire, tu vas la faire s'é.!** stop making her laugh, you'll make her choke *or* she'll choke!

étouffoir [etufwar] NM **1** *(pour la braise)* charcoal extinguisher **2** *Mus* damper **3** *Fam (lieu)* oven; **c'est un é. ici!** it's like an oven in here!

étoupe [etup] NF *Tech (lin, chanvre)* tow; **é. à calfater** oakum

étouper [3] [etupe] VT *Tech* to stop up with oakum

étoupille [etupij] NF **1** *Vieilli Mil (d'un canon)* slow-match **2** *(d'une fusée de feu d'artifice)* quick-match, squib; *Mines* fuse

étoupiller [3] [etupije] VT *Vieilli Mil (canon)* to fuse

étourderie [eturdəri] NF **1** *(faute)* careless mistake

2 *(caractère)* carelessness; **il est d'une é. incroyable** he is incredibly scatterbrained *or* *Fam* scatty; **faute d'é.** foolish mistake

❑ **par étourderie** ADV carelessly, without thinking

étourdi, -e [eturdi] **ADJ** *(personne)* careless; *(acte, réponse)* thoughtless
NM,F scatterbrain
❑ **à l'étourdie ADV** *Vieilli* thoughtlessly, foolishly

étourdiment [eturdimɑ̃] **ADV** thoughtlessly, carelessly, foolishly

étourdir [32] [eturdir] **VT 1** *(assommer)* to stun, to daze; **le coup l'avait un peu étourdi** he was slightly dazed by the blow
2 *(griser → sujet: vertige, sensation, alcool)* to make dizzy *or* light-headed; *(→ sujet: odeur)* to overpower; **le succès l'étourdissait** success had gone to his/her head; **cette perspective l'étourdissait** he/she was exhilarated at the prospect; **je suis toute étourdie** my head's spinning
3 *(abasourdir → sujet: bruit)* to deafen; **ces enfants m'étourdissent!** these children are deafening!
4 *Littéraire (calmer → douleur, chagrin)* to numb, to deaden
▸**s'étourdir VPR s'é. dans le plaisir** to live a life of pleasure; **s'é. de paroles** to get drunk on words

étourdissant, -e [eturdisɑ̃, -ɑ̃t] **ADJ 1** *(bruit)* deafening, ear-splitting; **nous roulions à une vitesse étourdissante** we were driving at breakneck speed **2** *(extraordinaire → beauté, créativité, activité)* stunning; **il a fait une prestation étourdissante dans 'Othello'** he was stunning in 'Othello'; **il est é. de beauté** he's stunningly handsome; **être é. d'esprit** to be very glib **3** *Littéraire (grisant → adulation, passion)* exciting, exhilarating

étourdissement [eturdismɑ̃] **NM 1** *(vertige)* fit of giddiness *or* dizziness, dizzy spell; *Méd* fainting fit, blackout; **avoir un é.** to feel giddy *or* dizzy; **cela me donne des étourdissements** it makes me feel giddy *or* dizzy, it makes my head spin *or* swim **2** *Littéraire (griserie)* exhilaration

étourneau, -x [eturno] **NM 1** *Orn* starling **2** *Fam (étourdi)* birdbrain

étrange [etrɑ̃ʒ] **ADJ** *(personne)* strange, odd; *(chose, fait)* strange, funny, odd; **quelle é. coïncidence!** what a strange coincidence!; **chose é., elle a dit oui** strangely enough, she said yes; **aussi é. que cela puisse paraître…** strange as it may seem…

'L'Étrange Noël de M. Jack' *Burton* 'The Nightmare before Christmas'

étrangement [etrɑ̃ʒmɑ̃] **ADV 1** *(bizarrement)* oddly, strangely; **elle était é. habillée** she was oddly dressed; **ressembler é. à qn/qch** to look suspiciously like sb/sth **2** *(inhabituellement)* strangely; **il est é. silencieux** he's strangely silent

étranger, -ère [etrɑ̃ʒe, -ɛr] **ADJ 1** *(d'un autre pays)* foreign
2 *(extérieur à un groupe)* outside; **le piquet de grève était renforcé par des éléments étrangers** the picket (line) had been reinforced by outside elements; **des éléments étrangers se sont introduits dans l'enceinte de l'école** outsiders entered the school premises; **je suis é. à leur communauté** I'm not a member of *or* I don't belong to their community; **elle est étrangère au projet** she isn't involved in the plan; **des personnes étrangères au service** non-members of staff; **entrée interdite à toute personne étrangère** no entry to unauthorized personnel
3 *(non familier → voix, visage, région, sentiment)* unknown, unfamiliar (**à** to); **parmi les odeurs de la maison, il discernait un parfum é.** he could discern *or* make out an unfamiliar odour amongst the house's usual smells
4 *(sans rapport)* **je suis complètement é. à cette affaire** I'm in no way involved in *or* I have nothing to do with this business; **développement é. au sujet** irrelevant development; **ce sont là des considérations étrangères à notre discussion** those points are irrelevant *or* extraneous to our discussion
5 é. à *(qui n'a pas le concept de)* closed *or* impervious to; *(inconnu de)* unknown to; **il est é. à la pitié** he's completely lacking in compassion; **la haine lui est étrangère** he/she doesn't know what hatred is; **la musique lui est étrangère** he/she has no knowledge of music, music is a closed book to him/her; **ce sentiment/visage ne m'est pas é.** that feeling/face is not unknown to me; **sa voix ne m'est pas étrangère** his/her voice is not unfamiliar
NM,F 1 *(habitant d'un autre pays)* foreigner, alien
2 *(inconnu)* stranger; **je suis devenu un é. pour elle** I'm like a stranger to her now; **je suis un é. ici** I'm a stranger here, I'm a foreigner in these parts
3 *(en français d'Afrique) (visiteur)* guest
NM l'é. *(pays)* foreign countries; **ça vient de l'é.** it comes from abroad
❑ **à l'étranger ADV** abroad; **aller/vivre à l'é.** to go/live abroad; **voyages à l'é.** foreign travel; **investissement à l'é.** foreign *or* outward investment

'L'Étranger' *Camus* 'The Outsider' (UK), 'The Stranger' (US)

étrangeté [etrɑ̃ʒte] **NF 1** *(singularité → d'un discours, d'un comportement)* strangeness, oddness **2** *Littéraire (remarque)* funny *or* strange *or* odd thing; *(incident)* strange *or* odd fact

étranglé, -e [etrɑ̃gle] **ADJ 1** *(rauque → voix, son)* tight, strangled **2** *(resserré → rue, passage)* narrow; *(taille)* nipped-in **3** *Méd (hernie)* strangulated

étranglement [etrɑ̃gləmɑ̃] **NM 1** *(strangulation)* strangling, strangulation; *(à la lutte)* stranglehold; **il est mort par é.** he died of strangulation, he was strangled; **ce n'est pas l'é. qui a provoqué la mort** strangulation was not the cause of death
2 *(étouffement, resserrement)* tightening, constriction; *(de la taille)* narrowing; **j'ai compris à l'é. de sa voix que…** the tightness in his/her voice told me that…
3 *(passage étroit)* bottleneck; *(d'une rivière)* narrow part, narrows; **il y a un é. dans la rue** the street forms a bottleneck; **grâce à l'é. du tuyau** owing to the narrower section of the pipe
4 *Littéraire (restriction → des libertés)* stifling
5 *Méd* strangulation; **é. herniaire** strangulated hernia
6 *Aut & Tech* throttling; **soupape d'é.** throttle valve

étrangler [3] [etrɑ̃gle] **VT 1** *(tuer → intentionnellement)* to strangle; *(→ par accident)* to strangle, to choke; **elle a été étranglée par son écharpe** she was strangled by her scarf
2 *(serrer)* to choke, to constrict; **ce col roulé m'étrangle** this turtleneck is choking me *or* is too tight around my neck; **elle avait la taille étranglée par une grosse ceinture** she had a wide belt pulled in tight around the waist
3 *(faire balbutier → sujet: colère, peur)* to choke; **la colère l'étrangle** he/she is choking with rage; **il répondit d'une voix étranglée par l'émotion** he replied in a voice choking *or* tight with emotion
4 *(ruiner)* to decimate, to squeeze out of existence; **les supermarchés ont étranglé le petit commerce** supermarkets have decimated small businesses; **les impôts m'étranglent** taxes are killing me
5 *Littéraire (restreindre → libertés)* to stifle
6 *Méd (vaisseau sanguin)* to strangulate
7 *Tech (vapeur etc)* to throttle; *Aut* **é. le moteur** to throttle (down) the engine
▸**s'étrangler VPR 1** *(personne)* to choke; **s'é. avec un os** to choke on a bone; **s'é. de rire/colère** to choke with laughter/anger; **s'é. d'indignation** to be speechless with indignation
2 *(voix)* to choke; **un sanglot s'étrangla dans sa gorge** a sob caught *or* died in his/her throat; **les mots se sont étranglés dans sa gorge** the words died on his/her lips, he/she couldn't get the words out
3 *(chemin, rue, vallée)* to form a bottleneck, to narrow (down); *(rivière)* to narrow

étrangleur, -euse [etrɑ̃glœr, -øz] **NM,F** strangler
NM *Aut & Tech* throttle

étrangloir [etrɑ̃glwar] **NM** *Naut (de voile)* throat brail; *(de chaîne)* compressor

étrave [etrav] **NF** *Naut* stem; **de l'é. à l'étambot** from stem to stern; **lame d'é.** bow wave

ÊTRE[1] [2] [ɛtr]

VI to be **A, B** ▪ to exist **A1** ▪ to go **C**
V IMPERSONNEL there is/are **1** ▪ to be **2, 3**
V AUX to have **1** ▪ to be **2** ▪ to have to **3**

VI A. *EXPRIME L'EXISTENCE, LA RÉALITÉ* **1** *(exister)* to be, to exist; **l'homme n'est pas sans le regard des autres** man only exists through others' eyes; **ne nie pas ce qui est** don't deny the facts; **parlons de ce qui est et non de ce qui a été** let's talk of what is and not of what used to be; **si Dieu est** if God exists; **si cela est** if (it is) so; *Littéraire* **mon fils n'est plus** my son is no more *or* passed away; **la nounou la plus patiente qui soit** the most patient nanny that ever was *or* in the world; **le plus petit ordinateur qui soit** the tiniest computer ever; **ê. ou ne pas ê.** to be or not to be; **on ne peut pas ê. et avoir été** you only live once
2 *Math* **soit une droite AB** let AB be a straight line
B. *RELIE L'ATTRIBUT, LE COMPLÉMENT AU SUJET* **1** *(suivi d'un attribut)* to be; **le boa est un serpent** the boa is a snake; **elle est professeur** she's a teacher; **le sac est trop lourd** the bag is too heavy; **ê. malade/déprimé** to be ill/depressed; **on est bien assis dans ce fauteuil** this armchair is comfortable; *Fam* **je ne te le prêterai pas! – comment** *ou* **comme tu es!** I won't lend it to you! – (you) see what you're like!; **je suis comme je suis** I am what I am; **comment es-tu ce matin?** how are you feeling this morning?; **Bruno/ce rôle est tout pour moi** Bruno/this part means everything to me; **elle n'est plus rien pour lui** she no longer matters to him; **le pain n'est plus ce qu'il était** bread isn't as good as it used to be; **elle n'est plus ce qu'elle était** she's not what she used to be; **qui suis-je?** who am I?; **qui était-ce?** who was it?; **qui est-il exactement?** who is he, exactly?
2 *(suivi d'une préposition)* **ê. à l'hôpital** to be in hospital; **je suis à la gare** I'm at the station; **où sommes-nous?** where are we?; **cela fait longtemps que je ne suis plus à Paris** I left Paris a long time ago; **le propriétaire? il est au troisième étage** the owner? he lives on the third floor; **j'y suis, j'y reste** here I am and here I stay; **je n'y suis pour personne** *(à la maison)* I'm not at home for anyone; *(au bureau)* I won't see anybody; **je suis à vous dans un instant** I'll be with you in a moment; **je suis à vous** *(je vous écoute)* I'm all yours; **la Sardaigne est au sud de la Corse** Sardinia is (situated) south of Corsica; **laisse la plante où elle est** leave the plant where it is; **ta chemise est au lavage** your shirt is in the wash; **tout le monde est à la page 15/au chapitre 9?** is everybody at page 15/chapter 9?; **vous êtes (bien) au 01.40.06.24.08** this is 01 40 06 24 08; **nous ne sommes qu'au début du tournoi** the tournament has just started; **ce livre est à moi** the book's mine; **il est tout à son travail** he's busy with his work; **il est toujours à me questionner** he's always asking me questions; **ê. contre** to be against; **ê. de** *(provenir de)* to be from, to come from; **je suis de la Martinique** I come from *or* was born in Martinique; **l'église est du XVIème** the church is from *or* dates back to the 16th century; **la lettre est du 12** the letter's dated the 12th; **les œufs sont d'hier** the eggs were laid yesterday; **ê. de** *(appartenir à)* to belong to, to be a member of; **êtes-vous du club?** do you belong to the club?, are you a member of the club?; **Bruno est de sa famille** Bruno is a member of his/her family *or* is a relative of his/hers; **le lys est de la famille des liliacées** the lily belongs to the family Liliaceae; **je suis de mariage le mois prochain** I've got (to go to) a wedding next month; **qui est de corvée de vaisselle?** who's on washing-up duty?; **acceptez-vous d'ê. (un) des nôtres?** would you care to join us?; **je regrette de ne pouvoir ê. des vôtres** I'm sorry I can't be with you; **ê. en prison/en France** to be in prison/in France; **la table est en chêne** the table is made of oak; **ê. en bonne santé** to be in good health; **ê. en forme** to be fit; **les dossiers qui sont en attente** the pending files; **vous n'êtes pas sans**

savoir que... I'm sure you're aware that...; **les joueurs en sont à deux sets partout** the players are two sets all; **j'en suis à la deuxième manche du pull** I'm doing *or* knitting the second sleeve of the jumper; **le projet n'en est qu'au début** the project has only just started; **Christian, où en sommes-nous dans le match?** Christian, what's the situation in the match?; **où en es-tu avec Michel?** how is it going with Michel?; **où en es-tu dans le livre?** how far have you got into the book?; **j'en suis au moment où il découvre le trésor** I've got to the part *or* the bit where he discovers the treasure; **où en étais-je?** *(après une interruption dans une conversation)* where was I?; **où en sont les travaux?** how's the work coming along?; **j'en suis à me demander si...** I'm beginning to wonder if...; **tu en es encore à lui chercher des excuses! – oh non, je n'en suis plus là!** you're still trying to find excuses for him/her! – oh no, I'm past that!; **je ne sais plus du tout où j'en suis dans tous ces calculs** I don't know where I am any more with all these calculations; **j'ai besoin de faire le point, je ne sais plus où j'en suis** I've got to take stock, I've completely lost track of everything; **tout le monde y est?** *(tout le monde est prêt?)* is everyone ready?; **vas-y, j'y suis** go on, I'm ready; **tu te souviens bien de Marie, une petite brune! – ah, oui, j'y suis maintenant!** but you must remember Marie, a brunette! – oh yes, I'm with you now!; **je n'y suis pas du tout!** I'm lost!; **mais non, vous n'y êtes pas du tout!** you don't understand!; **il est des nôtres!** he's one of us; *Fam* **en ê., ê. de ceux-là** *(être homosexuel)* to be one of them

3 *(dans l'expression du temps)* to be; **nous sommes le 8/jeudi** today is the 8th/Thursday; **quel jour sommes-nous?** what day is it today?; **on est déjà au mois de mars** we are in March already; **on était en avril** it was April; **on n'est qu'en février** it's only February; **imaginez, nous sommes en 1804** imagine it's (the year) 1804; **le mariage est en août** the wedding is in August

C. *SUBSTITUT DE "ALLER", "PARTIR"* to go; **tu y as déjà été?** have you already been there?; *Littéraire* **elle s'en fut lui porter la lettre** she went to take him/her the letter

V IMPERSONNEL1 *(exister)* **il est** *(il y a → suivi d'un singulier)* there is; *(→ suivi d'un pluriel)* there are; **il est une île où...** there's an island where...; **il est des romanciers qui...** there are novelists who..., some novelists...; **il est des parfums si entêtants que...** some perfumes are so heady that...; **il était une fois un prince...** once (upon a time) there was a prince...; **un escroc s'il en est** a crook if ever there was one

2 *(pour dire l'heure)* **il est 5 heures** it's 5 o'clock; **quelle heure est-il?** what time is it?

3 *(locutions)* **il en est ainsi** that's how it is; **il en est ainsi de toutes les démocraties** that's how it is in all democracies; **on a dit que vous vouliez démissionner – il n'en est rien** it was rumoured you wanted to resign – that's not true; **il n'est que de lire les journaux pour s'en rendre compte** you only have to read the newspapers to be aware of it

V AUX 1 *(sert à former les temps composés)* **je suis/j'étais descendu** I came/had come down; **dès qu'elle est apparue** as soon as she appeared; **serais-tu resté?** would you have stayed?; **tu te serais noyé si je n'avais pas été là!** you would have drowned if I hadn't been there!; **la tour s'est écroulée** the tower collapsed

2 *(sert à former le passif)* **des arbres ont été déterrés par la tempête** trees were uprooted during the storm

3 *(sert à exprimer une obligation)* **ce dossier est à préparer pour lundi** the file must be ready for Monday; **cela est à prouver** we have no proof of that yet

❑ **cela étant ADV** *(dans ces circonstances)* things being what they are; *(cela dit)* having said that

❑ **étant donné PRÉP** given, considering; **étant donné les circonstances** given *or* in view of the circumstances

❑ **étant donné que CONJ** since, given the fact that; **étant donné qu'il pleuvait...** since *or* as it was raining...

être² [ɛtr] **NM 1** *Biol & Phil* being; *Phil* **l'ê.** being; **des êtres venus d'ailleurs** beings *or* creatures from outer space; **un rêve peuplé d'êtres étranges** a dream full of strange creatures; **ê. humain** human being; **ê. de raison** rational being; **ê. vivant** living thing; *Littéraire* **un ê. de lumière/ténèbres** a creature of light/darkness

2 *Rel* **l'Ê. éternel** *ou* **infini** *ou* **suprême** the Supreme Being; **le Grand Ê.** the Great I Am

3 *(personne)* person; **c'est un ê. cruel** he's/she's a cruel person; **c'est un ê. hors du commun** he/she is someone out of the ordinary *or* is no common mortal; **c'est un ê. méprisable** he's/she's a despicable creature; **il était tout ému de tenir ce petit ê. dans ses bras** he was very moved holding the little thing in his arms; **nul ê. au monde ne t'a aimé plus que moi** no one in the world loved you more than I; **un ê. cher** a loved one; **je ne veux partager ce secret qu'avec un ê. cher** I want to share this secret only with someone close to me; **l'ê. aimé** the beloved

4 *(cœur, âme)* being, heart, soul; **tout mon ê. se révolte à cette idée** my entire being rebels at the idea; **je le crois de tout mon ê.** I believe it with all my heart; **au fond de son ê.** deep down in his/her heart; **du fond de son ê.** from the depths of his/her being; **il a été bouleversé jusqu'au fond de son ê.** he was profoundly moved; **il tremblait de tout son ê.** his whole being quivered *or* shuddered

'L'Être et le néant' *Sartre* 'Being and Nothingness'

étrécir [32] [etresir] **VT** *Vieilli* to shrink

étreindre [81] [etrɛ̃dr] **VT 1** *(serrer entre ses bras → ami, amant, adversaire)* to hug, to clasp, to embrace **2** *(oppresser → sujet: émotion, colère, peur)* to seize, to grip

▸**s'étreindre VPR** *(amis, amants)* to hug (each other), to embrace each other; *(lutteurs)* to grip each other, to have each other in a tight grip

étreinte [etrɛ̃t] **NF 1** *(embrassade)* hug, embrace

2 *(d'un boa)* constriction; *(d'un lutteur)* grip; **les troupes ennemies resserrent leur é. autour de la ville** the enemy troops are tightening their grip *or* stranglehold on the city

3 *Littéraire (oppression)* grip, grasp; **tu ne peux imaginer ce qu'est l'é. de la misère** you cannot imagine what it's like to be in the grip of poverty; **l'é. de la douleur se faisait sentir de plus en plus** the pain was strengthening its grip *or* hold

être-là [ɛtrəla] **NM INV** *Phil* being-there

étrenne [etrɛn] **NF** *Littéraire* **avoir l'é. de qch** to have the first use of sth

❑ **étrennes NFPL** *(cadeau)* New Year's Day present; **qu'est-ce que tu veux pour tes étrennes?** what would you like as a present for New Year's Day?; **les étrennes du facteur/de l'éboueur** New Year's tip *(given to postmen, dustmen, delivery men etc in the weeks running up to the New Year)*, *Br* ≃ Christmas box, *Am* ≃ Christmas bonus

étrenner [4] [etrene] **VT** *(machine)* to use for the first time; *(robe, chaussures)* to wear for the first time

VI *(souffrir)* **c'est toi qui vas é.!** YOU'RE going to catch it!

êtres [ɛtr] **NMPL** *Vieilli Littéraire (d'une maison)* layout (of the different parts)

étrésillon [etrezijɔ̃] **NM** *Constr* shore, strut, brace; *Mines* strut

étrésillonnement [etrezijɔnmɑ̃] **NM** *Constr* shoring (across), strutting, bracing; *Mines* strutting

étrésillonner [3] [etrezijɔne] **VT** *Constr* to shore, to strut, to brace; *Mines* to strut

étrette [etrɛt] **ADJ 1** *Vieilli ou Can Fam* narrow ▪ **2** *Can Fam (personne)* narrow-minded ▪

NF *Can Fam* narrow-minded person ▪

étrier [etrije] **NM 1** *Équitation* stirrup; **tenir l'é. à qn** to help sb mount; *Fig* to give sb a leg up; **vider les étriers** to be thrown; *Fig* to be thrown *or* disconcerted; *Fig* **avoir le pied à l'é.** *(être sur le départ)* to be on the point of leaving; *(être en bonne voie pour réussir)* to be off to a good start; *Fig* **mettre le pied à l'é. à qn** to give sb a helping hand; **boire** *ou* **prendre le coup de l'é.** to have one for the road

2 *Anat* stirrup, stirrup-bone

3 *Méd* **é. (de soutien)** stirrup, leg rest; **é. (de traction** *ou* **de réduction)** calliper

4 *(d'escalade) Br* étrier, *Am* stirrup

5 *Constr* stirrup

6 *Aut* stirrup, shackle; *(de frein)* caliper

étrille [etrij] **NF 1** *(peigne)* currycomb **2** *Zool* swimming crab

étriller [3] [etrije] **VT 1** *(cheval)* to curry, to currycomb **2** *Fam (vaincre)* to crush, to trounce **3** *Fam (critiquer)* to pan, *Br* to slate **4** *Fam (escroquer)* to swindle, to con **5** *Vieilli (frapper)* to trounce, to thrash

étripage [etripaʒ] **NM 1** *Culin (d'un poisson)* gutting; *(d'une volaille, d'un gibier)* drawing, cleaning **2** *Fam (tuerie)* slaughter ▪

étriper [3] [etripe] **VT 1** *Culin (poisson)* to gut; *(volaille, gibier)* to draw, to clean out **2** *Fam (tuer)* **je vais l'é., celui-là!** I'm going to make mincemeat of him *or Br* to have his guts for garters!

▸**s'étriper VPR** *Fam* to tear each other to pieces; **ils allaient s'é.** they were at each other's throats

étriqué, -e [etrike] **ADJ 1** *(trop petit → vêtement)* skimpy **2** *(mesquin → vie, habitudes, caractère)* mean, petty; *(→ perspective, esprit, vie)* narrow; *(→ avenir)* limited; **un point de vue très é.** a very narrow outlook

étriquer [3] [etrike] **VT** *Couture (vêtement)* to make too tight; **cette robe vous étrique** that dress is too tight on you

étrive [etriv] **NF** *Naut* throat-seizing

étriver [3] [etrive] **VT 1** *Naut (cordage)* to seize, to nip **2** *Can* to tease; **se faire é.** to get teased

étrivière [etrivjɛr] **NF** stirrup leather

étroit, -e [etrwa, -at] **ADJ 1** *(rue, bande, sentier, épaules, hanches)* narrow; *(vêtement)* tight

2 *(logement)* poky, cramped

3 *(mesquin → esprit)* narrow; *(→ idées)* limited; **être é. d'esprit, avoir l'esprit é.** to be narrow-minded; **avoir des vues étroites** to be limited in one's vision

4 *(liens, rapport, complicité, collaboration)* close; **je suis en rapport é. avec sa sœur** I am in close contact *or* touch with his/her sister; **travailler en étroite collaboration avec** to work closely *or* in close co-operation with

5 *(surveillance)* close, strict, tight; *(acception, interprétation)* narrow, strict; **sous étroite surveillance** under close surveillance; **un mot dans son sens le plus é.** the strictest sense of a word

❑ **à l'étroit ADV on est un peu à l'é. ici** it's rather cramped in here; **ils vivent** *ou* **sont logés à l'é.** they haven't much living space; **je me sens trop à l'é. dans ce jean** these jeans feel too tight, I'm bursting out of these jeans

étroitement [etrwatmɑ̃] **ADV 1** *(nouer, tenir)* tightly; **tenir qn/qch é. serré contre sa poitrine** to clasp sb/sth to one's breast

2 *(strictement → respecter)* strictly; **surveiller qn é.** to watch sb closely, to keep a close watch on sb

3 *(intimement → relier, collaborer)* closely; **être é. unis** to be closely allied, to have close links; **ces problèmes sont é. liés** these problems are closely *or* intimately linked

4 *(à l'étroit)* **être é. logé** to live in cramped conditions

étroitesse [etrwatɛs] **NF 1** *(d'une route, d'un couloir, d'épaules, de hanches)* narrowness **2** *(d'un logement, d'une pièce)* pokiness; **l'é. de ce bureau** the lack of space in this office **3** *(mesquinerie)* **é. d'esprit** *ou* **de vues** narrow-mindedness

étron [etrɔ̃] **NM** piece of excrement

Étrurie [etryri] **NF** *Hist* **l'É.** Etruria

étrusque [etrysk] **ADJ** Etruscan, Etrurian

NM *(langue)* Etruscan, Etrurian

❑ **Étrusque NMF** Etruscan, Etrurian

Ets *Com (abrév écrite* **établissements***)* **E. Legrand** Legrand (& Co)

ETSI [ətesi] **NM** *(abrév* **European Telecommunications Standards Institute***)* ETSI

ETTD, E.T.T.D. [ətetede] **NM** *Ordinat (abrév* **équipement terminal de traitement de données***)* DTE

-ette *voir* **-et**

étude [etyd] **NF 1** *(apprentissage)* study; **l'é. des langues** the study of languages; **aimer l'é.** to like studying; **elle a le goût de l'é.** she has a thirst for learning

2 *(analyse, essai)* study, paper; *Constr* survey; **une é. sur les mollusques** a study of *or* paper on molluscs; **procéder à l'é. d'une question, mettre une question à l'é.** to study *or* investigate *or* go into a question; *Mktg* **é. ad hoc** ad hoc survey; *Mktg & Com* **é. AIO** AIO research; **é. d'audience** audience research; **é. des besoins** needs study *or* analysis; **é. de cas** case study; *Mktg* **é. client** customer survey; **é. commerciale** marketing study; **é. du comportement** behavioural study; **é. du comportement du consommateur** consumer behaviour study; **é. auprès des consommateurs** consumer survey; **é. auprès des consommateurs finaux** end-user survey; *Fin* **é. de coût-efficacité** cost-volume-profit analysis; *Mktg* **é. des créneaux** gap analysis; **é. documentaire** desk research; *Mktg* **é. longitudinale** longitudinal study; **é. marketing** marketing study; *Mktg* **é. de mémorisation** recall study; *Mktg* **é. de motivation** motivational study; *Mktg* **é. de notoriété** awareness study; *Mktg* **é. de produit** product analysis; **é. qualitative** qualitative study; **é. quantitative** quantitative study; *Mktg* **é. de satisfaction de la clientèle** customer satisfaction survey; **é. sur le terrain** field study; **études sur les ventes** sales research; *Scol* **é. de texte** textual analysis

3 *(travail préparatoire)* study; **ce projet est à l'é.** this project is under study *or* being studied; *Mktg* **é. de faisabilité** feasability study; *Mktg* **é. d'impact** impact study; **é. de marché** market survey, market study; **faire une é. de marché** to do market research; **ce cabinet est spécialisé dans les études de marché** the company specializes in market research; *Mktg* **é. de marché standard** omnibus survey; **é. préliminaire** preliminary study; *Mktg* **é. prospective du marché** market study

4 *Scol (salle)* study *or Br* prep room; *(période)* study-time; **(salle d')é.** (private) study room, *Br* prep room; **pendant l'é.** during study-time; **elle reste à l'é. le soir** she stays on to study in the evenings; **je laisse mes enfants à l'é. jusqu'à 5 heures** ≃ I leave the children in homework class until 5 o'clock

5 *(bureau → gén)* office; *(→ d'un avocat, d'un notaire)* office, *Br* chambers; *(charge → d'un avocat, d'un notaire)* practice

6 *Mus* study, étude; **é. pour violon** violin study

7 *Beaux-Arts* study

▫ **études NFPL** *Scol & Univ* studies; **faire des études** to study; **faire des études de français/de droit** to study *or Br* read French/law; **faire de brillantes études** to do extremely well at university; **il a fait ses études à Eton/la Sorbonne** he was educated at Eton/he went to *or* studied at the Sorbonne; **arrêter ses études** *(par choix)* to give up studying; *(par rébellion)* to drop out; **j'ai arrêté mes études à 16 ans** I left school when I was 16; **payer ses études** to pay for one's education; **payer les études de qn** to pay for sb's education; **études commerciales** business studies; **études de communication** media studies; **études secondaires** secondary education; **études supérieures** higher education

étudiant, -e [etydjɑ̃, -ɑ̃t] **ADJ** student *(avant n)*

NM,F *Univ (avant la licence)* undergraduate, student; *(après la licence)* postgraduate, student; **é. en droit/médecine** law/medical student; **é. de première année** first-year (student); *Presse* **l'É.** = French monthly student magazine

étudié, -e [etydje] **ADJ 1** *(bien fait → plan, dessin)* specially *or* carefully designed; *(→ discours)* carefully composed; *(→ tenue)* carefully selected **2** *Com (prix)* reasonable **3** *(affecté → gestes)* studied; *(manières, sourires)* affected; **avoir un comportement é.** to have a studied manner

étudier [9] [etydje] **VT 1** *Scol & Univ (apprendre → matière)* to learn, to study; *(→ leçon)* to learn; *(→ instrument)* to learn (to play), to study; *(→ auteur, période, rôle)* to study; *(observer → insecte)* to study; **é. l'histoire** *Scol* to study history; *Univ* to study *or Br* to read history; **é. une matière en vue d'un examen** to read up on a subject for an examination

2 *(examiner → contrat, théorie)* to study, to examine; *(→ proposition)* to consider, to examine; *(→ liste, inventaire)* to go through, to check over; **nous étudierons votre suggestion** we'll consider your suggestion; **il faut é. toutes les éventualités** we have to look at *or* to examine all possible angles; **sa demande mérite d'être étudiée** his/her application merits examination; **é. le terrain** to survey the land

3 *(observer → passant, adversaire)* to watch, to observe; *(→ visage)* to study

4 *(concevoir → méthode)* to devise; *(→ modèle, maquette)* to design; **être très étudié** to be specially designed; *Fam* **c'est étudié pour** that's what it's for

5 *Péj (son apparence etc)* to study; **elle étudie ses poses** she strikes poses

VI 1 *(faire ses études)* to study, to be a student

2 *(travailler)* to study

▶**s'étudier VPR 1** *(se regarder soi-même)* to gaze at *or* to study oneself

2 *Péj (s'observer avec complaisance)* to admire oneself

3 *(se regarder l'un l'autre)* to observe each other; **ils se sont longuement étudiés** they took careful stock of each other

4 *(se donner une attitude)* to behave affectedly

étui [etɥi] **NM 1** *(gén)* case; *(de parapluie)* cover; **é. de cassette** cassette case; **é. à cigarettes** cigarette case; **é. à jumelles** binoculars case; **é. à lunettes** glasses case; **é. de revolver** holster; **é. à violon** violin case **2** *Mil* **é. de cartouche** cartridge case **3** *Naut* **é. de voile** sail cover

étuvage [etyvaʒ] **NM 1** *Culin* steaming **2** *(séchage)* drying, heating **3** *Tech* baking, stoving; *(stérilisation)* sterilization

étuve [etyv] **NF 1** *(sauna)* steam room; **é. humide** steam *or* vapour bath; **é. sèche** dry heat bath **2** *Tech (pour stériliser)* sterilizer, autoclave; *(pour sécher)* drier; **é. à incubation** *ou* **à cultures** incubator **3** *Fam (lieu où il fait trop chaud)* oven; **quelle é.** *ou* **c'est une vraie é. ici!** it's like an oven in here!

étuvée [etyve] **à l'étuvée ADJ** steamed *(in a tightly shut saucepan)*

ADV cuire à l'é. to steam *(in a tightly shut saucepan)*

étuvement [etyvmɑ̃] **NM 1** *Culin* steaming **2** *(séchage)* drying, heating **3** *Tech* baking, stoving; *(stérilisation)* sterilization

étuver [3] [etyve] **VT 1** *Culin* to steam **2** *(sécher)* to dry, to heat **3** *Tech* to bake, to stove; *(stériliser)* to sterilize **4** *Méd* to foment

étuveur [etyvœr] **NM 1** *Culin* steamer **2** *(dans un sauna)* steam room attendant

étuveuse [etyvøz] **NF** *Culin* steamer

étymologie [etimɔlɔʒi] **NF 1** *(discipline)* etymology, etymological research **2** *(origine)* etymology, origin; **l'é. d'un terme** the etymology *or* origin of a term

étymologique [etimɔlɔʒik] **ADJ** *Ling* etymological

étymologiquement [etimɔlɔʒikmɑ̃] **ADV** *Ling* etymologically

étymologiste [etimɔlɔʒist] **NMF** *Ling* etymologist

étymon [etimɔ̃] **NM** *Ling* etymon

E-U *(abrév écrite* **États-Unis***)* US

eu, -e [y] **PP** *voir* **avoir²**

E-U A *(abrév écrite* **États-Unis d'Amérique***)* USA

eubactérie [øbakteri] **NF** *Biol* eubacterium

Eubage [øbaʒ] **NM** *Hist* Celtic priest

Eubée [øbe] **NF** *Antiq & Géog* **l'E.** Euboea

eucalyptol [økaliptɔl] **NM** *Chim* eucalyptol, eucalyptole, cineole

eucalyptus [økaliptys] **NM** *Bot* eucalyptus

eucaride [økarid] *Zool* **NM** eucarid

▫ **eucarides NMPL** Eucarida

eucaryote [økarjɔt] *Biol* **ADJ** eucaryotic, eukaryotic

NM eucaryote, eukaryote

Eucharistie [økaristi] **NF l'E.** the Eucharist, Holy Communion

eucharistique [økaristik] **ADJ** Eucharistic

Euclide [øklid] **NPR** Euclid

euclidien, -enne [øklidjɛ̃, -ɛn] **ADJ** *Math* Euclidean, Euclidian; **non e.** non-Euclidean

eucologe [økɔlɔʒ] **NM** *Rel* eucologe

eudémis [ødemis] **NM** *Entom* eudemis moth

eudémonisme [ødemonism] **NM** *Phil* eudemonism

eudiomètre [ødjɔmɛtr] **NM** *Phys* eudiometer

eudiométrie [ødjɔmetri] **NF** *Phys* eudiometry

eudiométrique [ødjɔmetrik] **ADJ** *Phys* eudiometric, eudiometrical

eudiste [ødist] **NM** *Rel* Eudist

eugénate [øʒenat] **NM** *Chim & Méd* eugenolate, eugenate

eugénique [øʒenik] *Biol* **ADJ** eugenic

NF eugenics *(singulier)*

eugénisme [øʒenism] **NM** *Biol* eugenics *(singulier)*

eugéniste [øʒenist] **NMF** *Biol* eugenicist, eugenist

eugénol [øʒenɔl] **NM** *Chim* eugenol

euglène [øglɛn] **NF** *Bot* euglena

euh [ø] **EXCLAM** er

eumène [ømɛn] **NM** *Entom* potter wasp, eumenid

Euménides [ømenid] **NFPL** *Myth* Eumenides

'Les Euménides' *Eschyle* 'The Eumenides'

eunecte [ønɛkt] **NM** *Zool* anaconda, eunectes

eunuque [ønyk] **NM** eunuch

eupatoire [øpatwar] **NF** *Bot* eupatorium

eupatride [øpatrid] **NMF** *Antiq* eupatrid

eupepsie [øpɛpsi] **NF** *Physiol & Méd* eupepsia

eupeptique [øpɛptik] **ADJ** *Physiol & Méd* eupeptic

euphausiacé [øfozjase] *Zool* **NM** euphausiacean

▫ **euphausiacés NMPL** Euphausiacea

euphémique [øfemik] **ADJ** euphemistic

euphémiquement [øfemikmɑ̃] **ADV** euphemistically

euphémisme [øfemism] **NM** euphemism; **je dis "mauvais" mais c'est un e.** I say "bad" but it's an understatement

▫ **par euphémisme ADV** euphemistically

euphonie [øfɔni] **NF** *Ling* euphony

euphonique [øfɔnik] **ADJ 1** *(harmonieux)* euphonic, euphonious, harmonious **2** *Gram* **un "t" e.** a euphonic "t"

euphoniquement [øfɔnikmɑ̃] **ADV** *Ling* euphonically, harmoniously

euphonium [øfɔnjɔm] **NM** *Mus* euphonium

euphorbe [øfɔrb] **NF** *Bot* spurge, *Spéc* euphorbia; **e. des bois** wood spurge

euphorbiacée [øfɔrbjase] *Bot* **NF** member of the Euphorbiaceae

▫ **euphorbiacées NFPL** Euphorbiaceae

euphorie [øfɔri] **NF** euphoria

euphorique [øfɔrik] **ADJ** euphoric; **rendre e.** to make euphoric

euphorisant, -e [øfɔrizɑ̃, -ɑ̃t] **ADJ 1** *(médicament, drogue)* euphoriant **2** *(atmosphère, succès)* heady

NM *(médicament)* anti-depressant; *(drogue)* euphoriant

euphoriser [3] [øfɔrize] **VT** to make euphoric

euphotique [øfɔtik] **ADJ** euphotic

euphraise [øfrɛz] **NF** *Bot* eyebright

Euphrate [øfrat] **NM** *Géog* **l'E.** the (River) Euphrates

euphuisme [øfɥizm] **NM** *Littérature* euphuism

euplecte [øplɛkt] **NM** *Orn* bishop bird

euplectelle [øplɛktɛl] **NF** *Zool* Venus's flower basket, euplectella

-EUR, -EUSE [œr, øz] **SUFF**

- This suffix appears in adjectives and nouns derived from a verb, and gives the idea of a person WHO PERFORMS THE ACTION described by the verb. It can often be translated by the English suffix *-er*. It mostly refers to occupations or social activities, as well as traits of character, eg:

  un danseur, une danseuse a dancer; **un professeur, une professeur(e)** a teacher; **un serveur, une serveuse** a waiter, a waitress; **il est râleur, c'est un râleur** he never stops moaning; **elle est très bagarreuse** she's always ready for a scrap

- Note that not all names of occupations ending in **-eur** in the masculine have a feminine ending in **-euse**. The official recommendation for feminization of those nouns is the following:

When there is a verb in direct semantic relation to the noun, the feminine is **-euse**:
chercheur, chercheuse (from *chercher*); **enquêteur, enquêteuse** (from *enquêter*); **programmeur, programmeuse** (from *programmer*)

● When there is no corresponding verb or when the verb doesn't have a direct semantic link with the noun, the noun can either stay the same in the feminine or take an ending in **-e**. In both cases, the feminine article is used:
une ingénieur(e), une professeur(e), une proviseur(e)
See also **-TEUR, -TRICE**

---

eurafricain, -e[ørafrikɛ̃, -ɛn] ADJAfro-European

eurasiatique[ørazjatik] ADJEurasian

Eurasie[ørazi] NFl'E. Eurasia

eurasien, -enne[ørazjɛ̃, -ɛn] ADJEurasian
□ **Eurasien, -enne** NM,FEurasian

Euratom[øratɔm] NM*UE (abrév **European Atomic Energy Commission**)* Euratom

Eure[œr] NF*Géog* l'E. Eure

Eure-et-Loire [œrɛlwar] NF *Géog* l'E. Eure-et-Loire

eurêka[øreka] EXCLAMeureka!

eurent*voir* **avoir**[2]

EURIBOR [øribɔr] NM *Bourse (abrév **Euro Interbank Offered Rate**)* EURIBOR

Euripide[øripid] NPREuripides

euristique[øristik] *Phil* ADJheuristic
NFheuristics *(singulier)*

EURL [øyɛrɛl] NF *Com (abrév **entreprise unipersonnelle à responsabilité limitée**)* trader with limited liability

euro[øro] NM*UE (monnaie)* euro

euro-[øro] PRÉFEuro-

eurobanque[ørobɑ̃k] NF*Banque & Fin* Eurobank

eurocarte[ørokart] NF*Banque* eurocard

eurocentrique[ørosɑ̃trik] ADJEurocentric

eurocentrisme [ørosɑ̃trism] NM *Pol* Eurocentrism

euro-certificat [ørosɛrtifika] *(pl **euro-certificats**)* NM*Bourse* euro-certificate

eurochèque [øroʃɛk] NM *Banque & Fin* Eurocheque

eurocommunisme[ørokɔmynism] NMEurocommunism

eurocommuniste [ørokɔmynist] ADJ Eurocommunist
NMFEurocommunist

Eurocorps[ørokɔr] NM*Mil* Eurocorps

eurocrate[ørokrat] NMFEurocrat

eurocratie[ørokrasi] NFEurocracy

eurocratique[ørokratik] ADJEurocratic

eurocrédit[ørokredi] NM**1** *Com* eurocredit **2** *Fin* Euroloan

eurodéputé, -e[ørodepyte] NMF*Pol* Euro MP

eurodevise[ørodəviz] NFeurocurrency

Eurodisney® [ørodisnɛ] NM Disneyland® Paris, Eurodisney

eurodollar[ørodɔlar] NMeurodollar

eurofighter[ørofajtœr] NM*Aviat* Eurofighter

eurofranc [ørofrɑ̃] NM *Anciennement Banque & Fin* Eurofranc

Euroland, Eurolande[ørolɑ̃d] NFEuroland

euromarché[øromarʃe] NMEuromarket

euromissile[øromisil] NMeuromissile

euromonnaie[øromɔnɛ] NF*Fin* eurocurrency

euro-obligation [øroɔbligasjɔ̃] *(pl **euro-obligations**)* NF*Fin* eurobond

Europe[1][ørɔp] NPR*Myth* Europa

Europe[2][ørɔp] NF**1** *Géog* l'E. Europe; **l'E. centrale** Central Europe; **l'E. continentale** mainland Europe; **l'E. de l'Est** East *or* Eastern Europe; **l'E. du Nord** Northern Europe; **l'E. du Sud** Southern Europe; **l'E. sociale** social Europe *(a united Europe committed to a progressive social and welfare policy)*; **l'E. verte** European (community) agriculture; **ils ont parlé de l'E. verte** they discussed agriculture in the EU; **l'E. des 25** the European Union *(comprising 25 member states)*; **la nouvelle E.** New Europe; **la vieille E.** Old Europe **2** *Rad* **E. 1** = radio station broadcasting popular entertainment and general interest programmes; **E. 2** = radio station broadcasting mainly music

européanisation [ørɔpeanizasjɔ̃] NF Europeanization, Europeanizing *(UNCOUNT)*

européaniser[3] [ørɔpeanize] VTto Europeanize, to make European
▸**s'européaniser** VPRto become Europeanized

européanisme[ørɔpeanism] NMEuropeanism

européaniste[ørɔpeanist] ADJEuropeanist
NMFEuropeanist

européen, -enne[ørɔpeɛ̃, -ɛn] ADJEuropean; **les (élections) européennes** the European elections
□ **Européen, -enne** NM,FEuropean

européisme[ørɔpeism] NMEuropeanism

européocentrisme [ørɔpeosɑ̃trism] NMEurocentrism

europhile[ørɔfil] NMFEurophile

europhobe[ørɔfɔb] NMFEurophobe

europium[ørɔpjɔm] NM*Chim & Métal* europium

Europol[ørɔpɔl] NMEuropol

europudding[øropudiŋ] NM*Cin* europudding

euroscepticisme [ørosɛptisism] NM Euroscepticism

eurosceptique[ørosɛptik] NMFEurosceptic

Eurostar® [ørostar] NMEurostar®

Eurostat[ørostat] NM*UE* Eurostat

eurosterling[ørostɛrliŋ] NM*Fin* Eurosterling

Euro Stoxx[ørostɔks] NM*Bourse* Euro Stoxx; **l'E. 50** the Euro Stoxx 50 index

eurostratégique [ørostrateʒik] ADJ*Mil* Eurostrategic

eurotourisme[øroturism] NMEurotourism

Eurotunnel®[ørotynɛl] NMEurotunnel®

Eurovision® [ørovizjɔ̃] NF Eurovision®; **le concours E. de la chanson** the Eurovision® Song Contest

euroyen[ørwajɛ̃] NM*Fin* euroyen

eurozone[ørozon] NFEuro zone

Eurydice[øridis] NPR*Myth* Eurydice

euryhalin, -e[ørialɛ̃, -in] ADJ*Écol* euryhaline

euryhalinité[ørialinite] NF*Écol* euryhaline habits *or* conditions *or* state

eurytherme[øritɛrm] ADJ*Écol* eurythermal, eurythermic, eurythermous

eurythermie[øritɛrmi] NF*Écol* eurythermy

eurythmie[øritmi] NF **1** *(harmonie)* eurhythmy, eurythmy **2** *Méd* eurhythmia

eurythmique[øritmik] ADJeurhythmic, eurhythmical

-euse 1 *voir* **-eur, -euse 2** *voir* **-eux, -euse**

euskadi [œskadi] NM *(en basque)* the Basque Country

euskara [œskara], **euskera** [œskɛra] NMBasque, Euskara

euskarien, -enne [øskarjɛ̃, -ɛn] ADJ Euskarian, Basque
NM*(langue)* Euskara, Basque

eusse*etc voir* **avoir**[2]

eustache[østaʃ] NM*Fam Vieilli* clasp-knife

eustasie[østazi] NF*Géol* eustasy

eustatique[østatik] ADJ*Géol* eustatic

eustatisme[østatism] NM*Géol* eustasy

eusthenopteron [østɛnɔptərɔ̃] NM *Ich* Eusthenopteron

eut*etc voir* **avoir**[2]

eutectique[øtɛktik] ADJ*Phys* eutectic

eutexie[øtɛksi] NF*Phys* eutexia

euthanasie [øtanazi] NF euthanasia; **e. active/ passive** voluntary/passive euthanasia

euthanasier[9] [øtanazje] VTto euthanize, to put to sleep

euthanasique [øtanazik] ADJeuthanasic, euthanasia *(avant n)*

euthérien[øterjɛ̃] *Zool* NMeutherian
□ **euthériens** NMPLEutheria, Monodelphia, Placentalia

eutocie[øtɔsi] NF*Obst* eutocia

eutocique[øtɔsik] ADJ*Obst* eutocic

eutrophisation [øtrɔfizasjɔ̃] NF *Écol* eutrophication

eux [ø] PRON **1** *(sujet)* they; **e. l'ignorent encore** they still don't know about it; **si e. refusent, nous n'y pouvons rien** if they refuse, there's nothing we can do; **ils le savent bien, e.** they know it all right; **nous sommes invités, e. pas** *ou* **non** we are invited but they aren't *or* but not them; **ce sont e. les responsables** they are the ones *or* it is they who are responsible; **e. seuls connaissent la réponse** they alone *or* only they know the answer; **e., voter? cela m'étonnerait!** them? vote? I doubt it very much!; **e., plus**

craintifs, sont partis aussitôt they, being more afraid, left immediately; **nous sommes plus satisfaits qu'e.** we're happier than they are
2 *(après une préposition)* them; **nous irons sans e.** we'll go without them; **ne t'occupe pas d'e.** don't pay any attention to them; **avec e., on ne sait jamais** you never know with them; **comment me débarrasser d'e.?** how can I get rid of them?; **c'est à e.** it's theirs; **à e. seuls, ils n'y arriveront pas** they'll never manage on their own
3 *(en fonction de pronom réfléchi)* themselves; **ils ne pensent qu'à e.** they only think of themselves
4 *(suivi d'un nombre)* **e. deux** both *or* the two of them; **e. quatre/cinq** the four/five of them

---

-EUX, -EUSE[ø, øz] SUFF

● Adjectives and nouns ending in **-eux** or **-euse** refer to a QUALITY or PROPERTY. They are mostly derived from a noun, but also, rarely, from a verb. Possible variants are **-ieux, -ieuse** and **-ueux, -ueuse**, eg:
paresseux(euse) lazy/lazy person; **frileux(euse)** who feels the cold; **joyeux(euse)** joyful, merry; **boiteux(euse)** lame, who has a limp; **glamoureux(euse)** glamorous; **pâteux(euse)** doughy; **graisseux(euse)** greasy, fatty; **boueux(euse)** muddy; **capricieux(euse)** temperamental/fickle; **classieux(euse)** classy; **luxueux(euse)** luxurious
Note the use of the suffix -*y* in English to translate the French suffix when it refers to a natural property or texture.

● Medical vocabulary in particular contains numerous examples of words ending in **-eux** and **-euse**. Adjectives can often be translated by an English equivalent ending in -*ous*, eg:
cancéreux(euse) cancerous; **les cancéreux** cancer sufferers; **un lépreux** a leper; **nerveux(euse)** nervous; **veineux(euse)** venous
● There is a recent use of **-eux** and **-euse** in the creation of nouns applied to people who have as an OCCUPATION the thing described by the noun base. Those nouns are, as a rule, informal in register. They are usually found in the plural, as a generic and derogatory way of referring to a whole group of people, eg:
les modeux fashionistas; **les journaleux** hacks; **les théâtreux** luvvies, thespians; **les footeux** footballers

---

eux-mêmes[ømɛm] PRONthemselves

EV*(abrév écrite* **en ville***)* by hand

eV*(abrév écrite* **électron-volt***)* eV

évacuant, -e[evakɥɑ̃, -ɑ̃t] *Méd* ADJevacuant
NMevacuant

évacuateur, -trice[evakɥatœr, -tris] ADJevacuative, evacuation *(avant n)*; *(tuyau)* drainage
NM**é. (des eaux)** sluice

évacuatif, -ive[evakɥatif, -iv] *Méd* ADJlaxative, evacuant
NMlaxative, evacuant

évacuation[evakɥasjɔ̃] NF**1** *Physiol (de toxines)* elimination, eliminating *(UNCOUNT)*; *(du pus)* draining off
2 *(écoulement)* draining; **depuis les gelées, l'é. de l'eau ne se fait plus** since the frost came, the water no longer drains away; **une conduite assure l'é. des eaux usées** the waste water drains out through a pipe; **course d'é.** *(d'un moteur)* exhaust stroke
3 *(d'une ville, d'un lieu)* evacuation; *(d'une salle)* evacuation, clearing; *(d'un bateau)* abandoning; *Mil* **hôpital d'é.** clearing hospital
4 *(sauvetage)* evacuation, evacuating; **organiser/procéder à l'é. des habitants** to evacuate the local people; **é. de troupes par voie aérienne** airlifting of troops

évacuatrice[evakɥtris] *voir* **évacuateur**

évacué, -e[evakɥe] ADJ**personne évacuée** evacuee
NM,Fevacuee

évacuer[7] [evakɥe] VT**1** *Physiol (toxine)* to eliminate; *(excrément)* to evacuate; *(pus)* to drain off
2 *(faire s'écouler)* to drain; **les eaux usées sont évacuées par cette canalisation** the waste water drains out through this channel
3 *Mil (terrain)* to move off; *(position)* to retreat

eur-eva

from; *(place forte)* to leave; *(forteresse, ville)* to evacuate, to vacate

4 *(navire, hôpital)* to evacuate; **évacuez la salle!** please leave the room!; **craignant une explosion, ils ont fait é. la salle d'urgence** fearing an explosion, they had the room evacuated immediately; **faire é. un bâtiment** to evacuate *or* to clear a building; *Naut* **é. le bâtiment** to abandon ship

5 *(personne, population)* **é. qn de** to evacuate sb from; **il faut é. les enfants du premier étage** the children must be evacuated from the first floor; **faire é. tous les habitants** to evacuate all the inhabitants

6 *Fig (problème)* to get rid of, to solve; **c'est une question que je préférerais é. le plus vite possible** it's a matter I'd like to dispose of as soon as possible

évadé, -e [evade] ADJ escaped

NM,F escaped prisoner, escapee; **un é. de l'asile/de Fresnes** an escapee from the mental hospital/from Fresnes prison

évader [3] [evade] **s'évader** VPR **1** *(s'enfuir)* **s'é. de** to escape from, to break out of; **il les a fait s'é. contre de l'argent** he helped them to escape in exchange for money **2** *(pour oublier ses soucis)* to escape, to get away from it all; **aller s'é. à la campagne** to get out of town for a break; **j'ai besoin de m'é.** I need to get away from it all

évagination [evaʒinasjɔ̃] NF *Méd* evagination

évaginer [3] [evaʒine] VT *Méd* to evaginate

évaluable [evalɥabl] ADJ appraisable, assessable; **difficilement é.** *(dégâts, montant)* hard to appraise *or* to evaluate

évaluateur, -trice [evalɥatœr, -tris] NM,F *Can* valuer, assessor

évaluatif, -ive [evalɥatif, -iv] ADJ evaluative; **devis é.** quotation, cost estimate

évaluation [evalɥasjɔ̃] NF **1** *(estimation)* evaluation, assessment; *(d'une propriété, d'un bien)* valuation, appraisal; *(des dommages)* assessment; *(d'un poids, d'un nombre, des risques)* estimation; **faire l'é. d'un tableau** to estimate the value of *or* to value a painting; *Com* **é. du coût** cost assessment; *Com* **é. des coûts** cost analysis; *Com* **é. de la demande** demand assessment; *Com* **é. économique** economic appraisal; **é. financière** financial appraisal; *Com* **é. du marché** market appraisal; *Fin* **é. d'office** default assessment *(issued when taxpayers fail to supply the required tax return information on time)*; **é. des performances** *(d'un employé)* performance appraisal; *Com* **é. post-achat** post-purchase evaluation; **é. des risques** risk assessment; *Com* **é. des stocks** stock control

2 *(quantité évaluée)* estimation; *(d'une propriété, d'un bien)* valuation; *(des dommages)* assessment; *(d'un poids, d'un nombre, des risques)* estimate

évaluative [evalɥativ] *voir* **évaluatif**

évaluatrice [evalɥatris] *voir* **évaluateur**

évaluer [7] [evalɥe] VT **1** *(estimer → bijou, tableau)* to appraise, to assess; **faire é. qch** to have sth valued; **la propriété a été évaluée à trois millions** the estate has been valued at *or* the value of the estate has been put at three million

2 *(mesurer → volume, débit)* to estimate; *(→ dégâts, coût, besoin)* to assess, to estimate; **é. qch à** to estimate *or* to evaluate sth at; **à combien évalue-t-on le nombre des victimes?** what is the estimated number of victims?; **on évalue à 12 000 le nombre des victimes** the number of victims is estimated at 12,000; **on évalue les dégâts à 10 000 euros** the damage has been estimated at 10,000 euros; *Fin* **é. le coût** *ou* **les coûts de qch** to cost sth

3 *(estimer approximativement → distance)* to gauge; *(poids, nombre)* to estimate; **on évalue sa fortune à trois millions de dollars** his/her fortune is estimated at three million dollars

4 *(juger → qualité)* to evaluate, to gauge, to assess; **bien é. la difficulté d'un projet** to make a realistic assessment of the difficulty of a project; **mal é. les risques** to miscalculate the risks; **as-tu évalué les risques?** have you weighed up the risks?

évanescence [evanesɑ̃s] NF *Littéraire* evanescence

évanescent, -e [evanesɑ̃, -ɑ̃t] ADJ *Littéraire* evanescent

évangéliaire [evɑ̃ʒeljɛr] NM evangelistary, gospel-book

évangélique [evɑ̃ʒelik] ADJ **1** *(de l'Évangile)* evangelic, evangelical **2** *(protestant)* evangelical; **les chrétiens évangéliques** evangelical Christians

évangéliquement [evɑ̃ʒelikmɑ̃] ADV evangelically

évangélisateur, -trice [evɑ̃ʒelizatœr, -tris] ADJ evangelistic

NM,F evangelist

évangélisation [evɑ̃ʒelizasjɔ̃] NF evangelization, evangelizing

évangélisatrice [evɑ̃ʒelizatris] *voir* **évangélisateur**

évangéliser [3] [evɑ̃ʒelize] VT to evangelize

évangélisme [evɑ̃ʒelism] NM evangelism

évangéliste [evɑ̃ʒelist] NM *(prédicateur)* evangelist; *(auteur de l'un des Évangiles)* Evangelist

évangile [evɑ̃ʒil] NM **1** *Rel* **l'É.** the Gospel; **les Évangiles** the Gospels; **l'É. selon saint...** the Gospel according to Saint...; **l'é. du jour** the gospel for the day **2** *(credo)* gospel

évanoui, -e [evanwi] ADJ unconscious; **tomber é.** to fall down in a faint; **on l'a trouvé é.** he was found unconscious *or* in a (dead) faint

évanouir [32] [evanwir] **s'évanouir** VPR **1** *Méd* to faint, to pass out; **la chaleur l'a fait s'é.** he/she fainted in the heat **2** *(disparaître → personne, apparition, ombre)* to vanish (into thin air); *(→ craintes, illusions, doutes)* to vanish, to disappear; *(→ souvenir, rêve)* to fade (away); *(→ son)* to die away, to fade away; **s'é. dans la nature** to fade into the background

évanouissement [evanwismɑ̃] NM **1** *Méd (syncope)* fainting *(UNCOUNT)*, blackout; **avoir un é.** to (go into a) faint **2** *(disparition)* disappearance, disappearing, vanishing; *(d'un souvenir, d'un rêve)* fading **3** *Tél* fading **4** *Aut (de freins)* fade

évaporable [evapɔrabl] ADJ evaporable

évaporateur [evapɔratœr] NM *Tech* evaporator

évaporation [evapɔrasjɔ̃] NF evaporation

évaporatoire [evapɔratwar] ADJ evaporating

évaporé, -e [evapɔre] ADJ *(écervelé)* scatterbrained, birdbrained; **une blonde évaporée** a dumb blonde; **elle prend toujours des airs évaporés** she always acts like an airhead

NM,F dimwit

évaporer [3] [evapɔre] VT to evaporate

VI **faire é. un liquide** to evaporate a liquid

▸**s'évaporer** VPR **1** *(liquide)* to evaporate **2** *(colère, crainte)* to vanish, to disappear, *Littéraire* to evaporate **3** *Fam (disparaître)* to vanish (into thin air); **ces lunettes n'ont pas pu s'é.!** these glasses can't just have vanished (into thin air)!; **je me suis retourné et hop, il s'était évaporé!** I turned round and he'd gone *or* vanished, just like that!

évaporite [evapɔrit] NF *Géol* evaporite

évapotranspiration [evapɔtrɑ̃spirasjɔ̃] NF *Bot* evapotranspiration

évasé, -e [evaze] ADJ *(vêtement, manche)* flared; *(ouverture, tuyau)* funnel-shaped, splayed; *(récipient)* tapered; **le verre a une jolie forme évasée** the glass has a nice curved shape; **la jupe a une jolie forme évasée** the skirt flares out nicely

évasement [evazmɑ̃] NM *(d'une ouverture, d'un tuyau)* splay; *(d'un entonnoir)* widening-out; *(d'un vêtement, d'une manche)* flare

évaser [3] [evaze] VT *(vêtement, manche)* to flare; *(ouverture, tuyau)* to splay (out)

▸**s'évaser** VPR to widen, to open out; *(chenal)* to open out, to broaden; *(forme, vêtement)* to flare; *(tuyau)* to splay (out)

évasif, -ive [evazif, -iv] ADJ evasive, non-committal; **il s'est montré très é.** he was very evasive *or* non-committal; **je n'ai eu qu'une réponse évasive** all I got was a non-committal anwer; **d'un air é.** evasively

évasion [evazjɔ̃] NF **1** *(d'un prisonnier)* escape (**de** from); **tenter une é.** to try to escape; **réussir son é.** to succeed in escaping; **le roi de l'é.** the master escaper **2** *(distraction)* **l'é.** getting away from it all; **l'Égypte, l'é. totale garantie!** get away from it all in Egypt!, escape to exotic new surroundings in Egypt!; **j'ai besoin d'é.** I need to get away from it all **3** *Fin & Jur* **é. fiscale** tax avoidance **4** *Écon* **é. de capitaux** flight of capital

▫ **d'évasion** ADJ escapist; **cinéma d'é.** escapist films

évasive [evaziv] *voir* **évasif**

évasivement [evazivmɑ̃] ADV evasively; **"qui sait", répondit-il é.** "who knows," was his vague reply *or* he replied evasively

évasure [evazyr] NF funnel-shaped *or* splayed opening

Ève [ɛv] NPR *Bible* Eve; **je ne le connais ni d'È. ni d'Adam** I don't know him from Adam; **en costume** *ou* **en tenue d'È.** naked, in the altogether, in her birthday suit

évêché [eveʃe] NM *Rel* **1** *(territoire)* bishopric, diocese **2** *(demeure)* bishop's palace *or* house **3** *(ville)* cathedral town

évection [evɛksjɔ̃] NF *Astron* evection

éveil [evɛj] NM **1** *(fin du repos)* awakening

2 *(déclenchement)* **l'é. de** the awakening *or* early development *or* first stirrings of; **l'é. des sens/de la sexualité** the awakening of the senses/of sexuality; **l'é. du sentiment artistique** the first stirrings *or* glimmerings of a sense of aesthetics; **l'é. du sentiment national** the awakening *or* dawning *or* first stirrings of national feeling; **l'é. de la sensibilité motrice chez le nourrisson** the onset *or* early development of motor sensitivity in infants; **l'é. de qn à qch** sb's awakening to sth; **l'auteur raconte l'é. à l'amour d'une toute jeune fille** the author recounts the dawning of love in a young girl's heart

3 *Scol* **activité** *ou* **matière d'é.** = non-core subject covering topics such as arts, history, geography and biology

4 *(alerte)* **donner l'é.** to raise the alarm; **donner l'é. à qn** to arouse sb's suspicions, to put sb on their guard; **il s'est introduit dans la salle des coffres sans donner l'é.** he entered the strongroom without arousing anybody's suspicions

▫ **en éveil** ADV **1** *(sur ses gardes)* **être en é.** *(personne)* to be on the alert; *(esprit)* to be alert

2 *(actif)* **maintenant que ses soupçons sont en é.** now that his/her suspicions have been aroused; **à quatre ans, leur curiosité est en é.** by the time they're four, their curiosity is fully roused

éveillé, -e [eveje] ADJ **1** *(vif → enfant, esprit)* alert, bright, sharp; *(→ intelligence)* sharp; **garçon (à l'esprit) é.** bright boy **2** *(en état de veille)* awake; **tout é.** wide awake; **tenir qn é.** to keep sb awake; **se tenir é.** to stay awake

éveiller [4] [eveje] VT **1** *Littéraire (tirer du sommeil)* to awaken, to waken, to arouse

2 *(susciter → désir, jalousie, passion)* to kindle, to arouse; *(→ amour, méfiance)* to arouse; *(→ curiosité, soupçons)* to arouse, to awaken; *(→ espoir)* to awaken; *(→ attention, intérêt)* to attract

3 *(stimuler → intelligence)* to stimulate, to awaken

▸**s'éveiller** VPR **1** *(animal, personne)* to awaken, to wake up, to waken

2 *Littéraire (s'animer → campagne, village)* to come to life, to wake up

3 *(se révéler → intelligence, talent)* to reveal itself, to come to light

4 *(naître → curiosité, jalousie, méfiance)* to be aroused; *(→ amour)* to dawn, to stir

5 s'é. à un sentiment *(le ressentir)* to wake up to *or* to discover a feeling; **s'é. à l'amour** to discover love

éveilleur, -euse [evɛjœr, -øz] NM,F *Littéraire* = person who arouses a feeling or intellectual faculty

éveinage [evenaʒ] NM *Méd* stripping *(UNCOUNT)*; **se faire faire un é.** to have one's veins stripped

événement, évènement [evɛnmɑ̃] NM **1** *(fait)* event, occurrence, happening; **plus tard, les événements lui ont donné raison** what happened later *or* the later events proved him/her right; **vacances riches en événements** *Br* eventful holidays, *Am* an eventful vacation; **nous sommes débordés** *ou* **dépassés par les événements** we have been overtaken by events; **je suis complètement dépassé par les événements** this is all *or* all this is too much for

me; **attendre la suite des événements** to await the course of events

2 *Pol* **les événements d'Algérie** the Algerian War of Independence; **les événements de mai 68** the events of May 68

3 *(fait important)* event; **quand le cirque venait au village, c'était un (grand) é.** when the circus came to our village, it was quite an event *or* a big occasion; *Hum* **quand il fait la vaisselle, c'est (tout) un é.** when he does the dishes it's a cause for celebration *or* it's quite an event; **leur rencontre est un é. historique** their meeting is a historic event; **l'é. cinématographique/littéraire de cette année** the screen/literary event of this year; **é. médiatique** media event; **é. sportif** sporting event; **faire** *ou* **créer l'é.** to be news *or* a major event; **sa nomination a créé l'é.** his/her nomination was a major event; **sa démission fait l'é. dans tous les quotidiens** his/her resignation is making headlines in all the daily newspapers; **nous vous rappelons l'é. de la journée** here's the main news of the day again

4 *Presse* **l'É. du jeudi** = French weekly news magazine

événementiel, -elle, évènementiel, -elle [evɛnmɑ̃sjɛl] **ADJ** purely descriptive; *(histoire, programme télévisé)* factual

évent[1] [evɑ̃] **NM** **1** *Zool* blowhole, *Spéc* spiracle **2** *Tech* vent hole

évent[2] [evɑ̃] **NM** *(de nourriture, de vin, de parfum)* mustiness; *(de bière, de limonade)* flatness, staleness

éventail [evɑ̃taj] **NM** **1** *(accessoire)* fan **2** *(gamme)* range; **l'é. de son répertoire** the range *or* scope of his/her repertoire; **é. des prix** price range; **é. des salaires** salary range *or* spread; **l'é. politique** the political spectrum **3** *Com (de produits)* range

❑ **en éventail** **ADJ** fan-shaped; *(queue)* spread-out; **voûte en é.** fan vaulting; *Fam Fig* **elle est restée les doigts de pied en é. toute la matinée** she lazed around all morning

éventaire [evɑ̃tɛr] **NM** **1** *(étalage)* stall **2** *(plateau)* (street vendor's) tray

éventé, -e [evɑ̃te] **ADJ** **1** *(altéré → bière, limonade)* flat, stale; *(→ nourriture, vin, parfum)* musty, stale **2** *(connu → complot)* discovered; *(→ secret)* well-known

éventer [3] [evɑ̃te] **VT** **1** *(avec un éventail, un magazine)* to fan

2 *(aérer → vêtements)* to air; *(grain)* to aerate, to expose to the air; *(mine)* to ventilate

3 *(révéler → secret)* to disclose, to give away; **le secret est éventé** the secret is out

4 *Chasse* to scent, to get the scent of

▸**s'éventer** **VPR** **1** *(pour se rafraîchir)* to fan oneself; **s'é. avec un magazine** to fan oneself with a magazine

2 *(être divulgué → plan d'attaque, secret)* to get out, to become public knowledge

3 *(s'altérer → nourriture, vin, parfum)* to go musty *or* stale; *(→ bière, limonade)* to go flat *or* stale

éventration [evɑ̃trasjɔ̃] **NF** ventral rupture

éventrer [3] [evɑ̃tre] **VT** **1** *(personne → avec un couteau)* to disembowel, to eviscerate; **il a été éventré par le taureau** he was gored by the bull; **se faire é.** to be gored **2** *(canapé, outre, oreiller, sac)* to rip (open); *(boîte en carton)* to tear open; *(coffret)* to break open **3** *(champ)* to rip open, to rip holes in; *(immeuble)* to rip apart

▸**s'éventrer** **VPR** **1** to disembowel oneself **2** *(se fendre → oreiller, sac)* to burst open; **la barque s'est éventrée sur un récif** the boat hit a reef, ripping a hole in its hull

éventreur [evɑ̃trœr] **NM** ripper; **Jack l'É.** Jack the Ripper

éventualité [evɑ̃tɥalite] **NF** **1** *(possibilité)* possibility, contingency; **cette é. ne m'avait pas effleuré** this possibility hadn't occurred to me

2 *(circonstance)* eventuality, possibility, contingency; **pour parer** *ou* **être prêt à toute é.** to be ready for anything that might crop up; **il faut envisager toutes les éventualités** we must consider all the possibilities; **on pourrait donc me renvoyer – c'est une é.** so I could be fired – that's possible *or* that may happen; **dans cette é.** in such an *or* in this event, if this should happen

❑ **dans l'éventualité de** **PRÉP** in the event of; **dans l'é. d'une guerre** should a war break out, in the event of a war

éventuel, -elle [evɑ̃tɥɛl] **ADJ** possible; *(client)* potential, prospective; *(bénéfice)* possible, potential; **à titre é.** as a possibility

éventuellement [evɑ̃tɥɛlmɑ̃] **ADV** *(peut-être)* possibly; **tu me le prêterais? – é.** would you lend it to me? – maybe *or* possibly; **les entreprises qui pourraient é. nous racheter** the companies which might *or* could buy us out; **nous resterons le samedi et é. le dimanche** we'll stay Saturday and maybe Sunday; **il viendra avec sa cousine et é. avec sa tante** he'll come with his cousin and possibly with his aunt; **faites cet exercice en vous servant é. d'un dictionnaire** do this exercise using a dictionary if necessary; **j'aurais é. besoin de votre concours** I may need your help (later)

évêque [evɛk] **NM** *Rel* bishop; **é. suffragant** suffragan (bishop); **é. métropolitain** archbishop

Everest [evrɛst] **NM** *Géog* **l'E., le mont E.** Mount Everest

Everglades [evœrglad] **NMPL** *Géog* **les E.** the Everglades

éversion [evɛrsjɔ̃] **NF** *Méd* eversion

évertuer [7] [evɛrtɥe] **s'évertuer** **VPR** **s'é. sur qch** to struggle with sth; **s'é. à faire qch** to strive *or* to make every effort to do sth, to do one's utmost to do sth; **je m'évertue à lui répéter que c'est impossible** I'm tired of telling him/her that it's impossible; **je ne m'évertuerai pas à te convaincre** I won't waste energy trying to convince you

évhémérisme [evemerism] **NM** *Phil* euhemerism

Évian [evjɑ̃] **NF** *Géog* Evian

éviction [eviksjɔ̃] **NF** **1** *Jur (d'un locataire)* eviction; **procéder à l'é. d'un locataire** to evict a tenant; **é. illicite** ouster **2** *(expulsion → d'un rival, d'un leader)* ousting; **depuis son é. du parti** since his/her ousting *or* since being ousted from the party; **é. d'un poste** removal from a position; **é. scolaire** exclusion, expulsion **3** *Écon* **é. financière** crowding-out

évidage [evidaʒ] **NM** hollowing out

évidement [evidmɑ̃] **NM** **1** *(d'un fruit, d'un bloc de pierre, d'un tronc)* hollowing *or* scooping out *(UNCOUNT)* **2** *Méd* scraping out

évidemment [evidamɑ̃] **ADV** **1** *(bien entendu)* of course; *(manifestement)* obviously; **bien é.!** of course!; **tu me crois? – é.!** do you believe me? – of course (I do)! **2** *(avec colère, irritation)* needless to say, predictably enough; **é., elle n'a rien préparé!** needless to say she hasn't prepared a thing!; **j'ai oublié mes clés – é.!** *(ton irrité)* I've forgotten my keys – you would!

évidence [evidɑ̃s] **NF** **1** *(caractère certain)* obviousness; **l'é. d'un axiome** the obviousness of an axiom **2** *(fait manifeste)* obvious fact; **c'est une é., c'est l'é. même** it's obvious; **il n'a dit que des évidences** he just stated the obvious **3** *(ce qui est indubitable)* **l'é.** the obvious; **accepter** *ou* **se rendre à l'é.** to face facts; **c'est l'é. même!** it's quite obvious *or* evident!; **refuser** *ou* **nier l'é.** to deny the facts *or* the obvious

❑ **à l'évidence, de toute évidence** **ADV** evidently, obviously

❑ **en évidence** **ADV** *(chose, personne)* **ses décorations bien en é. sur le buffet** his/her medals lying conspicuously *or* there for all to see on the sideboard; **j'ai laissé le message bien en é. sur la table** I left the message on the table in a place where it couldn't be missed; **être en é.** *(objet)* to be in a prominent position, to be conspicuous; **mettre en é.** *(exposer)* to display (prominently); *(détail, talent)* to highlight, to bring out; *(idée)* to give prominence to, to underline; **les chercheurs ont mis en é. l'existence du virus** the researchers revealed the existence of the virus; **se mettre en é.** *(se faire remarquer)* to make oneself conspicuous

évident, -e [evidɑ̃, -ɑ̃t] **ADJ** **1** *(manifeste)* obvious, evident, self-evident; **son mépris n'est que trop é.** his/her contempt is only too obvious; **il était d'une mauvaise foi évidente** he was obviously *or* clearly insincere; **la réponse/solution me paraît évidente** the answer/solution seems obvious to me

2 *(certain)* obvious, certain; **il viendra? – pas é.!** will he come? – I wouldn't bet on it!; **l'issue du match semblait évidente** it seemed fairly certain what the result of the match would be; **c'est é.!** of course!, obviously!, that's obvious!; *Fam* **il a au moins 40 ans – c'est pas é., tu sais** he's at least 40 – don't be so sure; **il est é. que...** it's obvious *or* evident that...

3 *Fam (facile)* easy▪, simple▪; **ce n'est pas é.** *(difficile)* it's not that easy; *(problématique)* it's a bit of a problem; **ce n'est pas une décision évidente à prendre** it's not such an easy decision to make

évider [3] [evide] **VT** *(fruit, bloc de pierre, tronc)* to hollow *or* to scoop out

évidoir [evidwar] **NM** scooper, gouge

évidure [evidyr] **NF** hollow, cavity

évier [evje] **NM** (kitchen) sink; **é. à un bac** sink; **é. à deux bacs** double sink

évincé, -e [evɛ̃se] **ADJ** evicted

NM,F evictee

évincement [evɛ̃smɑ̃] **NM** **1** *(d'un concurrent, d'un rival)* ousting; **elle a obtenu leur é. du comité** she managed to have them ousted from *or* thrown off the committee **2** *Jur (d'un locataire)* eviction

évincer [16] [evɛ̃se] **VT** **1** *(concurrent, rival)* to oust, to supplant (**de** from); **é. qn d'un emploi** to oust sb from a job; **être évincé d'un comité** to be thrown off a committee; **se faire é.** to be ousted **2** *Jur (locataire)* to evict

éviscération [eviserasjɔ̃] **NF** *Méd* evisceration, eviscerating *(UNCOUNT)*

éviscérer [18] [evisere] **VT** *Méd* to eviscerate

évitable [evitabl] **ADJ** *(obstacle)* avoidable; *(accident)* preventable

évitage [evitaʒ] **NM** *Naut* **1** *(mouvement → d'un bateau)* swinging; **bassin d'é.** turning basin **2** *(espace)* room to swing, sea room

évitement [evitmɑ̃] **NM** **1** *(action d'éviter)* avoidance; **faire une manœuvre d'é.** to take evasive action; *Biol* **réaction d'é.** avoiding reaction **2** *Rail* shunting **3** *Belg Transp* diversion

❑ **d'évitement** **ADJ** **1** *Rail* **voie** *ou* **gare d'é.** siding; **ligne d'é.** loop line **2** *Psy (réaction)* avoidance *(avant n)*

éviter [3] [evite] **VT** **1** *(ne pas subir → coup)* to avoid, to dodge; *(→ danger)* to avoid, to steer clear of; *(→ corvée)* to avoid, to shun; **on ne pourra é. la guerre** war cannot be avoided; **la catastrophe a été évitée de justesse** a catastrophe was averted by a hair's breadth; **pour é. que la mayonnaise (ne) tourne** to prevent the mayonnaise from *or* to stop the mayonnaise curdling; **pour é. que le vent n'entre dans la maison** to prevent the wind getting into the house, to keep the wind out of the house; **évite que ça se sache** don't let it get out, prevent it getting out

2 *(ne pas heurter → ballon)* to avoid, to dodge, to stay out of the way of; *(→ obstacle)* to avoid; **je n'ai pas pu vous é.** I couldn't avoid you; **en essayant d'é. le chien** trying to avoid *or* to miss the dog

3 *(regard, personne)* to avoid, to shun; **é. le regard de qn** to avoid sb's eyes; **depuis notre querelle, il m'évite** since we quarrelled he's been avoiding me

4 *(lieu, situation)* to avoid; **en passant par là, on évite le carrefour** that way, you miss *or* avoid the junction; **j'évite les restaurants, ils sont trop enfumés** I avoid going into restaurants, they're too smoky; **elle évite la foule** she shies away from crowds

5 *(maladresse, impair)* to avoid; **j'évite les coups de téléphone après minuit** I avoid phoning after midnight; **évitez le franglais** try not to use franglais; **é. de faire qch** to avoid doing sth, to try not to do sth; **évite de laisser tes compacts par terre** try not to leave your CDs on the floor; **j'évite de me baisser** I avoid bending *or* I try not to bend down; **évite de recommencer!** don't start again!

6 *(aliment)* to avoid; **é. l'alcool/le sucre** to avoid *or* keep off alcohol/sugar; **maintenant j'évite les œufs** I try and avoid eating eggs now

7 *(épargner)* **é. qch à qn** to spare sb sth; **é. des ennuis à qn** to save *or* spare sb trouble; **évitons-lui tout souci** let's keep him/her from worrying (about anything) *or* spare him/her any worries;

je ne peux pas lui é. les déceptions I can't prevent him/her from experiencing disappointment; **cela lui évitera d'avoir à sortir** that'll save him/her having to go out

VI *Naut* **é. sur l'ancre** to swing at anchor; **évité au vent** riding the wind

▸**s'éviter** VPR **1** *(mutuellement)* to avoid each other *or* one another, to stay out of each other's way

2 s'é. qch to save *or* to spare oneself sth; **nous nous éviterons le détour en téléphonant d'abord** we'll save ourselves the detour by phoning first; **s'é. des tracas** to spare *or* to save oneself trouble

évocable [evɔkabl] ADJ *Jur* **cause é.** case that may be transferred to a superior court

évocateur, -trice [evɔkatœr, -tris] ADJ evocative, suggestive (**de** of)

évocation [evɔkasjɔ̃] NF **1** *(rappel → du passé, d'une personne, d'un paysage etc)* evocation, recalling; **la simple é. de cette scène la faisait pleurer** just recalling this scene made her weep; **je commencerai par une brève é. du passé de notre collège** I shall start with a brief recapitulation of the history of our college; **à l'é. de son premier amour** when he/she recalled his/her first love; *(mentionné par un tiers)* when reference was made to his/her first love; **le pouvoir d'é. d'un lieu/mot** the evocative power of a place/word

2 *(par la magie → d'un esprit)* evocation, calling forth, conjuring up

3 *Jur* evocation *(right of a higher court to give a ruling on a case transferred to it from a lower court)*, ≃ certiorari; **droit d'é.** right of evocation

évocatoire [evɔkatwar] ADJ *Littéraire* evocatory

évocatrice [evɔkatris] *voir* **évocateur**

évolué, -e [evɔlɥe] ADJ **1** *(civilisé → peuple, société)* advanced, sophisticated **2** *(progressiste → personne)* mature, broadminded; *(→ parents)* broadminded; *(→ idées)* progressive **3** *(méthode, technologie)* advanced, sophisticated **4** *Ordinat (langage)* high-level

évoluer [7] [evɔlɥe] VI **1** *(changer → maladie)* to develop; *(→ mœurs, circonstances)* to change, to develop; **la position du syndicat a évolué depuis hier** the union's position has changed since yesterday; **les chiffres n'ont pas évolué** the figures haven't changed; **les choses ont beaucoup évolué depuis le mois dernier** there have been many developments since last month; **ils cherchent à faire é. la situation** they are trying to get things to progress, they are trying to make some headway in the situation; **une maladie qui évolue lentement/rapidement** an illness which develops slowly/rapidly

2 *(progresser → pays)* to develop; *(→ civilisation, technique)* to develop, to advance; *(→ théorie)* to evolve, to develop; *(→ personne)* to mature; **ce stage l'a fait é. de manière significative** the traineeship really brought him on

3 *(se déplacer → danseur)* to perform; *(→ cerf-volant)* to fly around; *(→ poisson)* to swim (about); **elle évolue sur scène avec grâce** she glides across the stage; **ils évoluent sur scène en patins à roulettes** they move around the stage on roller-skates; **é. dans la haute société** to move in high society; *Fig* **les cercles dans lesquels elle évoluait** the circles in which she moved; **ce travail la faisait é. dans un milieu totalement différent** this job meant a complete change of environment for her

4 *Mil & Naut* to manoeuvre

5 *Biol* to evolve

6 *Ordinat* **faire é.** to upgrade

évolutif, -ive [evɔlytif, -iv] ADJ **1** *(poste)* with career prospects; **une situation évolutive** a situation which keeps developing, a fluid situation **2** *Méd (maladie)* progressive **3** *Ordinat* upgradable

évolution [evɔlysjɔ̃] NF **1** *(changement → de mœurs)* change; *(→ d'une institution, de la mode)* evolution; *(→ d'idées, d'événements, de l'économie, de la demande)* development; *(→ d'une situation, d'un conflit, du marché)* evolution, development

2 *(progrès → d'un pays)* development; *(→ d'une technique)* development, advancement, evolution; *(→ d'une théorie)* evolution; **suivre une lente é.** to evolve *or* develop slowly

3 *Méd (d'une maladie)* development, progression; *(d'une tumeur)* growth; **à é. lente/rapide** slow/rapidly developing

4 *Biol* **(la théorie de) l'é.** (the theory of) evolution

5 *(souvent pl) Sport* linked-up dance movements; **évolutions** *(d'un joueur, d'un patineur)* movements; *(des troupes)* manoeuvres; **évolutions aquatiques** water ballet

évolutionnisme [evɔlysjɔnism] NM *Biol* evolutionism, evolutionary theory

évolutionniste [evɔlysjɔnist] *Biol* ADJ **1** *(théorie etc)* evolutionist **2** *(biologie)* evolutionary

NMF evolutionist

évolutive [evɔlytiv] *voir* **évolutif**

évolutivité [evɔlytivite] NF *Ordinat* upgradability

évoquer [3] [evɔke] VT **1** *(remémorer → image, journée)* to conjure up, to evoke; *(→ souvenirs)* to call up, to recall, to evoke; **é. qch à qn** to remind sb of sth; **le nom ne lui évoquait rien** the name didn't ring any bells with *or* meant nothing to him/her

2 *(recréer → pays, atmosphère)* to call to mind, to conjure up, to evoke; **la chanson évoque la vie des bateliers du siècle dernier** the song conjures up the life of a bargee in the last century

3 *(rappeler par ressemblance)* to be reminiscent of; **un goût qui évoque un peu le romarin** a taste slightly reminiscent of rosemary; **elle m'évoque un peu ma tante** she reminds me of my aunt a little; **qu'est-ce que cela vous évoque?** what does that remind you of *or* conjure up for you?

4 *(aborder → affaire, question)* to refer to, to mention; **nous n'avons fait qu'é. le sujet** we've only touched on the subject

5 *(appeler → démon, fantôme)* to call up

6 *Jur* = to transfer from a lower to a higher court

evzone [ɛvzon] NM *Mil* evzone

ex [ɛks] NMF INV *Fam* ex; **un de mes ex** one of my exes

ex. *(abrév écrite* **exemple***)* eg, ex; **par e.** eg

ex- [ɛks] PRÉF ex-; **mon ex-mari** my ex-husband *or* former husband; **l'ex-champion du monde** the ex-world *or* former world champion

ex abrupto [ɛksabrypto] ADV abruptly, without warning

exacerbation [ɛgzasɛrbasjɔ̃] NF *(d'une douleur)* exacerbation, aggravation; *(d'une tension)* exacerbation, heightening

exacerbé, -e [ɛgzasɛrbe] ADJ exaggerated; **susceptibilité exacerbée** exaggerated sensitivity; **il est d'une susceptibilité exacerbée** he's extremely touchy; **nationalisme e.** extreme nationalism

exacerber [3] [ɛgzasɛrbe] VT *(douleur)* to exacerbate, to aggravate; *(colère, curiosité, désir, tension)* to exacerbate, to heighten; *(mépris, remords)* to deepen; **des mesures qui vont e. la concurrence** measures which will sharpen *or* heighten competition

▸**s'exacerber** VPR to intensify; **sa jalousie n'a fait que s'e.** he/she has become even more jealous

exact, -e [ɛgzakt] ADJ **1** *(conforme à la réalité → description, information, rapport)* exact, accurate; *(→ copie, réplique)* exact, true; *(→ prédiction, réponse)* correct, accurate; **c'est e., je t'avais promis de t'y emmener** quite right *or* true *or* correct, I'd promised I'd take you there; **il est e. que nous n'avions pas prévu son départ** true (enough), we hadn't anticipated (that) he'd/she'd leave; **il est e. que j'ai dit cela** it's quite true that I said that; **c'est e.** *(vrai)* it's quite true, it's a fact; **vous vous appelez bien Martin? – e.!** your name is Martin? – correct!

2 *(précis → mesure, poids, quantité)* exact, precise; *(→ expression, mot)* exact, right; **le lieu e. où cela s'est passé** the precise *or* exact place where it happened; **l'heure/la date exacte à laquelle...** the exact time/date when...; **as-tu l'heure exacte?** have you got the right *or* correct time?; **au moment e. où...** at the exact *or* precise *or* very moment when...; **pour être e., disons que...** to be accurate, let's say that...

3 *Math* right, correct, accurate; **l'addition n'est pas exacte** the figures don't add up (properly) *or* aren't right; **e. à un millimètre près** correct *or* accurate to within a millimetre

4 *(fonctionnant avec précision → balance, montre)* accurate

5 *(ponctuel)* punctual, on time; **être très e.** to be always on time *or* very punctual; **elle n'est jamais exacte à ses rendez-vous** she's never on time for her appointments; **il est e. à payer son loyer** he is punctual in paying his rent, he pays his rent on time

6 *Littéraire (strict → discipline, obéissance etc)* strict, rigorous

exactement [ɛgzaktəmɑ̃] ADV **1** *(précisément → calculer, placer)* exactly, precisely; *(fidèlement → rapporter, reproduire)* exactly, accurately; **c'est e. ici qu'on a retrouvé le corps** it's the exact place where the body was found; **je ne sais pas e. où ça se trouve** I don't exactly know where it is; **ce n'est pas e. ce que je cherchais** it's not exactly *or* quite what I was looking for; **mais c'est e. le contraire!** but it's exactly *or* precisely the opposite!; **il est très e. 2 heures 13** it is 2.13 precisely; **e. le même** exactly the same; **un effet e. contraire** a directly opposite effect

2 *(tout à fait)* **e.!** exactly!, precisely!

exacteur [ɛgzaktœr] NM exactor

exaction [ɛgzaksjɔ̃] NF exaction

❑ **exactions** NFPL violent acts, acts of violence *or* brutality; **se livrer à** *ou* **commettre des exactions (contre qn)** to perpetrate *or* to commit acts of violence (against sb)

exactitude [ɛgzaktityd] NF **1** *(conformité à la réalité)* exactness, accuracy; **l'e. historique** historical accuracy

2 *(expression précise → d'une mesure)* exactness, precision; *(→ d'une localisation)* exactness; **calculer/mesurer avec e.** to calculate/measure exactly *or* precisely; **je me souviens avec e. des mots de sa lettre** I can remember the precise *or* exact words he/she used in his/her letter

3 *(d'un instrument de mesure)* accuracy

4 *(justesse → d'une traduction, d'une réponse)* exactness, correctness

5 *(ponctualité)* punctuality; **être d'une parfaite e.** to be always perfectly on time; **avec e.** punctually; *Prov* **l'e. est la politesse des rois** punctuality is the politeness of kings

6 *(minutie)* punctiliousness, meticulousness; **faire son travail avec e.** to be punctilious in one's work

ex aequo, ex æquo [ɛgzeko] ADV placed equal; **être e. (avec)** to tie *or* to be placed equal (with); **être troisième e.** to tie for third place, to be placed equal third; **être e. avec qn** to tie with sb, to be placed equal with sb; **on trouve Lille et Nantes e. à la troisième place** Lille and Nantes come joint third; **elle est première e. avec la joueuse suédoise** she's placed equal first with the Swedish player; **premiers e., Maubert et Vuillet** *(à un concours)* the joint winners are Maubert and Vuillet; *(à l'école) Br* top marks *or Am* highest grades have been awarded to Maubert and to Vuillet

NMF INV **il y a deux e. pour la troisième place** there's a tie for third place; **séparer** *ou* **départager les e.** to break the tie

exagération [ɛgzaʒerasjɔ̃] NF **1** *(amplification)* exaggeration, overstating *(UNCOUNT)*; **tomber dans l'e.** to exaggerate; **en l'écoutant, il faut faire la part de l'e.** you must take what he/she says with a pinch of salt **2** *(écrit, parole)* exaggeration, overstatement **3** *(outrance → d'un accent, d'une attitude)* exaggeration

❑ **avec exagération** ADV exaggeratedly, excessively

❑ **sans exagération** ADV **tout le village a été détruit, sans e.** the whole village was destroyed, literally *or* and that's no exaggeration; **on peut dire sans e. que...** it is no exaggeration to say *or* one can say without exaggeration that...; **se montrer ferme sans e.** to be firm without overdoing it *or* going to extremes

exagéré, -e [ɛgzaʒere] ADJ **1** *(excessif → dépense, prix)* excessive; *(→ éloge, critique)* exaggerated, overblown; *(→ optimisme, prudence)* excessive, exaggerated; *(→ hâte, mécontentement)* undue; *(→ ambition, confiance en soi)* excessive, overweening; **confiance exagérée** overconfidence;

accorder une confiance exagérée à qn to place too much trust in sb; accorder une importance exagérée à qch to attach too much importance to sth, to exaggerate the importance of sth; 50 euros par personne, c'est un peu e.! 50 euros per person, that's a bit much!; il n'est pas e. de parler de menace it wouldn't be an overstatement to call it a threat; dire qu'il est bête, c'est un peu e. it's a bit much or a bit excessive to say that he's stupid

2 (outré → accent, attitude) exaggerated, overdone; en boitant de façon exagérée limping exaggeratedly

exagérément [ɛgzaʒeremã] ADV excessively, exaggeratedly; elle a e. tardé avant de répondre she delayed for far too long before replying; e. timide over-shy; e. méticuleux over-meticulous

exagérer [18] [ɛgzaʒere] VT 1 (amplifier → importance, dangers, difficultés) to exaggerate, to overemphasize, to overstate; (→ mérites, pouvoir) to exaggerate, to overrate, to overstate; (→ proportions, richesse, valeur) to exaggerate; tu exagères mon influence you're crediting me with more influence than I have; on a beaucoup exagéré l'importance de ce fait the significance of this fact has been overstated or greatly exaggerated, too much importance has been attached to this fact; il ne faut rien e., n'exagérons rien let's not get carried away

2 (outrer → accent, attitude) to overdo to, to exaggerate; e. son chagrin to put on a great show of grief; e. les précautions to be overcautious

USAGE ABSOLU (amplifier) il faut toujours que tu exagères! you always exaggerate!; sans e. without any exaggeration; sans e., elle mesurait bien deux mètres I'm not kidding, she was at least two metres tall

VI (abuser) ça fait deux heures que j'attends, il ne faut pas e.! I've been waiting for two hours, that's a bit much!; Fam ça fait ton troisième gâteau, (là) t'exagères! that's your third pastry, aren't you overdoing it a bit?; comment, tu ne veux plus y aller? alors là, tu exagères! what, you don't want to go any more? you can't be serious!; cette fois ils exagèrent, j'appelle la police! this time they've really gone too far, I'm calling the police!; encore un impôt supplémentaire? quand même, ils exagèrent! yet another tax? they must be joking! or that's a bit much!; Fam j'étais là avant vous, faut pas e.! I was there before you, you've got a nerve!

▸s'exagérer VPR s'e. qch to make too much of sth; s'e. les mérites de qn to exaggerate sb's merits

exaltant, -e [ɛgzaltã, -ãt] ADJ (expérience, perspective) exciting; (harangue) elating, stirring; sa prestation n'est pas très exaltante! his performance isn't particularly exciting!

exaltation [ɛgzaltasjɔ̃] NF 1 (excitation) (intense) excitement; (joie) elation; dans un état d'e. (excité) excited, overexcited; (euphorique) elated; e. mystique exaltation 2 (célébration → d'un talent, du travail) extolling, exalting, glorification 3 Psy (d'un malade mental) overexcitement 4 Méd overexcitement 5 Rel E. de la sainte Croix Exaltation of the Cross

exalté, -e [ɛgzalte] ADJ 1 (intense → désir, passion) inflamed 2 (excité → personne) elated, (very) excited; (→ esprit) excited, inflamed; (→ imagination) wild; (→ discours) wild, impassioned

NM,F Péj fanatic, hothead

exalter [3] [ɛgzalte] VT 1 (intensifier → désir) to excite, to kindle; (→ enthousiasme) to fire, to excite; (→ ressentiment, orgueil) to intensify; (→ imagination) to fire, to stimulate, to stir up; Littéraire (→ odeur) to intensify; la tiédeur de la pièce exaltait le parfum des fleurs the warmth of the room intensified the scent of the flowers

2 (exciter → foule, partisan) to excite; exalté à l'idée de carried away by the idea of

3 Littéraire (faire l'éloge de → beauté, bienfaits, talent) to glorify, to extol, to exalt

4 Littéraire (élever) to exalt, to ennoble

▸s'exalter VPR to become excited

exam [ɛgzam] NM Fam (abrév examen) exam▪

examen [ɛgzamɛ̃] NM 1 Scol & Univ examination, exam; tu as eu combien à l'e.? what did you get in the exam?; passer un e. (série d'épreuves) to take an exam; (écrit) Br to sit or Am to write a

paper; (oral) to take an oral (exam) or Br a viva; faire passer un e. à qn to examine sb; être reçu/refusé à un e. to pass/fail an exam; e. blanc Br mock exam, Am practice test; e. écrit written exam; e. d'entrée entrance exam; e. final final exam; e. de fin d'études final-year exam; e. oral oral (exam), Br viva; e. partiel (année) half-year exam; (semestre, trimestre) half-term exam, midterm exam; e. de passage end-of-year or Br sessional exam, Am final exam (for admission to the year above); e. spécial d'entrée à l'université university entrance exam

2 Méd (auscultation) e. (médical) (medical) examination; (analyse) test; e. médical complet complete checkup; examens complémentaires further tests; e. gynécologique gynaecological examination, internal; e. interne internal examination; e. neurologique neurological test; e. de personnalité personality test; e. prénuptial premarital checkup; e. préopératoire preoperative examination, Fam preop; e. radiologique X-rays; e. sérologique serological test; se faire faire un e./des examens to have a test/some tests done; faire faire des examens à un patient to send or to refer a patient for (further) tests; je vais chercher mes examens demain I'll go and pick up my test results tomorrow; e. de laboratoire test (of blood, urine etc); e. de la vue eye test, sight test

3 (inspection) inspection, examination; après e. du corps de la victime having examined the body of the victim; je viens faire l'e. de l'installation électrique I've come to inspect the wiring

4 (de documents, d'un dossier, d'un projet de loi) examination; (d'une requête) examination, consideration; (d'un texte) study; (d'une comptabilité) checking, inspection; son argumentation ne résiste pas à l'e. his/her arguments don't stand up to examination or under scrutiny; après un e. attentif de la situation/du problème after careful examination of the situation/problem; après e. (up)on examination; e. de conscience examination of (one's) conscience; faire son e. de conscience (réfléchir) to do some soul-searching, to search one's conscience; e. financier financial review; e. de la situation fiscale personnelle = inspection of personal finances

5 Jur e. contradictoire examination made in the presence of both parties to a contract; mise en e. indictment

❑ à l'examen ADV under consideration; mettre une question à l'e. to put a topic on the table for discussion

examinateur, -trice [ɛgzaminatœr, -tris] NM,F examiner; les examinateurs (jury) the examining panel; (réunion) the board of examiners

examiner [3] [ɛgzamine] VT 1 (réfléchir sur → dossier, documents) to examine, to go through; (→ circonstances) to examine, to go into; (→ requête) to examine, to consider; (→ affaire) to investigate, to examine, to go into; (→ comptes) to inspect, to go through

2 (regarder de près → meuble, signature etc) to examine; (→ emplacement, site) to examine, to inspect; (→ personne) to look carefully at, to study; (→ appartement) to have a close look around; (→ machine) to check; e. l'horizon to scan the horizon; e. les lieux to inspect the premises; e. minutieusement une écriture to scrutinize or to inspect a piece of handwriting; nous allons e. la question we're going to examine or look into the matter; e. une question de près to look at sth in detail; e. qch de plus près to take a closer look at sth; e. qch à la loupe to look at sth through a magnifying glass; Fig to have a very close look at sth, to scrutinize sth; e. qch dans le détail or en détail to examine sth in detail; elle m'a examiné de la tête aux pieds she eyed me from head to toe or looked me up and down

3 Méd (lésion, malade) to examine; se faire e. par un médecin to have oneself or be examined by a doctor; tu devrais te faire e. you should go and see a doctor; se faire e. les yeux to have one's eyes tested

4 Scol & Univ (candidat) to examine

▸s'examiner VPR 1 (emploi réfléchi) to examine oneself; s'e. dans un miroir to examine oneself or to look (closely) at oneself in the mirror

2 (emploi réciproque) to scrutinize one another or each other; ils s'examinaient avec méfiance they were eyeing each other up

ex ante [ɛksãte] ADJ ex ante

exanthématique [ɛgzãtematik] ADJ Méd exanthematous, exanthematic

exanthème [ɛgzãtɛm] NM Méd exanthema, exanthem; **exanthèmes** exanthemata, exanthemas, exanthems

exarchat [ɛgzarka] NM Rel exarchate

exarque [ɛgzark] NM Rel exarch

exaspérant, -e [ɛgzasperã, -ãt] ADJ exasperating, infuriating

exaspération [ɛgzasperasjɔ̃] NF 1 (colère) extreme annoyance, exasperation 2 Littéraire (d'un désir) exacerbation; (d'une émotion) heightening; (d'une douleur) aggravation, worsening

exaspérer [18] [ɛgzaspere] VT 1 (irriter) to exasperate, to infuriate; être exaspéré contre qn to be exasperated with sb 2 (intensifier → dépit, désir) to exacerbate; (→ douleur, tension) to aggravate

▸s'exaspérer VPR (désir, passion) to become exacerbated; (douleur) to worsen

exaucement [ɛgzosmã] NM fulfilment, granting

exaucer [16] [ɛgzose] VT 1 (vœu) to grant, to fulfil; (prière) to answer, to grant 2 (personne) to grant the wish of; Dieu m'avait exaucé God had answered or heard my prayer

ex cathedra [ɛkskatedra] ADV 1 Rel ex cathedra 2 (doctement) solemnly, with authority

excavateur, -trice [ɛkskavatœr, -tris] NM,F Tech excavator, digger

excavation [ɛkskavasjɔ̃] NF 1 (trou → artificiel) excavation, hole; (→ creusé par une bombe) crater; (→ naturel) hollow, cave; e. minière mine 2 (creusement) excavation, excavating, hollowing out

excavatrice [ɛkskavatris] voir excavateur

excaver [3] [ɛkskave] VT to excavate

excédant, -e [ɛksedã, -ãt] ADJ exasperating, infuriating

excédé, -e [ɛksede] ADJ exasperated, infuriated; j'étais e. I was exasperated, I had lost all patience

excédent [ɛksedã] NM 1 (surplus) surplus, excess; e. de blé/main-d'œuvre wheat/labour surplus; il y a un e. de personnel dans le service the department is overstaffed; e. de bagages excess luggage or baggage; vous avez un e. de bagages your luggage is overweight; vous avez deux kilos d'e. your luggage is two kilos overweight; payer 30 euros d'e. to pay 30 euros excess (charge); e. de poids excess weight

2 Écon & Fin (d'un budget) surplus; dégager un e. to show a surplus; excédents et déficits overs and shorts; e. de la balance commerciale balance of trade surplus; e. brut d'exploitation gross operating profit; e. budgétaire budget(ary) surplus; Compta e. de caisse cash overs; e. commercial trade surplus; e. de dépenses deficit; nous avons un e. de dépenses we are overspending; e. d'exploitation operating profit; excédents pétroliers excess oil production

❑ en excédent ADJ surplus (avant n), excess; budget en e. surplus budget; somme en e. sum in excess; la balance commerciale est en e. the trade balance shows a surplus, there is a trade surplus; vous avez deux kilos en e. your luggage is two kilos overweight or over

excédentaire [ɛksedãtɛr] ADJ (budget) surplus (avant n); (solde) positive; (poids) excess; (production) excess, surplus; on a stocké la récolte e. the surplus crop was stored away; cette année, la récolte est e. this year, the crop exceeds requirements; balance commerciale e. trade surplus

excéder [18] [ɛksede] VT 1 (dépasser → poids, prix) to exceed, to be over, to be in excess of; (→ durée) to exceed, to last more than; (→ limite) to go beyond; (→ quantité, somme, période) to exceed; les recettes excèdent les dépenses income is in excess of expenditure; nos pertes excèdent nos bénéfices our losses are greater than our profits; e. les moyens de qn to be beyond sb's means

2 *(outrepasser → pouvoirs, responsabilités)* to exceed, to go beyond, to overstep; *(→ forces, ressources)* to overtax; *(→ compétences)* to be beyond

3 *(exaspérer)* to exasperate, to infuriate

4 *(épuiser)* **excédé de fatigue** exhausted, overtired; **excédé de travail** overworked

excellemment [ɛkselamɑ̃] **ADV** excellently

excellence [ɛkselɑ̃s] **NF 1** *(qualité → d'une prestation, d'un produit)* excellence **2** *(titre)* **E.** Excellency; **Son/Votre E.** His/Your Excellency

❑ **par excellence ADV** par excellence, archetypal; **c'est le macho par e.** he's the archetypal male chauvinist, he's the male chauvinist par excellence

excellent, -e [ɛkselɑ̃, -ɑ̃t] **ADJ 1** *(très bon → artiste, directeur, nourriture)* excellent, first-rate (**en** at *or* in); *(→ article, devoir, note, idée)* excellent; *(→ santé)* excellent, perfect; **être en excellente santé** to be in the best of health, to be in excellent health; **il est e. en Méphisto** he's excellent as Mephisto **2** *Littéraire (d'une grande bonté)* **c'est un e. homme** he's a very good man

exceller [4] [ɛksele] **VI** to excel, to shine (**en** at *or* in); **pose-lui des questions en botanique, c'est là qu'il excelle** ask him questions on botany, that's where he shines; **e. dans** to excel in *or* at; **elle excelle dans la pâtisserie** she excels at baking, she's an excellent pastry cook; **je n'excelle pas en latin** Latin isn't my strong point; **e. à faire** to be particularly good at doing; **il excelle à préparer le poisson** he's an expert at (preparing) fish dishes

excentration [ɛksɑ̃trasjɔ̃] **NF** throwing off centre, setting over

excentré, -e [ɛksɑ̃tre] **ADJ 1** *Tech* thrown off centre, set over **2** *(quartier, stade)* outlying; **c'est très e.** it's quite a long way out

excentrer [3] [ɛksɑ̃tre] **VT 1** *Tech* to throw off centre, to set over **2** *(bâtiment, stade)* to build far from the town centre

excentricité [ɛksɑ̃trisite] **NF 1** *(attitude, acte)* eccentricity; **qu'est-ce que c'est encore que ces excentricités?** what's all this eccentric behaviour? **2** *Astron & Math* eccentricity **3** *(d'un quartier)* remoteness (from the town centre)

excentrique [ɛksɑ̃trik] **ADJ 1** *(bizarre)* eccentric **2** *Math* eccentric **3** *(quartier, habitation)* outlying

NMF *(personne)* eccentric

NM *Tech* eccentric

excentriquement [ɛksɑ̃trikmɑ̃] **ADV** eccentrically

excepté¹ [ɛksɛpte] **PRÉP** except, apart from; **tous les enfants ont eu les oreillons, e. le plus petit** all the children had the mumps, except *or* apart from the youngest; **il accepte tout, e. d'avoir à me rendre des comptes** he accepts everything, except having to be accountable to me; **il y va souvent, e. quand il n'a pas le temps** he often goes (there) except when he doesn't have the time; **tous les jours e. quand il pleut** every day except *or* apart from *or* with the exception of when it rains; **je viens avec toi, e. si tu y vas en train** I'll come with you, so long as you're not going by train *or* unless you're going by train

❑ **excepté que CONJ** except for *or* apart from the fact that; **tout s'est bien passé, e. qu'on a attendu trois heures** everything went well except for *or* apart from the fact that we had to wait three hours

excepté², -e [ɛksɛpte] **ADJ** *(après le nom)* **les femmes exceptées** except for *or* apart from the women; **vous deux exceptés** you two aside, except *or* apart from you two; **eux exceptés, personne n'en a entendu parler** no one heard about it apart from *or* except them; **j'aime tous leurs meubles, le bahut e.** I like all their furniture except for *or* apart from the sideboard

excepter [4] [ɛksɛpte] **VT** to except (**de** from); **si l'on excepte Marie, elles sont toutes là** with the exception of *or* except for Marie they are all here; **toute son œuvre, sans e. ses essais** all his/her work, including *or* not excluding his/her essays

exception [ɛksɛpsjɔ̃] **NF 1** *(chose, être ou événement hors norme)* exception; **la neige est une e. par ici** it rarely snows around here; **cette règle admet des exceptions** there are (some) exceptions to this rule; **ils sont tous très paresseux, à une e./quelques exceptions près** all of them with one exception/a few exceptions are very lazy; **à quelques rares exceptions près** with very few exceptions; **il n'accorde jamais d'interviews, c'était une e.** he never (normally) gives interviews, that was an exception; **faire e.** to be an exception; **être l'e.** to be the *or* an exception; **son cas est une** *ou* **fait e.** his/her case is an exception *or* is exceptional; **les collisions entre avions restent l'e.** plane collisions are still very rare; **l'e. confirme la règle, c'est l'e. qui confirme la règle** the exception proves the rule; **sauf e.** almost without exception; **sauf e., ils n'ont pas le droit de regarder la télé** they are only very rarely allowed to watch television; **e. culturelle** cultural exception; **l'e. française** the French exception

2 *(dérogation)* exception (**à** to); **faire une e. pour qn/qch** to make an exception for sb/sth; **faire une e. à** to make an exception to; **faire une e. à une règle** to make an exception to a rule; **nous ferons une e. à la règle** we'll bend the rules; **ce soir, je fais une petite e. à mon régime** I'll break my diet just for tonight; **faire e. de** *(exclure)* to make an exception of, to except; **si l'on fait e. des enfants** the children excepted, if you except the children

3 *Jur* plea; **e. de compétence** plea of incompetence; **e. dilatoire** dilatory plea; **e. d'illégalité/d'incompétence** plea of illegality/incompetence; **e. d'inexécution** = right not to perform a contract obligation due to non-performance by the other party; **e. d'ordre public** exception on the grounds of public policy; **e. péremptoire** peremptory plea; **opposer une e.** to put in a demurrer *or* plea

❑ **à l'exception de, exception faite de PRÉP** except (for), with the exception of

❑ **d'exception ADJ 1** *(mesure)* exceptional; *(loi)* emergency *(avant n)*

2 *(remarquable)* remarkable, exceptional; **c'est un être d'e.** *(homme)* he's an exceptional man; *(femme)* she's an exceptional woman

❑ **sans (aucune) exception ADV** without (any) exception; **sortez tous, sans e.!** out, every (single) one of you!

Culture

EXCEPTION FRANÇAISE

"L'exception française" is used to describe France's individual status in terms of economic development. It is characterized by a large public sector, by a larger degree of state intervention in the economy than in Britain or the US and by the persistence of a relatively generous welfare State coupled with greater investment in public services, all of which goes against the principles of market-driven economics. France is also keen to safeguard its film industry and has been campaigning in favour of "l'exception culturelle" – the notion that cultural products should not be treated in the same way as other commercial products and that consequently governments should be authorized to subsidize their film industries.

exceptionnalité [ɛksɛpsjɔnalite] **NF** exceptional character; **l'e. de ces mesures reflète l'e. de la situation** these exceptional *or* special measures reflect the exceptional situation

exceptionnel, -elle [ɛksɛpsjɔnɛl] **ADJ 1** *(très rare → faveur, chance, circonstances)* exceptional; *(→ accident, complication)* exceptional, rare; *(→ mesure)* exceptional, special; *(unique → concert)* special, *Br* one-off; *(→ offre, promotion)* special; **congé e.** special leave; **ouverture exceptionnelle dimanche 22 décembre** *(d'un magasin)* open Sunday 22 December

2 *(remarquable → intelligence, œuvre)* exceptional; *(→ personne)* remarkable, exceptional; **ne rien avoir d'e.** to be nothing special

3 *Pol (assemblée, conseil, mesures)* special, emergency *(avant n)*

NM l'e. the exceptional

exceptionnellement [ɛksɛpsjɔnɛlmɑ̃] **ADV 1** *(beau, doué)* exceptionally, extremely

2 *(contrairement à l'habitude)* exceptionally; **notre magasin sera ouvert lundi e.** next week only, our shop will be open on Monday; **nous ouvrirons e. le soir de Noël** we will open specially on Christmas Eve; **e., le square est fermé ce soir** for one night only, the park is closed this evening; **e. tu peux partir maintenant** just this once you can leave now

excès [ɛksɛ] **NM 1** *(surabondance)* surplus, excess; **e. de poids/calories** excess weight/calories; **un e. de potassium/sucre dans le sang** an excess of potassium/sugar in the blood; **les plantes souffrent d'un e. de chaleur/froid** plants can be damaged by excessive heat/cold; **c'est un peu un e. de précautions** these are rather excessive precautions; **e. de l'offre sur la demande** excess of supply over demand; **e. de prudence/rigueur/sévérité** excessive care/rigour/harshness; **e. de zèle** overzealousness; **faire de l'e. de zèle, pécher par e. de zèle** to go beyond the call of duty, to be overzealous; **pas d'e. de zèle!** there's no need to be overzealous!

2 *Transp* **e. de vitesse** speeding; **faire un e. de vitesse** to exceed *or* to break the speed limit, to speed

3 *(abus)* excess; **évitez tout e.** avoid overdoing things; *(alimentaire)* avoid overeating; **e. de langage** immoderate language; **se livrer à** *ou* **commettre des e. de langage** to use strong language; *Jur* **e. de pouvoir** abuse of power, *Spéc* action ultra vires

4 *(manque de mesure)* **tomber dans l'e.** to go to extremes, to overdo it; **sois plus lyrique mais sans tomber dans l'e.** be more lyrical but don't overdo it; **tomber dans l'e. inverse** to go to the opposite extreme; *Prov* **l'e. en tout est un défaut** moderation in all things

NMPL 1 e. (de table) overindulgence; **faire des e. (de table)** to eat and drink too much, to overindulge

2 *(violences, débauche)* excesses; **des e. de conduite** loose living

❑ **à l'excès ADV** to excess, excessively; **jusqu'à l'e.** to excess, excessively; **gentil/scrupuleux à l'e.** kind/scrupulous to a fault, overkind/overscrupulous; **critiquer à l'e.** to be excessive in one's criticism; **boire à l'e.** to drink to excess; **se dépenser à l'e.** to overexert oneself

❑ **avec excès ADV** to excess, excessively, immoderately; **manger avec e.** to overeat, to eat excessively *or* to excess; **dépenser avec e.** to overspend

❑ **sans excès ADV** with moderation, moderately

excessif, -ive [ɛksesif, -iv] **ADJ 1** *(chaleur, sévérité, prix, quantité)* excessive; *(colère)* undue; *(enthousiasme, optimisme)* undue, excessive; *(langage)* immoderate; *(opinion, idée)* extreme; **50 euros, ce n'est pas e.** 50 euros is quite a reasonable amount to pay; **des mois de travail e. l'ont rendu malade** he has become ill through months of overwork

2 *(personne)* extreme; **c'est quelqu'un de très e.** he's given to extremes of behaviour; **elle est excessive dans ses critiques** she overdoes her criticism

3 *(grand)* **sans excessive gentillesse** without being especially pleasant

excessivement [ɛksesivmɑ̃] **ADV 1** *(trop → raffiné)* excessively; **e. cher** overpriced; **manger e.** to overeat, to eat excessively *or* to excess; **il avait bu e.** he had been drinking to excess **2** *(extrêmement)* extremely; **il fait e. froid** it's hideously cold

exciper [3] [ɛksipe] **exciper de VT IND 1** *Jur* **e. de l'inconstitutionnalité d'une loi** to claim that a law is unconstitutional, to challenge the constitutionality of a law **2** *Littéraire* **e. de son ignorance/sa bonne foi** to plead ignorance/one's good faith

excipient [ɛksipjɑ̃] **NM** *Pharm* excipient, binder

excise [ɛksiz] **NF** excise

exciser [3] [ɛksize] **VT** *Méd* to excise

exciseur, -euse [ɛksizœr, -øz] **NM,F** *Méd* excisionist, excisor

excision [ɛksizjɔ̃] **NF** *Méd* excision

excitabilité [ɛksitabilite] **NF** excitability

excitable [ɛksitabl] **ADJ 1** *(facilement irrité)* **il est très e.** he gets worked up quickly *or* annoyed easily **2** *Physiol* excitable

excitant, -e [ɛksitɑ̃, -ɑ̃t] **ADJ 1** *(stimulant → boisson)* stimulating **2** *(aguichant → femme, homme, tenue)* arousing **3** *(passionnant → aventure,*

projet, vie) exciting, thrilling; *(→ film, roman)* exciting; **le match devient un peu plus e.** the match is warming up; **ce n'est pas très e.!** it's not very exciting!

NM stimulant

excitateur, -trice [ɛksitatœr, -tris] **NM,F** exciter, instigator (**de** of)

NM *Élec* discharger, (static) exciter

❑ **excitatrice NF** *Phys* exciter, exciting dynamo

excitation [ɛksitasjɔ̃] **NF 1** *(exaltation)* excitement; **ils étaient dans un tel état d'e.!** they were in such a state of excitement *or* such an excited state!; **en proie à une grande e.** very excited, in a state of great excitement; **dans l'e. du moment** in the heat of the moment

2 *(stimulation → d'un sens)* excitation; **e. (sexuelle)** (sexual) arousal *or* excitement

3 *(incitation)* incitement (**à** to); **e. à la révolte** incitement to rebellion; **e. des mineurs à la débauche** incitement of minors to commit immoral acts

4 *Physiol* excitation, stimulation

5 *Électron & Phys* excitation

excité, -e [ɛksite] **ADJ 1** *(enthousiasmé)* excited, thrilled; **nous étions tout excités à l'idée de la revoir** we were really excited at *or* thrilled by the idea of seeing her again; **ils sont sortis du bal complètement excités** they left the dance in a state of tremendous excitement

2 *(stimulé → sens, curiosité, imagination)* aroused, fired

3 *(agité → enfant, chien)* excited, restless; *(→ candidat)* tense, worked-up; **les animaux sont excités, ils pressentent l'orage** the animals are restless, they can feel the storm coming; **un jeune homme, passablement e., lançait des injures à la police** a young man, who was rather worked up, was shouting abuse at the police

4 *(sexuellement → organe, personne)* aroused, excited

NM,F *Péj* hothead; **les excités du volant** dangerous drivers

exciter [3] [ɛksite] **VT 1** *(exalter)* to excite, to exhilarate; **la vitesse l'excite** speed exhilarates him/her; *Fam* **les malheurs des autres, ça l'excite!** other people's misfortunes turn him/her on!; **n'excite pas les enfants avant le coucher** don't get the children excited before bed

2 *(rendre agité → drogue, café)* to overstimulate, to stimulate; **éviter les aliments susceptibles d'e. le malade** avoid foods which may overstimulate the patient

3 *(pousser)* to urge on; **e. qn à la révolte ou à se révolter** to urge sb to rebel, to incite sb to rebellion; **e. un chien à l'attaque** to egg a dog on to attack; **e. qn contre qn** to set sb against sb, to work sb up against sb; **e. la meute contre le gibier** to urge on the pack to hunt their quarry; **leur père les excite contre leur mère** their father gets them worked up against their mother

4 *(attiser → admiration, envie)* to provoke; *(→ curiosité, intérêt, soupçons)* to arouse, to stir up; *(→ amour, jalousie)* to arouse, to inflame, to kindle; **e. le rire** to provoke *or* cause mirth; **e. la pitié de qn** to move sb to pity, to arouse sb's pity

5 *(intensifier → appétit)* to whet; *(→ rage)* to whip up; *(→ désir)* to increase, to sharpen; *(→ douleur)* to intensify

6 *(sexuellement)* to excite, to arouse

7 *Fam (enthousiasmer)* to excite, to thrill, to get worked up; **cette perspective ne m'excite pas vraiment!** I can't say I'm thrilled *or* wild about the idea!

8 *Fam (mettre en colère)* to bug, to annoy; **tu commences à m'e.!** you're beginning to bug me!

9 *Physiol (nerf, muscle)* to excite, to stimulate; *Biol* to stimulate

10 *Électron* to excite

USAGE ABSOLU *(rendre agité)* **le café/le tabac excite** coffee/tobacco acts as a stimulant

▶**s'exciter VPR 1** *Fam (se mettre en colère)* to get worked up; **t'excite pas!** don't get worked up!, keep your shirt on!

2 *Fam (s'acharner)* **j'ai commencé à m'e. sur la serrure** I was losing my patience with the lock; **ne t'excite pas sur la fermeture Éclair®!** go easy on the *Br* zip *or Am* zipper!

3 *(s'exalter)* to get carried away *or* excited *or* overexcited; **ne t'excite pas trop, ce n'est qu'un petit rôle** don't get carried away, it's only a small part

exclamatif, -ive [ɛksklamatif, -iv] **ADJ** exclamatory; **à valeur exclamative** used as an exclamation; **proposition exclamative** exclamation

❑ **exclamative NF** exclamation

exclamation [ɛksklamasjɔ̃] **NF 1** *(cri)* exclamation, cry; **des exclamations de joie/surprise** cries of joy/surprise; **pousser une e. de joie/surprise** to cry out with joy/in surprise **2** *Ling* exclamation

exclamative [ɛksklamativ] *voir* **exclamatif**

exclamer [3] [ɛksklame] **s'exclamer VPR** to exclaim, to cry out; **"toi!" s'était-il exclamé** "you!" he had cried out *or* exclaimed; **il n'y a pas de quoi s'e., leur décision est connue depuis plusieurs jours** there's nothing to be surprised about, their decision has been known for several days; **s'e. de** *(surprise, admiration)* to exclaim *or* cry out in; *(douleur, colère)* to cry out in; **s'e. sur la beauté de qch** to cry out in admiration over the beauty of sth; **tous s'exclamaient sur le nouveau-né** they were all admiring the new-born baby; **s'e. sur la montée du chômage/de la violence** to make a lot of noise about rising unemployment/violence

exclu, -e [ɛkskly] **ADJ 1** *(non compris)* excluded, left out; **main-d'œuvre exclue, la facture s'élève à 58 euros** the bill amounts to 58 euros, labour excluded; **du 15 au 30 e.** from the 15th to the 30th exclusive; **le mois d'août jusqu'au 31 e.** the month of August excluding the 31st; **jusqu'à la ligne 22 exclue** up to line 21 inclusive, up to but excluding line 22; **prix des travaux, TVA exclue** the cost of the work, excluding VAT

2 *(rejeté → hypothèse, solution)* ruled out, dismissed, rejected; **l'hypothèse d'un meurtre n'est pas exclue** murder hasn't been ruled out; **une victoire de la gauche n'est pas exclue** a victory of the left is not to be ruled out; **il est e. que…** it's out of the question *or* impossible that…; **il est e. qu'il vienne avec nous** it's out of the question for him to come with us, *Fam* there's no way he's coming with us; **il est e. que je m'y rende** my going there is totally out of the question; **il n'est pas e. qu'on les retrouve** it's not impossible that they might be found

3 *(renvoyé → définitivement)* expelled; *(→ provisoirement)* suspended

NM,F le grand e. du palmarès à Cannes the big loser in the Cannes festival

❑ **exclus NMPL les exclus** *(gén)* the underprivileged; *(SDF)* the homeless; **les exclus de la société** social outcasts, the outcasts of society; **les exclus du progrès** those whom progress has ignored *or* passed by

exclure [96] [ɛksklyr] **VT 1** *(expulser → membre, élève)* to expel; *(→ étudiant)* to expel, *Br* to send down; *(→ sportif)* to ban, to expel; **e. qn de** *(parti, école)* to expel sb from; *(université)* to expel sb from, *Br* to send sb down from; *(équipe, compétition)* to ban *or* to expel sb from; *(fonction publique)* to remove from; *(salle, réunion)* to eject from; **elle a été exclue du comité** she was expelled from *or* thrown off the committee; **elle s'est fait e. de l'école pour trois jours** she's been suspended *or Br* excluded from school for three days

2 *(écarter)* to exclude (**de** from); **ils l'excluaient de leurs jeux** they used to exclude him/her from their games; **les enfants sont exclus de la bibliothèque** the library is out of bounds to the children; **e. le pain de son régime** to exclude *or* to cut out bread from one's diet; **e. l'alcool de sa table** not to allow alcohol in the house; **elle a exclu le rouge dans ses vêtements** she doesn't wear anything with red in it

3 *(mettre à part)* to exclude, to leave aside *or* out; **e. une facture de sa note de frais** to leave out *or* to exclude a bill from one's expenses; **sont exclus tous les internes** this doesn't apply to boarders; **si l'on exclut le mois de mars** March excluded; **si l'on exclut de petits incidents techniques** apart from a few minor technical hitches

4 *(être incompatible avec)* to exclude, to preclude; **la chimiothérapie n'exclut pas d'autres formes de traitement** chemotherapy doesn't preclude other forms of treatment; **l'un n'exclut pas l'autre** they're not mutually exclusive; **sa nomination exclut qu'elle vienne vous voir en octobre** her appointment will prevent her coming to see you in October; **cela n'exclut pas que vous puissiez enseigner** that doesn't rule out the possibility of your teaching

5 *(rejeter → hypothèse)* to exclude, to rule out, to reject; **e. l'hypothèse d'un suicide** to rule out suicide; **e. la possibilité d'un accord** to rule out the possibility of an agreement; **la possibilité de subvention est à e.** the possibility of obtaining subsidies is to be ruled out; **cette hypothèse est à e.** this possibility is out of the question

▶**s'exclure VPR 1** *(solutions, traitements)* to exclude *or* to preclude one another, to be incompatible *or* mutually exclusive

2 *(s'exposer au rejet)* to cut oneself off; **s'e. de** to cut oneself off from; **l'enfant brutal s'exclut par son comportement** bullies cut themselves off from the other children because of the way they behave

exclusif, -ive [ɛksklyzif, -iv] **ADJ 1** *(droit, modèle, privilège)* exclusive; *(agent, droits de reproduction, usage)* exclusive, sole; *(dépositaire, concessionnaire)* sole; **avoir la jouissance exclusive de** to be the sole user *or* possessor of; **avoir un intérêt e. pour qch** to be solely interested in sth; **pendant les vacances, son occupation exclusive a été de courir** during the holidays, running was his/her sole activity; **vente exclusive en pharmacie** sold exclusively in pharmacies; **propriété exclusive de l'auteur** exclusive property of the author

2 e. de *(incompatible avec)* exclusive of, incompatible with; **les services proposés ne sont pas exclusifs l'un de l'autre** the services offered are not mutually exclusive

3 *(absolu → amour, relation)* exclusive; **les jumeaux ont une relation exclusive** the twins relate to nobody outside each other; **il est e. en amour** he stays faithful to his partner, he believes in monogamy; **avoir un goût e. pour qch** to only like sth; **dans le but e. de faire qch** with the sole aim of doing sth

4 *(intolérant)* blinkered; **être e. dans ses goûts/amitiés** to be selective *or* discriminating in one's tastes/choice of friends

5 *(dossier, image, reportage)* exclusive; **une interview exclusive** an exclusive (interview)

6 *Ling & Math* disjunctive; **le "ou" e. de l'expression "ouvert ou fermé"** the disjunctive "or" in the phrase "open or shut"

❑ **exclusive NF** *(exclusion)* debarment; **frapper qn/un pays d'exclusive** to debar sb/a country; **jeter** *ou* **prononcer l'exclusive contre qn** to debar sb; **être l'objet d'une exclusive** to be debarred; **sans exclusive** without exception

exclusion [ɛksklyzjɔ̃] **NF 1** *(renvoi)* expulsion (**de** from); *(de la fonction publique)* removal (**de** from); *(d'une salle, d'une réunion)* ejection (**de** from); **demander l'e. de qn** to ask for sb to be expelled; **son e. du club** his/her expulsion from the club; **son e. du comité** his/her expulsion *or* exclusion from the committee; **son e. des fonctions de trésorière** her being debarred from continuing as treasurer; **e. temporaire** suspension; **pendant son e.** *(temporaire)* while he/she was suspended

2 *(mise à l'écart)* exclusion; **l'e. des femmes de la scène politique** the exclusion of women from the world of politics

3 *(dans la société)* **l'e. (sociale)** social exclusion; **les victimes de l'e. sociale** those rejected by society

4 *Math* exclusion

❑ **à l'exclusion de PRÉP** to the exclusion of; *(à l'exception de)* except, apart from, with the exception of; **tous les jours à l'e. de jeudi** every day apart from Thursday *or* Thursday excluded

exclusive [ɛksklyziv] *voir* **exclusif**

exclusivement [ɛksklyzivmɑ̃] **ADV 1** *(uniquement)* exclusively, solely; **ouvert le lundi e.** open on Mondays only; **parking e. réservé aux clients de l'hôtel** customer parking only; **il joue e. de la harpe** he only plays the harp **2** *(non inclus)* **du 1er au 10 e.** from the 1st to the 10th

exclusive **3** *(aimer)* exclusively, in an exclusive way; **il aime e. les opéras de Verdi** he likes Verdi's operas to the exclusion of all others

exclusivisme [ɛksklyzivism] **NM** exclusivism

exclusivité [ɛksklyzivite] **NF 1** *Com (droit)* sole *or* exclusive rights; **avoir l'e. de** to have the exclusive rights to; **avoir l'e. d'une interview** to have (the) exclusive coverage of an interview; **c'est notre journal qui a eu l'e. de son interview** our paper had an exclusive with him/her; **l'agence a l'e. des photos** the agency has exclusive rights to the pictures; **nous avons l'e. de la vente de ce produit** we have the (sole) rights for this product; **avoir un contrat d'e.** to have an exclusive contract; **e. à la marque** brand exclusivity

2 *(chose unique → article)* exclusive (article); *(→ interview)* exclusive (interview), scoop; *(→ film)* exclusive film; **ce modèle est une e.** this is an exclusive design; **c'est une e. Mercedes®** it's exclusive to Mercedes®

3 *TV (de film)* first run; *Cin* movie on general release

4 *(privilège exclusif)* **il n'a pas l'e. du talent** he doesn't have a monopoly on talent

❑ **en exclusivité ADV 1** *Com* exclusively; **ce modèle se trouve en e. chez...** this model is exclusive to *or* can only be found at...; **chemises Verpé en e. chez Flakk** Flakk, sole authorized distributor for Verpé shirts

2 *(diffusé, publié)* exclusively; **en e. sur notre chaîne** exclusively on our channel; **en e. dans 'le Figaro'** a 'Figaro' exclusive; **ses lettres ont été publiées en e. par le magazine 'Aujourd'hui'** his/her letters were published as an exclusive by 'Aujourd'hui' magazine

3 *Cin* **film en e.** movie on general release; **film en première e.** first showing

excommunication [ɛkskɔmynikasjɔ̃] **NF** *Rel* excommunication

excommunié, -e [ɛkskɔmynje] *Rel* **ADJ** excommunicated

NM,F excommunicated person, excommunicate

excommunier [9] [ɛkskɔmynje] **VT** *Rel* to excommunicate; **se faire e.** to be excommunicated

excoriation [ɛkskɔrjasjɔ̃] **NF** excoriation, scratch

excorier [9] [ɛkskɔrje] **VT** to excoriate, to scratch

ex-coupon [ɛkskupɔ̃] **ADV** *Bourse* ex coupon

excrément [ɛkskremɑ̃] **NM** excrement.

❑ **excréments NMPL** excrement, faeces

excrémenteux, -euse [ɛkskremɑ̃tø, -øz] **ADJ** *Vieilli* excremental

excrémentiel, -elle [ɛkskremɑ̃sjɛl] **ADJ** excremental

excréter [18] [ɛkskrete] **VT** to excrete

excréteur, -trice [ɛkskretœr, -tris] **ADJ** excretory

excrétion [ɛkskresjɔ̃] *Physiol* **NF** excretion

❑ **excrétions NFPL** *(substance)* excreta

excrétoire [ɛkskretwar] **ADJ** excretory

excrétrice [ɛkskretris] *voir* **excréteur**

excroissance [ɛkskrwasɑ̃s] **NF 1** *Méd* growth, *Spéc* excrescence **2** *Fig* excrescence

excursion [ɛkskyrsjɔ̃] **NF 1** *(voyage → en car)* excursion, trip; *(→ à pied)* ramble, hike; *(→ à bicyclette)* ride, tour; *(→ en voiture)* drive; *(→ lors d'une escale)* shore excursion, trip ashore; **faire une e., partir en e.** *(avec un véhicule)* to go on an excursion; *(à pied)* to go on *or* for a hike; **une e. dans le pays des vins** a tour of the vineyards; **e. d'un jour** day trip; **excursions de deux jours au pays de Galles** two-day tours *or* trips to Wales; **e. en car** coach trip; **e. en mer** boat trip; **e. en montagne** hill walk

2 *(sortie → scolaire)* outing, trip; **l'e. annuelle de l'école** the annual school outing *or* trip

excursionner [3] [ɛkskyrsjɔne] **VI** *(faire une excursion en car)* to go on an excursion *or* trip; *(→ à pied)* to go hiking *or* walking; *(faire des excursions)* to go touring

excursionniste [ɛkskyrsjɔnist] **NMF 1** *(en car, en bateau) Br* holiday-maker, *Am* vacationer; *(d'un jour)* day-tripper **2** *(randonneur)* hiker, rambler

excusable [ɛkskyzabl] **ADJ** excusable, forgivable; **tu n'es pas e.** you have no excuse; **ce n'est absolument pas e.** it's absolutely inexcusable *or* unforgivable; **allons, c'est e.!** come on, it's understandable!

excuse [ɛkskyz] **NF 1** *(motif allégué)* excuse, pretext; **j'étais fatigué – ce n'est pas une e.!** I was tired – that's no excuse!; **il a toujours une bonne e. pour ne pas téléphoner** he always has a good excuse for not phoning; **tu n'as aucune e.** you have no excuse; **sa conduite est sans e.** his/her behaviour is inexcusable, there's no excuse for his/her behaviour; **elle a donné pour e. le manque d'argent** she used lack of money as an excuse; **trouver une e. à qch/pour faire qch** to find an excuse for sth/for doing sth; **je ne trouve pas d'e. à votre retard** I can see no valid reason for your being late; **trouver des excuses à qn** to find excuses for *or* to excuse sb; *Ironique* **la belle e.!** what an *or* that's some excuse!; *Fam* **faites e.!** *(regrets)* I do apologize!; *(objection)* excuse me!; **mot d'e.** absence note

2 *Jur* **e. absolutoire** excuse involving acquittal; **excuses atténuantes** statutory extenuating circumstances; **e. légale** legal excuse

3 *(au tarot)* excuse

❑ **excuses NFPL** apology; **exiger des excuses** to demand an apology; **j'exige des excuses publiques** I want a public apology; **faire** *ou* **présenter ses excuses à qn** to offer one's apologies *or* to apologize to sb; **je vous fais mes plus plates excuses** *ou* **mes excuses les plus plates** you have my humble apologies; **tu me dois des excuses** you owe me an apology; **lettre d'excuses** letter of apology; **mille excuses!** *(dans une conversation)* I'm so sorry!; *(dans une lettre)* please accept my apologies!

excuser [3] [ɛkskyze] **VT 1** *(pardonner → conduite)* to excuse, to forgive; *(→ personne)* to forgive; **excusez ma curiosité mais...** excuse *or* forgive my curiosity but...; **excusez mon indiscrétion mais...** excuse my *or* forgive me for being indiscreet but...; **excuse-moi d'appeler si tard** forgive me *or* I do apologize for phoning so late; **excuse-moi de te déranger** I'm sorry to disturb you, excuse me for disturbing you; **excuse-moi de ne pas t'avoir téléphoné** I'm sorry I didn't phone you; **excusez-moi de vous le faire remarquer** excuse me for saying so, I hope you don't mind my mentioning it; **excusez-moi** *(regret)* forgive me, I'm sorry, I do apologize; *(interpellation, objection, après un hoquet)* excuse me; **oh, excusez-moi, je vous ai fait mal?** oh, sorry, did I hurt you?; **excusez-moi mais je suis pressé** excuse me *or* I'm sorry but I'm in a hurry; **je vous prie de** *ou* **veuillez m'e.** I (do) beg your pardon, I do apologize; **tu es tout excusé** you're forgiven, please don't apologize; *Ironique* **excusez du peu!** would you believe!, if you please!

2 *(justifier → attitude, personne)* to excuse, to find excuses *or* an excuse for; **tu l'excuses toujours!** you're always finding excuses for him/her!; **e. qn auprès de qn** to apologize for sb to sb; **l'ignorance n'excuse rien** ignorance is no excuse; **sa grossièreté ne peut être excusée** his/her rudeness is inexcusable, there is no excuse for his/her rudeness

3 *(accepter l'absence de)* to excuse; **se faire e.** to ask to be excused; **liste des présents, absents, excusés** list of those present, those absent and those from whom apologies have been received; **e. un juré** to excuse a juror (from attendance)

4 *(présenter les excuses de)* **excuse-moi auprès de lui** apologize to him for me

►**s'excuser VPR 1** *(demander pardon)* to apologize; **ne vous excusez pas** (please) don't apologize; *Ironique* **surtout ne t'excuse pas!** an apology wouldn't go amiss!; **tu pourrais t'e.!** it wouldn't hurt you to say sorry!; **s'e. auprès de qn** to apologize to sb; **s'e. de qch/de faire qch** to apologize for sth/for doing sth; **je m'excuse de mon retard/de vous interrompre** sorry for being late/for interrupting you; *Fam* **je m'excuse!** sorry!, excuse me!; *Prov* **qui s'excuse, s'accuse** he who excuses himself accuses himself

2 *(ton indigné)* **je m'excuse (mais...)!** excuse me *or* I'm sorry (but...)!; **je m'excuse mais je n'ai jamais dit ça!** excuse me but I never said that!

ex-dividende [ɛksdividɑ̃d] **ADV** *Fin* ex dividend

ex-droit [ɛksdrwa] **ADV** *Bourse* ex rights

exeat [egzeat] **NM INV** *Rel & Vieilli (permission)* exeat

exécrable [ɛgzekrabl] **ADJ 1** *(mauvais → dîner, goût, spectacle)* abysmal, awful, foul; *(→ temps)* awful, rotten, wretched; *(→ travail)* abysmal; **il est d'une humeur e. aujourd'hui** he's in a foul *or* filthy mood today; **avoir un caractère e.** to be foul-tempered; **elle a été e. avec moi** she was horrible to me **2** *(crime)* heinous

exécrablement [ɛgzekrabləmɑ̃] **ADV** abominably, abysmally

exécration [ɛgzekrasjɔ̃] **NF 1** *Littéraire (dégoût, horreur)* execration; **avoir qch en e.** to loathe *or* to abhor sth **2** *Arch (malédiction)* curse

exécrer [18] [ɛgzekre] **VT** *Littéraire* to loathe, to abhor

exécutable [ɛgzekytabl] **ADJ 1** *(réalisable)* possible, feasible; **être facilement/difficilement e.** to be easy/difficult to do; **ce n'est pas e. en trois jours** it can't possibly be done in three days **2** *Ordinat (programme)* executable

exécutant, -e [ɛgzekytɑ̃, -ɑ̃t] **NM,F 1** *(musicien)* performer **2** *Péj (subalterne)* subordinate, underling; **je ne suis qu'un simple e.** I only carry out orders; **il a commandité l'assassinat, mais ce n'est pas lui l'e.** he ordered the murder but did not carry it out

exécuter [3] [ɛgzekyte] **VT 1** *(mouvement, cabriole)* to do, to execute; **e. une manœuvre compliquée** *(en voiture)* to go through *or* to execute a complicated manoeuvre

2 *(confectionner → maquette, statue)* to make; *(→ tableau)* to paint; *(→ décor)* to produce, to execute

3 *(interpréter → symphonie)* to perform, to play; *(→ chorégraphie)* to perform, to dance

4 *(mener à bien → consigne, ordre, mission, plan)* to carry out, to execute; *(→ projet)* to carry out; **e. un projet jusqu'au bout** to see a project through to the end

5 *(commande)* to carry out

6 *(tuer → condamné)* to execute, to put to death; *(→ victime)* to execute, to kill

7 *Fam (vaincre → joueur)* to slaughter, to trounce; **elle s'est fait e. en 2 sets 6–1/6–0** she was disposed of in straight sets 6–1/6–0

8 *Fam (critiquer)* to pan, *Br* to slate; **à chaque fois qu'il ouvrait la bouche, il était exécuté** every time he opened his mouth, he was torn to pieces

9 *Jur (testament)* to execute; *(contrat)* to fulfil the terms of, to perform; *(arrêt, jugement, traité)* to enforce; *(débiteur)* to distrain upon

10 *Ordinat (programme)* to run; *(commande)* to execute, to carry out

11 *Bourse (spéculateur)* to hammer; *(client)* to sell out against

►**s'exécuter VPR** to comply, to do what one is told; **je lui demandai de sortir, il s'exécuta de mauvaise grâce** I asked him to go out, he did so *or* complied reluctantly; **il faudra bien vous e.** you'll have to bring yourself to do it

exécuteur, -trice [ɛgzekytœr, -tris] **NM,F 1** *Jur (d'un jugement)* enforcer; **e. testamentaire** executor; **exécutrice testamentaire** executrix **2** *Vieilli (d'un plan, d'une tâche)* executant

NM *Hist* **e. des hautes œuvres** executioner; *Hum* axeman; **e. des basses œuvres** henchman

exécutif, -ive [ɛgzekytif, -iv] **ADJ** executive; **le pouvoir e.** the executive (branch)

NM l'e. the executive

exécution [ɛgzekysjɔ̃] **NF 1** *(d'une maquette, d'une statue)* execution, making; *(d'un tableau)* execution, painting

2 *(d'une symphonie, d'une chorégraphie)* performance, performing; **difficultés d'e. d'un morceau de musique** difficulties in the execution of a piece of music; **droit d'e.** performing rights

3 *(d'une menace, d'un ordre, d'une décision)* carrying out; *(d'un projet)* execution; *(d'une promesse)* fulfilment; **mettre qch à e.** to carry sth out; **mettre un projet à e.** to put a plan into execution *or* operation, to carry out a plan; **travaux en voie d'e.** work in progress; *Mil* **e.!** at the double!; *Hum* **va ranger ta chambre, e.!** go and tidy your bedroom, NOW *or* on the double!

4 *(d'une commande)* carrying out

5 *(d'un condamné)* **e. (capitale)** execution; **ordre d'e.** death warrant

6 *Jur (d'un jugement, d'un traité)* enforcement;

(d'un débiteur) distraint (**de** upon); *(d'un contrat)* fulfilment, performance; **e. forcée** specific performance; **e. sur minute** = enforcement upon production of original document; **e. en nature** specific performance; **e. provisoire** provisional enforcement

7 *Bourse (d'un spéculateur)* hammering; **e. au prix du marché** execution at market

8 *Ordinat (d'un programme)* execution, running; *(d'une commande)* execution, carrying out

exécutive [ɛgzekytiv] *voir* **exécutif**

exécutoire [ɛgzekytwar] *Jur* **ADJ** *(jugement)* enforceable; **formule e.** executory formula; **mesure e.** binding measure; **titre e.** writ of execution

NM writ of execution

exécutoirement [ɛgzekytwarmɑ̃] **ADV** enforceably, effectively

exécutrice [ɛgzekytris] *voir* **exécuteur**

exèdre [ɛgzɛdr] **NF** *Antiq (salle, banc)* exedra, exhedra

exégèse [ɛgzeʒɛz] **NF** *Littérature* exegesis; **faire l'e. de** to write a critical interpretation of

exégète [ɛgzeʒɛt] **NMF** *Littérature* exegete

exégétique [ɛgzeʒetik] **ADJ** exegetical

exemplaire[1] [ɛgzɑ̃plɛr] **ADJ 1** *(qui donne l'exemple → conduite)* exemplary, perfect; *(→ personne)* exemplary, model; **d'une correction e.** perfectly correct

2 *(qui sert d'exemple → punition)* exemplary

exemplaire[2] [ɛgzɑ̃plɛr] **NM 1** *(d'un document)* copy; **e. gratuit** presentation copy; **en deux exemplaires** in duplicate; **en trois exemplaires** in triplicate; **photocopier un texte en 20 exemplaires** to make 20 photocopies of a text; **le contrat est fait en quatre exemplaires** there are four copies of the contract; **le livre a été tiré à 10 000 exemplaires** 10,000 copies of the book were published; **le journal tire à 150 000 exemplaires** the newspaper has a circulation of 150,000

2 *(d'un coquillage, d'une plante)* specimen, example

exemplairement [ɛgzɑ̃plɛrmɑ̃] **ADV** exemplarily; **elle a vécu e.** she led an exemplary life; **il a été puni e.** he was punished as an example to others

exemplarité [ɛgzɑ̃plarite] **NF** *Littéraire* exemplariness, exemplarity

exemplatif, -ive [ɛgzɑ̃platif, -iv] **ADJ** *Belg* **1** *(caractéristique)* typical **2 à titre e.** by way of an example, as an example

exemple [ɛgzɑ̃pl] **NM 1** *(d'architecture, d'un défaut, d'une qualité)* example; *(d'une situation)* example, instance; **donner qch en** *ou* **comme e.** to give sth as an example; **citer qn/qch en e.** to quote sb/sth as an example; **un bel e. de poterie égyptienne** a fine example of Egyptian pottery; **c'est un bel e. de coopération** that's a fine example *or* instance of cooperation

2 *(modèle)* example, model; **elle est l'e. de la parfaite secrétaire** she's a model secretary; **il est l'e. type du yuppie** he's a typical yuppie; **il est l'e. même du type qui ne sait pas ce qu'il veut** he's the perfect example of someone who doesn't know what he wants; **être l'e. même de la bêtise** to be stupidity itself *or* personified; **c'est l'e. même de la générosité** he's/she's the epitome of generosity; **donner l'e. (à qn)** to set an example (to sb); **faire un e.** to make an example; **prendre e. sur qn, prendre qn pour** *ou* **comme e.** to take sb as a model *or* an example, to model oneself on sb; **citer qn en e.** to hold sb up as an example; **servir d'e.** *(personne)* to be taken as an example; **servir d'e. à qn** *(réussite)* to be an example to sb; *(punition)* to be a lesson *or* a warning to sb; **que cela vous serve d'e.** let this be a warning to you; **suivre l'e. de qn** to follow sb's example, to take one's cue from sb; **la France a dit non et d'autres pays ont suivi son e.** France said no and other countries followed suit; **ne suivez pas le mauvais e. de vos prédécesseurs** don't follow the bad example set by your predecessors

3 *Gram & Ling (illustration d'une règle)* (illustrative) example; **donnez-moi des exemples à l'impératif** give me examples in the imperative; *Fam* **j'en connais plein: e., ma mère** I know lots: my mother, for example *or* for instance

❑ **à l'exemple de PRÉP à l'e. de son maître** following his master's example; **il couchait par terre, à l'e. de ses soldats** he slept on the bare earth, just like his soldiers

❑ **par exemple ADV 1** *(comme illustration)* for example *or* instance; **un de ces jours, par e. dimanche** one of these days, say *or* for example *or* for instance on Sunday

2 *(marque la surprise, l'indignation)* **(ça) par e., c'est Pierre!** Pierre! well I never!; **ça par e., le verre a disparu!** well, well, well, the glass has disappeared!; **ah non, par e.!** I should think not!

❑ **pour l'exemple ADV fusillé pour l'e.** shot as an example (to others)

❑ **sans exemple ADJ** unprecedented; **être d'une gentillesse/d'un égoïsme sans e.** to be of unparalleled kindness/selfishness

exemplification [ɛgzɑ̃plifikasjɔ̃] **NF** exemplification, exemplifying

exemplifier [9] [ɛgzɑ̃plifje] **VT** to exemplify

exempt, -e [ɛgzɑ̃, -ɑ̃t] **ADJ 1** *(dispensé)* **e. de** *(d'une obligation)* exempt from; **e. d'impôts** tax-exempt, exempt from tax; **produits exempts de taxes** duty-free *or* non dutiable goods; **e. de port** carriage free; **e. de droits (de douane)** free of duty, duty-free, non-dutiable; **e. de TVA** zero-rated

2 *(dépourvu)* **e. de danger** danger-free; **e. d'erreur** faultless; **son attitude n'était pas exempte d'un certain mépris** his/her attitude wasn't without contempt, there was a touch of contempt in his/her attitude; **sa remarque n'était pas exempte d'une certaine amertume** his/her remark was not without a trace of bitterness

NM *Hist* exempt

NM,F *(personne)* **les exempts d'éducation physique** pupils exempted from physical education

exempté, -e [ɛgzɑ̃te] **ADJ e. du service militaire** exempt from military service; **e. de corvée** exempt from duty

NM man exempt from military service

exempter [3] [ɛgzɑ̃te] **VT il a été exempté du service militaire** he has been exempted from doing military service; **il a réussi à se faire e. du service militaire** he managed to get out of military service; **e. un élève d'éducation physique** to exempt a pupil from physical education; **e. qn d'impôts** to exempt sb from taxes; **e. qn d'une obligation** to exempt sb from an obligation; **cette vie tranquille l'exemptait de tout souci** this quiet life freed him/her from all worries; **e. qn de faire qch** to exempt *or* to excuse sb from doing sth

▶**s'exempter VPR s'e. de qch/de faire qch** to get out of sth/of doing sth

exemption [ɛgzɑ̃psjɔ̃] **NF 1** *(dispense)* exemption (**de** from); **bénéficier de l'e. d'une taxe** to be exempt from a tax; **e. d'impôts, e. fiscale** tax exemption; **liste d'exemptions** *(de la douane)* free list **2** *Mil* exemption from military service **3** *Jur* **e. catégorielle** block exemption; **e. de peine** exemption from penalty

exequatur [ɛgzekwatyr] **NM INV** *Jur* **1** *(rendant exécutoire un jugement)* = proceedings to enforce a foreign judgement or an arbitrator's award **2** *(reconnaissant un consul)* (consul's) exequatur

exerçable [ɛgzɛrsabl] **ADJ** *Bourse (option)* exerciseable

exercé, -e [ɛgzɛrse] **ADJ** *(oreille, œil)* trained, keen; *(main)* practised; *(personne)* trained, experienced

exercer [16] [ɛgzɛrse] **VT 1** *(pratiquer → talent)* to exercise; *(→ profession)* to exercise; *(→ art)* to practise; **quel métier exercez-vous?** what's your job?; **e. le métier de dentiste/forgeron** to work as a dentist/blacksmith, to be a dentist by profession/a blacksmith by trade; **e. la médecine** to practise medicine; **e. des fonctions** to carry out duties; **il exerce ses talents en tant qu'avocat** he works as a lawyer

2 *(autorité, influence)* to exercise, to exert; *(droit, privilège)* to exercise; *(sanctions)* to carry out; **e. une action sur** to act on; **e. un attrait sur qn** *(sujet: personne)* to be attractive to *or* to attract sb; *(sujet: art, voyages)* to appeal *or* to be appealing to sb; **e. un contrôle sur** to control; **e. une influence sur** to exercise *or* to exert an influence on; **e. une pression sur qch** to press sth, to exert pressure on sth; **e. une pression sur qn** to put pressure on *or* to pressurize sb; **e. des sanctions contre** to carry out sanctions against; **e. des poursuites contre qn** to bring an action against sb, to take legal action against sb; **e. sa verve contre qn** to make sb the object of one's wit

3 *(entraîner → oreille, esprit, mémoire, corps)* to train, to exercise; **e. qn à faire qch** to train sb to do sth; **e. un chien à attaquer** *ou* **à l'attaque** to train a dog to attack; **e. son esprit à l'art de la rhétorique** to train one's mind in the art of rhetoric

4 *Littéraire (mettre à l'épreuve → patience)* to try (sorely)

5 *Bourse (option)* to exercise

USAGE ABSOLU *(sujet: dentiste, avocat, médecin)* to be in practice, to practise; **elle n'exerce plus** she doesn't practise any more

▶**s'exercer VPR 1** *(s'entraîner)* to practise; **s'e. à qch/à faire qch** to practise sth/doing sth; **s'e. au piano** to practise (playing) the piano

2 *(se manifester → autorité, pouvoir)* to make itself felt; **sa mauvaise foi s'exerce aussi contre ses proches** his/her close relations also feel the effects of his/her dishonesty

3 *(s'appliquer)* **s'e. sur** *(sujet: force, pression)* to be brought to bear on, to be exerted on; **l'attrait qui s'exerçait sur moi** the attraction I was feeling

exercice [ɛgzɛrsis] **NM 1** *(mouvement physique)* exercise; **exercices d'assouplissement/d'échauffement** stretching/warm-up exercises; **exercices respiratoires** (deep) breathing exercises; **exercices au sol** floor exercises; **c'est un excellent e. pour les pectoraux** it's an excellent exercise for the pectoral muscles; **faire des exercices** to exercise; **faire des exercices pour les abdominaux** to do exercises for *or* to exercise one's stomach muscles

2 *(sport)* **l'e. (physique)** (physical) exercise; **e. d'application** application *or* practice exercise; **faire** *ou* **prendre de l'e.** to take exercise, to exercise; **tu devrais faire plus d'e.** you should exercise more *or* take more exercise; **je manque d'e.** I don't take enough exercise; **faire des exercices au sol** to do floor exercises

3 *(pour l'apprentissage) & Scol* exercise; **faire un e.** to do an exercise; **e. de chimie** chemistry exercise; **exercices de grammaire/phonétique** grammar/phonetics exercises; **faire faire des exercices de grammaire/prononciation à qn** to give sb exercises in grammar/pronunciation; **faire des exercices au piano** to do (some) piano exercises; *Littérature* **e. de style** stylistic composition; *Fig* **son dernier recueil est un e. de style** his/her latest collection is an exercise in style; **e. d'évacuation en cas d'incendie** fire drill

4 *Mil* drill, exercise; **e. à la cible** target practice; **exercices de tir** shooting drill *or* practice; **faire l'e.** to drill

5 *(usage)* **l'e. du pouvoir/d'un droit** exercising power/a right; **l'e. de responsabilités** carrying out responsibilities; **dans l'e. de ses fonctions** in the exercise of one's duties

6 *(d'une profession)* practice; **l'e. d'un métier** plying a trade; **l'e. du métier d'avocat ne l'attirait guère** he/she wasn't keen on being a lawyer, the idea of being a lawyer didn't really appeal to him/her; **il prend sa retraite après 30 ans d'e.** *(dentiste, médecin, avocat)* he is retiring after 30 years in practice; *(fonctionnaire, enseignant)* he's retiring after 30 years in the profession; **être condamné pour e. illégal de la médecine** to be sentenced for practising medicine illegally

7 *Rel* **l'e. du culte** public worship

8 *Fin Br* financial year, *Am* fiscal year; **les impôts pour l'e. 2004** taxes for the 2004 fiscal *or* tax year; **fin de l'e.** end of the *Br* financial *or Am* fiscal year; **de fin d'e.** year-end; **en fin d'e.** at the end of the *Br* financial *or Am* fiscal year; **bilan en fin d'e.** end-of-year balance sheet; **e. bénéficiaire** profitable year; **e. budgétaire** budgetary year; **e. comptable** accounting year; **e. en cours** *Br* current financial year, *Am* current fiscal year; **e. écoulé** last *Br* financial *or Am* fiscal

exe–exi

year; **e. financier** *Br* financial *or Am* fiscal year; **e. fiscal** tax year

□ **à l'exercice** ADV *Mil* on parade

□ **en exercice** ADJ *(député, juge)* sitting; *(membre de comité)* serving; *(avocat, médecin)* practising; **être en e.** *(diplomate, magistrat)* to be in *or* to hold office; **le président en e.** the president in office

══════════════

'Exercices de style' *Queneau* 'Exercises in Style'

exerciseur [ɛgzɛrsisœr] NM *(gén)* exercise machine *or* bench; *(pour la poitrine)* chest expander

exérèse [ɛgzerɛz] NF *Méd* ablation

exergue [ɛgzɛrg] NM **1** *(au début d'un texte)* epigraph; *(sous une œuvre d'art)* inscription; **mettre une citation en e. à un** *ou* **d'un texte** to head a text with a quotation, to put in a quotation as an epigraph to a text; *Fig* **mettre un argument en e.** to underline *or* to stress an argument **2** *(sur une médaille → espace)* exergue; *(→ inscription)* epigraph

exfiltration [ɛksfiltrasjɔ̃] NF exfiltration

exfiltrer [3] [ɛksfiltre] VT to exfiltrate

exfoliant, -e [ɛksfɔljɑ̃, -ɑ̃t] ADJ exfoliating, exfoliative
   NM exfoliant

exfoliation [ɛksfɔljasjɔ̃] NF exfoliation, exfoliating *(UNCOUNT)*

exfolier [9] [ɛksfɔlje] VT *(arbre, ardoise, peau)* to exfoliate
   ▶**s'exfolier** VPR *(écorce, os, tendon)* to exfoliate, to scale off

exhalaison [ɛgzalɛzɔ̃] NF *(odeur → agréable)* fragrance, *Sout* exhalation; *(→ désagréable)* unpleasant odour, *Sout* exhalation; **les exhalaisons fétides des égouts** the fetid fumes from the sewers

exhalation [ɛgzalasjɔ̃] NF exhalation

exhaler [3] [ɛgzale] VT **1** *(dégager → parfum)* to exhale; *(→ gaz, effluves, vapeur)* to exhale, to give off; **les fromages qui séchaient exhalaient leur odeur sure** the drying cheeses gave off their sour smell
   2 *(émettre → soupir)* to breathe; *(→ gémissement)* to utter, *Littéraire* to give forth; *(→ chaleur)* to give off
   3 *Littéraire (être empreint de)* **la maison exhalait la mélancolie/le bonheur** the house exuded melancholy/radiated happiness
   4 *(en respirant)* to exhale
   ▶**s'exhaler** VPR *(odeur, vapeur)* to be given off, to waft **(de** from); *Fig (sensualité, autorité, force)* to emanate, to exude **(de** from)

exhaure [ɛgzɔr] NF *Mines* pumping (out), unwatering

exhaussement [ɛgzosmɑ̃] NM *Constr* raising

exhausser [3] [ɛgzose] VT *Constr (bâtiment, mur)* to raise; **le bâtiment a été exhaussé de deux étages** two floors were added to the building

exhausteur [ɛgzostœr] NM **1** *Tech* suction-pipe, aspirator **2 e. de goût** *ou* **de saveur** flavour enhancer

exhaustif, -ive [ɛgzostif, -iv] ADJ exhaustive

exhaustion [ɛgzostjɔ̃] NF **1** *Vieilli Tech* exhaust(ion) **2** *Math* **méthode d'e.** method of exhaustions

exhaustivement [ɛgzostivmɑ̃] ADV exhaustively

exhaustivité [ɛgzostivite] NF exhaustiveness

exhérédation [ɛgzeredasjɔ̃] NF *Jur* exheredation, disinheritance

exhéréder [18] [ɛgzerede] VT *Jur* to exheredate, to disinherit

exhiber [3] [ɛgzibe] VT **1** *Péj (afficher → décorations, muscles)* to display, to show off; *(→ richesses, savoir)* to show off, to flaunt **2** *(au cirque, à la foire)* to show, to exhibit **3** *(document officiel)* to produce, to show, to present
   ▶**s'exhiber** VPR *(parader)* to parade (around), to flaunt oneself; *(impudiquement)* to expose oneself

exhibition [ɛgzibisjɔ̃] NF **1** *Péj (comportement)* piece of provocative behaviour; **après cette e. ridicule, tu n'as plus qu'à t'excuser!** apologize for making such an absurd exhibition of yourself!
   2 *Péj (étalage)* display; *(de richesses, de savoir)*

flaunting, showing off; **une e. de pectoraux sur la plage** a display of muscular chests on the beach; *Jur* **e. sexuelle** indecent exposure
   3 *(compétition)* show; *(dans un concours)* showing; **e. de chiens de race** pedigree dog show; **e. de bétail** cattle show
   4 *(comme attraction)* exhibiting; **e. d'animaux de cirque** exhibiting circus animals
   5 *Sport* exhibition
   6 *(présentation → de documents)* presentation

exhibitionnisme [ɛgzibisjɔnism] NM exhibitionism

exhibitionniste [ɛgzibisjɔnist] ADJ exhibitionistic
   NMF exhibitionist

exhibo [ɛgzibo] NMF *Fam (abrév* **exhibitionniste***)* exhibitionist

exhilarant [ɛgzilarɑ̃] NM *Pharm* exhilarant

exhortation [ɛgzɔrtasjɔ̃] NF exhortation; **la foule, excitée par ses exhortations** the crowd, excited by his/her exhortations; **e. à** call for; **exhortations à la modération** calls for moderation

exhorter [3] [ɛgzɔrte] VT to urge; **e. qn à la patience** to urge *or* to exhort sb to be patient; **e. qn à la prudence** to urge *or* to exhort sb to be careful; **e. qn à faire qch** to exhort *or* to urge sb to do sth
   ▶**s'exhorter** VPR **s'e. à faire qch** to exhort oneself to do sth; **elle s'exhortait à la patience** she was exhorting herself to be patient

exhumation [ɛgzymasjɔ̃] NF **1** *(d'un cadavre)* exhumation; *(d'objets enfouis)* excavation, digging out **2** *Fig (de sentiments)* resurrection; *(de vieux documents)* unearthing

exhumer [3] [ɛgzyme] VT **1** *(déterrer → cadavre)* to exhume; *(→ objets enfouis)* to excavate, to dig out **2** *(sentiments)* to resurrect; *(vieux documents)* to unearth, to rescue from oblivion

exigeant, -e [ɛgziʒɑ̃, -ɑ̃t] ADJ **1** *(pointilleux → maître, professeur)* demanding, exacting; *(→ malade)* demanding; *(→ client)* demanding, particular, hard to please; **je suis très e. sur la qualité** I'm very particular about quality; **tu es trop exigeant avec tes amis** you ask too much of *or* expect too much from your friends; **être e. envers soi-même** to demand a lot of *or* to set high standards for oneself
   2 *(revendicateur)* **ne sois pas trop e., c'est ton premier emploi** don't be too demanding *or* don't expect too much, it's your first job; *Ironique* **je ne suis pas e.: je demande juste la fortune et la célébrité!** I don't want much: just fame and fortune!
   3 *(ardu → métier, travail)* demanding, exacting

exigence [ɛgziʒɑ̃s] NF **1** *(demande → d'un client)* requirement; *(→ d'un ravisseur)* demand; **satisfaire aux exigences de ses clients** to meet one's customers' requirements
   2 *(nécessité)* demand, requirement; **répondre aux exigences de qualité/sécurité** to meet quality/safety requirements; **les exigences de ma profession** the demands *or* requirements of my profession; **les exigences de la morale/du savoir-vivre** the demands of morality/of mannerliness; **l'e.** *ou* **les exigences de l'étiquette** the demands of etiquette
   3 *(caractère exigeant → d'un client)* particularity; *(→ d'un professeur, d'un parent)* strictness; **devant l'e. de son client** faced with such a demanding customer; **elle est d'une e. insupportable** she's intolerably demanding
   □ **exigences** NFPL *(salaire)* expected salary; **quelles sont vos exigences?** what salary do you expect?; **en donnant vos nom, adresse et exigences** stating your name, address and expected salary

exiger [17] [ɛgziʒe] VT **1** *(compensation, dû)* to demand, to claim; **j'exige réparation** I demand redress; **j'exige d'être payé immédiatement** I demand to be paid *or* I insist on being paid immediately, I demand *or* insist on immediate payment
   2 *(excuse, silence)* to require, to demand, to insist on; *(rançon)* to demand; **e. la plus grande honnêteté de la part de qn** to insist on scrupulous honesty from sb; **e. beaucoup/trop de qn** to expect a lot/too much from sb; **j'exige des excuses/que vous vous excusiez** I demand an apology/that you apologize

   3 *(déclarer obligatoire)* to require; **la connaissance du russe n'est pas exigée** knowledge of Russian is not a requirement; **le port du casque est exigé** hard hats must be worn; **aucun visa n'est exigé** no visa is needed; **e. qu'une chose soit faite** to insist on a thing being done, to demand that a thing be done
   4 *(nécessiter)* to require, to need; **un métier qui exige beaucoup de précision** a job requiring great accuracy; **un bateau exige beaucoup d'entretien** a boat needs *or* requires a lot of maintenance; **le poste exige beaucoup de déplacements** the post involves a lot of travelling; **nous interviendrons si la situation l'exige** we'll intervene if it becomes necessary *or* if the situation demands it; **prendre les mesures qu'exigent les circonstances** to take the necessary measures

exigibilité [ɛgziʒibilite] *Fin* NF payability; **date d'e.** due date; **e. de taxe** tax liability; **e. immédiate** immediately due
   □ **exigibilités** NFPL current liabilities

exigible [ɛgziʒibl] ADJ *(impôt)* due (for payment), payable; **cet impôt est e. en septembre** payment of this tax is due in September; **le paiement est e. dès réception de la facture** payment is due upon receipt of the invoice; **e. à vue** payable at sight

exigu, -ë [ɛgzigy] ADJ **1** *(appartement, pièce)* very small, tiny; *(couloir)* very narrow; **c'est un peu e. pour ma famille** it's a bit cramped *or* small for my family **2** *Vieilli (somme)* meagre, slender

exiguïté [ɛgzigɥite] NF **1** *(d'une pièce)* smallness; *(d'un couloir)* narrowness **2** *Vieilli (d'une somme)* meagreness

exil [ɛgzil] NM exile; **après plusieurs années d'e.** after several years in exile; **pendant son e. londonien** while he/she was living in exile in London; **terre e.** place of exile
   □ **en exil** ADJ exiled ADV *(vivre)* in exile; **envoyer qn en e.** to exile sb; **je me sens en e.** I feel like an exile

══════════════

'L'Exil et le royaume' *Camus* 'Exile and the Kingdom'

exilé, -e [ɛgzile] ADJ exiled
   NM,F exile

exiler [3] [ɛgzile] VT to exile **(de** from); *(d'une ville, de la cour)* to banish **(de** from); **le dictateur a fait e. tous les opposants au régime** the dictator had all the opponents of the regime sent into exile; *Fig* **on l'a exilé à l'autre bout de la classe** he was banished *or* exiled to the other end of the classroom
   ▶**s'exiler** VPR **1** *(quitter son pays)* to go into self-imposed exile; **s'e. à l'autre bout du monde** to go into self-imposed exile on the other side of the world **2** *(s'isoler)* to cut oneself off; **il s'est exilé à la campagne pour terminer son livre** he withdrew to the country to finish his book; **s'e. de la ville** to cut oneself off from the town

exinscrit, -e [ɛgzɛ̃skri, -it] ADJ *Géom* escribed (**à** in)

existant, -e [ɛgzistɑ̃, -ɑ̃t] ADJ *(modèle, loi, tarif)* existing, current, currently in existence
   NM *Com* **e. en caisse/en magasin** cash/stock in hand

existence [ɛgzistɑ̃s] NF **1** *(vie)* life, existence; **j'aurai travaillé toute mon e. pour rien** I'll have worked all my life *or* days for nothing; **que d'existences misérables!** so many wretched lives!; **dans l'e.** in life
   2 *(mode de vie)* lifestyle; **j'en ai assez de cette e.** I've had enough of this (kind of) life; **mener une e. tranquille** to lead a quiet existence *or* life
   3 *(durée → d'une constitution, d'une civilisation)* lifespan, lifetime; **il est improbable que ce gouvernement puisse dépasser un an d'e.** it's unlikely that this government can stay in existence for longer than a year
   4 *(réalité → d'un complot)* existence **(de** of); *(→ d'une substance)* presence, existence **(de** of)
   5 *(présence → d'une personne)* presence; **manifester** *ou* **signaler son e.** to make one's presence known
   6 *Phil (être)* existence, (state of) being
   7 *Compta* **existences en caisse** cash in hand

existentialisme [ɛgzistɑ̃sjalism] NM *Phil* existentialism

L'EXISTENTIALISME

Existentialism, whose main proponent was Jean-Paul Sartre (1905–1980), is the philosophy according to which existence precedes essence, so that human beings are free to choose what they are and have total responsibility for that choice. It became a fashion, especially for young people, in the years following the Second World War, offering freedom in their ideas and way of life, expressed notably in the cafés and nightclubs of Saint-Germain-des-Prés.

existentialiste [ɛgzistɑ̃sjalist] ADJ & NMF *Phil* existentialist

existentiel, -elle [ɛgzistɑ̃sjɛl] ADJ *Phil* existential

exister [3] [ɛgziste] VI 1 (*être réel*) to exist, to be real; **le père Noël n'existe pas!** Father Christmas doesn't exist!; **les roses noires, ça n'existe pas** there is no such thing as a black rose, black roses don't exist; **pour elle, l'amour/le danger, ça n'existe pas** love/danger doesn't exist for her; **ce personnage a bien existé, il vivait au XVIIème siècle** this character is real *or* did exist, he lived in the 17th century; *Fam* **le savon, ça existe!** there is such a thing as soap, you know!; *Hum* **si elle n'existait pas, il faudrait l'inventer!** if she didn't exist, we'd have to invent her!, what would we do without her!; **l'amour existe, je l'ai rencontré** love really does exist!

2 (*subsister*) to exist; **l'hôtel existe toujours/n'existe plus** the hotel is still there/isn't there anymore; **les vieilles pratiques religieuses qui existent toujours au village** the old religious practices still extant *or* which still exist in the village; **la galanterie, ça n'existe plus** (the age of) chivalry is dead

3 (*être important*) to matter; **seul son métier existe pour lui** his job's the only thing that matters to him; **il n'y a pas que l'argent qui existe!** money isn't everything (in life)!

4 (*vivre → personne*) to live; **tant que j'existerai** as long as I live; **fais comme si je n'existais pas** pretend I'm not here

5 (*article*) to be available; **ce modèle existe aussi en cuir/en rouge** this model is also available in leather/red

6 (*tournure impersonnelle*) **il existe** (*suivi d'un singulier*) there is, there's; (*suivi d'un pluriel*) there are; **il n'existe aucune directive à ce sujet** there are no guidelines for that; **il n'existe pas de meilleure explication** there is no better explanation; **il existe des appareils pour dénoyauter les fruits** there are machines for taking stones out of fruit; **existe-t-il une vie sur Mars?** does life exist on Mars?, is there life on Mars?

Si Dieu n'existait pas, il faudrait l'inventer

One of Voltaire's most familiar "bons mots", this phrase (meaning "If God didn't exist, we would have to invent Him") comes from the *Épître sur les trois imposteurs* of 1768. In modern French, as indeed in English, the formula is simply used when speaking of something that we find indispensable or that we love (for example, beer or the Internet).

exit [ɛgzit] ADV *Théât* exit; **e. les gardes** exit *or* *Sout* exeunt the guards; *Fig* **e. le Président** out goes the President; *Fig Hum* **e. les petits week-ends à Deauville!** no more weekend breaks in Deauville!, that's the end of the weekend breaks in Deauville!

ex-libris [ɛkslibris] NM INV ex-libris

ex navire [ɛksnavir] *Com* ADJ ex-ship
    ADV ex-ship

ex nihilo [ɛksniilo] ADV out of *or* from nothing, ex nihilo

exo [ɛgzo] NM *Fam* (*abrév* **exercice**) exercise ∎

exobiologie [ɛgzɔbjɔlɔʒi] NF exobiology

exobiologiste [ɛgzɔbjɔlɔʒist] NMF exobiologist

Exocet® [ɛgzɔsɛt] NM (*missile*) Exocet

exocet [ɛgzɔsɛt] NM *Ich* flying fish

exocrine [ɛgzɔkrin] ADJ *Physiol* exocrine

exode [ɛgzɔd] NM 1 (*départ*) exodus; **l'e. des Parisiens en août** the annual exodus of Parisians from the capital in August; **l'e. des cerveaux** the brain drain; *Fin* **l'e. des capitaux** the flight of capital; **l'e. rural** = the movement of populations from rural to urban areas; *Hist* **l'e.** = the flight southward and westward of French civilians before the occupying German army in 1940 2 *Bible* **l'E.** the Exodus; **(le livre de) l'E.** (the book of) Exodus

exoderme [ɛgzɔdɛrm] NM *Biol & Bot* exoderm

exogame [ɛgzɔgam] ADJ exogamous, exogamic
    NMF exogamous subject

exogamie [ɛgzɔgami] NF exogamy

exogamique [ɛgzɔgamik] ADJ exogamous, exogamic

exogène [ɛgzɔʒɛn] ADJ (*gén*), *Biol & Géol* exogenous

exon [ɛgzɔ̃] NM *Biol* exon

exonder [3] [ɛgzɔ̃de] **s'exonder** VPR *Géog* to emerge

exonération [ɛgzɔnerasjɔ̃] NF exemption, exempting (UNCOUNT) (**de** from); *Théât* (*place offerte*) complimentary ticket; **e. fiscale** *ou* **d'impôt** tax exemption; **e. de TVA** exemption from VAT; **e. de responsabilité** exemption from liability

exonérer [18] [ɛgzɔnere] VT 1 (*contribuable, revenus*) to exempt; **e. qn d'impôts** to exempt sb from income tax; **être exonéré d'impôts** to be exempt from tax; **e. des marchandises de taxes** to exempt goods from import duty; **marchandises exonérées** non-dutiable freight; **intérêt: 12 pour cent, exonéré d'impôts** 12 percent interest rate, non-taxable *or* free of tax; **exonéré de TVA** VAT-exempt, zero-rated

2 (*dégager*) **e. qn de** (*obligation*) to free sb from; (*responsabilité*) to exonerate *or* to free sb from

exonucléase [ɛgzɔnykleaz] NF *Biol & Chim* exonuclease

exophtalmie [ɛgzɔftalmi] NF *Méd* exophthalmos, exophtalmus

exophtalmique [ɛgzɔftalmik] ADJ *Méd* exophthalmic

exoplanète [ɛgzoplanɛt] NF *Astron* exoplanet

exopodite [ɛgzɔpɔdit] NM *Zool* exopodite

exorbitant, -e [ɛgzɔrbitɑ̃, -ɑ̃t] ADJ 1 (*trop cher*) exorbitant, extortionate 2 (*démesuré → requête*) outrageous; (*→ prétention*) absurd

exorbité, -e [ɛgzɔrbite] ADJ bulging; **les yeux exorbités** with bulging eyes, *Hum* with his/her eyes out on stalks

exorcisation [ɛgzɔrsizasjɔ̃] NF exorcizing

exorciser [3] [ɛgzɔrsize] VT 1 (*personne, lieu*) to exorcize; (*démon*) to cast out, to exorcize; (*fantôme*) to exorcize, to lay 2 *Fig* (*ses peurs, ses démons*) to exorcize
    USAGE ABSOLU to exorcize

exorcisme [ɛgzɔrsism] NM exorcism

exorciste [ɛgzɔrsist] NM exorcist

exorde [ɛgzɔrd] NM *Littérature* exordium

exoréique [ɛgzɔreik] ADJ *Géog* exoreic, exorheic

exoréisme [ɛgzɔreism] NM *Géog* exoreism, exorheism

exosmose [ɛgzɔsmoz] NF *Phys* exosmosis

exosphère [ɛgzɔsfɛr] NF *Géog* exosphere

exospore [ɛgzɔspɔr] NM *Bot* exospore

exosquelette [ɛgzɔskəlɛt] NM *Zool* exoskeleton

exostose [ɛgzɔstoz] NF 1 *Méd* exostosis 2 *Bot* knur

exotérique [ɛgzɔterik] ADJ exoteric

exothermie [ɛgzɔtɛrmi] NF *Chim & Phys* exothermia

exothermique [ɛgzɔtɛrmik] ADJ *Chim & Phys* exothermic, exothermal

exotique [ɛgzɔtik] ADJ (*produit, fruit, pays*) exotic; **une collection d'objets exotiques** a collection of exotica; **poisson e.** tropical fish

exotisme [ɛgzɔtism] NM exoticism

exotoxine [ɛgzɔtɔksin] NF *Biol* exotoxin

exotropie [ɛgzɔtrɔpi] NF *Méd* exotropia

expansé, -e [ɛkspɑ̃se] ADJ (*polystyrène*) expanded

expansibilité [ɛkspɑ̃sibilite] NF expansibility

expansible [ɛkspɑ̃sibl] ADJ expansible, liable to expand

expansif, -ive [ɛkspɑ̃sif, -iv] ADJ 1 (*caractère,*

personne*) expansive, exuberant, effusive; **il n'est pas très e. he's never very communicative *or* forthcoming 2 *Phys* expansive

expansion [ɛkspɑ̃sjɔ̃] NF 1 *Écon* **e. (économique)** (economic) growth; **taux d'e. économique** economic growth rate; *Fin* **e. monétaire** currency expansion; *Presse* **l'E.** = French weekly business magazine

2 (*augmentation → d'un territoire, de l'univers*) expansion, expanding (UNCOUNT); **e. coloniale** colonial expansion

3 (*propagation → d'une idéologie, d'une influence*) spread

4 *Chim & Phys* expansion, expanding (UNCOUNT)

5 *Littéraire* (*épanchement*) expansiveness, effusiveness; **avoir un besoin d'e.** to need to open out (to others)
    ❑ **en expansion** ADJ (*univers*) expanding
    ❑ **en (pleine) expansion** ADJ *Écon* expanding, booming; **être en pleine e.** (*économie, entreprise*) to be booming

expansionnisme [ɛkspɑ̃sjɔnism] NM expansionism

expansionniste [ɛkspɑ̃sjɔnist] ADJ expansionist
    NMF expansionist

expansive [ɛkspɑ̃siv] *voir* **expansif**

expansivité [ɛkspɑ̃sivite] NF expansiveness

expatriation [ɛkspatrijasjɔ̃] NF expatriation; *Fin* **e. de capitaux** movement of capital abroad

expatrié, -e [ɛkspatrije] ADJ expatriate
    NMF expatriate

expatrier [10] [ɛkspatrije] VT (*personne*) to expatriate; (*capitaux*) to move abroad
    ►**s'expatrier** VPR to become an expatriate, to leave one's country (of origin)

expectant, -e [ɛkspɛktɑ̃, -ɑ̃t] ADJ *Littéraire* expectant; **politique expectante** wait-and-see policy

expectative [ɛkspɛktativ] NF (*attente → incertaine*) state of uncertainty; (*→ prudente*) cautious wait; (*→ pleine d'espoir*) expectancy, expectation
    ❑ **dans l'expectative** ADV **être dans l'e.** (*espérer*) to be in a state of expectation; (*être incertain*) to be in a state of uncertainty; **rester dans l'e.** to wait and see

expectorant [ɛkspɛktɔrɑ̃] NM *Méd* expectorant

expectoration [ɛkspɛktɔrasjɔ̃] NF *Méd* expectoration

expectorer [3] [ɛkspɛktɔre] *Méd* VT to expectorate
    VI to expectorate

expédient, -e [ɛkspedjɑ̃, -ɑ̃t] ADJ *Littéraire* expedient; **il est e. de prendre les devants** it is advisable to take the initiative; **il est e. que vous soyez à l'heure** it is expedient *or* advisable that you be on time
    NM 1 (*moyen*) expedient; **se tirer d'une difficulté par un e.** to find an expedient for getting out of a difficulty 2 (*locutions*) **vivre d'expédients** to live by one's wits; **user d'expédients** to resort to evasion

expédier [9] [ɛkspedje] VT 1 (*envoyer → colis, lettre*) to send, to dispatch; **e. par avion** to send by air mail; **e. par bateau** (*marchandises*) to send by sea, to ship; **e. par coursier** to send by courier; **e. par la poste** to send through the mail *or Br* post; **e. par le train** to send by train *or* rail; **e. par fret aérien** to airfreight

2 (*se débarrasser de → objet*) to get rid of, to dispose of; (*→ personne*) to get rid of; **les colporteurs qui sonnent ici sont vite expédiés!** any hawkers ringing my bell soon get sent packing!; **je vais l'e. en colonie de vacances** I'm going to send *or* pack him/her off to a summer camp; **il a tendance à e. ses patients un peu vite** he tends to pack his patients out of the surgery rather quickly; *Fam* **e. qn dans l'autre monde** *ou* **au cimetière** to send sb off to meet their maker

3 (*bâcler, finir sans soin → dissertation, lettre*) to dash off; (*→ corvée, travail*) to make short work of, to dispatch; (*→ tâche*) to deal promptly with; **elle a expédié le match en deux sets** she wrapped up the match in two sets

4 (*avaler vite → repas*) to dispatch, to swallow; (*→ verre de vin*) to knock back; **e. son déjeuner** to make short work of one's lunch

5 *Jur* (*contrat, acte*) to draw up

6 *(locution)* **e. les affaires courantes** *(employé)* to deal with day-to-day matters (only); *(président)* to be a caretaker president

expéditeur, -trice [ɛkspeditœr, -tris] **ADJ** *(bureau, compagnie, gare)* dispatching, forwarding

NM,F 1 *(d'un colis, d'une lettre)* sender, forwarder **2** *Com (de marchandises)* shipper, consigner; *(par bateau)* shipper

expéditif, -ive [ɛkspeditif, -iv] **ADJ 1** *(efficace et rapide → procédé)* expeditious, quick; *(→ personne)* expeditious, prompt; **elle est plutôt expéditive!** she certainly wastes no time! **2** *Péj (trop rapide → procès, justice)* hasty; **il a des méthodes expéditives** he rushes through things

expédition [ɛkspedisjɔ̃] **NF 1** *(voyage)* expedition; *(équipe)* (members of the) expedition; **e. en Antarctique** expedition to the Antarctic; **partir en e.** to go on an expedition; **pour traverser la capitale, quelle e.!** it's quite an expedition to get across the capital!; **à chaque fois qu'on part en pique-nique, c'est une véritable e.** *ou* **c'est toute une e.** every time we go on a picnic, it's a real expedition

2 *Mil* expedition

3 *(raid)* **e. punitive** punitive raid *or* expedition

4 *(envoi de marchandises)* dispatch; **e. par avion** airfreighting; **e. par bateau** *ou* **par mer** shipping, shipment; **e. par chemin de fer** sending by rail, railfreighting; **e. par courrier** mailing, *Br* posting; **e. de détail** retail shipment; **e. exclusive** exclusive shipment; **e. maritime** maritime shipment; **e. par la poste** mailing, *Br* posting; *Com* **e. partielle** part shipment *or* consignment; *Com* **e. port à port** port to port shipment; **bulletin d'e.** waybill; *Com* **expéditions** *(service)* dispatch department, shipping department

5 *(cargaison)* consignment, shipment; **une e. de bananes** a consignment of bananas

6 *Admin* **il est chargé de l'e. des affaires courantes** he is in charge of day-to-day matters; **je préfère m'occuper d'abord de l'e. des affaires courantes** I prefer to deal with *or* get rid of the day-to-day matters first

7 *Jur (de contrat, d'acte)* copy; **première e.** first authentic copy; **en double e.** in duplicate

expéditionnaire [ɛkspedisjɔnɛr] **ADJ** *Mil* expeditionary

NMF *Com* forwarding agent

expéditive [ɛkspeditiv] *voir* **expéditif**

expéditivement [ɛkspeditivmɑ̃] **ADV 1** *(rapidement)* expeditiously **2** *(à la hâte)* hastily

expéditrice [ɛkspeditris] *voir* **expéditeur**

expérience [ɛksperjɑ̃s] **NF 1** *(connaissance)* experience; **sa grande e. des hommes** his/her long experience of men; **avec l'e., tu sauras que…** you'll find out with experience that…; **avoir de l'e. (en)** to have experience *or* to be experienced (in); **avoir l'e. de qch** to have experience of sth, to be experienced in sth; **il a l'e. des enfants/de ce genre de voitures** he is used to children/this kind of car; **manquer d'e.** to be inexperienced, to lack experience; **il nous faut quelqu'un qui a de l'e.** we need someone with experience; **il avait peu d'e. en amour** he wasn't an experienced lover; **plusieurs années d'e. en gestion seraient souhaitables** several years' experience in management *or* management experience would be desirable

2 *(apprentissage)* experience; **ses expériences amoureuses** his/her sexual experiences; **ses premières expériences amoureuses** his/her first sexual experiences; **j'ai eu plusieurs expériences malheureuses avec ce mixer** I've had several bad experiences with this blender; **raconte-nous tes expériences praguoises** tell us about your experiences in Prague; **tenter une e. de vie commune** to try living together; **faire l'e. de la haine/douleur** to experience hatred/pain; **je n'ai pas encore fait l'e. de la vie à deux** I've never lived with anyone; **je ne voudrais pas refaire l'e. d'une opération** I wouldn't like to go through an operation again; **j'en ai malheureusement fait l'e.** that has been my experience unfortunately, as I've discovered to my cost

3 *(test)* experiment; **e. de chimie** chemistry experiment; **e. en laboratoire** laboratory experiment; **e. sur le terrain** field experiment; **faire une e.** to carry out *or* do an experiment; **faire des expériences (sur des rats)** to carry out experiments *or* to experiment (on rats); *Fig* **nous avons décidé de tenter l'e.** we've decided to give it a try *or* a go

❑ **par expérience ADV** from experience

❑ **sans expérience ADJ** inexperienced; **un petit jeune sans e.** an inexperienced youngster, a youngster still wet behind the ears; **il est sans e. de la vie** he has no experience of life

expérimental, -e, -aux, -ales [ɛksperimɑ̃tal, -o] **ADJ 1** *(avion, médicament)* trial *(avant n)*, experimental **2** *(méthode, sciences)* experimental; **à titre e.** experimentally, as an experiment

expérimentalement [ɛksperimɑ̃talmɑ̃] **ADV** experimentally

expérimentateur, -trice [ɛksperimɑ̃tatœr, -tris] **NM,F** experimenter

expérimentation [ɛksperimɑ̃tasjɔ̃] **NF** experimentation; **e. animale** *(pratique)* animal experimentation; *(tests)* animal experiments; **e. sur l'homme** *(d'un vaccin, d'un médicament)* human experiments, tests on humans

expérimentatrice [ɛksperimɑ̃tatris] *voir* **expérimentateur**

expérimenté, -e [ɛksperimɑ̃te] **ADJ** experienced, practised

expérimenter [3] [ɛksperimɑ̃te] **VT** *(remède, vaccin, machine)* to try out, to test (**sur** on)

USAGE ABSOLU to experiment, to carry out experiments

expert, -e [ɛkspɛr, -ɛrt] **ADJ 1** *(agile)* expert; **d'une main experte** with an expert hand; **d'une oreille experte** with a trained ear; **pour un œil e.** to the trained *or* expert eye

2 *(savant)* highly knowledgeable (**en/dans** in); **être e. en la matière** to be an expert on *or* in the subject; **être e. en littérature chinoise** to be an expert on *or* a specialist in Chinese literature

NM 1 *(chargé d'expertise)* expert, specialist; *(en bâtiments)* surveyor; *(en assurances)* assessor; **e. financier/fiscal** financial/tax expert; **e. judiciaire** legal expert; **e. maritime** surveyor

2 *(comme adj; avec ou sans trait d'union)* **chimiste e.** expert in chemistry; **médecin e.** medical expert

3 *(connaisseur)* expert (**de** *ou* **en** on), connoisseur (**de** *ou* **en** of)

expert-comptable [ɛkspɛrkɔ̃tabl] *(pl* **experts-comptables**) **NM** *Compta Br* ≃ chartered accountant, *Am* ≃ certified public accountant

expert-conseil [ɛkspɛrkɔ̃sɛj] *(pl* **experts-conseils**) **NM** consultant

expertement [ɛkspɛrtəmɑ̃] **ADV** expertly

expertise [ɛkspɛrtiz] **NF 1** *(examen → d'un meuble, d'une voiture)* (expert) appraisal *or* evaluation *or* valuation; *Assur (de dommages)* (expert) assessment; **faire faire une e.** *(pour assurer un bien)* to have a valuation done; *Assur* **rapport d'e.** assessor's report, claims adjuster's report; *Naut* **e. d'avarie** damage survey; *Jur* **e. contradictoire** = valuation made in the presence of both parties to a contract; *Jur* **e. in futurum** pretrial judicial investigation; *Jur* **e. judiciaire** court-ordered appraisal; *Jur* **e. médicale et psychiatrique** expert opinion *(by a doctor)*; *Jur* **e. médico-légale** forensic examination

2 *Constr (document)* expert's *or* valuer's report

3 *(compétence)* expertise

expertiser [3] [ɛkspɛrtize] **VT** *(véhicule)* to value; *Assur (dommages, véhicule, meuble, tableau)* to assess; **faire e. une voiture** *(gén)* to have a car valued; *(après un accident)* to have the damage on a car looked at *(for insurance purposes)*

expert-répétiteur [ɛkspɛrrepetitœr] *(pl* **experts-répétiteurs**) **NM** *Fin* loss *or* average adjuster

expiable [ɛkspjabl] **ADJ** expiable, which can be atoned for; **tu as commis une faute, certes, mais elle est e.** yes, you made a mistake but you can make up *or* atone for it

expiateur, -trice [ɛkspjatœr, -tris] **ADJ** expiatory

expiation [ɛkspjasjɔ̃] **NF en e. de** in expiation of, in atonement for

expiatoire [ɛkspjatwar] **ADJ** expiatory

expier [9] [ɛkspje] **VT** *(crime, péché)* to expiate, to atone for; *(erreur, faute)* to pay *or* to atone for

expirant, -e [ɛkspirɑ̃, -ɑ̃t] **ADJ** *(personne, entreprise)* dying, expiring, moribund; *(voix)* faint

expirateur [ɛkspiratœr] **ADJ M** *Anat (muscle)* expiratory

expiration [ɛkspirasjɔ̃] **NF 1** *(d'air)* breathing out; **pendant** *ou* **sur l'e.** on exhalation, as you/he/*etc* exhale(s) *or* breathe(s) out; **fléchissez au moment de l'e.** flex your knees when you breathe out **2** *(fin)* expiration, expiry; **venir** *ou* **arriver à e.** to expire, to run out; **le bail arrive à e. le 30 août** the lease expires on 30 August; **date d'e.** expiry date

❑ **à l'expiration de PRÉP à l'e. du bail** when the lease expires; **à l'e. du délai** at the end of the stated period

expiratoire [ɛkspiratwar] **ADJ** *Physiol* expiratory

expirer [3] [ɛkspire] **VI 1** *(mourir)* to expire, to breathe one's last **2** *Littéraire (disparaître → lueur, son)* to expire, to die away; *(→ flamme, vague)* to die; *(→ feu)* to go out **3** *(aux avoir ou être) (cesser d'être valide → abonnement, bail, délai)* to expire, to end; *(→ carte de crédit)* to expire; **mon congé est expiré** my leave is up *or* has expired

VT *(air)* to breathe out

USAGE ABSOLU *(exhaler)* to breathe out; **expirez!** breathe out!

explant [ɛksplɑ̃] **NM** *Biol* explant

explantation [ɛksplɑ̃tasjɔ̃] **NF** *Biol* explantation

explanter [3] [ɛksplɑ̃te] **VT** *Biol* to explant

explétif, -ive [ɛkspletif, -iv] **ADJ** expletive, expletory; **le "ne" e.** "ne" used as an expletive

NM expletive

explicable [ɛksplikabl] **ADJ** explainable, explicable; **ces phénomènes ne sont explicables que par le paranormal** such phenomena can only be explained *or* accounted for in terms of the paranormal; **c'est un phénomène difficilement e.** it's a phenomenon which is difficult to explain *or* which is not easily explained

explicatif, -ive [ɛksplikatif, -iv] **ADJ 1** *(brochure, lettre)* explanatory; **notice** *ou* **note explicative** *(sur un emballage)* instructions *or* directions for use; *(dans un dossier)* explanatory note **2** *Gram* **proposition relative explicative** non-restrictive relative clause

explication [ɛksplikasjɔ̃] **NF 1** *(éclaircissement → d'un fait, d'une situation)* explanation; **demander des explications à qn** to ask sb for some explanations; **il a quitté sa femme sans (aucune) e.** he walked out on his wife without any explanation(s); **ça se passe d'e.** it's self-explanatory

2 *(motif → d'une attitude, d'un retard)* explanation; **donner l'e. de qch** to give the reason for sth, to explain sth; **j'exige des explications!** I demand an explanation!

3 *Scol & Univ (d'une œuvre)* commentary, analysis; **e. de texte** critical analysis, appreciation of a text

4 *(discussion)* discussion; *(querelle)* argument; **avoir une e. avec qn sur qch** *(discussion)* to talk sth over with sb; *(querelle)* to have an argument with sb about sth; **je crois qu'il va falloir que nous ayons une petite e. tous les deux** I think we're going to have to have a little talk, you and I

❑ **explications NFPL** *(mode d'emploi)* instructions *or* directions (for use); **je ne comprends pas les explications de la machine** I don't understand the instructions for the machine

explicative [ɛksplikativ] *voir* **explicatif**

explicitation [ɛksplisitasjɔ̃] **NF 1** *(d'intentions)* making explicit *or* plain **2** *(d'un texte)* clarifying, clarification

explicite [ɛksplisit] **ADJ** explicit (**sur** about); **en termes explicites** in explicit terms, plainly; **suis-je assez e.?** do I make myself plain (enough)?; **elle n'a pas été très e. sur ce point** she wasn't very clear on that point

explicitement [ɛksplisitmɑ̃] **ADV** explicitly; **formuler e. une demande** to make an explicit request

expliciter [3] [ɛksplisite] **VT 1** *(intentions)* to make explicit *or* plain **2** *(phrase, clause de contrat)* to clarify, to explain

expliquer [3] [ɛksplike] **VT 1** *(faire comprendre → événement, réaction, fonctionnement etc)* to explain; **e. qch à qn** to explain sth to sb; **cela ne se fait pas, je te l'ai expliqué mille fois!** I've explained it to *or* told you time and again, it just

isn't done!; **je lui ai fait e. clairement les termes du contrat** I asked him/her to be very clear on the terms of the contract; **je me suis fait e. la procédure** I asked someone to explain the procedure to me; **ce serait trop long à e.** it would take too long to explain; **je lui ai expliqué que je ne pouvais pas le faire** I explained to him/her *or* told him/her that I couldn't do it; **cela explique pourquoi/comment...** that explains why/how...; *Fam* **e. le pourquoi du comment** to explain the how and the why of it; *Fam* **on s'est pris un de ces savons, je t'explique pas...** you wouldn't have believed the telling-off we got

2 *(justifier → attitude, retard)* to explain, to account for; **cela explique qu'il se soit présenté en smoking** that explains why he turned up in *or* that accounts for his turning up in a dinner jacket; **ceci n'explique pas cela** that doesn't explain it

3 *Scol & Univ (texte)* to analyse, to make a critical analysis of, to comment on; *(doctrine, théorème, signification)* to explain

4 *(élucider → mystère)* to explain

▸**s'expliquer** VPR **1** *(être intelligible)* to be explained; **cela s'explique facilement** that's easily understandable *or* explainable; **il y a des choses qui ne s'expliquent pas** some things can't be explained; **c'est bizarre mais ça s'explique** it's strange but it can be explained *or* there's an explanation for it; **sa mort ne s'explique que par un suicide** his/her death can only be put down to suicide, suicide is the only explanation for his/her death; **le mauvais temps s'explique par la présence d'une dépression** the presence of a depression explains the bad weather; **tout s'explique!** that explains it!

2 *(s'exprimer)* to explain oneself, to make oneself clear; **explique-toi mieux** make yourself clearer; **elle s'explique bien/mal** she expresses herself well/badly; **me serais-je mal expliqué?** perhaps I didn't make myself clear *or* wasn't plain enough; **s'e. clairement** to explain oneself clearly; **je m'explique** this is what I mean, let me explain

3 *(se justifier)* to justify one's behaviour, to explain oneself; **s'e. sur ses intentions** *(éclaircir)* to make plain *or* to explain one's intentions; **pouvez-vous vous e. sur cette omission?** can you explain why this was omitted?; **elle s'est expliquée sur différents reproches qu'on lui faisait** she justified herself with regard to the things they reproached her with

4 *(comprendre)* to understand; **je ne m'explique pas pourquoi...** I can't understand why...; **je n'arrive pas à m'e. son silence** I can't understand why he/she is remaining silent

5 s'e. avec *(avoir une discussion avec)* to talk things over with; *(se disputer avec)* to have it out with; **expliquez-vous une bonne fois pour toutes** get it sorted out once and for all; **viens, on va s'e. dehors** come on, we'll settle this outside; **ils se sont expliqués au couteau** they settled it with knives

exploit [ɛksplwa] NM **1** *(acte → héroïque)* exploit; *(→ remarquable)* feat, achievement; **e. sportif** remarkable sporting achievement; **e. technique** technical feat *or* exploit; **ses exploits amoureux** his/her sexual exploits; **avoir réussi à la convaincre relève de l'e.!** it's no mean achievement to have convinced her!; *Hum* **il est arrivé à l'heure, tu te rends compte d'un e.!** he arrived on time, which was quite an achievement for him! **2** *Jur* **e. (d'huissier)** writ

exploitabilité [ɛksplwatabilite] NF *(d'un filon, d'un gisement)* workableness; **âge d'e.** *(d'une forêt)* age of maturity

exploitable [ɛksplwatabl] ADJ *(idée, mine, terre, etc)* exploitable, workable; *(énergie)* exploitable; **tes documents ne sont pas exploitables dans l'optique de mes recherches** I can't make use of your documentation for my research; **e. par ordinateur** machine readable; **corpus e. par ordinateur** computerized corpus

exploitant, -e [ɛksplwatɑ̃, -ɑ̃t] NM,F **1** *(d'une exploitation, d'une carrière → propriétaire)* owner; *(→ gérant)* operator; **e. (agricole)** farmer; **petit e.** small farmer, *Br* smallholder; **e. forestier** forestry agent **2** *Cin (propriétaire)* owner; *(directeur) Br* manager, *Am* exhibitor

exploitation [ɛksplwatasjɔ̃] NF **1** *(entreprise)* concern; **e. agricole** farm; **petite e. agricole** small farm, *Br* smallholding; **e. agricole à responsabilité limitée** = farm registered as a limited company; **e. à ciel ouvert** open-cast mine; **e. commerciale** business (concern); **e. familiale** family business; **e. forestière** forestry site; **e. industrielle** industrial concern; **e. minière** mine; **e. vinicole** *(vignes)* vineyard; *(société)* wine-producing establishment

2 *(d'un réseau ferroviaire)* running, operating; *(d'un cinéma)* running; *(d'une carrière, d'une forêt, d'une mine, d'un sol)* exploitation, working; *(d'une terre)* farming; *Com (d'un brevet)* commercialization; **l'e. forestière** forestry, lumbering; **mettre en e.** *(carrière, mine)* to exploit, to work; **mettre une terre en e.** to bring a piece of land under cultivation; **faire l'e. industrielle de qch** to produce sth on an industrial scale

3 *(utilisation → d'une idée, d'un talent)* exploitation, exploiting *(UNCOUNT)*, utilizing *(UNCOUNT)*; **elle a confié à une agence de publicité l'e. de son idée** she let an advertising agency make use of her idea

4 *(fait d'abuser)* exploitation, exploiting *(UNCOUNT)*; *(de la main-d'œuvre)* exploitation; **leur e. de la misère d'autrui** their exploitation of other people's wretchedness; **l'e. de l'homme par l'homme** man's exploitation of man; **six euros de l'heure, c'est de l'e.!** six euros per hour, that's sheer exploitation!

❑ **d'exploitation** ADJ *Fin & Ordinat* operating; **société d'e.** development company

exploité, -e [ɛksplwate] ADJ **1** *(ferme, carrière, sous-sol)* exploited **2** *(main-d'œuvre)* exploited

exploiter [3] [ɛksplwate] VT **1** *(mettre en valeur → forêt, mine etc)* to exploit, to work; *(→ ressources naturelles)* to exploit; *(→ brevet)* to commercialize; *(→ terre)* to farm, to work; *(→ invention)* to utilize

2 *(faire fonctionner → ferme, tunnel, réseau ferroviaire)* to run, to operate; *(→ entreprise, cinéma)* to run

3 *(tirer avantage de → talent)* to exploit, to make use of; *(→ thème)* to exploit; *(→ situation)* to exploit, to make capital out of, to make the most of

4 *Péj (abuser de)* to exploit, to take (unfair) advantage of; **e. la naïveté de qn** to take advantage of sb's naivety; **e. la serviabilité de qn** to exploit *or* to take advantage of sb's helpfulness

5 *Péj (main-d'œuvre)* to exploit; **se faire e.** to be exploited

exploiteur, -euse [ɛksplwatœr, -øz] NM,F exploiter

explorable [ɛksplɔrabl] ADJ explorable

explorateur, -trice [ɛksplɔratœr, -tris] NM,F explorer

exploration [ɛksplɔrasjɔ̃] NF **1** *Géog & Méd* exploration; **voyage d'e.** voyage of discovery; **partir en e.** to go off exploring *or* on an exploration **2** *(analyse)* exploration, examination; *Mktg* **e. des besoins et des désirs** needs-and-wants exploration

exploratoire [ɛksplɔratwar] ADJ exploratory, tentative

exploratrice [ɛksplɔratris] *voir* **explorateur**

explorer [3] [ɛksplɔre] VT **1** *(contrée, île)* to explore **2** *Méd* to explore **3** *(examiner → possibilité)* to explore, to examine; *(→ sujet)* to explore

exploser [3] [ɛksploze] VI **1** *(détoner → grenade, mine, maison, chaudière)* to explode, to blow up; *(→ bombe)* to explode, to go off; *(→ dynamite, gaz)* to explode; **faire e. une bombe** to set off *or* to explode *or* to detonate a bomb; **j'avais l'impression que ma tête/jambe allait e.** I felt as if my head/leg was going to explode *or* burst

2 *(augmenter → population)* to explode; *(→ prix)* to shoot up, to soar, to (sky)rocket

3 *(se révéler soudain → mécontentement, joie)* to explode; *(→ rage)* to explode, to burst out; *(→ rires)* to burst out; *Fam (→ artiste)* to burst onto the scene; **laisser e. sa colère/joie** to give vent to one's anger/joy; **la salle explosa en applaudissements** the audience burst into thunderous applause; *Fam* **ils ont explosé sur la scène rock il y a 20 ans** they burst onto the rock scene 20 years ago

4 *Fam (s'emporter)* to flare up, to lose one's temper *or* cool; **e. de colère** to explode, to blow one's top; **si tu continues, j'explose!** stop it *or* I'll lose my temper!

VT **1** *très Fam (battre)* **e. qn** *ou* **la gueule à qn** to smash sb's face in; **se faire e. la gueule** to get one's face smashed in

2 *Fam (détruire)* to smash up, *Br* to write off, *Am* to total; **il a explosé sa moto** *Br* he wrote off his motorbike, *Am* he totaled his motorcycle

3 *Fam* **être explosé (de rire)** to be killing oneself (laughing), to be cracking up, to be in stitches

4 *Fam* **elle explose l'écran** she has great screen presence, she fills the screen with her presence; **l'émission a explosé l'Audimat®** the programme scored record-breaking viewing figures; **elle a explosé le record du monde** she smashed the world record

exploseur [ɛksplozœr] NM blasting machine

explosibilité [ɛksplozibilite] NF explosiveness

explosible [ɛksplozibl] ADJ explosive

explosif, -ive [ɛksplozif, -iv] ADJ **1** *(mélange, puissance)* explosive; *(obus)* high-explosive **2** *(dangereux → situation, sujet, dossier)* explosive, highly sensitive; *(→ atmosphère)* explosive, charged **3** *(fougueux → tempérament)* fiery, explosive **4** *Ling* explosive, plosive

NM explosive

❑ **explosive** NF *Ling* explosive (consonant), plosive (consonant)

explosimètre [ɛksplozimɛtr] NM *Tech* explosimeter

explosion [ɛksplozjɔ̃] NF **1** *(détonation → d'une bombe, d'une chaudière, d'une mine)* explosion, blowing up; *(→ d'un gaz)* explosion; **faire e.** *(bombe)* to go off, to explode; *(obus)* to explode; **e. atomique** atomic explosion; **e. volcanique** volcanic explosion *or* eruption

2 *(manifestation)* **e. d'enthousiasme/d'indignation** burst of enthusiasm/indignation; **e. de joie** outburst *or* explosion of joy; **ce fut une e. de rire dans le public** the audience burst out into peals of laughter

3 *(accroissement)* **e. démographique** population boom *or* explosion; **l'e. démographique après la guerre** the post-war baby boom; **e. des naissances** baby boom

explosive [ɛksploziv] *voir* **explosif**

expo [ɛkspo] NF *Fam (abrév* **exposition***)* exhibition▪

exponentiel, -elle [ɛkspɔnɑ̃sjɛl] ADJ exponential; **de manière exponentielle** exponentially

exponentiellement [ɛkspɔnɑ̃sjɛlmɑ̃] ADV exponentially

export [ɛkspɔr] NM exportation; **l'e., le service e.** the export branch; *Ordinat* **e. de données** data export

exportable [ɛkspɔrtabl] ADJ *Com & Écon* exportable, which can be exported

exportateur, -trice [ɛkspɔrtatœr, -tris] ADJ *(pays)* exporting *(avant n)*; *(secteur)* export *(avant n)*; **être e. de qch** to be an exporter of sth, to export sth; **les pays exportateurs de pétrole/céréales** oil-/grain-exporting countries

NM,F exporter

exportation [ɛkspɔrtasjɔ̃] NF **1** *(sortie)* export, exportation; **faire de l'e.** to export; **réservé à l'e.** for export only, reserved for export; **ce produit marche très fort à l'e.** this product is doing very well on the export market; **e. de capitaux** export of capital; **e. kangourou** piggybacking

2 *Com & Écon* **exportations** *(marchandises)* exports; **exportations visibles/invisibles** visible/invisible exports

3 *Ordinat (d'un fichier)* exporting; *(données exportées)* exported data

❑ **d'exportation** ADJ export *(avant n)*; **articles d'e.** exports

exportatrice [ɛkspɔrtatris] *voir* **exportateur**

exporter [3] [ɛkspɔrte] VT **1** *Com & Écon* to export (**vers** to) **2** *(répandre à l'étranger → idées, culture)* to export, to spread abroad **3** *Ordinat* to export (**vers** to)

▸**s'exporter** VPR *(marchandises)* to be exported (**vers** to); **ces articles s'exportent mal** these

items are difficult to export *or* not good for exporting; *Fig* **ce genre de coutume s'exporte mal** this type of custom doesn't export *or* travel well; *Fig* **cette mode a été** *ou* **s'est exportée dans le monde entier** the fashion has spread throughout the world

exposant, -e [ɛkspozɑ̃, -ɑ̃t] **NM,F 1** *(dans une galerie, dans une foire)* exhibitor **2** *Jur* petitioner
NM 1 *Math* exponent **2** *Typ (chiffre, lettre)* superscript, superior; **3 en e.** superscript 3

exposé, -e [ɛkspoze] **ADJ 1** *(orienté)* **ce balcon est bien/mal e.** the balcony gets a lot of sun/doesn't get much sun; **jardin e. au sud** south-facing garden, garden with a southern aspect; **la chambre est exposée au nord** the room faces north
2 *(non abrité)* exposed, wind-swept; **champ très e.** very exposed field
3 *(montré)* on show, on display; **objet e.** *(dans une galerie, une foire)* item on show, exhibit; **les articles exposés en vitrine** the items on display in the window; **une des voitures exposées** one of the cars on show; **être e. (sur un lit de parade)** to lie in state
4 *(par les médias)* **le ministre est toujours très e.** the Minister is always in the public eye *or* gets a lot of media coverage
NM 1 *(compte rendu)* account, exposition; *(de faits, de situation)* statement, account, report; **faire un e. sur** to give an account of; **après un bref e. de la situation** after outlining the situation briefly; **e. verbal (de mission)** briefing
2 *Scol & Univ (écrit)* (written) paper; *(oral)* talk, presentation; **faire un e. (sur qch)** *(oral)* to give a talk *or* to read a paper (on sth); *(écrit)* to write a paper (on sth)
3 *Jur* **e. des motifs** exposition of motives
4 *Compta* **e. de la situation de l'entreprise** statement of the company's position

exposer [3] [ɛkspoze] **VT 1** *(dans un magasin)* to display, to put on display, to set out; *(dans une galerie, une foire)* to exhibit, to show; **e. des marchandises en vitrine** to display goods for sale
2 *(soumettre)* to expose; **e. qch à l'air/lumière** to expose sth to the air/light; **il faut e. cette plante à la lumière le plus possible** the plant must receive *or* get as much light as possible; **e. qch aux radiations** to expose *or* to subject sth to radiation; **e. qn à** *(critiques, ridicule)* to lay sb open to, to expose sb to
3 *(mettre en danger → honneur, vie)* to endanger, to put at risk; **e. qn** to put sb in danger
4 *(faire connaître → arguments, motifs)* to expound, to put forward; *(→ intentions)* to set forth *or* out, to explain; *(→ revendications)* to set forth, to put forward, to make known; *(→ griefs)* to air; **e. son point de vue à qn** to explain one's point of view to sb, to make one's point of view known to sb; **elle nous a exposé en détail ses projets** she explained to us in detail what her plans were; **je leur ai exposé ma situation** I explained my situation to them
5 *Hist (nouveau-né)* to expose
6 *Littérature & Mus* to set out; *(thème)* to introduce; **dialogue destiné à e. l'action** expository dialogue
7 *Phot* to expose; **e. un film à la lumière** to expose a film
USAGE ABSOLU nous exposerons à la foire du livre we'll be among the exhibitors at the Book Fair; **ça fait très longtemps qu'il n'a pas exposé** he hasn't exhibited anything for a very long time
►s'exposer VPR 1 *(se compromettre)* to leave oneself exposed; **il s'expose trop dans cette affaire** he's leaving himself far too exposed in this business; **s'e. à des critiques** to lay oneself open *or* to expose oneself to criticism; **s'e. à des poursuites judiciaires** to lay oneself open to *or* to run the risk of prosecution; **s'e. à des représailles** to expose oneself to retaliation
2 *(se placer)* **s'e. au soleil** to expose one's skin to the sun; **si tu t'exposes trop longtemps** if you stay in the sun too long

exposition [ɛkspozisjɔ̃] **NF 1** *(d'œuvres d'art)* show, exhibition; *(de produits manufacturés)* exhibition, exposition; **e. de peinture/photos** painting/photo exhibition; **e. de blanc** special linen week *or* event; **e. commerciale** trade

exhibition; **e. florale** flower show; **e. interprofessionnelle** trade exhibition *or* show; *Mktg* **e. sur le lieu de vente** point-of-sale display; *Mktg* **e. sur le marché** market exposure; **e. au public** audience exposure; **l'E. universelle** the World Fair; **salle d'e.** exhibition room
2 *(de marchandises, de fleurs)* display; **l'e. en vitrine a fané les tissus** the fabric has faded from being displayed in the window
3 *(d'un corps)* lying in state
4 *(d'arguments, de motifs)* exposition, expounding *(UNCOUNT)*; *(d'une situation, d'une théorie)* exposition; *Jur* **e. de la demande** statement of claims; **e. des faits** statement of the facts
5 *Littérature, Théât & Mus* exposition
6 *(soumission)* **e. à** *(danger, radiation, risque, froid)* exposure to; **éviter l'e. au soleil** do not stay in the sun; **il lui faut au minimum une heure d'e. (à la lumière) par jour** it needs at least an hour of light a day; *Fin* **e. aux risques** exposure
7 *(orientation)* orientation, aspect; **e. au sud** orientation to the south; **l'appartement a une double e. nord-sud** the *Br* flat *or* *Am* apartment has north-facing and south-facing windows
8 *Phot* exposure
❑ **d'exposition** **ADJ** expository, introductory; *Littérature & Théât* **scène d'e.** prologue

exposition-vente [ɛkspozisjɔ̃vɑ̃t] *(pl* **expositions-ventes)** **NF** *(gén)* display *(where the items are for sale)*; *(d'objets d'artisanat)* craft fair

ex post [ɛkspɔst] **ADJ** ex post facto

expo-vente [ɛkspovɑ̃t] *(pl* **expos-ventes)** **NF** *Fam (abrév* **exposition-vente)** *(gén)* display▪ *(where the items are for sale)*; *(d'objets d'artisanat)* craft fair▪

exprès¹ [ɛksprɛ] **ADV 1** *(délibérément)* on purpose, intentionally, deliberately; **c'est e. que j'ai employé ce mot** I used this word on purpose *or* intentionally *or* deliberately; **je ne l'ai pas fait e.** I didn't mean to do it, I didn't do it on purpose *or* intentionally *or* deliberately; **tu l'as vexé – je ne l'ai pas fait e.** you've offended him – I didn't mean to *or* it wasn't intentional; **elle fait e. de me contredire** she makes a point of contradicting me, she deliberately contradicts me; **j'ai déclenché l'alarme sans le faire e.** I set off the alarm without meaning to; **j'aurais voulu le faire e., je n'y serais pas arrivé** I couldn't have done it if I'd tried *or* if I'd wanted to; **c'est (comme) un** *ou* **on dirait un fait e.** you'd think it was done on purpose *or* was intentional; *Ironique* **comme (par) un fait e., il pleuvait** and of course *or* wouldn't you know it, it was raining; *Ironique* **comme (par) un fait e., il n'avait pas de monnaie** funnily enough, he had no change
2 *(spécialement)* especially, specially; **tu n'aurais pas dû venir e.** you shouldn't have come specially; **elle est sortie e. pour l'acheter** she went out specially *or* expressly to buy it; **c'est fait e. pour ranger des crayons** it's designed *or* meant for holding pencils; **il y a du papier à l'intérieur – c'est fait e.** there's some paper inside – it's meant to be like that

exprès², expresse [ɛksprɛ, ɛksprɛs] **ADJ** *(avertissement, autorisation, ordre)* express, explicit; *(recommandation)* express, strict; **défense expresse de fumer** smoking strictly prohibited

exprès³ [ɛksprɛs] **ADJ INV** *(lettre, paquet)* special delivery *(avant n)*
❑ **en exprès, par exprès** **ADV** **envoyer qch en e.** to send sth special delivery

express [ɛksprɛs] **ADJ INV 1** *Rail voir* **train 2** *(café)* espresso
NM 1 *Rail* express *or* fast train **2** *(café)* espresso (coffee) **3** *Presse* **l'E.** = French weekly news magazine

expressément [ɛkspresemɑ̃] **ADV 1** *(catégoriquement → défendre, ordonner)* expressly, categorically; *(→ conseiller, prévenir)* expressly **2** *(spécialement)* specially, specifically; **je l'ai fait e. pour toi** I did it specially for you

expressif, -ive [ɛkspresif, -iv] **ADJ 1** *(suggestif → style)* expressive, vivid; *(→ regard, visage)* expressive, meaningful; *(→ ton)* expressive; **sa mimique était expressive** the expression on his/her face said it all **2** *Ling* expressive

expression [ɛkspresjɔ̃] **NF 1** *(mot, tournure)* expression, phrase, turn of phrase; **avoir une e.**

malheureuse to use an unfortunate turn of phrase; **passez-moi l'e.** (if you'll) pardon the expression; **veuillez croire à l'e. de ma considération distinguée** *(à quelqu'un dont on connaît le nom)* *Br* yours sincerely, *Am* sincerely (yours); *(à quelqu'un dont on ne connaît pas le nom)* *Br* yours faithfully, *Am* sincerely (yours); **e. familière** colloquial expression, colloquialism; **e. figée** set phrase *or* expression, fixed expression, idiom; **e. toute faite** *(figée)* set phrase *or* expression; *(cliché)* hackneyed phrase, cliché
2 *(fait de s'exprimer)* expression, expressing *(UNCOUNT)*, voicing *(UNCOUNT)*; **nous condamnons l'e. d'opinions racistes** we condemn the voicing of racist opinions; **lutter pour l'e. de ses revendications** to fight for the right to make one's demands heard; **l'e. de nos idées doit se faire par le biais d'un journal** we must express our ideas in a newspaper
3 *(pratique de la langue)* **auteurs d'e. allemande** authors writing in German; **des enfants d'e. française** French-speaking children; **e. écrite/orale** written/oral expression
4 *(extériorisation → d'un besoin, d'un sentiment)* expression; **trouver son e. dans** to find (its) expression in; **au-delà de toute e.** *(employé comme adjectif)* inexpressible; *(employé comme adverbe)* inexpressibly; **e. corporelle** self-expression through movement
5 *(vivacité)* expression; **mets plus d'e. dans le dernier vers** put in more expression *or* feeling when you read the last line; **jouer avec e.** to play expressively; **geste/regard plein d'e.** expressive gesture/look
6 *(du visage)* expression, look; **si tu avais vu ton e.!** if you'd seen the look on your face!; **l'e. de son visage ne changea pas** his/her expression didn't change
7 *Math* expression; *Fig* **la famille, réduite à sa plus simple e.** the family, reduced to its simplest expression; *Fig* **un meublé dont le mobilier était réduit à sa plus simple e.** a furnished room that hardly merited the term
8 *Ordinat* expression; **e. logique** logical expression; **e. de sélection** selection command; **e. de tri** sort command
9 *Biol (d'un gène)* expression
❑ **sans expression** **ADJ** expressionless

expressionnisme [ɛkspresjɔnism] **NM** expressionism

expressionniste [ɛkspresjɔnist] **ADJ** expressionist
NMF expressionist

expressivement [ɛkspresivmɑ̃] **ADV** expressively

expressivité [ɛkspresivite] **NF** expressivity, expressiveness; **avec beaucoup d'e.** very expressively

expresso [ɛkspreso] **NM** *Culin* expresso, espresso

exprimable [ɛksprimabl] **ADJ** expressible; **ma joie est difficilement e.** my joy is difficult to express

exprimage [ɛksprimaʒ] **NM** *Tex* squeezing

exprimer [3] [ɛksprime] **VT 1** *(dire → sentiment)* to express; *(→ idée, revendication)* to express, to voice; **par là, elle exprime son désespoir** in this way she expresses *or* voices her despair; **comment vous e. toute mon admiration?** how can I tell you how much I admire you?; **je tiens à vous e. mon regret** I want to tell you how sorry I am; **mon émotion est difficile à e.** my emotion is difficult to put into words *or* to express
2 *(manifester → mécontentement, surprise)* to express, to show; **c'est comme ça que j'exprime mes sentiments** that's how I express my feelings
3 *(pour chiffrer une quantité, une somme)* to state, to express; *Math (quantité, valeur)* to express; **e. une quantité en kilos** to state a quantity in kilos; **e. une somme en dollars** to state a sum in dollars
4 *(extraire → jus, pus)* to express, to squeeze out *(de* from*)*
5 *Biol (gène)* to express
►s'exprimer VPR 1 *(se manifester → talent, sentiment)* to express *or* to show itself; **laisse ton cœur s'e.** let your heart speak; **tant de mélancolie s'exprime dans son poème** his/her poem expresses so much melancholy; **l'étonnement s'exprima sur son visage** his/her astonishment showed on his/her face

2 *(dire sa pensée)* to express oneself; **laissez-le s'e.** let him have his say *or* express himself; **chacun doit s'e.** all opinions must be heard; *Hum* **vas-y, exprime-toi!** come on, out with it!; **je me suis exprimée sur ce sujet** I've expressed myself *or* made my opinions known on the subject; **le président ne s'est pas encore exprimé sur ce sujet** the president has yet to voice an opinion on the matter; **s'e. par gestes/signes** to use sign language

3 *(choisir ses mots)* to express oneself; **exprime-toi clairement** express yourself clearly, make yourself clear; **non, je me suis mal exprimé** no, I've put it badly; **si je peux m'e. ainsi** if I can put it that way

4 *(manifester sa personnalité)* to express oneself; **s'e. par la danse/musique** to express oneself through dancing/music

expromission [ɛkspromisjɔ̃] NF expromission

expropriateur, -trice [ɛksproprijatœr, -tris] ADJ expropriating *(avant n)*

expropriation [ɛksproprijasjɔ̃] NF **1** *(d'une personne)* expropriation **2** *(d'une propriété)* compulsory purchase

exproprié, -e [ɛksproprije] ADJ expropriated

exproprier [10] [ɛksproprije] VT **1** *(personne)* to expropriate; **la municipalité a fait e. les occupants de l'immeuble** *Br* the local council placed a compulsory purchase order on the flats; **se faire e.** to be expropriated, *Br* to have a compulsory purchase order placed on one's property **2** *(maison, terre)* to expropriate, *Br* to place a compulsory purchase order on

expulsé, -e [ɛkspylse] ADJ expelled; *(locataire)* evicted

NM,F expellee

expulser [3] [ɛkspylse] VT **1** *(renvoyer → locataire)* to evict (**de** from), to throw out (**de** of); *(→ membre, participant, étudiant)* to expel (**de** from); *(→ immigrant)* to expel, to deport (**de** from); *(→ joueur)* to send off; **elle a été expulsée du terrain** she was sent off the field; **la propriétaire a fait e. ses locataires** the owner had the tenants thrown out; **se faire e.** to be thrown out **2** *Méd* to evacuate, to expel

expulsif, -ive [ɛkspylsif, -iv] ADJ *Méd* expulsive

expulsion [ɛkspylsjɔ̃] NF **1** *(d'un locataire)* eviction (**de** from); *(d'un membre de comité, d'un étudiant)* expulsion (**de** from); *(d'un immigrant)* expulsion, deportation (**de** from); *(d'un joueur)* sending off; **décider l'e. d'un élève** *(définitive)* to decide to exclude *or* expel a pupil; *(temporaire)* to decide to suspend a pupil **2** *Méd* expulsion, evacuation

expulsive [ɛkspylsiv] *voir* **expulsif**

expurgation [ɛkspyrgasjɔ̃] NF expurgation, bowdlerization

expurger [17] [ɛkspyrʒe] VT to expurgate, to bowdlerize; **une version très expurgée de cette histoire** an expurgated *or* sanitized version of the matter

exquis, -e [ɛkski, -iz] ADJ **1** *(saveur, vin, gentillesse etc)* exquisite; *(personne, temps)* delightful **2** *Méd (douleur)* exquisite

exquisément [ɛkskizemɑ̃] ADV *Littéraire* exquisitely

exquisité [ɛkskizite] NF *Littéraire* exquisiteness

ex-répartition [ɛksrepartisjɔ̃] ADV *Fin* ex allotment

exsangue [ɛksɑ̃g, ɛgzɑ̃g] ADJ **1** *Littéraire (pâle → figure, lèvres)* bloodless, livid **2** *(ayant perdu son sang → corps, victime)* bloodless; *Fig (pays)* bled white; *(œuvre, littérature)* anaemic, bloodless; *Fig* **après la guerre, notre industrie était e.** this country's industry was bled white by the war

exsanguination [ɛksɑ̃ginasjɔ̃] NF *Méd* exsanguination

exsanguino-transfusion [ɛksɑ̃ginotrɑ̃sfyzjɔ̃] *(pl* **exsanguino-transfusions**) NF *Méd* exchange transfusion

exstrophie [ɛkstrofi] NF *Méd* exstrophy, extrophy

exsudat [ɛksyda] NM *Biol, Bot & Méd* exudate

exsudation [ɛksydasjɔ̃] NF *Biol, Bot & Méd* exudation

exsuder [3] [ɛksyde] *Biol, Bot & Méd* VT to exude
VI to exude

exta [ɛksta] NF *Fam Arg* drogue E

extase [ɛkstaz] NF **1** *(exaltation)* ecstasy, rapture; **être** *ou* **rester en e. devant** to be in raptures *or*

ecstasies over; **tomber en e. devant qn/qch** to go into ecstasies at the sight of sb/sth **2** *Rel* ecstasy

extasié, -e [ɛkstazje] ADJ enraptured, ecstatic

extasier [9] [ɛkstazje] **s'extasier** VPR **s'e. devant/sur** to go into raptures *or* ecstasies over/about; **elle s'est longuement extasiée sur ses enfants/devant mes géraniums** she went into great raptures about her children/over my geraniums

extatique [ɛkstatik] ADJ *(de l'extase → vision, transport)* ecstatic; **état e.** ecstasy, trance **2** *(émerveillé)* enraptured

extemporané, -e [ɛkstɑ̃porane] ADJ *Méd* extemporaneous

extendeur [ɛkstɑ̃dœr] NM extender

extenseur [ɛkstɑ̃sœr] ADJ M *Anat* extensor
NM **1** *Anat* extensor **2** *(machine)* chest expander

extensibilité [ɛkstɑ̃sibilite] NF extensibility

extensible [ɛkstɑ̃sibl] ADJ **1** *(organe)* extensible; *(matière)* tensible, extensible; *(tissu)* stretch; *(liste)* extendable; *Fig (définition)* flexible; *Fig* **mon budget n'est pas e.** I can't stretch my budget any further, I can't make my budget go any further **2** *Ordinat* upgradeable; *(mémoire)* expandable, upgradeable

extensif, -ive [ɛkstɑ̃sif, -iv] ADJ **1** *Agr* extensive **2** *Phys (paramètre, force)* extensive **3 sens e.** *(d'un mot)* extended meaning

extension [ɛkstɑ̃sjɔ̃] NF **1** *(étirement → d'un élastique, d'un ressort, d'un muscle)* stretching; *(→ d'une matière)* extension; *Méd* traction, extension

2 *(agrandissement → d'un territoire)* expansion, enlargement; *(→ d'une entreprise, d'un marché, d'un réseau)* expansion, extension; *(→ de pouvoirs, d'un incendie, d'une maladie, d'une infection)* spreading, spread; *(→ d'une langue)* spread; *(→ de droits, de contrat)* extension; **prendre de l'e.** *(territoire)* to get bigger, to expand; *(secteur)* to grow, to develop; *(maladie, infection)* to spread, to extend; *(incendie)* to spread; **la maladie/l'incendie a pris une e. considérable** the disease/fire has spread considerably; **il faut éviter l'e. de l'épidémie/de l'incendie** the epidemic/fire must be prevented from spreading

3 *(élargissement)* **on a décidé l'e. des mesures à toute la population** it has been decided to extend the scope of the measures to include the entire population

4 *(partie ajoutée → d'un bâtiment, d'un réseau)* extension

5 *Ordinat (augmentation)* expansion; *(dispositif)* add-on; **carte d'e.** expansion board; **e. de nom de fichier** file name extension; **e. mémoire** memory expansion *or* upgrade

6 *Ling & Math* extension; *(d'un mot)* extended meaning

7 *Mktg* **e. de la gamme** range stretching; **e. de la ligne** line extension, line stretching; **e. de marché** market expansion; **e. de la marque** brand extension

8 *Belg & Can Tél (poste)* extension

▫ **en extension** ADJ **1** *(secteur)* developing, expanding; *(production)* increasing

2 *Anat (muscle, ressort)* stretched; **être en e.** *(ressort)* to be stretched *or* extended; *(gymnaste etc)* to be stretched out

▫ **par extension** ADV by extension; **le vocabulaire militaire sert, par e., à décrire ces manœuvres électorales** military terminology is used by extension to describe electoral manoeuvring; *Ling & Math* **définir par e.** to define by extension

'Extension du domaine de la lutte' *Houellebecq, Harel* 'Whatever'

extensionnel, -elle [ɛkstɑ̃sjɔnɛl] ADJ extensional

extensive [ɛkstɑ̃siv] *voir* **extensif**

extenso [ɛkstɛ̃so] *voir* **in extenso**

extensomètre [ɛkstɑ̃sɔmɛtr] NM *Tech* extensometer

exténuant, -e [ɛkstenɥɑ̃, -ɑ̃t] ADJ exhausting

exténuation [ɛkstenɥasjɔ̃] NF exhaustion

exténuer [7] [ɛkstenɥe] VT to exhaust, to tire out; **être exténué** to be worn out *or* exhausted

▶ **s'exténuer** VPR to exhaust oneself, to tire *or* to wear oneself out; **s'e. à faire qch** to exhaust

oneself doing sth; *Fam* **je m'exténue à lui dire de ne pas y aller** I'm tired of telling him/her not to go

ADJ outside **1, 4, 9** ■ outer **1** ■ external **1, 3–5, 7** ■ outlying **2** ■ outward **5** ■ superficial **6** ■ foreign **7** ■ exterior **8**
NM outside **1–3, 5, 7** ■ exterior **1, 6** ■ abroad **4** ■ outward appearance **6**

ADJ **1** *(escalier, bruit, éclairage, intérêts)* outside; *(cour, poche, mur, orbite, bord, boulevards)* outer; *(porte)* external, outer; **les bruits extérieurs la gênent** outside noises *or* noises from outside distract her; **avoir des activités extérieures** *(hors du foyer)* to have interests outside the home; *(hors du travail)* to have interests outside of work; **il habite dans un quartier e. à la ville** he lives outside the city

2 *(excentré → quartier)* outlying, out-of-town

3 *(non subjectif → réalité)* external; **le monde e.** the outside world

4 *(étranger à la personne, la chose considérée → influence, aide)* outside, external; **sans aide extérieure** without outside help; **ce sont des considérations extérieures** these are external considerations; **pour des raisons qui te sont complètement extérieures** for reasons that have absolutely nothing to do with you; **e. à** outside (of); **personnes extérieures à l'entreprise** persons not belonging to the staff; **une personnalité extérieure au cinéma** a personality outside the world of films; **développement e. au sujet** irrelevant development; **rester e. à une controverse/un débat** to remain aloof from *or* stay out of a controversy/debate

5 *(apparent)* external, surface *(avant n)*, outward; *(calme, joie, assurance)* outward, apparent; *(signe)* outward; **l'aspect e.** *(d'un édifice, d'un objet)* the outward appearance; *(d'une personne)* the exterior; **sa fragilité est toute extérieure** his/her vulnerability is all on the surface

6 *Péj (superficiel)* superficial, surface *(avant n)*, token *(avant n)*; **avec une compassion tout extérieure** with token *or* skin-deep compassion

7 *Écon & Pol (dette, commerce)* foreign, external; *(politique)* foreign

8 *Géom* exterior

9 *Tél* outside

NM **1** *(d'un bâtiment, d'une boîte)* exterior, outside

2 **l'e.** *(le plein air)* the outside *or* outdoors; **vernis pour l'e.** varnish for exterior use

3 **l'e.** *(à une personne)* the outside (world); **être tourné vers l'e.** to be outgoing

4 *Écon & Pol* **l'e.** abroad, foreign countries; **les relations avec l'e.** foreign relations

5 *(bord)* **l'e. de la chaussée** the outside (of the road)

6 *(apparence)* outward appearance, exterior; **il a un e. jovial** he's jolly on the outside; **sous un e. rébarbatif** under a forbidding exterior

7 *Sport* **l'e.** *(d'une piste, d'un circuit)* the outside

8 *Cin* location shot; **extérieurs tournés à Rueil** shot on location in Rueil; **il tourne en e.** he's on location; *TV* **émission en e.** outside broadcast, *Spéc* OB

9 *Belg Ftbl* winger

▫ **à l'extérieur** ADV **1** *(en plein air)* outside, outdoors; **manger à l'e.** *(en plein air)* to eat outside *or* outdoors; *(hors de chez soi)* to eat out

2 *(hors du système, du groupe)* outside; **nous allons d'abord consulter à l'e.** we shall first seek the opinion of outside consultants

3 *Sport (sur une piste)* on the outside; *(dans une autre ville)* away; **jouer à l'e.** to play away; **match (joué) à l'e.** away match

4 *Écon & Pol* abroad

5 *Tél* outside; **téléphoner à l'e.** to make an outside call

▫ **à l'extérieur de** PRÉP *(bâtiment)* outside (of); *(boîte)* on the outside of; **à l'e. de la gare/ville** outside the station/town; **à l'e. du parc** outside of the park; **à l'e. de l'Afrique** outside Africa

▫ **de l'extérieur** ADV **1** *(dans l'espace)* from (the)

outside; **vue de l'e., la maison paraît petite** seen from (the) outside, the house looks small; **vue de l'e., cette entreprise a l'air de bien marcher** judging by appearances, the company seems to be doing well

2 *(dans un système)* from the outside; **considérer un problème de l'e.** to look at a problem from the outside; **juger de l'e.** to judge by appearances; **des gens venus de l'e.** outsiders

extérieurement [εksterjœrmɑ̃] ADV **1** *(au dehors)* on the outside, externally **2** *(apparemment)* outwardly

extériorisation [εksterjɔrizasjɔ̃] NF **1** *(de sentiments)* expression, show, display **2** Psy exteriorization, externalization

extérioriser [3] [εksterjɔrize] VT **1** *(montrer → sentiment)* to express, to show **2** Psy to exteriorize, to externalize

USAGE ABSOLU **il n'extériorise pas assez** he doesn't show his feelings enough

▶**s'extérioriser** VPR *(joie, mécontentement)* to be expressed, to show; *(personne)* to show one's feelings; **il s'extériorise très peu** he shows little of what he's feeling

extériorité [εksterjɔrite] NF exteriority

exterminateur, -trice [εksterminatœr, -tris] ADJ *(ange)* exterminating; *(rage)* destructive ▪ NM,F exterminator

extermination [εksterminasjɔ̃] NF extermination

exterminatrice [εksterminatris] *voir* **exterminateur**

exterminer [3] [εstermine] VT **1** *(tuer → peuple, race)* to exterminate; **se faire e.** to be wiped out **2** Hum *(vaincre → adversaire)* to annihilate

externalisation [εksternalizasjɔ̃] NF Écon outsourcing

externaliser [3] [εksternalize] VT Écon to outsource

externalité [εksternalite] NF Écon externality

externat [εksterna] NM **1** Scol *(école)* day school; *(élèves)* day pupils; *(statut)* non-residency; **pour mes enfants, je préfère l'e.** I'd rather my children weren't boarders **2** *(en médecine)* non-resident (medical) studentship; **pendant mon e.** while I was Br a non-resident student or Am an extern; **faire son e.** to be Br a non-resident student or Am an extern

externe [εkstern] ADJ **1** *(cause, facteur)* external **2** *(partie, orbite, bord)* outer, external; **angle e.** exterior angle; Pharm **à usage e.** for external use only **3** Scol **élève e.** day pupil **4** Ordinat **dispositif e.** external device

▪ NMF **1** Scol day pupil, non-boarder **2** Méd **e. (des hôpitaux)** Br non-resident (medical) student, Am extern

extérocepteur [εksterɔsεptœr] NM Physiol exteroceptor

extéroceptif, -ive [εksterɔsεptif, -iv] ADJ Physiol exteroceptive

extéroceptivité [εksterɔsεptivite] NF Physiol exteroceptivity

exterritorialité [εksteritɔrjalite] NF Jur exterritoriality, extraterritoriality

extincteur, -trice [εkstɛ̃ktœr, -tris] ADJ extinguishing *(avant n)* ▪ NM (fire) extinguisher

extinctif, -ive [εkstɛ̃ktif, -iv] ADJ Jur extinctive

extinction [εkstɛ̃ksjɔ̃] NF **1** *(arrêt → d'un incendie)* extinction, extinguishment, putting out; **e. des feux** lights out; Aut **e. retardée** *(d'une lumière)* delayed cut-off

2 *(suppression → d'une dette)* extinguishment, discharge; **espèce animale menacée** ou **en voie d'e.** endangered animal species

3 *(affaiblissement)* **lutter jusqu'à l'e. de ses forces** to struggle until one has no strength left; Méd **e. de voix** loss of voice, Spéc aphonia; **avoir une e. de voix** to have lost one's voice

4 Chim *(de chaux)* slaking

5 Jur *(d'un droit)* extinguishment; *(d'un contrat)* termination; *(d'une hypothèque)* redemption

6 Biol & Méd **e. génique** gene silencing

extinctive [εkstɛ̃ktiv] *voir* **extinctif**

extinctrice [εkstɛ̃ktris] *voir* **extincteur**

extirpable [εkstirpabl] ADJ **1** *(extractible → tumeur)* removable; *(→ plante)* which can be rooted up or pulled out **2** *(destructible → mal)* eradicable

extirpateur [εkstirpatœr] NM Agr harrow

extirpation [εkstirpasjɔ̃] NF Méd *(extraction → d'une tumeur)* removal, removing, Spéc extirpation; *(→ d'une plante)* rooting up, pulling out, uprooting

extirper [3] [εkstirpe] VT **1** *(ôter → tumeur)* to remove, Spéc to extirpate; *(→ épine, racine)* to pull out; *(→ plante)* to root up or out, to uproot, to pull up; **e. qn du lit** to drag or to haul sb out of bed; **e. qn d'un fauteuil** to drag sb out of an armchair; **e. qn d'une situation impossible/d'un piège** to extricate sb from an impossible situation/from a trap; **je n'ai pas réussi à lui e. un mot** I couldn't drag or get a word out of him/her

2 *(détruire → préjugés, vice)* to eradicate, to root out

▶**s'extirper** VPR **s'e. du lit** to drag or to haul oneself out of bed; **s'e. de dessous la couette** to drag oneself from beneath the quilt; **s'e. de son pull/d'un enchevêtrement de racines** to extricate oneself from one's pullover/a tangle of roots

extorquer [3] [εkstɔrke] VT *(fonds)* to extort; **e. de l'argent à qn** to extort money from sb; **e. des aveux à qn** to wring a confession out of sb; **e. une signature à qn** to force a signature out of sb; **e. une promesse à qn** to extract or to extort a promise from sb; **elle s'est fait e. de l'argent par ses enfants** her children extorted money from her

extorqueur, -euse [εkstɔrkœr, -øz] NM,F extortionist

extorsion [εkstɔrsjɔ̃] NF extortion; **e. de fonds** extortion of money

extra [εkstra] ADJ INV **1** Fam *(exceptionnel → journée, personne, spectacle)* great, terrific, super; **tu viens passer le week-end avec nous? c'est e.!** you're spending the weekend with us? (that's) fantastic or terrific!

2 *(de qualité supérieure → vin, repas, vêtement)* first-class, first-rate; Com **beurre (de qualité) e.** finest-quality butter

3 Can Fam *(en supplément)* extra▪; **la taxe est e.** the tax is extra or on top

▪ NM **1** *(gâterie)* (special) treat; **faire** ou **s'offrir un e.** to give oneself a treat, to treat oneself; **on s'est fait un petit e. en achetant du homard** we gave ourselves a bit of a treat by buying lobster

2 *(frais)* extra cost or expenditure, incidental expenditure; **avec les extras, la semaine nous est revenue à 400 euros** if you include incidental expenditure or with (all) the extras, the week cost us 400 euros

3 *(emploi ponctuel)* **faire des extras chez qn** to do occasional work for sb; **faire des extras comme ouvreuse** to earn extra money by working (occasionally) as an usherette

4 *(serveur)* help; **pour la soirée, on prendra deux extras** we'll take on two extra people for the party

❑ extras NMPL Can Fam *(accessoires)* (optional) extras▪; **c'est plus cher avec les extras** it's much more expensive with the extras included

extra- [εkstra] PRÉF extra-

extrabudgétaire [εkstrabydʒetεr] ADJ extra-budgetary; **des dépenses extrabudgétaires** extra-budgetary costs, costs that have not been budgeted for

extracellulaire [εkstraselylεr] ADJ Biol extracellular

extra-comptable [εkstrakɔ̃tabl] ADJ Compta *(ajustement)* off-balance sheet

extraconjugal, -e, -aux, -ales [εkstrakɔ̃ʒygal, -o] ADJ extramarital

extracorporel, -elle [εkstrakɔrpɔrεl] ADJ extracorporeal

extra-courant [εkstrakurɑ̃] *(pl* extra-courants*)* NM Élec extra-current, self-induction current; **e. de rupture** break impulse

extra-crânien, -enne [εkstrakranjɛ̃, -εn] ADJ Anat extracranial

extracteur [εkstraktœr] NM **1** Mil, Chim & Méd extractor **2** Tech *(de miel)* extractor, centrifuge **3** Tech *(de fluides)* extractor

extractible [εkstraktibl] ADJ extractable; *(autoradio, disque)* removable

extractif, -ive [εkstraktif, -iv] ADJ extractive

extraction [εkstraksjɔ̃] NF **1** *(origine)* extraction, origin; **de basse e.** of humble birth; **de haute e.** highborn; **d'e. bourgeoise** from a bourgeois family **2** Mines & Pétr extraction; **e. à ciel ouvert** opencast mining; **l'e. de la pierre** quarrying (for stone); **l'e. du charbon** coal extraction or mining **3** *(d'une dent, d'une épine)* pulling out, extraction; *(d'une balle)* removal **4** Chim & Math extraction, extracting

extractive [εkstraktiv] *voir* **extractif**

extrader [3] [εkstrade] VT to extradite

extradition [εkstradisjɔ̃] NF extradition

extrados [εkstrado] NM **1** Archit extrados **2** Aviat upper surface *(of wing)*

extra-dry [εkstradraj] NM INV extra-dry champagne

extra-fin, -e, extrafin, -e [εkstrafɛ̃, -in] ADJ *(haricots, petits pois, papier)* extra-fine; *(collants)* sheer; *(chocolats)* superfine; *(beurre)* finest-quality; **de qualité extra-fine** ou **extrafine** extra fine

extrafort, -e [εkstrafɔr, -ɔrt] ADJ *(carton)* strong, stiff; *(colle)* extra-strong; *(moutarde)* hot ▪ NM bias-binding

extragalactique [εkstragalaktik] ADJ extragalactic

extra-hospitalier, -ère [εkstraɔspitalje, -εr] *(mpl* extra-hospitaliers, *fpl* extra-hospitalières*)* ADJ **soins extra-hospitaliers** home or Am non-hospital care; **en milieu e.** outside of hospital, in a non-clinical environment

extraire [112] [εkstrεr] VT **1** *(charbon)* to extract, to mine; *(pétrole)* to extract; *(pierre)* to extract, to quarry

2 *(ôter → dent, écharde, clou)* to extract, to remove, to pull out; *(→ balle)* to take out, to remove; *(→ blessés, corps)* to free (de from); **e. une balle d'une jambe** to extract or to remove a bullet from a leg; **e. un ticket de sa poche** to take or to dig a ticket out of one's pocket; **ils ont eu du mal à l'e. de sa voiture accidentée** they had great difficulty cutting him/her loose from the wreckage of his/her car; **e. un secret/des informations à qn** to worm a secret/information out of sb

3 Chim, Culin & Pharm to extract; *(en pressant)* to squeeze out; *(en écrasant)* to crush out; *(en tordant)* to wring out

4 Math to extract; **e. la racine carrée/cubique d'un nombre** to extract the square/cube root of a number

5 *(citer → passage, proverbe)* to extract, to excerpt (de from); **c'est extrait de la Genèse** it's taken from Genesis

▶**s'extraire** VPR **s'e. de qch** to climb or to clamber out of sth; **s'e. d'une voiture** *(rescapé d'un accident)* to extricate oneself from (the wreckage of) a car; **s'e. d'un puits** to climb out of a well

extrait [εkstrε] NM **1** *(morceau choisi)* extract; *(de livre, de discours, d'auteur)* extract, excerpt; *(de film)* extract, clip; **un e. de la conférence** an extract from the lecture; **un petit e. de l'émission d'hier soir** a short sequence from last night's programme; TV **extraits pré-enregistrés** recorded highlights; TV **extraits d'archives** archive footage

2 Admin **e. (d'acte) de naissance** birth certificate; **e. de casier judiciaire** extract from police records *(often used to show that one does not have a criminal record)*; **e. de compte** abstract of accounts; Compta statement of account; Banque bank statement

3 Culin & Pharm extract, essence; **e. de violette** extract or essence of violets; **e. de viande** meat extract or essence; **e. de café** coffee extract

extrajudiciaire [εkstraʒydisjεr] ADJ Jur extrajudicial

extralégal, -e, -aux, -ales [εkstralegal, -o] ADJ Jur extralegal, bordering on the illegal; **ils ont employé des méthodes extra-légales** they used methods that bordered on the illegal

extralinguistique [εkstralɛ̃gɥistik] ADJ Ling extralinguistic

extralucide [εkstralysid] ADJ clairvoyant ▪ NMF clairvoyant

extra-muros [εkstramyros] ADV outside the town, out of town; **Paris e.** outer Paris

extranéité [εkstraneite] NF Jur foreign origin, alien status

Extranet, extranet [εkstranεt] **NM** *Ordinat* Extranet

extraordinaire [εkstraɔrdinεr] **ADJ 1** *(inhabituel →* *histoire)* extraordinary, amazing; *(→ cas, personnage, intelligence)* extraordinary, exceptional; *(→ talent, courage)* extraordinary, exceptional, rare; *(→ circonstances)* extraordinary, special; *(→ messager, mission)* special; **mais, fait e., il connaissait la réponse** but, amazingly enough *or* would you believe it, he knew the answer; **frais** *ou* **dépenses extraordinaires** *(non prévues)* extras; *(uniques)* non-recurring expenditure

2 *Pol (mesures, impôt)* special; *(pouvoirs)* special, emergency *(avant n)*; **assemblée e.** special session, extraordinary meeting

3 *(remarquable → artiste, joueur, spectacle)* remarkable, outstanding; *(→ homme, femme, beauté, succès)* extraordinary, outstanding; *(→ temps)* wonderful; *(→ chaleur)* extraordinary

4 *Fam (très bon)* really good; **elle a fait un travail e.** she did outstanding work; **le repas n'avait rien d'e.** *ou* **n'était pas e.** there was nothing special about the meal

5 *(étrange)* extraordinary, strange; **cela n'a rien d'e.** that's nothing out of the ordinary; **cela n'a rien d'e. après ce que tu lui as dit** that's not surprising given what you said to him/her; **qu'y-a-t-il d'e. à cela?** what's so strange *or* special about that?; *Fam* **tu es e.!** you're amazing!; *Ironique* you're the limit!

❑ **par extraordinaire ADV** par e., il était chez lui ce soir-là he was at home that night, which was most unusual; **si par e. tu la voyais** if by some remote chance you should see her; **si par e. il arrivait que...** if by some unlikely chance it happened that...; **quand par e. il me rendait visite** on those rare occasions when he would visit me; **quand par e. nous nous rencontrons** when we meet, which we rarely do; *Fam* **comme par e., il était là** as if by magic, he was there

extraordinairement [εkstraɔrdinεrmɑ̃] **ADV 1** *(très)* extraordinarily, extremely, exceptionally **2** *(bizarrement)* extraordinarily, strangely, bizarrely

extraparlementaire [εkstraparləmɑ̃tεr] **ADJ** extraparliamentary

extrapatrimonial, -e, -aux, -ales [εkstrapatrimɔnjal, -o] **ADJ** *Jur* extrapatrimonial

extra petita [εkstrapetita] *Jur* **NM** excessive award
ADV statuer e. to adjudicate more than is asked for

extraplat, -e [εkstrapla, -at] **ADJ** extraflat, very slim, slimline; **une calculatrice extraplate** a slimline calculator

extrapolable [εkstrapɔlabl] **ADJ** that can be extrapolated

extrapolation [εkstrapɔlasjɔ̃] **NF** extrapolation

extrapoler [3] [εkstrapɔle] **VT** to extrapolate; **e. qch d'un fait** to extrapolate sth from a fact
VI to extrapolate; **e. à partir de qch** to extrapolate from sth

extrapyramidal, -e, -aux, -ales [εkstrapiramidal, -o] **ADJ** *Méd* extrapyramidal

extrarénal, -e, -aux, -ales [εkstrarenal, -o] **ADJ** *Méd* extrarenal

extrascolaire [εkstraskɔlεr] **ADJ** *(activités)* extra-curricular

extrasensible [εkstrasɑ̃sibl] **ADJ** ultrasensitive

extrasensoriel, -elle, extra-sensoriel, -elle [εkstrasɑ̃sɔrjεl] **ADJ** extrasensory

extrasolaire [εkstrasɔlεr] **ADJ** *Astron* extrasolar

extrastatutaire [εkstrastatytεr] **ADJ** extra-statutory

extrasystole [εkstrasistɔl] **NF** *Méd* extrasystole

extraterrestre [εkstratεrεstr] **ADJ** extraterrestrial
NMF extraterrestrial (being *or* creature)

extraterritorial, -e, -aux, -ales [εkstratεritɔrjal, -o] **ADJ** extraterritorial

extraterritorialité [εkstratεritɔrjalite] **NF** extraterritoriality

extra-utérin, -e [εkstrayterε̃, -in] *(mpl* **extra-utérins,** *fpl* **extra-utérines)* **ADJ** *Méd* extra-uterine; **grossesse extra-utérine** ectopic pregnancy

extravagance [εkstravagɑ̃s] **NF 1** *(outrance → d'une attitude, d'une personne, d'une réponse, d'une tenue)* extravagance; *(→ d'une demande)* extravagance, unreasonableness; *(→ de dépenses)* exorbitance; *(→ d'une tenue)* extravagance, eccentricity; *(→ d'un désir)* immoderateness; **des idées d'une telle e.** such extravagant ideas

2 *(acte)* extravagance; *(parole)* foolish thing (to say); **faire des extravagances** to behave extravagantly, to do eccentric things; **dire des extravagances** to talk wildly; **cette promesse était une e.** it was an extravagant promise to make

extravagant, -e [εkstravagɑ̃, -ɑ̃t] **ADJ 1** *(déraisonnable → attitude, personne, réponse, tenue)* extravagant; *(→ idée)* extravagant, wild, crazy; **de manière extravagante** extravagantly; **raconter des histoires extravagantes** to tell wild stories **2** *(excessif → demande, exigence, dépenses)* extravagant, unreasonable
NM,F eccentric (person)

extravaguer [3] [εkstravage] **VI** *Littéraire* to extravagate

extravaser [3] [εkstravaze] **s'extravaser VPR** *Physiol* to extravasate

extravéhiculaire [εkstraveikylεr] **ADJ** *Astron* extravehicular

extraversion [εkstravεrsjɔ̃] **NF** *Psy* extroversion

extraverti, -e [εkstravεrti] **ADJ** extroverted
NM,F extrovert

extrayait *etc voir* **extraire**

extrémal, -e, -aux, -ales [εkstremal, -o] **ADJ** extreme

extrême [εkstrεm] **ADJ 1** *(intense → confort, importance, soin etc)* extreme, utmost; *(→ froid)* extreme, intense; **j'ai l'e. regret de vous annoncer que...** to my deepest *or* very great regret, I have to tell you that...; **d'une complexité/maigreur e.** extremely complex/skinny

2 *(radical → idée)* extreme; *(→ mesures)* extreme, drastic; **être e. dans ses idées** to hold extreme views; **elle est e. en tout** she is extreme in everything; *Pol* **l'e. droite/gauche** the extreme *or* far right/left

3 *(exceptionnel → cas, exemple, situation)* extreme; **ne m'appelle qu'en cas d'e. urgence** only call me in cases of extreme urgency *or* if it's extremely urgent

4 *(le plus éloigné → point, limite)* far, extreme, farthest; **la limite e., l'e. limite** the furthest point; **à l'e. limite, j'accepterai d'attendre une semaine de plus** I'll agree to wait another week at the most *or* at the outside; **la partie e.** the furthest part; **la date e.** the final date

NM 1 *(cas limite)* extreme; **passer d'un e. à l'autre** to go from one extreme to the other *or* to another; **les extrêmes se rejoignent** extremes meet *or* join up

2 *Math* **extrêmes** *(termes)* extremes

❑ **à l'extrême ADV** extremely, in the extreme; **il est méticuleux à l'e.** he's conscientious in the extreme; **porter** *ou* **pousser les choses à l'e.** to take *or* to carry things to extremes

extrêmement [εkstrεmmɑ̃] **ADV** extremely

extrême-onction [εkstrεmɔ̃ksjɔ̃] *(pl* **extrêmes-onctions)* **NF** *Rel* extreme unction

Extrême-Orient [εkstrεmɔrjɑ̃] **NM l'E.** the Far East

extrême-oriental, -e *(mpl* **extrême-orientaux,** *fpl*

extrême-orientales)* [εkstrεmɔrjɑ̃tal, -o] **ADJ Far Eastern

❑ **Extrême-oriental, -e** *(mpl* **Extrême-Orientaux,** *fpl* **Extrême-Orientales)* **NM,F** Oriental

extremis [εkstremis] *voir* **in extremis**

extrémisme [εkstremism] **NM** extremism; **l'e. de droite/gauche** right-/left-wing extremism

extrémiste [εkstremist] **ADJ** extremist
NMF extremist; **les extrémistes de droite/gauche** right-/left-wing extremists

extrémité [εkstremite] **NF 1** *(d'un bâtiment, d'une table, d'une jetée, d'une corde)* end; *(d'un bâton)* end, tip; *(d'un doigt, de la langue, d'une aile)* tip; *(d'un champ)* edge, end; *(d'une aiguille, d'une épée)* point; *(d'un territoire)* (furthest) boundary; **aux extrémités de l'univers** at the outermost limits *or* on the edge of the universe

2 *Anat & Math* extremity; **les extrémités** *(pieds et mains)* the extremities, the hands and feet; **j'ai les extrémités glacées** my hands and feet are frozen

3 *(acte radical)* extreme act; **pousser qn à des extrémités** to drive sb to extremes; **en venir à des extrémités** to resort to extreme measures

4 *(brutalité)* act of violence; **en venir à des extrémités** to resort to violence; **il s'est porté à des extrémités regrettables** unfortunately he resorted to acts of violence

5 *(situation critique)* plight, straits, extremity; **dans cette e.** in this extremity; **être à la dernière e.** to be on the point of death; **être réduit à la dernière e.** to be in dire straits *or* in a dreadful plight

extremum [εkstremɔm] *(pl* **extremums)* **NM** *Math* extremum

extrinsèque [εkstrε̃sεk] **ADJ** extrinsic; **valeur e. d'une monnaie** face value of a currency

extrinsèquement [εkstrε̃sεkmɑ̃] **ADV** extrinsically

extrorse [εkstrɔrs] **ADJ** *Bot* extrorse

extroversion [εkstrovεrsjɔ̃] **NF** *Psy* extroversion

extroverti, -e [εkstrovεrti] **ADJ** extroverted

extruder [3] [εkstryde] **VT** *Ind* to extrude

extrudeuse [εkstrydøz] **NF** *Ind* extruder

extrusif, -ive [εkstryzif, -iv] **ADJ** *Géol* extrusive

extrusion [εkstryzjɔ̃] **NF 1** *Ind* extrusion, extruding **2** *Géol* extrusion

exubérance [εgzyberɑ̃s] **NF 1** *(entrain)* exuberance, joie de vivre; **avec e.** exuberantly **2** *Littéraire (action)* exuberant behaviour *(UNCOUNT)* **3** *(énergie, vigueur → d'une végétation, d'un style)* luxuriance; *(→ d'une imagination)* wildness, exuberance; *(→ de figures, de formes)* abundance, luxuriance

exubérant, -e [εgzyberɑ̃, -ɑ̃t] **ADJ 1** *(joyeux → attitude, personne)* exuberant **2** *(vigoureux → végétation, style)* luxuriant; *(→ imagination)* wild, exuberant

exulcération [εgzylserasjɔ̃] **NF** *Méd* ulceration

exultation [εgzyltasjɔ̃] **NF** *Littéraire* exultation, rejoicing

exulter [3] [εgzylte] **VI** to exult, to rejoice; **l'annonce de cette nouvelle la fit e.** when she heard the news she went wild with joy *or* was over the moon

exutoire [εgzytwar] **NM 1** *(dérivatif)* **un e. à** an outlet for **2** *(pour liquides)* outlet

exuvie [εgzyvi] **NF** *Zool* exuviae

ex vivo [εksvivo] *Méd* **ADJ** ex vivo
ADV ex vivo

ex-voto [εksvɔto] **NM INV** *Rel* ex voto

EXW [əiksdubləve] *Com (abrév* **ex-works)* EXW

eye-liner [ajlajnœr] *(pl* **eye-liners)* **NM** eyeliner

eyra [εra] **NM** *Zool* eyra

Ézéchiel [ezekjεl] **NPR** *Bible* Ezekiel

e-zine, ezine [izin] **NM** *Ordinat* e-zine, ezine

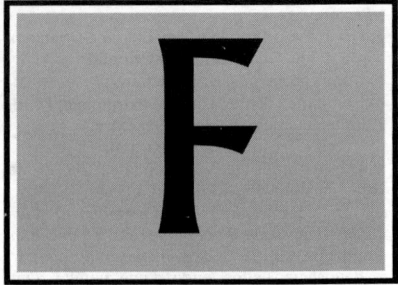

F¹, f [ɛf] NM INV **1** *(lettre)* F, f; **F comme François** ≃ F for Freddie **2** *Mus (note)* F **3** *(appartement)* **un F3** ≃ a two-bedroomed *Br* flat *or Am* apartment; **un F4** ≃ a three-bedroomed *Br* flat *or Am* apartment

F² [ɛf] NF *Sport (abrév* **Formule***)* F; **la F1** F1

F³ 1 *(abrév écrite* **franc***)* F; **500 F** 500 F, F 500 **2** *(abrév écrite* **fahrenheit***)* F **3** *(abrév écrite* **farad***)* F **4** *(abrév écrite* **femme***)* F

fa [fa] NM INV *(note)* F; *(quand on chante la gamme)* fa, fah; **en fa majeur/mineur** in F major/minor; **un fa bémol/dièse** an F flat/sharp; **en fa bémol/dièse** in F flat/sharp; **chantez-moi un fa** sing me an F; **chantez "ré, mi, fa"** sing "re, mi, fa *or* fah''; **clé de fa** key of F, bass clef

FAB [ɛfabe] ADJ INV & ADV *Com (abrév* **franco à bord***)* FOB, fob

fabacée [fabase] *Bot* NF member of the Fabaceae family

☐ **fabacées** NFPL Fabaceae

fable [fabl] NF **1** *Littérature* fable; **célèbre dans la f.** famous in fable **2** *Péj (invention)* lie, invention; **c'est une f.!** it's a fairytale! **3** *Littéraire (légende)* legend, tale **4** *Arch (locution)* **être la f. du village** to be the laughing stock of the village

fabliau, -x [fablijo] NM *Littérature* fabliau

fablier [fablije] NM *Littérature* book *or* collection of fables

fabricant, -e [fabrikɑ̃, -ɑ̃t] NM,F manufacturer, maker; **gros/petit f.** large/small manufacturer; **f. de voitures** car manufacturer; **f. de chaussures** shoemaker; **je suis f. de bougies** I make candles, I'm a candlemaker

fabricateur, -trice [fabrikatœr, -tris] NM,F **f. de fausse monnaie** counterfeiter; **f. de faux papiers** forger of documents; **f. de calomnies** slanderer; **f. de fausses nouvelles** scandal-monger

fabrication [fabrikasjɔ̃] NF **1** *(à la main)* making; *Ind* manufacture, production; **f. artisanale** production by craftsmen; **produits de f. artisanale** handmade products; **f. industrielle** industrial manufacture; **f. assistée par ordinateur** computer-aided *or* computer-assisted manufacturing; **f. intégrée par ordinateur** computer-integrated manufacturing; **f. par lots** batch production; **f. en série** mass production

2 *(contrefaçon → de fausses nouvelles)* fabrication; *(→ document)* counterfeiting, forging; **f. de fausse monnaie** counterfeiting; **f. de faux en écritures** forging of documents

3 *(production)* workmanship; **f. soignée** quality workmanship; **de f. maison** home-made; **article de f. française** article made in France, French-made article; **c'est de ta f.?** did you make it yourself?; **elle a apporté une tarte de sa f.** she brought along a tart she had made herself

4 *Péj* **la f. d'une vedette** the manufacturing of a star; **la f. d'un président** the making of a president

5 *Typ* layout

☐ **de fabrication** ADJ *(coûts, procédés)* manufacturing *(avant n)*; *(numéro)* serial *(avant n)*; **défaut de f.** manufacturing defect; **secret de f.** trade secret

fabricien, -enne [fabrisjɛ̃, -ɛn] *Belg Rel* ADJ of a (parochial) church council

NM,F member of a (parochial) church council, church warden

fabrique [fabrik] NF **1** *(établissement)* factory, works, mill; **f. de papier** paper mill **2** *(fabrication)* manufacture; **prix de f.** manufacturer's *or* factory price **3** *Rel* **conseil de f.**, *Belg* **F. d'Église** (parochial) church council

☐ **de fabrique** ADJ *(prix, secret)* manufacturer's, trade *(avant n)*; *(marque)* trade *(avant n)*

fabriqué, -e [fabrike] ADJ **1** *Écon (produit)* manufactured; **f. en France** made in France; **f. en série** mass-produced; **f. sur commande** made to order; **f. sur mesure(s)** made to measure **2** *(sans spontanéité → sentiment, réaction)* lacking in spontaneity

fabriquer [3] [fabrike] VT **1** *Ind* to make, to produce, to manufacture; *(gâteau, pull-over, guirlande)* to make; **f. des véhicules en série** to mass-produce vehicles

2 *(artisanalement)* to make; **nous fabriquons nos produits à la main** we make our products by hand; **cela a contribué à f. son personnage médiatique** that helped to turn him/her into a media figure *or* to make a media figure out of him/her

3 *Fam (faire)* to do■, to cook up; **je me demande ce qu'il peut f. toute la journée dans sa chambre** I wonder what he gets up to in his room all day (long); **mais qu'est-ce qu'il fabrique?** what's he up to?, what's he doing?; **qu'est-ce que tu fabriques, ces jours-ci?** what are you up to these days?; **ça alors, qu'est-ce que tu fabriques par ici?** what on earth are you doing here?; *Péj* **qu'est-ce que tu as encore fabriqué avec mes clefs?** now what have you gone and done with my keys?; **qu'est-ce qu'il fabrique, ce bus?** what's that bus doing?; **je me suis tout à coup demandé ce que je fabriquais là** I suddenly wondered what I was doing there

4 *Péj (histoire)* to concoct; *(personnalité)* to build up; **f. qch de toutes pièces** to make sth up, to fabricate sth; **c'est une histoire fabriquée de toutes pièces** it's a made-up story, the story is made-up from start to finish; **ils ont fabriqué (de toutes pièces) l'histoire du contrat soviétique** the Soviet contract story was a complete fabrication; **f. de la fausse monnaie** to counterfeit *or* forge money; **f. des faux papiers** to forge documents

▸**se fabriquer** VPR **1** *(être fabriqué)* to be made *or* manufactured; **ils se fabriquent facilement** they are easy to make, they are easily made *or* manufactured

2 se f. qch to build *or* make sth for oneself; **il s'était fabriqué une cabane** he had built a hut (for himself)

3 se f. qch *(s'inventer, se constituer)* to invent sth; **elle s'était fabriqué un passé d'actrice de cinéma** she had invented a past as a film actress for herself

fabulateur, -trice [fabylatœr, -tris] ADJ *Psy* confabulatory

NM,F fantasist; *Psy* confabulator

fabulation [fabylasjɔ̃] NF fabrication, fantasizing; *Psy* confabulation

fabuler [3] [fabyle] VI **1** *Psy* to confabulate **2** *Péj (mentir)* to tell tales; **des ours? – je crois qu'il fabule un peu** bears? – I think he's making it up

fabuleusement [fabyløzmɑ̃] ADV fabulously, fantastically

fabuleux, -euse [fabylø, -øz] ADJ **1** *(de légende)* fabulous, legendary; *(caractère, exploits)* mythical, legendary; **des animaux f.** fabulous beasts **2** *(hors du commun)* incredible, fabulous; **un destin f.** an incredible fate **3** *(élevé → prix, somme)* tremendous, astronomical; **elle gagne des sommes fabuleuses** she earns a tremendous amount of money

---

🎬

'Le Fabuleux destin d'Amélie Poulain' *Jeunet* 'Amélie' (UK), 'Amélie from Montmartre' (US)

fabuliste [fabylist] NMF *Littérature* fabulist, writer of fables

FAC [ɛfase] ADJ *Com (abrév* **franc d'avarie commune***)* FGA, fga

NM *Admin (abrév* **fonds d'aide et de coopération***)* = French government fund which administers economic and social projects in former colonies

fac [fak] NF *Fam (abrév* **faculté***)* university■, uni; **f. de droit/de lettres** faculty of law/arts■; **en f., à la f.** at university■ *or* college■, at uni; **être en f. d'allemand** to be studying German at uni

façade [fasad] NF **1** *(de bâtiment)* façade; **la f. du château** the front of the palace; **f. latérale** side (aspect); **f. principale** façade, (main) frontage; **hôtel sur la f. sur la place** hotel facing the square

2 *(paroi)* front wall *or* panel; **f. de quai** platform screen doors, platform-edge doors

3 *(apparence)* outward appearance, façade; *Péj (faux-semblant)* cover, pretence; **ce n'est qu'une f.** it's all show *or* a façade

4 *très Fam (visage)* mug, face■; **se refaire la f.** to touch up one's make-up; **se faire refaire la f.** to have a face-lift; **démolir la f. à qn** to smash sb's face in

5 *Géog* **la f. atlantique** the Atlantic coast

6 *Ordinat (d'un modem etc)* front panel

7 *Tél (d'un téléphone portable)* fascia

8 *Assur* fronting

☐ **de façade** ADJ **un optimisme de f.** a show of optimism; **une générosité/un patriotisme de f.** fake *or* sham generosity/patriotism

face [fas] NF **1** *(visage)* face; **il a reçu le coup en pleine f.** he was hit full in the face; **les muscles de la f.** facial muscles; **des lésions de la f.** lesions on the face; **f. contre terre** face down; **tomber f. contre terre** to fall flat on one's face; **arborer** *ou* **avoir une f. de carême** to have a long face; **il est arrivé avec une f. de carême** he turned up wearing a long face *or* looking very down in the mouth; *Can* **avoir une f. de mi-carême** *(avoir l'air émacié)* to look gaunt; *(avoir l'air déprimé)* to have a long face; *Can Fam* **avoir une f. de bœuf** *(avoir l'air fâché)* to look mad *or* pissed-off; *(avoir l'air abruti)* to look dazed■ *or* out of it; *Can Fam* **maudite f. de bœuf!** you moron!; *très Fam* **f. de crabe** *ou* **d'œuf** *ou* **de rat** *Br* face-ache, *Am* ratfink; **f. de lune** round face; **perdre/sauver la f.** to lose/to save face; **se voiler la f.** to delude oneself

2 *(aspect)* **la f. des choses** the face of things; **changer la f. de** to alter the face of; **examiner un problème sous toutes ses faces** to consider every aspect of a problem

3 *(côté → d'une médaille)* obverse; *(→ d'une pièce)* head, headside; *(→ d'un disque)* side; *(→ d'une montagne)* face; *(→ d'une lame d'épée)* flat; **la f. B d'un disque** the B-side *or* flipside of a record; **la f. cachée de la lune** the dark side of the moon; *Fig* **la f. cachée d'un problème** the hidden side *or* aspect of a problem; **à double f.** double-sided; **changer un disque de f.** to turn a record over; **f.!** *(en lançant une pièce)* heads!

4 *Littéraire (surface)* face; **la f. des eaux/de la terre** the face of the waters/of the earth

5 *Géom & Tech* face, side; **polyèdre à douze faces** twelve-sided polyhedron; **f. de guidage** guiding face; **f. portante** bearing face

6 *Ordinat* **disquette double f.** double-sided disk

7 *Couture* **double f.** double-faced; **tissu double f.** double-faced fabric

8 *(locutions)* **faire f.** to face up to things, to cope; **après l'accident, il lui a fallu faire f.** after the accident, he/she just had to cope; **faire f. à** *(être tourné vers)* to stand opposite to, to face; *(danger, difficultés)* to face up to; *(obligations, dépense)* to meet; **faire f. à la mer** to face the sea; **les fenêtres font f. au sud** the windows face south; **les deux maisons se font f.** the two houses face *or* are facing *or* are opposite each other; **faire f. aux critiques** to face one's critics; **faire f. à ses créanciers** to face up to one's creditors

❑ **à la face de** PRÉP *(devant)* **à la f. de son frère** to his/her brother's face; **jeter des accusations à la f. de qn** to throw accusations in sb's face; **elle lui a jeté à la f. qu'il était hypocrite** she told him straight to his face that he was a hypocrite; **à la f. du monde** *ou* **de tous** *(publiquement)* openly, publicly; **crier sa joie/son désespoir à la f. du monde** to shout out one's joy/despair to the world (at large); **à la f. de Dieu** before God

❑ **à sa face même** ADV *Can (à l'évidence)* evidently, clearly; **le tribunal a jugé que la demande était, à sa f. même, irrecevable** the court ruled that the claim was clearly inadmissible

❑ **de face** ADJ face *(avant n)*, facing; *Beaux-Arts & Phot* **photo/portrait de f.** full-face photograph/portrait; *Archit* **vue de f.** front view *or* elevation; *Tech* **clouage de f.** face nailing; *Théât* **loge de f.** box facing the stage; *Transp* **place de f.** seat facing the engine ADV **se présenter de f.** to be face on; **il l'a attaquée de f.** he attacked her from the front; *Fig* he attacked her openly

❑ **d'en face** ADJ **ceux d'en f.** *(adversaires)* the opposition; *(voisins)* the people opposite; **le garçon d'en f.** the boy from across the road; **la maison d'en f.** the house opposite

❑ **en face** ADV *(de front)* **avoir le soleil en f.** to have the sun (shining) in one's face; **regarder qn (bien) en f.** to look sb (full *or* straight) in the face; **regarder la mort en f.** to face up to death; **regarder les choses en f.** to face facts; **je lui ai dit la vérité en f.** I told him/her the truth to his/her face

❑ **en face de** PRÉP **juste en f. de moi** right in front of me; **sa maison est en f. de l'église** his house is opposite *or* faces the church; **les maisons en f. de l'école** the houses opposite *or* facing the school; **mettre qn en f. des réalités** to force sb to face reality; **en f. l'un de l'autre, l'un en f. de l'autre** face to face, opposite each other, facing each other; **nous sommes en f. d'un problème difficile** we are faced with a difficult problem

❑ **face à** PRÉP *(dans l'espace)* facing; **f. au public** in front of *or* facing the audience; **f. à l'ennemi/aux médias** faced with the enemy/media

❑ **face à face** ADV face to face; **nous étions enfin f. à f.** at last we had come face to face; **parler à qn f. à f.** to speak to sb face to face *or* in person; **mettre deux témoins f. à f.** to bring two witnesses face to face; **mettre qn f. à f. avec** to bring sb face to face with; **que feras-tu quand tu seras f. à f. avec lui?** what will you do when you're faced with *or* face to face with him?

face-à-face [fasafas] NM INV *(conversation)* (face-to-face) meeting; *(conflit)* (one-to-one) confrontation; **f. télévisé** television debate *(between two politicians)*

face-à-main [fasamɛ̃] *(pl* **faces-à-main)** NM lorgnette

face-texte [fastɛkst] *(pl* **faces-textes)** NM *Journ* facing matter

facétie [fasesi] NF *Littéraire (plaisanterie)* facetious remark, joke; *(trait d'esprit)* witticism, wisecrack; *(farce)* prank; **dire des facéties** to crack jokes; **épargne-nous tes facéties!** spare us your jokes!; **se livrer à des facéties** to fool around

facétieusement [fasesjøzmɑ̃] ADV facetiously, humorously

facétieux, -euse [fasesjø, -øz] ADJ facetious, humorous

NM,F joker, prankster

facette [fasɛt] NF 1 *Entom, Géol & (en joaillerie)* facet 2 *(aspect)* facet, aspect, side; **sa personnalité présente d'autres facettes** there are other sides to his/her personality; **examiner un problème sous toutes ses facettes** to examine a problem from every angle

❑ **à facettes** ADJ 1 *Entom, Géol & (en joaillerie)* multifaceted; **taillé à facettes** (cut) in facets, facetted 2 *(personnalité, talent)* multifaceted, many-sided

facetter [4] [fasete] VT *(en joaillerie)* to facet

fâché, -e [faʃe] ADJ 1 *(en colère)* angry, cross; **être f. contre qn** to be angry *or* annoyed with sb; **tu n'es pas f., au moins?** you're not angry, are you?; **avoir l'air f.** to look angry *or* cross

2 *(désolé)* sorry; **être f. de qch/pour qn** to be sorry about sth/for sb; **je suis f. de l'avoir manqué** I'm really sorry I missed him; **je ne serais pas f. d'avoir une réponse** I wouldn't mind getting an answer; **ils n'étaient pas fâchés de se retrouver chez eux** they were rather pleased to be home again; **je ne suis pas f. que ce soit terminé** I'm not sorry that it's finished

3 *(brouillé)* **ils sont fâchés** they're not on speaking terms; **être f. avec qn** to have fallen out with sb

4 *Fig Hum (sans goût pour)* **je suis f. avec les langues/les chiffres** languages/figures are not my thing; **il est f. avec le savon** he's allergic to soap; **tu es f. avec ton rasoir?** shaving doesn't come naturally to you, does it?

fâcher [3] [faʃe] VT 1 *(mettre en colère)* to annoy, to make angry, to anger; **un sujet qui fâche** a controversial topic

2 *Vieilli (contrarier)* to annoy, to vex; **acceptez, le contraire les fâcherait** say yes, they'd be offended if you didn't; **ce retard me fâche infiniment** I am extremely annoyed at this delay

▶**se fâcher** VPR 1 *(se brouiller)* to fall out *or* to quarrel (with each other *or* one another); **tes parents se sont fâchés?** did your parents quarrel?; **se f. avec qn** to quarrel *or* to fall out with sb

2 *(se mettre en colère)* to get cross *or* angry, to lose one's temper; **tes parents se sont fâchés?** did your parents get angry?; *Fam* **se f. tout rouge** to blow one's top; **se f. contre qn** to get angry with sb

fâcherie [faʃri] NF tiff; **entre eux, ce sont des fâcheries continuelles** they're always quarrelling (with each other *or* one another)

fâcheuse [faʃøz] *voir* **fâcheux**

fâcheusement [faʃøzmɑ̃] ADV *(malheureusement)* unfortunately; *(désagréablement)* unpleasantly; **il a été f. impressionné** he was not at all impressed

fâcheux, -euse [faʃø, -øz] ADJ regrettable, unfortunate; **une fâcheuse habitude** an unfortunate habit; **une fâcheuse coïncidence** an unfortunate coincidence; **une formulation fâcheuse** an unfortunate *or* a regrettable choice of words; **c'est f.!** it's rather a pity!; **il est f. qu'il soit parti si tôt** it's a pity (that) he left so early; **il a eu la fâcheuse idée de l'inviter à la soirée** he rather unfortunately invited him/her to the party

NM,F *Littéraire* bore

facho [faʃo] *Fam Péj* ADJ fascist■

NMF fascist■

facial, -e, -aux, -ales [fasjal, -o] ADJ *(muscle, angle)* facial; **massage f.** facial *or* face massage

faciès [fasjɛs] NM 1 *(traits)* facial aspect, features; *Méd* facies; **le f. caractéristique de Cro-Magnon** Cro-Magnon man's typical features 2 *Péj (visage)* face; **un f. grimaçant derrière le carreau** a grimacing face behind the windowpane 3 *Bot & Géol* facies

facile [fasil] ADJ 1 *(aisé)* easy; **essaie, c'est f. comme tout!** have a go, it's as easy as anything!; **rien de plus f.** nothing easier; **il ne m'est pas f. d'expliquer la situation** it's not easy for me to explain the situation; **f. à faire** easy to do, easily done; **f. à comprendre** easily understood, easy to understand; **f. à installer** easily installed; **f. à lire** (easily) readable, easy to read; **f. à retenir** easy to remember, (easily) memorable; **c'est f. à dire (mais moins f. à faire), c'est plus f. à dire qu'à faire** easier said than done; **f. d'accès** easy to reach, within easy reach; **la gare n'est pas f. d'accès** the station isn't easy to get to; **f. d'emploi** easy to use; **avoir la vie f.** to have an easy life; **c'est f. comme bonjour** *ou* **comme tout** it's as easy as pie; **ça n'est pas si f. que ça** it's not as easy as that, it's not all that easy

2 *(spontané, naturel)* **elle a la parole/plume f.** speaking/writing comes easily to her; **avoir l'argent f.** to be very casual about money; **avoir la larme f.** to be easily moved to tears; **avoir la gâchette f.** to be trigger-happy

3 *Péj (effet, humour)* facile; **avoir l'ironie f.** to be unnecessarily sarcastic

4 *(souple → caractère)* easy, easy-going; **être f. (à vivre)** to be easy-going; **tu n'as pas choisi quelqu'un de f. (à vivre)** you haven't exactly picked someone easy to get on with; **il n'a pas l'air f. en affaires** he doesn't seem an easy man to do business with; **c'est un enfant f.** this child is no problem

5 *Péj (libertin)* **une femme f.** *ou* **de mœurs faciles** a woman of easy virtue

ADV 1 *Fam (facilement)* **je te fais ça en deux heures f.** I can have it done for you in two hours, no problem; **d'ici à la maison, il reste 30 kilomètres f.** from here to the house, there's still a good 30 kilometres; **on met trois jours f. pour traverser l'île** it takes easily *or* at least three days to cross the island; **en trois jours, j'aurai lu f. deux livres** I'll easily read two books in three days

2 *Belg* **avoir f. à** *ou* **de faire qch** to find it easy to do sth, to have no problem doing sth

> *Allusion*
> **C'est facile et ça peut rapporter gros**
> This slogan was invented by the French national lottery board in 1980 to encourage people to take part in the lottery. It means "It's easy and there are big prizes to be won." When you want to persuade someone to do something, or explain to them why you are going to do it yourself, you can say this in a joking way.

facilement [fasilmɑ̃] ADV 1 *(sans difficulté)* easily, readily; **vous trouverez f., c'est à deux pas** you'll find it easily, it's not very far; **pas f. accessible** not readily accessible; **elle est f. déroutée par la critique** she's easily thrown off balance by criticism 2 *(au moins)* at least; **il fait f. trois fautes par page** he makes at least three mistakes per page; **je gagnerais f. le double** I would easily earn twice as much

facilitation [fasilitasjɔ̃] NF facilitation, facilitating

facilité [fasilite] NF 1 *(simplicité)* easiness; **selon le degré de f. des exercices** depending on how easy the exercises are; **d'une grande f. de lecture** very easy readable; *Péj* **céder à** *ou* **se laisser aller à** *ou* **choisir la f.** to take the easy way out *or* the easy option; *Péj* **c'est une solution de f.** it's the easy solution *or* way out; **f. d'emploi** *(d'un ordinateur etc)* user-friendliness, ease of use

2 *(possibilité)* opportunity; **avoir toute f.** *ou* **toutes facilités pour faire qch** to have every opportunity of doing sth

3 *(aisance)* ease; **f. de parole** fluency; **avoir beaucoup de f. pour** to have a gift for; **avec f.** easily, with ease; **avec une grande f.** with the greatest of ease; **parler avec f.** *(langue étrangère)* to speak fluently; **écrire avec f.** to write fluently *or* with ease; **il n'a pas la f. de son frère** things don't come as easily to him as they do to his brother; **les enfants comprennent l'informatique avec une f. déconcertante** children understand computers with disconcerting ease

4 *Com* **f. d'écoulement** *(d'un produit)* saleability; **f. de reprise** trade-in facility; **facilités de transport** transport facilities; **f. de vente** saleability

❑ **facilités** NFPL 1 *(capacités)* ability, aptitude; **avoir des facilités** to have ability *or* aptitude; **avoir des facilités en maths** to have great aptitude for maths; **votre enfant a des facilités** your child shows some aptitude

2 *Fin* facilities; **facilités de caisse** overdraft facilities; **facilités de crédit** credit facilities; **facilités d'endettement** borrowing capacity; **facilités de paiement** payment facilities, easy terms

faciliter [3] [fasilite] VT to ease, to help along, to make easier; **f. qch à qn** to make sth easier for sb; **ça ne va pas f. les choses entre eux** it won't make things easier *or* smoother between them; **cela ne va pas f. les choses** it won't make things (any) easier; **tu ne me facilites pas le travail!** you're not making things easy for me!; **le**

vent ne leur facilite pas la tâche the wind doesn't make it any easier for them; sa connaissance de la langue a facilité son insertion his/her knowledge of the language helped him/her to settle in (more easily); une influence qui a facilité ma carrière an influence which helped my career along

facing [fɛsiŋ] NM *Mktg* shelf facing

facob [fakɔb] NM *Assur* (*abrév* traité facultatif obligatoire) open cover

FAÇON [fasɔ̃]

manner 1 ▪ way 1, 2 ▪ making 3 ▪ cut 4

NF 1 (*manière*) manner, way; la phrase peut se comprendre de plusieurs façons the sentence can be interpreted in several ways; je l'empêcherai de le faire – et de quelle f.? I'll stop him/her doing it – how?; demande-lui de quelle f. il compte payer ask him how he wishes to pay; je n'aime pas la f. dont il me parle I don't like the way he talks *or* his way of talking to me; la f. dont l'anglais est enseigné the way (in which) English is taught; elle a raison, mais ce qui me dérange, c'est la f. dont elle le dit she's right but what bothers me is the way *or* manner in which she says it; d'une f. désordonnée in a disorderly fashion; d'une *ou* de f. générale generally speaking; de f. agréable pleasantly; de f. définitive definitively, finally; de f. systématique systematically; d'une f. ou d'une autre one way or another, somehow or other; en aucune f.! not at all!, by no means!; cela ne me dérange en aucune f. it doesn't bother me in the slightest; sa f. d'être the way he/she is; je ne tolérerai pas ces façons de parler I won't tolerate that sort of language; ce n'est pas une f. de parler à son père that's no way to speak to one's father; ce n'est pas une f. de parler pour un petit garçon that's no way for a little boy to speak; ce n'est qu'une f. de parler *ou* dire it's just a manner of speaking; *Fam* généreux, f. de parler, il ne m'a jamais donné un centime! generous, that's a funny way of putting it, he never gave me a penny!; tu pars en vacances? – oui, f. de parler, je vais garder mes neveux are you going on holiday? – yes, I suppose you could say that *or* in a manner of speaking *or* sort of, I'm looking after my nephews; je vais lui dire ma f. de penser, moi! I'll give him/her a piece of my mind!; elle a une curieuse f. de voir les choses she has a strange way of looking at things; ils n'ont pas les mêmes façons de voir they see things differently; ce n'est pas ma f. de faire it's not my way of doing things; avoir une f. à soi de faire qch to have one's own way of doing sth

2 (*moyen*) way; pour obtenir une audience de lui, il n'y a qu'une seule f. de s'y prendre there's only one way of getting *or* to get an audience with him; il n'y a pas trente-six façons de le faire there are no two ways of doing it

3 (*fabrication*) making, fashioning; (*facture*) craftsmanship, workmanship; (*main-d'œuvre*) labour; f. d'un manteau making (up) of a coat; matière et f. material and labour; compter 50 euros de f. to charge 50 euros for labour

4 *Couture* cut; f. et fournitures labour and material; de bonne f. well-made, (beautifully) tailored

5 *Suisse* avoir bonne/mauvaise f. to look good/bad, to create a good/bad impression; ne pas avoir de f. (*être inconvenant*) to be improper; (*manquer de savoir-vivre*) to be lacking in refinement; il n'a pas de f. avec cette vieille cravate he doesn't look very presentable in that old tie

6 *Can* avoir de la f. (*avoir des manières agréables*) to be pleasant; (*être beau parleur*) to be a smooth talker

7 *Agr* donner une f. à la terre to cultivate the soil

8 (*suivi d'un nom*) (*qui rappelle*) une nappe f. grand-mère a tablecloth like Grandma used to have; un dessin f. Dürer a drawing reminiscent of *or* in the style of Dürer; f. marbre/bois imitation marble/wood; un châle f. cachemire a paisley-patterned shawl; cuir f. porc imitation pigskin; sac f. cuir imitation leather bag

❑ façons NFPL (*manières*) manners, behaviour; en voilà des façons! watch your manners!, what a way to behave!; ce ne sont pas des façons! that's no way to behave!; avoir des façons engageantes to be charming; elle a des façons de petite vieille she behaves like an old woman; faire des façons (*se faire prier*) to make a fuss; (*se pavaner*) to put on airs; *Can* (*bien recevoir*) to entertain in style; on est entre nous, on ne va pas faire de façons we're all friends here, we won't stand on ceremony

❑ à façon ADJ (*artisan*) jobbing; (*travail*) contract (*avant n*); *Ordinat* centre de traitement *ou* travail à f. data processing *or* computer *or* service bureau ADV on travaille à f. (*dans une annonce*) customers' own materials made up

❑ à la façon de PRÉP like, in the manner of; à la f. des vieilles gens like old people; peindre à la f. des cubistes to paint in the manner *or* style of the Cubists; elle portait le paquet sur la tête, un peu à la f. d'une Africaine she was carrying the parcel on top of her head, much like an African woman would; ils vivent encore à la f. de leurs ancêtres they still live in the manner of their ancestors *or* as their ancestors did

❑ à ma façon, à sa façon *etc* ADJ une recette à ma/ta f. a recipe of mine/yours; un tour à sa f. one of his/her tricks; une invitation à leur f. their style of invitation ADV je le ferai à ma f. I'll do it my way; chante-le à ta f. sing it your way *or* any way you like

❑ de cette façon ADV 1 (*comme cela*) (in) this way, thus, in this manner; ouvre la boîte de cette f. open the box this way

2 (*par conséquent*) that way; nous irons demain, de cette f. ils ne seront pas déçus we'll go tomorrow, that way they won't be disappointed

❑ de façon à PRÉP so as to, in order to; de f. à pouvoir fermer la porte so as to be able to shut the door; j'ai fermé la fenêtre de f. à éviter les courants d'air I shut the window in order to prevent draughts; parlez de f. à vous faire comprendre speak so that you can be understood

❑ de façon (à ce) que CONJ so that; il s'est levé de bonne heure de f. à ce que tout soit prêt he got up early to make sure everything was ready in time; je lui ai donné un siège, de f. à ce qu'elle puisse attendre sans se fatiguer I gave her a seat so that she could wait without getting tired; elle parle de f. à ce que tout le monde l'entende she speaks in such a way that everyone can hear her

❑ de la belle façon ADV *Ironique* il s'est fait recevoir de la belle f.! he got the sort of reception he deserves!

❑ de la même façon ADV the same (way), identically, in like manner

❑ de la même façon que CONJ like, as, the same (way) as

❑ de ma/sa/*etc* ADJ une recette de ma/ta f. a recipe of mine/yours; un tour de sa f. one of his/her tricks; un poème de sa f. a poem of his/her own composition

❑ de telle façon ADV so, like that; pourquoi criez-vous de telle f.? why are you shouting like that?

❑ de telle façon que CONJ so that, in such a way that; écrivez de telle f. que le lecteur comprenne write in such a way that the reader understands; il pleuvait de telle f. que je fus obligé de rentrer it was raining so hard that I had to go home

❑ de toute façon, de toutes les façons ADV anyway, in any case

❑ d'une certaine façon ADV (*en quelque sorte*) in a way, in a manner of speaking, so to speak

❑ d'une façon ou d'une autre ADV somehow

❑ sans façon(s) ADJ (*style*) simple, unadorned; (*cuisine*) plain; (*personne*) simple ADV 1 (*familièrement*) elle m'a pris le bras sans f. *ou* façons she took my arm quite naturally; *Péj* il agit sans f. *ou* façons avec ses parents he's rather offhand *or* he behaves off-handedly with his parents

2 (*non merci*) no thank you; encore du fromage? – sans f. *ou* façons! more cheese? – no thank you!

❑ sans plus de façons ADV without further ado

faconde [fakɔ̃d] NF *Littéraire Péj* fluency, flow of words; être doué d'une belle f. to be a smooth talker; avoir de la f. to be fluent *or* voluble, *Péj* to be garrulous; quelle f.! he/she talks so much!

façonnage [fasɔnaʒ] NM 1 (*mise en forme*) shaping, working; (*sur un tour*) turning; (*de l'argile*) fashioning 2 (*fabrication* → *à la main*) making, fashioning; *Couture* making (up); *Ind* manufacturing 3 *Typ* forwarding

façonné, -e [fasɔne] *Tex* ADJ figured; étoffe façonnée figured fabric

NM figured fabric

façonnement [fasɔnmɑ̃] = façonnage

façonner [3] [fasɔne] VT 1 (*modeler* → *argile*) to shape, to fashion; (→ *métal, pierre, bois*) to shape, to work; *Agr* f. la terre to work the soil 2 *Fig* (*caractère*) to mould, to shape; f. qn à son image to mould sb in one's own image 3 (*fabriquer* → *à la main*) to make, to fashion; *Couture* to make (up); *Ind* to manufacture, to produce, to make; façonné à la main handmade

façonneur, -euse [fasɔnœr, -øz] NM,F maker, shaper, fashioner

façonnier, -ère [fasɔnje, -ɛr] ADJ 1 (*ouvrier*) jobbing 2 (*maniéré*) affected, mannered

NM,F jobbing worker

NM *Ordinat* computer bureau

fac-similé [faksimile] (*pl* fac-similés) NM 1 (*reproduction*) facsimile, exact copy 2 *Tél* (*technique*) facsimile; (*document*) facsimile, fax

factage [faktaʒ] NM 1 (*transport*) parcels cartage, carriage and delivery 2 (*frais*) carriage, transport costs; payer le f. to pay the carriage 3 (*distribution*) (postal) delivery

facteur[1] [faktœr] NM 1 *Math* coefficient, factor; mettre en facteurs to factorize; mise en facteurs factorization; f. aléatoire random factor; f. commun common factor; f. de sécurité coefficient of safety, safety factor; f. premier prime factor

2 *Physiol* f. VIII factor 8; f. Rhésus rhesus *or* Rh factor; f. Rhésus négatif/positif rhesus negative/positive; *Méd* f. de risque risk factor

3 (*élément*) element, factor; la courtoisie peut être un f. de réussite courtesy may be one of the ways to success; f. d'identification recognition factor; le f. chance the chance factor; f. coût cost factor; f. de demande demand factor; f. économique economic factor; le f. humain the human factor; *Mktg* f. de situation situational factor; le f. temps the time factor; f. vent windchill factor

4 (*manutentionnaire*) (transport) agent; f. en douane customs agent

5 *Mus* instrument maker; f. de pianos piano maker; f. d'orgues organ builder

facteur[2], **-trice** [faktœr, -tris] NM,F (*livreur de courrier*) *Br* postman, *f* postwoman, *Am* mailman, *f* mailwoman; est-ce que le f. est passé? has the *Br* postman *or Am* mailman been yet?

factice [faktis] ADJ 1 (*imité* → *diamant*) artificial, false; (→ *marchandise de présentation*) dummy (*avant n*); (→ *moustache, barbe*) false; les bouteilles de parfum en vitrine sont factices the bottles of perfume in the window are dummies 2 (*inauthentique* → *gentillesse, enthousiasme*) artificial, simulated, false; (→ *sourire*) forced; (→ *beauté*) artificial; une joie f. simulated happiness

facticement [faktismɑ̃] ADV artificially, factitiously

facticité [faktisite] NF 1 (*inauthenticité*) artificiality 2 *Phil* being a fact

factieux, -euse [faksjø, -øz] ADJ seditious

NM,F agitator, troublemaker

faction [faksjɔ̃] NF 1 (*groupe*) faction 2 *Mil* sentry *or* guard duty; être en *ou* de f. to be on sentry *or* guard duty; mettre qn en *ou* de f. to put sb on guard; mettre une sentinelle de f. devant la porte to post a sentry in front of the door; je suis resté en f. plusieurs heures devant sa porte I kept watch outside his/her door for hours 3 (*dans une entreprise*) (eight-hour) shift

factionnaire [faksjɔnɛr] NM *Mil* sentry, guard

NMF (*ouvrier*) shift worker

factitif, -ive [faktitif, -iv] *Gram* ADJ factitive, causative
NM causative verb

factorerie [faktɔrri] NF = office of a trading company abroad

factoriel, -elle [faktɔrjɛl] *Math* ADJ factorial, factor *(avant n)*; **analyse factorielle** factor analysis
□ **factorielle** NF factorial

factoring [faktɔriŋ] NM factoring

factorisation [faktɔrizasjɔ̃] NF *Math* factorization, factorizing

factoriser [3] [faktɔrize] VT *Math* to factorize

factotum [faktɔtɔm] NM factotum, handyman; **je ne suis pas ton f.!** I'm not your servant!

factrice [faktris] *voir* **facteur**[2]

factuel, -elle [faktɥɛl] ADJ *(gén) & Phil* factual

factum [faktɔm] NM **1** *(pamphlet)* controversial pamphlet **2** *Jur* statement of the facts (of a case), memorial, factum

facturation [faktyrasjɔ̃] NF *Com & Compta* **1** *(action)* invoicing, billing; **la f. interviendra le 10 du mois** you will be invoiced on the 10th of each month; **f. détaillée** itemized invoicing *or* billing; *Ordinat* **f. séparée** unbundling **2** *(service)* invoice department

facture[1] [faktyr] NF *Com & Compta* invoice, bill; **f. d'électricité/de gaz** electricity/gas bill; **fausse f.** fake *or* forged invoice; **établir** *ou* **faire** *ou* **dresser une f.** to make out an invoice; **payer** *ou* **régler une f.** to pay a bill, to settle an invoice; **conformément à la f., selon** *ou* **suivant f.** as per invoice; *Écon* **la f. pétrolière de la France** France's oil bill; **affaire des fausses factures** = fraud using fake invoices to disguise illegal cash transfers; *Fig* **c'est moi qui vais payer la f. comme d'habitude** I'm going to have to pay the price as usual; **f. d'achat** purchase invoice; **f. d'avoir** credit note; **f. certifiée** certified invoice; **f. client** guest bill; **f. commerciale** commercial invoice; **f. de confirmation** confirmation invoice; **f. de consignation** consignment invoice; **f. consulaire** consular invoice; **f. de débit** debit note; **f. détaillée** itemized invoice; **f. de doit** debit note; **f. douanière** customs invoice; **f. à l'exportation** export invoice; **f. originale** invoice of origin; **f. pro forma** *ou* **provisoire** pro forma invoice; **f. rectificative** amended invoice; **f. de transitaire** forwarding agent's invoice; **f. de vente** sales invoice

facture[2] [faktyr] NF **1** *(style → d'un morceau de musique, d'un poème, d'un tableau etc)* construction; *(→ d'un artiste etc)* style, technique; **d'une belle f.** *(meuble)* beautifully crafted; *(édifice)* beautifully proportioned; *(sculpture)* beautifully carved; *(peinture)* beautifully executed; *Beaux-Arts* **f. picturale** artistic style **2** *Mus (fabrication → gén)* making; *(→ d'orgues)* building

facturer [3] [faktyre] VT *(personne)* to invoice, to bill; *(produit, service)* to charge for; **f. qch à qn** to bill *or* to invoice sb for sth; **ils ne m'ont pas facturé la livraison** they didn't charge me for delivery; **le papier nous a été facturé 50 euros** we were invoiced 50 euros for the paper; *Ordinat* **f. séparément le matériel et le logiciel** to unbundle; **facturé à l'utilisation** pay-per-use

facturette [faktyrɛt] NF *Com* credit card sales voucher

facturier, -ère [faktyrje, -ɛr] NM,F invoice clerk; **f. d'entrée** purchase ledger clerk; **f. de sortie** sales ledger clerk
NM *(registre)* sales book; **f. d'entrée** purchase ledger; **f. de sortie** sales ledger
□ **facturière** NF *(machine)* invoicing machine

facule [fakyl] NF *Astron* facula

facultatif, -ive [fakyltatif, -iv] ADJ **1** *(au choix)* optional; **l'assurance est facultative** insurance is optional; **matière facultative** optional subject **2** *Transp (sur demande)* **arrêt f.** request stop

facultativement [fakyltativmɑ̃] ADV optionally, as an option

faculté [fakylte] NF **1** *(capacité)* ability, capability; **f. d'adaptation** adaptability, ability to adapt; **la f. de comprendre les enfants** the ability to understand children; **ne pas avoir la f. de marcher** to be unable to walk; **les humains possèdent la f. d'abstraction** mankind is capable of abstract thought
2 *(droit)* freedom, right; *(autorité)* power; *(possibilité)* option; **avoir la f. de faire qch** *(droit)* to have the right to do sth; *(autorité)* to be entitled to do sth; *(possibilité)* to have the option of doing sth; **vous avez la f. de refuser le contrat** you have the right to refuse to sign the contract; **il a la f. de rester s'il le désire** he may *or* he's free to stay if he wishes to; *Bourse* **f. du double** call of more; **f. de rachat** repurchase option; **avec f. d'achat ou de vente** with the option of purchase or sale
3 *Naut* **assurances sur corps et facultés** hull and cargo insurance
4 *Com* **facultés assurées** insured cargo
5 *Jur* **facultés contributives** ability to pay
6 *Univ (avant 1968)* university, college; *(depuis 1968)* faculty; **la f. des sciences** the science faculty; **on s'est connu à la** *ou* **en f.** we met at university *or* when we were students; **entrer en f.** to go to university; **cours/professeur de f.** university course/teacher; **des souvenirs de f.** memories of one's university *or* student days
7 *Vieilli* **la F.** the faculty of medicine; *(les médecins)* the medical profession; *Hum* **la F. m'interdit/me recommande de faire du sport** my doctors forbid me/encourage me to do sport *or Am* sports
□ **facultés** NFPL **1** *(esprit)* faculties, powers; **facultés intellectuelles** intellectual faculties; **facultés mentales** mental faculties; **avoir** *ou* **jouir de toutes ses facultés** to be of sound mind *or* in full possession of one's faculties; **il n'a pas toutes ses facultés** he's not in possession of all his faculties, he's not all there; **merci de faire confiance à mes facultés!** thank you for thinking I'm clever enough to do it!; **homme doué de grandes facultés** man of great abilities
2 *Vieilli (ressources)* resources, means; **dépenser au-dessus de ses facultés** to spend beyond one's means

fada [fada] *Fam (dans le sud de la France)* ADJ crazy, nuts, *Am* wacko
NMF nutcase, *Br* nutter, *Am* wacko; **les fadas de la moto** motorbike fanatics

fadaise [fadɛz] NF *(paroles)* piece of nonsense, silly remark; *(chose insignifiante)* trifle; **fadaises** drivel, nonsense, *Br* rubbish; **dire des fadaises** to talk drivel *or* nonsense

fadasse [fadas] ADJ *Fam Péj* **1** *(sans goût)* insipid■, bland■ **2** *(sans éclat)* dull■; **des couleurs fadasses** washed-out colours■; **c'est une fille assez f.** she's rather dull

fade [fad] ADJ **1** *(sans saveur)* insipid, bland; *(couleur)* drab, washed-out; *(beauté)* insipid **2** *(banal)* dull, pointless, vapid; **le compliment est plutôt f.** the compliment is rather flat

fadé, -e [fade] ADJ *Fam Ironique* **être f.** *(remarquable)* to beat them all, to take *Br* the biscuit *or Am* the cake

fadement [fadmɑ̃] ADV insipidly

fader [3] [fade] **se fader** VPR *très Fam* **se f. qn/qch** to get landed with sb/sth

fadeur [fadœr] NF **1** *(insipidité)* blandness, lack of flavour; *(d'une couleur)* drabness; *(d'une beauté)* insipidness **2** *(banalité)* blandness, vapidity; *(de compliments)* banality; *(de style)* dullness, dreariness
□ **fadeurs** NFPL *Vieilli (compliments)* banal *or* bland compliments; **dire des fadeurs à qn** to pay sb banal *or* bland compliments

fading [fadiŋ] NM *Rad* fading

fado [fado] NM *Mus* fado

faena [faena] NF faena

faf [faf] NMF *Fam* fascist■

fafiot [fafjo] NM *(billet de banque) Br* banknote■, *Am* greenback
□ **fafiots** NMPL *(papiers d'identité)* ID

fafouin, -e [fafwɛ̃, -in] *Can Fam* ADJ scatterbrained, *Br* scatty
NM,F scatterbrain; **arrête de faire le f., tu vas avoir un accident!** stop acting the fool *or* clowning around, you'll have an accident!

fagale [fagal] *Bot* NF beech, *Spéc* member of the Fagaceae
□ **fagales** NFPL Fagaceae

fagnard, -e [faɲar, -ard] *Belg* ADJ of/from the Fagnes region
NM,F = native or inhabitant of the Fagnes region

fagne [faɲ] NF *Belg* = marshland of the Ardennes plateau

fagot [fago] NM **1** *(branches)* bundle (of wood); **sentir le f.** *(personne)* to be a suspected heretic; *(opinion)* to smack of heresy **2** *(en Afrique)* firewood **3** *(locution)* **de derrière les fagots** very special; **une bouteille de derrière les fagots** a very special wine

fagotage [fagɔtaʒ] NM **1** *Péj (habillement)* ridiculous get-up **2** *(du bois)* bundling (up)

fagoté, -e [fagɔte] ADJ *Péj* **mal/bizarrement f.** badly/oddly dressed; **comme te voilà fagotée!** what a sight you are!, look at the state of you!; *Fam* **f. comme l'as de pique** wearing an outlandish rig-out, dressed up like a dog's dinner

fagoter [3] [fagɔte] VT **1** *(bois, branches)* to bind together, to tie up in bundles **2** *Péj (habiller)* **sa mère le fagote n'importe comment** his mother dresses him in the strangest outfits
►**se fagoter** VPR *Péj* **t'as vu comme elle se fagote!** have you seen some of the things she wears!

fagotier, -ère [fagɔtje, -ɛr] NM,F = person who ties wood in bundles

fagotin [fagɔtɛ̃] NM small bundle (of firewood)

Fahrenheit [farɛnajt] NPR **degré/échelle F.** Fahrenheit degree/scale

FAI [ɛfai] NM *Ordinat (abrév* **fournisseur d'accès à l'Internet***)* IAP

faiblard, -e [fɛblar, -ard] ADJ *Fam* **1** *(vieillard, convalescent)* weak■, frail■; **se sentir un peu f.** to feel a bit weak■ **2** *(excuse)* feeble■, lame■; *(argument)* feeble■; *(notes)* poor■; **en chimie, il est un peu f.** he's a bit weak■ *or* on the slow side in chemistry **3** *(lumière)* weak■, dim■

faible [fɛbl] ADJ **1** *(malade, vieillard)* weak, frail; **se sentir f.** to feel weak; **avoir la vue f.** to have weak *or* poor eyesight; **avoir le cœur/la poitrine f.** to have a weak heart/chest; **avoir les reins faibles** to have kidney trouble; **être de f. constitution** to have a weak constitution; **une f. femme** a helpless woman
2 *(étai, construction)* weak, flimsy, fragile; **la carlingue était trop f.** the cabin was too flimsy
3 *(esprit)* weak, deficient; *(intelligence)* low; **il n'a que de faibles moyens intellectuels** his intellectual capacities are rather weak
4 *(médiocre → étudiant, résultat)* weak, poor, mediocre; **une dissertation plutôt f.** a rather weak *or* poor essay; **être f. en qch** *(à l'école)* to be weak at sth; **elle est f. en maths** she's weak *or* not very good at *Br* maths *or Am* math
5 *(trop tempéré → style, argument, réforme)* weak; *(→ jugement)* mild; *(→ prétexte)* feeble, flimsy; **le mot est f.!** that's an understatement!; **...et le terme est f.!** ...and that's putting it mildly!
6 *(complaisant)* weak, lax; *(sans volonté)* weak, spineless; *(caractère)* weak; **il est f. avec ses enfants** he's lax *or* too lenient with his children; **être f. de caractère** to be weak-willed
7 *(impuissant → nation, candidat)* weak
8 *Com & Écon (demande)* slack; *(marge, revenus)* low; *(monnaie)* weak; *(ressources)* scant, thin
9 *(léger → lumière)* dim, faint; *(→ bruit)* faint; *(→ voix)* faint, quiet; *(→ brise)* light; *(→ odeur)* faint, slight
10 *(peu important → gén)* low, small; *(→ avantage, différence, chance, espoir)* slight; *(→ prix, revenu, loyer)* low; *(→ récolte, rendement)* poor; *(→ vitesse)* low, slow; **une f. quantité de sucre** a small quantity of sugar; **à f. débit** low-rate; **aller à f. vitesse** to proceed at low speed; **appareil de f. consommation** low-consumption appliance; **de f. encombrement** compact; **à une f. hauteur/profondeur** not very high up/deep down; **à f. émission** low-emission; **à f. teneur en minerai** of low mineral content, low-grade; **à f. teneur en alcool** low-alcohol; **f. en calories** low-calorie; **une f. différence entre deux ouvrages** a slight difference between two books; **avoir de faibles chances de succès** to have slight *or* slender chances of succeeding; **donner une f. idée de** to give a faint idea of
11 *Ling* weak, unstressed
NMF weak-willed person; **c'est un f.** he's weak-willed; **f. d'esprit** simpleton
NM **1** *(préférence)* **avoir un f. pour qch** to be partial to sth; **avoir un f. pour qn** to have a soft spot for sb

2 *Littéraire (point sensible)* weak spot; **prendre qn par son f.** to find sb's Achilles heel

□ **faibles** NMPL **les faibles** the weak

faiblement [fɛbləmɑ̃] ADV **1** *(sans force → résister, insister, protester)* weakly, feebly; *(→ parler)* quietly, faintly; **il protestait assez f.** he was protesting rather feebly **2** *(légèrement → gén)* faintly; *(→ éclairer)* faintly, dimly; **la cloche résonnait f. dans le lointain** the bell was ringing faintly in the distance

faiblesse [fɛblɛs] NF **1** *(manque de vigueur physique)* weakness, frailty; *(de la vue, de la poitrine)* weakness; **ressentir une grande f.** to feel very weak; **avoir une f. à l'œil droit** to have a weakness in the right eye; **je tombais de f.** I was ready to drop (with exhaustion); **la f. de sa constitution** his/her weak constitution

2 *(d'une construction)* weakness, flimsiness, fragility; *(d'une économie, d'un système)* weakness, fragility, vulnerability; *(d'un concurrent, d'un produit)* weakness; *(d'une voix, d'un son)* dimness, faintness; *(d'une lumière)* faintness; *(du vent)* lightness; **la f. de la monnaie/des marchés financiers** the weakness of the currency/the financial markets

3 *(médiocrité → d'un élève)* weakness; *(→ d'une œuvre, d'un argument)* feebleness, weakness; **étant donné la f. de ses notes, il devra redoubler** with such low marks, he will have to repeat a year; **il a des faiblesses à l'oral** his oral skills are weak; **f. d'esprit** feeble-mindedness

4 *(insignifiance → d'une différence, d'un écart)* insignificance; **la f. des effectifs** *(employés)* a shortage of staff; *(élèves)* insufficient numbers; **la f. de leurs revenus** their low income

5 *Littéraire (lâcheté)* weakness, spinelessness; **f. de caractère** weakness of character; **la f. humaine** human weakness *or* frailty; **un homme d'une grande f.** a weak man; **être d'une grande f. envers qn** *(trop indulgent)* to be overlenient with sb; **être d'une f. coupable envers qn** to be inexcusably soft with sb; **avoir la f. de faire qch** to be weak enough to do sth; **avoir la f. de croire/dire** to be foolish enough to believe/to say; **avoir un moment de f.** to have a moment of weakness; **dans un moment de f. je lui ai dit oui** in a moment of weakness I said yes to him/her; **un moment de f. et voilà une carrière politique gâchée** an entire political career ruined in a moment of weakness; **pour lui, l'amour filial est une f.** he considers that loving one's parents is a weakness

6 *(défaut → d'une personne)* weakness, shortcoming, failing; *(→ d'une œuvre d'art, d'une théorie)* weakness; **présenter plusieurs faiblesses** to have several weak points *or* weaknesses; **c'est là la grande f. du scénario** this is the major flaw of the script; **à chacun ses petites faiblesses** we all have our little weaknesses *or* shortcomings *or* failings

7 *(préférence)* weakness, partiality; **avoir une f. pour** to have a weakness for, to be partial to

8 *Littéraire (évanouissement)* fainting fit, dizzy spell; **avoir une** *ou* **être pris de f.** to feel faint

faiblir [32] [feblir] VI **1** *(perdre de sa force → personne, pouls)* to get weaker; *(→ mémoire, vue, mécanisme)* to fail; *(→ voix)* to lose its strength, to fail; **ses forces faiblissaient** he/she was getting weaker; **chez elle, c'est la mémoire qui faiblit** her memory is failing; **chez elle, c'est la tête qui faiblit** she's going weak in the head; **le moteur/la batterie faiblit** the engine/the battery is failing

2 *(diminuer → vent, orage, bourrasque)* to drop; *(→ lumière)* to dwindle; *(→ enthousiasme, colère, intérêt)* to wane, to dwindle; *(→ courage)* to fail, to flag; **le jour faiblit** it's getting dark; **l'intérêt du public faiblit** public interest is waning; **le succès de la pièce ne faiblit pas** the play continues to be a great success; **l'écart faiblit entre les coureurs** the gap between the runners is narrowing *or* closing

3 *(cesser d'être efficace → athlète, élève)* to get weaker; **son style n'a pas faibli** his/her style is as vigorous as ever; **j'ai faibli en langues à la fin de l'année** my marks in modern languages got weaker towards the end of the year; **le film faiblit vers la fin** the film falls off *or* tails off towards the end

4 *(plier → paroi, tige)* to show signs of weakening; *(→ résistance)* to weaken; **les premiers rangs de policiers faiblissaient sous l'assaut** the front ranks of the police were weakening under the assault

5 *(perdre de sa valeur → monnaie)* to get weaker

6 *Littéraire (défaillir)* to have a fainting fit

faiblissant, -e [fɛblisɑ̃, -ɑ̃t] ADJ **1** *(vieillard, malade)* weakening **2** *(lumière, vent)* failing **3** *(économie, pouvoir d'achat)* slackening

faïençage [fajɑ̃saʒ] NM *Tech* cracking, crazing

faïence [fajɑ̃s] NF **1** *(matière)* (glazed) earthenware, *Spéc* faience; **f. de Delft** Delft, delftware; **f. fine** china **2** *(objet)* piece of earthenware; **faïences** crockery, earthenware

faïencé, -e [fajɑ̃se] ADJ *(objet)* made to resemble pottery; *(tableau)* crackled

faïencerie [fajɑ̃sri] NF **1** *(usine)* pottery works **2** *(articles)* (glazed) earthenware **3** *(commerce)* pottery (trade)

faïencier, -ère [fajɑ̃sje, -ɛr] NM,F *(fabricant)* crockery *or* earthenware maker, potter; *(marchand)* crockery *or* earthenware dealer

faignant, -e [fɛɲɑ̃, -ɑ̃t] = **feignant**

faille[1] *voir* **falloir**

faille[2] [faj] NF **1** *Géol* fault **2** *(faiblesse)* flaw, weakness; *(incohérence)* inconsistency, flaw; *(dans une amitié)* rift, breach; **il y a une f. dans votre démonstration** your demonstration is flawed **3** *Tex* faille

□ **sans faille** ADJ *(logique)* faultless, flawless; *(fidélité, dévouement)* unfailing, unwavering; *(dévotion)* unfailing; **faire preuve d'une volonté sans f.** to be iron-willed, to have a will of iron

faillé, -e [faje] ADJ *Géol* faulted

failler [3] [faje] **se failler** VPR *Géol* to be affected by faults

failli, -e [faji] *Com* ADJ bankrupt

NM,F bankrupt; **f. concordataire** certificated bankrupt; **f. déchargé** discharged bankrupt; **f. non déchargé** undischarged bankrupt; **f. réhabilité** discharged bankrupt

faillibilité [fajibilite] NF fallibility

faillible [fajibl] ADJ fallible

faillir [46] [fajir] VI **1** *(être sur le point de)* **j'ai failli rater la marche** I nearly missed the step; **pendant un moment, j'ai failli y croire** I almost believed it for a moment; **il faillit être écrasé** he narrowly missed being run over; **j'ai bien failli me noyer** I (was) very nearly drowned; **tu l'as attrapé? – non, mais j'ai failli!** did you catch it? – not quite!; *Hum* **j'ai failli attendre** so you decided to come, did you?

2 *Littéraire (manquer à son devoir)* to fail in one's duty; *Euph* **elle a failli** she fell

3 *Littéraire (se démentir)* to waver, to falter; **dont la loyauté n'avait jamais failli** whose loyalty had never wavered *or* faltered

□ **faillir à** VT IND *Littéraire* **f. à une promesse/sa parole** to fail to keep a promise/one's word; **f. à son devoir** to fail in one's duty; **f. à un engagement** to fail to honour a commitment; **ne pas f. à sa réputation** to live up to one's reputation; **la mémoire me faut** my memory fails me

□ **sans faillir** ADV unfailingly

faillite [fajit] NF **1** *Com* bankruptcy, insolvency; **faire f.** to go bankrupt; **f. frauduleuse** fraudulent bankruptcy; **f. personnelle** personal bankruptcy; **f. simple** bankruptcy

2 *(échec)* failure; *Littéraire* **la f. de ses espoirs** the end *or* collapse of his/her hopes; **le spectacle a connu une f. complète** the show was a total failure; **les faits récents montrent la f. de cette politique** recent events demonstrate the failure of this policy; **le projet a fait f.** the project flopped *or* was a failure

□ **en faillite** *Com* ADJ bankrupt, insolvent; **être en (état de) f.** to be bankrupt; **déclarer qn en f.** to declare sb bankrupt ADV **mettre qn en f.** to declare sb bankrupt; **se mettre en f.** to file a petition for bankruptcy

faim [fɛ̃] NF **1** *(appétit)* hunger; **avoir f.** to be hungry; **avoir très** *ou* **grand f., avoir une grosse f.** to be *or* feel very hungry; **avoir un peu f.** to be *or* feel a bit hungry; **j'ai une petite f.** I'm feeling peckish; **avoir une f. de loup** to be ravenous; **j'ai une f. de loup** *ou* **à dévorer les montagnes** I could eat a horse, I'm ravenous; *Fam* **j'ai une de ces faims, je meurs de f., je crève de f.** I'm famished *or* starving; **je n'ai plus f. du tout** I'm not at all hungry any more; **merci, je n'ai plus f.** I've had enough, thank you; **ça me donne f.** it makes me hungry; *Fam* **il fait f.** I'm hungry; **manger à sa f.** to eat one's fill; **mangez à votre f.** eat as much as you like; **rester sur sa f.** to be still hungry; *Fig* to be left unsatisfied *or* frustrated; **tromper sa f.** to stave off hunger; *Prov* **la f. chasse le loup (hors)** *ou* **fait sortir le loup du bois** hunger drives the wolf out of the wood

2 *(famine)* **la f.** hunger, famine; **souffrir de la f.** to be starving *or* a victim of starvation; **mourir de f.** to starve to death, to die of starvation

3 *(envie)* **sa f. de tendresse** his/her yearning for tenderness; **avoir f. de paix** to hunger *or* to yearn for peace; **avoir f. de gloire/d'absolu** to hunger *or* to thirst after glory/absolutes

faine [fɛn] NF *Bot* beechnut

fainéant, -e [feneɑ̃, -ɑ̃t] ADJ idle, lazy

NM,F idler, layabout; **quel f.!** what a layabout!

fainéanter [3] [feneɑ̃te] VI to idle about *or* around; **il passe des heures à f.** he spends hours twiddling his thumbs *or* doing nothing

fainéantise [feneɑ̃tiz] NF idleness, laziness

FAIRE [109] [fɛr]

VT to make **A1, 3, B1, 2, D2** ▪ to build **A1** ▪ to have **A4** ▪ to do **B1–3, 5, 9, C1, 3, H** ▪ to carry out **B2** ▪ to study **B3** ▪ to write **B6** ▪ to say **B7** ▪ to clean **B8** ▪ to turn into **D2** ▪ to imitate **D6** ▪ to be **F2–4, G2** ▪ to cost **F2** ▪ to last **F6** ▪ to look (+ adj) **G1**
USAGE ABSOLU to go to the toilet
VI to do **1**
V IMPERSONNEL to be **1**
V AUXILIAIRE to make **1, 2** ▪ to have **2, 3**
NM doing **1** ▪ execution **2**

VT **A.** *FABRIQUER, RÉALISER* **1** *(confectionner → objet, vêtement, film, vin)* to make; *(→ construction)* to build; *(→ tableau)* to paint; *(→ repas, café)* to make, to prepare; *(→ gâteau, pain)* to make, to bake; *(→ bière)* to brew; **il m'a fait une poupée avec de la paille** he's made me a doll out of straw; **qu'as-tu fait (à manger) pour ce soir?** what have you prepared for dinner?; **je vais f. du café** I'm going to make some coffee; **c'est elle qui fait ses chansons** she writes her own songs; **f. une loi** to make a law; **f. un portrait** *(le peindre)* to paint a portrait; *(le dessiner)* to draw a portrait; **il a fait un portrait fidèle de la situation** he gave a very accurate description of the situation; **il sait tout f.** he can turn his hand to anything; *Fam* **grand-mère est super – oui, on n'en fait plus des comme ça!** grandma's great – yes, they broke the mould when they made her!; **ce pays fait d'excellents athlètes** this country produces excellent athletes; **les deux ou trois créateurs qui font la mode parisienne** the handful of designers who ARE Parisian fashion

2 *(produire, vendre)* **f. de l'élevage de bétail** to breed cattle; **f. du blé/de la vigne** to grow wheat/grapes; **f. une marque/un produit** to stock a make/an article; *Fam* **je vous fais les deux à 40 euros** you can have both for 40 euros, I'll take 40 euros for both

3 *(obtenir, gagner → bénéfices)* to make; **f. de l'argent** to earn *or* to make money

4 *(mettre au monde)* **f. un enfant** to have a child; **il veut que je lui fasse un enfant** he wants me to have his child; **il lui a fait deux enfants** he had two children with her; **la chatte a fait des petits** the cat has had kittens

5 *Euph* **f. ses besoins** to do one's business

B. *ACCOMPLIR, EXÉCUTER* **1** *(effectuer → mouvement, signe)* to make; *(→ saut périlleux, roue)* to do; **fais-moi un sourire/ un bisou** give me a kiss/a smile; **f. des grimaces** to make *or* to pull faces; **f. la grimace** to make a face; **f.** *Fam* **la tête** *ou très Fam* **la gueule** to sulk▪; to be in a huff

2 *(accomplir → choix, erreur, réforme, proposition)* to make; *(→ discours)* to deliver, to make, to give; *(→ conférence)* to give; *(→ inventaire, exercice, thèse, dissertation)* to do; *(→ recherches)* to do, to carry out; *(→ enquête)* to carry out; **f. ses études** to study; **il a fait ses études à la**

Sorbonne he studied at the Sorbonne; **tu as fait tes maths?** have you done your *Br* maths *or Am* math homework?; **f. son devoir** to do one's duty; **f. une blague à qn** to play a joke on sb; **f. des plaisanteries** to play tricks; **f. la cuisine** to cook; **f. le ménage** to do the housework; **f. son lit** to make one's bed; *Fam* **on ne me la fait pas, à moi!** *(plaisanterie)* you can't fool me!, there's no flies on me!; *Fam* **on me l'a déjà faite, celle-là** I know that one already; *Fam* **les voyages organisés, on me l'a déjà faite une fois et on ne me la fera plus!** one package tour was quite enough for me, thank you very much!; *Fam* **le** *ou* **la f. à l'esbroufe** *ou* **à l'épate** *ou* **au bluff** to bluff one's way through

3 *(étudier → matière, œuvre)* to study, to do; **il veut f. du droit** he wants to do law; *Fam* **f. sa médecine** to do *or* to study medicine■; **je n'ai jamais fait de musique** I've never studied music; **nous faisons Richard III cette année** we're doing *or* studying Richard III this year

4 *(suivre les cours de)* **f. l'ENA** to go to the ENA

5 *(pratiquer)* **f. de la poterie** to do pottery; **f. de la flûte/du violon** to play the flute/the violin; **f. de la danse** *(cours)* to go to dance classes; **il voulait f. de la danse** he wanted to be a dancer; **il a fait un peu de théâtre** he's done some acting; **je veux f. du théâtre** I want to be an actor *or* to go on the stage; **f. de l'équitation/de la natation/de la voile** to go horseriding/swimming/sailing; **f. du basket/du tennis** to play basketball/tennis

6 *(écrire → lettre)* to write; *(→ contrat, testament)* to write, to make; **fais mieux tes t** write your t's better

7 *(dire)* to say; **il fit oui de la tête** he nodded; **il fit non de la tête** he shook his head; **"non", fit-elle** "no," she said; **la vache fait "meuh!"** the cow goes "moo!"; **que fait le hibou?** what does the owl say?

8 *(nettoyer → chambre, vitres)* to clean, to do; *(→ chaussures)* to polish, to clean; *(tapisser, aménager → pièce, maison)* to do, to decorate

9 *(action non précisée)* to do; **que fais-tu dans la vie?** what do you do (for a living)?; **qu'est-ce qu'il t'a fait, ton frère?** what has your brother done to you?; **je ne t'ai jamais rien fait!** I've never done you any harm!; **que pouvais-je f. d'autre?** what else could I do?; **il a fort à f.** he's got lots to do; **tu es libre dimanche? – oui, je ne fais rien de spécial** are you free on Sunday? – yes, I'm not doing anything special; **tu fais quelque chose pour ton anniversaire?** are you doing anything (special) for your birthday?; **elle ne veut jamais rien f. sans lui** she never wants to do anything without him; **je fais ce que je peux!** I do what I can!, I do my best!; **elle ne fait que se plaindre** she does nothing but complain; **il ne fait que me harceler** he won't stop pestering me; **ils n'ont fait que chuchoter pendant tout le film** they kept whispering right through the film; **je ne veux rien avoir à f. avec eux!** I don't want anything to do with them!; **qu'ai-je fait de mes clefs?** what have I done with *or* where did I put my keys?; **que fais-tu de mes sentiments dans tout ça?** what about my feelings?, how do you think I feel?; **que vais-je f. de toi?** what am I going to do with you?; **elle fait ce qu'elle veut de lui** she can twist him round her little finger; **donne-le moi! – non, rien à f.!** give it to me! – nothing doing *or* no way!; **rien à f., le téléphone ne marche plus!** we're stuck, the phone doesn't work!; **tu lui as parlé? – oui, mais rien à f., il ne cédera pas** did you talk to him? – yes, but it's no use, he won't give in; **je vais vous raccompagner – n'en faites rien!** I'll take you back – there's really no need!; *Fam* **f. avec** to make do; **je n'ai que ce stylo – il faudra f. avec!** I've only got this pen – we'll/I'll have to make do with that!; **j'apprécie peu sa façon de travailler mais il faut bien f. avec!** I don't like the way he/she works but I suppose I'll just have to put up with it!; *Fam* **f. sans** to (make) do without; **j'ai oublié le livre chez moi – il faudra f. sans!** I've left the book at home – we'll just have to make do without it!; **autant que f. se peut** if possible, as far as possible; **je n'ai que f. de tes conseils** I can do without your advice; **mais bien sûr, tu n'as que f. de ma carrière!** but of course, my career matters very little to you! *or* you don't care about my career!; **pour ce f.** for that; **ce faisant** in so doing

C. *AVEC IDÉE DE DÉPLACEMENT* **1** *(se déplacer à la vitesse de)* **en marchant vite, tu peux f. dix kilomètres à l'heure** if you walk fast, you can do *or* cover ten kilometres in an hour; **le train peut f. jusqu'à 400 km/h** the train can do 400 km/h; **vous faisiez du 120 km/h** *(en voiture)* you were driving at *or* doing 120 km/h

2 *(couvrir → distance)* **le Concorde a fait Paris-New York en moins de cinq heures** Concorde went *or* flew from Paris to New York in less than five hours; **il y a des cars qui font Londres-Glasgow** there's a coach service between London and Glasgow; **sur tous les trains qui font Lyon-Marseille** on all the trains which run between Lyons and Marseille

3 *(visiter → pays, ville)* to do, to go to, to visit; **nous n'avons jamais fait le sud de l'Italie** we've never been to *or* done the south of Italy

4 *(inspecter, passer au crible)* **j'ai fait tous mes tiroirs, impossible de retrouver la photo** I searched through all my drawers, but I couldn't find the picture; **je n'ai pas envie de f. tous les dossiers!** I don't feel like searching *or* going through every single file!; **j'ai fait tous les étages avant de vous trouver** I looked on every floor before I found you; **j'ai fait tous les hôtels de la ville** *(j'y suis allé)* I did *or* went to *or* tried every hotel in town; *(j'ai téléphoné)* I called *or* did *or* tried every hotel in town; **f. les antiquaires** to go round the antique shops; **il fait les bars avant de rentrer chez lui** he goes round the bars before going home

D. *AVEC IDÉE DE TRANSFORMATION* **1** *(nommer)* **elle l'a fait baron** she gave him the title of Baron, she made him a baron; **elle l'a fait chevalier** she knighted him

2 *(transformer en)* **des rats, la fée fit des laquais** the fairy changed the rats into footmen; **ce film en a fait un sex-symbol** this film turned him/her into a sex symbol; **ce feuilleton en a fait une vedette** this series made him/her a star; **et ta robe bleue? – j'en ai fait une jupe** what about your blue dress? – I made it into a skirt; **garde les restes, j'en ferai une soupe** keep the leftovers, I'll make a soup with them; **ils ont fait trois appartements de leur grande maison** they converted *or* made their big house into three flats; **la prison en a fait un criminel** prison turned him into a criminal *or* made a criminal out of him; **c'était mon idée, mais il l'a faite sienne** it was my idea, but he took it from me *or* he made it his own; *Vieilli ou Hum* **quand je te ferai mienne** when I make you mine; **c'était un tyran et votre livre en fait un héros!** he was a tyrant, and your book shows *or* presents him as a hero!

3 *(devenir)* **"cheval" fait "chevaux" au pluriel** the plural of "cheval" is "chevaux"

4 *(servir de)* **une fois plié, le billard fait table** the billiard table, when folded, can be used *or* can serve as a normal table; **un canapé qui fait lit** a convertible settee; **une carotte fera le nez du bonhomme de neige** you can make the snowman's nose with a carrot; **cette peau fera un beau tapis** this animal skin will make a nice rug; **le gymnase fait aussi salle des fêtes** the gymnasium is also used as a community hall; **c'est un hôtel qui fait restaurant** it's a hotel with a restaurant

5 *(remplir le rôle de)* **il fera un bon mari** he'll make *or* be a good husband; **il fait le Père Noël dans les rues** he goes around the streets disguised as Father Christmas; *Théât* **qui fait le comte?** who plays the Count?; **il ferait un parfait Othello** he'd make *or* be a perfect Othello

6 *(imiter → personne)* to imitate, to take off, to impersonate; *(→ automate, animal)* to imitate; **il fait très bien le hibou** he imitates the owl very well, his imitation of the owl is very good; **ne fais pas l'idiot** don't be stupid; **ne fais pas l'innocent** don't play the innocent, *Br* don't come the innocent with me; **elle a fait l'étonnée** she pretended to be surprised *or* feigned surprise; **il faisait son intéressant** he was showing off

E. *INDIQUE UN RÉSULTAT* **1** *(provoquer)* **f. de la poussière** to raise dust; **ce charbon fait beaucoup de fumée** this coal makes a lot of smoke; **ça va f. une marque/une auréole** it will leave a mark/a ring; **l'accident a fait cinq morts** the accident left five dead *or* claimed five lives; **cela fait tout son charme** that's where his/her charm lies; **ce qui fait l'intérêt de son livre** what makes his/her book interesting; **f. de la peine à qn** to upset sb; **f. peur à qn** to frighten sb; **ces propos risquent de vous f. du tort** what you've said may well get you into trouble; **il fera votre malheur** he'll make life very difficult for you; **f. le désespoir de qn** to make sb despair; **f. quelque chose à qn** *(l'émouvoir)* to move sb, to affect sb; **ce n'était qu'un animal, mais ça m'a fait quelque chose quand il est mort** it was only an animal but it really affected me when it died; **ça m'a quand même fait quelque chose de le voir si triste** it did bother me to see him so sad; *Fam* **ça fait comment sur les montagnes russes?** what does it feel like *or* what is it like on a rollercoaster?; *Fam* **ça fait comment** *ou* **quoi de voir son nom sur une affiche?** what's it like to see your name on a poster?; **la vue du sang ne me fait rien** I don't mind the sight of blood, the sight of blood doesn't bother me; **si cela ne vous fait rien** if you don't mind; **la gravitation, force qui fait que les objets s'attirent** gravitation, the force which causes objects to be attracted towards each other; **ce qui fait que je suis arrivé en retard** which meant I was late

2 *(pour exprimer un souhait)* **faites qu'il ne lui arrive rien!** please don't let anything happen to him/her!

3 *(importer)* **qu'est-ce que cela peut f.?** what does it matter?, so what?; **qu'est-ce que cela peut te f.?** what's it to (do with) you?; **cela ne fait rien** it doesn't matter, never mind

4 *Fam (locutions)* **ça le fait** it's really cool, it's *Br* wicked *or Am* awesome; **ça le fait pas** it sucks; **ça le fait pas de se pointer avec une heure de retard le premier jour** it's just not on to show up an hour late on your first day; **le rouge sur du rose, ça le fait pas trop** red and pink just don't really work together

F. *INDIQUE UNE QUALITÉ, UNE FORME, UNE MESURE* **1** *(former)* **la route fait un coude** the road bends; **le circuit fait un huit** the circuit is (in the shape of) a figure of eight; **le tas fait une pyramide** the heap looks like a pyramid

2 *(coûter)* to be, to cost; **ça fait combien?** how much is it?; **ça fait trop cher** it's too expensive; **ça vous fait 60 euros en tout** that'll be 60 euros altogether

3 *(valoir, égaler)* to be, to make; **2 et 2 font 4** 2 and 2 are 4; **ça fait 23 en tout** that makes 23 altogether; **on a 15 euros, ça ne fait pas assez** we've got 15 euros, that's not enough

4 *(mesurer)* **le bateau fait 12 m de long/3 m de large** the boat is 12 m long/3 m wide; **la chambre fait 8m^2** the room is 8m^2; **il doit bien f. 1 m 90** he must be 1 m 90 tall; **je fais du 38** I take size 38; **je fais 56 kg** I weigh *or* am 56 kg; **cela (vous) fait une bonne livre** it's a bit over the pound

5 *(indique la durée, le temps)* **ça fait deux jours qu'il n'a pas mangé** he hasn't eaten for two days; **elle a téléphoné, cela fait bien une heure** she phoned at least an hour ago; *Fam* **on s'est rencontrés ça fait trois mois** we met three months ago, it's been three months since we met; *Fam* **cela faisait dix ans que je n'avais pas joué** I hadn't played for ten years

6 *Fam (durer → sujet: vêtement, objet)* to last■; **ton cartable te fera encore bien cette année** your schoolbag will last *or* do you this year; **cette robe m'a fait trois ans** this dress has lasted *or* done me three years; **une paire de chaussures ne me fait pas plus de six mois** I go through a pair of shoes in six months; **le ragoût m'a bien fait trois repas** I got three meals out of that stew; **il n'a pas fait deux mois dans cette entreprise** he didn't stay in the company more than two months

G. *VERBE ATTRIBUTIF* **1** *(paraître)* **la broche fait bien** *ou* **joli** *ou* **jolie sur ta robe** the brooch looks nice on your dress; **elle parle avec un léger accent, il paraît que ça fait bien!** she talks with a slight accent, it's supposed to be smart!; *Ironique* **j'ai un bleu sur la joue maintenant, ah ça fait bien!** I've got a bruise on my cheek now, that's lovely!; **ça fait bizarre** it looks strange; **il me faudrait un nom qui fasse artiste** I would need a name which sounds typically artistic; **je ne vais pas lui réclamer cinq euros, ça ferait mesquin** I'm not going to ask him/her for five euros, it'd be *or* look petty; **f. son âge** to look one's age; **elle ne fait pas son âge** she doesn't look her age

2 *Fam (devenir)* to be▪; **je veux f. pompier** I want to be *Br* a fireman *or Am* a firefighter

H. *VERBE DE SUBSTITUTION* **range ta chambre – je l'ai déjà fait** go and tidy up your room – I've already done it; **vous le lui expliquerez mieux que je ne saurais le f.** you'll explain it to him/her better than I could; **tu lui écriras? – oui, je le ferai** will you write to him/her? – yes I will; **puis-je prendre cette chaise? – (mais) faites donc!** may I take this chair? – please do *or* by all means!

USAGE ABSOLU *(faire ses besoins)* **tu as fait ce matin?** did you go to the toilet this morning?; *Fam* **il a fait dans sa culotte** he messed his pants

VI 1 *(agir)* to do; **fais comme chez toi** *(à l'arrivée de quelqu'un)* make yourself at home; **je peux prendre une douche? – bien sûr, fais comme chez toi** can I have a shower? – of course *or* by all means; *Ironique* **fais comme chez toi, surtout!** you've got a nerve!, don't mind me!; **faites comme vous voulez** do as you please; **fais comme tu veux!** *(ton irrité)* suit *or* please yourself!; **je le lui ai rendu – tu as bien fait!** I gave it back to him/her – you did the right thing *or* you did right!; **pourquoi l'as-tu acheté? – je croyais bien f.!** why did you buy it? – I thought it was a good idea!; **n'ai-je pas bien fait de lui répondre?** wasn't I right to answer him/her back?; **j'ai bien fait de me méfier** I was right to be suspicious; **tu ferais bien d'y réfléchir** you'd do well to *or* you should *or* you'd better think about it!; **pour bien f., il faudrait réserver aujourd'hui** the best thing would be to book today, ideally we should book today; **ça commence à bien f.!** enough is enough!; *Fam* **ça commence à bien f., tes reproches!** I've had quite enough of your criticism!

2 *Can Fam (être seyant)* **f. à qn** *(taille d'un vêtement)* to fit sb; *(style d'un vêtement)* to suit sb; **cette veste me fait** this jacket fits me

V IMPERSONNEL 1 *(pour exprimer le temps qu'il fait)* **il fait chaud/froid** it's hot/cold; **il faisait nuit** it was dark; **il fait (du) soleil** the sun is shining; **il fait bon au soleil** it's nice and warm in the sun; **il ne faisait pas bon avoir un nom à particule à cette époque** it wasn't a good thing to have an aristocratic-sounding name then

2 *(locutions)* **c'en est fait de vous** you've had it, you're done for; **c'est bien fait pour toi** it serves you right; *Can Fam* **ça va f.!, ça fait!** that's enough!

V AUX 1 *(provoquer une réaction)* **tu l'as fait rougir** you made him/her blush; **il sait f. bouger ses oreilles** he can make his ears move, he can move his ears; **le soleil a fait jaunir le papier** the sun has made the paper turn yellow; **les oignons, ça fait pleurer** onions make you cry; **ne la fais pas pleurer!** don't make her cry!; **ça me fait dormir** it puts *or* sends me to sleep

2 *(forcer à)* to make, to have; **fais-moi penser à le lui demander** remind me to ask him/her; **faites-le attendre** *(pour qu'il s'impatiente)* let him wait; *(en lui demandant)* ask him to wait; **faites-le asseoir** ask him to take a seat; **il faut le f. boire beaucoup** you should give him plenty to drink; **n'essaie pas de me f. croire que...** don't try to make *or* to have me believe that...; **il lui a fait avouer la vérité** he made him/her confess the truth; **ne me fais pas dire ce que je n'ai pas dit** don't put words into my mouth; **il me faisait f. ses dissertations** he had me write his essays for him

3 *(commander de)* **f. faire qch par qn** to have sb do *or* make sth, to have sth done *or* made by sb; **j'ai fait laver/vérifier ma voiture** I had my car washed/checked; **elle fait repasser son linge** she has her ironing done for her; **il fait f. ses costumes sur mesure** he has his suits tailor-made

NM 1 *(fait d'agir)* doing, making; **il y a loin du dire au f.** saying is one thing, doing is another

2 *Littéraire Beaux-Arts* execution; **un tableau d'un f. libre et élégant** a picture of free and elegant execution

□ **faire dans VT IND** *Fam* **il ne fait pas dans le détail** he doesn't bother about details; **son entreprise fait maintenant dans les produits de luxe** his/her company now produces luxury items; **certains cinéastes n'hésitent pas à f. dans le sordide** some film makers don't hesitate to show sordid scenes; **il fait dans le genre tragique** he makes everything sound so serious; **il fait dans le genre comique** he makes light of everything

▸**se faire VPR 1** *(réussir)* **elle s'est faite seule** she's a self-made woman

2 *(se forcer à)* **se f. pleurer/vomir** to make oneself cry/vomit

3 *(emploi réciproque)* **se f. la guerre** to wage war on each other

4 *(être à la mode)* to be fashionable, to be in fashion; **les salopettes ne se font plus** *Br* dungarees *or Am* overalls are out of fashion; **je ne sais pas ce qui se fait en ce moment** I don't know what's in fashion at the moment

5 *(être convenable)* **ça ne se fait pas de demander son âge à une femme** it's rude *or* it's not done to ask a woman her age; **ça ne se fait pas!** it's not done!, you (just) don't do that!; **tu peux dire merci, ça se fait!** you're allowed to say thank you, you know!

6 *(être réalisé)* **sans argent le film ne se fera pas** without money the film will never be made; **le projet ne se fera pas sans elle** the project won't go ahead without her; **finalement ça ne se fera pas** as it turns out, it's not going to happen; **les choses se font petit à petit** things evolve gradually; **la capitale où la mode se fait** the fashion capital; **je dois signer un nouveau contrat, mais je ne sais pas quand cela va se f.** I'm going to sign a new contract, but I don't know when that will be; **tu pourrais me prêter 50 euros? – ça pourrait se f.** could you lend me 50 euros? – that should be possible; **comment se fait-il que...?** how come *or* how is it that...?; **il pourrait se f. que...** it might *or* may be that..., it's possible that...; **c'est ce qui se fait de mieux en papiers peints lavables** it's the best washable wallpaper available

7 *(se former)* **les couples se font et se défont** people get together and separate

8 *(suivi d'un infinitif)* **se f. opérer** to have an operation; **se f. tuer** to get killed; **se f. photographier** *(par quelqu'un)* to get *or* to have one's picture taken; *(dans un Photomaton®)* to have some pictures (of oneself) done; **se f. couper les cheveux** to have one's hair cut; **il se fait f. ses vêtements chez un couturier** he gets his clothes tailor-made

9 *(devenir)* to become; **elle se fit toute douce** she became very gentle; **sa voix se fit plus grave** his/her voice became deeper; **les mesures de sécurité se sont faites plus rigoureuses** security measures have been tightened up *or* have become more stringent; **il s'est fait le porte-parole de toute une génération** he became the mouthpiece for a whole generation; **Dieu s'est fait homme** God took human form; *Fam* **s'il arrive à l'heure, je veux bien me f. nonne!** if he arrives on time, I'll eat my hat!; **il se fait tard** it's getting late

10 *(s'améliorer → fromage)* to ripen; *(→ vin)* to mature; **mes chaussures me serrent – elles vont se f.** my shoes feel tight – they'll stretch

11 *(fabriquer)* **se f. un gâteau** to make *or* to bake a cake (for oneself); **se f. un thé/un café** to make (oneself) a cup of tea/coffee; **elle se fait ses vêtements** she makes her own clothes

12 *(effectuer sur soi)* **il se fait ses piqûres seul** he gives himself his own injections; **je me suis fait une natte** I've plaited my hair; **se f. les ongles** to do one's nails; **se f. les yeux** to make up one's eyes

13 *Fam (gagner)* to make, to earn▪; **elle se fait 2000 euros par mois** she makes 2,000 euros per month, she gets 2,000 euros every month; **il ne se fait pas grand-chose** he doesn't earn *or* get much

14 *Fam (s'accorder)* **on se fait un film/un petit café?** what about going to see a film/going for a coffee?; **on s'est fait les trois musées dans la journée** we did the three museums in one day; **quand est-ce qu'on se le fait, ce match?** when are we going to have this game?

15 *Fam (supporter)* **il faut se la f.!** she's a real pain!

16 *Fam Arg crime (tuer)* to bump off; *(agresser)* to beat up; **se f. une banque** *(la voler)* to *Br* do over *or Am* boost a bank

17 *Vulg (posséder sexuellement)* to screw, *Br* to shag

18 se f. à *(s'habituer à)* to get used to; **elle ne t'aime plus, il faudra que tu t'y fasses** she doesn't love you any more, you'll have to get that into your head *or* get used to it; **il s'appelle Odilon – je ne m'y ferai jamais!** his name is Odilon – I'll never get used to it!

19 s'en f. *(s'inquiéter)* to worry; **si je lui en parle, elle va s'en f.** if I tell her about it she'll only worry; **je ne m'en fais pas pour lui** I'm not worried about him; **ne t'en fais pas pour le dîner, je m'en occupe** don't (you) worry about the dinner, I'll see to it; *Fam* **dans la vie faut pas s'en f.** you should take life easy; **elle s'en souviendra, ne t'en fais pas!** she'll remember, don't you worry!; **encore au lit? tu ne t'en fais pas!** still in bed? you're taking it easy, aren't you?; **il roule en Jaguar maintenant – il ne s'en fait pas!** he drives around in a Jaguar now – some people have all the luck!; *Fam* **tu as ouvert mon courrier? faut pas t'en f.!** you've opened my mail? you've got some nerve *or* don't mind me!

Allusion

Fais ce que voudras

In François Rabelais' *Gargantua* (1534), this is the motto of the Abbey of Thélème: "Do what you please". The Abbey represents a Utopian society, based on Humanist values. The motto is often wrongly interpreted to mean "Do whatever you like", an invitation to excess. This motto is forever associated with the name of Rabelais.

faire-part [fɛrpar] **NM INV 1** *(dans la presse)* announcement; **f. de décès** death notice; **f. de mariage** wedding announcement **2** *(carte)* = card sent to family or friends announcing a birth, wedding, death etc; **le présent avis tiendra lieu de f.** friends please accept this intimation

faire-valoir [fɛrvalwar] **NM INV 1** *(personne)* foil; *Théât (de comique)* stooge, straight man; **servir de f. à qn** to serve as a foil to sb, to act as a straight man to sb **2** *Agr* farming; **exploitation** *ou* **terres en f. direct** owner farm

fair-play [fɛrplɛ] **NM INV** fair play, fair-mindedness

ADJ INV fair-minded; **il est f.** *(joueur)* he plays fair; *Fig* he has a sense of fair play

fair-way [fɛrwɛ] **NM** *Sport* fairway

faisabilité [fəzabilite] **NF** *(d'un projet)* feasibility

faisable [fəzabl] **ADJ** *(réalisable)* feasible; *(possible)* possible, practicable; **c'est f.** it can be done; **ce n'est pas f. par un enfant** no child could do it; **tu peux être là à 14 heures? – c'est f.** can you come at 2 o'clock? – I should think so

faisait *etc voir* **faire**

faisan [fəzɑ̃] **NM 1** *(oiseau)* (cock) pheasant; **f. doré** golden pheasant **2** *Fam Péj (escroc)* crook, con-man

faisandage [fəzɑ̃daʒ] **NM** hanging (of meat)

faisandé, -e [fəzɑ̃de] **ADJ 1** *Culin* gamy, high **2** *Péj (goût, littérature, personne)* decadent; *(milieu politique)* corrupt

faisandeau, -x [fəzɑ̃do] **NM** young pheasant

faisander [3] [fəzɑ̃de] **VT** *Culin* to hang

▸**se faisander VPR 1** *Culin* to get high **2** *(pourrir)* to rot

faisanderie [fəzɑ̃dri] NF pheasant farm

faisane [fəzan] ADJ F **poule f.** (hen) pheasant
NF (hen) pheasant

faisant [fəzɑ̃] *voir* **faire**

faisceau, -x [fɛso] NM **1** *(rayon)* beam, ray; *Électron* **f. cathodique** cathode ray; *Électron & TV* **f. cathodique explorateur** scanning electron beam; *Électron & Phys* **f. d'électrons** *ou* **électronique** electron beam; *Électron & Phys* **f. hertzien** radio beam; **f. lumineux** *ou* **de lumière** light beam, beam of light, *Spéc* pencil of rays; *Phys* **f. de particules** particle beam; *Électron & Phys* **f. radar** radar beam

2 *(gerbe)* cluster, bundle; *(d'ampoules électriques)* cluster; **f. aimanté** bunch of magnets; **f. de fils** wiring harness; **f. de ressorts** cluster springs; *Fig* **f. de preuves** accumulation of evidence; *Archit* **colonne en f.** clustered column

3 *Mil (pyramide d'armes)* stack of arms; **former/rompre les faisceaux** to stack/to unstack arms

4 *Anat & Bot* fascicle

5 *Rail* **f. de voies** group of sidings

6 *Aut* **f. convergent** converging beam; **f. divergent** diverging beam; **f. parallèle** parallel beam; **f. du radiateur** radiator core

7 *Antiq & Hist* fasces; **les faisceaux consulaires** *ou* **des licteurs** the fasces of the consuls *or* lictors

faiseur, -euse [fəzœr, -øz] NM,F **1** *(artisan)* maker; **le bon f.** a first-class tailor; **ses costumes sortent de chez le bon f.** his suits are always smart and well-cut; **f. de dentelles** lacemaker; **f. de ponts** bridge builder

2 *(qui se livre à telle activité) Péj* **faiseuse d'anges** back-street abortionist; *TV & Rad* **f. d'Audimat®** = television/radio personality guaranteed to boost the ratings; *Péj* **f. d'embarras** fusspot, *Am* fussbudget; **faiseuse de mariages** matchmaker; **f. de miracles** miracle worker; **f. de tours** magician; *Péj* **f. de vers** poetaster

3 *Vieilli Péj (escroc)* swindler, dishonest businessman; *(hâbleur)* show-off, braggart

faisselle [fɛsɛl] NF *Culin* **1** *(récipient)* cheese basket **2** *(fromage)* fromage frais *(packaged in its own draining basket)*

FAIT[1] [fɛ]

act **1** ■ event **2** ■ fact **2, 3** ■ point **4**

NM **1** *(action)* act, deed; **le f. de boire** (the act of) drinking; **le f. du prince** *Jur* restraint of princes; *Pol* government action; **f. d'armes** feat of arms; **faits de guerre** exploits of war; **les faits et gestes de qn** everything sb says and does, sb's every move; **observer** *ou* **épier les (moindres) faits et gestes de qn** to watch sb's every move; **rendre compte de ses faits et gestes** to give an account of oneself; *(à la police)* to give an account of one's movements; **hauts faits** heroic deeds; **prendre qn sur le f.** to catch sb red-handed; **prendre f. et cause pour qn** to side with sb

2 *(événement)* event, fact, occurrence; **f. notoire** piece of common knowledge; **f. nouveau** new development; **les faits lui ont donné raison** he/she was proved right by events; **quels sont les faits?** *(dans un procès)* what are the facts?; **les faits qui lui sont reprochés** the charge laid against him/her; **quels sont les faits reprochés à mon client?** what is my client being accused of *or* charged with?; **où étiez-vous au moment des faits?** where were you at the time in question?; **racontez-nous les faits** tell us what happened; **niez-vous les faits?** do you deny the charge?; **de ce f.** thereby; **le contrat, de ce f., est résilié** the contract is thereby terminated; **il est pénalisé par le seul f. de son divorce** the very fact that he's divorced puts him at a disadvantage; **par le seul f. d'y être** by the mere fact of *or* simply by being there; **par le seul f. que** (solely) because of, due (solely) to the fact that; *Jur* **f. (juridique)** fact; *Jur* **f. concluant** conclusive evidence; *Jur* **faits constitutifs de délit** factors that constitute an offence

3 *(réalité)* fact; **c'est un f.** it's a (matter of) fact; **le f. est là** it's a fact; **le f. est que nous étions en retard** the fact is we were late; **f. accompli** fait accompli; **placer** *ou* **mettre qn devant le f. accompli** to present sb with a fait accompli; **considérer qch comme un f. acquis** to take sth for granted; **c'est loin d'être** *ou* **ce n'est pas un f. acquis** it's not a foregone conclusion; **état de f.** (inescapable) fact; **roi de nom plutôt que de f.** king in name rather than in fact; *Fam* **le f. est!** that's right!, you've said it!; **je n'ai pas eu le temps de le faire, le f. est!** I have to admit that I didn't have enough time to do it!

4 *(sujet, question)* point; **aller (droit) au f.** to go straight to the point; **en venir au f.** to come *or* to get to the point; **venons-en au f.** let's come *or* get to the point; **au f.!** get to the point!

5 *(locutions)* **dire son f. à qn** to give sb a piece of one's mind; **je vais lui dire son f., à ce goujat!** I'm going to give this lout a piece of my mind!; **être le f. de** to be characteristic of; **c'est le f. de tous les incapables que de se chercher des excuses** incompetents always try to find excuses for themselves; **la renaissance du judo français est le f. de quelques champions** the renaissance of judo in France is entirely due *or* attributable to a few champions; **l'erreur est de son f.** it was his/her mistake; **cela est du f. de Martin** this is Martin's doing; **parler n'était pas son f.** he/she was no talker; **la générosité n'est pas son f.** it's just not his/her way to be generous; *Littéraire* **ce n'est pas le f. d'un chevalier de** it does not become a knight to

❑ **au fait** ADV by the way, incidentally; **au f., je t'ai remboursé?** incidentally *or* by the way, did I pay you back?; **au f., on pourrait peut-être y aller à pied?** by the way, couldn't we walk there?

❑ **au fait de** PRÉP well aware of, fully informed about; **être au f. de** to know about, to be informed about *or* au fait with; **je ne suis pas très au f. de ce problème** I don't know much about this problem; **il est très au f. de ces questions** he's very well informed about such matters; **mettre qn au f. de la situation** to inform sb about the situation

❑ **de ce fait** ADV for that reason, on that account

❑ **de fait** ADJ **1** *Jur* actual, de facto; **possession de f.** actual possession

2 *(en affirmation)* **il est de f. que** it is true *or* a fact that; **il est de f. que je n'y avais pas pensé** it is true *or* a fact that it hadn't occurred to me

❑ **de fait** ADV in fact, actually, as a matter of fact; **en f., il n'est pas mon père** actually *or* in fact he isn't my father; **de f., je n'ai jamais compris ce qu'il voulait** actually *or* to be honest, I never understood what he wanted; **de f., cela est un refus** that is in effect a refusal

❑ **du fait de** PRÉP because of, due to, on account of

❑ **du fait que** CONJ because (of the fact that); **du f. qu'il boite** owing to the fact that *or* because he limps

❑ **en fait** = **de fait**

❑ **en fait de** PRÉP **1** *(en guise de)* by way of; **en f. de nourriture, il n'y a qu'une boîte de sardines** there's only a can of sardines by way of food

2 *(au lieu de)* instead of; **en f. de chien, c'était un loup** it wasn't a dog at all, it was a wolf

3 *(en matière de)* as regards, when it comes to; **expert en f. de vins** expert as regards wine *or* when it comes to wine

fait[2], -e [fɛ, fɛt] PP *voir* **faire**

ADJ **1** *(formé)* **être bien f. de sa personne** to be good-looking; **elle a la jambe bien faite** she's got shapely *or* nice legs; **une femme fort bien faite** a very good-looking woman; **f. au tour** shapely, well-turned; **une taille faite au tour** a well-turned waist, a shapely figure

2 *(adapté)* **être f. pour qn/qch** to be made for sb/sth; **cette voiture est faite pour la ville** this car is made *or* designed for town driving; **ils sont faits l'un pour l'autre** they're made for each other; **il est f. pour faire du cinéma/pour être avocat** he's cut out to act in films/to be a lawyer; *Fam* **on peut mettre un chapeau dans cette boîte – oui, c'est f. pour** you can put a hat in this box – yes, that's what it's for; **ça fait joli – c'est f. pour** that looks pretty – it's supposed *or* meant to; **sers-toi, c'est f. pour** help yourself, that's what it's there for

3 *(mûr)* mature, ripe; **un fromage f.** a fully ripened cheese; **trop f.** over-ripe

4 *(maquillé)* made-up; **avoir les ongles faits** to have nail polish on; **elle a les yeux faits** she's wearing eye make-up

5 *(prêt)* **tout f.** *(vêtement)* ready-made, ready-to-wear; *(tournure)* set, ready-made; **robes toutes faites** ready-to-wear *or Br* off-the-peg dresses; **une expression toute faite** a set phrase, a cliché; **une excuse toute faite** a ready-made excuse

6 *Fam (ivre)* blitzed, wasted, gassed

faîtage [fɛtaʒ] NM *Constr* **1** *(poutre)* ridgepole, ridgepiece **2** *(couverture)* ridge sheathing; *(tuiles)* ridge tiling

fait divers (*pl* **faits divers**), **fait-divers** (*pl* **faits-divers**) [fɛdivɛr] NM *Presse* **1** *(événement)* news story, news item

2 faits divers *(rubrique)* (news) in brief; *(page)* news in brief; **tenir la rubrique des faits divers** = to cover weddings and funerals; *Fam* **ne fréquente pas ces types-là si tu ne veux pas te retrouver dans les faits divers** don't mix with those types if you don't want to end up as a crime statistic

fait-diversier [fɛdivɛrsje] (*pl* **faits-diversiers**) NM *Presse* = journalist who covers short news items

faîte [fɛt] NM **1** *Géog* crest, top; **ligne de f.** watershed, crest line **2** *(sommet)* top, summit; **le f. des arbres était couvert de neige** the tops of the trees were covered with snow **3** *Constr* ridge **4** *(summum)* climax, acme; **le f. de la gloire** the height *or* pinnacle of glory; **atteindre le f. de sa carrière** to reach the climax of one's career

faîteau, -x [fɛto] NM *Constr* ridge tile

faites *voir* **faire**

faîtier, -ère [fɛtje, -ɛr] ADJ *Suisse (organisation, association)* umbrella

faîtière [fɛtjɛr] *Constr* ADJ *voir* **lucarne, tuile**
NF crest tile, ridge tile

faitout [fɛtu] NM stewpot, cooking pot

fait-tout [fɛtu] NM INV stewpot, cooking pot

faix [fɛ] NM **1** *Littéraire* burden, load; **le f. des ans** the weight of (advancing) years; **le f. des impôts** the burden of taxation; **ployer sous le f.** to bend beneath the load **2** *Obst* foetus and placenta

fakir [fakir] NM **1** *Rel* fakir **2** *(magicien)* conjurer

fakirisme [fakirism] NM practice of a fakir

falafel [falafɛl] NM *Culin* falafel

falaise [falɛz] NF cliff; **f. d'éboulement** secondary cliff; **f. littorale** *ou* **vive** sea cliff; **f. morte** ancient cliff

falarique [falarik] NF *Archéol* phalarica

falbalas [falbala] NM *Vieilli (volant de jupe)* flounce, furbelow

❑ **falbalas** NMPL *Péj* frills (and furbelows); **une architecture sans f.** an unadorned style of architecture

❑ **à falbalas** ADJ *(robe, rideau)* flouncy, frilly

falciforme [falsifɔrm] ADJ *Anat, Biol & Bot* falciform, falcate, sickle-shaped

falconidé [falkɔnide] *Orn* NM member of the falcon family *or* Falconidae

❑ **falconidés** NMPL Falconidae

fale [fal] NF *Can* **1** *(d'une volaille)* crop **2** *Fam (d'une personne, d'un animal → gorge)* throat■; *(→ poitrine)* chest■; **avoir la f. à l'air** *(gén)* to have one's chest uncovered■; *(femme)* to be showing a lot of cleavage■; *Fig* **avoir la f. basse** *(être abattu)* to be down-in-the-mouth; *(être affamé)* to be famished *or* ravenous

falerne [falɛrn] NM *Antiq* = wine from the Campania region of Italy, highly appreciated in ancient times

Falkland [folklɑ̃d] NFPL **les (îles) F.** the Falkland Islands, the Falklands; **aux îles F.** in the Falkland Islands

fallacieuse [falasjøz] *voir* **fallacieux**

fallacieusement [falasjøzmɑ̃] ADV deceptively, misleadingly; *(promettre)* misleadingly

fallacieux, -euse [falasjø, -øz] ADJ **1** *(trompeur)* deceptive, misleading, fallacious; *(apparence)* misleading; **promesses fallacieuses** false *or* deceptive promises; **l'espoir f. de les rencontrer** the illusory hope of meeting them; **sous un prétexte f.** on some pretext **2** *(spécieux)* insincere, specious; **des arguments f.** specious arguments

FALLOIR [69] [falwar] **V IMPERSONNEL A.** *EXPRIME LE BESOIN* **1** *(gén)* **pour ce tricot, il faut des aiguilles n° 6** to knit this jumper, you need number 6 needles; **il faut deux heures pour y aller** it takes two hours to get there; **faut-il vraiment tout ce matériel?** is all this equipment really necessary?; *Hum* **il est inspecteur des impôts – il en faut!** he's a tax inspector – someone has to do it!; **on a besoin d'un gros marteau – j'ai ce qu'il faut dans la voiture** we need a big hammer – I've got one in the car; **je bois deux litres d'eau par jour – c'est ce qu'il faut** I drink two litres of water a day – that's good; **ajoutez de la moutarde, juste ce qu'il faut** add some mustard, not too much; **je crois que nous avons trouvé l'homme qu'il nous faut** *(pour un poste)* I think we've found the right man for the job; **c'est un homme très tendre qu'il me faut** I need a man who is very loving; **ce n'est pas la femme qu'il te faut** she's not the right woman for you; **pour cette recette, il vous faut...** for this recipe, you need...; **c'est tout ce qu'il vous fallait?** *(dans une boutique)* was there anything else?; **il me faudrait deux filets de cabillaud, s'il vous plaît** I'd like two cod fillets, please; **j'ai plus d'argent qu'il n'en faut** I've got more money than I need; **j'ai plus de temps qu'il ne m'en faut** I've got time on my hands; **il ne lui en faut pas beaucoup pour se mettre en colère** it doesn't take a lot *or* much to make him/her angry; **il te faudrait une voiture** you need a car; *Hum* **j'aime les bonnes choses – oui, mais point trop n'en faut!** I like the good things in life – OK, but you shouldn't overindulge!; *Fam* **je voudrais que tu tapes la lettre en trois exemplaires – et puis qu'est-ce qu'il te faut encore?** I'd like you to type three copies of the letter – is there anything else while you're at it?; *Fam* **il t'a fait ses excuses, qu'est-ce qu'il te faut de plus?** he apologized, what more do you want?; *Fam* **il n'est pas très beau – qu'est-ce qu'il te faut!** he's not really good-looking – you're hard to please!; *Fam* **ce n'est pas très cher – qu'est-ce qu'il te faut!** it's not very expensive – well, what do you call expensive then?; *Fam* **je suis satisfait de lui – il t'en faut peu!** I'm satisfied with him – you're not hard to please!; *Fam* **elle a ce qu'il faut où il faut** she's got what it takes; *Fam* **il faut ce qu'il faut!** well, you might as well do things in style!

2 *(suivi d'une complétive au subj)* **il faudrait que nous nous réunissions plus souvent** we should have more regular meetings

B. *EXPRIME L'OBLIGATION* **1** *(gén)* **je ne veux pas me faire opérer – il le faut pourtant** I don't want to have an operation – you have no choice; **je lui ai dit – le fallait-il vraiment?** I told him/her – was it really necessary *or* did you really have to?; *Fam* **il ne fallait pas** *(en recevant un cadeau)* you shouldn't have; **s'il le faut** if I/we/*etc* must, if necessary; **nous irons jusque devant les tribunaux s'il le faut!** we'll take the matter to the courts if we must *or* if necessary!

2 *(suivi de l'infinitif)* **il faut m'excuser** please forgive me, you must forgive me; **il était furieux – il faut le comprendre** he was furious – that's understandable; **j'ai besoin d'aide – d'accord, que faut-il faire?** I need help – all right, what do you want me to do?; **je ne crois pas qu'il faille t'inquiéter** I don't think you should worry; **je n'ai pas envie – il faut pourtant le faire** I don't feel like it – still, it has to be done; **c'est un film qu'il faut voir (absolument)** this film's a must; **il faut bien se souvenir/se dire que...** it has to be remembered/said that...; **s'il fallait faire attention à tout ce que l'on dit!** if one had to mind one's Ps and Qs all the time!; **il ne fallait pas commencer!** you shouldn't have started!; **j'ai faim – il fallait le dire!** I'm hungry – why didn't you say so?; **qui faut-il croire?** who is to be believed?; **il me fallait lui mentir** I had to lie to him/her

3 *(suivi d'une complétive au subj)* **il faut absolument que je vous parle** I've got to speak to you; **il a fallu que je m'absente** I had to go out for a while; **il a bien fallu que je lui dise!** I had to tell him/her, didn't I?

4 *(au conditionnel, sens affaibli)* **il aurait fallu prévenir la police** the police should have been called; **attention, il ne faudrait pas que tu te trompes!** careful, you'd better not make any mistakes!; **ne dis rien, il ne faudrait pas que ça se sache** don't breathe a word, nobody should know about it; **il ne faudrait pas me prendre pour une idiote!** do you think I'm stupid?; **il faudrait pourtant que je m'achète une nouvelle voiture** I ought to buy a new car, really

5 *Fam (en intensif)* **il faut le voir pour le croire!** it has to be seen to be believed!; **c'était dangereux, il fallait y aller** *(ton admiratif)* it was dangerous, it took courage to do it; **il faut le faire!** *(en regardant un acrobate, un magicien)* that's amazing!; **ce qu'il a fait, il fallait le faire!** what he did was quite something!; **trois accidents en une semaine, il faut le faire!** three accidents in a week, that must be a record!; **ne pas fermer sa voiture, faut le faire!** it takes a fool *or* you've got to be completely stupid to leave your car unlocked!; **ça représente un cheval – il fallait le deviner!** it's supposed to be a horse – I'd never have known!; **il fallait l'entendre!** you should have heard him/her!; **il fallait le voir jouer Hamlet!** you should have seen him playing Hamlet!

C. *EXPRIME UNE FATALITÉ* **il a fallu que le téléphone sonne juste à ce moment-là!** the phone had to ring just then!; **je le lui avais défendu, mais non, il a fallu qu'elle le fasse** I'd told her not to, but she would have to do it

D. *POUR JUSTIFIER, EXPLIQUER* **il faut que tu aies fait mal à Rex pour qu'il t'ait mordu!** you must have hurt Rex to make him bite you!; **il fallait que le vase soit** *ou* **fût très fragile pour se casser aussi facilement** the vase must have been very fragile to break that easily

▸**s'en falloir V IMPERSONNEL il s'en faut de beaucoup qu'il n'ait fini!** he's far from finished!; **elle n'est pas de ton envergure, il s'en faut de beaucoup!** she's not in your league, far from it!; **peu s'en est fallu que je ne manque le train!** I very nearly *or* almost missed the train!; *Fam* **il s'en est fallu de rien** *ou* **d'un cheveu qu'il ne fût décapité** he came within inches of having his head chopped off; **tant s'en faut** far from it, not by a long way; **il n'est pas paresseux, tant s'en faut** he's far from being lazy

Fallope [falɔp] *voir* **trompe**

fallu [faly] **PP** *voir* **falloir**

falot[1] [falo] **NM 1** *(lanterne)* (hand) lantern **2** *Fam Arg mil* court martial▪

falot[2]**, -e** [falo, -ɔt] **ADJ** colourless, bland, vapid; **c'est un personnage assez f.** he's rather insipid

falsafa [falsafa] **NF** *Phil* falsafa

falsifiabilité [falsifjabilite] **NF** falsifiability

falsifiable [falsifjabl] **ADJ 1** *(signature, document)* falsifiable, forgeable **2** *Phil* which can be falsified

falsificateur, -trice [falsifikatœr, -tris] **NM,F** *(de documents, de comptes)* falsifier; *(d'une signature)* forger

falsification [falsifikasjɔ̃] **NF** *(de documents, de comptes)* falsification; *(de la vérité, des propos de quelqu'un)* misrepresentation; *(d'une signature)* forging, forgery; *(d'un vin)* adulteration; **f. des registres** tampering with registers

falsificatrice [falsifikatris] *voir* **falsificateur**

falsifier [9] [falsifje] **VT** *(document, comptes)* to forge, to falsify; *(vérité, propos de quelqu'un)* to misrepresent; *(signature)* to forge; *(vin)* to adulterate; **les comptes ont été falsifiés** the accounts have been falsified; **il a falsifié les résultats** he tampered with *or* falsified the results; *Fig* **f. la pensée de l'auteur** to misrepresent the author's thinking

faluche [falyʃ] **NF** *Vieilli* beret *(traditionally worn by French students)*

falun [falœ̃] **NM** *Agr* shell marl; *Géol* **faluns** shell beds, *Spéc* faluns

faluner [3] [falyne] **VT** *Agr* to manure with shell marl

falunière [falynjɛr] **NF** *Agr* shell-marl pit

falzar [falzar] **NM** *très Fam Br* trousers▪, keks, *Am* pants▪

Famagouste [famagust] **NM** Famagusta

famas [famas] **NM** *Mil (abrév* **fusil d'assaut de la manufacture d'armes de Saint-Étienne***)* Famas rifle *(type of French assault rifle)*

famé, -e [fame] *voir* **mal famé**

famélique [famelik] **ADJ** *(chat)* scrawny; *(prisonnier)* half-starved; **les ventres faméliques de l'Afrique** the starving of Africa

fameuse [famøz] *voir* **fameux**

fameusement [famøzmɑ̃] **ADV** *Fam Br* dead, *Am* real; **il est f. rusé!** he's *Br* dead *or Am* real crafty!; **on s'est f. bien amusé** we had a *Br* dead *or Am* real good time

fameux, -euse [famø, -øz] **ADJ 1** *(célèbre)* famous, renowned, well-known; *(ayant bonne réputation)* famous (**par** *ou* **pour** for); *(ayant mauvaise réputation)* notorious (**par** *ou* **pour** for); **f. entre tous** widely recognized

2 *Fam (bon → gén)* excellent, brilliant; *(→ repas, mets)* excellent, delicious; **ce fut une fameuse journée** it has been a memorable day; **f., ton gâteau** your cake is delicious; **j'ai bien une photo, mais elle n'est pas fameuse** I have got a photograph, but it's not that good; **l'image est bonne, mais la bande-son n'est pas fameuse** the picture is OK, but the soundtrack isn't brilliant; **son dernier roman n'est pas f.** his/her latest novel isn't up to much *or* isn't anything special

3 *(en intensif)* **c'est un f. mystère** it's quite a mystery; **un f. exemple de courage** an outstanding example of courage; **c'est un f. coquin, celui-là!** he's quite a lad!

4 *(dont on parle)* famous; **et où as-tu acheté ce f. bouquin?** where did you buy this book you keep mentioning?

5 *Ironique (soi-disant)* so-called; **c'est ça, ton f. trésor?** is THAT your famous treasure?; **montre-moi ce f. chef-d'œuvre** show me this so-called masterpiece

familial, -e, -aux, -ales [familjal, -o] **ADJ 1** *(de famille)* domestic, family *(avant n)*; *(usine, hôtel)* family-run, family-owned; **vie/réunion familiale** family life/meeting; **une atmosphère familiale** a friendly atmosphere; **entreprise familiale** family firm; **querelles familiales** domestic quarrels; **cet élève a des problèmes familiaux** this pupil has problems at home; **maladie familiale** hereditary disease *or* condition; **la cuisine familiale** home cooking; **quotient/revenu f.** family quotient/income

2 *Com* family-sized, economy *(avant n)*; **emballage f.** economy-size *or* family pack

▫ **familiale NF** *Br* estate (car), *Am* station wagon

familiarisation [familjarizasjɔ̃] **NF** familiarization

familiariser [3] [familjarize] **VT f. qn avec** to make sb familiar *or* to familiarize sb with, to get sb used to

▸**se familiariser VPR se f. avec qch** *(par la pratique)* to familiarize oneself with sth, to get to know sth; *(par habitude)* to get accustomed *or* used to sth; **se f. avec une technique/langue** to master a technique/language; **se f. avec un lieu** to get to know a place, to get to know one's way around; **peu familiarisé avec** unfamiliar *or* unacquainted with

familiarité [familjarite] **NF 1** *(désinvolture)* familiarity, casualness; **être d'une trop grande f. avec qn** to be too familiar *or* overfamiliar with sb; **je ne tolérerai aucune f. dans mes rapports avec les étudiants** I will not tolerate any familiarity in my relations with the students; **pas de f., je vous prie** please don't be familiar

2 *(connaissance)* **f. avec** familiarity with, knowledge of; **il a une grande f. avec l'œuvre de Proust** he has a close *or* an intimate knowledge of the work of Proust; **sa f. avec les oiseaux d'Europe du Nord** his/her knowledge of the birds of Northern Europe; **acquérir une certaine f. de l'anglais** to gain a certain knowledge of English

▫ **familiarités NFPL** liberties, undue familiarity; **s'autoriser** *ou* **prendre des familiarités avec qn** to take liberties *or* to be overfamiliar with sb

familier, -ère [familje, -ɛr] **ADJ 1** *(connu)* familiar; *(amical)* friendly; **un visage f.** a familiar face; **le problème m'est f.** I am familiar with the problem; **la maison lui était familière** he/she remembered the house quite clearly; **ce spectacle/bruit lui était f.** it looked/sounded familiar to him/her; **ta voix ne lui est pas familière** he/she doesn't know *or* recognize your voice

2 *(habituel)* usual; **une tâche familière** a routine task; **c'est l'une de ses attitudes familières**

it's one of his/her favourite poses; **il est préférable de les voir dans leur décor f.** you should see them in their usual surroundings; **ce genre de travail leur est f.** they are used to this kind of work

3 *(apprivoisé)* **animal f.** pet

4 *Péj (cavalier)* overfamiliar; **je n'aime pas leurs attitudes familières/les gens trop familiers** I don't like their offhand ways/people who are overfamiliar; **il s'est montré trop f.** he was too familiar, he was overfamiliar

5 *Ling* colloquial, informal

6 *(de la maison)* **dieux familiers** household gods

NM 1 *(ami)* familiar, friend; **elle se déplace en tournée avec tous ses familiers** she tours with her regular entourage; **un f. de la maison** a regular visitor to the house, an intimate friend of the household

2 *(client)* habitué, regular; **les familiers de ce café** this café's regulars

familièrement [familjɛrmɑ̃] **ADV 1** *(amicalement)* familiarly, informally, casually; **il lui donna f. une petite tape sur la joue** he gave him/her a friendly little pat on the cheek **2** *(couramment)* colloquially, in conversation; **la saxifrage, f. appelée mignonnette** saxifrage, commonly named London pride

familistère [familistɛr] **NM 1** *(coopérative)* coop, cooperative **2** *Hist* Fourierist co-operative

famille [famij] **NF 1** *(foyer)* family; *(ménage)* household; **la f. Laverne** the Laverne family, the Lavernes; **f. étendue/restreinte** extended/nuclear family; **revenu par f.** income per household; **il rentre dans sa f. tous les week-ends** he goes back home every weekend; **f. monoparentale** single-parent family; **f. nombreuse,** *Suisse* **grande f.** large family; **réduction f. nombreuse** family reduction *or* discount; **f. nucléaire** nuclear family; **f. patchwork** patchwork family, *Am* blended family *(consisting of children, parents etc of divorced parent's new spouse)*; *Fam* **f. tuyau de poêle** = family whose members have an incestuous relationship

2 *(enfants)* family, children; **comment va la petite f.?** how are the children?; **avec toute sa petite f.** with all his/her brood around him/her; *Can Fam* **être en f.** to be in the family way, to have a bun in the oven; *Can Fam* **partir pour la f.** to get knocked up, to get pregnant▪

3 *(tous les parents)* family, relatives; **une grande f. de France** one of the noblest families in France; **il n'est pas de ma f.** he's no relation of mine; **ils sont de la même f.** they're related; **prévenir la f.** to inform sb's relatives; *Jur* to inform the next of kin; **il faut que je vous présente à ma f.** *(parents)* I must introduce you to my parents; **c'est une f. de danseurs** they're all dancers in their family, they're a family of dancers; **je souhaite que mes bijoux ne sortent pas de la f.** I'd like my jewels to stay in the family; *Hum* **c'est ça, donne-lui ton rhume pour que ça ne sorte pas de la f.!** that's right, give him your cold, let's keep things in the family!; **les 200 familles** = the wealthiest families in France

4 *Bot, Ling & Zool (groupe)* family, group; *Chim & Phys* chain, family; **f. de langues** group of languages; **f. de mots/plantes** family of words/plants; **f. de l'uranium** uranium series; *Math & Mus* family; **la f. des instruments à vent** winds, the wind family

5 *Mktg (de produits)* family, line

6 *Typ* **f. de caractères** typeface

7 *(idéologie)* obedience, persuasion; **de la même f. politique** of the same political persuasion; **des gens appartenant à la même f. spirituelle que nous** our brothers in spirit

❑ **de bonne famille ADJ** well-bred, from a good family

❑ **de famille ADJ** *(cercle, médecin, biens)* family *(avant n)*; **charges de f.** dependants; **chef de f.** head of the family; *Admin* householder, head of the household; **soutien de f.** (main) wage earner, breadwinner; **fils de f.** young man of good social standing **ADV c'est** *ou* **cela tient de f.** it runs in the family, it's in the blood

❑ **des familles ADJ** *Fam* cosy, nice (little); **une petite soirée des familles** a cosy little party; **je vais nous faire un petit gigot des familles** I'm going to cook a nice little leg of lamb for us

❑ **en famille ADV 1** *(en groupe)* **passer Noël en f.** to spend Christmas with one's family *or* at home; **dîner/passer le week-end en f.** to dine/spend the weekend at home with one's family; **nous réglons toujours nos problèmes en f.** we always settle our problems within the family

2 *(en confiance)* **se sentir en f.** to feel at home; **ma petite Sylvie, vous êtes (comme) en f. ici!** my dear Sylvie, please consider yourself at home here!

famine [famin] **NF** famine, starvation; **ils souffrent de la f.** they're victims of the famine, they're starving; **crier f.** to plead poverty, to complain of hard times; **salaire de f.** starvation wages

fan [fan] **NMF** fan; **c'est un f. de jazz** he is a jazz fan; **je suis une f. de Victor Hugo!** I am one of Hugo's fervent admirers!

fana [fana] *Fam* **ADJ** crazy (**de** about), dead keen (**de** on); **il est f. de sport** he's crazy about sport

NMF fanatic; **f. du football/de la moto** football/motorbike fanatic *or* freak; **c'est une f. de cinéma** she's a real film buff

fanage [fanaʒ] **NM** *Agr (du foin)* tedding, tossing

fanaison [fanɛzɔ̃] **NF** drooping, withering

fanal, -aux [fanal, -o] **NM** lantern, lamp; *Naut (sur les côtes)* beacon, lantern; **f. de locomotive** headlight; *Naut* **f. de bord** ship's lantern, sidelight

fanatique [fanatik] **ADJ 1** *Péj (religieux)* fanatical, bigoted, zealous **2** *(passionné)* enthusiastic; **il est f. des jeux vidéo** he's mad about video games; **je ne suis pas f. de la bière** I'm not (that) keen on beer, I'm not a big fan of beer

NMF 1 *Péj* zealot **2** *(partisan)* fan, fanatic; **des fanatiques de Pavarotti** Pavarotti fans; **je ne suis pas un f. du poisson** I'm not mad *or* crazy about fish, I'm not a big fan of fish

fanatiquement [fanatikmɑ̃] **ADV** fanatically, zealously

fanatisation [fanatizasjɔ̃] **NF** fanaticization; **la f. des foules était due à une propagande très bien menée** extremely skilful propaganda turned the crowds into fanatics *or* made the crowds fanatical

fanatiser [3] [fanatize] **VT** to fanaticize, to make fanatical; **être fanatisé** to become fanatical; **suivi par une foule fanatisée** followed by a frenzied crowd; **des religieux fanatisés** religious fanatics

fanatisme [fanatism] **NM** fanaticism; *Pol & Rel* fanaticism, zealotry

fanchon [fɑ̃ʃɔ̃] **NF** kerchief, headscarf

fan-club [fanklœb] *(pl* **fans-clubs**) **NM 1** *(d'un artiste)* fan club **2** *Hum* admirers, supporters, *Fig* fan club

Fanconi [fɑ̃kɔni] **NPR** *Méd* **maladie** *ou* **anémie de F.** Fanconi anaemia

fancy-fair [fɑ̃sifɛr] *(pl* **fancy-fairs**) **NF** *Belg* charity fair

fandango [fɑ̃dɑ̃go] **NM** *Mus* fandango

fane [fan] **NF 1** *(de légumes)* top; **fanes de carotte/radis** carrot/radish tops; **fanes de pomme de terre** potato haulm **2** *(feuille morte)* (dead *or* fallen) leaf

faner [3] [fane] **VI 1** *Agr* to make hay; **ils sont en train de f.** they're at the haymaking **2** *(se flétrir)* to wither

VT 1 *Agr* to ted, to toss **2** *(décolorer)* to fade; **fané par le soleil** faded by the sun, sunbleached; **des couleurs fanées** faded *or* washed-out colours **3** *(fleur, plante)* to fade, to wither, to wilt

►**se faner VPR 1** *Bot* to fade, to wither **2** *(perdre son éclat)* to wane, to fade; **sa beauté s'est fanée** her beauty has lost its bloom *or* faded

faneur, -euse [fanœr, -øz] *Agr* **NM,F** haymaker, tedder

❑ **faneuse NF** *(machine)* tedder, tedding machine

fanfare [fɑ̃far] **NF** *(air)* fanfare; *(orchestre → civil)* brass band; *(→ militaire)* military band; **la f. du village** the village band

❑ **en fanfare ADV** *(réveiller)* noisily, brutally; **réveil en f.** brutal awakening; **annoncer la nouvelle en f.** to trumpet the news

fanfaron, -onne [fɑ̃farɔ̃, -ɔn] **ADJ** boastful, swaggering; **d'un air f.** boastfully

NM,F boaster, braggart, swaggerer; **faire le f.** to crow, to brag and boast; **ah, tu ne fais plus le f., maintenant?** ah, so you're not so pleased with yourself now?

fanfaronnade [fɑ̃farɔnad] **NF 1** *(acte)* bravado *(UNCOUNT)*; **par f.** out of (sheer) bravado **2** *(remarque)* boast **3 fanfaronnades** *(actes, propos)* bragging, boasting

fanfaronner [3] [fɑ̃farɔne] **VI** to boast, to brag, to swagger

fanfic [fanfik], **fanfiction** [fanfiksjɔ̃] **NF** fanfic

fanfreluches [fɑ̃frəlyʃ] **NFPL** *Péj* frills (and furbelows)

fange [fɑ̃ʒ] **NF** *Littéraire* mire; **vivre dans la f.** to live a life of degradation; **sortir de la f.** to climb out of the gutter; **élevé dans la f.** brought up in the gutter; **croupir dans la f.** to be living surrounded by filth

fangeux, -euse [fɑ̃ʒø, -øz] **ADJ** *Littéraire* **1** *(boueux)* miry **2** *(abject)* murky

fangothérapie [fɑ̃gɔterapi] **NF** *Méd* fangotherapy

fanion [fanjɔ̃] **NM** *(de club, bateau, corps d'armée etc)* pennant, pennon; *(balise)* flag; **des fanions** *(guirlandes)* bunting

fanny [fani] **ADJ INV** *(joueur de boules)* = beaten without having scored any points

fanon [fanɔ̃] **NM 1** *Zool (d'une baleine)* whalebone plate **2** *(bajoue → d'un bœuf)* dewlap; *(→ d'une dinde)* lappet, wattle **3** *(d'un cheval)* fetlock **4** *Rel* lappet (of a mitre)

fantaisie [fɑ̃tezi] **NF 1** *(originalité)* imagination; *Péj* fantasy; **avoir beaucoup de f.** to have a lively imagination; **donner libre cours à sa f.** to give free rein to one's imagination; **manquer de f.** *(personne)* to lack imagination; *(vie)* to be monotonous *or* uneventful; **vous interprétez le règlement avec beaucoup de f.** you have a rather imaginative interpretation of the rules; **elle était d'une f. rafraîchissante** she was refreshingly imaginative

2 *(lubie)* whim; **c'est sa dernière f.** it's his/her latest whim; **je ne sais quelle f. lui a pris** I don't know what came over him/her; **et s'il lui prend la f. de partir?** what if he/she should take it into his/her head to leave?; **il a eu** *ou* **il lui a pris la f. de se baigner** he took it into his head to go swimming, he had a sudden idea *or* notion to go swimming; **qu'est-ce que c'est que cette f.?** what's come over you?; **satisfaire une f.** to give in to a whim; **se passer une f.** to indulge a caprice; **il lui passe toutes ses fantaisies** he gives in to his/her every whim; **s'offrir une f.** to give oneself a treat, to treat oneself; **je m'offre une petite f., un week-end à Amsterdam** I'm giving myself a little treat, a weekend in Amsterdam; *Péj* **cette (petite) f. va vous coûter cher** you'll regret this little extravagance; **nous ne pouvons nous permettre aucune f.** we can't afford to indulge ourselves

3 *(bibelot)* fancy; **un magasin de fantaisies** a novelty shop

4 *Beaux-Arts & Littérature* (piece of) fantasy; *Mus* fantasy, fantasia; *(créativité)* fancy, imagination, imaginative power; **le récit relève de la plus haute f.** the story is highly imaginative

5 *(comme adj inv) (simulé)* imitation; *(peu classique)* fancy; **kirsch f.** imitation kirsch; **bijou f.** piece of costume jewellery; **des boutons f.** fancy buttons

❑ **de fantaisie ADJ 1** *(à bon marché)* novelty *(avant n)*; **article de f.** novelty; **pain de f.** fancy bread *(not sold by weight)*; **bijoux de f.** costume *or* novelty *or* fancy jewellery

2 *(imaginaire → œuvre, récit)* fantasy *(avant n)*, imaginative

3 *(non officiel)* **il portait un uniforme de f.** he was wearing a customized uniform

❑ **à la fantaisie de, selon la fantaisie de PRÉP n'en faire qu'à sa f.** to do exactly as one pleases; **chacun s'amusait à sa f.** everyone amused themselves as the fancy took them *or* as they pleased

fantaisiste [fɑ̃tezist] **ADJ 1** *(farfelu)* eccentric, unconventional; *(procédés, mode de vie)* unorthodox; **elle a des horaires fantaisistes** she keeps strange *or* odd hours **2** *(inventé)* fanciful; **un récit des plus fantaisistes** a most fanciful *or* whimsical account; **c'est une explication f.** that's a fanciful explanation; **les déclarations fantaisistes que vous avez faites à la presse**

your extremely fanciful statements to the press
NMF 1 *Théât* variety artist, sketcher 2 *Péj (dilettante)* joker, clown; **méfie-toi, c'est un f.** be careful, he's a bit of a joker

fantasia [fɑ̃tazja] NF fantasia

fantasmagorie [fɑ̃tasmagɔri] NF 1 *(féerie)* phantasmagoria 2 *(effets de style)* gothic effects; **des histoires pleines de fantasmagories** fantasies

fantasmagorique [fɑ̃tasmagɔrik] ADJ magical, *Littéraire* phantasmagorical

fantasmatique [fɑ̃tasmatik] ADJ fantasy *(avant n)*

fantasme [fɑ̃tasm] NM fantasy; **tu vis dans tes fantasmes** you're living in a fantasy world

fantasmer [3] [fɑ̃tasme] VI to fantasize; **f. sur qn/qch** to fantasize about sb/sth; **faire f. qn** *(sexuellement)* to turn sb on; **tu me fais f. avec tes récits de voyage** you make my imagination run wild talking about your trips

fantasque [fɑ̃task] ADJ 1 *(capricieux)* capricious, whimsical 2 *Littéraire (bizarre)* odd, weird

fantassin [fɑ̃tasɛ̃] NM foot soldier, infantry man

fantastique [fɑ̃tastik] ADJ 1 *(fabuleux → animal, personnage)* fantastical, fabulous, fantasy *(avant n)*

2 *(surnaturel → lumière, atmosphère)* weird, eerie; **roman f.** Gothic novel; **cinéma f.** science-fiction *or* fantasy films

3 *Fam (formidable)* great, brilliant; **j'ai gagné! n'est-ce pas f.?** I won! isn't it great *or* marvellous?; **c'est un type f.!** he's a great guy!

4 *Fam (étonnant)* extraordinary, unbelievable; **le f. essor des technologies** the extraordinary progress of technology; **une somme f.** a fantastic amount of money; **déployer un luxe f.** to make a display of fantastic luxury; **il a un courage f.** he's incredibly courageous

NM **le f.** *(l'étrange)* the fantastic, the supernatural; *(genre)* the Gothic (genre); *(littérature)* fantasy literature

fantastiquement [fɑ̃tastikmɑ̃] ADV fantastically, terrifically, amazingly

fantoche [fɑ̃tɔʃ] NM *Péj* puppet; *(comme adj)* **un gouvernement/souverain f.** a puppet government/king; **une armée f.** a non-existent army

Fantômas [fɑ̃tomas] NPR = a villainous hero of a series of adventure novels from the beginning of the 20th century

fantomatique [fɑ̃tɔmatik] ADJ phantom *(avant n)*, ghostly

fantôme [fɑ̃tom] NM 1 *(revenant)* ghost, phantom, spirit; **apparaître/disparaître comme un f.** to appear/to disappear as if by magic

2 *Littéraire (apparence)* ghostly image *or* shape, ghost; *Péj* **un f. de chef** a make-believe leader, a leader in name only; *Péj* **un f. de parti politique** a phantom political party; **ce n'est plus qu'un f.** *(très maigre)* he's just a skeleton, he's nothing but skin and bone

3 *(comme adj)* **cabinet f.** shadow cabinet; **des étudiants fantômes** non-existent students; **membre(-)f.** phantom limb; **société f.** bogus company; **train f.** ghost train; **ville f.** ghost town; **où est ce rapport f.?** where is this supposed report?

fanton [fɑ̃tɔ̃] NM *Constr* 1 *(tige de fer)* iron (tie) 2 *(cheville en bois)* dowel, pin, peg 3 *(matériau → fer)* strip iron; *(→ bois)* pegwood

fanum [fanɔm] NM *Archéol* fane, temple

fanzine [fɑ̃zin] NM fanzine

FAO [ɛfao] NF 1 *Ind (abrév* **fabrication assistée par ordinateur**) CAM 2 *(abrév* **Food and Agricultural Organization**) FAO

faon [fɑ̃] NM *Zool (cerf)* fawn, calf; *(daim)* fawn; *(chevreuil)* kid, fawn

FAP [ɛfape] ADJ *Assur (abrév* **franc d'avarie particulière**) FPA, fpa

FAQ [fak] *Ordinat (abrév* **frequently asked questions, foire aux questions**) FAQ

faquin [fakɛ̃] NM *Arch* knave, varlet

far [far] NM *Culin* **f. (breton)** = Breton custard tart with prunes

farad [farad] NM *Élec* farad

Faraday [faradɛ] *voir* **cage**

faradique [faradik] ADJ *Élec* faradic

faradisation [faradizasjɔ̃] NF *Vieilli Méd* faradization, faradism

faramineux, -euse [faraminø, -øz] ADJ *Fam (somme, fortune)* huge, tremendous; *(prix)* astronomical; **il a un aplomb f.!** he's got an awful nerve!; **c'est f. ce qu'elle a pu dépenser!** the amount of money she spent was incredible!; **il lui a fait des compliments pour le moins f.** his compliments were slightly over the top

farandole [farɑ̃dɔl] NF 1 *(danse)* farandole 2 *(au restaurant)* **et pour finir, la f. des fromages/desserts** to round off your meal, choose from our cheeseboard/dessert trolley

faraud, -e [faro, -od] *Fam Vieilli* ADJ boastful; **te voilà bien faraude avec ta robe neuve!** you look very pleased with yourself in your new dress!; **il n'était pas si f. pendant l'orage** he wasn't so cocky during the storm

NM,F swaggerer; **faire le f.** to show off

farce[1] [fars] NF 1 *(tour)* practical joke, prank, trick; **faire une f. à qn** to play a trick on sb; **quelqu'un t'a fait une f.** somebody has been pulling your leg; **une mauvaise f.** a joke gone wrong; *Can Fam* **f. plate** sick *or* tasteless joke; *Can Fam* **c'est pas des farces!** it's true!, I'm not joking! 2 *Littérature & Théât* farce; *Fig* **la vie n'est qu'une f.** life is nothing but a farce; *Fig* **la situation tournait à la f.** things were becoming farcical

ADJ *Vieilli* comical; **c'était assez f.!** it was hilarious!

❑ **farces et attrapes** NFPL jokes and novelties; **magasin de farces et attrapes** joke shop

farce[2] [fars] NF *Culin* forcemeat, stuffing

farceur, -euse [farsœr, -øz] ADJ mischievous; **il a l'œil f.** he has a waggish look; **ils sont farceurs** they like playing tricks

NM,F 1 *(qui fait des farces)* practical joker, prankster; **petit f.!** you rascal!; **je me demande qui est le petit f. qui m'a fait ça** I wonder who the joker is that I have to blame for this 2 *(blagueur)* joker, wag; **c'est un f. qui vous aura dit cela** somebody's been pulling your leg

farci, -e [farsi] *Culin* ADJ stuffed

NM stuffed vegetable

farcin [farsɛ̃] NM *Vét* farcy

farcir [32] [farsir] VT 1 *Culin* to stuff 2 *Fam (remplir)* **f. qch avec** *ou* **de** to fill sth chock-a-block with, to cram sth with; **cesse de lui f. le crâne avec ces sottises!** stop cramming his/her head full of this nonsense!; **elle avait la tête farcie de superstitions** her head was crammed full of superstitious beliefs

▸**se farcir** VPR **se f. qn** *Fam (le subir)* to have to put up with sb, to have to take sb; *Vulg (sexuellement)* to screw sb, *Br* to have it off with sb; *Fam* **se f. qch** *(le subir)* to get stuck *or Br* lumbered *or* landed with sth; *(le boire)* to knock sth back, to down sth; *(le manger)* to stuff oneself with sth; **son beau-frère, faut se le f.!** his/her brother-in-law is a real pain!

fard [far] NM 1 *(produit)* colour *(for make-up)*; **f. à joues** blusher; **f. à paupières** eyeshadow 2 *Vieilli (maquillage)* **le f.** *(gén)* make-up; *Théât* greasepaint

❑ **sans fard** ADJ straightforward, frank; **la vérité sans f.** the plain unvarnished truth ADV straightforwardly, frankly; **parler sans f.** to speak candidly *or* openly

fardage [fardaʒ] NM *Com* camouflage

farde [fard] NF *Belg* 1 *(cahier)* exercise book 2 *(chemise)* folder 3 *(cartouche)* carton *(of cigarettes)*

fardeau, -x [fardo] NM 1 *(poids)* burden, load 2 *(contrainte)* burden, millstone; **porter un f. sur les épaules** to carry *or* to bear a burden on one's shoulders; **être un f. pour qn** to be a burden to sb; **le f. des ans** *(la vieillesse)* old age; **f. de la dette** debt burden; *Fin* **le f. fiscal** the tax burden

farder [3] [farde] VT 1 *(maquiller)* to make up; **trop fardé** over-made up 2 *(cacher)* to conceal, to mask; **f. la réalité/ses sentiments** to disguise the truth/one's feelings 3 *Com* to camouflage

▸**se farder** VPR to make up one's face, to put one's make-up on; **se f. les yeux** to put eyeshadow on

fardier [fardje] NM *(gén)* trolley; *(pour le bois)* log transporter

fardoches [fardɔʃ] NFPL *Can* scrub, brushwood

faré [fare] NM = traditional house in Polynesia

farfadet [farfadɛ] NM imp, elf, goblin

farfelu, -e [farfəly] *Fam* ADJ crazy, strange, cranky
NM,F oddball, weirdo, crackpot

farfiner [3] [farfine] VI *Can* to be picky (about one's food)

farfineux, -euse [farfinø, -øz] *Can* ADJ picky
NM,F picky eater

farfouiller [3] [farfuje] *Fam* VI to grope *or* to rummage about; **elle farfouille dans sa valise/sous le lit** she's groping about in her suitcase/under the bed; **ils ont farfouillé dans tous les tiroirs** they've been rummaging about in all the drawers

VT *(chercher)* **qu'est-ce que tu farfouilles?** what are you after?

fargues [farg] NFPL *Naut (partie du bordé)* wash strakes; *(pavois de protection)* bow plate, spirketting plate, *Am* apron plate

faribole [faribɔl] NF *Littéraire* piece of nonsense; **dire** *ou* **raconter des fariboles** to talk nonsense; **et autres fariboles** and all that nonsense; **fariboles!** nonsense!

farigoule [farigul] NF *(en Provence)* thyme

farinacé, -e [farinase] ADJ farinaceous

farinage [farinaʒ] NM *(d'une peinture)* chalking

farine [farin] NF 1 *Culin* flour; **f. d'avoine** oatmeal; **f. de blé** wheat flour; **f. complète** wholewheat flour, *Br* wholemeal flour; **f. de froment** wheat flour; **f. de maïs** *Br* cornflour, *Am* cornstarch; **f. de manioc** cassava; **f. de poisson** fish meal; **f. de seigle** rye flour 2 *(poudre)* powder; **f. de forage** bore dust; **f. de moutarde** mustard powder 3 **farines animales** bone meal

❑ **de la même farine** ADJ of the same kind; *Littéraire* **ce sont tous gens de la même f.** they're all alike

fariner [3] [farine] VT to flour, to sprinkle flour over; **farinez le moule** dredge the tin with flour, flour the tin all over

farineux, -euse [farinø, -øz] ADJ 1 *(fariné)* floury, flour-covered 2 *(pâteux → poire)* mealy; *(→ pomme de terre)* floury 3 *(au goût de farine)* chalky, floury 4 *(féculent)* starchy, *Spéc* farinaceous

NM starchy food; **évitez les f. pendant quelque temps** avoid starch for a while

farlouche [farluʃ] NF *Can* = mixture of raisins and molasses used in pies

farlouse [farluz] NF *Orn* meadow pipit

Farnésine [farnezin] NF *Archit* **la F.** the Villa Farnesina

farnésol [farnesɔl] NM *Biol & Chim* farnesol

farniente [farnjɛnte, farnjɑ̃t] NM idleness, laziness; **amateur de f.** idler

faro [faro] NM = type of beer brewed in Brussels

farouch, farouche[1] [faruʃ] NM *Bot* crimson clover, French clover

farouche[2] [faruʃ] ADJ 1 *(caractère)* fierce, unflinching; *(résistance, regard)* fierce; **volonté f.** iron *or* unshakeable will; **elle a une méfiance f. à l'égard des religions** she is fiercely suspicious of all religion

2 *(animal)* wild; *(personne)* shy, coy; **un animal peu f.** a tame animal; **l'enfant est encore un peu f.** the child is still a bit shy; *Euph Hum* **c'est une femme/une fille peu f.** she is no model of virtue

3 *(brutal)* cruel, savage; **un combat f.** a savage fight

farouchement [faruʃmɑ̃] ADV 1 *(ardemment)* definitely, unquestionably; **je suis f. contre!** I am definitely against it!; **il est toujours f. décidé à ne pas bouger** he's still adamant he won't move 2 *(violemment)* fiercely, savagely; **se débattre f.** to kick and struggle

farrago [farago] NM *Agr* mixed corn

farsi [farsi] NM *(langue)* Farsi

fart [far(t)] NM *Ski* ski wax

fartage [fartaʒ] NM *Ski* waxing

farter [3] [farte] VT *Ski* to wax

Far-West [farwɛst] NM **le F.** the Far West

fasce [fas] NF 1 *Archit* fascia 2 *Hér* fess, fesse

fascé, -e [fase] ADJ *Hér* fessey

fascia [fasja] NM *Anat* fascia, aponeurosis

fasciation [fasjasjɔ̃] NF *Hort* fasciation

fascicule [fasikyl] NM 1 *(partie d'un ouvrage)* instalment, part, section; **publié par fascicules** published in parts 2 *(livret)* booklet, manual; **le calendrier figure dans un f. séparé** the timetable is given in a separate booklet; *Mil* **f. de mobilisation** mobilization instructions

fasciculé, -e [fasikyle] ADJ *Biol & Bot* fasciculate

fascié, -e [fasje] ADJ **1** *Zool* fasciated, banded, striped **2** *Bot* fasciate, fasciated

fascinage [fasinaʒ] NM **1** *(action)* protection with fascines **2** *(résultat)* fascine work

fascinant, -e [fasinɑ̃, -ɑ̃t] ADJ *(personne)* fascinating; *(beauté, yeux, sourire)* captivating

fascinateur, -trice [fasinatœr, -tris] ADJ fascinating

NM,F captivator

fascination [fasinasjɔ̃] NF fascination; **exercer une f. sur** to be fascinating to

fascinatrice [fasinatris] *voir* **fascinateur**

fascine [fasin] NF *Constr* fascine

fasciner[1] [3] [fasine] VT **1** *(sujet: serpent → proie)* to fascinate, to hypnotize **2** *(charmer → sujet: spectacle)* to captivate, to fascinate; **le spectacle les fascine** they're captivated by the show; **j'étais fasciné par l'adresse des marins dans les haubans** I was fascinated by the agility of the sailors up in the rigging; **elle est fascinée par ce garçon** she has been bewitched by that boy, she is under that boy's spell; **elle se laisse f. par l'argent** she lets herself be blinded *or* dazzled by money

fasciner[2] [3] [fasine] VT *Constr (rive)* to line with fascines, to fascine, *Am* to corduroy; **route fascinée** corduroy road

fascisant, -e [faʃizɑ̃, -ɑ̃t] ADJ *Pol* fascist, fascistic, pro-fascist

fascisation [faʃizasjɔ̃] NF **la f. d'une politique** the increasingly fascistic *or* fascist tendencies of a policy; **on assiste à la f. du régime** the regime is becoming more fascist

fasciser [3] [faʃize] VT **f. un État** to take a state towards fascism; **f. un régime/une politique** to make a regime/policy increasingly fascistic

fascisme [faʃism] NM **1** *(gén)* fascism **2** *Hist* Fascism

fasciste [faʃist] ADJ & NMF **1** *(gén)* fascist **2** *Hist* Fascist

faseyer [12] [faseje, fazeje] VI *Naut* to shiver

fashion [faʃœn] ADJ INV *Fam* trendy

fasse *etc voir* **faire**

faste [fast] ADJ **1** *(favorable → année)* good; *(→ jour)* good, lucky; **les années fastes, nous mangions de la viande tous les jours** in a good year, we would eat meat every day; **je paie la note, je suis dans une période f.!** I'll pay the bill, I'm in the money *or* I'm flush at the moment! **2** *Antiq* **jour f.** lawful day

NM *(luxe)* sumptuousness, splendour; **avec f.** sumptuously, with pomp (and circumstance), munificently; **sans f.** simply, quietly, plainly; **la cérémonie aura lieu sans f.** the ceremony will be a simple affair

❑ **fastes** NMPL **1** *Littéraire* pomp; **les fastes de l'État** the pomp and circumstance of great state occasions **2** *Antiq* annals

fast-food [fastfud] (*pl* **fast-foods**) NM fast-food restaurant

fastidieuse [fastidjøz] *voir* **fastidieux**

fastidieusement [fastidjøzmɑ̃] ADV boringly, dully, tediously

fastidieux, -euse [fastidjø, -øz] ADJ boring, tiresome, tedious

fastigié, -e [fastiʒje] ADJ *Bot* fastigiate

fastoche [fastɔʃ] ADJ *Fam* easy■; **c'était hyper f.** it was dead easy, it was a walk in the park

fastueuse [fastyøz] *voir* **fastueux**

fastueusement [fastɥøzmɑ̃] ADV sumptuously, with pomp (and circumstance), munificently

fastueux, -euse [fastɥø, -øz] ADJ magnificent, sumptuous, munificent

fat [fa(t)] *Littéraire* ADJ M bumptious, conceited, self-satisfied; **prendre un air f.** to look smug

NM smug person

fatal, -e, -als, -ales [fatal] ADJ **1** *(fixé par le sort)* fateful; **l'instant f.** the fatal moment; *Littéraire* **les déesses fatales** the Fates, the Parcae

2 *(désastreux)* disastrous, terrible; **cette erreur vous a été fatale** this mistake proved disastrous for you; *Ordinat* **erreur fatale** fatal error

3 *(mortel → collision, blessure)* fatal, mortal; **coup f.** deathblow; **porter un coup f. à** *(frapper)* to deliver a deadly *or* mortal blow to; *Fig* to administer the coup de grâce to; **le choc lui a été f.** the shock killed him/her

4 *(inévitable)* inevitable; **c'était f.** it was bound to happen, it was inevitable; **il est revenu, c'était f.** he came back, as was bound to happen

fatalement [fatalmɑ̃] ADV inevitably; **il devait f. perdre** he was bound to lose

fatalisme [fatalism] NM fatalism

fataliste [fatalist] ADJ fatalist, fatalistic; **il est f.** he's resigned to his fate

NMF fatalist

fatalité [fatalite] NF **1** *(sort)* destiny, fate; **poursuivi par la f.** pursued by fate; **c'est la f.** it's bad luck; **la f. s'acharne contre eux** they're dogged by misfortune; **il parle de l'analphabétisme comme si c'était une f.** he talks about illiteracy as if it were inevitable

2 *(circonstance fâcheuse)* mischance; **je le vois chaque fois que j'y vais, c'est une f.!** there must be a curse on me! every time I go there, I see him!; **par quelle f. était-il absent ce soir-là?** by what unfortunate coincidence did he happen to be away that evening?

3 *(inévitabilité)* inevitability

fatidique [fatidik] ADJ **1** *(marqué par le destin → date, jour)* fated, fateful **2** *(important)* crucial, momentous; **il est arrivé au moment f.** he arrived at the crucial moment; **c'est l'instant f.!** it's now or never!

fatigabilité [fatigabilite] NF fatigability

fatigable [fatigabl] ADJ **facilement f.** easily tired; **difficilement f.** untiring

fatigant, -e [fatigɑ̃, -ɑ̃t] ADJ **1** *(épuisant)* tiring, wearing; **c'est très f.** it's exhausting; **c'est f. pour le cœur** it strains the heart; **la lumière vive est fatigante pour les yeux** bright light is a strain on the eyes **2** *(agaçant)* tiresome, tedious, annoying; **c'est f., ce bourdonnement incessant** that endless buzzing is very annoying; **ce que tu peux être f.!** you're a real nuisance!; **il est f. avec ses questions** he's tiresome with his questions

fatigue [fatig] NF **1** *(lassitude)* tiredness, weariness; **ressentir une grande/légère f.** to feel very/a bit tired *or* weary; **tomber de f.** to be fit to drop; **je tombe** *ou* **je suis mort de f.** I'm dead on my feet; **va le coucher, il tombe de f.** put him to bed, he's fit to drop **2** *(tension → physique)* strain; *(→ nerveuse)* stress; **se remettre de la f.** *ou* **des fatigues de l'examen** to recover from the stress of the exam; **épargner** *ou* **éviter à qn la f. de qch/de faire qch** to save sb the strain *or* effort of sth/of doing sth; **f. intellectuelle** mental strain; **f. musculaire** stiffness; **f. nerveuse** nervous exhaustion; **f. oculaire** eyestrain **3** *Tech* **f. de l'acier** metal fatigue

fatigué, -e [fatige] ADJ **1** *(las → personne)* tired, weary; *(→ traits, regard, voix)* tired; *(→ yeux)* strained; **je suis f.** I'm tired; **je suis très f.** I'm exhausted; **je suis trop f. pour pouvoir m'endormir** I'm too tired to go to sleep; **je suis si f.!** I'm exhausted *or* so tired!; **f. de rester debout/d'attendre** tired of standing/of waiting; **f. par la promenade** tired from one's walk; **f. par le voyage** travel-worn, travel-weary; *Fig* **f. de qn/qch** tired *or* weary of sb/sth; **être f. de la vie** to be tired *or* weary of life; **f. de faire qch** tired *or* weary of doing sth

2 *(malade → personne)* suffering from fatigue; *(→ estomac, foie)* upset; *(→ cœur)* strained

3 *(usé → vêtement)* worn; *(→ livre)* well-thumbed; **un vieux manteau f.** a shabby old coat

fatiguer [3] [fatige] VT **1** *(épuiser → gén)* to tire *or* to wear out; *(→ cheval)* to tire; **f. le cœur/les yeux** to strain the heart/the eyes; **les transports en commun me fatiguent beaucoup** using public transport wears me out; *Hum* **si ça ne te fatigue pas trop** if you don't mind

2 *(lasser)* to annoy; **tu me fatigues avec tes critiques!** your constant criticism is getting on my nerves!; **ils nous fatiguent, à la fin, avec leurs publicités!** they're really getting on our nerves with their ads!; **tes mensonges continuels me fatiguent** you're wearing me out with your constant lying; **il commence à me f., celui-là!** he's beginning to annoy me!

3 *(user → machine, moteur)* to put a strain on; *(→ vêtements, chaussures etc)* to wear out; *(→ champ, sol)* to exhaust, to impoverish; **f. un livre** to give a book a lot of hard wear

4 *Fam (remuer)* **f. la salade** to toss the (green) salad

VI **1** *(peiner)* to grow tired, to flag; **dépêche-toi, je fatigue!** hurry up, I'm getting tired!; **je commence à f. sérieusement** I'm beginning to get really tired

2 *Tech (faiblir)* to become weakened; *(forcer)* to bear a heavy strain

3 *Naut* to ride hard

►**se fatiguer** VPR **1** *(s'épuiser → gén)* to get tired; *(→ en travaillant beaucoup)* to tire oneself out; **essaie de ne pas trop te f.** try not to get overtired; **les personnes âgées se fatiguent vite** old people tire *or* get tired very easily; **tu ne vas pas te f. à tout nettoyer!** don't tire yourself out cleaning everything!

2 *(faire un effort)* to push oneself; **ils ne se sont pas (trop) fatigués** they didn't exactly kill themselves

3 *(faire des efforts inutiles)* **ne te fatigue pas** don't waste your time; **ne te fatigue pas, je m'en occupe** don't bother, I'll see to it; **c'était bien la peine que je me fatigue!** I don't know why I bothered!; **c'était bien la peine que je me fatigue à préparer le repas** a fat lot of use it was me wearing myself out getting the meal ready; **ne te fatigue pas, je sais tout** don't bother *or* don't waste your breath, I already know everything; **se f. à faire qch** *(s'y appliquer)* to wear oneself out doing sth; **je me fatigue à le lui répéter** I wear myself out telling him/her

4 *(user)* **se f. la vue** *ou* **les yeux** to put a strain on *or* to strain one's eyes

5 se f. de *(se lasser de)* to get tired of; **se f. de qn/qch** to get tired *or* to tire of sb/sth; **se f. de faire qch** to get tired *or* to tire of doing sth; **elle se fatiguera vite de lui** she'll soon get tired of him

fatma [fatma] NF *Péj* North African woman

fatras [fatra] NM *Péj* **1** *(tas)* clutter, jumble; **tout un f. de vieux papiers** a clutter of old papers **2** *(mélange) Br* hotchpotch, *Am* hodgepodge; **un f. de connaissances** a confused mass of knowledge

fatrasie [fatrazi] NF *Littérature* = piece of medieval satirical nonsense verse

fatuité [fatɥite] NF complacency, conceit, smugness

fatum [fatɔm] NM *Littéraire* destiny, fate

fatwa [fatwa] NF *Rel* fatwa; **prononcer une f. contre qn** to declare *or* issue a fatwa against sb

fauber, faubert [fobɛr] NM *Naut* (deck) swab, mop

faubourg [fobur] NM **1** *(quartier périphérique)* suburb; **accent des faubourgs** (Parisian) working-class accent; **f. industriel** industrial suburb; **f. résidentiel** residential suburb; **les faubourgs de la ville** the outskirts of the city; **dans les faubourgs de Vienne** in the suburbs of Vienna **2** *(quartier de grande ville)* district; **le f. Saint-Antoine** = area in Paris famous for its furniture shops; **le f. Saint-Honoré** = area of Paris well-known for its luxury shops

faubourien, -enne [foburjɛ̃, -ɛn] ADJ suburban; **accent f.** working-class accent

NM,F working-class Parisian

faucard [fokar] NM long-handled scythe

faucarder [3] [fokarde] VT to clear out

fauchage [foʃaʒ] NM *Agr (du blé, d'un champ de blé)* reaping; *(de l'herbe, d'une prairie)* mowing, cutting; *(avec une faux)* scything

fauchaison [foʃɛzɔ̃] NF *Agr* **1** *(du blé, d'un champ de blé)* reaping; *(de l'herbe, d'une prairie)* mowing, cutting; *(avec une faux)* scything **2** *(saison → gén)* mowing time; *(→ du blé)* reaping time; *(→ des prés)* haymaking time

fauchard [foʃar] NM *Agr* double-edged slasher

fauche [foʃ] NF **1** *Fam (vol)* thieving■, (petty) theft■; *(dans un magasin)* shoplifting■; **méfie-toi, il y a de la f. au lycée** watch out, there's a lot of thieving going on at school■ **2** *Vieilli Agr (du blé, d'un champ de blé)* reaping; *(de l'herbe, d'une prairie)* mowing, cutting; *(avec une faux)* scything **3** *Fam (ruine)* **c'est la f.** I'm/he's/*etc* flat broke

fauché, -e [foʃe] ADJ **1** *Fam (sans argent)* broke, *Br* skint, strapped (for cash); **f. comme les blés** flat broke, *Br* stony broke **2** *Agr (blé)* cut; *(herbe)* mown; *(avec une faux)* scythed

NM,F *Fam* penniless individual■; **ce sont tous des fauchés** they haven't got a penny between them

faucher [3] [foʃe] **VT** **1** *Agr (blé, champ de blé)* to reap; *(herbe, prairie)* to mow, to cut; *(avec une faux)* to scythe

2 *(renverser brutalement → sujet: véhicule)* to knock *or* to mow down; *(→ sujet: arme)* to mow down; **les cyclistes ont été fauchés par un camion** the cyclists were knocked down by a lorry, a lorry ploughed into the cyclists; **se faire f. par une voiture** to be knocked down by a car; *Sport* **f. son homme** to bring down one's man

3 *(tuer → sujet: guerre, maladie)* to wipe out; **tous ces jeunes artistes fauchés à la fleur de l'âge** all these young artists struck down in the prime of life

4 *Fam (voler)* to pinch, to swipe; **qui a fauché le sel?** who's got the salt?▪; **je me suis encore fait f. mon briquet!** my lighter's been pinched again!

VI **1** *(cheval)* to dish

2 *Mil* to sweep the ground (with machine-gun fire)

fauchet [foʃɛ] **NM** *Vieilli* hay rake

fauchette [foʃɛt] **NF** billhook

faucheur, -euse [foʃœr, -øz] **NM,F** *Agr (personne → qui fauche le blé)* reaper; *(→ qui fauche les herbes)* mower

NM = **faucheux**

▫ **faucheuse** **NF** **1** *Agr* mechanical reaper **2** *Littéraire* **la Faucheuse** the Grim Reaper

faucheux [foʃø] **NM** *Entom* harvest spider, harvestman, *Am* daddy-long-legs

Fauchon [foʃɔ̃] **NM** = luxury food shop in Paris

fauchon [foʃɔ̃] **NM** *Agr (garni d'un râteau)* brush scythe; *(à lame courte)* sickle

faucille [fosij] **NF** sickle, reaping hook; **la f. et le marteau** the hammer and sickle

faucillon [fosijɔ̃] **NM** small sickle

faucon [fokɔ̃] **NM** **1** *Orn* falcon, hawk; **f. crécerelle** kestrel, *Br* windhover; **f. hagard** haggard; **f. hobereau** hobby; **f. des moineaux** (American) sparrowhawk; **f. pèlerin** peregrine falcon; **chasser au f.** to hawk; **chasse au f.** hawking, falconry **2** *Pol* hawk

'Le Faucon maltais' *Hammett, Huston* 'The Maltese Falcon'

fauconneau, -x [fokɔno] **NM** *Orn* young hawk

fauconnerie [fokɔnri] **NF** **1** *(activité)* hawking **2** *(abri)* hawk-house

fauconnier, -ère [fokɔnje, -ɛr] **NM,F** falconer

faucre [fokr] **NM** *Hist* fewter, rest *(for couched lance)*

faudra *etc voir* **falloir**

faufil [fofil] **NM** *Couture* basting *or* tacking thread

faufilage [fofilaʒ] **NM** *Couture* basting, tacking

faufiler [3] [fofile] **VT** *Couture* to baste, to tack

▸**se faufiler** **VPR** *(se frayer un chemin)* to weave one's way (**dans** *ou* **entre** through); *(s'introduire furtivement)* to slip in (**dans** *ou* **entre** through); **se f. dans la foule** to weave *or* thread one's way through the crowd; **se f. entre les voitures** to weave one's way through the traffic; **le chat s'est faufilé hors du jardin** the cat slipped out of the garden; **les enfants essayaient de se f. au premier rang** the children were trying to sneak up to the front; **il s'était faufilé parmi les invités** he had slipped in *or* sneaked in with the guests

faufilure [fofilyr] **NF** *Couture* basted *or* tacked seam

faune[1] [fon] **NF** **1** *Zool* fauna, animal life; **la f. et la flore** flora and fauna, wildlife **2** *Péj (groupe)* mob, bunch, crowd; **la f. prétentieuse des beaux quartiers** the snobbish residents of the fashionable districts; **on rencontre dans ce bar une f. étrange** you meet a strange crowd *or* bunch in this bar

faune[2] [fon] **NM** *Myth* faun

faunesque [fonesk] **ADJ** faunlike

faunesse [fonɛs] **NF** *Littéraire* female faun

faunique [fonik], **faunistique** [fonistik] **ADJ** faunal; **réserve f.** wildlife reserve

faussaire [fosɛr] **NMF** *(gén)* forger; *(faux-monnayeur)* forger, counterfeiter

fausse [fos] *voir* **faux**[2]

faussement [fosmɑ̃] **ADV** **1** *(à tort)* wrongfully **2** *(en apparence)* falsely, spuriously; **d'un air f. ingénu/intéressé** with feigned innocence/interest, pretending to look innocent/interested; **..., dit-il d'une voix f. inquiète** ..., he said, pretending to sound worried; **un sourire f. aimable** a deceptively pleasant smile; **avoir un air f. contrit** to pretend to look sorry, to assume a contrite look; **il prit un air f. désinvolte** he tried to look casual

fausser [3] [fose] **VT** **1** *(déformer → clef, lame)* to bend, to put out of true; *(détériorer → serrure)* to damage **2** *(réalité, résultat, fait)* to distort; *(comptes)* to falsify; **f. le sens d'une phrase** to distort the meaning of a sentence; **faire une présentation qui fausse la réalité** to present a distorted vision of reality **3** *(jugement, raisonnement)* to affect, to distort; *(esprit)* to warp, to twist **4** *(locution)* **f. compagnie à qn** to give sb the slip

VI *Can (chanter faux)* to sing out of tune *or* off-key; *(jouer faux)* to play out of tune *or* off-key

▸**se fausser** **VPR** **1** *(voix d'orateur)* to become strained; *(voix de chanteur)* to lose pitch **2** *(clé, serrure, axe etc)* to buckle, to bend

fausse-route [fosrut] *(pl* **fausses-routes***)* **NF** *Méd* **f. (alimentaire)** food choking

fausset[1] [fosɛ] **NM** *Mus* falsetto (voice)

fausset[2] [fosɛ] **NM** *Tech (d'un tonneau)* spigot, vent-peg; **trou de f.** vent-hole

fausseté [foste] **NF** **1** *(inexactitude)* falseness, falsity; **dénoncer la f. d'une assertion** to expose the fallacy of an argument **2** *(duplicité)* duplicity, treachery; **un comportement empreint de f.** deceitful behaviour

faustien, -enne [fostjɛ̃, -ɛn] **ADJ** Faustian

faut *voir* **falloir**

faute [fot] **NF** **1** *(erreur)* mistake, error; **faire une f.** to make a mistake; **j'ai fait une f. dans ton nom** I misspelt your name; **cet exercice est rempli de fautes** this exercise is full of mistakes; **f. d'accord** agreement error; **f. de conduite** driving error; **f. de copiste** clerical error; **f. d'étourderie** careless mistake *or* error; **f. de français** = grammatical mistake *or* error; **f. de frappe** typing error; *Ordinat* miskey, keying error, typo; **commettre une f. de goût** to show a lack of taste; **f. de grammaire** grammatical mistake *or* error; **f. d'impression** misprint; **f. d'inattention** careless mistake *or* error; **f. d'orthographe** spelling mistake; **f. de prononciation** pronunciation mistake; **il a fait quelques fautes de prononciation** he mispronounced a few words

2 *(manquement)* misdeed, transgression; **f. envers la religion/la morale** transgression against religion/morality; **commettre une f.** to do something wrong, to go wrong; **il n'a commis aucune f.** he did nothing wrong; **il a expié ses fautes** he paid dearly for his sins; **pour racheter les fautes de l'humanité** to redeem mankind; *Prov* **f. avouée est à moitié pardonnée** a fault confessed is half redressed

3 *(responsabilité)* fault; **c'est (de) ma/ta f.** it's my/your fault; **c'est bien sa f. s'il est toujours en retard** it's his own fault that he's always late; **tout ça, c'est (de) ta f.!** it's all your fault!; **c'est la f. de ton frère** *ou Fam* **à ton frère** it's your brother's fault; **ce n'est la f. de personne** it's nobody's fault, nobody's to blame; *Fam* **à qui la f.?, la f. à qui?** *(question)* who's to blame?, whose fault is it?; *(accusation)* and whose fault is that?, and who's to blame for that?; *Fam* **ce n'est quand même pas ma f. s'il pleut!** it's hardly my fault if it rains!, you can hardly blame me if it rains!; **la f. lui en incombe** the fault lies with him/her; **imputer la f. à qn** to lay the blame at sb's door; **aucune f. ne peut lui être imputée** no blame attaches to him/her, he/she deserves no blame; **la f. en revient à l'inflation** it's because of inflation, inflation's to blame; *Fam* **c'est la f. à pas de chance** it's just bad luck▪

4 *Admin & Jur* offence, misdemeanour; **commettre une f.** to commit an offence; **responsabilité des fautes et négligences du personnel** liability for the faults and defaults of the staff; **fait ou f. de l'assuré** act or fault of the insured; **f. par abstention** affirmative negligence; **f. commise dans l'exercice de fonctions officielles** instance of official misconduct; **f. contractuelle** failure to honour contractual obligations; **f. délictuelle** technical offence; **f. disciplinaire** breach of discipline; **f. grave** serious offence, high misdemeanour; **f. intentionnelle** deliberate transgression of duty; **f. légère** minor offence; **f. lourde** gross negligence; **f. partagée** contributory negligence; **f. professionnelle** professional misconduct; **f. professionnelle médicale** medical malpractice; **f. quasi-délictuelle** negligence

5 *(manque)* **le courage lui a fait f.** his/her courage failed him/her; **la main-d'œuvre nous fait f.** we're short of labour; **et pourtant ce n'est pas l'envie qui lui faisait f.** and yet it's not because he/she didn't want to; *Littéraire* **ne pas se faire f. de dire qch** to make no bones about saying sth; **ils ne se sont pas fait f. de nous prévenir** they did warn us several times; **je ne me suis pas fait f. de lui rappeler sa promesse** I didn't fail to remind him/her of his/her promise

6 *Vieilli (défaut)* **faire f. à qn** to break one's promise to sb

7 *Sport (au tennis)* fault; *(au football, au baseball etc)* foul; **commettre une f. sur qn** to foul sb; **f. de pied** foot fault; **f. de main** handball, handling the ball; **faire une f. de main** to handle the ball

▫ **en faute** **ADV** **être en f.** to be at fault; **prendre qn en f.** to catch sb in the act; **se sentir en f.** to feel that one is at fault *or* to blame

▫ **faute de** **PRÉP** for want of; **f. d'argent/de temps** for lack *or* want of money/of time; **f. de preuves** *(relâcher quelqu'un)* for lack of evidence; **f. d'ordres précis** in the absence of definite instructions; *Compta* **f. de provision** for lack of funds; **il n'a pas réussi, mais ce n'est pas f. d'essayer** he failed, but not for want of trying; **f. d'un plat plus grand, j'ai posé la tarte sur une assiette** I put the pie on a plate because I had no bigger dish; **f. de réponse satisfaisante** failing a satisfactory reply; **f. de paiement sous quinzaine, nous serons dans l'obligation de majorer notre facture de 10 pour cent** should payment not be made within fourteen days, we shall be obliged to add a 10 percent surcharge to your bill; **f. de mieux** for want of anything better; **f. de quoi** otherwise, failing which; **vous devez remplir personnellement l'imprimé, f. de quoi la demande ne sera pas valable** you must fill in the form yourself, otherwise *or* or else the application will be null and void; **f. de pouvoir aller au théâtre, il a regardé la télévision** since he couldn't go to the theatre, he watched television (instead); *Prov* **f. de grives, on mange des merles** half a loaf is better than no bread at all, beggars can't be choosers

▫ **par la faute de** **PRÉP** because of, owing to; **il a été puni par ma f.** it's my fault he was punished; **j'ai perdu du temps par la f. de cet imbécile** I wasted time because of that idiot

▫ **sans faute** **ADJ** faultless; **un parcours sans f.** *(dans une course)* a perfect race; *(dans un concours hippique)* a clear round; *Fig* **il a fait** *ou* **réussi un parcours sans f.** *(dans un quiz, à une série d'examens)* he got all the answers right; *(professionnellement)* he has had a remarkable career; *(scolairement)* he's sailed through school **ADV** without fail; **à demain sans f.** see you tomorrow without fail; **écris-moi sans f.** do write to me; **je le ferai sans f.** I'll do it without fail; **tu me donneras la clef sans f.** be sure and give me the key

Allusion

C'est la faute à Voltaire

The Enlightenment philosophers Voltaire and Rousseau were viewed by the French clergy in the 19th century as the root of all evil. In Victor Hugo's novel *Les Misérables* (1862), a character named Gavroche sings a satirical song with the line **C'est la faute à Voltaire, c'est la faute à Rousseau** ("It's Voltaire's fault, it's Rousseau's fault"). In modern French, this expression is used sarcastically in a context where someone is being blamed for something, but is not there to defend himself. The English equivalent would be, "That's right, it's somebody else's fault."

fauter [3] [fote] **VI** **1** *Euph Hum* to sin, to go astray; **f. avec qn** to be led astray by sb **2** *(en Afrique francophone) (en orthographe)* to make a spelling mistake; *(en français)* to make a grammatical mistake

fauteuil [fotœj] **NM** **1** *(meuble)* armchair; **f. à bascule** rocking chair; **f. club** club chair; **f. de**

dentiste dentist's chair; **f. de jardin** garden chair; **f. à oreillettes** wing chair; **f. pivotant** swivel chair; **f. pliant** folding chair; **f. roulant** wheelchair; **f. tournant** swivel chair; *Fam* **gagner** *ou* **arriver dans un f.** to win hands down

2 *Théât* **f. de balcon** dress-circle seat; **f. d'orchestre** seat in *Br* the stalls *or Am* the orchestra

3 *(présidence)* **occuper le f.** to be in the chair

4 *(à l'Académie française)* = numbered seat occupied by a member of the "Académie française"

fauteur, -trice [fotœr, -tris] NM,F **f. de guerre** warmonger; **f. de troubles** troublemaker

fautif, -ive [fotif, -iv] ADJ 1 *(défectueux → liste)* incorrect; *(→ citation)* inaccurate; **mémoire fautive** defective memory 2 *(coupable)* offending, responsible; **se sentir f.** to feel guilty

NM,F guilty party, culprit; **qui est le f.?** who's to blame?, who's the culprit?

fautivement [fotivmɑ̃] ADV erroneously, by mistake

fautrice [fotris] *voir* **fauteur**

fauve [fov] ADJ 1 *(couleur)* fawn-coloured, tawny 2 *(âpre → odeur)* musky 3 *Beaux-Arts* Fauve, Fauvist

NM 1 *Zool* big cat; **les grands fauves** big cats; *Fig Hum* **j'ai envoyé les fauves jouer dans le jardin** I sent the monsters out to play in the garden; *Fam* **sentir le f.** *(personne)* to stink; **ça sent le f. dans cette pièce** this room stinks 2 *(couleur)* fawn 3 *Beaux-Arts* Fauve, Fauvist

Culture

LES FAUVES

"Les fauves" were a group of French painters in 1905–7, including Matisse and Derain, who rejected classical conventions and explored the expressive potential of colour. They were derisively labelled "les fauves" by a critic who was shocked by their unconventionality, but this term, as well as "fauvisme", was soon used to officially refer to the movement which paved the way for cubism and modern expressionist art.

fauverie [fovri] NF big-cat house

fauvette [fovɛt] NF *Orn* warbler; **f. (d'Amérique) couronnée** ovenbird; **f. babillarde** lesser whitethroat; **f. couturière** tailorbird; **f. flamboyante** American redstart; **f. grisette** whitethroat; **f. d'hiver** hedge sparrow, dunnock; **f. des jardins** garden warbler; **f. passerine** subalpine warbler; **f. pitchou** Dartford warbler; **f. des roseaux** reed warbler; **f. à tête noire** blackcap

fauvisme [fovism] NM *Beaux-Arts* Fauvism

faux[1] [fo] NF 1 *Agr* scythe; **couper de l'herbe à la f.** to scythe through grass

2 *Anat* falx

FAUX², FAUSSE [fo, fos]

ADJ wrong **A1–3** ▪ false **A1–3, B1, 2, 5, 6** ▪ faulty **A2** ▪ out of tune **A4** ▪ imitation **B1** ▪ counterfeit **B2** ▪ feigned **B3** ▪ bogus **B4** ▪ deceitful **B5**

NM forgery **1, 2** ▪ falsehood **4**

ADV out of tune **1**

ADJ A. *CONTRAIRE À LA VÉRITÉ, À L'EXACTITUDE* 1 *(mensonger → réponse)* wrong; *(→ affirmation)* untrue; *(→ prétexte, nouvelle, promesse, témoignage)* false; **condamné pour f. serment** sentenced for perjury; **elle m'a donné un f. nom et une fausse adresse** she gave me a false name and address; *aussi Fig* **fausse alerte** false alarm

2 *(inexact → raisonnement)* false, faulty; *(→ calcul)* wrong; *(→ balance)* faulty; *Fam* **t'as tout f.** you're completely wrong■; *Sport & Fig* **f. départ** false start

3 *(non vérifié → argument)* false; *(→ impression)* mistaken, wrong, false; *(→ espoir)* false; **tu te fais une fausse idée de lui** you've got the wrong idea about him; **c'est un f. problème** *ou* **débat** this is not the issue

4 *Mus (piano, voix)* out of tune

5 *Cin & TV* **f. raccord** jump cut

B. *CONTRAIRE AUX APPARENCES* 1 *(dent, nez, barbe, plafond)* false; *(bijou, cuir, fourrure, marbre)* imitation; **du f. Boulle** imitation Boulle furniture; **f. chignon** hairpiece

2 *(falsifié → monnaie)* false, counterfeit, forged; *(→ carte à jouer)* trick *(avant n)*; *(→ papiers, facture)* forged, false; *(→ testament)* spurious; **une fausse pièce (de monnaie)** a forged *or* fake coin; **fabriquer de la fausse monnaie** to counterfeit money; **c'est un f. Renoir** it's a fake Renoir; **un trafic de f. tableaux** a traffic of forged *or* fake paintings; **f. bilan** fraudulent balance sheet; **fausse écriture** false entry; **fausse facture** false bill

3 *(feint → candeur, émotion)* feigned

4 *(pseudo → policier)* bogus; *(→ intellectuel)* pseudo

5 *(hypocrite → caractère, personne)* false, deceitful; *(→ regard)* deceitful, treacherous; *Ling* **f. ami** false friend; **f. frère** false friend

6 *Bot* false; **f. acacia** false acacia

NM 1 *Jur (objet, activité)* forgery; **c'est un f.** *(document, tableau)* it's a fake *or* a forgery; **inculper qn pour f. et usage de f.** to prosecute sb for forgery and use of forgeries 2 *Compta* **f. en écritures** forgery 3 *(imitation)* **c'est du cuir? – non, c'est du f.** is it leather? – no, it's imitation 4 *Phil* **le f.** falsehood ADV 1 *Mus (jouer, chanter)* out of tune, off-key; **sonner f.** *(excuse)* to have a hollow *or* false ring; **il riait d'un rire qui sonnait f.** he had a hollow laugh; **ça sonne f.** it doesn't ring true 2 *(locution)* **porter à f.** *(cloison)* to be out of plumb *or* true; *(objet)* to be precariously balanced; *(argument, raisonnement)* to be unfounded

❑ **fausse couche** NF *Méd* miscarriage; **faire une fausse couche** to have a miscarriage

❑ **faux jeton** *Fam* ADJ INV hypocritical■ NMF hypocrite■

❑ **faux pas** NM 1 *(en marchant)* **faire un f. pas** to trip, to stumble

2 *(erreur)* false move

3 *(maladresse)* faux pas, gaffe

faux-bord [fobɔr] *(pl* **faux-bords***)* NM *Naut* lopside

faux-bourdon [foburdɔ̃] *(pl* **faux-bourdons***)* NM 1 *Mus* faux-bourdon 2 *Entom* drone

faux-cul [foky] *(pl* **faux-culs***)* ADJ *très Fam* **il est f.** he's a two-faced bastard

NMF *très Fam* two-faced bastard, *f* two-faced bitch

NM *(vêtement)* bustle

faux-derche [fodɛrʃ] *(pl* **faux-derches***)* NM *très Fam* two-faced bastard

faux-facturier [fofaktyrje] *(pl* **faux-facturiers** *)* NM fake invoice fraudster

faux-filet [fofilɛ] *(pl* **faux-filets***)* NM *Culin* sirloin

faux-fuyant [fofɥijɑ̃] *(pl* **faux-fuyants***)* NM 1 *(prétexte)* excuse, subterfuge; **répondre par des faux-fuyants** to give evasive answers; **user de faux-fuyants** to prevaricate; **une réponse claire et nette, sans f.** a straight answer with no hedging *or* without any ifs and buts 2 *Arch (sentier)* bypath

faux-monnayeur [fomɔnɛjœr] *(pl* **faux-monnayeurs***)* NM forger, counterfeiter

'Les Faux-monnayeurs' *Gide* 'The Counterfeiters'

faux-pont [fopɔ̃] *(pl* **faux-ponts***)* NM *Naut* orlop deck

faux-semblant [fosɑ̃blɑ̃] *(pl* **faux-semblants***)* NM pretence, sham; **ne vous laissez pas abuser par des faux-semblants** don't let yourself be taken in by pretence

faux-sens [fosɑ̃s] NM INV *Ling* mistranslation

faux-titre [fotitr] *(pl* **faux-titres***)* NM *Typ* half-title

Favart [favar] NF **la salle F.** = the Opéra-Comique in Paris

favela [favɛla] NF favela, (Brazilian) shantytown

faverole [favrɔl] NF *Bot* field bean, horse bean

faveur [favœr] NF 1 *(plaisir)* favour; **faire une f. à qn** to do sb a favour; **faites-moi une f.** do me a favour; **nous feriez-vous la f. de venir dîner chez nous?** would you do us the honour of coming to have dinner with us?; **nous ferez-vous la f. de votre visite?** will you honour us with a visit?; **faites-moi la f. de l'inviter** do me a favour and invite him/her; **elle ne lui fit même pas la f. d'un sourire** she didn't even favour him/her with a smile; **faites-moi la f. de m'écouter quand je parle** would you mind listening when I speak?

2 *(bienveillance)* favour; **par f. spéciale** by special favour; **gagner la f. de qn** to gain sb's favour; **il a la f. du président** he's in the president's good books; **elle a eu la f. de la presse/du public** she found favour with the press/with the public; **être en (grande) f. auprès de qn** to be in (high) favour with sb

3 *(ruban)* ribbon, favour

❑ **faveurs** NFPL favours; *Euph* **accorder/refuser ses faveurs à qn** to give/to refuse sb one's favours; **elle lui a accordé ses faveurs** she obliged him/her with her favours

❑ **à la faveur de** PRÉP owing to, with the help of; **à la f. de la nuit** under cover of darkness

❑ **de faveur** ADJ preferential; **jours de f.** days of grace; **billet de f.** complimentary ticket; **prix de f.** preferential price

❑ **en faveur** ADV **être/ne pas être en f.** to be in/out of favour; **être en f. auprès de qn** to be in favour with sb; **cette mode a été remise en f.** this fashion has come back into vogue

❑ **en faveur de** PRÉP 1 *(à cause de)* on account of

2 *(au profit de)* to the benefit of, in favour of; **en ma/votre f.** in my/your favour; **se décider en f. de qch** to decide in favour of sth; **il a abdiqué en f. de son cousin** he abdicated in favour of his cousin; **quête en f. de qn/qch** collection in aid of sb/sth

3 *(pour)* in favour of; **plaider en f. de qn** to plead in sb's favour

favorable [favɔrabl] ADJ 1 *(propice)* favourable (**à** to), right (**à** for); *(situation, occasion, circonstances)* auspicious; *(vent)* favourable, fair; **arriver au moment f.** to arrive at the right moment; **saisir le moment f.** to take the opportunity; **recevoir un accueil f.** to be given a favourable reception, to be favourably received; **si le temps est f.** weather permitting, if the weather is favourable; **cette île est un lieu f. au repos** this island is an ideal place for resting; **politique f. à la paix** policy that favours peace *or* that is propitious to peace; **peu f.** unfavourable

2 *(bien disposé)* favourable; **se montrer sous un jour f.** to show oneself in a favourable light; **elle a présenté les choses sous un jour f.** she presented things in a favourable light *or* favourably; **préjugé f.** bias; **prêter à qn une oreille f.** to listen favourably to sb; **regarder qch d'un œil f.** to look favourably on sth; **f. à** in favour of; **je suis plutôt f. à son départ** I'm rather in favour of his/her going; **je suis f. à cette décision/à vos idées** I approve *or* I'm all in favour of this decision/of your ideas; **les taux de change ne vous sont pas favorables** the exchange rates are not in your favour

favorablement [favɔrabləmɑ̃] ADV favourably; **répondre f.** to say yes; **il a répondu f. à mon invitation** he accepted my invitation; **si les choses tournent f.** if things turn out all right

favori, -ite [favɔri, -it] ADJ *(personne, mélodie, dessert)* favourite; *(idée, projet)* favourite, pet *(avant n)*

NM,F 1 *Sport* favourite; **le grand f.** the odds-on *or* clear favourite 2 *(parmi les enfants)* favourite; **c'est elle la favorite** *(dans la famille)* she's the favourite; *(en classe)* she's the teacher's pet, she's the favourite

NM *Hist* (king's *or* royal) favourite

❑ **favorite** NF *Hist* **la favorite** the King's mistress

❑ **favoris** NMPL 1 *(chez un homme)* sideboards, sideburns 2 *Ordinat (sur l'Internet)* favorites

favorisant, -e [favɔrizɑ̃, -ɑ̃t] ADJ *(facteur)* predisposing; **facteurs favorisants de l'infection** factors that favour infection *or* that are conducive to infection

favorisé, -e [favɔrize] ADJ *(milieu)* fortunate; **les pays les plus favorisés** the most favoured nations; **parmi les classes les plus favorisées de la population** among the most privileged classes of the population

favoriser [3] [favɔrize] VT 1 *(traiter avantageusement)* to favour, to give preferential treatment to; **favorisé par le destin** blessed by fate; *Littéraire* **la nature l'a favorisé de ses dons** nature has favoured him with her gifts; *Littéraire* **f. qn d'un regard** to favour sb with a glance

2 *(être avantageux pour)* to favour, to be to the advantage of; **le partage favorisait traditionnellement l'aîné** traditionally, the distribution of property was to the eldest son's advantage; **le**

fait qu'elle soit une femme peut la f. the fact that she's a woman may work in her favour; **les événements l'ont/ne l'ont pas favorisé** events were in his favour *or* on his side/were not in his favour *or* were against him

3 *(faciliter, encourager)* to further, to promote; **f. les intérêts de la société** to further the interests of the firm; **f. le développement de l'économie** to promote economic development; **f. la fuite de qn** to help sb to escape; **l'obscurité a favorisé sa fuite** the darkness made it easier for him/her to escape; **des mesures pour f. le court-métrage** measures to promote the making of short films; **f. l'élection de qn** to help get sb elected

favorite [favɔrit] *voir* **favori**

favoritisme [favɔritism] NM favouritism; **faire du f.** to show favouritism; **on ne fait pas de f. ici** there's no favouritism here

favus [favys] NM *Méd* favus

fax [faks] NM *Tél (abrév* **Téléfax**) 1 *(machine)* fax (machine); **par f.** by fax; **envoyer qch par f.** to send sth by fax, to fax sth; **numéro de f.** fax number; *Ordinat* **f. modem** fax modem 2 *(message)* fax; **f. sur papier ordinaire** plain paper fax

faxer [3] [fakse] VT to fax

fayard [fajar] NM *Suisse Bot (dans les cantons de Genève et Vaud)* beech

fayot [fajo] NM *Fam* 1 *(haricot)* bean■ 2 *Péj (personne)* crawler, *Br* creep

fayotage [fajɔtaʒ] NM *Fam* crawling, *Br* creeping

fayoter [3] [fajɔte] VI *Fam* to crawl, *Br* to creep

fazenda [fazenda] NF *(au Brésil)* fazenda

FB *Anciennement (abrév écrite* **franc belge**) BF

FBI [ɛfbiaj] NM *(abrév* **Federal Bureau of Investigation**) FBI

FC [ɛfse] NM *(abrév* **Football Club**) FC

FCA [ɛfsea] *Com (abrév* **free carrier**) FCA

f.c.é.m. [ɛfseeɛm] NF *Élec (abrév* **force contre-électromotrice**) cemf, bemf, opposing emf

FCFA *(abrév écrite* **franc CFA**) = currency used in former French colonies in Africa

FCFP *(abrév écrite* **franc CFP**) = currency used in former French colonies in the Pacific

fco *Com (abrév écrite* **franco**) franco

FCP [ɛfsepe] NM *Fin (abrév* **fonds commun de placement**) investment company *or* trust, mutual fund

FCPE [ɛfsepeə] NM *Fin (abrév* **fonds commun de placement d'entreprise**) company investment fund

FCPR [ɛfsepeɛr] NM *Fin (abrév* **fonds commun de placement à risques**) VCT

FDR [ɛfdeɛr] NM *Fin (abrév* **fonds de roulement**) working capital

féal, -e, -aux, -ales [feal, -o] *Littéraire* ADJ faithful, trusty

NM devoted servitor, vassal

fébricule [febrikyl] NF *Méd* febricula

fébrifuge [febrifyʒ] *Pharm* ADJ antifebrile, antipyretic, febrifugal

NM antifebrile, antipyretic, febrifuge

fébrile [febril] ADJ 1 *Méd* febrile; **état f.** feverishness; **un patient f.** a patient who's running a fever 2 *(agité)* feverish, restless; **des préparatifs fébriles** feverish preparations; **déployer une activité f.** to be in fervent activity; **le village était f.** the village was in a state of excitement

fébrilement [febrilmɑ̃] ADV 1 *(avec inquiétude)* feverishly 2 *(avec hâte)* hastily

fébrilité [febrilite] NF feverish state, feverishness, *Spéc* febrility, febricity

fécal, -e, -aux, -ales [fekal, -o] ADJ faecal; **matières fécales** faeces

fécalome [fekalɔm] NM *Méd* fecaloma, faecaloma

fèces [fɛs] NFPL 1 *Physiol* faeces 2 *Chim* sediment, precipitate

fécial, -aux [fesjal, -o] NM *Antiq* fetial

FECOM [fekɔm] NM *Fin & UE (abrév* **Fonds européen de coopération monétaire**) EMCF

fécond, -e [fekɔ̃, -ɔ̃d] ADJ 1 *Biol* fecund, fertile

2 *(prolifique → terre)* rich, fertile; *(→ écrivain, inventeur)* prolific, productive; *(→ imagination)* lively, powerful; *Littéraire* **une idée féconde** a rich idea; *Littéraire* **puisse votre labeur être f.** may your labour bear much fruit; *Littéraire* **terre féconde en fruits de toute sorte** land rich in every kind of fruit; **une journée féconde en événements** an eventful day; **un feuilleton f. en rebondissements** a serial full of unexpected developments

fécondabilité [fekɔ̃dabilite] NF *Biol* fertility, *Spéc* fecundability; **taux de f.** fecundability rate

fécondable [fekɔ̃dabl] ADJ *Biol* fertilizable

fécondant, -e [fekɔ̃dɑ̃, -ɑ̃t] ADJ *Biol* fertilizing

fécondateur, -trice [fekɔ̃datœr, -tris] *Littéraire* ADJ fertilizing

NM fertilizer

fécondation [fekɔ̃dasjɔ̃] NF 1 *Biol (d'un mammifère)* impregnation; *(d'un ovipare, d'un ovule)* fertilization; **f. artificielle/in vitro** artificial/in vitro fertilization 2 *Bot* pollination, fertilization; **f. artificielle** artificial pollination

fécondatrice [fekɔ̃datris] *voir* **fécondateur**

féconder [3] [fekɔ̃de] VT 1 *Biol (mammifère)* to impregnate; *(ovipare, œuf)* to fertilize 2 *Bot* to pollinate, to fertilize 3 *Littéraire (terre, champ)* to make fertile 4 *Littéraire* **f. l'esprit/l'imagination/l'intelligence de qn** to enrich sb's mind/imagination/intelligence

fécondité [fekɔ̃dite] NF 1 *Biol* fertility, fecundity 2 *Littéraire (d'une terre, d'un jardin)* fruitfulness 3 *Littéraire (d'un créateur)* fertility

fécule [fekyl] NF starch; **f. (de maïs)** *Br* cornflour, *Am* cornstarch; **f. de pomme de terre** potato flour

féculence [fekylɑ̃s] NF 1 *Vieilli (d'une solution)* thickness, turbidity, feculence 2 *(d'un corps contenant de la fécule)* starchiness

féculent, -e [fekylɑ̃, -ɑ̃t] ADJ *(aliment)* starchy

NM starchy food, starch; **évitez les féculents** avoid starch *or* starchy foods

féculer [3] [fekyle] VT 1 *(extraire la fécule de)* to extract the starch from 2 *(additionner de fécule)* to add potato flour to

féculerie [fekylri] NF 1 *(fabrique)* starch mill, starch works 2 *(industrie)* starch industry

féculier, -ère [fekylje, -ɛr] ADJ starch *(avant n)*

FED [ɛfəde] NM *(abrév* **Fonds européen de développement**) EDF

fedayin, feddayin [fedajin] NM fedayee; **les fedayins** the Fedayeen

FEDER [fedɛr] NM *(abrév* **Fonds européen de développement régional**) ERDF

fédéral, -e, -aux, -ales [federal, -o] ADJ 1 *Pol* federal 2 *Suisse* federal *(relative to the Swiss Confederation)*

❑ **fédéraux** NMPL 1 *Hist* Federalist troops 2 **les fédéraux** *(le FBI)* the Feds

fédéraliser [3] [federalize] VT to federalize, to turn into a federation

fédéralisme [federalism] NM 1 *Pol* federalism 2 *Suisse* = political tendency defending the independence of the Swiss cantons from federal authority 3 *Can* federalism, = political ideology favouring a strong central government

fédéraliste [federalist] ADJ federalist, federalistic

NMF federalist, federal

fédérateur, -trice [federatœr, -tris] ADJ federative, federating; **élément/principe f.** unifying element/principle

NM,F unifier

fédératif, -ive [federatif, -iv] ADJ federative

fédération [federasjɔ̃] NF 1 *Pol (gén)* federation; *(au Canada)* confederation; **F. croato-musulmane** Bosnia-Herzegovina Federation, Muslim-Croat Federation; **F. de la gauche démocrate et socialiste** = former French socialist party; **la F. de Russie** the Federation of Russia

2 *(groupe)* federation; **F. de l'Éducation nationale** = teachers' trade union; **F. française de rugby** = French rugby federation; **F. internationale de football association** FIFA; **F. nationale des étudiants de France** = students' union; **F. nationale des syndicats d'exploitants agricoles** = farmers' union; **f. sportive** sports federation; **f. syndicale** trade union; **F. syndicale mondiale** World Federation of Trade Unions; **f. de syndicats (ouvriers)** amalgamated (trade) unions

fédérative [federativ] *voir* **fédératif**

fédératrice [federatris] *voir* **fédérateur**

fédéraux [federo] *voir* **fédéral**

fédéré, -e [federe] ADJ federated, federate

NM *Hist* federate

fédérer [18] [federe] VT to federate, to form into a federation

►**se fédérer** VPR to federate

fée [fe] NF fairy; **sa bonne f.** his/her good fairy, his/her fairy godmother; **la f. Carabosse** the wicked fairy; **pays des fées** fairyland; *Hum* **c'est une véritable f. du logis** she's a wonderful housewife; *Suisse* **f. verte** absinthe

'La Fée carabine' *Pennac* 'The Fairy Gunmother'

feed-back [fidbak] NM INV *Tech & Physiol* feedback

feeder [fidœr] NM 1 *Élec* feeder (cable) 2 *(de gaz)* (gas) pipeline

feeling [filiŋ] NM 1 *Mus* feeling 2 *Fam* **y aller** *ou* **faire qch au f.** to do sth by intuition■ *or* by gut feeling; **tout s'est passé** *ou* **s'est fait au f.** I/we/*etc* completely played it by ear; **je crois que ça va marcher, j'ai un bon f.** I think it's going to work, I have a good feeling about it

féerie [fe(e)ri] NF 1 *Théât* spectacular 2 *(merveille)* enchantment; **elle n'oubliera jamais la f. de cette nuit** she'll never forget the enchantment of that night; **le feu d'artifice était une f. de lumières** the firework display was pure enchantment; **une f. de couleurs** a riot of colour 3 *Vieilli (pouvoir des fées)* (power of) enchantment; *(monde des fées)* fairyland

féerique [fe(e)rik] ADJ 1 *Myth* fairy *(avant n)*, magic, magical 2 *(beau → vue, spectacle)* enchanting, magical

FEI [ɛfəi] NM *(abrév* **Fonds européen d'investissement**) EIF

feignait *etc voir* **feindre**

feignant, -e [fɛɲɑ̃, -ɑ̃t] *Fam* ADJ lazy■, idle

NM,F loafer

feignasse [fɛɲas] NF *Fam* lazy so-and-so, lazybones

feignasser [3] [fɛɲase] VI *Fam* to lounge *or* laze around

feindre [81] [fɛ̃dr] VT to feign; **f. la joie** to feign joy; **sa colère n'était pas feinte** he/she wasn't pretending to be angry, his/her anger wasn't feigned *or* was quite genuine

VI *Littéraire (dissimuler)* to pretend, to dissemble; **inutile de f.** it's no use pretending; **f. de faire qch** to pretend to do sth, to make a pretence of doing sth; **elle feint de s'intéresser à cette histoire** she pretends she's interested in this story

feint, -e [fɛ̃, fɛ̃t] ADJ 1 *(simulé → maladie, joie)* feigned, assumed, sham 2 *Archit (porte, fenêtre)* blind, dummy

❑ **feinte** NF 1 *(ruse)* ruse 2 *Littéraire (dissimulation)* dissembling *(UNCOUNT)*, dissimulation, pretence; **sans f.** frankly, without pretence 3 *Sport (en boxe, en escrime)* feint; *(au football, au rugby) Br* dummy, *Am* fake; **faire une f. (de passe)** to (sell a) dummy; **il a trompé l'arrière par une f.** *Br* he sold the full back a dummy, *Am* he faked out the full back 4 *Mil* feint, sham attack

feinter [3] [fɛ̃te] VT 1 *Sport* **f. l'adversaire** *(à la boxe, à l'escrime)* to feint at the opponent; **f. la passe** *(au football, au rugby) Br* to sell a dummy, *Am* to fake a pass 2 *Fam (duper)* to fool, to take in; **il t'a bien feinté!** he really took you in!; **feinté!** foiled again!

USAGE ABSOLU **f. du gauche** *(en boxe)* to feint *or* to make a feint with the left

VI *Fam* to fake

feinteur, -euse [fɛ̃tœr, -øz] NM,F dissembler

feintise [fɛ̃tiz] NF *Vieilli* pretence, dissembling

feld-maréchal [fɛldmareʃal] *(pl* **feld-maréchaux**) NM *Mil* field-marshal

feldspath [fɛldspat] NM *Minér* feldspar

feldspathique [fɛldspatik] ADJ *Minér* feldspathic

feldspathoïde [fɛldspatɔid] NM *Minér* feldspathoid

feldwebel [fɛldvebɛl] NM *Mil* = "adjudant" in the German army, ≃ staff sergeant

fêle [fɛl] NF blowpipe, blowtube

fêlé, -e [fele] ADJ 1 *(verre, porcelaine, os)* cracked 2 *(voix, son)* hoarse, cracked 3 *Fam (fou)* nuts, *Br* bonkers; **il est complètement f.!, il a le cerveau f.!** he's completely nuts!; **tu es complètement f. de le lui avoir dit!** you're absolutely crazy to have told him/her!

NM,F *Fam* nut, loony; **tous des fêlés!** they're all nuts *or Br* bonkers

fêler [4] [fele] **VT** to crack; *Fig Littéraire* **une amitié que jamais rien ne fêla** an undying friendship

▸**se fêler VPR** *(tasse, glace)* to crack; **se f. une côte** to fracture *or* to crack a rib; **se f. la hanche** to fracture one's hipbone

félibre [felibr] **NM** *Littérature* writer in the Provençal language

félibrée [felibre] **NF** *Littérature* meeting of the ''félibrige''

félibréen, -enne [felibreɛ̃, -ɛn] **ADJ** *Littérature* relating to the ''félibrige''

félibrige [felibriʒ] **NM** *Littérature* = society of poets and prose writers formed in 1854 with the object of preserving and purifying Provençal as a literary language

félicitations [felisitasjɔ̃] **NFPL** congratulation, congratulations; **(toutes mes) f.!** congratulations!; **adresser** *ou* **faire ses f. à qn (pour qch)** to congratulate sb (on sth); **recevoir les f. de qn pour qch** to be congratulated by sb on sth; *Univ* **avec les f. du jury** with the examining board's utmost praise, summa cum laude

félicité [felisite] **NF** *Littéraire* bliss, felicity

féliciter [3] [felisite] **VT** to congratulate; **f. qn de qch** to congratulate sb on sth; **f. qn d'avoir fait qch** to congratulate sb on having done sth; **je l'ai félicité d'avoir réussi son examen** I congratulated him on having passed his exam; **f. des jeunes mariés** to congratulate newly-weds; **permettez-moi de vous f.!** congratulations!; **je ne vous félicite pas!** you'll get no thanks from me!

▸**se féliciter VPR 1 se f. de qch/d'avoir fait qch** *(se réjouir de)* to be glad *or* pleased about sth/to have done sth; **tous se félicitaient de sa réussite** they were all pleased about his/her success *or* (that) he/she succeeded

2 se f. de qch/d'avoir fait qch *(se louer de)* to congratulate oneself on sth/on having done sth; **je me félicite d'être resté calme** I'm pleased to say I remained calm

félidé [felide] **NM** *Zool* feline

❏ **félidés NMPL les félidés** the cat family, *Spéc* the Felidae

félin, -e [felɛ̃, -in] **ADJ 1** *Zool* feline **2** *(regard, démarche, souplesse)* feline, catlike

NM 1 *(animal)* cat; **les félins** the cat family; **grand f.** big cat **2** *Bourse* stripped bond

félinité [felinite] **NF** *Littéraire* felinity, catlike quality

fellaga, fellagha [felaga] **NM** *Hist* fellagha *(name given by the French to Algerians fighting for independence)*

fellah [fela] **NM** fellah

fellation [felasjɔ̃] **NF** fellatio, fellation; **faire une f. à qn** to perform fellatio on sb

fellinien, -enne [felinjɛ̃, -ɛn] **ADJ** Felliniesque

félon, -onne [felɔ̃, -ɔn] **ADJ 1** *Littéraire (perfide)* disloyal, treacherous, felonious **2** *Hist* rebellious

NM 1 *Littéraire (traître)* traitor **2** *Hist* felon

félonie [feloni] **NF 1** *Littéraire (traîtrise)* disloyalty, treachery; *(acte)* act of treachery **2** *Hist* felony

félonne [felon] *voir* **félon**

felouque [fəluk] **NF** *Naut* felucca

Felquiste [fɛlkist] **NMF** *Can* member of the FLQ *(Front de Libération Québécois, pro-independence party abolished after the October crisis of 1970)*

feluette [fəlɥɛt] **ADJ** *Can Fam Péj (homme)* weedy; *(voix)* high■, reedy■

fêlure [felyr] **NF 1** *(d'un objet)* crack; **la surface de la jarre était couverte de mille petites fêlures** the surface of the jar was covered with a fine network of cracks; *Fig* **il y a une f. dans leur amitié** cracks are beginning to show in their friendship **2** *(de la voix)* crack **3** *Méd* fracture

femelle [fəmɛl] **ADJ 1** *Zool* female; *(éléphant, baleine)* cow *(avant n)*; *Orn* hen *(avant n)* **2** *Bot & Élec* female; **une prise f.** a socket

NF 1 *Zool* female **2** *très Fam Péj (femme)* female

femelot [fəmlo] **NM** *Naut* gudgeon

Fémina [femina] **NM le prix F.** = annual literary prize whose winner is chosen by a jury of women

féminin, -e [feminɛ̃, -in] **ADJ 1** *Biol (hormone)* female; **la morphologie féminine** the female body; **le sexe f.** the female sex

2 *(composé de femmes → population)* female; **notre main-d'œuvre féminine** our female workers; **l'équipe féminine** the women's team; **les conquêtes féminines d'un homme** a man's female conquests

3 *(typique de la femme → personne, charme)* feminine; **une réaction typiquement féminine** a typical female reaction; **elle est très féminine** she's very feminine; **il avait une voix féminine** he had a woman's voice

4 *(qui a rapport à la femme → magazine, presse)* women's; **mode féminine** women's fashions; **revendications féminines** women's demands; **le tennis f.** women's tennis

5 *Gram & Littérature (nom, rime)* feminine

NM 1 *Gram* feminine (gender); **ce mot est du f.** this word is feminine; **au f.** in the feminine

2 *voir* **éternel**

féminisant, -e [feminizɑ̃, -ɑ̃t] **ADJ** *Biol* feminizing

féminisation [feminizasjɔ̃] **NF 1** *Biol* feminization, feminizing *(UNCOUNT)* **2** *(augmentation du nombre de femmes)* **la f. d'une profession/d'un milieu** increased female participation in a profession/in a group; **depuis la f. de la profession** since women have entered the profession

Culture

LA FÉMINISATION DES NOMS

The feminization of nouns for professions, positions, ranks and titles has been official in France since March 1986. It is therefore perfectly correct to add the feminine ending, or use a feminine article, and refer to "une professeure", "une ambassadrice" and "madame la ministre" etc. However, despite government recommendations and the publication of a guide by the "Institut national de la langue française", these new feminine forms are not in widespread use – although they have been adopted more readily in Quebec, Switzerland and Belgium than in France.

féminiser [3] [feminize] **VT 1** *Biol* to feminize

2 *Gram (mot)* to put into the feminine gender

3 *(homme)* to make effeminate

4 *(augmenter le nombre de femmes dans)* **f. une profession** to bring *or* to introduce more women into a profession; **il faut f. ces professions** more women must be encouraged to enter those professions; **profession très féminisée** largely female profession, female-dominated profession

▸**se féminiser VPR 1** *Biol* to feminize

2 *(femme)* to become more feminine; *(homme)* to become effeminate

3 *(métier, profession)* **notre profession se féminise** more and more women are entering our profession; **le métier de médecin/détective se féminise** there are more and more women doctors/detectives

féminisme [feminism] **NM 1** *(mouvement)* feminism **2** *Biol* feminization

féministe [feminist] **ADJ** feminist

NMF feminist

féminité [feminite] **NF** femininity

femme [fam] **NF 1** *(personne)* woman; **parapluie de** *ou* **pour f.** lady's umbrella; **elle n'est pas f. à se plaindre** she's not the sort (of woman) to complain; *Fam* **une bonne f.** a woman; *Péj* **une vieille bonne f.** a little old woman; **contes/remèdes de bonne f.** old wives' tales/remedies; **f. d'affaires** businesswoman; **f. auteur** woman author, authoress; **f. de chambre** *(dans un hôtel)* chambermaid; *(chez des particuliers)* housemaid; *(attachée au service d'une dame)* (lady's) maid, (personal) maid; **f. de charge** housekeeper; **f. député** *(en France)* (female) deputy; *(en Grande-Bretagne)* (woman) MP; *(aux États-Unis)* Congresswoman; **f. écrivain** woman writer; **une f. enfant** a childlike woman; **f. fatale** femme fatale; *Can* **être une f. aux femmes** to be a lesbian; **une f. fleur** a delicate beauty; **f. ingénieur** woman engineer; *Belg* **f. à journée** cleaning lady, *Br* daily (woman), *Am* maid; **une f. de mauvaise vie** a scarlet *or* loose woman; **f. médecin** woman *or* lady doctor; **f. de ménage** cleaning lady, *Br* daily (woman), *Am* maid; **f. metteur en scène** woman *or* female director; **f. ministre** female minister; **f. du monde** socialite; *Belg* **f. d'ouvrage** cleaning lady, *Br* daily

(woman), *Am* maid; **une f. de parole** a reliable woman; **f. de petite vertu** woman of easy virtue; **une f. à poigne** a tough woman; **f. policier** policewoman, *Br* WPC; **f. politique** (female) politician; **f. de service** cleaner, *Br* charwoman; **f. soldat** woman soldier

2 *(adulte)* **c'est une f. maintenant** she's a woman now; **à treize ans elle fait déjà très f.** at thirteen she already looks very much a woman; **elle devient f.** she's growing up, she's becoming a woman

3 *(ensemble de personnes)* **la f., les femmes** woman, women, womankind; **la libération/les droits de la f.** women's liberation/rights; **l'émancipation de la f.** the emancipation of women

4 *(épouse)* wife; **prendre qn pour f.** to take sb as one's wife; **prendre f.** to take a wife; **il l'a prise pour f.** he took her as his wife; *Jur* **la f.** Dupont the wife of Dupont

5 *(comme adj) (féminine)* **être très f.** to be very feminine; **je me sens très f.** I feel very much a woman *or* very womanly; **être très f. du monde** to be a wonderful hostess

'**La Femme de mon pote**' Blier 'My Best Friend's Girl'

'**Le Journal d'une femme de chambre**' Renoir, Buñuel 'The Diary of a Chambermaid'

'**Une Femme est une femme**' Godard 'A Woman Is a Woman'

femmelette [famlɛt] **NF 1** *Péj (homme)* sissy, wimp, drip; **pas de femmelettes chez nous!** we don't want any sissies around here! **2** *(femme)* weak *or* frail woman

femme-objet [famɔbʒɛ] *(pl* **femmes-objets)** **NF** = woman seen *or* treated as an object

fémoral, -e, -aux, -ales [femoral, -o] **ADJ** thigh *(avant n)*, *Spéc* femoral

fémur [femyr] **NM** *Anat* thigh bone, *Spéc* femur

FEN [fɛn] **NF** *(abrév* **Fédération de l'Éducation nationale)** = teachers' trade union, *Br* ≃ NUT

fenaison [fənɛzɔ̃] **NF 1** *(récolte)* haymaking; *(époque)* haymaking time **2** *(fanage)* tedding, tossing

fendage [fɑ̃daʒ] **NM** *(du bois)* chopping; *(de l'ardoise)* splitting

fendant[1] [fɑ̃dɑ̃] **NM 1** *Escrime* sword thrust **2** *Suisse (raisin)* = chasselas grape variety **3** *Suisse (vin)* = white wine from the Valais canton made from the fendant grape variety

fendant[2]**, -e** [fɑ̃dɑ̃, -ɑ̃t] **ADJ** *Fam* hilarious, side-splitting

fendard[1] [fɑ̃dar] **ADJ** *Fam (amusant)* hysterical, side-splitting

fendard[2]**, fendart** [fɑ̃dar] **NM** *Fam Vieilli (pantalon) Br* trousers■, keks, *Am* pants■

fendeur [fɑ̃dœr] **NM** = worker specializing in splitting slates or wood

fendillé, -e [fɑ̃dije] **ADJ** *(miroir, peau, tableau, mur)* cracked; *(poterie, vernis, verre, émail)* crazed, crackled; *(bois)* split; **avoir les lèvres fendillées** to have chapped lips

fendillement [fɑ̃dijmɑ̃] **NM** *(d'un miroir, de la peau, d'un mur, d'un tableau)* cracking; *(du bois)* splitting, springing; *(du verre, de l'émail, du vernis, de la poterie)* crazing, crackling

fendiller [3] [fɑ̃dije] **VT** *(miroir, mur, tableau, peau)* to crack; *(bois)* to split; *(émail, verre, vernis, poterie)* to craze, to crackle

▸**se fendiller VPR** *(miroir, mur, tableau, peau)* to crack; *(bois)* to split; *(verre, poterie, émail, vernis)* to craze, to crackle

fendoir [fɑ̃dwar] **NM** chopper, cleaver

fendre [73] [fɑ̃dr] **VT 1** *(couper → bois, roche, diamant)* to split, to cleave; *(→ lèvre)* to cut *or* to split (open); **f. une bûche en deux** to split *or* to chop a log down the middle; **f. le crâne/la lèvre à qn** to split sb's skull/lip (open); **ça vous fend ou c'est à vous f. l'âme** *ou* **le cœur** it breaks your heart, it's heartbreaking, it's heart-rending; **la vue de cet enfant abandonné lui fendit le cœur** the sight of the abandoned child

broke his/her heart *or* made his/her heart bleed

2 *(fissurer → terre, sol, mur, plâtre)* to crack

3 *Couture (veste, jupe, robe)* to make a slit in

4 *(traverser → foule)* to push *or* to force one's way through; *Littéraire ou Hum* **f. les flots/l'air/le vent** to cleave through the seas/the air/the breeze

▶**se fendre** VPR **1** *(s'ouvrir → bois)* to split; *(→ terre, sol, mur)* to crack

2 *Fam (se ruiner)* **tu ne t'es pas trop fendu!** this really didn't ruin *or* break you, did it!; **se f. de 100 euros** to fork out *or* to shell out 100 euros; **il s'est fendu d'une bouteille de vin** he forked out *or* shelled out for a bottle of wine

3 *Fam (se fatiguer)* to wear *or* to tire oneself out▪; **tu ne t'es pas fendu!** you didn't exactly strain yourself!

4 *Escrime* to lunge

5 *(partie du corps)* **se f. le crâne** to crack one's skull (open); **elle s'est fendu la lèvre** she cut her lip (open); *Fam* **se f. la pêche** *ou* **la pipe** *ou* **la poire** *ou* **la gueule** *(rire)* to split one's sides; *(s'amuser)* to have a ball; *Can très Fam* **se f. le cul en quatre** *(travailler beaucoup)* to work one's arse off; *(se donner beaucoup de mal)* to bust a gut

fendu, -e [fɑ̃dy] ADJ *(robe, jupe)* slit; *(yeux)* almond-shaped; *(crâne, lèvre)* split; *(assiette)* cracked; *(sabot)* cloven; **une bouche fendue** *ou* **un sourire f. jusqu'aux oreilles** a broad grin *or* smile; **des yeux fendus en amande** almond-shaped eyes; **né avec le palais f.** born with a cleft palate; **vis à tête fendue** slotted screw

fenestrage [fənɛstraʒ] NM *Archit* fenestration; *Ordinat* windowing

fenestré, -e [fənɛstre] ADJ *Biol* fenestrated

Fenestron® [fənɛstrɔ̃] NM tail rotor

fenêtrage [fənɛtraʒ] NM *Archit* fenestration; *Ordinat* windowing

fenêtre [fənɛtr] NF **1** *Constr* window; **ouvrir/fermer la f.** to open/to close the window; **regarder par la f.** to look out of the window; **sauter par la f.** to jump out of the window; *Fig* **ouvrir une f. sur** to open a window on; *Fig* **une f. sur le monde/sur l'actualité** a window on the world/on current events; **f. à battants** casement window; **f. à coulisse** sliding window; **f. croisée** casement window; **f. en encorbellement** oriel window; **f. à guillotine** sash window; **f. mansardée** dormer window; **f. à meneaux** mullioned window; **f. en saillie** bay window; **f. à tabatière** skylight; **fausse f.** blind window; **une place côté couloir ou côté f.?** an aisle or a window seat?

2 *Anat* fenestra; **f. ovale/ronde** fenestra ovalis/rotunda

3 *Ordinat* window; **f. de lecture-écriture** read-write slot; **f. activée** active window; **f. d'aide** help window; **f. déroulante** pull-down window; **f. de dialogue** dialog(ue) window; **f. d'édition** editing *or* edit window; **f. flottante** floating window; **f. graphique** graphics window; **f. de saisie** text box

4 *TV* **f. d'observation** observation window

5 *(espace blanc)* space, blank

6 *(d'une enveloppe)* window

7 *Géol* inlier

8 *Astron* **f. atmosphérique** weather window; **f. de lancement** (launch) window

'Fenêtre sur cour' *Hitchcock* 'Rear Window'

fenêtrer [3] [fənetre] VT **1** *(bâtiment)* to put windows in **2** *Méd (bandage)* to fenestrate

fenian, -e [fenjɑ̃, -an] *Pol & Hist* ADJ Fenian

NM,F Fenian

fenil [fənil] NM hayloft

fennec [fenɛk] NM fennec

fenouil [fənuj] NM fennel; **f. doux** *ou* **de Florence** Florentine fennel

fente [fɑ̃t] NF **1** *(fissure → dans du bois)* cleft, split; *(→ dans un sol, un mur)* crack, fissure; *(→ dans une roche)* cleft **2** *(ouverture → d'une jupe, d'une poche, des volets)* slit; *(→ dans une boîte, sur une vis)* slot; *(→ dans une veste)* vent; *(→ pour passer les bras)* armhole **3** *Escrime* lunge

fenton [fɑ̃tɔ̃] = **fanton**

fenugrec [fənygrɛk] NM *Bot & Culin* fenugreek

féodal, -e, -aux, -ales [feɔdal, -o] ADJ feudal

NM *(propriétaire)* landlord; *(seigneur)* feudal lord

féodalement [feɔdalmɑ̃] ADV according to feudal law

féodalisme [feɔdalism] NM feudalism

féodalité [feɔdalite] NF **1** *(système)* feudal system

2 *Péj (puissance)* feudal power

FEOGA [feɔga] NM *(abrév* **Fonds européen d'orientation et de garantie agricole***)* EAGGF

fer [fɛr] NM **1** *Chim* iron *(UNCOUNT)*

2 *Métal* iron *(UNCOUNT)*; **f. doux** soft iron; **f. forgé** wrought iron

3 *(dans les aliments)* iron *(UNCOUNT)*

4 *(barre)* (iron) bar; **f. en T/U** T/U girder

5 *(partie métallique → d'une hache, d'une flèche)* head; *(→ d'une pelle)* blade; *(→ d'un lacet)* tag; *(lame)* blade; *aussi Fig* **f. de lance** spearhead; **le f. de lance de l'industrie française** the flagship of French industry; **tourner** *ou* **retourner le f. dans la plaie** to twist the knife in the wound; **par le f. et par le feu** by fire and sword

6 *(pour repassage)* **f. à repasser** iron; **f. à vapeur** steam iron; **f. électrique** (electric) iron; **donner un coup de f. à qch** to iron *or* to press sth; **passer un coup de f. sur un pantalon** to give a pair of trousers a quick iron; **ton pantalon a besoin d'un petit coup de f.** your trousers could do with a quick iron

7 *(instrument)* **f. à dorer** gilding iron; **f. à friser** curling *Br* tongs *or Am* iron; **f. à gaufrer** goffering iron; **f. à marquer** brand, branding iron; **f. rouge** brand; **f. à souder** soldering iron

8 *(de chaussure)* metal tip

9 *(pour cheval)* (horse)shoe; **mettre un f. à un cheval** to shoe a horse; **perdre un f.** to cast a shoe

10 *(de golf)* iron; **grand f.** driving iron; **f. droit** putter; **un f. 6** a (number) 6 iron

11 *Rail* **le f.** rail, the railway system, the railways; **acheminer/transporter par f.** to take/to carry by rail

12 *Littéraire (épée)* blade; **par le f. et par le feu** by force of arms

▫ **fers** NMPL *(chaînes)* irons, shackles; **mettre qn aux fers** to put sb in irons; *Fig* **briser ses fers** to throw off one's chains

▫ **de fer** ADJ *(moral, santé)* cast-iron *(avant n)*; *(discipline, volonté)* iron *(avant n)*; **homme de f.** man of iron *or* steel

▫ **fer à cheval** NM horseshoe; **en f. à cheval** *(escalier, table)* horseshoe-shaped, horseshoe *(avant n)*

fera *etc voir* **faire**

féra [fera] NF = type of whitefish found in Lake Geneva

fer-à-cheval [fɛraʃəval] *(pl* **fers-à-cheval***)* NM *Zool* horseshoe bat

féral, -e, -als *ou* **-aux, -ales** [feral, -o] ADJ feral

féralies [ferali] NFPL *Antiq* Feralia

fer-blanc [fɛrblɑ̃] *(pl* **fers-blancs***)* NM tin, tinplate

▫ **en fer-blanc** ADJ tin *(avant n)*; **boîte en f.** can, tin can

ferblanterie [fɛrblɑ̃tri] NF **1** *(manufacture)* tinplate making; *(industrie)* tinplate industry; *(commerce)* tinplate trade **2** *(objets)* tinware **3** *(boutique)* hardware store, *Br* ironmonger's (shop) **4** *Péj (décorations)* medals; **ils ont sorti toute leur f.** they had all their medals on display

ferblantier [fɛrblɑ̃tje] NM **1** *(ouvrier)* tinsmith **2** *(marchand)* hardware dealer, *Br* ironmonger

feria [ferja] NF fair *(yearly, in Spain and southern France)*

férial, -e, -aux, -ales [ferjal, -o] ADJ *Rel* ferial

férie [feri] NF **1** *Antiq* day of rest, holiday **2** *Rel* feria, weekday

férié, -e [ferje] ADJ **c'est un jour f.** it's a (public) holiday; **on ne travaille pas les jours fériés** we don't work on holidays; **demain, c'est f.** tomorrow's a (public) holiday

féringien, -enne [ferɛ̃ʒjɛ̃, -ɛn] ADJ Faroese, Faeroese

NM *(langue)* Faroese, Faeroese

▫ **Féringien, -enne** NM,F Faroese, Faeroese; **les Féringiens** the Faroese *or* Faeroese

férir [ferir] VT *(à l'infinitif seulement) Littéraire* **sans coup f.** without any problem *or* difficulty; **conquérir une région sans coup f.** to conquer a region without bloodshed

ferler [3] [fɛrle] VT *Naut* to furl

ferlouche [fɛrluʃ] NF *Can* = mixture of raisins and molasses used in pies

fermage [fɛrmaʒ] NM **1** *(location)* tenant farming **2** *(redevance)* farm rent

fermail, -aux [fɛrmaj, -o] NM *Arch* (ornamental) clasp

ferme[1] [fɛrm] NF **1** *(maison)* farmhouse; *(bâtiments)* farm buildings; *(exploitation)* farm; **f. d'élevage** cattle farm; **produits de la f.** farm produce

2 *Jur* **prendre à f.** to rent, to farm; **donner à f.** to let; **bail à f.** farm lease

3 *Archit* truss

4 *Théât* set piece

5 *Hist (de taxes)* farming (out)

ferme[2] [fɛrm] ADJ **1** *(dur → sol)* solid, firm; *(→ corps, chair, fruit, beurre, muscle)* firm; *(→ pâte)* stiff; **une viande un peu trop f.** slightly tough meat

2 *(stable)* **être f. sur ses jambes** to stand steady on one's legs *or* firm on one's feet

3 *(décidé → ton, pas)* firm, steady; **…, dit-elle d'une voix f.** …, she said firmly

4 *(inébranlable → volonté, décision)* firm; *(→ réponse)* definite; **des prix fermes et définitifs** firm *or* definite prices; **un engagement f.** a firm commitment; **il est resté f. sur le prix** he refused to bring the price down; **il faut être f. avec elle** you must be firm with her

5 *Écon* steady, firm; **le dollar est resté f.** the dollar stayed firm

6 *Com (achat, vente)* firm; **prendre un engagement f.** to enter into a firm undertaking; **vente/offre f.** firm sale/offer

ADV **1** *(solidement)* **tenir f.** *(clou)* to hold; *(personne, troupe)* to stand firm, to hold on

2 *(beaucoup → travailler)* hard; **batailler f.** to fight hard; **il boit f.** he's a heavy *or* a hard drinker

3 *(avec passion → discuter)* with passion, passionately

4 *Com* **acheter/vendre f.** to buy/to sell firm

fermé, -e [fɛrme] ADJ **1** *(passage)* closed, blocked; **col f.** *(panneau sur la route)* pass closed to traffic

2 *(porte, récipient)* closed, shut; *(à clef)* locked; **une porte fermée** a closed door; **j'ai laissé la porte à demi fermée** I left the door ajar *or* half-open; **une boîte fermée** a box which is shut, a closed box; **un local toujours f.** a room that's always locked; **f. à clef** locked; **f. à double tour** double-locked

3 *(radiateur, robinet)* off; *Élec (circuit)* closed

4 *(bouche, œil)* shut, closed (up); **dormir la bouche fermée** to sleep with one's mouth shut; *Fig* **c'est un très bon vin, tu peux y aller les yeux fermés** it's a very good wine, you needn't have any qualms about buying it; **je pourrais y aller les yeux fermés** I could get there blindfolded *or* with my eyes closed

5 *(magasin, bureau, restaurant)* closed; **vous restez f. pendant Noël?** will you be staying closed over Christmas?; **f. le lundi** closed on Mondays, closing day Monday

6 *Chasse & Pêche* closed

7 *(méfiant → visage)* closed, inscrutable, impenetrable; *(→ regard)* impenetrable; **une personnalité fermée** a secretive *or* an uncommunicative personality; **être f. à qch** to have no feeling for *or* no appreciation of sth

8 *(exclusif → milieu, ambiance)* exclusive, select

9 *(syllabe, voyelle)* closed

10 *Sport (jeu)* tight

11 *Ordinat & Math* closed

fermement [fɛrməmɑ̃] ADV **1** *(avec force)* firmly, solidly, steadily **2** *(résolument)* firmly, strongly

ferment [fɛrmɑ̃] NM **1** *Chim* ferment, leaven *(UNCOUNT)*; **ferments lactiques** = bacilli used in making yoghurt **2** *Littéraire (facteur)* **leur présence est un f. de haine** their presence stirs up hatred

fermentable [fɛrmɑ̃tabl] ADJ fermentable, fermentescible

fermentatif, -ive [fɛrmɑ̃tatif, -iv] ADJ fermentative

fermentation [fɛrmɑ̃tasjɔ̃] NF **1** *Chim* fermentation, fermenting **2** *Littéraire (agitation)* fermentation, commotion, unrest

▫ **en fermentation** ADJ *(raisin)* fermenting

fermentative [fɛrmɑ̃tativ] *voir* **fermentatif**

fermenté, -e [fɛrmɑ̃te] **ADJ** fermented

fermenter [3] [fɛrmɑ̃te] **VI 1** *Chim* to ferment; *(pâte)* to rise **2** *Littéraire (sentiment)* to be stirred; *(esprit)* to be in a ferment

fermentescible [fɛrmɑ̃tesibl] **ADJ** *Chim* fermentable, fermentescible

fermenteur [fɛrmɑ̃tœr] **NM** *Chim* fermenter

FERMER [3] [fɛrme]

> **VT** to close **1, 2, 5, 6, 10, 12** ■ to shut **1, 2** ■ to turn off **3** ■ to block **4** ■ to close down **6**
> **VI** to close **1–3** ■ to close down **2**
> **VPR** to close **2, 3** ■ to fasten **1**

VT 1 *(yeux, sac, valise, bocal, livre, parapluie)* to shut, to close; *(poing, doigts)* to close; *(enveloppe)* to seal, to shut, to close; *(éventail)* to fold, to close; *(col, jupe)* to fasten, to do up; **fermez vos cahiers** close your exercise books; **f. les rideaux** to draw the curtains (together), to pull the curtains shut; **ferme le tiroir** shut the drawer; **f. les yeux** to close *or* to shut one's eyes; **ferme très fort les yeux** screw your eyes up tight; **f. les yeux sur qch** to turn a blind eye to sth; **je n'ai pas fermé l'œil de la nuit** I didn't get a wink (of sleep) all night; **manger la bouche fermée** to eat with one's mouth closed *or* shut; *Fam* **f. sa bouche** *ou* **son bec** to shut up, to shut one's trap; *très Fam* **je le savais mais je l'ai fermée** I knew it but I didn't let on; *très Fam* **la ferme!** shut up!, shut your face!

2 *(porte, fenêtre)* to close, to shut; **f. une porte à clef** to lock a door; **f. une porte au verrou** to bolt a door; **f. une porte à double tour** to double-lock a door; **il a fermé la porte d'un coup de pied** he kicked the door shut; **il a fermé la porte d'un coup d'épaule** *(doucement)* he nudged the door shut with his shoulder; *(durement)* he banged the door shut with his shoulder; **f. violemment la porte** to slam *or* to bang the door (shut); *Fig* **f. la porte à qch** to close the door on sth; **f. ses portes** *(boutique, musée)* to shut, to close; **f. une maison** to shut up a house

3 *(éteindre → électricité, lumière, compteur)* to turn *or* to switch off; *(→ robinet)* to turn off; *Fam* **f. l'eau dans une maison** to turn the water off (at the mains) in a house■; **f. le gaz** to turn off the gas; *Fam* **ferme la télé** switch the TV off■; *Élec* **f. un circuit** to close a circuit; *Can* **f. la ligne** *(raccrocher le téléphone)* to hang up

4 *(rendre inaccessible → rue, voie)* to block, to bar, to obstruct; *Rail* **f. la voie** to close (off) the line

5 *(interdire → frontière, port)* to close; **f. l'entrée d'un port** to close a harbour; **f. son pays aux réfugiés politiques** to close one's borders to political refugees; **cette filière vous fermerait toutes les carrières scientifiques** this course would prevent you from following any scientific career

6 *(faire cesser l'activité de)* to close; **f. un restaurant/théâtre** *(pour un congé)* to close a restaurant/theatre; *(définitivement)* to close a restaurant/theatre (down); **ne fermez pas notre école!** don't close our school (down)!; **la police a fait f. l'établissement** the police had the place closed down; **f. boutique** *(pour un congé)* to shut up shop; *(pour cause de faillite)* to stop *or* to cease trading, to close down; *Fig* to give up

7 *(rendre insensible)* **f. son âme à qch** to harden one's heart to sth; **f. son cœur à qn** to harden one's heart to sb; **f. son esprit à qch** to close one's mind to sth; **c'est elle qui m'a fermée aux études** she's the one who turned *or* put me off studying

8 *(être à la fin de)* **f. la marche** to be at the back of the procession; **f. le bal** to be the last to leave the ball

9 *(délimiter)* **les montagnes qui ferment l'horizon/ferment la vue** the mountains which shut off the horizon/block the view

10 *Banque & Fin (compte, portefeuille d'actions)* to close

11 *Sport* **f. le jeu** to tighten up play

12 *Ordinat (fichier, fenêtre)* to close; *(commande)* to end

13 *TV & Cin* **f. par un volet** to wipe off

USAGE ABSOLU on ferme! closing now!

VI 1 *(se verrouiller → couvercle, fenêtre, porte)* to close; **le couvercle ferme mal** the lid doesn't shut *or* close properly; **le portail ferme mal** the gate is difficult to close *or* won't close properly; **le radiateur ferme mal** the radiator won't turn off properly

2 *(cesser son activité → temporairement)* to close; *(→ pour toujours)* to close down; **le musée/parc va f.** the museum/park will soon close; **la banque ferme le samedi** the bank closes Saturdays *or* is closed on Saturdays; **la chasse au faisan fermera la semaine prochaine** the pheasant season will close next week; **les usines ferment** factories are closing down

3 *Bourse (actions)* to close; **les actions ont fermé à 4,50 euros** shares closed at 4.50 euros

▶**se fermer VPR 1** *(être attaché → col, robe, veste)* to fasten, to do up

2 *(être verrouillé → porte, fenêtre)* to close; *Fig* **les frontières se fermaient devant lui** countries were closing their borders to him; **les sociétés occidentales se ferment à l'immigration** Western societies are closing their doors to immigrants; **son cœur s'est fermé à la pitié** he/she has become impervious to pity

3 *(se serrer, se plier → bras, fleur, huître, main)* to close (up); *(→ aile)* to fold; *(→ bouche, œil, paupière, livre, rideau)* to close; *(→ blessure)* to close (up), to heal; **mes yeux se ferment tout seuls** I can't keep my eyes open

4 *(être impénétrable)* **on ne peut pas lui parler, elle se ferme aussitôt** there's no talking to her, she just switches off *or* freezes up; **à cette demande, son visage se ferma** at this request, his/her face froze; **tu te fermes toujours quand on te parle de tes parents** you always clam up when people talk to you about your parents

5 *TV & Cin* **se f. en fondu** to fade out

fermeté [fɛrməte] **NF 1** *(solidité → d'un objet)* solidness, firmness; *(→ d'une pâte)* stiffness; *(→ d'un corps)* firmness **2** *(assurance → d'un geste)* assurance, steadiness; *(→ d'une voix)* firmness **3** *(autorité)* firmness; **faire preuve de f. à l'égard de qn** to be firm with sb; **avec f.** firmly, resolutely, steadfastly; **sans f.** irresolutely, waveringly; **le gouvernement agit sans f. aucune** the government is acting without any determination whatsoever **4** *Bourse* steadiness

fermette [fɛrmɛt] **NF 1** *(habitation)* small farm *or* farmhouse **2** *Constr* small truss

fermeture [fɛrmətyr] **NF 1** *(obstruction → de route, de frontière)* closing; **après la f. du puits/tunnel** once the well/tunnel is blocked off; **la f. du coffre se fera devant témoins** the safe will be locked *or* sealed in the presence of witnesses; *Élec* **f. du circuit** closing of the circuit

2 *(rabattement)* closing; **la f. des grilles avait lieu à midi** the gates were closed at noon; **ne pas gêner la f. des portes** *(dans le métro)* please do not obstruct the doors; **f. automatique des portières** *(dans le train)* doors close *or* shut automatically; *Aut* remote control locking; *Aut* **f. centralisée** central locking

3 *Com (d'un magasin, d'une entreprise → définitive)* closure, closing-down, *Am* closing-out; **les plus belles affaires se font à la f.** the best bargains are struck just before closing time *or* before the shop closes; **au moment de la f.** *(du bureau)* at the end of the day's work; *(de la banque, du magasin, du café)* at closing time; **il venait me chercher à la f. du bureau** he came for me after work; **f. annuelle** *(d'un magasin)* closed for annual holiday; **f. définitive** close-down; **jour de f.** *(hebdomadaire)* closing day; *(férié)* public holiday;

4 *Fin* closing; **pour faciliter la f. d'un compte courant** to make it easier to close a current account

5 *(fin → d'une session, d'un festival)* close, closing; *Chasse & Pêche* closing; *Fam* **demain, on fait la f. ensemble** we're going out on the last (official) day of shooting tomorrow; *Bourse* **à la f.** at the close of trading

6 *(dispositif)* **f. Éclair**® *ou* **à glissière** *Br* zip (fastener), *Am* zipper; **f. à rouleau** *(d'un magasin)* revolving shutter

7 *Ordinat (de fichier, de fenêtre)* closing; *(de commande)* ending; *(d'un ordinateur)* shutdown

8 *TV & Cin* fade; **f. en fondu** fade-out; **f. au noir** fade-out, fade-to-black

fermi [fɛrmi] **NM** fermi

fermier, -ère [fɛrmje, -ɛr] **ADJ 1** *Écon (compagnie, société)* farm *(avant n)* **2** *Com* **poulet/œuf f.** free-range chicken/egg; **lait/beurre f.** dairy milk/butter

NM 1 *Agr (locataire)* tenant farmer; *(propriétaire, agriculteur)* farmer **2** *Hist* **f. général** farmer general

❑ **fermière NF 1** *(épouse)* farmer's wife **2** *(cultivatrice)* woman farmer

fermion [fɛrmjɔ̃] **NM** *Phys* fermion

fermium [fɛrmjɔm] **NM** *Chim* fermium

fermoir [fɛrmwar] **NM** *(de collier, de sac)* clasp, fastener; *Can (fermeture à glissière) Br* zip, *Am* zipper

féroce [ferɔs] **ADJ 1** *(brutal → tyran, soldat)* cruel, bloodthirsty **2** *(acerbe → humour, examinateur)* cruel, harsh, ferocious; *(→ concurrence)* fierce; **dans une critique f. qui vient de paraître** in a ferocious *or* savage review just out **3** *(qui tue → animal, bête)* ferocious **4** *(extrême → appétit)* voracious; *(→ désir)* raging, wild

férocement [ferɔsmɑ̃] **ADV 1** *(brutalement)* cruelly **2** *(avec dureté)* harshly, ferociously

férocité [ferɔsite] **NF 1** *(brutalité)* cruelty, bloodlust **2** *(intransigeance)* harshness, ferociousness; **avec f.** ferociously **3** *(d'une bête)* ferocity

Féroé [ferɔe] **NFPL les (îles) F.** the Faroes *or* Faeroes, the Faroe *or* Faeroe Islands; **vivre aux F.** to live in the Faroes *or* Faeroes; **aller aux F.** to go to the Faroes *or* Faeroes

féroïen, -enne [ferɔjɛ̃, -ɛn] **ADJ** Faroese, Faeroese

NM *(langue)* Faroese, Faeroese

❑ **Féroïen, -enne NM,F** Faroese, Faeroese; **les Féroïens** the Faroese *or* Faeroese

ferrade [fɛrad] **NF** branding *(of cattle)*

ferrage [fɛraʒ] **NM 1** *(d'une roue)* rimming; *(d'une canne)* tipping with metal **2** *(d'un cheval, d'un bœuf)* shoeing **3** *Pêche* striking

ferraillage [fɛrajaʒ] **NM 1** *(action)* placing of reinforcement **2** *(armatures)* reinforcement

ferraille [fɛraj] **NF 1** *(débris)* **de la f.** scrap (iron); **un bruit de f.** a clanking noise; **marchand de f.** scrap merchant **2** *(rebut)* scrap; **mettre une machine à la f.** to sell a machine for scrap; **bon pour la** *ou* **à mettre à la f.** ready for the scrapheap, good for scrap **3** *Fam (monnaie)* small change■, *Br* coppers

ferraillement [fɛrajmɑ̃] **NM 1** *Péj (combat à l'épée)* sword rattling **2** *(bruit)* rattling, clanking

ferrailler [3] [fɛraje] **VT** *Constr (béton)* to reinforce

VI 1 *Escrime* to clash swords **2** *Fig (batailler)* to clash, to cross swords; **le gouvernement a ferraillé avec les syndicats** the government clashed with the unions **3** *(faire un bruit de ferraille)* to clank, to rattle

ferrailleur [fɛrajœr] **NM 1** *Constr* ≃ building worker *(in charge of iron frameworks)* **2** *(commerçant)* scrap merchant **3** *Arch (bretteur)* swashbuckler

ferralitique [feralitik] **ADJ** *Minér* lateritic

Ferrare [fɛrar] **NF** Ferrara

ferrate [fɛrat] **NM** *Chim & Minér* ferrate

ferratier [fɛratje] **NM** shoeing-smith's hammer

ferratisme [fɛratism] **NM** *Sport* via ferrata climbing

ferré, -e [fɛre] **ADJ 1** *(muni de fers → cheval)* shod; *(→ chaussure)* hobnailed; *(→ roue)* rimmed; *(→ lacets)* tagged; *(→ canne)* metal-tipped; **cheval f. à glace** roughshod horse **2** *Fam (locutions)* **être f. sur** *ou* **en qch** to be a genius at sth■; **elle est ferrée en chimie** she's a genius at chemistry■

ferrédoxine [feredɔksin] **NF** ferredoxin

ferrement [fɛrmɑ̃] **NM** *Constr* iron framework

ferrer [4] [fɛre] **VT 1** *(garnir → roue)* to rim; *(→ canne)* to tip with metal; *(→ chaussure)* to nail; *(→ lacet)* to tag **2** *(cheval, bœuf)* to shoe **3** *Pêche* to strike

ferret [fɛrɛ] **NM 1** *(de lacet)* aglet **2** *Ordinat* tag

ferretier [fɛrtje] **NM** shoeing-smith's hammer

ferreur [fɛrœr] **NM f. de chevaux** shoeing-smith, *Br* farrier

ferreux, -euse [fɛrø, -øz] **ADJ** *Chim* ferrous; **alliages f.** iron alloys, ferro-alloys

ferricyanure [fɛrisjanyr] NM *Chim* ferricyanide

ferrimagnétique [fɛrimaɲetik] ADJ ferrimagnetic

ferrimagnétisme [fɛrimaɲetism] NM *Phys* ferrimagnetism

ferrique [fɛrik] ADJ *Chim* ferric

ferrite [fɛrit] NM *Chim* ferrite
▻ NF *Métal* ferrite; *Ordinat* **mémoire à f.** ferrite core memory

ferro- [fɛro] PRÉF ferro-

ferroalliage [fɛroaljaʒ] NM *Métal* ferro-alloy, iron alloy

ferrocérium [fɛroserjɔm] NM *Métal* ferrocerium

ferrochrome [fɛrokrom] NM *Métal* ferrochromium, ferrochrome

ferrociment [fɛrosimã] NM *Constr* reinforced cement, ferroconcrete

ferrocyanure [fɛrosjanyr] NM *Chim & Minér* ferrocyanide

ferroélectricité [fɛroelɛktrisite] NF *Phys* ferroelectricity

ferroélectrique [fɛroelɛktrik] ADJ *Phys* ferroelectric

ferromagnétique [fɛromaɲetik] ADJ *Phys* ferromagnetic

ferromagnétisme [fɛromaɲetism] NM *Phys* ferromagnetism

ferromanganèse [fɛromãɡanɛz] NM *Métal* ferromanganese

ferromolybdène [fɛromolibdɛn] NM *Métal* ferromolybdenum

ferronickel [fɛronikɛl] NM *Métal* ferronickel

ferronnerie [fɛronri] NF 1 *(art)* **f. (d'art)** wrought-iron craft 2 *(ouvrage)* **une belle f. du XVIIIème siècle** a fine piece of 18th-century wrought ironwork *or* wrought-iron work; **des ferronneries, de la f.** wrought ironwork, wrought-iron work 3 *(métier)* ironwork 4 *(atelier)* ironworks *(singulier ou pluriel)*
▫ **de ferronnerie, en ferronnerie** ADJ wrought-iron *(avant n)*

ferronnier [fɛronje] NM 1 **f. (d'art)** wrought-iron craftsman 2 *(commerçant)* ironware dealer

ferronnière [fɛronjɛr] NF *(ornement)* ferronière, ferronnière

ferrosilicium [fɛrosilisjɔm] NM *Métal* ferrosilicon

ferrotitane [fɛrotitan] NM *Métal* ferrotitanium

ferrotungstène [fɛrotœ̃kstɛn] NM *Minér* ferrotungsten

ferroutage [fɛrutaʒ] NM *Transp* combined rail and road transport

ferrouter [3] [fɛrute] VT *Transp* to transport by rail and road

ferroviaire [fɛrovjɛr] ADJ *(trafic, tunnel, réseau)* rail *(avant n)*, *Br* railway *(avant n)*, *Am* railroad *(avant n)*; *(transports)* rail *(avant n)*

ferrugineux, -euse [fɛryʒinø, -øz] ADJ ferruginous, ferruginous; **source ferrugineuse** chalybeate spring

ferrure [fɛryr] NF 1 *(garniture)* metal hinge; **ferrures de porte** door fittings; **ferrures en cuivre** brass fittings 2 *(fait de ferrer)* shoeing *(UNCOUNT)* 3 *(fers)* horseshoes

ferry [fɛri] *(pl* ferries*)* NM *(pour voitures)* car-ferry, ferry; *(pour voitures ou trains)* ferry, ferry-boat; **f. roulier** roll-on roll-off ferry; **f. trans-Manche** cross-Channel ferry

ferry-boat [fɛribot] *(pl* ferry-boats*)* NM ferry, ferry-boat

ferté [fɛrte] NF *Arch* fortified town, fortress

fertile [fɛrtil] ADJ 1 *Agr & Géog* fertile, rich; **f. en** rich in; **région f. en agrumes** area rich in citrus fruit
2 *Fig (esprit, imagination)* fertile, inventive; **une année f. en événements** a very eventful year; **un épisode f. en rebondissements** an action-packed episode; **la semaine fut f. en discussions** the week was packed with discussions
3 *Biol (femelle, femme, couple)* fertile
4 *Nucl* fertile

fertilisable [fɛrtilizabl] ADJ *Agr* fertilizable

fertilisant, -e [fɛrtilizã, -ãt] ADJ *Agr* fertilizing
▻ NM fertilizer

fertilisation [fɛrtilizasjɔ̃] NF *Agr & Biol* fertilization, fertilizing

fertiliser [3] [fɛrtilize] VT *Agr* to fertilize

fertilité [fɛrtilite] NF 1 *Agr* fertility, fruitfulness 2 *Biol (d'un couple, d'une femme, d'une femelle)* fertility 3 *(d'un esprit, d'un cerveau)* fertility;

---

connu pour la f. de son imagination famous for his fertile imagination

féru, -e [fery] ADJ **être f. de qch** to be keen on *or* highly interested in sth; **être f. d'une idée** to be set on an idea; *Arch* **f. de qn** smitten with sb

férule [feryl] NF 1 *(fouet)* ferule, ferula; *Fig* **être sous la f. de qn** to be under sb's strict authority 2 *Bot* ferula

fervent, -e [fɛrvã, -ãt] ADJ fervent, ardent; *(amour)* ardent; *(prière)* fervent; *(approbation)* enthusiastic; *(catholique)* devout
▻ NM,F devotee, enthusiast, addict; **les fervents du rugby** rugby enthusiasts *or* fans; **c'est une fervente de romans policiers** she's a crime novel addict

ferveur [fɛrvœr] NF fervour, ardour, enthusiasm; **avec f.** *(prier)* fervently, earnestly; *(travailler)* with enthusiasm; *(aimer)* ardently; *(écouter)* eagerly

Fès [fɛz] NM Fez

fescennin, -e [fɛsenɛ̃, -in] ADJ *Littérature* **chants fescennins** Fescennine verses

fesse [fɛs] NF 1 *Anat* buttock; **les fesses** the buttocks; **un singe assis sur ses fesses** a monkey sitting on its behind; **avoir mal aux fesses** to have a sore bottom; **avoir de belles/grosses fesses** to have a nice/fat bottom; **cette actrice est toujours en train de montrer ses fesses** that actress is always appearing with no clothes on *or* in nude scenes; *Fam* **poser ses fesses quelque part** to sit down somewhere▪; *Fam* **pose tes fesses!** sit yourself down!; *Fam* **donner à qn un coup de pied aux fesses** to give sb a kick in the pants *or* up the backside; *très Fam* **occupe-toi de tes fesses!** mind your own damn business!
2 *très Fam* **la f.** *(le sexe)*▪ sex▪; *(la pornographie)* pornography▪, the porn industry; *Fam* **histoire de fesses** dirty story; *(aventure)* purely sexual affair▪; **raconter des histoires de fesses** to tell dirty jokes; *Fam* **magazine de fesses** porn *or* skin mag; *Can Vulg* **jouer aux fesses** to screw, *Br* to have it off
3 *Naut* tuck
▫ **aux fesses** ADV *Fam* **avoir qn aux fesses** to have sb on one's back; **s'il refuse, je lui mets la police aux fesses!** if he refuses, I'll have the law on him!; *très Fam* **coller aux fesses à qn** to stick to sb like glue; *(camion)* to sit on sb's tail

fessée [fese] NF 1 *(punition)* spanking; **avoir** *ou* **recevoir une f.** to get spanked; **donner une f. à qn** to spank sb 2 *Fig (défaite)* drubbing

fesse-mathieu [fɛsmatjø] *(pl* fesse-mathieux*)* NM *Arch* skinflint, miser

fesser [4] [fese] VT to spank

fessier, -ère [fesje, -ɛr] ADJ buttock *(avant n)*, *Spéc* gluteal; **poche fessière** *(de pantalon)* hip pocket
▻ NM 1 *Anat* buttocks, *Spéc* gluteus; **grand f.** gluteus maximus 2 *Fam (postérieur)* behind, bottom, *Br* bum

fessu, -e [fesy] ADJ *Fam* big-bottomed

festif, -ive [fɛstif, -iv] ADJ festive

festin [fɛstɛ̃] NM feast, banquet; **faire un f.** to have *or* to hold a feast; **quel f.!** what a feast!, what a spread!

festival, -als [fɛstival] NM festival; **f. du cinéma** film festival; **un f. de jazz** a jazz festival; *Fig* **un f. de qch** a brilliant display of sth; **on a eu droit à un f. de calembours** we were treated to pun after pun

festivalier, -ère [fɛstivalje, -ɛr] ADJ festival *(avant n)*
▻ NM,F *(participant)* festival participant; *(visiteur)* festival-goer

festive [fɛstiv] *voir* festif

festivités [fɛstivite] NFPL festivities

fest-noz [fɛstnɔz] *(pl inv ou* festoù-noz [fɛstunɔz]*)* NM = party with traditional Breton music and dancing

festoie *etc voir* festoyer

festoiement [fɛstwamã] NM feasting

feston [fɛstɔ̃] NM 1 *(guirlande) & Archit* festoon 2 *Couture* scallop; **à festons** scalloped; **point de f.** blanket stitch, buttonhole stitch

festonner [3] [fɛstone] VT 1 *Archit* to festoon 2 *Littérature (orner)* to adorn, to embellish 3 *Couture* to scallop; **f. un col** to trim a collar with fancy edging

---

festoyer [13] [fɛstwaje] VI to feast

féta, feta [feta] NF feta *(cheese)*

fêtard, -e [fɛtar, -ard] NM,F party animal

fête [fɛt] NF 1 *(célébration → civile)* holiday; *(→ religieuse)* feast; **demain, c'est f.** tomorrow is a special occasion; **la f. de l'Assomption** the feast (of) the Assumption; **f. légale** public holiday; **la f. des Mères** Mother's Day, *Br* Mothering Sunday; **f. mobile** movable feast; **la f. des Morts** All Souls' Day; **la f. nationale** *(gén)* the national holiday; *(en France)* Bastille Day; *(aux États-Unis)* Independence Day; **la f. de Noël** Christmas; **la f. des Pères** Father's Day; **la f. des Rois** Twelfth Night, Epiphany; **la f. du Travail** Labour Day
2 *(d'un saint)* saint's day, name day; **souhaiter sa f. à qn** to wish sb a happy saint's *or* name day; *Fam* **faire sa f. à qn** to give sb a good hiding; *Ironique* **on va lui faire sa f.!** we're going to teach him/her a lesson he/she won't forget!; **ça va être ta f.!** you'll *Br* cop it *or Am* catch hell!
3 *(réunion → d'amis)* party; **une f. de famille** a family celebration *or* gathering; **faire une f.** to have a party; **on donne** *ou* **organise une petite f. pour son anniversaire** we're having *or* giving a party for his/her birthday, we're giving him/her a birthday party; **être de la f.** to be one of the party; **vous serez de la f.?** will you be joining us/them?; *Fig* **il n'a jamais été à pareille f.** he's never had such a good time; *Ironique* **il n'était pas à la f.** it wasn't much fun for him; **le film est une vraie f. pour l'esprit/les sens** the film is really uplifting/a real treat for the senses; **que la f. commence!** let the festivities begin!
4 *(foire)* fair; *(kermesse)* fête, fete; *(festival)* festival, show; **f. champêtre** *ou* **de village** village fete *or* fair; **c'est la f. au village** *(forains de passage)* there's a fair in the village; *(organisée par le village)* the village fete is on; **(et) la f. continue!** the fun's not over yet!; **aujourd'hui, c'est la f.!** let's have fun today!; **ce n'est pas tous les jours (la) f.!** it's not every day you've got something to celebrate!; **faire la f.** to party; **la f. de la bière** the beer festival; **f. foraine** *(attractions) Br* funfair, *Am* carnival; **la f. de l'Humanité** *ou Fam* **de l'Huma** = annual festival organized by the Communist daily newspaper ''l'Humanité''; **la f. de la Musique** = annual music festival organized on 21 June throughout France; **f. à Neu-Neu** = large funfair held in the Bois de Boulogne every summer; **f. patronale** = town or village festival marking the patron saint's name
5 *(locutions)* **faire (la) f. à qn** to greet sb warmly; **mon chien m'a fait (la) f. quand je suis revenu** my dog was all over me when I got back; **se faire une f. de** to look forward eagerly to; **tu ne viens pas? elle qui s'en faisait une telle f.!** so you're not coming? she was so looking forward to it!
▫ **fêtes** NFPL 1 *(gén)* holidays; *(de Noël et du jour de l'an)* Christmas and New Year holidays, *Am* holidays; **pendant les fêtes** over the Christmas period, *Am* over the holidays; **les fêtes de fin d'année** the Christmas and New Year holidays, *Am* the holidays; **les fêtes juives/catholiques** the Jewish/Catholic holidays
2 *Beaux-Arts* **fêtes galantes** fêtes galantes
▫ **de fête** ADJ 1 **jour de f.** *Rel* feast day; *(jour férié)* public holiday
2 *(air, habits)* festive; **donnez un air de f. à votre table** give your table a festive appearance
▫ **en fête** ADV **la ville/les rues en f.** the festive town/streets; **le village était en f.** the village was in a festive mood; **regardez la nature en f.!** look! what a feast of nature!

⬒

'**La Fête du rosaire**' *Dürer* 'The Feast of the Rose Garlands'

Culture

FÊTE
The French traditionally wish "bonne fête" to a person who has the same name as the saint commemorated on that particular day.

Culture

FÊTE DE LA MUSIQUE

This annual event takes place throughout France on 21 June, the summer solstice. Both amateur and professional musicians take to the streets and there are many impromptu live performances, with bars and restaurants as well as museums and hospitals serving as free venues for all types of music. The festival was originally launched in 1982. Such is its success and popularity in France that the event has now spread to many other European countries.

Fête-Dieu [fɛtdjø] (*pl* **Fêtes-Dieu**) **NF la F.** Corpus Christi

fêter [4] [fete] **VT 1** (*célébrer → anniversaire, événement*) to celebrate; **f. ses soixante ans** to celebrate one's sixtieth birthday; **une promotion? il faut f. ça!** a promotion? that's worth celebrating! **2** (*accueillir → personne*) to fête, to fete; **ils l'ont fêté à son retour** they celebrated his return

fétial, -e, -aux, -ales [fesjal, -o] = **fécial**

fétiche [fetiʃ] **NM 1** (*objet de culte*) fetish, fetich **2** (*porte-bonheur*) mascot; (*comme adj*) lucky; **mon numéro f.** my lucky number **3** *Psy* fetish

féticheur [fetiʃœr] **NM** (*prêtre*) animist priest

fétichisme [fetiʃism] **NM 1** (*culte*) fetishism, fetichism **2** *Psy* fetishism, fetichism **3** (*admiration*) worship, cult; **le f. des sondages électoraux** the obsession with pre-election polls

fétichiste [fetiʃist] **ADJ 1** *Rel & Psy* fetishistic **2** (*admiratif*) worshipping

NMF *Rel & Psy* fetishist, fetichist

fétide [fetid] **ADJ** fetid

fétidité [fetidite] **NF** fetidness

fétu [fety] **NM f. (de paille)** (wisp of) straw; **comme un f.** like a feather

fétuque [fetyk] **NF** *Bot* fescue (grass)

feu¹, -x [fø] **NM 1** (*combustion*) fire; **le f. et l'eau** fire and water; **faire du** *ou* **un f.** to make a fire; **allumer un f.** (*gén*) to light a fire; (*dehors*) to light a bonfire *or* fire; **faire un bon f.** to get a good fire going; **assis autour du f./d'un bon f.** sitting round the fire/round a roaring fire; **au coin du f.** by the fire(side); **f. de bois** (wood) fire; **cuire qch au f. de bois** to cook sth in a wood-burning oven; **f. de braises** (glowing) embers; **f. de cheminée** chimney fire; **mettre le f. à une maison** to set a house on fire; *Can* **passer au f.** to burn down; *Fam* **flanquer** *ou très Fam* **foutre le f. à qch** to put a match to sth; **au f.!** fire!; **il y a le f. aux rideaux!** the curtains are on fire!; **f. de camp** campfire; **f. d'enfer** blazing fire; **f. de forêt** forest fire; **f. de joie** bonfire; *Belg* **f. ouvert** hearth; *Méd* **le f. Saint-Antoine** (St) Anthony's fire; *Fig* **f. de paille** flash in the pan; **f. de pinède** forest fire; **les feux de la Saint-Jean** = bonfires lit to celebrate Midsummer's Day; *Hist* **le f., l'épreuve du f.** ordeal by fire; **prendre f.** to catch fire; **le canapé a pris f.** the sofa caught fire; **sous un soleil de f.** under a blazing *or* fiery sun; *Hum* **il n'y a pas le f. (au lac)!** there's no need to panic!; **faire long f.** to hang fire; **elle n'a pas fait long f. dans l'entreprise** she didn't last long in the company; *Fig* **jouer avec le f.** to play with fire; **jeter** *ou* **lancer f. et flammes** to be raging *or* fuming; **il n'y a vu que du f.** he never saw a thing, he was completely taken in; **il se jetterait dans le f. pour lui/eux** he'd do anything for him/them; **avoir le f.** *Fam* **au derrière** *ou Vulg* **au cul** (*être pressé*) to be in a tearing hurry; (*sexuellement*) to be horny, *Br* to be gagging for it; *Can Fam* **prendre le f.**, *Vulg* **prendre le f. au cul** (*se fâcher*) to blow a fuse, to go mad

2 (*brûleur*) ring, burner; **cuisinière à trois/quatre feux** three-burner/four-burner stove; **à f. doux** (*plaque*) on a gentle *or* slow heat; (*four*) in a slow oven *or* heat; **mijoter** *ou* **faire cuire à petit f.** to cook slowly; *Fig* **tuer** *ou* **faire mourir qn à petit f.** to kill sb slowly; **à grand f.** *ou* **f. vif** on a fierce heat; **avoir qch sur le f.** to be (in the middle of) cooking sth; **j'ai laissé le lait sur le f.!** I've left the milk on!; **un plat/ramequin qui va sur le f.** a fireproof dish/ramekin

3 (*briquet*) **avoir du f.** to have a light; **il n'a jamais de f.** he's never got a light

4 (*en pyrotechnie*) **f. d'artifice** (*spectacle*) fireworks display; *Fig* **son récital, un vrai f. d'artifice!** his/her recital was a virtuoso performance!; **des feux d'artifice** fireworks; **f. de Bengale** Bengal light

5 *Mil* (*tir*) fire, shooting; (*combats*) action; **ouvrir le f. (sur)** to open fire (on), to start firing (at); **cesser le f.** to cease fire; **faire f. (sur qn/qch)** to fire *or* to shoot (at sb/sth); **f.!** fire!; **avoir vu le f.** to have seen action; **aller au f.** to go into battle *or* action; **un f. croisé, des feux croisés** a crossfire; *Fig* **pris dans le f. croisé de leurs questions** caught in the crossfire of their questions; **f. nourri** continuous *or* constant stream; *Fig* **un f. nourri de plaisanteries** a constant stream of jokes; **f. roulant** constant barrage; *Fig* **un f. roulant de commentaires** a running commentary; *Fig* **être entre deux feux** to be caught in the middle, to be in the crossfire; **mettre le f. aux poudres** to spark off an explosion; *Fig* to spark things off; *Fig* **c'est ce qui a mis le f. aux poudres** that's what sparked things off

6 *Transp* (*signal*) **f. (tricolore** *ou* **de signalisation)** traffic lights; **f. rouge/orange/vert** red/amber/green light; **à droite au troisième f. (rouge)** right at the third set of (traffic) lights; **attendre au f.** *ou* **aux feux** to wait at the lights; *Fig* **donner le f. vert à qn/qch** to give sb/sth the green light

7 *Aut, Aviat & Naut* light; **f. arrière** tail light; **f. à éclipses** occulting light; **f. de gabarit** side lamp; **f. à occultations** occulting light; **f. de plaque** number plate light; **f. de position** sidelight; **f. de recul** reversing light; **f. de stop** brake light; **f. de tribord** starboard light; **feux de balisage** boundary lights; **feux blancs** driving lights, headlights and sidelights; **feux de bord** *ou* **de navigation** navigation lights; **feux de brouillard** fog lamps; **feux de croisement** headlights; **feux de détresse** warning lights; **feux de freinage** brake lights; **feux de mouillage** (*d'un navire*) anchor lights; **feux de navigation** sailing lights; **feux de piste** runway lights; **feux (d'entrée) de port** harbour lights; **feux de route** headlights on full beam; **feux de stationnement** parking lights; **feux stop** brake lights; *Aut* **rouler tous feux éteints** to drive without (any) lights

8 *Rail* **f. d'avant** (*d'une locomotive*) headlight; **f. d'arrière** (*d'un train*) tail *or* rear light

9 *Cin & Théât* **les feux de la rampe** the footlights; **être sous le f. des projecteurs** to be in front of the spotlights; *Fig* to be in the limelight; **il est sous les feux de l'actualité** he's very much in the news at the moment

10 *Littéraire* (*ardeur*) fire, passion, ardour; **avoir le f. sacré** to burn with enthusiasm; **dans le f. de la discussion** in the heat of the debate; **Vénus et ses feux redoutables** Venus and the baleful passions that she kindles

11 *Littéraire* (*éclat, lumière*) fire, light; **le f. de son regard** his/her fiery eyes; **les feux de la ville** the city lights; **jeter des feux** to sparkle, to glitter; **les cristaux brillaient de tous leurs feux** the crystals sparkled brightly; **le f. d'un diamant** the blaze *or* fire of a diamond; **une pierre qui brille de mille feux** a stone that sparkles brilliantly; **faire f. des quatre fers** *ou* **pieds** (*cheval*) to make the sparks fly; *Fig* (*personne*) to go all out

12 (*sensation de brûlure*) burn; **le f. me monta au visage** I went *or* turned red, my face *or* I flushed; **le f. du rasoir** razor burn

13 *Arch* (*maison*) house, homestead; **un hameau de dix feux** a hamlet with ten houses *or* homes in it; **n'avoir ni f. ni lieu, être sans f. ni lieu** to have neither hearth nor home, to have nowhere to lay one's head

14 *Fam* (*pistolet*) gun, *Am* rod

15 *Can* **f. sauvage** cold sore

ADJ INV flame (*avant n*), tan, flame-coloured; **rouge f.** flame red; **un yorkshire noir et f.** a black and tan Yorkshire (terrier)

❑ **à feu et à sang ADV mettre une ville/un pays à f. et à sang** to put a town/country to fire and sword

❑ **avec feu ADV** passionately

❑ **dans le feu de PRÉP** in the heat of; **dans le f. de l'action** in the heat of the moment; **dans le f. de la discussion** in the heat of the debate

❑ **en feu ADJ 1** (*incendié*) blazing, burning; **une maison en f.** a house on fire, a burning house **2** (*brûlant*) **il avait le visage en f.** his face was bright red *or* flushed; **j'ai la bouche/gorge en f.** my mouth/throat is burning; **il entra, les joues en f.** he came in, cheeks ablaze

❑ **tout feu tout flamme ADJ** burning with enthusiasm

❑ **feu follet NM** will-o'-the-wisp

'Le Feu' *Barbusse* 'Under Fire'

'Le Feu follet' *Drieu La Rochelle, Malle* 'The Fire Within'

feu², feue [fø] **ADJ** (*inv avant l'article ou le possessif*) late; **f. la reine** the late Queen; **ma feue tante, f. ma tante** my late aunt; **fils de feue Berthe Dupont** son of the late Berthe Dupont, son of Berthe Dupont deceased

feudataire [fødatɛr] **NM** *Hist* feudatory

feudiste [fødist] **NM** *Jur* feudist, expert in feudal law

feuil [fœj] **NM** (thin) film

feuillage [fœjaʒ] **NM 1** (*sur l'arbre*) leaves, *Spéc* foliage; **là-haut dans le f.** (*d'un arbre*) up there amongst the leaves; (*de la forêt*) up in the canopy **2** (*coupé*) greenery, *Spéc* foliage

feuillaison [fœjɛzɔ̃] **NF 1** (*phénomène*) foliation **2** (*époque*) foliation period; **au moment de la f.** when trees foliate

feuillant [fœjɑ̃] **NM** Feuillant monk; *Hist* **les Feuillants** = political club consisting of constitutional monarchists which held its meetings in the former Feuillants' monastery in Paris from 1791 to 1792

feuillante [fœjɑ̃t] **NF** Feuillant nun

feuillantine [fœjɑ̃tin] **NF 1** *Culin* feuillantine pastry, puff pastry cake **2** *Rel* Feuillant nun

feuillard [fœjar] **NM 1** (*pour tonneau*) hoop wood **2** (*pour emballage*) strap

feuille [fœj] **NF 1** *Bot* leaf; **f. morte** dead *or* fallen leaf; **arbre à feuilles caduques/persistantes** deciduous/evergreen tree; **descendre** *ou* **tomber en f. morte** to make a falling-leaf roll; **f. d'acanthe** acanthus; **f. de chêne** (*laitue*) oakleaf; **f. de vigne** *Bot & Culin* vine leaf; *Beaux-Arts* fig leaf; *Culin* **feuilles de vigne farcies** dolmades, stuffed vine leaves

2 (*morceau de papier*) sheet; **les feuilles d'un cahier** the sheets *or* leaves *or* pages of a notebook; **f. intercalaire** slip sheet; **une f. de papier** a sheet (of paper), a piece of paper; **f. volante** *ou* **mobile** (loose) sheet of paper

3 *Presse* **f. de chou** rag; *Fam* **il a les oreilles en f. de chou** his ears stick out; **f. locale** local paper; **f. à sensations** gossip sheet

4 (*imprimé*) form, slip; **f. d'accompagnement** covering document; **f. des arrivées et des départs** (*d'un hôtel*) arrival and departure list, A & D list; *Jur* **f. d'audience** court records; *Compta* **f. d'avancement** flow sheet; *TV* **f. de conducteur** cue sheet; **f. de déplacement** *Mil* travel warrant; *Com* waybill; **f. d'émargement** pay sheet; *TV & Cin* **f. d'exposition** exposure sheet; **f. d'heures** time sheet; **f. d'impôts** tax form, tax return; *Compta* **f. de liquidation** settlement note; **f. de maladie** = claim form for reimbursement of medical expenses; *TV* **f. de mixage** cue sheet; **f. des mouvements** (*d'un hôtel*) arrival and departure list, A&D list; **f. d'occupation journalière** (*d'un hôtel*) daily density chart, daily forecast chart; *TV & Rad* **f. d'ordre de passage à l'antenne** rundown sheet; **f. de paie** payslip; **f. de présence** attendance sheet; (*d'un employé*) time sheet; **f. de réservation** reservation form, booking form; **f. des réveils** (*d'un hôtel*) call sheet; *Mil* **f. de route** travel warrant; *Com* waybill; **f. de service** (duty) roster; **f. de soins** = claim form for reimbursement of medical expenses; *Méd* **f. de température** temperature chart; *Banque* **f. de versement** paying-in slip

5 (*plaque*) leaf, sheet; **f. d'acétate** acetate foil; **f. de bois** thin board **f. d'étain** tinfoil; **f. de métal/d'or** metal/gold leaf;

6 *Ordinat* sheet; **f. de calcul** spreadsheet; **f. document** data sheet; **f. maîtresse** master data sheet; **f. programme** program sheet; **f. de style** style sheet

feuille-à-feuille [fœjafœj] **ADJ INV** sheet-fed

feuillée [fœje] NF *Littéraire (abri)* foliage bower; **sous la f.** under the leafy boughs
 ▫ **feuillées** NFPL *Mil* latrine
feuille-morte [fœjmɔrt] ADJ INV russet, yellowish-brown
feuiller [3] [fœje] VT *Menuis* to rabbet, to groove
 VI to break into leaf
feuilleret [fœjrɛ] NM *Menuis* rabbet plane
feuillet [fœjɛ] NM **1** *(d'un formulaire)* page, leaf; **à feuillets rechargeables** loose-leaf **2** *Biol* layer; **feuillets embryonnaires** germ layers **3** *Zool* manyplies **4** *Menuis* thin sheet of wood
feuilletage [fœjtaʒ] NM **1** *Culin (pâte)* puff pastry; **le f. de la pâte** rolling and folding pastry *(to produce puff pastry)* **2** *Géol* foliation
feuilleté, -e [fœjte] ADJ **1** *Culin* puff *(avant n)*; *(gâteau)* puff-pastry **2** *Géol* foliated **3** *Tech* laminated; **pare-brise (en verre) f.** laminated windscreen *or Am* windshield
 NM **1** *(dessert)* pastry **2** *(hors-d'œuvre)* puff pastry case; **f. aux asperges** asparagus in puff pastry
feuilleter [27] [fœjte] VT **1** *(album, magazine)* to leaf *or* to flip *or* to flick through, to skim (through) **2** *Culin* **f. de la pâte** to work the dough (into puff pastry) by rolling and folding it **3** *Ordinat* to scroll through; **f. en arrière** to page up, to scroll up; **f. en avant** to page down, to scroll down
feuilletis [fœjti] NM *(d'une pierre)* girdle
feuilleton [fœjtɔ̃] NM **1** *Journ (série)* series *(singulier)*, serial; *(rubrique)* (regular) column; **publier un roman en feuilletons** to serialize a novel **2** *TV & Rad* serial; *TV* **f. (télévisé)** *(sur plusieurs semaines)* TV serial; *(sur plusieurs années)* soap opera **3** *Littérature* feuilleton **4** *Fig (histoire à rebondissements)* saga
feuilletonesque [fœjtɔnɛsk] ADJ serial-like, soap-like, soap-opera-like; **ses aventures feuilletonesques avec le fisc** his/her saga with the tax people
feuilletoniste [fœjtɔnist] NMF *(auteur de romans-feuilletons)* serial writer; *(chroniqueur)* feature writer
feuillette *etc voir* **feuilleter**
feuillu, -e [fœjy] ADJ leafy, broad-leaved
 NM broad-leaved tree
feuillure [fœjyr] NF *Menuis* rabbet, rebate
feuj [føʒ] *Fam (verlan de* **juif**) ADJ Jewish ■
 NMF Jew ■
feulement [følmɑ̃] NM growl
feuler [3] [føle] VI to growl
feutrage [føtraʒ] NM felting; **lavez à l'eau froide pour empêcher le f.** wash in cold water to prevent felting
feutre [føtr] NM **1** *Tex (étoffe)* felt; **de** *ou* **en f.** felt **2** *(chapeau)* felt hat, fedora **3** *(stylo)* **(crayon** *ou* **stylo) f.** felt(-tip) pen, felt-tip; **couvert de traces de f.** covered in felt-tip
feutré, -e [føtre] ADJ **1** *(pull, vêtement)* felted **2** *(garni de feutre* → *bourrelet)* felt *(avant n)*; **porte feutrée** baize door **3** *(silencieux* → *salon, atmosphère)* hushed, quiet; *(*→ *voix)* muffled; **marcher à pas feutrés** to creep stealthily; **s'éloigner à pas feutrés** to steal away, to slip quietly away; **traverser une pièce à pas feutrés** to pad across a room
feutrer [3] [føtre] VT **1** *Tex* to felt **2** *(garnir* → *selle)* to pad *or* to line (with felt) **3** *(son)* to muffle
 VI to felt, to become felted *or* matted; **l'eau trop chaude fait f. les pulls** washing in very hot water makes jumpers lose their finish
 ▸**se feutrer** VPR to felt, to become felted *or* matted
feutrine [føtrin] NF felt; *(sur table de billard)* baize
fève [fɛv] NF **1** *Bot (graine)* bean; *(plante)* broad bean; **f. de cacao** cocoa bean; **f. de Calabar** Calabar bean; **f. tonka** tonka bean **2** *Can (haricot)* bean; **f. jaune** wax bean; **f. verte** string bean; **fèves au lard** baked beans with pork, *Am* pork beans **3** *(des Rois)* = lucky charm or token made of porcelain and hidden in a "galette des Rois"
féverole [fɛvrɔl] NF *Bot* field bean, horse bean
févier [fevje] NM *Bot* honey-locust (tree)
février [fevrije] NM February; *voir aussi* **mars**
fez [fɛz] NM fez
FF *Anciennement (abrév écrite* **franc français**) FF
FFA [ɛfɛfɑ] NFPL *(abrév* **Forces françaises en Allemagne**) = French forces in Germany
FFI [ɛfɛfi] NFPL *Hist (abrév* **Forces françaises de l'intérieur**) = French Resistance forces during World War II
FFL [ɛfɛfɛl] NFPL *Hist (abrév* **Forces françaises libres**) = free French Army during World War II
FFR [ɛfɛfɛr] NF *(abrév* **Fédération française de rugby**) = French rugby federation
fg *(abrév écrite* **faubourg**) suburb
FGA [ɛfʒea] NM *(abrév* **fonds de garantie automobile**) = fund financed through insurance premiums to compensate victims of uninsured losses
Fgaf [ɛfʒeaɛf] NF *Pol (abrév* **Fédération générale autonome des fonctionnaires**) = French civil servants' trade union
FGDS [ɛfʒedeɛs] NF *(abrév* **Fédération de la gauche démocrate et socialiste**) = former French socialist party
FGEN [ɛfʒeəɛn] NF *(abrév* **Fédération générale de l'Éducation nationale**) = teachers' trade union
fi [fi] EXCLAM *Hum* pooh!
 NM *(locution)* **faire fi de** *(mépriser)* to turn one's nose up at, to spurn; *(ignorer)* to ignore
fiabiliser [3] [fjabilize] VT *(dispositif, opération)* to safeguard
fiabilité [fjabilite] NF *(crédibilité)* reliability
fiable [fjabl] ADJ *(crédible)* reliable
FIAC [fjak] NF *(abrév* **Foire internationale d'art contemporain**) = annual international contemporary art fair in Paris
fiacre [fjakr] NM fiacre, (horse-drawn) carriage
fiançailles [fijɑ̃saj] NFPL **1** *(promesse)* engagement; **à quand tes f.?** when are you getting engaged? **2** *(cérémonie)* engagement party **3** *(durée)* engagement (period); **pendant leurs f.** while they were engaged, during their engagement
fiance [fjɑ̃s] NF *Can (en acadien)* trust
fiancé, -e [fijɑ̃se] NM,F fiancé, *f* fiancée; **les fiancés** the engaged couple, *Littéraire ou Hum* the betrothed
fiancer [16] [fijɑ̃se] VT to betroth; **il fiance sa fille** his daughter is getting engaged; **elle est fiancée à Paul** she's engaged to Paul, she and Paul are engaged
 ▸**se fiancer** VPR to get engaged; **se f. avec qn** to get engaged to sb; **ils se fiancent en mars** they are getting engaged in March
FIAS [fjas] NF *(abbr* **Force internationale d'assistance et de sécurité**) ISAF
fiasco [fjasko] NM **1** *(entreprise, tentative)* fiasco, flop; *(film, ouvrage)* flop; **faire f.** to flop, to be a (total) failure **2** *(échec sexuel)* failure to perform
fiasque [fjask] NF (Italian) wine flask
fibranne [fibran] NF *Tex* staple, bonded fibre
fibre [fibr] NF **1** *(filament)* fibre; *(du bois)* fibre, woodfibre; **dans le sens de la f.** going with the grain (of the wood); **panneau de fibres agglomérées** fibreboard; **riche en fibres (alimentaires)** rich in (dietary) fibre
 2 *Opt & Tech* fibre; **f. de carbone** carbon fibre; **f. de verre** fibreglass; **f. optique** fibre optics *(singulier)*; **fibres optiques** optical fibres; **câble en fibres optiques** fibre-optic cable
 3 *Tex* **une f. textile** a fibre; **les fibres naturelles/synthétiques** naturally-occurring/man-made fibres; **coton à fibres longues** long-staple cotton
 4 *(dans un muscle)* muscle fibre; **f. nerveuse** nerve fibre
 5 *(sentiment)* feeling; **avoir la f. commerçante** to be a born shopkeeper; **avoir la f. maternelle/paternelle** to have strong maternal/paternal feelings; **elle n'a pas la f. maternelle** she's not the maternal sort; **faire jouer** *ou* **vibrer la f. patriotique de qn** to play upon sb's patriotic feelings; *Littéraire* **les fibres du cœur** the heart-strings
fibreux, -euse [fibrø, -øz] ADJ **1** *(dur* → *viande)* stringy, tough **2** *(à fibres* → *tissu, muscle)* fibrous; *Méd* fibroid
fibrillaire [fibrijɛr] ADJ *Méd* fibrillar
fibrillation [fibrijasjɔ̃] NF *Méd* fibrillation, fibrillating *(UNCOUNT)*
fibrille [fibrij] NF **1** *(fibre* → *courte)* short fibre; *(*→ *fine)* thin fibre **2** *Biol & Bot* fibril, fibrilla
fibriller [3] [fibrije] VT *Méd* to fibrillate
fibrine [fibrin] NF *Biol* fibrin
fibrineux, -euse [fibrinø, -øz] ADJ *Biol* fibrinous
fibrinogène [fibrinɔʒɛn] NM *Biol* fibrinogen
fibrinolyse [fibrinɔliz] NF *Méd* fibrinolysis
fibrinolytique [fibrinɔlitik] *Méd* ADJ fibrinolytic
 NM fibrinolytic
fibroblaste [fibrɔblast] NM *Biol* fibroblast
Fibrociment® [fibrɔsimɑ̃] NM *Constr* Fibrociment®
fibrocyte [fibrɔsit] NM *Biol* fibrocyte
fibroferrite [fibrɔferit] NF *Minér* fibroferrite
fibroïne [fibrɔin] NF *Biol & Chim* fibroin
fibrokyste [fibrɔkist] NM *Méd* fibrocyst
fibrokystique [fibrɔkistik] ADJ *Méd* fibrocystic
fibromateux, -euse [fibrɔmatø, -øz] ADJ *Méd* fibromatous
fibromatose [fibrɔmatoz] NF *Méd* fibromatosis
fibrome [fibrom] NM *Méd (tumeur)* fibroma; *(dans l'utérus)* fibroid
fibromyalgie [fibromjalʒi] NF *Méd* fibromyalgia
fibromyome [fibrɔmjom] NM *Méd* fibromyoma
fibroscope [fibrɔskɔp] NM *Méd* fibrescope
fibroscopie [fibrɔskɔpi] NF *Méd* fibre-optic endoscopy
fibrose [fibroz] NF *Méd* fibrosis
fibrosite [fibrosit] NF *Méd* fibrositis
fibula [fibyla] NF *Anat* fibula
fibule [fibyl] NF *Archéol* fibula
fic [fik] NM *Vét (des bovins)* fig; *(des chevaux)* wart
ficaire [fikɛr] NF *Bot* pilewort, lesser celandine
ficelage [fislaʒ] NM **1** *(action)* tying up **2** *(liens)* string(s)
ficelé, -e [fisle] ADJ **1 bien f.** *(dossier)* well put together; *Fig (scénario)* well-crafted; *Fig* **c'est bien/mal f.** *(texte, histoire, film)* it hangs/doesn't hang together well **2** *Fam (habillé)* got up; **être f. comme l'as de pique** to be dressed like a scarecrow
ficeler [24] [fisle] VT to tie up; *Fig* **ficelé comme un saucisson** trussed up like a chicken
ficelle [fisɛl] NF **1** *(corde)* piece of string; **de la f.** string; *Fig* **la f. est un peu grosse** it sticks out like a sore thumb; **les ficelles du métier** the tricks of the trade; **connaître toutes les ficelles du métier** to know the ropes; **ça, c'est une des ficelles du métier** that's one of the tricks of the trade; **tirer les ficelles** to pull the strings **2** *(pain)* = very thin baguette **3** *Fam Arg mil* officer's stripe ■ **4** *Vieilli (comme adj) (malin)* cunning
ficellera *etc voir* **ficeler**
ficellerie [fisɛlri] NF string manufacture
fichage [fiʃaʒ] NM *(mise sur fichier)* filing, recording
fiche[1] [3] [fiʃ] *Fam* VT **1** = **ficher**[2]
 2 *(locutions)* **il n'en a rien à f.** he couldn't care less; **on n'en a rien à f., de leurs états d'âme!** we couldn't care less about their scruples!; **pour ce que j'en ai à f.!** a fat lot I care!; **va te faire f.!** get lost!
 ▫ **se fiche** = **se ficher**
 ▫ **se fiche de** = **se ficher de**
fiche[2] [fiʃ] NF **1** *(carton)* piece of (stiff) card, (index) card; **f. cartonnée** index card; **f. de compte** accounts card; **f. cuisine** recipe card; **f. de facture** account card; **f. à perforations marginales** edge punched card; **f. perforée** perforated card; *Com* **f. de pointage** clocking-in card; **f. en T** T-card; **mettre qch sur f.** to index *or Br* to card-index sth; **faire des fiches de lecture** to write notes *or* a commentary on a book
 2 *(papier)* sheet, slip; **f. client** customer record; **f.-contact** contacts file; **f. courrier** mail checklist *or* file; **f. dentaire** dental chart; **f. d'entretien** service record; **f. explicative** information sheet; **f. fournisseur** supplier file; **f. médicale** medical record (card); **f. d'observations** *(questionnaire d'évaluation)* comment card; **f. de paie** pay slip; **f. de poste** *(descriptif des tâches à accomplir)* task sheet; **f. de présence** *(de salarié)* attendance sheet; **f. prospect** potential-customer file; **f. signalétique** identification slip *or* sheet; **f. de stock** stock sheet; *Com* **f. technique** specifications sheet; **f. verticale suspendue** vertical suspension file; **f. à visibilité** visible card record
 3 *(formulaire)* form; **remplir une f.** to fill in *or* fill out a form; **mettre qn en** *ou* **sur f.** to open a file on sb; **lui, on l'a sur f.** we've got a file on

him, we've got him on file; **f. d'accueil** registration form; **f. d'appréciation** customer satisfaction questionnaire; **f. d'arrivée** registration form; *Ind* **f. de contrôle** checking form, *Br* docket; *Compta* **f. d'imputation** data entry form; **f. d'inscription** registration form; **f.-message** message form

4 *Admin* **f. anthropométrique** = (criminal) dossier; **f. d'état civil** = record of civil status *(birth details and marital status)*; **f. de police** = registration card to be filled in by hotel guests from non-EU countries; *(au débarquement)* landing card

5 *(d'un hôtel)* **remplir une f. d'hôtel** to register (with a hotel), to fill in a (hotel) registration card; **f. de blocage** block card, reservation rack card, room rack card; **f. client** room rack card; *(sur ordinateur)* guest folio, guest file; **f. d'hôtel** *(clé)* key card; **f. Kardex** guest history card; **f. d'occupation** room rack card; **f. voyageur** = hotel registration card for foreign guests; **f. Whitney** Whitney card

6 *(dans les jeux)* counter

7 *Ordinat* pin; **f. d'état** report form; **f. gigogne** dongle; **f. suiveuse** route card

8 *Constr* hinge; **f. de porte** door hinge

9 *Élec (prise)* plug; *(broche)* pin; **f. multiple** multiple adapter; **f. téléphonique** phone *or* jack plug; *(broche)* telephone jack; *(pour message)* telephone memo

ficher[1] [3] [fiʃe] **VT 1** *(enfoncer)* to drive *or* to stick (in); *(lame)* to plunge; *(épingle)* to stick in; **f. un pieu en terre** to drive a stake into the ground; **f. une épingle dans qch** to stick a pin into sth; **un couteau fiché entre les omoplates** a knife stuck right between the shoulder blades

2 *(information)* to file, to put on file; *(suspect)* to put on file; **il est fiché** the police have got a file on him

▶**se ficher VPR** to stick (**dans** in); **la flèche se ficha en plein milieu de la cible** the arrow hit the middle of the target; **la balle se ficha dans le mur** the bullet lodged in the wall

ficher[2] [3] [fiʃe] *Fam* **VT 1** *(mettre)* to stick, to shove, *Br* to bung; **fiche-le à la porte!** throw *or* kick him out!; **son patron l'a fichu à la porte** his boss fired him *or* threw him out *or Br* sacked him; **fiche ça dans le placard** throw *or* stick it in the closet; **ils l'ont fichu en prison** they threw him in jail; **fiche-moi ça dehors!** get rid of this!; **je lui ai fichu mon poing dans la figure** I punched him/her in the face; **qui a fichu ce rapport ici?** who stuck this report here?; **ce temps me fiche à plat** this weather really wipes me out; **son départ nous a tous fichus à plat** his/her departure took the wind out of our sails; **c'est cette phrase qui m'a fichu dedans** it was that phrase that got me into hot water; **ils ont essayé de nous f. dedans** they tried to land us right in it; **tu l'as fichue en l'air, sa lettre?** did you chuck out his/her letter?; **ce contretemps fiche tout en l'air** this last-minute hitch really messes everything up; **arrête, tu vas le f. en rogne!** stop it, you're going to make him lose his temper!; **c'est le genre de remarque qui me fiche en rogne** that's the kind of remark that drives me mad; **f. qch par terre** to chuck sth on the ground; **t'as tout fichu par terre** *(gâché)* you've messed everything up; **si c'est fermé mardi, ça fiche tout par terre!** if it's closed on Tuesday, everything's ruined!

2 *(faire)* to do; **qu'est-ce que tu fiches ici?** what on earth *or* the heck are you doing here?; **je n'ai rien fichu aujourd'hui** I haven't done a thing today; **il n'a rien fichu de la journée** he's done damn all all day, he hasn't done a thing all day; **bon sang, qu'est-ce qu'il fiche?** *(où est-il?)* for God's sake, where on earth is he?; *(que fait-il?)* what the heck is he doing?

3 *(donner)* **f. une gifle à qn** to give sb a slap in the face; **ça me fiche le cafard** it makes me feel down *or* depressed; **ça m'a fichu la chair de poule/la trouille** it gave me the creeps/the willies; **fiche-moi la paix!** leave me alone!; **je t'en ficherai, moi, du champagne!** champagne? I'll give you champagne!; **je t'en ficherai, tiens, moi, des petits copains à ton âge!** boyfriends at your age, what are you thinking of!; **je te fiche mon billet que...** I'll bet my bottom dollar that...

4 **ça la fiche mal (de ne pas y aller)** *(fait mauvais effet)* it looks really bad (not to go)

▶**se ficher VPR 1** *(se mettre)* **de désespoir, elle s'est fichue à la Seine** in despair, she threw herself *or* jumped into the Seine■; **ils se sont fichus dans un fossé** *(en voiture)* they drove into a ditch■; *(pour passer inaperçus)* they jumped into a ditch■; **se f. par terre** *(tomber)* to fall flat; **fais attention sur ce vélo, tu vas te f. par terre!** mind how you go on that bike or you'll fall off!; **se f. en l'air** *(se suicider)* to do oneself in; **se f. en colère** to see red, *Br* to lose one's rag; **se f. dedans** to screw up, to get it wrong■

2 **se f. de** *(railler)* to make fun of■; **elle n'arrête pas de se f. de lui** she's forever pulling his leg *or Br* winding him up; **tu te fiches de moi ou quoi?** are you kidding me?; **30 euros pour ça? il se fiche de toi!** 30 euros for this? he's trying to swindle you *or* he really takes you for a sucker!; **ils se fichent du monde dans ce restaurant!** *(c'est cher)* this restaurant is an absolute rip-off!; *(le service est mauvais)* they treat the customers like dirt in this restaurant!; **eh bien, tu ne t'es pas fichu de nous!** well, you've really done things in style!

3 **se f. de** *(être indifférent à)* not to give a damn about; **je m'en fiche (pas mal)** I don't give a damn, I couldn't care less; **je me fiche de ce que disent les gens** I don't give a damn about what people say; **elle s'en fiche que son père ne soit pas d'accord** she doesn't give a damn *or* couldn't care less if her father doesn't agree; **ils n'ont pas aimé notre spectacle – qu'est-ce qu'on s'en fiche!** they didn't like our show – so what *or* who cares!; **je m'en fiche comme de ma première chemise** *ou* **comme de l'an quarante** *ou* **complètement** I don't give a damn (about it), I couldn't care less

fichet [fiʃɛ] **NM** *(utilisé au trictrac)* peg

fichier [fiʃje] **NM 1** *(fiches)* (card index) file, catalogue; **pour enrichir mon f.** to add to my files; **f. (des) clients** client *or* customer file; *Ordinat* **f. de commandes** command file; *Journ* **f. de coupures** cuttings file; **f. en cours** current file; **f. des salariés** personnel files

2 *(meuble)* filing cabinet; *(à tiroirs)* card-index filing cabinet; *(boîte)* file; **f. Kardex** *(d'un hôtel)* guest history file; **f. rotatif** rotating card index, rotary (card) file

3 *Ordinat* file; **f. informatique** computer file; **volume du f.** file size; **f. à accès aléatoire** random access file; **f. à accès limité** restricted file; **f. actif** active file; **f. d'adresses** mailing list; *Ordinat* address file; **f. d'application** application file; **f. ASCII** ASCII file; **f. autoexec.bat** autoexec.bat (file); **f. de base de données** database file; **f. BAT** batch file; **f. batch** batch file; **f. binaire** binary file; **f. de commande** command file; **f. compte-rendu** log file; **f. config.sys** config.sys (file); **f. de cookies** command file; **f. en cours** current file; **f. de destination** target file; **f. de détail** detail file; **f. disque** disk file; **f. document** document file; **f. d'entrée** input file; **f. exécutable** executable *or* execute file; **f. FAQ** FAQ file; **f. à imprimer** print job; **f. indexé** indexed file; **f. d'intendance** control file; **f. joint** *(de courrier électronique)* attachment; **f. journal** logging file; **f. en lecture seule** read-only file; **f. lisez-moi** read-me file; **f. maître** master file; **f. non structuré** flat file; **f. par points** bitmap file; **f. principal** master file; **f. de sauvegarde** backup file; **f. de secours** backup file; **f. séquentiel** batch *or* sequential file; *Ordinat* **f. son** sound file; **f. de sortie** output file; **f. source** source file; **f. système** system file; *Can* **f. de témoins** cookie file; **f. (de) texte** text file; **f. de travail** scratch file

fichiste [fiʃist] **NMF** *(personne)* filing clerk

fichoir [fiʃwar] **NM** *Vieilli* clothes peg

fichtre [fiʃtr] **EXCLAM** *Fam Vieilli* (my) gosh!, my (my)!; **f. oui!** I should say so!, rather!; **f. non!** not likely!, no fear!

fichtrement [fiʃtrəmɑ̃] **ADV** *Fam Vieilli* darn; **tout cela est f. assommant** this is just too darn boring; **je n'en sais f. rien!** how the heck should I know!

fichu[1] [fiʃy] **NM** (large) scarf; *(couvrant les épaules)* fichu, (small) shawl

fichu[2], **-e** [fiʃy] **ADJ** *Fam* **1** *(perdu)* **il est f.** he's had it; **ma robe est fichue** my dress has had it; **ta voiture est fichue** your car's a write-off; **c'est f.!** *(sans espoir)* (we can) forget it!; **pour samedi soir, c'est f.** Saturday evening's *Br* up the spout *or Am* down the drain; **si tu renverses de l'eau sur le daim, c'est f.** if you spill water on suede, it ruins it■

2 *(avant le nom) (mauvais)* lousy, rotten; **quel f. temps!** what lousy weather!; **quel f. pays!** what a godforsaken country!; **je suis dans un f. état ce matin** I feel lousy this morning; **avoir un f. caractère** to have a lousy *or* filthy temper

3 *(avant le nom) (important)* **ça fait une fichue différence** that makes a heck of a difference; **j'ai un f. mal de dents** I've got one hell of a nasty toothache

4 *(capable)* **il n'est même pas f. de prendre un message correctement** he can't even take a message properly; **elle est fichue de partir!** she's quite capable of leaving!

5 *(habillé)* **être bien/mal f.** to be well/badly turned out *or* dressed

6 *(bâti, conçu)* **elle est vraiment bien fichue, cette fille** that girl's got a great body on her; **il est mal f.** he hasn't got a very nice body; **c'est bien/mal f.** it's well/badly designed■; **ce système est très bien f.** it's a very clever device; **leur manuel est mal f.** their handbook is lousy

7 **être mal f.** *(un peu malade)* to be out of sorts, *Br* to be off colour

8 *Can* **une fichue de belle maison/voiture** a gorgeous house/car■, a damn *or Br* bloody nice house/car; **un f. de beau garçon** a fine-looking *or* gorgeous-looking guy

fichument [fiʃymɑ̃] *Can* = **fichtrement**

fictif, -ive [fiktif, -iv] **ADJ 1** *(imaginaire)* imaginary, fictitious **2** *(faux* → *promesse)* false **3** *Fin* fictitious; *(compte)* dead; **valeur fictive** *(de billets)* face value

fiction [fiksjɔ̃] **NF 1** *(domaine de l'imaginaire)* **la f.** fiction; **film de f.** fictional film; **livre de f.** work of fiction; **un tel concept relève de la f.** a concept like this is sheer fiction; **la réalité dépasse la f.** truth is stranger than fiction; *Péj* **elle vit dans la f.** she's living in a dream world; **la politique-f.** political pie in the sky; **un livre de politique-f.** a political novel **2** *(histoire)* story, (piece of) fiction **3** *Jur* fiction; **f. légale** *ou* **de droit** legal fiction

fictionalisation [fiksjɔnalizasjɔ̃] **NF** fictionalization

fictionnel, -elle [fiksjɔnel] **ADJ** fictional

fictive [fiktiv] *voir* **fictif**

fictivement [fiktivmɑ̃] **ADV** fictitiously; **transposons-nous f. au XVIIIème siècle** let's imagine we're in the 18th century

fictivité [fiktivite] **NF** fictitiousness

ficus [fikys] **NM** *Bot* ficus; **f. elastica** rubber plant

fidéicommis [fideikɔmi] **NM** *Jur* trust

fidéicommissaire [fideikɔmisɛr] **NM** *Jur* trustee

fidéisme [fideism] **NM** *Phil & Rel* fideism

fidéiste [fideist] *Phil & Rel* **ADJ** fideistic

NMF fideist

fidéjusseur, -euse [fideʒysœr, -øz] **NM,F** *Jur* surety, guarantor

fidéjussion [fideʒysjɔ̃] **NF** *Jur* suretyship, guarantee

fidèle [fidɛl] **ADJ 1** *(constant* → *ami)* faithful, loyal, true; *(→ employé, animal)* loyal, faithful; *(→ conjoint)* faithful; *(→ client)* loyal; *(→ lecteur)* regular, loyal; **elle a été f. à sa parole** *ou* **promesse** she kept her word; **il est f. à la promesse qu'il nous a faite** he has kept faith with us, he has kept his promise to us; **rester f. à la mémoire de qn** to remain true *or* faithful to sb's memory; **être f. à ses engagements** to stand by one's commitments; **être f. à une idée** to stand by *or* to be true to an idea; **être f. à un médecin/commerçant** to be a regular patient/customer; **être/rester f. à une marque/un produit** to stick with a particular brand/product; *Mktg* **f. à la marque** brand-loyal; **f. à elle-même** true to herself; *Ironique* **f. à lui-même, il a oublié mon anniversaire** true to character *or* true to form, he forgot my birthday; **comment l'as-tu trouvé? – f. à lui-même** how did you find him? – his usual self; **être f. au poste** to be reliable; **elle est toujours f. au poste** you can always rely *or* depend on her

2 *(conforme → copie, description)* true, exact; *(→ traduction)* faithful, close; *(→ historien, narrateur)* faithful; *(→ mémoire)* reliable, correct; *(→ balance)* reliable, accurate; **livre f. à la réalité** book which is true to life; **la traduction n'est pas f. au texte** the translation is not faithful to the original

NMF 1 *Rel* believer; **les fidèles** *(croyants)* the believers; *(pratiquants)* the faithful; *(assemblée)* the congregation

2 *(adepte)* devotee, follower; *(client)* loyal customer; *(lecteur de journal)* regular *or* loyal reader; *TV* regular *or* loyal viewer; **je suis un f. de votre émission** I never miss one of your shows; *Mktg* **f. absolu** hard-core loyal

fidèlement [fidɛlmɑ̃] **ADV 1** *(régulièrement)* regularly; **père venait f. nous voir** father visited us regularly **2** *(loyalement)* faithfully, loyally; **suivre qn f.** to follow sb faithfully **3** *(conformément → copier)* exactly, faithfully; *(→ traduire, reproduire)* accurately, faithfully

❑ **fidèlement vôtre ADV** yours (ever)

fidélisation [fidelizasjɔ̃] **NF f. des clients** *ou* **d'une clientèle** building up *or* development of customer loyalty; **f. à la marque** creation of brand loyalty

fidéliser [3] [fidelize] **VT f. ses clients** *ou* **la clientèle** to build up *or* to develop customer loyalty; **f. un public** to maintain a regular audience *(by a commercial policy)*; **f. une équipe** to keep a team together

fidélité [fidelite] **NF 1** *(loyauté → d'un ami, d'un employé, d'un animal)* faithfulness, loyalty; *(→ d'un conjoint)* faithfulness, fidelity; *(→ d'un client, d'un lecteur)* loyalty; **sa f. à sa parole** *ou* **promesse** his/her faithfulness, his/her keeping faith; **f. à ses engagements** standing by one's commitments; *Mktg* **f. absolue** hard-core loyalty; *Mktg* **f. du client** customer loyalty; *Mktg* **f. du consommateur** consumer loyalty; *Mktg* **f. à la marque** brand loyalty; **f. à** *ou* **de la couleur** colour fidelity

2 *(exactitude → d'un récit, d'une description)* accuracy, faithfulness; *(→ de la mémoire)* reliability; *(→ d'un instrument)* accuracy, reliability

Fidji [fidʒi] **NFPL les (îles) F.** Fiji, the Fiji Islands; **vivre aux F.** to live in Fiji *or* the Fiji Islands; **aller aux F.** to go to Fiji *or* the Fiji Islands

fidjien, -enne [fidʒjɛ̃, -ɛn] **ADJ** Fijian

❑ **Fidjien, -enne NM,F** Fijian

fiduciaire [fidysjɛr] **ADJ** fiduciary; **monnaie f.** paper money; **avoirs en monnaie f.** *(d'une banque)* cash holdings; **une circulation f. excessive entraîne l'inflation** too much paper money in circulation leads to inflation; **société f.** trust company; *Jur* **en dépôt f.** in trust

NM *Jur* fiduciary, trustee

fiduciairement [fidysjɛrmɑ̃] **ADV** *Jur* in trust

fiducie [fidysi] **NF** *Jur* trust

fief [fjɛf] **NM 1** *Hist* fief **2** *(domaine réservé)* fief, kingdom; **n'entre pas dans la cuisine, c'est son f.!** don't go into the kitchen, it's his/her kingdom *or* domain!; **un f. électoral** a politician's fief; **un f. du parti socialiste** a socialist stronghold

fieffé, -e [fjefe] **ADJ 1** *Hist* enfeoffed **2** *Péj (extrême)* complete, utter; **un f. menteur/voleur** an arrant liar/thief; **un f. paresseux** a real old lazybones

fiel [fjɛl] **NM 1** *(bile)* gall, bile **2** *Littéraire (amertume)* rancour, bitterness, gall; *(méchanceté)* venom; **des propos pleins de f.** venomous words; **un sourire plein de f.** a twisted smile

fielleux, -euse [fjɛlø, -øz] **ADJ** *Littéraire* venomous, spiteful

fiente [fjɑ̃t] **NF de la f.** droppings

fienter [3] [fjɑ̃te] **VI** to leave droppings

fier[1] [9] [fje] **se fier VPR 1 se f. à qn/qch** *(avoir confiance en)* to trust sb/sth; **fiez-vous à moi, je le trouverai** leave it to me *or* trust me, I'll find him; **se f. à la parole de qn** to take sb's word for it, to believe sb; **je ne me fie pas à ce qu'il dit** I don't believe a word he says; **se f. aux apparences** to go by *or* on appearances; **ne vous y fiez pas!** don't be fooled by it/him/her/*etc*!

2 **se f. à qn/qch** *(compter sur)* to rely on *or* count on sb/sth; **ne te fie pas trop à ton assistant** don't rely too much on your assistant; **se f. à sa mémoire** to rely on one's memory

fier[2], **fière** [fjɛr] **ADJ 1** *(satisfait)* proud; **l'enfant était tout f.** the child was really proud; **être f. de qch/d'avoir fait qch** to be proud of sth/of having done sth; **j'étais f. d'avoir gagné** I was proud (that) I won; **je n'étais pas f. de moi** I wasn't pleased with *or* proud of myself; **il n'y a pas de quoi être f.** that's nothing to boast about *or* to be proud of

2 *(noble)* noble, proud; *Littéraire* **une âme fière** a noble mind; **ils sont trop fiers pour accepter de l'argent** they're too proud to take money

3 *(arrogant → personnage)* proud, arrogant, haughty; *(→ regard)* haughty, supercilious; **il est trop f. pour nous serrer la main** he's too proud to shake hands with us; **quand il a fallu sauter, il n'était plus tellement f.** when it came to jumping, he didn't seem so sure of himself; **alors, on est moins f., n'est-ce pas?** not quite so high and mighty now, are we?; *Fam* **c'est une fille pas fière** she's not a stuck-up girl; *Fam* **il n'est pas f. pour deux sous** he's not at all stuck-up; **avoir fière allure** to cut (quite) a dash; **être f. comme Artaban** *ou* **comme un coq** to be as proud as a peacock, to be puffed up with pride

4 *Littéraire (audacieux)* bold

5 *(avant le nom) Fam (extrême)* **tu as un f. culot!** you've got some nerve!; **c'est un f. imbécile!** what an idiot!

NM,F proud person; **faire le f.** to put on airs and graces; **ne joue pas le f. avec moi!** it's no use putting on your airs and graces with me!; **il fait le f. avec sa nouvelle voiture** he's showing off with his new car; **inutile de faire le f., ça sera pareil pour toi** it's no good giving yourself airs (and graces), it'll be the same for you

fier-à-bras [fjɛrabra] *(pl* **fiers-à-bras***)* **NM** braggart

fière [fjɛr] *voir* **fier**

fièrement [fjɛrmɑ̃] **ADV 1** *(dignement)* proudly

2 *Vieilli (d'une manière hautaine)* haughtily

3 *Vieilli (extrêmement)* famously

4 *Littéraire (avec audace)* boldly

fiérot, -e [fjɛro, -ɔt] *Fam* **ADJ** proud▪ **(de** of); **il était tout f.** he was as proud as a peacock

NM,F faire le f. to show off

fier-pet [fjɛrpɛ] *(pl* **fiers-pets***) Can Fam Péj* **ADJ** pompous▪, conceited▪

NM pompous ass

fierté [fjɛrte] **NF 1** *(dignité)* pride; **par f., je ne lui ai pas parlé** my pride wouldn't let me talk to him/her; **ravaler sa f.** to swallow one's pride; **elle n'a pas beaucoup de f.** she hasn't much pride *or* self-respect; **il a trop de f. pour demander de l'aide** he's too proud to ask for help; *Fam* **tu ne le lui as pas réclamé? – on a sa f.!** didn't you ask him/her to give it back? – I do have some pride!

2 *(arrogance)* arrogance, haughtiness, superciliousness

3 *(satisfaction)* (source of) pride; **tirer f.** *ou* **une grande f. de** to take (a) pride in, to pride oneself on; **ma fille/maison est ma f.** my daughter/house is my pride and joy; **la réussite de l'entreprise est notre f.** we pride ourselves on the success of the venture

❑ **avec fierté ADV** proudly; **c'est avec f. que je vous présente...** I'm proud to present to you..., I proudly present to you...

fiesta [fjɛsta] **NF** *Fam* (wild) party▪, *Br* rave-up; **faire la f.** to live it up

fieu [fjø] **NM** *Belg Fam* sonny

fièvre [fjɛvr] **NF 1** *Méd* fever, temperature; **avoir de la f.** to have a temperature *or* a fever; **avoir beaucoup de f.** to have a high temperature *or* a fever; **il a 40 de f.** his temperature is up to 40, he has a temperature of 40; **pour faire baisser la f.** (in order) to get the temperature down; *Fig Littéraire* **tomber de la f. en chaud mal** to fall from the frying pan into the fire; **f. amarile** yellow fever; *Vét* **f. aphteuse** foot and mouth disease; **f. bilieuse hémoglobinurique** blackwater fever, *Spéc* malarial haemoglobinuria; **f. hémorragique** haemorrhagic fever; **f. jaune** yellow fever; **f. de Lassa** Lassa fever; **f. de Malte** Malta fever; **f. miliaire** prickly heat, *Spéc* miliaria; **f. ondulante** undulant fever; **f. paludéenne** malaria; **f. proleptique** proleptic fever; *Vét & Méd* **f. Q** Q fever; **f. quarte** quartan fever; **f. de** *ou* **du Queensland** Q fever; **f. quinte** quintan fever; **f. subintrante** proleptic fever; **f. tierce** tertian fever; **f. typhoïde** typhoid fever

2 *(agitation)* excitement; **elle parlait avec f.** she spoke excitedly; **préparer un examen avec f.** to prepare feverishly for an exam; **la f. des présidentielles** the excitement of the presidential elections; **dans la f. de la campagne électorale** in the heat *or* excitement of the electoral campaign; **dans la f. du moment/des débats** in the heat of the moment/debates; **sans f.** calmly

3 *(désir)* **avoir la f. de l'or** to have a passion for gold

---

'La Fièvre du samedi soir' *Badham* 'Saturday Night Fever'

---

fiévreuse [fjevrøz] *voir* **fiévreux**

fiévreusement [fjevrøzmɑ̃] **ADV** *Méd & Fig* feverishly; *(attendre)* anxiously

fiévreux, -euse [fjevrø, -øz] **ADJ** *Méd & Fig* feverish, febrile; *(activité, préparations)* feverish, frantic; *(imagination)* feverish; *(attente)* anxious

FIF [ɛfiɛf] **NF** *(abrév* **Fédération internationale du film***)* FIF

FIFA [fifa] **NF** *(abrév* **Fédération internationale de football association***)* FIFA

fifi [fifi] **NM** *Can Fam* **1** *(petit garçon efféminé)* sissy **2** *(homosexuel)* pansy, *Br* poof, = offensive term used to refer to a homosexual

fifille [fifij] **NF** *Fam* little girl▪

fifine [fifin] **NF** *Can Fam* dyke, = offensive term used to refer to a lesbian

fifre [fifr] **NM 1** *(flûte)* fife **2** *(joueur)* fife player

fifrelin [fifrəlɛ̃] **NM** *Fam (locution)* **ça ne vaut pas un f.** it isn't worth a bean *or Am* a dime

fifty-fifty [fiftififti] **ADV** *Fam* fifty-fifty, half-and-half; **partager qch f.** to share sth fifty-fifty, to go dutch; **faisons f.** let's go halves

fig. *(abrév écrite* **figure***)* fig.

Figaro [figaro] **NPR** Figaro

NM *Presse* **le F.** = French daily newspaper with a right-wing bias

figaro [figaro] **NM** *Arch (coiffeur)* barber

figé, -e [fiʒe] **ADJ** set; *(sauce, huile)* congealed; *(sourire)* fixed; *(style)* stilted; *(société)* fossilized; **dans une attitude figée** motionless

figement [fiʒmɑ̃] **NM** *(de l'huile)* congealing; *(du sang)* coagulation, clotting

figer [17] [fiʒe] **VT 1** *(coaguler → huile)* to congeal; *(→ sang)* to coagulate, to clot; **des cris à vous f. le sang** bloodcurdling screams; **ce spectacle lui a figé le sang** the sight made his/her blood run cold

2 *(immobiliser → personne)* **la vue du tigre me figea sur place** I froze when I saw the tiger; **sa réponse m'a figé sur place** his/her answer struck me dumb

VI *(huile)* to congeal; *(sang)* to coagulate, to clot

▸**se figer VPR 1** *(être coagulé → huile)* to congeal; *(→ sang)* to coagulate, to clot; **mon sang s'est figé dans mes veines** my blood froze

2 *(s'immobiliser → attitude, sourire)* to stiffen; *(→ personne)* to freeze; **elle se figea sous l'effet de la terreur** she was rooted to the spot with fear; **se f. au garde-à-vous** to stand to attention; **se f. dans une attitude/un point de vue** to persist in an attitude/a point of view

fignolage [fiɲɔlaʒ] **NM** perfecting, touching up, polishing (up)

fignoler [3] [fiɲɔle] **VT** *(travail, dessin)* to perfect, to polish *or* to touch up; **un travail fignolé** a polished piece of work

USAGE ABSOLU to be meticulous; **il ne me reste plus qu'à f.** it's just a matter of adding the finishing touches now

fignoleur, -euse [fiɲɔlœr, -øz] **ADJ** meticulous, *Péj* finicky

NM,F meticulous *or Péj* finicky worker

figue [fig] **NF** fig; **f. de Barbarie** prickly pear; **f. caque** kaki, (Japanese) persimmon; **f. des Hottentots** Hottentot *or* sour fig

figueraie [figrɛ], **figuerie** [figri] **NF** fig garden, fig orchard

figuier [figje] **NM** fig tree; **f. banian** banyan; **f. de Barbarie** prickly pear, *Spéc* opuntia

figurant, -e [figyrɑ̃, -ɑ̃t] **NM,F** *Cin* extra; *Théât* extra, walk-on actor; *(en danse)* figurant; *Théât* **rôle de f.** walk-on (part), bit part; *Cin* bit part;

être réduit au rôle de f. ou à jouer les figurants (dans une réunion) to be a mere onlooker; (auprès d'une personne importante) to be a stooge

figuratif, -ive [figyratif, -iv] ADJ (art) figurative, representational; (artiste) representational; (plan) figurative

NM representational artist

figuration [figyrasjɔ̃] NF 1 (figurants) la f. Cin extras; Théât extras, walk-on actors; (en danse) figurants 2 (métier) la f. Cin being an or working as an extra; Théât doing a walk-on part; (en danse) being a or dancing as a figurant; faire de la f. Cin to work as an extra; Théât to do walk-on parts; (en danse) to dance as a figurant 3 (fait de représenter) representation, figuration; Beaux-Arts f. narrative narrative figuration

figurative [figyrativ] voir figuratif

figure [figyr] NF 1 (visage) face; (mine) face, features; jeter qch à la f. de qn to throw sth in sb's face; faire triste ou piètre f. to cut a sad figure, to be a sad or sorry sight; faire bonne f. to make a good impression; il faisait f. de riche he was looked on or thought of as a rich man; parmi tous ces imbéciles, il fait f. de génie! all those idiots make him look like a genius!; prendre f. to take shape; ne plus avoir f. humaine to be totally unrecognizable or disfigured; Hum le canapé n'avait plus f. humaine the sofa was totally worn out

2 (personnage) figure; une grande f. de la politique a great political figure; c'est une f.! he's quite a character!

3 (représentation) figures de cire waxworks, waxwork figures; Naut & Fig f. de proue figurehead

4 (illustration) figure, illustration; (schéma, diagramme) diagram, figure; f. géométrique geometrical figure

5 Cartes picture card, Am face card

6 (en danse, patinage et gymnastique) figure; figures libres freestyle; figures imposées compulsory figures

7 Mus figure

8 Ling f. de rhétorique rhetorical figure; f. de style stylistic device; Vieilli f. de mot figure of speech

figuré, -e [figyre] ADJ 1 (plan) diagrammatic 2 Ling (langage, sens) figurative

❑ au figuré ADV figuratively

figurément [figyremɑ̃] ADV figuratively

figurer [3] [figyre] VT 1 (représenter) to represent, to show, to depict; sur la carte, les villages sont figurés par des points villages are represented by dots on the map

2 (symboliser) to symbolize; la balance et le glaive figurent la justice scales and the sword symbolize or are the symbols of justice

VI 1 (apparaître) to appear; f. dans un catalogue/une bibliographie to be listed or to appear in a catalogue/a bibliography; votre nom ne figure pas sur la liste your name doesn't appear or isn't on the list; f. au nombre des élus to be among the successful candidates; voici les chevaux qui figurent à l'arrivée here are the names of the winning horses; f. en bonne place to be well placed, to be up among the winners; j'ai oublié de faire f. son nom sur l'affiche I forgot to include his/her name on the poster

2 Cin to be an extra; Théât to do a walk-on part

▶se figurer VPR 1 (imaginer) to imagine; figurez-vous une sorte de grande pièce imagine or picture a huge room

2 (croire) to believe; il se figure qu'il va gagner de l'argent he believes or thinks he's going to make money; figure-toi qu'il n'a même pas appelé! he didn't even call, can you believe it?; figure-toi que nous aussi, on a loué une maison dans ce village would you believe it, we've rented a house in that village as well; eh bien, figure-toi que moi non plus, je n'ai pas le temps! surprising though it may seem, I haven't got the time either!; je suis à sec, figure-toi believe it or not, I'm broke

figurine [figyrin] NF figurine, statuette

figuriste [figyrist] NMF (mouleur) maker of plaster figures

Fiji [fidʒi] = Fidji

fil [fil] NM 1 Tex (matière → de coton, de soie) thread; (→ de laine) yarn; (brin → de coton, de soie) piece of thread; (→ de laine) strand; cachemire trois/quatre fils three-ply/four-ply cashmere; f. à bâtir basting thread; f. de coton cotton thread; f. à coudre sewing thread; f. dentaire dental floss; f. d'Écosse lisle; chaussettes en f. d'Écosse lisle socks; f. de Nylon® nylon thread; Fig de f. en aiguille one thing leading to another; Fig donner du f. à retordre à qn to cause sb (no end of) trouble; Fig c'est cousu de f. blanc you can see right through it, it won't fool anybody

2 (lin) linen; draps de f. linen sheets

3 (filament → de haricot) string; haricots pleins de/sans fils stringy/stringless beans

4 (corde → à linge) line; (→ d'équilibriste) tightrope, high wire; (→ pour marionnette) string; Myth f. d'Ariane Ariadne's thread; f. conducteur ou d'Ariane (d'une enquête) (vital) lead; (dans une histoire) main theme; il n'y a pas de f. conducteur dans ce roman there's no unifying thread in this novel; le f. rouge the recurrent theme; débrouiller ou démêler les fils d'une intrigue to unravel the threads or strands of a plot; Fig sa vie ne tient qu'à un f. his/her life hangs by a thread; Fig il ne tenait qu'à un f. qu'il soit renvoyé it was touch and go whether he would be dismissed; Fig c'est lui qui tient les fils he's the one who holds (all) the strings; un f. de la Vierge a gossamer thread; des fils de la Vierge gossamer (threads); Fam avoir un f. à la patte to be tied down, to have one's hands tied

5 (câble) wire; f. (électrique) (electric) wire; f. (souple) lead, cord, Br flex; f. de cuivre/d'acier copper/steel wire; f. télégraphique/téléphonique telegraph/telephone wire; f. de masse ou de terre Br earth or Am ground wire; f. à couper le beurre cheesewire; f. de fer wire; f. de fer barbelé barbed wire; clôture en f. de fer (gén) wire fence; (barbelé) barbed wire fence; c'est un f. de fer, ce type! that guy's as thin as a rake!; f. à plomb plumbline; f. à souder soldering wire; f. de bougie (spark) plug lead

6 Fam (téléphone) au bout du f. on the phone■, on the line; à l'autre bout du f. on the other end of the line; donner ou passer un coup de f. à qn to give sb a call, to call sb (up), Br to give sb a ring, to ring sb (up); avoir ou recevoir un coup de f. de qn to get a (phone) call from sb■

7 (tranchant) edge; donner le f. à une lame to sharpen a blade; Littéraire passer qn au f. de l'épée to put sb to the sword; être sur le f. du rasoir to be on a knife-edge

8 (sens → du bois, de la viande) grain; dans le sens contraire au f., contre le f. against the grain; dans le sens du f. with the grain

9 (cours → de l'eau) current, stream; (→ de la pensée, d'une discussion) thread; Ordinat (→ d'un groupe de discussion) thread; le f. des événements the chain of events; perdre/reprendre le f. d'une histoire to lose/to pick up the thread of a story; perdre/reprendre le f. de la conversation to lose/to pick up the thread of the conversation; j'ai perdu le f., je ne sais plus où j'en suis I've lost the thread, I don't know where I am any more; suivre/interrompre le f. des pensées de qn to follow/to interrupt sb's train of thought

❑ au fil de PRÉP 1 (le long de) aller au f. de l'eau to go with the current or stream; se laisser aller au f. de l'eau to let oneself drift (with the current)

2 (au fur et à mesure de) au f. du temps as time goes by; au f. des semaines as the weeks go by, with the passing weeks; au f. de la discussion je m'aperçus que... as the discussion progressed I realized that...

❑ sans fil ADJ (télégraphie, téléphonie) wireless (avant n); (rasoir, téléphone) cordless

filable [filabl] ADJ Tex spinnable, suitable for spinning

fil-à-fil [filafil] NM INV Tex pepper-and-salt cloth

filage [filaʒ] NM 1 Tex spinning 2 Métal drawing 3 Théât run-through

filaire[1] [filɛr] Tél ADJ telegraphic; (téléphone) corded, plug-in

NM corded or plug-in phone

filaire[2] [filɛr] NF Méd & Zool filaria; f. de Médine Guinea worm

filament [filamɑ̃] NM 1 (fibre■) filament 2 Tex thread 3 Élec filament

filamenteux, -euse [filamɑ̃tø, -øz] ADJ filamentous, filamentary

filandière [filɑ̃djɛr] NF Arch spinner; Littéraire les sœurs filandières the Fates

filandre [filɑ̃dr] NF 1 (fil de la Vierge) gossamer 2 (dans un aliment) (tough) fibre

filandreux, -euse [filɑ̃drø, -øz] ADJ 1 (fibreux → viande) stringy 2 Péj (confus → style, discours) long-winded

filant, -e [filɑ̃, -ɑ̃t] ADJ 1 (qui file → liquide) free-running 2 Méd (pouls) (very) weak

❑ filante NF Belg (dans un collant) ladder, Am run

filao [filao] NM Bot filao

filariose [filarjoz] NF Méd filariasis

filasse [filas] NF tow; f. de chanvre hemp

ADJ INV Péj cheveux (blonds) f. dirty blond hair

filateur [filatœr] NM spinning-factory owner

filature [filatyr] NF 1 Tex (opérations) spinning; (usine) (spinning) mill; f. de coton cotton mill 2 (surveillance) shadowing, tailing; prendre qn en f. to shadow or to tail sb

fil-de-fériste, fildeferiste [fildəferist] (pl fil-de-féristes) NMF high wire acrobat

file [fil] NF 1 (suite → de véhicules) line, row; (→ de personnes) line; f. d'attente Br queue, Am line; se mettre en f. to line up, to stand in line, Br to queue up; prendre la f., se mettre à la f. to join the queue or Am line; marcher en ou à la f. to walk in line; entrer/sortir en f. ou à la f. to file in/out; en f. indienne in single file

2 Transp lane; la f. de droite the right-hand lane; sur deux files in two lanes; stationner en double f. to double-park; je suis en double f. I'm double-parked; ne changez pas de f. keep in lane

3 Mil file of soldiers

4 Ordinat f. d'attente print queue or list; mettre en f. d'attente to queue, to spool

❑ à la file ADV in a row, one after another or the other; il a bu trois verres à la f. he drank three glasses in a row or one after another

❑ de file ADV Suisse & Can (à la file) in a row, one after the other or another

filé [file] ADJ M 1 (bas, collant) with a run, Br laddered 2 verre f. spun glass

NM Tech & Tex thread; f. d'or gold thread

filer [3] [file] VT 1 Tech & Tex to spin; Fam f. un mauvais coton (être malade) to be in bad shape; (se préparer des ennuis) to be heading for trouble

2 Entom to spin

3 (dérouler → câble) to pay out; (→ amarre) to pay out, to slip

4 (développer → image, métaphore) to draw or to spin out; (tenir → note, son) to draw out

5 (carte) to palm off; f. les cartes (au poker) to show one's hand

6 (suivre → sujet: détective) to tail, to shadow

7 (déchirer → collant, bas) to run, Br to ladder

8 Fam (donner) f. qch à qn to give sb sth■; file-moi cinq euros give us five euros; f. une gifle à qn to give sb a slap, to smack or to slap sb in the face; f. un coup de main à qn to give sb a hand; file-moi un coup de main give us a hand; f. un coup de pied à qn to kick sb■; il m'a filé un coup de poing he Br landed or Am beaned me one; on m'a filé le sale boulot they Br landed or Am stuck me with the rotten job; je te file ma robe, je ne la mets jamais you can have my dress, I never wear it■; attends, je te file du papier wait, I'll let you have some paper■; elle m'a filé la grippe she's given me the flu■

9 (locutions) f. le parfait amour to live a great romance; f. des jours heureux to live very happily

VI 1 (liquide) to run, to flow; (fromage) to run

2 (flamme, lampe) to smoke

3 (se dérouler → câble) to run out; laisser f. un câble to pay out a cable

4 Naut f. (à) 20 nœuds to sail or to proceed at 20 knots

5 (collants, bas) to run, Br to ladder; (maille) to run; j'ai un bas qui file I've got a run or Br ladder

6 (passer vite → coureur) to dash; (→ véhicule, nuage) to fly (past); (→ temps) to fly; f. à toute vitesse (voiture) to bomb along; il a filé dehors

he dashed out; **il a filé dans sa chambre** *(gén)* he dashed *or* flew into his bedroom; *(après une réprimande)* he stormed off to his room; **elle a filé à travers le jardin** she dashed *or* flew across the garden; **il faut que je file si je veux avoir mon train** I must dash if I don't want to miss my train; **bon, je file!** right, I'm off!; **sa victime lui a filé entre les doigts** his/her victim slipped through his/her fingers; **l'argent lui file entre les doigts** money just slips through his/her fingers; **les journées filent à une vitesse!** the days are just flying by!

7 *Fam (disparaître → cambrioleur)* to scram, *Br* to scarper, *Am* to skedaddle; **f. (en douce)** to slip away *or* off; **quand je suis entré dans la boutique ils avaient filé!** when I went into the shop I found that they'd taken off!; **je t'ai assez vu, file!** I've had enough of you, scram! *or* clear off!; **f. à l'anglaise** to sneak off, to take French leave; *(pour éviter quelqu'un ou quelque chose)* to do a runner

8 *Fam (argent)* to go, to disappear, to vanish; **il a eu trois millions à la mort de son père mais tout a filé!** he inherited three million when his father died but now it's all gone!

9 *Can Joual (se sentir)* **f. bien/mal** to feel great/lousy

10 *(locution)* **f. doux** to behave oneself■; **avec sa tante, elle file doux!** she's as good as gold with her aunt!; **avec moi, tu as intérêt à f. doux!** just watch your step with me, that's all!

filet [filε] **NM 1** *Anat* fibre; **f. nerveux** nerve fibre; **f. de la langue** frenum linguae

2 *Bot (d'étamine)* filament

3 *(de reliure) & Archit* fillet

4 *Tech* thread

5 *Typ* rule; **f. maigre** hairline (rule)

6 *(petite quantité)* **un f. d'eau** a trickle of water; **un f. de bave** a dribble of saliva; **un f. de sang** a trickle of blood; **un f. d'air** a (light) stream of air; **un f. de lumière** a (thin) shaft of light; **un f. de fumée** a wisp of smoke; **un f. de citron/vinaigre** a dash of lemon/vinegar; **un (petit) f. de voix** a thin (reedy) voice

7 *Culin (de viande, de poisson)* fillet; **un morceau dans le f.** *(de bœuf)* ≃ a sirloin *or* porterhouse steak; **faire des filets de sole** to fillet a sole; **f. mignon** filet mignon

8 *(ouvrage à mailles)* net; **f. (à bagages)** (luggage) rack; *Mil* **f. de camouflage** camouflage net; **f. à cheveux** hair net; **f. dérivant** *ou* **flottant** drift net; *Pêche* **f. maillant** gill net; **f. à papillons** butterfly net; **f. (de pêche)** (fishing) net; **f. à provisions** string bag; *Fig* **attirer qn dans ses filets** to entrap *or* to ensnare sb; **tendre un f.** *Chasse* to set a snare; *Fig* to lay a trap; **un beau coup de f. pour la police** a good haul for the police

9 *Sport (au football, au hockey, au tennis)* net; *(d'acrobate)* safety net; **envoyer la balle dans le f.** to hit the ball into the net; **envoyer le palet au fond du f.** to slam the puck into the back of the net, to net the puck; **le petit f.** *(au football)* the side netting; **monter au f.** to come up to the net; **balle de f.** let (ball); **travailler sans f.** to perform without a safety net; *Fig* to take risks

filetage [filtaʒ] **NM** *Tech* **1** *(action)* threading **2** *(filets)* (screw) thread; **f. Acmé** Acme thread; **f. Whitworth** Whitworth thread

fileté [filte] **NM** *Tex* cotton fabric

fileter [28] [filte] **VT 1** *Tech* to thread; *(métal)* to wiredraw; *(fil)* to draw **2** *Culin* to fillet

fileur, -euse [filœr, -øz] **NM,F** *Tex* spinner

'Les Fileuses' *Velázquez* 'The Spinners'

filial, -e, -aux, -ales [filjal, -o] **ADJ** filial

▫ **filiale NF** subsidiary (company); **filiale consolidée** consolidated subsidiary; **filiale de distribution** marketing subsidiary; **filiale de vente** sales subsidiary

filialement [filjalmɑ̃] **ADV** filially

filialisation [filjalizasjɔ̃] **NF** division into subsidiary companies

filialiser [3] [filjalize] **VT** to divide *or* to make into subsidiary companies

filiation [filjasjɔ̃] **NF 1** *(entre individus)* line of descent, filiation; *Jur* filiation; **f. adultérine** adulterous filiation; **en f. directe** in direct line; **un descendant en f. directe** a direct descendant; **f. incestueuse** incestuous filiation; **f. légitime** legitimate filiation; **f. naturelle** natural filiation **2** *Littéraire (famille)* descendants **3** *(entre des mots, des idées)* relationship; **des théories en f. directe avec ce texte** theories directly related to this text

filicales [filikal] **NFPL** *Bot* Filicales, Filices

filicinée [filisine] *Bot* **NF** fern, *Spéc* member of the Filicineae

▫ **filicinées NFPL** ferns, *Spéc* Filicales, Filicineae

filicophyte [filikɔfit] *Bot* **NM** fern, *Spéc* member of the Filicophyta

▫ **filicophytes NMPL** ferns, *Spéc* Filicophyta

filicopside [filikɔpsid] **NF** *Bot* fern

filière [filjεr] **NF 1** *(procédures)* procedures, channels; **passer par la f. administrative** to go through administrative channels; **passer par** *ou* **suivre la f.** *(pour obtenir quelque chose)* to go through official channels; *(comme employé)* to work one's way up

2 *(réseau → de trafiquants, de criminels)* network, connection; **ils ont démantelé la f. française** they smashed the French connection; **remonter une f.** to trace a network back to its ringleaders

3 *Scol & Univ* **la f. technique/scientifique** technical/scientific subjects; **nous avons suivi la même f. jusqu'à 16 ans** we did the same subjects (as each other) until the age of 16; **il est passé par la f. classique pour devenir éditeur** he had the usual background and training of an editor

4 *Tech (pour fileter une vis)* screw plate; **f. (à machine)** *(pour étirage)* draw, drawing plate; *(pour tréfilage, filage)* die; **travailler un métal à la f.** to draw a metal

5 *Entom* spinneret

6 *Tex* spinneret

7 *Naut* guardrail

8 *Ind* industry; **la f. bois/électronique** the wood/electronics industry

9 *Can Fam (meuble)* filing cabinet■; *(dossier)* file■

filiforme [filifɔrm] **ADJ 1** *(maigre)* lanky, spindly **2** *Méd (pouls)* thready **3** *Entom* filiform, thread-like

filigrane [filigran] **NM 1** *(d'un papier)* watermark **2** *(en joaillerie)* filigree; **broche en f.** filigree brooch

▫ **en filigrane ADV** *(implicitement)* between the lines; **lire en f.** to read between the lines; **le problème du racisme apparaissait en f. dans la discussion** the problem of racism was implicit in the discussion

filigraner [3] [filigrane] **VT 1** *(papier)* to watermark; **du papier filigrané** watermarked paper **2** *(en joaillerie)* to filigree

filin [filε̃] **NM** rope

filipendule [filipɑ̃dyl] **NF** *Bot* dropwort, filipendula

filasse [fijas] **NF** *Péj Vieilli* slattern, sluttish *or* slatternly girl

fille [fij] **NF 1** *(enfant)* girl; **c'est une belle/gentille f.** she's a good-looking/nice girl; **tu es une grande f. maintenant** you're a big girl now; **une grande f. comme toi, ça ne pleure plus!** big girls like you don't cry!; **c'est encore une petite f.** she's still a little girl; **école de filles** girls' school; **c'est un jeu de filles** that's a girl's game; *Fig* **jouer la f. de l'air** to escape, to get out

2 *(jeune fille)* girl; *(femme)* woman; **c'est une f. que j'ai connue il y a 20 ans** I met that woman 20 years ago; **une f. de la campagne** a country girl; *Vieilli* **rester f.** to remain single *or* unmarried; *Péj* **f. facile** slut; **jeune f.** girl, young woman, *Littéraire* maiden, maid, *Arch* damsel, *Scot* lass; **f. mère** unmarried mother

3 *(descendante)* daughter; **les filles Richard ont toutes fait des études de droit** all the Richard girls *or* daughters studied law; *Fig* **la paresse est la f. de l'oisiveté** laziness is the daughter of idleness; **une f. de bonne famille** a respectable girl; **tu es bien la f. de ton père!** you're just like your father!

4 *(en appellatif)* **ma f.** (my) girl; **ça, ma f., je t'avais prévenue!** don't say I didn't warn you, (my) girl!

5 *Vieilli (employée)* **f. d'auberge** serving girl; **f. de cuisine** kitchen maid; **f. de ferme** farm girl; **f. de salle** *(dans les hôpitaux)* ward orderly; *(dans un hôtel)* waitress; **f. de service** maidservant

6 *Vieilli (prostituée)* whore; **aller chez les filles** to go to a brothel, to go whoring; *Littéraire* **f. publique** *ou* **de joie** *ou* **des rues** *ou* **perdue** whore, lady of the night; **f. à soldats** camp follower; **f. à matelots** prostitute *(whose customers are primarily sailors)*

7 *Hist* **f. d'honneur** maid of honour

8 *Rel* **les filles du Carmel** the Carmelite nuns; **les filles de Port-Royal** the sisters *or* nuns of Port-Royal

'La Fille aux cheveux de lin' *Debussy* 'The Girl with the Flaxen Hair'

fille-mère [fijmεr] *(pl* **filles-mères)** **NF** *Vieilli Péj* unmarried mother

fillette [fijεt] **NF 1** *(enfant)* little girl **2** *(bouteille)* small bottle *(for wine)*

filleul, -e [fijœl] **NM,F** godchild, godson, *f* goddaughter; *Mil* **f. de guerre** = soldier taken care of by a woman during a war

film [film] **NM 1** *Cin (pellicule)* film; *(œuvre)* movie, *Br* film; **tourner un f.** to shoot a movie *or Br* film; *Fam Fig* **il n'a rien compris au f.** he hasn't taken anything in; *Fam Fig* **se faire un f.** to be living in a dream world; **f. en noir et blanc/en couleur** black and white/colour movie *or Br* film; **f. d'action** action movie *or Br* film; **f. d'actualités** newsreel, news film; **f. d'animation** animated film, cartoon; **f. d'anthologie** anthology movie *or Br* film; **f. d'archives** library film; **f. d'art et d'essai** arthouse movie *or Br* film; **f. d'auteur** film d'auteur; **f. d'aventures** adventure movie *or Br* film; **f. biographique** biopic; **f. burlesque** slapstick comedy; **f. de cape et d'épée** swashbuckler; **f. catastrophe** disaster movie *or Br* film; **f. à clef** film based on real characters *(whose identities are disguised)*; **f. de cow-boys** cowboy movie *or Br* film; **f. culte** cult movie *or Br* film; **f. documentaire** documentary (film); **f. dramatique** drama; **f. d'entreprise** corporate film, corporate video; **f. d'épouvante** horror movie *or Br* film; **f. d'espionnage** spy movie *or Br* film; **f. ethnographique** ethnographic movie *or Br* film; **f. à faible budget** low-budget movie *or Br* film; **f. fantastique** supernatural thriller; **f. de fiction** fictional movie *or Br* film; **f. de genre** genre movie *or Br* film; **f. à grand spectacle** epic movie *or Br* film; **f. à gros succès** blockbuster; **f. de guerre** war movie *or Br* film; **f. d'horreur** horror movie *or Br* film; **f. institutionnel** corporate video; **f. long-métrage** feature-length movie, *Br* feature film; **f. de montage** film montage, compilation movie *or Br* film; **f. muet** silent movie *or Br* film; **f. noir** film noir; **f. parlant** talkie, talking film; **f. plat** two-dimensional movie *or Br* film; **f. policier** detective movie *or Br* film; *Fam* **f. porno** blue movie, skin flick; **f. pornographique** pornographic film, blue movie; **f. de poursuite** chase movie *or Br* film; **f. publicitaire** *(à la télévision)* commercial; *(au cinéma)* cinema advertisement; **f. en relief** 3D movie *or Br* film; **f. de science-fiction** science fiction movie *or Br* film; **f. semi-documentaire** docudrama; **f. de série B** B-movie; **f. sonore** sound film; **f. à succès** box-office hit; **f. à suspense** thriller; **f. télévisé** television movie *or Br* film, TV movie *or Br* film; **f. en 3D** 3D movie *or Br* film; **f. vidéo** video film; **f. de voyage** travelogue; **f. (classé) X** adults-only movie, *Br* '18' film

2 *Phot* film; **f. inversible** reversal film; **films définitifs** *(dans l'édition)* final film

3 *(couche)* film; **un f. d'huile** a film of oil; **f. dentaire** (dental) plaque

4 *(pellicule)* **sous f. plastique** shrink-wrapped; **f. transparent** transparency; **recouvert d'un f. protecteur** covered with a protective film; **f. alimentaire** *Br* clingfilm, *Am* Saran® wrap

5 *(déroulement)* sequence; **le f. des événements** the sequence of events; **quand elle retraçait le f. de sa vie** when she looked back on her life

filmage [filmaʒ] **NM** *Cin* filming

filmer [3] [filme] **VT** *(scène, événement)* to film, to shoot; *(personnage)* to film; **il a fait f. toute la**

scène sans le dire he got somebody to film the whole thing without telling anyone

filmique [filmik] **ADJ** cinematic

filmogène [filmɔʒɛn] **ADJ** *Tech* film-forming

filmographie [filmɔgrafi] **NF** filmography

filmologie [filmɔlɔʒi] **NF** cinema *or Br* film studies

filmothèque [filmɔtɛk] **NF** microfilm collection

filoche [filɔʃ] **NF** *Fam* shadowing, tailing

filocher [3] [filɔʃe] *Fam* **VT** *(suivre)* **f. qn** to tail sb
VI *(aller vite)* to skedaddle, *Br* to scarper

filoguidé, -e [filɔgide] **ADJ** *Mil* wire-guided

filon [filɔ̃] **NM 1** *Géol* seam, vein; *Fig* **ils ont déjà exploité ce f.** they have already exploited that gold mine
2 *Fam (locutions)* **il a trouvé le f. pour gagner de l'argent** *(moyen)* he found an easy way to make money▪; **trouver le f.** *(situation lucrative)* to strike it rich, *Am* to find the right connection; **j'ai enfin trouvé le f.** I've found a cushy number at last, *Am* I'm on the gravy train at last; **c'est un bon f.** it's a gold mine *or* a money-spinner; **j'ai un bon f. pour avoir des vidéos gratuites** I know where I can get free videos easily▪

filonien, -enne [filɔnjɛ̃, -ɛn] **ADJ 1** *Mines* seam *(avant n)* **2** *Géol* veined

filoselle [filɔzɛl] **NF** *Vieilli Tex* filoselle, filosella

filou [filu] **NM 1** *(voleur)* crook, rogue **2** *(ton affectueux)* rascal, scamp; **oh, le f., il a caché mon livre!** the little rascal's hidden my book!

filoutage [filutaʒ] **NM** *Fam* swindling

filouter [3] [filute] **VT** *Fam* **1** *(dérober)* to pinch, to swipe **2** *(escroquer)* to cheat▪, to swindle

filouterie [filutri] **NF** *Jur* fraud, swindle

fils [fis] **NM 1** *(enfant)* son, boy; **viens là, mon f.** come here my son *or* boy; *Fam* **tous les f. Fouillat ont mal tourné** all the Fouillat boys *or* sons went off the straight and narrow; **le f. de la maison** the son of the house; *Fam* **un f. à papa** a daddy's boy; **il est bien le f. de son père!** he's just like his father!; **un f. de famille** a wealthy young man; *Vulg* **f. de pute** son of a bitch; *Bible* **le f. prodigue** the prodigal son; **f. spirituel** spiritual son
2 *Com* **Brunet & F.** Brunet & Son *or* Sons; **je voudrais parler à M. Picard f.** I'd like to talk to Mr Picard junior
3 *Littéraire (descendant)* descendant; *(natif)* son; **la patrie reconnaissante à ses f. sacrifiés** *(sur monument aux morts)* lest we forget; **un f. du terroir** a son of the land
4 *Rel* **le F. de l'homme** *ou* **de Dieu** the son of man *or* of God; **mon f.** my son
5 *(locution)* **être f. de ses œuvres** to be a self-made man

'Le Fils ingrat' *Greuze* 'The Ungrateful Son'

filtrable [filtrabl] **ADJ** filterable, filtrable

filtrage [filtraʒ] **NM 1** *(d'un liquide)* filtering; *Chim* filtration **2** *(de l'information, de personnes)* screening **3** *Opt & Phot* filtering; **f. des images** image filtering

filtrant, -e [filtrɑ̃, -ɑ̃t] **ADJ** *(matériau, dispositif)* filtering *(avant n)*; *(verre)* filter *(avant n)*; *Méd* filterable, filtrable; **lunettes à verres filtrants** glasses with filter lenses; **une crème filtrante** a sunscreen

filtrat [filtra] **NM** *Chim* filtrate

filtration [filtrasjɔ̃] **NF** filtration, filtering

filtre [filtr] **ADJ** *(papier, cigarette, café)* filter *(avant n)*
NM filter; **f. à air** air filter; *Rad & TV* **f. antiparasites** interference filter *or* suppressor; *Ordinat* **f. antireflet** glare screen; **f. audio** audio filter; **f. à brouillard** *(pour une caméra)* fog filter; **f. à café** coffee filter; **f. à carburant** fuel filter; **f. au charbon** carbon filter; **f. à combustible** fuel filter; **f. correcteur** corrective filter; *Phot* **f. couleur** *ou* **de couleur** *ou* **coloré** colour filter; *Ordinat* **f. écran** screen filter; **f. à essence** petrol filter; *Ordinat* **f. d'exportation** export filter; **f. à huile** oil filter; *Ordinat* **f. d'importation** import filter; *TV & Cin* **f. pour objectif de caméra** camera lens filter; **f. à particules** dust filter; *Cin & TV* **f. polarisant** polarizing filter; **f. à pollen** pollen filter; *Rad* **f. séparateur** crossover; **f. solaire** sunscreen

filtre-presse [filtrəprɛs] *(pl* **filtres-presses)** **NM** filter press

filtrer [3] [filtre] **VT 1** *(liquide, air, lumière)* to filter **2** *(visiteurs, informations)* to screen
VI 1 *(liquide)* to seep, to filter (**à travers** through); *(lumière, bruit)* to filter (**à travers** through) **2** *(nouvelles)* to filter through; *(par accident)* to leak out; **ils n'ont rien laissé f. de ses déclarations** they have said nothing about his/her statement

FIN[1] [fɛ̃]

> end **1–4, 6, 7** ▪ death **3** ▪ purpose **4**

NF 1 *(terme → d'une période, d'un mandat)* end; *(→ d'une journée, d'un match)* end, close; *(→ d'une course)* end, finish; *(→ d'un film, d'un roman)* end, ending; *(→ d'un contrat, d'un bail)* expiry, expiration; **la f. de l'année/de sa vie/d'un concert** the end of the year/of his life/of a concert; **la f. de la journée** the end of the day; **à la f. de la journée** at the end of the day; **jusqu'à la f. des temps** *ou* **des siècles** until the end of time; **par une f. d'après-midi de juin** late on a June afternoon; **f. mai/2006** (at the) end of May/2006; **on se reverra f. mars** *ou* **à la f. de mars** we'll meet again at the end of March; **se battre/rester jusqu'à la f.** to fight/to stay to the very end; **mener qch à bonne f.** to carry sth off (successfully), to bring sth to a successful conclusion, to deal successfully with sth; **mettre f. à qch** to put an end to sth; **mettre f. à ses jours** to put an end to one's life, to take one's own life; **prendre f.** to come to an end; **tirer** *ou* **toucher à sa f.** to come to an end, to draw to a close; **nos vacances touchent à leur f.** our holidays are coming to an end *or* will soon be over; **le contrat touche à sa f.** the contract will expire soon; **f. de citation** end of quotation; **f. de semaine** end of the week; *(week-end)* weekend; **la f. du mois** the end of the month; *Com* **f. de mois** monthly statement; **de f. de mois** end-of-month; **assurer ses fins de mois** to make sure one has enough money at the end of the month; **avoir des fins de mois difficiles** to be always short of money at the end of the month, to find it hard to make ends meet (at the end of the month); **faire une f.** to settle down, to get married; **on n'en voit pas la f.** there doesn't seem to be any end to it; **tout ce travail, je n'en vois pas la f.!** I have so much work, there doesn't seem to be any end to it!; **ça y est, j'en vois la f.!** at last, I can see the light at the end of the tunnel!; **f.** *(d'un film)* The End
2 *(disparition)* end; **la f. de la civilisation inca** the end *or* death of Inca civilization; **la f. du monde** the end of the world; **ce n'est quand même pas la f. du monde!** it's not the end of the world, is it!; *Fam Hum* **c'est la f. de tout** *ou* **des haricots!** our goose is cooked!
3 *(mort)* death, end; **avoir une f. tragique/lente** to die a tragic/slow death; **connaître une f. prématurée** to come to *or* to meet an untimely end; **avoir une belle f.** to have a fine end; **il a eu une f. affreuse** he had a terrible end *or* death; **la f. approche** the end is near; **on sent bien que la f. n'est pas loin** you can tell the end is not far off *or* that it won't be long now; **vers la f., il n'était plus le même** he wasn't the same towards the end; **le lave-vaisselle est sur sa f.** the dishwasher is on its last legs
4 *(objectif)* end, purpose; **à cette f.** to this end, for this purpose, with that aim in mind; **à quelle f.?** for what purpose?, to what end?, with what end in view?; **à seule f. de faire** with the sole aim of doing, (simply) for the sake of doing, purely in order to do; *Jur* **aux fins de débauche** for immoral purposes; **aux fins de faire qch** with a view to doing sth; **arriver** *ou* **parvenir à ses fins** to achieve one's aim; **à des fins personnelles** for personal *or* private use; **à des fins politiques/religieuses** to political/religious ends; **f. en soi** end in itself; *Prov* **la f. justifie les moyens, qui veut la f. veut les moyens** the end justifies the means
5 *Jur* **f. de non-recevoir** demurrer; *Fig* **opposer une f. de non-recevoir à qn** to turn down sb's request bluntly; **renvoyé des fins de la plainte** discharged, acquitted
6 *Com* **f. courant** at the end of the current month; **payable f. courant/prochain** payable at the end of this/next month; **f. de série** *(d'articles)* discontinued line
7 *Compta* **f. d'exercice** year end, end of the financial year
8 *Ordinat* **f. de ligne** line end; **f. de page** page-break; **f. de page obligatoire** hard page break; **f. de paragraphe** paragraph break; **f. de session** logoff; **f. de session enregistrée à...** logoff timed at...

❑ **à la fin ADV 1** *(finalement)* in the end, eventually
2 *Fam (ton irrité)* **mais à la f., où est-il?** where on earth is it?; **tu es énervant à la f.!** you're beginning to get on my nerves!; **tu es stupide à la f.** you really are very stupid; **tu m'ennuies à la f.!** you're really annoying me!

❑ **à la fin de PRÉP** at the end *or* close of; **le glossaire est à la f. du livre** the glossary is at the back of the book

❑ **à toutes fins utiles ADV 1** *(pour information)* **je vous signale à toutes fins utiles que...** for your information, let me point out that...
2 *(le cas échéant)* just in case; **dans la boîte à gants, j'avais mis à toutes fins utiles une carte de France** I had put a map of France in the glove compartment, just in case

❑ **en fin de PRÉP en f. de soirée/match** towards the end of the evening/match; **en f. d'année** at the end of the year; **il a faibli en f. de trimestre** his work fell off towards the end of the term; **être en f. de liste** to be *or* to come at the end of the list; *Fig* **être en f. de course** *(athlète, président)* to be at the end of the road; *(vis)* to be screwed fully home; *(piston)* to have reached the end of its stroke; **être en f. de droits** to come to the end of one's entitlement *(to an allowance)*

❑ **en fin de compte ADV** *(après tout)* in the end, after all; *(tout bien considéré)* all things considered, taking everything into account; *(pour conclure)* finally, to conclude

❑ **fin de race ADJ** degenerate

❑ **fin de siècle ADJ** decadent, fin de siècle

❑ **sans fin ADJ 1** *(interminable)* endless, interminable, never-ending **2** *Tech* endless
ADV endlessly, interminably

'Fin de partie' *Beckett* 'Endgame'

'La Fin de Chéri' *Colette* 'The Last of Chéri'

FIN[2], -E [fɛ̃, fin]

> **ADJ** fine **1** ▪ delicate **2, 4** ▪ sharp **3, 6** ▪ high-quality **4** ▪ subtle **5**
> **ADV** finely **1** ▪ sharply **1**

ADJ 1 *(mince → sable, pinceau, aiguille, pointe, cheveu, fil)* fine; *(→ étoffe)* fine, thin; *(→ écriture)* fine, small; *(→ doigt, jambe, taille, main)* slim, slender; *(→ papier, tranche)* thin; *(→ collant, bas)* sheer; **pluie fine** drizzle; **haricots verts fins** dwarf beans
2 *(délicat → visage, traits)* delicate
3 *(aiguisé → pointe)* sharp
4 *(de qualité → aliments, produit)* high-quality, top-quality; *(→ mets, repas)* delicate, exquisite, refined; *(→ dentelle, lingerie)* delicate, fine; *(→ or, pierre, vin)* fine
5 *(subtil → observation, description)* subtle, clever; *(→ personne)* perceptive, subtle; *(→ esprit)* sharp, keen, shrewd; *(→ plaisanterie)* witty; **ce n'était pas très f. de ta part** it wasn't very smart *or* clever of you; **bien f. qui le prendra** it would take a smart man to catch him; **elle n'est pas très fine** she's not very bright; *Ironique* **c'est f.!** very clever!; **tu as l'air f. avec ce chapeau!** you look *Br* a right wally *or Am* a total jerk in that hat!
6 *(sensible → ouïe, vue)* sharp, keen, acute; *(→ odorat)* discriminating, sensitive; **avoir le nez f.** to have a keen sense of smell; *Fig* **elle a le nez f.** she's sharp
7 *Can (gentil)* nice, kind, sweet(-natured); **avoir l'air f.** *(beau)* to be good-looking

8 *(avant le nom) (extrême)* **dans le** *ou* **au f. fond du placard** at the very back of the closet; **au f. fond de la campagne** in the depths of the countryside, *Péj* in the middle of nowhere; **au f. fond de la Sibérie** in deepest Siberia; **le f. mot de l'histoire** the truth of the matter; **on ne connaîtra jamais le f. mot de l'histoire** we'll never know what really happened *or* the real story

9 *(avant le nom) (excellent)* **un f. connaisseur** a (great) connoisseur; **un f. connaisseur en vins** an expert on *or* a (great) connoisseur of wines; **une fine cuisinière** a gourmet cook; **un f. gourmet** a gourmet; **c'est une fine mouche** he's/she's a sharp customer; **un f. stratège** a fine *or* an expert strategist; **un f. tireur** a crack shot; **une fine lame** a fine swordsman, *f* swordswoman; **la fine équipe!** what a team!

NM 1 le f. du f. the ultimate, the nec plus ultra

2 jouer au (plus) f. to have a battle of wits; **ne joue pas au plus f. avec moi** don't try to outwit *or* to outsmart me

NM,F *Can Fam Ironique* **beau f./belle fine!** you fool!; **tu n'aurais pas dû mettre ton nez dans cette affaire, espèce de beau f.!** you should never have got mixed up in that business, you fool!

ADV 1 *(finement → moulu)* fine, finely; *(→ taillé)* sharp, sharply; **des crayons taillés f.** sharp-pointed pencils; **c'est écrit trop f.** it's written too small; **haché f.** *(herbes)* finely chopped

2 *(tout à fait)* **être f. prêt** to be ready; **nous sommes f. prêts** we're all set, we're ready; **être f. saoul** to be blind drunk

❑ **fine bouche NF 1** *(gourmet)* **c'est une fine bouche** he's/she's a gourmet

2 *(locution)* **tu ne vas pas faire la fine bouche!** don't be so choosy!

❑ **fine gueule NF** *Fam* gourmet■

---

finage [finaʒ] **NM** *Hist* **1** *(circonscription)* administrative area *(of a parish or village)* **2** *(en Bourgogne et en Franche-Comté)* cultivated land

final, -e, -als *ou* **-aux, -ales** [final, -o] **ADJ 1** *(qui termine)* final, end *(avant n)* **2** *Ling & Phil* final **3** *(règlement, solde)* final

NM *Mus & (en danse)* finale

❑ **finale NM** *Mus & (en danse)* finale

NF 1 *Ling (syllabe)* final syllable; *(voyelle)* final vowel **2** *Sport* final; **la finale de la coupe** the cup final; **aller/être en finale** to go *or* to get through to/to be in the finals

❑ **au final ADV** *Fam* in the end

final cut [fajnɔlkœt] **NM** *Cin* final cut

finalement [finalmɑ̃] **ADV 1** *(à la fin)* finally, eventually, in the end **2** *(tout compte fait)* after all, when all is said and done

finalisation [finalizasjɔ̃] **NF** finalization

finaliser [3] [finalize] **VT** to finalize

finalisme [finalism] **NM** *Phil* finalism

finaliste [finalist] **ADJ 1** *Sport* **l'équipe f.** the team of finalists; **candidat f.** *(dans un concours)* finalist **2** *Phil* finalistic

NMF *Phil, Sport & (dans un concours)* finalist

finalité [finalite] **NF 1** *(but)* aim, purpose, end **2** *Phil* finality **3** *Biol* adaptation

finançable [finɑ̃sabl] **ADJ** that can be financed *or* funded

finance [finɑ̃s] **NF** *(profession)* **la f., le monde de la f.** (the world of) finance; **entrer dans la f.** to enter the world of finance; **la haute f.** *(milieu)* high finance; *(personnes)* the financiers, the bankers; **f. d'entreprise** corporate finance; **f. internationale** global finance

❑ **finances NFPL 1** *Pol* **les Finances** *Br* ≃ the Exchequer, *Am* ≃ the Treasury Department; **finances publiques** public funds **2** *Fam (argent)* finances; **les finances de la société vont mal** the company's finances are in a bad state; **ça dépendra de mes finances** it will depend on whether I can afford it or not; **mes finances sont à zéro** my finances have hit rock bottom

financement [finɑ̃smɑ̃] **NM** financing *(UNCOUNT)*, finance; *(surtout d'un mécène)* (financial) backing; **le f. du projet sera assuré par la compagnie** the company will finance *or* fund the project; **f. à court terme** short-term financing; **f. de départ** start-up capital; **f. par emprunt** debt financing; **f. par endettement** debt financing; **f. d'entreprise** corporate financing; **f. initial** start-up capital; **f. à long terme** long-term financing; **f. à moyen terme** medium-term financing; **f. à taux fixe** fixed-rate financing

financement-relais [finɑ̃smɑ̃rəlɛ] *(pl* **financements-relais)** **NM** *Fin* bridge financing

financer [16] [finɑ̃se] **VT** *(journal, projet)* to finance, to back (financially), to put up the finance for; *(sujet: mécène)* to back, to put up the money for; **l'opération a été entièrement financée par emprunt** the transaction was hundred percent financed through borrowing; **BP financera le projet à 50 pour cent** BP will put up half of the funding for the project

USAGE ABSOLU *Fam* **une fois de plus, ce sont ses parents qui vont f.** once again, his/her parents will fork out

financier, -ère [finɑ̃sje, -ɛr] **ADJ** *(crise, politique)* financial; **problèmes financiers** *(d'un État)* financial problems; *(d'une personne)* money problems

NM 1 *Fin* financier; **f. d'entreprise** corporate finance manager **2** *Culin* financier *(rectangular sponge finger made with almonds)*

❑ **financière NF** *Culin* sauce financière, financière sauce *(made with sweetbreads, mushrooms etc)*

❑ **à la financière ADJ** *Culin* à la financière, with financière sauce

financièrement [finɑ̃sjɛrmɑ̃] **ADV** financially

finasser [3] [finase] **VI** *Fam* to scheme

finasserie [finasri] **NF** *Fam* scheming

finasseur, -euse [finasœr, -øz], **finassier, -ère** [finasje, -ɛr] **NM,F** *Fam Vieilli* trickster

finaud, -e [fino, -od] **ADJ** cunning, shrewd, wily

NM,F 1 *(malin)* **c'est un (petit) f.** he's a crafty *or* sly one **2** *Ordinat* hacker

finauderie [finodri] **NF** shrewdness, wiliness

fine [fin] **ADJ** *voir* **fin**[2]

NF 1 *(eau-de-vie)* ≃ brandy; **f. champagne** = variety of Cognac; **une f. à l'eau** = a brandy and soda **2** *(huître)* **fines de claire** = specially fattened greenish oysters

finement [finmɑ̃] **ADV 1** *(de façon fine → hacher, dessiner)* finely **2** *(subtilement)* subtly, with finesse

fines [fin] **NFPL** *Mines* fines

finesse [finɛs] **NF 1** *(délicatesse → d'un mets, d'un vin)* delicacy; *(→ d'une étoffe)* delicacy, fineness; *(→ du sable)* fineness; **un portrait d'une grande f. d'exécution** a very delicately painted portrait; **la f. du trait dans les dessins de Dürer** the delicate lines of *or* the finesse of Dürer's drawings; **jouer Chopin avec beaucoup de f.** to give a sensitive interpretation of Chopin

2 *(perspicacité)* flair, finesse, shrewdness

3 *(subtilité)* subtlety *(UNCOUNT)*; **une remarque pleine de f.** a very subtle remark; **f. d'esprit** shrewdness; **f. de goût** refined taste

4 *(acuité)* sharpness, keenness; **la f. avec laquelle il distingue les demi-tons** his good ear for the semi-tones; **f. d'ouïe/de l'odorat** keenness *or* acuteness of hearing/of smell

5 *(minceur → de la taille)* slenderness, slimness; *(→ des cheveux, d'une poudre)* fineness; *(→ du papier, d'un fil)* thinness; **la f. de ses traits** the fineness of his/her features; **des draps d'une grande f.** sheets of the finest cloth

6 *(d'une pointe, d'une image optique)* sharpness; *(d'une lame)* keenness

7 *Aviat* aerodynamic efficiency

8 *Naut* sharpness

❑ **finesses NFPL** *(subtilités)* subtleties, niceties; **les finesses du français** the subtleties of the French language; **les finesses de la diplomatie** diplomatic niceties; **il connaît toutes les finesses du métier** he knows all the tricks of the trade

finette [finɛt] **NF** *Tex* brushed cotton

fini, -e [fini] **ADJ 1** *(perdu)* finished; **c'est un homme f.** he's finished; **en tant que banquier, je suis f.** my banking career is finished

2 *Péj (en intensif)* complete, utter; **un imbécile f.** a complete *or* an utter fool; **un voleur f.** an out-and-out thief

3 *Math & Phil* finite

4 *(accompli, terminé)* finished; **c'est f. (tout cela), tout est f.** that's all over (and done with); **c'est f. entre nous** we're finished, it's all over between us; **(c'est) f. de rire** the fun's over

5 *(ouvrage → parfait)* well finished; **cette robe est mal finie** this dress is badly finished

NM 1 *(perfection)* finish

2 *Phil* **le f.** that which is finite

finir [32] [finir] **VT 1** *(achever → tâche, ouvrage)* to finish (off); *(→ guerre, liaison, vie)* to end; *(→ études)* to complete; *(→ période, séjour)* to finish, to complete; **f. un tableau/une sculpture** to finish (off) a picture/sculpture; **il a fini ses jours à Cannes** he ended his days in Cannes; **il a fini la soirée au poste** he wound up in a police cell (at the end of the evening); **finissez la vaisselle d'abord** first finish the dishes, get the dishes finished first; **mon travail est fini maintenant** my work's done now; **finis ta phrase** finish what you were saying; *Littéraire* **finissez mes craintes** put an end to my fears; **f. de faire qch** to finish doing sth; **il avait fini de travailler** he had finished working *or* work; **finis de faire tes devoirs** finish your homework; **j'ai presque fini de relire ma copie** I've almost finished rereading my paper

2 *(plat, boisson)* to finish (off *or* up); **qui a fini l'eau de Cologne?** who's used up all *or* finished off the Cologne?; *Fam* **finis ton assiette** eat up *or* finish off what's on your plate; **il a fini le gâteau/la bouteille** he finished off the cake/the bottle; **je finissais toujours les vêtements de mes aînés** I was always dressed in my elder brothers' hand-me-downs; **je vais f. ces chaussures** I'll wear these shoes out

3 *(en réprimande)* **vous n'avez pas fini de vous plaindre?** haven't you done enough moaning?, can't you stop moaning?; *Fam* **c'est pas bientôt fini, ce bazar?** is this racket going to stop soon?; **c'est fini, ce boucan?** stop that racket, will you!

USAGE ABSOLU 1 *(achever)* **laisse-moi seulement f.** just let me finish; **je n'ai pas fini!** I haven't finished (what I have to say)!; **tu n'as pas bientôt fini!** will you stop it!; **tu as fini, oui, ou c'est une claque!** stop it now or you'll get a smack!; **vous n'avez pas encore fini tous les deux!** are you two still at it!; **c'en est bien fini de mes rêves** that's the end of all my dreams; **finissons-en** let's get it over with; **elle a voulu en f.** *(se suicider)* she tried to end it all; **il faut en f., cette situation ne peut plus durer** it can't go on, we must do something to put an end to this state of affairs

2 en f. avec qn/qch to be *or* to have done with sb/sth; **il faut en f. avec ces idées reçues** we must break with *or* shake off these preconceived ideas; **il veut en f. avec la vie** he's had enough of life; **nous devons en f. avec la crise économique** we must end the slump; **j'en aurai bientôt fini avec lui** I'll be done with him soon

VI 1 *(arriver à son terme)* to finish, to end; **f. en pointe** to end in a point; **la route finit au pont** the road stops at the bridge; **la réunion a fini dans les hurlements** the meeting ended in uproar; **ça a fini par des embrassades** it ended in a lot of hugging and kissing; **le bal a fini sur une farandole** the ball ended with a farandole; **la leçon finit à quatre heures** the lesson finishes at four; **l'école finit en juin** school ends in June; **quand est-ce que ça finit?** when does it end *or* finish?; **quand finit ton stage?** when's the end of your placement?; **comment est-ce que ça a fini?** how did it end?; **à quelle heure tu finis?** what time do you finish?; **son bail finit à Pâques** his/her lease expires *or* lapses at Easter; **je finirai sur ce vers de Villon** let me end with this line from Villon; **pour f.** in the end, finally; **et pour f., voici le dessert** and to finish (with), here's dessert; **elle a marchandé mais pour f. elle n'a pas acheté le tapis** she haggled over the price of the carpet but in the end she didn't buy it; **f. par faire qch** to end up (by) doing sth; **il a fini par renoncer/réussir** he finally gave up/succeeded; **elle finira par t'oublier/s'y habituer** she'll forget you/get used to it in the end *or* eventually; **la justice finit par triompher** justice triumphs in the end *or* in the long run *or* eventually; **ça finit par coûter cher** it costs a lot of money in the end; **tu finis par m'agacer** you're beginning to annoy me; **tu vas f. par le faire pleurer** you'll end up (by) making him cry; *Fam* **et maintenant, fini de se croiser les bras!** and now let's see some action!; **en janvier, fini de rigoler, tu te remets au travail** come January

fin–fin

there'll be no more messing around, you're going to have to get down to some work; **son discours n'en finit pas** his/her speech is never-ending; **cette journée n'en finit pas** there's no end to this day; **cela n'en finit pas** there's no end to it; **il n'en finit plus de se préparer dans la salle de bain** he's taking ages in the bathroom getting ready; **si on tient compte des exceptions, on ne va plus en f.!** we'll never see the end of this if we take exceptions into account!; **cette route n'en finit pas** this road seems to go on (and on) forever; *Hum* **un grand adolescent qui n'en finit pas** a big kid; **à n'en plus f.** endless, never-ending, interminable; **elle a des jambes à n'en plus f.** she has incredibly long legs; **des plaintes à n'en plus f.** endless *or* never-ending complaints; *Fam* **f. en queue de poisson** to fizzle out

2 *(avoir telle issue)* **elle a fini juge** she ended up a judge; **il a mal fini** *(délinquant)* he came to a bad end; **une histoire qui finit bien/mal** a story with a happy/sad ending; **un roman qui finit bien/mal** a novel with a happy/sad ending; **l'histoire ne finit pas là** that's not the end of the story; **comment tout cela va-t-il f.?** where *or* how will it all end?; **ça va mal f.** no good will come of it, it will all end in disaster; *Prov* **tout est bien qui finit bien** all's well that ends well

3 *(mourir)* to die; **f. à l'hôpital** to end one's days *or* to die in hospital; **f. sous un autobus** to end up under a bus

finish [finiʃ] NM INV *Sport* finish; **jouer un match/une partie au f.** to play a match/a game to the finish; *Fam Fig* **je l'ai eu au f.** I got him in the end

finissage [finisaʒ] NM *Tech* finishing

finissant, -e [finisɑ̃, -ɑ̃t] ADJ **1** *Littéraire* finishing; *(société)* in decline; **au jour f.** at dusk **2** *Can (élève)* in his/her last year at school

NM,F *Can* final-year student

finisseur, -euse [finisœr, -øz] NM,F *(gén) & Sport* finisher; **on peut lui faire confiance pour le marathon, c'est un f.!** we can count on him in the marathon, he's a finisher!

NM *(dans les travaux publics)* finisher

finissure [finisyr] NF casing-in

Finistère [finistɛr] NM **le F.** Finistère

finition [finisjɔ̃] NF **1** *(détail)* **la f. de l'anorak est très bien faite** the anorak's nicely finished; **les finitions** the finishing touches; *Couture* **je déteste faire les finitions** I hate the sewing up **2** *(perfectionnement)* finishing off *(UNCOUNT)*; **les travaux de f. prendront plusieurs jours** it will take several days to finish off the work

finitisme [finitism] NM *Math* finitism

finitude [finityd] NF finiteness

finlandais, -e [fɛ̃lɑ̃dɛ, -ɛz] ADJ Finnish

❑ **Finlandais, -e** NM,F Finn

Finlande [fɛ̃lɑ̃d] NF **la F.** Finland; **vivre en F.** to live in Finland; **aller en F.** to go to Finland

finlandisation [fɛ̃lɑ̃dizasjɔ̃] NF Finlandization

finnois, -e [finwa, -az] ADJ Finnish

❑ **Finnois, -e** NM,F Finn

NM *(langue)* Finnish

finno-ougrien, -enne [finougrijɛ̃, -ɛn] (*mpl* **finno-ougriens,** *fpl* **finno-ougriennes**) *Ling* ADJ Finno-Ugric, Finno-Ugrian

NM Finno-Ugric, Finno-Ugrian

FINUL, Finul [finyl] NF (*abrév* **Forces intérimaires des Nations unies au Liban**) UNIFIL

fiole [fjɔl] NF **1** *(bouteille)* phial, vial **2** *très Fam (tête)* nut, *Br* bonce; *(visage)* mug; **se payer la f. de qn** to make a fool of sb

fion [fjɔ̃] NM **1** *Vulg (postérieur) Br* arse, *Am* ass; **se casser le f. (pour faire qch)** to bust a gut *or Am* one's ass (doing sth) **2** *Vulg (anus) Br* arsehole, *Am* asshole **3** *Vulg (chance)* luck▪; **avoir du f.** to be lucky▪ *or Br* jammy; **ne pas avoir de f.** to be unlucky▪ **4** *très Fam* **donner le coup de f. à** to put the finishing touch to **5** *(pique)* taunt; **lancer des fions à qn** to taunt sb

Fionie [fjɔni] NF *Géog* Fyn

fioritures [fjɔrityr] NFPL **1** *(décorations)* embellishments; *(d'une écriture)* flourishes; **une lettre pleine de f.** a flowery letter **2** *Mus* fioritura

❑ **sans fioritures** ADJ plain, unadorned

fiotte [fjɔt] NF *Vulg* queer, *Br* poof, *Am* fag

fioul [fjul] NM fuel oil, heating oil

FIP [fip] NF (*abrév* **France Inter Paris**) = Paris radio station broadcasting continuous music and traffic information

firewall [fajœrwol] NM *Ordinat* firewall

FireWire® [fajœrwajœr] NM INV *Ordinat* FireWire®

firmament [firmamɑ̃] NM *Littéraire* firmament, heavens; *Fig* **au f. de sa gloire** at the zenith *or* height of his fame

firman [firmɑ̃] NM *Hist* firman

firme [firm] NF firm, company; **f. multinationale** multinational company

firmware [fœrmwɛr] NM *Ordinat* firmware

FIS [fis] NM (*abrév* **Front islamique du salut**) **le F.** the FIS, the Islamic Salvation Front

fisc [fisk] NM *Br* ≃ Inland Revenue, *Am* ≃ Internal Revenue, IRS; **avoir des ennuis avec le f.** to have problems with the *Br* taxman *or Am* IRS; **les employés du f.** tax officials; **frauder le f.** to evade tax

fiscal, -e, -aux, -ales [fiskal, -o] ADJ *Fin* fiscal, tax *(avant n)*; **dans un but f.** for tax purposes; **pression** *ou* **charge fiscale** tax burden; **l'administration fiscale** the tax authorities; **conseiller f.** tax adviser; **abri f.** tax shelter

fiscalement [fiskalmɑ̃] ADV fiscally, from the point of view of taxation; **dans quel pays êtes-vous f. domicilié?** in which country do you pay tax?

fiscalisation [fiskalizasjɔ̃] NF *Fin* taxing, taxation

fiscaliser [3] [fiskalize] VT *Fin* to tax

fiscaliste [fiskalist] NMF *Fin* tax specialist, tax consultant

fiscalité [fiskalite] NF *Fin (système, législation)* tax system; **f. écologique** green taxation; **f. des entreprises** corporate taxation; **f. directe** direct taxation; **f. indirecte** indirect taxation; **f. locale** local taxation; **optimiser la f. de qch** to improve the tax efficiency of sth, to make sth more tax efficient

fish-eye [fiʃaj] (*pl* **fish-eyes**) NM fish-eye lens

fissa [fisa] ADV *Fam* **faire f.** to get a move on, to get one's skates on

fissible [fisibl], **fissile** [fisil] ADJ *Minér & Nucl* fissile

fission [fisjɔ̃] NF fission; **f. nucléaire** nuclear fission; **f. de l'atome** atomic fission, splitting of the atom

fissionner [3] [fisjɔne] VT to split

fissuration [fisyrasjɔ̃] NF cracking, *Spéc* fissuring

fissure [fisyr] NF **1** *(fente)* crack, *Spéc* fissure; **les fissures du mur** the cracks in the wall **2** *Méd* fissure **3** *Fig (défaut)* fissure, crack, chink; **il y a des fissures dans son raisonnement** his/her argument doesn't hold water

fissurer [3] [fisyre] VT *(mur, paroi)* to crack, *Spéc* to fissure

▸**se fissurer** VPR to crack

fiston [fistɔ̃] NM *Fam* sonny; **allez f.!** now then, young fellow *or* my lad *or* sonny!

fistot [fisto] NM *Fam Arg mil* first-year naval cadet▪

fistulaire [fistylɛr] ADJ *Méd* fistular, fistulate

fistule [fistyl] NF *Méd* fistula

fistuleux, -euse [fistylø, -øz] ADJ *Méd* fistulous

fistuline [fistylin] NF *Bot* fistulina, beefsteak fungus

fit *etc voir* **faire**

fitness [fitnɛs] NM fitness; **salle de f.** fitness room; **centre de f.** gym; **cours de f.** fitness class

FIV [ɛfive] NF (*abrév* **fécondation in vitro**) IVF

FIVETE, fivete [fivɛt] NF (*abrév* **fécondation in vitro et transfert d'embryon**) GIFT; **une F.** a test-tube baby

fixage [fiksaʒ] NM **1** *Phot* fixing; **bain de f.** fixing bath **2** *Bourse* fixing

fixateur, -trice [fiksatœr, -tris] ADJ fixative; **bactéries fixatrices d'azote** nitrogen-fixing bacteria

NM **1** *Phot* fixer **2** *(pour les cheveux)* setting lotion **3** *Biol* fixative **4** *Beaux-Arts* fixative

fixatif, -ive [fiksatif, -iv] ADJ fixative *(avant n)*

NM fixative

fixation [fiksasjɔ̃] NF **1** *(accrochage)* fixing, fastening; **quel est le système de f. des étagères?** how are the shelves fixed to the wall?; **f. par bride** *ou* **par collier** clamping

2 *(établissement → d'un prix, d'un salaire)* setting; *(→ d'un rendez-vous)* making, fixing; **être chargé de la f. de l'impôt** to be responsible for setting tax levels; **f. de prix** *ou* **des prix** price fixing, pricing; **f. concertée des prix** common pricing, common price fixing; **f. du prix unitaire** unit pricing; **f. d'un prix d'appel** loss-leader pricing; **f. d'un prix de soumission** sealed-bid pricing; **f. de l'impôt** tax assessment; **f. du prix en fonction du coût** cost-plus pricing; **f. du prix en fonction du taux de rentabilité souhaité** target-return pricing; **f. du prix optimal** optimal pricing

3 *Chim & Biol* fixation

4 *Beaux-Arts & Phot* fixing

5 *Psy* fixation, obsession; **la f. au père/à la mère** father/mother fixation; **faire une f. sur qch** to be obsessed with *or* by sth; *Fam* **il fait une f. sur les examens** he's obsessed by exams

6 *(de ski)* binding

7 *Tech* attachment, anchor

fixative [fiksativ] *voir* **fixatif**

fixatrice [fiksatris] *voir* **fixateur**

fixe [fiks] ADJ **1** *(invariable → repère)* fixed; **prendre un médicament à heure f.** to take (a) medicine at a set time; **prendre ses repas à heure f.** to eat at fixed *or* set times; *Ordinat* **virgule f.** fixed point

2 *Mil* **(à vos rangs,) f.!** attention!

3 *(immobile → œil, regard)* fixed, staring

4 *(durable → emploi)* permanent, steady

5 *Écon, Fin & Jur (droit)* fixed duty *(avant n)*; *(prix)* set; *(revenu, salaire)* fixed; **à prix f.** at fixed prices; **assignation à jour f.** fixed summons

6 *Tél (ligne)* fixed; *(poste)* landline *(avant n)*

NM **1** *(salaire)* (fixed *or* regular) salary; **toucher un f.** to be on a fixed salary

2 *Tél (poste fixe)* fixed phone, landline phone

3 *Fam (de drogue)* fix *(of drug)*

fixé, -e [fikse] ADJ **1** *(date, heure, jour)* agreed, appointed; **à la date fixée** on the agreed *or* appointed day **2 être f. sur qch** *(décidé)* to have made up one's mind about sth; **je ne suis pas f.** I haven't made my mind up yet; **la voilà enfin fixée sur ton compte** she's finally been set straight about you; **te voilà f.!** now you know!

fixement [fiksəmɑ̃] ADV fixedly; **elle le regarde f.** she's staring at him

fixer [3] [fikse] VT **1** *(accrocher → gén)* to fix; *(→ par des épingles, des punaises)* to pin (on); *(→ avec de l'adhésif)* to tape (on); *(→ avec un fermoir, un nœud)* to fasten; **f. un tableau au mur** to put up a painting on a wall; **f. un badge sur un vêtement** *(avec une épingle)* to pin a badge on (to) a garment; *(en le cousant)* to sew a badge on (to) a garment; **les vis qui fixent la serrure** the screws that hold the lock

2 *(en regardant)* to stare; **f. qn du regard** to stare at sb; **f. les yeux** *ou* **son regard sur qn/qch** to stare at sb/sth; *(scruter)* to look hard *or* intently at sb/sth; **tout le monde avait les yeux fixés sur elle** everybody was staring at her; **il la fixe droit dans les yeux** he's staring straight into her eyes

3 *(concentrer)* **f. son attention/esprit sur qch** to fix one's attention/mind on sth; **f. son choix sur qch** to decide *or* to settle on sth; **il a enfin fixé son choix sur une montre** he finally decided on a watch; **f. qch dans sa mémoire** to implant sth in one's memory

4 *(définir → date, lieu)* to fix, to set, to decide on; *(→ conditions)* to fix, to lay down; *(→ prix, impôt)* to fix, to set; *(→ délai)* to set; **f. le prix des matières premières** to fix a price for *or* the price of raw materials; **f. le prix de** to price; **f. le prix d'une réparation** to cost a repair job; **f. un rendez-vous à qn** to arrange a meeting with sb; **vous fixerez votre heure** you decide on the time that suits you (best)

5 *(informer)* **f. qn sur qch** to put sb in the picture about sth; **cette conversation m'a fixé sur son compte** that conversation set me straight about him/her

6 *(établir)* **f. son domicile à Paris** to take up (permanent) residence *or* to settle (down) in Paris

7 *(stabiliser)* to fix; **f. la langue/l'orthographe** to standardize the language/the spelling

8 *Beaux-Arts, Chim & Phot* to fix

9 *Bourse* **f. un cours** to make a price

▸**se fixer** VPR **1** *(s'accrocher)* to be fixed *or* fastened; **ça se fixe facilement sur le ski** it

fastens easily onto the ski; **ça se fixe avec une courroie** you attach it with a strap, you strap it on

2 *(s'installer)* to settle; **elle s'est fixée en Irlande** she settled (permanently) in Ireland

3 *(se stabiliser)* to settle down; **il s'est fixé après son mariage** he settled down after he got married; **l'orthographe du mot se fixe au XVIIIème siècle** the spelling of the word became fixed in the 18th century

4 *très Fam Arg drogue (s'injecter de la drogue)* to shoot up

5 *(se donner)* **il s'est fixé un objectif dans la vie, réussir** he has (set himself) one aim in life, to succeed; **fixons-nous trois tâches** let's set ourselves three tasks

6 se f. sur *(choisir)* to decide on; **il s'est fixé sur une cravate bleue** he decided on a blue tie; **elle s'est fixée sur cette idée** she's got the idea in her head (and nothing will shift it)

fixette [fiksɛt] NF *Fam* **faire une f. sur qn/qch** to be obsessed with sb/sth ▪, *Br* to have sb/sth on the brain

fixeur [fiksœr] NM *Bourse* **f. de prix** price maker

fixing [fiksiŋ] NM *Bourse* fixing *(of the price of gold)*

fixisme [fiksism] NM creationism

fixiste [fiksist] ADJ creationistic
   NM,F creationist

fixité [fiksite] NF *(d'une disposition)* fixity, unchangeableness; *(du regard)* fixedness, steadiness

fjeld [fjɛld] NM *Géog* fjeld

fjord [fjɔrd] NM *Géog* fjord

FL *(abrév écrite* **florin***)* Fl, F, G

fl. *(abrév écrite* **fleuve***)* R

fla [fla] NM flam

flabellé, -e [flabɛle], **flabelliforme** [flabɛlifɔrm] ADJ *Biol* flabellate, flabelliform

flac [flak] ONOMAT splash!; **faire f.** to splash, to go splash

flaccidité [flaksidite] NF flaccidity, flaccidness

flache [flaʃ] NF **1** *(creux)* pothole **2** *(flaque)* puddle **3** *(sur un arbre)* blaze

flacherie [flaʃri] NF *(maladie des vers à soie)* flacherie

flacheux, -euse [flaʃø, -øz] ADJ *(planche)* waney; *(bois)* dull-edged

flacon [flakɔ̃] NM *(de parfum, de solvant)* (small) bottle; *(de spiritueux, de laboratoire)* flask; **f. à parfum** perfume bottle; **f. à liqueur** liqueur decanter

---

Allusion

Qu'importe le flacon pourvu qu'on ait l'ivresse

This is a fragment of a couplet, from Alfred de Musset's *Il ne faut jurer de rien* of 1836, and its meaning is "What does the mistress matter? It's being in love that counts! What does the bottle matter? It's getting drunk that counts." In other words, it is the contents that matter, not the packaging. **Qu'importe le flacon** has become a very common expression in modern French when one wants to stress what is really most essential in a given situation.

---

flaconnage [flakɔnaʒ] NM **1** *(fabrication)* bottle making **2** *(flacons)* set of flasks, (small) bottles

flacon-pompe [flakɔ̃pɔ̃p] *(pl* **flacons-pompes***)* NM spray bottle

fla-fla [flafla] *(pl* **fla-flas***) Fam* NM *Vieilli* **faire du f.** to make a huge fuss
   ▫ **sans fla-flas** ADV simply ▪, without fuss ▪

flagada [flagada] ADJ INV *Fam* pooped, washed-out

flagellaire [flaʒɛlɛr] ADJ *Biol* flagellar

flagellant [flaʒɛlɑ̃] NM *Hist* flagellant

flagellateur, -trice [flaʒɛlatœr, -tris] NM,F scourger

flagellation [flaʒɛlasjɔ̃] NF flogging, whipping; *(sur soi-même)* flagellation

flagellatrice [flaʒɛlatris] *voir* **flagellateur**

flagelle [flaʒɛl] NM *Biol* flagellum

flagellé, -e [flaʒɛle] *Biol* ADJ flagellate, flagellated
   NM flagellate

flageller [flaʒɛle] VT **1** *(battre)* to whip **2** *Littéraire (dénoncer)* to flagellate
   ▶ **se flageller** VPR to scourge oneself

flageolant, -e [flaʒɔlɑ̃, -ɑ̃t] ADJ *(jambe)* shaking, trembling, wobbly; **j'ai les jambes flageolantes** my legs are shaking *or* trembling

flageoler [3] [flaʒɔle] VI *(jambes)* to shake, to tremble, to wobble; **il flageolait sur ses jambes** *(de peur)* he was shaking *or* quaking at the knees; *(de fatigue)* he was dead on his feet, his legs were trembling *or* shaking

flageolet¹ [flaʒɔlɛ] NM *Mus* flageolet

flageolet² [flaʒɔlɛ] NM *Bot & Culin* flageolet (bean)

flagorner [3] [flagɔrne] VT *Littéraire* to fawn on

flagornerie [flagɔrnəri] NF *Littéraire* fawning, flattering, toadying

flagorneur, -euse [flagɔrnœr, -øz] NM,F *Littéraire* flatterer, toady

flagrance [flagrãs] NF *Jur* flagrancy

flagrant, -e [flagrã, -ãt] ADJ **1** *(évident)* blatant, obvious, flagrant; **de façon flagrante** blatantly; **il apparaît de façon flagrante que...** it is blatantly obvious that...; **avec une mauvaise volonté flagrante** with obvious reluctance; **elle ne voulait pas le voir, c'était f.** she didn't want to see him, that much was obvious

2 *Jur* **f. délit** flagrante delicto; **en f. délit** in flagrante delicto; *Fig* in the act, red-handed; **pris en f. délit** caught in the act, caught red-handed; **pris en f. délit d'adultère** caught in flagrante; **pris en f. délit de mensonge** caught lying; **surpris en f. délit de chapardage** caught stealing

flair [flɛr] NM **1** *(odorat)* scent, (sense of) smell, nose; **avoir du f.** to have a good sense of smell **2** *Fig (perspicacité)* intuition, sixth sense; **avoir du f.** to have intuition *or* a sixth sense

flairer [4] [flɛre] VT **1** *(humer → sujet: chien)* to scent, to sniff at; *(→ sujet: personne)* to smell; **le chien flairait sa pâtée/le gibier** the dog sniffed (at) its food/scented the game **2** *(deviner)* to sense; **f. le danger** to have a sense of impending danger; **f. le mensonge** to detect a lie; **il a flairé qu'il y avait une astuce** he could see there was a trick; **f. le vent** to see which way *or* how the wind blows **3** *Belg Fam Péj (empester)* to stink *or* reek of

flaireur, -euse [flɛrœr, -øz] ADJ *(nez)* keen (-scented)
   NM,F smeller, scenter

flamand, -e [flamã, -ãd] ADJ Flemish
   NM *(langue)* Flemish
   ▫ **Flamand, -e** NM,F Fleming; **les Flamands** the Flemish

flamant [flamã] NM flamingo; **f. rose** (pink) flamingo

flambage [flãbaʒ] NM **1** *Culin (d'une omelette, d'une crêpe)* flambéing; *(d'un poulet)* singeing **2** *(d'un instrument)* sterilization **3** *Tex* singeing **4** *Tech (déformation)* buckling

flambant, -e [flãbã, -ãt] ADJ *Littéraire (bois, fagot)* burning, blazing; *Mines (houille)* bituminous
   ADV **1** *(locution)* **f. neuf** brand new **2** *Can Fam (complètement)* completely ▪, totally ▪, **f. nu** stark naked ▪, starkers
   NM *Mines* bituminous coal

flambard, flambart [flãbar] NM *Fam Vieilli* braggart ▪, **faire le f.** to show off ▪

flambe [flãb] NF **1** *Bot* **f. d'eau** (yellow) water flag, yellow iris **2** *(feu)* blaze, fire **3** *(épée)* kris

flambé, -e [flãbe] ADJ **1** *Culin* flambéed; **des crêpes flambées** flambéed pancakes **2** *Fam (personne)* ruined ▪, **il est f.** *(ruiné)* he's all washed up; *(dans une situation sans issue)* he's had it, his goose is cooked
   ▫ **flambée** NF **1** *(feu)* blaze, fire; **faire une petite flambée** to light a small fire; **faire une bonne flambée** to get a roaring fire going **2** *Fig (poussée)* **une flambée de colère** an outburst of anger; **une flambée de violence** an outbreak or a sudden wave of violence; **la flambée des prix** the leap in prices

flambeau, -x [flãbo] NM **1** *(torche)* torch; *(chandelier)* candlestick; *Fig* torch; **à la lumière** *ou* **à la lueur des flambeaux** by torchlight; **marche** *ou* **retraite aux flambeaux** torchlit procession; *Fig* **passer** *ou* **transmettre le f.** to pass on the torch; *Fig* **reprendre le f.** to take up the torch; *Fig* **se passer** *ou* **se transmettre le f. (de génération en génération)** to pass the tradition down (from generation to generation)

2 *Littéraire (lumière)* **le f. du rationalisme/de la foi** the light of rationalism/faith

flambement [flãbmã] NM *Tech* buckling

flamber [3] [flãbe] VT **1** *Culin (lapin, volaille)* to singe; *(omelette, crêpe)* to flambé **2** *(stériliser)* **f. une aiguille** to sterilize a needle (in a flame) **3** *Fam (dilapider)* to blow, to throw away; **il a de l'argent à f.** he has money to burn
   VI **1** *(se consumer)* to burn (brightly); **f. comme une allumette** to burn like matchwood **2** *(briller)* to flash **3** *Fam (augmenter)* to rocket; **les prix ont flambé** prices rocketed **4** *Fam (jouer)* to gamble (for big stakes) ▪ **5** *Tech (se déformer)* to buckle

flamberge [flãbɛrʒ] NF flamberge, flamberg; *Littéraire ou Hum* **mettre f. au vent** to draw one's sword

flambeur, -euse [flãbœr, -øz] NM,F *Fam* big-time gambler

flamboie *etc voir* **flamboyer**

flamboiement [flãbwamã] NM *(d'un incendie)* blaze; *(du regard)* flashing

flamboyance [flãbwajãs] NF *Littéraire* flamboyance

flamboyant, -e [flãbwajã, -ãt] ADJ **1** *(brillant → foyer)* blazing, flaming; *(→ regard)* flashing **2** *Archit* flamboyant; **le gothique f.** high Gothic style
   NM *Bot* flamboyant

flamboyer [13] [flãbwaje] VI **1** *(être en flammes)* to blaze *or* to flare (up); **dans l'âtre qui flamboie** in the blazing hearth **2** *(briller → œil, regard)* to flash; **f. de colère** *(yeux)* to blaze *or* flash with anger

flamenco, -ca [flamɛnko, -ka] ADJ flamenco
   NM flamenco

flamiche [flamiʃ] NF leek pie *or* quiche

flamine [flamin] NM *Antiq* flamen

flamingant, -e [flamɛ̃gã, -ãt] ADJ Flemish-speaking
   NM,F **1** *Ling* Flemish speaker **2** *Pol* Flemish nationalist

flamingantisme [flamɛ̃gãtism] NM *Pol* Flemish nationalism

flamme [flam] NF **1** *(feu)* flame; **faire une f.** to flare *or* to blaze up; **cracher** *ou* **jeter** *ou* **lancer des flammes** *(dragon)* to breathe fire; *(canon)* to flare; **passer qch à la f.** to singe sth; **la f. du tombeau du Soldat inconnu** the Eternal Flame

2 *Littéraire (éclat)* fire; **dans la f. de son regard** in his/her fiery eyes; **la f. de son intelligence** the brilliance of his/her intellect

3 *(ferveur)* fire; **discours plein de f.** impassioned speech

4 *Arch & Littéraire (amour)* ardour; **déclarer sa f. à une femme** to declare one's love for a woman

5 *(fanion → d'un navire de guerre)* pennant, pennon; *(→ de la cavalerie)* pennon

6 *(sur une lettre)* slogan

7 *Élec* **(ampoule) f.** candle bulb
   ▫ **flammes** NFPL **les flammes** fire; **périr dans les flammes** to burn to death, to be burnt alive; *Fig* **les flammes éternelles** *ou* **de l'enfer** hellfire
   ▫ **à la flamme de** PRÉP by the light of; **lire une inscription à la f. d'un briquet** to read an inscription by the light of a cigarette lighter
   ▫ **avec flamme** ADV passionately
   ▫ **en flammes** ADJ burning, blazing; **un château en flammes** a blazing castle; **mettre le pays en flammes** to set the country ablaze ADV **l'avion est tombé en flammes** the plane went down in flames; *Fam* **descendre un auteur/une pièce en flammes** to pan an author/a play

flammé, -e [flame] ADJ *(céramique)* flambé

flammèche [flamɛʃ] NF *(flying)* spark

flammerole [flamrɔl] NF will-o'-the-wisp

flan [flã] NM **1** *Culin* custard tart; **f. à la vanille** vanilla(-flavoured) custard tart **2** *Typ* flong **3** *Métal (d'une pièce, d'un disque)* flan **4** *Fam (locutions)* **c'est du f.!** it's a load of bunkum *or* bunk!; **en rester comme deux ronds de f.** to be flabbergasted; **y aller au f.** to try it on, to bluff; **j'ai dit ça au f.** I said it just for the sake of it *or* just for something to say
   ▫ **à la flan** ADJ *Fam* **des arguments à la f.** *Br* waffle, *Am* hooey

flanc [flã] NM **1** *Anat (entre les côtes et le bassin)* flank; *(côté du corps)* side **2** *Zool* flank, side;

battre des flancs (cheval) to heave, to pant 3 (côté → d'un navire) side; (→ d'une colline) side, slope; le navire se présentait de f. the ship was broadside on 4 Mil flank; par le f. droit! by the right!; attaquer de f. to attack on the flank 5 Littéraire (ventre maternel) womb 6 Hér flank 7 (locution) tirer au f. to be bone-idle

❑ à flanc de PRÉP à f. de coteau on the hillside

❑ sur le flanc ADJ être sur le f. (épuisé) to be exhausted; (malade) to be laid up ADV (sur le côté) on one's side; il s'est retourné et s'est mis sur le f. he rolled over on to his side; mettre qn sur le f. to exhaust sb; ça m'a mis sur le f. it really took it out of me

flanc-garde [flɑ̃gard] (pl flancs-gardes) NF Mil flank guard, flanker

flancher [3] [flɑ̃ʃe] VI 1 (faiblir) to give out, to fail; j'ai la mémoire qui flanche my memory's giving out on or failing me; son cœur a flanché his/her heart gave out on him/her 2 (manquer de courage) to waver; ce n'est pas le moment de f. this is no time for weakness

flanchet [flɑ̃ʃɛ] NM flank

flanc-mou [flɑ̃mu] (pl flancs-mous) NMF Can Fam lazybones, shirker

Flandre [flɑ̃dr] NF (la) F., (les) Flandres Flanders; (la) F.-Occidentale Western Flanders; (la) F.-Orientale Eastern Flanders; en F. ou Flandres in Flanders

flandricisme [flɑ̃drisism] NM loan word from Flemish

flandrin [flɑ̃drɛ̃] NM Arch un grand f. a lanky fellow

flâne [flan] NF Vieilli Littéraire 1 (oisiveté) idleness 2 (promenade) stroll

flanelle [flanɛl] NF Tex flannel; f. (de) coton flannelette; pantalon de f. grise grey flannels

flâner [3] [flane] VI 1 (se promener) to stroll or to amble (along) 2 Péj (perdre son temps) to hang about, to lounge around, to idle; on n'a pas le temps de f. avant les examens there's no time for hanging about before the exams

flânerie [flanri] NF stroll, wander

flâneur, -euse [flanœr, -øz] NM,F 1 (promeneur) stroller 2 (oisif) idler, loafer

flannelette [flanlɛt] NF Can flannelette; drap de f. flannelette sheet

flanquement [flɑ̃kmɑ̃] NM Mil flanking manoeuvre

flanquer[1] [3] [flɑ̃ke] VT 1 (être à côté de) to flank; deux bougeoirs flanquaient le miroir a candleholder stood on either side of the mirror

2 Fam Péj (accompagner) elle est arrivée, flanquée de ses deux frères she came in with her two brothers at her side■ or flanked by her two brothers

3 Mil to flank

flanquer[2] [3] [flɑ̃ke] Fam VT 1 (lancer) to fling, to chuck; il lui a flanqué son verre d'eau à la figure he threw or chucked his glass of water in his/her face; elle m'a flanqué son parapluie dans les mollets she jabbed me in the shins with her umbrella; f. qn dehors ou à la porte (l'expulser) to kick sb out; (le licencier) Br to sack or Am to can sb; il a flanqué les bouquins par terre (volontairement) he chucked the books on the floor; (par maladresse) he knocked the books onto the floor■; Fig j'ai tellement voulu réussir et toi tu vas tout f. par terre I wanted to succeed so badly and now you're going to mess it all up (for me)

2 (donner) f. un P-V à qn to give sb a ticket; f. une gifle à qn to smack or to slap sb■; f. un coup de poing à qn to punch sb■; f. un coup de pied à qn to kick sb■; f. la trouille ou la frousse ou les jetons à qn to scare the pants off sb; ça m'a flanqué le cafard it really got me down

►se flanquer VPR 1 (tomber) se f. par terre to take a tumble; se f. la figure ou la gueule par terre to fall flat on one's face

2 (se jeter) se f. par la fenêtre to throw oneself out of the window; elle s'est flanquée dans le ravin she plunged into the ravine

3 (se donner) ils se sont flanqué des coups they exchanged blows■, they had a punch-up; je me suis flanqué une bonne indigestion I gave myself a real dose of indigestion

flapi, -e [flapi] ADJ Fam dead beat, bushed, Br knackered

flaque [flak] NF puddle; une large f. d'huile a pool of oil

flaser [3] [flaze] Can Vieilli VT (broder) to embroider

VI Fam to make small talk■, Am to shoot the breeze

flash [flaʃ] (pl flashs ou flashes) NM 1 Phot (éclair) flash; (ampoule) flash bulb; prendre une photo au f. to take a picture using a flash; Fam avoir un f. to have a brainwave; f. asservi slave flash unit; f. électronique electronic flash; f. TTL TTL flash 2 Rad & TV f. (d'informations) newsflash; f. spécial (special) newsflash 3 Cin & TV (plan) flash; f. publicitaire commercial 4 très Fam Arg drogue rush (after taking drugs)

flashage [flaʃaʒ] NM Typ imagesetting

flash-back [flaʃbak] NM INV flashback; elle utilise beaucoup les f. dans ses romans there are a lot of flashbacks in her novels

flasher [3] [flaʃe] VI 1 (clignoter) to flash (on and off) 2 Fam (craquer) elle me fait f., cette nana! that girl really turns me on! 3 Fam Arg drogue to get a rush

❑ flasher sur VT IND Fam to go crazy over, to fall for in a big way; elle a vraiment flashé sur cette robe she fell in love with or just went crazy over this dress

flasheuse [flaʃøz] NF Typ imagesetter

flasque[1] [flask] ADJ 1 (muscle, peau) flaccid, flabby 2 (veule) spineless; c'est un être f. he has no backbone

flasque[2] [flask] NM 1 Tech (d'une machine) flange, end-plate; Aut hubcap, wheel disc; (d'une roue) flange 2 Mil cheek (of gun carriage)

flasque[3] [flask] NF (pour whisky) (hip) flask; (à mercure) flask

flat [flat] NM 1 Belg & Can (appartement) (small) Br flat or Am apartment 2 Can Joual (crevaison) flat tyre■, flat

flatter [3] [flate] VT 1 (encenser) to flatter; f. qn sur son bel esprit to flatter sb on his/her wit; n'essaie pas de me f.! flattery will get you nowhere!; tu me flattes, je ne pense pas avoir si bien réussi you flatter me, I don't think I did that well; f. bassement qn to fawn upon sb

2 (embellir) to be flattering to; cette coupe ne la flatte pas that style doesn't flatter her; peintre qui flatte ses modèles painter who flatters his sitters; ce portrait la flatte plutôt this portrait of her is rather flattering

3 (toucher) to touch, to flatter; il sera flatté de ou par tes remarques he will be very touched by what you said; je suis flatté de votre proposition I am flattered by your proposal; j'ai été flatté qu'on me confie cette responsabilité I was very touched or flattered to be entrusted with this responsibility

4 Littéraire (encourager) to encourage; f. les caprices de qn to pander to sb's whims; f. la vanité de qn to indulge sb's vanity

5 Littéraire (tromper) to delude; f. qn de l'espoir de qch to hold out false hopes of sth to sb

6 (caresser → animal) to stroke; (→ cheval) to pat

7 (être agréable à → vue, odorat) to delight, to be pleasing to; un vin qui flatte le palais a (wonderfully) smooth wine

►se flatter VPR to flatter oneself; sans vouloir me f., je crois que j'ai raison though I say it myself, I think I'm right; elle se flatte de savoir recevoir she prides herself on knowing how to entertain or on her skills as a hostess; je me flatte que personne d'autre n'y ait pensé I pride myself on being the only person to have thought of it, I take pride in the fact that nobody else thought of it; elle se flattait de réussir she flattered herself or felt sure that she would succeed

flatterie [flatri] NF 1 (adulation) flattery 2 (propos) flattering remark; flatteries sweet talk; ce ne sont que de viles flatteries it's just base flattery

flatteur, -euse [flatœr, -øz] ADJ (remarque, portrait, couleur) flattering; (personne) full of flattery; peu f. unflattering; il a fait un tableau f. de la situation he painted a rosy picture of the situation; sans vouloir être f. à ton égard, c'est vraiment du beau travail without wishing to flatter you, you did a really nice job

NM,F flatterer

flatteusement [flatøzmɑ̃] ADV flatteringly

flatulence [flatylɑ̃s] NF flatulence; avoir des flatulences to suffer from flatulence

flatulent, -e [flatylɑ̃, -ɑ̃t] ADJ flatulent

flatuosité [flatɥozite] NF Méd flatus

flavescent, -e [flavɛsɑ̃, -ɑ̃t] ADJ Littéraire flavescent

flaveur [flavœr] NF flavour

flavine [flavin] NF Chim flavin

Flavius [flavjys] NPR F. Josèphe Flavius Josephus

flavone [flavɔn] NF Chim flavone

FLB [ɛfɛlbe] NM (abrév Front de libération de la Bretagne) = Breton liberation front

ADJ INV & ADV Com (abrév franco long du bord) FAS

FLE [flə] NM (abrév français langue étrangère) French as a foreign language

fléau, -x [fleo] NM 1 (désastre) curse, plague; Hist Attila, le f. de Dieu Attila the Hun, the scourge of God 2 Fam (cause de désagréments) pain; sa fille est un véritable f. his/her daughter is a pain or pest; ces baladeurs, quel f.! personal stereos are a real pain! 3 (d'une balance) beam 4 Agr flail 5 Mil f. d'armes flail

fléchage [fleʃaʒ] NM signposting (with arrows); le f. de l'itinéraire bis n'est pas terminé they haven't finished marking out or signposting the alternative route yet

flèche[1] [flɛʃ] NF 1 (projectile) arrow, Littéraire shaft; (d'un canon) trail; partir comme une f. to shoot off; Fig faire f. de tout bois to use all available means, to use all means at one's disposal

2 (en balistique) f. d'une trajectoire highest point of a trajectory

3 (signe) arrow; suivez la f. follow the arrow; f. lumineuse (pour projection) pointer

4 Archit (d'un arc) broach; (d'un clocher) spire

5 (d'une balance) pointer

6 Tech (d'une grue) boom

7 (d'un câble) sag, dip

8 Ordinat pointer, arrow; f. de défilement scroll arrow; f. vers la droite right arrow; f. vers la gauche left arrow; f. vers le bas down arrow; f. vers le haut up arrow; flèches verticales up and down arrow keys

9 Sport (au ski) = giant slalom proficiency test

10 Aviat sweep-back; avion à f. variable sweep-wing aircraft

11 Bot f. d'eau arrowhead

12 Géog f. littorale spit

13 (timon) shaft

14 cheval de f. leader, leading horse

15 Littéraire (raillerie) broadside, jibe; ses flèches ne m'atteignent pas I pay no heed to his/her jibes; la f. du Parthe the Parthian or parting shot

16 Belg (dans un collant) run, Br ladder

❑ en flèche ADJ rising; des cinéastes en f. rising film-makers, film-makers on the way up ADV 1 (spectaculairement) monter ou grimper en f. to go straight up (like an arrow), to shoot up; Fig to shoot up; les tarifs montent en f. prices are rocketing; au début de sa carrière, il est monté en f. he shot up at the beginning of his career; partir en f. to go off like an arrow, to shoot off; Fig to shoot off 2 (atteler) bœufs/chevaux attelés en f. oxen/horses harnessed in tandem

flèche[2] [flɛʃ] NF (de lard) flitch

flèche[3] [flɛʃ] NM Fam j'ai pas un f. I'm totally broke or Br skint or strapped

fléché, -e [fleʃe] ADJ signposted; itinéraire f. arrowed or signposted route; suivez la déviation fléchée follow the detour signs

flécher [18] [fleʃe] VT to mark with arrows, to signpost

fléchette [fleʃɛt] NF dart; jouer aux fléchettes to play darts

fléchi, -e [fleʃi] ADJ Ling inflected

fléchir [32] [fleʃir] VT 1 (ployer) to bend, to flex; fléchissez l'avant-bras flex your forearm; f. le genou devant qn to bow the knee to sb

2 (apitoyer → juge, tribunal) to move to pity; se laisser f. to relent, to let oneself be swayed

VI 1 (se ployer) to bend; (jambes) to give way; (câble, poutre) to sag; elle sentait ses genoux f. sous elle she could feel her knees giving way

2 (baisser) to fall; (marché, devises) to weaken; (prix, cours, demande) to fall, to drop; le dollar a

de nouveau fléchi the dollar has fallen again; **le chômage fléchit** unemployment is falling

3 *(céder)* to weaken; **nous ne fléchirons pas devant la menace** we will not give in to threats; **leur père ne fléchissait jamais** their father was utterly inflexible

fléchissement [fleʃismɑ̃] **NM 1** *(flexion → d'une partie du corps)* flexing, bending; *(→ d'une poutre)* yielding, bending; *(→ d'un câble)* sagging **2** *(affaiblissement → des genoux)* sagging; *(→ de la nuque)* drooping **3** *(baisse)* fall; *(du marché, d'une devise)* weakening; *(des prix, des cours, de la demande)* fall, drop; **un f. de la production/de la natalité** a fall in production/in the birthrate **4** *(de la volonté)* failing

fléchisseur [fleʃisœr] *Anat* **ADJ M muscle f.** flexor
NM flexor

flegmatique [flɛgmatik] **ADJ** phlegmatic
NMF phlegmatic person

flegmatiquement [flɛgmatikmɑ̃] **ADV** phlegmatically

flegme [flɛgm] **NM 1** phlegm, composure; **le f. britannique** British phlegm; **perdre son f.** to lose one's composure **2** *Méd* phlegm

❑ **avec flegme ADV** coolly, phlegmatically

flegmon [flɛgmɔ̃] = **phlegmon**

flein [flɛ̃] **NM** punnet, chip-basket

flémingite [flemɛ̃ʒit] **NF** *Fam Hum* laziness■, lazy-itis; **il fait de la f. aiguë** he's suffering from acute laziness

flemmard, -e [flɛmar, -ard] *Fam* **ADJ** idle■, lazy■, workshy■
NM,F idler, loafer, lazy so-and-so

flemmarder [3] [flɛmarde] **VI** *Fam* to loaf about; **f. au lit** to laze in bed■

flemmardise [flɛmardiz] **NF** *Fam* idleness■, laziness■

flemme [flɛm] **NF** *Fam* laziness■; **j'ai vraiment la f. d'y aller** I just can't be bothered to go; **je me sens comme une grosse f. ce matin** I feel like loafing around this morning; **tirer sa f.** to be bone idle; **il tire une de ces flemmes aujourd'hui!** he's been loafing around all day!

fléole [fleɔl] = **phléole**

flet [flɛ] **NM** *Ich* flounder

flétan [fletɑ̃] **NM** *Ich* halibut

flétri, -e [fletri] **ADJ 1** *(plante, feuille)* withered **2** *Littéraire (peau)* wrinkled, withered; *(beauté)* faded; **un visage tout f.** a wizened face

flétrir[1] [32] [fletrir] **VT 1** *Bot* to wither, to wilt

2 *Littéraire (ôter l'éclat de → couleur)* to fade; *(→ teint, peau)* to wither; **les soucis ont flétri sa beauté** anxiety has destroyed his/her good looks, he/she looks careworn

3 *Littéraire (avilir → ambition, espoir)* to sully, to corrupt, to debase; **la vie a flétri en eux tout ce qu'il y avait d'innocence** life has robbed them of their innocence

▶ **se flétrir VPR 1** *Bot* to wither, to wilt

2 *Littéraire (peau)* to wither; *(couleur, beauté)* to fade

flétrir[2] [32] [fletrir] **VT 1** *Hist (criminel)* to brand

2 *Littéraire (condamner)* to condemn, to denounce; **f. l'injustice** to denounce injustice

3 *(la réputation de quelqu'un)* to blacken, to sully, to stain

flétrissure[1] [fletrisyr] **NF 1** *Bot* wilting **2** *Littéraire (altération → du teint, de la peau)* withering *(UNCOUNT)*

flétrissure[2] [fletrisyr] **NF** *Littéraire (déshonneur)* stain; **l'ignoble f. dont vous l'avez marquée** the foul stain you placed upon her honour

flette [flɛt] **NF** *Naut* **1** *(péniche)* shallop, barge **2** *(barque)* punt

fleur [flœr] **NF 1** *Bot* flower; *(d'un arbre)* blossom; **les fleurs du cerisier** the cherry blossom; **le langage des fleurs** the language of flowers; **fleurs des champs** wild flowers; **f. de lotus** lotus blossom; **f. d'oranger** *(fleur)* orange flower; *(essence)* orange flower water; **f. de la Passion** passion flower; **fraîche comme une f.** as fresh as a daisy; **jolie comme une f.** as pretty as a picture; **ni fleurs, ni couronnes** *(dans une annonce nécrologique)* no flowers by request

2 *Fig (le meilleur de)* **la f. de l'âge** the prime of life; **f. de farine** fine wheat flour; **la f. de la jeunesse** the full bloom of youth; **dans la première f. de la jeunesse** in the first flush *or* flower of youth; **c'est la fine f. de l'école** he's/she's the pride of his/her school; **la fine f. de la canaille** a prize swine

3 *Biol* **f. de vin/vinaigre** flower of wine/vinegar

4 *Hér* **f. de lis** *ou* **lys** fleur-de-lis

5 *Vieilli Chim* **f. d'arsenic** flowers of arsenic; **f. de soufre** flowers of sulphur

6 *Vieilli (virginité)* virginity; **perdre sa f.** to lose one's virtue

7 *Can (farine)* flour

8 *Fam (locutions)* **faire une f. à qn** to do sb an unexpected favour *or* a favour■; **arriver comme une f.** to turn up out of the blue; **faire qch comme une f.** to do sth almost without trying■; **c'est passé comme une f.** it was as easy as pie

❑ **fleurs NFPL 1** *Littérature* **fleurs de rhétorique** flowers of rhetoric, rhetorical flourishes; **sans fleurs de rhétorique** in plain language

2 *(louanges)* **couvrir qn de fleurs** to praise sb highly; *Fam* **s'envoyer** *ou* **se jeter des fleurs** *(mutuellement)* to sing one another's praises, to pat one another on the back; *(à soi-même)* to pat oneself on the back

❑ **à fleur de PRÉP** on the surface of; **à f. d'eau** just above the surface (of the water); **des yeux à f. de tête** prominent eyes; **une sensibilité à f. de peau** hypersensitivity; **avoir les nerfs à f. de peau** to be all on edge

❑ **à fleurs ADJ** *(papier, tapisserie, nappe)* floral, flowery; **tissu à fleurs** floral *or* flowery material; **une robe à fleurs** a floral *or* flowery dress, a dress with a flower motif

❑ **en fleur, en fleurs ADJ** *(rose, pivoine)* in flower *or* bloom, blooming; *(arbre, arbuste)* blossoming, in blossom

❑ **fleur bleue ADJ INV** sentimental, romantic; **un roman f. bleue** a sentimental novel; **il adore tout ce qui est f. bleue** he's an incurable romantic

---

'Les Fleurs du mal' *Baudelaire* 'The Flowers of Evil'

Allusion

Les jeunes filles en fleurs

This is a shortened version of the title of the second volume of Marcel Proust's *À la recherche du temps perdu, À l'ombre des jeunes filles en fleurs.* This volume deals with the narrator's adolescence, the girls in question being Albertine and Gilberte, who will later play important roles in his life. When the phrase is used allusively today, it refers to the attractiveness of young girls in the first bloom of youth, at the stage when they suddenly blossom into young women with an awareness of their budding sensuality.

fleurage [flœraʒ] **NM** *(sur un tissu, sur un tapis)* floral pattern

fleurdelisé, -e [flœrdəlize] **ADJ** decorated with fleurs-de-lis; *Hér* fleury, flory
NM *Can (drapeau du Québec)* flag of Quebec

fleurer [5] [flœre] **VT** *Littéraire* to smell of; **la chambre fleure le bois de pin** the bedroom smells of pinewood; *Fig* **son histoire fleure le scandale** his/her story smacks of scandal
VI f. bon to smell nice

fleuret [flœrɛ] **NM 1** *Escrime* foil; **à fleurets mouchetés** *(discussion, attaque)* = where the attacker holds back **2** *Mines* borer, drill (bit)

fleureter [3] [flœrte] **VI** *Vieilli* to whisper sweet nothings

fleurette [flœrɛt] **NF** small flower, floweret, floret

fleurettiste [flœrɛtist] **NMF** foilsman, *f* foilswoman

fleuri, -e [flœri] **ADJ 1** *(arbre, arbuste)* in bloom *or* blossom

2 *(orné de fleurs)* flowered, flowery; *(papier peint, tapis, vêtement)* floral; *(vaisselle)* flower-patterned; **une nappe fleurie** a flowery tablecloth; **un balcon f.** a balcony decorated with flowers; **Rouen, ville fleurie** *(sur panneau)* Rouen, town in bloom; **village f.** = village taking part in a flower competition; **avoir la boutonnière fleurie** to have a flower in one's buttonhole; *(décoré)* to wear a decoration; **l'empereur à la barbe fleurie** Charlemagne

3 *Littéraire (teint)* florid

4 *(conversation, style)* flowery, overornate

fleurir [32] [flœrir] **VI 1** *Bot (fleur)* to flower, to bloom; *(arbre, arbuste)* to flower, to blossom; **les arbres ont entièrement fleuri** the trees are in full bloom; *Fig Littéraire* **des visages butés où fleurissait un rare sourire** stubborn faces across which a smile would occasionally spread

2 *(apparaître)* to burgeon; **les antennes paraboliques qui fleurissent sur tous les toits** the satellite dishes mushrooming *or* burgeoning all over every roof

3 *(se développer → affaire, commerce)* to flourish, to thrive

VT to decorate with flowers; *(boutonnière)* to put a flower in; **les villageois ont fleuri leurs maisons** the villagers have decorated their houses with flowers; **f. une table** to decorate a table with flowers; **f. la tombe de qn** to put flowers on sb's grave; **f. qn** to pin a flower on sb's lapel

fleurissement [flœrismɑ̃] **NM** = decorating with flowers, particularly a public place

fleuriste [flœrist] **NMF 1** *(vendeur)* florist; **f. artificiel** dealer in artificial flowers **2** *(cultivateur)* flower grower

fleuron [flœrɔ̃] **NM 1** *(ornement → de reliure)* flower, fleuron; *Archit* finial; *Fig* **le (plus beau) f. de...** the jewel of...; **cette bouteille est le plus beau f. de ma cave** this is the finest bottle in my cellar; **on a volé le f. de sa collection d'émeraudes** the finest emerald in his/her collection has been stolen **2** *Bot* floret

fleuronné, -e [flœrɔne] **ADJ 1** *Bot* floreted **2** *(ornement)* ornamented with flower-work *or* with fleurons, flowered **3** *Archit* with finials

Fleury-Mérogis [flœrimerɔʒis] **NF** = town near Paris well-known for its prison

fleuve [flœv] **NM 1** *(rivière)* river *(flowing into the sea)*; **f. international** = river going across national borders; **f. côtier** coastal river; **le f. Jaune** the Yellow River; **le f. Zaïre** the (River) Zaïre

2 *(écoulement)* **un f. de boue** a river of mud, a mudslide; **un f. de larmes** a flood of tears

3 *(comme adj; avec ou sans trait d'union)* **une lettre f.** a very long letter; **roman-f.** saga; **discours-f.** lengthy speech

flexibiliser [1] [flɛksibilize] **VT** to make flexible

flexibilité [flɛksibilite] **NF 1** *(d'un matériau)* pliability; *(du corps)* flexibility, suppleness, litheness **2** *Psy* flexible *or* adaptable nature **3** *(d'un arrangement, d'un horaire)* flexibility, adaptability; *(d'un dispositif)* versatility; *(d'une entreprise, de la main-d'œuvre)* flexibility

flexible [flɛksibl] **ADJ 1** *(pliable)* pliable, flexible **2** *Psy* flexible, adaptable, amenable to change; *(accommodant)* accommodating **3** *(variable → arrangement, horaire)* flexible; *(→ dispositif)* versatile; **avoir des horaires flexibles** to have a flexible schedule

NM 1 *(tuyau)* flexible tube **2** *Tech* flexible shaft; *Aut* **f. de frein** brake hose

flexicurité [flɛksikyrite] **NF** flexicurity, = social model combining a flexible labour market with good job security and benefits

flexion [flɛksjɔ̃] **NF 1** *(d'un arc, d'un ressort)* bending *(UNCOUNT)*, flexion; *Tech* **effort de f.** bending stress **2** *(des membres)* flexing *(UNCOUNT)*; **f., extension!** bend, stretch!; *Gym* **f. du corps** trunk exercise **3** *Ling* inflection; **langue à flexions** inflected language; **f. nominale** noun inflection

flexionnel, -elle [flɛksjɔnɛl] **ADJ** *Ling (langue, langage)* inflected

flexographie [flɛksɔgrafi] **NF** *Typ* flexography

flexueux, -euse [flɛksɥø, -øz] **ADJ** *Littéraire* flexuous, winding

flexuosité [flɛksɥozite] **NF** *Littéraire* flexuosity

flexure [flɛksyr] **NF** *Géol* flexure, fold; **f. continentale** shelf edge

flibuste [flibyst] **NF la f.** *(piraterie)* freebooting; *(pirates)* freebooters

flibuster [3] [flibyste] **VI** to freeboot, to buccaneer
VT *Fam Vieilli* to pinch, to pilfer

flibustier [flibystje] **NM 1** *Hist* freebooter, buccaneer **2** *Fam & Arch (escroc)* cheat■, crook■

flic [flik] **NM** *Fam* cop, policeman■

flicage [flikaʒ] **NM** *Fam Péj (par la police)* heavy policing■; *Fig* **ils craignent le f. du courrier électronique par la direction** they are afraid that the management are checking their e-mails■

flicaille [flikaj] **NF** *très Fam Péj* **la f.** the pigs, the cops, *Br* the filth

flic flac [flikflak] **ONOMAT** splash splash, splish splosh; *(d'un fouet)* crack

flingot [flɛ̃go], **flingue** [flɛ̃g] **NM** *très Fam* shooter, *Am* piece

flinguer [3] [flɛ̃ge] *très Fam* **VT 1** *(tuer)* to blow away, to waste **2** *(abîmer)* to wreck, to bust, *Br* to knacker **3** *(critiquer sévèrement)* to shoot down, to savage

▸**se flinguer VPR** to blow one's brains out; **c'est à se f.!, il y a de quoi se f.!** it's enough to drive you to suicide!

flint [flint], **flint-glass** [flintglas] *(pl* **flint-glasses**) **NM** flint glass

flip [flip] **NM** *Fam* **1** *(déprime)* **être en plein f.** to be on a real downer; **c'est le f.!** what a downer! **2** *(après absorption de drogue)* depression■, downer *(as the after-effect of taking cocaine or amphetamines)*

flip-flap [flipflap] *(pl* **flips-flaps**) **NM** *Gym* back(-ward) flip

flipot [flipo] **NM** *Menuis* Dutchman, strengthening piece

flippant, -e [flipɑ̃, -ɑ̃t] **ADJ** *très Fam (déprimant)* depressing■; *(inquiétant)* worrying■; *(effrayant)* creepy; **c'était f.!** it was a real downer!

flipper[1] [flipœr] **NM** *(appareil)* pinball (machine); *(jeu)* pinball; **jouer au f.** to play pinball

flipper[2] [3] [flipe] **VI** *très Fam* **1** *(être déprimé)* to feel down; **lui raconte pas tes malheurs, tu vas le faire f.** don't go telling him your troubles, it'll only get him down

2 *(paniquer)* to flip, to freak out; **ça me fait f.** that freaks me out; **elle flippe à cause de son travail** she's cracking up under her workload

3 *(après absorption de drogue)* to come down *(as the after-effect of taking cocaine or amphetamines)*

fliquer [3] [flike] **VT** *Fam* to police heavily■; **fliqué** *(endroit)* overrun with cops; *Fig* **au bureau, on a vraiment l'impression d'être fliqués** in the office we really feel we're being watched like criminals■; *Fig* **il flique complètement sa femme** he watches his wife like a hawk

flirt [flœrt] **NM** *Vieilli* **1** *(relation)* (little) fling; **ce n'est qu'un petit f. entre eux** they are just having a fling **2** *(ami)* boyfriend; *(amie)* girlfriend; **un de ses anciens flirts** an old flame

flirter [3] [flœrte] **VI** *(badiner)* to flirt; **elle aime f.** she's a flirt, she loves flirting; **f. avec qn** to have a little fling with sb; *Fig* **f. avec qn/qch** to flirt with sb/sth; **f. avec le danger** to flirt with danger; **il a longtemps flirté avec le socialisme** he had a long flirtation with socialism

flirteur, -euse [flœrtœr, -øz] **ADJ** flirting

NM,F flirt

FLN [ɛfɛlɛn] **NM** *Hist (abrév* **Front de libération nationale**) = one of the main political parties in Algeria, established as a resistance movement in 1954 at the start of the war for independence

FLNC [ɛfɛlɛnse] **NM** *(abrév* **Front de libération nationale corse**) = Corsican liberation front

FLNKS [ɛfɛlɛnkaɛs] **NM** *(abrév* **Front de libération nationale kanak et socialiste**) = Kanak independence movement in New Caledonia

flo [flo] **NMF** *Can Fam* teenager■, teen

floc [flɔk] **ONOMAT** splash!

flocage [flɔkaʒ] **NM 1** *Tex* flocking **2** *Constr* insulation, lining

floche [flɔʃ] **ADJ** flossy; **fil/soie f.** floss thread/silk

NF *Belg (gland)* tassel

flock-book [flɔkbuk] *(pl* **flock-books**) **NM** *Agr* flock book

flocon [flɔkɔ̃] **NM** *(parcelle → de laine, de coton)* flock; *(→ de neige)* snowflake, flake; **flocons d'avoine** oatmeal *(UNCOUNT)*; **flocons de maïs** cornflakes; **purée en flocons** instant mashed potato

floconner [3] [flɔkɔne] **VI** to go fluffy

floconneux, -euse [flɔkɔnø, -øz] **ADJ** fluffy

floculant [flɔkylɑ̃] **NM** *Chim* flocculant, flocculating agent

floculation [flɔkylasjɔ̃] **NF** *Chim* flocculation, flocculating

floculer [3] [flɔkyle] **VI** *Chim* to flocculate

floe [flo] **NM** (ice) floe

flonflon [flɔ̃flɔ̃] **NM** oompah; **on entendait les flonflons du bal** music could be heard coming from the dance

flop [flɔp] **NM** *Fam* flop; **faire un f.** to be a flop

flopée [flɔpe] **NF** *Fam* **une f.** *ou* **des flopées (de qch)** loads *or* masses (of sth)

flops [flɔps] **NM** *Ordinat (abrév* **floating point operations per second**) FLOPS

floquer [3] [flɔke] **VT** *Tex* to flock; *Constr* to insulate, to line

floraison [flɔrɛzɔ̃] **NF 1** *Bot (éclosion)* blooming, blossoming, flowering; *(saison)* flowering time; **quand les arbres sont en pleine f.** when the trees are in full bloom **2** *(apparition → d'artistes, d'œuvres)* **une f. de** a boom in; **il y a actuellement une f. de publicités pour des banques** at present there is something of a rash of advertisements for banks

floral, -e, -aux, -ales [flɔral, -o] **ADJ** *(décor)* floral; **composition florale** flower arrangement; **exposition florale** flower show; **parc f.** flower garden

floralies [flɔrali] **NFPL** flower show

flore [flɔr] **NF 1** *(végétation)* flora **2** *(ouvrage)* flora **3** *Biol & Méd* **f. bactérienne** bacterial flora; **f. intestinale** intestinal flora

floréal [flɔreal] **NM** = 8th month of the French Revolutionary calendar (from 21 April to 20 May)

Florence [flɔrɑ̃s] **NM** Florence

florence [flɔrɑ̃s] **NF** *Pêche* **(crin de) f.** silkworm gut, silk gut

florentin, -e [flɔrɑ̃tɛ̃, -in] **ADJ** Florentine

▫ **Florentin, -e NM,F** Florentine

NM Florentine *(biscuit containing almonds and candied fruit with a chocolate base)*

▫ **florentine NF** *Culin* **à la florentine** Florentine *(cooked with spinach)*

florès [flɔrɛs] **NM** *Littéraire* **faire f.** to enjoy great success, to be a huge success; **elle a fait f. dans les années vingt** she was a roaring success in *or* the toast of the twenties

floricole [flɔrikɔl] **ADJ** flower-dwelling

floriculture [flɔrikyltyr] **NF** flower-growing, *Spéc* floriculture

Floride [flɔrid] **NF la F.** Florida; **en F.** in Florida

floridée [flɔride] *Bot* **NF** red alga, *Spéc* member of the Florideae

▫ **floridées NFPL** red algae, *Spéc* Florideae

florifère [flɔrifɛr] **ADJ** flowering, *Spéc* floriferous; **plante très f.** prolific flowerer

florilège [flɔrilɛʒ] **NM** anthology

florin [flɔrɛ̃] **NM** *Anciennement* florin

florissait *etc voir* **fleurir**

florissant, -e [flɔrisɑ̃, -ɑ̃t] *voir* **fleurir**

ADJ *(affaire, plante)* thriving, flourishing; *(santé, mine)* blooming; **être d'une santé florissante** to be in the best of health

floristique [flɔristik] **ADJ** floristic

flot [flo] **NM 1** *(de larmes, de paroles)* flood; *(de sang, d'injures)* torrent, stream; *(de boue, de voitures)* stream; **un f. de gens** a stream of people; *Littéraire* **un f. de cheveux blonds** flowing blond hair; **un f. de dentelle/rubans** a cascade of lace/ribbons; **faire couler des flots d'encre** to cause much ink to flow; **déverser des flots de bile** to pour out one's gall

2 *(marée)* **le f.** the incoming *or* rising tide

▫ **flots NMPL** *Littéraire* **les flots** the waves; **les flots bleus** the ocean blue

▫ **à flot ADV 1** *Naut* **être à f.** to be afloat; **mettre un navire à f.** to launch a ship; **remettre un bateau à f.** to refloat a boat

2 *(sorti de difficultés financières)* **être à f.** *(personne)* to have one's head above water; **je suis à f. maintenant** I'm back on an even keel now; **remettre à f.** *(personne, entreprise)* to get back on an even keel

▫ **à flots ADV** in floods *or* torrents; **la pluie ruisselle à flots sur les toits** the rain is running down the rooftops in torrents; **la lumière du soleil entre à flots dans la chambre** sunlight is flooding *or* streaming into the bedroom; **le champagne coulait à flots** champagne flowed freely

flottabilité [flɔtabilite] **NF** buoyancy; **caisson** *ou* **réservoir de f.** buoyancy tank

flottable [flɔtabl] **ADJ 1** *(bois)* buoyant **2** *(fleuve)* floatable

flottage [flɔtaʒ] **NM** *(du bois, du verre)* floating; **bois de f.** raft wood; **train de f.** timber raft

flottaison [flɔtɛzɔ̃] **NF 1** *(sur l'eau)* buoyancy; **f. en charge** load line; **f. lège** light waterline **2** *Fin* floating

flottant, -e [flɔtɑ̃, -ɑ̃t] **ADJ 1** *(sur l'eau → épave, mine)* floating

2 *(ondoyant → chevelure)* flowing; *(→ drapeau)* billowing; **elle préfère les robes un peu flottantes** she prefers loose-fitting dresses

3 *(hésitant → caractère, pensée)* irresolute; **électeur f.** floating voter; **le raisonnement est un peu f. dans le dernier chapitre** the line of argument loses its way slightly in the final chapter

4 *(variable)* fluctuating, variable; **les effectifs sont flottants** the numbers fluctuate *or* go up and down

5 *Fin (dette, capitaux, taux de change, police d'assurance)* floating

6 *Anat (côte, rein)* floating

NM 1 *(short)* pair of baggy shorts

2 *Bourse* float

flottard [flɔtar] **NM** *Fam Arg mil* naval cadet■

flottation [flɔtasjɔ̃] **NF** flotation

flotte [flɔt] **NF 1** *Aviat & Naut* fleet; **f. de ligne** *ou* **de combat** battle fleet; **f. de commerce** merchant fleet; **f. aérienne** air fleet; **f. marchande** merchant marine **2** *Fam (pluie)* rain■; *(eau)* water■; **on a eu de la f. pendant un mois** it poured for a month; **des fraises pleines de f.** watery strawberries; **c'est de la f., ce café!** this coffee's like water!

flottement [flɔtmɑ̃] **NM 1** *(incertitude)* indecisiveness, wavering *(UNCOUNT)*; **on note un certain f. dans ses réponses** his/her answers seem hesitant *or* indecisive; **il y eut un moment de f.** there was a moment's hesitation

2 *(imprécision)* looseness, imprecision; **il y a du f. dans la boîte de vitesses** the gears are a bit loose

3 *(ondoiement)* flapping, fluttering

4 *(d'une chaîne, d'une roue)* wobble

5 *(fluctuation → d'une monnaie)* floating; *(→ de chiffres)* fluctuation; **il y a du f. dans les effectifs** numbers keep fluctuating *or* going up and down; **f. dirigé** managed float

6 *Mil* swaying

flotter [3] [flɔte] **VI 1** *(surnager)* to float; **réussir à faire f. un modèle réduit de bateau** to keep a model boat afloat, to get a model boat to float

2 *(être en suspension)* to hang; **une bonne odeur de soupe flottait dans la cuisine** the kitchen was filled with a delicious smell of soup; **f. dans l'air** *(idée, rumeur)* to be going around

3 *(ondoyer → banderole)* to flap, to flutter; **ses cheveux flottent au vent/sur ses épaules** his/her hair is streaming in the wind/hangs loose over his/her shoulders

4 *(être trop large)* to flap (around); **un short qui flottait autour de ses cuisses** a pair of shorts flapping around his/her thighs

5 *(être au large)* **elle flotte dans sa robe** she's lost in that dress, her dress is too big for her

6 *Littéraire (errer)* to wander, to roam; **laissez f. votre imagination** let your imagination roam, give free rein to your imagination; **un vague sourire flottait sur ses lèvres** a faint smile crossed his/her lips

7 *Fin (monnaie)* to float; **faire f. la livre** to float the pound

VT f. du bois to float timber *(down a stream)*; **bois flotté** driftwood

V IMPERSONNEL *Fam (pleuvoir)* to rain■; **il a flotté toute la nuit** it poured *or Br* it bucketed down all night long

flotteur [flɔtœr] **NM 1** *(ouvrier)* raftsman *(in charge of timber raft)* **2** *(d'une canne à pêche, d'un hydravion, d'un carburateur)* float **3** *(d'un robinet)* ball; **robinet à f.** ballcock

flottille [flɔtij] **NF 1** *Naut* flotilla; **f. de pêche** fishing fleet **2** *Aviat* squadron

flou, -e [flu] **ADJ 1** *(imprécis → souvenir)* blurred, hazy; *(→ renseignements, argumentation)* vague; *(→ horizon)* hazy; *(→ idée)* hazy, vague

2 *Cin & Phot* out of focus

3 *(souple → vêtement)* ample, flowing, loose-fitting; *(→ coiffure)* soft

NM 1 *Cin & Phot* blurredness, fuzziness; **f. artistique** soft-focus effect; *Fig* **c'est un peu le f. artistique en ce moment** things are very much

up in the air at the moment; *Fig* **il entretient un certain f. artistique** he's being fairly vague about it **2** *(imprécision)* vagueness; *(→ de l'horizon)* haziness; *(→ d'une idée)* haziness, vagueness; **rester dans le f.** to remain vague **3** *(des cheveux)* softness, fluffiness; *(d'une robe)* looseness **ADV je vois f.** I can't focus properly

flouche [fluʃ] **NMF** *Can Fam* teenager■, *Am* teen

flouer [6] [flue] **VT** *Fam* to rook, to con; **il s'est fait f.** he was conned

floune [flun] *Can Fam* = **flouche**

flouse [fluz] **NM** *Fam* cash, *Br* dosh, *Am* bucks

flouter [3] [flute] **VT** *Phot & TV (image)* to blur

flouve [fluv] **NF** *Bot* (sweet) vernal grass

flouze [fluz] = **flouse**

FLQ[1] [ɛfɛlky] **ADJ INV** *Com (abrév* **franco long du quai**) FAQ

FLQ[2] [ɛfɛlky] **NM** *(abrév* **Front de Libération Québécois**) = militant political movement in favour of Quebec's independence in the 1960s

fluage [flyaʒ] **NM** *Métal* creep, drift

fluatation [flyatasjɔ̃] **NF** *Constr* surface waterproofing

fluctuant, -e [flyktɥɑ̃, -ɑ̃t] **ADJ** fluctuating

fluctuation [flyktɥasjɔ̃] **NF** fluctuation; **f. des prix** price fluctuation; **f. saisonnière** seasonal fluctuation; *Écon* **bande** *ou* **marge de f.** fluctuation band *or* margin; *Élec* **fluctuations de tension** voltage fluctuations

fluctuer [7] [flyktɥe] **VI** to fluctuate; **la production de pétrole fait f. les cours mondiaux** oil production affects trading prices all over the world

fluent, -e [flyɑ̃, -ɑ̃t] **ADJ 1** *Méd* bleeding **2** *Littéraire (mouvant)* flowing

fluer [7] [flye] **VI** *Littéraire (liquide)* to flow; *(odeur)* to waft

fluet, -ette [flyɛ, -ɛt] **ADJ** *(personne)* slender, slim; *(voix)* reedy

fluide [flɥid] **ADJ 1** *(liquide)* fluid

2 *(qui coule facilement)* fluid, smooth; *Fig* **la circulation est f.** there are no hold-ups (in the traffic); *Fig* **en un style f.** in a flowing style; *Fig* **en une langue f.** fluently

3 *(fluctuant → situation)* fluctuating, changeable; *(→ pensée)* elusive

4 *(flou → forme, blouse, robe)* flowing

NM 1 *(liquide)* fluid; *Chim* **f. aéré** aerated fluid; *Aut* **f. d'embrayage** clutch fluid; *Aut* **f. de frein** brake fluid; **f. glacial** = ice-cold liquid used by children for pranks; **f. moteur** engine fluid; **f. de nettoyage** cleaning fluid; *Chim* **f. pénétrant** penetrating fluid, penetrant; **f. de refroidissement** coolant

2 *(d'un médium)* aura; **il a du f.** he has occult powers

fluidifiant, -e [flɥidifjɑ̃, -ɑ̃t] *Méd* **ADJ** expectorant

NM expectorant

fluidification [flɥidifikasjɔ̃] **NF** fluidization

fluidifier [9] [flɥidifje] **VT** to fluidize

fluidique [flɥidik] **ADJ** fluidic

NF fluidics *(singulier)*

fluidisation [flɥidizasjɔ̃] **NF** *Tech* fluidization

fluidiser [3] [flɥidize] **VT** *Tech* to fluidize

fluidité [flɥidite] **NF 1** *(qualité → d'une crème, d'une sauce)* smoothness, fluidity; **grâce à la f. de la circulation** because there were no hold-ups in the traffic, because the traffic was flowing smoothly **2** *(flou → d'une forme, d'un vêtement)* fluid *or* flowing contours **3** *Écon (de la main-d'œuvre)* flexibility

fluo [flyo] **ADJ INV** *Fam* fluorescent■, Day-Glo®■

fluographie [flyɔgrafi] **NF** fluorography

fluor [flyɔr] **NM** fluorine; **dentifrice au f.** fluoride toothpaste

fluoration [flyɔrasjɔ̃] **NF** *(de l'eau)* fluoridation

fluoré, -e [flyɔre] **ADJ** fluoridated

fluorène [flyɔrɛn] **NM** *Chim* fluorene

fluorescéine [flyɔresein] **NF** fluorescein, fluoresceine

fluorescence [flyɔresɑ̃s] **NF** fluorescence

fluorescent, -e [flyɔresɑ̃, -ɑ̃t] **ADJ** fluorescent; **rose/vert f.** fluorescent pink/green

fluorhydrique [flyɔridrik] **ADJ** *(acide)* hydrofluoric

fluorine [flyɔrin], **fluorite** [flyɔrit] **NF** fluor, fluorspar, *Am* fluorite

fluoroacétate [flyɔroasetat] **NM** *Chim* fluoroacetate

fluoroscope [flyɔrɔskɔp] **NM** *Méd* fluoroscope

fluoroscopie [flyɔrɔskɔpi] **NF** *Méd* fluoroscopy

fluorose [flyɔroz] **NF** *Méd* fluorosis

fluorure [flyɔryr] **NM** *Chim* fluoride; **f. d'hydrogène** hydrofluoric acid

fluotournage [flyɔturnaʒ] **NM** rotary extrusion

fluoxétine [flyɔksetin] **NF** *Pharm* fluoxetine

flush [flœʃ, flɔʃ] *(pl* **flushes**) **NM** *Cartes* flush; **quinte f.** running flush; **f. royal** royal flush

flusher [3] [flœʃe] **VT** *Can Joual* **1 f. la toilette** to flush the toilet■ **2** *(se séparer de → employé)* to fire; *(→ petit ami)* to dump, *Br* to chuck **3** *Ordinat* to flush **4** *(supprimer)* **ils ont décidé de f. l'émission** they decided to pull the plug on the programme

flustre [flystr] **NF** *Zool* sea mat, flustra

flûte [flyt] **NF 1** *(instrument)* flute; **f. à bec** recorder; **f. de Pan** panpipe; **f. traversière, grande f.** flute; **petite f.** piccolo

2 *(verre)* flute (glass); **f. à champagne** champagne flute

3 *(pain)* = thin loaf of French bread

4 *Suisse (biscuit salé)* breadstick

EXCLAM *Fam* drat!, bother!; **f. alors, il est déjà parti!** blow it *or* drat it, he's gone already!; **oh, et puis f., je serai mouillée** to hell with it, I'll just have to get wet!

❑ **flûtes NFPL** *Fam (jambes) Br* pegs, *Am* gams; **jouer** *ou* **se tirer des flûtes** to show a clean pair of heels, to take to one's heels

'La Flûte enchantée' *Mozart* 'The Magic Flute'

flûté, -e [flyte] **ADJ** *(rire, voix)* reedy

flûteau [flyto] **NM** *Bot* water plantain

flûtiau, -x [flytjo] **NM** tin *or* penny whistle

flûtiste [flytist] **NMF** flautist

flutter [flœtœr] **NM** *Aviat & Méd* flutter

fluvial, -e, -aux, -ales [flyvjal, -o] **ADJ** *(érosion)* fluvial; *(navigation)* river *(avant n)*; **alluvions fluviales** fluvial deposits

fluviatile [flyvjatil] **ADJ** fluviatile; **mollusques fluviatiles** river *or* freshwater molluscs

fluvio-glaciaire [flyvjɔglasjɛr] *(pl* **fluvio-glaciaires**) **ADJ** fluvioglacial

fluviographe [flyvjɔgraf], **fluviomètre** [flyvjɔmɛtr] **NM** fluviograph, fluviometer

fluviométrique [flyvjɔmetrik] **ADJ** *(mesure)* fluviometric

flux [fly] **NM 1** *(marée)* incoming tide, floodtide; **le f. et le reflux** the ebb and flow; **le f. et le reflux de la foule** the ebbing and flowing of the crowd

2 *(écoulement → d'un liquide)* flow; *(→ du sang menstruel)* menstrual flow; **un f. menstruel abondant/léger** a heavy/light flow; *Can* **avoir le f.** to have diarrhoea

3 *(abondance)* **noyé dans un f. de paroles** carried away by a torrent of words; **devant ce f. de recommandations** faced with this string of recommendations

4 *Phys* flux; **f. de courant** current flow; **f. électrique** electric flux; **f. électronique** electron flow *or* stream; **f. lumineux** luminous flux; **f. magnétique** magnetic flux; **f. vidéo** video flux

5 *Com* **distribution à f. tendus** just-in-time distribution; **méthode des f. tendus** just-in-time method

6 *Métal* flux

7 *Fin* **f. circulaire des revenus** circular flow of income; **f. monétaire** flow of money, cash flow; **f. de fonds** flow of funds; **f. de trésorerie** cash-flow; **f. de trésorerie disponible** free cash flow

fluxion [flyksjɔ̃] **NF** *Méd* inflammation, *Spéc* fluxion; **f. dentaire** gumboil, *Spéc* parulis; *Vieilli* **f. de poitrine** pneumonia

fluxmètre [flymɛtr] **NM** fluxmeter

Fluxus [flyksys] **NM** Fluxus; *Beaux-Arts* **le mouvement F.** the Fluxus movement

flyé, -e [flaje] *Can Joual* **ADJ** *(drogué)* spaced-out, spacey; *(excentrique)* extravagant■, over-the-top

NM,F *(paumé)* space cadet; *(drogué)* junkie

flyer [flajœr] **NM** *Fam (prospectus de club)* flier■, flyer■

flysch [fliʃ] **NM** *Géol* flysch

FM [ɛfɛm] **NF** *(abrév* **frequency modulation**) FM

FME [ɛfɛmə] **NM** *(abrév* **Fonds monétaire européen**) EMF

Fme *(abrév écrite* **femme**) F

FMI [ɛfɛmi] **NM** *(abrév* **Fonds monétaire international**) IMF

FMP [ɛfɛmpe] **NM** *Cin (abrév* **full motion picture**) FMP

FMV [ɛfɛmve] **NM** *Cin (abrév* **full motion vision**) FMV

FN [ɛfɛn] **NM** *(abrév* **Front national**) Front National *(French extreme right-wing political party)*

FNA [ɛfɛna] **NF** *(abrév* **Fédération nationale de l'artisanat automobile**) = French car mechanics' trade union

FNAC, Fnac [fnak] **NF** *(abrév* **Fédération nationale des achats des cadres**) = chain of large stores selling hi-fi, books etc

Fnap [fnap] **NF** *(abrév* **Fédération nationale autonome de la police**) = French police trade union

FNE [ɛfɛnə] **NM** *(abrév* **Fonds national de l'emploi**) = state fund providing aid to jobseekers and workers who accept lower-paid work to avoid redundancy

FNEF, Fnef [fnɛf] **NF** *(abrév* **Fédération nationale des étudiants de France**) = students' union, *Br* ≃ NUS

FNGS [ɛfɛnʒeɛs] **NM** *(abrév* **Fonds national de garantie des salaires**) = national guarantee fund for the payment of salaries

FNI [ɛfɛni] **NFPL** *Mil (abrév* **Forces nucléaires intermédiaires**) INF

FNSEA [ɛfɛnɛsəa] **NF** *(abrév* **Fédération nationale des syndicats d'exploitants agricoles**) = farmers' union, *Br* ≃ NFU

FO [ɛfo] **NF** *(abrév* **Force ouvrière**) = moderate workers' union (formed out of the split with Communist CGT in 1948)

FOB [fɔb, ɛfobe] **ADJ INV** *Com (abrév* **free on board**) FOB; **vente F.** FOB sale

foc [fɔk] **NM** *Naut* jib; **grand f.** main *or* outer jib; **petit f.** inner jib; **f. d'artimon** mizzen-topmast staysail

focal, -e, -aux, -ales [fɔkal, -o] **ADJ 1** *(central)* **point f. d'un raisonnement** main *or* central point in an argument **2** *Math, Opt & Phot* focal

❑ **focale NF** *Opt & Phot* focal distance *or* length; **f. fixe** fixed focus lens

focalisation [fɔkalizasjɔ̃] **NF 1** *Opt & Phys* focalization, focussing **2** *(concentration)* focussing **3** *Mktg* targeting; **f. stratégique** strategic targeting

focaliser [3] [fɔkalize] **VT 1** *Opt & Phys* to focus **2** *(concentrer)* to focus (**sur** on) **3** *Mktg* to target

►**se focaliser VPR se f. sur** to be focussed *or* to focus on

focimètre [fɔsimɛtr], **focomètre** [fɔkɔmɛtr] **NM** *Opt* focimeter

focusser [3] [fɔkyse] *Can Joual* **VT 1** *Opt & Phys* to focus■ **2** *(concentrer)* to focus (**sur** on)■

fœhn [føn] **NM 1** *(vent)* foehn, föhn **2** *Suisse* hairdryer

foène, foëne [fwɛn] **NF** *Pêche* fishgig

fœtal, -e, -aux, -ales [fetal, -o] **ADJ** foetal

fœto-maternel, -elle [fetɔmatɛrnɛl] *(mpl* **fœto-maternels**, *fpl* **fœto-maternelles**) **ADJ** foetomaternal

fœtopathie [fetɔpati] **NF** foetopathy

fœtoscopie [fetɔskɔpi] **NF** foetoscopy

fœtus [fetys] **NM** foetus

fofolle [fɔfɔl] *voir* **foufou**

foggara [fɔgara] **NF** irrigation tunnel

föhn [føn] = **fœhn**

foi [fwa] **NF 1** *Rel* faith; **avoir la f.** to have faith; *Hum* **il faut avoir la f. pour travailler avec elle** you have to be really dedicated to work with her; **acte/article de f.** act/article of faith; *Fig* **faire sa profession de f.** to set out one's ideas and beliefs; *Rel* **avoir la f. du charbonnier** to have a naive belief in God; *Fig* to be naively trusting; **n'avoir ni f. ni loi, être sans f. ni loi** to fear neither God nor man; *Hum* **il n'y a que la f. qui sauve!** faith is a wonderful thing!

2 *(confiance)* faith, trust; **ajouter** *ou* **accorder f. à des rumeurs** to give credence to rumours; **il faut toujours garder f. en soi-même** you must always trust (in) yourself; **avoir f. en** *ou* **dans qn** to have faith in *or* to trust (in) sb; **elle a une f. aveugle en lui** she trusts him blindly; **avoir f. en l'avenir** to have confidence in the future

3 *Littéraire (parole)* pledged word; **elle n'a pas respecté la f. conjugale** she has broken her

marital vows; **f. d'honnête homme!** on my word of honour!; *Hum* **la robe sera prête demain, f. de couturière!** I give you my word as a seamstress that the dress will be ready tomorrow!

4 *(preuve)* **faire f.** to be valid; **il n'y a qu'une pièce officielle qui fasse f.** only an official paper is valid; **les coupons doivent être envoyés avant le 1er septembre, le cachet de la poste faisant f.** the coupons must be postmarked no later than 1 September; **les bandes magnétiques ne font pas f. au tribunal** tape recordings are not admissible evidence in court

5 *(locutions) Jur* **en f. de quoi** in witness whereof; **il avait dit qu'il viendrait, en f. de quoi j'ai préparé un petit discours** he had said he would come, on the strength of which I have prepared a little speech; **ma f.!** well!; **viendrez-vous? – ma f. oui!** will you come? – why, certainly!; **c'est ma f. possible, qui sait?** it might be possible, who knows?

❑ **bonne foi** NF **être de bonne f.** to be sincere; **les gens de bonne f.** honest people, decent folk; **témoin de bonne f.** truthful witness; **il a agi en toute bonne f.** he acted in good faith

❑ **mauvaise foi** NF **être de mauvaise f.** to be insincere; **témoin de mauvaise f.** untruthful witness; **écoutez-le, il est de mauvaise f.!** listen to him, he doesn't mean a word he's saying!

❑ **sous la foi de** PRÉP **sous la f. du serment** on *or* under oath

❑ **sur la foi de** PRÉP **sur la f. de leur déclaration/réputation** on the strength of their statement/reputation

foie [fwa] NM **1** *Anat* liver

2 *Culin* liver; **f. de broutard** calf's liver *(from an animal that has started grazing)*; **f. de génisse** cow's liver; **f. gras** foie gras; **f. de veau** calf's liver *(from a milk-fed animal)*; **f. de volaille** chicken liver

❑ **foies** NMPL *Fam* **se ronger** *ou* **se manger les foies** to be climbing the walls, to go berserk; *très Fam* **avoir les foies** to be scared stiff; *très Fam* **il m'a foutu les foies** he scared the pants off me

foie-de-bœuf [fwadəbœf] *(pl* **foies-de-bœuf***)* NM beefsteak fungus

foil [fɔjl] NM *Naut* hydrofoil, foil

foin [fwɛ̃] NM **1** *Agr* hay; **tas de f.** haycock; **meule de f.** haystack; **rentrer le f.** to bring in the hay; **c'est la saison des foins** it's haymaking season; **faire les foins** to make hay; **avoir du f. dans ses bottes** to have a fair bit (of money) tucked away; *Fig* **chercher une aiguille** *ou* **une épingle dans une botte** *ou* **une meule de f.** to look for a needle in a haystack; *Can Fam* **avoir du f.** to be loaded; *Can Fam* **il a du f. à vendre** he's flying low, his flies are undone■

2 *(d'un artichaut)* choke

3 *Fam (locution)* **faire du f.** *(être bruyant)* to make a din; *(faire un scandale)* to kick up a fuss

❑ **foin de** EXCLAM *Littéraire* **f. de l'argent et de la gloire!** the Devil take money and glory!

foirade [fwarad] NF *très Fam Br* cock-up, balls-up, *Am* ball-up

foirail [fwaraj] *(pl* **foirails***)* NM fairground

foire [fwar] NF **1** *(marché)* fair; **f. agricole** agricultural show; **f. aux bestiaux** cattle fair *or* market; **la f. à la ferraille et au jambon** = annual second-hand goods fair in the suburbs of Paris; **champ de f.** fairground; *Ordinat* **f. aux questions** frequently asked questions

2 *(exposition)* trade fair; **f. commerciale** trade show; **f. internationale** international (trade) fair; **f. professionnelle** trade fair; **f. commerciale de Marseille** Marseilles trade fair

3 *(fête foraine)* funfair; **la f. du Trône** = large annual funfair on the outskirts of Paris

4 *Fam (désordre)* mess; **c'est la f. dans cette maison!** this house is a real dump!; *(bruit)* it's a madhouse *or Br* it's bedlam in here!; **qu'est-ce que c'est que cette f., voulez-vous bien faire vos devoirs!** will you stop messing about and get down to your homework!; **faire la f.** to live it up

5 *(locutions)* **f. d'empoigne** free-for-all; **c'était une vraie f. d'empoigne dans les vestiaires** there was an absolute free-for-all in the cloakroom; *Vulg Vieilli* **avoir la f.** to have the runs

foire-échantillon [fwareʃɑ̃tijɔ̃] *(pl* **foires-échantillons***)* NF trade fair

foire-expo [fwarɛkspo] *(pl* **foires-expos***)* NF *Fam (abrév* **foire-exposition***)* trade fair■

foire-exposition [fwarɛkspozisjɔ̃] *(pl* **foires-expositions***)* NF trade fair

foirer [3] [fware] VI **1** *très Fam (rater)* to be a *Br* cock-up *or* balls-up *or Am* ball-up; **la mission/le plan/la soirée a complètement foiré** the mission/the plan/the evening was a complete *Br* cock-up *or* balls-up *or Am* ball-up; **il a tout fait f.** he *Br* ballsed *or* cocked *or Am* balled everything up **2** *(fusée, obus)* to fail **3** *(vis)* to slip

VT *très Fam (rater)* to make a *Br* cock-up *or* balls-up *or Am* ball-up of

foireux, -euse [fwarø, -øz] ADJ **1** *Fam Péj (mal fait)* hopeless, useless; **leur espèce de festival f.** their washout of a festival; **c'est un plan f.** that plan is going to be a *Br* cock-up *or* balls-up *or Am* ball-up **2** *Fam (poltron)* yellow-bellied, chicken; **quel mec f.!** what a chicken! **3** *Vulg (diarrhéique)* shitty

foirolle [fwarɔl] NF *Bot* annual mercury

fois [fwa] NF **1** *(exprime la fréquence)* **une f.** once; **deux f.** twice; **trois f.** three times, *Littéraire* thrice; **payez en six f.** pay in six instalments; **ça a raté tellement de f. que je n'essaie même plus** it went wrong so many times I don't even try any more; **une autre f., il avait oublié ses gants** another time he'd left his gloves behind; **une autre f. peut-être** *(pour refuser une invitation)* some other *or* another time maybe; **une f. et une seule** just the once, once and once only; **c'est la seule f. où j'ai regretté** that's the only time when *or* that I had regrets; **il faut le boire en une f.** you must drink it at *or* in one go; **d'autres f.** at other times; **bien des f.** many times, often; **encore une f.** once more, once again; **que de f. te l'ai-je dit!** how many times have I told you!; **combien de f.?** how many times?, how often?; **neuf f. sur dix, quatre-vingt-dix-neuf f. sur cent** nine times out of ten, ninety-nine times out of a hundred; *Littéraire* **par deux f.** twice, not once but twice; *Littéraire* **par trois f.** three times, thrice; **pour la énième f.** for the umpteenth time; **pour une f.** for once; **pour une f. que je peux y aller, il faut qu'il vienne aussi!** it's the one time I can go *or* for once I can go and he has to come as well!; **allez, viens en boîte, pour une f.!** come to a club for once!; **une (bonne) f. pour toutes** once and for all; **la première/deuxième f.** the first/second time; **c'est la première f. que j'en fais** it's my first time, it's the first time I've done it; **une dernière f., arrête!** for the last time, stop it!; **cette f.** this time; **cette f., je gagnerai** this time, I'll win; **cette f., je vais me mettre en colère!** I'm really going to get cross this time!; **pour cette f.** this once; **ça ira pour cette f., mais ne recommencez pas** it's all right this once, but don't do it again; **(à) chaque f. que, toutes les f. que** every *or* each time; **chaque f. que j'essaie, je rate** every time I try, I fail; **la f. suivante** *ou* **d'après** the time after that; **il y a des f. où je me demande à quoi tu penses** there are times when I wonder what you're thinking about; **cent euros une f., deux f., trois f., adjugé, vendu!** a hundred euros, going, going, gone!; **une f. n'est pas coutume** just the once won't hurt; **il était une f. un roi** once upon a time there was a king

2 *(dans les comparaisons)* time; **c'est trois f. plus grand** it's three times as big; **il y a dix f. moins de spectateurs que l'année dernière** there are ten times fewer spectators than last year

3 *(comme distributif)* **deux f. par jour** twice daily *or* a day; **deux f. par mois** twice a month; **une f. par semaine** once a week; **trois f. par an, trois f. l'an** three times a year

4 *Math* times; **trois f. quatre font douze** three times four is twelve; **deux** *ou* **trois f. rien** virtually nothing, hardly anything; **ma maladie? trois f. rien** my illness? it was nothing really; **il faut du beurre? – oui, mais trois f. rien** do you need some butter? – yes, but the smallest amount *or* but hardly any; **je l'ai acheté pour trois f. rien** I bought it for next to nothing

5 *(locutions)* **une f. nettoyé, il sera comme neuf** once *or* after it's been cleaned, it'll be as good as new; **tu n'as qu'à venir une f. ton travail terminé** just come as soon as your work is finished; **nous aurons plus de temps une f. installés** we'll have more time when we've settled in; **une f. que tu auras compris, tout sera plus facile** once you've understood, you'll find everything's easier; *Fam* **des f.** *(parfois)* sometimes■; **des f., elle est plutôt bizarre** she's a bit strange sometimes■; **non mais des f.!** honestly!; **dis donc, tu trouves pas que tu exagères des f.?** hey, don't you think you're pushing your luck?; **tu n'aurais pas vu mon livre, des f.?** you wouldn't happen to have seen my book anywhere, would you?; *Fam* **des f. que** (just) in case; **je préfère l'appeler, des f. qu'elle aurait oublié** I'd rather call her in case she's forgotten

❑ **à la fois** ADV together, at a time, at the same time; **versez la farine et le sucre à la f.** add the flour and (the) sugar at the same time; **à la f. utile et pas cher** both useful and inexpensive; **pas tous à la f.!** one at a time!, not all at once!; **pas trop vite, une chose à la f.** slow down, one thing at a time

❑ **(tout) à la fois** ADV both; **il rit et pleure (tout) à la f.** he's laughing and crying at (one and) the same time; **elle est (tout) à la f. auteur et traductrice** she's both an author and a translator

❑ **une fois** ADV *Belg* indeed; **venez une f. voir** *(donc)* just come and see

foison [fwazɔ̃] NF *Arch* abundance, plenty

❑ **à foison** ADV *Littéraire* galore, plenty; **des pommes à f.** apples in abundance, apples galore; **il y en a à f.** there are plenty of them, they are abundant; **il y a de quoi boire à f.** there's drinks galore

foisonnant, -e [fwazɔnɑ̃, -ɑ̃t] ADJ abundant

foisonnement [fwazɔnmɑ̃] NM **1** *(abondance)* abundance, proliferation **2** *Chim & Tech* expansion

foisonner [3] [fwazɔne] VI **1** *(abonder)* to abound; **une œuvre où les idées foisonnent** a work rich in ideas; **le gibier foisonne ici** game is plentiful here; **f. de** *ou* **en qch** to abound in sth, to be full of sth; **notre littérature foisonne en jeunes auteurs de talent** our literature abounds in *or* is full of talented young authors **2** *Chim & Tech* to expand

fol [fɔl] *voir* **fou**

folasse [fɔlas] *Fam Vieilli* ADJ batty, nutty

NF nutcase, madwoman■

folâtre [fɔlatr] ADJ *(enjoué)* frisky, frolicsome; **être d'humeur f.** to be in a playful mood

folâtrer [3] [fɔlatre] VI *(personne)* to romp, to frolic; *(animal)* to gambol, to frolic, to frisk about

folâtrerie [fɔlatrəri] NF *Littéraire* **1** *(de tempérament → d'un agneau)* friskiness; *(→ d'un chaton, d'un enfant)* playfulness **2** *(action)* frolicking

foldingue [fɔldɛ̃g] ADJ *Fam* crazy, batty

folerie [fɔləri] NF *Can Fam* **elle a fait une f. en épousant cet homme** she was crazy *or* mad■ to marry that man; **faire des foleries** *(faire le clown)* to clown about; *(dépenser beaucoup)* to be extravagant■

foliacé, -e [fɔljase] ADJ foliaceous, foliate

foliaire [fɔljɛr] ADJ foliar

foliation [fɔljasjɔ̃] NF *Bot & Géol* foliation

folichon, -onne [fɔliʃɔ̃, -ɔn] ADJ *Fam* playful■, lighthearted■; **pas f.** not much fun; **un après-midi pas bien f.** a pretty dull afternoon; **on ne peut pas dire que ses amis soient très folichons** his/her friends weren't exactly a bundle of laughs *or* a laugh a minute; **elle n'est pas du genre f.** she's a bit strait-laced

folie [fɔli] NF **1** *Psy (démence)* madness; **un accès** *ou* **une crise de f.** a fit of madness

2 *(déraison)* madness, lunacy; **c'est pure f.** it's utter madness *or* sheer folly; **elle a la f. du ski** she's mad about skiing; **elle a la f. du jeu** she's got the gambling bug; **c'est de la f. douce que de vouloir la raisonner** it's sheer lunacy to try to reason with her; **sortir par ce temps, c'est de la f. furieuse!** it's (sheer) madness to go out in weather like this!; **avoir la f. des grandeurs** to suffer from *or* to have delusions of grandeur

3 *(acte déraisonnable)* crazy thing to do, *Littéraire* folly; **il a eu la f. de céder** he was mad enough to give in; **ce sont des folies de jeunesse** those are just the crazy things you get up to when you're young; **j'ai fait une f. en achetant ce manteau** I was crazy *or* mad to buy that

foi–fol

coat; **faire des folies** (*dépenser*) to be extravagant; *Hum* **faire des folies de son corps** to put oneself about; **dire des folies** to talk wildly, to say crazy things

4 *Hist (maison)* folly

□ **à la folie** ADV passionately, to distraction; **aimer qn à la f.** to be madly in love with sb, to love sb to distraction

folié, -e [folje] ADJ foliate

Folies-Bergères [foliberʒɛr] NFPL **les F.** = famous cabaret and music hall in Paris

folio [foljo] NM folio

foliole [foljɔl] NF *Bot* leaflet

foliot [foljo] NM foliot

foliotage [foljotaʒ] NM foliation

folioter [3] [foljote] VT to folio, to foliate; *(par page)* to paginate

folioteur [foljotœr] NM page-numbering machine

folique [folik] ADJ M **acide f.** folic acid

folk [folk] ADJ folk *(avant n)*
NM folk music

folkeux, -euse [folkø, -øz] NM,F *Fam* folk music fan■, folkie

folklo [folklo] ADJ INV *Fam* bizarre, weird and wonderful; *(personne)* eccentric■, loopy, off-the-wall, *Am* kooky

folklore [folklor] NM **1** *Mus & (en danse)* **le f.** folklore **2** *Fam Péj* **c'est du f.** it's a load of nonsense

folklorique [folklorik] ADJ **1** *Mus & (en danse)* folk *(avant n)*; *(costume)* traditional **2** *Fam (insolite, ridicule)* bizarre, weird; **tu l'aurais vu avec tous ses sacs en plastique, c'était f.!** you should have seen him with all those plastic bags, it was just too much!

folkloriste [folklorist] NMF folklorist, specialist in folklore

folksong [folksɔg] NM folk (music)

folle [fol] ADJ F *voir* **fou**
NF *Pêche* wide-mesh fishing net

folle-blanche [folblɑ̃ʃ] *(pl* **folles-blanches***)* NF Folle Blanche, Gros Plant *(variety of white grape used formerly to make cognac)*

follement [folmɑ̃] ADV **1** *(excessivement)* madly; **il l'aime f.** he's madly in love with him/her; **s'amuser f.** to have a great time; **le prix en est f. élevé** the price is ridiculously high; **ce n'est pas f. gai** it's not that much fun **2** *(déraisonnablement)* madly, wildly

follet [folɛ] *voir* **esprit, feu, poil**

folliculaire [folikylɛr] ADJ follicular
NM *Vieilli Péj* penny-a-liner, hack writer

follicule [folikyl] NM *Anat & Bot* follicle

folliculeux, -euse [folikylø, -øz] ADJ *Anat & Bot* follicular

folliculine [folikylin] NF *Biol* folliculin, oestrone

folliculite [folikylit] NF *Med* folliculitis

fomentateur, -trice [fomɑ̃tatœr, -tris] NM,F *Littéraire* agitator, troublemaker

fomentation [fomɑ̃tasjɔ̃] NF *Méd & Littéraire* fomenting, fomentation

fomentatrice [fomɑ̃tatris] *voir* **fomentateur**

fomenter [3] [fomɑ̃te] VT *Méd & Littéraire* to foment

fonçage [fɔ̃saʒ] NM **1** *(de tonneau)* bottoming, heading **2** *Mines (de puits)* boring, sinking

fonçaille [fɔ̃saj] NF *(de tonneau)* head

foncé, -e [fɔ̃se] ADJ dark, deep

foncer [16] [fɔ̃se] VI **1** *(s'élancer)* to charge; **f. contre** *ou* **sur son adversaire** to rush at one's adversary; **f. droit devant soi** to go straight ahead; *Fam* **f. dans le tas** to charge in, to pile in

2 *Fam (se déplacer très vite)* to speed along; **les coureurs foncent vers la victoire** the runners are sprinting on to victory; **il a foncé à l'hôpital** he rushed straight to the hospital

3 *Fam (se hâter)* **il a fallu f. pour boucler le journal** we had to work flat out to get the newspaper out on time; *Fig* **il a toujours su f.** he has always been the dynamic type; **f. dans le brouillard** to forge ahead (without worrying about the consequences)

4 *Fam (s'y mettre)* to get one's head down; **ne te pose pas de questions, fonce!** don't ask any questions, just do it!

5 *(s'assombrir → cheveux)* to go darker
VT 1 *(teinte)* to make darker, to darken
2 *(mettre un fond à)* to (fit with a) bottom

3 *Culin (au lard)* to line with bacon fat; *(avec de la pâte)* to line with pastry

4 *Mines (pieu)* to sink, to drive (in); *(puits)* to bore, to sink

fonceur, -euse [fɔ̃sœr, -øz] *Fam* ADJ dynamic■
NM,F dynamic type

foncier, -ère [fɔ̃sje, -ɛr] ADJ **1** *Admin & Fin (impôt, politique, problème)* land *(avant n)*; **biens fonciers** (real) property, real estate; **crédit f.** land bank; **droit f.** ground law; **propriétaire f.** landowner; **propriété foncière** land ownership, ownership of land

2 *(fondamental)* fundamental, basic
NM land *or* property tax; **f. bâti** landed property; **f. non bâti** land for development

foncièrement [fɔ̃sjɛrmɑ̃] ADV **1** *(fondamentalement)* fundamentally, basically; **l'argument est f. vicieux** the argument is basically flawed **2** *(totalement)* deeply, profoundly; **il est f. ignorant** he's profoundly ignorant

fonction [fɔ̃ksjɔ̃] NF **1** *(emploi)* office; **entrer en f.** *ou* **fonctions, prendre ses fonctions** to take up one's post *or* one's duties; *(président, ministre)* to take up office; **être en f.** to be in office; **faire f. de** to act as; **ce couteau fera f. de tournevis** this knife will do instead of a screwdriver; **il a pour f. d'écrire les discours du président** his job is to write the president's speeches; **il occupe de hautes fonctions** he has important responsibilities; **est-ce que cela entre dans tes fonctions?** is this part of your duties?; **remplir ses fonctions** to carry out one's job *or* functions; **elle remplit les fonctions d'interprète** she acts as interpreter; **se démettre de ses fonctions** to resign one's post *or* from one's duties; **démettre qn de ses fonctions** to dismiss sb (from his/her duties)

2 *(rôle)* function; **fonctions de nutrition** nutritive functions; **c'est la première f. de l'estomac** it's the main function of the stomach; **la pièce a pour f. de maintenir l'équilibre de la balance** the part serves to keep the scales balanced; **faire f. de gérant** to act as manager; **les fonctions de directeur** the functions of a director; **fonctions d'encadrement** executive functions; **cette table fait f. de table à café** this table acts *or* serves as a coffee table; **adjectif qui fait f. d'adverbe** adjective that is used *or* functions as an adverb; **la f. crée l'organe** necessity is the mother of invention

3 *être f. de (dépendre de)* **sa venue est f. de son travail** whether he/she comes or not depends on his/her work

4 *Chim, Ling & Math* function; **en f. inverse de** in inverse ratio to; **être f. de** to be a function of; *Écon & Mktg* **f. de la demande** demand function, market demand function

5 *Ordinat* function, facility; **f. booléenne** Boolean function; **f. de comptage de mots** word count facility; **f. de contrôle** control function; **f. couper-coller** cut-and-paste function *or* facility; **f. d'éditeur de texte** text editing feature; **f. multimédia** multimedia facility; **f. multitâche** multitasking facility; **f. de recherche et remplacement** search and replace function *or* facility; **f. de recopie** copy function *or* facility; **f. de répétition** repeat function; **f. de sauvegarde** save function *or* facility; **f. de vérité** truth function

□ **de fonction** ADJ **appartement** *ou* **logement de f.** accommodation that goes with the job, *Br* tied accommodation; **voiture de f.** company car

□ **en fonction de** PRÉP according to; **payé en f. de sa contribution au projet** paid according to one's contribution to the project; **exprimer une quantité en f. d'une autre** to express one quantity in terms of *or* as a function of another; **les prix varient en f. de la demande** prices vary in accordance with *or* according to demand

□ **fonction publique** NF **la f. publique** ≃ the civil *or* public service

fonctionnaire [fɔ̃ksjɔnɛr] NMF ≃ civil servant; **f. détaché** ≃ civil servant *Br* on secondment *or* *Am* on a temporary assignment; **f. municipal** local government official; **haut f.** senior civil servant, senior official; **petit f.** minor official, *Péj* **avoir une mentalité de petit f.** to have a petty bureaucratic mentality, *Br* to be a jobsworth

Culture

FONCTIONNAIRE

This term covers a broader range of public service employees than the term "civil servant", from high-ranking members of the state administration to public-sector teachers and post office workers. "Fonctionnaires", of whom there are more than four and a half million in France, are normally recruited through competitive state examination and enjoy greater job security and other privileges to which private sector employees are not automatically entitled.

fonctionnaliser [3] [fɔ̃ksjɔnalize] VT *(ameublement, cuisine)* to make more functional

fonctionnalisme [fɔ̃ksjɔnalism] NM functionalism

fonctionnaliste [fɔ̃ksjɔnalist] ADJ functionalist, functionalistic
NMF functionalist

fonctionnalité [fɔ̃ksjɔnalite] NF practicality, functionality
□ **fonctionnalités** NFPL *Ordinat* functions, features

fonctionnariat [fɔ̃ksjɔnarja] NM employment by the state

fonctionnarisation [fɔ̃ksjɔnarizasjɔ̃] NF **1** *(d'un employé)* moving an employee into the public *or* civil service **2** *(d'une profession)* making a profession part of the public *or* civil service

fonctionnariser [3] [fɔ̃ksjɔnarize] VT to make part of the civil service

fonctionnarisme [fɔ̃ksjɔnarism] NM *Péj* officialdom, bureaucracy

fonctionnel, -elle [fɔ̃ksjɔnɛl] ADJ **1** *Math, Méd & Psy* functional **2** *(adapté)* practical, functional; **des meubles fonctionnels** functional furniture **3** *Ling* **linguistique fonctionnelle** functional linguistics; **mot f.** function word

fonctionnellement [fɔ̃ksjɔnɛlmɑ̃] ADV functionally

fonctionnement [fɔ̃ksjɔnmɑ̃] NM *(d'un mécanisme, d'un engin)* running, working; *(du métro, d'un véhicule)* running; *(d'une entreprise)* running, functioning; **en (bon) état de f.** in (good) working order; **pour assurer le bon f. de votre machine à laver** to keep your washing machine in good working order; **pour le bon f. du service, il est préférable que tous les employés aient les mêmes horaires** if the department is to run efficiently it is preferable that all staff have the same working hours; **ça vient d'un mauvais f. de la prise** it's due to a fault in the plug; **la panne est due à un mauvais f. du carburateur** the breakdown is due to a malfunction in the *or* a malfunctioning carburettor; *Ordinat* **f. en réseau** networking

fonctionner [3] [fɔ̃ksjɔne] VI *(mécanisme, engin)* to run, to work; *(métro, véhicule)* to run; *(personne)* to function, to operate; *(entreprise)* to run, to function; *Ordinat* to run; **le moteur fonctionne mal/bien** the engine isn't/is working properly; **les freins n'ont pas fonctionné** the brakes failed, the brakes didn't work; **mon cœur fonctionne encore bien!** my heart is still going strong!; **faire f. une machine** to operate a machine; **je n'arrive pas à faire f. la machine à laver** I can't get the washing machine to work; **ça fonctionne avec des pièces de deux euros** it works with two-euro coins, you need two-euro coins to work it; *Élec* **f. sur courant continu** to operate *or* to run on direct current; **f. sur piles** to run on batteries, to be battery-operated; **f. au gaz** to be gas-powered, to run on gas

FOND [fɔ̃]

bottom **1** ■ back **1** ■ depths **2** ■ heart **3** ■ core **3** ■ background **5** ■ drop **7** ■ long-distance running **10**		

NM 1 *(d'un récipient)* bottom; *(d'un placard)* back; *(extrémité)* bottom, far end; *(de la gorge)* back; *(d'une pièce)* far end, back; *(d'un jardin)* far end, bottom; *(d'un océan)* bottom, bed; *(d'un chapeau)* crown; *(d'une chaise)* seat; *(d'un tonneau)* bottom, head; **sans f.** bottomless; **bateau à f. plat** flat-bottomed boat; **le f. d'un puits** the bottom of a well; **regarde bien dans le f. du**

placard take a good look at the back of the cupboard; **le f. de sa gorge est un peu rouge** the back of his/her throat is a bit red; **la salle du f.** the room at the end, the far room; **au fin f. du désert** in the middle of the desert; **au fin f. de la campagne irlandaise** in the depths of the Irish countryside; **il y a cinq mètres de f.** *(de profondeur)* the water is five metres deep *or* in depth; **aller par le f.** to sink; **envoyer par le f.** to send to the bottom, to sink; **couler par 100 mètres de f.** to sink to a depth of 100 metres; **prendre f.** *(d'une ancre)* to bite, to grip; **il n'y a pas assez de f. pour plonger/pour jeter l'ancre** the water isn't deep enough for diving/ for dropping anchor; **f. de cylindre/chaudière** cylinder/boiler head; **f. de culotte** *ou* **de pantalon** seat (of one's pants); *Méd* **le f. d'œil** the back of the eye; *Méd* **faire un examen du f. d'œil** to have an ophthalmoscopy; **les grands fonds marins** the depths of the ocean; **à f. de cale** at rock bottom; **tous les mutins furent enfermés à f. de cale** the mutineers were all locked away in the bottom of the hold; *Fam Fig* **gratter** *ou* **vider** *ou* **racler les fonds de tiroir** to scrape around *(for money, food etc)*

2 *Fig* depths; **atteindre le f. de la misère** to reach the depths of poverty; **toucher le f. (du désespoir)** to reach the depths of despair, to hit rock bottom; **il connaît le f. de mon cœur/âme** he knows what's in my heart/soul; **je vous remercie du f. du cœur** I thank you from the bottom of my heart; **il faut aller jusqu'au f. de ce mystère** we must get to the bottom of this mystery

3 *(cœur, substance)* heart, core, nub; **voilà le f. du problème** here is the core *or* the root of the problem; **le f. de notre politique** the essential features of our policy; **puis-je te dire le f. de ma pensée?** can I tell you what I really think?; *Littérature* **le f. et la forme** substance and form; **sur le f., vous avez raison** you're basically right; *Jur* **juger sur le f.** to decide on the substance

4 *(tempérament)* **il a un bon f.** he's basically a good *or* kind person; **elle n'a pas vraiment un mauvais f.** she's not a bad person really

5 *(arrière-plan)* background; **le f. de la toile est jaune** the background is yellow; **des fleurs sur f. blanc** flowers on a white background; **sur un f. de violons** with violins in the background; **il y a un f. de vérité dans ce que vous dites** there's some truth in what you're saying; **f. sonore** *ou* **musical** background music; **bruit de f.** background noise; **il y avait du jazz en f. sonore** there was jazz playing in the background; **le f. de l'air est frais** there's a chill *or* nip in the air

6 *Typ* **f. perdu** bleed; **à f. perdu** bleeding; **(blanc de) petit f.** back margin, gutter; **(blanc de) grand f.** fore-edge, gutter

7 *(reste)* drop; **il reste un f. de café** there's a drop of coffee left; **boire** *ou* **vider le f. d'une coupe de champagne** to empty one's champagne glass; **boire** *ou* **vider les fonds de bouteilles** to drink up the dregs; **le f. du panier** the leftovers

8 *Culin* **f. de sauce/soupe** base for a sauce/ soup; **f. d'artichaut** artichoke heart; **f. de tarte** pastry case

9 *Mines* **travailler au f.** to work at the coal face; **descendre au f. de la mine** to go down the pit; **les mineurs de f.** the men in the pits

10 *Sport* **le f.** long-distance running; **course de (grand) f.** long-distance race; *Ski* cross-country race; **cheval qui a du f.** horse with staying power

11 *(locution)* **faire f. sur** to put one's trust in

□ **à fond** ADV in depth; **enfoncer un clou à f.** to hammer a nail home, to drive a nail all the way in; **respirer à f.** to breathe deeply; *Fam* **faire le ménage à f. dans la maison** to clean the house thoroughly■, to spring-clean■; *Fam* **se consacrer** *ou* **se donner à f. à qch** to give one's all to sth, to devote all one's energy to sth■; **il s'est donné à f. dans son travail** he threw himself completely into his work; *Fam* **s'engager à f. dans une aventure** to get deeply involved in an adventure■; **il s'est engagé à f. dans le combat écologique** he committed himself wholeheartedly *or* body and soul to the struggle for the environment; *Fam* **apprendre** *ou* **connaître une langue à f.** to acquire *or* to have a thorough knowledge of a language■

□ **à fond de train** ADV *Fam* (at) full tilt

□ **à fond la caisse, à fond les manettes** ADV *Fam* (at) full tilt

□ **au fond** ADV basically; **au f., c'est mieux comme ça** it's better that way, really; **au f., on pourrait y aller en janvier** in fact, we could go in January; **au f., elle n'est pas méchante** she's not a bad sort at heart *or* deep down, she's basically not a bad sort; **au f., c'est ce qu'il voulait** (deep down) that's what he really wanted; **au f. il était très flatté** in his heart of hearts he was extremely flattered

□ **au fond de** PRÉP **au f. de soi-même** deep down; **c'est au f. du couloir/de la salle** it's at the (far) end of the corridor/of the hall; **au f. de la rivière** at the bottom of the river; **regarder qn au f. des yeux** to look deeply into sb's eyes

□ **dans le fond** PRÉP = **au fond**

□ **de fond** ADJ 1 *Sport (épreuve, coureur, course)* long-distance *(avant n)*; **ski de f.** cross-country skiing 2 *(analyse, remarque, texte, question)* basic, fundamental; **article de f.** feature (article)

□ **de fond en comble** ADV *(nettoyer, fouiller)* from top to bottom; *Fig* **revoir un texte de f. en comble** to revise a text thoroughly

□ **fond de robe** NM slip

□ **fond de teint** NM foundation

---

fondamental, -e, -aux, -ales [fɔ̃damɑ̃tal, -o] ADJ 1 *(théorique → science)* fundamental, basic; **la recherche fondamentale** basic *or* fundamental research

2 *(de base)* elementary, basic; **couleurs fondamentales** primary colours; **ce sont des choses fondamentales que vous devriez connaître** these are fundamental *or* basic things you should know

3 *(important)* fundamental, essential, crucial; **il est f. que nous réparions notre erreur** it's crucial *or* fundamental that we should correct our mistake

4 *Phys (niveau)* fundamental

5 *Mus* fundamental; **son f.** *(d'une corde)* root, generator

□ **fondamentale** NF *Mus* fundamental

□ **fondamentaux** NMPL **les fondamentaux de qch** the basics *or* fundamentals of sth

fondamentalement [fɔ̃damɑ̃talmɑ̃] ADV fundamentally; **c'est f. la même chose** it's basically the same thing; **f. opposés** radically opposed

fondamentalisme [fɔ̃damɑ̃talism] NM (religious) fundamentalism

fondamentaliste [fɔ̃damɑ̃talist] ADJ fundamentalist, fundamentalistic

NMF 1 *(scientifique)* scientist engaged in basic research 2 *Rel* fundamentalist

fondant, -e [fɔ̃dɑ̃, -ɑ̃t] ADJ 1 *(glace, neige)* melting, thawing 2 *(aliment)* **une poire fondante** a pear that melts in the mouth; **un rôti f.** a tender roast; **un bonbon/chocolat f.** a sweet/chocolate that melts in the mouth

NM 1 *Culin (bonbon, gâteau)* fondant; **un f. au chocolat** a chocolate fondant 2 *Métal* flux

fondateur, -trice [fɔ̃datœr, -tris] NM,F 1 *(gén)* founder 2 *Jur* incorporator

fondation [fɔ̃dasjɔ̃] NF 1 *(création → d'une ville, d'une société)* foundation; *(→ d'une bourse, d'un prix)* establishment, creation; **f. d'une entreprise** setting up of a business 2 *(fonds)* endowment (fund), foundation 3 *(institution)* foundation; **la F. de France** = charitable organization for the needy

□ **fondations** NFPL *Constr* foundations

fondatrice [fɔ̃datris] *voir* **fondateur**

fondé, -e [fɔ̃de] ADJ 1 *(argument, peur)* justified; **mes craintes ne sont que trop fondées** my fears are only too justified; **vos craintes ne sont pas fondées** your fears are groundless *or* unfounded *or* unjustified; **qu'est-ce qu'il y a de f. dans ces bruits?** is there any truth in these reports?, is anything in these reports justified?; **un reproche non f.** an unjustified reproach; **mal f.** ill-founded

2 *(créé)* founded; **établissement f. en 1850** established 1850

3 *(locution)* **je serais f. à croire qu'il y a eu malversation** I would be justified in thinking *or* I would have grounds for believing that embezzlement has taken place

□ **fondé de pouvoir** NM agent *(holding power of attorney)*; *(mandant)* proxy; *(directeur de banque)* manager with signing authority; **il est le f. de pouvoir (de)** he holds power of attorney (for)

fondement [fɔ̃dmɑ̃] NM 1 *(base)* foundation; **jeter les fondements d'une nouvelle politique** to lay the foundations of a new policy 2 *Hum (derrière)* derrière, behind, backside; *(anus)* back passage 3 *Phil* fundament

□ **sans fondement** ADJ *(crainte, rumeur)* groundless, unfounded

fonder [3] [fɔ̃de] VT 1 *(construire → ville, empire, parti)* to found; **f. un foyer** *ou* **une famille** to start a family; **f. un hôpital** *(en donnant un legs)* to found a hospital

2 *Com (société, journal)* to found, to set up; **fondé en 1928** established in 1928

3 *(appuyer)* **f. qch sur** to base *or* to found *or* to pin sth on; **f. ses espérances sur qch** to base *or* build one's hopes on sth; **elle fondait tous ses espoirs sur son fils** she pinned all her hopes on her son

4 *(légitimer → réclamation, plainte)* to justify

▸ **se fonder** VPR 1 **se f. sur qn/qch** *(se prévaloir de)* to base oneself on sb/sth; **sur quoi te fondes-tu pour affirmer pareille chose?** what grounds do you have for such a claim?

2 **se f. sur** *(remarque, théorie)* to be based on

fonderie [fɔ̃dri] NF 1 *(extraction → de minerai)* smelting; *(fusion → de métaux)* founding, casting 2 *(usine)* smelting works 3 *(atelier)* foundry

fondeur[1], -euse[1] [fɔ̃dœr, -øz] NM,F *Sport* cross-country skier, langlaufer

fondeur[2], -euse[2] [fɔ̃dœr, -øz] NM,F 1 *(maître de forges)* ironmaster 2 *(ouvrier → de bronze)* caster; *(→ de l'or, de l'argent)* smelter; *(→ de fusion)* (metal) founder; **f. en cuivre** brass founder; **f. en caractères, f. typographe** type founder

□ **fondeuse** NF *(machine)* smelter

fondis [fɔ̃di] NM *Mines* subsidence

fondoir [fɔ̃dwar] NM rendering plant

fondouk [fɔ̃duk] NM fonduk

fondre [75] [fɔ̃dr] VT 1 *(rendre liquide → minerai)* to smelt; *(→ métal)* to melt down; *(→ sucre)* to dissolve; *(→ neige, cire)* to melt; **f. de l'or/de l'argent** to smelt gold/silver; **f. des pièces** to melt coins down

2 *(fabriquer → statue, canon, cloche)* to cast, to found

3 *(dissoudre)* to dissolve

4 *(combiner → couleurs)* to blend, to merge; *(→ sociétés)* to merge, to amalgamate, to combine; **f. deux livres en un seul** to combine two books in one *or* in a single volume

5 *TV* to fade; **f. des teintes** to blend colours

VI 1 *(se liquéfier)* to melt; *(de la neige)* to melt, to thaw; **la glace fond au-dessus de 0°C** ice thaws at 0°C; **faites f. le chocolat** melt the chocolate; **f. comme cire** *ou* **comme neige au soleil** *ou Belg* **comme beurre sur la poêle** to vanish into thin air; *Élec* **faire f. un fusible** to blow a fuse

2 *(se dissoudre)* to dissolve; **faire f. du sucre** to dissolve sugar; **f. dans la bouche** to melt in the mouth

3 *(s'affaiblir → animosité, rage)* to melt away, to disappear; **il sent son cœur f. quand il voit ses enfants** he can feel his heart melting when he sees his children; **mon cœur fondit (de pitié)** my heart melted (with pity); **je fonds** my heart melts; **le général a vu sa division f. en quelques heures** the general saw his entire division vanish in a few hours; **f. en larmes** to dissolve into tears

4 *Fam (maigrir)* to get thin■; **il fond à vue d'œil** the weight's dropping off him; **j'ai fondu de trois kilos** I've lost three kilos■

5 **f. sur** *(se jeter sur → sujet: personne, avion, rapace)* to swoop down on

▸ **se fondre** VPR 1 *(se liquéfier)* to melt

2 *(se mêler)* to merge, to mix; **les couleurs se fondent à l'arrière-plan du tableau** the colours merge into the background of the painting; **se f.**

dans la nuit/le brouillard to disappear into the night/the mist; **se f. dans la foule** to merge *or* to blend into the crowd; **se f. dans la masse** to melt *or* to disappear into the crowd; **se f. dans l'anonymat** to hide under the cloak of anonymity

fondrière [fɔ̃drijɛr] **NF 1** *(sur une route)* pothole **2** *(marécage)* bog, quagmire; *Can* **f. de mousse** muskeg

fonds [fɔ̃] **NM 1** *(propriété)* business; **un f. de commerce** a business; **f. de commerce à vendre** business for sale (as a going concern); **un f. de boulangerie** a bakery business; **f. de clientèle** customer base

2 *Fin* fund; **f. d'amortissement** sinking fund; **f. de caisse** cash in hand, float; **f. de capital-risque maison** captive fund; **f. commun de placement** investment company *or* trust, *Am* mutual fund; **f. commun de placement d'entreprise** company investment fund; **f. commun de placement à risques** venture capital trust; **f. dédié** captive fund; **f. de dotation** endowment fund; **f. d'entreprise** occupational pension scheme; **f. d'épargne-retraite** retirement savings fund; **f. éthique** ethical fund; **F. européen de coopération monétaire** European Monetary Cooperation Fund; **F. européen de développement** European Development Fund; **F. européen de développement régional** European Regional Development Fund; **f. à faible frais d'entrée** low-load fund; **f. de garantie** guarantee fund; **f. de garantie automobile** = emergency fund to compensate victims of accidents caused by uninsured drivers; **f. géré** managed fund; **f. à gestion indicielle** index *or* tracker fund; **f. de groupe** occupational pension scheme; **f. indiciel** index *or* tracker fund; **f. indiciel négociable en bourse** exchange-traded fund; **f. d'investissement** investment fund; **f. monétaire** money market fund; **F. monétaire européen** European Monetary Fund; **F. monétaire international** International Monetary Fund; **F. national de l'emploi** = French national employment fund; **F. national de garantie des salaires** = national guarantee fund for the payment of salaries; **F. national de solidarité** = support scheme for the old and needy; **f. obligatoire** bond fund; **f. off shore** offshore funds; *Can* **f. de parité** equalization fund; **f. de pension** pension fund; **f. perdus** annuity; **placer son argent à f. perdus** to purchase an annuity; **f. de placements spéculatifs** dynamic fund; **f. de placement sur le marché monétaire** money market fund; **f. de prévoyance** contingency fund; **f. de réserve** reserve fund; **f. de retraite maison** occupational pension scheme; **f. de roulement** working capital; **f. social** company funds; **F. social européen** European Social Fund; **f. de stabilisation des changes** exchange equalization account; **f. structuré** structured fund; **f. structurel** structural fund

3 *(ressources)* collection; **notre bibliothèque a un f. très riche d'ouvrages du XVIIIème siècle** our library has a very rich collection of 18th-century books; **c'est un f. inestimable pour les chercheurs** it is an invaluable resource for researchers; **le f. commun de toutes les langues indo-européennes** the common stock of all Indo-European languages

4 *Jur* **f. dominant** dominant tenement; **f. servant** servient tenement

NMPL 1 *Fin* funds; **réunir des f.** to raise funds; **des f. ont été détournés** funds were embezzled; **être en f.** to be in funds; **rentrer dans ses f.** to recoup one's costs; **je n'ai pas les f. suffisants pour ouvrir un magasin** I don't have the (necessary) funds *or* capital to open a shop; *Hum* **mes f. sont au plus bas** funds are low; **prêter de l'argent à f. perdus** to loan money without security; **collecte de f.** financial appeal, fund-raising *(UNCOUNT)*; **organiser un dîner pour une collecte de f.** to organize a fund-raising dinner; **la mise de f. initiale a été de 10 millions de livres** the venture capital *or* seed money was 10 million pounds; **f. communs** pool; **f. disponibles** liquid assets, available funds; **f. fédéraux** federal funds; **f. liquides** available funds; **f. propres** shareholders' *or* stockholders' equity; **les f. publics** public funds; **f. secrets** secret funds

2 *(argent)* money; **je n'ai pas les f. sur moi** I don't have the ready cash with *or* on me

3 *Bourse* stocks, securities; **f. consolidés** consolidated stock, *Br* consols; **f. d'État, f. publics** government stock(s)

fondu, -e [fɔ̃dy] **PP** *voir* **fondre**

ADJ 1 *(liquéfié)* melted; *Métal* molten; **de la neige fondue** *(qui tombe)* sleet; *(par terre)* slush

2 *(ramolli)* melted

3 *Beaux-Arts (teinte)* blending

4 *Fam (fou)* round the bend, out to lunch

NM 1 *Cin* dissolve; **faire un f.** to fade; **faire un f. au noir** to fade to black; **s'ouvrir en f.** to fade in; **ouverture en f.** fade-in; **fermeture en f.** fade-out; **les personnages apparaissent/disparaissent en f.** the characters fade in/out; **f. enchaîné** (lap-)dissolve, fade-in fade-out; **faire un f. enchaîné** to (lap-)dissolve, to fade in-fade out; **f. enchaîné automatique** auto-dissolve; *Rad* **f. enchaîné sonore** cross-fade; **f. en ouverture** fade-in; **f. en fermeture** fade-out; **f. sonore** *(au début)* fade-in; *(à la fin)* fade-out; **f. par ondulation** ripple dissolve; **f. par passage au flou** defocus dissolve

2 *Beaux-Arts* blend

3 *Fam (passionné)* fanatic, freak; **un f. d'informatique/de skateboard** he's a computer/skateboard freak

4 *Belg Culin* cheese croquette

❑ **fondue NF** *Culin* fondue; **fondue bourguignonne** fondue bourguignonne, = fondue consisting of cubes of raw beef cooked in hot oil; **fondue de légumes** vegetable fondue; **fondue savoyarde** cheese fondue

fongibilité [fɔ̃ʒibilite] **NF** fungibility

fongible [fɔ̃ʒibl] **ADJ** fungible

fongicide [fɔ̃ʒisid] **ADJ** fungicidal

NM fungicide

fongiforme [fɔ̃ʒifɔrm] **ADJ** fungiform

fongique [fɔ̃ʒik] **ADJ** fungal, fungous

fongoïde [fɔ̃gɔid] **ADJ** fungoid

fongosité [fɔ̃gozite] **NF** *Méd* fungoid growth

fongueux, -euse [fɔ̃gø, -øz] **ADJ** fungous

fonio [fɔnjo] **NM** fonio

fonne [fɔn] **NM** *Can Joual* fun■; **avoir du f.** to have fun■; **être du f.** *(personne)* to be fun, to be a laugh

font *voir* **faire**

fontaine [fɔ̃tɛn] **NF 1** *(édifice)* fountain; **f. Wallace** = dark green ornate drinking fountain (typical of Paris) **2** *(petit réservoir)* cistern; **f. filtrante** *ou* **de ménage** (household) filter **3** *(source)* spring; **la F. de Jouvence** the Fountain of Youth; *Prov* **il ne faut pas dire: f. je ne boirai pas de ton eau** never say never

fontainebleau [fɔ̃tɛnblo] **NM** *Culin* = soft cheese whipped with cream

fontainier [fɔ̃tenje] **NM** hydraulic engineer

fontanelle [fɔ̃tanɛl] **NF** fontanelle

fontange [fɔ̃tɑ̃ʒ] **NF** *Hist* fontange

fonte[1] [fɔ̃t] **NF 1** *Métal* cast iron; **(fer de) f., f. de fer** cast iron; **f. d'acier** cast steel; **poêle en f.** cast-iron stove

2 *(fusion → gén)* melting; *(→ des neiges, de glace)* thawing, melting; *(→ d'objet en or ou argent)* melting down; *(→ du métal, de minerai)* smelting; *(→ de cloche, de statue)* casting, founding; **pièces de f.** castings; **à la f. des neiges/glaces** when the snow/ice thaws

3 *Typ & Ordinat* font; **f. bitmap** bitmap font; **f. de caractère** character font; **f. écran** screen font; **f. imprimante** printer font; **f. reconnue optiquement** OCR-font; **f. vectorielle** outline font

4 *Agr & Hort* **f. des semis** damping off seedlings

5 *Méd* **f. musculaire** wasting of muscle

fonte[2] [fɔ̃t] **NF** *(d'une selle)* holster

fontine [fɔ̃tin] **NF** Fontina

fontis [fɔ̃ti] **NM** *Mines* subsidence

fonts [fɔ̃] **NMPL f. (baptismaux)** (baptismal) font; **tenir un enfant sur les f. baptismaux** to be godfather/godmother to a child

foot [fut] **NM** *Fam* soccer■, *Br* football■, footie; **jouer au f.** to play soccer *or Br* football

football [futbol] **NM** soccer, *Br* football; **jouer au f.** to play soccer *or Br* football; **f. américain** *Br* American football, *Am* football

footballeur, -euse [futbolœr, -øz] **NM,F** soccer *or Br* football player, *Br* footballer

footballistique [futbolistik] **ADJ** soccer *(avant n)*, *Br* football *(avant n)*

footeux [futø] **NM** *Fam (joueur)* soccer *or Br* football player■, *Br* footballer■; *(supporter)* soccer *or Br* football fan■

footing [futiŋ] **NM le f.** jogging; **faire un f.** to go jogging, to go for a jog

foqué, -e [fɔke] *Can Joual Vulg* **ADJ** fucked-up

NM,F basket case

foquer [3] [fɔke] **VT** *Can Joual Vulg (voiture)* to smash up, to wreck■; *Fig (personne, famille)* to fuck up

FOR *(abrév écrite* **forint)** F, Ft

for [fɔr] **NM en** *ou* **dans son f. intérieur** in one's heart of hearts; **en mon f. intérieur** deep down *or* inside, in my heart of hearts

forage [fɔraʒ] **NM** *Tech* **1** *(creusement → d'un puits de pétrole)* boring, drilling; *(→ d'un puits, d'une mine)* sinking; **f. pétrolier** drilling oil wells; **effectuer un f.** *(de puits de pétrole)* to drill an oil well; *(de puits)* to sink a well **2** *(diamètre d'un cylindre, du canon d'un fusil)* bore

forain, -e [fɔrɛ̃, -ɛn] **ADJ 1** *(boutique)* fairground *(avant n)*; **marchand f.** stallholder; **spectacle f.** travelling show; **hercule f.** strongman *(at a fair)*; **baraque foraine** fairground stall **2** *Naut* **mouillage f.** open berth

NM,F stallholder

foraminé, -e [fɔramine] **ADJ** *Bot & Zool* foraminate

foraminifère [fɔraminifɛr] *Zool* **NM** foraminifer, *Spéc* member of the Foraminifera

❑ **foraminifères NMPL** foraminifers, *Spéc* Foraminifera

forban [fɔrbɑ̃] **NM 1** *(pirate)* freebooter **2** *Péj (escroc)* crook

forçage [fɔrsaʒ] **NM 1** *Archit & Hort* forcing **2** *Aut* **introduction d'air par f.** ram-air induction

forçat [fɔrsa] **NM** *Hist (sur une galère)* galley slave; *(dans un bagne)* convict; **travailler comme un f.** to work like a slave; **mener une vie de f.** to have a hard life; **la maçonnerie est un métier de f.** building work is really backbreaking

FORCE [fɔrs]

> **NF** strength **1, 2, 4, 7, 13** ■ force **1, 3, 8**
> **ADV** many

NF 1 *(puissance → d'une tempête, d'un coup)* strength, force; *(→ d'un sentiment)* strength; *(→ d'une idée, d'un argument)* strength, power; **avec f.** forcefully; **ce qui fait votre f., c'est...** your strength is...; **dans toute la f. du mot** *ou* **terme** in the strongest sense of the word *or* term; *Météo* **un vent (de) f. 7** a force 7 wind; **la f. de l'habitude** force of habit; **les forces de la nature** the forces of nature; **les forces du mal** the forces of evil; **f. vitale** life force

2 *(vigueur physique)* strength; **avoir beaucoup de f.** to be very strong; **être d'une f. herculéenne** to be as strong as an ox; **avoir la f. de** to have the strength to; **il sent sa f. l'abandonner avec l'âge** he feels himself growing weaker with age; **elle était sans f.** she had no strength, she was bereft of strength; **la maladie le laissa sans f.** the illness left him (feeling) weak, the illness sapped his strength; **sentir ses forces décliner** to feel one's strength ebbing; **elle n'avait plus la f. de répondre** she didn't have the strength (left) to answer, she had no strength left to answer; **je ne me sens pas/ne suis pas de f. à faire cela** I don't feel/I'm not up to *or* equal to doing it; **elle ne se sentait pas la f. de lui en parler** she didn't feel up to talking to him/her about it; **donner des forces à qn** to give sb strength; **reprendre des forces** to regain one's strength; **de f. égale, de même f.** equally matched, well matched; **c'est au-dessus de mes forces** it's beyond me; **de toutes mes/ses forces** with all my/his/her strength, with all my/his/her might; **j'ai poussé la porte de toutes mes forces** I pushed the door with all my might; **je le veux de toutes mes forces** I want it with all my heart; **j'essaie de toutes mes forces de le convaincre** I'm trying as hard as I can to convince him; **ne pas sentir** *ou* **connaître sa f.** not to know one's own strength; **être bâti en f.** to be stocky, to be strongly built; **f. motrice** *(personne)* prime mover; **être une f. de la**

nature to be a mighty force; **être dans la f. de l'âge** to be in the prime of life; **les forces vives de la nation** the nation's resources

3 *(contrainte, autorité)* force; **vaincre par la f.** to win by (using) force; **avoir recours à la f.** to resort to force; **nous ne céderons pas à la f.** we will not yield to force; *Jur* **f. exécutoire** legal force; **avoir f. exécutoire** to be enforceable; **avoir f. de loi** to have the force of law; *Jur* **f. majeure** force majeure; **c'est un cas de f. majeure** it's completely unavoidable; **il y a (cas de) f. majeure** there are circumstances beyond one's control; *Pol & Écon* **un coup de f.** a takeover by force; *Jur* **f. obligatoire** imperativeness; **la f. prime le droit** might is right; *Jur* **f. probante** probative force

4 *(puissance morale)* strength; **ce qui fait sa f., c'est sa conviction politique** his/her political commitment is his/her strength; **f. d'âme** spiritual strength; **f. de caractère** strength of character; **elle a une sacrée f. de caractère** she has incredible strength of character

5 *(niveau)* **c'est un orateur de première f.** he's a first-class speaker; **elles sont de la même f. en sciences** they're well matched in science; **je ne suis pas de f. à lui faire concurrence** I'm no match for him/her

6 *Admin & Mil* **F. d'action rapide** = section of the French armed forces responding immediately in emergencies; **la f. nucléaire stratégique** *ou* **la f. de frappe** *ou* **la f. de dissuasion de la France** France's nuclear strike capacity; **les forces armées** the (armed) forces; **Forces françaises en Allemagne** = French forces in Germany; *Hist* **Forces françaises de l'intérieur** = French Resistance forces during World War II; *Hist* **Forces françaises libres** = free French Army during World War II; **Forces intérimaires des Nations unies au Liban** UNIFIL; **les forces navales/aériennes** the naval/air forces; **forces nucléaires intermédiaires** intermediate-range nuclear forces; **la f. publique, les forces de l'ordre** *ou* **de police** the police; **f. tactique** *ou* **d'intervention** task force

7 *(suprématie)* strength, might; **occuper une position de f.** to be in a position of strength; **f. est restée à la loi** the law prevailed

8 *Phys* force; **f. centrifuge/centripète** centrifugal/centripetal force; **forces de cisaillement** shear forces; **f. électromotrice** electromotive force; **f. d'inertie** force of inertia; **f. motrice** motive power; *Fig* driving force; **f. de traction** traction *or* tractive force; *Aut* **forces en virage** cornering force; **f. vive** kinetic energy, momentum

9 *Pol* **F. ouvrière** = trade union

10 *Typ* **f. de corps** body size

11 *Naut* **faire f. de rames** to ply the oars; **faire f. de voiles** to cram on sail

12 *Constr* **(jambe de) f.** force piece, strut; **f. de résistance à la tension** tensile strength

13 *(d'un produit, d'un concurrent)* strength; *Com* **f. de vente** sales force; *Écon* **les forces du marché** market forces; *Mktg* **forces, faiblesses, opportunités et menaces** strengths, weaknesses, opportunities and threats, SWOT

14 *(locutions)* **f. est de constater que...** there is no choice but to accept that...; **f. me fut d'accepter sa décision** I had no choice but to accept his/her decision; **f. lui fut d'obéir** he/she was obliged to obey, he/she had no option but to obey; **par la f. des choses/de l'habitude** by force of circumstance/of habit

ADV *Littéraire ou Hum* many; **nous avons mangé f. gigots** we ate a great many legs of lamb; **je le lui ai expliqué avec f. exemples** I explained it to him/her by giving numerous examples

❑ **à force ADV** *Fam* **tu vas le casser, à f.!** you'll break it if you go on like that!; **il va se lasser, à f.** he'll get tired of it eventually; **à f., je suis fatigué** I'm getting tired

❑ **à force de PRÉP** by dint of; **à f. de parler** by dint of talking; **à f. de travailler** by (dint of) hard work; **à f. de répéter** by constant repetition; **à f. d'explications** by dint of explanation; **à f. de volonté** by sheer willpower; **il s'est enroué à f. de crier** he shouted himself hoarse

❑ **à la force de PRÉP** by the strength of; **grimper à la f. des bras** to climb by the strength of one's arms; *Fig* **s'élever à la f. du poignet** to go up in the world by the sweat of one's brow

❑ **à toute force ADV** at all costs

❑ **de force ADV** by force; **il est entré de f.** he forced his way in; **entrer** *ou* **pénétrer de f. dans une maison** to force one's way into a house; **faire entrer qch de f. dans qch** to force sth into sth; **on les a fait sortir de f.** they were made to leave

❑ **en force ADV 1** *(en nombre)* in force, in large numbers; **ils sont arrivés en f.** they arrived in force *or* in great numbers **2** *(sans souplesse)* **faire qch en f.** to do sth by brute force

❑ **par force ADV par f. nous nous sommes résignés à son départ** we were forced to accept *or* we had to resign ourselves to his/her departure

---

'La Force de l'âge' *de Beauvoir* 'The Prime of Life'

Allusion

La force tranquille

Advertising man Jacques Séguéla coined this slogan for François Mitterrand's 1981 successful presidential election campaign. It appeared on posters, with the candidate in the foreground and a background showing a typical French village set in a green and rustic landscape. This supposedly conveyed an image of solidity and serenity: **La force tranquille** ("Strength in tranquillity"). The expression stuck and people use it jokingly of themselves and others. It suggests "the strong, silent type" but the allusion to the Mitterrand poster remains strong.

---

forcé, -e [fɔrse] **ADJ 1** *(obligé)* forced; *(emprunt)* forced, compulsory; *(cours, vente)* forced; **consentement/mariage f.** forced consent/marriage; **atterrissage f.** emergency *or* forced landing; **liquidation forcée** compulsory liquidation; **contraint et f.** under duress

2 *(inévitable)* inevitable; **ça n'a pas marché, c'est f., il était mal préparé** it didn't work out, which isn't surprising because he wasn't properly prepared

3 *(involontaire)* **prendre un bain f.** to fall in (the water)

4 *(sans spontanéité)* strained; **un rire/un sourire f.** a forced laugh/smile; **comparaison forcée** artificial comparison

forcement [fɔrsəmɑ̃] **NM** forcing; **f. de blocus** blockade running

forcément [fɔrsemɑ̃] **ADV** inevitably, necessarily; **pas f.** not necessarily; **ça devait f. arriver** it was bound to happen; **elle sera f. déçue** she's bound to be disappointed; **l'herbe est verte, f., il a plu tous les jours** the grass is green but it's not surprising, it has been raining every day; **f.!** of course!; **elle est très mince – f., elle ne mange rien!** she's very slim – that's hardly surprising, she never eats a thing!

forcené, -e [fɔrsəne] **ADJ 1** *(passionné)* fanatical, frenzied; **un goût f. du travail** a fanatical liking for work; **c'est un admirateur f. de Mozart** he's an ardent fan of Mozart

2 *(violent)* frenzied; **frapper des coups forcenés à la porte** to knock frenziedly at the door; **une haine forcenée** a fanatical hatred

NM,F 1 *(fou)* maniac

2 *(passionné)* **un f. de** a fanatic of; **un f. du karaté** a karate fanatic *or* maniac; **crier comme un f.** to scream like a madman/madwoman

forceps [fɔrsɛps] **NM** forceps; **accouchement au f.** forceps delivery

forcer [16] [fɔrse] **VT 1** *(obliger)* to compel, to force; **f. qn à faire qch** to force *or* to compel sb to do sth, to make sb do sth; **l'ennemi a forcé l'avion à atterrir** the enemy forced the plane down; **il l'a forcée à quitter la société** he forced her out of the firm; **sans vouloir te f. il faudrait faire la vaisselle** I don't want to force you, but the washing-up has to be done; **être forcé de faire qch** to be forced to do sth; **je suis forcée de rester au lit** I have (no choice but) to stay in bed; **écoute, personne ne te** *ou* **ne t'y force!** listen, nobody's forcing you!; **f. la main à qn** to force sb's hand; **on lui a forcé la main** he/she was made to do it, his/her hand was forced; *Littéraire Vieilli* **je ne veux point f. ton inclination** I want to leave you free to marry whom you choose, I don't want to force a husband on you

2 *(ouvrir de force → tiroir, valise)* to force (open); *(→ serrure, mécanisme)* to force; **f. un coffre-fort** to force a safe open; **f. la caisse** to force open the till, to break into the till; **f. une porte** to force (open) *or* break open a door; *Fig* **f. la porte de qn** to barge *or* to force one's way into sb's house; **f. le passage** to push (one's way) through

3 *(outrepasser) Pharm* **f. la dose** to prescribe too large a dose; *Fig* to go too far; **f. la note** to overdo it

4 *Arch (violer → personne)* to violate

5 *(susciter)* **f. le respect/l'admiration (de qn)** to command (sb's) respect/admiration

6 *(influencer → événements)* to influence; **f. le destin** to force the hand of destiny

7 *(presser)* **f. le pas** *ou* **l'allure** to force the pace; *Équitation* **f. son cheval** to overtax *or* to override one's horse

8 *Agr & Hort* to force

9 *(pousser trop loin)* **f. sa voix** to strain one's voice; **f. sa nature** to go against one's true nature; **il n'a pas besoin de f. sa nature pour jouer les pères autoritaires** playing the heavy father comes naturally to him; **f. le sens d'un texte** to distort the meaning of a text

10 *Chasse* to run down; **f. un cerf** to run down a stag, to bring a stag to bay

11 *Ordinat (justification, coupure de page)* to force

VI *(en faire trop)* to strain oneself, to overdo it; *(pousser, tirer)* to force it; **ne force pas, tu vas casser le mécanisme** don't force it, you'll break the mechanism; **pliez la jambe sans f.** bend your leg very gently *or* without straining; **il y est arrivé sans f.** he managed without straining himself *or* without too much effort; **ne force pas, ça doit se fermer tout seul!** don't force it, it has to close by itself!; *Naut* **f. de voiles** to crowd on sail; **le vent force** the wind is rising

❑ **forcer sur VT IND** to overdo; **ne forcez pas sur les abdominaux** don't do too many stomach exercises; **il force sur les somnifères** he overdoes the sleeping pills; **je crains d'avoir forcé sur le poivre** I'm afraid I've overdone (it with) the pepper; *Fam Hum* **f. sur la bouteille** to be fond of the bottle; **il avait un peu forcé sur la bouteille** he'd had one too many *or Br* one over the eight; **f. sur les avirons** to strain at the oars; *Cartes* **f. sur l'annonce de qn** to overcall *or* to overbid sb

►**se forcer VPR** *(gén)* to make an effort; *(en mangeant)* to force oneself; **se f. à lire/à travailler** to force oneself to read/to work

forcerie [fɔrsəri] **NF** *Hort* forcing house

forces [fɔrs] **NFPL** *Vieilli* shears

forcing [fɔrsiŋ] **NM** *Sport* pressure; **faire le f.** to put the pressure on; *Fam Fig* **faire du f.** to use fair means and foul; **avoir qn au f.** to pressurize sb, to put pressure on sb

forcipressure [fɔrsiprɛsyr] **NF** *Méd* forcipressure

forcir [32] [fɔrsir] **VI 1** *(personne)* to get bigger **2** *(tempête, vent)* to pick up, to get stronger

forclore [fɔrklɔr] **VT** *(à l'infinitif et au participe passé seulement) Jur* to debar

forclos, -e [fɔrklo, -oz] *Jur* **PP** *voir* **forclore**

ADJ foreclosed

forclusion [fɔrklyzjɔ̃] **NF** *Jur* debarment

forçure [fɔrsyr] **NF** *Can (abats)* pluck; *(plat)* fried liver dish

fordisme [fɔrdism] **NM** Fordism, Ford system of mass production

forer [3] [fɔre] **VT** *(roche, puits de pétrole)* to bore, to drill; *(puits, mine)* to sink

forestage [fɔrɛstaʒ] **NM** forestry

foresterie [fɔrɛstəri] **NF** forestry

forestier, -ère [fɔrɛstje, -ɛr] **ADJ** *(chemin, code)* forest *(avant n)*; **chemin f.** forest road; **essences forestières** forest trees; **une exploitation forestière** a forestry development

NM,F forester

❑ **forestière NF** *Culin* **poulet/champignons à la forestière** chicken/mushrooms forestière

for–for

foret [fɔrɛ] NM **1** *(vrille)* drill **2 f. à bois** gimlet; **f. de charpentier** auger **3** *(vilebrequin)* (brace) bit

forêt [fɔrɛ] NF **1** *(arbres)* forest; **f. vierge** virgin forest; **région couverte de forêts** forest(ed) region **2** *(multitude)* **une f. de** a forest of

foretage [fɔrtaʒ] NM rent for quarrying rights

forêt-galerie [fɔrɛgalri] *(pl* **forêts-galeries***)* NF gallery forest

Forêt-Noire [fɔrɛnwar] NF *Géog* **la F.** the Black Forest

forêt-noire [fɔrɛnwar] *(pl* **forêts-noires***)* NF *(gâteau)* Black Forest gateau

foreur [fɔrœr] ADJ M *(ingénieur, ouvrier)* drilling *(avant n)*
NM *Tech* driller; *Pétr* **f. d'exploration** oil prospector, *Am Fam* wildcatter

foreuse [fɔrøz] NF drill; *Mines* rock drill; **f. à main** hand drill

forfaire [109] [fɔrfɛr] **forfaire à** VT IND *Littéraire* to be false to; **f. à son devoir** to fail in one's duty; **f. à l'honneur** to forfeit one's honour; **f. à sa parole** to break one's word

forfait[1] [fɔrfɛ] NM **1** *(abonnement → de transport, à l'opéra)* season ticket; *(→ au ski)* (ski-)pass; **le f. comprend les frais de location et d'entretien du matériel** the package *or* the price includes the cost of hire and maintenance of the equipment; **et pour un f. de 70 euros...** and for an all-in *or* all-inclusive price of 70 euros..., and for 70 euros all in...; **f. train + hôtel** package deal including train ticket and hotel reservation; **f. avion + location de voiture** fly drive; **f. week-end** weekend package; **f.(-voyage)** package (deal)
2 *Com* flat rate *or* fee, fixed rate; **payer qn au f.** to pay sb a flat *or* fixed rate; **travailler au f.** to work for a flat rate *or* fee; **vente à f.** outright sale; **f. de port** carriage forward
3 *Fin* **être au f.** to be taxed on estimated income

forfait[2] [fɔrfɛ] NM *Littéraire (crime)* infamy, (heinous) crime

forfait[3] [fɔrfɛ] NM *Sport (somme)* forfeit, fine; *(renoncement à participer)* withdrawal; **gagner par f.** to win by default; **déclarer f. pour un cheval** to scratch a horse; **déclarer f.** *(athlète, concurrent)* to scratch; *Fig* to throw in the towel; **l'équipe a déclaré f.** the team withdrew

forfaitaire [fɔrfɛtɛr] ADJ inclusive; **marché f.** fixed-price contract; **montant f.** lump sum; **paiement f.** lump sum; **prix f.** all-inclusive *or* all-in price; **somme f.** lump sum; **voyage à prix f.** package tour; **indemnités forfaitaires** basic allowance

forfaitairement [fɔrfɛtɛrmɑ̃] ADV *Fin* in a lump sum; *(facturer)* in a lump sum, in one amount

forfaiture [fɔrfɛtyr] NF **1** *Jur* abuse of authority; **f. au devoir** failure in duty; **f. à l'honneur** breach of honour **2** *Hist* forfeiture

forfait-vacances [fɔrfɛvakɑ̃s] *(pl* **forfaits-vacances***)* NM package holiday

forfanterie [fɔrfɑ̃tri] NF *Littéraire* boastfulness

forficule [fɔrfikyl] *Entom* NF earwig, *Spéc* member of the Forficulidae
❑ **forficules** NFPL earwigs, *Spéc* Forficulidae

forge [fɔrʒ] NF **1** *(atelier)* forge, smithy; **f. (de maréchal-ferrant)** smithy; **mener un cheval à la f.** to take a horse to the blacksmith's; **f. de serrurier** locksmith's workshop; **pièce de f.** forging **2** *(fourneau)* forge
❑ **forges** NFPL *Vieilli (usine sidérurgique)* steel works

forgeable [fɔrʒabl] ADJ *Tech* forgeable

forgeage [fɔrʒaʒ] NM *Tech* forging

forger [17] [fɔrʒe] VT **1** *Tech* to forge; **f. à chaud** to hot-forge; *Fig Littéraire* **f. les chaînes de qn** to forge bonds for sb; *Prov* **c'est en forgeant qu'on devient forgeron** practice makes perfect
2 *(inventer → alibi)* to make up; *(→ phrase, mot)* to coin; *(→ accusation)* to trump up; *(→ vision)* to conjure up; **une histoire forgée de toutes pièces** a fabricated *or* a cock-and-bull story
3 *(fabriquer → document, preuve)* to forge
4 *(aguerrir → personnalité)* to form, to forge; *(→ caractère)* to build, to form; **f. un homme** to build *or* form a man's character
► **se forger** VPR **se f. une réputation** to earn oneself a reputation; **se f. un idéal** to build *or* create an ideal for oneself; **se f. un idéal de vie** to create an ideal lifestyle for oneself; **se f. le caractère** to build up one's character

forgeron [fɔrʒərɔ̃] NM blacksmith

forgeur[1]**, -euse** [fɔrʒœr, -øz] NM,F *Littéraire (de mots, de phrases)* coiner; *(de documents)* forger

forgeur[2] [fɔrʒœr] NM *Littéraire (forgeron)* metal worker

forgeuse [fɔrʒøz] *voir* **forgeur**[1]

forint [fɔrint] NM forint

forjeter [27] [fɔrʒəte] *Archit* VT to construct so as to project (outwards)
VI to project, to jut out

forlancer [16] [fɔrlɑ̃se] VT *Chasse* to start

forlane [fɔrlan] NF *(danse)* forlana, furlana

forligner [3] [fɔrliɲe] VI **1** *Vieilli (déshonorer ses ancêtres)* to disgrace one's ancestors *or* ancestry **2** *Littéraire (se déshonorer)* to forfeit one's honour

forlonger [17] [fɔrlɔ̃ʒe] VT *Chasse* to get ahead of

formage [fɔrmaʒ] NM **1** *Métal* forming **2** *(de plastique)* moulding

formaldéhyde [fɔrmaldeid] NM formaldehyde

formalisation [fɔrmalizasjɔ̃] NF formalization

formaliser [3] [fɔrmalize] VT *(idée, théorie)* to formalize; **logique formalisée** formal logic
► **se formaliser** VPR **se f. de** to take offence at

formalisme [fɔrmalism] NM **1** *(attitude)* respect for etiquette; **faire preuve de f.** to be a stickler for etiquette *or* form **2** *Beaux-Arts, Phil & Littérature* formalism

formaliste [fɔrmalist] ADJ **1** *(guindé)* strict about etiquette **2** *Beaux-Arts, Littérature & Phil* formalistic
NMF **1** *(personne guindée)* stickler for etiquette *or* form **2** *Beaux-Arts, Littérature & Phil* formalist

formalité [fɔrmalite] NF **1** *Admin* formality; **formalités administratives/douanières** administrative/customs formalities
2 *(acte sans importance)* formality; **cet examen n'est qu'une f.** this medical test is a mere formality; **notre enquête n'est qu'une simple** *ou* **pure f.** we're just making routine enquiries; **les formalités d'usage** the usual formalities
3 *(cérémonial)* formality; **sans autre f., sans plus de formalités** without further ado

formant [fɔrmɑ̃] NM formant

formariage [fɔrmarjaʒ] NM *Hist* = marriage outside of one's rank or condition

format [fɔrma] NM **1** *(dimension)* size; *Phot* size, format; **photo petit f.** small (format) print; *Phot* **f. normal** enprint; **f. de poche** pocket size
2 *Typ* format; **livre en f. de poche** paperback (book); **f. berlinois** = paper format measuring 32 x 47 cm; **f. d'impression** print format; **f. in-folio** folio; **f. oblong** oblong format; **f. de papier** paper format; **f. rogné** trimmed page size, TPS; **f. tabloïd** tabloid; **papier f. A4/A3** A4/A3 paper
3 *Ordinat* format; **f. ASCII** ASCII format; **f. d'écran** screen format; **f. de fichier** file format; **f. graphique** image format; **f. d'impression** print format; **f. de page** page format *or* setup; **f. de paragraphe** paragraph format; **f. TIFF** TIFF
4 *TV & Cin* **f. de l'image** aspect ratio; **f. de présentation** show format

formatage [fɔrmataʒ] NM **1** *Ordinat* formatting; **f. de bas niveau** low-level formatting; **f. de haut niveau** high-level formatting; **f. logiciel** soft sectoring **2** *Fig* tailoring

formater [3] [fɔrmate] VT **1** *Ordinat* to format **2** *Fig* to tailor

formateur, -trice [fɔrmatœr, -tris] ADJ *(rôle, influence, expérience)* formative; **ce stage en entreprise a été très f.** this placement was very instructive
NM,F trainer

formatif, -ive [fɔrmatif, -iv] ADJ formative

formation [fɔrmasjɔ̃] NF **1** *(naissance)* development, formation, forming; **la f. d'un volcan/des dunes** the forming of a volcano/of (sand) dunes; **la f. du goût/de la personnalité** the development of taste/of the personality; **volcan en voie** *ou* **en cours de f.** volcano in the process of formation
2 *(groupe)* group; **f. musicale** *(classique)* orchestra; *(moderne)* band; **f. paramilitaire** paramilitary group; **f. politique** political group; **f. syndicale** (trade) union
3 *(apprentissage)* training *(UNCOUNT)*; *(connaissances)* cultural background; **il faut que nous leur donnions une f.** we must train them; **suivre une f.** to do *or* take a training course; **avoir une excellente f.** to have an excellent training; **elle a une bonne f. littéraire/scientifique** she has a good literary/scientific background; **il n'a aucune f. musicale** he has no musical training; **il est technicien de f.** he trained as a technician; **architecte de f., elle est devenue cinéaste** having trained as an architect, she turned to making films; **être en f.** to be undergoing training; **f. en alternance** *ou* **alternée** = training given partly in an educational institution and partly in the workplace; **f. continue** *ou* **permanente** continuing education; **f. des maîtres** *ou* **pédagogique** *Br* teacher training, *Am* teacher education; **f. courte** *ou* **accélérée** intensive training; **f. dans l'entreprise** in-house training; **f. interne** in-house training; **f. professionnelle** vocational training; **f. professionnelle pour adultes** adult education; **f. sur le tas** *ou* **par la pratique** on-the-job training
4 *Mil (détachement)* unit; *(disposition)* formation; **f. serrée** close formation
5 *Sport & (en danse)* formation
6 *Physiol* puberty; **au moment de la f.** when puberty occurs
7 *Géol* formation
8 *Ling* **la f. du vocabulaire** vocabulary formation; **la f. du féminin/pluriel** the formation of the feminine/plural; **mot de f. savante** word of learned origin

formative [fɔrmativ] *voir* **formatif**

formatrice [fɔrmatris] *voir* **formateur**

forme [fɔrm] NF **1** *(configuration)* shape, form; **donner une f. courbe à un vase** to give a curved shape to a vase; **un dessin de f. géométrique** a geometrical pattern; **la Terre a la f. d'une sphère** the Earth is spherical; **sans f.** shapeless; **ne plus avoir f. humaine** to be unrecognizable; **mettre en f.** *(texte)* to format; **mettez vos idées en f.** give your ideas some shape; **mettre un écrit en f.** to structure a piece of writing; **prendre la f. de** to take (on) the form of, to assume the shape of; **prendre f.** to take shape, to shape up
2 *(état)* form; **se présenter sous f. gazeuse** to come in gaseous form *or* in the form of a gas; **c'est le même sentiment sous plusieurs formes** it's the same feeling expressed in several different ways; **nous voulons combattre la misère sous toutes ses formes** we want to fight poverty in all its forms; **l'histoire racontée sous une nouvelle f.** history told in a new way; **présenter les choses sous une autre f.** to present things in a different *or* in another way
3 *(silhouette)* figure, shape; **une vague f. apparut dans le brouillard** a hazy figure appeared in the fog
4 *(type)* form; **la f. de gouvernement qui convient au pays** the form *or* type of government (best) suited to the country; **la f. monarchique/républicaine** the monarchical/republican form of government; **des formes de vie différentes sur d'autres planètes** different forms of life on other planets
5 *(style)* form; **sacrifier à la f.** to put form above content; **une f. plus concise serait préférable** a more concise form would be preferable
6 *Mus* form; **f. sonate** sonata form
7 *Ling* form; **mettre un verbe à la f. interrogative/négative** to put a verb into the interrogative/in the negative (form); **la f. progressive** the progressive; **les formes du futur** future tense forms
8 *Jur* form; **respecter la f. légale** to respect legal procedures; **arrêt cassé pour vice de f.** judgment quashed on a technical point
9 *(condition physique)* form; **f. physique** physical fitness; **être en bonne f. physique** to be fit; *Fam* **avoir** *ou* **tenir la f.** to be in great shape; **je n'ai** *ou* **ne tiens pas la f.** I'm in poor shape; **il tient la grande f. en ce moment** he's in great form at the moment; **être en f.** to be on form; **être au mieux** *ou* **sommet de sa f., être en pleine f.** to be on top form; **c'est bon pour la f.** it's good for you, it'll do you good; *Fam* **alors, c'est la f.?** how are you doing?
10 *(moule → gén)* former, forming block; *(→ pour chapeau)* block; *(→ pour chaussure)* last;

(→ *pour élargir*) shoe tree; (→ *pour fromage*) mould
11 *Psy* **théorie de la f.** gestalt theory
12 *Typ* forme
13 *Vét* ringbone
14 *Math* quantic
15 *Naut* dock
16 *Chasse (de lièvre)* form
17 *Com* **f. sociale** type of company
❏ **formes** NFPL **1** (*physique* → *d'un bateau*) lines; (→ *d'une personne*) figure; (→ *d'une femme*) curves; **avoir des formes** to have a shapely figure; **avoir des formes généreuses** to be curvaceous; **vêtement qui épouse les formes** close-fitting *or* figure-hugging garment; **les formes d'un tableau** the lines of a picture; **les formes d'un paysage** the shapes of a landscape **2** (*convention*) **les formes** the conventions *or* proprieties; **y mettre les formes** to be tactful; **elle n'a pas su y mettre les formes** she wasn't very tactful about it; **elle a toujours respecté les formes** she has always respected convention
❏ **dans les formes** ADV according to form; **faire qch dans les formes** to do sth in the accepted way; **avertir qn dans les formes** to give sb formal *or* due warning
❏ **de pure forme** ADJ purely formal; **vérification de pure f.** routine check
❏ **en bonne (et due) forme** ADJ (*contrat*) bona fide ADV (*établir un document*) in due form, according to the proper form; **faire une réclamation en bonne et due f.** to use the correct procedure in making a complaint
❏ **en forme de** PRÉP (*ressemblant à*) **en f. de poisson** shaped like a fish, fish-shaped; **en f. d'œuf** egg-shaped; **en f. de croix** in the shape of a cross; **yeux en f. de billes** eyes like marbles
❏ **pour la forme** ADV for the sake of form, as a matter of form
❏ **sans autre forme de procès** ADV without further ado
❏ **sans forme** ADJ shapeless
❏ **sous forme de, sous la forme de** PRÉP in the form of, as; **un médicament qui existe sous f. de comprimés** a drug available in tablet form; **sous la f. d'une nymphe** in the form *or* shape of a nymph; **statistiques sous f. de tableau** statistics in tabular form; **sous toutes ses formes** in all its forms *or* guises

formé, -e [fɔrme] ADJ **1** *Physiol* fully formed, fully developed **2 un personnel bien f.** well-trained staff
❏ **formée** ADJ F (*jeune fille*) pubescent

formel, -elle [fɔrmɛl] ADJ **1** (*net* → *ordre, refus*) definite; (→ *démenti*) flat, categorical; (→ *interdiction*) strict; (→ *identification, preuve*) positive; **je suis f., il ne viendra pas** I'm positive he won't come; **le médecin a été f., pas de laitages!** no milk products, the doctor was quite clear about that!; **il a été tout à fait f. sur ce point** he was quite adamant *or* definite on this point **2** (*de la forme*) formal; **la beauté formelle d'une nouvelle** the formal beauty of a short story **3** (*superficiel*) **leur protestation était purement formelle** their protest was purely for the sake of form **4** *Phil* formal

formellement [fɔrmɛlmɑ̃] ADV **1** (*nettement*) categorically; **s'engager f. à régler ses dettes** to vow to pay off one's debts; **accuser f. qn** to specifically accuse sb; **je vous le dis f., je refuserai de signer** I'm telling you categorically that I'll refuse to sign; **il m'a f. interdit de fumer** he strictly forbade me to smoke; **l'homme a été f. reconnu** the man was positively identified **2** (*stylistiquement*) formally; **une argumentation f. inattaquable** an argument that cannot be attacked on formal grounds **3** *Phil* formal

former [3] [fɔrme] VT **1** (*donner un contour à* → *lettre*) to shape, to form; (→ *phrase*) to put together, to shape; *Bible* **Dieu forma l'homme à son image** God made man in his own image **2** (*créer* → *gouvernement, association*) to form; **f. une unité de combat** to form a combat unit; **f. un train** to make up a train **3** (*se constituer en*) to form; **ils ont formé un**

cortège/attroupement they formed a procession/a mob **4** (*dessiner*) to form; **les murs forment un carré** the walls form a square; **le nuage forme un cœur** the cloud is shaped like a heart *or* is heart-shaped; **tout cela forme un amas confus dans ma mémoire** all that's just a confused blur in my memory; **les collines alentour forment une vaste cuvette** the surrounding hills form a vast basin **5** (*constituer*) to form; **nous ne formions qu'un seul être** we were as one; **ils forment un couple uni** they're a united couple; **ils forment un couple étrange** they make a strange couple; **ils forment une bonne équipe** they make a good team **6** (*faire apparaître*) to make, to form; **le froid forme du givre sur les vitres** the cold makes frost form on the windowpanes **7** (*créer, faire par la pensée*) **f. un projet** to think up a plan; **nous avons formé le dessein de nous marier** we are planning to marry; **f. des vœux pour le succès de qn/qch** to wish sb/sth success; **tous les espoirs que nous formons pour eux** all the hopes we place in them **8** *Ling* to form; **formez le pluriel de "marteau-piqueur"** form *or* give the plural of "marteau-piqueur"; **formez le conditionnel sur le futur** form the conditional tense using the future tense as a model **9** *Hort* **f. un poirier en fuseau** to train a pear tree into a cone-shape **10** *Ind & Scol* to train; **f. les jeunes en entreprise** to give young people industrial training; **cette université a formé des hommes remarquables** this university has turned out *or* produced some remarkable men; **f. qn à qch** to train sb in sth; **f. son personnel à l'informatique** to train one's staff to use computers; **formé à la gestion** trained in management (techniques) **11** (*développer* → *caractère, goût*) to develop; **un exercice qui forme l'oreille** an exercise which trains *or* develops the ear; **f. l'esprit de qn** to develop sb's mind; **cela forme le caractère** it's character-forming *or* character-building **12** *Tech* **f. par roulage** to roll
▶ **se former** VPR **1** (*apparaître* → *croûte, pellicule, peau*) to form; (→ *couche, dépôt*) to form, to build up; **ces montagnes se sont formées à l'ère tertiaire** these mountains were formed during the Tertiary period **2** (*se perfectionner*) to train oneself; (*s'instruire*) to educate oneself; **elle s'est surtout formée au contact du public** she has learnt most of what she knows through dealing with the public; **se f. sur le tas** to learn on the job *or* as one goes along; **se f. aux affaires** to acquire a business training **3 une jeune fille qui se forme** a girl who is developing **4 se f. en** (*se placer en*) to form, to make; **se f. en cortège** to form a procession; **se f. en carré** to form a square **5** (*se constituer*) **se f. une opinion** to form an opinion

formeret [fɔrmərɛ] *Archit* ADJ **M arc f.** wall-rib, formeret
NM wall-rib, formeret

formiate [fɔrmjat] NM *Chim* formate

Formica® [fɔrmika] NM Formica®; **en F.** Formica®

formicant, -e [fɔrmikɑ̃, -ɑ̃t] ADJ *Méd* formicant

formication [fɔrmikasjɔ̃] NF *Méd* formication

formidable [fɔrmidabl] ADJ **1** (*imposant*) tremendous, *Littéraire* formidable; **elle a une volonté f., elle réussira!** she has tremendous willpower, she'll succeed! **2** *Fam* (*invraisemblable*) incredible, unbelievable"; **tu n'en as jamais entendu parler, c'est f., ça!** it's incredible, you've never heard of it!; *Ironique* **tu es f.!** you're incredible! **3** *Fam* (*admirable*) great, wonderful; **c'est un type f.** he's a great guy **4** *Littéraire* (*effrayant*) fearsome, formidable

formidablement [fɔrmidabləmɑ̃] ADV **1** *Fam* (*admirablement*) tremendously; **nous avons été f. accueillis** we were given a tremendous *or* fantastic welcome; **elle sait f. bien s'occuper des enfants** she's great *or* marvellous with children

2 *Littéraire* (*de manière effrayante*) formidably, fearsomely

formique [fɔrmik] ADJ *Chim* formic

formol [fɔrmɔl] NM *Chim* formalin

formoler [3] [fɔrmɔle] VT to use formalin on

formosan, -e [fɔrmɔzɑ̃, -an] ADJ Formosan
❏ **Formosan, -e** NM,F Formosan

Formose [fɔrmoz] NF *Anciennement* Formosa; **vivre à F.** to live in Formosa; **aller à F.** to go to Formosa

formulable [fɔrmylabl] ADJ **la proposition n'est pas encore f.** the proposal can't yet be formulated; **f. en termes de droit** expressible in legal terms; **une théorie f. en termes clairs** a theory that can be clearly formulated; **une opinion difficilement f.** an opinion that is difficult to formulate

formulaire [fɔrmylɛr] NM **1** (*document*) form; *Anciennement* **f. E111** form E111; **f. d'appréciation** customer satisfaction questionnaire; **f. d'assurance** insurance form; **f. de candidature** (job) application form; **f. de détaxe** tax-free shopping form; **f. de recensement** census return; *Ordinat* **f. de saisie** input form **2** (*recueil*) formulary; (*de pharmaciens*) formulary, pharmacopoeia

formulation [fɔrmylasjɔ̃] NF formulation, wording; **la f. de votre problème est incorrecte** you formulated your problem incorrectly, the way you formulated your problem is incorrect

formule [fɔrmyl] NF **1** (*tournure*) expression, (turn of) phrase; **trouver la f. qui convient** to find the right expression; **elle a terminé sa lettre par une belle f./une f. toute faite** she ended her letter with a well-turned phrase/a ready-made phrase; **f. consacrée** accepted expression; **selon la f. consacrée** as the expression goes; **la f. magique** the magic words; *Suisse Pol* = name given to the coalition that forms the executive body of the Swiss government; **f. de politesse** (*dans une lettre*) standard letter ending **2** (*imprimé*) form; **f. de chèque** *Br* cheque form, *Am* blank check; **f. de demande de crédit** credit application form; **f. de réponse** reply form; *Com* **f. de soumission** tender form; **f. de télégramme** telegram form **3** *Chim & Math* formula; **la f. pour convertir les degrés Fahrenheit en degrés Celsius** the formula for converting degrees Fahrenheit into degrees Celsius; **f. empirique** empirical formula **4** *Pharm* formula, composition **5** (*solution*) formula, trick; **ils ont (trouvé) la f. pour ne pas avoir d'ennuis** they've found a way of avoiding problems **6** (*méthode*) way; **une f. économique pour vos vacances** an economical way to spend your holidays; **c'est la f. idéale pour les vacances en famille** it's the ideal formula for a family holiday; **nous vous proposons plusieurs formules de crédit** we offer you several credit options; **formules de paiement** methods of payment, payment options; **formules de remboursement** repayment options; **nouvelle f.** (*menu, abonnement*) new-style; **une nouvelle f. de spectacle/restaurant** a new kind of show/restaurant; **notre restaurant vous propose sa f. à 20 euros ou sa carte** our restaurant offers you a set menu at 20 euros or an à la carte menu **7** *Aut* formula; **f. 1/2/3** formula 1/2/3; **courir en f. 3** to compete in formula 3 races **8** *Méd* **f. dentaire** dental formula

formuler [3] [fɔrmyle] VT **1** (*exprimer* → *doctrine, revendication*) to formulate, to express; (→ *souhait*) to express; (→ *proposition*) to formulate, to put into words; (→ *plainte*) to lodge; **elle m'a regardé sans oser f. sa question** she looked at me without daring to ask her question **2** (*rédiger* → *théorème*) to formulate; (→ *décret, acte*) to draw up

fornicateur, -trice [fɔrnikatœr, -tris] NM,F *Littéraire ou Hum* fornicator

fornication [fɔrnikasjɔ̃] NF *Littéraire ou Hum* fornication

fornicatrice [fɔrnikatris] *voir* **fornicateur**

forniquer [3] [fɔrnike] VI *Littéraire ou Hum* to fornicate

FORPRONU [fɔrprɔny] NF (*abrév* **Forces de protection des Nations unies**) UN-profor

fors [fɔr] **PRÉP** *Arch* except, save; **tout est perdu, f. l'honneur** all is lost save honour

forsure [fɔrsyr] **NF** *Can (abats)* pluck; *(plat)* fried liver dish

forsythia [fɔrsisja] **NM** forsythia

FORT, -E [fɔr, fɔrt]

> **ADJ** strong **A1, 4, 6, B3, 4** ■ hard **A1, 6** ■ powerful **A4, 5** ■ big **B1** ■ thick **B1** ■ broad **B1** ■ pronounced **B2** ■ loud **B2** ■ intense **B3**
> **ADV** hard **1** ■ loud **3** ■ loudly **3** ■ very **4**
> **NM** forte **2** ■ fort **3**

ADJ A. *QUI A DE LA PUISSANCE, DE L'EFFET* **1** *(vigoureux → personne, bras)* strong, sturdy; *(→ vent)* strong, high; *(→ courant, jet)* strong; *(→ secousse)* hard; *(→ pluies)* heavy; *Météo* **mer forte** rough sea; **f. comme un Turc** *ou* **un bœuf** as strong as an ox

2 *(d'une grande résistance morale)* **une âme forte** a steadfast soul; **rester f. dans l'adversité** to remain strong *or* to stand firm in the face of adversity

3 *(autoritaire, contraignant → régime)* strong-arm *(avant n)*

4 *(puissant → syndicat, parti, économie)* strong, powerful; *(→ monnaie)* strong, hard; *(→ carton, loupe, tranquillisant)* strong; **l'as est plus f. que le roi** the ace is higher than the king; **colle (très) forte** (super) *or* extra strong glue; **tes lunettes sont trop fortes pour moi** your glasses are too strong for me; **c'est plus f. que moi** I can't help it; **je l'ai frappé, c'était plus f. que moi** I couldn't help hitting him; **f. de son expérience** with a wealth of experience behind him; **f. de leur protection** reassured by their protection; **une équipe forte de 40 hommes** a 40-strong team; **l'homme f. du parti** the strong man of the party

5 *(de grand impact → œuvre, film)* powerful; *(→ argument)* weighty, powerful, forcible; **le moment le plus f. de la pièce** the most powerful moment in the play

6 *Ling (formation, verbe)* strong; *(consonne)* hard

B. *MARQUÉ* **1** *(épais, corpulent → jambes)* big, thick; *(→ personne)* stout, large; *(→ hanches)* broad, large, wide; **avoir la taille forte** to be big around the waist; **ils ont de jolis modèles pour les femmes fortes** they've got nice outsize designs

2 *(important quantitativement → dénivellation)* steep, pronounced; *(→ accent)* strong, pronounced, marked; *(→ fièvre, taux)* high; *(→ hausse)* large; *(→ somme)* large, big; *(→ concentration)* high; *(→ bruit)* loud; *(→ différence)* great, big; **il est prêt à payer le prix f.** he's willing to pay the full price; **au prix f., le lave-linge vous coûterait 800 euros** if you had to pay the full price, the washing machine would cost you 800 euros; **baisse le son, c'est trop f.** turn the sound down, it's too loud

3 *(grand, intense → amour, haine)* strong, intense; *(→ douleur)* intense, great; *(→ influence)* strong, big, great; *(→ propension)* marked; **il recherche les sensations fortes** he's after big thrills; **avoir une forte volonté** to be strong-willed, to have a strong will; **elle a une forte personnalité** she's got a strong personality

4 *(café, thé, moutarde, tabac)* strong; *(sauce)* hot, spicy; *(odeur)* strong; **ces oignons sont très forts** these onions are really strong

5 *Fam (locutions)* **c'est un peu f. (de café)** that's a bit rich; **et c'est moi qui devrais payer? alors ça, c'est trop f.!** and I should pay? that's a bit much!; **le plus f., c'est qu'il avait raison!** the best of it is that he was right!; **trop f.!** cool!, *Br* wicked!, *Am* awesome!

C. *HABILE* **son frère est magicien/acrobate, il est très f.** his/her brother's a magician/an acrobat, and a very good one; **le marketing, c'est là qu'il est f./que sa société est forte** marketing is his/his company's strong point; **trouver plus f. que soi** to meet one's match; **pour faire des gaffes, tu es forte!** when it comes to making blunders, you take some beating!; **pour donner des leçons, elle est très forte!** she's very good at lecturing people!; **f. en** very good at; **f. en gymnastique/en langues** very good at gymnastics/at languages; **il est très f. à la volée** he volleys very well; **encore plus f., il va vous dire le numéro de votre passeport!** better still, he's going to tell you what your passport number is!

ADV 1 *(avec vigueur → taper, tirer)* hard; **pousse plus f.** push harder

2 *Fam (avec intensité)* **il pleut f.** it's pelting down; **sentir f.** to smell; **mets le gaz plus/moins f.** turn the gas up/down; **le gaz est trop f.** the gas is too high; **tu y vas un peu f.!** you're going a bit far!

3 *(bruyamment → parler)* loudly, loud; **parle plus f., on ne t'entend pas** speak up, we can't hear you; **parle moins f.** lower your voice; **ne chante pas si f.** don't sing so loud; **mets le son plus/moins f.** turn the sound up/down

4 *(très)* very; **f. désagréable** most disagreeable; **f. joli** very pretty; **c'est f. bien dit!** well said!; **f. bien, partons à midi!** very well, let's leave at noon!; *Hum* **j'en suis f. aise!** I'm very pleased to hear it!

5 *(locution)* **faire f.** to do really well■, to excel oneself■; **là, tu as fait très f.!** you've really excelled yourself!

NM 1 *(physiquement, moralement)* **les forts et les faibles** the strong and the weak; **un f. en thème** *(intellectuellement) Br* a swot, *Am* a grind

2 *(spécialité)* forte; **la cuisine, ce n'est pas ton f.!** cooking isn't your forte!; **la politesse n'est pas son f.!** politeness isn't his/her strongest point!

3 *(forteresse)* fort; **le f. Chabrol** = name given to the building in the rue de Chabrol where members of the anti-Dreyfusard "Grand Occident" held out in a hopeless show of resistance against the police in 1899

❑ **au (plus) fort de PRÉP au (plus) f. de l'hiver** in the depths of winter; **au (plus) f. de l'été** in the height of summer

---

fort-à-bras [fɔrabra] *(pl* **forts-à-bras***)* **NM** *Can (fanfaron)* braggart, boaster; *(lutteur)* strongman, wrestler; *(videur)* bouncer, heavy

fortage [fɔrtaʒ] = **foretage**

Fort-de-France [fɔrdəfrɑ̃s] **NM** Fort-de-France

forte [fɔrte] **ADJ & NM INV** *Mus* forte

fortement [fɔrtəmɑ̃] **ADV 1** *(avec force)* hard; **appuyer f. sur les deux bords pour les coller** press both ends tight to glue them together; **f. salé** heavily salted; **f. épicé** highly spiced; **f. charpenté** solidly built

2 *(avec netteté)* strongly; **des traits f. marqués** strongly marked features

3 *(beaucoup → souhaiter, influencer)* strongly; **il désire f. vous rencontrer** he wishes very much to meet you; **être f. tenté** to be sorely tempted; **être f. intéressé par qch** to be most interested in sth; **être f. impressionné (par qn/qch)** to be most impressed (by sb/sth); **insister f. sur qch** to insist firmly *or* strongly on sth; **f. critiqué** strongly *or* highly criticized; **f. irrité** greatly *or* extremely irritated; **c'est f. conseillé** it's strongly advised

forteresse [fɔrtərɛs] **NF 1** *(citadelle)* fortress **2** *(prison)* fortress **3** *Aviat* **f. volante** flying fortress **4** *Fig* wall, barrier; **f. de préjugés** wall of prejudice

fortiche [fɔrtiʃ] **ADJ** *Fam* clever■, smart■; **elle est f. en anglais!** she's *Br* dead *or Am* real good at English!

fortifiant, -e [fɔrtifjɑ̃, -ɑ̃t] **ADJ 1** *(nourriture)* fortifying; *(climat)* bracing, invigorating **2** *Littéraire (édifiant)* uplifting

NM tonic

fortification [fɔrtifikasjɔ̃] **NF 1** *(mur)* fortification, wall **2** *(action)* **la f. d'une ville** the fortification of a town

fortifier [9] [fɔrtifje] **VT 1** *(affermir → muscle, santé)* to fortify, to strengthen; *(→ amitié, volonté, opinion, impression)* to strengthen; *(→ mur)* to fortify, to strengthen; **il m'a fortifié dans ma décision** he strengthened me in my decision; **ainsi fortifié dans ses préjugés, il reprit la lecture du journal** with his prejudices thus confirmed, he went back to reading the paper

2 *(protéger)* to fortify; **une ville fortifiée** a walled *or* fortified town

►**se fortifier VPR 1** *(emploi passif)* **la ville s'est fortifiée au XIIème siècle** the town was fortified *or* walls were built around the town in the 12th century

2 *Mil* to raise a line of defences; *(en creusant des tranchées)* to dig oneself in

3 *(devenir plus fort)* to get *or* to become stronger; *(muscle)* to firm up, to grow stronger; *(amitié, amour)* to grow stronger; **l'exercice aide le corps à se f.** exercise helps the body grow stronger

4 se f. le dos/les chevilles to strengthen one's back/ankles

fortifs [fɔrtif] **NFPL** *Fam* **les f.** = the old defence works around Paris, once a favourite area for criminals

fortin [fɔrtɛ̃] **NM** small fort

fortiori [fɔrsjɔri] *voir* **a fortiori**

fortissimo [fɔrtisimo] *Mus* **ADV** *(tempo)* fortissimo **NM** *(morceau de musique)* fortissimo

fortitude [fɔrtityd] **NF** *Littéraire* fortitude

Fortran [fɔrtrɑ̃] **NM** Fortran, FORTRAN

fortuit, -e [fɔrtɥi, -it] **ADJ** *(événement)* fortuitous; **faire une rencontre fortuite** to meet somebody by chance, to have a chance encounter *or* meeting; **dans cette affaire, rien n'est f.** nothing is fortuitous *or* nothing can be put down to chance in this matter; *Jur* **cas f.** act of God

fortuitement [fɔrtɥitmɑ̃] **ADV** by chance, fortuitously

fortune [fɔrtyn] **NF 1** *(biens)* wealth, fortune; **une f. personnelle** private wealth, a private fortune; **sa f. est importante** he/she has a considerable fortune, he/she has considerable wealth; **toute sa f. est en biens immobiliers** his/her entire fortune is in property *or* real estate; *Fam* **ça lui a rapporté une (petite) f.** it brought him/her a nice little sum; **c'était une f. à l'époque** it was a lot of money at the time; *Hum* **voici 20 euros, c'est toute ma f.!** here's 20 euros, it's all my worldly wealth!; **son père est une grosse f.** his father is a very wealthy man; **avoir de la f.** to be wealthy; **faire f.** to make one's fortune; **valoir une f.** to be worth a fortune

2 *Littéraire (hasard)* good fortune, luck; **il a eu la bonne** *ou* **l'heureuse f. de la connaître** he was fortunate enough to know her; **il a eu la mauvaise f. de tomber malade** he was unlucky enough *or* he had the misfortune to fall ill; **un homme en bonnes fortunes** a Don Juan; **être en bonne f.** to be successful *(with women)*; **faire contre mauvaise f. bon cœur** to make the best of a bad job; *Prov* **la f. sourit aux audacieux** fortune favours the bold; **la f. vient en dormant** good luck comes when you least expect it; **dîner à la f. du pot** to take pot luck; **inviter qn à la f. du pot** to invite sb to take pot luck; **viens, ce sera à la f. du pot!** come and take pot luck!

3 *Littéraire (sort)* fortune; **leurs livres ont connu des fortunes très diverses** their books had varying success

4 *Naut* **f. de mer** *(biens)* property at sea; *(risques)* perils of the sea; **voile de f.** crossjack; **mât de f.** jury mast

❑ **de fortune ADJ** *(lit, moyens)* makeshift; *(installation, réparation)* temporary

❑ **sans fortune ADJ** with no hope of an inheritance

fortuné, -e [fɔrtyne] **ADJ 1** *(riche)* rich, wealthy **2** *Littéraire (heureux)* fortunate, blessed

forum [fɔrɔm] **NM** *Antiq & Archit* forum; *(débat)* forum; *Ordinat* **f. de discussion** forum; **F. économique mondial** World Economic Forum; **f. sur l'éducation** forum *or* symposium on education; **le F. des Halles** = shopping complex at Les Halles in Paris; *Rad* **f. populaire** vox pop; **F. social mondial** World Social Forum

forure [fɔryr] **NF** *(gén)* bore hole; *(d'une clé)* pipe

fosa [foza] **NM** *Zool* fossa

fosbury-flop [fɔsbœriflɔp] *(pl* **fosbury-flops***)* **NM** *Sport* Fosbury flop

fosse [fos] **NF 1** *(cavité)* pit; **f. à fumier/à purin** manure/slurry pit; **f. (d'aisances)** cesspool; **f. aux lions** lions' den; *Fig* **descendre dans la f. aux lions** to enter the lions' den; **f. aux ours** bear pit; **f. septique** septic tank

2 *Aut & Sport* pit; *Aut* **f. (de réparation)** inspection pit
3 *Mus* **f. d'orchestre** orchestra pit
4 *(tombe)* grave; **f. commune** common grave; **creuser sa f. avec ses dents** = to eat oneself into an early grave; **avoir un pied dans la f.** to have one foot in the grave
5 *Anat* fossa; **fosses nasales** nasal fossae
6 *Géol* trough; *(abyssale)* trench; **f. sous-marine** deep-sea *or* ocean trench; **les animaux des grandes fosses** animals living on the ocean bed
7 *Mines* pit
8 *Golf* **f. de sable** sand trap, bunker

fossé [fose] **NM** 1 *(tranchée)* ditch; *(douve)* moat; **finir** *ou* **se retrouver dans le f.** to end up in a ditch; *Mil* **f. antichar** antitank ditch; *Aut* **f. d'inspection** inspection pit
2 *Fig* gulf, gap; **f. culturel** culture gap; **le f. qui nous sépare** the gulf between us; **le f. ne cesse de se creuser entre eux** there is an ever-widening gulf between them; **le f. des générations** the generation gap
3 *Géol* trough; **f. tectonique** *ou* **d'effondrement** graben

fossette [fosɛt] **NF** dimple

fossile [fosil] **ADJ** fossil *(avant n)*; *Fig* fossil-like, fossilized
NM *aussi Fig* fossil; *Fam* **un vieux f.** an old fossil

fossilifère [fosilifɛr] **ADJ** fossiliferous

fossilisation [fosilizasjɔ̃] **NF** fossilization

fossiliser [3] [fosilize] **VT** to fossilize
▶**se fossiliser VPR** to become fossilized

fossoir [foswar] **NM** *Agr (charrue)* vineyard plough; *(houe)* hoe

fossoyer [13] [foswaje] **VT** *Littéraire* to dig

fossoyeur [foswajœr] **NM** gravedigger; *Fig Littéraire* **les fossoyeurs de la révolution** the destroyers *or* gravediggers of the revolution

fou, folle [fu, fɔl]

> **fol** is used before masculine singular nouns beginning with a vowel or h mute.

ADJ 1 *(dément)* insane, mad; **devenir f.** to go mad *or* insane; **je ne suis pas f. tout de même, je l'ai bien vu hier** I'm not crazy *or* mad you know, I really did see him yesterday; **il y a de quoi devenir f.!** it's enough to drive you mad!; **un regard un peu f.** a somewhat crazed look; **être f. de bonheur/joie/douleur** to be beside oneself with happiness/joy/grief; **être f. d'inquiétude** to be mad with worry; **être f. d'amour pour qn, être f. amoureux de qn** to be madly in love with sb; **être f. furieux** *ou* **à lier** to be (stark) raving mad
2 *(déraisonnable)* mad; **tu serais f. de ne pas accepter** you'd be mad *or* crazy not to accept; **je ne suis pas assez f. pour y aller tout seul** I'm not mad *or* crazy enough to go by myself; **ton projet est complètement f.** your plan is completely crazy *or* mad; **un fol espoir** a foolish *or* mad hope; **avoir de folles pensées** to have wild thoughts; **il n'est pas f.** he's no fool; *Fam* **pas folle, la guêpe!** he's/she's not stupid!; **souvent femme varie, (bien) fol qui s'y fie** woman is fickle, man beware!
3 *(hors de soi)* wild, mad; **des diamants? mais tu es f.!** diamonds? you're mad *or* crazy!; **rendre qn f.** to drive *or* to send sb mad; **il est encore en retard, ça me rend folle!** he's late again, it drives me wild *or* mad!; **cette musique/situation me rend f.** the music/situation is driving me mad
4 *(passionné)* **être f. de qn/qch** to be mad *or* wild about sb/sth; **elle est folle de football** she's crazy about *or Br* mad keen on football
5 *(intense)* mad, wild; **nous avons passé une folle soirée** we had a wild evening; **entre eux, c'est l'amour f.** they're crazy about each other, they're madly in love
6 *(incontrôlé)* wild; **se lancer dans une course folle** to embark on a headlong chase; **camion/train f.** runaway truck/train; **boussole folle** crazy compass needle; **folle avoine** wild oats; **folles illusions** wild delusions; **avoir des mèches folles** to have wild *or* straggly hair; **f. rire** (uncontrollable) giggle *or* giggles; **avoir** *ou* **être pris d'un f. rire** to have a fit of the giggles; *Bible* **les vierges folles** the foolish virgins; *Littéraire* **les tourbillonnements fols des feuilles** the wild whirlings of the leaves
7 *Fam (très important)* tremendous; **il y avait un monde f.** there was a huge crowd■; **un prix f.** an extortionate price■; **un succès f.** a tremendous *or* wild success; **mettre un temps f. à faire qch** to take absolutely ages to do sth; **nous avons mis un temps f. pour venir** it took us ages to get here; **ça dure un temps f.** it goes on for ages; **gagner un argent f.** to make piles *or* a lot of money; **à une allure folle** at breakneck speed; **d'une gaieté folle** wildly happy; *Fam* **c'est f. ce que c'est grand!** it's incredible how big it is!
8 *(incroyable)* incredible; **c'est une histoire complètement folle!** it's the most incredible story!; **c'est f., ce qui lui est arrivé** what happened to him/her is incredible
9 *Jur* **folle enchère** irresponsible bid
NM,F 1 *(dément)* madman, *f* madwoman; *Vieilli* **envoyer qn chez les fous** to have sb locked up *or* put away; **vous n'avez pas vu le feu rouge, espèce de f.?** didn't you see the red light, you stupid fool?; **tais-toi, vieille folle!** shut up, you crazy old woman!; **comme un f.** dementedly; *(intensément)* like mad *or* crazy; **c'est une histoire de fous** I can't make head (n)or tail of it; **c'est un f. fou** he's a raving lunatic
2 *(excité)* lunatic, fool; **ce jeune f. va nous entraîner dans une catastrophe** that young fool will ruin us; **faire le f.** to act the fool *or* idiot
3 *(passionné)* **c'est un f. de moto** he's mad on *or* crazy about bikes; **f. du volant** reckless driver
NM 1 *Échecs* bishop
2 *Hist* **f. (du roi)** (court) jester
3 *Orn* booby; **f. brun** brown booby; **f. de Bassan** gannet
4 *(locution)* **plus on est de fous plus on rit** the more the merrier
❑ **folle NF** 1 *Fam Péj (homosexuel)* queen; **grande folle** screaming queen 2 *Littéraire (locution)* **la folle du logis** a vivid imagination

> *Allusion*
> **Ils sont fous ces Romains**
> Obélix, the famous cartoon character from *Astérix*, makes this comment every time the Romans do something he does not understand. It means "These Romans are crazy!" When French people do not understand an unfamiliar aspect of a foreign culture (or when they disapprove of it), they will use this expression or a variant of it. For example, of the fact that the English put mint sauce on their lamb – **Ils sont fous ces Anglais!**

fouace [fwas] = **fougasse**

fouacier [fwasje] **NM** *Vieilli* = person who bakes or sells "fougasses"

fouage [fwaʒ] **NM** *Hist* hearth-tax

fouaille [fwɑj] **NF** *Chasse* fourail

fouailler [3] [fwaje] **VT** *Littéraire* to whip, to lash; **la pluie leur fouaillait le visage** the rain lashed at their faces

foucade [fukad] **NF** *Littéraire* whim, passing fancy

fouchtra [fuʃtra] **EXCLAM** *très Fam* = swear word presumed to be used by people in the Auvergne

foudre[1] [fudr] **NM** 1 *(tonneau)* tun 2 *Myth* thunderbolt
❑ **foudre de guerre NM** 1 *(guerrier)* great warrior 2 *Fig Hum* **ce n'est pas un f. de guerre** he wouldn't say boo to a goose; *Fig* **f. d'éloquence** powerful orator

foudre[2] [fudr] **NF** *Météo* lightning; *Bible* thunderbolt; **être frappé par la f.** to be struck by lightning; **il est resté comme frappé par la f.** he looked as if he had been struck by lightning; **prompt** *ou* **rapide comme la f.** (as) quick as lightning
❑ **foudres NFPL** *Littéraire* wrath, ire; **il a tout fait pour s'attirer les foudres du public** he did everything to bring down the public's wrath upon him *or* to incur the public's wrath

foudroiement [fudrwamɑ̃] **NM** 1 *(fait de foudroyer)* striking 2 *(fait d'être foudroyé)* being struck

foudroyage [fudrwajaʒ] **NM** *Mines* caving

foudroyant, -e [fudrwajɑ̃, -ɑ̃t] **ADJ** 1 *(soudain)* violent; *(attaque, nouvelles)* devastating; **une crise cardiaque foudroyante** a massive coronary; **une mort foudroyante** (an) instant death; **un poison f.** a devastatingly lethal poison
2 *(extraordinaire)* striking, lightning *(avant n)*; **faire des progrès foudroyants** to make lightning progress; **la pièce a connu un succès f.** the play was a massive success; **à une vitesse foudroyante** with lightning speed
3 *(furieux → regard)* thunderous; **jeter des regards foudroyants à qn** to look daggers at sb

foudroyer [13] [fudrwaje] **VT** 1 *Météo* to strike; **être foudroyé** to be struck by lightning
2 *(tuer)* to strike down; **la sentinelle a été foudroyée par une balle perdue** the sentry was struck by a stray bullet; **foudroyé par une crise cardiaque** struck down by a heart attack; **foudroyé par une décharge électrique** killed by an electric shock, electrocuted; *Fig* **f. qn du regard** *ou* **des yeux** to look daggers at sb
3 *(anéantir)* to strike down; **la mort de ses parents l'a foudroyé** he was crushed by his parents' death; **la division fut foudroyée par la puissance de feu de l'ennemi** the division was decimated by enemy fire power

fouëne [fwɛn] = **foène**

fouet [fwɛ] **NM** 1 *(instrument)* whip; **donner le f. à qn** to whip *or* to flog sb; **coup de f.** lash, stroke; *Fig* fillip, stimulus; **l'air de la mer lui a donné un coup de f.** the sea air has perked him/her up *or* given him/her a lift; **donner un coup de f. à l'économie** to stimulate *or* to boost the economy, to give a fillip to the economy 2 *Culin* whisk 3 *Orn* **f. de l'aile** wing tip 4 *Naut (d'une poulie)* tail

fouettard [fwɛtar] *voir* **père**

fouetté, -e [fwete] **ADJ** *(crème)* whipped
NM *(en danse)* fouetté

fouettement [fwɛtmɑ̃] **NM** *(de la pluie, de la grêle)* lashing; *(d'une voile)* flapping

fouette-queue [fwɛtkø] (*pl* **fouette-queues**) **NM** agamid

fouetter [4] [fwete] **VT** 1 *(frapper)* to whip, to flog; **f. son cheval** to whip one's horse; **fouette, cocher!** don't spare the horses!; **il n'y a pas de quoi f. un chat** there's nothing to get excited about
2 *Culin (crème)* to whip; *(blanc d'œuf)* to beat, to whisk
3 *(cingler → sujet: pluie)* to lash
4 *Fig (exciter)* to excite, to stimulate; **vent qui fouette le sang** wind that makes the blood tingle; **le sang fouetté par le désir** spurred on *or* stimulated by desire; **l'air glacé lui fouettait le sang** the icy air got his/her circulation going
VI 1 *(câble)* to lash, to whip; *(voile)* to flap; **la pluie fouette contre les vitres** the rain is lashing (against) the panes
2 *très Fam (empester)* to stink■, *Br* to pong; **ça fouette par ici!** there's a hell of a stink *or Br* a pong in here!
3 *très Fam (avoir peur)* to wet oneself

foufou, fofolle [fufu, fɔfɔl] **ADJ** *Fam* crazy, loopy

foufoune [fufun], **foufounette** [fufunɛt] **NF** *Vulg (sexe de femme)* pussy, *Br* fanny
❑ **foufounes NFPL** *Can Fam (en langage enfantin)* bum, botty

fougasse [fugas] **NF** = flat loaf traditionally cooked in wood-ash and sometimes flavoured with olives or anchovies

fouger [17] [fuʒe] **VI** *Chasse* to root, to rout

fougeraie [fuʒrɛ] **NF** patch of ferns

fougère [fuʒɛr] **NF** fern; **f. aigle** bracken; **f. arborescente** tree fern

fougue [fug] **NF** 1 *(ardeur)* passion, spirit, ardour; **la f. de la jeunesse** youthful high spirits; **cheval plein de f.** spirited horse; **un discours rempli** *ou* **plein de f.** a fiery speech; **il s'est lancé dans cette aventure avec la f. de ses vingt ans** he threw himself into this adventure with all the ardour of his twenty years; **se battre avec f.** to fight with spirit, to put up a spirited fight; **répondre avec f.** to answer with brio
2 *Naut* topgallant (mast)

fougueuse [fugøz] *voir* **fougueux**

fougueusement [fugøzmɑ̃] **ADV** ardently, with brio, with passion; *(s'élancer)* impetuously; *(s'embrasser)* passionately

fougueux, -euse [fugø, -øz] **ADJ** *(personne)*

ardent, fiery, impetuous; *(cheval)* spirited; *(réponse, résistance)* spirited, lively; **tempérament f.** fiery temperament

fouillage [fujaʒ] **NM** *Agr* burrowing

fouille [fuj] **NF 1** *(d'un lieu)* search; **passer à la f.** to be searched; **f. corporelle** *(rapide)* frisking; *(approfondie)* body search

2 *Agr* digging (up)

3 *Mines* exploration, search; **travail en f.** earth digging; **f. à ciel ouvert** open pit

4 *très Fam (poche)* pocket■; *Fig* **se remplir les fouilles, s'en mettre plein les fouilles** to line one's pockets

5 *Can (chute)* fall; **prendre une f.** to fall, to have a fall

❑ **fouilles NFPL** *Archéol* dig, excavations; **faire des fouilles** to carry out excavations *or* a dig; **participer à des fouilles** to take part in a dig

fouillé, -e [fuje] **ADJ** *(enquête)* thorough, wide-ranging; *(étude)* detailed; *(détails)* elaborate

fouille-merde [fujmɛrd] **NMF INV** *très Fam* nosey parker

fouiller [3] [fuje] **VT 1** *(explorer → tiroir)* to search (through); *(→ valise)* to go through; *(→ au cours d'une vérification)* to search, to go through; **nous avons fouillé toute la maison/région** we searched the entire house/area; **fouille un peu tes poches, tu vas sûrement le retrouver!** have a look in your pockets, you're bound to find it!; **la police a fouillé tous les bagages** the police went through all the luggage; **f. qn** *(rapidement)* to frisk sb; *(de façon approfondie)* to search sb; **ses yeux fouillaient la salle** his/her eyes *or* he/she scanned the room

2 *(creuser → sujet: cochon, taupe)* to dig; **f. la terre** to root in *or* to burrow in *or* to dig the earth; *Archéol* **f. un site** to excavate a site

3 *(approfondir)* to go deeply *or* thoroughly into; **il aurait fallu f. la question** the question should have been researched more thoroughly

VI 1 *(creuser → gén)* to dig; *(→ lapin)* to burrow; *(→ cochon)* to root; **c'est là qu'il vous faut f.** this is where you must dig

2 *(faire une recherche)* **f. dans qch** *(légitimement)* to go through sth, to search sth; *(par indiscrétion)* to go through sth, *Péj* to rifle through sth; **f. dans une armoire/dans sa poche** to search *or* to rummage in a cupboard/in one's pocket; **f. dans les papiers de qn** to search through *or* to go through sb's papers; **f. dans les librairies pour trouver un livre** to search around in bookshops for a book; **f. dans sa mémoire** to search one's memory; **f. dans son esprit** to rack one's brains; **f. dans le passé de qn** to delve into sb's past

3 *Can (tomber)* to fall, to tumble (over)

▸**se fouiller VPR 1** *(emploi réfléchi)* **se f. les poches** to go through one's pockets

2 *Fam* **tu peux toujours te f.!** dream on!, nothing doing!; **une participation? il peut se f.!** let him have a share in the profits? he can whistle for it *or* not likely!

fouilleur, -euse [fujœr, -øz] **NM,F 1** *Archéol* excavator **2** *(policier)* searcher; *(à la douane)* officer who carries out body-searches **3** *(fouineur)* rummager, searcher; **un f. de brocantes/bibliothèques** an avid frequenter of second-hand shops/libraries

❑ **fouilleuse NF** *Agr* subsoil plough

fouillis [fuji] **NM** jumble; **faire du f.** *(personne)* to make a mess; **range ton f.** put away your mess; **quel f. dans ta chambre!** what a mess *or* dump *or* shambles your room is!; **un f. de** a mass *or* a jumble of; **le jardin n'est qu'un f. de ronces** the garden's nothing but a mass of brambles; **se perdre dans un f. de détails** to get bogged down in (a mass of) details

ADJ messy, untidy; **ce que tu peux être f.!** you're so messy!; *Fam* **faire f.** to look messy

❑ **en fouillis** *Fam* **ADJ** in a mess; **une chambre en f.** a messy room; **des dossiers en f.** muddled-up files **ADV laisser un lieu en f.** to leave a place in a mess

fouinard, -e [fwinar, -ard] *Fam* **ADJ** nosey, prying

NM busybody, *Br* nosey parker

fouine [fwin] **NF 1** *Zool* stone *or* beech marten; **avoir un visage de f.** to be weasel-faced **2** *Fam (fouineur)* busybody, *Br* nosey parker; **avoir un air de f.** to look like a right nosey parker **3** *Pêche* fishgig

fouiner [3] [fwine] **VI** *Fam* **1** *(explorer)* **f. au marché aux puces** to go hunting for bargains at the flea market **2** *Péj (être indiscret)* to nose about *or* around; **il est toujours à f. dans les affaires des autres** he keeps poking his nose into other people's business

fouineur, -euse [fwinœr, -øz] *Fam* **ADJ** nosey, prying

NM,F 1 *(indiscret)* busybody, *Br* nosey parker **2** *(chez les brocanteurs)* bargain hunter **3** *Offic Ordinat (pirate informatique)* hacker

fouir [32] [fwir] **VT** to burrow, to dig

fouissage [fwisaʒ] **NM** burrowing, digging

fouisseur, -euse [fwisœr, -øz] **ADJ** burrowing *(avant n)*, *Spéc* fossorial

NM burrower, *Spéc* fossorial animal

foulage [fulaʒ] **NM 1** *(du raisin)* pressing, treading; *(d'une peau)* tanning; *(d'un tissu)* fulling **2** *Typ* impression

foulant, -e [fulɑ̃, -ɑ̃t] **ADJ 1** *Fam (fatigant)* backbreaking, *Br* knackering; **c'est pas f.!** it's not exactly backbreaking work! **2** *voir* **pompe**

foulard [fular] **NM 1** *(pièce d'étoffe)* scarf; **le F. islamique** Muslim headscarf **2** *Tex* foulard

> *Culture*
> **LE FOULARD ISLAMIQUE**
> The issue of the wearing of the Muslim headscarf in state schools and other public buildings has been a source of huge controversy and debate in France for a number of years. The principle of secularism has long been a cornerstone of the French educational system (see box on "école laïque" at entry "école"), but the question of deciding whether it was acceptable for female Muslim pupils to wear the headscarf at school had been left to the discretion of school heads. Given the growing number of incidents involving girls being banned from school for insisting on wearing the headscarf and refusing to take part in activities such as physical education on religious grounds, the government passed a law in 2004 prohibiting the display of *any* obvious religious signs at school (as well as in state jobs that involve contact with the public). This measure was described as an attempt to safeguard the principle of secularism and to keep issues of ethnicity and religion from being a divisive factor among children.

foule [ful] **NF 1** *(gens)* crowd, *Péj* mob, *Littéraire* throng; *Fam* **il y a f.** there are crowds *or* masses of people; *Fam* **il n'y a pas f.** there's hardly anyone around; **fuir la f.** to flee the crowds; **mouvement de f.** *ou* **de foules** movement in the crowd; **quelle f. dans les rues!** how crowded the streets are!

2 *(masses populaires)* **la f., les foules** the masses; **un président qui plaît aux foules** a popular president

3 *(grand nombre)* **une f. de gens** a crowd of people; **une f. d'amis** a host of friends; **j'ai une f. de choses à te raconter** I've got lots of things to tell you; **il m'a donné une f. de détails** he gave me a whole mass of details

❑ **en foule ADV** *(venir, se présenter)* in huge numbers; **entrer en f.** to crowd in

foulée [fule] **NF 1** *(enjambée)* stride; **avancer à longues foulées** to stride along; **courir à petites foulées** to trot along **2 foulées** *(d'animaux sauvages)* track(s), spoor

❑ **dans la foulée ADV** *Fam* **dans la f., j'ai fait aussi le repassage** I did the ironing while I was at it

❑ **dans la foulée de PRÉP** *Sport* **rester dans la f. de qn** to stay close on sb's heels

fouler [3] [fule] **VT 1** *(écraser → raisin)* to press, to tread; *(→ céréale)* to tread

2 *(marcher sur)* to tread *or* to walk on; *Littéraire* **f. le sol natal** to tread the native soil; **nous foulions pour la première fois le sol de Grèce** we were setting foot for the first time on Greek soil; **f. qch aux pieds** to trample on sth

3 *(cuir, peau)* to tan

4 *Tex* to full

▸**se fouler VPR 1** *Fam* **se f. (la rate)** *(se fatiguer)* to strain oneself, to overexert oneself; **tu ne t'es pas beaucoup foulé** you didn't exactly strain *or* overexert yourself, did you?

2 *(se faire mal)* **se f. le poignet** to sprain one's wrist; **se f. la cheville** to sprain *or* to twist one's ankle

foulerie [fulri] **NF** *Tex* **1** *(atelier)* fulling mill, fullery **2** *(machine)* fulling machine

fouleur, -euse [fulœr, -øz] **NM,F 1** *(de tissu)* fuller; *(de cuir)* tanner **2** *(de raisins)* winepresser *(person)*

fouloir [fulwar] **NM 1** *(pour le raisin)* wine press **2** *Tex* fulling mill **3** *(de tanneur)* tanning drum

foulon [fulɔ̃] **NM 1** *Tex (machine)* **(moulin à) f.** fulling mill; *(ouvrier)* fuller **2** *(de tanneur)* tanning drum **3 terre à f.** fuller's earth

foulonner [3] [fulɔne] **VT** *Tex (cuir)* to tan

foulque [fulk] **NF** *Orn* **f. (macroule)** coot; **f. américaine** American coot

foultitude [fultityd] **NF** *Fam* **une f. de** loads *or* masses of; **avoir une f. de choses à faire** to have loads of things to do

foulure [fulyr] **NF** sprain; **f. du poignet/de la cheville** sprained wrist/ankle

four [fur] **NM 1** *Culin* oven; **un plat allant au f.** an ovenproof dish; **de la vaisselle allant au f.** ovenware; **faire cuire au f.** *(pain)* to bake; *(viande)* to roast; **avoir qch au f.** to have sth cooking (in the oven); *Fig* to have sth in the pipeline *or Br* on the go; **f. de boulanger** baker's oven; **f. à catalyse** = oven fitted with catalytic liners; **f. à chaleur tournante** fan-assisted oven; **f. combiné** combi-oven; **f. électrique** electric oven; **f. à gas** gas oven; **f. à micro-ondes** microwave oven; **f. multifonctions** combi-oven; **f. à pain** baker's oven; **f. à pyrolyse** pyrolitic oven; **ouvrir la bouche comme un f.** to open one's mouth wide; **il fait chaud comme dans un f.** it's like an oven (in here); **on ne peut pas être à la fois au f. et au moulin** you can't be in two places at the same time

2 *Tech* furnace, kiln; **f. à briques** brick kiln; **f. à céramique** pottery kiln; **f. à chaux** lime kiln; **f. à émaux** enamelling kiln; **f. solaire** solar furnace

3 *Hist* **f. crématoire** gas oven *(in the Nazi concentration camps)*

4 *Fam (fiasco)* flop; **sa pièce a été** *ou* **a fait un f.** his/her play was a flop

fourbe [furb] *Littéraire* **ADJ** deceitful, treacherous

NMF cheat, treacherous *or* false-hearted person

fourberie [furbəri] **NF** *Littéraire* **1** *(duplicité)* treacherousness **2** *(acte)* treachery

> **'Les Fourberies de Scapin'** *Molière* 'That Scoundrel Scapin'

fourbi [furbi] **NM** *Fam* **1** *(désordre)* shambles *(singulier)*, mess; **quel f.! je ne retrouve rien!** what a muddle *or* mess! I can't find anything! **2** *(affaires)* stuff, *Br* gear; *(de soldat)* kit; **et tout le f.** the whole (kit and) caboodle **3** *(truc)* thingy

fourbir [32] [furbir] **VT 1** *(nettoyer)* to polish (up) **2** *Fig Littéraire* **f. ses armes** to prepare for war; **f. ses arguments** to line up one's arguments

fourbissage [furbisaʒ] **NM** polishing (up)

fourbisseur [furbisœr] **NM** (sword) furbisher

fourbu, -e [furby] **ADJ 1** *(personne)* exhausted; **je suis f.** I'm tired out *or* exhausted **2** *(cheval)* foundered

fourbure [furbyr] **NF** *Vét* founder, laminitis

fourche [furʃ] **NF 1** *Agr* fork; **f. à foin** pitchfork, hayfork; **remuer le sol à la f.** to fork the ground

2 *(embranchement)* fork; *Aut* Y-junction; **la route fait une f.** the road forks

3 *(d'une bicyclette, d'un arbre)* fork

4 *Aut* **f. d'attelage** trailer hitch

5 *Belg Scol* break, gap *(in one's timetable)*

6 *(de cheveux)* split end; **j'ai des fourches** I've got split ends

7 *Antiq* **les fourches Caudines** the Caudine Forks; *Fig* **passer sous les fourches Caudines** to be humiliated

8 *Hist* **les fourches patibulaires** the gallows

fourchée [furʃe] **NF** *Vieilli (de foin)* pitchforkful

fourcher [3] [furʃe] **VI 1** *Arch* to fork, to divide; **j'ai les cheveux qui fourchent** I've got split ends **2** *(locutions)* **sa langue a fourché** he/she made a slip (of the tongue); **excusez-moi, ma langue a fourché** sorry, it was a slip of the tongue

VT *(sol)* to fork

fourchet [furʃɛ] **NM** *Vét* foot rot

fourchette [furʃɛt] **NF 1** *(pour manger)* fork; **f. à dessert** dessert fork; **f. à escargots** snail fork; **f. à huîtres** oyster fork; **f. à poisson** fish fork; **être une bonne f.** to be a hearty eater; **elle a un bon coup de f.** she's a hearty eater; *Hum* **la f. du père Adam** the fingers

2 *(écart)* bracket; **une f. comprise entre 1000 et 1500 euros** prices ranging from 1,000 to 1,500 euros; *Bourse* **f. de cotation** trading range; *Bourse* **f. de cours de clôture** closing range; *Bourse* **f. de cours d'ouverture** opening range; **f. d'imposition** tax bracket; **f. de prix** price bracket *or* range; **dans une f. de prix acceptable** within an acceptable price range *or* bracket; **f. de salaire** wage bracket; **f. de taux** rate band

3 *Mil* bracket; **prendre une cible en f.** *ou* **à la f.** to bracket a target

4 *Anat* **f. sternale** jugular notch; **f. vulvaire** fourchette

5 *Zool (du cheval)* frog; *(de l'oiseau)* wishbone, *Spéc* furcula

6 *Cartes* tenace; *Échecs* fork

7 *(de balance)* beam support

8 *Tech* belt guide, shifter; **f. de débrayage** clutch throw-out fork; **f. d'embrayage** clutch fork

fourchon [furʃɔ̃] **NM** prong, tine

fourchu, -e [furʃy] **ADJ 1** *(cheveux)* **avoir les cheveux fourchus** to have split ends **2** *(tronc, route)* forked; *(bâton)* cleft **3** *(pied)* cloven; *(sabot)* cloven, cleft; *(menton)* cleft; **aux pieds fourchus** cloven-hoofed

fourgon [furgɔ̃] **NM 1** *(voiture)* van; *Br* **f. cellulaire** police van, *Am* patrol *or* police wagon; *Br* **f. de déménagement** removal *or Am* moving van; **f. funèbre** *ou* **funéraire** *ou* **mortuaire** hearse; **f. postal** mail van

2 *Rail* coach, *Br* wagon; *Br* **f. à bagages** luggage van, *Am* baggage car; **f. à bestiaux** *ou* **à bétail** cattle truck; **f. de queue** rear (brake) van, guard's van, *Am* caboose

3 *(tige de métal)* poker

fourgonner [3] [furgɔne] **VT** *(feu, poêle)* to poke, to rake

VI *Fam (fouiller)* to poke *or* to rummage about

fourgonnette [furgɔnɛt] **NF** (small) van

fourgon-pompe [furgɔ̃pɔ̃p] *(pl* **fourgons-pompes***)* **NM** fire engine

fourgue [furg] **NM** *Fam Arg crime* fence

fourguer [3] [furge] **VT** *Fam* **1** *Arg crime (vendre)* to fence **2** *Péj (donner)* to unload; **f. qch à qn** *(vendre)* to flog sth to sb; *(placer)* to unload sth on sb, to palm sth off on sb **3** *(dénoncer)* to squeal on, *Br* to grass on, to shop, *Am* to rat on

fouriérisme [furjerism] **NM** Fourierism

fouriériste [furjerist] **ADJ 1** *(relatif au fouriérisme)* Fourieristic, associationistic **2** *(partisan du fouriérisme)* of Fourierism

NMF Fourierist, associationist

fourme [furm] **NF** = hard cheese made in central France; **f. d'Ambert** Fourme d'Ambert (blue) cheese

fourmi [furmi] **NF 1** *Entom* ant; **f. blanche** termite; **f. légionnaire** army ant; **f. pharaon** sugar ant; **f. rouge** red ant

2 *(personne)* busy bee; **ma tante a toujours été une (vraie) f.** my aunt has always been a busy little bee

3 *Fam Arg crime (passeur)* (small-time) pusher

4 *(locution)* **avoir des fourmis dans les jambes** to have pins and needles in one's legs

❑ **de fourmi ADJ** *(travail)* meticulous, painstaking

fourmilier [furmilje] **NM 1** *Zool* anteater; **grand f.** giant anteater; **petit f.** lesser *or* collared anteater; **f. marsupial rayé** numbat, banded anteater **2** *Orn* antbird

fourmilière [furmiljɛr] **NF 1** *Entom* anthill, antheap; *Fig* **donner des coups de pied dans la f.** to stir things up **2** *Fig (lieu animé)* hive of activity; **l'aéroport s'est transformé en une véritable f.** the airport was bustling with activity; **cette banlieue est une véritable f. (humaine)** this suburb is swarming *or* teeming with people

fourmilion, fourmi-lion [furmiljɔ̃] *(pl* **fourmis-lions***)* **NM** *Entom* ant lion

fourmillement [furmijmɑ̃] **NM 1** *(picotement)* tingle, *Méd* formication; **j'ai des fourmillements dans les doigts** I've got pins and needles in my fingers **2** *(foisonnement → d'insectes, de promeneurs)* swarm; *(→ d'idées)* welter; **il fut pris de panique devant ce f. d'insectes** he panicked when he saw the swarm of insects *or* the swarming insects; **un f. de détails** a mass *or* wealth of detail

fourmiller [3] [furmije] **VI 1** *(s'agiter)* to swarm; **les vers fourmillaient dans ce fromage** the cheese was alive with maggots

2 *(être abondant)* to abound; **un documentaire où fourmillent les révélations intéressantes** a documentary full of *or* teeming with interesting revelations; **f. de** *(insectes, personnes)* to swarm with; *(fautes)* to be full of, to be riddled with; *(idées)* to be bursting with, to be full of

3 *(picoter)* to tingle; **j'ai les doigts qui fourmillent** I have pins and needles in my fingers, my fingers are tingling

fournaise [furnɛz] **NF 1** *Littéraire (feu)* blaze **2** *Can (poêle à bois)* (wood-burning) stove; *(poêle au charbon)* (coal-burning) stove; *(chaudière de chauffage central) Br* boiler, *Am* (central heating) furnace; **f. à l'huile** oil boiler **3** *(lieu caniculaire)* **la ville/cette chambre est une (vraie) f. en été** the city/this room is like an oven in the summer

fourneau, -x [furno] **NM 1** *(cuisinière)* stove; **f. de cuisine** (kitchen) range; **f. à gaz** gas stove *or Br* cooker; **être aux** *ou* **derrière les fourneaux** to be cooking; **c'est David qui est aux fourneaux ce soir** David is the chef this evening; **toujours à ses fourneaux!** always slaving over a hot stove!

2 *Métal* furnace; **haut f.** blast furnace

3 *(d'une pipe)* bowl

4 *(pour explosif)* mine chamber

fournée [furne] **NF 1** *(du boulanger)* batch; **faire deux fournées de pain dans la matinée** to bake two batches of bread in the morning; **aujourd'hui nous n'avons fait qu'une f.** today we only baked one batch **2** *Fam Fig (ensemble de choses)* batch; *(ensemble de personnes)* lot; **le métro dégorge sa dernière f.** the last lot of passengers leave the metro

fourni, -e [furni] **ADJ 1** *(touffu → cheveux)* thick; *(→ barbe)* heavy, thick; *(→ sourcils)* bushy; *(→ haie)* luxuriant; **barbe peu fournie** sparse *or* thin beard **2** *(approvisionné)* **abondamment** *ou* **bien f.** well-stocked; **mal f.** poorly stocked

fournier [furnje] **NM** *Orn* ovenbird

fournil [furni] **NM** bakehouse, bakery

fourniment [furnimɑ̃] **NM 1** *Mil* pack, equipment **2** *Fam (attirail)* gear, paraphernalia

fournir [32] [furnir] **VT 1** *(approvisionner)* to supply; **f. qch à qn** to supply sb with sth; **il n'y a plus de quoi f. les troupes** there's nothing left to feed the army; **f. qn en** to supply sb with; **f. une entreprise en matières premières** to supply a firm with raw materials; **c'est eux qui me fournissent en pain** I buy (my) bread from them

2 *(procurer)* to provide; **f. qch à qn** to provide sb with sth; **c'est la France qui leur fournit des armes** it's France who is providing *or* supplying them with weapons; **f. du travail aux chômeurs** to provide the unemployed with work; **il pourra peut-être te f. du travail** he might be able to give you some work; **vous devez nous f. un devis/une pièce d'identité** you must provide us with an estimate/some form of identification; **voici la liste des pièces à f.** here is a list of required documents; **f. un alibi à qn** to provide sb with an alibi; **f. des renseignements à qn** to supply *or* to provide *or* to furnish sb with information; **la brochure vous fournira tous les renseignements nécessaires** the brochure will give you all the necessary information; **fournissez-moi l'argent demain** let me have the money tomorrow

3 *(produire)* to produce; **ces vignes fournissent un vin de qualité moyenne** this vineyard produces a wine of average quality; **les régions du sud fournissent les agrumes et les olives** the southern regions produce citrus fruits and olives

4 *(accomplir)* **f. un effort** to make an effort

5 *Cartes* **f. la couleur demandée** to follow suit; **f. à trèfle** to follow suit in clubs

USAGE ABSOLU 1 *(approvisionner)* **qui fournit la famille royale?** who is the Royal Family's supplier?, who supplies the Royal Family?

2 *Hum (produire)* **je ne peux plus f., moi!** I can't cope any more!

❑ **fournir à VT IND** *Vieilli* **f. aux besoins de qn** to provide for sb's needs; **f. à la dépense** to defray the cost; **f. aux frais** to defray expenses

▸**se fournir VPR se f. chez qn** to get one's supplies from sb; **je me fournis toujours chez le même boucher** I always shop at the same butcher's, I get all my meat from the same place; **se f. en qch** to get in supplies of sth; **ils se fournissent (en vin) chez ce négociant** they get their supplies (of wine) from this merchant; **il se fournit chez nous** he is a customer of ours, he's one of our customers

fournissement [furnismɑ̃] **NM** *Fin* contribution *(in shares)*

fournisseur, -euse [furnisœr, -øz] **NM,F 1** *(établissement, marchand)* supplier; **fournisseurs de l'armée** army contractors; **f. de navires** *ou* **de la marine** ships' chandler; *Fin* **f. en capitaux** funder, supplier of capital; **f. exclusif** sole supplier; **f. principal** main supplier; **f. secondaire** secondary supplier; **quel est votre f. habituel?** who's your usual supplier?; **c'est le plus gros f. de papier de tout le pays** he's the biggest supplier of paper in the whole country

2 *Ordinat* **f. d'accès (à Internet)** (Internet) access provider; **f. de contenu** content provider

ADJ les pays fournisseurs de la France the countries that supply France (with goods), France's suppliers

fourniture [furnityr] **NF** *(action)* supplying, providing

❑ **fournitures NFPL** *(objets)* materials; **fournitures de bureau** office supplies; **fournitures de navires** ships' chandlery; **fournitures scolaires** school stationery

fourrage [furaʒ] **NM 1** *Agr* fodder; **f. sec** hay; **f. vert** silage; **rentrer du f.** to harvest forage **2** *(d'un vêtement → action)* lining; *(→ peau)* lining fur

fourrager[1] [17] [furaʒe] **VI** *(faire du fourrage)* to make fodder; *(se nourrir de fourrage)* to feed

VT 1 *Fam (papiers)* to rummage through **2** *Arch (pays)* to pillage, to ravage

❑ **fourrager dans VT IND** *Fam* to rummage through

fourrager[2]**, -ère** [furaʒe, -ɛr] **ADJ** fodder *(avant n)*; **plantes fourragères** fodder crops

❑ **fourragère NF 1** *Mil (décoration)* fourragère **2** *(champ)* field *(in which a fodder crop is grown)* **3** *(charrette)* cart *(for fodder)*

fourrageur [furaʒœr] **NM** *Arch Mil* **1** *(qui enlève le fourrage)* forager **2** *(cavalier)* = member of the cavalry in open order; **en fourrageurs** in open *or* extended order

fourre [fur] **NF** *Suisse (d'un oreiller)* pillowcase; *(pour un édredon)* quilt cover; *(d'un disque)* sleeve; *(d'un livre)* jacket

fourré[1] [fure] **NM** *(bois)* thicket; *(à la chasse)* cover; **il disparut dans les fourrés** he disappeared into the undergrowth *or* bushes

fourré[2]**, -e** [fure] **ADJ 1** *(doublé de fourrure)* fur-lined; **des chaussons/gants fourrés** lined slippers/gloves **2** *Culin* filled; **bonbons fourrés à la fraise** *Br* sweets *or Am* candy with strawberry-flavoured centres; **des dates fourrées à la pâte d'amandes** marzipan-filled dates, dates stuffed with marzipan; **chocolats fourrés** chocolate creams **3** *Fig Vieilli* **paix fourrée** hollow *or* mock peace

fourreau, -x [furo] **NM 1** *(d'une arme)* sheath; *(d'un parapluie)* cover; **remettre son épée au f.** to sheathe one's sword **2** *(robe)* sheath dress **3** *Élec* sleeve

ADJ jupe/robe f. pencil skirt/sheath dress

fourrer [3] [fure] **VT 1** *(doubler de fourrure)* to line with fur

2 *Culin (fruit, gâteau)* to fill; **f. un chocolat/une crêpe de qch** to fill a chocolate/a pancake with sth; **f. une dinde de marrons** to stuff a turkey with chestnuts

3 *Fam (mettre)* to stick, to shove; **f. qch dans qch** to stuff sth in *or* into sth; **je les avais fourrés dans le coin** I'd stuck them in the corner; **ne fourre pas tes affaires dans le sac, range-les** don't just shove your things into the bag, put them in neatly; *Fig* **f. qch dans la tête à qn** to get sth into sb's head; **ils lui ont fourré dans la tête**

que... they managed to get it into his/her head that...; **mais où ai-je bien pu f. ça?** where on earth have I stuck it?; **f. ses mains dans ses poches** to stick *or* to shove one's hands into one's pockets; **avoir les mains fourrées dans les poches** to have one's hands (deep) in one's pockets; **f. son doigt dans son nez** to stick one's finger up one's nose; *Fig* **f. son nez partout** to poke *or* to stick one's nose into everything; *Can Joual Vulg* **f. le chien** to screw around, to waste time mucking about

4 *Fam (laisser → papier, vêtement)* to put■, to leave■; **f. qch quelque part** to stick *or* to leave sth somewhere; **où as-tu fourré ce dossier?** where have you put *or* left that file?; **mon assistant fourre tout n'importe où** my assistant sticks things any old where

5 *Fam (placer → personne, animal)* to stick, to put■; **on l'a fourré en prison** *ou* **au trou** they stuck him in jail; **on m'a fourré aux archives** I've been stuck away *or* dumped in the archives section; **il est toujours fourré chez ses parents/à l'église** he's always at his parents'/in church■; **il est toujours fourré au bistrot** he's always stuck in the pub; **ce chat/gosse, toujours fourré dans mes jambes** *ou* **pattes!** that cat/kid is always under my feet!

6 *Vulg (posséder sexuellement)* to shaft, to poke

7 *Can Joual Vulg (tromper)* to screw, to shaft; **se faire f.** to get screwed *or* shafted

8 *Tech (jointure)* to pack

►**se fourrer** VPR *Fam* 1 *(se mettre)* **se f. au lit/sous les couvertures/dans son sac de couchage** to snuggle down in bed/under the blankets/into one's sleeping bag; **il s'est fourré dans le coin/sous le lit** he got into the corner/under the bed; **où est-il allé se f.?** wherever has he got to?, wherever has he hidden himself?; **il ne savait plus où se f.** he didn't know where to put himself

2 *(s'engager)* **se f. dans une sale affaire** to get mixed up in a nasty business; **se f. dans un (vrai) guêpier** to land oneself in real trouble

3 *(se mettre)* **se f. un doigt dans le nez** to stick one's finger up one's nose; **se f. une idée dans la tête** to get an idea into one's head; *Fig* **il s'est fourré dans le crâne que...** he's got it into his head that...; *Fig* **si tu crois que je vais l'attendre, tu te fourres le doigt dans l'œil (jusqu'à la clavicule)** if you think I'm going to wait for him/her, you've got another think coming

fourre-tout [furtu] NM INV 1 *(pièce)* junk room; *(placard)* junk cupboard 2 *(sac léger) Br* holdall, *Am* carryall; *(trousse)* pencil case 3 *Fig* jumble, ragbag; **cette loi est un (vrai) f.** this law is a real mess

ADJ INV **sac f.** *Br* holdall, *Am* carryall; **placard f.** junk cupboard; *Péj* **une loi f.** a mishmash *or* ragbag of a law

fourreur [furœr] NM furrier

fourrier [furje] NM 1 *Mil & Naut* quartermaster 2 *Littéraire* **être le f. de** to be a harbinger of 3 *Hist & Mil (responsable de la nourriture)* quartermaster sergeant; *(responsable du logement)* billeting officer

fourrière [furjɛr] NF *(pour chiens, pour voitures)* pound; **mettre une voiture en** *ou* **à la f.** to impound a car

fourrure [furyr] NF 1 *(vêtement)* fur; **un manteau/une veste de f.** a fur coat/jacket; **f. polaire** fleece 2 *(peau préparée)* fur 3 *Zool* fur, coat; **l'ours blanc a une épaisse f.** the polar bear has thick fur *or* a thick coat 4 *(commerce)* **la f.** the fur trade 5 *Tech* packing; *Aut* **f. de frein** brake lining 6 *Hér* fur

fourvoiement [furvwamɑ̃] NM *Littéraire* going astray

fourvoyer [13] [furvwaje] VT *Littéraire* to lead astray, to mislead

►**se fourvoyer** VPR *(s'égarer)* to lose one's way, to go astray; *Fig (se tromper)* to be mistaken, to be in error; **tu te fourvoies si tu crois qu'il va y renoncer** you're mistaken *or* you're making a mistake if you think he'll give it up; **se f. dans qch** to get oneself involved in sth; **je me suis encore fourvoyé dans une drôle d'histoire** I got myself involved in some funny business again; **où donc est-elle allée se f.?** where on earth has she got to?

fous *etc voir* **foutre**[1]

foutage [futaʒ] NM *très Fam* **c'est du f. de gueule!** you/they/*etc* gotta be kidding!, *Br* that's just taking the piss!

foutaise [futɛz] NF *très Fam* crap, *Am* bull; **tout ça, c'est de la f.!** that's just a load of crap *or Am* bull!; **arrête de raconter des foutaises!** stop talking crap *or Am* bull

fouteur, -euse [futœr, -øz] NM,F *très Fam* **f. de merde** shit-stirrer, *Am* buttinski

foutimasser [3] [futimase] VI *Suisse Fam (perdre son temps)* to mess about; *(faire quelque chose de douteux)* to be up to something

foutoir [futwar] NM *très Fam* dump, *Br* tip; **sa chambre est un vrai f.** his/her room is a complete tip

foutou [futu] NM *Culin (en Afrique)* fou-fou

foutral, -e, -als, -ales [futral] ADJ *Fam Vieilli* super, *Br* smashing

foutraque [futrak] ADJ *Fam* nuts, *Br* crackers

foutre[1] [116] [futr] *très Fam* ADV **je n'en sais f. rien** *Br* I'm buggered if I know, *Am* the hell if I know; **personne n'en sait f. rien** fuck knows

VT 1 *(envoyer, mettre)* **fous-le dans la valise** bung it in the case; **je me demande où elle a pu le f.** where the hell has she put it?; **f. qch par la fenêtre** to chuck sth out of the window; **f. qn par terre** to throw sb to the ground■; **f. une pile de livres par terre** to knock a pile of books to the ground■; *Fig* **f. un rêve/un projet par terre** to wreck a dream/a project; **f. qn dehors** to kick sb out; **f. qn à la porte** to throw *or* to chuck sb out; **il s'est fait f. à la porte** he was chucked *or* thrown out; **f. qch en l'air** to screw sth up; **f. sur la gueule à qn** to bash *or* to smash sb's face in; **ils ont foutu le feu à l'église** they set fire to the church■; *Suisse* **f. qch bas** *(démolir)* to knock sth down■; *Suisse* **f. qn bas** *(tuer)* to kill sb■, *Br* to do sb in

2 *(donner)* to give; **f. une claque à qn** to give sb a slap; **f. la trouille à qn** to give sb the creeps; **f. le cafard à qn** to get sb down; **f. la paix à qn** to leave sb alone■, to get out of sb's hair; **f. une (bonne) raclée à qn** to thump sb; **il m'a foutu une raclée au tennis** he thrashed me at tennis; **f. la trouille à qn** to put the wind up sb, to scare sb stiff; **elle m'a foutu la honte** *(d'elle)* I was ashamed of her■; *(de moi)* she made me ashamed of myself■; **ça nous a foutu un coup** it gave us a nasty shock■; **qu'est-ce qui m'a foutu un empoté pareil!** what an absolute oaf you are!

3 *(faire)* to do; **il ne fout rien de la journée** he doesn't do a damn *or Br* bloody thing all day; **il n'a pas l'air de f. grand-chose** he doesn't seem to do much at all; **qu'est-ce que tu fous là?** what the hell are you doing here?; **qu'est-ce que tu fous, on est pressés!** what the (bloody) hell are you doing, we're in a hurry!; **qu'est-ce que ça peut f.?** what the hell difference does that make?; **qu'est-ce que ça peut f. qu'on soit en retard?** so what if we're late, what the hell does it matter if we're late?; **qu'est-ce que ça peut te/lui f.?** what the hell does it matter to you/him/her?; **je ne sais pas quoi f. de lui/de cette vieille table** I don't know what the hell to do with him/with this old table; **il en a rien à f.** he couldn't give a damn *or Br* a toss *or* a monkey's; **rien à f., de leur bagnole!** who cares about their damn car?

4 *Vulg Vieilli (posséder sexuellement)* to fuck

5 *(locutions)* **ça la fout mal** it looks pretty bad; **il va falloir en f. un coup si on veut avoir fini demain!** we'll have to get a bloody move on if we want to be finished by tomorrow!; **mon mec a foutu le camp** my man's *Br* buggered off (and left me) *or Am* run out on me; **fous le camp de chez moi!** get the hell out of my house!; **y'a ta barrette qui fout le camp** your *Br* hair slide's *or Am* barrette's falling out■; **tout fout le camp!** this place is going to the dogs!; **je te fous mon billet qu'ils sont déjà partis** I'll bet you anything you like they've already left; **rembourser? je t'en fous, il ne remboursera jamais!** you think he's going to pay you back? you'll be lucky!; **je t'en foutrai, moi, du caviar!** caviar? I'll give you bloody caviar!; *Vulg* **va te faire f.!** fuck off!; **qu'il aille se faire f.!** he can fuck off *or Br* piss off!

►**se foutre** VPR 1 **se f. entre les pattes de qn** to fall into sb's clutches; **il s'est foutu par terre** he fell flat on his face; **se f. dedans** to blow it; **il s'est encore foutu dedans** he blew it yet again; **il s'est encore foutu dans une affaire louche** he's got (himself) mixed up in some shady business again; **se f. en colère** to lose one's rag, to go spare; **se f. à crier/pleurer/rire** to start shouting/crying/laughing; **se f. sur la gueule** to beat the living daylights out of each other; **se f. en l'air** to top oneself

2 **il s'est foutu de la peinture sur son pantalon** he spilt paint all over his trousers; **s'en f. plein la lampe** to make a pig of oneself; **s'en f. plein les poches** to line one's pockets

3 **se f. de** *(se moquer de)* to laugh at, to make fun of; **se f. de la gueule de qn** to take the piss *or Br* the mickey out of sb; **tu te fous de moi ou quoi!** are you taking the piss?; **ils se foutent du monde!** they really take people for idiots!; **c'est vraiment se f. (de la gueule) du monde!** he/they/*etc* must think we're absolute idiots!; **40 euros pour une heure de spectacle, ils se foutent de nous!** 40 euros for an hour-long show, what kind of morons do they take us for?

4 **se f. de** *(être indifférent à)* not to give a damn *or Br* a toss about; **je me fous de ce qu'il fera** I don't give a damn *or Br* a toss about what he'll do; **il se fout de l'argent** he doesn't give a damn about money; **je m'en fous** I don't give a damn

5 *Suisse (se suicider)* to commit suicide■, *Br* to top oneself

foutre[2] [futr] NM *Vulg (sperme)* cum, *Br* spunk

foutrement [futrəmɑ̃] ADV *très Fam* really■, damn, *Br* bloody; **c'est f. bon** it's damn good; **elle sait f. bien qu'il ne l'épousera jamais** she knows damn well he'll never marry her; **je n'en sais f. rien** I know damn all *or Br* bugger all about it

foutriquet [futrikɛ] NM *Vieilli Fam Péj* little squirt

foutu, -e [futy] *très Fam* PP *voir* **foutre**[1]

ADJ 1 *(abîmé) Br* buggered, *Am* screwed-up; *(gâché)* ruined■; **une voiture foutue** a write-off; **encore un collant (de) f.!** another pair of *Br* tights *or Am* pantihose ruined!; **encore des vacances foutues à cause de la grève!** another holiday ruined on account of the strike■; **ma bagnole est foutue** my car's had it; **il est f.** he's had it, he's done for; **c'est f.!** forget it!; **pour la fête de demain, c'est f.** you can forget the party tomorrow; **c'est f. pour mon augmentation** I can forget *or* it's goodbye to my pay rise

2 *(avant le nom) (considérable)* damned, *Br* bloody; **tu as eu une foutue chance** you were damned lucky; **il lui a fallu une foutue volonté pour rester** he/she needed a hell of a lot of willpower to stay

3 *(avant le nom) (détestable)* god-awful, *Br* bloody; **elle a un f. caractère** she's so damn(ed) *or Br* bloody difficult; **quel f. temps!** what shitty *or Br* bloody awful weather!

4 *(locutions)* **c'est bien/mal f.** *(bien conçu)* it's well/badly designed■; **cette machine est bien foutue** what a clever machine; **elle est plutôt bien foutue, sa pièce** his/her play is pretty good; **une fille très bien foutue** a girl with a great body; **il est mal f.** *(de corps)* he's not well-built■, he doesn't have a good body■; *(malade)* he feels rotten; **f. de** *(en mesure de)* **il est f. de réussir** he just might succeed; **elle serait foutue de le lui dire** she's quite likely to tell him/her; **ne pas être f. de faire qch** to be incapable of doing sth■; **elle est pas foutue d'être à l'heure!** she can't even be bothered to be on time!■, *Br* she can't even be on bloody time!

fovéa [fɔvea] NF *Anat* fovea

fox [fɔks] NM INV fox terrier

foxé, -e [fɔkse] ADJ foxy

fox-hound [fɔksaund] *(pl* **fox-hounds***)* NM foxhound

fox-terrier [fɔkstɛrje] *(pl* **fox-terriers***)* NM fox terrier

fox-trot [fɔkstrɔt] NM INV fox-trot

foyard [fwajar] NM *Suisse Bot* beech

foyer [fwaje] NM 1 *(chez soi)* home; *(domicile)* household; *Fin & Mktg* household unit; **rentrer dans** *ou* **regagner ses foyers** *(pays natal)* to go back to one's own country; *(domicile)* to return home; **renvoyer qn dans ses foyers** to send sb home; **f. conjugal** marital home; **femme** *ou* **mère au f.** housewife; **être mère au f.** to be a housewife and mother; **il est père au f.** he keeps

house and looks after the children, he's a house husband

2 *(résidence collective)* hall; **f. pour le troisième âge** retirement home; **f. d'accueil et d'hébergement** *(pour les gens à la rue)* hostel for the homeless; **f. d'étudiants** student hostel; **f. d'immigrés** immigrant workers' hostel; **f. des jeunes travailleurs** = hostel for young workers

3 *(lieu de réunion → gén)* hall; *(→ pour le public d'un théâtre)* foyer; *(→ de lycée)* common room; **f. des artistes** greenroom; **f. socio-éducatif** ≃ community centre

4 *(âtre)* hearth

5 *(dans une machine)* firebox; **f. de chaudière** boiler furnace

6 *(centre)* seat, centre; *(de chaleur)* source; **le f. d'agitation** the centre of the disturbance; **un f. d'incendie** the source of a fire; **f. d'intrigue** hotbed of intrigue; **le f. de la rébellion** the centre of the rebellion

7 *Méd* **f. infectieux** *ou* **d'infection** source of infection; **f. tuberculeux** tubercle

8 *Opt & Phys* focus, focal point; **des lunettes à double f.** bifocals; **des verres à double f.** bifocal lenses, bifocals; **lentilles à f. variable** variable focus lenses

9 *Géom* focus

10 *Admin* **f. fiscal** household *(as a tax unit)*

FP *(abrév écrite* **franchise postale***)* PP

FPA [ɛfpeɑ] **NF** *(abrév* **formation professionnelle pour adultes***)* adult education

FPLP [ɛfpeɛlpe] **NM** *(abrév* **Front populaire de libération de la Palestine***)* PFLP

FPU [ɛfpey] **NF** *Ordinat (abrév* **floating-point unit***)* FPU

FR3 [ɛfɛrtrwa] **NF** *(abrév* **France Régions 3***)* = former French state-owned television channel (now France 3)

frac [frak] **NM** tailcoat; **en f.** wearing tails

fracas [fraka] **NM** *(bruit)* crash, roar; *(de l'orage)* din; *(des armes)* clash; *(vacarme)* racket, din; **le f. des vagues contre la falaise** the crashing of the waves against the cliff; **le f. de la circulation sur l'avenue** the roar of the traffic on the avenue; **faire du f.** *(d'un événement)* to create a sensation; **elle sortit avec f.** she stormed out
❑ **à grand fracas ADV 1** *(bruyamment)* with a great deal of crashing and banging **2** *(spectaculairement)* with a lot of fuss

fracassant, -e [frakasɑ̃, -ɑ̃t] **ADJ 1** *(assourdissant)* deafening, thunderous; **la porte s'ouvrit avec un bruit f.** the door opened with a deafening crash **2** *(qui fait de l'effet)* sensational, staggering; *(succès)* resounding; **faire une déclaration fracassante** to make a sensational statement

Fracasse [frakas] **NPR le Capitaine F.** = swashbuckling hero created by Théophile Gautier

fracassement [frakasmɑ̃] **NM** *(d'une voiture)* smashing

fracasser [3] [frakase] **VT** to smash; **f. qch en mille morceaux** to smash sth into pieces; **f. une porte** *(volontairement)* to smash a door in, to break a door down; **il aurait pu avoir la tête fracassée** *(lors d'une agression)* he could have had his head smashed in; *(dans un accident)* he could have smashed his head in

►**se fracasser VPR 1** *(s'écraser)* to smash; **se f. contre** *ou* **sur** to smash into; **aller se f. contre qch** *(voiture, personne)* to smash *or* slam into sth; **le bateau est allé se f. contre les rochers** the boat was smashed to pieces on the rocks

2 se f. le crâne to crack one's head

fractal, -e, -als, -ales [fraktal] **ADJ** fractal
❑ **fractale NF** fractal

fraction [fraksjɔ̃] **NF 1** *Math* fraction; **par 10 euros ou f. de 10 euros** for each 10 euros or fraction thereof; **f. ordinaire** vulgar fraction; **f. décimale** decimal fraction; **f. périodique** recurring decimal

2 *(partie)* fraction, part; *Pol* splinter group; **une large f. de la population** a large proportion of the population; **une f. de seconde** a fraction of a second; *Compta* **f. imposable** part subject to tax; **f. d'intérêt** interest accrued

3 *Rel* breaking of the bread

4 *Suisse* = parliamentary committee

fractionnaire [fraksjɔnɛr] **ADJ** *Math* fractional; **nombre f.** improper fraction

fractionné, -e [fraksjɔne] **ADJ** *Chim (mélange)* fractionated

fractionnel, -elle [fraksjɔnɛl] **ADJ** divisive

fractionnement [fraksjɔnmɑ̃] **NM 1** *Chim* fractionation; *(d'huiles minérales)* cracking **2** *(morcellement)* splitting *or* dividing up; *(des paiements)* spreading (out) **3** *Com* breaking bulk **4** *Bourse (des actions)* splitting **5** *Jur* **f. de la peine** split sentence

fractionner [3] [fraksjɔne] **VT 1** *(diviser)* to divide, to split up; **vous pouvez f. le remboursement** you may pay in instalments; **la propriété a été fractionnée entre les héritiers** the estate was divided up between the heirs

2 *Chim* to fractionate; *(huiles minérales)* to crack

3 *Bourse (actions)* to split

►**se fractionner VPR** to split (up); **le groupe se fractionne en deux** the group splits *or* divides in two

fractionnisme [fraksjɔnism] **NM** *(tactique)* divisive tactics; *(caractère)* factionalism

fractionniste [fraksjɔnist] **ADJ** factionalist
NMF factionalist

fracturation [fraktyrasjɔ̃] **NF** *Géol* fracturing

fracture [fraktyr] **NF 1** *Méd* fracture; **f. du crâne** fractured skull; **il a eu une f. du crâne** his skull was fractured; **f. en bois vert** greenstick fracture; **f. comminutive** comminuted fracture; **f. de Dupuytren** Pott's fracture; **f. fermée** closed *or* simple fracture; **f. multiple** compound fracture; **f. ouverte** open fracture; **f. de Pouteau-Colles** Colles' fracture; **f. simple** simple *or* closed fracture; **f. spiroïde** spiral fracture; **f. transversale** transverse fracture

2 *Vieilli (effraction)* breaking open *(UNCOUNT)*; **y a-t-il eu f. du coffre?** was the safe broken open *or* broken into?

3 *Géol* fracture

4 *Fig (écart)* split; **f. Nord-Sud** North-South divide; **f. numérique** digital divide; **la f. sociale** the social divide

fracturer [3] [fraktyre] **VT 1** *(briser)* to break open; **f. un coffre-fort à l'explosif** to blow a safe **2** *(os)* to fracture **3** *Pétr* to fracture

►**se fracturer VPR se f. le bras/poignet** to fracture one's arm/wrist

fragile [fraʒil] **ADJ 1** *(peu solide)* fragile; **attention, f.** *(sur un colis)* fragile, handle with care; **avoir les cheveux fragiles** to have brittle hair; **c'est une pendule très f.** it's a very delicate clock

2 *(constitution)* frail; **un enfant f.** a frail child; **avoir l'estomac f.** to have a delicate stomach; **avoir les yeux fragiles** to have sensitive eyes; **être f. des poumons/de la gorge** to have delicate lungs/a delicate throat; **il est de santé f.** his health is rather delicate

3 *(personnalité)* delicate; **une adolescente f. qui est souvent déprimée** a sensitive teenager who is often depressed; **ne la brutalise pas, elle est encore f.** don't treat her roughly, she's still (feeling) fragile

4 *(équilibre)* fragile, frail; **un bonheur f.** a fragile *or* precarious happiness; **un pays à l'économie f.** a country with a shaky *or* precarious economy; **une hypothèse/argumentation f.** a flimsy hypothesis/argument

fragilisation [fraʒilizasjɔ̃] **NF 1** *(affaiblissement)* weakening **2** *Métal* embrittling

fragiliser [3] [fraʒilize] **VT 1** *(affaiblir)* to weaken; **la mort de son père l'a beaucoup fragilisé** his father's death affected him deeply; **le régime a été fragilisé par une série de scandales** the regime has been weakened *or* damaged *or* undermined by a series of scandals **2** *Métal* to embrittle

fragilité [fraʒilite] **NF 1** *(d'une horloge, d'une construction)* fragility, weakness; *(du verre)* fragility; *(des cheveux)* brittleness; **l'effondrement de l'immeuble est dû à la f. des fondations** the building collapsed because of its weak foundations

2 *(d'un organe, d'un malade)* weakness

3 *(d'un sentiment, d'une conviction, d'une victoire)* fragility; *(d'une hypothèse, d'une argumentation)* shakiness, flimsiness; *(d'un équilibre)* delicacy; *(d'un bonheur)* precariousness, fragility; *(d'une économie)* weakness, shakiness

fragment [fragmɑ̃] **NM 1** *(débris)* chip, fragment, piece; *(d'os)* fragment, splinter; **des fragments de verre** bits of shattered glass, shards of glass

2 *(morceau → d'une œuvre en partie perdue)* fragment; *(→ d'un air, d'une conversation)* snatch; **il nous a lu quelques fragments de son dernier roman** he read a few extracts of his last novel for us; **seuls ont survécu des fragments de l'inscription** only fragments of the inscription have survived; **des fragments d'une symphonie de Mahler provenaient d'une maison voisine** snatches of a Mahler symphony could be heard coming from a nearby house; **f. de vérité** shred of truth

fragmentaire [fragmɑ̃tɛr] **ADJ** fragmentary, sketchy, incomplete

fragmentairement [fragmɑ̃tɛrmɑ̃] **ADV** sketchily

fragmentation [fragmɑ̃tasjɔ̃] **NF** *(fractionnement)* division, splitting up; *Ordinat* fragmentation

fragmenter [3] [fragmɑ̃te] **VT** to divide, to split (up); **f. la publication d'un ouvrage** to publish a work in parts; **le film a été fragmenté en deux épisodes pour la télévision** the film was divided *or* split into two parts for television; **avoir une vision fragmentée des choses** to have a fragmented view of things

►**se fragmenter VPR** to fragment, to split

fragon [fragɔ̃] **NM** *Bot* ruscus

fragrance [fragrɑ̃s] **NF** *Littéraire* fragrance

fragrant, -e [fragrɑ̃, -ɑ̃t] **ADJ** *Littéraire* fragrant

frai[1] [frɛ] **NM 1** *(œufs)* spawn **2** *(poissons)* fry **3** *(période)* spawning season

frai[2] [frɛ] **NM** *(de pièces de monnaie)* abrasion, wear

fraîche [frɛʃ] *voir* **frais**

fraîchement [frɛʃmɑ̃] **ADV 1** *(nouvellement)* freshly, newly; **f. repeint** freshly *or* newly painted; **f. coupé** *(herbe)* new-mown; **fleurs f. cueillies** freshly picked flowers; **f. marié/divorcé/arrivé** newly *or* recently married/divorced/arrived

2 *(froidement)* coolly; **il nous a reçus plutôt f.** he greeted us rather coolly

3 *Fam (locution)* **ça va plutôt f. aujourd'hui** it's a bit chilly today▪

fraîcheur [frɛʃœr] **NF 1** *(température)* coolness; **dans la f. du petit jour/du soir** in the cool of early dawn/of the evening; **une sensation de f.** a feeling of freshness; **rechercher un peu de f.** to seek out a cool spot; **la f. de la maison est agréable en été** the coolness of the house is pleasant in summer

2 *(bonne qualité)* freshness; **pour conserver la f. de vos légumes** to keep your vegetables fresh

3 *(intensité → des couleurs)* freshness, brightness; **les coloris des rideaux ont gardé toute leur f.** the curtains have retained their fresh *or* crisp colours; *Fam* **la robe n'est plus de la première f.** the dress isn't exactly brand new

4 *(éclat)* freshness; **dans toute la f. de ses vingt ans** with all the freshness of his/her youth; **elle a perdu sa f. d'esprit** she has lost her freshness of mind

5 *(indifférence)* coolness; **la f. de son accueil nous a surpris** his/her cool reception was a surprise to us

fraîchin [frɛʃɛ̃] **NM** briny smell, smell of the sea

fraîchir [32] [frɛʃir] **VI 1** *(se refroidir)* to get cooler; **les jours fraîchissent, il faut vous couvrir** the weather is getting cooler, you'd better put on warm clothing **2** *Naut (vent)* to freshen, to get stronger

fraie *etc voir* **frayer**

frais[1] [frɛ] **NMPL 1** *(dépenses)* expenses, costs; **j'ai eu beaucoup de f. ce mois-ci** I've had a lot of expense(s) this month; **cela lui a occasionné des f.** it cost him/her a certain amount (of money); **les f. du ménage** a family's everyday expenses *or* expenditure; **faire des f.** to go to great expense; **faire des f. de toilette** to spend money on clothes; **à f. communs** sharing the expense; **à grands f.** at great expense; **à moindre f.** less expensively, at a cheaper price; **à peu de f.** cheaply; *Fam* **aux f. de la princesse** at the firm's/government's/*etc* expense▪; **exempt de f., sans f.** free of charge; *(sur une lettre de change)* no expenses; **tous f. payés** all expenses paid; **rentrer dans** *ou* **faire ses f.** to break even, to recoup one's expenses; **se mettre en f.** to spend money; **tu ne t'es pas mis en f.** you didn't exactly *Br* splash out *or Am* put yourself out of pocket; **se mettre en f. de politesse** to go out of one's way to be polite; **faire**

qch à ses f. to do sth at one's own expense; **en être pour ses f.** to be out of pocket; *Fig* to waste one's time; **il en a été pour ses f.** he didn't even break even; *Fig* he was let down; *Fig* **j'en suis pour mes f.** it's been a lot of trouble for nothing, I've been wasting my time; *Fig* **faire les f. de qch** to pay the price for sth; **faire les f. de la conversation** to be the main topic of conversation; **j'ai fait les f. de la plaisanterie** the joke was at my expense; **faire les f. d'une politique** to pay the price for a policy; **f. accessoires** incidental costs *or* expenses; **f. d'achat** purchase costs; **f. de camionnage** haulage; **f. de commercialisation** marketing costs; **f. commerciaux** selling costs; **f. de constitution** *(de société)* start-up costs; *(de compte)* set-up fee; *Bourse* **f. de courtage** brokerage, commission; **f. de déplacement** travelling expenses; **f. directs** direct costs; **f. de distribution** distribution costs; **f. de douane** customs duties; **f. d'entretien** maintenance costs; **f. d'envoi** carriage costs; *(par courrier)* postage; **f. d'établissement** start-up costs; **f. d'expédition** carriage costs; *(par courrier)* postage; **f. d'exploitation** operating costs; **f. extraordinaires** extraordinary expenses; **f. fixes** fixed costs; **f. de fonctionnement** operating costs; **f. de garde** child-minding costs; **f. de gestion** running costs; **f. d'habillement** clothing expenses; **f. inclus** inclusive of costs; **f. d'installation** initial expenses; **f. de lancement** set-up *or* start-up costs; **f. de liquidation** closing-down costs; **f. de livraison** delivery charges; **f. de main-d'œuvre** labour costs; **f. de manutention** handling charges; **f. de mission** travelling expenses; **f. de port** *(de marchandises)* carriage; *(de lettres, de colis)* postage; **f. de port et d'emballage** postage and packing; **f. de portage** porterage; **f. de production** production costs; **f. professionnels** professional expenses; **f. de publicité** advertising costs; **f. de recouvrement** collection fees; **f. de représentation** entertainment allowance; **f. de sortie** exit charges, back-end load; **f. de transport** carriage; **f. de trésorerie** finance costs; *Can Tél* **appeler qn à f. virés** *Br* to make a reverse-charge call to sb, *Am* to call sb collect; **f. de voyage** travelling expenses

2 *Compta* outgoings; **f. accumulés** accrued expenses; **f. d'amortissement** amortization *or* depreciation charges; **f. bancaires** *ou* **de banque** bank charges; **f. différés** deferred charges; **f. divers** miscellaneous costs; **f. facturables** chargeable expenses; **f. financiers** interest charges; **f. fixes** fixed charges; **f. généraux** *Br* overheads, *Am* overhead; **f. variables** variable costs; **f. de tenue de compte** account charges; *(de compte bancaire)* bank charges; **faux f.** incidental costs

3 *Jur* **f. (de justice)** (legal) costs; **être condamné aux f.** to be ordered to pay costs; **devoir payer les f. d'un procès** to have to pay (legal) costs

4 *Admin* fees; **f. d'abonnement** standing charges; **f. d'adhésion** membership fee; **f. d'administration** administrative costs; *(en échange d'un service)* handling charge; **f. d'administration générale** *Br* general overheads, *Am* general overhead; **f. d'agence** agency fee; **f. d'annulation** cancellation charge; **f. de Bourse** transaction costs; **f. consulaires** consular fees; **f. de dossier** administration charges; **f. d'encaissement** collection charges *or* fees; **f. d'entrée** *(d'une sicav)* front-end *or* front-load fees; *Bourse* commission on purchase of shares; **f. d'inscription** registration fee, membership fee; *Ordinat* set-up charge, set-up fee; **f. de réservation** booking fee, reservation charge; **f. de scolarité** school fees; **f. de tenue de compte** account charges; *(de compte bancaire)* bank charges

frais², **fraîche** [frɛ, frɛʃ] **ADJ 1** *(un peu froid)* cool, fresh; **l'air est f. ce soir** it's chilly tonight

2 *(rafraîchissant)* cooled, chilled; **des boissons fraîches** cold drinks

3 *(récent → œuf, huître)* fresh; *(→ encre, peinture)* wet; *(→ souvenir)* recent, fresh; **œufs f. de ce matin** eggs newly laid this morning; **les croissants sont tout f. de ce matin** the croissants are fresh this morning; **peinture fraîche** *(sur panneau)* wet paint; **il y avait des fleurs fraîches sur la table** there were freshly cut

flowers on the table; **des huîtres pas fraîches** oysters which are no longer fresh; **j'ai reçu des nouvelles fraîches** I've got some recent news; **la blessure** *ou* **la plaie est encore fraîche** the wound is still fresh; **cette robe n'est plus très fraîche, mais elle fera l'affaire** this dress isn't very fresh any more, but it will do; **de fraîche date** recent, new; **des amis de fraîche date** recent friends

4 *(agréable)* fresh, sweet; **un f. parfum de lavande** a sweet smell of lavender; **avoir la bouche** *ou* **l'haleine fraîche** to have sweet breath

5 *(reposé)* fresh; **envoyer des troupes fraîches sur le front** to send fresh troops to the front; *Fam* **je ne me sens pas trop f. ce matin** I don't feel too good *or* well this morning; **être f. et dispos, f. comme un gardon** to be on top form; **f. et dispos, f. comme une rose** as fresh as a daisy

6 *(éclatant)* fresh; **avoir une peau jeune et fraîche** to have a young and fresh looking skin; **avoir le teint f.** to have a fresh complexion

7 *Fig (indifférent → accueil, réception)* cool

8 *Fam (en mauvais état)* **être f.** to be in the soup; **me voilà f.!** I'm in a mess!

9 *Can Fam Péj (vaniteux, arrogant)* stuck up, snooty

10 *Écon* **argent f.** ready cash; **avoir de l'argent f.** to have new money

11 *Naut* fresh

ADV 1 *(nouvellement)* newly, freshly; **des fleurs f.** *ou* **fraîches coupées** freshly cut flowers; **herbe f.** *ou* **fraîche coupée** freshly *or* newly cut grass; **il est f. débarqué de sa province** he is fresh from the country; **f. émoulu de la faculté de droit** freshly graduated from law school **2** *(froid)* **il fait f.** it's cool *or* fresh; **il fait f. dans la maison** it's chilly in the house; **boire f.** *(sur brick, bouteille)* drink chilled; **servir f.** *(sur etiquette)* serve cold *or* chilled **NM 1** *(air frais)* **le f.** the fresh air; **prendre le f.** to take some *or* a breath of (fresh) air; **si on allait prendre un peu le f. à la campagne?** how about going to the countryside for a breath of (fresh) air? **2** *Météo & Naut* **grand f.** gale; **avis de grand f.** gale warning **3** *Can Fam Péj* **faire le f.** to show off ▪, to be full of oneself ▪

▫ **fraîche NF 1** *(heure)* cool (of evening); **attendre la fraîche pour sortir** to wait for it to cool down before going out; **à la fraîche** in the cool evening air; *Can* **prendre la fraîche** *(sortir prendre l'air)* to go for a stroll; *(prendre froid)* to catch a chill **2** *Fam Arg* crime cash

▫ **au frais ADV 1** *(dans un lieu froid)* in a cool place; **à conserver au f.** *(sur etiquette)* to be kept cool *or* in a cool place, store in a cool place; **mettre le vin au f.** to put the wine to cool **2** *Fam Arg* crime *(en prison)* in the cooler; **mettre qn au f.** to throw sb in the cooler

▫ **de frais ADV habillé de f.** wearing a fresh set of clothes *or* clean clothes; **rasé de f.** having recently had a shave

fraisage [frɛzaʒ] **NM 1** *(usinage)* milling **2** *(élargissement → d'un trou)* reaming; *(→ pour vis)* countersinking **3** *(par le dentiste)* drilling

frais-chié, -e [frɛʃje] *(mpl* **frais-chiés,** *fpl* **frais-chiées) NM,F** *Can très Fam Péj* cocky bastard *or* upstart

fraise [frɛz] **NF 1** *Bot* strawberry; **f. des bois** wild strawberry; *Fig* **aller aux fraises** to go (off) for a roll in the hay

2 *Fam (visage)* mug; **un coup en pleine f.** a punch in the kisser; **amène ta f.!** get yourself *or* très *Fam* your arse over here!; **il est tout le temps à ramener sa f.** he's always sticking his oar in

3 *(pour couper)* mill, cutter; **f. (conique)** countersink

4 *(pour faire → un trou)* reamer; *(→ un trou de vis)* countersink (bit)

5 *(en odontologie)* drill

6 *Orn* wattle

7 *Culin (de veau)* caul

8 *Hist (collerette)* ruff

9 *Méd* strawberry (mark)

ADJ INV strawberry (pink), strawberry-coloured; **f. écrasée** crushed strawberry

▫ **à la fraise, aux fraises ADJ** strawberry *(avant n)*, strawberry-flavoured; **tarte aux fraises** strawberry tart

---

'Les Fraises sauvages' *Bergman* 'Wild Strawberries'

---

fraiser [4] [frɛze] **VT 1** *(usiner)* to mill; *(évaser → trou)* to ream; *(→ trou de vis)* to countersink, to knead **2** *(dent)* to drill

fraiseraie [frɛzrɛ] **NF** strawberry field

fraiseur, -euse [frɛzœr, -øz] **NM,F** milling machine operator

▫ **fraiseuse NF** milling machine

fraiseur-outilleur [frɛzœrutijœr] *(pl* **fraiseurs-outilleurs) NM** milling machine operator

fraiseuse [frɛzøz] *voir* **fraiseur**

fraisier [frɛzje] **NM 1** *Bot* strawberry plant **2** *Culin* strawberry cream cake

fraisière [frɛzjɛr] **NF** strawberry field

fraisil [frɛzi(l)] **NM** coal cinders

fraisure [frɛzyr] **NF** countersink (hole)

framboise [frãbwaz] **NF 1** *Bot* raspberry **2** *(alcool)* raspberry liqueur

    ADJ INV raspberry *(avant n)*

framboiser [3] [frãbwaze] **VT** to flavour with raspberry liqueur

framboisier [frãbwazje] **NM 1** *Bot* raspberry cane **2** *(gâteau)* raspberry cream cake

framée [frame] **NF** *Hist* framea, javelin

franc¹ [frã] **NM** *(monnaie)* franc; *Anciennement* **ancien/nouveau f.** old/new franc; *Anciennement* **f. belge** Belgian franc; *Anciennement* **f. français** French franc; *Anciennement* **f. luxembourgeois** Luxembourg franc; **f. suisse** Swiss franc; **f. CFA** = currency used in former French colonies in Africa; **f. CFP** = currency used in former French colonies in the Pacific area; **f. constant** constant *or* inflation-adjusted francs; **exprimé en francs courants** in real terms; **f. or** gold value of the franc; **f. pacifique** = currency used in former French colonies in the Pacific area; *Anciennement* **f. symbolique** nominal sum; *Anciennement* **un f. symbolique de dommages et intérêts** token damages; *Anciennement* **f. vert** green franc; **je l'ai eu pour trois francs six sous** I got it for next to nothing; *Anciennement* **le f. fort** = the policy of the French government of not devaluing the franc, whatever the pressure

franc², **franche** [frã, frãʃ] **ADJ 1** *(honnête → réponse)* frank, honest; *(→ conversation)* frank, candid; **un rire f.** an open laugh; **un regard f.** an open look; **sois f. avec moi** be honest *or* frank with me; **pour être f. (avec vous)** to be frank *or* honest with you; **il a l'air f.** he looks like an honest person, he has an honest look (about him); **être f. comme l'or** to be as honest as the day is long; **être f. du collier** to be straightforward; **sa réponse a au moins le mérite d'être franche** at least he/she answered frankly *or* candidly; **jouer f. jeu (avec qn)** to play fair (with sb); **il n'a pas joué f. jeu** he didn't play fair, he played dirty

2 *(pur)* strong; *(rupture)* clean; **un rouge f.** a strong red; **un album aux couleurs franches** an album in strong colours

3 *(avant le nom) (parfait, extrême)* utter; **un f. scélérat, une franche canaille** a downright scoundrel; **l'ambiance n'était pas à la franche gaieté** the atmosphere wasn't exactly a happy

one; **ça a été une franche rigolade** it was an absolute scream; **rencontrer une franche hostilité** to encounter outright hostility; **huit jours francs** eight clear days

4 *Bot* **f. de pied** ungrafted; **arbre f.** cultivar; *Agr* **terre franche** loam

5 *Jur* **le jugement est exécutable au bout de trois jours francs** the decision of the court to be carried out within three clear days; **f. d'avarie** free from average

6 *Com & Fin (gratuit)* free; **port f.** free port; **f. de tout droit** duty-free, free of duty; **f. d'avarie commune** free of general average, FGA; **f. d'avarie particulière** free of particular average, FPA; **f. de casse** free of breakage; **f. de douane** duty paid; **f. d'impôts** tax free, free of tax; **f. de port** carriage paid, carriage free; **f. de port (et d'emballage)** postage paid; **f. de toute avarie** free of average; *Hist* **ville franche** free city; **zone franche** free zone

ADV je préfère te parler f. I prefer to be frank with you; **parlons f.** let's be frank (with each other)

franc[3]**, franque** [frɑ̃, frɑ̃k] *Hist* **ADJ** Frankish

❑ **Franc, Franque NM,F** Frank

français, -e [frɑ̃sɛ, -ɛz] **ADJ** French; **c'est une attitude bien française** that's a typically French attitude

ADV acheter f. to buy French; **rouler/boire/manger f.** to drive French cars/drink French wine/eat French food

❑ **Français, -e NM,F** Frenchman, *f* Frenchwoman; **les F.** *(la population)* French people, the French; *(les hommes)* Frenchmen; **les Françaises** French women; **le F. n'aime pas...** the average Frenchman *or* French person doesn't like...

NM *(langue)* French; **en bon f.** in proper French; **parler f.** to speak French; *(correctement)* to speak properly; **f. langue étrangère** French as a foreign language; *Fam* **tu ne comprends pas le f.?** ≃ don't you understand (plain) English?

❑ **à la française ADJ** *(jardin, parquet)* French, French-style **ADV** (in) the French way; **imprimer à la française** to print portrait

> *Allusion*
>
> **Français, encore un effort**
>
> In the Marquis de Sade's *La Philosophie dans le boudoir* (1795), this allusion in its entirety reads **Français, encore un effort si vous voulez être républicains** ("A final effort, people of France, if you wish to become republicans"). Today, **Français, encore un effort** is frequently used as an encouragement to the nation, in articles about sport or the economic situation, for example.

franc-alleu [frɑ̃kaløl] *(pl* **francs-alleux)** **NM** *Hist & Jur* allodium, alodium

franc-bord [frɑ̃bɔr] *(pl* **francs-bords)** **NM** *Naut* freeboard

franc-bourgeois [frɑ̃burʒwa] *(pl* **francs-bourgeois)** **NM** *Hist* freeman

franc-comtois, -e [frɑ̃kɔ̃twa, -az] *(mpl* **francs-comtois,** *fpl* **franc-comtoises)** **ADJ** of/from Franche-Comté

❑ **Franc-Comtois, -e NM,F** = inhabitant of or person from Franche-Comté

France [frɑ̃s] **NF la F.** France; **vivre en F.** to live in France; **aller en F.** to go to France; **la F. est sa patrie** France is his/her homeland; **les vins de F.** French wines; **l'histoire de F.** French history, the history of France; *Fig* **la F. d'en bas** the French underclass; *TV* **F. 2** = French state-owned television channel; *TV* **F. 3** = French state-owned television channel; *Télécom* **F. Télécom** = state-owned company which runs all telecommunications services, until 1991 part of the PTT; *TV* **F. Télévision** = the state-owned television channels France 2, France 3 and La Cinquième

NM *(navire)* **le F.** the "France", = French transatlantic luxury liner

❑ **vieille France ADJ INV être** *ou* **faire (très) vieille F.** to be rather old-fashioned

France-Culture [frɑ̃skyltyr] **NF** = radio station broadcasting mainly arts programmes

France-Dimanche [frɑ̃sdimɑ̃ʃ] **NM** *Presse* = popular French Sunday newspaper

France-Infos [frɑ̃sɛ̃fo] **NF** = 24-hour radio news station

France-Inter [frɑ̃sɛ̃tɛr] **NF** = radio station broadcasting mainly current affairs programmes, interviews and debates

France-Musique [frɑ̃smyzik] **NF** = radio station playing classical music

France-Soir [frɑ̃sswar] **NM** *Presse* = French daily newspaper with right-wing tendencies

franc-fief [frɑ̃fjɛf] *(pl* **francs-fiefs)** **NM** *Hist (taxe)* frank-fee; *(fief)* freehold

Francfort [frɑ̃kfɔr] **NM F.(-sur-le-Main)** Frankfurt (am Main)

franche [frɑ̃ʃ] *voir* **franc**[2]

Franche-Comté [frɑ̃ʃkɔ̃te] **NF la F.** Franche-Comté

franchement [frɑ̃ʃmɑ̃] **ADV 1** *(sincèrement)* frankly; **parlons f.** let's be frank; **je vais te parler f.** I'll be frank with you; **pour vous parler f., je ne sais pas de quoi il s'agit** to be honest with you, I don't know what it's all about; **f., je ne sais que faire** I honestly don't know what to do; **écoute, f., tu crois vraiment qu'il le fera?** listen, do you honestly think he'll do it?; **il me l'a dit f.** he told me openly

2 *(sans équivoque)* clearly, definitely; **il a pris f. parti pour son Premier ministre** he came down unequivocally on the side of his Prime Minister

3 *(résolument)* boldly; **appuie f. sur le bouton** press firmly on the button; **vas-y f., appuie sur la manette** go on, push the joystick hard; **ils y sont allés f.** *(dans un projet)* they got right down to it; *(dans une conversation, dans une négociation)* they didn't mince words

4 *(vraiment)* really; **elle est devenue f. jolie** she became really pretty; **il est f. insupportable** he's downright unbearable; **j'en suis f. dégoûté** I'm absolutely sick of it; **non, mais f.!** no, honestly *or* really!; **tu as de ces idées, f.!** the ideas you have, honestly *or* really!

franchir [32] [frɑ̃ʃir] **VT 1** *(passer par-dessus* → *barrière, mur)* to get over; *(*→ *rapides)* to shoot, to cross; **il a franchi le fossé d'un bond** he jumped over the ditch; **la panthère franchit le mur d'un seul bond** the panther cleared *or* jumped over the wall in one bound; *Fig* **f. un obstacle** to get over an obstacle; **f. une difficulté** to overcome a difficulty

2 *(outrepasser* → *ligne, limite, frontière, date)* to cross; *(*→ *porte)* to pass *or* walk through; **au moment de f. le seuil, je m'arrêtai** I halted just as I was stepping across the threshold; **f. la ligne d'arrivée** to cross the finishing line; **f. le mur du son** to break the sound barrier; **il y a certaines limites à ne pas f.** there are certain limits which should not be overstepped; *Fig* **f. un cap** to reach a milestone *or* turning point; **f. le cap de la trentaine/cinquantaine** to turn thirty/fifty; **f. la barre des 3 millions** to pass the 3 million mark

3 *(dans le temps)* to last through; **sa renommée a franchi les siècles** his/her reputation has lasted *or* come down intact through the centuries

franchisage [frɑ̃ʃizaʒ] **NM** franchising

franchise [frɑ̃ʃiz] **NF 1** *Com & Fin (exploitation)* franchise agreement; *(exonération)* exemption; **f. de bagages** baggage allowance; **f. douanière** exemption from customs duties; **f. fiscale** tax exemption; **f. de TVA** VAT exemption, zero-rating; **importer/faire entrer qch en f.** to import sth duty-free; **en f. d'impôt** exempt from tax, tax-free; **en f. postale** official paid; **bagages en f.** baggage allowance; **en f. de TVA** VAT-exempt, zero-rated

2 *Com (de commerce)* franchise; **ouvrir un magasin en f.** to open a franchise

3 *(d'une assurance) Br* excess, *Am* deductible

4 *(honnêteté)* frankness, straightforwardness; *(franc-parler)* plain speaking, outspokenness; **avec f.** frankly, straightforwardly; **en toute f.** quite frankly, to be honest with you

franchisé, -e [frɑ̃ʃize] **ADJ magasin f.** franchise

NM,F franchisee

franchiser [3] [frɑ̃ʃize] **VT** to franchise

franchiseur, -euse [frɑ̃ʃizœr, -øz] **NM,F** franchiser

franchising [frɑ̃ʃajziŋ] **NM** franchising

franchissable [frɑ̃ʃisabl] **ADJ** *(route)* passable; *(col de montagne)* negotiable; *(obstacle)* surmountable; **un mur difficilement f.** a wall which is difficult to climb

franchissement [frɑ̃ʃismɑ̃] **NM** *(d'une barrière, d'un mur)* getting over; *(d'une rivière)* crossing; *(de fossé)* jumping; *(d'un obstacle, d'une difficulté)* getting over, overcoming

franchouillard, -e [frɑ̃ʃujar, -ard] *Fam Péj* **ADJ** typically French▪

NM,F typical Frenchman, *f* Frenchwoman▪

francien [frɑ̃sjɛ̃] **NM** *Ling* = dialect spoken in northern France during the Middle Ages, which developed into the French language

francilien, -enne [frɛsiljɛ̃, -ɛn] **ADJ** of/from the Île-de-France *(region around Paris)*

❑ **Francilien, -enne NM,F** = inhabitant of or person from the Île-de-France

francique [frɑ̃sik] **ADJ** Frankish

NM *(langue)* Frankish

francisant, -e [frɑ̃sizɑ̃, -ɑ̃t] **NM,F** French specialist, specialist in French language and literature

francisation [frɑ̃sizasjɔ̃] **NF 1** *Ling (d'un mot)* gallicizing, gallicization **2** *Naut* registering as French

franciscain, -e [frɑ̃siskɛ̃, -ɛn] **ADJ & NM,F** *Rel* Franciscan

franciser [3] [frɑ̃size] **VT 1** *Ling (mot, terme)* to gallicize; **f. un nom propre** to give a proper name a French spelling **2** *Naut (navire)* to register as French

francisque [frɑ̃sisk] **NF** francisc, francesque; **f. gallique** = double-headed battle-axe (symbol of the Vichy government)

franciste [frɑ̃sist] **NMF** specialist in French language and literature

francité [frɑ̃site] **NF** Frenchness

francium [frɑ̃sjɔm] **NM** *Chim* francium

franc-jeu [frɑ̃ʒø] *(pl* **francs-jeux)** **NM** fair play

franc-maçon, -onne [frɑ̃masɔ̃, -ɔn] *(mpl* **francs-maçons,** *fpl* **franc-maçonnes)** **NM,F** Free-mason

franc-maçonnerie [frɑ̃masɔnri] *(pl* **franc-maçonneries)** **NF** *(société secrète)* **la f.** Freemasonry

franc-maçonnique [frɑ̃masɔnik] **ADJ** Masonic

franco [frɑ̃ko] **ADV 1** *Com (dans un envoi)* **f. (de port)** carriage paid; **livraison f. frontière française** delivered free as far as the French border; **livré f.** delivered free; **échantillons f. sur demande** free samples available on request; **f. à bord** FOB, fob; **f. (à) domicile** delivery free, carriage paid; **f. allège** free over side; **f. d'emballage** free of packing charges; **f. de douane** free of customs duty; **f. frontière** free at frontier; **f. gare** free on rail; **f. gare de réception** free on rail; **f. le long du navire** free alongside ship; **f. long du bord** free alongside ship; **f. long du quai** free alongside quay; **f. de port et d'emballage** postage and packing paid; **f. rendu** free at; **f. de tous frais** free of all charges; **f. transporteur** free carrier; **f. wagon** free on rail, FOR

2 *Fam (franchement)* **y aller f.** to go straight *or* right ahead; **elle lui a dit ce qu'elle pensait de lui et elle y est allée f.** she told him what she thought of him and she didn't mince her words

franco- [frɑ̃ko] **PRÉF** Franco-

franco-allemand, -e [frɑ̃koalmɑ̃, -ɑ̃d] *(mpl* **franco-allemands,** *fpl* **franco-allemandes)** **ADJ** Franco-German

franco-britannique [frɑ̃kobritanik] *(pl* **franco-britanniques)** **ADJ** Anglo-French

franco-canadien, -enne [frɑ̃kokanadjɛ̃, -ɛn] *(mpl* **franco-canadiens,** *fpl* **franco-canadiennes)** **ADJ** French Canadian

NM *Ling* Canadian French

franco-français, -e [frɑ̃kofrɑ̃sɛ, -ɛz] *(mpl* **franco-français,** *fpl* **franco-françaises)** **ADJ** pure French; **une entreprise franco-française** a hundred percent French-owned company

francogène [frɑ̃kɔʒɛn] **NMF** *Can* = person of French origin whose main language is no longer French

François [frɑ̃swa] **NPR** Francis; **F. 1er** Francis I

François-Joseph [frɑ̃swaʒɔzɛf] **NPR** Franz Josef

francolin [frɑ̃kɔlɛ̃] **NM** *Orn* black partridge, francolin

franconiser [3] [frɑ̃kɔnize] **VT** *Can* **f. des employés/un service** to train employees/a department to be able to function in French

francophile [frɑ̃kɔfil] **ADJ** Francophil, Francophile
NMF Francophile

francophilie [frɑ̃kɔfili] **NF** love of (all) things French

francophobe [frɑ̃kɔfɔb] **ADJ** Francophobe
NMF Francophobe

francophobie [frɑ̃kɔfɔbi] **NF** Francophobia, dislike of (all) things French

francophone [frɑ̃kɔfɔn] **ADJ** Francophone, French-speaking
NMF Francophone, French speaker

francophonie [frɑ̃kɔfɔni] **NF la f.** = the speaking and promotion of French around the world

franco-provençal, -e, -aux, ales [frɑ̃kɔprɔvɑ̃sal, -o] *Ling* **ADJ** Franco-Provençal
NM Franco-Provençal

franc-parler [frɑ̃parle] (*pl* **francs-parlers**) **NM** outspokenness; **il a son f.** he doesn't mince (his) words

franc-quartier [frɑ̃kartje] (*pl* **francs-quartiers**) **NM** *Hér* quarter

franc-tireur [frɑ̃tirœr] (*pl* **francs-tireurs**) **NM 1** *Mil* franc-tireur, irregular (soldier) **2** *(indépendant)* maverick

frange [frɑ̃ʒ] **NF 1** *(de cheveux) Br* fringe, *Am* bangs **2** *(de tissu)* fringe **3** *(minorité)* fringe; **la f. des indécis** the waverers **4** *(bordure)* (fringed) edge **5** *Opt* **franges d'interférence** interference fringes
▫ **à franges ADJ** fringed

frangeant [frɑ̃ʒɑ̃] *voir* **récif**

franger [17] [frɑ̃ʒe] **VT** *(vêtement, tissu)* to (edge with a) fringe

frangin [frɑ̃ʒɛ̃] **NM** *Fam* bro, brother■

frangine [frɑ̃ʒin] **NF** *Fam* **1** *(sœur)* sis, sister■ **2** *(femme)* chick

frangipane [frɑ̃ʒipan] **NF 1** *Culin (crème, gâteau)* frangipane **2** *(fruit)* frangipani

frangipanier [frɑ̃ʒipanje] **NM** *Bot* frangipani (tree)

franglais [frɑ̃glɛ] **NM** Franglais

franque [frɑ̃k] *voir* **franc**[3]

franquette [frɑ̃kɛt] **NF** *Fam* **à la bonne f.** simply■, informally■; **recevoir qn à la bonne f.** to have sb round for a simple meal (among friends)■; **on mangera à la bonne f.** we'll have a simple meal■

franquisme [frɑ̃kism] **NM** Francoism

franquiste [frɑ̃kist] **ADJ** pro-Franco
NMF Franco supporter

fransquillon [frɑ̃skijɔ̃] **NM** *Belg* **1** *Péj (personne affectée)* = Belgian who speaks French with an affected accent **2** *(Flamand francophone)* = French-speaking Flemish person

fransquillonner [3] [frɑ̃skijɔne] **VI** *Belg Péj* = to speak French with an affected accent

frappadingue [frapadɛ̃g] **ADJ** *Fam* crazy, bonkers, *Br* mental

frappage [frapaʒ] **NM 1** *Métal* stamping; *(d'une médaille)* striking; *(de la monnaie)* minting **2** *(d'une boisson)* chilling

frappant, -e [frapɑ̃, -ɑ̃t] **ADJ** *(ressemblance, exemple)* striking

frappe [frap] **NF 1** *(d'une secrétaire, d'un pianiste)* touch; *(sur une machine à écrire)* typing; *(sur un ordinateur)* keying; **donner son texte à la f.** to give one's text (in) to be typed; **vitesse de f.** typing/keying speed; *Ordinat* **f. au kilomètre** continuous input; *Ordinat* **f. en continu** type-ahead; **f. de touche** keystroke
2 *(copie)* typed copy, typescript; **lire la première f.** to read the top copy
3 *(d'une monnaie)* minting
4 *Sport (d'un footballeur)* shot; *(d'un boxeur)* punch
5 *très Fam (voyou)* hooligan, hoodlum; **une petite f.** a young hooligan
▫ **frappes NFPL** *(bombardements)* strikes; **frappes aériennes** air-strikes; **frappes militaires** military strikes; **frappes de précision** precision strikes

frappé, -e [frape] **ADJ 1** *(boisson)* iced; **café f.** iced coffee; **champagne f.** chilled champagne; **servir bien f.** *(sur étiquette)* serve chilled **2** *Tex* embossed **3** *Fam (fou)* crazy; **il est un peu f.** he's a bit touched **4** *(bien exprimé)* **parole bien frappée** well-chosen word

frappement [frapmɑ̃] **NM** knock, knocking *(UNCOUNT)*

frapper [3] [frape] **VT 1** *(battre → adversaire)* to hit, to strike; **je ne frappe jamais un enfant** I never hit *or* smack a child; **ne me frappe pas!** don't hit me!; **f. qn à la tête** to hit sb on the head; **frappé à mort** mortally wounded
2 *(donner)* to hit, to strike; *Fig* **f. un grand coup** *ou* **un coup décisif** to strike a decisive blow; *Théât* **f. les trois coups** = to give three knocks to announce the start of a theatrical performance
3 *(percuter)* to hit; **f. les touches d'un clavier** to strike the keys on a keyboard; **f. la terre** *ou* **le sol du pied** to stamp (one's foot); **les grêlons frappaient durement la fenêtre** hailstones were lashing the windowpane; **f. légèrement** to tap; **être frappé d'une balle au front** to be hit *or* struck by a bullet in the forehead; *Can Fam Fig* **f. un nœud** to hit a snag
4 *(affecter)* to strike *or* to bring down, to hit; **le cancer a frappé le père et le fils** cancer struck down both father and son; **le deuil/mal qui nous frappe** the bereavement/pain we are suffering; **être frappé par une maladie** to be struck down by a disease; **être frappé par le malheur** to be struck by misfortune; **être frappé de mutisme** to be struck dumb; **f. qn d'étonnement** to strike sb with amazement
5 *(s'appliquer à → sujet: loi, sanction, taxe)* to hit; **un châtiment qui frappe les coupables** a punishment which falls on the guilty
6 *(surprendre)* to strike; *(impressionner)* to upset, to shock; **un style qui frappe l'œil/l'oreille** a striking visual/musical style; **ce qui me frappe chez lui, c'est sa désinvolture** what strikes me about him is his offhandedness; **ce qui m'a frappé le plus, c'était son sang-froid** what struck *or* impressed me most was his/her coolness; **je fus frappé par leur ressemblance** I was struck by their resemblance; **j'ai été frappé de sa pâleur** I was shocked by his/her pallor; **être frappé de stupeur** to be stupefied *or* struck dumb; **je suis frappé de le retrouver dans cette situation** I'm surprised to find him in this situation
7 f. qn/qch de *(le soumettre à)* **f. qn d'anathème** to put an anathema on sb; **f. qn d'une interdiction de séjour** to ban sb; **f. l'alcool d'un impôt spécial** to put a special tax on alcohol
8 *Can (entrer en collision avec)* to hit
9 *Can Fam (trouver → emploi, affaire)* to land
10 *Littéraire (entacher)* **attitude frappée de pédanterie** attitude tinged with pedantry
11 *(refroidir)* to ice; *(boisson)* to chill; **f. le champagne** to put the champagne on ice; **faut-il ou non f. le champagne?** should champagne be chilled or not?
12 *Beaux-Arts & Tex* to emboss; *(motif)* to punch (out), to cut out; *(cuir)* to block
13 *Métal* to stamp; *(médaille)* to strike; *(pièces de monnaie)* to strike, to mint; *Fig* **frappé au coin de** bearing the mark *or* hallmark of; **une remarque frappée au coin du bon sens** a common-sensical remark
14 *(lettre)* to type; *Ordinat* to key; *Ordinat* **f. au kilomètre** to input continuously
USAGE ABSOLU *Hum* **le voleur de parapluies a encore frappé!** the umbrella thief strikes again!
VI 1 *(pour entrer)* to knock; **f. à la porte/fenêtre** to knock on the door/window; **on a frappé** someone knocked at the door; **f. doucement** *ou* **légèrement à la porte** to tap on *or* at the door; **la prochaine fois vous pourrez entrer sans f.** next time you can come in without knocking; *Fig* **f. à toutes les portes** to try every avenue; *Fig* **f. à la bonne/mauvaise porte** to go to the right/wrong place; **tu es sûr que tu nous as fait f. à la bonne porte?** are you sure you gave us the right door number?
2 *(pour exprimer un sentiment)* **f. des mains** *ou* **dans ses mains** to clap one's hands; **f. du poing sur la table** to bang one's fist on the table; **f. du pied** to stamp one's foot
3 *(cogner)* to strike; **les branches frappent contre la vitre** the branches are tapping against the windowpane; **f. dur** *ou* **sec** to strike hard; **f. fort** to hit hard; *Fig* to hit hard, to act decisively; *Fig* **f. à la tête** to aim for the top
4 *Fam (agir)* to strike; **le gang a encore frappé** the gang has struck again; **la grippe va f. durement** the flu will hit everyone hard
5 *(footballeur)* to shoot, to take a shot; **il frappe du pied gauche** he kicks with his left foot
►**se frapper VPR 1** *(emploi réfléchi)* to hit oneself; **se f. la poitrine** to beat one's chest; **se f. le front** to slap one's forehead
2 *(emploi réciproque)* to hit one another *or* each other
3 *Fam (s'inquiéter)* to get (oneself) worked up, to panic■; **ne te frappe pas pour si peu!** don't get all worked up about such a little thing!
4 *Can (entrer en collision)* to collide

frappeur [frapœr] **ADJ M** *voir* **esprit**
NM *Métal* striker; *(de papier peint)* embosser

fraser [3] [fraze] = **fraiser**

frasil [frazi] **NM** *Can* frazil

frasque [frask] **NF** escapade, prank; **des frasques de jeunesse** youthful indiscretions; **faire des frasques** to get up to mischief *or* to no good

fraternel, -elle [fratɛrnɛl] **ADJ** brotherly, fraternal; **amour f.** brotherly love; **geste f.** friendly gesture; **ils sont unis par des liens quasi fraternels** they're almost as close as brothers

fraternellement [fratɛrnɛlmɑ̃] **ADV** fraternally; **agir f. envers qn** to act in a brotherly way towards sb; **nous nous embrassâmes f.** we kissed like brothers

fraternisation [fratɛrnizasjɔ̃] **NF** fraternizing; **la f. entre les peuples** fraternization between peoples

fraterniser [3] [fratɛrnize] **VI** to fraternize

fraternité [fratɛrnite] **NF** *(lien)* brotherhood, fraternity; **f. d'armes** brotherhood of arms; **on constate une certaine f. d'esprit entre eux** you can see a certain kinship of spirit between them

fratricide [fratrisid] **ADJ** *(guerre, haine)* fratricidal
NMF *(meurtrier)* fratricide
NM *(meurtre)* fratricide

fratrie [fratri] **NF** brothers and sisters

fraude [frod] **NF 1** *(tromperie)* fraud; **la f. aux examens** cheating at exams
2 *Jur* **f. électorale** electoral fraud, vote *or* ballot rigging; **f. fiscale** tax evasion *or* fraud; **f. sur les produits** fraudulent trading
▫ **en fraude ADV** *(vendre)* fraudulently; **entrer/sortir en f.** to sneak in/out; **passer qch en f.** to smuggle sth in; **il entra en f. dans le pays** he entered the country illegally *or* unlawfully

frauder [3] [frode] **VT** *(état)* to defraud; **f. le fisc** to evade taxation; **f. la douane** to defraud customs, to smuggle
VI to cheat; **f. à** *ou* **dans un examen** to cheat in an exam; **f. sur le poids** to cheat on the weight, to give short measure; **il a l'habitude de f. dans le métro** he always avoids buying a ticket for the underground

fraudeur, -euse [frodœr, -øz] **ADJ** *(attitude, tempérament)* cheating
NM,F *(envers le fisc)* tax evader; *(à la douane)* smuggler; *(à un examen)* cheat; *(dans le métro, dans le bus)* fare-dodger

fraduleuse [frodyløz] *voir* **frauduleux**

frauduleusement [frodyløzmɑ̃] **ADV** fraudulently; **faire entrer/sortir qch f.** to smuggle sth in/out

frauduleux, -euse [frodylø, -øz] **ADJ** fraudulent; **édition frauduleuse** pirate edition

fraxinelle [fraksinɛl] **NF** fraxinella

frayée [frɛje] **NF** wheel rut

frayement [frɛjmɑ̃] **NM** *Vét* galling

frayer [11] [frɛje] **VT 1** *(route, voie)* to clear; **f. un chemin en abattant les arbres** to clear a path by felling the trees; *Fig* **f. la voie à qn/qch** to pave the way for sb/sth
2 *(sujet: cerf → tête)* to scrape, to rub, to fray; *Vét (sujet: cheval)* to gall
VI *Ich* to spawn
▫ **frayer avec VT IND** to associate with; **je ne fraye pas avec des gens de cette espèce** I don't mix with that sort of people
►**se frayer VPR se f. un passage** to clear a way (for oneself); **se f. un chemin** *ou* **un passage dans la foule** to force *or* to push one's way through the crowd; *Fig* **se f. un chemin** *ou* **une route vers la gloire** to work one's way towards fame

frayère [frɛjɛr] **NF** spawning ground *(of fish)*

frayeur [frɛjœr] **NF** fright; **avoir des frayeurs nocturnes** to suffer from night terrors; **faire une f. à qn** to give sb a fright; **tu m'as fait une de ces**

frayeurs! you really frightened me!, you gave me such a fright!; **vous me donnez des frayeurs** you're getting me worried; **j'ai eu une f., j'ai cru que j'avais oublié mes clés** I had or got a fright, I thought I had forgotten my keys; **se remettre de ses frayeurs** to recover from one's fright

frazil [frazi] = **frasil**

FRBG [ɛfɛrbeʒe] NM (*abrév* **fonds pour risques bancaires généraux**) FGBR

freak [frik] NM *Fam* dropout

fredaine [frədɛn] NF escapade, prank; **faire des fredaines** to get into or up to mischief; *(amoureuses)* to carry on

Frédéric [frederik] NPR **F. le Grand** Frederick the Great

Frédéric-Guillaume [frederikgijom] NPR Frederick William

fredonnement [frədɔnmã] NM humming

fredonner [3] [frədɔne] VT *(air, chanson)* to hum VI to hum

free-jazz [fridʒaz] NM INV *Mus* free jazz

free-lance [frilãs] *(pl* **free-lances)** ADJ INV freelance NMF freelance, freelancer NM freelancing, freelance work; **travailler** ou **être en f., faire du f.** to work on a freelance basis or as a freelancer, to freelance

free-martin [frimartin] *(pl* **free-martins)** NM *Vét* freemartin

free-shop [friʃɔp] *(pl* **free-shops)** NM duty-free shop

freesia [frezja] NM freesia

Freetown [fritawn] NM Freetown

freeware [friwɛr] NM *Ordinat* freeware; **freewares** freeware programs

freezer [frizœr] NM freezer compartment

frégatage [fregataʒ] NM *Naut* tumblehome

frégate [fregat] NF 1 *Orn* frigate bird 2 *Naut* frigate

frégater [3] [fregate] VT *Naut* to streamline the hull of

frein [frɛ̃] NM 1 *Aut* brake; **actionner les freins** to brake; *Fam* **mettre le f.** to pull on the handbrake; *Fig* **mettre un f. à qch** to curb sth; **mettre un f. aux désirs de qn** to curb or to bridle sb's desires; **mettre un f. à la montée de la colère/du chômage** to stem or to check or to curb the rising tide of anger/rising unemployment; *Fig* **f. à l'expansion** brake on growth; **donner un brusque coup de f.** to brake sharply or suddenly; *Fig* **un coup de f. à la création d'entreprises** a check or curb on the creation of new companies; *Fig* **c'est un coup de f. à l'économie** this will act as a brake on the economy; **f. à air comprimé** airbrake; **freins arrière** rear brakes; **freins assistés** power brakes; **freins avant** front brakes; **freins à bande** band brakes; *Can* **f. à bras** handbrake, *Am* parking brake; **f. à disque** disc brake; **f. sur échappement** exhaust brake; **f. d'embrayage** clutch stop; *Écon* **f. fiscal** fiscal drag; **f. hydraulique** hydraulic brake; **f. à main** handbrake; **f. moteur** engine brake; **utilisez votre f. moteur** *(sur panneau)* engage low gear; **f. à pédale** footbrake; **f. au pied** footbrake; **f. secondaire** emergency brake; **f. de stationnement** handbrake, *Am* parking brake; **f. à tambour** drum brake; **f. sur transmission** transmission brake; **f. à vide** vacuum brake

2 *Anat* fraenum, frenum

3 *(mors)* bit; **ronger son f.** *(cheval) & Fig (personne)* to champ at the bit

☐ **sans frein** ADJ unbridled

freinage [frɛnaʒ] NM 1 *(action)* braking; **distance de f.** braking distance; **traces de f.** skid marks; *Aviat* **parachute de f.** brake parachute 2 *(système)* brake system, brakes 3 *(de l'inflation)* curbing; *(de production)* cutting back; *(des importations, des salaires)* reduction

freiner [4] [frene] VT 1 *(ralentir → véhicule)* to slow down; *(→ évolution)* to check; **des arbres ont freiné sa chute** trees broke his/her fall

2 *(amoindrir → impatience)* to curb; *(→ enthousiasme)* to dampen; *(→ inflation, production)* to curb, to check; *(→ importations, salaires)* to reduce

3 *(personne)* to restrain

VI *(conducteur, auto)* to brake; **ta voiture freine bien/mal** your car brakes are good/bad; *Fig* **il voudrait moderniser l'usine mais son père freine des quatre fers** he'd like to modernize the factory, but his father's holding him back

▸ **se freiner** VPR *Fig* to keep oneself in check, to restrain oneself

freinte [frɛ̃t] NF *Com* = loss in volume or weight *(during transit or manufacture)*

frelatage [frəlataʒ] NM adulteration

frelaté, -e [frəlate] ADJ 1 *(nourriture, vin)* adulterated 2 *Fig Littéraire* artificial; **un mode de vie f.** an artificial way of life

frelater [3] [frəlate] VT *(lait, vin, huile)* to adulterate

frêle [frɛl] ADJ 1 *(fragile → corps, santé)* frail, fragile; *(→ voix)* thin, reedy; *(→ embarcation, cabane)* flimsy, frail; **tout repose sur ses frêles épaules** everything rests on his/her frail shoulders 2 *(ténu → espoir)* frail, flimsy

frelon [frəlɔ̃] NM hornet

freluquet [frəlykɛ] NM 1 *Fam (homme chétif)* pipsqueak, (little) runt 2 *Littéraire (prétentieux) (young)* whippersnapper

frémille [fremil] NF *Can Fam* ant■

frémir [32] [fremir] VI 1 *(trembler → de froid)* to shiver, to shudder; *(→ de peur)* to shake, to tremble, to shudder, to quake; **je frémis encore en y pensant** thinking about it still sends shivers down my spine; **f. de colère** to shake or to tremble or to quiver with anger; **f. d'impatience** to tremble or to quiver with impatience; **f. de plaisir/de joie** to quiver with pleasure/happiness

2 *Littéraire (vibrer → tige, herbe)* to quiver, to tremble; *(→ surface d'un lac)* to ripple; *(→ vitres)* to shake, to rattle; *(→ feuilles)* to rustle; *(→ vent)* to sigh; **l'air frémissait encore des échos d'une flûte lointaine** the air was still vibrating to the echoes of a distant flute

3 *(avant l'ébullition)* to simmer

frémissant, -e [fremisɑ̃, -ɑ̃t] ADJ 1 *(avant l'ébullition)* simmering

2 *Littéraire (feuilles)* quivering, rustling; *(surface d'un lac)* quivering; *(chair)* quivering, trembling

3 *(en émoi)* quivering, trembling; **une sensibilité frémissante** a trembling sensitivity; **être f. de colère** to be shaking or trembling or quivering with anger; **être f. d'impatience** to be trembling or quivering with impatience; **être f. de plaisir/joie** to be quivering with pleasure/happiness

frémissement [fremismɑ̃] NM 1 *(d'indignation, de colère)* quiver, shiver, shudder; *(de peur)* shudder; **un f. de colère** a quiver of anger; **un f. d'impatience la parcourut** a thrill of impatience ran through her; **un f. parcourut le public** a shudder ran through the audience; **avec un f. de crainte** shaking or quaking with fear; **avec un f. dans la voix** with a trembling or shaky voice

2 *Littéraire (des feuilles)* rustling; *(de la surface d'un lac)* rippling; *(du vent)* sighing; **le f. des champs de blé sous la brise** the wheatfields quivering in the breeze

3 *(avant l'ébullition)* simmer, simmering

frênaie [frɛnɛ] NF ash plantation

frénateur, -trice [frenatœr, -tris] ADJ *Méd* inhibitor *(avant n)*

french cancan [frɛnʃkɑ̃kɑ̃] *(pl* **french cancans)** NM *(French)* cancan

frêne [frɛn] NM 1 *(arbre)* ash (tree) 2 *(bois)* ash

frénésie [frenezi] NF frenzy; **f. d'achat** shopping spree; **être pris d'une f. de voyages** to have a strong urge to travel, to have the travel bug; **avec f.** frantically, frenetically, wildly; **travailler/parler avec f.** to work/talk frenziedly

frénétique [frenetik] ADJ *(agitation, hurlement)* frantic; *(activité)* frenzied, frantic; *(joie, passion)* frenzied; *(rythme)* frenetic, frenzied; **des applaudissements frénétiques** frenzied applause

frénétiquement [frenetikmɑ̃] ADV frantically, frenetically, wildly

Fréon® [freɔ̃] NM Freon®

fréquemment [frekamɑ̃] ADV frequently, often

fréquence [frekɑ̃s] NF 1 *(périodicité)* frequency; **quelle est la f. des trains sur cette ligne?** how many trains a day run on this line?; *Mktg* **f. d'achat** purchase frequency; **f. d'utilisation** usage frequency

2 *Méd* **f. du pouls** ou **cardiaque** fast pulse rate

3 *(en acoustique)* frequency; *(de son)* tone; *Tél*

wavelength, (wave) band, frequency; **basse/moyenne/haute f.** low/middle/high frequency; **f. cumulée** cumulative frequency; **f. porteuse** carrier frequency; **f. radio** radio frequency; **f. réglée** adjusted frequency; **f. relative** relative frequency; **f. du signal** signal frequency; **f. vocale** vocal frequency; **f. sonore** audio frequency

4 *(en statistique)* frequency; **f. absolue** absolute frequency; **f. cumulée** cumulative frequency

5 *Ordinat* **f. d'horloge** clock speed or frequency; **f. d'horloge du microprocesseur** microprocessor clock frequency; **f. de rafraîchissement** refresh rate

fréquencemètre [frekɑ̃smɛtr] NM frequency meter

fréquent, -e [frekɑ̃, -ɑ̃t] ADJ 1 *(répété)* frequent; **peu f.** infrequent; **il est f. de voir des jeunes couples divorcer** you frequently or often see young couples getting divorced; **il est peu f. que...** it is not very often that... 2 *Méd* **pouls f.** fast pulse

fréquentable [frekɑ̃tabl] ADJ **sa famille n'est guère f.** his/her family isn't exactly the kind you'd care to associate with; **c'est un endroit bien peu f.** it's not the sort of place you'd like to be seen in

fréquentatif, -ive [frekɑ̃tatif, -iv] ADJ *Ling* frequentative

fréquentation [frekɑ̃tasjɔ̃] NF 1 *(d'un lieu)* frequenting (**de** of); **f. des théâtres** theatre-going; **la f. des cinémas a baissé** cinema-going has decreased

2 *(relation)* acquaintance; **quelles sont ses fréquentations?** who does he/she associate with?; **avoir de mauvaises fréquentations** to keep bad company; **surveillez ses fréquentations** keep a watch on the company he/she keeps; **ce ne sont pas des fréquentations pour une jeune fille** these are not the sort of people a young girl should be associating with; **ce garçon n'est pas une f. pour toi** you shouldn't associate with this boy

3 *Littéraire (lecture)* **la f. des bons auteurs/de la littérature italienne** acquaintance with the great authors/Italian literature, reading good books/Italian literature

fréquentative *voir* **fréquentatif**

fréquenté, -e [frekɑ̃te] ADJ busy; **un endroit bien/mal f.** a place with a good/bad reputation; **c'est un café très f. par les jeunes** it's a café that's very popular with young people; **un endroit peu f.** a place hardly anyone ever goes to

fréquenter [3] [frekɑ̃te] VT 1 *(lieu)* to frequent

2 *(voir régulièrement)* to see frequently, to associate with; **elle n'a jamais fréquenté sa belle-famille** she never sees her in-laws; **nous ne nous fréquentons plus beaucoup** we don't see much of each other any more; **je fréquente peu ce genre de personnes** I don't associate much with that type of person; **qui fréquente-t-il?** who does he go around with?, what company does he keep?; **je t'interdis de f. les voisins** I forbid you to speak to the neighbours; **parmi tous ceux que je fréquente** amongst all my acquaintances

3 *Vieilli (courtiser)* **elle fréquente mon frère depuis un an** she's been going out with my brother for a year

4 *Littéraire (lire)* **f. les bons écrivains/la littérature italienne** to read good books/Italian literature

USAGE ABSOLU *Fam Vieilli* **il paraît qu'elle fréquente** there are rumours she's courting

VI *Arch* ou *Littéraire* **f. chez qn/dans des familles riches** to be on visiting terms with sb/with wealthy people

▸ **se fréquenter** VPR *Vieilli* **ils se fréquentent depuis deux ans** they've been going out for two years; **ils se fréquentent assez peu** they don't see much of each other

fréquentiel, -elle [frekɑ̃sjɛl] ADJ frequential

frère [frɛr] NM 1 *(dans une famille)* brother; **tu es un (vrai) f. pour moi** you're like a brother to me; **mon grand/petit f.** *(de deux)* my older/younger brother; *(de plusieurs)* my oldest/youngest brother; **tu vas avoir un petit f.** you are going to have a little or baby brother; **se ressembler comme des frères** to be like two peas (in a

pod); **s'aimer comme des frères** to love each other like brothers; **en frères** as brothers; **partager en frères** to share fairly; **ce sont des frères ennemis** a friendly rivalry exists between them; **f. aîné/cadet** older/younger brother; **f. jumeau** twin brother; **f. de lait** foster brother; **f. de sang** blood brother; *Fam* **f. Trois-points** freemason

2 *(compagnon)* brother; *Fam* **salut, vieux f.!** hello, old pal!; *Fam Hum* **j'ai un bougeoir qui a perdu son f.** I've got one candle-holder but I've lost its companion; **frères d'armes** brothers in arms; **frères de race** brothers

3 *Rel* brother, friar; **aller à l'école chez les frères** to go to a Catholic boys' school; **mes bien chers frères** dearly beloved brethren; **f. lai** lay brother; **frères mineurs** Franciscans, Franciscan monks; **frères pêcheurs** Dominican monks *or* friars; **le f. Dominique** Brother Dominic

4 *(au sein d'une communauté)* brother

5 *(comme adj) (groupe, parti, pays)* sister *(avant n)*

Allusion

Si ce n'est toi, c'est donc ton frère

In La Fontaine's fable *Le Loup et l'Agneau* ("The Wolf and the Lamb"), a wolf sets out to kill a lamb. The wolf puts forward a series of false accusations, notably that the lamb has been speaking ill of him. When the lamb protests that he was not even born at the time, the wolf says: **Si ce n'est toi, c'est donc ton frère** ("Well, if it wasn't you, it was your brother"), drags him into the woods and kills him. The phrase is used today when two similar people or things are mistaken for each other, or when summary justice is meted out to an innocent person.

---

frérot [frero] NM *Fam* kid brother, little brother■; **alors, f., ça va?** so how's it going, little brother *or* bro?

Fresnes [frɛn] NM = town in the Paris suburbs with a well-known prison

fresque [frɛsk] NF **1** *Beaux-Arts* fresco; **peindre à f.** to paint in fresco **2** *(description)* panorama, detailed picture; **ce roman est une f. historique** this novel is a historical epic; **le film est une f. sociale sur l'Italie des années 50** the film is a social portrait of Italy in the 50s

fresquiste [frɛskist] NMF fresco painter

fressure [fresyr] NF pluck; *Culin* fry

fret¹ [frɛ] NM **1** *(chargement → d'un avion, d'un navire)* cargo, freight; *(→ d'un camion)* load; **avion de f.** charter aircraft; **donner à f.** to freight; **prendre à f.** to charter; **f. aérien** air-freight; **expédier par f. aérien** to airfreight; **f. d'aller** outward freight; **f. par conteneur** containerized freight; **f. express** express freight; **f. à forfait** through freight; **f. intérieur** inland freight; **f. maritime** sea *or* ocean freight; **f. payé** freight paid; **f. au poids** freight by weight; **f. de retour** home freight

2 *(prix → par air, mer)* freight (charges), freightage; *(→ par route)* carriage; **payer le f.** to pay the freight charges *or* freightage

fret², **frette** [frɛt] *Can Fam* ADJ freezing

    ADV **il fait f.** it's freezing cold

    NM **le f.** the cold■, **il fait un f. noir** it's freezing cold

fréter [18] [frete] VT *(avion)* to charter; *(navire)* to freight; *(camionnette)* to hire

fréteur [fretœr] NM freighter; *(armateur)* shipowner; **f. et affréteur** owner and charterer

frétillant, -e [fretijã, -ãt] ADJ *(ver, poisson)* wriggling; *(queue)* wagging; *Fig (personne)* lively; *Fig* **tout f. d'impatience** quivering with impatience; **elle était toute frétillante à l'idée de le revoir** she couldn't keep still at the thought of seeing him again

frétillement [fretijmã] NM *(de la queue)* wagging; *(de vers, de poissons)* wriggling; *Fig* fidgeting

frétiller [3] [fretije] VI *(ver, poisson)* to wriggle; *(queue)* to wag; **le chien frétille de la queue** the dog is wagging its tail; *Fig* **il frétille**

d'impatience/de joie he's quivering with impatience/joy

fretin [frətɛ̃] NM fry; *Fig* **(menu) f.** small fry

frettage [frɛtaʒ] NM *Tech* fitting a hoop *or* collar *(de* **on**)

frette¹ [frɛt] NF **1** *Tech* hoop, collar; **f. de moyeu** nave ring **2** *Mus* fret

frette² [frɛt] NF *Archit & Hér* fret

frette³ [frɛt] ADJ *voir* **fret²**

fretter [3] [frete] VT to hoop; **béton fretté** hooped concrete

freudien, -enne [frødjɛ̃, -ɛn] ADJ & NM,F Freudian

freudisme [frødism] NM Freudianism

freudo-marxisme [frødomarksism] *(pl* **freudo-marxismes**) NM Freudian Marxism

freux [frø] NM *Orn* rook; **colonie de f.** rookery

friabilité [frijabilite] NF *(d'une roche)* friableness, friability; *(d'un biscuit)* crumbliness

friable [frijabl] ADJ *(roche)* crumbly, friable; *(biscuit)* crumbly

friand, -e [frijã, -ãd] ADJ **1** *Vieilli (gourmand)* fond of delicacies **2 f. de** *(sucreries)* fond of; **il est très f. de chocolat** he's very fond of chocolate; *Fig* **être f. de compliments** to enjoy receiving compliments

    NM **1** *(salé)* ≃ meat pie (made with puff pastry); **f. au fromage** ≃ cheese pie (made with puff pastry) **2** *(sucré)* ≃ almond *Br* biscuit *or Am* cookie

friandise [frijãdiz] NF sweetmeat, (sweet) delicacy, titbit; **aimer les friandises** to have a sweet tooth

Fribourg [fribur] NM *(en Allemagne)* Freiburg; *(en Suisse)* Fribourg; **le canton de F.** Fribourg

fribourg [fribur] NM Fribourg cheese

Fribourg-en-Brisgau [friburãbrizgo] NM Freiburg

fric [frik] NM *Fam* cash, dough; **gagner plein de f.** to make loads of money; **il est bourré de f.** he's loaded; **j'ai plus de f.!** I'm broke *or* skint!

fricadelle [frikadɛl] NF *Belg* meatball

fricandeau, -x [frikãdo] NM *Culin* fricandeau

fricandelle [frikãdɛl] NF *Belg* meatball

fricasse [frikas] NF *Suisse Fam (grand froid)* freeze■

fricassée [frikase] NF **1** *(ragoût)* fricassee; *Fam Hum* **f. de museaux** exchange of kisses■; **au moment de partir, c'est la f. de museaux!** just before leaving, everybody goes all kissy-kissy! **2** *Belg* ≃ eggs and bacon

fricasser [3] [frikase] VT to fricassee; **faire des champignons** to fricassee mushrooms

fricatif, -ive [frikatif, -iv] *Ling* ADJ fricative

    ▫ **fricative** NF fricative

fric-frac [frikfrak] NM INV *très Fam* burglary■, break-in■

friche [friʃ] NF **1** *Agr* piece of fallow land, fallow; *Fig* **une idée/un projet qui est** *ou* **reste en f.** an idea/a plan which has not yet been taken up **2** *Ind* **f. industrielle** industrial wasteland

    ▫ **en friche** ADJ **1** *Agr* **terre en f.** plot of fallow land; **rester** *ou* **être en f.** to lie fallow, to remain uncultivated

2 *(inactif)* unused; **avoir l'esprit en f.** to have intellectual capacities which go unused; **avoir des dons en f.** to have hidden talents; **une idée/un projet qui est** *ou* **reste en f.** an idea/a plan which has not yet been taken up

frichti [friʃti] NM *Fam* **1** *(nourriture) Br* grub, chow **2** *(repas)* cooked meal■

fricot [friko] NM *Fam* **1** *(ragoût)* stew■ **2** *(cuisine) Br* grub, *Am* chow; **faire le f.** to cook■

fricotage [frikotaʒ] NM *Fam Péj* scheming■

fricoter [3] [frikɔte] *Fam* VT **1** *(cuisiner)* to stew■

2 *(manigancer)* to cook up; **je me demande ce qu'il fricote** I wonder what he's up to *or* what he's cooking up

    VI **1** *(trafiquer)* to be on the fiddle

2 *(avoir des relations sexuelles)* **ils fricotent ensemble** they're sleeping together

    ▫ **fricoter avec** VT IND **1** *(sexuellement)* to knock around with

2 *(être complice de)* to cook something up with

fricoteur, -euse [frikɔtœr, -øz] NM,F *Fam (trafiquant)* fiddler

friction [friksjɔ̃] NF **1** *(frottement)* chafing

2 *(massage → gén)* rub (down); *(→ du cuir chevelu)* scalp massage

3 *Fig (désaccord)* friction; **il y a des frictions**

entre eux they don't see eye to eye; **cela reste un point de f.** that remains a bone of contention

4 *Géol & Tech* friction; **embrayage à f.** friction clutch; **entraînement par f.** *(d'une imprimante)* friction feed; **réduire les frictions** to reduce friction

frictionnel, -elle [friksjɔnɛl] ADJ *Tech* frictional; *(chômage)* temporary

frictionner [3] [friksjɔne] VT to rub (down); **f. qn** to rub sb down, to give sb a rubdown; **f. la tête de qn** to massage sb's scalp, to give sb a scalp massage

    ►**se frictionner** VPR to rub oneself; **frictionne-toi bien** give yourself a good rub down; **se f. le bras/la jambe** to rub one's arm/leg

fridolin [fridɔlɛ̃] NM *très Fam* Kraut, Fritz, = offensive term used to refer to a German person; **les fridolins** Jerry

Frigidaire® [friʒidɛr] NM **1** *(portant la marque)* Frigidaire® (refrigerator) **2** *(appareil quelconque)* refrigerator, fridge; *Fig* **mettre qch au Frigidaire®** to put sth on the back burner, to shelve sth

frigidarium [friʒidarjɔm] NM *Antiq* frigidarium

frigide [friʒid] ADJ frigid; *Littéraire (cœur, caractère)* cold, icy

frigidité [friʒidite] NF frigidity

frigo [frigo] NM *Fam* **1** *(réfrigérateur)* fridge■ **2** *(chambre froide)* cold room■

frigorie [frigɔri] NF *Vieilli Phys* negative kilocalorie

frigorifié, -e [frigɔrifje] ADJ frozen; *Fam Fig* frozen stiff

frigorifier [9] [frigɔrifje] VT to refrigerate; *Fam Fig* **la promenade m'a complètement frigorifié** I'm frozen stiff after that walk

frigorification [frigɔrifikasjɔ̃] NF refrigerating, refrigeration

frigorifique [frigɔrifik] ADJ refrigerated; **appareil f.** refrigerator; **mélange f.** freezing mixture; **camion f.** refrigerated lorry; **wagon f.** refrigerator van; **entrepôt f.** cold store

    NM **1** *(établissement)* cold store **2** *(appareil)* refrigerator

frigorigène [frigɔriʒɛn] ADJ **fluide f.** refrigerating fluid

    NM refrigerant

frigoriste [frigɔrist] NMF refrigerating engineer

frileuse [friløz] *voir* **frileux**

frileusement [friløzmã] ADV **s'envelopper f. dans des couvertures** to wrap oneself in blankets

frileux, -euse [frilø, -øz] ADJ **1** *(qui a froid)* sensitive to (the) cold; **je suis très f.** I really feel the cold **2** *(prudent)* timid, unadventurous **3** *Arch & Littéraire (temps, jour)* cold

    NM,F = person who feels the cold

frilosité [frilozite] NF *Littéraire* sensitivity to the cold; *Fig* nervousness, hesitancy; **la f. des marchés financiers** the nervousness of the financial markets

frimaire [frimɛr] NM = 3rd month of the French Revolutionary calendar (from 22 November to 21 December)

frimas [frima] NM *Littéraire* hoar frost

frime [frim] NF *Fam* **1** *(fanfaronnade)* **les lunettes noires, c'est pour la f.** sunglasses are just for posing in; **bon, t'arrêtes ta f.?** will you stop showing off!; **tu l'aurais vu avec son nouveau cuir, la f.!** you should have seen him in his new leather jacket, what a poser! **2** *(comportement trompeur)* **c'est de la f.** it's all an act, it's all put on

frimer [3] [frime] VI *Fam* to show off, to put on an act

frimeur, -euse [frimœr, -øz] *Fam* ADJ *(attitude, ton)* showy

    NM,F show-off

frimousse [frimus] NF **1** *Fam* (sweet) little face■ **2** *Ordinat (smiley)* smiley

fringale [frɛ̃gal] NF *Fam* **1** *(faim)* hunger■; **avoir la f.** to be ravenous *or* starving *or* famished; **j'ai une de ces fringales!** I'm starving! **2** *(désir)* **une f. de** a craving for

fringant, -e [frɛ̃gã, -ãt] ADJ **1** *(personne)* dashing; **encore f.** (still) spry; **je ne me sens pas trop f. aujourd'hui** I don't feel too good *or* well today **2** *(cheval)* frisky, spirited

fringillidé [frɛ̃ʒilide] *Orn* NM finch, *Spéc* member of the Fringillidae

    ▫ **fringillidés** NMPL finches, *Spéc* Fringillidae

fringue [frɛ̃g] **NF** *Fam* piece of clothing■; **j'ai plus une f. à me mettre** I haven't a thing to wear; **j'ai envie d'aller m'acheter une f.** I want to go and buy something to wear; **des fringues** clothes■, threads, *Br* gear

fringuer [3] [frɛ̃ge] **VT** *Fam* to dress■; **être bien/mal fringué** to be well/badly dressed■; **elle est fringuée n'importe comment!** she's got no dress sense!

VI *Arch ou Can Fam* to prance about, to skip about

▶**se fringuer VPR** *Fam* **1** *(s'habiller)* to get dressed■; **fringue-toi, on y va!** get some clothes on (you), we're off!; **elle se fringue très seventies** she dresses really seventies **2** *(s'habiller bien)* to get done up *or* dolled up

Frioul-Vénétie Julienne [friulvenesiʒyljɛn] **NM** *Géog* **le F.** Friuli-Venezia Giulia

fripe [frip] **NF la f., les fripes** second-hand clothes

fripé, -e [fripe] **ADJ** *Can Fam* exhausted■, beat, *Br* knackered

friper [3] [fripe] **VT 1** *(chiffonner)* to crumple *or* to crease (up); **son pantalon était tout fripé aux genoux** his/her trousers were all creased around the knee **2** *(rider)* **avoir un visage tout fripé** to have crease-marks all over one's face

▶**se friper VPR** to crumple, to get crumpled

friperie [fripri] **NF 1** *(boutique)* second-hand clothes *Br* shop *or Am* store **2** *(vêtements)* secondhand clothes

fripier, -ère [fripje, -ɛr] **NM,F** second-hand clothes dealer

fripon, -onne [fripɔ̃, -ɔn] **ADJ** *(enfant)* mischievous, roguish; *(sourire)* roguish

NM,F rogue; **tu n'es qu'un petit f.!** you little rogue *or* scamp!

friponnerie [fripɔnri] **NF** *Vieilli (caractère)* roguery, knavery; *(action)* mischievous prank

fripouille [fripuj] **NF 1** *Péj (scélérat)* rascal, rogue **2** *(ton affectueux)* **(petite) f.!** you little rogue! **3** *Arch (racaille)* rabble, riff-raff

fripouillerie [fripujri] **NF** *Fam* roguishness

friqué, -e [frike] **ADJ** *Fam (person)* loaded; *(quartier)* rich■, *Br* posh; **c'est un mec vachement f.** *Br* he's rolling in it, *Am* he's rolling in dough

friquet [frikɛ] **NM** *Orn* tree sparrow

frire [115] [frir] **VT** *Culin* to fry; *(en friteuse, dans un bain d'huile)* to deep-fry; **poisson frit** fried fish

VI to fry; **faire f. des poissons** to fry fish

frisage [frizaʒ] **NM 1** *(des cheveux)* curling, waving **2** *Métal* crimping

frisant, -e [frizɑ̃, -ɑ̃t] **ADJ** *(lumière)* oblique

Frisbee® [frizbi] **NM** Frisbee®

Frise [friz] **NF la F.** Friesland

frise [friz] **NF 1** *Archit & Beaux-Arts* frieze **2** *Théât* border **3 f. chronologique** timeline

frisé, -e [frize] **ADJ 1** *(barbe, cheveux)* curly; *(personne)* curly-haired; **être f. comme un mouton** to have curly *or* frizzy hair **2** *(chicorée)* curly

NM,F *Fam* **1** *(personne)* curly-haired person■; *(enfant)* curly-haired child **2** *Fam* Kraut, Fritz, *Br* Jerry, = offensive term used to refer to German people

▫ **frisée NF** *(chicorée)* curly endive; **frisée aux lardons** = curly endive salad with fried bacon pieces

friselis [frizli] **NM** *Littéraire (des feuilles)* rustling; *(de l'eau)* quivering

friser [3] [frize] **VT 1** *(barbe, cheveux)* to curl; **se faire f. (les cheveux)** to have one's hair curled

2 *(effleurer)* to graze, to skim; **le ballon a frisé la vitre** the ball skimmed past the window

3 *(être proche de)* **elle doit f. la quarantaine** she must be getting on for forty; **nous avons frisé la catastrophe** we came within an inch of disaster; **cela frise l'impertinence** it's verging on the impertinent

4 *Métal* to crimp

5 *Can (gicler)* to spurt

VI to have curly hair; **f. naturellement** to have naturally curly hair

frisette [frizɛt] **NF 1** *(de cheveux)* small curl; **avoir des frisettes** to have curly hair **2** *Menuis* narrow plank; **faire poser de la f. sur un mur** to panel a wall

frisolée [frizɔle] **NF** *Hort (de pommes de terre)* crinkle

frison[1] [frizɔ̃] **NM** *(de cheveux)* curl; *(de bois, de papier etc)* shaving

frison[2], **-onne** [frizɔ̃, -ɔn] **ADJ** Friesian, Frisian; **vache frisonne** Friesian cow

NM *(langue)* Friesian, Frisian

▫ **Frison, -onne NM,F** Frisian

▫ **frisonne NF** *(vache)* **frisonne (pie-noire)** *Br* Friesian, *Am* Holstein

frisottant, -e [frizɔtɑ̃, -ɑ̃t] **ADJ** *(cheveux)* frizzy

frisotter [3] [frizɔte] **VT** to frizz

VI to be frizzy; **la pluie fait f. mes cheveux** the rain makes my hair go all frizzy

frisottis [frizɔti] **NM** *Littéraire (de cheveux)* small curl

frisquet, -ette [friskɛ, -ɛt] **ADJ** *Fam (temps, vent)* chilly; **il fait plutôt f. aujourd'hui** it's rather chilly *or* there's a nip in the air today

frisson [frisɔ̃] **NM 1** *(de froid, de fièvre)* shiver; *(de peur)* shudder; *(de plaisir)* thrill; **avoir des frissons** to shiver, *Fam* to have the shivers; **être pris** *ou* **saisi de frissons** to get the shivers; **ton livre m'a donné des frissons** your book gave me the shivers; **j'en ai des frissons** it makes me shudder; **ça me donne des frissons rien que d'y penser** it makes me shudder just thinking of it; **ça a été le grand f.** it was a big thrill

2 *Littéraire (bruissement* → *de l'eau)* ripple; *(*→ *des feuilles)* rustle

frissonnant, -e [frisɔnɑ̃, -ɑ̃t] **ADJ 1** *(eau)* simmering **2** *(personne)* shivering; **être f. de froid/fièvre** to be shivering with cold/fever

frissonnement [frisɔnmɑ̃] **NM 1** *(de froid, de fièvre)* shiver; *(de peur)* shudder; **un f. de plaisir** a thrill of pleasure; **un f. lui parcourut le corps** a shiver ran through his/her body **2** *Littéraire (de la surface d'un étang)* ripple, rippling *(UNCOUNT)*; *(des feuilles)* rustling *(UNCOUNT)*

frissonner [3] [frisɔne] **VI 1** *(de froid, de fièvre)* to shiver; *(de peur)* to shudder; *(de joie)* to quiver; **elle frissonnait de bonheur** she was trembling with happiness; **ça me fait f. rien que d'y penser** the very thought of it gives me the creeps **2** *Littéraire (feuilles)* to rustle; *(surface d'un étang)* to ripple

frisure [frizyr] **NF** curls; **elle a une f. légère** her hair is slightly curly

frit, frite[1] [fri, frit] **PP** *voir* **frire**

ADJ 1 *Culin* fried **2** *Fam* **il est f.** he's had it, his goose is cooked

frite[2] [frit] **NF 1** *Culin Br* chip, *Am* French fry; **des frites** *Br* chips, *Am* French fries **2** *Fam (sur les fesses)* **faire une f. à qn** to flick sb on the bottom **3** *Fam (locutions)* **avoir la f.** to be on top form, to have bags of energy; **ne pas avoir la f.** not to be on top form; **ça va te donner la f.** that'll perk you up

friter [3] [frite] *Fam* **VT** *(battre)* **f. qn** to beat sb up, to kick sb's head in

▶**se friter VPR** to have a fistfight *or Br* punch-up

friterie [fritri] **NF** *(restaurant)* ≃ fast-food restaurant; *(ambulante) Br* ≃ chip van, *Am* ≃ French fry vendor

friteuse [fritøz] **NF** deep fryer, *Br* chip pan; **f. électrique** electric fryer

fritillaire [fritilɛr] **NF 1** *Entom (papillon)* fritillary; **f. panachée** variegated fritillary **2** *Bot* fritillary;

▫ **fritillaires NFPL** *Bot* Fritillaria

fritons [fritɔ̃] **NMPL** *Culin* crackling

frittage [fritaʒ] **NM 1** *Métal* sintering **2** *(du verre)* fritting

fritte [frit] **NF** frit

fritter [3] [frite] **VT 1** *Métal* to sinter **2** *(verre)* to frit

friture [frityr] **NF 1** *(aliments frits)* fried food; *(poissons)* fried fish; **acheter de la f.** to buy (small) fish for frying; **petite f.** small fry **2** *Culin (cuisson)* frying; *(matière grasse)* deep fat **3** *(en acoustique)* static; **(bruits de) f.** crackling (noise), interference; **il y a de la f.** we're getting some interference **4** *Belg (friterie) Br* ≃ chip van, *Am* ≃ French fry vendor

fritz [frits] **NM** *très Fam Vieilli* Kraut, = offensive term used with reference to Germans

frivole [frivɔl] **ADJ** *(personne, sujet)* frivolous

frivolement [frivɔlmɑ̃] **ADV** frivolously

frivolité [frivɔlite] **NF 1** *(légèreté)* frivolity, frivolousness; *(manque de sérieux* → *d'un projet, d'une œuvre)* triviality **2** *(vétille)* trifle; **perdre son temps à des frivolités** to waste time in frivolous pursuits *or* frivolities

▫ **frivolités NFPL** *Vieilli* fancy goods, novelties

froc [frɔk] **NM 1** *Fam (pantalon) Br* trousers■, keks, *Am* pants■; *aussi Fig* **faire dans son f.** to shit *or* to crap oneself; **baisser son f.** to demean oneself■ **2** *Rel (habit)* habit, frock; **prendre le f.** to become a monk; **porter le f.** to be a monk; **jeter son f. aux orties** to leave holy orders

frœbélien, -enne [frœbeljɛ̃, -ɛn] **NM,F** *Belg* nursery school teacher

froid, -e [frwa, frwad] **ADJ 1** *(boisson, temps, moteur, bain)* cold; **un vent f.** a cold wind; **un jour d'hiver f. et sec** a crisp winter day; **par un matin très f.** on a raw morning; **maintenant, les radiateurs sont froids** now the radiators have gone cold; **mange donc!, ça va être f.!** eat up or it'll be cold!

2 *(indifférent* → *personne)* cold, insensitive, unfeeling; *(*→ *tempérament)* cold; *(*→ *accueil)* cold, chilly; *(*→ *réponse)* cold, cool; *(*→ *attitude)* cold, unfriendly; *(*→ *style)* cold, unemotional; **ton/regard f.** hostile tone/stare; **se montrer** *ou* **être f. avec** *ou* **envers qn** to be cold towards sb, to treat sb coldly *or* coolly; **devant ce spectacle, il est resté f.** he was unmoved by the sight; **ça me laisse f.** it leaves me cold; **style f.** bloodless *or* cold style; **colère froide** cold fury; **f. comme le marbre** as cold as marble

3 *(triste)* cold, bleak; **des murs froids et nus** cold bare walls

4 *(couleur)* cold, cool

5 *(ancien)* cold, dead; **la piste est froide** the scent is cold, the trail's gone dead

NM 1 *(température)* **le f.** *(climat)* cold weather, the cold; *(air)* the cold (air); **les grands froids** the coldest part of the winter; **par ce f.** in this cold; **les plantes qui supportent le f.** plants that can endure the cold; **conserver qch au f.** to store sth in a cold place; **coup de f.** cold spell *or* snap; **il fait un f. de canard** *ou* **de loup** *ou* **sibérien** it's freezing *or* bitterly cold

2 *(sensation)* **avoir f.** to be *or* to feel cold; **j'ai f. aux mains** my hands are cold; **attraper** *ou* **prendre f.** to get *or* to catch a cold; **je meurs de f.** I'm freezing (cold); *Fig* **avoir f. dans le dos** to feel one's blood run cold; **ça me donne f. dans le dos** it makes my blood run cold, it sends shivers down my spine; **une histoire qui fait f. dans le dos** a chilling *or* creepy story; *Fig* **il n'a pas f. aux yeux** he's bold *or* plucky

3 *(malaise)* **il y a un f. entre eux** things have gone cool between them; **cela a jeté un f.** it cast a chill over the proceedings; **être en f. avec qn** to be on bad terms with sb; **ils sont en f.** they've fallen out, things are a bit strained between them

4 l'industrie du f. the refrigerating industry; **le f. industriel** refrigeration; **la chaîne du f.** the refrigeration chain

ADV il fait f. dehors it's cold out; **en janvier, il fait f.** the weather's cold in January; **boire f.** *(habituellement)* to drink cold drinks; **remuez et buvez f.** stir and chill before drinking; **manger f.** *(habituellement)* to have one's food cold; **assaisonnez et mangez f.** season and leave to cool before eating

▫ **à froid ADJ** *voir* **opération ADV 1** *(sans émotion)* calmly, dispassionately; **je te dis cela à f., mais j'ai pleuré quand je l'ai appris** I'm telling you this calmly but I cried when I first heard it

2 *(sans préparation)* **je ne peux pas répondre à f.** I can't answer off the top of my head; **prendre qn à f.** to catch sb unawares *or* off guard

3 *Tech & Métal* cold; **laminer à f.** to cold roll; **démarrer à f.** to start from cold; **soluble à f.** soluble when cold; **lavage à f.** cold water rinse

4 *Méd* **intervenir** *ou* **opérer à f.** to operate between attacks

froidement [frwadmɑ̃] **ADV 1** *(avec réserve)* coldly, coolly; *(répondre)* coolly; **recevoir qn f.** to give sb a cool reception **2** *(lucidement)* dispassionately; **raisonner f.** to use cold logic **3** *(avec indifférence)* cold-bloodedly; **abattre qn f.** to shoot down sb in cold blood **4** *Fam (locution)* **ça va f.!** I'm fine but a bit chilly!

froideur [frwadœr] **NF 1** *(indifférence méprisante)* coldness, cold indifference; **il est toujours d'une très grande f. avec moi** he is always very cold towards me

2 *(manque de sensualité)* coldness

3 *Littéraire (au toucher)* feel; **son front avait la f. du marbre** his/her forehead was cold as marble

❑ **avec froideur** ADV coldly, indifferently; **accueillir qn avec f.** to give sb a chilly welcome

froidure [frwadyr] NF 1 *Littéraire (temps)* intense cold; *(saison)* cold season *or* weather; **par ces temps de f.** in this cold weather 2 *Méd* frostbite

froissable [frwasabl] ADJ creasable; **robe trop f.** dress that creases (too) easily

froissant, -e [frwasɑ̃, -ɑ̃t] ADJ hurtful, wounding

froissé, -e [frwase] ADJ 1 *(chemise, tissu)* creased 2 *(personne)* hurt

froissement [frwasmɑ̃] NM 1 *(plis → d'un papier, d'une étoffe)* crumpling, creasing 2 *(bruit)* rustling, rustle 3 *Littéraire (vexation)* hurt feelings; **un f. d'amour-propre** a blow to one's pride 4 *Méd* straining *(UNCOUNT)*

froisser [3] [frwase] VT 1 *(friper → tissu)* to crease, to crumple; *(→ papier)* to crumple, to crease 2 *(carrosserie)* to dent 3 *(blesser → orgueil)* to ruffle, to bruise; *(→ personne)* to offend 4 *Méd* to strain

➤**se froisser** VPR 1 *(vêtement)* to crush, to crease 2 *(personne)* to take offence (**de** at), to be offended (**de** by) 3 **se f. un muscle** to strain a muscle

froissure [frwasyr] NF crease, rumple, wrinkle

frôlement [frolmɑ̃] NM 1 *(frottement)* brush, light touch; **j'ai senti le f. du chat contre ma jambe** I felt the cat brushing *or* rubbing against my leg 2 *(bruit)* rustle, swish, rustling sound

frôler [3] [frole] VT 1 *(effleurer)* to brush, to touch lightly, to graze; **l'avion a frôlé les arbres** the plane skimmed *or* grazed the treetops; **il m'a frôlé la joue du doigt** he stroked my cheek lightly; **la balle lui frôla la joue** the bullet grazed his/her cheek; **la branche lui a frôlé les cheveux** the branch brushed against his/her hair 2 *(passer très près de)* to come close to touching; **f. les murs** to hug the walls; **la livre a frôlé la barre des 1,50 euros** the pound was hovering just short of the 1.50 euro mark 3 *(échapper à)* to come within a hair's breadth *or* an ace of, to escape narrowly; **f. la mort** to come within a hair's breadth of death *or* dying; **mon métier m'a fait f. la mort plusieurs fois** I've diced with death more than once in my job; **f. la catastrophe** to come within a hair's breadth of disaster; **f. la rupture** to nearly split up, to come close to splitting up; **ton attitude frôle le ridicule** your attitude verges on *or* borders on the ridiculous

➤**se frôler** VPR to brush against *or* to jostle each other; **les passants se frôlent** passers-by brush against *or* jostle each other; **les deux voitures se sont frôlées** the two cars brushed past each other

frôleur, -euse [frolœr, -øz] ADJ *(geste)* stroking

NM pervert *(who likes to rub up against women in crowds)*

❑ **frôleuse** NF temptress, seductress

frolic [frɔlik] NM *Can (en acadien)* = local festival or celebration

froliquer [3] [frɔlike] VI *Can (en acadien)* to party

fromage [frɔmaʒ] NM 1 *(laitage)* cheese; **un f. a** cheese; **du f.** cheese; **prenez du f.** have some cheese; **plusieurs sortes de fromages** several kinds of cheese; **f. de vache/brebis/chèvre** cow's/sheep's/goat's milk cheese; **f. blanc** fromage frais; **f. blanc battu** smooth fromage frais; **f. fondu** cheese spread; **f. frais** fromage frais; **f. à pâte molle/dur** soft/hard cheese; **f. à pâte persillée** blue(-veined) cheese; **f. à pâte pressée** hard cheese; **f. à tartiner** cheese spread; *Fam* **en faire tout un f.** to kick up a (huge) fuss, to make a mountain out of a molehill; **pas la peine d'en faire un f.** it's not worth making a fuss about

2 *Fam* **un (gentil petit) f.** *(sinécure)* a cushy job *or* number, a nice little earner

3 *Fam Fig* **f. blanc** *(Français de souche)* = French person of native stock as opposed to immigrants *or* their descendants

❑ **au fromage** ADJ *(omelette, soufflé, sandwich)* cheese *(avant n)*; **des pâtes au f.** pasta with cheese

❑ **fromage de tête** NM *Br* brawn, *Am* headcheese

fromageon [frɔmaʒɔ̃] NM goat's milk cheese *(from the South of France)*

fromager, -ère [frɔmaʒe, -ɛr] ADJ cheese *(avant n)*

NM,F 1 *(commerçant) Br* cheesemonger, *Am* cheese seller 2 *(fabricant)* cheese maker, dairyman, *f* dairywoman

NM 1 *(récipient)* cheese mould 2 *Bot* kapok, silk-cotton tree, *Spéc* ceiba

fromagerie [frɔmaʒri] NF 1 *(boutique)* cheese *Br* shop *or Am* store 2 *(fabrique)* dairy

fromegi [frɔmʒi] NM *Fam* cheese■

froment [frɔmɑ̃] NM wheat

fromental, -aux [frɔmɑ̃tal, -o] NM tall oat-grass

frometon, fromton [frɔmtɔ̃] NM *Fam* cheese■

fromgi [frɔmʒi] = **fromegi**

fromton [frɔmtɔ̃] = **frometon**

fronce [frɔ̃s] NF *(de tissu)* gather; **faire des fronces à un tissu** to gather a piece of material ❑ **à fronces** ADJ gathered

froncement [frɔ̃smɑ̃] NM **f. de sourcils** frown

froncer [16] [frɔ̃se] VT 1 *Couture* to gather 2 *(rider)* **f. le nez** to wrinkle one's nose; **f. les sourcils** to knit one's brow, to frown; **sa remarque lui fit f. les sourcils** his/her remark brought a frown to his/her face *or* made him/her frown

froncis [frɔ̃si] NM *Couture* gathers, gathering *(UNCOUNT)*

frondaison [frɔ̃dɛzɔ̃] NF 1 *(feuillage)* foliage, leaves 2 *(époque)* foliation

fronde¹ [frɔ̃d] NF 1 *(arme)* sling 2 *(lance-pierres) Br* catapult, *Am* slingshot 3 *Littéraire (révolte)* rebellion, revolt; *Hist* **la F.** the Fronde rebellion

---

Culture

LA FRONDE

This refers to a civil war (1648–1653) which took place during Louis XIV's minority, and was directed initially against his chief minister, Mazarin. The revolt of the "Parlement" and the erection of barricades in Paris – known as the "**journées des Barricades**" (see box at entry **barricade**) – was followed by the "Fronde des Princes", when a coalition under the Prince de Condé fought against royal troops under Turenne.

---

fronde² [frɔ̃d] NF *Bot* frond

fronder [3] [frɔ̃de] VT *Littéraire* to revolt against; *(critiquer)* to lampoon

VI 1 *Hist* to belong to the Fronde; *Fig* to rebel 2 *Arch* to use one's sling

frondeur, -euse [frɔ̃dœr, -øz] ADJ insubordinate, rebellious; **elle est d'un tempérament f.** she has a rebellious nature

NM,F 1 *Hist* member of the Fronde, Frondeur 2 *(rebelle)* rebel, troublemaker

front [frɔ̃] NM 1 *Anat* forehead, brow; **baisser le f.** to lower one's head; *Fig* **baisser** *ou* **courber le f.** to submit; **relever le f.** to regain confidence; **le f. haut** proudly, with one's head held high; *Littéraire* **avoir le f. d'airain** to be cruel

2 *(d'une montagne)* face; *(de colline)* brow; *(d'un monument)* frontage, façade; **f. de mer** seafront; **villa sur le f. de mer** villa on the seafront *or* facing the sea

3 *(audace)* **avoir le f. de faire qch** to have the audacity *or* impudence to do sth

4 *Pol* front; **F. islamique du salut** Islamic Salvation Front; **F. de libération de la Bretagne** = Breton liberation front; **F. de libération nationale** = one of the main political parties in Algeria, established as a resistance movement in 1954, at the start of the war for independence; **F. de libération nationale corse** = Corsican liberation front; **F. de libération nationale kanak et socialiste** = Kanak independence movement in New Caledonia; **F. de Libération Québécois** = militant political movement in favour of Quebec independence in the 1960s; **le F. national** the National Front *(extreme rightwing French political party)*; **le F. populaire** the Popular Front; **F. populaire de libération de la Palestine** PFLP; **f. uni** united front; **faire f.** to form a united front, to close ranks; **faire f. devant l'adversaire** to present a united front to the enemy; **faire f. commun contre qn/qch** to make common cause against sb/sth; **faire f. à qn/qch** to face up to *or* stand up to sb/sth; **je ne suis pas sûr qu'il puisse faire f. seul** I'm not sure he'll be able to cope alone; **tu vas devoir faire f.** you'll have to face up to it

5 *Mil (zone)* front; *(ligne)* front line; **partir sur le** *ou* **au f.** to go (up) to the front; **ils ont été** envoyés au f. *ou* sur le f. they were sent to the front; **des nouvelles du f.** news from the front

6 *Mines (gén)* face; *(dans une houillère)* coalface; **f. de taille** working face

7 *Météo* front; **f. froid/chaud** cold/warm front

8 *Can (impudence)* **avoir du f. (tout le tour de la tête)** to be very rude

❑ **de front** ADV 1 *(attaquer)* head-on; **attaquer qn de f.** to attack sb from the front; *Fig* to attack sb head-on; **aborder une difficulté de f.** to tackle a problem head-on

2 *(en vis-à-vis)* head-on; **heurter qn/qch de f.** to run head-on into sb/sth; **se heurter de f.** *(véhicules)* to collide head-on; *(adversaires)* to come into direct confrontation

3 *(côte à côte)* abreast; **on ne peut pas passer de f.** you can't get through side by side; **nous marchions de f.** we were walking next to one another; **rouler à trois voitures de f.** to drive three (cars) abreast; *Mil* **marche de f.** march in line; *Naut* **en ligne de f.** line abreast

4 *(en même temps)* at the same time, at a time; **faire marcher deux affaires de f.** to run two businesses at once *or* at a time; **mener plusieurs choses de f.** to have several things on the go at once

---

Culture

LE FRONT POPULAIRE

This coalition of socialists, radicals and communists came to power in 1936 under Léon Blum. Within a remarkably short period, it established the 40-hour week and holidays with pay for commerce and industry, and passed a range of laws relating to the rights of trade unions.

---

frontail [frɔ̃taj] NM forehead strap, headband

frontal, -e, -aux, -ales [frɔ̃tal, -o] ADJ 1 *Anat* & *Géom* frontal; *Mines* **lampe frontale** cap lamp 2 *(conflit, attaque, collision)* head-on; *(concurrence)* direct 3 *Ordinat* front-end; **ordinateur f.** front end

NM 1 *Anat* frontal bone 2 *Com* facing; **f. de rayonnage** shelf facing

❑ **frontale** NF *Com* shelf facing

frontalier, -ère [frɔ̃talje, -ɛr] ADJ border *(avant n)*

NM,F *(habitant)* inhabitant of the frontier zone; *(travailleur)* cross-border commuter

frontalité [frɔ̃talite] NF *Beaux-Arts* frontality

fronteau, -x [frɔ̃to] NM 1 *Archit* small pediment 2 *Rel (de nonne)* frontlet

frontière [frɔ̃tjɛr] NF 1 *Pol* border; **incident de f.** border incident; **au-delà de la f.** over the border; **dans nos frontières** within our borders; **poste/ville/zone f.** border post/town/area

2 *Fig (démarcation)* boundary; **la f. entre la veille et le sommeil** the borderline between sleeping and waking; **aux frontières de la vie et de la mort** between life and death; **f. naturelle/linguistique** natural/linguistic boundary

3 *Fig (limite)* frontier; **reculer les frontières de l'inconnu** to roll back the frontiers of the unknown; **faire reculer les frontières du savoir** to roll back the frontiers of knowledge; **dépasser les frontières du possible** to go beyond the bounds of what is possible; **son imagination n'a pas de f.** he/she has a boundless imagination; **ma liberté ne connaît pas de f.** my freedom knows no bounds

4 *Math* **(point) f.** frontier

frontignan [frɔ̃tiɲɑ̃] NM Frontignan (wine)

frontispice [frɔ̃tispis] NM *(titre, illustration)* frontispiece

frontiste [frɔ̃tist] *Pol* ADJ of the (French) National Front

NMF member of the (French) National Front

front-office [frɔ̃tɔfis] *(pl* **front-offices)** NM *Banque* front office

fronton [frɔ̃tɔ̃] NM 1 *Archit* pediment 2 *Sport (mur)* fronton; *(court)* pelota court

frottage [frɔtaʒ] NM 1 *(frottement)* rubbing, scrubbing; *(des sols)* polishing 2 *Beaux-Arts* frottage

frottant, -e [frɔtɑ̃, -ɑ̃t] ADJ *(surface)* rubbing

frottée [frɔte] NF 1 *Fam Vieilli (volée)* beating, thrashing 2 *Culin* **f. (d'ail)** = bread which has been toasted and then rubbed with a clove of garlic

frotte-manche [frɔtmɑ̃ʃ] (*pl* **frotte-manches**) **NMF** *Belg Fam* bootlicker, toady

frottement [frɔtmɑ̃] **NM 1** *(friction)* rubbing *(UNCOUNT)*, friction; **le f. a fait un trou à ma chaussette** I've worn a hole in my sock; *Phot* **marques de f.** stress marks

2 *(bruit)* rubbing *or* scraping noise

3 *Méd* friction murmur; **f. à deux temps** to and fro sound; **f. pleural** pleural rub

4 *Tech* friction; *(de freins)* binding; **f. de glissement** sliding friction; **usure par f.** abrasion

❑ **frottements NMPL** *(mésentente)* dispute, disagreement; **il y a des frottements entre eux** there is some friction between them

frotter [3] [frɔte] **VT 1** *(pour nettoyer)* to rub, to scrub; *(avec une brosse)* to brush; *(cuivre)* to polish; **f. une tache avec une brosse/avec du savon** to scrub a stain with a brush/with soap; **f. une casserole** to scour a saucepan; **f. ses chaussures pour enlever la boue** to scrape the mud off one's shoes

2 *(pour enduire)* to rub; **f. une table** to polish a table; **f. d'ail des croûtons** to rub croûtons with garlic; *Belg Fam* **f. la manche à** *ou* **de qn** to soft-soap sb

3 *(mettre en contact)* **f. deux pierres l'une contre l'autre** to rub *or* to scrape two stones together; **f. une allumette** to strike a match; **f. un mur avec sa main** to rub one's hand against a wall; *Fam Vieilli* **être frotté de latin** to have a smattering of Latin

4 *(frictionner)* to rub; **f. le dos à qn** to give sb's back a rub, to rub sb's back

VI to scrape, to rub; **il y a quelque chose qui frotte sous la voiture** there's something under the car making a scraping noise; **le frein de mon vélo frotte** the brakes on my bike keep sticking

▸**se frotter VPR 1** *(se frictionner)* to rub oneself (down); **se f. avec une serviette** to rub oneself (down) *or* to give oneself a rub-down with a towel; **se f. contre qn/qch** to rub (up) against sb/sth; **se f. les yeux** to rub one's eyes; **se f. les mains** to rub one's hands (together); *Fig* to rub one's hands

2 se f. à qn/qch *(effleurer)* to rub (up) against sb/sth; *Fam Fig* **se f. à qn** *(fréquenter)* to rub shoulders with sb; **le chat se frotte à ma jambe** the cat rubs (up) against my leg; *Fig* **ne te frotte pas à lui quand il est en colère** steer clear of him when he's angry; **ne vous y frottez pas, c'est trop dangereux** don't interfere *or* meddle, it's too dangerous; **qui s'y frotte s'y pique** if you meddle you'll get your fingers burnt; *Fam Fig* **depuis le temps que je me frotte aux artistes, je les connais!** I've been around artists for long enough to know what they're like!

3 se f. à qch *(se confronter à)* to face sth; **elle a dû très vite se f. au monde des affaires** she soon had to face the business world

frotteur, -euse [frɔtœr, -øz] **ADJ** rubbing

NM 1 *Élec* brush spring, wiper; **f. de contact** contact finger **2** *Rail* carbon sliding, slip contact; *Aut* slipper **3** *(personne)* floor polisher **4** *Fam (frôleur)* pervert▪ *(who likes to rub up against women in crowds)*

frotti-frotta [frɔtifrɔta] **NM** *Fam* **faire du f.** to rub up against each other

frottis [frɔti] **NM 1** *Méd* smear; **f. vaginal** cervical smear, smear test; **se faire faire un f. (vaginal)** to have a smear test *or* a cervical smear **2** *Beaux-Arts* scumbling

frottoir [frɔtwar] **NM** *(sur une boîte d'allumettes)* striking surface; *(ustensile)* rubber; *(brosse)* scrubbing brush; *(de dynamo)* brush

frouer [6] [frue] **VI** *Chasse* = to imitate the call of an owl (in order to ensnare birds)

froufrou, frou-frou [frufru] (*pl* **frous-frous**) **NM** *(bruit)* swish, rustle, frou-frou

❑ **froufrous, frous-frous NMPL** *(ornement de vêtement)* frills (and furbelows)

froufroutant, -e [frufrutɑ̃, -ɑ̃t] **ADJ 1** *(bruissant)* rustling, swishing **2** *(à volants → robe, jupe)* frilly, flouncy

froufroutement [frufrutmɑ̃] **NM** rustle, swish

froufrouter [3] [frufrute] **VI** to rustle, to swish

frouiller [3] [fruje] **VI** *Suisse Fam* to cheat▪

froussard, -e [frusar, -ard] *Fam* **ADJ** cowardly▪, chicken, yellow-bellied

NM,F coward▪, chicken, yellow-belly

frousse [frus] **NF** *Fam* fright▪; **avoir la f.** to be scared▪; **elle ne veut plus se présenter à l'examen, elle a la f.** she won't take the exam, she's got cold feet; **avoir la f. de faire qch** to be scared to do *or* of doing sth▪; **donner** *ou* **flanquer la f. à qn** to scare sb▪, to give sb the willies, *Br* to put the wind up sb; **ça m'a donné** *ou* **flanqué** *ou* **foutu la f.** it scared the pants off me

fructidor [fryktidɔr] **NM** = 12th month of the French Revolutionary calendar (from 18/19 August to 17/18 September)

fructifère [fryktifɛr] **ADJ** *Bot* fruit-bearing, *Spéc* fructiferous; **corps f.** fruit body

fructification [fryktifikasjɔ̃] **NF 1** *(processus)* fructification **2** *(période)* fruitage

fructifier [9] [fryktifje] **VI 1** *Agr* to be productive; *Bot* to bear fruit, to fructify **2** *Écon* to yield a profit; **faire f. son capital** to make one's capital yield a profit; **il sait faire f. son argent** he knows how to get a return on his money **3** *(produire des résultats)* to bear fruit, to be productive *or* fruitful; **une idée qui fructifie** an idea that bears fruit

fructose [fryktoz] **NM** fructose, fruit sugar

fructueuse [fryktɥøz] *voir* **fructueux**

fructueusement [fryktɥøzmɑ̃] **ADV** *(avantageusement)* fruitfully, productively, successfully

fructueux, -euse [fryktɥø, -øz] **ADJ 1** *(fécond)* fruitful, productive; **vos recherches ont-elles été fructueuses?** were your investigations fruitful *or* successful?; **tout ce travail n'a pas été très f.** all this work yielded very few results **2** *(profitable)* profitable; **une opération fructueuse** a profitable deal

fructus [fryktys] **NM** *Jur* = right to derive income from property

frugal, -e, -aux, -ales [frygal, -o] **ADJ 1** *(simple)* frugal; **un repas f.** a frugal *or* plain meal **2** *(qui mange peu)* frugal

frugalement [frygalmɑ̃] **ADV** frugally

frugalité [frygalite] **NF** frugality

frugivore [fryʒivɔr] **ADJ** fruit-eating, *Spéc* frugivorous

NM fruit-eater, *Spéc* frugivore

fruit[1] [frɥi] **NM 1** *Bot* **manger un f.** to eat some fruit *or* a piece of fruit; **après ton fromage, veux-tu un f.?** would you like some fruit *or* a piece of fruit after your cheese?; **des fruits** fruit; **manger des fruits** to eat (some) fruit; **des arbres chargés de fruits** trees heavy with fruit; **porter des fruits** *(d'un arbre)* to bear fruit; *Fig* **porter ses fruits** *(d'une action, d'un investissement)* to bear fruit; **la tomate est un f.** the tomato is a (type of) fruit; **fruits des bois,** *Suisse* **petits fruits** fruits of the forest; **fruits confits** candied *or* crystallized fruit; **f. défendu** forbidden fruit; **fruits déguisés** = prunes, dates etc stuffed with almond paste; **f. du dragon** dragon fruit, pitahaya; **fruits jumeaux** double fruits; **f. de la passion** passion fruit; **fruits rafraîchis** (chilled) fruit salad; **fruits rouges** red berries, red fruits; **un f. sec** a piece of dried fruit; *Fig* a failure; *Fig* **un f. vert** an immature young girl; *Prov* **c'est au f. qu'on connaît l'arbre** = the tree is known by its fruit

2 *Culin* **fruits de mer** seafood

3 *(résultat)* fruit; **le f. de son travail** the fruit *or* result of his/her labours; **le f. d'un mariage** the offspring of a marriage; **le f. de leurs amours** the fruit of their love; *Littéraire* **le f. de ses entrailles** the fruit of her womb; **cela a porté ses fruits** it bore fruit; **les fruits de la Terre** the fruits *or* bounty of the Earth; *Littéraire* **avec f.** fruitfully, profitably

4 *Jur* **fruits civils** income derived from capital; **fruits industriels** income derived from work; **fruits naturels** emblements

fruit[2] [frɥi] **NM** *Constr* batter; **avoir du f.** to batter

fruité, -e [frɥite] **ADJ** fruity; **ce vin est très f.** this wine is very fruity

fruiterie [frɥitri] **NF 1** *(boutique) Br* fruit shop, *Am* fruit store **2** *(dépôt)* storeroom (for fruit)

fruiticulteur, -trice [frɥitikyltœr, -tris] **NM,F** fruit grower

fruitier, -ère [frɥitje, -ɛr] **ADJ** fruit *(avant n)*

NM,F fruiterer, *Br* greengrocer, *Am* fruit seller

NM 1 *(verger)* orchard **2** *(arbre)* fruit tree **3** *(local)* storeroom (for fruit)

❑ **fruitière NF** cooperative cheese dairy

frumentaire [frymɑ̃tɛr] **ADJ** *Antiq* **lois frumentaires** wheat (distribution) laws

frusques [frysk] **NFPL** *Fam* threads, *Br* gear; **prends tes f. et file!** take your things *or* gear and get out!

fruste [fryst] **ADJ 1** *(grossier → personne)* uncouth, rough **2** *(sans élégance → style)* unpolished, crude, rough **3** *(pièce, statue)* worn **4** *Méd* mild

frustrant, -e [frystrɑ̃, -ɑ̃t] **ADJ** frustrating

frustration [frystrasjɔ̃] **NF 1** *Psy* frustration **2** *(d'un légataire)* cheating, defrauding

frustré, -e [frystre] **ADJ** frustrated

NM,F frustrated person; **c'est un f.** he's so frustrated; **"les Frustrés"** = cartoon characters created by Claire Bretécher representing modern middle-class intellectuals

frustrer [3] [frystre] **VT 1** *(décevoir)* to frustrate, to thwart; **être frustré dans ses espoirs** to be thwarted in one's hopes **2** *(priver)* **f. qn de qch** to rob *or* to deprive sb of sth; **ils ont été frustrés de la victoire** they were robbed of their victory **3** *Psy* to frustrate; **il a été frustré par son échec** he was frustrated by his failure **4** *Jur* **f. qn de** to defraud sb of

frutescent, -e [frytɛsɑ̃, -ɑ̃t] **ADJ** frutescent, fruticose

FS *(abrév écrite* **franc suisse***)* SFr

FSB [ɛfɛsbe] **NM** *(organisme qui a remplacé le KGB, en Russie)* FSB

FSE [ɛfɛsə] **NM 1** *(abrév* **foyer socio-éducatif***)* ≃ community centre **2** *(abrév* **Fonds social européen***)* ESF

FSM [ɛfɛsɛm] **NF** *(abrév* **Fédération syndicale mondiale***)* WFTU

NM *(abrév* **Forum social mondial***)* WSF

FSU [ɛfɛsy] **NF** *(abrév* **Fédération syndicale unitaire***)* = French association of teachers' and lecturers' trade unions

FTP [ɛftepe] **NM** *Ordinat (abrév* **File Transfer Protocol***)* FTP

NMPL *Hist (abrév* **Francs-tireurs et partisans***)* = Communist resistance during World War II

fucales [fykal] **NFPL** *Bot* Fucales

fuchsia [fyʃja] **ADJ INV** fuchsia

NM fuchsia

fuchsine [fyksin] **NF** fuchsine, fuchsin, magenta

fucus [fykys] **NM** wrack, *Spéc* fucus; **f. vésiculeux** bladderwrack

fuégien, -enne [fɥeʒjɛ̃, -ɛn] **ADJ** of/from Tierra del Fuego

❑ **Fuégien, -enne NM,F** = inhabitant of or person from Tierra del Fuego

fuel [fjul], **fuel-oil** [fjulɔjl] (*pl* **fuel-oils**) **NM** (fuel *or* heating) oil; **f. domestique** domestic heating oil

fuero [fwero] **NM** *Hist* fuero *(urban charter granted to Spanish towns in the Middle Ages)*

fufute [fyfyt] **ADJ** *Fam* **il n'est pas très f.** he's a bit thick, he's not the brightest star in the sky

fugace [fygas] **ADJ** *(beauté)* transient, evanescent, ephemeral; *(impression, souvenir, pensée)* transient, fleeting; *(parfum)* elusive, fleeting

fugacité [fygasite] **NF** *Littéraire* transience, fleetingness

fugitif, -ive [fyʒitif, -iv] **ADJ 1** *(en fuite)* runaway *(avant n)*, fugitive *(avant n)* **2** *(fugace → vision, idée)* fleeting, transient; *(→ bonheur)* short-lived; *(→ souvenir)* elusive; *(→ ombre)* fleeting

NM,F runaway, fugitive

fugitivement [fyʒitivmɑ̃] **ADV** fleetingly, briefly

fugue [fyg] **NF 1** *Mus* fugue **2** *(fuite)* **faire une f.** *(de chez soi)* to run away from home; *(d'une pension)* to run away from boarding school; *(pour se marier)* to elope

fugué, -e [fyge] **ADJ** fugato

fuguer [1] [fyge] **VI** *Fam* to clear off, *Br* to do a bunk, *Am* to split

fugueur, -euse [fygœr, -øz] **ADJ être f.** to keep running away; **c'était un enfant f.** as a child, he used to run away repeatedly

NM,F runaway

Führer [fyrœr] **NM le F.** the Führer

fuie [fɥi] **NF** *Littéraire ou (dans l'ouest de la France)* dovecot

fuir [35] [fɥir] **VI 1** *(s'enfuir)* to run away, to flee (**devant** from); **les animaux fuyaient à notre approche** the animals fled *or* ran away as we came near; **f. de son pays** to flee the country; **faire f. qn** to frighten sb away, to put sb to flight;

f. à toutes jambes to run for dear *or* one's life; **f. devant le danger** to flee in the face of danger; **laid à faire f.** as ugly as sin; **bête à faire f.** as stupid as can be; **son agressivité fait f. tout le monde** he puts everyone off by being so aggressive

2 *(s'éloigner)* to vanish, to recede; **des lignes qui fuient vers l'horizon** lines that converge towards the horizon; **le paysage fuyait par la vitre du train** the landscape flashed past the window of the train

3 *Littéraire (passer)* to fly, to slip away; **le temps fuit** time flies

4 *(se dérober)* to run away; **f. devant ses responsabilités** to shirk *or* to evade one's responsibilities; *Naut* **f. devant le vent** to scud *or* to run before the wind; **il a le regard qui fuit** he has shifty eyes

5 *(se répandre → eau)* to leak; *(→ gaz)* to leak, to escape; **f. à petites gouttes** to seep *or* to ooze (through)

6 *(perdre son contenu → tonneau, stylo)* to leak, to be leaky; **un tuyau qui fuit** a leaky pipe

VT 1 *(abandonner)* to flee (from); **f. son pays** to flee one's country; **elle a fui le pays** she fled the country

2 *(éviter)* to avoid, to shun; **il me fuit** he's avoiding me; **f. les gens** to avoid contact with other people; **f. sa famille** to shun one's family; **f. le monde** to flee society; **f. le regard de qn** to avoid looking sb in the eye; **f. le danger** to keep away from *or* to avoid danger

3 *(se soustraire à, s'éloigner de)* to shirk, to evade; **f. la tentation** to flee from *or* to avoid temptation

4 *(résister à)* to elude; **le sommeil le fuyait** he couldn't sleep, sleep would not come to him

fuite [fɥit] NF 1 *(départ)* escape, flight (**devant** from); **prendre la f.** *(prisonnier)* to run away, to (make one's) escape; **le chauffard a pris la f.** it was a hit-and-run accident; **être en f.** to be on the run; **mettre qn/un animal en f.** to put sb/an animal to flight; **l'action du gouvernement est considérée par certains comme une f. en avant** some people accuse the government of blindly refusing to come to terms with the problem; **la f. des cerveaux** the brain drain; **la F. à Varennes** = the attempt by Louis XVI and Marie-Antoinette to escape from France in 1791, which was stopped at Varennes

2 *Fig (devant des difficultés, des problèmes)* evasion, avoidance

3 *Fin* **f. de capitaux** flight of capital (abroad); **f. devant l'impôt** tax evasion

4 *(écoulement → de liquide)* leak, leakage; *(→ de gaz)* leak; *(→ de courant)* escape; **f. de gaz** gas leak; *Littéraire* **la f. du temps** the passage *or* passing of time

5 *(d'un pneu)* puncture; *(d'une canalisation, d'un récipient)* leak; **boucher une f. dans une bouée** to stop a rubber ring leaking; **as-tu trouvé la f.?** did you find the leak?

6 *(indiscrétion)* leak; **il y a eu des fuites en histoire** some of the history questions leaked out

7 *Beaux-Arts* **point de f.** vanishing point

fuitif, -ive [fɥitif, -iv] ADJ *Littéraire* fleeting, fugitive

Fuji-Yama [fuʒijama] NM **le (mont) F.** Fujiyama, Mount Fuji

fulgurance [fylgyrɑ̃s] NF *Littéraire* piercing *or* blinding quality

fulgurant, -e [fylgyrɑ̃, -ɑ̃t] ADJ 1 *(rapide → réponse, attaque)* lightning *(avant n)*; *(→ idée)* sudden; *(→ carrière)* dazzling; **j'ai eu une idée fulgurante** an idea flashed *or* shot through my mind; **elle a connu un succès f.** she was brilliantly successful

2 *(intense → douleur)* shooting, *Spéc* fulgurating; *(→ lumière)* blinding, dazzling, fulgurant

3 *Littéraire (éclatant → éclair)* flashing; *(→ regard)* blazing, flashing; *(→ beauté)* dazzling; **lancer un regard f. à qn** to look daggers at sb

fulguration [fylgyrasjɔ̃] NF 1 *Météo* heat lightning 2 *Méd* fulguration

fulgurer [3] [fylgyre] VI *Littéraire* to flash, to blaze

fuligineux, -euse [fyliʒinø, -øz] ADJ 1 *(qui produit de la suie)* sooty, smoky, *Spéc* fuliginous 2 *Fig Littéraire* fuliginous

fuligule [fyligyl] NM *Orn* **f. milouin** pochard; **f. milouinan** scaup (duck); **f. morillon** tufted duck; **f. nyroca** ferruginous duck; **f. aux yeux rouges** canvasback

full [ful] NM *Cartes* full house

full-contact [fulkɔ̃takt] *(pl* **full-contacts***)* NM *Sport* full-contact karate, American boxing

fullerène [fylrɛn] NM *Chim* fullerene

full-time, full time [fultajm] NM *Belg & Can (emploi)* full-time job; *(travailleur)* full-time worker

fulmicoton [fylmikɔtɔ̃] NM guncotton

fulminant, -e [fylminɑ̃, -ɑ̃t] ADJ 1 *Littéraire (menaçant → regard)* furious, enraged, irate; *(→ lettre)* venomous, vituperative 2 *(soudain → douleur)* fulminant 3 *Chim* fulminating

fulminate [fylminat] NM *Chim* fulminate

fulmination [fylminasjɔ̃] NF 1 *Rel* fulmination 2 *Littéraire (colère)* ire, wrath

fulminer [3] [fylmine] VI *Littéraire* to fulminate, to rail; **f. contre le gouvernement** to fulminate *or* to rail against the government

VT 1 *Littéraire (proférer)* to thunder, to roar, to utter; **f. des menaces à l'égard de qn** to thunder *or* to roar threats at sb 2 *Rel* to fulminate

fulminique [fylminik] ADJ fulminic

fumable [fymabl] ADJ smokable

fumage[1] [fymaʒ] NM *Culin* smoking, curing

fumage[2] [fymaʒ] NM *Agr* manuring, dunging

fumagine [fymaʒin] NF *Hort* fumagine

fumaison [fymɛzɔ̃] NF *Agr* manuring, dunging

fumant, -e [fymɑ̃, -ɑ̃t] ADJ 1 *(cheminée, feu)* smoking, smoky; *(cendres, décombres)* smouldering

2 *(liquide, nourriture)* steaming; **assis autour de la soupe fumante** sitting around a steaming bowl of soup; *Fig Littéraire* **mains encore fumantes de sang** hands still reeking with blood

3 *(furieux)* fuming; **être f. de colère** to flare up with anger

4 *Fam (remarquable)* amazing, incredible; **coup f.** a masterstroke[■]; **faire un coup f. (à qn)** to play a dirty trick (on sb)

5 *Chim* fuming

▫ **fumantes** NFPL *très Fam (chaussettes)* socks[■]

fumariacée [fymarjase] *Bot* NF fumitory, *Spéc* member of the Fumariaceae

▫ **fumariacées** NFPL fumitories, *Spéc* Fumariaceae

fumasse [fymas] ADJ *Fam* furious[■], fuming; **elle était f.!** she was furious!

fumé, -e [fyme] ADJ 1 *(poisson, viande etc)* smoked, smoke-cured 2 **verre f.** smoked glass; **verres fumés** dark lenses; *(lunettes)* dark glasses, sunglasses

NM *(aliment)* smoked food; **évitez de consommer du f.** avoid smoked foods

fume-cigare [fymsigar] NM INV cigar holder

fume-cigarette [fymsigarɛt] NM INV cigarette holder

fumée [fyme] ADJ *voir* **fumé**

NF 1 *(de combustion)* smoke; **partir** *ou* **s'en aller en f.** to go up in smoke; *Prov* **il n'y a pas de f. sans feu** there's no smoke without fire; **la f. (du tabac) vous gêne-t-elle?** do you mind my smoking? 2 *(vapeur)* steam; *(du charbon de bois)* fumes

▫ **fumées** NFPL *Littéraire* stupor; **dans les fumées de l'ivresse** *ou* **du vin** in a drunken stupor

fumer[1] [3] [fyme] VT 1 *(tabac)* to smoke; **f. la pipe** to smoke a pipe; **f. cigarette sur cigarette** to chain-smoke; *Fam* **en f. une** to have a smoke[■]; **c'est lui qui m'a fait f. ma première cigarette** it was he who first introduced me to *or* started me smoking

2 *Culin* to smoke

3 *très Fam Arg crime (battre)* to clobber, to thump; *(tuer)* to kill[■], *Br* to do in

USAGE ABSOLU *(personne)* to smoke; **je ne fume plus** I don't smoke any more, I've given up smoking; **f. comme un pompier** *ou* **un sapeur** to smoke like a chimney

VI 1 *(feu, cheminée)* to smoke, to give off smoke; *(cendres, décombres)* to smoke, to smoulder; **cheminée qui fume** smoky chimney

2 *(liquide, nourriture)* to steam, to give off steam; **vois la bonne soupe qui fume** look at the lovely steaming bowl of soup; **on voyait f. les flancs des chevaux** you could see the steam coming *or* rising off the horses' flanks

3 *Chim* to fume, to give off fumes

4 *Fam (être furieux)* to fume, *Am* to be mad

fumer[2] [3] [fyme] VT *(terre)* to manure, to dress, to dung

fumerie [fymri] NF opium den

fumerolle [fymrɔl] NF fumarole

fumerollien, -enne [fymerɔljɛ̃, -ɛn] ADJ fumarolic

fumeron [fymrɔ̃] NM piece of half-kilned charcoal, smoky charcoal

fumet [fymɛ] NM 1 *(odeur → d'un plat)* (pleasant) smell, aroma; *(→ d'un vin)* bouquet 2 *Culin* stock, fumet 3 *Chasse* scent

fumeterre [fymtɛr] NF *Bot* fumitory

fumette [fymɛt] NF *Fam* getting stoned; **c'est un habitué de la f.** he gets stoned regularly; **il y a que la f. qui l'intéresse** all he's/she's interested in is getting stoned

fumeur, -euse[1] [fymœr, -øz] NM,F 1 *(adepte du tabac)* smoker; **un gros f.** a heavy smoker; **f. de pipe/cigares** pipe/cigar smoker; **f. d'opium** opium smoker; **les fumeurs** smokers, people who smoke; **compartiment fumeurs** smoking compartment *or Am* car 2 *Ind* curer

fumeux, -euse[2] [fymø, -øz] ADJ 1 *(confus)* hazy; **idée fumeuse** vague *or* nebulous idea; **il a l'esprit f.** his ideas are a bit woolly, he's woolly-minded 2 *(bougie, lampe)* smoky

fumier [fymje] NM 1 *(engrais)* manure, dung; **fosse à f.** slurry pit 2 *(tas)* dunghill, manure 3 *très Fam (personne)* bastard; **espèce de f.!** you bastard!; **le f.!, il m'a menti!** he lied to me, the bastard!

fumière [fymjɛr] NF dung heap, midden

fumigateur [fymigatœr] NM 1 *Agr* fumigator 2 *Méd* inhaler

fumigation [fymigasjɔ̃] NF 1 *(pour un local)* fumigation; **faire des fumigations de désinfectant** to fumigate with disinfectant 2 *Agr & Méd* fumigation

fumigatoire [fymigatwar] ADJ fumigating, fumigatory

fumigène [fymiʒɛn] ADJ smoke *(avant n)*; *Mil* **grenade f.** smoke grenade

NM smoke generator

fumiste [fymist] NM 1 *(installateur)* heating specialist 2 *(ramoneur)* chimney sweep

ADJ *Fam Péj (attitude, personne)* lazy[■]; **il est un peu f.** he's a bit of a shirker

NMF *Fam Péj* shirker, *Br* layabout; **c'est un f.** he doesn't exactly kill himself working

fumisterie [fymistəri] NF 1 *Fam Péj* humbug, sham, farce; **une vaste f.** an absolute farce 2 *(métier → d'installateur)* boiler installation *or* fitting; *(→ de ramoneur)* chimney sweeping

fumivore [fymivɔr] ADJ *(appareil)* smoke extracting; *(combustion)* smokeless

NM smoke extractor

fumoir [fymwar] NM 1 *(pour fumeurs) Br* smoking room, *Am* smoke room 2 *(pour aliments)* smokehouse

fumure [fymyr] NF 1 *(engrais)* manure, fertilizer 2 *(fertilisation)* manuring, fertilizing

fun [fœn] ADJ INV *Fam* funny

NM 1 *Fam* **le f.** entertainment[■] 2 *Sport* funboard 3 *Can Joual* = **fonne**

funambule [fynɑ̃byl] NMF tightrope walker, funambulist

funambulesque [fynɑ̃bylɛsk] ADJ 1 **l'art f.** the art of tightrope walking; **acrobatie f.** high-wire acrobatics 2 *Fig (idées, projet etc)* fantastic, bizarre

funboard [fœnbɔrd] NM funboard

Funchal [funʃal] NM *Géog* Funchal

funèbre [fynɛbr] ADJ 1 *(relatif aux funérailles)* funeral *(avant n)*; **cérémonie f.** funeral service; **chant f.** dirge; **veillée f.** deathwatch, wake 2 *(lugubre)* gloomy, lugubrious, funereal

funérailles [fyneraj] NFPL funeral; **f. nationales** state funeral

EXCLAM *Fam* heavens!, *Br* blimey!

funéraire [fynerɛr] ADJ funeral *(avant n)*, *Spéc* funerary; **urne/chambre f.** funeral *or* funerary urn/chamber; **site f.** burial site; **l'art f. égyptien** Egyptian funerary art

funérarium [fynerarjɔm] NM funeral parlour, *Am* funeral home

funeste [fynɛst] ADJ 1 *(désastreux)* disastrous, catastrophic; **erreur f.** fatal *or* disastrous *or* catastrophic error; **le jour f. où je l'ai rencontré** that fateful *or* ill-fated day when I met him; **l'ignorance est souvent f.** ignorance is often

dangerous *or* harmful; **suites funestes** tragic *or* disastrous *or* dire consequences; **être f. à qn** to have terrible consequences for sb; **être f. à qch** to be fatal to sth
2 *Littéraire (triste)* lugubrious; **un récit f.** a sad tale
3 *Littéraire (mortel)* fatal, lethal

funestement [fynɛstəmɑ̃] ADV *Littéraire* disastrously, catastrophically

funiculaire [fynikylɛr] ADJ funicular
NM funicular (railway)

funicule [fynikyl] NM *Bot* funicle, funiculus

funk [fœnk] ADJ INV funk
NM INV **le f.** funk

Funk Art [fœnkart] NM *Beaux-Arts* Funk Art

funky [fœnki] ADJ INV funky
NM jazz funk

FUNU, Funu [fyny] NF (*abrév* **Force d'urgence des Nations unies**) UNEF

fur [fyr] **au fur et à mesure** ADV gradually; **donnez-les-moi au f. et à mesure** give them to me gradually *or* as we go along; **il s'adaptera au f. et à mesure** he'll get used to it in time; **je préfère faire mon travail au f. et à mesure plutôt que de le laisser s'accumuler** I prefer to do my work as and when it comes rather than letting it pile up; **au f. et à mesure, j'ai compris comment ça fonctionnait** I understood how it worked as I went along *or* bit by bit
▫ **au fur et à mesure de** PRÉP as; **au f. et à mesure de l'avance des travaux** as work proceeds; **au f. et à mesure des besoins** as needed; **au f. et à mesure de ses recherches** as he progressed with his/her research; **je vous les enverrai au f. et à mesure de leur disponibilité** I'll send them to you as and when they are available
▫ **au fur et à mesure que** CONJ as; **au f. et à mesure que le temps passe, l'angoisse augmente** as time goes by, anxiety grows; **l'eau s'écoule au f. et à mesure que je remplis l'évier** the water drains away as (soon as) I fill up the sink; **les oiseaux mangent les cerises au f. et à mesure qu'elles mûrissent** the birds eat the cherries as (soon as *or* fast as) they get ripe

furanne [fyran] NM furan

furax [fyraks] ADJ INV *Fam* livid, hopping mad

furcula [fyrkyla] NF *Orn* furcula, wishbone

furet [fyrɛ] NM **1** *Zool* ferret; **aller à la chasse au f.** to go ferreting **2** *Vieilli (curieux)* snoop **3** *(jeu)* pass the slipper

furetage [fyrtaʒ] NM **1** *(recherche)* ferreting (around *or* about), nosing (around *or* about) **2** *Chasse* ferreting

fureter [28] [fyrte] VI **1** *(fouiller)* to ferret (around *or* about), to snoop (around *or* about); **f. dans le sac de qn** to ferret around in sb's bag; **f. dans les armoires** to ferret (about) *or* to rummage (about) in the cupboards; **je suis allé f. dans sa chambre** I had a snoop around his/her room; **les journalistes ont fureté dans mon passé** journalists pried into my past **2** *Chasse* to ferret

fureteur, -euse [fyrtœr, -øz] ADJ *Péj* prying; **regard f.** inquisitive look
NM,F **1** *Péj (indiscret)* snooper **2** *(fouilleur)* **elle a trouvé des merveilles au grenier/à la brocante, c'est une fureteuse** she found some real treasures in the attic/junk-shop, she loves poking around **3** *(chasseur)* ferreter
NM *Can Ordinat* browser

fureur [fyrœr] NF **1** *(colère)* rage, fury; **accès de f.** fit of anger *or* rage; **f. noire** blind anger *or* rage; **se mettre dans une f. noire** to fly into a rage; **quand sa f. s'est calmée** when his/her anger had died down
2 *(passion)* passion; **la f. du jeu** a mania *or* passion for gambling; **la f. de vivre** a lust for life; **faire f.** to be all the rage
3 *Littéraire (violence)* rage, fury, wrath; **la f. des flots** the wrath of the sea
▫ **avec fureur** ADV **1** *(colériquement)* furiously **2** *(passionnément)* passionately
▫ **en fureur** ADJ furious, enraged ADV **entrer en f.** to fly into a rage *or* fury; **mettre qn en f.** to send sb wild with rage, to enrage sb

'La Fureur de vivre' *Ray* 'Rebel Without a Cause'

furfuracé, -e [fyrfyrase] ADJ *Méd* furfuraceous

furfural [fyrfyral] NM *Chim* furfural, furfuraldehyde

furia [fyrja] NF *(d'une foule)* frenzy; **ils n'ont pas pu résister à la f. bordelaise** they were overwhelmed by the Bordeaux team's furious onslaught

furibard, -e [fyribar, -ard] ADJ *Fam* hopping mad, livid

furibond, -e [fyribɔ̃, -ɔ̃d] ADJ furious; **être f. contre qn** to be furious with sb; **elle lui a lancé un regard f.** she glared at him/her

Furie [fyri] NPR *Myth* Fury

furie [fyri] NF **1** *(colère)* fury, rage
2 *(mégère)* fury; **elle s'est jetée sur lui comme une f.** she flew at him like a fury
▫ **avec furie** ADV **1** *(avec colère)* furiously, angrily
2 *(ardemment)* ardently, passionately, furiously; **elle écrivait avec f.** she wrote furiously
3 *(violemment)* furiously, wildly, savagely
▫ **en furie** ADJ furious, enraged; *Littéraire* **les éléments en f.** the raging elements

furieuse [fyrjøz] *voir* **furieux**

furieusement [fyrjøzmɑ̃] ADV **1** *(avec colère)* furiously, angrily **2** *(violemment)* furiously, wildly, savagely **3** *(extrêmement)* hugely, tremendously, extremely; **avoir f. envie de** to have a tremendous urge to

furieux, -euse [fyrjø, -øz] ADJ **1** *(enragé → personne)* furious, (very) angry; *(→ geste, cri)* furious; *(→ taureau)* mad, raging; **cela me rend f.** it makes me furious; **d'un air f.** looking like thunder; **être f. contre qn** to be furious with sb; **je suis furieuse contre moi-même** I'm furious with myself; **être f. de son échec** to be enraged *or* infuriated at one's failure; **il est f. d'apprendre que tout a été fait sans lui** he's furious to hear that it's all been done without him; **il est f. d'avoir attendu** he's furious at having been kept waiting; **elle est furieuse qu'on ne l'ait pas prévenue** she's furious that nobody told her
2 *Littéraire (violent)* raging, wild; **tempête furieuse** raging storm; **les flots f.** the raging seas
3 *Littéraire (passionné)* furious; **une haine furieuse** a furious *or* wild hatred
4 *(extrême)* tremendous; **avoir une furieuse envie de dormir** to have an overwhelming desire to go to sleep
NM,F madman, *f* madwoman, maniac

furoncle [fyrɔ̃kl] NM boil, *Spéc* furuncle

furonculeux, -euse [fyrɔ̃kylø, -øz] ADJ furuncular, furunculous
NM,F furunculosis sufferer

furonculose [fyrɔ̃kyloz] NF furunculosis

furtif, -ive [fyrtif, -iv] ADJ **1** *(comportement)* furtive; *(geste, action)* furtive, surreptitious, stealthy; *(regard)* furtive, sly; *(sourire)* quiet, secret; *(larme)* hidden **2** *Mil (avion)* stealth *(avant n)*, low-observable

furtivement [fyrtivmɑ̃] ADV stealthily, surreptitiously, furtively; **entrer/sortir f.** to steal in/out, to enter/leave furtively

furtivité [fyrtivite] NF *Mil* low-observability, low-observable *or* stealth characteristics

fusain [fyzɛ̃] NM **1** *Bot* spindle (tree) **2** *Beaux-Arts (crayon)* piece of charcoal; *(dessin)* charcoal
▫ **au fusain** ADJ charcoal *(avant n)* ADV *(dessiner, illustrer)* in charcoal

fusainiste [fyzɛnist] NMF charcoal artist *or* sketcher

fusant, -e [fyzɑ̃, -ɑ̃t] ADJ *(qui ne détonne pas)* fusing; **obus f.** time shell
NM time shell

fusariose [fyzarjoz] NF *Hort* fusariosis, fusariose

fuscine [fysin] NF *Antiq & Myth* trident

fuseau, -x [fyzo] NM **1** *(bobine)* spindle; *(pour la dentelle)* bobbin; **dentelle/ouvrage aux fuseaux** bobbin lace/needlework **2** *(pantalon)* stirrup pants **3** *Géom* lune **4** *Biol* spindle
▫ **en fuseau** ADJ tapered, spindle-shaped; **jambes en f.** slender legs ADV **tailler qch en f.** to taper sth
▫ **fuseau horaire** NM time zone; **changer de f. horaire** to go into a different time zone

fusée [fyze] NF **1** *Astron* rocket; **f. à étages multiples, fusées gigognes** multiple-stage rocket; **f. à trois étages** three-stage rocket; **f. d'appoint** booster; **f. interplanétaire** space rocket; **f. orbitale** orbital rocket; **lancer une f.** to launch a rocket; **partir comme une f.** to be off like a shot, to shoot off
2 *(signal)* rocket; **f. de détresse** flare; **f. éclairante** flare; **f. à pétard** maroon; *Naut* **f. porte-amarre** life(-saving) rocket; **f. de signalisation** signal (sky) rocket
3 *(projectile)* rocket, missile; *(détonateur)* fuse; **f. air-air** air-to-air missile; **f. anti-engin** antimissile missile; **f.-engin** missile; **f. percutante** percussion fuse; **f. porteuse** carrier rocket; **f. à temps** time fuse
4 *Méd* sinus *(of boil)*
5 *(d'arbre, d'axe)* spindle; *(de roue)* stub axle; **f. de direction** stub axle
6 *(en horlogerie)* fusee, fuzee
7 *Hér* fusil

fusée-détonateur [fyzedetɔnatœr] (*pl* **fusées-détonateurs**) NF fuse

fusée-sonde [fyzesɔ̃d] (*pl* **fusées-sondes**) NF probe, sounding rocket

fusel [fyzɛl] NM **(huile de) f.** fusel oil

fuselage [fyzlaʒ] NM fuselage

fuselé, -e [fyzle] ADJ **1** *(doigt)* slender, tapered, tapering; *(jambe)* slender; *(muscle)* well-shaped; *(colonne)* tapered, tapering, spindle-shaped; *Aut* streamlined **2** *Hér* fusilly

fuseler [24] [fyzle] VT **1** *(former en fuseau)* to taper
2 *Aviat, Aut & Naut* to streamline

fuséologie [fyzeɔlɔʒi] NF rocketry

fuser [3] [fyze] VI **1** *(jaillir → vapeur)* to gush *or* to spurt (out); *(→ liquide)* to jet *or* to gush *or* to spurt (out); *(→ lumière)* to stream out; *(→ étincelle)* to fly; **un projectile a fusé dans l'espace** a missile shot through the air
2 *(retentir → rire, voix)* to burst out; **des rires fusèrent de toutes parts** there were bursts of laughter from all sides, laughter erupted from all sides; **des cris/des remarques fusèrent de toutes parts** cries/comments were suddenly heard from all sides
3 *(bougie)* to melt; *(poudre)* to burn slowly; *(sels)* to crackle

fusette [fyzɛt] NF reel, spool

fusibilité [fyzibilite] NF fusibility

fusible [fyzibl] ADJ **1** *(qui peut fondre)* fusible, meltable **2** *(à point de fusion bas)* fusible
NM fuse; *(fil métallique)* fuse wire; **un f. a grillé** a fuse blew; **où sont les fusibles?** where is the fuse box?; **f. à cartouche** cartridge fuse; **f. de sûreté** safety fuse, cut-out

fusiforme [fyzifɔrm] ADJ spindle-shaped, *Spéc* fusiform

fusil [fyzi] NM **1** *(arme)* gun, rifle; **f. à air comprimé** air gun; **f. d'assaut** assault rifle; **f. automatique** automatic rifle; **f. à canon scié** sawn-off shotgun; **f. à canons basculants** break-open shotgun; **f. à canons juxtaposés** side-by-side shotgun; **f. à canons superposés** over-and-under shotgun; **f. à chargeur** magazine rifle; **f. de chasse** shotgun; **f. à chiens extérieurs** exposed hammer shotgun; **f. à chiens intérieurs** hammerless shotgun; **f. à deux coups** double-barrelled *or* double barrel shotgun; **f. harpon** harpoon gun; **f. à lunette** rifle with telescopic sight; **f. à pompe** pump-action rifle; **f. rayé** rifle; **f. à répétition** repeating rifle; **f. semi-automatique** semi-automatic rifle; **f. sous-marin** speargun; *Fig* **changer son f. d'épaule** to change (one's) tack; *Can* **partir/entrer en coup de f.** to storm out/in
2 *(tireur)* **un bon f.** a good shot
3 *(affiloir)* **f. (à aiguiser)** steel

fusilier [fyzilje] NM rifleman, *Br* fusilier; **f. marin** marine

fusillade [fyzijad] NF **1** *(bruit)* shooting *(UNCOUNT)*, gunfire; **j'ai entendu une f.** I heard a volley of shots **2** *(combat)* gunfight, gun battle **3** *(exécution)* shooting

fusiller [3] [fyzije] VT **1** *(exécuter)* to shoot; *Fig* **f. qn du regard** to look daggers *or* to glare at sb **2** *Fam (détruire)* to wreck, to bust, *Br* to knacker; **il a loupé le virage et fusillé sa bagnole** he missed the turn and *Br* wrote his car off *or Am* totaled his car **3** *Fam (dépenser)* to blow

fusilleur [fyzijœr] NM executioner

fusil-mitrailleur [fyzimitrajœr] (*pl* **fusils-mitrailleurs**) NM light machine gun

fusiniste [fyzinist] NMF charcoal artist *or* sketcher

fusion [fyzjɔ̃] NF **1** *Métal* fusion, melting; **f. froide, f. à froid** cold fusion **2** *Mines* smelting **3** *(dissolution → du sucre, de la glace)* melting **4** *Nucl* **f. (nucléaire)** fusion; **f. du cœur** nuclear meltdown **5** *Fig (union → d'idées, de sentiments)* fusion; *(→ de groupes)* fusion, merging; *(→ de peuples, de cultures)* fusion, merging **6** *Écon* merger, merging, amalgamation; **f. horizontale** horizontal merger; **f. verticale** vertical merger; **fusions-rachats** *ou* **fusions-acquisitions** mergers and acquisitions **7** *Ordinat* merge, merging; **f. de fichiers** file merge □ **en fusion** ADJ *Métal* molten ADV **mettre deux éléments en f.** to fuse two elements (together)

fusionnel, -elle [fyzjɔnɛl] ADJ *Psy (relation)* intense, intensely close; *(amour)* intense

fusionnement [fyzjɔnmɑ̃] NM **1** *Écon* amalgamation, merger **2** *(rassemblement → de groupes, de cultures)* merging, fusion

fusionner [3] [fyzjɔne] VT **1** *(sociétés)* to merge, to amalgamate **2** *Ordinat (fichiers)* to merge ▶ VI **1** *Écon* to merge, to amalgamate **2** *Ordinat* to merge

fusse *etc voir* **être**[1]

fustanelle [fystanɛl] NF fustanella

fuste [fyst] NF *Suisse* = long large barrel for transporting picked grapes to the press

fustet [fystɛ] NM *Bot* fustet, Venetian sumach

fustigation [fystigasjɔ̃] NF *Littéraire* **1** *(correction)* thrashing, beating **2** *(critique → d'une personne)* censure; *(→ d'un vice)* castigation, censure

fustiger [17] [fystiʒe] VT *Littéraire* **1** *(battre)* to thrash **2** *(critiquer → personne, attitude)* to censure, to criticize harshly; *(→ vice)* to castigate

fut *etc voir* **être**[1]

fût [fy] NM **1** *(d'un arbre)* bole **2** *(tonneau)* cask; *(pour l'huile)* drum; **tirer de la bière du f.** to draw beer from the wood *or* cask *or* barrel **3** *(partie → d'une vis, d'un poteau)* shaft; *(→ d'une colonne)* shaft, body; *(→ de candélabre)* stem; *(→ de rivet)* shank **4** *(d'un canon)* stock **5** *(d'un tambour)* barrel, body **6** *(de scie, de raquette)* handle

futaie [fytɛ] NF forest, *Am* (piece of) timberland; **haute** *ou* **vieille f.** established *or* mature forest; **arbre de haute f.** full-grown tree

futaille [fytaj] NF cask, barrel

futaine [fytɛn] NF *Tex* fustian

futal, -als [fytal], **fute** [fyt] NM *Fam Br* trousers▪, *Am* pants▪

futé, -e[1] [fyte] ADJ sharp, smart, clever; *aussi Ironique* **ça, c'est f.!** that was clever!; **il n'est pas très f.** he's not very bright ▶ NM,F sharp *or* smart person; **c'est une futée** she's very sharp *or* shrewd; **hé, petit f., comment tu l'enlèves maintenant?** hey, smarty-pants, now how are you going to get it off again?

futée[2] [fyte] NF *Menuis* wood putty *or* cement

fute-fute [fytfyt] = **fufute**

futile [fytil] ADJ **1** *(frivole → raison)* frivolous, trifling; *(→ occupation, lecture, personne)* frivolous; *(→ prétexte)* idle **2** *(sans valeur → vie)* pointless, futile; **il serait f. d'essayer** it would be futile *or* pointless to attempt it

futilement [fytilmɑ̃] ADV pointlessly

futilité [fytilite] NF *(caractère futile)* triviality; **il perd son temps à des futilités** he wastes his time in trivial pursuits; **ils ne se racontaient que des futilités** their conversation consisted of nothing but trivialities; **s'occuper à des futilités** to fritter away one's time

futon [fytɔ̃] NM futon

futur, -e [fytyr] ADJ **1** *(à venir → difficulté, joie)* future *(avant n)*; **les générations futures** future *or* coming generations; *Rel* **la vie future** the afterlife **2** *(avant le nom)* **une future mère** a mother-to-be; **mon f. mari** my future husband, my husband-to-be; **les futurs époux** the engaged couple, the bride-and-groom-to-be; **mes futurs collègues** my future colleagues; **un f. client** a prospective client; **un f. acheteur** a prospective buyer; **un f. mathématicien** a future *or* budding mathematician; **un f. artiste** a budding artist; **mon f. emploi/appartement** my next job/flat ▶ NM,F *Hum* intended, husband-to-be, *f* wife-to-be ▶ NM **1** *(avenir)* **le f.** the future; **quel f. pour l'Europe?** what will Europe's future be? **2** *Gram* **le f.** the future (tense); **au f.** in the future; **f. antérieur** future perfect; **le f. proche** the immediate future

futurisme [fytyrism] NM futurism

futuriste [fytyrist] ADJ **1** *(d'anticipation)* futuristic **2** *Beaux-Arts & Littérature* futurist ▶ NMF futurist

futurologie [fytyrɔlɔʒi] NF futurology

futurologue [fytyrɔlɔg] NMF futurologist

Futuroscope [fytyrɔskɔp] NM **le F.** = futuristic theme park near Poitiers

fuyait *etc voir* **fuir**

fuyant, -e [fɥijɑ̃, -ɑ̃t] ADJ **1** *(insaisissable → caractère)* elusive; *(→ regard)* shifty, elusive; **avoir le regard f.** to have shifty eyes, to be shifty-eyed **2** *(menton, front)* receding; **un homme au menton f.** a weak-chinned man **3** *Beaux-Arts* vanishing; **ligne fuyante** receding line **4** *Littéraire (fugitif)* fleeting, transient ▶ NM vanishing perspective

fuyard, -e [fɥijar, -ard] ADJ *Arch* shy, timid ▶ NM,F runaway, fugitive ▶ NM *Mil* retreating soldier

FV *(abrév écrite* **fréquence vocale**) VF

Fyn [fin] NM *Géog* Fyn

G

G¹, g¹ [ʒe] NM INV **1** (*lettre*) G, g; **G comme Gaston** ≃ G for George **2** *Mus* (*note*) G **3** *Phys* (*accélération de l'apesanteur*) g; **une force égale à plusieurs G** a force of several G **4** *Psy* **facteur g** g factor

G² [ʒe] NM *Belg Fam* (*abrév* **GSM**) *Br* mobile, *Am* cell

g² 1 (*abrév écrite* **gramme**) g **2** *Phys* (*abrév écrite* **gauss**) G **3** (*abrév écrite* **giga**) G **4** (*abrév écrite* **gauche**) L

G7 [ʒesɛt] NM (*abrév* **Groupe des Sept**) le G7 G7

G8 [ʒeɥit] NM (*abrév* **Groupe des Huit**) le G8 G8

GAB [gab] (*abrév* **guichet automatique de banque**) *Br* ≃ Minibank, *Am* ≃ ATM

GABA [gaba] NM *Méd* GABA

gabardine [gabardin] NF **1** (*tissu*) gabardine, gaberdine **2** (*vêtement*) gabardine (coat)

gabare [gabar] NF **1** *Naut* (*sailing*) barge; (*pour charger, décharger un navire*) lighter; (*chaland*) scow, store ship **2** *Pêche* dragnet

gabariage [gabarjaʒ] NM *Naut* templating

gabarier¹ [gabarje] NM *Naut* **1** (*capitaine*) skipper (*of barge*) **2** (*manœuvre*) lighterman, bargee

gabarier² [10] [gabarje] VT *Métal* to gauge

gabarit [gabari] NM **1** (*dimension*) size; **de g. réglementaire** regulation size; **hors g.** (*panneau sur la route*) heavy vehicles

2 *Fam* (*carrure*) size ▪, build ▪, **il a un g. impressionnant** he is very heavily built ▪, **c'est un tout petit g.** he/she is very slightly built ▪, (*stature*) he's/she's a bit on the short side

3 *Fam Fig* calibre; **elle a/n'a pas le g.** she is/isn't up to it; **ils sont bien du même g.** it's six of one and half a dozen of the other

4 *Tech* (*pour mesure*) gauge; (*maquette*) & *Ordinat* template; (*d'un bateau*) model; (*d'une pièce de bateau*) mould; *Constr* (*d'un bâtiment*) outline; **g. d'assemblage** assembly jig, assembling gauge; *Rail* **g. de chargement** loading gauge; **g. d'écartement (des voies)** rail *or* track gauge; *Typ* **g. de mise en page** (filmsetting) grid

gabarre [gabar] = **gabare**

gabarrier [gabarje] = **gabarier¹**

gabbro [gabro] NM *Géol* gabbro

gabegie [gabʒi] NF (*mauvaise gestion*) mismanagement; (*désordre*) muddle, chaos; **la g. administrative** bureaucratic waste

gabelle [gabɛl] NF *Hist* salt tax (*in France*)

gabelou [gablu] NM **1** *Péj Hum* customs officer **2** *Hist* salt-tax collector (*in France*)

gabie [gabi] NF *Hist & Naut* half-top

gabier [gabje] NM **1** *Naut* deckhand; **g. breveté** able(-bodied) seaman **2** *Hist* topman

gabion [gabjɔ̃] NM **1** *Mil* & (*en travaux publics*) gabion **2** *Chasse Br* hide, *Am* blind

gabionnage [gabjɔnaʒ] NM *Mil* gabionage, gabions; (*fortification*) gabionade; (*en travaux publics*) gabion installation

gabionner [3] [gabjɔne] VT *Mil* to gabion; (*en travaux publics*) to gabion, to install gabions along

gâble, gable [gabl] NM (*pignon*) (Gothic) gable; (*charpente*) (triangular) window canopy

Gabon [gabɔ̃] NM **le G.** Gabon; **vivre au G.** to live in Gabon; **aller au G.** to go to Gabon

gabonais, -e [gabonɛ, -ɛz] ADJ Gabonese
□ **Gabonais, -e** NM,F Gabonese; **les G.** the Gabonese

Gaborone [gabɔrɔn] NM Gaborone

gâchage [gaʃaʒ] NM **1** *Constr* mixing **2** (*gaspillage*) waste **3 g. des prix** price undercutting

gâche¹ [gaʃ] NF **1** (*pour le plâtre*) trowel **2** (*de pâtissier*) spatula

gâche² [gaʃ] NF **1** (*d'une serrure*) (box) staple, keeper; (*d'une fenêtre*) (latch) catch; (*de crémone*) (espagnolette) plate; (*d'un pêne*) striking box *or* plate, strike box; **g. automatique** remote control lock; *Aut* **g. de porte** striker plate **2** *Tech* (*pour cliquet*) notch

gâcher [3] [gaʃe] VT **1** (*gaspiller* → *argent, talent, temps*) to waste; **c'est de la nourriture gâchée** it's a waste of food; **il n'est pas très bon photographe, il aime surtout g. de la pellicule** he's not very good at taking photos, he's just snaphappy; **g. sa vie** to waste one's life

2 (*abîmer*) to spoil, to ruin; *Fam* **il m'a gâché mon dessin!** he messed up *or* spoiled my drawing!; **ne dis rien, tu risques de tout g.!** keep quiet or you might spoil *or* ruin everything!; *Fam* **ne va pas me g. le plaisir** don't go spoiling *or* ruining it for me; **il a gâché la soirée** he spoiled the evening; **g. ses chances de succès** to spoil one's chances; **g. le métier** to spoil it for the others (*by undercutting prices or working for lower wages*)

3 *Constr* (*plâtre, ciment*) to mix; **g. la chaux** to slack lime

gâchette [gaʃɛt] NF **1** (*d'arme à feu*) trigger; **appuyez sur la g.** pull the trigger; **avoir la g. facile/rapide** to be trigger-happy/quick on the draw **2** (*tireur*) **la meilleure g. de l'Ouest** the fastest gun in the West **3** *Électron* (*de semi-conducteur*) gate; (*de tube*) grid (electrode) **4** (*de serrure*) spring catch **5** *Tech* pawl

gâcheur, -euse [gaʃœr, -øz] ADJ wasteful
NM,F (*gaspilleur*) wasteful person, wastrel; (*bâcleur*) bungler, botcher
NM *Constr Br* plasterer's mate, *Am* plasterer's helper

gâchis [gaʃi] NM **1** (*gaspillage*) waste; **je ne supporte pas le g.** I can't stand waste *or* wastefulness; **tout ce pain jeté, quel g.!** what a waste of all that bread!; **vous avez fait un beau g. dans la cuisine!** you've made a right mess in the kitchen!; **sa vie est un véritable g.** his/her life has been completely wasted

2 (*désordre*) mess; **faire du g.** to make a mess; **g. politique** political muddle

3 (*mortier*) wet mortar

gade [gad] = **gadidé**

gadelle [gadɛl] NF *Can Bot* currant; **g. blanche** white currant; **g. noire** blackcurrant; **g. rouge** redcurrant

gadget [gadʒɛt] NM **1** (*appareil*) gadget; **une cuisine pleine de gadgets** a kitchen full of gadgets **2** (*idée, projet*) gimmick; **g. publicitaire** advertising gimmick **3** (*comme adj; avec ou sans trait d'union*) **une mesure g.** a gimmicky measure; **une réforme g.** a token reform

gadgétisation [gadʒetizasjɔ̃] NF **la g. croissante de la vie moderne** the increasing use of gadgetry in modern life

gadgétisé, -e [gadʒetize] ADJ gadgety

gadgétiser [3] [gadʒetize] VT to add gadgets to; **g. une voiture** to customize a car (with gadgets)

gadidé [gadide] *Ich* NM gadid, gadoid, *Spéc* member of the Gadidae
□ **gadidés** NMPL gadids, gadoids, *Spéc* Gadidae

gadin [gadɛ̃] NM *très Fam* **prendre** *ou* **ramasser un g.** to fall flat on one's face, *Br* to come a cropper

gadjo [gadʒo] (*pl* **gadjé** [gadʒe] *ou* **gadjos**) NM non-gypsy

gadolinium [gadɔlinjɔm] NM *Chim* gadolinium

gadoue [gadu] NF (*boue*) mud, muck
□ **gadoues** NFPL *Agr* treated sewage

gadouille [gaduj] NF *très Fam* mud ▪, sludge

gad'zart [gadzar] NM *Fam* = student of the "École des Arts et Métiers"

GAEC, G.A.E.C. [gaɛk] NM (*abrév* **groupement agricole d'exploitation en commun**) = farm run as a semi-cooperative

gaélique [gaelik] ADJ Gaelic
NM *Ling* Gaelic; **g. d'Écosse** Scots Gaelic; **g. d'Irlande** Irish

gaffe [gaf] NF **1** *Fam* (*bêtise* → *en paroles*) gaffe; (→ *en actions*) blunder, *Br* boob, *Am* goof, booboo; **faire une g.** to put one's foot in it, to make a blunder; **tu as fait une g. en le lui racontant** you put your foot in it *or Br* you dropped a clanger *or Am* you goofed when you told him/her that

2 *Naut* boathook, hook

3 *Pêche* gaff; *Fam* **avaler sa g.** to die, to kick the bucket

4 *Fam Arg* crime screw, prison warder ▪

5 *Fam* (*locution*) **faire g.** (*faire attention*) to be careful ▪, **fais g. à toi!** (*prends soin de toi*) take care of yourself!; (*menace*) be careful!, watch it!; **fais g., c'est chaud!** watch out *or* careful, it's hot!; **fais g. à ce que tu dis!** be careful *or* watch what you say!

gaffer¹ [gafœr] NM *TV & Cin* gaffer

gaffer² [3] [gafe] VI **1** *Fam* (*commettre une bévue* → *en parlant*) to make a gaffe, *Br* to drop a clanger; (→ *en agissant*) to put one's foot in it, *Br* to boob, *Am* to goof

2 *très Fam* (*surveiller*) **va g. au coin de la rue** go and keep a lookout at the corner of the street
VT **1** *très Fam* (*regarder*) **gaffe un peu ça!** get a load of this!; **gaffez si les flics s'amènent pas** keep an eye open for the cops

2 (*objet flottant*) to hook; *Pêche* (*poisson*) to gaff
► **se gaffer** VPR *Suisse Fam* to watch out ▪

gaffeur¹, -euse [gafœr, -øz] *Fam* ADJ **être g.** to be always putting one's foot in it
NM,F blunderer; **son g. de frère** his/her blundering idiot of a brother; **c'est une gaffeuse née** she's always putting her foot in it

gaffeur² [gafœr] NM *TV & Cin* grip gator clip

gaffeuse [gaføz] *voir* **gaffeur²**

gag [gag] NM gag, joke; **du coup, j'ai laissé mes clefs à l'intérieur, c'est le g.!** now I've gone and locked myself out, what a farce this is!; **tu es renvoyé – c'est un g.?** you're fired – you're kidding *or* joking!; **son pantalon a craqué au milieu de la réunion, le g.!** his/her trousers split during the meeting, what a scream!; *Cin* **g. à répétition** running gag

gaga [gaga] *Fam* ADJ senile ▪, gaga; **il est complètement g., le vieux** he's a senile old fool
NM,F **un vieux g.** a doddering old fool

gagaku [gagaku] NM *Mus* gagaku

Gagarine [gagarin] NPR **Iouri G.** Yuri Gagarin

gage [gaʒ] NM **1** (*caution*) security, collateral (UNCOUNT); (*au mont-de-piété*) pledge; **laisser qch en g.** to leave sth as security; **mettre qch en g.** to pawn *or Am* to hock sth; **mise en g.** pawning; **ma montre est en g.** my watch is in pawn; **rester en g.** to remain as surety; **lettre de g.** debenture bond; (*pour hypothèque*) mortgage bond; *Jur* **g. mobilier** mortgage over assets, mortgage over property

2 *Fig* (*garantie*) guarantee; **sa compétence sera le g. d'une bonne gestion** his/her competence will guarantee *or* secure good management; **votre parole sera le meilleur des gages** your word will be the best guarantee

3 (*témoignage*) proof, token; **g. d'amour** token of love, love token; **en g. de** as proof of; **en g. de**

mon amour as proof *or* a pledge of my love; **en g. de ma bonne volonté** as a token of my goodwill; **je t'offre ce livre en g. de notre amitié** I offer you this book as a token of our friendship; **son premier film est le g. d'un grand talent** his/her first film gives proof *or* shows evidence of great talent

4 *(dans un jeu)* forfeit

❑ **gages** NMPL *Vieilli (salaire)* wages, pay; **être aux gages de qn** to be in sb's employ (as a servant); **il est aux gages de la Mafia** he's on the mafia payroll *or* in the pay of the Mafia

gagé, -e [gaʒe] ADJ **1** *(objet)* pledged, pawned; **meubles gagés** furniture under distraint; **recettes non gagées** unassigned *or* unpledged revenue **2** *(emprunt)* secured; **g. sur l'or** backed by gold

gager [17] [gaʒe] VT **1** *Fin (emprunt)* to secure, to guarantee **2** *Littéraire (parier)* to wager; **gageons qu'il l'épousera** I wager he'll marry her

gageur, -euse [gaʒœr, -øz] NM,F *Com & Jur* pledger, pawner

gageure [gaʒyr] NF **1** *(action difficile)* challenge; **c'est une g. de vouloir la raisonner** trying to reason with her is quite a challenge; **pour le gouvernement, c'est une g.** the government is attempting the impossible; **soutenir la g.** to take up the challenge; **réussir la g. de faire qch** to succeed in the difficult task of doing sth **2** *Littéraire (pari)* wager, *Can* bet

gageuse [gaʒøz] *voir* **gageur**

gagiste [gaʒist] NMF *Jur* pledgee, secured creditor

gagman [gagman] (*pl* **gagmen** [-mɛn]) NM gag writer, gag-man

gagnable [gaɲabl] ADJ winnable; **le match est encore g.** the match can still be won

gagnage [gaɲaʒ] NM *Vieilli* **1** *Agr* pasturage **2** *Chasse* browsing land, feeding ground

gagnant, -e [gaɲɑ̃, -ɑ̃t] ADJ *(ticket, coupon)* winning *(avant n)*; **il est donné g.** he is favourite *or* has been tipped to win; **il fallait jouer Fleur de Lys g.** you should have backed Fleur de Lys to win; **coup g.** *(au tennis)* winner *(shot)*; *Fig* **elle part gagnante** all the odds are in her favour; *Fig* **jouer g.** to hold all the trump cards

NM,F winner; *Fig* **c'est toi le grand g. de l'histoire** you've come out on top, you've got the best of the bargain

gagne [gaɲ] NF *Fam* winning edge■; **jouer la g.** to play to win

gagne-pain [gaɲpɛ̃] NM INV livelihood; **ces traductions sont son g.** these translations are his/her livelihood; **c'est mon seul g.** it's my only means of existence

gagne-petit [gaɲpəti] NMF INV *Péj* **1** *(qui gagne peu)* **les g.** the low-paid; **ce sont des g.** they work for a pittance **2** *(qui manque d'ambition)* small-time operator, small-timer

GAGNER [3] [gaɲe]

> **VT** to win **1, 6** ■ to earn **2** ■ to make **2** ■ to gain **3, 5** ■ to save **4** ■ to win over **6** ■ to overcome **7** ■ to reach **9**
> **VI** to win **1** ■ to gain ground **2**
> **VPR** to win **2** ■ to earn **2**

VT **1** *(partie, match, élection, prix)* to win; *aussi Fig* **g. le gros lot** to win *or* to hit the jackpot; **g. un procès** to win a (court) case; *Fig* **la partie n'est pas gagnée** we haven't won yet; **ce n'est pas gagné d'avance** it's a bit early to start talking about success; **c'est un pari gagné d'avance** it's in the bag; *Ironique* **c'est gagné!** now you've got what you asked for!

2 *(argent → comme rémunération)* to earn, to make; *(→ comme récompense)* to earn; *(→ dans une transaction)* to make a profit of, to make; **combien gagne-t-elle par mois?** how much does she earn a month?; *Fam* **g. gros** to earn *or* to make big money; *(société)* to make large profits; **il a gagné gros avec son dernier roman** he made a packet *or Br* a bomb on his last novel; **il ne gagne presque rien** he earns next to nothing; **elle a gagné 500 euros sur la vente du tableau** she made 500 euros on the sale of the painting; **g. une fortune à la loterie** to win a fortune on the lottery; *aussi Fig* **allez, prends, tu l'as bien gagné!** go on, take it, you've earned it!; **g. des mille et des cents** to earn a fortune; *Fam* **g. sa vie** *ou* **son pain** *ou* **son bifteck** *ou* **sa croûte** to earn a living *or* one's daily bread; **g. qch à la sueur de son front** to earn sth with the sweat of one's brow; **g. de quoi vivre** to earn a living, to earn enough to live on; *Fam Ironique* **eh bien, j'ai gagné ma journée!** I should have stayed in bed today!

3 *(obtenir → avantage)* to gain; *(→ part de marché)* to capture; **il y a tout à g. à faire cette démarche** there's everything to gain *or* to be gained from making this move; **nous ne gagnerons rien à attendre** there is nothing to be gained *or* we'll gain nothing by waiting; **et si j'accepte, qu'est-ce que j'y gagne?** and if I accept, what do I get out of it?; **qu'est-ce que tu gagnes à tout changer?** what's the point of changing everything?; **il y a gagné un bras cassé/une réputation de menteur** all he got out of it was a broken arm/a reputation for being a liar; **nous n'y avons gagné que des problèmes** all it brought us was problems; **c'est toujours ça de gagné!, c'est autant de gagné!** that's something, anyway!

4 *(économiser)* to save; **g. de la place** to save space; **en enlevant la porte on gagne 10 cm** if you take the door off you gain an extra 10 cm; **g. du temps** *(en allant très vite)* to save time; *(en atermoyant)* to play for time; **chercher à g. du temps** to play for time; **j'ai gagné trois places dans la queue** I've moved up three places in the queue

5 *Bourse* to gain; **l'indice a gagné deux points** the index has gone up by *or* has gained two points

6 *(conquérir → ami)* to win; *(→ partisan)* to win over; **g. l'appui de qn** to win sb's support; **g. la confiance/l'estime/l'amitié de qn** to win *or* to gain sb's confidence/respect/friendship; **g. qn à une cause** to win sb over (to a cause); **g. qn à une idée** to sell sb an idea

7 *(sujet: sentiment, sensation)* to overcome; *(sujet: épidémie, infection, feu, nuages)* to spread to; **je sentais la panique me g.** I could feel panic coming *or* creeping over me; **la faim nous gagnait** we were getting hungry; **le cancer gagne l'autre poumon** the cancer is spreading to the other lung; **s'ils se laissent g. par le froid, ils sont perdus** if they allow the cold to take a grip of *or* to get to them, they are finished; **j'ai fini par me laisser g. par son enthousiasme** I ended up being infected by his/her enthusiasm; **le rire gagna l'assemblée tout entière** the laughter spread through the whole audience

8 *(avancer)* **g. du terrain** *Naut & Fig* to gain ground; *Naut (sur la mer)* to reclaim land; **la mer gagne du terrain** the sea is encroaching on the land; **nos concurrents gagnent du terrain** our competitors are gaining ground

9 *(rejoindre)* to reach, to get to; **nous gagnerons Paris/le refuge avant la nuit** we will reach Paris/the refuge before nightfall; **il gagna la sortie** he made his way to the exit; *Naut* **g. le port** to reach port, *Spéc* to fetch into port; **le ferry gagna le large** the ferry got out into the open sea

10 *Naut (rattraper)* **g. un navire** to gain on *or* overhaul a ship; **g. le devant** to forge ahead, to take the lead; **g. le vent** to make *or* to fetch to windward; **g. le vent d'une pointe** to weather a headland; **g. de l'avant** to forge ahead

VI **1** *(l'emporter)* to win; **on a gagné (par) 3 buts à 2** we won (by) 3 goals to 2, we won 3–2; **g. aux points** to win on points; **g. aux courses** to win at the races; **g. aux échecs** to win at chess; **g. aux élections** to win the election; **tu as gagné, on fera ce que tu demandes** you win, we'll do as you say; **à ce petit jeu, ce n'est pas toi qui gagneras** you're not going to beat me/him/*etc* at that little game; **à tous les coups l'on** *ou* **on gagne!** everyone's a winner!

2 *(avancer → incendie, érosion)* to gain ground; **g. sur** to gain *or* to advance on; **ses concurrents gagnent sur lui** his competitors are gaining on him; **la mer gagne sur la côte** the sea is eating away at the coastline; **g. en** to increase *or* to gain in; **g. en longueur** to increase in length, to grow longer; **g. en vigueur** to become stronger; **notre production gagne en qualité** the quality of our product is improving

3 *Naut* **g. au vent** to make *or* to fetch to windward

❑ **gagner à** VT IND **g. à qch/à faire qch** to benefit from sth/from doing sth; **elle gagne à être connue** once you get to know her a bit she grows on you; **vin qui gagne à vieillir** wine for laying down *or* which improves with age; **ils gagneraient à ce que nul ne l'apprenne** it would be to their advantage if nobody found out; **accepte, tu y gagnes** *ou* **tu gagnes au change** say yes, it's to your advantage *or* you get the best of the deal

▶**se gagner** VPR **1** *(emploi passif)* **l'argent ne se gagne pas si facilement** it isn't so easy to make money

2 se g. qch to win *or* to earn sth; **se g. l'estime de qn** to win sb's esteem; **se g. le respect de qn** to earn sb's respect; **se g. un adepte** to win over a follower

gagneur, -euse [gaɲœr, -øz] NM,F winner, go-getter; **avoir un tempérament de g.** to be a winner; **c'est un g. né** he's a born winner

❑ **gagneuse** NF *très Fam (prostituée)* pro

gaguesque [gagyɛsk, gagɛsk] ADJ *Fam* comical■, farcical■

gai, -e [gɛ] ADJ **1** *(personne)* cheerful, merry, lively, in good spirits; *(mine, décor, personnalité)* cheerful, happy; *(musique)* cheerful, jolly; *(voix)* cheerful, cheery; *(couleur)* bright, cheerful; **g. comme un pinson** happy as a lark *or Br* as a sandboy; **tu es bien g. ce matin!** you're cheerful this morning!; **sa vie n'a pas toujours été très gaie** his/her life hasn't always been much fun *or* a happy one; **cette couleur rend la pièce plus gaie** this colour makes the room look more cheerful; **encore une panne! ça n'est vraiment pas g.!** another breakdown! that's (just) great!; **tout cela n'est pas très g.** it's all a bit depressing; *Ironique* **il vérifie en permanence ce que je fais, c'est g.** he's continually checking what I'm doing, it's charming *or* really nice; *Ironique* **il pleut encore, c'est g.!** great, it's raining again!

2 *(un peu ivre)* merry, tipsy

3 *Belg (agréable)* nice, pleasant

4 *(homosexuel)* = **gay**

NM,F = **gay**

'Le Gai Savoir' *Nietzsche* 'The Gay Science'

gaïac [gajak] NM *Bot* guaiacum

gaïacol [gajakɔl] NM *Chim* guaiacol

gaiement [gemɑ̃] ADV **1** *(avec joie)* cheerfully, cheerily **2** *(avec enthousiasme)* cheerfully, heartily; **allons-y g.!** let's get on with it!

gaieté [gete] NF **1** *(bonne humeur)* cheerfulness, gaiety; **elle a retrouvé sa g.** she's cheered up again; **tu n'es pas d'une g. folle ce matin** you're not exactly a bundle of fun this morning; **un accès de g.** a burst of merriment **2** *(d'une couleur)* brightness, gaiety

❑ **gaietés** NFPL *Ironique* **les gaietés du métro aux heures de pointe** the delights of the underground in the rush hour

❑ **de gaieté de cœur** ADV willingly, gladly; **je ne l'ai pas fait de g. de cœur!** it's not something I enjoyed doing!

gaillac [gajak] NM Gaillac *(wine from south-west France)*

gaillard, -e [gajar, -ard] ADJ **1** *(grivois)* bawdy, lewd, ribald

2 *(vigoureux)* lusty; **se sentir g.** to feel in good form, *Br* to be full of beans; **il est encore g.** he is still sprightly *or* lively; **un petit vent g.** a good stiff breeze, a lively breeze

NM,F *(personne forte)* fellow; **un grand et solide g.** a great strapping man; **tu ne vas pas pleurer, un grand g. comme toi!** you're not going to cry, a big guy like you!; **c'est un sacré g.!** *(homme viril)* he's a lusty *or* red-blooded fellow!; *(costaud)* he's a great strapping lad!; **c'est une (rude) gaillarde** she's no shrinking violet; **c'est une grande gaillarde** she's a big strapping girl *or Br* lass

NM **1** *Fam* **toi, mon g., tu n'as pas intérêt à bouger!** *(avec menace)* you'd better not move,

Br mate *or Am* buddy!; **c'est un g. qui promet** *(avec amitié)* he's a promising boy *or Br* lad

2 *Naut* **g. d'avant** forecastle, fo'c'sle; **g. d'arrière** poop; **haut de g.** deep-waisted

❑ **gaillarde** NF *Mus & (danse)* galliard

gaillardement [gajardəmɑ̃] ADV **1** *(gaiement)* cheerfully, good-humouredly; **elle accepte/supporte tout ça g.** she accepts/bears it all cheerfully **2** *(vaillamment)* valiantly, gamely; **on se mit en marche g.** we set off boldly *or* in good spirits; **elle va g. sur ses 70 ans** she'll soon be a sprightly 70

gaillardise [gajardiz] NF *Vieilli* **1** *(bonne humeur)* cheerfulness, good humour **2** *(grivoiserie)* ribald *or* risqué remark; **conter des gaillardises** to tell risqué *or* off-colour stories

gaillet [gajɛ] NM *Bot* bedstraw

gaillette [gajɛt] NF *(large)* lump of coal

gaîment [ɡɛmɑ̃] *Arch* = **gaiement**

gain [ɡɛ̃] NM **1** *(succès)* winning; **elle a eu** *ou* **obtenu g. de cause** *(dans un procès)* she won the case; *Fig* it was agreed that she was in the right; **donner g. de cause à qn** to decide in favour of sb

2 *(économie)* saving; **un g. de place/temps** a saving of space/time; **cela permet un (énorme) g. de place/temps** it saves (a lot of) space/time; **gains de productivité** productivity gains

3 *(progrès)* benefit; **un g. de 30 sièges aux élections** a gain of 30 seats in the elections

4 *(bénéfice financier)* profit, gain; *(rémunération)* earnings; *(au jeu)* winnings; **faire des gains importants à la Bourse** to make a big profit on the stock exchange; **gains illicites** illicit earnings; **gains invisibles** invisible earnings; **l'amour du g.** the love of gain; **avoir l'amour du g.** to love making money; *Compta* **g. latent** unrealized gain

5 *Électron* gain; **commande automatique de g.** automatic gain control; **g. en courant** current gain; **g. en tension** voltage magnification; **g. d'étage** stage gain; *Nucl* **g. de régénération** breeding gain

6 *Jur* **gains de survie** (stipulated *or* contractual) rights of survivorship

7 *Suisse* **par g. de paix** as a conciliatory gesture

gainage [ɡɛnaʒ] NM *(de câble)* sheathing; *(de cylindre, de tuyau)* lagging, cladding

gaine [ɡɛn] NF **1** *(étui → de poignard)* sheath; *(→ de parapluie)* cover; **g. métallique** metallic sheath *or* sleeve; **g. souple** flexible sheath; **câble sous g.** sheathed cable

2 *Anat & Bot* sheath

3 *(d'amorce)* priming tube

4 *Beaux-Arts (piédestal)* plinth

5 *Constr (conduit vertical)* shaft, duct; *(de climatisation)* duct; **g. d'aération** ventilation shaft; **g. d'ascenseur** *Br* lift shaft, *Am* elevator shaft; **g. de ventilation** ventilation shaft

6 *Électron* jacket

7 *Naut* tabling

8 *Nucl* can; **g. d'électrons/d'ions** electron/ion sheath

9 *(sous-vêtement)* girdle

gaine-culotte [ɡɛnkylɔt] *(pl* **gaines-culottes**) NF panty girdle

gainer [4] [ɡene] VT *(câble)* to sheathe, to encase *(de* in); *(cylindre, tuyau)* to lag, to clad; **le corps gainé de vinyle bleu** his/her body sheathed in blue vinyl; **flacon gainé de cuir** leather-cased flask

gainerie [ɡɛnri] NF **1** *(fabrication d'étuis)* case-making; *(fabrication de fourreaux)* sheath-making, scabbard-making **2** *(commerce)* casing trade

gainier [ɡenje] NM *Bot* Judas tree

gaîté [ɡete] *Arch* = **gaieté**

Gaius [ɡajys] NPR Gaius

gaize [ɡɛz] NF *Minér* gaize

Gal *(abrév écrite* **Général)** Gen

gal, -als [ɡal] NM *Phys* gal

gala [ɡala] NM gala; **dîner en grand g.** to dine in state, to dine with great ceremony; **g. de charité** charity gala

❑ **de gala** ADJ gala *(avant n)*; **en habit** *ou* **tenue de g.** in gala dress, in full dress

Galaad [ɡalaad] NM *Géog, Bible & Myth* Galahad

galactique [ɡalaktik] ADJ galactic

galactogène [ɡalaktɔʒɛn] ADJ galactagogue, galactogenetic

    NM galactagogue, galactogenetic

galactophore [ɡalaktɔfɔr] ADJ *Anat* **canal g.** galactophore, milk duct

galactose [ɡalaktoz] NM galactose

galago [ɡalaɡo] NM *Zool* bushbaby

galalithe [ɡalalit] NF galalith

galamment [ɡalamɑ̃] ADV gallantly; *Littéraire (noblement)* honourably; **que c'est g. dit!** there speaks a *or* spoken like a true gentleman!

galandage [ɡalɑ̃daʒ] NM *Constr* brick-on-edge partition

galant, -e [ɡalɑ̃, -ɑ̃t] ADJ **1** *(courtois)* gallant, gentlemanly; **un homme g.** a gentleman; **sois g., porte-lui son paquet** be a gentleman and carry her parcel for her; **un g. homme** an honourable man, a gentleman; **se conduire en g. homme** to behave like a gentleman

2 *Littéraire (amoureux)* **un rendez-vous g.** a date, a rendezvous, *Vieilli* a lover's tryst; **en galante compagnie** in the company of the opposite sex; **une femme galante** a woman of easy virtue

3 *(en Afrique francophone) (chic, à la mode)* trendy

    NM *Vieilli* suitor, admirer; *Littéraire* **un vert g.** an ageing beau; **faire le g. auprès d'une dame** to court *or* to pay court to a lady; *(flirter)* to flirt with a lady

galanterie [ɡalɑ̃tri] NF **1** *(courtoisie)* courteousness, gallantry, chivalry; **la g. se perd!** the age of chivalry is dead! **2** *(compliment)* gallant remark, gallantry; **dire des galanteries à qn** to pay sb compliments **3** *(intrigue)* love affair, intrigue

galantin [ɡalɑ̃tɛ̃] NM *Péj Vieilli* ladies' man

galantine [ɡalɑ̃tin] NF *Culin* galantine

Galápagos [ɡalapaɡos] NFPL **les (îles) G.** the Galapagos Islands; **vivre aux G.** to live in the Galapagos Islands; **aller aux G.** to go to the Galapagos Islands

galapiat [ɡalapja] NM *Fam Vieilli (polisson)* rapscallion, rascal; *(vaurien)* good-for-nothing

Galatée [ɡalate] NF *Myth* Galatea

galathée [ɡalate] *Zool* NF squat lobster, *Spéc* member of the Galatheidae

❑ **galathées** NFPL squat lobsters, *Spéc* Galatheidae

galaxie [ɡalaksi] NF galaxy; *Astron* **la G.** the Galaxy

galbe [ɡalb] NM curve; **des jambes d'un g. parfait** shapely legs

galbé, -e [ɡalbe] ADJ **1** *(commode, poterie)* curved, with a curved outline; **les pieds galbés d'une commode** the curved legs of a chest of drawers **2** *(mollet → de femme)* shapely; *(→ de sportif)* muscular

galber [3] [ɡalbe] VT *(vase, commode)* to give curves to

gale [ɡal] NF **1** *Méd* scabies; **g. bédouine** prickly heat; **la g. du ciment** bricklayer's itch; *Fam* **embrasse-le, il n'a pas la g.!** give him a kiss, you won't catch anything!; **mauvais** *ou* **méchant comme la g.** wicked as sin **2** *Fam (personne odieuse)* rat, *Br* nasty piece of work **3** *Vét (du chien, du chat)* mange; *(du mouton)* scab **4** *Bot* scab **5** *Can (escharre)* scab

galéace, galéasse [ɡaleas] NF *Naut & Hist* large Venetian galley, galleass

galée [ɡale] NF *(en imprimerie)* galley

galéjade [ɡaleʒad] NF *Fam (en Provence)* tall story; **raconter** *ou* **dire des galéjades à qn** to pull sb's leg, to spin sb a yarn

galéjer [18] [ɡaleʒe] VI *Fam* to spin a yarn; **tu galèjes!** a likely story!

galène [ɡalɛn] NF *Minér* galena, galenite

galénique [ɡalenik] ADJ *Pharm* Galenical; **médicament g.** Galenical

galénisme [ɡalenism] NM Galenism

galéopithèque [ɡaleɔpitɛk] NM *Zool* flying lemur

galère [ɡalɛr] NF **1** *(navire)* galley; **condamné** *ou* **envoyé aux galères** sent to the galleys; *Naut* **avirons en g.!** rest on your oars!

2 *Fam (situation pénible)* hassle, mess; **après des années de g.** after years of hardship■, **c'est la g. pour obtenir des places de théâtre** it's a real hassle getting theatre tickets; **vivre à Los Angeles sans voiture, c'est une vraie g.** life in Los Angeles without a car is the pits *or* is a real hassle; **c'est la g.!, quelle g.!** what a pain *or* drag *or* hassle!; *très Fam* **se foutre dans une g.** to get oneself into a mess

    ADJ *Fam* **il est vraiment g., ce mec** he's nothing but trouble; **c'est un peu g.** it's a bit of a hassle; **c'est g. de trouver une cabine téléphonique dans cette ville** it's a (real) hassle to find a phone box in this town; **lui et ses plans galères!** him and his lousy ideas!

Allusion

Qu'allait-il faire dans cette galère?

This is a quotation from Molière's *Les Fourberies de Scapin*, act II, scene 7. A crafty, cheeky valet called Scapin is trying to get some money out of a character named Géronte by telling him that his son is a galley slave on a Turkish galley, and can only be freed on payment of a ransom. The miserly father cannot bear to think of paying up, and repeats several times **Que diable allait-il faire dans cette galère?** ("What the devil was he doing in the galleys?"), expressing exasperation rather than concern. Today the expression is used allusively when questioning how someone has got involved in something, eg **Mais qu'allais-tu faire dans cette galère?** ("Why on earth did you get mixed up in this?"). The word "galère" has itself taken on the sense of "mess", in the sense of a bad situation.

---

galérer [18] [ɡalere] VI *Fam (avoir du mal)* to have a hard time (of it); **on a galéré deux heures en banlieue** we wasted two whole hours driving around the suburbs; **j'ai galéré toute la journée pour m'inscrire** I've been running around (like mad) all day sorting out my enrolment; **elle a vraiment galéré avant d'être connue** she had a hard time of it before she made it

galerie [ɡalri] NF **1** *(local → d'expositions, de ventes)* (art) gallery, private gallery; **g. d'art** *ou* **de peinture** *ou* **de tableaux** art gallery; **g. de portraits** portrait gallery; *Fig* rogue's gallery

2 *(salle d'apparat)* hall, gallery; **la g. des Glaces** the Hall of Mirrors

3 *(passage couvert)* gallery; *(arcade)* arcade; **g. marchande** *(passage couvert)* shopping arcade; *(centre commercial) Br* shopping centre, *Am* shopping mall

4 *Can (véranda)* porch

5 *Théât* **la g.** the gallery, the balcony; **les deuxièmes galeries** *(qui ne sont pas les plus hautes)* the dress circle; *(les plus hautes)* the upper circle; **la troisième g.** the gallery, *Fam* the gods; **jouer pour la g.** to play to the gallery; *Fig* **tout ce qu'il fait, c'est pour la g.** everything he does is to show off *or* is calculated to impress; *Fig* **amuser la g.** to play for laughs

6 *(souterrain → de taupe)* tunnel; *(→ de termites)* gallery

7 *Mines* gallery, level; **g. d'avancement** heading

8 *Aut* roof rack

9 *(sur meuble)* cornice

10 *Élec* **g. des câbles** cable tunnel

galérien [ɡalerjɛ̃] NM galley slave; **travailler comme un g.** to work like a (galley) slave *or* a horse *or* a Trojan; **mener une vie de g.** to lead a dog's life

galeriste [ɡalrist] NMF gallery owner

galerne [ɡalɛrn] NF north-west wind

galéruque [ɡaleryk] NF *Entom* (chrysomelid) beetle

galet [ɡalɛ] NM **1** *(caillou)* pebble; **sur les galets** on the shingle *or* the pebble beach **2** *(roue)* roller; *Tech* roller; *Ordinat (de souris)* wheel; *Aut* **g. de direction** roller; **g. de guidage** jockey wheel; **g. de roulement** travelling *or* running wheel **3** *Mil* **g. porteur** track-supporting roller **4** *Archéol* **g. aménagé** pebble tool

galetage [ɡaltaʒ] NM *Tech* rolling

galetas [ɡalta] NM **1** *Littéraire (logement)* hovel **2** *Suisse & (en français régional) (grenier)* attic, garret

galeter [27] [ɡalte] VT *Tech* to roll

galetouse [ɡaltuz] NF *très Fam* mess tin, dixie

galette [ɡalɛt] NF **1** *(crêpe → épaisse)* pancake, griddle cake; *(→ de froment, de sarrasin, de blé noir)* buckwheat pancake; *(pain azyme)* matzo

bread; *(biscuit)* butter biscuit; **g. de maïs** corn bread *(UNCOUNT)*; **g. de pommes de terre** potato pancake; **la g. des Rois** = pastry traditionally eaten on Twelfth Night *(in France)*

  2 *très Fam (argent)* dough, *Br* dosh; **ils se sont tirés avec la g.** they did a disappearing act with the dough; **elle a de la g.** she's rolling in it

  3 *Belg (gaufrette)* wafer

  4 *Fam (disque, CD)* disc■

galetteux, -euse [galɛtø, -øz] ADJ *Fam Vieilli* loaded, rolling in it

galeux, -euse [galø, -øz] ADJ **1** *(qui a la gale)* mangy; *(arbre)* scabby; *Méd* **plaie galeuse** sore caused by scabies **2** *(dégoûtant → façade, bâtisse)* scruffy, dingy; *(→ quartier)* squalid, seedy; **murs g.** peeling *or* flaking walls

  NM,F *Péj* **on y trouve réunis tous les g. de la terre** all the scum of the earth is there

galgal, -als [galgal] NM *Archéol* cairn, barrow

galhauban [galobã] NM *Naut* back stay

galibot [galibo] NM *Mines* pit boy

Galice [galis] NF **la G.** Galicia

Galicie [galisi] NF **la G.** Galicia; **G. occidentale/orientale** Polish/Russian Galicia

galicien, -enne [galisjɛ̃, -ɛn] ADJ *(de Galice, de Galicie)* Galician

  NM *(langue de Galice)* Galician

  ❑ **Galicien, -enne** NM,F *(de Galice, de Galicie)* Galician

Galilée[1] [galile] NF *Géog* **la G.** Galilee

Galilée[2] [galile] NPR Galileo

galiléen, -enne [galileɛ̃, -ɛn] ADJ Galilean

  ❑ **Galiléen, -enne** NM,F Galilean

  ❑ **Galiléen** NM **le G.** the Galilean

galimatias [galimatja] NM gibberish *(UNCOUNT)*, gobbledegook *(UNCOUNT)*, nonsense *(UNCOUNT)*

galion [galjɔ̃] NM *Naut* galleon

galiote [galjɔt] NF *Naut* **1** *Hist* galliot, galiot; **g. à bombe** bomb-ketch **2** *(bateau hollandais)* (covered-in) canal barge **3** *(traverse)* hatch beam

galipette [galipɛt] NF *Fam* forward roll■, somersault■; **galipettes** somersaults; *Hum (ébats amoureux)* (bedroom) romps■; **faire des galipettes** *(faire des sauts)* to do somersaults■; *(gambader)* to romp about■; *Hum (ébats amoureux)* to have a roll around; **les enfants dévalaient la colline en faisant des galipettes** the children were tearing down the hill doing somersaults

galipot [galipo] NM **1** *(résine)* galipot, white resin **2** *Naut* blacking

galipote [galipɔt] NF *Can Fam* **courir la g.** to chase women

galipoter [3] [galipɔte] VT *Naut* to black down

galle [gal] NF *Bot* gall; **g. de chêne** oak apple

gallec [galɛk] ADJ INV = of/from the part of Brittany where the "Gallo" dialect is spoken

  NM *(dialecte)* = dialect spoken in the non-Breton-speaking part of Brittany

  ❑ **Gallec** NMF INV = inhabitant of or person from the part of Brittany where the "Gallo" dialect is spoken

gallérie [galeri] NF *Entom* wax moth, bee moth

Galles [gal] NM **le pays de G.** Wales; **vivre au pays de G.** to live in Wales; **aller au pays de G.** to go to Wales

galleux, -euse [galø, -øz] ADJ *Chim & Minér* gallic

gallican, -e [galikã, -an] *Rel* ADJ Gallican

  ❑ **Gallican, -e** NM,F Gallican

gallicanisme [galikanism] NM *Rel* Gallicanism

gallicisme [galisism] NM *Ling (calque du français)* Gallicism; *(emprunt au français)* French idiom, Gallicism

gallicole [galikɔl] ADJ *Entom* gallicolous

Galliera [galjɛra] NM **le palais G.** = mansion housing the Paris museum of fashion and costume

galliforme [galiform] *Orn* NM galliform *or* gallinaceous bird

  ❑ **galliformes** NMPL Galliformes, gallinaceous birds

gallinacé, -e [galinase] *Orn* ADJ gallinaceous, gallinacean

  NM gallinacean

  ❑ **gallinacés** NMPL chicken family, *Spéc* Gallinaceae

gallinule [galinyl] NF *Orn* moorhen, *Spéc* gallinule

Gallipoli [galipoli] NM *Géog* Gallipoli

---

gallique[1] [galik] ADJ *Chim & Minér* gallic; **acide g.** gallic acid

gallique[2] [galik] ADJ *Hist* Gallic

gallium [galjɔm] NM *Chim* gallium

gallo [galo] ADJ INV **pays g.** = area in which the "Gallo" dialect is spoken

  NM *(dialecte)* = dialect spoken in the non-Breton-speaking part of Brittany

  ❑ **Gallo** NMF INV = inhabitant of or person from the part of Brittany where the "Gallo" dialect is spoken

gallois, -e [galwa, -az] ADJ Welsh

  NM *(langue)* Welsh

  ❑ **Gallois, -e** NM,F Welshman, *f* Welshwoman; **les G.** the Welsh

gallon [galɔ̃] NM gallon; **un g. aux 30 miles** 30 miles to the *or* per gallon; **le g. américain** the US gallon; **le g. impérial** the imperial *or* British gallon

gallo-romain, -e [galɔrɔmɛ̃, -ɛn] *(mpl* **gallo-romains,** *fpl* **gallo-romaines)** ADJ Gallo-Roman

  ❑ **Gallo-Romain, -e** NM,F Gallo-Roman

gallo-roman, -e [galɔrɔmã, -an] *(mpl* **gallo-romans,** *fpl* **gallo-romanes)** ADJ *Ling* Gallo-Romance, Gallo-Roman

galoche [galɔʃ] NF **1** *(chaussure)* wooden-soled shoe, clog *(with leather uppers)* **2** *Naut* snatch block **3** *très Fam* French kiss; **rouler une g. à qn** to French-kiss sb, *Br* to snog sb

galon [galɔ̃] NM **1** *Tex (ruban)* braid *(UNCOUNT)*, trimming *(UNCOUNT)*; **un g. doré** a piece of gold braid; **g. de finition** *(d'ameublement)* upholstery binding **2** *Mil (insigne)* stripe; **il a mis du temps pour gagner ses galons d'officier** it took him a long time to earn his stripes; *Fig* **prendre du g.** to take a step up the ladder, to get a promotion **3** *Can* **g. (à mesurer)** tape measure, *Br* measuring tape

galonné [galɔne] NM *Fam Arg mil (officier)* officer■, *Br* brass hat; *(sous-officier)* NCO■; **les galonnés** the top brass

galonner [3] [galɔne] VT *Couture* to braid, to trim *(with braid)*; **col galonné de velours** velvet-trimmed collar

galonnier [galɔnje] NM *Couture* trimmer

galop [galo] NM **1** *Équitation* gallop; **prendre le g.** to break into a gallop; **petit g.** canter; **grand g.,** **triple g.** full gallop; **g. de manège** hand gallop; **g. d'essai** warm-up gallop; *Fig* dry run; *(examen blanc)* mock exam

  2 *(en danse)* galop

  3 *Méd* **bruit de g.** gallop *or* cantering rhythm

  ❑ **au galop** ADV at a gallop; **mettre sa monture au g.** to put one's horse into a gallop; **partir au (grand ou triple) g.** to gallop away; **il a descendu la colline au g.** he galloped down the hill; **va m'acheter le journal, et au g.!** go and buy me the newspaper, and be quick about it!; *Fig* **au triple g.** at top speed; **arriver au (grand ou triple) g.** to come like a shot

galopade [galɔpad] NF **1** *(course)* (mad) rush; **on est arrivés à l'heure, mais après quelle g.!** we got there on time, but it was a real scramble *or* dash! **2** *(bruit)* stampede **3** *Équitation* lope

galopant, -e [galɔpã, -ãt] ADJ *(consommation, inflation)* galloping; *(urbanisation)* uncontrolled, unplanned; **démographie galopante** rapid population growth; **le flot g. des vagues** the rushing waves

galope [galɔp] NF hatching iron

galoper [3] [galɔpe] VI **1** *Équitation* to gallop; **se mettre à g.** to break into a gallop; **il faudrait faire g. un peu la jument** the mare needs a good gallop

  2 *(aller trop vite → idées, images)* to race; *(→ enfants)* to charge; *(çà et là)* to gallop *or* rush around; **ne galopez pas dans les escaliers!** don't charge up and down the stairs!; *Fam* **g. après qn/qch** to chase (around) after sb/sth; *Fam* **j'ai galopé toute la matinée** I've been rushing about all morning

  VT *(cheval)* to gallop

galopeur [galɔpœr] NM *Équitation* galloper

galopin [galɔpɛ̃] NM *Fam* (street) urchin, scamp; **espèce de petit g.!** you little devil!, you little brat!

galoubet [galubɛ] NM *Mus* three-holed fipple flute

galuchat [galyʃa] NM *(gén)* shagreen; *(de requin)* sharkskin

---

galure [galyr], **galurin** [galyrɛ̃] NM *Fam* hat■

galvanique [galvanik] ADJ *Méd* galvanic; **courant g.** galvanic current **2** *Métal* electroplating *(avant n)*; **plaqué g.** electroplate; **dorure g.** electrogilding

galvanisation [galvanizasjɔ̃] NF **1** *Méd* galvanization **2** *Métal* galvanization

galvaniser [3] [galvanize] VT **1** *Méd* to galvanize **2** *Métal* to electroplate, to galvanize, to zinc-plate **3** *Fig (stimuler)* to galvanize *or* to spur into action; **g. les foules** to whip up *or* to provoke the crowds; **ça l'a galvanisé** *(après une catastrophe)* it galvanized *or* spurred him into action; *(après une bonne nouvelle)* it lifted his spirits

galvanisme [galvanism] NM *Méd* galvanism

galvano [galvano] NM *Fam Typ* electro

galvanocautère [galvanokotɛr] NM *Méd* galvanocautery

galvanomètre [galvanɔmɛtr] NM galvanometer

galvanoplastie [galvanɔplasti] NF electroplating, electrodeposition; *Typ* electrotyping

galvanoplastique [galvanɔplastik] ADJ electroplating *(avant n)*, *Spéc* galvanoplastic

galvanotropisme [galvanɔtrɔpism] NM *Biol* galvanotropism

galvanotype [galvanotip] NM *Typ* electrotype

galvanotypie [galvanotipi] NF *Typ* electrotyping

galvaudage [galvodaʒ] NM *(de dons, de qualités)* prostituting

galvaudé, -e [galvode] ADJ *(mot)* hackneyed, commonplace, clichéd; *(plaisanterie)* corny

galvauder [3] [galvode] VT **1** *(réputation, nom)* to sully, to tarnish

  2 *(don, qualité)* to prostitute; **un vrai musicien ne galvaude pas son talent pour de l'argent** a true musician won't prostitute his talent for the sake of money

  3 *(mot, sens)* to debase; **le mot a été galvaudé** the word has become clichéd *or* hackneyed through overuse

  VI *Vieilli ou Can (ne rien faire)* to idle (about)

  ▸**se galvauder** VPR to demean *or* to lower oneself

gamay [gamɛ] NM *(cépage)* Gamay (grape); *(vin)* Gamay (wine)

gamba [gãba, gãmba, *pl* gãbas, gãmbas] NF = type of large Mediterranean prawn

gambade [gãbad] NF *(cabriole)* leap, caper; **faire des gambades** *(chien)* to frisk about; *(enfant)* to skip about

gambader [3] [gãbade] VI to gambol, to leap *or* to caper about; **les enfants gambadaient de joie autour de l'arbre de Noël** the children were gleefully capering around the Christmas tree

gambe [gãb] *voir* **viole**

gamberge [gãbɛrʒ] NF *Fam* **il est en pleine g.** *(il combine quelque chose)* he's plotting something; *(il rêvasse)* he's daydreaming■

gamberger [17] [gãbɛrʒe] *Fam* VI *(penser)* to think hard■; **j'ai gambergé** *(j'ai réfléchi)* I've been mulling things over■; *(je me suis inquiété)* I've been brooding■; **ça m'a fait g., cette histoire** that business really made me think■

  VT *(combiner)* **je me demande ce qu'il gamberge** I wonder what he's up to; **ne t'en fais pas, j'ai tout bien gambergé** don't worry, I've got it all figured out *or* sewn up; **c'est lui qui a gambergé le coup de la banque** he's the one who masterminded the bank job

gambette[1] [gãbɛt] NM *(oiseau)* redshank

gambette[2] [gãbɛt] NF *Fam (jambe)* leg■, *Br* pin, *Am* gam; **jouer ou tricoter des gambettes** to go off like a shot, to leg it

Gambie [gãbi] NF **1** *(pays)* **la G.** the Gambia; **vivre en G.** to live in the Gambia; **aller en G.** to go to the Gambia **2** *(fleuve)* **la G., le fleuve G.** the Gambia (River)

gambien, -enne [gãbjɛ̃, -ɛn] ADJ Gambian

  ❑ **Gambien, -enne** NM,F Gambian

gambiller [3] [gãbije] VI *Fam Vieilli* to jig about, to dance■

gambit [gãbi] NM *Échecs* gambit; **g. du roi/de la reine** king's/queen's gambit

gambusie [gãbyzi] NF *Ich* gambusia

gamelan [gamlã] NM *Mus* gamelan

gamelle [gamɛl] NF **1** *(récipient → d'un soldat)* mess tin; *(→ d'un ouvrier)* lunch *Br* box *or Am* pail; *(→ d'animal)* bowl; *Fam* **passe-moi ta g.** *(assiette)* give me your plate■

2 *Mil & Naut* mess; **la g. des officiers** the officers' mess
3 *Fam (projecteur)* spot, spotlight■
4 *Belg Fam (baderne)* (old) stick-in-the-mud
5 *très Fam (baiser)* French kiss; **rouler une g. à qn** to French-kiss sb, *Br* to snog sb
6 *très Fam (locutions)* **ramasser** *ou* **(se) prendre une g.** to fall flat on one's face, *Br* to come a cropper

gamète [gamɛt] **NM** *Biol* gamete
gamétique [gametik] **ADJ** *Biol* gametic
gamétocyte [gametɔsit] **NM** *Biol* gametocyte
gamétogenèse [gametɔʒənɛz] **NF** *Biol* gametogenesis
gamétophyte [gametɔfit] **NM** *Bot* gametophyte
gamin, -e [gamɛ̃, -in] **NM,F** *Fam* kid; **une gamine de dix ans** a girl of ten■
ADJ *(puéril)* childish■; *(espiègle)* childlike■, impish, playful■; **elle est encore gamine** she's still just a child■; **quand j'étais gamine** when I was a young girl *or* a child■
gaminer [3] [gamine] **VI** *Littéraire* to behave like a child
gaminerie [gaminri] **NF** *(acte)* childish *or* silly prank; *(comportement)* childishness *(UNCOUNT)*, infantile behaviour *(UNCOUNT)*; **ses gamineries m'exaspéraient** his/her childish ways were driving me mad; **ce ne sont que des gamineries** this is just childish, this is all very infantile; **il a passé l'âge de ces gamineries** he's too old to behave so childishly *or* in such a childish way
gamique [gamik] **NF** *Can Joual (combine)* game; *Fig* **connaître la g.** to know the score
gamma [gama] **NM INV** gamma
gammaglobuline [gamaglɔbylin] **NF** *Biol* gamma globulin
gammagraphie [gamagrafi] **NF** *Tech* gammaradiography
gamma-hydroxybutyrate [gamaidrɔksibytirat] **NM** *Chim* gamma hydroxybutyrate
gammare [gamar] **NM** *Zool* freshwater shrimp
gammathérapie [gamaterapi] **NF** *Méd* gamma-ray therapy
gamme [gam] **NF 1** *Mus* scale, *Spéc* gamut; **gammes chromatiques** chromatic scales; **g. montante/descendante** rising/falling scale; **faire des gammes** to do *or* practise scales; **faire ses gammes** to play one's scales; *Fig* to go through the basics, to learn the ropes
2 *(de produits)* range, series; *(de prix, de couleurs)* range; *(de sentiments)* gamut; **étendre sa g. de produits** to widen one's product range; **une nouvelle g. de produits de beauté** a new range of beauty products; **une g. de beiges, du plus clair au plus foncé** all shades of beige, from the lightest to the darkest; **le film joue sur toute la g. des sentiments humains** the film runs the (whole) gamut of human feelings; **g. de prix** price range
3 *Com* **bas de g.** *(de qualité inférieure)* bottom-of-the-range; *(peu prestigieux)* downmarket; **haut de g.** *(de qualité supérieure)* top-of-the-range; *(prestigieux)* upmarket; **un téléviseur haut de g.** an upmarket *or* a top-of-the-range TV; **milieu de g.** middle-of-the-range; **un ordinateur d'entrée de g.** an entry-level computer
4 *Aut* **g. moyenne** mid-range; *Aut* **g. de transmission** driving range
gammée [game] *voir* **croix**
gamopétale [gamɔpetal] *Bot* **ADJ** gamopetalous
▫ **gamopétales NFPL** Gamopetalae
gamosépale [gamɔsepal] **ADJ** *Bot* gamosepalous
gan [gan] **NM** *(dialecte)* Gan, Kan
ganache [ganaʃ] **NF 1** *Péj* **une (vieille) g.** an old codger **2** *(du cheval)* lower jaw, cheek **3** *Culin* ganache, = cake filling made from chocolate, butter and cream
ganaderia [ganaderija] **NF** (cattle) ranch
Gand [gɑ̃] **NM** Ghent
gandin [gɑ̃dɛ̃] **NM** *(dandy)* dandy, fop
gandoura [gɑ̃dura] **NF** gandoura
gang[1] [gɑ̃g] **NM** *(bande)* gang; **guerre des gangs** gang warfare
gang[2] [gaŋ] **NF** *Can Joual (bande)* band■, group■; **une g. de bandits** a gang
ganga [gɑ̃ga] **NM** *Orn* sand grouse
Gange [gɑ̃ʒ] **NM le G.** the (River) Ganges
gangétique [gɑ̃ʒetik] **ADJ** Gangetic
ganglion [gɑ̃glijɔ̃] **NM** *Méd* ganglion; **g. lymphatique** lymph gland; **g. nerveux** ganglion cell; *Fam* **avoir des ganglions** to have swollen glands
ganglionnaire [gɑ̃glijɔnɛr] **ADJ** *Méd* ganglionic, ganglial; **neurone g.** ganglioneuron
ganglioplégique [gɑ̃glijɔpleʒik] *Méd* **ADJ** ganglioplegic
NM ganglion-blocking agent
gangrené, -e [gɑ̃grəne] **ADJ 1** *Méd* gangrenous, gangrened **2** *Fig* corrupt
gangrène [gɑ̃grɛn] **NF 1** *Méd* gangrene; **g. sèche/humide/gazeuse** dry/moist/gas gangrene; **avoir la g.** to have gangrene **2** *Fig (corruption)* scourge, canker; **la g. du terrorisme** the scourge of terrorism
gangrener [19] [gɑ̃grəne] **VT 1** *Méd* to cause to become gangrenous, to gangrene **2** *Fig (corrompre)* to corrupt, to rot
▸**se gangrener VPR 1** *Méd* to become gangrenous; **la jambe risque de se g.** the leg may become gangrenous *or* may get gangrene **2** *Fig* to become corrupt
gangreneux, -euse [gɑ̃grənø, -øz] **ADJ** *Méd* gangrenous
gangster [gɑ̃gstɛr] **NM 1** *(bandit)* gangster; **un film de gangsters** a gangster movie *or Br* film **2** *(escroc)* cheat, swindler
gangstérisme [gɑ̃gsterism] **NM** gangsterism
gangue [gɑ̃g] **NF 1** *Mines (d'une pierre précieuse, d'un minerai)* gangue **2** *(couche)* coating; **recouvert d'une g. de glace** coated with ice **3** *Fig* **ils sont enfermés dans une g. de préjugés** they are hidebound with prejudice; **il n'a jamais pu sortir de la g. de son éducation/de la religion** he was never able to free himself from the straitjacket of his education/of religion
ganoïde [ganɔid] *Ich* **ADJ** ganoid
NM ganoid, *Spéc* member of the Ganoidei
▫ **ganoïdes NMPL** *Vieilli* ganoids, *Spéc* Ganoidei
ganse [gɑ̃s] **NF 1** *Couture* braid *or* twine binding **2** *Can (passant)* belt loop; *Fig* **tenir qn par la g.** to have a hold on sb
gansé, -e [gɑ̃se] **ADJ** *(vêtement)* braided
ganser [3] [gɑ̃se] **VT** *(robe, tissu)* to braid, to trim; *(chapeau)* to trim; **des canotiers gansés de velours** velvet-trimmed boaters; **g. une couture** to pipe a seam
gansette [gɑ̃sɛt] **NF** *Tex* mesh
gant [gɑ̃] **NM** *(accessoire)* glove; **mettre ses gants** to put one's gloves on; **g. de boxe** boxing glove; **g. de crin** massage glove; **g. d'escrime** fencing glove; **g. de fauconnier** falconer's gauntlet; **g. de motard** motorcycle glove; **g. de Neptune** glove sponge; **g. de toilette** *Br* flannel, facecloth, *Am* washcloth; **gants de ménage** rubber gloves, *Br* washing-up gloves; **ça te va comme un g.** it fits you like a glove; *Fig* **se donner les gants de qch** to claim credit for sth; *Fig* **mettre** *ou* **prendre des gants avec qn** to handle sb with kid gloves; **tu as intérêt à prendre** *ou* **mettre des gants pour le lui dire** you'd do well to tell him/her gently; *Fig* **jeter le g. (à qn)** to throw down the gauntlet (to sb); *Fig* **relever** *ou* **ramasser le g.** to take up the gauntlet, to accept the challenge
ganté, -e [gɑ̃te] **ADJ** *(personne)* wearing gloves; *(main)* gloved
gantelée [gɑ̃tle] **NF** *Bot* **1** *(digitale pourprée)* foxglove **2** *(campanule)* throatwort, nettle-leaved bell-flower
gantelet [gɑ̃tlɛ] **NM 1** *Hist & Sport* gauntlet **2** *Ind* gauntlet, hand leather
ganteline [gɑ̃tlin] **NF** *Bot* rose-tipped clavaria, red-tipped coral fungus
ganter [3] [gɑ̃te] *Littéraire* **VT** to glove; **ses mains étaient gantées de dentelle noire** her hands were gloved in black lace, she was wearing black lace gloves
VI vous gantez du combien? what size gloves do you take?
▸**se ganter VPR** *(mettre ses gants)* to put on *or* to slip on one's gloves
ganterie [gɑ̃tri] **NF 1** *(industrie)* glove-making industry; *(fabrique)* glove factory **2** *(négoce)* **la g.** the glove trade **3** *(boutique)* glove *Br* shop *or Am* store, glover's; *(rayon)* glove counter *or* department
gantier, -ère [gɑ̃tje, -ɛr] **NM,F** glover
gantois, -e [gɑ̃twa, -az] **ADJ** of/from Ghent
▫ **Gantois, -e NM,F** = inhabitant of or person from Ghent
Ganymède [ganimɛd] **NPR** *Myth* Ganymede
GAO [ʒeao] **NF** *(abrév* **gestion assistée par ordinateur**) CAM, computer-aided management
gaperon [gapərɔ̃] **NM** = garlic-flavoured cow's milk cheese from the Auvergne
gâpette [gapɛt] **NF** *Fam* cap■
garage [garaʒ] **NM 1** *(de voitures)* garage; *(de bateaux)* boathouse; *(de vélos)* shed; *(d'avions)* shed, hangar; *(de bus)* garage, depot; **la voiture est au g.** the car is in the garage; **j'ai mis la voiture au g.** I've put the car in the garage **2** *(atelier) Br* garage, *Am* car repair shop; **ma voiture est au g.** my car is at the garage **3** *Rail* siding; **g. de machines** engine shed
garagiste [garaʒist] **NMF** *(propriétaire)* garage owner; *(gérant)* garage manager; *(mécanicien)* (garage) mechanic; *Fam* **j'emmène la voiture chez le g.** I'm taking the car to the garage
garamond [garamɔ̃] **NM** *Typ* Garamond
garançage [garɑ̃saʒ] **NM** madder dyeing, dyeing with madder
garance [garɑ̃s] **NF 1** *Bot* madder; **g. voyageuse** wild madder **2** *(teinture)* madder (dye)
ADJ INV *(rouge)* ruby red; **les uniformes** *ou* **pantalons g.** French uniforms *(in use until the 1914–18 war)*
garancer [16] [garɑ̃se] **VT** to madder, to dye with madder
garant, -e [garɑ̃, -ɑ̃t] **ADJ 1** *Jur* **être g. d'une dette** to stand guarantor *or* surety for a debt
2 *(responsable)* **être/se porter g. de qn** to vouch *or* to answer for sb; *(devant la justice)* to go bail for sb; *(à la banque)* to stand guarantor for sb; **elle viendra, je m'en porte g.** she'll come, I can vouch for that; **les pays garants d'un traité** countries acting as guarantors of a treaty; **désormais, vous serez g. de ses faits et gestes** from now on, you'll be answerable *or* responsible for his/her conduct
NM,F 1 *(personne)* **tu es la garante de notre réussite** thanks to you, we are assured of success
2 *(responsable)* guarantor; **les membres du GATT sont les garants de la liberté des échanges** the members of GATT are the guarantors of free trade
NM 1 *Jur (personne)* guarantor; *(somme, bien, document)* surety, security; **être le g. de qn** to stand surety for sb; **g. solidaire** joint and several guarantor
2 *(garantie)* guarantee, warranty; **la réputation d'un commerçant est le meilleur g. de son honnêteté** a tradesman's reputation is the best guarantee of his honesty
3 *Naut* (tackle) fall
garanti [garɑ̃ti] **NM** *Jur* guarantee
garantie [garɑ̃ti] **NF 1** *Com (assurance)* guarantee, warranty (**contre** against); **j'ai acheté une voiture d'occasion avec six mois de g.** I've bought a second-hand car with a six-month guarantee *or* warranty; **prendre des garanties contre le vol/les risques d'incendie** to take precautions against theft/fire risk; **contrat de g.** guarantee; **rupture de g.** breach of warranty; **lettre de g. d'indemnité** letter of indemnity; **g. accessoire** collateral security; **g. de bonne exécution** *ou* **de bonne fin** performance bond; **g. contractuelle** contractual guarantee; **g. conventionnelle** contractual cover; **g. de crédit acheteur** buyer credit guarantee; **g. de crédit à l'exportation** export credit guarantee; **g. décennale** = ten-year guarantee on newly built property; **g. illimitée** unlimited warranty; **g. légale** legal guarantee; **g. limitée** limited warranty; **g. de parfait achèvement** = one-year guarantee on new property by which the builder must carry out repairs due to construction faults; **g. pièces et main-d'œuvre** parts and labour warranty; **g. prolongée** extended warranty; **g. de remboursement** money-back guarantee; **g. retour atelier** return-to-base warranty *or* guarantee; **g. sur site** on-site warranty *or* guarantee; **g. totale** full warranty; **g. des vices** guarantee against hidden defects *or* faults
2 *Jur (obligation)* guarantee; **g. bancaire** bank guarantee; *Bourse* **g. de cours** hedging; **g.**

d'exécution contract bond; **g. de paiement** guarantee of payment

3 *(gage)* guarantee; **demander des garanties à qn** to ask sb for guarantees; **il me faut des garanties sérieuses** I need some reliable guarantees; **c'est sans g.!** I'm not promising *or* guaranteeing anything!; **elle m'a donné toutes les garanties que…** she gave me every guarantee that…; **fonds déposés** *ou* **détenus en g.** funds lodged *or* held as security

4 *Pol* **g. individuelle, garanties individuelles** guarantee of individual liberties

❑ **sous garantie** ADJ under guarantee; **un appareil sous g.** an appliance under guarantee

garantique [garɑ̃tik] NF *(technique)* computer security technology; *(théorie)* data protection

garantir [32] [garɑ̃tir] VT 1 *(veiller sur)* to guarantee, to safeguard; **la Constitution garantit les libertés civiques** the Constitution guarantees *or* safeguards civil liberties

2 *(assurer → produit, service)* to guarantee; **cet appareil est garanti deux ans** this appliance is guaranteed for two years *or* has a two-year guarantee; **l'antiquaire me l'a garanti d'époque** the antique dealer assured me *or* guaranteed me it's a period piece; **le pull est garanti 100 pour cent coton** the sweater is guaranteed 100 percent cotton; **nous garantissons un délai de livraison d'une semaine** we guarantee delivery within seven days

3 *(promettre)* to guarantee, to assure; **suis mes conseils et je te garantis le succès** take my advice and I guarantee you'll succeed *or* I guarantee you success; **il m'a garanti que ça serait livré demain, il m'a garanti la livraison pour demain** he assured me that it would be delivered tomorrow, he guaranteed delivery for tomorrow; **je ne te garantis pas le soleil** I can't guarantee *or* promise you any sun; **je te garantis que tu le regretteras!** I can assure you you'll regret it!; **je te garantis que je l'ai aperçu dans la foule** I can vouch for the fact that I spotted him in the crowd; **je peux te g. qu'il ne reviendra pas** I can guarantee you he won't come back, he won't come back, I warrant you; **elle m'a garanti qu'elle serait à l'heure** she gave me a guarantee that she'd be on time; **je te le garantis** I can vouch for it

4 *(protéger)* **g. qn de qch** to protect sb from sth; **ce double vitrage va vous g. du froid** this double-glazing will protect *or* shield you from the cold

5 *Jur* **g. qn contre qch** to cover sb against sth; **mon assurance me garantit contre l'incendie** my insurance covers me against fire, I'm covered against fire

6 *Fin (paiement, dette)* to guarantee; *(emprunt)* to guarantee, to secure; *(créance)* to secure; *(émission d'actions)* to underwrite

7 *Assur* to cover; **son assurance le garantit contre le vol** his insurance covers him against theft

▸**se garantir** VPR **se g. contre le froid/le vent** to protect oneself from the cold/the wind

garbure [garbyr] NF *Culin* = Béarnaise vegetable broth with goose

garce [gars] NF *très Fam* 1 *Péj* bitch, *Br* cow; **sale g.!** you rotten bitch!; **j'en ai marre de cette g. de vie!** I'm fed up with this shitty life! 2 *Vieilli (prostituée)* whore, hooker

garcette [garsɛt] NF *Naut* gasket

garçon [garsɔ̃] NM 1 *(enfant)* boy; **école de/vestiaire des garçons** boys' school/cloakroom; **nous avons un g. et une fille** we've got a boy and a girl; **un grand g. comme toi, ça ne pleure pas** big boys like you don't cry; **tu es un grand g. maintenant** you're a big boy now; **petit g.** little boy; **se sentir un petit g. à côté de qn** to feel like a child beside sb, to feel dwarfed by sb; **g. manqué** tomboy

2 *(homme)* boy, young man; **elle sort trop avec les garçons** she goes out too much with boys; **c'est un g. qui connaît très bien l'entreprise** that chap knows the company very well; **g. d'honneur** best man; **il est plutôt beau** *ou* **joli g.** he's quite good-looking; **c'est un bon** *ou* **brave g.** he's a good sort; **c'est un mauvais g.** he's bad news, *Br* he's a bad lot

3 *(fils)* boy, son

4 *(célibataire)* bachelor

5 *(employé)* **g. d'ascenseur** *Br* liftboy, lift attendant, *Am* elevator operator; **g. boucher** butcher's boy *or* assistant; **g. de bureau** office boy; *Naut* **g. de cabine** (cabin) steward; **g. coiffeur** *Br* junior *(in a hairdressing salon)*, *Am* hairdresser's assistant; **g. de courses** errand boy; **g. d'écurie** stableboy; **g. d'étage** floor waiter; **g. de ferme** farm hand; *Naut* **g. de pont** deck steward; **g. de recette** bank messenger

6 *(serveur)* waiter; **g. (de café** *ou* **de salle)** waiter; **g., une bière, s'il vous plaît!** waiter, one beer please!

7 *Fam (en appellatif)* **attention, mon g.!** watch it, sonny!

ADJ M 1 *(célibataire)* unmarried; **il est resté g.** he remained unmarried *or* single *or* a bachelor

2 *(qui a une apparence masculine)* boyish; **ça fait très g., cette coiffure** that haircut looks very boyish

garçonne [garsɔn] NF *Hist* **les garçonnes des années vingt** the flappers

❑ **à la garçonne** ADV **coiffée à la g.** with an Eton crop; **habillée à la g.** dressed like a (twenties) flapper

garçonnet [garsɔnɛ] NM 1 *(petit garçon)* (little) boy 2 *(comme adj)* **rayon g.** boyswear (department); **taille g.** boy's size

garçonnier, -ère [garsɔnje, -ɛr] ADJ boyish; **des manières garçonnières** boyish ways

❑ **garçonnière** NF bachelor pad

Gard [gar] NM **le G.** Gard

Garde [gard] *voir* **lac**

GARDE¹ [gard]

guarding **A1** ■ care **A2** ■ duty **A3** ■ custody **A4** ■ guard **B, C** ■ hilt **D**

NF **A.** 1 *(surveillance → d'un bien, d'un lieu)* guarding; **je te confie la g. du manuscrit** I am entrusting you with the manuscript, I am leaving the manuscript in your safekeeping *or* care; **assurer la g. d'un immeuble** *(police)* to guard a building; *(concierge)* to look after a building, to be caretaker of a building; **ils dressent des chiens pour la g.** they train guard dogs; **on te prête la maison pour le week-end, mais fais bonne g.** we'll let you use our house for the weekend, but look after it carefully; **affecté à la g. du palais présidentiel** on guard duty at the presidential palace; **monter la g.** to stand guard

2 *(protection → d'un enfant, d'un animal)* care; **je confierai la g. des enfants à ma tante** I will leave the children in the care of my aunt; **puis-je te confier la g. de mon chien pendant deux jours?** would you take care of *or* look after my dog for two days?

3 *Méd (service de surveillance)* **interne qui fait des gardes** *Br* locum, locum tenens, *Am* intern on duty; **g. de nuit** night duty

4 *Jur* custody; **la g. des enfants fut confiée à la mère** the mother was given custody of the children, the children were left in the custody of their mother; **g. à vue** police custody; **placé en g. à vue** put into police custody; **droit de g.** (right of) custody; **g. alternée** *(d'enfant)* alternating custody

B. *Sport* guard; **tenir la g. haute** to keep one's guard up; **fermer/ouvrir sa g.** to close/to open one's guard; **baisser sa g.** to drop one's guard; **ne pas baisser sa g. (devant qn)** to remain on one's guard (with sb)

C. 1 *(escorte, milice)* guard; **g. (d'honneur)** guard of honour; **g. mobile** (State) security police; **la G. républicaine** the Republican Guard *(on duty at French state occasions)*; *Hist* **G. nationale** national guard *(civil militia, 1789–1871)*; **la vieille g.** the old guard *(of a political party)*

2 *(soldats en faction)* guard; **g. montante/descendante** relief/old guard

D. *(d'une arme blanche)* hilt; *Fig* **jusqu'à la g.** up to the hilt; **il s'est enferré dans ses mensonges jusqu'à la g.** he got completely tangled up in his own lies

E. *(locutions) Arch & Littéraire* **n'avoir g. de faire qch** to take good care not to do sth; **je n'aurai g. de vous contredire** I'll take good care not to contradict you; **prends g.!** watch out!; **prenez g. à la marche** *Br* mind *or Am* watch the step; **prenez g. de ne rien oublier** make sure *or* take care you don't leave anything behind; **je prendrai g. à ce qu'il ne parle pas** I shall ensure *or* make sure he doesn't talk; **prends g. qu'on ne te voie pas** make sure nobody sees you

❑ **gardes** NFPL guard *(civil militia, 1789–1871)*; **être/se tenir sur ses gardes** to be/to stay on one's guard

❑ **de garde** ADJ 1 *voir* **chien**

2 *(qui se conserve)* **fromage de (bonne) g.** cheese that keeps well; **vin de g.** wine for keeping *or* laying down

3 *Méd* duty *(avant n)*; **médecin de g.** duty doctor, doctor on duty; **elle est de g. trois nuits par semaine** she's on duty three nights a week; **je suis de g. demain soir** I'm on night duty tomorrow

❑ **en garde** ADV 1 *Mil & Sport* **en g.!** on (your) guard!; **mettez-vous en g.** take your guard

2 *(sous surveillance)* **ils prennent des animaux en g. l'été** they board pets during the summer

3 *Jur Br* in care, *Am* in custody; **le juge a placé les enfants en g.** the judge made the children wards of court, *Br* the judge had the children put into care

4 *(locution)* **mettre qn en g.** to warn sb; **je l'avais mise en g. contre les dangers du tabac** I had warned her against the dangers of smoking

❑ **sous bonne garde** ADV **le stade est sous bonne g.** the stadium is under (heavy) guard; **ton argent est sous bonne g.** your money is in safe hands

garde² [gard] NMF 1 *(personne)* **une g. d'enfants** a baby-sitter; **la g. des enfants est une jeune Allemande** the baby-sitter *or Br* childminder is a young German girl

2 **g. des Sceaux** (French) Minister of Justice, *Br* ≃ Lord Chancellor, *Am* ≃ Attorney General

NM 1 *(surveillant)* warden; **g. champêtre** = council employee with various minor duties including, traditionally, informing townspeople of news and events; **g. du corps** bodyguard; **g. forestier** *Br* forest warden, *Am* forest ranger; **g. maritime** coastguard; **g. mobile** member of the (State) security police; **g. de nuit** *(pour un malade)* night nurse *(privately employed)*; *Mil* night watchman; **g. républicain** Republican guardsman *(on duty at French state occasions)*

2 *(soldat → en faction)* guard; *(→ en service d'honneur)* guardsman; *Hist* **g. rouge** Red Guard

NF *Méd* nurse

garde-à-vous [gardavu] NM INV *Mil* (position of) attention; **des soldats au g.** soldiers standing at *or* to attention; **g., fixe!** attention!, 'shun!; **se mettre au g.** to stand to attention

garde-barrière [gardəbarjɛr] *(pl* **gardes-barrière** *ou* **gardes-barrières)** NMF *Br* level-crossing keeper, *Am* grade-crossing keeper

NF *Ordinat* firewall

garde-bœuf [gardəbœf] *(pl* **inv** *ou* **garde-bœufs** [-bø]) NM *Orn* cattle egret

garde-boue [gardəbu] NM INV mudguard

garde-cendre(s) [gardəsɑ̃dr] *(pl* **garde-cendres)** NM *(devant un foyer)* fender

garde-chasse [gardəʃas] *(pl* **gardes-chasse** *ou* **gardes-chasses)** NM gamekeeper

garde-chiourme [gardəʃjurm] *(pl* **gardes-chiourme** *ou* **gardes-chiourmes)** NM 1 *Hist* warder *(in charge of a gang of convicts)* 2 *Péj (surveillant brutal)* martinet, disciplinarian

garde-corps [gardəkɔr] NM INV 1 *(balustrade)* railing, handrail; *(parapet)* parapet 2 *Naut (le long d'une vergue)* lifeline; *(sur le pont)* manrope; **g. arrière** stern rail

garde-côte¹ [gardəkot] *(pl* **garde-côtes)** NM *(bateau)* coastguard vessel

garde-côte² [gardəkot] *(pl* **gardes-côtes)** NM *Vieilli (soldat)* coastguard

garde-feu [gardəfø] *(pl* **inv** *ou* **garde-feux)** NM 1 *(grille)* fireguard, firescreen 2 *Can (personne)* fire ranger

garde-fou [gardəfu] *(pl* **garde-fous)** NM 1 *(barrière)* railing, guardrail; *(talus)* (raised) bank; *(mur)* parapet, balustrade 2 *Fig (défense)* **servir de g. (contre)** to safeguard (against)

garde-française [gardəfrɑ̃sɛz] *(pl* **gardes-françaises)** NM *Hist* = soldier of the "gardes

françaises" (infantry regiment of the King's household, disbanded in 1789)

garde-frontière, garde-frontières [gardəfrɔ̃tjɛr] (*pl* **gardes-frontières**) **NM** border guard

garde-magasin [gardmagazɛ̃] (*pl* **gardes-magasin** *ou* **gardes-magasins**) **NM** warehouseman; *Mil* storekeeper, quartermaster

garde-malade [gardəmalad] (*pl* **gardes-malade** *ou* **gardes-malades**) **NMF** nurse

garde-manger [gardəmɑ̃ʒe] **NM INV** *(placard)* food *or* meat safe; *(réserve)* pantry, larder

garde-meuble, garde-meubles [gardəmœbl] (*pl* **garde-meubles**) **NM** storehouse *or Br* furniture depository; **mettre qch au g.** to put sth in storage

garde-mite, garde-mites [gardəmit] (*pl* **gardes-mites**) **NM** *Fam Mil* warehouseman▪, storekeeper▪, quartermaster▪

Gardénal® [gardenal] **NM** *Pharm Br* phenobarbitone, *Am* phenobarbital

gardénia [gardenja] **NM** *Bot* gardenia

garden-party [gardɛnparti] (*pl* **garden-partys** *ou* **garden-parties**) **NF** garden party

garde-pêche [gardəpɛʃ] **NM** (*pl* **gardes-pêche**) *(personne) Br* water bailiff, *Am* fish warden

NM INV *(bateau → en mer)* fisheries protection vessel; *(→ sur rivière) Br* bailiff's boat, *Am* fish warden's boat

garde-place [gardəplas] (*pl* **garde-places**) **NM** *Rail* reservation holder; *(ticket)* reservation ticket

garde-port [gardəpɔr] (*pl* **gardes-port** *ou* **gardes-ports**) **NM** wharfmaster *(on river)*

GARDER [3] [garde]

> **VT** to look after **A1** ▪ to guard **A2** ▪ to save **A3, C5** ▪ to keep **C1, 2, 4–7, 9, 11** ▪ to keep on **C3**
> **VPR** to keep **1** ▪ to be careful not to **3** ▪ to beware of **4**

VT A. 1 *(veiller sur → personne, animal)* to look after; *(→ boutique)* to keep an eye on, to mind; **il a fallu trouver quelqu'un pour g. le bébé** we had to find someone to look after the baby; **elle garde des enfants** she does some baby-sitting *or Br* childminding; **les moutons sont gardés par des chiens** the sheep are guarded by dogs; **pourriez-vous g. mes affaires un instant?** would you mind keeping an eye on my things for a minute?; **elle m'a demandé de g. la boutique** she asked me to keep an eye on *or* to mind the shop for her; **il doit faire g. les enfants le soir** he has to get somebody to look after the children in the evening; *Fam* **on n'a pas gardé les cochons ensemble!** don't be so familiar!

2 *(surveiller → personne, lieu)* to guard; **le stade était gardé par des hommes en armes** the stadium was guarded by armed men; **un cyprès garde l'entrée du cimetière** a cypress stands guard at the entrance to the cemetery

3 *Littéraire (prémunir)* **g. qn de qch** to protect *or* to save sb from sth; **cette sage parole m'a gardé de bien des erreurs** this sound advice has kept *or* saved me from many a mistake

4 *Jur* **g. qn à vue** to keep *or* to hold sb in custody

B. 1 *(sujet: malade)* **g. le lit** to be confined to bed, to be laid up; **elle garde la chambre** she is confined to her room *or* staying in her room

2 *Mil* **g. les arrêts** to remain under arrest

C. 1 *(conserver → aliment)* to keep; **on peut g. ce gâteau plusieurs mois** you can keep this cake *or* this cake will keep for several months; **g. à l'abri de la chaleur et de la lumière** *(sur emballage)* store in a cool dark place

2 *(ne pas se dessaisir de)* to keep; **j'ai gardé toutes ses lettres** I kept all his/her letters; **garde-le, un jour il aura de la valeur** hold on to it, one day it will be valuable

3 *(conserver sur soi)* to keep on; **puis-je g. mon chapeau/manteau?** may I keep my hat/coat on?

4 *(conserver en dépôt)* to keep; **la voisine garde mon courrier pendant mon absence** my neighbour keeps my mail for me when I'm away

5 *(réserver)* to save, to keep; **je t'ai gardé du poulet** I've saved you some chicken, I've kept some chicken for you; **ne te fatigue pas trop, il faut g. des forces pour ce soir** don't overtire yourself, save some of your energy for tonight; **garde-moi une place pour le cas où j'arriverais en retard** keep a seat for me in case I'm late; **attends que je termine mon histoire, j'ai gardé le meilleur pour la fin** wait for me to finish my story, I've kept the best bit until last; *Fig* **g. une poire pour la soif** to keep something for a rainy day

6 *(retenir → personne)* to keep; **tu es pressé, je ne te garderai pas longtemps** as you're in a hurry, I won't keep you long; **g. qn à dîner** to have sb stay for dinner; **il a gardé sa secrétaire** he kept his secretary on; **il a gardé le même dentiste toute sa vie** he kept the same dentist all his life; **on les a gardés au commissariat** they were held at the police station; **va-t-elle g. le bébé?** is she going to keep the baby?

7 *(ne pas révéler)* to keep; **g. un secret** to keep a secret; **g. le secret sur qch** to keep sth secret; **tu ferais bien de g. ça pour toi** you'd better keep that to yourself

8 *(avoir à l'esprit)* **elle garde de son enfance une image heureuse** she has happy memories of her childhood; **je n'ai pas gardé de très bons souvenirs de cette époque** my memories of that time are not very happy ones; **g. qch présent à l'esprit** to bear *or* to keep sth in mind

9 *(maintenir → attitude, sentiment)* to keep; **g. l'anonymat** to remain anonymous; **g. son calme** to keep calm *or* cool; **g. son sérieux** to keep a straight face; **g. le silence** to keep silent; **g. rancune à qn de qch** to bear *or* to harbour a grudge against sb for sth; **g. la tête froide** to keep one's head *or* a cool head; **g. les yeux baissés** to keep one's eyes lowered

10 *(observer, respecter → règle, loi)* **g. le jeûne** to observe a fast; **g. ses distances** to keep one's distance

11 *(ne pas perdre → qualité)* to keep; **le mot garde encore toute sa valeur** the word still retains its full meaning

▶**se garder VPR 1** *(emploi passif) (aliment)* to keep; **les framboises ne se gardent pas (longtemps)** raspberries do not keep (long); **ça se garde une semaine au congélateur** it will keep for a week in the freezer; **des denrées qui se gardent six mois** foodstuffs with a shelf life of six months *or* that will keep for six months

2 *(emploi réfléchi)* **les enfants sont grands, ils se gardent tout seuls maintenant** the children are old enough to be left without a baby-sitter now

3 se g. de faire qch *(éviter de)* to be careful not to do sth; **je me garderai bien de lui en parler** I'll be very careful not to talk to him/her about it; **garde-toi bien de le vexer** be very careful not to offend him

4 se g. de *(se méfier de)* to beware of *or* be wary of; **il faut se g. des gens trop expansifs** one should beware *or* be wary of over-effusive people; **gardons-nous de nos tendances égoïstes** let us try to curb our selfish tendencies

garderie [gardəri] **NF 1** *(de quartier) Br* day nursery, *Am* day-care center; *(liée à une entreprise) Br* crèche, *Am* baby-sitting services; *(le soir, après l'école)* childminding service **2** *(étendue de bois)* (forest ranger's) beat

garde-rivière [gardərivjɛr] (*pl* **gardes-rivière** *ou* **gardes-rivières**) **NM** riverkeeper, river patrolman, *Br* waterways board official

garde-robe [gardərɔb] (*pl* **garde-robes**) **NF 1** *(vêtements)* wardrobe; **g. d'hiver** winter wardrobe; **il serait temps que je renouvelle ma g.** it's high time I bought myself some new clothes **2** *(penderie)* wardrobe

garde-temps [gardətɑ̃] **NM INV** chronometer, timing apparatus

gardeur, -euse [gardœr, -øz] **NM,F** *Littéraire (d'animaux)* keeper; **g. d'oies** gooseherd; **g. de vaches** cowherd; **g. de cochons** pig keeper, *Fam Vieilli* swineherd

garde-voie [gardəvwa] (*pl* **gardes-voie** *ou* **gardes-voies**) **NM** *Rail* track watchman, lineman, line guard

garde-vue [gardəvy] **NM INV** *Vieilli* eyeshade

gardian [gardjɑ̃] **NM** herdsman *(in the Camargue)*

gardien, -enne [gardjɛ̃, -ɛn] **NM,F 1** *(surveillant → d'une usine, d'une société)* (security) guard; *(→ d'un immeuble, d'un cimetière)* caretaker; *(→ d'un domaine)* warden; *(→ d'un zoo)* keeper; *(→ d'un musée, d'un parking)* attendant; **g. d'immeuble** *Br* caretaker, porter, *Am* janitor; **g. de musée** museum attendant; **g. de nuit** night watchman; **g. de parking** *Br* car park *or Am* parking lot attendant; **g. de phare** lighthouse keeper; **g. de prison** prison officer *or Br* warder, *Am* prison guard; **g. de square** park attendant

2 *Fig (protecteur)* guardian, custodian; **le g. de nos libertés/de la tradition/du patrimoine** the guardian of our freedom/of tradition/of our heritage; **se poser en g. de l'ordre** to set oneself up as a guardian *or* an upholder of public order

3 *Can* childminder

NM g. de but goalkeeper; **g. de la paix** = low-ranking police officer; *Fig* **g. du temple** *(défenseur)* gatekeeper

▫ **gardienne NF 1 gardienne d'enfants** nursery help *or Br* helper, *Am* day-care assistant

2 *Belg (école)* nursery school, kindergarten, *Br* infant school

gardiennage [gardjɛnaʒ] **NM** *(d'un bâtiment)* caretaking; **assurer le g. d'un entrepôt** to be in charge of security in a warehouse; **assurer le g. d'une résidence** *Br* to be the caretaker *or* porter in a block of flats, *Am* to be the doorman *or* janitor in an apartment block; **société de g.** security firm

gardiennat [gardjɛna] **NM** *Belg* childminding

gardienne [gardjɛn] *voir* **gardien**

gardon [gardɔ̃] **NM** *Ich* roach

gare[1] [gar] **NF 1** *Rail (installations et voies)* station; *(hall)* (station) concourse; *(bâtiments)* station building *or* buildings; **de quelle g. part le train pour Calais?** which station does the train to Calais leave from?; **entrer** *ou* **arriver en g.** *(d'un train)* to arrive in *or* come into the station; **le train de 14h 30 à destination de Paris va entrer en g. voie 10** the train now arriving at platform 10 is the two-thirty to Paris; **g. d'arrivée** *(pour passagers)* arrival station; *(pour marchandises)* receiving station; **g. de départ** *(pour passagers)* departure station; **g. expéditrice, g. d'expédition** forwarding station, dispatch station; **g. frontière** border station; **g. de marchandises** goods station; **g. maritime** harbour station; **g. de passage/transbordement** through/transshipment station; **g. de triage** *Br* marshalling yard, *Am* switchyard; **g. de voyageurs** passenger station; **romans de g.** cheap *or* trashy novels; **café/hôtel de la g.** station café/hotel

2 *(garage à bateaux)* (river) basin; *(d'un canal)* passing place; **g. fluviale** dock

3 *Transp* **g. routière** *(de poids lourds)* haulage depot; *(de cars)* bus station, *Br* coach station; **g. routière de marchandises** road haulage depot; **g. de péage** (motorway) toll station

gare[2] [gar] **EXCLAM** *Fam* **g. à toi!, g. à tes fesses!** you just watch it!; **si je te reprends à voler du gâteau, g. à tes fesses!** if I catch you stealing cake again, you've had it *or Br* you're for it!; **g. à vous si vous rentrez après minuit!** if you come home after midnight, there'll be trouble!, you'd better be in by midnight, or else!; **g. à toi si on l'apprend** woe betide you if anyone finds out; **g. à tes doigts avec ce couteau** watch your fingers with that knife; **g. dessous!** look out *or* watch out down below!

garenne [garɛn] **NF 1** *(lieu boisé)* (rabbit) warren

2 *(de pêche)* fishing preserve

NM *Zool* wild rabbit

garer [3] [gare] **VT 1** *(véhicule)* to park; **j'ai garé la voiture pas trop loin d'ici** I've parked the car not too far from here; **bien/mal garé** parked legally/illegally; **garé en double file** double-parked

2 *Transp (canot)* to dock, to berth; *(avion léger → dans un hangar)* to put away; *(→ sur la piste)* to park

3 *Rail* to shunt, to move into a siding, *Am* to switch

▶**se garer VPR 1** *(en voiture)* to park; **se g. facilement** to have no trouble parking; **trouver à se g.** to find a parking place *or* space; **tu trouveras à te g. dans le quartier** you'll find somewhere to park in the area; **j'ai eu de la peine à me g.** I had trouble parking

2 *Fam (s'écarter)* **gare-toi!** get out of the way!

gar–gar

3 se g. de *(éviter)* to steer clear of; **se g. d'un danger** to steer clear of a danger; **garez-vous de ces gens-là** give those people a wide berth, steer clear of those people

Gargantua [gargɑ̃tɥa] NPR = the giant in Rabelais' novel of the same name (1534)

'(La Vie inestimable du grand) Gargantua' *Rabelais* 'Gargantua and Pantagruel'

gargantua [gargɑ̃tɥa] NM **un (véritable) g.** a glutton

gargantuesque [gargɑ̃tɥɛsk] ADJ gargantuan

gargariser [3] [gargarize] **se gargariser** VPR **1** *(se rincer la gorge)* to gargle **2 se g. de** to delight in; **il se gargarise volontiers de mots à la mode/de noms célèbres** he delights in trotting out fashionable words/in dropping famous names

gargarisme [gargarism] NM *(rinçage)* gargling; *(produit)* mouthwash; **faire des gargarismes** to gargle

gargote [gargɔt] NF *Péj* cheap restaurant

gargotier, -ère [gargɔtje, -ɛr] NM,F *Péj* **1** *(propriétaire)* **demande au g.** ask the guy who runs this cheap joint **2** *(mauvais cuisinier)* bad cook

gargoton [gargɔtɔ̃] NM *Can* *(pomme d'Adam)* Adam's apple; *(gosier)* gullet; *Fig* **se mouiller le g.** to wet one's whistle

gargouillade [gargujad] NF *(en danse)* gargouillade

gargouille [garguj] NF **1** *(de gouttière)* waterspout **2** *Archit* gargoyle

gargouillement [gargujmɑ̃] NM **1** *(d'une fontaine)* gurgling *(UNCOUNT)* **2** *(de l'estomac)* rumbling *(UNCOUNT)*; **j'ai des gargouillements (dans le ventre)** my stomach's rumbling

gargouiller [3] [garguje] VI **1** *(liquide)* to gurgle **2** *(estomac)* to rumble

gargouillis [garguji] = **gargouillement**

gargoulette [gargulɛt] NF **1** *(cruche)* goglet **2** *très Fam Vieilli (gosier)* throat■, gullet, craw

gargousse [gargus] NF cartridge bag

gari [gari] NM *(en Afrique francophone)* manioc, gar(r)i

gariguette [garigɛt] NF gariguette, = French aromatic variety of strawberry

garnement [garnəmɑ̃] NM brat, rascal; **le vilain g., il s'est encore enfui** that little rascal has run away again

garni, -e [garni] ADJ **1** *Culin (plat du jour, viande)* with vegetables; **panier g.** food hamper, hamper of food

2 bien g. *(bourse)* well-lined; *(compte en banque)* healthy; *(magasin)* well-stocked; *(maison)* well-appointed; **il est bien g., ton frigo!** your fridge is very well stocked!

3 *Vieilli (chambre, logement, hôtel)* furnished

NM *Vieilli* furnished rooms *or* accommodation

Garnier [garnje] NM **le palais G.** = the old Paris Opera House

garniérite [garnjerit] NF *Minér* garnierite

garnir [32] [garnir] VT **1** *(décorer)* to trim (**de** with); **ils ont garni la table de fleurs et de bougies** they decorated the table with flowers and candles; **il faudrait quelques bibelots pour g. les étagères** the shelves would look much nicer with a few ornaments (on them); **l'arbre sera garni de cheveux d'anges** the tree will be hung *or* decorated with Christmas floss; **revers garnis de vison** mink-trimmed lapels; **une robe garnie de dentelle** a dress trimmed with lace, a lace-trimmed dress; **la passementerie qui garnit cette veste est très colorée** the braid trimming on that jacket is very colourful

2 *(remplir)* to fill (**de** with); *(cave)* to stock; **nous vendons la corbeille garnie de fruits** the basket is sold (complete) with an assortment of fruit; **la trousse de toilette est vendue entièrement garnie** the *Br* sponge bag *or Am* toilet case comes complete with toiletries

3 *(munir de ce qui protège, renforce etc)* to fit out (**de** with); **les semelles sont garnies de pointes d'acier** the soles are steel-tipped

4 *Aut & Rail (aménager → intérieur d'un véhicule)* to fit

5 *(de tissu → siège) (rembourrer)* to stuff; *(couvrir)* to cover, to upholster; *(→ vêtement, coffret, tiroir)* to line; **elle a garni la robe d'une doublure en satin** she lined the dress with satin; **je vais g. les tiroirs de papier de soie** I'll line the drawers with tissue paper; **garni de feutre** felt-lined

6 *Culin (plat)* to garnish; *(remplir)* to fill; **toutes nos viandes sont garnies de pommes sautées** all our meat dishes come with *or* are served with sautéed potatoes

7 *(remplir du nécessaire)* to fill (up); **g. la chaudière pour la nuit** to stoke *or* to fill (up) the boiler for the night

▸**se garnir** VPR **1** *(se remplir)* to fill up; **le théâtre se garnissait de personnalités connues** the theatre was filling up with celebrities

2 *(se couvrir)* **les murs du nouveau musée se garnissent peu à peu** the walls of the new museum are gradually becoming lined with exhibits

garnison [garnizɔ̃] NF garrison; **le régiment est en g. à Nancy** the regiment is garrisoned *or* stationed in Nancy

❑ **de garnison** ADJ garrison *(avant n)*

garnissage [garnisaʒ] NM **1** *(remplissage → d'un coussin, d'une couette)* stuffing; *(décoration → d'un manteau)* trimming; *(→ d'un chapeau)* trim **2** *Aut (intérieur d'un véhicule)* (interior) trim; **g. de plafond** headliner, headlining; **g. de siège** seat trim **3** *(matériau)* packing, stuffing; *Métal* **g. acide/basique** acid/basic lining **4** *Tech (d'un piston)* packing; *(d'une chaudière)* lining

garnissement [garnismɑ̃] NM *Jur (de lieux)* = obligation of a tenant to furnish a property

garniture [garnityr] NF **1** *(ensemble)* (matching) set; **une g. de boutons** a set of buttons; **g. de foyer** *ou* **de feu** set of fire irons; **une g. de bureau** a set of desk accessories; **g. de cheminée** (set of) mantelpiece ornaments; **une g. de lit** a matching set of sheets and pillowcases; **g. de toilette** toilet set

2 *(ornementation → d'un chapeau, d'une robe)* trimming, decoration; **avec une g. de dentelle** trimmed with lace; **la g. d'une automobile** the interior trim *or* the upholstery of a car

3 *(protection → de joint)* packing; *(→ de piston)* stuffing (piece); *(→ de chaudière)* lagging; *Typ* furniture; *Aut* **g. d'embrayage** clutch lining; *Aut* **g. de frein** brake lining; *(de disque de frein)* brake pad; **g. de porte** door liner

4 *Culin (d'un feuilleté)* filling; *(accompagnement → décoratif)* garnish; *(→ légumes)* vegetables; **pour la g., vous avez le choix entre des haricots verts ou des frites** to go with it, you have a choice of green beans or chips; **que servez-vous comme g. avec le poisson?** what does the fish come with?, what is the fish served with?; **c'est servi sans g.** it's served without vegetables *or* on its own; **tout changement de g. entraîne un supplément** *(sur la carte d'un restaurant)* there is an extra charge if you wish an alternative side order

❑ **garnitures** NFPL *(d'une serrure)* wards

garnotte [garnɔt] NF *Can Joual (gravier)* gravel■

garonnais, -e [garɔnɛ, -ɛz] ADJ of the Garonne basin

Garonne [garɔn] NF **la G.** the (River) Garonne

garou [garu] NM *Bot* spurge flax

garrigue [garig] NF scrubland, garigue; **ça sent bon la g.** it smells of Provence

garrochage [garɔʃaʒ] NM *Can* throwing; **pas de g.!** don't throw things!

garrocher [3] [garɔʃe] *Can* VT to throw

▸**se garrocher** VPR to rush, to hurry; **se g. sur qn** *(attaquer)* to throw oneself on sb

garrot[1] [garo] NM **1** *Méd* tourniquet; **mettre** *ou* **poser un g.** to apply a tourniquet **2** *Hist (supplice)* garrotte **3** *(de scie)* toggle

garrot[2] [garo] NM *Zool (d'animal)* withers; **mesurer 1,20 m au g.** to be 12 hands high

garrot[3] [garo] NM *Orn* **g. arlequin** harlequin duck; **g. à l'œil d'or** goldeneye

garrottage [garɔtaʒ] NM **1** *Méd (d'une blessure)* putting a tourniquet on **2** *(supplice)* garrotting

garrotte [garɔt] NF *Hist* gar(r)otte, gar(r)otting

garrotter [3] [garɔte] VT **1** *(attacher)* to tie up, to bind; *Méd* to put a tourniquet on **2** *Fig (priver de liberté)* to stifle, to muzzle; **tous les partis d'opposition ont été garrottés** the opposition parties have all been stifled *or* muzzled **3** *(supplicier)* to garrotte

gars [gɑ] NM *Fam* **1** *(garçon, fils)* boy■, *Br* lad; **qu'est-ce qui ne va pas, mon petit g.?** what's the matter, kid *or* sonny? **2** *(jeune homme)* boy■, guy, *Br* lad; **allons-y, les g.** let's go, boys; **c'est un g. bizarre** he's a weird guy *or Br* bloke; **salut, les g.** hi, guys!, *Br* hi, lads!

gas [gas] NM *Can Joual (essence) Br* petrol■, *Am* gas■

Gascogne [gaskɔɲ] NF **la G.** Gascony; **le golfe de G.** the Bay of Biscay

gascon, -onne [gaskɔ̃, -ɔn] ADJ Gascon

NM *(dialecte)* Gascon (dialect)

❑ **Gascon, -onne** NM,F Gascon; **une offre** *ou* **une promesse de G.** an empty promise

gasconnade [gaskɔnad] NF *Littéraire (vantardise)* **des gasconnades** bragging *(UNCOUNT)*; **raconter des gasconnades** to brag

gasconne [gaskɔn] *voir* **gascon**

gas-oil, gasoil [gazɔjl, gazwal] *(pl* **gas-oils**) = **gazole**

gaspacho [gaspatʃo] = **gazpacho**

Gaspar(d) [gaspar] NPR *Bible* Caspar

gaspard [gaspar] NM *Fam* rat■

gaspillage [gaspijaʒ] NM *(action → de nourriture, temps)* wasting; *(→ d'argent)* wasting, squandering; *(résultat)* waste; **un g. de temps et d'argent** a waste of time and money; **évitez le g. de nourriture/d'électricité** don't waste food/electricity; **j'ai horreur du g.** I hate waste, I hate wasting things; **c'est du g.** it's a waste, it's wasteful; **pas de g.!** don't be wasteful!

gaspiller [3] [gaspije] VT *(denrée, temps, talent, énergie)* to waste; *(économies)* to squander; **en une semaine, ils gaspillèrent les économies d'une année** they threw away *or* squandered a year's savings in one week; **il a gaspillé son talent** he has squandered his talent; **elle me fait g. mon temps et mon argent** she wastes both my time and my money; **arrête de me faire g. mon temps** stop wasting my time

gaspilleur, -euse [gaspijœr, -øz] ADJ wasteful; **il est incroyablement g.** he's unbelievably wasteful *or* extravagant

NM,F squanderer, spendthrift

gastérale [gasteral] *Bot* NF gasteromycete, *Spéc* member of the Gasteromyceteae

❑ **gastérales** NFPL gasteromycetes, *Spéc* Gasteromyceteae

gastéromycète [gasterɔmisɛt] NM = **gastérale**

gastéropode [gasterɔpɔd] *Zool* NM gastropod, gasteropod, *Spéc* member of the Gastropoda

❑ **gastéropodes** NMPL the snail family, *Spéc* Gastropoda

Gaston Lagaf' [gastɔ̃lagaf] NPR = clumsy youth in a cartoon strip of the same title

gastos [gastos] NM *Fam (bistrot)* bar■, *Br* boozer

gastralgie [gastralʒi] NF *Méd* stomach pains, *Spéc* gastralgia

gastralgique [gastralʒik] ADJ *Méd* gastralgic

gastrectomie [gastrɛktɔmi] NF *Méd* gastrectomy

gastrique [gastrik] ADJ gastric, stomach *(avant n)*; **embarras/lésion g.** stomach trouble/lesion

gastrite [gastrit] NF *Méd* gastritis

gastro-duodénal, -e [gastrɔdɥɔdenal, -o] *(mpl* **gastro-duodénaux**, *fpl* **gastro-duodénales**) ADJ *Anat* gastroduodenal; **ulcère g.** gastroduodenal ulcer

gastro-entérite [gastrɔɑ̃terit] *(pl* **gastro-entérites**) NF *Méd* gastroenteritis *(UNCOUNT)*

gastro-entérologie [gastrɔɑ̃terɔlɔʒi] NF *Méd* gastroenterology

gastro-entérologue [gastroɑ̃terɔlɔg] *(pl* **gastro-entérologues**) NMF *Méd* gastroenterologist

gastrofibroscopie [gastrɔfibrɔskɔpi] NF *Méd* gastric endoscopy

gastro-hépatite [gastrɔepatit] *(pl* **gastro-hépatites**) NF *Méd* gastrohepatitis *(UNCOUNT)*

gastro-intestinal, -e [gastrɔɛ̃tɛstinal, -o] *(mpl* **gastro-intestinaux**, *fpl* **gastro-intestinales**) ADJ *Anat* gastrointestinal

gastromycète [gastrɔmisɛt] = **gastéromycète**

gastronome [gastrɔnɔm] NMF gastronome, gourmet

gastronomie [gastrɔnɔmi] NF gastronomy; **ça ne va pas être de la haute g., je fais un poulet rôti** don't expect anything fancy, I'm only doing roast chicken

gastronomique [gastrɔnɔmik] ADJ gastronomic, gastronomical; **buffet g.** gourmet buffet

gastroparésie [gastrɔparezi] NF *Med* gastroparesis
gastropode [gastrɔpɔd] = **gastéropode**
gastroscope [gastrɔskɔp] NM *Méd* gastroscope
gastroscopie [gastrɔskɔpi] NF *Méd* gastroscopy
gastrotomie [gastrɔtɔmi] NF *Méd* gastrotomy
gastrula [gastryla] NF *Biol* gastrula
gastrulation [gastrylasjɔ̃] NF *Biol* gastrulation
gâté [gɑte] ADJ **1** *(pourri → fruit)* damaged, spoilt; *(→ dents)* rotten, decayed; **viande gâtée** meat that has gone off *or* is bad, bad meat **2** *Fig* **enfant g.** spoilt *or* pampered child; **l'enfant g. de la famille/de la littérature russe** the blue-eyed boy of the family/of Russian literature; **tu n'es qu'une enfant gâtée!** a spoilt brat, that's what you are!
gâteau, -x [gɑto] NM **1** *Culin (pâtisserie)* cake; *(biscuit) Br* biscuit, *Am* cookie; **faire un g.** to make *or* bake a cake; **donne-moi une petite part/tranche de g.** give me a small piece/slice of cake; *Fam* **avoir sa part du g.** to have one's slice *or* share of the cake; *Can* **g. des anges** angel cake; **g. d'anniversaire** birthday cake; **g. apéritif** *Br* savoury biscuit, *Am* cracker *(to eat with drinks)*; **g. éponge** sponge cake; **g. marbré** marble cake; **g. aux noix** walnut cake; **g. de riz** rice pudding; **g. de Savoie** sponge cake; **g. sec** *Br* (sweet) biscuit, *Am* cookie; **g. de semoule** ≃ semolina pudding; *Fam* **ça n'est pas du g.** it isn't as easy as it looks; *Fam* **c'est du g.** it's a piece of cake *or Am* a walkover
2 *Suisse Culin* tart
3 *(masse pressée)* cake; *(de fulmicoton)* disc; **g. de miel** *ou* **de cire** honeycomb
ADJ INV *Fam* **c'est un papa g.** he's a soft touch with his children; **j'ai eu un tonton g.** I had an uncle who spoilt me rotten; **marraine g.** fairy godmother
gâte-bois [gɑtbwɑ] NM INV *Entom* goat moth
gatekeeper [gɛjtkipœr] NM *TV* gatekeeper
gâter [3] [gɑte] VT **1** *(combler → ami, enfant)* to spoil; **j'aime bien les g. à Noël** I like to spoil them at Christmas; **j'ai été gâté aujourd'hui, j'ai eu trois offres d'emploi** today was my lucky day, I had three job offers; **du champagne! vous nous avez gâtés!** champagne! you shouldn't have!; **quel beau temps, nous sommes vraiment gâtés** we're really lucky with the weather; *Ironique* **nous sommes gâtés avec cette pluie!** lovely weather for ducks!; *Fam* **tu as vu ce qu'il y a à la télé ce soir, on n'est pas gâtés!** have you seen what's on TV tonight, great, isn't it?; **la vie ne les avait pas gâtés** life hadn't treated them kindly; **il n'est pas gâté par la nature** nature wasn't very kind to him
2 *(abîmer)* to spoil; **l'humidité gâte les fruits** moisture makes fruit go bad *or* spoils fruit; **les mouches gâtent la viande** flies infect meat; **la sauce a bouilli, ça l'a gâtée** the sauce boiled, that's what spoiled it; **la pluie a gâté la récolte** the rain has spoiled *or* ruined the harvest; **elle a beaucoup de dents gâtées** she's got a lot of bad teeth
3 *(gâcher)* to spoil; **ce qui ne gâte rien** which is no bad thing; **il est beau et riche, ce qui ne gâte rien** he's good-looking and he's wealthy to boot, he's good-looking and wealthy into the bargain
► **se gâter** VPR **1** *(pourrir → viande, poisson, lait)* to go bad *or Br* off; *(→ fruit)* to go bad
2 *(se carier → dent)* to decay, to go rotten
3 *(se détériorer → situation)* to take a turn for the worse, to deteriorate; **nos relations ont commencé à se g.** our relationship is starting to go wrong *or* sour; *Fam* **voilà ses potes, attention, ça va se g.** here come his/her mates, things are going to get nasty; **regarde le ciel, le temps se gâte** look at the sky, it's starting to cloud over *or* the weather's changing for the worse
gâterie [gɑtri] NF **1** *(cadeau)* treat, present; **laisse-moi t'offrir une petite g.** let me treat you to a little something, let me buy you a little treat **2** *(friandise)* treat, titbit **3** *très Fam Hum* **faire une petite g. à qn** to go down on sb
gâte-sauce [gɑtsos] *(pl inv ou* **gâte-sauces***)* NM kitchen help; *Péj* bad cook
gâteux, -euse [gɑtø, -øz] ADJ **1** *(sénile)* doddering, doddery; **un vieillard g.** an old dodderer **2** *Fam (stupide)* gaga; **le bébé les rend tous g.** they are all completely besotted by the baby, they all go gaga over the baby
NM,F *Péj* **un vieux g.** a doddering old fool
gateway [gɛjtwɛ] NM *Ordinat* gateway
gâtifier [9] [gɑtifje] VI *Fam* **1** *(devenir gâteux)* to go soft in the head **2** *(bêtifier)* **autour du bébé, tout le monde gâtifie** everyone goes gaga over the baby
gâtine [gɑtin] NF *(dans le Poitou)* barren marshland
gâtion, -onne [gɑtjɔ̃, -ɔn] NM,F *Suisse Fam* spoilt brat
gâtisme [gɑtism] NM *Méd* senility; *Péj* **il se répète, c'est du g.!** he's repeating himself, he must be going senile!
GATT, Gatt [gat] NM *(abrév* **General Agreement on Tariffs and Trade***)* GATT
gatte [gat] NF *Naut* manger
gatter [3] [gate] VT *Suisse Fam Arg scol (cours)* to skip, to cut; **g. l'école** to play *Br* truant *or Am* hooky
gattilier [gatilje] NM *Bot* agnus castus, chaste tree, monk's pepper
gauche [goʃ] ADJ **1** *(dans l'espace)* left; **la partie g. du tableau est endommagée** the left *or* left-hand side of the painting is damaged
2 *(maladroit → adolescent)* awkward, gawky; *(→ démarche)* ungainly; *(→ manières)* awkward, gauche; *(→ geste, mouvement)* awkward, clumsy; **qu'il est g.!** *Br* he's all fingers and thumbs!, *Am* he's all thumbs!; **ses excuses étaient encore plus gauches que sa gaffe** his/her apologies were even clumsier *or* more awkward than his/her blunder
3 *Constr* warped
4 *Math* **courbe g.** skew curve
NM **1** *Sport (pied gauche)* **marquer un but du g.** to score a goal with one's left (foot)
2 *Sport (poing gauche)* left; **il a un g. imparable** he has an unstoppable left
3 *Constr* warping
NF **1** *(côté gauche)* **la g.** the left *or* left-hand side; **il confond sa droite et sa g.** he mixes up (his) right and left; **la page de g.** the left-hand page; **le tiroir de g.** the left-hand drawer; **le magasin de g.** the shop on the left; **mon voisin de g.** my left-hand neighbour; **l'homme assis à ma g.** the man seated on my left; **il y a deux ascenseurs, prenez celui de g.** there are two lifts, take the one on your *or* on the left; **l'église est à g. de l'hôtel** the church is to the left of the hotel; **la deuxième rue sur votre g.** the second street on your left; **sur votre g., vous pouvez voir la tour Eiffel** on your left(-hand side) you can see the Eiffel Tower; **l'arabe s'écrit de droite à g.** Arabic is written from right to left
2 *Pol* **la g.** the left; **quand la g. est arrivée au pouvoir** when the left came to power; **voter à g.** to vote (for the) left; **être très à g.** to be very left-wing; **à droite comme à g., on condamne les essais nucléaires** right and left both condemn nuclear testing; *Fam* **la g. caviar** champagne socialism; **la g. dure** the hard left; **la g. modérée** the soft left; **la g. plurielle** = the rainbow coalition of socialists, communists and ecologists in the government of Lionel Jospin *(elected in 1997)*
❑ **à gauche** EXCLAM **1** *Mil* **à g., g.!** left (turn)!
2 *Naut* **à g.!** left!; **à g. toute!** hard to port!; **à g. tout doucement!** left hand down and slow! ADV **1** *(sur le côté gauche)* on the left; **conduire/doubler à g.** to drive/overtake on the left; **tournez à g.** turn left; **la première rue à g.** the first street on the left
2 *Fam (locutions)* **mettre de l'argent à g.** to put *or* to tuck some money away; **heureusement, elle avait de l'argent à g.** fortunately, she had some money put aside *or* tucked away
❑ **à gauche de** ADV **à g. de la porte d'entrée/de Marie** on *or* to the left of the entrance/of Marie
❑ **de gauche** ADJ *Pol* left-wing; **idées/parti de g.** left-wing ideas/party; **homme de g.** man of the left; **être de g.** to be left-wing *or* a left-winger
❑ **jusqu'à la gauche** ADV *Fam* to the end, to the last; **on s'est fait arnaquer jusqu'à la g.** we got completely ripped off, they cheated us good and proper; **il est compromis jusqu'à la g. dans cette affaire** he's involved right up to the hilt in this business
gauchement [goʃmɑ̃] ADV clumsily
gaucher, -ère [goʃe, -ɛr] ADJ left-handed; **il n'est pas g.!** he is (rather) good with his hands!
NM,F *(gén)* left-hander; *(boxeur)* southpaw; **g. contrarié** = natural left-hander brought up to be right-handed
gaucherie [goʃri] NF **1** *(attitude)* clumsiness *(UNCOUNT)*; **ils ont fait preuve d'une g. inhabituelle dans cette affaire** they have handled this case with unusual clumsiness
2 *(acte, geste)* awkwardness *(UNCOUNT)*; *(expression)* tactless *or* insensitive statement; **des gaucheries typiques d'un garçon de quinze ans** awkwardness typical of a fifteen-year-old boy; **bon exposé, malgré quelques gaucheries** a good essay, despite some clumsy turns of phrase
3 *Méd (prévalence manuelle)* left-handedness
gauchir [32] [goʃir] VT **1** *Constr* to warp **2** *Aviat* **g. l'aileron** to bank **3** *Fig (altérer)* to distort; **les préjugés gauchissent la réalité** prejudice distorts reality; **il accuse les journalistes d'avoir gauchi ses propos** he accuses the journalists of distorting *or* misrepresenting his words
VI to warp
► **se gauchir** VPR to warp
gauchisant, -e [goʃizɑ̃, -ɑ̃t] *Pol* ADJ **être g.** to have left-wing tendencies, to be a left-winger
NM,F **c'est un g.** he's a left-winger, he's got left-wing tendencies
gauchisme [goʃism] NM *Pol (gén)* leftism; *(depuis 1968)* New Leftism
gauchissement [goʃismɑ̃] NM **1** *Constr* warping **2** *Aviat* banking **3** *Fig* distortion, misrepresentation
gauchiste [goʃist] *Pol* ADJ *(gén)* left; *(depuis 1968)* (New) Leftist
NMF *(gén)* leftist; *(depuis 1968)* (New) Leftist
gaucho[1] [goʃo] NM *(gardien de troupeaux)* gaucho
gaucho[2] [goʃo] *Fam Péj Pol* ADJ INV lefty, pinko
NMF lefty, pinko
gaude [god] NF *Bot* yellow-weed, dyer's weed *or* weld
❑ **gaudes** NFPL *Culin* polenta *(UNCOUNT)*, *Am* cornmeal mush *(UNCOUNT)*
gaudriole [godrijɔl] NF *Fam* **1** *(plaisanterie)* bawdy joke **2** *(sexe)* **il ne pense qu'à la g.** he's got a one-track mind
gaufrage [gofraʒ] NM **1** *(relief → sur du cuir, du métal)* embossing; *(→ sur une étoffe)* diapering; **g. à froid** blind embossing **2** *(plissage d'un tissu)* goffering **3** *Typ* goffering
gaufre[1] [gofr] NF **1** *Culin* waffle **2** *(de cire)* honeycomb
gaufre[2] [gofr] NM *Zool* (pocket) gopher
gaufré, -e [gofre] ADJ *Typ* embossed
gaufrer [3] [gofre] VT **1** *(imprimer un relief sur → cuir, métal)* to emboss, to boss; *(→ papier, étoffe)* to emboss **2** *(plisser → tissu)* to goffer; *(→ cheveux)* to crimp; **elle s'est fait g. les cheveux** she had her hair crimped
gaufrerie [gofrəri] NF *Can* waffle shop
gaufrette [gofrɛt] NF *Culin* wafer (biscuit)
gaufreur, -euse [gofrœr, -øz] NM,F **1** *(de cuir, de métaux)* embosser **2** *(de tissu)* gofferer
❑ **gaufreuse** NF embossing press
gaufrier [gofrije] NM waffle iron
gaufroir [gofrwar] NM goffer
gaufrure [gofryr] NF **1** *(sur du métal, du cuir, du papier, de l'étoffe)* embossed design **2** *(plissure → du tissu)* goffering
gaulage [golaʒ] NM beating *(of a tree, to bring down fruit or nuts)*; **le g. des noix** = beating walnuts down from trees
Gaule [gol] NF *Hist* **la G.** Gaul
gaule [gol] NF **1** *(perche)* pole; *Vulg* **avoir la g.** to have a hard-on **2** *Pêche* fishing rod
gaulé, -e [gole] ADJ *très Fam* **être bien/mal g.** to have/not to have a great bod
gauleiter [gawlajtœr] NM *Hist* gauleiter
gauler [3] [gole] VT **1** *(arbre)* to beat; *(fruit)* to beat down (from the tree) **2** *Fam (locution)* **se faire g.** to be *Br* nicked *or Am* busted
gaulis [goli] NM *Bot* **1** *(jeune plantation)* sapling wood *or* plantation **2** *(branche)* branch fit for cutting
gaullien, -enne [goljɛ̃, -ɛn] ADJ of de Gaulle, de

Gaulle's; **l'éloquence gaullienne** de Gaulle's eloquence

gaullisme [golism]**NM** Gaullism

GAULLISME
The political ideology inspired by the ideas of General de Gaulle includes nationalism, independence from foreign powers, and a strong executive. Gaullists are strongly committed to the defence of France's prestige on the international scene.

gaulliste [golist]**ADJ** Gaullist
NMF Gaullist

gaulois, -e [golwa, -az]**ADJ 1** *Hist* Gallic, Gaulish **2** *(grivois)* bawdy; **plaisanterie gauloise** bawdy joke; **l'humour g.** bawdy humour
NM *(langue)* Gaulish
□ **Gaulois, -e NM,F** Gaul
□ **gauloise®** *NF (cigarette)* Gauloise®

gauloisement [golwazmã]**ADV** bawdily

gauloiserie [golwazri] **NF 1** *(plaisanterie)* bawdy joke; *(remarque)* bawdy remark **2** *(attitude)* bawdiness

Gault et Millau [goemijo] **NM** le **G.** = annual guide to hotels and restaurants

gaultheria [goterja] **NM** *Bot* wintergreen, *Spéc* gaultheria

gaulthérie [goteri]**NF** *Bot* wintergreen, *Spéc* gaultheria

gaupe [gop]**NF** *Fam Vieilli* slut, trollop

gauphre [gofr] = **gaufre²**

gaur [gɔr]**NM** *Zool* gaur

gauss [gos]**NM** *Élec* gauss

gausser [3] [gose] **se gausser VPR** *Littéraire* to mock; **gaussez-vous donc, braves gens!** well may you mock, good people!; **vous vous gaussez!** you jest!

gaussien, -enne [gosjɛ̃, -ɛn]**ADJ** Gaussian

gavage [gavaʒ] **NM 1** *Agr* force-feeding, gavage; **le g. des oies pour Noël** the fattening (up) of geese for Christmas **2** *Méd* tube-feeding

gave [gav] **NM** (mountain) stream *(in south-west France)*

Gaveau [gavo] **NM la salle G.** = concert hall in Paris

gaver [3] [gave]**VT 1** *Agr* to force-feed
2 *(bourrer → personne) (de nourriture)* to fill up, to stuff **(de** with); **on l'a gavé d'antibiotiques** he has been stuffed with antibiotics; **j'ai été gavé de littérature classique** I had classical literature crammed into me; **la télévision nous gave de publicités** we get an overdose of commercials on television
▸**se gaver VPR** to stuff oneself **(de** with); **ils se sont gavés de fraises** they stuffed themselves with strawberries; *Fig* **cet été, je me suis gavé de romans policiers** this summer I indulged myself with detective stories

gaveur, -euse [gavœr, -øz] **NM,F** *(de volailles)* (poultry) crammer
NM *Aviat* booster pump
□ **gaveuse NF** (poultry) crammer, cramming machine

gavial, -als [gavjal]**NM** *Zool* gavial

gavotte [gavɔt]**NF** *Mus & (danse)* gavotte

gavroche [gavrɔʃ]**ADJ** *(air, expression)* mischievous, impish
NM un vrai petit g. a typical Parisian urchin *(from character in Victor Hugo's 'Les Misérables')*

gay [gɛ]**ADJ** gay *(homosexual)*; **il/elle est g.** he's/she's gay
NMF gay *(homosexual)*

gayal, -als [gajal]**NM** *Zool* gayal

gaz [gaz]**NM INV 1** *(pour le chauffage, l'éclairage)* gas *(UNCOUNT)*; **avoir le g.** to have gas, *Br* to be on gas; **cuisiner au g.** to cook with gas, to use a gas cooker; **se chauffer au g.** to have gas-powered heating; **allumer/couper le g.** to light/turn off the gas; **il n'y a pas le g. ici** we don't have gas in this place; **l'employé du g.** the gasman; **g. d'éclairage** town gas; **G. de France** = the French gas board; **g. de ville** town gas; **la cuisinière est-elle branchée sur le g. de ville?** is the stove connected to the mains gas?
2 *Chim* gas; **g. ammoniac** ammonia gas; **g. asphyxiant** asphyxiant gas; **g. carbonique** carbon dioxide; *Mil* **g. de combat** poison gas; **g. CS** CS gas; *Chim* **g. délétères** after-damp; **des g. à effet de serre** greenhouse gases; **g. hilarant** laughing gas; **g. inerte** inert gas; **g. innervant** nerve gas; **g. lacrymogène** tear gas; **g. des marais** marsh gas; **g. naturel** natural gas; **g. neurotoxique** nerve gas; **g. parfait** ideal gas; **g. de pétrole liquéfié** liquefied petroleum gas; **g. propulseur** propellant; **g. rare** rare gas; **g. toxique** poison *or* toxic gas
3 *Méd* **g. (anesthésique** *ou* **anesthésiant)** *(pour anesthésie)* gas
4 *Fam (locution)* **être dans le g.** to be out of it
NMPL 1 *Physiol* **avoir des g.** to have *Br* wind *or* *Am* gas
2 *(carburant)* **g. d'admission** air-fuel mixture; **g. brûlés** *ou* **d'échappement** exhaust fumes; *Fam* **mettre les g.** *(en voiture)* *Br* to put one's foot down, *Am* to step on the gas; *(en avion)* to open up the throttle■; *Fam* **on roulait (à) pleins g.** we were going flat out *or* at full speed■
□ **à gaz ADJ** gas *(avant n)*; **réchaud à g.** *(portable)* gas stove; **usine à g.** gasworks; *Fig* overly complicated system

Gaza [gaza] **NM** Gaza; **la bande de G.** the Gaza Strip

gazage [gazaʒ] **NM 1** *Tex* singeing **2** *Mil* gassing

gaze [gaz] **NF 1** *Tex* gauze; **g. métallique** wire gauze **2** *Méd* gauze; **g. stérilisée** aseptic gauze

gazé, -e [gaze]**ADJ** gassed; **soldats gazés** soldiers killed by (poison) gas
NM,F (poison) gas victim

gazéification [gazeifikasjɔ̃] **NF 1** *Chim* gasification **2** *Mines* **g. souterraine** underground gasification; **g. du charbon** (ex situ) coal distillation **3** *(de l'eau)* aeration; *(avec du gaz carbonique)* carbonation

gazéifier [9] [gazeifje]**VT 1** *Chim* to gasify **2** *(eau)* to aerate; *(avec du gaz carbonique)* to carbonate

gazelle [gazɛl] **NF** *Zool* gazelle; **g. dorcas** dorcas gazelle; **g. girafe** gerenuk, Waller's gazelle; **g. de Thomson** Thomson's gazelle; *Fig* **avoir des yeux de gazelle** to be doe-eyed

gazer [3] [gaze]**VT 1** *(asphyxier)* to gas; **il a été gazé** *(dans une chambre à gaz)* he died in a gas chamber; *(sur le champ de bataille)* he was a victim of poison gas **2** *Tex* to singe
VI *Fam* **1** *(aller bien)* **alors, ça gaze? – ça gaze!** how's things *or* how's it going? – great!; **ça ne gaze pas du tout en ce moment** things aren't too great at the moment **2** *(foncer)* **allez, gaze!** step on it!, get a move on!

gazetier, -ère [gaztje, -ɛr] **NM,F 1** *Arch* gazette proprietor, gazetteer **2** *Péj* hack

gazette [gazɛt]**NF 1** *Arch (journal)* gazette, newspaper; *Presse* **la G. de Lausanne** = Swiss daily newspaper **2** *Fam Vieilli (bavard)* **son mari est une vraie g.!** her husband knows everybody's business *or* all the latest gossip!

gazeux, -euse [gazø, -øz]**ADJ 1** *Chim* gaseous **2** *(boisson)* fizzy, carbonated; *(eau)* sparkling, fizzy; **eau gazeuse naturelle** naturally carbonated water **3** *Méd* gas *(avant n)*

gazier, -ère [gazje, -ɛr]**ADJ** gas *(avant n)*
NM 1 *(employé du gaz)* gasman; *(dans une usine à gaz)* gasworks employee **2** *très Fam (individu)* guy, *Br* bloke, *Am* dude

gazinière [gazinjɛr]**NF** gas stove, *Br* gas cooker

gazoduc [gazɔdyk]**NM** gas pipeline

gazogène [gazɔʒɛn] **NM** *(appareil)* gas producer; **gaz de g.** producer gas

gazole [gazɔl] **NM 1** *(pour moteur Diesel)* diesel (oil), *Br* derv **2** *(combustible)* **g. de chauffe** (domestic) fuel oil

gazoline [gazɔlin]**NF** gasoline, gasolene

gazomètre [gazɔmɛtr]**NM** gasholder, gasometer

gazométrie [gazɔmetri]**NF** gasometry

gazon [gazɔ̃] **NM 1** *(herbe)* **du g.** turf **2** *(pelouse)* lawn; **g. anglais** well-kept lawn, smooth lawn; **défense de marcher sur le g.** *(sur panneau)* keep off the grass **3** *(motte de terre)* turf, sod **4** *Bot* **g. mousse** mossy saxifrage

gazonnage [gazɔnaʒ]**NM** turfing, grassing (over)

gazonnant, -e [gazɔnã, -ãt]**ADJ** tufty, grassy

gazonnement [gazɔnmã] **NM** turfing, planting with turf

gazonner [3] [gazɔne]**VT** to turf, to grass (over)
VI *(terrain)* to become covered with grass

gazouillant, -e [gazujã, -ãt]**ADJ 1** *(oiseau)* chirp-ing, warbling **2** *(bébé)* babbling, gurgling **3** *Littéraire (eau)* babbling; **ruisseau g.** babbling brook

gazouillement [gazujmã] **NM 1** *(d'oiseau)* chirping *(UNCOUNT)*, warbling *(UNCOUNT)* **2** *(d'un bébé)* babbling *(UNCOUNT)*, gurgling *(UNCOUNT)* **3** *Littéraire (de l'eau)* babbling *(UNCOUNT)*; **on n'entendait que le g. d'une fontaine** all that could be heard was the babbling of a fountain

gazouiller [3] [gazuje] **VI 1** *(oiseau)* to chirp, to warble **2** *(bébé)* to babble, to gurgle **3** *Littéraire (ruisseau, eau)* to babble, to murmur, to gurgle

gazouilleur, -euse [gazujœr, -øz] **ADJ 1** *(oiseau)* chirping, warbling **2** *(bébé)* babbling, gurgling; **ruisseau g.** babbling brook

gazouillis [gazuji] **NM 1** *(d'oiseau)* chirping *(UNCOUNT)*, warbling *(UNCOUNT)* **2** *(d'un bébé)* babbling *(UNCOUNT)*, gurgling *(UNCOUNT)* **3** *Littéraire (de l'eau)* babbling *(UNCOUNT)*; **on n'entendait que le g. d'une fontaine** all that could be heard was the babbling of a fountain

gazpacho [gazpatʃo]**NM** *Culin* gazpacho

GB, G-B *(abrév écrite* **Grande-Bretagne)** GB

gd *(abrév écrite* **grand)** lg.

Gdańsk [gdãsk]**NM** Gdańsk

GDB [ʒedebe] **NF** *Fam (abrév* **gueule de bois)** hangover

GDF [ʒedeɛf] **NM** *(abrév* **Gaz de France)** = the French gas board

geai [ʒɛ]**NM** *Orn* jay; **g. bleu** blue jay

géant, -e [ʒeã, -ãt]**ADJ 1** *(énorme)* giant *(avant n)*; *(carton, paquet)* giant-sized; **une ville géante** a gigantic town; **un écran g.** a giant screen; **une clameur géante** an almighty clamour
2 *Astron* giant *(avant n)*
3 *Fam (formidable)* **c'est g.!** it's wicked *or* brill!
NM,F 1 *(personne, chose de grande taille)* giant; *Littéraire* **le chêne, g. de la forêt** the oak, giant of the forest; **le projet avance à pas de g.** the project is *Br* coming on *or* *Am* moving along in leaps and bounds
2 *Fig* **les géants de la littérature classique** the giants *or* great names of classical literature; **le g. du cyclisme français** the star of French cycling; **ils ont couronné un g.** they have given the award to one of the all-time greats; *Écon* **c'est un des géants de l'électronique** it's one of the giants of the electronics industry
3 *Myth* giant, *f* giantess
□ **géante NF** *Astron* giant; **géante rouge** red giant

géaster [ʒeaster]**NM** *Bot* geaster, geastrum

gecko [ʒeko]**NM** *Zool* gecko

gégène [ʒeʒɛn] *Fam* **ADJ** brilliant, great, terrific
NF = torture by electric shock

Géhenne [ʒeɛn]**NF** *Bible* **la G.** Gehenna

GEIE, G.E.I.E. [ʒeɔia] **NM** *(abrév* **groupement européen d'intérêt économique)** EEIG

Geiger [ʒeʒɛr]**NPR** **compteur (de) G.** Geiger counter

geignait *etc voir* **geindre**

geignard, -e [ʒɛɲar, -ard] *Fam* **ADJ** *(personne, voix)* whining, *Br* whingeing, *Am* whiny; **"et moi?" dit-il d'une voix geignarde** "what about me?" he whined
NM,F *(enfant)* crybaby; *(adulte)* moaner, *Br* whinger, *Am* bellyacher

geignement [ʒɛɲmã]**NM** moaning *(UNCOUNT)*, groaning *(UNCOUNT)*

geindre [81] [ʒɛ̃dr]**VI 1** *(gémir)* to groan, to moan; **g. de douleur** to moan *or* groan with pain **2** *Fam (pour des riens)* to whine, to gripe **3** *Littéraire (vent)* to moan

geisha [gɛʃa]**NF** geisha (girl)

gel [ʒɛl]**NM 1** *Météo* frost; **persistance du g. sur toute la moitié ouest** it will stay frosty in the west
2 *(suspension)* **le g. des opérations militaires** the suspension of military operations; **g. des négociations** suspension of negotiations; *UE* **g. des terres** set-aside
3 *Écon* freeze; **g. des crédits** credit freeze; **g. des prix** price freeze; **ce n'est pas le g. des prix qui nous aidera** freezing prices won't help us; **g. des salaires** wage freeze
4 *Chim* gel; **g. coiffant** hair gel; **se mettre du g.** to put gel on one's hair; **g. douche** shower gel; **dentifrice en g.** gel toothpaste

gélatine [ʒelatin] NF **1** *Culin* gelatine; **g. de poisson** isinglass, fish glue; **feuille de g.** sheet of gelatine **2** *Phot* **une plaque enduite de g.** a gelatine-coated plate **3** *(explosif)* **g. explosive** blasting gelatine

gélatiné, -e [ʒelatine] ADJ *Phot* **papier g.** gelatine paper; **plaque gélatinée** gelatinized plate

gélatineux, -euse [ʒelatinø, -øz] ADJ **1** *(contenant de la gélatine)* gelatinous; **substance gélatineuse** gelatinous substance; **solution gélatineuse** gelatine solution **2** *(flasque)* gelatinous, jellylike, flaccid

gélatiniforme [ʒelatinifɔrm] ADJ *Méd* gelatiniform, gelatinoid

gélatiniser [3] [ʒelatinize] VT to gelatinize

gélatino-bromure [ʒelatinobrɔmyr] *(pl* **gélatino-bromures)** NM *Phot* gelatino-bromide; **papier au g.** bromide paper

gélatino-chlorure [ʒelatinoklɔryr] *(pl* **gélatino-chlorures)** NM *Phot* gelatino-chloride

gelé, -e [ʒəle] ADJ **1** *Agr & Météo (sol)* frozen; *(pousse, bourgeon)* frostbitten, frozen; *(arbre)* frozen

2 *Fig (glacé)* frozen; **des draps gelés** ice-cold sheets; **être g. jusqu'aux os** to be frozen to the bone, to be frozen stiff; **je suis complètement g.** I'm absolutely frozen *or* freezing

3 *Méd* frostbitten; **il a eu les orteils gelés** his toes were frostbitten, he got frostbite in his toes; **mourir g.** to freeze to death

4 *Écon & Fin* frozen

5 *(hostile)* icy, stone-cold

6 *Can Fam (drogué)* wasted; *(anesthésié)* under
☐ **gelée** NF **1** *Météo* frost; **gelée blanche** white frost, hoarfrost; **forte gelée** hard frost
2 *Culin* jelly; **gelée de groseilles** redcurrant jelly *or* preserve
☐ **en gelée** ADJ *Culin* in jelly; **volaille en gelée** chicken in aspic *or* jelly
☐ **gelée royale** NF royal jelly

geler [25] [ʒəle] VT **1** *(transformer en glace → eau, sol)* to freeze; *(→ route)* to make icy; **le froid a gelé la rivière** the cold has frozen the river (over)

2 *(bloquer → tuyau, serrure)* to freeze up

3 *(détruire → plante, tissu organique)* to freeze; **le froid a gelé les premières fleurs** the cold has frozen *or* nipped the first flowers

4 *(transir → visage)* to chill, to numb; *(→ membres)* to freeze

5 *(paralyser → négociations)* to halt; *(→ projet)* to halt, to block; *Fin (→ capitaux, salaires, prix)* to freeze; **tous les crédits sont gelés jusqu'à nouvel ordre** all funding has been frozen until further notice

VI **1** *(eau, liquide)* to freeze; *(lac, rivière)* to freeze over

2 *(tuyau, serrure)* to freeze up

3 *(pousses, légumes)* to freeze, to be nipped by the frost

4 *Fig (personne)* to freeze; **je gèle** I'm frozen (stiff); **on gèle dans cette salle** it's freezing in this room; **ferme la porte, on gèle ici** shut the door, it's freezing in here

V IMPERSONNEL **il gèle** it's freezing; **il a gelé cette nuit** it was below freezing *or* zero last night; **il a gelé blanc** there's been a frost; **il gèle à pierre fendre** it is freezing hard

▶**se geler** VPR **1** *(personne)* **je me suis gelé là-bas** I got (absolutely) frozen down there

2 *très Fam* **on se les gèle** it's damned cold, *Br* it's brass monkey weather

gélif, -ive [ʒelif, -iv] ADJ *Géol* susceptible to frost heave **2** *Agr (champ)* susceptible to spring frosts; *(sol)* susceptible to frost heave; *(arbre)* frost-cleft

gélifiant, -e [ʒelifjɑ̃, -ɑ̃t] ADJ gelling *(avant n)* NM gelling agent

gélification [ʒelifikasjɔ̃] NF *Bot & Chim* gelation, gelling

gélifier [9] [ʒelifje] VT **1** *Chim* to gel **2** *Culin* to make into a jelly, to jellify
▶**se gélifier** VPR to gel

gélifraction [ʒelifraksjɔ̃] NF *Géol (de roches)* frost shattering

gélignite [ʒeliɲit] NF gelignite

gélinotte [ʒelinɔt], **gelinotte** [ʒəlinɔt] NF *Orn* **g. (des bois)** hazel grouse, hazel hen; **g. des prairies** prairie chicken

gélisol [ʒelisɔl] NM frozen ground

géliturbation [ʒelityrbasjɔ̃] NF *Géol* cryoturbation

gélivation [ʒelivasjɔ̃] NF *Géol* congelifraction, frost weathering

gélive [ʒeliv] *voir* **gélif**

gélivité [ʒelivite] NF *Constr* gelivity, liability to crack *(due to frost)*

gélivure [ʒelivyr] NF *(de la pierre, de la terre)* cleft; *(du bois)* heart shake

gélose [ʒeloz] NF agar

gélule [ʒelyl] NF *Pharm* capsule

gelure [ʒəlyr] NF *Méd* frostbite *(UNCOUNT)*

gémeau, -elle, -aux, -elles [ʒemo, -ɛl] ADJ *Vieilli* twin
NM,F *Vieilli* twin
☐ **Gémeaux** NMPL **1** *Astron* Gemini **2** *Astrol* Gemini; **être G.** to be Gemini *or* a Geminian

gémellaire [ʒemelɛr] ADJ twin *(avant n)*, *Spéc* gemellary; **grossesse g.** twin pregnancy

gémellipare [ʒemelipar] ADJ gemelliparous

gémelliparité [ʒemeliparite] NF twin pregnancy

gémellité [ʒemelite] NF **le taux de g. varie selon les pays** the number of twin births varies from country to country

gémination [ʒeminasjɔ̃] NF *Ling & Méd* gemination

géminé, -e [ʒemine] ADJ **1** *(double)* twin *(avant n)*, *Spéc* geminate; *Archit* **arcades géminées** twin or dual arcades; **fenêtres géminées** paired or gemel windows **2** *Ling* **consonne géminée** geminate consonant
☐ **géminée** NF *Ling* geminate

géminer [3] [ʒemine] VT **1** *(gén)* to geminate, to twin **2** *Ling* to geminate

gémir [32] [ʒemir] VI **1** *(blessé, malade)* to moan, to groan; **g. de douleur** to groan or moan with pain **2** *(vent)* to moan, to wail; *(parquet, gonds)* to creak **3** *(se plaindre)* to moan, to whine **4** *Littéraire (souffrir)* **g. dans les fers** to languish in irons; **g. sous le joug de la tyrannie** to groan under the yoke of tyranny **5** *(colombe, tourterelle)* to coo

gémissant, -e [ʒemisɑ̃, -ɑ̃t] ADJ *(blessé, malade)* moaning, groaning; *(voix)* wailing; *Fig* **les accents gémissants d'un violon** the wailing strains of a violin; **les accents gémissants de la bise** the moaning of the north wind; **essieu g.** creaking axle

gémissement [ʒemismɑ̃] NM **1** *(gén)* moan, groan; **pousser un g.** to (utter a) groan; **le g. du vent** the moaning or wailing of the wind; **gémissements** *(plaintes)* whimpering *(UNCOUNT)*, whining *(UNCOUNT)* **2** *(de la tourterelle, de la colombe)* cooing *(UNCOUNT)*

gemmage [ʒemaʒ] NM tapping *(of a pine tree)*

gemmail, -aux [ʒemaj, -o] NM *Archit* non-leaded stained glass (window)

gemmation [ʒemasjɔ̃] NF *Biol* gemmation

gemme [ʒem] NF **1** *(pierre précieuse)* gem **2** *(résine)* (pine) resin **3** *Arch Bot* (leaf) bud
ADJ *voir* **sel**

gemmé, -e [ʒeme] ADJ *Littéraire* gemmed, jewelled

gemmer [4] [ʒeme] VT *(arbre)* to tap *(pine trees)*

gemmeur, -euse [ʒemœr, -øz] NM,F tapper *(of pine trees)*

gemmifère [ʒemifɛr] ADJ *Biol* gemmate

gemmipare [ʒemipar] ADJ *Biol* gemmiparous

gemmiparité [ʒemiparite] NF *Biol* gemmiparous reproduction

gemmologie [ʒemɔlɔʒi] NF gemology, gemmology

gemmologiste [ʒemɔlɔʒist], **gemmologue** [ʒemɔlɔg] NM,F gemologist, gemmologist

gemmothérapie [ʒemɔterapi] NF *Méd* gemmotherapy

gemmule [ʒemyl] NF *Biol* gemmule

gémonies [ʒemoni] NFPL **1** *Antiq* the Gemonies **2** *Littéraire (locutions)* **traîner** ou **vouer qn aux g.** to pillory sb; **traîner** ou **vouer qch aux g.** to hold sth up to public ridicule

gemsbok [ʒemzbɔk] NM *Zool* gemsbok

gênant, -e [ʒenɑ̃, -ɑ̃t] ADJ **1** *(qui bloque le passage)* in the way; *(qui est encombrant)* cumbersome; **enlève ce fauteuil, il est g.** move that armchair, it's in the way

2 *(ennuyeux → situation, lumière, bruit)* annoying, irritating; **les bus sont en grève? c'est g.,** ça so the buses are on strike? what a nuisance or

how annoying; **c'est g. qu'elle ne soit pas là** it's annoying or it's a bit of a nuisance that she's not here; **ce n'est pas g.** it doesn't matter; **est-ce que c'est g.?** does it matter?

3 *(embarrassant → situation, silence)* awkward, embarrassing; *(→ témoin)* awkward; **c'est g. d'y aller sans avoir été invité** I feel a bit awkward or uncomfortable about going there without an invitation; **j'ai trouvé extrêmement g. que tu abordes ce sujet** it was extremely embarrassing of you to mention the subject

gencive [ʒãsiv] NF *Anat* gum; **j'ai les gencives enflées** my gums are swollen; *Fam* **prendre un coup dans les gencives** to get socked in the jaw, to get a kick in the teeth; **prends ça dans les gencives!** take that!; **qu'est-ce qu'il s'est pris dans les gencives!** he really got it in the neck!; **elle lui a envoyé dans les gencives que...** she told him/her straight to his/her face that...

gendarme [ʒãdarm] NM **1** *(policier)* gendarme, policeman; **g. mobile** = member of the riot police; **gendarmes mobiles** riot police; **gendarmes à cheval** mounted police; **gendarmes motocyclistes** motorcycle police; **jouer au g. et au voleur** ou **aux gendarmes et aux voleurs** to play cops and robbers; *Fam Aut* **g. couché** sleeping policeman

2 *Fam (personne autoritaire)* **faire le g.** to lay down the law; **leur mère est un vrai g.** their mother's a real or *Br* right battle-axe

3 *Fam (hareng)* smoked herring ∎

4 *(saucisse)* = dry, flat sausage

5 *(pointe rocheuse)* gendarme

6 *(d'une pierre précieuse)* flaw

7 *(d'une montagne)* needle

gendarmer [3] [ʒãdarme] **se gendarmer** VPR **se g. (contre)** *(protester)* to kick up a fuss (about); *(s'indigner)* to get on one's high horse (about); **il n'y a pas de quoi se g.** there's nothing to get worked up about

gendarmerie [ʒãdarməri] NF **1** *(corporation)* gendarmerie, police force; **g. mobile** (anti-)riot police; **g. nationale** = national police force, gendarmerie; **la G. royale du Canada** the Royal Canadian Mounted Police **2** *(bureaux)* gendarmerie, police station; *(caserne)* police or gendarmerie barracks

gendre [ʒãdr] NM son-in-law

gène [ʒɛn] NM gene; **structure du g.** gene structure; **banque de gènes** gene bank; **famille de gènes** gene family; **g. aberrant** rogue gene

gêne [ʒɛn] NF **1** *(matérielle)* inconvenience; **je resterais bien un jour de plus si ça ne vous cause aucune g.** I would like to stay for another day if it doesn't put you to any trouble or if that's no bother; **sa présence parmi nous est une g.** his/her being here with us is a bit awkward; **nous prions nos clients de bien vouloir excuser la g. occasionnée par les travaux** we apologize to customers for the inconvenience caused by the work

2 *(morale)* embarrassment; **ressentir ou éprouver de la g.** to feel embarrassed; **éprouver une certaine g. à parler en public** to feel rather ill at ease or embarrassed when speaking in public; **j'éprouvais une grande g. à lui annoncer qu'il était renvoyé** I felt deeply embarrassed having to tell him that he was dismissed; **il a accepté l'argent avec une certaine g.** he was uncomfortable about taking the money; **il a accepté l'argent sans la moindre g.** he took the money without the slightest qualm; **un moment de g.** an awkward moment; **il y a une certaine g. dans leurs relations** relations between them are rather strained; **où (il) y a de la g., (il n')y a pas de plaisir** there's no need to stand on ceremony; *Ironique (ton indigné)* don't mind me

3 *(physique)* difficulty, discomfort; **éprouver ou avoir de la g. à faire qch** to find it difficult to do sth; **sentir une g. respiratoire** ou **pour respirer** to have difficulty (in) breathing

4 *(pauvreté)* **être dans la g.** to be in need; **sa mort nous a mis dans la g.** his death has left us in financial straits

5 *Arch (physique, morale)* torture
☐ **sans gêne** ADJ inconsiderate

gêné, -e [ʒene] ADJ **1** *(personne, sourire)* embarrassed; **silence g.** embarrassed or awkward or

uneasy silence; **pourquoi prends-tu cet air g.?** why are you looking so embarrassed?; *Fam* **il n'est pas g., lui!** he's got a nerve *or Br* a cheek!

2 *(serré)* ill at ease, uncomfortable; **il se sentait g. dans son nouvel uniforme** he felt uncomfortable in his new uniform; *Fig* **être g. aux entournures** *(mal à l'aise)* to feel ill at ease *or* self-conscious

3 *(financièrement)* in financial difficultes; **les personnes momentanément gênées peuvent demander une avance** people with temporary financial difficulties can ask for an advance

généalogie [ʒenealɔʒi] NF **1** *(ascendance)* ancestry; *(d'un cheval, d'un chien)* pedigree; **faire** *ou* **dresser sa g.** to trace one's ancestry *or* family tree **2** *(science)* genealogy

généalogique [ʒenealɔʒik] ADJ genealogical; **livre g.** *(de chevaux)* stud book; *(du bétail)* herd book

généalogiste [ʒenealɔʒist] NMF genealogist

génépi [ʒenepi], **genépi** [ʒənepi] NM **1** *Bot* wormwood **2** *(liqueur)* genipi *(absinthe liqueur)*

gêner [4] [ʒene] VT **1** *(incommoder → sujet: chose)* to bother; **j'ai une poussière dans l'œil qui me gêne** there's a speck of dust in my eye that's bothering me; **est-ce que la fumée vous gêne?** does the smoke bother you?; **la lanière de mes sandales me gêne quand je marche** the straps on my sandals are uncomfortable when I walk; **mes lunettes me gênent pour mettre mon casque** my glasses get in the way when I put my helmet on; **j'ai oublié mes lunettes, ça me gêne pour lire** I've left my glasses behind and I'm finding it difficult to read; **ça me gêne dans mon travail** it disturbs me when I'm trying to work; **j'ai été gêné par le manque de temps/ma méconnaissance du milieu** I was hindered *or* hampered by the lack of time/my ignorance of the milieu; **j'ai été gêné par le bruit/la lumière/le monde** I was disturbed by the noise/the light/the people; **ce qui me gêne, c'est que...** what bothers me is that...; **le froid ne me gêne pas** I don't mind the cold

2 *(encombrer)* to be in the way of; **g. le passage** to be in the way; **ma valise vous gêne-t-elle?** is my case in your way?; **ne bougez pas, vous ne me gênez pas du tout** don't move, you're not in my *or* the way at all; **recule-toi, tu me gênes pour passer** move back, you're in my way *or* you're stopping me from getting past; **si tu pouvais te pousser, tu me gênes pour passer les vitesses** could you move over, I can't change gear with you there

3 *(empêcher → activité)* to interfere with; **ce camion gêne la circulation** that lorry is holding up the traffic; **la neige gênait la visibilité** visibility was hindered *or* impaired by the snow; **je suis gêné dans mon métier par mes lacunes en mathématiques** the gaps in my knowledge of mathematics are a handicap *or* a drawback in my line of business

4 *(importuner → sujet: personne)* to put out, to bother, to inconvenience; **ça ne le gênerait pas que j'arrive après minuit?** would it bother him *or* put him out if I arrived after midnight?; **ça vous gêne si j'ouvre la fenêtre?** do you mind if I open the window?; **ça ne me gêne pas de le lui dire** I don't mind telling him/her (about it); **cela ne te gênerait pas de me prêter ta voiture?** would you mind lending me your car?; **cela vous gênerait-il que je revienne demain?** would it disturb you *or* bother you *or* put you out if I came back tomorrow?; *Fam* **oui, pourquoi, ça te gêne?** yes, why, what's it to you *or* got any objections?

5 *(intimider)* to embarrass; **les plaisanteries de son ami la gênaient** her friend's jokes embarrassed her *or* made her feel uncomfortable; **cela me gênerait de le rencontrer** it would be awkward for me to meet him, I would feel uncomfortable meeting him; **sa présence me gêne** I feel awkward *or* embarrassed in his/her presence, his/her presence makes me feel ill at ease; **ça me gêne qu'il écoute** I feel uneasy with him listening; *Can* **être gêné** to be shy

6 *(serrer)* **mes souliers me gênent** my shoes pinch *or* are too tight; **cette ceinture/ce col me gêne** this belt/this collar is too tight; **cette jupe trop étroite me gêne pour marcher** I find it hard to walk in this tight skirt

7 *(mettre en difficulté financière)* **en ce moment, cela me gênerait un peu de vous prêter cet argent** I can't really afford to lend you the money at the moment

USAGE ABSOLU **1** *(encombrer)* **c'est le placard qui gêne pour ouvrir la porte** the door won't open because of the cupboard; **pousse-toi, tu vois bien que tu gênes!** move along, you can see you're in the way!

2 *(importuner)* **ça ne gêne pas que tu viennes, il y a de la place** it'll be no bother *or* trouble at all if you come, there's enough room

▸**se gêner** VPR **1** *(emploi réciproque)* **la chambre est trop petite, on se gêne les uns les autres** the room is too small, we're in each other's way; **il y a beaucoup de place, nous ne nous gênerons pas** there's a lot of room, we won't be in each other's way

2 *Fam* **je vais me g., tiens!** just watch me!; **tu aurais tort de te g.!** why should you worry *or* care?▪; **il ne se gêne pas avec nous** he doesn't stand on ceremony with us; **continuez votre repas, ne vous gênez pas pour moi** go on with your meal, don't mind me; **je ne me suis pas gêné pour le lui dire** I didn't hesitate to tell him/her so▪, I made no bones about telling him/her so; **ne te gêne pas pour le lui faire remarquer** go right ahead and point it out to him/her▪; *Ironique* **vous avez pris ma place, surtout ne vous gênez pas!** go on, take my seat, don't mind me!; **il y en a qui ne se gênent pas!** some people have got a nerve!

3 *Suisse (être intimidé)* to be shy

général, -e, -aux, -ales [ʒeneral, -o] ADJ **1** *(d'ensemble)* general; **les caractéristiques générales du texte** the general features of the text; **la situation générale** the general *or* overall situation; **le phénomène est g.** the phenomenon is widespread, it's a general phenomenon; **le sens g. d'un mot** the general *or* broad meaning of a word; **état g.** general *or* overall condition; **l'état g. du malade est bon** the patient's overall condition is good

2 *(imprécis)* general; **il s'en est tenu à des remarques générales** he confined himself to generalities *or* to some general remarks

3 *(collectif)* general, common; **le bien g.** the common good; **à la surprise/l'indignation générale** to everybody's surprise/indignation

4 *(total)* general; **amnistie générale** general amnesty

5 *Admin & Pol (assemblée, direction)* general; **il a été nommé directeur g.** he's been appointed managing director

6 *(discipline, science)* general; **linguistique générale** general linguistics *(singulier)*

NM **1** *Mil* general; **g. d'armée** general; **g. d'armée aérienne** *Br* air chief marshal, *Am* general; **g. de brigade** *Br* brigadier, *Am* brigadier general; **g. de brigade aérienne** *Br* air commodore, *Am* brigadier general; **g. en chef** commander in chief; **g. de corps aérien** *Br* air marshal, *Am* lieutenant general; **g. de corps d'armée** lieutenant general; **g. de corps d'armée aérienne** *Br* air marshal, *Am* lieutenant general; **g. de division** major general; **g. de division aérienne** *Br* air vice-marshal, *Am* major general

2 *Rel* general

3 *(toujours au singulier)* general; **aller du g. au particulier** to move from the general to the particular

❑ **Général** NPR **le G.** General de Gaulle

❑ **générale** NF **1** *Théât* (final) dress rehearsal

2 *Mil* alarm call; **battre** *ou* **sonner la générale** *Mil* to sound the alarm; *Naut* to beat to quarters

3 *(épouse du général)* general's wife; **bonjour, madame la générale** *(qui s'appelle Leclerc)* hello, Mrs Leclerc

❑ **Générale** NF **la Générale des Eaux** = water utility

❑ **en général** ADV **1** *(habituellement)* generally, as a rule; **en g. elle se couche tôt** she goes to bed early as a rule, she generally goes to bed early; **en g., il me prévient quand il rentre tard** he generally *or* usually lets me know if he's going to be late (home)

2 *(globalement)* in general; **le genre humain en g.** mankind in general, the great majority of mankind; **on parlait de l'amour en g.** we were talking about love in general; **tu parles en g. ou (tu parles) de nous?** are you talking generally *or* in general terms or (are you talking) about us?; **est-ce que vous êtes d'accord avec ses propos? – en g., non!** do you agree with what he says? – generally speaking, no!

généralat [ʒenerala] NM *Rel* generalate

généralement [ʒeneralmɑ̃] ADV **1** *(habituellement)* generally, usually; **les magasins sont g. fermés le dimanche** (the) shops are generally closed on Sundays **2** *(globalement)* generally; **g. parlant** generally speaking; **on croit g. que...** there is a widespread belief that..., it is widely believed that...

généralisable [ʒeneralizabl] ADJ that can be generalized; **l'expérience/la théorie est intéressante, mais est-elle g.?** it's an interesting experiment/theory, but can it be generalized *or* applied more generally?

généralisateur, -trice [ʒeneralizatœr, -tris] ADJ *(esprit, méthode)* generalizing; **c'est un livre trop g.** the book generalizes too much *or* indulges in too many generalizations

généralisation [ʒeneralizasjɔ̃] NF **1** *(propos, idée)* generalization; **faire des généralisations** to make generalizations, to generalize; **avoir tendance à la g.** to tend to make generalizations *or* to generalize; **une g. hâtive** a sweeping generalization **2** *(extension)* generalization; **nous assistons à la g. du conflit/de la maladie** the conflict/the disease is spreading

généralisatrice [ʒeneralizatris] *voir* **généralisateur**

généralisé, -e [ʒeneralize] ADJ *(conflit, crise)* widespread, generalized; **il a un cancer g.** the cancer has spread through his whole body

généraliser [3] [ʒeneralize] VT **1** *(répandre)* **cette méthode/interdiction a été généralisée** this method/ban now applies to everybody; **cette mesure a été généralisée en 1969** this measure was extended across the board in 1969

2 *(globaliser)* to generalize; **il a tendance à tout g.** he tends to generalize; **tu n'as pas le droit de g.** you have no right to generalize; **ne généralise pas ton cas personnel** don't generalize from your own experience

USAGE ABSOLU to generalize; **on ne peut pas g.** you can't generalize

▸**se généraliser** VPR *(crise, famine)* to become widespread; *(usage, conflit, grève)* to spread; **l'usage de la carte de crédit s'est généralisé** credit cards are now in general use; **la crise économique s'est généralisée à tous les pays occidentaux** the economic crisis has spread to all countries in the West

généralissime [ʒeneralisim] NM generalissimo

généraliste [ʒeneralist] ADJ **une chaîne de télévision g.** a general-interest TV channel; **le caractère g. de l'entreprise** the diversity of the company's activities

NMF *Méd Br* general practitioner, GP, *Am* family practitioner

généralité [ʒeneralite] NF **1** *(universalité)* generality

2 *(majorité)* **dans la g. des cas** in most cases

❑ **généralités** NFPL *(points généraux)* general remarks; *(banalités)* generalities; **s'en tenir à des généralités** to confine oneself to generalities *or* to general remarks; **exposer quelques généralités dans un cours d'introduction** to present some general ideas in an introductory course

générateur, -trice [ʒeneratœr, -tris] ADJ **1** *(machine)* generating; *(force, organe)* generative; *Élec* **station** *ou* **usine génératrice** generating station *or* plant; **chaudière génératrice** steam boiler

2 *(créateur)* **être g. de** to generate; **la nouvelle politique salariale sera génératrice d'emplois** the new wages policy will create jobs *or* generate employment; **une industrie génératrice d'emplois** a job-creating industry; **un fanatisme g. de violence** a fanaticism that breeds violence; **un colorant alimentaire g. de troubles gastriques** a food colouring which causes gastric problems

3 *Math* **ligne génératrice d'une surface** line which generates a surface

NM **1** *Élec* generator; **g. d'électricité** electricity

generator; *Électron* **g. d'impulsions** pulse generator; *Électron* **g. de signaux** signal *or* signalling generator; **g. de vapeur** steam generator

2 *Nucl* **g. isotopique** radioisotopic (power) generator

3 *Ordinat* generator; **g. automatique de programmes** report program generator; **g. de caractères** character generator; **g. d'effets numériques** digital effects generator; **g. d'états** report generator; **g. graphique** graphics generator; **g. de menus** menu builder; **g. de programmes** (program) generator; **g. de système expert** generic expert system tool

4 *TV & Cin* **g. de couleur** colour synthesizer; **g. d'effets spéciaux** (special) effects generator, SEG; **g. de signaux** colour coder; **g. de synchro** *ou* **de synchronisation** synchronizing generator, sync pulse generator, SPG; **g. de titres graphiques** graphic titler

❑ **génératrice** NF **1** *Élec* generator; *Nucl* **génératrice nucléaire** nuclear power reactor

2 *Math* generatrix

génératif, -ive [ʒeneratif, -iv] ADJ generative

génération [ʒenerasjɔ̃] NF **1** *Biol* generation; **les organes de la g.** the reproductive organs; **g. spontanée** spontaneous generation

2 (*action de générer*) generation; (*de vapeur*) generation, production; (*de métaux*) formation

3 (*groupe d'âge*) generation; **la g. actuelle** the present generation; **la g. électronique** the e-generation; **la jeune g.** the younger generation; **la g. montante** the new generation; **les jeunes de ma g.** young people my age *or* of my generation; **de g. en g.** from generation to generation, through the generations; **quatre générations vivent sous le même toit** four generations live under the same roof; **des immigrés de la seconde g.** second-generation immigrants; *Fig* **la g. perdue** the lost generation; **g. X** generation X; **g. Y** generation Y

4 (*durée*) generation; **entre le grand-père et le petit-fils il y a deux générations** there are two generations between the grandfather and the grandson; **il y a environ trois générations par siècle** there are approximately three generations per century

5 (*d'une technique*) **la nouvelle g. de machines à laver** the new generation of washing machines; **les lecteurs de disques compacts de la quatrième g.** fourth-generation compact disc *or* CD players

6 *Ordinat* generation; **g. automatique de textes** automatic generation of texts; **g. d'écrans** screen generation; **g. de langage/machine/système** language/computer/system generation

7 *Pol* **G. Écologie** = one of the two green parties in France

générationnel, -elle [ʒenerasjɔnɛl] ADJ generational

générative [ʒenerativ] *voir* **génératif**

génératrice [ʒeneratris] *voir* **générateur**

générer [18] [ʒenere] VT **1** (*faire naître* → *idées, images, profits*) to generate; *Ordinat* **généré par ordinateur** computer-generated **2** (*produire* → *électricité, vapeur*) to generate, to produce

généreuse [ʒenerøz] *voir* **généreux**

généreusement [ʒenerøzmɑ̃] ADV **1** (*avec libéralité*) generously; **g. rétribué** generously rewarded **2** (*avec noblesse*) generously; **il a g. offert de nous aider** he generously offered to help us **3** (*en grande quantité*) **se servir à manger g.** to help oneself to a generous portion; **se verser g. à boire** to pour oneself a good measure

généreux, -euse [ʒenerø, -øz] ADJ **1** (*prodigue*) generous; **être** *ou* **se montrer g. (avec** *ou* **envers qn)** to be generous (with sb); **il a été très g.** he gave very generously, he was very generous; **laisser un pourboire g.** to leave a generous *or* handsome tip

2 (*noble* → *geste, tempérament, âme*) noble; **des sentiments g.** unselfish *or* noble sentiments

3 (*fertile* → *terre*) generous, fertile

4 (*abondant* → *portion*) generous; (→ *repas*) lavish

5 (*plantureux*) **aux formes généreuses** curvaceous; **une femme à la poitrine généreuse** a woman with an ample bosom

6 (*vin* → *riche en alcool*) high in alcohol; (→ *riche en saveur*) full-bodied

générique [ʒenerik] ADJ (*publicité, marché, produit*) generic; **produit g.** no-name *or* generic product; **médicament g.** generic drug

NM **1** *Cin & TV* credits; **figurer au g.** to appear in the credits, to get a credit; **au g. de notre émission ce soir...** and tonight we have for you, and tonight's programme includes...; **g. de début** opening credits; **g. de fin** closing credits, end titles; **g. déroulant** rolling titles

2 (*indicatif musical*) signature tune

générosité [ʒenerozite] NF **1** (*largesse*) generosity **2** (*bonté*) generosity, kindness; **avec g.** generously; **je l'ai fait dans un élan de g.** I did it in a sudden fit of kindness; **tu fais ça par (pure) g.?** are you doing this out of the kindness of your heart? **3** (*d'un vin*) full body **4** (*des formes*) opulence

❑ **générosités** NFPL (*cadeaux*) gifts, liberalities

Gênes [ʒɛn] NM Genoa

genèse [ʒɔnɛz] NF **1** (*élaboration*) genesis; **la g. d'un livre** the genesis *or* origin of a book; **faire la g. de qch** to trace the evolution of sth **2** *Bible* **la G.** (the Book of) Genesis

génésiaque [ʒenezjak] ADJ Genesitic, Genesiac, Genesiacal

génésique [ʒenezik] ADJ generative

genet [ʒɔnɛ] NM *Zool* jennet (*horse*)

genêt [ʒɔnɛ] NM *Bot* broom (UNCOUNT)

généthliaque [ʒenetljak] ADJ *Astrol* genethliac, genethliacal

généticien, -enne [ʒenetisjɛ̃, -ɛn] NM,F geneticist

genêtière [ʒɔnɛtjɛr] NF broom field

génétique [ʒenetik] ADJ genetic; **fond g. commun** gene pool

NF genetics (*singulier*)

génétiquement [ʒenetikmɑ̃] ADV genetically; **g. modifié** genetically modified

génétisme [ʒenetism] NM *Psy* geneticism

génétiste [ʒenetist] *Psy* ADJ geneticist

NMF geneticist

genette [ʒɔnɛt] NF *Zool* genet

gêneur, -euse [ʒenœr, -øz] NM,F nuisance; **il ne cesse de m'appeler, quel g.!** he keeps phoning me, what a nuisance (he is)!

Genève [ʒɔnɛv] NM Geneva; **le lac de G.** Lake Geneva; **le canton de G.** Geneva

Geneviève [ʒɔnvjɛv] NPR **G. de Brabant** = a symbol of virtue persecuted but triumphant, based on a medieval legend

genevois, -e [ʒɔnvwa, -az] ADJ Genevan, Genevese

❑ **Genevois, -e** NM,F Genevan, Genevese; **les G.** the Genevans, the Genevese

genévrier [ʒɔnevrije] NM *Bot* juniper

Gengis Khan [ʒɛ̃ʒiskɑ̃] NPR Genghis Khan

génial, -e, -aux, -ales [ʒenjal, -o] ADJ **1** (*qui a du génie*) of genius; **Mozart était un compositeur g.** Mozart was a composer of genius

2 (*ingénieux*) brilliant; **ce fut une invention géniale** it was a brilliant invention

3 *Fam* (*extraordinaire*) brilliant, great, fantastic; **un film g.** a great *or* brilliant *or* fantastic film; **un mec g.** a great guy; **elle est géniale, ta copine** your girlfriend is great *or* fantastic; **je n'ai pas trouvé cette exposition géniale** I didn't think much of that exhibition; **pas g.** not exactly brilliant; **tu as vu le film hier soir? pas g., hein?** did you see the film last night? no great shakes *or* not up to much, was it?; **tu as gagné aux courses? mais c'est g.!** you've won on the horses? that's great *or* fantastic *or* brilliant!

EXCLAM brilliant!, great!

génialement [ʒenjalmɑ̃] ADV with genius, masterfully, brilliantly

génialité [ʒenjalite] NF genius, brilliancy

génie [ʒeni] NM **1** (*don*) genius; **avoir du g.** to be a genius; **avoir le g. de qch/pour faire qch** to have a genius *or* gift for sth/for doing sth; **elle a le g. des affaires** she has a genius for business; *Ironique* **tu as vraiment le g. pour te mettre dans des situations impossibles!** you have a real gift for *or* the knack of always getting into difficult situations!

2 (*personne*) genius; **c'est loin d'être un g.** he's/she's no genius; **à 15 ans, c'était déjà un g. de l'électronique** at 15 he/she was already an electronics wizard

3 (*essence*) genius; **le g. de la langue française** the genius *or* spirit of the French language; **le g. d'un peuple** the genius of a people

4 *Littérature & Myth* (*magicien*) genie; (*esprit*) spirit; **g. des airs** spirit of the air; **être le bon/mauvais g. de qn** to be a good/bad influence on sb; **le petit g. de la forêt** the forest sprite

5 *Tech* **le G.** engineering; **les officiers du g.** *Br* ≃ the Royal Engineers, *Am* ≃ the (Army) Corps of Engineers; **soldat du g.** engineer, *Br* sapper; **g. aéroporté** airborne engineers; **g. de l'air** aviation engineers; **g. atomique** nuclear engineering; **g. biologique** bioengineering; **g. chimique** chemical engineering; **g. civil** civil engineering; **g. électronique** electronic engineering; **g. génétique** genetic engineering; **g. industriel** industrial engineering; **g. logiciel** systems engineering; **g. maritime** marine engineering; **g. militaire** military engineering; **g. rural** agricultural engineering

❑ **de génie** ADJ (*musicien, inventeur*) of genius; (*idée*) brilliant

'**Génie du christianisme**' *Chateaubriand* 'The Genius of Christianity'

genièvre [ʒɔnjɛvr] NM **1** *Bot* (*arbre*) juniper; (*fruit*) juniper berry; **grain de g.** juniper berry **2** (*eau-de-vie*) geneva

génique [ʒenik] ADJ genic; **thérapie g.** gene therapy

génisse [ʒenis] NF *Zool* heifer

génistéine [ʒenistein] NF *Biol & Chim* genistein

génital, -e, -aux, -ales [ʒenital, -o] ADJ *Anat* genital; **appareil g.** genitalia

géniteur, -trice [ʒenitœr, -tris] NM,F *Hum* progenitor, parent

NM *Zool* sire

génitif [ʒenitif] NM *Gram* genitive (case); **au g.** in the genitive

génito-urinaire [ʒenitɔyrinɛr] (*pl* **génito-urinaires**) ADJ genito-urinary

génitrice [ʒenitris] *voir* **géniteur**

génocidaire [ʒenɔsidɛr] ADJ genocidal

NMF genocide

génocide [ʒenɔsid] NM genocide

génois, -e [ʒenwa, -az] ADJ Genoese, Genovese

NM **1** (*dialecte*) Genoese *or* Genovese (dialect) **2** *Naut* Genoa (jib)

❑ **Génois, -e** NM,F Genoese, Genovese; **les G.** the Genoese, the Genovese

❑ **génoise** NF *Culin* sponge cake; **une génoise fourrée aux abricots** an apricot sponge (cake)

génome [ʒenom] NM *Biol* genome

génomique [ʒenɔmik] *Biol* ADJ genomic, genome (*avant n*)

NF genomics (*singulier*)

génothérapie [ʒenɔterapi] NF *Biol* genotherapy, gene therapy

génotypage [ʒenɔtipaʒ] NM *Biol* genotyping

génotype [ʒenɔtip] NM *Biol* genotype

genou, -x [ʒɔnu] NM **1** *Anat* knee; **on était dans la neige jusqu'aux genoux** we were knee-deep *or* up to our knees in snow; **sa robe lui arrivait au-dessus du g./aux genoux** her dress came down to just above the knee/to her knees; **cette année les jupes s'arrêtent au g.** knee-length skirts are the fashion this year; **mon jean est troué aux genoux** my jeans have got holes at *or* in the knees; **avoir les genoux en dedans** to be knock-kneed; **mettre un g. à terre** to go down on one knee; **assis sur les genoux de sa mère** sitting on his/her mother's lap *or* knee; **plier** *ou* **fléchir** *ou* **ployer le g. devant qn** to bow down *or* to kneel before sb; **faire du g. à qn** to play footsie with sb; **être sur les genoux** to be exhausted; **être aux genoux de qn** to be at sb's feet

2 *Tech* (*joint*) ball-and-socket joint

3 *Couture* knee pad

❑ **à genoux** ADV **1** (*sur le sol*) **se mettre à genoux** to kneel (down), to go down on one's knees; **se mettre à genoux devant qn** to go down on one's knees to sb; **elle lavait le sol à genoux** she was cleaning the floor on her hands and knees

2 *Fig* **être à genoux devant qn** (*lui être soumis*) to be on one's knees before sb; (*être en adoration devant lui*) to worship sb; **le public français**

est à genoux devant lui French audiences worship him; **c'est à tomber** *ou* **se mettre à genoux tellement c'est beau** it's so beautiful it bowls you over; **je ne vais pas me mettre à genoux devant lui** *(le supplier)* I'm not going to go down on my knees to him; **demander qch à genoux** to ask for sth on bended knee; **je te le demande à genoux** I beg of you

'Le Genou de Claire' *Rohmer* 'Claire's Knee'

genouillé, -e [ʒənuje] **ADJ** *Anat* **corps g.** geniculate body

genouillère [ʒənujɛr] **NF 1** *(protection)* knee pad **2** *(bandage)* knee bandage *or* support **3** *(pièce d'armure)* knee piece, genouillère **4** *Tech* **articulation à g.** toggle joint

genre [ʒɑ̃r] **NM 1** *(sorte, espèce)* kind, sort, type; **on y trouve des livres de tous les genres** all sorts *or* kinds *or* types of books are found there; **quel g. de femme est-elle?** what kind of woman is she?; **quel g. de vie mène-t-il?** what kind *or* sort of (a) life does he lead?; **ce n'est pas le g. à renoncer** he's/she's not the sort to give up *or* who gives up; **partir sans payer, ce n'est pas son g.** it's not like him/her to leave without paying; **sa nouvelle copine est du g. pot de colle** his new girlfriend's the clinging sort *or* kind; **c'est ce qu'on fait de mieux dans le g.** it's the best of its kind; **un g. de** *(une sorte de)* a kind *or* sort of; **un peu dans le g. de...** rather *or* a bit like...; **elle m'a répondu quelque chose du g. "je ne suis pas ta bonne"** she answered something along the lines of "I'm not here to wait on you"; **un vin blanc g. sauternes** a Sauternes-type white wine; **étui g. maroquin** case in imitation morocco

2 *(comportement, manières)* type, style; **le g. intellectuel** the intellectual type; **c'est le g. star** he's/she's the film star type; **avoir un drôle de g.** to be an odd sort; **leurs enfants ont vraiment bon g.** their children really know how to behave; **elle a mauvais g.** she's a bit vulgar; **dans le g. vulgaire, on ne fait pas mieux!** beat that for vulgarity!; **il a exigé qu'on lui rembourse le dessert, tu vois le g.!** he had the dessert deducted from the bill, you know the sort!; **il est romantique, tout à fait mon g.!** he's a romantic, just my type!; **faire du g., se donner un g.** to put on airs, to give oneself airs; **g. de vie** lifestyle

3 *Biol* genus; **le g. humain** mankind, the human race

4 *Beaux-Arts* genre; **le grand g.** historical painting; **peinture de g.** genre painting

5 *Gram* gender; **s'accorder en g. et en nombre** to agree in gender and number

6 *Littérature* genre; **le g. policier** the detective genre, detective stories; **le g. romanesque** the novel; **le g. comique** comedy; **le g. tragique** tragedy

▫ **dans son genre ADV** *(à sa façon)* in his/her (own) way; **c'est un artiste dans son g.** he's/she's an artist in his/her (own) way

▫ **en son genre ADV** *(dans sa catégorie)* **un voyage vraiment unique en son g.** a journey unique of its kind; **elle est unique en son g.** she's in a class of her own

▫ **en tout genre, en tous genres ADV** of all kinds; **fournitures de bureau en tout g.** office equipment of all kinds; **travaux en tous genres** all kinds of work undertaken

gens[1] [ʒɛ̃s] *(pl* **gentes** [ʒɛ̃tɛs]) **NF** *Antiq (groupe de familles)* gens; **la g. Cornelia** the gens Cornelia

gens[2] [ʒɑ̃]

Any adjective before **gens** will be in the feminine; any adjective coming after will be in the masculine.

NMPL OU NFPL 1 *(personnes)* people; **les vieilles g.** old people, old folk; **les g. sont de plus en plus pressés** people are in more and more of a hurry; **que vont dire les g.?** what will people say?; **beaucoup de g., bien des g.** many people, a lot of people; **il y avait peu de g. dans la salle** there were not many people in the hall; **il y a des g. qui demandent à vous voir** there are some people who want to see you; **des g. de la campagne** country folk *or* people; **les g. d'ici, les g. du pays** people from around here, the locals; **les g. du monde** society people; **des g. simples** ordinary folk *or* people; **les g. de la ville** townspeople, townsfolk; **petites g.** people of limited means; **les bonnes g. murmurent que...** people are saying *or* whispering that...

2 *(corporation)* **comme disent les g. du métier** as the experts *or* the professionals say; **les g. d'Église** clergymen, the clergy, the cloth; **g. de lettres** men and women of letters; **g. de maison** servants, domestic staff; **g. de mer** seafarers; *Littéraire* **les g. de robe** the legal profession; **g. du spectacle** stage *or* showbusiness people; **g. de théâtre** theatre *or* theatrical people; **les g. du voyage** *(artistes)* travelling players *or* performers; *(gitans)* travellers

3 *(nation)* **le droit des g.** the law of nations

4 *Vieilli (domestiques)* servants, domestics; *(de roi)* retinue

gent [ʒɑ̃] **NF** *Hum (espèce)* race, tribe; **la g. ailée** our feathered friends; **la g. masculine/féminine** the male/female sex

gentamicine [ʒɑ̃tamisin] **NF** gentamicin

gentes [ʒɛ̃tɛs] *voir* **gens**[1]

gentiane [ʒɑ̃sjan] **NF 1** *Bot* gentian; **g. amère** autumn gentian; **g. champêtre** field gentian; **g. printanière** spring gentian; **g. pneumonante** marsh gentian **2** *(liqueur)* gentian bitters

gentil, -ille [ʒɑ̃ti, -ij] **ADJ 1** *(serviable)* kind; **ils sont gentils avec moi** they're kind *or* nice to me; **sois g., apporte-moi mes lunettes** do me a favour and get my glasses for me; **vous serez g. de me prévenir de leur arrivée** be kind enough to let me know when they are arriving; **merci, c'est g.** thanks, that's very kind of you

2 *(aimable)* nice, sweet; **tu es bien g. de m'aider** it's very nice *or* kind *or* good of you to help me; **c'est g. de votre part (de m'écrire)** it is kind *or* good of you (to write to me); **je l'aime bien, il est g.** I like him, he's nice; **ils ont écrit sur moi des choses gentilles** they wrote some very nice things about me; **elle a pris mon idée sans me le dire, ce n'est pas très g.** she stole my idea without telling me, that's not very nice (of her); **il est g. comme un cœur** he's an absolute angel; **g. membre** holidaymaker *(at Club Méditerranée)*; **g. organisateur** group leader *(at Club Méditerranée)*

3 *(joli)* nice, pretty, cute; **un g. petit village** a nice *or* pretty little village; **un g. petit minois** a cute little face; **c'est g. par ici** it's nice *or* pleasant around here

4 *(exprimant l'impatience)* **c'est bien g., mais...** that's all very well, but...; **c'est bien g., tout ça, mais si on parlait affaires?** that's all very well, but what about getting down to business?; **tu es bien g., mais quand est-ce que je vais récupérer mon argent?** that's all very well but when do I get my money back?; **elle est bien gentille mais elle n'y comprend rien** she's means well but she hasn't got a clue

5 *(obéissant)* good; **il a été g.?** was he good?; **si tu es g./gentille** if you're a good boy/girl; **en voilà un g. garçon!** there's a good boy!

6 *(avant le nom) (considérable)* **une gentille somme** a tidy *or* fair sum

NM *(non-juif)* Gentile; **les gentils** the Gentiles

gentilé [ʒɑ̃tile] **NM** *Gram (nom)* gentile noun; *(adjectif)* gentile adjective

gentilhomme [ʒɑ̃tijɔm] *(pl* **gentilshommes** [ʒɑ̃tizɔm]) **NM 1** *Hist* nobleman, gentleman; **g. campagnard** (country) squire, country gentleman; **g. de la Chambre du Roi** gentleman of the Privy Chamber; **g. de la garde** gentleman-at-arms **2** *Littéraire (gentleman)* gentleman; **il se conduit toujours en g.** he always behaves like a gentleman

gentilhommière [ʒɑ̃tijɔmjɛr] **NF 1** *(demeure)* country seat, manor house **2** *(en Belgique)* boarding house for men

gentilité [ʒɑ̃tilite] **NF** *Hist & Rel* Gentiles

gentille [ʒɑ̃tij] *voir* **gentil**

gentillesse [ʒɑ̃tijɛs] **NF 1** *(d'une personne)* kindness *(UNCOUNT)*; **elle a fait cela par g.** she did that out of kindness; **elle a eu la g. de venir elle-même** she was kind enough to come herself; **j'étais touché par la g. de leur accueil** I was moved by their kind welcome

2 *(dans des formules de politesse)* **auriez-vous la g. de me prévenir à l'avance?** would you be so kind as to let me know beforehand?

3 *(parole)* kind word; **il lui chuchotait des gentillesses à l'oreille** he whispered kind words *or* sweet nothings in her ear; *Ironique* **échanger des gentillesses** to exchange insults

4 *(acte)* act of kindness; **elle est toujours prête à toutes les gentillesses** she's always ready to help people out

gentillet, -ette [ʒɑ̃tijɛ, -ɛt] **ADJ 1** *(mignon)* rather *or* quite nice; **il est g., leur appartement** they've got a lovely little *Br* flat *or Am* apartment **2** *Péj* **c'est un film g., sans plus** it's a pleasant enough film, but that's about it

gentilshommes [ʒɑ̃tizɔm] *voir* **gentilhomme**

gentiment [ʒɑ̃timɑ̃] **ADV 1** *(aimablement)* kindly; **ils nous ont g. proposé de nous raccompagner** they kindly offered to drive us home; **elle m'a g. tenu compagnie** she was kind enough to keep me company, she kindly kept me company; **les retardataires se sont fait g. taper sur les doigts** the latecomers got a rap on the knuckles; **je leur ai g. expliqué que c'était trop tard** I politely explained to them that it was too late

2 *(sagement)* nicely; **on discutait g. quand...** we were chatting away nicely *or* quietly chatting away when...

3 *Suisse (sans précipitation)* **fais-le g., tu as tout le temps** take your time, there's no hurry

gentleman [dʒɛntləman] *(pl* **gentlemen** [-mɛn]) **NM 1** *(homme distingué)* gentleman; **en parfait g.** like a true gentleman **2** *Courses de chevaux* amateur jockey

gentleman-farmer [dʒɛntləmanfarmœr] *(pl* **gentlemen-farmers** [-mɛn-]) **NM** gentleman farmer

gentleman-rider [dʒɛntləmanrajdœr] *(pl* **gentlemen-riders** [-mɛn-]) **NM** *Courses de chevaux* amateur jockey

gentleman's agreement [dʒɛntləmansagrimɛnt] *(pl* **gentlemen's agreements** [-mɛns-]) **NM** gentleman's agreement

gentlemen [dʒɛntləmɛn] *voir* **gentleman**

gentry [dʒɛntri] **NF** gentry

génuflexion [ʒenyflɛksjɔ̃] **NF** genuflection; **faire une g.** to genuflect

géo [ʒeo] **NF** *Fam Arg scol* geog, geography

géo- [ʒeɔ] **PRÉF** geo-

géobiologie [ʒeɔbjɔlɔʒi] **NF** geobiology

géocentrique [ʒeɔsɑ̃trik] **ADJ** geocentric

géocentrisme [ʒeɔsɑ̃trism] **NM** geocentrism

géochimie [ʒeɔʃimi] **NF** geochemistry

géochimique [ʒeɔʃimik] **ADJ** geochemical

géochimiste [ʒeɔʃimist] **NMF** geochemist

géochronologie [ʒeɔkrɔnɔlɔʒi] **NF** geochronology

géochronologique [ʒeɔkrɔnɔlɔʒik] **ADJ** geochronological

géocroiseur [ʒeɔkrwazœr] **NM** *Astron* near-earth asteroid

géode [ʒeɔd] **NF 1** *Géol & Méd* geode **2** *(à Paris)* **la G.** the Géode *(the spherical building housing a cinema at the Cité des Sciences in Paris)*

géodémographie [ʒeɔdemɔgrafi] *Mktg* **NF 1** *(données)* geodemographics **2** *(discipline)* geodemography

géodémographique [ʒeɔdemɔgrafik] **ADJ** *Mktg* geodemographic

géodésie [ʒeɔdezi] **NF** geodesy, geodetics *(singulier)*

géodésien, -enne [ʒeɔdezjɛ̃, -ɛn] **NM,F** geodesist

géodésique [ʒeɔdezik] **ADJ 1** *Math* geodesic; **point g.** triangulation point **2** *Géog* geodetic

NF *Math & Geog* geodesic (line)

géodiversité [ʒeɔdivɛrsite] **NF** geodiversity

géodynamique [ʒeɔdinamik] **ADJ** geodynamic

NF geodynamics *(singulier)*

géoglyphe [ʒeɔglif] **NM** *Archéol* geoglyph

géographe [ʒeɔgraf] **NMF** geographer

géographie [ʒeɔgrafi] **NF 1** *(science)* geography; **g. humaine/physique/politique** human/physical/political geography **2** *(livre)* geography book

géographique [ʒeɔgrafik] **ADJ** geographic, geographical; **carte g.** map; **dictionnaire g.** gazetteer

géographiquement [ʒeɔgrafikmɑ̃] **ADV** geographically

géoïde [ʒeɔid] **NM** geoid

geôle [ʒol] **NF** *Arch ou Littéraire* jail, *Br* gaol

geôlier, -ère [ʒolje, -ɛr] **NM,F** *Arch ou Littéraire* jailer, *Br* gaoler; *Fig* **les lois ne doivent pas être les geôlières de la liberté** the law must not fetter liberty

géologie [ʒeɔlɔʒi] **NF** geology

géologique [ʒeɔlɔʒik] **ADJ** geologic, geological

géologiquement [ʒeɔlɔʒikmã] **ADV** geologically

géologue [ʒeɔlɔg] **NMF** geologist

géomagnétique [ʒeɔmaɲetik] **ADJ** geomagnetic

géomagnétisme [ʒeɔmaɲetism] **NM** geomagnetism

géomancie [ʒeɔmãsi] **NF** geomancy

géomarketing [ʒeɔmarketiŋ] **NM** geomarketing

géométral, -e, -aux, -ales [ʒeɔmetral, -o] **ADJ** flat, plane
  NM flat projection

géomètre [ʒeɔmɛtr] **NMF 1** *Math* geometer, geometrician **2** *(arpenteur)* land surveyor
  NM *Entom (chenille)* measuring worm, looper; *(papillon)* geometer moth

géométride [ʒeɔmetrid], **géométridé** [ʒeɔmetride] *Entom* **NM** geometer moth, *Spéc* member of the Geometridae
  ◻ **géométrides, géométridés NMPL** geometer moths, *Spéc* Geometridae

géométrie [ʒeɔmetri] **NF 1** *Math* geometry; **g. analytique** analytical *or* co-ordinate geometry; **g. euclidienne/non euclidienne** Euclidean/non-Euclidean geometry; **g. plane/dans l'espace** plane/solid geometry **2** *(livre)* geometry book
  ◻ **à géométrie variable ADJ 1** *(avion)* swing-wing *(avant n)* **2** *Fig (susceptible d'évoluer)* flexible, adaptable

géométrique [ʒeɔmetrik] **ADJ 1** *Math* geometric, geometrical; **progression/suite g.** geometric progression/series **2** *Beaux-Arts* geometric; **abstraction g.** geometrical abstraction; **ornementation g.** geometric decorative style **3** *Fig (précision)* mathematical; **être d'une rigueur toute g.** to be extremely rigorous

géométriquement [ʒeɔmetrikmã] **ADV** geometrically

géométrisation [ʒeɔmetrizasjɔ̃] **NF** geometrization

géométriser [3] [ʒeɔmetrize] **VT** to geometrize

géomorphologie [ʒeɔmɔrfɔlɔʒi] **NF** geomorphology

géomorphologique [ʒeɔmɔrfɔlɔʒik] **ADJ** geomorphological

géomorphologue [ʒeɔmɔrfɔlɔg] **NMF** geomorphologist

géophage [ʒeɔfaʒ] **ADJ** geophagous
  NMF geophagist

géophagie [ʒeɔfaʒi] **NF** geophagy

géophile [ʒeɔfil] **NM** *Entom* geophilus

géophone [ʒeɔfɔn] **NM** geophone

géophysicien, -enne [ʒeɔfizisjɛ̃, -ɛn] **NM,F** geophysicist

géophysique [ʒeɔfizik] **ADJ** geophysical
  NF geophysics *(singulier)*

géopolitique [ʒeɔpɔlitik] **ADJ** geopolitical
  NF geopolitics *(singulier)*

Georgetown [dʒɔrʒtaun] **NM** Georgetown

georgette [ʒɔrʒɛt] **NF** *Tex* **crêpe g.** georgette (crepe)

Géorgie [ʒeɔrʒi] **NF** **la G.** Georgia; **vivre en G.** to live in Georgia; **aller en G.** to go to Georgia

georgien, -enne [ʒeɔrʒjɛ̃, -ɛn] **ADJ** *Archit* Georgian

géorgien, -enne [ʒeɔrʒjɛ̃, -ɛn] **ADJ** *Géog* Georgian
  NM *(langue)* Georgian
  ◻ **Géorgien, -enne NM,F** Georgian

géorgique [ʒeɔrʒik] **ADJ** *Littérature* georgic

Géorgiques [ʒeɔrʒik] **NFPL**

'Les Géorgiques' *Virgile* 'The Georgics'

---

géoscience [ʒeɔsjãs] **NF** geoscience, earth science; **les géosciences** geoscience, earth sciences

géosmine [ʒeɔsmin] **NF** *Chim* geosmin

géosphère [ʒeɔsfɛr] **NF** geosphere

géostationnaire [ʒeɔstasjɔnɛr] **ADJ** *Astron* **satellite g.** geostationary satellite

géostatique [ʒeɔstatik] **ADJ** geostatic
  NF geostatics *(singulier)*

géostatistique [ʒeɔstatistik] **NF** *Mines* geostatistics *(singulier)*

géostratégie [ʒeɔstrateʒi] **NF** geostrategy

géostratégique [ʒeɔstrateʒik] **ADJ** geostrategic

géostrophique [ʒeɔstrɔfik] **ADJ** *Météo* geostrophic

géosynchrone [ʒeɔsɛ̃kron] **ADJ** geosynchronous

géosynclinal, -aux [ʒeɔsɛ̃klinal, -o] **NM** geosyncline

géotechnicien, -enne [ʒeɔtɛknisjɛ̃, -ɛn] **NM,F** geotechnician

géotechnique [ʒeɔtɛknik] **ADJ** geotechnical
  NF geotechnics *(singulier)*

géotectonique [ʒeɔtɛktɔnik] **ADJ** geotectonic

géotextile [ʒeɔtɛkstil] **NM** geotextile

géothermie [ʒeɔtɛrmi] **NF** geothermal science, geothermics *(singulier)*

géothermique [ʒeɔtɛrmik] **ADJ** geothermic, geothermal

géothermomètre [ʒeɔtɛrmɔmɛtr] **NM** geothermometer

géotropique [ʒeɔtrɔpik] **ADJ** geotropic

géotropiquement [ʒeɔtrɔpikmã] **ADV** geotropically

géotropisme [ʒeɔtrɔpism] **NM** *Bot* geotropism

géotrupe [ʒeɔtryp] **NM** *Entom* geotrupes

gérable [ʒerabl] **ADJ** manageable; **un problème/une situation difficilement g.** a problem/a situation which is difficult to deal with *or* to manage

gérance [ʒerãs] **NF 1** *(fonction)* management; **assurer la g. de** to be (the) manager of, to manage; **prendre/reprendre un fonds en g.** to take on/to take over the management of a business; **donner la g. d'un commerce à qn** to appoint sb manager of a business; **mettre un fonds en g.** to appoint a manager to a business; **une g. de cinq ans** a five-year managership; **g. libre** lease management; **g. de portefeuille** portfolio management
  2 *(période)* management, managership; **pendant sa g.** during his/her time as manager, under his/her management

géraniacée [ʒeranjase] *Bot* **NF** member of the Geraniaceae family
  ◻ **géraniacées NFPL** Geraniaceae

géranium [ʒeranjɔm] **NM** *Bot* geranium; *(sauvage)* crane's bill; **g. des bois** wood crane's bill; **g. brun** dusky crane's bill; **g. colombin** long-stalked crane's bill; **g. découpé** cut-leaved crane's bill; **g. fluet** small-flowered crane's bill; **g. luisant** shining crane's bill; **g. mou** dove's-foot crane's bill; **g. des prés** meadow crane's bill; **g. des Pyrénées** hedge-row crane's bill; **g. sanguin** bloody crane's bill

géranium-lierre [ʒeranjɔmljɛr] *(pl* **géraniums-lierres)** **NM** *Bot* ivy-leaved geranium

gérant, -e [ʒerã, -ãt] **NM,F** manager; *(d'un journal)* managing editor; **g. d'affaires** business manager; **g. de fonds** fund manager; **g. d'hôtel** hotel manager; **g. d'immeubles** managing agent *(for an apartment block)*; **g. de magasin** store manager; **g. majoritaire** manager with a controlling interest; **g. minoritaire** manager with a minority interest; **g. non associé** salaried manager, manager with no holding in a business; **g. de portefeuille** portfolio manager; **g. de société** managing director *(of a company)*

gerbage [ʒɛrbaʒ] **NM 1** *(du blé)* binding, sheaving **2** *(de fûts, de paquets)* stacking, piling

gerbe [ʒɛrb] **NF 1** *(de blé)* sheaf; *(de fleurs)* spray; **lier le blé en gerbes** to sheave the corn, to bind the corn into sheaves; **g. de fleurs** spray of flowers; **déposer une g. au pied d'un monument aux morts** to lay a wreath at a war memorial
  2 *(de feu d'artifice)* spray, *Spéc* gerbe
  3 *(jaillissement → d'eau)* spray; *(→ d'étincelles)* shower; **une g. de flammes** a blaze, a burst of flame; **la voiture faisait jaillir des gerbes d'eau sur son passage** the car sent up a spray of water as it went by
  4 *Astron & Phys* shower
  5 *Mil* cone of fire
  6 *Vulg* **avoir la g.** *(avoir envie de vomir)* to feel like throwing up *or* puking; *(vomir)* to puke, to throw up; **foutre la g. à qn** to make sb want to throw up *or* puke

gerbée [ʒɛrbe] **NF 1** *(paille)* fodder straw **2** *(fourrage)* corn cut in the green

gerber [3] [ʒɛrbe] **VT 1** *(blé)* to bind, to sheave, to bind into sheaves **2** *(fûts, paquets)* to pile (up), to stack (up)
  VI 1 *Vulg (vomir)* to throw up, to puke; **ça me**

fait g. it makes me want to throw up *or* puke **2** *(feu d'artifice)* to shower, to fan out

gerbera [ʒerbera] **NM** *Bot* gerbera

gerbeur [ʒɛrbœr] **NM** stacker, stacking machine

gerbeuse [ʒɛrbøz] **NF** stacker, stacking machine

gerbier [ʒɛrbje] **NM** stack, rick

gerbière [ʒɛrbjɛr] **NF 1** *(charrette)* harvest wagon **2** *(meule)* pile of sheaves

gerbille [ʒɛrbij] **NF** *Zool* gerbil

gerboise [ʒɛrbwaz] **NF** *Zool* jerboa

gerce [ʒɛrs] **NF 1** *Métal* crack **2** *(dans le bois)* crack, flaw

gercé, -e [ʒɛrse] **ADJ** cracked; *(mains, lèvres)* chapped

gercement [ʒɛrsmã] **NM** *(du bois)* cracking *(UNCOUNT)*; *(de la peau, des mains, des lèvres)* chapping *(UNCOUNT)*, cracking *(UNCOUNT)*

gercer [16] [ʒɛrse] **VI 1** *(peau, mains, lèvres)* to chap, to crack; **chaque hiver, j'ai les mains qui gercent** every winter I get chapped hands **2** *(bois, métal, enduit)* to crack
  VT to chap, to crack
  ▶ **se gercer VPR** *(peau, mains, lèvres)* to chap, to get chapped, to crack; *(terre)* to crack

gerçure [ʒɛrsyr] **NF 1** *(des mains, des lèvres)* crack, chapping *(UNCOUNT)*; **j'ai des gerçures aux mains/lèvres** I've got chapped hands/lips **2** *Tech (d'un métal, d'un enduit)* hairline crack; *(d'un diamant, du bois)* flaw; *(d'un tronc)* heart shake

géré, -e [ʒere] **ADJ 1** *(affaire, entreprise)* **bien g.** well managed; **mal g.** poorly managed **2** *Ordinat* **g. par ordinateur** computer-assisted, computer-controlled; **g. par le système** system-maintained

gérénuk [ʒerenyk] **NM** *Zool* gerenuk, Waller's gazelle

gérer [18] [ʒere] **VT 1** *(budget, fortune, ville)* to administer, to manage; *(finances, conflit, situation difficile)* to manage; **elle a bien géré ses comptes** she managed her accounts well; **mal g. qch** to mismanage sth; **g. une tutelle** to administer the estate of a ward; *Fig* **ils se contentent de g. la crise** they're (quite) happy to sit out the crisis
  2 *(entreprise, hôtel, magasin)* to manage, to run; *(stock, production)* to control
  3 *(ménage)* to administer; *(temps)* to organize
  4 *Ordinat* to manage; **g. des données/un fichier** to manage data/a file

gerfaut [ʒɛrfo] **NM** *Orn* gyrfalcon

gériatre [ʒerjatr] **NMF** geriatrician, geriatrist

gériatrie [ʒerjatri] **NF** geriatrics *(singulier)*

gériatrique [ʒerjatrik] **ADJ** geriatric

germain, -e [ʒɛrmɛ̃, -ɛn] **ADJ 1** *(ayant un grand-parent commun)* **cousine germaine** first cousin **2** *(du même père et de la même mère)* **frère g.** full brother; **sœur germaine** full sister **3** *(d'Allemagne)* Germanic, German
  NM,F **cousin issu de g.** second cousin
  ◻ **Germain, -e NM,F** German, Teuton; **les Germains** the Germans *or* Teutons

germandrée [ʒɛrmãdre] **NF** *Bot* germander

Germanie [ʒɛrmani] **NF** *Hist* **la G.** Germania

germanique [ʒɛrmanik] **ADJ 1** *Hist* Germanic **2** *(allemand)* Germanic, German; **à consonance g.** German-sounding
  NM *Ling* Germanic; *Hist & Ling* Germanic, Proto-Germanic

germanisant, -e [ʒɛrmanizã, -ãt] **NM,F** Germanist

germanisation [ʒɛrmanizasjɔ̃] **NF** Germanization

germaniser [3] [ʒɛrmanize] **VT** to Germanize

germanisme [ʒɛrmanism] **NM** Germanism

germaniste [ʒɛrmanist] **NMF** Germanist

germanium [ʒɛrmanjɔm] **NM** *Chim* germanium

germanophile [ʒɛrmanɔfil] **ADJ** German-loving, Germanophile
  NMF Germanophile

germanophilie [ʒɛrmanɔfili] **NF** love of Germany, Germanophilia

germanophobe [ʒɛrmanɔfɔb] **ADJ** German-hating, Germanophobic
  NMF Germanophobe

germanophobie [ʒɛrmanɔfɔbi] **NF** hatred towards Germany, Germanophobia

germanophone [ʒɛrmanɔfɔn] **ADJ** German-speaking
  NMF German speaker; **les germanophones** German-speaking people *or* peoples

germanopratin, -e [ʒɛrmanɔpratɛ̃, -in] ADJ of/from Saint-Germain-des-Prés; **les bars germanopratins** the bars in Saint-Germain-des-Prés
NM,F = resident of Saint-Germain-des-Prés

germe [ʒɛrm] NM **1** *Anat, Biol & Méd* germ; **g. dentaire** tooth bud; **germes pathogènes** pathogenic bacteria
2 *(pousse → de pomme de terre)* eye; **g. de blé** wheat germ; **germes de soja** (soya) bean sprouts
3 *(origine)* **le g. d'une idée** the germ of an idea; **les germes de la révolution/corruption** the seeds of revolution/corruption
❑ **en germe** ADV **contenir qch en g.** to contain the seeds of sth; **la théorie était déjà présente en g. dans leur premier manifeste** the theory was already there in embryonic form in their first manifesto

germé, -e [ʒɛrme] ADJ *(pomme de terre)* sprouting; *(blé)* germinated

germen [ʒɛrmɛn] NM *Biol* germ cells

germer [3] [ʒɛrme] VI **1** *Agr & Hort (graine)* to germinate; *(bulbe, tubercule)* to shoot, to sprout; **faire g. du blé** to germinate corn **2** *Fig (idées)* to germinate; **l'idée de révolte a mis du temps à g.** the idea of revolt took some time to germinate *or* to develop; **le concept a d'abord germé dans l'esprit des urbanistes** the notion first took shape in the minds of town planners

germicide [ʒɛrmisid] ADJ germicidal
NM germicide

germinal, -e, -aux, -ales [ʒɛrminal, -o] ADJ *Biol* germinal; **cellule germinale** reproductive *or* germ cell; **lignée germinale** germ line *or* track
NM = 7th month of the French revolutionary calendar (from 22 March to 20 April)

germinateur, -trice [ʒɛrminatœr, -tris] ADJ germinative

germinatif, -ive [ʒɛrminatif, -iv] ADJ *Biol* **1** *(du germe)* germinative **2** *(du germen → pouvoir)* germinal; *(→ cellule, plasma)* germ *(avant n)*

germination [ʒɛrminasjɔ̃] NF *Biol* germination

germinative [ʒɛrminativ] *voir* **germinatif**

germinatrice [ʒɛrminatris] *voir* **germinateur**

germoir [ʒɛrmwar] NM *Biol* **1** *(pot)* seed tray **2** *(bâtiment)* germination area **3** *(d'une brasserie)* malt house, malting

germon [ʒɛrmɔ̃] NM *Ich* albacore, long-finned tuna

gérome [ʒerɔme] NM = cow's milk cheese made in Alsace and the Vosges

gérondif [ʒerɔ̃dif] NM *Ling* **1** *(en latin)* gerundive; **au g.** in the gerundive **2** *(dans d'autres langues)* gerund

Gérone [ʒerɔn] NM Gerona

géronte [ʒerɔ̃t] NM *Antiq* gerontocrat

gérontisme [ʒerɔ̃tism] NM senile decay, dotage

gérontocratie [ʒerɔ̃tɔkrasi] NF gerontocracy

gérontologie [ʒerɔ̃tɔlɔʒi] NF gerontology

gérontologue [ʒerɔ̃tɔlɔg] NMF gerontologist

gérontophile [ʒerɔ̃tɔfil] ADJ gerontophile
NMF gerontophile

gérontophilie [ʒerɔ̃tɔfili] NF gerontophilia

gerris [ʒeris] NM *Entom* pond skater

Gers [ʒɛr] NM **le G.** Gers

gerseau, -x [ʒɛrso] NM *Naut* grummet, grommet

gésier [ʒezje] NM gizzard

gésine [ʒezin] NF *Littéraire ou Vieilli* **en g.** in labour *or* childbirth

gésir [49] [ʒezir] VI **1** *(être étendu)* to lie, to be lying; **de nombreux blessés gisent encore parmi les décombres** many of the injured are still lying among the ruins; **elle gisait là, comme endormie** there she lay (dead), as if asleep; **il gisait dans son sang** he was lying *or* weltering in his blood
2 *(être épars)* to lie; **ce qui restait de la statue gisait sur le sol** what was left of the statue was lying on the ground
3 *Littéraire (résider)* **c'est là que gît la difficulté** therein lies the difficulty; *Fig* **c'est là que gît le lièvre** that's the crux of the matter, there's the rub

gesse [ʒɛs] NF *Bot* vetch; **g. odorante** sweet pea; **g. des prés** meadow vetchling

Gestalt [geʃtalt] NF *Psy* Gestalt

gestaltisme [geʃtaltism] NM *Psy* Gestalt (psychology)

gestaltiste [geʃtaltist] *Psy* ADJ Gestaltist
NMF Gestaltist

gestalt-thérapie [geʃtaltterapi] NF *Psy* Gestalt therapy

Gestapo [gɛstapo] NF **la G.** the Gestapo; **un officier de la G.** a Gestapo officer

gestation [ʒɛstasjɔ̃] NF **1** *Biol* gestation; **la g. n'est que de 21 jours** gestation takes only 21 days; **période de g.** gestation period; **g. utérine** uterogestation **2** *Fig (d'une œuvre)* gestation (period)
❑ **en gestation** ADJ **1** *Biol (fœtus)* gestating **2** *Fig* **un roman en g.** a novel in preparation

geste [ʒɛst] NM **1** *(mouvement)* movement; *(signe)* gesture; **ses gestes étaient d'une grande précision** his/her movements were very precise; **faire un g.** to make a gesture; **faire un g. de la main** to gesture (with one's hand); *(pour saluer)* to wave; **faire des gestes en parlant** to speak with one's hands; **faire un g. approbateur** to nod one's assent *or* approval; **d'un g. de la main, il refusa le whisky** he waved aside the glass of whisky; **d'un g., il nous a fait sortir/entrer** he motioned *or* gestured to us to go out/come in; **il lui montra la porte d'un g.** he gestured him/her towards the door; **d'un g., elle m'indiqua où se trouvait le coffre-fort** she gestured to where the safe was; **il me le fit comprendre d'un g.** he indicated it to me with a gesture; **d'un g. de la main** with a wave of the hand; **je te l'indiquerai d'un g. de la main** I'll indicate it to you; **à grand renfort de gestes, elle appela le maître d'hôtel** she waved the head waiter over; **saluer qn d'un g.** to wave to sb; **avoir un g. de surprise** to start, to look startled; **avoir un g. malheureux** to make a clumsy gesture *or* movement; **il eut un g. de résignation** he gave a shrug of resignation, he shrugged in resignation; **congédier qn d'un g.** to dismiss sb with a wave of the hand; **encourager qn de la voix et du g.** to cheer sb on; **sans un g.** without moving; **pas un g., ou je tire!** don't move or I'll shoot!; **faites** *ou* **ayez le g. qui sauve** learn how to give first aid; **il épie mes moindres gestes** *ou* **tous mes gestes** he watches my every move
2 *(action)* gesture; **un g. politique/diplomatique** a political/diplomatic gesture; **faire un beau g.** to make a noble gesture; **un g. lâche** a cowardly act *or* deed; **allez, fais un g.!** come on, do something!; **vous n'avez qu'un g. à faire** you only have to say the word; **elle n'a pas fait un g. (pour l'aider)** she didn't do a thing *or* lift a finger (to help him); **il a eu un g. touchant, il m'a apporté des fleurs** a rather touching thing he did was to bring me some flowers; **joindre le g. à la parole** to suit the action to the word
NF *Littérature* gest, geste

gesticulant, -e [ʒɛstikylɑ̃, -ɑ̃t] ADJ gesticulating

gesticulation [ʒɛstikylasjɔ̃] NF gesticulation; **cesse tes gesticulations!** stop gesticulating!, stop waving your arms about!

gesticuler [3] [ʒɛstikyle] VI to gesticulate, to wave one's arms about

gestion [ʒɛstjɔ̃] NF **1** *Com & Ind* management; **chargé de la g. de l'hôtel** in charge of running *or* managing the hotel; **par une mauvaise g.** through bad management, through mismanagement; **techniques de g.** management techniques *or* methods; **g. actif-passif** assets and liabilities management; **g. administrative** administration, administrative management; **g. d'affaires** (day-to-day) running of affairs *or* business; **g. assistée par ordinateur** computer-aided management; **g. budgétaire** budgetary control; **g. de capital** asset management; **g. de la chaîne logique** supply-chain management; **g. du changement** change management; **g. du circuit de distribution** distribution channel management; **g. de comptes-clés** key-account management; **g. des connaissances** knowledge management; **g. par consensus** consensus management; **g. des coûts** cost management; **g. de la distribution** distribution management; **g. de la distribution physique** physical distribution management; **g. de division** divisional management; **g. des droits numériques** digital rights management; **g. des effectifs** manpower management; **g. d'entreprise** business management; **g. financière** financial management; **g. de fonds** fund management; **g. hôtelière** hotel administration *or* management, hospitality management; **g. indicielle** indexed portfolio; **g. des investissements** investment management; **g. logistique** logistics management; **g. marketing** marketing management; **g. de marque** brand management; **g. des matières** materials management; **g. par objectifs** management by objective; **g. passive** passive management; **g. des performances** performance management; **g. de portefeuille** portfolio management; **g. prévisionnelle** forward planning; **g. de la production** production management; **g. de produits** product management; **g. (de** *ou* **de la) qualité** quality control, quality management; **g. de la qualité totale** total quality management, TQM; **g. des ressources humaines** human resources management; **g. des risques** risk management; **g. des sociétés** business management; **g. sonore** sound handling, sound management; **g. de stock** *ou* **des stocks** *Br* stock *or Am* inventory control; **g. stratégique** strategic management; **g. de taux** yield management; **g. du temps de travail** time management; **g. de trésorerie** cash management
2 *Ordinat* management; **g. de bases de données** database management; **système de g. de base de données** database management system; **g. des césures** hyphenation control; **g. des couleurs** colour management; **g. des disquettes** disk management; **g. de données** data management; **g. de fichiers** file management; **g. intégrée** integrated management; **g. de mémoire** memory management; **g. multifeuille** *(de tableur)* multi-spreadsheet handling; **g. de parc réseau** network management; **g. des performances** performance monitoring *or* tuning; **g. des projets** project scheduling; **g. des systèmes d'information** information systems management; **g. des travaux** job scheduling

gestionnaire [ʒɛstjɔnɛr] ADJ administrative, managing, management *(avant n)*
NMF **1** *Admin* administrator
2 *Com & Ind* manager, administrator; **g. de fonds** fund manager; **g. de fonds obligatoire** bond fund manager; **g. de portefeuille** portfolio manager; **g. de risques** risk manager; **g. de stock** *ou* **des stocks** *Br* stock controller, *Am* inventory controller
NM *Ordinat* manager; **g. de base de données** database administrator; **g. de fichiers** file manager; **g. de fichiers et de répertoires** filer; **g. de mémoire** memory manager; **g. de périphérique** device driver; **g. de projets** project management package; **g. de réseau** network manager; **g. de la souris** mouse driver; **g. de tâches** task scheduler

gestrinone [ʒɛstrinɔn] NF *Pharm* gestrinone

gestualité [ʒɛstɥalite] NF non-verbal behaviour *or* communication, body language

gestuel, -elle [ʒɛstɥɛl] ADJ gestural; **langage g.** gestural language
❑ **gestuelle** NF **1** *(gén)* non-verbal behaviour *or* communication, body language **2** *Théât & (en danse)* gesture

Gethsémani [ʒɛtsemani] NM *Bible* Gethsemane

getter [getɔr] NM *Électron* getter

gewurztraminer [gevyrstraminɛr] NM Gewürztraminer *(variety of white grape)*

geyser [ʒɛzɛr] NM geyser

GFU [ʒeɛfy] NM *Tél (abrév* **groupe fermé d'utilisateurs***)* CUG

Ghana [gana] NM **le G.** Ghana; **vivre au G.** to live in Ghana; **aller au G.** to go to Ghana

ghanéen, -enne [ganeɛ̃, -ɛn] ADJ Ghanaian, Ghanian
❑ **Ghanéen, -enne** NM,F Ghanaian, Ghanian

Ghats [gat] NMPL *Géog* **les G.** the Ghats; **les G. occidentaux** the Western Ghats; **les G. orientaux** the Eastern Ghats

GHB [ʒeaʃbe] NM *Chim (abrév* **gamma-hydroxybutyrate***)* GHB

ghetto [gɛto] NM ghetto

ghettoïsation [gɛtoizasjɔ̃] NF ghettoization

ghilde [gild] = **gilde**

GI, G.I. [dʒiaj] NM INV *Mil (abrév* **Government Issue***)* GI

GIA [ʒeia] NM *(abrév* **Groupes islamiques armés***)* GIA

giaour [ʒjaur] NM *Péj* giaour

giardiase [ʒjardjaz] NF*Méd* giardiasis

gibbérelline [ʒiberelin] NF*Biol* gibberellin

gibbeux, -euse [ʒibø, -øz] ADJ *Astron* gibbous **2** *(animal)* humpbacked, *Spéc* gibbous

gibbon [ʒibɔ̃] NM*Zool* gibbon

gibbosité [ʒibozite] NF*Anat* hump, *Spéc* gibbosity

gibbsite [ʒibsit] NF*Minér* gibbsite

gibecière [ʒibsjɛr] NF **1** *Chasse* game bag, gamekeeper's pouch **2** *Vieilli (d'un écolier)* satchel

gibelet [ʒiblɛ] NM*Menuis* auger

gibelin, -e [ʒiblɛ̃, -in] *Hist* ADJGhibelline NM,FGhibelline

gibelotte [ʒiblɔt] *Culin* NF **1** *(ragoût de lapin)* rabbit stew *(made with white wine)* **2** *Can (mets régional)* = dish from the Sorel region made from perch or loach **3** *Can Fam (mets peu appétissant)* rubbish, pigswill
□ **en gibelotte** ADJstewed in white wine

giberne [ʒibɛrn] NF cartridge pouch; *Prov* **tout soldat a un bâton de maréchal dans sa g.** = every private has the makings of a general

gibet [ʒibɛ] NM **1** *(potence)* gibbet, gallows *(singulier)* **2** *Rel* **le g.** the Rood

gibier [ʒibje] NM **1** *(animaux)* game (UNCOUNT); **gros/petit g.** big/small game; **g. d'eau** waterfowl; **g. à plumes** game birds or fowl (UNCOUNT); **g. à poils** game animals
2 *Culin (viande)* game; **manger du g.** to eat game; **il aime le g. faisandé** he likes well-hung game; **pâté de g.** game pâté
3 *Fam (personne)* quarry, prey; **ces types-là, c'est du gros g.** these guys are in the big-time; **un g. de potence** a gallows bird

giboulée [ʒibule] NF shower; **giboulées de mars** ≃April showers

giboyeux, -euse [ʒibwajø, -øz] ADJabounding or rich in game, well stocked with game

Gibraltar [ʒibraltar] NM Gibraltar; **vivre à G.** to live in Gibraltar; **aller à Gibraltar** to go to Gibraltar; **le détroit de G.** the Strait of Gibraltar

gibus [ʒibys] NMopera or crush hat

GIC [ʒeise] NM **1** *(abrév* **grand invalide civil)** severely disabled person; **macaron G.** disabled sticker **2** *(abrév* **Groupe interministériel de contrôle)** interdepartmental regulatory committee

giclée [ʒikle] NF **1** *(de liquide)* jet, spurt, squirt **2** *très Fam (coup de feu)* burst (of machine-gun fire)▪ **3** *Suisse (petite quantité)* spot, smidgen, touch **4** *Suisse (averse)* (rain) shower **5** *Suisse (chute)* fall *(with rebound)*

giclement [ʒikləmɑ̃] NM *(gén → d'un liquide)* spurting (UNCOUNT), squirting (UNCOUNT); *(→ du sang)* spurting (UNCOUNT)

gicler [3] [ʒikle] VI **1** *(liquide → gén)* to spurt, to squirt; *(→ sang)* to spurt; **faire g. de l'eau avec un pistolet à eau** to squirt water out of a water pistol; **arrête de faire g. de l'eau!** stop splashing or squirting water!; **et ça m'a giclé à la figure** and it splashed into my face
2 *Fam (partir)* to be off, to push off, *Am* to split **3** *Suisse (être projeté)* **g. en l'air** to be thrown into the air
4 *Suisse (précipiter)* to rush; *(être mis à la porte)* to get fired, *Br* to get the sack **5** *Suisse (pleuvoir)* to rain
VT*Suisse (asperger, projeter)* to spray

gicleur [ʒiklœr] NM *Aut* (carburettor) jet; **g. de pompe** pump nozzle; **g. de ralenti** idling jet

gidien, -enne [ʒidjɛ̃, -ɛn] ADJ*Littérature* of André Gide

GIE, G.I.E. [ʒeiə] NM*(abrév* **groupement d'intérêt économique)** economic interest group

GIEC [geiʒœk] NM*(abrév* **Groupement intergouvernemental de l'étude du climat)** IPPC

GIF [geif] NM *Ordinat (abrév* **Graphics Interchange Format)** GIF; **G. animé** animated GIF

gifle [ʒifl] NF **1** *(coup)* slap (in the face); **donner une g. à qn** to slap sb's face, to box sb's ears; **prendre ou recevoir une g.** to get a slap (in the face); **une fameuse g.** a real smack in the face **2** *Fig (humiliation)* (burning) insult, slap in the face

gifler [3] [ʒifle] VT **1** *(sujet: personne)* **g. qn** to slap sb's face or sb in the face; **elle le gifla à toute volée** she caught him an almighty slap in the face; **tu vas te faire g. si tu continues!** you'll get a slap in the face if you carry on like that!
2 *(sujet: pluie, vent)* to lash; **la bourrasque lui giflait le visage** the wind lashed his/her face

3 *Fig (humilier)* to humiliate; **ses paroles m'avaient giflé** his/her words had humiliated or mortified me

GIG, G.I.G. [ʒeiʒe] NM *(abrév* **grand invalide de guerre)** = war invalid

giga [ʒiga] ADJ INV *Fam* wicked, *Br* fab, *Am* awesome

GIGA- [ʒiga] PRÉF

This prefix of scientific origin has come to prominence with the advent of mass computing and its *gigabytes* (**gigaoctets**) of memory. It has since passed into colloquial language as an INTENSIFIER, used as a prefix but also on its own, as a term of appreciation:
on a fait une giga-teuf we had a massive party; **il a poussé un giga coup de gueule** he yelled really loud; **c'est giga marrant** it's hysterical; **c'est giga (cool)!** wicked!
It is worth noting that, in colloquial computing speak, **gigaoctet** is often abbreviated to just **giga** (translated in English as *gig*), as in **un disque dur de 120 gigas** a 120 gig hard disk

gigahertz [ʒigaɛrts] NMgigahertz

gigantesque [ʒigɑ̃tɛsk] ADJ **1** *(animal, plante, ville)* gigantic, giant *(avant n)*; **d'une taille g.** gigantic, of a gigantic size **2** *(projet)* gigantic, giant *(avant n)*; *(erreur)* huge, gigantic

gigantisme [ʒigɑ̃tism] NM **1** *Méd, Bot & Zool* gigantism, giantism **2** *Fig* gigantic size; **une ville atteinte de g.** a city that has grown to enormous proportions

gigantomachie [ʒigɑ̃tɔmaʃi] NF *Myth (bataille)* gigantomachia, battle of the giants; *Beaux-Arts* gigantomachy

gigantostracé [ʒigɑ̃tɔstrase] NM*Zool* eurypterid

gigaoctet [ʒigaɔktɛ] NM*Ordinat* gigabyte

gigathérapie [ʒigaterapi] NF*Méd* = multitherapy treatment for HIV

GIGN [ʒeiʒɛɛn] NM *(abrév* **Groupe d'intervention de la gendarmerie nationale)** = special crack force of the gendarmerie, *Br* ≃ SAS, *Am* ≃ SWAT

gigogne [ʒigɔɲ] *voir* **lit, poupée, table**

gigolette [ʒigɔlɛt] NF **1** *Fam Vieilli (fille délurée)* floozy **2** *Culin* leg of turkey

gigolo [ʒigɔlo] NM*Fam* gigolo

gigondas [ʒigɔ̃das] NM Gigondas *(wine from south-east France)*

gigot [ʒigo] NM **1** *Culin* leg; **g. (d'agneau)** leg of lamb; **g. de chevreuil** haunch of venison **2** *(d'un cheval)* hind leg **3** *Hum (d'une personne)* leg, thigh

gigoté, -e [ʒigɔte] ADJ**bien/mal g.** *(cheval, chien)* strong/weak in the hind legs

gigotement [ʒigɔtmɑ̃] NM wriggling (UNCOUNT), fidgeting (UNCOUNT)

gigoter [3] [ʒigɔte] VI **1** *(bébé)* to wriggle (about); *(enfant)* to fidget **2** *(animal à l'agonie)* to give a convulsive jerk

gigue¹ [ʒig] NF **1** *(danse)* gigue, jig; **danser la g.** to jig; *Fig* to wriggle about, to jig up and down **2** *Mus* gigue

gigue² [ʒig] NF **1** *Culin* **g. de chevreuil** haunch of venison **2** *Fam (jambe)* leg▪, **les gigues** legs▪, *Br* pins **3** *Fam (personne)* **une grande g.** a beanpole

giguer [3] [ʒige] VI*Can* to jig

gigueur, -euse [ʒigœr, -øz] NM,F*Can* jig dancer

gilde [gild] NF*Hist* guild

gilet [ʒilɛ] NM **1** *(vêtement → taillé)* Br waistcoat, *Am* vest; *(→ tricoté)* Br cardigan, *Am* cardigan sweater **2** *(sous-vêtement)* Br vest, *Am* undershirt **3** *(protection)* **g. d'armes** fencing jacket; **g. pare-balles** bulletproof vest; **g. de sauvetage** life jacket

giletier, -ère [ʒiltje, -ɛr] NM,F*Br* waistcoat maker, *Am* vest maker
□ **giletière** NFfob (chain)

Gilles [ʒil] NMPL = figures of giants in carnival parades in Belgium

gimblette, gimbelette [ʒɛblɛt] NF *Culin* jumble, ring-biscuit

gimmick [gimik] NM **1** *Fam* gimmick **2** *Can* gamique

gin [dʒin] NMgin

gindre [ʒɛ̃dr] NMbaker's assistant

gin-fizz [dʒinfiz] NM INVgin fizz

gingembre [ʒɛ̃ʒɑ̃br] NM ginger; **racine de g.** root ginger, fresh ginger; **biscuits au g.** ginger biscuits

gingival, -e, -aux, -ales [ʒɛ̃ʒival, -o] ADJ*Anat* gum *(avant n)*, *Spéc* gingival

gingivite [ʒɛ̃ʒivit] NF*Méd* gum disease, *Spéc* gingivitis

gingko [ʒinko] NM*Bot* gingko

gin-rami [dʒinrami] *(pl* **gin-ramis**), **gin-rummy** [dʒinrœmi] *(pl* **gin-rummys**) NM *Cartes* gin rummy

ginseng [ʒinsɛn] NM*Bot* ginseng

gin-tonic [dʒintɔnik] *(pl* **gin-tonics**) NM gin and tonic

giobertite [ʒɔbɛrtit] NF*Minér* giobertite, magnesite

giorno [dʒiɔrno] *voir* **a giorno**

girafe [ʒiraf] NF **1** *Zool* giraffe; *Fig* **avoir un cou de g.** to have a long neck **2** *Fam (personne)* beanpole **3** *Fam Rad & TV* boom▪

girafeau, -x [ʒirafo] NM*Zool* baby giraffe

girafidé, giraffidé [ʒirafide] *Zool* NM member of the Giraffidae family
□ **girafidés, giraffidés** NMPLGiraffidae

girafon [ʒirafɔ̃] = **girafeau**

girandole [ʒirɑ̃dɔl] NF **1** *(chandelier)* girandole, candelabra; *(feux d'artifice)* girandole **2** *(grappe → de fleurs)* cluster; *(→ de bijoux)* girandole

girasol [ʒirasɔl] NMgirasol, girasole

giration [ʒirasjɔ̃] NF gyration; *Naut* **cercle de g.** turning circle

giratoire [ʒiratwar] ADJgyrating, gyratory
NM*Suisse (rond-point)* Br roundabout, *Am* traffic circle

giraumon, giraumont [ʒiromɔ̃] NMpumpkin

giraviation [ʒiravjasjɔ̃] NF *Aviat* rotary-wing aviation

giravion [ʒiravjɔ̃] NM*Aviat* gyroplane, rotorcraft

girelle [ʒirɛl] NF*Ich* rainbow wrasse

giries [ʒiri] NFPL *Fam Vieilli (plaintes)* whining (UNCOUNT), bellyaching (UNCOUNT); *(manières)* (affected) airs; **faire des g.** *(se plaindre)* to whine, to bellyache; *(faire des manières)* to put on airs

girl [gœrl] NFchorus or show girl

girodyne [ʒirodin] NM*Aviat* autogyro

girofle [ʒirɔfl] NMclove; **huile de g.** oil of cloves

giroflée [ʒirɔfle] NF **1** *Bot* stock, gillyflower; **g. des murailles** wallflower, gillyflower **2** *Fam Fig* **une g. à cinq feuilles** *(une gifle)* a stinging slap

giroflier [ʒirɔflije] NMclove (tree)

girolle [ʒirɔl] NFchanterelle

giron [ʒirɔ̃] NM **1** *(d'une personne)* lap; **dans le g. de sa mère** in his/her mother's lap **2** *Littéraire (communauté)* bosom; **le g. familial** the family fold; **accepté dans le g. de l'Église** accepted into the fold or the bosom of the Church **3** *(d'une marche)* tread **4** *Hér* giron, gyron

girond, -e [ʒirɔ̃, -ɔ̃d] ADJ *Fam Vieilli* plump▪, buxom▪, well-padded; **une femme plutôt gironde** a buxom or plump woman

Gironde [ʒirɔ̃d] NF **1** *Géog* **la G.** *(département, fleuve)* the Gironde; *(estuaire)* the Gironde estuary **2** *Hist* **la G.** the Girondist Party

girondin, -e [ʒirɔ̃dɛ̃, -in] ADJ **1** *(gén)* of/from the Gironde; **le vignoble g.** the vineyards of the Gironde **2** *Hist* Girondist
□ **Girondin, -e** NM,F**1** *(personne)* = inhabitant of or person from the Gironde **2** *Hist* Girondist **3** *Sport* **les Girondins (de Bordeaux)** = the Bordeaux football team

---

Culture

LES GIRONDINS

"Les Girondins" were a party occupying the right wing of the "**Convention**" from 1791 to 1793 in opposition to the left-wing "Montagne". With a power base in the south of France, they opposed the execution of the king and advocated a federalist structure for France. They were supplanted by the "**Montagnards**", and many of their leaders were executed during the Terror.

---

gironné, -e [ʒirɔne] ADJ **1** *Constr* **marches gironnées** winding steps; **tuile gironnée** triangular tile **2** *Hér* gyronny

girouette [ʒirwɛt] NF **1** *(sur un toit)* weathercock, weather vane **2** *Naut* telltale, dog vane **3** *Fam*

(*personne*) weathercock; **c'est une vraie g.!** he keeps changing his mind!, he's a real weathercock!

gis *etc voir* **gésir**

gisait *etc voir* **gésir**

gisant, -e [ʒizɑ̃, -ɑ̃t] **ADJ** *Littéraire (corps)* lifeless, motionless

NM *Beaux-Arts* recumbent figure *or* statue

giscardien, -enne [ʒiskardjɛ̃, -ɛn] **ADJ** of Giscard d'Estaing

NM,F = supporter of Giscard d'Estaing

giselle [ʒizɛl] **NF** *Tex* giselle

gisement [ʒizmɑ̃] **NM 1** *Géol & Mines* deposit; **g. aurifère** goldfield; **g. crayeux** chalk deposit; **g. houiller** *(filon)* coal deposit *or* measures; *(bassin)* coalfield; **g. d'or** goldfield; **g. de pétrole, g. pétrolifère** oilfield

2 *Aviat & Naut* bearing; **relever/tracer un g.** to take/to plot a bearing; **g. à la boussole** compass bearing

3 *Com* **g. de clientèle** pool of customers, potential customers

4 *Archéol* **g. préhistorique** prehistoric site

gît *voir* **gésir**

gitan, -e [ʒitɑ̃, -an] **ADJ** Gypsy *(avant n)*

❑ **Gitan, -e NM,F** Gypsy

❑ **Gitane**® **NF** Gitane® (cigarette)

gîte[1] [ʒit] **NM 1** *(logement)* lodging, resting place; *(foyer)* home; **retrouver son g.** to get back home; **ne pas avoir de g.** to be homeless; **le g. et le couvert** room and board; **offrir le g. et le couvert** to provide board and lodging; **g. camping-caravaning à la ferme** campsite in close proximity to a farm; **g. chambre d'hôte** bed and breakfast; **g. d'enfants** holiday placements for children with a rural family; **g. équestre** rural gîte with horses for hire; **g. d'étape** *(pour randonneurs)* halt; **g. rural** gîte; **g. rural communal** = gîte communally owned by a village or group of villages

2 *Chasse (de gibier)* lair; *(de lièvre)* form; **être/se mettre au g.** *(lièvre)* to be sitting/to be lying in its form; **trouver un lièvre au g.** to find a hare sitting

3 *(viande) Br* shin *or Am* shank (of beef); **g. de derrière** shank; **g. de devant** *Br* shin, *Am* shank; **g. à la noix** *Br* topside, *Am* round

4 *Mines* bed, deposit

gîte[2] [ʒit] **NF** *Naut* list; **avoir** *ou* **prendre de la g.** to list, to heel; **donner de la g.** to list; **donner de la g. sur tribord** to list to starboard

gîte-gîte [ʒitʒit] *(pl* **gîtes-gîtes***)* **NM** *Br* shin *or Am* shank (of beef)

gîter [3] [ʒite] **VI 1** *Vieilli ou Littéraire (loger)* to lodge; *(voyageur)* to stay **2** *(animal)* to find shelter; *(lapin)* to couch; *(oiseau)* to perch **3** *Naut* to list

►**se gîter VPR** *Chasse (lièvre)* to lie in the form

gîtologie [ʒitɔlɔʒi] **NF** *Géol* metallogeny

giton [ʒitɔ̃] **NM** *Littéraire* catamite

givrage [ʒivraʒ] **NM 1** *Aviat* icing; **à 9000 mètres, on risque le g.** at 9,000 metres icing may occur **2** *(sur un verre)* frosting

givrant, -e [ʒivrɑ̃, -ɑ̃t] **ADJ brouillard g.** freezing fog

givre [ʒivr] **NM 1** *(glace)* frost; **couvert de g.** frosted over **2** *(en joaillerie)* white fleck

givré, -e [ʒivre] **ADJ 1** *(arbre)* covered with frost; *(serrure)* iced up; **les ailes de l'avion étaient givrées** the plane's wings were iced up **2** *(verre)* frosted *(with sugar)* **3** *Culin* **orange givrée** orange *Br* sorbet *or Am* sherbet *(served inside the fruit)* **4** *Fam (fou)* crackers, nuts; **il est complètement g.!** he's completely nuts *or* off his head!

givrer [3] [ʒivre] **VT 1** *(avec du sucre)* to frost **2** *(couvrir de givre)* to cover with frost

VI *Aviat* to ice up

►**se givrer VPR** *(se couvrir de givre)* to frost *or* to ice up

givreux, -euse [ʒivrø, -øz] **ADJ** *(en joaillerie)* with icy flecks, flawed

givrure [ʒivryr] **NF** white fleck *(in a gem)*

Gizeh [giʒɛ] **NF** (El) Gîza

glabelle [glabɛl] **NF** *Anat* glabella

glabre [glabr] **ADJ 1** *(imberbe)* smooth-chinned; *(rasé)* clean-shaven; **le visage g.** with a smooth face **2** *Bot* glabrous, hairless

glaçage [glasaʒ] **NM 1** *(d'un tissu, du cuir, du papier, de photos)* glazing; *Ind (polissage)* surfacing, burnishing **2** *Culin (d'un gâteau) Br* icing, *Am* frosting; *(de bonbons)* sugar coating; *(de légumes, d'un poisson, d'une viande)* glazing

glaçant, -e [glasɑ̃, -ɑ̃t] **ADJ** *(regard, attitude)* cold, frosty; *Vieilli (vent)* icy

glace [glas] **NF 1** *(eau gelée)* ice; **g. flottante** floating ice, drift ice; **g. de fond** bottom ice; *Can* **g. noire** black ice; **g. pilée** crushed ice; *Fig* **rompre** *ou* **briser la g.** to break the ice; **une fois la g. rompue, elle s'est révélée charmante** once we'd broken the ice she turned out to be charming; *Can* **sur g.** *(boisson)* on the rocks

2 *(crème glacée)* ice cream; *(sucette) Br* ice lolly, *Am* Popsicle®; *(cône)* ice cream (cone); **g. à la vanille/à l'abricot** vanilla/apricot ice cream; **g. à l'eau** *Br* water ice, *Am* sherbet; **g. à la crème** *Br* dairy ice cream, *Am* iced-milk ice cream; **g. portative** ice-cream cake, ice-cream gateau

3 *Culin Br* icing, *Am* frosting; *(de viande)* glaze; **g. royale** royal icing

4 *(miroir)* mirror; **se regarder dans la g.** to look at oneself in the mirror; **une g. sans tain** a two-way mirror

5 *(vitre* → *d'un véhicule, d'une boutique)* window

6 *Tech* sheet of plate glass; **g. flottée** float glass; *Aut* **g. de custode** quarterlight, quarterwindow

7 *(en joaillerie)* (white) fleck *or* flaw

8 *Ind* **g. sèche** *ou* **carbonique** dry ice

❑ **glaces NFPL** *(du pôle)* ice fields; *(sur un fleuve)* ice sheets; *(en mer)* ice floes, drift ice; **le navire est pris dans les glaces** the ship is icebound

❑ **de glace ADJ** *(accueil, visage, regard)* icy, frosty; **être** *ou* **rester de g.** to remain unmoved; **tu as un cœur de g.** you've got a heart of stone

glacé, -e [glase] **ADJ 1** *(transformé en glace)* frozen

2 *(lieu)* freezing *or* icy (cold); **les plages glacées du nord** the icy cold beaches of the north

3 *(personne)* frozen, freezing cold; **j'ai les pieds glacés** my feet are frozen

4 *(hostile)* frosty, icy; **d'une politesse glacée** with icy politeness; **regard g.** cold stare

5 *Culin (dessert, soufflé, café)* iced; *(petit-four)* glacé; *(oignon, viande, poisson)* glazed; **cerises glacées** glacé cherries

6 *(brillant* → *photo)* glossy; *(*→ *papier)* glazed; *(*→ *cuir, soie)* glazed, glacé; **gants glacés** glacé kid gloves; **soie glacée** watered silk, glazed thread

NM glaze, gloss

glacer [16] [glase] **VT 1** *(transformer en glace)* to freeze

2 *(refroidir* → *bouteille)* to chill

3 *(transir)* **le vent me glace** the wind is icy; **un froid qui vous glace jusqu'aux os** weather that chills you to the bone

4 *Fig (pétrifier)* **son regard me glace** the look in his/her eye turns me cold; **ça m'a glacé le sang (dans les veines)** it made my blood run cold; **un hurlement à vous g. le sang** a blood-curdling scream; **ce souvenir me glace encore le cœur** the memory still sends shivers down my spine; **g. qn d'effroi/de terreur** to paralyse *or* freeze sb with fear/terror

5 *Culin (petit-four, oignon, poisson etc)* to glaze; *(gâteau) Br* to ice, *Am* to frost

6 *Ind & Tech* to glaze, to glacé

►**se glacer VPR leur sang se glaça dans leurs veines** their blood ran cold

glacerie [glasri] **NF 1** *(fabrication de glaces)* ice-cream making; *(commerce)* ice-cream trade **2** *(fabrique de verre)* glassworks *(singulier)*; *(commerce)* glass trade

glaceur [glasœr] **NM** glazer

glaceuse[1] [glasøz] **NF** glazing machine, print drier

glaceux, -euse[2] [glasø, -øz] **ADJ** *(diamant)* with icy flecks, flawed

glaciaire [glasjɛr] **ADJ** glacial

NM le g. the Ice Age, the Glacial Period *or* Epoch

Glacial [glasjal] **ADJ** *Vieilli* **l'océan G. Arctique/Antarctique** the (Arctic/Antarctic) polar sea

glacial, -e, -als *ou* **-aux, -ales** [glasjal, -o] **ADJ 1** *(climat)* icy, freezing; *(vent)* bitter, freezing; *(pluie)* freezing (cold) **2** *(accueil, ambiance)* frosty, icy; *(sourire)* frosty; *(abord, personne)* cold; **elle est vraiment glaciale** she's really cold *or* a real iceberg

ADV il fait g. it's freezing cold

glacialement [glasjalmɑ̃] **ADV** frostily, icily

glaciation [glasjasjɔ̃] **NF** glaciation; **pendant la g.** during the Ice Age

glaciel, -elle [glasjɛl] **ADJ** drift-ice *(avant n)*

glacier [glasje] **NM 1** *Géol* glacier; **g. de vallée** valley *or* Alpine glacier; **g. continental** continental ice sheet **2** *(confiseur)* ice-cream man *or* salesman; *(fabricant)* ice-cream maker; **g.-confiseur** confectioner and ice-cream seller

glacière [glasjɛr] **NF 1** *(local)* cold-room **2** *(armoire)* refrigerated cabinet; *(récipient)* cool box, *Austr* Esky®, *NZ* chilly bin; *(de réfrigérateur)* freezer compartment, icebox; *Fig* **mon bureau est une vraie g.!** my office is like a fridge *or* an icebox!

glaciérisme [glasjerism] **NM** glacier climbing

glaciériste [glasjerist] **NMF** glacier climber

glaciologie [glasjɔlɔʒi] **NF** glaciology

glaciologique [glasjɔlɔʒik] **ADJ** glaciological

glaciologue [glasjɔlɔg] **NMF** glaciologist

glacis [glasi] **NM 1** *Hist* **le g. soviétique** the Soviet buffer zone **2** *Constr* ramp; **g. d'écoulement** weathering **3** *Beaux-Arts* glaze, scumble **4** *Mil* glacis **5** *Géog* glacis; **g. d'érosion** pediment

glaçon [glasɔ̃] **NM 1** *Géog & Météo (sur un fleuve)* block of ice, ice floe; *(sur un étang)* patch of ice; *(en mer)* ice floe; *(pendant)* icicle; **glaçons** *(sur une rivière)* drift *or* broken ice; *Fam* **j'ai le nez comme un g.** my nose is like a block of ice *or* is frozen

2 *(pour boisson)* ice cube; **sucer un g.** to suck an ice cube; **voulez-vous un g.?** would you like some ice?; **servi avec des glaçons** served with ice *or* on the rocks

3 *Fig* **cette fille est un g.** that girl's a real ice queen

glaçure [glasyr] **NF** *Cér* glaze; **g. plombifère** lead glaze

gladiateur [gladjatœr] **NM** *Antiq* gladiator; **combat de gladiateurs** gladiatorial combat

glagolitique [glagɔlitik] **ADJ** *Ling* Glagolitic

glaïeul [glajœl] **NM** *Bot* gladiolus; **des glaïeuls** gladioli; **g. des marais** (sword) flag

glaire [glɛr] **NF 1** *Physiol* mucus; **g. cervicale** cervical mucus **2** *(d'œuf)* white **3** *(pour le cuir)* glair

glairer [4] [glɛre] **VT** to glair

glaireux, -euse [glɛrø, -øz] **ADJ** glairy, glaireous

glairure [glɛryr] **NF** *Typ* glair

glaise [glɛz] **NF** clay

ADJ F terre g. (potter's) clay

glaiser [3] [gleze] **VT 1** *(amender avec de la glaise)* to clay, to dress with clay **2** *(enduire de glaise)* to line with clay

glaiseux, -euse [glɛzø, -øz] **ADJ** clayey, clay *(avant n)*

glaisière [glɛzjɛr] **NF** clay pit

glaive [glɛv] **NM** broadsword, *Arch* glaive; *Littéraire* **le g. de la Justice** the sword of justice

glamour [glamur] *Fam* **ADJ INV** *(personne, allure)* glam

NM le g. glamour▪

glanage [glanaʒ] **NM le g.** gleaning, gathering

gland [glɑ̃] **NM 1** *Bot (du chêne)* acorn; **glands** *(pour les cochons)* mast **2** *Couture* tassel; **orné de glands** tasselled **3** *Anat* glans **4** *très Fam (imbécile) Br* prat, *Am* jerk

glandage [glɑ̃daʒ] **NM 1** *(lieu)* area where acorns are gathered **2** *(ramassage)* gathering acorns

glande [glɑ̃d] **NF 1** *Anat* gland; **glandes de Bartholin** Bartholin's glands; **glandes endocrines** endocrine glands; **glandes exocrines** exocrine glands; **g. lacrymale** tear gland; **g. parotide** parotid gland; **g. salivaire** salivary gland; **g. sébacée** sebaceous gland; **g. surrénale** suprarenal gland; **g. uropygienne** oil gland **2** *Anat (ganglion)* (neck) gland **3** *Vulg* **avoir les glandes** *(être énervé)* to be hacked off *or* cheesed off; *(être triste)* to be upset▪; **foutre les glandes à qn** *(énerver)* to hack *or* cheese sb off; *(attrister)* to upset sb▪

glandée [glɑ̃de] **NF** acorn crop *or* harvest; **mener les cochons à la g.** to take the pigs to forage for acorns

glander [3] [glɑ̃de] **VI** *très Fam* **1** *(ne rien faire)* to

loaf about; **mais qu'est-ce qu'il glande, il devait arriver à trois heures!** where the hell is he, he was supposed to be here at three; **il a glandé toute l'année** he's done nothing but loaf about all year; **ça fait deux ans qu'il glande** that's two years now he's been loafing around *or* doing sweet FA; **arrête de g. et fais quelque chose d'utile** *(ne rien faire)* get off your backside and do something useful; *(ne rien faire d'utile)* stop mucking around and do something useful
2 *(attendre)* to hang around; **ça fait trois heures que je glande** I've been hanging around for three hours
3 *(locution)* **j'en ai rien à g.** I don't give a damn

glandeur, -euse [glɑ̃dœr, -øz] **NM,F** *très Fam* layabout, *Am* goldbrick; **c'est un vrai g., ce mec-là** he's a complete layabout, that guy

glandouiller [glɑ̃duje] = **glander**

glandouilleur, -euse [glɑ̃dujœr, -øz] **NM,F** *très Fam* layabout, *Am* goldbrick; **c'est un vrai g., ce mec-là** he's a complete layabout, that guy

glandu [glɑ̃dy] **NM** *très Fam* halfwit, dope

glandulaire [glɑ̃dylɛr], **glanduleux, -euse** [glɑ̃dylø, -øz] **ADJ** glandular; **infection glanduleuse** glandular infection

glane [glan] **NF 1** *(ramassage)* **la g.** gleaning; **faire la g.** to glean **2** *(tresse)* **g. d'oignons** string of onions

glaner [3] [glane] **VT 1** *(ramasser → épis)* to glean; *(→ bois)* to gather; *(→ fruits)* to gather, to pick up; **g. du petit bois** to gather sticks **2** *Fig (renseignements, détails)* to glean, to gather; **il y a toujours quelque chose à g. dans ses cours** there is always something to be got out of *or* gleaned from his classes

glaneur, -euse [glanœr, -øz] **NM,F** gleaner

'Les Glaneurs et la glaneuse' *Varda* 'The Gleaners and I'

glanure [glanyr] **NF** *Arch* gleanings

glaouis [glawi] **NMPL** *très Fam* balls, nuts, *Br* bollocks

glapir [32] [glapir] **VI 1** *(renard)* to bark; *(chiot)* to yelp, to yap **2** *(personne)* to yelp, to squeal
VT to shriek

glapissant, -e [glapisɑ̃, -ɑ̃t] **ADJ** *(chien)* yapping, yelping; *(voix)* shrill

glapissement [glapismɑ̃] **NM 1** *(du chien)* yelp; *(du renard)* bark **2** *(de personne, de tempête, du vent)* shrieking *(UNCOUNT)*; **les enfants surexcités poussaient des glapissements** the children were squealing *or* shrieking *(UNCOUNT)* with excitement

glaréole [glareɔl] **NF** *Orn* pratincole; **g. à collier** (collared) pratincole; **g. à ailes noires** black-winged pratincole

Glaris [glaris] **NM** *(ville)* Glarus; **le canton de G.** Glarus

glas [glɑ] **NM** knell; **on sonne le g. pour notre cousin** the bell is tolling *or* they are tolling the knell for our cousin; *Fig* **cette nouvelle sonne le g. de toutes ses espérances** this news sounds the death knell for all his/her hopes

'Pour qui sonne le glas' *Hemingway* 'For Whom the Bell Tolls'

glasnost [glasnɔst] **NF** *Hist* glasnost

glass [glas] **NM** *Fam Vieilli* drink■, snifter

glatir [32] [glatir] **VI** *(aigle)* to scream

glaucomateux, -euse [glokɔmatø, -øz] **ADJ** *Méd* glaucomatous

glaucome [glokom] **NM** *Méd* glaucoma

glauconie [glokɔni], **glauconite** [glokɔnit] **NF** *Minér* glauconite, green earth

glauque [glok] **ADJ 1** *(verdâtre)* bluish-green, *Littéraire* glaucous **2** *(trouble → eau)* murky **3** *Fam (lugubre → pièce)* dreary; *(→ film, plaisanteries)* tasteless, in bad taste; **je suis partie très vite, l'ambiance était g.** I left very quickly since the atmosphere was pretty heavy; **il est un peu g., son copain** his/her friend's a bit creepy

glauquerie [glokri] **NF** *Fam (d'une pièce, d'une maison)* dreariness; *(d'un film, d'une plaisanterie)* bad taste

glaviot [glavjo] **NM** *très Fam* gob of spit

glavioter [3] [glavjɔte] **VI** *très Fam* to spit■, *Br* to gob

glèbe [glɛb] **NF 1** *Littéraire (sol cultivé)* soil, glebe **2** *Hist (domaine)* feudal land, glebe

gléchome, glécome [glekɔm] **NM** *Bot* ground ivy, glechoma, glecoma

glène[1] [glɛn] **NF** *Anat* socket

glène[2] [glɛn] **NF** *Naut* coil (of rope)

gléner [18] [glene] **VT** *Naut* to coil

glénoïdal, -e, -aux, -ales [glenɔidal, -o], **glénoïde** [glenɔid] **ADJ** *Anat* glenoid

glial, -e, -aux, -ales [glijal, -o] **ADJ** *Biol* glial

glie [gli] **NF** *Biol* glia

gliomatose [glijomatoz] **NF** *Méd* gliomatosis

gliome [glijom] **NM** *Méd* glioma

gliose [glijoz] **NF** *Méd* gliosis

glissade [glisad] **NF 1** *(jeu)* sliding *(UNCOUNT)*; **faire une g./des glissades** to slide; **pas de glissades sur la rampe** no sliding down the bannister **2** *(en danse)* glissade **3** *Aviat* **g. sur l'aile** sideslip; **g. sur la queue** tail slide **4** *(glissoire)* slide **5** *Can (pente)* = icy slope for sledging; *(toboggan)* slide

glissage [glisaʒ] **NM le g. du bois** = sliding timber down a mountainside

glissance [glisɑ̃s] **NF** slipperiness

glissando [glisɑ̃do, glisando] *Mus* **ADV** glissando
NM glissando

glissant, -e [glisɑ̃, -ɑ̃t] **ADJ 1** *(sol)* slippery; *Fig* **être sur une pente glissante/sur un terrain g.** to be on a slippery slope/on slippery ground **2** *(coulissant)* sliding; **joint g.** sliding joint, slip joint **3** *Math* **vecteur g.** sliding vector

glisse [glis] **NF** *(d'un ski)* friction coefficient; **sports de g.** = generic term referring to sports such as skiing, snowboarding, surfing etc

glissé [glise] **ADJ M pas g.** glissé
NM glissé

glissement [glismɑ̃] **NM 1** *(déplacement)* sliding *(UNCOUNT)*; **pour favoriser le g. des skis/de la porte** to help the skis glide faster/the door slide more smoothly
2 *(évolution)* shift; **la politique du gouvernement a connu un net g. à droite** there's been a marked shift to the right in government policy
3 *Ling* **g. de sens** shift in meaning
4 *Géol* **g. de terrain** landslide; *(moins important)* landslip
5 *Écon (d'une monnaie, des salaires)* slide; **une progression annuelle de 4 pour cent en g.** a yearly 4 percent slide
6 *Aviat* sideslipping
7 *Électron* **g. de fréquence** frequency variation

glisser[1] [3] [glise] **VI 1** *(déraper → personne)* to slip; *(→ voiture)* to skid; **mon pied a glissé** my foot slipped
2 *(s'échapper accidentellement)* to slip; **ça m'a glissé des mains** it slipped out of my hands; *aussi Fig* **g. entre les mains** *ou* **les doigts de qn** to slip through sb's fingers
3 *(tomber)* to slide; **faire g.** *(pièce de machine)* to slide; **elle fit g. sa robe sans un mot** she stepped out of her dress without saying a word; **il se laissa g. à terre** he slid to the ground; **se laisser g. le long d'une corde** to slide down a rope
4 *(avancer sans heurt → skieur, patineur)* to glide along; *(→ péniche, ski)* to glide; *Aviat* **g. sur l'aile** to sideslip
5 *(passer)* **son regard glissa de la fenêtre à mon fauteuil** his/her eyes drifted from the window to my chair; **un sourire ironique glissa sur ses lèvres** an ironic smile stole over his/her face; **g. sur** *(sujet)* to touch lightly on, to skip over; **glissons (sur ce sujet)!** let's say no more about it!; **sur toi, tout glisse comme sur les plumes d'un canard** it's like water off a duck's back with you; **l'épée lui glissa sur les côtes** the sword glanced off his/her ribs; **une larme glissa sur sa joue** a tear slid *or* ran down his/her cheek
6 *(avoir une surface glissante)* to be slippery; **la chaussée glisse beaucoup** the road is very slippery; **attention, ça glisse par terre** watch out, it's slippery underfoot *or* the ground's slippery
7 *Fig (s'orienter)* **g. à** *ou* **vers** to shift to *or* towards; **g. dans le sommeil** to fall asleep; **g. vers le désespoir** to slide *or* slip into despair; **une partie de l'électorat a glissé à gauche** part of the electorate has shifted *or* moved to the left; **le sens du mot a glissé vers autre chose** the meaning of the word has shifted towards something else; **il glisse vers le mélodrame** he is slipping into melodrama; **ce parti glisse vers le fascisme** this party is moving *or* edging towards fascism
8 *(en danse)* to glissade
9 *Écon (salaires, monnaie)* to slip, to slide
10 *Ordinat* **faire g.** *(pointeur)* to drag
VT 1 *(introduire)* to slip; **g. une lettre sous la porte** to slip a letter under the door; **g. qch dans la poche de qn** to slip sth into sb's pocket
2 *(confier)* **g. un petit mot/une lettre à qn** to slip sb a note/a letter; **g. un mot à qn** to have a quick word with sb; **g. à qn que...** to whisper to sb that...; **g. qch à l'oreille de qn** to whisper sth in sb's ear
3 *(mentionner)* **j'ai glissé ton nom dans la conversation** I managed to slip *or* to drop your name into the conversation; **essaie de g. quelques citations dans ta dissertation** try to slip a few quotations into your essay
4 *(locution)* **g. un œil dans une pièce** to peep *or* to peek into a room; **les enfants devraient dormir, glisse un œil** the children should be asleep, have a (quick) look *or* just have a peep
▶**se glisser VPR 1** *(se faufiler)* to slip (**dans** into); **se g. au premier rang** *(rapidement)* to slip into the front row; **se g. jusqu'à sa place** *(en se cachant)* to slip into one's seat; **glisse-toi là** *(sans prendre de place)* squeeze (yourself) in there; **se g. dans son lit** to slip *or* creep into bed
2 *(erreur)* **des fautes ont pu se g. dans l'article** some mistakes may have slipped *or* crept into the article
3 *(sentiment)* **le doute s'est peu à peu glissé en lui** little by little, doubt crept into his mind; **la haine s'était glissée dans son cœur** hatred had crept into his/her heart

glisser[2] [glise] **NM** *Ordinat* **g. d'icônes** icon drag

glisser-lâcher [giiselaʃe] **NM INV** *Ordinat* drag and drop; **g. d'icônes** icon drag and drop

glisseur [glisœr] **NM** *Math* sliding vector

glissière [glisjɛr] **NF 1** *Tech* slide, runner; **à g.** sliding; **porte à g.** sliding door; **banc à glissières** *(en aviron)* sliding seat **2** *(en travaux publics)* **g. de sécurité** crash barrier **3** *Ind (pour le charbon)* chute

glissoir [gliswar] **NM 1** *(d'une machine)* slide, sliding block **2** *(pour le bois)* timber chute

glissoire [gliswar] **NF** slide *(on ice)*

global, -e, -aux, -ales [glɔbal, -o] **ADJ** *(résultat, vision)* overall, global; *(somme, budget, demande)* total; *(paiement)* lump; *(production)* aggregate; *(revenu)* gross; **as-tu une idée globale du coût?** have you got a rough idea of the cost?; **avoir une vue** *ou* **vision globale d'une situation** to have an overview *or* an overall view; **le budget g. de publicité excède les coûts de production** the total publicity budget is higher than the production costs

globalement [glɔbalmɑ̃] **ADV** all in all, overall; **les résultats sont g. positifs** all in all *or* overall, the results are positive; **g., l'entreprise se porte bien** all in all *or* by and large, the company is doing well

globalisant, -e [glɔbalizɑ̃, -ɑ̃t], **globalisateur, -trice** [glɔbalizatœr, -tris] **ADJ** *(approche)* inclusive; *(concept)* all-encompassing; **vision globalisante** all-embracing view, overview

globalisation [glɔbalizasjɔ̃] **NF** *(d'un marché, d'un conflit)* globalization

globalisatrice [glɔbalizatris] *voir* **globalisateur**

globaliser [3] [glɔbalize] **VT 1** *(réunir)* **le syndicat a globalisé ses revendications** the union is putting forward its demands en bloc **2** *(mondialiser)* to globalize

globalisme [glɔbalism] **NM** globalism

globalité [glɔbalite] **NF** *(ensemble)* **prendre un problème dans sa g.** to tackle a problem as a whole; **envisageons le processus dans sa g.** let's view the process as a whole

globe [glɔb] **NM 1** *(sphère)* globe; **le g.** *(la Terre)* the globe, the world; **sur toute la surface du g.** all over the globe; **une région déshéritée du g.** a poor part of the world; **faire le tour du g.** to go

round the world; **g. céleste** celestial globe; **le g. terrestre** the terrestrial globe

2 *(d'une lampe)* (glass) globe; *(d'une pendule)* glass dome *or* cover

3 *(pour protéger)* glass dome; **conserver qch sous g.** to keep sth under glass; *Fig* **c'est une idée géniale, il faut la mettre sous g.!** that's a brilliant idea, we must keep it under wraps!

4 *Anat* globe; **g. oculaire** eye

globe-trotter [glɔbtrɔtœr] *(pl* **globe-trotters**) **NM** globe-trotter

globicéphale [glɔbisefal] **NM** *Zool* pilot whale, blackfish

globigérine [glɔbiʒerin] **NF** *Zool* globigerina; *Géol* **boue à globigérines** globigerina ooze

globine [glɔbin] **NF** *Biol & Chim* globin

globique [glɔbik] **ADJ** globoid, globular; **vis g.** hourglass *or* globoid worm

globulaire [glɔbylɛr] **ADJ 1** *(sphérique)* globular, globe-shaped **2** *Biol & Physiol* corpuscular

globule [glɔbyl] **NM 1** *Biol & Physiol* corpuscle; **g. blanc** white corpuscle; **g. polaire** polar body; **g. rouge** red corpuscle, red blood cell **2** *Pharm* (spherical) capsule **3** *Vieilli (d'air, d'eau)* globule

globuleux, -euse [glɔbylø, -øz] **ADJ 1** *(forme)* globular, globulous **2** *(œil)* protruding, bulging

globuline [glɔbylin] **NF** globulin

glockenspiel [glɔkənʃpil] **NM** *Mus* glockenspiel

gloire [glwar] **NF 1** *(renom)* fame; **connaître la g.** to find fame; **g. éphémère** short-lived fame; **au faîte** *ou* **sommet de sa g.** at the height *or* pinnacle of his/her fame; **ne t'attends pas à être payé, on fait ça pour la g.** don't expect payment, we're doing it for love; **cette salle est la g. du musée du Louvre** this gallery is the (crowning) glory of the Louvre museum; **elle a eu son heure de g.** she has had her hour of glory

2 *(mérite)* glory, credit; **toute la g. vous en revient** the credit is all yours; **tirer g. de qch** to glory in sth, to pride oneself on sth; **se faire g. de** to boast about; *Fam* **c'est pas la g.** it's not exactly brilliant

3 *(éloge)* praise; **écrit à la g. de...** written in praise of...; **rendre g. au courage de qn** to praise sb's courage; **g. à Dieu** praise be to *or* glory to God; **g. aux soldats morts pour la France!** glory to the soldiers who died for France!

4 *(personne)* celebrity; **il est la g. de notre école** he is the pride of our school

5 *Beaux-Arts (auréole)* aureole; *(ciel décoré)* glory

6 *(splendeur) & Rel* glory; **la famille royale dans toute sa g.** the royal family in all its splendour; **la g. éternelle** eternal glory; **le séjour de g.** the Kingdom of Glory

glome [glɔm] **NM** *Vét* glome

gloméris [glɔmeris] **NM** *Entom* pill millipede

glomérule [glɔmeryl] **NM** *Anat* glomerulus; *Bot* glomerule

glomérulonéphrite [glɔmerylɔnefrit] **NF** *Vieilli Méd* glomerulonephritis

glomérulopathie [glɔmerylɔpati] **NF** *Méd* glomerulopathy

gloria[1] [glɔrja] **NM INV** *Rel* Gloria

gloria[2] [glɔrja] **NM** *Fam Vieilli (café)* = coffee served with spirits

gloriette [glɔrjɛt] **NF** *(pavillon)* gazebo

glorieuse [glɔrjøz] *voir* **glorieux**

glorieusement [glɔrjøzmã] **ADV** gloriously

glorieux, -euse [glɔrjø, -øz] **ADJ 1** *(remarquable)* glorious; **il a eu une mort glorieuse** he died a glorious death; **porter un nom g.** to have an illustrious name; **un g. général** a glorious *or* triumphant general; **une page peu glorieuse de notre histoire** an event in our history we can be less than proud of

2 *Littéraire (fier)* **g. de sa victoire** priding himself on his victory; **être g. de sa naissance** to be proud of one's birth

3 *Rel* glorious

4 *Fam Fig* **ce n'est pas g.** it's not exactly brilliant

5 *Can Péj (en acadien) (vaniteux)* proud

□ **Glorieuse NF** *Hist* **les Trente Glorieuses** = the thirty years following the Second World War; **les Trois Glorieuses** = the three-day Revolution in 1830 (27, 28 and 29 July)

LES TRENTE GLORIEUSES

"Les Trente glorieuses" was originally the title of an essay published in 1979 by the French economist Jean Fourastié. The term has since been used to refer to the period of unparalleled consumer prosperity that France experienced between 1945 and 1973, which began during the reconstruction programme of the post-war years and continued until the oil crisis in 1973. During this era of full employment, raw materials were cheap and the building trade flourished. Economic growth averaged at 5 percent per year, buoyed up by soaring consumption, the easy availability of credit and the baby boom. The standard of living for ordinary French people increased greatly at this time.

---

glorificateur, -trice [glɔrifikatœr, -tris] **ADJ** glorifying

NM,F glorifier

glorification [glɔrifikasjɔ̃] **NF** glorification

glorificatrice [glɔrifikatris] *voir* **glorificateur**

glorifier [9] [glɔrifje] **VT** *(exploit, qualité, héros)* to glorify, to praise; *(Dieu)* to glorify

▸**se glorifier VPR se g. de qch** to glory in sth; **se g. d'avoir fait qch** to boast of having done sth

gloriole [glɔrjɔl] **NF** vainglory; **faire qch par g.** to do sth to show off *or* for show; **pour la g.** for the kudos of it

glose [gloz] **NF** *Ling* gloss; **g. marginale** marginal note

□ **gloses NFPL** *Vieilli (commérages)* gossip *(UNCOUNT)*; **faire des gloses sur qn** to gossip about sb

gloser [3] [gloze] **VT** *(annoter)* to annotate, to gloss

□ **gloser sur VT IND 1** *(discourir sur)* **g. sur qch** to ramble on about sth **2** *(jaser sur)* **g. sur qn/qch** to gossip about sb/sth

gloss [glɔs] **NM** *(pour les lèvres)* lip gloss; *(pour les joues)* highlighter

glossaire [glɔsɛr] **NM** glossary, vocabulary

glossectomie [glɔsɛktɔmi] **NF** *Méd* glossectomy

Glossette® [glɔsɛt] **NF** *Pharm* sublingual tablet

glossine [glɔsin] **NF** *Entom* glossina

glossite [glɔsit] **NF** *Méd* glossitis

glossodynie [glɔsɔdini] **NF** *Méd* glossodynia

glossolalie [glɔsɔlali] **NF** glossolalia

glosso-pharyngien, -enne [glɔsɔfarɛ̃ʒjɛ̃, -ɛn] *(mpl* **glosso-pharyngiens,** *fpl* **glosso-pharyngiennes)* **ADJ** glossopharyngeal

NM glossopharyngeal nerve

glossotomie [glɔsɔtɔmi] **NF** *Méd* glossotomy

glottal, -e, -aux, -ales [glɔtal, -o] **ADJ** glottal

glotte [glɔt] **NF** *Anat* glottis; *Ling* **coup de g.** glottal stop

glottique [glɔtik] **ADJ** glottal, glottic

glouglou [gluglu] **NM 1** *Fam (d'une fontaine)* gurgle, gurgling *(UNCOUNT)*; *(d'une bouteille)* glug-glug; **faire g.** *(fontaine)* to gurgle; *(bouteille)* to go glug-glug **2** *(du dindon)* gobbling *(UNCOUNT)*

glouglouter [3] [gluglute] **VI 1** *Fam (fontaine)* to gurgle; *(bouteille)* to go glug-glug **2** *(dindon)* to gobble

gloussant, -e [glusã, -ãt] **ADJ** clucking

gloussement [glusmã] **NM 1** *(d'une personne)* chuckle; **gloussements** chuckling *(UNCOUNT)*; **pousser un g. de satisfaction** to chuckle with satisfaction **2** *(d'une poule)* clucking *(UNCOUNT)*

glousser [3] [gluse] **VI 1** *(personne)* to chuckle **2** *(poule)* to cluck

glouteron [glutrɔ̃] **NM** *Bot* burdock

glouton, -onne [glutɔ̃, -ɔn] **ADJ** greedy, gluttonous; **que ce bébé est g.!** what a greedy baby!

NM,F glutton

NM *Zool* wolverine, glutton

gloutonnement [glutɔnmã] **ADV** greedily, gluttonously; **il dévora g. son déjeuner** he devoured his lunch greedily

gloutonnerie [glutɔnri] **NF** gluttony

glu [gly] **NF 1** *(substance visqueuse)* birdlime; **prendre des oiseaux à la g.** to lime birds **2** *(colle)* glue **3** *Fam (personne)* **c'est une vraie g.** she sticks to you like glue

---

gluant, -e [glyã, -ãt] **ADJ** *(collant)* sticky; *(boue, limace, paroi, poisson)* slimy; **riz g.** sticky rice

gluau, -x [glyo] **NM** lime twig

glucagon [glykagɔ̃] **NM** *Chim* glucagon

glucide [glysid] **NM** carbohydrate

glucidique [glysidik] **ADJ** carbohydrate *(avant n)*

glucine [glysin] **NF** *Chim* beryllia, beryllium oxide

glucinium [glysinjɔm] **NM** *Vieilli Chim* glucinium

glucocorticoïde [glykɔkɔrtikɔid] **NM** glucocorticoid

glucomètre [glykɔmɛtr] **NM** saccharimeter, saccharometer

gluconique [glykɔnik] **ADJ** **acide g.** gluconic acid

glucosamine [glykɔzamin] **NF** *Pharm* glucosamine

glucose [glykoz] **NM** glucose; **g. sanguin** blood sugar

glucosé, -e [glykoze] **ADJ** containing glucose; **une solution glucosée** a glucose solution

glucoserie [glykɔzri] **NF 1** *(usine)* glucose factory **2** *(industrie)* glucose industry

glucoside [glykɔzid] **NM** glucoside

glucosurie [glykɔsyri] **NF** *Méd* glucosuria

glume [glym] **NF 1** *(des graminées)* glume **2** *(du blé)* chaff

glumelle [glymɛl] **NF** *Bot* glumella, lemma

gluon [glyɔ̃] **NM** gluon

glutamate [glytamat] **NM** glutamate; **g. de sodium** monosodium glutamate

glutamique [glytamik] **ADJ** *Chim* glutamic

gluten [glytɛn] **NM** gluten; **sans g.** gluten-free

glutineux, -euse [glytinø, -øz] **ADJ** glutinous

glycémie [glisemi] **NF** blood-sugar level, *Spéc* glycaemia

glycéride [gliserid] **NM** glyceride

glycérie [gliseri] **NF** glyceria, sweet grass

glycérine [gliserin] **NF** glycerin, glycerine

glycériner [3] [gliserine] **VT** to treat with glycerine

glycérique [gliserik] **ADJ** glyceric

glycérol [gliserɔl] **NM** *Chim* glycerol

glycérolé [gliserɔle] **NM** *Pharm* glycerite

glycérophtalique [gliserɔftalik] **ADJ** glycerophtalic

glycéryle [gliseril] **NM** *Chim* glyceryl

glycine [glisin] **NF 1** *Bot* wisteria **2** *Biol & Chim* glycine, glycocoll

glycocolle [glikɔkɔl] **NM** *Vieilli Chim* glycine, glycocoll

glycogène [glikɔʒɛn] **NM** glycogen

glycogenèse [glikɔʒənɛz] **NF** glycogenesis

glycogénique [glikɔʒenik] **ADJ** glycogenetic

glycol [glikɔl] **NM** glycol

glycolipide [glikɔlipid] **NM** *Biol & Chim* glycolipid

glycolique [glikɔlik] **ADJ** glycolic

glycolyse [glikɔliz] **NF** *Biol & Chim* glycolysis

glycoprotéine [glikɔprɔtein] **NF** *Biol & Chim* glycoprotein

glycorégulation [glikɔregylasjɔ̃] **NF** glycoregulation

glycosurie [glikɔzyri] **NF** *Méd* glycosuria

glycosurique [glikɔzyrik] **ADJ** glycosuric

glyphe [glif] **NM** *Archit* glyph

glyptique [gliptik] **NF** glyptics *(singulier)*

glyptodon [gliptɔdɔ̃], **glyptodonte** [gliptɔdɔ̃t] **NM** glyptodon

glyptographie [gliptɔgrafi] **NF** glyptography

glyptologie [gliptɔlɔʒi] **NF** glyptology

glyptothèque [gliptɔtɛk] **NF 1** *(de pierres gravées)* collection of carved gems **2** *(de sculpture)* archaeological museum, museum of statuary

GM [ʒeɛm] **NM 1** *(abrév* **gentil membre)** holiday-maker *(at Club Méditerranée)* **2** *Com (abrév* **grand magasin)** department store

GMS [ʒeɛmɛs] **NFPL** *Com (abrév* **grandes et moyennes surfaces)** large and medium-sized commercial outlets

GMT [ʒeɛmte] **ADJ INV** *(abrév* **Greenwich Mean Time)** GMT

gnangnan [nãnã] *Fam Péj* **ADJ INV 1** *(personne)* drippy **2** *(œuvre, style)* **j'ai vu le film, que c'était g.!** I saw the film, it was so soppy!

NF drip, wimp

gnaque [nak] = **gniac**

gnaquer [3] [nake] **VT** *Fam (mordre)* to bite

gnaule [ɲol] = **gnôle**

gneiss [gnɛs] **NM** gneiss

gneisseux, -euse [gnɛsø, -øz], **gneissique** [gnɛsik] **ADJ** *Géol* gneissic

gnète [gnɛt] NF *Bot* Gnetum

gnétophyte [gnetofit] *Bot* NF gnetophyte, *Spéc* member of the Gnetophyta

❑ **gnétophytes** NFPL Gnetophyta

gnetum [gnetɔm] NM *Bot* Gnetum

gniac [njak] NF *Fam* fighting spirit∎, drive∎; **avoir la g., être plein de g.** to have plenty of drive

gniole [nɔl] = **gnôle**

GNL [ʒeɛnɛl] NM (*abrév* **gaz naturel liquéfié**) LNG

gnocchi [nɔki] (*pl inv ou* **gnocchis**) NM piece of gnocchi; **des g., des gnocchis** gnocchi

gnognote, gnognotte [nɔnɔt] NF *Fam* **c'est de la g.** (*c'est facile*) it's a cinch; (*c'est sans valeur*) it's *Br* rubbish *or Am* garbage; **c'est pas de la g.** it's the real McCoy; **c'est pas de la g., cette voiture** that car is quite something

gnôle, gnole [nɔl] NF *très Fam* firewater

gnome [gnom] NM **1** (*génie*) gnome **2** (*nabot*) dwarf, gnome

gnomique [gnɔmik] ADJ gnomic

gnomon [gnɔmɔ̃] NM gnomon

gnomonique [gnɔmɔnik] NF gnomonics (*singulier*)

gnon [nɔ̃] NM *Fam* **1** (*coup*) thump; **se prendre un g.** to get thumped *or* walloped; **elle lui a flanqué un sacré g.** she gave him/her a real thump **2** (*enflure*) bruise∎

gnose [gnoz] NF **1** *Rel* (*mouvement*) gnosticism **2** *Vieilli* (*mode de connaissance*) gnosis

gnoséologie [gnozeolɔʒi] NF gnoseology

gnoséologique [gnozeolɔʒik] ADJ gnoseological

gnosie [gnozi] NF gnosis

gnosticisme [gnɔstisism] NM Gnosticism

gnostique [gnɔstik] ADJ Gnostic

NMF Gnostic

gnou [gnu] NM *Zool* wildebeest, gnu

gnouf [nuf] NM **1** *Fam Arg mil* (*prison*) glasshouse; **au g.** in the glasshouse **2** *Fam Arg* crime (*poste de police*) police station∎, cop shop; (*cellule*) police cell∎

GO [ʒeo] NFPL *Rad* (*abrév* **grandes ondes**) LW

NM (*abrév* **gentil organisateur**) group leader (*at Club Méditerranée*)

Go NM *Ordinat* (*abrév écrite* **gigaoctet**) GB

go [go] NM INV go; **le jeu de go** go

❑ **tout de go** ADV *Fam* (*dire, annoncer etc*) straight out; **répondre tout de go** to answer straight off *or* straight out; **ne le lui annonce pas tout de go** don't tell him/her straight out; **il est entré tout de go** he went straight in

Goa [goa] NM Goa

goal [gol] NM (*gardien*) goalkeeper

goal-average [golavɛredʒ] (*pl* **goal-averages**) NM goal difference

gobelet [gɔblɛ] NM **1** (*timbale*) tumbler, beaker; **g. jetable** (*en carton*) paper cup; (*en plastique*) plastic cup **2** (*au jeu*) shaker

gobeleterie [gɔblɛtri] NF **1** (*commerce*) hollow glass trade **2** (*articles*) hollow glassware

Gobelins [gɔblɛ̃] NMPL **la manufacture des G.** = the factory in Paris where Gobelin tapestries are made

gobe-mouches [gɔbmuʃ] NM INV **1** *Orn* flycatcher; **g. gris** spotted flycatcher; **g. noir** pied flycatcher **2** *Fam Vieilli* (*naïf*) gull

gober [3] [gɔbe] VT **1** (*avaler → nourriture*) to gulp down; (*→ huître*) to swallow; (*→ œuf*) to suck; (*→ insecte*) to catch (and eat)

2 *Fam* (*croire*) to swallow; **alors, elle a gobé ton histoire?** so, did she swallow *or* buy it?; **ils ont tout gobé!** they swallowed it (all), hook, line and sinker!; **il gobe tout ce qu'on lui dit** he believes everything he's told∎, he'll swallow anything

3 *Fam* (*supporter*) **je n'ai jamais pu la g.!** I never could stand *or Br* stick her!

4 *Fam* (*location*) **ne reste pas là à g. les mouches** don't just stand there gawping!, don't just stand there like a *Br* lemon *or Am* lump!

USAGE ABSOLU *Fam* (*prendre un cachet d'ecstasy*) to drop an E

▸**se gober** VPR *Fam* to fancy oneself; **qu'est-ce qu'il se gobe, celui-là!** he really fancies himself!, he really thinks he's something special!

goberge [gɔbɛrʒ] NF *Can Ich* pollack, pollock

goberger [17] [gɔbɛrʒe] **se goberger** VPR *Fam* **1** (*se prélasser*) to laze (about), to take it easy **2** (*faire bonne chère*) to indulge oneself∎

gobeur, -euse [gɔbœr, -øz] NM,F (*de nourriture*) gulper, swallower; *Fam Fig* **c'est un g.** he's very gullible∎, he'll swallow anything

Gobi [gɔbi] NM **le désert de G.** the Gobi Desert

gobie [gɔbi] NM *Ich* goby; **g. marcheur** *ou* **des marais** mudskipper, *Br* mudhopper

godage [gɔdaʒ] NM *Couture* pucker

godailler [3] [gɔdaje] VI *Couture* to pucker, to be puckered; **g. aux genoux** to bag at the knees

godasse [gɔdas] NF *Fam* shoe∎

godelureau, -x [gɔdlyro] NM *Hum* (*young*) Romeo, ladies' man

godemiché [gɔdmiʃe] NM dildo

godendard, godendart [gɔdɑ̃dar] NM *Can Vieilli* two-handed saw

goder [3] [gɔde] VI *Couture* to pucker, to be puckered; **g. aux genoux** to bag at the knees

godet [gɔdɛ] NM **1** (*petit récipient*) jar; (*verre*) tumbler; **un g. en étain** a pewter mug; **g. à huile** (*d'une machine*) waste oil cup; *Fam* **on va boire un g. ?** let's have a drink∎ *or Br* jar

2 (*pour peinture*) pot

3 (*d'une pipe*) bowl

4 (*nacelle → d'une noria*) scoop; (*→ d'une roue à eau, en manutention*) bucket; *Tech* (*au pied d'une machine*) socket; *Mines* skip

5 *Couture* (*à ondulation*) flare; (*à découpe*) gore; (*défaut*) pucker, ruck

❑ **à godets** ADJ *Couture* flared; (*à lés*) gored

GODF [ʒeodeɛf] NM (*abrév* **Grand Orient de France**) = principal masonic lodge of France, *Br* ≃ United Grand Lodge of England

godiche [gɔdiʃ] *Fam* ADJ (*maladroit*) oafish; (*niais*) silly, *Am* dumb; **ce qu'il peut être g.!** he's such an oaf!

NF (*maladroite*) clumsy thing; (*niaise*) silly thing

godichon, -onne [gɔdiʃɔ̃, -ɔn] ADJ *Fam* (*maladroit*) oafish; (*niais*) silly, *Am* dumb; **ce qu'il peut être g.!** he's such an oaf!

godille [gɔdij] NF **1** *Naut* (*rame*) (stern-mounted) scull; **avancer à la g.** to scull **2** (*en ski*) wedeln; **descendre en g., faire la g.** to wedeln

godiller [3] [gɔdije] VI **1** *Naut* to scull **2** (*au ski*) to wedeln

godilleur [gɔdijœr] NM *Naut* sculler

godillot [gɔdijo] NM **1** (*chaussure → de soldat*) boot; *Fam* (*chaussure de marche*) clodhopper **2** *Fam* (*personne*) party-liner, yes-man

godiveau, -x [gɔdivo] NM veal forcemeat (*UNCOUNT*)

godron [gɔdrɔ̃] NM **1** *Beaux-Arts* gadroon, godroon; **à godrons** gadrooned, godrooned **2** *Tex* (*pli*) pleat, goffer **3** *Archit* flute

goéland [gɔelɑ̃] NM *Orn* seagull; **g. argenté** herring gull; **g. brun** lesser black-backed gull; **g. cendré** common gull; **g. marin** great black-backed gull

goélette [gɔelɛt] NF schooner; **(voile) g.** trysail

goémon [gɔemɔ̃] NM wrack

goethite [gɔtit] NF *Minér* goethite, göthite

goétie [gɔesi] NF *Antiq* goety, black magic

goger [17] [gɔʒe] *Suisse* VI to soak (in water); **faire g. un bateau** to sink a boat

VT **g. une maladie** to be coming down with *or* getting an illness

goglu [gogly] NM *Can Orn* bobolink

gogo [gogo] *Fam* NM sucker, *Br* mug, *Am* patsy; **c'est pour les gogos, leur publicité** you'd have to be a real sucker to fall for their advert

❑ **à gogo** ADV galore; **il y avait des frites à g.** there were *Br* chips *or Am* fries galore

gogol [gɔgɔl] = **gol**

goguenard, -e [gɔgnar, -ard] ADJ mocking, jeering; **un œil g.** a mocking look

goguenardise [gɔgnardiz] NF mocking, jeering; **regarder qn avec g.** to eye sb mockingly

goguenots [gɔgno], **gogues** [gɔg] NMPL *très Fam Br* loo, *Am* john

goguette [gɔgɛt] **en goguette** ADJ tipsy, *Br* merry; **être en g.** to be (a bit) tight *or Br* merry; (*faire la noce*) to be out for a good time; **des commerciaux en g.** some salesmen having a boozy get-together

goï [gɔj] = **goy**

goïm [gɔjim] *voir* **goy**

goinfre [gwɛ̃fr] *Fam* NMF pig, *Br* greedy guts, gannet, *Am* hog; **manger comme un g.** to eat like a pig

ADJ greedy∎, piggish

goinfrer [3] [gwɛ̃fre] **se goinfrer** VPR *Fam* to pig *or* to stuff oneself; **se g. de qch** to stuff oneself with sth

goinfrerie [gwɛ̃frəri] NF *Fam* piggishness; **arrête de manger, c'est de la g.** stop eating, you're just being a pig *or* making a pig of yourself

goitre [gwatr] NM *Méd* goitre

goitreux, -euse [gwatrø, -øz] *Méd* ADJ goitrous

NM,F = person with a goitre

gol [gɔl] NMF *Fam* spaz, *Br* mong

Golan [gɔlɑ̃] NM **le (plateau du) G.** the Golan Heights

Goldberg [gɔldbɛrg] NPR

🎵

'Les Variations Goldberg' *Bach* 'The Goldberg Variations'

golden [gɔldɛn] NF Golden Delicious

goldo [gɔldo] NF *Fam* = Gauloise® cigarette

Goldorak [gɔldorak] NPR = Japanese cartoon hero once immensely popular among French children

gold-point [gɔldpɔjnt] (*pl* **gold-points**) NM *Fin* gold point

golem [gɔlɛm] NM golem

golf [gɔlf] NM **1** *Sport* **le g.** golf; **jouer au g.** to play golf **2** (*terrain*) golf course; **g. miniature** miniature golf, mini-golf

Golfe [gɔlf] NM **le G.** the Gulf; **les États du G.** the Gulf States

golfe [gɔlf] NM gulf; **le g. d'Aden** the Gulf of Aden; **le g. d'Alaska** *ou* **de l'Alaska** the Gulf of Alaska; **le g. d'Aqaba** the Gulf of Aqaba; **le g. du Bengale** the Bay of Bengal; **le g. du Bénin** the Bight of Benin; **le g. de Botnie** the Gulf of Bothnia; **le g. de Cadix** the Gulf of Cadiz; **le g. de Californie** the Gulf of California; **le g. de Carpentarie** the Gulf of Carpentaria; **le g. de Corinthe** the Gulf of Corinth; **le g. de Finlande** the Gulf of Finland; **le g. de Gascogne** the Bay of Biscay; **le g. de Gênes** the Gulf of Genoa; **le g. de Guinée** the Gulf of Guinea; **le g. du Lion** the Gulf of Lions; **le g. du Maine** the Gulf of Maine; **le g. du Mexique** the Gulf of Mexico; **le g. d'Oman** the Gulf of Oman; **le g. de Panamá** the Gulf of Panama; **le g. Persique** the Persian Gulf; **le g. de Riga** the Gulf of Riga; **le g. de Suez** the Gulf of Suez; **le g. de Tarente** the Gulf of Taranto; **le g. de Thaïlande** the Gulf of Thailand, *Anciennement* the Gulf of Siam; **le g. de Venise** the Gulf of Venice

golfer [3] [gɔlfe] VI *Can* to play golf

golfeur, -euse [gɔlfœr, -øz] NM,F golfer

Golgi [gɔlʒi] NPR Golgi; *Méd* **appareil de G.** Golgi body

Golgotha [gɔlgɔta] NM **le G.** Golgotha

Goliath [gɔljat] NPR *Bible* Goliath

golmote, golmotte [gɔlmɔt] NF *Bot* (*amanite*) blusher, reddish amanita; (*lépiote*) parasol mushroom

gombo [gɔbo] NM *Bot* (*plante*) gumbo; (*cosse*) gumbo, lady's finger; *Culin* (*potage*) gumbo

Gomina® [gɔmina] NF brilliantine, ≃ Brylcreem®

gominé, -e [gɔmine] ADJ **avoir les cheveux gominés** to have one's hair slicked back with Brylcreem® *or* hair cream

gominer [3] [gɔmine] **se gominer** VPR to put Brylcreem® *or* hair cream on

gommage [gɔmaʒ] NM **1** (*effacement*) erasing **2** (*de la peau*) exfoliation; **se faire faire un g.** to have one's skin deep-cleansed; **g. pour le corps** body scrub **3** (*encollage*) gumming; *Tech* (*des valves, des pistons*) sticking, gumming

gommant [gɔmɑ̃] ADJ **crème gommante, soin g.** face scrub

gomme [gɔm] NF **1** (*pour effacer*) eraser, *Br* rubber; **g. à crayon** eraser, *Br* rubber; **g. à encre** ink eraser *or Br* rubber

2 (*substance*) gum; **g. adragante** tragacanth; **g. arabique** gum arabic

3 *Méd* gumma

4 (*friandise*) gum; **g. à mâcher** chewing-gum

5 *Fam* (*locutions*) **à la g.** lousy; **des conseils à la g.** lousy advice; **son installation électrique est à la g.** his/her lousy *or* crummy wiring; **mettre (toute) la g.** (*en voiture*) to put one's foot down; (*au travail*) to pull out all the stops

gom-gor

gommé, -e [gɔme] ADJ *(papier, enveloppe)* gummed

gomme-gutte [gɔmgyt] *(pl* **gommes-guttes)** NF gamboge

gomme-laque [gɔmlak] *(pl* **gommes-laques)** NF lac

gommer [3] [gɔme] VT **1** *(avec une gomme)* to erase, *Br* to rub out

2 *(faire disparaître)* to chase away, to erase; **g. les cellules mortes de la peau** to remove dead skin

3 *(estomper)* **g. les contours** to soften the outline; **g. une partie de son passé/un souvenir pénible** to erase part of one's past/a painful memory; *Fig* **le reportage a gommé les moments les plus pénibles** the report played down *or* glossed over the toughest moments

4 *(encoller)* to gum; *Tech* to stick, to gum; **piston gommé** gummed piston

gomme-résine [gɔmrezin] *(pl* **gommes-résines)** NF gum resin

gommette [gɔmɛt] NF (small) sticker

gommeux, -euse [gɔmø, -øz] ADJ **1** *Bot* gum-yielding, *Spéc* gummiferous **2** *Méd* gummatous **3** *(collant)* gummy, sticky
▪ NM *Vieilli* young fop
❑ **gommeuse** NF gumming machine

gommier [gɔmje] NM *Bot* gum tree, *Spéc* gummiferous tree

gommifère [gɔmifɛr] ADJ *Bot* gum-bearing, gum-yielding, *Spéc* gummiferous

gommose [gɔmoz] NF *Hort* gommosis, gum

Gomorrhe [gɔmɔr] *voir* **Sodome**

gon [gɔ̃] NM *Géom* grade

gonade [gɔnad] NF gonad

gonadique [gɔnadik] ADJ gonadal

gonadostimuline [gɔnadɔstimylin] NF gonadotropin, gonadotrophin

gonadotrope [gɔnadɔtrɔp] ADJ gonadotropic, gonadotrophic

gonadotrophine [gɔnadɔtrɔfin] NF gonadotropin, gonadotrophin

gonange [gɔnɑ̃ʒ] NM *Zool* gonophore

gonarthrose [gɔnartroz] NF arthritis of the knee

Goncourt [gɔ̃kur] NM **le prix G.** = prestigious annual literary prize awarded by the Académie Goncourt

gond [gɔ̃] NM hinge; **mettre une porte sur ses gonds** to hang a door; *Fig* **sortir de ses gonds** to blow one's top, to fly off the handle

gondolage [gɔ̃dɔlaʒ] NM *(du bois)* warping; *(d'une tôle)* buckling; *(du papier)* cockling, curling

gondolant, -e [gɔ̃dɔlɑ̃, -ɑ̃t] ADJ *Fam Vieilli* hysterical, side-splitting

gondole [gɔ̃dɔl] NF **1** *Naut* gondola **2** *Mktg (présentoir)* gondola; **tête de g.** gondola end

gondolement [gɔ̃dɔlmɑ̃] NM *(du bois)* warping; *(d'une tôle)* buckling; *(du papier)* cockling, curling

gondoler [3] [gɔ̃dɔle] VI *(bois)* to warp, to get warped; *(tôle)* to buckle; *(papier)* to crinkle, to curl, to cockle
▪ VT *(papier)* to crinkle, to curl, to cockle; *(disque)* to warp
▸ **se gondoler** VPR **1** *(se déformer → bois)* to warp; *(→ papier)* to crinkle, to curl, to cockle; *(→ tôle)* to buckle; **mon disque s'est gondolé à la chaleur** the heat has warped my record

2 *très Fam (rire)* to fall about (laughing); **ils se sont tous gondolés quand je le leur ai dit** when I told them they all fell about (laughing) *or* they were all in stitches

gondolier, -ère [gɔ̃dɔlje, -ɛr] NM,F *Com* merchandise assistant
▪ NM *(batelier)* gondolier

gonelle [gɔnɛl] NF *Ich* gunnel, butterfish

gonfalon [gɔ̃falɔ̃] NM *Hist* gonfalon, gonfanon

gonfalonier [gɔ̃falɔnje] NM *Hist* gonfalonier

gonfanon [gɔ̃fanɔ̃] = **gonfalon**

gonfanonier [gɔ̃fanɔnje] NM *Hist* **1** *(porteur du gonfalon)* gonfalonier **2** *(en Italie)* gonfalonier

gonflable [gɔ̃flabl] ADJ *(canot)* inflatable; *(ballon, poupée)* blow-up

gonflage [gɔ̃flaʒ] NM **1** *(d'un pneu)* inflating; *(d'un ballon)* blowing up; **vérifie le g. des pneus** check the tyre pressure **2** *Cin & Phot* blow-up process

gonflant, -e [gɔ̃flɑ̃, -ɑ̃t] ADJ **1** *(bouffant → jupon)*

full; *(→ manche)* puffed **2** *très Fam (irritant)* maddening, irritating; **c'est g.!** what a drag!; **qu'il est g. à toujours être en retard!** it's so annoying the way he's always late!
▪ NM *(d'un tissu)* volume; *(d'une chevelure)* volume, body; **donner du g. à ses cheveux** to give body *or* volume to one's hair

gonfle [gɔ̃fl] NF *Suisse (congère)* snowdrift

gonflé, -e [gɔ̃fle] ADJ **1** *(enflé)* swollen, puffed up; *(yeux)* swollen, puffy; *(visage)* bloated, swollen, puffy; *(estomac)* bloated, swollen; *(pieds, chevilles)* swollen; **enfants faméliques au ventre g.** starving children with distended *or* swollen stomachs; **torrent g. par les pluies** torrent swollen by the rains; *Fig* **être g. d'orgueil** to be puffed up with pride; **elle avait les yeux gonflés de larmes** her eyes were swollen with tears; **g. comme une outre** full to bursting (point)

2 *Naut (voile)* full

3 *Fam (locutions)* **t'es g.!** *(effronté)* you've got a nerve *or* some cheek!; *(courageux)* you've got guts!; **c'est g. ce qu'il a fait là** what he did there took some nerve; **être g. à bloc** to be raring to go

gonflement [gɔ̃fləmɑ̃] NM **1** *(de pneu, de ballon)* inflating, inflation **2** *(grosseur)* swelling **3** *(augmentation → des prix)* inflation; *(→ des statistiques)* exaggeration; *(→ des impôts)* excessive increase *(de* in)

gonfler [3] [gɔ̃fle] VT **1** *(remplir d'un gaz → bouée, pneu)* to inflate, to blow up; *(→ poumons)* to fill; **g. les joues** to puff out one's cheeks; **avoir le cœur gonflé de peine/de chagrin/de joie** to be heartbroken/grief-stricken/overjoyed

2 *(faire grossir)* **gonfle tes muscles** flex your muscles; **un abcès lui gonflait la joue** his/her cheek was swollen with an abscess; **la brise gonflait sa jupe** her skirt was billowing in the breeze; **le vent gonfle les voiles** the wind is filling the sails; **la fonte des neiges gonfle les torrents** the thaw swells the torrents *or* makes the torrents swell; **les yeux gonflés de sommeil/de larmes** eyes swollen with sleep/with tears

3 *(faire augmenter de volume)* to swell; *(prix, devis)* to inflate, to push up; *(frais, statistiques)* to exaggerate, to inflate; *(impact, conséquences)* to exaggerate, to blow out of all proportion; **g. l'importance de qn/qch** to exaggerate *or* overstress the importance of sb/sth; **le prof a gonflé les notes** the teacher bumped up the marks

4 *Fam Aut (moteur)* to hot up, to soup up

5 *Cin* to blow up, to enlarge

6 *très Fam (irriter)* **g. qn** to get on sb's nerves *or Br* wick; **il commence à me g.** he's starting to get on my nerves *or Br* on my wick; **il nous les gonfle avec ses matchs de foot** he really gets on our nerves *or* he's a real pain in the neck with his football matches
▪ VI **1** *Culin (pâte)* to rise; *(riz)* to swell (up)

2 *(enfler)* to be puffed up *or* bloated; **le bois a gonflé** the wood has warped; **la bière fait g. l'estomac** beer bloats the stomach
▸ **se gonfler** VPR **1** *(d'air, de gaz)* to inflate; **les poumons se gonflent** the lungs fill; **ce matelas se gonfle à l'aide d'une pompe** this air bed can be blown up *or* inflated with a pump

2 *(voile)* to swell; *(éponge)* to swell up

3 *Fig* **se g. de colère** to be bursting with rage; **son cœur se gonfle d'allégresse** his/her heart is bursting with joy

gonflette [gɔ̃flɛt] NF *Fam Péj* pumping iron; **faire de la g.** to pump iron

gonfleur [gɔ̃flœr] NM *(air)* pump

gong [gɔ̃g] NM **1** *Mus* gong **2** *Sport* bell; *Fig* **sauvé par le g.** saved by the bell

gongorisme [gɔ̃gɔrism] NM *Littérature* gongorism

goniomètre [gɔnjɔmɛtr] NM goniometer

goniométrie [gɔnjɔmetri] NF goniometry

goniométrique [gɔnjɔmetrik] ADJ goniometric

gonnelle [gɔnɛl] = **gonelle**

gonochorique [gɔnɔkɔrik] ADJ *Biol* gonochorismal

gonochorisme [gɔnɔkɔrism] NM *Biol* gonochorism

gonococcie [gɔnɔkɔksi] NF *Méd* gonococcal infection

gonocoque [gɔnɔkɔk] NM *Méd* gonococcus; **des gonocoques** gonococci

gonocyte [gɔnɔsit] NM *Biol* gonocyte

gonophore [gɔnɔfɔr] NM *Zool* gonophore

gonorrhée [gɔnɔre] NF gonorrhoea

gonosome [gɔnɔsɔm] NM *Biol* gonosome

gonozoïde [gɔnɔzɔid] NM *Zool* gonozooid

gonze [gɔ̃z] NM *très Fam* guy, *Br* bloke

gonzesse [gɔ̃zɛs] NF *très Fam* **1** *(femme) Br* bird, *Am* chick **2** *(homme)* sissy, *Am* pantywaist

goodyère [gudjɛr] NF *Bot* **g. rampante** creeping lady's tresses

gopak [gɔpak] NM *(danse ukrainienne)* gopak

gopher [gɔfɛr] NM *Ordinat* gopher

gopura [gɔpyra] NM gopura, gopuram

goral, -als [gɔral] NM *Zool* goral

Gorbatchev [gɔrbatʃɛf] NPR **Mikhaïl G.** Mikhail Gorbachov

gord [gɔr] NM kiddle, stake net

gordien [gɔrdjɛ̃] *voir* **nœud**

gore [gɔr] *Fam* ADJ INV *(film)* gory
▪ NM *(genre)* gore (cinema); *(film)* gore movie *or Br* film

goret [gɔrɛ] NM **1** *(porcelet)* piglet **2** *Fam (personne)* **petit g.!** you grubby little pig!; **manger comme un g.** to eat like a pig

Gore-Tex® [gɔrtɛks] NM *Tex* Gore-Tex®

gorfou [gɔrfu] NM *Orn* crested penguin, rock hopper

gorge [gɔrʒ] NF **1** *(gosier)* throat; **avoir mal à la g.**, **avoir un mal de g.** to have a sore throat; **j'ai la g. sèche** my throat is dry *or* parched; **l'arête m'est restée en travers de la g.** the bone got stuck in my throat; *Fig* **son refus m'est resté en travers de la g.** his/her refusal stuck in my throat; **avoir la g. nouée** *ou* **serrée** to have a lump in one's throat; **parler avec la g. serrée par la peine/l'angoisse** to speak in a voice trembling with sorrow/anguish; **l'odeur/la fumée vous prenait à la g.** the smell/smoke made you gag; **crier à pleine g.** *ou* **à g. déployée** to shout at the top of one's voice; **rire à g. déployée** to roar with laughter; **on lui enfoncera** *ou* **lui fera rentrer ses mots dans la g.** we'll make him/her eat his/her words; **prendre qn à la g.** to grab *or* to take sb by the throat; *Fig* **pris à la g., ils ont dû emprunter** they had a gun to their heads, so they had to borrow money; **tenir qn à la g.** to hold sb by the throat; *Fig* to have a stranglehold on sb; **faire rendre g. à qn** to force sb to pay *or* to cough up; **faire des gorges chaudes de qn/qch** to have a good laugh about sb/sth; **quand ils sauront, ils vont en faire des gorges chaudes** when they find out, they'll have a good laugh about it

2 *Littéraire (poitrine → d'une femme)* bosom, breast; *(→ d'un pigeon)* breast

3 *Géog* gorge

4 *Archit* groove, glyph, quirk; **moulure à g.** grooved moulding

5 *Constr (d'une cheminée)* throat; *(d'une fenêtre)* groove

6 *Tech (d'une poulie)* groove, score; *(d'une serrure)* tumbler; *(d'un écrou)* furrow; *(d'un pistolet, d'un étui à cartouches)* neck; **roue** *ou* **poulie à g.** sheave

gorgé [gɔrʒe] ADJ **une éponge gorgée d'eau** a sponge full of water; **sol g. d'eau** sodden soil; **champs gorgés d'eau** waterlogged fields; **des fruits gorgés de soleil** sun-kissed fruit; **g. de sang** gorged with blood

gorge-bleue [gɔrʒblø] *(pl* **gorges-bleues)** NF *Orn* bluethroat

gorge-de-pigeon [gɔrʒdəpiʒɔ̃] ADJ INV dove-coloured

gorgée [gɔrʒe] NF mouthful; **à petites gorgées** in little sips; **boire qch à petites gorgées** to sip sth; **à grandes gorgées** in great gulps; **d'une seule g.** in one gulp

gorgeon [gɔrʒɔ̃] NM *Fam* drink

gorger [17] [gɔrʒe] VT *(oies)* to cram; **g. un enfant de sucreries** to stuff a child full of sweets
▸ **se gorger** VPR **se g. (de qch)** *(se remplir de)* to stuff oneself (with sth); **se g. d'eau** *(terre, rizière)* to become waterlogged; *Fig* **elle semblait se g. de sa présence** it seemed as if she couldn't see enough of him/her

gorgerin [gɔrʒərɛ̃] NM **1** *Hist (d'un casque)* gorget, throat-piece **2** *Archit* gorgerin, necking

gorget [gɔrʒɛ] NM **1** *(rabot)* moulding plane **2** *(moulure)* quirk

gorgonaires [gɔrgɔnɛr] NMPL *Zool* Gorgonacea

gorgone [gɔrgɔn] NF **1** *Littéraire (femme)* gorgon, virago **2** *Zool* gorgonian

Gorgones [gɔrgɔn] NFPL *Myth* **les G.** the Gorgons

gorgonzola [gɔrgɔ̃zɔla] NM Gorgonzola (cheese)

gorille [gɔrij] NM **1** *Zool* gorilla **2** *Fam (garde)* gorilla, bodyguard▪

Gorki [gɔrki] NPR **Maxime G.** Maxim Gorky

gosette [gozɛt] NF *Belg* = fruit-filled pastry

gosier [gozje] NM *(gorge)* throat, gullet; **rire à plein g.** to laugh loudly *or* heartily; *Fam* **j'ai le g. sec** I could do with a drink, I'm parched; *Fam* **ça m'est resté en travers du g.** it really stuck in my throat; *Fam* **avoir le g. en pente** to have a permanent thirst, to like one's drink

gospel [gɔspɛl] NM gospel (music)

gosse [gɔs] NMF *Fam* **1** *(enfant)* kid; **sale g.!** you brat!; **c'est un/une brave g.** he's/she's a nice kid; **c'est une g. de la rue** she grew up in the street; **g. de riches** rich kid **2** *(fils, fille)* kid; **ses trois gosses** his/her three kids **3** *(jeune)* **il est beau g.** he's a good-looking guy; **une belle g.** a good-looking girl▪ **4** *Can Vulg* **gosses** balls, nuts, *Br* bollocks

Göteborg [gøtəbɔrg] NM Gothenburg, Göteborg

gotha [gɔta] NM *(aristocratie)* aristocracy; *(élite)* élite; **le g. de l'édition** the leading lights of the publishing world; **tout le g. de la mode était là** (all) the big names in fashion were there; **le g.** *(almanach)* ≃ Burke's Peerage

gothique [gɔtik] ADJ **1** *Beaux-Arts & Hist* Gothic; **écriture g.** Gothic script **2** *Littérature* Gothic **3** *Aviat* Gothic

NM **1** *Beaux-Arts* **le g.** the Gothic style **2** *Littérature* **le g.** Gothic

NF Gothic (type); **écrire en g.** to write in Gothic script

Goths [go] NMPL **les G.** the Goths

gotique [gɔtik] NM *Ling* Gothic

Gotland [gɔtlɑ̃d] NM *Géog* Gothland, Gotland

goton [gɔtɔ̃] NF *Fam Vieilli* floozy, tart

gouache [gwaʃ] NF gouache; **peindre à la g.** to paint in *or* with gouache; **quelques belles gouaches** some beautiful gouaches

gouacher [3] [gwaʃe] VT to paint in gouache

gouaille [gwaj] NF *Vieilli* cheeky humour; **elle répliqua avec une g. bien parisienne** she replied with typical Parisian humour

gouailler [3] [gwaje] VI *Vieilli* to joke

gouaillerie [gwajri] NF *Vieilli* mocking *or* cheeky remark

gouailleur, -euse [gwajœr, -øz] ADJ *Vieilli* mocking, cheeky

goualante [gwalɑ̃t] NF *Fam Vieilli* popular song▪

goualeuse [gwaløz] NF *Fam Vieilli* street singer▪

gouape [gwap] NF *Fam Vieilli* hoodlum, hood

gouda [guda] NM Gouda (cheese); **vieux g.** mature Gouda

goudrelle [gudrɛl], **goudrille** [gudrij] NF = spout for collecting maple sap

goudron [gudrɔ̃] NM tar; **g. bitumineux** bitumen; **g. de bois/houille** wood/coal tar; **g. minéral** asphalt, bitumen

❑ **goudrons** NMPL (cigarette) tar

goudronnage [gudrɔnaʒ] NM tarring, surfacing

goudronné, -e [gudrɔne] ADJ **papier g.** tar-lined paper; **route goudronnée** tarred road

goudronner [3] [gudrɔne] VT **1** *(route)* to tar, to surface (with tar) **2** *(bateau)* to pay

goudronneur [gudrɔnœr] NM *(ouvrier)* tar sprayer *or* spreader

goudronneux, -euse [gudrɔnø, -øz] ADJ tarry

❑ **goudronneuse** NF *(machine)* tar tank *or* spreader

gouet [gwɛ] NM **1** *(outil)* billhook **2** *(arum)* wild arum, lords and ladies

gouffre [gufr] NM *Géol (dû à l'effondrement)* trough fault (valley); *(dû à un fleuve)* swallow hole; *(abîme)* chasm, abyss, pit; **un g. béant** a yawning *or* gaping chasm; **g. sous-marin** oceanic abyss; *Fig* **être au bord du g.** to be on the edge of the abyss; *Littéraire* **tombé dans le g. de l'oubli/du désespoir** fallen into the depths of oblivion/despair; *Fig* **c'est un g. d'ignorance** the depths of his/her ignorance are unfathomable; *Fig* **cette voiture est un g.** this car just swallows up money, with this car it's like pouring money into a bottomless pit; **cette affaire sera un g. financier** this business will just swallow up money, we'll have to keep on pouring money into this business; *Mktg* **g. financier** *(produit)* financial disaster, dog

gouge [guʒ] NF **1** *(ciseau à bois)* gouge; *(pour évider)* hollow chisel **2** *(de cordonnier)* paring gouge

gougère [guʒɛr] NF gougère *(choux pastry filled with Gruyère cheese)*

gougnafier [guɲafje] NM *Fam Vieilli (individu grossier)* yokel, peasant, *Am* hick; *(bon à rien)* good-for-nothing, *Br* waster, *Am* slacker; *(mauvais ouvrier)* careless workman▪, *Br* cowboy

gougoune [gugun] NF *Can Br* flip-flop, *Am* thong; **des gougounes** (a pair of) *Br* flip-flops *or Am* thongs

gouille [guj] NF *Suisse (flaque d'eau)* puddle; *(étang, mare)* pond

gouine [gwin] NF *très Fam* dyke, = offensive term used to refer to a lesbian

goujat [guʒa] NM boor

goujaterie [guʒatri] NF boorishness, uncouthness; **quelle g.!** how uncouth!

goujon[1] [guʒɔ̃] NM **1** *Ich* gudgeon **2** *Culin* **g. de sole** sole goujon *(small piece of fillet)*

goujon[2] [guʒɔ̃] NM **1** *Constr (gén)* pin; *(de bois)* dowel; *(de métal)* gudgeon; *Menuis* **g. perdu, g. prisonnier** dowel (pin) **2** *Tech (de poulie)* pin; **g. de jonction** assembling pin, bolt; **g. de charnière** hinge pin; **g. d'arbre** shaft gudgeon

goujonner [3] [guʒɔne] VT **1** *Constr* to joggle; *(bois)* to dowel; *(métal)* to bolt **2** *Tech* to bolt (with gudgeons)

goujonnette [guʒɔnɛt] NF *Culin* goujon

goujonnière [guʒɔnjɛr] NF *Pêche* bait kettle

goulache [gulaʃ] NM goulash

goulafre [gulafr] *Belg* ADJ greedy

NMF greedy person

goulag [gulag] NM Gulag

goulasch [gulaʃ] = **goulache**

goule [gul] NF ghoul

goulée [gule] NF *Fam* **1** *(de liquide)* gulp▪; **vider son verre à grandes goulées** to gulp down one's drink **2** *(d'air)* **prendre une g. d'air** to take in a lungful of air; **il tira sur son havane, et aspira une grosse g.** he drew deeply on his cigar

goulet [gulɛ] NM **1** *(rétrécissement)* narrowing; **la rue fait un g.** the road narrows; **g. d'étranglement** bottleneck **2** *Géol* gully, (narrow) gorge **3** *(chenal)* channel; **le G. de Brest** the Brest Channel

goulette [gulɛt] NF *(en travaux publics)* race, conduit

gouleyant, -e [gulejɑ̃, -ɑ̃t] ADJ *(vin)* lively

goulot [gulo] NM **1** *(de bouteille)* neck; **boire au g.** to drink straight from the bottle **2** *Fig* **g. d'étranglement** bottleneck **3** *Vulg* **refouler du g.** to have foul breath

goulotte [gulɔt] NF *(conduit)* conduit; *(rigole)* channel; *(d'un wagonnet à charbon)* spout

goulu, -e [guly] ADJ greedy, gluttonous; *(regards)* hungry, greedy

NM,F **1** *(glouton)* glutton **2** *Fam Vieilli (qui a une grande bouche)* = person with a big mouth

goulûment [gulymɑ̃] ADV greedily; *(regarder)* hungrily, greedily; **manger g.** to eat greedily, to gobble (down) one's food

goum [gum] NM *Mil & Hist* goum, Arab unit

goumier [gumje] NM *Mil & Hist* goum, goumier

Goupil [gupi] NPR *Littérature* Reynard the Fox

goupil [gupi] NM *Arch* fox

goupille [gupij] NF (joining) pin, cotter (pin); **g. fendue** split pin; **g. d'arrêt** stop bolt

goupiller [3] [gupije] VT **1** *Tech* to pin, to (fix with a) cotter

2 *Fam (combiner)* to set up; **bien/mal goupillé** well/badly organized; **ils avaient tout goupillé d'avance!** they had it all set up *or* worked out!; **je voudrais bien savoir ce qu'elle est en train de g.** I'd really like to know what she's up to; **elle avait bien goupillé son coup** she'd set it up neatly *or* planned it just right

▸**se goupiller** VPR *Fam (se dérouler)* to turn out; **ça dépend comment les choses vont se g.** it depends how things turn *or* work out; **ça s'est bien/mal goupillé** things turned out well/badly

goupillon [gupijɔ̃] NM **1** *(brosse)* bottle-brush **2** *Rel* aspersorium

gour [gur] NM *Géog* eroded hill, gara

goura [gura] NM *Orn* goura

gourami [gurami] NM *Ich* gourami, paradise fish

gourance [gurɑ̃s], **gourante** [gurɑ̃t] NF *très Fam Br* boob, bloomer, *Am* goof; **faire une g.** *Br* to (make a) boob, to make a bloomer, *Am* to goof

gourbet [gurbɛ] NM *Bot* beach grass, marram (grass)

gourbi [gurbi] NM **1** *Fam (taudis)* dump, hovel **2** *(en Afrique du Nord)* gourbi, shack

gourd, -e[1] [gur, gurd] ADJ *(engourdi)* numb, stiff; **j'ai les doigts gourds** my fingers are numb *or* stiff (with cold)

gourdasse [gurdas] NF *Fam* blockhead, twit

gourde[2] [gurd] NF **1** *(récipient → en peau)* leather flask, wineskin; *(→ en métal ou plastique)* bottle, flask **2** *(courge)* gourd **3** *Fam (personne)* blockhead, twit; **c'est une vraie g.!** he's a real blockhead *or* twit!

ADJ *Fam* dopey, thick

gourde[3] [gurd] NF *(monnaie de Haïti)* gourde

gourdin [gurdɛ̃] NM **1** *(arme)* cudgel **2** *Vulg (pénis)* dick, prick, *Br* knob; **avoir le g.** to have a hard-on

gouren [gurɛ̃] NM Gouren *(traditional Breton wrestling)*

gourer [3] [gure] **se gourer** VPR *Fam* **1** *(se tromper) Br* to boob, to make a boob *or* bloomer, *Am* to goof; **se g. d'adresse** to get the address wrong; **se g. de jour** to get the day wrong; **je me suis gouré dans les horaires** I got the times mixed up; **tu t'es complètement gouré!** you've got it all mixed up *or* all wrong! **2** *(se douter)* **je m'en gourais!** I thought as much!

gouret [gure] NM *Can* hockey stick

gourgandine [gurgɑ̃din] NF *Vieilli Péj* hussy

gourgane [gurgan] NF *Can* broad bean

gourmand, -e [gurmɑ̃, -ɑ̃d] ADJ **1** *(personne → gén)* who likes his/her food; *(→ à l'excès)* greedy; **g. de chocolat** fond of chocolate; **cet enfant est très g.** *(de sucreries)* that child has a sweet tooth

2 *(gastronomique)* **notre page gourmande** our food *or* gastronomy page; **pause gourmande** snack; **les petites recettes gourmandes de Julie** Julie's special *or* tasty recipes

3 *(bouche)* greedy; *(lèvres)* eager; *(regard)* greedy, eager

4 *(État, fisc)* greedy

5 *Hort* **branche gourmande** sucker

NM,F person who loves his/her food, *Sout* gourmand; **c'est vrai, je suis une gourmande** *(gén)* I must admit I am rather fond of my food; *(de sucreries)* I must admit I've got a bit of a sweet tooth

NM *Bot* sucker

gourmander [3] [gurmɑ̃de] VT to rebuke, to castigate, to upbraid

gourmandise [gurmɑ̃diz] NF **1** *(caractère)* greediness, greed **2** *(sucrerie)* delicacy

gourme [gurm] NF **1** *(du cheval)* strangles *(singulier)*, equine distemper **2** *Vieilli Méd* impetigo **3** *Fam Vieilli (locution)* **jeter sa g.** to sow one's wild oats

gourmé, -e [gurme] ADJ *Littéraire* stiff, starched

gourmet [gurmɛ] NM gourmet, epicure

gourmette [gurmɛt] NF **1** *(chaînette)* (chain) bracelet; *(d'une montre)* chain **2** *(pour cheval)* curb (chain)

gournable [gurnabl] NF *Naut* treenail

gourou [guru] NM **1** *Rel* guru **2** *Fig* guru, mentor

gousse [gus] NF **1** *(de haricot)* pod, husk; *(de petit pois)* pod; **g. d'ail** clove of garlic; **g. de cardamome** cardamom pod; **g. de vanille** vanilla pod **2** *Vulg (lesbienne)* dyke, = offensive term used to refer to a lesbian

gousset [gusɛ] NM **1** *Couture (de gilet)* waistcoat pocket; *(de pantalon)* fob pocket; *Fig* **il a le g. bien garni** his pockets are well lined **2** *Constr (traverse)* support; *(plaque)* gusset, plate

GOÛT [gu] NM **1** *(sens)* taste; **perdre le g.** to lose one's sense of taste

2 *(saveur)* taste; **avoir un drôle de g.** to taste funny; **ne pas avoir de g.** to be tasteless, to have no taste; **ça a un g. très épicé** it tastes very hot; **ça a un g. de miel/moutarde** it tastes of honey/mustard; **ce vin a un g. de bouchon** this wine is corked; **ça n'a aucun g.** it's tasteless, it's got no taste; **avec ce rhume, je ne trouve aucun g. à**

la nourriture I can't taste my food (properly) because of this cold; **donner du g. à un mets** to give a dish flavour

3 *(préférence)* taste; **sucrez selon votre g.** add sugar to taste; **tu choisiras selon ton g.** you'll choose what you like *or* whatever appeals to you; **un g. marqué** *ou* **particulier pour...** a great liking *or* fondness for...; **avoir des goûts de luxe** to have expensive tastes; **avoir des goûts bizarres** to have strange tastes; **c'est (une) affaire** *ou* **question de g.** it's a matter of taste; **à chacun son g., chacun ses goûts** each to his own; **tous les goûts sont dans la nature** it takes all sorts (to make a world); *Prov* **des goûts et des couleurs, on ne discute pas** there's no accounting for taste

4 *(intérêt)* taste, liking; **avoir du g. pour** *ou* **le g. de qch** to have a taste *or* liking for sth; **il faut leur donner le g. des maths** we've got to give them a taste *or* a liking for maths; **prendre g. à qch** to develop a taste for sth; **avec le temps, elle y a pris g.** it grew on her, she developed a liking for it; **ne plus avoir g. à qch** to have lost one's taste for sth; **elle n'a plus (de) g. à rien** she no longer wants to do anything; **reprendre g. à la lecture/à la musique** to regain one's taste for reading/music; **reprendre g. à la vie** to regain one's zest for living, to find life worth living again; **faire qch par g.** to do sth out of *or* by inclination; **je ne le fais pas par g.** I don't do it from choice; **je le fais par g. du travail bien fait** I do it because I like to see work well done; *Fig* **je vais lui faire passer le g. du pain** *(tuer)* I'm going to do away with him/her; *(dissuader)* I'm going to cure him/her (of that) once and for all; **je vais lui faire passer le g. du mensonge** I'm going to put a stop to his/her lying once and for all

5 *(jugement esthétique)* taste; **les gens de g.** people of taste; **une femme de g.** a woman of taste; **avoir du g.** to have (good) taste; **elle a bon/mauvais g.** she has good/bad taste; **elle n'a aucun g.** she has no taste; **s'habiller avec g.** to have (a) good dress sense, to have good taste in clothes; **une décoration de bon g.** a tasteful decoration; **il serait de bon g. de nous retirer** *ou* **que nous nous retirions** it would be proper to take our leave; **il a eu le (bon) g. de se taire** he had the sense to remain silent; **cette plaisanterie est d'un g. douteux** that joke is in poor *or* doubtful taste; **une remarque de mauvais g.** a remark in poor *or* bad taste; **une robe de mauvais g.** a tasteless dress

6 *(mode)* **c'était le g. de l'époque** it was the style of the time; **c'est le g. du jour** it is the current fashion; **être au g. du jour** to be in line with current tastes; **remettre qch au g. du jour** to update sth; *Littéraire* **un opéra dans le g. de Verdi** an opera in the style of Verdi; **c'était une fourrure en renard, ou quelque chose dans ce g.-là** it was a fox fur, or something of the sort

❑ **à mon/son/***etc* **goût** ADJ & ADV to my/his/*etc* liking; **trouver qn/qch à son g.** to find sb/sth to one's taste *or* liking; **le décor est tout à fait à mon g.** the decor is exactly to my liking; **à mon/son g., on est trop lents** we're not going fast enough for my/his liking

goûter[1] [3] [gute] VT **1** *(aliment, boisson)* to taste, to try; **voulez-vous g. ma sauce?** would you like to taste *or* try my sauce?; **fais-moi g.** let me have a taste, give me a taste; **ils m'ont fait g. les spécialités de la région** they had me try the local delicacies

2 *(apprécier)* to savour, to enjoy; **goûtons ensemble le calme du soir** let's savour *or* enjoy the peace of the evening together; **elle n'a pas goûté l'humour de leurs commentaires** she didn't appreciate their witticisms

3 *Belg & Can (avoir un goût de)* to taste of; **ce fruit goûte le pourri** this fruit tastes rotten

VI **1** *(prendre une collation)* to have an afternoon snack, *Br* to have tea; **venez g., les enfants!** come and have your snack, children!; **il goûte toujours d'une pomme et d'un verre de lait** he always has an apple and a glass of milk for his afternoon snack

2 *Belg (avoir bon goût)* to taste nice

❑ **goûter à** VT IND **1** *(manger)* to taste, to try; **tu ne dois pas g. au gâteau avant le dessert** you mustn't take any cake before the dessert; **goûtez donc à ces biscuits** do try some of these biscuits

2 *(faire l'expérience de)* to have a taste of; **maintenant qu'elle a goûté à la célébrité** now that she's tasted *or* had a taste of fame

3 *Belg (plaire à)* **ça ne me goûte pas** I don't like it

❑ **goûter de** VT IND **1** *(plat)* to taste, to try; **puis-je g. un peu de ce fromage?** may I taste *or* try some of this cheese?

2 *(faire l'expérience de)* to have a taste of; **depuis qu'elle a goûté du piano, c'est une passionnée** since she's had a taste of piano playing, she's become an enthusiast

goûter[2] [gute] NM *(collation)* = afternoon snack for children, typically consisting of bread, butter, chocolate, and a drink; *(fête)* children's party; **g. d'anniversaire** (children's) birthday party; **l'heure du g.** = time for the children's afternoon snack

goûteur, -euse[1] [gutœr, -øz] NM,F taster

goûteux, -euse[2] [gutø, -øz] ADJ tasty

goutte [gut] NF **1** *(d'eau, de lait, de sang)* drop; *(de sueur)* drop, bead; *(de pluie)* drop (of rain), raindrop; **il est tombé une g. (ou deux)** there was a drop (or two) of rain; **il tombait quelques gouttes** it was spitting with rain; **passer entre les gouttes** *Hum* to dodge the raindrops; *Fig* to come through unscathed *or* without a scratch; **g. d'eau** drop of water; *(bijou)* drop; **g. de rosée** dewdrop; **boire qch jusqu'à la dernière g.** to drink every last drop of sth; **avoir la g. au nez** to have a runny nose; **c'est une g. d'eau dans la mer** it's a drop in the ocean; **c'est la g. d'eau qui fait déborder le vase** it's the straw that broke the camel's back

2 *(petite quantité)* **une g. de** a (tiny) drop of; **une g. de vin?** a drop of wine?; **boire une g. de cognac après le repas** to have a drop *or* nip of brandy after one's meal; *Fam* **boire la g.** to have a nip

3 *Méd (maladie)* gout; **avoir la g.** to suffer from *or* have gout, to be gouty

4 *Archit* drop, gutta

5 *Fam (eau-de-vie)* **la g.** the hard stuff

❑ **gouttes** NFPL *Pharm* **gouttes pour le nez/les oreilles/les yeux** nose/ear/eye drops; **prendre des gouttes** to take drops

❑ **goutte à goutte** ADV drop by drop; **tomber g. à g.** to drip; *Fig* **ils laissent filtrer les informations g. à g.** they are letting the news filter out bit by bit

❑ **ne... goutte** ADV *Arch* **je n'y comprends** *ou* **entends g.** I can't understand a thing; **je n'y vois g.** I can't see a thing

'La Goutte d'or' *Tournier* 'The Golden Droplet'

goutte-à-goutte [gutagut] NM INV *Méd Br* drip, *Am* IV; **ils lui ont mis un g.** they've put him/her on *Br* a drip *or Am* an IV

Goutte d'Or [gutdɔr] NF **la G.** = working-class area of Paris with a large immigrant population

gouttelette [gutlɛt] NF droplet

goutter [3] [gute] VI to drip

gouttereau, -x [gutro] ADJ M *Archit* **mur g.** wall that carries the gutter

goutteur [gutœr] NM trickler

goutteux, -euse [gutø, -øz] ADJ gouty

NM,F gout-sufferer

gouttière [gutjɛr] NF **1** *Constr* gutter; **g. verticale** drainpipe **2** *Méd* splint **3** *Anat (d'un os)* groove **4** *Typ (de page)* gutter **5** *Suisse (fente, eau)* leak *(in roof or ceiling)*

gouvernable [guvɛrnabl] ADJ governable; **ce pays n'est pas g.** it's impossible to govern this country, this country is ungovernable

gouvernail [guvɛrnaj] NM **1** *Naut* rudder; **g. automatique/compensé** automatic/balanced rudder; *Aviat* **g. de direction** rudder; *Naut* **g. de plongée** *(d'un sous-marin)* horizontal rudder; **g. de profondeur** *(d'un sous-marin)* hydroplane; **roue du g.** (steering) wheel

2 *Fig* **être au** *ou* **tenir le g.** to call the tune; **tenir le g. de l'État/d'une affaire** to be at the helm of the state/a business

gouvernance [guvɛrnɑ̃s] NF **1** *(action de gouverner)* government **2** *(manière de gérer)* governance, government; **g. mondiale** global governance

gouvernant, -e [guvɛrnɑ̃, -ɑ̃t] ADJ ruling *(avant n)*; **les classes gouvernantes** the ruling classes

NM,F man, *f* woman in power; **il n'a pas une âme de g.** he was not born for government; **les gouvernants** the people in power, the Government

❑ **gouvernante** NF **1** *(préceptrice)* governess

2 *Vieilli (domestique)* housekeeper

3 *(d'un hôtel)* **gouvernante d'étage** floor housekeeper; **gouvernante générale** executive *or* head housekeeper; **gouvernante du soir** turndown housekeeper

gouverne [guvɛrn] NF **1** *(instruction)* **pour ma/ta g.** for my/your information; **sache pour ta g. que je ne mens pas** for your information, please remember that I don't lie **2** *Naut* steering; **aviron de g.** stern *or* steering oar **3** *Aviat* control surface; **gouvernes** control surfaces; **g. compensée** balanced surface; **g. de direction** (tail) rudder; **g. de profondeur** elevator

gouvernement [guvɛrnəmɑ̃] NM **1** *(régime)* government; **sous le g. socialiste** under the socialist government; **g. central** central government; **g. de coalition** coalition government; **g. démocratique** democratic government; **g. d'État** state government; **g. fantoche** puppet government; **g. fédéral** federal government; **g. majoritaire** majority government; **g. minoritaire** minority government; **g. monarchique** monarchic government; **g. provisoire** provisional government; **g. représentatif** representative government; **g. de transition** interim government

2 *(ensemble des ministres)* Government; **le Premier ministre a formé son g.** the Prime Minister has formed his government *or* cabinet; **le g. a démissionné** the Government has resigned; **il est au g. depuis 15 ans** he has been in government *or* in power for 15 years; **sous le g. Raffarin** during Raffarin's term of office, during Raffarin's administration; **g. de cohabitation** = government in which the President and the parliamentary majority are from different parties

3 g. d'entreprise corporate governance

gouvernemental, -e, -aux, -ales [guvɛrnəmɑ̃tal, -o] ADJ *(parti)* ruling *(avant n)*, governing *(avant n)*; *(presse)* pro-government; *(politique, décision, crise)* government *(avant n)*; **des dispositions gouvernementales** measures taken by the government; **l'équipe gouvernementale** the Government *or Br* Cabinet *or Am* Administration

gouverner [3] [guvɛrne] VT **1** *Pol* to rule, to govern; **le pays n'était plus gouverné** the country no longer had a government

2 *Littéraire (maîtriser)* to govern, to control; **g. ses passions** to control one's passions; **ne nous laissons pas g. par la haine** let us not be governed *or* ruled by hatred

3 *Naut* to steer; **faire g.** to con; **g. sur un port** to steer *or* stand *or* head for a port, to bear in with a port; **g. à la lame** to steer by the sea

4 *Gram* to govern

5 *Tech* **mouvement gouverné par un pendule** movement regulated *or* governed *or* controlled by a pendulum

6 *Vieilli (régir)* to manage, to administer; **bien g. ses ressources** to husband one's resources

7 *Suisse (soigner → bétail)* to look after, to tend

USAGE ABSOLU *Pol* to govern; **un parti qui gouverne depuis des années** a party which has governed *or* has been in government for years; **g., c'est prévoir** to govern is to foresee

VI *Naut* to steer; **g. à la lame/à tribord** to steer by the sea/to starboard; **g. de l'arrière** to steer aft; **navire qui ne gouverne plus** ship that no longer answers to her helm; **bateau qui gouverne bien** boat that steers well; **gouvernez droit!** steady!

▸**se gouverner** VPR **1** *Pol* to govern oneself; **le droit des peuples à se g. eux-mêmes** the right of peoples to self-government

2 *(se maîtriser)* to control oneself

gouvernés [guvɛrne] NMPL **les g.** those who are governed

gouverneur, -e [guvɛrnœr] NM,F *Admin & Pol* governor; *Mil (d'une position fortifiée)* commanding officer; **le G. de la Banque de France** the Governor of the Bank of France; *Can* **G. général** Governor General

goy [gɔj] *(pl* **goyim** *ou* **goïm** [gɔjim]) **ADJ** goyish
NMF goy; **les goyim** goyim, goys
goyave [gɔjav] **NF** guava
goyavier [gɔjavje] **NM** guava (tree)
goyim [gɔjim] *voir* **goy**
Gozo [gozo] **NM** Gozo; **vivre à Gozo** to live in Gozo; **aller à Gozo** to go to Gozo
GPAO [ʒepeao] **NF** *Ordinat (abrév* **gestion de production assistée par ordinateur**) computer-aided production management
GPL [ʒepeɛl] **NM** *(abrév* **gaz de pétrole liquéfié**) LPG
GPRS [ʒepeɛrɛs] **NM** *Tél (abrév* **General Packet Radio Service**) GPRS
GPS [ʒepeɛs] **NM** *Tél (abrév* **global positioning system**) GPS
GQG [ʒekyʒe] **NM** *(abrév* **grand quartier général**) GHQ
GR® [ʒeɛr] **NM** *(abrév* **sentier de grande randonnée**) long-distance hiking path
gr *(abrév écrite* **grade**) grade, mark
Graal [gral] **NM le G.** the (Holy) Grail
grabat [graba] **NM** pallet, litter
grabataire [grabatɛr] **ADJ** bedridden
NMF (bedridden) invalid; **les grabataires** the bedridden
grabatisation [grabatizasjɔ̃] **NF** *Méd* **à cause de sa g. il avait besoin d'une infirmière à domicile** because he was bedridden he needed a full-time nurse
graben [grabən] **NM** *Géol* graben, rift valley
grabons [grabɔ̃] **NMPL** *Suisse (dans les cantons de Genève, Vaud et Fribourg)* = leftover fat from cooked pork, fried and used as an ingredient in certain Swiss dishes
grabuge [grabyʒ] **NM** *Fam* **il y avait du g.** there was a bit of a rumpus; **ça va faire du g.** that's going to cause havoc; **il y a eu du g.?** was there any trouble *or Br* bother?
grâce [gras] **NF 1** *(beauté → d'un paysage)* charm; *(→ d'une personne)* grace; **avoir de la g.** to be graceful; **avec g.** gracefully; **plein de g.** graceful; **sans g.** graceless; **la vue n'est pas sans g.** the view is not without charm
2 *(volonté)* **de bonne g.** with good grace, willingly; **avoir la bonne g. de dire/faire** to have the grace to say/to do; **de mauvaise g.** grudgingly, with bad grace; **vous auriez mauvaise g. à** *ou* **de vous plaindre** it would be ungracious of you to complain
3 *(faveur)* favour; **je te le demande comme une g.** I'm asking you this as a favour; **être en g. auprès de qn** to be in favour with sb; **rentrer en g. auprès de qn** to come back into sb's favour; **fais-moi la g. de m'écouter** do me the favour of listening to me; **faites-moi la g. d'oublier cette histoire** do me the favour *or* kindness of forgetting this matter; **nous ferez-vous la g. de signer votre dessin?** would you do us the honour of signing your drawing?; **trouver g. aux yeux de qn** to find favour with sb; **rien/personne ne trouve g. à ses yeux** nothing/nobody finds favour in his/her eyes; **c'est (toute) la g. que je vous souhaite** that is what I would wish for you
4 *(sursis → de peine)* pardon; *(→ dans un délai)* grace; **lettre(s) de g.** reprieve; **accorder sa g. à qn** to pardon sb; **crier** *ou* **demander g.** to beg for mercy; **je te fais g. des centimes** I'll let you off the cents; **je te fais g. du reste** I'll spare you the rest; *(ne m'en dites ou n'en faites pas plus)* you needn't do/say any more; **je vous fais g. des détails** I'll spare you the details; **je vous fais g. cette fois-ci** I'll let you off this time; **une semaine/un mois de g.** one week's/month's grace; **g. amnistiante** free pardon; **g. présidentielle** presidential pardon; *Com* **jours** *ou* **terme de g.** days of grace
5 *Rel* grace; **la g. divine** divine grace; **avoir la g.** to be inspired; **en état de g.** in a state of grace; **par la g. de Dieu** by the grace of God; **à la g. de Dieu** *(advienne que pourra)* come what may; *(n'importe comment)* any old way
6 *(pour exprimer la reconnaissance)* **rendre g.** *ou* **grâces à Dieu** to give thanks to God; **(rendons) g. à Dieu!** thanks be to God!
7 *(titre)* **Sa G.** His/Her Grace; **Votre G.** Your Grace
EXCLAM *Arch* mercy!; **ah, g.!** have mercy!; **de g.!** for God's *or* pity's sake!
❑ **grâces** **NFPL 1** *(faveurs)* **rechercher les bonnes grâces de qn** to curry favour with sb, to seek sb's favour; **être/entrer dans les bonnes grâces de qn** to be/to get in favour with sb
2 *(manières)* **faire des grâces à qn** to make up to sb; **faire des grâces** to put on airs (and graces)
3 *Rel* **dire les grâces** to give thanks (after eating)
❑ **grâce à** **PRÉP** *(avec l'aide de)* **g. à qn/qch** thanks to sb/sth; **g. à votre aide** thanks to your help; **g. à Dieu** with God's help, by God's grace
Grâces [gras] **NFPL les trois G.** the three Graces
graciable [grasjabl] **ADJ** pardonable
gracier [9] [grasje] **VT** to reprieve
gracieuse [grasjøz] *voir* **gracieux**
gracieusement [grasjøzmɑ̃] **ADV 1** *(joliment)* gracefully **2** *(aimablement)* graciously, kindly; **il m'a accueilli le plus g. du monde** he greeted me very amiably **3** *(gratuitement)* free (of charge), gratis; **un repas vous sera servi g.** you will be served a free meal
gracieuseté [grasjøzte] **NF 1** *(parole aimable)* pleasantry **2** *Vieilli (cadeau)* gratuity
gracieux, -euse [grasjø, -øz] **ADJ 1** *(joli)* charming, graceful; **qu'il est g., ce bébé!** what a charming baby!
2 *(aimable)* affable, amiable, gracious; **sa lettre était écrite sur le ton le plus g.** his/her letter was most amiable
3 *(gratuit)* free (of charge); **à titre g.** gratis, free of charge; **exemplaire envoyé à titre g.** complimentary *or* presentation copy
4 *(pour exprimer le respect)* **notre g. souverain** our gracious Sovereign
gracile [grasil] **ADJ** *Littéraire* slender
gracilité [grasilite] **NF** *Littéraire* slenderness, slimness
Gracques [grak] **NPR les G.** the Gracchi
gradation [gradasjɔ̃] **NF 1** *(progression)* gradation; **il y a une g. dans nos exercices** we grade our exercises; **avec une g. lente** gradually, by degrees; **g. ascendante/descendante** gradual increase/decrease **2** *(étape)* stage; **procédons par gradations** let's proceed step by step *or* gradually
grade [grad] **NM 1** *(rang)* rank; **il a le g. de capitaine** his rank is captain; **avancer** *ou* **monter en g.** to be promoted; *Fam* **en prendre pour son g.** to get hauled over the coals, *esp Br* to get it in the neck **2** *(niveau)* **g. universitaire** degree **3** *Belg Scol & Univ (mention)* distinction **4** *Géom* (centesimal) grade **5** *Chim* grade
gradé, -e [grade] **ADJ militaire g.** non-commissioned officer, NCO
NM,F 1 *Mil* non-commissioned officer, NCO; **tous les gradés** all ranks **2** *Naut* **les gradés** the petty officers
grader [3] [grade] **VI** *Suisse* to be promoted
gradient [gradjɑ̃] **NM 1** *Météo* gradient; **g. thermique** temperature gradient **2** *Math* **g. d'une fonction** gradient of a function **3** *Élec* **g. de potentiel** voltage gradient
gradin [gradɛ̃] **NM 1** *(dans un amphithéâtre)* tier, (stepped) row of seats; **les gradins** *(dans un stade)* the terraces **2** *Géog* step, terrace; **à gradins** stepped **3** *Agr* terrace; **à gradins** terraced; **les vergers s'élèvent en gradins** the orchards rise in terraces **4** *(d'un autel)* gradin, gradine **5** *Élec* **disposer les balais en gradins** to stagger the brushes *(of a dynamo)*
gradine [gradin] **NF** *Archit* (toothed) chisel
gradiomètre [gradjɔmɛtr] **NM** gradiometer
gradualisme [gradɥalism] **NM** *Biol* (evolutionary) gradualism
graduat [gradɥa] **NM** *Belg (diplôme)* technical diploma *(just below university level)*
graduateur [gradɥatœr] **NM** graduator
graduation [gradɥasjɔ̃] **NF 1** *(repère)* mark; **verser le liquide jusqu'à la deuxième g.** pour the liquid up to the second mark **2** *(échelle de mesure)* scale; **la g. va jusqu'à 20** the scale goes up to 20 **3** *(processus)* graduation
gradué, -e [gradɥe] **ADJ 1** *(à graduations)* graduated **2** *(progressif)* graded; **exercices gradués** graded exercises
NM,F *Belg* graduate *(having passed the "graduat")*
graduel, -elle [gradɥɛl] **ADJ** gradual, progressive
NM gradual
graduellement [gradɥɛlmɑ̃] **ADV** gradually
graduer [7] [gradɥe] **VT 1** *(augmenter)* to increase gradually; **il faut g. la difficulté des tests** the tests should become gradually more difficult **2** *(diviser)* to graduate
graff [graf] **NM** *Fam* graffiti▪ *(using a spray can)*
graffeur, -euse [grafœr, -øz] **NM,F** graffiti artist *(using a spray can)*
graffiter [3] [grafite] **VT** to cover with graffiti
graffiteur, -euse [grafitœr, -øz] **NM,F** graffiti artist
graffiti [grafiti] *(pl* **inv** *ou* **graffitis**) **NM 1** *(inscription)* graffiti *(UNCOUNT)*; **un g.** a piece of graffiti; **des g., des graffitis** graffiti **2** *Archéol* graffito
grafigne [grafiɲ] **NF** *Can Fam* scratch▪
grafigner [3] [grafiɲe] **VT** *Can Fam* to scratch▪; **se faire g.** to get scratched▪
grafignure [grafiɲyr] **NF** *Can Fam* scratch▪
graille [graj] **NF** *très Fam (aliments)* food▪, grub, nosh
graillement [grajmɑ̃] **NM** *Vieilli* **1** *(de corneille)* cawing *(UNCOUNT)* **2** *(de la voix)* hoarseness *(UNCOUNT)*; *(causé par la glaire)* huskiness *(UNCOUNT)* **3** *(son rauque)* hoarse sound, croak
grailler [3] [graje] **VI 1** *(corneille)* to caw **2** *(personne)* to speak hoarsely *or* throatily **3** *très Fam (manger)* to eat▪; **venez g.!** *esp Br* grub's up!, *Am* come chow down!
VT *très Fam* to eat▪; **il n'y a plus rien à g.** there's no grub left
graillon [grajɔ̃] **NM 1** *Fam (friture)* **une odeur de g.** a smell of burnt fat▪; **sentir le g.** to smell of burnt fat; **avoir un goût de g.** to taste greasy▪ **2** *très Fam (crachat)* gob (of spit)
graillonner [3] [grajɔne] **VI 1** *(sentir la friture)* to smell of greasy food **2** *Fam (cracher en toussant)* to hawk (up), *Br* to gob; *(parler)* to speak hoarsely▪ *or* huskily▪
grain[1] [grɛ̃] **NM 1** *(de sel, de sable)* grain, particle; *(de riz, de poudre)* grain; *(de poussière)* speck; *Fig* **un g. de cruauté** a touch of cruelty; *Fig* **un g. de lucidité** a grain *or* flicker of understanding; *Fig* **un g. de folie** a touch of madness; *Fig* **un g. de coquetterie/d'originalité** a touch *or* hint of coquetry/originality; *Fig* **il n'a pas un g. de bon sens** he hasn't got an ounce *or* a grain of common sense; *Fig* **donner du g. à moudre à qn** to give sb food for thought; *Fam* **mettre son g. de sel** to stick one's oar in; *Fam* **elle a un g.** she's got a screw loose
2 *(céréales)* **le g., les grains** (cereal) grain; **alcool** *ou* **eau-de-vie de g.** grain alcohol
3 *(d'un fruit, d'une plante)* **g. de blé** grain of wheat; **g. de café** *(avant torréfaction)* coffee berry; *(après torréfaction)* coffee bean; **g. de cassis** blackcurrant (berry); **g. de grenade** pomegranate seed; **g. de groseille** redcurrant (berry); **g. de moutarde** mustard seed; **g. d'orge** barleycorn, grain of barley; **g. de poivre** peppercorn; **g. de raisin** grape
4 *(perle)* bead; **g. de chapelet** rosary bead; **un collier à grains d'ambre** an amber necklace
5 *(aspect → de la peau)* grain, texture; *(→ du bois, du papier)* grain; *(→ de la peau, d'un animal)* rough side; **à gros g.** coarse-grained; **ruban gros g.** petersham; **à petit g.** close-grained, fine-grained; **à grains fins/serrés** fine-/close-grained; **aller/travailler dans le sens du g.** to go/to work with the grain; **contre le g.** against the grain
6 *Phot* grain; **la photo a du g.** the photo is *or* looks grainy
7 *Pharm* pellet
❑ **en grains** **ADJ** *(café)* unground, whole; **moulu ou en grains?** ground or not?, ground or whole?; **poivre en grains** whole peppercorns
❑ **grain de beauté** **NM** beauty spot, mole

'Si le grain ne meurt' *Gide* 'If it die…'

grain[2] [grɛ̃] **NM** *Météo* squall; **essuyer un g.** to meet with a squall; **g. en ligne** line squall
grainage [grɛnaʒ] **NM 1** *(d'une surface)* graining **2** *(d'une substance)* graining, granulation
graine [grɛn] **NF 1** *(semence)* seed; **g. d'anis**

goy–gra

aniseed; **g. de lin** linseed; **graines (pour oiseaux)** birdseed; **monter en g.** to go to seed; *Fig (personne → grandir)* to shoot up; *(femme → rester célibataire)* to be (left) on the shelf; **casser la g.** to have a bite to eat; **c'est de la mauvaise g., ce garçon-là!** that boy is bad news!; **son frère, c'est de la g. de voyou!** his brother has the makings of a hooligan!; *Fam* **ton frère a réussi tous ses examens, prends-en de la g.** your brother has passed all his exams, take a leaf out of his book

2 *(du ver à soie)* silkworm eggs, graine

3 *Can Vulg (pénis)* dick, cock

grainer [4] [gʀene]**VI** *Agr* to seed

VT 1 *(réduire en grains → poudre à canon)* to granulate; *(→ cire)* to shred; *(→ sel)* to grain **2** *(donner un aspect grené à → papier, cuir)* to grain

graineterie [gʀɛntʀi]**NF 1** *(commerce)* seed trade **2** *(magasin)* seed merchant's

grainetier, -ère [gʀɛntje, -ɛʀ]**ADJ le commerce g.** the seed trade

NM,F *(marchand → de graines)* seed merchant; *(→ de grain)* corn chandler

grainier, -ère [gʀenje, -ɛʀ] **ADJ** seed *(avant n)*; **rendement g.** seed yield

grais [gʀɛ]**NMPL** *Zool* upper tusks, whetters *(of a wild boar)*

graissage [gʀesaʒ] **NM 1** *Aut & Tech (avec de l'huile)* oiling, lubrication; *(avec de la graisse)* greasing, lubrication; **faire faire un g.** to have one's car lubricated; **circuit de g.** lubrication system **2** *Typ* emboldening

graisse [gʀɛs]**NF 1** *(corps gras)* fat; **régime pauvre en graisses** low-fat diet; **évitez les graisses** cut down on fat; *Fam* **prendre de la g.** to put on weight"; *Fam* **faire de la g.** to pile on the pounds; **il a de la g. en trop!** he's too fat!; **g. animale/végétale** animal/vegetable fat; **g. de baleine/phoque** whale/seal blubber; **g. à chaussures** dubbin, dubbing; **g. de porc** lard; **g. de rognon** suet; *Fam* **il lui a raconté des boniments à la g. d'oie!** he told him/her a load of tall stories!

2 *Tech* grease; **pistolet** *ou* **pompe** *ou* **injecteur à g.** grease gun; **g. pour engrenages** gear lubricant; **g. pour essieux** axle grease; **g. lubrifiante** lubricant; **g. minérale** crude paraffin, mineral jelly; **g. au silicone** silicone grease

3 *(en œnologie)* ropiness; **tourner à la g.** to become ropy

4 *Typ* thickness, boldness; *(de caractère)* weight

graisser [4] [gʀese] **VT 1** *(enduire → moteur)* to lubricate; *(→ pièce, mécanisme)* to grease, to oil; *(→ fusil)* to grease; *(→ chaussures)* to dub; *(→ moule)* to grease; **une crème qui ne graisse pas les mains** a non-greasy cream; **g. la patte à qn** to grease sb's palm; **il a graissé la patte aux témoins** he bribed the witnesses

2 *(tacher)* to grease, to soil with grease

3 *Typ* to embolden

VI 1 *(devenir gras)* **ses cheveux graissent très vite** his/her hair gets greasy very quickly

2 *(rendre quelque chose gras)* **onguent qui ne graisse pas** non-greasy ointment

3 *(en œnologie)* to become ropy

▸**se graisser VPR se g. les mains avec une crème** to rub cream into one's hands

graisseur, -euse[1] [gʀesœʀ, -øz]**ADJ** greasing, lubricating; **godet g.** grease box; **pistolet g.** grease gun

NM 1 *(appareil)* lubricator, oiler **2** *Aut* grease nipple **3** *(ouvrier)* greaser, oiler

graisseux, -euse[2] [gʀesø, -øz] **ADJ 1** *(cheveux, col)* greasy **2** *(tumeur)* fatty; **bourrelet g.** roll of fat

Gram [gʀam]**NM INV** *Biol* Gram; **G. positif** Gram-positive; **G. négatif** Gram-negative

gramen [gʀamɛn] **NM** *Vieilli ou Littéraire* lawn grass

graminée [gʀamine] *Bot***ADJ** **F** graminaceous

NF grass, *Spéc* member of the Gramineae

❑ **graminées** **NFPL** grasses, *Spéc* Gramineae

grammage [gʀamaʒ]**NM** grammage

grammaire [gʀamɛʀ]**NF 1** *(règles)* grammar; **la g.** grammar; **règle de g.** grammatical rule; **g. générative** generative grammar; **g. normative** normative grammar **2** *(livre)* grammar (book) **3** *Fig*

la **g. du cinéma/dessin** the grammar of cinema/drawing

grammairien, -enne [gʀamɛʀjɛ̃, -ɛn] **NM,F** grammarian

grammatical, -e, -aux, -ales [gʀamatikal, -o]**ADJ 1** *(de grammaire)* grammatical; **loi grammaticale** law of grammar; **exercice g.** grammar exercise; **catégorie grammaticale** part of speech **2** *(correct)* grammatical; **non g.** ungrammatical

grammaticalement [gʀamatikalmɑ̃] **ADV** grammatically

grammaticalisation [gʀamatikalizasjɔ̃] **NF** grammaticalization

grammaticaliser [3] [gʀamatikalize] **VT** to grammaticalize

grammaticalité [gʀamatikalite]**NF** grammaticality, grammaticalness, grammatical correctness

gramme [gʀam]**NM** gramme; **elle n'a pas un g. de graisse** she hasn't got an ounce of fat (on her); **je n'ai pas pris/perdu un g. pendant les vacances!** I didn't put on/lose an ounce over the holidays!; *Fig* **pas un g. de bon sens/de compassion** not an ounce of common sense/of compassion

gramophone [gʀamɔfɔn]**NM** gramophone

grana [gʀana]**NM** *Culin* grana *(Italian hard cheese similar to Parmesan)*

GRAND, -E [gʀɑ̃, gʀɑ̃d]

| **ADJ** tall A1 ■ big A1–4, B7 ■ large A2, 7 ■ long A2, 5 ■ grown-up A4 ■ great A6, 7, 10, B1, 2, 8, 10, C ■ greater A9 ■ major B1 ■ top B3 |
| **NM,F** grown-up 2 ■ tall person 3 |

ADJ A. *ASPECT QUANTITATIF* **1** *(de taille élevée → adulte)* tall; *(→ enfant)* tall, big; **une grande femme maigre** a tall thin woman; **il est maintenant aussi g. que son frère** he's now as big as his brother; *Can Fam Fig* **g. comme ma main** knee high to a grasshopper

2 *(de grandes dimensions → objet, salle, ville)* big, large; *(→ distance)* long; **un g. cercle** a big circle; **une grande pendule** a big clock; **il te faudrait un g. couteau** you'll need a big or long knife; **g. A/B/C** capital A/B/C; **une grande tour** a high or tall tower; **la grande pyramide de Khéops** the Great Pyramid of Cheops; **un g. désert** a big desert; **dans toutes les grandes villes** in all the big or major towns; **de grandes forêts** large areas of forest; **un g. fleuve** a long or big river; **c'est un instrument plus g. que le violon** it's a bigger or larger instrument than the violin; **l'univers est plus g. qu'on ne peut l'imaginer** the universe is bigger than or more vast than one can possibly imagine; **une statue plus grande que nature** a large-scale statue; **de grandes jambes** long legs; **un g. front** a prominent forehead; **avoir de grands pieds** to have big or large feet; **ses grands yeux bleus** his/her big blue eyes; **marcher à grands pas** to walk with great or long strides; **ouvrir la bouche toute grande** to open one's mouth wide; **g. ensemble** *Br* housing scheme, *Am* housing project; **g. magasin** department store; **grande surface** superstore, hypermarket; **grandes et moyennes surfaces** large and medium commercial outlets; **grande surface spécialisée** specialist superstore; *Cin & TV* **g. écran** widescreen; *Rad* **grandes ondes** long wave; **sur grandes ondes** on long wave

3 *(d'un certain âge → être humain)* big; **tu es un g. garçon maintenant** you're a big boy now; **être assez g. pour faire qch** to be old or big enough to do sth; **tu es assez g. pour comprendre** you're old enough to understand

4 *(aîné → frère, sœur)* big; *(au terme de sa croissance → personne)* grown-up; *(→ animal)* fully grown, adult; **quand je serai g.** when I'm grown-up or big; **elle a de grands enfants** she has grown-up children

5 *(qui dure longtemps)* long; **pendant un g. moment** for quite some time; **une grande explication** a long explanation; **une grande période de beau temps** a long or lengthy spell of good weather

6 *(intense, considérable)* great; **un g. cri** a loud

cry; **un g. remue-ménage/vacarme** a great commotion/noise; **les risques sont grands** there are considerable risks; **un g. mouvement de protestation** a great or big or widespread protest movement; **de grande diffusion** widely distributed; *Com* **grande distribution** mass distribution; **une grande fortune** great wealth, a large fortune; **faire de grands frais** to go to great expense; **ils ont marié leur fille à grands frais** they married off their daughter at great or vast expense; **il y avait une grande affluence à la poste** there was a great or an enormous crush at the post office; **rincer à grande eau** to rinse thoroughly; **les grands froids** intense cold; **pendant les grandes chaleurs** in high summer, in or at the height of summer; **un g. vent soufflait du nord** a strong wind was blowing from the north; **nous avons fait un g. feu** we made a big fire; **un g. incendie** a major or great fire; **ce sont des articles de grande consommation** they are everyday consumer articles; **(à l'époque des) grandes marées** (at) spring tide; **au g. jour** in broad daylight; **le g. public** the general public, the public at large; **une émission g. public** a programme designed to appeal to a wide audience; **un livre g. public** a mass-market book; **un film g. public** a mainstream movie or *Br* film; **musique g. public** middle-of-the-road music

7 *(pour qualifier une mesure)* large, great; **la grande majorité de** the great or vast majority of; **son g. âge explique cette erreur** this mistake can be put down to his/her being so old; **des arbres d'une grande hauteur** very tall trees; **ils plongent à une grande profondeur** they dive very deep or to a great depth; **un g. nombre de passagers** a large number of passengers; *Phot* **grande profondeur de champ** deep focus

8 *(entier)* **une grande cuillerée de sucre** a heaped spoonful of sugar; **elle m'a fait attendre une grande heure/semaine** she made me wait a good hour/a good week

9 *Bot* greater; **grande chélidoine** greater celandine; **grande plantain** greater plantain

10 *Géog* **la Grande Baie Australienne** the Great Australian Bight; **Grande Canarie** Gran Canaria; **le G. Canyon** the Grand Canyon; **le G. Désert de Sable** the Great Sandy Desert; **le G. Lac des Esclaves** Great Slave Lake; **le G. Lac de l'Ours** Great Bear Lake; **le G. Lac Salé** the Great Salt Lake; **les Grands Lacs** the Great Lakes; **le G. Lyon** = syndicate of local authorities in the Lyons area; **les Grandes Plaines** the Great Plains

11 *Géom* **g. axe** major axis; **g. cercle** great circle

12 *Zool* **les grands animaux** (the) larger animals; **grands chiens** big dogs

B. *ASPECT QUALITATIF* **1** *(important)* great, major; **de grands progrès** great progress or strides; **les grands thèmes de son œuvre** the major themes in his/her work; **les grands problèmes de notre temps** the main or major or key issues of our time; **grande école** = higher education establishment with competitive entrance, specializing in professional training

2 *(acharné, invétéré)* great, keen; **un g. amateur de livres rares** a great or keen collector of rare books; **c'est une grande cruciverbiste** *(assidue)* she loves doing crosswords; *(douée)* she is very good at (doing) crosswords; **c'est un g. travailleur** he's a hard worker, he's hard-working; **tu n'es qu'une grande menteuse** you're just a big liar; **c'est une grande timide** she's really shy; **ce sont de grands amis** they're great or very good friends; **un g. buveur** a heavy drinker; **grands fumeurs** heavy smokers; **g. invalide civil** severely disabled person; **les grands blessés/brûlés/invalides** the seriously wounded/burned/disabled; **les grands handicapés** the severely handicapped

3 *(puissant, influent → banque)* top; *(→ industriel)* top, leading, major; *(→ propriétaire, famille)* important; *(→ personnage)* great

4 *(dans une hiérarchie)* **les grands dignitaires du régime** the leading or important dignitaries

of the regime; **g. écuyer** Master of the (Royal) Horse; *Pol* **grands électeurs** *(en France)* = body electing members of the (French) Senate; *(aux États-Unis)* presidential electors; *Écon* **le G. Marché (européen)** the European Market; **le G. rabbin (de France)** the Chief Rabbi (of France); **les grands corps de l'État** the major public bodies

5 *(noble)* **de grande naissance** of high *or* noble birth; **avoir g. air** *ou* **grande allure** to carry oneself well, to be imposing

6 *(généreux)* **c'est un g. cœur** his/her heart is in the right place; **il a un g. cœur** he's big-hearted, he has a big heart; **une grande âme** a noble soul

7 *(exagéré)* big; **de grands gestes** extravagant gestures; **de grandes promesses** big promises; **grands mots** high-sounding words, high-flown language; **grandes phrases** high-flown phrases

8 *(fameux, reconnu)* great; **un g. homme** a great man; **un g. journaliste** a great *or* top journalist; **un des plus grands spécialistes** one of the greatest *or* top experts; **un g. esprit/talent** a great mind/talent; **il a accompli de grandes choses** he has accomplished great things; **un disque des grands airs de Verdi** a record of great Verdi arias; **une grande œuvre d'art** a great work of art; **son dernier essai est un g. texte** his/her latest essay is a brilliant piece of writing; **les grands textes classiques** the classics; **il ne descend que dans les grands hôtels** he only stays in the best hotels *or* the most luxurious hotels; **le g. film de la soirée** tonight's big *or* feature film; **le g. jour** the big day; **les grandes dates de l'histoire de France** the great *or* most significant dates in French history; **un g. nom** a great name; **un g. nom de la peinture contemporaine** one of today's great painters; **les grands couturiers** the top fashion designers

9 *Hist* **la Grande Armée** the Grande Armée; **la Grande Catherine** Catherine the Great; **le G. Moghol** the Great Mogul; **le G. Turc** the Grand Turk

10 *(omnipotent, suprême)* great; **Dieu est g.** God is great

C. *EN INTENSIF* great; **avec une (très) grande facilité** with (the greatest of) ease; **sans g. enthousiasme/intérêt** without much enthusiasm/interest; **sa grande fierté, c'est son jardin** he's/she's very proud of *or* he/she takes great pride in his/her garden; **quel g. bonheur de t'avoir parmi nous!** how happy we all are to have you with us!; **c'était un g. moment** it was a great moment; **il était dans un g. état de fatigue** he was extremely tired; **un g. merci à ta sœur** lots of thanks to *or* a big thank you to your sister; **c'est le g. amour!** it's true love!; **Robert fut son g. amour** Robert was the love of her life; **tu aurais g. avantage à la prévenir** you'd be well advised to warn her; **cette cuisine a g. besoin d'être nettoyée** this kitchen really needs *or* is in dire need of a clean; **ça m'a fait le plus g. bien** it did me a power of *or* the world of good; **il en a pensé le plus g. bien** he thought most highly of it; **g. bien lui fasse!** much good may it do him/her!; **faire g. cas de** to set great store by; **toute la famille au g. complet** the whole family, every single member of the family; **à sa grande honte** to his/her great shame; **jamais, au g. jamais je n'accepterai** never in a million years will I accept; **il n'y a pas g. mal à demander des précisions** there's no harm in asking for further details; **il n'y a pas g. mal** there's no great harm done; **il est parti de g. matin** he left at the crack of dawn; **il n'y avait pas g. monde à son concert** there weren't many people at his/her concert; **pour notre plus g. plaisir** to our (great) delight; **prendre g. soin de** to take great care of; **à sa grande surprise** much to his/her surprise, to his/her great surprise; **il est g. temps que tu le lises** it's high time you read it

NM,F 1 *(enfant d'un certain âge)* **l'école des grands** primary school; **merci, mon g.!** *(en appellatif)* thanks, son!; **allons, ma grande, ne**

pleure pas! come on now, love, don't cry!; **je me débrouillerai tout seul, comme un g./toute seule, comme une grande** I'll manage on my own, like a big boy/a big girl

2 *(adulte)* grown-up, adult; **un jeu pour petits et grands** a game for young and old (alike); **alors, ma grande, tu as pu te reposer un peu?** well dear, did you manage to get some rest?

3 *(personne de grande taille)* **pour la photo, les grands se mettront derrière** for the photo, tall people *or* the taller people will stand at the back

NM 1 *voir* **infiniment**

2 *(entrepreneur, industriel)* **un g. de la mode** a leading light in the fashion business; **les grands de l'automobile** the major *or* leading car manufacturers

3 *Hist* **G. d'Espagne** (Spanish) grandee *or* Grandee

ADV 1 *(dans l'habillement)* **c'est un modèle qui chausse g.** this is a large-fitting shoe; **ça devrait vous aller, ça taille g.** it should fit you, it's cut large

2 *(largement)* **g. ouvert** wide-open; **elle dort la fenêtre g. ouverte** *ou* **grande ouverte** she sleeps with the window wide open *or* open wide; **il avait maintenant les yeux g.** *ou* **grands ouverts** now he had his eyes wide open

3 *Beaux-Arts* **représenter qch plus g. que nature** to enlarge sth

4 *(locution)* **voir g.** *(avoir de vastes projets)* to think big; **ils ont vu trop g.** they bit off more than they could chew; **elle voit g. pour son fils** she's got great hopes for her son; **deux rôtis! tu as vu g.!** two roasts! you don't do things by halves!

❑ **grande NF** *Can Aut* top (gear); *Fig* **en grande** at top speed, in a rush

❑ **grands NMPL** *Écon & Pol* **les grands** *(les puissants)* the rich (and powerful); **les grands de ce monde** the people in (positions of) power *or* in high places; *Pol* **les deux Grands** the two superpowers

❑ **en grand ADV 1** *(complètement)* on a large scale; **il faut aérer la maison en g.** the house needs a thorough *or* good airing; *Fig* **il a fait les choses en g.** he really did things properly

2 *Naut* **gouverner en g.** to make a heading; **navire en g. sur un bord** ship listing heavily to one side

3 *Can (beaucoup)* a lot; *(très)* very; **il est laid en g.** he's very *or* really ugly

---

🎬

'**La Grande illusion**' *Renoir* 'The Great Illusion'

📖

'**Le Grand Meaulnes**' *Alain-Fournier* 'The Lost Domain'

🎬

'**Le Grand chantage**' *Mackendrick* 'Sweet Smell of Success'

GRANDES ÉCOLES
These are highly selective establishments which exist in parallel to the universities. Admission is usually only possible after two years of intensive preparatory studies ("**écoles préparatoires**") and a competitive examination ("**concours**"). Graduates from these institutions typically go on to work in senior and executive posts in the civil service or the private sector. The "grandes écoles" include HEC (management), Polytechnique, Centrale, the École des Mines and the École des Ponts et Chaussées (engineering), the ENA (senior civil service) and the École normale supérieure (humanities or science). Having been to a "grande école" is comparable in prestige to having an Oxbridge degree in Britain or a degree from Harvard or Yale in the US.

---

grand-angle [grɑ̃tɑ̃gl] *(pl* **grands-angles** [grɑ̃zɑ̃gl])**, grand-angulaire** [grɑ̃tɑ̃gylɛr] *(pl* **grands-**

angulaires [grɑ̃zɑ̃gylɛr]) **NM** *Phot* wide-angle lens

grand-chose [grɑ̃ʃoz] **PRON INDÉFINI pas g.** not much; **ce ne sont que quelques fleurs, ce n'est pas g.** it's just a few flowers, nothing much; **ce que je te demande, ce n'est pas g.** I'm not asking for much; **je n'y comprends pas g.** I don't understand much of it; **plus g.** not much (left); **il ne me reste plus g. à dire** there's not much more (left) to say; **il n'y a plus g. à manger** there's not much left to eat

grand-croix [grɑ̃krwa] *(pl* **grands-croix**)**NF** Grand Cross *(in various orders, including the "Légion d'honneur")*
NMF holder *or* Knight of the Grand Cross

grand-duc [grɑ̃dyk] *(pl* **grands-ducs**)**NM 1** *(titre)* grand duke **2** *Orn* eagle owl

grand-ducal, -e, -aux, -ales [grɑ̃dykal, -o] **ADJ 1** *(du grand-duc)* grand-ducal **2** *(du grand-duché)* of the grand duchy

grand-duché [grɑ̃dyʃe] *(pl* **grands-duchés**) **NM** grand duchy

Grande-Bretagne [grɑ̃dbrətaɲ] **NF la G.** (Great) Britain; **vivre en G.** to live in Great Britain; **aller en G.** to go to Great Britain

grande-duchesse [grɑ̃dyʃɛs] *(pl* **grandes-duchesses**)**NF** grand duchess

grandelet, -ette [grɑ̃dlɛ, -ɛt]**ADJ** *Fam Vieilli* tallish

grandement [grɑ̃dmɑ̃] **ADV 1** *(largement)* absolutely; **si c'est là votre opinion, vous vous trompez g.!** if that is what you believe, you are very much mistaken!; **vous avez g. raison/tort** you are quite right/wrong; **nous avons g. le temps** we have ample time; **avoir g. de quoi vivre** to have plenty to live on

2 *(beaucoup)* a great deal, greatly; **il m'a g. aidée** he helped me a great deal, he's been a great help to me; **être g. reconnaissant à qn de qch** to be truly grateful to sb for sth

3 *(généreusement)* **vous avez fait les choses g.!** you've done things in great style!; **ils ne seront pas g. logés** their accommodation will be nothing grand *or* special

4 *(noblement)* grandly, nobly

grandesse [grɑ̃dɛs]**NF** grandeeship

grandet, -ette [grɑ̃dɛ, -ɛt] **ADJ** *Vieilli* tallish, biggish

grandeur [grɑ̃dœr] **NF 1** *(taille)* size; *(d'un arbre)* height, size; **une poupée de la g. d'un enfant de deux ans** a doll the size of *or* as big as a two-year-old child; **deux vases de la même g.** two vases (of) the same size; **dimensions données en vraie g.** full-size measurement; **(en) g. nature** life-size

2 *(importance)* importance; *(d'un amour, d'une folie)* greatness; **se donner des airs de g.** to give oneself airs (and graces)

3 *(noblesse)* greatness; **avec g.** nobly; **la g. de son sacrifice** the greatness *or* the beauty of his/her sacrifice; **la g. humaine** the greatness of man; **g. d'âme** generosity of spirit, magnanimity

4 *(splendeur)* grandeur, splendour; **la g. de Rome** the grandeur *or* greatness of Rome; **g. et décadence de Byzance** rise and fall of Byzantium

5 *Arch* **Votre G.** Your Grace; **Sa G. l'archevêque** His Grace the Archbishop

6 *Astron* magnitude; **étoile de première g.** star of the first magnitude

7 *Math & Phys* **chiffres de la même g.** figures of the same magnitude; **g. de sortie** output; **grandeurs énergétiques** energy consumption and supply

8 *Can (d'un vêtement, de chaussures)* size

9 *Can* **à la g. de** throughout

grand-guignol [grɑ̃giɲɔl]**NM** *Fam* **c'est du g.** it's all blood and thunder

grand-guignolesque [grɑ̃giɲɔlɛsk] *(pl* **grand-guignolesques**) **ADJ** *(personne)* blood-and-thunder; *(pièce de théâtre, film)* gruesome

grandiloquence [grɑ̃dilɔkɑ̃s] **NF** grandiloquence, *Péj* pomposity

grandiloquent, -e [grɑ̃dilɔkɑ̃, -ɑ̃t] **ADJ** grandiloquent, *Péj* pompous

grandiose [grɑ̃djoz]**ADJ** *(cérémonie, proportions)* imposing, grandiose; *(spectacle, vue)* imposing, awe-inspiring; **la gaffe était g.** it was an incredible blunder

grandir [32] [grɑ̃dir] VI **1** *(devenir grand)* to grow; **elle a grandi** she has grown, she is taller; **ton fils a beaucoup grandi** your son has grown a lot; **cet enfant n'arrête pas de g.** that child is shooting up; **sa fille a grandi de cinq centimètres** her daughter is five centimetres taller (than when I last saw her); **je te trouve grandie** you've grown *or* you look taller since I last saw you; **un enfant qui aurait grandi trop vite** a lanky child; **un arbre qui grandit vite** a tree which grows quickly, a fast-growing tree; **un arbre qui aurait grandi trop vite** a spindly tree; **la soupe, ça fait g.** soup makes you big and strong

2 *(mûrir)* to grow up; **j'ai compris en grandissant** I understood as I grew up *or* older

3 *(s'intensifier → bruit)* to increase, to grow louder; *(→ influence, importance)* to increase; **une inquiétude qui grandit** a growing *or* an increasing feeling of unease; **sa faim allait grandissant** he/she grew more and more hungry

4 *(s'étendre → ville)* to spread

5 *Fig* **g. en force/sagesse/beauté** to get stronger/wiser/more beautiful, to grow in strength/wisdom/beauty; **il a grandi dans mon estime** he has gone up in my esteem

VT **1** *(faire paraître plus grand)* **ces talons hauts la grandissent encore** these high-heeled shoes make her (look) even taller

2 *(surestimer)* **g. l'importance de qch** to exaggerate *or* overstate the importance of sth

3 *(ennoblir)* **notre profession sort grandie de cette longue lutte** our profession emerges from this long struggle with greater prestige; **il est sorti grandi de ce conflit/de cette épreuve** he came out of this conflict/the ordeal a stronger person; **ses malheurs l'ont grandi** his misfortunes have made him stronger; *(aux yeux des autres)* his misfortunes have increased his stature; **cela ne la grandit pas à mes yeux** that does not improve her standing in my eyes

▸**se grandir** VPR **1** *(vouloir paraître plus grand)* to make oneself (look) taller; *(vouloir paraître plus important)* to show oneself in the best possible light; **se g. en se haussant sur la pointe des pieds** to make oneself taller by standing on tiptoe

2 *(s'élever en dignité)* **elle s'est grandie en ne révélant rien** she has improved her reputation *or* people's opinion of her by disclosing nothing

grandissant, -e [grɑ̃disɑ̃, -ɑ̃t] ADJ *(effectifs, douleur, renommée)* growing, increasing; *(vacarme)* growing; *(pénombre)* deepening

grandissement [grɑ̃dismɑ̃] NM **1** *Opt* magnification **2** *Vieilli (fait d'agrandir)* growth, increase

grandissime [grɑ̃disim] ADJ *Hum* extraordinary, marvellous; **le g. favori** the firm favourite

grand-livre [grɑ̃livr] *(pl* **grands-livres***)* NM ledger; **porter qch au g.** to enter sth in the ledger; **g. d'achats** purchase ledger; **g. auxiliaire** subledger; **le g. (de la dette publique)** the National Debt register; **g. général** nominal ledger; **g. de ventes** sales ledger

grand-maman [grɑ̃mamɑ̃] *(pl* **grand-mamans** *ou* **grands-mamans***)* NF *Suisse & Can (en langage enfantin)* granny, grandma

grand-mère [grɑ̃mɛr] *(pl* **grand-mères** *ou* **grands-mères***)* NF **1** *(aïeule)* grandmother **2** *Fam (vieille femme)* little old lady, *Péj* old biddy

grand-messe [grɑ̃mɛs] *(pl* **grand-messes** *ou* **grands-messes***)* NF **1** *Rel* High Mass **2** *Fig* **la g. du parti** the party jamboree

grand-monde [grɑ̃mɔ̃d] NM *Can (adultes)* grown-ups

grand-oncle [grɑ̃tɔ̃kl] *(pl* **grands-oncles** [grɑ̃zɔ̃kl]*)* NM great-uncle

grand-papa [grɑ̃papa] *(pl* **grands-papas***)* NM *Suisse & Can (en langage enfantin)* grandpa, grandad; *Fam Fig* **le commerce/tourisme de g.** old-fashioned ways of doing business/of holidaying

grand-peine [grɑ̃pɛn] **à grand-peine** ADV with great difficulty

grand-père [grɑ̃pɛr] *(pl* **grands-pères***)* NM **1** *(parent)* grandfather **2** *Fam (vieil homme) Br* grandad, *Am* old-timer

▫ **grand-pères** NMPL *Can Culin* = maple syrup dumplings

grand-route [grɑ̃rut] *(pl* **grand-routes***)* NF main road

grand-rue [grɑ̃ry] *(pl* **grand-rues***)* NF high *or Br* main street, *Am* mainstreet

grands-parents [grɑ̃parɑ̃] NMPL grandparents

grand-tante [grɑ̃tɑ̃t] *(pl* **grand-tantes** *ou* **grands-tantes***)* NF great-aunt

grand-vergue [grɑ̃vɛrg] *(pl* **grand-vergues** *ou* **grands-vergues***)* NF *Naut* main yard

grand-voile [grɑ̃vwal] *(pl* **grand-voiles** *ou* **grands-voiles***)* NF mainsail

grange [grɑ̃ʒ] NF barn

grangée [grɑ̃ʒe] NF barnful

granit, granite [granit] NM *Géol* granite; **de g.** *(indestructible)* granitelike, made of granite; *(insensible)* of stone

granité, -e [granite] ADJ granitelike

NM **1** *(sorbet)* granita **2** *Tex* pebble-weave fabric *or* cloth

graniter [3] [granite] VT to paint in imitation of granite

graniteux, -euse [granitø, -øz] ADJ granitic

granitique [granitik] ADJ granitic, granite *(avant n)*

granitoïde [granitɔid] ADJ granitoid

NM granitoid

granivore [granivɔr] ADJ seed-eating, *Spéc* granivorous

NM seedeater, *Spéc* granivore

granny-smith [granismis] NF INV Granny Smith *(apple)*

granoclassement [granɔclasmɑ̃] NM graded bedding

granulaire [granylɛr] ADJ granular, granulous

granulat [granyla] NM aggregate

granulation [granylasjɔ̃] NF **1** *(d'une substance)* graining, granulation **2** *Méd* granulation **3** *Astron* **g. solaire** granulation of the sun, photospheric granulation **4** *Phot* grain, graininess

granule [granyl] NM **1** *(particule)* (small) grain, granule; *(pour animaux)* pellet **2** *Pharm* (small) tablet, pill

NF *Astron* granule

granulé, -e [granyle] ADJ *(surface)* granular; *(présentation)* granulated

NM granule; **un médicament en granulés** a medicine in granule form

granuler [3] [granyle] VT to granulate

granuleux, -euse [granylø, -øz] ADJ **1** *(aspect)* granular, grainy **2** *Méd* granular; *Biol* **cellule granuleuse** granule cell

granulie [granyli] NF *Méd* granulitis

granulite [granylit] NF *Minér* granulite

granulocyte [granylɔsit] NM *Biol* granulocyte

granulome [granylom] NM *Méd* granuloma

granulométrie [granylɔmetri] NF granulometry

grape-fruit, grapefruit [grɛpfrut] *(pl* **grape-fruits** *ou* **grapefruits***)* NM grapefruit

graphe [graf] NM **1** *Math* graph **2** *Ordinat* graph; **g. complet/non orienté** complete/indirected graph **3** *Mktg* graph, chart; **g. en ligne** line chart

graphème [grafɛm] NM *Ling* grapheme

grapheur [grafœr] NM *Ordinat* graphics package

graphie [grafi] NF *Ling* written form

graphiose [grafjoz] NF *Hort* Dutch elm disease

graphique [grafik] ADJ **1** *(relatif au dessin)* graphic

2 *(relatif à l'écriture)* written

3 *Ordinat* **informatique g.** computer graphics *(singulier)*

4 *Math* graphical

NM **1** *(schéma)* graph, chart; **tracer un g.** to plot a graph; **faire le g. de qch** to chart sth; **g. d'acheminement** flow chart; **g. des activités** activity chart; **g. à** *ou* **en barres** bar chart; **g. circulaire** pie chart; **g. en colonnes** bar chart; **g. d'évolution** flow chart; **g. de gestion** management chart; **g. à secteurs** pie chart; **g. à tuyaux d'orgue** bar chart; **g. de type camembert** pie chart; **g. de type lignes** line chart

2 *(de température)* chart

3 *Ordinat* graphic

NF graphics *(singulier)*

graphiquement [grafikmɑ̃] ADV graphically

graphisme [grafism] NM **1** *(écriture)* handwriting; **un g. exubérant** elaborate handwriting **2** *(dessin)* **un g. vigoureux** a vigorously executed drawing; **le g. de Dürer** Dürer's draughtsmanship **3** *Ordinat* **graphismes** graphics

graphiste [grafist] NMF graphic artist

graphitage [grafitaʒ] NM *Tech* graphitization

graphite [grafit] NM graphite; **lubrifiant au g.** graphite lubricant

graphiter [3] [grafite] VT **1** *(transformer)* to graphitize **2** *(enduire)* to graphitize, to impregnate with graphite **3 huile graphitée** graphite oil

graphiteux, -euse [grafitø, -øz], **graphitique** [grafitik] ADJ graphitic

graphitisation [grafitizasjɔ̃] NF **1** *Chim* graphitization **2** *Métal* graphitization (treatment)

graphologie [grafɔlɔʒi] NF graphology

graphologique [grafɔlɔʒik] ADJ graphological

graphologue [grafɔlɔg] NMF graphologist

graphomètre [grafɔmɛtr] NM graphometer

grappa [grapa] NF grappa

grappe [grap] NF **1** *(de fruits)* bunch; *(de fleurs)* cluster; **g. de glycine** wisteria flowerhead; **g. de raisins** bunch of grapes; *Fig* **grappes humaines** clusters of people **2** *Bot* raceme **3** *Ordinat (de terminaux)* cluster **4** *Vulg* **lâche-moi la g.!** piss off!

▫ **en grappe(s)** ADV *(tomber → fleurs)* in bunches

grappillage [grapijaʒ] NM **1** *(de raisin)* gleaning **2** *(d'argent) Br* fiddling, *Am* chiseling

grappiller [3] [grapije] VI **1** *Littéraire (après la vendange)* to glean, to gather grapes left after the harvest

2 *(faire de petits profits)* to be on the take *or Br* the fiddle; **il est bien le seul à ne pas g.** he's the only one who's not on the take

VT **1** *Littéraire (cerises, prunes)* to pick; *(brindilles)* to gather; *(fleurs)* to pick, to gather

2 *(argent) Br* to fiddle, *Am* to chisel

3 *(temps)* **elle grappille tous les jours une demi-heure sur l'horaire** she sneaks off half an hour early every day

4 *(renseignements)* to pick up; **on n'a pu g. que quelques détails insignifiants** we could only pick up a few minor clues

grappilleur, -euse [grapijœr, -øz] NM,F *(profiteur) Br* fiddler, *Am* chiseler

grappillon [grapijɔ̃] NM small bunch *or* cluster

grappin [grapɛ̃] NM **1** *Naut (ancre)* grapnel; *(d'abordage)* grappling iron **2** *(de levage)* grab; *(d'une grue)* clutch **3** *(pour grimper)* grappler, climbing iron **4** *Fam (locution)* **mettre le g. sur qn/qch** to get one's hands on *or* get hold of sb/sth; **il m'a mis le g. dessus à la sortie** he grabbed me on the way out; **attends que je lui mette le g. dessus!** wait till I get my hands on him/her!

graptolite [graptɔlit] *Zool* NM graptolite, *Spéc* member of the Graptolitoidea

▫ **graptolites** NMPL graptolites, *Spéc* Graptolitoidea

GRAS, GRASSE [gra, gras]

ADJ	fatty **A1, 6** ▪ fat **A2** ▪ greasy **A3, 4** ▪ crude **A5** ▪ sticky **B1** ▪ slippery **B2** ▪ throaty **B3** ▪ thick **B5**
NM	fat **1** ▪ fleshy part **2** ▪ grease **3**

ADJ **A. 1** *Culin* fatty; **ne mettez pas trop de matière grasse** do not add too much fat; **fromage g.** full-fat cheese; **bouillon g.** fatty stock; **évitez la cuisine grasse** avoid fatty foods

2 *(dodu)* fat, plump; **il est très g.** he's very fat; **elle est plutôt grasse** she's rather plump *or* fat; **être g. comme une caille** *ou* **un chanoine** *ou* **un cochon** *ou* **un moine, être g. à lard** to be as round as a barrel

3 *(huileux)* greasy, oily; *(taché)* greasy

4 *(peau, cheveux)* greasy

5 *(vulgaire)* crude, coarse

6 *Chim* fatty; **série grasse** acyl group

7 *Rel* **jours g.** meat days

B. 1 *(terre, boue)* sticky, slimy

2 *(pavé)* slippery

3 *(voix, rire)* throaty

4 *Littéraire (abondant → récompense)* generous; *(→ pâturage)* rich; *Fam* **ce n'est pas g.** *(peu de chose)* that's not much; *(profit médiocre)* it's not a fortune; **l'herbe grasse était douce sous le pied** the thick grass was soft underfoot

5 *(épais → gén)* thick; *(→ trait)* bold; *(→ caractère)* bold, bold-faced; *Typ* **en g.** in bold (type)

6 *Méd (toux)* phlegmy

7 *(vin, bierre etc)* ropy

8 *(locution)* **faire la grasse matinée** to stay in bed (very) late, *Br* to have a long lie-in

□ **gras** NM **1** *(d'une viande)* fat; **le g. de jambon** ham fat; *Culin* **au g.** cooked with meat stock **2** *(du corps)* fleshy part; **le g. de la jambe** the calf **3** *(substance)* grease; **j'ai les doigts pleins de g.** my fingers are covered in grease; **des taches de g.** greasy stains ADV **1** *(dans l'alimentation)* **il mange trop g.** he eats too much fatty food **2** *Rel* **faire g.** to eat meat **3** *(en grasseyant)* **parler g.** to pronounce one's Rs from the back of the throat, to use Parisian Rs **4** *Fam (beaucoup)* **il n'y a pas g. à manger** there's not much to eat; **il y a pas g. de monde dans les rues aujourd'hui** there's not many people out today

gras-double [gradubl] *(pl* **gras-doubles**) NM *Culin* (ox) tripe

grasse [gras] *voir* **gras**

grassement [grasmɑ̃] ADV **1** *(largement)* handsomely; **g. payé** *ou* **rémunéré** generously *or* handsomely paid; *Littéraire* **vivre g.** to live off the fat of the land; **il vit g. de ses terres** he makes a handsome living from the land he owns **2** *(vulgairement)* coarsely, crudely; **plaisanter g.** to make coarse *or* crude jokes

grasserie [grasri] NF grasserie, jaundice

grasset, -ette [grasɛ, -ɛt] ADJ *Can* plump, chubby NM *Anat* stifle, stifle joint

□ **grassette** NF *Bot* butterwort

grasseyant, -e [grasɛjɑ̃, -ɑ̃t] ADJ **avoir un parler/ rire g.** to speak/to laugh from the back of one's throat

grasseyement [grasɛjmɑ̃] NM **le g. des Parisiens** = the Parisian way of pronouncing Rs from the back of the throat

grasseyer [12] [grasɛje] VI to pronounce one's Rs from the back of the throat, to use Parisian Rs VT *Ling* **un R grasseyé** a uvular R

grassouillet, -ette [grasujɛ, -ɛt] ADJ *Br* podgy, *Am* pudgy

grateron [gratrɔ̃] NM *Bot* goose-grass, cleavers *(singulier)*

graticiel [gratisjɛl] NM *Ordinat* freeware

gratifiant, -e [gratifjɑ̃, -ɑ̃t] ADJ gratifying, rewarding

gratification [gratifikasjɔ̃] NF **1** *(pourboire)* tip; *(prime)* bonus; **g. de fin d'année** Christmas *or* end-of-year bonus **2** *(satisfaction)* gratification (UNCOUNT)

gratifier [9] [gratifje] VT **1** *(satisfaire)* to gratify; **sa réussite a beaucoup gratifié ses parents** his/ her success was very gratifying for his/her parents

2 g. qn d'une récompense to grant sb a reward; *Ironique* **être gratifié d'une amende** to be landed with a fine; **elle m'a gratifié d'un sourire** she favoured me with a smile; *Ironique* **je ne vois pas pourquoi tu devrais nous g. de ta mauvaise humeur!** I can't see what we've done to deserve your bad temper!; **et je fus gratifié d'une paire de gifles** and my reward was a slap in the face

gratin [gratɛ̃] NM **1** *Culin (plat → recouvert de fromage)* gratin *(dish with a topping of toasted cheese)*; *(→ recouvert de chapelure)* = dish with a crispy topping; **un g. de pâtes/de poisson** a pasta/fish gratin; **g. dauphinois** gratin dauphinois, = sliced potatoes baked with cream and browned on top; **g. de macaronis** *Br* macaroni cheese, *Am* macaroni and cheese

2 *(croûte → de fromage)* cheese topping; *(→ de chapelure)* crispy topping

3 *Fam (élite)* **le g.** the upper crust; **tout le g. parisien** everybody who's anybody in Paris

□ **au gratin** ADJ au gratin, (cooked) with (breadcrumbs and) grated cheese; **chou-fleur au g.** ≃ cauliflower cheese

gratiné, -e [gratine] ADJ **1** *Culin (doré)* browned; *(cuit au gratin)* (cooked) au gratin **2** *Fam (addition)* huge; *(examen, problème)* tough; **elle va avoir droit à un savon g.!** she's in for a real telling-off!; **dans le genre paresseux, il est g.!** he's as lazy as they come!, for laziness he takes the *Br* biscuit *or Am* cake!

□ **gratinée** NF French onion soup

gratiner [3] [gratine] VT *(cuire en gratin)* to cook au gratin; *(dorer)* to brown

VI to brown; **faire g. qch, mettre qch à g.** to brown sth; **faire g. avant de servir** brown under the grill before serving; **ça n'a pas tout à fait fini de g.** the top is not quite brown yet

gratiole [grasjɔl] NF *Bot* gratiola, hedge-hyssop

gratis [gratis] *Fam* ADV free (of charge)ⁿ; **il a fait la réparation g.** he repaired it for nothingⁿ ADJ free ⁿ; **un spectacle g.** a free show

gratitude [gratityd] NF gratitude, gratefulness

gratos [gratɔs] ADJ *Fam* free (of charge)ⁿ

gratouiller [3] [gratuje] = **grattouiller**

grattage [grataʒ] NM *(avec des griffes, des ongles, une plume)* scratching; *(avec quelque chose de dur)* scraping; **effacer qch par g.** to scratch sth out; **au g., on s'aperçoit que la couche de peinture était très mince** when you scrape off the paint you can see that it was put on very thinly; **gagner au g.** *(à la loterie)* to win on the scratch cards

gratte [grat] NF **1** *Fam (profit)* **faire de la g.** to make a bit on the side **2** *Fam (guitare)* guitarⁿ **3** *Can (outil)* scraper; *(machine) Br* snowplough, *Am* snow-pusher **4** *Belg (griffure)* scratch; *(éraflure)* scratch, scrape

gratte-ciel [gratsjɛl] NM INV skyscraper

gratte-cul [gratky] NM INV *Fam* rosehipⁿ

gratte-dos [gratdo] NM INV backscratcher

grattement [gratmɑ̃] NM scratching; **elle entendit un léger g. à la porte** she heard a gentle scratching at the door

gratte-papier [gratpapje] NM INV *Fam Péj* pen-pusher

gratte-pieds [gratpje] NM INV shoe scraper, metal doormat

gratter [3] [grate] VT **1** *(avec des griffes, des ongles, une plume)* to scratch; *(avec quelque chose de dur)* to scrape; *(avec un sabot)* to paw; **g. la terre du pied** *(sujet: cheval)* to paw the ground; **g. le dos à qn** to scratch sb's back; **elle grattait doucement la tête de son chat** she was gently scratching her cat's head

2 *(frotter → allumette)* to strike; *(→ métal oxydé)* to scrape, to rub; *(→ couche de saleté)* to scrape *or* to rub off; **g. une vieille peinture/du vieux papier peint** to scrape off old paint/old wallpaper; **g. un mur à la brosse métallique** to wire-brush a wall

3 *(effacer)* to scratch out; *(tache)* to scrape off

4 *(irriter)* **une chemise/un pull-over qui gratte la peau** a shirt/sweater which makes you itch; *Fam* **ça me gratte** it's itchy; *Fam* **un gros rouge qui gratte la gorge** a rough red wine which catches in the throat

5 *Fam (grappiller) Br* to fiddle, *Am* to chisel; **il n'y a pas grand-chose à g.** there's not much to be made out of that, there isn't much money in that

6 *Fam (devancer)* to overtakeⁿ; **on s'est fait g. par la concurrence** we were overtaken by our competitors

VI **1** *(plume)* to scratch; **prête-moi une plume, la mienne gratte** lend me a pen, mine keeps scratching (the paper)

2 *(faire du bruit)* **g. à la porte** to tap lightly at the door; **ces vieux disques grattent beaucoup** these old records are very scratchy *or* crackly

3 *(tissu, laine, pull)* to itch, to be itchy

4 *Fam (jouer de)* **g. du violon** to scrape away at the violin

5 *Fam (approfondir)* **il a l'air très cultivé, mais si tu grattes un peu...** he has a very cultured air, but if you scratch away his veneer a bit...; **pas besoin de g. beaucoup pour s'apercevoir qu'il est bête** it soon becomes pretty obvious that he's stupid

6 *Fam (travailler)* to workⁿ, to do odd jobs; *(écrire)* to scribble; **il gratte quelques heures par semaine chez un avocat** he does a few hours a week at a solicitor's office

▶ **se gratter** VPR to scratch (oneself), to have a scratch; **se g. la tête/le bras** to scratch one's head/arm; *très Fam* **tu peux toujours te g.!** you'll be lucky!

gratteron [gratrɔ̃] = **grateron**

gratteur [gratœr] NM *Tech* reclaiming scraper; **g. de sable** sand scraper

gratteux, -euse [gratø, -øz] *Fam* ADJ *Can* stingy, mean NM,F **1** *Can (avare)* miser **2** *(joueur de guitare)* guitaristⁿ

grattoir [gratwar] NM **1** *(de bureau)* erasing-knife **2** *(de graveur)* scraper; *Typ* slice **3** *(de boîte d'allumettes)* striking surface **4** *Archéol* grattoir **5** *Can (pour déneiger)* scraper

grattons [gratɔ̃] NMPL crackling (UNCOUNT)

grattouiller [3] [gratuje] VT *Fam* **1** *(démanger)* **ça me grattouille** it makes me itchⁿ **2** *(guitare)* to strum away on

gratture [gratyr] NF scrapings, scratchings

gratuiciel [gratyisjɛl] = **graticiel**

gratuit, -e [gratɥi, -it] ADJ **1** *(en cadeau)* free; **entrée gratuite** *(concert, musée)* admission free; **c'est g.** it's free, there's no charge; **à titre g.** gratis, free of charge

2 *(sans fondement)* unwarranted, unfounded; **tu fais là une supposition tout à fait gratuite** your assumption is absolutely unwarranted *or* unfounded

3 *(absurde → acte, violence)* gratuitous; *(→ cruauté)* wanton, gratuitous

4 *(désintéressé)* **aide gratuite** free help; **il est rare que les éloges soient gratuits** praise is rarely disinterested

NM *(magazine)* free magazine

gratuité [gratɥite] NF **1** *(accès non payant)* **nous voulons la g. de l'enseignement/des livres scolaires** we want free education/school-books; **g. de la justice** proceedings being free of administrative charges

2 *(absence de motif → d'une accusation, d'un acte violent)* gratuitousness; *(→ d'une supposition)* unwarranted *or* unfounded nature; **la g. d'un tel acte** the gratuitousness of such an act

3 *(désintéressement)* disinterestedness; **la g. de ses éloges** the disinterestedness *or* the dis-interested nature of his/her praise

gratuitement [gratɥitmɑ̃] ADV **1** *(sans payer)* free (of charge); **pour deux disques achetés, ils en donnent un g.** if you buy two records, they give you one free

2 *(sans motif)* gratuitously, for no reason; **vous l'agressez g., elle ne vous a rien fait!** you're attacking her for no reason, she hasn't done you any harm!; **ils ont tout saccagé g.** they destroyed everything just for the sake of it

grau, -s [gro] NM *(dans le Languedoc)* **1** *(chenal)* channel *(linking a lake or a river to the sea)* **2** *(estuaire)* estuary

gravatier [gravatje] NM rubble carter

gravats [grava] NMPL **1** *(décombres)* rubble (UNCOUNT) **2** *(de plâtre)* screenings

grave [grav] ADJ **1** *(après le nom) (solennel)* grave, solemn; **il la dévisageait, l'air g.** he stared at her gravely; **votre ami est toujours tellement g.!** your friend is always so solemn *or* serious!

2 *(sérieux → motif, problème, blessure, maladie)* serious; *(→ opération)* serious, major; **une faute g.** a grave error; **l'heure est g.** this is a critical moment; **ce n'est pas g.!** never mind!, it doesn't matter!; **c'est g.!** it's serious!; **elle a eu une g. maladie** she's been seriously ill; **c'est g., docteur?** is it serious, doctor?; **hélas!, il y avait plus g.** alas! there was worse to come

3 *Mus & (en acoustique → note)* low; *(→ voix)* deep; **un son g.** a bass *or* low note

4 *(accent)* grave

5 *Fam (dérangé)* **il est g.** he's not all there, he's off his rocker *or Br* head

6 *Arch (lourd)* heavy; *Phys* **corps g.** heavy body NM *Mus* **le g.** the low register; **les graves et les aigus** low and high notes, the low and high registers

NF *(en travaux publics)* aggregate

ADV *Fam* in a bad way; **il me prend la tête g.** he really *or Br* seriously bugs me

□ **graves** NM *(vin)* Graves (wine) NFPL *(terrain)* gravel beach *or* strand

graveleux, -euse [gravlø, -øz] ADJ **1** *(grivois)* smutty **2** *Géog* gravelly **3** *(fruit)* gritty

gravelle [gravɛl] NF **1** *Arch Méd* gravel **2** *Can Joual (gravier)* gravelⁿ

gravelot [gravlo] NM *Orn* **grand g.** ringed plover; **petit g.** little ringed plover

Gravelotte [gravlɔt] NF Gravelotte

gra–gre

gravelure [gravlyr] NF smuttiness (UNCOUNT)

gravement [gravmã] ADV **1** (solennellement) gravely, solemnly **2** (en intensif) **g. handicapé** severely handicapped; **g. malade/blessé** seriously ill/injured; **être g. menacé** to face a serious threat; **tu t'es g. trompé** you've made a serious or big mistake; **vous êtes g. coupable de l'avoir laissé sortir seul** the burden of guilt lies with you for having let him go out alone

graver [3] [grave] VT **1** (tracer → sur métal, sur pierre) to carve, to engrave; (→ sur bois) to carve

  2 Fig **à jamais gravé (en lettres d'or) dans mon esprit/mon souvenir** indelibly printed on my mind/memory; **cela reste gravé dans ma mémoire ou en moi** it is engraved on my memory; **la souffrance était gravée sur son visage** suffering was written on his/her face; Hum **ce n'est pas gravé sur son front** you can't tell from looking at him/her

  3 Typ (imprimer) to print

  4 Beaux-Arts to engrave; **g. à l'eau-forte** to etch

  5 (disque) to cut; **le dernier album qu'ils ont gravé n'a pas marché** the last album they made wasn't a success

  6 Ordinat (CD-ROM) to write, to burn

gravettien, -enne [gravetjẽ, -ɛn] Archéol ADJ Gravettian

  NM **le g.** the Gravettian period, Gravettian culture

graveur, -euse [gravœr, -øz] NM,F (personne) engraver, carver; **g. sur bois** wood engraver or cutter; **g. à l'eau-forte** etcher

  NM **1** (pour disques) cutter **2** Ordinat (de CD-ROM) writer, burner; **g. de CD** CD burner or writer; **g. de CD-ROM** CD-ROM burner

gravide [gravid] ADJ Méd pregnant, Spéc gravid; **truie g.** sow in pig

gravidique [gravidik] ADJ Méd gravidic

gravidité [gravidite] NF Méd gravidness, gravidity

gravier [gravje] NM **1** Géol grit, gravel **2** (petits cailloux) gravel; **couvrir une allée de g.** to gravel a path; **allée de g.** gravel path

gravière [gravjɛr] NF gravel pit

gravifique [gravifik] ADJ Phys **l'attraction g.** the force of gravity

gravillon [gravijɔ̃] NM **1** (caillou) piece of gravel or grit **2** (revêtement) grit (UNCOUNT), fine gravel; **gravillons** (panneau sur la route) loose chippings, Am gravel

gravillonnage [gravijɔnaʒ] NM gritting

gravillonner [3] [gravijɔne] VT to grit

gravimètre [gravimɛtr] NM gravimeter

gravimétrie [gravimetri] NF gravimetry

gravimétrique [gravimetrik] ADJ gravimetric, gravimetrical

gravir [32] [gravir] VT **1** (grimper) to climb; (échelle) to climb, to mount; **g. une montagne/un escalier** to climb up a mountain/a staircase; **il gravit les marches d'un pas lourd** he trudged up the steps

  2 Fig (dans une hiérarchie) **g. les échelons** to climb the ladder; **il faut g. (tous) les échelons** you must go up through the ranks; **quand elle aura gravi tous les échelons** once she's got to the top; **disons qu'il m'a fait g. les échelons plus rapidement** let's just say he helped me to make my way up more quickly

gravisphère [gravisfɛr] NF gravisphere

gravissime [gravisim] ADJ extremely serious

gravitation [gravitasjɔ̃] NF Phys gravitation

gravitationnel, -elle [gravitasjɔnɛl] ADJ gravitational; **force gravitationnelle** force of gravity

gravité [gravite] NF **1** (sérieux, dignité) seriousness, solemnity; **son visage exprimait une profonde g.** he/she looked very solemn or serious; **l'enfant la dévisagea avec g.** the child stared at her solemnly

  2 (importance) seriousness, gravity; **tu ne**

perçois pas la g. du problème you don't realize the seriousness or gravity of the problem

  3 (caractère alarmant) seriousness; (d'une blessure) severity; **un accident sans g. s'est produit en gare d'Orléans** there was a minor accident at the station in Orléans; **une blessure sans g.** a slight or minor wound; **une chute sans g.** a minor fall; **une maladie sans g.** a minor ailment

  4 (pesanteur) gravity; **g. spécifique** specific gravity; **alimentation par g.** gravity feed

  5 Mus lowness

graviter [3] [gravite] VI **1** Astron **g. autour de** to revolve or to orbit around; **g. autour de la terre** to orbit the earth **2** Fig (évoluer) **g. autour de qn** to hover around sb; **il a toujours gravité dans les sphères gouvernementales** he has always moved in government circles **3** Vieilli (tendre) to gravitate (**vers** towards)

graviton [gravitɔ̃] NM Phys graviton

gravois [gravwa] = gravats

gravure [gravyr] NF **1** (tracé en creux) engraving; **g. en creux** intaglio engraving; **g. sur bois** (procédé) woodcutting; (objet) woodcut; **g. sur pierre** stone carving; **g. sur verre** glass engraving

  2 Typ (processus) engraving, imprinting; **g. sur cuivre** (procédé) copperplating; (plaque) copperplate; **g. directe** hand cutting; **g. à l'eau-forte** etching; (image) engraving, etching; **g. en taille-douce** copperplate engraving; **une g. de Dürer** an engraving by Dürer; **g. de mode** fashion plate; **habillé ou vêtu comme une g. de mode** dressed like a model in a fashion magazine; **g. en couleurs** colour print; **g. hors texte** full-page plate; **g. avant la lettre** proof before letters

  3 (d'un disque) cutting; **g. directe** direct cut; **disque à g. universelle ou compatible** stereo compatible record

gray [grɛ] NM Phys gray

grayé, -e [greje] ADJ Can (pour faire quelque chose) well-equipped; Fam (bien monté) well-hung

gré [gre] NM **1** (goût, convenance) **à mon g., selon mon g.** to my liking, to my taste; **prenez n'importe quelle chaise, à votre g.** sit down wherever you wish or please; **la chambre est-elle à votre g.?** is the room to your liking?; **il est trop jeune à mon g.** he's too young for my liking; **trouver qch à son g.** to find sth to one's liking

  2 (volonté, accord) **à mon g., selon mon g.** as I please or like; **de mon propre g., de mon plein g.** of my own free will, of my own accord; **elle a toujours agi à son g.** she has always done as she pleases; **je m'habille à mon g.** I dress to please myself; **de bon g.** willingly, gladly; **de mauvais g.** reluctantly; **il la suivit de bon g.** he followed her willingly or of his own accord; **on l'a fait signer contre son g.** they made him/her sign against his/her will; **se marier contre le g. de son père** to get married against one's father's wishes; **bon g. mal g., il faudra que tu m'écoutes** whether you like it or not, you'll have to listen to me; **ramenez-le de g. ou de force!** bring him back by fair means or foul!; **il le fera, de g. ou de force** he'll do it whether he likes it or not, he'll have to do it willy-nilly

  3 Sout (gratitude) **savoir g. à qn de qch** to be grateful to sb for sth; **je vous saurais g. de bien vouloir me faire parvenir...** I should be grateful if you would kindly send me...; Vieilli **savoir mauvais g. à qn de qch** to be annoyed with sb about sth; **on vous saura mauvais g. d'avoir dit la vérité** you'll get little reward or people won't thank you for having spoken the truth

  □ **au gré de** PRÉP **le bail est renouvelable au g. du locataire** the lease is renewable at the tenant's request; **au g. des flots** at the mercy of the waves; **se laisser aller au g. du courant** to let oneself drift along with the current; **ballotté au g. des événements** tossed about or buffeted by events; **changer d'avis au g. des circonstances** to change one's mind according to the circumstances

  □ **de gré à gré** ADV Jur by mutual agreement; **vendre de g. à g.** to sell by private contract, to sell privately

grèbe [grɛb] NM Orn grebe; **petit g., g. castagneux**

little grebe, dabchick; **g. à cou noir** black-necked grebe; **g. esclavon** Slavonian grebe; **g. huppé** great crested grebe; **g. oreillard** Slavonian grebe

grébiche [grebiʃ], **grébige** [grebiʒ] NF **1** Typ (numéro d'ordre) file number **2** Typ (classeur) loose-leaf binder **3** (en maroquinerie) metallic edging or trimming

grec, grecque [grɛk] ADJ Greek; **profil g.** Grecian profile

  NM (langue) Greek; **le g. ancien** ancient Greek; **le g. moderne** modern or demotic Greek

  □ **Grec, Grecque** NM,F Greek

  □ **grecque** NF **1** Archit & Beaux-Arts (Greek) fret, Greek key pattern

  2 Typ (scie) bookbinder's saw

  □ **à la grecque** ADJ (champignons, oignons) (cooked) à la grecque (in olive oil and spices)

Grèce [grɛs] NF **la G.** Greece; **vivre en G.** to live in Greece; **aller en G.** to go to Greece; **la G. antique** Ancient Greece

gréciser [3] [gresize] VT (mot) to give a Greek turn to

grécité [gresite] NF Graecism, Hellenism

Greco [greko] NPR **le G.** El Greco; **un tableau du G.** a painting by El Greco

gréco- [greko-] PRÉF Graeco-

gréco-bouddhique [grekɔbudik] (pl **gréco-bouddhiques**) ADJ Vieilli Graeco-Buddhist

gréco-latin, -e [grekɔlatẽ, -in] (mpl **gréco-latins**, fpl **gréco-latines**) ADJ Graeco-Latin

gréco-romain, -e [grekɔrɔmẽ, -ɛn] (mpl **gréco-romains**, fpl **gréco-romaines**) ADJ Graeco-Roman

grecque [grɛk] voir grec

grecquer [4] [greke] VT to sew the back of (a book)

gredin, -e [grədẽ, -in] NM,F rascal, rogue

gredinerie [grədinri] NF Littéraire **1** (caractère) roguishness **2** (acte) roguish act

gréé, -e [greje] ADJ Can **1** être bien g. pour faire qch to be equipped or ready to do sth; **les enfants sont gréés pour l'école** the children are dressed and ready for school **2** très Fam (homme) well-hung; (femme) well-stacked

gréement [gremã] NM **1** (voilure) rigging (UNCOUNT), rig; (équipement) gear (UNCOUNT); (processus) rigging; **g. courant/dormant** running/standing rigging **2** (disposition des mâts et des voiles) rig; **g. marconi** Marconi rig **3** Can (ustensiles) gear (UNCOUNT), equipment (UNCOUNT); **un g. de ferme** farm equipment

green [grin] NM Golf green

Greenwich [grinwitʃ] N Greenwich; **le méridien de G.** the Greenwich Meridian

gréer [15] [gree] VT (navire) to rig; (hamac, filets) to sling; **gréé en carré** square-rigged; **g. une vergue** to send up a yard

gréeur [greœr] NM Naut rigger

greffage [grɛfaʒ] NM Hort grafting

greffe[1] [grɛf] NM **1** Jur clerk's office, clerk of the court's office; **g. du tribunal de commerce** commercial court **2** Fin (de société par actions) registry **3** Suisse (secrétariat) town hall secretary's office; (secrétaire) town hall secretary

greffe[2] [grɛf] NF **1** Hort (processus) grafting; (pousse) graft; **g. en couronne/écusson/fente** crown/shield/cleft grafting; **g. par œil détaché** budding **2** Méd (d'un organe, de moelle osseuse) transplant; (d'un os) graft; **g. du cœur** heart transplant; **g. cœur-poumon** heart-lung transplant; **g. de la cornée** corneal graft; **g. de peau** skin graft; **g. du rein** kidney transplant; **g. xénogénique** xenotransplant

greffé, -e [grɛfe] NM,F transplant patient; **les greffés du cœur** heart-transplant patients

greffer [4] [grɛfe] VT **1** Hort to graft; **g. sur franc/sauvageon** to graft onto a hybrid/stock

  2 Méd (os, peau) to graft; (organe, moelle osseuse) to transplant; **on lui a greffé une cornée** he/she had a cornea transplant, he/she was given a new cornea; **se faire g. un rein** to have a kidney transplant

  ▸ **se greffer** VPR **le problème de la santé vient se g. sur celui du logement** the problem of the health service has now come on top of the housing problem; **puis d'autres problèmes sont venus se g. là-dessus** then additional problems came along or arose

greffeur [grɛfœr] NM Hort grafter

greffier [grɛfje]NM

> Note that it is no longer considered a mistake to feminize this word and to say **une greffière** in sense 1. Some French speakers nonetheless regard this form as unacceptable, especially in France. See also the entry **féminisation**.

1 *Jur* clerk (of the court), registrar; **g. en chef** registrar; **g. du tribunal de commerce** clerk of the commercial court **2** *Fam (chat)* puss, moggy

greffoir [grɛfwar]NM grafting knife

greffon [grɛfɔ̃]NM **1** *Hort* graft; *Spéc* scion **2** *Méd (tissu)* graft; *(organe)* transplant

grégaire [greger]ADJ gregarious; **l'instinct g.** the herd instinct

grégarine [gregarin]NF *Zool* gregarine

grégarisme [gregarism]NM gregariousness, herd instinct

grège [grɛʒ]ADJ *(soie)* raw, unbleached, undyed
    ADJ INV *(couleur)* greyish-beige, beigey-grey
    NM greyish-beige, beigey-grey

grégeois [greʒwa]ADJ M *Hist & Mil* **feu g.** Greek fire

Grégoire [gregwar]NPR **G. de Tours** Gregory of Tours; **G. le Grand** Gregory the Great

grégorien, -enne [gregorjɛ̃, -ɛn]ADJ Gregorian
    NM Gregorian chant

grègues [grɛg]NFPL *Arch* trunk hose, breeches

grêle¹ [grɛl] ADJ **1** *(mince et long → jambes)* spindly, thin; *(→ personne)* skinny; *(→ tige, silhouette)* slender **2** *(aigu → voix)* reedy

grêle² [grɛl] NF **1** *Météo* hail; **la récolte a été détruite par la g.** the harvest was ruined by hail; **il est tombé de la g. hier** it hailed yesterday; **une averse de g.** a hailstorm **2** *Fig* **une g. de coups** a shower of blows; **une g. de flèches** a hail *or* shower of arrows; **une g. d'insultes** a volley of insults

grêlé, -e [grele]ADJ *(peau, visage)* pockmarked, pitted

grêler [4] [grele]V IMPERSONNEL **il grêle** it's hailing
    VT *(cultures)* to damage by hail; **l'orage a grêlé les vignes** the vines suffered hail damage in the storm

grêleux, -euse [grelø, -øz]ADJ **le temps est souvent g. en mars** it often hails in March

grelin [grəlɛ̃]NM hawser

grêlon [grɛlɔ̃]NM hailstone

grelot [grəlo] NM **1** *(clochette)* (small sleigh *or* jingle) bell; *(de traîneau)* sleigh bell; **attacher le g. (au cou du chat)** to bell the cat **2** *Fam (téléphone)* **passe-moi un coup de g.** give me a buzz *or Br* a tinkle
    ▫ **grelots** NMPL *très Fam* **1** *(testicules)* balls, nuts, *Br* bollocks **2** *(locution)* **avoir les grelots** to have the heebie-jeebies

grelottant, -e [grəlɔtɑ̃, -ɑ̃t]ADJ **1** *(tremblant)* shivering; **g. de froid** shivering with cold; **tout g.** shivering all over **2** *(chevrotant)* trembling **3** *(sonnant)* jingling, tinkling

grelottement [grəlɔtmɑ̃]NM **1** *(tremblement)* shivering **2** *(sonnerie)* jingling

grelotter [3] [grəlɔte]VI **1** *(avoir froid)* **ferme la fenêtre, on grelotte** shut the window, it's freezing in here **2** *(trembler)* **g. de froid** to shiver *or* to tremble with cold; **g. de peur** to shake with fear; **g. de fièvre** to shiver with fever **3** *(cloche)* to jingle

greluche [grəlyʃ]NF *très Fam Péj* chick, *Br* bird

greluchon [grəlyʃɔ̃] NM *Fam Vieilli* = kept woman's lover

grémil [gremil]NM *Bot* gromwell

grémille [gremij]NF *Ich* pope, ruff(e)

grenache [grənaʃ]NM **1** *(cépage)* Grenache plant *or* vine **2** *(vin)* Grenache (wine)

grenadage [grənadaʒ]NM *Mil* grenading (**de** of), attack with hand grenades (**de** on); *(d'un sousmarin)* depth-charging

Grenade [grənad]NF **1** *(île)* **la G.** Grenada; **à la G.** in Grenada **2** *(ville d'Espagne)* Granada

grenade [grənad] NF **1** *(projectile)* grenade; **g. d'exercice** training grenade; **g. fumigène/ incendiaire/lacrymogène** smoke/incendiary/ tear-gas grenade; **g. à fusil/à main** rifle/hand grenade; **g. sous-marine** depth charge **2** *(écusson militaire)* grenade ornament **3** *Bot* pomegranate

grenader [3] [grənade]VT *Mil* to attack with grenades; *(sous-marin)* to depth-charge

grenadeur [grənadœr]NM depth-charge rails

grenadier [grənadje]NM **1** *Mil* grenadier; *(femme)* tall and masculine woman; **boire comme un g.** to drink like a fish **2** *Bot* pomegranate tree

grenadière [grənadjɛr] NF **1** *Hist (sac)* grenade pouch **2** *(de fusil)* band

grenadille [grənadij]NF granadilla

grenadin¹ [grənadɛ̃] NM **1** *Culin* grenadine (of veal) **2** *Bot* grenadin

grenadin², -e¹ [grənadɛ̃, -in]ADJ *(de la Grenade)* Grenadian
    ▫ **Grenadin, -e** NM,F Grenadian

grenadine² [grənadin] NF **1** *(sirop)* grenadine *(bright red fruit syrup used in making drinks)*; **une g.** *(boisson)* a (glass of) grenadine **2** *Tex* grenadine

grenage [grənaʒ]NM **1** *(d'une surface)* graining **2** *(d'une substance)* graining, granulation

grenaillage [grənajaʒ]NM shot-blasting, steel grit blasting

grenaille [grənaj] NF **1** *Métal* shot *(UNCOUNT)*, steel grit *(UNCOUNT)*; **en g.** grained, granulated **2** *(plomb de chasse)* shot; **g. de plomb** lead shot **3** *(pour la volaille)* refuse grain *(UNCOUNT)*, tailings **4** *Belg (revêtement)* grit *(UNCOUNT)*, fine gravel *(UNCOUNT)*; **grenailles errantes** *(sur panneau)* loose chippings, *Am* gravel

grenailler [3] [grənaje]VT to granulate

grenaison [grənɛzɔ̃]NF *Agr* seeding, corning

grenat [grəna]NM *(pierre, couleur)* garnet
    ADJ INV garnet, garnet-coloured

grené, -e [grəne] ADJ *(dessin)* stippled; *(cuir)* grainy
    NM *(de dessin)* stipple; *(de cuir)* grain

greneler [24] [grɛnle]VT to grain

Grenelle [grənɛl] *voir* **accord**

grener [19] [grəne]VI *(céréales)* to seed
    VT **1** *(réduire en grains → poudre à canon)* to granulate; *(→ cire)* to shred; *(→ sel)* to grain **2** *(donner un aspect grené à → papier, cuir)* to grain

grènetis [grɛnti]NM milled edge

grenier [grənje]NM **1** *(combles)* attic; **g. aménagé** converted loft **2** *(à grain)* loft; *(pour grain, fourrage)* granary; **g. à foin** hayloft; **g. à blé** granary; *Fig* **le g. à blé de la France** the granary of France

Grenoble [grənɔbl]NM Grenoble

grenoblois, -e [grənɔblwa, -az]ADJ of/from Grenoble
    ▫ **Grenoblois, -e** NM,F = inhabitant of or person from Grenoble

grenouillage [grənujaʒ] NM *Fam* jiggery-pokery *(UNCOUNT)*, skullduggery *(UNCOUNT)*; **il y a du g. ou des grenouillages là-dessous** there's some funny business going on there

grenouille [grənuj]NF **1** *Zool* frog; **g. verte/rousse** edible/common frog; **g. taureau ou mugissante** bullfrog; *Fam Fig Péj* **g. de bénitier** *(homme)* Holy Joe; *(femme)* Holy Mary; **c'est une vraie g. de bénitier** he's/she's very churchy **2** *Fam (cagnotte)* kitty, cash-box■; **manger** *ou* **faire sauter la g.** to make off with the kitty

---

Allusion

La grenouille qui veut se faire aussi grosse que le bœuf
This is the title of a La Fontaine fable *The frog who wants to become as big as the ox*. In this fable, a frog admires an ox for its size, swells up in an attempt to emulate it, and bursts. The expression is used of someone who appears overly ambitious, claims to be something they are not, or gives themselves airs.

---

grenouiller [3] [grənuje]VI *Fam* to scheme, to connive

grenouillère [grənujɛr]NF **1** *(pyjama)* sleepsuit, sleeping-suit **2** *(lieu)* frog pond

grenouillette [grənujɛt] NF **1** *Méd* ranula **2** *Bot* water crowfoot

grenu, -e [grəny] ADJ **1** *(blé etc)* grainy, full of grain **2** *(surface)* grainy, grained; *(cuir, peau)* grained **3** *Géol* granulose

grenure [grənyr]NF *(du cuir)* grain

grès [grɛ] NM **1** *Géol* sandstone **2** *(vaisselle)* **g. (céramе)** stoneware; **des assiettes en g.** stoneware plates
    NMPL *Zool* upper tusks, whetters *(of a wild boar)*

grésage [grezaʒ]NM polishing (with sandstone)

gréser [18] [greze]VT to polish (with sandstone)

gréseux, -euse [grezø, -øz]ADJ sandstone *(avant n)*

grésil [grezil]NM fine hail

grésillement [grezijmɑ̃]NM **1** *(de l'huile)* sizzling *(UNCOUNT)*; *(de la flamme)* sputtering *(UNCOUNT)*; *(de téléphone, de radio)* crackling *(UNCOUNT)*; **il y a des grésillements sur la ligne** there's some interference on the line, the line's crackling **2** *(cri du grillon)* chirping *(UNCOUNT)*

grésiller [3] [grezije]V IMPERSONNEL **il grésille** it's hailing
    VI **1** *(huile)* to sizzle; *(flamme)* to sputter; *(feu, téléphone, radio)* to crackle; **ça grésille** *(téléphone, radio)* it's all crackly **2** *(grillon)* to chirp

grésoir [grezwar]NM *(sandstone)* smoother

gressin [gresɛ̃] NM grissino, bread stick; **des gressins** grissini, bread sticks

GRETA, Greta [greta] NM *(abrév* **groupements d'établissements pour la formation continue***)* = state body organizing adult training programmes

greubons [grøbɔ̃] NMPL *Suisse (dans les cantons de Vaud, Neuchâtel, Berne et Jura)* = leftover fat from cooked pork, fried and used as an ingredient in certain Swiss dishes

grevé, -e [grəve]ADJ burdened, encumbered

grève [grɛv]NF **1** *(cessation d'une activité)* strike; **g. des cheminots/des Postes** train/postal strike; **être en g., faire g.** to be on strike, to strike; **se mettre en g.** to go on strike; **g. d'avertissement** warning strike; **g. bouchon** disruptive strike; **g. de la faim** hunger strike; **commencer une g. de la faim** to go on hunger strike; **g. générale** general strike; **g. illégale** wildcat strike; **g. partielle** partial or localized strike; **g. perlée** *Br* goslow, *Am* slowdown; **g. avec préavis** official strike; **g. de protestation** protest strike; **g. sauvage** wildcat strike; **g. de solidarité** sympathy strike; **ils font une g. de solidarité** they've come out in sympathy; **g. surprise** lightning strike; **g. sur le tas** sit-down strike; **g. tournante** staggered strike; **g. du zèle** work-to-rule; **faire la g. du zèle** to work to rule
    2 *Littéraire (plage)* shore, strand; *(rive)* bank, strand; **les grèves de la Loire** the sandbanks of the Loire; *Hist* **la (place de) G.** = open space on the banks of the Seine where dissatisfied workmen used to assemble

grever [19] [grəve]VT **1** *(économie)* to put a strain on; *(succession)* to burden, to encumber; **l'inflation a grevé le pouvoir d'achat** inflation has restricted or put a squeeze on purchasing power; **les vacances ont grevé mon budget** the holidays have put a severe strain on my finances; **grevé d'impôts** weighed down or burdened with tax **2** *Jur* **sa propriété est grevée d'hypothèques** he's/she's mortgaged up to the hilt

Grévin [grevɛ̃]NM **le musée G.** = wax museum in Paris

Grévisse [grevis] NM **le G.** = reference book on the correct use of the French language

gréviste [grevist]NMF striker, striking worker; **g. de la faim** hunger striker
    ADJ striking; **les étudiants grévistes** the striking students

greyé, -e [greje] = **gréé**

GRH [ʒeɛraʃ] NF *(abrév* **gestion des ressources humaines***)* HRM

gribiche [gribiʃ]ADJ **sauce g.** = flavoured mayonnaise with chopped hard-boiled egg and capers
    NF **1** *Suisse & Can Fam (femme acariâtre)* shrew **2** *Typ (de manuscrit)* file number **3** *(classeur)* loose-leaf binder

gribouillage [gribujaʒ] NM **1** *(dessin)* doodle; **faire des gribouillages** to doodle **2** *(écriture illisible)* scrawl, scribble

gribouille [gribuj] NM **1** *Fam Vieilli (personne)* simpleton, nitwit **2** *Can (dispute)* quarrel, fight

gribouiller [3] [gribuje]VT to scribble
    VI to doodle, to scribble

gribouilleur, -euse [gribujœr, -øz]NM,F scribbler

gribouillis [gribuji] NM **1** *(dessin)* doodle; **faire des g.** to doodle **2** *(écriture illisible)* scrawl, scribble

gre-gri

grief [grijɛf] **NM** *Littéraire* grievance; **mes griefs sont nombreux** I have numerous grievances; **faire** *ou* **tenir g. à qn de qch** to hold sth against sb; **on lui a fait g. d'avoir épousé un banquier** they resented her marrying a banker; **on lui a fait g. de ne pas se mêler aux autres** it was held against him/her that he/she didn't mix with the others

grièvement [grijɛvmɑ̃] **ADV** *(blessé)* severely, seriously; **g. brûlé/touché** severely burned/wounded; **quinze blessés dont trois g.** fifteen wounded, three of them seriously

griffade [grifad] **NF** *Vieilli* scratch

griffe [grif] **NF 1** *(d'un animal)* claw; *(d'un faucon)* claw, talon; **faire ses griffes** *(chat)* to sharpen its claws; *Fig* to cut one's teeth; **rentrer/sortir ses griffes** to draw in/to show one's claws; *Fig* **le voilà qui montre ses griffes** now he's showing his claws; **tomber dans les griffes de qn** to fall into sb's clutches; *Fig* **arracher qn des griffes de qn** to snatch sb out of sb's clutches; **il faut l'arracher des griffes de sa mère** he/she needs to be rescued from his/her mother's clutches; **coup de g.** scratch; **donner un coup de g. à qn** to scratch *or* to claw sb; *Fig* **elle a reçu de nombreux coups de griffes** she was the victim of quite a bit of backbiting

2 *(de vêtement)* label; **une grande g.** a famous *(designer)* label

3 *(empreinte)* stamped signature; *(ce qui sert à faire cette empreinte)* (signature) stamp; *Fig (d'un auteur, d'un artiste)* stamp; **on reconnaît la g. de Zola dans ce roman** the novel bears Zola's stamp; **cet article porte la g. de Monsieur Dubois** this article is written in Mr Dubois's unmistakable style; **on reconnaît la g. de Saint Laurent** you can recognize the Saint Laurent style

4 *Bot (de l'asperge)* crown; *(du lierre, de la vigne)* tendril

5 *(en joaillerie)* claw

6 *Belg (rayure)* scratch

7 *Tech* claw, clip, clamp; *(outil)* dog; **accouplement/embrayage à griffes** claw coupling/clutch; **griffes de monteur** climbing irons

8 *Phot* **g. du flash** hot shoe

griffé, -e [grife] **ADJ** *(vêtement)* designer *(avant n)*

griffer [grife] **VT 1** *(sujet: personne, animal)* to scratch; **Marie m'a griffé** Marie scratched me; **g. la joue à qn** to scratch sb's cheek, to scratch sb on the cheek **2** *(sujet: couturier)* to put one's label on; **Chanel a griffé cette veste** this jacket bears the Chanel label

▸**se griffer** **VPR** to scratch oneself; **je me suis griffé au rosier** I scratched myself on the rosebush

griffeur, -euse [grifœr, -øz] **ADJ** *(animal)* that scratches

NM,F scratcher

griffon [grifɔ̃] **NM 1** *Myth* griffin **2** *Zool (chien)* griffon **3** *Orn* griffon (vulture)

griffonnage [grifɔnaʒ] **NM 1** *(écrit)* scribble; **griffonnages** scribbling **2** *(dessin)* rough sketch

griffonnement [grifɔnmɑ̃] **NM** *Beaux-Arts (en cire)* wax model; *(en terre)* clay model

griffonner [grifɔne] **VT 1** *(noter → adresse)* to scribble (down); *(→ plan)* to sketch roughly, to do a quick sketch of; *Beaux-Arts (dessiner)* to sketch quickly **2** *(mal écrire)* to scribble; **les pages étaient toutes griffonnées au crayon noir** the pages were all scribbled over in black pencil

USAGE ABSOLU *(gribouiller)* to scribble

griffonneur, -euse [grifɔnœr, -øz] **NM,F 1** *(écrivant mal)* scribbler **2** *(dessinant mal)* scrawler

griffton [griftɔ̃] = **griveton**

griffu, -e [grify] **ADJ** clawed; **main griffue** claw-like hand

griffure [grifyr] **NF** *(d'une personne, d'une ronce)* scratch; *(d'un animal)* scratch, claw mark

grifton [griftɔ̃] = **griveton**

grignard, -e [griɲar, -ard] **ADJ** *Zool* with a protrusive lower jaw, prognathic

grigne [griɲ] **NF 1** *(dans le pain)* slash **2** *Tex* kink, pucker

grigner [griɲe] **VI** to crease, to wrinkle

grignotage [griɲɔtaʒ] **NM** nibbling; *Fig* wearing away, erosion; **le g. des voix par l'opposition**

the gradual loss of votes to the opposition; **le g. de nos droits** the gradual whittling away of our rights

grignotement [griɲɔtmɑ̃] **NM** nibbling

grignoter [3] [griɲɔte] **VT 1** *(ronger)* to nibble (at *or* on)

2 *Fig (amoindrir)* to erode; **g. son capital/ses économies** to eat into one's capital/one's savings

3 *(acquérir)* to acquire gradually; **ils ont réussi à g. pas mal d'avantages** they gradually managed to win quite a few advantages; **la jument est en train de g. du terrain sur ses adversaires** the mare is gaining on *or* gradually catching up with the other horses

VI to nibble; **ne grignotez pas entre les repas** don't eat between meals

grignoteuse [griɲɔtøz] **NF** nibbling machine

grigou [grigu] **NM** *Fam* skinflint; **quel vieux g.!** what an old skinflint *or* Scrooge!

gri-gri *(pl* **gris-gris***)*, **grigri** [grigri] **NM** grigri, gris-gris

gril [gril] **NM 1** *Culin* grill, *Am* broiler; **faire cuire du poisson sur le g.** to grill fish, *Am* to broil fish; *Fam Fig* **être sur le g.** to be on tenterhooks **2** *Tech* grating *(protecting sluice gate)*; *Rail & Naut* gridiron; *Théât* grid, gridiron **3** *Anat* **g. costal** rib cage

grill [gril] **NM 1** *(restaurant)* grill-room, grill **2** *TV (pour l'éclairage)* pipe grid

grillade [grijad] **NF** grill, grilled meat; **achète des grillades** get some meat for grilling; **leurs grillades sont renommées** their grills have quite a reputation; **faire des grillades** to have a barbecue

grilladin[1] [grijadɛ̃] **NM** grill cook

grillage[1] [grijaʒ] **NM 1** *(matériau)* wire netting *or* mesh **2** *(clôture)* wire fence *or* fencing; **poser un g. électrifié** to put up an electrified fence **3** *(d'une fenêtre)* wire screen **4** *Élec (de plaque d'accumulateur)* grid, frame

grillage[2] [grijaʒ] **NM 1** *Culin* roasting **2** *Métal (de minerai)* calcining, roasting **3** *Tex* singeing

grillagé, -e [grijaʒe] **ADJ** *(fenêtre)* covered with wire mesh; *(jardin)* surrounded with a wire fence *or* with wire fencing

grillager [17] [grijaʒe] **VT 1** *(fenêtre)* to put wire mesh on **2** *(terrain, jardin)* to put a wire fence *or* wire fencing around

grillardin[1] [grijardɛ̃] **NM** grill cook

grille [grij] **NF 1** *(porte)* (iron) gate; *(barrière)* railing; *(clôture basse)* railings; *(d'une fenêtre)* bars

2 *(d'un égout, d'un foyer)* grate; *(d'un parloir, d'un comptoir)* grill, grille; **g. d'entrée d'air** air vent; **g. de réchauffeur** heater matrix

3 *Can Aut (calandre)* grille

4 *Élec (d'un accumulateur, d'un tube à électrons)* grid; **courant de g.** grid current

5 *(programme)* schedule; **voici notre nouvelle g. pour l'été** here's our new summer schedule; *Rad & TV* **g. généraliste** general-interest programmes; *Rad & TV* **g. des programmes** programme schedule *or* grid

6 *(au jeu)* **une g. de mots croisés** a crossword grid *or* puzzle; **la g. du Loto** Loto card

7 *(en travaux publics)* (frame) grate

8 *Jur & Écon* **g. des salaires** pay *or* salary scale; **g. indiciaire** salary structure *or* scale; *(de la fonction publique)* wage index; **g. d'avancement** career structure; **g. de gestion** managerial grid; *Compta* **g. d'imputation** table of account codes; **g. produit/marché** product/market grid; **g. de rémunération** salary scale

9 *Ordinat* **g. de saisie** input grid

grillé, -e [grije] **ADJ 1** *(amandes, noisettes)* roasted; *(viande)* grilled; **une tartine grillée** a piece of toast **2** *(ampoule, fusible)* blown

3 *Fam (ampoule, fusible)* to blow; *(moteur)* to burn out

4 *Métal (minerai)* to roast, to calcine

5 *Tex* to singe

6 *Fam (dépasser)* **le bus a grillé mon arrêt** the bus went right past my stop; **g. un feu rouge** to jump the lights, to jump *or* go through a red light; **g. les étapes** *(dans sa carrière)* to shoot up the ladder; *(dans un travail)* to cut corners; **g. quelques étapes** to jump a few stages; **g. qn (à l'arrivée)** *Br* to pip sb at the post, *Am* to beat sb out; **g. un concurrent** to leave a competitor standing

7 *Fam (fumer)* **g. une cigarette, en g. une** to have a smoke

8 *Fam (compromettre)* **il est grillé** *(dévoilé)* his game's up; *(fini)* he's had it; **il nous a grillés auprès du patron** he's really landed us in it with the boss; **il s'est fait g. en train de tricher à l'examen** he got *Br* nabbed or *Am* busted for cheating in the exam

VI 1 *Culin* **faire g. du pain** to toast some bread; **faire g. du café** to roast coffee beans; **faire g. de la viande** to grill meat, *Am* to broil meat

2 *Élec (sauter → fusible)* to blow

3 *Fam (avoir trop chaud)* to roast, to boil; **ouvre la fenêtre, on grille ici** open the window, it's boiling in here

4 *Fam (brûler)* **la ferme a entièrement grillé** the farmhouse was burnt to the ground

5 *Fig* **g. de curiosité** to be consumed with curiosity; **je grille (d'envie ou d'impatience) de la rencontrer** I'm itching *or* dying to meet her

6 *Can Fam (se bronzer)* to tan

▸**se griller** **VPR** *Fam* **1** *(se démasquer)* **il s'est grillé en disant cela** he gave himself away by saying that; **se g. auprès de qn** to blot one's copybook with sb

2 **se g. au soleil** to roast in the sun; *Can (se bronzer)* to tan

3 **se g. les orteils devant la cheminée** to toast one's feet in front of the fire; **on s'en grille une?** how about a (quick) smoke?

griller[2] [3] [grije] **VT** *(fermer d'une grille)* to put bars on; **les fenêtres de la chapelle ont été grillées** they have put bars on the chapel windows

grilloir [grijwar] **NM** grill, *Am* broiler

grillon [grijɔ̃] **NM** *Entom* cricket

grill-room [grilrum] *(pl* **grill-rooms***)* **NM** grill-room, grill

grimaçant, -e [grimasɑ̃, -ɑ̃t] **ADJ** *(sourire)* painful; *(bouche)* twisted; *(visage)* contorted; *(clown, gargouille)* grimacing

grimace [grimas] **NF 1** *(expression → amusante)* funny face; *(→ douloureuse)* grimace; **faire une g.** *(pour faire rire)* to make a funny face; *(de douleur)* to wince; *(de peur)* to grimace; **une g. de dégoût** a disgusted look; **faire la g.** to make a face **2** *(faux-pli)* pucker; **faire une g.** to pucker ▢ **grimaces** **NFPL** *Littéraire (manières)* airs

grimacer [16] [grimase] **VI 1** *(de douleur)* to grimace, to wince; *(de dégoût)* to make a face; **il grimaça en goûtant l'anchois** he screwed up his face when he tasted the anchovy; **g. de douleur** to grimace *or* wince with pain **2** *(pour faire rire)* to make a funny face **3** *(robe)* to pucker

VT malgré la douleur, elle grimaça un sourire she forced a smile in spite of the pain

grimacier, -ère [grimasje, -ɛr] **ADJ 1** *(grotesque)* grimacing **2** *Littéraire (maniéré)* affected

grimage [grimaʒ] **NM** *(action)* making up; *(résultat)* make-up

grimaud [grimo] **NM** *Vieilli (homme inculte)* ignoramus; *(mauvais écrivain)* scribbler

grimer [3] [grime] **VT** to make up; **grimé en vieillard/chat** made up as an old man/a cat

▸**se grimer** **VPR** to put one's make-up on; **se g. en** to make oneself up as

grimoire [grimwar] **NM 1** *(livre de sorcellerie)* book of magic spells **2** *(écrit illisible)* illegible scrawl *or* scribble; *(ouvrage confus)* piece of gibberish *or* mumbo-jumbo

grimpant, -e [grɛ̃pɑ̃, -ɑ̃t] **ADJ** *(arbuste)* climbing *(fraisier)* creeping

NM *Fam Arg* crime *Br* trousers, keks, *Am* pants

grimpe [grɛ̃p] **NF** rock-climbing; **faire de la g.** to go rock-climbing

grimpée [grɛ̃pe] NF *(pente, montée)* stiff *or* steep climb
grimper [3] [grɛ̃pe] VI **1** *(personne, animal, plante)* to climb; **g. à une échelle/un mur** to climb up a ladder/wall; **g. à un arbre** to climb (up) a tree; **g. sur une table** to climb on (to) a table; **grimpe dans la voiture** get into the car; **grimpe dans ton lit/sur le tabouret** climb into bed/(up) on the stool; **le lierre grimpe le long du mur** the ivy climbs up the wall; *Fam* **g. aux rideaux** to hit the *Br* roof *or Am* ceiling; **g. à quatre pattes** *(en alpinisme)* to scramble; **g. en tête** *(en alpinisme)* to lead; **g. en second** *(en alpinisme)* to follow
2 *(s'élever en pente raide)* to climb; **la route grimpe beaucoup à cet endroit** the road climbs steeply here; **ça grimpe!** it's steep!; **ça grimpe à cet endroit-là** there's a steep climb at that point
3 *(température, inflation)* to soar; **la température a grimpé à 35°** the temperature rocketed *or* soared to 35°
VT **1** *(escalier, pente)* to climb (up); **il grimpe l'escalier difficilement** he has difficulty climbing the stairs
2 *très Fam (posséder sexuellement)* to screw, *Br* to shag
NM *Sport* rope-climbing; **l'épreuve de g. aura lieu le matin** the rope-climbing event will be held in the morning
grimpereau, -x [grɛ̃pro] NM *Orn* **g. (des bois)** treecreeper; **g. des jardins** short-toed treecreeper; **g. des murailles** wallcreeper
grimpette [grɛ̃pɛt] NF *Fam* steep *or* stiff climb▪
grimpeur, -euse [grɛ̃pœr, -øz] ADJ *Orn* scansorial
NM,F **1** *Sport* climber; *(de rocher)* rock-climber; *(en cyclisme)* hill climber; **c'est un bon/mauvais g.** *(cycliste)* he's good/bad on hills **2** *Orn* **les grimpeurs** scansorial birds
grimpion, -onne [grɛ̃pjɔ̃, -ɔn] NM,F *Suisse Fam* careerist
grinçant, -e [grɛ̃sɑ̃, -ɑ̃t] ADJ **1** *(porte, parquet)* squeaking, creaking **2** *(voix, musique)* grating **3** *(humour)* sardonic
grincement [grɛ̃smɑ̃] NM *(bruit)* grating, creaking; **dans un g. de freins** with a squeal of brakes; *Fig* **il y a eu des grincements de dents** there was much gnashing of teeth
grincer [16] [grɛ̃se] VI **1** *(bois)* to creak; *(frein)* to squeal; *(métal)* to grate; *(ressort)* to squeak; **la girouette grinçait au vent** the weather vane was creaking in the wind **2** *(personne)* **g. des dents** to gnash one's teeth; *Fig* **le bruit de la craie sur le tableau me fait g. des dents** the noise the chalk makes on the board sets my teeth on edge
grinche [grɛ̃ʃ] ADJ *Suisse* grumpy, grouchy
grincheux, -euse [grɛ̃ʃø, -øz] ADJ grumpy, grouchy; **être d'une humeur grincheuse** to be grumpy *or* in a grumpy mood
NM,F grumbler; **un vieux g.** an old grouch *or* moaner
gringalet [grɛ̃galɛ] NM *(enfant)* puny child; *(adulte)* puny man; *Littérature* **G.** = name of Gawain's horse in Chrétien de Troyes' 'Légende du roi Arthur'
ADJ M puny
gringe [grɛ̃ʒ] ADJ *Suisse* grumpy, grouchy
gringo [griŋgo] NM *Péj* gringo
gringue [grɛ̃g] NM *très Fam* **faire du g. à qn** to come on to sb, *Br* to chat sb up, *Am* to hit on sb
griot [grijo] NM griot *(in Africa, a travelling poet and musician)*
griotte [grijɔt] NF **1** *Bot* morello (cherry) **2** *(marbre)* (griotte) marble
griottier [grijɔtje] NM morello cherry tree
grip [grip] NM *Sport (position de la main, revêtement)* grip
grippage [gripaʒ] NM *Tech* jamming, seizing (up); **pour éviter le g. du piston** to stop the piston from seizing up *or* jamming
grippal, -e, -aux, -ales [gripal, -o] ADJ flu *(avant n)*, *Spéc* influenzal; **état g.** influenza, flu; **soulage les états grippaux** *(sur médicament)* relieves flu symptoms
grippe [grip] NF **1** *Méd* flu, *Spéc* influenza; **attraper/avoir la g.** to catch/have (the) flu; **ce n'est qu'une petite g.** it's just a touch of flu; **g. asiatique** Asian flu; *Méd* **g. aviaire** bird flu, *Spec* avian flu; **g. intestinale** gastric flu **2 prendre qn/qch en g.** to take a (strong) dislike to sb/sth
grippé, -e [gripe] ADJ **1** *Méd* **être g.** to have (the) flu; **elle est un peu grippée** she's got a touch of the flu **2** *Tech* seized (up), jammed **3** *Méd (visage)* pinched, drawn
Grippeminaud [gripɛmino] NM *Vieilli* **1** *(chat)* cat, *Arch* grimalkin **2** *(personne)* sly character
gripper [3] [gripe] VT to block, to jam; **la grève a grippé les rouages de l'administration** the strike has blocked the workings of the administration
VI **1** *(se coincer)* to jam, to seize up; *Fig* **les rouages de l'État commencent à g.** the wheels of state are beginning to seize up **2** *(se froisser)* to crinkle (up), to wrinkle, to pucker
▸**se gripper** VPR to jam, to seize up
grippe-sou [gripsu] *(pl* **grippe-sous***)* *Fam* NM skinflint; **un vieux g.** an old Scrooge
ADJ INV money-grabbing
gris, -e [gri, griz] ADJ **1** *(couleur)* grey; **g. acier/anthracite/ardoise/argent/fer/perle** steel/charcoal/slate/silver/iron/pearl grey; **g. clair** light grey; **g. pommelé** dapple-grey; **g. souris** mouse-coloured; **g. bleu/vert** bluish/greenish grey; **une robe g. foncé** a dark grey dress; **avoir les cheveux g.** to be grey-haired; **il est déjà tout g.** he's grey-haired *or* he's gone grey already
2 *Météo* overcast; **il fait g. ce matin** it's cloudy *or* dull *or* overcast this morning, it's a grey *or* dull morning; **ciel g. sur tout le pays** skies will be grey *or* overcast over the whole country; **nous sommes partis par un matin g.** we left on a dull (grey) morning
3 *(terne)* dull, grey; **son existence a été plutôt grise et monotone** his/her life was dull and dreary; **en apprenant la nouvelle, il a fait grise mine** his face fell when he heard the news
4 *Fam (ivre)* tipsy
5 *(en œnologie)* **vin g.** rosé (wine)
❑ **gris** NM **1** *(couleur)* grey; **porter du g.** to wear grey **2** *(tabac)* = French caporal tobacco in grey packet, ≃ shag **3** *(cheval)* grey (horse) ADV **il a fait g. toute la journée** it's been grey *or* dull all day
grisaille [grizaj] NF **1** *(morosité)* dullness, greyness **2** *Météo* dull weather; **encore de la g. pour aujourd'hui** today will again be dull (and overcast) **3** *Beaux-Arts* grisaille; **une marine en g.** a seascape in shades of grey
grisailler [3] [grizaje] VT *Beaux-Arts* to paint in grisaille
VI to turn *or* to become grey
grisant, -e [grizɑ̃, -ɑ̃t] ADJ **1** *(enivrant)* intoxicating, heady **2** *(excitant)* exhilarating
grisard [grizar] NM grey poplar
grisâtre [grizatr] ADJ **1** *(couleur)* greyish **2** *(monotone)* **une vie g.** a dull life
grisbi [grizbi] NM *Fam Arg crime* dough, cash
grise [griz] *voir* **gris**
grisé [grize] NM grey tint; *Ordinat* grey tone; **en g.** *(article)* dimmed
Grisélidis [grizelidis] NF *Littérature* Griselda
griséofulvine [grizeofylvin] NF *Chim* griseofulvin
griser [3] [grize] VT **1** *(colorer)* to tint; *(rendre gris)* to make grey
2 *(enivrer)* to intoxicate
3 *Fig (étourdir, exciter)* to intoxicate, to fascinate; **grisé par le succès** carried away *or* intoxicated by *or* with success; **grisé par son sourire** fascinated by his/her smile; **grisé par la vitesse** intoxicated by speed; **le luxe ambiant l'a grisé** the luxuriousness of the place went to his head
4 *Ordinat* to shade
▸**se griser** VPR to get drunk; **se g. de qch** to get drunk on sth; **se g. des paroles de qn/de musique** to get carried away by sb's words/by music
griserie [grizri] NF **1** *(ivresse)* intoxication **2** *Fig (exaltation)* exhilaration, excitement; **se laisser porter par la g. du succès** to let success go to one's head
griset [grizɛ] NM *Ich* black (sea) bream
grisette [grizɛt] NF *Vieilli* grisette
gris-gris [grigri] = **gri-gri**
grisoller [3] [grizɔle] VI *(alouette)* to sing
grison, -onne [grizɔ̃, -ɔn] ADJ of/from the Graubünden
❑ **Grison, -onne** NM,F = inhabitant of or person from the Graubünden
grisonnant, -e [grizɔnɑ̃, -ɑ̃t] ADJ greying; **elle est grisonnante, elle a les cheveux grisonnants** she's going grey; **avoir les tempes grisonnantes** to be greying at the temples
grisonne [grizɔn] *voir* **grison**
grisonnement [grizɔnmɑ̃] NM greying
grisonner [3] [grizɔne] VI *(barbe, cheveux)* to be going grey; **elle grisonne** she's going grey
Grisons [grizɔ̃] NMPL **les G.** the Graubünden; **viande des G.** = thinly sliced dried beef, traditionally served with raclette
grisou [grizu] NM firedamp; **coup de g.** firedamp explosion
grisoumètre [grizumɛtr] NM firedamp indicator
grisouteux, -euse [grizutø, -øz] ADJ **une mine grisouteuse** a mine full of firedamp
grive [griv] NF *Orn* thrush; **g. draine** mistle-thrush; **g. fauve** veery; **g. à gorge noire** black-throated thrush; **g. à joues grises** grey-cheeked thrush; **g. litorne** fieldfare; **g. mauvis** redwing; **g. musicienne** song thrush; **g. de Swainson** Swainson's thrush
grivelé, -e [grivle] ADJ speckled with grey
griveler [24] [grivle] VI = to eat a meal or to stay at a hotel and deliberately leave without paying
grivèlerie [grivɛlri] NF = offence of leaving a restaurant or a hotel without having paid
grivelure [grivlyr] NF grey speckled colour
grivet [grivɛ] NM *Zool* grivet monkey
griveton [grivtɔ̃] NM *Fam Arg mil Br* ≃ squaddy, *Am* ≃ grunt
grivois, -e [grivwa, -az] ADJ risqué, bawdy
grivoiserie [grivwazri] NF **1** *(caractère)* bawdiness **2** *(histoire)* bawdy story; *(plaisanterie)* risqué *or* saucy joke; *(acte)* rude gesture
grizzli, grizzly [grizli] NM grizzly (bear)
grœnendael [grɔnɛndal] NM Groenendael (sheepdog)
Groenland [grɔɛnlɑ̃d] NM **le G.** Greenland; **vivre au G.** to live in Greenland; **aller au G.** to go to Greenland
groenlandais, -e [grɔɛnlɑ̃dɛ, -ɛz] ADJ of/from Greenland, Greenland *(avant n)*
❑ **Groenlandais, -e** NM,F Greenlander
grog [grɔg] NM hot toddy; **g. au rhum** rum toddy
groggy [grɔgi] ADJ INV **1** *(boxeur)* groggy **2** *Fam (abruti)* stunned, dazed
grognard [grɔɲar] NM **1** *Hist* = soldier of Napoleon's Old Guard **2** *(militant traditionnaliste)* member of the old guard **3** *Vieilli (grincheux)* grouch, curmudgeon
grognasse [grɔɲas] NF *très Fam* old bag, old bat
grognasser [3] [grɔɲase] VI *Fam* to grumble, *Br* to whinge
grogne [grɔɲ] NF dissatisfaction, discontent; **c'est la g. chez les ouvriers/dans le milieu étudiant** the workers/the students are grumbling
grognement [grɔɲmɑ̃] NM **1** *(d'une personne)* grunt, growl; **pousser des grognements** to grunt, to growl; **"on verra", dit-elle dans un g.** "we'll see," she growled *or* grunted **2** *(d'un cochon)* grunt, grunting *(UNCOUNT)*; *(d'un chien)* growl, growling *(UNCOUNT)*; **pousser des grognements** *(cochon)* to grunt; *(chien)* to growl
grogner [3] [grɔɲe] VI **1** *(personne)* to grumble, to grouse; *Fam* **ça ne sert à rien de g. après** *ou* **contre ton patron** it's no use grumbling *or* moaning about your boss **2** *(cochon)* to grunt; *(chien)* to growl
VT *(réponse, phrase)* to grunt (out)
grognerie [grɔɲri] NF grumbling, grousing *(UNCOUNT)*
grogneur, -euse [grɔɲœr, -øz] ADJ grumbling, grousing; **figure grogneuse** sulky *or* disagreeable face
NM,F grumbler, grouser
NM *Ich* pigfish
grognon, -onne [grɔɲɔ̃, -ɔn] *Fam* ADJ grumpy, crotchety; **un air g.** a surly look; **ce matin, elle est g.** *ou* **grognonne** she's grumpy this morning
NM,F grumbler, moaner; **c'est une vraie grognonne** she's such a moaner
grognonner [3] [grɔɲɔne] VI *Fam* to grumble, *Br* to whinge
groin [grwɛ̃] NM **1** *(d'un porc)* snout **2** *Fam (visage laid)* mug
groisil [grwazi, grwazil] NM *Tech* cullet
grole, grolle [grɔl] NF *très Fam* shoe▪; **mets des groles** put something on your feet

:mmeler [24] [grɔmle] **VI 1** *(personne)* to :mble, to mutter **2** *(sanglier)* to snort
/T to mutter

:mmellement [grɔmɛlmɑ̃] **NM 1** *(du sanglier)* :norting **2** *(d'une personne)* grumbling, mutter- :ng; **quelques grommellements indistincts** a :ew inaudible mutters *or* mutterings

:rommellera *etc voir* **grommeler**

grondant, -e [grɔ̃dɑ̃, -ɑ̃t] **ADJ** rumbling; **une foule grondante** a crowd muttering discontentedly

grondement [grɔ̃dmɑ̃] **NM 1** *(du tonnerre, du métro)* rumbling; *(d'un torrent de montagne, des vagues, d'un moteur)* roar(ing); *(de canons)* booming; **le g. de la foule se fit de plus en plus fort** the angry murmur of the crowd grew louder and louder **2** *(d'un chien)* growling

gronder [3] [grɔ̃de] **VI 1** *(rivière, tonnerre, métro)* to rumble; *(canons)* to boom; *(vagues)* to roar
2 *(chien)* to growl
3 *Littéraire (révolte)* to be brewing; **la colère gronde chez les étudiants/les ouvriers** students/workers are becoming increasingly discontented, there are rumblings of discontent among students/workers
VT *(réprimander)* to scold, to tell off; **se faire g.** to get told off

gronderie [grɔ̃dri] **NF** scolding, telling-off

grondeur, -euse [grɔ̃dœr, -øz] **ADJ 1** *(personne, voix)* scolding, grumbling; **d'un ton g.** in a tone of reproof **2** *(orage, torrent)* rumbling

grondin [grɔ̃dɛ̃] **NM** *Ich* gurnard; **g. perlon** sapphirine gurnard

Groningue [grɔnɛ̃g] **NM** Groningen

groom [grum] **NM 1** *(employé d'hôtel)* bellboy **2** *Arch Équitation* groom

---

GROS, GROSSE [gro, gros]

> **ADJ** large **1** ■ big **1–3, 5, 6** ■ fat **2** ■ heavy **3, 4** ■ hearty **3**
> **NM,F** fat person
> **NM** most part **1** ■ bulk **1** ■ wholesale **2** ■ rich person **3**
> **NF** engrossment **1** ■ gross **2**

ADJ 1 *(grand)* large, big; *(épais, solide)* big, thick; **une grosse boîte de haricots** a large *or* big can of beans; **le paquet est/n'est pas (très) g.** the parcel is/isn't (very) big; **une orange grosse comme le poing** an orange the size of *or* as big as your fist; **prends-le par le g. bout** pick it up by the thick *or* thicker end; **écrire qch en g. caractères** to write sth in big *or* large letters; **un g. crayon** a (big) thick pencil; **de grosses chaussures** heavy shoes; **de grosses chaussettes** thick *or* heavy socks; **un g. pull** a thick *or* heavy jumper; **g. drap** coarse linen; **de grosses lèvres** thick lips; **une grosse limace** a big fat slug; **g. trait de crayon** thick pencil mark; **une grosse tranche** a thick slice; *Fam* **un bon g. sandwich** a nice big sandwich; **g. morceau** big *or* large piece, lump; *Fig* **l'examen de statistiques, voilà le g. morceau** the statistics exam is the big one; *Ordinat* **g. système** mainframe; *Typ* **g. corps** headings type, headline type; *Journ* **g. titre** banner headline; **en g. titres** in banner headlines

2 *(corpulent)* big, fat; **un g. bébé** a big *or* fat baby; **un homme grand et g.** a tall fat man; **une grosse dame** a big *or* fat lady; **de grosses jambes** fat *or* stout legs

3 *(en intensif)* **un g. appétit** a big *or* hearty appetite; **les grosses chaleurs** the hot season, the height of summer; *Fam* **un g. bisou** a big kiss; **un g. bruit** a loud *or* big noise; **un g. kilo** a good kilo; **une grosse récolte** a bumper harvest; **un g. sanglot** a big *or* heavy sob; **un g. soupir** a big *or* heavy sigh; **un g. mangeur** a big *or* hearty eater; **un g. buveur** a heavy drinker; **un g. utilisateur** a heavy user; **g. bêta!** you great ninny!; *Fam* **le plus g. buteur du championnat** the highest scorer in the championship

4 *(abondant)* heavy; **une grosse averse** a heavy shower; **de grosses pluies/chutes de neige** heavy rainfall/snowfall; **son usine a de g. effectifs** his/her factory employs large numbers of people *or* has a large workforce

5 *(important)* big; **le g. avantage des supermarchés** the big *or* major advantage of supermarkets; **un g. consommateur de pétrole** a major oil consumer; **de g. dégâts** extensive *or* widespread damage; **une grosse entreprise** a large *or* big company; **une grosse erreur** a big *or* serious mistake; **une grosse faute** a serious *or* gross mistake; **une grosse commande** a bulk order; **une grosse somme** a large sum of money; **de g. frais** heavy expenses; **avoir de g. moyens** to have a large income *or* considerable resources; **de g. progrès** considerable progress, a lot of progress; **de g. profits** big *or* fat profits; **il y a de g. travaux à faire dans cette maison** that house needs a lot (of work) done to it; **la plus grosse partie de nos affaires/notre personnel** the bulk of our business/our staff; **une grosse angine** a (very) sore throat; **un g. rhume** a bad *or* heavy cold; **une grosse fièvre** a high fever; **un g. choc psychologique** a serious psychological shock; **de g. ennuis** serious trouble, lots of trouble; **une grosse journée (de travail)** a hard day's work; **de grosses pertes** heavy losses; **g. œuvre** structural work, *Spéc* carcass

6 *(prospère)* big; **un g. commerçant** a major retailer; **un g. producteur d'Hollywood** a big Hollywood producer; **un g. propriétaire (terrien)** a big landowner; **une grosse héritière** a wealthy heiress; **les g. actionnaires** the major shareholders

7 *(rude)* **une grosse voix** a rough *or* gruff voice; **un g. rire** coarse laughter; **l'astuce/la supercherie était un peu grosse** the trick/the hoax was a bit obvious; **grosse blague** crude joke

8 *(exagéré)* **j'ai trouvé ça un peu g.!** I thought it was a bit much!; **un g. drame** a big tragedy *or* catastrophe; **une grosse indélicatesse** a gross impropriety; **ne lui dis pas, sinon ça va faire une grosse histoire** don't tell him/her or you'll never hear the end of it; **ce n'est pas une grosse affaire** it's no big deal; *Fam* **tout de suite, les grosses menaces!** so it's threats already, is it?

9 *Météo* **par g. temps/grosse mer** in heavy weather/seas; **g. vent** gale

10 *(rempli)* **un ciel g. d'orage** stormy skies; **yeux g. de larmes** eyes moist with tears; **un cœur g. de tendresse** a heart full of tenderness; **un regard g. de menaces** a threatening look; **un choix g. de conséquences** a choice fraught with implications

11 *Cin & TV* **g. plan** close-up, close-shot; **g. plan de tête** head shot

NM,F fat person; **les g.** fat people; **un petit g.** a fat little man; *Fam* **ça va, mon g.?** all right, old boy *or Br* chap?

NM 1 *(la plus grande partie)* **le g. de la classe a du mal à suivre** most of the class has trouble keeping up; **le g. des étudiants** most of the students; **le g. du débat sera télévisé** the main part of the debate will be televised; **le g. de l'hiver est passé** the worst of the winter is over; **le g. du chargement/personnel** the bulk of the cargo/staff; **le g. de l'armée** the main body *or* the bulk of the army; **g. d'un mât** thick end of a mast; **le plus g. est fait** the biggest part of the job is done **2** *Com* wholesale (trade); **ils ne vendent/font que du g.** they only sell/deal wholesale **3** *Fam (riche)* rich person■; **les g.** the rich

ADV couper g. to cut in large slices; **écrire g.** to write big; **coûter/gagner g.** to cost/to win a lot (of money); *aussi Fig* **ça va vous coûter g.** it'll cost you dear; **ça peut rapporter g.** it can bring in a lot; **il y a g. à parier qu'il ne viendra pas!** a hundred to one he won't come!; **jouer g.** to play for high stakes; *Fig* **jouer** *ou* **miser** *ou* **risquer g.** to take *or* to run a big risk, to stick one's neck out; **elle donnerait g. pour savoir qui a fait ça** she'd give her right arm *or* anything to know who did it

❑ **grosse NF 1** *Jur* engrossment **2** *Com* gross **3** *Arch (écriture)* roundhand (writing) **ADJ F** *Vieilli (enceinte)* pregnant

❑ **de gros ADJ** *Com* wholesale *(avant n)*

❑ **en gros ADJ** bulk *(avant n)* **ADV 1** *(approximativement)* roughly; **il y avait en g. quinze personnes** there were roughly *or* about fifteen people there; **je sais en g. de quoi il s'agit** I know roughly what it's about; **voilà, en g., ce dont il s'agit** that's the long and the short of it **2** *(en lettres capitales)* **c'est imprimé en g.** it's printed in big letters **3** *Com* wholesale; **acheter en g.** to buy wholesale; *(en grosse quantité)* to buy in bulk; **vendre en g.** to sell wholesale

❑ **gros bonnet NM** *Fam* bigwig, big shot; **tous les g. bonnets de la finance** all the financial bigwigs

❑ **grosse légume NF** *Fam (personne influente)* bigwig, big shot; *(officier)* brass hat; **les grosses légumes du régiment** the top brass (of the regiment)

---

gros-bec [grobɛk] *(pl* **gros-becs***)* **NM** *Orn* hawfinch, grosbeak

groschen [grɔʃɛn] **NM INV** groschen

gros-cul [groky] *(pl* **gros-culs***)* **NM** *Fam* truck■, *Br* lorry■

groseille [grozɛj] **NF g. (blanche)** white currant; **g. rouge** redcurrant; **sirop de g.** redcurrant syrup; **g. à maquereau** gooseberry
ADJ INV light red

groseillier [grozeje] **NM** currant bush; **g. rouge** redcurrant bush; **g. blanc** white currant bush; **g. à maquereau** gooseberry bush

gros-grain [grogrɛ̃] *(pl* **gros-grains***)* **NM** *Tex* grosgrain

Gros-Jean [groʒɑ̃] **NM INV se retrouver** *ou* **être G. comme devant** to feel deflated *(by failure)*

gros-plant [groplɑ̃] *(pl* **gros-plants***)* **NM** Grosplant (wine)

gros-porteur [groportœr] *(pl* **gros-porteurs***)* **NM** jumbo, jumbo jet

grosse [gros] *voir* **gros**

grosserie [grosri] **NF 1** *Vieilli (commerce de gros)* wholesale trading **2** *(taillanderie)* edge tools **3** *(vaisselle d'argent)* silver tableware

grossesse [grosɛs] **NF** pregnancy; **pendant ma g.** when I was pregnant; **g. extra-utérine** ectopic pregnancy; **g. gémellaire** twin pregnancy; **g. môlaire** molar pregnancy; **g. nerveuse** phantom pregnancy; **g. à risque** high-risk pregnancy

grosseur [grosœr] **NF 1** *(taille)* size; **de la g. d'une noix** the size of a walnut; **des grêlons de la g. de mon poing** hailstones as big as *or* the size of my fist **2** *(obésité)* weight, fatness **3** *Méd* lump

grossier, -ère [grosje, -ɛr] **ADJ 1** *(approximatif)* rough, *Péj* crude; **c'est du travail g.** it's shoddy work; **un dessin g.** a rough sketch; **je n'ai qu'une idée grossière de l'endroit où il se trouve** I've only got a rough idea (of) where he is

2 *(peu raffiné)* coarse, rough; **de la toile grossière** coarse linen; **des traits grossiers** coarse features

3 *(impoli)* rude, crude (**envers** to); **il est vraiment g.** he's so rude *or* impolite; **il a été on ne peut plus g.** he was extremely rude; **il est devenu g.** he started using strong language

4 *(vulgaire)* vulgar, uncouth; *(langage, plaisanterie)* coarse, crude; *(plaisirs)* base; **(quel) g. personnage!** what a vulgar individual!; **c'est un esprit g.** he's/she's ignorant, he's/she's a Philistine

5 *(erreur)* gross, stupid; *(ignorance)* gross, crass; **une ruse grossière** a very obvious trick; **les ficelles de l'intrigue sont vraiment grossières** the plot is really obvious

grossièrement [grosjɛrmɑ̃] **ADV 1** *(approximativement)* roughly (speaking); **j'ai évalué g. les frais** I made a rough estimate of the costs; **voilà, g., comment je vois les choses** roughly (speaking), that's how I see things

2 *(sans délicatesse)* roughly; **un visage g. dessiné** a face that has been roughly sketched

3 *(injurieusement)* rudely; **elle m'a parlé g.** she was rude to me; **insulter qn g.** to be insultingly rude to sb

4 *(beaucoup)* **tu te méprends g.** you're grossly *or* wildly mistaken

grossièreté [grosjɛrte] **NF 1** *(impolitesse)* rudeness; **il est d'une incroyable g.** he is incredibly rude

2 *(manque de finesse → d'une personne)* coarseness; *(→ d'une chose)* crudeness, coarseness; **la g. de ses traits** the coarseness of his/her features

3 *(gros mot)* coarse remark; **je me suis retenu pour ne pas lui dire des grossièretés** I had to bite my tongue to avoid swearing at him/her

4 *(obscénité)* rude joke; **il aime raconter des grossièretés** he likes telling rude jokes; **allons, pas de grossièretés!** come on now, keep it clean!

grossir [32] [grosir] **VI** 1 *(prendre du poids → personne)* to put on weight, to get fatter; *(→ animaux, fruits)* to get bigger *or* larger; **elle a beaucoup grossi** she's put on a lot of weight; **j'ai grossi d'un kilo** I've put on a kilo; **ça fait g.** it's fattening

2 *(augmenter)* to grow; *(mer)* to get rough, to rise; *(rivière)* to swell; **la foule grossissait sans cesse** the crowd was constantly getting bigger *or* growing; **les bourgeons grossissent** the buds are swelling; **le bruit grossit** the noise is getting louder

VT 1 *(faire paraître gros)* **ta robe te grossit** your dress makes you look fatter

2 *(augmenter)* to raise, to swell; **des pluies diluviennes ont grossi la rivière** the river has been swollen by torrential rain; **torrent grossi par les pluies** torrent swollen by the rain; **g. le nombre/les rangs des manifestants** to join the growing numbers of demonstrators/swell the ranks of the demonstrators; **g. sa voix pour se faire entendre** to raise one's voice *or* to speak up in order to make oneself heard

3 *(exagérer)* to exaggerate, to overexaggerate; **g. l'importance de qch/le rôle de qn dans une action** to exaggerate the importance of sth/sb's part in an action; **les journaux ont grossi les conséquences de la grève** the newspapers exaggerated *or* magnified the consequences of the strike; **on a grossi l'affaire** the affair was blown up out of all proportion

4 *(à la loupe)* to magnify, to enlarge; **objet grossi trois fois** object magnified three times

grossissant, -e [grosisɑ̃, -ɑ̃t] **ADJ** 1 *(verre)* magnifying 2 *Littéraire (qui s'accroît)* growing, swelling

grossissement [grosismɑ̃] **NM** 1 *(augmentation de taille)* increase in size 2 *(d'une tumeur)* swelling, growth 3 *(avec une loupe)* magnifying 4 *(capacité d'un instrument d'optique)* magnification, magnifying power 5 *(exagération)* exaggeration

grossiste [grosist] **NMF** wholesaler; **g. généraliste** general wholesaler; **g. importateur** import wholesaler

grosso modo [grosomodo] **ADV** roughly, more or less; **g., c'est une comédie** roughly speaking *or* broadly speaking, it's a comedy; **laisse-moi t'expliquer l'histoire g.** let me give you a rough idea of the story

grossoyer [13] [groswaje] **VT** *Jur (document)* to engross

grotesque [grɔtɛsk] **ADJ** 1 *(burlesque)* ridiculous

2 *(absurde)* ridiculous, ludicrous; **ne sois pas g.!** don't be absurd *or* ridiculous!

3 *Beaux-Arts (personnage)* grotesque

NM 1 *Beaux-Arts & Littérature* **le g.** the grotesque

2 *(absurdité)* ludicrousness, preposterousness; **cet homme/cette situation est d'un g.!** the man's/the situation's ludicrous *or* ridiculous!

❑ **grotesques NFPL** *Beaux-Arts* grotesques

grotesquement [grɔtɛskəmɑ̃] **ADV** ludicrously, ridiculously

grotte [grɔt] **NF** 1 *Géol* cave; **g. naturelle/préhistorique** natural/prehistoric cave; **les grottes de Lascaux** the Lascaux Caves 2 *Archit* grotto

'La Grotte de Fingal' *Mendelssohn* 'Fingal's Cave'

grouillant, -e [grujɑ̃, -ɑ̃t] **ADJ** swarming, teeming; **les rues grouillantes de monde** the streets swarming *or* teeming with people; **il y avait une foule grouillante sur la place** the square was teeming with people

grouillement [grujmɑ̃] **NM** swarming; **un g. d'insectes** a swarm of insects; **un g. de vers** a wriggling mass of worms; **le g. de la foule** the bustling *or* milling *or* seething crowd

grouiller [3] [gruje] **VI** 1 *(clients, touristes)* to mill *or* to swarm about; **la foule grouille sur les boulevards** the boulevards are bustling with people; **les vers grouillent sur la viande** the meat is crawling with maggots

2 **g. de** *(être plein de)* to be swarming *or* crawling with; **les rues grouillent de monde** the streets are swarming with people; **la pomme grouillait de vers** the apple was crawling with worms; *Fig* **ce texte grouille de termes techniques** this text is crammed with technical terms; **ce bouquin grouille de bonnes idées** this book is teeming with good ideas; **ça grouille de vie dans tous les nids** all the nests are teeming with life; **il y grouille une foule de jeunes artistes** the place is swarming with young artists

3 *très Fam (se dépêcher)* **allez, grouillez, ça commence dans cinq minutes** come on, get cracking *or* get a move on, it starts in five minutes

4 *Fam Vieilli (bouger)* to move▪

▸**se grouiller VPR** *Fam* to get a move on; **grouille-toi, on est en retard** get a move on, we're late

grouillot [grujo] **NM** 1 *Fam (employé qui fait les courses)* errand boy 2 *Bourse* messenger (boy), runner 3 *TV & Cin* best boy, runner

groundé, -e [grunde] *Can Joual* 1 *Élec Br* earthed▪, *Am* grounded▪ 2 *Fig (qui a les pieds sur terre)* grounded, down to earth; **malgré tout son succès, elle reste pas mal groundée** despite all her success, she's still very grounded *or* down to earth

groupage [grupaʒ] **NM** 1 *Com (de paquets)* bulking; *(de commandes, d'envois, de livraisons)* bundling; **le g. des commandes** bulk ordering

2 *Méd* (blood) grouping

groupal, -e, -aux, -ales [grupal, -o] **ADJ** *Psy* group *(avant n)*, collective; **imaginaire g.** collective imagination

groupe [grup] **NM** 1 *(de gens, d'objets)* group; **ils sont venus par groupes de quatre ou cinq** they came in groups of four or five *or* in fours and fives; **se mettre par groupes de trois** to get into *or* form groups of three; **g. dissident** splinter *or* dissident group; **g. hospitalier** hospital complex; **g. d'intérêt** interest group; **g. scolaire** *(bâtiments)* school complex; *(élèves)* school party; **g. familial** family group; *Pol* **g. marginal** fringe group; **g. parlementaire** parliamentary group; **g. d'âge** age group; *Scol* **g. de niveau** stream; **g. de pression** pressure group; **g. de réflexion** think tank; **g. de rock** rock band *or* group; **g. socio-économique** socio-economic group; **g. de travail** working group *or* party; *Pol* **g. de contact** contact group; **g. d'intervention de la gendarmerie nationale** special task force of the gendarmerie; **G. interministériel de contrôle** interdepartmental regulatory committee; **Groupes islamiques armés** GIA; **le g. de l'Abbaye** = group of artists and writers, including Georges Duhamel and Charles Vildrac, who moved to live and work in Créteil (Paris suburb) in 1906

2 *Écon* group; **les grands groupes de l'édition** the big publishing groups; **g. de détaillants** retailer co-operative; **g. industriel** industrial group; **g. de presse** press consortium *or* group; **g. multimédia** multimedia group, communications conglomerate; *Pol & Écon* **le G. des Sept** the Group of Seven; **le G. des Huit** the Group of Eight; **G. des États d'Afrique, des Caraïbes et du Pacifique** African, Caribbean and Pacific Group of States

3 *Mktg* **g. de consommateurs** consumer group; **g. de prospects** prospect pool; **g. de référence** reference group; **g. suivi** control group; **g. témoin** focus group; **g. test de consommateurs** consumer test group; **g. volontaire** voluntary group

4 *Beaux-Arts* group

5 *Élec* set; **g. électrogène** generator; *Aut* **g. moto-propulseur** powerplant

6 *Ling* **g. consonantique** consonant cluster; **g. de mots** word group; **g. du verbe** *ou* **verbal** verbal group; **g. du nom** *ou* **nominal** nominal group

7 *Math* group

8 *Méd* **g. sanguin** blood group; **quel est votre g. sanguin?** what's your blood group?, what blood group are you?; **g. à risque** risk group

9 *Mil* group; **g. de combat** squad; **demi-g.** section, *Am* half squad; **g. d'artillerie** battery, *Am* battalion; **g. d'intervention** task force; **g. d'aviation** squadron *(of transport aircraft)*

10 *Bot & Zool (classification)* group

11 *Ordinat* **g. de discussion** discussion group; **g. de nouvelles** newsgroup

❑ **de groupe ADJ** group *(avant n)*; **billet de g.** group ticket; **psychologie/psychothérapie de g.** group psychology/therapy

❑ **en groupe ADV** in a group

groupé, -e [grupe] **ADJ** 1 *(commandes, envois, livraisons)* grouped, consolidated 2 *Ordinat* blocked 3 *Sport voir* **saut**

groupe-cible [grupsibl] *(pl* **groupes-cibles)** **NM** target group

groupement [grupmɑ̃] **NM** 1 *(association)* group; **g. d'achat (commercial)** bulk-buying group, purchasing group; **g. agricole d'exploitation en commun** = farm run as a semi-cooperative; **g. de défense des consommateurs** consumers' association; **groupements d'établissements pour la formation continue** = state body organizing adult training programmes; *Écon* **G. européen d'intérêt économique** European Economic Interest Group; **g. d'intérêt économique** economic interest group; **G. intergouvernemental de l'étude du climat** Intergovernmental panel on climate change; **g. de détaillants** retailers' group

2 *(rassemblement)* grouping; *Com & Ind (d'intérêts)* pooling; **g. des enfants d'après l'âge** classification of children by age groups; **on a procédé au g. des commandes** all the orders have been grouped together

3 *Mil* group, formation; **g. d'infanterie** brigade group, *Am* battle group; **g. tactique** task force

grouper [3] [grupe] **VT** 1 *(réunir → personnes)* to group together; *(→ ressources)* to pool; **groupons nos forces** let's pool our resources; **les dépendances groupées autour du corps de ferme** the outbuildings clustered around the main farm building

2 *(classer)* to put *or* to group together; **on peut g. ces articles sous la même rubrique** we can put all these articles together under the same heading

3 *Com (commandes, envois, livraisons)* to consolidate, to group; *(paquets)* to bulk

4 *Méd* to determine the blood group of

5 *Sport* **groupez les genoux sous le menton** bring your knees up to your chin

▸**se grouper VPR** 1 *(dans un lieu)* to gather; **la foule s'est groupée sous le balcon** the crowd gathered under the balcony; **rester groupés** to keep together

2 *(dans une association)* to join together; **nous devons nous g. pour mieux défendre nos droits** we must band together *or* join together to protect our rights; **se g. autour d'un chef** to join forces under one leader

groupe-témoin [gruptemwɛ̃] *(pl* **groupes-témoins)** **NM** *Mktg* focus group, control group, consumer panel

groupeur [grupœr] **NM** *Com* consolidator; **g. de fret aérien** air freight consolidator; **g. maritime** maritime freight consolidator; **g. routier** road haulage consolidator

groupie [grupi] **NMF** *Fam* 1 *(d'un chanteur)* groupie 2 *(inconditionnel)* avid follower▪, groupie

groupusculaire [grupyskylɛr] **ADJ** *(qui tient du groupuscule)* small-scale; **la gauche g.** *(formée de groupuscules)* the small (splinter) groups of the left

groupuscule [grupyskyl] **NM** *Péj Pol* small group; **les groupuscules gauchistes** small left-wing (splinter) groups

grouse [gruz] **NF** *Orn* (red) grouse

Groznyï [grɔzni] **NM** Grozny

gruau [gryo] **NM** 1 **g. (d'avoine)** groats; **farine de g.** fine wheat flour; **pain de g.** fine wheaten bread 2 *Can Culin* porridge

grue [gry] **NF** 1 *Tech* crane; **g. automotrice** motor-driven crane; **g. fixe** fixed *or* stationary crane; **g. à flèche** jib crane; **g. flottante** floating crane; **g. à flotteur** pontoon crane; **g. de levage** wrecking crane; **g. à pivot** revolving crane; **g. à portique** gantry crane; **g. à volée** jib crane; *Rail* **g. d'alimentation** (water) crane

2 *Cin & TV* crane; **g. de prise de vue** camera crane; **g. hydraulique** simon crane

3 *Orn* crane; **g. antigone** sarus crane; **g. blanche américaine** whooping crane; **g. du Canada** sandhill crane; **g. de Numidie** demoiselle crane

4 *très Fam Vieilli (prostituée) Br* tart, *Am* hooker
5 *Fam Vieilli (femme stupide)* silly goose

grugeoir [gryʒwar] **NM** notcher

gruger [17] [gryʒe] **VT 1** *Littéraire (tromper)* to deceive, to swindle; **se faire g.** to get swindled **2** *Tech* to shape the edges of **3** *Fam* **g. la place de qn** *(dans une file d'attente)* to push in in front of sb▪; *Can* **g. l'avance de qn** *(dans un sondage)* to eat into sb's lead

gruiforme [gryifɔrm] **NM** *Orn* crane

grulette [grylɛt] **NF** *Suisse Fam* **avoir la g.** to have the jitters

grume [grym] **NF** trunk, log; **bois en g.** unhewn *or* undressed wood

grumeau, -x [grymo] **NM 1** *(boule)* lump; **plein de grumeaux** lumpy; **sans grumeaux** smooth; **faire des grumeaux** to go lumpy, to form lumps **2 grumeaux de sel** specks of salt

grumeler [24] [grymle] **se grumeler VPR 1** *(sauce)* to go lumpy **2** *(lait)* to curdle, to clot

grumeleux, -euse [grymlø, -øz] **ADJ 1** *(sauce)* lumpy **2** *(lait)* curdled **3** *(peau)* uneven; *(surface)* granular **4** *(fruit)* gritty

grumelle *etc voir* **grumeler**

grumelure [grymlyr] **NF** *Métal* pipe (fault)

grumier [grymje] **NM** timber lorry

gruon [gryɔ̃] **NM** young crane

gruppetto [grupɛto] *(pl* **gruppetti** [-ti]) **NM** *Mus* gruppetto, turn

gruter [3] [gryte] **VT** to raise *or* move with a crane

grutier [grytje] **NM** crane driver *or* operator

gruyère [gryjɛr] **NM g., fromage de g.** Gruyère (cheese); **crème de g.** = processed Gruyère (cheese)

gryphée [grife] **NF** *Zool* gryphaea

GSM [ʒeɛsɛm] **NM** *Tél (abrév* **global system for mobile communications) 1** *(système)* GSM; **réseau G.** GSM network **2** *Belg (téléphone portable) Br* mobile phone, *Am* cellphone

GSS [ʒeɛsɛs] **NF** *Com (abrév* **grande surface spécialisée)** specialist superstore

guacamole [gwakamɔl] **NM** guacamole

guachero [gwatʃɛro] **NM** oilbird

Guadeloupe [gwadlup] **NF la G.** Guadeloupe; **à la** *ou* **en G.** in Guadeloupe

guadeloupéen, -enne [gwadlupeɛ̃, -ɛn] **ADJ** Guadeloupean

❑ **Guadeloupéen, -enne NM,F** Guadeloupean

guai, guais [gɛ] **ADJ M** *Pêche* **hareng guais** shotten herring

guanaco [gwanako] **NM** *Zool* guanaco

Guangzhou [gwangʒu] **NM** Guangzhou

guanine [gwanin] **NF** *Biol & Chim* guanine

guano [gwano] **NM** guano

guarani [gwarani] **NM** *(langue)* Guarani

Guatemala [gwatemala] **NM le G.** Guatemala; **vivre au G.** to live in Guatemala; **aller au G.** to go to Guatemala

guatémaltèque [gwatemaltɛk] **ADJ** Guatemalan

❑ **Guatémaltèque NMF** Guatemalan

Gud, GUD [gyd] **NM** *(abrév* **Groupe union défense)** = extreme right-wing student group

gué [ge] **NM** *(passage)* ford; **passer un ruisseau à g.** to ford a stream; **là, on peut passer à g.** there's a ford there, we can cross there; *Fig* **même son plus fidèle allié l'a abandonné au milieu du g.** even his most faithful ally left him in the lurch; **il a changé d'avocat au milieu du g.** he changed lawyers in midstream; **la nouvelle loi est au milieu du g.** the new law doesn't go far enough

EXCLAM *Arch* **oh g.!** hey nonny no!

guéable [geabl] **ADJ** fordable

guèbre [gɛbr] **NMF** *Rel* Guebre, Gheber

guède [gɛd] **NF** *Bot* woad, pastel

guéer [15] [gee] **VT** to ford

guéguerre [gegɛr] **NF** *Fam* (little) war, squabble; **se faire la g.** to squabble, to bicker; **la g. entre les chefs de service** the squabbling *or* bickering between the heads of department

Gueldre [gɛldrə] **NM** *Géog* Guelderland, Gelderland

guelfe [gɛlf] **ADJ** Guelphic, Guelfic

NMF Guelph, Guelf

guelte [gɛlt] **NF** *Vieilli Com* commission, percentage *(on sales)*

Guenièvre [gənjɛvr] **NPR** *Littérature* Guinever(e)

guenille [gənij] **NF 1** *(vêtements)* **guenilles** rags (and tatters); **être vêtu de guenilles** to be wearing old rags **2** *Littéraire (loque humaine)* wreck **3** *Can (chiffon)* cloth; *(serpillière)* floor cloth; *Fig* **c'est de la g.** it's rubbish

guenilloux, -ouse [gəniju, -uz] *Can Fam* **ADJ 1** *(négligé)* scruffy▪ **2** *(de mauvaise qualité)* cheap▪

NM,F *(personne mal habillée)* scruffy person▪, scruff; *(marchand)* rag dealer▪

guenon [gənɔ̃] **NF 1** *Zool* female monkey, she-monkey **2** *très Fam Péj (femme)* dog, *Br* boot, *Am* beast

guépard [gepar] **NM** cheetah

'Le Guépard' *Visconti* 'The Leopard'

guêpe [gɛp] **NF 1** *Entom* wasp **2** *Vieilli (femme rusée)* **c'est une fine g.** she's very sharp

guêpier [gepje] **NM 1** *(nid de guêpes)* wasp's nest **2** *Fig (situation périlleuse)* sticky situation; **il s'est fourré** *ou* **mis dans un beau g.** he got himself into a sticky situation **3** *Orn* bee-eater

guêpière [gepjɛr] **NF** basque

guère [gɛr] **ADV 1** *(employé avec "ne")* **ne... g.** *(pas beaucoup)* not much; *(pas longtemps)* hardly, scarcely; **il n'est g. aimable** he's not very nice; **je ne suis g. contente de vous** I'm not terribly pleased with you; **je ne l'aime g.** I don't care much for him/her; **je n'aime g. cela** I don't much like that, I don't like that much; **elle n'y voit plus g.** she can hardly see any more; **je n'ai g. dormi** I didn't get much sleep, I hardly slept, I didn't sleep much; **il n'a g. apprécié votre remarque** he didn't appreciate your remark much; **il ne nous en parle g.** he hardly *or* scarcely talks to us about it; **il n'est g. plus aimable qu'elle** he's not much nicer than she is; **il n'y a g. de monde** there's hardly anyone; **il n'a g. d'argent/d'amis** he hasn't much money/many friends; **je n'ai g. de temps libre** I don't have much *or* I hardly have any free time; **je n'en sais g. plus** I hardly know anything more about it, I don't know much more about it; **ça ne durera g. longtemps** it won't last very long; **le beau temps ne dura g.** the fine weather lasted hardly any time at all *or* didn't last very long; **cela ne se dit plus g.** you don't hear that much now, hardly anybody says that now; **il n'en reste plus g.** *(non comptable)* there's hardly any left; *(comptable)* there are hardly any left; **il ne vient g. nous voir** he hardly ever comes to see us; **on ne tarda g. à entendre parler de lui dans les journaux** it wasn't long before he was mentioned in the newspapers; **il n'y a plus g. de noyers dans la région** there are hardly *or* scarcely any walnut trees left in this area; **il n'a g. plus de vingt ans** he is barely *or* scarcely twenty years old; **il ne nous reste g. que deux heures à attendre** we have barely two hours left to wait; **je ne suis plus g. qu'à une heure de Paris** I'm only an hour away from Paris; **il n'y a g. que moi qui m'en soucie** I'm practically the only one who cares about it; **il ne se déplace plus g. qu'avec une canne** he can hardly walk without a stick any more

2 *(dans une réponse)* **aimez-vous l'art abstrait? – g.** do you like abstract art? – not really; **la voyez-vous? – g.!** do you see her? – hardly ever!; **comment allez-vous? – g. mieux** how are you? – not much better *or* hardly any better; **tu as mieux dormi qu'hier? – oh, g. mieux!** did you sleep better than yesterday? – hardly!

guéret [gerɛ] **NM** *(non ensemencé)* fallow land; *(non labouré)* balk

guéréza [gereza] **NM** *Zool* guereza

guéri, -e [geri] **ADJ** cured (**de** of); *(rétabli)* better, recovered; **elle est guérie de sa rougeole** she's cured of *or* recovered from her measles; *Fig* **être g. d'une peur/d'un préjugé** to be cured of a fear/a prejudice; **il est g. de sa timidité** he is cured of *or* he has got over his shyness; **l'amour, il en est g.!** you won't catch him falling in love again!; **elle est guérie de l'amour** she's got over being in love; **je ne pense plus à lui, je suis guérie** I don't think of him any more, I've got over him

guéridon [geridɔ̃] **NM** *(table)* occasional table

guérilla [gerija] **NF 1** *(guerre)* guerrilla warfare; *Com* guerrilla attack; **g. urbaine** urban guerrilla warfare; **la g. parlementaire de l'opposition** the guerrilla tactics employed by the opposition in parliament **2** *(soldats)* group of guerrillas, guerrilla unit

guérillero [gerijero] **NM** guerrilla

guérir [32] [gerir] **VT 1** *Méd (malade, maladie)* to cure; *(blessure)* to heal; **g. un malade de son cancer** to cure a patient of his cancer

2 *Fig* **g. qn d'une habitude** to cure *or* break sb of a habit; **il saura g. ta timidité** he'll know how to cure *or* to help you get rid of your shyness; **je vais le g. de cette manie** I'll cure him of that habit; **le temps seul guérit les grands chagrins** only time can heal deep grief

VI 1 *Méd (convalescent)* to recover, to be cured; **il n'en guérira pas** he won't recover from it

2 *(blessure)* to heal, to mend; **son épaule guérit lentement** his/her shoulder is healing *or* mending slowly; **un chagrin qui ne guérit pas** an incurable grief, a grief that cannot be cured

3 *Fig* **il n'en guérira pas** he won't get over it

▸**se guérir VPR 1** *(malade)* to cure oneself; **il s'est guéri grâce à l'homéopathie** he cured himself thanks to homeopathy

2 *(maladie)* **est-ce que ça se guérit facilement?** is it easy to cure?

3 se g. de qch *(timidité, habitude)* to cure oneself of sth; **il ne s'est jamais guéri de sa jalousie** he never got over his jealousy

guérison [gerizɔ̃] **NF 1** *Méd (d'un patient)* recovery; *(d'une blessure)* healing; **il est maintenant en voie de g.** he's now on the road to recovery; **attends la g. complète avant de sortir** wait until you are completely recovered before going out **2** *Fig* **la g. sera lente après une telle déception** it'll take a long time to get over such a disappointment

guérissable [gerisabl] **ADJ 1** *Méd (patient, mal)* curable; *(blessure)* that can be healed **2** *Fig* **son chagrin n'est pas g.** there is no cure for his/her sorrow

guérisseur, -euse [gerisœr, -øz] **NM,F** healer, *Péj* quack

NM *(d'une tribu)* medicine man

guérite [gerit] **NF 1** *(sur un chantier)* site office **2** *Mil* sentry box

guerlot [gɛrlo] *Can Fam* **ADJ M 1** *(fou)* crazy▪, nuts **2** *(un peu ivre)* tipsy, merry; *(ivre) Br* pissed, *Am* bombed

NM *(idiot) Br* nutter, *Am* screwball

Guernesey [gɛrnəzɛ] **NF** Guernsey; **vivre à G.** to live on Guernsey; **aller à G.** to go to Guernsey

guernesiais, -e [gɛrnəzjɛ, -ɛz] **ADJ** of/from Guernsey, Guernsey *(avant n)*

❑ **Guernesiais, -e NM,F** = inhabitant of or person from Guernsey

Guernica [gɛrnika] **NM** *Beaux-Arts & Géog* Guernica

guerre [gɛr] **NF 1** *(conflit)* war; **en temps de g.** in wartime; **être en g. (contre)** to be at war (with); **pays en g.** country at war; **des pays en g.** countries at war, warring countries; **faire la g. (à)** to wage war (against); *Fig* to battle (with); **il a fait la g. en Europe** he was in the war in Europe; **faire la g. aux inégalités** to wage war on inequality; **je fais la g. aux moustiques/fumeurs** I've declared war on mosquitoes/smokers; **elle lui fait la g. pour qu'il mange plus lentement** she's always (nagging) on at him to eat more slowly; *Fam* **mes chaussures/gants ont fait la g.** my shoes/gloves have been in the wars; **partir en g. (contre)** to go to war (against); *Fig* to launch an attack (on); *Fig* **partir en g. contre la drogue/l'injustice** to declare war on drugs/injustice; **entrer** *ou* **se mettre en g. (contre)** to go to war (with); **déclarer la g. (à)** to declare war (against *or* on); **la g. a éclaté entre...** war has broken out between...; **on entre dans une logique de g.** war is the only logical outcome; **maintenant, entre Jeanne et moi, c'est la g.** Jeanne and I are at each other's throats all the time now; *Fam* **à la g. comme à la g.** well, you just have to make the best of things; *Prov* **c'est de bonne g.** all's fair in love and war; **de g. lasse, je l'ai laissé sortir** in the end I let him go out, just to have some peace (and

quiet); **crime de g.** war crime; **g. aérienne** air war; **g. atomique** atomic war; **la g. de Cent Ans** the Hundred Years War; **g. civile** civil war; *Écon* **g. commerciale** trade war; **la g. de Corée** the Korean War; **la g. de Crimée** the Crimean War; **g. des Deux-Roses** War of the Roses; **g. d'embuscade** guerrilla war; **la g. des étoiles** Star Wars; **la g. franco-allemande** the Franco-Prussian War; **la g. froide** the cold war; **g. des gangs** gang warfare; **la g. du Golfe** the Gulf War; **la g. d'Indochine** the first Indo-Chinese War *(1946–1954)*; **la g. du Kippour** the Yom Kippur War; **g. larvée** undeclared war; **g. mondiale** world war; *Fig* **g. des nerfs** war of nerves; **g. nucléaire** nuclear war; **g. à outrance** all-out war; **g. ouverte** open war; **g. préventive** pre-emptive *or* preventive war; **g. des prix** price war; **g. de religion** war of religion; **g. sainte** Holy War; **la g. de Sécession** the American Civil War; **la g. des sexes** the battle of the sexes; **la g. des Six Jours** the Six-Day War; **la g. de 70** the Franco-Prussian War; **g. des tarifs** price war; **g. totale** total war; **g. de Trente Ans** Thirty Years' War; **la g. de Troie** the Trojan War; **g. d'usure** war of attrition; **g. zéro-mort** casualty-free war; **la Grande G., la Première G. (mondiale), la g. de 14** the Great War, the First World War, World War I; **la Seconde G. mondiale, la g. de 40** World War II, the Second World War

2 *(technique)* warfare; **g. asymétrique** asymmetric warfare; **g. atomique** atomic warfare; **g. bactériologique** germ warfare; **g. biologique** biological warfare; **g. chimique** chemical warfare; **g. conventionnelle** conventional warfare; **g. éclair** blitzkrieg; **g. économique** economic warfare; **g. électronique** electronic warfare; **g. des ondes** radio propaganda warfare; **g. de positions** static warfare; **la g. presse-bouton** push-button warfare; **g. psychologique** psychological warfare; **g. de tranchées** trench warfare

'Guerre et paix' *Tolstoï* 'War and Peace'

'La Guerre des étoiles' *Lucas* 'Star Wars'

'La Guerre de Troie n'aura pas lieu' *Giraudoux* 'Tiger at the Gates'

'La Guerre sans nom' *Tavernier* 'The Undeclared War'

'La Guerre des Mondes' *Wells, Spielberg* 'War of the Worlds'

guerrier, -ère [gɛrje, -ɛr] ADJ *(peuple)* warlike; **un chant g.** a battle song *or* chant; **une danse guerrière** a war dance; **être d'humeur guerrière** to be in a belligerent mood

NM warrior

guerroyer [13] [gɛrwaje] VI to (wage) war (**contre** against); *Fig* **g. contre l'inégalité/l'hypocrisie** to struggle against *or* wage war on inequality/hypocrisy

guet [gɛ] NM 1 *(action)* watch; **faire le g.** to be on the lookout; **poste de g.** lookout post 2 *Hist (patrouille)* watch

guetali [getali] NM *(à la Réunion)* garden veranda

guet-apens [gɛtapɑ̃] *(pl* **guets-apens** [gɛtapɑ̃]) NM ambush, trap; **tendre un g. à qn** to set a trap *or* an ambush for sb; **tomber dans un g.** to fall into a trap, to be ambushed; **c'était un g.** it was a trap

guète [gɛt] = **guette**

guêtre [gɛtr] NF 1 *(bande de cuir)* gaiter; *Fam* **traîner ses guêtres** to wander about *or* around■ 2 *(en tricot)* leggings 3 *Belg (locutions)* **il a la police à ses guêtres** the police are after him, the police are on his tail *or* hot on his heels; **avoir qch à ses guêtres** to get the blame *or* be blamed for sth

guêtrer [3] [getre] VT to gaiter, to put gaiters on

▸**se guêtrer** VPR to put on one's gaiters

guêtron [gɛtrɔ̃] NM short gaiter, spat

guette [gɛt] NF *Hist* 1 *(tourelle)* watchtower 2 *(trompette)* alarum (trumpet)

guetter [4] [gete] VT 1 *(surveiller)* to watch; **il guette chacun de ses mouvements** he studies his/her every move

2 *Fig (menacer)* **la mort le guette** death is lying in wait for him; **l'embonpoint te guette** you need to watch your weight; **l'infarctus la guette** she's liable to have a heart attack; **les ennuis la guettent** there's trouble in store for her; **le surmenage/la dépression le guette** overwork/depression will get him in the end

3 *(attendre)* to watch out for; **le chat guette la souris** the cat is watching for the mouse; **le guépard guettait sa proie** the cheetah was lying in wait for its prey; **il guette le facteur** he is on the lookout for the postman; **g. l'arrivée/la sortie/le passage de qn** to watch out for sb arriving/leaving/going past; **g. l'occasion propice** to watch out for the right opportunity

USAGE ABSOLU *(surveiller)* **tu vas g. pendant qu'on entre** you keep watch while we go in

guetteur, -euse [getœr, -øz] NM 1 *Mil* lookout; *Hist* watch, watchman 2 *(gén)* lookout

gueulante [gœlɑ̃t] NF *très Fam* **pousser une g.** to kick up a stink, to hit the *Br* roof *or Am* ceiling

gueulard, -e [gœlar, -ard] ADJ 1 *très Fam (personne)* loud, loudmouthed; *(radio, chanson)* bawling, noisy■ 2 *Fam (gourmand)* greedy■ 3 *très Fam (couleur)* loud

NM,F 1 *très Fam (adulte)* loudmouth; *(bébé)* bawler 2 *Fam (gourmand)* greedy guts

NM 1 *Métal* (blast furnace) throat *or* shaft 2 *Naut* loudhailer

gueule [gœl] NF 1 *très Fam (bouche) Br* gob, *Am* yap; **un whisky/curry qui emporte** *ou* **arrache la g.** a whisky/curry that takes the roof off your mouth; **s'en mettre plein la g.** to make a pig of oneself; **se soûler** *ou* **se bourrer la g.** to get *Br* pissed *or Am* juiced; **pousser un coup de g.** to yell out■; **c'est une grande g.** *ou* **un fort en g.** he's a big mouth *or* a loudmouth, he's always shooting his mouth off; **il faut toujours qu'il ouvre sa grande g.!** he always has to open his big mouth!; **(ferme) ta g.!** shut your mouth *or* trap!; **vos gueules!** shut up(, you lot)!

2 *très Fam (visage)* mug, face■; **avoir une sale g.** *(être moche)* to have an ugly mug; *(avoir mauvaise mine)* to look rotten; *(avoir l'air déprimé)* to look down in the mouth; **il va faire une sale g. quand il saura la vérité** he's going to be mad *or* livid when he finds out the truth; **bien fait pour ta sale g.!** (it) serves you damn well right!; **je te pète la g.!** I'll smash your face in!; **sa g. ne me revient pas** I don't like the look of him/her; **t'aurais vu sa g.!** you should have seen his/her face!; **avoir** *ou* **faire une drôle de g.** to look funny *or* weird; **avoir une belle g.** to have a pretty face; **faire la g.** to sulk; **faire la g. à qn** to be in a huff *or* a bad mood with sb; **il nous fait la g. depuis notre arrivée** he's been in a huff *or* in a bad mood with us ever since we arrived; **faire une g. d'enterrement** to look thoroughly depressed; **elle a fait une de ces gueules en trouvant la porte fermée!** you should have seen her face when she saw the door was shut!; **se foutre de** *ou* **se payer la g. de qn** to take the piss out of sb; **(s')en prendre plein la g.** *(se faire insulter)* to get a right mouthful (of abuse); *(se faire frapper)* to get one's face smashed in; *(se faire critiquer)* to get torn to pieces; **g. cassée** World War I veteran *(with bad facial injuries)*■; **g. noire** miner■; **g. de raie** fish face

3 *Fam (apparence)* **ce fromage a une bonne g.** I like the look of this cheese■; **cette pizza a une sale g.** that pizza looks gross *or Br* minging

4 *très Fam (charme)* **elle n'est pas belle, mais elle a de la g.** she's not beautiful, but she's got something about her; **il a de la g., ce type** that guy's really got something; **ce tableau a de la g.** that's some picture; **leur maison a vraiment de la g.** their house really has got style

5 *(d'un animal)* mouth; **se jeter dans la g. du loup** to throw oneself into the lion's mouth *or* jaws

6 *(d'un canon, d'un fusil)* muzzle; *(d'un four)* mouth

▫ **gueule de bois** NF *Fam* hangover; **se réveiller avec/avoir la g. de bois** to wake up with/have a hangover

gueule-de-loup [gœldəlu] *(pl* **gueules-de-loup**) NF 1 *Bot* snapdragon 2 *Constr* (chimney) cowl, chimney jack 3 *(de machine)* (exhaust) muffler

gueulement [gœlmɑ̃] NM *Fam* bawl, yell; **pousser des gueulements** to yell, to bawl

gueuler [5] [gœle] *Fam* VI 1 *(personne → de colère)* to shout■; *(→ de douleur)* to yell out; *(protester)* to kick up a fuss; **arrête de g., on va t'aider** stop shouting, we're going to help you■; **quand il a su ça, il a gueulé** when he found out he blew his top *or* he hit the roof; **si je suis en retard, ça va g. à la maison** if I'm late I'll get bawled out at home; **faudrait g.!** we should kick up a fuss!; **g. sur qn** to shout at sb; **g. comme un putois** to shout one's head off

2 *(radio, haut-parleur)* to blare out; **faire g. sa radio** to turn one's radio up full blast

3 *(chien)* to howl■

VT *(chanson, ordres)* to bellow out, to bawl out; **g. qn** to bawl sb out, to roar at sb

gueules [gœl] NM *Hér* gules

gueuleton [gœltɔ̃] NM *Fam (repas)* blowout, *Br* nosh-up; **faire un bon petit g. entre amis** to have a good blowout with some friends

gueuletonner [3] [gœltɔne] VI *Fam* to have a blowout, *Br* to have a nosh-up

gueuse [gøz] NF 1 *voir* **gueux** 2 *(bière)* = **gueuze**

gueuser [5] [gøze] *Fam Vieilli* VT **g. son pain** to beg for *or* to cadge one's bread

VI to beg■, to be a beggar■

gueuserie [gøzri] NF *Arch ou Littéraire* 1 *(état)* beggary *(UNCOUNT)* 2 *(action)* foul deed

gueux, -euse [gø, gøz] NM,F *Arch ou Littéraire* 1 *(mendiant)* beggar; **les g.** the wretched 2 *(fripon)* rascal, rogue

▫ **gueuse** NF 1 *Métal* pig (mould) 2 *Arch ou Littéraire (femme de mauvaise vie)* harlot, strumpet 3 *Hist* **la Gueuse** = name given to the French Republic by Royalists during the Third Republic

gueuze [gøz] NF gueuze *(variety of strong Belgian beer)*

guèze [gɛz] NM *Ling* Ethiopic

gugusse [gygys] NM *Fam* clown; **faire le g.** to fool around

gui [gi] NM 1 *Bot* mistletoe; **boules de g.** clumps of mistletoe 2 *Naut* boom

guib [gib] NM *Zool* bushbuck

guibolle, guibole [gibɔl] NF *très Fam Br* pin, *Am* gam; **j'en ai plein les guibolles** my legs have had it; *Vieilli* **jouer des guibolles** to stir one's stumps

guibre [gibr] NF *Hist & Naut (pour attacher le beaupré)* cutwater, knee of the (ship's) head

guiche [giʃ] NF *(mèche de cheveux) Br* kiss curl, *Am* spit curl

guichet [giʃɛ] NM 1 *(d'une banque)* counter; *(d'un théâtre)* ticket office; *(d'une poste)* counter, window; **allez au g. numéro 2 pour les renseignements** go to window *or* position number 2 for information; **g. fermé** *(dans une banque, à la poste)* position closed; **g. automatique (de banque)** *Br* cashpoint, *Am* ATM, automated teller machine; **jouer à guichets fermés** to play to packed houses; **on joue à guichets fermés** the performance is sold out

2 *(porte)* hatch, wicket

3 *(judas)* judas; *(d'un confessionnal)* shutter

4 *Sport (en cricket)* wicket; **gardien de g.** wicketkeeper

guichetier, -ère [giʃtje, -ɛr] NM,F *(de gare)* ticket clerk; *(de poste, de banque)* counter clerk, teller

guidage [gidaʒ] NM 1 *Tech (d'une pièce mobile)* guiding; *(sur un tour de forage)* centring; *Aut* steering; **système de g.** guiding system 2 *Électron (d'un avion)* guidance; **tête de g.** homing head; **g. par radio-maillage** *ou* **par radio-mailles** grid guidance; **g. de missile** missile guidance *or* tracking

guidance [gidɑ̃s] NF guidance; **centre de g.** child guidance clinic

guide [gid] NMF 1 *(personne)* guide, leader; *(pour touristes)* (tour) guide; **g. (de haute montagne)** mountain guide

2 *(principe)* guiding principle

3 *(livre)* guidebook; **G. Bleu** = detailed tourist guide; **g. de conversation** phrase book; **g. gastronomique** restaurant guide, good food guide; **g. touristique** guidebook; *Ordinat* **g. de l'utilisateur** instruction manual; **G. Vert** Michelin guide

4 *Tél* **g. d'ondes** (wave) guide; **g. d'ondes optiques** fibre optics system

5 *Aut* **g. chaîne** chain guide; *Tech* **g. de courroie** belt guide

6 *Typ* **g. de caractères** type book; **g. du style maison** stylebook, style guide

7 *Belg* (indicateur de chemin de fer) railway timetable; (annuaire) telephone book

NF 1 (scout) *Br* girl guide, *Am* girl scout; **g. aînée** ranger

2 (rêne) rein

guide-âne [gidan] (*pl* **guide-ânes**) **NM** *Vieilli* (basic) handbook

guideau, -x [gido] **NM 1** *Pêche* kiddle **2** (barrage) guide vane

guide-bande [gidbãd] (*pl* **guide-bandes**) **NM** tape guide

guide-classement [gidklasmã] (*pl* **guide-classements**) **NM** file divider

guide-conférencier, -ère [gidkɔ̃ferãsje, -ɛr] (*mpl* **guides-conférenciers**, *fpl* **guides-conférencières**) **NM,F** guide

guide-fil [gidfil] (*pl* **guide-fils**) **NM 1** *Tex* thread guide **2** (de planche à repasser) cord loop *or* guide

guide-interprète [gidɛ̃tɛrprɛt] (*pl* **guides-interprètes**) **NMF** bilingual tour guide

guide-lame [gidlam] **NM INV 1** (d'une faucheuse) blade guide **2** (d'une scie à ruban) fence

guide-papier [gidpapje] (*pl* **guide-papiers**) **NM** (d'une imprimante) paper guide

guider [3] [gide] **VT 1** (diriger) to guide; **le chien guide l'aveugle** the dog is guiding the blind man; **g. un avion par radar** to guide an aircraft by radar; **guidé par radio** radio-controlled **2** (conseiller) to guide; **guidée par son expérience** guided by his/her experience; **se laisser g. par son intuition** to be guided by one's intuition; **seul le profit le guide** he is guided only by profit; **nous sommes là pour vous g. dans vos recherches** we're here to help you find what you're looking for; **j'ai besoin d'être guidé** I need some guidance

▶**se guider** **VPR** **il s'est guidé sur le soleil** he used the sun as a guide; **il s'est guidé sur l'exemple de son maître** he modelled himself on his master

guiderope [gidrɔp] **NM** *Aviat* trail rope, drag

guide-ruban [gidrybã] (*pl* **guide-rubans**) **NM** (d'une imprimante) ribbon guide

guide-sortie [gidsɔrti] (*pl* **guide-sorties**) **NM** *Ordinat* (d'une fiche) file extraction marker

guidon [gidɔ̃] **NM 1** (d'un vélo) handlebars; *Fig* **avoir la tête** *ou* **le nez dans le g.** to have one's nose to the ground; **moustaches en g. de bicyclette** handlebar moustache **2** *Mil & Naut* (pavillon) guidon **3** (d'une arme à feu) foresight

guidoune [gidun] **NF** *Can Fam* tart, slapper

guifette [gifɛt] **NF** *Orn* tern; **g. à ailes blanches** white-winged black tern; **g. épouvantail** black tern; **g. à moustaches** whiskered tern; **g. noire** black tern

guignard, -e [giɲar, -ard] **ADJ** *Fam* (malchanceux) jinxed, unlucky▪

guigne¹ [giɲ] **NF** *Bot* sweet cherry; **se soucier de qn/qch comme d'une g.** not to give a fig about sb/sth

guigne² [giɲ] **NF** *Fam* (malchance) bad luck▪; **il porte la g. à toute sa famille** he's the bane of his family; **avoir la g.** to be jinxed, to have rotten luck

guigner [3] [giɲe] **VT** to sneak a look at; *Fig* **il guigne l'argent de son oncle depuis des années** he has had his eye on his uncle's money for years; *Cartes* **g. le jeu du voisin** to sneak a look at one's opponent's hand

guignette [giɲɛt] **NF 1** (petite serpe) billhook **2** *Naut* (outil) caulking iron **3** (mollusque) periwinkle, winkle

guignier [giɲje] **NM** gean

guignol [giɲɔl] **NM 1** (pantin) (glove) puppet; (théâtre) puppet theatre; (spectacle) ≃ Punch and Judy show; **on va au g.** ≃ we're off to see Punch and Judy

2 *Fam Fig* clown, joker; **faire le g.** to clown around, to play the fool; **ce nouveau ministre est un g.** that new minister is a (real) clown ▫ **Guignol NPR** (Mister) Punch; *TV* **les Guignols**

(de l'info) = satirical television programme featuring latex puppets representing political figures and celebrities

guignolade [giɲɔlad] **NF** (situation grotesque) farcical situation, farce; (farce) trick; **il faudrait qu'ils arrêtent leurs guignolades** they should stop their nonsense *or* stop fooling around

guignolée [giɲɔle] **NF** *Can* = Christmas charity collection to help the poor

guignolet [giɲɔlɛ] **NM** = liqueur made from cherries

guignon [giɲɔ̃] **NM** *Fam Vieilli* bad luck▪

guilde [gild] **NF 1** (club) club **2** *Hist* guild

guili-guili [giligili] **NM INV** (en langage enfantin) tickle; **faire g. à qn** to tickle sb

Guillaume [gijom] **NPR G. le Conquérant** William the Conqueror; **G. d'Orange** William of Orange; **G. le Roux** William Rufus; **G. Tell** William Tell

guillaume [gijom] **NM** *Menuis* rabbet plane; **g. à onglet** mitre plane

guilledou [gijdu] *voir* **courir**

guillemet [gijmɛ] **NM** quotation mark, *Br* inverted comma; **ouvrir/fermer les guillemets** to open/to close (the) quotation marks *or Br* inverted commas; **ouvrez/fermez les guillemets** (en dictant) quote/unquote, open/close quotation marks *or Br* inverted commas; **entre guillemets** in quotation marks, in quotes, *Br* in inverted commas; **tu connais son sens de la "justice", entre guillemets** you know his/her so-called sense of justice; *Typ* **guillemets fermants** closing quote marks; *Typ* **guillemets ouvrants** opening quote marks; *Typ* **guillemets simples** single quotes

guillemeter [27] [gijmete] **VT** to put in quotation marks *or Br* inverted commas

guillemot [gijmo] **NM** *Orn* guillemot; **g. à miroir blanc** black guillemot

guilleret, -ette [gijrɛ, -ɛt] **ADJ 1** (gai) jolly, cheerful; **d'un air g.** jauntily **2** (léger → plaisanterie) risqué

guillochage [gijɔʃaʒ] **NM** (processus) ornamenting with guilloche, guilloching; (résultat) guilloche (pattern)

guilloche [gijɔʃ] **NF** graver (for guilloche work)

guillocher [3] [gijɔʃe] **VT** to guilloche, to ornament with guilloches

guillochis [gijɔʃi] **NM** guilloche (pattern)

guillochure [gijɔʃyr] **NF** guilloche (pattern)

guillon [gijɔ̃] **NM** *Suisse* spigot

guillotine [gijɔtin] **NF** guillotine; **aller à la g.** to go to the guillotine

guillotiné, -e [gijɔtine] **ADJ** guillotined **NM,F** guillotined person

guillotiner [3] [gijɔtine] **VT** to guillotine

guillotineur [gijɔtinœr] **NM** guillotiner

guimauve [gimov] **NF 1** *Bot & Culin* marshmallow; **g. rose** hollyhock **2** *Fig Péj* **ses chansons, c'est de la g.** his/her songs are all soppy *or* schmaltzy

guimbarde [gɛ̃bard] **NF 1** *Fam* (voiture) jalopy, *Br* (old) banger **2** *Mus* Jew's-harp **3** (outil) router plane, grooving plane

Guimet [gimɛ] **NM** **le musée G.** = museum of Far Eastern art in Paris

guimpe [gɛ̃p] **NF 1** (chemisier) chemisette **2** (d'une religieuse) wimple

guincher [3] [gɛ̃ʃe] **VI** *Fam Vieilli* to bop, to dance▪

guindage [gɛ̃daʒ] **NM** lifting, hoisting

guindaille [gɛ̃daj] **NF** *Belg Fam* student party▪

guindailler [3] [gɛ̃daje] **VI** *Belg Fam* to attend a student party▪

guindailleur, -euse [gɛ̃dajœr, -øz] **NM,F** *Belg Fam* fast-living student

guindant [gɛ̃dã] **NM** *Naut* hoist

guindé, -e [gɛ̃de] **ADJ** (personne) stiff, starchy; (discours) stilted; (atmosphère) strained; (langage) affected; (style) stilted, stiff; (réception) posh; **d'un air g.** starchily, stiffly; **prendre un ton g.** to speak in a stilted manner

guindeau, -x [gɛ̃do] **NM** *Naut* windlass

guinder [3] [gɛ̃de] **VT 1** (personne) **son costume le guinde** he looks very stiff and starchy in that suit **2** *Tech* to hoist; *Naut* (mât) to send up, to sway up

▶**se guinder** **VPR** (personne, ambiance) to become stiff; (style) to become stilted *or* stiff

guinderesse [gɛ̃drɛs] **NF** *Naut* mast *or* top rope

Guinée [gine] **NF** **la G.** Guinea; **vivre en G.** to live

in Guinea; **aller en G.** to go to Guinea; **la G.-Bissau** Guinea-Bissau; **la G.-Équatoriale** Equatorial Guinea

guinée [gine] **NF** (monnaie) guinea

guinéen, -enne [gineɛ̃, -ɛn] **ADJ** Guinean ▫ **Guinéen, -enne NM,F** Guinean

guingois [gɛ̃gwa] **de guingois ADJ l'affiche est de g.** the poster is lopsided **ADV marcher de g.** to walk lopsidedly; *Fig* **aller de g.** to go haywire

guinguette [gɛ̃gɛt] **NF** = open-air café *or* restaurant with dance floor

guipage [gipaʒ] **NM 1** *Tex* covering **2** *Élec* insulating, binding

guiper [3] [gipe] **VT 1** *Tex* to cover (with silk, cotton etc) **2** *Élec* to insulate with material

guipon [gipɔ̃] **NM** *Naut* tar brush *or* mop, pitch mop

guipure [gipyr] **NF 1** *Tex* guipure (lace) **2** *Littéraire* (givre) tracery

guirlande [girlãd] **NF 1** (de fleurs) garland; **des guirlandes de chèvrefeuille** garlands of honeysuckle

2 (de papier) paper chain *or* garland; **g. de Noël** (length of) tinsel (UNCOUNT)

3 (de lumières) **g. électrique** (de Noël) Christmas tree lights, fairy lights; (pour une fête) fairy lights; **g. lumineuse** string of lights

4 (de personnes) string; **une g. de danseurs** a string *or* chain of dancers

5 *Ordinat* **connecté en g.** in a token ring configuration

guisarme [gɥizarm] **NF** *Hist* guisarme

guise [giz] **à ma/ta**/etc **guise ADV** as I/you/etc please; **il n'en fait qu'à sa g.** he just does as he pleases *or* likes ▫ **en guise de PRÉP** by way of; **en g. de dîner, nous n'avons eu qu'un peu de soupe** for dinner, we just had a little soup

guitare [gitar] **NF 1** *Mus* guitar; **avec Christophe Banti à la g.** with Christophe Banti on guitar; **g. basse** bass guitar; **g. classique** classical guitar; **g. électrique** electric guitar; **g. hawaïenne** Hawaiian guitar; **g. sèche** acoustic guitar **2** *Ich* **g. de mer** guitarfish

guitariste [gitarist] **NMF** guitar player, guitarist

guitoune [gitun] **NF 1** *Fam* (tente) tent▪ **2** *Fam Arg mil* dugout▪, shelter▪

guivre [givr] **NF** *Hér* serpent devouring a babe

guivré, -e [givre] **ADJ** *Hér* bearing a "guivre"

Guizèh [gize] = **Gizeh**

gulden [guldɛn] **NM** guilder

Gulf Stream [gœlfstrim] **NM** **le G.** the Gulf Stream

gummifère [gɔmifɛr] **ADJ** *Bot* gummiferous, gum-bearing, gum-yielding

gunitage [gynitaʒ] **NM** *Constr* guniting

gunite [gynit] **NF** *Constr* gunite

guniter [3] [gynite] **VT** *Constr* to gunite

günz [gynz] **NM** *Géol* Günz

guppy [gypi] **NM** *Ich* guppy

guru [guru] = **gourou**

gus, gusse [gys] **NM** *Fam* guy, *Br* bloke

gustatif, -ive [gystatif, -iv] **ADJ** gustatory, gustative

gustation [gystasjɔ̃] **NF** tasting, *Spéc* gustation

gustative [gystativ] *voir* **gustatif**

Gustave [gystav] **NPR** (roi) Gustav; **G. Adolphe** Gustavus Adolphus

gutta-percha [gytapɛrka] (*pl* **guttas-perchas**) **NF** gutta-percha

guttiféracée [gytiferase] *Bot* **NF** member of the Guttiferae family ▫ **guttiféracées NFPL** Guttiferae

guttifères [gytifɛr] **NMPL** *Bot* Guttiferae

guttural, -e, -aux, -ales [gytyral, -o] **ADJ 1** (ton) guttural; (voix) guttural, throaty; *Anat* **artère gutturale** carotid artery **2** *Ling* guttural ▫ **gutturale NF** *Ling* guttural

Guyana [gɥijana] **NF** *ou* **NM** **la** *ou* **le G.** Guyana; **vivre en G.** to live in Guyana; **aller en G.** to go to Guyana

guyanais, -e [gɥijanɛ, -ɛz] **ADJ 1** (région, département) Guianese, Guianian **2** (république) Guyanan, Guyanese ▫ **Guyanais, -e NM,F 1** (région, département) Guianese, Guianian; **les G.** the Guianese, the Guianians **2** (république) Guyanan, Guyanese; **les G.** the Guyanans, the Guyanese

Guyane [gɥijan] **NF** **la G., les Guyanes** Guiana,

the Guianas; **la G. française** French Guiana; **vivre en G.** to live in Guiana; **aller en G.** to go to Guiana; **la G. hollandaise** Dutch Guiana; *Hist* **la G. britannique** British Guiana

Guyenne [gɥijɛn]**NF la G.** Guyenne, Guienne

guyot¹ [gɥijo]**NM** *Géog* guyot

guyot² [gɥijo]**NF** *Bot* guyot pear

guzla [guzla]**NF** *Mus* gusla, gusle

gym [ʒim] **NF** *(à l'école)* PE; *(pour adultes)* gym; **aller à la g.** *(gén)* to go to gym class; *(à l'école)* to go to PE (class); **faire de la g.** to do exercises; **un cours de g.** a gym class

gymkhana [ʒimkana]**NM 1** *Sport* rally; **g. motocycliste** motorcycle rally, *Br* scramble **2** *Fam Fig* obstacle course▪

gymnase [ʒimnaz]**NM 1** *(salle)* gym, gymnasium **2** *Suisse (lycée)* = state school attended by pupils between ages of 15 and 19, *Br* ≃ secondary school, *Am* ≃ high school

gymnasial, -e, -aux, -ales [ʒimnazjal, -o] **ADJ** *Suisse Br* ≃ secondary school *(avant n)*, *Am* ≃ high school *(avant n)*

gymnaste [ʒimnast]**NMF** gymnast

gymnastique [ʒimnastik] **NF 1** *Sport* physical education, gymnastics *(singulier)*; **professeur de g.** gymnastics *or* PE teacher; **faire de la g.** to do exercises; **faire sa g. matinale** to do one's morning exercises; **g. corrective** remedial gymnastics; **g. respiratoire** breathing exercises; **g. rythmique** rhythmic gymnastics; **au pas (de) g.** at a jog trot

2 *Fig* gymnastics *(singulier)*; **g. mentale** *ou* **intellectuelle** mental gymnastics; **il faut faire toute une g. pour sortir de cette auto** you have to be a contortionist to get out of this car; **ça a été toute une g. pour obtenir des billets** getting tickets was a real hassle

gymnique [ʒimnik]**ADJ** gymnastic

gymnocarpe [ʒimnɔkarp]**ADJ** *Bot* gymnocarpous

gymnosperme [ʒimnɔspɛrm] *Bot* **NF** gymnosperm

❑ **gymnospermes** **NFPL** gymnosperms, *Spéc* member of the Gymnospermae

gymnote [ʒimnɔt] **NM** *Ich* electric eel, *Spéc* gymnotus

gynandre [ʒinãndr]**ADJ** *Bot* gynandrous

gynandromorphisme [ʒinãdrɔmɔrfism] **NM** *Entom* gynandromorphism

gynécée [ʒinese] **NM 1** *Antiq* gynaeceum **2** *Bot* gynoecium

gynéco [ʒineko] **NMF** *Fam (abrév* **gynécologue***)* gynaecologist▪

gynécologie [ʒinekɔlɔʒi]**NF** gynaecology

gynécologique [ʒinekɔlɔʒik]**ADJ** gynaecological

gynécologue [ʒinekɔlɔg]**NMF** gynaecologist

gynécomastie [ʒinekɔmasti] **NF** *Méd* gynaecomastia

gynérium [ʒinerjɔm]**NM** *Bot* pampas grass

gynodioïque [ʒinodiɔik]**ADJ** *Bot* gynodioecious

gypaète [ʒipaɛt] **NM** *Orn* **g. barbu** lammergeier, bearded vulture

gyps [ʒi]**NM** *Suisse* plaster

gypse [ʒips]**NM** gypsum

gypserie [ʒipsœri]**NF** *Archit* (decorative) plasterwork

gypseux, -euse [ʒipsø, -øz]**ADJ** gypseous

gypsier [ʒipsje]**NM** *Suisse* plasterer

gypsophile [ʒipsɔfil]**NF** *Bot* gypsophila

gyrin [ʒirɛ̃] **NM** *Entom* whirligig beetle, *Spéc* gyrinid

gyrocompas [ʒirɔkɔ̃pa]**NM** gyrocompass

gyrolaser [ʒirolazɛr]**NM** gyrolaser

gyromagnétique [ʒirɔmaɲetik] **ADJ** gyromagnetic

gyromètre [ʒirɔmɛtr]**NM** gyrometer

gyromitre [ʒiromitr]**NM** *Bot* gyromitra

gyrophare [ʒirɔfar]**NM** rotating light *or* beacon

gyropilote [ʒiropilɔt]**NM** *Aviat* gyropilot, automatic pilot

gyroscope [ʒirɔskɔp] **NM** gyroscope; *Aviat* **g. directionnel** directional gyroscope

gyrostat [ʒirɔsta]**NM** gyrostat, gyrostabilizer

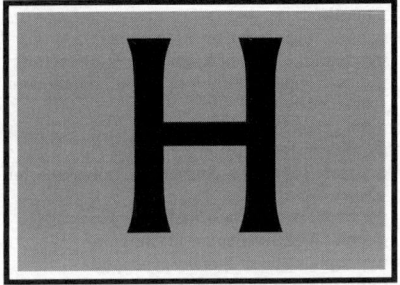

h-hab

H¹, h¹ [aʃ] NM INV *(lettre)* H, h; **H comme Henri** ≃ H for Harry

H² [aʃ] NM INV *Fam (abrév* **haschisch***)* hash, *Br* blow

H³ *(abrév écrite* **homme***)* M

h² **1** *(abrév écrite* **heure***)* hr; **2 h** 2 hrs; **à 2h** *(du matin)* at 2 am; *(du soir)* at 2 pm **2** *(abrév écrite* **hecto***)* h

ha¹ *(abrév écrite* **hectare***)* ha

ha² [a] EXCLAM **1** *(surprise)* **h., vous partez déjà?** what, (are you) leaving already?; *(ironie, suspicion)* **ha, ha, je t'y prends!** aha! caught you! **2** *(rire)* **ha, ha, que c'est drôle!** ha-ha, very funny!

hab. *(abrév écrite* **habitants***)* **50 000 h.** pop. 50,000

***habanera** [abanera] NF habanera

habeas corpus [abeaskɔrpys] NM INV **l'h.** habeas corpus

habie [abi] EXCLAM *Belg* quick!

habile [abil] ADJ **1** *(adroit)* skilful; **il est très h. aux échecs** he's very good at chess; **il est h. en affaires** he's got good business sense; **être h. de ses mains** to be good *or* clever with one's hands; **il n'est pas encore bien h. de ses mains** *(bébé)* his manual skills are still not fully developed; *(accidenté)* he still hasn't fully recovered his manual skills; **h. dans son travail** good at one's work

2 *(intelligent, fin → personne)* clever, bright; *(→ film, roman)* clever; **sa présentation des faits est très h.** his/her presentation of the facts is very clever

3 *(rusé)* clever, cunning; **la réponse est h.** it's a clever answer; **une manœuvre h.** a clever move; **il est h. à se décharger de ses responsabilités** he is good *or* very clever at offloading his responsibilities

4 *Jur* **h. à tester** fit to make out one's will; **h. à succéder** entitled to inherit

habilement [abilmɑ̃] ADV *(travailler)* cleverly, skilfully; *(répondre)* cleverly; **elle a négocié h.** she negotiated skilfully; **les négociations ont été h. menées** the negotiations were conducted with skill; **elle a h. tiré son épingle du jeu** she cleverly *or* skilfully managed to wriggle out of it

habileté [abilte] NF **1** *(dextérité)* skill, dexterity *(UNCOUNT)*; **un orfèvre d'une grande h.** a very skilful goldsmith, a goldsmith of great skill

2 *(ingéniosité)* cleverness, smartness; **son h. en affaires est bien connue** his/her business sense *or* flair is well known; **il lui fallut mettre toute son h. au service de cette démarche** he/she had to use all her artfulness to do this

habilitant, -e [abilitɑ̃, -ɑ̃t] ADJ enabling

habilitation [abilitasjɔ̃] NF **1** *Jur* capacitation **2** *Univ* accreditation, habilitation

habilité, -e [abilite] ADJ *Jur* **h. à** fit to; **toute personne habilitée à signer** any person who is entitled to sign; **je suis h. à parler en son nom** I'm legally entitled *or* empowered to speak in his/her name

❏ **habilité** NF *Jur* capacity, entitlement

habiliter [3] [abilite] VT **1** *Jur* to entitle, to empower *(à faire qch* to do sth) **2** *Univ* to accredit, to authorize, to habilitate

habillable [abijabl] ADJ **1** *(personne)* **il est difficilement h.** it's difficult to find clothes to fit him **2** *(meuble)* **ce lave-linge est h.** the washing machine may be panelled as part of a fitted kitchen

habillage [abijaʒ] NM **1** *(revêtement → d'une machine)* casing; *(→ d'un produit)* packaging; *(→ d'un ordinateur)* cabinetry; *Aut (→ d'un siège)* covering; *(→ d'un plafond)* lining; *(→ d'un intérieur)* trim; *Mktg* **h. transparent** *(emballage)* blister pack

2 *Culin (de la viande, du gibier à plumes)* dressing; *(d'un poisson)* cleaning; **l'h. d'un poulet** cleaning and trussing a chicken

3 *(d'un acteur)* dressing

4 *(montage → d'une montre, d'une horloge)* assembly, putting together

5 *Hort (des arbres)* pruning, trimming

6 *TV & Rad* **h. chaîne** station identification *(including on-air promos, transitions and titles)*

7 *Compta (d'un bilan)* window-dressing

❏ **en habillage** ADJ *Typ* **texte en h.** text wrap

habillé, -e [abije] ADJ *(vêtements)* smart, dressy; **dîner h.** dinner in evening dress

habillement [abijmɑ̃] NM **1** *(vêtements)* clothes, clothing; *(action d'habiller)* dressing, clothing; **magasin d'h.** *Br* clothes shop, *Am* clothing store; **il a de grosses dépenses d'h.** he spends a lot on clothes **2** *(industrie)* *Br* clothing trade, *Am* garment industry

habiller [3] [abije] VT **1** *(vêtir)* to dress; **elle a habillé sa fille d'une salopette rouge** she dressed her daughter in a pair of red dungarees; **toujours habillé de** *ou* **en vert** always dressed in green; **il est mal habillé** *(sans goût)* he's badly dressed; **le roi se faisait h. par ses valets** the king was dressed by his manservants; *Fam Fig* **h. qn pour l'hiver** to bad-mouth sb, *Br* to slag sb off

2 *(équiper → famille, groupe)* to clothe; *(→ skieur, écolier)* to kit out; **j'habille toute la famille** I make clothes for all the family; **la somme devrait suffire à h. toute la famille** the money should be enough to keep the entire family in clothes

3 *(sujet: couturier, tailleur)* to design clothes for; **elle se fait h. par un grand couturier** she gets her clothes from a top designer

4 *(déguiser)* **h. qn en** to dress sb up as; **elle a habillé sa fille en Zorro** she dressed her daughter up as Zorro

5 *(décorer, recouvrir)* to cover; **h. un mur de toile de jute** to cover a wall with hessian; **h. des meubles de housses** to put loose covers on furniture; **tableau de bord habillé de cuir** leather-padded dashboard

6 *Mktg* to package (and present)

7 *Compta (bilan)* to window-dress

8 *Culin (viande, gibier à plumes)* to dress; *(volaille)* to clean and truss; *(poisson)* to clean

9 *(monter → montre, horloge)* to assemble, to put together

▸**s'habiller** VPR **1** *(se vêtir)* to get dressed, to dress; **habille-toi vite!** hurry up and get dressed!; **il s'habille tout seul maintenant** he's able to dress himself now; **tu devrais t'h. plus jeune** you should wear younger clothes; **tu t'habilles mal** you have no dress sense; **je n'aime pas la façon dont elle s'habille** I don't like her taste in clothes *or* the way she dresses; **comment vous habillez-vous pour la soirée?** what are you wearing to the party?; **habille-toi chaudement** wrap up well *or* warm; **il s'intéresse à la façon dont je m'habille** he notices what I wear; **il s'habille chez un jeune couturier** he buys his clothes from a young fashion designer; **s'h. sur mesure** to have one's clothes made *or* tailor-made; **s'h. en** *(se déguiser en)* to dress up as; **s'h. en page** to dress up as a pageboy

2 *(se parer)* to dress up; **j'aime m'h. pour sortir le soir** I like dressing up to go out in the evening; **s'h. pour le dîner** to dress for dinner

habilleur, -euse [abijœr, -øz] NM,F *Cin, Théât & TV* dresser

habit [abi] NM **1** *(déguisement)* costume, outfit; **un h. de fée/sorcière** a fairy/witch outfit; **h. d'arlequin** Harlequin suit *or* costume

2 *(vêtement de cérémonie)* **h. (de soirée)** tails; **l'h. est de rigueur** tails must be worn; **en h.** wearing tails; **se mettre en h.** to wear tails; **h. de cour** court dress; **l'h. de lumière** the bullfighter's outfit; **l'h. vert** = regalia (hat, jacket and sword) worn by members of the ''Académie française''; **porter l'h. vert** to be a member of the ''Académie française''

3 *Rel* habit; **l'h. ecclésiastique** ecclesiastical dress; **prendre l'h.** *(femme)* to take the veil; *(homme)* to go into holy orders; **quitter l'h.** to leave orders; *Prov* **l'h. ne fait pas le moine** you can't judge a book by its cover

NM OU NF *Can* suit; **h. de neige** snowsuit; **h. de skidoo** snowmobile suit

❏ **habits** NMPL clothes; **mettre ses habits du dimanche** to put on one's Sunday best

'Les Habits neufs de l'empereur' *Andersen* 'The Emperor's New Clothes'

habitabilité [abitabilite] NF **1** *(d'un véhicule)* capacity **2** *(d'un lieu)* habitability

habitable [abitabl] ADJ habitable; **la maison est tout à fait h.** the house is perfectly habitable

habitacle [abitakl] NM **1** *Aviat* cockpit **2** *Aut* passenger compartment **3** *Littéraire (demeure)* abode, dwelling **4** *Naut* binnacle

habitant, -e [abitɑ̃, -ɑ̃t] NM,F **1** *(d'une ville, d'un pays)* inhabitant; *(d'un immeuble)* occupant; *(d'un quartier)* inhabitant, resident; **une ville de 30 000 habitants** a town of 30,000 inhabitants; **nous avons logé chez l'h.** we stayed with a family; **par h.** per person, per capita

2 *(gén pl) Littéraire (animal)* denizen; **les habitants des bois/de l'onde/des airs** the denizens of the forest/of the deep/of the air

3 *(gén pl) (être humain)* dweller; **les habitants des cavernes** cave-dwellers; **les habitants de la terre** earthlings

4 *Can (cultivateur)* farmer; *Péj Br* country bumpkin, *Am* hick; *Hist* = early French-Canadian settler, owner of farmland

ADJ *Can* **1** *(nourriture, objets)* rustic

2 *Péj (personne)* uneducated; **il est un peu h. sur les bords** he's a bit of a *Br* country bumpkin *or Am* hick

habitat [abita] NM **1** *Bot & Zool* habitat **2** *(en anthropologie et sociologie)* settlement; **h. dispersé** open settlement **3** *(conditions de logement)* housing; **amélioration de l'h.** better housing (conditions)

habitation [abitasjɔ̃] NF **1** *(immeuble)* house, building; **groupe d'habitations** housing *Br* estate *or Am* development; **h. à loyer modéré** *(immeuble) Br* ≃ block of council flats, *Am* ≃ public housing unit; *(appartement) Br* ≃ council flat, *Am* ≃ (apartment in a) public housing unit; *(maison) Br* ≃ council house, *Am* ≃ low-rent house

2 *(domicile)* residence; **h. principale** main residence

3 *(action d'habiter)* living, *Sout* habitation; **les conditions d'h. sont très difficiles** living *or* housing conditions are very hard; **locaux à usage d'h.** premises for residential use

The symbol * indicates that the initial **h** is aspirate and that hence there is no liaison, eg **les haricots** [leariko] and not [lezariko], or contraction in spelling, eg **la haine** and not **l'haine**.

4 *(aux Antilles → maison)* plantation house; *(→ domaine)* plantation, estate

habité, -e [abite] ADJ *(maison)* occupied; *(planète, région)* inhabited; **engin spatial h.** manned spacecraft

habiter [3] [abite] VT **1** *(maison, ville, quartier)* to live in; *(ferme)* to live on; **qui habite au** *ou* **le numéro 22?** who lives at number 22?

2 *Fig* to inhabit, to be *or* to dwell in; **les craintes/démons qui l'habitent** the fears/demons within him/her; **elle est habitée par la haine** she is full of hatred

3 *(sujet: animaux)* to inhabit; **les oiseaux qui habitent nos forêts** the birds which inhabit our forests

VI to live; **h. Paris** *ou* **à Paris** to live in Paris; **h. en Italie** to live in Italy; **j'habite au 3, place des Cardeurs** I live at number 3, place des Cardeurs; **h. à l'hôtel** to live *or* to stay in a hotel; **h. chez des amis** to be staying with friends; **vous habitez chez vos parents?** do you live at home?; *Hum* ≃ do you come here often?; **où habite-t-elle?** where does she live?

habituation [abitɥasjɔ̃] NF *Biol & Psy* habituation

habitude [abityd] NF **1** *(manière d'agir)* habit; **j'ai l'h. de me coucher tôt** I normally *or* usually go to bed early; **je n'ai pas l'h. d'attendre!** I am not in the habit of being kept waiting!; **elle a l'h. de la conduite sur circuit** she's used to racetrack driving; **ça ne la gênera pas, elle a l'h.** that won't bother her *or* she won't mind, she's used to it; **avoir pour h. de faire qch** to be in the habit of doing sth; **prendre l'h. de faire qch** to get into the habit of doing sth; **ce sont de bonnes/mauvaises habitudes** those are good/bad habits; **prendre de mauvaises habitudes** to get into bad habits, to pick up bad habits; **elle a ses petites habitudes** she's got her own (little) ways *or* habits; **ce n'est pas dans mes habitudes d'insister ainsi** I don't usually insist on things like that; **à** *ou* **selon** *ou* **suivant son h.** as is his/her wont, as usual; **tu n'as rien préparé, comme à ton h.!** you didn't get a thing ready, as usual *or* as always!; *Prov* **l'h. est une seconde nature** = habits are just like instincts; *Com* **habitudes d'achat** buying habits, purchasing habits

2 *(pratique)* experience; **avoir une longue h. du travail en commun** to have long experience of working together

3 *(usage)* custom; **c'est l'h. chez nous** it's a custom with us, it's our custom

▫ **d'habitude** ADV usually; **d'h., je suis d'accord avec elle** I usually *or* generally agree with her; **comme d'h.** as usual; **plus tôt que d'h.** earlier than usual

▫ **par habitude** ADV out of habit; **oh pardon, j'ai fait ça par h.!** sorry, I did it automatically *or* out of sheer habit!

habitué, -e [abitɥe] NM,F regular; **ça va déplaire aux habitués** the regulars won't like it

habituel, -elle [abitɥɛl] ADJ **1** *(traditionnel)* usual, regular; **le public h. des concerts de jazz était là** the usual *or* regular jazz audience was there; **il nous reçut avec sa ponctualité habituelle** he received us with his usual punctuality; **cette attitude ne lui est pas habituelle** this is not his/her usual attitude, he/she doesn't usually take this attitude; *Fam* **c'est le coup h.** it's the same old story, it's par for the course

2 *(ordinaire, courant)* usual; **au sens h. du terme** in the everyday sense of the term

habituellement [abitɥɛlmɑ̃] ADV usually, normally; **h. il se lève à huit heures** he usually *or* generally gets up at eight

habituer [7] [abitɥe] VT to accustom; **h. qn à qch** to get sb used to sth, to accustom sb to sth; **il faut h. les enfants à manger un peu de tout** one should get children used to eating a little bit of everything; **on l'a habitué à se taire** he's been taught to keep quiet; **il est habitué** *(il a l'habitude)* he's used to it; **c'est facile quand on est habitué** it's easy once you're used to it *or* once you get used to it; **elle est habituée à rester seule** she's used to being alone

►**s'habituer** VPR **s'h. à** to get *or* to grow *or* to become used to; **elle a fini par s'h. à notre petite ville** she eventually got used to our little town; **je ne pourrai jamais m'y h.** I'll never get used to it

habitus [abitys] NM *Méd* habitus

***hâbler** [3] [ɑble] VI *Littéraire* to boast, to brag

***hâblerie** [ɑbləri] NF *Littéraire (parole)* boast; **ce n'était qu'une h. de sa part** he/she was only bragging

***hâbleur, -euse** [ɑblœr, -øz] *Littéraire* ADJ boastful

NM,F boaster, braggart

***Habsbourg** [abzbur] NPR Hapsburg, Habsburg

***hachage** [aʃaʒ] NM *(gén)* chopping (up); *Culin (de la viande) Br* mincing, *Am* grinding

***hache** [aʃ] NF **1** *(instrument tranchant)* axe; **abattre un arbre à la h.** to chop a tree down; **h. d'abordage** scuttling axe; **h. d'armes** battleaxe; **h. à main** hatchet; **la h. du bourreau** the executioner's axe; **h. de guerre** tomahawk; *Fig* **enterrer la h. de guerre** to bury the hatchet; *Fig* **déterrer la h. de guerre** to be on the warpath (again); *Archéol* **h. de silex** flint axe **2** *Fig* **fait** *ou* **taillé à coups de h.** *(ouvrage)* rough-hewn, crudely worked; *(visage)* rough-hewn, rugged

***haché, -e** [aʃe] ADJ **1** *Culin (légume, amandes)* chopped; *(viande) Br* minced, *Am* ground; *Fig* **un film h. par des publicités** a film interspersed with adverts **2** *(style, tirade)* jerky; **son débit était trop h.** his/her delivery was too jerky

NM *Culin Br* mince, *Am* ground meat

***hache-légumes** [aʃlegym] NM INV vegetable chopper

hachement [aʃmɑ̃] = **hachage**

Hachémite [aʃemit] ADJ Hashimite, Hashemite

NMF Hashimite, Hashemite

***hache-paille** [aʃpaj] NM INV *Agr* chaffcutter

***hacher** [3] [aʃe] VT **1** *Culin (légumes, fines herbes)* to chop (up); *(viande) Br* to mince, *Am* to grind; **le persil doit être haché menu** the parsley should be chopped finely; *Fig* **je vais le h. menu comme chair à pâté** I'll make mincemeat (out) of him; **il se ferait h. (menu** *ou* **en morceaux) plutôt que de reconnaître ses torts** he'd die (screaming) rather than admit he was wrong; **elle se ferait h. (menu** *ou* **en morceaux) pour ses enfants** she would go through hell and high water for her children

2 *(mettre en pièces, lacérer)* to cut to pieces; **la grêle a haché la vigne** the hail ripped the vines to pieces; **les mitraillettes ennemies ont haché le bataillon** the enemy submachine-guns mowed down *or* cut down the battalion

3 *(saccader)* to break up; **il hachait toutes ses phrases, je n'y comprenais rien** all his sentences were so broken up *or* jerky that I didn't understand a thing

4 *(hachurer)* to hatch

***hachereau, -x** [aʃro] NM *(outil)* hatchet

***hachette** [aʃɛt] NF *(outil)* hatchet

***hacheur** [aʃœr] NM *Électron* chopper

***hache-viande** [aʃvjɑ̃d] NM INV *Br* mincer, *Am* grinder

***hachis** [aʃi] NM *Culin (de viande) Br* mince, *Am* ground meat; *(pour farce)* (meat) stuffing, forcemeat; *(de légumes)* chopped vegetables; **h. de veau** minced veal; **h. d'herbes** chopped herbs; **h. Parmentier** hachis Parmentier *(dish similar to shepherd's pie)*

***hachisch** [aʃiʃ] = **haschisch**

***hachoir** [aʃwar] NM **1** *(couteau)* chopping knife, chopper; **h. berceuse** mezzaluna **2** *(planche)* chopping board; *(machine) Br* mincer, *Am* grinder

***hachure** [aʃyr] NF **1** *(en cartographie et dessin industriel)* hachure **2** *(sur un dessin, une gravure)* hatching *(UNCOUNT)*

***hachurer** [3] [aʃyre] VT **1** *(carte)* to hachure **2** *(dessin, gravure)* to hatch

hacienda [asjɛnda] NF hacienda

***hacker** [akœr] NM *Ordinat* hacker

***hadal, -e, -aux, -ales** [adal, -o] ADJ **profondeurs hadales** depths of over 6000 metres

***haddock** [adɔk] NM *Culin* smoked haddock

***Hadès** [adɛs] NPR *Myth* Hades

***hadith** [adit] NMPL *Rel* Hadith

***hadj** [adʒ] NM INV *Rel* **1** *(pèlerinage)* Hajj **2** *(pèlerin)* Hadji, Hajji

***hadjdj** [adʒ] = **hadj 1**

***hadji** [adʒi] = **hadj 2**

Hadrien [adrijɛ̃] NPR Hadrian

hadron [adrɔ̃] NM *Phys* hadron

***Haendel** [ɛndɛl] NPR Handel

***hafnium** [afnjɔm] NM *Chim* hafnium

***hagard, -e** [agar, -ard] ADJ wild, crazed; **il me regardait avec des yeux hagards** he was looking at me with wild *or* staring eyes; **avoir l'air h.** to look crazed, to have a wild look in one's eyes

NM *Orn* haggard

***haggis** [agis] NM *Culin* haggis

hagiographe [aʒjɔgraf] NMF hagiographer

hagiographie [aʒjɔgrafi] NF *Rel & Fig* hagiography

hagiographique [aʒjɔgrafik] ADJ hagiographic, hagiographical

***Hague** [ag] NF **la H.** la Hague

Culture

LA HAGUE

Note that la Hague is a peninsula in Normandy, well-known for its nuclear waste processing plants; it is not to be confused with La Haye (The Hague, in the Netherlands).

***hahnium** [anjɔm] NM *Chim* hahnium

***haï, -e** [ai] PP *voir* **haïr**

***haïdouk** [ajduk] NM *Hist* heyduck

***haie** [ɛ] NF **1** *Hort* hedge; **h. morte** paling *or* dead hedge; **h. vive** quickset hedge **2** *Sport* hurdle; **courir le 400 mètres haies** to run the 400 metres hurdles **3** *Équitation* fence; **cheval de haies** hurdler, hurdle; **course de haies** hurdles race **4** *(file de gens)* line, row; **les spectateurs ont fait une h. pour laisser passer les coureurs** the spectators all drew back to let the runners go through; **h. d'honneur** guard of honour

***haïe** [ai] *voir* **haïr**

***Haïfa, *Haiffa** [ajfa] NM Haifa

***haïk** [aik] NM *(voile)* haick, haik

***haïkaï** [ajkaj] NM *Littérature* haikai

***haïku** [ajku] NM *Littérature* haiku

***haillonneux, -euse** [ajɔnø, -øz] ADJ *Littéraire* **1** *(vêtement)* in rags; **des vêtements h.** rags, torn and tattered clothes **2** *(personne)* ragged; **un vieil homme h.** a ragged old man

***haillons** [ajɔ̃] NMPL rags, torn and tattered clothes; **être vêtu de h.** to be dressed in rags; **être en h.** to be in rags

***Hainaut** [ɛno] NM **le H.** Hainaut

***haine** [ɛn] NF hatred, hate; **sa h. de la guerre** his/her hatred of war; **avoir de la h. pour qn/qch** to hate *or* detest sb/sth; **être plein de h. envers qn** to be full of hatred *or* filled with hatred for sb; **prendre qn/qch en h.** to take an immense dislike to sb/sth; **sans h.** without hatred, with no hatred; *Fam* **avoir la h.** to be full of rage

▫ **par haine de** PRÉP out of hatred for

***haineuse** [ɛnøz] *voir* **haineux**

***haineusement** [ɛnøzmɑ̃] ADV with hatred; **il la regarda h.** he looked at her with hatred

***haineux, -euse** [ɛnø, -øz] ADJ full of hatred *or* hate; **d'un ton h.** with a voice full of hate

***hainuyer, -ère** [ɛnɥije, -ɛr] ADJ of/from Hainaut

▫ **Hainuyer, -ère** NM,F = inhabitant of or person from Hainaut

***Haiphong** [ajfɔ̃g] NM Haiphong

***haïr** [33] [air] VT **1** *(personne)* to hate; **il me hait de lui avoir menti** he hates me for having lied to him **2** *(attitude, comportement)* to hate, to detest; **h. l'hypocrisie** to hate *or* to detest hypocrisy

►**se haïr** VPR *(soi-même)* to hate oneself; *(mutuellement)* to hate each other; **je me hais de lui mentir** I hate myself for lying to him/her

***haire** [ɛr] NF *Hist* hair shirt

***haïssable** [aisabl] ADJ *(préjugé, attitude, personne)* hateful, loathsome, detestable

***haïssait** *etc voir* **haïr**

Haïti [aiti] NM Haiti; **vivre à H.** to live in Haiti; **aller à H.** to go to Haiti

haïtien, -enne [aisjɛ̃, -ɛn] ADJ Haitian

▫ **Haïtien, -enne** NM,F Haitian

***haka** [aka] NM *(chant)* haka

***hakka** [aka] NM *(dialecte)* hakka

***halage** [alaʒ] NM *Naut (traction)* hauling; *(remorquage)* warping, towing

The symbol * indicates that the initial **h** is aspirate and that hence there is no liaison, eg **les haricots** [leariko] and not [lezariko], or contraction in spelling, eg **la haine** and not **l'haine**.

hal–han

*halakha, *halakhah [alaka] NF *Rel* Halakah, Halachah

*halal [alal] ADJ INV *Rel (viande)* halal

*halbi [albi] NM = fermented drink made of apples and pears

*halbran [albrɑ̃] NM *Orn* flapper

*halbrené, -e [albrəne] ADJ **1** *Chasse (faucon)* broken-feathered **2** *Fam Vieilli (épuisé)* knackered, fagged out

HALDE [ald] NF *(abrév* **Haute Autorité de Lutte contre les Discriminations et pour l'Égalité)** = independent authority set up to fight discrimination in France

*hâle [al] NM suntan, tan

*hâlé, -e [ɑle] ADJ suntanned, tanned

haleine [alɛn] NF **1** *(mouvement de respiration)* breath, breathing; **hors d'h.** out of breath; **reprendre h.** to get one's breath back; **tenir qn en h.** to keep sb in suspense *or* on tenterhooks; **courir à perdre h.** to run until one is out of breath
⯈ **2** *(air expiré)* breath; **avoir mauvaise h.** to have bad breath; **elle a l'h. fraîche** her breath smells sweet
❑ **de longue haleine** ADJ long-term; **des recherches de longue h.** long-term research

*halener [19] [alne] VT *Chasse* to scent

*haler [3] [ale] VT *Naut* **1** *(tirer → bateau)* to haul; *(remorquer → bateau)* to warp, to tow **2** *(tirer sur → cordage)* to pull, to haul in, to heave; **h. bas une voile** to let a sail down

*hâler [3] [ɑle] VT **1** *(peau, corps)* to tan **2** *Tex* to sun-dry

*haletant, -e [altɑ̃, -ɑ̃t] ADJ *(chien)* panting; **sa respiration haletante l'empêche de parler** he's/she's so out of breath he/she can't talk; **il est entré, tout h.** he came in, all out of breath; **son père était h. de fureur** his/her father was choking with anger

*halètement [alɛtmɑ̃] NM **1** *(respiration saccadée)* panting *(UNCOUNT)* **2** *(rythme saccadé)* **le h. de la locomotive** the puffing of the locomotive

*haleter [28] [alte] VI **1** *(chien)* to pant; *(asthmatique)* to gasp for breath; *(pendant l'accouchement)* to breathe hard, to pant; **h. d'émotion** to be breathless with emotion; **h. de colère** to choke with anger **2** *(faire un bruit saccadé)* to sputter; **la locomotive haletait** the locomotive was puffing

*haleur, -euse [alœr, -øz] NM,F *Naut (personne)* tower, hauler
⯈ NM *(remorqueur)* tug

*half court [alfkurt] *(pl* **half courts)** NM *Sport* half-court tennis

*half-track [alftrak] *(pl* **half-tracks)** NM half-track (vehicle)

*halicte [alikt] NM *Entom* halictus

halieutique [aljøtik] ADJ halieutic; **ressources halieutiques** fish resources *or* stocks
⯈ NF halieutics *(singulier)*

haliotide [aljɔtid] NF *Ich* haliotis, ear-shell

halite [alit] NF *Minér* halite, rock salt

*hall [ol] NM **1** *(d'un hôtel)* hall, lobby, foyer; *(d'une banque)* lobby, hall; **h. d'accueil** reception, lobby; **h. d'entrée** entrance hall; **h. de gare** concourse; **je t'attendrai dans le h. de la gare** I'll wait for you inside the station; **roman de h. de gare** trashy novel; **c'est un vrai h. de gare ici!** it's like Piccadilly Circus here!; **h. d'exposition** exhibition hall **2** *Ind* **h. de montage** assembly area

*hallage [alaʒ] NM *Com* market trader's dues

hallali [alali] NM **1** *Chasse* **l'h.** *(sonnerie)* the mort; **sonner l'h.** to sound the mort **2** *Fig (défaite)* (death) knell; **sonner l'h. de qn/qch** to sound the death knell for sb/sth

*halle [al] NF **1** *(marché)* (covered) market; **h. au blé** corn exchange; **h. aux poissons** fish market; **le marché sous la h.** the covered market; **elle fait ses courses aux halles** she goes to the central food market to do her shopping **2 les Halles** = the Paris wholesale food market until 1968 (now a shopping centre) **3** *Suisse (bâtiment)* hall; **h. d'exposition** exhibition centre; **h. de fête** community centre; **h. de gymnastique** sports centre, sports hall; **h. polyvalente** community centre; **h. de sport** sports centre, sports hall; **h. de tennis** tennis club

*hallebarde [albard] NF **1** *(arme)* halberd, halbert **2** *Fam (locution)* **il pleut** *ou* **il tombe des hallebardes** it's raining cats and dogs

*hallebardier [albardje] NM halberdier

*hallier [alje] NM *Chasse* thicket, (brush) covert; **battre les halliers** to beat the thicket *or* covert

*Halloween [alɔwin] NF Hallowe'en

*hallstattien, -enne [alstatjɛ̃, -ɛn] ADJ *Archéol* Hallstatt *(avant n)*, Hallstattian

hallu [aly] NF *Fam (abrév* **hallucination)** hallucination■; **je dois avoir des hallus!** I must be seeing things!

hallucinant, -e [alysinɑ̃, -ɑ̃t] ADJ **1** *(frappant)* unbelievable, incredible; **un paysage d'une beauté hallucinante** strikingly beautiful scenery **2** *(hallucinogène)* hallucinatory

hallucination [alysinasjɔ̃] NF hallucination; **avoir des hallucinations** to hallucinate; *Fam* **j'ai des hallucinations (ou quoi)!** I must be seeing things!; **une h. collective** a collective hallucination

hallucinatoire [alysinatwar] ADJ hallucinatory

halluciné, -e [alysine] ADJ *(regard)* wild-eyed, crazed
⯈ NM,F visionary, *Péj* lunatic; **comme un h.** like a madman

halluciner [3] [alysine] VI **1** *Psy* to hallucinate, to suffer from *or* to have hallucinations
⯈ **2** *Fam Fig* **mais j'hallucine ou quoi?** I don't believe this!
⯈ VT *Littéraire* **h. qn** to make sb hallucinate; **halluciné par le manque de sommeil** seeing double through lack of sleep

hallucinogène [alysinɔʒɛn] ADJ hallucinogenic
⯈ NM hallucinogen

hallucinose [alysinoz] NF *Psy* hallucinosis

*halo [alo] NM **1** *Astron* halo, corona **2** *Phot* halo, halation **3** *Littéraire* aureole, halo; **un h. de lumière/de gloire** a halo of light/of glory; **entouré d'un h. de mystère** shrouded in mystery

halochimie [alɔʃimi] NF *Chim* halology

halogénation [alɔʒenasjɔ̃] NF *Chim* halogenation

halogène [alɔʒɛn] ADJ halogenous
⯈ NM **1** *Chim* halogen **2** *(éclairage)* **(lampe à) h.** halogen lamp

halogéné, -e [alɔʒene] ADJ *Chim* halogenated

halogéner [18] [alɔʒene] VT *Chim* to halogenate

halogénure [alɔʒenyr] NM *Chim* halide

halographie [alɔgrafi] NF *Chim* halography

haloïde [alɔid] ADJ & NM haloid

*hâloir [ɑlwar] NM = place where soft cheeses are left to mature

halomètre [alɔmɛtr] NM *Chim* halometer

halométrie [alɔmetri] NF *Chim* halometry

halon [alɔ̃] NM *Chim* halon

halopéridol [alɔperidɔl] NM *Pharm* haloperidol

halophile [alɔfil] ADJ *Bot* halophytic

halophyte [alɔfit] NF *Bot* halophyte

halothane [alɔtan] NM *Méd* halothane

*halte [alt] NF **1** *(arrêt)* stop, break; **faire h.** to halt, to stop; **faire une h.** to have a break, to pause; **nous disons h. à la guerre** we are calling for a halt *or* an end to the war
⯈ **2** *(répit)* pause, break; **le gouvernement a décidé une h. dans le programme spatial** the government decided to call a temporary halt to the space programme
⯈ **3** *(lieu)* stopping *or* resting place; *Rail* halt; *Can (aire de repos → côtière)* viewpoint, *Am* scenic overlook; *(→ routière)* *Br* service area, *Am* rest area, rest stop
⯈ EXCLAM stop!; *Mil* halt!; **h. à la pollution!** no

more pollution!; **h., qui va là?** halt, who goes there?; **h.-là, ne t'emballe pas trop** hold on, don't get carried away

*halte-garderie [altəgardəri] *(pl* **haltes-garderies)** NF ≃ day nursery

haltère [altɛr] NM **1** *(avec des sphères)* dumbbell; *(avec des disques)* barbell; **faire des haltères** to do weight-lifting **2** *Antiq* halterer

haltérophile [alterɔfil] NMF weight-lifter

haltérophilie [alterɔfili] NF weight-lifting

*halva [alva] NM *Culin* halva

*hamac [amak] NM hammock

*hamada [amada] NF *Géol* hamada, hammada

hamadryade [amadrijad] NF **1** *Myth* hamadryad, dryad, wood nymph **2** *Zool* king cobra

hamadryas [amadrijas] NM *Zool* hamadryas baboon

hamamélis [amamelis] NM *Bot* witch hazel *(UNCOUNT)*

*Hambourg [ɑbur] NM Hamburg

*hambourgeois, -e [ɑ̃burʒwa, -az] ADJ of/from Hamburg
❑ **Hambourgeois, -e** NM,F = inhabitant of or person from Hamburg

*hamburger [ɑ̃bœrgœr] NM hamburger

*hameau, -x [amo] NM hamlet

hameçon [amsɔ̃] NM (fish) hook

*hammam [amam] NM Turkish *or* steam bath, hammam

*hammerless [amɛrlɛs] NM INV *(fusil)* hammerless shotgun

*hampe [ɑ̃p] NF **1** *(d'un drapeau)* pole **2** *Pêche & (d'une arme)* shaft **3** *Typ (d'une lettre)* stem; **h. montante** ascender **4** *(d'un pinceau)* handle **5** *Bot* **h. florale** scape **6** *(du bœuf)* flank; *(du cerf)* breast

*hamster [amstɛr] NM hamster

*han [ɑ̃] NM INV oof; **pousser des h.** to grunt *(with effort)*

*hanafisme [anafism] NM *Jur* Hanafism

*hanap [anap] NM hanap, goblet

*hanbalisme [anbalism] NM Hanbalism

*hanche [ɑ̃ʃ] NF **1** *Anat* hip; **avoir les hanches larges/étroites** to have broad/narrow hips; **être large des hanches** to have broad hips; **mettre les mains** *ou* **les poings sur les hanches** to put one's hands on one's hips **2** *Zool* haunch, hindquarter **3** *Entom* coxa **4** *Naut (d'un navire)* quarter; **par la h.** on the quarter

*hanchement [ɑ̃ʃmɑ̃] NM **1** *Littéraire* jutting (out) of the hip **2** *Beaux-Arts* slouch

*hancher [3] [ɑ̃ʃe] **se hancher** VPR *Littéraire* to stick out one's hip

*hand [ɑ̃d] NM *Fam Sport* handball■

*handball [ɑ̃dbal] NM handball

*handballeur, -euse [ɑ̃dbalœr, -øz] NM,F handball player

*handicap [ɑ̃dikap] NM **1** *(gén) & Sport* handicap; **son poids est un grand h.** his/her weight is a great handicap **2** *(comme adj; avec ou sans trait d'union)* handicap *(avant n)*

*handicapant, -e [ɑ̃dikapɑ̃, -ɑ̃t] ADJ **c'est (très) h.** it's a (great) handicap

*handicapé, -e [ɑ̃dikape] ADJ *(physique)* handicapped, disabled; **enfants handicapés mentaux** mentally handicapped children
⯈ NM,F *(physique)* handicapped *or* disabled person; **les handicapés** the disabled; **h. mental** mentally handicapped person; **un h. moteur** a spastic

*handicaper [3] [ɑ̃dikape] VT to handicap; **il sera handicapé par son poids** his weight will be a handicap; **ça l'a handicapé dans sa carrière** it was a handicap to his career

*handicapeur [ɑ̃dikapœr] NM *Courses de chevaux (official)* handicapper

*handisport [ɑ̃dispɔr] ADJ INV **activité/jeux h.** sport/games for the disabled

*hangar [ɑ̃gar] NM *(gén)* shed; *(pour avions)* (aircraft) hangar; *(pour locomotives, bus)* depot; **h. à bateaux** boathouse; **un h. à charbon** a coal shed

*hanneton [antɔ̃] NM *Entom* cockchafer, May bug, June bug; **h. vert** rose beetle

*hannetonnage [antɔnaʒ] NM clearing of cockchafers *or* May bugs *or* June bugs

*hannetonner [3] [antɔne] VT to clear of cockchafers *or* May bugs *or* June bugs

VI to destroy cockchafers *or* May bugs *or* June bugs

Hannibal [anibal]**NPR** Hannibal

*****Hanoi** [anɔj]**NM** Hanoi

*****Hanoukka** [anuka]**NF** *Rel* Hanukkah

*****Hanovre** [anɔvr]**NM** Hanover

*****hanovrien, -enne** [anɔvrijɛ̃, -ɛn]**ADJ** Hanoverian
  ◻ **Hanovrien, -enne NM,F** Hanoverian

*****hansart** [ɑ̃sart]**NM** *(dans l'ouest de la France) Br* mincer, *Am* grinder

*****hanse** [ɑ̃s] *Hist* **NF** Hanse, Hansa; **la H.** the Hanseatic League

*****hanséatique** [ɑ̃seatik]**ADJ** Hanseatic

*****hantavirus** [ɑ̃tavirys]**NM** *Méd* hantavirus

*****hanté, -e** [ɑ̃te]**ADJ** *(maison, forêt)* haunted

*****hanter** [3] [ɑ̃te] **VT 1** *(sujet: fantôme, esprit)* to haunt; **ce souvenir le hante** he's haunted by the memory; **hanté par de vieux souvenirs** haunted *or* obsessed by old memories **2** *Littéraire (fréquenter)* to haunt; *Prov* **dis-moi qui tu hantes et je te dirai qui tu es** a man is known by the company he keeps
  USAGE ABSOLU *Belg (couple → sortir ensemble)* to go out together; *(→ flirter)* to flirt together
  ◻ **hanter avec VT IND** *Belg* to go out with

*****hantise** [ɑ̃tiz]**NF** obsession, obsessive fear; **avoir la h. de la mort** to be haunted *or* obsessed by the fear of death; **j'ai la h. de ce genre de réunion** I dread this kind of meeting; **sa h. d'un accident l'empêche de conduire** his/her obsessive fear of accidents stops him/her from driving; **chez lui, c'est une h.** he's obsessed by it, it's an obsession with him

haoussa, haousa [ausa]**NM** *(langue)* Hausa

hapax [apaks] **NM** *Ling* nonce word, *Spéc* hapax (legomenon)

haplodiploïde [aplɔdiplɔid]**ADJ** *Biol* haplodiploid

haplographie [aplɔgrafi]**NF** *Ling* lipography

haploïde [aplɔid]**ADJ** *Biol* haploid

haplologie [aplɔlɔʒi]**NF** *Ling* haplology

*****happe** [ap]**NF** *Menuis* cramp *or* clamp iron

*****happement** [apmɑ̃]**NM** snapping *(with the mouth)*

*****happening** [apəniŋ]**NM** *(spectacle)* happening

*****happer** [3] [ape]**VT 1** *(avec le bec ou la bouche)* to snap up; *(avec la main ou la patte)* to snatch, to grab; **la machine a happé sa main** his/her hand got caught in the machine **2** *(accrocher violemment)* to strike *or* to hit violently; **être happé par un train/une voiture** to be mown down *or* hit by a train/car

*****happy end** [apiɛnd] *(pl* **happy ends)** **NM** happy ending

*****happy few** [apifju] **NMPL** happy few; **une soirée réservée à quelques h.** a reception for a few selected guests

haptène [aptɛn]**NM** *Biol & Chim* hapten, haptene

haptine [aptin]**NF** *Biol & Chim* hapten, haptene

haptique [aptik] *Psy***ADJ** haptic
  NF haptics *(singulier)*

haptoglobine [aptɔglɔbin]**NF** *Biol & Chim* haptoglobin

haptonomie [aptɔnɔmi] **NF** *Obst* = technique of communication with foetus through sensory stimulation

*****haquebute** [akbyt]**NF** *Arch* hackbut, harquebus

*****haquenée** [akne]**NF** *Arch* palfrey

*****haquet** [akɛ]**NM** narrow dray

*****hara-kiri** [arakiri] *(pl* **hara-kiris)** **NM** hara-kiri; **(se) faire H.** to commit hara-kiri; *Presse* **H.** = former French monthly satirical magazine

*****harangue** [arɑ̃g] **NF 1** *(discours solennel)* harangue **2** *Péj (sermon)* sermon

*****haranguer** [3] [arɑ̃ge]**VT** to harangue

*****harangueur, -euse** [arɑ̃gœr, -øz] **NM,F 1** *Vieilli* orator, speaker **2** *Littéraire Péj* speechifier, tubthumper

*****Harare** [arar]**NM** Harare

*****haras** [ara]**NM** stud farm

*****harassant, -e** [arasɑ̃, -ɑ̃t]**ADJ** exhausting, wearing

*****harasse** [aras]**NF** (large) crate

*****harassé, -e** [arase] **ADJ** exhausted, worn out; **avoir l'air h.** to look exhausted

*****harassement** [arasmɑ̃]**NM** *Littéraire* exhaustion, fatigue

*****harasser** [3] [arase]**VT** to exhaust, to wear out

*****harcelant, -e** [arsəlɑ̃, -ɑ̃t] **ADJ 1** *(obsédant)* haunting **2** *(importun)* harassing, pestering

*****harcèlement** [arsɛlmɑ̃]**NM** harassment; **h. moral** moral harassment; **h. sexuel** sexual harassment

*****harceler** [25] [arsəle] **VT** *(personne)* to harass; *(animal)* to bait; **h. qn de questions** to plague *or* to pester sb with questions; **cesse de me h.!** stop pestering *or* bothering me!; **h. l'ennemi** to harass *or* to harry the enemy; **les remords le harcèlent** he's tormented *or* plagued by remorse; **h. qn sexuellement** to sexually harass sb

*****harceleur, -euse** [arsəlœr, -øz] **NM,F** pest; **h. téléphonique** telephone pest

*****hard** [ard] *Fam* **1 = hard-core 2 = hard-rock 3 = hardware**

*****hard bop** [ardbɔp]**NM INV** *Mus* hard bop

*****hard-core** [ardkɔr]**ADJ INV** hard-core; **un film h.** a hard-core (porn) movie
  NM INV *(genre)* hard-core porn

*****harde** [ard] **NF 1** *(d'animaux sauvages)* herd **2** *Chasse (lien)* leash; *(chiens liés)* set (of coupled hounds)

*****harder** [3] [arde]**VT** *Chasse (chiens)* to couple in fours/sixes

*****hardes** [ard]**NFPL** *Littéraire Péj* rags, tatters

*****hardeur, -euse**[1] [ardœr, -øz]**NM,F** hardcore porn star

*****hardeux, -euse**[1] [ardø, -øz]**NM,F** *Fam (homme)* rocker; *(femme)* rock chick

*****hardi, -e** [ardi] **ADJ 1** *(intrépide)* bold, daring; *(original)* bold; **nos hardis explorateurs** our bold *or* intrepid explorers **2** *(téméraire)* rash; *Fig* **l'hypothèse est un peu hardie** the supposition is a bit rash *or* hasty **3** *(licencieux)* daring, bold; **on a censuré les passages les plus hardis** the most daring *or* the most risqué *or* the raciest parts were cut out
  ◻ **hardi EXCLAM** *Arch* **h., les gars!** go to it, boys!

*****hardiesse** [ardjɛs] **NF 1** *(intrépidité)* boldness, daring, audacity; *(originalité → du style, d'une figure)* boldness **2** *(témérité)* **avoir la h. de faire qch** to be forward *or* daring enough to do sth; **auriez-vous la h. de réclamer un pourcentage?** would you have the audacity to ask for a commission? **3** *(acte, parole)* **h. de langage** bold turn of phrase; **des hardiesses de langage** *(propos crus)* bold language; *(effets de style)* daring stylistic effects; **se permettre des hardiesses avec qn** to take liberties with sb **4** *(indécence)* boldness, raciness; **la h. de certaines scènes peut choquer** you may find the explicitness of some of the scenes offensive

*****hardiment** [ardimɑ̃]**ADV 1** *(avec audace)* boldly, daringly, fearlessly **2** *(avec effronterie)* impudently; *(à la légère)* rashly

*****hardos** [ardos] **NM** *Fam (musicien de hard-rock)* hard rocker; *(amateur de hard-rock)* hard rocker, metalhead

*****hard-rock** [ardrɔk]**NM INV** *Mus* hard rock, heavy metal

*****hard-top** [ardtɔp] *(pl* **hard-tops)** **NM** hardtop (roof)

*****hardware** [ardwɛr]**NM** *Ordinat* hardware

*****harem** [arɛm]**NM** harem

*****hareng** [arɑ̃] **NM 1** *(poisson)* herring; **h. fumé** kipper; **h. saur** smoked herring, kipper **2** *très Fam (souteneur)* pimp

*****harengaison** [arɑ̃gɛzɔ̃]**NF** *Pêche* **1** *(activité)* herring fishing **2** *(saison)* herring season

*****harengère** [arɑ̃ʒɛr] **NF 1** *(marchande)* fishwife, fishwoman **2** *Fam Vieilli (femme querelleuse et grossière)* fishwife, harridan

*****harenguet** [arɑ̃gɛ]**NM** *Ich* sprat

*****harenguier** [arɑ̃gje]**NM** *Pêche* **1** *(bateau)* herring boat **2** *(personne)* herring fisherman

*****haret** [arɛ]**ADJ M** chat h. feral cat
  NM feral cat

*****harfang** [arfɑ̃] **NM** *Orn* great white owl; **h. des neiges** snowy owl

*****hargne** [arɲ]**NF** aggressiveness; **avec h.** aggressively, cantankerously; **des propos pleins de h.** aggressive remarks

*****hargneuse** [arɲøz] *voir* **hargneux**

*****hargneusement** [arɲøzmɑ̃] **ADV** aggressively, cantankerously

*****hargneux, -euse** [arɲø, -øz] **ADJ 1** *(caractère)* aggressive, quarrelsome; **une femme hargneuse** a shrew, an ill-tempered woman; **un vieil homme h.** a cantankerous old man **2** *(ton, paroles)* aggressive **3** *(combatif)* aggressive; **il est h. dans les sprints** he's an aggressive sprinter **4** *(animal)* vicious

*****haricot** [ariko]**NM 1** *(légume)* bean; **h. beurre =** yellow variety of string bean; **h. blanc** white (haricot) bean; **h. d'Espagne** scarlet runner; **h. flageolet** flageolet; **h. de Lima** Lima bean; **h. mange-tout** runner *or* string bean; **h. noir** black bean; **h. rouge** red *or* kidney bean; **h. vert** string *or* green *or Br* French bean; **haricots fins/extra-fins** high-quality/superfine green *or Br* French beans; **haricots à écosser** shell beans; **haricots en grains** dried beans **2** *Culin (ragoût)* **h. de mouton** mutton haricot *or* stew **3** *Méd (cuvette)* kidney tray *or* dish
  ◻ **haricots NMPL** *Fam* des haricots not a thing, *Am* zilch; **cette affaire m'a rapporté des haricots** I hardly made a *Br* penny *or Am* cent out of that business; **travailler pour des haricots** to work for peanuts

*****haridelle** [aridɛl] **NF 1** *(cheval)* jade, nag **2** *(femme)* beanpole

*****harissa** [arisa]**NF** harissa (sauce)

*****harki** [arki] **NM =** Algerian who fought for the French during the Franco-Algerian War and who was subsequently given French nationality

*****harle** [arl] **NM** *Orn* merganser; **h. bièvre** goosander; **h. couronné** hooded merganser, *Am* smew; **h. huppé** red-breasted merganser; **h. piette** smew

harmattan [armatɑ̃]**NM** *(vent)* harmattan

harmonica [armɔnika] **NM** harmonica, mouth organ; **h. de verres** glass harmonica

harmoniciste [armɔnisist] **NMF** harmonica player, mouth organ player

harmonie [armɔni] **NF 1** *(élégance)* harmony; **l'h. du corps humain** the beauty of the human body **2** *(entente)* harmony; **il régnait dans leur couple une grande h.** the couple lived together in great harmony **3** *Mus (accord)* harmony; *(instruments à vent et percussions)* wind section with percussion; *(fanfare)* brass band **4** *Ling* **h. vocalique** vowel harmony; **h. consonantique** consonant drift **5** *Littérature* **h. imitative** onomatopoeia
  ◻ **en harmonie ADV** in harmony, harmoniously; **en parfaite h.** in perfect harmony **ADV** in harmony; **le tapis n'est pas en h. avec les meubles** the carpet doesn't go with *or* match the furniture; **quand les sentiments de l'un sont en h. avec ceux de l'autre** when two people feel the same way

harmonieuse [armɔnjøz] *voir* **harmonieux**

harmonieusement [armɔnjøzmɑ̃] **ADV** harmoniously, in harmony

harmonieux, -euse [armɔnjø, -øz] **ADJ 1** *(mélodieux → son, instrument)* harmonious; *(→ voix)* harmonious, tuneful, melodious **2** *(équilibré)* harmonious, balanced; **des teintes harmonieuses** well-matched colours; **un visage h.** well-balanced features; **un couple h.** a well-matched *or* happy couple

harmonique [armɔnik] **ADJ** *Math & Mus & (en acoustique)* harmonic; **analyse/moyenne h.** harmonic analysis/mean; **série/progression h.** harmonic series/progression; **son h.** harmonic **NM 1** *Mus & (en acoustique)* harmonic **2** *Phys* harmonic, overtone

harmoniquement [armɔnikmɑ̃]**ADV** *Mus* harmonically

harmonisation [armɔnizasjɔ̃] **NF 1** *(mise en accord)* harmonization; **réclamer l'h. des salaires du public et du privé** to demand that public sector salaries be brought into parity *or* line

with those in the private sector; **h. fiscale** tax harmonization **2** *Mus* harmonizing **3** *Ling* **h. vocalique** vowel harmony

harmoniser [3] [armɔnize] **VT** *Mus* to harmonize; *(styles, couleurs)* to match; **h. les théories en présence** to reconcile the various opposing theories; **h. les salaires du public et du privé** to bring public and private sector salaries into line; **h. les rideaux avec la moquette** to match the curtains with the carpet, to match up the curtains and the carpet

▸**s'harmoniser VPR s'h. avec** to harmonize with; **ces couleurs s'harmonisent bien entre elles** these colours go together well

harmoniste [armɔnist] **NMF** *Mus* **1** *(musicien)* harmonist **2** *Tech* tuner

harmonium [armɔnjɔm] **NM** *Mus* harmonium

***harnachement** [arnaʃmɑ̃] **NM 1** *(d'un cheval → équipement)* harness; *(→ action)* harnessing **2** *Hum (accoutrement)* outfit, get-up; *(attirail)* paraphernalia

***harnacher** [3] [arnaʃe] **VT 1** *(cheval)* to harness **2** *Hum (accoutrer)* to deck *or* to rig out; *(équiper)* to kit out; **il fallait voir comment elle était harnachée** you should have seen the ridiculous outfit she was wearing **3** *Can (cours d'eau)* to harness

▸**se harnacher VPR** *(s'équiper)* to get kitted out; **ils s'étaient harnachés de cordes et de piolets pour l'ascension** they were kitted out with ropes and ice axes for the climb

***harnais** [arnɛ] **NM 1** *(d'un cheval)* harness **2** *(sangles)* **h. (de sécurité)** (safety) harness; **mettre le h. (de sécurité) à qn** to strap sb in **3** *Tech* backgear; **h. d'engrenage** (back) gear train **4** *Tex* healds, harness **5** *Arch (armure)* armour

***harnois** [arnwa] **NM** *Littéraire* **blanchi sous le h.** gone grey in the saddle

***haro** [aro] **NM crier h. sur qn** to raise a hue and cry against sb; **on a crié h. sur le baudet** there was a hue and cry

***Harold** [arɔld] **NPR** Harold

Harpagon [arpagɔ̃] **NM** *Littéraire* Scrooge, skinflint

> *Allusion*
> **C'est un Harpagon**
> Harpagon is the name of the miser in Molière's play *l'Avare*, whose servants ultimately make a fool of him. Today, if someone is very tight-fisted or obsessed with accumulating wealth, one can say this of them.

***harpail** [arpaj] **NM** herd of hinds and young deer

***harpaille** [arpaj] **NF** herd of hinds and young deer

***harpe** [arp] **NF 1** *Mus* harp; **h. celtique** Celtic harp; **h. éolienne** wind *or* aeolian harp **2** *Zool (mollusque)* harp (shell) **3** *Constr (pierre en saillie)* toothing (stone)

***Harpie** [arpi] **NF** *Myth* Harpy

***harpie** [arpi] **NF 1** *(mégère)* shrew, harpy **2** *Hér* harpy **3** *Orn (aigle)* harpy eagle; *(chauve-souris)* harpy bat

***harpiste** [arpist] **NMF** harpist

***harpon** [arpɔ̃] **NM 1** *Pêche* harpoon **2** *Constr* (wall) staple **3** *Archéol* harping iron, harpoon

***harponnage** [arpɔnaʒ], ***harponnement** [arpɔnmɑ̃] **NM 1** *Pêche* harpooning **2** *Constr* stapling

***harponner** [3] [arpɔne] **VT 1** *Pêche* to harpoon **2** *Fam (accaparer)* to grab, to collar; **harponne-le à la sortie de la réunion** grab him when he comes out of the meeting; **je me suis fait h. par un collègue juste avant de partir** I got collared by a colleague just as I was about to leave **3** *Fam (arrêter)* to pick up, to nab; **les flics l'ont harponné à la sortie du club** the cops nabbed him outside the club

***harponneur** [arpɔnœr] **NM** *Pêche* harpooner

'Harry, un ami qui vous veut du bien' *Moll* 'Harry, He's Here to Help'

'Harry Potter à l'école des sorciers' *Rowling, Columbus* 'Harry Potter and the Philosopher's Stone' (UK), 'Harry Potter and the Sorcerer's Stone' (US)

***hart** [ar] **NF 1** *(lien d'osier)* band, binder **2** *Arch* rope, noose

haruspice [aryspis] **NM** *Antiq* haruspex

***hasard** [azar] **NM 1** *(providence)* chance, fate; **s'il gagne, c'est le h.** if he wins, it's by sheer luck *or* chance; **s'en remettre au h.** to leave it to chance, to trust to luck; **ne rien laisser au h.** to leave nothing to chance; **le h. a voulu que je sois à l'étranger** as it happened, I was abroad; **le h. fait bien les choses** there are some lucky coincidences; **le h. faisant bien les choses, ils se retrouvèrent quelques années plus tard** as chance would have it, they met again some years later

2 *(incident imprévu)* **quel heureux h.!** what a stroke of luck *or* piece of good fortune!; **un h. malheureux** a piece of bad luck

3 *(coïncidence)* **quel heureux h.!** what a fantastic coincidence!; **un heureux h. a fait qu'il a été muté dans la même région que moi** by a stroke of luck he was transferred to the same area as me; **c'est un (pur) h. que vous m'ayez trouvé chez moi à cette heure-ci** it's sheer luck that you've found me in at this time of day; **par un curieux h., il était né le même jour** by a strange coincidence he was born on the same day; **par quel h. étiez-vous là ce jour-là?** how come you happened to be there that day?; **par le plus grand des hasards** by the most extraordinary *or* incredible coincidence; **tu n'aurais pas, par le plus grand des hasards, vu mes lunettes?** you wouldn't by any chance have happened to see my glasses, would you?

4 *(jeu)* **jeu de h.** game of chance; *Fig* **l'amour est un jeu de h.** love is like a game of chance

5 *(en statistique)* chance; **échantillonnage/nombres au h.** random sampling/numbers

▫ **hasards NMPL 1** *(aléas)* **les hasards de la vie** life's ups and downs, life's vicissitudes **2** *Littéraire (périls)* hazards, dangers; **les hasards de la guerre** the hazards *or* dangers of war

▫ **à tout hasard ADV** on the off chance, just in case

▫ **au hasard ADV** at random; **j'ai ouvert le livre au h.** I opened the book at random; **aller** *ou* **marcher au h.** *(par indifférence)* to walk aimlessly; *(par plaisir)* to go where one's fancy takes one; **tirez** *ou* **piochez une carte au h.** pick a card(, any card)

▫ **au hasard de PRÉP toute sa vie, elle a pris des notes au h. de ses lectures** throughout her life, she took notes of things she happened to come across in her reading; **je me suis fait des amis au h. de mes voyages** I made friends with people I happened to meet on my travels

▫ **de hasard ADJ** chance *(avant n)*; **une rencontre de h.** a chance meeting; **des amours de h.** brief encounters

▫ **par hasard ADV** by chance *or* accident; **je l'ai appris par h.** I heard about it completely by chance; **si par h. vous la voyez** if by any chance you should see her, should you happen to see her; **je suis entré par h. et je l'ai pris la main dans le sac** I went in quite by chance and caught him red-handed; **tu ne l'as pas vu, par h.?** you haven't seen it by any chance, have you?; *Ironique* **comme par h.!** that's a surprise!, surprise, surprise!; **comme par h., elle n'a rien entendu!** surprisingly enough, she didn't hear a thing!

***hasardé, -e** [azarde] = **hasardeux**

***hasarder** [3] [azarde] **VT** *(opinion, démarche)* to hazard, to venture, to risk; **h. un orteil dans l'eau glacée** to cautiously dip one toe into the icy water; **je me permettrai de h. une question** I'll venture a question, I'll take the liberty of asking a question; **les soldats hasardent leur vie à la guerre** soldiers risk their lives *or* put their lives at stake at war

▸**se hasarder VPR 1** *Arch (s'exposer au danger)* to venture forth **2** *(s'aventurer)* to venture; **il se hasarda dans l'obscurité** he ventured into the darkness; **la nouvelle élève se hasarda à répondre** the new student plucked up courage to answer; **je ne m'y hasarderais pas** I wouldn't risk it *or* chance it

***hasardeux, -euse** [azardø, -øz] **ADJ 1** *(douteux)* dubious; **l'issue en est hasardeuse** the outcome of all this is uncertain **2** *(dangereux)* hazardous, dangerous; **une affaire hasardeuse** a risky business

***has been** [azbin] **NMF INV** *Fam* has-been

***hasch** [aʃ] **NM** *Fam* hash

***haschisch, *haschich** [aʃiʃ] **NM** hashish

***hase** [ɑz] **NF** *Zool* doe

Hasmonéens [asmɔneɛ̃] **NMPL** *Hist* Hasmoneans

***hassid** [asid] *(pl* **hassidim** [-dim]*)* **NM** *Rel* Hasid, Hasidic Jew

***hassidique** [asidik] **ADJ** *Rel* Hasidic

***hassidisme** [asidism] **NM** *Rel* Hasidism

***hassium** [asjɔm] **NM** *Chim* hassium

hast [ast] **NM** *Arch* shaft; **arme d'h.** shafted weapon

hastaire [astɛr] **NM** *Antiq* spearman

hastati [astati] **NMPL** *Antiq* = first line of Roman army in order of battle

hasté, -e [aste] **ADJ** *Bot* hastate

***hâte** [ɑt] **NF 1** *(précipitation)* haste, hurry, rush; **dans sa h., il a oublié ses clés** he was in such a hurry *or* rush (that) he left his keys behind; **mettre trop de h. à faire qch** to be in too great a hurry *or* too much of a hurry to do sth; **avec h.** hastily, hurriedly; **sans h.** at a leisurely pace, without hurrying; **sans grande h.** with no great haste, unhurriedly **2** *(être impatient)* **avoir h. de faire qch** to be looking forward to doing sth; **j'ai h. que vous veniez/que Noël arrive** I can't wait for you to come/for Christmas to come round; **pourquoi avez-vous h. de partir?** why are you in (such) a hurry *or* rush to leave?; **il n'a qu'une h., c'est d'avoir un petit-fils** he's dying to have a grandson

▫ **à la hâte ADV** hurriedly, hastily, in a rush; **faire qch à la h.** to do sth hastily

▫ **en hâte, en grande hâte, en toute hâte ADV** hurriedly, in (great) haste; **envoyez votre réponse en toute h. à l'adresse suivante** send your reply without delay to the following address

***hâtelet** [ɑtlɛ] **NM** *Vieilli* skewer

***hâtelette** [ɑtlɛt] **NF** *Vieilli Culin* skewered chunk of meat

***hâter** [3] [ɑte] **VT 1** *(accélérer)* to speed up, to hasten; **h. le pas** to quicken one's pace, to walk quicker **2** *(avancer → date)* to bring forward; *(→ naissance, mort, mariage)* to precipitate; **je dois h. mon départ** I must go sooner than I thought

▸**se hâter VPR** to hurry (up), to hasten, to make haste; **les travailleurs se hâtaient vers les gares** the workers were hurrying towards the stations; **hâtez-vous de me répondre** answer me posthaste; **elle s'est hâtée de répandre la nouvelle** she hastened to spread the news; **hâte-toi lentement** more haste, less speed

***hâtier** [ɑtje] **NM** spit-rack

***hâtif, -ive** [ɑtif, -iv] **ADJ 1** *(rapide → travail, repas)* hurried, rushed; *(→ décision)* hasty, rash **2** *(précoce → croissance, fruit)* early

***hâtiveau, -x** [ɑtivo] **NM** *Vieilli Bot* early variety

***hâtivement** [ɑtivmɑ̃] **ADV** hastily, hurriedly, in a rush; **le livre a été écrit un peu h.** the book was written in somewhat of a rush

***hattéria** [aterja] **NM** *Zool* tuatara, *Spéc* sphenodon

***hauban** [obɑ̃] **NM 1** *Aviat & Naut* shroud **2** *Tech* stay

***haubanage** [obanaʒ] **NM 1** *Naut* staying **2** *Aviat* shrouds

***haubaner** [3] [obane] **VT** *Naut (mât)* to stay (with shrouds)

***haubert** [obɛr] **NM** *Hist* hauberk, shirt of mail

***hausse** [os] **NF 1** *(augmentation)* rise, increase (**de** in); **la h. du coût de la vie** the rise in the cost of living; **les prix ont subi une forte h.** prices have increased sharply, prices have shot up; **une h. de 4 pour cent** a 4 percent rise; **une h. des prix** a price increase; *Bourse* **h. des cours** stock market rise; *Bourse* **provoquer une h. factice** to rig the market **2** *(élévation)* rise **3** *(d'une arme)* back-sight **4** *(d'une ruche)* superhive

▫ **à la hausse ADV 1** *(au maximum)* **réviser le budget à la h.** to increase the budget, to revise the budget upwards **2** *Bourse* **à la h.** *(tendance, marché, position)* bullish; **être à la h.** to go up; **le marché évolue** *ou* **est à la h.** there is an upward trend in the market; **jouer à la h.** to speculate on the rising market *or* on the bull market; **pousser à la h.** to bull; **pousser les actions à la h.** to bull the market; **les cours sont orientés à la h.** there

The symbol * indicates that the initial **h** is aspirate and that hence there is no liaison, eg **les haricots** [leariko] and not [lezariko], or contraction in spelling, eg **la haine** and not **l'haine**.

is an upward trend in share prices; **vendre à la h.** to sell in a rising market, *Spéc* to contrary sell ▫ **en hausse** ADJ increasing, rising; **être en h.** to be on the increase, to be rising; **des prix en h.** rising prices; **les vols de voitures sont en h. de 30 pour cent sur l'année dernière** car thefts are up 30 percent on last year

*hausse-col [oskɔl] (*pl* **hausse-cols**) NM *Hist* gorget

*haussement [osmã] NM **avec un h. d'épaules** with a shrug (of one's shoulders); **avec un h. de sourcils** with raised eyebrows

*hausser [3] [ose] VT 1 *Écon* to raise, to increase, to put up; **le prix a été haussé de 10 pour cent** the price has been increased *or* has gone up by 10 percent; **h. ses prétentions** to aim higher 2 *Constr* to raise; **l'immeuble a été haussé d'un étage** the building was made higher by adding another floor; *Fig* **h. qn au niveau de** to raise sb up to the level of 3 (*partie du corps*) **h. les épaules** to shrug (one's shoulders); **h. les sourcils** to raise one's eyebrows 4 (*intensifier*) **h. la voix** *ou* **le ton** to raise one's voice
VI to rise; **faire h. les prix** to force up prices
▸ **se hausser** VPR 1 (*se hisser*) **se h. sur la pointe des pieds** to stand on tiptoe; **je me suis haussé jusqu'à la fenêtre** I stretched up to the window; *Fig* **se h. du col** to show off 2 (*atteindre un degré supérieur*) **se h. à** to attain, to reach; **elle est parvenue à se h. au niveau de la classe** she managed to reach the level of the other students in her class

*haussier, -ère[1] [osje, -ɛr] *Bourse* ADJ **un marché h.** a rising *or* bull market
NM,F bull

*haussière[2] [osjɛr] NF *Naut* hawser; **h. de halage** warp; **h. de touée** stream-cable; **cordage commis en h.** hawser-laid rope

*Haussmann [osman] NPR Haussmann

*haussmannien, -enne [osmanjẽ, -ɛn] ADJ (*immeuble, architecture etc*) Haussmann (*avant n*), Haussmann-style (*avant n*)

*HAUT, -E [o, ot]

ADJ high **1–8** ▪ tall **1** ▪ top **5**	
NM top **1, 2** ▪ top end **5**	
ADV high **1, 4–6** ▪ far (back) **2** ▪ above **2** ▪ aloud **3**	

ADJ 1 (*de grande dimension → bâtiment*) high, tall; (→ *tige, tronc*) tall; (→ *qui a poussé*) high; **les hautes colonnes du temple** the lofty *or* towering columns of the temple; **un homme de haute taille** a tall man; **les pièces sont hautes de plafond** the rooms have high ceilings; **j'aime les fleurs hautes** I like long-stemmed *or* tall flowers; **les roseaux sont hauts** the reeds are high 2 (*d'une certaine dimension*) high; **la maison est haute de trois mètres** the house is three metres high
3 (*situé en hauteur*) high; **le soleil est h. dans le ciel** the sun is high (up) in the sky; **la mer était haute** the tide was in *or* high; **un véhicule h. sur roues** a vehicle with a high (wheelbase) clearance; **une robe à taille haute** a high-waisted dress; **sur les hautes branches** on the top *or* topmost branches; **en haute montagne** high in the mountains; **la partie haute de l'arbre** the top of the tree; **le H. Nil** the upper (reaches of the) Nile
4 (*extrême, intense*) high; **c'est de la plus haute importance** it's of the utmost *or* greatest importance; **à h. risque** high-risk; **à haute température** high-temperature; **c'était du plus h. comique** it was high farce; **c'était de la plus**

haute fantaisie it was most fanciful; *Ordinat & Tél* **h. débit** broadband; *TV* **haute définition** high definition; *Ordinat* **haute densité** high density; **haute fréquence** high frequency; **de haute précision** high-precision; **haute pression** high pressure; **haute technologie** high technology; **haute tension** high tension
5 (*dans une hiérarchie*) high, top (*avant n*); **de h. niveau** top-level, high-level; **des officiers de h. niveau** high-ranking officers; **de hauts dignitaires** eminent *or* leading dignitaries; *Jur* **les hautes parties contractantes** the sovereign contracting parties; **la haute coiffure** haute coiffure, designer hairdressing; **la haute cuisine** haute cuisine; *Suisse* **haute école** = higher education establishment (university, technical college or "grande école"); **de hautes études commerciales/militaires** advanced business/military studies; **Hautes études commerciales** = prestigious business school in Paris; **les hauts fonctionnaires** top *or* top-ranking civil servants; **les hauts salaires** the highest *or* top salaries; **politique des hauts salaires** high income policy
6 (*dans une échelle de valeurs*) high; **d'une haute intelligence** highly intelligent; **avoir une haute idée de soi-même** to have a high opinion of oneself; **tenir qch en haute estime** to hold sb/sth in high esteem
7 *Bourse & Com* high; **la livre est à son niveau le plus h.** the pound is at its highest level *or* has reached a high
8 *Mus & Ling* high; **une note/voyelle haute** a high note/vowel
9 *Ling* **le h. allemand** (Old) High German; *Hist* **le h. Moyen Âge** the Early Middle Ages; *Art & Hist* **la haute Renaissance** the High Renaissance
10 *Littéraire* (*noble*) lofty, high-minded; **cette haute pensée/âme** this exalted thought/soul
NM 1 (*partie supérieure → gén*) top; (→ *de robe*) bodice; **vers le h.** upwards; **h.** (*sur une caisse*) (this way *or* side) up; *Compta* **h. de bilan** (*fonds propres*) shareholders' funds
2 (*vêtement*) top
3 (*hauteur*) **un mur d'un mètre de h.** a one-metre (high) wall; **le mur fait six mètres de h.** the wall is six metres high; **regarder qn de (tout) son h.** to look down on sb; **tomber de tout son h.** (*chuter*) to fall headlong; (*être déçu*) to come down (to earth) with a bump; (*être surpris*) to be flabbergasted
4 *Can* (*d'un immeuble*) top floor
5 *Mktg* (*du marché*) high end, top end
ADV 1 (*dans l'espace*) high; **h. dans les airs** high (up) in the air; **levez h. la jambe** raise your leg (up) high *or* high up; **plus h., les genoux!** get those knees up!; **l'aigle monte h. dans le ciel** the eagle soars (high up) in the sky
2 (*dans le temps*) far (back); (*dans un livre, un article*) above; **remonter plus h. (dans le temps)** to go further back; **voir plus h.** see above; **comme il est dit plus h.** as mentioned above; **l'exemple cité plus h.** the example given above
3 (*fort, avec puissance*) **(tout) h.** aloud; **dire tout h. ce que tout le monde pense tout bas** to say out loud what everyone else is thinking; **penser tout h.** to think aloud *or* out loud; **parlez plus h.** speak up, speak louder; **dites-le h. et clair** *ou* **bien h.** tell (it to) everyone, say it out loud; **parler h. et clair** to speak one's mind
4 *Mus* high; **elle monte très h. dans les aigus** she gets up to the really high notes; **tu prends la deuxième mesure un peu trop h.** (*chanteur*) you're singing the second bar a bit sharp *or* high; (*musicien*) you're playing the second bar a bit sharp *or* high
5 (*dans une hiérarchie*) high; **être h. placé** to be highly placed, to hold high office; **des amis h. placés** friends in high places; **nous l'avons toujours placé très h. dans notre estime** we've always held him in high regard
6 *Bourse & Com* high; **les enchères sont montées très h.** the bidding went sky high *or* hit the roof; **le prix de la réparation risque de monter très h.** the cost of the repairs could be enormous

▫ **hauts** NMPL 1 (*dans des noms de lieux*) heights
2 *Naut* (*partie émergée*) topsider; (*du gréement*) top *or* higher rigging
3 (*locution*) **avoir** *ou* **connaître des hauts et des bas** to have one's ups and downs
▫ **haute** NF *Fam* **la haute** high society■, the upper crust; **les gens de la haute** upper crust people
▫ **de haut** ADV 1 (*d'un lieu élevé*) from a great height; **regarder qch de h.** to look down on sth; **tomber de h.** to fall from a great height; *Fig* (*être surpris*) to be flabbergasted; (*être déçu*) to come down (to earth) with a bump
2 (*avec détachement*) casually, unconcernedly; **prendre** *ou* **regarder** *ou* **voir les choses de h.** to look at things with an air of detachment
3 (*avec mépris*) **prendre qch de h.** to be high and mighty about sth; **regarder qn de h.** to look down on sb; **traiter qn de h.** to treat sb high-handedly
▫ **de haut en bas** ADV 1 (*sans mouvement*) from top to bottom; **nettoyer la maison de h. en bas** to clean the house from top to bottom
2 (*avec mouvement, vers le bas*) from top to bottom, downwards; **il faut toujours se raser de h. en bas** you must always shave with a downward movement
3 (*avec mépris*) **regarder** *ou* **considérer qn de h. en bas** to look sb up and down
▫ **d'en haut** ADV 1 (*depuis la partie élevée*) from above; **d'en h. on voit la mer** you can see the sea from up there
2 *Fig* (*dans la hiérarchie*) from on high; **le bon exemple doit venir d'en h.** people in positions of authority must give the lead; **la directive est venue d'en h.** the directive came from the top *or* from on high
▫ **du haut** ADJ (*de l'étage supérieur*) upstairs; **les gens du h.** the people upstairs; **les fenêtres du h.** the upstairs windows; **les chambres du h.** the upstairs bedrooms; **l'étage du h.** the top floor
▫ **du haut de** PRÉP (*échelle, colline*) from the top of; **du h. de la colline, on voit toute la ville** you can see the whole town from the top of the hill; **elle est tombée du h. de l'escalier** she fell all the way down the stairs; *Fig* **il nous regarde du h. de sa grandeur** he looks down his nose at us
▫ **en haut** ADV 1 (*à l'étage supérieur*) upstairs
2 (*dans la partie élevée*) at the top; **regarde dans le placard, les verres sont en h.** look in the cupboard, the glasses are at the top; **nous sommes passés par en h.** (*par la route du haut*) we came along the high road; **tout en h.** at the very top, right at the top
3 (*en l'air*) up; **lancer qch en h.** to throw sth (up) in the air
▫ **en haut de** PRÉP at the top of; **regarde en h. de l'armoire** look at the top of the wardrobe; **grimper en h. d'un arbre** to climb (up) to the top of a tree; **arriver en h. de la côte** to reach the top of the hill; **tout en h. d'une colline** high up on a hill
▫ **haut lieu** NM **le h. lieu de...** the Mecca of..., a Mecca for...; **en août, la ville devient un h. lieu de la musique** in August, the town is THE place *or* a major centre for music

'Les Hauts de Hurlevent' Emily Brontë 'Wuthering Heights'

*hautain[1], -e [otẽ, -ɛn] ADJ haughty; **d'une façon hautaine** haughtily
*hautain[2] [otẽ] = **hautin**
*hautbois [obwa] NM 1 (*instrument*) oboe; **h. alto** cor anglais, English horn 2 (*instrumentiste*) oboe (player)
*hautboïste [obɔist] NMF *Mus* oboist, oboe (player)
*Haut-Canada [okanada] NM *Hist* Upper Canada *voir aussi l'encadré sous* **Bas-Canada**
*haut-commissaire [okɔmisɛr] (*pl* **hauts-commissaires**) NM high commissioner
*haut-commissariat [okɔmisarja] (*pl* **hauts-commissariats**) NM 1 (*fonction*) high commissionership 2 (*bureaux*) high commission

*haut-de-chausses, *haut-de-chausse [odʃos] (*pl* **hauts-de-chausse** *ou* **hauts-de-chausses**) NM knee-breeches, breeches, trunk hose

*haut-de-forme [odfɔrm] (*pl* **hauts-de-forme**) NM top hat

*haute [ot] *voir* **haut**

*Haute-Autriche [ototriʃ] NF la H. Upper Austria

*haute-contre [otkɔ̃tr] (*pl* **hautes-contre**) NF (*voix*) countertenor (voice)
NM (*chanteur*) countertenor

*Haute-Corse [otkɔrs] NF la H. Haute-Corse

*haute-fidélité [otfidelite] (*pl* **hautes-fidélités**) NF
1 (*technique*) high fidelity, hi-fi 2 (*comme adj*) high-fidelity (*avant n*), hi-fi

*Haute-Garonne [otgarɔn] NF la H. Haute-Garonne

*Haute-Loire [otlwar] NF la H. Haute-Loire

*Haute-Marne [otmarn] NF la H. Haute-Marne

*hautement [otmɑ̃] ADV 1 (*fortement*) highly, extremely; **c'est h. improbable** it's highly unlikely; **ce qu'elle dit est h. sujet à caution** you should be extremely wary of what she says 2 *Vieilli* (*ouvertement*) openly

*Haute-Normandie [otnɔrmɑ̃di] NF la H. Haute-Normandie

*Hautes-Alpes [otzalp] NF les H. Hautes-Alpes

*Haute-Saône [otson] NF la H. Haute-Saône

*Haute-Savoie [otsavwa] NF la H. Haute-Savoie

*Hautes-Pyrénées [otpirene] NFPL les H. Hautes-Pyrénées

*hauteur [otœr] NF 1 (*mesure verticale*) height; **quelle est la h. du mur?** how high is the wall?; **l'immeuble a une h. de 40 mètres** the building is 40 metres high; **la pièce fait trois mètres de h.** (**sous plafond**) the ceiling height in the room is three metres; **il est tombé de toute sa h.** he fell headlong; **de faible h.** low; *Constr* **h. sous clef** rise; *Constr* **à h. d'appui** at elbow height; **h. libre** *Constr* headroom; *Rail* overhead clearance; *Ordinat* **h. de ligne** line height; *Typ* **h. de page** page depth; *Constr* **h. de passage** headroom; **h. sous plafond** ceiling height; **quelle est la h. sous plafond?** what is the height of *or* how high is the ceiling?
2 (*altitude*) height, altitude; **prendre de la h.** to gain altitude *or* height; **une occupation qui sied à la h. de son rang** a post in keeping with his/her high rank; **n'étant plus mandaté, je me permets de voir les choses avec (une certaine) h.** as I'm no longer in office, I can afford to look upon things with a certain detachment
3 *Mus & Ling* height, pitch; **deux notes/voyelles de la même h.** two equally pitched notes/vowels
4 (*noblesse*) loftiness; **rien n'égala la h. de vues** *ou* **de pensées de ce monarque** nothing could equal the loftiness of this monarch's ideas
5 (*arrogance*) haughtiness, arrogance; **un refus plein de h.** a haughty refusal
6 *Sport* **la h.** the high jump; **recordman du monde de h.** world record holder for the men's high jump
7 *Géom* (*d'un triangle*) altitude
8 *Couture* length
9 *Mil & Nucl* **h. d'éclatement** height of burst
10 *Astron* **h. d'un astre** height of a star
❏ **hauteurs** NFPL heights; **il y a de la neige sur les hauteurs** there's snow on the higher slopes; **l'aigle s'envola vers les hauteurs** the eagle soared high up (into the sky *or* air); **les hauteurs de Montmartre** the top of Montmartre
❏ **à hauteur de** PRÉP **h. des yeux** at eye level; **à h. d'homme** about six feet off the ground; **vous serez remboursé à h. de 1000 euros** you'll be reimbursed up to 1,000 euros; **un actionnaire à h. de 5 pour cent** a shareholder with 5 percent of the shares
❏ **à la hauteur** ADJ *Fam* **tu ne t'es pas montré à la h.** you weren't up to it *or* equal to the task; **elle a été tout à fait à la h.** she coped beautifully
❏ **à la hauteur de** PRÉP 1 (*au niveau de*) up to; **l'eau nous arrivait à la h. des épaules** the water came up to our shoulders
2 (*à côté de*) **arrivé à sa h., je m'aperçus qu'il parlait tout seul** when I was *or* drew level with him, I noticed he was talking to himself; **elle habite à la h. de l'église** she lives near the church *or* up by the church; **arrivés à la h. du**

---

cap when we were in line with *or* when we were off the cape; **à la h. de Grenoble, il faudra commencer à penser à mettre les chaînes** when you get to Grenoble, you will have to start thinking about putting the snow chains on; **il y a des embouteillages à la h. de l'échangeur de Rocquencourt** there are traffic jams at the Rocquencourt interchange
3 (*digne de*) worthy of; **une carrière à la h. de ses ambitions** a career commensurate with his/her ambitions; **être** *ou* **se montrer à la h. d'une tâche** to be *or* to prove equal to *or* up to a task; **être à la h. de la situation** to be equal to *or* up to the situation
❏ **en hauteur** ADV 1 (*debout*) upright; **mettez-le en h.** stand it upright *or* on its end
2 (*dans un endroit élevé*) **nous avons installé les étagères en h.** we put the shelves high up on the wall; **ça ne vous ennuie pas d'habiter en h.?** doesn't living high up bother you?

*Haute-Vienne [otvjɛn] NF la H. Haute-Vienne

*Haute-Volta [otvɔlta] NF la H. Upper Volta

*haut-fond [ofɔ̃] (*pl* **hauts-fonds**) NM shallow, shoal

*haut-fourneau [ofurno] (*pl* **hauts-fourneaux**) NM blast furnace

*hautin [otɛ̃] NM *Agr* espalier-trained vine

*Haut-Karabakh [okarabak] NM Nagorno-Karabakh

*haut-le-cœur [olkœr] NM INV 1 (*nausée*) **avoir un/des h.** to retch 2 *Fig* **une attitude aussi lâche me donne des h.** such cowardly behaviour makes me (feel) sick

*haut-le-corps [olkɔr] NM INV start, jump; **avoir un h.** to start, to jump

*haut-parleur [oparlœr] (*pl* **haut-parleurs**) NM loudspeaker, speaker; **h. d'aigus** tweeter; **h. de graves** woofer

*haut-relief [orəljɛf] (*pl* **hauts-reliefs**) NM *Beaux-Arts* high relief

*Haut-Rhin [orɛ̃] NM le H. Haut-Rhin

*Hauts-de-Seine [odsɛn] NMPL les H. Hauts-de-Seine

*hauturier, -ère [otyrje, -ɛr] ADJ deep-sea (*avant n*); **navigation hauturière** ocean navigation; **pêche hauturière** deep-sea fishing

*haüyne [oin] NF *Minér* haüyne

*havage [avaʒ] NM *Mines* cutting, hewing

*havanais, -e [avanɛ, -ɛz] ADJ of/from Havana
❏ **Havanais, -e** NM,F = inhabitant of or person from Havana
❏ **havanaise** NF habanera

*Havane [avan] NF La H. Havana

*havane [avan] NM 1 (*tabac*) Havana 2 (*cigare*) Havana
ADJ INV Havana brown

*hâve [ɑv] ADJ haggard; (*joues*) sunken

*haveneau, -x [avno], ***havenet** [avnɛ] NM *Pêche* shrimping net

*haver [3] [ave] VT *Mines* to cut, to hew

*Havers [avɛrs] NPR *Anat* **systèmes de H.** Haversian canals

*haveur [avœr] NM *Mines* hewer, coal-cutter, cutter

*haveuse [avøz] NF *Mines* cutting machine, cutter

*havrais, -e [avrɛ, -ɛz] ADJ of/from Le Havre
❏ **Havrais, -e** NM,F = inhabitant of or person from Le Havre

*Havre [avr] NM Le H. Le Havre; **au H.** in Le Havre

*havre [avr] NM *Littéraire* haven, harbour; **un h. de paix** a haven of peace

*havresac [avrəsak] NM (*de campeur*) haversack, knapsack; (*de militaire*) haversack, kitbag

*havrits [avri] NMPL *Mines* rashings

hawaïen, -enne [awajɛ̃, -ɛn] = **hawaiien**

Hawaii [awaj] NM Hawaii; **vivre à H.** to live in Hawaii; **aller à Hawaii** to go to Hawaii

hawaiien, -enne [awajɛ̃, -ɛn] ADJ Hawaiian
NM (*langue*) Hawaiian
❏ **Hawaiien, -enne** NM,F Hawaiian

Haydn [ajdən] NPR Haydn

*Haye [ɛ] NF La H. The Hague

*hayon [ajɔ̃] NM 1 (*de voiture*) hatchback, tailgate; (*d'une charrette*) tailboard 2 *Tech* **h. élévateur** (fork) lift

*HCR [aʃseɛr] NM (*abrév* **Haut-Commissariat des Nations unies pour les réfugiés**) UNHCR

HD *Ordinat* (*abrév écrite* **haute densité**) HD

---

*HDL-cholestérol [aʃdeɛlkɔlɛsterɔl] NM *Méd* HDL cholesterol, high-density lipoproteins

*HD MAC [aʃdemak] NM (*abrév* **High Definition Multiplexed Analogue Components**) HD MAC

hdr (*abrév écrite* **heures des repas**) = at lunchtime or in the evening (*used in newspaper advertisements*)

*hé [e] EXCLAM 1 (*pour interpeller quelqu'un*) hey!; **hé, vous, là!** hey! you!; **hé! arrêtez!** hey! *or* oi! stop it! 2 (*d'étonnement*) hey!, well (well, well)!; **hé hé, quelle surprise!** well(, well, well), what a surprise!; **hé, la voilà qui arrive!** hey, here she comes!

*heaume [om] NM *Hér & Hist* helm, helmet

*heaumier, -ère [omje, -ɛr] NM,F maker of helmets

hebdo [ɛbdo] NM *Fam Journ* weekly ■; **h. télé** TV magazine ■

hebdomadaire [ɛbdɔmadɛr] ADJ weekly; **un feuilleton/salaire h.** a weekly serial/wage
NM weekly

hebdomadairement [ɛbdɔmadɛrmɑ̃] ADV weekly, once a week

hebdomadier, -ère [ɛbdɔmadje, -ɛr] NM,F *Rel* hebdomadary

hébéphrène [ebefrɛn] *Psy* ADJ hebephreniac
NMF hebephreniac

hébéphrénie [ebefreni] NF *Psy* hebephrenia

hébéphrénique [ebefrenik] ADJ *Psy* hebephrenic

héberge [ebɛrʒ] NF *Jur* point of disjunction

hébergement [ebɛrʒəmɑ̃] NM 1 (*lieu*) lodgings, accommodation 2 (*action*) lodging; **l'h. est en chalet** chalet accommodation is provided 3 *Ordinat* (*de site Web*) hosting

héberger [17] [ebɛrʒe] VT 1 (*loger* → *pour une certaine durée*) to lodge, to accommodate; (→ *à l'improviste*) to put up; (→ *réfugié, vagabond*) to take in, to shelter; (→ *criminel*) to harbour, to shelter; **notre bâtiment hébergera le secrétariat pendant les travaux** the secretarial department will be housed in our building during the alterations 2 *Ordinat* (*site Web*) to host

hébergeur [ebɛrʒœr] NM *Ordinat* (*de site Web*) host

hébertisme [ebɛrtism] NM = developing the body through open-air games and sports, such as walking and swimming

hébertiste [ebɛrtist] *Hist* ADJ of Jacques Hébert (*politician during the French Revolution*)
NMF follower of Jacques Hébert

hébété, -e [ebete] ADJ dazed, in a daze; **il avait un air h.** he looked dazed
NM,F **il était là comme un h.** he stood there looking stunned

hébétement [ebetmɑ̃] NM stupor; **son h. est dû à l'alcool** he's in a drunken stupor

hébéter [18] [ebete] VT to daze; **hébété par l'alcool/la drogue** in a drunken/drug-induced stupor; **hébété de douleur** numb with grief

hébétude [ebetyd] NF 1 *Littéraire* stupor, stupefaction 2 *Psy* hebetude

heboïdophrénie [ebɔidofreni] NF *Psy* heboidophrenia

hébraïque [ebraik] ADJ Hebraic, Hebrew (*avant n*)

hébraïsant, -e [ebraizɑ̃, -ɑ̃t] NM,F Hebraist, Hebrew scholar

hébraïser [3] [ebraize] VT to Hebraize

hébraïsme [ebraism] NM *Ling* Hebraism

hébraïste [ebraist] NMF Hebraist, Hebrew scholar

hébreu, -x [ebrø] ADJ m Hebrew; **l'État h.** the Hebrew State, Israel
NM 1 (*langue*) Hebrew 2 *Fam* (*locution*) **pour moi, c'est de l'h.** I can't make head or tail of it, it's all Greek to me
❏ **Hébreux** NMPL **les Hébreux** the Hebrews

Hébrides [ebrid] NFPL (**les îles**) H. the Hebrides; **vivre aux H.** to live in the Hebrides; **aller aux H.** to go to the Hebrides; **les H. extérieures** the Outer Hebrides; **les H. intérieures** the Inner Hebrides

*Hébron [ebrɔ̃] NF Hebron

HEC [aʃəe] 1 NF (*abrév* **Hautes études commerciales**) = prestigious business school in Paris
2 NMF = graduate of the ''HEC'' business school

hécatombe [ekatɔ̃b] NF 1 (*carnage*) slaughter, massacre; **l'h. annuelle des blessés de la route** the carnage that occurs every year on the roads 2 *Fig* **ça a été une h. cette année aux examens!**

---

hau-hec

the exam results were disastrous this year! **3** *Antiq* hecatomb

hectare [ɛktar] NM hectare

hectique [ɛktik] ADJ *Méd* **fièvre h.** hectic fever

hecto [ɛkto] NM *Fam* **1** (*abrév* **hectogramme**) hectogramme▪, hectogram▪ **2** (*abrév* **hectolitre**) hectolitre▪

hectogramme [ɛktɔgram] NM hectogramme, hectogram; **un h.** a hundred grams, a hectogram

hectolitre [ɛktɔlitr] NM hectolitre; **un h.** a hundred litres, a hectolitre

hectomètre [ɛktɔmɛtr] NM hectometre; **un h.** a hundred metres, a hectometre

hectométrique [ɛktɔmetrik] ADJ hectometre (*avant n*)

hectopascal, -als [ɛktɔpaskal] NM millibar

Hector [ɛktɔr] NPR *Myth* Hector

hectowatt [ɛktɔwat] NM hectowatt; **un h.** a hundred watts, a hectowatt

hédéracée [ederase] *Bot* NF member of the Hedera genus
  ❏ **hédéracées** NFPL Hedera

hédonisme [edɔnism] NM hedonism

hédoniste [edɔnist] ADJ hedonist, hedonistic NMF hedonist

hédonistique [edɔnistik] ADJ hedonistic

hégélianisme [egeljanism] NM *Phil* Hegelianism

hégélien, -enne [egeljɛ̃, -ɛn] *Phil* ADJ Hegelian NM,F Hegelian

hégémonie [eʒemɔni] NF hegemony; **l'h. des USA sur le monde** the USA's position of hegemony in the world

hégémonique [eʒemɔnik] ADJ hegemonic

hégémonisme [eʒemɔnism] NM hegemonic tendencies

hégire [eʒir] NF *Rel* **l'h.** the hegira, the hejira

*****heiduque** [edyk, ɛdyk] NM *Hist* heyduck

*****hein** [ɛ̃] EXCLAM *Fam* **1** (*quoi?*) **h.?** eh?, what? **2** (*n'est-ce pas?*) eh?; **c'est drôle, h.!** funny, eh *or* isn't it!; **tu ne vas pas le répéter, h.?** you won't say anything, will you?▪, you won't tell anyone, will you?▪; **h. qu'il fait bien la cuisine!** he's a good cook, isn't he?▪ **3** (*exprimant la colère*) OK!, right!; **on se calme, h.!** cool it, will you!, that's enough, OK?; **tu te tais, h.!** just shut up, OK?▪

*****hei tiki** [ejtiki] NM (*pendentif*) tiki (*Maori pendant made of jade*)

*****hélas** [elas] EXCLAM unfortunately, unhappily, *Littéraire* alas; **h., je ne pourrai pas venir** unfortunately *or* I'm afraid I won't be able to come; **h., trois fois h.!** alas, alack!

Hélène [elɛn] NPR **1** *Myth* Helen; **H. de Troie** Helen of Troy **2** *Hist* (*mère de Constantin*) Helena

hélépole [elepɔl] NF *Hist* helepole, helepolis

*****héler** [18] [ele] VT (*personne*) to call out to, to hail; (*taxi, porteur*) to hail

hélianthe [eljɑ̃t] NM *Bot* sunflower, *Spéc* helianthus

hélianthème [eljɑ̃tɛm] NM *Bot* rockrose, *Spéc* helianthemum

hélianthine [eljɑ̃tin] NF *Chim* methyl orange

héliaque [eljak] ADJ *Astron* heliacal

héliaste [eljast] NM *Antiq* Heliast

hélice [elis] NF **1** *Tech & Naut* propeller, screw, screwpropeller; **h. d'avion** air screw, aircraft propeller **2** *Archit & Math* helix; **escalier en h.** spiral staircase

héliciculteur, -trice [elisikyltœr, -tris] NM,F snail breeder

héliciculture [elisikyltyr] NF snail breeding

hélico [eliko] NM *Fam* (*abrév* **hélicoptère**) chopper

hélicoïdal, -e, -aux, -ales [elikɔidal, -o] ADJ **1** (*en forme de vrille*) helical, spiral; **escalier h.** spiral staircase **2** *Math & Tech* helicoidal, helicoidal

hélicoïde [elikɔid] *Math* ADJ helicoid NM helicoid

hélicon [elikɔ̃] NM helicon

héliconia [elikɔnja] NM *Bot* heliconia

hélicoptère [elikɔptɛr] NM helicopter; **h. d'attaque** attack helicopter; **h. de combat** helicopter gunship

héligare [eligar] NF heliport

hélio [eljo] NF *Fam* (*abrév* **héliogravure**) heliogravure▪

héliocentrique [eljɔsɑ̃trik] ADJ heliocentric

héliocentrisme [eljɔsɑ̃trism] NM heliocentrism

héliodore [eljɔdɔr] NM *Minér* heliodor

héliographe [eljɔgraf] NM *Météo* heliograph

héliographie [eljɔgrafi] NF *Typ* heliography

héliograveur, -euse [eljɔgravœr, -øz] NM,F photo-engraver

héliogravure [eljɔgravyr] NF heliogravure

héliomarin, -e [eljɔmarɛ̃, -in] ADJ (*cure*) involving sunshine and sea air therapy; (*établissement*) offering sunshine and sea air therapy

hélion [eljɔ̃] NM *Phys* helion, helium nucleus

héliophile [eljɔfil] ADJ sun-loving, *Spéc* heliophilous

Hélios [eljos] NPR *Myth* Helios

héliostat [eljɔsta] NM *Phys* heliostat

héliosynchrone [eljɔsɛ̃krɔn] ADJ *Astron* heliosynchronous

héliothérapie [eljɔterapi] NF *Méd* heliotherapy; **h. artificielle** sunray treatment

héliotrope [eljɔtrɔp] NM *Bot & Minér* heliotrope

héliotropine [eljɔtrɔpin] NF *Chim* heliotropin, piperonal

héliotropisme [eljɔtrɔpism] NM *Biol* heliotropism

héliport [elipɔr] NM heliport

héliportage [elipɔrtaʒ] NM helicopter transportation

héliporté, -e [elipɔrte] ADJ **1** (*transporté par hélicoptère*) helicoptered; **troupes héliportées** airborne troops (*brought in by helicopter*) **2** (*exécuté par hélicoptère*) **une opération héliportée** a helicopter mission

héliski [eliski] NM heliskiing

hélisurface [elisyrfas] NF *Naut* helideck; (*sur un immeuble*) helipad

hélitransporté, -e [elitrɑ̃spɔrte] ADJ transported by helicopter, helicoptered

hélitreuillage [elitrœjaʒ] NM winching up (into a helicopter)

hélitreuiller [5] [elitrœje] VT to winch up (into a helicopter)

hélium [eljɔm] NM *Chim* helium

hélix [eliks] NM *Anat & Zool* helix

helladique [eladik] ADJ *Archéol* Helladic

hellébore [elebɔr] NM *Bot* hellebore; **h. fétide** stinking hellebore

helléborine [eleborin] NF *Bot* helleborine

hellène [elɛn] ADJ Hellenic
  ❏ **Hellène** NMF Hellene

hellénique [elenik] ADJ *Antiq* (*des Hellènes*) Hellenic; (*de la Grèce moderne*) Greek

hellénisant, -e [elenizɑ̃, -ɑ̃t] NM,F Hellenist

hellénisation [elenizasjɔ̃] NF Hellenization

helléniser [3] [elenize] VT to Hellenize

hellénisme [elenism] NM **1** (*civilisation*) Hellenism **2** *Ling* Hellenism, Graecism

helléniste [elenist] NMF Hellenist

hellénistique [elenistik] ADJ Hellenistic

*****hello** [ɛlo] EXCLAM hello!

helminthe [ɛlmɛ̃t] NM *Biol & Méd* helminth

helminthiase [ɛlmɛ̃tjaz] NF *Méd* helminthiasis

helminthique [ɛlmɛ̃tik] *Méd* ADJ helminthic NM helminthic

helminthologie [ɛlmɛ̃tɔlɔʒi] NF *Biol & Entom* helminthology

hélodée [elɔde] NF *Bot* water thyme, *Spéc* elodea

héloderme [elɔdɛrm] NM *Zool* gila monster, *Spéc* heloderma

Héloïse [elɔiz] NPR **H. et Abélard** Héloïse and Abelard

*****Helsinki** [ɛlsiŋki] NM Helsinki

helvelle [ɛlvɛl] NF *Bot* turban-top

helvète [ɛlvɛt] ADJ Helvetian
  ❏ **Helvète** NMF Helvetian

Helvétie [ɛlvesi] NF *Hist* **l'H.** Helvetia

helvétique [ɛlvetik] ADJ Swiss

helvétisme [ɛlvetism] NM = characteristic word or expression used by French-speaking Swiss

*****hem** [ɛm] EXCLAM **1** (*exprimant le doute*) hum, ahem, mmm; (*exprimant une hésitation*) hum, er **2** (*pour attirer l'attention*) ahem!

héma- [ema] PRÉF *Méd* haema-

hémal [emal] NM *Physiol* haemal

hémangiome [emɑ̃ʒjom] NM *Méd* haemangioma

hémarthrose [emartroz] NF *Méd* haemarthrosis

hématémèse [ematemɛz] NF *Chim & Physiol* haematemesis

hématie [emasi] NF *Biol* erythrocyte

hématine [ematin] NF *Biol* haem, haematin

hématique [ematik] ADJ *Physiol* haematic

hématite [ematit] NF *Minér* haematite

hémato- [emato] PRÉF *Méd* haemato-

hématoblaste [ematɔblast] NM *Physiol* haematoblast

hématocèle [ematɔsɛl] NM *Méd* haematocele

hématocrite [ematɔkrit] NM *Physiol* haematocrit

hématographie [ematɔgrafi] NF *Méd* haematography

hématologie [ematɔlɔʒi] NF *Méd* haematology

hématologique [ematɔlɔʒik] ADJ *Méd* haematological, haematologic

hématologiste [ematɔlɔʒist], **hématologue** [ematɔlɔg] NMF *Méd* haematologist

hématome [ematom] NM bruise, *Spéc* haematoma; **se faire un h.** to bruise oneself

hématophage [ematɔfaʒ] ADJ *Zool* haematophagous

hématopoïèse [ematɔpɔjez] NF *Physiol* haemopoiesis

hématopoïétique [ematɔpɔjetik] ADJ *Physiol* haematopoietic

hématose [ematoz] NF *Physiol* haematosis

hématozoaire [ematozɔɛr] NM *Zool* haematozoon

hématurie [ematyri] NF *Méd* haematuria

hème [ɛm] NM *Biol & Chim* haem

héméralope [emeralɔp] *Méd* ADJ nyctalopic NMF nyctalopic

héméralopie [emeralɔpi] NF *Méd* night blindness, *Spéc* nyctalopia

héméralopique [emeralɔpik] ADJ *Méd* nyctalopic

hémérobe [emerɔb] NM *Entom* lacewing

hémérocalle [emerɔkal] NF *Bot* hemerocallis, day-lily

hémialgie [emialʒi] NF *Méd* hemialgia

hémianopsie [emianɔpsi] NF *Méd* hemianopia

hémicordé [emikɔrde] *Zool* NM member of the Hemichordata *or* Hemichordata group
  ❏ **hémicordés** NMPL Hemichordata, Hemichorda

hémicrânie [emikrɑni] NF *Méd* hemicrania (migraine)

hémicycle [emisikl] NM **1** (*espace en demi-cercle*) semicircle; **l'abside de l'église est un h.** the apse of the church is semicircular **2** (*salle garnie de gradins*) semicircular amphitheatre; *Pol* **l'H.** (*Assemblée*) the French National Assembly; (*salle*) = the benches chamber of the French National Assembly

hémièdre [emiɛdr] ADJ *Phys* hemihedral

hémiédrie [emiedri] NF *Phys* hemihedrism

hémine [emin] NF *Biol* haemin

hémione [emjɔn] NM *Zool* hemione, dziggetai, kiang

hémioxyde [emjɔksid] NM *Chim* **h. d'azote** dinitrogen oxide

hémiplégie [emipleʒi] NF *Méd* hemiplegia

hémiplégique [emipleʒik] *Méd* ADJ hemiplegic NMF hemiplegic

hémiptère [emiptɛr] *Vieilli* = **hémiptéroïde**

hémiptéroïde [emipterɔid] *Entom* NM hemipteron, *Spéc* member of the Hemiptera order
  ❏ **hémiptéroïdes** NMPL Hemiptera

hémisphère [emisfɛr] NM hemisphere; **l'h. Nord/Sud** the Northern/Southern hemisphere; **h. cérébral** cerebral hemisphere

hémisphérique [emisferik] ADJ hemispheric, hemispherical

hémistiche [emistiʃ] NM *Littérature* hemistich

hémitropie [emitrɔpi] NF *Minér* hemitropism, hemitropy

hémo- [emo] PRÉF *Méd* haemo-

hémochromatose [emɔkromatoz] NF *Chim* haemochromatosis, bronze diabetes

hémocompatible [emɔkɔ̃patibl] ADJ *Biol* haemocompatible

hémoculture [emɔkyltyr] NF *Méd* blood culture

hémocyanine [emɔsjanin] NF *Physiol* haemocyanin

hémodialyse [emɔdjaliz] NF *Méd* haemodialysis

hémodynamique [emɔdinamik] NF *Chim & Méd* haemodynamics (*singulier*)

hémoglobine [emɔglɔbin] NF **1** *Physiol* haemoglobin **2** *Fam* (*sang*) gore, blood and guts

hémoglobinopathie [emɔglɔbinɔpati] NF *Méd* haemoglobinopathy

hémoglobinurie [emɔglɔbinyri] NF *Méd* haemoglobinuria

hec-hem

hémogramme [emɔgram] **NM** *Méd* haemogram, CBC
hémolyse [emɔliz] **NF** *Chim & Méd* haemolysis
hémolysine [emɔlizin] **NF** *Biol & Chim* haemolysin
hémolytique [emɔlitik] **ADJ** *Chim & Méd* haemolytic
hémopathie [emɔpati] **NF** *Méd* blood disease
hémophile [emɔfil] *Méd* **ADJ** haemophiliac
NM haemophiliac
hémophilie [emɔfili] **NF** *Méd* haemophilia; **être atteint d'h.** to suffer from haemophilia, to be a haemophiliac
hémoptysie [emɔptizi] **NF** *Méd* haemoptysis
hémorragie [emɔraʒi] **NF 1** *Méd* haemorrhage, bleeding *(UNCOUNT)*; **h. cérébrale** cerebral haemorrhage; **h. interne/externe** internal/external haemorrhage; **faire une h.** to haemorrhage
2 *Fig (perte)* drain; **les universités connaissent une véritable h. depuis la crise** the universities have been drained of their manpower since the beginning of the crisis; **l'h. des cerveaux** the brain drain; **l'h. des capitaux** the drain *or* haemorrhage of capital
hémorragique [emɔraʒik] **ADJ** *Méd* haemorrhagic
hémorroïdaire [emɔrɔidɛr] *Méd* **ADJ** *(gén)* haemorrhoidal; *(malade)* suffering from haemorrhoids
NMF haemorrhoids sufferer
hémorroïdal, -e, -aux, -ales [emɔrɔidal, -o] **ADJ** *Méd* haemorrhoidal
hémorroïdes [emɔrɔid] **NFPL** *Méd* haemorrhoids; **avoir des h.** to suffer from haemorrhoids, to have piles
hémostase [emɔstaz] **NF** *Physiol* haemostasis
hémostatique [emɔstatik] *Physiol* **ADJ** haemostatic
NM haemostatic
hémotoxine [emɔtɔksin] **NF** *Physiol* haemotoxin
hémotoxique [emɔtɔksik] **ADJ** *Physiol* haemotoxic
hémovigilance [emɔviʒilɑ̃s] **NF** *Méd* haemovigilance
hendécagonal, -e, -aux, -ales [ɛ̃dekagɔnal, -o] **ADJ** *Géom* hendecagonal
hendécagone [ɛ̃dekagɔn] **NM** *Géom* hendecagon
hendécasyllabe [ɛ̃dekasilab] **ADJ** hendecasyllabic
NM hendecasyllable
hendiadyin [ɛndjadin], **hendiadys** [ɛndjadis] **NM** *Ling* hendiadys
***henné** [ene] **NM** henna; **se faire un h.** to henna one's hair, to give one's hair a henna rinse; **les cheveux teints au h.** hennaed hair
***hennin** [enɛ̃] **NM** *Hist* hennin
***hennir** [32] [enir] **VI 1** *(cheval)* to neigh, to whinny **2** *(personne)* to bray
***hennissant, -e** [enisɑ̃, -ɑ̃t] **ADJ 1** *(cheval)* neighing **2** *(rire)* braying
***hennissement** [enismɑ̃] **NM 1** *(d'un cheval)* neigh, whinny **2** *(d'une personne)* braying *(UNCOUNT)*
***hennuyer, -ère** [ɛnɥije, -ɛr] = **hainuyer**
Henri [ɑ̃ri] **NPR 1** *(roi de France)* Henry; **H. IV** Henry the Fourth **2** *(roi d'Angleterre)* Henry; **H. VIII** Henry the Eighth
Henriette-Marie [ɑ̃rjɛtmari] **NPR H. (de France)** Henrietta Maria
***henry** [ɑ̃ri] *(pl* **henrys)** **NM** *Élec* henry
***hep** [ɛp] **EXCLAM** hey!; **h. ! taxi!** hey! taxi!
héparine [eparin] **NF** *Pharm* heparin
hépatalgie [epatalʒi] **NF** *Méd* hepatalgia
hépatectomie [epatɛktɔmi] **NF** *Méd* hepatectomy
hépatique [epatik] **ADJ** *Physiol & Méd* hepatic, liver *(avant n)*
NMF *Méd* = person suffering from a liver ailment
NF *Bot* liverwort, hepatic
hépatisation [epatizasjɔ̃] **NF** *Méd* hepatization
hépatite [epatit] **NF** *Méd* hepatitis; **h. infectieuse** infectious hepatitis; **h. virale** viral hepatitis; **h. A/B/C** hepatitis A/B/C
hépatocyte [epatɔsit] **NM** *Biol* hepatocyte
hépatologie [epatɔlɔʒi] **NF** *Méd* hepatology
hépatologue [epatɔlɔg] **NMF** *Méd* hepatologist
hépatomégalie [epatɔmegali] **NF** *Méd* hepatomegaly
hépatonéphrite [epatɔnefrit] **NF** *Méd* hepatonephritis
hépatopancréas [epatɔpɑ̃kreas] **NM** *Zool & Anat* hepatopancreas
Héphaïstos [efaistos] **NPR** *Myth* Hephaestus
heptaèdre [ɛptaɛdr] **NM** *Géom* heptahedron
heptaédrique [ɛptaedrik] **ADJ** *Géom* heptahedral
heptagonal, -e, -aux, -ales [ɛptagɔnal, -o] **ADJ** *Géom* heptagonal
heptagone [ɛptagɔn] **NM** *Géom* heptagon
heptane [ɛptan] **NM** *Chim* heptane
heptasyllabe [ɛptasilab] *Littérature* **ADJ** heptasyllabic
NM heptasyllabic verse
heptathlon [ɛptatlɔ̃] **NM** heptathlon
Héra [era] **NPR** *Myth* Hera
Héraclès [eraklɛs] **NPR** *Myth* Heracles
Héraclite [eraklit] **NPR** Heraclitus
Héraklion [eraklijɔ̃] **NF** Heraklion
héraldique [eraldik] **ADJ** heraldic
NF heraldry
héraldiste [eraldist] **NMF** heraldry specialist, heraldist
Hérault [ero] **NM l'H.** Hérault
***héraut** [ero] **NM 1** *Hist* herald; **h. d'armes** officer *or* herald of arms **2** *Fig Littéraire* herald, messenger
herbacé, -e [ɛrbase] **ADJ** *Bot* herbaceous
herbage [ɛrbaʒ] **NM** *(prairie)* grazing land, pasture (land); *(herbe)* grass, pasture
❑ **herbages NMPL 1** *Pêche* coral fishing nets **2** *Can (herbes)* medicinal herbs; *(racines)* medicinal roots
herbager[1] [17] [ɛrbaʒe] **VT** *Vieilli* to graze, to put out to grass
herbager[2], **-ère** [ɛrbaʒe, -ɛr] **NM,F** grazier
herbe [ɛrb] **NF 1** *(plante, gazon)* grass; **faire de l'h.** *(pour les lapins)* to cut grass; **laisser un champ en h.** to leave a field under grass; *Bot* **h. de blé** wheatgrass; *Bot* **h. à chats** catmint, catnip; *Bot* **h. à éternuer** sneezewort; *Bot* **herbes folles** wild grass; **herbes marines** seaweed; *Bot* **h. à puces** poison ivy; *Bot* **h. à Robert** herb Robert; *Bot* **h. sacrée** wild vervain; *Bot* **h. à sétons** green hellebore; *Bot* **h. à tous les maux** wild vervain; **hautes herbes** tall grass; **une mauvaise h.** a weed; **de la mauvaise h.** weeds; *Fam Fig* **je connais ce type, c'est de la mauvaise h.** I know this guy, he's no good *or* bad news; **comme de la mauvaise h.** like wildfire; **couper** *ou* **faucher l'h. sous le pied à qn** to cut the ground *or* to pull the rug from under sb's feet; *Prov* **l'h. du voisin est toujours plus verte** the grass is always greener on the other side (of the fence)
2 *(aromatique, médicinale)* herb; *Culin* **fines herbes** herbs, fines herbes; **herbes de Provence** mixed herbs
3 *Fam (marihuana)* grass, weed
❑ **en herbe ADJ** *Bot* green; *Fig* in the making; **c'est un musicien en h.** he has the makings of a musician, he's a budding musician
herbe-aux-chats [ɛrboʃa] *(pl* **herbes-aux-chats)** **NF 1** *(cataire)* catnip, catmint **2** *(valériane)* valerian
herbette [ɛrbɛt] **NF** *Arch* (green)sward
herbettes [ɛrbɛt] **NFPL** *Suisse* mixed herbs
herbeux, -euse [ɛrbø, -øz] **ADJ** grassy
herbicide [ɛrbisid] **ADJ** herbicidal
NM weedkiller, *Spéc* herbicide
herbier [ɛrbje] **NM 1** *(collection)* dried flower collection, *Spéc* herbarium; *(lieu)* herbarium; **faire un h.** to build up a collection of dried plants **2** *Géog* aquatic plant habitat
herbivore [ɛrbivɔr] **ADJ** herbivorous
NM herbivore
herborisation [ɛrbɔrizasjɔ̃] **NF** botanizing, plant-collecting
herboriser [3] [ɛrbɔrize] **VI** to botanize, to collect plants
herboriste [ɛrbɔrist] **NMF** *Méd & Pharm* herbalist, herb doctor
herboristerie [ɛrbɔristəri] **NF** herbalist's (shop)
herbu, -e [ɛrby] **ADJ** grassy
***herchage** [ɛrʃaʒ] **NM** *Mines* haulage
***hercher** [3] [ɛrʃe] **VI** *Mines* to haul coal
***hercheur** [ɛrʃœr] **NM** *Mines* haulage man
Herculanum [ɛrkylanɔm] **NF** *Géog* Herculaneum
Hercule [ɛrkyl] **NPR** *Myth* Hercules
hercule [ɛrkyl] **NM 1** *(homme fort)* Hercules; **il est bâti en h.** he's as strong as an ox **2 h. (de foire)** strong man
herculéen, -enne [ɛrkyleɛ̃, -ɛn] **ADJ** *(tâche)* Herculean; *(force)* Herculean, superhuman
hercynien, -enne [ɛrsinjɛ̃, -ɛn] **ADJ** *Géol* Hercynian
***herd-book** [œrdbuk] *(pl* **herd-books)** **NM** herd book
***hère** [ɛr] **NM 1** *Littéraire* **un pauvre h.** a poor wretch **2** *Zool* (yearling) stag
héréditaire [ereditɛr] **ADJ 1** *Jur* hereditary **2** *Biol* inherited, hereditary; *Hum* **il est toujours grincheux, c'est h.!** he's always moaning, he was born like that!
héréditairement [ereditɛrmɑ̃] **ADV** hereditarily, through heredity
hérédité [eredite] **NF 1** *Biol* heredity; **h. liée au sexe** sex-linkage; **elle a une h. chargée** *ou* **une lourde h.** her family history has a lot to answer for; *Hum* **c'est l'h. qui veut ça!** it's in the blood! **2** *Jur* **action en pétition d'h.** = claim to succeed to an estate held by a third party
***hereford** [ɛrfɔrd] **NMF** *(bovin)* Hereford cow
hérésiarque [erezjark] **NMF** heresiarch
hérésie [erezi] **NF 1** *(erreur)* sacrilege, heresy; **une table Régence dans la cuisine, c'est de l'h.!** a Regency table in the kitchen, that's (a) sacrilege! **2** *Rel* heresy
hérétique [eretik] **ADJ** heretical
NMF heretic
***hérissé, -e** [erise] **ADJ 1** *(cheveux, poils → naturellement raides)* bristly; *(→ dressés de peur)* bristling, standing on end; **un chien à l'échine hérissée** a dog with its hackles up **2** *(parsemé)* **h. de** *(clous, pointes)* covered in, bristling with; *(citations, fautes)* full of; **un texte h. de difficultés** a text full of difficult points **3** *Bot* spiny
***hérissement** [erismɑ̃] **NM** *(du pelage)* bristling
***hérisser** [3] [erise] **VT 1** *(dresser)* **le chat hérissait ses poils** the cat's fur was bristling; **le chien hérissait ses poils** the dog's hackles were rising *or* up; **le perroquet hérissait ses plumes** the parrot was ruffling its feathers; **les cheveux hérissés par le vent** his/her hair sticking up with the wind **2** *(irriter)* **cette question le hérisse** *ou* **lui hérisse le poil** that question gets his back up *or* really makes his hackles rise **3** *(remplir)* **h. un texte de citations/de jeux de mots** to fill a text with quotations/puns
►**se hérisser VPR 1** *(se dresser → pelage)* to bristle; *(→ cheveux)* to stand on end **2** *(dresser son pelage)* **le chat se hérisse** the cat's coat is bristling; **le chien se hérisse** the dog's hackles are up **3** *(s'irriter)* to bristle; **elle se hérisse facilement** she's easily ruffled
***hérisson** [erisɔ̃] **NM 1** *Zool* hedgehog; **h. de mer** sea urchin **2** *Fam (personne)* **c'est un vrai h.** he's really prickly **3** *Mil* cheval-de-frise; **défense en h.** hedgehog **4** *Constr (pointes)* spiked wall strip; *(fondation)* placed foundation (stone); *(d'une route)* cobblestone road foundation **5** *(égouttoir)* bottle drainer **6** *(brosse)* flue brush, chimney sweep's brush **7** *Agr (d'un épandeur)* beater **8** *Tex* urchin
***hérissonne** [erisɔn] **ADJ F chenille h.** furry *or* hairy caterpillar
héritabilité [eritabilite] **NF** heritability
héritage [eritaʒ] **NM 1** *Jur (destiné à une personne)* inheritance; *(destiné à une institution)* bequest; **faire un h.** to inherit; **faire un gros h.** to come into a fortune; **elle m'a laissé ses bijoux en h.** she left me her jewels; **avoir eu qch en h.** to have inherited sth; **sa part de l'h.** his/her part of the inheritance; **mon oncle/cousin à h.** my rich uncle/cousin
2 *Fig* heritage, legacy; **notre h. culturel** our cultural heritage; **nos problèmes sont l'h. de la décennie précédente** our problems are the legacy of the previous decade
hériter [3] [erite] **VI** to inherit; **h. de qch** *(recevoir en legs)* to inherit sth; **h. d'un château** to inherit a château; *Fig* **nous héritons d'une longue tradition humaniste** we are the inheritors of a long-standing tradition of humanism; **comment as-tu hérité de cette toile?** how did you come into possession of *or* come by *or* acquire this canvas?; **j'ai hérité de son vieux pantalon** I was given his/her old trousers; **j'espère que le bébé n'héritera pas de ton sale caractère!** I hope the baby won't inherit your foul temper!
VT 1 *Jur (bien matériel)* to inherit; **h. qch de qn**

hem–her

to inherit sth from sb **2** *(trait physique ou moral)* **elle a hérité sa bonne humeur de sa famille paternelle** she inherited her even temper from her father's side of the family

USAGE ABSOLU *Jur* **h. de qn** to inherit from sb; **elle a hérité de sa mère** she received an inheritance *or* a legacy from her mother

héritier, -ère [eritje, -ɛr]NM,F **1** *Jur* heir, *f* heiress; **l'h. d'une fortune/d'une grosse entreprise** the heir to a fortune/to a big firm; **l'unique** *ou* **le seul h.** the sole heir; **l'h. apparent** the heir apparent; **h. indirect** collateral heir; **h. légitime** rightful heir; **l'h. naturel** the heir-at-law; **l'h. présomptif** the heir presumptive; **h. réservataire** = heir who cannot be totally disinherited; **h. testamentaire** devisee, legatee **2** *Hum (enfant)* heir; *(fils)* son and heir; *(fille)* daughter **3** *(disciple)* heir, follower

hermandad [ɛrmãda(d)]NF *Hist* hermandad
hermaphrodisme [ɛrmafrɔdism]NM *Biol* hermaphroditism
Hermaphrodite [ɛrmafrɔdit] NPR *Myth* Hermaphroditus
hermaphrodite [ɛrmafrɔdit] *Biol*ADJ hermaphrodite, hermaphroditic
 NMF hermaphrodite
herméneutique [ɛrmenøtik] *Rel & Phil* ADJ hermeneutic, hermeneutical
 NF hermeneutics *(singulier)*
Hermès [ɛrmɛs]NPR *Myth* Hermes
hermès [ɛrmɛs]NM INV *Beaux-Arts* herm, herma; **buste en h.** herm bust
herméticité [ɛrmetisite] NF *(à l'eau)* watertightness; *(à l'air)* airtightness
hermétique [ɛrmetik]ADJ **1** *(étanche → gén)* hermetically sealed, hermetic; *(→ à l'eau)* watertight; *(→ à l'air)* airtight
 2 *(doctrine)* Hermetic
 3 *(incompréhensible)* abstruse
 4 *(impénétrable → visage)* inscrutable, impenetrable; **son expression était parfaitement h.** his/her face was totally expressionless
 5 *(insensible)* **être h. à** to be unreceptive *or* impervious to; **je suis complètement h. à l'art moderne** modern art is a closed book to me
hermétiquement [ɛrmetikmã]ADV hermetically; **fermer un bocal h.** to hermetically seal a jar
hermétisme [ɛrmetism]NM **1** *(doctrine)* alchemy **2** *(caractère incompréhensible)* abstruseness, reconditeness
hermétiste [ɛrmetist]NMF *Arch* alchemist
hermine [ɛrmin] NF **1** *Zool (brune)* stoat; *(blanche)* ermine **2** *(fourrure)* ermine *(UNCOUNT)*; *(sur une robe de magistrat)* ermine **3** *Hér* ermine
herminette [ɛrminɛt]NF *(hache)* adze
Hermione [ɛrmjɔn]NF *Myth* Hermione
***herniaire** [ɛrnjɛr]ADJ hernial
***hernie** [ɛrni]NF **1** *Méd* hernia, rupture; **h. discale** slipped disc, *Spéc* prolapsed invertebral disc; **h. étranglée/hiatale** strangulated/hiatus hernia **2** *(d'un pneu)* bulge
***hernié, -e** [ɛrnje]ADJ *Méd* herniated, ruptured
***hernieux, -euse** [ɛrnjø, -øz] *Méd* ADJ **1** *(organe)* herniated **2** *(malade)* suffering from a hernia
 NM,F hernia sufferer
Héro [ero]NPR *Myth* Hero
héro [ero]NF *Fam (abrév héroïne)* smack, skag
Hérode [erɔd]NPR *Bible* Herod; **vieux comme H.** as old as Methuselah *or* the hills
Hérodiade [erɔdjad]NPR *Bible* Herodias
Hérodote [erɔdɔt]NPR *Bible* Herodotus
héroïcité [erɔisite]NF heroic nature, heroicness
héroï-comique [erɔikɔmik] *(pl* **héroï-comiques)** ADJ mock-heroic
héroïde [erɔid]NF *Littérature* heroic verse
héroïne [erɔin] NF **1** *(drogue)* heroin **2** *(femme) voir* **héros**
héroïnomane [erɔinɔman]NMF heroin addict
héroïnomanie [erɔinɔmani]NF heroin addiction
héroïque [erɔik]ADJ **1** *(courageux)* heroic; *Hum* **je lui ai opposé un refus h.** I heroically refused his/her offer **2** *Littérature* heroic **3** *(mémorable)* **l'époque h. des machines volantes** the pioneering *or* great days of the flying machines; *Antiq* **les temps héroïques, l'âge h.** the heroic age
héroïquement [erɔikmã]ADV heroically
héroïsme [erɔism]NM heroism; *Hum* **épouser un**

---

homme comme ça, mais c'est de l'h.! marrying a man like that is nothing short of heroic!
***héron** [erɔ̃] NM *Orn* heron; **h. à aigrette** tufted heron; **h. bihoreau** night heron; **h. cendré** grey heron; **h. crabier** squacco heron; **h. garde-boeufs** cattle egret; **h. pourpre** purple heron
***héronneau, -x** [erɔno]NM young heron
***héronnière** [erɔnjɛr] NF **1** *(lieu)* heronry **2** *(colonie)* colony of herons
***héros, héroïne** [ero, erɔin]NM,F hero, *f* heroine; **les h. de Dickens** Dickens' heroes (and heroines); **il est mort en h.** he died a hero's death *or* like a hero; **tu ne t'es pas comporté en h.** you weren't exactly heroic
 NM *Antiq* **les dieux et les h. grecs** the gods and heroes of Greece
***herpe** [ɛrp] NF *Naut* **h. de poulaine** head-rail; **h. de guibre** headboard
 ❏ **herpes** NFPL *Vieilli Jur* **herpes marines** *(objets échoués)* flotsam and jetsam; *(corail, ambre gris etc)* = natural treasures thrown up by the sea
herpès [ɛrpɛs]NM *Méd* herpes *(UNCOUNT)*; **avoir de l'h. à la bouche** to have a cold sore (on one's mouth)
herpétique [ɛrpetik] ADJ *Méd* herpes *(avant n)*, *Spéc* herpetic
herpétologie [ɛrpetɔlɔʒi] = **erpétologie**
herpétologique [ɛrpetɔlɔʒik] = **erpétologique**
herpétologiste [ɛrpetɔlɔʒist] = **erpétologiste**
***hersage** [ɛrsaʒ]NM *Agr* harrowing
***herschage** [ɛrʃaʒ] = **herchage**
***herscher** [ɛrʃe] = **hercher**
***herscheur** [ɛrʃœr] = **hercheur**
***herse** [ɛrs] NF **1** *Agr* harrow; **h. roulante** revolving harrow **2** *(d'un château)* portcullis; *(pour barrer la route)* cheval-de-frise **3** *Théât* batten **4** *Rel* candle-holder
***herser** [3] [ɛrse]VT *Agr* to harrow
***herseuse** [ɛrsøz]NF *Agr* harrow
***hertz** [ɛrts]NM hertz
***hertzien, -enne** [ɛrtsjɛ̃, -ɛn] ADJ *TV* terrestrial; *Rad* hertzian; *TV* **par voie hertzienne** terrestrially; *Rad* **réseau h.** radio relay system
 NM *TV* **le h.** terrestrial (broadcasting)
Hésiode [ezjɔd]NPR Hesiod
hésitant, -e [ezitã, -ãt]ADJ **1** *(indécis)* hesitant; **je suis encore un peu h.** I haven't quite made up my mind yet; **les réponses sont encore un peu hésitantes** the answers are still rather hesitant **2** *(peu assuré)* hesitant, faltering; **une voix hésitante** a faltering voice
hésitation [ezitasjɔ̃] NF **1** *(atermoiement)* hesitation; **après quelques minutes d'h.** after hesitating for a few minutes, after a few minutes' hesitation; **après bien des hésitations** after much hesitation; **pas d'h., vas-y!** no dithering, off you go!
 2 *(arrêt)* pause; **marquer** *ou* **avoir une h.** to pause, to hesitate
 3 *(doute)* doubt; **pas d'h., c'est lui!** it's him, no doubt about it *or* without a doubt!; **il lui confia ses hésitations** he confided his doubts *or* misgivings to him/her
 ❏ **sans hésitation** ADV unhesitatingly, without hesitation; **c'est sans h. que je lui ai menti** I had no hesitation in lying to him/her; **je préfère le ciné à la télé, sans h.** I prefer cinema to television any day
hésiter [3] [ezite] VI **1** *(être dans l'incertitude)* to hesitate; **je ne sais pas, j'hésite** I don't know, I can't make up my mind *or* I'm undecided; **sans h.** without hesitating *or* hesitation; **il n'y a pas à h.** why wait?; **elle hésite encore sur la pointure** she's still not sure about the size; **l'enfant hésitait entre le rire et les larmes** the child didn't know whether to laugh or cry; **j'ai longtemps hésité avant de prendre ma décision** I hesitated for a long time before making up my mind
 2 *(être réticent)* **h. à faire qch** to hesitate to do sth; **n'hésitez pas à m'appeler** don't hesitate to call me; **j'hésite à le lui dire** I'm not sure whether to tell him/her; **il hésite à s'engager dans la marine** he's unsure *or* hesitant about joining the Navy
 3 *(marquer un temps d'arrêt)* to pause, to falter; **son pas hésita un instant dans l'escalier** his/her footsteps paused for a moment on the stairs; **il a hésité en prononçant le nom** he faltered *or*

---

stumbled over the name; **h. devant l'obstacle** *(cheval)* to refuse a fence
hespéride [ɛsperid] = **hespérie**
Hespérides [ɛsperid] NFPL **1** *Myth (nymphes)* **les H.** the Hesperides **2** *(îles)* **les H.** the Hesperides, the Islands of the Blessed
hespérie [ɛsperi]NF *Entom* skipper (butterfly)
hespéritine [ɛsperitin]NF *Chim* hesperitin
***Hesse** [ɛs]NF **la H.** Hesse
hessois, -e [ɛswa, -az]ADJ of/from Hesse
 ❏ **Hessois, -e** NM,F = inhabitant of or person from Hesse
hésychasme [ezikasm]NM *Rel* Hesychasm
hétaïre [etair]NF *Littéraire & Antiq* hetaera, hetaira
hétairie [eteri]NF *Antiq & Hist* hetairia
hétéro [etero] *Fam (abrév* **hétérosexuel)** ADJ hetero, straight
 NMF hetero, straight
hétérocerque [eterɔsɛrk]ADJ *Ich* heterocercal
hétérochromosome [eterɔkrɔmozom] NM *Biol* sex chromosome
hétéroclite [eterɔklit] ADJ disparate; **il y avait là toutes sortes d'objets hétéroclites** there was a strange collection *or* assortment of disparate objects; **tout le mobilier est h.** none of the furniture matches
hétérocycle [eterɔsikl]NM *Chim* heterocycle
hétérocyclique [eterɔsiklik] ADJ *Chim* heterocyclic
hétérodonte [eterɔdɔ̃t]ADJ *Zool* heterodont
hétérodoxe [eterɔdɔks] ADJ **1** *Rel* heterodox **2** *(non conformiste)* heterodox, unorthodox
 NMF **les hétérodoxes ne sont pas très bien vus dans ce pays** unorthodox believers are frowned upon in this country
hétérodoxie [eterɔdɔksi]NF heterodoxy
hétérodyne [eterɔdin] NF *Rad* heterodyne (generator)
hétérogame [eterɔgam]ADJ *Biol* heterogamous
hétérogamétique [eterɔgametik]ADJ *Biol* heterogametic
hétérogamie [eterɔgami] NF **1** *Biol* heterogamy **2** *(en sociologie)* **l'h. est fréquente** mixed marriages are common
hétérogène [eterɔʒɛn] ADJ **1** *(mêlé)* heterogeneous, mixed **2** *Chim* heterogeneous
hétérogénéité [eterɔʒeneite] NF heterogeneousness, heterogeneity
hétérogreffe [eterɔgrɛf]NF *Méd (de tissu)* heterograft; *(d'un organe)* heterotransplant
hétérométabole [eterɔmetabɔl]ADJ *Entom* heterometabolic, heterometabolous
hétéromorphe [eterɔmɔrf] ADJ *Biol* heteromorphic, heteromorphous
hétéromorphie [eterɔmɔrfi] NF *Biol* heteromorphism
hétéromorphisme [eterɔmɔrfism] NM heteromorphism
hétéronome [eterɔnɔm]ADJ heteronomous
hétéronomie [eterɔnɔmi]NF heteronomy
hétérophorie [eterɔfɔri]NF *Opt* heterophoria
hétéroplastie [eterɔplasti]NF *Méd* heteroplasty
hétéroprotéine [eterɔprɔtein] NF *Chim & Biol* conjugated protein
hétéroptère [eterɔptɛr] *Entom* NM member of the Heteroptera suborder
 ❏ **hétéroptères** NMPL Heteroptera
hétérosexualité [eterɔsɛksyalite] NF heterosexuality
hétérosexuel, -elle [eterɔsɛksyɛl] ADJ heterosexual
 NM,F heterosexual
hétéroside [eterɔzid]NM *Chim* heteroside
hétérosis [eterɔzis]NF *Biol* heterosis
hétérosphère [eterɔsfɛr]NF *Géog* heterosphere
hétérotherme [eterɔtɛrm]*Zool* ADJ poikilothermal, poikilothermic
 NM poikilotherm
hétérotransplantation [eterɔtrãsplãtasjɔ̃] NF *Méd* xenotransplant
hétérotrophe [eterɔtrɔf] *Biol*ADJ heterotrophic
 NM heterotroph
hétérotrophie [eterɔtrɔfi]NF *Biol* heterotrophy
hétérotypique [eterɔtipik] ADJ *Biol* heterotypic, heterotypical
hétérozygote [eterɔzigɔt] *Biol*ADJ heterozygous
 NMF heterozygote

The symbol * indicates that the initial **h** is aspirate and that hence there is no liaison, eg **les haricots** [lariko] and not [lezariko], or contraction in spelling, eg **la haine** and not **l'haine**.

an [ɛtmɑ̃] **NM** *Hist* (Cossack) hetman

aie [ɛtrɛ] **NF** beech grove

e [ɛtr] **NM 1** *Bot* beech (tree) **2** *Menuis* beech od)

[ø] **EXCLAM 1** *(exprime le doute)* hmmm, um, **2** *(exprime l'hésitation)* er, um; **h., h., je ne s pas** er, er, I don't know

heur [œr] **NM** *Littéraire* good fortune; **je n'ai pas eu l'h. de lui plaire** I did not have the good fortune to please him/her; **je n'ai pas l'h. de la connaître** I have not the pleasure of her acquaintance

HEURE [œr]

hour **1–3, 6–8** ▪ time **4, 5**

NF 1 *(unité de temps)* hour; **une h. d'horloge** an hour by the clock, a whole hour; **j'attends depuis une bonne h.** I've been waiting for a good *or* full hour; **il faut deux bonnes heures** it takes a good two hours; **revenez dans une petite h.** be *or* come back in less than *or* in under an hour; **les heures passent vite/sont longues** the hours fly past/drag by; **à 45 km à l'h.** at 45 km an *or* per hour; **faire du 100 kilomètres h.** to do 100 kilometres an hour; **24 heures sur 24** round-the-clock, 24 hours a day; **pharmacie ouverte 24 heures sur 24** all-night *or* 24-hour chemist; **d'h. en h.** by the hour; **la situation s'aggrave d'h. en h.** the situation is getting worse by the hour

2 *(durée d'un trajet)* hour; **à deux heures (de voiture** *ou* **de route) de chez moi** two hours(' drive) from my home; **il y a trois heures de marche/vol** it's a three-hour walk/flight

3 *(unité de travail ou de salaire)* hour; **un travail payé à l'h.** a job paid by the hour; **dix euros de l'h.** ten euros an *or* per hour; **une h. de travail** an hour's work, an hour of work; **le coût de trente heures de travail** the cost of thirty man-hours *or* thirty hours of work; **sans compter les heures de main-d'œuvre** excluding labour (costs); **la semaine de 35 heures, les 35 heures** the 35-hour week; *Scol* **une h. de chimie** a chemistry period *or* class; **elle a dix heures de cours par semaine** she has ten periods *or* ten hours of lessons a week; **une h. supplémentaire** an *or* one hour's overtime; **des heures supplémentaires** overtime; **faire des heures supplémentaires** to do *or* work overtime

4 *(point précis de la journée)* time; **il n'est pas la même h. à Rome qu'à Tokyo** it's not the same time *or* the time's not the same in Rome as it is in Tokyo; **15 h h. locale** 3 pm local time; **il est deux heures** it's two o'clock; **cinq heures moins dix** ten (minutes) to *or Am* of five; **vingt heures quarante** eight forty pm; **le train de neuf heures** the nine o'clock train; *Fam* **elle est passée sur le coup de huit heures** she dropped in at about eight; **à la même h.** at the same time; **que fais-tu debout à cette h.-ci?** what are you doing up at this time?; **où serai-je demain à cette h.-ci?** where will I be this time tomorrow?; **à cette h.-ci je devrais déjà être parti** I should have left by now; **c'est l'h.!** *(de partir)* it's time (to go)!; *(de rendre sa copie)* time's up!; **c'est l'h. de partir** it's time to go; **l'h., c'est l'h.** on time is on time; *Fam* **quand c'est l'h., c'est l'h.!** when you've got to go, you've got to go!; **avant l'h.** before time; *Fam* **avant l'h., c'est pas l'h., après l'h. c'est plus l'h.** there's a right time for everything; **quelle h. est-il?** what time is it?, what's the time?; **vous avez l'h.?** do you have the time?; **quelle h. avez-vous?** what time do you make it?; **est-ce que vous avez l'h. exacte** *ou* **juste?** do you have the right time?; **tu as vu l'h. (qu'il est)?** have you any idea what time it is?; **il ne sait pas encore lire l'h.** he can't tell the time yet; **il y a une h. pour tout, chaque chose à son h.** there's a time (and a place) for everything; **il n'y a pas d'h. pour les braves!** when a man's got to go, a man's got to go!; **il n'a pas d'h., avec lui il n'y a pas d'h.** *(il n'est pas ponctuel)* he just turns up when it suits him; *Fam* **jusqu'à pas d'h.** until some ungodly hour; *Fam* **se coucher à pas d'h.** to go to bed at all hours; *Fam* **elle est rentrée à pas d'h.** she didn't get home until some ungodly hour; **h. d'arrivée** arrival time; **h. probable d'arrivée** expected time of arrival; **h. probable de départ** expected time of departure; **l'h. d'été** *Br* British Summer Time, *Am* daylight (saving) time; **passer à l'h. d'été/d'hiver** to put the clocks forward/back; **l'h. de Greenwich** Greenwich Mean Time, GMT; **l'h. H** zero hour

5 *(moment)* time; **à une h. avancée** at a late hour; **à une h. indue** at some ungodly *or* godforsaken hour; **ce doit être ma tante qui appelle, c'est son h.** that must be my aunt, this is her usual time for calling *or* she usually calls about now; **ton h. sera la mienne** (you) choose *or* name a time; **elle est romancière à ses heures** she writes the odd novel (now and again); *Journ* **nouvelles de dernière h.** latest news, stop-press (news); **un partisan de la dernière h.** a late convert to the cause, *Fam* a Johnny-come-lately; **un partisan de la première h.** a supporter from the word go; *Fam* **ils ont dû atterrir à l'h. qu'il est** they must have landed by now; **à l'h. qu'il est** *ou* **à l'h. actuelle, je ne sais pas si les otages ont été libérés** at this (point in) time I don't know whether the hostages have been freed; **l'h. d'aller au lit** bedtime; **l'h. du déjeuner** lunchtime; **l'h. du dîner** dinnertime; **l'h. du repas** mealtime; **l'h. du thé** teatime; **les heures d'affluence** the rush hour; **heures de bureau** office hours; *Bourse* **heures de cotation** trading time; **les heures creuses** *(sans foule)* off-peak period; *(sans clients)* slack period; *Transp, Élec & Tél* off-peak hours; **heures d'écoute** *Rad* listening time; *TV* viewing hours; **heures de grande écoute** *Rad* peak listening time; *TV* peak viewing time, prime time; **heures de fermeture** closing times; **h. limite** deadline; **les heures de pointe** *(où il y a foule)* peak time, the rush hour; **heures d'ouverture** opening hours; **pendant les heures d'ouverture** *Com* when the shops are open, during (normal) opening hours; *Admin* during (normal) office *or* working hours; **h. de table** lunch break

6 *(période d'une vie)* hour; **l'h. est grave** things are serious; **l'h. est à l'action** now is the time for action; **c'est sa dernière h.** his/her time is near; **dis-toi que ce n'était pas ton h.** don't worry, your time will come; **son h. est venue** his/her time has come; **son h. de gloire** his/her moment of glory; **l'h. de vérité** the moment of truth

7 *Ind* **h. machine** machine-hour

8 *Astron* hour

▫ **heures NFPL** *Rel* hours; **heures canoniales** canonical hours; **livre d'heures** Book of Hours

▫ **à la bonne heure ADV** good; **elle est reçue, à la bonne h.!** so she passed, good *or* marvellous!; *Ironique* **tu as perdu tes clés, à la bonne h.!** you've lost your keys!, marvellous!

▫ **à l'heure ADJ 1** *(personne)* on time; **être à l'h.** to be on time

2 *(montre)* **la montre est à l'h.** the watch is keeping good time; **ma montre n'est pas à l'h.** my watch is wrong **ADV mettre sa montre/une pendule à l'h.** to set one's watch/a clock right; **les trains partent à l'h.** the trains leave on time; **le Japon à l'h. anglaise** the Japanese go British

▫ **à l'heure de PRÉP** in the era *or* age of; **nous vivons à l'h. de la robotique** we're living in the age of robots

▫ **à toute heure ADV** at any time, at all hours of the day, round the clock; **ouvert à toute h.** open 24 hours (a day); **repas chauds à toute h.** hot meals 24 hours a day; **à toute h. du jour ou de la nuit** round the clock

▫ **de bonne heure ADV** *(tôt)* early; *(en avance)* in good time; **de très bonne h.** very early

▫ **pour l'heure ADV** for now *or* the time being *or* the moment

▫ **sur l'heure ADV** *Littéraire* straightaway, at once

▫ **tout à l'heure ADV 1** *(dans un moment)* later, in a (short *or* little) while; **je passerai la voir tout à l'h.** I'll go and see her a bit later on *or* in a little while; **à tout à l'h.!** see you later!

2 *(il y a un moment)* a little while ago; **je l'ai vu tout à l'h.** I saw him a little while ago

heure-homme [œrɔm] *(pl* **heures-hommes)** **NF** man-hour

heureuse [œrøz] *voir* **heureux**

heureusement [œrøzmɑ̃] **ADV 1** *(par chance)* fortunately, luckily; **il les a invités à l'improviste, mais h. j'avais fait des courses** he asked them to dinner without warning me, but fortunately I'd done some shopping; **je le surveillais, et h.!** I was keeping an eye on him, and just as well *or* and a good thing too!; **il a freiné à temps – oh, h.!** he braked in time – thank God *or* goodness for that!; **il m'a remboursé et s'est même excusé – eh bien, h.!** he paid me back and even apologized – I should hope *or* think so too!; **la soirée fut une catastrophe, h. que tu n'es pas venu** the party was a total flop, (it's a) good thing you didn't come

2 *(avec succès)* successfully; **le débat fut h. mené** the debate went off smoothly; **des textures h. assorties** well-matched textures

3 *(favorablement)* well; **le procès s'est terminé h.** the trial ended satisfactorily

4 *(dans le bonheur)* happily; **vivre h.** to live happily

heureux, -euse [œrø, -øz] **ADJ 1** *(qui éprouve du bonheur)* happy; **rendre qn h.** to make sb happy; **elle a tout pour être heureuse** she has everything going for her; **h. en ménage** happily married; **h. (celui) qui…** happy is he who…; **ils vécurent h. et eurent beaucoup d'enfants** they lived happily ever after

2 *(satisfait)* happy, glad; **être h. de** to be happy with; **je suis heureuse de cette conclusion** I'm happy *or* pleased it ended like this; **il était trop h. de partir** he was only too glad to leave; **h. de te revoir** glad *or* pleased to see you again; **(très) h. de faire votre connaissance** pleased *or* nice to meet you

3 *(chanceux)* lucky, fortunate; **il est h. que…** it's fortunate *or* it's a good thing that…; **l'h. élu** the lucky man *(to be married or recently married)*; **l'heureuse élue** the lucky girl *(to be married or recently married)*; *Prov* **h. au jeu, malheureux en amour** lucky at cards, unlucky in love

4 *(bon)* good; *Euph* **un h. événement** a happy event; **h. anniversaire!** happy birthday!; **bonne et heureuse année!** happy new year!

5 *(réussi)* good, happy, *Sout ou Hum* felicitous; **c'est un choix h.** it's well chosen; **ce n'est pas très h. comme prénom pour une fille** it's a rather unfortunate name for a girl; **la formulation n'est pas toujours très heureuse dans ce texte** this text is not always very well worded

NM,F happy man, *f* woman; **faire des h.** to make some people happy; **le changement ne fera pas que des h.** the change won't suit everybody *or* be to everybody's liking; **si tu le lui donnes, tu vas faire un h.** if you give it to him, you will make him a happy man

heuristique [øristik] **ADJ** heuristic

NF heuristics *(singulier)*

***heurt** [œr] **NM 1** *(choc → léger)* bump, knock, collision; *(→ violent)* crash, collision **2** *(contraste)* clash; **le h. de deux caractères** the clash of two personalities **3** *(conflit)* clash, conflict; **il y a eu des heurts entre le président et le secrétaire** the chairman and the secretary crossed swords; **le concert/débat s'est déroulé sans heurts** the concert/debate went off smoothly; **leur collaboration ne va pas sans heurts** their collaboration has its ups and downs *or* its rough patches

***heurté, -e** [œrte] **ADJ 1** *(couleurs, sons)* clashing **2** *Littéraire (style)* jerky, abrupt **3** *(mouvement)* halting, jerky

***heurter** [3] [œrte] **VT 1** *(cogner)* to strike, to hit, to knock; **en descendant du train, je l'ai heurté avec mon sac** I caught him with my bag *or* I bumped into him with my bag as I got off the train; **l'hélice l'a heurté de plein fouet** he was hit with the full force of the propeller; **son front a violemment heurté le carrelage** he/she banged her forehead on the tiled floor; **h. qn du coude** to jostle sb with one's elbow; **h. qch du coude** to bump sth with one's elbow **2** *(aller à l'encontre de)* to run counter to, to go against; **son discours risque de h. l'opinion publique** his/her speech is likely to go against public opinion; **ce sont des idées qui heurtent ma conception de**

The symbol * indicates that the initial **h** is aspirate and that hence there is no liaison, eg **les haricots** [leariko] and not [lezariko], or contraction in spelling, eg **la haine** and not **l'haine**.

la justice those are ideas which offend my sense of justice 3 *(choquer)* to shock, to offend; **sa grossièreté m'a toujours heurtée** I've always been shocked by his/her rudeness; **h. la sensibilité de qn** to hurt sb's feelings

VI *Suisse ou Littéraire* to knock; **h. à la porte** to knock at the door

▫ **heurter contre VT IND** to bump into; **dans le noir j'ai heurté contre le mur de la cave** in the dark I bumped into the cellar wall; **le voilier a heurté contre un récif** the sailing boat struck a reef

►**se heurter VPR 1** *(passants, véhicules)* to collide, to bump or to run into each other; **les deux voitures se sont heurtées** the two cars collided (with each other)

2 *(être en désaccord)* to clash (with each other); **nous nous sommes heurtés à la dernière réunion** we crossed swords or clashed at the last meeting

3 se h. à *ou* **contre qch** *(se cogner)* to bang into sth, to bump into sth

4 *Fig* **se h. à qch** *(rencontrer)* to come up against sth; **l'entreprise va se h. à de gros problèmes économiques** the company is going to come up against severe economic difficulties; **il s'est heurté à un refus catégorique** he met with a categorical refusal

*****heurtoir** [œrtwar] **NM 1** *(de porte)* (door) knocker **2** *Tech* stop, stopper **3** *(dans une écluse)* striking plate **4** *Rail* buffer

hévéa [evea] **NM** hevea

hexachlorocyclohexane [εgzaklɔrɔsikloεgzan] **NM** *Chim* hexachlorocyclohexane

hexachlorophène [εksaklɔrɔfεn] **NM** *Chim* hexachlorophene

hexachlorure [εgzaklɔryr] **NM** *Chim* hexachloride

hexacoralliaire [εgzakɔraljer] *Zool* **NM** hexacoral, *Spéc* member of the Hexacoralla

▫ **hexacoralliaires NMPL** Hexacoralla

hexacorde [εgzakɔrd] **NM** *Mus* hexachord

hexadécane [εgzadekan] **NM** *Chim* hexadecane

hexadécimal, -e, -aux, -ales [εgzadesimal, -o] **ADJ** hexadecimal

hexaèdre [εgzaεdr] *Géom* **ADJ** hexahedral
  NM hexahedron

hexaédrique [εgzaedrik] **ADJ** *Géom* hexahedral

hexafluorure [εgzaflyɔryr] **NM** *Chim* hexafluoride

hexagonal, -e, -aux, -ales [εgzagɔnal, -o] **ADJ 1** *Géom* hexagonal **2** *Fig (français)* French; *Péj* chauvinistically French

hexagone [εgzagɔn] **NM 1** *Géom* hexagon **2** *Fig* **l'H.** *(la France)* France

hexamètre [εgzamεtr] **ADJ** hexametric, hexametrical
  NM hexameter

hexamidine [εgzamidin] **NF** *Pharm* = powerful bactericidal antiseptic

hexane [egzan] **NM** *Chim* hexane

hexapode [εgzapɔd] *Zool* **ADJ** hexapod
  NM hexapod

hexastyle [egzastil] **ADJ** *Archit* hexastyle

hexavalent, -e [egzavalã, -ãt] **ADJ** *Chim* hexavalent

hexogène [εgzɔʒεn] **NM** *Chim* hexogen

hexose [egzoz] **NM** *Biol* & *Chim* hexose

HF *Tél (abrév écrite* **hautes fréquences***)* HF

*****hi** [i] **EXCLAM** hi hi! ha ha!; **hi hi, que c'est drôle!** ha ha, that's funny!

hiatal, -e, -aux, -ales [jatal, -o] **ADJ** *Méd* hiatal

hiatus [jatys] **NM 1** *(interruption)* break, hiatus, gap **2** *Ling* hiatus **3** *Méd* hiatus; **h. œsophagien** hiatus oesophageus; **h. de Winslow** foramen of Winslow, epiploic foramen

hibernal, -e, -aux, -ales [ibεrnal, -o] **ADJ 1** *Bot* hibernal; **germination hibernale** hibernal germination **2** *Zool* winter *(avant n)*; **pendant leur sommeil h.** during their hibernation or their winter sleep

hibernant, -e [ibεrnã, -ãt] **ADJ** *Zool* hibernating

hibernation [ibεrnasjɔ̃] **NF 1** *Zool* hibernation; *Fig* **l'industrie textile est en état d'h.** the textile industry is in the doldrums **2** *Méd* **h. artificielle** induced hypothermia

▫ **en hibernation** *Fig* in mothballs; **mettre un projet en h.** to shelve or to mothball a project

hiberner [3] [ibεrne] **VI** *Zool* to hibernate

hibernie défeuillante [ibεrnidefœjãt] **NF** *Entom* mottled umber moth

hibiscus [ibiskys] **NM** *Bot* hibiscus

*****hibou, -x** [ibu] **NM** owl; **h. des marais** shorteared owl; **h. moyen-duc** long-eared owl; **h. petit-duc** scops owl; *Fig* **un vieux h.** a grumpy old recluse

*****hic** [ik] **NM INV** *Fam* snag; **c'est bien là** *ou* **voilà le h.** there's the rub, that's the trouble; **il y a un h. quelque part** there's a snag or catch somewhere

*****hic et nunc** [ikεtnɔ̃k] **ADV** here and now

*****hickory** [ikɔri] **NM** *Bot* hickory

hidalgo [idalgo] **NM** hidalgo; **un bel h.** a dark handsome man *(with Latin looks)*

*****hideur** [idœr] **NF** *Littéraire* hideousness

*****hideuse** [idøz] *voir* **hideux**

*****hideusement** [idøzmã] **ADV** hideously

*****hideux, -euse** [idø, -øz] **ADJ** hideous

*****hidjab** [idʒab] **NM** hidjab *(veil worn by Muslim woman)*

*****hie** [i] **NF** *(pour pavés)* beetle, rammer; *(pour pilotis)* pile driver

hièble [jεbl] **NF** dwarf elder

hiémal, -e, -aux, -ales [jemal, -o] **ADJ** *Littéraire* winter *(avant n)*

hier [ijεr] **ADV 1** *(désignant le jour précédent)* yesterday; **h. matin** yesterday morning; **h. (au) soir** yesterday evening; **le journal d'h.** yesterday's paper; **j'y ai consacré la journée/l'après-midi d'h.** I spent all (day) yesterday/all yesterday afternoon doing it; **je m'en souviens comme si c'était h.** I remember it as if it were yesterday

2 *(désignant un passé récent)* **la technologie d'h.** outdated or outmoded technology; **h. encore, on ignorait tout de cette maladie** until very recently, this disease was totally unknown; **ça ne date pas d'h.** that's nothing new
  NM **tu avais tout h. pour te décider** you had all (day) yesterday to make up your mind

*****hiérarchie** [jerarʃi] **NF 1** *Admin (structure)* hierarchy; **la h. des salaires** the wage ladder; **la h. des valeurs sociales** the scale of social values **2** *Fam (supérieurs)* **la h.** the top brass **3** *Ordinat* **h. de mémoire** memory hierarchy, hierarchical memory structure

*****hiérarchique** [jerarʃik] **ADJ** hierarchic, hierarchical; **passer par la voie h.** to go through official channels; **c'est mon supérieur h.** he's my immediate superior

*****hiérarchiquement** [jerarʃikmã] **ADV** hierarchically; **dépendre h. de qn** to report to sb

*****hiérarchisation** [jerarʃizasjɔ̃] **NF 1** *(action)* establishment of a hierarchy; *(structure)* hierarchical structure; **la h. des fonctions** the grading of jobs **2** *(de tâches)* prioritization

*****hiérarchisé, -e** [jerarʃize] **ADJ** *(gén)* & *Ordinat* hierarchical

*****hiérarchiser** [3] [jerarʃize] **VT 1** *Admin* to organize along hierarchical lines; **h. les salaires** to introduce wage differentials **2** *(classer →* données*)* to structure, to classify; *(→* besoins*)* to grade or to assess according to importance; *(→* tâches*)* to prioritize

*****hiérarque** [jerark] **NM** hierarch

hiératique [jeratik] **ADJ 1** *(sacré)* hieratic **2** *(geste)* solemn

hiératiquement [jeratikmã] **ADV** *Littéraire* hieratically

hiératisme [jeratism] **NM** *Littéraire* hieratic character

hiérodule [jerodyl] **NM** *Antiq* hierodule

hiérogamie [jerɔgami] **NF** *Rel* hierogamy

*****hiéroglyphe** [jerɔglif] **NM** hieroglyph

  ▫ **hiéroglyphes NMPL** *Hum (écriture illisible)* hieroglyphics

*****hiéroglyphique** [jerɔglifik] **ADJ 1** *Archéol* hieroglyphic, hieroglyphical **2** *(illisible)* scrawled, illegible

hiéronymite [jerɔnimit] **NM** *Rel* Hieronymite

hiérophante [jerɔfãt] **NM** *Antiq* hierophant

*****hi-fi** [ifi] **NF INV** hi-fi; **magasin de h.** hi-fi shop

*****high-8** [ajɥit] **ADJ** *Tech* high-8

*****highlander** [ajlãdœr] **NM 1** *(habitant)* highlander **2** *(soldat)* = soldier from a Scottish regiment where Highland dress is worn on ceremonial occasions

*****Highlands** [ajlãds] **NMPL** **les H.** the Highlands; **les H. du Sud** the Southern Uplands

*****high-tech** [ajtεk] **NM INV** high tech
  ADJ INV high-tech

higoumène [igumεn] **NM** *Rel* hegumen

*****hi-han** [iã] **EXCLAM** hee-haw!
  NM INV hee-haw

*****hi-hi** [ii] **EXCLAM 1** *(rire →* gén*)* tee-hee!; *(→* méchant*)* snigger snigger! **2** *(pleurs)* boo-hoo!

*****hilaire** [ilεr] **ADJ** *Anat* hilar

hilarant, -e [ilarã, -ãt] **ADJ** *(drôle)* hilarious

hilare [ilar] **ADJ** laughing, smiling, joyful; **un visage h.** a laughing or merry face

hilarité [ilarite] **NF** hilarity, mirth, gaiety; **provoquer l'h. générale** to cause general hilarity

*****hile** [il] **NM** *Anat* & *Bot* hilum

hiloire [ilwar] **NF** *Naut* hatch coaming

hilote [ilɔt] **NM** *Antiq* helot

hilotisme [ilɔtism] **NM** *Antiq* helotism

Himalaya [imalaja] **NM** **l'H.** the Himalayas

himalayen, -enne [imalajε̃, -εn] **ADJ** Himalayan

himation [imatjɔn] **NM** *Antiq (manteau)* himation

hinayana [inajana] **ADJ INV** *Rel* hinayana

*****hindi** [indi] **NM** *(langue)* Hindi

hindou, -e [ε̃du] **ADJ** hindu
  ▫ **Hindou, -e NM,F** Hindu

hindouisme [ε̃duism] **NM** Hinduism

hindouiste [ε̃duist] **ADJ** Hindu
  NMF Hindu

Hindoustan [ε̃dustã] **NM** **l'H.** Hindustan

hindoustani [ε̃dustani] **NM** *Ling* Hindustani

Hindu Kuch [induku ʃ] **NM** **l'H.** the Hindu Kush

hinterland [intεrlãd] **NM** *Géog* hinterland

*****hip** [ip] **EXCLAM** **h., h., h., hourra!** hip, hip, hooray!

*****hip-hop** [ipɔp] **ADJ INV** hip-hop
  NM INV hip-hop

hipparion [iparjɔ̃] **NM** *Archéol* & *Zool* hipparion

Hipparque [ipark] **NPR** Hipparchus

*****hippie** [ipi] **ADJ** hippie, hippy
  NMF hippie, hippy

hippique [ipik] **ADJ** horse *(avant n)*; **concours h.** horse trials or show; **course h.** *(activité)* horse racing; *(épreuve)* horse race; **sport h.** equestrian sports

hippisme [ipism] **NM** equestrian sports, equestrianism

hippocampe [ipɔkãp] **NM 1** *Zool* seahorse **2** *Myth (animal mythologique)* hippocampus **3** *Anat* hippocampus (major)

hippocastanacée [ipɔkastanase] **NF** *Bot* horse chestnut, *Spéc* member of the Hippocastanaceae

hippocastanacées NFPL horse chestnuts, *Spéc* Hippocastanaceae

Hippocrate [ipɔkrat] **NPR** Hippocrates; **le serment d'H.** the Hippocratic oath

hippocratique [ipɔkratik] **ADJ** Hippocratic

hippocratisme [ipɔkratism] **NM 1** *(doctrine)* hippocratism **2** *Méd* **h. digital** hippocratic fingers

hippocrépide [ipɔkrepid] **NF** *Bot* **h. à toupet** horseshoe vetch

hippodrome [ipɔdrom] **NM 1** *(champ de courses)* racecourse **2** *Antiq* hippodrome

hippogriffe [ipɔgrif] **NM** hippogriff, hippogryph

hippologie [ipɔlɔʒi] **NF** = scientific study of horses

hippologique [ipɔlɔʒik] **ADJ** equestrian

Hippolyte [ipɔlit] **NPR** *Myth* Hippolytus

Hippolyté [ipɔlite] **NPR** *Myth* Hippolyta

hippomobile [ipɔmɔbil] **ADJ** horsedrawn

hippophaé [ipɔfae] **NM** *Bot* hippophaë

hippophagie [ipɔfaʒi] **NF** **l'h. n'est pas très répandue en Angleterre** horsemeat is only rarely eaten in England

hippophagique [ipɔfaʒik] **ADJ** **boucherie h.** horsemeat butcher's

hippopotame [ipɔpotam] **NM 1** *Zool* hippopotamus; **h. nain** pygmy hippopotamus **2** *Fam (personne)* elephant; **c'est un vrai h.!** what an elephant!

hippopotamesque [ipɔpotamεsk] **ADJ** *Fam* hippolike; **une grâce h.** the grace of a hippo

hippotechnie [ipɔtεkni] **NF** horse breeding and training

hippotrague [ipɔtrag] **NM** *Zool* hippotrague, roan antelope; **h. noir** sable antelope

hippurique [ipyrik] **ADJ** hippuric

*****hippy** [ipi] = **hippie**

hiragana [iragana] **NM** hiragana

hircin, -e [irsε̃, -in] **ADJ** hircine, goatish

hirondeau, -x [irɔ̃do] **NM** young swallow

hirondelle [irɔ̃dεl] **NF 1** *Orn* swallow; **h. de cheminée** swallow, *Am* barn swallow; **h. de fenêtre**

house martin; **h. de mer** tern; **h. pourprée** purple martin; **h. de rivage** sand martin; **h. des rochers** crag martin; *Prov* **une h. ne fait pas le printemps** one swallow doesn't make a summer **2** *Ich (grondin)* grey gurnard **3** *Fam Vieilli (policier) Br* bobby, *Am* cop

Hiroshima [iʀɔʃima] NM Hiroshima

hirsute [iʀsyt] ADJ **1** *(échevelé)* bushy-haired; *(touffu → sourcils)* bushy; *(→ barbe, cheveux)* unkempt **2** *Biol* hirsute, hairy

hirsutisme [iʀsytism] NM *Méd* hirsutism

hirudine [iʀydin] NF *Biol* hirudin

hirudinée [iʀydine] *Zool* NF leech, *Spéc* member of the Hirudinea
□ **hirudinées** NFPL Hirudinea

Hispaniola [ispanjɔla] NF Hispaniola

hispanique [ispanik] ADJ **1** *(gén)* Hispanic **2** *(aux États-Unis)* Spanish-American
□ **Hispanique** NMF *(aux États-Unis)* Spanish American

hispanisant, -e [ispanizɑ̃, -ɑ̃t] NM,F Hispanicist

hispanisation [ispanizasjɔ̃] NF Hispanicization

hispaniser [3] [ispanize] VT to Hispanicize

hispanisme [ispanism] NM *Ling* Hispanicism

hispaniste [ispanist] NMF Hispanicist

hispano-américain, -e [ispanɔameʀikɛ̃, -ɛn] *(mpl* **hispano-américains,** *fpl* **hispano-américaines)** ADJ Spanish-American
□ **Hispano-Américain, -e** NM,F Spanish American

hispano-arabe [ispanɔaʀab] *(pl* **hispano-arabes)** ADJ Hispano-Moorish

hispano-mauresque *(pl* **hispano-mauresques),** **hispano-moresque** *(pl* **hispano-moresques)** [ispanɔmɔʀɛsk] ADJ Hispano-Moorish

hispanophone [ispanɔfɔn] ADJ Spanish-speaking NMF Spanish speaker

hispide [ispid] ADJ *Bot* hispid

*****hisse** [is] EXCLAM **ho h.!** heave!, heave-ho!

*****hisser** [3] [ise] VT **1** *(lever → drapeau)* to run up; *(→ voile)* to hoist; *(→ ancre)* to raise; *(→ épave)* to raise, to haul up; *(soulever → personne)* to lift up; **h. qn sur ses épaules** to lift sb onto one's shoulders **2** *Fig* **h. qn au poste de directeur** to raise sb to the position of manager; **h. une petite entreprise au rang des meilleures** to push a small company to the top
▶ **se hisser** VPR **1** *(s'élever)* to hoist oneself; **se h. sur la pointe des pieds** to stand up on tiptoe; **se h. sur une balançoire** to heave *or* to hoist oneself (up) onto a swing **2** *Fig* **elle s'est hissée au poste d'adjointe de direction** she worked her way up to the position of assistant manager; **l'équipe s'est hissée en deuxième division** the team clawed its way into the second division

histamine [istamin] NF *Biol & Chim* histamine

histaminique [istaminik] ADJ *Biol & Chim* histamine *(avant n)*, histaminic

histidine [istidin] NF *Biol & Chim* histidine

histiocytaire [istjɔsitɛʀ] ADJ *Biol* histiocytic, histiocyte *(avant n)*

histiocyte [istjɔsit] NM *Biol* histiocyte

histochimie [istoʃimi] NF *Biol & Chim* histochemistry

histocompatibilité [istɔkɔ̃patibilite] NF *Biol* histocompatibility

histogenèse [istɔʒɔnɛz] NF *Biol* histogenesis

histogramme [istɔgʀam] NM histogram, column graph

HISTOIRE [istwaʀ]

---

history **1–4** ■ story **5, 6, 8** ■ plot **6** ■ history book **7** ■ fib **8** ■ trouble **9, 10**

NF **1** *(passé)* history; **un lieu chargé d'h.** a place steeped in history; **les hommes et les femmes qui ont fait l'h.** the men and women who have made history; **l'h. d'une croyance** the history of a belief

2 *(mémoire, postérité)* history; **ces faits appartiennent à l'h.** these facts are history; **rester dans l'h.** to go down in history *or* in the history books; **l'h. dira si nous avons eu raison** only time will tell whether we were right

3 *(période précise)* history; **l'h. et la préhistoire** history and prehistory

4 *(discipline)* history; **l'H. avec un grand H** History with a capital H; **l'h. de l'art/la littéra-**

art/literary history; **l'h. de France** the history of France, French history; **l'h. ancienne/du Moyen Âge** ancient/medieval history; *Fig* **tout ça, c'est de l'h. ancienne** that's all ancient history; **l'h. contemporaine** contemporary history; **h. événementielle** factual history; *Vieilli & Biol* **h. naturelle** natural history; **l'H. sainte** Biblical history; **licence d'h.** ≃ BA in History, *Br* ≃ History degree; **pour la petite h.** for the record; **je te le dis pour la petite h.** I'm (only) telling you so you'll know; **sachez, pour la petite h., qu'elle fut la maîtresse du roi** let me tell you, by the way *or* for the record, that she was the king's mistress; **sais-tu, pour la petite h., qu'il est né au Pérou?** do you know that he was born in Peru, by the way?

5 *(récit, écrit)* story; **je leur raconte une h. tous les soirs** every night I tell them a story; **écrire des histoires pour enfants** to write children's stories; **c'est une h. vraie** it's a true story; **c'est une longue h.** it's a long story; **nous avons vécu ensemble une belle h. d'amour** we had a wonderful romance; **attends, je ne t'ai pas encore dit le plus beau** *ou* **le meilleur de l'h.!** wait, the best part *or* bit is still to come!; **une h. drôle** a joke, a funny story; *Fam* **h. à dormir debout** cock-and-bull story, tall story

6 *(intrigue → d'une pièce, d'un film)* plot, story; *(→ d'une chanson)* story

7 *(livre)* history book; **une h. d'Allemagne** a history of Germany; **elle a écrit une h. du village** she wrote a history of the village

8 *Fam (mensonge)* fib, (tall) story; **tout ça, c'est des histoires** that's a load of (stuff and) nonsense, that's all hooey *or Am* baloney; **tu crois encore ses histoires?** do you still believe his/her nonsense?; **raconter des histoires** to tell tall stories; **allez, tu me racontes des histoires!** come on, you're pulling my leg!; **ne me raconte pas d'histoires, je t'ai vu** don't tell me any stories, I saw you; **je t'assure, je ne te raconte pas d'histoires!** I assure you, I'm not making it up!

9 *Fam (complications)* trouble, fuss; **faire des histoires** to make a fuss; **il n'a pas fait d'histoires pour accepter le chèque?** did he make any fuss about accepting the cheque?; **ça va faire toute une h.** there'll be hell to pay; **ç'a été toute une h.** it was quite a business *or* a to-do; **pour faire venir l'électricien, ç'a été toute une h.** we had the devil's own job getting the electrician to come; **c'est toute une h. tous les matins pour la coiffer** what a palaver *or* struggle doing her hair every morning; **elle en a fait toute une h.** she kicked up a (huge) fuss about it; **sans faire d'h.** *ou* **d'histoires** without (making) a fuss; **vous allez me suivre au poste, et pas d'h.** *ou* **d'histoires!** you're coming with me to the station and I don't want any trouble (from you)!

10 *(ennuis)* trouble; **faire des histoires (à qn)** to cause *or* to make trouble (for sb); **si tu ne veux pas avoir d'histoires** if you want to keep *or* to stay out of trouble; **tu vas nous attirer** *ou* **nous faire avoir des histoires** you'll get us into trouble; **je ne veux pas d'histoires dans mon hôtel, moi!** I'm having no monkey business in my hotel!; **taisez-vous toutes les trois, j'en ai assez de vos histoires!** shut up you three, I've had enough of you going on like that!

11 *(question, problème)* **pourquoi démissionne-t-elle? – oh, une h. de contrat** why is she resigning? – oh, something to do with her contract; **se fâcher pour une h. d'argent** to fall out over a question of money; **c'est une h. de fous!** it's crazy!; **il m'arrive une sale h.** something terrible's happened (to me); **ne pensons plus à cette h.** let's forget the whole thing *or* business; **qu'est-ce que c'est que cette h.?** what's this I hear?, what's all this about?; **c'est toujours la même h.** it's always the same (old) story; **c'est une (toute) autre h.** that's quite a different matter

12 *Fam (locution)* **h. de** *(afin de)* just to; **on va leur téléphoner, h. de voir s'ils sont là** let's ring them up, just to see if they're there; **faire qch h. de rigoler** to do sth just for a laugh; **h.**

de dire quelque chose for the sake of saying something
□ **à histoires** ADJ **c'est une femme à histoires** she's nothing but trouble
□ **sans histoires** ADJ *(gens)* ordinary; *(voyage)* uneventful, trouble-free

---

'**Histoires extraordinaires**' *Poe* 'Tales of the Grotesque and Arabesque'

'**L'Histoire d'Adèle H**' *Truffaut* 'The Story of Adele H'

'**L'Histoire du soldat**' *Stravinsky* 'The Soldier's Tale'

'**L'Histoire sans fin**' *Ende, Petersen* 'The Neverending Story'

---

histologie [istɔlɔʒi] NF *Biol* histology

histologique [istɔlɔʒik] ADJ *Biol* histologic, histological

histologiste [istɔlɔʒist] NMF *Biol* histologist

histolyse [istɔliz] NF *Physiol* histolysis

histon [istɔ̃] NM, **histone** [istɔn] NF *Biol & Chim* histone

histopathologie [istɔpatɔlɔʒi] NF *Biol* histopathology

histoplasmose [istɔplasmoz] NF *Méd* histoplasmosis

historicisme [istɔʀisism] NM historicism

historiciste [istɔʀisist] ADJ historicist NMF historicist

historicité [istɔʀisite] NF historicity

historié, -e [istɔʀje] ADJ **1** *(manuscrit)* storiated, historiated **2** *Archit* historied

historien, -enne [istɔʀjɛ̃, -ɛn] NM,F **1** *(spécialiste)* historian; **se faire l'h. d'un village/d'une institution** to tell the story of a village/an institution; **h. d'art** art historian **2** *(étudiant)* history student

historier [9] [istɔʀje] VT *(décorer)* to decorate, to embellish

historiette [istɔʀjɛt] NF anecdote

historiographe [istɔʀjɔgʀaf] NM historiographer

historiographie [istɔʀjɔgʀafi] NF historiography

historique [istɔʀik] ADJ **1** *(relatif à l'histoire → méthode, roman)* historical; *(→ fait, personnage)* historical

2 *(célèbre)* historic; **une émission/poignée de main h.** a historic programme/handshake; **la parole** *ou* **le mot h. de Pu Yi** Pu Yi's famous remark

3 *(mémorable)* historic; **c'est un moment/match h.** this is a historic moment/match; **nous avons atteint le cours h. de 42 dollars l'once** we've reached the record *or* unprecedented level of 42 dollars an ounce
NM **1** *(chronologie)* background history, (historical) review; **faire l'h. des événements** to give a chronological account of events; **faire l'h. des jeux Olympiques** to trace the (past) history of the Olympic Games
2 *Ordinat (d'un document)* log; *(dans un logiciel de navigation)* history list

historiquement [istɔʀikmɑ̃] ADV historically; **le fait n'est pas h. prouvé** it's not a historically proven fact

historisme [istɔʀism] NM historicism

histrion [istʀijɔ̃] NM **1** *Antiq* histrion **2** *Hist (jongleur)* wandering minstrel, troubadour **3** *Fig Péj* exhibitionist; **un h. politique** a politician who likes to play to the crowd

histrionique [istʀijɔnik] ADJ **1** *Littéraire* thespian **2** *Psy* histrionic

histrionisme [istʀijɔnism] NM *Psy* histrionism

*****hit** [it] NM *(succès)* hit song

hitlérien, -enne [itlɛʀjɛ̃, -ɛn] ADJ Hitlerian, Hitlerite NM,F Hitlerite

hitlérisme [itlɛʀism] NM Hitlerism

*****hit-parade** [itpaʀad] *(pl* **hit-parades)** NM **1** *Mus* charts; **ils sont premiers** *ou* **numéro un au h.** they're (at the) top of *or* they're number one in the charts **2** *Fig (classement)* **placé au h. des**

The symbol * indicates that the initial **h** is aspirate and that hence there is no liaison, eg **les haricots** [leaʀiko] and not [lezaʀiko], or contraction in spelling, eg **la haine** and not **l'haine**.

hir-hit

hommes politiques among the top *or* leading politicians

*hittite [itit] ADJ Hittite
  NM *(langue)* Hittite
  ❏ **Hittite** NMF **les Hittites** the Hittites

*HIV [aʃivɛ] NM *(abrév* **human immunodeficiency virus**) HIV; **être atteint du H.** to be HIV-positive

hiver [ivɛʀ] NM **1** *(saison)* winter; **en h.** *ou* **l'h., on rentre les géraniums** we bring in the geraniums in (the) winter; **l'h. dernier** last winter; **l'h. prochain** next winter; **l'h. fut précoce/tardif** winter came early/late; **tout l'h.** all winter long, all through the winter; **au cœur de l'h.** in the middle of winter, in midwinter; *Fam* **elle ne passera pas l'h.** she won't make it through the winter; **h. nucléaire** nuclear winter
  2 *Fig Littéraire* **à l'h. de sa vie** in the twilight *or* evening of his/her life
  ❏ **d'hiver** ADJ *(ciel, paysage, temps)* wintry; *(quartiers, vêtements, fruits)* winter *(avant n)*; **le palais d'h.** the Winter Palace

hivernage [ivɛʀnaʒ] NM **1** *Agr (activité)* wintering, winter feeding; *Vieilli (fourrage)* winter fodder **2** *Météo* winter season *(in tropical regions)* **3** *Naut (activité)* wintering; *(port)* winter harbour **4** *(d'oiseaux, d'animaux)* (over)wintering; **zone d'h.** winter range

hivernal, -e, -aux, -ales [ivɛʀnal, -o] ADJ *(propre à l'hiver)* winter *(avant n)*; *(qui rappelle l'hiver)* wintry; **journées/températures hivernales** winter days/temperatures; **un temps h.** wintry weather; **un ciel h.** a wintry sky
  ❏ **hivernale** NF winter ascent

hivernant, -e [ivɛʀnɑ̃, -ɑ̃t] ADJ wintering
  NM,F winter tourist

hivernement [ivɛʀnəmɑ̃] NM *Can Agr* wintering

hiverner [3] [ivɛʀne] VI *(passer l'hiver)* to (over)-winter
  VT *Agr* to winter

hl *(abrév écrite* **hectolitre**) hl

*HLM [aʃɛlɛm] NM OU NF *(abrév* **habitation à loyer modéré**) *(immeuble) Br* ≃ block of council flats, *Am* ≃ public housing unit; *(appartement) Br* ≃ council flat, *Am* ≃ (apartment in a) public housing unit; *(maison) Br* ≃ council house, *Am* ≃ low-rent house

hm *(abrév écrite* **hectomètre**) hm

HO ADJ *Archit (abrév écrite* **hors œuvre**) out of alignment, projecting

*ho [o] EXCLAM **1** *(de surprise)* oh! **2** *(pour interpeller)* hey!

*hoazin [oazin] NM *Orn* hoatzin

*Hobart [obart] Hobart

*hobby [ɔbi] *(pl* **hobbys** *ou* **hobbies**) NM hobby

*hobereau, -x [ɔbʀo] NM **1** *Péj (gentilhomme)* country squire **2** *Orn* hobby

*hobo [ɔbo] NM *Can Joual* tramp▪, *Am* hobo

*hocco [ɔko] NM *Orn* curassow; **h. commun** crested curassow; **h. à casque** galeated curassow, cashew bird

*hochement [ɔʃmɑ̃] NM **h. de tête** *(approbateur)* nod; *(désapprobateur)* shake of the head; **accepter d'un h. de tête** to accept with a nod; **refuser d'un h. de tête** to refuse with a shake of the head

*hochepot [ɔʃpo] NM *Culin* **h. (à la flamande)** (Flemish) hotchpotch *(stew of meat and vegetables)*

*hochequeue [ɔʃkø] NM *Orn* wagtail

*hocher [3] [ɔʃe] VT **h. la tête** *(pour accepter)* to nod; *(pour refuser)* to shake one's head; **il hocha la tête en signe d'acquiescement** he nodded in agreement; **il hocha la tête en signe de refus** he refused with a shake of the head

*hochet [ɔʃɛ] NM **1** *(jouet)* rattle **2** *Fig Littéraire* gewgaw

*Hô Chi Minh-Ville [oʃiminvil] NM Ho Chi Minh City

*hockey [ɔkɛ] NM hockey; **h. sur glace** *Br* ice hockey, *Am* hockey; **h. sur gazon** *Br* hockey, *Am* field hockey

*hockeyeur, -euse [ɔkɛjœʀ, -øz] NM,F hockey player

*Hodgkin [ɔdʒkin] NPR **maladie de H.** Hodgkin's disease

hodjatoleslam [ɔdʒatɔleslam] NM *Rel* Hodjatoleslam

*Hoggar [ogaʀ] NM **le H.** the Hoggar; **dans le H.** in the Hoggar Mountains

---

hoir [waʀ] NM *Vieilli Jur* direct heir

hoirie [waʀi] NF *Jur* **1 avancement d'h.** advancement *(of an inheritance)* **2** *Suisse Vieilli (héritage)* joint legacy; **l'h.** *(ensemble des héritiers)* the legatees

*Hokkaido [ɔkaido] NF Hokkaido

*holà [ɔla] EXCLAM hey!, whoa!; **h.! attention!** hey *or* whoa, be careful!
  NM **mettre le h. à qch** to put a stop to sth; **il se remet à boire trop, il faut que j'y mette le h.** he's drinking too much again, I must put a stop to it *or* put my foot down

*holding [ɔldiŋ] NM OU NF *Fin* holding company

*hold-up [ɔldœp] NM INV raid, hold-up; **un h. à la banque/poste** a bank/post office raid

*holisme [ɔlism] NM *Méd & Phil* holism

*holiste [ɔlist] *Méd & Phil* ADJ holistic
  NMF holist

*holistique [ɔlistik] ADJ *Méd & Phil* holistic

*hollandais, -e [ɔlɑ̃dɛ, -ez] ADJ Dutch
  NM *(langue)* Dutch
  ❏ **Hollandais, -e** NM,F Dutchman, *f* Dutchwoman; **les H.** the Dutch
  ❏ **hollandaise** NF **1** *Culin* hollandaise *(sauce)* **2** *(vache)* Friesian

*Hollande [ɔlɑ̃d] NF **la H.** Holland; **vivre en H.** to live in Holland; **aller en H.** to go to Holland

*hollande [ɔlɑ̃d] NM **1** *Culin* Dutch cheese *(Edam or Gouda)* **2** *(papier)* Dutch paper
  NF **1** *Culin* Dutch potato **2** *Tex* holland **3** *(porcelaine)* Dutch porcelain

*Hollande-Méridionale [ɔlɑ̃dmeridjɔnal] NF **la H.** South Holland

*Hollande-Septentrionale [ɔlɑ̃dsɛptɑ̃trional] NF **la H.** North Holland

*hollywoodien, -enne [ɔliwudjɛ̃, -ɛn] ADJ *(de Hollywood)* Hollywood *(avant n)*; *(évoquant Hollywood)* Hollywood-like; **un luxe h.** Hollywood-style *or* ostentatious luxury

holmium [ɔlmjɔm] NM *Chim* holmium

holocauste [ɔlɔkost] NM **1** *Hist* **l'h., l'H.** the Holocaust **2** *(massacre)* holocaust, mass murder **3** *Rel* burnt offering; **offrir un animal en h.** to offer an animal in sacrifice **4** *(victime)* sacrifice

holocène [ɔlɔsɛn] *Géol* ADJ **la période h.** the Holocene, the Recent (epoch)
  NM **l'h.** the Holocene, the Recent

holocristallin, -e [ɔlɔkristalɛ̃, -in] ADJ *Géol* holocrystalline

hologramme [ɔlɔgram] NM *Phot* hologram

holographe [ɔlɔgraf] NM *Jur* holograph

holographie [ɔlɔgrafi] NF *Phot* holography

holographique [ɔlɔgrafik] ADJ *Phot* holographic

holométabole [ɔlɔmetabɔl] ADJ *Entom* holometabolous

holomorphe [ɔlɔmɔrf] ADJ *Math* holomorphic, analytic

Holopherne [ɔlɔfɛrn] NPR *Bible* Holofernes

holophrastique [ɔlɔfrastik] ADJ *Ling* holophrastic

holoplancton [ɔlɔplɑ̃ktɔ̃] NM *Biol* holoplankton

holoprotéine [ɔlɔprotein] NF *Chim & Biol* simple protein

holoside [ɔlɔzid] NM *Biol* holoside

holostéen [ɔlɔsteɛ̃] *Ich* NM member of the Holostei order
  ❏ **holostéens** NMPL Holostei

holothurie [ɔlɔtyri] NF *Zool* sea cucumber, sea slug, *Spéc* holothurian

holotype [ɔlɔtip] NM *Biol* holotype

*holster [ɔlstɛr] NM holster

*Homais [ɔmɛ] NPR = the pharmacist in Flaubert's *Madame Bovary* (1857), self-satisfied freethinker and epitome of ignorant faith in scientific progress

*homard [ɔmaʀ] NM lobster; *Culin* **h. à la nage** lobster cooked in court-bouillon

*homarderie [ɔmardəri] NF lobster ground

*home [om] NM **1** *(centre d'accueil)* **h. d'enfants** residential leisure centre (for children); *Belg* **h. d'étudiants** student hall of residence *or Am* dormitory, student hostel; *Belg* **h. pour personnes âgées** old people's home, retirement home **2** *Vieilli (chez-soi)* home; **ici, c'est mon h.** here is where I feel at home

*HomeCam® [omkam] NF HomeCam®

*home cinéma [omsinema] *(pl* **home cinémas**) NM home cinema

*homeland [omlɑ̃d] NM homeland, Bantustan

---

homélie [ɔmeli] NF **1** *Rel* homily **2** *(sermon)* lecture, sermon; **suivi une longue h. sur les dangers du tabac** there then followed a long lecture on the dangers of smoking

homéomorphe [ɔmeɔmɔrf] ADJ *Minér & Math* homeomorphic, homeomorphous

homéomorphisme [ɔmeɔmɔrfism] NM *Minér & Math* homeomorphism

homéopathe [ɔmeɔpat] *Méd* NMF homeopath, homeopathist
  ADJ **médecin h.** homeopathic doctor

homéopathie [ɔmeɔpati] NF *Méd* homeopathy

homéopathique [ɔmeɔpatik] ADJ *Méd* homeopathic

homéostasie [ɔmeɔstazi] NF *Physiol* homeostasis

homéostat [ɔmeɔsta] NM homeostat

homéostatique [ɔmeɔstatik] ADJ *Physiol* homeostatic

homéotherme [ɔmeɔtɛrm] *Physiol* ADJ warm-blooded, *Spéc* homoiothermic, homothermal
  NM warm-blooded organism, *Spéc* homoiotherm

homéothermie [ɔmeɔtɛrmi] NF *Physiol* warm-bloodedness, *Spéc* homoiothermia

Homère [ɔmɛr] NPR Homer

homérique [ɔmerik] ADJ **1** *Littérature* Homeric **2** *(phénoménal)* Homeric

*homespun [omspœn] NM *Tex* homespun cloth

*home-trainer [omtrɛnœr] NM *Sport* exercise bicycle

homicide [ɔmisid] ADJ *Littéraire* homicidal
  NMF *Littéraire (personne)* homicide
  NM **1** *(acte)* killing *(UNCOUNT)* **2** *Jur* homicide; **commettre un h.** to commit homicide; **h. involontaire** *Br* ≃ manslaughter, *Am* ≃ second-degree murder, *Scot* ≃ culpable homicide; **h. par imprudence** *Br* ≃ reckless manslaughter, *Am* ≃ second-degree murder, *Scot* ≃ culpable homicide; **h. volontaire** murder

hominidé [ɔminide] *Zool* NM hominid, member of the Hominidae family
  ❏ **hominidés** NMPL Hominidae

hominien [ɔminjɛ̃] NM *(en paléontologie)* hominoid

hominisation [ɔminizasjɔ̃] NF *(en anthropologie)* hominization

hominoïde [ɔminɔid] *Zool* ADJ hominoid
  NM hominoid

hommage [ɔmaʒ] NM **1** *(marque de respect)* tribute, homage; **recevoir l'h. de qn** to receive sb's tribute; **rendre h. à** to pay homage *or* (a) tribute to; **ce soir nous rendons h. à Édith Piaf** tonight we pay tribute to Edith Piaf; **il faut rendre h. à sa perspicacité** you have to admire his/her clear-sightedness
  2 *(don)* **h. de l'éditeur** complimentary copy
  3 *Hist* homage
  ❏ **hommages** NMPL **être sensible aux hommages** to appreciate receiving compliments; **(je vous présente) mes hommages, Madame** my respects, Madam; **mes hommages à votre épouse** please give my regards to your wife; **veuillez agréer, Madame, mes hommages respectueux** *ou* **mes respectueux hommages** *(à quelqu'un dont on connaît le nom) Br* yours sincerely, *Am* sincerely (yours); *(à quelqu'un dont on ne connaît pas le nom) Br* yours faithfully, *Am* sincerely (yours)
  ❏ **en hommage à** PRÉP in tribute *or* homage to

hommasse [ɔmas] ADJ *Péj* mannish, masculine; **elle a des manières hommasses** she has very masculine ways

homme [ɔm] NM **1** *(individu de sexe masculin)* man; **l'h. a une espérance de vie plus courte que celle de la femme** men have a shorter life expectancy than women; **alors, t'es un h. (ou un lâche)?** what are you, a man or a mouse?; **sors si t'es un h.!** step outside if you're a man!; **le service militaire en a fait un h.** national service made a man of him; **un magazine pour hommes** a men's magazine; *Com* **rayon hommes** men's department, menswear; **il est h. à démissionner si besoin est** he's the sort (of man *or* person) who'll resign if necessary; **je ne suis pas h. à croire les gens sur parole** I'm not the sort of man who blindly believes what I'm told; **trouver son h.** *(pour un travail)* to find one's man; **si vous voulez quelqu'un de tenace, Lambert est votre h.** if you want somebody who'll stick at it, then Lambert's just the

hit–hom

person; **une double page sur l'h. du jour** a two-page spread on the man of the moment; **c'est l'h. fort du parti** he is the kingpin of the party; **une discussion d'h. à h.** a man-to-man talk; **je n'ai que des professeurs hommes** all my teachers are male *or* men; **h. d'action** man of action; **h. d'affaires** businessman; **h. d'Église** man of the Church *or* cloth; **h. d'État** statesman; **h. à femmes** lady's *or* ladies' man, *Péj* womanizer; **Can être un h. aux hommes** to be a homosexual; **Suisse h. du feu** *Br* fireman, *Am* fire fighter; **h. de loi** lawyer, man of law; **h. de main** henchman; **c'est un parfait h. du monde** he's a real gentleman; **h. de paille** man of straw, figurehead; **h. de peine** labourer; **h. politique** politician; **h. de science** scientist, man of science; **h. à tout faire** odd-job man, handyman; **les hommes du Président** the President's men; **comme un seul h.** as one man; *Prov* **un h. averti en vaut deux** forewarned is forearmed; **les hommes naissent libres et égaux en droit** ≃ all men are born equal; **le musée de l'H.** = the Museum of Mankind in the Palais de Chaillot in Paris

2 *(être humain)* man; **un h. sur la Lune** a man on the Moon; **l'h.** man, mankind, humankind; **les hommes** man, mankind, human beings; **l'h. est-il plus sujet aux maladies que l'animal?** is man *or* are humans more prone to disease than animals?; **l'h. descend du singe** human beings are *or* man is descended from the apes; **h. des cavernes** caveman; **l'h. de Cro-Magnon** Cro-Magnon Man; **l'h. de Neandertal** Neanderthal Man; **l'h. de la rue** the man in the street; *Prov* **l'h. propose, Dieu dispose** man proposes, God disposes

3 *Fam (amant, époux)* **mon/son h.** my/her man; **elles laissent leurs hommes à la maison** they leave their men at home; **où est mon petit h.?** *(fils)* where's my little man?; **l'h. idéal** Mr Right; **elle a rencontré l'h. de sa vie** she's met the love of her life

4 *Naut (marin)* **h. de barre** helmsman; **h. d'équipage** crew member, crewman; **h. de quart** man *or* sailor on watch; **h. de vigie** lookout; **un h. à la mer!** man overboard!

5 *Mil* **les officiers et leurs hommes** the officers and their men; **h. de troupe** private, ordinary soldier

6 *Hist* **h. d'armes** man-at-arms; **h. lige** liege (man)

7 *Aviat* crewman, crew member

8 *Bot* **h. pendu** man orchid

─────📖─────
'Les Hommes de bonne volonté' *Romains* 'Men of Goodwill'

─────📖📽─────
'L'Homme au masque de fer' *Dumas, Wallace* 'The Man in the Iron Mask'

─────🖼─────
'L'Homme au turban rouge' *Van Eyck* 'The Man in the Red Turban'

─────📽─────
'L'Homme qui aimait les femmes' *Truffaut* 'The Man Who Loved Women'

─────📽─────
'L'Homme qui venait d'ailleurs' *Roeg* 'The Man Who Fell to Earth'

─────📖─────
'L'Homme révolté' *Camus* 'The Rebel'

─────📖─────
'L'Homme sans qualités' *Musil* 'The Man Without Qualities'

─────📽─────
'L'Homme tranquille' *Ford* 'The Quiet Man'

─────📽─────
'Les Hommes du Président' *Pakula* 'All the President's Men'

homme-grenouille [ɔmgrənuj] (*pl* **hommes-grenouilles**) NM frogman, diver

homme-orchestre [ɔmɔrkɛstr] (*pl* **hommes-orchestres**) NM **1** *Mus* one-man band **2** *Fig* jack-of-all-trades

homme-sandwich [ɔmsãdwitʃ] (*pl* **hommes-sandwichs**) NM sandwich man

homo[1] [ɔmo] NM INV *Zool* Homo

homo[2] [ɔmo] *Fam (abrév* **homosexuel**) ADJ gay
  NMF gay

homocentre [ɔmosãtr] NM *Géom* common centre

homocentrique [ɔmosãtrik] ADJ *Géom* homocentric

homocerque [ɔmosɛrk] ADJ *Ich* homocercal

homochromie [ɔmokrɔmi] NF *Écol* cryptic coloration

homocinétique [ɔmosinetik] ADJ *Tech* **joint h.** Hooke's joint

homocyclique [ɔmosiklik] ADJ *Chim* homocyclic

homodonte [ɔmodɔ̃t] ADJ *Zool* homodont

homofocal, -e, -aux, -ales [ɔmofɔkal, -o] ADJ **1** *Opt* homofocal **2** *Géom* confocal

homogamétique [ɔmogametik] ADJ *Biol* homogametic

homogamie [ɔmogami] NF *(en sociologie)* homogamy

homogène [ɔmɔʒɛn] ADJ **1** *(substance, liquide, marché, produits)* homogeneous; **jusqu'à obtention d'une pâte bien h.** until you have a nice smooth mixture **2** *(gouvernement, classe)* uniform, consistent, coherent **3** *Chim & Math* homogeneous **4** *Mktg (marché, produits)* homogeneous

homogénéisateur, -trice [ɔmɔʒeneizatœr, -tris] ADJ homogenizing
  NM,F homogenizer

homogénéisation [ɔmɔʒeneizasjɔ̃] NF **1** *(d'une substance)* homogenization **2** *Fig (uniformisation)* standardization; **on constate une h. des modes de paiement** payment methods are being standardized

homogénéisatrice [ɔmɔʒeneizatris] *voir* **homogénéisateur**

homogénéisé, -e [ɔmɔʒeneize] ADJ homogeneous, homogenized; *(lait)* homogenized

homogénéiser [3] [ɔmɔʒeneize] VT to make homogeneous; *(lait)* to homogenize

homogénéité [ɔmɔʒeneite] NF **1** *(d'une substance)* homogeneity, homogeneousness **2** *(d'une œuvre, d'une équipe)* coherence, unity

homographe [ɔmograf] ADJ homographic
  NM homograph

homographie [ɔmografi] NF homography

homographique [ɔmografik] ADJ homographic

homogreffe [ɔmogrɛf] NF *(de tissu)* homograft; *(d'un organe)* homotransplant

homologation [ɔmɔlɔgasjɔ̃] NF **1** *(déclaration de conformité)* accreditation **2** *Jur (entérinement)* ratification, approval; *(d'un testament)* probate **3** *Sport* ratification; **l'h. d'un record** the ratification of a record

homologie [ɔmɔlɔʒi] NF *Math, Biol & Chim* homology

homologue [ɔmɔlɔg] ADJ **1** *(équivalent)* homologous, homologic, homological; **amiral est le grade h. de général** an admiral is equal in rank to a general **2** *Biol & Chim* homologous **3** *Math* homologous, homologic, homological
  NMF *(personne)* counterpart, opposite number
  NM *Biol & Chim* homologue

homologuer [3] [ɔmɔlɔge] VT **1** *(déclarer conforme)* to approve, to accredit; **prix homologué** authorized price **2** *Jur (entériner)* to sanction, to ratify; *(testament)* to probate **3** *Sport* to ratify

homomorphe [ɔmɔmɔrf] *Biol* ADJ homomorphic, homomorphous
  NM homomorph

homomorphisme [ɔmɔmɔrfism] NM **1** *Biol* homomorphism, homomorphy **2** *Math* homomorphism

homoncule [ɔmɔ̃kyl] = **homuncule**

homonyme [ɔmɔnim] ADJ homonymous
  NMF *(personne, ville)* namesake
  NM homonym

homonymie [ɔmɔnimi] NF homonymy

homonymique [ɔmɔnimik] ADJ homonymic

homoparental, -e, -aux, -ales [ɔmoparãtal, -o] ADJ relating to gay parenting, *Spéc* homoparental; **famille homoparentale** family with gay parents

homoparentalité [ɔmoparãtalite] NF gay parenting

homophobe [ɔmofɔb] ADJ homophobic
  NMF homophobe

homophobie [ɔmofɔbi] NF homophobia

homophone [ɔmofɔn] ADJ **1** *Ling* homophonous **2** *Mus* homophonic
  NM *Ling* homophone

homophonie [ɔmofɔni] NF *Ling & Mus* homophony

homophonique [ɔmofɔnik] ADJ *Mus* homophonic

homoptère [ɔmɔptɛr] *Entom* NM homopteran, member of the Homoptera order
  ❏ **homoptères** NMPL Homoptera

homosexualité [ɔmosɛksɥalite] NF homosexuality

homosexuel, -elle [ɔmosɛksɥɛl] ADJ homosexual, gay
  NM,F homosexual, gay

homosphère [ɔmosfɛr] NF *Géog* homosphere

homothétie [ɔmotesi] NF *Math* homothetic transformation

homothétique [ɔmotetik] ADJ *Math* homothetic

homozygote [ɔmozigɔt] *Biol* ADJ homozygous
  NMF homozygote

homozygotie [ɔmozigɔsi] NF *Biol* homozygosis

homuncule [ɔmɔ̃kyl] NM **1** *(en alchimie)* homunculus **2** *Fam Vieilli (petit homme)* squirt

*****honchets** [ʃʃɛ] NMPL *Vieilli* spillikins

*****Honduras** [ɔdyras] NM **le H.** Honduras; **vivre au H.** to live in Honduras; **aller au H.** to go to Honduras; **le H. britannique** British Honduras

*****hondurien, -enne** [ɔdyrjɛ̃, -ɛn] ADJ Honduran
  ❏ **Hondurien, -enne** NM,F Honduran

*****Hongkong, *Hong Kong** [ɔgkɔ̃g] NM Hong Kong

*****hongre** [ɔgr] ADJ M gelded
  NM gelding

*****hongrer** [3] [ɔgre] VT *Vét* to geld, to castrate

*****hongreur** [ɔgrœr] NM gelder

*****Hongrie** [ɔgri] NF **la H.** Hungary; **vivre en H.** to live in Hungary; **aller en H.** to go to Hungary

*****hongroierie** [ɔgrwari] NF tawing

*****hongrois, -e** [ɔgrwa, -az] ADJ Hungarian
  NM *(langue)* Hungarian, Magyar
  ❏ **Hongrois, -e** NM,F Hungarian

*****hongroyage** [ɔgrwajaʒ] NM tawing

*****hongroyer** [13] [ɔgrwaje] VT to taw

*****hongroyeur, -euse** [ɔgrwajœr, -øz] NM,F tawer

*****honing** [ɔniŋ] NM *Tech* honing

honnête [ɔnɛt] ADJ **1** *(scrupuleux → vendeur, associé)* honest; **le procédé n'est pas très h. mais j'ai besoin d'argent** it's a rather unscrupulous *or* dishonest thing to do but I need the money; **ils ont employé des moyens peu honnêtes pour arriver à leurs fins** they used rather unscrupulous *or* dishonest means to get what they wanted

2 *(franc)* honest; **soyons honnêtes** let's be honest; **il faut être h., elle n'a aucune chance de réussir** let's face it *or* we might as well face facts, she hasn't got a hope of succeeding; **être h. avec soi-même** to be honest with oneself

3 *(acceptable → prix)* fair, reasonable; *(→ résultat)* decent, reasonable; *(→ repas)* decent; **12 sur 20, c'est h.** 12 out of 20, that's not bad; **une note plus qu'h.** a perfectly respectable mark

4 *(respectable)* honest, respectable, decent; **des gens honnêtes** respectable people; *Littéraire* **un h. homme** ≃ a gentleman

5 *Arch (poli)* courteous, polite, well-bred

honnêtement [ɔnɛtmã] ADV **1** *(sincèrement)* honestly, frankly, sincerely; **répondez h.** answer honestly, give an honest answer; **h., je ne la connais pas!** honestly, I don't know her!; **non mais, h., tu la crois?** come on now, be honest, do you believe her?

2 *(décemment)* fairly, decently; **je connais cet endroit, on y mange h.** I know that place, the food they serve is quite decent; **elle a terminé h. son année scolaire** she finished the year with reasonable marks

3 *(de façon morale)* honestly; **vivre h.** to live *or* to lead an honest life; **c'est de l'argent h. gagné** it's money honestly earned; **il a relaté les faits h.** he told the story honestly *or* candidly

4 *Arch (avec courtoisie)* courteously, politely

honnêteté [ɔnɛtte] NF **1** *(franchise)* honesty, candour; **avec h.** honestly, candidly; **il a reconnu**

son erreur avec h. he admitted honestly that he was wrong

2 *(intégrité → d'une conduite)* honesty, decency; *(→ d'une personne)* integrity, decency

3 *Arch (décence)* decency, propriety, decorum

4 *Arch (courtoisie)* courtesy, politeness

❑ **en toute honnêteté** ADV **1** *(avec sincérité)* in all honesty, frankly; **répondez en toute h.** give an honest answer

2 *(pour être honnête)* to tell the truth, to be perfectly honest

honneur [ɔnœr] NM **1** *(dignité)* honour; **homme d'h.** man of honour, honourable man; **mon h. est en jeu** my honour is at stake; **l'h. est sauf** my/his/*etc* honour is saved *or* intact; **c'est une question d'h.** it's a matter of honour; **mettre un point d'h. à** *ou* **se faire un point d'h. de faire qch** to make a point of honour of doing sth; **venger l'h. de qn** to avenge sb's honour; **rendre l'h. à une femme** to restore a woman's honour; **je finirai la partie pour l'h.** I'll play to the end (even though I've lost); **se faire h. de** to pride oneself on *or* upon

2 *(mérite)* **c'est tout à son h.** it's entirely to his/her credit; **l'h. vous en revient** the credit is yours; **être l'h. de sa nation** to be a credit *or* an honour to one's country; **faire h. à qn** to do sb credit; **ces sentiments ne lui font pas h.** these feelings do him/her no credit

3 *(marque de respect)* honour; *(dans des formules de politesse)* privilege, honour; **vous me faites trop d'h.** you're being too kind (to me); **c'est lui faire trop d'h.** he/she doesn't deserve such respect; **à vous l'h.!** after you!; **h. aux dames!** ladies first!; **c'est un h. pour moi de vous présenter...** it's a great privilege for me to introduce to you...; **j'ai l'h. de solliciter votre aide** I would be most grateful for your assistance; **nous avons l'h. de vous informer que...** we have the pleasure of informing you that...; **faites-nous l'h. de venir nous voir** would you honour us with a visit?; **me ferez-vous l'h. de m'accorder cette danse?** may I have the honour of this dance?; **à qui ai-je l'h.?** to whom do I have the honour (of speaking)?

4 *(titre)* **votre/son H.** Your/His Honour

5 *(locutions)* **faire h. à qch** *(signature, chèque, facture, traite)* to honour; **faire h. à ses engagements** to honour one's commitments; **ils ont fait h. à ma cuisine/mon gigot** they did justice to my cooking/leg of lamb

❑ **honneurs** NMPL **1** *(cérémonie)* honours; **les honneurs dus à son rang** the honours due to his/her rank; **honneurs funèbres** last honours; **enterré avec les honneurs militaires** buried with (full) military honours; **rendre les honneurs à qn** *Mil (saluer)* to present arms to sb, to give *or* pay (military) honours to sb; *(funèbres)* to pay sb one's last respects; *Mil* **les honneurs de la guerre** the honours of war; *Fig* **avec les honneurs de la guerre** honourably

2 *(distinction)* **briguer** *ou* **rechercher les honneurs** to seek public recognition; **avoir les honneurs de la première page** to get a write-up on the front page; **faire à qn les honneurs de qch** to show sb round sth; **permettez que je vous fasse les honneurs de la cave** do let me show you round the cellar

3 *Cartes* honours

❑ **à l'honneur** ADJ **être à l'h.** to have the place of honour; **ce soir, c'est vous qui êtes à l'h.** tonight is in your honour; **les organisateurs de l'exposition ont voulu que la sculpture soit à l'h.** the exhibition organizers wanted sculpture to take pride of place

❑ **d'honneur** ADJ *(invité, place, tour)* of honour; *(membre, président)* honorary; *(cour, escalier)* main

❑ **en honneur** ADJ in favour; **mettre qch en h.** to bring sth into favour

❑ **en l'honneur de** PRÉP in honour of; **en l'h. de notre ami Maurice** in honour of our friend Maurice; **une fête en mon/son h.** a party for me/him/her

❑ **en quel honneur** ADV *Fam* **il faut que tu m'aides – ah bon, et en quel h.?** you've got to help me – give me one good reason why I should!; *Fam Hum* **ce regard noir, c'est en quel h.?** what's that scowl in aid of?, what's that scowl for?

❑ **sur l'honneur** ADV upon *or* on one's honour; **jurer sur l'h.** to swear on one's honour

---

'L'Honneur perdu de Katharina Blum' *Böll, Schlöndorff* 'The Lost Honor of Katharina Blum'

***honnir** [32] [ɔnir] VT *Littéraire* to despise; **un dictateur honni** a hated dictator; **honni soit qui mal y pense** honi soit qui mal y pense, shame be to him who thinks evil of it

Honolulu [ɔnɔlyly] NM Honolulu

honorabilité [ɔnɔrabilite] NF respectability

honorable [ɔnɔrabl] ADJ **1** *(digne de respect)* respectable, honourable; **les citoyens honorables** respectable *or* upright citizens; **ses motifs ne sont pas des plus honorables** his/her intentions are less than honourable

2 *(avant le nom) Hum* **mon h. collègue** my esteemed colleague; **j'en appelle à l'h. compagnie** I appeal to this honourable company

3 *(satisfaisant)* fair, decent; **son bulletin scolaire est tout à fait h./est h. sans plus** her school report is quite satisfactory/is just satisfactory

honorablement [ɔnɔrabləmɑ̃] ADV **1** *(de façon respectable)* decently, honourably; **h. connu** known and respected; **vivre h.** to lead a respectable life **2** *(de façon satisfaisante)* creditably, honourably; **gagner h. sa vie** to earn a decent living

honoraire [ɔnɔrɛr] ADJ **1** *(conservant son ancien titre)* **professeur h.** professor emeritus **2** *(ayant le titre mais non les fonctions)* honorary

honoraires [ɔnɔrɛr] NMPL fee, fees; **il demande des h. raisonnables** he charges reasonable fees *or* a reasonable fee

honorariat [ɔnɔrarja] NM *(titre)* honorary title; **obtenir** *ou* **recevoir l'h.** to become an honorary member

honoré, -e [ɔnɔre] ADJ **1** *(honorable)* **mes chers et honorés confrères** most honourable and esteemed colleagues **2** *(lors de présentations)* **très h.!** I'm (greatly) honoured!

❑ **honorée** NF *Vieilli Com* **par votre honorée du 20 avril** by your letter of 20 April

honorer [3] [ɔnɔre] VT **1** *(rendre hommage à)* to honour; **honorons nos héros disparus** let us pay tribute to our dead heroes; **h. qn de sa confiance** to honour sb with one's confidence; *Hum* **elle ne nous a même pas honorés d'un regard** she never even honoured us with a glance

2 *(respecter, estimer)* to honour; **nous honorons tous l'homme qui a pris cette décision** the man who made that decision is held in great esteem by us all; **tu honoreras ta famille** you will respect your family

3 *(contribuer à la réputation de)* to honour, to be a credit *or* an honour to; **votre sincérité vous honore** your sincerity does you credit

4 *(gratifier)* to honour; **votre présence m'honore** you honour me with your presence

5 *(s'acquitter de → facture, chèque, traite, engagements, signature)* to honour

6 *Rel* **h. Dieu** to honour *or* to praise God

7 *Hum (sexuellement)* to make love to

▸**s'honorer** VPR **s'h. de** to be proud of, to take pride in, to pride oneself upon; **je m'honore de votre amitié** *ou* **d'être votre ami** I'm honoured *or* proud to be your friend

honorifique [ɔnɔrifik] ADJ honorary; **c'est un poste h.** it's an honorary position

***honoris causa** [ɔnɔriskoza] ADJ **être docteur h.** to be the holder of an honorary doctorate

Honshu [ɔnʃu] NM *Géog* Honshu

***honte** [ɔ̃t] NF **1** *(sentiment d'humiliation)* shame; **avoir h. (de qn/qch)** to be *or* to feel ashamed (of sb/sth); **vous devriez avoir h.!** you should be ashamed!; **n'as-tu pas h.?** aren't you ashamed?; **j'ai h. d'arriver les mains vides** I feel *or* I'm ashamed at arriving empty-handed; **faire h. à qn** to make sb (feel) ashamed, to shame sb; **il fait h. à son père** *(il lui est un sujet de mécontentement)* his father is ashamed of him; *(il lui donne un sentiment d'infériorité)* he puts his father to shame; **ne me fais pas h. devant nos invités** please don't show me up in front of our guests; **trois ans plus tard, toute h. bue, il recommençait son trafic** three years later, totally lacking in any sense of shame, he started up his little racket again; *Fam* **(c'est) la h.!** the shame of it!; *Fam* **avoir la h.** to be embarrassed■ *or* mortified

2 *(indignité, scandale)* disgrace, (object of) shame; **être la h. de sa famille** to be a disgrace to one's family; **la société laisse faire, c'est une h.!** it's outrageous *or* it's a crying shame that society just lets it happen!

3 *(déshonneur)* shame, shamefulness; **essuyer** *ou* **subir la h. d'un refus** to suffer the shame of a rebuff; **à ma grande h.** to my shame; **h. à celui/celle qui...** shame on him/her who...; **h. à toi!** shame on you!; **il n'y a pas de h. à être au chômage** being unemployed is nothing to be ashamed of

4 *(peur)* fear; **tu as h. de venir me dire bonjour?** are you afraid to come and say hello?

5 *(pudeur)* **fausse h.** bashfulness; **n'ayez pas de fausse h. à parler au médecin** don't feel bashful *or* self-conscious about talking to the doctor

❑ **sans honte** ADV shamelessly, without shame, unashamedly; **vous pouvez parler sans h.** you may talk quite openly

***honteuse** [ɔ̃tøz] *voir* **honteux**

***honteusement** [ɔ̃tøzmɑ̃] ADV **1** *(avec gêne)* shamefully, ashamedly; **elle cacha h. son visage dans ses mains** she hid her face in shame **2** *(scandaleusement)* shamefully, disgracefully; **on les exploite h.** they are disgracefully *or* scandalously exploited

***honteux, -euse** [ɔ̃tø, -øz] ADJ **1** *(déshonorant)* shameful, disgraceful; **de h. secrets** shameful secrets; **un passé h.** a shameful past, an inglorious past; **maladie honteuse** venereal disease

2 *(scandaleux → exploitation, politique)* disgraceful, outrageous, shocking; **des loyers aussi élevés, c'est h.** such high rents are a disgrace; **c'est h. de lui prendre le peu qu'elle a** it's disgraceful *or* a disgrace to take from her the little she has; **ils continuent leur h. trafic de stupéfiants** they keep up their vile drug trafficking

3 *(qui a des remords)* ashamed; **être h. de qch/d'avoir fait qch** to be ashamed of sth/of having done sth

4 *(qui cache ses opinions)* closet *(avant n)*

***hoodia gordonii** [udjagɔrdɔni] NM *Bot* hoodia

***hooligan** [uligan] NM (football) hooligan

***hooliganisme** [uliganism] NM (football) hooliganism

***hop** [ɔp] EXCLAM **allez, h.!** *(à un enfant)* come on, upsadaisy!; **allez h., on s'en va!** (right,) off we go!; **h.-là!** oops(-a-daisy)!

***hopak** [ɔpak] NM *(danse)* gopak

hôpital, -aux [ɔpital, -o] NM **1** *(établissement)* hospital; **il est très bien soigné à l'h.** he is being very well cared for in hospital; **h. de campagne** field hospital; **h. de jour** outpatient clinic, *Br* day hospital; **h. naval** naval hospital; **h. psychiatrique** psychiatric hospital; **c'est l'h. qui se moque de la Charité** it's the pot calling the kettle black **2** *(comme adj; avec ou sans trait d'union)* hospital *(avant n)*; **navire h.** hospital ship

hoplite [ɔplit] NM *Antiq* hoplite

***hoquet** [ɔkɛ] NM **1** *(spasme)* hiccup, hiccough; **avoir le h.** to have the hiccups; **mon h. m'a repris** my hiccups have come back again; **dans un h. de dégoût** with a gasp of disgust **2** *(d'un appareil)* chug, gasp; **le moteur eut un dernier h. et rendit l'âme** the engine gave a final splutter and died

***hoqueter** [27] [ɔkte] VI **1** *(personne)* to hiccup, to have (the) hiccups **2** *(appareil)* to judder; **le moteur hoqueta, puis s'arrêta** the engine spluttered to a halt

***hoqueton** [ɔktɔ̃] NM *Hist* **1** *(d'homme d'armes)* haqueton, acton **2** *(de paysan, de berger)* smock-frock

Horace [ɔras] NPR *(poète)* Horace

❑ **Horaces** NMPL *(frères romains)* **les Horaces** the Horatii

horaire [ɔrɛr] ADJ hourly

NM **1** *(de travail)* schedule, timetable; *(d'un magasin)* opening hours; **j'ai un h. réduit** I work shorter hours; **nos horaires sont chargés** we

The symbol * indicates that the initial **h** is aspirate and that hence there is no liaison, eg **les haricots** [leariko] and not [lezariko], or contraction in spelling, eg **la haine** and not **l'haine**.

work a busy *or* heavy schedule *or* a lot of hours; **nous n'avons pas les mêmes horaires** we don't work the same hours; **je n'ai pas d'h.** I don't have any particular schedule; **h. individualisé** *ou* **souple** *ou* **à la carte** flexible working hours, *Br* flexitime, *Am* flextime; **nous avons un h. à la carte** we have flexible working hours, we work *Br* flexitime *or Am* flextime; **horaires de bureau/ de travail** office/working hours

2 *(de train, d'avion)* schedule, timetable; **horaires d'avion** flight timetable; **je ne connais pas l'h. des trains** I don't know the train times; **être en retard sur l'h.** to be running late

***horde** [ɔrd] **NF** horde; **des hordes de gens affamés assaillaient les trains** hordes *or* throngs of hungry people mobbed the trains

hordéacé, -e [ɔrdease] **ADJ** *Bot* hordeaceous

hordéine [ɔrdein] **NF** *Biol* hordein

Horeca [ɔreka] **NM** *Belg (abrév* **hôtels, restaurants, cafés**) = hotels, cafés and restaurants *(collectively)*

***horion** [ɔrjɔ̃] **NM** *Littéraire* blow, punch; **les horions pleuvaient de partout** fists were flying

horizon [ɔrizɔ̃] **NM 1** *(ligne)* horizon; *aussi Fig* **à l'h.** on the horizon; **le soleil disparaît à l'h.** the sun is disappearing below the horizon; **le ciel se dégage à l'h.** the sky *or* the weather is clearing on the horizon; **on voit encore le bateau à l'h.** the ship is still visible on the horizon; *aussi Fig* **rien à l'h.** nothing in sight *or* view; *Fam* **pas le moindre petit boulot à l'h.** no job anywhere to be had, nothing doing jobwise

2 *(paysage)* horizon, view, vista; **un h. de toits et de coupoles** a skyline of rooftops and domes; **changer d'h.** to have a change of scene *or* scenery

3 *(domaine d'activité)* horizon; **élargir ses horizons** to broaden one's horizons; **h. intellectuel** intellectual horizons *or* boundaries

4 *(perspectives d'avenir)* **notre h. est janvier 2010** our objective is *or* we are working towards January 2010; **les prévisions à l'h. 2010** the forecast for 2010; **ouvrir des horizons** to open up new horizons *or* prospects; **h. économique/ politique** economic/political prospects

5 *Astron* (celestial) horizon

6 *Géol* horizon; **h. A/B/C** A/B/C horizon

7 *Aviat* **h. artificiel** artificial horizon

8 *Beaux-Arts* **ligne/plan d'h.** horizon line/plane

horizontal, -e, -aux, -ales [ɔrizɔ̃tal, -o] **ADJ 1** *(position)* horizontal; **mettez-vous en position horizontale** lie down (flat); **le un h.** *(aux mots croisés)* one across **2** *Écon (concentration, intégration)* horizontal

❑ **horizontale NF** horizontal

❑ **à l'horizontale ADV** horizontally, in a horizontal position; **placer qch à l'horizontale** to lay sth down (flat)

horizontalement [ɔrizɔ̃talmɑ̃] **ADV** horizontally; **pose l'échelle h.** lay the ladder down flat; **h. un: en six lettres, oiseau** *(aux mots croisés)* one across: six letters, bird

horizontalité [ɔrizɔ̃talite] **NF** horizontalness, horizontality

horloge [ɔrlɔʒ] **NF 1** *(pendule)* clock; **il est deux heures à l'h.** it's two by the clock; **j'ai attendu une bonne heure d'h.** I waited a full *or* solid hour by the clock; **h. atomique** atomic clock; **h. biologique** body *or* biological clock; *Can* **h. grand-père** grandfather *or* longcase clock; **h. horodatrice** time clock; **h. interne** body *or* biological clock; **h. mystérieuse** mystery clock; **h. normande** grandfather *or* longcase clock; **h. parlante** *Br* speaking clock, *Am* time (telephone) service; **h. de parquet** grandfather *or* longcase clock; **h. pointeuse** time clock; *Ordinat* **h. du système** system clock; *Ordinat* **h. en temps réel** real-time clock

2 *Entom* **h. de la mort** deathwatch beetle

horloger, -ère [ɔrlɔʒe, -ɛr] **ADJ** clock-making; **la production horlogère** clock and watch making

NM,F watchmaker, clockmaker; **h. bijoutier** jeweller

'L'Horloger de Saint-Paul' *Tavernier* 'The Clockmaker of St Paul' (US), 'The Watchmaker of St Paul' (UK)

horlogerie [ɔrlɔʒri] **NF 1** *(technique, métier)* clock (and watch) *or* timepiece making; **pièce d'h.** *(interne)* clock component; *(horloge)* timepiece **2** *(boutique)* watchmaker's, clockmaker's; **h. (bijouterie)** *Br* jewellery shop, *Am* jewelry store **3** *(articles)* clocks and watches

***hormis** [ɔrmi] *Littéraire* **PRÉP** save (for); **le stade était vide, h. quelques rares spectateurs** the stadium was empty, save for *or* apart from a handful of spectators

❑ **hormis que CONJ** *(à part que)* except *or* save that; *Can (à moins que)* unless

hormonal, -e, -aux, -ales [ɔrmɔnal, -o] **ADJ** *(gén)* hormonal; *(traitement, crème)* hormone *(avant n)*

hormone [ɔrmɔn] **NF** *Biol* hormone; **h. de croissance** growth hormone; **h. folliculo-stimulante** follicle-stimulating hormone, FSH; **h. lutéinisante** luteinizing hormone; **aux hormones** *(animaux)* hormone-fed

hormonothérapie [ɔrmɔnɔterapi] **NF** *Méd* hormone therapy, *Spéc* hormonotherapy

Hormuz [ɔrmuz] **NM le détroit d'H.** the strait of Hormuz

***Horn** [ɔrn] **NM le cap H.** Cape Horn

***hornblende** [ɔrnblɛ̃d] **NF** *Minér* hornblende

horodaté, -e [ɔrɔdate] **ADJ** *(ticket)* stamped *(with the date and time)*; **stationnement h.** pay-and-display parking zone

horodateur, -trice [ɔrɔdatœr, -tris] **ADJ** time-stamping

NM *(administratif)* time-stamp; *(de parking)* ticket machine

horokilométrique [ɔrɔkilɔmetrik] **ADJ rendement h.** time-distance ratio

horoscope [ɔrɔskɔp] **NM** horoscope

horreur [ɔrœr] **NF 1** *(effroi)* horror; **saisi** *ou* **rempli d'h.** horror-stricken, filled with horror; **hurler/ reculer d'h.** to cry out/to shrink away in horror; **avoir qch en h.** *(dégoût)* to have a horror of *or* to loathe sth; **avoir qn en h.** to loathe sb; **avoir h. de** to loathe, to hate; **j'ai h. des araignées** I hate *or* I'm terrified of spiders; **elle a h. des huîtres** she hates *or* can't stand oysters; **j'ai h. qu'on me dérange** I hate *or* I can't stand being disturbed; **faire h. à qn** to horrify *or* to terrify sb, to fill sb with horror; **rien que l'idée de manger des escargots me fait h.** the very idea of eating snails fills me with horror *or* disgust; *Fam* **c'est l'h.** it's the pits, it sucks, *Am* it bites; **film d'h.** horror movie *or Br* film

2 *(cruauté)* horror, ghastliness; **l'h. des images était insoutenable** the pictures were unbearably horrific; **il décrit la guerre des tranchées dans toute son h.** he describes trench warfare in all its horror

3 *Fam (chose ou personne laide)* **c'est une h.** *(personne)* he's/she's repulsive; *(objet)* it's hideous; **jette-moi toutes ces vieilles horreurs** throw away all these horrible old things

4 *(dans des exclamations)* **oh, quelle h.!** that's awful *or* terrible!; **quelle h., cette odeur!** what a disgusting *or* vile smell!; *Hum* **une goutte de bière sur mon tapis neuf, l'h.!** a drop of beer on my new carpet, oh, no!

❑ **horreurs NFPL 1** *(crimes)* horrors; **les horreurs de la guerre** the horrors of war; **les horreurs dont il est responsable** the horrible *or* dreadful deeds he is responsible for

2 *(calomnies)* **on m'a raconté des horreurs sur lui** I've heard horrible things about him

horrible [ɔribl] **ADJ 1** *(effroyable* → *cauchemar)* horrible, dreadful; *(*→ *mutilation, accident)* horrible, horrific; *(*→ *crime)* horrible, ghastly; *(*→ *cri)* horrible, frightful; **ce fut une guerre particulièrement h.** it was a particularly horrific war

2 *(laid* → *personne)* horrible, hideous, repulsive; *(*→ *vêtement)* ghastly, frightful; *(*→ *décor, style)* horrible, hideous, ghastly; **une espèce d'h. chapeau** a really ghastly hat

3 *(méchant)* horrible, nasty, horrid; **être h. avec qn** to be nasty *or* horrible to sb; **raconter des histoires horribles sur qn** to say horrible *or* nasty things about sb

4 *(infect)* horrible, disgusting; **la nourriture était h.** the food was disgusting

5 *(très désagréable* → *temps)* terrible; *(*→ *douleur)* terrible, awful; **un vacarme h.** a horrible noise; **des douleurs horribles** excruciating pain

horriblement [ɔribləmɑ̃] **ADV 1** *(en intensif)* horribly, terribly, awfully; **nous étions h. déçus** we were terribly disappointed; **je suis h. confus** I'm terribly sorry; **faire qch h. mal** to do sth very badly indeed; **h. mal habillé** appallingly dressed; **ça fait h. mal** it hurts terribly **2** *(atrocement)* horribly

horrifiant, -e [ɔrifjɑ̃, -ɑ̃t] **ADJ** horrifying, terrifying

horrifier [9] [ɔrifje] **VT h. qn** to horrify sb, to fill sb with horror; **être horrifié par** to be horrified at; **elle recula, horrifiée** she shrank back in horror

horrifique [ɔrifik] **ADJ** *Littéraire* horrific, horrendous, horrifying

horripilant, -e [ɔripilɑ̃, -ɑ̃t] **ADJ** *Fam* infuriating, exasperating, irritating; **ne fais pas grincer ta craie, c'est h.** don't grate your chalk on the board, it sets my teeth on edge; **il est h., avec sa manie de jeter les journaux!** he gets on my nerves, always throwing out the papers!

horripilateur [ɔripilatœr] **ADJ M** *Anat* **muscle h.** erector pili muscle

horripilation [ɔripilasjɔ̃] **NF 1** *Physiol* gooseflesh, goose pimples *or* bumps, *Spéc* horripilation **2** *Fam (exaspération)* exasperation, irritation

horripiler [3] [ɔripile] **VT 1** *Fam (exaspérer)* to exasperate; **ses petites manies m'horripilaient** his/her annoying little habits were getting on my nerves; **ne te balance pas sur ta chaise, ça m'horripile** don't rock your chair, it's driving me mad **2** *Physiol* to horripilate

***HORS** [ɔr] **PRÉP 1** *Littéraire (hormis)* except (for), save (for); **personne h. les initiés** no one save *or* but the initiated

2 *(locutions) Rad & TV* **h. antenne** off the air, off-air; **h. barème** off-scale, unquoted; *Compta* **h. bilan** off-balance sheet; **h. Bourse** after hours; **h. budget** not included in the budget; *Admin* **h. cadre** seconded, on secondment; **h. catégorie** outstanding, exceptional; *TV & Cin* **h. champ** out of vision, out of shot; **mettre une lampe h. circuit** to disconnect a lamp; *Fig* **être h. circuit** to be out of circulation; **h. commerce** not for sale to the general public; **il est h. concours** *(exclu)* he's been disqualified; *Fig* he is in a class of his own; **le film a été présenté h. concours** the movie *or Br* film was exempted from the competition; **être h. course** to be out of touch; *Sport* **il est h. jeu** he's offside; **h. ligne** *(exceptionnel)* exceptional, outstanding; **mettre qn h. la loi** to declare sb an outlaw, to outlaw sb; **se mettre h. la loi** to place oneself outside the law; **h. les murs** *(festival)* out of town; **h. normes** non-standard; *Archit* **h. œuvre** out of alignment, projecting; **h. pair** exceptional, outstanding; **une cuisinière h. pair** an exceptional *or* outstanding cook; **skier h. piste** to ski off piste; **h. saison** off-season; **louer h. saison** to rent in the off-season; **h. série** *(remarquable)* outstanding, exceptional; *(personnalisé)* custom-built, customized; **numéro h. série** *(publication)* special issue; **h. service** out of order; **mettre qch h. service** to decommission sth; *Fam* **mettre qn h. service** to knock sb out; **h. sujet** irrelevant, off the subject; **h. taxe** *ou* **taxes** excluding tax; *(à la douane)* duty-free; *Typ* **planche h. texte** plate; **h. tout** overall; **h. TVA** net of VAT

❑ **hors de PRÉP 1** *(dans l'espace* → *à l'extérieur de)* out of, outside; *(*→ *loin de)* away from; **h. de la ville** out of town, outside the town; **h. de mon monde/de mes habitudes** away from my surroundings/my routine; **h. de ma vue** out of my sight; **h. d'ici!** get out of here!

2 *(dans le temps)* **h. de saison** out of season; **h. du temps** timeless; **elle est** *ou* **elle vit h. de son temps** she lives in a different age

3 *(locutions)* **il était h. de lui** he was beside himself; **elle m'a mis h. de moi** she infuriated me, she made me furious *or* mad; **mettre qch h. d'action** to disable sth; **être h. d'affaire** to have come *or* pulled through; **te voilà h. d'affaire!** that's you over the worst!; **être h. de combat** *Sport* to be knocked out *or* hors de combat; *Fig* to be out of the game *or* running; **mettre qn h. de combat** to disable sb; **mettre qn h. de cause** to exonerate sb; **h. du commun** outstanding, exceptional; **ici, vous êtes h. de danger** you're safe *or* out of harm's reach here; **la victime n'est pas encore h. de danger** the victim isn't out of

danger yet; **il est h. de doute que…** it's beyond doubt that…; **il est h. d'état de nuire** he's been rendered harmless; *Euph (tué)* he's been taken care of; *Archit* **h. d'œuvre** out of alignment, projecting; **h. de portée (de)** *(trop loin)* out of reach *or* range (of); *Fig* out of reach (of); **h. de prix** prohibitively *or* ruinously expensive; **h. de propos** inopportune, untimely; **c'est h. de question** it's out of the question; **h. d'usage** out of service; **h. de l'Église, point de salut** there is no salvation outside the Church

***horsain** [ɔrsɛ̃] **NM** *(en Normandie)* outsider

***hors-bord** [ɔrbɔr] **NM INV** **1 (moteur) h.** outboard motor **2** *(bateau)* speedboat, outboard

***hors-cote** [ɔrkɔt] *Bourse* **ADJ INV** unlisted
NM INV *(marché)* unlisted securities market

***hors-d'œuvre** [ɔrdœvr] **NM INV** **1** *Culin* starter, hors d'œuvre; **h. variés** (assorted) cold meats and salads **2** *Fig* **et ce n'était qu'un h.** and that was just the beginning **3** *Archit* annexe, outwork

horse-ball** [ɔrsbol] *(pl* **horse-balls)* **NM** *Sport* horse ball

horse-guard** [ɔrsgard] *(pl* **horse-guards)* **NM** *Br* Horse Guard

***horse power** [ɔrspɔwœr] **NM INV** horsepower

***horsin** [ɔrsɛ̃] = **horsain**

***hors-jeu** [ɔrʒø] **ADJ INV** offside; **le joueur est h.** the player is offside
NM INV offside; **h. de position** offside *(where the player is not interfering with play)*

***hors-la-loi** [ɔrlalwa] **NM INV** outlaw

***hors-média** [ɔrmedja] *Mktg* **ADJ INV** *(publicité, promotion, coûts)* below-the-line
NM INV below-the-line advertising

***hors-micro** [ɔrmikro] **ADV** *Rad* off-mike

***hors-piste, *hors-pistes** [ɔrpist] **NM INV** **faire du h.** to ski off piste
ADJ INV **le ski h.** off-piste skiing

hors-série** [ɔrseri] *(pl* **hors-séries)* *Presse* **ADJ INV** special
NM special edition

***hors-sol** [ɔrsɔl] *Agr* **ADJ INV** = using feed which has come from other farms
NM INV = method of rearing farm animals using feed which has come from other farms

***hors statut** [ɔrstaty] **ADJ INV** *Admin* = not covered by the conditions and regulations usually applicable to a particular area of work

***hors-statut** [ɔrstaty] **NM INV** *Admin* = employee not covered by the conditions and regulations usually applicable to his or her area of work

***horst** [ɔrst] **NM** *Géol* horst

***hors-texte** [ɔrtɛkst] **NM INV** *Typ* (inset) plate, tip-in

hortensia [ɔrtɑ̃sja] **NM** hydrangea

horticole [ɔrtikɔl] **ADJ** horticultural; **exposition h.** flower show

horticulteur, -trice [ɔrtikyltœr, -tris] **NM,F** horticulturist

horticulture [ɔrtikyltyr] **NF** horticulture

hortillonnage [ɔrtijɔnaʒ] **NM** *(terme picard)* = marshy land which has been canalized for agricultural use

hosanna [ozana] **NM** *Littéraire Rel* hosanna

hospice [ɔspis] **NM** **1** *(asile)* **h. (de vieillards)** (old people's) home; **finir à l'h.** to end up in the poorhouse **2** *Rel* hospice

hospitalier, -ère [ɔspitalje, ɛr] **ADJ** **1** *Admin (frais, service, personnel)* hospital *(avant n)*; **en milieu h.** in a hospital environment; **établissement h.** hospital **2** *(accueillant → personne, peuple, demeure)* hospitable, welcoming; *(→ rivage, île)* inviting **3** *Rel* **frère h.** Hospitaller; **ordre h.** Hospitaller order; **sœur hospitalière** Hospitaller
NM,F hospital worker; **les hospitaliers** hospital staff *or* workers
NM *Rel* Hospitaller

hospitalisation [ɔspitalizasjɔ̃] **NF** hospitalization; **son état nécessite une h. immédiate** in his/her state, he/she should be admitted to hospital immediately; **pendant mon h.** while I was in hospital; **h. à domicile** home care

hospitalisé, -e [ɔspitalize] **NM,F** hospital patient

hospitaliser [3] [ɔspitalize] **VT** to hospitalize; **se faire h.** to be admitted *or* taken to hospital; **le médecin veut le faire h.** the doctor wants to send him to hospital *or* to have him admitted to hospital *or* to hospitalize him; **elle est hospitalisée à La Salpêtrière** she's in hospital at La Salpêtrière; **il est resté hospitalisé pendant plusieurs mois** he was in hospital for several months

hospitalisme [ɔspitalism] **NM** *Psy* separation anxiety

hospitalité [ɔspitalite] **NF** **1** *(hébergement)* hospitality; **offrir/donner l'h. à qn** to offer/to give sb hospitality **2** *(cordialité)* **nous vous remercions de votre h.** *(après un séjour, un repas)* thank you for making us (feel) welcome; **avoir le sens de l'h.** to be hospitable **3** *(asile)* **donner l'h. à des réfugiés politiques** to give shelter to *or* to take in political refugees

hospitalo-universitaire [ɔspitalɔynivɛrsitɛr] *(pl* **hospitalo-universitaires***)* **ADJ** **centre h.** teaching *or* university hospital; **enseignement h.** clinical teaching

hospodar [ɔspɔdar] **NM** *Hist* hospodar

host [ɔst] **NM** *Hist (à l'époque féodale)* army

hostellerie [ɔstɛlri] **NF** country inn

hostie [ɔsti] **NF** **1** *Rel* host **2** *Vieilli & Littéraire (victime)* victim, offering *(for sacrifice)*
EXCLAM *Can très Fam Br* bloody hell!, *Am* goddammit!

hostile [ɔstil] **ADJ** **1** *(inamical)* hostile, unfriendly; **un regard h.** a hostile look; *Littéraire* **cette nature/ce rivage h.** this hostile *or* unfriendly environment/shore **2** *(opposé)* hostile; **être h. à** to be hostile to *or* opposed to *or* against **3** *École* hostile

hostilement [ɔstilmɑ̃] **ADV** hostilely, with hostility

hostilité [ɔstilite] **NF** hostility; **manifester de l'h. envers** to show hostility to *or* towards
▫ **hostilités** **NFPL** *Mil* **les hostilités** hostilities; **reprendre les hostilités** to reopen *or* to resume hostilities

hosto [ɔsto] **NM** *Fam (hôpital)* hospital ▪

***hot** [ɔt] *Mus* **ADJ INV** *(jazz)* hot
NM INV hot jazz

hot dog** [ɔtdɔg] *(pl* **hot dogs)* **NM** hot dog

hôte, hôtesse [ot, otɛs] **NM,F** *(personne qui reçoit)* host, *f* hostess; **notre h.** our host
NM **1** *(invité)* guest; *(client dans un hôtel)* patron, guest; **un h. de marque** an important guest; **h. payant** paying guest
2 *Littéraire (habitant)* **les hôtes des bois/lacs** the denizens of the woodlands/lakes
3 *Biol* host
4 *Ordinat* host (computer)
▫ **hôtesse** **NF** *(responsable de l'accueil → dans un hôtel)* receptionist; *(→ dans une exposition)* hostess; **hôtesse d'accueil** receptionist; **demande à l'hôtesse** ask at reception; **hôtesse de l'air** stewardess

hôtel [otɛl] **NM** **1** *(établissement commercial)* hotel; **h. de charme** country house hotel; *(en ville)* = hotel of distinctive character; **h. tout confort** hotel with all *Br* mod cons *or Am* modern conveniences; **h. social** hostel *(for people who are homeless or in difficulty)*; **h. de tourisme** basic hotel; **on ne trouve pas d'hôtels dans la région à cette saison** there is no hotel accommodation available in the area at this time of year; *Fam* **on n'est pas dans un h. ici!** stop treating this place like a hotel!; **h. de passe** = hotel used for prostitution
2 *(bâtiments administratifs)* **l'h. de Brienne** = building in Paris where the French Ministry of Defence is situated; **l'h. Drouot** = salerooms in Paris where auctions are held; **h. des impôts** tax office; **l'h. des Invalides** = building constructed by Louis XIV for wounded soldiers, now housing a military museum and the remains of Napoléon I, which lie under the dome; **l'h. de la Monnaie** = the French Mint, in Paris; **l'h. de Sens** = historic building, now a museum, in the Marais district of Paris, a fine example of late medieval architecture famous for its associations with Marguerite de Valois; **l'h. de Soubise** = eighteenth-century house in the Marais district of Paris, home of the national archives since 1808; **h. des ventes** saleroom, salerooms, auction room *or* rooms; **h. de ville** town *or* city hall
▫ **hôtel particulier** **NM** (private) mansion, town house

hôtel-Dieu [otɛldjø] *(pl* **hôtels-Dieu***)* **NM** *Arch* general hospital

hôtelier, -ère [otəlje, -ɛr] **ADJ** *(relatif à l'hôtellerie)* hotel *(avant n)*; **le personnel h.** hotel staff; **gestion hôtelière** hotel management; **la qualité de l'accueil h.** the standards of hotel accommodation; **l'infrastructure hôtelière** hotel facilities; **l'industrie hôtelière** the hotel industry *or* trade
NM,F hotelier, hotel manager
NM *Rel* Hospitaller

hôtellerie [otɛlri] **NF** **1** *Com* hotel trade *or* business *or* industry; **l'h. de plein air** the camping and caravanning business **2** *Rel* hospice **3** *(hôtel)* country inn

hôtel-restaurant [otɛlrɛstɔrɑ̃] *(pl* **hôtels-restaurants***)* **NM** hotel and restaurant

hôtesse [otɛs] *voir* **hôte**

hot line** [ɔtlajn] *(pl* **hot lines)* **NF** hot line

***hot money** [ɔtmɔnɛ] **NF INV** *Fin* hot money

***hotte** [ɔt] **NF** **1** *(de cheminée, de laboratoire)* hood; **h. aspirante** *ou* **filtrante** *(de cuisine)* extractor hood **2** *(de vendangeur)* basket; **la h. du Père Noël** Father Christmas's sack; *Fam* **en avoir plein la h.** to be bushed *or Br* knackered *or Am* beat

***hottentot, -e** [ɔtɑ̃to, -ɔt] **ADJ** Hottentot
▫ **Hottentot, -e** **NM,F** Hottentot; **les Hottentots** the Hottentots, the Hottentot

***hotter** [3] [ɔte] **VT** to carry in a basket

***hottereau, -x** [ɔtro], ***hotteret** [ɔtrɛ] **NM** small basket

hottonie [ɔtɔni] **NF** *Bot* **h. des marais** water violet

***hotu** [ɔty] **NM** *Ich* beaked carp, nose-carp

***hou** [u] **EXCLAM** *(pour effrayer)* boo!; *(pour faire honte)* shame!

***houache** [waʃ], ***houaiche** [wɛʃ] **NF** *Naut* wake

***houari** [uari] **NM** *Naut* shoulder-of-mutton sail, sliding-gunter sail

***houblon** [ublɔ̃] **NM** *Bot* hop (plant); *(de bière)* hops

***houblonnage** [ublɔnaʒ] **NM** hopping

***houblonner** [3] [ublɔne] **VT** to hop

***houblonnier, -ère** [ublɔnje, ɛr] *Agr* **ADJ** *(région)* hopgrowing; *(industrie)* hop *(avant n)*
NM,F hop grower
▫ **houblonnière** **NF** *(champ de houblon)* hop field *or* garden

***houdan** [udɑ̃] **NF** *Agr* Houdan

***houe** [u] **NF** **1** *Hort* hoe; *Agr* (drag) hoe; **h. rotative** rotary (motor) hoe **2** *Constr* pestle

***houer** [6] [we] **VT** *Vieilli Agr* to hoe

***houille** [uj] **NF** **1** *Mines* coal; **h. flambante** bituminous coal; **h. maigre/grasse** lean/bituminous coal **2** *(énergie)* **h. rouge/d'or** geothermal/solar energy; **h. blanche** hydroelectric power *(from waterfalls)*; **h. bleue** wave and tidal power; **h. incolore** wind power; **h. verte** hydroelectric power *(from rivers)*

***houiller, -ère** [uje, ɛr] **ADJ** *Mines (bassin, production)* coal *(avant n)*; *(sol, roche)* coal-bearing, *Spéc* carboniferous
NM *(en Europe)* Upper Carboniferous; *(aux États-Unis)* Pennsylvanian
▫ **houillère** **NF** coalmine

***houka** [uka] **NM** hookah

***houle** [ul] **NF** *(mouvement de la mer)* swell; **grosse** *ou* **grande h.** heavy swell; **il y a de la h.** the sea's rough

***houlette** [ulɛt] **NF** **1** *Arch (d'un berger)* crook **2** *Hort* trowel
▫ **sous la houlette de** **PRÉP** under the leadership *or* direction *or* aegis of

***houleux, -euse** [ulø, -øz] **ADJ** **1** *(mer)* rough, choppy **2** *(débat, réunion)* stormy

***houligan** [uligan] = **hooligan**

***houliganisme** [uliganism] = **hooliganisme**

***houlque** [ulk] **NF** *Bot* holcus; **h. laineuse** velvet-grass, meadow soft-grass

***houmous** [umus] **NM** houmous, hummus

***houp** [up] = **hop**

***houppe** [up] **NF** **1** *(à maquillage)* powder puff **2** *(de cheveux)* tuft (of hair) **3** *(décorative)* tassel **4** *Orn* tuft

***houppelande** [uplɑ̃d] **NF** *Arch* mantle

***houpper** [3] [upe] **VT** **1** *(garnir de houppes)* to tassel **2** *Tex* to comb

***houppette** [upɛt] **NF** powder puff

***houppier** [upje] **NM** *Bot* crown *(of tree)*

***houque** [uk] = **houlque**

hor–hou

The symbol * indicates that the initial **h** is aspirate and that hence there is no liaison, eg **les haricots** [leariko] and not [lezariko], or contraction in spelling, eg **la haine** and not **l'haine**.

*hourd [ur] NM Hist **1** (fortification) hoarding **2** (estrade pour tournoi) scaffold, covered stand

*hourdage [urdaʒ] NM Constr roughcasting

*hourder [3] [urde] VT Constr to roughcast

*hourdis [urdi] NM Constr roughcast

*houri [uri] NF Littéraire Rel houri

*hourque [urk] NF Naut howker, hooker

*hourra [ura] EXCLAM hurrah!, hooray!
NM cheer (of joy); **pousser des hourras** to cheer

*hourvari [urvari] NM **1** Chasse (ruse) doubling back **2** Littéraire (tumulte) uproar, tumult

*house [awz] NF Mus **la h. (music)** house music

*houseau, -x [uzo] NM Hist greave

*house-boat [awsbot] (pl **house-boats**) NM houseboat

*houspiller [3] [uspije] VT to tell off, to scold; **se faire h.** to get told off

*houspilleur, -euse [uspijœr, -øz] NM,F scolder

*houssaie [usɛ] NF holly plantation, holly grove

*housse [us] NF **1** (de machine à écrire) dust cover; (de coussin) cover; (de meubles → pour protéger) dustsheet; (→ pour décorer) Br cover, Am slipcover; (de vêtements) suit carrier; (de voiture) seat cover; **h. (de protection)** cover; **h. de couette** duvet or quilt cover; **h. de rangement** cover **2** Tech roughcasting

*housser [3] [use] VT to put a (dust) cover on, to cover (up)

*houssine [usin] NF Vieilli switch of holly

*houssiner [3] [usine] VT Vieilli to beat with a switch of holly

*houssoir [uswar] NM Vieilli broom

*houx [u] NM holly; **petit h.** butcher's broom

hovercraft [ɔvœrkraft] NM hovercraft

hoverport [ɔvœrpɔr] NM hoverport

*hoyau, -x [wajo, ojo] NM **1** Agr mattock, grubbing-hoe **2** Mines pickaxe

HP¹ [aʃpe] NM Fam (abrév **hôpital psychiatrique**) psychiatric hospital▪

HP² (abrév écrite **haut-parleur**) loudspeaker

HPA [aʃpea] NF Aviat (abrév **heure probable d'arrivée**) ETA

HPD [aʃpede] NF Aviat (abrév **heure probable de départ**) ETD

HR (abrév écrite **heures des repas**) = at lunchtime or in the evening (used in newspaper advertisements)

*HS [aʃɛs] ADJ Fam (abrév **hors service**) (appareil) out of order▪; (personne) Br knackered, shattered, Am bushed; **la télé est complètement H.** Br the telly's on the blink, Am the TV's on the fritz

HT ADJ Com (abrév écrite **hors taxe**) not including tax, exclusive of tax; **200 euros HT** 200 euros plus VAT
NF (abrév écrite **haute tension**) HT

HTML [aʃteɛmɛl] NM Ordinat (abrév **Hyper Text Markup Language**) HTML

HTTP [aʃtetepe] NM Ordinat (abrév **Hyper Text Transfer Protocol**) HTTP

Huang He [waŋə], **Huang-ho** [waŋo] NM Huang-Ho

*huard, *huart [qar] NM **1** Orn (rapace) osprey, Am fish hawk **2** Can Orn (plongeon) Br black-throated diver, Am loon **3** Can Fam Hum (pièce de monnaie) = humorous name for a Canadian one-dollar coin, Can loonie

*hub [œb] NM Ordinat & Transp hub

*hublot [yblo] NM (de bateau) porthole; (d'avion) window; (de machine à laver) (glass) door
❏ **hublots** NMPL Fam **mes hublots** my specs

*huche [yʃ] NF chest; **h. à pain** bread bin; **h. à pétrir** kneading trough

*hucher [3] [yʃe] VT Vieilli to call out to

*huchet [yʃɛ] NM Arch hunting-horn; Hér hunter's horn (without sling)

Hudson [ytsɔn] NM **l'H.** the Hudson River

*hue [y] EXCLAM gee up!; **allez h., cocotte!** gee up!, giddy up!
❏ **à hue et à dia** ADV tirer **à h. et à dia** to pull or to tug in opposite directions (at once)

*Huê [qe] NM Hué, Huê

*huée [qe] NF Chasse hallooing, halloos
❏ **huées** NFPL boos, booing; **il quitta la scène sous les huées** he was booed or hissed off stage

*huer [7] [qe] VT **1** (par dérision) to boo **2** Chasse to halloo
VI (hibou) to hoot; (héron) to croak

---

*huerta [wɛrta] NF = irrigated plain in Spain

*huguenot, -e [ygno, -ɔt] ADJ Huguenot
NM,F Huguenot

hui [qi] ADV Arch today; **dès h.** this very day; Jur **ce jour d'h.** today, this day

huilage [qilaʒ] NM oiling, lubrication

huile [qil] NF **1** Culin oil; **faire frire qch à l'h.** to fry sth in oil; **pommes à l'h.** potatoes in an oil dressing; **h. d'arachide/de coco/de colza/ d'olive/de maïs/de noix/de tournesol** groundnut/ coconut/rapeseed or colza/olive/corn/walnut/ sunflower oil; **h. pour assaisonnement** salad oil; **h. de cuisson** cooking oil; **h. de table** (salad) oil; **h. végétale** vegetable oil; **h. vierge** unrefined or virgin oil; Fig **jeter** ou **mettre** ou **verser de l'h. sur le feu** to add fuel to the flames
2 (pour chauffer, pour lubrifier) oil; Can **h. (de) chauffage** domestic fuel, heating oil; Fam **h. de coude,** Can **h. de bras** elbow grease; **h. de graissage** lubricating or lubrication oil; **h. minérale** mineral oil; **h. (pour) moteur** engine oil; **h. de vidange** waste (lubricating) oil; Fig **mettre de l'h. dans les rouages de** to oil the wheels of
3 Pharm **h. d'amandes douces/amères** sweet/ bitter almond oil; **h. de bain** bath oil; **h. pour bébés** baby oil; **h. de cade** oil of cade; **h. pour le corps** body oil; **h. essentielle** essential oil; **h. de foie de morue** cod-liver oil; **h. de lin** linseed oil; **h. de paraffine** paraffin oil; **h. de ricin** castor oil; **h. solaire** suntan oil; **h. de vaseline** paraffin oil; **h. volatile** essential oil
4 Rel **les saintes huiles** the holy oils
5 Beaux-Arts (œuvre) oil (painting); **un portrait à l'h.** a portrait in oils
6 Fam (personne importante) bigwig, big shot; **les huiles du régiment** the regimental (top) brass or big shots
❏ **d'huile** ADJ (mer) glassy; **la mer était d'h.** the sea was like glass or a mill pond

huilé, -e [qile] ADJ **1** (enduit d'huile) oiled **2** (qui fonctionne) **bien h.** well-oiled

huiler [3] [qile] VT to oil, to lubricate

huilerie [qilri] NF (fabrique) oil works or factory; (commerce) oil trade

huileux, -euse [qilø, -øz] ADJ **1** (substance) oily **2** (cheveux, doigts) oily, greasy

huilier, -ère [qilje, ɛr] ADJ oil (avant n)
NM **1** (ustensile de table) oil and vinegar set; (avec moutardier) cruet (stand), condiment set **2** (fabricant) oil manufacturer

*huis [qi] NM Littéraire door
❏ **huis clos** NM Jur **demander le h. clos** to ask for proceedings to be held in camera; Jur **le procès se déroulera à h. clos** the trial will be held in camera; **avoir une discussion à h. clos** to have a discussion behind closed doors

---

'Huis clos' Sartre 'In Camera'

huisserie [qisri] NF Constr (de porte) (door) frame; (de fenêtre) (window) frame

huissier [qisje] NM

Note that it is no longer considered a mistake to feminize this word and to say **une huissière**. Some French speakers nonetheless regard this form as unacceptable, especially in France. See also the entry **féminisation**.

1 (gardien, appariteur) usher **2** Jur **h. (de justice)** ≃ court bailiff; **h. d'audience** court crier, usher

*huit [qit, before consonant qi] ADJ eight; **h. jours** (une semaine) a week; **donner ses h. jours à qn** to give sb their notice; **page/numéro h.** page/ number eight
PRON eight
NM INV **1** (gén) eight; **aujourd'hui en h.** this time next week; **jeudi en h.** a week from or Br on Thursday **2** (numéro d'ordre) number eight **3** (chiffre écrit) eight **4** Cartes eight **5** (dessin) figure of eight; **l'ivrogne avançait en faisant des h.** the drunk was reeling or staggering along **6** (en patinage) figure of eight **7** (en aviron) eight; **h. de pointe** eight **8** (attraction) **le grand h.** rollercoaster (in figure of eight); voir aussi **cinq**

'Huit et demi' Fellini 'Eight and a Half'

*huitain [qitɛ̃] NM Littérature octave

*huitaine [qitɛn] NF **une h.** around or about eight, eight or so; **une h. (de jours)** about a week, a week or so; **sous h.** within a week; **remis à h.** postponed for a week

*huitante [qitɑ̃t] Suisse (dans les cantons de Vaud, du Valais et de Fribourg) ADJ **1** (gén) eighty **2** (dans des séries) eightieth; **page/numéro h.** page/number eighty
PRON eighty
NM INV **1** (gén) eighty **2** (numéro d'ordre) number eighty **3** (chiffre écrit) eighty; voir aussi **cinquante**

*huitantième [qitɑ̃tjɛm] Suisse (dans les cantons de Vaud, du Valais et de Fribourg) ADJ eightieth
NMF **1** (personne) eightieth **2** (objet) eightieth (one)
NM **1** (partie) eightieth **2** (étage) Br eightieth floor, Am eighty-first floor; voir aussi **cinquième**

*huitième [qitjɛm] ADJ eighth; **le h. art** television; **la h. merveille du monde** the eighth wonder of the world
NMF **1** (personne) eighth **2** (objet) eighth (one)
NM **1** (partie) eighth **2** (étage) Br eighth floor, Am ninth floor **3** (arrondissement de Paris) eighth (arrondissement)
NF Anciennement Scol Br = fourth year of primary school, Am ≃ fourth grade; voir aussi **cinquième**
❏ **huitièmes** NMPL Sport **les huitièmes de finale** the round before the quarterfinals, the last sixteen

*huitièmement [qitjɛmmɑ̃] ADV eighthly, in eighth place

huître [qitr] NF **1** Zool & Culin oyster; **h. de Marennes** Marennes oyster; **h. perlière** pearl oyster; **h. plate** flat or native oyster; **h. portugaise** Portuguese oyster **2** Fam Vieilli (personne stupide) twit

*huit-reflets [qiʀəflɛ] NM INV Vieilli top hat

huîtrier, -ère [qitrije, ɛr] ADJ oyster (avant n)
NM Orn oystercatcher
❏ **huîtrière** NF (banc) oyster bed; (parc) oyster farm or bed

*hulotte [ylɔt] NF Orn brown owl

*hululement [ylylmɑ̃] NM hooting; **des hululements** hooting

*hululer [3] [ylyle] VI to hoot

*hum [œm] EXCLAM **1** (marquant le doute) er, um, h'mm **2** (pour signaler sa présence) ahem

Huma [yma] NF Fam Presse **l'H.** = nickname of l'Humanité newspaper

*humage [ymaʒ] NM inhalation, breathing in

humagne [ymaɲ] NM OU NF Suisse **h. (blanc** ou **blanche)** = former grape variety from the Valais canton and white wine made from it; **h. rouge** = grape variety from the Valais canton and red wine made from it

humain, -e [ymɛ̃, -ɛn] ADJ **1** (propre à l'homme → corps, race, condition) human; **il cherche à se venger, c'est h.** he's looking for revenge, it's only human; **nous faire travailler par cette chaleur, ce n'est pas h.** forcing us to work in this heat is inhuman; **une ville nouvelle aux dimensions humaines** a new town planned with people in mind or on a human scale
2 (bienveillant) humane; **il est très h.** he's very understanding; **être h. avec qn** to act humanely towards sb, to treat sb humanely
NM **1** (être) **un h.** a human (being); **les humains** mankind, humans, human beings
2 Littéraire **l'h.** (nature) human nature; (facteur) the human element or factor; **perdre le sens de l'h.** to lose one's sense of humanity

humainement [ymɛnmɑ̃] ADV **1** (avec bienveillance) humanely; **traiter qn h.** to treat sb humanely **2** (par l'homme) humanly; **faire tout ce qui est h. possible** to do everything that is humanly possible

humanisation [ymanizasjɔ̃] NF humanization; **aujourd'hui, on vise à une h. des rapports dans l'entreprise** today, the aim is to make relationships in the company more human

humaniser [3] [ymanize] VT (environnement) to humanize, to adapt to human needs; (personne) to make more human

---

The symbol * indicates that the initial **h** is aspirate and that hence there is no liaison, eg **les haricots** [leariko] and not [lezariko], or contraction in spelling, eg **la haine** and not **l'haine**.

▶**s'humaniser VPR** to become more human; **l'environnement industriel s'est humanisé** the industrial environment has a more human face

humanisme [ymanism] **NM** humanism

humaniste [ymanist] **ADJ** humanist, humanistic
NMF humanist

humanitaire [ymanitɛr] **ADJ** humanitarian; **organisation h.** relief *or* aid organization
▪ **NMF** *(personne)* humanitarian (aid) worker
▪ **NM l'humanitaire** the humanitarian sector

humanitarisme [ymanitarism] **NM** *Péj* humanitarianism

humanitariste [ymanitarist] *Péj* **ADJ** humanitarian
▪ **NMF** humanitarian

humanité [ymanite] **NF 1** *(êtres)* **l'h.** humanity, mankind, humankind
2 *(compassion)* humanity, humaneness; **traiter qn avec h.** to treat sb humanely
3 *Rel* humanity
4 *Presse* **l'H.** = French communist daily newspaper
◽ **humanités NFPL 1** *Belg Scol* = the three years leading to the baccalauréat examination in Belgium
2 *Vieilli Univ* **les humanités** the classics

humanoïde [ymanɔid] **ADJ** humanoid
▪ **NMF** humanoid

humble [œbl] **ADJ 1** *(effacé → personne)* humble, meek; **d'un ton h.** humbly, meekly
2 *(par déférence)* humble; **veuillez accepter mes humbles excuses** please accept my most humble apologies; **à mon h. avis** in my humble opinion
3 *(pauvre, simple → demeure, origine)* humble; *(→ employé)* humble, lowly, obscure
◽ **humbles NMPL** *Littéraire* **les humbles** those of humble extraction

humblement [œbləmɑ̃] **ADV 1** *(sans prétention)* humbly; **je vous ferai h. remarquer que...** may I humbly point out that...? **2** *(sans richesse)* humbly; **vivre h.** to live modestly *or* humbly

humectage [ymɛktaʒ] **NM** *(d'un linge)* dampening; *(du visage → avec un liquide)* moistening; *(→ avec un linge mouillé)* dampening

humecter [4] [ymɛkte] **VT** *(linge)* to dampen; *(visage → avec un liquide)* to moisten; *(→ avec un linge mouillé)* to dampen; **la sueur humectait son front** his/her forehead was damp with perspiration
▶**s'humecter VPR s'h. les lèvres** to moisten one's lips; *Fam* **s'h. le gosier** to wet one's whistle

humecteur [ymɛktœr] **NM** *(de papier, d'étoffe)* dampener

*****humer** [3] [yme] **VT** *(sentir)* to smell; *(inspirer)* to inhale, to breathe in

huméral, -e, -aux, -ales [ymeral, -o] **ADJ** *Anat* humeral

humérus [ymerys] **NM** *Anat* humerus

humeur [ymœr] **NF 1** *(état d'esprit)* mood; **être d'h. à faire qch** to be in the mood to do sth *or* for doing sth; **je ne suis pas d'h. à écouter ses commérages** I am not in the mood to listen to *or* I am in no mood for listening to his/her gossip; **selon l'h. du jour** it depends (on) how the mood takes me/him/*etc*; **être d'h. changeante** to be moody; **être de bonne/mauvaise h.** to be in a good/bad mood; **la bonne h. régnait dans la maison** the whole household was in a good mood; **un livre/film plein de bonne h.** a good-humoured book/film; **passer sa mauvaise h. sur** to take one's bad mood out on; **être d'une h. de dogue** to be like a bear with a sore head; **être d'une h. noire** to be in a foul mood
2 *(caractère)* temper; **être d'h. chagrine** to be bad-tempered *or* sullen; **être d'h. égale/inégale** to be even-tempered/moody
3 *Littéraire (acrimonie)* bad temper, ill humour; **montrer de l'h.** to show ill temper; **répondre avec h.** to answer testily *or* moodily; **accès/mouvement d'h.** outburst/fit of temper
4 *(caprice)* **il a ses humeurs** he has his whims
5 *Méd* **h. aqueuse/vitrée** aqueous/vitreous humour
◽ **humeurs NFPL** *Arch* humours

humide [ymid] **ADJ** *(linge, mur)* damp; *(éponge)* damp, moist; *(cave)* damp, dank; *(chaussée)* wet; *(chaleur, air, climat)* humid; *(terre)* moist;

j'ai les mains humides my hands are damp; **la terre doit toujours être un peu h.** always keep the soil slightly moist; **temps chaud et h.** muggy weather; **il fait h.** it *or* the weather is humid; **les yeux humides de larmes** eyes moist with tears; **elle me lançait des regards humides** she was looking at me with moist eyes

humidificateur [ymidifikatœr] **NM** *(gén)* humidifier; *(pour les cigares)* humidor

humidification [ymidifikasjɔ̃] **NF 1** *(de l'air)* humidifying, moisturizing, *Spéc* humidification **2** *(du linge)* dampening, moistening

humidifier [9] [ymidifje] **VT 1** *(air)* to humidify, to moisturize **2** *(linge)* to dampen, to moisten

humidimètre [ymidimɛtr] **NM** *(en peinture industrielle)* hygrometer

humidité [ymidite] **NF 1** *(de l'air chaud)* humidity, moisture; *(de l'air froid, d'une terre)* dampness; *(d'une cave)* dampness, dankness; **il faut beaucoup d'h. à cette plante** this plant needs a lot of moisture; **il y a des taches d'h. au plafond** there are damp patches on the ceiling; **la pièce sent l'h.** the room smells (of) damp; **craint l'h.** *(sur un paquet)* keep dry, store in a dry place
2 *Phys* **h. absolue/relative** absolute/relative humidity

humification [ymifikasjɔ̃] **NF** humification

humiliant, -e [ymiljɑ̃, -ɑ̃t] **ADJ** humiliating; **critique humiliante** galling *or* mortifying criticism

humiliation [ymiljasjɔ̃] **NF** humiliation; **infliger une h. à qn** to humiliate sb; **subir les pires humiliations** to suffer the deepest humiliation

humilié, -e [ymilje] **ADJ** humiliated
▪ **NM,F** humiliated person; **les humiliés** the humiliated, the humbled

humilier [9] [ymilje] **VT 1** *(abaisser)* to humiliate, to shame **2** *Vieilli (rendre humble)* to humble
▶**s'humilier VPR 1** *(s'abaisser)* to humiliate oneself **2** *Vieilli* **s'h. devant** *(être humble)* to humble oneself before

humilité [ymilite] **NF 1** *(d'une personne)* humility, humbleness, modesty; **avec h.** humbly; **une leçon d'h.** a lesson in humility **2** *Littéraire (d'une tâche)* humbleness, lowliness
◽ **en toute humilité ADV** in all humility

humique [ymik] **ADJ** humic

humoral, -e, -aux, -ales [ymoral, -o] **ADJ** *Méd* humoral

humorisme [ymorism] **NM** *Hist* humoralism

humoriste [ymorist] **ADJ** humorous
▪ **NMF** humorist

humoristique [ymoristik] **ADJ** *(récit, ton)* humorous

humour [ymur] **NM** humour; **avec h.** humorously; **il a pris ça avec (beaucoup d')h.** he took it in (very) good part; **plein d'h.** humorous; **il n'y a aucun h. dans le scénario** the script is totally humourless; **avoir de** *ou* **le sens de l'h.** to have a sense of humour; **faire de l'h.** to make jokes; **h. noir** black humour

humus [ymys] **NM** humus

*****Hun** [œ̃] **NMF** Hun; **les Huns** (the) Hun

*****Hunan** [ynan] **NF** Hunan

*****hune** [yn] **NF** *Arch Naut* top

*****hunier** [ynje] **NM** *Arch Naut* topsail

*****hunnique** [ynik] **ADJ** *Hist* Hunnic, Hunnish

*****hunter** [œ̃tœr] **NM** *Équitation* **1** *(cheval)* hunter **2** *(discipline)* showjumping

*****huppe** [yp] **NF** *Orn* **1** *(oiseau)* hoopoe **2** *(plumes)* crest; *(chez certains pigeons)* tuft, tufts

*****huppé, -e** [ype] **ADJ 1** *Fam (personne, restaurant, soirée)* smart■, *Br* posh; **les gens huppés** the upper crust, the smart set **2** *Orn* crested

*****hurdler** [œrdlœr] **NM** *Sport* hurdler

*****hure** [yr] **NF 1** *Zool* head *(of wild boar, fish etc)* **2** *Culin* brawn, *Am* headcheese

*****hurlant, -e** [yrlɑ̃, -ɑ̃t] **ADJ 1** *(foule)* yelling, howling **2** *(couleur → voyante)* garish; *(→ qui jure)* clashing

*****hurlement** [yrləmɑ̃] **NM 1** *(humain)* yell, roar; **des hurlements de joie** whoops of joy; **des hurlements d'indignation** howls of indignation; **pourquoi tous ces hurlements?** what is all this shouting about? **2** *(d'un chien, d'un loup)* howl; **des hurlements** howling **3** *Littéraire (de la tempête)* roar; *(du vent)* howling (UNCOUNT); *(d'une sirène)* wail

*****hurler** [3] [yrle] **VI 1** *(crier)* to yell, to scream; **h. de douleur** to howl with pain; **h. de joie** to

whoop *or* to shout with joy; **h. de rage** to howl with rage; **h. de rire** to scream with laughter; **c'était à h. de rire** it was screamingly funny, it was a scream; **ça me fait h. d'entendre ça!** it makes me so mad to hear things like that!; *Fam* **il me fait h. de rire, ce mec!** he creases me up, that guy! **2** *(parler fort → personne)* to shout, to bellow; *(avoir un niveau sonore élevé → radio)* to blare; **avec lui il faut h., sinon il n'entend pas** you have to shout or he won't hear you **3** *(singe)* to howl, to shriek; *(chien, loup)* to howl; **h. à la mort** *ou* **à la lune** to bay at the moon; *Fig* **h. avec les loups** to follow the pack **4** *Littéraire (tempête)* to roar; *(vent)* to howl; *(sirène)* to shriek, to wail **5** *(jurer → couleur)* to clash
▪ **VT 1** *(ordre, réponse, chanson)* to bawl out, to bellow out **2** *(douleur, indignation)* to howl out

*****hurleur, -euse** [yrlœr, -øz] **ADJ 1** *(personne)* howling, bawling, yelling **2** *Zool* **singe h.** howler monkey
▪ **NM,F** howler, bawler
▪ **NM** *(singe)* howler (monkey)

hurluberlu, -e [yrlybɛrly] **NM,F** *Fam* crank, weirdo

*****huron, -onne** [yrɔ̃, ɔn] **ADJ** Huron
▪ **NM** *(langue)* Huron
◽ **Huron, -onne NM,F** Huron
◽ **Huron NM le lac H.** Lake Huron

*****huronien, -enne** [yrɔnjɛ̃, -ɛn] **ADJ** *Géol* Huronian

*****hurrah** [ura] = **hourra**

*****hurricane** [yrikan] **NM** hurricane *(in West Indies and Central America)*

*****husky** [œski] **NM** *(chien)* husky

*****hussard** [ysar] **NM** hussar

*****hussarde** [ysard] **NF** *Fam* **à la h.** roughly, brutally

*****hussite** [ysit] **NM** *Hist & Rel* Hussite

*****hutinet** [ytinɛ] **NM** cooper's mallet

*****hutte** [yt] **NF 1** *(abri)* hut, cabin **2** *Chasse Br* hide, *Am* blind; **chasse à la h.** shooting from a *Br* hide *or Am* blind

hyacinthe [jasɛ̃t] **NF 1** *Vieilli Bot* hyacinth **2** *Minér* hyacinth, jacinth

hyalin, -e [jalɛ̃, -in] **ADJ** *Minér* transparent, glassy; **quartz h.** rock crystal

hyalite [jalit] **NF 1** *Minér* hyalite, water opal **2** *Méd* hyalitis

hyaloclastite [jaloklastit] **NF** *Géol* hyaloclastite

hyaloïde [jalɔid] **ADJ** *Anat* hyaloid

hyaloplasme [jaloplasm] **NM** *Biol* hyaloplasm

hybridation [ibridasjɔ̃] **NF** *Biol* hybridization

hybride [ibrid] **ADJ 1** *Bot, Zool & Ling* hybrid **2** *(mêlé)* hybrid, mixed; **une solution un peu h.** a rather hybrid solution; **une architecture h.** a patchwork of architectural styles; **un album h.** a crossover album
▪ **NM** hybrid

hybrider [3] [ibride] **VT** *Biol* to hybridize

hybridisme [ibridism] **NM** *Biol* hybridism

hybridité [ibridite] **NF** *Biol* hybridity

hybridome [ibridom] **NM** *Biol* hybridoma

hydarthrose [idartroz] **NF** *Méd* hydrarthrosis

hydatide [idatid] **NF** *Méd* hydatid (larva)

hydatique [idatik] **ADJ** *Méd* hydatid

hydne [idn] **NM** *Bot* hydnum

hydracide [idrasid] **NM** *Chim* hydracid

hydraire [idrɛr] **NM** *Zool* hydroid
◽ **hydraires NMPL** Hydroidea

hydramnios [idramnjɔs] **NM** *Obst* hydramnios, hydramnion

hydrant [idrɑ̃] **NM** *Suisse Br* fire hydrant, *Am* fireplug

hydrante [idrɑ̃t] **NF** = **hydrant**

hydranthe [idrɑ̃t] **NM** *Zool* hydranth

hydrargie [idrarʒi], **hydrargyrisme** [idrarʒirism] **NM** *Méd* mercurialism

hydrastis [idrastis] **NM** *Bot & Méd* hydrastis

hydratable [idratabl] **ADJ** *Chim* hydratable

hydratant, -e [idratɑ̃, -ɑ̃t] **ADJ 1** *(crème, lotion)* moisturizing **2** *Chim* hydrating
▪ **NM** moisturizer

hydratation [idratasjɔ̃] **NF 1** *(de la peau)* moisturizing **2** *Chim* hydration

hydrate [idrat] **NM** *Chim* hydrate; *Vieilli* **h. de carbone** carbohydrate

hydraté, -e [idrate] **ADJ 1** *(peau)* moisturized **2** *Chim* hydrous

hydrater [3] [idrate] **VT 1** *(peau)* to moisturize **2** *Chim* to hydrate

hum–hyd

▶s'hydrater VPR **1** *(peau)* to become moisturized **2** *Chim* to become hydrated, to hydrate

hydraule [idrol] NF *Hist & Mus* hydraulus, hydraulic organ

hydraulicien, -enne [idrolisjɛ̃, -ɛn] NM,F hydraulic engineer

hydraulique [idrolik] ADJ hydraulic
  NF hydraulics *(singulier)*

hydravion [idravjɔ̃] NM seaplane, hydroplane, *Am* float plane

hydrazine [idrazin] NF *Chim* hydrazine

Hydre [idr] NF *Myth* **l'H. de Lerne** the Lernean Hydra

hydre [idr] NF **1** *Zool* hydra **2** *Littéraire* **l'h. de l'anarchie** the hydra of anarchy

hydrémie [idremi] NF *Méd* hydraemia

hydrie [idri] NF *Antiq* hydria, water pitcher

hydrille [idrij] NM *Bot* **h. verticillé** water thyme, *Spéc* hydrilla

hydrique [idrik] ADJ *Chim* hydric

hydrobase [idrobaz] NF *Aviat* seaplane *or* hydroplane base

hydrocarbonate [idrokarbonat] NM *Chim* hydrocarbonate

hydrocarboné, -e [idrokarbone] ADJ *Chim* hydrocarbonaceous

hydrocarbure [idrokarbyr] NM *Chim* hydrocarbon

hydrocèle [idrosɛl] NF *Méd* hydrocele

hydrocéphale [idrosefal] *Méd* ADJ hydrocephalic, hydrocephalous
  NMF hydrocephalic

hydrocéphalie [idrosefali] NF *Méd* hydrocephalus, hydrocephaly

hydrocharitacée [idrokaritase] *Bot* NF hydrocharitacea
  ❏ **hydrocharitacées** NFPL Hydrocharitaceae

hydroclasseur [idroklasœr] NM *Ind* hydraulic classifier

hydrocoralliaire [idrokoraljɛr] *Zool* NM hydrocorallina
  ❏ **hydrocoralliaires** NMPL Hydrocorallinae

hydrocortisone [idrokortizon] NF *Méd* hydrocortisone

hydrocotyle [idrokotil] NF *Bot* pennywort, watercup, *Spéc* hydrocotyle

hydrocracking [idrokrakiŋ], **hydrocraquage** [idrokrakaʒ] NM *Pétr* hydrocracking

hydrocuté, -e [idrokyte] NM,F drowned person *(as a result of immersion syncope)*

hydrocution [idrokysjɔ̃] NF immersion syncope

hydrodésulfuration [idrodesylfyrasjɔ̃] NF *Pétr* hydrodesulphurization

hydrodistillation [idrodistilasjɔ̃] NF *Chim* hydrodistillation

hydrodynamique [idrodinamik] ADJ hydrodynamic
  NF hydrodynamics *(singulier)*

hydrodynamisme [idrodinamism] NM hydrodynamism

hydroélectricité [idroelɛktrisite] NF hydroelectricity

hydroélectrique [idroelɛktrik] ADJ hydroelectric

hydrofilicale [idrofilikal] NF *Bot* water fern

hydrofoil [idrofojl] NM *Naut* hydrofoil

hydrofugation [idrofygasjɔ̃] NF waterproofing

hydrofuge [idrofyʒ] ADJ waterproof, water-repellent
  NM water-repellent

hydrofuger [17] [idrofyʒe] VT to waterproof

hydrogel [idroʒɛl] NM *Chim* hydrogel

hydrogénation [idroʒenasjɔ̃] NF *Chim* hydrogenation, hydrogenization

hydrogène [idroʒɛn] NM *Chim & Phys* **1** *(élément)* hydrogen; **h. lourd** heavy hydrogen, deuterium **2** *(comme adj)* hydrogen *(avant n)*

hydrogéné, -e [idroʒene] ADJ *Chim* hydrogenated

hydrogéner [8] [idroʒene] VT *Chim* to hydrogenate

hydrogénocarbonate [idroʒenokarbonat] NM *Chim* hydrogen carbonate

hydrogéologie [idroʒeoloʒi] NF hydrogeology

hydrogéologue [idroʒeolog] NMF hydrogeologist

hydroglisseur [idrogliscœr] NM hydroplane (boat)

hydrographe [idrograf] NMF hydrographer

hydrographie [idrografi] NF hydrography

hydrographique [idrografik] ADJ hydrographic, hydrographical

---

hydrolase [idrolaz] NF *Biol & Chim* hydrolase

hydrolat [idrola] NM *Pharm* medicated water

hydrolithe [idrolit] NF *Chim* hydrolith

hydrologie [idroloʒi] NF hydrology

hydrologique [idroloʒik] ADJ hydrologic, hydrological

hydrologiste [idroloʒist], **hydrologue** [idrolog] NMF hydrologist

hydrolysable [idrolizabl] ADJ *Chim* hydrolyzable

hydrolyse [idroliz] NF *Chim* hydrolysis

hydrolyser [3] [idrolize] VT *Chim* to hydrolyse

hydromécanique [idromekanik] ADJ hydromechanic, hydromechanical
  NF hydromechanics *(singulier)*

hydromel [idromɛl] NM *(non fermenté)* hydromel; *(fermenté)* mead

hydrométallurgie [idrometalyrʒi] NF hydrometallurgy

hydromètre [idromɛtr] NM *Phys (pour densité)* hydrometer; *(de réservoir)* depth gauge
  NF *Entom* water measurer

hydrométrie [idrometri] NF *Phys* hydrometry

hydrominéral, -e, -aux, -ales [idromineral, -o] ADJ mineral water *(avant n)*

hydromoteur, -trice [idromotœr, -tris] ADJ water-driven

hydronéphrose [idronefroz] NF *Méd* hydronephrosis

hydropathie [idropati] NF *Méd* hydropathy

hydroperoxyde [idroperoksid] NM *Chim* hydroperoxide

hydrophile [idrofil] ADJ *Chim* hydrophilic
  NM *Entom* scavenger beetle

hydrophobe [idrofob] ADJ *Chim & Méd* hydrophobic

hydrophobie [idrofobi] NF **1** *Méd* hydrophobia, rabies **2** *Chim* hydrophobic property

hydrophone [idrofon] NM *Phys* hydrophone

hydropique [idropik] *Méd* ADJ dropsical
  NMF dropsical patient

hydropisie [idropizi] NF *Méd* dropsy

hydropneumatique [idropnømatik] ADJ hydropneumatic

hydroponique [idroponik] ADJ *Agr* hydroponic

hydroposie [idropozi] NF *Méd* dropsy

hydropote [idropot] NM *Zool* Chinese water deer

hydropropulseur [idropropylscœr] NM water jet attachment *(for electric toothbrush)*

hydroptère [idroptɛr] NM *Naut* hydrofoil

hydroquinone [idrokinon] NF *Chim & Phot* hydroquinone

hydrosilicate [idrosilikat] NM *Chim* hydrated silicate

hydrosol [idrosol] NM *Chim* hydrosol

hydrosoluble [idrosolybl] ADJ *Chim* water-soluble

hydrosphère [idrosfɛr] NF hydrosphere

hydrostatique [idrostatik] *Phys* ADJ hydrostatic
  NF hydrostatics *(singulier)*

hydrothérapie [idroterapi] NF *Méd* **1** *(cure)* hydrotherapy **2** *(science)* hydrotherapeutics *(singulier)*

hydrothérapique [idroterapik] ADJ *Méd* hydrotherapeutic, hydrotherapy *(avant n)*

hydrothermal, -e, -aux, -ales [idrotɛrmal, -o] ADJ hydrothermal

hydrothorax [idrotoraks] NM *Méd* hydrothorax

hydrotimétrie [idrotimetri] NF hydrotimetry

hydrotraitement [idrotrɛtmɑ̃] NM *Pétr* hydrotreating

hydrotropisme [idrotropism] NM hydrotropism

hydroxyde [idroksid] NM *Chim* hydroxide

hydroxylamine [idroksilamin] NF *Chim* hydroxylamine

hydroxyle [idroksil] NM *Chim* hydroxyl

hydrozoaire [idrozoɛr] *Zool* NM hydrozoon
  ❏ **hydrozoaires** NMPL Hydrozoa

hydrure [idryr] NM *Chim* hydride; **h. lourd** deuteride

***hyène** [jɛn] NF *Zool* hyena; **h. brune** brown hyena; **h. tachetée** spotted hyena

Hygiaphone® [iʒjafon] NM speaking grille

hygiène [iʒjɛn] NF **1** *(principes)* hygiene; **pour l'h. des pieds/du cuir chevelu** to keep feet/the scalp clean *or* in good condition; **il n'a aucune h.** he doesn't bother about personal hygiene; **h. alimentaire/corporelle** food/personal hygiene; **avoir une mauvaise h. alimentaire** to have bad eating habits *or* a poor diet; **h. mentale/publi-**

---

que mental/public health; **avoir une bonne h. de vie** to live healthily
  2 *(science)* hygienics *(singulier)*, hygiene
  3 *Jur* **h. et sécurité du travail** industrial hygiene and safety

hygiénique [iʒjenik] ADJ hygienic; **ce n'est pas h.** it's unhygienic; **un mode de vie h.** a healthy lifestyle; **une promenade h.** a constitutional

hygiéniquement [iʒjenikmɑ̃] ADV hygienically

hygiéniste [iʒjenist] NMF hygienist, hygeist, hygieist

hygroma [igroma] NM *Méd* hygroma; **h. du genou** housemaid's knee

hygromètre [igromɛtr] NM *Phys* hygrometer

hygrométrie [igrometri] NF *Météo* hygrometry

hygrométrique [igrometrik] ADJ *Phys* hygrometric

hygrophile [igrofil] ADJ *Biol* hygrophilous; **plantes hygrophiles** hygrophiles

hygrophore [igrofor] NM *Bot* waxy cap

hygroscope [igroskop] NM *Phys* hygroscope

hygroscopie [igroskopi] NF *Météo* hygroscopy

hygroscopique [igroskopik] ADJ *Phys* hygroscopic

hygrostat [igrosta] NM *Phys* hygrostat

hylochère [iloʃɛr] NM *Zool* giant forest hog

hylozoïsme [ilozoism] NM *Phil* hylozoism

Hymen [imɛn] NPR *Myth* Hymen

hymen [imɛn] NM **1** *Anat* hymen **2** *Littéraire* (bonds of) marriage

hyménée [imene] NM *Littéraire* (ties *or* bonds of) marriage

hyménium [imenjom] NM *Bot* hymenium

hyménomycètes [imenomisɛt] NMPL *Bot* hymenomycetes

hyménoptère [imenoptɛr] *Entom* ADJ hymenopterous
  NM hymenopteran, hymenopteron
  ❏ **hyménoptères** NMPL Hymenoptera

hymne [imn] NM **1** *Littérature & Rel* hymn; **h. national** national anthem **2** *Littéraire (glorification)* hymn; **un h. à l'amour** a hymn *or* paean to love

'Hymne à la joie' *Beethoven* 'Ode to Joy'

hyoïde [joid] *Anat* ADJ *(os)* hyoid
  NM hyoid (bone)

hyoïdien, -enne [joidjɛ̃, -ɛn] ADJ *Anat* hyoidean, hyoidal

hyoscine [josin] NF *Chim* hyoscine

hypallage [ipalaʒ] NF *Ling* hypallage

hyper [ipɛr] NM *Fam (abrév* **hypermarché***)* hypermarket■, superstore■

HYPER- [ipɛr] PRÉF

This very productive prefix acts as an INTENSIFIER.

- It appears in nouns and adjectives belonging to science and in particular medicine:
  hypermétrope farsighted, longsighted; **hyperglicémie** hyperglycaemia; **hypertension** high blood pressure; **hyperactif** hyperactive; **hyperbole** hyperbole/hyperbola; **hypermarché** (sometimes abbreviated colloquially to **hyper**) superstore
- It is widely used in colloquial French as an adverb, to intensify an adjective with positive connotations. It can be translated by **really, dead, well** etc, eg:
  il est hyper-sympa he's dead nice; **un bar hyper-branché** a really trendy bar; **un film hyper-marrant** a hysterical film; **c'est hyper-grand chez elle** her place is massive

---

hyperacidité [iperasidite] NF *Méd* hyperacidity

hyperacousie [iperakuzi] NF *Méd* hyperacousia

hyperactif, -ive [iperaktif, -iv] ADJ hyperactive

hyperactivité [iperaktivite] NF hyperactivity

hyperalgésie [iperalʒezi] NF *Méd* hyperalgesia

hyperazotémie [iperazotemi] NF *Méd* uraemia

hyperbare [iperbar] ADJ *Tech* hyperbaric

hyperbate [iperbat] NF *Ling* hyperbaton, inversion

hyperbole [iperbol] NF **1** *(figure de style)* hyperbole **2** *Géom* hyperbola

hyperbolique [iperbolik] ADJ *Ling & Géom* hyperbolic

---

hyperboloïde [ipɛrbɔlɔid] *Math* **ADJ** hyperboloïdal
   NM hyperboloid

hyperboréen, -enne [ipɛrbɔreɛ̃, -ɛn] **ADJ** *Littéraire* hyperborean

hypercalcémie [ipɛrkalsemi] **NF** *Méd* hypercalcaemia

hypercalorique [ipɛrkalɔrik] **ADJ** hypercalorific

hypercapnie [ipɛrkapni] **NF** *Méd* hypercapnia

hypercharge [ipɛrʃarʒ] **NF** *Chim* hypercharge

hyperchlorhydrie [ipɛrklɔridri] **NF** *Méd* hyperchlorhydria

hypercholestérolémie [ipɛrkɔlɛsterɔlemi] **NF** *Méd* hypercholesteraemia, hypercholesterolaemia

hypercontinental, -e, -aux, -ales [ipɛrkɔ̃tinãtal, -o] **ADJ** *(climat)* extreme continental

hypercorrection [ipɛrkɔrɛksjɔ̃] **NF** *Ling* hypercorrection

hypercritique [ipɛrkritik] **ADJ** *Fam* hypercritical∗

hyperdulie [ipɛrdyli] **NF** *Rel* hyperdulia

hyperémie [ipɛremi] **NF** *Méd* hyperaemia, congestion

hyperémotivité [ipɛremɔtivite] **NF** hyperemotivity, hyperemotionality

hyperéosinophilie [ipɛreɔzinɔfili] **NF** *Méd* hyperinosis

hyperespace [ipɛrɛspas] **NM** hyperspace

hyperesthésie [ipɛrɛstezi] **NF** *Méd* hyperaesthesia

hyperfocal, -e, -aux, -ales [ipɛrfɔkal, -o] **ADJ** hyperfocal

hyperfolliculinie [ipɛrfɔlikylini] **NF** *Méd* folliculin excess

hyperfonctionnement [ipɛrfɔ̃ksjɔnmã] **NM** hyperfunctioning *(UNCOUNT)*

hyperfréquence [ipɛrfrekãs] **NF** ultra-high frequency

hypergamie [ipɛrgami] **NF** *(en anthropologie)* hypergamy

hyperglycémiant, -e [ipɛrglisemjã, -ãt] **ADJ** *Méd* hyperglycaemic

hyperglycémie [ipɛrglisemi] **NF** *Méd* hyperglycaemia

hypergol [ipɛrgɔl] **NM** *Chim* hypergol, hypergolic rocket fuel

hyperhémie [ipɛremi] = **hyperémie**

hyperhydrose [ipɛridroz] **NF** *Méd* hyperhydrosis

hypéricacées [iperikase] **NFPL** *Bot* Hypericaceae

hyperinflation [ipɛrɛ̃flasjɔ̃] **NF** *Écon* hyperinflation

Hypérion [iperjɔ̃] **NPR** *Myth* Hyperion

hyperkaliémie [ipɛrkaljemi] **NF** *Méd* hyperkalaemia

hyperkinétique [ipɛrkinetik] **ADJ** *Méd* **syndrome h. de l'enfant** attention deficit hyperactivity disorder

hyperleucocytose [ipɛrløkɔsitoz] **NF** *Méd* hyperleucocytosis

hyperlien [ipɛrljɛ̃] **NM** *Ordinat* hyperlink

hyperlipémie [ipɛrlipemi], **hyperlipidémie** [ipɛrlipidemi] **NF** *Méd* hyperlipaemia

hypermarché [ipɛrmarʃe] **NM** hypermarket, superstore

hypermédia [ipɛrmedja] **NM** *Ordinat* hypermedia

hypermètre [ipɛrmɛtr] **ADJ** *Littérature* hypermetric(al)

hypermétrope [ipɛrmetrɔp] *Opt* **ADJ** farsighted, longsighted, *Spéc* hypermetropic
   NMF farsighted *or Spéc* hypermetropic person

hypermétropie [ipɛrmetrɔpi] **NF** *Opt* farsightedness, longsightedness, *Spéc* hypermetropia

hypermnésie [ipɛrmnezi] **NF** *Psy* hypermnesia

hypernatrémie [ipɛrnatremi] **NF** *Méd* hypernatraemia

hypernerveux, -euse [ipɛrnɛrvø, -øz] **ADJ** overexcitable
   NM,F overexcitable person

hypernervosité [ipɛrnɛrvozite] **NF** overexcitability, *Spéc* hyperexcitability

hypernova [ipɛrnova] *(pl* **-ae)** **NM** *Astron* hypernova

hyperœstrogénie [ipɛrɛstrɔʒeni] **NF** *Méd* hyperoestrogenism

hypéron [iperɔ̃] **NM** *Phys* hyperon

hyperonyme [iperɔnim] **NM** *Ling* hypernym, superordinate (term)

hyperparasite [ipɛrparazit] **NM** *Biol* hyperparasite

hyperpiésie [ipɛrpjezi] **NF** *Méd* hyperpiesis

hyperplan [ipɛrplã] **NM** *Géom* hyperplane

hyperplaquettose [ipɛrplakɛtoz] **NF** *Méd* thrombocytosis

hyperplasie [ipɛrplazi] **NF** *Méd* hyperplasia

hyperpnée [ipɛrpne] **NF** *Méd* hyperventilation

hyperpronation [ipɛrprɔnasjɔ̃] **NF** overpronation

hyperpuissance [ipɛrpɥisãs] **NF** *Pol* hyperpower

hyperpyrexie [ipɛrpirɛksi] **NF** *Méd* hyperpyrexia

hyperréalisme [ipɛrrealism] **NM** *Beaux-Arts* hyperrealism

hyperréaliste [ipɛrrealist] *Beaux-Arts* **ADJ** hyperrealistic
   NMF hyperrealist

hypersécrétion [ipɛrsekresjɔ̃] **NF** *Méd* hypersecretion

hypersegmentation [ipɛrsɛgmãtasjɔ̃] **NF** hypersegmentation

hypersensibilité [ipɛrsãsibilite] **NF** hypersensitivity, hypersensitiveness

hypersensible [ipɛrsãsibl] **ADJ** hypersensitive
   NMF hypersensitive (person)

hypersomniaque [ipɛrsɔmniak] **ADJ** hypersomniac
   NMF hypersomnia sufferer

hypersomnie [ipɛrsɔmni] **NF** hypersomnia

hypersonique [ipɛrsɔnik] **ADJ** hypersonic

hyperstatique [ipɛrstatik] **ADJ** hyperstatic

hypersupination [ipɛrsypinasjɔ̃] **NF** underpronation

hypersustentateur [ipɛrsystãtatœr] *Aviat* **ADJ M** high-lift
   NM high-lift device

hypersustentation [ipɛrsystãtasjɔ̃] **NF** *Aviat* high-lift capability

hypertélie [ipɛrteli] **NF** *Zool* hypertely

hypertendu, -e [ipɛrtãdy] **ADJ** *Méd* suffering from high blood pressure, *Spéc* hypertensive
   NM,F person suffering from high blood pressure, *Spéc* hypertensive

hypertenseur [ipɛrtãsœr] **ADJ M** *Méd* hypertensive

hypertensif, -ive [ipɛrtãsif, -iv] **ADJ** *Méd* = relating to high blood pressure, *Spéc* hypertensive

hypertension [ipɛrtãsjɔ̃] **NF** *Méd* high blood pressure, *Spéc* hypertension

hypertensive [ipɛrtãsiv] *voir* **hypertensif**

hypertexte [ipɛrtɛkst] **NM** *Ordinat* hypertext

hyperthermie [ipɛrtɛrmi] **NF** *Méd* hyperthermia

hyperthyroïdie [ipɛrtiroidi] **NF** *Méd* hyperthyroidism; **faire de l'h.** to have an overactive thyroid

hyperthyroïdien, -enne [ipɛrtiroidjɛ̃, -ɛn] *Méd* **ADJ** hyperthyroid
   NM,F hyperthyroid sufferer

hypertoile [ipɛrtwal] **NF** *Ordinat* World Wide Web

hypertonie [ipɛrtɔni] **NF 1** *Chim & Phys* hypertonicity **2** *Méd* hypertonicity, hypertonia

hypertonique [ipɛrtɔnik] **ADJ** *Méd (symptôme)* hypertonic; *(patient)* suffering from hypertonicity

hypertrophie [ipɛrtrɔfi] **NF 1** *Méd* hypertrophia, hypertrophy **2** *Fig* exaggeration; **une h. de l'amour-propre** an inflated sense of self-importance

hypertrophié, -e [ipɛrtrɔfje] **ADJ** *Méd* abnormally enlarged, *Spéc* hypertrophied

hypertrophier [9] [ipɛrtrɔfje] **VT** *Méd* to enlarge abnormally, *Spéc* to hypertrophy
   ▸**s'hypertrophier** **VPR** *Méd* to become abnormally large, *Spéc* to hypertrophy

hypertrophique [ipɛrtrɔfik] **ADJ** *Méd* abnormally enlarged, *Spéc* hypertrophic

hypertropie [ipɛrtrɔpi] **NF** *Méd* hypertropia

hyperventilation [ipɛrvãtilasjɔ̃] **NF** *Méd* hyperventilation

hypervitaminose [ipɛrvitaminoz] **NF** *Méd* hypervitaminosis

hypervolémie [ipɛrvɔlemi] **NF** *Med* hypervolemia

hyphe [if] **NF** *Bot* hypha

hypholome [ifɔlom] **NM** *Bot* hypholoma

hypnagogique [ipnagɔʒik] **ADJ** *Psy* hypnagogic

hypne [ipn] **NF** *Bot* hypnea

hypnoïde [ipnɔid] **ADJ** *Psy* hypnoid, hypnoidal

hypnologie [ipnɔlɔʒi] **NF** *Psy* hypnology

hypnose [ipnoz] **NF** *Psy* hypnosis; **sous h.** under hypnosis; **être en état d'h.** to be under hypnosis, to be in a hypnotic trance

hypnothérapeute [ipnɔterapøt] **NMF** *Psy* hypnotherapist

hypnothérapie [ipnɔterapi] **NF** *Psy* hypnotherapy

hypnotique [ipnɔtik] **ADJ** *Psy* hypnotic
   NM hypnotic (drug)

hypnotiser [3] [ipnɔtize] **VT 1** *Psy* to hypnotize **2** *(fasciner)* to fascinate
   ▸**s'hypnotiser** **VPR** **s'h. sur** to become obsessed with

hypnotiseur, -euse [ipnɔtizœr, -øz] **NM,F** *Psy* hypnotist

hypnotisme [ipnɔtism] **NM** *Psy* hypnotism

hypoacousie [ipoakuzi] **NF** *Méd* hypoacusis

hypoallergénique [ipoalɛrʒenik] **ADJ** = **hypoallergique**

hypoallergique [ipoalɛrʒik] **ADJ** hypoallergenic
   NM hypoallergenic

hypocalcémie [ipokalsemi] **NF** *Méd* hypocalcaemia

hypocalorique [ipokalɔrik] **ADJ** *(régime)* low-calorie

hypocapnie [ipokapni] **NF** *Méd* hypocapnia

hypocauste [ipokost] **NM** *Antiq* hypocaust

hypocentre [iposãtr] **NM** hypocentre

hypochloreux [ipoklɔrø] **ADJ M** *Chim* hypochlorous

hypochlorhydrie [ipoklɔridri] **NF** *Méd* hypochlorhydria

hypochlorite [ipoklɔrit] **NM** *Chim* hypochlorite

hypochrome [ipokrom] **ADJ** *Méd* hypochromic

hypocondre [ipokɔ̃dr] **NM** *Anat* hypochondrium
   NMF *Vieilli* hypochondriac

hypocondriaque [ipokɔ̃drijak] *Méd* **ADJ** hypochondriac, hypochondriacal
   NMF hypochondriac

hypocondrie [ipokɔ̃dri] **NF** *Méd* hypochondria; **être atteint d'h.** to be a hypochondriac, to suffer from hypochondria

hypocoristique [ipokɔristik] *Ling* **ADJ** hypocoristic
   NM hypocorism, hypocoristic

hypocras [ipokras] **NM** *Arch (alcool)* hippocras

hypocrisie [ipokrizi] **NF 1** *(attitude)* hypocrisy **2** *(action)* hypocritical act; **assez d'hypocrisies** let's stop this pretence

hypocrite [ipokrit] **ADJ 1** *(sournois → personne)* hypocritical, insincere **2** *(mensonger → attitude, regard)* hypocritical; *(→ promesse)* hollow
   NMF hypocrite; **faire l'h.** to be a hypocrite

hypocritement [ipokritmã] **ADV** hypocritically

hypocycloïdal, -e, -aux, -ales [iposiklɔidal, -o] **ADJ** *Tech & Géom* hypocycloidal

hypocycloïde [iposiklɔid] **NF** *Géom* hypocycloid

hypoderme [ipodɛrm] **NM 1** *Anat* hypodermis **2** *Entom* botfly, *Spéc* hypoderm

hypodermique [ipodɛrmik] **ADJ** *Anat* hypodermic

hypodermose [ipodɛrmoz] **NF** *Vét* hypodermosis

hypoesthésie [ipoɛstezi] **NF** *Méd* hypoaesthesia

hypogastre [ipogastr] **NM** *Anat* hypogastrium

hypogastrique [ipogastrik] **ADJ** *Anat* hypogastric

hypogé, -e[1] [ipoʒe] **ADJ** *Bot* hypogeal, hypogeous

hypogée[2] [ipoʒe] **NM** *Archéol* underground (burial) vault, *Spéc* hypogeum

hypoglosse [ipoglos] **ADJ** *Anat* hypoglossal

hypoglycémiant, -e [ipoglisemjã, -ãt] **ADJ** *Méd* hypoglycaemic
   NM hypoglycaemic

hypoglycémie [ipoglisemi] **NF** *Méd* hypoglycaemia; **je suis en h.** my blood sugar's low

hypogyne [ipoʒin] **ADJ** *Bot* hypogynous

hypoïde [ipoid] **ADJ** *Tech* **engrenage h.** crown-wheel and pinion, hypoid (gear)

hypokaliémie [ipokaljemi] **NF** *Méd* hypokalaemia

hypokhâgne [ipokaɲ] **NF** *Fam Arg scol* = first year of a two-year arts course, preparing for entrance to the "École normale supérieure"

hypolaïs [ipolais] **NM** *Orn* **h. pâle** olivaceous warbler; **h. polyglotte** melodious warbler; **h. russe** booted warbler

hypomanie [ipomani] **NF** *Psy* hypomania

hyponatrémie [iponatremi] **NF** *Méd* hyponatraemia

hyponeurien [iponœrjɛ̃] *Zool* **ADJ M** protostomian
   NM protostome

hyponomeute [iponɔmøt] **NM** *Entom* ermine moth

hyponyme [iponim] **NM** hyponym

hypoœstrogénie [ipoɛstrɔʒeni] **NF** *Méd* hypooestrogenism

The symbol ∗ indicates that the initial **h** is aspirate and that hence there is no liaison, eg **les haricots** [leariko] and not [lezariko], or contraction in spelling, eg **la haine** and not **l'haine**.

hypophosphite [ipɔfɔsfit] NM *Chim* hypophosphite

hypophosphoreux [ipɔfɔsfɔrø] ADJ M *Chim* hypophosphorous

hypophysaire [ipɔfizer] ADJ *Physiol* hypophyseal

hypophyse [ipɔfiz] NF *Physiol* hypophysis, pituitary gland

hypoplasie [ipɔplazi] NF *Méd* hypoplasia

hyposécrétion [ipɔsekresjɔ̃] NF *Méd* hyposecretion

hyposodé, -e [ipɔsɔde] ADJ *Méd* low-salt

hypospadias [ipɔspadjas] NM *Méd* hypospadias

hypostase [ipɔstaz] NF *Phil, Rel & Méd* hypostasis

hypostasier [9] [ipɔstazje] VT *Phil* to hypostasize, to hypostatize

hypostatique [ipɔstatik] ADJ *Rel* hypostatic

hypostyle [ipɔstil] ADJ *Archit* hypostyle, pillared

hyposulfite [ipɔsylfit] NM *Chim* hyposulphite

hyposulfureux [ipɔsylfyrø] ADJ M *Chim* hyposulphurous

hypotaupe [ipɔtop] NF *Fam Arg scol* = first year of advanced mathematics or physics prior to the competitive examination for the ''École normale supérieure''

hypotendu, -e [ipɔtɑ̃dy] *Méd* ADJ suffering from low blood pressure, *Spéc* hypotensive
▪ NM,F person suffering from low blood pressure, *Spéc* hypotensive

hypotenseur [ipɔtɑ̃sœr] *Méd* ADJ M hypotensive ▪ NM hypotensive (drug)

hypotensif, -ive [ipɔtɑ̃sif, -iv] ADJ *Méd* = relating to low blood pressure, *Spéc* hypotensive

hypotension [ipɔtɑ̃sjɔ̃] NF low blood pressure, *Spéc* hypotension

hypoténuse [ipɔtenyz] NF hypotenuse

hypothalamique [ipɔtalamik] ADJ *Anat* hypothalamic

hypothalamus [ipɔtalamys] NM hypothalamus

hypothécable [ipɔtekabl] ADJ *Jur* mortgageable

hypothécaire [ipɔtekɛr] ADJ *Jur* mortgage *(avant n)*

hypothécairement [ipɔtekɛrmɑ̃] ADV *Jur* by *or* on mortgage

hypothénar [ipɔtenar] *Anat* ADJ INV **éminence h.** hypothenar
▪ NM hypothenar

hypothèque [ipɔtɛk] NF 1 *Jur* mortgage; **franc** *ou* **libre d'hypothèques** unmortgaged; **prendre une h.** to take out a mortgage; **emprunter sur h.** to borrow on mortgage; **lever une h.** to raise a mortgage; **purger une h.** to pay off *or* to clear *or* to redeem a mortgage; **h. générale** blanket mortgage; **h. judiciaire** judicial mortgage; **h. légale** legal mortgage; **h. de premier rang** first legal mortgage; **propriété grevée d'hypothèques** encumbered estate 2 *Fig* **prendre une h. sur l'avenir** to count one's chickens before they're hatched; **lever l'h.** to remove the stumbling block *or* the obstacle

hypothéquer [18] [ipɔteke] VT 1 *Jur (propriété)* to mortgage; *(dette)* to secure by mortgage 2 *Fig* **h. son avenir** to mortgage one's future

hypothermie [ipɔtɛrmi] NF *Méd* hypothermia

hypothèse [ipɔtɛz] NF 1 *(supposition)* hypothesis, assumption; **dans la meilleure des hypothèses** at best; **dans l'h. où il refuserait, que feriez-vous?** supposing he refuses, what would you do?; **dans l'h. d'un tremblement de terre** in the event of an earthquake; **selon cette h.** on this assumption; **ce n'est pas une simple h. d'école** it's not just a speculative hypothesis; **h. de travail** working hypothesis; *Écon* **h. du cycle de vie** life-cycle hypothesis 2 *Ling* hypothesis
▫ **en toute hypothèse** ADV in any event, whatever the case

hypothético-déductif, -ive [ipɔtetikodedyktif, -iv] *(mpl* **hypothético-déductifs,** *fpl* **hypothético-déductives)** ADJ hypothetico-deductive

hypothétique [ipɔtetik] ADJ 1 *(supposé)* hypothetical, assumed 2 *(peu probable)* hypothetical, unlikely, dubious; **c'est très h.** it's extremely doubtful 3 *Ling* hypothetical

hypothétiquement [ipɔtetikmɑ̃] ADV hypothetically

hypothyroïdie [ipɔtirɔidi] NF *Méd* hypothyroidism; **faire de l'h.** to have an underactive thyroid

hypothyroïdien, -enne [ipɔtirɔidjɛ̃, -ɛn] *Méd* ADJ hypothyroid
▪ NM,F hypothyroid sufferer

hypotonie [ipɔtɔni] NF 1 *Chim* hypotonicity 2 *Méd* hypotonia

hypotonique [ipɔtɔnik] *Méd* ADJ *(muscle)* hypotonic; *(personne)* suffering from hypotonicity
▪ NMF person in a hypotonic condition

hypotrophie [ipɔtrɔfi] NF *Méd* underdevelopment, hypotrophy

hypoventilation [ipɔvɑ̃tilasjɔ̃] NF *Méd* hypoventilation

hypovitaminose [ipɔvitaminoz] NF *Méd* hypovitaminosis

hypovolémie [ipɔvɔlemi] NF *Méd* hypovolaemia

hypoxémie [ipɔksemi] NF *Méd* hypoxaemia

hypoxie [ipɔksi] NF *Méd* hypoxia

hypsomètre [ipsɔmɛtr] NM *Phys* hypsometer

hypsométrie [ipsɔmetri] NF hypsometry; *(représentation des altitudes)* hypsography

hypsométrique [ipsɔmetrik] ADJ hypsometric, hypsometrical; **carte h.** contour map

hysope [izɔp] NF *Bot* hyssop

hystérectomie [isterɛktɔmi] NF *Méd* hysterectomy

hystérésis [isterezis] NF *Phys* hysteresis

hystérie [isteri] NF hysteria; **je ne veux pas de crise d'h.** I don't want any hysterics; **h. collective** mass hysteria

hystériforme [isterifɔrm] ADJ hysteroid

hystérique [isterik] *Psy* ADJ hysterical
▪ NMF hysteric

hystérisation [isterizasjɔ̃] NF **l'h. du débat sur l'immigration** the mounting hysteria surrounding the issue of immigration '

hystérographie [isterɔgrafi] NF *Méd* hysterography, uterography

hystérométrie [isterɔmetri] NF *Méd* hysterometry

hystérosalpingographie [isterɔsalpɛ̃gɔgrafi] NF *Méd* hysterosalpingography, uterosalpingography

hystéroscopie [isterɔskɔpi] NF *Méd* hysteroscopy

hystérotomie [isterɔtɔmi] NF *Obst* hysterotomy

Hz *(abrév écrite* **hertz)** Hz

I

I, i [i] NM INV *(lettre)* I, i; **I comme Irma** ≃ I for Ivor; *Fig* **mettre les points sur les i** to dot the i's and cross the t's

IA [ia] NF *Ordinat (abrév* **intelligence artificielle)** AI

IAC [iɑse] NF *(abrév* **insémination artificielle entre conjoints)** AIH

IAD [iɑde] NF *(abrév* **insémination artificielle par donneur extérieur)** DI, AID

iambe [jɑ̃b] NM *(pied)* iamb, iambus; *(vers)* iambic
  □ **iambes** NMPL *(pièce satirique)* iambic

iambique [jɑ̃bik] ADJ iambic

IAO [iao] NF *(abrév* **ingénierie assistée par ordinateur)** CAE

IATA [jata] NF *(abrév* **Association internationale des transporteurs aériens)** IATA

iatrogène [jatrɔʒɛn], **iatrogénique** [jatrɔʒenik] ADJ *Méd* iatrogenic

ibère [ibɛr] ADJ Iberian
  □ **Ibère** NMF Iberian

ibéride [iberid] NF *Bot* candytuft, *Spéc* iberis

Ibérie [iberi] NF *(l')*l. Iberia

ibérique [iberik] ADJ Iberian

ibéris [iberis] NM *Bot* Iberis

Ibiza [ibiza] NM Ibiza

ibid. *(abrév écrite* **ibidem)** ibid

ibidem [ibidɛm] ADV ibidem

ibijau [ibiʒo] NM *Orn* potoo

ibis [ibis] NM *Orn* ibis; **i. falcinelle** glossy ibis; **i. rouge** scarlet ibis; **i. sacré** sacred ibis

---

-IBLE [ibl] SUFF

● This suffix expresses the idea of POSSIBILITY and is used to create adjectives, mainly from transitive verbs but also sometimes intransitive verbs or nouns. Its equivalent in English is, in many cases, *-ible* or *-able*. When there isn't an equivalent suffix form, the translation often includes an expression like "which can be…" or "easy to…", eg:
  accessible accessible/affordable; **audible** audible; **convertible** convertible; **flexible** flexible; **lisible** legible/readable; **9 est divisible par 3** 9 can be divided by 3

● The suffix **-ible** is often found in conjunction with a base and the prefix **in-** (or **im-**), with the idea of IMPOSSIBILITY, even if there isn't an equivalent positive form:
  incompréhensible incomprehensible; **incorrigible** incorrigible; **invincible** invincible; **impassible** impassive; **indéfectible** staunch, unfailing

---

iboga [ibɔga] NM *Bot* iboga

ibogaïne [ibɔgain] NF *Méd* ibogaine

ibuprofène [ibyprɔfɛn] NM *Pharm* ibuprofen

IC [ise] NM *Math (abrév* **intervalle de confiance)** IC

icaque [ikak] NF *Bot* icaco, coco plum

icaquier [ikakje] NM *Bot* icaco, coco plum (tree)

Icare [ikar] NPR *Myth* Icarus

icarien, -enne [ikarjɛ̃, -ɛn] ADJ **jeux icariens** trapeze acrobatics

icaunais, -e [ikonɛ, -ɛz] ADJ of/from the Yonne
  □ **Icaunais, -e** NM,F = inhabitant of or person from the Yonne

ICBM [isebeɛm] NM INV *(abrév* **Intercontinental Ballistic Missile)** ICBM

iceberg [ajsbɛrg] NM 1 *(glace)* iceberg 2 *Fig* **la partie cachée** *ou* **immergée de l'i.** the hidden aspects of the problem; **la partie visible de l'i.** the tip of the iceberg

ice-cream [ajskrim] *(pl* **ice-creams)** NM ice cream, ice-cream

icefield [ajsfild] NM *Géog* icefield

icelle [isɛl] *Arch* PRON DÉMONSTRATIF *(personne)* she; *(objet)* it
  ADJ DÉMONSTRATIF this

icelui [isəlɥi] *(pl* **iceux** [isø]) *Arch* PRON DÉMONSTRATIF *(personne)* he; *(objet)* it
  ADJ DÉMONSTRATIF this

ice-shelf [ajsʃɛlf] *(pl* **ice-shelfs** *ou* **ice-shelves)** NM *Géog* ice-shelf

ichneumon [iknømɔ̃] NM 1 *Vieilli Zool* ichneumon, Pharaoh's rat, Egyptian mongoose 2 *Entom* ichneumon (fly)

ichnologie [iknɔlɔʒi] NF ichnology

ichthus [iktys] NM *Rel* ichthys

ichtyocolle [iktiɔkɔl] NF isinglass, fish glue

ichtyoïde [iktjɔid] ADJ ichthyoid

ichtyol [iktjɔl] NM *Chim* ichthammol

ichtyologie [iktjɔlɔʒi] NF ichthyology

ichtyologique [iktjɔlɔʒik] ADJ *(science)* ichthyological; *(traité)* ichthyology *(avant n)*; **étude i. du Saint-Laurent** study of the fish life of the Saint Lawrence River

ichtyologiste [iktjɔlɔʒist] NMF ichthyologist

ichtyophage [iktjɔfaʒ] ADJ ichthyophagous

ichtyornis [iktjɔrnis] NM *Archéol* ichthyornis

ichtyosaure [iktjɔzɔr] NM *Ich & Archéol* ichthyosaurus

ichtyose [iktjoz] NF *Méd* fishskin disease, *Spéc* ichthyosis

ichtyostéga [iktjɔstega] NM *Zool* ichthyostega

ICI [isi] ADV 1 *(dans ce lieu, à cet endroit)* here; *(dans un écrit, un discours)* here, at this point; **posez-le i.** put it here; **i. même** on this very spot, in this very place; **il fait beau i.** the weather's nice here; **vous i.!** what are you doing here?; **i. et là** here and there; **vous êtes i. chez vous** make yourself at home; **pour toute demande, s'adresser i.** please enquire within; **c'est i. que j'ai mal** this is where it hurts; **c'est i. que ça s'est passé** this is the place where it happened; **viens, d'i. on voit mieux** come on, you can see better from here; **il y a 11 km d'i. au village** it's 11 km from here to the village; **c'est à cinq minutes/15 km d'i.** it's five minutes/15 km from here; **c'est loin/près d'i.** it's a long way from here/near here; **les gens d'i.** the locals, the people from around here; **je ne suis pas d'i.** I'm a stranger here, I'm not from around here; **le car vient jusqu'i.** the bus comes as far as here *or* as far as this; **Descartes écrit i. que…** Descartes writes here that…; **je voudrais souligner i. l'importance de cette décision** here *or* at this point I would like to emphasize the importance of this decision

2 *(dans le temps)* **d'i. (à) lundi, on a le temps** we've got time between now and Monday; **d'i. demain ce sera terminé** it will be finished by tomorrow; **d'i. peu** before (very) long; **d'i. là, tout peut arriver!** in the meantime *or* until then *or* between now and then anything can happen!; **vous serez guéri d'i. là** you'll be better by then; **d'i. à ce que vous ayez fini, je serai parti** by the time you've finished, I'll have gone; **Fam d'i. à ce qu'il se décide** by the time he makes up his mind; **d'i. à ce qu'il rechange d'avis, il n'y a pas loin** *ou* **il n'y a qu'un pas!** it won't be long before he changes his mind again!; **je vois ça d'i.!** I can just see that!; *Fam* **tu vois d'i. la pagaille!** you can (just) imagine the mess!

3 *(au téléphone, à la radio)* **allô, i. Paul** hello, (it's) Paul here *or* Paul speaking; **i. France Culture** this is *or* you are listening to France Culture
  □ **par ici** ADV 1 *(dans cette direction)* this way; **venez par i.** come this way; **tourne-toi par i.** turn round this way; **regarde par i.** look over here; **par i. la visite guidée** this way for the guided tour; **par i. la sortie** this way out, the exit is this way; **elle est passée par i. avant d'aller à la gare** she stopped off here on her way to the station; *Hum* **par i. la monnaie!** pay attention; *Fam Hum* **par i. la monnaie!** come on now, cough up!

2 *(dans les environs)* around here; **j'habitais par i. autrefois** I used to live around here

---

ici-bas [isiba] ADV here below, on earth

ici-dans [isidã], **ici-dedans** [isidədã] ADV *Can* here; **qu'est-ce qu'il fait froid i.i.!** it's freezing in here!

icit, icitte [isit] ADV *Can* here

icône [ikon] NF 1 *Rel* icon 2 *(image, symbole)* icon; *Ordinat* **i. de la corbeille** wastebasket icon, *Am* trash icon

iconique [ikɔnik] ADJ iconic

iconoclasme [ikɔnɔklasm] NM iconoclasm

iconoclaste [ikɔnɔklast] ADJ iconoclastic
  NMF iconoclast

iconographe [ikɔnɔgraf] NMF *(spécialiste)* iconographer; *(dans l'édition)* art *or* picture editor

iconographie [ikɔnɔgrafi] NF 1 *(étude théorique)* iconography 2 *(illustrations)* artwork

iconographique [ikɔnɔgrafik] ADJ iconographical

iconologie [ikɔnɔlɔʒi] NF iconology

iconologique [ikɔnɔlɔʒik] ADJ iconological

iconoscope [ikɔnɔskɔp] NM *TV* iconoscope

iconostase [ikɔnɔstaz] NF *Rel* iconostasis

iconothèque [ikɔnɔtɛk] NF 1 *(dans un musée)* iconography department *(of a museum)* 2 *(dans une bibliothèque)* photo *or* picture library

icosaèdre [ikɔzaɛdr] NM *Géom* icosahedron

ictère [iktɛr] NM *Méd* jaundice, *Spéc* icterus

ictérique [ikterik] *Méd* ADJ jaundice *(avant n)*, *Spéc* icteric
  NMF jaundice *or Spéc* icterus sufferer

ictus [iktys] NM *Méd & Littérature* ictus

id. *(abrév écrite* **idem)** id

IDA [idea] NF *Méd (abrév* **insémination par donneur anonyme)** = AID

Idaho [idao] NM **l'I.** Idaho; **dans l'I.** in Idaho

ide [id] NM *Ich* ide, orfe

idéal, -e, -als *ou* **-aux, -ales** [ideal, -o] ADJ 1 *(demeure, société, solution)* ideal, best, perfect; **ce n'est pas le comédien i. pour le rôle de Falstaff** he's not the ideal actor for playing Falstaff
  2 *(pureté, bonheur)* absolute
  3 *Math* ideal
  NM 1 *(modèle parfait)* ideal; **l'i. de la beauté chez les Grecs** the Greek ideal of beauty
  2 *(valeurs)* ideal; **tous ces jeunes sans i.** *ou* **qui n'ont pas d'i.!** all these young people with no ideal in life!
  3 *(solution parfaite)* **c'est l'i. pour se remettre en forme** it's the ideal thing for getting back into shape; **l'i. serait de/que…** the ideal *or* best solution would be to/if…; **dans l'i.** ideally; **camper quand il pleut, ce n'est pas l'i.!** when it's raining, camping isn't exactly ideal!
  4 *Math* ideal

idéalement [idealmã] ADV ideally; **i. situé à proximité de la plage** ideally situated *or* situated in an ideal position close to the beach; **les Vierges de Raphaël sont i. belles** Raphael's Madonnas are the very embodiment of beauty

idéalisateur, -trice [idealizatœr, -tris] ADJ **il est i.** he is an idealizer, he idealizes things

idéalisation [idealizasjɔ̃] NF idealization
idéalisatrice [idealizatris] *voir* **idéalisateur**
idéaliser [3] [idealize] VT to idealize
idéalisme [idealism] NM *(gén) & Phil* idealism
idéaliste [idealist] ADJ **1** *(gén)* idealistic **2** *Phil* idealist
NMF idealist
idéalité [idealite] NF ideality
idéation [ideasjɔ̃] NF *Psy* ideation
idée [ide] NF **1** *(pensée)* idea; **j'ai jeté quelques idées sur le papier** I've jotted down a few ideas; **c'est une i. de génie!** that's a brilliant idea!; **bonne i.!** good idea!; **c'était une bonne i. de l'emmener au restaurant** it was a good idea to take him/her out to eat; **je ne peux pas supporter l'i. qu'il est malheureux** I can't bear the idea *or* thought of him being unhappy; **se faire à l'i. (de/que…)** to get used to the idea (of/that…); *Fam* **j'ai l'i. que…** I've got the feeling that…; *Fam* **on n'a pas i. de faire des choses pareilles!** whoever heard of doing things like that!; **heureusement qu'il a eu l'i. d'éteindre le gaz** luckily he thought of turning the gas off *or* it occurred to him to turn the gas off; **avoir la bonne i. de faire qch** to have the bright idea of doing sth; *Hum* **il a eu la bonne i. de ne pas venir** he was quite right not to come; **qu'est-ce qui vous a donné l'i. de venir?** what gave you the idea *or* made you think of coming?; **rien qu'à l'i. de la revoir, je tremble** the mere thought *or* the very idea of seeing her again makes me nervous; **je me faisais une autre i. de la Tunisie/de sa femme** I had imagined Tunisia/his wife to be different; **moi, t'en vouloir? en voilà une i.** *ou* **quelle drôle d'i.!** me, hold it against you? where did you get that idea (from)?; **se faire des idées** to imagine things; **s'il croit obtenir le rôle, il se fait des idées** if he thinks he's going to get the part, he's deceiving himself; **se faire des idées sur qn** to have the wrong idea about sb; **donner des idées à qn** to give sb ideas *or* to put ideas in *or* into sb's head; **l'i., c'est de se débarrasser de ses cartes le plus vite possible** the idea *or* aim (of the game) is to get rid of one's cards as quickly as possible; **avoir une i. derrière la tête** to be up to sth; **avoir des idées noires** to be down in the dumps, to have the blues; **une certaine i. de la France** a certain idea of France
2 *(inspiration, création)* idea; **qui a eu l'i. du barbecue?** whose idea was it to have *or* who suggested having a barbecue?; **d'après une i. originale de** *(dans un film)* based on an (original) idea by; **je tiens l'i. d'un spectacle** I've got an idea for a show
3 *(imagination)* ideas, imagination; **avoir de l'i.** to be quite inventive; *Fam* **aie un peu d'i.!** try and use your head *or* imagination a bit!; *Fam* **pas mal ce dessin, il y a de l'i.** it's not bad this drawing, it's got something; **il y a de l'i. mais le plan du devoir laisse à désirer** the idea is good but your presentation leaves something to be desired
4 *(gré, convenance)* **fais à ton i.** do as you see fit *or* as you please; **elle n'en fait toujours qu'à son i.** she always does just what she wants
5 *(esprit)* **avoir dans l'i. que…** to have an idea that…, to think that…; **avais-tu dans l'i. d'acheter des actions?** were you thinking of buying shares?; **tu la connais, quand elle a dans l'i. de faire quelque chose!** you know her, when she's got it into her head to do something *or* when she's set her mind on doing something!; **se mettre dans l'i. de/que…** to get it into one's head to/that…; **t'est-il jamais venu à l'i. que…?** has it never occurred to you *or* entered your head that…?; **il ne me viendrait jamais à l'i. de le frapper** it would never cross my mind *or* occur to me to hit him; *Fam* **on va au concert ce soir? ça m'était complètement sorti de l'i.** we're going to the concert tonight? it had gone clean *or* right out of my mind
6 *(point de vue, opinion)* **l'i. qu'il a du travail** his idea *or* notion of work; **il a une i. un peu étrange de l'amour** he has rather a strange idea of love; **on a tous une i. différente sur la question** we all have a different opinion *or* view on the matter; **avoir des idées bien arrêtées sur** to have set ideas *or* definite views about; **je préfère me faire une i. (par) moi-même** I prefer to make up my own mind; **je préfère me faire moi-même une i. de la situation** I'd rather assess the situation for myself; **à ton i., je raccourcis la robe?** what do you think, should I shorten the dress?; **changer d'i.** to change one's mind; **i. fixe** idée fixe, obsession; **c'est une i. fixe chez toi!** it's an obsession with you!; **elle a une i. fixe** she's got a fixed idea *or* an idée fixe; **i. reçue** commonplace, received idea, idée reçue; **idées préconçues** preconceived ideas, preconceptions; **avoir les idées larges/étroites** to be broad-/narrow-minded; **avoir une haute i. de qn/qch** to have a high opinion of sb/sth, to think highly of sb/sth; **avoir sa petite i. sur qch** to have one's own little ideas about sth
7 *(aperçu, impression)* idea; **une vague** *ou* **petite i.** an inkling; **donnez-moi une i. du prix que ça va coûter/du temps que ça va prendre** give me a rough idea *or* some idea of the price/of the time it will take; **as-tu (une) i.** *ou* **la moindre i. du prix que ça coûte?** have you any idea how much it costs?; **tu n'as pas i. de son entêtement!** you have no idea *or* you can't imagine how stubborn he is!; *Fam* **elle est belle, t'as pas i.!** you wouldn't believe how beautiful she is; **je n'en ai pas la moindre i.** I haven't the slightest *or* faintest idea; **aucune i.!** I haven't a clue!, no idea!
8 *(en composition; avec ou sans trait d'union)* idea; **une i.-cadeau** a gift idea; **une i.-rangement astucieuse** a clever storage idea; **une i.-repas** an idea for a meal
idée-force [idefɔrs] *(pl* **idées-forces***)* NF *(point principal)* crux, nub, mainstay; *(point fort)* strong point
idéel, -elle [ideɛl] ADJ *Phil* ideal
idem [idɛm] ADV idem, ditto; *Fam* **je suis venu en voiture et lui i.** I came by car and so did he *or* and he did too
idempotent, -e [idɛmpɔtɑ̃, -ɑ̃t] ADJ *Math* idempotent
identifiable [idɑ̃tifjabl] ADJ identifiable; **difficilement i.** difficult to identify; **aisément i. à son plumage bleuté** easily identified by its bluish feathers
identifiant [idɑ̃tifjɑ̃] NM *Ordinat* identifier; **i. biométrique** biometric identifier
identificateur [idɑ̃tifikatœr] NM **1** *Ordinat* identifier **2** *Mktg* **i. de marque** brand identifier
identification [idɑ̃tifikasjɔ̃] NF **1** *(assimilation)* identification (**à** with); **son i. à son père est complète** he/she completely identifies with his/her father; *Psy* **i. projective** projective identification **2** *(d'un cadavre)* identification; *(d'un tableau)* identification, attribution **3** *Tél* **i. d'appel** caller identification, *Fam* caller ID; *Ordinat* **i. de l'utilisateur** user identification **4** *Mktg* **i. de la marque** brand recognition
identificatoire [idɑ̃tifikatwar] ADJ identifying
identifier [9] [idɑ̃tifje] VT **1** *(reconnaître)* to identify; **il a été identifié comme étant le voleur** he was identified as the robber; **le tableau n'a jamais été identifié** the painting was never attributed *or* identified; **se faire i.** to give one's identity, to identify oneself **2** *(assimiler)* **i. qn/qch à** *ou* **avec** to identify sb/sth with
►**s'identifier** VPR **s'i. à qn/qch** to identify oneself with sb/sth; **elle s'est complètement identifiée à son personnage** she's got right into the part; **je ne m'identifie à aucun parti** I don't identify myself with any particular party
identifieur [idɑ̃tifjœr] = **identificateur**
identique [idɑ̃tik] ADJ identical; **i. à qn/qch** identical to sb/sth; **le village est resté i.** the village has stayed much the same; **elle reste i. à elle-même** she's still the same as she always *or* ever was
❑ **à l'identique** ADV identically; **j'en ai fait un à l'i.** I made an identical one
identiquement [idɑ̃tikmɑ̃] ADV identically
identitaire [idɑ̃titɛr] ADJ **obsession i.** obsession with issues of identity; **les revendications identitaires des minorités ethniques** ethnic minorities' demands for recognition; **l'afflux d'immigrants a donné lieu à un phénomène de repli i.** the large influx of immigrants has caused people to cling to their idea of cultural identity
identité [idɑ̃tite] NF **1** *(personnalité, état civil)* identity; **sous une fausse i.** under an assumed name; **établir son i.** to prove one's identity; **elle est encore à la recherche de sa véritable i.** she's still trying to find *or* to discover her true identity; **l'i. des victimes n'a pas été révélée** the names of the victims haven't been released; **contrôle** *ou* **vérification d'i.** (police) identity check
2 *(similitude)* identity, similarity; **l'i. d'humeur entre eux** the similarity in their characters
3 *Ling, Math & Psy* identity
4 *Jur* **I. judiciaire** ≃ Criminal Record Office
5 *Mktg* **i. graphique** logo; **i. de marque** brand identity
idéogramme [ideɔgram] NM ideogram
idéographie [ideɔgrafi] NF ideography
idéographique [ideɔgrafik] ADJ ideographic, ideographical
idéologie [ideɔlɔʒi] NF ideology
idéologique [ideɔlɔʒik] ADJ ideological
idéologisation [ideɔlɔʒizasjɔ̃] NF ideologization
idéologue [ideɔlɔg] NMF ideologist
❑ **Idéologues** NMPL *Phil* **les Idéologues** the Ideologues
idéomoteur, -trice [ideɔmɔtœr, -tris] ADJ *Psy* ideomotor
ides [id] NFPL *Antiq* ides; **prends garde aux i. de mars** beware the ides of March
id est [idɛst] CONJ ie
IDH [ideaʃ] NM *Écon (abrév* **indicateur de développement humain***)* HDI
IDHEC [idɛk] NM *Anciennement (abrév* **Institut des hautes études cinématographiques***)* = former French film school
idiolecte [idjɔlɛkt] NM *Ling* idiolect
idiomatique [idjɔmatik] ADJ idiomatic; **une expression** *ou* **une tournure i.** an idiom, an idiomatic expression
idiome [idjom] NM idiom
idiopathique [idjɔpatik] ADJ *Méd* idiopathic
idiosyncrasie [idjɔsɛ̃krazi] NF idiosyncrasy
idiot, -e [idjo, -ɔt] ADJ **1** *(stupide → individu, réponse, sourire)* idiotic, stupid; *(→ accident, mort)* stupid; **un ricanement i.** a silly *or* foolish snigger; **ça n'est pas i. du tout, ton système** that's quite a smart system you've got; **ce serait vraiment i. de ne pas en profiter** it would be foolish *or* stupid not to take advantage of it; *Hum* **dis-moi comment faire, je ne veux pas mourir i.** tell me how to do it, I don't want to be a complete ignoramus
2 *Vieilli Méd* idiotic
NM,F **1** *(imbécile)* idiot; **arrête de faire l'i.!** *(de faire le pitre)* stop fooling around *or* about!; *(à un enfant)* stop being stupid!; *(à un simulateur)* stop acting stupid!; **ne fais pas l'i., range ce couteau!** don't be stupid, put that knife away!; **tu me prends pour un i.?** what kind of idiot do you take me for?, do you take me for a complete idiot?
2 *Vieilli Méd* idiot; **l'i. du village** the village idiot

'L'Idiot' *Dostoïevski* 'The Idiot'

idiotement [idjɔtmɑ̃] ADV idiotically, stupidly; **ricaner i.** to snigger like an idiot
idiotie [idjɔsi] NF **1** *(caractère)* idiocy, stupidity **2** *(acte, parole)* stupid thing; **arrête de dire des idioties** stop talking nonsense; **il y en a des idioties à la télé!** there's such a lot of nonsense on TV!; **aïe! j'ai fait une i.!** oh dear, I've done something stupid! **3** *Vieilli Méd* idiocy
idiotisme [idjɔtism] NM idiom, idiomatic phrase, idiomatic expression
idoine [idwan] ADJ *Littéraire* appropriate; **jusqu'à ce que nous trouvions la solution i.** until we find the appropriate solution
idolâtre [idɔlatr] ADJ **1** *Rel* idolatrous **2** *(fanatique)* adulatory; **un public i.** an idolizing *or* adulatory public
NMF **1** *Rel* idolater, *f* idolatress **2** *(fanatique)* devotee
idolâtrer [3] [idɔlatre] VT **1** *Rel* to idolize **2** *(adorer)* to idolize
idolâtrie [idɔlatri] NF **1** *Rel* idolatry, idol worshipping **2** *(fanatisme)* **il l'aime jusqu'à l'i.** he idolizes her
idolâtrique [idɔlatrik] ADJ idolatrous

idole [idɔl] NF **1** *Rel* idol; **les idoles des temples païens** the idols in pagan temples **2** *(personne)* idol; **mon frère était mon i.** I used to idolize my brother; **c'est l'i. des jeunes** he's/she's a teenage idol

Idoménée [idɔmene] NPR *Myth* Idomeneus

IDS [ideɛs] NF *Mil (abrév* **initiative de défense stratégique)** SDI

idylle [idil] NF **1** *(poème)* idyll **2** *(amourette)* romantic idyll

idyllique [idilik] ADJ **1** *Littérature* idyllic **2** *(amour, couple, paysage)* idyllic, perfect; **se faire une idée i. de qch** to have an idealized view of sth

-IE [i] SUFF

• Among its various uses, the suffix **-ie** can be found at the end of names of countries or regions (**la Normandie, l'Andalousie, la Roumanie** etc). It also appears in words referring to types of government, eg **monarchie** (monarchy), **tyrannie** (tyranny).

• It is a combination of these two features that has given rise in recent years to a humorous use of the suffix **-ie**, mostly in combination of names of political leaders. This type of neologism is mostly used in newspaper headlines, eg:
bienvenue en Chiraquie welcome to Chirac's world; **ouragan sur la Chiraquie** storm hits the Chirac camp; **les déçus de la Mitterrandie** the people disappointed by the Mitterrand era
• The word **ovalie** follows the same pattern, but is derived from the word "ovale" (as in the shape of a rugby ball) as opposed to a proper noun. Again, it refers to the world of rugby in general, to rugby players as a whole or even to the sport itself, eg:
votre voyage en Ovalie va durer six semaines [about the rugby world cup] welcome to six weeks of rugby; **il a quitté l'ovalie** he left rugby
• Note that, like a lot of recent coinages, the spelling for **ovalie, chiraquie, jospinie** etc can fluctuate between the capitalized and uncapitalized forms.

IED [iəde] NM *(abrév* **investissement étranger direct)** FDI

-IEN, -IENNE [jɛ̃, jɛn] SUFF

This suffix has a wide variety of uses, some of which are particularly productive.

• It appears in names of INHABITANTS of countries, regions, cities or even planets, where it is often translated by the English suffix *-ian*, eg:
parisien(ne)/Parisien(ne) Parisian; **italien(ne)/Italien(ne)** Italian; **la banlieue londonienne** the London suburbs; **les Londoniens** Londoners; **les Terriens** inhabitants of the Earth, Earthlings; **un martien** a Martian
• The same word can be used to refer to the language spoken by such inhabitants, eg:
elle parle bien italien she speaks good Italian
• When added to a noun referring to a particular field, it takes on the meaning of PERSON WHO SPECIALIZES IN....., eg:
un(e) chirurgien(ne) a surgeon; **un(e) comédien(ne)** an actor; **un(e) généticien(ne)** a geneticist; **un(e) électricien(ne)** an electrician
• In the medical world, **-ien, -ienne** is used to form adjectives with the meaning of RELATING TO. Their English equivalents are often *-ian* or *-ial*, eg:
coronarien(ne) coronary; **microbien(ne)** microbial/bacterial; **rachidien(ne)** rachidian, rachidial
• This same, rather vague meaning, is also contained in adjectives and nouns derived from people's names, and it is in this area that the suffix **-ien, -ienne** becomes most productive as it can be added to the name of virtually any politician, writer etc, eg:
l'inconscient freudien the Freudian unconscious; **l'école platonicienne** the Platonic school; **l'univers faulknérien** the world of Faulkner; **la période mitterrandienne** the Mitterand period; **les jospiniens** Jospin supporters; **un fervent chiraquien** a diehard Chirac supporter

léna [jena] NM Jena

lenisseï [jenisei] NM **l'l.** the (River) Yenisei

-ienne *voir* **-ien**

IEP [iəpe] NM *(abrév* **Institut d'études politiques)** = "grande école" for political science

-IER, -IÈRE [je, jɛr] SUFF

Among the many uses of this suffix, three are particularly productive.

• A lot of nouns describing a person's JOB, TRADE OR STATUS end in **-ier, -ière**. The most common English equivalent is probably the suffix *-er*, eg:
un(e) jardinier(ère) a gardener; **un plombier(ère)** a plumber; **un(e) ouvrier(ère)** a worker; **un(e) prisonnier(ère)** a prisoner; **un(e) cuisinier(ère)** a cook; **un(e) écolier(ère)** a schoolboy/schoolgirl
• The idea of PRODUCTION is an important one with this suffix. It appears in masculine names of trees or plants bearing a particular fruit (**prunier** plumtree; **poirier** pear tree; **fraisier** strawberry plant; **olivier** olive tree), as well as in feminine names of places where a particular plant or tree grows or where a mineral is produced (**sapinière** fir plantation; **rizière** rice field).
• When added to nouns describing a food item or cosmetic, **-ier, -ière** carries the idea of CONTAINER, eg:
poudrier powder compact; **cendrier** ashtray; **soupière** soup tureen; **cafetière** coffee pot; **salière** saltcellar

-ieux, -ieuse *voir* **-eux, -euse**

if [if] NM **1** *Bot* yew (tree) **2** *Menuis* yew **3** *(égouttoir)* **if (à bouteilles)** (bottle draining) rack

-IF [if] SUFF

In French "traditional" argot, this suffix is added to nouns, sometimes along with an extra consonant and sometimes also with the base noun truncated, eg:
calcif (from **caleçon**) underpants; **porcif** (from **portion**) portion; **soutif** (from **soutien-gorge**) bra; **beaujolpif** Beaujolais

IFOP, Ifop [ifɔp] NM *Mktg (abrév* **Institut français d'opinion publique)** = French market research institute

Ifremer [ifrəmɛr] NM *(abrév* **Institut français de recherche pour l'exploitation de la mer)** = French research establishment for marine resources

IG [iʒe] NM *Méd (abrév* **index glycémique)** GI

IGEN [iʒeɛn] NM *Scol (abrév* **Inspecteur général de l'Éducation nationale)** = high-ranking education inspector

IGF [iʒeɛf] NM INV *Anciennement Fin (abrév* **impôt sur les grandes fortunes)** wealth tax

IGH [iʒeaʃ] NM *(abrév* **Immeuble de grande hauteur)** = very high building

igloo, iglou [iglu] NM igloo

IGN [iʒeɛn] NM *(abrév* **Institut géographique national)** = French national geographical institute, *Br* ≃ Ordnance Survey, *Am* ≃ United States Geological Survey

---

Culture

IGN
Created in 1940, this state agency is responsible for the official map of France and for keeping a geographical database. It is organized into regional offices and sponsors a school which trains 200 students a year.

Ignace [iɲas] NPR **I. de Loyola** Ignatius Loyola

igname [iɲam] NF *Bot* yam

ignare [iɲar] ADJ ignorant, uncultivated
NMF ignoramus

igné, -e [igne, iɲe] ADJ **1** *Phys* heat-engendered; *Chim* pyrogenic; *Géol* igneous **2** *Littéraire (en feu)* fiery, burning, flaming

ignifugation [ignifygasjɔ̃, iɲifygasjɔ̃] NF fireproofing

ignifuge [ignifyʒ, iɲifyʒ] ADJ *(qui ne brûle pas)* fireproof; *(qui brûle difficilement)* fire-retardant
NM *(pour protéger du feu)* fireproof substance; *(pour ralentir la propagation)* fire-retardant substance

ignifugé, -e [ignifyʒe, iɲifyʒe] ADJ *(matériau)* fireproofed

ignifugeant, -e [ignifyʒã, -ãt, iɲifyʒã, -ãt] ADJ *(qui ne brûle pas)* fireproof; *(qui brûle difficilement)* fire-retardant

ignifuger [17] [ignifyʒe, iɲifyʒe] VT to fireproof

ignimbrite [ignɛ̃brit] NF *Minér* ignimbrite

ignipuncture [ignipɔ̃ktyr, iɲipɔ̃ktyr] NF *Méd* heat cauterization, ignipuncture

ignition [ignisjɔ̃, iɲisjɔ̃] NF *Phys* ignition

ignitron [ignitrɔ̃, iɲitrɔ̃] NM *Électron* ignitron

ignivome [ignivom, iɲivom] ADJ *Littéraire (volcan, dragon etc)* ignivomous, fire-emitting

ignoble [iɲɔbl] ADJ **1** *(vil → individu)* low, base; *(→ crime)* infamous, heinous; *(→ accusation)* shameful; *(→ conduite)* unspeakable, disgraceful, shabby; **tu as vraiment été i. avec elle** you were really vile to her **2** *Fam (bâtisse)* hideous; *(nourriture)* revolting, vile; *(logement)* squalid; **d'ignobles taudis** squalid hovels

ignoblement [iɲɔbləmã] ADV vilely, disgracefully

ignominie [iɲɔmini] NF **1** *(caractère vil)* ignominy, infamy; *(déshonneur)* ignomony, *(public)* disgrace *or* dishonour; **se couvrir d'i.** to disgrace oneself **2** *(action)* disgraceful act; *(parole)* disgraceful remark; **commettre une i.** to behave ignominiously *or* disgracefully; **dire des ignominies** to say disgraceful *or* hateful things; **c'est une i.!** it's a disgrace!, it's shameful!

ignominieusement [iɲɔminjøzmã] ADV *Littéraire* ignominiously, disgracefully

ignominieux, -euse [iɲɔminjø, -øz] ADJ *Littéraire* ignominious

ignorance [iɲɔrãs] NF ignorance; **être dans l'i. de qch** to be unaware of sth; **tenir qn dans l'i. de qch** to keep sb in ignorance of sth; **j'avoue mon i. en géologie** I must confess my ignorance of geology; **pécher par i.** to err through ignorance

ignorant, -e [iɲɔrã, -ãt] ADJ **1** *(inculte)* ignorant, uncultivated **2** *(incompétent)* ignorant about; **il est i. en informatique** he doesn't know anything about computers **3** *(pas au courant)* **i. de** ignorant *or* unaware of
NM,F ignoramus; **ne fais pas l'i.** don't pretend you don't know

ignorantin [iɲɔrãtɛ̃] *Rel* ADJ M **frère i.** Ignorantine friar
NM Ignorantine

ignoré, -e [iɲore] ADJ **1** *(cause, événement)* unknown; **être i. de qn** to be unknown to sb **2** *(artiste)* unrecognized

ignorer [3] [iɲore] VT **1** *(cause, événement etc)* to be unaware of; **j'ignore ton adresse/où il est/quand elle revient** I don't know your address/where he is/when she's coming back; **il ignorait tout de mon passé/d'elle** he knew nothing about my past/her; **j'ignorais qu'il était malade** I was unaware that he was ill; **personne n'ignore que...** everybody knows that...; **elle ignorait vous avoir blessé** she didn't realize she had hurt your feelings; **nous n'ignorons pas les difficultés qu'elle rencontre** we are not unaware of her difficulties
2 *(personne, regard)* to ignore, to take no notice of; *(avertissement, panneau)* to ignore, to take no heed of; *(ordre, prière)* to ignore; **ignore-le** ignore him
3 *(faim, pauvreté)* to have had no experience of; **nous ignorons la faim** we don't know what it is to be hungry; **il ignore la peur** he knows no fear, he doesn't know the meaning of fear
▸ **s'ignorer** VPR **1** *(mutuellement)* to ignore each other
2 *(soi-même)* **c'est un comédien qui s'ignore** he is unaware of his talent as an actor, he's an actor without knowing it

IGP [iʒepe] NF *Com (abrév* **indication géographique protégée)** = designation of a product which guarantees its authentic place of origin and gives the name protected status

IGPN [iʒepeɛn] NF *(abrév* **Inspection générale de la police nationale)** = police disciplinary body, *Br* ≃ Police Committee

IGS [iʒeɛs] NF *(abrév* **Inspection générale des services)** = police disciplinary body for Paris, *Br* ≃ Metropolitan Police Commission

Iguaçu [igwasu] NM **les chutes d'I.** the Iguaçu Falls

iguane [igwan] NM *Zool* iguana; **i. marin/terrestre** marine/land iguana; **i. vert** common *or* green iguana

iguanodon [igwanɔdɔ̃] **NM** *Zool & Archéol* iguanodon

igue [ig] **NF** *Géol (dans le Quercy)* sinkhole, *Br* swallow hole

IHS [iaʃɛs] **NM** *Rel (abrév* **Iesus Homimum Salvator**) IHS

IJsselmeer [esəlmir] **NM l'I.** the IJsselmeer

ikat [ikat] **NM** *Tex* ikat

ikebana [ikebana] **NM** ikebana

il [il] *(pl* **ils**) **PRON 1** *(sujet d'un verbe → homme)* he; *(→ animal, chose)* it; *(→ animal de compagnie)* he; **ils** they; **ils ont augmenté l'essence/les impôts** they've put petrol/taxes up; **viendra-t-il?** will he come?

2 *(dans des tournures impersonnelles)* **il pleut** it's raining; **il faut que tu viennes** you must come; **il me faut du pain** I need some bread; **il faut patienter** you/we have to wait; **il commence à se faire tard** it's getting late; **il manque deux élèves** two pupils are missing; **il suffit de patienter** all you/we have to do is wait; **il est facile de s'en assurer** it's easy to make sure

3 *(emphatique)* **ton père est-il rentré?** has your father come back?; **Paul a-t-il appelé?** has Paul called?; **qu'il est joli, ce foulard!** what a pretty scarf (that is)!

ilang-ilang [ilɑ̃ilɑ̃] = **ylang-ylang**

île [il] **NF 1** *Géog* island, isle; **une petite î.** an islet; **les habitants de l'î.** the islanders; **vivre sur** *ou* **dans une î.** to live on an island; **aller sur une î.** to go to an island; **aborder une î.** to land on an island; **î. déserte** desert island; **les îles d'Åland** the Åland Islands; **les îles Aléoutiennes** the Aleutian Islands; **les îles de l'Amirauté** the Admiralty Islands; **les îles Andaman** the Andaman Islands; **les îles Anglo-Normandes** the Channel Islands; **les îles Australes** the Tubuai *or* Austral Islands; **les îles Bahrayn** *ou* **Bahreïn** the Bahrain *or* Bahrein Islands; **les îles Baléares** the Balearic Islands; **l'î. de Beauté** Corsica; **les îles Britanniques** the British Isles; **les îles Canaries** the Canary Islands; **les îles du Cap Vert** the Cape Verde Islands; **les îles Carolines** the Caroline Islands; **les îles Cayman** the Cayman Islands; **l'î. Christmas** Christmas Island; **l'î. de la Cité** = island on the Seine in Paris where Notre-Dame stands; **les îles Comores** the Comoros; **les îles Cook** the Cook Islands; **l'î. d'Elbe** Elba; **l'î. d'Ellesmere** Ellesmere Island; **les îles Éoliennes** the Aeolian Islands; **les îles Falkland** the Falkland Islands, the Falklands; **les îles Féroé** the Faeroes; **les îles Fidji** the Fiji Islands; **les îles Frisonnes orientales** the East Frisian Islands; **les îles Galapagos** the Galapagos Islands; **les îles Gilbert** the Gilbert Islands; **les îles Hébrides** the Hebrides; **les îles Ioniennes** the Ionian Islands; **les îles Kouriles** the Kuril *or* Kurile Islands; **l'î. Krakatoa** Krakatau, Krakatoa; **les îles de la Ligne** the Line Islands; **les îles Lipari** the Lipari Islands; **les îles Maldives** the Maldives; **les îles Malouines** the Falkland Islands, the Falklands; **l'î. de Man** the Isle of Man; **les îles Mariannes** the Mariana Islands; **les îles Marquises** the Marquesas Islands; **les îles Marshall** the Marshall Islands; **l'î. Maurice** Mauritius; **les îles de la mer Égée** the Aegean *or* Greek Islands; **les îles Moluques** the Molucca Islands, the Moluccas; **l'î. du Nord** North Island; **l'î. d'Ouessant** (the Isle of) Ushant; **l'î. de Pâques** Easter Island; **l'î. du Prince-Édouard** Prince Edward Island; **les îles de la Reine-Élisabeth** Queen Elizabeth Islands; **les îles Salomon** the Solomon Islands; **l'î. de Sein** the Ile de Sein; **les îles Shetland** the Shetland Islands, the Shetlands; **les îles de la Société** the Society Islands; **les îles de la Sonde** the Sunda Islands; **les îles Sorlingues** the Scilly Isles; **les îles Sous-le-Vent** *(aux Antilles)* the Netherlands (and Venezuelan) Antilles; *(en Polynésie)* the Leeward Islands, the Western Society Islands; **l'î. du Sud** South Island; **l'î. de la Trinité** Trinidad; **les îles Turks et Caicos** the Turks and Caicos Islands; **l'î. de Vancouver** Vancouver Island; **les îles du Vent** *(aux Antilles)* the Windward Islands; *(en Polynésie)* the Eastern Society Islands; **l'î. Victoria** Victoria Island; **les îles Vierges** the Virgin Islands; **l'î. de Wight** the Isle of Wight

2 *Littéraire ou Vieilli (colonie)* **les Îles** the Caribbean (Islands), the West Indies

3 *Culin* **î. flottante** floating island

'L'Île du Docteur Moreau' *Wells* 'The Island of Dr Moreau'

'L'Île au trésor' *Stevenson* 'Treasure Island'

iléal, -e, -aux, -ales [ileal, -o] **ADJ** *Anat & Méd* ileal

Île-de-France [ildəfrɑ̃s] **NF l'Î.** the Île-de-France; **en Î.** in the Île-de-France region

iléite [ileit] **NF** *Méd* ileitis

iléo-cæcal, -e, -aux, -ales [ileɔsekal, -o] **ADJ** *Anat* ileocæcal

iléon [ileɔ̃] **NM** *Anat* ileum

iléostomie [ileɔstɔmi] **NF** *Méd* ileostomy

iléus [ileys] **NM** *Méd* ileus

Iliade [iljad] **NF**

'L'Iliade' *Homère* 'The Iliad'

iliaque [iljak] **ADJ** *Anat* iliac; **artère i.** iliac artery; **fosses iliaques** iliac fossae; **os i.** hip bone

îlien, -enne [iljɛ̃, -ɛn] **NM,F** islander *(especially from the islands off Brittany)*

ilion [iljɔ̃] **NM** *Anat* pelvic bone, *Spéc* ilium

Ille-et-Vilaine [ilevilɛn] **NF l'I.** Ille-et-Vilaine

illégal, -e, -aux, -ales [ilegal, -o] **ADJ** *(contre la loi)* illegal, unlawful; *(sans autorisation)* illicit; **de façon illégale** illegally; **c'est maintenant i.** it's now illegal, it's now against the law; **détention illégale** unlawful detention

illégalement [ilegalmɑ̃] **ADV** illegally, unlawfully

illégalité [ilegalite] **NF 1** *(caractère)* illegality, unlawfulness; **être dans l'i.** to be in breach of the law; **vivre dans l'i.** to live outside the law, to be an outlaw **2** *(délit)* illegal *or* unlawful act; **commettre une i.** to break the law

illégitime [ileʒitim] **ADJ 1** *Jur (enfant, acte)* illegitimate; *(mariage)* unlawful **2** *(requête, prétention)* illegitimate; *(frayeur, soupçons)* groundless

illégitimement [ileʒitimmɑ̃] **ADV 1** *Jur* illegitimately, unlawfully **2** *(injustement)* unwarrantedly, unjustifiably

illégitimité [ileʒitimite] **NF 1** *Jur (d'un enfant, d'un acte)* illegitimacy; *(d'un mariage)* unlawfulness **2** *(injustice)* unwarrantedness, unfoundedness

illettré, -e [iletre] **ADJ 1** *(qui ne peut ni lire ni écrire)* functionally illiterate **2** *(ignorant)* uncultivated, uneducated

NM,F 1 *(personne qui ne peut ni lire ni écrire)* functionally illiterate person, functional illiterate **2** *(ignorant)* uncultivated *or* uneducated person

illettrisme [iletrism] **NM** functional illiteracy

illicéité [iliseite] **NF** illicitness, unlawfulness

illicite [ilisit] **ADJ** illicit; **gains illicites** unlawful gains

illicitement [ilisitmɑ̃] **ADV** illicitly

illico [iliko] **ADV i. (presto)** right away, pronto

illimité, -e [ilimite] **ADJ 1** *(en abondance → ressources, espace)* unlimited; *(→ patience, bonté)* boundless, limitless **2** *(non défini → durée)* unlimited, indefinite; **en congé i.** on indefinite leave **3** *Math* unrestricted; *Géom* unbounded **4** *Ordinat* **accès i.** unrestricted access

Illinois [ilinwa] **NM l'I.** Illinois; **dans l'I.** in Illinois

illisibilité [ilizibilite] **NF** illegibility

illisible [ilizibl] **ADJ 1** *(écriture)* illegible, unreadable **2** *(écrivain, roman)* unreadable **3** *Ordinat (fichier, disquette)* unreadable

illisiblement [ilizibləmɑ̃] **ADV** illegibly

illogique [ilɔʒik] **ADJ** illogical; **de façon i.** illogically

illogiquement [ilɔʒikmɑ̃] **ADV** illogically

illogisme [ilɔʒism] **NM** illogicality, absurdity

illumination [ilyminasjɔ̃] **NF 1** *(d'un monument)* floodlighting **2** *(lumière)* illumination, lighting (up) **3** *(idée)* flash of inspiration *or* understanding; *(révélation)* illumination **4** *Rel* illumination

▫ **illuminations NFPL** illuminations, lights; **les illuminations de Noël** the Christmas lights

illuminé, -e [ilymine] **ADJ** *(monument)* lit up, floodlit, illuminated; *(rue)* lit up, illuminated

NM,F 1 *(visionnaire)* visionary, *Arch* illuminate; *Hist* **les Illuminés** the Illuminati **2** *Péj (fou)* lunatic

illuminer [3] [ilymine] **VT 1** *(ciel → sujet: étoiles, éclairs)* to light up; *(monument)* to floodlight; *(pièce)* to light; *Fig* **cet événement a illuminé sa vie** this event has lit up his/her life **2** *(visage, regard)* to light up; **un sourire illumina son visage** a smile lit up his/her face **3** *Rel* to enlighten

►**s'illuminer VPR 1** *(ciel, regard, visage)* to light up; **s'i. de** to light up with **2** *(vitrine)* to be lit up; *(guirlande)* to light up

illuminisme [ilyminism] **NM** *Rel & Psy* illuminism

illusion [ilyzjɔ̃] **NF 1** *(idée fausse)* illusion; **ne lui donne pas d'illusions** don't give him/her (any) false ideas; **perdre ses illusions** to lose one's illusions; **faire perdre ses illusions à qn** to disillusion sb; **se faire des illusions** to delude oneself; **je ne me fais pas d'illusions là-dessus** I have no illusions *or* I'm not deluding myself about it; **si tu crois qu'elle va revenir, tu te fais des illusions** if you imagine she's going to come back you're deluding yourself; **se bercer d'illusions** to delude oneself, to harbour illusions

2 *(erreur de perception)* illusion, trick; **c'est une i. due à la lumière** it's a trick of the light; **le miroir donne une i. de profondeur** the mirror gives an illusion of depth; **en donnant** *ou* **créant une i. de stabilité** with an outward show of stability; **Mirax, le roi de l'i.!** Mirax, the great illusionist!; **faire i.** to fool people; **c'est un vieux manteau mais il fait i.** it's an old coat but it still passes for new *or* but you wouldn't think so to look at it; **son aisance fait i.** his/her apparent ease is deceptive; **i. d'optique** optical illusion

'Illusions perdues' *Balzac* 'Lost Illusions'

illusionner [3] [ilyzjɔne] **VT** to delude

►**s'illusionner VPR** to delude *or* to deceive oneself; **tu t'illusionnes sur ses intentions** you're deluding yourself *or* you're mistaken about his/her intentions; **ne t'illusionne pas sur sa détermination** make no mistake about his/her determination

illusionnisme [ilyzjɔnism] **NM 1** *Beaux-Arts* illusionism **2** *(prestidigitation)* conjuring tricks; *(truquage)* illusionism

illusionniste [ilyzjɔnist] **NMF** conjurer, illusionist

illusoire [ilyzwar] **ADJ** *(promesse)* deceptive, illusory; *(bonheur, victoire)* illusory, fanciful; **il serait i. de croire que...** it would be wrong *or* mistaken to believe that...

illusoirement [ilyzwarmɑ̃] **ADV** *Littéraire* illusorily, deceptively

illustrateur, -trice [ilystratœr, -tris] **NM,F** illustrator

illustratif, -ive [ilystratif, -iv] **ADJ** illustrative

illustration [ilystrasjɔ̃] **NF 1** *(image, activité)* illustration; *(ensemble d'images)* illustrations; **texte et illustrations de ...** text and illustrations by ...; **l'i. de cette édition est somptueuse** this book is lavishly illustrated **2** *Fig (démonstration)* illustration; *(exemple)* illustration, example

illustrative [ilystrativ] *voir* **illustratif**

illustratrice [ilystratris] *voir* **illustrateur**

illustre [ilystr] **ADJ** illustrious; **une ville au passé i.** a town with an illustrious *or* a glorious past; **l'i. compagnie** the Académie française; *Hum* **qui est cet i. inconnu?** who is this famous person I've never heard of?

illustré, -e [ilystre] **ADJ** illustrated

NM pictorial, illustrated magazine; *(pour enfants)* comic

illustrer [3] [ilystre] **VT 1** *(livre)* to illustrate **2** *(définition, théorie)* to illustrate (**de** *ou* **par** with) **3** *Littéraire (rendre prestigieux)* to lend distinction to; **Molière a illustré la langue française** Molière contributed to the greatness of the French language

►**s'illustrer VPR** to become renowned *or* famous; **elle s'est illustrée par son interprétation de Carmen** she won fame through her performance of Carmen; **les Français se sont illustrés en natation** the French distinguished themselves at swimming

Illustre-Théâtre [ilystrəteatr] **NM l'I.** = name of the theatre company of which Molière was a member as a young man

illustrissime [ilystrisim] **ADJ** *Hum* most illustrious

illuvial, -e, -aux, -ales [ilyvjal, -o] ADJ *Géol* illuvial

illuviation [ilyvjasjɔ̃] NF *Géol* illuviation

illuvium [ilyvjɔm] NM *Géol* illuvium

ILM [iɛlɛm] NM (*abrév* **immeuble à loyer moyen**) = apartment building with low-rent accommodation (more expensive than an HLM)

ilménite [ilmenit] NF *Minér* ilmenite

ILN [iɛlɛn] NM (*abrév* **immeuble à loyer normal**) = apartment building with low-rent accommodation

îlot [ilo] NM **1** *Géog* small island, islet **2** *(espace)* island; **un î. de verdure** an island of greenery; **dans l'î. de calme où je travaille** in the island *or* oasis of peace where I work; **î. de résistance** pocket of resistance **3** *(pâté de maisons)* block; *(pour surveillance policière)* patrol area, beat **4** *(sur une route)* **î. directionnel** traffic *or* lane divider **5** *(dans un magasin)* gondola; **î. de vente** (display) stand, island **6** *Naut* island **7** *Méd* islet

îlotage [ilɔtaʒ] NM **1** *(d'un quartier)* community policing **2** *Élec* grid sectioning

ilote [ilɔt] NM **1** *Antiq* Helot **2** *Fig Littéraire* helot

îlotier [ilɔtje] NM community policeman, policeman on the beat

ilotisme [ilɔtism] NM **1** *Antiq* helotism **2** *Fig* helotism

ils [il] *voir* **il**

ILV [iɛlve] NF *Mktg* (*abrév* **information sur le lieu de vente**) point-of-sale information

IMA [ima] NM (*abrév* **Institut du monde arabe**) = Arab cultural centre and library in Paris holding regular exhibitions of Arab art

image [imaʒ] NF **1** *(illustration → gén)* picture; *(→ comme récompense scolaire)* ≃ gold star; **l'i. fournie par le satellite** the satellite picture; *Fig* **l'i. de** the picture of; **elle était l'i. du malheur/de la bonne santé** she was the very picture of tragedy/health; **i. de la mère/du père** mother/father figure; **i. d'Épinal** = popular 19th-century print showing idealized scenes of French and foreign life, well-known characters or heroic events, named after the city where these prints were manufactured; *Fig* **c'est une véritable i. d'Épinal** it's a very stereotyped image; **i. pieuse** holy image; **livre d'images** picture book

2 *(reflet)* image, reflection; *Phys* image; **i. réelle/virtuelle** real/virtual image

3 *(au cinéma → plan)* frame; *(à la télévision → réception)* picture; **25 images par seconde** 25 frames per second; **l'i. est floue** *(télévision)* the picture is fuzzy; **il n'y a plus d'i.** there's nothing on screen; **certaines scènes du roman sont difficiles à mettre en images** some scenes from the novel are difficult to adapt for the screen; **i. d'archive** library picture; *Cin, TV* library shot; *TV* **i. fantôme** ghosting; **i. multiple** multiple image; *Phot* **i. de solarisation** solarized image; **images de synthèse** computer-generated images, CGI; **i. de télévision** television picture; **i. tramée** raster image; **i. virtuelle** virtual image

4 *Littérature* image; **les images de Hugo** Hugo's imagery; **ce n'est qu'une i.** it's just an image

5 *(idée)* image, picture; **quelle i. te fais-tu de lui?** how do you picture him?; **donner une fausse i. de qch** to misrepresent sth, to give a false impression of sth; **soigner son i.** to cultivate one's image; *Littéraire* **son i. me hante** his/her face haunts me; *Compta* **i. fidèle** true and fair view; *Psy* **i. mentale** mental image

6 *Math* image

7 *Ordinat (imprimée)* hard copy; *(sur l'écran)* image; **i. bitmap** bitmap image; **i. cliquable** clickable image; **i. digitalisée** digitized image; **i. intégrée** inline image; **i. mémoire** dump; **prendre une i. mémoire** to take a hard copy, to dump; **images de synthèse** computer-generated images, CGI; **i. vectorielle** outline image

8 *Mktg* **i. de l'entreprise** *ou* **institutionnelle** corporate image; **i. de marque** *(d'un produit)* brand image; *(d'une entreprise)* corporate image; *(d'une personnalité, d'une institution)* (public) image; **i. de marque personnelle** personal brand; **i. de produit** product image; **images à compléter** picture completion

❑ **à l'image de** PRÉP **Dieu créa l'homme à son i.** God created man in His own image; **cet enfant est tout à fait à l'i. de sa mère** this child is the very image of his mother; **ce jardin est à l'i. de son propriétaire** this garden is the reflection of its owner

imagé, -e [imaʒe] ADJ full of imagery; **elle a un langage très i.** she uses colourful imagery; **parler de façon imagée** to use picturesque speech

imager [17] [imaʒe] VT *Littéraire (style, discours)* to colour

imagerie [imaʒri] NF **1** *(ensemble d'images)* prints, pictures; **l'i. napoléonienne** the imagery of the Napoleonic era **2** *(commerce)* coloured print trade; *(fabrication)* printing **3** *Météo* satellite photography **4** *Méd* **i. cérébrale** brain imaging *or* scanning; **i. médicale** medical imaging; **i. par résonance magnétique** magnetic resonance imaging; **i. par résonance magnétique fonctionnelle** functional magnetic resonance imaging; **i. par résonance magnétique nucléaire** nuclear magnetic resonance imaging **5** *Ordinat* imagery **6** *Tech* imaging; **i. infrarouge** infrared imaging; **i. radar** radar imagery

imageur, -euse [imaʒœr, -øz] ADJ *(radar, radiomètre)* imaging

NM *Ordinat* imager; **i. documentaire** document imager

Imagier® [imaʒje] NM picture book

imagier, -ère [imaʒje, -ɛr] NM,F **1** *(dessinateur)* drawer *or* painter *(of popular pictures)*; *Vieilli (imprimeur)* printer *(of popular pictures)*; *Vieilli (vendeur)* print seller **2** *(sculpteur)* sculptor *(of human figures or animals)*

imaginable [imaʒinabl] ADJ imaginable, conceivable; **ce n'est pas i. d'être aussi têtu!** you're/he's *etc* unbelievably stubborn!; **c'est difficilement i.** it's hard to imagine; **ce n'est plus i. à notre époque** it's just unthinkable nowadays

imaginaire [imaʒinɛr] ADJ **1** *(fictif → pays, personnage)* imaginary **2** *Math* imaginary

NM imagination; **le domaine de l'i.** the realm of fancy; *Psy* **l'i. collectif** the collective imagination

imaginal, -e, -aux, -ales [imaʒinal, -o] ADJ *Entom* imaginal; **disques imaginaux** imaginal discs, buds

imaginatif, -ive [imaʒinatif, -iv] ADJ imaginative, fanciful

imagination [imaʒinasjɔ̃] NF **1** *(faculté)* imagination; **essaie d'avoir un peu d'i.** try using your imagination; **avoir beaucoup d'i.** to have a lot of imagination, to be very imaginative; **tu as vraiment trop d'i.!** you imagine things!; **tu manques d'i.!** you have no imagination!; **tu as l'i. fertile** you have a fertile *or* good imagination; **son récit frappe l'i.** his/her story strikes the imagination; **les derniers événements dépassent l'i.** the latest incidents defy the imagination *or* beggar belief; **elle lui parlait en i.** she imagined herself talking to him/her; **c'est de l'i. pure et simple** it's sheer *or* pure imagination **2** *(chimère)* **ce sont de pures imaginations** that's pure fancy; **imaginations que tout cela!** those are just imaginings!

imaginative [imaʒinativ] *voir* **imaginatif**

imaginer [3] [imaʒine] VT **1** *(concevoir)* to imagine; **c'est l'homme le plus gentil qu'on puisse i.** he is the kindest man imaginable; **je n'imaginais pas que cela soit faisable** I didn't think it could be done; **la maison est plus grande que je l'imaginais** the house is bigger than I imagined it (to be); **tu imagines sa tête quand je lui ai dit ça!** you can imagine *or* picture his/her face when I told him/her that!; **tu l'imagines avec des enfants!** can you imagine *or* picture him/her with children?; **on imagine facilement qu'elle n'était pas ravie** as you can imagine, she wasn't very pleased; **on imagine mal la suite** it's hard to imagine what happened next; **tu n'imagines tout de même pas que je vais céder?** you don't really think *or* imagine I'm going to give in, do you?; **que vas-tu i. là?** how can you think such a thing?

2 *(supposer)* to imagine, to suppose; **imaginons qu'il refuse** supposing he refuses; **tu veux de l'argent, j'imagine!** you want some money, I suppose!

3 *(inventer → personnage)* to create, to imagine; *(→ gadget, mécanisme)* to devise, to think up

▸**s'imaginer** VPR **1** *(soi-même)* to imagine oneself; **elle s'imagine déjà danseuse étoile!** she already imagines *or* pictures herself as a prima ballerina!; **j'ai du mal à m'i. grand-mère** I have a hard job picturing *or* seeing myself as a grandmother

2 *(se représenter)* to imagine, to picture; **imaginez-vous un petit chalet blotti dans la montagne** picture, if you will, a little chalet nestling in the mountains; **je me l'imaginais bien plus grand** I imagined him much taller; **il est bien plus grand que je ne me l'imaginais** he's much taller than I imagined; **comme vous pouvez vous l'i.** as you can (well) imagine; **s'i. que...** to imagine *or* to think that...; **si tu t'imagines que je vais démissionner, tu te trompes** if you think that I'm going to resign, you're mistaken; **tu t'imagines bien que je n'ai pas vraiment apprécié** as you can imagine, I wasn't too pleased; **il s'imagine tout savoir** he thinks he knows everything; **si je m'imaginais te rencontrer ici!** fancy meeting you here!

imago [imago] NM *Entom* imago

NF *Psy* imago

imam [imam] NM *Rel* imam

imamat [imama] NM *Rel* imamate

IMAO [imao] NM *Pharm* (*abrév* **inhibiteur de la monoamine-oxydase**) MAOI

Imax [imaks] NM *Cin* IMAX

imbattable [ɛ̃batabl] ADJ unbeatable

imbécile [ɛ̃besil] ADJ **1** *(niais)* stupid **2** *Vieilli Méd* imbecilic

NMF **1** *(niais)* idiot, fool; **ne fais pas l'i.** *(ne fais pas le pitre)* stop fooling about *or* around; *(ne simule pas)* stop acting stupid *or* dumb; *Fam* **le premier i. venu peut comprendre ça** any (old) fool can understand that; *Fam* **espèce d'i. heureux!** you stupid idiot! **2** *Vieilli Méd* imbecile

imbécilement [ɛ̃besilmɑ̃] ADV idiotically, stupidly

imbécillité [ɛ̃besilite] NF **1** *(caractère)* stupidity, idiocy **2** *(parole)* nonsense *(UNCOUNT)*; *(acte)* stupid behaviour *(UNCOUNT)*; **n'écoute pas ces imbécillités!** don't listen to this nonsense!; **qu'est-ce qu'il t'a dit? – une i.** what did he say to you? – something stupid; **avec ses imbécillités il va finir par se faire prendre** his foolish behaviour is going to land him in trouble one of these days **3** *Vieilli Méd* imbecility

imberbe [ɛ̃bɛrb] ADJ beardless

imbibé, -e [ɛ̃bibe] ADJ *Fam* tanked up, *Br* sozzled, *Am* soused

imbiber [3] [ɛ̃bibe] VT to soak; **imbibez les biscuits de kirsch** soak the biscuits in kirsch; **i. une éponge d'eau** to soak a sponge with water; **la terre est imbibée d'eau** the earth is completely waterlogged

▸**s'imbiber** VPR **1** *(s'imprégner)* to become soaked; **s'i. de** *(sujet: gâteau)* to become soaked with *or* in; *(sujet: terre)* to become saturated with **2** *Fam (boire)* to booze

imbibition [ɛ̃bibisjɔ̃] NF **1** *(action)* soaking; *(absorption)* absorption, absorbing **2** *Phys* imbibition

imbitable, imbittable [ɛ̃bitabl] ADJ *très Fam Br* bloody *or Am* goddamn incomprehensible

imbrication [ɛ̃brikasjɔ̃] NF **1** *(d'écailles, de pièces, de tuiles)* overlapping, *Spéc* imbrication **2** *(de considérations, d'hypothèses)* interweaving, overlapping; *(de questions)* overlapping, interlinking **3** *Ordinat* embedding; *(de commandes)* nesting

imbriqué, -e [ɛ̃brike] ADJ **1** *(écailles, pièces, tuiles)* overlapping, *Spéc* imbricated **2** *(considérations, hypothèses)* interwoven, overlapping; *(questions)* overlapping, interlinked **3** *Ordinat* embedded; *(commandes)* nested

imbriquer [3] [ɛ̃brike] VT **1** *(pièces)* to fit into *or* over each other; *(tuiles)* to overlap; **il faut i. les différents morceaux les uns dans les autres** the different pieces have to be fitted into each other **2** *Ordinat* to embed; *(commandes)* to nest

▸**s'imbriquer** VPR **1** *Constr (pièces)* to fit into *or* over each other; *(tuiles, feuilles, écailles)* to overlap, *Spéc* to imbricate **2** *(être lié)* to be interlinked *or* closely linked; **des questions**

pratiques sont venues s'i. dans les considérations esthétiques practical problems began to interfere with the purely aesthetic considerations; **le scénariste a fait s'i. les vies de tous les personnages** the screenwriter linked the lives of all his characters together

imbroglio [ɛ̃brɔljo] NM *(gén) & Théât* imbroglio

imbrûlé, -e [ɛ̃bryle] ADJ unburnt, non-combusted

□ **imbrûlés** NMPL unburnt residue

imbu, -e [ɛ̃by] ADJ **être i. de sa personne** *ou* **de soi-même** to be full of oneself, to be full of a sense of one's own importance; **être i. de préjugés** to be imbued with prejudices

imbuvable [ɛ̃byvabl] ADJ **1** *(boisson)* undrinkable **2** *Fam (individu)* unbearable■; **je le trouve i., ce mec** I can't stand (the sight of) that guy, I can't stomach *or Br* stick that guy

IMC [iɛmse] *Méd* NM **1** *(abrév* **indice de masse corporelle)** BMI **2** *(abrév* **infirme moteur cérébral)** person suffering from cerebral palsy

NF *(abrév* **infirmité motrice cérébrale)** cerebral palsy

IME [iɛmə] NM **1** *Écon (abrév* **Institut monétaire européen)** EMI **2** *(abrév* **Institut médico-éducatif)** special needs school

imide [imid] NM *Chim* imide

imine [imin] NF *Chim* imine

imipramine [imipramin] NF *Pharm* imipramine

imitable [imitabl] ADJ imitable; **difficilement i.** hard to imitate

imitateur, -trice [imitatœr, -tris] NM,F imitator; *(de personnalités connues)* impersonator, mimic; *(de cris d'animaux)* imitator, mimic

ADJ *(moutonnier)* imitating, mimicking

imitatif, -ive [imitatif, -iv] ADJ imitative, mimicking

imitation [imitasjɔ̃] NF **1** *(parodie)* imitation, impression; **elle a un talent d'i.** she's a talented mimic; **elle fait d'excellentes imitations** she does excellent imitations, she's an excellent mimic

2 *Beaux-Arts* imitation, copy; *Littérature* imitation

3 *(matière artificielle)* imitation; **i. marbre** imitation marble; **ce n'est pas du liège, c'est de l'i.** it's not genuine cork, it's only imitation; **des bijoux en i. or** imitation gold jewels

4 *Mus & Psy* imitation

5 *(contrefaçon* → *d'un produit)* imitation; *(*→ *d'une signature, d'un billet)* forgery

□ **à l'imitation de** PRÉP in imitation of

imitative [imitativ] *voir* **imitatif**

imitatrice [imitatris] *voir* **imitateur**

imiter [3] [imite] VT **1** *(copier* → *bruit, personne)* to imitate; *(*→ *mouvements, façon de parler)* to imitate, to mimic; *(*→ *produit)* to imitate; **Jacques imite très bien ses collègues** Jacques does good impressions of his colleagues; **i. la signature de qn** to imitate sb's signature; *(à des fins criminelles)* to forge sb's signature; **le peintre et le poète imitent les couleurs de la nature** the painter and the poet reproduce the colours of nature

2 *(suivre l'exemple de)* to imitate, to copy; **si elle démissionne, d'autres l'imiteront** if she resigns, others will do the same *or* follow suit *or* do likewise

3 *(ressembler à)* to look like; **c'est une matière qui imite le liège** it's imitation cork; **un style imité du Berlin des années 30** a style modelled on Berlin in the thirties

immaculé, -e [imakyle] ADJ *(blanc, neige)* immaculate; *(nappe, draps)* immaculately *or* spotlessly clean; *(réputation)* immaculate, unsullied, spotless; *Rel* **l'Immaculée Conception** the Immaculate Conception

immanence [imanɑ̃s] NF *Phil* immanence

immanent, -e [imanɑ̃, -ɑ̃t] ADJ *Phil* immanent

immanentisme [imanɑ̃tism] NM *Phil* immanentism

immangeable [ɛ̃mɑ̃ʒabl] ADJ uneatable, inedible

immanquable [ɛ̃mɑ̃kabl] ADJ **1** *(inévitable)* inevitable **2** *(infaillible)* sure, reliable, infallible

immanquablement [ɛ̃mɑ̃kabləmɑ̃] ADV without fail

immarcescible [ɛ̃marsesibl] ADJ *Littéraire* unfading, incorruptible

immatérialité [imaterjalite] NF immateriality

immatériel, -elle [imaterjɛl] ADJ **1** *Phil* immaterial **2** *Littéraire (léger)* ethereal **3** *Fin (actif, valeurs)* intangible

immatriculation [imatrikylasjɔ̃] NF registration; **numéro d'i.** *(d'une voiture) Br* registration number, *Am* license number; **numéro d'i. à la Sécurité sociale** *Br* ≃ National Insurance number, *Am* ≃ Social Security number

Culture

IMMATRICULATION

The last two numbers on French number plates refer to the "département" where the vehicle was registered. Vehicles from the Val-de-Marne, for example, bear the number 94.

immatriculer [3] [imatrikyle] VT **(faire) i. qch** to register sth; **car immatriculé 75** coach with the *Br* registration *or Am* license number ending in 75; **car immatriculé à Paris** coach with a Paris *Br* registration *or Am* license number; *Fam* **je ne suis plus immatriculé 92** my *Br* registration *or Am* license number no longer ends in 92; **elle n'est pas immatriculée à la Sécurité sociale** ≃ she has no *Br* National Insurance number *or Am* Social Security number

immaturation [imatyrasjɔ̃] NF *Psy* immaturity, immatureness

immature [imatyr] ADJ immature

immaturité [imatyrite] NF **1** *(d'une personne, d'une attitude)* immaturity **2** *(d'un fruit)* unripeness

immédiat, -e [imedja, -at] ADJ **1** *(avenir)* immediate; *(réponse)* immediate, instantaneous; *(effet)* immediate, direct; *(soulagement)* immediate, instant; **sa mort fut immédiate** he/she died instantly **2** *(voisins)* immediate, next-door *(avant n)*; *(environs)* immediate; **dans mon voisinage i.** in close proximity to *or* very near where I live; **supérieur i.** direct superior **3** *Chim & Phil* immediate

□ **dans l'immédiat** ADV for the time being, for the moment, for now; **nous n'effectuerons pas de changement dans l'i.** we will introduce no immediate changes *or* no changes in the immediate future

immédiatement [imedjatmɑ̃] ADV **1** *(dans le temps)* immediately, at once, *Sout ou Hum* forthwith; **viens ici i.!** come here at once!; **la nouvelle disposition prend effet i.** the new measure comes into immediate effect *or* into effect immediately **2** *(dans l'espace)* directly, immediately; **tournez à gauche i. après le prochain feu** turn left immediately *or Br* straight after the next traffic lights

immédiateté [imedjatte] NF **1** *(instantanéité)* immediacy, immediateness **2** *Phil* immediacy

immelmann [imɛlman] NM *Aviat (acrobatie)* Immelmann turn

immémorial, -e, -aux, -ales [imemɔrjal, -o] ADJ *Littéraire* age-old, immemorial; **de temps i.** from time immemorial; **remonter à des temps immémoriaux** to date from time immemorial

immense [imɑ̃s] ADJ *(forêt, bâtiment, plaine)* vast, huge; *(talent)* immense, towering; *(acteur, écrivain)* great, tremendous; *(soulagement, impact)* immense, great, tremendous; *(sacrifice, dévotion)* immense, boundless; *(succès)* huge, great; **c'est un i. acteur/écrivain** he's a tremendous *or* great actor/writer

immensément [imɑ̃semɑ̃] ADV immensely, hugely; **ce cadeau me fait i. plaisir** this gift gives me tremendous *or* great pleasure, this gift pleases me greatly

immensité [imɑ̃site] NF **1** *(d'un lieu)* immensity, vastness; *(de la mer)* immensity; *Littéraire* **dans l'i.** in infinity, in infinite space **2** *(d'une tâche, d'un problème)* enormity; *(d'un talent, d'un chagrin)* immensity

immergé, -e [imɛrʒe] ADJ **1** *(au-dessous de l'eau)* submerged; **la majeure partie d'un iceberg est immergée** the bulk of an iceberg is underwater; **l'épave est immergée par 500 m de fond** the wreck is lying 500 m underwater *or* under 500 m of water; **plante immergée** aquatic plant; **terres immergées** submerged areas of land **2** *Fig* **l'économie immergée** the underground economy

immerger [17] [imɛrʒe] VT *(oléoduc, bombes)* to lay under water, to submerge; *(produits radioactifs)* to dump *or* to deposit at sea; *(cadavre)* to bury at sea

►**s'immerger** VPR *(sous-marin)* to dive, to submerge

immérité, -e [imerite] ADJ undeserved, unmerited

immersif, -ive [imɛrsif, -iv] ADJ *Tech* by immersion, by means of immersion

immersion [imɛrsjɔ̃] NF **1** *(gén)* immersion; *(d'un sous-marin)* diving, submersion; *(d'un oléoduc, de bombes)* underwater laying, submersion; *(de déchets)* dumping at sea; *(d'un cadavre)* burying at sea **2** *Astron & Rel* immersion

immettable [ɛ̃metabl] ADJ *(vêtement* → *abîmé)* no longer fit to wear; *(*→ *indécent)* unwearable

immeuble [imœbl] ADJ *Jur* immovable, real; **biens immeubles** immovables, real estate

NM **1** *Archit (gén)* building; **i. de bureaux** office building *or Br* block; **i. commercial** rented office building *or Br* block; **i. de grande hauteur** = very high building; **i. d'habitation** residential building, *Br* block of flats, *Am* apartment building; **i. à loyer moyen** = apartment building with low-rent accommodation (more expensive than an "HLM"); **i. à loyer normal** = apartment building with low-rent accommodation; **i. miroir** building glazed with reflective glass; **i. de rapport** investment property, rental property; **i. à usage locatif** *(résidentiel) Br* block of rented flats, *Am* rental apartment building

2 *Jur* real estate, landed property, *Am* realty; **placer son argent en immeubles** to invest in property; **i. par destination** fixture

immigrant, -e [imigrɑ̃, -ɑ̃t] ADJ immigrant

NM,F immigrant

immigration [imigrasjɔ̃] NF immigration; **i. choisie** selective immigration policy; **les populations issues de l'i.** immigrant populations; **les Français issus de l'i.** = French citizens from ethnic minorities

immigré, -e [imigre] ADJ immigrant; **travailleur i.** immigrant worker, guest worker

NM,F immigrant; **i. clandestin** illegal immigrant

immigrer [3] [imigre] VI to immigrate; **i. en France/aux États-Unis** to immigrate to France/ to the (United) States

imminence [iminɑ̃s] NF imminence

imminent, -e [iminɑ̃, -ɑ̃t] ADJ imminent, impending; **c'est i.** it's imminent, it won't be long (now); **sa décision est imminente** he's/she's about to make a decision

immiscer [16] [imise] **s'immiscer** VPR **1** *(intervenir)* to interfere; **s'i. dans une affaire** to interfere with *or* in a matter; **elle s'immisce toujours dans la conversation** she's always interrupting **2** *Jur* **s'i. dans une succession** to enter into *or* to assume a succession

immixtion [imiksjɔ̃] NF **1** *Littéraire* interference, interfering **2** *Jur* assumption

immobile [imɔbil] ADJ **1** *(mer, surface)* still, calm; *(nuit, air)* still; *(feuillage, animal, personne)* still, motionless; *(visage)* immobile; **gardez votre bras i.** keep your arm still **2** *Littéraire (temps)* immobile; *(institution, dogme)* unchanging, changeless

immobilier, -ère [imɔbilje, -ɛr] ADJ *Com & Jur Br* property *(avant n)*, *Am* real-estate *(avant n)*

NM *Com* **l'i.** the *Br* property *or Am* real-estate business; **l'i. de bureaux** the office *Br* property *or Am* real-estate business; **l'i. de loisir** the *Br* holiday *or Am* vacation rentals business; **l'i. d'entreprise** the commercial *Br* property *or Am* real-estate business; **l'i. locatif** the *Br* property *or Am* real-estate rental business

immobilisation [imɔbilizasjɔ̃] NF **1** *(arrêt* → *d'un adversaire, de forces armées)* immobilization; **le manque à gagner dû à l'i. des machines** losses through downtime; **attendre l'i. complète du train** wait until the train comes to a complete stop *or* standstill

2 *Fin (de capital)* locking up, tying up, immobilization; *(d'actif, de valeurs)* freezing

3 *Jur* conversion *(of personalty into realty)*; **i. des fruits** = distribution of profits among creditors; **i. de véhicule** = judgment preventing a car owner from using his/her vehicle for six months; **i. d'un véhicule terrestre à moteur** = clamping of a debtor's car on demand from a legally recognized creditor

4 *Sport* hold

5 *Méd* immobilization

❑ **immobilisations** NFPL fixed *or* capital assets; **faire de grosses immobilisations** to carry heavy stocks; **immobilisations capitaux** tied-up capital, capital assets; **immobilisations corporelles** tangible (fixed) assets; **immobilisations financières** long-term investments; **immobilisations incorporelles** intangible (fixed) assets; **immobilisations non financières** physical fixed assets

immobiliser [3] [imɔbilize] VT **1** *(membre)* to strap up, to immobilize; *(adversaire, forces armées)* to immobilize; *(balancier)* to stop; *(circulation)* to bring to a standstill *or* to a halt; **les véhicules sont immobilisés à la sortie du tunnel** the vehicles have been brought to a standstill at the tunnel exit; *Méd* **être immobilisé** *(personne)* to be laid up; **il est resté immobilisé au lit pendant cinq semaines** he was laid up in bed for five weeks

2 *Fin (capitaux)* to tie up, to immobilize; *(actifs, valeurs)* to freeze

3 *Jur* to convert *(personalty into realty)*

▸**s'immobiliser** VPR *(personne)* to stand still *or* stock-still; *(véhicule)* to come to a halt, to pull up; **la libellule s'immobilisa sur la fleur** the dragonfly came to rest *or* settled on the flower

immobilisme [imɔbilism] NM **1** *(gén)* opposition to change **2** *Pol* immobilism

immobiliste [imɔbilist] ADJ conservative, *Spéc* immobilist; **la politique i. du gouvernement** the government's conservative policies

NMF conservative, upholder of the status quo

immobilité [imɔbilite] NF *(d'un lac, d'une personne)* stillness, motionlessness; *(d'un regard)* immobility, steadiness; **je suis contraint à l'i. totale** I've been told not to move at all

immodéré, -e [imɔdere] ADJ immoderate, inordinate

immodérément [imɔderemɑ̃] ADV immoderately, excessively

immodeste [imɔdɛst] ADJ *Littéraire* immodest

immodestie [imɔdɛsti] NF *Littéraire* immodesty

immolateur [imɔlatœr] NM *Littéraire* immolator

immolation [imɔlasjɔ̃] NF immolation

immoler [3] [imɔle] VT **1** *Rel (sacrifier)* to immolate; **i. qn à** to sacrifice sb to **2** *Littéraire (exterminer)* to kill **3** *Fig Littéraire (renoncer à)* to sacrifice

▸**s'immoler** VPR *Littéraire* to sacrifice oneself; **s'i. par le feu** to set fire to oneself

immonde [imɔ̃d] ADJ **1** *Rel (impur)* unclean, impure **2** *(sale)* foul, filthy, obnoxious **3** *(ignoble → crime, pensées, propos)* sordid, vile, base; *(→ individu)* vile, base, obnoxious **4** *(laid)* vile

immondice [imɔ̃dis] NF *Vieilli (chose sale ou impure)* unclean thing

❑ **immondices** NFPL refuse, *Br* rubbish, *Am* trash

immoral, -e, -aux, -ales [imɔral, -o] ADJ immoral

immoralement [imɔralmɑ̃] ADV immorally

immoralisme [imɔralism] NM immoralism

immoraliste [imɔralist] ADJ immoralist

NMF immoralist

═══════════════

📖

'**L'Immoraliste**' *Gide* 'The Immoralist'

═══════════════

immoralité [imɔralite] NF immorality

immortalisation [imɔrtalizasjɔ̃] NF immortalization

immortaliser [3] [imɔrtalize] VT to immortalize

▸**s'immortaliser** VPR to gain immortality, to win everlasting fame (**par** through *or* with)

immortalité [imɔrtalite] NF immortality; **son œuvre lui a assuré l'i.** his/her work won him/her everlasting fame *or* immortality; **entrer dans l'i.** to gain immortality, to win everlasting fame

immortel, -elle [imɔrtɛl] ADJ *(dieu)* immortal; *(bonheur, gloire)* immortal, everlasting, eternal

NM,F **1** *Myth* Immortal **2** *(académicien)* **les Immortels** = the members of the "Académie française"

❑ **immortelle** NF *Bot* everlasting (flower), immortelle

immotivé, -e [imɔtive] ADJ **1** *(attaque, décision, demande)* unmotivated; *(peur, allégation)* groundless **2** *Ling* unmotivated

immuabilité [imɥabilite] NF *Jur* immutability

immuable [imɥabl] ADJ *(principes, vérités, amour)* immutable, unchanging; *(sourire)* unchanging, fixed; *(politesse)* eternal, unfailing; *(opinion)* unwavering, unchanging

immuablement [imɥablmɑ̃] ADV eternally, perpetually, immutably; **une ville i. brumeuse** a perpetually foggy town

immun, -e [imœ̃, -yn] ADJ *Méd* immune

immunisant, -e [imynizɑ̃, -ɑ̃t] ADJ *Méd* immunizing

immunisation [imynizasjɔ̃] NF *Méd* immunization

immuniser [3] [imynize] VT *Méd* to immunize; **i. qn contre qch** to immunize sb against sth; **depuis le temps qu'elle me critique, je suis immunisé!** she's been criticizing me for so long, I'm immune to it now!; **son échec l'a immunisé contre l'aventurisme politique** his failure has cured him of political adventurism

immunitaire [imynitɛr] ADJ *Biol* immune; **réaction i.** immune reaction; **système i.** immune system

immunité [imynite] NF **1** *Jur* immunity; **i. diplomatique** diplomatic immunity; **i. d'exécution** immunity from execution; **i. fiscale** immunity from taxation; **i. de juridiction** immunity from jurisdiction; **i. parlementaire** parliamentary privilege; **i. souveraine** sovereign immunity **2** *Biol* immunity; **acquérir une i. (à)** to become immune (to) *or* immunized (against); **i. acquise** acquired immunity; **i. à médiation cellulaire** cell-mediated immunity; **i. naturelle** natural immunity; **i. passive** passive immunity

immunochimie [imynoʃimi] NF *Méd* immunochemistry

immunocompétent, -e [imynokɔ̃petɑ̃, -ɑ̃t] ADJ *Biol* immunocompetent

immunodéficience [imynodefisjɑ̃s] NF *Méd* immunodeficiency

immunodéficitaire [imynodefisitɛr] ADJ *Méd* immunodeficient

immunodépresseur [imynodeprɛsœr] NM *Méd* immunodepressant, immunosuppressive

immunodépressif, -ive [imynodepresif, -iv] ADJ *Méd* immunodepressive, immunosuppressive

immunodépression [imynodepresjɔ̃] NF *Méd* immunodepression

immunodéprimé, -e [imynodeprime] *Méd* ADJ immunodepressed

NM,F person with immunodepression

immuno-essai [imynoɛsɛ] (*pl* **immuno-essais**) NM *Biol* immunoassay

immunofluorescence [imynoflyɔresɑ̃s] NF *Biol* immunofluorescence

immunogène [imynoʒɛn] ADJ *Biol & Med* immunogenic

immunogénétique [imynoʒenetik] NF immunogenetics *(singulier)*

immunoglobuline [imynoglɔbylin] NF *Biol* immunoglobulin

immunologie [imynolɔʒi] NF immunology

immunologique [imynolɔʒik] ADJ immunological

immunologiste [imynolɔʒist] NMF immunologist

immunopathologie [imynopatɔlɔʒi] NF *Méd* immunopathology

immunostimulant, -e [imynostimylɑ̃, -ɑ̃t] *Biol* ADJ immunostimulatory

NM immunostimulant

immunosuppresseur [imynosyprɛsœr] NM *Méd* immunosuppressant

immunosuppressif, -ive [imynosypresif, -iv] ADJ *Méd* immunosuppressive

immunosuppression [imynosypresjɔ̃] NF *Méd* immunosuppression

immunothérapie [imynoterapi] NF immunotherapy

immunotransfusion [imynotrɑ̃sfyzjɔ̃] NF *Méd* immunotransfusion

immunsérum [imynserɔm] NM *Méd* immune serum

immutabilité [imytabilite] NF *Jur* immutability

impact [ɛ̃pakt] NM **1** *(choc → de corps)* impact, collision; *(→ de projectiles)* impact; **au moment de l'i.** on impact; **point d'i.** point of impact **2** *(influence, effet → de mesures)* impact, effect; *(→ d'une publicité, d'une campagne)* impact; *(→ d'un mouvement, d'un artiste)* impact, influence; **les sondages ont-ils un grand i. sur le résultat des élections?** do opinion polls have a major impact on election results?; *Écol* **étude d'i. (sur l'environnement)** environmental

impact assessment; **i. à long terme** long-term impact

impactite [ɛ̃paktit] NF *Minér* impactite

impair, -e [ɛ̃pɛr] ADJ **1** *(chiffre)* odd, uneven; **les jours impairs** odd *or* odd-numbered days; **les années impaires** odd *or* odd-numbered years; **le côté i.** *(dans la rue)* the uneven numbers **2** *Littérature (vers)* irregular *(having an odd number of syllables)* **3** *Anat* single, *Spéc* azygous **4** *Rail (voie, train)* down

NM **1** *(bévue)* blunder; **faire** *ou* **commettre un i.** to (make a) blunder **2** *(au jeu)* **l'i.** odd numbers; *(à la roulette)* impair

impala [impala] NM *Zool* impala

impalpable [ɛ̃palpabl] ADJ impalpable, intangible

impaludation [ɛ̃palydasjɔ̃] NF *Méd* malarial infection; **i. thérapeutique** malaria therapy

impaludé, -e [ɛ̃palyde] ADJ *(région)* malaria-infested, malarious

impaluder [3] [ɛ̃palyde] VT *Méd* to give malaria therapy to

impanation [ɛ̃panasjɔ̃] NF *Rel* impanation

imparable [ɛ̃parabl] ADJ **1** *(coup, ballon)* unstoppable **2** *(argument)* unanswerable; *(logique)* irrefutable

impardonnable [ɛ̃pardɔnabl] ADJ *(erreur, oubli)* unforgivable, inexcusable; **tu es i. d'avoir oublié son anniversaire** it's unforgivable *of or* inexcusable for you to have forgotten his/her birthday; **j'ai encore pris votre parapluie, je suis i.!** I've taken your umbrella again, how unforgivable of me!

imparfait, -e [ɛ̃parfɛ, -ɛt] ADJ **1** *(incomplet)* imperfect, partial; **une connaissance imparfaite du problème** imperfect *or* insufficient knowledge of the problem; **guérison imparfaite** incomplete recovery **2** *(personne)* imperfect; **l'homme est une créature imparfaite** Man is an imperfect creature **3** *(inexact)* inaccurate; **une image imparfaite de la réalité** an inaccurate picture of reality

NM *Ling* **l'i.** the imperfect (tense); **l'i. du subjonctif** the imperfect subjunctive; **à l'i.** in the imperfect

imparfaitement [ɛ̃parfɛtmɑ̃] ADV imperfectly

imparidigité, -e [ɛ̃paridiʒite] *Zool* ADJ imparidigitate

NM imparidigitate animal

imparipenné, -e [ɛ̃paripɛne] ADJ *Bot* imparipinnate

imparisyllabique [ɛ̃parisilabik] *Ling* ADJ imparisyllabic

NM *(nom)* imparisyllabic noun; *(adjectif)* imparisyllabic adjective

imparité [ɛ̃parite] NF imparity, oddness

impartageable [ɛ̃partaʒabl] ADJ *(expérience)* which cannot be shared; *(domaine)* indivisible

impartial, -e, -aux, -ales [ɛ̃parsjal, -o] ADJ impartial, unprejudiced, unbiased

impartialement [ɛ̃parsjalmɑ̃] ADV impartially, without prejudice *or* bias

impartialité [ɛ̃parsjalite] NF impartiality, fairness; **juger avec i.** to judge impartially

impartir [32] [ɛ̃partir] VT **1** *(temps)* **i. un délai à qn** to grant sb an extension; **le temps qui vous était imparti est écoulé** you have used up the time allotted to you **2** *Littéraire (don)* to bestow (**à** on); **en vertu des pouvoirs qui me sont impartis** by virtue of the powers (that are) vested in me **3** *Jur (droit, faveur)* to grant (**à** to)

impartition [ɛ̃partisjɔ̃] NF *Écon* subcontracting

impasse [ɛ̃pas] NF **1** *(rue)* dead end, cul-de-sac; **i.** *(sur panneau)* no through road

2 *(situation)* impasse, blind alley; **nous sommes dans l'i.** we have reached an impasse *or* a stalemate; **il faut absolument faire sortir les négociations de l'i.** we must break the deadlock in the negotiations; *Fin* **i. budgétaire** budget deficit

3 *Fam Arg scol* **j'ai fait une i. sur la Seconde Guerre mondiale** I *Br* missed out *or Am* skipped (over) World War II in my revision

4 *Cartes* finesse; **faire une i.** to (make a) finesse; **j'ai fait l'i. au roi** I finessed against the king

impassibilité [ɛ̃pasibilite] NF impassiveness, impassivity, composure; **être d'une grande i.** to show great composure

impassible [ɛ̃pasibl] ADJ impassive, imperturbable

impassiblement [ɛ̃pasibləmɑ̃] ADV impassively, imperturbably

impatiemment [ɛ̃pasjamɑ̃] ADV impatiently; **nous attendons i. le résultat** we eagerly await the result

impatience [ɛ̃pasjɑ̃s] NF impatience; **avec i.** impatiently, with impatience; **sans i.** patiently; **donner des signes d'i.** to show signs of impatience

impatiens [ɛ̃pasjɑ̃s] NF *Bot* balsam, *Br* busy lizzie, *Spéc* impatiens

impatient, -e [ɛ̃pasjɑ̃, -ɑ̃t] ADJ (*personne, geste*) impatient; **d'un air i.** impatiently; **i. de commencer** impatient to start; **êtes-vous i. de rentrer?** are you anxious *or* eager to get home?
□ **impatiente** NF *Bot* balsam, *Br* busy lizzie, *Spéc* impatiens

impatienter [3] [ɛ̃pasjɑ̃te] VT to annoy, to irritate; **son entêtement a fini par m'i.** his/her stubbornness made me lose my patience in the end, I finally lost patience with his/her stubbornness
▸**s'impatienter** VPR (*dans une attente*) to grow or to become impatient; (*dans une discussion*) to lose one's patience; **j'ai fini par m'i.** I lost patience in the end; **s'i. de qch** to get impatient with sth; **s'i. contre qn** to get impatient with sb

impatronisation [ɛ̃patrɔnizasjɔ̃] NF *Littéraire* imposing one's authority

impatroniser [3] [ɛ̃patrɔnize] **s'impatroniser** VPR *Littéraire* to impose one's authority

impavide [ɛ̃pavid] ADJ *Littéraire* impassive, unruffled, composed

impayable [ɛ̃pɛjabl] ADJ *Fam* priceless; **il est vraiment i.!** he's priceless *or* a scream!

impayé, -e [ɛ̃pɛje] ADJ (*facture*) unpaid; (*dette*) outstanding; (*comptes*) unsettled; (*effet*) dishonoured; **tous les effets impayés le 8 mai** all bills not settled by 8 May
NM (*somme*) outstanding payment

impeachment [impitʃmɛnt] NM impeachment

impec [ɛ̃pɛk] *Fam* ADJ (*très propre*) spotless; (*parfait*) perfect▪
ADV perfectly▪; **tout s'est passé i.** everything went off like a dream; **ils nous ont reçus i.** they made us incredibly welcome; **c'est du travail de pro, il a fait ça i.** it's a really professional job, his work was faultless▪

impeccable [ɛ̃pekabl] ADJ **1** (*propre et net → intérieur, vêtement*) spotless, impeccable; (*→ coiffure, ongles*) impeccable; **et que les escaliers soient impeccables!** and I don't want to see a speck of dirt on the stairs!
2 (*parfait → manières, travail*) impeccable, flawless, perfect; **il parle un espagnol i.** he speaks impeccable *or* perfect Spanish; **d'une propreté i.** impeccably clean; *Fam* **10 heures, ça te va? – oui, i.!** would 10 o'clock suit you? – yes, great *or* perfect!
3 *Rel* impeccable

impeccablement [ɛ̃pekabləmɑ̃] ADV impeccably; **elle parle i. russe** she speaks impeccable *or* perfect Russian

impécunieux, -euse [ɛ̃pekynjø, -øz] ADJ *Littéraire* impecunious, penurious

impécuniosité [ɛ̃pekynjozite] NF *Littéraire* impecuniosity, penury

impédance [ɛ̃pedɑ̃s] NF *Phys* impedance; **i. acoustique** sound *or* acoustic impedance; **i. du vide** *ou* **de l'espace** (intrinsic) impedance in the vacuum

impedimenta [ɛ̃pedimɛ̃ta] NMPL *Mil & Littéraire* impedimenta

impénétrabilité [ɛ̃penetrabilite] NF (*d'une forêt, d'une citadelle, d'un texte, d'un mystère*) impenetrability; (*d'une personne, d'un air, d'un visage*) inscrutability

impénétrable [ɛ̃penetrabl] ADJ (*forêt, citadelle, texte, mystère*) impenetrable; (*personne, air, visage*) inscrutable

impénitence [ɛ̃penitɑ̃s] NF *Rel* impenitence, impenitent state

impénitent, -e [ɛ̃penitɑ̃, -ɑ̃t] ADJ **1** *Rel* impenitent, unrepentant **2** (*buveur, fumeur*) inveterate

impensable [ɛ̃pɑ̃sabl] ADJ (*inconcevable*) unthinkable, inconceivable; (*incroyable*) unbelievable; **ç'aurait été i. il y a dix ans** it would have been unthinkable ten years ago

impenses [ɛ̃pɑ̃s] NFPL *Jur* expenses

imper [ɛ̃pɛr] NM *Fam* raincoat▪, *Br* mac

impératif, -ive [ɛ̃peratif, -iv] ADJ **1** (*qui s'impose → mesure, intervention*) imperative, urgent, vital; (*→ besoin, date*) imperative; **il est i. de...** it is imperative *or* essential to... **2** (*de commandement → appel, geste, voix*) imperative, peremptory **3** *Ling* imperative
NM **1** (*souvent pl*) (*exigence*) requirement, necessity; **savoir nager est un i.** it is essential to be able to swim; **les impératifs de la mode** the dictates of fashion; **les impératifs du direct** the constraints of live broadcasting; *Phil* **l'i. catégorique** the (categorical) imperative **2** *Ling* **l'i.** the imperative (mood); **à l'i.** in the imperative

impérativement [ɛ̃perativmɑ̃] ADV **il faut que je termine i. pour ce soir** it's essential that I should finish tonight

impératrice [ɛ̃peratris] NF empress

imperceptibilité [ɛ̃persɛptibilite] NF imperceptibility

imperceptible [ɛ̃persɛptibl] ADJ imperceptible (à to); **de manière i.** imperceptibly; **elle eut un sourire i.** she gave a barely perceptible smile; **i. à l'œil nu** imperceptible to the naked eye

imperceptiblement [ɛ̃persɛptibləmɑ̃] ADV imperceptibly; **sourire i.** to give a barely perceptible smile

imperdable [ɛ̃perdabl] ADJ **ce match est i.!** this is a match you can't lose!
NF *Suisse* safety pin

imperfectible [ɛ̃perfɛktibl] ADJ non-perfectible

imperfectif, -ive [ɛ̃perfɛktif, -iv] *Ling* ADJ imperfective
NM **l'i.** the imperfective; **à l'i.** in the imperfective

imperfection [ɛ̃perfɛksjɔ̃] NF **1** (*défaut → d'un tissu, d'un cuir*) imperfection, defect; (*→ d'une personne*) imperfection, shortcoming; (*→ d'un style, d'une œuvre*) imperfection, weakness; (*→ d'un système*) shortcoming; **toutes les petites imperfections de la peau** all the small blemishes on the skin **2** (*état*) imperfection

imperfective [ɛ̃perfɛktiv] *voir* **imperfectif**

imperforation [ɛ̃perfɔrasjɔ̃] NF *Méd* imperforation

impérial, -e, -aux, -ales [ɛ̃perjal, -o] ADJ **1** *Hist & Pol* imperial **2** *Fig* (*allure, manières*) imperial, majestic **3** *Com* imperial, of superior quality
□ **impériale** NF **1** (*étage*) top deck; **bus/rame à impériale** double-decker bus/train **2** (*dais*) crown; (*de lit*) (domed) tester **3** *Cartes* royal flush **4** (*barbe*) imperial

impérialement [ɛ̃perjalmɑ̃] ADV imperially, majestically

impérialisme [ɛ̃perjalism] NM imperialism

impérialiste [ɛ̃perjalist] ADJ imperialist
NMF imperialist

impériaux [ɛ̃perjo] NMPL *Hist* **les I.** the Imperials

impérieuse [ɛ̃perjøz] *voir* **impérieux**

impérieusement [ɛ̃perjøzmɑ̃] ADV **1** (*de façon pressante*) urgently **2** (*autoritairement*) imperiously, peremptorily

impérieux, -euse [ɛ̃perjø, -øz] ADJ **1** (*irrésistible → désir*) urgent, compelling, pressing; **un besoin i.** a pressing need **2** (*de commandement → appel, personne, voix*) imperious, peremptory; **d'un ton i.** in a commanding tone

impérissable [ɛ̃perisabl] ADJ (*vérité*) eternal, *Sout* imperishable; (*splendeur*) undying; (*gloire*) everlasting, eternal; (*souvenir*) enduring; **garder un souvenir i. de qch** to have an enduring memory of sth; **ce film ne me laissera pas un souvenir i.** that film's pretty forgettable

impéritie [ɛ̃perisi] NF *Littéraire* incompetence

imperium [ɛ̃perjɔm] NM *Antiq* imperium

imperméabilisant, -e [ɛ̃pɛrmeabilizɑ̃, -ɑ̃t] ADJ waterproofing
NM waterproofing (substance)

imperméabilisation [ɛ̃pɛrmeabilizasjɔ̃] NF waterproofing

imperméabiliser [3] [ɛ̃pɛrmeabilize] VT to (make) waterproof *or* rainproof

imperméabilité [ɛ̃pɛrmeabilite] NF **1** (*gén*) & *Géol* impermeability **2** (*incompréhension*) imperviousness (à to)

imperméable [ɛ̃pɛrmeabl] ADJ **1** *Géol* impermeable **2** (*combinaison de plongée*) waterproof;

(*enduit intérieur*) waterproof, *Spéc* water-resistant; (*vêtement, chaussure, enduit extérieur*) waterproof, rainproof **3** (*insensible*) **être i. à** to be impervious to
NM (*vêtement*) raincoat

impersonnalité [ɛ̃persɔnalite] NF impersonality

impersonnel, -elle [ɛ̃persɔnɛl] ADJ **1** (*atmosphère, décor, ton*) impersonal, cold; **de manière impersonnelle** impersonally **2** (*approche, texte*) impersonal **3** *Ling* impersonal

impersonnellement [ɛ̃persɔnɛlmɑ̃] ADV impersonally

impertinence [ɛ̃pertinɑ̃s] NF **1** (*caractère*) impertinence, impudence, effrontery; **avec i.** impertinently; **quelle i.!** how impertinent *or* impudent! **2** (*parole*) impertinence, impertinent remark; **dire des impertinences à qn** to speak impertinently to sb **3** (*manque d'à-propos*) irrelevance, inappropriateness

impertinent, -e [ɛ̃pertinɑ̃, -ɑ̃t] ADJ **1** (*impudent*) impertinent, impudent **2** (*question, remarque*) irrelevant
NM,F impertinent person; **un petit i.** an impertinent little boy

imperturbabilité [ɛ̃pertyrbabilite] NF imperturbability

imperturbable [ɛ̃pertyrbabl] ADJ (*personne*) imperturbable; (*optimisme*) unshakeable; **il restait i.** he remained impassive *or* unruffled

imperturbablement [ɛ̃pertyrbabləmɑ̃] ADV imperturbably

impesanteur [ɛ̃pəzɑ̃tœr] NF weightlessness; **en état d'i., en i.** in weightless conditions

impétigineux, -euse [ɛ̃petiʒinø, -øz] ADJ *Méd* impetiginous

impétigo [ɛ̃petigo] NM *Méd* impetigo

impétrant, -e [ɛ̃petrɑ̃, -ɑ̃t] NM,F *Jur* recipient

impétration [ɛ̃petrasjɔ̃] NF *Jur* impetration

impétrer [18] [ɛ̃petre] VT *Jur* to impetrate

impétueuse [ɛ̃petɥøz] *voir* **impétueux**

impétueusement [ɛ̃petɥøzmɑ̃] ADV *Littéraire* impetuously, impulsively

impétueux, -euse [ɛ̃petɥø, -øz] ADJ **1** (*personne*) impetuous, impulsive; (*tempérament*) fiery, impetuous; (*amour*) impetuous **2** *Littéraire* (*flot, rythme*) impetuous, wild; (*torrent*) raging

impétuosité [ɛ̃petɥozite] NF **1** (*d'une personne, d'un tempérament*) impetuousness, impetuosity, foolhardiness **2** *Littéraire* (*des flots, d'un rythme*) impetuosity, impetuousness

impie [ɛ̃pi] *Littéraire* ADJ impious; **des paroles impies** blasphemy
NMF impious *or* ungodly person

impiété [ɛ̃pjete] NF *Littéraire* **1** (*caractère*) impiety, ungodliness **2** (*parole, acte*) impiety

impignoration [ɛ̃piɲɔrasjɔ̃] NF impignoration, pawning

impitoyable [ɛ̃pitwajabl] ADJ (*juge, adversaire*) merciless, pitiless; (*haine, combat*) merciless, relentless

impitoyablement [ɛ̃pitwajabləmɑ̃] ADV mercilessly, ruthlessly, pitilessly

implacabilité [ɛ̃plakabilite] NF *Littéraire* implacability, relentlessness

implacable [ɛ̃plakabl] ADJ **1** (*acharné, inflexible*) implacable; **une haine i.** implacable hatred **2** *Littéraire* (*inéluctable*) relentless, implacable; **avec une logique i.** with relentless logic

implacablement [ɛ̃plakabləmɑ̃] ADV implacably, mercilessly, relentlessly

implant [ɛ̃plɑ̃] NM *Méd* implant; **i. dentaire** (dental) implant; **implants capillaires** hair graft; **il s'est fait faire des implants** he had a hair graft; **implants mammaires** breast implants

implantable [ɛ̃plɑ̃tabl] ADJ *Méd* implantable

implantation [ɛ̃plɑ̃tasjɔ̃] NF **1** (*établissement → d'une entreprise*) establishment, setting up; (*→ d'un parti politique*) establishment; (*→ d'une mode, d'une coutume*) introduction; **l'i. d'une usine a permis la création de cent emplois** the setting up of a factory has led to the creation of one hundred jobs
2 (*d'un magasin, d'un rayon*) location
3 (*des cheveux*) hairline
4 *Méd* (lateral) implantation; (*en odontologie*) implant
5 *Électron* implantation; **i. ionique** ion implantation

implanté, -e [ɛ̃plɑ̃te] ADJ **une tradition bien implantée** a well-established tradition; **une croyance/habitude bien implantée** an ingrained belief/habit; **notre société est implantée dans dix pays** our company operates in ten countries

implanter [3] [ɛ̃plɑ̃te] VT **1** *(bâtiment, magasin, rayon)* to locate; *(entreprise)* to set up, to establish, to locate; *(idées)* to implant; *(coutumes, mode)* to introduce; *(parti politique)* to establish; **i. un produit sur le marché** to establish a product on the market **2** *Méd* to implant **3** *Constr (tracer)* to stake out

▸**s'implanter** VPR *(entreprise, ville, rayon)* to be set up *or* located *or* established; *(peuple)* to settle; *(coutumes, mode)* to become established; **s'i. sur un marché** to establish oneself in a market

implantologie [ɛ̃plɑ̃tɔlɔʒi] NF *(odontologie)* implant dentistry

implexe [ɛ̃plɛks] ADJ *Littéraire* intricate, complex

implication [ɛ̃plikasjɔ̃] NF **1** *(participation)* involvement, implication **2** *Phil & Math* implication

❑ **implications** NFPL implications, consequences

implicite [ɛ̃plisit] ADJ **1** *(tacite)* implicit **2** *Ordinat (option, valeur)* default *(avant n)*

implicitement [ɛ̃plisitmɑ̃] ADV **1** *(tacitement)* implicitly **2** *Ordinat* **toutes les variables prennent i. la valeur 0** all the variables have the default value 0

impliqué, -e [ɛ̃plike] ADJ involved; **être i. dans qch** to be involved in sth; **les personnes impliquées** the people involved

impliquer [3] [ɛ̃plike] VT **1** *(compromettre)* to implicate, to involve; **i. qn dans qch** to implicate sb in sth; **elle ne se sent pas très impliquée dans son travail** she's not very involved in her work **2** *(supposer → sujet: terme, phrase)* to imply **3** *(entraîner → dépenses, remaniements)* to imply, to involve, to entail; **ce poste implique d'être souvent en déplacement** the job involves a lot of travelling **4** *Math* **p implique q** if p then q

▸**s'impliquer** VPR **s'i. dans qch** to get (oneself) involved in sth

implorant, -e [ɛ̃plɔrɑ̃, -ɑ̃t] ADJ *Littéraire (voix, regard, geste)* imploring, beseeching; **d'un ton i.** imploringly, beseechingly

imploration [ɛ̃plɔrasjɔ̃] NF *Littéraire* entreaty

implorer [3] [ɛ̃plɔre] VT **1** *(solliciter)* to implore, to beseech; **i. le pardon de qn** to beg sb's forgiveness **2** *(supplier)* **i. qn de faire qch** to implore *or* to beg sb to do sth; **i. qn du regard** to give sb an imploring look

imploser [3] [ɛ̃ploze] VI to implode

implosif, -ive [ɛ̃plozif, -iv] *Ling* ADJ implosive

❑ **implosive** NF implosive

implosion [ɛ̃plozjɔ̃] NF *Ling & Phys* implosion

implosive [ɛ̃ploziv] *voir* **implosif**

impluvium [ɛ̃plyvjɔm] NM *Antiq* impluvium

impolarisable [ɛ̃polarizabl] ADJ *Élec* unpolarizable

impoli, -e [ɛ̃pɔli] ADJ impolite, rude, uncivil; **être i. envers qn** to be impolite *or* rude to sb

NM,F impolite *or* ill-mannered person

impoliment [ɛ̃pɔlimɑ̃] ADV impolitely, rudely

impolitesse [ɛ̃pɔlitɛs] NF **1** *(caractère)* impoliteness, rudeness; **avec i.** impolitely, rudely; **quelle i.!** how rude!; **il est d'une i.!** he's so rude! **2** *(acte, parole)* impolite thing; **commettre une i.** to do something rude *or* impolite; **dire des impolitesses** to be impolite *or* rude, to say impolite things

impolitique [ɛ̃pɔlitik] ADJ impolitic, unwise

impondérabilité [ɛ̃pɔ̃derabilite] NF imponderability

impondérable [ɛ̃pɔ̃derabl] ADJ imponderable

NM *(gén pl)* imponderable; **les impondérables** the imponderables

impopulaire [ɛ̃pɔpylɛr] ADJ *(mesure, dirigeant)* unpopular

impopularité [ɛ̃pɔpylarite] NF unpopularity

import [ɛ̃pɔr] NM **1** *Com* importation **2** *Belg (montant)* amount; **une facture d'un i. de 3000 euros** a bill for 3,000 euros **3** *Ordinat* **i. de données** data import

importable [ɛ̃pɔrtabl] ADJ **1** *Écon* importable **2** *(habit)* unwearable

importance [ɛ̃pɔrtɑ̃s] NF **1** *(qualitative → d'une décision, d'un discours, d'une personne)* importance, significance; **de peu d'i.** of little importance, of no great significance; **avoir de l'i.** to be of importance, to matter; **tout ceci a de l'i.** all this is of importance; **tout ceci n'a plus d'i.** none of this matters any longer; **cela a beaucoup d'i. pour moi** it's very important to me, it matters a lot to me; **sans i.** *(personne)* unimportant, insignificant; *(fait)* of no importance, irrelevant; *(somme)* insignificant, trifling; **la date est sans i.** the date is irrelevant *or* is of no importance; **que disais-tu? – c'est sans i.** what were you saying? – it's of no importance *or* it doesn't matter; **accorder** *ou* **attacher trop d'i. à qch** to attach too much importance *or* significance to sth; **et alors, quelle i.?** so, what does it matter?; **se donner de l'i.** to act important

2 *(quantitative → d'un effectif, d'une somme, d'une agglomération)* size; *(→ de dégâts, de pertes)* extent; **prendre de l'i.** *(entreprise)* to expand; *(mouvement)* to gain ground; **notre coopérative prend de plus en plus d'i.** our cooperative is expanding *or* is getting bigger and bigger; **une entreprise d'i. moyenne** a medium-sized business

❑ **d'importance** ADJ important ADV *Littéraire* soundly, thoroughly; **il s'est fait rosser d'i.** he was soundly thrashed

important, -e [ɛ̃pɔrtɑ̃, -ɑ̃t] ADJ **1** *(qualitativement → découverte, témoignage, rencontre, personnalité)* important; *(→ date, changement)* important, significant; *(→ conséquence)* important, serious, far-reaching; *(→ position)* important, high; **peu i.** unimportant; **j'ai quelque chose de très i. à te dire** I've got something very important to tell you; **il est i. que tu viennes** it's important (that) you come; **ta carrière n'est-elle pas importante pour toi?** isn't your career important to you?; **c'est i. pour moi de connaître la vérité** finding out the truth matters *or* is important to me

2 *(quantitativement → collection, effectif)* sizeable, large; *(→ ville)* large, major; *(→ augmentation, proportion)* substantial, significant, large; *(→ somme)* substantial, considerable, sizeable; *(→ retard)* considerable; *(→ dégâts)* considerable, extensive; **peu i.** small

3 *(présomptueux)* **prendre** *ou* **se donner des airs importants** to act important, to give oneself airs

NM,F *(personne)* **faire l'i.** to act important

NM **l'i., c'est de…** the important thing is to…, the main thing is to…; **l'i., c'est que tu sois satisfait** the important *or* main thing is for you to be satisfied

importateur, -trice [ɛ̃pɔrtatœr, -tris] ADJ importing; **les pays importateurs de pétrole** oil-importing countries

NM,F importer; **c'est l'i. exclusif de cette marque pour la France** they are the sole French importers of this brand

importation [ɛ̃pɔrtasjɔ̃] NF **1** *Écon (action)* importing; *(produit)* import, importation; **produit d'i.** imported product, import; **droits/licence d'i.** import duties/licence; **i. en franchise** duty-free import; **i. temporaire** temporary importation **2** *(d'un mouvement, d'une invention)* introduction, importation; *(d'un animal)* importing

❑ **importations** NFPL *Com* imports; **nos importations dépassent nos exportations** we import more than we export; **importations grises** grey imports; **importations invisibles** invisible imports; **importations parallèles** parallel imports; **importations visibles** visible imports

importatrice [ɛ̃pɔrtatris] *voir* **importateur**

importer [3] [ɛ̃pɔrte] VT **1** *(marchandises, main-d'œuvre, brevets)* to import; *(mode)* to introduce, to import; *(animal, végétal)* to import, to introduce into the country; *(idée)* to import, to bring in; **i. des marchandises des États-Unis en France** to import goods from the United States into France; **musique importée des États-Unis** music imported from the United States **2** *Ordinat* to import (**depuis** from)

VI *(avoir de l'importance)* to matter (**à** to); **son âge importe peu** his/her age is of little importance *or* doesn't matter much; **ton opinion m'importe beaucoup** your opinion is very important *or* matters a lot to me; **peu importe** *(ce n'est pas grave)* it doesn't matter; *(ça m'est égal)* I don't mind; **peu importe le prix** the price isn't important *or* doesn't matter; **peu importe que le voile soit blanc ou écru** it doesn't matter much whether the veil is white or beige; **qu'importe!** what does it matter!; **qu'importe qu'il vienne ou non?** what does it matter whether he comes or not?; **ce qui importe avant tout c'est que tu sois heureuse** the most important thing *or* what matters most is your happiness; **peu m'importe!** it doesn't matter to me!

V IMPERSONNEL **il importe de ne pas faire d'erreurs** it's important not to make mistakes; **il importe qu'elle soit consciente de ses responsabilités** it's important that she should be aware of her responsibilities; **il importe que vous y soyez** it's important that you're there

import-export [ɛ̃pɔrɛkspɔr] *(pl* **imports-exports***)* NM import-export; **il travaille dans l'i.** he works in the import-export business

importun, -e [ɛ̃pɔrtœ̃, -yn] ADJ *(personne, visiteur, question)* importunate; *(arrivée, remarque)* ill-timed; **je crains d'être i. en restant** I would not wish to outstay my welcome; **les insectes importuns l'agaçaient** the troublesome insects irritated him/her

NM,F pest, nuisance

importunément [ɛ̃pɔrtynemɑ̃] ADV *Littéraire* **1** *(fâcheusement)* irritatingly, importunately **2** *(mal à propos)* inopportunely

importuner [3] [ɛ̃pɔrtyne] VT *(sujet: musique, insecte)* to bother, to disturb, to annoy; *(sujet: personne → ennuyer)* to importune, to bother; *(→ déranger)* to disturb; **j'espère que je ne vous importune pas** I hope I'm not disturbing you; **de crainte de les i. avec mes problèmes** for fear of bothering them with my problems

importunité [ɛ̃pɔrtynite] NF *Littéraire (d'une question, d'une arrivée)* untimeliness, importunity

imposable [ɛ̃pozabl] ADJ *(revenu)* taxable; *(personne)* liable for tax; *(propriété)* rateable; **non i.** *(revenu, personne)* not liable for tax

imposant, -e [ɛ̃pozɑ̃, -ɑ̃t] ADJ imposing, impressive; **une imposante majorité** an impressive majority

imposé, -e [ɛ̃poze] ADJ **1** *Sport voir* **figure** **2** *Com voir* **prix** **3** *(soumis à l'impôt)* taxed; **être lourdement i.** to be heavily taxed

NM,F *(contribuable)* taxpayer

NM *Sport (exercice)* compulsory exercise

❑ **imposée** NF *Sport (figure)* compulsory figure

imposer [3] [ɛ̃poze] VT **1** *(fixer → règlement, discipline)* to impose, to enforce; *(→ méthode, délai, corvée)* to impose; **i. qch à qn** to force sth on sb; **i. le silence à qn** to impose silence on sb; **le règlement nous impose le secret absolu** the rules compel us to absolute secrecy; **i. un effort à qn** to force sb to make an effort; **i. sa volonté/son point de vue** to impose one's will/one's ideas; **i. sa loi (à qn)** to lay down the law (to sb); **il a imposé son fils dans l'entreprise** he foisted his son on the company

2 *(provoquer)* **i. l'admiration/le respect** to command admiration/respect; **cette affaire impose la prudence/la discrétion** this matter requires prudence/discretion

3 *(rendre célèbre)* **i. son nom** *(personne)* to make oneself known; *(entreprise)* to become established

4 *Fin (personne, revenu)* to tax; *(propriété)* to levy a rate on; **i. qn/qch** to tax sb/sth; **imposé à 33 pour cent** taxed at 33 percent; **i. des droits sur qch** to impose *or* to put a tax on sth, to tax sth

5 *Typ* to impose

6 *Rel* **i. les mains** to lay on hands

7 *(locutions)* **en i.** to be impressive; **elle en impose par son savoir-faire** her know-how is impressive; **en i. à qn** to impress sb; **s'en laisser i.** to let oneself be intimidated

▸**s'imposer** VPR **1** *(se faire accepter de force)* to impose oneself; **de peur de s'i.** for fear of being in the way *or* of imposing

2 *(se faire reconnaître)* to stand out; **elle s'impose actuellement comme la meilleure cycliste** she has established herself as today's top cyclist; **Bordeaux s'est imposé (par) 5 à 2** Bordeaux won 5–2; **s'i. dans un domaine** to make a name for oneself in a field; **elle s'est imposée par sa compétence** she made a name for herself through sheer ability; **la solution s'impose comme la seule viable** this stands out as the only viable solution; **cette solution s'est imposée d'elle-même** it seemed the obvious solution

3 *(être inévitable)* to be necessary; **les modifications qui s'imposent** the adjustments that have to be made; **je crois qu'une lettre à leur service commercial s'impose** I think a letter to their sales department is called for; **cette dernière remarque ne s'imposait pas** that last remark was unnecessary *or* uncalled for; **une coupe de champagne s'impose!** this calls for champagne!

4 s'i. qch *(se fixer)* to impose sth on oneself; **s'i. un effort/un sacrifice** to force oneself to make an effort/a sacrifice; **s'i. la discrétion** to make it a rule to be discreet; **s'i. un régime sévère** to follow a strict diet; **s'i. de faire qch** to make it a rule to do sth

imposeur [ɛ̃pozœr] **NM** *Typ* form setter, imposer

imposition [ɛ̃pozisjɔ̃] **NF** *Fin (procédé)* taxation; *(impôt)* tax; **i. en cascade** cascade taxation; **i. des entreprises** business taxation; **i. forfaitaire** basic-rate taxation; **i. progressive** progressive taxation; **i. régressive** regressive taxation; **i. à la source** taxation at source **2** *Typ* imposition **3** *Rel* **i. des mains** laying on *or* *Sout* imposition of hands

impossibilité [ɛ̃posibilite] **NF** impossibility; **se heurter à une i.** to come up against an insurmountable problem; **être** *ou* **se trouver dans l'i. de faire qch** to be unable to do sth; **je suis dans l'i. de me déplacer** I'm unable to travel, it's impossible for me to travel; **vu l'i. dans laquelle je me trouve d'assister à la réunion** since I'm unable to attend the meeting, since it's impossible for me to attend the meeting

impossible [ɛ̃posibl] **ADJ 1** *(infaisable)* impossible; **i. à déchiffrer** impossible to decipher; **ton problème est i. à résoudre** there is no answer to your problem; **il est i. de...** it's impossible *or* not possible to...; **il est i. qu'il revienne avant lundi** he can't possibly be back before Monday; **il m'est i. de te répondre** it's impossible for me to give you an answer, I can't possibly answer you; **désolé, cela m'est i.** I'm sorry but I can't (possibly); **il n'est pas i. que je vienne aussi** I might (just) *or* there's a chance I might come too; **est-ce que tu vas venir? – ce n'est pas i.** are you going to come? – it's not impossible *or* I might; **i. n'est pas français** there's no such word as ''can't''

2 *(insupportable → personne)* impossible, unbearable; *(→ situation)* impossible, intolerable; **vous lui rendez la vie i.** you're making life impossible for him/her, you're making his/her life a misery

3 *Fam (extravagant)* impossible, ridiculous, incredible; **il t'arrive toujours des trucs impossibles** the weirdest *or* wildest things are always happening to you; **à des heures impossibles** at the most ungodly hours; **un nom i.** a preposterous name

NM l'i. *(l'irréalisable)* the impossible; **tenter l'i.** to attempt the impossible; **ne me demande pas l'i.** don't ask me to do the impossible *or* to perform miracles; **nous ferons l'i.** we will do our utmost, we will move heaven and earth; *Prov* **à l'i. nul n'est tenu** = nobody is expected to do the impossible

❏ **par impossible ADV si par i.** if by any (remote) chance *or* by some miracle

imposte [ɛ̃pɔst] **NF 1** *Archit (pierre en saillie)* impost **2** *Menuis (d'une porte, d'une fenêtre) Br* fanlight, *Am* transom

imposteur [ɛ̃pɔstœr] **NM** impostor

imposture [ɛ̃pɔstyr] **NF** *Littéraire* fraud, (piece of) trickery, deception

impôt [ɛ̃po] **NM 1** *(prélèvement)* tax; **l'i.** taxation, taxes; **les impôts** *(sur le revenu)* income tax; **payer des impôts** to pay (income) tax; **payer 200 euros d'i.** to pay 200 euros in taxes *or* (in) tax; **c'est déductible des impôts** it's tax-deductible; *Fam* **écrire/aller aux impôts** *(à l'hôtel des impôts)* to write to/to go and see the tax people; **financé par l'i.** paid for out of taxes *or* with the taxpayers' money; **après/avant impôts** after/before tax; **i. sur les bénéfices** profit tax; **i. de Bourse** transaction tax; **i. sur le capital** capital tax; **i. sur le chiffre d'affaires** turnover *or* *Br* cascade tax; **i. à la consommation** output tax; **i. dégressif** sliding scale taxation, degressive taxation; **i. déguisé** hidden tax; **i. différé** deferred taxation; **i. direct** direct tax; **i. sur les dividendes** dividend tax; **i. sur les donations et les successions** gift and inheritance tax; **i. extraordinaire** emergency tax; **i. foncier** property tax; **i. forfaitaire** basic-rate tax; **i. sur les gains exceptionnels** windfall tax; *Anciennement* **i. sur les grandes fortunes** wealth tax; **i. indiciaire** wealth tax; **i. indirect** indirect tax; **impôts locaux** *Br* ≃ council tax, *Am* ≃ local property tax; **i. de luxe** tax on luxury goods; **i. sur la masse salariale** payroll tax; **i. négatif sur le revenu** negative income tax; **i. sur les plus-values** capital gains tax; **i. à la production** input tax; **i. progressif** progressive tax; *(sur le revenu)* graduated income tax; **i. proportionnel** proportional tax; **i. de quotité** coefficient tax; **i. retenu à la source** withholding tax; **i. sur le revenu** income tax; **i. sur le revenu des personnes physiques** income tax; **i. sur les sociétés** *Br* corporation tax, *Am* corporate income tax; **i. de solidarité sur la fortune** wealth tax; **i. sur le transfert des capitaux** capital transfer tax; **i. sur le travail** payroll tax

2 *Fig Littéraire* **l'i. du sang** the duty to serve one's country

impotence [ɛ̃pɔtɑ̃s] **NF** loss of mobility *(through old age)*, infirmity

impotent, -e [ɛ̃pɔtɑ̃, -ɑ̃t] **ADJ** *(personne)* infirm; *(membre)* withered

NM,F *(personne)* cripple

impraticabilité [ɛ̃pratikabilite] **NF 1** *(d'un col)* impassability; *(d'un terrain de sport)* unplayable condition; *(d'une route)* impracticability **2** *Littéraire (d'une méthode, d'une idée)* impracticability

impraticable [ɛ̃pratikabl] **ADJ 1** *(col)* inaccessible, impassable; *(fleuve)* unnavigable; *(aérodrome)* unfit for use; *(route)* impassable; *(terrain de sport)* unfit for play; **un chemin i. pour les voitures** a road unfit for cars **2** *Littéraire (méthode, idée)* unfeasible, unworkable, impracticable

imprécateur, -trice [ɛ̃prekatœr, -tris] **NM,F** *Littéraire* imprecator

imprécation [ɛ̃prekasjɔ̃] **NF** *Littéraire* imprecation, curse; **proférer des imprécations à l'encontre de qn** to call down curses upon sb's head, to inveigh against sb

imprécatoire [ɛ̃prekatwar] **ADJ** *Littéraire* imprecatory, damning

imprécatrice [ɛ̃prekatris] *voir* **imprécateur**

imprécaution [ɛ̃prekosjɔ̃] **NF** *Littéraire (absence de précaution)* want of precaution; *(imprudence)* incautiousness

imprécis, -e [ɛ̃presi, -iz] **ADJ 1** *(témoignage, souvenir, contours)* vague, imprecise **2** *(appareil, instrument)* imprecise, inaccurate

imprécision [ɛ̃presizjɔ̃] **NF 1** *(d'un souvenir, d'un témoignage)* vagueness, imprecision; *(de contours)* lack of definition **2** *(d'un appareil, d'un instrument)* inaccuracy, lack of precision

imprédictibilité [ɛ̃prediktibilite] **NF** unpredictability

imprédictible [ɛ̃prediktibl] **ADJ** unpredictable

imprégnation [ɛ̃preɲasjɔ̃] **NF 1** *(d'une matière)* impregnation, saturation; *(d'un esprit)* impregnation, inculcation, imbuing; **i. alcoolique** blood alcohol level **2** *Constr* treating, impregnation **3** *Menuis* steeping, *Spéc* impregnation **4** *Métal* impregnation **5** *Zool* imprinting

imprégner [18] [ɛ̃preɲe] **VT 1** *(imbiber)* to soak (**de** in), to impregnate (**de** with); **un coton imprégné d'alcool** a piece of *Br* cotton wool *or* *Am* absorbent cotton impregnated with alcohol; *Fig* **il est encore imprégné du souvenir de la guerre** his mind is still filled with memories of the war; **imprégné de préjugés** full of prejudice

2 *(être présent dans)* to permeate, to pervade, to fill; **cette odeur imprègne toute la maison** the smell permeates *or* pervades *or* fills the whole house; **l'odeur du tabac imprègne ses vêtements** his/her clothes reek of tobacco

▸ **s'imprégner VPR s'i. de** *(éponge, bois)* to become soaked *or* impregnated with; *(air)* to become permeated *or* filled with; *(personne, esprit)* to become immersed in *or* imbued with; **ils se sont imprégnés de culture orientale** they immersed themselves in Eastern culture

imprenable [ɛ̃prənabl] **ADJ 1** *Mil (ville)* impregnable; *(position)* unassailable **2** *(vue)* unobstructed; **avec vue i. sur la baie** with an unobstructed view of the bay

impréparation [ɛ̃preparasjɔ̃] **NF** unpreparedness, lack of preparation

imprésario, impresario [ɛ̃presarjo] *(pl* **impresarii** [-ri]) **NM** impresario

imprescriptibilité [ɛ̃prɛskriptibilite] **NF** *Jur* imprescriptibility, indefeasibility

imprescriptible [ɛ̃prɛskriptibl] **ADJ 1** *Jur* imprescriptible, indefeasible **2** *(éternel)* eternal

impressif, -ive [ɛ̃presif, -iv] **ADJ** *Littéraire* impressive

impression [ɛ̃presjɔ̃] **NF 1** *(effet, réaction)* impression; **premières impressions** first impressions; **faire bonne/mauvaise i. (sur qn)** to make a good/a bad impression (on sb); **faire une forte** *ou* **grosse i.** to make quite a strong impression; **il ne m'a pas fait une grande i.** he did not make a great impression on me; **faire i.** to make an impression, to be impressive; **il me fait l'i. de savoir ce qu'il veut** he strikes me as someone who knows what he wants; **il donne l'i. de s'ennuyer** he seems to be bored

2 *(sensation)* feeling; **une i. de bien-être** an impression *or* a feeling of well-being; **ça fait une drôle d'i. de s'entendre parler** it's a funny feeling, hearing yourself speak; **cela m'a fait une drôle d'i.** it really had a funny effect on me; **avoir l'i. que** *(croire)* to have a feeling that; **j'ai l'i. qu'elle ne viendra plus** I have a feeling (that) she won't come; **j'ai l'i. qu'elle est assez timide** I have the impression that *or* my impression of her is that she's rather shy; *Fam* **j'ai comme l'i. qu'il mentait** I have a hunch he was lying; **j'ai l'i. de l'avoir déjà vue** I've a feeling that I've seen her before

3 *Vieilli (empreinte)* impression, mark; **l'i. d'un cachet dans la cire** the impression *or* imprint of a seal on wax

4 *(motif, dessin)* pattern; **tissu à impressions géométriques** cloth with a geometrical pattern *or* print

5 *Typ* printing; **envoyer un manuscrit à l'i.** to send a manuscript off to press *or* the printer's; **le livre est à l'i.** the book is with the printer's *or* in (the) press; **la troisième i. d'un livre** the third impression *or* printing of a book; **i. continue** web-offset printing; **i. couleur** colour printing; **i. en deux couleurs** two-tone printing; **i. polychrome** chromatic printing; **i. en quadrichromie** process colours *or* four-colour printing; **i. en relief** relief printing; **i. en retiration** backing up; **i. sans presse** plateless printing; **i. en surcharge** overprinting; **i. en taille-douce** intaglio printing; **i. tête à queue** work and tumble; **i. tremblée** slurring; **i. au verso** backing up

6 *Ordinat* printing; **i. en arrière-plan** background (mode) printing; **i. bidirectionnelle** bidirectional printing; **i. en colonnes** column printing; **i. à la demande** print on demand; **i. écran** screen dump; **i. numérique** digital printing; **i. ombrée** shadow printing **i. en qualité brouillon** draft quality printing

7 *Phot* exposure

8 *(en peinture)* priming, ground

≡⬛≡

'Impression : soleil levant' *Monet* 'Impression: Sunrise'

impressionnabilité [ɛ̃presjɔnabilite] **NF 1** *Littéraire (émotivité)* impressionability **2** *Phot* (photo)sensitivity

impressionnable [ɛ̃presjɔnabl] **ADJ 1** *(émotif)* easily upset; **c'est quelqu'un de facilement i.** he's/she's very easily upset **2** *Phot* (photo)sensitive

impressionnant, -e [ɛ̃presjɔnɑ̃, -ɑ̃t] **ADJ 1** *(imposant → œuvre, personnalité)* impressive; *(→ portail, temple)* awe-inspiring; *(→ exploit)* impressive, stunning, sensational; *(→ somme)* considerable **2** *(bouleversant)* disturbing, upsetting

impressionner [ɛ̃presjɔne] **VT 1** *(frapper)* to impress; **être impressionné par qch** to be impressed by sth; **si tu crois que tu m'impressionnes!** don't think you impress me!; **se laisser i.** to let oneself be impressed **2** *(bouleverser)* to distress, to upset; **la vue du sang m'impressionne toujours** the sight of blood always upsets *or* distresses me **3** *Phot* to expose **4** *Physiol* to act on

impressionnisme [ɛ̃presjɔnism] **NM** impressionism

impressionniste [ɛ̃presjɔnist] **ADJ 1** *Beaux-Arts* impressionist **2** *(subjectif)* impressionistic
NMF impressionist

imprévisibilité [ɛ̃previzibilite] **NF** unpredictability

imprévisible [ɛ̃previzibl] **ADJ** *(temps, réaction, personne)* unpredictable; *(événement)* unforeseeable

imprévision [ɛ̃previzjɔ̃] **NF** lack of foresight

imprévoyance [ɛ̃prevwajɑ̃s] **NF** *(gén)* lack of foresight; *(financière)* improvidence

imprévoyant, -e [ɛ̃prevwajɑ̃, -ɑ̃t] **ADJ** *(gén)* lacking (in) foresight; *(financièrement)* improvident
NM,F improvident person

imprévu, -e [ɛ̃prevy] **ADJ** *(inattendu)* unexpected, unforeseen; **des dépenses imprévues** unforeseen expenses; **un dénouement i.** an unexpected *or* a surprise ending; **de manière imprévue** unexpectedly
NM 1 **l'i.** *(les surprises)* the unexpected; **un séjour plein d'i.** a stay full of surprises **2** *(événement)* unexpected event; **sauf i.** *ou* **à moins d'un i., je serai à l'heure** unless anything unforeseen happens *or* barring accidents, I'll be on time; **prévenez-moi en cas d'i.** let me know if anything crops up; **les imprévus de la vie** life's little surprises **3** *(dépense)* unforeseen *or* hidden expense

imprimabilité [ɛ̃primabilite] **NF** printability

imprimable [ɛ̃primabl] **ADJ** printable

imprimante [ɛ̃primɑ̃t] **NF** *Ordinat* printer; **i. à barre** bar printer; **i. à bulles (d'encre)** bubblejet printer; **i. à chaîne** chain printer; **i. couleur** colour printer; **i. feuille à feuille** sheet-fed printer; **i. graphique** graphics printer; **i. à impact** impact printer; **i. à jet d'encre** ink-jet printer; **i. (à) laser** laser printer; **i. (ligne) par ligne** line printer; **i. à marguerite** daisy-wheel printer; **i. matricielle** dot matrix printer; **i. parallèle** parallel printer; **i. par points** dot matrix printer; **i. photo** photo printer; **i. PostScript®** PostScript® printer; **i. à roues** wheel printer; **i. série** serial printer; **i. thermique, i. thermoélectrique** thermal printer

imprimatur [ɛ̃primatyr] **NM INV** imprimatur

imprimé [ɛ̃prime] **NM 1** *(brochure, livre)* printed book *or* booklet; **imprimés** *(sur une enveloppe)* printed matter; **i. publicitaire** advertising leaflet, publicity handout **2** *(formulaire)* (printed) form **3** *(étoffe)* printed fabric *or* material; **un i. à fleurs/à motifs géométriques** a flower/geometric print

imprimer [ɛ̃prime] **VT 1** *Typ (fabriquer)* to print (out); *(publier)* to print, to publish; **i. en offset** to offset
  2 *Tex* to print
  3 *Ordinat* to print (out); **i. un écran** to do a print screen
  4 *(transmettre)* to transmit, to impart, to give; **i. un mouvement à qch** to impart *or* to transmit a movement to sth

5 *Littéraire (marquer)* to imprint; **des traces de pas imprimées dans la neige** footprints in the snow; **il voulait i. tous ces détails dans sa mémoire** he wanted to impress all these details on his memory
  ▸**s'imprimer** **VPR** to be printed; *Ordinat (document)* to print

imprimerie [ɛ̃primri] **NF 1** *(technique)* printing
  2 *(établissement)* printing works *(singulier)*, printer's; *(atelier)* printing office *or* house; *Presse* print room; **le livre est parti à l'i.** the book's gone to the printer's; **i. intégrée** in-house printing office; **l'I. nationale** = the French government stationery office, *Br* ≃ HMSO, *Am* ≃ the Government Printing Office
  3 *(matériel)* printing press *or* machines; *(jouet)* printing set
  4 *(industrie)* **l'i.** the printing industry

imprimeur [ɛ̃primœr] **NM** *(industriel)* printer; *(ouvrier)* printer, print worker

impro [ɛ̃pro] **NF** *Fam Mus & Théât (abrév* **improvisation***)* improv

improbabilité [ɛ̃prɔbabilite] **NF** unlikelihood, improbability

improbable [ɛ̃prɔbabl] **ADJ** unlikely, improbable; **dans le cas très i. où...** in the very unlikely event that...

improbateur, -trice [ɛ̃prɔbatœr, -tris] *Littéraire* **ADJ** disapproving; **murmure i.** murmur of disapproval
  NM,F disapprover, censurer

improbation [ɛ̃prɔbasjɔ̃] **NF** *Littéraire* disapproval; **sa conduite a encouru l'i. générale** his/her conduct has incurred universal censure

improbatrice [ɛ̃prɔbatris] *voir* **improbateur**

improbité [ɛ̃prɔbite] **NF** *Littéraire* **1** *(manque de probité)* dishonesty, improbity **2** *(acte)* dishonest act

improductif, -ive [ɛ̃prɔdyktif, -iv] **ADJ** unproductive; *(capital)* unproductive, idle
  NM,F unproductive person; **les improductifs** the nonproductive members of society

improductivité [ɛ̃prɔdyktivite] **NF** unproductiveness, nonproductiveness

impromptu, -e [ɛ̃prɔ̃pty] **ADJ** *(improvisé → gén)* impromptu, unexpected, surprise *(avant n)*; *(→ repas)* impromptu; *(→ discours)* impromptu, off-the-cuff; **une visite impromptue** a surprise *or* an unexpected visit
  ADV *(faire un discours)* off the cuff, impromptu; *(répondre)* off the cuff
  NM *Littérature, Mus & Théât* impromptu

imprononçable [ɛ̃prɔnɔ̃sabl] **ADJ** unpronounceable

impropre [ɛ̃prɔpr] **ADJ 1** *(personne, produit)* unsuitable, unsuited, unfit; **il est i. à ce type de travail** he's unsuited to *or* unsuitable for this kind of work; **produits impropres à la consommation** products not fit *or* unfit for human consumption **2** *(terme)* inappropriate

improprement [ɛ̃prɔprəmɑ̃] **ADV** incorrectly, improperly

impropriété [ɛ̃prɔprijete] **NF 1** *(caractère)* incorrectness, *Sout* impropriety **2** *(terme)* mistake, *Sout* impropriety

improuvable [ɛ̃pruvabl] **ADJ** unprovable

improvisateur, -trice [ɛ̃prɔvizatœr, -tris] **ADJ** improvisational, improvising
  NM,F improviser, improvisor; **avoir un talent d'i.** to have a talent for improvising

improvisation [ɛ̃prɔvizasjɔ̃] **NF 1** *(gén)* improvisation, improvising **2** *Mus & Théât* improvisation; *(d'un comique)* ad-libbing; **faire de l'i.** to improvise; *(comique)* to ad-lib

improvisatrice [ɛ̃prɔvizatris] *voir* **improvisateur**

improvisé, -e [ɛ̃prɔvize] **ADJ** *(discours)* improvised, *Sout* extempore; *(explication)* off-the-cuff, ad hoc; *(mesure, réforme)* hurried, makeshift,

improvised; *(décision)* snap; **un repas i.** a makeshift meal

improviser [ɛ̃prɔvize] **VT** to improvise; **i. un repas** to improvise a meal, to throw a meal together; **i. un discours** to improvise a speech, to make an extempore speech; **i. une explication** to give an off-the-cuff explanation; **on l'a improvisé trésorier** they set him up as treasurer ad hoc
  VI 1 *(parler spontanément)* to improvise; *(comique)* to ad-lib; **i. autour d'un** *ou* **sur un thème** to improvise on a theme
  2 *Mus* to improvise; **i. au piano** to improvise on the piano
  ▸**s'improviser** **VPR 1** *(s'inventer)* to be improvised; **l'orthographe, ça ne s'improvise pas** you can't just make spelling up as you go along; **un départ en vacances, ça ne s'improvise pas** going on holiday isn't something you can do just like that
  2 *(devenir)* **s'i. journaliste/photographe** to act as a journalist/photographer; **on ne s'improvise pas peintre** you don't become a painter overnight *or* just like that

improviste [ɛ̃prɔvist] **à l'improviste ADV** unexpectedly, without warning; **arriver à l'i.** to turn up unexpectedly *or* without warning; **prendre qn à l'i.** to take *or* to catch sb unawares *or* by surprise

imprudemment [ɛ̃prydamɑ̃] **ADV** *(gén)* recklessly, carelessly, imprudently; *(conduire)* recklessly, carelessly; **agir i.** to act foolishly *or* unwisely

imprudence [ɛ̃prydɑ̃s] **NF 1** *(caractère)* imprudence, carelessness, foolhardiness; **i. au volant** careless driving; **l'i. des skieurs hors-piste** the imprudence *or* foolhardiness of off-piste skiers
  2 *(acte)* careless act *or* action; **commettre une i.** to do something stupid *or* thoughtless *or* careless; **il a commis l'i. d'en parler aux journalistes** he was stupid enough to talk to the press about it; **pas d'imprudences!** be careful!, don't do anything silly!
  ❏ **par imprudence** **ADJ** *Jur* **blessures par i.** (non-malicious) wounding; **homicide par i.** = manslaughter

imprudent, -e [ɛ̃prydɑ̃, -ɑ̃t] **ADJ 1** *(conducteur)* careless; *(joueur)* reckless **2** *(acte, comportement)* unwise, imprudent; *(remarque)* foolish, careless, unwise; *(projet)* foolish, ill-considered; *(décision)* rash, unwise, ill-advised; **il serait très i. de la laisser partir seule** it would be very unwise to let her go off on her own
  NM,F *(personne)* careless *or* reckless person

impubère [ɛ̃pyber] **ADJ** prepubescent
  NMF prepubescent; *Jur* minor

impuberté [ɛ̃pyberte] **NF** *Jur* underage status *(for marriage)*

impubliable [ɛ̃pyblijabl] **ADJ** unpublishable, unprintable

impudemment [ɛ̃pydamɑ̃] **ADV** impudently, insolently, brazenly; **il ment i.** he's a brazen *or* shameless liar

impudence [ɛ̃pydɑ̃s] **NF 1** *(caractère)* impudence, insolence, brazenness; **il est d'une i.!** he is so impudent!; **il n'aura pas l'i. de revenir** he won't have the impudence *or* be impudent enough to come back **2** *(action)* impudent act; *(remarque)* impudent remark

impudent, -e [ɛ̃pydɑ̃, -ɑ̃t] **ADJ** impudent, insolent, brazen
  NM,F impudent person

impudeur [ɛ̃pydœr] **NF 1** *(immodestie)* immodesty, shamelessness **2** *(impudence)* brazenness, shamelessness

impudicité [ɛ̃pydisite] **NF** *Littéraire* **1** *(immodestie)* immodesty, shamelessness, impudicity **2** *(caractère, acte, parole)* indecency

impudique [ɛ̃pydik] **ADJ 1** *(immodeste)* immodest, shameless **2** *(indécent)* shameless, indecent

impudiquement [ɛ̃pydikmɑ̃] **ADV 1** *(sans modestie)* immodestly, shamelessly **2** *(de façon indécente)* shamelessly, indecently

impuissance [ɛ̃pɥisɑ̃s] **NF 1** *(faiblesse)* powerlessness, helplessness; **un sentiment d'i.** a feeling of helplessness; **réduire qn à l'i.** to render sb helpless *or* powerless **2** *(incapacité)* inability, powerlessness; **i. à faire qch** inability to do sth **3** *Méd & Physiol* impotence

imp-imp

impuissant, -e [ɛ̃pɥisɑ̃, -ɑ̃t] **ADJ 1** *(inutile)* power-less, helpless; **on est i. devant un tel malheur!** one is powerless in the face of such a misfortune!; **être i. à faire qch** to be powerless to do sth; **des efforts impuissants** unsuccessful *or* ineffectual *or* futile efforts **2** *Méd & Physiol* impotent

NM *Méd & Physiol* impotent (man)

impulser [3] [ɛ̃pylse] **VT 1** *(activité)* to boost, to stimulate **2** *(personnes)* to set in motion, to drive on, to spur

impulsif, -ive [ɛ̃pylsif, -iv] **ADJ** impulsive
NM,F impulsive person

impulsion [ɛ̃pylsjɔ̃] **NF 1** *Tech & Phys* impulse; *Électron* pulse, impulse; **radar à impulsions** pulse radar; *TV* **i. de synchro** sync pulse
2 *Fig (dynamisme)* impetus, impulse; **donner une i. au commerce** to give an impetus to *or* to boost trade; **sous l'i. des dirigeants syndicaux** spurred on by the union leaders
3 *(élan)* impulse; **céder à une i.** to give in to an impulse; **sous l'i. de la haine** spurred on *or* driven by hatred; **sur** *ou* **sous l'i. du moment** on the spur of the moment
4 *Psy* impulsion

impulsive [ɛ̃pylsiv] *voir* **impulsif**

impulsivement [ɛ̃pylsivmɑ̃] **ADV** impulsively

impulsivité [ɛ̃pylsivite] **NF** impulsiveness

impunément [ɛ̃pynemɑ̃] **ADV** with impunity; **je vais vous prouver qu'on ne se moque pas i. de moi!** I'll show you that you can't laugh at me and get away with it!

impuni, -e [ɛ̃pyni] **ADJ** unpunished

impunité [ɛ̃pynite] **NF** impunity; **en toute i.** with impunity

impur, -e [ɛ̃pyr] **ADJ 1** *(pensée, sentiment)* impure, unclean; *(air, eau)* impure, foul; *(style)* impure; *(race)* mixed, mongrel; **les esprits impurs** the demons **2** *Rel (viande, personne)* unclean **3** *Métal* impure

impurement [ɛ̃pyrmɑ̃] **ADV** impurely

impureté [ɛ̃pyrte] **NF 1** *(caractère)* impurity, foulness; **l'i. de l'air** the impurity of the air **2** *(élément)* impurity; **l'eau contient de nombreuses impuretés** the water contains numerous impurities **3** *Littéraire (impudicité)* lewdness **4** *Électron* impure atom **5** *Rel (souillure)* uncleanness

imputabilité [ɛ̃pytabilite] **NF** imputability

imputable [ɛ̃pytabl] **ADJ 1** *(attribuable)* **i. à** imputable *or* ascribable *or* attributable to **2** *Fin (crédit)* chargeable (**sur** to); *(débit)* to be debited (**sur** from)

imputation [ɛ̃pytasjɔ̃] **NF 1** *(accusation)* charge, *Sout* imputation **2** *Fin* charging (**à** to); **l'i. d'une somme au crédit/débit d'un compte** crediting an amount to/debiting an amount from an account; **imputations budgétaires** budget allocations; **i. des charges** cost allocation

imputer [3] [ɛ̃pyte] **VT 1** *(attribuer)* **i. un crime à qn** to impute a crime to sb; **i. ses échecs à la malchance** to put one's failures down to bad luck **2** *Fin* **i. des frais à un budget** to deduct expenses from a budget; **i. une somme à un budget** to allocate a sum to a budget; **i. des frais à un compte** to charge expenses to an account

imputrescibilité [ɛ̃pytresibilite] **NF** rot-resistance

imputrescible [ɛ̃pytresibl] **ADJ** rot-resistant, anti-rot

in [in] **ADJ INV** *Fam* in, hip, trendy; **l'endroit le plus in de Paris** the trendiest *or* hippest spot in Paris
NM *(au Festival d'Avignon)* **le in** the official festival; **au programme du in** on the official festival programme

INA [ina] **NM 1** *(abrév* **Institut national de l'audiovisuel)** = national television archive **2** *(abrév* **Institut national d'agronomie)** = "grande école" for agricultural studies

inabordable [inabɔrdabl] **ADJ 1** *(lieu)* inaccessible; **l'île/le port est i. par mauvais temps** the island/the harbour is inaccessible in bad weather **2** *(personne)* unapproachable, inaccessible; **sa fonction le rendait i.** his position made him inaccessible *or* unapproachable **3** *(prix)* prohibitive; *(produit, service)* prohibitively expensive

inabouti, -e [inabuti] **ADJ** unsuccessful, failed

inabrité, -e [inabrite] **ADJ** unprotected, unsheltered

inabrogeable [inabrɔʒabl] **ADJ** *Jur* unrepealable

inaccentué, -e [inaksɑ̃tɥe] **ADJ** *(voyelle)* unstressed; *(syllabe)* unstressed, unaccentuated; *(pronom)* atonic

inacceptable [inaksɛptabl] **ADJ** *(mesure, proposition)* unacceptable; *(propos, comportement)* unacceptable, intolerable, inadmissible

inacceptation [inaksɛptasjɔ̃] **NF** *Littéraire ou Fin* non-acceptance

inaccessibilité [inaksesibilite] **NF** inaccessibility

inaccessible [inaksesibl] **ADJ 1** *(hors d'atteinte → sommet)* inaccessible, out-of-reach, unreachable
2 *(irréalisable → objectif, rêve)* unfeasible, unrealizable
3 *(inabordable → personne)* unapproachable, inaccessible
4 *(obscur → ouvrage)* inaccessible, opaque; **c'est un texte très spécialisé, i. au grand public** it's a very specialized text which will be inaccessible to the general public
5 *(indifférent)* **être i. à la pitié** to be incapable of feeling pity

inaccompli, -e [inakɔ̃pli] **ADJ 1** *(inachevé)* unaccomplished **2** *(non réalisé → rêve, vœu)* unfulfilled **3** *Ling* imperfective
NM *Ling* imperfective

inaccomplissement [inakɔ̃plismɑ̃] **NM** *Littéraire* nonfulfilment; **l'i. d'une promesse** the nonfulfilment of a promise

inaccordable [inakɔrdabl] **ADJ 1** *Mus* untunable **2** *(grâce, permission)* that cannot be granted; *(requête)* inadmissible

inaccoutumance [inakutymɑ̃s] **NF 1** *Arch & Littéraire* unaccustomedness **2** *Méd* **i. à un médicament** non-addictive quality of a drug

inaccoutumé, -e [inakutyme] **ADJ 1** *(inhabituel)* unusual, unaccustomed **2** *Littéraire (non habitué)* **i. à obéir** unused *or* unaccustomed to obeying

inachevé, -e [inaʃve] **ADJ** *(non terminé)* unfinished, uncompleted; *(incomplet)* incomplete

inachèvement [inaʃɛvmɑ̃] **NM** incompletion

inacquitté, -e [inakite] **ADJ** *Fin (effet)* unreceipted

inactif, -ive [inaktif, -iv] **ADJ 1** *(personne → oisive)* inactive, idle; *(→ sans travail)* non-working; **rester i.** to be idle
2 *(traitement, produit)* ineffective
3 *Bourse & Com (marché)* slack, slow, sluggish
4 *Opt* (optically) inactive
5 *Fin (fonds)* unemployed, idle
6 *Géol* **volcan i.** dormant volcano
7 *Chim* inert
NM,F **les inactifs** the non-working population, those not in active employment

inactinique [inaktinik] **ADJ** *Opt* inactinic; *Phot* **éclairage i.** safe light; *Phot* **lampe i.** safe lamp

inaction [inaksjɔ̃] **NF** *(absence d'activité)* inaction; *(oisiveté)* idleness, lethargy; **je ne supporte pas l'i.** I can't bear being idle *or* having nothing to do; **sa maladie l'a réduit à l'i. pendant plusieurs mois** his illness put him out of action for several months

inactivation [inaktivasjɔ̃] **NF** inactivation

inactive [inaktiv] *voir* **inactif**

inactiver [3] [inaktive] **VT** to inactivate

inactivité [inaktivite] **NF 1** *(oisiveté)* inactivity; **une période d'i.** a slack period; *Admin & Mil* **en i.** not in active service **2** *Bourse & Com (du marché)* slackness, slowness, sluggishness **3** *Chim* inertness

inactualité [inaktɥalite] **NF** out-of-dateness

inactuel, -elle [inaktɥɛl] **ADJ** out-of-date, behind the times

inadaptable [inadaptabl] **ADJ** not adaptable

inadaptation [inadaptasjɔ̃] **NF** maladjustment; **i. à la vie scolaire** failure to adapt to school life; **l'i. du réseau routier aux besoins actuels** the inadequacy of the road system to cope with present-day traffic

inadapté, -e [inadapte] **ADJ 1** *(enfant)* with special needs; **enfants inadaptés au système scolaire** children who fail to adapt to the educational system; *Psy* **enfance inadaptée** children with special needs **2** *(outil, méthode)* **i. à** unsuited *or* not adapted to; **du matériel i. aux besoins actuels** equipment unsuited to *or* unsuitable for today's needs
NM,F *(adulte)* person with social difficulties, *Péj* social misfit; *(enfant)* child with special needs

inadéquat, -e [inadekwa, -at] **ADJ** *(insuffisant)* inadequate (**à** for); *(mal adapté)* unsuitable, inappropriate (**à** for)

inadéquation [inadekwasjɔ̃] **NF** *(insuffisance)* inadequacy; *(inadaptation)* unsuitability, inappropriateness; **étant donné l'i. des moyens au problème** given the unsuitability of the means used to deal with the problem; **il y a i. entre développement économique et progrès social** there is a contradiction between economic development and social progress

inadmissibilité [inadmisibilite] **NF** inadmissibility

inadmissible [inadmisibl] **ADJ** *(intolérable → attitude, erreur)* inadmissible, intolerable, unacceptable; *(irrecevable → demande, proposition)* unacceptable

inadvertance [inadvɛrtɑ̃s] **NF** *Littéraire* oversight, inadvertence
□ **par inadvertance** **ADV** inadvertently, by mistake

inaffectivité [inafɛktivite] **NF** *Psy* lack of emotional response

inaliénabilité [inaljenabilite] **NF** *Jur* inalienability

inalliable [inaljabl] **ADJ** *Métal* that cannot be alloyed, non-alloyable

inaliénable [inaljenabl] **ADJ** *Jur* inalienable

inaliénation [inaljenasjɔ̃] **NF** *Jur* inalienability

inalpage [inalpaʒ] **NM** *(en Savoie)* = moving of cattle up to higher mountain pastures at the beginning of summer

inalpe [inalp] **NF** *Suisse* = **inalpage**

inalper [3] [inalpe] **s'inalper** **VPR** *(en Savoie)* = to move cattle up to higher mountain pastures at the beginning of summer

inaltérabilité [inalterabilite] **NF 1** *(à la lumière)* fade-resistance; *(au lavage)* fastness; *(d'une couleur)* permanence **2** *Métal* stability **3** *Phot* light stability

inaltérable [inalterabl] **ADJ 1** *(couleur)* permanent, fast; *(peinture)* non-fade; **i. à l'air** air-resistant **2** *Métal* stable **3** *(amitié)* steadfast; *(haine)* eternal; *(espoir)* unfailing, steadfast; *(bonne humeur, courage)* unfailing; *(optimisme)* steadfast, unshakeable; *(calme)* unwavering

inaltéré, -e [inaltere] **ADJ 1** *(bois, pierre)* unweathered **2** *(sentiment)* unchanged

inamical, -e, -aux, -ales [inamikal, -o] **ADJ** unfriendly, inimical

inamissible [inamisibl] **ADJ** *Rel* inamissible

inamovibilité [inamɔvibilite] **NF** *Admin (d'une personne)* irremovability, security of tenure *or* office

inamovible [inamɔvibl] **ADJ 1** *Admin (fonctionnaire)* permanent, irremovable; *Hum* **il est i.** he's a permanent fixture **2** *(fixé)* fixed

inanalysable [inanalizabl] **ADJ** unanalysable, inexplicable

inanimé, -e [inanime] **ADJ 1** *(mort)* lifeless; *(évanoui)* unconscious; **tomber i.** to faint, to fall down in a faint; *Littérature* **style i.** lifeless *or* flat style **2** *Ling* inanimate; **objets inanimés** inanimate objects

inanité [inanite] **NF** *Littéraire (manque d'intérêt → d'une conversation)* inanity; *(inutilité)* futility, pointlessness; **des conversations d'une i. terrifiante** incredibly inane conversations

inanition [inanisjɔ̃] **NF** *(faim)* starvation; *(épuisement)* total exhaustion, *Spéc* inanition; **tomber/mourir d'i.** to faint with/to die of hunger; *Fig Hum* to be starving

inapaisable [inapɛzabl] **ADJ** *Littéraire (soif)* unquenchable; *(faim)* voracious, insatiable; *(chagrin, souffrance)* unappeasable

inapaisé, -e [inapeze] **ADJ** *Littéraire (soif)* unquenched; *(faim)* unsatiated; *(chagrin, souffrance)* unappeased

inaperçu, -e [inapɛrsy] **ADJ** unnoticed; **passer i.** to go unnoticed

inapparent, -e [inaparɑ̃, -ɑ̃t] **ADJ** invisible; *Méd* symptomless

inappétence [inapetɑ̃s] **NF 1** *Méd (perte d'appétit)* loss of appetite, *Spéc* inappetence **2** *Littéraire (perte du désir)* diminishing desire

inapplicable [inaplikabl] **ADJ** inapplicable, not applicable; *(loi, décret)* unenforceable

inapplication [inaplikasjɔ̃] **NF 1** *(d'une loi, d'un décret)* non-enforcement **2** *(d'une personne)* lack of application *or* concentration

inappliqué, -e [inaplike] ADJ **1** *(loi, décret)* not enforced **2** *(personne)* lacking in application

inappréciable [inapresjabl] ADJ **1** *(précieux)* invaluable, priceless **2** *(difficile à évaluer)* inappreciable, imperceptible

inapprécié, -e [inapresje] ADJ unappreciated, not appreciated

inapprivoisable [inaprivwazabl] ADJ untameable

inapprivoisé, -e [inaprivwaze] ADJ untamed

inapprochable [inaprɔʃabl] ADJ **il est vraiment i. en ce moment** you can't say anything to him at the moment

inapproprié, -e [inaprɔprije] ADJ inappropriate; **i. à qch** inappropriate to *or* unsuitable for sth

inapte [inapt] ADJ **1** *(incapable → intellectuellement)* unsuitable; *(→ pour raisons médicales)* unfit; **être i. à qch** to be unsuitable/unfit for sth; **être i. à faire qch** to be unfit to do sth; **il est i. à occuper ce poste** he's ill-suited to the job **2** *Mil* **i. (au service militaire)** unfit (for military service)

NMF *Mil* army reject

inaptitude [inaptityd] NF **1** *(incapacité → physique)* incapacity, unfitness; *(→ intellectuelle)* (mental) inaptitude; **i. à qch** unfitness for sth; **i. à faire qch** unfitness for doing *or* to do sth **2** *Mil* unfitness (for military service)

inarrangeable [inarɑ̃ʒabl] ADJ **1** *(dispute)* irreconcilable **2** *(montre)* beyond repair

inarticulé, -e [inartikyle] ADJ inarticulate

inassimilable [inasimilabl] ADJ *(substance)* indigestible, *Spéc* unassimilable; *(connaissances)* impossible to take in; *(population)* which cannot become integrated

inassimilé, -e [inasimile] ADJ unassimilated

inassouvi, -e [inasuvi] ADJ **1** *(soif)* unquenched; *(faim)* unappeased, unsatiated **2** *(passion)* unappeased, unsatiated; *(désir)* unfulfilled; *(vengeance)* unsatisfied, unassuaged

inassouvissement [inasuvismɑ̃] NM *Littéraire* **i. d'un désir** failure to quench *or* to satisfy a desire

inattaquable [inatakabl] ADJ **1** *(personne)* beyond reproach *or* criticism; *(conduite)* unimpeachable, irreproachable; *(argument, preuve)* unassailable, irrefutable, unquestionable; *(forteresse, lieu)* impregnable **2** *Métal* corrosion-resistant

inatteignable [inatɛɲabl] ADJ unreachable

inattendu, -e [inatɑ̃dy] ADJ *(personne)* unexpected; *(réflexion, événement)* unexpected, unforeseen; **c'est assez i. de votre part** I didn't quite expect this from you

inattentif, -ive [inatɑ̃tif, -iv] ADJ inattentive; **vous êtes trop i. (à)** you don't pay enough attention (to)

inattention [inatɑ̃sjɔ̃] NF lack of attention *or* concentration, inattentiveness; **un moment** *ou* **une minute d'i.** a momentary lapse of concentration; **faute** *ou* **erreur d'i.** careless mistake

inattentive [inatɑ̃tiv] *voir* **inattentif**

inaudible [inodibl] ADJ **1** *(imperceptible)* inaudible **2** *(insupportable)* unbearable

inaugural, -e, -aux, -ales [inogyral, -o] ADJ *(discours, cérémonie)* opening *(avant n)*, inaugural; *(voyage)* maiden *(avant n)*

inauguration [inogyrasjɔ̃] NF **1** *(d'une route, d'une exposition)* inauguration; *(d'une statue, d'un monument)* unveiling **2** *(commencement)* beginning, inauguration, initiation

inaugurer [3] [inogyre] VT **1** *(route, exposition)* to inaugurate; *(statue, monument)* to unveil; *Fig (système, méthode)* to initiate, to launch **2** *(marquer le début de)* to usher in; **le changement de gouvernement inaugurait une ère de liberté** the change of government ushered in an era of freedom

inauthenticité [inotɑ̃tisite] NF inauthenticity

inauthentique [inotɑ̃tik] ADJ inauthentic

inavouable [inavwabl] ADJ unmentionable, shameful

inavoué, -e [inavwe] ADJ secret, unconfessed

in-bord [inbɔr, inbɔrd] ADJ INV *(moteur)* inboard

NM INV inboard boat

INC [iɛnse] NM *(abrév* **Institut national de la consommation**) = national institute for consumer advice, *Br* ≃ National Consumer Council

inca [ɛ̃ka] ADJ Inca

▫ **Inca** NMF Inca; **les Incas** the Inca, the Incas

▫ **Inca** NM *(souverain)* Inca

incalculable [ɛ̃kalkylabl] ADJ **1** *(considérable)* incalculable, countless; **des fortunes incalculables** incalculable *or* untold wealth; **un nombre i. de fois/d'erreurs** countless times/mistakes **2** *(imprévisible)* incalculable; **des conséquences incalculables** incalculable *or* far-reaching consequences

incandescence [ɛ̃kɑ̃desɑ̃s] NF incandescence; **être en i.** to be incandescent; **porté à i.** heated until glowing, incandescent; **i. résiduelle** afterglow

incandescent, -e [ɛ̃kɑ̃desɑ̃, -ɑ̃t] ADJ incandescent; *Fig (imagination)* ardent

incanescent, -e [ɛ̃kanɛsɑ̃, -ɑ̃t] ADJ *Biol* canescent

incantation [ɛ̃kɑ̃tasjɔ̃] NF incantation

incantatoire [ɛ̃kɑ̃tatwar] ADJ incantatory; **formule i., paroles incantatoires** incantation

incapable [ɛ̃kapabl] ADJ **1** *(par incompétence)* incapable, incompetent, inefficient; **être i. de faire qch** to be incapable of doing sth; **elle était i. de répondre** she was unable to answer, she couldn't answer; **je serais bien i. de le dire** I really wouldn't know, I really couldn't tell you

2 *(par nature)* **être i. de qch** to be incapable of sth; **il est i. d'un effort** he's incapable of making an effort; **être i. d'attention** to be incapable of paying attention; **elle est i. d'amour** she's incapable of loving *or* love; **elle est i. de méchanceté** there's no malice in her; **être i. de faire** to be incapable of doing; **elle est i. de tricher** she's incapable of cheating

3 *Jur* incompetent

NMF **1** *(incompétent)* incompetent; **ce sont des incapables** they're all incapable *or* incompetent

2 *Jur* person who is legally incompetent; **i. majeur** person under disability

incapacitant, -e [ɛ̃kapasitɑ̃, -ɑ̃t] ADJ *Mil* incapacitating

NM *Méd & Mil* incapacitant

incapacité [ɛ̃kapasite] NF **1** *(impossibilité)* incapacity, inability; **être dans l'i. de faire qch** to be unable to do sth; **son i. à se décider** his/her incapacity *or* inability to make up his/her mind **2** *(incompétence)* incapacity, incompetence, inefficiency **3** *Méd* disablement, disability; **i. permanente** permanent disablement *or* disability **4** *Jur* (legal) incapacity; **i. de travail** industrial disablement; **i. temporaire de travail** temporary disability; **i. électorale** legal incapacity to vote; **i. permanente partielle** permanent partial disability

incarcération [ɛ̃karserasjɔ̃] NF imprisonment, jailing, *Sout* incarceration; **i. provisoire** remand

incarcérer [18] [ɛ̃karsere] VT to imprison, to jail; **il est incarcéré à la prison des Baumettes** he is (being held) in Baumettes prison

incarnadin, -e [ɛ̃karnadɛ̃, -in] *Littéraire* ADJ incarnadine

NM incarnadine

incarnat, -e [ɛ̃karna, -at] ADJ incarnadine

NM incarnadine; *(du teint)* rosiness

incarnation [ɛ̃karnasjɔ̃] NF **1** *Myth & Rel* incarnation **2** *(manifestation)* embodiment; **elle est l'i. de la bonté** she's the embodiment *or* personification of goodness

incarné, -e [ɛ̃karne] ADJ **1** *(personnifié)* incarnate, personified; **le diable i.** the devil incarnate **2** *Méd (ongle)* ingrowing, ingrown

incarner [3] [ɛ̃karne] VT **1** *(symboliser)* to embody, to personify **2** *(interpréter → personnage)* to play

▸**s'incarner** VPR **1** *Rel* to become incarnate **2** *(se matérialiser)* to be embodied; **en toi s'incarne la beauté idéale** you are the embodiment of ideal beauty **3** *Méd* **un ongle qui s'incarne** an ingrowing toenail

incartade [ɛ̃kartad] NF **1** *(écart de conduite)* misdemeanour, escapade; **à la moindre i., vous serez puni** put one foot wrong and you'll be punished **2** *(d'un cheval)* swerve

incasique [ɛ̃kazik] ADJ Inca

incassable [ɛ̃kasabl] ADJ unbreakable

incendiaire [ɛ̃sɑ̃djɛr] ADJ **1** *(balle, bombe)* incendiary **2** *(propos)* incendiary, inflammatory

NMF arsonist, *Br* fire-raiser

incendie [ɛ̃sɑ̃di] NM **1** *(feu)* fire; **maîtriser un i.** to bring a fire *or* blaze under control; **i. criminel** (act of deliberate) arson; **i. de forêt** forest fire; **i. involontaire** involuntary destruction of property by fire; **i. volontaire** arson **2** *Littéraire (lumière)* blaze, glow **3** *Fig (violence)* fire; **l'i. de la révolte** the frenzy of revolt

incendié, -e [ɛ̃sɑ̃dje] ADJ **1** *(ville, maison)* burnt (down), destroyed by fire; **les familles incendiées seront dédommagées** the families affected by the fire will be given compensation; **les bâtiments incendiés** the buildings gutted by fire **2** *Littéraire (éclairé)* ablaze, aglow

NM,F fire victim

incendier [9] [ɛ̃sɑ̃dje] VT **1** *(mettre le feu à)* to set fire to, to set on fire; **la forêt a été incendiée** the forest was set on fire

2 *Fam (invectiver)* **i. qn** to give sb hell; **tu vas te faire i.!** you'll be in for it!

3 *Fig (brûler)* to burn; **une vodka qui incendie la gorge** a vodka that burns one's throat

4 *(esprit, imagination)* to stir; **des discours destinés à i. les esprits** inflammatory speeches

5 *Littéraire (illuminer)* to light up; **le soleil couchant incendiait les champs** the setting sun gave the fields a fiery glow

incertain, -e [ɛ̃sɛrtɛ̃, -ɛn] ADJ **1** *(peu sûr → personne)* uncertain, unsure; **être i. de qch** to be uncertain *or* unsure of sth

2 *(indéterminé → durée, date, quantité)* uncertain, undetermined; *(→ résultat)* uncertain; *(→ fait)* uncertain, doubtful

3 *(aléatoire → gén)* uncertain; *(→ temps)* unsettled

4 *(vague → contour)* indistinct, vague, blurred; *(→ lumière)* poor; *(→ couleur)* indeterminate

5 *(mal équilibré → démarche, appui)* unsteady, uncertain, hesitant; **il avançait vers sa mère d'un pas i.** he walked unsteadily *or* tottered towards his mother

NM *Bourse & Fin* variable exchange; **coter l'i.** to quote on the exchange rate

incertitude [ɛ̃sɛrtityd] NF **1** *(doute, précarité)* uncertainty; **nous sommes dans l'i.** we're uncertain, we're not sure; **vivre dans l'i.** to live in a state of uncertainty; **il est seul face à ses incertitudes** he's left alone with his doubts; **il reste encore bien des incertitudes dans cette affaire** there are still a great many uncertainties *or* unresolved questions in the matter **2** *Math & Phys* uncertainty **3** *(en métrologie)* **i. absolue** absolute uncertainty; **i. relative** relative uncertainty

incessamment [ɛ̃sesamɑ̃] ADV **1** *(bientôt)* very soon; **il doit arriver i.** he'll be here any minute now; *Hum* **i. sous peu** very soon **2** *Arch (sans cesse)* unceasingly, incessantly

incessant, -e [ɛ̃sesɑ̃, -ɑ̃t] ADJ *(effort)* ceaseless, continual; *(bruit, bavardage)* incessant, ceaseless, continual; *(douleur, pluie)* unremitting, constant

incessibilité [ɛ̃sesibilite] NF *Jur (d'un privilège)* non-transferability; *(d'un droit)* inalienability, indefeasibility

incessible [ɛ̃sesibl] ADJ *Jur (privilège)* non-transferable; *(droit)* inalienable, indefeasible

inceste [ɛ̃sɛst] NM incest

incestueux, -euse [ɛ̃sɛstɥø, -øz] ADJ **1** *(personne, relation)* incestuous **2** *(né d'un inceste)* **enfant i.** child born of an incestuous relationship; **l'enfant i. de** the incestuous child of

inchangé, -e [ɛ̃ʃɑ̃ʒe] ADJ unchanged, unaltered

inchangeable [ɛʃɑ̃ʒabl] ADJ unchangeable

inchantable [ɛ̃ʃɑ̃tabl] ADJ unsingable; **c'est i.** it's unsingable, it can't be sung

inchauffable [ɛ̃ʃofabl] ADJ impossible to heat

inchavirable [ɛ̃ʃavirabl] ADJ non-capsizing, self-righting

inchiffrable [ɛ̃ʃifrabl] ADJ unquantifiable, immeasurable; **les dégâts sont inchiffrables** it's impossible to put a figure on the damage

inchoatif, -ive [ɛ̃kɔatif, -iv] ADJ *Ling* inchoative, ingressive

NM *Ling* inchoative, ingressive

incidemment [ɛ̃sidamɑ̃] ADV *(accessoirement)* incidentally, in passing; *(par hasard)* by chance; **il a été i. question du problème des retards** the problem of lateness came up in passing *or* incidentally

incidence [ɛ̃sidɑ̃s] NF **1** *(répercussion)* effect, repercussion, impact; *Écon* **i. fiscale** fiscal effect; **avoir une i. sur** to affect **2** *Méd (d'une maladie)* incidence **3** *Aviat & Phys* incidence

incident[1] [ɛ̃sidɑ̃] **NM** **1** *(événement)* incident, event; *(accrochage)* incident; **sans i.** without a hitch, without incident, smoothly; **i. diplomatique/de frontière** diplomatic/border incident; **i. technique** technical hitch *or* incident; **avoir un i. de parcours** to come across a hitch (on the way); **sa démission n'est qu'un i. de parcours** his/her resignation is only a minor incident; **l'i. est clos** the matter is (now) closed

2 *Jur* **i. (de procédure)** objection (on a point of law); **soulever un i.** to raise an objection

3 *Littérature* (little) episode

incident[2], **-e** [ɛ̃sidɑ̃, -ɑ̃t] **ADJ** **1** *(accessoire → remarque)* incidental **2** *Ling* interpolated, parenthetical **3** *Phys* incident **4** *Jur* incidental; **demande incidente** accessory claim

▫ **incidente** **NF** *Gram* parenthetical clause

incinérateur [ɛ̃sineratœr] **NM** incinerator

incinération [ɛ̃sinerasjɔ̃] **NF** *(de linge, de papiers)* incineration; *(de cadavres)* cremation

incinérer [18] [ɛ̃sinere] **VT** *(linge, papiers)* to incinerate; *(cadavres)* to cremate

incipit [ɛ̃sipit] **NM INV** incipit

incirconcis [ɛ̃sirkɔ̃si] **ADJ** uncircumcised

incise [ɛ̃siz] **NF** **1** *Ling* interpolated clause **2** *Mus* phrase

inciser [3] [ɛ̃size] **VT** **1** *Méd* to incise, to make an incision in; *(furoncle, abcès)* to lance **2** *Bot & Hort* to incise, to cut (a notch into); *(pour extraire la résine)* to tap

incisif, -ive[1] [ɛ̃sizif, -iv] **ADJ** *(ironie, remarque, ton)* cutting, incisive, biting; *(personne, style)* incisive; *(regard)* piercing

incision [ɛ̃sizjɔ̃] **NF** **1** *Méd (action, coupure → de gencive)* incision; *(→ d'un furoncle, d'un abcès)* lancing **2** *Bot & Hort* incision; *(pour extraire la résine)* tapping; **i. annulaire** ringing

incisive[2] [ɛ̃siziv] **ADJ** *voir* **incisif**

NF incisor

incisure [ɛ̃sizyr] **NF** **1** *Anat* incisure **2** *Bot* incising

incitant, -e [ɛ̃sitɑ̃, -ɑ̃t] **ADJ** inciting, stimulating

NM *Méd* stimulant

incitateur, -trice [ɛ̃sitatœr, -tris] **ADJ** inciting, incentive

NM,F inciter

incitatif, -ive [ɛ̃sitatif, -iv] **ADJ** inciting

incitation [ɛ̃sitasjɔ̃] **NF** **1** *(encouragement)* incitement, encouragement; **c'est une i. à la violence** it's incitement to *or* it encourages violence; **i. au crime** abetting, abetment; *Fin* **i. fiscale** tax incentive; *Jur* **i. à la haine raciale** incitement to racial hatred; *Jur* **i. de mineurs à la débauche** corruption of minors **2** *Mktg* incentive; **i. à l'achat** buying incentive; **i. à la vente** sales incentive

incitative [ɛ̃sitativ] *voir* **incitatif**

incitatrice [ɛ̃sitatris] *voir* **incitateur**

inciter [3] [ɛ̃site] **VT** **1** *(encourager)* **i. qn à faire qch** to prompt *or* to encourage sb to do sth; **son succès l'incita à continuer** his/her success encouraged *or* prompted him/her to continue; **cela m'incite à penser qu'une réforme est nécessaire** that leads me to think that a reform is needed; **cela incite à la réflexion/prudence** it makes you stop and think/makes you cautious

2 *Jur* to incite

incivil, -e [ɛ̃sivil] **ADJ** discourteous

incivilisable [ɛ̃sivilizabl] **ADJ** which cannot be civilized

incivilité [ɛ̃sivilite] **NF** **1** *(manque de courtoisie)* discourteousness **2** *(acte, comportement)* discourtesy

incivique [ɛ̃sivik] **ADJ** *Vieilli* lacking in civic *or* public spirit, lacking in public-mindedness; **il tient des propos inciviques** what he says isn't very public-spirited

NMF *Belg Hist* = collaborator with the Nazis during WWII

incivisme [ɛ̃sivism] **NM** **1** *Vieilli* lack of civic *or* public spirit, lack of public-mindedness **2** *Belg Hist (politique)* collaborationist policy; *(période)* collaboration

inclassable [ɛ̃klasabl] **ADJ** unclassifiable; **un film/peintre i.** a film/painter that/who cannot be pigeonholed

inclassifiable [ɛ̃klasifjabl] **ADJ** *Méd* untypable

inclémence [ɛ̃klemɑ̃s] **NF** *Littéraire* **1** *(manque d'indulgence)* mercilessness, pitilessness **2** *(rigueur → du climat)* inclemency

inclément, -e [ɛ̃klemɑ̃, -ɑ̃t] **ADJ** *Littéraire* **1** *(qui manque d'indulgence)* merciless, pitiless **2** *(rigoureux → climat)* inclement

inclinable [ɛ̃klinabl] **ADJ** *(siège, dossier)* reclining; *(table, plan)* tilting

inclinaison [ɛ̃klinɛzɔ̃] **NF** **1** *(d'un plan)* incline, slant; *(d'un avion)* tilt, tilting; *(d'un toit, des combles, d'un pignon)* pitch, slope; *(d'un navire)* list, listing; **la faible/forte i. du jardin** the gentle slope/the steepness of the garden; **l'i. de la tour de Pise** the angle at which the Tower of Pisa leans; **l'i. de la voie** *(route, chemin de fer)* the gradient, the incline

2 *(d'une partie du corps)* **l'i. de la tête** the tilt of the head

3 *Géom* inclination, angle

4 *Astron* declination; **i. magnétique** inclination, magnetic dip

inclination [ɛ̃klinasjɔ̃] **NF** **1** *(tendance)* inclination, tendency; *(goût)* inclination, liking; **avoir une i. pour la musique** to have a liking for music, to be musically inclined; **une i. à douter** a tendency to doubt things; **suivre son i.** to follow one's (natural) inclination

2 *(mouvement → de la tête)* bow, inclination; *(→ du corps)* bow; *(signe d'acquiescement)* nod; **d'une légère i. de la tête** with a slight bow of the head

3 *Littéraire (attirance)* **avoir de l'i. pour qn** to have a liking for sb; **un mariage d'i.** a love match

incliné, -e [ɛ̃kline] **ADJ** **1** *(en pente)* sloping; *(penché → mur)* leaning; *(→ dossier, siège)* reclining; **le poteau est légèrement i.** the stake is at a bit of an angle; **la tête inclinée** *(sur le côté)* with one's head (tilted) to one side; *(en avant)* with bowed head **2** *(enclin)* **une nature inclinée au mal** a character inclined *or* disposed to evil

incliner [3] [ɛ̃kline] **VT** **1** *(courber)* to bend; **i. la tête** *ou* **le front** *(en avant)* to bow *or Littéraire* to incline one's head; *(pour acquiescer ou saluer)* to nod (one's head); *(sur le côté)* to tilt one's head to one side; **i. le corps (en avant)** to bend forward; *(pour saluer)* to bow

2 *(pencher → dossier, siège)* to tilt; **être incliné** *(avion)* to tilt; *(bateau)* to list

3 *(inciter)* **i. qn à faire** to encourage *or* to prompt sb to do; **cette information m'incline à revoir mon point de vue** this news leads me *or* makes me inclined to reconsider my position; **i. qn à la rigueur** to encourage sb to be strict; **ceci ne les incline pas à la clémence/au travail** this makes them disinclined to be lenient/to work

▫ **incliner à** **VT IND** to tend to *or* towards, to incline towards; **j'incline à penser qu'elle a tort** I'm inclined to think she's wrong

▸**s'incliner** **VPR** **1** *(se courber → personne)* to bend forward; *(→ personne qui salue)* to bow; *(→ cime d'arbre)* to bend (over)

2 *(pencher → mur)* to lean (over); *(→ toit, route)* to slope; *(→ avion)* to tilt, to bank; *(→ navire)* to list; *(→ siège)* to tilt

3 *Fig (se soumettre)* **s'i. devant le talent** to bow before talent; **s'i. devant les faits** to submit to *or* to accept the facts; **s'i. devant la supériorité de qn** to yield to sb's superiority; *Sport* **le Racing s'est incliné devant Toulon par 15 à 12** Racing Club lost *or* went down to Toulon 15 to 12; **leur équipe a finalement dû s'i.** their team had to give in *or* had to admit defeat eventually

4 *(se recueillir)* **s'i. devant la dépouille mortelle de qn** to pay one's last respects to sb

inclinomètre [ɛ̃klinɔmɛtr] **NM** *Tech* inclinometer

inclure [96] [ɛ̃klyr] **VT** **1** *(ajouter)* to include, to add, to insert; **i. de nouvelles données dans une liste** to include new data in a list **2** *(joindre)* to enclose **3** *(comporter)* to include; **le contrat inclut une nouvelle clause importante** the contract includes *or* comprises an important new clause; **cet accord inclut une autre condition** the agreement includes a further condition

4 *Jur (introduire → clause)* to insert

inclus, -e [ɛ̃kly, -yz] **ADJ** **1** *(contenu)* enclosed; **le reçu i. dans ce courrier** the receipt enclosed with this letter

2 *(compris)* included; **le service est i.** service is included; **20, les enfants i.** 20, including the children; **du 1er au 12 juin i.** from 1 June to 12 June inclusive, *Am* from June 1 through June 12; **jusqu'à la page 32 incluse** up to and including page 32; **jusqu'au dimanche i.** up to and including Sunday; **il travaille tous les jours, dimanche i.** he works every day, including Sundays

3 *Math* **l'ensemble X est i. dans l'ensemble Z** the set X is included in the set Z *or* is a subset of Z

4 *Méd* **dent incluse** impacted tooth

inclusif, -ive [ɛ̃klyzif, -iv] **ADJ** inclusive; **prix i.** all-inclusive price

inclusion [ɛ̃klyzjɔ̃] **NF** **1** *(action)* inclusion; *(dans un courrier)* enclosure (**dans** with) **2** *(objet décoratif)* = flower, shell etc set into plastic and used as paperweight, ornament, jewellery etc **3** *Méd* impaction **4** *Math & Métal* inclusion **5** *Ordinat (de fichier)* insertion

inclusive [ɛ̃klyziv] *voir* **inclusif**

inclusivement [ɛ̃klyzivmɑ̃] **ADV** up to and including, *Am* through; **jusqu'au 14 mars i.** up to and including 14 March, *Am* through March 14

incoagulable [ɛ̃kɔagylabl] **ADJ** non-coagulating

incoercibilité [ɛ̃kɔɛrsibilite] **NF** irrepressibility, *Sout* incoercibility

incoercible [ɛ̃kɔɛrsibl] **ADJ** irrepressible, *Sout* incoercible

incognito [ɛ̃kɔɲito] **ADV** incognito

NM incognito; **garder l'i.** to remain anonymous *or* incognito

incohérence [ɛ̃kɔerɑ̃s] **NF** **1** *(manque d'unité → d'une attitude, d'une personne)* inconsistency, incoherence; *(→ d'un discours, d'idées)* incoherence **2** *(contradiction)* inconsistency, contradiction, discrepancy; **le film est plein d'incohérences** the film is full of inconsistencies

incohérent, -e [ɛ̃kɔerɑ̃, -ɑ̃t] **ADJ** **1** *(d'une attitude, d'une personne)* incoherent, inconsistent; *(d'un discours, d'idées)* incoherent; **de manière incohérente** incoherently; **tenir des propos incohérents** to speak incoherently **2** *(disparate)* divided

incoiffable [ɛ̃kwafabl] **ADJ** *(cheveux)* unmanageable

incollable [ɛ̃kɔlabl] **ADJ** **1** *Culin* **riz i.** non-stick rice **2** *Fam (connaisseur)* unbeatable▪; **elle est i. en géographie** you can't catch her out in geography

incolore [ɛ̃kɔlɔr] **ADJ** **1** *(transparent → liquide)* colourless; *(→ vernis, verre)* clear; *(→ cirage)* neutral **2** *Fig (terne → sourire)* wan; *(→ style)* colourless, bland, nondescript; **i., inodore et sans saveur** deadly dull

incomber [3] [ɛ̃kɔ̃be] **incomber à** **VT IND** **1** *(revenir à)* **les frais de déplacement incombent à l'entreprise** travelling expenses are to be paid by the company; **à qui en incombe la responsabilité?** who is responsible for it?; **cette tâche vous incombe** this task is your responsibility

2 *(tournure impersonnelle)* **il vous incombe de la recevoir** it's your duty *or Sout* it is incumbent upon you to see her; **il vous incombe de le faire** the onus is on you to do it

3 *Jur (être rattaché)* **cette pièce incombe au dossier Falon** this document belongs in the Falon file

incombustibilité [ɛ̃kɔ̃bystibilite] **NF** incombustibility

incombustible [ɛ̃kɔ̃bystibl] **ADJ** non-combustible

incommensurabilité [ɛ̃kɔmɑ̃syrabilite] **NF** **1** *(immensité)* immeasurableness **2** *Math* incommensurability

incommensurable [ɛ̃kɔmɑ̃syrabl] **ADJ** **1** *(énorme)* immeasurable; **il est d'une bêtise i.** he's immensely *or* inordinately stupid **2** *Math* incommensurable

incommensurablement [ɛ̃kɔmɑ̃syrabləmɑ̃] **ADV** **1** *(très)* immeasurably; **il est i. stupide** he's immensely *or* inordinately stupid **2** *Math* incommensurably

incommodant, -e [ɛ̃kɔmɔdɑ̃, -ɑ̃t] **ADJ** *(chaleur)* unpleasant, uncomfortable; *(bruit)* irritating, irksome; *(odeur)* offensive, nauseating

incommode [ɛ̃kɔmɔd] **ADJ** **1** *(peu pratique → outil)* impractical, awkward; *(→ livre)* unwieldy, impractical; *(→ maison)* inconvenient; *(→ horaire, arrangement)* inconvenient, awkward **2** *(inconfortable → position)* uncomfortable, awkward; *(→ fauteuil)* uncomfortable

incommoder [3] [ɛ̃kɔmɔde] **VT** to bother; **la chaleur commence à m'i.** the heat is beginning to

bother me *or* to make me feel uncomfortable; *Vieilli* **être incommodé** *(souffrant)* to feel unwell *or* off colour

incommodité [ɛ̃kɔmɔdite] NF *(d'un outil)* inconvenience, impracticability, unsuitability; *(d'un meuble, d'une posture, d'un trajet)* uncomfortableness, discomfort; *(d'un horaire, d'un arrangement)* inconvenience, awkwardness

incommunicabilité [ɛ̃kɔmynikabilite] NF incommunicability

incommunicable [ɛ̃kɔmynikabl] ADJ incommunicable

incommutabilité [ɛ̃kɔmytabilite] NF *Jur* non-transferability

incommutable [ɛ̃kɔmytabl] ADJ *Jur* non-transferable

incomparable [ɛ̃kɔ̃parabl] ADJ 1 *(très différent)* not comparable, unique, singular; **nos deux situations sont incomparables** you can't compare our two situations; **vous sentez la différence? c'est i.!** do you feel the difference? there's just no comparison! 2 *(inégalable)* incomparable, matchless, peerless

incomparablement [ɛ̃kɔ̃parabləmɑ̃] ADV incomparably; **il est i. plus beau que moi** he's incomparably *or* infinitely more handsome than me

incompatibilité [ɛ̃kɔ̃patibilite] NF 1 *(opposition)* incompatibility; **i. d'humeur** mutual incompatibility; **il y a une totale i. entre eux** they are totally incompatible 2 *Bot, Méd & Ordinat* incompatibility

incompatible [ɛ̃kɔ̃patibl] ADJ incompatible; **ces deux solutions sont incompatibles** these two solutions are mutually exclusive

incompétence [ɛ̃kɔ̃petɑ̃s] NF 1 *(incapacité)* incompetence 2 *(ignorance)* ignorance, lack of knowledge; **son i. en informatique** his/her ignorance about *or* lack of knowledge of computers 3 *Jur* incompetence, incompetency, *(legal)* incapacity; **i. d'attribution** lack of subject-matter jurisdiction; **i. territoriale** lack of territorial jurisdiction

incompétent, -e [ɛ̃kɔ̃petɑ̃, -ɑ̃t] ADJ 1 *(incapable)* incompetent, inefficient 2 *(ignorant)* ignorant; **je suis i. en la matière** I'm not qualified *or* competent to speak about this; **je suis i. en informatique** I know nothing *or* I am ignorant about computers 3 *Jur & Pol* incompetent
  NM,F incompetent

incomplet, -ète [ɛ̃kɔ̃plɛ, -ɛt] ADJ *(fragmentaire)* incomplete; *(inachevé)* unfinished

incomplètement [ɛ̃kɔ̃plɛtmɑ̃] ADV incompletely, not completely

incomplétude [ɛ̃kɔ̃pletyd] NF 1 *Littéraire (inassouvissement)* nonfulfilment 2 *Math* **théorème d'i.** incompleteness theorem

incompréhensibilité [ɛ̃kɔ̃preɑ̃sibilite] NF incomprehensibility

incompréhensible [ɛ̃kɔ̃preɑ̃sibl] ADJ incomprehensible, impossible to understand; **de manière i.** incomprehensibly; **c'est i., je les avais posées là!** I don't understand it, I put them right there!

incompréhensiblement [ɛ̃kɔ̃preɑ̃sibləmɑ̃] ADV incomprehensibly

incompréhensif, -ive [ɛ̃kɔ̃preɑ̃sif, -iv] ADJ unsympathetic, unfeeling

incompréhension [ɛ̃kɔ̃preɑ̃sjɔ̃] NF lack of understanding *or* comprehension; **leur i. était totale** they found it totally impossible to understand

incompréhensive [ɛ̃kɔ̃preɑ̃siv] *voir* **incompréhensif**

incompressibilité [ɛ̃kɔ̃presibilite] NF 1 *Phys* incompressibility 2 *(de dépenses, d'un budget)* irreducibility

incompressible [ɛ̃kɔ̃presibl] ADJ 1 *Phys* incompressible 2 *(dépenses)* which cannot be reduced; **notre budget est i.** we can't cut down on our budget 3 *Jur (peine)* irreducible

incompris, -e [ɛ̃kɔ̃pri, -iz] ADJ 1 *(méconnu)* misunderstood *or (énigmatique)* impenetrable; **un texte qui jusqu'à ce jour était resté i.** a text which had not been understood until today
  NM,F *Hum* **je suis un éternel i.** nobody ever understands me

inconcevable [ɛ̃kɔ̃svabl] ADJ inconceivable, unthinkable, unimaginable; **avec un aplomb i.** with an incredible *or* amazing nerve

inconcevablement [ɛ̃kɔ̃svabləmɑ̃] ADV incredibly, inconceivably

inconciliable [ɛ̃kɔ̃siljabl] ADJ *(incompatible)* incompatible, irreconcilable; **des intérêts inconciliables** incompatible interests; **des points de vue inconciliables** irreconcilable points of view; **i. avec qch** incompatible with sth

inconditionnalité [ɛ̃kɔ̃disjɔnalite] NF *(d'un partisan)* unreservedness, wholeheartedness; **l'i. de notre soutien** our unwavering *or* unconditional support

inconditionné, -e [ɛ̃kɔ̃disjɔne] ADJ *Phil* unconditioned

inconditionnel, -elle [ɛ̃kɔ̃disjɔnɛl] ADJ 1 *(partisan)* staunch, unwavering; *(appui)* unconditional, unreserved, wholehearted; *(reddition)* unconditional 2 *Psy* unconditioned
  NM,F **un i. de** a fan of; **je suis une inconditionnelle de l'Espagne** I am mad about *or* I adore Spain; **pour les inconditionnels de l'informatique** for computer buffs *or* enthusiasts

inconditionnellement [ɛ̃kɔ̃disjɔnɛlmɑ̃] ADV unconditionally, unreservedly, wholeheartedly

inconduite [ɛ̃kɔ̃dɥit] NF *(dévergondage)* loose living; *(mauvaise conduite)* misconduct

Inconel® [ɛ̃kɔnɛl] NM *Métal* Inconel®

inconfort [ɛ̃kɔ̃fɔr] NM *(d'une maison)* lack of comfort; *(d'une posture)* discomfort; *(d'une situation)* awkwardness

inconfortable [ɛ̃kɔ̃fɔrtabl] ADJ 1 *(maison, siège)* uncomfortable 2 *(situation, posture)* uncomfortable, awkward

inconfortablement [ɛ̃kɔ̃fɔrtabləmɑ̃] ADV uncomfortably

incongelable [ɛ̃kɔ̃ʒlabl] ADJ which cannot be deep-frozen

incongru, -e [ɛ̃kɔ̃gry] ADJ *(remarque, réponse)* inappropriate, out of place; *(bruit)* rude; *(tenue)* extravagant; *Vieilli (personne)* uncouth

incongruité [ɛ̃kɔ̃grɥite] NF 1 *(d'une remarque, d'une réponse)* inappropriateness; *(d'une tenue)* extravagance 2 *(parole)* inappropriate remark; *(action)* inappropriate action

incongrûment [ɛ̃kɔ̃grymɑ̃] ADV inappropriately

inconnaissable [ɛ̃kɔnɛsabl] ADJ unknowable
  NM **l'i.** the unknowable

inconnu, -e [ɛ̃kɔny] ADJ 1 *(personne → dont on ignore l'existence)* unknown; **il est né de père i.** the name of his father is not known; **i. à cette adresse** *(sur une enveloppe ou un colis)* not known at this address
  2 *(destination)* unknown
  3 *(étranger)* unknown; **il m'était i.** I didn't know him, he was a stranger to me; **ce visage ne m'est pas i.** I've seen that face before; **c'est un problème qui lui est totalement i.** the problem is totally foreign to him/her, it's a problem he/she knows absolutely nothing about; *Fam* **i. au bataillon** never heard of him
  4 *(sans notoriété)* unknown
  NM,F 1 *(étranger)* unknown person, stranger; **ne parle pas aux inconnus** don't talk to strangers
  2 *(personne sans notoriété)* unknown person; **une pièce jouée par des inconnus** a play with a cast of unknowns; **c'est un i. qui a remporté le prix Nobel** someone no one has ever heard of has won the Nobel prize
  NM **l'i.** the unknown; **un saut dans l'i.** a leap in the dark
  ❑ **inconnue** NF 1 *(élément ignoré)* unknown quantity *or* factor; **il y a trop d'inconnues pour que je prenne une décision** there are too many unknown factors for me to decide
  2 *Math* unknown

🎬

'**L'Inconnu du Nord-Express**' *Hitchcock* 'Strangers on a Train'

---

inconsciemment [ɛ̃kɔ̃sjamɑ̃] ADV *(machinalement)* unconsciously, unwittingly; *(dans l'inconscient)* unconsciously

inconscience [ɛ̃kɔ̃sjɑ̃s] NF 1 *(insouciance)* recklessness, irresponsibility; *(folie)* madness, craziness; **faire preuve d'i.** to be reckless *or* irresponsible; **c'est de l'i.!** it's sheer madness! 2 *(perte de connaissance)* unconsciousness; **sombrer** *ou* **tomber dans l'i.** to lose consciousness

inconscient, -e [ɛ̃kɔ̃sjɑ̃, -ɑ̃t] ADJ 1 **être i. de qch** *(ne pas s'en rendre compte)* to be unaware of sth 2 *(insouciant)* reckless, rash; *(fou)* mad, crazy 3 *(automatique)* mechanical, unconscious; *Psy* unconscious 4 *(évanoui)* unconscious
  NM,F *(personne insouciante)* reckless *or* irresponsible person; *(personne folle)* mad person, crazy person
  NM *Psy* **l'i.** the unconscious; **l'i. collectif** the collective unconscious

inconséquemment [ɛ̃kɔ̃sekamɑ̃] ADV *Littéraire (de façon → incohérente)* incoherently, inconsistently; *(→ imprudente)* thoughtlessly, unthinkingly, recklessly

inconséquence [ɛ̃kɔ̃sekɑ̃s] NF 1 *(manque de cohérence)* incoherence, inconsistency; *(manque de prudence)* thoughtlessness, carelessness, recklessness 2 *(action imprudente)* reckless *or* irresponsible act; *(parole illogique)* non sequitur

inconséquent, -e [ɛ̃kɔ̃sekɑ̃, -ɑ̃t] ADJ 1 *(incohérent)* incoherent, inconsistent; **être i. dans ses propos** to contradict oneself, to speak illogically 2 *(imprudent)* thoughtless, unthinking, reckless

inconsidéré, -e [ɛ̃kɔ̃sidere] ADJ *(acte, remarque)* thoughtless, rash, foolhardy; *(dépenses)* reckless

inconsidérément [ɛ̃kɔ̃sideremɑ̃] ADV *(agir, parler)* rashly, thoughtlessly, unwisely; *(dépenser)* recklessly

inconsistance [ɛ̃kɔ̃sistɑ̃s] NF 1 *(d'un roman, d'un argument)* flimsiness, shallowness; *(d'une personne, du caractère)* shallowness, superficiality; **le film/roman était d'une i. telle que...** the film/novel was so lacking in substance that... 2 *(de la boue, de la vase)* softness; *(d'une crème, d'un enduit)* thinness, runniness; *(d'une soupe)* wateriness

inconsistant, -e [ɛ̃kɔ̃sistɑ̃, -ɑ̃t] ADJ 1 *(roman, argument)* flimsy, weak, shallow; *(personne, caractère)* shallow, superficial 2 *(boue, vase)* soft; *(crème, enduit)* thin, runny; *(soupe)* watery

inconsolable [ɛ̃kɔ̃sɔlabl] ADJ inconsolable

inconsolé, -e [ɛ̃kɔ̃sɔle] ADJ *(peine, chagrin)* unconsoled; *(personne)* disconsolate

inconsommable [ɛ̃kɔ̃sɔmabl] ADJ unfit for consumption

inconstance [ɛ̃kɔ̃stɑ̃s] NF *(infidélité, variabilité)* inconstancy, fickleness 2 *Littéraire* **l'i. du succès** the fickleness of fortune

inconstant, -e [ɛ̃kɔ̃stɑ̃, -ɑ̃t] ADJ 1 *(infidèle, d'humeur changeante)* inconstant, fickle; **être i. en amour** to be fickle 2 *Littéraire (changeant → temps)* changeable, unsettled
  NM,F fickle person

inconstatable [ɛ̃kɔ̃statabl] ADJ impossible to ascertain, unascertainable

inconstitutionnalité [ɛ̃kɔ̃stitysjɔnalite] NF *Jur* unconstitutionality

inconstitutionnel, -elle [ɛ̃kɔ̃stitysjɔnɛl] ADJ *Jur* unconstitutional

inconstitutionnellement [ɛ̃kɔ̃stitysjɔnɛlmɑ̃] ADV *Jur* unconstitutionally

inconstructible [ɛ̃kɔ̃stryktibl] ADJ **zone i.** site without development approval, *Am* permanently restricted zone

incontestabilité [ɛ̃kɔ̃tɛstabilite] NF *(d'une preuve, d'un argument)* indisputability

incontestable [ɛ̃kɔ̃tɛstabl] ADJ incontestable, indisputable, undeniable; **sa compétence est i.** his/her competence is indisputable *or* beyond question; **il a fait un gros effort, c'est i.** there's no denying the fact that he put in a lot of effort

incontestablement [ɛ̃kɔ̃tɛstabləmɑ̃] ADV indisputably, undeniably, beyond any shadow of (a) doubt; **i. coupable** unquestionably guilty

incontesté, -e [ɛ̃kɔ̃tɛste] ADJ uncontested, undisputed; **c'est un expert i.** he's an unchallenged *or* undisputed expert

incontinence [ɛ̃kɔ̃tinɑ̃s] NF 1 *Méd* incontinence; **i. nocturne** bed-wetting 2 *Littéraire (débauche)* debauchery 3 *(dans le discours)* **i. verbale** logorrhoea, *Hum* verbal diarrhoea

incontinent, -e [ɛ̃kɔ̃tinɑ̃, -ɑ̃t] ADJ 1 *Méd* incontinent 2 *Littéraire (débauché)* debauched 3 *Littéraire (dans ses propos)* unrestrained (in one's speech)
  ❑ **incontinent** ADV *Arch* forthwith, straightaway, directly

incontournable [ɛ̃kɔ̃turnabl] ADJ **c'est un problème i.** this problem can't be ignored; **son argument était i.** there was no getting away from his/her argument; **son œuvre est i.** his/her work cannot be overlooked *or* has exercised a major influence; **son dernier film est absolument i.** his/her latest movie *or Br* film is absolutely unmissable *or* is an absolute must

incontrôlable [ɛ̃kɔ̃trolabl] ADJ **1** *(sentiment, colère)* uncontrollable, ungovernable, wild; *(personne)* out of control; **l'incendie/la foule était i.** the fire/crowd was out of control; **des éléments incontrôlables** rowdy elements; *Can* **circonstances incontrôlables** circumstances beyond one's control **2** *(non vérifiable → affirmation)* unverifiable, unconfirmable

incontrôlé, -e [ɛ̃kɔ̃trole] ADJ **1** *(bande, groupe)* unrestrained, unruly, out of control; **des éléments incontrôlés** unruly elements **2** *(non vérifié → nouvelle)* unverified, unconfirmed

inconvenance [ɛ̃kɔ̃vnɑ̃s] NF **1** *(caractère)* impropriety, indecency; **vous avez été d'une i. choquante** you behaved in a most unseemly manner **2** *(parole)* impropriety, rude remark; *(acte)* impropriety, rude gesture; **dire/commettre une i.** to say/to do something improper

inconvenant, -e [ɛ̃kɔ̃vnɑ̃, -ɑ̃t] ADJ *(déplacé)* improper, indecorous, unseemly; *(indécent)* indecent, improper; **rien d'i. ne s'est passé entre eux** nothing improper *or* untoward passed between them

inconvénient [ɛ̃kɔ̃venjɑ̃] NM *(désagrément)* disadvantage, drawback, inconvenience; *(danger)* risk; **les avantages et les inconvénients** the advantages and disadvantages, the pros and cons; **les inconvénients qu'il y a à vivre si loin de la ville** the disadvantages *or* drawbacks *or* inconvenience of living so far from town; **je ne vois pas d'i. à ce que tu y ailles** I can see nothing against your going; **y voyez-vous un i.?** *(désagrément)* can you see any difficulties *or* drawbacks in this?; *(objection)* do you have any objection to this?, do you mind?; **l'i., c'est que...** the problem is that...

inconvertibilité [ɛ̃kɔ̃vɛrtibilite] NF *Fin* inconvertibility

inconvertible [ɛ̃kɔ̃vɛrtibl] ADJ **1** *Fin* inconvertible **2** *Rel* unconvertible

incoordination [ɛ̃koɔrdinasjɔ̃] NF **1** *(incohérence → de la pensée, d'un discours)* lack of coordination **2** *(des mouvements)* uncoordination, lack of coordination, *Spéc* ataxia

incorporable [ɛ̃kɔrpɔrabl] ADJ **1** *Mil Br* recruitable, *Am* draftable **2** *(parcelle, matériau)* incorporable

incorporation [ɛ̃kɔrpɔrasjɔ̃] NF **1** *Mil* recruitment, *Br* conscription, *Am* induction; **j'attends mon i.** I'm waiting to be called up **2** *Psy* incorporation **3** *(d'un produit)* blending, mixing (**dans** into *or* with); *(d'un territoire)* incorporation; **l'i. de Calais à l'Angleterre a eu lieu en 1347** Calais was incorporated into England in 1347 **4** *Fin* **i. des réserves au capital** capitalization of reserves

incorporé, -e [ɛ̃kɔrpɔre] ADJ **1** built-in, integrated; **avec cellule photoélectrique incorporée** with built-in light meter **2** *Journ (journaliste, reporter)* embedded

NM *Mil* recruit, *Am* inductee

incorporéité [ɛ̃kɔrpɔreite] NF incorporeity

incorporel, -elle [ɛ̃kɔrpɔrɛl] ADJ **1** *(intangible)* insubstantial, incorporeal **2** *Jur (actif, valeurs)* intangible; **bien i.** intangible property; **propriété incorporelle** incorporeal hereditaments

incorporer [3] [ɛ̃kɔrpɔre] VT **1** *Culin (mêler)* to blend, to mix; **incorporez le sucre peu à peu** gradually mix in the sugar; **incorporez le fromage râpé aux jaunes d'œufs** blend *or* mix the grated cheese with the egg yolks **2** *Mil Br* to recruit, *Am* to draft, to induct **3** *(intégrer)* to incorporate, to integrate; **quand la Savoie a été incorporée à la France** when Savoy became part of France; **incorporez quelques citations dans le texte** add a few quotations to the text

▸**s'incorporer** VPR **s'i. à** *(groupe)* to join

incorrect, -e [ɛ̃kɔrɛkt] ADJ **1** *(erroné)* incorrect, wrong; **l'emploi i. d'un mot** the incorrect *or* improper use of a word **2** *(indécent)* improper, impolite, indecent; **dans une tenue incorrecte** improperly dressed **3** *(impoli)* rude, discourteous, impolite **4** *(irrégulier)* underhand, irregular, unscrupulous; **c'était i. de leur part de ne pas nous prévenir** it was wrong of them not to warn us; **il a été très i. avec ses concurrents** he behaved quite unscrupulously towards his competitors

incorrectement [ɛ̃kɔrɛktəmɑ̃] ADV **1** *(de façon erronée)* wrongly, incorrectly; **mots orthographiés i.** wrongly spelt words, misspelt words **2** *(indécemment)* improperly, impolitely, indecently **3** *(impoliment)* rudely, discourteously, impolitely **4** *(irrégulièrement)* underhand, irregularly, unscrupulously

incorrection [ɛ̃kɔrɛksjɔ̃] NF **1** *(caractère → indécent)* impropriety, indecency; *(→ impoli)* rudeness, impoliteness; **elle est d'une i.!** she's incredibly rude! **2** *(propos)* impropriety, improper remark; *(acte)* improper act; **à la suite d'une grave i. envers un professeur** after being extremely rude to a teacher **3** *(emploi fautif)* impropriety

incorrigibilité [ɛ̃kɔriʒibilite] NF incorrigibility

incorrigible [ɛ̃kɔriʒibl] ADJ **1** *(personne)* incorrigible; **c'est un i. paresseux** he's incorrigibly lazy **2** *(défaut)* incorrigible

incorrigiblement [ɛ̃kɔriʒibləmɑ̃] ADV incorrigibly

incorruptibilité [ɛ̃kɔryptibilite] NF **1** *(honnêteté)* incorruptibility **2** *(inaltérabilité → d'un métal)* stability; *(→ d'un bois)* incorruptibility, rot-resistance

incorruptible [ɛ̃kɔryptibl] ADJ **1** *(honnête)* incorruptible; **on la sait i.** everybody knows she wouldn't take a bribe **2** *(inaltérable → métal)* stable; *(→ bois)* non-decaying

NMF incorruptible; **c'est un i.** he's incorruptible

incoté, -e [ɛ̃kɔte] ADJ *Bourse* unquoted

incoterms [ɛ̃kɔtɛrm] NMPL *Com* incoterms

incrédibilité [ɛ̃kredibilite] NF incredibleness, incredibility

incrédule [ɛ̃kredyl] ADJ **1** *(sceptique)* incredulous, disbelieving; **d'un air i.** incredulously, in disbelief **2** *Rel (incroyant)* unbelieving

NMF *Rel (incroyant)* nonbeliever, unbeliever

incrédulité [ɛ̃kredylite] NF **1** *(doute)* incredulity, disbelief, unbelief; **avec i.** incredulously, in disbelief **2** *Rel (incroyance)* lack of belief, unbelief

incréé, -e [ɛ̃kree] ADJ *Littéraire* uncreated

incrément [ɛ̃kremɑ̃] NM *Ordinat* increment

incrémenter [3] [ɛ̃kremɑ̃te] VT *Ordinat* to increment

incrémentiel, -elle [ɛ̃kremɑ̃sjɛl] ADJ *Ordinat* incremental

increvable [ɛ̃krəvabl] ADJ **1** *(pneu, ballon)* puncture-proof **2** *Fam (personne)* tireless■; **les gosses sont increvables** kids never seem to get tired; **à cet âge-là, j'étais i.** at that age, I never got tired; **cette voiture est i.** this car will last for ever

incriminable [ɛ̃kriminabl] ADJ *Littéraire* impeachable, condemnable

incrimination [ɛ̃kriminasjɔ̃] NF incrimination, accusation

incriminer [3] [ɛ̃krimine] VT **1** *(rejeter la faute sur)* to put the blame on, to incriminate **2** *(accuser → décision, négligence)* to (call into) question; *(→ personne)* to accuse; **il avait déjà été incriminé dans une affaire de drogue** he'd previously been implicated in a drugs case

incristallisable [ɛ̃kristalizabl] ADJ uncrystallizable, non-crystallizing

incrochetable [ɛ̃krɔʃtabl] ADJ *(serrure)* unpickable; *(coffre)* burglar-proof

incroyable [ɛ̃krwajabl] ADJ **1** *(peu vraisemblable)* incredible, unbelievable; **quelle histoire i.!** what an incredible story!; **il est i. que...** it's incredible *or* hard to believe that...

2 *(étonnant)* incredible, amazing; **tu es vraiment i., pourquoi ne veux-tu pas venir?** you're unbelievable, why don't you want to come?; **j'ai eu une chance i.** I was incredibly lucky, I had incredible luck; **d'une bêtise i.** incredibly stupid; **c'est quand même i., ce retard!** this delay is getting ridiculous!; **c'est i., ça!** I don't believe it!; **ils sont incroyables de suffisance** they're unbelievably self-important

NMF *Hist* Incroyable, dandy

incroyablement [ɛ̃krwajabləmɑ̃] ADV incredibly, unbelievably, amazingly

incroyance [ɛ̃krwajɑ̃s] NF unbelief

incroyant, -e [ɛ̃krwajɑ̃, -ɑ̃t] ADJ unbelieving

NM,F unbeliever

incrustant, -e [ɛ̃krystɑ̃, -ɑ̃t] ADJ incrusting, coating

incrustation [ɛ̃krystasjɔ̃] NF **1** *(décoration)* inlay; *(procédé)* inlaying; **avec incrustations de nacre** inlaid with mother-of-pearl **2** *Géol (action)* encrusting; *(résultat)* incrustation **3** *Couture* insertion **4** *TV* (image) inlay, cut-in; **i. couleur** chroma key **5** *(dépôt → sur une chaudière)* fur, scale

incruste [ɛ̃kryst] NF *Fam* **si on l'invite, il va encore taper l'i.** if we invite him, we'll never get rid of him; **il a tapé l'i. à ma soirée** he gatecrashed my party

incruster [3] [ɛ̃kryste] VT **1** *(orner)* to inlay; **i. qch de** to inlay sth with; **un bracelet incrusté d'émeraudes** a bracelet inlaid with emeralds **2** *(recouvrir → gén)* to incrust, to coat; *(→ de calcaire)* to fur up **3** *Constr (pierre)* to insert **4** *TV* to inlay

▸**s'incruster** VPR **1** *(se couvrir de calcaire)* to become incrusted, to become covered in scale, to fur up **2** *(adhérer)* to build up; **enlever le calcaire qui s'est incrusté** to remove the build-up of scale **3** *Fam (personne)* **l'ennui, c'est que si on l'invite, il s'incruste** the problem is that if we ask him over, he'll overstay his welcome; **ne t'incruste pas** don't stick around too long; **ils font une fête, on s'incruste?** they're having a party, let's gatecrash

incubateur, -trice [ɛ̃kybatœr, -tris] ADJ *Biol* incubating

NM *Méd & Écon* incubator

incubation [ɛ̃kybasjɔ̃] NF **1** *(d'œufs)* incubation **2** *(d'une maladie)* incubation; **l'i. dure trois jours, il y a une période d'i. de trois jours** the incubation period is three days

incubatrice [ɛ̃kybatris] *voir* **incubateur**

incube [ɛ̃kyb] NM *(démon)* incubus

incuber [3] [ɛ̃kybe] VT *(œuf)* to incubate

incuit [ɛ̃kɥi] NM *Tech* unburned part

inculcation [ɛ̃kylkasjɔ̃] NF *Littéraire* inculcation, instilling

inculpable [ɛ̃kylpabl] ADJ chargeable

inculpation [ɛ̃kylpasjɔ̃] NF indictment, charge; **le juge lui a notifié son i.** the judge informed him/her that he/she was being charged; **sous l'i. d'assassinat** charged with murder; **être sous le coup d'une i. (pour)** to be indicted (for) *or* on a charge (of)

inculpé, -e [ɛ̃kylpe] NM,F **l'i.** the accused

inculper [3] [ɛ̃kylpe] VT to charge (**de** *ou* **pour** with)

inculquer [3] [ɛ̃kylke] VT to inculcate; **i. qch à qn** to inculcate sth in sb

inculte [ɛ̃kylt] ADJ **1** *(campagne, pays)* uncultivated **2** *(esprit, intelligence, personne)* uneducated, uncultured, uncultivated; **ils sont complètement incultes** they're totally ignorant **3** *(cheveux)* unkempt, dishevelled; *(barbe)* untidy

incultivable [ɛ̃kyltivabl] ADJ unworkable, uncultivable; **des terres incultivables** wasteland; **ces landes sont incultivables** these moors are no use for farming *or* as farmland

incultivé, -e [ɛ̃kyltive] ADJ *Littéraire (région, terre)* uncultivated

inculture [ɛ̃kyltyr] NF *(d'une personne)* lack of culture *or* education

incunable [ɛ̃kynabl] ADJ *(édition)* incunabular

NM incunabulum, incunable; **les incunables** the incunabula

incurabilité [ɛ̃kyrabilite] NF *Méd* incurability, incurableness

incurable [ɛ̃kyrabl] ADJ **1** *Méd* incurable **2** *(incorrigible → personne, défaut)* incurable, inveterate; **d'une paresse/bêtise i.** incurably lazy/stupid

NMF *Méd* incurable

incurablement [ɛ̃kyrabləmɑ̃] ADV **1** *Méd* incurably **2** *(irrémédiablement)* incurably, desperately, hopelessly

incurie [ɛ̃kyri] NF *Sout* negligence; **faire preuve d'i.** to be negligent, to be guilty of negligence

incurieux, -euse [ɛ̃kyrjø, -øz] ADJ *Littéraire* incurious (**de** of), lacking in curiosity

incuriosité [ɛ̃kyrjozite] NF *Littéraire* incuriosity, lack of curiosity

incursion [ɛ̃kyrsjɔ̃] NF 1 *Mil* foray, raid 2 *(exploration → d'un domaine)* foray, incursion 3 *(entrée soudaine)* intrusion; **faire une i. dans une réunion** to burst into a meeting

incurvation [ɛ̃kyrvasjɔ̃] NF bending, curving, incurvation

incurvé, -e [ɛ̃kyrve] ADJ curved, bent, incurved

incurver [3] [ɛ̃kyrve] VT to curve (inwards), to make into a curve
▸ **s'incurver** VPR 1 *(trajectoire)* to curve (inwards or in), to bend 2 *(étagère)* to sag

incus, -e [ɛ̃ky, -yz] ADJ incuse
❑ **incuse** NF *(médaille)* incuse medal; *(pièce de monnaie)* incuse coin

indaguer [3] [ɛ̃dage] VI *Belg Jur* to carry out an investigation

indatable [ɛ̃databl] ADJ *(manuscrit, ruines)* undatable, undateable

Inde [ɛ̃d] NF **l'I.** India; **vivre en I.** to live in India; **aller en I.** to go to India

indé, -e [ɛ̃de] ADJ *Fam (abrév **indépendant**)* indie; **le rock i.** indie (rock)

indéboulonnable [ɛ̃debulɔnabl] ADJ *Hum* **il est i.!** they'll never be able to sack him!

indébrouillable [ɛ̃debrujabl] ADJ *(écheveau, procès)* hopelessly entangled, inextricable

indécelable [ɛ̃desəlabl] ADJ undetectable, indiscernible

indécemment [ɛ̃desamɑ̃] ADV indecently

indécence [ɛ̃desɑ̃s] NF 1 *(manque de pudeur)* indecency 2 *(propos, acte)* indecency, impropriety

indécent, -e [ɛ̃desɑ̃, -ɑ̃t] ADJ 1 *(honteux)* indecent; **c'est un gaspillage presque i.** the waste is almost obscene 2 *(licencieux)* indecent, obscene

indéchiffrable [ɛ̃deʃifrabl] ADJ 1 *(code)* undecipherable, indecipherable; **aucun code n'est i.** there's no code that can't be broken or cracked 2 *(écriture)* illegible, unreadable 3 *(visage, mystère, pensée)* inscrutable, impenetrable

indéchirable [ɛ̃deʃirabl] ADJ tear-resistant

indécidable [ɛ̃desidabl] ADJ *Ling & Math* undecidable

indécis, -e [ɛ̃desi, -iz] ADJ 1 *(flou)* vague, indistinct; **on apercevait quelques formes indécises dans le brouillard** a few blurred shapes could be made out in the fog
2 *(incertain)* undecided, unsettled; **la victoire est restée indécise jusqu'à la fin** victory was uncertain until the very end; **le temps est i.** the weather is unsettled
3 *(hésitant → momentanément)* undecided, unsure, uncertain; *(→ de nature)* indecisive, irresolute; **je suis i. (sur la solution à choisir)** I'm undecided (as to the best solution), I can't make up my mind (which solution is the best); **il a toujours été i.** he's always been indecisive, he never has been able to make up his mind
NM,F indecisive person; *(électeur)* floating voter, don't-know; **c'est un i.** he can never make his mind up; **le vote des i.** the floating vote

indécision [ɛ̃desizjɔ̃] NF *(caractère irrésolu)* indecisiveness; *(hésitation)* indecision; **être dans l'i. (quant à)** to be undecided or unsure (about)

indéclinable [ɛ̃deklinabl] ADJ indeclinable; **le mot est i.** the word does not decline

indécodable [ɛ̃dekɔdabl] ADJ 1 *(impossible à décoder)* undecodable, that cannot be decoded 2 *Ordinat* undecodable

indécollable [ɛ̃dekɔlabl] ADJ non-removable; *(revêtement)* permanent

indécomposable [ɛ̃dekɔ̃pozabl] ADJ *(corps, ensemble)* indecomposable

indécrottable [ɛ̃dekrɔtabl] ADJ *Fam* hopeless; **c'est un i. imbécile!** he's hopelessly stupid!; **un i. réactionnaire** an out-and-out reactionary

indéfectibilité [ɛ̃defɛktibilite] NF 1 *(d'une amitié, du soutien)* staunchness, unfailingness 2 *Rel* indefectibility

indéfectible [ɛ̃defɛktibl] ADJ *(amitié, soutien)* staunch, unfailing, unshakeable; *(confiance)* unshakeable; *(mémoire)* unfailing; **une i. volonté** staunch determination; **une foi i. en l'informatique** an unshakeable faith in computers; **avec une ambition i.** with unflagging or unfailing ambition 2 *Rel* indefectible

indéfectiblement [ɛ̃defɛktiblamɑ̃] ADV staunchly, unfailingly, unshakeably

indéfendable [ɛ̃defɑ̃dabl] ADJ 1 *(condamnable → personne, comportement)* indefensible 2 *(insoutenable → théorie, opinion)* indefensible, untenable

indéfini, -e [ɛ̃defini] ADJ 1 *(sans limites)* indefinite, unlimited; **un temps i.** an undetermined length of time 2 *(confus)* ill-defined, vague; **un trouble i. l'envahit** a vague feeling of uneasiness crept over him/her 3 *Ling* indefinite
NM *Ling* indefinite

indéfiniment [ɛ̃definimɑ̃] ADV indefinitely, for ever; **répéter qch i.** to say sth over and over again, to keep repeating sth

indéfinissable [ɛ̃definisabl] ADJ indefinable

indéformable [ɛ̃defɔrmabl] ADJ *(chapeau, vêtement)* which cannot be pulled out of shape; *(semelle)* rigid; *(acier)* that does not buckle

indéfrichable [ɛ̃defriʃabl] ADJ *(sol, terre)* unclearable

indéfrisable [ɛ̃defrizabl] NF *Vieilli* perm, permanent wave

indéhiscent, -e [ɛ̃deisɑ̃, -ɑ̃t] ADJ *Bot* indehiscent

indélébile [ɛ̃delebil] ADJ 1 *(ineffaçable → encre)* indelible, indelible; *(→ tache)* indelible 2 *(indestructible → souvenir)* indelible

indélébilité [ɛ̃delebilite] NF indelibility

indélicat, -e [ɛ̃delika, -at] ADJ 1 *(grossier)* coarse, indelicate, rude 2 *(véreux)* dishonest, unscrupulous

indélicatement [ɛ̃delikatmɑ̃] ADV 1 *(grossièrement)* coarsely, indelicately 2 *(malhonnêtement)* dishonestly, unscrupulously

indélicatesse [ɛ̃delikatɛs] NF 1 *(des manières)* indelicacy, coarseness 2 *(caractère malhonnête)* dishonesty, unscrupulousness 3 *(acte malhonnête)* dishonest or unscrupulous act; **commettre une i.** to behave dishonestly

indémaillable [ɛ̃demajabl] ADJ *(bas, collant)* runproof, *Br* ladderproof; *(pull, tissu)* run-resistant, runproof
NM non-run or runproof fabric

indémêlable [ɛ̃demelabl] ADJ *(cheveux)* hopelessly entangled; *(intrigue)* inextricable, entangled

indemne [ɛ̃dɛmn] ADJ 1 *(physiquement)* unhurt, unharmed; **ma sœur est sortie i. de la collision** my sister was unhurt in the collision 2 *(moralement)* unscathed; **il est sorti i. du scandale** he emerged unscathed from the scandal

indemnisable [ɛ̃dɛmnizabl] ADJ *(propriétaire, réfugié)* entitled to compensation, *Am* compensable

indemnisation [ɛ̃dɛmnizasjɔ̃] NF 1 *(argent)* compensation, indemnity; **il a reçu 5000 euros d'i.** he received 5,000 euros compensation 2 *(procédé)* compensating; **l'i. des sinistrés prendra plusieurs mois** it will take several months to compensate the disaster victims

indemnisé, -e [ɛ̃dɛmnize] ADJ compensated for
NM,F person receiving compensation

indemniser [3] [ɛ̃dɛmnize] VT 1 *(après un sinistre)* to compensate, to indemnify; **ils seront tous indemnisés** they will all receive compensation; **elle a réussi à faire i. la famille de la victime** she managed to obtain compensation for the victim's family; **se faire i.** to receive compensation
2 *(après une dépense)* **être indemnisé de ses frais** to have one's expenses paid for or reimbursed; **quand je voyage, je suis indemnisé (de mes frais)** when I travel, it all goes on expenses

indemnitaire [ɛ̃dɛmnitɛr] ADJ compensative, compensatory
NMF *(recevant une allocation)* recipient of an allowance 2 *(après un sinistre)* person awarded compensation

indemnité [ɛ̃dɛmnite] NF 1 *(après un sinistre)* compensation; *(dommages et intérêts)* damages; **i. en argent** cash compensation; **i. de clientèle** compensation for loss of custom; **i. de caractère personnel** compensation for personal loss; **i. compensatrice** compensation; **i. compensatrice de congés payés** pay in lieu of holidays; **i. d'éviction** compensation for eviction; **i. d'expropriation** compensation for expropriation; **i. de retard** late payment penalty; **i. de rupture** severance pay; **i. de rupture abusive** compensation for breach of contract
2 *(allocation)* allowance; **i. de cherté de vie** cost of living allowance, *Br* weighting; **i. de**

chômage unemployment benefit; **i. complémentaire** additional allowance; **i. conventionnelle** contractual allowance; **i. de déménagement** relocation grant or allowance; **i. de départ** severance pay; **i. de déplacement** travel or transport allowance; **i. journalière** daily allowance; **i. kilométrique** = mileage allowance; **i. de licenciement** redundancy payment; **i. de logement** accommodation allowance; **i. de maladie** sickness benefit; **i. parlementaire** *Br* ≃ member of parliament's salary; **i. de représentation** entertainment allowance; **i. de résidence** housing allowance; **i. de retard** late payment penalty; **i. de séjour** living expenses; **i. de transport** travel allowance or expenses; **i. viagère de départ** = severance money for retiring farmers; **i. de vie chère** cost of living allowance

indémodable [ɛ̃demodabl] ADJ perennially fashionable; **un tailleur i.** a classic suit, a suit that will never go out of fashion

indémontable [ɛ̃demɔ̃tabl] ADJ *(jouet, serrure)* which cannot be taken apart or dismantled; *(étagère)* fixed

indémontrable [ɛ̃demɔ̃trabl] ADJ 1 *Ling & Math* indemonstrable 2 *(non prouvable)* unprovable

indène [ɛ̃dɛn] NM *Chim* indene

indéniable [ɛ̃denjabl] ADJ undeniable; **il est i. que...** it cannot be denied that..., there's no denying that...

indéniablement [ɛ̃denjablamɑ̃] ADV undeniably

indénombrable [ɛ̃denɔ̃brabl] ADJ innumerable, uncountable

indénouable [ɛ̃denwabl] ADJ that cannot be untied

indentation [ɛ̃dɑ̃tasjɔ̃] NF 1 *(échancrure)* indentation; **les indentations du littoral** the ragged coastline 2 *Typ* indent; **i. à droite/gauche** right/left indent

indenter [ɛ̃dɑ̃te] VT *Typ* to indent

indépassable [ɛ̃depasabl] ADJ *(crédit, limite)* unextendable, fixed; *(coureur)* unbeatable

indépendamment [ɛ̃depɑ̃damɑ̃] ADV *(séparément)* independently
❑ **indépendamment de** PRÉP *(outre, mis à part)* apart from; *(en faisant abstraction de)* regardless of; **i. de son salaire, il a des rentes** apart from his salary he has a private income; **i. l'un de l'autre** independently of one another; **i. du résultat** regardless of the result

indépendance [ɛ̃depɑ̃dɑ̃s] NF 1 *(d'un pays, d'une personne)* independence; **prendre son i.** to assume one's independence; **le jour de l'I.** Independence Day; **il a une grande i. d'esprit** he's very independently minded, he's good at thinking for himself 2 *(absence de relation)* independence

indépendant, -e [ɛ̃depɑ̃dɑ̃, -ɑ̃t] ADJ 1 *(gén) & Pol* independent; **pour des raisons indépendantes de notre volonté** for reasons beyond our control
2 *(distinct)* **ces deux problèmes sont indépendants l'un de l'autre** these two problems are separate or distinct from each other; **une chambre indépendante** a self-contained room; **avec salle de bains indépendante** with own or separate bathroom
3 *(traducteur, photographe)* freelance; *(député)* independent
4 *Ling & Math* independent
5 *Biol* free-living
NM,F 1 *Pol* independent
2 *(travailleur)* self-employed worker; *(traducteur, journaliste, photographe)* freelancer
❑ **indépendante** NF *Gram* independent clause
❑ **en indépendant** ADV **travailler en i.** to work freelance or on a freelance basis

indépendantisme [ɛ̃depɑ̃datism] NM **l'i.** the independence or separatist movement

indépendantiste [ɛ̃depɑ̃datist] ADJ **mouvement i.** independence or separatist movement
NMF separatist

indépensé, -e [ɛ̃depɑ̃se] ADJ *Fin* unspent

indéracinable [ɛ̃derasinabl] ADJ 1 *(préjugé, habitude)* entrenched, ineradicable 2 *Fam (personne)* **deux ou trois poivrots indéracinables** two or three drunks who couldn't be shifted

indéréglable [ɛ̃dereglabl] ADJ *(mécanisme, montre)* extremely reliable

Indes [ɛ̃d] **NFPL** Indies; *Hist* **les I. occidentales/orientales** the West/East Indies; *Hist* **la Compagnie des I. orientales** the East India Company; **aux I.** *(en Inde)* in India

'Les Indes galantes' *Rameau* 'The Gallant Indes'

indescriptible [ɛ̃dɛskriptibl] **ADJ** indescribable

indésirable [ɛ̃dezirabl] **ADJ** undesirable, unwanted; **une présence i.** an undesirable *or* unwanted presence; **effets indésirables: assoupissements, nausées** may cause drowsiness or nausea

NMF undesirable; **on nous traite comme des indésirables** we are treated as though we were not wanted

Indes-Occidentales [ɛ̃dɔksidɑ̃tal] **NFPL** the (British) West Indies

indestructibilité [ɛ̃dɛstryktibilite] **NF** indestructibility, indestructibleness

indestructible [ɛ̃dɛstryktibl] **ADJ** *(bâtiment, canon)* indestructible, built to last; *(amour, lien)* indestructible

indétectable [ɛ̃detɛktabl] **ADJ** undetectable

indéterminable [ɛ̃detɛrminabl] **ADJ** indeterminable; **sa date de naissance est i.** his/her date of birth cannot be determined (with any certainty)

indétermination [ɛ̃detɛrminasjɔ̃] **NF 1** *(approximation)* vagueness **2** *(indécision → momentanée)* indecision; *(→ de nature)* indecisiveness **3** *Math* indeterminacy **4** *Phil* indetermination

indéterminé, -e [ɛ̃detɛrmine] **ADJ 1** *(non défini)* indeterminate, unspecified; **à une date indéterminée** at an unspecified date; **dans une direction indéterminée** in an unknown direction; **pour une raison indéterminée** for some unknown reason; **l'origine du mot est indéterminée** the origin of the word is uncertain *or* not known **2** *Math* indeterminate **3** *Phil* indeterminate

❑ **indéterminée NF** *Math* indeterminate variable

indéterminisme [ɛ̃detɛrminism] **NM** *Phil* indeterminism

index [ɛ̃dɛks] **NM 1** *(doigt)* index finger, forefinger **2** *(repère)* pointer **3** *(liste)* index **4** *Hist* **l'I.** the Index; **mettre qn/qch à l'i.** to blacklist sb/sth **5** *Ordinat* (fixed) index **6** *Méd* **i. glycémique** glycaemic index **7** *Belg Écon* **i. (des prix)** price index

indexage [ɛ̃dɛksaʒ] **NM** indexing, indexation

indexation [ɛ̃dɛksasjɔ̃] **NF 1** *(classement)* indexation, indexing **2** *Écon (des prix, des salaires)* indexation, index-linking (**sur** to)

indexé, -e [ɛ̃dekse] **ADJ** *Écon (prix, salaires)* indexed, index-linked (**sur** to); *Ordinat (valeur)* indexed

indexer [4] [ɛ̃dɛkse] **VT 1** *(ouvrage)* to index **2** *Écon* to index, to index-link (**sur** to) **3** *Ordinat* to index

indexeur [ɛ̃deksœr] **NM** indexer

Indiana [indjana] **NM l'I.** Indiana; **dans l'I.** in Indiana

Indianapolis [indjanapɔlis] **NM** Indianapolis

indianisme [ɛ̃djanism] **NM** *(mot)* Indian word; *(expression)* Indian turn of phrase

indianiste [ɛ̃djanist] **NMF** specialist on India

indianologie [ɛ̃djanɔlɔʒi] **NF** Amerindian studies

indic [ɛ̃dik] **NM** *Fam* squealer, *Br* grass, *Am* rat

indican [ɛ̃dikɑ̃] **NM** *Chim* indican

indicateur, -trice [ɛ̃dikatœr, -tris] **ADJ** indicative

NM,F *(informateur)* (police) informer *or* spy

NM 1 *(plan, liste)* **i. des rues** street guide *or* directory; **i. des chemins de fer** *Br* railway *or Am* railroad timetable

2 *(appareil)* indicator, gauge; **i. d'altitude** altimeter; *Tech* **i. de crête** peak programme meter; **i. de changement de direction** (directional *or* direction) indicator; **i. de niveau de carburant** fuel gauge; **i. de pression** pressure gauge; **i. de vitesse** speedometer

3 *(indice)* indicator, pointer; **i. d'activité** activity indicator; **indicateurs d'alerte** economic indicators, business indicators; **i. clé** key indicator; **i. de développement humain** Human Development Index; **i. (d'activité) économique** economic indicator; **i. de marché** market indicator; **i. statistique** statistical indicator; *Bourse* **i. de tendance** market indicator

4 *Chim & Ling* indicator; *Chim* **i. universel de pH** universal indicator

5 *Nucl* (radioactive) indicator *or* tracer

indicatif, -ive [ɛ̃dikatif, -iv] **ADJ** *(état, signe)* indicative; *Gram (mode)* indicative

NM 1 *Gram* indicative **2** *Rad & TV* **i. (musical)** signature *or Br* theme tune **3** *Tél (de zone)* (dialling) code; **i. du pays** international dialling code; **i. de zone** area code **4** *Ordinat* **i. d'appel** ident; **i. de fichier** filename; **i. de tri** sort key; **i. (du) DOS** DOS prompt

indication [ɛ̃dikasjɔ̃] **NF 1** *(action d'indiquer)* indication, indicating, pointing out; **l'i. de la date de péremption est obligatoire** the use-by date must be shown *or* indicated

2 *(recommandation)* instruction; **j'ai suivi toutes vos indications** I followed all your instructions; **sauf i. contraire** unless otherwise specified; **les indications du mode d'emploi** the directions for use; **les indications de montage** the assembly instructions; **indications scéniques** stage directions

3 *(information, renseignement)* information *(UNCOUNT)*, piece of information; **il a été arrêté sur les indications d'un complice** he was arrested on information given by an accomplice

4 *(signe)* sign, indication

5 *(aperçu)* indication; **c'est une excellente i. sur l'état de l'économie** it's an excellent indication of the state of the economy

6 *Méd & Pharm* **sauf i. contraire du médecin** unless otherwise stated by the doctor; **indications (thérapeutiques)** indications; **indications:...** *(sur notice)* suitable for...

7 *Com* **i. d'origine** label of origin; *Com* **i. géographique protégée** = designation of a product which guarantees its authentic place of origin and gives the name protected status

8 *Jur* **i. de paiement** = recognition of part-payment of a debt made in writing by the creditor

indicative [ɛ̃dikativ] *voir* **indicatif**

indicatrice [ɛ̃dikatris] *voir* **indicateur**

indice [ɛ̃dis] **NM 1** *(symptôme → d'un changement, d'un phénomène)* indication, sign; *(→ d'une maladie)* sign, symptom; **aucun i. ne laissait présager le drame** there was no sign of the impending tragedy; **la presse s'accorde à y voir l'i. de proches négociations** all the papers agree that this is evidence *or* a sign that negotiations are imminent

2 *(d'une enquête policière)* clue; *(d'une énigme)* clue, hint

3 *(chiffre indicateur) Écon, Opt & Phys* index; *Bourse* index, average; **i. d'activité industrielle** industrial activity index; *Mktg* **i. ad hoc** specific indicator; **i. boursier** share index; **l'i. CAC 40** the CAC 40 index; *Pétr* **i. de cétane** cetane number; **i. de confiance** consumer confidence index; *Bourse* **i. composé, i. composite** composite index; *Écon* **i. corrigé des variations saisonnières** seasonally adjusted index; *Bourse* **i. non-corrigé des variations saisonnières** non-seasonally adjusted index; *Écon* **i. des cours d'actions** share price index; **i. du coût de la vie** cost of living index; *Écon* **i. de croissance** index of growth; *Bourse* **l'i. DAX** the Dax index; *Écon* **i. de développement humain** Human Development Index; *Bourse* **l'i. Dow Jones** the Dow Jones index; *Bourse* **l'i. FTSE des 100 valeurs** the FTSE 100 share index; *Bourse* **l'i. Hang Seng** the Hang Seng index; **l'i. de l'INSEE** ≃ the retail price index; *Phot* **i. de lumination** exposure value *or* index; *Méd* **i. de masse corporelle** body mass index; *Bourse* **l'i. MidCAC** = Paris stock exchange index of 100 medium range shares, *Am* ≃ MidCap index; *Bourse* **l'i. Nikkei** the Nikkei index; *Pétr* **i. d'octane** octane rating; *Aut* **i. d'octane moteur** motor octane numbers; *Pétr* **i. d'octane recherche** research octane number; **i. pollinique (de l'air)** pollen count; **i. pondéré** weighted index; **i. pondéré par le commerce extérieur** trade-weighted index; **i. des prix (à la consommation)** (consumer) price index; **i. des prix de détail** retail price index; **i. des prix de gros** wholesale price index; *Écon* **i. des prix et des salaires** wage and price index; **i. des prix à la production** producer price index; **i. de profit** profit indicator; **i. de refroidissement (au vent)** windchill factor; *Admin* **i. de rémunération** salary grading; **i. de rentabilité** profitability index; *Écon* **i. de richesse vive** consumer purchasing power index; *Bourse* **l'i. SBF** the SBF index *(broad-based French Stock Exchange index)*; *Bourse* **i. des titres** stock average; *Admin* **i. de traitement** salary grading; **i. des valeurs boursières** share index; **l'i. Xetra-Dax** the Xetra-Dax index

4 *Rad & TV* **l'i. d'écoute** the audience rating, the ratings; **avoir un mauvais i. d'écoute** to have a low (audience) rating, to get bad ratings

5 i. de protection *(d'une crème solaire)* sun protection factor

6 *Math* index; *Typ* subscript; **b i. 3** b subscript *or* index 3; **3 en i.** subscript 3

7 *Ling* index

indiciaire [ɛ̃disjɛr] **ADJ 1** *Écon* index-based; **impôt i.** wealth-related tax **2** *Admin* grade-related

indicible [ɛ̃disibl] **ADJ** indescribable, unutterable

indiciblement [ɛ̃disibləmɑ̃] **ADV** ineffably

indiciel, -elle [ɛ̃disjɛl] **ADJ 1** *Écon & Math* index *(épith)* **2** *Ling* contextual, deictic

indiction [ɛ̃diksjɔ̃] **NF 1** *Antiq & Hist* indiction, cycle *or* era of indiction **2** *Rel (d'un concile)* convocation

indien, -enne [ɛ̃djɛ̃, -ɛn] **ADJ 1** *(de l'Inde)* Indian **2** *(d'Amérique)* American Indian, Native American

❑ **Indien, -enne NM,F 1** *(de l'Inde)* Indian **2 I. (d'Amérique)** American Indian, Native American

❑ **indienne NF 1** *Tex Br* printed (Indian) cotton, *Am* printed calico **2** *(nage)* overarm stroke

indie-rock [indirɔk] **NM INV** indie music

indifféremment [ɛ̃diferamɑ̃] **ADV 1** *(aussi bien)* **elle joue i. de la main droite ou de la main gauche** she plays equally well with her right or left hand; **la radio marche i. sur piles ou sur secteur** the radio can run on batteries or be plugged into the mains **2** *(sans discrimination)* indiscriminately; **il regarde toutes les émissions i.** he watches television whatever is on

indifférence [ɛ̃diferɑ̃s] **NF** *(détachement → envers une situation, un sujet)* indifference, lack of interest; *(→ envers quelqu'un)* indifference; **son roman est paru dans la plus grande i.** the publication of his/her novel went completely unnoticed; **faire qch avec i.** to do sth indifferently *or* with indifference; *Fam* **il me fait le coup de l'i.** he's pretending not to notice me; **i. pour qch** lack of concern for sth; **son i. totale pour la politique** his/her total lack of interest in *or* complete indifference to politics

indifférenciable [ɛ̃diferɑ̃sjabl] **ADJ** indistinguishable; **ces jumeaux sont indifférenciables** it's impossible to tell those twins apart

indifférenciation [ɛ̃diferɑ̃sjasjɔ̃] **NF 1** *Physiol* absence of differentiation; **pendant l'i. sexuelle de l'embryon** while the embryo is still sexually undifferentiated **2** *Méd* anaplasia

indifférencié, -e [ɛ̃diferɑ̃sje] **ADJ 1** *Physiol (organisme)* undifferentiated; *(cellule)* unspecialized **2** *Méd* anaplastic

indifférent, -e [ɛ̃diferɑ̃, -ɑ̃t] **ADJ 1** *(insensible, détaché)* indifferent; **leur divorce me laisse i.** their divorce is of no interest to me *or* is a matter of indifference to me; **sa mort ne laissera personne i.** his/her death will leave no one indifferent; **ta requête ne pourra pas le laisser i.** he can't fail to respond to your request; **elle me laisse i.** she leaves me cold; **elle ne le laisse pas i.** he's not blind *or* indifferent to her charms; **être i. à la politique** to be indifferent towards politics; **il a été i. à tous mes arguments** he was unmoved by my arguments; **elle est restée indifférente à ses avances** she was indifferent to his advances, his advances left her cold

2 *(d'intérêt égal)* indifferent, immaterial; **âge i.** *(dans les petites annonces)* age unimportant *or* immaterial; **religion/race indifférente** *(dans les petites annonces)* religion/race no barrier

3 *(insignifiant)* indifferent, uninteresting, of no interest; **parler de choses indifférentes** to talk about this and that; **ça m'est i.** it's (all) the same to me, I don't care either way; **la mort ne m'est pas/m'est complètement indifférente** I do care/don't care if I live or die; **il lui était i. de partir (ou non)** it didn't matter *or* it was immaterial to

him/her whether he/she left or not; **la suite des événements m'est indifférente** what happens next is of no concern *or* interest to me

NM,F indifferent *or* apathetic person; **il fait l'i.** *ou* **joue les indifférents** he's feigning indifference

indifférentisme [ɛ̃diferɑ̃tism] **NM** *Pol & Rel* indifferentism

indifférer [18] [ɛ̃difere] **indifférer à VT IND 1** *(n'inspirer aucun intérêt à)* **il m'indiffère complètement** I'm totally indifferent to him, I couldn't care less about him; **tout l'indiffère** he/she takes no interest in anything **2** *(être égal à)* to be of no importance to; **le prix m'indiffère** the price is of no importance (to me); **ça m'indiffère** I don't mind, it's all the same to me

indigénat [ɛ̃diʒena] **NM 1** *Hist* = before 1945, special system of administration applying to the native populations of the French colonies **2** *Suisse (droit de cité)* citizenship

indigence [ɛ̃diʒɑ̃s] **NF 1** *(matérielle)* poverty, *Sout* indigence; **vivre dans l'i.** to be destitute **2** *(intellectuelle)* paucity, poverty

indigène [ɛ̃diʒɛn] **ADJ 1** *(d'avant la colonisation → droits, pratique)* native, indigenous; *(→ coutumes)* native **2** *(autochtone → population)* native, indigenous **3** *Bot & Zool* indigenous, native (**de** to); **la faune i. de ces régions** the fauna indigenous to these regions

NMF 1 *(colonisé)* native **2** *(autochtone)* native **3** *Bot & Zool* indigen, indigene, native **4** *Suisse* citizen

indigénisme [ɛ̃diʒenism] **NM** nativism

indigent, -e [ɛ̃diʒɑ̃, -ɑ̃t] **ADJ 1** *(pauvre)* destitute, poor, *Sout* indigent **2** *(insuffisant)* poor; **un esprit i.** an impoverished mind; **avoir une imagination indigente** to be totally lacking in imagination

NM,F pauper; **les indigents** the destitute, the poor

indigeste [ɛ̃diʒɛst] **ADJ 1** *(nourriture)* indigestible, heavy; **je trouve la choucroute très i.** I find sauerkraut very heavy on the stomach **2** *(livre, compte-rendu)* indigestible; **je trouve ce livre i.** this book is heavy going

indigestion [ɛ̃diʒɛstjɔ̃] **NF 1** *Méd* indigestion *(UNCOUNT)*; **avoir une i.** to have indigestion; **se donner une i.** to give onself indigestion; **j'ai mangé tellement de chocolat que je m'en suis donné une i.** I ate so much chocolate that I made myself ill **2** *Fig* **avoir une i. de qch** to be sick of sth

indigète [ɛ̃diʒɛt] **ADJ** *Antiq* **dieux indigètes** local patron deities

indignation [ɛ̃diɲasjɔ̃] **NF** indignation; **protester avec i.** to protest indignantly; **un regard d'i.** an indignant look; **à l'i. de tous** to the indignation of everyone present

indigne [ɛ̃diɲ] **ADJ 1 i. de** *(honneur, confiance)* unworthy of; **i. d'un tel honneur** unworthy *or* undeserving of such an honour; **un mensonge i. de lui** a lie unworthy of him; **ce travail est i. de lui** this work is not good enough for him *or* is beneath him; **des médisances indignes d'une sœur** malicious gossip one doesn't expect from a sister; **il est i. de succéder à son père** he's not fit to take his father's place

2 *(choquant → action, propos)* disgraceful, outrageous, shameful; **avoir une attitude i.** to behave shamefully *or* disgracefully

3 *(méprisable → personne)* unworthy; **c'est une mère i.** she's not fit to be a mother; **un fils i.** an unworthy son

4 *Jur* **être i. d'hériter** to be judicially debarred from inheriting

NMF *Jur* (judicially) disinherited person

indigné, -e [ɛ̃diɲe] **ADJ** indignant, shocked, outraged; **d'un air/ton i.** indignantly

indignement [ɛ̃diɲəmɑ̃] **ADV** disgracefully, shamefully

indigner [3] [ɛ̃diɲe] **VT** to make indignant, to incense, to gall

▸**s'indigner VPR** *(se révolter)* to be indignant; **il y a de quoi s'i.!** there's good reason to be indignant!; **s'i. de qch** to be indignant about sth; **je m'indigne de voir ce crime impuni** it makes me indignant to see this crime go unpunished; **s'i. contre l'injustice** to cry out *or* to inveigh against injustice

indignité [ɛ̃diɲite] **NF 1** *(caractère indigne)* unworthiness, disgracefulness **2** *(acte)* shameful *or* disgraceful act **3** *Jur* **i. successorale** judicial debarment from succession **4** *Hist* **i. nationale** loss of citizenship rights *(for having collaborated with Germany during WWII)*

indigo [ɛ̃digo] **ADJ INV** indigo (blue)

NM indigo; **i. bleu** indigotin

indigotier [ɛ̃digɔtje] **NM** *Bot* indigo (plant)

indigotine [ɛ̃digɔtin] **NF** *Chim* indigotin

indiqué, -e [ɛ̃dike] **ADJ 1** *(recommandé → conduite)* advisable; **dans ton état, ce n'est pas très i. de fumer!** in your condition, smoking isn't really advisable *or* isn't really a sensible thing to do!; **dans votre cas, un séjour à la montagne me paraît tout à fait i.** a stay in the mountains seems to me to be just the thing you need

2 *(approprié → personne, objet)* **un vérin serait tout i.** what we need is a jack; **tu es tout i. pour le rôle** you're exactly the right person *or* the obvious choice for the part; **voilà une carrière tout indiquée pour un homme ambitieux** that's the obvious *or* very career for an ambitious man; **ce médicament est/n'est pas i. dans ce cas** this drug is appropriate/inappropriate in this case

3 *(date, jour)* agreed; *(endroit)* agreed, appointed; *(heure)* appointed

indique-fuites [ɛ̃dikfɥit] **NM INV** leak detector

INDIQUER [3] [ɛ̃dike]

> to show **1–3, 8** ▪ to point out **1** ▪ to show the way to **2** ▪ to indicate **3, 8** ▪ to note down **4** ▪ to mark **4** ▪ to suggest **5** ▪ to prescribe **5** ▪ to tell **6** ▪ to name **7**

VT 1 *(montrer d'un geste → chose, personne, lieu)* to show, to point out; **i. qch de la tête** to nod towards sth, to indicate sth with a nod; **i. qch de la main** to point out *or* to indicate sth with one's hand; **i. qn/qch du doigt** to point at sb/sth; **elle m'avait indiqué le suspect du regard** she'd shown me the suspect by looking at him; **il indiqua la porte avec son revolver** he pointed to the door with his gun; **je ne pourrais pas t'i. la ville avec précision sur la carte** I couldn't pinpoint the town on the map for you; **i. une fuite à qn** to show sb where a leak is

2 *(musée, autoroute, plage)* to show the way to; *(chemin)* to indicate, to show; **pouvez-vous m'i. (le chemin de) la gare?** could you show me the way to *or* direct me to the station?; **il ne s'est trouvé personne pour m'i. où se trouvait la galerie** nobody could tell me where the gallery was *or* show me the way to the gallery; **je me suis fait i. la station de métro la plus proche** I asked someone to tell me where the nearest underground station was

3 *(sujet: carte, enseigne, pancarte, statistiques)* to show, to say, to indicate; *(sujet: flèche, graphique)* to show; *(sujet: horaire)* to show, to say, to give; *(sujet: dictionnaire)* to say, to give; **l'aiguille de la boussole indique toujours le nord** the compass needle always points North; **le cadran indique la vitesse** the speed is shown on the dial; **le panneau vert indique la sortie** the green panel indicates the exit; **l'horloge indique 6 heures** the clock says 6 o'clock; **qu'indique le devis?** what does the estimate say?, how much does it say in the estimate?

4 *(noter → date, prix)* to note *or* to write (down); *(→ repère)* to mark, to draw; **indiquez votre adresse ici** write your address here; **ce n'est pas indiqué dans le contrat** it's not written down *or* mentioned in the contract; **la loi oblige à i. le prix des marchandises en vitrine** by law, you have to show the price of goods displayed in the window; **il indiqua la cache d'une croix sur la carte** he marked the hiding place with a cross on the map; **indique sur la liste les achats qui sont déjà faits** tick off on *or* mark on the list the items that have already been bought

5 *(conseiller → ouvrage, professionnel, restaurant)* to suggest, to recommend; *(→ traitement)* to prescribe, to give; **tu peux m'i. un bon coiffeur?** can you recommend a good hairdresser?; **une auberge qu'elle m'avait indiquée** a hostel she'd told me about

6 *(dire → marche à suivre, heure)* to tell; **je t'indiquerai comment faire** I'll tell you how to do it; **pourriez-vous m'i. le prix de ce vase?** could you tell me how much the vase is?; **le réceptionniste nous a indiqué nos chambres** the receptionist told us which rooms we had been given

7 *(fixer → lieu de rendez-vous, jour)* to give, to name; **indique-moi où et quand, j'y serai** tell me where and when *or* name the place and the time and I'll be there; **à l'heure indiquée** at the appointed *or* agreed time

8 *(être le signe de → phénomène)* to point to, to indicate; *(→ crainte, joie)* to show, to betray; **des signes qui indiquent un redressement économique** signs of economic recovery; **tout indique que nous allons vers une crise** everything suggests that we are heading towards a crisis; **ce cri indique que l'animal va attaquer** this cry indicates *or* means that the animal is going to attack

9 *Beaux-Arts* to sketch out; *Littérature* to outline

indirect, -e [ɛ̃dirɛkt] **ADJ 1** *(itinéraire, critique)* indirect; *(approche)* indirect, roundabout; *(influence)* indirect; **j'ai appris la nouvelle de façon indirecte** I heard the news in an indirect way; **faire allusion à qch de façon indirecte** to refer obliquely *or* indirectly to sth; **elle m'a fait des reproches indirects** she told me off in a roundabout way

2 *Jur* **héritier i.** collateral heir

3 *Com (coûts, vente)* indirect

4 *Gram* **complément i.** *(d'un verbe transitif)* indirect complement; *(d'un verbe intransitif)* prepositional complement; **discours** *ou* **style i.** indirect *or* reported speech

indirectement [ɛ̃dirɛktəmɑ̃] **ADV** indirectly; **je suis i. responsable** I'm indirectly responsible; **je l'ai su i.** I heard about it indirectly *or* in a roundabout way; **dire les choses i.** to say things in an indirect *or* a roundabout way; **nous sommes i. apparentés** we are indirectly related

indiscernable [ɛ̃disɛrnabl] **ADJ** indiscernible

indiscipline [ɛ̃disiplin] **NF** *(dans un groupe)* lack of discipline, indiscipline; *(d'un enfant)* disobedience; *(d'un soldat)* insubordination; **faire preuve d'i.** *(écoliers)* to be undisciplined; *(militaires)* to defy orders

indiscipliné, -e [ɛ̃disipline] **ADJ** *(dans un groupe)* undisciplined, unruly; *(enfant)* unruly, disobedient; *(soldat)* undisciplined, insubordinate; *Fig (cheveux)* unmanageable; *(mèches)* flyaway

indiscret, -ète [ɛ̃diskrɛ, -ɛt] **ADJ 1** *(curieux → personne)* inquisitive; *(→ demande, question)* indiscreet; *(→ regard)* inquisitive, prying; **sans (vouloir) être i., combien est-ce que ça vous a coûté?** could I possibly ask you how much you paid for it?; **comment le lui demander sans avoir l'air i.?** how could I ask him/her without seeming indiscreet *or* as though I'm prying?; **loin des oreilles indiscrètes** far from *or* out of reach of eavesdroppers; **à l'abri des regards indiscrets** safe from prying eyes

2 *(révélateur → propos, geste)* indiscreet, telltale; *(→ personne)* indiscreet, garrulous; **trahi par des langues indiscrètes** given away by wagging tongues; **des témoins indiscrets en ont parlé aux journalistes** witnesses have leaked it to the press

NM,F 1 *(personne curieuse)* inquisitive person

2 *(personne bavarde)* indiscreet person

indiscrètement [ɛ̃diskrɛtmɑ̃] **ADV 1** *(sans tact)* indiscreetly **2** *(avec curiosité)* inquisitively

indiscrétion [ɛ̃diskresjɔ̃] **NF 1** *(d'une personne)* inquisitiveness, curiosity; *(d'une question)* indiscreetness, tactlessness; **pardonnez mon i.** forgive me for asking; **il a poussé l'i. jusqu'à demander des détails** he was so indiscreet as to ask for details; **sans i., avez-vous des enfants?** if you don't mind my asking, do you have children?

2 *(révélation)* indiscretion; **nous savons par des indiscrétions que...** we know unofficially that..., it's been leaked that...; **commettre une i.** to commit an indiscretion, to say something one shouldn't

indiscutable [ɛ̃diskytabl] **ADJ** indisputable, unquestionable; **vous avez raison, c'est i.** you're indisputably *or* unquestionably right

indiscutablement [ɛ̃diskytabləmã] **ADV** indisputably, unquestionably

indiscuté, -e [ɛ̃diskyte] **ADJ** undisputed; **le maître i. de la cuisine japonaise** the undisputed *or* uncontested master of Japanese cooking; **ses vertus curatives sont indiscutées** its curative powers are unquestioned

indispensable [ɛ̃dispɑ̃sabl] **ADJ** *(fournitures, machine)* essential, indispensable; *(mesures)* essential, vital, indispensable; *(précautions)* essential, required, necessary; *(personne)* indispensable; **cette entrevue est-elle vraiment i.?** is this interview really necessary?, do I really have to go through with this interview?; **tu te crois i.?** so you think you're indispensable?; **tes réflexions n'étaient pas indispensables!** we could have done without your remarks!; **des connaissances en électricité sont indispensables** some knowledge of electricity is essential; **anglais i.** *(dans une offre d'emploi)* English indispensable *or* essential; **il est i. de/que...** it's essential to/that...; **son fils lui est i.** he/she can't do without his/her son; **tu ne m'es pas i., tu sais!** I can do without you, you know!; **i. à tous les sportifs!** essential *or* a must for all sportsmen!; **mes lunettes me sont désormais indispensables** I can't do without my glasses now; **ce document m'est i. pour continuer mes recherches** this document is absolutely vital *or* essential if I am to carry on my research; **l'ordinateur est i. à l'édition** computers are vital in publishing; **tu n'es pas/tu es i. au projet** the project can/can't proceed without you

  NM l'i. *(le nécessaire)* the essentials; **n'emporte que l'i.** only take what you really need

indisponibilité [ɛ̃disponibilite] **NF 1** *(d'une machine)* downtime; *(d'une marchandise, d'une personne, de fonds)* non-availability, unavailability **2** *Jur* inalienability

indisponible [ɛ̃disponibl] **ADJ 1** *(marchandise, personne, fonds)* not available, unavailable; **elle est i. actuellement, rappelez plus tard** she's not available at the moment, please call back later; **je suis i. jusqu'à 19 heures** I'm not free until 7 o'clock **2** *Jur* inalienable

indisposé, -e [ɛ̃dispoze] **ADJ** *(légèrement souffrant)* unwell, *Sout* indisposed

  ❑ **indisposée ADJ** *f Euph* **je suis indisposée** it's my *or* that time of the month

indisposer [3] [ɛ̃dispoze] **VT 1** *(irriter)* to annoy; **elle a l'art d'i. les gens** she's got a talent for rubbing people up the wrong way *or* putting people's backs up; **je ne sais pas pourquoi je l'indispose** I don't know why he/she finds me irritating; **i. qn contre qn** to set sb against sb **2** *(rendre malade)* to upset, to make (slightly) ill, *Sout* to indispose

indisposition [ɛ̃dispozisjɔ̃] **NF 1** *(malaise)* discomfort, ailment, *Sout* indisposition; **j'ai eu une i. passagère** I felt slightly off colour for a little while **2** *Euph (menstruation)* period

indissociable [ɛ̃disosjabl] **ADJ** indissociable, inseparable (**de** from)

indissolubilité [ɛ̃disolybilite] **NF** indissolubility

indissoluble [ɛ̃disolybl] **ADJ** *(lien, union)* indissoluble

indissolublement [ɛ̃disolybləmã] **ADV** *(allier, unir)* indissolubly

indistinct, -e [ɛ̃distɛ̃(kt), -ɛ̃kt] **ADJ** *(chuchotement)* indistinct, faint; *(forme)* indistinct, unclear, vague; **prononcer des paroles indistinctes** to mumble inaudibly

indistinctement [ɛ̃distɛ̃ktəmã] **ADV 1** *(confusément → parler)* indistinctly, unclearly; *(→ se souvenir)* indistinctly, vaguely; **les sommets m'apparaissaient i.** I could just make out the mountain tops **2** *(sans distinction)* indiscriminately; **recruter i. hommes et femmes** to recruit people regardless of sex

indium [ɛ̃djɔm] **NM** *Chim & Métal* indium

individu [ɛ̃dividy] **NM 1** *(personne humaine)* individual **2** *(quidam)* individual, person; **deux individus ont été aperçus par le concierge** the porter saw two men *or* individuals; **un drôle d'i.** a strange character; **un sinistre i.** a sinister individual **3** *Biol, Bot & Phil* individual

individualisation [ɛ̃dividɥalizasjɔ̃] **NF 1** *(d'une espèce animale, d'une langue)* individualization; *(d'un système)* adapting to individual

requirements **2** *Jur* **i. de la peine** = sentencing depending upon the individual requirements or characteristics of the defendant

individualisé, -e [ɛ̃dividɥalize] **ADJ 1** *(enseignement)* individualized **2** *(méthode, caractère)* distinctive; *(groupe)* separate, distinct

individualiser [3] [ɛ̃dividɥalize] **VT 1** *(système)* to adapt to individual needs, to tailor **2** *Jur* **i. les peines** to tailor sentencing to fit offenders' needs

  ▶**s'individualiser VPR** to acquire individual characteristics

individualisme [ɛ̃dividɥalism] **NM** individualism

individualiste [ɛ̃dividɥalist] **ADJ** individualistic

  NMF individualist

individualité [ɛ̃dividɥalite] **NF 1** *(caractère → unique)* individuality; *(→ original)* originality **2** *(style)* **une forte i.** a strong personal *or* individual style

individuation [ɛ̃dividɥasjɔ̃] **NF** *Phil & Psy* individuation

individuel, -elle [ɛ̃dividɥɛl] **ADJ 1** *(personnel)* individual, personal; **c'est votre responsabilité individuelle** it's your personal responsibility; **faire qch à titre i.** to do sth independently **2** *(particulier)* individual, private; **chambre individuelle** (private) single room; **compartiment i.** private compartment; **éclairage i.** individual light; **cas i.** individual case; *Tél* **ligne individuelle** private line **3** *Sport* **épreuve individuelle** individual event

  NM,F *Sport (gén)* individual sportsman, *f* sportswoman; *(athlète)* individual athlete

individuellement [ɛ̃dividɥɛlmã] **ADV 1** *(séparément)* individually, separately, one by one; **chaque cas sera examiné i.** each case will be examined individually **2** *(de façon personnelle)* individually, personally; **vous êtes tous i. responsables** you are all personally responsible **3** *Jur* severally; **responsables i.** severally liable

indivis, -e [ɛ̃divi, -iz] **ADJ** *Jur (domaine, succession)* joint, undivided; *(propriétaires)* joint

  ❑ **en indivis, par indivis ADV** *Jur* in common; **posséder une propriété en i.** to own a property jointly

indivisaire [ɛ̃divizɛr] **NMF** *Jur (propriétaire)* joint owner

indivisément [ɛ̃divizemã] **ADV** *Jur* jointly

indivisibilité [ɛ̃divizibilite] **NF** indivisibility

indivisible [ɛ̃divizibl] **ADJ** indivisible

indivision [ɛ̃divizjɔ̃] **NF** *Jur* joint ownership; **propriété/biens en i.** jointly-owned property/goods

in-dix-huit [indizɥit] *Typ* **ADJ INV** octodecimo, eighteenmo

  NM INV octodecimo, eighteenmo

indo-aryen, -enne [ɛ̃doarjɛ̃, -ɛn] *(mpl* **indo-aryens,** *fpl* **indo-aryennes) ADJ** Indo-Aryan

  NM *Ling* Indo-Aryan

Indochine [ɛ̃doʃin] **NF l'I.** Indochina; **la guerre d'I.** the Indo-Chinese War

indochinois, -e [ɛ̃doʃinwa, -az] **ADJ** Indo-Chinese

  ❑ **Indochinois, -e NM,F** Indo-Chinese

indocile [ɛ̃dosil] **ADJ** disobedient, recalcitrant, *Sout* indocile

  NMF rebel

indocilité [ɛ̃dosilite] **NF** disobedience, recalcitrance

indo-européen, -enne [ɛ̃doœrɔpeɛ̃, -ɛn] *(mpl* **indo-européens,** *fpl* **indo-européennes) ADJ** Indo-European

  NM *Ling* Indo-European

  ❑ **Indo-Européen, -enne NM,F** Indo-European

indole [ɛ̃dɔl] **NM** *Chim* indole

indole-acétique [ɛ̃dɔlasetik] *(pl* **indole-acétiques) ADJ** *Chim & Biol* **acide i.** indoleacetic acid

indolemment [ɛ̃dɔlamã] **ADV** indolently, lazily

indolence [ɛ̃dɔlãs] **NF 1** *(mollesse → dans le travail)* indolence, apathy, lethargy; *(→ dans l'attitude)* indolence, languidness; **une pose pleine d'i.** a languid posture **2** *Méd* indolence, benignancy

indolent, -e [ɛ̃dɔlã, -ãt] **ADJ 1** *(apathique)* indolent, apathetic, lethargic **2** *(languissant)* indolent, languid **3** *Vieilli Méd* indolent, benign

indolore [ɛ̃dɔlɔr] **ADJ** painless

indomptable [ɛ̃dɔ̃tabl] **ADJ 1** *(animal)* untamable, untameable **2** *Fig (nation)* indomitable; *(volonté)* indomitable, invincible; *(passion)* ungovernable, uncontrollable

indompté, -e [ɛ̃dɔ̃te] **ADJ 1** *(sauvage)* untamed, wild; **cheval i.** unbroken horse **2** *Fig (nation)* unvanquished; *(volonté)* unbroken; *(passion)* ungoverned, uncontrolled

Indonésie [ɛ̃donezi] **NF l'I.** Indonesia; **vivre en I.** to live in Indonesia; **aller en I.** to go to Indonesia

indonésien, -enne [ɛ̃donezjɛ̃, -ɛn] **ADJ** Indonesian

  NM *(langue)* Indonesian

  ❑ **Indonésien, -enne NM,F** Indonesian

indoor [indor] **ADJ INV** *Sport* indoor

indophénol [ɛ̃dofenol] **NM** *Chim* indophenol

in-douze [induz] *Typ* **ADJ INV** duodecimo, twelvemo

  NM INV duodecimo, twelvemo

Indre [ɛ̃dr] **NM l'I.**

Indre-et-Loire [ɛ̃drelwar] **NM l'I.** Indre-et-Loire

indri [ɛ̃dri] **NM** *Zool* indri

indu, -e [ɛ̃dy] **ADJ 1** *(inconvenant)* undue, excessive; **à une heure indue** at an ungodly hour; **il rentre à des heures indues** he comes home at all hours of the night **2** *Jur (non fondé → réclamation)* unjustified, unfounded

  NM *Jur* sum not owed

indubitable [ɛ̃dybitabl] **ADJ** undoubted, indubitable, undisputed; **c'est i.** it's beyond doubt *or* dispute; **il est i. que...** there's no doubt that...

indubitablement [ɛ̃dybitabləmã] **ADV** undoubtedly, indubitably

inductance [ɛ̃dyktãs] **NF** *Phys* inductance; *Aut* induction; **i. mutuelle** mutual inductance; **i. propre** self-inductance

inducteur, -trice [ɛ̃dyktœr, -tris] **ADJ** *Phys (capacité, champ)* inductive; *(courant)* inducing

  NM 1 *Phys* inductor **2** *Biol & Chim* inducer

inductif, -ive [ɛ̃dyktif, -iv] **ADJ** *Phil & Phys* inductive

induction [ɛ̃dyksjɔ̃] **NF** *Phil & Phys* induction; **procéder** *ou* **raisonner par i.** to employ inductive reasoning, to induce; **par i., nous pouvons conclure que...** by induction we may conclude that...; **courant d'i.** induced current

inductive [ɛ̃dyktiv] *voir* **inductif**

inductrice [ɛ̃dyktris] *voir* **inducteur**

induire [98] [ɛ̃dɥir] **VT 1** *(inciter)* **i. qn en erreur** to mislead sb; **i. qn en tentation** to lead sb into temptation; *Littéraire* **i. qn à faire qch** to induce sb to do sth **2** *(avoir pour conséquence)* to lead to **3** *(conclure)* to infer, to induce; **que pouvez-vous en i.?** what can you infer from that? **4** *Phys, Phil & Nucl* to induce

induit, -e [ɛ̃dɥi, -it] **ADJ 1** *Élec (circuit)* induced, secondary; *(courant)* induction *(avant n)* **2** *(demande, investissement)* induced

  NM *(circuit)* induced circuit; *(rotor)* rotor

indulgence [ɛ̃dylʒãs] **NF 1** *(clémence)* leniency, tolerance, *Sout* indulgence; **avec i.** indulgently, leniently; **un regard plein d'i.** an indulgent look; **je fais appel à votre i.** I'm asking you to make allowances; **faire preuve d'i. envers qn** to be indulgent with sb, to make allowances for sb; **elle a été d'une i. coupable avec ses enfants** she was far too over-indulgent with her children **2** *Rel* indulgence

  ❑ **sans indulgence ADJ** *(traitement, critique)* severe, harsh; *(regard)* stern, merciless **ADV** *(traiter, critiquer)* severely, harshly; *(regarder)* sternly, mercilessly

indulgencier [9] [ɛ̃dylʒãsje] **VT** *Rel* to attach an indulgence to, to indulgence

indulgent, -e [ɛ̃dylʒã, -ãt] **ADJ 1** *(qui pardonne)* lenient, forgiving; **soyons indulgents** let's forgive and forget **2** *(sans sévérité → personne)* indulgent, lenient; *(→ verdict)* lenient; **tu es trop i. avec eux** you're not strict enough with them; **sois i. avec elle** go easy on her

ind-ind

induline [ɛ̃dylin] **NF** *Chim* indulin, induline
indult [ɛ̃dylt] **NM** *Rel* indult
indûment [ɛ̃dymɑ̃] **ADV** unjustifiably, without due *or* just cause; **tu te l'es i. approprié** you had no right to take it; **il réclame i. une somme colossale** he's claiming a huge sum of money to which he is not entitled
induration [ɛ̃dyrasjɔ̃] **NF** *Géol & Méd* induration
induré, -e [ɛ̃dyre] **ADJ** *Géol & Méd* indurate
indurer [3] [ɛ̃dyre] *Géol & Méd* **VT** to indurate
▶**s'indurer VPR** to become indurate
Indus [ɛ̃dys] **NM l'I.** the (River) Indus
industrialisation [ɛ̃dystrijalizasjɔ̃] **NF** industrialization; **économie en voie d'i.** industrializing economy
industrialisé, -e [ɛ̃dystrijalize] **ADJ** *(pays)* industrialized; *(agriculture)* industrial
industrialiser [3] [ɛ̃dystrijalize] **VT 1** *(doter d'industries)* to industrialize **2** *(mécaniser)* to mechanize, to industrialize
▶**s'industrialiser VPR 1** *(se doter d'industries)* to industrialize, to become industrialized **2** *(se mécaniser)* to become mechanized *or* industrialized
industrialisme [ɛ̃dystrijalism] **NM** *Écon* industrialism
industrie [ɛ̃dystri] **NF 1** *(secteur de production)* industry; **travailler dans l'i.** to work in industry *or* in manufacturing; **i. alimentaire** food (processing) industry; **i. automobile** *Br* car *or Am* automobile industry; **i. de base** basic industry; **i. chimique** chemical industry; **i. clé** key industry; **i. de consommation** consumer goods industry; **i. en croissance rapide** growth industry; **i. extractive** mining industry; **i. de l'énergie** power industry; **i. laitière** dairying; **i. légère** light industry; **i. lourde** heavy industry; **i. de luxe** luxury goods industry; **i. manufacturière** manufacturing industry; **i. minière** mining industry; **i. nationalisée** nationalized *or* state-owned industry; **i. pétrolière** oil industry; **i. de pointe** high-tech industry; **i. de précision** precision tool industry; **i. primaire** primary industry; **i. secondaire** secondary industry; **i. de services** service industry; **i. sidérurgique** iron and steel industry; **i. subventionnée** subsidized industry; **i. textile** textile industry; **i. de transformation** processing industry
2 *(secteur commercial)* industry, trade, business; **l'i. hôtelière** the hotel industry *or* trade *or* business; **l'i. du livre** publishing; **l'i. du spectacle** the entertainment business; **l'i. des loisirs** the leisure industry; **les industries de la langue** the language professions; **l'i. du crime** organized crime
3 *(équipements)* plant, industry
4 *(entreprise)* industrial concern
5 *Hum (profession)* **elle exerçait** *ou* **pratiquait de nuit sa douteuse i.** at night, she plied her dubious trade
6 *Arch (ingéniosité)* ingenuity, cleverness
industriel, -elle [ɛ̃dystrijɛl] **ADJ 1** *(procédé, secteur, zone, révolution, société)* industrial; *(pays)* industrial, industrialized **2** *(destiné à l'industrie → véhicule, équipement, rayonnages)* industrial, heavy, heavy-duty **3** *(non artisanal)* mass-produced, factory-made; **des crêpes industrielles** ready-made *or* factory-made pancakes
NM industrialist, manufacturer
industriellement [ɛ̃dystrijɛlmɑ̃] **ADV** industrially; **fabriqué i.** factory-made, mass-produced
industrieux, -euse [ɛ̃dystrijø, -øz] **ADJ** *Littéraire* industrious
inébranlable [inebrɑ̃labl] **ADJ 1** *(ferme)* steadfast, unshakeable, unwavering; **ma décision est i.** my decision is final; **elle a été i.** there was no moving her, she was adamant **2** *(solide → mur)* immovable, (rock) solid
inébranlablement [inebrɑ̃labləmɑ̃] **ADV** steadfastly, unshakeably, unwaveringly
inéchangeable [ineʃɑ̃ʒabl] **ADJ** non-exchangeable
inécoutable [inekutabl] **ADJ** unbearable, impossible to listen to
inécouté, -e [inekute] **ADJ rester i.** to remain unheeded *or* ignored
INED, Ined [inɛd] **NM** *(abrév* **Institut national d'études démographiques***)* = national institute for demographic research

inédit, -e [inedi, -it] **ADJ 1** *(correspondance, auteur)* (hitherto) unpublished; **ce film est i. en France** this film has never been released in France **2** *(jamais vu)* new, original
NM 1 *(œuvre)* unpublished work; **un i. de Gide** an unpublished work by Gide **2** *(nouveauté)* **c'est de l'i. pour nos trois alpinistes** it's a first for our three climbers
inéducable [inedykabl] **ADJ** unteachable, *Spéc* ineducable
ineffable [inefabl] **ADJ** *Littéraire* **1** *(indicible)* ineffable, indescribable **2** *(amusant)* hilarious
ineffablement [inefabləmɑ̃] **ADV** *Littéraire (indiciblement)* ineffably, indescribably
ineffaçable [inefasabl] **ADJ** *(marque)* indelible; *(souvenir, traumatisme)* unforgettable, enduring
inefficace [inefikas] **ADJ** *(méthode, médicament)* ineffective; *(personne)* ineffective, ineffectual; *(dans son travail)* inefficient
inefficacement [inefikasmɑ̃] **ADV** ineffectively, ineffectually; *(travailler)* inefficiently
inefficacité [inefikasite] **NF** *(d'une méthode, d'un médicament)* inefficacy, ineffectiveness; *(d'une personne)* ineffectuality; *(dans son travail)* inefficiency; **d'une totale i.** totally ineffective
inégal, -e, -aux, -ales [inegal, -o] **ADJ 1** *(varié → longueurs, salaires)* unequal, different; *(mal équilibré)* uneven, unequal; **leurs chances sont inégales** their chances are not equal, they haven't got equal chances; **le combat était i.** the fight was one-sided
2 *(changeant → écrivain, élève, pouls)* uneven, erratic; *(→ humeur)* changeable, uneven; **la qualité est inégale** it varies in quality; **le livre est i.** the book is uneven
3 *(rugueux)* rough, uneven, bumpy
inégalable [inegalabl] **ADJ** incomparable, matchless, peerless
inégalé, -e [inegale] **ADJ** *(personne, qualité)* unequalled, unmatched, unrivalled; *(record)* unbeaten
inégalement [inegalmɑ̃] **ADV 1** *(différemment)* unequally; **le film a été i. apprécié par les critiques** the film received mixed reviews from the critics **2** *(irrégulièrement)* unevenly
inégalitaire [inegalitɛr] **ADJ** non-egalitarian, elitist
inégalité [inegalite] **NF 1** *(disparité)* difference, disparity; **i. entre deux variables/nombres** difference between two variables/numbers; **i. de l'offre et de la demande** imbalance between supply and demand
2 *(injustice)* inequality (**entre** between); **l'i. des salaires** the difference *or* disparity in wages; **l'i. des chances** the lack of equal opportunities; **les inégalités sociales** social inequalities
3 *(qualité variable → d'une surface)* roughness, unevenness; *(→ d'un travail, d'une œuvre)* uneven quality, unevenness; *(→ du caractère)* changeability; **les inégalités de terrain** the unevenness of *or* the bumps in the ground; **elle a des inégalités d'humeur** she's moody
4 *Math* inequality
inélastique [inelastik] **ADJ** *Phys* inelastic
inélégamment [inelegamɑ̃] **ADV** inelegantly
inélégance [inelegɑ̃s] **NF 1** *(d'allure)* inelegance, ungainliness; *(d'une méthode, de manières)* inelegance; **le procédé était d'une grande i.** his/her behaviour was most ungracious **2** *(acte, tournure)* impropriety
inélégant, -e [inelegɑ̃, -ɑ̃t] **ADJ 1** *(qui manque d'élégance → allure)* inelegant, ungainly; *(→ méthode, manières)* inelegant **2** *(indélicat)* indelicate, inelegant; **ce fut très i. de ta part** that was very indelicate of you
inéligibilité [ineliʒibilite] **NF** *Jur* ineligibility; **i. absolue** disqualification; **i. relative** = disqualification from standing for office in certain constituencies
inéligible [ineliʒibl] **ADJ** *Jur* ineligible
inéluctabilité [inelyktabilite] **NF** *Sout* ineluctability
inéluctable [inelyktabl] **ADJ** inevitable, unavoidable, *Littéraire* ineluctable
inéluctablement [inelyktabləmɑ̃] **ADV** inevitably, inescapably, unavoidably

inemploi [inɑ̃plwa] **NM** *Euph* unemployment
inemployable [inɑ̃plwajabl] **ADJ 1** *(ressources, matériaux)* unusable; *(méthode)* useless, unserviceable **2** *(travailleur)* unemployable
inemployé, -e [inɑ̃plwaje] **ADJ** *(ressources, talent)* dormant, untapped; *(énergie)* untapped, unused
inénarrable [inenarabl] **ADJ** hilarious; **si tu avais vu le tableau, c'était i.!** I wish you'd seen it, I can't tell you how funny it was!
inentamé, -e [inɑ̃tame] **ADJ** *(économies)* intact, untouched; *(bouteille, boîte)* unopened; *(pain, camembert, gâteau)* uncut
inenvisageable [inɑ̃vizaʒabl] **ADJ** inconceivable, unthinkable
inéprouvé, -e [inepruve] **ADJ 1** *(non mis à l'épreuve)* untried, untested **2** *(non ressenti)* unknown
inepte [inɛpt] **ADJ** *(personne)* inept, incompetent; *(réponse, raisonnement)* inept, foolish; *(plan)* inept, ill-considered
ineptie [inɛpsi] **NF 1** *(caractère d'absurdité)* ineptitude, stupidity **2** *(acte, parole)* piece of nonsense; **dire des inepties** to talk nonsense; **c'est une i. de dire que...** it's idiotic *or* absurd to say that...
inépuisable [inepɥizabl] **ADJ 1** *(réserves)* inexhaustible, unlimited; *(courage)* endless, unlimited; *(imagination)* limitless **2** *(bavard)* inexhaustible; **elle est i. sur mes imperfections** once she gets going about my faults, there's no stopping her
inépuisablement [inepɥizabləmɑ̃] **ADV** inexhaustibly, endlessly
inépuisé, -e [inepɥize] **ADJ** not yet used up *or* exhausted
inéquation [inekwasjɔ̃] **NF** *Math* inequality, *Spéc* inequation
inéquitable [inekitabl] **ADJ** unjust, unfair, *Littéraire* inequitable
inerme [inɛrm] **ADJ 1** *Bot* inerm, inermous **2** *Zool* unarmed; **ténia i.** unarmed tapeworm
inertage [inɛrtaʒ] **NM** *(de déchets)* encapsulation
inerte [inɛrt] **ADJ 1** *(léthargique → personne)* inert, apathetic, lethargic; *(→ visage)* expressionless **2** *(semblant mort)* inert, lifeless **3** *Chim & Phys* inert
inerter [3] [inɛrte] **VT** *(déchets)* to encapsulate
inertie [inɛrsi] **NF 1** *(passivité)* lethargy, inertia, passivity **2** *Chim, Math, Méd, Phot & Phys* inertia
inertiel, -elle [inɛrsjɛl] **ADJ** *Phys* inertial
inescomptable [inɛskɔ̃tabl] **ADJ** *Fin* undiscountable
inespéré, -e [inɛspere] **ADJ** unhoped-for; **c'est pour moi un bonheur i.** it's a pleasure I hadn't dared hope for
inesthétique [inɛstetik] **ADJ** unsightly, unattractive
inestimable [inɛstimabl] **ADJ 1** *(impossible à évaluer)* incalculable, inestimable; **les dégâts sont inestimables** it's impossible to work out the extent of the damage; **des bijoux d'une valeur i.** priceless jewels **2** *(précieux)* inestimable, invaluable, priceless
inétendu, -e [inetɑ̃dy] **ADJ** *Littéraire* unextended, exiguous
inévitable [inevitabl] **ADJ 1** *(auquel on ne peut échapper)* unavoidable, inevitable; **et ce fut l'i. catastrophe** and then came the inevitable catastrophe; **c'était i.!** it was bound to happen *or* inevitable! **2** *(avant le nom) (habituel)* inevitable; **l'i. pilier de bar** the inevitable figure propping up the bar; **l'i. Lulu était là** Lulu was there as per usual
NM l'i. the inevitable
inévitablement [inevitabləmɑ̃] **ADV** inevitably, predictably; **et i., elle se décommanda à la dernière minute** and predictably *or* sure enough, she cancelled at the last minute; **si on passe par là, il va i. nous voir** if we go that way he's bound to see us
inexact, -e [inɛgza(kt), -akt] **ADJ 1** *(erroné)* inexact, incorrect, inaccurate; **le calcul est i.** there's a mistake in the calculations; **une version inexacte des faits** an inaccurate version of the facts; **il serait i. de dire...** it would be wrong *or* incorrect to say...; **non, c'est i.** no, that's wrong *or* incorrect **2** *(en retard)* unpunctual, late; **il est très i.** he's always late

inexactement [inɛgzaktəmɑ̃] ADV inaccurately, incorrectly

inexactitude [inɛgzaktityd] NF **1** *(d'un raisonnement)* inaccuracy, imprecision; *(d'un récit)* inaccuracy, inexactness; *(d'un calcul)* inaccuracy, inexactitude **2** *(erreur)* inaccuracy, error **3** *(manque de ponctualité)* unpunctuality, lateness

inexaucé, -e [inɛgzose] ADJ *(demande)* unanswered; *(vœu)* unfulfilled

inexcitabilité [inɛksitabilite] NF *(gén) & Physiol* unexcitability

inexcitable [inɛksitabl] ADJ *(gén) & Physiol* unexcitable

inexcusable [inɛkskyzabl] ADJ *(action)* inexcusable, unforgivable; *(personne)* unforgivable

inexécutable [inɛgzekytabl] ADJ *(plan, programme)* unworkable, impractical; *(tâche)* unfeasible, impossible; *(ordre)* impossible to carry out *or* to execute; *(musique)* unplayable; *(pas de danse)* undanceable

inexécuté, -e [inɛgzekyte] ADJ *(ordre, travaux)* not (yet) carried out *or* executed; *(contrat)* unfulfilled; **l'ordre de tirer sur les civils resta i.** the order to shoot civilians was not carried out *or* executed; **le projet resta i.** the project did not go ahead

inexécution [inɛgzekysjɔ̃] NF *(d'un contrat)* nonfulfilment; **i. des travaux** failure to carry out work

inexercé, -e [inɛgzɛrse] ADJ *(recrue, novice)* untrained, inexperienced; *(oreille, main)* unpractised, untrained, untutored

inexigibilité [inɛgziʒibilite] NF *Jur* **à cause de l'i. de la dette** as the debt cannot be exacted *or* recovered

inexigible [inɛgziʒibl] ADJ *Jur (dette, impôt)* irrecoverable, *Sout* inexigible

inexistant, -e [inɛgzistɑ̃, -ɑ̃t] ADJ **1** *(très insuffisant)* nonexistent, inadequate; **devant un public i.** in front of a nearly empty house; **un service d'ordre i.** inadequate stewarding; **ce bonhomme est totalement i.** this guy's a complete non-entity; **lors de la réunion, il a été i.** at the meeting he didn't utter a word; **les structures de base sont inexistantes** the basic structures are lacking, there are hardly any basic structures **2** *(irréel → monstre, peur)* imaginary

inexistence [inɛgzistɑ̃s] NF **1** *(de Dieu)* nonexistence; *(de preuves, de structures)* lack, absence; **l'i. de structures économiques** the complete lack *or* absence of economic structure **2** *(manque de valeur)* uselessness **3** *Jur* nullity

inexorabilité [inɛgzɔrabilite] NF *Littéraire* inexorability

inexorable [inɛgzɔrabl] ADJ **1** *(inévitable)* inexorable, inevitable **2** *(impitoyable)* inexorable

inexorablement [inɛgzɔrabləmɑ̃] ADV **1** *(inévitablement)* inexorably, inevitably **2** *(impitoyablement)* inexorably

inexpérience [inɛksperjɑ̃s] NF lack of experience

inexpérimenté, -e [inɛksperimɑ̃te] ADJ **1** *(sans expérience → personne)* inexperienced; **avec des gestes inexpérimentés** with unpractised hands **2** *(non testé)* (as yet) untested

inexpert, -e [inɛkspɛr, -ɛrt] ADJ inexpert, untrained, untutored; **confié à des mains inexpertes** placed in the hands of a novice

inexpiable [inɛkspjabl] ADJ **1** *(inexcusable)* inexpiable; **un crime i.** an unpardonable crime **2** *Littéraire (impitoyable)* **une lutte i.** a merciless struggle

inexpié, -e [inɛkspje] ADJ unexpiated

inexplicable [inɛksplikabl] ADJ *(comportement)* inexplicable; *(raison, crainte)* inexplicable, unaccountable

NM **l'i.** the inexplicable

inexplicablement [inɛksplikabləmɑ̃] ADV inexplicably, unaccountably

inexpliqué, -e [inɛksplike] ADJ *(décision)* unexplained; *(phénomène)* unexplained, unsolved; *(agissements, départ)* unexplained, mysterious; **une disparition restée inexpliquée jusqu'à ce jour** a disappearance that remains a mystery to this day

inexploitable [inɛksplwatabl] ADJ *(ressources)* unexploitable; *(mine, terres)* unworkable; *(idée)* impractical, unfeasible

inexploité, -e [inɛksplwate] ADJ *(richesses)* undeveloped, untapped; *(mine, terres)* unworked; *(idée, talent)* untapped, untried; *(technique)* unexploited, untried; **laisser un don i.** to fail to exploit a latent talent

inexplorable [inɛksplɔrabl] ADJ unexplorable

inexploré, -e [inɛksplɔre] ADJ unexplored; **cette branche de la science est encore inexplorée** this branch of science is still unexplored

inexplosible [inɛksplozibl] ADJ nonexplosive

inexpressif, -ive [inɛkspresif, -iv] ADJ *(visage, regard)* inexpressive, expressionless, blank; **il a gardé un visage i. pendant tout le match** his face remained impassive throughout the match

inexprimable [inɛksprimabl] ADJ inexpressible, ineffable, indescribable

inexprimé, -e [inɛksprime] ADJ unspoken; **une rancœur inexprimée** unspoken resentment

inexpugnable [inɛkspygnabl] ADJ *Littéraire (forteresse)* unassailable, impregnable; *(vertu)* inexpugnable

inextensibilité [inɛkstɑ̃sibilite] NF *Tech (d'un appareil, d'un câble)* non-stretchability, inextensibility; *(d'un tissu)* non-stretchability

inextensible [inɛkstɑ̃sibl] ADJ *Tech (appareil, câble)* non-stretchable, inextensible; *(tissu)* non-stretch

in extenso [inɛkstɛ̃so] ADV in full, *Sout* in extenso; **recopie le paragraphe i.** copy out the paragraph in full *or* the whole paragraph

inextinguible [inɛkstɛ̃gibl] ADJ **1** *Littéraire (feu)* inextinguishable **2** *(soif, désir)* inextinguishable, unquenchable; *(amour)* undying **3** *(rire)* uncontrollable

inextirpable [inɛkstirpabl] ADJ *(fléau)* which cannot be eliminated; *(paresse, ignorance)* deep-rooted, entrenched

in extremis [inɛkstremis] ADV **1** *(de justesse)* at the last minute, in the nick of time, at the eleventh hour; **réussir qch i.** to (only) just manage to do sth; **vous avez réussi? – oui, mais i.!** did you manage? – yes, but it was a close call! **2** *(avant la mort)* in extremis; **baptiser un enfant/un adulte i.** to christen a child before he dies/an adult on his deathbed

inextricable [inɛkstrikabl] ADJ *(situation, problème, conflit)* inextricable; *(labyrinthe)* inescapable; **cette affaire est i.** this matter is a real tangle; **tu t'es mise dans une situation i.** you've got yourself into an impossible position

inextricablement [inɛkstrikabləmɑ̃] ADV inextricably

infaillibiliste [ɛ̃fajibilist] *Rel* ADJ infallibilist

NMF infallibilist

infaillibilité [ɛ̃fajibilite] NF *(gén) & Rel* infallibility

infaillible [ɛ̃fajibl] ADJ **1** *(efficace à coup sûr)* infallible; **c'est un remède i. contre la toux** it's an infallible cure for coughs **2** *(certain)* infallible, reliable, guaranteed; **c'est la marque i. d'une forte personnalité** it's a sure sign of a strong personality **3** *(qui ne peut se tromper)* infallible; **nul n'est i.** no one is infallible, everyone makes mistakes

infailliblement [ɛ̃fajibləmɑ̃] ADV **1** *(inévitablement)* inevitably, without fail **2** *Littéraire (sans se tromper)* infallibly

infaisable [ɛ̃fəzabl] ADJ *(choix)* impossible; **c'est i.** *(projet, mots croisés)* it can't be done

infalsifiable [ɛ̃falsifjabl] ADJ *(carte d'identité)* forgery-proof

infamant, -e [ɛ̃famɑ̃, -ɑ̃t] ADJ **1** *(déshonorant → acte, crime)* heinous, infamous, abominable; *(→ propos, accusation)* defamatory, slanderous; **tu peux réclamer ton argent, ce n'est pas i.** you can go and ask for your money, there's no shame in that **2** *Jur voir* **peine**

infâme [ɛ̃fam] ADJ **1** *(vil → crime)* despicable, loathsome, heinous; *(→ criminel)* vile, despicable; *(→ traître)* despicable **2** *(répugnant → odeur, nourriture)* revolting, vile, foul; *(→ endroit)* disgusting, revolting; **une i. odeur de putréfaction** a foul stench of rotting

infamie [ɛ̃fami] NF **1** *(déshonneur)* infamy, disgrace; **il a couvert sa famille d'i.** he has brought disgrace upon his family

2 *(caractère abject → d'une action, d'une personne)* infamy, vileness

3 *(acte révoltant)* infamy, loathsome deed; **au nom de la religion, on a souvent commis des infamies** in the name of religion many heinous crimes *or* many infamies have been committed

4 *(propos)* piece of (vile) slander, smear; **dire des infamies de qn** to vilify *or* to slander sb

infant, -e [ɛ̃fɑ̃, -ɑ̃t] NM,F infante, *f* infanta

infanterie [ɛ̃fɑ̃tri] NF infantry; **soldat d'i.** infantryman, foot soldier; **i. aéroportée/motorisée** airborne/motorized infantry; **i. divisionnaire** tank division; **i. légère** light infantry; **i. de ligne** heavy infantry; **i. de marine** marine corps, marines

infanticide [ɛ̃fɑ̃tisid] ADJ infanticidal

NMF *(personne)* child killer, *Jur & Littéraire* infanticide

NM infanticide

infantile [ɛ̃fɑ̃til] ADJ **1** *Méd & Psy* child *(avant n)*, *Spéc* infantile **2** *Péj (puéril)* infantile, childish; **se comporter de façon i.** to behave childishly

infantilisant, -e [ɛ̃fɑ̃tilizɑ̃, -ɑ̃t] ADJ patronizing; **ils ont un discours i.** they talk to people as if they were children

infantilisation [ɛ̃fɑ̃tilizasjɔ̃] NF infantilization

infantiliser [3] [ɛ̃fɑ̃tilize] VT to infantilize; **la télévision infantilise les gens** television reduces people to the level of two-year-olds

infantilisme [ɛ̃fɑ̃tilism] NM **1** *Péj (puérilité)* infantilism, immaturity; **elle a refusé! – c'est de l'i.!** she said no! – how childish! **2** *Méd & Psy* infantilism

infarci, -e [ɛ̃farsi] ADJ *Méd* infarcted

infarctus [ɛ̃farktys] NM *Méd* infarct; **avoir un i.** to have a heart attack *or* a coronary; **i. médullaire** myelomalacia; **i. du myocarde** myocardial infarction; **i. pulmonaire** pulmonary (embolism) infarctus

infatigable [ɛ̃fatigabl] ADJ **1** *(toujours dispos)* tireless, untiring, *Sout* indefatigable **2** *(indéfectible → énergie, courage)* inexhaustible, unwavering, unflagging; *(→ détermination)* dogged, unflagging; *(→ dévouement)* unstinting, unflagging; **elle a mené une lutte i. contre l'injustice** she fought tirelessly against injustice; *Littéraire* **i. à faire le bien** never wearied in well-doing

infatigablement [ɛ̃fatigabləmɑ̃] ADV tirelessly, untiringly, *Sout* indefatigably

infatuation [ɛ̃fatɥasjɔ̃] NF *Littéraire* conceit, self-importance

infatué, -e [ɛ̃fatɥe] ADJ **1** *Littéraire (vaniteux)* self-satisfied, conceited, bumptious; **i. de sa personne** self-important, full of oneself **2** *Vieilli (entiché)* **i. de qn/qch** infatuated with sb/sth

infatuer [7] [ɛ̃fatɥe] **s'infatuer** VPR **1** *Littéraire (être content de soi)* to be conceited **2** *Vieilli (s'enticher de)* **s'i. de** to become infatuated with

inféconde, -e [ɛ̃fekɔ̃, -ɔ̃d] ADJ *Littéraire* **1** *(sol, femme)* infertile, barren **2** *Fig (pensée)* sterile, barren, unproductive

infécondité [ɛ̃fekɔ̃dite] NF *Littéraire* **1** *(d'un sol, d'une femme)* infertility, infecundity, barrenness **2** *Fig (d'une pensée)* sterility, barrenness, unproductiveness

infect, -e [ɛ̃fɛkt] ADJ **1** *(répugnant → repas)* rotten, revolting, disgusting; *(→ odeur)* foul, rank, putrid; *(→ lieu)* filthy; **il y a une odeur infecte ici** it smells foul in here; **il est i., leur vin** their wine's revolting *or* disgusting **2** *Fam (très laid, très désagréable)* foul, lousy; **c'est un type i.** he's absolutely revolting; **les enfants ont été infects ce matin** the kids were terrible *or* awful this morning; **être i. avec qn** to be rotten to sb

infectant, -e [ɛ̃fɛktɑ̃, -ɑ̃t] ADJ *Méd* infectious, infective

infecter [4] [ɛ̃fɛkte] VT **1** *Méd* to infect; **plaie infectée** septic wound **2** *(rendre malsain)* to contaminate, to pollute **3** *Littéraire (empester)* **l'usine infecte toute la région** the factory pollutes the whole area **4** *Ordinat (fichier, disque)* to infect

► **s'infecter** VPR *Méd* to become infected, to go septic

infectieux, -euse [ɛ̃fɛksjø, -øz] ADJ *Méd (maladie)* infectious; **un sujet i.** a carrier

infectiologie [ɛ̃fɛksjɔlɔʒi] NF *Méd* infectiology

infection [ɛ̃fɛksjɔ̃] NF **1** *Méd* infection; **i. nosocomiale** nosocomial *or* hospital-acquired infection; **i. nosocomiale à bactéries multirésistantes** MRSA, *Fam* superbug **2** *(puanteur)* (foul) stench; **c'est une i., ce marché!** this

market stinks (to high heaven)! **3** *Ordinat* infection

infectiosité [ɛ̃fɛktjɔsite] **NF** *Méd* infectiveness

infélicité [ɛ̃felisite] **NF** *Littéraire* unhappiness, misfortune

inféodation [ɛ̃feɔdasjɔ̃] **NF 1** *Pol* subservience, subjection (**à** to) **2** *Hist* enfeoffment, infeudation

inféodé, -e [ɛ̃feɔde] **ADJ 1** *Pol (soumis)* subservient (**à** to); **un pays i. à une grande puissance** a country subjugated by a great power **2** *Hist* enfeoffed **3** *Écol (insecte)* dependent (**à** on)

inféoder [3] [ɛ̃feɔde] **VT 1** *(soumettre)* to subjugate; **être inféodé à** to be subservient to **2** *Hist* to enfeoff

▸**s'inféoder VPR** *Pol* **s'i. à** to become subservient to

infère [ɛ̃fɛr] **ADJ** *Bot* inferior

inférence [ɛ̃ferɑ̃s] **NF** inference

inférer [18] [ɛ̃fere] **VT** *Littéraire* to infer, to gather (**de** from)

inférieur, -e [ɛ̃ferjœr] **ADJ 1** *(du bas → étagères, membres)* lower; *(→ lèvre, mâchoire)* lower, bottom *(avant n)*; **la partie inférieure de la colonne** the bottom *or* lower part of the column

2 *(situé en dessous)* lower down, below; **c'est à l'étage i.** it's on the floor below *or* on the next floor down; **la couche inférieure** the layer below *or* beneath; **être i. à** to be lower than *or* below

3 *(moins bon → niveau)* lower; *(→ esprit, espèce)* inferior, lesser; *(→ qualité)* inferior, poorer; **les gens d'un rang i.** people of a lower rank *or* lower in rank; **se sentir i. (par rapport à qn)** to feel inferior (to sb); **i. à** inferior to; **je me sens vraiment inférieure à elle** she makes me feel really inferior; **en physique il est très i. à sa sœur** he's not nearly as good as his sister at physics; **je préfère jouer contre quelqu'un qui ne m'est pas i.** I'd rather play against someone who's at least as good as I am; *Littéraire* **il est i. à sa tâche** he is not equal to the task, he is not up to the job

4 *(plus petit → chiffre, salaire)* lower, smaller; *(→ poids, vitesse)* lower; *(→ taille)* smaller; **nous (leur) étions inférieurs en nombre** there were fewer of us (than of them); **i. à** *(chiffre)* lower *or* smaller *or* less than; *(rendement)* lower than, inferior to; **a est i. ou égal à 3** a is less than or equal to 3; **des températures inférieures à 10°C** temperatures below 10°C *or* lower than 10°C; **les notes inférieures à douze** marks below twelve

5 *(dans une hiérarchie → le plus bas)* lower; *Bot & Zool* **animaux/végétaux inférieurs** lower animals/plants

6 *Astron* inferior

7 *Géog (cours, région)* lower

NM,F *(gén)* inferior; *(subalterne)* inferior, subordinate, *Péj* underling; **il les considère comme ses inférieurs** he regards them as his inferiors

inférieurement [ɛ̃ferjœrmɑ̃] **ADV** *(moins bien)* less well; **i. entretenu/approvisionné/conçu** less well-maintained/-stocked/-designed

infériorisation [ɛ̃ferjɔrizasjɔ̃] **NF l'i. d'un enfant** making a child feel inferior

inférioriser [3] [ɛ̃ferjɔrize] **VT 1** *(dévaloriser)* **i. qn** to make sb feel inferior **2** *(minimiser)* to minimise the importance of

infériorité [ɛ̃ferjɔrite] **NF 1** *(inadéquation → en grandeur, en valeur)* inferiority; **i. numérique** *ou* **en nombre** numerical inferiority, inferiority in numbers **2** *(handicap)* weakness, inferiority, deficiency; **être en situation d'i.** to be in a weak position; **je me sens en situation d'i.** I feel that I'm in a weak position

infernal, -e, -aux, -ales [ɛ̃fɛrnal, -o] **ADJ 1** *Fam (terrible)* infernal, hellish, diabolical; **cet enfant est i.!** that child's a real terror!; **elle est infernale, à toujours se plaindre** she's really awful, she's always complaining; **il faisait une chaleur infernale** the heat was infernal; **nous dévalions la pente à une vitesse infernale** we hurtled down the slope at breakneck speed; **ils mettent de la musique toute la nuit, c'est i.** they've got music on all night, it's absolute hell

2 *Littéraire (de l'enfer)* infernal; **les puissances infernales** the infernal powers

3 *(diabolique → engrenage, logique)* infernal, devilish, diabolical; **la machination infernale qui devait le conduire à la mort** the diabolical scheme which was to lead him to his death; **cycle i.** vicious circle

infertile [ɛ̃fɛrtil] **ADJ** *Littéraire* **1** *(terre)* infertile, barren **2** *(imagination, esprit)* infertile, uncreative, sterile

infertilité [ɛ̃fɛrtilite] **NF** *Littéraire* **1** *(de la terre, de l'imagination)* infertility **2** *(d'une femme)* infertility, barrenness

infestation [ɛ̃fɛstasjɔ̃] **NF 1** *Méd (infection)* infection **2** *(de parasites, de moustiques)* infestation

infester [3] [ɛ̃fɛste] **VT 1** *(sujet: rats)* to infest, to overrun; *(sujet: pillards)* to infest; **la région est infestée de sauterelles/moustiques** the area is infested with locusts/mosquitoes; **chien infesté de puces** flea-ridden dog; **rues infestées de marchands de souvenirs** streets swarming with souvenir sellers **2** *Méd* to infest

infeutrable [ɛ̃føtrabl] **ADJ** *Tex* **ce tissu est i.** this fabric won't mat *or* felt

infibulation [ɛ̃fibylasjɔ̃] **NF** infibulation

infichu, -e [ɛ̃fiʃy] **ADJ** *Fam (incapable)* **être i. de faire qch** to be incapable of doing sth▪

infidèle [ɛ̃fidɛl] **ADJ 1** *(gén)* disloyal, unfaithful; *(en amour)* unfaithful, *Littéraire* untrue; *(en amitié)* disloyal; **être i. à son seigneur** to be disloyal to one's liege; **être i. à sa parole** to go back on one's word **2** *(inexact → témoignage, texte)* inaccurate, unreliable; *(→ traduction)* unfaithful, inaccurate; *(→ mémoire)* unreliable **3** *Rel* infidel

NMF *Rel* infidel

NF *Littérature* **belle i.** = well-turned but inaccurate translation (term used in 17th-century literature)

infidèlement [ɛ̃fidɛlmɑ̃] **ADV** *(inexactement)* inaccurately, unfaithfully

infidélité [ɛ̃fidelite] **NF 1** *(inconstance)* infidelity, unfaithfulness; *(aventure adultère)* infidelity, affair; **commettre une i.** to be unfaithful; **faire une i. à qn** to be unfaithful to sb; *Hum* **j'ai fait une i. à mon coiffeur** I deserted my usual hairdresser

2 *(déloyauté)* disloyalty, unfaithfulness; **son i. à l'idéal de notre jeunesse** his/her disloyalty to our youthful ideal; **l'i. à la parole donnée** being untrue to *or* breaking one's word

3 *(caractère inexact)* inaccuracy, unreliability; *(erreur)* inaccuracy, error; **le scénario est truffé d'infidélités à Molière** the screenplay is full of departures from Molière's original

infiltrat [ɛ̃filtra] **NM** *Chem & Méd* infiltrate

infiltration [ɛ̃filtrasjɔ̃] **NF 1** *Méd* injection; **se faire faire des infiltrations dans le genou** to have injections in the knee; **i. anesthésique** infiltration anaesthesia

2 *(gén) & Méd* infiltration; **il y a eu une i. de fluide dans les tissus musculaires** there has been infiltration of fluid into the muscle tissue; **on observe des infiltrations au niveau des plinthes** there is some damp around the skirting boards; **il y a des infiltrations dans le plafond** there are leaks in the ceiling, water is leaking *or* seeping through the ceiling; *Géol* **eaux d'i.** percolated water

3 *(d'une idée)* penetration, *Littéraire* percolation; *(d'un agitateur)* infiltration

infiltrer [3] [ɛ̃filtre] **VT 1** *Méd* to inject (**dans** into), *Spéc* to infiltrate **2** *(organisation, réseau)* to infiltrate

▸**s'infiltrer VPR 1** *(air, brouillard, eau)* to seep in; *(lumière)* to filter in; **s'i. dans qch** *(sujet: air, brouillard, eau)* to seep into sth; *(sujet: lumière)* to filter into sth; **quand l'eau s'infiltre dans le sable** when the water seeps (through) into the sand **2** *Fig (pénétrer)* **s'i. dans les lieux** to get into the building; **s'i. dans un réseau d'espions** to infiltrate a spy network; *Littéraire* **un soupçon s'infiltra dans mon esprit** a suspicion crept *or* found its way into my mind

infime [ɛ̃fim] **ADJ** *(quantité, proportion, différence)* infinitesimal, minute, tiny; *(détail)* minor

infini, -e [ɛ̃fini] **ADJ 1** *(étendue)* infinite, vast, boundless; *(ressources)* infinite, unlimited

2 *(extrême → générosité, patience, reconnaissance)* infinite, boundless, limitless; *(→ charme, douceur)* infinite; *(→ précautions)* infinite, endless; *(→ bonheur)* infinite, immeasurable; *(→ difficulté, peine)* immense, extreme; **vous m'avez fait un plaisir i. en venant me voir** you have given me enormous pleasure in coming to see me; **auriez-vous l'infinie bonté de me donner l'heure, monsieur?** would you do me the great kindness of telling me the time, sir?; **mettre un soin i. à faire qch** to take infinite pains to do sth

3 *(interminable)* never-ending, interminable, endless; **j'ai dû attendre un temps i.** I had to wait interminably

4 *Math* infinite

NM 1 *Math, Opt & Phot* infinity; *Phot* **faire la mise au point sur l'i.** to focus to infinity; *Math* **tendre vers l'i.** to tend towards infinity; **plus/moins l'i.** plus/minus infinity

2 *Phil* **l'i.** the infinite; *Littéraire* **l'i. de cette vaste plaine** the immensity of this endless plain

❑ **à l'infini ADV 1** *(discuter, reproduire)* endlessly, ad infinitum; *(varier)* infinitely; *(s'étendre)* endlessly

2 *Math* to *or* towards infinity

infiniment [ɛ̃finimɑ̃] **ADV 1** *(extrêmement → désolé, reconnaissant)* extremely; *(→ généreux)* immensely, boundlessly; *(→ agréable, douloureux)* immensely, extremely; *(→ long, grand)* infinitely, immensely; *(→ petit)* infinitesimally; **je vous remercie i.** thank you so much; **je regrette i.** I'm extremely sorry; **c'est i. mieux/pire que la dernière fois** it's infinitely better/worse than last time; **elle est i. plus brillante** she's far *or* infinitely brighter; **avec i. de patience/de précautions** with infinite patience/care

2 *Math* infinitely; **l'i. grand** the infinite, the infinitely great; **l'i. petit** the infinitesimal

infinité [ɛ̃finite] **NF 1** *(très grand nombre)* **une i. de** an infinite number of; **on me posa une i. de questions** I was asked endless *or* a great many questions **2** *Littéraire* **l'i. de l'espace** the infinity of space

infinitésimal, -e, -aux, -ales [ɛ̃finitezimal, -o] **ADJ** infinitesimal

infinitif, -ive [ɛ̃finitif, -iv] *Gram* **ADJ** infinitive

NM infinitive (mood); **i. de narration** infinitive of narration

❑ **infinitive NF** infinitive (clause)

infinitude [ɛ̃finityd] **NF** *Littéraire* infinitude

infirmatif, -ive [ɛ̃firmatif, -iv] **ADJ** *Jur* invalidating

infirmation [ɛ̃firmasjɔ̃] **NF** *Jur* invalidation

infirme [ɛ̃firm] **ADJ 1** *(handicapé)* disabled, crippled; **i. du bras gauche** crippled in the left arm; **il est resté i. à la suite de son accident** his accident left him disabled *or* crippled *or* a cripple **2** *Littéraire (faible → esprit, corps, etc)* weak, feeble, frail; **l'esprit est prompt mais la chair est i.** the spirit is willing but the flesh is weak

NMF disabled person; **les infirmes** the disabled; **i. moteur cérébral** person suffering from cerebral palsy, *Vieilli* spastic

infirmer [3] [ɛ̃firme] **VT 1** *(démentir)* to invalidate, to contradict **2** *Jur (arrêt)* to revoke; *(jugement)* to quash

infirmerie [ɛ̃firməri] **NF** *(dans une école, une entreprise)* sick bay *or* room; *(dans une prison)* infirmary; *(dans une caserne)* infirmary, sick bay; *(sur un navire)* sick bay

infirmier, -ère [ɛ̃firmje, -ɛr] **NM,F** male nurse, *f* nurse; **elle fait un stage d'infirmière** she's doing a nursing course; **i. en chef, infirmière en chef** *Br* charge nurse, *Am* head nurse; **i. militaire** medical orderly; **i. de nuit** night nurse; **infirmière diplômée (d'État)** registered nurse; **infirmière visiteuse** district nurse

ADJ nursing *(avant n)*

infirmité [ɛ̃firmite] **NF 1** *(invalidité)* disability, handicap; **la vieillesse et son cortège d'infirmités** old age and the infirmities that come with it; *Méd* **i. motrice cérébrale** cerebral palsy **2** *Littéraire (faiblesse)* failing, weakness; **i. de l'esprit** weakness of the mind

infixe [ɛ̃fiks] **NM** *Ling* infix

inflammabilité [ɛ̃flamabilite] **NF** inflammability, flammability

inflammable [ɛ̃flamabl] **ADJ 1** *(combustible)* inflammable, flammable; **gaz i.** flammable gas;

matériaux inflammables inflammable materials **2** *Littéraire (impétueux)* inflammable; **un tempérament i.** a fiery temperament

inflammation [ɛ̃flamasjɔ̃] **NF** *Méd* inflammation; **j'ai une i. au genou** my knee is inflamed

inflammatoire [ɛ̃flamatwar] **ADJ** *Méd* inflammatory

inflation [ɛ̃flasjɔ̃] **NF 1** *Écon* inflation; **i. par la demande/les coûts** demand-pull/cost-push inflation; **i. fiduciaire** inflation of the currency; **i. galopante** galloping inflation; **i. larvée** creeping inflation; **i. monétaire** monetary inflation; **i. des prix** price inflation; **i. des salaires** wage inflation; **des investissements à l'abri de l'i.** inflation-proof investments

2 *(accroissement → des effectifs)* **l'i. du nombre des bureaucrates** the inflated *or* swelling numbers of bureaucrats

inflationnisme [ɛ̃flasjɔnism] **NM** *Écon* inflationism

inflationniste [ɛ̃flasjɔnist] *Écon* **ADJ** *(tendance)* inflationary; *(politique)* inflationist

NMF inflationist

inflatoire [ɛ̃flatwar] **ADJ** *Belg Écon (tendance)* inflationary; *(politique)* inflationist

infléchi, -e [ɛ̃fleʃi] **ADJ 1** *(phonème)* inflected **2** *Archit* **arc i.** inflected arch

infléchir [32] [ɛ̃fleʃir] **VT 1** *(courber)* to bend, to inflect

2 *(influer sur)* to modify, to influence; **i. le cours des événements** to affect *or* to influence the course of events

3 *Bourse (faire diminuer)* to cut, to reduce

►**s'infléchir VPR 1** *(décrire une courbe → gén)* to bend, to curve (round); *(→ rayon)* to be inflected *or* bent; *(→ plancher, poutre)* to sag, to bow; **le chemin s'infléchit à cet endroit** the path curves here; **la courbe de température s'infléchit** *(vers le bas)* the temperature curve is dipping (slightly); *(vers le haut)* the temperature curve is climbing *or* rising (slightly)

2 *Fig (changer de but)* to shift, to change course; **la politique du gouvernement s'infléchit dans le sens du protectionnisme** government policy is shifting *or* veering towards protectionism

3 *Bourse (diminuer → cours)* to fall

infléchissement [ɛ̃fleʃismɑ̃] **NM** shift, change of course; **i. d'une politique** change of emphasis *or* shift in policy

inflexibilité [ɛ̃flɛksibilite] **NF 1** *(d'un matériau)* inflexibility, rigidity **2** *(d'une personne)* inflexibility, firmness, resoluteness

inflexible [ɛ̃flɛksibl] **ADJ 1** *(matériau)* rigid, inflexible **2** *(personne)* inflexible, rigid, unbending; *(volonté)* iron *(avant n)*, unbending; **il est resté i.** he wouldn't change his mind **3** *(loi, morale)* rigid, hard-and-fast; *(règlement, discipline)* strict

inflexiblement [ɛ̃flɛksibləmɑ̃] **ADV** *Littéraire* inflexibly, rigidly

inflexion [ɛ̃flɛksjɔ̃] **NF 1** *(modulation → de la voix)* inflection, modulation

2 *(de courbe, rayon)* inflection

3 *(changement de direction)* shift, change of course; **on constate une i. de la politique vers la détente** there has been a change in policy in favour of détente

4 *Ling & Math* inflection; **point d'i.** point of inflection

5 *(inclination)* **avec une gracieuse i. de la tête** with a graceful nod; **une i. du buste** a bow

6 *Bourse (diminution)* reduction, fall

infliger [17] [ɛ̃fliʒe] **VT i. une punition/une défaite/des souffrances/des pertes à qn** to inflict a punishment/a defeat/sufferings/losses on sb; **i. une amende/corvée à qn** to impose a fine/chore on sb; **i. une humiliation à qn** to put sb down, to humiliate sb; **tel est le châtiment infligé aux traîtres** such is the punishment meted out to traitors; **i. sa compagnie** *ou* **présence à qn** to inflict one's company *or* presence on sb

inflight [inflajt] **NM** *Presse* inflight magazine

inflorescence [ɛ̃flɔrɛsɑ̃s] **NF** *Bot* inflorescence

influençable [ɛ̃flyɑ̃sabl] **ADJ** easily influenced *or* swayed

influence [ɛ̃flyɑ̃s] **NF 1** *(marque, effet)* influence; **on voit tout de suite l'i. de Kokoschka dans ses tableaux** it's easy to spot the influence of Kokoschka on *or* in his/her paintings; **l'i. du climat sur la végétation** the influence of the climate on the vegetation; **cela n'a eu aucune i. sur ma décision** it didn't influence my decision at all, it had no bearing (at all) on my decision

2 *(emprise → d'une personne, d'une drogue, d'un sentiment)* influence; **avoir de l'i. sur qn** to have influence over sb; **avoir une bonne i. sur** to be *or* to have a good influence on; **avoir une grande i. sur** to have a great influence on; **j'ai beaucoup d'i. sur lui** I've got a lot of influence over him; **subir l'i. de qn** to be influenced by sb; **être sous l'i. de la boisson/drogue** to be under the influence of drink/drugs; **être sous l'i. de la jalousie** to be possessed by jealousy; **il a agi sous l'i. de la colère** he acted in the grip of *or* in a fit of anger; **être sous i.** *(drogué)* to be under the influence of drugs

3 *Psy* influence

4 *(poids social ou politique)* influence; **avoir de l'i.** to have influence, to be influential

5 *Élec* static induction

influencer [16] [ɛ̃flyɑ̃se] **VT** to influence; **ne te laisse pas i. par la publicité** don't let advertising influence you, don't let yourself be influenced by advertising; **il se laisse facilement i.** he's easily influenced; **ses arguments m'influençaient toujours au moment du vote** his/her arguments always used to sway me just before a vote; **sa peinture fut très influencée par les fauves** his/her painting was heavily influenced by the Fauvists; **la lune influence les marées** the moon affects the tide

influenceur [ɛ̃flyɑ̃sœr] **NM** *Mktg* influencer

influent, -e [ɛ̃flyɑ̃, -ɑ̃t] **ADJ** influential; **c'est une personne influente** he's/she's a person of influence *or* an influential person; **les gens influents** people in positions of influence, influential people

influenza [ɛ̃flyɑ̃za, ɛ̃flyɛ̃za] **NF** *Vieilli* influenza

influer [7] [ɛ̃flye] **influer sur VT IND** to have an influence on, to influence, to affect

influx [ɛ̃fly] **NM** *Physiol* **i. nerveux** nerve impulse

info [ɛ̃fo] *Fam* **NF** info *(UNCOUNT)*; **c'est lui qui m'a donné cette i.** I got the info from him

▫ **infos NFPL les infos** the news■ *(UNCOUNT)*; **je l'ai entendu aux infos** I heard it on the news

infodominance [ɛ̃fodɔminɑ̃s] **NF** *Mil* information dominance

infogérance [ɛ̃foʒerɑ̃s] **NF** facilities management

infographe [ɛ̃fɔgraf] **NMF** graphics artist

infographie® [ɛ̃fɔgrafi] **NF** *Ordinat* computer graphics

infographique [ɛ̃fɔgrafik] **ADJ** graphics *(avant n)*

infographiste [ɛ̃fɔgrafist] **NMF** graphics artist

in-folio [infɔljo] *Typ* **ADJ INV** folio

NM INV folio

infomercial, -aux [ɛ̃fɔmɛrsjal, -o] **NM** infomercial

infondé, -e [ɛ̃fɔ̃de] **ADJ** unfounded, groundless

informateur, -trice [ɛ̃fɔrmatœr, -tris] **NM,F** *(gén)* informant; *(de police)* informer

informaticien, -enne [ɛ̃fɔrmatisjɛ̃, -ɛn] **ADJ** *voir* **ingénieur**

NM,F *(dans une entreprise)* data processor; *(à l'université)* computer scientist; **son fils est i.** his/her son works in computers

informatif, -ive [ɛ̃fɔrmatif, -iv] **ADJ** informative

information [ɛ̃fɔrmasjɔ̃] **NF 1** *(renseignement)* piece of information; **des informations** (some) information; **on manque d'informations sur les causes de l'accident** we lack information about the cause of the accident; **demander des informations sur** to ask (for information) about, to inquire about; **je vais aux informations** I'll go and find out; **nous vous adressons ce catalogue à titre d'i.** we are sending you this catalogue for your information

2 l'i. *(mise au courant)* information; **réunion d'i.** briefing session; **l'i. circule mal entre les services** there's poor communication between departments; **nous demandons une meilleure i. des consommateurs sur leurs droits** we want consumers to be better informed about their rights; **pour ton i., sache que...** for your (own) information, you should know that...; *Mktg* **i. commerciale** market intelligence; *Mktg* **i. sur le lieu de vente** point-of-sale information; *Mktg* **informations primaires** primary data; *Mktg* **informations secondaires** secondary data

3 *Presse, Rad & TV* news item, piece of news; **voici une i. de dernière minute** here is some last-minute news; **des informations de dernière minute semblent indiquer que le cessez-le-feu est intervenu** latest reports seem to indicate that a ceasefire has been declared; **des informations économiques** economic news; **l'i. financière de la journée** the day's financial news; **pour finir, je rappelle l'i. la plus importante de notre journal** finally, here is our main story *or* main news item once again; **l'i.** the news; **la liberté d'i., le droit à l'i.** freedom of information; **place à l'i.** priority to current affairs; **qui fait l'i.?** who decides what goes into the news?; **journal d'i.** quality newspaper

4 *Ordinat* **l'i.** data, information; **les sciences de l'i.** information science, informatics *(singulier)*; **protection de l'i.** data protection; **traitement de l'i.** data processing

5 *Aut & Transp* **i. embarquée** on-board information, *(dans une voiture)* in-car information

6 *Jur* **i. (judiciaire)** *(enquête)* inquiry; *(instruction préparatoire)* preliminary investigation; **ouvrir une i.** to set up a preliminary investigation

▫ **informations NFPL** *Rad & TV (émission)* **les informations** the news (bulletin); **informations régionales** local news; **informations télévisées/radiodiffusées** television/radio news; **c'est passé aux informations** it was on the news; **je l'ai vu/entendu aux informations** I saw/heard it on the news

informationnel, -elle [ɛ̃fɔrmasjɔnɛl] **ADJ** informational; **le contenu i. d'un document** the information content of a document

informatique [ɛ̃fɔrmatik] **ADJ** computer *(avant n)*; **un système i.** a computer system

NF *(science)* computer science, information technology; *(traitement des données)* data processing; **travailler dans l'i.** to work *or* to be in computing; **société/magazine d'i.** computer company/magazine; **cours d'i.** computer course; **i. documentaire** (electronic) information retrieval; **i. d'entreprise** business data processing; **i. familiale** home computing; **i. de gestion** *(dans une administration)* administrative data processing; *(dans une entreprise)* business data processing, business applications; **i. grand public** mass (consumer) computing; **i. individuelle** personal computing

informatiquement [ɛ̃fɔrmatikmɑ̃] **ADV** by *or* on computer; **toutes les données sont traitées i.** all the data is processed by *or* on computer

informatisable [ɛ̃fɔrmatizabl] **ADJ** computerizable

informatisation [ɛ̃fɔrmatizasjɔ̃] **NF** computerization

informatisé, -e [ɛ̃fɔrmatize] **ADJ** *(secteur, système)* computerized; *(enseignement)* computer-based; *(gestion)* computer-aided, computer-assisted

informatiser [3] [ɛ̃fɔrmatize] **VT** to computerize

►**s'informatiser VPR** to become computerized; **la bibliothèque s'est informatisée** the library catalogue has been computerized; **depuis que je me suis informatisé** since I got a computer

informative [ɛ̃fɔrmativ] *voir* **informatif**

informatrice [ɛ̃fɔrmatris] *voir* **informateur**

informe [ɛ̃fɔrm] **ADJ 1** *(inesthétique → vêtement, sculpture)* shapeless **2** *(qui n'a plus de forme → chaussure)* shapeless, battered **3** *(sans contours nets)* formless, shapeless; *Biol & Chim* amorphous; **une masse i. de cellules** an amorphous mass of cells **4** *(ébauché)* rough, unfinished, undeveloped; **ce n'est qu'une esquisse i.** it's only a rough sketch

informé, -e [ɛ̃fɔrme] **ADJ** well-informed, informed; **dans les milieux informés** in informed circles; **les gens bien informés** well-informed people; **de source bien informée** from a well-informed *or* an authoritative source; **c'est son amant – tu m'as l'air bien** *ou* **très i.!** he's her lover – you seem to know a lot!; **nous sommes mal informés** *(peu renseignés)* we don't get enough information, we're not sufficiently informed; *(avec de fausses informations)* we're being misinformed; **se tenir i. de** to keep oneself informed about; **tenir qn i. (de qch)** to keep sb informed (of sth)

NM *Jur* (judicial *or* legal) inquiry; **jusqu'à plus ample i.** pending further information

informel, -elle [ɛ̃fɔrmɛl] ADJ **1** (non officiel, décontracté) informal **2** Beaux-Arts informal; **art i.** art informel

NM Beaux-Arts informal artist

informer [3] [ɛ̃fɔrme] VT **1** (aviser) **i. qn de** to inform or to tell or to advise sb of; **si le notaire téléphone, vous voudrez bien m'en i.** if the solicitor phones, will you please let me know or inform me; **elle a démissionné – on vient de m'en i.** she's resigned – I've just been informed of it or told about it; **i. qn que...** to inform or to tell sb that...; **l'a-t-on informé qu'il est muté?** has he been informed or notified of his transfer?; **nous informons Messieurs les voyageurs que...** passengers are informed that...; **j'ai fait i. son père de votre décision** I've made sure that his/her father has been informed of your decision

2 (renseigner) to inform, to give information to; **nous sommes là pour i. le public** our job is to inform the public; **les consommateurs ne sont pas assez informés de** ou **sur leurs droits** consumers are not informed enough or don't know enough about their rights; **on vous a mal informé, vous avez été mal informé** you've been misinformed or wrongly informed

3 Phil to inform

VI Jur **i. contre qn** to start investigations concerning sb; **i. sur un crime** to investigate a crime, to inquire into a crime

▶ **s'informer** VPR **1** (se renseigner) to get information, to ask, to inquire; **je me suis informé auprès de mon avocat/de la mairie** I asked my lawyer/at the Br town hall or Am city hall; **s'i. de** (droit, horaire, résultats) to inquire or to ask about; **s'i. de la santé de qn** to inquire after sb's health; **s'i. sur** to inform oneself about; **je vais m'i. sur la marche à suivre** I'm going to find out what the procedure is

2 (se tenir au courant) to keep oneself informed

informulé, -e [ɛ̃fɔrmyle] ADJ unformulated, unspoken

inforoute [ɛ̃fɔrut] NF Can Ordinat information superhighway, infohighway

infortune [ɛ̃fɔrtyn] NF Littéraire **1** (événement) misfortune; **ce jour-là fut la plus grande i. de ma vie** that day was the greatest misfortune in my life **2** (malheur) misfortune; **dans son i., elle a au moins une consolation** she has at least one consolation in the midst of her misfortune; Euph **i. conjugale** infidelity

infortuné, -e [ɛ̃fɔrtyne] Littéraire ADJ (avant le nom) unfortunate, luckless

NM,F (unfortunate) wretch

infos [ɛ̃fo] NFPL Fam **les i.** the news▪

infospectacle [ɛ̃fɔspɛktakl] NF infotainment

infosphère [ɛ̃fɔsfɛr] NF infosphere

infotainment [ɛ̃fɔtɛjnmənt] NM infotainment

infoutu, -e [ɛ̃futy] ADJ très Fam **être i. de faire qch** to be downright incapable of doing sth▪

infra [ɛ̃fra] ADV **voir i.** see below

infraction [ɛ̃fraksjɔ̃] NF **1** Jur breach of the law, offence; **i. au code de la route** driving offence; **être en i.** to be in breach of the law; **je n'ai jamais été en i.** I've never committed an or any offence; **i. complexe** = infraction where the actus reus is a complex operation; **i. continue** continuing offence; **i. continuée** = series of similar offences committed on one occasion; **i. formelle** = action carried out with criminal intent, irrespective of the outcome; **i. d'habitude** = offence consisting of the repetition of individually inoffensive acts; **i. impossible** = attempted crime that fails; **i. instantanée** = violation that cannot be prolonged in time; **i. internationale** breach of international law; **i. militaire** military offence; **i. mineure** non-indictable offence; **i. obstacle** regulatory offence; **i. permanente** = instantaneous offence, the effects of which continue as a result of the passive attitude of the offender; **i. politique** ≃ offence or offences against the state; **i. praeterintentionnelle** = offence resulting in more serious consequences than intended; **i. purement matérielle** strict-liability offence; **i. putative** putative offence **2** (transgression) infringement, transgression; **i. à** breach of, transgression against

infraétatique [ɛ̃fraetatik] ADJ infrastate

infraliminaire [ɛ̃fraliminɛr] ADJ Psy subliminal

infranchissable [ɛ̃frɑ̃fisabl] ADJ **1** (col) impassable; (rivière) which cannot be crossed **2** (difficulté) insuperable, insurmountable

infrangible [ɛ̃frɑ̃ʒibl] ADJ Littéraire infrangible

infra petita [ɛ̃frapetita] NM insufficient award

ADV **statuer i.** to adjudicate less than is asked for

infrarouge [ɛ̃fraruʒ] ADJ infrared

NM infrared (radiation)

infrason [ɛ̃frasɔ̃] NM infrasound

infrasonore [ɛ̃frasɔnɔr] ADJ infrasonic

infrastructure [ɛ̃frastryktyr] NF **1** (ensemble d'équipements) infrastructure; **i. routière/touristique** road/tourist infrastructure; **l'i. commerciale de la ville** the town's shopping facilities **2** Constr substructure

infréquentable [ɛ̃frekɑ̃tabl] ADJ **ils sont infréquentables** they're not the sort of people you'd want to associate with; **tu es i.!** you're a disgrace!

infroissabilité [ɛ̃frwasabilite] NF crease resistance

infroissable [ɛ̃frwasabl] ADJ crease-resistant

infructueusement [ɛ̃fryktɥøzmɑ̃] ADV fruitlessly, unsuccessfully

infructueux, -euse [ɛ̃fryktɥø, -øz] ADJ **1** (vain) fruitless, unsuccessful **2** Vieilli (arbre, terre) barren

infumable [ɛ̃fymabl] ADJ unsmokable

infundibuliforme [ɛ̃fɔ̃dibylifɔrm] ADJ Bot infundibular, infundibuliform

infuse [ɛ̃fyz] **voir science**

infuser [3] [ɛ̃fyze] VT **1** (faire macérer → thé) to brew, to infuse; (→ tisane) to infuse; **le thé est assez infusé** the tea has brewed or infused for long enough **2** Littéraire (insuffler) **i. qch à qn** to infuse or to inject sb with sth, to infuse or to inject sth into sb

VI (aux être ou avoir) (macérer → thé) to brew, to infuse; (→ tisane) to infuse; **faire i.** to brew; **laissez i. quelques minutes** leave to infuse for a few minutes

Infusette® [ɛ̃fyzɛt] NF **I. de thé** tea bag; **I. de tisane** herbal tea bag

infusibilité [ɛ̃fyzibilite] NF Tech infusibility

infusible [ɛ̃fyzibl] ADJ Tech infusible

infusion [ɛ̃fyzjɔ̃] NF **1** (boisson) herbal tea, infusion; **une i. de camomille** some camomile tea, an infusion of camomile **2** (macération → de thé) brewing, infusion; (→ de tisane) infusion, infusing; **le thé n'a pas besoin d'être passé après i.** the tea doesn't need straining after brewing

infusoire [ɛ̃fyzwar] Vieilli ADJ Biol & Géol infusorial

NMPL Zool infusoria

-ING [iŋ] SUFF

Although this English suffix has been legitimately integrated into French through the use of whole English words in their original sense (**marketing**, **shopping**, **jogging**, **canyoning** etc), it also appears in a lot of "fake" anglicisms which may make an English speaker smile, eg:

un camping a camp site; **un parking** a car park; **faire le forcing** to put the pressure on; **un pressing** a dry cleaner's; **faire du footing** to go jogging; **un mailing** a mailshot; **le zapping** channel-hopping; **le surbooking** (a hybrid made up of a French prefix and an English word) overbooking, double-booking

---

ingagnable [ɛ̃ganabl] ADJ unwinnable, which can't be won; **la partie est i. pour l'Angleterre** England can't win (the game)

ingambe [ɛ̃gɑ̃b] ADJ Littéraire nimble, spry, sprightly; **il est resté i. jusqu'à la fin** he remained very active to the end

ingénier [9] [ɛ̃ʒenje] **s'ingénier** VPR **s'i. à** to try hard or to endeavour or to strive to; **s'i. à trouver une solution** to work hard at finding or to do all one can to find a solution; **s'i. à plaire** to strive to please; **on dirait qu'il s'ingénie à me nuire** it's as if he's going out of his way to do me down

ingénierie [ɛ̃ʒeniri] NF engineering; **i. assistée par ordinateur** computer-assisted engineering; **i. financière** financial engineering; **i. génétique** genetic engineering; **i. informatique** systems engineering; **i. logicielle** software engineering;

i. de systèmes systems engineering; **i. de systèmes assistée par ordinateur** computer-aided software engineering, CASE

ingénieriste [ɛ̃ʒenirist] NMF Vieilli specialist engineer

ingénieur [ɛ̃ʒenjœr] NM

engineer; **i. agronome** agricultural engineer; **i. commercial** sales engineer; **i. électricien** electrical engineer; **i. électronicien** electronics engineer; **i. du génie civil** civil engineer; **i. informaticien** computer scientist; **i. mécanicien** mechanical engineer; **i. de méthodes** methods engineer; **i. des ponts et chaussées** civil engineer; **i. du son** sound engineer; **i. système** systems engineer; **i. des travaux publics** civil engineer

ingénieur-conseil [ɛ̃ʒenjœrkɔ̃sɛj] (pl **ingénieurs-conseils**) NM engineering consultant, consultant engineer

ingénieuse [ɛ̃ʒenjøz] **voir ingénieux**

ingénieusement [ɛ̃ʒenjøzmɑ̃] ADV ingeniously

ingénieux, -euse [ɛ̃ʒenjø, -øz] ADJ (personne) ingenious, clever, inventive; (plan, appareil, procédé) ingenious

ingéniosité [ɛ̃ʒenjozite] NF ingenuity, inventiveness, cleverness

ingénu, -e [ɛ̃ʒeny] ADJ ingenuous, naive

NM,F ingenuous or naive person

◻ **ingénue** NF Théât ingenue or ingénue (role); Fig **cesse de jouer les ingénues** stop acting or playing the innocent

ingénuité [ɛ̃ʒenɥite] NF ingenuousness, naivety

ingénument [ɛ̃ʒenymɑ̃] ADV ingenuously, naively

ingérable [ɛ̃ʒerabl] ADJ Fam unmanageable▪

ingérence [ɛ̃ʒerɑ̃s] NF interference; Pol interference, intervention; Presse **i. rédactionnelle** editorial interference

ingérer [18] [ɛ̃ʒere] VT to absorb, to ingest

▶ **s'ingérer** VPR **s'i. dans** to interfere in; **s'i. dans la vie privée de qn** to meddle in sb's private life; **s'i. dans les affaires intérieures d'un autre pays** to interfere in the domestic affairs of another country

ingestion [ɛ̃ʒɛstjɔ̃] NF ingestion

ingouvernable [ɛ̃guvɛrnabl] ADJ ungovernable

ingrat, -e [ɛ̃gra, -at] ADJ **1** (sans grâce → visage) unattractive, unpleasant, coarse; **avoir un physique i.** to be unattractive or graceless **2** (tâche, travail, sujet, rôle) unrewarding; (terre) unproductive **3** (sans reconnaissance → personne) ungrateful (**avec** ou **envers** to, towards)

NM,F ungrateful person

ingratitude [ɛ̃gratityd] NF **1** (d'une personne) ingratitude, ungratefulness; **faire preuve d'i.** to behave with ingratitude **2** (d'une tâche) thanklessness

ingrédient [ɛ̃gredjɑ̃] NM **1** (dans une recette, un mélange) ingredient **2** Fig (élément) ingredient; **les ingrédients du bonheur** the recipe for happiness

ingresque [ɛ̃grɛsk] ADJ Beaux-Arts Ingresque

ingrisme [ɛ̃grism] NM Beaux-Arts art of Ingres and his imitators

inguérissable [ɛ̃gerisabl] ADJ (malade, maladie) incurable; (chagrin) inconsolable

inguinal, -e, -aux, -ales [ɛ̃gɥinal, -o] ADJ Anat (canal, hernie) inguinal

ingurgitation [ɛgyrʒitasjɔ̃] NF swallowing, Spéc ingurgitation

ingurgiter [3] [ɛ̃gyrʒite] VT Fam **1** (avaler → aliments) to wolf or to gulp down; (→ boisson) to gulp down, to knock back; **il ingurgita un gros morceau de viande** he wolfed down a huge piece of meat **2** Fig to take in; **avec tout ce qu'on leur fait i. avant l'examen** with all the stuff they have to cram (into their heads) before the exam!; **faire i. des faits/dates à qn** to stuff sb's head full of facts/dates

inhabile [inabil] ADJ **1** (sans aptitude) inept, unskilful; **elle n'est pas i. mais elle manque d'expérience** she's not inept but she lacks

experience; **i. à** unfit for **2** *(maladroit → mouvement)* clumsy, awkward; *(→ propos, méthode)* inept, clumsy; **il traça un cercle d'une main i.** he clumsily drew a circle; **une déclaration i.** a bungling statement **3** *Jur* (legally) incapable; **i. à témoigner/à tester** incompetent to stand as a witness/to make a will

inhabileté [inabilte] NF *Littéraire* ineptitude, ineptness, clumsiness

inhabilité [inabilite] NF *Jur* (legal) incapacity (**à** to)

inhabitable [inabitabl] ADJ *(maison, grenier)* uninhabitable; *(quartier)* unpleasant to live in

inhabité, -e [inabite] ADJ **1** *(maison, chambre)* uninhabited, unoccupied; *(contrée)* uninhabited; **des villages inhabités** uninhabited villages; **de vastes contrées inhabitées s'étendent vers le nord** vast empty tracts of land lie to the north **2** *Astron (vol)* unmanned

inhabituel, -elle [inabitɥɛl] ADJ unusual, odd

inhalateur, -trice [inalatœr, -tris] ADJ inhaling, breathing

NM **1** *(pour inhalations)* inhaler **2** *Aviat* oxygen mask

inhalation [inalasjɔ̃] NF **1** *(respiration)* breathing in, *Spéc* inhalation **2** *(traitement)* (steam) inhalation; **je (me) fais des inhalations avec ce produit** I use this product as an inhalant; **le mieux pour les rhumes, c'est de faire des inhalations** inhaling steam is the best thing for a cold

inhalatrice [inalatris] *voir* **inhalateur**

inhaler [3] [inale] VT to inhale, to breathe in

inhalothérapeute [inaloterapøt] NMF *Can* inhalotherapist

inhalothérapie [inaloterapi] NF *Can* inhalotherapy

inharmonieux, -euse [inarmɔnjø, -øz] ADJ *(tons)* inharmonious, jarring; *(musique)* inharmonious, discordant

inhérence [inerɑ̃s] NF inherence

inhérent, -e [inerɑ̃, -ɑ̃t] ADJ inherent; **i. à** inherent in

inhibant, -e [inibɑ̃, -ɑ̃t] ADJ inhibiting

inhibé, -e [inibe] ADJ inhibited, repressed

NM,F inhibited *or* repressed person

inhiber [3] [inibe] VT to inhibit

inhibiteur, -trice [inibitœr, -tris] ADJ *Physiol & Psy* inhibitive, inhibitory

NM **1** *Pharm & Physiol* inhibitor **2** *Écon* inhibitor; **i. de croissance** growth inhibitor

inhibitif, -ive [inibitif, -iv] ADJ *Physiol & Psy* inhibitive, inhibitory

inhibition [inibisjɔ̃] NF *Physiol & Psy* inhibition; **le traumatisme a provoqué une i. de la parole chez l'enfant** the child had speech difficulties after the shock

inhibitive [inibitiv] *voir* **inhibitif**

inhibitrice [inibitris] *voir* **inhibiteur**

inhomogène [inɔmɔʒɛn] ADJ inhomogeneous

inhospitalier, -ère [inɔspitalje, -ɛr] ADJ inhospitable

inhumain, -e [inymɛ̃, -ɛn] ADJ inhuman; **un cri i.** an inhuman *or* unearthly cry

NM,F *Arch & Littéraire* **ma belle inhumaine** my fair cruel one

inhumainement [inymɛnmɑ̃] ADV inhumanly, inhumanely

inhumanité [inymanite] NF *Littéraire* inhumanity

inhumation [inymasjɔ̃] NF burial, *Sout* interment, inhumation; **l'i. aura lieu à 14 heures** the burial *or* interment will take place at 2 p.m.

inhumer [3] [inyme] VT to bury, to inter

inimaginable [inimaʒinabl] ADJ unimaginable; **un paysage d'une beauté i.** an unbelievably beautiful landscape

inimitable [inimitabl] ADJ inimitable

inimité, -e [inimite] ADJ which has still to be imitated, unique

inimitié [inimitje] NF enmity, hostility; **regarder qn avec i.** to look at sb hostilely

ininflammable [inɛ̃flamabl] ADJ *(produit)* nonflammable; *(revêtement)* flame-proof

inintelligemment [inɛ̃teliʒamɑ̃] ADV unintelligently

inintelligence [inɛ̃teliʒɑ̃s] NF **1** *(stupidité)* lack of intelligence; **elle a eu l'i. de photocopier la lettre** rather unintelligently, she photocopied the letter **2** *(incompréhension)* incomprehension, lack of understanding; **une profonde i. des difficultés** a total lack of insight into the problems

inintelligent, -e [inɛ̃teliʒɑ̃, -ɑ̃t] ADJ unintelligent

inintelligibilité [inɛ̃teliʒibilite] NF unintelligibility

inintelligible [inɛ̃teliʒibl] ADJ unintelligible, impossible to understand

inintelligiblement [inɛ̃teliʒibləmɑ̃] ADV unintelligibly

inintéressant, -e [inɛ̃terɛsɑ̃, -ɑ̃t] ADJ uninteresting

inintérêt [inɛ̃terɛ] NM *Littéraire* disinterest, lack of interest

ininterrompu, -e [inɛ̃tɛrɔ̃py] ADJ *(série, flot)* unbroken, uninterrupted; *(bruit)* continuous; *(tradition)* continuous, unbroken; *(efforts)* unremitting, steady; *(bavardage)* continuous, ceaseless; **une nuit de sommeil i.** a night of unbroken sleep; **nous diffusons aujourd'hui cinq heures de musique ininterrompue** today we are broadcasting five hours of non-stop *or* uninterrupted music

inique [inik] ADJ *Littéraire* iniquitous, unjust, unfair; **une loi i.** an unjust law

iniquement [inikmɑ̃] ADV *Littéraire* iniquitously, unjustly, unfairly

iniquité [inikite] NF *Littéraire* iniquity, injustice; **commettre des iniquités** to commit wrongs

initial, -e, -aux, -ales [inisjal, -o] ADJ initial; **le choc i.** the initial shock; **une erreur initiale de dosage** a dosage error in the initial *or* early stages; *Bot* **cellules initiales** initial cells

❑ **initiale** NF *(première lettre)* initial; **une trousse à vos initiales** a pencil-case with your initials on it; **il a signé le document de ses initiales** he signed the document with his initials, he initialled the document; *Beaux-Arts* **initiale ornée** ornamented initial (letter)

initialement [inisjalmɑ̃] ADV initially, at first, originally

initialer [3] [inisjale] VT *Can* to initial

initialisation [inisjalizasjɔ̃] NF *Ordinat* initialization

initialiser [3] [inisjalize] VT *Ordinat* to initialize

initiateur, -trice [inisjatœr, -tris] ADJ initiatory

NM,F **1** *(maître)* initiator; **elle a été son initiatrice en amour/musique** it was thanks to her that he/she discovered love/music **2** *(novateur)* pioneer; **les initiateurs de la biologie/du structuralisme** the founders of biology/of structuralism

initiation [inisjasjɔ̃] NF **1** *(approche)* initiation, introduction; **son i. à l'amour eut lieu à l'âge de 20 ans** he was initiated into the ways of love when he was 20; **i. à la psychologie/au russe** introduction to psychology/to Russian **2** *Chim & Phys* initiating, setting off **3** *(en anthropologie)* initiation

initiatique [inisjatik] ADJ *(rite)* initiatory, initiation *(avant n)*

initiative [inisjativ] NF **1** *(esprit de décision)* initiative; **avoir de l'i.** to have initiative *or* drive; **manquer d'i.** to lack initiative; **faire preuve d'i.** to show great initiative; **esprit d'i.** initiative; **plein d'i.** enterprising

2 *(idée)* initiative; **l'i. du concert est venue d'elles** the original idea for the concert came from them; **à** *ou* **sur l'i. de qn** on sb's initiative; **il a été hospitalisé sur mon i.** he was sent to hospital on my initiative; **les négociations ont été organisées à l'i. du Brésil** the negotiations were initiated by Brazil *or* organized on Brazil's initiative; **prendre l'i. de qch** to initiate sth, to take the initiative for sth; **prendre l'i. de faire qch** to take the initiative in doing sth; *Mil* **i. de défense stratégique** strategic defence initiative; **i. gouvernementale** governmental prerogative to propose legislation; **i. parlementaire** parliamentary prerogative to legislate; **i. populaire** democratic right to petition; **i. privée** *Écon* private initiative; *Jur & Pol* initiative

3 *(action spontanée)* initiative; **faire qch de sa propre i.** to do sth on one's own initiative; **prendre une i.** to take an initiative; **prendre des initiatives** to show initiative; **elle nous laisse prendre des initiatives** she allows us freedom of action; **prendre l'i. de faire qch** to take the initiative in doing sth; *Pol* **i. de paix** peace initiative *or* overture

initiatrice [inisjatris] *voir* **initiateur**

initié, -e [inisje] ADJ initiated

NM,F **1** *(connaisseur)* initiated person, initiate; **les initiés** the initiated; **pour les initiés** not for the uninitiated **2** *(en anthropologie)* initiate **3** *Bourse* insider

initier [9] [inisje] VT **1** *(novice)* to initiate; **i. qn à qch** to initiate sb into sth, to introduce sb to sth **2** *(en anthropologie)* to initiate **3** *(faire démarrer)* to initiate, to get going; **i. un processus** to initiate a process

►**s'initier** VPR **s'i. à qch** to learn the basics of sth, to get to know sth; **j'ai besoin de deux semaines pour m'i. au traitement de texte** I need two weeks to teach myself *or* to learn how to use a word processor

injectable [ɛ̃ʒɛktabl] ADJ injectable

injecté, -e [ɛ̃ʒɛkte] ADJ **1** *(rougi)* **yeux injectés de sang** bloodshot eyes **2** *Méd* injected **3** *Tech* injection-moulded

injecter [4] [ɛ̃ʒɛkte] VT **1** *Constr, Géol & Méd* to inject (**dans** into); **on cherche des cobayes qui acceptent de se faire i. le virus** we're looking for people who would agree to be injected with the virus

2 *(introduire)* to inject, to infuse, to instil; *Fin (argent, capitaux)* to inject (**dans** into); **il faudrait i. quelques idées nouvelles dans ce projet** we need to inject *or* to infuse a few new ideas into the project; **i. de l'enthousiasme à une équipe** to instil enthusiasm into a team; **i. des millions dans une affaire** to inject *or* to pump millions into a business

3 *Tech* to inject

4 *Astron* **i. un engin sur orbite** to inject a spacecraft (into its orbit)

►**s'injecter** VPR *(yeux)* to become bloodshot

injecteur, -trice [ɛ̃ʒɛktœr, -tris] ADJ injection *(avant n)*

NM injector

injectif, -ive [ɛ̃ʒɛktif, -iv] ADJ injective

injection [ɛ̃ʒɛksjɔ̃] NF **1** *Constr, Géol & Méd* injection **2** *Fin (apport → d'argent)* injection (**dans** into) **3** *Tech voir* **moulage 4** *Tech* injection; **à i.** (fuel) injection *(avant n)* **5** *Astron & Math* injection

injectrice [ɛ̃ʒɛktris] *voir* **injecteur**

injoignable [ɛ̃ʒwaɲabl] ADJ **j'ai essayé de l'appeler toute la matinée mais il était i.** I tried to phone him all morning, but I couldn't get through (to him) *or* get hold of him

injonctif, -ive [ɛ̃ʒɔ̃ktif, -iv] ADJ *Gram* injunctive

injonction [ɛ̃ʒɔ̃ksjɔ̃] NF **1** *(ordre)* order; **sur l'i. de qn** at sb's behest; *Bourse* **i. à la vente** sell order **2** *Jur* injunction, (judicial) order; **i. d'assigner un jury** venire; **i. de faire** mandatory injunction; **i. de payer** order to pay; **i. thérapeutique** drug rehabilitation order, *Br* ≃ Drug Treatment and Testing Order

injonctive [ɛ̃ʒɔ̃ktiv] *voir* **injonctif**

injouable [ɛ̃ʒwabl] ADJ unplayable; **le premier acte est i.** the first act is impossible to stage; **la sonate est i.** the sonata is impossible to play; **la balle est i.** the ball is unplayable

injure [ɛ̃ʒyr] NF **1** *(insulte)* insult, abuse *(UNCOUNT)*; **un chapelet d'injures** a stream of abuse *or* insults; **il se mit à lâcher des injures** he started hurling abuse; **accabler** *ou* **couvrir qn d'injures** to heap abuse on sb; *Jur* **i. publique** ≃ slander without special damage

2 *(affront)* affront, insult; **c'est une i. à la nation** it's an insult to our country; **vous me feriez i. en refusant** you would offend me by refusing; **il m'a fait l'i. de refuser mon invitation** he insulted me by refusing my invitation

3 *Littéraire (dommage)* **l'i. du temps** the ravages of time

injurier [9] [ɛ̃ʒyrje] VT **1** *(adresser des insultes à)* to insult, to abuse; **il n'arrête pas de l'i.** he's always insulting him/her; **on s'est carrément fait i. par la voisine** we came in for a real stream of abuse from our neighbour **2** *Littéraire (offenser moralement)* to be an insult to; **il injurie la mémoire de son père** he is an insult to his father's memory

►**s'injurier** VPR to insult each other; **les chauffeurs de taxi se sont injuriés** the taxi drivers hurled insults at each other *or* swore at one another

injurieusement [ɛ̃ʒyrjøzmɑ̃] ADV abusively, insultingly

injurieux, -euse [ɛ̃ʒyrjø, -øz] ADJ abusive, insulting, offensive; **des propos i.** abusive *or* offensive language; **être i. envers qn** to be abusive *or* insulting to sb; **cela n'a rien d'i.!** no offence meant *or* intended!

injuste [ɛ̃ʒyst] ADJ **1** *(décision)* unjust, unfair; **une sentence i.** an unjust sentence; **ce que vous dites est i.** what you're saying is unfair **2** *(personne)* unfair, unjust; **ne sois pas i.!** be fair!, don't be unfair!; **être i. envers qn** to do sb an injustice

injustement [ɛ̃ʒystəmɑ̃] ADV **1** *(avec iniquité)* unfairly, unjustly; **punir i.** to punish unjustly **2** *(sans raison)* without reason; **se plaindre i.** to complain without just cause *or* for no good reason

injustice [ɛ̃ʒystis] NF **1** *(caractère inique)* injustice, unfairness; **l'i. sociale** social injustice; **c'est l'i. du sort!** that's the luck of the draw! **2** *(acte inique)* injustice, wrong; **commettre une i. envers qn** to do sb wrong *or* an injustice; **c'est une i.!** that's unfair!

injustifiable [ɛ̃ʒystifjabl] ADJ unjustifiable

injustifié, -e [ɛ̃ʒystifje] ADJ *(critique, punition)* unjustified, unwarranted; *(crainte)* unfounded, groundless; *(absence)* unexplained

inlandsis [inlɑ̃tsis] NM *(glacier)* ice sheet

inlassable [ɛ̃lasabl] ADJ *(infatigable → personne)* indefatigable, tireless, untiring; *(→ énergie)* tireless; **elle est d'un dévouement i.** her devotion is untiring

inlassablement [ɛ̃lasabləmɑ̃] ADV indefatigably, tirelessly, untiringly; **elle répétait i. le même mot** she kept repeating the same word over and over again

inlay [inlɛ] NM *(en odontologie)* (dental) inlay

inné, -e [ine] ADJ **1** *(don)* inborn, innate **2** *Phil* innate

innéisme [ineism] NM *Phil* innatism

innéité [ineite] NF *Phil* innateness

innervant [inɛrvɑ̃] ADJ M **gaz i.** nerve gas

innervation [inɛrvasjɔ̃] NF *Physiol* innervation

innervé, -e [inɛrve] ADJ *Bot* nerveless

innerver [3] [inɛrve] VT *Physiol* to innervate

innocemment [inɔsamɑ̃] ADV innocently; **j'ai posé la question i.** I asked the question in all innocence, I meant no harm by my question

innocence [inɔsɑ̃s] NF **1** *(gén)* innocence; **en toute i.** in all innocence, quite innocently **2** *Rel* innocence; **en état d'i.** in a state of innocence **3** *Jur* innocence; **établir** *ou* **prouver l'i. de qn** to establish *or* to prove sb's innocence

Innocent [inɔsɑ̃] NPR *(pape)* Innocent

innocent, -e [inɔsɑ̃, -ɑ̃t] ADJ **1** *(non responsable → inculpé, victime)* innocent; *Jur* **déclarer qn i.** to find sb innocent *or* not guilty; **être i. de qch** to be innocent of sth; **tant de sang i. versé** so much innocent blood spilt

2 *(plaisanterie, question, plaisirs)* innocent, harmless; *(baiser, jeune fille)* innocent

3 *(candide → enfant, âge)* innocent; **on est encore i. à cet âge** they're still innocent at that age; **i. comme l'agneau** *ou* **l'enfant qui vient de naître** as innocent as a newborn lamb *or* a babe in arms

4 *(niais)* innocent, simple

NM,F **1** *(personne non coupable)* innocent person

2 *(personne candide)* innocent; **faire l'i.** to play *or* to act the innocent; **ne joue pas l'i.** *ou* **les innocents avec moi!** don't come the innocent with me!; **tu as été un bel i. de la croire!** you were pretty naive to believe her!; **c'est un grand i.!** he's a bit naive!; **aux innocents les mains pleines** the meek shall inherit the earth

3 *(niais)* simpleton; **innocente, va!** you (great big) ninny!; **l'i. du village** the village idiot

innocenter [3] [inɔsɑ̃te] VT **1** *Jur (sujet: jury)* to clear, to find innocent *or* not guilty; *(sujet: témoignage, document)* to prove innocent, to show to be innocent; **il réussit à faire i. son client** he managed to get his client cleared **2** *(excuser)* to excuse; **i. la conduite de qn** to excuse sb's behaviour

innocuité [inɔkɥite] NF harmlessness, inoffensiveness, *Méd & Sout* innocuousness

innombrable [inɔ̃brabl] ADJ innumerable, countless; **d'innombrables mouches** huge numbers of flies; **une foule i.** a vast *or* huge crowd

innomé, -e [inɔme] ADJ **1** *(sans nom)* unnamed **2** *Antiq & Jur* **contrat i.** innominate contract

innominé, -e [inɔmine] ADJ innominate

innommable [inɔmabl] ADJ unspeakable, loathsome, nameless

innommé, -e [inɔme] = **innomé**

innovant, -e [inɔvɑ̃, -ɑ̃t] ADJ innovative

innovateur, -trice [inɔvatœr, -tris] ADJ innovative, groundbreaking

NM,F innovator; *Mktg* **i. continu** continuous innovator; *Mktg* **i. tardif** laggard

innovation [inɔvasjɔ̃] NF **1** *(créativité)* innovation **2** *(changement)* innovation; **il y a eu des innovations ici depuis que tu es parti** there have been a few changes around here since you left **3** *Com* innovation; *Mktg* **i. continue** continuous innovation; **i. de produit** product innovation; **i. technologique** technological innovation

innovatrice [inɔvatris] *voir* **innovateur**

innover [3] [inɔve] VI to innovate; **depuis des années, les banques n'ont pas innové** the banks haven't come up with any new ideas *or* haven't innovated for years; **i. en (matière de)** to break new ground *or* to innovate in (the field of)

Innsbruck [inzbryk] NM Innsbruck

inobservable [inɔpsɛrvabl] ADJ **1** *(imperceptible par la vue)* unobservable **2** *(inexécutable)* **des recommandations inobservables** recommendations that cannot be observed *or* carried out

inobservance [inɔpsɛrvɑ̃s] NF *Littéraire* **l'i. des traditions** disregard for tradition; **l'i. du règlement** non-compliance with the regulations

inobservation [inɔpsɛrvasjɔ̃] NF *Littéraire & Jur* **i. d'une loi** non-compliance *or* failure to comply with a law; **i. d'un contrat** breach of contract

inobservé, -e [inɔpsɛrve] ADJ *Littéraire & Jur* unobserved

inocclusion [inɔklyzjɔ̃] NF *Méd* malocclusion

inoccupation [inɔkypasjɔ̃] NF inactivity, idleness

inoccupé, -e [inɔkype] ADJ **1** *(vide → maison, local)* unoccupied, empty **2** *(vacant → poste)* unoccupied, vacant, available; *(→ taxi, fauteuil)* empty, free; **choisissez parmi les places/tables inoccupées** take one of the empty seats/tables **3** *(inactif)* inactive, unoccupied, idle; **elle est longtemps restée inoccupée** for a long time she had nothing to do; **ne laisse pas les enfants inoccupés** don't leave the children with nothing to do

in-octavo [inɔktavo] *Typ* ADJ INV octavo

NM INV octavo, eightvo; **des i.** octavos

inoculable [inɔkylabl] ADJ *Méd* inoculable

inoculation [inɔkylasjɔ̃] NF **1** *Méd (vaccination)* inoculation; *(contamination)* infection **2** *Métal* inoculation

inoculer [3] [inɔkyle] VT **1** *Méd* to inoculate; **on inocule le virus à un cobaye** a guinea pig is injected with the virus; **les volontaires se font i. le vaccin** the volunteers are injected with the vaccine **2** *(transmettre → enthousiasme, manie)* to infect, to pass on to; **elle m'a inoculé la passion du jeu** she passed on her love of gambling to me

inocybe [inɔsib] NM *Bot* inocybe

inodore [inɔdɔr] ADJ **1** *(sans odeur)* odourless **2** *(sans intérêt)* uninteresting, commonplace

inoffensif, -ive [inɔfɑ̃sif, -iv] ADJ *(personne)* harmless, inoffensive; *(animal)* harmless; *(remarque)* innocuous

inondable [inɔ̃dabl] ADJ liable to flooding

inondation [inɔ̃dasjɔ̃] NF **1** *(eau)* flood, flooding, *Sout* inundation; *(action)* flooding, *Sout* inundation **2** *Fig* flood, deluge; *(du marché)* flooding; **on assiste à une i. du marché par les voitures étrangères** foreign cars are flooding *or* inundating the market **3** *Méd* **i. péritonéale** flooding of the peritoneal cavity

inondé, -e [inɔ̃de] ADJ **1** *(champ, maison, cave)* flooded; **on voit qu'il a pris une douche, la salle de bains est inondée!** you can tell he's had a shower, the bathroom's flooded out!; **populations inondées** flood victims

2 *Fig* **être i. de réclamations/de mauvaises nouvelles** to be inundated with complaints/with bad news; **une pièce inondée de soleil** a room flooded with *or* bathed in sunlight; **être i. de joie** to be overcome *or* overwhelmed by joy; **le visage i. de larmes** with tears streaming down his/her face

NM,F flood victim

inonder [3] [inɔ̃de] VT **1** *(champs, maison, ville)* to flood, *Sout* to inundate; **tu ne peux donc pas prendre un bain sans tout i.?** can't you have a bath without flooding the bathroom?; **j'ai été inondé par les gens du dessus** my apartment has been flooded by the people upstairs

2 *(tremper)* to soak; **les larmes inondaient ses joues** his/her cheeks were streaming with *or* bathed in tears; **les yeux inondés de pleurs** his/her eyes full of *or* swimming with tears; **le front inondé de sueur** his/her forehead bathed in sweat

3 *Fig (envahir → marché)* to flood (**de** with); *(→ sujet: foule)* to flood into, to swarm; *(→ sujet: lumière)* to flood *or* to pour into, to bathe; *(→ sujet: bonheur)* to flood; **ses fans l'inondent de lettres** he/she is inundated with fan mail; **le marché des produits de luxe est inondé de contrefaçons** the luxury goods market is flooded with imitation products

▸**s'inonder** VPR **s'i. de qch** to flood *or* to douse onself in sth; **chaque matin il s'inonde d'eau de Cologne** every morning he douses himself with eau de Cologne

inopérable [inɔperabl] ADJ *Méd* inoperable

inopérant, -e [inɔperɑ̃, -ɑ̃t] ADJ inoperative, ineffective

inopiné, -e [inɔpine] ADJ *(inattendu)* unexpected

inopinément [inɔpinemɑ̃] ADV unexpectedly

inopportun, -e [inɔpɔrtœ̃, -yn] ADJ ill-timed, inopportune, untimely; **sa remarque était plutôt inopportune** he/she timed his/her remark rather badly

inopportunément [inɔpɔrtynemɑ̃] ADV *Littéraire* inopportunely

inopportunité [inɔpɔrtynite] NF *Littéraire* inopportuneness, untimeliness

inopposabilité [inɔpozabilite] NF *Jur* unenforceability

inopposable [inɔpozabl] ADJ *Jur* unenforceable

inorganique [inɔrganik] ADJ inorganic

inorganisable [inɔrganizabl] ADJ unorganizable

inorganisation [inɔrganizasjɔ̃] NF lack of organization, disorganization

inorganisé, -e [inɔrganize] ADJ **1** *(désordonné)* disorganized, unorganized **2** *(non syndiqué)* unorganized **3** *Biol* unorganized

NM,F *(travailleur non syndiqué)* non-union member, unorganized worker

inotrope [inɔtrɔp] ADJ *Physiol* inotropic

inoubliable [inublijabl] ADJ unforgettable, never to be forgotten; **elle fut une i. Antigone** she was an unforgettable Antigone

inouï, -e [inwi] ADJ **1** *(incroyable)* incredible, amazing, unbelievable; **il a une assurance inouïe** it's incredible *or* extraordinary how confident he is; **c'est i. ce que cet enfant peut faire comme dégâts!** you wouldn't believe how much havoc that child can cause!; **tu es i.!** you're incredible *or* unbelievable! **2** *Littéraire (sans précédent → prouesse, performance)* unheard of, unprecedented

Inox® [inɔks] ADJ INV stainless steel *(avant n)*

NM INV stainless steel; **couverts en I.** stainless steel cutlery

inoxydable [inɔksidabl] ADJ **1** *(qui résiste à l'oxydation)* stainless; **couteau i.** stainless steel knife **2** *Fam (inaltérable)* enduring; **les dessins animés de Tex Avery, c'est i., c'est toujours aussi amusant qu'il y a 50 ans** Tex Avery's cartoons have stood the test of time; they're as funny now as they were 50 years ago

NM stainless steel

in pace, in-pace [inpase] NM INV *Hist* = dungeon in a convent, where prisoners were locked up for life

in partibus [inpartibys] ADJ *Rel* in partibus

in petto [inpeto] ADV *Littéraire* privately, in petto; **je pensais i. que...** I was thinking to myself that...

INPI [iɛnpei] NM *(abrév* **Institut national de la propriété intellectuelle***)* French National Patent Office

inj–inp

in-plano [inplano] *Typ* ADJ INV full sheet *(avant n)*, broadsheet *(avant n)*
NM INV full sheet; **des i.** books printed on full sheets
input [input] NM *Écon* input
inqualifiable [ɛ̃kalifjabl] ADJ unspeakable; **un acte i.** an unspeakable act; **ce que tu as fait est i.** there are no words for what you've done
inquart [ɛ̃kar] NM *Métal* quartation
inquartation [ɛ̃kartasjɔ̃] NF *Métal* quartation
in-quarto [inkwarto] *Typ* ADJ INV quarto
NM INV quarto; **des i.** quartos
inquiet, -ète [ɛ̃kjɛ, -ɛt] ADJ **1** *(personne)* worried, anxious, concerned; *(regard)* worried, uneasy, nervous; *(attente)* anxious; *(sommeil)* uneasy, troubled, broken; **elle est inquiète de ne pas avoir de nouvelles** she's worried *or* anxious at not having any news; **il est toujours i.** he's always worried about something; **tu es toujours inquiète!** you're always worried!, you're such a worrier!; **être i. de qch** to be worried about sth; **je suis i. de son silence** I'm worried about not having heard from him/her; **il est i. de la montée du racisme** he's worried about the rise of racism
2 *Littéraire (activité, curiosité)* restless
NM,F worrier
inquiétant, -e [ɛ̃kjetɑ̃, -ɑ̃t] ADJ **1** *(alarmant)* worrying, disquieting, disturbing; **la situation est inquiétante** the situation is worrying *or* gives cause for concern **2** *(qui effraie → air, sourire)* frightening; **la drogue provoquait des fantasmes inquiétants** the drug caused disturbing fantasies
inquiéter [18] [ɛ̃kjete] VT **1** *(troubler → sujet: personne, situation)* to worry, to trouble; **son état de santé m'inquiète** I'm worried about his/her state of health; **son silence m'inquiète beaucoup** his/her silence is worrying me; **qu'est-ce qui t'inquiète?** what are you worried about?, what's worrying you?; **il n'est pas encore arrivé? tu m'inquiètes!** hasn't he arrived yet? you've got me worried now!
2 *(ennuyer, harceler)* to disturb, to bother, to harass; **s'ils viennent t'i. chez toi, préviens-moi** if they come to bother *or* harass you at home, let me know; **le magistrat ne fut jamais inquiété par la police** the police never troubled the magistrate; **ils ont vidé les coffres sans être inquiétés** they were able to empty the safes without being disturbed *or* interrupted; **il n'a jamais inquiété le champion du monde** he's never posed any threat to the world champion; **c'est la première fois que notre gardien de but est sérieusement inquiété** it's the first time that our goalkeeper has been really worried *or* in real trouble
USAGE ABSOLU *(troubler)* **ces nouvelles ont de quoi i.** this news is quite disturbing *or* worrying *or* alarming
▶**s'inquiéter** VPR **1** *(être soucieux)* to worry, to be worried; **il y a de quoi s'i.** that's something to be worried about, there's real cause for concern; **s'i. au sujet de** *ou* **pour qn** to be worried *or* concerned about sb; **ne t'inquiète pas pour elle!** don't (you) worry about her!; **je m'inquiète beaucoup de le savoir seul** it worries *or* troubles me a lot to know that he's alone
2 s'i. de *(tenir compte de)* to bother *or* to worry about; **elle achète sans s'i. du prix** she buys things regardless of the price *or* without worrying about the price
3 s'i. de *(s'occuper de)* to see to sth; **et son cadeau? – je m'en inquiéterai plus tard** what about her present? – I'll see about that *or* take care of that later; **t'es-tu inquiété de réserver les places?** did you think of booking?; **elle ne s'est jamais inquiétée de savoir si j'avais besoin de quelque chose** she never bothered *or* troubled *or* took the trouble to find out if I needed anything; *Fam* **où tu vas? – t'inquiète!** where are you off to? – mind your own business! *or* what's it to you?
4 s'i. de *(se renseigner sur)* to inquire *or* to ask about
inquiétude [ɛ̃kjetyd] NF **1** *(souci)* worry, anxiety, concern; **avec i.** anxiously, fretfully, nervously; **un sujet d'i.** a cause for concern *or* anxiety; **n'ayez aucune i., soyez sans i.** rest easy, have no fear; **avoir des inquiétudes** to be worried *or* concerned **2** *Arch (agitation)* agitation, restlessness
inquilin, -e [ɛ̃kɥilɛ̃, -in] *Zool* ADJ inquiline, inquilinous
NM inquiline
inquilisme [ɛ̃kɥilism] NM *Zool* inquilinism, inquilinity
inquisiteur, -trice [ɛ̃kizitœr, -tris] ADJ inquisitive, prying
NM inquisitor; **le Grand I.** the Inquisitor General
inquisition [ɛ̃kizisjɔ̃] NF **1** *Hist* **la (Sainte) I.** the (Holy) Inquisition **2** *Péj (ingérence)* inquisition
inquisitoire [ɛ̃kizitwar] ADJ *Jur* inquisitorial
inquisitorial, -e, -aux, -ales [ɛ̃kisitɔrjal, -o] ADJ **1** *(méthode)* inquisitorial, high-handed **2** *Hist* inquisitorial, Inquisition *(avant n)*
inquisitrice [ɛ̃kizitris] *voir* **inquisiteur**
INR [iɛnɛr] NM *Belg* (*abrév* **Institut national de radiodiffusion**) = Belgian broadcasting company
INRA, Inra [inra] NM (*abrév* **Institut national de la recherche agronomique**) = national institute for agronomic research
inracontable [ɛ̃rakɔ̃tabl] ADJ *(trop grivois)* unrepeatable; *(trop compliqué)* too complicated for words; **je me suis débattu avec le fisc, c'est i.!** I can't even begin to tell you what a struggle I had with the tax people!
inratable [ɛ̃ratabl] ADJ *(spectacle)* unmissable
inrayable [ɛ̃rɛjabl] ADJ non-scratch
insaisissabilité [ɛ̃sezisabilite] NF *Jur* exemption from seizure
insaisissable [ɛ̃sezisabl] ADJ **1** *(imprenable → terroriste, voleur)* elusive **2** *(imperceptible)* imperceptible, intangible; **elle distingue des détails pour moi insaisissables** she picks out details I can't even see **3** *(fuyant)* unfathomable, elusive; **caractère i.** elusiveness; **c'est quelqu'un d'i., tu n'auras pas de réponse nette de sa part** he's/she's very evasive, you won't get a straight answer from him/her **4** *Jur* exempt from seizure
insalifiable [ɛ̃salifjabl] ADJ *Chim* not salifiable
insalissable [ɛ̃salisabl] ADJ stain-resistant
insalivation [ɛ̃salivasjɔ̃] NF insalivation
insalubre [ɛ̃salybr] ADJ *(immeuble)* insalubrious; *(climat)* insalubrious, unhealthy
insalubrité [ɛ̃salybrite] NF *(d'un immeuble)* insalubrity; *(du climat)* insalubrity, unhealthiness
insane [ɛ̃san] ADJ **1** *Littéraire (insensé)* nonsensical, insane **2** *Psy* insane
insanité [ɛ̃sanite] NF **1** *(folie)* insanity; *Jur* **i. d'esprit** insanity **2** *(remarque)* insane *or* nonsensical remark; *(acte)* insane act, insane thing to do; **proférer des insanités** to say insane things; **tu n'es pas forcé d'écouter ses insanités** you don't have to listen to his/her ravings
insatiabilité [ɛ̃sasjabilite] NF insatiability
insatiable [ɛ̃sasjabl] ADJ insatiable; **d'une curiosité i.** insatiably curious
insatiablement [ɛ̃sasjabləmɑ̃] ADV insatiably
insatisfaction [ɛ̃satisfaksjɔ̃] NF dissatisfaction
insatisfaisant, -e [ɛ̃satisfəzɑ̃, -ɑ̃t] ADJ unsatisfactory
insatisfait, -e [ɛ̃satisfɛ, -ɛt] ADJ **1** *(inassouvi → curiosité, besoin)* unsatisfied, frustrated **2** *(mécontent → personne)* unsatisfied, dissatisfied, displeased; **être i. de** to be unhappy about
NM,F discontented person; **les insatisfaits** the discontented; **c'est un éternel i.** he's never satisfied *or* happy
insaturé, -e [ɛ̃satyre] ADJ unsaturated
inscriptible [ɛ̃skriptibl] ADJ inscribable
inscription [ɛ̃skripsjɔ̃] NF **1** *(ensemble de caractères)* inscription, writing *(UNCOUNT)*; **il y avait une i. sur le mur** there was an inscription *or* something written on the wall; **des tablettes portant des inscriptions** inscribed tablets; **i. comptable** accounting entry
2 *(action d'écrire)* **l'i. d'un slogan sur un mur** daubing *or* writing a slogan on a wall; **l'i. d'une épitaphe sur une tombe** inscribing *or* engraving an epitaph on a tombstone
3 *(action d'inclure → dans un journal, un registre)* entering, recording; **une question dont l'i. à l'ordre du jour s'impose** a question which must go (down) *or* be placed on the agenda; **l'i. des dépenses au budget** the listing of expenses in the budget
4 *(formalité)* **i. à** *(cours, concours)* registration for, enrolment in; *(club, parti)* enrolment in, joining (of); **i. à l'université** university registration *or* enrolment, *Br* university matriculation; **i. sur les listes électorales** *Br* registration on the electoral roll, *Am* voter registration; **au moment de l'i. de votre enfant à l'école** when it's time to enrol *or* to register your child for school; **j'ai demandé mon i. sur une liste d'attente** I've asked for my name to go on *or* to be added to a waiting list; **dernière date pour les inscriptions** *(à l'université)* closing date for enrolment *or* registration; *(dans un club)* closing date for enrolment; *Univ* **dossier d'i.** admission form, *Br* ≃ UCAS form; *Univ* **droits d'i.** registration fees; *Univ* **service des inscriptions** admissions office
5 *(personne inscrite)* **il y a une trentaine d'inscriptions au club/pour le rallye** about 30 people have joined the club/entered the rally
6 *Jur* **i. de faux** challenge *(to the validity of a document)*; **i. hypothécaire** mortgage registration
7 *Fin* scrip; **i. de rente** *ou* **sur le grand-livre** Treasury scrip
8 *Bourse* quotation (privilege); **i. à la cote** quotation on the (official) list; **faire une demande d'i. à la cote** to apply for admission to the official list, to seek a share quotation
9 *Compta (dans un livre de comptes)* entry; **i. comptable** accounting entry
10 *Hist & Naut* **l'I. maritime** ≃ (naval) Seamen's Register
inscrire [99] [ɛ̃skrir] VT **1** *(écrire → chiffre, détail)* to write *or* to note (down); *(→ en gravant)* to engrave, to inscribe; **inscrivez votre adresse ici** write down *or* enter your address here; **inscris ton nom au tableau/sur la feuille** write your name (up) on the board/(down) on the sheet; **quelqu'un avait inscrit une phrase à la peinture sur le mur** somebody had painted some words on the wall; **les données inscrites sur l'écran** the data displayed on (the) screen; **je ferai i. son nom sur la tombe** I'll have his/her name engraved *or* inscribed on the tombstone; *Fig* **son visage reste inscrit dans ma mémoire** his/her face remains etched in my memory
2 *(enregistrer → étudiant)* to register, to enrol; *(→ électeur, membre)* to register; *Ordinat (→ logiciel)* to register; **i. un enfant à l'école** to register *or* to enrol a child for school, to put a child's name down for school; **il faut vous (faire) i. à l'université avant le 15 octobre** you must register *or* enrol for university before 15 October; **les étudiants inscrits à l'examen** the students entered for the exam, *Br* the students sitting the exam; **les étudiants inscrits en droit** the students enrolled *Br* on *or Am* in the law course; **se faire i. sur les listes électorales** to register as a voter, to put one's name on the electoral register; **être inscrit au registre du commerce** to be on the trade register; **je vais l'i. au cours de danse** I'm putting him/her down for the dance class; **être inscrit à un club** to be a member of a club; **j'inscris ma fille au club de tennis** I'm putting my daughter's name down to join the tennis club; **i. qn pour un rendez-vous** to put sb *or* sb's name down for an appointment; **je vous inscris sur la liste d'attente** I'll put your name *or* you (down) on the waiting list; **et la liste des passagers? – il n'y est pas inscrit non plus** what about the passenger list? – he's not listed there *or* his name's not on it either
3 *(inclure)* to list, to include; **i. qch au budget** to include sth in the budget; **ces sommes sont inscrites au budget de la culture** these amounts are listed in the arts budget; **son style l'inscrit dans la tradition italienne** his/her style places *or* situates him/her within the Italian tradition; **i. un prix littéraire/un disque d'or à son palmarès** to add a literary prize/a gold disc to one's list of achievements; **on n'a fait qu'i. dans la législation une coutume solidement établie** all they have done is to write a firmly established custom into the legislation; **i. une question à l'ordre du jour** to put *or* to place a question on the agenda; **parmi les sujets inscrits à l'ordre du jour** among the subjects on the agenda
4 *Sport (but, essai)* to score
5 *Math* to inscribe (**dans** in)

▶**s'inscrire** VPR **1 s'i. à** (club, parti) to join, to enrol as a member of; (bibliothèque) to join; (université) to register or to enrol at; (concours, rallye) to enter or to put one's name down for; (cours, atelier) to put oneself or one's name down for, to enrol for; **s'i. au chômage** to register as unemployed; **s'i. sur une liste électorale** to register to vote, to have one's name put on the electoral roll

2 (apparaître) to appear, to come up; **le numéro de téléphone va s'i. sur vos écrans** the phone number will come up or be displayed or appear on your screens; Fig **l'âge s'inscrit sur nos visages** age leaves its mark on our faces

3 Jur **s'i. en faux contre** to lodge a challenge against; Fig **s'i. en faux contre une politique/des allégations** to strongly denounce a policy/deny allegations

4 Bourse **s'i. en hausse/baisse** to be (marked) up/down; **les valeurs industrielles s'inscrivent en baisse de 13 points à la clôture** industrial shares closed 13 points down

5 (appartenir) **cette mesure s'inscrit dans le cadre de notre campagne** this measure comes or lies within the framework of our campaign; **son action s'inscrit tout à fait dans la politique de notre parti** his/her action is totally in keeping or in line with our party's policy; **il s'inscrit dans la lignée des grands metteurs en scène réalistes** he is in the tradition of the great realist directors; **son œuvre s'inscrit dans la tradition romantique** his/her work belongs to the Romantic tradition; **l'architecture moderne s'inscrit bien dans le site** contemporary architecture fits in very well with the site

inscrit, -e [ɛ̃skri, -it] ADJ **1** (étudiant, membre d'un club) enrolled, registered, Br matriculated; (chômeur) registered; Pol (candidat, électeur) registered; (orateur) scheduled

2 Banque & Fin registered; **créancier i.** Br ≃ member of the Finance Houses' Association

3 Math inscribed

4 Bourse **i. à la cote officielle** listed; **non inscrite** unlisted

NM,F (sur une liste) registered person; (à un club, à un parti) registered member; (étudiant) registered student; (candidat) registered candidate; (électeur) registered elector; **au consulat, nous avons de moins en moins d'inscrits chaque année** fewer and fewer people register with the consulate each year; Pol **les inscrits au prochain débat** the scheduled speakers for the next debate; Naut **i. maritime** registered seaman

inscrivait etc voir **inscrire**

inscrivant, -e [ɛ̃skrivɑ̃, -ɑ̃t] NM,F applicant for mortgage registration

insculper [3] [ɛ̃skylpe] VT (gén) to stamp; (orfèvrerie) to hallmark

INSEAD [insead] NM (abrév **Institut européen d'administration**) = European business school in Fontainebleau

insécabilité [ɛ̃sekabilite] NF indivisibility

insécable [ɛ̃sekabl] ADJ indivisible

insectarium [ɛ̃sɛktarjɔm] NM insectarium

insecte [ɛ̃sɛkt] NM insect

insecticide [ɛ̃sɛktisid] ADJ insecticide (avant n), insecticidal; **poudre i.** insecticide or insect powder

NM insecticide

insectifuge [ɛ̃sɛktifyʒ] NM insect repellent

insectivore [ɛ̃sɛktivɔr] ADJ insectivorous

NM insectivore; **les insectivores** the Insectivora

insécurité [ɛ̃sekyrite] NF **1** (manque de sécurité) lack of safety; **l'i. qui règne dans les grandes villes** the collapse of law and order in big cities, the climate of fear reigning in big cities; **le gouvernement veut prendre des mesures contre l'i.** the government wants to introduce measures to improve public safety **2** (précarité → de l'emploi) insecurity, precariousness; (→ de l'avenir) uncertainty **3** (angoisse) insecurity; **un sentiment d'i.** a feeling of insecurity

INSEE, Insee [inse] NM (abrév **Institut national de la statistique et des études économiques**) = French national institute for statistical and economic studies

in-seize [insɛz] Typ ADJ INV sextodecimo

NM INV sextodecimo, sixteenmo; **des i.** sextodecimos

inselberg [inselbɛrg] NM Géol inselberg

inséminateur, -trice [ɛ̃seminatœr, -tris] ADJ inseminating

NM,F inseminator

insémination [ɛ̃seminasjɔ̃] NF insemination; **i. artificielle** artificial insemination; **i. artificielle entre conjoints/par donneur anonyme/par donneur extérieur** artificial insemination by husband/by anonymous donor/by donor

inséminatrice [ɛ̃seminatris] voir **inséminateur**

inséminer [3] [ɛ̃semine] VT to inseminate

insensé, -e [ɛ̃sɑ̃se] ADJ **1** (déraisonnable → projet, initiative) foolish, insane; (→ espoir) unrealistic, mad; **ses idées sont littéralement insensées** his/her ideas are literally crazy; **il est complètement i. de penser que...** it is utterly foolish or absurd to think that...; **c'est i.!** this is absurd or preposterous!; **c'est i. ce qu'il peut boire!** it's crazy the amount he can drink!

2 (excessif) enormous, considerable; **une somme insensée** an excessive or a ludicrous amount of money; **un travail i.** an enormous or unbelievable amount of work

NM,F Littéraire madman, f madwoman

insensibilisation [ɛ̃sɑ̃sibilizasjɔ̃] NF local anaesthesia

insensibiliser [3] [ɛ̃sɑ̃sibilize] VT **1** Méd to anaesthetize; **il m'a insensibilisé la mâchoire** he anaesthetized my jaw **2** (endurcir) to harden; **être insensibilisé aux souffrances d'autrui** to be hardened or to have become immune to the sufferings of others

insensibilité [ɛ̃sɑ̃sibilite] NF **1** (absence de réceptivité) **i. à** insensitiveness or insensitivity to; **i. à la beauté/musique** lack of receptiveness to beauty/music; **i. à la souffrance des autres** insensitivity to the suffering of others **2** Méd insensitivity, numbness

insensible [ɛ̃sɑ̃sibl] ADJ **1** (privé de sensation, de sentiment) **i. à** insensitive to; **i. à la douleur** insensitive to pain; **elle est i. au froid** she's insensitive to or she doesn't feel the cold; **elle est i. à mes reproches** she's impervious or immune to my reproaches; **je suis i. à son mépris** I'm unaffected by or impervious to his/her contempt; **elle demeura i. à ses prières** she remained indifferent to or unmoved by his/her pleas

2 (imperceptible) imperceptible; **progrès insensibles** imperceptible progress

insensiblement [ɛ̃sɑ̃siblǝmɑ̃] ADV imperceptibly, gradually

inséparable [ɛ̃separabl] ADJ inseparable; **ces deux-là, ils sont inséparables** those two are inseparable; **le vice et le crime sont inséparables** vice and crime are inseparable or go hand in hand

□ **inséparables** NMFPL (personnes) **deux inséparables** a pair of inseparable friends NMPL Orn **un couple d'inséparables** a pair of lovebirds

inséparablement [ɛ̃separablǝmɑ̃] ADV inseparably

insérable [ɛ̃serabl] ADJ insertable

insérer [18] [ɛ̃sere] VT **1** (ajouter → chapitre, feuille) to insert (**dans/entre** into/between); (mettre → publicité, annonce) to place (**dans** in); **faire i. une clause dans un contrat** to have a clause added to or put in or inserted into a contract; **i. une annonce dans un journal** to insert or to put an advertisement in a paper

2 (introduire → clé, lame) to insert; **i. qch dans** to insert sth into

3 Ordinat to insert

▶**s'insérer** VPR **1 s'i. dans** (socialement) to become integrated into; **les jeunes ont souvent du mal à s'i. dans le monde du travail** young people often find it difficult to find their place in or to fit into a work environment; **être bien/mal inséré dans la société** to be well/poorly integrated into society

2 s'i. dans (s'inscrire dans) to be part of; **ces mesures s'insèrent dans le cadre d'une politique globale** these measures come within or are part of an overall policy

INSERM, Inserm [insɛrm] NM (abrév **Institut national de la santé et de la recherche médicale**) = national institute for medical research

insermenté [ɛ̃sɛrmɑ̃te] Hist ADJ M non-juring

NM non-juring priest

insert [ɛ̃sɛr] NM **1** Cin & TV cut-in, insert **2** Tech moulding

insertion [ɛ̃sɛrsjɔ̃] NF **1** (introduction) insertion, introduction; **i. d'une page dans un livre** inserting a page into a book

2 (intégration) integration; **l'i. des jeunes dans le monde du travail** the integration of young people into a work environment; **i. sociale** social integration

3 Presse & Mktg advertisement; **i. publicitaire** advertisement; **tarif des insertions** advertising rates; **frais d'i.** advertising charge

4 Ordinat insertion; **mode d'i.** insert mode; **i. de caractères** character insert; **i. de ligne** line insert

5 Jur correction; **i. forcée** publication (of reply) by order of the court

6 Anat insertion

insidieuse [ɛ̃sidjøz] voir **insidieux**

insidieusement [ɛ̃sidjøzmɑ̃] ADV insidiously

insidieux, -euse [ɛ̃sidjø, -øz] ADJ **1** (perfide → question) insidious, treacherous; Littéraire (→ personne) insidious; **un raisonnement i.** a specious argument **2** (sournois → odeur, poison) insidious **3** Méd insidious

insight [insajt] NM insight

insigne [ɛ̃siɲ] ADJ Littéraire (remarquable) remarkable, noteworthy; **faveur i.** signal favour; **j'ai eu l'i. honneur d'être invité à sa table** I had the great honour of being invited to his/her table; **pour les services insignes rendus à la Couronne** for outstanding services to the Crown; **mensonge/calomnie i.** unparalleled lie/slander

NM (marque distinctive → d'un groupe) badge, emblem, symbol; (→ d'une dignité) insignia; **les insignes de la royauté** royal insignia; **l'i. du club sur sa cravate** the club emblem on his tie

insignifiance [ɛ̃siɲifjɑ̃s] NF insignificance, unimportance

insignifiant, -e [ɛ̃siɲifjɑ̃, -ɑ̃t] ADJ **1** (sans intérêt) insignificant, trivial; **nous parlions de choses insignifiantes** we were engaged in idle chatter; **des gens insignifiants** insignificant or unimportant people **2** (minime → gén) insignificant, negligible; (→ erreur) unimportant; (→ somme) trifling, petty

insincère [ɛ̃sɛ̃sɛr] ADJ Littéraire insincere, hypocritical

insincérité [ɛ̃sɛ̃serite] NF Littéraire insincerity, hypocrisy

insinuant, -e [ɛ̃sinɥɑ̃, -ɑ̃t] ADJ (personne, ton) ingratiating; **il avait un odieux sourire i.** he had a horrible fawning smile

insinuation [ɛ̃sinɥasjɔ̃] NF **1** (allusion) insinuation, innuendo; **quelles sont ces insinuations?** what are you hinting at or insinuating or trying to suggest?; **il procède toujours par i.** he always speaks in innuendos **2** Jur insinuation

insinuer [7] [ɛ̃sinɥe] VT to insinuate; **que veut-elle i.?** what's she hinting at or trying to insinuate?; **insinuez-vous que je mens?** are you insinuating or implying that I'm lying?

▶**s'insinuer** VPR **elle parvient à s'i. partout** she gets everywhere; **s'i. dans** (sujet: arôme, gaz) to creep in; (sujet: eau) to filter or to seep in; (sujet: personne) to make one's way in, to infiltrate, to penetrate; **il a réussi a s'i. jusque dans les plus hautes sphères du pouvoir** he managed to worm his way into the higher reaches of power; **s'i. dans les bonnes grâces de qn** to insinuate oneself into sb's favour, to curry favour with sb; **le doute/une idée diabolique s'insinua en lui** doubt/an evil thought crept into his mind

insipide [ɛ̃sipid] ADJ **1** (sans goût) insipid, tasteless; **l'eau est i.** water has no taste or doesn't taste of anything **2** Fig (sans relief → personne) insipid, bland; (→ conversation, livre) uninteresting, dull

insipidité [ɛ̃sipidite] NF **1** (absence de goût) insipidness, tastelessness **2** Fig (ennui) insipidness, tediousness

insistance [ɛ̃sistɑ̃s] NF (obstination) insistence; **il lui demanda avec i. de chanter** he insisted that he/she should sing; **regarder qn avec i.** to stare at sb insistently; **son i. à refuser** his/her insistence on refusing

insistant, -e [ɛ̃sistɑ̃, -ɑ̃t] ADJ **1** (persévérant) insistent; **elle se faisait de plus en plus insistante**

she was growing more and more insistent *or* demanding; **les sonneries insistantes du téléphone** the insistent ringing of the telephone **2** *(fort → parfum)* pervasive, intrusive

insister [3] [ɛ̃siste] **VI 1** *(persévérer)* to insist; **je ne vous dirai rien, inutile d'i.!** I'm not telling you anything, so there's no point pressing me any further!; **ça ne répond pas – insistez!** there's no answer – keep trying *or* try again!; **il a tellement insisté que j'ai fini par accepter** he was so insistent about it that I ended up accepting; **il était en colère, alors je n'ai pas insisté** he was angry, so I didn't push the matter (any further) *or* I didn't insist; **elle a essayé la planche à voile mais elle n'a pas insisté** she tried windsurfing but soon gave (it) up; **insiste, sinon la tache ne partira jamais** keep rubbing or the stain will never come out; **très bien, si vous insistez!** all right, if you insist!

2 *(demander instamment)* to insist; **j'insiste pour que vous m'écoutiez jusqu'au bout** I insist that you hear me out; **elle a insisté pour que nous dormions sur place** she insisted on our staying the night; **vous devez i. auprès du directeur pour qu'on vous accorde un congé** you have to talk to the manager and insist that you get leave

❑ **insister sur VT IND 1** *(mettre l'accent sur → idée, problème)* to stress, to emphasize, to underline; **on ne saurait trop i. sur cette différence** this difference cannot be overemphasized; **si j'étais toi, je n'insisterais pas trop sur le salaire** if I were you, I wouldn't lay too much emphasis on the salary; **dans notre école, nous insistons beaucoup sur la discipline** in our school, we attach great importance to *or* lay great stress on discipline

2 *(s'attarder sur → anecdote)* to dwell on; *(→ tache, défaut)* to pay particular attention to; **mes années d'école, sur lesquelles je n'insisterai pas** my school years, which I'd rather not dwell on; **appliquez ce produit sur votre tapis en insistant bien sur les taches** apply the product to your carpet, paying particular attention to stains

in situ [insity] **ADV** in situ

insituable [ɛ̃sitɥabl] **ADJ** unclassifiable, uncategorizable; **c'est un artiste i.** he's an artist who cannot be categorized *or* pigeonholed

insociable [ɛ̃sɔsjabl] **ADJ** *(farouche)* unsociable; *(asocial)* antisocial

in-soixante-quatre [inswasɑ̃tkatr] *Typ* **ADJ** sixty-fourmo

NM sixty-fourmo

insolation [ɛ̃sɔlasjɔ̃] **NF 1** *Méd* sunstroke, *Spéc* insolation; **attraper une i.** to get sunstroke **2** *Météo* sunshine, *Spéc* insolation; **avoir une faible i.** to get very little sunshine **3** *Phot* exposure (to the light)

insolemment [ɛ̃sɔlamɑ̃] **ADV 1** *(avec arrogance)* insolently, arrogantly **2** *(avec effronterie)* unashamedly

insolence [ɛ̃sɔlɑ̃s] **NF 1** *(irrespect)* insolence; **il était d'une telle i. que nous l'avons renvoyé** he was so insolent that we fired him; **avec i.** insolently **2** *(remarque)* insolent remark; *(acte)* insolent act **3** *(orgueil)* arrogance; **l'i. de l'argent** the arrogance that comes with wealth

insolent, -e [ɛ̃sɔlɑ̃, -ɑ̃t] **ADJ 1** *(impoli)* insolent; **d'un ton i.** insolently, impertinently, impudently **2** *(arrogant)* arrogant; **l'insolente arrogance de l'argent** the arrogance that comes with wealth **3** *(extraordinaire → luxe, succès)* outrageous; **vous avez eu une chance insolente** you've been incredibly lucky

NM,F insolent person; **petit i.!** you impudent *or* impertinent little boy!; **petite insolente!** you impudent *or* impertinent little girl!

insoler [3] [ɛ̃sɔle] **VT** to expose to light, *Spéc* to insolate

insolite [ɛ̃sɔlit] **ADJ** unusual, strange

NM l'i. the unusual, the bizarre

insolubiliser [3] [ɛ̃sɔlybilize] **VT** to make insoluble

insolubilité [ɛ̃sɔlybilite] **NF** *(d'une substance)* insolubility; *(d'un problème)* insolvability

insoluble [ɛ̃sɔlybl] **ADJ 1** *Chim* insoluble **2** *(problème)* insoluble, insolvable; **le problème est i. si l'on utilise de telles méthodes** the problem can't be solved with such methods; **c'est une situation i.** there's no solution to this situation

insolvabilité [ɛ̃sɔlvabilite] **NF** insolvency

insolvable [ɛ̃sɔlvabl] **ADJ** insolvent

NMF insolvent

insomniaque [ɛ̃sɔmnjak] **ADJ** insomniac

NMF insomniac

insomnie [ɛ̃sɔmni] **NF** insomnia *(UNCOUNT)*; **des nuits d'i.** sleepless nights; **avoir des insomnies** to have insomnia; **souffrir d'insomnies** to suffer from insomnia

insondable [ɛ̃sɔ̃dabl] **ADJ 1** *(impénétrable → desseins, mystère)* unfathomable, impenetrable; *(→ regard, visage)* inscrutable **2** *(très profond)* unfathomable; **une crevasse i.** a seemingly bottomless crevasse **3** *(infini)* abysmal; **il est d'une bêtise i.** he's abysmally stupid

insonore [ɛ̃sɔnɔr] **ADJ** soundproof, *Spéc* sound-insulated

insonorisation [ɛ̃sɔnɔrizasjɔ̃] **NF** soundproofing, *Spéc* (sound) insulation

insonoriser [3] [ɛ̃sɔnɔrize] **VT** to soundproof, *Spéc* to (sound) insulate; **studio d'enregistrement insonorisé** soundproof recording studio; **pièce mal insonorisée** inadequately soundproofed room

insonorité [ɛ̃sɔnɔrite] **NF** lack of sonority

insouciance [ɛ̃susjɑ̃s] **NF** lack of concern, carefree attitude, casualness; **avec i.** blithely, casually; **vivre dans l'i.** to live a carefree *or* untroubled existence; **en ce qui concerne l'argent, elle est d'une totale i.** she's got a totally carefree attitude towards money; **son i. à l'égard de ses études** his/her lack of concern for *or* his/her easy-going attitude towards his studies; **l'i. de la jeunesse** the frivolity of youth

insouciant, -e [ɛ̃susjɑ̃, -ɑ̃t] **ADJ 1** *(nonchalant)* carefree, unconcerned, casual; **êtes-vous toujours aussi i. lorsqu'il s'agit d'argent?** are you always so casual with money? **2** *(indifférent)* **i. du danger** oblivious of *or* to the danger; **i. de l'avenir** indifferent to *or* unconcerned about the future; **i. de sa santé** unconcerned about one's health

insoucieux, -euse [ɛ̃susjø, -øz] **ADJ** *Littéraire* carefree, unconcerned; **être i. du lendemain** to be unmindful *or* heedless of what tomorrow may bring

insoumis, -e [ɛ̃sumi, -iz] **ADJ 1** *(indiscipliné → jeunesse, partisan)* rebellious; *(→ enfant)* unruly, *Sout* refractory **2** *(révolté → tribu)* rebel, rebellious; *(→ pays)* unsubdued, undefeated, rebellious **3** *Mil* **soldat i.** *(réfractaire au service militaire)* draft-dodger; *(déserteur)* soldier absent without leave

NM *(réfractaire au service militaire)* draft-dodger; *(déserteur)* soldier absent without leave

insoumission [ɛ̃sumisjɔ̃] **NF 1** *(indiscipline)* rebelliousness, insubordination **2** *(révolte)* rebelliousness, rebellion; **un régiment était encore en état d'i.** one regiment was still in open rebellion **3** *Mil (objection)* draft-dodging; *(désertion)* absence without leave

insoupçonnable [ɛ̃supsɔnabl] **ADJ 1** *(personne)* above suspicion; **il est d'une probité i.** his integrity is beyond question **2** *(invisible → retouche, sous-vêtement)* invisible

insoupçonné, -e [ɛ̃supsɔne] **ADJ** *(vérité)* unsuspected; *(richesses)* undreamt-of, unheard-of; **des trésors d'une valeur insoupçonnée** treasure which nobody expected to be so valuable

insoutenable [ɛ̃sutnabl] **ADJ 1** *(insupportable → douleur, scène, température)* unbearable, unendurable; *(→ lumière)* blinding **2** *(impossible à soutenir → concurrence, lutte)* unsustainable **3** *(indéfendable → opinion, thèse)* unsustainable; *(→ position)* indefensible

NM l'i. the unbearable; **à la limite de l'i.** verging on the unbearable

'L'Insoutenable légèreté de l'être' *Kundera* 'The Unbearable Lightness of Being'

inspecter [4] [ɛ̃spɛkte] **VT 1** *(contrôler → appartement, bagages, engin, travaux)* to inspect, to examine; *(→ marchandises)* to examine; *(troupes)* to review, to inspect; *(→ école, professeur)* to inspect **2** *(scruter)* to inspect; **i. qn des pieds à la tête** to examine sb from head to foot

inspecteur, -trice [ɛ̃spɛktœr, -tris] **ADJ** *Jur* **magistrat i.** visiting magistrate

NM,F 1 *(contrôleur)* inspector; **i. des contributions directes** tax inspector; **i. des contributions indirectes** customs and excise official; *Mil* **i. général** inspector general; **i. (général) des Finances** *Br* ≃ general auditor *(of the Treasury, with special responsibilities)*, *Am* ≃ Comptroller General; *Fin* **i. des impôts** tax inspector; **i. des mines** inspector of mines; **i. du travail** factory inspector; *Fig Hum* **c'est un vrai i. des travaux finis!** he always turns up when the work's done!; **i. sanitaire (public)** health inspector; **i. de la TVA** VAT inspector

2 *(policier)* inspector, detective; **excusez-moi i., mais j'ai trouvé la balle** excuse me, inspector, but I've found the bullet; **i. de la police judiciaire** = inspector belonging to the criminal investigation department, *Br* ≃ CID inspector; **i. de police** *Br* detective sergeant, *Am* lieutenant; **i. principal** ≃ detective inspector

3 *Scol* **i. d'Académie** *Br* ≃ inspector of schools, *Am* ≃ Accreditation officer; **i. de l'Éducation nationale** = education inspector (mainly for the primary sector); **I. pédagogique régional** = locally-based education inspector

inspection [ɛ̃spɛksjɔ̃] **NF 1** *(vérification)* inspection; *(surveillance)* overseeing, supervising; **faire l'i. de** to inspect; **ils se livrèrent à une i. de la voiture** they inspected the car; **ils se livrèrent à une i. détaillée du véhicule** they searched the vehicle thoroughly; **les douaniers soumirent la valise/le passager à une i. en règle** the customs officers subjected the suitcase/the passenger to a thorough search; **après i., le dossier se révéla être un faux** on inspection, the file turned out to be a forgery; **passer une i.** *(l'organiser)* to carry out an inspection, to inspect; *(la subir)* to undergo an inspection, to be inspected; **passer l'i.** *(être en règle)* to pass (the test); *Mil* **prêt pour l'i.!** ready for inspection!

2 *Admin* inspectorate; **i. académique** *Br* ≃ Schools Inspectorate, *Am* ≃ Accreditation Agency; **entrer à l'i. académique** to become a school inspector; **i. générale des Finances** = government department responsible for monitoring the financial affairs of state bodies; **I. générale de la police nationale** = police disciplinary body, *Br* ≃ Police Committee; **I. générale des services** = police disciplinary body for Paris, *Br* ≃ Metropolitan Police Commission; **i. des impôts** *Br* ≃ Inland Revenue, *Am* ≃ Internal Revenue Service; **i. du travail** *Br* ≃ Health and Safety Executive, *Am* ≃ Labor Board

3 *(inspectorat)* inspectorship

inspectorat [ɛ̃spɛktɔra] **NM** *(charge)* inspectorate; *(durée)* inspectorship; **pendant son i.** while he/she was an inspector

inspectrice [ɛ̃spɛktris] *voir* **inspecteur**

inspirant, -e [ɛ̃spirɑ̃, -ɑ̃t] **ADJ** *Fam* inspiring▪; **je ne trouve pas ça très i.** I don't find it very inspiring

inspirateur, -trice [ɛ̃spiratœr, -tris] **ADJ 1** *(inspirant)* inspiring **2** *Anat* inspiratory; **muscles inspirateurs** inspiratory muscles

NM,F 1 *(guide)* inspirer; **la religion est la principale inspiratrice de leur mouvement** religion is the main driving force behind their movement **2** *(instigateur)* instigator; **l'i. d'un complot** the instigator of *or* the person behind a plot

❑ **inspiratrice NF** *(égérie)* muse, inspiration

inspiration [ɛ̃spirasjɔ̃] **NF 1** *(esprit créatif)* inspiration; **tirer son i. de, trouver son i. dans** to draw (one's) inspiration from; **elle a manqué d'i.** she lacked inspiration *or* wasn't much inspired; **je n'ai pas d'i. ce matin** I don't feel inspired *or* I don't have any inspiration this morning; **elle est pour lui une source d'i.** she's his muse; **musique pleine d'i.** inspired music

2 *(idée, envie)* inspiration, (bright) idea; **agir selon l'i. du moment** to act on the spur of the moment; **j'ai eu l'i. de rentrer au bon moment** I had the bright idea of coming home at the right time

3 *(influence)* influence, instigation; **l'architecture d'i. nordique** architecture with a Scandinavian influence, Scandinavian-inspired architecture

4 *Physiol* breathing in, *Spéc* inspiration

5 *Rel* inspiration

inspiratoire [ɛ̃spiratwar] ADJ inspiratory

inspiratrice [ɛ̃spiratris] *voir* **inspirateur**

inspiré, -e [ɛ̃spire] ADJ **1** *(artiste, air, livre)* inspired **2** *(avisé)* **j'ai été bien i. de lui résister** I was well-advised to resist him, I did the right thing in resisting him; **tu as été bien i. de venir me voir aujourd'hui** you did well to come and see me today

NM,F **1** *(mystique)* mystic, visionary **2** *Péj (illuminé)* eccentric

inspirer [3] [ɛ̃spire] VT **1** *(provoquer → décision, sentiment)* to inspire; *(→ remarque)* to inspire, to give rise to; *(→ conduite)* to prompt; *(→ complot)* to instigate; **i. de la haine/du mépris à qn** to inspire sb with hatred/with contempt; **i. de l'admiration à qn** to fill sb with admiration; **i. confiance à qn** to inspire confidence in sb, to inspire sb with confidence; **cette viande ne m'inspire pas confiance!** I don't much like the look of that meat!; **i. le respect** to inspire respect; **son état n'inspire pas d'inquiétude** his/her health gives no cause for concern; **cette réponse lui a été inspirée par la jalousie** his/her answer was inspired *or* prompted by jealousy; **le texte m'inspire plusieurs réflexions** the text leads me to make several remarks; **ma fille m'a inspiré mes plus belles chansons** my daughter inspired me to write my best songs

2 *(influencer → œuvre, personne)* to inspire; **le fait historique qui l'a inspiré pour ce dessin** the historical event which inspired him to do this drawing; **le sujet de dissertation ne m'inspire guère!** the subject of the essay doesn't really fire my imagination!; **une toile inspirée de Bosch** a painting inspired by Bosch; **l'histoire est largement inspirée de la vie du grand homme** the story is largely drawn from *or* based upon the great man's life

3 *(aspirer → air, gaz)* to breathe in, *Spéc* to inspire; **i. de l'air** to breathe air

VI to breathe in, *Spéc* to inspire

► **s'inspirer** VPR **s'i. de** to draw one's inspiration from, to be inspired by

instabilité [ɛ̃stabilite] NF **1** *(précarité → d'une situation, d'un emploi)* instability, precariousness; *(→ d'un régime politique, d'un marché, des prix, de la personnalité, d'une population)* instability; *(→ du temps)* unsettled nature **2** *Chim, Phys & Psy* instability

instable [ɛ̃stabl] ADJ **1** *(branlant)* unsteady, unstable; *(glissant → terrain)* unstable, shifting; **être en équilibre i.** to be balanced precariously **2** *(précaire → situation, emploi)* unstable, precarious; *(→ régime politique, marché, prix, personnalité)* unstable; *(→ population)* shifting, unsettled, unstable; *(→ temps)* unsettled; **la paix est encore i.** the peace is still fragile *or* uncertain **3** *Chim, Phys & Psy* unstable

NMF unreliable *or* unsteady person; *Psy* unstable person

installateur, -trice [ɛ̃stalatœr, -tris] NM,F *(d'appareils sanitaires)* fitter; *Élec, Rad & TV* installer

installation [ɛ̃stalasjɔ̃] NF **1** *(dispositif, équipement)* installation; *(aménagement)* set-up; **une i. de fortune** a makeshift set-up; **i. électrique** wiring; **i. informatique** computer facility; **i. téléphonique** telephone installation

2 *(d'un dentiste, d'un médecin)* setting up (practice); *(d'un ecclésiastique, d'un magistrat)* installation, induction; *(d'un commerçant)* opening, setting up (shop); *(d'un locataire)* moving in; **je fais une fête pour célébrer mon i.** I'm having a housewarming (party); **comment s'est passée votre i.?** how did the move go?

3 *(mise en service → de l'électricité, du gaz, du chauffage)* installation, installing, putting in; *(→ d'un appareil ménager)* installation, installing; *(→ d'une grue)* setting up; *(→ d'une antenne)* installing; *(→ d'une cuisine, d'un atelier, d'un laboratoire)* fitting out; **qui a fait l'i. de la prise/du lave-linge?** who wired the socket/ plumbed in the washing machine?; **refaire l'i. électrique (d'une maison)** to rewire (a house)

4 *(implantation → d'une usine)* setting up

5 *Ordinat* installation; **programme d'i.** installation program; **i. en réseau** network installation

6 *(œuvre d'art)* installation; **i. vidéo** video installation

▫ **installations** NFPL *(dans une usine)* machinery and equipment; *(complexe, bâtiment)* installations; **installations portuaires** port installations; **installations sanitaires** sanitary installations *or* fittings

installatrice [ɛ̃stalatris] *voir* **installateur**

installé, -e [ɛ̃stale] ADJ **1** *(aisé)* well-off, established; **les gens installés** the comfortably well-off **2** *(aménagé)* **un laboratoire bien/mal i.** a well/badly equipped laboratory; **elle est bien installée** she's got a really nice place; **ils sont mal installés** their place is really uncomfortable

INSTALLER [3] [ɛ̃stale]

> **VT** to install **1, 8** ▪ to put in **1, 2** ▪ to set up **2, 5, 7** ▪ to put **3, 6** ▪ to fit out **4**
> **VPR** to sit down **1** ▪ to be set up **2** ▪ to set up **2, 3** ▪ to become established **4**

VT **1** *(mettre en service → chauffage, eau, gaz, électricité, téléphone)* to install, to put in; *(→ appareil ménager, logiciel)* to install; **nous avons dû faire i. l'eau/le gaz/l'électricité** we had to have the water laid on/the gas put in/the house wired

2 *(mettre en place → meuble)* to put in; *(→ tente)* to put up, to pitch; *(→ barrière)* to put up, to erect; *(→ campement)* to set up; *(→ troupes)* to position; **j'ai installé deux appliques au-dessus du lit** I've put in *or* fixed *or* installed two wall-lamps above the bed; **où va-t-on i. le buffet?** where are we going to put the sideboard?; **il a installé son ordinateur dans sa chambre à coucher** he set up *or* put his computer in his bedroom

3 *(faire asseoir, allonger)* to put, to place; **n'installez pas les enfants sur la banquette avant** don't put the children in the front; **installez-le sur la civière** lay him down on the stretcher; **une fois qu'il est installé devant la télévision, il n'y a plus moyen de lui parler** once he's settled himself down *or* installed (himself) in front of the TV, there's no talking to him

4 *(pièce, logement → aménager)* to fit out; *(→ disposer)* to lay out; *(usine, atelier → équiper)* to fit up *or* out, to equip; **nous avons installé la salle de jeu au grenier** we've turned the attic into a playroom; **comment le dortoir est-il installé?** how is the dormitory laid out?

5 *(établir → jeune couple)* to set up

6 *(loger)* to put; **je les ai installés dans la chambre bleue** I've put them in the blue room; **les blessés furent installés dans la tour** the wounded were put in the tower

7 *(implanter → usine)* to set up

8 *Admin* to install; **i. qn dans ses fonctions** to install sb in his/her post

► **s'installer** VPR **1** *(s'asseoir, s'allonger)* **il s'est installé à la terrasse d'un café** he sat down outside a pavement café; **installez-vous comme il faut, je reviens tout de suite** make yourself comfortable *or* at home, I'll be right back; **s'i. au volant** to sit at the wheel; **s'i. dans un canapé/devant la télévision** to settle down on a couch/in front of the television

2 *(s'implanter → cirque, marché)* to (be) set up; *(→ usine)* to be set up; **s'i. à la campagne** *(emménager)* to set up house *or* to go and live *or* to settle in the country; **s'i. dans une maison** to move into a house; **je m'installai dans un petit hôtel** I put up at a small hotel; **s'i. dans de nouveaux bureaux** *(entreprise)* to move into new offices; *(employés)* to move into one's new offices; **si ça continue, elle va finir par s'i. chez moi!** if this goes on, she'll end up moving in (permanently)!

3 *(pour exercer → médecin, dentiste)* to set up a practice; *(→ commerçant)* to set up shop; **s'i. à son compte** to set up one's own business *or* on one's own; **quand je me suis installé, la clientèle était rare** when I started, there weren't many customers

4 *(se fixer → statu quo)* to become established; *(→ maladie)* to take hold *or* a grip; *(→ doute, peur)* to creep in; *(→ silence)* to take over; **il s'est installé dans le mensonge** he's become an habitual liar, he's well used to lying; **l'idée de la mort s'installa en elle et ne la quitta plus** the thought of death took hold of her mind and never left her again; **un climat d'insécurité s'est installé dans le pays** a climate of insecurity has taken hold of the country; **le pays s'installe peu à peu dans la crise** the country is sliding *or* sinking into a recession

instamment [ɛ̃stamɑ̃] ADV insistently; **je vous demande i. de revenir sur votre décision** I beg *or* urge you to reconsider your decision

instance [ɛ̃stɑ̃s] NF **1** *(organisme)* authority; **les instances économiques/communautaires** the economic/EU authorities; **les plus hautes instances du parti** the leading bodies of the party; **le dossier sera traité par une i. supérieure** the file will be dealt with at a higher level *or* by a higher authority

2 *Jur* (legal) proceedings; **introduire une i.** to start *or* to institute proceedings; **en première i.** on first hearing; **en seconde i.** on appeal; **i. d'appel** appeal proceedings

3 *Littéraire (insistance)* insistence; **avec i.** earnestly, with insistence

4 *Psy* psychic apparatus

▫ **instances** NFPL entreaties; **sur** *ou* **devant les instances de son père, il finit par accepter** in the face of his father's entreaties *or* pleas, he eventually accepted

▫ **en dernière instance** ADV in the last analysis

▫ **en instance** ADJ *(dossier)* pending, waiting to be dealt with; *Jur (affaire)* pending, *Br* sub judice; *(courrier)* ready for posting

▫ **en instance de** PRÉP **être en i. de divorce** to be waiting for a divorce *or* in the middle of divorce proceedings; **prisonnier en i. de libération** prisoner waiting for *or* pending release

instant[1] [ɛ̃stɑ̃] NM **1** *(courte durée)* moment, instant; **il a eu un i. d'inattention** he had a momentary lapse of concentration; **nous n'avons pas un i. à perdre** we don't have a moment to lose; **pendant un i., j'ai cru que c'était elle** for a moment *or* an instant, I thought it was her; **il s'arrêta un i.** he stopped for a moment; **j'ai pensé, pendant un i.** *ou* **l'espace d'un i., que...** for half a minute *or* for a split second, I thought that...; **as-tu pensé un i. au danger?** didn't it cross your mind for one moment that it was dangerous?; **il ne s'est pas demandé un i. ce qui pouvait arriver** he never asked himself once what might happen; **je n'en doute pas un seul i.** I don't doubt it at all, I've never doubted it for a minute; **(attendez) un i.!** just a moment!, just a second!; **je reviens dans un i.** I'll be right back, I'll be back in a minute; **c'est l'affaire d'un i.** it won't take a minute; **c'est prêt en un i.** it's ready in an instant *or* in no time at all

2 *(moment précis)* moment; **l'i. suprême** the supreme moment

▫ **à chaque instant** ADV all the time

▫ **à l'instant (même)** ADV this instant, this minute; **je suis rentré à l'i. (même)** I've just come in this minute *or* second; **je l'apprends à l'i. (même)** I've just this moment heard about it; **nous devons partir à l'i. (même)** we must leave right now *or* this instant *or* this very minute; **à l'i. (même) où je m'apprêtais à partir** just as I was about to leave

▫ **à tout instant** ADV *(continuellement)* all the time; *(d'une minute à l'autre)* any time (now), any minute

▫ **dans l'instant** ADV at this moment, instantly

▫ **de tous les instants** ADJ constant

▫ **dès l'instant que** CONJ *(si)* if; *(puisque)* since; *(aussitôt que)* as soon as, from the moment

▫ **d'un instant à l'autre** ADV any moment now

▫ **par instants** ADV at times, from time to time

▫ **pour l'instant** ADV for the moment, for the time being

instant[2], **-e** [ɛ̃stɑ̃, -ɑ̃t] ADJ *Littéraire* **1** *(imminent → péril)* pressing

2 *(pressant → prière)* pressing, insistent

instantané, -e [ɛ̃stɑ̃tane] ADJ **1** *(immédiat)* instantaneous; **la mort a été instantanée** death was instantaneous; **sa réponse a été instantanée** his/her answer was immediate **2** *(soluble → café, soupe)* instant **3** *Phot* **cliché i.** snapshot

NM snap, snapshot

instantanéité [ɛ̃stɑ̃taneite] NF instantaneity

instantanément [ɛ̃stɑ̃tanemɑ̃] ADV instantly, instantaneously; **ce produit se dissout i. dans l'eau** this product dissolves instantly in water

ins–ins

instar [ɛ̃star] **à l'instar de** PRÉP following (the example of); **à l'i. de ses parents, il sera enseignant** like his parents, he's going to be a teacher

instaurateur, -trice [ɛ̃stɔratœr, -tris] NM,F *Littéraire* founder, creator

instauration [ɛ̃stɔrasjɔ̃] NF institution, foundation

instauratrice [ɛ̃stɔratris] *voir* **instaurateur**

instaurer [3] [ɛ̃stɔre] VT *(système, régime, contrôle)* to introduce, to set up; *(dialogue)* to initiate, to institute; *(mode)* to introduce, to start; **i. le couvre-feu dans une ville** to impose a curfew in a town; **afin d'i. un climat de confiance** to create an atmosphere of trust

▸**s'instaurer** VPR to be established

instigateur, -trice [ɛ̃stigatœr, -tris] NM,F instigator; **il nie être l'i. du crime** he denies being behind the crime *or* being the instigator of the crime; **l'association ainsi créée sera l'instigatrice d'une nouvelle politique** the association thus created will initiate new policy decisions

instigation [ɛ̃stigasjɔ̃] NF instigation; **à** *ou* **sur l'i. de qn** at sb's instigation

instigatrice [ɛ̃stigatris] *voir* **instigateur**

instiguer [3] [ɛ̃stige] VT *Belg* to incite; **ils ont été instigués à se mettre en grève** they were incited to go on strike

instillation [ɛ̃stilasjɔ̃] NF instillation

instiller [3] [ɛ̃stile] VT **1** *Méd* to instil; **i. un liquide dans l'œil** to drop a liquid into the eye **2** *Littéraire (insuffler)* to instil; **i. le doute dans l'esprit de qn** to instil doubt in sb's mind

instinct [ɛ̃stɛ̃] NM **1** *Psy & Zool* instinct; **i. de conservation** instinct of self-preservation; **i. maternel** maternal instinct **2** *(intuition)* instinct; **il eut l'i. de parer le coup** he instinctively fended off the blow; **se fier à son i.** to trust one's instincts *or* intuition **3** *(don)* instinct; **elle a l'i. de la scène** she has a natural talent for the stage

▫ **d'instinct** ADV instinctively, by instinct

▫ **par instinct** ADV **1** *Psy & Zool* instinctively, by instinct **2** *(intuitivement)* instinctively

instinctif, -ive [ɛ̃stɛ̃ktif, -iv] ADJ **1** *(inconscient → réaction, antipathie)* instinctive; **si je vois un gâteau, je le mange, c'est i.!** if I see a cake, I eat it, I can't help it! **2** *(impulsif)* instinctive, impulsive; **c'est un être i.** he's/she's a creature of instinct

NM,F instinctive person

instinctivement [ɛ̃stɛ̃ktivmɑ̃] ADV instinctively

instinctuel, -elle [ɛ̃stɛ̃ktɥɛl] ADJ instinctual

instit [ɛ̃stit] NMF *Fam (de maternelle)* (nursery school) teacher▪; *(d'école primaire)* (primary school) teacher▪

instituer [7] [ɛ̃stitɥe] VT **1** *(règlement, système)* to introduce, to establish; *(impôt)* to institute; *(commission d'enquête)* to set up **2** *Jur (désigner → héritier)* to institute, to appoint **3** *Rel (évêque, cardinal)* to institute

▸**s'instituer** VPR **1** *(se désigner)* to set oneself up; **il s'est institué (comme) arbitre de leur querelle** he set himself up as the arbitrator of their quarrel **2** *(s'établir)* to be *or* to become established; **des relations durables se sont instituées entre les deux pays** a lasting relationship was established between the two countries

institut [ɛ̃stity] NM *(organisme)* institute; **i. de recherches/scientifique** research/scientific institute; **i. de beauté** beauty salon; *Banque* **i. d'émission** central note-issuing authority; **i. monétaire** lender of last resort; **i. de sondage** polling company; **l'I. catholique de Paris** = large private university in Paris; **l'I. d'Études politiques** = "grande école" for political sciences in Paris, commonly known as "Sciences-Po"; **I. européen d'administration** = European business school in Fontainebleau; *Mktg* **I. français d'opinion publique** = French market research institute; **I. français de recherche pour l'exploitation de la mer** = French research establishment for marine resources; **l'I. de France** the Institut de France, *Br* ≃ the Royal Society, *Am* ≃ the National Science Foundation; **I. géographique national** = French national geographical institute, *Br* ≃ Ordnance Survey, *Am* ≃ United States Geological Survey; *Anciennement* **I. des hautes études cinématographiques** = former French film school; **l'I. du Monde Arabe** = Arab cultural centre and library in Paris holding regular exhibitions of Arab art; **l'I. monétaire européen** the European Monetary Institute; **I. national d'agronomie** = "grande école" for agricultural studies; **I. national de l'audiovisuel** = national television archive; **I. national de la consommation** = French consumer research organization; **I. national d'études démographiques** = national institute for demographic research; *Belg* **I. national de radiodiffusion** = Belgian broadcasting company; **I. national de la recherche agronomique** = national institute for agronomic research; **I. national de la santé et de la recherche médicale** = national institute for medical research; **I. national de la statistique et des études économiques** = French national institute of statistics and information about the economy; *Anciennement* **I. de préparation aux enseignements du second degré** training college *(for secondary school teachers)*; **I. universitaire de formation des maîtres** = teacher-training college; **I. universitaire professionnel** = business school; **I. universitaire de technologie** = vocational higher education college

Culture

L'INSTITUT DE FRANCE

"L'Institut", as it is commonly known, is the learned society which includes the five "Académies" (the **Académie française** being one of them). Its headquarters are in the building of the same name on the banks of the Seine in Paris.

instituteur, -trice [ɛ̃stitytœr, -tris] NM,F **1** *(de maternelle)* (nursery school) teacher; *(d'école primaire)* (primary school) teacher; **demande à ton institutrice** ask your teacher **2** *Vieilli (précepteur, gouvernante)* tutor, *f* governess

institution [ɛ̃stitysjɔ̃] NF **1** *(établissement)* institution; **i. pour les aveugles** institution *or* school for the blind; **ils ont mis la vieille dame dans une i.** they put the old lady into a home; **i. religieuse** *(catholique)* Catholic school; *(autre)* denominational school; **i. financière** financial institution

2 *(coutume)* institution; **l'i. du mariage** the institution of marriage; **ici le repos dominical est une véritable i.** Sunday as a day of rest is a real institution here

3 *(mise en place)* institution, establishment; *(d'une loi)* introduction; *(d'une règle)* laying down

4 *Jur (d'un héritier)* appointment, institution; **i. contractuelle** conventional designation *(of an heir)*

5 *Rel (d'un évêque, d'un cardinal)* institution; **i. canonique** institution

▫ **institutions** NFPL institutions; **les institutions politiques** political institutions; **se battre contre les institutions (établies)** to fight the established institutions

institutionnalisation [ɛ̃stitysjɔnalizasjɔ̃] NF institutionalization

institutionnaliser [3] [ɛ̃stitysjɔnalize] VT to institutionalize

institutionnalisme [ɛ̃stitysjɔnalism] NM institutionalism

institutionnel, -elle [ɛ̃stitysjɔnɛl] ADJ institutional

NM institutional investor

institutrice [ɛ̃stitytris] *voir* **instituteur**

instructeur, -trice [ɛ̃stryktœr, -tris] NM,F instructor

NM *Aviat* (flying) instructor; *Mil* instructor

ADJ M **juge i.** examining magistrate; **sergent i.** drill sergeant

instructif, -ive [ɛ̃stryktif, -iv] ADJ informative, instructive; **j'ai trouvé l'émission instructive** I thought the programme was informative *or* instructive; *Hum* **c'est très i. d'écouter aux portes!** you learn a lot listening at keyholes!

instruction [ɛ̃stryksjɔ̃] NF **1** *Vieilli (culture)* (general) education; **il a une solide i.** he has a good general level of education; **elle a beaucoup d'i.** she's well-educated; **manquer d'i.** to be uneducated, to lack education

2 *(formation)* education, teaching; **il se charge de l'i. de ses enfants** he is taking care of his children's education himself; **l'i. que j'ai reçue à l'école** the teaching *or* education I was given at school; **i. civique** civics; *Mil* **i. militaire** military training; **i. professionnelle** vocational training; **i. primaire** primary education; **i. religieuse** religious instruction; **i. secondaire** secondary education

3 *Jur* preliminary investigation *or* inquiry *(of a case by an examining magistrate)*; **qui est chargé de l'i.?** who's setting up the inquiry?

4 *Ordinat* instruction; **jeu d'instructions** instruction set

5 *(ordre)* instruction; **donner/recevoir des instructions** to give/to receive instructions; **sur les instructions de ses supérieurs** following orders from his/her superiors

6 *Admin (circulaire)* directive

▫ **instructions** NFPL *(d'un fabricant)* instructions, directions; **instructions de montage** instructions *or* directions for assembly; **conformément aux instructions** as directed

instructive [ɛ̃stryktiv] *voir* **instructif**

instructrice [ɛ̃stryktris] *voir* **instructeur**

instruire [98] [ɛ̃strɥir] VT **1** *(enseigner à)* to teach, to instruct; *(former)* to educate; *Mil (recrue)* to train; **une émission destinée à i. en distrayant** a programme designed to be both entertaining and educational; **instruit par l'expérience** taught by experience

2 *(aviser)* **i. qn de qch** to inform sb of sth, to acquaint sb with sth; **il était à peine instruit de la situation** he was barely acquainted with the situation

3 *Jur* **i. une affaire** *ou* **un dossier** to set up a preliminary inquiry

VI *Jur* **i. contre qn** to set up a preliminary inquiry against sb

▸**s'instruire** VPR **1** *(se cultiver)* to educate oneself; **il s'est instruit tout seul** he's self-educated **2** *(apprendre)* to learn; **on s'instruit à tout âge** it's never too late to learn

3 s'i. de qch to obtain information about sth, to find out about sth; **s'i. de qch auprès de qn** to ask sb about sth, to inquire of sb about sth

instruit, -e [ɛ̃strɥi, -it] ADJ well-educated, educated; **un homme i.** an educated man

instrument [ɛ̃strymɑ̃] NM **1** *(outil, matériel)* instrument; **i. tranchant** edged *or* cutting tool; **naviguer aux instruments** to fly on instruments; **instruments aratoires** ploughing implements; **instruments de bord** instruments; **i. de mesure/d'observation** measuring/observation instrument; **un i. de torture** an instrument of torture; **i. de travail** tool; **c'est un de mes instruments de travail** it's a tool of my trade; **i. de vente** sales tool; **c'est un i. d'analyse de l'inflation** it's a tool for analysing inflation

2 *Mus* **i. (de musique)** (musical) instrument; **i. à cordes/à percussion/à vent** string/percussion/wind instrument

3 *Fig (agent)* instrument, tool; **la télévision est-elle un i. de propagande?** is television an instrument of propaganda?; **être l'i. de qn** to be sb's instrument *or* tool; **être l'i. de** to bring about; **il fut l'i. de leur ruine** he brought about their ruin; **il fut l'un des instruments de leur ruine** he was instrumental in their ruin

4 *(document, acte authentique)* instrument; *Jur* (legal) instrument; **i. de commerce** instrument of commerce; **i. de couverture** hedging instrument; **i. de crédit** instrument of credit; **i. dérivé** derivative; **i. financier** financial instrument; **i. financier à terme** financial future; **i. négociable** negotiable instrument; **i. de négociation** trading instrument; **i. de placement** investment instrument

instrumentaire [ɛ̃strymɑ̃tɛr] *voir* **témoin**

instrumental, -e, -aux, -ales [ɛ̃strymɑ̃tal, -o] ADJ instrumental

NM *Ling* instrumental (case)

instrumentalisation [ɛ̃strymɑ̃talizasjɔ̃] NF instrumentalization

instrumentaliser [3] [ɛ̃strymɑ̃talize] VT to use for one's own ends

instrumentalisme [ɛ̃strymɑ̃talism] NM instrumentalism

instrumentation [ɛ̃strymɑ̃tasjɔ̃] NF 1 *Mus* orchestration, instrumentation 2 *Tech* instrumentation

instrumenter [3] [ɛ̃strymɑ̃te] VI *Jur* to draw up an official document; **i. contre qn** to order proceedings to be taken against sb

VT 1 *Mus* to orchestrate, to score (for instruments) 2 *(en travaux publics)* to instrument

instrumentiste [ɛ̃strymɑ̃tist] NMF 1 *Mus* instrumentalist 2 *Méd* theatre nurse

insu [ɛ̃sy] **à l'insu de** PRÉP 1 *(sans être vu de)* without the knowledge of, unbeknown *or* unbeknownst to; **sortir à l'i. de ses parents** to go out without one's parents' knowing *or* knowledge; **à l'i. de tout le monde, il s'était glissé dans la cuisine** he'd slipped unnoticed into the kitchen

2 **à mon/son i.** *(sans m'en/s'en apercevoir)* unwittingly, without being aware of it; **lentement, presque à mon i., je m'habituais à la pauvreté** gradually, almost without realizing it *or* without my being aware of it, I was growing accustomed to poverty

insubmersibilité [ɛ̃sybmɛrsibilite] NF insubmersibility

insubmersible [ɛ̃sybmɛrsibl] ADJ *(canot)* insubmersible; *(jouet)* unsinkable

insubordination [ɛ̃sybɔrdinasjɔ̃] NF insubordination

insubordonné, -e [ɛ̃sybɔrdɔne] ADJ insubordinate

insuccès [ɛ̃syksɛ] NM failure; **l'i. de la pièce** the failure of the play; **son i. aux élections l'a découragé** his/her poor performance at the polls has discouraged him/her

insuffisamment [ɛ̃syfizamɑ̃] ADV insufficiently, inadequately; **i. nourri** underfed; **la lettre était i. affranchie** the letter had insufficient postage; **des vêtements i. rincés** clothes that haven't been thoroughly rinsed; **le chapitre sur l'Amérique latine est i. documenté** the chapter on Latin America isn't sufficiently documented

insuffisance [ɛ̃syfizɑ̃s] NF 1 *(manque)* insufficiency, deficiency; **i. de ressources** lack of *or* insufficient resources; **l'i. de la production industrielle** the shortfall in industrial production; **i. de capitaux** insufficient capital; **i. d'espèces** cash shortage; **i. de personnel** staff shortage; **i. de provision** insufficient funds *(to meet cheque)* 2 *(point faible)* weakness, deficiency; **ses insuffisances en matière de pathologie** his/her lack of knowledge of pathology 3 *Méd* deficiency; **elle est morte d'une i. cardiaque** she died from heart failure; **i. hormonale** hormone deficiency; **i. organique** organic insufficiency *or* dysfunction; **i. rénale** kidney failure *or Spéc* insufficiency; **i. respiratoire** respiratory insufficiency *or* failure

insuffisant, -e [ɛ̃syfizɑ̃, -ɑ̃t] ADJ 1 *(en quantité)* insufficient; **nous avons des effectifs insuffisants** our numbers are too low, we're understaffed; **c'est i. pour ouvrir un compte** it's not enough to open an account; **nous disposons de médicaments mais en quantité insuffisante** we have drugs at our disposal but not enough of them

2 *(en qualité)* inadequate; **des résultats insuffisants en mathématiques** inadequate results in mathematics

3 *(inapte)* incompetent; **on l'a jugé i. pour ce travail** he's been deemed incompetent *or* unfit for this job; **la plupart de nos élèves sont insuffisants en langues** most of our pupils are poor *or* weak at languages

insufflateur [ɛ̃syflatœr] NM 1 *Méd* insufflator 2 *Tech* blower

insufflation [ɛ̃syflasjɔ̃] NF *Méd* insufflation

insuffler [3] [ɛ̃syfle] VT 1 *Méd* to insufflate; **i. de l'air dans un corps** to blow *or* to insufflate air into a body 2 *(inspirer)* **i. qch à qn** to instil sth in sb, to infuse sb with sth; **la terreur lui insuffla du courage** terror inspired him/her to be brave; **ce succès a insufflé un nouvel élan à l'entreprise** this success gave the company a new lease of life *or* breathed new life into the company

insula [insula] NF *Antiq* insula

insulaire [ɛ̃sylɛr] ADJ island *(avant n)*, insular; **la population i.** the population of the island, the island population

NMF islander

insularité [ɛ̃sylarite] NF 1 *Géog* insularity; **leur i. en fait des gens à part** the fact that they live on an island sets them apart 2 *Péj (étroitesse d'esprit)* insularity

insulinase [ɛ̃sylinaz] NF *Biol* insulinase

insuline [ɛ̃sylin] NF insulin

insulinique [ɛ̃sylinik] ADJ insulin *(avant n)*

insulinodépendant, -e [ɛ̃sylinɔdepɑ̃dɑ̃, -ɑ̃t] ADJ insulin-dependent

insulinothérapie [ɛ̃sylinɔterapi] NF insulin *or* insulin-based treatment *(for diabetes)*

insultant, -e [ɛ̃syltɑ̃, -ɑ̃t] ADJ insulting; **c'est i. pour moi** I'm insulted; **il s'est comporté de façon insultante à mon égard** the way he treated me was an insult

insulte [ɛ̃sylt] NF 1 *(parole blessante)* insult; **je n'ai pas relevé l'i.** I didn't react; **lancer des insultes à qn** to hurl abuse at sb 2 *Fig (atteinte, outrage)* insult; **c'est une i. à sa mémoire** it's an insult to his/her memory; **une i. au bon sens** an insult to common sense; **il nous a fait l'i. de refuser** he insulted us by refusing

insulté, -e [ɛ̃sylte] ADJ insulted; **tu crois qu'elle s'est sentie insultée?** do you think she felt insulted *or* offended?

NM,F **l'i.** the injured party

insulter [3] [ɛ̃sylte] VT to insult; **il m'a insulté** he insulted me; **i. la mémoire de qn** to insult sb's memory; **se faire i.** to be insulted

▸**s'insulter** VPR to exchange insults, to insult each other

insulteur, -euse [ɛ̃syltœr, -øz] NM,F insulter

insupportable [ɛ̃sypɔrtabl] ADJ 1 *(insoutenable → démangeaison, douleur, vision)* unbearable; *(→ bruit)* unbearable; *(→ lumière)* unbearably bright; *(→ situation)* intolerable; **il fait une chaleur i.** it's unbearably hot; **sans toi, la vie m'est i.** without you, life is more than I can bear *or* is too hard to bear; **l'idée de tuer un animal lui est i.** he/she can't bear the idea of killing an animal

2 *(turbulent → enfant, élève)* impossible, insufferable, unbearable; **tu es i., si tu continues tu vas au lit!** you're being impossible, if you don't stop you're off to bed!

insupportablement [ɛ̃sypɔrtabləmɑ̃] ADV unbearably

insupporter [3] [ɛ̃sypɔrte] VT **il m'insupporte!** I can't stand him!

insurgé, -e [ɛ̃syrʒe] ADJ insurgent *(avant n)*

NM insurgent

insurger [17] [ɛ̃syrʒe] **s'insurger** VPR **s'i. contre qn** to rise up *or* to rebel against sb; **s'i. contre qch** *(se rebeller)* to rebel against sth; *(critiquer)* to protest strongly against sth; **la nature humaine ne peut que s'i. devant un tel crime** human nature cannot but rise up in protest before such a crime

insurmontable [ɛ̃syrmɔ̃tabl] ADJ 1 *(infranchissable → obstacle)* insurmountable, insuperable 2 *(invincible → aversion, angoisse)* uncontrollable, unconquerable; **il m'inspire un dégoût i.** I cannot overcome *or* conquer the disgust I feel for him

insurpassable [ɛ̃syrpasabl] ADJ unsurpassable

insurrection [ɛ̃syrɛksjɔ̃] NF 1 *(révolte)* insurrection; **le pays était en pleine i.** the country was in a state of open insurrection; **i. armée** armed insurrection 2 *Littéraire (indignation)* revolt

insurrectionnel, -elle [ɛ̃syrɛksjɔnɛl] ADJ insurrectionary, insurrectional

intact, -e [ɛ̃takt] ADJ *(réputation, économies)* intact; **le paquet est arrivé i.** the parcel arrived in one piece *or* intact; **je veux garder mon capital i.** I want to keep my capital intact, I don't want to touch my capital; **le problème reste i.** the problem remains unsolved

intaille [ɛ̃taj] NF intaglio

intailler [3] [ɛ̃taje] VT to intaglio

intangibilité [ɛ̃tɑ̃ʒibilite] NF intangibility; **i. d'une loi** inviolability of a law

intangible [ɛ̃tɑ̃ʒibl] ADJ 1 *(impalpable)* intangible 2 *(inviolable)* inviolable, sacred, sacrosanct

intarissable [ɛ̃tarisabl] ADJ 1 *(inépuisable → source)* inexhaustible, unlimited; *(→ mine)* inexhaustible; *(→ imagination)* inexhaustible, boundless, limitless; *(→ bavardage)* endless 2 *(bavard)* unstoppable; **sur le vin, il est i.** if you get him talking on wine, he'll go on for ever

intarissablement [ɛ̃tarisabləmɑ̃] ADV inexhaustibly; **il discourait i.** he was going on and on (and on)

intégrable [ɛ̃tegrabl] ADJ *Math* integrable

intégral, -e, -aux, -ales [ɛ̃tegral, -o] ADJ 1 *(complet)* complete; **édition intégrale des poèmes de Donne** collected poems of Donne; **remboursement i. d'une dette** full *or* complete repayment of a debt; **la somme intégrale de vos dépenses s'élève à 480 euros** your expenses amount to 480 euros; **paiement i.** payment in full; **texte i.** unabridged version; **version intégrale** *(film)* uncut version

2 *Hum (en intensif)* utter, complete; **c'est un parasite i.** he's a complete parasite

❑ **intégrale** NF 1 *(œuvre)* complete works; **l'intégrale des œuvres de Shakespeare** the complete works of Shakespeare; **l'intégrale des quatuors à cordes de Chostakovitch** the complete set of Shostakovich string quartets

2 *Math* integral

intégralement [ɛ̃tegralmɑ̃] ADV in full, fully, completely; **vous serez i. remboursé** you'll get all your money back, you'll be fully reimbursed; *Fin* **i. libéré** fully paid up

intégralité [ɛ̃tegralite] NF whole; **l'i. de la dette** the entire debt, the debt in full; **l'i. de son salaire a été payée aujourd'hui** his/her whole *or* entire salary was paid today; **elle a résolu le problème dans son i.** she solved the entire problem; **la presse dans son i. protesta** the press protested as a body *or* en bloc

intégrant, -e [ɛ̃tegrɑ̃, -ɑ̃t] ADJ **partie intégrante de** integral part of; **faire partie intégrante de qch** to be an integral part of sth

intégrateur [ɛ̃tegratœr] NM integrator

intégratif, -ive [ɛ̃tegratif, -iv] ADJ *Physiol* integrative

intégration [ɛ̃tegrasjɔ̃] NF 1 *(insertion)* integration; **i. raciale** racial integration

2 *(entrée dans une école, une organisation)* entry

3 *Math, Phys & Psy* integration

4 *Écon* integration; **i. en amont** *ou* **ascendante** backward integration; **i. en aval** forward integration; **i. descendante** forward integration; **i. économique** economic integration; **i. européenne** European integration; **i. financière** financial integration; **i. horizontale** horizontal integration; **i. latérale** lateral integration; **i. sociale** social integration; **i. verticale** vertical integration

5 *Ordinat* integration; **i. de bases de données** database integration

intègre [ɛ̃tɛgr] ADJ 1 *(honnête)* honest 2 *(équitable, impartial)* upright, upstanding

intégré, -e [ɛ̃tegre] ADJ 1 *(appareil)* built-in 2 *(entreprise)* integrated 3 *Nucl* integrated 4 *Ordinat (fax, modem)* integrated; **traitement i. de l'information** integrated (data) processing; **avec système i.** with an in-house system

intègrement [ɛ̃tɛgrəmɑ̃] ADV 1 *(honnêtement)* honestly 2 *(équitablement, impartialement)* uprightly, upstandingly

intégrer [8] [ɛ̃tegre] VT 1 *(inclure)* to integrate (**à** *ou* **dans** in), to incorporate, to include (**à** *ou* **dans** in); **i. un nouveau paragraphe dans un chapitre** to insert a new paragraph into a chapter; **notre société intègre différents secteurs d'activité** our company takes in *or* covers various areas of activity; **des activités destinées à i. les petits à la classe** activities designed to bring *or* to integrate the younger children into the group

2 *(assimiler → enseignement, notion)* to assimilate; **j'ai complètement intégré les préceptes de mes parents** I've totally assimilated the principles my parents taught me

3 *Math* to integrate

4 *(entrer à → école)* to get into, to enter; *(→ entreprise)* to enter; *(→ club)* to join; **i. les Mines** to be admitted to the School of Mining Engineers

VI *Fam Arg scol* = to get into a "Grande École"; **i. aux Mines** to get into the School of Mining Engineers

▸**s'intégrer** VPR 1 *(élément d'un kit)* to fit; **s'i. à** to fit into; **les pièces s'intègrent les unes aux autres** the pieces fit together

ins–int

2 *(personne)* to become integrated *or* assimilated; **ils se sont mal intégrés à la vie du village** they never really fitted into village life

intégrisme [ɛ̃tegrism] NM *Rel* fundamentalism

intégriste [ɛ̃tegrist] *Rel* ADJ fundamentalist
NMF fundamentalist

intégrité [ɛ̃tegrite] NF 1 *(totalité)* integrity; **dans son i.** as a whole, in its integrity; **i. territoriale** *ou* **du territoire** territorial integrity 2 *(état originel)* soundness, integrity; **malgré son âge, elle a conservé l'i. de ses facultés** despite her age, she is still of sound mind 3 *(honnêteté)* integrity, honesty 4 *Ordinat* **i. des données** data integrity

intellect [ɛ̃telɛkt] NM intellect, understanding

intellection [ɛ̃telɛksjɔ̃] NF *Phil* intellection

intellectualisation [ɛ̃telɛktɥalizasjɔ̃] NF intellectualization

intellectualiser [3] [ɛ̃telɛktɥalize] VT to intellectualize

intellectualisme [ɛ̃telɛktɥalism] NM intellectualism

intellectualiste [ɛ̃telɛktɥalist] ADJ intellectualistic
NMF intellectualist

intellectualité [ɛ̃telɛktɥalite] NF intellectuality

intellectuel, -elle [ɛ̃telɛktɥɛl] ADJ 1 *(mental → capacité)* intellectual, mental; **facultés intellectuelles** intellectual faculties; **puissance intellectuelle** brainpower 2 *(cérébral → personne)* intellectual, cerebral; **c'est une approche très intellectuelle de la mise en scène** it's a very intellectual approach to directing 3 *(non manuel → travail)* non-manual
NM,F intellectual

intellectuellement [ɛ̃telɛktɥɛlmɑ̃] ADV intellectually

intelligemment [ɛ̃teliʒamɑ̃] ADV intelligently, cleverly

intelligence [ɛ̃teliʒɑ̃s] NF 1 *(intellect, discernement)* intelligence; **il n'est pas d'une grande i.** he's not very intelligent *or* bright *or* clever; **ils ont l'i. vive** they are sharp-witted *or* quick, they have sharp minds; **elle est d'une i. supérieure** she's of above-average intelligence; **avec i.** intelligently; **il a eu l'i. de ne pas recommencer** he was intelligent enough not to try again
2 *(personne)* **c'est une grande i.** he's/she's a great mind *or* intellect
3 *(compréhension)* **pour l'i. de ce qui va suivre** in order to understand *or* to grasp what follows; **elle a l'i. des affaires** she has a good understanding *or* grasp of business; **mon i. de l'informatique est très limitée** my understanding of computing is very limited; **avoir l'i. du cœur** to be highly intuitive
4 *(relation)* **vivre en bonne/mauvaise i. avec qn** to be on good/bad terms with sb
5 *Ordinat* **i. artificielle** artificial intelligence
6 *Mktg* **i. marketing** marketing intelligence
▫ **intelligences** NFPL contacts; **elle a des intelligences dans le milieu** she has contacts in the underworld; **entretenir des intelligences avec qn** to have secret dealings *or* contacts with sb
▫ **d'intelligence** ADJ *(complice)* **regard/sourire d'i.** knowing look/smile; **faire des signes d'i. à qn** to give sb a knowing look ADV in collusion; **être d'i. avec qn** to be in collusion *or* in league with sb; **agir d'i. avec qn** to act in (tacit) agreement with sb

intelligent, -e [ɛ̃teliʒɑ̃, -ɑ̃t] ADJ 1 *(gén)* intelligent, bright, clever; **enfin une analyse intelligente!** an intelligent analysis at last!; **avoir l'air i.** to look intelligent; *Ironique* **c'est i.!** brilliant!, that was clever! 2 *Ordinat* intelligent; **terminal i.** intelligent terminal 3 *Mil* smart; **armes intelligentes** smart weapons

intelligentsia [ɛ̃teliʒɛnsja, ɛ̃teligɛnsja] NF **l'i.** the intelligentsia

intelligibilité [ɛ̃teliʒibilite] NF intelligibility, *Sout* intelligibleness

intelligible [ɛ̃teliʒibl] ADJ 1 *(compréhensible → explication, raisonnement)* intelligible, comprehensible; **je ne sais pas si mes propos sont intelligibles** I don't know if what I'm saying makes sense to you; **il ne s'exprime pas de façon très i.** he doesn't express himself very clearly 2 *(audible)* intelligible, clear, audible; **parler à haute et i. voix** to speak loudly and clearly

intelligiblement [ɛ̃teliʒibləmɑ̃] ADV 1 *(de façon compréhensible)* intelligibly 2 *(de façon audible)* intelligibly, clearly, audibly

intello [ɛ̃telo] *Fam Péj* ADJ highbrow▪
NMF intellectual▪, egghead

intempérance [ɛ̃tɑ̃perɑ̃s] NF 1 *Littéraire (de comportement)* immoderation, intemperance, excess; **ses intempérances de langage** his/her immoderate *or* excessive *or* unrestrained language 2 *(dans la vie sexuelle)* debauchery, intemperance; *(dans le manger, le boire)* lack of moderation, intemperance

intempérant, -e [ɛ̃tɑ̃perɑ̃, -ɑ̃t] ADJ excessive, intemperate

intempéries [ɛ̃tɑ̃peri] NFPL bad weather; **exposé aux i.** exposed to the elements

intempestif, -ive [ɛ̃tɑ̃pɛstif, -iv] ADJ inopportune, untimely; **sa remarque était intempestive** his/her comment was out of place

intempestivement [ɛ̃tɑ̃pɛstivmɑ̃] ADV at an untimely moment, inopportunely

intemporalité [ɛ̃tɑ̃pɔralite] NF 1 *(immuabilité)* timelessness 2 *(immatérialité)* immateriality

intemporel, -elle [ɛ̃tɑ̃pɔrɛl] ADJ 1 *(immuable)* timeless 2 *(immatériel)* immaterial

intenable [ɛ̃tənabl] ADJ 1 *(insupportable)* unbearable, intolerable; **c'est devenu i. au bureau** it's become unbearable *or* intolerable at the office 2 *(indiscipliné)* uncontrollable, unruly, badly-behaved; **elle est i. en classe** she's unruly at school 3 *(non défendable → thèse)* untenable; *(→ position)* indefensible

intendance [ɛ̃tɑ̃dɑ̃s] NF 1 *Mil (pour l'ensemble de l'armée de terre)* Supply Corps; *(dans un régiment)* quartermaster stores 2 *Scol (service, bureau)* (domestic) bursar's office; *(gestion)* school management; **nous avons eu des problèmes d'i.** we had supply problems 3 *(gestion → d'un domaine)* stewardship; *(des finances)* management

intendant, -e [ɛ̃tɑ̃dɑ̃, -ɑ̃t] NM,F 1 *(administrateur)* steward, bailiff 2 *Univ* bursar
NM 1 *Hist* intendant 2 *Mil* quartermaster
▫ **intendante** NF 1 *(d'un couvent)* Mother Superior 2 *Hist* intendant's wife

intense [ɛ̃tɑ̃s] ADJ 1 *(extrême → chaleur, froid)* intense, extreme; *(→ son)* loud, intense; *(→ lumière)* intense, bright; *(→ douleur)* intense, severe, acute; *(→ plaisir, désir, passion, émotion)* intense; *(→ regard)* intent, intense; **vivre de façon i.** to be intense
2 *(très vif → couleur)* intense, bright, strong; **rouge i.** bright red; **des yeux d'un bleu i.** intensely blue eyes, deep blue eyes
3 *(abondant, dense → circulation, bombardement)* heavy

intensément [ɛ̃tɑ̃semɑ̃] ADV intensely

intensif, -ive [ɛ̃tɑ̃sif, -iv] ADJ 1 *(soutenu)* intensive; **cours intensifs** crash *or* intensive course 2 *Ling (pronom, verbe)* intensive; *(préfixe)* intensifying 3 *Agr & Écon* intensive
NM intensifier

intensification [ɛ̃tɑ̃sifikasjɔ̃] NF *(gén)* intensification; *(d'échanges commerciaux)* strengthening

intensifier [9] [ɛ̃tɑ̃sifje] VT *(gén)* to intensify, to step up; *(échanges commerciaux)* to increase, to step up
▸ **s'intensifier** VPR *(passion, recherche)* to intensify, to become *or* to grow more intense; *(douleur)* to become more intense, to worsen; *(bombardements, circulation)* to become heavier

intensionnel, -elle [ɛ̃tɑ̃sjɔnɛl] ADJ intensional

intensité [ɛ̃tɑ̃site] NF 1 *(de la chaleur, du froid)* intensity; *(d'un son)* loudness; *(de la lumière)* intensity, brightness; *(d'une douleur)* intensity, acuteness; *(du plaisir, du désir, de la passion, d'une émotion)* intensity; *(d'une couleur)* intensity, depth, strength; *(d'un regard)* intentness, intensity; *(des bombardements)* severity; **l'i. de la circulation** the heavy traffic; **l'i. de la lumière était telle que…** the light was so intense *or* bright that…; **il y a dans ce spectacle des moments d'une grande i.** there are some very intense moments in the show
2 *Opt & Phys* intensity; **i. d'un champ magnétique** magnetic field strength *or* intensity; *Géol* **i. d'un tremblement de terre** earthquake magnitude *or* intensity; **i. acoustique** intensity level; *Élec* **i. de courant** current; **i. énergétique** radiant intensity; **i. lumineuse/de rayonnement** luminous/radiant intensity; **i. lumineuse d'un télescope/microscope** light-transmitting capacity of a telescope/microscope; *Rad, Tél & TV* **i. du signal** signal strength

intensive [ɛ̃tɑ̃siv] *voir* **intensif**

intensivement [ɛ̃tɑ̃sivmɑ̃] ADV intensively

intenter [3] [ɛ̃tɑ̃te] VT **i. une action en justice à** *ou* **contre qn** to bring an action against sb; **i. un procès à** *ou* **contre qn** to institute (legal) proceedings against sb, to take sb to court

intention [ɛ̃tɑ̃sjɔ̃] NF intention; **quelles sont vos intentions?** what are your intentions?, what do you intend to do?; **avoir de bonnes/mauvaises intentions** to be well-/ill-intentioned, to have good/bad intentions; **il est plein de bonnes intentions** he's full of good intentions; **elle vous a offert ces fleurs dans la meilleure i.** she gave you these flowers with the best of intentions; **c'est l'i. qui compte** it's the thought that counts; **avoir l'i. de faire qch** to intend to do sth, to have the intention of doing sth; **elle a la ferme i. de rester ici** she's determined to stay here, she's intent on staying here; **il n'a pas l'i. de se laisser faire** he doesn't intend to be cheated; **n'avoir aucune i. de faire qch** to have no intention of doing sth; **il n'est pas** *ou* **il n'entre pas dans mes intentions de l'acheter maintenant** I have no intention of buying it now; **dans l'i. de faire qch** with the intention of *or* with a view to doing sth; **avec i.** on purpose, intentionally; **sans i.** without meaning to, unintentionally; *Jur* **i. délictueuse** criminal intent; *Jur* **sans i. de donner la mort** without intent to kill; *Jur* **sans i. de nuire** with no ill intent; *Mktg* **i. d'achat** intention to buy; **intentions de vote** voting intentions; **ils enregistrent 28 pour cent des intentions de vote** 28 percent of those polled said that they would vote for them
▫ **à cette intention** ADV for that purpose, with this intention
▫ **à l'intention de** PRÉP for; **film à l'i. des enfants** film for *or* aimed at children; **brochure à l'i. des consommateurs** brochure for (the information of) consumers; **collecte à l'i. des aveugles** fund-raising for (the benefit of) *or* in aid of the blind; **messe/prière à l'i. du défunt** mass/prayer for the deceased; **ils ont organisé un banquet à l'i. de leurs invités** they organized a banquet in honour of their guests; *Météo* **(avis) à l'i. de tous les bateaux** warning to all shipping

intentionnalité [ɛ̃tɑ̃sjɔnalite] NF *Phil* intentionality

intentionné, -e [ɛ̃tɑ̃sjɔne] ADJ **bien/mal i.** well-/ill-intentioned

intentionnel, -elle [ɛ̃tɑ̃sjɔnɛl] ADJ intentional, deliberate

intentionnellement [ɛ̃tɑ̃sjɔnɛlmɑ̃] ADV intentionally, deliberately; **c'est i. que je ne l'ai pas invitée** I deliberately didn't invite her, I didn't invite her on purpose

inter [ɛ̃tɛr] NM 1 *Vieilli Tél* long-distance call, *Br* trunk call; **j'ai eu du mal à obtenir l'i.** I had trouble getting the long-distance operator *or Br* making a trunk call; **faire l'i.** to make a long-distance call, *Br* to put in a trunk call 2 *Sport* inside-forward; **i. droit/gauche** inside right/left

inter- [ɛ̃tɛr] PRÉF inter-

interactif, -ive [ɛ̃tɛraktif, -iv] ADJ 1 *(gén)* interactive 2 *Ordinat* interactive

interaction [ɛ̃tɛraksjɔ̃] NF 1 *(gén)* interaction, interplay 2 *Phys* interaction

interactionnel, -elle [ɛ̃tɛraksjɔnɛl] ADJ interactional

interactionnisme [ɛ̃tɛraksjɔnism] NM interactionism

interactive [ɛ̃tɛraktiv] *voir* **interactif**

interactivité [ɛ̃tɛraktivite] NF interactivity

interafricain, -e [ɛ̃tɛrafrikɛ̃, -ɛn] ADJ Pan-African

interagir [32] [ɛ̃tɛraʒir] VI to interact

interallemand, -e [ɛ̃tɛralmɑ̃, -ɑ̃d] ADJ between the two Germanies

interallié, -e [ɛ̃tɛralje] ADJ allied

interaméricain, -e [ɛ̃tɛramerikɛ̃, -ɛn] ADJ Pan-American, Inter-American

interarabe [ɛ̃tɛrarab] ADJ Pan-Arab

interarmées [ɛ̃tɛrarme] ADJ INV **opération i.** inter-service *or* joint service operation; **état-major i.** joint staff

interarmes [ɛ̃tɛrarm] ADJ INV *(opération, manœuvre)* combined
interatomique [ɛ̃tɛratɔmik] ADJ interatomic
interattraction [ɛ̃tɛratraksjɔ̃] NF mutual attraction
interbancaire [ɛ̃tɛrbɑ̃kɛr] ADJ *(relations)* interbank; **le marché i.** the money markets
interblocage [ɛ̃tɛblɔkaʒ] NM *Ordinat* deadlock
intercalaire [ɛ̃tɛrkalɛr] ADJ **1** *(feuille)* **feuillet i.** inset, insert; **fiche i.** divider **2** *(date)* **jour/année i.** intercalary day/year **3** *Bot* intercalary
NM **1** *(feuillet)* inset, insert **2** *(fiche)* divider **3** *Géol* intercalated bed
intercalation [ɛ̃tɛrkalasjɔ̃] NF **1** *(dans le calendrier)* intercalation **2** *(de feuilles)* insertion; *(de termes)* interpolation
intercaler [3] [ɛ̃tɛrkale] VT **1** *Typ* to insert, to inset **2** *(insérer)* to insert, to fit *or* to put in; **des coupures de journaux intercalées dans un dossier** newspaper clippings inserted into a file; **la fédération a intercalé trois jours de repos entre les matches** the league fitted in three rest days between the matches **3** *(dans le calendrier)* to intercalate
▸**s'intercaler** VPR **s'i. entre** to come (in) *or* to fit in between; **la voiture s'est intercalée entre deux ambulances** the car came *or* slipped in between two ambulances
intercantonal, -e, -aux, -ales [ɛ̃tɛrkɑ̃tɔnal, -o] ADJ *Suisse (entre cantons)* inter-canton, between cantons; *(qui concerne plusieurs cantons)* cross-canton
intercéder [8] [ɛ̃tɛrsede] VI **i. (auprès de qn) en faveur de qn** to intercede (with sb) for *or* on behalf of sb
intercellulaire [ɛ̃tɛrselylɛr] ADJ *Biol* intercellular
intercepter [4] [ɛ̃tɛrsɛpte] VT **1** *(arrêter → véhicule)* to stop; *(→ lettre, message)* to intercept; *(→ fugitif)* to stop, to intercept; **le store intercepte la lumière** the blind blocks out the light *or* stops the light coming in **2** *Mil (avion)* to intercept **3** *Sport (ballon)* to intercept
intercepteur [ɛ̃tɛrsɛptœr] NM *Mil* interceptor
interception [ɛ̃tɛrsɛpsjɔ̃] NF interception; **avion d'i.** interceptor (aircraft)
intercesseur [ɛ̃tɛrsesœr] NM *Littéraire* intercessor
intercession [ɛ̃tɛrsesjɔ̃] NF *Littéraire* intercession
interchangeabilité [ɛ̃tɛrʃɑ̃ʒabilite] NF interchangeability
interchangeable [ɛ̃tɛrʃɑ̃ʒabl] ADJ interchangeable
intercirculation [ɛ̃tɛrsirkylasjɔ̃] NF intercarriage access
interclasse [ɛ̃tɛrklas] NM *Scol Br* break, *Am* recess; **à l'i.** at *or* during the *Br* break *or Am* recess
interclassement [ɛ̃tɛrklasmɑ̃] NM *Ordinat* merging
interclasser [3] [ɛ̃tɛrklase] VT *Ordinat* to merge
interclasseuse [ɛ̃tɛrklasøz] NF collator
interclubs [ɛ̃tɛrklœb] ADJ *Sport* interclub
intercom [ɛ̃tɛrkɔm] NM *Can Joual* entryphone
intercommunal, -e, -aux, -ales [ɛ̃tɛrkɔmynal, -o] ADJ intermunicipal; **projet i.** joint project *(between two or more French communes)*; **hôpital i.** ≃ County *or* Regional Hospital
□ **intercommunale** NF *Belg* = public or semi-public body which is run by several communes
intercommunalité [ɛ̃tɛrkɔmynalite] NF = co-operation between neighbouring communes
intercommunautaire [ɛ̃tɛrkɔmynotɛr] ADJ inter-community; **projet i.** joint project *(between two or more communities)*; **relations intercommunautaires** relations between EU countries
intercommunication [ɛ̃tɛrkɔmynikasjɔ̃] NF intercommunication
intercompréhension [ɛ̃tɛrkɔ̃preɑ̃sjɔ̃] NF *Ling* mutual comprehension
interconnectable [ɛ̃tɛrkɔnɛktabl] ADJ interconnectable
interconnecter [4] [ɛ̃tɛrkɔnɛkte] VT to interconnect, to interlink, to connect together
interconnexion [ɛ̃tɛrkɔnɛksjɔ̃] NF **1** *Élec* interconnection **2** *(de réseaux, systèmes)* interconnectivity
intercontinental, -e, -aux, -ales [ɛ̃tɛrkɔ̃tinɑ̃tal, -o] ADJ intercontinental
intercostal, -e, -aux, -ales [ɛ̃tɛrkɔstal, -o] ADJ *(muscle)* intercostal; **il a des douleurs intercostales** he has a pain in his side
NM intercostal muscle
intercotidal, -e, -aux, -ales [ɛ̃tɛrkɔtidal, -o] ADJ *Géog* intertidal
intercours [ɛ̃tɛrkur] NM *Belg Scol Br* break, *Am* recess; **à l'i.** at *or* during the *Br* break *or Am* recess
interculturel, -elle [ɛ̃tɛrkyltyrɛl] ADJ cross-cultural
intercurrent, -e [ɛ̃tɛrkyrɑ̃, -ɑ̃t] ADJ *Méd* intercurrent
interdépartemental, -e, -aux, -ales [ɛ̃tɛrdepartəmɑ̃tal, -o] ADJ interdepartmental; **projet i.** joint project *(between two or more French départements)*
interdépendance [ɛ̃tɛrdepɑ̃dɑ̃s] NF interdependence; **l'i. des salaires et des prix** the interdependence of prices and wages
interdépendant, -e [ɛ̃tɛrdepɑ̃dɑ̃, -ɑ̃t] ADJ *(gén)* interdependent, mutually dependent; *(problèmes)* linked, related
interdiction [ɛ̃tɛrdiksjɔ̃] NF **1** *(prohibition → résultat)* ban; *(→ action)* banning; **passer outre à/lever une i.** to ignore/to lift a ban; **malgré l'i. des ventes** in spite of the ban on sales *or* of sales being prohibited; **i. d'exportation** export ban; **i. d'importation** import ban; **l'i. du livre en 1953 a assuré son succès** the banning of the book in 1953 guaranteed its success; **obtenir l'i. du site aux touristes** to get an order forbidding tourists access to the site; **nous apprenons l'i. de la manifestation** we've just heard that the demonstration has been banned; **et maintenant, i. d'utiliser la voiture!** and now you're banned from driving the car!; **i. m'avait été faite d'en parler** I'd been forbidden to talk about it; **i. est faite aux employés de passer par la grande porte** employees are not allowed through *or* are forbidden to use the main entrance; **i. de faire demi-tour** *(sur panneau)* no U-turn; **i. de marcher sur les pelouses** *(sur panneau)* keep off the grass, do not walk on the grass; **i. de pêcher** *(sur panneau)* fishing prohibited; **i. de stationner** *(sur panneau)* no parking; **i. de déposer des ordures** *(sur panneau)* no dumping; **i. (formelle** *ou* **absolue) de fumer** *(sur panneau)* (strictly) no smoking, smoking (strictly) prohibited; **et i. absolue de toucher à mon ordinateur!** and don't touch my computer!
2 *(suspension → d'un fonctionnaire)* suspension (from duty); *(→ d'un aviateur)* grounding; *(→ d'un prêtre)* interdict, interdiction; **il a une i. de vol** he's been grounded; **frapper un prêtre d'i.** to place a priest under (an) interdict *or* interdiction; **i. bancaire** stopping of payment on all cheques; **vous risquez une i. bancaire** you could have your chequebook taken away; *Ordinat* **i. d'écriture** write lockout; **le document est en i. d'écriture** the document is write-protected; *Jur* **i. des droits civils, civiques et de famille** = forfeiture of civic, civil and family rights; *Jur* **i. légale** (temporary) deprivation of legal rights; **i. de séjour** banning order
interdigital, -e, -aux, -ales [ɛ̃tɛrdiʒital, -o] ADJ interdigital
interdire [103] [ɛ̃tɛrdir] VT **1** *(défendre)* to forbid; **i. l'alcool/le tabac à qn** to forbid sb to drink/to smoke; **i. à qn de faire qch** *(sujet: personne)* to forbid sb to do sth; *(sujet: règlement)* to prohibit sb from doing sth; **le règlement du bureau nous interdit de fumer** office rules prohibit smoking *or* prohibit us from smoking; **ils ont décidé d'i. l'accès du club aux femmes/aux mineurs** they've decided to ban women/minors from the club; **je lui ai interdit ma porte** *ou* **ma maison** I will not allow him/her into my home, I have banned him/her from my home
2 *(tournure impersonnelle)* **il est interdit de...** it's forbidden to...; **il m'est interdit d'en dire plus** I am not allowed *or* at liberty to say any more; **il est interdit de fumer ici** smoking is forbidden *or* isn't allowed here
3 *(prohiber → circulation, stationnement, arme à feu, médicament)* to prohibit, to ban; *(→ manifestation, revue, parti politique)* to ban; **i. qch d'exportation/d'importation** to impose an export/import ban on sth; **la loi l'interdit, c'est interdit par la loi** it's illegal, *Sout* it's prohibited by law; **le gouvernement a fait i. toute manifestation de rue** the government issued a ban on all street demonstrations
4 *(empêcher)* to prevent, to preclude; **le mauvais temps interdit toute opération de sauvetage** bad weather is preventing any rescue operations; **sa maladie lui interdit tout effort** his/her illness doesn't allow him/her to make any physical effort
5 *(suspendre → magistrat)* to suspend; *(→ prêtre)* to (lay under an) interdict
▸**s'interdire** VPR **s'i. l'alcool/le tabac** to abstain from drinking/smoking; **elle s'interdit tout espoir de la revoir** she denies herself all hope of seeing her again; **il s'interdit d'y penser** he doesn't let himself think about it

> *Allusion*
>
> **Il est interdit d'interdire**
>
> This is a student slogan from the riots of May 1968. It means literally "It is forbidden to forbid", or "No saying no". The students saw French society as hedged about with all sorts of restrictions and stifled by convention. The expression is used today in a humorous way, when someone will not grant a request, or forbids a course of action; it is a jocular refusal to take "no" for an answer.

interdisciplinaire [ɛ̃tɛrdisiplinɛr] ADJ interdisciplinary
interdisciplinarité [ɛ̃tɛrdisiplinarite] NF interdisciplinarity
interdisez *etc voir* **interdire**
interdit, -e [ɛ̃tɛrdi, -it] PP *voir* **interdire**
ADJ **1** *(non autorisé)* forbidden; **ne t'assieds pas sur la pelouse, c'est i.** don't sit on the lawn, it's not allowed; **décharge/baignade interdite** *(sur panneau)* no dumping/bathing; **affichage i.** *(sur panneau)* (stick *or* post) no bills; **zone interdite** *(sur panneau)* no-go area; **le pont est i. aux voyageurs** the bridge is closed to passengers; **la zone piétonne est interdite aux véhicules** vehicles are not allowed in the pedestrian area; **i. au public** *(sur panneau)* no admittance; *Cin* **i. aux moins de 18 ans** adults only, *Br* ≃ 18, *Am* ≃ NC-17; *Cin* **i. aux moins de 13 ans** *Br* ≃ 12, *Am* ≃ PG-13
2 *(privé d'un droit) Jur* **i. de séjour en France** banned *or* prohibited from entering France; **être i. bancaire** *ou* **de chéquier** to have one's *Br* chequebook facilities *or Am* checking privileges withdrawn; *Ordinat* **i. d'écriture** *(disquette)* write-protected; **appareil/pilote i. de vol** grounded aircraft/pilot
3 *(frappé d'interdiction → film, revue)* banned
4 *(stupéfait)* dumbfounded, flabbergasted; **laisser qn i.** *(très surpris)* to take sb aback; *(perplexe)* to disconcert sb; **elle le dévisagea, interdite** she stared at him in bewilderment; **ils étaient là, interdits, devant les ruines de leur maison** they stood speechless before the wreckage of their home
NM,F *Jur* **i. de séjour en Suisse** person banned from *or* not allowed to enter Switzerland
NM **1** *(de la société)* (social) constraint; *(tabou)* taboo; **il brave tous les interdits** he defies all social taboos; **lever un i.** to lift a restriction
2 *(condamnation)* **jeter l'i. sur** *ou* **contre qn** to cast sb out, to exclude sb
3 *(en anthropologie)* prohibition
4 *Rel* interdict; **des interdits alimentaires** food forbidden by dietary law
5 *Banque* **i. bancaire** ban on writing cheques; **être frappé d'i. bancaire** to have one's *Br* chequebook facilities *or Am* checking privileges withdrawn
interentreprises [ɛ̃tɛrɑ̃trəpriz] ADJ INV intercompany
intéressant, -e [ɛ̃teresɑ̃, -ɑ̃t] ADJ **1** *(conversation, œuvre, personne, visage etc)* interesting; **de manière intéressante** interestingly; **elle cherche toujours à se rendre intéressante** she's always trying to attract attention, she's an attention-seeker; **il n'est vraiment pas i.** he's not worth bothering with; *Hum Vieilli* **être dans une situation intéressante** *ou* **dans un état i.** *ou* **dans une position intéressante** to be in the family way
2 *(avantageux)* attractive, favourable; *(lucratif)* profitable, worthwhile; **c'est une affaire très intéressante** it's a very good deal; **cette carte n'est intéressante que si tu voyages beaucoup** this card is only worth having if you

travel a lot; **il serait plus i. pour vous de changer de banque** you'd be better off banking with somebody else; **pas i.** *(offre, prix)* not attractive, not worthwhile; *(activité)* not worthwhile, unprofitable

NM,F *Péj* **faire l'i.** *ou* **son i.** to show off

intéressé, -e [ɛ̃terese] **ADJ 1** *(égoïste → personne)* self-interested, self-seeking, calculating; *(→ comportement, conseil)* motivated by self-interest; **amour i.** cupboard love; **je ne suis pas du tout i.** I'm not doing it out of self-interest

2 *(concerné)* concerned, involved; **les parties intéressées** *(gén)* the people concerned *or* involved; *Jur* the interested parties; **les puissances intéressées dans le conflit** the powers involved in the conflict

3 *(financièrement)* **être i. dans une affaire** to have a stake *or* a financial interest in a business

NM,F l'i. the person concerned; **les premiers/principaux intéressés** the persons most closely concerned *or* most directly affected; **elle est la première** *ou* **principale intéressée** she's the person principally involved *or* concerned; **les intéressés** the persons concerned, the interested parties

intéressement [ɛ̃terɛsmɑ̃] **NM i. (aux résultats)** profit-sharing scheme; **l'i. des salariés aux bénéfices de l'entreprise** profit-sharing

intéresser [4] [ɛ̃terese] **VT 1** *(passionner → sujet: activité, œuvre, professeur etc)* to interest; **la politique les intéresse peu** they're not very interested in politics, politics doesn't interest them very much; **notre offre peut peut-être vous i.** our offer might interest you *or* might be of interest to you; **le débat ne m'a pas du tout intéressé** I didn't find the debate at all interesting; **elle sait i. ses élèves** she knows how to gain her pupils' interest *or* how to interest her pupils; **continue, tu m'intéresses!** go on, you're starting to interest me!; **j'ai l'impression que ma sœur l'intéresse beaucoup!** I've got the feeling that he's very interested in my sister!; **ça m'intéresserait de savoir ce qu'il en pense** I'd be interested to know what he thinks; **je revends mon ordinateur, ça t'intéresse?** I'm selling my computer, are you interested?

2 *(concerner → sujet: loi, réforme)* to concern, to affect; **ces mesures intéressent essentiellement les mères célibataires** these measures mainly affect single mothers; **un problème qui intéresse la sécurité du pays** a problem which is relevant to *or* concerns national security

3 *Écon & Fin* **i. qn aux bénéfices** to give sb a share of the profits; **notre personnel est intéressé aux bénéfices** our staff gets a share of our profits, we operate a profit-sharing scheme; **être intéressé dans une entreprise** to have a stake *or* a financial interest in a company

4 *(dans un jeu)* **jouons un euro le point, pour i. la partie** let's play for one euro per point, to make the game more interesting

▶**s'intéresser VPR s'i. à qn/qch** to be interested in sb/sth; **elle ne s'intéresse à rien** she is not interested *or* she takes no interest in anything; **à quoi vous intéressez-vous?** what are your interests (in life)?; **je m'intéresse vivement à sa carrière** I take great *or* a keen interest in his/her career; **elle s'intéresse énormément à mon frère** she's very interested in my brother, she shows a great deal of interest in my brother; **un jeune romancier qui mérite qu'on s'intéresse à lui** a young novelist who merits some attention; **personne ne s'intéresse à moi!** nobody cares about me!, nobody's interested in me!; **ce n'est pas facile de les faire s'i. à ce sujet** it's not easy getting them interested in this subject

intérêt [ɛ̃terɛ] **NM 1** *(attention, curiosité)* interest; *(bienveillance)* interest, concern; **avoir** *ou* **éprouver de l'i. pour qch** to be interested *or* to take an interest in sth; **je n'éprouve aucun i. pour le théâtre** I'm not at all interested in the theatre, the theatre doesn't interest me at all; **manifester de l'i. pour qn/qch** to show an interest in sb/sth; **prendre de l'i. à qch** to take an interest in sth; **j'ai pris (un) grand i. à suivre votre émission, j'ai suivi votre émission avec (un) grand i.** I watched your programme with great interest; **elle a perdu tout i. pour son travail** she has lost all interest in her work; **porter de l'i. à qn** to take an interest in sb; **témoigner de l'i. à qn** to show an interest in sb, to show concern for sb

2 *(ce qui éveille l'attention)* interest; **une architecture/ville pleine d'i.** architecture/a town of great interest; **son essai offre peu d'i.** his/her essay is of no great interest

3 *(utilité)* point, idea; **l'i. d'un débat est que tout le monde participe** the point *or* idea of having a debate is that everybody should join in; **tout l'i. de cette décision réside dans le gain de place réalisé** the whole point *or* idea of this decision is to save space; **je ne vois pas l'i. de continuer cette discussion** I see no point in carrying on this discussion

4 *(importance)* importance, significance; **ses observations sont du plus haut** *ou* **grand i.** his/her comments are of the greatest interest *or* importance

5 *(avantage)* interest; **elle sait où se trouve son i.** she knows what's in her best interests; **agir dans/contre son i.** to act in/against one's own interest; **il n'est pas dans ton i. de vendre maintenant** it's not in your interest to sell now; **dans l'i. général** in the general interest; **dans l'i. de tous** in the interest of everyone; **dans l'i. public** in the public interest; **dans l'i. de mon travail/ma santé** in the interest of my job/my health; **d'i. public** of public interest; **elle a tout i. à se taire** she'd be well advised to remain silent; **quel i. aurait-elle à te nuire?** why should she want to harm you?; **je n'ai aucun i. à le faire** it's not at all in my interest; **on a i. à réserver si on veut avoir des places** we'd better book if we want seats; *Fam* **tu as i. à te faire tout petit!** you'd be well advised to *or* you'd better keep your head down!; *Fam* **t'as i. à te grouiller!** you *or* you'd better get a move on!; *Fam* **si elle va me rembourser? (il) y a i.!** will she pay me back? you bet (she will)!; **i. du consommateur** consumer welfare

6 *(égoïsme)* self-interest; **il l'a fait par i. (personnel)** he did it out of self-interest

7 *Écon & Banque* interest; **laisser courir des intérêts** to allow interest to accumulate; **payer des intérêts** to pay interest; **rapporter des intérêts** to yield *or* to bear interest; **placer son argent à 7 pour cent d'i.** to invest one's money at 7 percent interest; **prêt à i.** loan with interest, interest-bearing loan; **prêt sans i.** interest-free loan; **emprunter/prêter à i.** to borrow/to lend at interest; **cela rapporte des intérêts** it yields *or* bears interest; **intérêts arriérés** back interest; **i. bancaire** bank interest; **i. du capital** interest on capital; **intérêts compensatoires** damages; **i. composé** compound interest; **i. conventionnel** contractual interest rate; **intérêts courus** accrued interest; **intérêts débiteurs** debit interest; **intérêts dus** interest due; **intérêts échus** accrued interest; **intérêts exigibles** interest payable; **i. fixe** fixed interest; **i. légal** statutory (rate of) interest; **intérêts moratoires** default interest, penalty interest; **i. négatif** negative interest; *Bourse* **i. de report** contango; **i. de retard** interest on arrears; **i. simple** simple interest; **i. à taux flottant** floating-rate interest; **i. variable** variable-rate interest

❑ **intérêts NMPL** *(d'une personne, d'un pays)* interests; **nos intérêts économiques/vitaux** our economic/vital interests; **servir les intérêts de qn/d'une société** to serve sb's/a company's interests; *Jur* **les intérêts fondamentaux de la nation** the fundamental interests of the nation; *Écon & Fin* **avoir des intérêts dans une société** to have a stake *or* a financial interest in a company

❑ **sans intérêt ADJ** *(exposition, album)* uninteresting, of no interest, devoid of interest; **ne va pas au festival, c'est sans i.** don't go to the festival, it's not worth it; **que disais-tu? – c'est sans i.** what were you saying? – it's not important *or* it doesn't matter; **c'est sans i. pour la suite de l'enquête** it's of no importance for *or* relevance to the rest of the inquiry **ADV** uninterestedly, without interest; **je fais mon travail sans i.** I take no interest in my work

interétatique [ɛ̃teretatik] **ADJ** interstate

interethnique [ɛ̃terɛtnik] **ADJ** inter-ethnic

intereuropéen, -enne [ɛ̃tɛrørɔpeɛ̃, -ɛn] **ADJ** Pan-European

interfaçage [ɛ̃tɛrfasaʒ] **NM** *Ordinat* interfacing

interface [ɛ̃tɛrfas] **NF 1** *Ordinat* interface; **i. commune de passerelle** common gateway interface, CGI; **i. de communication** communication interface; **i. graphique** graphics interface; **i. d'imprimante** printer interface; **i. numérique** digital interface; **i. parallèle** parallel interface; **i. série** serial interface; **i. utilisateur** user interface; **i. utilisateur graphique** graphical user interface; **i. vidéo numérique** digital video interface; **i. WIMP** WIMP **2** *(intermédiaire)* interface

interfacer [16] [ɛ̃tɛrfase] **VT** *Ordinat* to interface

interfécond, -e [ɛ̃tɛrfekɔ̃, -ɔ̃d] **ADJ** *Biol* interfertile

interférence [ɛ̃tɛrferɑ̃s] **NF 1** *Météo, Rad & Phys* interference *(UNCOUNT)*; **il y a des interférences** there is interference **2** *(interaction)* interaction; **il y a i. entre l'évolution climatique et l'équilibre écologique de la région** there's an interaction between climatic changes and the ecological balance of the area

interférent, -e [ɛ̃tɛrferɑ̃, -ɑ̃t] **ADJ** interfering, interference *(avant n)*

interférentiel, -elle [ɛ̃tɛrferɑ̃sjɛl] **ADJ** interferential

interférer [18] [ɛ̃tɛrfere] **VI 1** *Phys* to interfere **2** *(se mêler)* to interact, to combine; **le courant A risque d'i. avec le courant B** current A may interact *or* combine with current B; **les deux courants interfèrent** the two currents interact with each other **3** *(intervenir)* **i. dans la vie de qn** to interfere *or* to meddle in sb's life

interféromètre [ɛ̃tɛrferɔmɛtr] **NM** *Phys* interferometer

interférométrie [ɛ̃tɛrferɔmetri] **NF** interferometry

interféron [ɛ̃tɛrferɔ̃] **NM** interferon

interfinancement [ɛ̃tɛrfinɑ̃smɑ̃] **NM** *Fin* cross-subsidization

interfluve [ɛ̃tɛrflyv] **NM** interfluve

interfoliage [ɛ̃tɛrfɔljaʒ] **NM i. d'un manuscrit/livre** interleaving of a manuscript/book

interfolier [9] [ɛ̃tɛrfɔlje] **VT** to interleave

interfrange [ɛ̃tɛrfrɑ̃ʒ] **NM** *Opt* distance between interference rings

intergalactique [ɛ̃tɛrgalaktik] **ADJ** intergalactic

intergénérationnel, -elle [ɛ̃tɛrʒenerasjɔnɛl] **ADJ** intergenerational

interglaciaire [ɛ̃tɛrglasjɛr] **ADJ** interglacial

intergouvernemental, -e, -aux, -ales [ɛ̃tɛrguvɛrnəmɑ̃tal, -o] **ADJ** intergovernmental

intergroupe [ɛ̃tɛrgrup] **NM** *Pol* joint committee

interhumain, -e [ɛ̃terymɛ̃, -ɛn] **ADJ** *Méd* interhuman

INTÉRIEUR, -E [ɛ̃terjœr]

> **ADJ** inside **1** ▪ inner **1, 2** ▪ interior **1, 6** ▪ internal **1, 3, 4** ▪ domestic **3** ▪ inland **5**
> **NM** inside **1** ▪ interior **1–4** ▪ home **3**

ADJ 1 *(du dedans → escalier)* inside, inner; *(→ cour)* inner; *(→ poche)* inside; *(→ partie)* inside, internal; **la pochette intérieure du disque** the inner sleeve of the record; **l'emballage i.** the inside wrapping; **les peintures intérieures de la maison** the interior decoration of the house

2 *(sentiment, vie)* inner; **un grand calme/bonheur i.** a great (feeling of) inner peace/happiness; **des voix intérieures** inner voices

3 *(national → ligne aérienne, politique)* domestic; *(→ marché)* domestic, home; *(→ vol)* domestic, internal; **le gouvernement est aux prises avec des difficultés intérieures** the government is battling against difficulties at home *or* domestic problems; **la dette intérieure** the national debt

4 *(interne)* internal; **les problèmes intérieurs d'un parti** a party's internal problems

5 *Géog (désert, mer)* inland

6 *Géom* interior

NM 1 *(d'un bâtiment, d'un véhicule)* inside, interior; *(d'un four, d'un récipient, d'une boîte)* inside; **ne pas utiliser de tampon abrasif pour nettoyer l'i.** do not use abrasive pads to clean the inside; **i. cuir** *(de voiture)* leather trim

2 *(d'un pays, d'une région)* interior; **l'i. (des terres)** the interior; **l'i. de l'île** the interior of the island, the hinterland; **demain, nous irons visiter l'i.** tomorrow we'll visit the interior; **dans**

l'i. du pays inland; les villages de l'i. inland villages

3 (foyer, décor) interior, home; **un i. douillet** a cosy interior or home; **son i. est parfaitement bien tenu** his/her housekeeping is perfect; **visiter un i. 1900 reconstitué** to visit a recreated 1900s interior; **femme d'i.** houseproud housewife; **scène d'i.** interior; **veste d'i.** indoor jacket

4 Cin interior (shot); **entièrement tourné en i.** shot entirely indoors

5 Fam **le Ministère de l'I., l'I.** Br ≃ the Home Office, Am ≃ the Department of the Interior

6 Sport inside-forward; **i. droit/gauche** inside right/left

◻ **à l'intérieur** ADV **1** (dedans) inside; **il y a une graine à l'i.** there's a seed inside

2 (dans la maison) inside, indoors; **à l'i. il fait plus frais** it's cooler inside

◻ **à l'intérieur de** PRÉP **1** (lieu) in, inside; **la pluie pénètre à l'i. du garage** the rain is coming into the garage; **reste à l'i. de la voiture** stay in or inside the car; **à l'i. des frontières** within or inside the frontiers; **à l'i. des murs** within the walls; **à l'i. des terres** inland

2 (groupe) within; **à l'i. d'une famille/d'un petit groupe** within a family/small group

◻ **de l'intérieur** ADV **1** (d'un lieu) from (the) inside; **verrouiller la portière de l'i.** to lock the door from (the) inside

2 (d'un groupe) from the inside, from within; **il veut transformer le parti de l'i.** he wants to change the party from the inside or from within

intérieurement [ɛ̃terjœrmɑ̃] ADV **1** (à l'intérieur) inside, within **2** (secrètement) inwardly; **il se félicitait i.** he was congratulating himself inwardly

intérim [ɛ̃terim] NM **1** (période) interim (period); **dans l'i.** meanwhile, in the meantime, Sout in the interim **2** (remplacement) Pol **assurer l'i.** to take over on a caretaker basis; **j'assure l'i. de la secrétaire en chef** I'm deputizing or covering for the chief secretary **3** (emploi) temporary work; **faire de l'i.** to do temporary work, to temp; **agence d'i.** temping agency

◻ **par intérim,** Belg **ad intérim, ad interim** ADJ (président, trésorier) interim (avant n), acting (avant n); (secrétaire) acting (avant n); (gouvernement) caretaker (avant n) ADV in a temporary capacity, temporarily; **gouverner par i.** to govern in the interim or for an interim period

intérimaire [ɛ̃terimɛr] ADJ **1** (assurant l'intérim → directeur, trésorier, ministre) acting; (→ personnel, employé) temporary; (→ gouvernement, cabinet) caretaker; **secrétaire i.** temporary secretary, temp **2** (non durable → fonction) interim (avant n); (→ commission) provisional, temporary

NMF (cadre) deputy; (secrétaire) temp; **travailler comme i.** to temp, to do temping work; **elle a beaucoup travaillé comme i.** she's done a lot of temping

interindividuel, -elle [ɛ̃terɛ̃dividɥɛl] ADJ interpersonal; **psychologie interindividuelle** psychology of personal relationships

interindustriel, -elle [ɛ̃terɛ̃dystrijɛl] ADJ between industries

intériorisation [ɛ̃terjɔrizasjɔ̃] NF internalization, interiorization

intérioriser [3] [ɛ̃terjɔrize] VT **1** Psy to internalize, to interiorize **2** (garder pour soi) to keep in; **elle a intériorisé sa colère** she kept her anger in, she bottled up her anger **3** Théât **vous devez i. le rôle** you have to get inside the part

intériorité [ɛ̃terjɔrite] NF inwardness, interiority

interjectif, -ive [ɛ̃terʒɛktif, -iv] ADJ interjectional

interjection [ɛ̃terʒɛksjɔ̃] NF **1** (exclamation) interjection **2** Jur **i. d'appel** lodging of an appeal

interjective [ɛ̃terʒɛktiv] voir **interjectif**

interjeter [27] [ɛ̃terʒəte] VT **i. appel** to lodge an appeal

interlettrage [ɛ̃terletraʒ] NM Typ leading

interlettrer [3] [ɛ̃terletre] VT Typ to letterspace

interleukine [ɛ̃terløkin] NF Biol interleukin

interlignage [ɛ̃terliɲaʒ] NM Typ leading, line spacing; **i. double** double spacing; **i. simple** single spacing

interligne [ɛ̃terliɲ] NM **1** (blanc) space (between

the lines); Ordinat & Typ line spacing; **simple/double i.** single/double spacing; **tapé en simple/double i.** typed with single/double spacing, single-/double-spaced; **i. réglable** adjustable line space **2** (ajout) interlineation **3** Mus space

NF Typ (lame) lead

interligner [3] [ɛ̃terliɲe] VT **1** (séparer) to space **2** (écrire) to interline, to interlineate, to write between the lines; **i. un mot dans le texte** to interline a word in the text

interlinéaire [ɛ̃terlineɛr] ADJ Typ (texte) interlinear

interlock [ɛ̃terlɔk] NM **1** (tricot) interlock **2** (machine) interlock machine

interlocuteur, -trice [ɛ̃terlɔkytœr, -tris] NM,F **1** (gén) = person speaking or being spoken to; Ling speaker, Sout interlocutor; (dans un débat) speaker; **mon i. n'avait pas compris** the man I was talking to hadn't understood

2 (dans une négociation) negotiating partner; **les États-Unis ont toujours été l'i. privilégié de la Grande-Bretagne** the United States has always had a special relationship with Great Britain; **nous ne considérons plus le ministre comme un i. valable** we no longer consider the minister to be an acceptable negotiating partner; **nous avions un i. de premier plan** we were dealing with a first-rate negotiator

interlocutoire [ɛ̃terlɔkytwar] ADJ interlocutory

NM interlocutory judgement

interlocutrice [ɛ̃terlɔkytris] voir **interlocuteur**

interlope [ɛ̃terlɔp] ADJ **1** (frauduleux) unlawful, illegal, illicit; **commerce i.** illicit trade **2** (louche) shady, dubious; **relations ou amitiés interlopes** underworld connections

interloquer [3] [ɛ̃terlɔke] VT (décontenancer) to take aback, to disconcert; (stupéfier) to stun; **cette réponse l'a interloqué** the answer stunned or nonplussed him; **elle resta interloquée** she was dumbfounded or flabbergasted or stunned

interlude [ɛ̃terlyd] NM interlude

intermède [ɛ̃termɛd] NM **1** Mus interlude, intermedio, Spéc intermezzo; Théât interlude, interval piece; **un i. comique** a comic interlude **2** Fig interlude, interval; **notre liaison ne fut qu'un agréable i.** our affair was just a pleasant interlude

intermédiaire [ɛ̃termedjɛr] ADJ **1** (moyen → gén) intermediate, intermediary; (→ pointure) in between; **couleur i. entre le bleu et le vert** colour halfway between blue and green; **solution i.** compromise (solution)

2 Scol intermediate; **niveau i.** intermediate level

3 Cin, Géol & Métal intermediate

NMF **1** (médiateur) intermediary, go-between; **servir d'i.** to act as an intermediary or as a go-between

2 Com intermediary, middleman; **les fournisseurs et les intermédiaires** the suppliers and the middlemen; **i. agréé** authorized dealer; **i. négociateur** trading member

3 Banque **i. agréé** authorized intermediary; **i. financier** financial intermediary

4 Bourse market maker; **i. remisier (en Bourse)** intermediate broker

◻ **par l'intermédiaire de** PRÉP (personne) through, via; **par votre i.** through you; **il a appris l'anglais par l'i. de la radio** he learnt English from the radio

◻ **sans intermédiaire** ADV (directement) directly; **je préfère vendre sans i.** I prefer to sell directly to the customer

intermédiation [ɛ̃termedjasjɔ̃] NF intermediary financing

intermétallique [ɛ̃termetalik] ADJ intermetallic

intermezzo [ɛ̃termedzo] NM intermezzo

interminable [ɛ̃terminabl] ADJ interminable, neverending, endless; **un discours i.** an interminable speech; **la route lui paraissait i.** he/she thought the road would never end

interminablement [ɛ̃terminabləmɑ̃] ADV interminably, endlessly, without end

interministériel, -elle [ɛ̃terministerjɛl] ADJ interdepartmental, Br joint ministerial; **Groupe i. de contrôle** = official body controlling the use of telephone-tapping

intermission [ɛ̃termisjɔ̃] NF **1** Méd (period of)

remission, intermission **2** Can Théât intermission

intermittence [ɛ̃termitɑ̃s] NF **1** (irrégularité → gén) intermittence, irregularity; (→ d'un signal lumineux) irregular flashing; (→ de la production) irregularity **2** Méd intermission, remission

◻ **par intermittence** ADV intermittently; **travailler par i.** to work in fits and starts or intermittently

intermittent, -e [ɛ̃termitɑ̃, -ɑ̃t] ADJ **1** (irrégulier → tir) intermittent, sporadic; (→ travail) casual, occasional; (→ pulsation) irregular, periodic; (→ éclairage) intermittent; (→ averses) occasional **2** Méd **fièvre intermittente** intermittent fever; **pouls i.** irregular pulse

NM **les intermittents du spectacle** = people working in the performing arts (and thus entitled to social security benefits designed for people without regular employment)

intermodal, -e, -aux, -ales [ɛ̃termɔdal, -o] ADJ **1** (gare) intermodal **2** Psy intermodal

intermoléculaire [ɛ̃termɔlekylɛr] ADJ intermolecular

intermusculaire [ɛ̃termyskylɛr] ADJ intermuscular

internalisation [ɛ̃ternalizasjɔ̃] NF Écon internalization; **i. du recrutement** recruiting in-house, in-house or internal recruitment

internaliser [3] [ɛ̃ternalize] VT Écon to internalize

internat [ɛ̃terna] NM **1** Scol (école) boarding school; (régime) boarding school system **2** Méd (concours) = competitive examination for Br a housemanship or Am an internship; (stage) hospital training, Br time as a houseman, Am internship

international, -e, -aux, -ales [ɛ̃ternasjɔnal, -o] ADJ **1** (gén) international **2** Archit **style i.** international style

NM,F international (player or athlete)

NM Écon **l'i.** world markets; **ces entreprises réalisent tout leur chiffre d'affaires à l'i.** these companies make all their profits in international trade or on the international market

◻ **internationaux** NMPL Sport internationals; **les internationaux de France de tennis** the French Open

Internationale [ɛ̃ternasjɔnal] NF **1** (chant) **l'I.** the Internationale **2** (groupement) **l'I.** the International

internationalement [ɛ̃ternasjɔnalmɑ̃] ADJ internationally

internationalisation [ɛ̃ternasjɔnalizasjɔ̃] NF internationalization

internationaliser [3] [ɛ̃ternasjɔnalize] VT to internationalize

▸ **s'internationaliser** VPR to take on an international dimension; **le conflit s'est internationalisé** the conflict took on an international dimension

internationalisme [ɛ̃ternasjɔnalism] NM internationalism

internationaliste [ɛ̃ternasjɔnalist] ADJ internationalist

NMF **1** Pol internationalist **2** Jur international lawyer

internationalité [ɛ̃ternasjɔnalite] NF internationality

internaute [ɛ̃ternot] NMF Internet user, (Net) surfer; **i. novice** Internet novice, Fam newbie

interne [ɛ̃tern] ADJ **1** (intérieur → paroi) internal, inside; (→ face, structure, conflit, difficultés) internal; (→ raison, cause, logique) internal, inner; (de l'entreprise → personnel) in-house; **il a fallu radiographier le côté i. de la jambe/du pied** the inner part of the leg/foot had to be X-rayed **2** Méd (hémorragie, organe) internal

NMF **1** Méd **i. (des hôpitaux)** Br houseman, junior hospital doctor, Am intern; **i. en pharmacie** student pharmacist (in a hospital) **2** Scol boarder; **il est i.** he's at boarding school

◻ **en interne** ADV (dans l'entreprise) on an in-house basis

interné, -e [ɛ̃terne] ADJ **1** Méd committed, Br sectioned **2** (emprisonné) interned

NM,F **1** Méd committed or Br sectioned patient **2** (prisonnier) internee

internégatif [ɛ̃ternegatif] NM internegative

internement [ɛ̃ternəmɑ̃] NM **1** Méd commitment, Br sectioning **2** (emprisonnement) internment; **i.**

int–int

abusif illegal internment; **i. administratif** internment without trial

interner [3] [ɛ̃tɛrne] **VT 1** *Méd* to commit, *Br* to section **2** *Pol* to intern

Internet [ɛ̃tɛrnɛt] **NM** Internet; **sur (l')I.** on the Internet; **naviguer sur (l')I.** to surf the Internet; **acheter/vendre qch sur (l')I.** to buy/to sell sth over the Internet; **I. utile** the Internet as a practical tool

internonce [ɛ̃tɛrnɔ̃s] **NM** *Rel* internuncio

interocéanique [ɛ̃tɛrɔseanik] **ADJ** interoceanic

interoceptif, -ive [ɛ̃tɛrɔsɛptif, -iv] **ADJ** *Physiol* interoceptive

interœstrus [ɛ̃tɛrɛstrys] **NM** *Physiol* anoestrus

interopérabilité [ɛ̃tɛrɔperabilite] **NF** interoperability

interosseux, -euse [ɛ̃tɛrɔsø, -øz] **ADJ** interosseous

interparlementaire [ɛ̃tɛrparləmɑ̃tɛr] **ADJ** interparliamentary; **commission i.** joint committee

interpellateur, -trice [ɛ̃tɛrpelatœr, -tris] **NM,F 1** *Pol (questionneur)* questioner, *Spéc* interpellator **2** *(personne qui apostrophe)* = person calling out; **mon i.** the person calling out to me

interpellation [ɛ̃tɛrpelasjɔ̃] **NF 1** *(apostrophe)* call, shout **2** *(par la police)* (arrest for) questioning; **la police a procédé à plusieurs interpellations** several people were detained *or* taken in by police for questioning **3** *Pol* question, *Spéc* interpellation

interpellatrice [ɛ̃tɛrpelatris] *voir* **interpellateur**

interpeller [26] [ɛ̃tɛrpəle] **VT 1** *(appeler)* to call out to, to hail **2** *(sujet: police)* to stop for questioning **3** *(concerner)* to touch; *Hum* **ça m'interpelle quelque part** I can relate to that **4** *Pol* to put a question to

▸**s'interpeller VPR** *(s'appeler)* to call out to *or* to hail one another

interpénétration [ɛ̃tɛrpenetrasjɔ̃] **NF** interpenetration

interpénétrer [18] [ɛ̃tɛrpenetre] **s'interpénétrer VPR** to interpenetrate, to penetrate mutually; **des cultures qui s'interpénètrent** intermingling cultures

interpersonnel, -elle [ɛ̃tɛrpɛrsɔnɛl] **ADJ** interpersonal, person-to-person

interphase [ɛ̃tɛrfaz] **NF** interphase

Interphone® [ɛ̃tɛrfɔn] **NM** *(dans un bureau)* intercom; *(à l'entrée d'un immeuble)* entry *or* security phone; **elle a appelé sa secrétaire à l'interphone** she called her secretary on the intercom

interplanétaire [ɛ̃tɛrplanetɛr] **ADJ** interplanetary; **voyage i.** space flight

INTERPOL, Interpol [ɛ̃tɛrpɔl] **NM** Interpol

interpolateur, -trice [ɛ̃tɛrpɔlatœr, -tris] **NM,F** interpolator

interpolation [ɛ̃tɛrpɔlasjɔ̃] **NF** interpolation, insertion

interpolatrice [ɛ̃tɛrpɔlatris] *voir* **interpolateur**

interpoler [3] [ɛ̃tɛrpɔle] **VT 1** *(texte)* to insert, to fit in *or* into, *Spéc* to interpolate; **i. un paragraphe dans un texte** to insert a paragraph into a text; **i. une phrase dans un discours** to add a sentence to a speech **2** *Math* to interpolate

interposer [3] [ɛ̃tɛrpoze] **VT** to place, to insert (**entre** between); **ils ont pu se contacter par personne interposée** they were able to make contact through an intermediary

▸**s'interposer VPR 1** *(faire écran)* **s'i. entre** to stand between; **il s'est interposé entre la lumière et mon appareil** he stood between the light and my camera **2** *(intervenir)* to intervene, to step in, *Sout* to interpose oneself; **il s'est interposé pour l'empêcher de me frapper** he stepped in *or* intervened to stop him/her hitting me

interpositif [ɛ̃tɛrpozitif] **NM** interpositive

interposition [ɛ̃tɛrpozisjɔ̃] **NF 1** *(d'un objet, de texte)* interposition, interposing **2** *(intervention)* interposition, intervention; *Mil* **forces d'i.** intervention forces **3** *Jur* **i. de personnes** defrauding to the advantage of a third party *(by drawing up a contract)*

interprétable [ɛ̃tɛrpretabl] **ADJ** interpretable; **c'est i. de deux façons** this may be interpreted *or* taken in two ways

interprétariat [ɛ̃tɛrpretarja] **NM** interpreting; **diplôme d'i.** diploma in interpreting; **faire de l'i.** to work as an interpreter

interprétatif, -ive [ɛ̃tɛrpretatif, -iv] **ADJ 1** *(explicatif)* expository, interpretative, interpretive **2** *Ordinat* interpretive **3** *Psy* interpretative

interprétation [ɛ̃tɛrpretasjɔ̃] **NF 1** *(exécution → d'une œuvre musicale)* interpretation, performance; *(→ d'un rôle)* interpretation; *(→ d'un texte)* reading

2 *(analyse)* interpretation, analysis; **c'est une drôle d'i. de la situation** it's a strange way of looking at *or* interpreting the situation; **il a donné une fausse i. de mes déclarations** he gave an incorrect interpretation of *or* he misinterpreted my statements

3 *(interprétariat)* interpreting

4 *Psy* **i. des rêves** interpretation of dreams

5 *Ordinat* interpretation

6 *Jur* **i. stricte** strict interpretation

interprète [ɛ̃tɛrprɛt] **NMF 1** *(musicien, acteur)* performer, player; *(chanteur)* singer; *(danseur)* dancer; **l'i. de Giselle** the dancer of the title role in 'Giselle'; **les interprètes** *(d'un film, d'une pièce)* the cast; **une pause pour donner aux interprètes le temps de se changer** a break to allow the performers to change; **il est devenu l'i. par excellence de Beckett** he became the foremost interpreter of Beckett's work; **l'i. de Cyrano n'était pas à la hauteur** the actor playing Cyrano wasn't up to the part; **les interprètes de ce concerto sont...** the concerto will be played by...

2 *(traducteur)* interpreter; **servir d'i. à** to act as interpreter for; **i. de conférence** conference interpreter

3 *(représentant)* spokesperson, spokesman, *f* spokeswoman; **être** *ou* **se faire l'i. de qn auprès des autorités** to speak to the authorities on sb's behalf

interpréter [18] [ɛ̃tɛrprete] **VT 1** *(exécuter, jouer)* to perform, *Sout* to interpret; **i. un rôle** to play a part; **elle interprète Madame Butterfly** she plays (the part of) Madame Butterfly; **i. une sonate au piano** to play a sonata on the piano; **j'aime la façon dont il interprète Hamlet/la cantate** I like the way he performs Hamlet/the cantata; **i. un air** to perform *or* to sing a tune; **elle va maintenant nous i. un prélude de Schubert** she will now perform *or* play a prelude by Schubert for us

2 *(comprendre → texte, paroles, rêve, geste)* to interpret; **mal i. qch** to misinterpret sth; **i. qch en bien/mal** to take sth well/the wrong way

3 *(traduire)* to interpret

▸**s'interpréter VPR** *(être compris)* to be interpreted; **son refus peut s'i. de plusieurs façons** his/her refusal can be interpreted in several ways

interpréteur [ɛ̃tɛrpretœr] **NM** *Ordinat* interpreter

interprofession [ɛ̃tɛrprɔfɛsjɔ̃] **NF** joint-trade organization

interprofessionnel, -elle [ɛ̃tɛrprɔfɛsjɔnɛl] **ADJ** interprofessional

interquartile [ɛ̃tɛrkwartil] **ADJ** *Math* interquartile

interracial, -e, -aux, -ales [ɛ̃tɛrrasjal, -o] **ADJ** interracial

interrégional, -e, -aux, -ales [ɛ̃tɛrreʒjɔnal, -o] **ADJ** interregional

interrègne [ɛ̃tɛrrɛɲ] **NM** interregnum

interro [ɛ̃tero] **NF** *Fam Arg scol (abrév* **interrogation**) test■

interrogateur, -trice [ɛ̃terɔgatœr, -tris] **ADJ** *(regard)* inquiring, questioning; **d'un air i.** interrogatively, questioningly; **sur un ton i.** questioningly, searchingly

NM,F *Scol* (oral) examiner

interrogatif, -ive [ɛ̃terɔgatif, -iv] **ADJ 1** *(interrogateur)* questioning, inquiring; **d'un ton i.** questioningly **2** *Ling* interrogative

NM interrogative (word); **l'i.** the interrogative

▫ **interrogative NF** interrogative *or* question clause

interrogation [ɛ̃terɔgasjɔ̃] **NF 1** *(questionnement → gén)* questioning; *(→ d'un témoin)* questioning, interrogation; **sur son visage se lisait une muette i.** there was a questioning expression on his/her face

2 *Scol* test; **i. écrite/orale** written/oral test

3 *Ling* **i. directe/indirecte** direct/indirect question

4 *Tél* search

5 *Ordinat (d'une base de données)* inquiry, query; *(activité)* interrogation; **i. à distance** remote access

interrogative [ɛ̃terɔgativ] *voir* **interrogatif**

interrogativement [ɛ̃terɔgativmɑ̃] **ADV 1** *Ling* interrogatively **2** *(en demandant)* questioningly, inquiringly

interrogatoire [ɛ̃terɔgatwar] **NM 1** *(par la police → d'un prisonnier, d'un suspect)* interrogation, questioning; **subir un i. en règle** to undergo a thorough questioning *or* interrogation; *Fam* **faire subir à qn un i. serré** to grill sb; *Fam* **faire subir à qn un i. musclé** to work sb over *(to obtain information)* **2** *Jur (dans un procès)* examination, cross-examination; *(par un juge d'instruction)* hearing; *(procès-verbal)* statement; **i. de première comparution** first examination *(in which the suspect is told of the charges against him/her)*

interrogatrice [ɛ̃terɔgatris] *voir* **interrogateur**

interrogeable [ɛ̃terɔʒabl] **ADJ i. à distance** *(répondeur)* with remote-access facility

interroger [17] [ɛ̃terɔʒe] **VT 1** *(questionner → ami)* to ask, to question; *(→ guichetier)* to ask, to inquire of; *(→ suspect)* to question, to interrogate, to interview; **i. qn pour savoir si...** to ask sb whether..., *Sout* to inquire of sb whether...; **i. qn sur qch** to ask sb questions about sth; **i. qn du regard** to look questioningly *or* inquiringly at sb; **il y a là un monsieur qui m'a interrogé à votre sujet** there is a gentleman here inquiring about you *or* asking questions about you; **ils l'ont interrogé sans ménagement** they put him through a gruelling interrogation

2 *Fig (sa conscience)* to examine; **i. sa mémoire** to try to remember

3 *Mktg (par un questionnaire)* to interview, to poll, to question; **60% des personnes interrogées ont déclaré n'avoir jamais entendu parler de ce produit** 60% of those questioned said that they had never heard of this product; **personne interrogée** respondent

4 *Scol & Univ (avant l'examen)* to test, to quiz; *(à l'examen)* to examine; **j'ai été interrogé sur la guerre de 14–18** I was asked questions on the 1914–18 war; **être interrogé par écrit/oral** to be given a written/an oral test *or* exam

5 *Ordinat & Tél* to interrogate, to query

6 *Jur* to examine, to cross-examine

▸**s'interroger VPR s'i. sur qch** to wonder about sth; **je ne sais pas si je vais l'acheter, je m'interroge encore** I don't know whether I'll buy it, I'm still wondering (about it) *or* I haven't made up my mind yet

interrompre [78] [ɛ̃tɛrɔ̃pr] **VT 1** *(perturber → personne, conversation, études)* to interrupt; **il fut interrompu par l'arrivée de son père** he was interrupted by the arrival of his father; **je ne voulais pas vous i. dans votre travail** I didn't want to interrupt you while you were working; **n'interrompez pas la conversation** don't interrupt the conversation; **ses études furent interrompues par la guerre** his/her studies were interrupted by the war; **j'en ai assez de me faire i.!** I'm fed up with being interrupted!

2 *(faire une pause dans → débat)* to stop, to suspend; *(→ session)* to interrupt, to break off; *(→ voyage)* to break; **l'athlète a interrompu son entraînement pendant deux mois** the athlete stopped training for two months; **i. ses études pendant un an** to take a year off from one's studies

3 *(définitivement)* to stop; **i. sa lecture/son repas** to stop reading/eating; **le match a été interrompu par la pluie** rain stopped play; **i. une grossesse** to terminate a pregnancy

4 *Com (produit)* to discontinue

▸**s'interrompre VPR** *(dans une conversation)* to break off, to stop; *(dans une activité)* to break off

interro-négatif, -ive [ɛ̃teronegatif, -iv] **ADJ** *Gram* negative interrogative

interrupteur, -trice [ɛ̃teryptœr, -tris] **NM,F** *Littéraire (personne)* interrupter

NM *(dispositif)* switch; **i. à bascule** toggle switch; *Ordinat* **i. DIP** *ou* **à plusieurs positions** DIP switch; **i. horaire** time switch; **i. principal** master switch

interruption [ɛ̃terypsjɔ̃] **NF 1** *(arrêt définitif → de négociations, de relations diplomatiques)* breaking off; **sans i.** continuously, uninterruptedly,

without stopping; **ouvert sans i. de 9 h à 20 h** *(sur la vitrine d'un magasin)* open all day 9 a.m. to 8 p.m.; *Méd* **i. illégale de grossesse** illegal abortion; **i. volontaire de grossesse** termination *(of pregnancy)*

2 *(pause → dans un spectacle)* break; **après une brève i., le spectacle reprit** after a short break, the show started up again

3 *(perturbation)* interruption; **des interruptions continuelles l'empêchaient de travailler** continual interruptions prevented him/her from working; **veuillez nous excuser pour cette i. momentanée de l'image/du son** we apologize for the momentary loss of picture/of sound; *Élec* **i. de courant** power cut

4 *Ordinat* **fonction d'i.** interrupt function

5 *Jur* **i. de l'instance** abatement of proceedings

interruptrice [ɛ̃teryptris] *voir* **interrupteur**

intersaison [ɛ̃tɛrsɛzɔ̃] NF off season

interscolaire [ɛ̃tɛrskɔlɛr] ADJ interschools

intersecté, -e [ɛ̃tɛrsɛkte] ADJ *Archit* intersecting; *Géom* intersected

intersection [ɛ̃tɛrsɛksjɔ̃] NF **1** *(de routes)* intersection, junction; **i. avec une route secondaire** intersection with a minor road; **à l'i. des deux routes** where the two roads intersect *or* meet; **à l'i. de plusieurs courants politiques** where several different political tendencies meet *or* come together **2** *Math (de droites, de plans)* intersection; *(d'ensembles)* set

intersession [ɛ̃tɛrsesjɔ̃] NF *Pol* recess

intersexualité [ɛ̃tɛrsɛksɥalite] NF intersexuality

intersexué, -e [ɛ̃tɛrsɛksɥe] ADJ intersexual

intersidéral, -e, -aux, -ales [ɛ̃tɛrsideral, -o] ADJ intersideral; **espace i.** deep space

intersigne [ɛ̃tɛrsiɲ] NM mysterious connection

interspécifique [ɛ̃tɛrspesifik] ADJ interspecific

interstellaire [ɛ̃tɛrstelɛr] ADJ interstellar; **espace i.** deep space

interstice [ɛ̃tɛrstis] NM crack, chink, *Sout* interstice

interstitiel, -elle [ɛ̃tɛrstisjɛl] ADJ interstitial

NM interstitial

intersubjectif, -ive [ɛ̃tɛrsybʒɛktif, -iv] ADJ intersubjective

intersubjectivité [ɛ̃tɛrsybʒɛktivite] NF *Psy* intersubjectivity

intersyndical, -e, -aux, -ales [ɛ̃tɛrsɛ̃dikal, -o] ADJ interunion, joint union

❏ **intersyndicale** NF interunion committee

intertexte [ɛ̃tɛrtɛkst] NM *Littérature* intertext

intertextualité [ɛ̃tɛrtɛkstɥalite] NF *Littérature* intertextuality

intertextuel, -elle [ɛ̃tɛrtɛkstɥɛl] ADJ *Littérature* intertextual

intertidal, -e, -aux, -ales [ɛ̃tɛrtidal, -o] ADJ *Géog* intertidal

intertitre [ɛ̃tɛrtitr] NM **1** *Presse* subheading **2** *Cin* insert title

intertrigo [ɛ̃tɛrtrigo] NM intertrigo

intertropical, -e, -aux, -ales [ɛ̃tɛrtrɔpikal, -o] ADJ intertropical

interuniversitaire [ɛ̃teryniversitɛr] ADJ interuniversity

interurbain, -e [ɛ̃teryrbɛ̃, -ɛn] ADJ *(gén)* intercity, interurban; *Vieilli Tél* long-distance *(avant n)*, *Br* trunk *(avant n)*

NM *Vieilli* long-distance telephone service, *Br* trunk call service

intervalle [ɛ̃tɛrval] NM **1** *(durée)* interval; **un i. de trois heures** a three-hour interval *or* gap; **ils se sont retrouvés à trois mois d'i.** they met again after an interval of three months; **à intervalles réguliers** at regular intervals; **par intervalles** intermittently, at intervals, now and again; **dans l'i., je ferai le nécessaire** meanwhile *or* in the meantime I'll do what has to be done; **dans l'i., j'étais revenu** I had come back by then *or* by that time

2 *(distance)* interval, space; **laissez deux mètres d'i. entre chaque piquet** leave a gap of two metres *or* a two-metre gap between each stake; **plantés à intervalles de trois mètres** *ou* **à trois mètres d'i.** planted three metres apart; **l'i. entre les deux maisons** the distance between the two houses

3 *(brèche)* gap

4 *Math, Mil & Mus* interval; *Math* **i. de confiance** confidence interval; *Math* **i. ouvert/fermé** open/closed interval

intervenant, -e [ɛ̃tɛrvənɑ̃, -ɑ̃t] ADJ intervening

NM,F **1** *(dans un débat, un congrès)* participant, speaker; **i. principal** keynote speaker **2** *Jur* intervening party **3** *Mktg* **i. sur le marché** market participant

intervenir [40] [ɛ̃tɛrvənir] VI **1** *(agir)* to intervene, to step in; **i. en faveur de qn** to intercede *or* to intervene on sb's behalf; **i. auprès de qn pour** to intercede with sb in order to; **il était temps d'i.** it was time to do something about it *or* to act; **on a dû faire i. la police** the police had to be brought in *or* called in; **l'État a dû i. pour renflouer la société** the state had to intervene to keep the company afloat

2 *Méd* to operate

3 *(prendre la parole)* to speak; **vous ne devez pas i. dans ce débat** you mustn't speak in this debate

4 *Mil* to intervene

5 *(jouer un rôle → circonstance, facteur)* **i. dans** to influence, to affect; **le prix n'intervient pas dans mon choix** the price has no bearing on *or* doesn't affect my choice

6 *(survenir → accord, décision)* to be reached; *(→ incident, changement)* to take place; **le changement/la mesure intervient au moment où...** the change/measure comes at a time when...

7 *Jur* to intervene

intervention [ɛ̃tɛrvɑ̃sjɔ̃] NF **1** *(entrée en action)* intervention; **il a fallu l'i. des pompiers** the fire brigade had to be called in *or* brought in; **malgré l'i. rapide des secours** despite swift rescue action; **malgré son i. auprès du ministre** despite his/her having spoken to the minister; **i. en faveur de qn** intervention in sb's favour; **grâce à votre bienveillante i.** thanks to your good offices

2 *Mil* intervention; **l'i. des forces armées** military intervention; **i. aérienne** air strike; **i. armée** armed intervention

3 *(ingérence)* interference; *Pol* intervention; **i. de l'État** state intervention; **i. gouvernementale** government intervention

4 *(discours)* talk, *Univ* paper; **faire une i. dans un colloque** to give a talk *or* paper at a conference; **i. principale** keynote speech; **j'ai fait deux interventions** I spoke twice; **j'ai approuvé son i.** I agreed with his/her contribution *or* what he/she said

5 *Méd* **i. (chirurgicale)** (surgical) operation, surgery *(UNCOUNT)*; **procéder à une i. chirurgicale** to operate

6 *Agr & Écon* **beurre d'i.** subsidized butter; **prix d'i.** intervention price

7 *Jur* intervention

interventionnel, -elle [ɛ̃tɛrvɑ̃sjɔnɛl] ADJ *Méd (examen radiologique)* interventional

interventionnisme [ɛ̃tɛrvɑ̃sjɔnism] NM interventionism

interventionniste [ɛ̃tɛrvɑ̃sjɔnist] ADJ interventionist; **non i.** non-interventionist

NMF interventionist

intervenu, -e [ɛ̃tɛrvəny] PP *voir* **intervenir**

interversion [ɛ̃tɛrvɛrsjɔ̃] NF inversion; **i. de chiffres** transposition of figures; **i. des rôles** role reversal

intervertébral, -e, -aux, -ales [ɛ̃tɛrvɛrtebral, -o] ADJ intervertebral

intervertir [32] [ɛ̃tɛrvɛrtir] VT to invert (the order of); **i. les rôles** to reverse roles

intervient *etc voir* **intervenir**

interview [ɛ̃tɛrvju] NF OU NM *Presse & TV* interview; **une i. exclusive** an exclusive (interview); **i. radio** radio interview; **i. télévisée** television interview

interviewé, -e [ɛ̃tɛrvjuve] *Presse & TV* ADJ interviewed

NM,F interviewee

interviewer[1] [3] [ɛ̃tɛrvjuve] VT *Presse & TV* to interview

interviewer[2] [ɛ̃tɛrvjuvœr] NM *Presse & TV* interviewer

intervieweur, -euse [ɛ̃tɛrvjuvœr, -øz] NM,F *Presse & TV* interviewer

intervint *etc voir* **intervenir**

intervocalique [ɛ̃tɛrvɔkalik] ADJ intervocalic

intestat [ɛ̃tɛsta] ADJ INV intestate; **mourir i.** to die intestate

NMF intestate

intestin[1] [ɛ̃tɛstɛ̃] NM *Anat* intestine, bowel; **les intestins** the intestines, the bowels; **i. grêle** small intestine; **gros i.** large intestine; **cancer de l'i.** bowel cancer

intestin[2], **-e** [ɛ̃tɛstɛ̃, -in] ADJ *(interne)* internal; **luttes intestines** internecine struggles

intestinal, -e, -aux, -ales [ɛ̃tɛstinal, -o] ADJ intestinal; **douleurs intestinales** stomach pains

intifada [intifada] NF intifada

intimation [ɛ̃timasjɔ̃] NF **1** *(d'un ordre)* notification **2** *Jur (assignation)* summons *(before a high court)*; **signifier une i.** to issue *or* to serve a summons; **i. d'appel** notice of appeal

intime [ɛ̃tim] ADJ **1** *(proche)* close; **un ami i.** a close friend, *Sout* an intimate; **ils sont (très) intimes** they are (very) close

2 *(privé → pensée, vie)* intimate; **conversation i.** private conversation; **chagrin i.** personal *or* intimate grief; **avoir des relations intimes avec qn** to be intimate with sb, to be on intimate terms with sb; **univers i.** secret world

3 *Euph (génital)* **hygiène i.** personal hygiene; **parties intimes** private parts

4 *(discret)* quiet, intimate; **cérémonie/mariage i.** quiet ceremony/wedding; **soirée i.** *(entre deux personnes)* quiet dinner; *(entre plusieurs)* quiet get-together; **restaurant i.** quiet little restaurant

5 *(profond)* inner, intimate; **les recoins les plus intimes de l'âme** the innermost *or* deepest recesses of the soul; **le sens i. d'un texte** the underlying *or* deeper meaning of a text; **il a une connaissance i. de la langue** he has a thorough knowledge of the language, he knows the language inside out

6 *(avant le nom)* **j'ai l'i. conviction qu'il ment** I am utterly convinced that he's lying

NMF *(ami)* close friend, *Sout* intimate; **ses intimes** his/her closest friends (and relations); **moi, c'est Madeleine, Mado pour les intimes** I'm Madeleine, Mado to my friends *or* my friends call me Mado

intimé, -e [ɛ̃time] ADJ **partie intimée** respondent party

NM,F respondent

intimement [ɛ̃timmɑ̃] ADV *(connaître)* intimately; **ces deux faits sont i. liés** these two facts are closely connected; **i. convaincu** *ou* **persuadé** utterly convinced

intimer [3] [ɛ̃time] VT **1** *(signifier)* **i. à qn l'ordre de faire qch** to order sb to do sth **2** *Jur (en appel)* to summon; *(faire savoir)* to notify

intimidable [ɛ̃timidabl] ADJ easily intimidated; **ce n'est pas quelqu'un de facilement i.** he's/she's not someone who is easily intimidated

intimidant, -e [ɛ̃timidɑ̃, -ɑ̃t] ADJ intimidating

intimidateur, -trice [ɛ̃timidatœr, -tris] ADJ intimidating

intimidation [ɛ̃timidasjɔ̃] NF intimidation; **céder à des intimidations** to give in to intimidation; **ils ont usé d'i. pour l'obliger à céder** they used intimidation to force him/her into submission

intimidatrice [ɛ̃timidatris] *voir* **intimidateur**

intimidé, -e [ɛ̃timide] ADJ nervous

intimider [3] [ɛ̃timide] VT **1** *(faire pression sur)* to intimidate; **vous croyez m'i.?** do you think you can frighten me? **2** *(troubler)* to intimidate, to overawe; **il s'est laissé i. par elle** he allowed her to intimidate him; **elle ne se laisse pas facilement i.** she is not easily intimidated

intimisme [ɛ̃timism] NM *Beaux-Arts & Littérature* intimism

intimiste [ɛ̃timist] ADJ *Beaux-Arts & Littérature* intimist; **un film i.** a film that explores the world of feelings

intimité [ɛ̃timite] NF **1** *(vie privée, caractère privé)* privacy; **l'i. du foyer** the privacy of one's own home; **envahir l'i. de qn** to invade sb's privacy; **nous fêterons son succès dans l'i.** we'll celebrate his/her success with just a few close friends; **ils se sont mariés dans la plus stricte i.** they were married in the strictest privacy

2 *(familiarité)* intimacy; **l'i. conjugale** the intimacy of married life; *Euph* **vivre dans l'i. avec qn** to be on intimate terms with sb

3 *(confort)* intimacy, cosiness, snugness; **dans l'i. de la cuisine** in the warmth of the kitchen

4 *Littéraire (profondeur)* intimacy; **dans l'i. de la prière** in the privacy *or* intimacy of prayer;

dans l'i. de nos âmes in the innermost depths of our souls

intitulé [ɛ̃tityle] NM **1** *(d'un livre)* title; *(d'un chapitre)* heading; *(d'un article)* title **2** *Jur (d'un acte)* premises; *(d'un titre)* abstract (of title); *(d'une loi)* long title; **i. d'inventaire** preliminary record of inventory **3** *(d'un compte)* name

intituler [3] [ɛ̃tityle] VT to call; **comment a-t-il intitulé le roman?** what did he call the novel?, what title did he give the novel?; **un film intitulé 'M'** a film called *or* entitled 'M'; **un article intitulé...** an article headed..., an article with the heading...

▸**s'intituler** VPR **1** *(personne)* to give oneself the title of, to call oneself **2** *(œuvre)* to be entitled *or* called

intolérable [ɛ̃tɔlerabl] ADJ **1** *(insupportable)* intolerable, unbearable **2** *(inadmissible)* intolerable, inadmissible, unacceptable; **vos retards sont intolérables** your lateness will not be tolerated; **il est i. que seul l'aîné y ait droit** it's unacceptable that only the older one should be entitled to it

intolérablement [ɛ̃tɔlerabləmɑ̃] ADV intolerably

intolérance [ɛ̃tɔlerɑ̃s] NF **1** *(sectarisme)* intolerance; **i. politique/religieuse** political/religious intolerance **2** *Méd* intolerance; **i. aux analgésiques** intolerance to painkillers; **i. à l'alcool** lack of tolerance to alcohol; **i. alimentaire** allergy (to food); **i. au lait** lactic intolerance

intolérant, -e [ɛ̃tɔlerɑ̃, -ɑ̃t] ADJ intolerant; **une secte intolérante** an intolerant sect; **des parents intolérants** intolerant parents

NM,F intolerant person, bigot

intonatif, -ive [ɛ̃tɔnatif, -iv] ADJ intonational

intonation [ɛ̃tɔnasjɔ̃] NF **1** *(inflexion de la voix)* tone, intonation; **une voix aux intonations très douces** a very soft voice **2** *Ling* intonation

intouchable [ɛ̃tuʃabl] ADJ *(qui ne peut être* → *touché, sanctionné)* untouchable; *(*→ *critiqué)* untouchable, beyond criticism, uncriticizable

NMF *(paria)* untouchable

intox [ɛ̃tɔks] NF *Fam* propaganda▪, brainwashing▪; **tout ça, c'est de l'i.** all that's just propaganda

intoxicant, -e [ɛ̃tɔksikɑ̃, -ɑ̃t] ADJ poisonous, toxic

intoxication [ɛ̃tɔksikasjɔ̃] NF **1** *Méd* poisoning; **i. alimentaire** food poisoning **2** *Fig (propagande)* propaganda, brainwashing

intoxiqué, -e [ɛ̃tɔksike] ADJ **1** *Méd* poisoned; *(par un aliment)* suffering from food poisoning; **i. par l'alcool** intoxicated, drunk; **il fume beaucoup trop, il est complètement i.!** he smokes far too much, he's totally addicted! **2** *(manipulé)* indoctrinated, brainwashed

NM,F **1** *(drogué)* (drug) addict **2** *(endoctriné)* indoctrinated *or* brainwashed person

intoxiquer [3] [ɛ̃tɔksike] VT **1** *Méd* to poison **2** *Fig* to brainwash, to indoctrinate; **une propagande qui intoxique les esprits** propaganda which poisons the mind

▸**s'intoxiquer** VPR to poison oneself; **s'i. avec de la viande/des fraises** to get food poisoning from (eating) meat/strawberries

intra-atomique [ɛ̃traatɔmik] *(pl* **intra-atomiques***)* ADJ intra-atomic

intracardiaque [ɛ̃trakardjak] ADJ *Méd* intracardiac

intracellulaire [ɛ̃traselylɛr] ADJ *Biol* intracellular

intracérébral, -e, -aux, -ales [ɛ̃traserebral, -o] ADJ intracerebral

intracervical, -e, -aux, -ales [ɛ̃traservikal, -o] ADJ *Méd* intracervical

intracommunautaire [ɛ̃trakɔmynotɛr] ADJ *UE* intra-Community

intracrânien, -enne [ɛ̃trakranjɛ̃, -ɛn] ADJ intracranial

intradermique [ɛ̃tradɛrmik] ADJ *Anat* intradermal, intracutaneous

NF *Méd* intradermal *or* intracutaneous injection

intradermo-réaction [ɛ̃tradɛrmɔreaksjɔ̃] *(pl* **intradermo-réactions***)* NF intradermal test

intrados [ɛ̃trado] NM **1** *Aviat* lower surface *(of a wing)* **2** *Archit* intrados

intraduisible [ɛ̃tradɥizibl] ADJ **1** *(texte, mot)* untranslatable; **c'est i.** it's impossible to translate, it can't be translated; **le mot est i.** there is no translation for the word **2** *(indicible)* inexpressible, indescribable

intraitable [ɛ̃trɛtabl] ADJ uncompromising, inflexible; **il est resté i. sur ce point** he remained adamant on this point; **il est i. sur le chapitre de la propreté** he is a stickler for cleanliness

intrajournalier, -ère [ɛ̃traʒurnalje, -ɛr] ADJ *Bourse* intra-day

intramoléculaire [ɛ̃tramɔlekylɛr] ADJ intramolecular

intramontagnard, -e [ɛ̃tramɔ̃taɲar, -ard] ADJ intramontane

intra-muros [ɛ̃tramyros] ADJ INV **quartiers i.** districts within the city boundaries; **Vérone i.** the walled city of Verona; **Londres i.** inner London

ADV **habiter i.** to live in the city itself

intramusculaire [ɛ̃tramyskylɛr] ADJ intramuscular

NF intramuscular injection

Intranet [ɛ̃tranɛt] NM Intranet

intransférabilité [ɛ̃trɑ̃sferabilite] NF untransferability, nontransferability

intransférable [ɛ̃trɑ̃sferabl] ADJ untransferable, not transferable; *Jur (droit)* unassignable

intransigeance [ɛ̃trɑ̃ziʒɑ̃s] NF intransigence; **faire preuve d'i.** to be uncompromising *or Sout* intransigent

intransigeant, -e [ɛ̃trɑ̃ziʒɑ̃, -ɑ̃t] ADJ *(personne)* uncompromising, *Sout* intransigent; *(code moral, ligne de conduite)* uncompromising, strict; **se montrer i. envers** *ou* **vis-à-vis de qn** to take a hard line *or* to be uncompromising with sb; **il est i. sur la discipline** he's a stickler for discipline

NM,F hardliner, uncompromising person

intransitif, -ive [ɛ̃trɑ̃zitif, -iv] ADJ intransitive

NM intransitive (verb)

intransitivement [ɛ̃trɑ̃zitivmɑ̃] ADV intransitively

intransitivité [ɛ̃trɑ̃zitivite] NF intransitivity, intransitiveness

intransmissibilité [ɛ̃trɑ̃smisibilite] NF **1** *Biol* intransmissibility **2** *Jur* untransferability, nontransferability, *Spéc* untransmissibility

intransmissible [ɛ̃trɑ̃smisibl] ADJ **1** *Biol* intransmissible **2** *Jur* untransferable, nontransferable, unassignable

intransportable [ɛ̃trɑ̃spɔrtabl] ADJ **1** *(objet)* untransportable; **c'est i.** it can't be moved *or* transported **2** *(blessé)* **il est i.** he shouldn't be moved, he's unfit to travel

intrant [ɛ̃trɑ̃] NM *Écon* input

intranucléaire [ɛ̃tranykleɛr] ADJ intranuclear

intraoculaire [ɛ̃traɔkylɛr] ADJ intraocular

intra-utérin, -e [ɛ̃trayterɛ̃, -in] *(mpl* **intra-utérins,** *fpl* **intra-utérines***)* ADJ intrauterine; **la vie intra-utérine** life in the womb, *Sout* life in utero

intravasculaire [ɛ̃travaskylɛr] ADJ *Méd* intravascular

intraveineux, -euse [ɛ̃travɛnø, -øz] ADJ intravenous

▫ **intraveineuse** NF intravenous injection

intra vires [ɛ̃travirɛs] ADV *Jur* intra vires

in-trente-deux [intrɑ̃ddø] *Typ* ADJ thirty-twomo

NM thirty-twomo

in-trente-six [intrɑ̃tsis] *Typ* ADJ thirty-sixmo

NM thirty-sixmo

intrépide [ɛ̃trepid] ADJ **1** *(courageux)* intrepid, bold, fearless **2** *(persévérant)* unashamed, unrepentant; **un buveur i.** a hardened drinker; **un bavard i.** a terrible chatterbox; **un menteur i.** a barefaced liar

NMF intrepid *or* brave person

intrépidement [ɛ̃trepidmɑ̃] ADV intrepidly, boldly, fearlessly

intrépidité [ɛ̃trepidite] NF **1** *(courage)* intrepidness, boldness, *Sout* intrepidity; **il s'était battu avec i.** he had fought fearlessly **2** *(persévérance)* **mentir avec i.** to lie shamelessly

intrication [ɛ̃trikasjɔ̃] NF intricacy, intricateness

intrigant, -e [ɛ̃trigɑ̃, -ɑ̃t] ADJ scheming, conniving

NM,F schemer, plotter, *Sout* intriguer

intrigue [ɛ̃trig] NF **1** *(scénario)* plot; **rebondissement de l'i.** twist in the plot; **i. compliquée** intricate plot; **i. policière** detective story; **i. secondaire** subordinate plot, sub-plot **2** *(complot)* intrigue, plot, scheme; **déjouer une i.** to foil a plot; **nouer une i. contre qn** to hatch a plot against sb; **intrigues politiques** political intrigues **3** *Littéraire (liaison amoureuse)* (secret) love affair, *Sout* intrigue

intriguer [3] [ɛ̃trige] VT to intrigue, to puzzle; **son appel m'a intrigué** his/her call puzzled me; **ça m'intrigue** that intrigues me

VI to scheme, to plot, *Sout* to intrigue

intrinsèque [ɛ̃trɛ̃sɛk] ADJ intrinsic

intrinsèquement [ɛ̃trɛ̃sɛkmɑ̃] ADV intrinsically

intriqué, -e [ɛ̃trike] ADJ intricate, entangled

intriquer [3] [ɛ̃trike] VT to confuse

▸**s'intriquer** VPR to become confused

intro [ɛ̃tro] NF *Fam (abrév* **introduction***)* intro; *(musicale)* theme tune▪

introducteur, -trice [ɛ̃trɔdyktœr, -tris] NM,F **1** *(auprès de quelqu'un)* **il fut mon i. auprès de Michel** he was the person who introduced me to Michel **2** *(d'une idée, d'une mode)* initiator; **il fut l'i. du tabac en Europe** he introduced tobacco (in)to Europe

introductif, -ive [ɛ̃trɔdyktif, -iv] ADJ introductory; **cours i.** foundation course; **discours i.** opening remarks

introduction [ɛ̃trɔdyksjɔ̃] NF **1** *(préambule)* introduction; **une i. à la littérature** an introduction to literature; **quelques mots d'i.** a few introductory remarks; **un cours d'i.** an introductory lecture

2 *(contact)* introduction; **j'ai besoin d'introductions** I need to be introduced to people; **après leur i. auprès de l'attaché** after they were introduced to the attaché

3 *(importation)* importing; *(adoption* → *d'un mot, d'un règlement)* introduction; **i. en France de techniques nouvelles/de drogues dures** introducing new techniques/smuggling hard drugs into France

4 *(insertion)* insertion (**dans** into)

5 *Bourse (de valeurs)* introduction; **i. en Bourse** flotation, listing on the Stock Market, *Am* initial public offering

6 *Ordinat* **i. de données** data input

7 *(au rugby)* put-in

introductive [ɛ̃trɔdyktiv] *voir* **introductif**

introductrice [ɛ̃trɔdyktris] *voir* **introducteur**

introduire [98] [ɛ̃trɔdɥir] VT **1** *(insérer)* to insert (**dans** into); **i. une clé dans une serrure** to put *or* to insert a key into a lock

2 *(faire adopter* → *idée, mot)* to introduce, to bring in; *(*→ *règlement)* to institute; *(*→ *mode, produit)* to introduce, to launch; *(illégalement)* to smuggle in; **i. un sujet dans une conversation** to introduce a topic into a conversation; *Jur* **i. une instance** to institute an action at law, to institute legal proceedings; **i. des valeurs en Bourse** to list shares on the stock market; *Écon* **i. un produit sur le marché** to bring out *or* to launch a product onto the market; **i. clandestinement** *(marchandises)* to smuggle in; **i. des armes dans un pays/en France** to smuggle *or* to bring weapons into a country/into France

3 *(présenter)* to introduce; *(faire entrer* → *visiteur)* to show in; **i. qn auprès de** to introduce sb to; **il l'a introduit dans un petit cercle d'amis** he introduced him to a small circle of friends; **on introduisit le visiteur dans la pièce** the visitor was let into *or* shown into the room; **veuillez i. cette dame** please show the lady in; **il fut introduit auprès de la reine** he was ushered in *or* shown in to see the Queen

4 *Ordinat* **i. des données** to input *or* to enter data

5 *Sport* **i. le ballon** to put the ball in

▸**s'introduire** VPR **1 s'i. dans** *(pénétrer dans* → *sujet: clé, piston)* to go *or* to fit into; *(*→ *sujet: eau)* to filter *or* to seep into; *(*→ *sujet: cambrioleur)* to break into; *Fig (*→ *sujet: erreur)* to creep into; **le doute s'est peu à peu introduit dans mon esprit** I began to have doubts; *Ordinat* **s'i. en fraude dans un réseau** to hack into a network

2 s'i. dans *(être accepté par* → *sujet: idée)* to penetrate (into), to spread throughout, *Péj* to infiltrate; **l'expression s'est introduite dans la langue** the expression entered the language

3 s'i. dans *(se faire admettre dans* → *sujet: postulant)* to gain admittance to; *(*→ *sujet: intrigant)* to worm one's way into, to infiltrate

introduit, -e [ɛ̃trɔdɥi, -it] ADJ **il est très bien i. dans ce milieu** he's well established in these circles

introït [ɛ̃trɔit] NM introit

introjection [ɛ̃trɔʒɛksjɔ̃] NF *Psy* introjection

intromission [ɛ̃trɔmisjɔ̃] NF intromission

intron [ɛ̃trɔ̃] **NM** *Biol & Chim* intron
intronisation [ɛ̃trɔnizasjɔ̃] **NF** **1** *(d'un roi, d'un évêque)* enthronement **2** *Fig (mise en place)* establishment; *Pol* **l'i. du nouveau gouvernement** the establishment of the new government
introniser [3] [ɛ̃trɔnize] **VT** **1** *(roi, évêque)* to enthrone; **il s'est fait i. à l'âge de 60 ans** *(roi)* he came to the throne when he was 60; *(évêque)* he was made bishop at the age of 60 **2** *Fig (établir)* to establish; **i. une mode** to establish a fashion
introrse [ɛ̃trɔrs] **ADJ** *Bot* introrse
introspectif, -ive [ɛ̃trɔspɛktif, -iv] **ADJ** introspective
introspection [ɛ̃trɔspɛksjɔ̃] **NF** introspection
introspective [ɛ̃trɔspɛktiv] *voir* **introspectif**
introuvable [ɛ̃truvabl] **ADJ** *(objet égaré)* nowhere to be found; **elle reste i.** she's still missing, her whereabouts are still unknown; **ces pendules sont introuvables aujourd'hui** you can't get hold of these clocks anywhere these days
introversion [ɛ̃trɔvɛrsjɔ̃] **NF** introversion
introverti, -e [ɛ̃trɔvɛrti] **ADJ** introverted
NM,F introvert
introvertir [32] [ɛ̃trɔvɛrtir] **VT** to introvert
intrus, -e [ɛ̃try, -yz] **ADJ** intrusive
NM,F intruder; **elle considère son gendre comme un i.** she treats her son-in-law like an outsider *or* an unwelcome guest; **cherchez l'i.** *(dans une liste de mots)* find the odd one out
intrusif, -ive [ɛ̃tryzif, -iv] **ADJ** intrusive
intrusion [ɛ̃tryzjɔ̃] **NF** **1** *(ingérence)* intrusion; **c'est une i. dans ma vie privée** it's an intrusion into *or* it's a violation of my privacy; **faire i. dans une réunion** to interrupt a meeting; **faire i. dans la vie privée de qn** to intrude upon *or* to invade sb's private life **2** *Géol* intrusion
intubation [ɛ̃tybasjɔ̃] **NF** *Méd* intubation
intuber [3] [ɛ̃tybe] **VT** *Méd* to intubate
intuitif, -ive [ɛ̃tɥitif, -iv] **ADJ** **1** *(perspicace)* intuitive, instinctive **2** *Phil* intuitive
NM,F intuitive person; **c'est un i.** he's very intuitive
intuition [ɛ̃tɥisjɔ̃] **NF** **1** *(faculté)* intuition; **suivre son i.** to follow one's intuition; *Fam* **j'y allais à l'i.** I was acting intuitively; **par i.** intuitively, by intuition; **l'i. féminine** feminine intuition **2** *(pressentiment)* **avoir l'i. d'un drame** to have a premonition of tragedy; **il en a eu l'i.** he knew it intuitively, *Sout* he intuited it; **j'ai l'i. qu'il est rentré** I have a suspicion *or* an inkling *or* a hunch (that) he's home
intuitionnisme [ɛ̃tɥisjɔnism] **NM** intuitionalism
intuitive [ɛ̃tɥitiv] *voir* **intuitif**
intuitivement [ɛ̃tɥitivmɑ̃] **ADV** intuitively, instinctively
intuitivité [ɛ̃tɥitivite] **NF** *Ordinat (de logiciel, d'interface)* intuitiveness
intumescence [ɛ̃tymesɑ̃s] **NF** swelling, *Spéc* intumescence
intumescent, -e [ɛ̃tymesɑ̃, -ɑ̃t] **ADJ** swelling, *Spéc* intumescent
intussusception [ɛ̃tyssysɛpsjɔ̃] **NF** *Méd* intussusception, introsusception
inuit [inɥit] **ADJ INV** Inuit
□ **Inuit NMF INV** Inuit; **les I.** the Inuit *or* Inuits
inuktitut [inuktitut] **NM** Inuktitut
inule [inyl] **NF** *Bot* inula, elecampane; **i. conyze** ploughman's spikenard
inuline [inylin] **NF** *Biol & Chim* inulin
inusable [inyzabl] **ADJ** which will never wear out, hardwearing; **achetez-en une paire, c'est i.!** buy a pair, they'll last (you) forever!
inusité, -e [inyzite] **ADJ** **1** *Ling (mot)* uncommon, not in use (any longer); **le terme est i. de nos jours** the word is no longer used; **les formes inusitées d'un verbe** the rare forms of a verb **2** *Littéraire (inhabituel)* unusual, uncommon; **un bruit i.** an uncommon *or* a strange noise
inusuel, -elle [inyzɥɛl] **ADJ** *Littéraire* unusual, inhabitual
in utero [inytero] **ADJ** in utero
ADV in utero
inutile [inytil] **ADJ** **1** *(qui ne sert à rien → gadget)* useless; *(→ digression, argument)* pointless; *(→ effort)* useless, pointless, vain; *(→ remède)* useless, ineffective; **(il est) i. de m'interroger** there's no point in questioning me; **i. de mentir!** it's no use lying!, lying is useless!; **j'ai écrit, téléphoné, tout s'est révélé i.** I wrote, I phoned, (but) all to no avail
2 *(superflu)* needless, unnecessary; **ces précautions sont inutiles** these precautions serve no purpose; **quelques précisions ne seront pas inutiles** a few explanations will come in useful; **une leçon de conduite supplémentaire ne serait pas i. avant l'examen** an extra driving lesson wouldn't go amiss before the test; **ne me raccompagne pas, c'est i.** you don't have to bring me back, there's no need; **i. de préciser qu'il faut arriver à l'heure** I hardly need to point out that *or* needless to say you have to turn up on time; **i. de demander, sers-toi** just help yourself, there's no need to ask; **i. d'insister, je ne viendrai pas** don't go on about it, I'm not coming
NMF *Péj* useless person; **c'est un i.** he's no use
inutilement [inytilmɑ̃] **ADV** needlessly, unnecessarily, to no purpose
inutilisable [inytilizabl] **ADJ** unusable, useless; **après l'accident, la voiture était i.** the car was *Br* a write-off *or Am* totaled after the accident
inutilisé, -e [inytilize] **ADJ** *(gén)* unused; *(ressources)* untapped, unused
inutilité [inytilite] **NF** *(d'un objet)* uselessness; *(d'une digression, d'un argument)* pointlessness; *(d'un effort, d'une tentative)* uselessness, pointlessness; *(d'un remède)* uselessness, ineffectiveness
□ **inutilités NFPL** *(futilités)* useless information *(UNCOUNT)*
inv. *(abrév écrite* **invariable***)* inv
invagination [ɛ̃vaʒinasjɔ̃] **NF** *Biol & Méd* invagination; **i. intestinale** intestinal intussusception
invaginer [3] [ɛ̃vaʒine] **s'invaginer VPR** *Biol & Méd* to invaginate
invaincu, -e [ɛ̃vɛ̃ky] **ADJ** *(équipe)* unbeaten, undefeated; *(armée)* unvanquished, undefeated; *(maladie)* unconquered
invalidant, -e [ɛ̃validɑ̃, -ɑ̃t] **ADJ** incapacitating, disabling
invalidation [ɛ̃validasjɔ̃] **NF** *(d'une élection)* invalidation, quashing; *(d'une décision juridique)* quashing; *(d'un contrat)* nullification; *(d'un élu)* removal from office
invalide [ɛ̃valid] **ADJ** **1** *(infirme)* disabled **2** *Jur* invalid, null and void **3** *Ordinat (mot de passe, nom du fichier)* invalid
NMF *(infirme)* disabled person, invalid; **i. du travail** = person disabled in an industrial accident
NM **grand i. civil** = officially recognized severely disabled person; **(grand) i. de guerre** = officially recognized war invalid
invalider [3] [ɛ̃valide] **VT** *(élection)* to invalidate, to make invalid, to nullify; *(décision juridique)* to quash; *(élu)* to remove from office
invalidité [ɛ̃validite] **NF** disability, disablement
Invar® [ɛ̃var] **NM** *Métal* Invar®
invariabilité [ɛ̃varjabilite] **NF** invariability
invariable [ɛ̃varjabl] **ADJ** **1** *(constant)* invariable, unchanging; **d'une i. bonne humeur** invariably good-humoured; **rester i. dans ses opinions** to remain unchanging *or* unswerving in one's opinions **2** *Gram* invariable
invariablement [ɛ̃varjabləmɑ̃] **ADV** invariably
invariance [ɛ̃varjɑ̃s] **NF** invariance, invariancy
invariant, -e [ɛ̃varjɑ̃, -ɑ̃t] **ADJ** invariant
NM invariant
invasif, -ive [ɛ̃vazif, -iv] **ADJ** *Méd (traitement)* invasive
invasion [ɛ̃vazjɔ̃] **NF** **1** *Mil* invasion; **armée/troupes d'i.** invading army/troops **2** *(arrivée massive)* invasion, influx; **une i. de rats** an invasion of rats; **l'i. de produits étrangers sur le marché** the flooding of the market by foreign products; **une i. de touristes dans les hôtels** an influx of tourists into the hotels **3** *Méd* **(période d')i.** invasion
invasive [ɛ̃vaziv] *voir* **invasif**
invective [ɛ̃vɛktiv] **NF** invective *(UNCOUNT)*, insult; **il s'est répandu en invectives contre moi** he started hurling abuse at me
invectiver [3] [ɛ̃vɛktive] **VT** to curse, to insult, to heap insults *or* abuse upon
□ **invectiver contre VT IND** to curse
invendable [ɛ̃vɑ̃dabl] **ADJ** unsaleable, unmarketable; **vous m'apportez toujours des marchandises invendables** you always bring me goods that don't sell
invendu, -e [ɛ̃vɑ̃dy] **ADJ** unsold
NM *(gén)* unsold article *or* item; *(journal)* unsold copy; **les invendus** (the) unsold copies
inventaire [ɛ̃vɑ̃tɛr] **NM** **1** *(liste)* inventory; **faire** *ou* **dresser un i.** to draw up an inventory; **nous avons fait l'i. avec la propriétaire** we went through the inventory with the landlady; **l'i. de ses biens** the inventory *or* a detailed list of his/her possessions; **faire l'i. des ressources d'un pays** to assess a country's resources; *Fig* **si je fais l'i. de mes souvenirs** if I take stock of my memories; **i. supplémentaire des monuments historiques** register of listed buildings
2 *Com (procédure)* stocktaking; *(liste)* stocklist, *Am* inventory; **faire** *ou* **dresser un i.** *Br* to stocktake, *Am* to take the inventory; **faire l'i. de la marchandise** to take stock of the goods; **i. d'entrée/de sortie** incoming/outgoing inventory; **i. extracomptable** stocks, *Br* stock-in-trade, *Am* inventories; **i. intermittent** periodical inventory; **i. périodique** periodic inventory; **i. permanent** perpetual inventory; **i. physique** physical inventory; **i. théorique** theoretical inventory; **livre d'i.** inventory *or* stock book
3 *Compta* **i. (comptable)** book inventory; **i. de fin d'année** accounts for the end of the *Br* financial *or Am* fiscal year
4 *Fin (d'un portefeuille de titres)* valuation
5 *Jur* inventory; **dresser l'i. d'une succession** to draw up an inventory of an estate
6 *Naut* inventory

> *Allusion*
> **Un inventaire à la Prévert**
> Jacques Prévert's poem "Inventaire" (from *Paroles*, 1946) consists of a long list of objects, apparently associated at random. This expression is used when describing a lot of miscellaneous items all together in one place, ie a mixed bag.

inventer [3] [ɛ̃vɑ̃te] **VT** **1** *(créer → machine)* to invent; *(→ mot)* to coin; **il n'a pas inventé la poudre** *ou* **l'eau chaude** *ou* **l'eau tiède** *ou* **le fil à couper le beurre** he'll never set the world on fire
2 *(imaginer → jeu)* to think up, to make up, to invent; *(→ système)* to think up, to dream up, to work out, *Péj* to concoct; **je ne sais plus quoi i. pour les amuser** I've run out of ideas trying to keep them amused; *Fam* **ils ne savent plus quoi i.!** what will they think of next!; **qu'est-ce que tu vas i. là?** whatever gave you that idea?, where on earth did you get that idea from?
3 *(forger)* to think up, to make up, to invent; **invente une excuse!** just make up *or* invent some excuse!; **je n'invente rien!** I'm not inventing a thing!; **une histoire inventée de toutes pièces** an entirely made-up story, a complete fabrication
4 *Jur (trésor)* to discover, to find
▸**s'inventer VPR** **1** **ça ne s'invente pas** *(ça ne peut qu'être vrai)* nobody could make up a thing like that, you couldn't make it up
2 **s'i. un passé/de multiples maîtresses** to invent a past/several mistresses for oneself
inventeur, -trice [ɛ̃vɑ̃tœr, -tris] **NM,F** **1** *(d'un appareil, d'un système)* inventor **2** *Jur (d'un trésor)* finder, discoverer **3** *(de fausses nouvelles)* fabricator
inventif, -ive [ɛ̃vɑ̃tif, -iv] **ADJ** inventive, creative, resourceful; **les enfants sont très inventifs** children have a lot of imagination
invention [ɛ̃vɑ̃sjɔ̃] **NF** **1** *Tech & (gén)* invention; **le robot ménager, quelle formidable i.!** what a wonderful invention food processors are!; **grâce à l'i. du laser** thanks to the invention of lasers
2 *(créativité)* inventiveness, creativeness; **avoir de l'i.** to be inventive *or* creative; **manquer d'i.** to be unimaginative; **de mon/ton i.** invented by me/you; **un modèle de mon i.** a pattern I designed myself, one of my own designs
3 *(idée)* invention; **leur liaison est une i. de l'auteur** their love affair was made up by the author *or* is the author's own invention
4 *(mensonge)* invention, fabrication; **c'est (de**

la) pure i. it's all made up *or* sheer invention *or* pure fabrication; **elle n'en est pas à une i. près pour justifier ses retards** she'll make up any excuse to justify being late

5 *Jur (d'un trésor)* finding, discovering

6 *Mus* **inventions à deux voix** two-part inventions

inventive [ɛ̃vɑ̃tiv] *voir* **inventif**

inventivité [ɛ̃vɑ̃tivite] NF inventiveness

inventoriage [ɛ̃vɑ̃tɔrjaʒ] NM stocktaking

inventorier [9] [ɛ̃vɑ̃tɔrje] VT **1** *(gén)* to list, to make a list of **2** *Com* to make a stocklist *or* inventory of **3** *Jur* to make an inventory of, *Sout* to inventory

inventrice [ɛ̃vɑ̃tris] *voir* **inventeur**

invérifiable [ɛ̃verifjabl] ADJ unverifiable, uncheckable

inversable [ɛ̃vɛrsabl] ADJ that cannot be knocked over

inverse [ɛ̃vɛrs] ADJ **1** *(opposé)* opposite; **les voitures qui viennent en sens i.** cars coming the other way *or* from the opposite direction; **dans l'ordre i.** in (the) reverse order, the other way round; **dans le sens i. des aiguilles d'une montre** *Br* anticlockwise, *Am* counterclockwise; **être en proportion** *ou* **raison i. de** to be inversely proportional *or* in inverse proportion to

2 *Géol* reversed

3 *Math* inverse

NM **1** *(contraire)* **l'i.** the opposite, the reverse; **c'est l'i.** it's the other way round; **mais l'i. n'est pas vrai** but the reverse *or* contrary isn't true; **c'est parce que sa femme l'a quitté qu'il s'est mis à boire et non l'i.** he started drinking because his wife left him and not the other way round *or* and not vice versa; **j'aurais dû faire l'i.** I should have done the opposite (of what I did); **supposons l'i. de cette théorie** let's consider the converse of this theory

2 *Math* inverse; **l'i. d'un nombre** the inverse *or* reciprocal of a number

3 *Chim* **i. optique** optical antipode

□ **à l'inverse** ADV conversely

□ **à l'inverse de** PRÉP contrary to, unlike; **à l'i. de ce que tu crois** contrary to what you think; **à l'i. de mon collègue, je pense que...** unlike my colleague, I think that...

inversé, -e [ɛ̃vɛrse] ADJ **1** *Phot* reverse, reversed **2** *Aviat & Géog* inverted

inversement [ɛ̃vɛrsəmɑ̃] ADV **1** *(gén)* conversely; **vous pouvez l'aider, et i. il peut vous renseigner** you can help him, and in return he can give you some information; **i., on pourrait conclure que...** conversely, you could conclude that...; **...ou i.** ...or the other way round, ...or vice versa **2** *Math* inversely; **i. proportionnel à** inversely proportional to

inverser [3] [ɛ̃vɛrse] VT **1** *(intervertir → ordre, tendance)* to reverse; *(→ deux mots)* to invert; *(→ rôles)* to swap; **les rôles ont été totalement inversés** there's been a complete role reversal **2** *Élec & Phot* to reverse

inverseur [ɛ̃vɛrsœr] NM **1** *Élec* reversing switch; **i. de pôles** pole changing switch **2** *Tech* **i. (de marche)** reversing gear **3** *Aviat* **i. de poussée** thrust reverser

inversible [ɛ̃vɛrsibl] ADJ **1** *Math* invertible **2** *Phot* reversible

inversif, -ive [ɛ̃vɛrsif, -iv] ADJ *Gram* inversive

inversion [ɛ̃vɛrsjɔ̃] NF **1** *(changement)* reversal, inversion; **i. des rôles** role reversal **2** *Ling* inversion **3** *Élec* reversal **4** *Aviat* **i. de poussée** thrust reversal; *Géog* **i. de relief** inverted relief; *Ordinat* **i. vidéo** reverse mode; *Chim* **i. de Walden** Walden inversion; *Phot* **pellicule par i.** reversal film **5** *Psy & Vieilli* inversion, homosexuality

invertase [ɛ̃vɛrtaz] NF *Biol & Chim* invertase, sucrase

invertébré, -e [ɛ̃vɛrtebre] ADJ invertebrate

NM invertebrate; **les invertébrés** the invertebrates *or Spéc* Invertebrata

inverti, -e [ɛ̃vɛrti] ADJ *Biol & Chim* **sucre i.** invert sugar

NM,F *Vieilli (homosexuel)* homosexual, invert

invertine [ɛ̃vɛrtin] NF *Biol & Chim* invertase, sucrase

invertir [32] [ɛ̃vɛrtir] VT **1** *(inverser)* to reverse, to invert **2** *Chim* to invert

investigateur, -trice [ɛ̃vɛstigatœr, -tris] ADJ **1** *(avide de savoir)* inquiring, inquisitive, probing; **un esprit fin et i.** a sharp, inquisitive mind **2** *(scrutateur → regard)* searching, scrutinizing; **son regard i. pesait sur moi** I could feel his/her searching gaze

NM,F investigator

investigation [ɛ̃vɛstigasjɔ̃] NF investigation; **investigations** *(policières)* inquiries, investigation; *(scientifiques)* research, investigations

investigatrice [ɛ̃vɛstigatris] *voir* **investigateur**

investiguer [3] [ɛ̃vɛstige] VI to investigate, to research

investir [32] [ɛ̃vɛstir] VT **1** *Fin* to invest (**dans** in); **capital investi** invested capital

2 *(engager → ressources, temps, énergie)* to invest; **j'avais beaucoup investi dans notre amitié** I had invested a lot in our friendship

3 *(d'un pouvoir, d'une fonction)* **i. qn d'une dignité** to invest sb with a function; **i. qn d'un honneur** to bestow an honour upon sb; **i. qn de sa confiance** to place one's trust in sb; **par l'autorité dont je suis investi** by the authority vested in *or* conferred upon me; **elle se sentait investie d'une mission** she felt she'd been entrusted with a mission

4 *(encercler → sujet: armée)* to surround, to besiege; *(→ sujet: police)* to block off, to surround

USAGE ABSOLU *Fin* **i. à court/long terme** to make a short-/long-term investment; **i. dans la pierre** to invest (money) *Br* in bricks and mortar *or Am* in real estate; *Hum* **il est temps que j'investisse dans l'achat d'une nouvelle cravate** it's time I invested in a new tie

►**s'investir** VPR **s'i. dans qch** to put a lot into sth; **s'i. dans son métier** to be involved *or* absorbed in one's job; **une actrice qui s'investit entièrement dans ses rôles** an actress who throws herself heart and soul into every part she plays; **je me suis énormément investie dans le projet** I really put a lot into *or* invested a lot in the project

investissement [ɛ̃vɛstismɑ̃] NM **1** *Fin (action)* investing, investment; *(somme)* investment; **un gros i. de départ** a big initial investment *or* outlay; *Fig* **ne te plains pas d'avoir appris l'arabe, c'est un i. (pour l'avenir)** don't be sorry that you learnt Arabic, it'll stand you in good stead (in the future); **i. de capitaux** capital investment; **i. à court terme** short-term investment; **i. direct** direct investment; **i. éthique** ethical investment; **i. à l'étranger** outward *or* foreign investment; **i. de l'étranger** inward investment; **i. étranger direct** foreign direct investment; **i. immobilier** investment in real estate, property investment; **i. indirect** indirect investment; **i. institutionnel** institutional investment; **i. locatif** investment in rental property; **i. privé** private investment; **i. de productivité** productivity investment; **i. à revenu fixe** fixed-rate investment; **i. à revenu variable** floating-rate investment; **i. en valeurs de redressement** *ou* **de retournement** failure investment

2 *(effort)* investment, commitment; **un important i. en temps** a big commitment in terms of time

3 *Mil (encerclement)* surrounding, siege

□ **d'investissement** ADJ *Fin (société, banque)* investment *(avant n)*; *(dépenses)* capital *(avant n)*

investisseur, -euse [ɛ̃vɛstisœr, -øz] ADJ investing

NM investor; **i. à contre-courant** contrarian investor; **i. institutionnel** institutional investor; **i. minoritaire** minority investor; **i. privé** private investor; **i. providentiel** business angel

investiture [ɛ̃vɛstityr] NF **1** *Pol (d'un candidat)* nomination, selection; *(d'un gouvernement)* vote of confidence **2** *Hist & Rel* investiture

invétéré, -e [ɛ̃vetere] ADJ *(mal, habitude)* ingrained, deep-rooted; *(préjugé)* deeply-held, deep-seated, confirmed; *(buveur)* inveterate, habitual; *(coureur)* inveterate, incorrigible

invétérer [18] [ɛ̃vetere] **s'invétérer** VPR *(mal, habitude)* to become ingrained *or* deep-rooted

invigilant, -e [ɛ̃viʒilɑ̃, -ɑ̃t] ADJ *Littéraire* unwatchful

invincibilité [ɛ̃vɛ̃sibilite] NF invincibility, invincibleness

invincible [ɛ̃vɛ̃sibl] ADJ **1** *(imbattable → héros, nation)* invincible, unconquerable; **avec un courage i.** with invincible courage **2** *(insurmontable → dégoût)* insuperable, insurmountable; *(→ passion)* irresistible **3** *(irréfutable → argument)* invincible, unbeatable

invinciblement [ɛ̃vɛ̃sibləmɑ̃] ADV invincibly, irresistibly

inviolabilité [ɛ̃vjɔlabilite] NF **1** *(gén)* inviolability **2** *Pol* immunity; **l'i. parlementaire** *Br* Parliamentary privilege, *Am* congressional immunity; **i. diplomatique** diplomatic immunity **3** *Jur* **l'i. du domicile** inviolability of the home **4** *Ordinat (de données)* (data) protection

inviolable [ɛ̃vjɔlabl] ADJ **1** *(droit, serment)* inviolable **2** *(parlementaire, ministre)* untouchable, immune **3** *(imprenable)* impregnable, *Sout* inviolable

inviolé, -e [ɛ̃vjɔle] ADJ **1** *(non enfreint → loi)* inviolate, unviolated **2** *(non forcé → lieu)* unforced, inviolate; *(→ forêt)* virgin; **un refuge i.** an inviolate refuge; **le sommet i. de la montagne** the unconquered summit of the mountain

invisibilité [ɛ̃vizibilite] NF invisibility

invisible [ɛ̃vizibl] ADJ **1** *(imperceptible)* invisible; **i. à l'œil nu** invisible *or* not visible to the naked eye **2** *(occulte)* hidden, secret; **une menace i.** a hidden threat **3** *(non disponible)* unavailable; **tu es devenu i. dernièrement** you've been rather elusive recently

□ **invisibles** NMPL *Écon* **les invisibles** *(échanges)* invisibles, invisible trade; *(exportations)* invisibles, invisible exports; **la balance des invisibles** the balance of invisible trade

invisiblement [ɛ̃vizibləmɑ̃] ADV invisibly

invitant, -e [ɛ̃vitɑ̃, -ɑ̃t] ADJ **puissance invitante** host country

invitation [ɛ̃vitasjɔ̃] NF **1** *(requête)* invitation; **une i. à un cocktail** an invitation to a cocktail party; **à** *ou* **sur l'i. de nos amis** at the invitation of our friends; **venir sans i.** to come uninvited; **répondre à une i.** to reply to an invitation; **sur i.** by invitation only; **carton d'i.** invitation card; **lettre d'i.** letter of *or* written invitation

2 *(incitation)* invitation, provocation; **ton sac grand ouvert est une i. au vol** leaving your bag wide open is an (open) invitation to thieves; **ce film est une i. au voyage** this film makes you want to travel

invite [ɛ̃vit] NF **1** *(invitation)* invitation, request; **répondre aux invites de qn** to respond to sb's requests **2** *Cartes* lead **3** *Ordinat* prompt; **i. du DOS** DOS prompt; **i. du système** system prompt

invité, -e [ɛ̃vite] NM,F guest; **i. de marque** distinguished guest; **i. d'honneur** guest of honour

inviter [3] [ɛ̃vite] VT **1** *(ami, convive)* to invite; **i. qn à déjeuner** to invite *or* to ask sb to lunch; **i. qn chez soi** to invite sb (over) to one's house; **je ne les inviterai plus** I won't invite *or* ask them (round) again; **demain nous sommes invités** we've been invited out tomorrow; **je regrette, je suis déjà invité** I'm sorry, but I have a previous engagement; **puis-je vous i. à danser?** may I have this dance?; **on s'est fait i. à la première par un copain** we were invited to the premiere by a friend; **tu ne peux pas t'arranger pour te faire i.?** can't you swing it so that you get invited?

2 *(inciter)* **i. qn à entrer** to ask sb (to come) in; **d'un signe de la tête, il m'invita à me taire** he nodded to me to keep quiet; **je vous invite à observer une minute de silence** I call upon you to observe a minute's silence; **j'invite tous les locataires mécontents à écrire à l'association** may I suggest that all dissatisfied tenants write to the association; **vous êtes invités à me suivre** would you be so kind as to follow me; **vous êtes invités à sortir par l'autre porte** please use the other door when leaving; **les passagers à destination de Rome sont invités à se présenter à la porte d'embarquement numéro deux** passengers for Rome are requested to proceed to gate number two; **i. à la réflexion** to be thought-provoking; **ce temps invite à la paresse** this weather tends to make you feel lazy

USAGE ABSOLU *Fam (payer)* **allez, c'est moi qui invite!** it's on me!

VI *Cartes* to lead

►**s'inviter** VPR to invite oneself

in vitro [invitro] ADJ INV in vitro
  ADV in vitro
invivable [ɛ̃vivabl] ADJ **1** *(personne)* impossible, unbearable, insufferable **2** *(situation)* unbearable, intolerable **3** *(habitation)* **cette maison est devenue i.** this house has become impossible to live in
in vivo [invivo] ADJ INV in vivo
  ADV in vivo
invocateur, -trice [ɛ̃vɔkatœr, -tris] NM,F invoker
invocation [ɛ̃vɔkasjɔ̃] NF invocation; **i. aux Muses** invocation to the Muses
  ❏ **sous l'invocation de** PRÉP *Rel (dédié à → sujet: lieu de culte)* dedicated to, under the protection of
invocatoire [ɛ̃vɔkatwar] ADJ invocatory
invocatrice [ɛ̃vɔkatris] *voir* **invocateur**
involontaire [ɛ̃vɔlɔ̃tɛr] ADJ **1** *(machinal)* involuntary; **j'eus un mouvement de recul i.** I recoiled involuntarily *or* instinctively
  2 *(non délibéré)* unintentional; **c'était i.** it was unintentional, I didn't do it on purpose; **une erreur i.** an inadvertent error
  3 *(non consentant)* unwilling, reluctant; **j'ai été le témoin i. de sa déchéance** I was the reluctant witness of his/her downfall
  4 *Anat & Physiol* involuntary
  5 *Jur* involuntary
involontairement [ɛ̃vɔlɔ̃tɛrmɑ̃] ADV unintentionally, unwittingly, without meaning to; **être i. mêlé à une affaire de contrebande** to be unwittingly involved in a smuggling operation; **si je vous ai vexé, c'est tout à fait i.** if I've offended you, it really wasn't intentional *or* I really didn't mean to
involucelle [ɛ̃vɔlysɛl] NM *Bot* involucel
involucre [ɛ̃vɔlykr] NM *Bot* involucre
involuté, -e [ɛ̃vɔlyte] ADJ involuted
involutif, -ive [ɛ̃vɔlytif, -iv] ADJ **1** *Math* involutional **2** *Méd* involutionary
involution [ɛ̃vɔlysjɔ̃] NF involution
invoquer [3] [ɛ̃vɔke] VT **1** *(avoir recours à → argument, prétexte)* to put forward; *(→ article de loi)* to refer to, to cite; **i. son ignorance** to plead ignorance **2** *(en appeler à → personne)* to invoke, to appeal to; *(→ dieu, esprit)* to invoke; *(→ aide)* to call upon; **i. la Muse** to invoke the Muse
invraisemblable [ɛ̃vrɛsɑ̃blabl] ADJ **1** *(improbable → hypothèse, excuse)* unlikely, improbable, implausible **2** *(incroyable → histoire)* incredible, unbelievable, amazing **3** *(bizarre → tenue, personne)* weird, incredible, extraordinary **4** *(en intensif)* **elle a un toupet i.!** she has an amazing cheek!
  NM **l'i.** the incredible
invraisemblablement [ɛ̃vrɛsɑ̃blabləmɑ̃] ADV improbably, incredibly, unbelievably
invraisemblance [ɛ̃vrɛsɑ̃blɑ̃s] NF **1** *(caractère improbable)* unlikelihood, unlikeliness, improbability **2** *(fait)* improbability; **le scénario est truffé d'invraisemblances** the script is filled with implausible details
invulnérabilité [ɛ̃vylnerabilite] NF invulnerability
invulnérable [ɛ̃vylnerabl] ADJ **1** *(physiquement)* invulnerable **2** *(moralement)* invulnerable; **le temps l'a rendue i. aux critiques** with the passage of time she's become invulnerable *or* immune *or* impervious to criticism **3** *(socialement)* invulnerable; **du fait de ses relations, il est i.** because of his contacts he is unassailable
Io [jo] NPR *Myth* Io
iodate [jɔdat] NM *Chim* iodate
iode [jɔd] NM *Chim* iodine
iodé, -e [jɔde] ADJ *Chim* iodized, iodated
ioder [3] [jɔde] VT *Chim* to iodize, to iodate
iodhydrique [jɔdidrik] ADJ M *Chim* hydriodic
iodique [jɔdik] ADJ M *Chim* iodic
iodisme [jɔdism] NM *Méd* iodism
iodler [jɔdle] = **jodler**
iodoforme [jɔdɔfɔrm] NM *Méd & Pharm* iodoform
iodure [jɔdyr] NM *Chim* iodide
ioduré, -e [jɔdyre] ADJ *Chim* iodized
iodurer [3] [jɔdyre] VT *Chim* to iodinate
IOM [ioɛm] NM *Pétr (abrév* **indice d'octane moteur**) MON
ion [jɔ̃] NM ion
ionien, -enne [jɔnjɛ̃, -ɛn] ADJ **1** *(de l'Ionie → gén)*

Ionian; *(→ dialecte)* Ionic **2** *Mus* **mode i.** Ionian mode
  NM *(dialecte)* Ionic
  ❏ **Ionien, -enne** NM,F Ionian
ionique [jɔnik] ADJ **1** *(de l'Ionie)* Ionic **2** *Archit* Ionic **3** *Chim & Phys* ionic **4** *Élec* ionic, ion *(avant n)* **5** *Astron* ion *(avant n)*
ionisant, -e [jɔnizɑ̃, -ɑ̃t] ADJ *Chim & Phys* ionizing
ionisation [jɔnizasjɔ̃] NF *Chim & Phys* ionization
ionisé, -e [jɔnize] ADJ *Chim & Phys* ionized
ioniser [3] [jɔnize] VT *Chim & Phys* to ionize
ioniseur [jɔnizœr] NM *Chim & Phys* ionizer
ionogramme [jɔnɔgram] NM ionogram
ionomère [jɔnɔmɛr] NM *Chim* ionomer
ionone [jɔnɔn] NF *Chim* ionone
ionoplastie [jɔnɔplasti] NF cathode sputtering
ionosphère [jɔnɔsfɛr] NF ionosphere
ionosphérique [jɔnɔsferik] ADJ ionospheric
ionotropique [jɔnɔtrɔpik] ADJ *Physiol (récepteur)* ionotropic
IOR [ioɛr] NM *Pétr (abrév* **indice d'octane recherche**) RON
iota [jɔta] NM INV iota; **ne changez pas votre article d'un i.** *ou* **un i. dans votre article** don't change your article one iota *or* a thing in your article; **il n'a pas bougé d'un i.** *(dans ses convictions)* he didn't shift *or* budge an inch
iouler [jule] = **jodler**
iourte [jurt] = **yourte**
Iowa [ajowa] NM **l'I.** Iowa; **dans l'I.** in Iowa
IP [ipe] NM *(abrév* **indice de protection**) SPF
IPC [ipese] NM *Mktg (abrév* **indice des prix à la consommation**) CPI
ipé [ipɛ] NM ipé *(rainforest hardwood tree)*
ipéca [ipeka], **ipécacuan(h)a** [ipekakwana] NM ipecac, ipecacuanha
Iphigénie [ifiʒeni] NPR *Myth* Iphigenia

'Iphigénie en Aulide' *Gluck* 'Iphigenia in Aulis'

'Iphigénie en Tauride' *Gluck* 'Iphigenia in Tauris'

iPod® [ipɔd] NM iPod®
ipomée [ipɔme] NF *Bot* ipomea
IPP [ipepe] NM *Écon (abrév* **indice des prix à la production**) PPI
ippon [ipɔn] NM ippon
IPR [ipeɛr] NM *(abrév* **Inspecteur pédagogique régional**) = locally-based education inspector
ipséité [ipseite] NF *Phil* ipseity
ipso facto [ipsofakto] ADV ipso facto, by that very fact
ipso jure [ipsoʒyre] ADV *Jur* ipso jure, by the law itself
Ipsos [ipsos] NM = French market research institute

-IQUE [ik] SUFF

This suffix containing the idea of RELATING TO, BELONGING TO is a very productive one, especially in the areas of science and technology, where it is used to create words that can sometimes be both adjectives and nouns.

● It can be added to a noun, itself sometimes ending in the suffix **-ie** or **-isme**, and is often, in that case, translated by the English suffix *-ic*, eg: **économique** (from *économie*) economical, economic; **bureaucratique** (from *bureaucratie*) bureaucratic; **sadique** (from *sadisme*) sadistic; **alcoolique** (from *alcool*) alcoholic
● It can also be found at the end of a noun to form a feminine noun from the field of science or technology. The English equivalent is often *-ics*, eg: **robotique** robotics; **domotique** home automation; **avionique** avionics
● The suffixation can be based directly on a Latin or Greek radical. The English translation often sounds less specialized than the French word, eg: **domotique** (from the Latin *domus*, house) home automation; **ludique** (from the Latin *ludus*, game) play (adj); **bionique** (from the Greek *bios*, life) bionics
● The suffix **-ique** is used quite productively in French slang to form derogatory adjectives such as: **merdique** rubbish, shitty; **chiatique: t'es vraiment chiatique!** you're a bloody pain!; **bordélique** messy, chaotic

IR [iɛr] ADJ *(abrév* **infrarouge**) IR
IRA [ira] NF *(abrév* **Irish Republican Army**) IRA; **l'I. provisoire** the Provisional IRA
ira *etc voir* **aller²**
Irak [irak] NM **l'I.** Iraq; **vivre en I.** to live in Iraq; **aller en I.** to go to Iraq
irakien, -enne [irakjɛ̃, -ɛn] ADJ Iraqi
  NM *(langue)* Iraqi
  ❏ **Irakien, -enne** NM,F Iraqi
Iráklion [irakliɔ̃] NM Iraklion
Iran [irɑ̃] NM **l'I.** Iran; **vivre en I.** to live in Iran; **aller en I.** to go to Iran
iranien, -enne [iranjɛ̃, -ɛn] ADJ Iranian
  NM *(langue)* Iranian
  ❏ **Iranien, -enne** NM,F Iranian
Iraq [irak] = **Irak**
iraquien [irakjɛ̃] = **irakien**
irascibilité [irasibilite] NF irritability, testiness, *Sout* irascibility
irascible [irasibl] ADJ short-tempered, testy, *Sout* irascible
IRBM [iɛrbeɛm] NM *(abrév* **intermediate range ballistic missile**) IRBM
IRC [iɛrse] NM *Ordinat (abrév* **Internet Relay Chat**) IRC
ire [ir] NF *Littéraire* ire, wrath
irénique [irenik] ADJ irenic
irénisme [irenism] NM *Rel* irenicism
iridacée [iridase] *Bot* NF member of the iris family *or Spéc* the Iridaceae
  ❏ **iridacées** NFPL iris family, *Spéc* Iridaceae
iridectomie [iridɛktɔmi] NF *Méd* iridectomy
iridescent, -e [iridɛsɑ̃, -ɑ̃t] ADJ iridescent
iridié, -e [iridje] ADJ *Chim* iridic
iridien, -enne [iridjɛ̃, -ɛn] ADJ *Méd* iridian
iridium [iridjɔm] NM *Chim* iridium
iridodiagnostique [iridodjagnɔstik] NM = **iridologie**
iridologie [iridɔlɔʒi] NF iridology
iridologue [iridɔlɔg] NMF iridologist
irien, -enne [irjɛ̃, -ɛn] ADJ *Méd* iridian
Iris [iris] NPR *Myth* Iris
iris [iris] NM **1** *Anat* iris **2** *Bot* iris, flag; **i. fétide** stinking iris; **i. de Florence** orris; **i. jaune** *ou* **des marais** yellow flag *or* iris **3** *Phot* iris (diaphragm) **4** *Littéraire* (arc-en-ciel) iris, rainbow
irisable [irizabl] ADJ *Opt* capable of iridescence *or Spéc* irisation
irisation [irizasjɔ̃] NF *Opt* iridescence, *Spéc* irisation
irisé, -e [irize] ADJ iridescent
iriser [3] [irize] VT to make iridescent, *Spéc* to irisate
  ▸ **s'iriser** VPR to become iridescent
irish-coffee, irish coffee [ajriʃkɔfi] *(pl* **irish(-)coffees**) NM Irish coffee
irish-terrier [ajriʃterje] *(pl* **irish-terriers**) NM Irish terrier
iritis [iritis] NF *Méd* iritis
irlandais, -e [irlɑ̃dɛ, -ɛz] ADJ Irish
  NM *(langue)* Irish
  ❏ **Irlandais, -e** NM,F Irishman, *f* Irishwoman; **les I. the Irish; un I. du Nord** = a Northern Irish person; **les I. du Nord** the Northern Irish
Irlande [irlɑ̃d] NF **l'I.** Ireland; **vivre en I.** to live in Ireland; **aller en I.** to go to Ireland; **l'I. du Nord/Sud** Northern/Southern Ireland; **la mer d'I.** the Irish Sea; **la République d'I.** the Irish Republic
IRM [iɛrɛm] NF *Méd (abrév* **imagerie par résonance magnétique**) MRI
IRMf [iɛrɛmɛf] NF *Méd (abrév* **imagerie par résonance magnétique fonctionnelle**) fMRI
IRMN [iɛrɛmɛn] NF *Méd (abrév* **imagerie par résonance magnétique nucléaire**) NMRI
irone [irɔn] NF *Chim* irone
ironie [irɔni] NF irony; **l'i. du sort a voulu que je le rencontre** as fate would have it, I bumped into him
ironique [irɔnik] ADJ ironic, ironical; **regarder qn d'un air i.** to look at sb quizzically
ironiquement [irɔnikmɑ̃] ADV ironically; **répondre i. à une question** to answer a question tongue-in-cheek *or* ironically
ironiser [3] [irɔnize] VI to be sarcastic; **i. sur** to be sarcastic about; **il ne cesse d'i. sur les intentions du parti** he keeps being sarcastic about the party's intentions
ironiste [irɔnist] NMF ironist

iroquoien, -enne [irɔkɔjɛ̃, -ɛn] *Ling* **ADJ** Iroquoian
NM,F Iroquoian

iroquois, -e [irɔkwa, -az] **ADJ** Iroquois, Iroquoian
NM *(langue)* Iroquoian
▫ **Iroquois, -e NM,F** Iroquois
▫ **iroquoise NF** mohican (hairstyle); **coiffé à l'iroquoise** with a mohican (hairstyle)

IRPP [iɛrpepe] **NM** *(abrév* **impôt sur le revenu des personnes physiques***)* income tax

irrachetable [iraʃtabl] **ADJ** unredeemable, unreturnable

irradiant, -e [iradjɑ̃, -ɑ̃t] **ADJ** irradiant

irradiation [iradjasjɔ̃] **NF 1** *(rayonnement)* radiation, irradiation **2** *(exposition → d'une personne, d'un tissu)* irradiation, exposure to radiation; **il y a des risques d'i.** there is a risk of irradiation *or* of being exposed to radiation **3** *Méd (traitement)* irradiation **4** *Physiol* **irradiations douloureuses** radiating pain **5** *Anat* radiation **6** *Phot* halation

irradier [9] [iradje] **VI 1** *Phys* to radiate; **les rayons du foyer lumineux irradient de tous côtés** light waves radiate in all directions **2** *(se propager)* to spread; **la douleur irradiait dans toute la jambe** the pain spread to the whole leg **3** *Littéraire (se diffuser → bonheur)* to radiate; **la joie irradie autour d'elle** she radiates joy
VT 1 *(soumettre à un rayonnement)* to irradiate; **se faire i.** to be exposed to radiation **2** *Littéraire (répandre → bonheur)* to radiate

irraisonné, -e [irɛzɔne] **ADJ** unreasoned, irrational

irrationalisme [irasjɔnalism] **NM** irrationalism

irrationaliste [irasjɔnalist] **ADJ** irrationalist
NMF irrationalist

irrationalité [irasjɔnalite] **NF** irrationality

irrationnel, -elle [irasjɔnɛl] **ADJ** *(gén) & Math* irrational; **de façon irrationnelle** irrationally
NM 1 *(gén)* **l'i.** the irrational **2** *Math* irrational (number)

irrattrapable [iratrapabl] **ADJ** *(erreur)* irredeemable, which cannot be rectified; *(retard)* which cannot be made up

irréalisable [irealizabl] **ADJ** *(ambition)* unrealizable, unachievable; *(idée, projet)* unworkable, unfeasible, impracticable; *Fin (valeurs)* unrealizable

irréalisé, -e [irealize] **ADJ** unrealized, unachieved; **un espoir i.** an unrealized hope

irréalisme [irealism] **NM** lack of realism

irréaliste [irealist] **ADJ** unrealistic
NMF unrealistic person, (pipe) dreamer

irréalité [irealite] **NF** unreality

irrecevabilité [irəsəvabilite] **NF 1** *(d'un argument)* unacceptability **2** *Jur* inadmissibility

irrecevable [irəsəvabl] **ADJ 1** *(inacceptable)* unacceptable **2** *Jur* inadmissible

irréconciliable [irekɔ̃siljabl] **ADJ** *(ennemis, adversaires)* irreconcilable, unreconcilable; *(haine)* implacable; **ils sont irréconciliables** nothing can reconcile them

irrécouvrable [irekuvrabl] **ADJ** irrecoverable

irrécupérable [irekyperabl] **ADJ 1** *(argent)* irrecoverable **2** *(irréparable → objet)* beyond repair **3** *(personne)* irremediable, beyond redemption

irrécusabilité [irekyzabilite] **NF** *(de preuves)* indisputability, unchallengeability; *(d'un témoignage, d'un juge)* unimpeachability

irrécusable [irekyzabl] **ADJ 1** *(indéniable → signe, vérité)* undeniable; *(→ preuves)* indisputable **2** *Jur (témoignage, juge)* unimpeachable

irrédentisme [iredɑ̃tism] **NM** *Pol* irredentism

irrédentiste [iredɑ̃tist] *Pol* **ADJ** irredentist
NMF irredentist

irréductibilité [iredyktibilite] **NF 1** *(d'un obstacle)* insurmountability, intractability; *(d'un ennemi)* implacability **2** *Chim & Math* irreducibility

irréductible [iredyktibl] **ADJ 1** *(insurmontable → conflit, différence)* insurmountable, intractable, insoluble; *(→ obstacle)* insurmountable
2 *(inflexible)* invincible, implacable, uncompromising; **il s'est fait quelques ennemis irréductibles** he's made himself a few implacable enemies; **derrière cette réussite, il y a la détermination i. d'une femme** this success is based on the invincible *or* indomitable determination of a woman; **leur opposition au pouvoir en place est i.** their opposition to the powers that be is implacable
3 *Math & Chim* irreducible; **fraction i.** irreducible fraction
NMF diehard, hardliner; **les irréductibles de (la) gauche/droite** the left-wing/right-wing diehards

irréductiblement [iredyktibləmɑ̃] **ADV** implacably

irréel, -elle [ireɛl] **ADJ** unreal; **des paysages irréels** unreal landscapes
NM 1 *(gén) & Phil* **l'i.** the unreal **2** *Gram* **l'i. du présent/passé** the hypothetical present/past

irréfléchi, -e [irefleʃi] **ADJ** *(acte, parole)* rash, reckless; *(geste, mouvement)* instinctive; *(personne)* unthinking, rash, reckless

irréflexion [ireflɛksjɔ̃] **NF** rashness, recklessness; **faire preuve d'i.** to be rash *or* reckless

irréformable [irefɔrmabl] **ADJ** *Jur (décision)* final, unchallengeable

irréfragabilité [irefragabilite] **NF** irrefutability

irréfragable [irefragabl] **ADJ** indisputable, *Sout* irrefragable

irréfragablement [irefragabləmɑ̃] **ADV** irrefutably

irréfutabilité [irefytabilite] **NF** irrefutability, indisputability

irréfutable [irefytabl] **ADJ** irrefutable, indisputable; **il a prouvé de manière i. que…** he proved irrefutably *or* indisputably that…

irréfutablement [irefytabləmɑ̃] **ADV** indisputably, irrefutably

irréfuté [irefyte] **ADJ** unrefuted

irrégularité [iregylarite] **NF 1** *(de forme, de rythme)* irregularity, unevenness; *(d'un terrain, d'une surface)* unevenness; **une i. du rythme cardiaque** an irregular heartbeat
2 *(en qualité)* unevenness, patchiness; **l'i. de son visage** the irregularity of his/her features; **l'i. de votre travail ne permet pas le passage dans le groupe supérieur** (the quality of) your work is too uneven *or* erratic for you to move up into the next group
3 *(surface irrégulière → bosse)* bump; *(→ creux)* hole; **les irrégularités du sol** the unevenness of the ground; **les irrégularités du relief** the hilliness of the area
4 *(infraction)* irregularity; **une i. dans son permis de séjour** something irregular in his/her residence permit; **il y a des irrégularités dans les comptes** there are a few irregularities *or* discrepancies in the accounts; **i. comptable** accounting irregularity
5 *Jur* **i. de fond** substantial irregularity; **i. de forme** formal irregularity

irrégulier, -ère [iregylje, -ɛr] **ADJ 1** *(dessin, rythme)* irregular, uneven; *(terrain, surface)* uneven; *(traits, écriture, pouls)* irregular; *(respiration)* erratic, irregular; *(expansion)* uneven, erratic; **je m'entraîne de façon irrégulière** I train intermittently *or* sporadically; **nous avons des horaires irréguliers** we don't work regular hours
2 *(qualité, travail)* uneven; **vos prestations sont irrégulières** your work is uneven *or* erratic; **j'étais un étudiant i.** my work was erratic when I was a student
3 *(illégal)* irregular; **ils sont en situation irrégulière dans le pays** their residence papers are not in order; **des retraits de fonds irréguliers** unauthorized withdrawals
4 *Mil* irregular; **les soldats des troupes irrégulières** the irregulars
5 *Bot, Géom & Gram* irregular
NM *Mil* irregular (soldier)

irrégulièrement [iregyljɛrmɑ̃] **ADV 1** *(de façon non uniforme)* irregularly, unevenly **2** *(de façon illégale)* irregularly, illegally **3** *(de façon inconstante)* irregularly, erratically

irréligieux, -euse [ireliʒjø, -øz] **ADJ** irreligious

irréligion [ireliʒjɔ̃] **NF** irreligion

irremboursable [irɑ̃bursabl] **ADJ** *(obligation)* irredeemable

irrémédiable [iremedjabl] **ADJ** *(rupture)* irreparable, irretrievable; *(dégâts)* irreparable, irreversible; *(maladie)* incurable, fatal; **son mal est i.** his/her illness is incurable *or Sout* irremediable; **les conséquences pour l'environnement sont irrémédiables** the effects on the environment are irreparable *or* irreversible
NM l'i. a été commis irreversible harm has been done

irrémédiablement [iremedjabləmɑ̃] **ADV** irremediably, irretrievably; **tout espoir de le retrouver est i. perdu** we have definitely lost all hope of (ever) finding him

irrémissible [iremisibl] **ADJ** *Littéraire* **1** *(impardonnable)* unpardonable, *Sout* irremissible **2** *(inexorable)* implacable, inexorable

irrémissiblement [iremisibləmɑ̃] **ADV** *Littéraire* relentlessly, inexorably, *Sout* irremissibly

irremplaçable [irɑ̃plasabl] **ADJ** irreplaceable; **personne n'est i.** no one is indispensable

irréparable [ireparabl] **ADJ 1** *(montre, voiture)* unrepairable, beyond repair; **ma radio est i.** my radio is beyond repair **2** *(erreur, tort, perte)* irreparable; *(affront)* unpardonable
NM commettre l'i. to go beyond the point of no return

irréparablement [ireparabləmɑ̃] **ADV** *(définitivement)* irreparably; **sa réputation est i. atteinte** his/her reputation has suffered an irreparable blow

irrépréhensible [ireprеɑ̃sibl] **ADJ** *Littéraire* irreproachable, irreprehensible

irrépressible [irepresibl] **ADJ** irrepressible

irréprochable [ireprɔʃabl] **ADJ 1** *(personne, conduite)* irreproachable; **personne n'est i.** nobody's beyond *or* above reproach **2** *(tenue)* impeccable; *(travail)* impeccable, faultless; **d'une propreté i.** immaculate; **des ongles irréprochables** immaculate nails

irréprochablement [ireprɔʃabləmɑ̃] **ADV** irreproachably, impeccably, faultlessly

irrésistible [irezistibl] **ADJ 1** *(séduisant)* irresistible; **un sourire i.** an irresistible smile **2** *(irrépressible → besoin)* compelling, pressing; *(→ envie)* irresistible, uncontrollable, compelling; **elle fut prise d'une i. envie de rire** she had an irresistible urge to laugh

irrésistiblement [irezistibləmɑ̃] **ADV** irresistibly; **i. tenté par le gâteau** irresistibly tempted by the cake

irrésolu, -e [irezɔly] **ADJ 1** *(personne)* indecisive, unresolved, *Sout* irresolute **2** *(problème)* unsolved, unresolved
NM,F irresolute person, *Péj* ditherer

irrésolution [irezɔlysjɔ̃] **NF** irresoluteness, indecisiveness

irrespect [irɛspɛ] **NM** disrespect, lack of respect; **leur i. envers leur mère/l'autorité** their lack of respect for their mother/of authority

irrespectueuse [irɛspɛktɥøz] *voir* **irrespectueux**

irrespectueusement [irɛspɛktɥøzmɑ̃] **ADV** disrespectfully

irrespectueux, -euse [irɛspɛktɥø, -øz] **ADJ** disrespectful, lacking in respect (**envers** towards)

irrespirable [irɛspirabl] **ADJ 1** *(air → trop chaud)* stifling, stuffy; *(→ toxique)* unsafe, not fit to breathe; **aère ta chambre, c'est i. ici!** air your room, it's stifling in here! **2** *(oppressant → ambiance)* unbearable, stifling; **j'ai trouvé l'ambiance i. à la maison** I found the atmosphere unbearable at home

irresponsabilité [irɛspɔ̃sabilite] **NF 1** *(légèreté)* irresponsibility; **agir avec une totale i.** to behave totally irresponsibly **2** *(du chef de l'État)* non-accountability; **i. du chef de l'État** = immunity of the Head of State; **i. parlementaire** *Br* parliamentary privilege, *Am* congressional immunity

irresponsable [irɛspɔ̃sabl] **ADJ 1** *(inconséquent)* irresponsible; **de manière i.** irresponsibly **2** *Jur* (legally) incapable
NMF irresponsible person; **espèce d'i.!** you irresponsible idiot!

irrétrécissabilité [iretresisabilite] **NF** unshrinkable nature

irrétrécissable [iretresisabl] **ADJ** unshrinkable

irrévérence [ireverɑ̃s] **NF 1** *(irrespect)* irreverence; **avec i.** irreverently **2** *(remarque)* irreverent remark; *(acte)* irreverent act

irrévérencieuse [ireverɑ̃sjøz] *voir* **irrévérencieux**

irrévérencieusement [ireverɑ̃sjøzmɑ̃] **ADV** irreverently

irrévérencieux, -euse [ireverɑ̃sjø, -øz] **ADJ** irreverent

irréversibilité [irevɛrsibilite] **NF** irreversibility

irréversible [irevɛrsibl] **ADJ** *(gén) & Chim & Phys* irreversible; **le processus est i.** the process is irreversible

irréversiblement [irevɛrsibləmɑ̃] ADV irreversibly
irrévocabilité [irevɔkabilite] NF irrevocability, finality
irrévocable [irevɔkabl] ADJ *(gén)* irrevocable; *(verdict)* irrevocable, final
irrévocablement [irevɔkabləmɑ̃] ADV irrevocably
irrigable [irigabl] ADJ irrigable, suitable for irrigation
irrigateur [irigatœr] NM *Agr & Méd* irrigator
irrigation [irigasjɔ̃] NF **1** *Agr & Méd* irrigation **2** *Physiol* **l'i. des tissus par les vaisseaux sanguins** the supply of blood to the tissues by blood vessels
irriguer [3] [irige] VT **1** *Agr & Méd* to irrigate **2** *Physiol* **si le cerveau n'est pas irrigué pendant plus de trois minutes** if there is no blood supply to the brain for more than three minutes
irritabilité [iritabilite] NF **1** *(irascibilité)* irritability, quick temper **2** *Méd* irritability
irritable [iritabl] ADJ **1** *(colérique)* irritable, easily annoyed **2** *Méd* irritable
irritant, -e [iritɑ̃, -ɑ̃t] ADJ **1** *(agaçant)* irritating, annoying, aggravating **2** *Méd* irritant
NM **1** *Méd* irritant **2** *Can (source de mécontentement)* irritating aspect *or* point
irritatif, -ive [iritatif, -iv] ADJ irritative
irritation [iritasjɔ̃] NF **1** *(agacement)* irritation, annoyance; **avec i.** irritably, petulantly **2** *Méd* irritation; **i. cutanée** skin irritation
irrité, -e [irite] ADJ **1** *(exaspéré)* irritated, annoyed (**contre** with); **d'un ton i.** irritably, peevishly; **d'un air i.** irritably **2** *Méd* irritated
irriter [3] [irite] VT **1** *(agacer)* to irritate, to annoy; **ses petites manies m'irritent** his/her little quirks get on my nerves **2** *Méd* to irritate **3** *Littéraire (exacerber → passion, désir)* to inflame, to arouse; *(→ curiosité)* to excite
▸**s'irriter** VPR **1** *(s'énerver)* to get annoyed *or* irritated (**contre qn/de qch** with sb/at sth) **2** *Méd* to become irritated
irruption [irypsjɔ̃] NF **1** *(entrée)* breaking *or* bursting *or* storming in; **ils n'ont pas pu empêcher l'i. des spectateurs sur le terrain** they were unable to stop spectators from storming *or* invading the *Br* pitch *or Am* field; **l'i. des eaux dans les cultures** the (sudden) flooding of the fields; **faire i. chez qn** to burst in on sb; **faire i. dans** to burst *or* to barge into
2 *(émergence)* upsurge, sudden development; **l'i. du fondamentalisme dans le monde** the worldwide upsurge of fundamentalism
IRSM [iɛrɛsɛm] NM *Mktg (abrév* **impact sur la rentabilité de la stratégie marketing**) PIMS
ISA [iɛsa] NM *Mktg (abrév* **imprimé sans adresse**) mailshot
Isaac [izaak] NPR *Bible* Isaac
isabelle [izabɛl] ADJ INV *(cheval)* Isabella-coloured
NM Isabella-coloured horse
ISAF [izaf] NF *(abrév* **International Sailing Federation**) ISAF
Isaïe [izai] NPR *Bible* Isaiah
isallobare [izalɔbar] NF *Météo* isallobar

-ISANT, -ISANTE [izɑ̃, izɑ̃t] SUFF

This suffix is used to form adjectives and – more rarely – nouns with the idea of having a TENDENCY or a LEANING towards, mostly, an ideology. In English, the suffix *-istic* can sometimes be used as an equivalent, eg:
communisant(e) Communistic, with Communist sympathies; **socialisant(e)** left-leaning, with left-wing tendencies; **fascisant(e)** fascistic, pro-fascist

isard [izar] NM *Zool* izard, Pyrenean chamois

-ISATION, -ISER [izasjɔ̃, izer] SUFF

• Like their English equivalents (*-ization, -ize*), these two suffixes are widely used to suggest a TRANSFORMATION, either in noun or verb form. A noun ending in **-isation** often corresponds to a verb ending in **-iser**, which can be transitive or reflexive. The base for derivation is either an adjective or a noun, the idea being that of "becoming...", eg:
se clochardiser (to become destitute/to be made homeless) and **clochardisation** (becoming destitute/making homeless); **diaboliser** (to demonize) and **diabolisation** (demonization); **(se) marginaliser** (to marginalize/to become marginalized) and **marginalisation** (marginalization); **ringardiser** (to make tacky) and **ringardisation** (making/becoming tacky)
• A particular trend in recent times has been to add **-isation** to a proper noun, often from the political or cultural arena, eg:
l'hollywoodisation du cinéma mondial the Hollywoodization of world cinema; **la disneylandisation d'un lieu** the Disneyfication of a place; **la macdonaldisation de l'alimentation** the McDonaldization of food; **la lepénisation des esprits** the influence of Le Pen (the French far-right politician) on people's ideas

isatis [izatis] NM **1** *Bot* isatis **2** *Zool (renard)* Arctic *or* blue fox; *(fourrure)* (blue) isatis, blue fox
isba [izba] NF isba
ISBN [iɛsbeɛn] NM *(abrév* **International standard book number**) **(numéro) I.** ISBN
Iscariote [iskarjɔt] NPR *Bible* Iscariot
ischémie [iskemi] NF *Méd* ischaemia
ischémique [iskemik] ADJ *Méd* ischaemic
ischiatique [iskjatik] ADJ ischiatic
ischion [iskjɔ̃] NM ischium
isentropique [izɑ̃trɔpik] ADJ isentropic
Isère [izɛr] NF **l'I.** Isère
Iseut [izø] NPR Isolde
ISF [iɛsɛf] NM *Fin (abrév* **impôt de solidarité sur la fortune**) wealth tax
Ishtar [iʃtar] NPR *Myth* Astarte
isiaque [izjak] ADJ Isiac, Isiacal
Isis [izis] NPR *Myth* Isis
Islam [islam] NM **l'I.** *(civilisation)* Islam
islam [islam] NM **l'i.** *(religion)* Islam
Islamabad [islamabad] NM Islamabad
islamique [islamik] ADJ Islamic
islamisation [islamizasjɔ̃] NF Islamization
islamiser [3] [islamize] VT to Islamize
islamisme [islamism] NM Islamism
islamiste [islamist] ADJ Islamic
NMF Islamic fundamentalist
islamologie [islamɔlɔʒi] NF Islamology, Islamic studies
islamophobe [islamɔfɔb] ADJ Islamophobic
NMF Islamophobe
islamophobie [islamɔfɔbi] NF Islamophobia
islandais, -e [islɑ̃dɛ, -ɛz] ADJ Icelandic
NM *(langue)* Icelandic
▫ **Islandais, -e** NM,F Icelander
Islande [islɑ̃d] NF **l'I.** Iceland; **vivre en I.** to live in Iceland; **aller en I.** to go to Iceland
Ismaël [ismaɛl] NPR *Bible* Ishmael
ismaélien, -enne [ismaeljɛ̃, -ɛn] NM,F Ismaili
ismaélisme [ismaelism] NM Ismailism
ismaélites [ismaelit] NMPL Ishmaelites
ismaïlien, -enne [ismailjɛ̃, -ɛn] = **ismaélien**
ismaïlisme [ismailism] = **ismaélisme**

-ISME, -ISTE [ism, ist] SUFF

• The main use of these suffixes, whose English equivalents are, in a lot of cases, *-ism* and *-ist*, consists in forming nouns and adjectives related to ATTITUDES, social, political or religious MOVEMENTS or DOCTRINES and their FOLLOWERS. The base for suffixation can be an adjective, a noun, a proper noun or even a verb, eg:
libéralisme (from *libéral*) liberalism/free-market economics; **racisme/raciste** (from *race*) racism/racist; **catholicisme** (from *catholique*) Catholicism; **narcissisme** (from *Narcisse*) narcissism; **gaullisme** (from *Général de Gaulle*) Gaullism; **arrivisme/arriviste** (from *arriver*) pushiness/careerist; **dirigisme/dirigiste** (from *diriger*) state intervention/interventionist
• A recent, humorous and colloquial trend has been to add **-isme** or **-iste** to a whole expression, which is held together with hyphens, eg:
je-m'en-foutisme (from *je m'en fous !* I couldn't give a damn!) couldn't-care-less attitude; **il est très je-m'en-foutiste** he's a couldn't-give-a-damn sort of person; **jusqu'au-boutisme** (from *jusqu'au bout* to the end) hard-line attitude; **les jusqu'au-boutistes** the hard-liners; **à-quoi-bonisme** (from *à quoi bon?* what's the point?) what's-the-point attitude; **une génération d'à-quoi-bonistes** a generation who don't see the point of anything
• The term **âgisme** (ageism) is a modern coinage due to the influence of the word **racisme**, both in form and meaning. **Jeunisme**, however, although similar in form, has the opposite idea: it refers to the cult of youth rather than discrimination against young people.

ISMH [iɛsɛmaʃ] NM *(abrév* **inventaire supplémentaire des monuments historiques**) register of listed buildings; **château classé I.** = château classed as a listed building
ISO [izo] NF *Phot (abrév* **International Standards Organization**) ISO
isobare [izɔbar] ADJ *Météo & Phys* isobaric
NM *Phys* isobar
NF *Météo* isobar
isobathe [izɔbat] ADJ isobathic
NF isobath
isobutane [izɔbytan] NF *Chim* isobutane
isocalorique [izɔkalɔrik] ADJ *Méd* isocaloric
isocarde [izɔkard] NM *Zool* isocardia
isocèle [izɔsɛl] ADJ isosceles; **triangle i.** isosceles triangle
isochore [izɔkɔr] ADJ *Phys* isochoric
isochromatique [izɔkrɔmatik] ADJ isochromatic
isochrone [izɔkron] ADJ isochronal, isochronous
NF isochron, isochronal line
isochronique [izɔkrɔnik] ADJ isochronal, isochronous
isochronisme [izɔkrɔnism] NM isochronism
isoclinal, -e, -aux, -ales [izɔklinal, -o] ADJ *Géol* isoclinal
isocline [izɔklin] *Phys* ADJ *(ligne)* isoclinal
NF isocline, isoclinal line
isodome [izɔdɔm] ADJ *Archit* isodomic, isodomous
isodynamie [izɔdinami] NF *Physiol* isodynamia
isodynamique [izɔdinamik] ADJ isodynamic
isoédrique [izɔedrik] ADJ isohedral
isoélectrique [izɔelɛktrik] ADJ isoelectric
isoète [izɔɛt] NM *Bot* isoetes, quill-wort
isoflavone [izoflavɔn] NF *Chim* isoflavone
isogame [izɔgam] ADJ *Bot* isogamous
isogamie [izɔgami] NF *Bot* isogamy
isoglosse [izɔglɔs] ADJ isoglossal, isoglottic
NF isogloss
isoglucose [izɔglykɔz] NM isoglucose
isogone [izɔgɔn] ADJ *Géom & Géol* isogonal, isogonic
NF *Géol* isogonal (line), isogonic (line)
isogreffe [izɔgrɛf] NF *Méd* isograft, isotransplant
isohyète [izɔjɛt] *Météo* ADJ isohyetal
NF isohyet
isohypse [izɔips] NF isohypse
isoïonique [izɔjɔnik] ADJ isoionic
isolable [izɔlabl] ADJ isolable, isolatable; **un virus difficilement i.** a virus (which is) difficult to isolate
isolant, -e [izɔlɑ̃, -ɑ̃t] ADJ **1** *(thermique, électrique)* insulating; *(acoustique)* soundproofing; **bouteille isolante** vacuum flask **2** *Ling* isolating
NM *(thermique, électrique)* insulating material; *(acoustique)* soundproofing (material); **i. thermique/électrique** thermal/electrical insulator
isolat [izɔla] NM isolate
isolateur, -trice [izɔlatœr, -tris] ADJ insulating
NM *Élec & Phys* insulator
isolation [izɔlasjɔ̃] NF **1** *Constr* insulation; **i. thermique** heat *or* thermal insulation; **i. phonique** *ou* **acoustique** soundproofing, *Spéc* sound insulation **2** *Élec* insulation **3** *Psy* isolation
isolationnisme [izɔlasjɔnism] NM isolationism
isolationniste [izɔlasjɔnist] ADJ isolationist
NMF isolationist
isolatrice [izɔlatris] *voir* **isolateur**
isolé, -e [izɔle] ADJ **1** *(unique → cas, exemple)* isolated; **généraliser à partir d'un ou deux cas isolés** to generalize from one or two isolated examples; **heureusement, il s'agit d'un problème i.** fortunately, this is an isolated problem
2 *(coupé du monde → personne)* isolated; *(→ hameau)* isolated, cut-off, remote; *(→ maison)* isolated, secluded, remote; *(→ forêt)* remote, lonely; **il vit trop i.** he lives too much in isolation, he leads too isolated a life; **quelques arbres isolés visibles à l'horizon** a few lonely trees dotted along the horizon
3 *(seul → activiste)* maverick
4 *Géom & Phys* isolated
NM,F **1** *(personne)* isolated individual
2 *Pol* maverick, isolated activist; **ce sont les**

irr–iso

iso-iti

revendications de quelques **isolés** only a few isolated people are putting forward these demands

NM *Mil* = soldier awaiting posting

isolement [izɔlmɑ̃] **NM 1** *(éloignement → géographique)* isolation, seclusion, remoteness; *(→ affectif)* isolation, loneliness; *(sanction)* solitary *(confinement)*; *Écon & Pol* isolation; **vivre dans l'i.** to live in isolation **2** *Biol & Méd* isolation; **l'i. du virus** isolating the virus **3** *Élec* insulation **4** *Constr (contre le bruit)* insulation, soundproofing; *(contre le froid, la chaleur)* insulation; **i. thermique** (thermal) insulation

isolément [izɔlemɑ̃] **ADV** *(l'un de l'autre)* separately, individually; **le malfaiteur a agi i.** the criminal acted in isolation *or* on his own

isoler [3] [izɔle] **VT 1** *(séparer)* to isolate, to separate off *or* out, to keep separate *(de* from); **i. une citation de son contexte** to lift a quotation out of context, to isolate a quotation from its context

2 *(couper du monde → personne)* to isolate, to leave isolated; *(→ endroit)* to isolate, to cut off; **sa maladie l'isole** his/her illness cuts him/her off from other people; **les inondations ont isolé des dizaines de villages** dozens of villages have been cut off by the flood

3 *(distinguer)* to isolate, to single *or* to pick out; **on n'a pas pu i. la cause de la déflagration** it was not possible to identify the cause of the explosion; **i. un cas parmi d'autres** to pick out an isolated case

4 *Constr (du froid, de la chaleur)* to insulate; *(du bruit)* to insulate (against sound), to soundproof **5** *Élec* to insulate **6** *Méd (malade, virus)* to isolate **7** *Chim* to isolate **8** *Admin (prisonnier)* to put into *or* to place in solitary confinement

▸**s'isoler VPR** to isolate oneself, to cut oneself off; **s'i. pour travailler** to find somewhere private to work; **s'i. dans son bureau** to shut oneself (up) in one's office; **le jury s'isola pour délibérer** the jury withdrew to consider its verdict; **elles s'isolèrent** *(pour voter)* they went into separate booths; **pourrions-nous nous i. un instant?** is there somewhere we could talk privately *or* in private for a moment?

isoleucine [izɔløsin] **NF** *Chim* isoleucine

isoloir [izɔlwar] **NM** *Pol* voting booth, polling booth

isomérase [izɔmeraz] **NF** *Biol & Chim* isomerase

isomère [izɔmɛr] *Chim & Phys* **ADJ** isomeric

NM isomer

isomérie [izɔmeri] **NF** *Chim & Phys* isomerism

isomérique [izɔmerik] **ADJ** *Chim & Phys* isomeric

isomérisation [izɔmerizasjɔ̃] **NF** *Chim & Phys* isomerization

isomériser [3] [izɔmerize] **VT** *Chim & Phys* to isomerize

isométrie [izɔmetri] **NF** isometry

isométrique [izɔmetrik] **ADJ** isometric

isomorphe [izɔmɔrf] **ADJ** *Biol, Chim, Math & Ling* isomorphic, isomorphous

NM *Biol & Chim* isomorph

isomorphisme [izɔmɔrfism] **NM** *Biol, Chim, Math & Ling* isomorphism

isoniazide [izɔnjazid] **NF** *Méd* isoniazid

isonomie [izɔnɔmi] **NF** *Jur* isonomy

isopentane [izɔpɛ̃tan] **ADJ** *Chim* isopentane

isopet [izɔpɛ] = **ysopet**

isopode [izɔpɔd] *Zool* **ADJ** isopodous

NM isopod

❑ **isopodes NMPL** Isopoda

isoprène [izɔprɛn] **NM** *Chim* isoprene

isopropyle [izɔprɔpil] **NM** *Chim* isopropyl

isoptère [izɔptɛr] *Entom* **NM** = member of the Isoptera order

❑ **isoptères NMPL** Isoptera

Isorel® [izɔrɛl] **NM** hardboard

isoséiste [izɔseist], **isosiste** [izɔsist] *Géol* **ADJ** isoseismal, isoseismic

NF isoseist, isoseismal

isostasie [izɔstazi] **NF** *Géol* isostasy, isostacy

isostatique [izɔstatik] **ADJ** *Géol* isostatic

isosyllabique [izɔsilabik] **ADJ** isosyllabic

isothérapie [izɔterapi] **NF** *Méd* isotherapy

isotherme [izɔtɛrm] **ADJ** isothermal; **bouteille i.** vacuum flask; **sac i.** cool bag

NF isotherm

---

isothermie [izɔtɛrmi] **NF** constant temperature, *Spéc* isothermia

isotonie [izɔtɔni] **NF** isotonicity

isotonique [izɔtɔnik] **ADJ** isotonic

isotope [izɔtɔp] *Phys* **ADJ** isotopic

NM isotope

isotopique [izɔtɔpik] **ADJ** *Phys* isotopic

isotron [izɔtrɔ̃] **NM** *Phys* isotron

isotrope [izɔtrɔp] **ADJ** *Chim & Phys* isotropic, isotropous

isotropie [izɔtrɔpi] **NF** *Chim & Phys* isotropy, isotropism

isotropique [izɔtrɔpik] **ADJ** *Chim & Phys* isotropic, isotropous

isotype [izɔtip] **NM** *Biol* isotype

Ispahan [ispaɑ̃] **NM** Isfahan

Israël [israɛl] **NM** Israel **vivre en I.** to live in Israel; **aller en I.** to go to Israel

israélien, -enne [israeljɛ̃, -ɛn] **ADJ** Israeli

❑ **Israélien, -enne NM,F** Israeli

israélite [israelit] **ADJ 1** *(juif)* Jewish **2** *Bible* Israelite

❑ **Israélite NMF 1** *(juif)* Jew, *f* Jewess **2** *Bible* Israelite

ISRS [iɛsɛrɛs] **NM** *Pharm (abrév* **inhibiteur sélectif de recapture de la sérotonine)** SSRI

issant, -e [isɑ̃, -ɑ̃t] **ADJ** *Hér* issuant

-ISSIME [isim] **SUFF**

● This very productive suffix is derived from Latin or Italian and acts as a SUPERLATIVE when added to adjectives. Its use always gives a slightly humorous tone to the sentence, especially when the resulting adjective is entirely made up and does not appear in dictionaries. As there is no direct equivalent in English, the translation will have to include a similarly superlative turn of phrase, usually with an adverb, eg:

richissime fantastically wealthy; **rarissime** extremely rare; **nullissime** completely useless; **simplissime** easy as pie; **élégantissime** incredibly elegant; **ringardissime** unbelievably tacky; **glamourissime** amazingly glamorous

(It is worth noting that, contrary to the other words listed above, the adjectives *richissime* and *rarissime* have existed for a very long time and have no humorous or colloquial overtones.)

● It is even possible to add **-issime** to a proper noun when describing something or somebody as typical of what the person represents, especially in the field of arts or literature, eg:

un film allenissime (from the American director Woody Allen) a Woody Allen-ish film; **une description proustissime** (from the XIXth century French writer Marcel Proust) a Proustian description

---

ISSN [iɛsɛsɛn] **NM** *(abrév* **International standard serial number) (numéro) I.** ISSN

issu, -e[1] [isy] **ADJ être i. de** *(résulter de)* to stem *or* to derive *or* to spring from; **la révolution est issue du mécontentement populaire** the revolution stems from popular discontent; **être i. d'une famille pauvre/nombreuse** to be born into a poor/large family; **enfant i. d'un second mariage** child from a second marriage; **cousins issus de germains** second cousins

issue[2] [isy] **NF 1** *(sortie)* exit; *(déversoir)* outlet; **i. de secours** emergency exit **2** *(solution)* solution, way out; **trouver** *ou* **se ménager une i.** to find a way out *or* a loophole; **il n'y a pas d'autre i. que de se rendre** there's no other solution *or* we have no alternative but to surrender **3** *(fin)* outcome; **cet épisode a eu une i. heureuse/ tragique** the incident had a happy/tragic ending

❑ **issues NFPL** *(des animaux)* abattoir byproducts; *(des céréales)* mill offals

❑ **à l'issue de PRÉP** at the end *or* close of; **à l'i. du cinquième round** at the end of the fifth round

❑ **sans issue ADJ 1** *(sans sortie)* with no way out; **ruelle sans i.** dead end; **sans i.** *(sur une porte)* no exit **2** *(voué à l'échec)* hopeless, doomed; *(discussions)* deadlocked; **une situation sans i.** a dead end

IST [iɛste] **NF** *(abrév* **infection sexuellement transmissible)** STI

Istanbul [istɑ̃bul] **NM** Istanbul

isthme [ism] **NM** *Anat & Géog* isthmus; **l'i. de**

Panama the Isthmus of Panama; **l'i. de Suez** the Isthmus of Suez

isthmique [ismik] **ADJ 1** *Géog* isthmian **2** *Antiq* **Jeux Isthmiques** Isthmian Games

Istrie [istri] **NF** *Géog* **l'I.** Istria

italianisant, -e [italjanizɑ̃, -ɑ̃t] **ADJ** *(style)* Italianate

NM,F 1 *Univ* Italianist, Italian scholar **2** *Beaux-Arts* Italianizer

italianiser [3] [italjanize] **VT** to Italianize

italianisme [italjanism] **NM** Italianism

italianiste [italjanist] **NMF** Italianist

Italie [itali] **NF l'I.** Italy; **vivre en I.** to live in Italy; **aller en I.** to go to Italy

italien, -enne [italjɛ̃, -ɛn] **ADJ** Italian

NM *(langue)* Italian

❑ **Italien, -enne NM,F** Italian

❑ **à l'italienne ADJ 1** *Culin (sauce)* à l'italienne *(cooked with mushrooms, ham and herbs)*; *(pâtes)* al dente **2** *Théât* proscenium arch *(avant n)* **3** *Typ* landscape; **imprimer qch à l'i.** to print sth in landscape

italique [italik] **ADJ 1** *Typ* italic **2** *Hist & Ling* Italic

NM 1 *Typ* italics; **écrire un mot en i.** to write a word in italics, to italicize a word **2** *Hist & Ling* Italic

---

-ITE [it] **SUFF**

● The feminine suffix **-ite** originally belongs to the medical world and means INFLAMMATION of the organ referred to by the noun base. Its equivalent in English is *-itis*, eg:

gastrite gastritis; **appendicite** appendicitis; **pharyngite** pharyngitis

● It has also been given a humorous twist in words like **réunionnite** or **espionnite**, with the implication of some sort of MANIA or obsession, eg:

une réaction contre la réunionnite des années 90 a reaction against the meeting mania of the 90s; **une vague d'espionnite aiguë** a strong wave of spymania

Note the use of **aigu**, which emphasizes the fake medical tone of the expression. It can also be found in **flemmingite aiguë**, a colloquial way of describing a bout of laziness:

j'ai fait une pause de plusieurs heures pour cause de flemmingite aiguë I took a few hours' break due to an attack of laziness

---

-ITÉ [ite] **SUFF**

When added to adjectives, this suffix is used to create feminine nouns referring to the QUALITY expressed by the root word. In the majority of cases, its English equivalent is *-ity*, but note also the use of *-ness* in some examples below, eg:

féminité femininity; **masculinité** masculinity, manliness; **la laïcité** secularism; **la mixité** (in schools) coeducational system; **la parité** parity, equality; **la francité** Frenchness; **la latinité** Latinity/the Latin world

● With the advent of all things electronic, a number of words have been coined or resurrected with a new meaning, often under the influence of English. Eg:

jouabilité playability (of a computer game); **connectivité, connectabilité** connectivity, connectability; **fonctionnalités** functions, features (of a piece of software, a website etc)

---

item[1] [itɛm] **ADV** *Com* ditto

item[2] [itɛm] **NM** *Ling & Psy* item

ITER [iter] **NM** *Phys (abrév* **International Thermonuclear Experimental Reactor)** ITER

itératif, -ive [iteratif, -iv] **ADJ 1** *(répété)* repeated, reiterated, *Sout* iterated **2** *Ordinat & Ling* iterative

itération [iterasjɔ̃] **NF 1** *(répétition)* iteration, repetition **2** *Typ & Ling* iteration

itérative [iterativ] *voir* **itératif**

itérativement [iterativmɑ̃] **ADV** iteratively, repeatedly

Ithaque [itak] **NF** Ithaca

ithyphallique [itifalik] **ADJ** *Antiq* ithyphallic

itinéraire [itinerɛr] **NM 1** *(trajet)* itinerary, route; **i. bis** = alternative route recommended when roads are highly congested, especially at peak holiday times; **i. de dégagement** alternative route; **i. touristique** tourist route; **i. vert** nature

trail **2** *(cheminement → professionnel)* career, path; **i. politique** political career; **il a eu un i. sentimental mouvementé** his love life has had its ups and downs

Itinéraire d'un enfant gâté
This is the title of Claude Lelouch's hit film of 1988, starring Jean-Paul Belmondo and Richard Anconina. The expression is often used in newspaper articles. The translation is "The making of a spoilt child". In modern French, other words are substituted for **enfant gâté** in alluding to, for example, the career of a successful actor or politician. A French magazine article entitled **L'itinéraire d'un acteur comblé** might be translated "The making of a totally happy actor", and would chart his progress along the road to success.

itinérance [itinerɑ̃s] NF *Tél* roaming

itinérant, -e [itinerɑ̃, -ɑ̃t] ADJ *(main-d'œuvre)* itinerant, travelling; *(inspecteur)* peripatetic; *(pasteur)* itinerant; *(ambassadeur)* roving; *(comédien, exposition)* travelling; **camp i.** = children's holiday camp which moves between various locations

itinérer [18] [itinere] VI **1** *(se déplacer)* to travel from place to place **2** *Tél* to roam

itou [itu] ADV *Fam Vieilli* likewise, ditto; **et moi i.!** me too!

ITP [itepe] NM *(abrév* **ingénieur des travaux publics***)* civil engineer

-ITUDE [ityd] SUFF
● This suffix is similar in meaning to **-ité**, in that it denotes a QUALITY or STATE, mostly based on an adjective but also sometimes on a Latin radical ending in **-i**, eg:
altitude altitude; **aptitude** ability, aptitude; **ingratitude** ingratitude, ungratefulness; **certitude** certainty

● One recent, colloquial word formed on this model is **branchitude**, ie all that is *branché* or trendy, eg:
un haut lieu de la branchitude parisienne one of the hippest hangouts in Paris; **Berlin, capitale de la branchitude** Berlin, capital of cool
● There is also a series of words in **-itude** which refer to national or racial identity, as did **négritude** (negritude, blackness), coined in the 1970s by L.S. Senghor, A. Césaire and other black writers. Those words sometimes have an equivalent ending in **-ité** with the same meaning, like **francité** (Frenchness). In both cases, the English equivalent is usually *-ness*, eg:
la francitude Frenchness; **l'anglitude** Englishness

IUFM [iyɛfɛm] NM *(abrév* **Institut universitaire de formation des maîtres***)* = teacher-training college

iule [jyl] NM iulus, julus

IUP [iype] NM *(abrév* **Institut universitaire professionnel***)* = business school

IUT [iyte] NM *(abrév* **Institut universitaire de technologie***)* = institute of technology offering two-year vocational courses leading to the DUT qualification

IV [ive] ADJ *Méd (abrév* **intra-veineux***)* IV

Ivan [ivɑ̃] NPR **I. le Grand** Ivan the Great; **I. le Terrible** Ivan the Terrible

Ivanhoé [ivanɔe] NPR Ivanhoe

ive [iv], **ivette** [ivɛt] NF *Bot* iva, ground-pine

IVG [iveʒe] NF *(abrév* **interruption volontaire de grossesse***)* termination *(of pregnancy)*

ivoire [ivwar] NM **1** *(matière)* ivory (UNCOUNT); **statuette d'i.** *ou* **en i.** ivory statuette **2** *(objet)* (piece of) ivory **3** *Bot* **i. végétal** vegetable ivory, ivory nut
▫ **d'ivoire** ADJ *Littéraire* **1** *(blanc)* ivory *(avant n)*, ivory-coloured **2** *(ayant l'aspect de l'ivoire)* ivory-like

ivoirerie [ivwarri] NF **1** *(objets)* ivories *(pluriel)* **2** *(art)* ivory work

ivoirien, -enne [ivwarjɛ̃, -ɛn] ADJ of/from the Ivory Coast
▫ **Ivoirien, -enne** NM,F = inhabitant of or person from the Ivory Coast

ivoirier, -ère [ivwarje, -ɛr] NM,F ivory sculptor

ivoirin, -e [ivwarɛ̃, -in] ADJ *Littéraire* **1** *(blanc)* ivory *(avant n)*, ivory-coloured **2** *(ayant l'aspect de l'ivoire)* ivory-like

ivraie [ivrɛ] NF *Bot* **i. commune** darnel; **i. vivace** rye grass **2** *(locution)* **séparer le bon grain de l'i.** to separate the wheat from the chaff

ivre [ivr] ADJ **1** *(saoul)* drunk, intoxicated; **i. mort** blind drunk **2** *Fig* **être i. de joie** to be deliriously happy; **i. de haine** blinded by hatred; **être i. de colère/bonheur** to be beside oneself with anger/happiness; **i. de fatigue** dead tired; **être i. de sang** to be thirsting for blood

ivresse [ivrɛs] NF **1** *(ébriété)* drunkenness, intoxication; **il était en état d'i.** he was drunk *or* intoxicated **2** *(excitation)* ecstasy, euphoria, exhilaration; **la vitesse procure un sentiment d'i.** speed is exhilarating; **emporté par l'i. des mots** *(poésie)* enraptured by these words; *(discours politique)* carried away by this heavy talk *or* rhetoric; **dans l'i. du moment** in the excitement of the moment; **i. poétique** poetic frenzy **3** *Sport* **i. des profondeurs** (diver's) staggers

ivressomètre [ivrɛsomɛtr] NM *Can Br* breathalyser, *Am* Breathalyzer®

ivrogne [ivrɔɲ] NMF drunk, drunkard

ivrognerie [ivrɔɲri] NF drunkenness

ivrognesse [ivrɔɲɛs] NF *Vieilli* drunken woman

iwan [iwan] NM *Archit* iwan

ixia [iksja] NF *Bot* ixia

ixième [iksjɛm] ADJ umpteenth, nth; **pour la i. fois** for the umpteenth time

ixode [iksɔd] NM *Entom* tick, *Spéc* ixodid

Izmir [izmir] NM Izmir

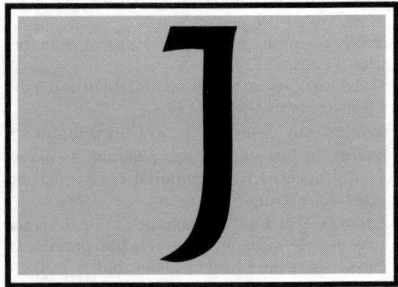

J¹, j [ʒi] NM INV (lettre) J, j; **J comme Joseph** ≃ J for John

J² [ʒi] NM (abrév **jour**) day; Hist & Fig **le jour J** D-day

J³ (abrév écrite **joule**) J

j' [ʒ] voir **je**

jabiru [ʒabiry] NM Orn jabiru

jable [ʒabl] NM 1 (rainure) croze 2 (partie de la douve) chimb

jabler [3] [ʒable] VT to croze

jablière [ʒablijɛr] NF croze

jabloir [ʒablwar] NM croze

jabloire [ʒablwar] = **jablière**

jaborandi [ʒabɔrɑ̃di] NM Bot jaborandi

jabot [ʒabo] NM 1 Orn crop 2 (ornement) ruffle, frill

jaboter [3] [ʒabɔte] VI 1 (oiseau) to gobble 2 Fam Vieilli to jabber, to chatter

jaboteur, -euse [ʒabɔtœr, -øz] NM,F Fam Vieilli chatterer, jabberer

JAC, Jac [ʒiase] NF (abrév **Jeunesse agricole chrétienne**) = Christian youth organization

jacana [ʒakana] NM Orn jacana

jacaranda [ʒakarɑ̃da] NM Bot jacaranda (tree)

jacasse [ʒakas] NF Orn magpie

jacassement [ʒakasmɑ̃] NM 1 Orn chatter 2 Péj (bavardage) chatter (UNCOUNT), prattle (UNCOUNT); **leurs incessants jacassements** their constant chatter or prattle

jacasser [3] [ʒakase] VI 1 Orn to chatter 2 Péj (bavarder) to chatter, to prattle; **j. comme une pie** to chatter like a magpie, to jabber away

jacasserie [ʒakasri] NF Péj chatter (UNCOUNT), prattle (UNCOUNT); **leurs incessantes jacasseries** their constant chatter or prattle

jacasseur, -euse [ʒakasœr, -øz] Péj ADJ chattering, prattling
   NM,F chatterbox

jacée [ʒase] NF Bot brown radiant knapweed; **petite j.** wild pansy

jacent [ʒasɑ̃] ADJ Vieilli Jur unclaimed

jachère [ʒaʃɛr] NF 1 (pratique) (practice of) fallowing land; **mettre la terre en j.** to let the land lie fallow; **rester en j.** to lie fallow; **laisser en j.** (talent) to leave undeveloped or untapped 2 (champ) fallow (land)

jacinthe [ʒasɛ̃t] NF hyacinth; **j. sauvage** ou **des bois** bluebell, wild hyacinth

jaciste [ʒasist] ADJ belonging to the "JAC"
   NMF member of the "JAC"

jack [dʒak] NM 1 Tél jack 2 Tex jack (lever)

jackpot [dʒakpɔt] NM 1 (combinaison) jackpot; **j. roulant** rollover jackpot; aussi Fig **toucher le j.** to hit the jackpot 2 (machine) slot machine

jaco [ʒako] = **jacquot**

Jacob [ʒakɔb] NPR Bible Jacob

jacobée [ʒakɔbe] NF ragwort (UNCOUNT), Spéc jacobaea

jacobin, -e [ʒakɔbɛ̃, -in] ADJ 1 Hist Jacobinic, Jacobinical, Jacobin (avant n) 2 Pol radical, Jacobin (avant n) 3 Rel Dominican
   NM,F Dominican
   ▢ **Jacobin** NM Hist Jacobin

jacobinisme [ʒakɔbinism] NM Jacobinism

jacobite [ʒakɔbit] ADJ Jacobite (avant n), Jacobitic
   NMF Hist & Rel Jacobite

jaconas [ʒakɔnas] NM jaconet

jacquard [ʒakar] NM 1 (pull) Jacquard or Jacquard-style sweater 2 Tex (machine) Jacquard loom, jacquard; (tissu) Jacquard weave
   ADJ pull j. Jacquard or Jacquard-style sweater

jacquemart [ʒakmar] NM = **jaquemart**

jacquerie [ʒakri] NF peasants' revolt, jacquerie; Hist **la J.** the Jacquerie (peasant uprising in Picardy against the nobility in May 1358)

Jacques [ʒak] NPR (roi d'Angleterre) James; **saint J.** Saint James; **Maître J.** = Harpagon's servant who acts both as a coachman and as a cook in Molière's 'l'Avare' (1668), hence a term for a Jack-of-all-trades
   NM 1 Hist (rebelle) = peasant taking part in "la Jacquerie" 2 Vieilli (paysan) peasant

'**Jacques le Fataliste et son maître**' Diderot 'Jacques the Fatalist and his Master'

jacques [ʒak] NM Fam 1 Vieilli (niais) fool, simpleton 2 **faire le j.** (faire le fou) to play the fool, to clown around; (se donner en spectacle) to make an exhibition of oneself

jacquet [ʒakɛ] NM (jeu) backgammon; (tablette) backgammon (board)

jacquier [ʒakje] = **jaquier**

jacquot [ʒako] NM Orn African grey parrot

jactance [ʒaktɑ̃s] NF 1 très Fam (baratin) chattering 2 Littéraire (infatuation) conceit (UNCOUNT), self-praise (UNCOUNT), Arch vainglory (UNCOUNT)

jacter [3] [ʒakte] très Fam VT (parler → langue) to jabber away in; **j. chinois** to jabber away in Chinese
   VI 1 (avouer) to squeal, to come clean 2 (médire) **ça va faire j. si on nous voit ensemble** people will talk if we're seen together 3 (parler) to chatter, Br to witter (on), to natter

jaculatoire [ʒakylatwar] ADJ Rel **oraison j.** ejaculatory prayer

Jacuzzi® [ʒakuzi] NM Jacuzzi®

jade [ʒad] NM 1 (matière) jade; **bague de j.** jade ring 2 (objet) jade (object) or artefact

jadéite [ʒadeit] NF Minér jadeite

jadis [ʒadis] Littéraire ADV long ago, in bygone days; **il y avait j. un prince** there was once a prince, once upon a time there was a prince; **la ville a conservé sa splendeur de j.** the town has kept its former splendour
   ADJ **au temps j.** in days of old, in bygone days; **contes du temps j.** tales of long ago, tales of yesteryear

Jaffa [ʒafa] NM Jaffa

jaguar [ʒagwar] NM Zool jaguar

jaguarondi [ʒagwarɔ̃di] NM Zool jaguarundi

Jahvé [ʒave] NPR Bible Yahweh

jaillir [32] [ʒajir] VI 1 (personne, animal) to spring or to shoot or to bolt out; **il jaillit de derrière le mur** he sprang or leapt out from behind the wall; **ils jaillissaient de tous les coins de rue** they were pouring out of all the side streets

2 (liquide, sang, source) to spurt (out), to gush (forth), to spout; (flamme) to leap or to shoot or to spring up; (larmes) to gush, to start flowing; **la lumière d'un projecteur jaillit dans l'obscurité** a spotlight suddenly shone out in the darkness; **des étincelles jaillissaient du moteur** sparks were flying from the engine; **une pluie de cendres jaillie du volcan** a plume of ash sent up by the volcano; Fig **les gratte-ciel jaillissent au-dessus de la ville** skyscrapers soar or tower above the city

3 (surgir → doute) to spring up, to arise (suddenly); (→ rires) to burst out or forth; **une pensée jaillit dans son esprit** a thought suddenly came into his/her mind; **des réponses jaillirent de tous côtés** there was a volley of replies; **il n'eut pas plus tôt mis les pieds dans la salle que les premières plaisanteries jaillirent** as soon as he set foot in the room the jokes came thick and fast

jaillissant, -e [ʒajisɑ̃, -ɑ̃t] ADJ (liquide) spurting, gushing, spouting; (étincelles) flying, shooting

jaillissement [ʒajismɑ̃] NM (jet) spurting (UNCOUNT), gushing (UNCOUNT); **un j. d'idées** an outpouring of ideas

jaïn, -e [ʒaɛ̃] ADJ Jain, Jaina
   NM,F Jain, Jaina

jaïna [ʒaina] ADJ INV & NMF INV = **jaïn**

jaïnisme [ʒainism] NM Jainism

Jaipur [ʒaipur] NM Jaipur

jais [ʒɛ] NM Minér jet; **des perles de j.** jet beads; Fig **des yeux de j.** jet-black eyes

jaja [ʒaʒa] NM Fam vino, wine

Jakarta [dʒakarta] = **Djakarta**

jalap [ʒalap] NM Bot jalap

jalon [ʒalɔ̃] NM 1 (piquet) marker

2 (référence) milestone, landmark; **quelques jalons pour vous aider à comprendre l'histoire de la Révolution** a few reference points or milestones to help you to grasp the history of the Revolution; **cette décision est un j. dans l'histoire des relations est-ouest** this decision is a landmark or a watershed in East-West relations; Fig **planter** ou **poser des jalons** to pave the way, to prepare the ground; **poser les jalons d'un accord** to pave the way for or to prepare the ground for an agreement

jalon-mire [ʒalɔ̃mir] (pl **jalons-mires**) NM target levelling-rod

jalonnement [ʒalɔnmɑ̃] NM 1 (de terrain) marking or staking out 2 Mil marking

jalonner [3] [ʒalɔne] VT 1 (terrain) to mark out or off 2 (longer) to line; **des bouées jalonnent le chenal** a line of buoys marks the channel; **de charmants petits villages jalonnent le littoral** the coastline is dotted with lovely little villages; **la route est jalonnée de jolies maisons** the road is lined with pretty houses; **une carrière jalonnée de succès** a career punctuated by a series of successes 3 Mil to mark
   VI (poser des jalons) to set out markers

jalonneur [ʒalɔnœr] NM (ouvrier, militaire) marker

jalouse [ʒaluz] voir **jaloux**

jalousement [ʒaluzmɑ̃] ADV 1 (avec jalousie) jealously; **regarder qn j.** to watch sb jealously, to keep a jealous eye on sb 2 (soigneusement) jealously; **un secret j. gardé** a closely or jealously guarded secret; **je protège j. mon indépendance** I jealously guard my independence

jalouser [3] [ʒaluze] VT to be jealous of

jalousie [ʒaluzi] NF 1 (envie) jealousy, envy; (possessivité) jealousy; **éprouver de la j. envers qn** to be or to feel jealous of sb; **tourmenté par la j.** tormented by jealousy 2 (store) Venetian blind, jalousie

jaloux, -ouse [ʒalu, -uz] ADJ 1 (possessif) jealous; **rendre qn j.** to make sb jealous; **être j. de qn** to be jealous of sb; **j. comme un tigre** horribly jealous

2 (envieux) jealous, envious (**de** of); **il est j. des notes que tu as obtenues** he is jealous of the Br marks or Am grades you got; **elle est jalouse de**

moi parce que je pars en Italie she's jealous (of me) because I'm off to Italy

3 *(attaché)* **la France, jalouse de sa réputation en matière de vins** France, jealous of her reputation for good wine; **la profession est jalouse de ses prérogatives** the profession guards its privileges jealously

4 *(extrême)* **garder qch avec une attention jalouse** to keep a jealous watch over sth; **mettre un soin j. à faire qch** to do sth with the utmost care

NM,F jealous person; **faire des j.** to make people jealous *or* envious

jamaïcain, -e, jamaïquain, -e [ʒamaikɛ̃, -ɛn] **ADJ** Jamaican

❑ **Jamaïcain, -e, Jamaïquain, -e NM,F** Jamaican

Jamaïque [ʒamaik] **NF la J.** Jamaica; **vivre à la J.** to live in Jamaica; **aller à la J.** to go to Jamaica

JAMAIS [ʒamɛ] **ADV 1** *(sens négatif)* never; **il n'est j. trop tard** it's never too late; **il n'a j. su à quoi s'en tenir** he never knew where he stood; **il n'a j. fait aussi froid** it has never been this cold; **je suis heureuse comme j. je ne l'avais été** I'm happier than I have ever been; **il travaille sans j. s'arrêter** he works without ever stopping; *Fam* **j. tu dis bonjour?** don't you ever say hello?■; **vous ne le verrez plus j., plus j. vous ne le verrez** you'll never (ever) see him again; **comme plus j.** *ou* **j. plus vous n'en reverrez** the like of which you'll never see again; **ah non! plus j. ça!** oh no, never again!; **j. je n'aurais pensé ça de lui** I would never have thought it of him; **j. (une) si grande émotion ne m'avait envahi** never before had I been so overcome with emotion; *Littéraire* **j. homme ne fut plus comblé** there was never a happier man; **n'as-tu j. aimé?** haven't you ever *or* have you never loved?; **la maison est très calme: j. un bruit** the house is very quiet: (there's) never a noise; **presque j.** hardly ever, almost never; **on ne le voit presque j.** we hardly ever see him; **une équipe j. vaincue** an undefeated team; **un rêve j. réalisé** an unfulfilled dream; **c'est du j. vu!** it's never happened before!, it's totally unheard of!; **c'est le moment ou j.!, c'est maintenant ou j.!** it's now or never!; **c'est le moment ou j. d'y aller** now is the best time to go; **on ne sait j.!** you never know!, who knows?; **tu lui pardonneras? – j.!** will you forgive him/her? – never!; **j. le dimanche** never on a Sunday; **vous prenez un petit verre, commissaire? – j. pendant le service!** you'll have a quick one, superintendent? – never while I'm on duty!; **j. deux sans trois** everything comes in threes, if it's happened twice, it'll happen a third time; **j. de la vie!** not on your life!; **j., au grand j.!** never in a month of Sundays!; **j., au grand j., je n'ai fait une telle promesse!** I never ever made such a promise!, I never made such a promise, never on your life!; **il ne faut j. dire j.** never say never

2 *(sens positif)* ever; **a-t-on j. vu pareille splendeur?** have you ever seen such splendour?; **si j'ai j. eu peur, c'est bien cette fois-là** if I was ever frightened, it was that time (then); **c'est à se demander si tu as j. appris à lire** it makes me wonder if you ever learnt to read; **je désespère de j. y arriver** I've lost all hope of ever succeeding; **si j. tu le rencontres, dis-lui de m'appeler** if ever you meet him, tell him to call me; **si j. vous venez** if ever you come, if you ever come; **si j. il revenait** if he ever came back, if ever he came back; **si j. il reste des places, tu en veux?** if by any chance there are tickets left, do you want any?; **si j. je t'y reprends!** if I ever catch you at it again!; **plus/moins/pire que j.** more/less/worse than ever; **on s'amuse plus que j.** we're having more fun than ever, we're enjoying ourselves more than ever; **il est moins que j. décidé à changer d'entreprise** he is less decided than ever about changing firms; **le seul/le plus beau que j'aie j. vu** the only one/the most beautiful I have ever seen

3 *(en corrélation avec "que")* **ce n'est j. qu'à 20 minutes à pied** it's only 20 minutes' walk; **ce n'est j. qu'un film** it's only a film (after all); **ce n'est j. qu'un homme (comme vous et moi)** he's only human (after all); **il n'a j. fait qu'obéir aux ordres** all he did was follow orders, he was only following orders; **elle n'a j. fait que se plaindre toute sa vie** she's done nothing *or* never done anything but complain all her life

❑ **à jamais ADV** for good, forever; **c'est fini à j.** it's finished for ever *or* for good; **ils se sont dit adieu à j.** they said goodbye forever; **des souvenirs à j. envolés** memories gone forever

❑ **à tout jamais ADV** forever, *Littéraire* for evermore; **il y a renoncé à tout j.** he has given it up forever *or Littéraire* for evermore; **je renonce à tout j. à connaître le fin mot de l'histoire** I've given up ever trying to get to the bottom of the matter; **nous avons à tout j. perdu l'espoir de le revoir** we have lost all hope of ever seeing him again

❑ **pour jamais ADV** forever; **adieu pour j.** goodbye forever; **il partit pour j.** he left forever *or* never to return

---

jamais-vu [ʒamɛvy] **NM INV c'est du j.** that's a first

jambage [ʒɑ̃baʒ] **NM 1** *Archit (piédroit)* jamb; *(pilier)* jamb, post; **j. de cheminée** fireplace cheek **2** *(trait d'une lettre → vers le bas)* downstroke; *(→ vers le haut)* upstroke; *(→ au-dessous de la ligne)* tail, descender

jambart [ʒɑ̃bar] **NM** greave

jambe [ʒɑ̃b] **NF 1** *Anat* leg; **avoir de grandes** *ou* **longues jambes** to have long legs; **avoir les jambes nues** to be bare-legged; **elle est tout en jambes** she's all legs; **elle a de bonnes jambes** she's got a good (strong) pair of legs; **j'ai de mauvaises jambes maintenant** my legs aren't as good *or* strong as they used to be; **il a (encore) des jambes de vingt ans** he's still very spry; **j. artificielle/de bois** artificial/wooden leg; *Sport* **il a un bon jeu de jambes** his footwork is good; **je n'ai plus de** *ou* **je ne sens plus mes jambes** I'm totally exhausted, my legs have gone; **avoir dix kilomètres dans les jambes** to have walked ten kilometres; *Fam* **en avoir plein les jambes** to be *Br* knackered *or Am* beat; **il avait les jambes en coton** his legs were like jelly *or* cotton wool; **en rentrant, j'avais les jambes en marmelade** my legs were killing me on the way home; **il est toujours dans mes jambes** *(enfant)* he's always under my feet *or* in my way; **ça me/lui fait une belle j.!** a fat lot of good that does me/him/her!; **la peur lui donnait des jambes** fear drove him/her on; **prendre ses jambes à son cou** to take to one's heels; **détaler** *ou* **s'enfuir à toutes jambes** to make a bolt for it; **se mettre en jambes** to warm up, to do a warm-up; *Fam* **tenir la j. à qn** to drone on (and on) at sb; **tirer dans les jambes à qn** to aim (a shot) at sb's legs; *Fig* to create (all sorts of) problems for sb; **traiter qn par-dessus la j.** to treat sb offhandedly; **un travail fait par-dessus la j.** sloppy *or* slipshod work; *très Fam* **une partie de jambes en l'air** a bit of nooky

2 *(du cheval)* leg

3 *(de pantalon)* (trouser) leg

4 *(d'un compas)* leg

5 *Constr* prop; **j. de force** *(d'une poutre)* strut; *(d'un comble)* joist stay

6 *Aut* radius rod; *Vieilli* **j. de force** torque rod

7 *Aviat* **j. de train d'atterrissage** landing gear strut

8 *Tech* **j. de suspension** MacPherson strut

jambette [ʒɑ̃bɛt] **NF 1** *Constr (d'un entrait)* tie-beam strut; *(d'un arbalétrier)* principal rafter post **2** *Naut* **j. de pavois** bulwark stay **3** *Can* **donner une j. à qn** *(croc-en-jambe)* to trip sb up

jambier [ʒɑ̃bje] **ADJ M** leg *(avant n)*

NM 1 *Anat* leg muscle; **j. antérieur/postérieur** anterior/posterior leg muscle **2** *(à l'abattoir)* gambrel

jambière [ʒɑ̃bjɛr] **NF 1** *(pour la danse)* legwarmer **2** *(pour le football)* (shin) pad **3** *(guêtre)* legging, gaiter **4** *Équitation* pad, gaiter **5** *(pièce d'armure)* greave, jambeau

jambon [ʒɑ̃bɔ̃] **NM 1** *(viande)* ham; **j. de Bayonne** Bayonne ham; **j. blanc** boiled *or* cooked ham; **j. cru** cured ham; **j. fumé** smoked ham; **j. à l'os** ham on the bone; **j. de Paris** boiled *or* cooked ham; **j. de Parme** Parma ham; **j. de pays** cured ham; **j. salé** salted ham; **j. d'York** boiled ham on the bone; **des œufs au j.** ≃ ham and eggs; **un j. beurre** a ham sandwich *(in buttered baguette)*; **un j. fromage** a ham and cheese sandwich *(in buttered baguette)* **2** *Fam (cuisse)* thigh■

jambonneau, -x [ʒɑ̃bɔno] **NM 1** *(petit jambon)* knuckle of ham **2** *Fam (cuisse)* thigh■ **3** *(mollusque)* fan mussel

jamboree [ʒɑ̃bɔri] **NM** jamboree

jambose [ʒɑ̃boz] **NF** rose apple (fruit)

jambosier [ʒɑ̃bozje] **NM** rose apple (tree)

James [dʒɛms] *voir* **baie**[2]

jam-session [dʒamseʃœn] *(pl* **jam-sessions***)* **NF** jam session

jan [ʒɑ̃] **NM** *(table)* backgammon board

jangada [ʒɑ̃gada] **NF** jangada

janissaire [ʒanisɛr] **NM** janissary

jansénisme [ʒɑ̃senism] **NM 1** *Rel* **le j.** Jansenism **2** *Littéraire (piété austère)* puritanism

Culture

LE JANSÉNISME

This term refers to a movement within the Catholic Church founded by Jansenius, Bishop of Ypres, that propounded views on grace and predestination comparable to those of the Calvinists. Its centre was at Port Royal. Very influential in the 17th century, when its doctrines were espoused by such illustrious figures as Pascal and Racine, it is now associated with an austere moral emphasis in religious matters.

janséniste [ʒɑ̃senist] **ADJ 1** *Rel* Jansenist, Jansenistic **2** *Littéraire (austère)* puritanical

NMF 1 *Rel* Jansenist **2** *Littéraire (moraliste)* puritan

jante [ʒɑ̃t] **NF** (wheel) rim; *Aut* **jantes en aluminium** (aluminium) alloy wheels; *Fam Fig* **rouler sur la j.** to be going round the bend, to be losing one's marbles

Janus [ʒanys] **NPR** *Myth* Janus

janvier [ʒɑ̃vje] **NM** January; *voir aussi* **mars**

JAPD [ʒiapede] **NF** *(abrév* **journée d'appel de préparation à la défense***)* = day during which young people are introduced to issues connected with national security

Japon [ʒapɔ̃] **NM le J.** Japan; **vivre au J.** to live in Japan; **aller au J.** to go to Japan

japon [ʒapɔ̃] **NM** *(papier)* Japanese paper; *(porcelaine)* Japanese porcelain

japonais, -e [ʒapɔnɛ, -ɛz] **ADJ** Japanese

NM *(langue)* Japanese

❑ **Japonais, -e NM,F** Japanese (person); **les J.** Japanese people, the Japanese

japonaiserie [ʒapɔnɛzri], **japonerie** [ʒapɔnri] **NF** Japanese artefact

japonisant, -e [ʒapɔnizɑ̃, -ɑ̃t] **ADJ** *Beaux-Arts* inspired by Japanese art

NM,F specialist in Japanese studies

japonisme [ʒapɔnism] **NM** *Beaux-Arts* japonism

japoniste [ʒapɔnist] **NMF** collector of Japanese artefacts

jappement [ʒapmɑ̃] **NM** *(d'un chien)* yelp, yap; *(du chacal)* bark; **des jappements** yelping *(UNCOUNT)*, yapping *(UNCOUNT)*

japper [3] [ʒape] **VI** *(chien)* to yelp, to yap; *(chacal)* to bark

jappeur, -euse [ʒapœr, -øz] **ADJ** yelping, yapping

NM,F yelper, yapper

jaque [ʒak] **NM** *Bot* jackfruit

jaquelin [ʒaklɛ̃] **NM** large-bellied bottle

jaquemart [ʒakmar] **NM** clock jack

jaquette [ʒakɛt] **NF 1** *(vêtement → d'homme)* morning coat; *(→ de femme)* jacket **2** *(de livre)* (dust) cover *or* jacket, book jacket **3** *(couronne dentaire)* crown **4** *Tech* jacket, casing **5** *Can (chemise de nuit)* nightdress **6** *Suisse (en tricot)* cardigan **7** *très Fam* = offensive term used to refer to male homosexuals; **la j. (flottante)** *Br* poofs, *Am* fags; **être** *ou* **refiler de la j. (flottante)** to be a *Br* poof *or Am* fag

jaquier [ʒakje] **NM** jackfruit (tree)

jar, jard [ʒar] **NM** *Géog* = shifting sand or silt that accumulates in the Loire river

jarde [ʒard] **NF** *Vét* bog spavin

jardin [ʒardɛ̃] **NM 1** *(terrain clos → gén)* garden; *(→ d'une maison)* garden, *Am* yard; **il est dans le** *ou* **au j.** he's in the garden; **les jardins du château de Windsor** the grounds of Windsor Castle; **j. d'acclimatation** zoological garden *or* gardens, zoo; **j. à l'anglaise** landscape garden; **j. botanique** botanical garden *or* gardens; **j. à la française** formal garden; **j. fruitier** orchard; **j. d'hiver** winter garden; **j. japonais** miniature

(Japanese) garden; **j. maraîcher** market garden; *Bible* **le j. des Oliviers** the Garden of Gethsemane; **j. ouvrier** allotment; **j. paysager** landscaped garden; **j. potager** vegetable *or* kitchen garden; **j. public** park, public garden *or* gardens; **j. de rapport** market garden; **c'est mon j. secret** that's my little secret; **jardins suspendus** hanging gardens; **j. zoologique** zoological garden *or* gardens, zoo; **mobilier de j.** garden furniture; **le J. d'Acclimatation** (*à Paris*) = children's park and zoo in the Paris suburbs; **le J. des Plantes** (*à Paris*) = botanical garden in Paris with a small zoo (la Ménagerie) and Natural History Museum

2 *Littéraire* (*région fertile*) garden; **c'est le j. de l'Angleterre** it's the garden of England
▫ **jardin d'enfants** NM kindergarten, playgroup, *Br* pre-school nursery

'**Le Jardin des délices**' *Bosch* 'The Garden of Earthly Delights'

jardinage[1] [ʒardinaʒ] NM 1 (*d'un potager, de fleurs*) gardening; **faire un peu de j.** to do a bit of gardening 2 (*de forêts*) selective working
▫ **de jardinage** ADJ (*outil, magasin*) gardening (*avant n*), garden (*avant n*)
jardinage[2] [ʒardinaʒ] NM (*d'une pierre précieuse*) cloud
jardiner [3] [ʒardine] VI to garden; **j'aime j.** I like gardening; **elle est dehors en train de j.** she's out doing some gardening
VT to select, to cull
jardinerie [ʒardinri] NF garden centre
jardinet [ʒardinɛ] NM small garden
jardineux, -euse [ʒardinø, -øz] ADJ (*pierre précieuse*) cloudy
jardinier, -ère [ʒardinje, -ɛr] ADJ 1 *Hort* garden (*avant n*) 2 (*de forêts*) selective
NM,F gardener
▫ **jardinière** NF 1 (*sur un balcon*) window box; (*pour fleurs coupées*) jardinière; (*meuble*) plant holder 2 *Culin* **jardinière (de légumes)** (diced) mixed vegetables, jardinière
▫ **jardinière d'enfants** NF nursery-school *or* kindergarten teacher, *Br* playgroup assistant

'**La Belle Jardinière**' *Raphaël* 'La Belle Jardinière'

jardon [ʒardɔ̃] NM *Vét* bog spavin
jargon [ʒargɔ̃] NM 1 (*langage incorrect*) jargon; (*langage incompréhensible*) jargon, mumbo-jumbo 2 (*langue spécialisée*) jargon; **le j. administratif** officialese, official jargon; **le j. communautaire** Eurospeak; **le j. des journalistes** journalese; **le j. judiciaire** legalese, legal jargon; **le j. du métier** trade jargon; **le j. des publicitaires, le j. publicitaire** advertising jargon 3 (*cri du jars*) honk
jargonaphasie [ʒargɔnafazi] NF jargon aphasia
jargonner [3] [ʒargɔne] VI 1 (*s'exprimer* → *en jargon*) to use jargon, to talk (in) jargon; (→ *de façon incompréhensible*) to talk gibberish, to jabber away 2 (*jars*) to honk
jargonneux, -euse [ʒargɔnø, -øz] ADJ *Péj* jargony, full of jargon
Jarnac [ʒarnak] NPR **coup de J.** stab in the back
jarnicoton [ʒarnikɔtɔ̃] EXCLAM *Vieilli* gadzooks!
jarnigoine [ʒarnigwan] NF *Can Vieilli* wits, intelligence; **il lui en a fallu de la j. pour sortir de ce pétrin-là!** he/she needed all his/her wits to get out of that mess!
jarovisation [ʒarɔvizasjɔ̃] NF *Agr* vernalization
jarre [ʒar] NF 1 (*vase*) (earthenware) jar 2 *Can* (*bocal*) (preserving) jar
NM (*poil*) overhair
jarret [ʒarɛ] NM 1 *Anat* back of the knee, ham; *Zool* hock; *Culin* **j. de veau** knuckle of veal, veal shank; **j. de bœuf** shin of beef; *Fam* **avoir du j. ou des jarrets d'acier** to have a good, sturdy pair of legs 2 *Constr* (*imperfection*) bulge 3 (*coude*) knee joint
jarreté, -e [ʒarte] ADJ 1 (*cheval*) close-hocked 2 (*danseur*) with legs turned in 3 *Constr* bulging
jarretelle [ʒartɛl] NF *Br* suspender, *Am* garter
jarreter[1] [27] [ʒarte] VT to garter
jarreter[2] [27] [ʒarte] VI *Constr* to bulge
jarretière [ʒartjɛr] NF 1 (*bande élastique*) garter; **la**

j. de la mariée the bride's garter (*worn on the wedding day, removed by the best man and auctioned off to the guests*) 2 *Ich* (*cépole*) red band fish
jars [ʒar] NM 1 *Zool* gander 2 *Can* **faire le j.** to show off, to swagger (about)
jas [ʒa] NM 1 (*bergerie, en Provence*) sheepfold 2 *Naut* (anchor) stock
jasant, -e [ʒazɑ̃, -ɑ̃t] ADJ *Can Fam* (*bavard*) chatty; (*cancanier*) gossipy
jase [ʒaz] = **jasette**
jaser [3] [ʒaze] VI 1 (*médire*) to gossip (**sur** about); **ça va faire j. dans le quartier** that'll set the neighbours' tongues wagging 2 *Fam* (*avouer*) to squeal, to blab; **on n'aime pas les gens qui jasent** we don't like squealers 3 (*gazouiller* → *pie, geai*) to chatter; (→ *ruisseau, bébé*) to babble; (→ *personne*) to chatter
jaseran [ʒazrɑ̃] NM 1 *Hist* shirt *or* coat of mail 2 *Vieilli* (*chaîne*) gold chain
jasette [ʒazɛt] NF *Can Fam* chat, conversation■; **faire une petite j., piquer une j.** to have a chat *or* chinwag, *Am* to shoot the breeze
jaseur, -euse [ʒazœr, -øz] NM,F (*bavard*) chatterbox; (*mauvaise langue*) gossip, scandal-monger
ADJ 1 (*oiseau*) chattering 2 (*personne* → *qui bavarde*) chattering; (→ *qui médit*) gossiping, gossipy
NM *Orn* waxwing
jasione [ʒazjɔn] NF **j. des montagnes** sheep's bit
jasmin [ʒasmɛ̃] NM jasmine; **thé au j.** jasmine tea; **j. d'hiver** winter jasmine
Jason [ʒazɔ̃] NPR *Myth* Jason
jaspe [ʒasp] NM 1 *Minér* jasper; **j. noir** touchstone; **j. sanguin** bloodstone 2 (*objet en jaspe*) jasper object 3 *Géol* jasperoid
jasper [3] [ʒaspe] VT 1 (*marbrer*) to marble, to mottle, to speckle 2 *Typ* to marble, to jasper
jaspiner [3] [ʒaspine] VI *très Fam* to rattle on, to chatter away; **ça a fait j. toute l'école** it had *or* set the whole school talking
jaspure [ʒaspyr] NF 1 (*d'une arme*) mottling (UNCOUNT) (*due to quenching*) 2 *Typ & Tex* marbling (UNCOUNT)
jass [jas] NM *Suisse* = popular Swiss card game
jasser [3] [jase] VI *Suisse* to play "jass"
jasseur, -euse [jasœr, -øz] NM,F *Suisse* "jass" player
JAT [ʒiate] ADJ (*abrév* **juste-à-temps**) JIT
jataka [ʒataka] NM INV *Rel* Jataka
jatte [ʒat] NF 1 (*petite*) bowl; (*grande*) basin; **une j. de lait** a bowl of milk 2 *Belg* (*récipient*) coffee cup; (*contenu*) cup of coffee
jattée [ʒate] NF (*petite*) bowlful; (*grande*) basinful
jauge [ʒoʒ] NF 1 (*pour calibrer*) gauge; **j. d'épaisseur** thickness *or* feeler gauge; **j. extensométrique** strain gauge; **j. de filetage** (standard) wire gauge; **j. de profondeur** depth gauge
2 (*indicateur*) gauge; **j. de pression/vapeur** pressure/steam gauge; *Aut* **j. d'essence** *Br* petrol gauge, *Am* gas gauge; *Aut* **j. (de niveau) d'huile** (*sur le tableau de bord*) oil-level indicator; (*manuelle*) dipstick
3 (*contenance* → *d'un réservoir*) capacity; (*tonnage*) tonnage, burden; **j. brute/nette** gross/net (registered) tonnage
4 *Agr* trench
5 *Menuis & Phys* gauge
jaugeage [ʒoʒaʒ] NM gauging, measuring; *Naut* measurement (of tonnage)
jauger [17] [ʒoʒe] VT 1 (*mesurer* → *fil*) to gauge; (→ *réservoir*) to gauge (the capacity of); (→ *liquide*) to gauge (the volume of); (→ *navire*) to measure the tonnage *or* burden of
2 *Littéraire* (*juger* → *dégâts*) to assess; (→ *personne*) to size up; (→ *situation*) to size up, to weigh up; **comment j. sa personnalité?** how can we assess *or* judge *or* determine what sort of a personality he/she has?
VI *Naut* **un navire qui jauge 600 tonneaux** a ship with a tonnage of *or* measuring 600 tons; **j. deux mètres d'eau** to draw two metres of water
jaugeur [ʒoʒœr] NM 1 (*personne*) gauger 2 (*instrument*) gauge
jaumière [ʒomjɛr] NF *Naut* rudder trunk *or* tube
jaunâtre [ʒonatr] ADJ (*couleur*) yellowish, yellowy; (*teint*) yellowish, sallow, waxen
jaune [ʒon] ADJ 1 (*couleur*) yellow; **avoir le teint j.**

to look yellow *or* sallow; **j. canari** canary yellow; **j. citron** lemon yellow; **j. moutarde** mustard-coloured; **j. d'or** golden yellow; **j. paille** straw-coloured; **j. comme un citron** *ou* **un coing** (as) yellow as a lemon
2 *très Fam Vieilli* (*d'Asie*) Oriental, = offensive term used to refer to an Oriental person
NMF 1 (*non-gréviste*) strikebreaker
2 *Can* (*lâche*) yellowbelly
NM 1 (*couleur*) yellow; **elle aime s'habiller en j.** she likes to wear yellow
2 *Culin* **j. (d'œuf)** (egg) yolk
3 *Fam* (*apéritif anisé*) pastis■
▫ **Jaune** NMF *très Fam Vieilli* Oriental, = offensive term used to refer to an Oriental person
jaunet, -ette [ʒonɛ, -ɛt] ADJ *Littéraire* yellowish, yellowy
NM **j. d'eau** yellow water lily
jaunir [32] [ʒonir] VT 1 (*rendre jaune*) to turn yellow; **ses dents sont jaunies par le tabac** his/her teeth have been turned yellow by smoking 2 (*défraîchir*) to yellow, to turn yellow; **le soleil a jauni les pages** the sun has made the pages go *or* turn yellow
VI 1 (*devenir jaune*) to turn *or* to become yellow, to yellow 2 (*se défraîchir*) to fade; **quelques photos jaunies** a few yellowed *or* faded photographs; **l'encre a jauni** the ink has faded
jaunissant, -e [ʒonisɑ̃, -ɑ̃t] ADJ yellowing; **blés jaunissants** ripening corn
jaunisse [ʒonis] NF *Méd* jaundice; **le bébé a la j.** the baby has jaundice; *Fam* **tu ne vas pas en faire une j.!** there's no need to get into a state *or* to get worked up about it!
jaunissement [ʒonismɑ̃] NM yellowing
Java[1] [ʒava] NF Java; **vivre à J.** to live in Java; **aller à Java** to go to Java
Java®[2] [ʒava] NM *Ordinat* Java®
java [ʒava] NF 1 (*danse*) = type of dance popular in the "bals musettes" at the beginning of the 20th century 2 *Fam* (*fête*) party■, shindig, *Br* knees-up; **faire la j.** to party■
javanais, -e [ʒavanɛ, -ɛz] ADJ Javanese
NM *Ling* 1 (*langue indonésienne*) Javanese 2 (*argot*) = slang using -av- or -ad- as an infix before each vowel sound 3 *Fam* (*langage incompréhensible*) **c'est du j.** that's gobbledegook
▫ **Javanais, -e** NM,F Javanese; **les J.** the Javanese
javart [ʒavar] NM *Vét* ulcerous sore
JavaScript® [ʒavaskript] NM *Ordinat* JavaScript®
javeau, -x [ʒavo] NM sandbank, silt deposit
Javel [ʒavɛl] NM **de l'eau de J., de la J.** bleach
javelage [ʒavlaʒ] NM laying in swaths
javeler [24] [ʒavle] VT to lay in swaths
javeleur, -euse [ʒavlœr, -øz] NM,F harvester
javeline [ʒavlin] NF javelin
javelle [ʒavɛl] NF swath; **mettre le blé en javelles** to lay wheat in swaths
javellisation [ʒavelizasjɔ̃] NF *Chim* chlorination
javelliser [3] [ʒavelize] VT *Chim* to chlorinate
javelot [ʒavlo] NM javelin
jazz [dʒaz] NM jazz; **musicien de j.** jazz musician; **le j. Nouvelle-Orléans** New Orleans jazz; **le j. classique** traditional *or* mainstream jazz
jazz-band [dʒazbɑ̃d] (*pl* **jazz-bands**) NM jazz band
jazzique [dʒazik], **jazzistique** [dʒazistik] ADJ jazz (*avant n*)
jazzman [dʒazman] (*pl* **jazzmans** *ou* **jazzmen** [dʒazmɛn]) NM jazzman, jazz player *or* musician
jazz-rock [dʒazrɔk] NM jazz-rock
jazzy [dʒazi] ADJ INV *Fam* jazzy
J.-C. (*abrév écrite* **Jésus-Christ**) J.C.; **en (l'an) 180 avant/après J.-C.** in (the year) 180 BC/AD 180
JCR [ʒiseɛr] NF (*abrév* **Jeunesse communiste révolutionnaire**) = Communist youth movement
je [ʒə]

j' is used before a word beginning with a vowel or h mute.

PRON I; **j'y vais demain** I'm going there tomorrow; **puis-je me joindre à vous?** may I join you?; **que vois-je?** what do I see?; **puissé-je me tromper!** let us hope I am wrong!; *Fam* **et que je bavarde, et que je me fais un petit café...** (*pour commenter les actions d'autrui*)

and there he/she was, chatting away, making coffee…

NM INV le je *Ling* the first person; *Phil* the self

Jean [ʒɑ̃] **NPR** *Bible* John; *Hist* **J. sans Terre** John Lackland

jean [dʒin] **NM 1** *(tissu)* **(toile de) j.** denim; **un blouson en j.** a denim jacket **2** *(pantalon)* (pair of) jeans

jean-foutre [ʒɑ̃futr] **NM INV** *très Fam* layabout, *Br* waster

jean-le-blanc [ʒɑ̃ləblɑ̃] **NM INV** short-toed eagle

Jeanne [ʒan] **NPR J. d'Arc** *ou* **la Pucelle** Joan of Arc; **elle est coiffée à la J. d'Arc** she wears her hair in a pageboy cut

'Jeanne la Pucelle' *Rivette* 'Joan of Arc'

jeannette [ʒanɛt] **NF 1** *(pour repasser)* sleeve-board **2** *(croix)* gold cross *(worn around the neck)*; *(chaîne)* gold chain *(for wearing a cross)* **3** *(scout) Br* Brownie, *Am* Girl Scout **4** *(plante)* **j. jaune** daffodil **5** *Belg Fam Péj (homosexuel)* queer, fairy, *Am* fag, = offensive term used to refer to a male homosexual

jeans [dʒins] = **jean 2**

JEC, Jec [ʒiəse] **NF** *(abrév* **Jeunesse étudiante chrétienne**) = Christian youth organization

jéciste [ʒesist] **ADJ** belonging to the "JEC"

NMF member of the "JEC"

Jeep® [dʒip] **NF** Jeep®

Jéhovah [ʒeɔva] **NPR** Jehovah; **les témoins de J.** the Jehovah's Witnesses

jéjunal, -e, -aux, -ales [ʒeʒynal, -o] **ADJ** *Anat* jejunal

jéjuno-iléon [ʒeʒynɔileɔ̃] *(pl* **jéjuno-iléons**) **NM** *Anat* jejunoileum

jéjunostomie [ʒeʒynɔstɔmi] **NF** *Méd* jejunostomy

jéjunum [ʒeʒynɔm] **NM** *Anat* jejunum

je-m'en-fichisme [ʒmɑ̃fiʃism] *(pl* **je-m'en-fichismes**) **NM** *Fam* couldn't-care-less attitude; **faire preuve de j.** to show one couldn't care less

je-m'en-fichiste [ʒmɑ̃fiʃist] *(pl* **je-m'en-fichistes**) *Fam* **ADJ** couldn't care less *(avant n)*, devil-may-care *(avant n)*

NMF couldn't care less *or* devil-may-care sort of person

je-m'en-foutisme [ʒmɑ̃futism] *(pl* **je m'en foutismes**) **NM** *Fam* couldn't-care-less attitude; **regarde comment il a écrit ça, c'est vraiment du j.!** look how he's written that, he really couldn't give a damn!

je-m'en-foutiste [ʒmɑ̃futist] *(pl* **je-m'en-foutistes**) *Fam* **ADJ** couldn't give a damn *(avant n)*

NMF couldn't-give-a-damn sort of person

je-ne-sais-quoi [ʒənsekwa] **NM INV un j.** a certain je ne sais quoi, a certain something; **un j. de qch** a hint of sth

jennérien, -enne [ʒenerjɛ̃, -ɛn] **ADJ** Jennerian

jenny [dʒeni] **NF** *Tex* spinning jenny

jérémiades [ʒeremjad] **NFPL** *(lamentations)* wailing; **assez de j.!** stop whining *or* moaning *or* complaining!; **avec lui, ce ne sont que des j.** all you ever get from him is moaning

Jérémie [ʒeremi] **NPR** *Bible* Jeremiah

jerez [gzerɛs] = **xérès**

Jéricho [ʒeriko] **NM** Jericho

jerk [dʒɛrk] **NM** *(danse)* jerk

jerker [3] [dʒɛrke] **VI** to dance the jerk

Jéroboam [ʒerɔbɔam] **NPR** *Bible* Jeroboam

jéroboam [ʒerɔbɔam] **NM** jeroboam

jerrican(e), jerrycan [ʒerikan] **NM** jerrycan

Jersey [ʒɛrzɛ] **NF** Jersey; **vivre à J.** to live in *or* on Jersey; **aller à J.** to go to Jersey

jersey [ʒɛrzɛ] **NM 1** *Vieilli (pull)* jersey, sweater **2** *(tissu)* jersey, jersey knit; **j. de laine** wool jersey; **j. de soie** silk jersey

jersiais, -e [ʒɛrzjɛ, -ɛz] **ADJ** of/from Jersey; **vache jersiaise** Jersey (cow); **race jersiaise** Jersey breed

❑ **Jersiais, -e NM,F** = inhabitant of or person from Jersey

❑ **jersiaise NF** Jersey (cow)

Jérusalem [ʒeryzalɛm] **NM** Jerusalem; **la nouvelle J., la J. céleste** the New Jerusalem

jésuite [ʒezɥit] **ADJ 1** *Rel* Jesuit **2** *Péj (hypocrite)* Jesuitical

NMF *Péj (hypocrite)* Jesuit, casuist; **agir en vrai j.** to be as crafty as a Jesuit

NM *Rel* Jesuit; **les jésuites** the Jesuits

jésuitique [ʒezɥitik] **ADJ 1** *Rel* Jesuitic, Jesuitical **2** *Péj (hypocrite)* Jesuitic, Jesuitical, casuistic

jésuitiquement [ʒezɥitikmɑ̃] **ADV** Jesuitically, casuistically

jésuitisme [ʒezɥitism] **NM 1** *(système moral)* Jesuitism **2** *Péj (hypocrisie)* casuistry, Jesuitry

Jésus [ʒezy] **NPR** Jesus; **le petit J.** baby Jesus; **(doux) J.!, J. Marie!** sweet Jesus!, in the name of Jesus!; **Compagnie** *ou* **Société de J.** Society of Jesus

jésus [ʒezy] **NM 1** *(représentation)* (figure of the) infant *or* baby Jesus; **mets le j. dans la crèche** put the baby Jesus into the crib **2** *Culin* pork liver sausage *(from Franche-Comté and Switzerland)*; **j. de Lyon** ≃ pork salami **3** *Typ* **grand j.** ≃ imperial; **petit j.** ≃ super royal **4** *Fam (chérubin)* cherub, angel; **viens, mon j.!** come along, my (little) angel!

Jésus-Christ [ʒezykri] **NPR** Jesus Christ; **en (l'an) 180 avant/après J.** in (the year) 180 BC/AD 180

jet[1] [dʒɛt] **NM** *Aviat* jet (plane)

jet[2] [ʒɛ] **NM 1** *(embout)* nozzle; *(lance → de pompier)* nozzle, fire (hose); *(→ de jardinier)* (garden) hose; **laver** *ou* **passer qch au j.** to hose sth down

2 *(jaillissement → de flammes, de sang)* spurt, jet; *(→ d'eau, de vapeur)* jet, gush; *(→ de gaz)* gush; **un j. de salive** a jet of saliva

3 *(lancer → de cailloux, d'une balle etc)* throwing *(UNCOUNT)*; **des jets de pierres** stone-throwing; **à un j. de pierre** a stone's throw away

4 *Sport* throw

5 *(ébauche)* **premier j.** *(d'un tableau, d'un dessin)* first *or* rough sketch; *(d'une œuvre littéraire)* first *or* rough draft

6 *Bot (d'arbre)* young shoot

7 *Aviat* jet

8 *Métal (coulage)* cast, casting; *(veine libre)* (pouring) stream; *(arête)* dead head

9 *(entrave → d'un faucon)* jess

10 *Belg (pousse)* **j. de pomme de terre** eye; **j. de soja** (soya) bean sprouts

❑ **à jet continu ADV** non-stop, without a break

❑ **d'un (seul) jet ADV** *Métal* in one piece; *Fig* in one go; **elle nous raconta tout d'un seul j.** she told us everything in one go *or* breath

❑ **jet d'eau NM** *(filet d'eau)* fountain, spray; *(mécanisme)* fountain; *Menuis* weather strip; *Aut* drip moulding

jetable [ʒətabl] **ADJ** *(couche, briquet, gobelet etc)* disposable

jetage [ʒətaʒ] **NM 1** *Vét* running at the nostrils, gleet **2** *(jet)* throwing

jeté[1] [ʒəte] **NM 1** *(danse)* jeté; **petit j.** jeté; **grand j.** grand jeté **2** *Sport* jerk **3** *(maille)* **j. (simple), 1 j.** make 1 **4** *(couverture)* **j. de lit** bedspread; **j. de table** table runner

jeté[2]**, -e**[1] [ʒəte] **ADJ** *Fam* crazy, nuts

jetée[2] [ʒəte] **NF 1** *(en bord de mer)* pier, jetty **2** *(dans une aérogare)* passageway

'La Jetée' *Marker* 'The Jetty' *or* 'The Pier'

JETER [27] [ʒəte]

VT to throw **1–3, 6** ■ to cast **1, 3, 10** ■ to give out **3** ■ to jot down **5** ■ to throw out **7** ■ to lay **9**

VPR to throw oneself **2, 4** ■ to rush **3** ■ to run **5**

VT 1 *(lancer → balle, pierre)* to throw; *(→ filets, dés)* to cast; **elle m'a jeté la balle** she threw me the ball, she threw the ball to me; **j. qch par terre** to throw sth down (on the ground); **ne jetez pas de papiers par terre** don't drop litter; **il a jeté le ballon par-dessus le mur** he threw the ball over the wall; **il a jeté son hochet** he threw down his rattle; **elle lui a jeté sa lettre à la figure** she threw the letter in his/her face; **comme on jette un os à un chien** as you would throw a dog a bone; *Fig* **j. l'éponge** to throw in the sponge *or* towel; *Fam* **n'en jetez plus (la cour est pleine)!** you're making me blush!, don't overdo it!; *Ironique* give it a rest!

2 *(avec un mouvement du corps)* to throw; **l'enfant jeta ses bras autour de mon cou** the child threw *or* flung his/her arms around my neck; **j. la tête/les épaules en arrière** to throw one's head/one's shoulders back; **j. la jambe en l'air** to kick one's leg up; **j. un (coup d')œil sur** *ou* **à qch** to cast a glance *or* to have a (quick) look at sth; **elle jeta un œil las/soupçonneux sur le document** she glanced wearily/suspiciously at the document; **jette un œil sur les enfants** have a quick look *or* check to see if the children are all right; **j. les yeux** *ou* **un regard sur qn/qch** to glance at sb/sth; **elle lui jetait des regards désespérés** she glanced at him/her despairingly *or* in despair, she cast despairing glances at him/her

3 *(émettre → étincelle)* to throw *or* to give out; *(→ lumière)* to cast, to shed; *(→ ombre)* to cast; *(→ son)* to let *or* to give out; **j. un cri** to let out *or* to utter a cry; *Fam* **elle en jette, ta moto!** that's some *or Am* a neat bike you've got there!; *Fam* **elle en jetait dans sa robe de satin noir!** she looked really something in her black satin dress!

4 *(dire brusquement)* **le genre de petites phrases jetées par les ministres aux journalistes** the kind of soundbite that ministers throw at the press; **"venez!", me jeta-t-elle de son bureau** "come here!" she called out to me from her office; **elle leur jeta à la figure qu'ils étaient des incapables** she told them straight (to their faces) that they were incompetent; **j. des injures à la tête de qn** to hurl *or* to fling insults at sb; **il nous jeta quelques ordres secs** he barked out a few orders at us

5 *(écrire rapidement)* to jot down, to scribble (down); **elle jeta quelques remarques sur le papier** she scribbled down a few notes

6 *(mettre)* to throw; **j. qn dehors** *ou* **à la porte** to throw sb out; **j. qn à terre** to throw sb down *or* to the ground; **j. qn en prison** to throw sb into jail *or* prison; **j. qn à la rue** to throw sb out into the street; **j. qn à l'eau** *(à la piscine, sur la plage)* to throw sb in *or* into the water; *(d'un bateau)* to throw sb overboard; **il a jeté sa voiture contre un mur** he ran his car into a wall; **j. une lettre à la boîte** to drop *or* to pop a letter into the postbox; **j. quelques affaires dans un sac** to throw a few things in a bag; **j. son bulletin dans l'urne** to drop *or* to pop one's ballot paper into the box; **j. un châle sur ses épaules** to throw on a shawl; **j. bas** to throw *or* to cast *or* to hurl down; **la statue du dictateur a été jetée bas** the dictator's statue was hurled to the ground; *Fig* **ils ont jeté bas les idoles** they threw down their idols

7 *(mettre au rebut → ordures, vêtements)* to throw away *or* out; **j. qch à la poubelle** to throw sth into the *Br* dustbin *or Am* trashcan; **j. qch au feu** to throw sth into *or* on the fire; **il jeta la boulette de papier dans les flammes** he threw *or* tossed the crumpled piece of paper into the fire; **les lettres de réclamation sont directement jetées au panier** letters of complaint are thrown straight into the wastepaper basket; **jette l'eau dans le caniveau** pour the water (out) into the gutter; **il n'y a rien à j. dans ce livre** this book's as good as you'll get; **c'est bon à j.** it's fit for the *Br* dustbin *or Am* trashcan; *Fig* **j. le bébé avec l'eau du bain** to throw the baby out with the bathwater

8 *(plonger)* **j. qn dans l'embarras** to throw *or* to plunge sb into confusion; **j. qn dans le désarroi/les affres de la jalousie** to plunge sb into despair/the torments of jealousy; **j. qn dans de terribles fureurs** to drive sb into paroxysms of anger

9 *(établir → fondations)* to lay; *(→ passerelle)* to set up; *(→ pont)* to throw; **j. les fondements d'une loi/politique** to lay the foundations of a law/policy; **le traité jette les bases de la nouvelle Europe** the treaty lays the foundations for the new Europe

10 *(répandre → doute)* to cast; **cela a jeté la consternation dans la famille** it filled the whole family with dismay; **j. le discrédit sur qn/qch** to discredit sb/sth, to bring sb/sth into disrepute; **j. le doute dans les esprits** to sow *or* to cast doubt in people's minds; **j. le trouble chez qn** to disturb *or* to trouble sb

11 *Fam (expulser)* **se faire j.** to get kicked out; **on a essayé d'aller en boîte mais on s'est fait**

j. par un videur we tried to get into a nightclub but the bouncer kicked us out; **ce n'est pas le moment de lui demander, tu vas te faire j.!** now is not the time to ask him/her, he'll/she'll just send you packing!; **il s'est fait j. par sa copine** he's been chucked by his girlfriend

VI 1 *Belg (graine)* to germinate; *(bulbe, tubercule)* to shoot, to sprout

2 *Fam* **ça jette!** it looks fantastic!

▶se jeter VPR 1 *(être jetable)* **un rasoir qui se jette** a disposable razor

2 *(sauter)* to throw *or* to hurl oneself, to leap; **se j. à bas de son cheval** to leap from one's horse; **se j. dans le vide** to throw oneself into the void; **se j. par la fenêtre** to throw oneself out of the window; **elle s'est jetée du haut du pont** she hurled herself *or* threw herself from the top of the bridge; **un homme s'est jeté sous la rame** a man threw himself *or* hurled himself in front of the train; **je n'ai pas pu l'éviter, il s'est jeté sous mes roues** I couldn't avoid him, he just leapt out in front of my car; **se j. de côté** to leap aside, to take a sideways leap; **se j. à l'eau** to leap into the water; *Fig* to take the plunge; **jette-toi à l'eau, propose-lui le mariage** go on, take the plunge and ask him/her to marry you

3 *(se précipiter)* to rush (headlong); **se j. aux pieds de qn** to throw oneself at sb's feet; **se j. dans la foule** to plunge into the crowd; **se j. sur qn** to set about *or* to pounce on sb; **ils se sont tous jetés sur moi** *(pour me frapper)* they all set about *or* pounced on me; *(pour me questionner)* they all pounced on me; **il avait tellement faim qu'il s'est jeté sur la nourriture** he was so hungry he fell on the food; **les chiens se sont jetés sur la viande** the dogs devoured the meat; **ne vous jetez pas sur les biscuits!** don't eat the biscuits all at once!; **elle se jeta sur son lit** she threw herself on (to) her bed; **le canot s'est jeté dans les rapides** the canoe plunged into the rapids; **elle se jeta dans un taxi** she leapt into a taxi; **elles se jetèrent sous le premier porche venu** they scurried *or* rushed into the nearest doorway; **vous vous êtes tous jetés sur la question B** you all went for question B; **se j. à la tête de qn** to throw oneself at sb

4 *(entreprendre)* **se j. dans qch** to throw *or* to fling oneself into sth; **se j. à corps perdu dans une aventure** to fling oneself body and soul into an adventure

5 *(cours d'eau)* **se j. dans** to run *or* to flow into; **là où la Marne se jette dans la Seine** where the Marne meets the Seine, at the confluence of the Marne and the Seine

6 *très Fam (locution)* **s'en j. un (derrière la cravate)** to have a quick drink *or* a quick one; **on s'en jette un dernier?** let's have one for the road!

---

jeteur, -euse [ʒətœr, -øz] **NM,F j. de sort** wizard, *f* witch

jeton [ʒətɔ̃] **NM 1** *(pièce)* token; **j. de téléphone** token for the telephone

2 *(au jeu)* counter; *(à la roulette)* chip, counter, jetton

3 *(dans une entreprise)* **j. (de présence)** director's fees; **il n'est là que pour toucher ses jetons** he's just a timeserver, all he does is draw his salary

4 *très Fam (coup de poing)* whack; **(se) prendre un j.** to get a whack in the face

▫ jetons NMPL *très Fam* **avoir les jetons** to be scared stiff; **foutre les jetons à qn** to give sb the willies, *Br* to put the wind up sb

jet-set [dʒɛtsɛt] *(pl* **jet-sets)** **NF OU NM** jet set; **membre de la j.** jet-setter

jet-ski [dʒɛtski] *(pl* **jet-skis)** **NF** jet ski; **faire du j.** to go jet-skiing

jet society [dʒɛtsɔsajti] **NF** = **jet-set**

jet-stream [dʒɛtstrim] *(pl* **jet-streams)** **NM** *Météo* jet stream

jettatura [dʒɛtatura] **NF** evil eye

jette *etc voir* **jeter**

JEU, -X [ʒø]

game **1, 4–6** ▪ hand **2** ▪ set **3** ▪ play **1, 5, 11, 13** ▪ acting **9** ▪ gambling **10**

NM 1 *(gén)* game; **le j.** *(activité)* play; **ce n'est qu'un j.!** it's only a game!, it's only for fun!; **c'est le j.!** it's fair (play)!; **ce n'est pas de** *ou* **du j.!** that's not fair!; **le j. d'échecs** the game of chess; **l'enfant s'exprime par le j.** a child expresses himself/herself by playing *or* through play; **par j.** for fun, in play; **les chiots ne mordent que par j.** puppies only bite in play; **j. d'adresse** game of skill; **j. éducatif** educational game; **j. électronique** computer game; **j. d'entreprise** management simulation (game); **j. de hasard** game of chance; **j. informatique** computer game; **j. interactif** interactive game; **j. de l'oie** ≃ snakes and ladders; **j. de plein air** outdoor game; **j. radiophonique** (radio) game show; *(avec questions)* (radio) quiz (show); **j. en réseau** network game; **j. de rôle** role-playing; **j. de société** *(charades, devinettes)* parlour game; *(petits chevaux, jeu de l'oie)* board games; **j. télévisé** game show; *(avec questions)* (television) quiz (show); **j. vidéo** video game; **c'est un j. d'enfant!** this is child's play!; **se faire un j. de faire qch** to make light *or* easy work of doing sth; **il s'est fait un j. de démolir tous nos arguments** it was child's play for him to destroy all our arguments; **jeux de mains, jeux de vilains** all this fooling around is going to end in tears

2 *(cartes)* hand; **avoir du j.** *ou* **un bon j.** to have a good hand; **ne pas avoir de j., avoir un mauvais j.** to have a bad hand; **il avait tout le j.** he had all the good cards; **ne montre pas ton j.!** don't show your hand *or* your cards!; **étaler son j.** to lay down one's hand *or* cards; **le grand j.** *(d'une cartomancienne)* (complete) Major Arcana; **elle nous a joué** *ou* **sorti le grand j.** she pulled out all the stops with *or* on us; **avoir beau j. (de faire qch)** to have no trouble (in doing sth), to find it easy (to do sth); **il a eu beau j. de montrer qu'elle avait tort** it was easy for him to prove her wrong; *Fig* **montrer** *ou* **dévoiler son j.** to show one's hand; *Fig* **il a bien caché son j.** he played (his cards) very close to his chest

3 *(ensemble de pièces)* set; **j. de (32/52) cartes** *Br* pack *or Am* deck of (32/52) cards; **un j. de dames/d'échecs/de loto/de quilles** a draughts/chess/lotto/skittles set; **un j. de clés/tournevis** a set of keys/screwdrivers; *Ordinat* **j. de caractères** character set; *Ordinat* **j. d'essai** sample data *or* deck; *Ordinat* **j. de fiches** card index; *Mus* **j. d'orgue** organ stop

4 *(manigances)* game; **c'est un (petit) j. dangereux!** this is a dangerous (little) game you're playing!; **qu'est-ce que c'est que ce petit j.?, à quel j. joues-tu?** *(ton irrité)* what are you playing at?, what's your game?; **entrer dans le j. de qn** to go along with sb; **faire le j. de qn** to play into sb's hands; **être pris à son propre j.** to be caught at one's own game; **se (laisser) prendre au j.** to get caught up *or* involved in what's going on; **voir clair** *ou* **lire dans le j. de qn** to see through sb's little game, to see what sb is up to

5 *(activité sportive, partie)* game; *(action)* play; **les jeux d'équipe** team games; **le j. à XIII** rugby league; **le j. s'est accéléré** the play *or* the game has livened up a bit; **le j. est très ouvert/fermé** the game is very open/tight; **où en est le j.?** what's the score?; **il y a eu du beau j.** there was some very good play; **notre équipe a fait tout le j.** our team had the upper hand; **faire j. égal** to be evenly matched; **il a fait j. égal avec le champion** the champion met his match in him

6 *(au tennis)* game; **j. Federer!** game to Federer!; **deux jeux partout** two games all; **j. blanc** love game; **j., set et match** game, set and match

7 *(terrain)* **la balle est sortie du j.** the ball has gone out (of play); **j. de boules** *(sur gazon)* bowling green; *(de pétanque)* ground *(for playing boules)*; **j. de quilles** skittle alley

8 *(style d'un sportif)* game, way of playing; **il a un j. défensif/un j. offensif** he plays a defensive/an attacking game; **elle a un j. de fond de court** she's got a baseline game; **il a un bon j. de volée** he's a good volleyer, he volleys well

9 *(interprétation → d'un acteur)* acting; *(→ d'un musicien)* playing; **la pièce exige un j. tout en nuances** the play requires subtle acting

10 *(activité du parieur)* **le j.** gambling; **elle a tout perdu au j.** she gambled her entire fortune away, she lost her whole fortune (at) gambling; **j. de Bourse** gambling on the Stock Exchange, Stock Exchange speculation

11 *(effets)* play; **j. d'eau** fountain; **j. de jambes** *(d'un boxeur, d'un joueur de tennis)* footwork; **jeux de lumière** *(naturels)* play of light; *(artificiels)* lighting effects; **j. de mots** play on words, pun; **j. d'ombres** play of shadows

12 *(espace)* **la vis a** *ou* **prend du j.** the screw is loose; **il y a du j.** there's a bit of play *or* of a gap; **donner du j. à qch** to loosen sth up; *Fig* **donner** *ou* **laisser du j. à qn** to allow sb (some) freedom *or* leeway; **je leur laisse un certain j. au niveau du budget** I give them some freedom of action *or* some leeway where the budget is concerned

13 *(action)* play; **le j. du piston dans le cylindre** the action of the piston inside the cylinder; *Littéraire* **le j. des vagues sur les rochers** the play of waves on the rocks; **c'est un j. de ton imagination/ta mémoire** it's a trick of your imagination/your memory; **laisser faire le j. de la concurrence** to allow the free play of competition; **le marché s'est agrandi grâce au j. de forces économiques nouvelles** the market has expanded because new economic forces have come into play; **ils sont parvenus à un accord par le j. subtil de la diplomatie** they reached an agreement through the subtle use of diplomacy; **il n'a obtenu le siège que par le j. des alliances électorales** he won the seat only through the interplay *or* working of electoral alliances

14 *Compta* **j. d'écritures** paper transaction; **par un j. d'écritures** by some creative accounting

15 *Littérature* = tragedy or comedy in verse, performed during the Middle Ages

▫ jeux NMPL 1 *(mise)* **faites vos jeux(, rien ne va plus)** place your bets, faites vos jeux(, rien ne va plus); **les jeux sont faits** no more bets, les jeux sont faits; *Fig* the die is cast, there's no going back now

2 *Sport* **les Jeux, les jeux Olympiques** the (Olympic) Games, the Olympics; **les Jeux d'hiver, les jeux Olympiques d'hiver** the Winter Olympics; **les jeux Olympiques pour handicapés, les jeux Paralympiques** the Paralympic Games, the Paralympics; *Antiq* **les jeux du cirque** the (games of the) circus

▫ en jeu ADJ 1 *(en question)* at stake; **l'avenir de l'entreprise n'est pas en j.** the company's future is not at stake *or* at risk **2** *(en action)* at play; **les forces en j. sur le marché** the competing forces *or* the forces at play *or* the forces at work on the market; **les intérêts en j.** the interests at stake *or* at issue *or* involved **3** *(parié)* at stake; **la somme en j.** the money at stake *or* which has been staked **ADV 1** *Ftbl* **mettre le ballon en j.** to throw in the ball **2** *(en pariant)* **mettre une somme en j.** to place a bet; **mettre qch en j.** *(risquer qch)* to put sth at stake; **mettre son avenir en j.** to put one's future at stake, to stake one's future; **entrer en j.** *(intervenir)* to come into play; **les institutions religieuses sont entrées en j. pour s'opposer à l'avortement** the religious institutions entered the fray to oppose abortion

▫ jeu de massacre NM Aunt Sally; *Fig* **le débat s'est transformé en j. de massacre** the debate turned into a slanging match

'Jeux interdits' *Clément* 'Forbidden Games'

'Le Jeu de l'amour et du hasard' *Marivaux* 'The Game of Love and Chance'

Culture

LE JEU DES MILLE FRANCS

This radio programme was originally broadcast in the 1950s and has become a national institution. The quiz, whose top prize was originally one thousand francs, consists of a series of questions sent in by listeners. Today, the prize is one thousand euros, and the show's name has been updated to *le Jeu des mille euros*.

jeu-concours [ʒøkɔ̃kur] (pl **jeux-concours**) NM competition

jeudi [ʒødi] NM Thursday; **le J. noir** Black Thursday (day of the Wall Street Crash, 1929); **le j. saint** Holy Thursday, Br Maundy Thursday; Fam **la semaine des quatre jeudis,** Can **dans la semaine des trois jeudis** never in a month of Sundays; voir aussi **mardi**

jeun [ʒœ̃] **à jeun** ADJ **il est à j.** (il n'a rien mangé) he hasn't eaten anything; (il n'a rien bu) he's sober ▪ ADV on an empty stomach; **il faut venir à j.** (avant une opération, avant une piqûre) you have to fast beforehand; **venez à j.** don't eat anything before you come; **trois comprimés à j.** three tablets to be taken on an empty stomach

---

JEUNE [ʒœn]

| ADJ young 1, 4, 5–7 ▪ younger 2 ▪ early 4 ▪ young-looking 5 ▪ youthful 5 ▪ new 6, 7 |
| NM young man |
| NF young girl |

ADJ **1** (peu avancé en âge → personne, génération, population) young; **mourir j.** to die young; **réussir j.** to succeed at a young age; **il n'est plus très j.** he's not that young any more, he's not as young as he used to be; **tout j.** very young; Fam **ma voiture n'est plus toute j.** my car's got quite a few miles on the clock now; **j. arbre** sapling, young tree; **j. chien** puppy, young dog; **un j. homme** a young man, a youth; **eh bien, j. homme, où vous croyez-vous?** I say, young man, where do you think you are?; **faire le j. homme** to act the young man; **une j. femme** a young woman; **un j. garçon** (enfant) a boy, a youngster; (adolescent) a youth, a teenager; **une j. fille** a girl, a young woman; **j. oiseau** fledgling, young bird; **j. fille au pair** au pair (girl); **j. personne** young lady; **de jeunes enfants** young or small children; **jeunes gens** (garçons) young men; (garçons et filles) youngsters, young people; **un j. Français/Anglais** a French/an English boy; **une j. Indienne** an Indian girl; **être plus/moins j. que** to be younger/older than; **je suis plus j. que lui de deux mois** I'm younger than him by two months, I'm two months younger than him; **ma j. sœur** my youngest sister; **ils font j. ou jeunes** they look young; **faire ou paraître plus j. que son âge** to look younger than one's age or one's years or one is; Fam **c'est j., ça ne sait pas!** he's/she's (still) young or wet behind the ears, he'll/she'll learn!

2 (en comparaison) younger; **mon j. frère** my younger brother

3 (débutant) **on reparlera de ce j. metteur en scène** we haven't heard the last of this young director; **cherchons j. ingénieur** (dans les petites annonces) recently qualified engineer required; **être j. dans le métier** to be new to the trade or business

4 (du début de la vie) young, early; **mes jeunes années** my youth; **il a passé ses jeunes années en Provence** he spent his early years or youth in Provence; Littéraire **dans notre j. âge** in our youth, when we were young; **étant donné son j. âge** given his/her youth or how young he/she is; Fam **dans mon j. temps** when I was a youngster

5 (d'aspect → personne) young, young-looking, youthful; (→ apparence, allure) youthful; (→ couleur, coiffure) young, youthful; **pour avoir l'air toujours j., pour rester j.** to stay young or young-looking; **être j. d'esprit ou de caractère** to be young at heart; **être j. d'allure** to be young-looking, to be youthful-looking, to have a youthful appearance

6 (récent → discipline, entreprise, État) new, young; **leur histoire d'amour est encore j.** their (love) affair is still young or hasn't matured yet; **les jeunes États d'Afrique** the new or young African States

7 (vin) young, new; (fromage) young

8 Fam (juste) **ça fait ou c'est un peu j.!** (somme d'argent) that's a bit mean!; (temps) that's cutting it a bit fine!; (dimensions) that's a bit on the small side!; (poids) that's a bit on the light side!; **c'est un peu j. comme argument** it's a bit of a flimsy argument

▪ ADV (comme les jeunes) **s'habiller j.** to wear young-looking clothes; **se coiffer j.** to have a young-looking hairstyle

▪ NM (garçon) young man, youngster; Fam **petit j.** young guy; **les jeunes de cette génération-là sont morts dans les tranchées** the youngsters or young men of that generation died in the trenches

▪ NF (fille) (young) girl; Fam **petite j.** young girl ▪ □ **jeunes** NMPL (garçons et filles) **les jeunes** youngsters, young people, the young; **les jeunes d'aujourd'hui** young people today; **les jeunes ont préféré manger sur la terrasse** the youngsters chose to eat out on the terrace; **une bande de jeunes** a bunch of kids

---

'La Jeune fille à la perle' Chevalier, Webber 'Girl with a Pearl Earring'

'La Jeune fille au turban' ou 'La jeune fille à la perle' Vermeer 'Girl with Turban' or 'Girl with a Pearl Earring'

---

jeûne [ʒøn] NM **1** (période) fast; **le j. du ramadan** the fasting at Ramadan **2** (pratique) fast, fasting (UNCOUNT); **observer une semaine de j.** to fast for a week; **un petit j. ne lui fera pas de mal** it won't do him/her any harm to go without food or to fast for a while

jeunement [ʒœnmɑ̃] ADV **1** Arch youthfully **2** Chasse **cerf dix cors j.** stag just turned five years

jeûner [3] [ʒøne] VI **1** Rel to fast **2** (ne rien manger) to go without food

jeunesse [ʒœnɛs] NF **1** (juvénilité → d'une personne) youth, youthfulness; (→ d'une génération, d'une population) youthfulness, young age; (→ d'un arbre, d'un animal) young age; (→ des traits, d'un style) youthfulness; **elle m'a rendu ma j.** she made me feel young again; **tous furent impressionnés par la j. de l'équipe gouvernementale** they were all impressed by how young the government ministers were; **j'apprécie la j. d'esprit ou de caractère** I appreciate a youthful outlook or frame of mind; **l'important, c'est d'avoir la j. du cœur** what matters is to remain young at heart

2 (enfance → d'une personne) youth; (→ d'une science) early period, infancy; **dans ma ou au temps de ma j.** in my youth, when I was young, in my early years; **la génétique est encore dans sa j.** genetics is still in its infancy; **il n'est plus de la première j.** (personne) he's not as young as he was, he's getting on a bit; (objet) it's seen better days; Prov **il faut que j. se passe** youth will have its fling

3 (jeunes gens) **la j.** young people, the young; **la j. américaine** American youth, young Americans; **la j. étudiante** young students, student youth; **la j. ouvrière** young workers, working-class youth; **émissions pour la j.** TV programmes for young viewers; Rad programmes for young listeners; Fam **alors, la j., on se dépêche!** come on, you youngsters or young folk, hurry up!; **la j. dorée** gilded youth; Prov **si j. savait, si vieillesse pouvait** if youth but knew and age but could

4 Vieilli (jeune fille) (young) girl; **ce n'est plus une j.** she's no longer young

5 Can Fam (jeune personne) young person ; **je me sens vieux parmi toutes ces jeunesses!** I feel old among all these young people!

6 (d'un vin) youthfulness, greenness

7 (groupe) **J. agricole chrétienne** = Christian youth organization; **J. communiste révolutionnaire** = Communist youth movement; **J. étudiante chrétienne** = Christian youth organization; **J. ouvrière chrétienne** = Christian youth organization

□ **jeunesses** NFPL (groupe) youth; **les jeunesses hitlériennes** the Hitler Youth; **les jeunesses communistes/socialistes** Young Communists/Socialists; **les Jeunesses musicales de France** = association promoting music for the young

□ **de jeunesse** ADJ **ses amours/œuvres/péchés de j.** the loves/works/sins of his/her youth

jeunet, -ette [ʒœnɛ, -ɛt] ADJ youngish, rather

young; **elle est un peu jeunette pour faire ce travail** she's a bit on the young side to do this job

jeune-turc, jeune-turque [ʒœntyrk] (mpl **jeunes-turcs,** fpl **jeunes-turques**) NM,F Hist & Pol Young Turk

jeûneur, -euse [ʒønœr, -øz] NM,F faster

jeunisme [ʒœnism] NM Péj cult of youth

jeunot, -otte [ʒœno, -ɔt] ADJ youngish, rather young; **il est un peu j.** he's a bit on the young side

▪ NM,F youngster; **un petit j.** a young lad

Jézabel [ʒezabɛl] NPR Bible Jezebel

JF, jf 1 (abrév écrite **jeune fille**) girl **2** (abrév écrite **jeune femme**) young woman

JH, jh (abrév écrite **jeune homme**) young man

jigger [ʒigɛr] NM **1** Élec jigger, oscillation transformer **2** Tex jigger

jingle [dʒingœl] NM jingle

jingxi [ʒiŋksi] NM ching-hsi, Pinyin jingxi

jinisme [ʒinizm] NM = **jaïnisme**

jiu-jitsu [ʒjyʒitsu] NM ju-jitsu, jiu-jitsu

Jivaro [ʒivaro] NM,F Jivaro; **les Jivaros** the Jivaro

JMF [ʒiɛmɛf] NFPL (abrév **Jeunesses musicales de France**) = association promoting music for the young

JO [ʒio] NM Admin (abrév **Journal Officiel**) = French government publication giving information to the public about new laws, parliamentary debates, government business and new companies, Br ≃ Hansard, Am ≃ Federal Register; voir aussi l'encadré sous **journal**

▪ NMPL (abrév **jeux Olympiques**) Olympic Games

joaillerie [ʒoajri] NF **1** (art) **la j.** jewelling; **la j. du XVème siècle** the art of the jeweller in the 15th century **2** (commerce) **la j.** the jewel trade, jewellery **3** (magasin) Br jeweller's shop, Am jeweler's store **4** (articles) **la j.** jewellery

joaillier, -ère [ʒoaje, -ɛr] ADJ jewel (avant n) ▪ NM,F jeweller

Job [ʒɔb] NPR Bible Job; **pauvre comme J.** as poor as Job, as poor as a church mouse

job [dʒɔb] Fam (emploi) job ; **elle a un bon j.** she's got a good job

▪ NF Can Joual (travail) job ; **il a fait une bonne j. sur sa maison** he's done a good job on his house

jobard, -e [ʒɔbar, -ard] Fam ADJ (très naïf) gullible, naive

▪ NM,F sucker, Br mug, Am patsy

jobarder [3] [ʒɔbarde] VT Fam Vieilli to fool , to hoax

jobarderie [ʒɔbardri], **jobardise** [ʒɔbardiz] NF Fam (crédulité) gullibility, naivety

jobine [ʒobin], **jobinette** [ʒobinɛt] NF Can Fam casual job ; **faire des jobines** to do odd jobs or casual work

jobiste [ʒobist] NMF Belg Fam student with a casual job

JOC, Joc [ʒiose] NF (abrév **Jeunesse ouvrière chrétienne**) = Christian youth organization

jocasse [ʒokas] NF Orn fieldfare

Jocaste [ʒokast] NPR Myth Jocasta

jociste [ʒosist] ADJ related to the "JOC" ▪ NMF member of the "JOC"

jockey [ʒokɛ] NM jockey

Joconde [ʒokɔ̃d] NF

'La Joconde' de Vinci 'The Mona Lisa'

---

jocrisse [ʒokris] NM Vieilli dupe, Br gull

Jodhpur [ʒodpur] NM Jodhpur

jodhpurs [ʒodpyr] NMPL jodhpurs

jodler [3] [ʒodle] VI to yodel

jogger[1] [dʒɔgœr] NM ou NF (chaussure) jogging shoe, trainer

jogger[2] [3] [dʒɔge] VI to jog

joggeur, -euse [dʒɔgœr, -øz] NM,F jogger

jogging [dʒɔgiŋ] NM **1** (activité) jogging; (course) run; **faire du j.** to go jogging, to jog; **faire son j. matinal** to go for one's morning jog; **ils ont organisé un j.** they organized a run **2** (survêtement) tracksuit

Johannesburg [ʒoanɛsbur] NM Johannesburg

johannique [ʒoanik] ADJ Rel Johannine

johannisberg [ʒoanisbɛrg] NM (vin) = white wine from the Valais canton

johannite [ʒoanit] Rel ADJ Johannite ▪ NMF Johannite

joice [ʒwas] *très Fam* = **jouasse**

joie [ʒwa] **NF 1** *(bonheur)* joy, delight; **être fou de j.** to be wild with joy; **elle ne se sentait plus de j.** she was beside herself with joy; **pousser un cri de j.** to shout *or* to whoop for joy; **sauter** *ou* **bondir de j.** to jump *or* to leap for joy; **être au comble de la j.** to be overjoyed; **quelle a été votre plus grande j.?** what has been your greatest joy?; **travailler dans la j. et la bonne humeur** to work cheerfully and good-humouredly; **pour la plus grande j. de ses parents, elle a obtenu la bourse** much to the delight of her parents *or* to her parents' great delight, she won the scholarship; **j. de vivre** joie de vivre, enjoyment of life; **déborder de j. de vivre** to be full of the joys of spring; *Fam* **c'est pas la j. à la maison** life at home isn't exactly a laugh a minute *or* a bundle of laughs

2 *(plaisir)* pleasure; **c'est une j. de le voir rétabli** it's a joy *or* a delight to see him on his feet again; **avec j.!** with great pleasure!; **il a accepté avec j.** he was delighted to accept; **nous avons la j. d'avoir M. Dupont parmi nous** we have the pleasure of having Mr Dupont with us; **nous avons la j. de vous annoncer la naissance de Charles** we are happy to announce the birth of Charles; **quand vais-je avoir la j. de faire sa connaissance?** when will I have the pleasure of making his/her acquaintance?; **je suis tout à la j. de revoir mes amis** I'm overjoyed at the idea of *or* I'm greatly looking forward to seeing my friends again; **des films qui ont fait la j. de millions d'enfants** films which have given pleasure to *or* delighted millions of children; **la petite Émilie fait la j. de sa mère** little Émilie is the apple of her mother's eye *or* is her mother's pride and joy; **il se faisait une telle j. de venir à ton mariage** he was so delighted at the idea of *or* so looking forward to coming to your wedding; *Hum* **je me ferai une j. de lui dire ses quatre vérités** I shall be only too pleased to tell him/her a few home truths; **cette nouvelle l'a mis en j.** he is delighted by the news; **tu m'as fait une fausse j.** you got me all excited for nothing; **ne me fais pas de fausse j.** don't build up my hopes

❑ **joies NFPL** *(plaisirs)* joys; **les joies de la vie/retraite** the joys of life/retirement

joignable [ʒwaɲabl] **ADJ je suis j. à ce numéro** I can be reached at this number

JOINDRE [82] [ʒwɛ̃dr]

> **VT** to join **1** ▪ to put together **2** ▪ to link **3,** **5** ▪ to add **4** ▪ to enclose **4** ▪ to attach **4** ▪ to combine **5** ▪ to contact **6**
> **VPR** to get through to each other **1** ▪ to make contact **1** ▪ to join **3**

VT 1 *(attacher → ficelles, tuyaux)* to join (together); *(→ câbles)* to join, to connect; **j. deux lattes, j. une latte à une autre** to put two boards together, to join one board to another; *Fig* **j. les deux bouts** to make ends meet

2 *(rapprocher)* to put *or* to bring together; **j. les mains** *(pour prier)* to put one's hands together

3 *(points, lieux)* to link

4 *(ajouter)* to add (**à** to); *(dans une lettre, un colis)* to enclose (**à** with); *Ordinat (à un courrier électronique)* to attach (**à** to); **joignez une photocopie à votre dossier** add a photocopy to *or* put a photocopy in your file; **veuillez j. CV et photo d'identité** please enclose *or* attach a copy of your *Br* CV *or Am* résumé and a photograph; **l'échantillon joint à votre lettre** the sample enclosed with your letter; **je joins à ce pli un chèque de 300 euros** please find enclosed a cheque for 300 euros; **ils ont renvoyé le manuscrit sans j. la moindre explication** they sent the manuscript back without (adding) the slightest explanation; **voulez-vous j. une carte aux fleurs?** would you like to send a card with the flowers?; **j. sa voix aux protestations** to add one's voice to *or* to join in the protests

5 *(associer)* to combine, to link; **j. la technique à l'efficacité** to combine technical know-how and efficiency; **le bon sens joint à l'intelligence** common sense combined with intelligence; **les servitudes jointes à l'élargissement de nos activités** the constraints associated *or* connected *or* that come with an increase in the scope of our activities

6 *(contacter)* to contact, to get in touch with; **j. qn par téléphone** to get through to sb on the phone, to contact sb by phone; **j. qn par lettre** to contact sb in writing; **où pourrai-je vous j.?** how can I get in touch with you *or* contact you?; **tu peux toujours me j. à la maison** you can always reach *or* contact me at home

VI *(porte, planches, battants)* **des volets qui joignent bien/mal** shutters that close/don't close properly; **des lattes de plancher qui joignent bien** tightly fitting floorboards

▸**se joindre VPR 1** *(se contacter → par téléphone)* to get through to each other; *(→ par lettre)* to make contact

2 *(se nouer)* **leurs mains se sont jointes** their hands came together *or* joined

3 se j. à *(s'associer à)* to join; **quelques touristes se sont joints à la foule des manifestants** a few tourists joined in with *or* mingled with the crowd of demonstrators; **tu veux te j. à nous?** would you like to join us?; **se j. à une conversation/partie de rami** to join in a conversation/game of rummy; **puis-je me j. à vous pour acheter le cadeau de Pierre?** may I contribute to Pierre's present?; **Lisa se joint à moi pour vous souhaiter la bonne année** Lisa and I wish you *or* Lisa joins me in wishing you a Happy New Year

joint, -e [ʒwɛ̃, -ɛ̃t] **ADJ 1** *(rapproché)* **agenouillé, les mains jointes** kneeling with his hands (clasped) together

2 *(attaché)* **planches mal/solidement jointes** loose-/tight-fitting boards

3 *(documents, échantillons)* enclosed, attached

NM 1 *Constr & Menuis (garniture d'étanchéité)* joint; *(ligne d'assemblage)* join; **les joints d'un mur** the pointing of a wall; **j. de chantier** temporary *or* makeshift joint; **j. de dilatation/retrait/rupture** expansion/contraction/breaking joint; **j. saillant** raised joint

2 *Tech (ligne d'assemblage)* joint; **j. abouté** butt joint; **j. articulé** knuckle (joint); **j. biseauté** scarf joint; **j. à brides** flange joint; **j. brisé** universal *or* cardan joint, coupling; **j. de cardan** universal *or* cardan joint, coupling; *Aut* **j. de culasse** (cylinder) head gasket; **j. à rotule** ball(-and-socket) joint; **j. tournant** revolving joint; **j. universel** universal joint

3 *Tech* **j. (d'étanchéité)** seal, gasket; **j. à lèvre** lip seal; **j. torique** O-ring

4 *Rail* (rail) joint

5 *(de robinet)* washer

6 *Géol* joint

7 *Fam (moyen)* **trouver le j.** to come up with a solution▪; **il cherche un j. pour payer moins d'impôts** he's trying to find a clever way of paying less tax

8 *(intermédiaire)* **faire le j. (entre deux personnes)** to act as a go-between (between two people)

9 *Fam (drogue)* joint

jointif, -ive [ʒwɛ̃tif, -iv] **ADJ** *Menuis* butt-jointed

jointoiement [ʒwɛ̃twamɑ̃] **NM** *Constr* pointing

jointoyer [13] [ʒwɛ̃twaje] **VT** *Constr* to point (up)

jointure [ʒwɛ̃tyr] **NF 1** *Anat* joint; *(chez le cheval)* pastern joint, fetlock; **jointures des doigts** knuckles **2** *(assemblage)* joint; *(point de jonction)* join

joint-venture [dʒɔjntvɛntʃər] (*pl* **joint-ventures**) **NM** joint venture

jojo [ʒoʒo] *Fam* **ADJ INV** *(beau, correct)* **pas j.** not very nice▪; **il est pas j., son petit ami** his/her boyfriend's no oil painting; **c'est pas j. ce qu'il a fait là** what he did there wasn't very nice

NM *(enfant)* **ce gamin est un affreux j.** that child is a little horror

jojoba [ʒoʒoba] **NM** jojoba

joker [ʒokɛr] **NM 1** *Cartes* joker; *Fig* **sortir son j.** to play one's trump card **2** *Ordinat* wild card

joli, -e [ʒoli] **ADJ 1** *(voix, robe, sourire)* pretty, lovely, nice; *(poème)* pretty, lovely; *(voyage, mariage)* lovely, nice; *(personne)* pretty; **très j.** *(enfant, vêtement)* lovely; **une très jolie femme** a very pretty woman; **ces deux bleus ensemble, ça n'est pas j.** these two blues don't look nice together; **il est j. garçon** he's nice-looking *or* attractive; **le j. mois de mai** the merry month of May; *Fam* **ce n'était pas j. à voir, ce n'était pas j. j.**, it wasn't a pretty *or* pleasant sight; **ce n'est pas j. de mentir** it's not nice to tell lies; **être j. comme un cœur** *ou* **j. à croquer** to be (as) pretty as a picture; **faire le j. cœur** to flirt

2 *(considérable)* **une jolie (petite) somme, un j. (petit) pécule** a nice *or* tidy *or* handsome (little) sum of money; **elle s'est taillé un j. succès** she's been most *or* very successful; **de très jolis résultats** very good *or* fine results

3 *(usage ironique)* **elle est jolie, la politique!** what a fine *or* nice thing politics is, isn't it?; *Fam* **tu nous as mis dans un j. pétrin** you got us into a fine mess *or* pickle; **j. monsieur!** what a charming individual!; **tout ça c'est bien j., mais...** that's all very well *or* that's all well and good, but...

NM,F lovely; **viens, ma jolie!** come here, honey *or* darling *or* lovely!

❑ **joli NM** *Ironique* **1** *(action blâmable)* **tu l'as cassé? c'est du j.!** you broke it? that's great!; **c'est du j. d'avoir filé!** that's nice, running away! **2** *(locution)* **quand il va voir les dégâts, ça va faire du j.!** when he sees the damage, there'll be all hell to pay! **ADV faire j.** to look nice *or* pretty

joliesse [ʒoljɛs] **NF** *Littéraire* prettiness, charm, grace

joliet, -ette [ʒoljɛ, -ɛt] **ADJ** rather pretty *or* attractive

joliment [ʒolimɑ̃] **ADV 1** *(élégamment)* prettily, nicely; **j. dit** nicely *or* neatly put; **table j. présentée** nicely decorated table

2 *Fam (en intensif)* pretty, *Br* jolly; **c'est j. compliqué** it's pretty *or* awfully complicated; **elle est j. énervée!** she's really *or Am* darn annoyed!; **elle s'est j. fait enguirlander** she got a real *or Br* right telling-off

3 *Ironique (très mal)* **on s'est fait j. accueillir!** a fine *or* nice welcome we got there!; **te voilà j. arrangé!** you're in a right mess *or* state!

joliotium [ʒoljɔtjɔm] **NM** *Chim* joliotium

jomon [ʒomɔ̃] **NM** Jomon

Jonas [ʒonas] **NPR** *Bible* Jonah, Jonas

Jonathan [ʒonatɑ̃] **NPR** *Bible* Jonathan

jonc [ʒɔ̃] **NM 1** *Bot* rush; **j. à balais** broom; **j. des chaisiers** bulrush; **j. fleuri** flowering rush; **j. marin** gorse **2** *(canne)* (Malacca-)cane, rattan **3 j. d'or** *(bague)* gold ring; *(bracelet)* gold bangle *or* bracelet; *Can Vieilli (alliance)* (gold) wedding ring

joncacée [ʒɔ̃kase] *Bot* **NF** member of the Juncaceae family

❑ **joncacées NFPL** Juncaceae

joncer [16] [ʒɔ̃se] **VT j. une chaise** to rush the bottom of a chair

jonchaie [ʒɔ̃ʃɛ] **NF** (area of) rushes

jonchée [ʒɔ̃ʃe] **NF** *Littéraire* **une j. de pétales** a carpet of petals; **une j. d'herbe coupée** a swath of cut grass

joncher [3] [ʒɔ̃ʃe] **VT** *(couvrir)* to strew; **les corps jonchaient le sol** the bodies lay strewn on the ground; **jonché de détritus** littered with *Br* rubbish *or Am* garbage; **jonché de pétales** strewn with petals

jonchère [ʒɔ̃ʃɛr], **joncheraie** [ʒɔ̃ʃrɛ] **NF** (area of) rushes

jonchet [ʒɔ̃ʃɛ] **NM** spillikin; **jouer aux jonchets** to play spillikins

jonction [ʒɔ̃ksjɔ̃] **NF 1** *(réunion → action)* joining; *(→ résultat)* junction; **opérer la j. de deux câbles** to join up two cables; **opérer la j. de deux armées** to combine two armies; **(point de) j.** meeting point *or* junction; **à la j.** *ou* **au point de j. des deux cortèges** where the two processions meet; **à la j. des deux routes** at the junction (of the two roads)

2 *Jur* **j. d'instance** joinder (of causes of action)

3 *Électron, Ordinat, Rail & Tél* junction

jongler [3] [ʒɔ̃gle] **VI 1** *(avec des balles)* to juggle; *Ftbl* **j. avec le ballon** to juggle with the ball **2** *Fig* **j. avec** *(manier avec aisance)* to juggle with; **elle aime j. avec les mots** she likes to juggle *or* to play with words; **j. avec la loi** to juggle with the law **3** *Can (rêvasser)* to daydream

jonglerie [ʒɔ̃gləri] **NF 1** *(action, art)* juggling; *(tour de passe-passe)* juggling trick **2** *(ruse)* juggling, trickery

joi–jon

jongleur, -euse[1] [ʒɔ̃glœr, -øz] ADJ *Can (rêveur)* dreamy; *(pensif)* pensive, thoughtful
NM,F **1** *(qui fait des tours)* juggler **2** *Can (rêveur)* daydreamer
NM *Hist* (wandering) minstrel, jongleur

jongleux, -euse[2] [ʒɔ̃glø, -øz] *Can* ADJ *(rêveur)* dreamy; *(pensif)* pensive, thoughtful
NM,F daydreamer

jonque [ʒɔ̃k] NF junk

jonquille [ʒɔ̃kij] NF *Bot* (wild) daffodil, jonquil
ADJ INV bright *or* daffodil yellow

joran [ʒɔrɑ̃] NM *Suisse* = cold north-westerly wind that blows over the Jura and Lake Geneva

Jordanie [ʒɔrdani] NF **la J.** Jordan; **vivre en J.** to live in Jordan; **aller en J.** to go to Jordan

jordanien, -enne [ʒɔrdanjɛ̃, -ɛn] ADJ Jordanian
❑ **Jordanien, -enne** NM,F Jordanian

jos [dʒo] = **djos**

jos-connaissant [djokɔnɛsɑ̃] *(pl* **jos-connaissants)** NM *Can Fam Péj* know-all

Joseph [ʒozɛf] NPR **J. d'Arimathie** Joseph of Arimathia

Joséphine [ʒozefin] NPR **l'impératrice J.** the Empress Josephine

joséphisme [ʒozefism] NM *Hist* Josephism

Josias [ʒozjas] NPR *Bible* Josiah

Josué [ʒozɥe] NPR *Bible* Joshua

jota [xɔta] NF *(lettre, danse)* jota

jottereau, -x [ʒɔtro] NM *Naut* cheek, hound

jouabilité [ʒwabilite] NF *(d'un jeu vidéo)* playability

jouable [ʒwabl] ADJ **1** *Mus* playable; *Théât (pièce)* stageable, that can be performed; **sa dernière pièce n'est pas j.** his/her last play can't be staged; **ce rôle n'est pas j.** this role is impossible to perform; **ce jeu vidéo est j. sur plusieurs consoles** this video game can be played on *or* runs on several different consoles **2** *Sport (coup)* which can be played, feasible; **le coup n'est pas j.** it's not feasible, it's impossible

jouailler [3] [ʒwaje] VI *Fam* **1** *(jouer petit jeu)* to play for small stakes▪ **2** *(jouer d'un instrument)* to play badly▪

joual [ʒwal] NM joual, = dialectal form of Canadian French; *Can Fig* **passer du j. à cheval** = to change one's way of speaking from joual to standard French
ADJ *(origines)* working-class

> *Culture*
>
> **JOUAL**
>
> Joual (derived from vernacular French Canadian pronunciation of the word "cheval") is the traditional working-class variant of French used in Quebec. Initially derided by purists as a bastardized and highly anglicized form of French, the reputation of "joual" was rehabilitated in the sixties when it was championed by Quebec intellectuals as a symbol of Quebecois identity. Popularized in the 1970s by the songs of Robert Charlebois, it gained a new respectability with the publication of literary works written in "joual" (most notably Michel Tremblay's play, *Les Belles-sœurs*, in 1968).

joualerie [ʒwalri] NF *Can (langage vulgaire)* coarse *or* vulgar language; *(comportement vulgaire)* uncouthness

joualisant, -e [ʒwalizɑ̃, -ɑ̃t] ADJ who speaks "joual"
NM,F *(personne qui parle joual)* "joual" speaker; *(personne qui préconise le joual)* advocate of "joual"

joualiser [3] [ʒwalize] *Can* VI to speak "joual"
▸**se joualiser** VPR to adopt the "joual" dialect

jouasse [ʒwas] ADJ *Fam* pleased▪, *Br* chuffed; **qu'est-ce que t'as, t'es pas j.?** got a problem?

joubarbe [ʒubarb] NF *Bot* houseleek, sempervivum

joue [ʒu] NF **1** *Anat* cheek; **j. contre j.** cheek to cheek; **ce bébé a de bonnes joues** this baby's got really chubby cheeks; *très Fam* **se caler** *ou* **se remplir les joues** to stuff oneself
2 *Culin* **j. de bœuf** ox cheek; **j. de raie** = part of the head of a skate, considered a delicacy
3 *Tech (d'une poulie)* cheek; *(d'un rabot)* fence
4 *(d'un fauteuil, d'un canapé)* side
❑ **joues** NFPL *Naut* bows
❑ **en joue** ADV **coucher un fusil en j.** to take aim with *or* to aim a rifle; **coucher** *ou* **mettre qn/qch en j.** to (take) aim at sb/sth; **tenir qn/qch en j.** to hold sb/sth in one's sights; **en j.!** take aim!

jouée [ʒwe] NF *Archit* reveal

JOUER [6] [ʒwe]

> **VI** to play **1, 2, 5, 9** ▪ to gamble **3** ▪ to act **4** ▪ to perform **4, 5** ▪ to be of consequence **6** ▪ to apply **6** ▪ to warp **7** ▪ to work **8**
> **VT** to play **1, 4** ▪ to bet (on) **2** ▪ to stake **2, 3** ▪ to act **4** ▪ to perform **4** ▪ to put on **5** ▪ to fool **6**
> **VPR** to play **5** ▪ to be on **1** ▪ to be performed **1** ▪ to be played **1, 2**

VI **1** *(s'amuser)* to play; **j. avec qn** to play with sb; **elle joue dehors** she's playing outside; **j. au ballon/au train électrique/à la poupée** to play with a ball/an electric train/a doll; **j. à la guerre** to play soldiers; **j. aux petits soldats** to play (at) soldiers; **j. à la marchande/au docteur** to play (at) shops/doctors and nurses; **j. aux charades** to play (at) charades; **on ne joue pas avec un fusil!** a gun isn't a toy!; **il jouait avec sa gomme** he was playing *or* fiddling with his eraser; **elle jouait avec ses cheveux** she was playing with her hair; *Can Fam* **j. dans les cheveux de qn** to pull a fast one on sb; *Can Fam* **se faire j. dans les cheveux** to be had; *Can Fam* **ne joue pas dans mes plates-bandes** mind your own business; **j. avec les sentiments de qn** to play *or* to trifle with sb's feelings; **tu joues avec ta santé/vie** you're gambling with your health/life; **il a passé sa soirée à faire j. le chien avec la balle** he spent the evening throwing the ball around for the dog; **sois gentil, fais j. ta petite sœur avec vous** be a good boy and let your little sister play with you; **je ne joue plus** I'm not playing any more; *Fig* I don't want to have any part in this any more; **comme un chat joue avec une souris** as a cat plays with a mouse

2 *Sport & (aux cartes, à un jeu de société)* to play; **j. au golf/football/squash** to play golf/football/squash; **j. aux cartes/au billard** to play cards/billiards; **elle joue bien/mal au badminton** she's a good/poor badminton player, she's good/not very good at badminton; **on joue demain à Marseille** we're playing tomorrow in Marseilles; **il joue à l'avant/à l'arrière** he plays up front/in defence; **j. ailier droit** to play on the right wing; **(c'est) à toi de j.** *(aux cartes)* (it's) your turn; *(aux échecs)* (it's) your move; *Fig* it's up to you; **bien/mal j.** to be a good/bad player, to play well/badly; **ils ont bien joué en deuxième mi-temps** there was some good play in the second half; *Fam* **les gars ont joué dur** the lads played a tough game; **j. contre qn/une équipe** to play (against) sb/a team; **à quel jeu joues-tu?** what do you think you're playing at?; **j. au plus fin** *ou* **malin avec qn** to try to outsmart sb; **ne joue pas au plus fin avec moi!** don't try to be smart *or* clever with me!; *très Fam* **j. au con** to act like a *Br* prat *or Am* jerk

3 *(parier → au casino)* to gamble; *(→ aux courses)* to bet; **j'ai joué dans la deuxième course** I had a bet on the second race; **j'ai joué sur le 12** I played (on) number 12; **j. à la roulette** to play roulette; **j. aux courses** to bet on horses; **j. au loto sportif** *Br* ≃ to do the pools, *Am* ≃ to play the pools; **j. à la Bourse** to gamble on *or* to speculate on *or* to play the Stock Exchange; **j. à la hausse** to gamble on a rise in prices, to bull the market; **j. à la baisse** to gamble on a fall in prices, to bear the market; **je ne joue jamais** *(au casino)* I'm not a gambler, I never gamble; *(aux courses)* I never bet, I'm not a betting man/woman; **il ne joue qu'à coup sûr** he only lays sure *or* safe bets; *Can Fam* **j. fessier** *(aux cartes, au casino)* to play like a miser▪, to play for miserly stakes▪

4 *Cin & Théât (acteur)* to act; *(troupe)* to perform; **j. dans un film/une pièce** to be in a film/a play; **elle joue dans une pièce de Brecht** she's got a part in *or* she's in a Brecht play; **j'ai déjà joué avec lui** I've already worked with him; **nous jouons à l'Apollo en ce moment** at the moment, we're playing at *or* our play is on at the Apollo; **bien/mal j.** *(gén)* to be a good/bad actor; *(dans un film, une pièce)* to give a good/bad performance; **elle joue vraiment bien** she's a really good actress; **ce soir-là, ils ont particulièrement bien joué** they gave a particularly good *or* fine performance that night

5 *Mus* to play, to perform; **bien/mal j.** *(gén)* to be a good/bad musician; *(dans un concert)* to give a good/bad performance, to play well/badly; **il a mal joué hier soir** he played badly last night; **les flûtes jouaient en sourdine** the flutes were playing softly; **j. d'un instrument** to play an instrument; **tu joues d'un instrument?** do *or* can you play an instrument?; **j. de l'accordéon/de l'orgue/du violon** to play the accordeon/the organ/the violin; **elle joue très bien du piano/de la clarinette** she's a very good pianist/a very good clarinet player

6 *(intervenir → facteur)* to be of consequence *or* of importance; *(→ clause)* to apply; **l'âge joue peu** age is of little consequence; **les événements récents ont joué dans leur décision** recent events have been a factor in *or* have affected *or* have influenced their decision; **il a fait j. la clause 3 pour obtenir des indemnités** he had recourse to *or* he made use of clause 3 to obtain compensation; **faire j. ses relations** to make use of one's connections; **il a fait j. ses relations pour obtenir le poste** he pulled some strings to get the job; **j. pour** *ou* **en faveur de qn** to work in sb's favour; **la réputation d'Yvonne a joué en faveur de sa promotion** Yvonne's reputation helped her to get promoted; **j. contre** *ou* **en défaveur de qn** to work against sb; **le temps joue en notre faveur/défaveur** time is on our side/is against us; **ma jeunesse a joué en ma défaveur** the fact that I'm young worked against me *or* put me at a disadvantage

7 *(se déformer → bois)* to warp; *(avoir du jeu)* to work loose; **le bois a joué sous l'effet de l'humidité** the wood has warped with the damp; **les chevilles ont joué** the dowels have worked loose

8 *(fonctionner)* to work; **le mécanisme de sécurité n'a pas joué** the safety mechanism didn't work *or* operate; **faire j. une clé (dans une serrure)** *(pour ouvrir la porte)* to turn a key (in a lock); *(pour l'essayer)* to try a key (in a lock); **fais j. le pêne** get the bolt to slide; **faire j. un ressort** to trigger a spring

9 *(faire des effets)* to play; **le soleil jouait sur le lac** the sunlight was playing *or* dancing on the lake; **une brise légère jouait dans ses cheveux** a gentle breeze was ruffling *or* playing with his/her hair

10 *(s'appliquer)* to be operative, to operate; **l'augmentation des salaires joue depuis le 1er janvier** the rise in salaries has been effective since 1 January

11 *Suisse (convenir)* to be all right; **cela ne joue pas** it's not right; **avec un peu de chance ça pouvait j.** with a bit of luck it could work out

VT **1** *Sport (match, carte)* to play; *(pièce d'échecs)* to move, to play; **j. la finale** to play in the final; **j. la revanche/belle** to play the return match/decider; **ils jouent la balle de match** it's match point; **ils ont joué le ballon à la main** they passed the ball; **jouons encore une autre partie** let's play another game; **j'ai joué cœur** I played hearts; **c'était un coup facile/difficile à j.** *(au ballon)* it was an easy/a difficult shot to play; *(dans un jeu)* it was an obvious/a difficult move; **bien joué!** *Cartes & Sport* well played!; *(à un jeu)* good move!; *Fig* well done!; *Fig* **il joue un drôle de jeu** he's playing a strange *or* funny (little) game; **laisse-la j. son petit jeu, nous ne sommes pas dupes** let her play her little game, she won't fool us; **j. le jeu** to play the game; **rien n'est encore joué** nothing has been decided yet

2 *(au casino → somme)* to stake, to wager; *(→ numéro)* to bet on; *(au turf → somme)* to bet, to stake; *(→ cheval)* to bet on, to back; **je ne joue jamais d'argent** I never play for money; **il joue d'énormes sommes** he gambles vast sums, he plays for high stakes *or* big money; **j'ai joué 20 euros sur le 12** I bet *or* put 20 euros on number 12; **j. 50 euros sur un cheval** to bet 50 euros on

a horse; **jouons les consommations!** the loser pays for the drinks!; *aussi Fig* **j. gros jeu** to play for high stakes *or* big money; *Bourse* **j. la livre à la baisse/à la hausse** to speculate on a falling/rising pound

3 *(risquer → avenir, réputation)* to stake; **il joue sa vie dans cette aventure** he's putting his life in the balance; *Fam* **je joue ma peau** I'm risking my neck

4 *(interpréter → personnage)* to play (the part of), to act; *(→ concerto)* to play, to perform; **il a très bien joué Cyrano/la fugue** he gave an excellent performance as Cyrano/of the fugue; **l'intrigue est passionnante mais c'est mal joué** the plot is gripping but the acting is poor; **j. Brecht** *(acteur)* to play Brecht, to be in a Brecht play; *(troupe)* to play Brecht, to put on a Brecht play; **j. du Chopin** to play (some) Chopin; **j. un morceau à la flûte** to play a piece on a flute; **il joue toujours les jeunes premiers** he always plays the lead *or* gets the leading role; **elle ne sait pas j. la tragédie** she's not a good tragic actress; *Fig* **j. les martyrs** to play *or* to act the martyr; **ne joue pas les innocents!** don't play the innocent *or* don't act innocent (with me)!; **j. la prudence** to play it safe; **j. l'étonnement/le remords** to pretend to be surprised/sorry; *Mus* **j. sa partie** to play one's part; *aussi Fig* **j. un rôle** to play a part; **la lecture joue un grand rôle dans l'acquisition de l'orthographe** reading plays a large part in learning to spell

5 *(montrer → film, pièce)* to put on, to show; **qu'est-ce qu'on joue en ce moment?** what's on at the moment?; **on ne joue rien d'intéressant** there's nothing interesting on; **la Comédie-Française ne joue que les classiques** only classical drama is performed *or* played at the Comédie-Française; **la pièce a toujours été jouée en anglais** the play has always been performed in English; **on joue beaucoup Bernanos en ce moment** Bernanos is being performed a lot at the moment; **ça fait longtemps que sa pièce est jouée** his/her play has had a long run *or* has been on for a long time; *Fam* **où t'as vu j. ça?** are you mad?, are you off your rocker?

6 *(berner)* to fool, to deceive; **une fois de plus, nous avons été joués!** we've been deceived *or* fooled again!; **nul n'a jamais pu le j.** no one could ever get the better of him

▫ **jouer de** VT IND **1** *(se servir de)* to make use of, to use; **j. du couteau/marteau** to wield a knife/hammer; **elle joue de son infirmité** she plays on *or* uses the fact that she's disabled; *très Fam* **j. des jambes** *ou* **flûtes** *(s'enfuir)* to take to one's heels, *Br* to scarper, *Am* to hightail (it); *(courir)* to run *Br* like the clappers *or Am* like the dickens; **j. des poings** to use one's fists

2 *(être victime de)* **j. de malchance** *ou* **malheur** to be dogged by misfortune *or* bad luck; **décidément nous jouons de malheur** *ou* **malchance!** it's just one thing after another at the moment!

▫ **jouer sur** VT IND *(crédulité, sentiment)* to play on; **ils jouent sur la naïveté des gens** they play on *or* exploit people's gullibility; **il nous faut j. à plein sur le mécontentement populaire** we must capitalize on people's discontent; **j. sur les mots** to play with words

▸ **se jouer** VPR **1** *(film)* to be on, to be shown; *(pièce)* to be on, to be performed; *(morceau de musique)* to be played *or* performed; **sa nouvelle trilogie se jouera à Paris en octobre prochain** his/her new trilogy is on in Paris next October; **ce passage se joue legato** this passage should be played legato; **bien des drames se sont joués derrière ces murs** these walls have witnessed many a dramatic scene

2 *(sport, jeu)* to be played; **le football se joue avec deux équipes de onze joueurs** football is played with two teams of eleven players; **le match se jouera la semaine prochaine** the match will be played next week

3 *(être en jeu)* **des sommes considérables se jouent chaque soir** huge amounts of money are played for every night

4 *(se décider)* **son sort est en train de se j.** his/her fate is hanging in the balance; **mon sort va se j. sur cette décision** my fate hangs on this decision; **l'avenir du pays se joue dans cette négociation** the fate of the country hinges *or* depends on the outcome of these negotiations

5 *(produire un effet)* to play; **la surface lisse du lac où se joue un rayon de lune** the still surface of the lake on which a shaft of moonlight is dancing *or* playing

6 *Fam* **se la j.** to show off, to pose

7 se j. de *(ignorer)* to ignore; **se j. des lois/du règlement/des ordres** to pay no heed to the law/rules/orders; **se j. des obstacles/problèmes** to make light of the difficulties/problems

8 *Littéraire* **se j. de** *(duper)* to deceive, to dupe, to fool

9 *(locution)* **(comme) en se jouant** with the greatest of ease

jouet [ʒwɛ] NM **1** *(d'enfant)* toy **2** *(victime)* plaything; **il croyait être le j. des dieux** he felt he was sport *or* a plaything for the gods; **j'ai été le j. de leur machination** I was a pawn in their game; **tu as été le j. d'une illusion** you've been the victim of an illusion **3** *Équitation* curb chain

jouette [ʒwɛt] *Belg* ADJ playful, fun-loving

NF *(personne qui ne pense qu'à s'amuser)* fun-loving person

joueur, -euse [ʒwœr, -øz] ADJ **1** *(chaton, chiot)* playful **2** *(parieur)* **être j.** to be fond of gambling

NM,F **1** *Mus & Sport* player; **j. de basket/flûte** basketball/flute player; **joueurs de cartes/d'échecs** card/chess players; **j. de golf/cricket** golfer/cricketer; **j. de tambour** drummer; **j. de trompette** trumpeter; **être beau/mauvais j.** to be a good/bad loser *or* sport **2** *(pour de l'argent)* gambler **3** *Bourse* speculator; **un j. à la baisse** a bear; **un j. à la hausse** a bull

'Le Joueur de vielle' *La Tour* 'The Hurdy-Gurdy Player'

'Les Joueurs de cartes' *Cézanne* 'The Card Players'

joufflu, -e [ʒufly] ADJ *(bébé)* chubby-cheeked; **un visage j.** a chubby face

NM *Fam (postérieur)* butt, *Br* bum, *Am* fanny

joug [ʒu] NM **1** *Agr* yoke **2** *Littéraire (assujettissement)* yoke; **être sous le j. d'un tyran** to be under the yoke of a tyrant; **secouer le j.** to throw off one's yoke **3** *(d'une balance)* beam

jouir [32] [ʒwir] VI **1** *(sexuellement)* to come

2 *Fam (prendre du plaisir)* **ça me fait j.** I get a kick out of it

3 *Fam (souffrir)* to go through hell

▫ **jouir de** VT IND **1** *(profiter de → vie, jeunesse)* to enjoy, to get pleasure out of

2 *(se réjouir de → victoire)* to enjoy, to delight in

3 *(avoir → panorama)* to command; *(→ ensoleillement, droit)* to enjoy, to have; *(→ privilège, réputation)* to enjoy; **j. d'une bonne santé** to enjoy good health; **il ne jouit pas de toutes ses facultés** he isn't in full possession of his faculties

jouissance [ʒwisɑ̃s] NF **1** *(plaisir)* enjoyment, pleasure; *(orgasme)* climax, orgasm; **les jouissances de la vie** life's pleasures

2 *Jur (usage)* use; **avoir la j. de qch** to have the use of sth; **entrer en j. de qch** to enter *or* to come into possession of sth; **à vendre avec j. immédiate** *(dans une petite annonce)* for sale with immediate possession; **avoir la (pleine) j. de ses droits** to enjoy one's (full) rights; **j. en commun** *(d'un bien)* communal tenure; **j. légale** legal enjoyment; **j. locative** tenure; **j. à temps partagé** timeshare; **la période de j. est de sept ans** the period of tenure is seven years; **entrée en j.** coming into *or* assumption of possession; *Fin* **j. d'intérêts** entitlement to interest

jouissant, -e [ʒwisɑ̃, -ɑ̃t] ADJ *Fam Vieilli* cheering

jouisseur, -euse [ʒwisœr, -øz] NM,F pleasure-seeker

jouissif, -ive [ʒwisif, -iv] ADJ *Fam* fun; **ce film, c'était j.!** that film was a treat!; *Ironique* **je suis allée chez le dentiste, c'était j.!** I went to the dentist's, what a barrel of laughs!

joujou, -x [ʒuʒu] NM *(jouet)* toy, plaything; *Fam* **faire j. avec** to play with; **va faire j.** go and play

joujouthèque [ʒuʒutɛk] NF *Can* games library

joule [ʒul] NM joule; **effet J.** Joule effect

JOUR [ʒur]

day **A1–4** ▪ daylight **B1** ▪ light **B2** ▪ gap **C1** ▪ opening **C2, 4**

NM **A.** *DIVISION TEMPORELLE* **1** *(division du calendrier)* day; **les jours raccourcissent/rallongent** the days are getting shorter/longer; **les jours de la semaine** the days of the week; **j. de semaine** weekday; **un mois de trente jours** a thirty-day month; **un j. de deuil/joie** a day of mourning/joy; **j. astronomique** astronomical day; *Admin* **j. chômable, j. chômé** public holiday; **j. de congé** day off; **j. de l'échéance** due date; **j. férié** public holiday; **j. franc** clear day; *Fin* **jours d'intérêt** interest days; *Com* **j. non ouvrable** non-trading day; **j. ouvrable** working day; **j. de paie** pay day; **j. plein** clear day; **un j. de repos** a rest day; **j. sidéral/solaire** sidereal/solar day; **un j. de travail** a workday, *Br* a working day; **il me reste des jours à prendre avant la fin de l'année** I still have some (days') leave (to take) before the end of the year; **à dix jours de là** ten days later; **dans deux/quelques jours** in two/a few days' time; **il est resté des jours entiers sans sortir** he didn't go out for days on end; **il y a deux/dix jours** two/ten days ago; **tout le j.** all day long; **tous les jours** every day; **au j. le j.** *(sans s'occuper du lendemain)* from day to day; *(précairement)* from hand to mouth; **de j. en j.** *(grandir)* daily, day by day; *(varier)* from day to day, from one day to the next; **je note des progrès de j. en j.** I can see there is daily progress; **d'un j. à l'autre** *(incessamment)* any day (now); *(de façon imprévisible)* from one day to the next; **j. après j.** *(constamment)* day after day; *(graduellement)* day by day; **j. par j.** day by day; **sa lettre fait j. par j. le récit de leur voyage** his/her letter gives a day-by-day account of their trip; **j. pour j.** to the day; **cela fait deux ans j. pour j.** it's two years to the day

2 *(exprime la durée)* day; **un bébé d'un j.** a day-old baby; **c'est à un j. de marche/voiture** it's one day's walk/drive away; **nous avons eu trois jours de pluie** we had rain for three days *or* three days of rain; **j'en ai pour deux jours de travail** the work's going to take me two days; **ça va prendre un j. de lessivage et trois jours de peinture** it'll take one day to wash down and three days to paint; **il nous reste deux jours de vivres/d'eau/de munitions** we've got two days' (worth of) food/water/ammunition left; **emporte trois jours de ravitaillement** take enough provisions for three days; *Naut* **jours de planche** *ou* **de starie** lay days; *Littéraire* **leur beauté n'est que d'un j.** their beauty is ephemeral *or* is but for one day

3 *(date précise)* day; **fixer un j. pour qch/pour faire qch** to fix a day *or* date for sth/for doing sth; **quel j. sommes-nous?** what day (of the week) is it (today)?; **depuis ce j.** since that day, from that day on *or* onwards; **l'autre j.** the other day; **le j. où** the day *or* time that; **le j. où on a besoin de lui, il est malade!** the (one) day *or* time you need him, he's ill!; **le j. précédent** *ou* **d'avant** the previous day, the day before; **le j. suivant** *ou* **d'après** the following day, the next day, the day after; **dès le premier j.** from the very first day; **ils sont amoureux comme au premier j.** they're as much in love as when they first met; **le j. est loin où j'étais heureux** it's a long time since I've been happy; **le j. n'est pas loin où tu pourras y aller tout seul** it won't be long before you can go alone; **le j. viendra où...** the day will come when...; **un j.** one day; **un j. que...** one day when...; *Scol* **le j. de la rentrée** the first day (back) at school; *Scol* **le j. de la sortie** the last day of school; **le vendredi, c'est le j. de Valérie/c'est le j. du poisson** Friday is Valérie's day/is the day we have fish; **le j. de mes 20 ans** my 20th birthday; **le j. de l'an** New Year's Day; **le j. des Cendres** Ash Wednesday; **le j. des élections** election *or* polling day; **le j. du Jugement dernier** doomsday, Judgement Day; **le j. des morts** All Souls' Day; **le j. de Noël** Christmas

Day; **le j. de la Pentecôte** Whit Sunday; **le j. des Rameaux** Palm Sunday; **le j. des Rois** Twelfth Night, Epiphany; **le j. du scrutin** election or polling day; **le j. du Seigneur** the Lord's Day, the Sabbath; **j. de valeur** value date or day; **mon/son (grand) j.** my/his/her (big) day; **le grand j. pour lui/elle** his/her big day; **son manteau des grands jours** the coat he/she wears on important occasions; **son discours des grands jours** the speech he/she makes on important occasions; **de tous les jours** everyday (avant n); **mes chaussures de tous les jours** my everyday or ordinary shoes, the shoes I wear every day; **elle attend son j.** she's biding her time or marking time; **ce n'est pas mon j.!** it's not my day!; Ironique **ce n'est (vraiment) pas le j.!, tu choisis bien ton j.!** you really picked your day!; **elle est dans un bon j.** she's having one of her good days; **il est dans un mauvais j.** he's having one of his off or bad days; **je t'invite, c'est mon j. de bonté** my treat, I'm feeling generous today; Fam **il y a les jours avec et les jours sans** there are good days and (there are) bad days, there are days when everything goes right and others when everything goes wrong; **un beau j.** one (fine) day; **et un beau j., elle disparut** then, one fine day, she vanished; **un de ces jours, un j. ou l'autre** one of these days; **à un de ces jours!** see you soon!; **à ce j.** to this day, to date; **à ce j. la facture que nous vous avons envoyée reste impayée** to date the invoice we sent you remains unpaid; **intérêts à ce j.** interest to date; Fam **au j. d'aujourd'hui** in this day and age; **il a au lendemain** overnight; **il a changé d'avis du j. au lendemain** he changed his mind overnight

4 Bourse day; **j. de Bourse** trading day; **j. de la déclaration des noms** ticket day; **j. de grâce** day of grace; **j. de la liquidation** account day, settlement day; **j. d'option** option date; **j. de paiement, j. de règlement** payment day, settlement day; **j. de la réponse des primes** option day; **j. du terme** term day; **j. de valeur** value day

B. CLARTÉ **1** (lumière) daylight; **un faible j. éclairait la cuisine/la scène** the kitchen/the stage was lit by weak daylight; **le j. baisse** it's getting dark; **il fait (encore) j.** it's still light; **l'été, il fait j. à 4h30** in the summer it gets light at 4.30; **il faisait grand j.** it was broad daylight; Fig **faire qch au grand j.** to do sth openly or in broad daylight; **l'affaire fut étalée au grand j.** the affair was brought out into the open; **le j. se lève** the sun is rising; **avant le j.** before dawn or daybreak; **au petit j.** at dawn or daybreak; **j. et nuit, nuit et j.** day and night, night and day; **je dors le j.** I sleep during the day or in the daytime; **examine-le au** ou **en plein j.** look at it in the daylight; **vous me cachez le j.** you're in my light; **mets-toi face au j.** face the light; **j. artificiel** artificial daylight; **elle et son mari, c'est le j. et la nuit** she and her husband are like chalk and cheese

2 (aspect) light; **sous un certain j.** in a certain light; **présenter qn/qch sous un j. favorable** to show sb/sth in a favourable light; **se présenter sous un j. positif** to come across well; **le marché apparaît sous un j. défavorable** the market does not look promising; **apparaître sous un meilleur j.** to appear in a better light; **enfin, il s'est montré sous son vrai j.!** he's shown his true colours at last!; **voir qn sous son vrai** ou **véritable j.** to see what sb's really like; **voir qch sous son vrai** ou **véritable j.** to see sth in its true light; **sous un faux j.** in a false light; **pendant longtemps, nous l'avons vue sous un faux j.** for a long time we didn't see her for what she really was

3 (locutions) **donner le j. à** (enfant) to give birth to, to bring into the world; (projet) to give birth to; (mode, tendance) to start; **jeter un j. nouveau sur** to throw or to cast new light on; **mettre au j.** to bring to light; **voir le j.** (bébé) to be born; (journal) to come out; (théorie, invention) to appear; (projet) to see the light of day; **ces tableaux n'ont jamais vu le j.** these paintings have never seen the light of day

C. OUVERTURE **1** (interstice → entre des planches) gap, chink; (→ dans un feuillage) gap; **il fallut percer un j. dans le mur de devant** an opening had to be made in the front wall

2 Archit opening; Beaux-Arts light; **balcon/cloison à j.** openwork balcony/partition

3 (fenêtre) **j. de souffrance** window (looking on to an adjacent property and subject to legal specifications); **faux j.** interior window

4 Couture opening (made by drawing threads); **des jours** openwork, drawn work; **à jours** (passementerie, tricot, chemisier) openwork; **jours de Venise** Venetian stitch

5 Mines surface installations; **ouvrier de j.** surface worker

6 (location) **se faire j.** to emerge, to become clear; **pour que la vérité se fasse j.** for the truth to emerge or to come out; **sa personnalité a mis longtemps à se faire j.** it took a long time for his/her personality to come out or to reveal itself; **l'idée s'est fait j. dans son esprit** the idea dawned on him/her

❑ **jours** NMPL **1** (vie) days, life; **il a fini ses jours dans l'opulence** he ended his days or life a wealthy man; **mettre fin à ses jours** to put an end to one's life; **ses jours sont comptés** his/her days are numbered; **ses jours ne sont plus en danger** no longer fear for his/her life; Littéraire **jours filés d'or et de soie** life of happiness and prosperity

2 (époque) **de la Rome antique à nos jours** from Ancient Rome to the present day; **passer des jours heureux** to have a good time; **les mauvais jours** (les moments difficiles) unhappy days, hard times; (les jours où rien ne va) bad days; **il a sa tête des mauvais jours** it looks like he's in a bad mood; **ce manteau a connu des jours meilleurs** this coat has seen better days; **ses vieux jours** his/her old age; **pense à tes vieux jours** think of your old age; **de nos jours** these days, nowadays; **de nos jours on n'en fait plus des comme ça** they don't make them anymore nowadays or these days; **les beaux jours** (printemps) springtime; (été) summertime; **ah, c'étaient les beaux jours!** (jeunesse) ah, those were the days!

❑ **à jour** ADJ (cahier, travail) kept up to date; (rapport) up-to-date, up-to-the-minute; **être à j. de ses cotisations** to have paid one's subscription; ADV up to date; **tenir/mettre qch à j.** to keep/to bring sth up to date; **mettre son journal intime à j.** to update one's diary, to bring one's diary up to date; **mettre sa correspondance à j.** to catch up on one's letter writing; **ce qui presse le plus, c'est la mise à j. des registres** updating the ledgers is the most urgent task

❑ **de jour** ADJ (hôpital, unité) day, daytime (avant n); (infirmière) day (avant n); Mil (officier) duty (avant n) ADV (travailler) during the day; (conduire) in the daytime, during the day; **être de j.** to be on day duty or on days; **de j. comme de nuit** day and night

❑ **du jour** ADJ (mode, tendance, préoccupation) current, contemporary; (homme) of the moment; **as-tu lu le journal du j.?** have you read today's paper?; **quelles sont les nouvelles du j.?** what's today's news?; **un œuf du j.** a freshly laid egg; **le poisson est-il du j.?** is the fish fresh (today)?

❑ **d'un jour** ADJ short-lived, Sout ephemeral, transient

❑ **par jour** ADV a day, per day; **travailler cinq heures par j.** to work five hours a day; **trois fois par j.** three times a day

'Le Jour se lève' Carné 'Daybreak'

jour-amende [ʒuʀamɑ̃d] (pl **jours-amendes**) NM Jur = fine that is payable daily for a set number of days

Jourdain [ʒuʀdɛ̃] NM **le J.** the (River) Jordan
NPR **Monsieur J.** = main character in Molière's 'le Bourgeois Gentilhomme' (1670), who takes lessons in his attempt to become a gentleman; best remembered for his amazed discovery that

he has been speaking prose all his life (see box at **prose**)

journal, -aux [ʒuʀnal, -o] NM **1** (publication) paper, newspaper; (spécialisé) journal; **j. du matin/soir/dimanche** morning/evening/Sunday paper or newspaper; **c'est dans** ou **sur le j.** it's in the paper; **j. d'annonces** advertising newspaper; **j. sur CD-ROM** CD-ROM newspaper; Presse **le J. du dimanche** = French tabloid Sunday newspaper; **j. électronique** electronic newspaper; **j. d'entreprise** staff magazine, company magazine; **j. grand format** broadsheet; **j. gratuit** free paper, freesheet; **j. interne** (du personnel) staff magazine or newsletter; (de l'entreprise) company magazine or newsletter; Can **j. jaune** scandal sheet; **j. en ligne** electronic newspaper; Pol **le J. officiel (de la République Française)** = French government publication giving information to the public about new laws, parliamentary debates, government business and new companies, Br ≃ Hansard, Am ≃ Federal Register; **j. professionnel** trade journal; **j. à scandale** ou **à sensation** scandal sheet

2 (bureau) office, paper; (équipe) newspaper (staff)

3 Rad & TV (informations) **j. parlé/télévisé** radio/television news; **ce j. est présenté par...** the news is presented by or Br read by...; Fam **ils l'ont dit au j.** they said so on the news

4 (carnet) Br diary, Am journal; Ordinat log; **j. (intime)** Br diary or Am journal; **tenir un j.** to keep a Br diary or Am journal; **j. de bord** Naut log, logbook; Belg **j. de classe** (d'élève) homework Br diary or Am journal; (de professeur) (work) record book; **j. de voyage** travel diary

5 Compta ledger, account book; **j. des achats** purchase ledger, bought ledger; **j. analytique** analysis ledger; Fin **j. de banque** bank book; **j. de caisse** cash book; **j. des effets à payer** bills payable ledger; **j. des effets à recevoir** bills receivable ledger; Compta **j. factures-clients** sales invoice ledger; Compta **j. factures-fournisseurs** purchase invoice ledger; **j. de paie** wages ledger; **j. des rendus** returns ledger or book; **j. de trésorerie** cash book; **j. des ventes** sales ledger

6 Anciennement Agr ≃ acre

'Le Journal d'un curé de campagne' Bernanos, Bresson 'The Diary of a Country Priest'

'Le Journal d'un voleur' Genet 'A Thief's Journal'

Culture
LE JOURNAL OFFICIEL
This bulletin prints information about new laws and summaries of parliamentary debates, and informs the public of any important government business. When new companies are established, they are obliged by law to publish an announcement in the "Journal officiel".

journaleux, -euse [ʒuʀnalø, -øz] NM,F Fam Péj hack (journalist)

journalier, -ère [ʒuʀnalje, -ɛʀ] ADJ daily NM,F Agr day labourer

journaliser [3] [ʒuʀnalize] VT Compta to enter, to write up in the books

journalisme [ʒuʀnalism] NM journalism; **faire du j.** to be a journalist; **je fais un peu de j. de temps en temps** I write the odd article; **il a 30 ans de j. politique derrière lui** he's been a political journalist for 30 years; **j. électronique** electronic news gathering; **j. d'enquête, j. d'investigation** investigative journalism; **j. de radio** radio journalism; **j. sportif** sports journalism; **j. de télévision** television journalism

journaliste [ʒuʀnalist] NMF journalist; **elle est j. au Monde** she's a journalist for or with Le Monde; **assaillie par les journalistes** mobbed by reporters; **les journalistes de la rédaction** the editorial staff; **j. politique/sportif/économique** political/sports/economics correspondent or journalist; **j. embarqué** ou **incorporé** ou **intégré** embedded journalist; **j. d'investigation** investigative journalist; **j. parlementaire** parliamentary correspondent, lobby correspondent

journalistique [ʒurnalistik] **ADJ** journalistic

journée [ʒurne] **NF 1** *(durée)* day; **par une belle j. d'été** on a beautiful summer *or* summer's day; **à quoi occupes-tu tes journées?** how do you spend your days?, what do you do during the day?; **je n'ai rien fait de la j.** I haven't done a thing all day; **dans la j.** in the course of the day, during the day; **en début de j.** early in the morning *or* day; **en fin de j.** at the end of the day, in the early evening; **toute la j.** all day (long), the whole day; **bonne j.!** have a good *or* nice day!; **à une j./deux journées d'ici** one day's/two days' journey away; **j. verte/orange/rouge/noire** = day with little/some/severe/very severe traffic congestion

2 *Écon & Ind* **une j. de travail** a day's work; **la j. de huit heures** the eight-hour day; **faire des journées de 12 heures** to work a 12-hour day *or* 12 hours a day; **faire de longues journées** to work long hours; **je commence/finis ma j. à midi** I start/stop work at noon; **embauché/payé à la j.** employed/paid on a daily basis; **j. de travail** working day; **faire des journées (chez)** *(femme de ménage)* to work as *Br* a daily *or Am* a maid (for); **j. d'action** day of (industrial) action; **j. comptable** accounting day; **faire la j. continue** *(entreprise)* to work a continuous shift; *(magasin)* to stay open over the lunch hour; *(personne)* to work through lunch; **journées de travail perdues** lost working days

3 *(salaire)* day's pay *or* wages

4 *(activité organisée)* day; **la j. des enfants/du cinéma** children's/film day; **les journées du cancer** *(séminaire)* the cancer (research) conference; *(campagne)* cancer research (campaign) week; *Pol* **les journées (parlementaires) du parti** *Br* ≃ the (Parliamentary) Party conference, *Am* ≃ the party convention; **j. d'appel de préparation à la défense** = day during which young people are introduced to issues connected with national security; **j. d'études** study day; **j. portes ouvertes** *Br* open day, *Am* open house; **les Journées du Patrimoine** European Heritage Day, *Br* ≃ Doors Open Day

journellement [ʒurnɛlmã] **ADV 1** *(chaque jour)* daily, every day **2** *(fréquemment)* every day

joute [ʒut] **NF 1** *Hist* joust, tilt; *Sport* **j. nautique** *ou* **lyonnaise** water jousting **2** *Littéraire (rivalité)* joust; *(dialogue)* sparring match; **j. littéraire** literary contest; **j. oratoire** debate; **j. d'esprit** battle of wits

jouter [3] [ʒute] **VI 1** *(combattre)* to joust **2** *Littéraire (rivaliser)* to spar

jouteur, -euse [ʒutœr, -øz] **NM,F 1** *Hist* jouster, tilter; *Sport* water jouster **2** *Fig* adversary, opponent

jouvence [ʒuvãs] *voir* **bain, eau, fontaine**

jouvenceau, -x [ʒuvãso] **NM** *Hum* youngster, youth, stripling; **ce n'est qu'un j.** he's a mere stripling; **je ne suis plus un j.** I'm no spring chicken

jouvencelle [ʒuvãsɛl] **NF** *Hum* damsel, maiden; **ce n'est qu'une j.** she's a mere slip of a lass

jouxter [3] [ʒukste] **VT** to be adjacent to, to adjoin

jovial, -e, -als *ou* **-aux, -ales** [ʒɔvjal, -o] **ADJ** *(visage)* jovial, jolly; *(rire)* jovial, hearty; *(caractère)* jovial, cheerful

jovialement [ʒɔvjalmã] **ADV** jovially

jovialité [ʒɔvjalite] **NF** joviality, cheerfulness; **sa j. le rendait très populaire** his cheerful manner made him very popular

jovien, -enne [ʒɔvjɛ̃, -ɛn] **ADJ** Jovian

joyau, -x [ʒwajo] **NM 1** *(bijou)* gem, jewel; **les joyaux de la couronne** the crown jewels **2** *Fig (monument)* gem; *(œuvre d'art)* jewel; **le j. de la marine française** the jewel *or* showpiece of the French Navy; **le j. de la poésie romantique** the jewel of Romantic poetry; **le manoir de Luré, véritable petit j. de la Renaissance** the Manor at Luré, a real little Renaissance gem

joyeuse [ʒwajøz] *voir* **joyeux**

joyeusement [ʒwajøzmã] **ADV** joyfully, gladly; **elle accepta j.** she gladly accepted

joyeuseté [ʒwajøzte] **NF** *Fam (plaisanterie)* pleasantry

joyeux, -euse [ʒwajø, -øz] **ADJ** joyful, joyous, merry; **une joyeuse nouvelle** glad tidings; *Ironique* **et elle vient avec lui? c'est j.!** so she's

coming with him? that'll be nice for you!; **c'est un j. drille** he's a jolly fellow

   ❑ **joyeuses NFPL** *Vulg (testicules)* balls, nuts, *Br* bollocks

═══ 🌼 ═══

'Les Joyeuses Commères de Windsor' *Shakespeare* 'The Merry Wives of Windsor'

joystick [dʒɔjstik] **NM** *Ordinat* joystick

JPEG [ʒipɛg] **NM** *Ordinat (abrév* **Joint Photographic Experts Group**) JPEG

JRI [ʒiɛri] **NMF** *Presse (abrév* **journaliste reporter d'images**) reporter-cameraman

JT [ʒite] **NM** *(abrév* **journal télévisé**) TV news

jubarte [ʒybart] **NF** *Zool* humpback whale

jubé [ʒybe] **NM** jube, rood screen

jubilaire [ʒybilɛr] **ADJ** jubilee *(avant n)*; **année j.** jubilee year

   NMF *Belg & Suisse* guest of honour, = person fêted at a "jubilé"

   NM *Belg (célébration de 50 ans d'existence)* jubilee; *(anniversaire)* = celebration marking the anniversary of a club, the arrival of a member of staff in a company etc

jubilant, -e [ʒybilã, -ãt] **ADJ** *Fam* jubilant, exultant

jubilation [ʒybilasjɔ̃] **NF** jubilation, exultation; **avec j.** jubilantly

jubilatoire [ʒybilatwar] **ADJ** exhilarating

jubilé [ʒybile] **NM 1** *(célébration de 50 ans d'existence)* jubilee **2** *Suisse* = celebration marking the anniversary of a club, the arrival of a member of staff in a company etc

jubiler [3] [ʒybile] **VI** to be jubilant, to rejoice, to exult; *(méchamment)* to gloat; **il jubilait de me voir humilié** he gloated over my humiliation

juchée [ʒyʃe] **NF** pheasants' roost, pheasants' roosting place

jucher [3] [ʒyʃe] **VT** to perch; **juchée sur les épaules de son père** perched on her father's shoulders; **une casquette juchée sur le crâne** a cap perched on his/her head; **j. qn/qch en haut d'un mur** to perch sb/sth on top of a wall

   VI 1 *(faisan, poule)* to perch **2** *Fam (personne)* to live; **il juche au cinquième** he lives (up) on the fifth floor

   ▸ **se jucher VPR** **se j. sur** to perch (up) on

juchoir [ʒyʃwar] **NM** *(endroit)* roost(ing place); *(perche)* perch

Juda [ʒyda] **NPR** *Bible* Judah

judaïcité [ʒydaisite] **NF** Jewishness

judaïque [ʒydaik] **ADJ** Judaic, Judaical

judaïser [3] [ʒydaize] **VT** to Judaize

judaïsme [ʒydaism] **NM** Judaism

Judas [ʒyda] **NPR** *Bible* **J. (Iscariote)** Judas (Iscariot)

judas [ʒyda] **NM 1** *(ouverture)* judas (hole); **j. optique** peephole **2** *(traître)* Judas

Jude [ʒyd] **NPR** *Bible* Jude

Judée [ʒyde] **NF** **la J.** Judaea, Judea

judéité [ʒydeite] **NF** Jewishness

judelle [ʒydɛl] **NF** *Orn* coot

judéo-allemand, -e [ʒydeoalmã, -ãd] *(mpl* **judéo-allemands**, *fpl* **judéo-allemandes**) **ADJ** Judaeo-German

   NM *(langue)* Judaeo-German

judéo-chrétien, -enne [ʒydeokretjɛ̃, -ɛn] *(mpl* **judéo-chrétiens**, *fpl* **judéo-chrétiennes**) **ADJ** Judaeo-Christian

   ❑ **Judéo-Chrétien, -enne NM,F** Judaeo-Christian

judéo-christianisme [ʒydeokristjanism] **NM** Judaeo-Christianity

judéo-espagnol, -e [ʒydeoɛspaɲɔl] *(mpl* **judéo-espagnols**, *fpl* **judéo-espagnoles**) **ADJ** Judaeo-Spanish

   NM *(langue)* Judaeo-Spanish

judicature [ʒydikatyr] **NF** judicature

judiciaire [ʒydisjɛr] **ADJ** *(pouvoir, enquête, acte)* judicial; *(aide, autorité, frais)* legal; **vente j.** sale by order of the court

judiciairement [ʒydisjɛrmã] **ADV** judicially

judiciarisation [ʒydisjarizasjɔ̃] **NF** judicialization; **on assiste à une j. des conflits familiaux** we're seeing more and more family disputes being taken to court; **la j. des procédures d'internement psychiatrique** the fact of giving the courts more power in the procedures for sectioning psychiatric patients

judiciariser [3] [ʒydisjarize] **VT** to judicialize; **j. un conflit** to take a dispute to court; **il faut éviter de j. la relation entre un parent et un enfant** we should avoid turning parent-child relationships into a legal issue; **il faudrait j. davantage les procédures d'internement psychiatrique** the courts should have more power in the procedures for sectioning psychiatric patients

judicieuse [ʒydisjøz] *voir* **judicieux**

judicieusement [ʒydisjøzmã] **ADV** *(décider)* judiciously, shrewdly; *(agencer, organiser)* cleverly

judicieux, -euse [ʒydisjø, -øz] **ADJ** *(personne, esprit)* judicious, shrewd; *(manœuvre, proposition, décision)* shrewd; *(choix)* judicious; *(plan)* well thought-out; **peu j.** ill-advised; **il serait j. de téléphoner avant d'y aller** it would be sensible *or* wise to phone before going

judo [ʒydo] **NM** judo

judogi [ʒydɔgi] **NM** judogi

judoka [ʒydɔka] **NMF** judoka

jugal, -e, -aux, -ales [ʒygal, -o] **ADJ** jugal, zygomatic

juge [ʒʒ] **NMF**

1 *Jur* judge; **le j. X** Judge X; **Madame/Monsieur le J. X** *Br* ≃ Mrs/Mr Justice X, *Am* ≃ Judge X; **jamais, Monsieur le j.!** never, Your Honour!; **les juges** ≃ the Bench; **être nommé j.** to be appointed judge, *Br* ≃ to be raised to the Bench, *Am* ≃ to be appointed to the Bench; **aller/se retrouver devant le j.** to appear/to end up in court; **j. ad hoc** specially appointed judge; **j. aux affaires familiales** family court judge; **j. aux affaires matrimoniales** divorce court judge; **j. de l'application des peines** = judge responsible for the terms and conditions of sentences; **j. consulaire** = judge in a commercial court; **j. départiteur** arbitrator; **j. des enfants** children's judge, *Br* juvenile magistrate; **j. de l'exécution** = judge with jurisdiction to decide issues related to the execution of judgments; **j. de l'expropriation** expropriations judge; **j. informateur** investigating judge; *Vieilli* **j. d'instance** Justice of the Peace; **j. d'instruction** investigating judge, *Br* ≃ examining magistrate *or* justice, *Am* ≃ committing magistrate; **j. des libertés et de la détention** = judge empowered to grant or refuse bail; **j. des loyers** = judge dealing with disputes between owners and tenants of commercial premises; **j. de la mise en état** pre-trial judge; **j. de paix** stipendiary magistrate; **j. de proximité** = lay judge who hears small claims; **j. rapporteur** judge rapporteur; **j. des référés** ≃ judge in chambers; **j. des tutelles** = judge responsible for guardianship orders; **on ne peut être à la fois j. et partie** you can't both judge and be judged

2 *(personne compétente)* **j'en suis seul j.** I am sole judge (of the matter); **je te laisse j. de la situation** I'll let you be the judge of the situation; **être bon/mauvais j. en matière de** to be a good/bad judge of

3 *Sport* judge; **j. d'arrivée** finishing judge; **j. de chaise** umpire; **j. de filet/de fond** net cord/foot fault judge; **j. de ligne** linesman; **j. de touche** *Ftbl* linesman; *(au rugby)* linesman, touch judge

4 *Bible* **le Livre des Juges, les Juges** the (Book of) Judges

jugé [ʒyʒe] **au jugé ADV** at a guess; **au j., je dirais que...** at a guess, I would say that...; **tirer au j.** to fire blind

jugeable [ʒyʒabl] **ADJ** *Jur* judicable

juge-arbitre [ʒyʒarbitr] *(pl* **juges-arbitres**) **NM** referee

juge-commissaire [ʒyʒkɔmisɛr] *(pl* **juges-commissaires**) **NM** = judge designated by a commercial court in France to preside over certain cases, for example bankruptcy hearings

jugement [ʒyʒmã] **NM 1** *Jur (procès)* trial; *(verdict)* sentence, ruling, decision; **j. demain** the sentence will be passed tomorrow, a decision is expected tomorrow; **porter un j. prématuré sur qch** to judge sth too hastily; **prononcer** *ou*

rendre un j. to pass sentence, to give a ruling; **faire passer qn en j.** to bring sb to (stand) trial; **passer en j.** to stand trial; **j. avant dire droit** interlocutory judgment; **j. constitutif** = judgment creating or altering status; **j. contentieux** judgment in disputed matter; **j. contradictoire** = judgment rendered in the presence of the parties involved; **j. déclaratif** declaratory judgment; **j. déclaratif de faillite** adjudication in bankruptcy; **j. déclaratoire** declaratory judgment; **j. par défaut** judgment in absentia *or* default; **j. définitif** final judgment; **j. en dernier ressort** judgment of last resort; **j. de donner acte** = judgment confirming the entry of a fact in the record; **j. étranger** foreign judgment; **j. d'exécution de paiement** money judgment; **j. exécutoire** enforceable judgment; **j. d'expédient** consent judgment; **j. gracieux** = decision in non-contentious proceedings; **j. irrévocable** irrevocable judgment; **j. mis en délibéré** reserved judgment; **j. mixte** = final judgment that decides the issue of liability and appoints an expert to assess the damages; **j. en premier ressort** trial court judgment; **j. préparatoire** preparatory judgment; **j. provisoire** interlocutory judgment; **j. sur le fond** judgment on the merits; **j. sur pièces** judgment based on evidence; **j. susceptible d'opposition** judgment liable to stay of execution

2 *Rel* **le j. dernier** the Last Judgment, the Day of Judgment, Judgment Day; **le jour du J. dernier** Judgment Day, doomsday; *Hist* **le j. de Dieu** the Ordeal

3 *(discernement)* judgment, flair; **erreur de j.** error of judgment; **faire preuve/manquer de j.** to show/lack sound *or* good judgment; **elle a du/n'a aucun j. (en matière de...)** she's a good/no judge (of...)

4 *(opinion)* judgment; **j. préconçu** prejudgment, preconception; **un j. téméraire** a rash judgment; **formuler un j. sur qn/qch** to express an opinion about sb/sth; **porter un j. sur qn/qch** to pass judgment on sb/sth; **soumettre qch au j. de qn** to submit sth to sb for his/her judgment; **c'est un j. sans appel** it's a harsh verdict; **le j. de l'histoire/la postérité** the verdict of history/posterity; **j. de valeur** value judgment

jugeote [ʒyʒɔt] NF *Fam* common sense■

juger [17] [ʒyʒe] VT **1** *Jur (accusé)* to try; *(affaire)* to judge, to try; **être jugé pour vol** to be tried *or* to stand trial for theft; **elle a été jugée coupable/non coupable** she was found guilty/not guilty; **il s'est fait j. pour atteinte à la vie privée** he had to stand trial for violation of privacy

2 *(trancher)* to judge, to decide; **à toi de j. (si/quand...)** it's up to you to decide *or* to judge (whether/when...); **j. un différend** to arbitrate in a dispute; **j. qui a tort** to judge *or* to decide who's wrong

3 *(se faire une opinion de)* to judge; **vous n'avez pas le droit de me j.!** you have no right to judge me!; **j. qn/qch à sa juste valeur** to form a correct opinion of sb/sth

4 *(considérer)* to consider, to judge; **j. qn capable/incompétent** to consider sb capable/incompetent; **son état est jugé très préoccupant** his/her condition is believed to be serious; **jugé bon pour le service** declared fit to join *or* fit for the army; **j. qch utile/nécessaire** to consider *or* to judge sth to be useful/necessary; **mesures jugées insuffisantes** measures deemed inadequate; **j. qn bien/mal** to have a good/poor opinion of sb; **vous me jugez mal** *(à tort)* you're misjudging me; **j. bon de faire qch** to think fit to do sth; **agissez comme vous jugerez bon** do as you think fit *or* appropriate; **j. que** to think *or* to consider that, to be of the opinion that

USAGE ABSOLU **l'histoire/la postérité jugera** history/posterity will judge; **moi, je ne juge pas** I'm not in a position to judge, I'm not making any judgment; **j. par soi-même** to judge for oneself; **il ne faut pas j. sur** *ou* **d'après les apparences** don't judge from *or* go by appearances

□ **juger de** VT IND **1** à **en j. par son large sourire** if his/her broad smile is anything to go by; **autant qu'on puisse en j.** as far as one can judge; **si j'en juge par ce que j'ai lu** judging from *or* by what I've read, if what I've read is anything to go by; **jugez-en vous-même** judge *or* see for yourself; **jugez de mon indignation**

imagine my indignation, imagine how indignant I felt

▸**se juger** VPR **1** *(se considérer)* **elle se juge sévèrement** she has a harsh opinion of herself; **les commerçants se jugent lésés** shopkeepers consider *or* think themselves hard done by

2 *(se mesurer)* to be judged; **le succès d'un livre se juge aux ventes** a book's success is judged by the numbers of copies sold; *Jur* **l'affaire se jugera mardi** the case will be heard on Tuesday

jugeur, -euse [ʒyʒœr, -øz] NM,F *Péj Littéraire* self-appointed judge

juglandacée [ʒyglɑ̃dase] *Bot* NF member of the Juglandaceae family

□ **juglandacées** NFPL Juglandaceae

jugulaire [ʒygylɛr] ADJ *Anat* jugular; **glandes/veines jugulaires** jugular glands/veins

NF **1** *Anat* jugular (vein) **2** *(bride)* chin strap

juguler [3] [ʒygyle] VT **1** *(arrêter → hémorragie, maladie)* to halt, to check; *(→ sanglots)* to suppress, to repress; *(→ chômage, inflation)* to curb, to check **2** *(étouffer → révolte)* to quell

juif, -ive [ʒɥif, -iv] ADJ Jewish

NM *Fam* **le petit j.** the funny bone

□ **Juif, -ive** NM,F Jew

'Le Juif errant' *Sue* 'The Wandering Jew'

juillet [ʒɥijɛ] NM July; **la monarchie de j.** the July Monarchy; **le quatorze j.** *(fête nationale)* Bastille Day; *voir aussi* **mars**

Culture
LA FÊTE DU 14 JUILLET
The celebrations to mark the anniversary of the storming of the Bastille begin on 13 July with outdoor public dances ("les bals du 14 Juillet") and firework displays, and continue on the 14th with a military parade in the morning. Firework displays are also held in the evening of "Bastille Day".

juillettiste [ʒɥijetist] NMF = person who goes on holiday in July

juin [ʒɥɛ̃] NM June; *voir aussi* **mars**

juive [ʒɥiv] *voir* **juif**

juiverie [ʒɥivri] NF **1** *(quartier juif)* Jewish quarter **2** *Fam* **la j.**, = the Jewry, = offensive term used to refer to the Jewish community

jujitsu, ju-jitsu [ʒyʒitsy] = jiu-jitsu

jujube [ʒyʒyb] NM **1** *(fruit)* jujube (fruit) **2** *Can (friandise)* jujube, gumdrop

jujubier [ʒyʒybje] NM jujube (tree)

juke-box [dʒukbɔks] *(pl inv ou juke-boxes)* NM jukebox

Jules [ʒyl] NPR *(pape)* Julius; **J. César** Julius Caesar

jules [ʒyl] NM *très Fam* **1** *(amant)* boyfriend■, man, *Br* bloke; *(mari)* old man **2** *(souteneur)* pimp

Julien [ʒyljɛ̃] NPR **J. l'Apostat** Julian the Apostate

julien, -enne¹ [ʒyljɛ̃, -ɛn] ADJ *(année, période)* Julian *(avant n)*

juliénas [ʒyljenas] NM Julienas (wine)

julienne² [ʒyljɛn] ADJ *voir* **julien**

NF **1** *Culin* **j. (de légumes)** *(garniture)* (vegetable) julienne; *(soupe)* julienne (consommé) **2** *Ich* ling **3** *Bot* dame's violet

jumbo [dʒœmbo] NM *Tech* jumbo drill

jumbo-jet [dʒœmbodʒɛt] *(pl jumbo-jets)* NM jumbo (jet)

jumeau, -elle, -aux, -elles [ʒymo, -ɛl] ADJ **1** *Biol* twin *(avant n)*; *(fruits)* double **2** *(symétrique)* twin *(avant n)*, identical; **les flèches jumelles de la cathédrale** the twin spires of the cathedral

NM,F **1** *Biol* twin; **jumeaux conjoints** conjoined twins; **vrais/faux jumeaux** identical/fraternal twins **2** *(sosie)* double

NM **1** *Anat* gemellus muscle **2** *Culin* neck of beef

□ **jumelle** NF *Aut* **jumelle de ressort** (spring) shackle

jumel [ʒymɛl] ADJ M *Tex* **coton j.** Egyptian cotton, Nile (Jumel) cotton

jumelage [ʒymlaʒ] NM **1** *(association)* twinning **2** *Rail* paired running

jumelé, -e [ʒymle] ADJ **1** *(fenêtres)* double; *(colonne)* twin *(avant n)*; **villes jumelées** twinned towns/cities, *Am* sister cities **2** *Naut* twin *(avant n)*

NM *(pari)* first and second forecast

jumeler [24] [ʒymle] VT **1** *(villes)* to twin, *Am* to make sister cities; **être jumelé à** to be twinned with, *Am* to be a sister city with **2** *(moteurs)* to couple; *(poutres)* to join

jumelle [ʒymɛl] ADJ *voir* **jumeau**

NF **1** *(sœur, sosie)* voir **jumeau 2** *Aut* (spring) shackle

jumellerai etc voir **jumeler**

jumelles [ʒymɛl] ADJ PL *voir* **jumeau**

NFPL **1** *Opt* binoculars; **visible aux j.** visible through binoculars; **j. de théâtre** *ou* **spectacle** opera glasses; **j. de campagne** field glasses **2** *Naut* fishes, fish pieces

jument [ʒymɑ̃] NF mare; **j. poulinière** brood mare

'La Jument verte' *Aymé* 'The Green Mare'

jumping [dʒœmpiŋ] NM *Équitation* showjumping

jungien, -enne [junʒɛ̃, -ɛn] ADJ *Phil & Psy* Jungian

jungle [ʒœ̃gl] NF **1** *Géog* jungle **2** *Fig* jungle; **la j. des villes** the concrete jungle; **la j. des affaires** the jungle of the business world

junior [ʒynjɔr] ADJ INV **1** *(fils)* junior; **Douglas Fairbanks j.** Douglas Fairbanks Junior **2** *(destiné aux adolescents → mode)* junior; **les nouveaux blousons j.** the new jackets for teenagers **3** *(débutant)* junior

ADJ *Sport* junior; **les équipes juniors** the junior teams

NM,F *Sport* junior

Junior-Entreprise® [ʒynjɔrɑ̃trəpriz] *(pl Junior-Entreprises)* NF = association set up by students who carry out paid work for companies in fields related to their studies

junk bond [dʒœkbɔnd] *(pl junk bonds)* NM *Fin* junk bond

junker [junkər] NM Junker

junkie [dʒœnki] NMF *très Fam* junkie, junky

Junon [ʒynɔ̃] NPR *Myth* Juno

junonien, -enne [ʒynɔnjɛ̃, -ɛn] ADJ Junonian, Junoesque

junte [ʒœ̃t] NF junta

jupe [ʒyp] NF **1** *(vêtement)* skirt; **j. droite** straight skirt; **j. évasée, j. à godets** flared skirt; **j. plissée** pleated skirt; **j. portefeuille** wrapover *or* wraparound (skirt); **il est toujours dans les** *ou* **accroché aux jupes de sa mère** he's tied to his mother's apron strings **2** *Tech (d'un aéroglisseur)* skirt, apron; *(d'un piston, d'un rouleau)* skirt

jupe-culotte [ʒypkylɔt] *(pl jupes-culottes)* NF (pair of) culottes

jupette [ʒypɛt] NF short skirt; **j. de tennis** tennis skirt

jupier, -ère [ʒypje, -ɛr] NM,F *Vieilli* = tailor or dressmaker specializing in cutting skirts

Jupiter [ʒypitɛr] NF *Astron* Jupiter

NPR *Myth* Jupiter, Jove

jupitérien, -enne [ʒypiterjɛ̃, -ɛn] ADJ Jovian

jupon [ʒypɔ̃] NM petticoat, slip, underskirt

juponner [1] [ʒypone] VT **1** *(robe)* to sew a petticoat on, to fit with an underskirt **2** *(table)* to cover with a long tablecloth

Jura [ʒyra] NM **1** *(en France)* **le J.** *(chaîne montagneuse)* the Jura (Mountains); *(département)* the Jura **2** *(en Suisse)* **le canton du J.** Jura, the Jura canton

jurançon [ʒyrɑ̃sɔ̃] NM Jurançon wine *(from southern France)*

jurande [ʒyrɑ̃d] NF *Hist* **1** *(fonction)* guild-mastership, wardenship **2** *(corporation)* guild

jurassien, -enne [ʒyrasjɛ̃, -ɛn] ADJ of/from the Jura

□ **Jurassien, -enne** NM,F = inhabitant of or person from the Jura

jurassique [ʒyrasik] ADJ Jurassic

NM **le j.** the Jurassic period

jurat [ʒyra] NM *Hist* jurat, alderman

juratoire [ʒyratwar] *voir* **caution**

juré, -e [ʒyre] ADJ **1** *(assermenté → expert, traducteur)* sworn **2** *(ennemi)* sworn; **je ne recommencerai plus – (c'est) j.?** I won't do it again – do you swear?

NM,F *Jur* member of a jury, juror; **les jurés ont**

délibéré the jury has *or* have reached a verdict; **elle a été convoquée comme j.** she's had to report for *Br* jury service *or Am* jury duty

jurement [ʒyrmɑ̃] **NM** *Vieilli* oath, swear word

jurer [3] [ʒyre] **VT** *aussi Jur (promettre)* to swear; **je ne l'ai jamais vue, je le jure!** I've never seen her, I swear it!; **j. allégeance/fidélité/obéissance à qn** to swear *or* to pledge allegiance/loyalty/obedience to sb; **il a juré ma perte** he has sworn *or* vowed to bring about my downfall; **je te jure que c'est vrai** I swear it's true; **je jurerais que c'est vrai** I'd swear to it; **j'aurais juré que c'était elle** I could have sworn it was her; **j. de faire qch** to swear to do sth; **j'ai juré de garder le secret** I'm sworn to secrecy; **elle m'a fait j. de garder le secret** she swore me to secrecy; **elle a juré de ne plus jouer/boire** she's sworn *or* pledged to give up gambling/drink; **jurez-vous de dire la vérité, toute la vérité, rien que la vérité?** do you swear to tell the truth, the whole truth and nothing but the truth?; **dites je le jure – je le jure** do you so swear? – I swear *or* I do; **j. ses grands dieux que…** to swear to God that…

USAGE ABSOLU j. sur la Bible/devant Dieu to swear on the Bible/to God; **j. sur l'honneur** to swear on one's honour; **je ne l'ai jamais vu, je le jure sur la tête de mon fils** I swear on my mother's grave I've never seen him

VI 1 *(blasphémer)* to swear, to curse; **j. après qn/qch** to curse *or* to swear at sb/sth; **j. comme un charretier** to swear like a trooper

2 *(détonner → couleurs, architecture)* to clash, to jar; **le foulard jure avec la robe** the scarf clashes with the dress

3 *Fig* **jurer par** to swear by; **elle ne jure que par l'huile de foie de morue** she swears by cod-liver oil; **ils ne jurent que par leur nouvel entraîneur** they swear by their new coach

❑ **jurer de VT IND 1** *(affirmer)* **j. de son innocence** to swear to one's innocence; **j. de sa bonne foi** to swear that one is sincere; **il ne faut j. de rien** you never can tell

2 *(au conditionnel)* **j'en jurerais** I'd swear to it; **c'est peut-être mon agresseur, mais je n'en jurerais pas** he might be the man who attacked me but I wouldn't swear to it

▸**se jurer VPR 1** *(l'un l'autre)* **se j. fidélité** to swear *or* to vow to be faithful to each other

2 *(à soi-même)* **se j. de faire** to swear *or* to vow to do; **se j. que** to swear *or* to vow that

jureur [ʒyrœr] **NM 1** *Jur* swearer **2** *Vieilli (blasphémateur)* swearer

juridicité [ʒyridisite] **NF** juridicity

juridiction [ʒyridiksjɔ̃] **NF 1** *(pouvoir)* jurisdiction; **exercer sa j.** to exercise one's power; *Jur* **pleine j.** full jurisdiction, unlimited jurisdiction; **tomber sous la j. de** to come under the jurisdiction of; **j. commerciale** commercial jurisdiction **2** *(tribunal)* court (of law); *(tribunaux)* courts (of law); **j. administrative** administrative court; **j. d'annulation** annulment jurisdiction; **j. arbitrale** arbitration jurisdiction; **j. d'attribution** = administrative court of limited jurisdiction; **j. consulaire** commercial court; **j. de droit commun** ordinary courts, courts of general jurisdiction; **j. échevinale** = court in which professional judges sit with lay judges or a jury; **j. d'exception** court of limited jurisdiction; **j. gracieuse** voluntary jurisdiction; **j. d'instruction** examining courts; **j. judiciaire** judicial courts; **j. de jugement** penal courts; **j. de la libération conditionnelle** parole jurisdiction; **j. militaire** ≃ military courts; **j. obligatoire** compulsory jurisdiction; **j. de l'ordre administratif** administrative court; **j. de l'ordre judiciaire** ordinary court; **j. de premier degré** court of first instance; **j. de second degré** *Br* ≃ Court of Appeal, *Am* ≃ Appellate Court

juridictionnel, -elle [ʒyridiksjɔnɛl] **ADJ** jurisdictional

juridique [ʒyridik] **ADJ** *(vocabulaire)* legal, juridical; *(conseiller, texte, frais)* legal; *(système, environnement)* legal, judicial; **il a une formation j.** he studied law; **situation j.** legal situation

juridiquement [ʒyridikmɑ̃] **ADV** legally, juridically

juridisme [ʒyridism] **NM** legalism

jurisconsulte [ʒyriskɔ̃sylt] **NM** jurisconsult

jurisprudence [ʒyrisprydɑ̃s] **NF** *(source de droit)* case law; **faire j.** *(décision, jugement, arrêt)* to set *or* to create a (legal) precedent; **cas/affaire qui fait j.** test case

jurisprudentiel, -elle [ʒyrisprydɑ̃sjɛl] **ADJ** *(principe)* of case law; *(décision)* that sets a legal precedent; *(conflit)* regarding case law; **droit j.** case law

juriste [ʒyrist] **NMF** *(qui pratique)* lawyer, *Am* jurist; *(auteur)* jurist; **j. d'entreprise** company lawyer

juron [ʒyrɔ̃] **NM** swear word, oath; **proférer des jurons** to swear, to curse

jury [ʒyri] **NM 1** *Jur* jury; **membre du j.** juror, member of the jury; **il fait partie du j.** he sits on the jury; **j. partagé** hung jury **2** *Scol* board of examiners, jury **3** *Beaux-Arts & Sport* panel *or* jury *(of judges)* **4** *Mktg* **j. de consommateurs** focus group

jus [ʒy] **NM 1** *(boisson)* juice; **j. de citron/tomate** lemon/tomato juice; **ces oranges rendent** *ou* **donnent beaucoup de j.** these oranges are very juicy; **j. de fruit** *ou* **fruits** fruit juice; **le j. de la treille** wine

2 *Culin (de viande)* juice(s); **mon rôti n'a pas fait beaucoup de j.** my roast hasn't given off *or* produced much juice; *très Fam* **cuire** *ou* **mijoter dans son j.** to stew in one's (own) juice; *Fam* **c'est du j. de chaussettes, leur café** their coffee tastes like dishwater; *Can Fam* **j. de bras** elbow grease; *Can Fam* **il y en a du j. de bras là-dedans!** a lot of work *or* effort went into that!▪

3 *Fam (café)* coffee▪ ; **tu prends un j.?** are you having a cup (of coffee)?

4 *Fam (courant électrique)* juice; **attention, tu vas prendre le j.!** watch out, you'll get a shock!

5 *Fam (eau)* **tout le monde au j.!** everybody in (the water)!▪ ; **ils ont mis Paul au j.** they've thrown Paul in *or* into the water; **il est allé au j.** *(matelot)* he fell into the drink

6 *Fam Arg mil* **c'est 16 jours au j.** *Br* it's 16 days to demob (day), *Am* it's only 16 days until I'm/we're discharged▪

7 *Beaux-Arts* glaze

8 *Fam (locution)* **être au j.** *(au courant)* to know▪

jusant [ʒyzɑ̃] **NM** ebb tide

jusée [ʒyze] **NF** tanning liquor, ooze

jusqu'au-boutisme [ʒyskobutism] *(pl* **jusqu'au-boutismes***)* **NM** *Fam (d'un individu)* hardline attitude; *Pol* hardline policy

jusqu'au-boutiste [ʒyskobutist] *(pl* **jusqu'au-boutistes***)* *Fam* **ADJ** hardline

NMF *Pol* hardliner; **c'est un j.** he's a hardliner

JUSQUE [ʒyskə]

as far as **1** ▪ up to **1** ▪ until **2** ▪ even **3**

jusqu', or in literary language **jusques**, is used before a word beginning with a vowel or h mute.

PRÉP 1 *(dans l'espace)* **elle m'a suivi j. chez moi** she followed me all the way home; **les nuages s'étendront j. vers la Bourgogne** the clouds will spread as far as Burgundy; **je suis monté jusqu'en haut de la tour** I climbed (right) up to the top of the tower; *Littéraire* **du haut jusques en bas** from top to bottom; **jusqu'où?** how far?; **jusqu'où iront-ils?** (just) how far will they go?; **jusqu'où peut aller la bêtise/cruauté!** (just) how stupid/cruel can people be!; **jusques et y compris** up to and including; **jusques et y compris la page 15** up to and including page 15

2 *(dans le temps)* until, till; **j'attendrai j. vers 11 heures** I'll wait till *or* until about 11 o'clock; **jusqu'en avril** until *or* till April; **jusqu'alors** (up) until *or* till then; **j. tard** until *or* till late; **j. tard dans la nuit** until *or* till late at night

3 *(même, y compris)* even; **il y avait du sable j. dans les lits** there was even sand in the beds; **j'ai cherché j. sous les meubles** I even looked underneath the furniture

❑ **jusqu'à PRÉP 1** *(dans l'espace)* **jusqu'à Marseille** as far as Marseilles; **le train va-t-il jusqu'à Nice?** does the train go all the way to Nice *or* as far as Nice?; **lisez jusqu'à la page 30 incluse** read up to and including page 30; **il a rempli les verres jusqu'au bord** he filled the glasses (right up) to the brim; **jusqu'au bout de la rue** (right) to the end of the street; **le sous-marin peut plonger jusqu'à 3000 m de profondeur** the submarine can dive (down) to 3,000 m; **elle avait de l'eau jusqu'aux genoux** she was up to her knees in water, she was knee-deep in water; **il y a 300 m de chez nous jusqu'à la gare** it's 300 m from our house to the station

2 *(dans le temps)* until; **la pièce dure jusqu'à quelle heure?** what time does the play finish?; **jusqu'à 15 ans** up to the age of 15, up to 15 (years old); **je suis en congé jusqu'au 17 juillet (inclus)** I'm on holiday until 17 July (inclusive); **jusqu'à quand peut-on s'inscrire?** when's the last (possible) date for registering?; **tu vas attendre jusqu'à quand?** how long are you going to wait?; **il ne veut pas porter de casque, jusqu'au jour où il aura un accident!** he won't wear a helmet, until he has an accident one day!; **jusqu'à nouvel ordre** until further notice; **jusqu'à preuve du contraire** as far as I know; **jusqu'à plus ample informé** pending further information, until further information is available; **de lundi jusqu'à mardi** from Monday to *or* until *or* till Tuesday; **de 15 h jusqu'à 18 h** from 3 p.m. to *or* until *or* till 6 p.m.; **j'ai jusqu'à demain pour finir mon rapport** I've got (up) until *or* till tomorrow to finish my report; **jusqu'à hier** (up) until *or* till yesterday; **jusqu'à maintenant, jusqu'à présent** up to now, until now, till now; **jusqu'à aujourd'hui, jusqu'aujourd'hui** (up) until *or* till today

3 *(indiquant le degré)* **jusqu'à quel point peut-on lui faire confiance?** to what extent *or* how far can we trust him/her?; **jusqu'à un certain point** up to a certain point, to a certain extent; **jusqu'à 60 pour cent de réduction sur les fourrures!** up to 60 percent off furs!; **elle peut soulever jusqu'à 150 kg** she can lift up to 150 kg; **un amour maternel qui allait jusqu'à l'adoration** motherly love bordering on adoration; **sa désinvolture va jusqu'à l'insolence** he's/she's relaxed to the point of insolence; **il se montrait sévère jusqu'à la cruauté** he was severe to the point of cruelty; **aller jusqu'à faire qch** to go as far as to do sth; **j'irais jusqu'à dire que c'était délibéré** I would go as far as to say it was done on purpose; **j'irai jusqu'à 30 euros, pas plus** I'll go up to 30 euros, no more; **jusqu'à concurrence de 1000 euros** up to 1,000 euros maximum, up to (a limit of) 1,000 euros; *Fam* **il nous aura embêtés jusqu'à la fin** *ou* **la gauche!** he will have been a nuisance to us (right) to the bitter end!

4 *(même, y compris)* even; **il n'est pas jusqu'aux enfants qui ne se battent** even the children are fighting; **il n'est pas jusqu'aux puits qui ne soient pollués** even wells have been polluted; **ils ont tout emporté, jusqu'aux meubles** they took everything away, even the furniture *or* furniture and all; **tout en lui, jusqu'à son sourire, a changé** everything about him, right down to *or* even his smile, has changed; **il a mangé tous les bonbons jusqu'au dernier** he's eaten every last *or* single sweet

❑ **jusqu'à ce que CONJ** until; **je les aiderai jusqu'à ce qu'ils soient tirés d'affaire** I'll help them until they've sorted themselves out; **tout allait bien jusqu'à ce qu'il arrive** everything was going fine until he turned up

❑ **jusqu'à tant que CONJ** until

❑ **jusqu'au moment où CONJ** until; **je t'ai attendu jusqu'au moment où j'ai dû partir pour mon rendez-vous** I waited for you until I had to go to my meeting

❑ **jusque-là ADV 1** *(dans le présent)* up to now, (up) until *or* till now; *(dans le passé)* up to then, (up) until *or* till then; **j.-là, tout va bien** so far so good; **tout s'était bien passé j.-là** everything had gone well up until *or* till *or* to then

2 *(dans l'espace)* **je ne suis pas allé j.-là pour rien** I didn't go all that way for nothing; **ils sont arrivés j.-là et puis ils sont repartis** they got so far and then they went back; **on avait de l'eau j.-là** the water was up to here; **je n'ai pas encore lu**

j.-là I haven't got *or* read that far yet; *Fam* **j'en ai j.-là de tes caprices!** I've had it up to here with your whims!, I'm sick and tired of your whims!; *Fam* **s'en mettre j.-là** to stuff one's face *or* oneself; **on s'en est mis j.-là** we stuffed ourselves *or* our faces

◻ **jusqu'ici** ADV **1** (*dans l'espace*) (up) to here, as far as here; **approchez-vous jusqu'ici** come as far as here; **je ne suis pas venu jusqu'ici pour rien!** I haven't come all this way *or* as far as this for nothing!

2 (*dans le temps*) so far, until now, up to now; **nous n'avons pas eu de nouvelles jusqu'ici** up to now *or* so far we haven't had any news; **jusqu'ici, rien de grave** nothing serious so far

jusquiame [ʒyskjam] NF *Bot* **j. noire** henbane
jussiée [ʒysje] NF *Bot* primrose willow
jussieua [ʒysjøa] NM *Bot* primrose willow
jussion [ʒysjɔ̃] NF *Hist* **lettres de j.** jussive letter, peremptory order
justaucorps [ʒystokɔr] NM **1** (*de gymnaste, de danseur*) leotard **2** *Hist* jerkin

---

JUSTE [ʒyst]

> **ADJ** ▪ fair **1** ▪ just **2** ▪ legitimate **2** ▪ right **3, 4, 7** ▪ accurate **3** ▪ tight **5** ▪ relevant **7** ▪ good **8** ▪ in tune **9**
> **ADV** correctly **1** ▪ exactly **2** ▪ just **2, 3** ▪ only **3**
> **NM** just man

ADJ 1 (*équitable → partage, décision, personne*) fair; **être j. envers** *ou* **avec qn** to be fair to sb; **elle n'a pas eu de chance, soyons justes!** she hasn't had any luck, let's be fair!; **pour être j. envers elle** in fairness to her, to be fair to her; **il ne serait que j. qu'il soit remboursé** it would only be fair *or* right for him to get his money back; *Fam* **c'est pas j.!** it's not fair *or* right!

2 (*justifié → cause, récompense, punition*) just; (→ *requête*) legitimate; (→ *colère*) righteous, legitimate; **il est en colère, et à j. titre!** he's angry, and quite rightly (so) *or* and with good reason!

3 (*exact → calcul, compte, réponse*) right; (→ *horloge*) accurate, right; (→ *balance*) accurate, true; **as-tu l'heure j.?** have you got the right *or* exact time?; **à l'heure j.** right on time

4 (*précis → terme, expression*) appropriate, right
5 (*serré → habit*) tight; (→ *chaussures*) tight, small; **la nappe est un peu j. en longueur/largeur** the tablecloth is a bit on the short/narrow side

6 (*qui suffit à peine*) **trois bouteilles pour sept personnes, c'est un peu j.!** three bottles for seven people, that's not very much!; **70 euros pour une semaine, c'est un peu j.!** 70 euros for one week, it's a bit on the short side!; **une heure pour aller à l'aéroport, c'est trop j.** an hour to get to the airport, that's cutting it a bit fine; **ses notes sont trop justes pour que vous le laissiez passer** his marks are too borderline for you to pass him; **elle a réussi l'examen, mais c'était j.** she passed her exam, but it was a close thing; *Fam* **on est un peu justes en ce moment** (*financièrement*) we're a bit pushed for money *or* strapped for cash at the moment

7 (*sensé, judicieux → raisonnement*) sound; (→ *objection, observation*) relevant, apt; **ta remarque est tout à fait j.!** your comment is quite right!; **très j.!** quite right!, good point!; **j'ai moins d'expérience que lui – c'est j.** I'm less experienced than he is – that's true *or* right

8 (*compétent*) good; **avoir l'oreille/le coup d'œil j.** to have a good ear/eye

9 *Mus* (*voix, instrument*) true, in tune; (*note*) true, right; **le piano n'est pas j.** the piano is out of tune

10 (*approprié*) **apprécier qch à son j. prix** to appreciate the true value *or* worth of sth; **apprécier qn à sa j. valeur** to appreciate the true worth *or* value of sb

ADV 1 (*avec justesse*) **chanter j.** to sing in tune; **deviner j.** to guess correctly *or* right; **tu as vu** *ou* **deviné j.!** you guessed correctly *or* right!;

tomber j. to guess right, to hit the nail on the head; **sa remarque a touché** *ou* **frappé j.** his/her remark struck home

2 (*exactement*) exactly, just; **il a fait j. ce qu'il fallait** he did just *or* exactly what he had to; **il est neuf h j.** it's exactly nine o'clock; **arriver à dix heures j.** to arrive at exactly ten o'clock, to arrive at ten o'clock sharp; **arriver j. à l'heure** to arrive just in time *or* in the nick of time; **le train part à deux h j.** the train leaves at two o'clock exactly; **ça fait j. huit euros, ça fait huit euros tout j.** that comes to exactly eight euros; **la balle est passée j. à côté du poteau** the ball went just past the post; **c'est j. là** it's just there; **j. au milieu** right in the middle; **c'est j. ce qu'il me fallait** it's just what I wanted, it's the very thing, it's just the job; **tu arrives j. à temps** you've come just in time; **j. quand** *ou* **comme le téléphone sonnait** just as *or* when the phone was ringing; **il s'est fait renvoyer? – tout j.!** so he was dismissed? – he was indeed!

3 (*à peine, seulement*) just, only; **il vient j. d'arriver** he's just arrived (this minute); **il est j. 9 heures, vous n'allez pas partir déjà** it's only 9 o'clock, you're not going to leave already; **je voudrais j. de quoi faire une jupe** I'd like just enough to make a skirt; **j'ai bu j. une gorgée pour goûter** I just *or* only drank a mouthful to get the taste; **c'est j. que je ne voulais pas te déranger** it's only *or* just that I didn't want to disturb you; **j'ai tout j. le temps de prendre un café** I've just about enough *or* I've just got enough time to have a cup of coffee; **j'ai tout j. eu le temps de m'abriter** I only just had (enough) time to run for cover; **ils ont (tout) j. fini de manger** they've only just finished eating; **c'est tout j. s'il ne m'a pas frappé** he very nearly *or* all but hit me; **c'est tout j. s'il sait lire** he can only just *or* he can barely read; **c'est tout j. s'il dit bonjour** he hardly bothers to say hello, you're lucky if he says hello; **il ne manque jamais son train, mais c'est tout j.** he never misses his train, but he cuts it fine

4 (*en quantité insuffisante*) **un gâteau pour huit, ça fait (un peu) j.** one cake for eight people, that won't go very far; **voir** *ou* **prévoir** *ou* **calculer trop j.** not to allow enough, to allow too little; **tu as coupé le tissu un peu j.** you've cut the material a bit on the short side

5 *Com* **j. à temps** (*achat, distribution, production*) just-in-time

NM just man; **les justes** the just

◻ **au juste** ADV exactly; **combien sont-ils au j.?** how many (of them) are there exactly?; **qu'est-ce que ça veut dire au j.?** what does that mean exactly?

◻ **au plus juste** ADV **calculer qch au plus j.** to calculate sth to the nearest penny; **le budget a été calculé au plus j.** the budget was calculated down to the last penny

◻ **comme de juste** ADV of course, needless to say; **comme de j., elle avait oublié** she'd forgotten, of course; **et comme de j., tu n'as pas d'argent!** and of course *or* needless to say, you haven't got any money!

◻ **juste ciel, juste Dieu** EXCLAM good heavens!, heavens (above)!

justement [ʒystəmɑ̃] ADV **1** (*à ce moment précis, d'ailleurs*) **voilà j. Paul** talking of Paul, here he is; **j'ai j. besoin d'une secrétaire** actually *or* as it happens, I need a secretary; **j'allais j. te téléphoner** I was just going to phone you; **j., à ce propos, je voulais te dire que...** well, while we're on the subject, I wanted to tell you that...

2 (*pour renforcer un énoncé*) quite, just so; **il se met vite en colère – j., ne le provoque pas!** he loses his temper very quickly – quite *or* exactly *or* that's right, so don't provoke him!; **tu ne vas pas partir sans lui dire au revoir? – si, j.!** you're not going without saying goodbye to him/her? – that's precisely *or* exactly what I'm doing *or* indeed I am!

3 (*exactement*) exactly, precisely; **j'ai j. ce qu'il vous faut** I've got exactly *or* just what you need; **c'est j. pour cela que je lui en veux** that's precisely *or* exactly why I'm annoyed with him/her

4 (*pertinemment*) rightly, justly; **comme tu l'as dit si j.** as you (so) rightly said

5 (*avec justice*) rightly, justly; **elle fut j. récompensée/condamnée** she was justly rewarded/condemned

justesse [ʒystɛs] NF **1** (*d'un raisonnement, d'un jugement*) soundness; (*d'une observation, d'un terme, d'un ton*) appropriateness, aptness; **elle raisonne avec j.** her reasoning is sound **2** *Math & Mus* accuracy; (*d'un mécanisme, d'une horloge, d'une balance*) accuracy, precision

◻ **de justesse** ADV just, barely, narrowly; **il a gagné de j.** he won by a narrow margin *or* by a hair's breadth; **j'ai eu mon permis de j.** I only just passed my driving test; **on a eu le train de j.** we caught the train with only moments to spare, we only just caught the train; **on a évité la collision de j.** we very nearly had a crash

justice [ʒystis] NF **1** (*équité*) justice, fairness; **il traite ses hommes avec j.** he treats his men fairly *or* justly *or* with fairness; **en bonne j.** in all fairness; **ce n'est que j.** it's only fair; **ce n'est que j. qu'elle obtienne le rôle** it's only fair *or* just that she should get the part; *Hum* **il n'y a pas de j.!** there's no justice (in the world)!; **j. sociale** social justice

2 *Jur* **la j.** the law; **rendre la j.** to administer *or* to dispense justice; **avoir la j. pour soi** to have the law on one's side; **avoir des démêlés avec la j.** to fall foul of the law; **il fuit la j. de son pays** he's on the run from the law in his country; **il a fait des aveux à la j.** he confessed to the law; **la j. administrative** administrative law; **la j. civile** civil law; **j. expéditive** summary justice; **la j. militaire** military law; **j. de paix** Justice of the Peace; **j. politique** political law; **j. sommaire** summary justice

3 (*réparation*) justice; **demander j.** to ask for justice to be done; **obtenir j.** to obtain justice; **nous voulons que j. soit faite!** we want justice to be done!; **faire j.** (*venger une faute*) to take the law into one's own hands; **j. est faite** justice is done; **faire j. de qch** (*montrer que c'est nocif*) to prove sth to be bad; (*le réfuter*) to prove sth wrong, to give the lie to sth; **se faire j.** (*se venger*) to take the law into one's own hands; (*se tuer*) to take one's (own) life; **rendre** *ou* **faire j. à qn** to do sb justice; **rendons-lui cette j. qu'elle a fait beaucoup d'efforts** she made a big effort, let's be fair *or* let's grant her that; **la postérité rendra j. à son courage** posterity will recognize his/her courage; **la J.** (*symbole, allégorie*) Justice; **j. immanente** poetic justice

◻ **de justice** ADJ **un homme de j.** a man of the law

◻ **en justice** ADV *Jur* **aller en j.** to go to court; **passer en j.** to stand trial, to appear in court

justiciabilité [ʒystisjabilite] NF *Jur* amenability
justiciable [ʒystisjabl] ADJ **1** (*responsable*) **j. de** answerable for, responsible for; **pour ses électeurs, il est j. de sa politique** he is answerable to the electorate for his policies; **pour les héritiers, je suis j. de la gestion des biens** as far as the heirs are concerned, I am legally responsible for the management of the estate

2 **j. de** (*qui requiert*) requiring; **maladie j. d'hydrothérapie** illness requiring *or* which calls for hydrotherapy

3 *Jur* **il est j. des tribunaux pour enfants** he is subject to *or* comes under the jurisdiction of the juvenile courts

NMF person liable *or* subject to trial; **les justiciables** those due to be tried

justicier, -ère [ʒystisje, -ɛr] ADJ **1** (*qui rend la justice*) justiciary (*avant n*) **2** (*qui fait justice lui-même*) **le jury a condamné le mari j.** the jury found the husband who had taken the law into his own hands guilty; **emporté par sa fougue justicière** carried away by his burning desire to enforce justice

NM,F (*redresseur de torts*) righter of wrongs; **il faut toujours qu'elle s'érige en justicière** she's always setting herself up as a righter of wrongs

NM *Hist* justiciar

justifiable [ʒystifjabl] ADJ justifiable; **tous vos arguments doivent être justifiables** you must be able to justify *or* to substantiate every one of your arguments; **sa négligence n'est pas j.** his/her negligence is unjustifiable *or* cannot be justified

justifiant, -e [ʒystifjɑ̃, -ɑ̃t]**ADJ** *Rel* saving *(avant n)*
justificateur, -trice [ʒystifikatœr, -tris] **ADJ** *(témoignage)* justifying, justificatory
  NM *Typ & Ordinat* justifier
justificatif, -ive [ʒystifikatif, -iv] **ADJ** *(rapport)* justificatory, supporting; *(facture)* justificatory; **document j. d'identité** (written) proof of one's identity
  NM 1 *Admin* written proof *or* evidence; *Compta* receipt; **à adresser à la Comptabilité avec justificatifs** to be sent to the accounts department with all necessary receipts; **j. de domicile** proof of address **2** *Presse* free copy *(of newspaper sent to those who have an advertisement or a review etc in it)*
justification [ʒystifikasjɔ̃] **NF 1** *(motivation → d'une attitude, d'une politique)* justification; **j. de la violence** apology for *or* justification of violence; **il n'y a pas de j. possible à un acte aussi barbare** there is no possible justification for such a barbaric act
  2 *(explication)* justification, reason; **demander/chercher des justifications** to demand/ seek justification; **vos justifications ne m'intéressent pas** I'm not interested in your reasons *or Péj* excuses
  3 *Admin* (written) proof *(of expenses incurred)*; **j. d'identité** proof of identity; **j. de paiement** proof of payment
  4 *Ordinat & Typ* justification; **j. à droite/gauche** right/left justification; *Typ* **j. de tirage** limitation notice; **j. verticale** vertical justification

justificative [ʒystifikativ] *voir* **justificatif**
justificatrice [ʒystifikatris] *voir* **justificateur**
justifié, -e [ʒystifje] **ADJ** *(conduite, réaction, colère)* justified, justifiable
justifier [9] [ʒystifje] **VT 1** *(motiver → conduite, mesure, dépense)* to justify; **rien ne saurait j. de tels propos** there's no possible justification for speaking in such terms
  2 *(confirmer → crainte, théorie)* to justify, to confirm, to back up; **il a tout fait pour j. ses dires** he did everything to try and back up his statements
  3 *(prouver → affirmation)* to prove, to justify; *(→ versement)* to give proof *or* evidence of
  4 *(innocenter)* to vindicate
  5 *Typ & Ordinat* to justify; **le paragraphe est justifié à gauche/droite** the paragraph is left-/ right-justified
  ◻ **justifier de VT IND j. de son identité** to prove one's identity; **pouvez-vous j. de ce diplôme?** can you provide evidence that *or* can you prove that you are the holder of this qualification?
  ▶**se justifier VPR** to justify oneself; **je n'ai pas à me j. devant toi** I don't have to justify myself to you, I don't owe you any explanations; **se j. d'une accusation** to clear oneself of an accusation, to clear one's name
Justinien [ʒystinjɛ̃] **NPR** Justinian
jute [ʒyt]**NM** jute; **de** *ou* **en j.** jute *(avant n)*
juter [3] [ʒyte] **VI 1** *(fruit)* to ooze with juice; *(viande)* to give out *or* to release a lot of juice;

ce sont des oranges qui jutent beaucoup these oranges are very juicy *or* are full of juice **2** *Vulg (éjaculer)* to come■ , to get one's rocks off
juteux, -euse [ʒytø, -øz]**ADJ 1** *(fruit, viande)* juicy **2** *Fam (transaction)* lucrative■ ; **c'est une affaire bien juteuse!** that business is a real gold mine!
  NM *Fam Arg mil Br* warrant officer class II■ , *Am* warrant officer (junior grade)■
Jütland [ʒytlɑ̃d]**NM le J.** Jutland
Juvénal [ʒyvenal]**NPR** Juvenal
juvénat [ʒyvena]**NM** *Rel* juvenate
juvénile [ʒyvenil] **ADJ 1** *(jeune → silhouette)* young, youthful; *(→ ardeur, enthousiasme)* youthful; **il avait toujours gardé une passion j. pour les motos** he'd always kept his youthful passion for motorbikes **2** *Physiol* juvenile **3** *Géol & Minér* juvenile **4** *Entom* **hormone j.** juvenile hormone
juvénilité [ʒyvenilite] **NF** *Littéraire* youthfulness, juvenility
juxtalinéaire [ʒykstalineɛr] **ADJ** line-by-line, (placed) parallel
juxtaposable [ʒykstapozabl] **ADJ** that can be placed side by side; **mobilier à éléments juxtaposables** unit furniture
juxtaposé, -e [ʒykstapoze]**ADJ** juxtaposed
juxtaposer [3] [ʒykstapoze] **VT** to juxtapose, to place side by side; **j. un mot à un autre** to juxtapose two words
juxtaposition [ʒykstapozisjɔ̃]**NF** juxtaposition
Jylland [ʒilɑ̃d] = **Jütland**

K¹, k¹ [ka] NM INV (*lettre*) K, k; **K pour Kléber** ≃ K for Kevin

K² *Ordinat* (*abrév écrite* **kilo-octet**) K

k² (*abrév écrite* **kilo**) k

K2 [kadø] NM **le K2** K2

K7 [kasɛt] NF (*abrév* **cassette**) cassette; **radio-K7** radiocassette

ka [ka] NM *Phys* kaon

kabbale [kabal] = **cabale 2**

kabbaliste [kabalist] = **cabaliste**

kabbalistique [kabalistik] = **cabalistique**

Kaboul [kabul] NM Kabul

kabuki [kabuki] NM kabuki

Kabul [kabul] = **Kaboul**

kabyle [kabil] ADJ Kabyle
◇ NM (*langue*) Kabyle
◻ **Kabyle** NMF Kabyle

Kabylie [kabili] NF **la K.** Kabylia; **la Grande K.** Great Kabylia

kaddish [kadiʃ] NM *Rel* Kaddish

Kadhafi [kadafi] NPR Gaddafi

kafkaïen, -enne [kafkajɛ̃, -ɛn] ADJ Kafkaesque

kaïnite [kainit] NF *Minér* kainite

Kaiser [kajzɛr] NM **le K.** the Kaiser

kakatoès [kakatɔɛs] = **cacatoès**

kakemono [kakemɔno] NM *Beaux-Arts* kakemono (*Japanese wall-picture*)

kaki [kaki] ADJ INV (*couleur*) khaki
◇ NM 1 (*couleur*) khaki 2 *Bot* (*arbre*) (Japanese) persimmon, kaki; (*fruit*) persimmon, sharon fruit

kakou [kaku] NMF *Fam* **faire le k.** to act smart

kala-azar [kalaazar] (*pl* **kala-azars**) NM *Méd* kala-azar, visceral leishmaniasis

kalachnikov [kalaʃnikɔf] NM OU NF kalashnikov

Kalahari [kalaari] NM **le (désert du) K.** the Kalahari Desert

kalanchoe [kalãkɔe] NM kalanchoe

kalé [kale] ADJ INV gypsy (*avant n*)
◇ NMF INV gypsy

kaléidoscope [kaleidɔskɔp] NM *Opt & Fig* kaleidoscope

kaléidoscopique [kaleidɔskɔpik] ADJ kaleidoscopic

kali [kali] NM 1 *Bot* prickly saltwort 2 *Chim* potash

kaliémie [kaljemi] NF *Méd* kaliaemia

Kalinine [kalinin] NPR Kalinin

kalmouk, -e [kalmuk] ADJ Kalmuck
◇ NM (*langue*) Kalmuck
◻ **Kalmouk, -e** NM,F Kalmuck; **les Kalmouks** the Kalmucks *or* Kalmuck

kamala [kamala] NM kamala

Kama Sutra [kamasutra] NM **le K.** the Kama Sutra

kami [kami] NM INV kami

kamichi [kamiʃi] NM *Orn* screamer

kamikaze [kamikaz] ADJ kamikaze; *Fig* **être k.** to have a death wish
◇ NM kamikaze

kammerspiel [kamərʃpil] NM *Cin & Théât* Kammerspiel

Kampala [kãpala] NM Kampala

Kampuchéa [kãputʃea] NM **le K.** Kampuchea

kampuchéen, -enne [kãputʃeɛ̃, -ɛn] ADJ Kampuchean

Kamtchatka [kamtʃatka] NM *Géog* **le K.** (*péninsule*) the Kamchatka peninsula; (*rivière*) the Kamchatka (river)

kan [kã] = **khan**

kana [kana] NM INV kana

kanak, -e [kanak] = **canaque**

Kandinsky [kãdinski] NPR Kandinsky

kandjar [kãdʒar] NM handjar, khanjar

Kandy [kãdi] NM Kandy

kangourou [kãguru] NM 1 *Zool* kangaroo 2 (*comme adj*) *Rail* **technique k.** rail-road transport

kanji [kãdʒi] NM INV kanji

kannara [kanara] NM Kannada, Kanarese

Kansas [kãsas] NM **le K.** Kansas; **au K.** in Kansas

kantien, -enne [kãsjɛ̃, -ɛn] ADJ Kantian

kantisme [kãtism] NM Kantianism

kaoliang [kaɔljã] NM kaoliang

kaolin [kaɔlɛ̃] NM kaolin

kaolinisation [kaɔlinizasjɔ̃] NF kaolinization

kaolinite [kaɔlinit] NF *Minér* kaolinite

kaon [kaɔ̃] NM *Phys* kaon

kapo [kapo] NM *Hist* kapo, = prisoner placed in charge of other prisoners in Nazi concentration camps

kapok [kapɔk] NM kapok

kapokier [kapɔkje] NM ceiba (tree), kapok tree

Kaposi [kapozi] NPR *Méd* **maladie** *ou* **sarcome de K.** Kaposi's sarcoma

kappa [kapa] NM INV kappa

kaput [kaput] ADJ *Fam* kaput; **la téloche est k., impossible de regarder le match!** the TV's kaput, we can't watch the match!

Karachi [karaʃi] NM Karachi

karaïte [karait] ADJ Karaite
◇ NMF Karaite

Karakorum [karakɔrum], **Karakoram** [karakɔram] NM **le K.** the Karakoram Range

karakul [karakyl] = **caracul**

karaoké [karaɔke] NM karaoke

karaté [karate] NM karate

karatéka [karateka] NMF karate expert, karateka

karbau, -x [karbo] NM water buffalo

karité [karite] NM (*arbre*) shea (tree); (*substance*) shea; **beurre de k.** shea butter

karma [karma], **karman** [karman] NM karma

Karnak [karnak] NM Karnak

Karpathes [karpat] = **Carpates**

karst [karst] NM *Géol* karst

karstification [karstifikasjɔ̃] NF *Géol* karstification

karstique [karstik] ADJ *Géol* karstic

kart [kart] NM kart, go-kart; **faire du k.** to go-kart, to go karting

karting [kartiŋ] NM karting, go-karting; **faire du k.** to go-kart, to go karting

kasba(h) [kazba] = **casbah**

kasher [kaʃɛr] ADJ INV kosher

kashrout [kaʃrut] NF Kashrut, Kashruth

kassite [kasit] ADJ *Antiq* Kassite

kata [kata] NM kata

katakana [katakana] NM katakana

Katanga [katãga] NM Katanga

Katar [katar] NM **le K.** Katar, Qatar

katchina [katʃina] NM kachina

kathakali [katakali] NM Kathakali

Katmandou [katmãdu] NM Katmandu, Kathmandu

Katowice [katɔvitse] NM Katowice

kava [kava] = **kawa 1**

kawa [kawa] NM 1 *Bot* kawakawa, pepper tree 2 *Fam* (*café*) coffee ■, *Am* java

Kawasaki [kawazaki] NF Kawasaki

kayak [kajak] NM (*embarcation*) kayak; (*sport*) kayaking; **k. de mer** (*embarcation*) sea kayak; (*sport*) sea kayaking; **faire du k.** to go kayaking; **faire du k. de mer** to go sea kayaking

kayakable [kajakabl] ADJ *Can* (*lac, rivière*) suitable for kayaking on

kayakisme [kajakism] NM kayaking

kayakiste [kajakist] NMF kayaker

kazakh, -e [kazak] ADJ Kazakh
◇ NM (*langue*) Kazakh
◻ **Kazakh, -e** NM,F Kazakh

Kazakhstan [kazakstã] NM **le K.** Kazakhstan; **vivre au K.** to live in Kazakhstan; **aller au K.** to go to Kazakhstan

Kb (*abrév écrite* **kilobit**) Kb

keeper [kipər, kɛpɛr] NM *Belg* (*gardien*) goalkeeper

keepsake [kipsɛk] NM *Hist* annual gift-book, keepsake

keffieh [kefje] NM keffiyeh, kaffiyeh

kéfir [kefir] = **képhir**

keiretsu [kɛjrɛtsu] NM *Écon* keiretsu

keirin [kerin] NM *Sport* keirin

kelvin [kɛlvin] NM *Phys* kelvin

kémalisme [kemalism] NM *Hist* Kemalism

kendo [kɛndo] NM kendo

kénotron [kenɔtrɔ̃] NM *Électron* kenotron

kentia [kɛntja, kɛnsja] NM *Bot* kentia

Kentucky [kãtyki] NM **le K.** Kentucky; **dans le K.** in Kentucky

Kenya [kenja] NM **le K.** Kenya; **vivre au K.** to live in Kenya; **aller au K.** to go to Kenya

kényan, -e [kenjã, -an] ADJ Kenyan
◻ **Kényan, -e** NM,F Kenyan

kenyapithèque [kenjapitɛk] NM Kenyapithecus

kepa [kepa] NM *Fam* (*verlan de* **paquet**) (*de cocaïne*) bindle

képhir [kefir] NM kefir, kephir

képi [kepi] NM kepi

kérabau, -x [kerabo] NM *Zool* water buffalo

kératectomie [keratɛktɔmi] NF *Méd* keratectomy

kératine [keratin] NF *Biol* keratin

kératinisation [keratinizasjɔ̃] NF *Biol* keratinization

kératinisé, -e [keratinize] ADJ *Biol* keratinized

kératite [keratit] NF *Méd* keratitis

kératocône [keratɔkon] NM *Méd* keratoconus

kératogène [keratɔʒɛn] ADJ *Physiol* keratogenous

kératoplastie [keratɔplasti] NF *Méd* keratoplasty

kératose [keratoz] NF *Méd & Physiol* keratosis

kératotomie [keratɔtɔmi] NF *Méd* keratotomy; **faire une k.** to couch a cataract

Kerguelen [kɛrgelɛn] NFPL **les (îles) K.** the Kerguelen Islands

kerma [kɛrma] NM *Phys & Méd* kerma

kermès [kɛrmɛs] NM 1 *Entom* kermes 2 *Bot* (**chêne**) **k.** kermes oak 3 *Minér* **k. minéral** kermesite

kermesse [kɛrmɛs] NF 1 *Belg* kermis, kirmess 2 (*de charité*) charity fête, bazaar; **k. paroissiale** church fête; **k. de l'école** school fête

kern [kɛrn] NM *Belg Pol* inner cabinet

kérogène [kerɔʒɛn] NM kerogen

kérosène [kerɔzɛn] NM kerosene, kerosine

kerria [kerja] NM *Bot* kerria, Jew's mallow

ket [kɛt] NM *Belg Fam* (*enfant*) kid (*from Brussels*)

ketch [kɛtʃ] NM ketch

ketchup [kɛtʃœp] NM ketchup

ketmie [kɛtmi] NF *Bot* ketmia

keuf [kœf] NM *très Fam* (*verlan de* **flic**) cop; **les keufs** the fuzz, the cops

keum [kœm] NM *Fam* (*verlan de* **mec**) guy, *Br* bloke

keV (*abrév écrite* **kiloélectronvolt**) keV

Kevlar® [kevlar] NM Kevlar®

keylogging [kilɔgiŋ] NM *Ordinat* keylogging

keynésianisme [kenezjanism] NM *Écon* Keynesianism

keynésien, -enne [kenezjẽ, -ɛn] ADJ Keynesian

KF [kaɛf] NM *Anciennement* (*abrév* **kilofranc**) thousand francs; **son salaire annuel est de 100 KF** he/she earns 100,000 francs a year

kg (*abrév écrite* **kilogramme**) kg

KGB [kaʒebe] NM KGB

khâgne [kaɲ] NF *Fam Arg scol* = second year of a two-year arts course preparing for entrance to the ''École normale supérieure''

khâgneux, -euse [kaɲø, -øz] NM,F *Fam Arg scol* = student in ''khâgne''

khalifat [kalifa] = **califat**

khalife [kalif] = **calife**

khalkha [kalka] NM Khalkha

khamsin [xamsin] NM khamsin

khan [kɑ̃] NM (*titre, abri*) khan

khanat [kana] NM khanate

Khaniá [kanja] NM Khaniá

kharidjisme [karidʒism] NM *Rel* Kharijism, Kharidjism

kharidjite [karidʒit] *Rel* ADJ Kharijite, Kharidjite NMF Kharijite, Kharidjite

Kharkov [karkɔf] NM Kharkov

Khartoum [kartum] NM Khartoum

khat [kat] = **qat**

Khatchatourian [katʃaturjɑ̃] NPR Khachaturian

khédival, -e, -aux, -ales [kedival, -o] ADJ khedival, khedivial

khédivat [kediva] NM khedivate, khediviate

khédive [kediv] NM khedive

khédivial, -e, -aux, -ales [kedivjal, -o] ADJ khedivial, khedivial

khédiviat [kedivja] NM khedivate, khediviate

Khéops [keɔps] NPR Cheops; **la grande pyramide de K.** the Great Pyramid of Cheops

khi [ki] NM INV chi

khmer, -ère [kmɛr] ADJ Khmer NM (*langue*) Khmer
□ **Khmer, -ère** NM,F Khmer; **les Khmers** the Khmers; **les Khmers rouges** the Khmer Rouge

khoin [kɔɛ̃], **khoisan** [kwazɑ̃] *Ling* Khoisan

khôl [kol] NM kohl

Khrouchtchev [krutʃef] NPR **Nikita K.** Nikita Khrushchev

kHz (*abrév écrite* **kilohertz**) kHz

kiang [kiɑ̃] NM *Zool* kiang

kibboutz [kibuts] (*pl inv ou* **kibboutzim** [-tsim]) NM kibbutz; **travailler dans un k.** to work on a kibbutz

kick [kik] NM kick-starter, kick-start; **j'ai démarré au k.** I kick-started the motorbike

kicker [kikœr] NM *Belg Br* table football, *Am* foosball

kick-starter [kikstartɛr] NM = **kick**

kid [kid] NM *Fam* (*gamin*) kid

kidnapper [3] [kidnape] VT (*personne*) to kidnap

kidnappeur, -euse [kidnapœr, -øz] NM,F kidnapper

kidnapping [kidnapiŋ] NM kidnapping

kief [kjɛf] NM *Littéraire* = period of rest observed at midday in the East

kieselguhr, kieselgur [kizɛlgur, kizɛlgyr] NM *Minér* kieselguhr

kiesérite [kjezerit] NF *Minér* kieserite

Kiev [kjɛv] NM Kiev

kif [kif] NM (*haschisch*) kif, kef

kiffer [3] [kife] VT *Fam* **1** (*prendre du plaisir à*) to get a kick out of **2** (*aimer*) to be crazy about; **je la kiffe trop, cette fille** I'm totally crazy about this girl

kif-kif [kifkif] ADJ INV *Fam* **c'est k. (bourricot)** it's all the same, it's six of one and half a dozen of the other, *Br* it makes no odds

kikajon [kikaʒɔ̃] = **quicageon**

kiki [kiki] NM *Fam* **1** (*cou*) neck▪; (*gorge*) throat▪; **serrer le k. à qn** to throttle *or* to strangle sb▪ **2** (*en langage enfantin* → *pénis*) willy **3** (*locution*) **c'est parti, mon k.!** here we go!

kil [kil] NM *très Fam* bottle (of wine)▪; **un k. de rouge** a bottle of cheap red wine *or Br* (red) plonk

kilim [kilim] NM kilim

Kilimandjaro [kilimɑ̃dʒaro] NM **le (mont) K.** (Mount) Kilimanjaro

kilo [kilo] NM *Fam* (*abrév* **kilogramme**) kilo

kilobar [kilobar] NM kilobar

kilobaud [kilobo] NM *Ordinat* kilobaud

kilobit [kilɔbit] NM *Ordinat* kilobit

kilocalorie [kilɔkalɔri] NF kilocalorie

kilocycle [kilɔsikl] NM *Ordinat* kilocycle

kilofranc [kilɔfrɑ̃] NM *Anciennement* thousand francs

kilogramme [kilɔgram] NM kilogramme

kilohertz [kilɔɛrts] NM kilohertz

kilojoule [kilɔʒul] NM kilojoule

kilométrage [kilɔmetraʒ] NM **1** (*d'un véhicule*) ≃ mileage; **k. illimité** ≃ unlimited mileage **2** (*d'une voie*) marking out (*in kilometres*)

kilomètre [kilɔmɛtr] NM (*distance*) kilometre; **100 kilomètres à l'heure, 100 kilomètres-heure** 100 kilometres per *or* an hour; *Fig* **des kilomètres de pellicule** miles of film; **avoir dix kilomètres dans les jambes** to have walked ten kilometres; **k. carré** square kilometre; **k. zéro** = point near Notre-Dame from which distances from Paris are measured; *Sport* **k. arrêté** standing-start kilometre **2** *Ordinat* **frappe** *ou* **saisie au k.** straight keying

kilomètre-passager [kilɔmɛtrpasaʒe] (*pl* **kilomètres-passagers**) NM passenger-kilometre

kilométrer [18] [kilɔmetre] VT to mark with kilometric reference points

kilomètre-voyageur [kilɔmɛtrvwajaʒœr] (*pl* **kilomètres-voyageurs**) NM passenger-kilometre

kilométrique [kilɔmetrik] ADJ **au point k. 21** at km 21; **distance k.** distance in kilometres

kilo-octet [kilɔɔktɛ] (*pl* **kilo-octets**) NM *Ordinat* kilobyte

kilotonne [kilɔtɔn] NF kiloton

kilotonnique [kilɔtɔnik] ADJ kiloton (*avant n*)

kilovolt [kilɔvɔlt] NM kilovolt

kilowatt [kilɔwat] NM kilowatt

kilowattheure [kilɔwatœr] NM kilowatt-hour

kilt [kilt] NM (*d'Écossais, de femme*) kilt

kimbanguisme [kimbɑ̃gism] NM *Rel* Kimbanguist Church

kimberlite [kɛ̃bɛrlit] NF *Géol* kimberlite; **pipe de k.** kimberlite pipe

kimono [kimɔnɔ] NM kimono
ADJ INV **manches k.** kimono *or* loose sleeves

kinase [kinaz] NF *Biol & Chim* kinase

kiné [kine] NMF *Fam* (*abrév* **kinésithérapeute**) physio

kinescopage [kinɛskɔpaʒ] NM kinescope transfer, kinescope recording

kinescope [kinɛskɔp] NM kinescope

kinésie [kinezi] NF kinesis

kinésiologie [kinezjɔlɔʒi] NF kinesiology

kinésiste [kinezist] NMF *Belg Br* physiotherapist, *Am* physical therapist

kinésithérapeute [kineziterapøt] NMF *Br* physiotherapist, *Am* physical therapist

kinésithérapie [kineziterapi] NF *Br* physiotherapy, *Am* physical therapy

kinesthésie [kinɛstezi] NF *Méd* kinaesthesia, kinaesthesis

kinesthésique [kinɛstezik] ADJ *Méd* kinaesthetic

kinétoscope [kinetɔskɔp] NM *Cin* kinetoscope

king-charles [kiɲʃarl] NM INV King Charles spaniel

Kingston [kiŋstɔn] NM Kingston

Kingstown [kiŋztaun] NM Kingstown

kinine [kinin] NF *Biol & Bot* kinin

kinkajou [kɛ̃kaʒu] NM *Zool* kinkajou

kinois, -e [kinjwa, -az] ADJ of/from Kinshasa NM,F **vivre au K.** inhabitant of or person from Kinshasa

Kinshasa [kinʃasa] NM Kinshasa

kiosque [kjɔsk] NM **1** (*boutique*) **k. à journaux** newspaper stand, news-stand; **k. à fleurs** flower stall **2** (*édifice → dans un jardin*) pavilion; **k. à musique** bandstand **3** *Naut* (*d'un navire*) wheelhouse; (*d'un sous-marin*) conning tower **4** *Tél* **K.®** (*d'un Minitel®*) ≃ (telephone) viewdata service **5** *Can* (*stand de foire*) stand (*at an exhibition*)

kiosquier, -ère [kjɔskje, -ɛr] NM,F newspaper seller, newsvendor; **il est k.** he runs a news-stand

kip [kip] NM (*monnaie*) kip

kippa [kipa] NF kippa

kipper [kipœr] NM kipper

Kippour [kipur] NM **le K.** the Kippur

kir [kir] NM kir (*white wine with crème de cassis*); **k. royal** kir royal (*champagne with crème de cassis*)

kirghiz, -e [kirgiz] ADJ Kirghiz, Kirgiz NM (*langue*) Kirghiz
□ **Kirghiz, -e** NM,F Kirghiz, Kirgiz; **les K.** the Kirghiz *or* Kirgiz

Kirghizie [kirgizi] NF **la K.** Kirghizia, Kirgizia

Kirghizistan [kirgizistɑ̃] NM **le K.** Kirghizia, Kirgizia; Kirghizia *or* Kirgizia, *or* Kirgizia; **aller au K.** to go to Kirghizia *or* Kirgizia

Kiribati [kiribati] NF Kiribati

kirsch [kirʃ] NM kirsch

kit [kit] NM kit; **meubles en k.** flatpack furniture, furniture for self-assembly; **vendu en k.** sold in kit form; (*meubles*) sold in flatpack form; **acheter une table en k.** to buy a table in flatpack form *or* for self-assembly; *Pharm* **k. de dépistage** home-testing kit; *Ordinat* **k. d'accès, k. de connexion** connection kit; **k. d'extension** *ou* **d'évolution** upgrade kit; **k. de téléchargeur** download kit

kit-bag [kitbag] (*pl* **kit-bags**) NM *Belg* (*sac → de marin, de soldat*) kit bag; (*→ de sport*) kit bag, gear bag

kitch [kitʃ] = **kitsch**

kitchenette [kitʃənɛt] NF kitchenette

kitsch [kitʃ] ADJ INV kitsch (*avant n*), kitschy NM INV kitsch

kiwi [kiwi] NM **1** *Bot* (*fruit*) kiwi (fruit), Chinese gooseberry; (*arbre*) kiwi tree **2** *Orn* kiwi **3** *Sport* kiwi

kJ (*abrév écrite* **kilojoule**) kJ

Klaxon® [klaksɔn] NM horn; **coup de K.** (*fort*) hoot; (*moins fort*) toot, beep; **donner un coup de K.** to sound *or* honk one's horn, *Br* to hoot (one's horn)

klaxonner [3] [klaksɔne] VI to sound *or* honk one's horn, *Br* to hoot (one's horn)
VT **il m'a klaxonné** he honked *or Br* hooted at me

klébard [klebar] NM *Fam* mutt

Kléber® [klebɛr] NM = tyre manufacturer; **guide K.** = former tourist guide published by the Kléber firm

klebs [klɛps] NM *Fam* mutt

Kleenex® [klinɛks] NM (paper) tissue, paper handkerchief, Kleenex®

kleenex [klinɛks] ADJ *Fam Fig* **emploi k.** job with no security; **salarié k.** disposable employee

klephte [klɛft] NM *Hist* klepht, (Greek) brigand

kleptomane [klɛptoman] NMF kleptomaniac

kleptomanie [klɛptomani] NF kleptomania

klippe [klip] NF *Géol* klippe, outlier

klondike [klɔndajk] NM *Can Fam* high-paying job▪, plum job

klystron [klistrɔ̃] NM *Électron* klystron

km (*abrév écrite* **kilomètre**) km

km/h (*abrév écrite* **kilomètre par heure**) kmph

knickerbockers [nikœrbɔkœr], **knickers** [nikœr] NMPL *Br* knickerbockers, *Am* knickers

knock-down [nɔkdawn] NM INV *Sport* knockdown

knock-out [nɔkawt] NM INV knockout; **k. technique** technical knockout
ADJ INV knocked out, out for the count; **mettre qn k.** to knock sb out

knöpflis [knœpfli] NMPL *Suisse Culin* small dumplings

knout [knut] NM knout

know-how [noaw] NM INV *Écon* know-how

KO [kao] NM *Ordinat* (*abrév* **kilo-octet**) K, KB; **une disquette de 720 KO** a 720K diskette

K-O [kao] (*abrév* **knock-out**) NM INV KO; **K. technique** technical knockout
ADJ INV **1** *Sport* KO'd; **mettre qn K.** to knock sb out; **être K.** to be out for the count **2** *Fam* (*épuisé*) all in, dead beat, *Br* shattered; **mettre qn K.** to exhaust sb▪

koala [kɔala] NM *Zool* koala (bear)

kob [kɔb] NM *Zool* kob

Kobe [kɔbe] NF Kobe

kobold [kɔbɔld] NM *Myth* kobold

Koch [kɔk] *voir* **bacille**

kodiak [kɔdjak] NM *Zool* Kodiak (bear)

kohol [kɔɔl] NM kohl

koinè [kɔjnɛ] NF *Ling* **1** (*dialecte attique*) Koine **2** (*langue commune*) koine, lingua franca

kola [kɔla] NM cola, kola

kolatier [kɔlatje] NM cola (tree), kola (tree)

kolinski [kɔlɛ̃ski] NM kolinsky

kolkhoz(e) [kɔlkoz] NM kolkhoz

kolkhozien, -enne [kɔlkozjɛ̃, -ɛn] **ADJ** kolkhoz *(avant n)*
 NM,F kolkhoznik
Komintern [kɔmintɛrn] **NM** Comintern
kommandantur [kɔmɑ̃dɑ̃tur] **NF** German military command
komsomol [kɔmsɔmɔl] **NMF** Komsomol member
kondo [kɔ̃do] **NM** kondo
konzern [kɔ̃zɛrn, kɔntsɛrn] **NM** *Com & Fin* trust
kop [kɔp] **NM** *Belg Sport (club de supporters)* supporters' club, fan club; *(groupement de supporters)* fans
kopeck [kɔpɛk] **NM** kopeck; *Fam* **ça ne vaut pas un k.** it's not worth *Br* a brass farthing *or Am* a red cent
kora [kɔra] **NF** kora
korê [kɔrɛ] **NF** kore
korrigan, -e [kɔrigɑ̃, -an] **NM,F** mischievous dwarf *or* goblin *(in Breton legends)*, ≃ leprechaun
ko/s *Ordinat (abrév écrite* **kilo-octets par seconde)** kbps
kosovar, -e [kɔsɔvar] **ADJ** Kosovan
 ❏ **Kosovar, -e NM,F** Kosovan
Kosovo [kɔsɔvo] **NM le K.** Kosovo; **vivre au K.** to live in Kosovo; **aller au K.** to go to Kosovo
kot [kɔt] **NM** *Belg* **1** *(chambre d'étudiant)* bedroom *(for student)* **2** *(abri)* shack, hut
kotch, kotche [kɔtʃ] **NM** *Belg (cagibi)* storeroom
koter [3] [kɔte] **VI** *Belg Fam* to rent a room ■, to be in rented accommodation ■
koteur, -euse [kɔtœr, -øz] **NM,F** *Belg Fam* = student in rented accommodation ■
kotje [kɔtʃ] **NM** = **kotch**
koto [kɔto] **NM** *Mus* koto
koubba [kuba] **NF** = monument over a marabout's tomb
koudou = **coudou**
kougelhof, kouglof [kuglɔf] **NM** kugelhopf *(cake)*
kouign-amann [kwiɲaman] **NM** *INV Culin* = large butter biscuit caramelized on top
koukri [kukri] **NM** kukri, Gurkha knife
koulak [kulak] **NM** kulak
koulibiac [kulibjak] **NM** *Culin* coulibiac
koumis, koumys [kumis] **NM** koumiss, kumiss

kourgane [kurgan] **NM** *Hist* kurgan
Kouriles [kuril] **NFPL les (îles) K.** the Kuril *or* Kurile Islands
kouros [kurɔs] **NM** kouros
Kourou [kuru] **NM** Kourou
Koursk [kursk] **NM** Kursk
Koweït [kɔwɛjt] **NM** *(pays)* **le K.** Kuwait, Koweit; **vivre au K.** to live in Kuwait; **aller au K.** to go to Kuwait
 NF *(ville)* = **Koweït City**
Koweït City [kɔwɛjtsiti] **NM** *(ville)* Kuwait, Kuwait City, Koweit
koweïtien, -enne [kɔwɛjtjɛ̃, -ɛn] **ADJ** Kuwaiti
 ❏ **Koweïtien, -enne NM,F** Kuwaiti
kraal [krɑl] **NM** kraal
krach [krak] **NM** *Fin* crash; **k. (boursier)** (stock market) crash; **le k. de Wall Street** the Wall Street Crash
kraft [kraft] **NM** brown wrapping paper, kraft paper
 ADJ INV papier k. brown wrapping paper, kraft paper; **pâte k.** kraft pulp
krak [krak] **NM** *Hist* = fortress built by European crusaders in Syria and Palestine in the 12th and 13th centuries
kraken [krakɛn] **NM** *Myth* kraken
KRD *(abrév écrite* **couronne danoise)** Kr, DKr
Kremlin [krɛmlɛ̃] **NM le K.** the Kremlin
kremlinologie [krɛmlinɔlɔʒi] **NF** Kremlinology, Kremlin watching
kremlinologue [krɛmlinɔlɔg] **NMF** Kremlinologist, Kremlin watcher
kreuzer [krøtzɛr, krødzɛr] **NM** kreutzer
kriek [krik] **NF** *Belg* kriek, = beer made from cherries
krill [kril] **NM** krill
krishnaïsme [kriʃnaism] **NM** *Rel* Krishnaism
kriss [kris] **NM** kris
KRN *(abrév écrite* **couronne norvégienne)** Kr, NKr
kronprinz [krɔnprints] **NM** *Hist* Crown Prince (of Prussia)
kroumir [krumir] **NM 1** *(chausson)* pump **2** *Fam* **(vieux) k.** old fogey, *Am* geezer
KRS *(abrév écrite* **couronne suédoise)** Kr, SKr
Kruger [krugœr] **N Parc National Kruger** K. National Park

krypton [kriptɔ̃] **NM** *Chim* krypton
ksar [ksar] *(pl* **ksour** [ksur]) **NM** = North African fortified village
kshatriya, ksatriya [kʃatrija] **NM** *INV* Kshatriya
ksour [ksur] *voir* **ksar**
Kuala Lumpur [kwalalumpur] **NM** Kuala Lumpur
kufique [kufik] = **coufique**
Ku Klux Klan [kyklyksklɑ̃] **NM le K.** the Ku Klux Klan
kummel [kymɛl] **NM** kümmel (liqueur)
kumquat [kumkwat] **NM** kumquat
kung-fu [kuɲfu] **NM** *INV* kung fu
kurde [kyrd] **ADJ** Kurdish
 NM *(langue)* Kurdish
 ❏ **Kurde NMF** Kurd
Kurdistan [kyrdistɑ̃] **NM le K.** Kurdistan; **vivre au K.** to live in Kurdistan; **aller au K.** to go to Kurdistan
kuru [kuru] **NM** *Méd* kuru
kvas [kvas] **NM** kvass, kvas
kW *(abrév écrite* **kilowatt)** kW
kwa [kwa] **NM** *Ling* Kwa
kwas [kvas] **NM** kvass, kvas
kwashiorkor [kwaʃjorkɔr] **NM** *Méd* kwashiorkor
K-way® [kawɛ] **NM** *INV* cagoule; **pantalon de K.** waterproof *Br* trousers *or Am* pants
kWh *(abrév écrite* **kilowattheure)** kW/hr
kyat [kjat] **NM** kyat
kymographe [kimɔgraf] **NM** *Méd* kymograph
Kyoto [kjɔto] **NM** Kyoto
Kyrie [kirije] **NM** *INV Rel* Kyrie (eleison)
kyrielle [kirjɛl] **NF** *Fam* **une k. de bambins** a whole bunch *or* swarm of kids; **une k. d'insultes** a string of insults; **une k. de mensonges** a pack of lies; **elle a toute une k. d'amis** she has masses of friends
kyste [kist] **NM** *Méd* cyst; **k. sébacé** sebaceous cyst, *Spéc* wen
kystique [kistik] **ADJ** *Méd* cystic
kyudo [kjudo] **NM** kyudo
Kyushu [kjuʃu] **NF** *Géog* Kyushu

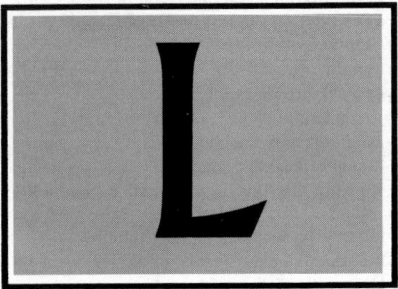

L, l¹ [ɛl] NM INV **1** (*lettre*) L, l; **L comme Louis** ≃ L for Larry **2** (*forme*) L (shape) **3** *Can Univ* **L ès L** (*licencié ès lettres*) *Br* ≃ BA, *Am* ≃ AB
▫ **en L** ADJ L-shaped

l² (*abrév écrite* **litre**) l

l' [l] *voir* **le¹**

la¹ [la] *voir* **le¹**

la² [la] NM INV *Mus* A; (*chanté*) lah; **donner le la** to give the *or* an A; *Fig* to set the tone

LÀ [la] ADV **1** (*dans l'espace* → **là-bas**) there; (→ **ici**) here; **elle habite Paris maintenant, c'est là qu'elle a trouvé du travail** she lives in Paris now, that's where she found work; **il est à la poste? – qu'est-ce qu'il fait là?** he's at the post office? – what's he doing there?; **c'est là, je reconnais la maison** there it is (over there), I recognize the house; **de là au village il y a un kilomètre** it's one kilometre from there to the village; **à quelques kilomètres de là** a few kilometres away; **là où vous êtes** where you are; **là en bas/en haut** down/up there; **déjà là?** (are you) here already?; **je ne peux rien faire, il est toujours là** I can't do anything, he's always around; **viens là!** come here!; **est-ce qu'il est là?** is he in?; **ne t'inquiète pas, je suis là pour t'aider si tu en as besoin** don't worry, I'm here to help you if you need me; **je ne suis là pour personne** if anybody asks I'm not in *or* here; **je suis là pour vous répondre** it's my job to answer your questions; **allez, on n'est pas là pour bavarder** come on now, we're not here to chat

2 (*dans le temps*) **c'est là que j'ai paniqué** that's when I panicked; **attendons demain et là nous déciderons** let's wait until tomorrow and then (we'll) decide; **à partir de là** from then on, from that moment on; **là, je n'ai pas le temps de lui en parler** I don't have time to tell him/her about it right now; **à quelque temps de là** some time after; **à quelques jours/mois de là** a few days/months later; **c'est là où tu m'as le plus étonné** that's where you most surprised me; **il est anxieux là où il faudrait être calme** he gets worked up (just) when he should remain calm

3 (*dans cette situation*) **là tu exagères** now you're exaggerating; **vous n'avez fait là que ce qui était nécessaire** you only did what was necessary; **c'est justement là où je ne vous suis plus** that's just where you've lost me; **nous n'en sommes pas encore là** we haven't reached that stage yet; **pour l'instant nous en sommes là** that's how things stand at the moment; **j'en étais là de mes réflexions quand le téléphone a sonné** I'd got that far with my thinking when the phone rang; **comment en es-tu arrivé là?** how did you manage to let things go so far?; **je n'ai pas l'intention d'en rester** *ou* **demeurer là** I don't intend leaving it at that

4 (*dans cela*) **il n'y a là rien d'étonnant** there's nothing surprising about that; **je ne vois là aucune raison de s'inquiéter** I don't see that there's anything to worry about; **ne voyez là aucune malice de ma part** please don't take it the wrong way; **c'est bien là le problème** that's the problem; **la santé, tout est là** (good) health is everything

5 (*pour renforcer*) **ce sont là mes amis** those are my friends; **c'est là mon intention** that's my intention *or* what I intend to do; **c'est là le problème/la difficulté** that's where the problem/the difficulty lies

6 (*emploi expressif*) **oui, j'ai refusé ce travail, là, tu es content?** yes, I turned down the job,

now are you satisfied?; **alors là, je ne sais pas!** well that I really don't know!; **alors là, tu exagères!** you've got a nerve!; **c'est une belle grippe que tu as là!** that's quite a bout of flu you've got there!; *Fam* **que me chantes-tu là?** what are you on about?; **malheureux, qu'as-tu fait là!** what have you gone and done now?; **qu'est-ce que je vois là! mais ce sont mes gants!** if it isn't my gloves!; **là, là, calme-toi!** now, now *or* there, there, calm down!; **hé là!** *ou* **oh là! doucement!** gently does it!
▫ **de-ci de-là** ADV *Littéraire* here and there
▫ **de là** ADV **1** (*dans l'espace*) from there; **de là je me suis dirigée vers l'église** from there I headed towards the church; **de là jusqu'à la poste il y a 500 m** it's 500 m from there to the post office; *Fig* **de là à dire que c'est un criminel, il y a loin** there's a big difference between that and saying he's a criminal; **mais de là à dire qu'ils sont tous antipathiques!** but I wouldn't go as far as to say they're all unpleasant!; **mais de là à ce qu'il nous donne son accord...** but as to giving us his agreement...

2 (*marquant la conséquence*) **de là son amertume** that's why he's/she's bitter, that explains his/her bitterness, hence his/her bitterness; **on peut déduire de là que...** from that we can deduce that...
▫ **là contre** ADV **c'est votre droit, je n'ai rien à dire là contre** it's your right, I have nothing to say in opposition
▫ **par là** ADV **1** (*dans l'espace*) **c'est par là** it's over there; **quelque part par là** somewhere around here/there; **vous devriez passer par là** you should go that way

2 *Fig* **si tu vas par là** if you go along that road; **qu'entendez-vous** *ou* **que voulez-vous dire par là?** what do you mean by that?; **il faut en passer par là!** there's no alternative!, it can't be helped!

-là [la] ADV **1** (*lié à un nom introduit par un adjectif démonstratif*) (*singulier*) that; (*pluriel*) those; **cette femme-là** that woman; **ce stylo-là** that pen; **dans ces endroits-là** in those places; *Péj* **tu fréquentes ces gens-là?** are those the kind of people you go around with?; **ne fais pas cette tête-là!** you needn't look like that!; *très Fam* **il est taré, ce mec-là!** the guy's crazy!

2 (*lié à un pronom*) **quel livre voulez-vous? – celui-là** which book do you want? – that one; **celui-là, alors!** honestly, that one!

3 (*exprimant le passé*) **ce matin-là** that morning; **en ce temps-là** in those days, at that time

labanotation [labanɔtasjɔ̃] NF labanotation

labarum [labarɔm] NM *Hist* labarum

là-bas [lɑba] ADV **1** (*en bas*) down *or* under there; **l. dans la vallée** down there in the valley **2** (*en un lieu éloigné*) there; **une fois arrivés l., nous nous arrangerons** we'll sort it out when we get there

labbe [lab] NM *Orn* skua; **grand l., l. cataracte** great skua; **l. longicaude** long-tailed skua; **l. parisite** Arctic skua

labdanum [labdanɔm] NM labdanum, ladanum

label [label] NM **1** (*étiquette*) label; **l. NF** *ou* **norme française** French industry standards label; **l. d'origine** label of origin; **l. de garantie** guarantee label; **l. de qualité/d'exportation** quality/export label; **il fera probablement campagne sous le l. socialiste** he will probably campaign as a Socialist **2** (*maison de disques*) label; **l. indépendant** independent *or* indie record label **3** *Ordinat* **l. de volume** volume label

labéliser [3] [labelize] VT to label

labelle [labɛl] NM **1** *Bot* labellum **2** (*de coquillage*) lip

labelliser [labelize] = **labéliser**

labeur [labœr] NM **1** *Littéraire* (*travail pénible*) toil, labour; (*effort*) hard work; **une vie de l.** a life of toil **2** *Typ* bookwork; **imprimerie de l.** bookwork printers

labferment [labfɛrmɑ̃] NM *Biol* rennet, rennin

labial, -e, -aux, -ales [labjal, -o] ADJ **1** *Anat* lip (*avant n*), labial **2** *Ling* labial
▫ **labiale** NF labial (consonant)

labialisation [labjalizasjɔ̃] NF (*d'une voyelle*) rounding; (*d'une consonne*) labialization

labialiser [3] [labjalize] VT (*voyelle*) to round; (*consonne*) to labialize

labié, -e [labje] *Bot* ADJ labiate
▫ **labiée** NF labiate, *Spéc* member of the Labiatae
▫ **labiées** NFPL labiates, *Spéc* Labiatae

labile [labil] ADJ **1** *Chim & Psy* labile **2** *Littéraire* (*peu stable*) unstable, temperamental

labilité [labilite] NF *Chim & Psy* lability

labiodental, -e, -aux, -ales [labjɔdɑ̃tal, -o] ADJ labiodental
▫ **labiodentale** NF labiodental (consonant)

labiolecture [labjɔlɛktyr] NF lip-reading

labium [labjɔm] NM labium

labo [labo] NM *Fam* (*abrév* **laboratoire**) lab; **l. de langues** language lab; **l. photo** darkroom

laborantin, -e [labɔrɑ̃tɛ̃, -in] NM,F laboratory assistant, *Am* laboratory operator

laboratoire [labɔratwar] NM **1** (*lieu*) laboratory; (*équipe*) (research) team; **l. d'analyses (médicales)** analytical laboratory; **L. européen pour la physique des particules** European laboratory for particle physics; **l. expérimental** testing laboratory; **l. de recherche** research laboratory; **l. d'idées** think tank

2 *Scol* **l. de langues** language laboratory

3 *Métal* heating chamber

4 *Phot* (*salle*) processing room; (*usine*) processing works; *Cin & Phot* **l. de film** film laboratory
▫ **en laboratoire** ADV in the laboratory, under laboratory conditions; **embryon végétal obtenu en l.** plant embryo obtained in the laboratory *or* under laboratory conditions

laborieuse [labɔrjøz] *voir* **laborieux**

laborieusement [labɔrjøzmɑ̃] ADV (*péniblement*) laboriously, with great difficulty

laborieux, -euse [labɔrjø, -øz] ADJ **1** (*long et difficile* → *procédure, tâche, manœuvre*) laborious

2 (*lourd* → *style*) heavy, laboured; **trois heures pour faire une lettre, ce fut l.!** three hours to write a letter, that's slow going!; **j'ai réussi à la convaincre, mais ç'a été l.** I managed to convince her but it was a laborious task *or* but it was heavy going!; **dans un anglais l.** in halting English; **lecture/récitation laborieuse** laboured reading/recitation

3 (*industrieux*) hardworking, industrious; **la classe laborieuse** the working *or* labouring class

labour [labur] NM **1** *Agr* tilling (UNCOUNT), ploughing (UNCOUNT); **les labours** the ploughed fields; **commencer les labours** to start ploughing **2** *Hort* digging (over)

labourable [laburabl] ADJ ploughable; **des terres labourables** arable land

labourage [labura3] NM **1** *Agr* tilling, ploughing **2** *Hort* digging over

labourer[3] [labure] VT 1 *Agr* to plough; *Hort* to dig (over) 2 *(entailler)* to dig into, to lacerate, to scratch; **les sangles labouraient les flancs du cheval** the straps were digging into the horse's flanks; **un terrain labouré par les obus** land churned up by artillery shells; **un visage labouré de rides** a face furrowed with wrinkles; **les policiers lui ont labouré les côtes** the cops beat him/her up; **l'ancre labourait le fond** the anchor was dragging along the bottom

laboureur [laburœr] NM 1 *Littéraire* ploughman 2 *Hist* husbandman, ≃ yeoman

Labrador [labradɔr] NM le L. Labrador

labrador [labradɔr] NM 1 *Minér* labradorite 2 *Zool* Labrador retriever, labrador; **l. doré/noir/chocolat** golden/black/chocolate labrador

labre [labr] NM 1 *Ich* wrasse 2 *(d'arthropode, de mollusque)* labrum

labri(t) [labri] NM Pyrenean sheepdog

labyrinthe [labirɛ̃t] NM 1 *(dédale)* labyrinth, maze; **la vieille ville est un l. de ruelles étroites** the old (part of) town is a maze of narrow streets 2 *Fig* maze; **le l. des lois** the intricacies of the law 3 *Anat* labyrinth

labyrinthique [labirɛ̃tik] ADJ labyrinthine, maze-like

labyrinthite [labirɛ̃tit] NF *Méd* labyrinthitis

labyrinthodonte [labirɛ̃tɔdɔ̃t] NM labyrinthodont

lac [lak] NM *(pièce d'eau)* lake; **l. artificiel/de barrage** artificial/barrier lake; **l. de cirque** cirque lake; **la région des Lacs** the Lakes, the Lake District; *Fig* **c'est tombé dans le l.** it has fallen through; **le l. Baïkal** Lake Baikal; **le l. Balaton** Lake Balaton; **le l. de Cabora Bassa** *ou* **Cahora Bassa** Lake Cabora Bassa, Lake Cahora Bassa; **le l. de Côme** Lake Como; **le l. de Constance** Lake Constance; **le l. Érié** Lake Erie; **le l. de Garde** Lake Garda; **le l. Huron** Lake Huron; **le l. Kariba** Lake Kariba; **le l. Ladoga** Lake Ladoga; **le l. Léman** Lake Geneva; **le l. de Lugano** Lake Lugano; **le l. Majeur** Lake Maggiore; **le l. Malawi** Lake Malawi; **le l. Michigan** Lake Michigan; **le l. Mobutu** Lake Mobutu; **le l. Nasser** Lake Nasser; **le l. de Neuchâtel** Lake Neuchâtel; **le l. Ontario** Lake Ontario; **le l. Peïpous** Lake Peipus; **le l. Supérieur** Lake Superior; **le l. Tanganyika** Lake Tanganyika; **le l. Tchad** Lake Chad; **le l. de Tibériade** the Sea of Galilee; **le l. Titicaca** Lake Titicaca; **le l. Turkana** Lake Turkana; **le l. Victoria** Lake Victoria; **le l. Volta** Lake Volta; **le l. Winnipeg** Lake Winnipeg; **le l. de Zoug** Lake Zug; **le l. de Zurich** Lake Zürich

'Le Lac des cygnes' *Tchaïkovski* 'Swan Lake'

laçage [lasaʒ] NM *(de chaussures, de bottes)* lacing up, tying up; *(de vêtement)* lacing (up)

laccase [lakaz] NF *Biol & Chim* laccase

laccolite, laccolithe [lakɔlit] NM *Géol* laccolite, laccolith

Lacédémone [lasedemɔn] NF Lacedaemonia

lacédémonien, -enne [lasedemɔnjɛ̃, -ɛn] ADJ Lacedaemonian

❑ **Lacédémonien, -enne** NM,F Lacedaemonian

lacement [lasmɑ̃] NM *(de chaussures, de bottes)* lacing up, tying up; *(de vêtement)* lacing (up)

lacer [16] [lase] VT *(vêtement)* to lace (up); *(chaussure)* to lace up, to tie up

►**se lacer** VPR to lace (up); **comment cette botte se lace-t-elle?** how do you lace (up) this boot?

lacération [laserasjɔ̃] NF 1 *Méd* laceration, gash 2 *(fait de déchirer → gén)* ripping, tearing, slashing; *(→ de sièges)* slashing; **la l. des affiches est monnaie courante en période électorale** during election time posters often get slashed

lacérer [18] [lasere] VT 1 *(affiche, rideau, siège)* to slash; **le chat a lacéré le fauteuil avec ses griffes** the cat has clawed the armchair to pieces 2 *(blesser)* to lacerate, to gash; **la douleur lui lacère le dos** the pain is like a knife in his/her back, he/she has a lacerating pain in his/her back

lacerie [lasri] NF fine openwork basketry *or* wickerwork

lacertilien [lasɛrtiljɛ̃] *Zool* NM lacertilian, lacertian, *Spéc* member of the Lacertilia

❑ **lacertiliens** NMPL lacertilians, lacertians, *Spéc* Lacertilia

lacet [lasɛ] NM 1 *(de chaussure, de corset)* lace 2 *(piège)* snare; **poser** *ou* **tendre des lacets** to set snares 3 *(d'une route)* hairpin bend; **faire des lacets** *(route)* to twist and turn 4 *Aviat* yaw 5 *Couture* tie 6 *Rail (mouvement)* hunting

❑ **à lacets** ADJ *(chaussure)* with laces, lace-up *(avant n)*

❑ **en lacets** ADJ *(route)* winding, twisting ADV **la route monte en lacets** the road winds *or* twists upwards

laceur, -euse [lasœr, -øz] NM,F net maker

lâchage [lɑʃaʒ] NM 1 *(rupture)* failure; **c'est dû au l. des freins** it's due to brake failure 2 *Fam (abandon)* **c'est un l. en règle de leur part** they've really let us down

lâche [lɑʃ] ADJ 1 *(poltron)* cowardly, spineless; **être l.** to be cowardly; **se montrer l.** to behave like a coward

2 *(avant le nom) (méprisable)* cowardly; **un l. attentat** a cowardly *or* despicable attack

3 *(non serré → nœud)* loose, slack; *(→ vêtement)* loose, baggy

4 *(imprécis → dialogue, scénario)* weak; *(→ raisonnement)* woolly, slipshod

5 *(sans rigueur → règlement, discipline)* lax, overlenient

6 *Tex (étoffe)* loose, loosely woven; *(tricot)* loose-knit

NMF coward

lâché, -e [lɑʃe] ADJ *Beaux-Arts* sloppy, careless

lâchement [lɑʃmɑ̃] ADV 1 *(sans courage)* in a cowardly manner 2 *(sans tension)* loosely, slackly

lâcher [3] [lɑʃe] VT 1 *(desserrer)* to loosen, to slacken; **il a lâché sa ceinture d'un cran** he let out *or* he loosened his belt a notch; **l. la vapeur** to let off steam; **l. la bonde** *ou* **les bondes à** to give vent to; **l. la bride à un cheval** to give a horse its head; *Fig* **l. la bride à qn** to allow sb more freedom of movement

2 *(cesser de tenir)* to let go of; *(laisser tomber)* to drop; **l. la pédale du frein** to take one's foot off the brake (pedal); **elle a lâché la pile d'assiettes** she dropped the pile of plates; **il roule en lâchant le guidon** he rides with no hands; **lâche-moi!** let me go!, let go of me!; **ne lâche pas la rampe, l'escalier est glissant** don't let go of the banister, the stairs are slippery; **elle ne la lâchait pas des yeux** *ou* **du regard** she didn't take her eyes off her for a moment; **l. prise** to let go; **cette idée ne m'a pas lâché** I couldn't get this idea out of my mind; *Fam* **il ne m'a pas lâché d'une semelle** he stuck to me like a leech; *Fam* **tu me lâches, oui?** leave me alone!, get off my back *or* case!; *Fam* **lâche-moi les baskets!** leave me alone!, get off my back *or* case!; *Fam* **les l.** *(payer)* to fork out; *Fam* **il les lâche avec un élastique** he's a stingy *or* tight-fisted old so-and-so; **l. la proie pour l'ombre** to chase rainbows; *aussi Fig* **l. pied** to give way

3 *Aviat (bombe)* to drop; *(ballon)* to launch

4 *Ordinat (icône)* to drop

5 *(libérer → oiseau)* to let loose, to release, to let go; *(→ chien)* to let off, to unleash; *(→ animal dangereux)* to set loose; *(→ meute, faucon)* to slip; **l. les chiens sur qn** to set the dogs on sb; *Fam* **le prof nous a lâchés plus tôt** the teacher let us out early; *Can Fam* **l. son fou** to let one's hair down, to let off steam

6 *Fam (abandonner → ami)* to drop; *(→ amant, mari, famille)* to walk out on▪; *(→ emploi)* to chuck in; **l. ses études** to drop out of school; **le moteur nous a lâchés le deuxième jour** the engine died *or* packed in on us on the second day

7 *(émettre → cri, juron)* to let out; *(→ plaisanterie, sottise)* to come out with; **l. un soupir de soulagement** to let out a sigh of relief; *Fam* **l. un pet** to break wind

8 *Sport (distancer → concurrent)* to leave behind, to get a lead on; **l. le peloton** to leave the rest of the field behind, to break from the pack

VI 1 *(se casser → câble)* to snap, to break, to give (way); *(→ embrayage, frein)* to fail; *Fam (→ organe)* to give out, to pack in; **les freins ont lâché** the brakes failed; **ses nerfs ont fini par l.** he/she eventually cracked up *or* had a breakdown

2 *(abandonner)* **le coureur a lâché dans la dernière montée** the runner gave up the fight in the middle of the last climb

NM 1 *(fait de laisser partir)* release; **ils ont fait un l. de ballons/de colombes** they released balloons/a flock of doves

2 *Ordinat* **l. d'icônes** icon drop

►**se lâcher** VPR *Littéraire* to let oneself go, to throw off all restraint

lâcheté [lɑʃte] NF 1 *(manque de courage)* cowardice 2 *(caractère vil)* baseness, lowness; *(procédé vil)* low *or* dirty trick; **commettre une l.** to do something despicable

lâcheur, -euse [lɑʃœr, -øz] NM,F *Fam* **quel l., il n'est pas venu!** what an unreliable so-and-so, he didn't come!

lacinié, -e [lasinje] ADJ laciniate

lacis [lasi] NM 1 *(labyrinthe)* maze, web; **un l. de ruelles** a maze of little streets 2 *(entrelacement)* lattice, network, tracery; **l. veineux** network of veins

lackeman, lackman, lackment, lacment [lakmɑ̃] = **lacquement**

laconique [lakɔnik] ADJ *(lettre, réponse)* terse, *Sout* laconic; *(personne)* laconic

laconiquement [lakɔnikmɑ̃] ADV tersely, *Sout* laconically

laconisme [lakɔnism] NM terseness, *Sout* laconism

La Corogne [lakɔrɔɲ] NF La Coruña, Corunna

lacquement [lakmɑ̃] NM *Belg* = wafer biscuit with a sweet filling, eaten hot

lacrima-christi [lakrimakristi] NM INV lachryma Christi (wine)

lacrymal, -e, -aux, -ales [lakrimal, -o] ADJ tear *(avant n)*, *Spéc* lachrymal, lacrimal

lacrymogène [lakrimɔʒɛn] ADJ *(gaz)* tear *(avant n)*, *Spéc* lachrymatory, lacrymogenic; *(grenade)* tear-gas *(avant n)*

lacrymo-nasal, -e [lakrimɔnazal, -o] *(mpl* **lacrymo-nasaux**, *fpl* **lacrymo-nasales)** ADJ nasolachrymal, nasolacrimal

lacs [lɑ] NM 1 *(piège)* snare 2 *aussi Hér* **l. d'amour** *(motif décoratif)* love knot, true-lover's knot 3 *Méd (ruban)* corrective strap

lactaire [laktɛr] ADJ *Physiol* lacteal

NM *Bot* milk cap; **l. délicieux** saffron milk cap

lactalbumine [laktalbymin] NF *Chim* lactalbumin

lactame [laktam] NM *Chim* lactam

lactarium [laktarjɔm] NM milk bank

lactase [laktaz] NF *Physiol* lactase

lactate [laktat] NM *Chim* lactate

lactation [laktasjɔ̃] NF lactation

lacté, -e [lakte] ADJ 1 *(contenant du lait)* milky, *Spéc* lacteal; **farine lactée** milk-enriched cereal; **produits lactés** milk *or* milky foods; **régime l.** milk diet 2 *Littéraire (pareil au lait)* milky, lacteous

lactescence [laktesɑ̃s] NF lactescence

lactescent, -e [laktesɑ̃, -ɑ̃t] ADJ 1 *(contenant du lait)* lactescent 2 *Littéraire (d'un blanc laiteux)* milky-white, lacteous

lactifère [laktifɛr] ADJ lactiferous

lactique [laktik] ADJ *Chim* lactic

lactodensimètre [laktɔdɑ̃simɛtr] NM lactometer

lactoflavine [laktɔflavin] NF riboflavin, vitamin B2

lactomètre [laktɔmɛtr] NM lactometer

lactone [laktɔn] NF *Chim* lactone

lactose [laktoz] NM lactose

lactosérum [laktɔserɔm] NM whey

lacunaire [lakynɛr] ADJ 1 *(incomplet)* incomplete, *Littéraire* lacunary; **il a des connaissances/des fichiers lacunaires** his knowledge is/his files are full of gaps 2 *Anat & Bot (système)* lacunar; *(tissu)* lacunal

lacune [lakyn] NF 1 *(omission)* gap; **de vieux manuscrits pleins de lacunes** old manuscripts with many parts missing *or* full of gaps; **les lacunes de la loi sur cette question** the gaps in the law regarding this matter; **ma mémoire a des lacunes** there are gaps in my memory; **il y a des lacunes dans cette encyclopédie** there are some omissions in this encyclopedia; **j'ai des lacunes en mathématiques** there are gaps in my knowledge of mathematics 2 *Anat, Biol & Géol* lacuna

lacuneux, -euse [lakynø, -øz] ADJ 1 *Littéraire (incomplet)* lacunary 2 *Bot* lacunose

lacustre [lakystr] ADJ **1** *Biol & Bot* lacustrine **2** *Constr & Archit* **cité l.** lakeside pile-dwelling settlement; **habitation l.** lakeside dwelling
lad [lad] NM stableboy, *Br* stable lad
ladang [ladɑ̃g] NM ladang
ladanum [ladanɔm] NM ladanum, labdanum
là-dedans [laddɑ̃] ADV **1** *(ici)* in here; *(là-bas)* in there; **le tiroir est sens dessus dessous, je ne trouve rien l.** the drawer is in a mess, I can't find anything in here; *Fam* **debout l.!** rise and shine!
2 *(dans ce texte)* in here; **il y a l. des choses qui m'échappent** *(dans ce qui est dit)* there are things that escape me in what was said; **il y a du vrai l.** there's some truth in it; **ça ne m'étonnerait pas qu'elle soit impliquée l.** it wouldn't surprise me if she was involved (in it); **il n'a rien à voir l.!** he's got nothing to do with it!
3 *Fam Hum (locution)* **il y en a, l.!** he's/she's got a lot up top!
là-dessous [ladsu] ADV **1** *(sous cet objet-ci)* under here; *(sous cet objet-là)* under there **2** *(dans cette affaire)* **il y a quelque chose de bizarre l.** there's something strange *or* odd about all this; **qu'est-ce qui se cache l.?** what's behind all this *or* behind it all?
là-dessus [ladsy] ADV **1** *(sur cet objet-ci)* on here; *(sur cet objet-là)* on there; **ne t'appuie pas l.!** don't lean on it!; *Fam* **monte l. et tu verras Montmartre** up you get *(when encouraging child up on to chair etc)* **2** *(sur ce sujet)* **je n'en sais pas plus que toi l.** I don't know any more than you about it; **nous reviendrons l.** we'll come back to that; **c'est l. qu'il faut se concentrer** that's what you/we/*etc* have to concentrate on **3** *(sur ce)* **l. je vous dis bonsoir** at this point *or* with that, I'll say goodnight; **l., elle se tut** at which point *or Sout* whereupon she stopped talking
ladies [lɛdiz] *voir* **lady**
ladin [ladɛ̃] NM Ladin
ladino [ladino] NM *(langue)* Ladino
ladite [ladit] *voir* **ledit**
ladre [ladr] ADJ **1** *Vét* measly, measled **2** *Littéraire (avare)* miserly, measly **3** *Arch (lépreux)* leprous
NMF **1** *Littéraire (avare)* miser, skinflint **2** *Arch (lépreux)* leper
NM *Vét* **tache de l.** bare patch
ladrerie [ladrəri] NF **1** *Littéraire (avarice)* miserliness **2** *Vét* measles **3** *Arch (lèpre)* leprosy; *(léproserie)* leper hospital *or* house
lady [lɛdi] *(pl* **ladys** *ou* **ladies** [lɛdiz]) NF lady; **elle se prend pour une l.** she thinks she's really something
Lagarde et Michard [lagardemiʃar] NM = series of school books each describing a period of literary history through illustrations, historical notes and extracts from literary works, known to generations of French schoolchildren
lagomorphe [lagɔmɔrf] *Zool* NM lagomorph, *Spéc* member of the Lagomorpha order
❑ **lagomorphes** NMPL lagomorphs, *Spéc* Lagomorpha
lagon [lagɔ̃] NM (coral reef) lagoon
lagopède [lagɔpɛd] NM *Orn* **l. des Alpes** ptarmigan; **l. (rouge) d'Écosse** (red) grouse; **l. d'Écosse femelle** moorhen; **l. des saules** willow grouse
Lagos [lagos] NM Lagos
lagotriche [lagɔtriʃ], **lagothrix** [lagɔtriks] NM *Zool* woolly monkey, *Spéc* lagothrix
laguiole [lajɔl] NM **1** *(couteau)* = distinctively shaped knife **2** *(fromage)* = cheese produced in the Aubrac, similar to Cantal
laguis [lagi] NM *Naut* running bowline
lagunage [lagynaʒ] NM *Agr* lagooning
lagunaire [lagynɛr] ADJ lagoonal
lagune [lagyn] NF lagoon
lahar [laar] NM lahar
là-haut [lao] ADV **1** *(au-dessus)* up there; *(à l'étage)* upstairs; **leur maison est l. sur la colline** their house is up there on the hill; **tout l.** way up there, all the way up there **2** *(aux cieux)* up there, (up) in Heaven, *Sout* on high
lai, -e [lɛ] ADJ *Rel* **frère l.** lay brother; **sœur laie** lay sister
NM *Littérature* lay
laïc, laïque [laik] ADJ **1** *(non clérical)* secular, lay, *Littéraire* laic; **l'esprit l.** secularism; **habit l.** lay dress
2 *(indépendant du clergé)* secular; **l'école laïque** secular education; **un État l.** a secular state
NM,F layman, *f* laywoman; **les laïcs** the laity
❑ **laïque** ADJ **1** *(non clérical)* secular, lay, *Littéraire* laic; **habit laïque** lay dress
2 *(indépendant du clergé)* **un État laïque** a secular state NF *Vieilli* state; **la laïque** = the state educational system (in France)
laïcat [laika] NM laity
laîche [lɛʃ] NF sedge
laïcisation [laisizasjɔ̃] NF secularization, laicization
laïciser [3] [laisize] VT to secularize, to laicize
laïcisme [laisism] NM secularism
laïciste [laisist] ADJ secularist
NMF secularist
laïcité [laisite] NF secularism; **la défense de la l.** defence of secular education *(in France)*
laid, -e [lɛ, lɛd] ADJ **1** *(inesthétique → bâtisse)* ugly, unsightly; *(→ vêtement, tableau, décoration)* ugly, unattractive, awful; *(→ personne)* unattractive, ugly; **en bleu, c'est très l.** it looks awful in blue; **il est/c'est très l.** he's/it's hideous; **l. comme un pou** *ou* **un singe, l. à faire peur** *ou* **fuir** (as) ugly as sin **2** *(impoli)* rude, unseemly; **c'est l. de faire des grimaces aux gens** it's rude *or* not nice to pull faces at people
NM *(valeur esthétique)* **le l.** ugliness
laidement [lɛdmɑ̃] ADV **1** *(de façon laide)* unattractively **2** *(ignoblement)* dirtily, *Littéraire* basely
laideron [lɛdrɔ̃] NM ugly girl
laideur [lɛdœr] NF **1** *(physique → d'une personne, d'une chose)* ugliness; **d'une l. repoussante** repulsively ugly **2** *(chose laide)* monstrosity **3** *(morale → d'un crime)* heinousness; *(→ d'une accusation)* meanness, *Littéraire* baseness; **il a dépeint l'hypocrisie dans toute sa l.** he portrayed hypocrisy in all its ugliness
laie [lɛ] ADJ *voir* **lai**
NF **1** *Zool* wild sow **2** *Agr (trouée)* (compartment) line; *(sentier)* forest path **3** *Tech* bush hammer
laimargue [lɛmarg] NF Greenland shark
lainage [lɛnaʒ] NM **1** *Tex (tissu)* woollen fabric *or* material; *(procédé)* napping; **une robe de** *ou* **en l.** a woollen dress **2** *(pull)* woollen sweater *or Br* jumper; *(gilet)* wool cardigan; **mets un l.** put on a sweater *or Br* jumper; **des lainages** woollens **3** *(toison)* fleece
laine [lɛn] NF **1** *(poil → du mouton, de l'alpaga etc)* wool; **l. vierge** new wool; **il se laisserait manger** *ou* **tondre la l. sur le dos** he'd let you take the shirt off his back; *Can* **être (un Québécois) pure l.** = to be a descendant of the first French settlers in Canada
2 *Tex (tissu)* wool; **un tapis en l. peignée** a worsted rug; **l. des Pyrénées** = warm, fleecy woollen material *(made in the Pyrenees)*; **l. à tricoter** knitting wool
3 *Fam (vêtement)* **(petite) l.** sweater■, *Br* woolly
4 *(isolant)* **l. de bois** wood wool *or* fibre; **l. de laitier** slag wool; **l. minérale** mineral wool; **l. de roche** rock wool; **l. de verre** glass wool
❑ **de laine** ADJ wool *(avant n)*, woollen; **bonnet/chaussettes de l.** woollen hat/socks; **robe de l.** wool *or* woollen dress
lainé, -e [lɛne] ADJ **peau lainée** sheepskin
lainer [4] [lɛne] VT *Tex (tissu)* to nap
lainerie [lɛnri] NF **1** *(fabrication)* manufacture of woollens **2** *(usine, atelier)* woollen mill **3** *(magasin de gros)* (wholesale) wool shop
laineur, -euse[1] [lɛnœr, -øz] NM,F napper
❑ **laineuse** NF napping machine, raising machine
laineux, -euse[2] [lɛnø, -øz] ADJ **1** *(tissu)* woollen; *(mouton, cheveux)* woolly **2** *Bot* woolly, *Spéc* piliferous
lainier, -ère [lɛnje, -ɛr] ADJ *(production)* wool *(avant n)*; *(usine)* wool-producing
NM,F **1** *(industriel)* wool manufacturer **2** *(ouvrier)* wool worker **3** *(commerçant)* wool stapler
laïque [laik] *voir* **laïc**
laird [lɛrd] NM laird
lais [lɛ] NMPL (exposed) foreshore
laisse [lɛs] NF **1** *(lien)* leash, lead; **tirer sur la l.** to strain at the leash; **tenir un chien en l.** to keep a dog on the leash *or* lead; *Fig* **mener** *ou* **tenir qn en l.** to keep a tight rein on sb, to have sb (well) under one's thumb **2** *Géog (partie de plage)* foreshore; *(ligne)* tidemark, high-water mark; **l. de basse/haute mer** low/high tidemark
laissées [lese] NFPL *Chasse* wild boar droppings
laissé-pour-compte, laissée-pour-compte [lesepurkɔ̃t] *(mpl* **laissés-pour-compte,** *fpl* **laissées-pour-compte)** ADJ *Com (article, marchandise)* rejected, returned
NM,F *(personne)* social reject *or* outcast; **les laissés-pour-compte de l'industrialisation** the casualties *or* victims of industrialization
NM *Com* reject, return

LAISSER [4] [lese]

> to leave **A1–4, 6, 7, B1, 2, 4, 5, C** ■ to lose **A5** ■ to let have **B3** ■ to let, to allow **D1, 2**
> **VPR** to let oneself

VT **A.** *ABANDONNER* **1** *(ne pas prendre, renoncer à)* to leave; **elle a laissé son dessert** she left her pudding (untouched), she didn't touch her pudding; **laisse quelques fruits pour eux** leave them some fruit, leave some fruit for them; **c'est à prendre ou à l.** (it's) take it or leave it; **il y a à prendre et à l.** *(il y a du bon et du mauvais)* you have to pick and choose; *(il y a du vrai et du faux)* you have to be selective; **laissez toute espérance, vous qui entrez** abandon hope all ye who enter here
2 *(quitter momentanément → personne, chose)* to leave; **j'ai laissé mes enfants chez mon frère** I left my children at my brother's; **n'oubliez pas de l. vos manteaux au vestiaire** don't forget to leave your coats in the cloakroom; **j'ai laissé la voiture à la maison** I left the car at home; **laisse-nous à la gare** drop us off *or* leave us at the station; **laisse-nous, nous avons à parler** leave us (alone), we have things to talk about; **merci, vous pouvez nous l.** thank you, that will be all; **allez, je vous laisse** I'll be off now; **je vous laisse** *(au téléphone)* I must hang up *or* go now; *(dans une lettre)* that's all for now, I'll leave you now; **l. là qn** to leave sb in the lurch
3 *(quitter définitivement)* to leave, to abandon; *(après sa mort → famille)* to leave; **il s'est expatrié, laissant sa famille, ses amis** he emigrated, leaving his family and his friends; **il a laissé femme et enfants** he abandoned his wife and children, he walked out on his wife and children; **il laisse une femme et deux enfants en bas âge** he leaves a wife and two young children
4 *(oublier)* to leave; **j'ai laissé mon sac à la maison** I left my bag at home; **ne laissez rien dans les voitures** don't leave anything in your car; **l. des fautes dans un texte** to leave mistakes in a text
5 *(perdre → membre, personne, bien matériel)* to lose; **il a laissé sa fortune dans cette aventure** he lost all his money in this affair, this affair has lost him all his money; **il y a laissé beaucoup d'argent** he lost a lot of money in it; **y l. la vie** *ou* **sa vie** to lose one's life; **y l. sa santé** to ruin one's health
6 *(derrière soi → trace, marque)* to leave; **la mer a laissé des algues sur la plage** the tide left some seaweed (behind) on the beach; **l. une marque/auréole** to leave a mark/ring; **ce vin laisse un arrière-goût désagréable** this wine has an unpleasant aftertaste; **l. une impression** to leave *or* to make an impression; **il laisse un bon/un mauvais souvenir** we have good/bad memories of him; **elle laisse le souvenir d'une femme énergique** she will be remembered as an energetic woman; **partir sans l. d'adresse** to go away without leaving one's address; **il est mort sans l. de descendance** *ou* **d'héritiers** he died without leaving any heirs; **il laisse beaucoup de dettes** he has left considerable debts (behind him); **elle a laissé une œuvre considérable** she left (behind her) a vast body of work
7 *(négliger)* to leave; **laisse ton livre et viens avec moi** put down *or* leave your book and come with me; **laissez la direction de Paris sur la gauche et tournez à droite** go past the road to Paris on your left and turn right; **laisse tes soucis et viens avec nous** forget your worries and

lac–lai

come with us; **laissons les détails et occupons-nous de l'essentiel** let's leave the details aside and concentrate on the essentials

8 *Littéraire* **cette déclaration ne laisse pas d'être inquiétante** one cannot but be worried by this statement; **l'intérêt qu'il me manifeste ne laisse pas de me flatter** the interest he shows in me is nothing if not flattering (to me); **cette réponse ne laisse pas de m'étonner** I can't help but be surprised by this answer

B. *DONNER, CÉDER* **1** *(accorder)* to leave; **l. qch à qn** to leave sth for sb, to leave sb sth; **laisse-moi un peu de gâteau** leave some cake for me; **l. un pourboire au garçon** to leave the waiter a tip; **ils ont laissé les enfants à la grand-mère** they left the children with their grandmother; **le juge lui a laissé les enfants** the judge gave him/her custody of the children; **c'est tout ce que les cambrioleurs m'ont laissé** it's all the burglars left me (with); **après l'insurrection, il dut l. le pouvoir à son fils** after the rebellion, he had to hand over power to his son; **laissez la priorité à droite** give way to the right; **laissez le passage à l'ambulance** let the ambulance through; **l. sa place à qn** *(siège)* to give up one's seat to sb; **laisse-nous un peu de place!** let us have *or* leave us some room!; **laisse-lui le temps de le faire** leave *or* give him/her time to do it; **ils m'ont laissé une semaine pour le finir** they left *or* allowed me a week in which to finish it

2 *(confier)* to leave; **l. des consignes à qn** to leave instructions with sb, to leave sb with instructions; **l. un message à la secrétaire** to leave a message with the secretary; **laissez les clés chez le gardien** drop the keys off at the caretaker's, leave the keys with the caretaker; **il m'a laissé sa voiture pendant son absence** he left me his car while he was away; *Vieilli* **l. sa carte** to leave one's card; **je lui laisse les travaux pénibles** I leave him/her the heavy work, I leave the heavy work to him/her; **tu me laisses tout le travail!** you're leaving me with all the work!; **l. qch à faire à qn** to leave sb to do sth, to leave sth for sb to do; **je vous laisse les lettres à envoyer** I'll leave you to send the letters

3 *(vendre)* to let have; **je vous le laisse pour dix euros** I'll let you have it for ten euros

4 *(léguer)* to leave, *Sout* to bequeath; **il a laissé d'immenses propriétés à sa famille** he left his family vast estates; **elle a laissé tous ses biens à une œuvre de charité** she left *or Sout* bequeathed all her property to charity

5 *(réserver)* to leave; **laissez une marge pour les corrections** leave a margin for corrections; **l. qch pour la fin** to leave sth till last *or* till the end; **l. le meilleur pour la fin** to leave *or* save the best till last

6 l. à penser que *(sujet: chose)* to make one think *or* suppose that, to lead one to believe that; **cette note laisse à penser qu'elle est fâchée** this message would lead you to believe *or* from this message you would think she's angry; **ta lettre laisse à penser que tu ne pourras pas venir** your letter implies that you won't be coming; **je vous laisse à imaginer s'ils étaient surpris** I'll leave you to imagine how surprised they were; *aussi Ironique* **je vous laisse à penser comme cela nous a fait plaisir** I hardly need to tell you *or* you can just imagine how pleased we were; **elle n'est pas là, cela laisse à penser** she's not here, it makes you wonder

C. *DANS UN ÉTAT, UNE SITUATION (faire demeurer)* to leave; **elle a laissé son mari planté sur le trottoir** she left her husband standing on the pavement looking like a fool; **laisse la fenêtre fermée/ouverte** leave the window shut/open; **l. un crime impuni** to let a crime go unpunished, to leave a crime unpunished; **ceci me laisse sceptique** I remain sceptical (about it); **cela me laisse froid** *ou* **indifférent** it leaves me cold *or* unmoved; **vous n'allez pas me l. tout seul?** you're not going to leave me (all) on my own?; **l. qn tranquille** *ou* **en paix** to leave sb alone *or* in peace; **l. qch tranquille** to leave sth alone; **je vous laisse libre d'agir** you are free to do as you like; **l. qn dans l'ignorance de qch** to let sb remain ignorant of sth, to leave sb in the dark about sth; **je ne peux pas te l. dans cet état-là!** I can't leave you in this state!; **je ne te laisserai pas dans la misère** I won't let you want for anything; **l. une maison à l'abandon** to let a house go to rack and ruin; **laissez le nom en blanc** leave the name blank, do not write the name in; **l. des terres en friche** to let land lie fallow; **l. qn/qch sans surveillance** to leave sb/sth unattended; **les corps ont été laissés sans sépulture** the bodies remained *or* were left unburied; *aussi Fig* **l. derrière soi** to leave behind; **l. derrière soi tous ses concurrents** to leave all one's competitors behind; **il a laissé le peloton loin derrière** he left the pack well behind him; **elle laisse les autres loin derrière elle** *(elle les surpasse)* she puts all the others to shame, she leaves all the others way behind; **l. la bride sur le cou à un cheval** to give a horse its head; *Fig* **l. la bride sur le cou à qn** to give sb free rein

D. *SUIVI D'UN INFINITIF* **1** *(autoriser)* to let, to allow; **l. qn faire qch** to let sb do sth, to allow sb to do sth; **le gardien les laisse jouer dans la cour** the caretaker lets them play *or* allows them to play in the yard; **ils ne m'ont pas laissé lui parler** they didn't allow me to *or* they didn't let me speak to him/her

2 *(ne pas empêcher de)* to let, to allow; **l. qn faire** to let sb do, to leave sb to do, to allow sb to do; **laisse-le dormir** let him sleep, leave him to sleep; **laissez-moi passer** let me past *or* through; **laissez-le faire!** leave it to him!, let him get on with it!; **laisse-moi le lui dire** let me tell him/her (about it); **je te laisse imaginer la suite** I'll leave the rest to your imagination; **le toit laissait passer la pluie** the roof let the rain in; **l. tomber qch** to drop sth; **l. voir qch à qn** *(lettre, photo)* to let sb have a look at sth, to let sb see sth; **l. voir** *(montrer)* to show, to reveal; **son décolleté laissait voir une peau satinée** her plunging neckline revealed skin like satin; **l. voir son émotion** to show one's emotion; **l. voir ses intentions** to reveal one's intentions; **ils ont laissé le prisonnier s'échapper** they let the prisoner escape; **l. condamner un innocent** to allow an innocent man to be punished; **tu me laisseras aller avec toi, dis?** let me come with you, go on!; **l. échapper un cri de douleur** to let out a cry of pain; **elle laissa échapper un soupir** she gave a sigh; **l. sécher la colle** to leave *or* to allow the glue to dry; **laissez bouillir quelques secondes** let it boil for a few seconds; **elle laisse trop paraître ses sentiments** she doesn't hide her feelings enough; **il ne laisse rien paraître de ses intentions** it's impossible to know what he has in mind; **ne rien l. deviner** to give nothing away; **l. vieillir un vin** to allow a wine to age; **ceci laisse supposer que...** this implies that..., this makes one think that...

3 *(locutions) Fam* **laisse aller, ce n'est pas grave** don't worry, it doesn't matter; *Fam* **laisse courir** leave it, forget it; **laissez dire et faites ce que vous avez à faire** let them talk and do what you have to do; **bien faire et l. dire, c'est ma devise** do what you think best and don't worry about what people say, that's my motto; **on n'y peut rien, il faut l. faire** there's nothing we can do (about it), you just have to let things take their course; **laisse faire, ce n'est pas grave!** don't worry, it doesn't matter!; **tu t'imagines que je vais l. faire ça?** do you think I'm just going to stand by and watch while this happens?; **l. faire le temps** to let time take its course; *Fam* **l. tomber qn** *(ami)* to drop sb; *(petit ami)* to give sb *Br* the push *or Am* the dump; *Fam* **tu devrais l. tomber, ça ne marchera jamais** you should give up *or* drop it *or* forget it, it'll never work; *Fam* **je te dois encore cinq euros – laisse tomber** I still owe you five euros – forget it *or* don't worry about it

USAGE ABSOLU *(s'abstenir d'intervenir)* **laisse, je vais le faire** leave it, I'll do it myself; **laisse, ça va aller** I'll be all right; **laissez, je vous en prie** please don't bother (with that); **laisse, c'est moi qui paie** put your money away, I'll pay for this; **laisse, c'est ma tournée** no, it's my round

▶**se laisser** VPR to let oneself; **elle s'est laissé accuser injustement** she allowed herself to be *or* she let herself be unjustly accused; **il ne s'est pas laissé accuser** he refused to let them pin the blame on him; **se l. décourager** to let oneself be discouraged; **il refuse de se l. photographier** he refuses to be photographed; **il s'est laissé séduire** he let himself be seduced; **il s'est laissé mourir** he just gave up living; **ils se sont laissé surprendre par la nuit** they were caught out by nightfall; **se l. tomber sur une chaise/dans un fauteuil** to collapse onto a chair/into an armchair; **se l. aller** *(se négliger)* to let oneself go; *(se détendre)* to let oneself go, to relax; **depuis la mort de sa femme, il se laisse aller** since his wife's death, he's let himself go; **se l. aller au découragement** to let oneself become discouraged; **se l. aller au pessimisme** to give way to pessimism; **se l. aller à faire qch** to go as *or* so far as to do sth; **il s'est laissé aller à injurier son père** he went so far as to insult his father; **se l. dire que** to have heard (it said) that; **je me suis laissé dire qu'elle avait démissionné** I heard she'd resigned; **on l'accuse injustement et elle se laisse faire** she's unjustly accused, and she just stands by and lets it happen; **ne te laisse pas faire!** stand up for yourself!, don't let yourself be taken advantage of!; **la proposition est tentante, je crois que je vais me l. faire** it's an attractive offer, I think I'll give in to temptation; **laisse-toi faire, ça nous fait plaisir de te l'offrir** do take it *or* come on, we'd love to give it to you; *Fam* **se l. vivre** to take life as it comes; **ça se laisse regarder** *(à la télévision)* it's watchable; **il se laisse boire, ton petit vin** your wine goes down nicely *or* is very drinkable; **ça se laisse manger** it's rather tasty

---

laisser-aller [lesеale] NM INV **1** *(désinvolture)* casualness **2** *(relâchement → dans le travail)* carelessness, sloppiness; **il y a du l. dans cette maison!** things are a bit too easy-going *or* slack in this house!; **il y a du l. dans sa tenue** he/she dresses a bit too casually, he's/she's a bit of a sloppy dresser

laisser-courre [lesekur] NM INV *Chasse* slipping

laisser-faire, laissez-faire [lesefɛr] NM INV *Écon* laissez-faire, non-interventionism

laissez-passer [lesepase] NM INV **1** *(autorisation)* pass **2** *Com* carnet **3** *Naut* transire

lait [lɛ] NM **1** *(des mammifères)* milk; **avec ou sans l.?** with or without milk?, *Br* black or white?; *Belg* **l. battu** buttermilk; **l. caillé** curdled *or* soured milk; **l. concentré** *ou* **condensé non sucré** evaporated milk; **l. concentré** *ou* **condensé sucré** (sweetened) condensed milk; **l. cru** unpasteurized milk; **l. demi-écrémé** *Br* semi-skimmed milk, *Am* two percent milk; **l. écrémé** *Br* skimmed milk, *Am* skim milk; **l. entier** whole milk, *Br* full-cream milk; **l. fraise** = milk with strawberry syrup; **l. homogénéisé** homogenized milk; **l. longue conservation** long-life milk; **l. maternel** mother's *or* breast milk; **l. maternisé** baby formula (milk); **l. en poudre** dried *or* powdered milk; **l. stérilisé** sterilized milk

2 *(de certains fruits)* milk; **l. d'amande** almond milk; **l. de coco** coconut milk

3 *(boisson préparée)* **l. de palme** date palm leaf syrup; **l. de poule** eggnog

4 *(pour la toilette)* milk; **l. démaquillant** *ou* **de toilette** cleansing milk

5 *Constr* **l. de chaux** slaked lime wash

▫ **au lait** ADJ with milk

▫ **de lait** ADJ **1** *(ayant la même nourrice)* foster *(avant n)* **2** *(qu'on allaite encore)* suckling *(avant n)* **3** *(semblable au lait)* milky; **un teint de l.** a milky *or* milk-white complexion

laitage [lɛtaʒ] NM dairy product

laitance [lɛtɑ̃s] NF **1** *Ich* milt **2** *Culin* (soft) roe

laité, -e [lete] ADJ *(poisson)* soft-roed

laiterie [lɛtri] NF **1** *(fabrique, ferme, magasin)* dairy **2** *(secteur d'activité)* dairy industry *or* farming

laiteron [lɛtrɔ̃] NM *Bot* sow thistle, milkweed

laiteux, -euse [lɛtø, -øz] ADJ **1** *(semblable au lait)* milky; **un liquide l.** a milky *or* cloudy liquid **2** *(de la couleur du lait)* milk-white, milky-white; **un teint l.** a milky-white complexion

laitier, -ère [lɛtje, -ɛr] **ADJ 1** *(du lait)* dairy *(avant n)*; **des produits laitiers** dairy produce **2** *(bête)* milk *(avant n)*
NM,F 1 *(livreur)* milkman, *f* milkwoman; **l'heure du l.** *(l'aurore)* the crack of dawn **2** *(crémier)* dairyman, *f* dairywoman **3** *(éleveur)* dairy farmer
NM *Métal* slag
❑ **laitière NF 1** *(ustensile)* milk pail, *Br* milk can, *Am* milk bucket **2** *(vache)* milk *or* milch *or* dairy cow; **ces vaches sont de bonnes laitières** these cows are good milkers
laiton [lɛtɔ̃] **NM** brass; **un fil de l.** a piece of brass wire
laitonnage [lɛtɔnaʒ] **NM** brass plating
laitonner [3] [lɛtɔne] **VT** to brass plate
laitue [lety] **NF** lettuce; **l. pommée** round lettuce
laïus [lajys] **NM** *Fam* long spiel, long-winded speech; **ne me fais pas tout un l.!** give me the short version!
laïusser [3] [lajyse] **VI** *Fam* to ramble (on) endlessly
laïusseur, -euse [lajysœr, -øz] *Fam* **ADJ** long-winded, *Br* waffling
NM,F windbag, *Br* waffler
laize [lɛz] **NF 1** *(d'un tissu, d'un papier peint)* width **2** *(d'une jupe)* gore
lakiste [lakist] *Littérature* **ADJ un poète l.** one of the Lake poets; **les poètes lakistes** the Lake poets
NM un l. one of the Lake poets; **les lakistes** the Lake poets
lallation [lalasjɔ̃] **NF 1** *Ling* lallation **2** *(d'un bébé)* babbling
lama [lama] **NM 1** *Rel* lama; **le Grand l.** the Dalai Lama **2** *Zool* llama
lamage [lamaʒ] **NM** *Métal* facing
lamaïque [lamaik] **ADJ** *Rel* lamaistic
lamaïsme [lamaism] **NM** *Rel* Lamaism
lamaïste [lamaist] **NMF** *Rel* Lamaist
lamanage [lamanaʒ] **NM** *Naut* harbour piloting
lamaneur [lamanœr] **NM** *Naut* harbour pilot
lamantin [lamɑ̃tɛ̃] **NM** manatee
lamarckisme [lamarkism] **NM** Lamarckism
lamaserie [lamazri] **NF** lamasery
lambada [lɑ̃bada] **NF** lambada
lambda [lɑ̃bda] **ADJ INV** *Fam* **un individu l.** your average person■ *or Br* bloke *or Am* Joe; **le contribuable l.** the average *or* ordinary taxpayer■
NM INV *(lettre)* lambda
lambdoïde [lɑ̃bdɔid] **ADJ** *Anat (suture)* lambdoid, lambdoidal
lambeau, -x [lɑ̃bo] **NM 1** *(morceau)* scrap, strip, bit; **des lambeaux de chair** strips of flesh; **des lambeaux de conversation** scraps *or* fragments of conversation **2** *Méd* flap
❑ **en lambeaux ADJ** *(déchiré)* in tatters, in shreds; **le tapis est en lambeaux** the carpet is in tatters *or* in shreds **ADV les affiches partent** *ou* **tombent en lambeaux** the posters are getting really tattered; **mettre qch en lambeaux** to tear sth to shreds *or* to pieces
lambel [lɑ̃bɛl] **NM** *Hér* label
Lambert [lɑ̃bɛr] **NPR projection L.** Lambert projection; *Opt* **loi de L.** Lambert's law
lambi [lɑ̃bi] **NM** stromb
lambic, lambick [lɑ̃bik] **NM** lambic, lambick *(strong Belgian ale)*
lambin, -e [lɑ̃bɛ̃, -in] *Fam* **ADJ** dawdling, slow■; **ce qu'il peut être l.!** he can be such a dawdler *or Br* slowcoach *or Am* slowpoke!
NM,F dawdler, *Br* slowcoach, *Am* slowpoke
lambiner [3] [lɑ̃bine] **VI** *Fam* to dawdle; **pas le temps de l.** no time to dawdle *or* to hang around
lambineur, -euse [lɑ̃binœr, -øz], **lambineux, -euse** [lɑ̃binø, -øz] *Can Fam* = **lambin**
lamblia [lɑ̃blia] **NM** *Biol* Giardia
lambliase [lɑ̃bljaz] **NF** *Méd* giardiasis
lambourde [lɑ̃burd] **NF 1** *Bot* fruit-tree shoot **2** *Constr (pour solives)* wall plate; *(frise)* (joist) backing strip
lambouri [lɑ̃buri] **NM** *Can (en acadien)* navel
lambrequin [lɑ̃brɔkɛ̃] **NM 1** *(motif décoratif)* lambrequin **2** *Constr* (eaves) cornice **3** *(d'un lit)* valance; *(d'une fenêtre) Br* pelmet, *Am* lambrequin
❑ **lambrequins NMPL** *Hér* mantle, mantling
lambris [lɑ̃bri] **NM 1** *(en bois)* panelling *(UNCOUNT)*; **l. de chêne** oak panelling; **sous les l. dorés du ministère** in the gilded halls of the ministry; *Littéraire* **né sous des l. dorés** born in marble halls **2** *(en marbre, en stuc)* casing *(UNCOUNT)*
lambrissage [lɑ̃brisaʒ] **NM** *(en bois)* panelling, wainscot(t)ing; *(en marbre, en stuc)* casing
lambrisser [3] [lɑ̃brise] **VT** *(en bois)* to panel, to wainscot; *(en marbre, en stuc)* to case; **lambrissé de chêne** oak-panelled
lambruche [lɑ̃bryʃ], **lambrusque** [lɑ̃brysk] **NF** *Vieilli* wild vine
lambswool [lɑ̃bswul] **NM** lamb's wool
lame [lam] **NF 1** *(de couteau, d'épée)* blade; *(de scie)* web; *(de tournevis)* shaft; **l. de rasoir** razor blade; **il a le visage en l. de couteau** he's hatchet-faced
2 *Littéraire (épée)* sword; **une bonne** *ou* **fine l.** *(personne → homme)* a fine swordsman; *(→ femme)* a fine swordswoman
3 *Aut (de ressort)* leaf
4 *Constr (de store)* slat; *(en bois)* lath, strip; **l. de parquet** floorboard
5 *Géol* **l. mince** thin plate *or* section
6 *Opt* slide
7 *(de champignon)* lamella, gill
8 *Tex (de lisses)* leaf
9 *(vague)* wave; *aussi Fig* **l. de fond** ground swell; **une l. de fond électorale** a ground swell of electoral support
lamé, -e [lame] **ADJ** spangled, lamé
NM lamé; **une robe en l.** a spangled *or* lamé dress; **l. or** gold lamé
lamellaire [lamɛlɛr] **ADJ** lamellar, lamellate
lamelle [lamɛl] **NF 1** *Bot* lamella, gill **2** *Culin (de viande)* thin strip; *(de fromage, de pomme)* thin slice, sliver; **couper en (fines) lamelles** to cut into (wafer-)thin slices **3** *(de fer, de plastique etc)* thin strip; *(de minéral)* flake, *Spéc* lamella **4** *Opt* coverslip, cover glass
❑ **en lamelles ADJ** *Culin* sliced
lamellé, -e [lamɛle] **ADJ** lamellate, lamellated, lamellar
lamellé-collé [lamɛlekɔle] *(pl* **lamellés-collés)** **NM** laminated wood
lamellibranche [lamɛlibrɑ̃ʃ] *Zool* **NM** lamellibranch, *Spéc* member of the Lamellibranchia
❑ **lamellibranches NMPL** Lamellibranchia
lamellicorne [lamɛlikɔrn] *Entom* **ADJ** lamellicorn
NM lamellicorn, *Spéc* member of the Lamellicornia
❑ **lamellicornes NMPL** lamellicornes, *Spéc* Lamellicornia
lamelliforme [lamɛlifɔrm] **ADJ** lamelliform
lamellirostre [lamɛlirɔstr] **ADJ** lamellirostral
lamellophone [lamɛlɔfɔn] **NM** *Mus* lamellophone, thumb piano
lamentable [lamɑ̃tabl] **ADJ 1** *(désolant → accident)* deplorable, frightful; *(pitoyable → plainte, vie)* pitiful; *(→ état)* awful, terrible; **il est dans un état l. depuis la mort de sa femme** he's been in an awful *or* a terrible state since his wife died **2** *(mauvais → performance, résultat)* pathetic, appalling; **vous avez été lamentables!** you were useless! **3** *(triste → voix, ton)* mournful, woeful
lamentablement [lamɑ̃tabləmɑ̃] **ADV** miserably, dismally
lamentation [lamɑ̃tasjɔ̃] **NF 1** *(pleurs)* wailing *(UNCOUNT)*, lamentation **2** *(récrimination)* moaning *(UNCOUNT)*, complaining *(UNCOUNT)*; **cesse tes lamentations** stop your moaning *or* complaining; **se répandre en lamentations** to burst into a torrent of complaints
❑ **lamentations NFPL** *Rel* **les lamentations** the Lamentations of Jeremiah; **le livre des Lamentations** the Book of Lamentations
lamenter [3] [lamɑ̃te] **se lamenter VPR 1** *(gémir)* to moan, to whine; **se l. sur qch** to moan about sth, *Sout* to bemoan sth; **il se lamente sur la dégradation des valeurs morales** he deplores the decline in moral values; **se l. sur son sort** to bemoan *or* to lament one's fate; **elle se lamentait d'avoir perdu son bracelet** she was moaning about having lost her bracelet, she was bemoaning the loss of her bracelet **2** *(pleurer)* to wail
lamento [lamɛnto] **NM** lament
lamer [3] [lame] **VT 1** *Métal* to face **2** *(broder)* to spangle
lamiacée [lamjase] *Bot* **NF** labiate, *Spéc* member of the Labiatae
❑ **lamiacées NFPL** labiates, *Spéc* Labiatae
lamie [lami] **NF 1** *Myth* lamia **2** *Ich* mackerel shark, porbeagle
lamier [lamje] **NM** *Bot* dead-nettle; **l. à feuilles embrassantes** henbit dead-nettle; **l. hybride** cut-leaved dead-nettle
lamifié, -e [lamifje] **ADJ** laminated
NM laminated wood
laminage [laminaʒ] **NM 1** *(du plastique, du métal, du verre)* rolling, laminating; *(du caoutchouc, du papier)* calendering; **l. à chaud/à froid** hot-/cold-rolling **2** *(réduction → des revenus)* erosion; *(→ des effectifs)* decimation **3** *Fam (anéantissement → d'un parti)* near annihilation■
laminaire [laminɛr] **ADJ** *voir* **régime**
NF *(algue)* oarweed, laminarian
laminectomie [laminɛktɔmi] **NF** *Méd* laminectomy
laminer [3] [lamine] **VT 1** *(plastique, métal, verre)* to roll, to laminate; *(caoutchouc, papier)* to calender **2** *(réduire → revenus)* to erode; *(→ effectifs)* to decimate **3** *Fam (personne → épuiser)* to exhaust; **la gauche a été laminée aux législatives** the left were nearly annihilated in the parliamentary elections■
lamineur, -euse [laminœr, -øz] **ADJ** laminating; **cylindre l.** roller
NM,F millhand *(in a roller mill)*
❑ **lamineuse NF** roller *(for glass)*
lamineux [laminø] **ADJ M** laminose, laminous; *Anat* **tissu l.** loose connective tissue
laminoir [laminwar] **NM 1** *Métal* rolling mill; **passer au l.** to be put through the mill; **(faire) passer qn au l.** to put sb through the mill **2** *(à papier)* calender
lampadaire [lɑ̃padɛr] **NM 1** *(dans une maison) Br* standard lamp, *Am* floor lamp **2** *(dans la rue)* streetlamp, streetlight
lampant, -e [lɑ̃pɑ̃, -ɑ̃t] **ADJ** lamp *(avant n)*; **pétrole l.** paraffin (oil), *Am* kerosene
lamparo [lɑ̃paro] **NM 1** *(lampe)* (fishing) lamp; **aller à la pêche au l.** to go fishing by lamplight **2** *(bateau)* lamplight fishing boat
lampas [lɑ̃pa(s)] **NM 1** *(tissu)* lampas **2** *Vét* lampas, lampers
lampassé, -e [lɑ̃pase] **ADJ** *Hér* langued
lampe [lɑ̃p] **NF 1** *(luminaire)* lamp, light; **à la lumière de la l.** by lamplight; **l. à acétylène** acetylene lamp *or Am* torch; **l. à arc** arc lamp *or* light; **l. (d')architecte** *ou* **articulée** anglepoise lamp; **l. de bureau** desk lamp; **l. de chevet** bedside lamp; **l. à gaz** gaslight; **l. halogène** halogen lamp; **l. à huile** oil lamp; *Phot* **l. inactinique** safelight; **l. à incandescence** incandescent lamp; **l. au néon** fluorescent *or* neon light; **l. à pétrole** *Br* paraffin lamp, *Am* kerosene lamp; **l. de poche** *Br* torch, *Am* flashlight; **à la lumière d'une l. de poche** *Br* by torchlight, *Am* by flashlight; **l. témoin** warning light
2 *(appareil)* **l. à alcool** spirit lamp; **l. à bronzer** sunlamp; **l. à souder** *Br* blowlamp, *Am* blowtorch
3 *Mines* **l. de sûreté** safety lamp
4 *Rad* valve (tube)
5 *Fam* **s'en mettre** *ou très Fam* **s'en foutre plein la l.** to stuff oneself *or* one's face, to pig out
lampée [lɑ̃pe] **NF** *Fam* swig, gulp; **boire qch à grandes lampées** to gulp sth down
lamper [3] [lɑ̃pe] **VT** *Fam* to swig, to gulp down
lampe-tempête [lɑ̃ptɑ̃pɛt] *(pl* **lampes-tempête)** **NF** storm lantern
lampion [lɑ̃pjɔ̃] **NM** paper *or* Chinese lantern; **scander des slogans sur l'air des lampions** to chant slogans
lampiste [lɑ̃pist] **NM 1** *Vieilli (d'un théâtre)* light maintenance man; *(des chemins de fer)* lampman **2** *Fam (subalterne)* underling, menial, *Br* dogsbody; **ce sont toujours les lampistes qui trinquent** it's always the little people that get the blame
lampisterie [lɑ̃pistəri] **NF** *Vieilli* = place where lamps are stored and repaired in a mine
lampourde [lɑ̃purd] **NF** cocklebur
lamprillon [lɑ̃prijɔ̃] **NM** *Ich (larve)* larval lamprey
lamproie [lɑ̃prwa] **NF** *Ich* lamprey; **l. de rivière** lampern, river lamprey
lamprophyre [lɑ̃prɔfir] **NM** *Minér* lamprophyre

lampyre [lɑ̃pir] NM glow-worm

lançage [lɑ̃saʒ] NM *Constr* = use of a monitor to facilitate pile-driving

lance [lɑ̃s] NF **1** *(pique)* spear; **transpercer qn d'un coup de l.** to spear sb, to run sb through with a spear **2** *(tuyau)* **l. d'arrosage** water hose; **l. à eau** hosepipe; **l. d'incendie** fire hose **3** *Métal* **l. à oxygène** oxygen lance

lancé, -e [lɑ̃se] ADJ **1** *(personne)* **le voilà l.!** he's made it! **2** *Sport* **départ l.** flying start

  □ **lancée** NF **1** *(vitesse acquise)* momentum **2** *Suisse (douleur)* shooting pain

  □ **sur ma/sa/etc lancée** ADV **il courait, et sur sa lancée il a dribblé ses deux adversaires** he ran up the field, dribbling around two attackers as he went; **sur sa lancée, il s'en prit même à son père** he even took his father to task while he was at it; **j'ai fait les exercices 5 et 6, et sur ma lancée j'ai aussi fait le 7** I did exercises 5 and 6, and while I was at it I did 7 as well; **continuer sur sa lancée** to keep going

lance-amarre [lɑ̃samar] *(pl* **lance-amarres)** NM line-throwing gun

lance-bombe, lance-bombes [lɑ̃sbɔ̃b] *(pl* **lance-bombes)** NM bomb-dropping gear

lancée [lɑ̃se] *voir* **lancé**

lance-flamme, lance-flammes [lɑ̃sflam] *(pl* **lance-flammes)** NM flame-thrower

lance-fusée, lance-fusées [lɑ̃sfyze] *(pl* **lance-fusées)** NM rocket launcher

lance-grenade, lance-grenades [lɑ̃sgrənad] *(pl* **lance-grenades)** NM grenade launcher; **lance-grenades sous-marines** depth-charge launcher

---

'Lancelot ou le Chevalier à la charrette'
Chrétien de Troyes 'Lancelot, or the Knight of the Cart'

---

lancement [lɑ̃smɑ̃] NM **1** *Astron & Naut* launch, launching; **nous allons procéder au l.** we will now proceed with the launch; **créneau** *ou* **fenêtre de l.** firing *or* launch window **2** *Tech (d'un pont)* throwing **3** *(en publicité → opération)* launching; *(→ cérémonie, réception)* launch; *(d'un projet, d'une société, d'un produit)* launch; **prix de l.** launch price; *Mktg* **l. sur le marché** market entry; *Mktg* **l. tardif** late entry **4** *Bourse (d'une société)* flotation; *(de titres boursiers, d'un emprunt)* issuing, issue; *(d'une souscription)* start **5** *(projection)* throwing **6** *Ordinat (d'impression)* start; *(de programme)* running **7** *Belg* stabbing pain

lance-missile, lance-missiles [lɑ̃smisil] *(pl* **lance-missiles)** NM missile launcher

lancéolé, -e [lɑ̃seɔle] ADJ **1** *Bot* lanceolate **2** *Archit* **arc l.** lancet arch

lance-pierre, lance-pierres [lɑ̃spjɛr] *(pl* **lance-pierres)** NM **1** *(fronde)* catapult **2** *Fam (locutions)* **déjeuner/manger au** *ou* **avec un l.** to gulp one's lunch/meal (down); **être payé au** *ou* **avec un l.** to be paid peanuts *or Am* chump change

lancequiner [3] [lɑ̃skine] VI *très Fam* **1** *(pleuvoir)* **il lancequine** it's pissing down **2** *(uriner)* to pee, to piss, *Br* to have a slash

---

LANCER [16] [lɑ̃se]

VT	to throw **A1, 2, 6** ■ to shoot **A2** ■ to launch **A2, B2, 4, 7, 8** ■ to let out **A3** ■ to send out **A4** ■ to issue **A4** ■ to cast **A7** ■ to get going **B3, 5**
VI	to stab
NM	casting **1** ■ throw, pitch **2**
VPR	to throw at one another **1** ■ to throw oneself **2** ■ to embark on **5**

VT A. *ENVOYER, ÉMETTRE* **1** *(jeter)* to throw; **elle m'a lancé la balle** she threw me the ball, she threw the ball to me; **lancez les bras en arrière puis en avant** swing *or* throw your arms backwards then forwards; **l. la jambe en l'air** to kick one's leg up; **l. des pierres à qn** to throw stones at sb; **l. le disque/javelot/marteau** to throw the discus/javelin/hammer; **l. le poids** to put the shot; **l. un regard haineux à qn** to give sb a look

full of hate; **ils nous lançaient des regards curieux** they looked at us curiously; **l. qch à la figure à qn** to throw sth in sb's face; **l. son poing dans la figure à qn** to smash one's fist into sb's face; **le cheval lança une ruade** the horse kicked out

2 *(flèche)* to shoot; *(fusée, torpille)* to launch; *(bombe)* to drop; *(grenade)* to throw, to launch; **l. des flèches avec un arc** to fire (off) *or* to shoot arrows from a bow; **l. un projectile téléguidé** to fire a remote-controlled missile; **l. des bombes sur un objectif** to drop bombs on a target; **l. une fusée** to launch a rocket; **ils ont lancé des satellites pendant dix ans** they sent up *or* launched satellites for ten years; **avec leurs sarbacanes, ils lançaient des boulettes de papier** with their peashooters they were firing *or* shooting little balls of paper; **l. des torpilles** to fire (off) torpedoes; **l. un signal de détresse** to fire off a distress signal

3 *(émettre → cri)* to let out; *(→ remarque)* to make; *(→ proposition, idée)* to throw out; *(→ juron)* to let out; *(→ étincelles)* to throw off; **l. un cri de terreur** to let out a cry of terror; **les mouettes lançaient leurs appels aigus** the gulls were screeching *or* were crying shrilly; **l. un bon mot** to crack a joke; **l. des injures à qn** to hurl insults at sb; **l. des questions** to fire questions; **le volcan lance des flammes** the volcano is throwing out flames; **les joyaux lançaient mille feux** the jewels were sparkling brightly; **ses yeux lançaient des éclairs** his/her eyes flashed

4 *(diffuser → décret, consigne)* to send out, to put out, to issue; **l. des invitations** *(par courrier)* to send invitations; *(oralement)* to give out invitations; **l. un SOS/un appel à la radio** to send out an SOS/an appeal on the radio; **l. un appel d'offres** to invite tenders; **l. un mandat d'amener/un ultimatum** to issue a summons/an ultimatum; **l. un emprunt** to float *or* to issue a loan; **l. une souscription** to start a fund

5 *Bourse (société)* to float; *(titres boursiers, emprunt)* to issue; *(souscription)* to start; **l. des titres sur le marché** to issue shares

6 *Constr* to throw; **l. un pont** to throw a bridge

7 *Pêche* to cast; **l. sa ligne** to cast one's line

B. *METTRE EN MARCHE, FAIRE DÉBUTER* **1** *(faire partir brusquement)* **les cavaliers lancèrent leurs chevaux** the riders set off at full speed on their horses; **ils lancèrent les chiens sur les rôdeurs** they set the dogs on the prowlers; **l. des troupes à l'attaque** to send troops into the attack

2 *(mettre en train → campagne)* to launch; *(→ affaire)* to set up; *(→ idée)* to float; *(→ mode)* to start; **l. un mouvement de protestation** to launch a protest campaign, to get a protest campaign going

3 *(faire fonctionner → gén)* to get going *or* started, to start; *Ordinat (programme, impression)* to start, to run; **l. un balancier** to set a pendulum swinging; **l. un moteur** to start an engine; **une fois le moteur lancé** once the engine is running; **la voiture était lancée à toute vitesse** the car was going at full speed; **le train était lancé à 150 km/h quand...** the train was hurtling along at 150 km/h when...

4 *(faire connaître → projet, société, produit, modèle)* to launch; **l. un nouveau produit sur le marché** to launch a new product on the market; **c'est ce roman/cette émission qui l'a lancé** this novel/programme made him famous; **une fois lancé dans le cyclisme professionnel** once he'd embarked on his career as a professional cyclist; **maintenant qu'il est lancé il pourra demander plus cher** now that he's made a name for himself he can ask for more money

5 *Fam (orienter → discussion)* to get going; **une fois qu'il est lancé sur ce sujet, on ne peut plus l'arrêter** once he gets going on the subject, there's no stopping him; **si on le lance sur la course automobile, il est intarissable** if you start him off on motor racing, there's no stopping him

6 *(engager)* to lead; **vous lancez le pays dans**

l'aventure you're leading the country into unknown territory

7 *Mil* to launch; **l. une attaque** to launch an attack; **l. une contre-attaque** to launch a counter-attack, to counter-attack

8 *Naut (navire)* to launch

9 *Chasse (cerf)* to dislodge, to unharbour; *(lièvre)* to start

VI *(élancer → douleur)* to stab; **ça me lance dans l'épaule, l'épaule me lance** I've got a sharp stabbing pain in my shoulder

NM **1** *Pêche* casting; **l. léger/lourd** fixed/free reel casting

2 *Sport* throw; *(au base-ball)* pitch; **le l. du disque** the discus; **le l. du javelot** the javelin; **le l. du poids** the shot; **pratiquer le l. du disque/javelot** to throw the discus/javelin; **pratiquer le l. du poids** to put the shot; **l. franc** *(au basket)* free throw

▶ **se lancer** VPR **1** *(mutuellement)* to throw at one another; **ils se lançaient des assiettes à la figure** they were throwing plates at each other; **elles se lançaient des injures** they were hurling insults at each other, they were exchanging insults

2 *(se précipiter)* to throw oneself; *(courir)* to rush (headlong), to dash; **ce week-end, les citadins vont se l. sur les routes** this weekend, city dwellers will take to the roads; **se l. à l'attaque** to throw oneself into the attack; **se l. à la poursuite de** to set off in pursuit of; **se l. dans le vide** to jump *or* to throw oneself into empty space

3 *(se mettre à parler)* **se l. sur un sujet** to get going on a topic

4 *(prendre l'initiative)* **allez, lance-toi et demande une augmentation** go on, take the plunge and ask for a rise; **le bébé s'est lancé et a traversé la pièce** the baby set off and crossed the room; **allez, lance-toi, tu verras ce n'est pas si difficile** go on, off you go, you'll soon see it's not so hard

5 **se l. dans** *(s'aventurer dans → explication, aventure)* to embark on; **ne te lance pas dans de grosses dépenses** don't go spending a lot of money; **se l. dans une entreprise hasardeuse** to get oneself involved in *or* to embark on a dangerous undertaking; **il s'est lancé dans des digressions interminables** he went off into endless digressions

6 *(débuter)* **se l. dans les affaires** to launch out into the world of business; **se l. dans la politique/la peinture** to take up politics/painting; **la France se lance alors dans la troisième croisade** France then threw itself into the Third Crusade

7 *Com & Mktg* **se l. sur le marché** to enter the market

lance-roquette, lance-roquettes [lɑ̃srɔkɛt] *(pl* **lance-roquettes)** NM *(hand-held)* rocket launcher *or* gun

lance-torpille, lance-torpilles [lɑ̃stɔrpij] *(pl* **lance-torpilles)** NM torpedo *(launching)* tube

lancette [lɑ̃sɛt] NF *Archit & Méd* lancet, lance

lanceur, -euse [lɑ̃sœr, -øz] NM,F **1** *Sport (au base-ball)* pitcher; *(au cricket)* bowler; **l. de javelot** javelin thrower; **l. de poids** shot putter **2** *(promoteur)* promoter, originator; **un l. d'affaires** a business promoter

NM *Astron* launch vehicle, launcher

lanceur-d'engins [lɑ̃sœrdɑ̃ʒɛ̃] NM INV nuclear warhead submarine, missile launcher

lanceuse [lɑ̃søz] *voir* **lanceur**

lancier [lɑ̃sje] NM **1** *Mil* lancer **2 les lanciers** *(quadrille)* the lancers

lancinant, -e [lɑ̃sinɑ̃, -ɑ̃t] ADJ **1** *(douleur)* throbbing **2** *(obsédant → souvenir)* haunting; *(→ regret)* nagging **3** *(répétitif)* nerve-shattering; **une musique lancinante** pounding music

lancination [lɑ̃sinasjɔ̃] NF throbbing pain

lancinement [lɑ̃sinmɑ̃] NM throbbing pain; *Fig* laceration

lanciner [3] [lɑ̃sine] VT *(obséder)* to obsess, to haunt, to plague; *(tourmenter)* to harass, to badger, to pester

lançon [lɑ̃sɔ̃] NM *Ich* launce, sand eel *or* lance

lançure [lɑ̃syr] NF *Belg (élancement)* shooting *or* stabbing pain

Land [lɑ̃d] *(pl* **Länder** [lɛndœr]) **NM** Land; **les Länder allemands** the German Länder

landais, -e [lɑ̃dɛ, -ɛz] **ADJ** of/from the Landes

❑ **Landais, -e NM,F** = inhabitant of or person from the Landes

landammann [lɑ̃daman] **NM** *Suisse* landammann, = chairman of the governing body of a canton

land art [lɑ̃dart] **NM** land art

landau, -s [lɑ̃do] **NM 1** *(pour bébés) Br* pram, *Am* baby carriage **2** *(attelage)* landau

landaulet [lɑ̃dolɛ] **NM** *Aut* landaulet, landaulette

landaulette [lɑ̃dolɛt] **NF** *Aut* landaulet, landaulette

lande [lɑ̃d] **NF** moor; **la l. bretonne** the moors of Brittany

Länder [lɛndœr] *voir* **Land**

Landernau, Landerneau [lɑ̃dɛrno] **NPR cela fera du bruit dans L.** it will be the talk of the town

Landes [lɑ̃d] **NFPL les L.** *(région, département)* the Landes

landgrave [lɑ̃dgrav] **NM** *Hist* landgrave

landgraviat [lɑ̃dgravja] **NM** *Hist* landgraviate

landier [lɑ̃dje] **NM** firedog, andiron

Landru [lɑ̃dry] **NPR l'affaire L.** = the trial of the well-known serial killer Landru in 1921

Landsgemeinde [lɑ̃dsgemajndə] **NF INV** *Suisse* = open-air annual citizens' assembly in some German-speaking Swiss cantons

Landtag [lɑ̃dtag] **NM** Landtag

laneret [lanrɛ] **NM** lanneret

langage [lɑ̃gaʒ] **NM 1** *Ling & Psy* language; **l'acquisition du l.** language acquisition; **le l. enfantin** baby talk; **l. écrit/parlé** written/spoken language; **troubles du l.** speech *or* language disorders

2 *(code)* language; **le l. des animaux** animal language; **le l. des abeilles** the language of bees; **le l. du corps** body language, body talk; **le l. des fleurs** the language of flowers; **le l. musical** the musical idiom; **le l. de la peinture** the idiom of painting; **le l. des signes** *ou* **le l. des sourds-muets** sign language

3 *(jargon)* language; **le l. des juristes** legal language; **l. administratif/technique** administrative/technical language

4 *(style)* language; **l. familier/populaire** colloquial/popular language; **l. correct/incorrect** *(d'après la bienséance)* polite/impolite language; **l. argotique** slang; **l. imagé** colourful *or* picturesque language; **l. poétique** poetic language; **il a un l. très grossier** his language is very coarse; **qu'est-ce que c'est que ce l.?** what kind of language is that?; **le beau l.** educated speech

5 *(discours)* language, talk; **tu tiens un drôle de l. depuis quelque temps** you've been coming out with *or* saying some very odd things recently; **tenir un tout autre l.** to change one's tune; **voilà un l. qui me plaît!** that's what I like to hear!; **parler le l. de la franchise/vérité** to speak frankly/truthfully; **c'est le l. de la raison** that's a sensible thing to say

6 *Ordinat & Tél* language; **l. assembleur** *ou* **d'assemblage** assembly language; **l. auteur** authoring language; **l. chiffré** cipher; **l. de commande** command language; **l. de description de page** page description language; **l. évolué** high-level language; **l. d'imprimante par pages** page printer language; **l. d'interrogation** query language; **l. JavaScript®** JavaScript®; **l. machine** internal *or* machine language; **l. naturel** natural language; **l. à objets** object-oriented language; **l. de programmation** programming language; **l. source** source language; **l. utilisateur** user language

langagier, -ère [lɑ̃gaʒje, -ɛr] **ADJ** linguistic, language *(avant n)*

lange [lɑ̃ʒ] **NM** *(pour bébé)* baby blanket

❑ **langes NMPL** swaddling clothes

❑ **dans les langes ADJ** *Fig (à ses débuts)* in its/their infancy; **le cinéma était encore dans les langes** cinema was still in its infancy

langer [17] [lɑ̃ʒe] **VT 1** *(emmailloter)* to swaddle **2** *(changer → bébé)* to change

langoureuse [lɑ̃gurøz] *voir* **langoureux**

langoureusement [lɑ̃gurøzmɑ̃] **ADV** languorously

langoureux, -euse [lɑ̃gurø, -øz] **ADJ** *(alangui)* languishing; *(mélancolique)* languid, languorous; **un regard l.** a languid look

langouste [lɑ̃gust] **NF** *Zool* (sea) crayfish *or Am* crawfish; *Culin* (spiny) lobster

langoustier [lɑ̃gustje] **NM 1** *(bateau)* lobster (fishing) boat **2** *(filet)* crayfish *or Am* crawfish net

langoustine [lɑ̃gustin] **NF** langoustine, Dublin bay prawn

langres [lɑ̃gr] **NM** Langres cheese *(from Burgundy)*

langue [lɑ̃g] **NF A.** *ORGANE* **1** *Anat* tongue; **se mordre/se brûler la l.** to bite/burn one's tongue; **avoir la l. blanche** *ou* **chargée** to have a coated *or* furred tongue; *Fig* **une mauvaise l., une l. de vipère** a malicious gossip; **les mauvaises langues prétendent que...** some (ill-intentioned) gossips claim that...; **mauvaise l.!** that's a bit nasty of you!, that's a rather nasty thing to say!; **les langues vont bon train** tongues are wagging; **tirez la l. et dites "ah"** put *or* stick your tongue out and say "aah"; **tirer la l. à qn** to stick one's tongue out at sb; *Fam Fig* **tirer la l.** *(avoir soif)* to be gasping (for a drink); *(avoir du mal)* to have a hard *or* rough time; *(être fatigué)* to be worn out; *(être dans le besoin)* to be strapped for cash; **tu as avalé** *ou* **perdu ta l.?** have you lost *or* (has the) cat got your tongue?; *Fam* **avoir la l. bien affilée** *ou* **bien pendue** to have the gift of the gab; *Fig* **avoir la l. fourchue** to speak with a forked tongue; *Fig* **avoir la l. trop longue** to have a big mouth; **coup de l.** lick; **donner des coups de l. à qn/qch** to lick sb/sth; *Fig Littéraire* **coups de l.** spiteful gossip; **délier** *ou* **dénouer la l. à qn** to loosen sb's tongue; **le vin délie les langues** wine always gets people chatting; *Fam* **elle n'a pas la l. dans sa poche** she's never at a loss for something to say *or* for words; **donner sa l. au chat** to give up (guessing); **prendre l. avec qn** to contact sb, to make contact with sb; **tenir sa l.** to keep a secret; **il ne sait pas tenir sa l.** he can't keep a secret; *Fam* **tourne sept fois ta l. dans ta bouche avant de parler** think twice before you open your mouth

2 *Culin* tongue; **l. de bœuf** *(chaude)* boiled ox tongue; *(froide)* (cold) tongue

B. *Ling* **1** *(moyen de communication)* language, *Littéraire* tongue; **les ressources de la l.** the resources of the language; **l. commune** common language; **décrire une l.** to describe a language; **elle connaît bien sa l.** she knows her language well; **pendant le festival, on entend parler toutes les langues** you can hear all sorts of languages during the festival; **ce métier exige la connaissance des langues** this job requires a knowledge of languages; **un professeur de langues** a (foreign) language teacher; **l'anglais est la l. internationale** English is the international language; **les passagers de l. anglaise** English-speaking passengers; **langues anciennes** classical languages; **l. d'arrivée** target language; **l. cible** target language; **l. de départ** source language; **l. écrite** written language; **langues étrangères** foreign languages; *Univ* **langues étrangères appliquées** = applied modern languages; **l. maternelle** mother tongue; **langues mortes** dead languages; **l. nationale** national language; **Langues O** *(institut)* = centre for Oriental studies in Paris; *Hist* **l. d'oc** = medieval French dialect spoken in southern France; **l. officielle** official language; *Hist* **l. d'oïl** = medieval French dialect spoken in northern France; **l. parlée** spoken language; **dans la l. parlée** colloquially; **l. des signes française** = official name of the sign language used in France; **langues sœurs** sister languages; **l. source** source language; **l. de travail** working language; **l. véhiculaire** lingua franca; **la l. vernaculaire** the vernacular; **les langues vivantes** *Scol* modern languages; *(utilisées de nos jours)* living languages

2 *(jargon)* language; **dans la l. du barreau** in the language of the courts, *Sout* in legal parlance; **l. de bois** hackneyed phrases; **la l. de bois des politiciens** the clichés politicians come out with; **la l. littéraire** literary language; **la l. populaire** popular language; *Hist* **l. savante** *(latin)* language of learning; **la l. verte** slang; *Hist* **l. vulgaire** *(langue du peuple)* vernacular

3 *(style → d'une époque, d'un écrivain)* language; **la l. de la Renaissance** Renaissance language; **la l. de James Joyce** the language of James Joyce; **dans la l. de Molière/Shakespeare** in French/English

C. *FORME* **1** *(gén)* tongue; **des langues de feu léchaient le mur** tongues of flame were licking the wall

2 *Géog* **une l. de terre** a strip of land, a narrow piece of land; **une l. glaciaire** a spur of ice

langué, -e [lɑ̃ge] **ADJ** *Hér* langued

langue-de-bœuf [lɑ̃gdəbœf] *(pl* **langues-de-bœuf) NF** *Bot* beefsteak fungus

langue-de-cerf [lɑ̃gdəsɛr] *(pl* **langues-de-cerf) NF** *Bot* hart's-tongue

langue-de-chat [lɑ̃gdəʃa] *(pl* **langues-de-chat) NF** *Culin* langue de chat, thin finger biscuit

langue-de-chien [lɑ̃gdəʃjɛ̃] *(pl* **langues-de-chien) NF** *Bot* hound's-tongue

langue-de-serpent [lɑ̃gdəsɛrpɑ̃] *(pl* **langues-de-serpent) NF** *Bot* adder's-tongue

Languedoc [lɑ̃gdɔk] **NM le L.** Languedoc

languedocien, -enne [lɑ̃gdɔsjɛ̃, -ɛn] **ADJ** of/from the Languedoc (region)

❑ **Languedocien, -enne NM,F** = inhabitant of or person from the Languedoc (region)

Languedoc-Roussillon [lɑ̃gdɔkrusijɔ̃] **NM le L.** Languedoc-Roussillon

languette [lɑ̃gɛt] **NF 1** *(petite bande)* strip; **les dossiers sont séparés par une l. de papier** the files are separated by a strip of paper *or* a paper marker **2** *(de chaussure)* tab, stem **3** *(d'une canette)* ring pull, tab **4** *(de balance)* pointer **5** *Tech (tenon)* tongue **6** *Mus (d'orgue)* languet; *(d'instrument à anche)* reed **7** *Ordinat* slider

langueur [lɑ̃gœr] **NF 1** *(apathie)* languidness **2** *(mélancolie)* languor; **un sourire plein de l.** a languid *or* languorous smile **3** *Vieilli (asthénie)* wasting disease

langueyer [12] [lɑ̃geje] **VT 1** *Vét* to examine the tongue of **2** *Mus* to tongue

languide [lɑ̃gid] **ADJ** *Littéraire* languid, languishing

languier [lɑ̃gje] **NM** *Culin* = smoked pig's tongue and throat

languir [32] [lɑ̃gir] **VI 1** *Littéraire (personne, animal)* to languish, to pine; **la petite fille languit loin de sa mère** the little girl is pining for her mother; **l. (d'amour) pour qn** to be consumed *or* languishing with love for sb; **l. en prison** to languish in prison

2 *(plante)* to wilt; **le rosier languit sous le mur** the rose tree isn't doing (very) well under the wall

3 *(conversation, situation)* to flag; **la conversation languissait** the conversation was flagging; **les affaires languissent** business is slack

4 *(attendre)* **faire l. qn** to keep sb waiting; *Littéraire* **je languis d'être avec vous** I am longing *or* pining to be with you

❑ **languir après VT IND** to languish *or* to pine for

▸**se languir VPR** *(personne)* to pine; **il se languit de toi** he's pining for you; **je me languis de la Provence** I'm longing to go back to Provence

languissamment [lɑ̃gisamɑ̃] **ADV** *Littéraire* languidly, languishingly

languissant, -e [lɑ̃gisɑ̃, -ɑ̃t] **ADJ 1** *Littéraire (qui dépérit)* failing, dwindling; **santé languissante** failing health **2** *Littéraire (amoureux)* languishing, lovelorn, lovesick **3** *(sans vigueur)* languid, listless **4** *(morne → conversation)* dull; **le commerce est l.** business is slack

langur [lɑ̃gyr] **NM** *Zool* langur

lanice [lanis] **ADJ bourre l.** flock of wool

lanier [lanje] **NM** *Orn* lanner

lanière [lanjɛr] **NF 1** *(bande)* strap; **découper qch en lanières** to cut sth into strips **2** *(d'un fouet)* lash

lanifère [lanifɛr], **lanigère** [laniʒɛr] **ADJ** *Zool & Bot* wool-bearing

laniste [lanist] **NM** *Antiq* lanista

lanlaire [lɑ̃lɛr] **ADV** *Fam Vieilli* **envoyer qn se faire l.** to send sb packing *or* to Jericho

lanoline [lanɔlin] **NF** lanolin, lanoline

lansquenet [lɑ̃skənɛ] **NM** *Hist, Mil & Cartes* lansquenet

lantana [lɑ̃tana], **lantanier** [lɑ̃tanje] **NM** *Bot* lantana

lanterne [lɑ̃tɛrn] **NF 1** *(lampe)* lantern; **l. chinoise**

Chinese lantern; **l. sourde/vénitienne** dark/Chinese lantern; **les aristocrates à la l.!** string the aristocrats up!
 2 *Cin* projector
 3 *Constr* lantern
 4 *Phot* **l. magique** magic lantern
 5 *Zool* **l. d'Aristote** Aristotle's lantern
 ❑ **lanternes** NFPL *Aut Br* sidelights, *Am* parking lights
 ❑ **lanterne rouge** NF **1** *Rail* rear *or* tail light **2** *(locution)* **être la l. rouge** *(gén)* to bring up the rear; *Sport (dans une course)* to come (in) last; *(équipe)* to get the wooden spoon; *(à l'école)* to be bottom of the class

lanterneau, -x [lɑ̃tɛrno] NM skylight, roof light

lanterner [3] [lɑ̃tɛrne] VI *Fam* **1** *(perdre son temps)* to dawdle, to drag one's feet; **il est toujours à l.** he is always dawdling **2** *(attendre)* **faire l. qn** to keep sb hanging about *or* waiting

lanternon [lɑ̃tɛrnɔ̃] NM lantern (tower *or* turret)

lanthane [lɑ̃tan] NM *Chim* lanthanum

lanthanide [lɑ̃tanid] NM *Chim* lanthanide

lanugineux, -euse [lanyʒinø, -øz] ADJ lanuginous, downy

lao [lao] NM *(langue)* Lao, Laotian

laogai [laogaj] NM Laogai *(China's forced-labour camps)*

Laos [laos] NM **le L.** Laos; **vivre au L.** to live in Laos; **aller au L.** to go to Laos

laotien, -enne [laɔsjɛ̃, -ɛn] ADJ Laotian
 NM *(langue)* Lao, Laotian
 ❑ **Laotien, -enne** NM,F Laotian

La Palice [lapalis] NPR **une vérité de L.** a truism

lapalissade [lapalisad] NF truism; **c'est une l.** that's self-evident, that's stating the obvious

Allusion

Lapalissade

This word comes from La Palice, the name of a 16th-century Marshal of France. When he died, his soldiers composed a song in his honour containing the truism: **Un quart d'heure avant sa mort, il était encore en vie** ("A quarter of an hour before his death he was still alive"). It has since been used whenever somebody is only stating the obvious.

laparoscopie [laparɔskɔpi] NF *Méd* laparoscopy

laparotomie [laparɔtɔmi] NF *Méd* laparotomy

La Paz [lapaz] NF La Paz

lapement [lapmɑ̃] NM lapping *(UNCOUNT)*

laper [3] [lape] VT to lap (up)
 VI to lap

lapereau, -x [lapro] NM young rabbit

lapiaz [lapjaz] NM *Géog* lapiés

lapicide [lapisid] NMF *Archéol* lapidary

lapidaire [lapidɛr] ADJ **1** *(concis)* terse, *Sout* lapidary; **un style l.** a pithy *or* succinct style **2** *Minér* lapidary; **art l.** lapidary art
 NM **1** *(artisan)* lapidary **2** *(commerçant)* gem merchant

lapidation [lapidasjɔ̃] NF stoning, *Sout* lapidation

lapider [3] [lapide] VT **1** *(jeter des pierres à)* to stone, to throw stones at; *(tuer)* to stone to death, *Sout* to lapidate **2** *Littéraire (critiquer)* to lambast

lapié [lapje] NM *Géog* lapiés

lapilli [lapili] NMPL lapilli

lapin [lapɛ̃] NM **1** *Zool* rabbit; **l. mâle** buck (rabbit); **l. de choux** *ou* **de clapier** *ou* **domestique** tame *or* domestic rabbit; **l. de garenne** wild rabbit; *(aux États-Unis)* cottontail (rabbit); **l. tête de lion** lionhead rabbit; *Fam* **poser un l. à qn** to stand sb up; *Can Fam* **en criant l.** in a flash, *Br* before you could say Jack Robinson
 2 *Culin* rabbit; **civet/pâté de l.** rabbit stew/pâté
 3 *(fourrure) Br* rabbit (skin), *Am* cony (skin)
 4 *Fam (terme d'affection) Br* poppet, *Am* honey; **ça va, mon petit l.?** all right, honey *or Br* poppet?

lapine [lapin] NF doe (rabbit); *Fam Fig* **c'est une vraie l.** she breeds like a rabbit

lapiner [3] [lapine] VI to litter

lapinière [lapinjɛr] NF rabbit hutch

lapinisme [lapinism] NM *Fam Péj* excessive fertility■

lapis-lazuli [lapislazyli], **lapis** [lapis] NM INV lapis lazuli

La Plata [laplata] NF *Géog* La Plata

lapon, -e *ou* **-onne** [lapɔ̃, -ɔn] ADJ Lapp, Lappish
 NM *(langue)* Lappish, Lapp
 ❑ **Lapon, -e** *ou* **-onne** NM,F Lapp, Laplander

Laponie [lapɔni] NF **la L.** Lapland

Laponne, laponne [lapɔn] *voir* **lapon**

lapping [lapiŋ] NM *Tech* lapping

laps [laps] NM **un l. de temps** a lapse of time, a while

lapsi [lapsi] NMPL *Rel* **les l.** the lapsed

lapsus [lapsys] NM **1** *(faute)* **l. (linguae)** slip (of the tongue), *Spéc* lapsus linguae; **l. (calami)** slip of the pen **2** *Psy* Freudian slip; **l. révélateur** Freudian slip

laquage [lakaʒ] NM **1** *Tech* lacquering **2** *Méd* **l. du sang** haemolysis

laquais [lakɛ] NM **1** *(valet)* footman **2** *Littéraire Péj (homme servile)* lackey; **âme de l.** servile *or* cringing nature

laque [lak] NF **1** *(vernis)* lacquer; **en l.** lacquered; **l. de Chine** japan **2** *(pour cheveux)* hairspray **3** *(peinture)* gloss (paint) **4** lac
 NM *(objet)* piece of lacquerwork; **des laques** lacquerware *(UNCOUNT)*, lacquerwork *(UNCOUNT)*

laqué, -e [lake] ADJ **1** *Beaux-Arts* lacquered **2** *Constr* **cuisine laquée (en) rouge** kitchen in red gloss **3** *(cheveux)* lacquered **4** *Culin voir* **canard**
 NM *(peinture)* (high) gloss paint; *(enduit) Br* varnish, *Am* enamel

laquelle [lakɛl] *voir* **lequel**

laquer [3] [lake] VT **1** *(objet, meuble)* to lacquer; *(ongles)* to varnish **2** *(cheveux)* to put hairspray on

laqueur [lakœr] NM lacquerer

laqueux, -euse [lakø, -øz] ADJ lacquer-like

laraire [larɛr] NM *Antiq* lararium

larbin [larbɛ̃] NM *Fam Péj aussi Fig* flunkey■; **je ne suis pas ton l., débrouille-toi tout seul!** I'm not your servant, sort it out yourself!

larcin [larsɛ̃] NM **1** *(petit vol)* petty theft; **commettre de menus larcins** to engage in petty theft **2** *(objet volé)* **le grenier était plein de ses larcins** the attic was filled with his/her spoils *or* booty

lard [lar] NM **1** *Culin* bacon; **omelette au l.** bacon omelette; **l. fumé** smoked bacon; **l. gras, gros l.** fat bacon; **l. maigre, petit l., l. de poitrine** streaky bacon; **l. salé** salt pork
 2 *Fam (locutions)* **faire du l.** to sit around and get fat; **avec eux, on se demande** *ou* **on ne sait pas si c'est du l. ou du cochon** with that lot, you never know where you are; **rentrer dans le l. à qn** to lay into sb; *très Fam* **un gros l.** a fatso, a fat slob

larder [3] [larde] VT **1** *Culin* to lard **2** *(poignarder)* **l. qn de coups de couteau** to stab sb repeatedly **3** *(truffer)* **l. une lettre de citations** to pepper a letter with quotations **4** *Tech* **l. un morceau de bois** to stud a piece of wood with nails

lardoire [lardwar] NF **1** *Culin* larding needle *or* pin **2** *Fam (épée)* sword■

lardon [lardɔ̃] NM **1** *Culin* piece of diced bacon, lardon; **achète des lardons pour le ragoût** buy some lardons for the stew **2** *très Fam (enfant)* kid

lardonner [3] [lardɔne] VT **1** *Culin (lard)* to cut into lardons, to dice **2** *Arch (railler)* to jibe at

lare [lar] ADJ **dieux lares** lares
 NM household god; *Littéraire* **transporter ailleurs ses lares et pénates** to move with all one's belongings; **abandonner ses lares** to desert one's home

larfeuil, larfeuille [larfœj] NM *Br Fam* wallet■, *Am* billfold■

largable [largabl] ADJ releasable; **réservoir l.** releasable tank

largage [largaʒ] NM **1** *(par parachute)* dropping; *(de troupes, de matériel)* dispatching, dropping; **opération de l.** drop; **point de l.** drop point **2** *(d'une bombe)* dropping, releasing

large [larʒ] ADJ **1** *(grand → gén)* broad, wide; *(→ plaine)* big, wide; *(→ rue)* broad; *(→ tache)* large; **l. de 5 cm** 5 cm wide; **un nez l.** a broad nose; **un chapeau à larges bords** a wide-brimmed hat; **la Dordogne est l. à Libourne** the Dordogne gets wider at Libourne; **l. d'épaules** broad-shouldered; **percer une l. ouverture dans qch** to make a big hole in sth; **un l. mouvement du bras** a sweeping gesture with the arm; **d'un geste l.** with a sweeping gesture; **peindre à larges traits** to paint with broad brushstrokes; **un l. sourire** a broad smile
 2 *(ample → vêtement)* big, baggy; *(→ chaussures)* wide
 3 *(considérable)* large; **elle a une l. part de responsabilité** she must bear a large *or* major share of the blame; **ils font une part très l. à l'esprit d'initiative** they place a lot of importance on *or* they attach a lot of importance to initiative; **jouissant d'une l. autonomie** enjoying a large amount of independence; **jouissant d'une l. diffusion** widely distributed; **avoir un l. vocabulaire** to have a wide *or* wide-ranging vocabulary; **elle a fait de larges concessions/un l. tour d'horizon** she made generous concessions/an extensive survey of the situation; **les journaux ont publié de larges extraits de son discours** the papers quoted extensively from his/her speech
 4 *(général)* **prendre un mot dans son sens l.** to take a word in its broadest sense
 5 *(généreux)* generous; **elle est l. avec le personnel** she's generous with the staff; **de larges gratifications** generous bonuses
 6 *(ouvert)* open; **leur père a l'esprit l.** their father is open-minded *or* broad-minded
 7 *(excessif)* **ton estimation était un peu l.** your estimate was a bit wide of the mark
 NM **1** *(dimension)* width; **ici la rivière a** *ou* **fait 2 km de l.** here the river is 2 km wide; **être au l.** to have plenty of room; *(financièrement)* to be well off
 2 *Naut* **le l.** the open sea; **respirer l'air du l.** to breathe the sea air; **vent du l.** offshore wind; **au l.** offshore, at sea; **au l. de Hong Kong** off Hong Kong; *Fig* **se tenir au l. de qch** to stand clear of sth; **gagner** *ou* **prendre le l.** to head for the open sea; *Fam Fig* **il est temps de prendre le l.** it's time we beat it; *Fam* **du l.!** beat it!, clear off!
 ADV **calculer** *ou* **prévoir l.** to allow a good margin for error; **voir l.** to think big; **cette robe taille l.** this dress is loose-fitting
 ❑ **en large** ADV widthways; **mets les tables en l.** turn the tables widthways

largement [larʒəmɑ̃] ADV **1** *(amplement)* **gagner l. sa vie** to make a good living; **tu auras l. le temps** you'll easily have enough time, you'll have more than enough time; **elle a l. 60 ans** she's well over 60; **il y en a l. assez** there's more than enough; **des pouvoirs l. accrus** considerably increased powers; **une opinion l. répandue** a widely held opinion; **il s'est l. inspiré de Rabelais** he drew a great deal of inspiration from Rabelais; **il était l. cinq heures** it was well past five; **il vit l. au-dessus de ses moyens** he lives well beyond his means
 2 *(généreusement)* generously; **donner l. (à une collecte)** to give generously (to a collection); **on l'a l. récompensé** he has been amply *or* handsomely rewarded
 3 *(de beaucoup)* greatly; **la demande excède l. notre capacité** demand greatly exceeds our capacity
 4 *(facilement)* easily; **il vaut l. son frère** he's easily as good as his brother; **je gagne l. le double** I make at least *or* I easily earn twice that
 5 *(en grand)* **ouvrir l. une porte** to open a door wide

largesse [larʒɛs] NF *(magnanimité)* generosity, *Sout* largesse; **il fait toujours preuve de l.** he's always very generous; **traiter qn avec l.** to be generous to sb
 ❑ **largesses** NFPL *(présents)* gifts, *Sout* liberalities; **il ne faisait pas de telles largesses avec tous** he wasn't so generous to everybody

larget [larʒɛ] NM *Métal* sheet bar

largeur [larʒœr] NF **1** *(dimension → gén)* width; *(→ d'une voie ferrée)* gauge; **quelle est la l. de la pièce?** how wide is the room?; **la route a une l. de 5 m** *ou* **a 5 m de l.** the road is 5 m wide; **une remorque barrait la route dans** *ou* **sur toute sa l.** there was a trailer blocking the entire width of the road; **déchiré dans** *ou* **sur toute la l.** torn all the way across; *Transp* **l. hors tout** overall width; *Ordinat* **l. de papier** paper width
 2 *Fig* broadness, breadth; **l. d'esprit** *ou* **de vues** broadness of mind, broadmindedness
 3 *Com* **grande l.** double-width
 4 *Typ* breadth, set, width; **l. de la colonne** column width
 5 *Ordinat* **l. de bande** bandwidth
 ❑ **dans les grandes largeurs** ADV *Fam* **ça a été un fiasco dans les grandes largeurs!** that

turned out to be a fiasco with a capital F!; **on s'est fait avoir dans les grandes largeurs!** we were well and truly taken for a ride!

❑ **en largeur** ADV widthways, widthwise, crosswise; **la table fait 30 cm en l.** the table is 30 cm widthways *or* across

larghetto [largɛto] *Mus* ADV larghetto

NM larghetto

largo [largo] *Mus* ADV largo

NM largo

largonji [largɔ̃ʒi] NM = type of slang formed by replacing the initial consonant of a word with the letter "l" and moving the original consonant to the end of the word, followed by a vowel to aid pronunciation (eg "à poil" becomes "à lolipé")

largue [larg] *Naut* ADJ *(cordage)* loose, slack; *(vent)* free

NM **petit l.** fine reach; **grand l.** quartering wind

largué, -e [large] ADJ *Fam* **être l.** *(ne pas comprendre)* to be out of one's depth; *(plus à la page)* to be out of touch

larguer [3] [large] VT **1** *Naut (voile)* to slip, to let out, to unfurl; *(amarre)* to slip

2 *Aviat (bombe, charge, parachutiste)* to drop; *(réservoir)* to jettison; *(fusée)* to release

3 *très Fam (abandonner → poste)* to quit▪, to walk out on, *Br* to chuck (in); *(→ vieillerie, projet) Br* to chuck, to bin, *Am* to trash; *(→ amant)* to dump, to jilt; *(→ personne avec qui l'on vit, associé)* to walk out on; **se faire l.** to be dumped; **il a tout largué pour partir vivre aux Caraïbes** he chucked everything in and went to live in the Caribbean

USAGE ABSOLU *Naut* **larguez!** let go!

VI *très Fam (émettre des gaz intestinaux)* to fart, *Br* to let off, *Am* to lay one

largueur [largœr] NM *(de matériel)* dispatcher

lariforme [larifɔrm] *Orn* NM larid, *Spéc* member of the Laridae

❑ **lariformes** NMPL larids, *Spéc* Laridae

larigot [larigo] *voir* **tire-larigot**

larme [larm] NF **1** *Physiol* tear; **retenir ses larmes** to hold back one's tears; **être en larmes** to be in tears; **ses yeux s'emplirent de larmes** his/her eyes filled with tears; **être au bord des larmes** to be on the verge of tears; **avec des larmes dans la voix** with *or* in a tearful voice; **ça vous fait venir les larmes aux yeux** it brings tears to your eyes; **il y a de quoi vous arracher** *ou* **vous tirer des larmes** it's enough to make you burst into tears; **avoir les larmes aux yeux** to have tears in one's eyes; **il a toujours la l. à l'œil, il a la l. facile** he cries easily; *Littéraire* **mêler ses larmes à celles de quelqu'un** to share someone's sorrow; **pleurer** *ou* **verser des larmes de joie** to cry for joy, to shed tears of joy; **il y est allé de sa (petite) l.** he shed a tear; **une grosse l.** a big tear; **larmes de crocodile** crocodile tears; *Littéraire* **larmes de sang** tears of blood

2 *(petite quantité)* **une l. (de)** a drop (of); **une l. de cognac** a drop of brandy; **oh, juste une l.!** the tiniest drop, please!

3 *(d'un cerf)* tear

larme-de-Job [larmdəʒɔb] *(pl* **larmes-de-Job***)* NF *Bot* Job's tears *(singulier)*

larmichette [larmiʃɛt] NF *Fam* tiny drop▪

larmier [larmje] NM **1** *Archit* dripstone, larmier **2** *Zool (du cerf)* tear pit; *(du cheval)* temple **3** *Anat* inner corner of the eye, *Spéc* inner canthus

larmoie *etc voir* **larmoyer**

larmoiement [larmwamɑ̃] NM *Physiol* watering

❑ **larmoiements** NMPL *Littéraire (pleurnicheries)* tears, snivelling *(UNCOUNT)*

larmoyant, -e [larmwajɑ̃, -ɑ̃t] ADJ **1** *Physiol* watery **2** *Péj (éploré)* **le récit l. de ses malheurs** the sorry tale of his/her misfortunes; **d'une voix larmoyante, elle nous annonça...** she told us in a tearful voice... **3** *(sentimental → film, mélo)* mawkish **4** *Littérature* **comédie larmoyante** sentimental comedy

larmoyer [13] [larmwaje] VI **1** *Physiol (œil)* to water **2** *Péj (se lamenter)* to weep, to snivel, to whimper

larron [larɔ̃] NM **1** *Arch (voleur)* robber, thief **2** *Bible* thief; **le bon l. et le mauvais l.** the penitent thief and the impenitent thief

❑ **larrons** NMPL *Typ* hickeys

larsen [larsɛn] NM **effet l.** feedback

larvaire [larvɛr] ADJ **1** *Zool* larval **2** *Fig* embryonic, unformed; **le projet était encore à l'état l.** the plan was still in its early stage *or* in embryo

larve [larv] NF **1** *Zool (d'amphibien, de poisson)* larva; *(d'insecte)* grub **2** *Fam (fainéant)* lazybones, slob **3** *Péj* **l. (humaine)** worm **4** *Antiq* spectre

larvé, -e [larve] ADJ **1** *Méd* latent, *Spéc* larvate **2** *(latent)* latent, concealed; **en 1964 il y avait déjà une révolte larvée** a rebellion was already brewing in 1964; **une guerre larvée** a latent war

larver [3] [larve] VI *Fam* to veg (out), to slob about *or* around; **j'ai passé la journée à l. devant la télé** I spent the day vegging (out) in front of the TV

larvicide [larvisid] ADJ larvicidal

NM larvicide

laryngé, -e [larɛ̃ʒe] ADJ *Anat* laryngal, laryngeal

laryngectomie [larɛ̃ʒɛktɔmi] NF *Méd* laryngectomy

laryngien, -enne [larɛ̃ʒjɛ̃, -ɛn] ADJ *Anat* laryngal, laryngeal

laryngite [larɛ̃ʒit] NF *Méd* laryngitis

laryngologie [larɛ̃gɔlɔʒi] NF *Méd* laryngology

laryngologiste [larɛ̃gɔlɔʒist], **laryngologue** [larɛ̃gɔlɔg] NMF *Méd* throat specialist, *Spéc* laryngologist

laryngoscope [larɛ̃gɔskɔp] NM *Méd* laryngoscope

laryngoscopie [larɛ̃gɔskɔpi] NF *Méd* laryngoscopy

laryngotomie [larɛ̃gɔtɔmi] NF *Méd* laryngotomy

larynx [larɛ̃ks] NM *Anat* voice box, *Spéc* larynx

las[1] [lɑs] EXCLAM *Littéraire* alas!

las[2], **lasse** [lɑ, lɑs] ADJ **1** *Littéraire (fatigué)* weary; **je me sens l. après cette marche** I feel quite weary after that walk **2** *(découragé, écœuré)* weary; **être l. de qch/de faire qch** to be weary of sth/of doing sth

lasagnes [lazaɲ] NFPL lasagne *(UNCOUNT)*

lascar [laskar] NM *Fam* **1** *(individu rusé)* rogue; **celui-là, c'est un drôle de l.!** he's a shady character!; **tu vas le regretter, mon l.!** *(homme)* you'll be sorry, buster *or* pal!; *(enfant)* you'll be sorry, you little rascal! **2** *(individu quelconque)* character, customer; **qui c'est, ce l.?** who's that character?; **un grand l.** a big chap

lascif, -ive [lasif, -iv] ADJ **1** *(sensuel)* lascivious, sensual **2** *(lubrique)* lustful, lewd

lascivement [lasivmɑ̃] ADV lustfully

lascivité [lasivite], **lasciveté** [lasivte] NF **1** *(sensualité)* wantonness, lasciviousness **2** *(lubricité)* lust, lewdness

laser [lazɛr] NM laser; **traitement au l.** laser treatment; **enregistrement l.** *(procédé)* laser recording; *(disque)* laser disc; **faisceau l.** laser beam

Las Palmas [laspalmas] NF Las Palmas

lassant, -e [lasɑ̃, -ɑ̃t] ADJ tedious; **tu es l. à la fin!** you're beginning to irritate me!

lasse [las] *voir* **las**[2]

lasser [3] [lase] VT **1** *(exténuer)* to weary; **lassée par ce long voyage** weary after that long journey

2 *(importuner)* to bore, to tire, *Sout* to weary; **tu me lasses avec tes problèmes** I'm tired of hearing about your problems; **parlons d'autre chose, ne lassons pas nos invités** let's talk about something else, let's not bore our guests

3 *(décourager)* to tax, to exhaust, *Sout* to fatigue; **l. l'attention de l'auditoire** to overtax the audience's attention; **l. la patience de qn** to try sb's patience

USAGE ABSOLU **ses jérémiades finissent par l.** his/her moaning gets a bit trying after a while

►**se lasser** VPR to get tired, *Sout* to (grow) weary; **se l. de qn/qch/de faire qch** to get tired of sb/sth/of doing sth; **je ne me lasse jamais de te voir** I never tire of seeing you; **je ne me lasse jamais de tes visites** I never get tired of your visits; **elle se lassera vite de lui** she'll soon get tired of him; **je ne me lasse pas d'écouter du Mozart** I never get tired of listening to Mozart; **sans se l.** tirelessly

lasserie [lasri] NF fine openwork basketry, wickerwork

lassis [lasi] NM **1** *(bourre de soie)* flock of silk **2** *(étoffe)* flock silk

lassitude [lasityd] NF **1** *(fatigue)* tiredness *(UNCOUNT)*, weariness *(UNCOUNT)*, *Littéraire* lassitude *(UNCOUNT)* **2** *(découragement)* weariness; **être pris d'une immense l.** to be overcome by weariness

lasso [laso] NM lasso, *Am* lariat; **attraper** *ou* **prendre une bête au l.** to lasso an animal

Lastex® [lastɛks] NM Lastex®

lasting [lastiŋ] NM *Tex* lasting(s)

lasure [lazyr] NF varnish, wood sealant

Las Vegas [lasvegas] NF Las Vegas

lat. *(abrév écrite* **latitude***)* lat

latanier [latanje] NM latania

latence [latɑ̃s] NF latency; **période de l.** latency period

latent, -e [latɑ̃, -ɑ̃t] ADJ latent; **à l'état l.** in the making

latéral, -e, -aux, -ales [lateral, -o] ADJ **1** *(sur le côté)* lateral, side *(avant n)*; **porte/rue/sortie latérale** side door/street/exit **2** *(annexe)* minor; **canal l.** minor canal **3** *Tél* **bande latérale** sideband **4** *Ling* **consonne latérale** lateral (consonant)

❑ **latérale** NF *Ling* lateral

latéralement [lateralmɑ̃] ADV sideways, laterally; **se déplacer l.** to move sideways *or* crabwise; **la lumière de la bougie l'éclairait l.** the light from the candle fell on him/her from the side

latéralisation [lateralizasjɔ̃] NF lateralization; **l. à droite/à gauche** right-/left-handedness

latéralisé, -e [lateralize] ADJ lateralized

latéralité [lateralite] NF laterality

latérite [laterit] NF *Géol* laterite

latéritique [lateritik] ADJ *Géol* lateritic

latéritisation [lateritizasjɔ̃] NF *Géol* laterization

latex [latɛks] NM latex

laticifère [latisifɛr] *Bot* ADJ laticiferous, latex-bearing

NM laticiferous element *or* cell

laticlave [latiklav] NM *Antiq* laticlave

latifolié, -e [latifɔlje] ADJ *Bot* latifoliate, broad-leaved

latifundia [latifɔ̃dja] *voir* **latifundium**

latifundiste [latifɔ̃dist] NM latifundista

latifundium [latifɔ̃djɔm] *(pl* **latifundia** [-dja]*)* NM latifundium

latin, -e [latɛ̃, -in] ADJ **1** *Antiq* Latin; **le monde l.** the Latin world

2 *Ling (appartenant au latin)* Latin; *(issu du latin)* Romance *(avant n)*; **les langues latines** the Romance *or* Latin languages

3 *(en sociologie)* Latin; **les peuples latins** the Latin races; **le tempérament l.** the Latin temperament

4 *Rel* Latin; **l'Église latine** the Latin Church

5 *(à Paris)* **le Quartier l.** the Latin Quarter *(area on the Left Bank of the Seine, traditionally associated with students and artists)*

❑ **Latin, -e** NM,F Latin; **les Latins** the Latin people, the Latins NM *(langue)* Latin; **l. classique** classical Latin; **bas l.** low Latin; **l. de cuisine** dog Latin

latinisant, -e [latinizɑ̃, -ɑ̃t] ADJ Latinizing; **pour ceux qui sont latinisants** for those who know Latin, for the Latin scholars

latinisation [latinizasjɔ̃] NF Latinization

latiniser [3] [latinize] VT to Latinize

latinisme [latinism] NM **1** *(idiotisme du latin)* Latinism **2** *(emprunt au latin)* Latin phrase

latiniste [latinist] NMF *(spécialiste)* Latin scholar, Latinist; *(étudiant)* Latin student, student of Latin

latinité [latinite] NF **1** *(caractère)* Latinity **2** *(civilisation)* Latin world

latino [latino] *Fam* ADJ Latino▪

NMF Latino▪

latino-américain, -e [latinoamerikɛ̃, -ɛn] *(mpl* **latino-américains**, *fpl* **latino-américaines***)* ADJ Latin American

❑ **Latino-Américain, -e** NM,F Latin American

latitude [latityd] NF **1** *(liberté)* latitude, scope; **j'ai toute l. pour mener mon enquête** I have full scope *or* a free hand to conduct my enquiry; **vous avez toute l. de dire oui ou non** you are completely free *or* at liberty to say yes or no; **une certaine l. pour agir** some freedom of action *or* movement

2 *Astron & Géog* latitude; **cette ville est à 70° de l. Nord** this city is situated at latitude 70° North; **par 70° de l. Nord** in latitude 70° North; **basses/hautes latitudes** low/high latitudes

3 *(région, climat)* **sous d'autres latitudes** in other parts of the world

latitudinaire [latitydinɛr] ADJ latitudinarian

NMF latitudinarian

Latium [lasjɔm] NM **le L.** Latium

latomies [latɔmi] NFPL Antiq latomies, = stone quarries used in Syracuse as prisons

lato sensu [latosɛ̃sy] ADV loosely or broadly speaking

latrie [latri] NF Rel culte de l. latria

latrines [latrin] NFPL latrine

latrodecte [latrɔdɛkt], **latrodectus** [latrɔdɛktys] NM Entom black widow

lats [lats] NM (monnaie) lat

lattage [lataʒ] NM 1 (action) lathing, battening 2 (lattis) lathwork (UNCOUNT)

latte [lat] NF 1 Constr lath; (pour chevronnage) roof batten; **l. de plancher** floorboard 2 Naut batten 3 très Fam (pied) foot ◾; (chaussure) shoe ◾; **prendre un coup de l.** to get kicked 4 Belg (règle plate) ruler 5 Belg Ftbl (barre) crossbar; (passe) cross

latter [3] [late] VT 1 Constr to lath, to batten 2 Fam to kick ◾, to boot, Br to put the boot into

lattis [lati] NM Constr lathwork (UNCOUNT)

laudanum [lodanɔm] NM Pharm laudanum

laudateur, -trice [lodatœr, -tris] NM,F Littéraire laudator

laudatif, -ive [lodatif, -iv] ADJ (discours, article) laudatory; **il a été très l.** he was full of praise

laudatrice [lodatris] voir **laudateur**

laudes [lod] NFPL lauds

lauracée [lɔrase] Bot NF lauraceous plant, Spéc member of the Lauraceae

□ **lauracées** NFPL lauraceous plants, Spéc Lauraceae

laure [lɔr] NF laura, lavra (large Orthodox monastery)

lauré, -e [lɔre] ADJ Littéraire laureate (avant n)

lauréat, -e [lɔrea, -at] ADJ prizewinning
NM,F prizewinner, laureate; **l. du prix Nobel** Nobel prizewinner; **l. du prix Goncourt** winner of the "prix Goncourt"

'Le Lauréat' Nichols 'The Graduate'

Laurent [lɔrɑ̃] NPR **L. le Magnifique** Lorenzo the Magnificent

Laurentides [lɔrɑ̃tid] NFPL 1 Géog Laurentides, Laurentian Mountains 2 Admin (au Québec) Laurentides

laurentien, -enne [lɔrɑ̃sjɛ̃, -ɛn] ADJ 1 Géog Laurentian 2 (personne) of/from the Laurentian Mountains/the Laurentides
NM,F = inhabitant of or person from the Laurentian Mountains/the Laurentides

lauréole [lɔreɔl] NF Bot daphne

laurier [lɔrje] NM 1 Bot (bay) laurel, (sweet) bay; **l. de Saint-Antoine** rosebay willowherb, fireweed 2 Culin **mettre du l. dans une sauce** to flavour a sauce with bay leaves; **feuille de l.** bay leaf

□ **lauriers** NMPL (gloire) laurels; **il est revenu couvert de lauriers** he came home covered in glory

laurier-cerise [lɔrjesəriz] (pl **lauriers-cerises**) NM Bot cherry laurel

laurier-rose [lɔrjeroz] (pl **lauriers-roses**) NM Bot rosebay, oleander

laurier-sauce [lɔrjesos] (pl **lauriers-sauce**) NM Bot bay tree

laurier-tin [lɔrjetɛ̃] (pl **lauriers-tins**) NM Bot laurustinus

Lausanne [lozan] NM Lausanne

lausannois, -e [lozanwa, -az] ADJ of/from Lausanne

□ **Lausannois, -e** NM,F = inhabitant of or person from Lausanne

lause, lauze [loz] NF 1 (pour toits) roofing stone 2 (pour dallage) flat paving stone

LAV [ɛlave] NM Méd (abrév lymphadenopathy associated virus) LAV

lavable [lavabl] ADJ washable; **l. en machine** machine-washable

lavabo [lavabo] NM 1 (évier) Br washbasin, Am washbowl 2 Rel lavabo

□ **lavabos** NMPL (toilettes) toilets, Am washroom

lavage [lavaʒ] NM 1 (nettoyage → du linge) washing (UNCOUNT); (→ d'une surface) scrubbing (UNCOUNT); **faites deux lavages séparés pour la laine et le coton** wash wool and cotton separately; **il a fallu trois lavages pour venir à bout des taches** it took three washes to get rid of the stains; **son jean a besoin d'un bon l.** his/

her jeans need a good wash; **le carrelage a besoin d'un bon l.** the tiles need a good scrub; **l. à grande eau** sluicing; **l. en machine** (sur l'étiquette d'un vêtement) machine wash; **l. à la main** (sur l'étiquette d'un vêtement) hand wash (only); **l. au poids** washing by weight; **instructions de l.** (sur l'étiquette d'un vêtement) washing instructions

2 Méd lavage; **l. d'estomac** pumping out (of) the stomach, Spéc gastric lavage; **faire un l. d'estomac à qn** to pump (out) sb's stomach; **l. interne** douche; **l. du sperme** sperm washing

3 Métal & Tex washing

□ **au lavage** ADV in the wash; **tes chemises sont au l.** your shirts are in the wash; **la tache est partie/n'est pas partie au l.** the stain came out/ didn't come out in the wash; **ma chemise a rétréci/déteint au l.** my shirt has shrunk/run in the wash

□ **lavage de cerveau** NM brainwashing (UNCOUNT); **subir un l. de cerveau** to be brainwashed; **faire un l. de cerveau à qn** to brainwash sb

lavallière [lavaljɛr] NF = necktie with a large bow

lavande [lavɑ̃d] NF Bot lavender; **(eau de) l.** lavender water; **l. de mer** sea lavender
ADJ INV lavender blue

lavandière [lavɑ̃djɛr] NF 1 Littéraire (blanchisseuse) washerwoman 2 Orn (white) wagtail

lavandin [lavɑ̃dɛ̃] NM hybrid lavender

lavaret [lavare] NM Ich powan

lavasse [lavas] Péj ADJ (sans éclat) watery
NF Fam (café, bière, soupe) dishwater; **son café, c'est de la l.** his/her coffee tastes like dishwater

lave [lav] NF lava

□ **de lave** ADJ lava (avant n)

lavé, -e [lave] ADJ 1 (délayé → couleur) faded, washed-out; **un bleu un peu l.** a slightly washed-out blue 2 Beaux-Arts **dessin l.** wash drawing

lave-auto [lavoto] (pl **lave-autos**) NM Can car wash

lave-dos [lavdo] NM INV back-scrubber

lave-glace [lavglas] (pl **lave-glaces**) NM Br windscreen washer, Am windshield washer

lave-linge [lavlɛ̃ʒ] NM INV washing machine; **l. à chargement frontal** front-loading washing machine

lave-mains [lavmɛ̃] NM INV Br wash-hand basin, Am small washbowl

lavement [lavmɑ̃] NM 1 Méd (remède) enema; **l. baryté** barium enema 2 Méd (procédé) lavage 3 Bible **le l. des pieds** the washing of the Apostles' feet

lave-pont [lavpɔ̃] (pl **lave-ponts**) NM scrubbing brush, (floor) scrubber

laver [3] [lave] VT 1 (vêtement, tissu) to wash; (tache) to wash out or off; (surface) to wash down; (avec une brosse) to scrub; **l. à grande eau** to swill out or down; **l. qch à l'éponge** to sponge sth (down); **la voiture a besoin d'être lavée** the car needs washing or a wash; **l. la vaisselle** to wash or to do the dishes, Br to wash up, to do the washing-up; Fig **il vaut mieux l. son linge sale en famille** don't wash your dirty linen in public

2 (faire la toilette de) to wash; **l. la tête** ou **les cheveux à qn** to wash sb's hair; Fam Fig **l. la tête à qn** to give sb a good dressing-down

3 (expier → péché) to wash away; (dégager) to clear; **l. sa conscience** to clear one's conscience; **l. qn d'une accusation** to clear sb's name of an accusation; **l. qn d'une faute** to forgive sb an offence; **être lavé de tout soupçon** to be clear of all suspicion; **l. un affront dans le sang** to avenge an insult (by fighting)

4 Beaux-Arts (dessin) to wash; (couleur) to dilute, to wash

5 Méd (plaie) to bathe, to cleanse; (estomac) to wash or to pump out

6 (minerai) to wash

USAGE ABSOLU (nettoyer) **cette lessive lave très bien** this powder washes very well; **l. en machine** (sur l'étiquette d'un vêtement) machine wash; **l. à la main** (sur l'étiquette d'un vêtement) hand wash (only)

▸ **se laver** VPR 1 (emploi réfléchi) to (have a) wash; **lave-toi tout seul, comme un grand** you're old enough to wash yourself; **se l. la**

figure/les **mains** to wash one's face/hands; **se l. les dents** to clean or to brush one's teeth; Fig **je m'en lave les mains** I wash my hands of the entire matter

2 (emploi passif) **ça se lave très bien** it's very easy to wash, it washes very well; **comment ça se lave, la viscose?** how should viscose be washed?

3 **se l. d'un soupçon** to clear oneself of suspicion; **se l. de ses péchés** to cleanse oneself of one's sins

laverie [lavri] NF 1 (blanchisserie) **l. (automatique)** self-service laundry, Br launderette, Am Laundromat® 2 Mines washing plant

lave-tête [lavtɛt] NM INV shampoo basin

lavette [lavɛt] NF 1 (chiffon) dishcloth; (brosse) Br washing-up brush, Am dish mop 2 Fam (personne) drip, wimp, wuss 3 Belg & Suisse (gant de toilette) Br face flannel, Am washcloth

laveur, -euse [lavœr, -øz] NM,F (de vaisselle) washer, dishwasher; (de linge) washerman, f washerwoman; (de voiture) car washer; **l. de carreaux** ou **de vitres** window cleaner
NM 1 Agr drum washer 2 Tech washer 3 Zool voir **raton**

lave-vaisselle [lavvɛsɛl] NM INV dishwasher

lave-vitre [lavvitr] (pl **lave-vitres**) NM Aut Br windscreen or Am windshield washer

lavis [lavi] NM 1 (technique) washing (UNCOUNT) 2 (dessin) wash drawing

lavoir [lavwar] NM 1 (établissement) washhouse; (bassin) (cement) washtub 2 Mines (atelier) washing plant; (machine) washer 3 Belg (blanchisserie) **l. (automatique)** self-service laundry

lavomatic [lavomatik] NM Br launderette, Am Laundromat®

lavra [lavra] NF laura, lavra (large Orthodox monastery)

lavure [lavyr] NF slops, dishwater

Lawrence [lɔrɑ̃s] NPR **L. d'Arabie** Lawrence of Arabia

lawrencium [lɔrɑ̃sjɔm] NM Chim lawrencium

laxatif, -ive [laksatif, -iv] ADJ laxative (avant n)
NM laxative

laxisme [laksism] NM 1 (tolérance excessive) laxity, permissiveness 2 Rel laxism

laxiste [laksist] ADJ 1 (trop tolérant) soft, lax 2 Rel laxist
NM,F 1 (gén) overlenient person 2 Rel laxist

laxité [laksite] NF (d'un ligament) laxity, relaxed state; (d'une corde) slackness

layer [11] [leje] VT 1 (forêt) to cut a path into 2 Constr to bush-hammer

layette [lɛjɛt] NF baby clothes, layette; Com babywear; **bleu/rose l.** baby blue/pink

layon [lɛjɔ̃] NM Agr (division) (compartment) line; (sentier) forest path

Lazare [lazar] NPR Bible Lazarus

lazaret [lazarɛ] NM (lieu d'isolement) lazaretto, lazaret

lazariste [lazarist] NM Lazarist (priest)

lazulite [lazylit] NF Minér lazulite

lazurite [lazyrit] NF Minér lazurite

lazzi [ladzi] (pl inv ou **lazzis**) NM jeer, gibe

l/c Banque (abrév écrite **lettre de crédit**) L/C

LCD [ɛlsede] NM Électron (abrév **liquid crystal display**) LCD; **écran LCD** LCD screen

LCE [ɛlseø] NM Univ (abrév **Langue et civilisation étrangères**) espagnol/anglais **L.** Spanish/English language and civilization

LCR [ɛlseɛr] NF 1 Fin (abrév **lettre de change relevé**) bills of exchange statement 2 Pol (abrév **ligue communiste révolutionnaire**) = militant Trotskyist organization

LDL-cholestérol [ɛldeɛlkɔlɛsterɔl] NM Méd (abrév **low-density lipoprotein-cholesterol**) LDL-cholesterol

LDR [ɛldeɛr] NM Électron (abrév **light dependent resistor**) LDR

LE[1], LA[1], LES[1] [lə, la, le]

| the **1, 2, 10, 12** ◾ a **3–5** ◾ what a **6** ◾ one's **7** |

l' is used instead of **le** or **la** before a word beginning with a vowel or h mute.

ART DÉFINI 1 (avec un nom commun) the; **le soleil, la lune et les étoiles** the sun, the moon and the

stars; **c'était touchant de voir le père et le fils ensemble** it was touching to see father and son together; **ouvre la fenêtre** open the window; **le chemin le plus court** the shortest route; **l'arbre qui est derrière la maison** the tree behind the house; **l'été de la sécheresse** the summer there was a drought; **l'idée qu'il allait partir...** the idea that he was going to leave...; **la salade du chef** the chef's salad

2 *(dans le temps)* **le sixième jour** the sixth day; **la troisième fois** the third time; **pendant les vacances** during the holidays; **l'été dernier** last summer; **l'été 1976** the summer of 1976; **le premier juillet** the first of July; **le 15 janvier 1991** 15 January 1991; **il est passé nous voir le 15 août** he came to see us on the 15th of August *or* on August the 15th; *(par écrit)* he came to see us on 15 August

3 *(dans les fractions)* a; **le quart/tiers de** a quarter/third of; **la moitié de** (a) half of

4 *(avec un sens distributif)* **j'y vais le soir** I go there in the evening; **elle vient deux fois la semaine** she comes twice a week; **2 euros le kilo** 2 euros a *or* per kilo; **le docteur reçoit le lundi et le vendredi** *ou* **les lundis et vendredis** the doctor sees patients on Monday and Friday *or* Mondays and Fridays

5 *(avec valeur d'adjectif démonstratif)* **l'affaire est grave** the matter is serious, it's a serious matter; **on sait que le problème est difficile** we know that it's a difficult problem

6 *(avec une valeur expressive)* what a; **la belle moto!** what a beautiful bike!; **l'idiot!** what an idiot!, (the) idiot!; *Fam* **vise un peu la tenue!** look at that get-up!; **alors, les amis, comment ça va?** well, folks, how are you?; **debout, les enfants!** time to get up, children!

7 *(avec les parties du corps)* **le chapeau sur la tête** his/her/*etc* hat on his/her/*etc* head; **se laver les mains** to wash one's hands; **il est parti le livre sous le bras** he went off with the book under his arm; **elle a les yeux bleus** she has blue eyes; **elle ferma les yeux** she closed her eyes

8 *(avec une valeur généralisante)* **les hommes et les femmes** men and women; **tous les hommes** all men; **la femme est l'égale de l'homme** woman is man's equal; **les jeunes** young people; **le cheval, comme d'autres mammifères...** the horse *or* horses, like other mammals...; **le cauchemar chez l'enfant de six à dix ans** nightmares in children between six and ten years old; **j'apprends le français** I'm learning French; **j'étudie l'économie/la physique** I'm studying economics/physics; **aimer la musique/la littérature/le football** to like music/literature/football; **aller au théâtre/au cinéma** to go to the theatre/the cinema; **la paresse est un des sept péchés capitaux** sloth is one of the seven deadly sins; **l'important dans tout ça** the important thing (in all this); **les petits et les grands** *(par la taille)* small people and tall people; **ne fais pas l'idiot** don't be an idiot

9 *(marquant l'approximation)* **ça vaut dans les 100 euros** it's worth around 100 euros; **vers les quatre heures** about *or* around four o'clock; **sur les deux heures** at about two o'clock; **il va sur la quarantaine** he's getting on for forty

10 *(avec un nom propre)* the; **nous sommes invités chez les Durand** we are invited to the Durands' (house); **les Bourbons** the Bourbons; *Fam* **la Marie** Marie■ ; **ce n'est plus la Sophie que nous avons connue** she's no longer the Sophie (that) we used to know; **la Callas** Callas; **le Racine des 'Plaideurs'** the Racine of *or* who wrote 'Les Plaideurs'; **le Descartes/Sophocle du XXème siècle** the Descartes/Sophocles of the 20th century; **le Paris de l'après-guerre** post-war Paris; **le Paris que nous aimions** the Paris we knew and loved; **l'Amérique de Mark Twain n'existe plus** Mark Twain's America no longer exists; **les Raphaël des Offices** the Raphaels in the Uffizi

11 *(avec les jours de fête)* **la Toussaint** All Saints' Day; **quand tombe la Saint-Simon?** what day does Saint Simon's day fall on?; *Fam* **à la Noël** at Christmas

12 *(avec un adjectif)* the; **je vous donne les livres neufs et je reprends les vieux** I'll give you the new books and take back the old ones; **tu préfères la rouge ou la jaune?** do you prefer the red (one) or the yellow (one)?

LE², LA², LES² [lə, la, le]

l' is used instead of **le** or **la** before a word beginning with a vowel or h mute.

PRON 1 *(complément d'objet → homme)* him; *(→ femme, nation, bateau)* her; *(→ chose, animal)* it; *(→ nouveau-né, animal domestique mâle)* him, it; *(→ nouveau-née, animal domestique femelle)* her, it; **l'addition? je l'ai payée** the bill? I've paid it; **ce bordeaux, je l'ai déjà goûté** I've already tasted this *or* that Bordeaux; **Jean est malade, je vais l'appeler** Jean is ill, I'm going to call him; **il l'a probablement oublié, ton livre** he's probably forgotten your book *or* that book of yours; **combien de fois on l'a vu, ce garçon?** how many times have we seen that boy?

2 *(représentant une proposition)* **elle est partie hier soir, du moins je l'ai entendu dire** she left last night, at least that's what I've heard; **il m'a insulté mais, crois-moi, il ne le refera pas** he insulted me but, believe me, he won't do it again; **elle a été récompensée comme elle le mérite** she got her just deserts; **allez, dis-le-lui** go on, tell him (about it); **je le pense aussi** I think so too; **il est plus riche que vous ne le pensez** he's richer than you think (he is); **puisque je te le disais que ce n'était pas possible!** but I TOLD you it was impossible!

3 *(comme attribut)* **êtes-vous satisfaite? – je le suis** are you satisfied? – I am; **son frère est médecin, il voudrait l'être aussi** his brother is a doctor, he would like to be one too; **malheureux, je l'étais certainement** I certainly was unhappy; **pour être timide, ça, il l'est!** boy, is he shy!, talk about shy!

lé [le] **NM 1** *(d'un tissu, d'un papier peint)* width **2** *(d'une jupe)* gore

LEA [ɛləa] **NFPL** *Univ (abrév* **langues étrangères appliquées**) = applied modern languages

lead [lid] **NM** *Journ (d'un article)* introductory paragraph

leader [lidœr] **NM 1** *(chef)* leader; **le l. du parti socialiste** the leader of the socialist party; **l. de la majorité** majority leader

2 *Com (entreprise, produit)* (market) leader; **le l. mondial de la micro-informatique** the world leader in microcomputing; **l. sur le marché** market leader; **l. d'opinion** opinion former, opinion leader

3 *Presse* leader, leading article

4 *Sport* **le l. du championnat de France** the team at the top of the French league

5 *(comme adj)* **c'est le produit l. de la gamme** it's the leading product in the range

leadership [lidœrʃip] **NM** *(fonction de leader)* leadership; *(position dominante)* leading position

Léandre [leɑ̃dr] **NPR** *Myth* Leander

leasing [liziŋ] *Banque* **NM** leasing

❑ **en leasing ADV** on lease, as part of a leasing contract

lebel [ləbɛl] **NM** Lebel rifle

lécanore [lekanɔr] **NF** *Bot* lecanora

léchage [leʃaʒ] **NM 1** *(gén)* licking; *Fam* **l. de bottes** bootlicking **2** *Fam (fignolage)* finishing touches■

léché, -e [leʃe] **ADJ** *Fam* **du travail l.** a highly polished piece of work; **un roman policier bien l.** a neat little detective novel

lèche [lɛʃ] **NF** *très Fam* bootlicking; **faire de la l.** to be a bootlicker; **faire de la l. à qn** to suck up to sb, to lick sb's boots

lèche-bottes [lɛʃbɔt] **NMF INV** *Fam* bootlicker

lèche-cul [lɛʃky] **NMF INV** *Vulg* brown-nose, *Br* arse-licker, *Am* ass-licker

lèchefrite [lɛʃfrit] **NF 1** *(pour recevoir le jus de viande) Br* dripping pan, *Am* broiler pan **2** *Can (moule à gâteau)* cake tin; *(moule à pain)* loaf tin **3** *Can (marmite)* maple syrup boiler

lèchement [lɛʃmɑ̃] = **léchage**

lécher [18] [leʃe] **VT 1** *(passer la langue sur)* to lick; **l. ses plaies** to lick one's wounds; *Fam* **l. les bottes à qn** to lick sb's boots; *Vulg* **l. le cul à qn** to lick sb's *Br* arse *or Am* ass

2 *(confiture, miel)* to lick up; *(lait, crème)* to lap up; **l'enfant lécha la cuillère** the child licked the spoon clean

3 *Fam (perfectionner)* to polish up; **le réalisateur a trop léché les images au détriment du scénario** the director spent too much time on the camera work and not enough on the script

4 *(effleurer → sujet: feu)* to lick at; **les flammes léchaient déjà le mur** the flames were already licking at the wall; **les vagues léchaient le sable** the waves were lapping on the sand

►**se lécher VPR** to lick oneself; **le chiot se léchait les pattes** the puppy was licking its paws; **se l. les doigts** to lick one's fingers; **c'est à s'en l. les doigts** *ou* **les babines!** it's scrumptious!, it's really yummy!

lécheur, -euse [leʃœr, -øz] **NM,F** *Fam Péj* bootlicker, groveller■

ADJ M suctorial

lèche-vitrines [lɛʃvitrin] **NM INV** window-shopping; **faire du l.** to go window-shopping

lechwe [lɛʃwe] **NM** *Zool* lechwe

lécithine [lesitin] **NF** *Chim* lecithin

leçon [ləsɔ̃] **NF 1** *Scol (cours)* lesson; **donner/prendre des leçons de français** to give/to take French lessons; **il faut que je prépare ma l. de géographie pour demain** I've got to prepare for tomorrow's geography lesson; **prenez la l. sur la digestion à la page 50** turn to the lesson on digestion on page 50; **la couture en 15 leçons** needlework in 15 (easy) lessons; **l. de choses** object lesson; **l. de conduite** driving lesson; **tu ne vas pas me faire une l. de morale?** you're not going to start moralizing at me, are you?; **leçons particulières** private lessons, private tuition

2 *(devoirs)* homework *(UNCOUNT)*; **apprendre sa l.** *ou* **ses leçons** to do one's homework; *Fig* **ils avaient bien appris leur l.** they had learnt their lines well, they had rehearsed what to say very well; **sais-tu ta l. pour demain?** have you learnt what you were set for tomorrow's lesson?

3 *(cours privé)* lesson; **prendre des leçons de danse/piano** to take dance/piano lessons

4 *(conseil)* advice; **en matière de politesse, il pourrait te donner des leçons** as far as being polite is concerned, he could easily teach you a thing or two; **je n'ai de leçons à recevoir de personne!** I don't need advice from you or anybody else!, nobody's going to tell ME what to do!; **faire la l. à qn** to tell sb what to do

5 *(avertissement)* lesson; **donner une (bonne) l. à qn** to teach sb a lesson; **ça lui donnera une (bonne) l.!, ça lui servira de l.!** that'll teach him/her!; **que ceci vous serve de l.!** let this *or* that be a lesson to you!; *Fig* **recevoir une (bonne) l.** to learn one's lesson; **espérons qu'il retiendra la l.** let's hope he's learnt his lesson

6 *(de manuscrit)* reading

7 *Rel* lesson

Allusion

Cette leçon vaut bien un fromage

This is a line from La Fontaine's famous fable *Le Corbeau et le renard* ("The Fox and the Crow"). A fox wants a piece of cheese that a crow has in his beak. The fox flatters the crow by asking to hear him sing: the crow opens his beak, the cheese drops and the fox grabs it, pronouncing the moral of the story: **Mon bon Monsieur, apprenez que tout flatteur vit aux dépens de celui qui l'écoute; cette leçon vaut bien un fromage sans doute.** ("Let me tell you, dear Sir, that all flatterers live off the people they flatter; undoubtedly, this lesson is well worth a piece of cheese.") People might quote this line from the fable when someone learns a hard lesson.

'La Leçon d'anatomie du Dr Tulp' *Rembrandt* 'The Anatomy Lesson of Dr Nicolaes Tulp'

lecteur, -trice [lɛktœr, -tris] **NM,F 1** *(personne qui lit)* reader; **l. de journaux** newspaper reader;

c'est un grand l. de BD he reads a lot of comics; **nos lecteurs** our readers, our readership
2 (*récitant*) reader
3 (*correcteur*) reader
4 *Scol* foreign language assistant (*at university*); **l. de français** French foreign-language assistant
5 *Typ* proofreader
6 *Rel* lay reader
NM **1** (*de sons, de disques*) player; **l. audio portable** portable music player, portable jukebox; **l. de cassettes** cassette player; **l. de CD** CD player; **l. de disques compacts** *ou* **laser** CD player; **l. de DVD** DVD player; **l. de MiniDiscs®** MiniDisc® player; **l. MP3** MP3 player
2 *Ordinat* reader; (*de disques, de disquettes*) drive; **l. de bandes** tape drive *or* reader; **l. de bande audionumérique** DAT drive; **l. Bernoulli®** Bernoulli® drive; **l. biométrique** biometric reader; **l. de cartes magnétiques** magnetic card reader; **l. de carte à mémoire** smart card reader, card reader; **l. de carte à puce** smart card reader; **l. de cassettes** cassette drive; **l. de CD-ROM** CD-Rom drive; **l. de CD-ROM double vitesse** double-speed CD-ROM drive; **l. de code (à) barres** bar code reader; **l. de courrier** mail reader; **l. DAT** DAT drive; **l. par défaut** default drive; **l. de destination** destination drive; **l. de disque dur** hard disk drive; **l. de disque optique** CD-ROM drive; **l. de disquettes** disk drive; **l. de documents** document reader; **l. Jaz®** Jaz® drive; **l. de microforme** microform reader; **l. OCR** OCR reader; **l. optique** optical reader *or* scanner; **l. optique de caractères** optical character reader; **l. de pages** page scanner; **l. Zip®** Zip® drive

lecteur-encodeur [lɛktœrãkɔdœr] (*pl* **lecteurs-encodeurs**) NM *Ordinat* reader-encoder
lectisterne [lɛktistɛrn] NM *Antiq* lectisternium
lectorat [lɛktɔra] NM **1** *Presse* readership, readers **2** *Scol* foreign language assistantship
lectrice [lɛktris] *voir* **lecteur**
lecture [lɛktyr] NF **1** (*déchiffrage* → *d'un texte, d'une carte*) reading; **la photocopie ne facilite pas la l. du plan** the plan is more difficult to read because it has been photocopied; **la l. d'un message en morse** the reading of a message in Morse; **seule une l. attentive permet de s'en apercevoir** you'll only notice it if you read it carefully; **il est occupé à la l. du scénario** he's busy reading the script; **à la l. de sa lettre, elle a souri** on reading his/her letter, she smiled; **un livre d'une l. agréable** a book that makes pleasant reading; **j'aime la l.** I like reading; *Typ* **l. des épreuves** proofreading; **l. rapide** speed reading
2 (*capacité*) reading; **l'apprentissage de la l.** learning to read; **leçon de l.** reading lesson
3 (*à voix haute*) reading; **une l. publique de qch** a public reading of sth; **donner l. de qch à** to read sth out; **faire la l. à qn** to read to sb
4 (*interprétation*) reading, interpretation; **une l. psychanalytique d'un film** a psychoanalytical interpretation *or* reading of a film; **la l. de Gaulle par Malraux** Malraux's interpretation of de Gaulle
5 (*ce qu'on lit*) reading matter, something to read; **un peu de l., monsieur?** would you like something to read, sir?; **lectures pour la jeunesse** reading *or* books for young people; **à cette époque mes lectures étaient plutôt classiques** at that time I was mostly reading the classics; **il a de mauvaises lectures** he reads things he shouldn't
6 (*de sons, de disques*) reading
7 *Ordinat* read-out; **l. destructive** destructive read-out; **l. sur disque** reading to disk; **l. optique** optical reading, optical character recognition; **l. au scanner** scan; **en l. seule** in read-only mode
8 *Mus* reading; **l. à vue** sight-reading
9 *Pol* reading; **le texte a été adopté en première l.** the bill was passed on its first reading
10 *Rel* reading; **faire une l.** to do a reading
lecture-écriture [lɛktyrekrityr] NF *Ordinat* read-write (mode); **en l.** in read-write mode
lécythe [lesit] NM *Archéol* lecythus
LED [ɛløde] NF*Électron* (*abrév* **light emitting diode**) LED
Léda [leda] NPR*Myth* Leda

lèdge [lɛdʒ] ADJ *Fam* (*excuse*) lame; **deux bouteilles pour quatre, ça va faire un peu l., non?** two bottles for four people, that's going to be cutting it a bit fine, don't you think?
ledit, ladite [lədi, ladit] (*mpl* **lesdits** [ledi], *fpl* **lesdites** [ledit]) ADJ*Jur* the aforementioned, the aforesaid
légal, -e, -aux, -ales [legal, -o] ADJ *Jur* (*disposition, procédure*) legal; (*héritier*) lawful; **est-il l. de vendre des biens sans payer d'impôts?** is it legal to sell goods without paying taxes?; **employer des moyens légaux contre qn** to take legal action against sb; **adresse légale** registered address
légalement [legalmã] ADV legally, lawfully
légalisation [legalizasjɔ̃] NF **1** (*action de légaliser*) legalization **2** (*authentification*) certifying, *Sout* ratification
légaliser [3] [legalize] VT **1** (*rendre légal*) to legalize **2** (*authentifier*) to certify, to authenticate; **une signature légalisée** a certified signature
légalisme [legalism] NM legalism
légaliste [legalist] ADJ legalistic, legalist
NMF legalist
légalité [legalite] NF **1** (*caractère légal*) legality; **l. d'un acte/d'une procédure** legality of an act/a procedure; **l. des poursuites** principle of mandatory prosecution **2** (*actes autorisés par la loi*) **la l.** the law; **rester dans/sortir de la l.** to keep within/to break the law; **agir en toute l.** to act within the law; **il l'a ainsi dépouillé de ses biens en toute l.** he thus stripped him of his possessions quite legally
légat [lega] NM **1** *Antiq* legate **2** *Rel* **l. du Pape** papal legate; **l. a latere** legate a latere
légataire [legatɛr] NMF legatee; **l. universel** sole legatee
légation [legasjɔ̃] NF **1** (*représentation diplomatique*) legation **2** (*résidence*) legation, legate's residence **3** (*charge*) legateship
legato [legato] ADV legato
NM legato
lège [lɛʒ] ADJ **1** *Naut* light **2** = **lèdge**
légendaire [leʒãdɛr] ADJ **1** (*mythique*) legendary; **un passé/héros l.** a legendary past/hero **2** (*connu de tous*) **elle est d'une discrétion l.** she's well known for her discretion
légende [leʒãd] NF **1** (*récit mythique*) legend, tale; **légendes irlandaises** Irish legends *or* folk tales **2** (*renommée*) **la l.** legend; **entrer dans la l.** to become a legend **3** (*commentaire* → *d'un dessin, d'une photo*) caption; (→ *d'une carte*) legend, key **4** (*d'une médaille, d'une monnaie*) legend □ **de légende** ADJ fairytale (*avant n*); **un chevalier de l.** a knight out of a fairy tale; **un mariage de l.** a fairytale wedding
légender [3] [leʒãde] VT (*photo, dessin*) to caption; (*plan, carte*) to provide with a key; **images copieusement légendées** pictures with a wealth of caption material

LÉGER, -ÈRE [leʒe, -ɛr]

light 1–7, 10	■ thin 3	■ moderate 5	■ faint 5
■ slight 5, 6	■ mild 6, 7	■ minor 6	■ weak 7	■ irresponsible 8

ADJ **1** (*de peu de poids*) light; **un gaz plus l. que l'air** a gas that is lighter than air; **construction trop légère** flimsy building; *Fig* **je me sens plus l.** I feel (as though) a great weight's been lifted off my shoulders; **d'un cœur l.** with a light heart; **l. comme une plume** *ou* **bulle** (as) light as a feather
2 (*gracieux* → *danseur*) light, nimble; (→ *démarche*) light, springy
3 (*fin* → *couche*) thin; (→ *brouillard*) light; (→ *robe*) light, flimsy
4 (*mobile* → *artillerie, industrie, matériel*) light; **escadre légère** flotilla
5 (*modéré* → *consommation*) moderate; (→ *bruit, odeur*) faint, slight; (→ *ondée, brise*) light, slight; (→ *maquillage*) light, discreet; **peindre par touches légères** to paint with light strokes; **une légère tristesse/ironie** a hint of sadness/irony; **le beurre a un l. goût de rance** the butter tastes slightly rancid
6 (*sans gravité* → *blessure, perte*) minor; (→ *peine*) light; (→ *responsabilité*) light, undemanding;

(→ *erreur*) slight, minor, unimportant; (→ *douleur, picotement*) slight; (→ *grippe*) mild; **il n'y a eu que des blessés légers** there were only minor injuries
7 (*peu concentré* → *café, thé*) weak; (→ *crème, vin*) light; (→ *tabac*) mild; **un repas l.** a snack, a light meal
8 (*irresponsable* → *personne, conduite*) irresponsible, thoughtless, unthinking; (*insuffisant* → *excuse, justification, raison*) flimsy; **vous avez été un peu l.** it was a bit thoughtless *or* careless of you; **c'est un peu l. comme résultat** there's not much to show for it
9 (*immoral* → *femme, mœurs*) loose; (→ *plaisanterie*) risqué; (→ *ton*) light-hearted
10 *Mus* (*opéra, ténor*) light
ADV **manger l.** to avoid rich food, to eat lightly □ **à la légère** ADV **agir à la légère** to act thoughtlessly *or* rashly; **parler à la légère** to speak unthinkingly *or* thoughtlessly; **prendre qch à la légère** to make light of sth, to treat sth lightly

légèrement [leʒɛrmã] ADV **1** (*un peu*) slightly; **l. blessé/teinté** slightly hurt/tinted; **loucher/boiter l.** to have a slight squint/limp; **brun tirant l. sur le roux** brown with a slight hint of auburn; **il est l. paranoïaque** he's a bit paranoid; **une boisson l. alcoolisée** a slightly alcoholic drink; **un gâteau l. parfumé au citron** a cake with a hint of lemon flavouring
2 (*avec grâce*) nimbly, gracefully
3 (*inconsidérément*) lightly; **on ne peut pas parler du cancer l.** one cannot talk lightly about cancer; **agir l.** to act thoughtlessly *or* without thinking
4 (*frugalement*) **déjeuner/manger l.** to have a light lunch/meal
5 (*avec des vêtements légers*) **être habillé l.** to be wearing light clothes
légèreté [leʒɛrte] NF **1** (*poids*) lightness
2 (*grâce*) lightness, nimbleness; **marcher avec l.** to walk lightly
3 (*finesse* → *de la dentelle, d'une pâtisserie, d'un vin*) lightness; (→ *d'un parfum*) discreetness, subtlety
4 (*désinvolture*) casualness; **il a fait preuve d'une certaine l. dans ses propos** what he said was somewhat irresponsible; **avec l.** casually
5 (*faiblesse* → *d'une mesure*) slightness; (→ *de la brise*) lightness, gentleness; (→ *du tabac*) mildness; (→ *d'un vin*) lightness; (→ *du thé, du café*) weakness; (→ *d'un son, d'une nuance*) faintness
6 (*clémence* → *d'une punition*) lightness
léger-vêtu, -e [leʒevety] (*mpl* **léger-vêtus**, *fpl* **léger-vêtues**) ADJ *Littéraire* lightly clad; **des nymphes léger-vêtues** lightly clad nymphs
leggings [legiŋs] NFPL leggings
leghorn [legɔrn] NF Leghorn
légiférer [18] [leʒifere] VI to legislate
légion [leʒjɔ̃] NF **1** *Mil* **la L. (étrangère)** the (French) Foreign Legion **2** (*décoration*) **la L. d'honneur** the Légion d'Honneur, the Legion of Honour **3** *Antiq* legion **4** (*grand nombre*) **une l. de cousins** an army of cousins; **ses admirateurs sont l.** his/her admirers are legion

légionelle [leʒjonɛl] NF *Biol* Legionella pneumophila

lec-leg

légionellose [leʒjɔnɛloz] NF *Méd* legionnaire's disease

légionnaire [leʒjɔnɛr] NM 1 *(de la Légion étrangère)* legionnaire 2 *Antiq* legionary
NMF *(membre de la Légion d'honneur)* member of the Légion d'honneur

législateur, -trice [leʒislatœr, -tris] ADJ law-making
NM,F lawmaker, legislator
NM **le l.** the legislature

législatif, -ive [leʒislatif, -iv] ADJ 1 *(qui fait les lois)* legislative; **les instances législatives** legislative bodies; **des réformes législatives** legislative reforms 2 *(de l'Assemblée) Br* ≃ parliamentary, *Am* ≃ Congressional
NM **le l.** the legislature
▫ **législatives** NFPL *Br* ≃ general election, *Am* ≃ Congressional election

législation [leʒislasjɔ̃] NF legislation; **la l. en vigueur** current legislation; **l. antitrust** *Br* anti-monopoly *or Am* antitrust legislation; **l. bancaire** banking legislation; **l. douanière** customs legislation; **l. européenne** EU legislation; **l. fiscale** tax laws; **la l. française/anglaise** French/English legislation *or* laws; **la l. viticole** the laws surrounding the wine trade; **l. du travail** labour laws

législative [leʒislativ] *voir* **législatif**

législativement [leʒislativmɑ̃] ADV legislatively

législatives [leʒislativ] *voir* **législatif**

législatrice [leʒislatris] *voir* **législateur**

législature [leʒislatyr] NF 1 *(durée du mandat)* term (of office); **les crises qui ont agité la précédente l.** the crises in the previous administration 2 *(corps)* legislature, legislative body

légiste [leʒist] ADJ *voir* **médecin**
NMF legist

légitimation [leʒitimasjɔ̃] NF 1 *Jur (d'un enfant)* legitimization 2 *(reconnaissance)* recognition; *(justification)* justification

légitime [leʒitim] ADJ 1 *(légal → gén)* lawful, legal; *(→ mariage)* lawful; *(→ enfant)* legitimate; **le gouvernement l. de la France** the lawful government of France
2 *(justifié → revendication)* legitimate; **son refus l. d'obéir** his/her rightful refusal to obey; **une colère l.** a justifiable *or* justified anger; **il est tout à fait l. de se plaindre** he is/they are/*etc* quite justified in complaining
NF *très Fam (épouse)* missus; **ma l.** the missus, my old lady
▫ **légitime défense** NF self-defence; **il était en état de l. défense** he was acting in self-defence

légitimé, -e [leʒitime] *Jur* ADJ *(enfant)* legitimized
NM,F legitimized child

légitimement [leʒitimmɑ̃] ADV 1 *(justement)* legitimately, justifiably; **vous auriez l. pu vous plaindre** you would have been justified in complaining; **on peut l. penser que...** we have good reason *or* good cause to believe that... 2 *Jur* legitimately, lawfully

légitimer [3] [leʒitime] VT 1 *Jur (enfant)* to legitimate; *(accord, union, titre)* to (make) legitimate, to legitimize, to legitimatize 2 *(justifier)* to justify, to legitimate; **n'essaie pas de l. son comportement** don't try to find excuses for *or* to justify his/her behaviour; **on ne peut pas l. la prise du pouvoir par la force** taking power by force is indefensible

légitimisme [leʒitimism] NM legitimism

légitimiste [leʒitimist] ADJ legitimist
NMF legitimist

légitimité [leʒitimite] NF 1 *Jur & Pol* legitimacy 2 *(bien-fondé)* rightfulness; **tu ne peux nier la l. de ses réclamations** you cannot say that his/her complaints aren't justified *or* well-founded

Lego® [lego] NM (set of) Lego®

Le Greco [ləgreko] NPR El Greco

legs [lɛg] NM 1 *Jur* legacy, bequest; **faire/recevoir un l.** to leave/receive a legacy; **faire un l. à qn** to leave a legacy to sb, to leave sb a legacy; **l. rémunératoire** legacy in consideration of service rendered; **l. à titre particulier** specific bequest *or* legacy; **l. à titre universel** residuary bequest *or* legacy, residue of one's estate; **l. universel** general legacy 2 *(héritage)* legacy, heritage

léguer [18] [lege] VT 1 *Jur* to bequeath, to leave; **l. qch à qn** to bequeath *or* to leave sth to sb; **son père lui a légué une énorme fortune** his/her father bequeathed *or* left him/her a huge fortune 2 *Fig* to hand down, to pass on; **il lui a légué son goût pour la musique** he passed on his love of music to him/her

légume [legym] NM 1 *Bot & Culin* vegetable; **tu ne manges pas assez de légumes** you don't eat enough vegetables; **soupe de légumes** vegetable soup; **légumes secs** dried vegetables; **légumes verts** green vegetables 2 *Fam (personne)* vegetable
NF *Fam* **grosse l.** bigwig, big shot

légumier, -ère [legymje, -ɛr] ADJ vegetable *(avant n)*
NM,F 1 vegetable grower 2 *Belg (commerçant)* greengrocer
NM *(plat)* vegetable dish

légumine [legymin] NF *Chim* legumin

légumineuse [legyminøz] NF *Bot* leguminous plant, legume, *Spéc* member of the Leguminosae
ADJ F leguminous
▫ **légumineuses** NFPL leguminous plants, legumes, *Spéc* Leguminosae

legustrum [legystrɔm] = **ligustrum**

lei [lɛ] *voir* **leu**

leibnizien, -enne [lɛbnitsjɛ̃, -ɛn] ADJ Leibnizian

Leinster [lɛnstɛr] NM **le L.** Leinster

léiomyome [lejɔmjom] NM *Méd* leiomyoma

léipoa [leipoa] NM *Orn* leipoa

Leipzig [lɛpsig] NM Leipzig

leishmanie [lɛʃmani] NF *Biol* leishmania

leishmaniose [lɛʃmanjoz] NF *Méd* leishmaniasis, leishmaniosis

leitmotiv [lajtmɔtif, lɛtmɔtiv] *(pl* **leitmotivs** *ou* **leitmotive)** NM 1 *Littérature & Mus* leitmotiv, leitmotif 2 *Fig* hobbyhorse; **elle dit qu'elle n'aime pas la capitale, c'est son l.** she's always harping on about not liking the capital

lek [lɛk] NM 1 *(monnaie)* lek 2 *Orn* lek

lem [lɛm] NM *Astron* lunar excursion module, LEM

Léman [lemɑ̃] NM **le lac L.** Lake Geneva

lémanique [lemanik] ADJ of/from Lake Geneva

lemme [lɛm] NM *Math & Phil* lemma

lemming [lɛmiŋ] NM *Zool* lemming

lemnacée [lɛmnase] *Bot* NF member of the Lemnaceae family
▫ **lemnacées** NFPL Lemnaceae

lemniscate [lɛmniskat] NF *Géom* lemniscate

lempira [lɛmpira] NM *(monnaie)* lempira

lémur [lemyr] NM *Zool* lemur; **l. catta** ring-tailed lemur

lémure [lemyr] NM *Antiq* lemur

lémurien [lemyrjɛ̃] NM *Zool* lemurine

lendemain [lɑ̃dmɛ̃] NM 1 *(le jour suivant)* **le l.** the next *or* the following day, the day after; **le l. matin** the next *or* the following morning; **le l. de son anniversaire** the day after his/her birthday; **le l. de son arrestation** the day after he/she was arrested; **les lendemains de fête sont souvent difficiles** it's often hard to get through the morning after the night before; *Prov* **il ne faut pas remettre au l. ce qu'on peut faire le jour même** never put off till tomorrow what you can do today
2 *(futur)* **le l.** tomorrow, the future; **il dépense son argent sans penser au l.** he spends his money without thinking of the future
▫ **lendemains** NMPL 1 *(avenir)* future; **son arrivée au pouvoir annonçait de sombres lendemains** his/her coming to power heralded a dark future *or* dark days to come; **délinquant à onze ans, ça nous promet de beaux lendemains!** eleven years old and already a delinquent, he's got a bright future ahead of him!; **des lendemains difficiles** a bleak future; **des lendemains qui chantent** a brighter future
2 *(conséquences)* consequences; **avoir d'heureux lendemains** to have happy consequences
▫ **au lendemain de** PRÉP **au l. de la Révolution** immediately *or* just after the Revolution; **au l. de son élection** in the days (immediately) following his/her election
▫ **sans lendemain** ADJ short-lived

lendit [lɑ̃di] NM *Hist* = medieval fair held in Saint-Denis

lénifiant, -e [lenifjɑ̃, -ɑ̃t] ADJ 1 *Méd* calming 2 *Fig (images, paroles)* soothing, lulling, *Sout* assuaging

lénifier [9] [lenifje] VT 1 *Méd* to calm 2 *Fig (calmer)* to soothe, to lull, *Sout* to assuage

Lénine [lenin] NPR Lenin

Leningrad [leningrad] NM Leningrad

léninisme [leninism] NM Leninism

léniniste [leninist] ADJ Leninist
NMF Leninist

lénitif, -ive [lenitif, -iv] ADJ 1 *Méd* calming 2 *Fig Littéraire* soothing

lent, -e[1] [lɑ̃, lɑ̃t] ADJ 1 *(pas rapide → mouvement, film)* slow; *(→ circulation)* slow, sluggish; *(→ animal)* slow-moving; **à combustion lente** slow-burning; **il a une digestion lente** it takes him a long time to digest his food; **avoir l'esprit l.** to be slow-witted; **la justice est tellement lente!** the legal system is so slow!; **il est l. à comprendre** he's slow on the uptake; **la fin est lente à venir** the end is a long time coming; *Can* **l. comme la mort** painfully slow
2 *(progressif → agonie)* lingering; *(→ effritement, évolution)* slow, gradual; *(→ poison)* slow-acting

lente[2] [lɑ̃t] NF *Entom* nit

lentement [lɑ̃tmɑ̃] ADV slowly; **marcher l.** to walk slowly *or* at a slow pace; **il travaille l.** he's a slow worker; **l. mais sûrement** slowly but surely

lenteur [lɑ̃tœr] NF slowness; **avec l.** slowly; **d'une l. désespérante** appallingly slow; **l. d'esprit** slowness; **tu es d'une l.!** you're so slow!; **devant la l. avec laquelle elle a réagi** faced with her slowness in reacting *or* her sluggish reaction; **lenteurs administratives** administrative delays; **les lenteurs de la justice** the slowness of the courts, the slow course of justice

lenticelle [lɑ̃tisɛl] NF *Bot* lenticel

lenticulaire [lɑ̃tikylɛr] ADJ lenticular

lenticule [lɑ̃tikyl] NF *Bot* duckweed

lenticulé, -e [lɑ̃tikyle] = **lenticulaire**

lentigine [lɑ̃tiʒin] NF freckle, *Spéc* lentigo

lentigo [lɑ̃tigo] NM freckle, *Spéc* lentigo

lentille [lɑ̃tij] NF 1 *Bot & Culin* lentil; **l. d'eau** duckweed *(UNCOUNT)* 2 *Opt & Phys* lens; **lentilles cornéennes** *ou* **de contact** contact lenses; **lentilles souples** soft (contact) lenses; *Can Phot* **l. télescopique** telescopic lens

lentillon [lɑ̃tijɔ̃] NM *Bot* (variety of) small red lentil

lentisque [lɑ̃tisk] NM *Bot* lentisk

lentivirus [lɑ̃tivirys] NM *Biol* lentivirus

lento [lɛnto] *Mus* ADV lento
NM lento

léonard, -e [leonar, -ard] ADJ of/from the Léon area of Brittany
NM,F = inhabitant of or person from the Léon area of Brittany

Léonard de Vinci [leɔnardəvɛ̃si] NPR Leonardo da Vinci

léonin, -e [leɔnɛ̃, -in] ADJ 1 *Jur (commission, partage)* unfair, one-sided; *(contrat)* leonine 2 *(de lion)* leonine 3 *(vers)* Leonine

léonure [leɔnyr] NM *Bot* leonurus, motherwort

léopard [leɔpar] NM 1 *Zool* leopard; **l. de mer** leopard seal; **l. des neiges** snow leopard, ounce 2 *(fourrure)* leopard skin; **veste en l.** leopard-skin jacket 3 *(en apposition)* leopard-skin *(avant n)*; *Mil* **tenue l.** camouflage battle dress 4 *Hér* lion passant guardant

léopardé, -e [leɔparde] ADJ *Hér* **lion l.** lion passant, leopard

Léopold [leɔpɔld] NPR *(empereur)* Leopold

LEP, Lep [lɛp] NM 1 *Anciennement (abrév* **lycée d'enseignement professionnel**) = former name for a "lycée professionnel" 2 *Banque (abrév* **livret d'épargne populaire**) = special tax-exempt savings account 3 *(abrév* **Large Electron-Positron collider**) LEP

lepeniste [ləpenist] NMF *Pol* = supporter of Jean-Marie Le Pen

lépidodendron [lepidɔdɛ̃drɔ̃] NM lepidodendron

lépidolite, lépidolithe [lepidɔlit] NM *Minér* lepidolite

lépidoptère [lepidɔptɛr] *Entom* ADJ lepidopteran, lepidopterous
NM lepidopteran, *Spéc* member of the Lepidoptera order
▫ **lépidoptères** NMPL Lepidoptera

lépidoptériste [lepidɔpterist] NMF *Entom* lepidopterist

lépidosirène [lepidɔsirɛn] NM *Ich* lepidosiren

lépidostée [lepidɔste] NM *Ich* gar (pike)
lépiote [lepjɔt] NF *Bot* parasol mushroom
lépisme [lepism] NM *Entom* silverfish, lepisma
lépisostée [lepizɔste] NM *Ich* gar (pike)
léporidé [lepɔride] *Zool* NM leporid, *Spéc* member of the Leporidae
❑ **léporidés** NMPL Leporidae
lèpre [lɛpr] NF **1** *Méd* leprosy **2** *Littéraire (moisissure)* **mur rongé par la l.** wall eaten away by damp **3** *Fig (fléau)* blight, scourge; **la drogue, l. de notre époque** drugs, the scourge of our age
lépreux, -euse [leprø, -øz] ADJ **1** *Méd* leprous **2** *Littéraire (mur)* flaking, peeling; **des baraquements l.** crumbling shacks
NM,F *Méd* leper; **traiter qn comme un l.** to ostracize sb, *Br* to send sb to Coventry
léprologie [leprɔlɔʒi] NF leprosy research, leprology
lépromateux, -euse [leprɔmatø, -øz] ADJ *Méd* lepromatous
léprome [leprom] NM *Méd* leproma
léproserie [leprozri] NF leper hospital, leprosarium
lepte [lɛpt] NM *Zool* leptus
leptine [lɛptin] NF *Biol* leptin
leptocéphale [lɛptɔsefal] NM *Ich* leptocephalus
lepton [lɛptɔ̃] NM *Phys* lepton
leptonique [lɛptɔnik] ADJ leptonic
leptosome [lɛptɔzɔm] ADJ leptosomic, leptosomatic
NM leptosome
leptospire [lɛptɔspir] NM *Biol* leptospira
leptospirose [lɛptɔspiroz] NF *Méd* leptospirosis
leptotène [lɛptɔtɛn] NM *Biol* leptotene
lepture [lɛptyr] NM *Entom* leptura

LEQUEL, LAQUELLE [ləkɛl, lakɛl], *(mpl* **lesquels** [lekɛl], *fpl* **lesquelles** [lekɛl])

> **lequel** and **lesquel(le)s** contract with **à** to form **auquel** and **auxquel(le)s**, and with **de** to form **duquel** and **desquel(le)s**.

PRON RELATIF **1** *(sujet → personne)* who; *(→ chose)* which; **il était avec sa sœur, laquelle m'a reconnu** he was with his sister, who recognized me; **elle habitait une ferme, laquelle n'existe plus** she lived in a farmhouse which is no longer there

2 *(complément → personne)* whom; *(→ chose)* which; **un ami auprès duquel trouver un réconfort** a friend (who) one can find comfort with, a friend with whom one can find comfort; **un ami avec l. il sort souvent** a friend with whom he often goes out, a friend (who) he often goes out with; **la dame chez laquelle je l'ai rencontré** the lady at whose house I met him; **l'ami sans l. il n'aurait pas réussi** the friend without whom he wouldn't have succeeded; **une réaction à laquelle je ne m'attendais pas** a reaction (which *or* that) I wasn't expecting; **la maison dans laquelle j'ai grandi** the house where *or* in which I grew up, the house (that) I grew up in; **le moyen par l. il compte réussir** the means by which he intends to succeed; **il y avait là beaucoup de jeunes gens, parmi lesquels...** there were a lot of young people there, amongst whom...; **c'est une personne dans laquelle je n'ai aucune confiance** he/she is someone (who) I have no confidence in, he/she is someone in whom I have no confidence; **les gens au nom desquels je parle** the people on whose behalf I am speaking; **un dispositif au moyen duquel on peut...** a device whereby *or* by means of which it is possible to...; **l'homme sans l'avis duquel on ne peut rien faire** the man without whose advice one can do nothing; **le livre à la rédaction duquel il se consacre** the book that he is writing

ADJ RELATIF **il avait contacté un deuxième avocat, l. avocat avait également refusé de le défendre** he contacted another lawyer who also refused to defend him; **auquel cas** in which case; **il se pourrait que j'échoue, auquel cas je repasserai l'examen l'année prochaine** I might possibly fail, in which case I'll resit the exam next year

PRON INTERROGATIF which (one); **l. est-ce?** which (one) is it?; **l. d'entre vous a gagné?** which (one) of you won?; **l. de ces chapeaux préférez-vous?** which (one) of these hats do you prefer?; **laquelle veux-tu?** which (one) would you like?; **laquelle est ta valise?** which is your suitcase?, which suitcase is yours?; **difficile de dire laquelle me plaît le plus** difficult to say which (one) I like best; **j'ai rencontré un de ses collaborateurs, je ne sais plus l.** I met one of his/her colleagues, I can't remember which (one); **de laquelle de ces deux régions êtes-vous originaire?** which (one) of these two regions do you come from?

---

lerche [lɛrʃ] ADV *Fam* **il y en a pas l.** there isn't much/aren't many■
Lermontov [lɛrmɔntɔf] NPR Lermontov
lérot [lero] NM *Zool* garden dormouse
les [le] *voir* **le**[1]
lès [lɛ] = **lez**
lesbianisme [lɛsbjanism] NM lesbianism
lesbien, -enne [lɛsbjɛ̃, -ɛn] ADJ lesbian
❑ **lesbienne** NF lesbian
lesdites [ledit], **lesdits** [ledi] *voir* **ledit**
lésé, -e [leze] *Jur* ADJ injured, wronged
NM,F injured party
lèse-majesté [lɛzmaʒɛste] NF INV lese-majesty, lèse-majesté
léser [18] [leze] VT **1** *(désavantager → personne)* to wrong; **l. les intérêts de qn** to harm sb's interests; **elle s'estime lésée par rapport aux autres** she feels badly done by *or* unfavourably treated compared with the others **2** *Jur* **l. les droits de qn** to encroach *or* to infringe upon sb's rights; **partie lésée** injured party **3** *Méd* to injure
lésine [lezin] NF *Littéraire* miserliness, stinginess
lésiner [3] [lezine] **lésiner sur** VT IND to skimp on; **ils lésinent sur tout** they're stingy with everything; **ne pas l. sur** to be generous with; **tu n'as pas lésiné sur le sel!** you got a bit carried away with *or* you were a bit too generous with the salt!; **il n'a pas lésiné sur les critiques!** he didn't spare his criticism!
lésinerie [lezinri] NF *Littéraire* miserliness, stinginess
lésineur, -euse [lezinœr, -øz] *Vieilli* ADJ miserly, niggardly
NM,F miser, niggard
lésion [lezjɔ̃] NF **1** *Méd* injury, *Spéc* lesion; **à appliquer sur les lésions tous les soirs** *(sur la notice d'une pommade ou d'une lotion)* apply to the affected area every evening; **l. par écrasement/souffle** crush/blast injury **2** *Jur* wrong
lésionnaire [lezjɔnɛr] ADJ *Jur* prejudicial, detrimental
lésionnel, -elle [lezjɔnɛl] ADJ *Méd (résultant d'une lésion)* due to a lesion; *(causant lésion)* lesion-causing
Lesotho [lezɔto] NM **le L.** Lesotho; **vivre au L.** to live in Lesotho; **aller au L.** to go to Lesotho
lesquelles [lekɛl], **lesquels** [lekɛl] *voir* **lequel**
lessivable [lɛsivabl] ADJ washable
lessivage [lɛsivaʒ] NM **1** *(d'un mur, d'un plancher)* scrubbing, washing; *(du linge)* washing; *Fig* **c'est le grand l. dans la société** there's a big clear-out (of personnel) going on in the company **2** *Géol* leaching
lessive [lɛsiv] NF **1** *(poudre)* detergent, washing *or* soap powder; *(liquide)* (liquid) detergent
2 *(linge)* washing *(UNCOUNT)*, laundry *(UNCOUNT)*; *(contenu d'une machine)* (washing-machine) load; **étendre la l.** to hang out the washing; **je t'ai apporté ma l.** I've brought you my washing *or* my laundry; **et mon jean? – ce sera pour la prochaine l.** what about my jeans? – they'll go in with the next wash *or* load
3 *(lavage)* wash; **faire la l.** to do the washing *or* the laundry; **faites deux lessives séparées pour la laine et le coton** wash wool and cotton separately; **j'ai fait trois lessives ce matin** I've done three washes this morning
4 *Fam (épuration)* clean-up (operation)
5 *Chim* lye
lessiver [3] [lɛsive] VT **1** *(laver → vêtement, tissu)* to wash; *(→ mur)* to wash down **2** *Fam (épuiser)* to wear out; **je suis lessivé** I'm washed out *or* all in **3** *Fam (ruiner)* to clean out **4** *très Fam (éliminer)* **se faire l.** to get knocked out **5** *Chim & Géol* to leach (out)
lessiveuse [lɛsivøz] NF **1** *Anciennement* boiler *(for clothes)* **2** *Belg (machine à laver)* washing machine
lessiviel, -elle [lɛsivjɛl] ADJ detergent *(avant n)*, *Spéc* detersive
lessivier [lɛsivje] NM detergent manufacturer
lest [lɛst] NM *Aviat & Naut* ballast; **navire sur l.** ship in ballast; **jeter** *ou* **lâcher du l.** to dump ballast; *Fig* **lâcher du l.** to make concessions, to yield some ground
lestage [lɛstaʒ] NM *Aviat & Naut* ballasting
leste [lɛst] ADJ **1** *(souple et vif → personne)* nimble; *(→ animal)* agile, nimble; *(→ mouvement)* brisk, nimble; **il est encore l. malgré son âge** he's still sprightly for his age **2** *(désinvolte → ton)* offhand, disrespectful **3** *(libre → plaisanterie, propos)* risqué, crude
lestement [lɛstəmɑ̃] ADV **1** *(avec souplesse)* nimbly **2** *(avec désinvolture)* offhandedly, casually **3** *(hardiment)* **il plaisantait un peu l.** he was making rather risqué jokes
lester [3] [lɛste] VT **1** *Aviat & Naut* to ballast **2** *Fam (charger)* **l. qch de** to fill *or* to cram sth with; **les poches lestées de bonbons** pockets filled *or* crammed with sweets
▸**se lester** VPR *Fam* **se l. (l'estomac)** to stuff oneself
let [lɛt] ADJ INV *Sport* let; **balle l.** let (ball)
létal, -e, -aux, -ales [letal, -o] ADJ *Méd* lethal
létalité [letalite] NF *Méd* lethality
letchi [lɛtʃi] NM lychee, litchi
léthargie [letarʒi] NF **1** *Méd* lethargy; **tomber en l.** to fall into a lethargic state, to become lethargic **2** *Fig (mollesse → physique)* lethargy; **tirer qn de sa l.** to shake sb out of his/her lethargy
léthargique [letarʒik] ADJ *Méd & Fig* lethargic
lette [lɛt] NM *(langue)* Latvian, Lettish
letton, -e *ou* **-onne** [lɛtɔ̃, -ɔn] ADJ Latvian
NM *(langue)* Latvian, Lettish
❑ **Letton, -e** *ou* **-onne** NM,F Latvian, Lett
Lettonie [lɛtɔni] NF **la L.** Latvia; **vivre en L.** to live in Latvia; **aller en L.** to go to Latvia
Lettonne, lettonne [lɛtɔn] *voir* **letton**
lettrage [lɛtraʒ] NM *Typ* lettering
lettre [lɛtr] NF **A.** *CARACTÈRE* **1** *(d'un alphabet)* letter; **un mot de neuf lettres** a nine-letter word; **l. majuscule** capital (letter); **l. minuscule** small letter; **écrit en lettres de feu** written in letters of fire; **leur abnégation est gravée en lettres d'or dans nos cœurs** their self-sacrifice is engraved indelibly in our hearts; **cette page d'histoire est imprimée en lettres de sang dans notre mémoire** this page of history has left a bloody impression in our memory
2 *Typ (forme en plomb)* character, letter; **l. ornée** initial
B. *ÉCRIT* **1** *(correspondance)* letter; **suite à votre l. du...** further to your letter of...; **je lui ai envoyé une petite l. pour son anniversaire** I sent him/her a note for his/her birthday; **pas de lettres pour moi?** no mail *or* no letters for me?; **mettre une l. à la poste** to post a letter; *Fam* **passer comme une l. à la poste** *(boisson, aliment)* to go down a treat; *(demande, mesure)* to go off without a hitch, to go off smoothly; **la nouvelle est passée comme une l. à la poste** the news was received without any fuss; **l. d'accompagnement** covering letter; *Bourse* **l. d'allocation** letter of allotment; **l. d'amour** love letter; **l. anonyme** anonymous letter; **l. d'avis** advice note, letter of advice; **l. de château** thank-you letter; **l. commerciale** business letter; **l. de démission** resignation letter; **l. d'embauche** written offer of employment; **apportez une l. d'excuse de vos parents** bring a note from your parents; **l. exprès** express letter; **l. d'injures** abusive letter; **l. d'intention** letter of intent; **l. d'introduction** letter of introduction; **l. de licenciement** letter of dismissal; **l. de menace** threatening letter; *Belg* **l. de mort** announcement of death; **l. de motivation** covering letter *(sent with job application)*; **l. de rappel** reminder; **l. de réclamation** letter of complaint; **l. de recommandation** letter of recommendation, reference; **l. recommandée** *Br* recorded delivery letter, *Am* letter sent by certified mail; *(avec objets de valeur)* registered letter; **l. recommandée avec accusé de réception** = recorded delivery letter with confirmation of receipt; *(avec objets de valeur)* =

registered letter with confirmation of receipt; **l. de référence** letter of reference; **l. de relance** follow-up letter; **l. de remerciements** letter of thanks, thank-you letter; **elle m'a écrit une l. de rupture** she wrote to tell me she was leaving me; **l. type** *(pour mailing)* form letter; **l. de vente** sales letter

2 *Banque & Fin* **l. accréditive** letter of credit; **l. d'aval** letter of guaranty; **l. de change** bill of exchange; **l. de change à l'extérieur** foreign bill; **l. de change relevé** bills of exchange statement; **l. de créance** letter of credit; **l. de crédit** letter of credit; **l. de crédit circulaire** circular letter of credit; **l. de crédit documentaire** documentary letter of credit; **l. de crédit irrévocable** irrevocable letter of credit; **l. de gage** debenture bond; *(pour hypothèque)* mortgage bond; **l. de garantie** letter of guarantee; **l. de garantie bancaire** bank guarantee; **l. de garantie d'indemnité** letter of indemnity; **l. de nantissement** letter of hypothecation; **l. de relance des impayés** debt-chasing letter; *Bourse* **l. de souscription** letter of application

3 *Jur* **l. d'intention** letter of intent; **l. missive** missive; **l. de provision** exequatur; **l. de voiture** waybill, consignment note

4 *Hist* **l. de cachet** letter of cachet, = order under the King's private seal; **lettres de noblesse** letters patent (of nobility); *Fig* **conquérir** *ou* **recevoir ses lettres de noblesse** to gain respectability; **lettres patentes** letters patent

5 *Pol* **lettres de créance** credentials; **lettres réversales** letters of mutual concessions

6 *Presse* **l. ouverte (à)** open letter (to)

C. *SENS STRICT* letter; **respecter la l. de la loi** to respect *or* to observe the letter of the law; **rester l. morte** to go unheeded, to be disregarded; **le cessez-le-feu est devenu l. morte** the ceasefire is no longer being observed

❑ **lettres** NFPL **1** *Scol* **les lettres** the arts, the humanities; **étudiant en lettres** arts student; **faculté de lettres** faculty of arts *or* humanities; **lettres classiques** classics, Latin and Greek; **lettres modernes** modern literature; **lettres supérieures** = preparatory class leading to the "École normale supérieure" and lasting two years

2 *Littérature* **les lettres** literature; **le monde des lettres** the literary world; **avoir des lettres** to be well-read; **un homme/une femme de lettres** a man/a woman of letters

❑ **à la lettre, au pied de la lettre** ADV *(suivre)* to the letter; **suivez l'ordonnance du médecin à la l.** follow the doctor's prescription to the letter; **ne prends pas ce qu'il dit au pied de la l.** don't take what he says at face value

❑ **avant la lettre** ADV **c'était un surréaliste avant la l.** he was a surrealist before the term was ever invented

❑ **en toutes lettres** ADV **1** *(entièrement)* in full; **écrire qch en toutes lettres** to write sth (out) in full; **écrivez la somme en toutes lettres** write the amount in words

2 *(très clairement)* clearly, plainly; **c'est écrit en toutes lettres dans le contrat** it's written in black and white *or* it's spelt out plainly in the contract

'Lettres de mon moulin' *Daudet* 'Letters from My Mill'

'Lettres persanes' *Montesquieu* 'Persian Letters'

'Lettre sur les aveugles' *Diderot* 'Letter on the Blind'

lettré, -e [lɛtre] ADJ **1** *(cultivé)* well-read **2** *Belg* *(sachant lire et écrire)* **il est l.** he can read and write

NM,F **1 c'est un fin l.** he's extremely well-read *or* scholarly **2** *Belg (personne sachant lire et écrire)* = person who can read and write

lettre-transfert [lɛtrətrɑ̃sfɛr] *(pl* **lettres-transferts***)* NF Letraset® (letter)

lettrine [lɛtrin] NF **1** *Ordinat & Typ* drop cap **2** *(d'un dictionnaire)* running initial

lettrisme [lɛtrism] NM *Littérature* lettrism

leu [lø] *(pl* **lei** [lɛ]*)* NM *(monnaie)* leu; **15 lei** 15 lei

leucanie [løkani] NF *Entom* leucania, army-worm moth

leucémie [løsemi] NF *Méd* leukaemia; **l. myéloblastique** myeloblastic leukaemia

leucémique [løsemik] *Méd* ADJ leukaemic

NMF leukaemia sufferer

leucine [løsin] NF *Biol & Chim* leucine, leucin

leucistique [løsistik] ADJ *Zool* leucistic

leucite [løsit] NF *Minér* leucite

leucoblaste [løkɔblast] NM *Biol* leucoblast

leucobryum [løkɔbrijɔm] NM *Bot* cushion moss, white moss, *Spéc* Leucobryum

leucocytaire [løkɔsitɛr] ADJ *Biol* leucocytic

leucocyte [løkɔsit] NM *Biol* leucocyte

leucocytose [løkɔsitoz] NF *Méd* leucocytosis

leucoderme [løkɔdɛrm] *Méd* ADJ leucodermal, leucodermic

NMF person with leucodermia

leucodermie [løkɔdɛrmi] NF *Méd* leucodermia

leuco-encéphalite [løkɔɑ̃sefalit] *(pl* **leuco-encéphalites***)* NF *Méd* leucoencephalitis

leucome [løkom] NM *Méd* leucoma, albugo

leucopénie [løkɔpeni] NF *Méd* leucopenia

leucophlegmasie [løkɔflɛgmazi] NF *Méd* white-leg

leucoplasie [løkɔplazi] NF *Méd* leucoplakia, leucoplasia

leucopoïèse [løkɔpɔjɛz] NF *Méd* leucopoiesis, leucocytopoiesis

leucorrhée [løkɔre] NF *Méd* leucorrhoea

leucose [løkoz] NF *Méd* leucosis

leucotomie [løkɔtɔmi] NF *Méd* leucotomy, lobotomy

leude [lød] NM *Hist* leud, feudatory, feudal vassal

leur [lœr] PRON to them; **je voudrais l. parler avant qu'ils ne partent** I'd like to speak to them before they leave; **je l. ai donné la lettre** I gave them the letter, I gave the letter to them; **je l. ai serré la main** I shook their hands; **il l. a jeté une pierre** he threw a stone at them; **je la l. ai montrée** I showed it to them, I showed them it; **donnez-le-l.** give it to them, give them it; **ça ne l. rapporte rien** they aren't getting anything out of it; **il l. est difficile de venir** it's difficult for them to come

ADJ POSSESSIF their; **c'est l. tour** it's their turn; **l. oncle et l. tante** their uncle and aunt; **ce sont leurs enfants** these are their children; **une de leurs amies** a friend of theirs, one of their friends; **ils ont eu l. vendredi** they got Friday off; **avec cette aisance qui a toujours été l.** with that characteristic ease of theirs; **ils ont fait l. la langue anglaise** they made the English language their own

❑ **le leur, la leur, les leurs** PRON theirs; **c'est notre problème, pas le l.** it's our problem, not theirs; **nos enfants et les leurs** our children and theirs; **ils ont pris une valise qui n'était pas la l.** they took a suitcase that wasn't theirs *or* their own; **ils n'en ont pas besoin, ils ont le l.** they don't need it, they've got their own; **les leurs** *(leur famille)* their family; **être (un) des leurs** to belong to their group, to be one of them; **je ne me suis jamais senti l'un des leurs** I never felt that I was one of them; **serez-vous aussi des leurs dimanche?** will you be there on Sunday too?; **ils ont été aidés, mais ils y ont mis beaucoup du l.** they were helped, but they put a lot of effort into it (themselves)

leurre [lœr] NM **1** *(illusion)* delusion, illusion; **ce serait un l. d'espérer qu'il réponde à votre demande** you would be deceiving yourself if you thought that he might comply with your demands **2** *(tromperie)* deception; **son grand projet n'est qu'un l.** his/her great plan is just a trick **3** *Mil* decoy; **l. thermique** heat decoy **4** *Chasse* decoy, lure; *(en fauconnerie)* lure **5** *Pêche* lure; *(vivant)* bait

leurrer [5] [lœre] VT **1** *(tromper)* to deceive, to delude; **ne te laisse pas l. par ses beaux discours** do not be deceived *or* taken in by his/her fine words; **il se laisse facilement l.** he is easily taken in

2 *(en fauconnerie)* to lure

▸**se leurrer** VPR *(se laisser abuser)* to delude oneself (**sur** about); **ne te leurre pas, elle ne t'aime plus** don't delude yourself, she doesn't love you any more; **il ne faut pas se l., on va perdre** let's not fool ourselves, we're going to lose

lev [lev] *(pl* **leva** [leva]*)* NM *(monnaie)* lev

levage [ləvaʒ] NM **1** *Tech* lifting; **appareil de l.** lifting tackle *(UNCOUNT) or* appliance **2** *Culin* raising, rising; **après le deuxième l.** *(du pain)* after the dough has risen a second time

levain [ləvɛ̃] NM **1** *Culin (substance, pâte)* leaven, leavening; **pain au/sans l.** leavened/unleavened bread **2** *Fig Littéraire* **le l. de la révolte** the seeds of revolt

Levant [ləvɑ̃] NM **le L.** the Levant

levant [ləvɑ̃] ADJ *voir* **soleil**

NM **le l.** the east; **baie exposée au l.** east-facing bay; **du l. au couchant** from east to west

levantin, -e [ləvɑ̃tɛ̃, -in] ADJ Levantine

❑ **Levantin, -e** NM,F Levantine

levé, -e[1] [ləve] ADJ *Belg Fam* **bien/mal l.** in a good/bad mood

NM survey; **faire le l. d'un champ** to survey a field

levée[2] [ləve] NF **1** *(ramassage → du courrier, des impôts)* collection; **il y a deux levées par jour** the *Br* post *or Am* mail is collected twice a day, there are two collections a day; **la l. est faite** the post has been collected *or* has gone

2 *(cessation → de sanctions)* lifting; *(→ d'une séance)* adjournment; **il a demandé la l. des sanctions/de l'embargo** he asked for the sanctions/the embargo to be lifted; **demander la l. de la séance** to ask for an adjournment; **cela nécessiterait la l. de son immunité parlementaire** this would involve withdrawing his/her parliamentary immunity

3 *Jur* **l. d'écrou** release (from prison); **l. de jugement** transcript (of the verdict); **l. des scellés** removal of the seals

4 *Cartes* trick; **son roi de pique fait la l.** his/her king of spades takes *or* wins the trick

5 *Géol* levee

6 *Constr* **l. de terre** levee

7 *Mil (de troupes)* levying; *(d'un siège)* raising; **l. en masse** levy en masse; *Fig* **l. de boucliers** outcry, uproar; **ça a provoqué une l. de boucliers chez les féministes** it provoked an outcry from feminists

8 *Fin* **l. d'option/d'actions** taking up of the option/stock; *Banque* **levées de compte** personal withdrawals

9 *(cérémonie)* **la l. du corps** taking the body from the house *(for the funeral)*; **la l. du corps aura lieu à 15 h** the funeral procession will gather at the house at 3 o'clock

lève-glace [lɛvglas] *(pl* **lève-glaces***)* NM window winder; **l. électrique** electric window

lever[1] [ləve] NM **1** *(apparition)* **le l. du soleil** sunrise; **le l. du jour** daybreak, dawn

2 *(fait de quitter son lit)* **programme de la journée: l. 6 h 30, petit-déjeuner 7 h 30** today's schedule: rise *or* get up at 6.30, breakfast at 7.30; **il se met au travail dès son l.** he starts working as soon as he gets up; **elle boit un grand verre d'eau au l.** she drinks a big glass of water as soon as she gets up *or* first thing in the morning; **le l. du roi** the levee of the king

3 *Théât* **au l. de rideau** when the curtain goes up *or* rises; **un l. de rideau** *(pièce)* a curtain-raiser

4 *(d'un plan)* survey

LEVER[2] [19] [ləve]

> **VT** to raise **A1, 2, B1, C3** ▪ to lift **A1, 2, B4** ▪ to collect **B1** ▪ to draw (up) **B2** ▪ to close **B4** ▪ to remove **B4** ▪ to get up **A3** ▪ to pick up **B6, C2**
> **VI** to come up **1** ▪ to rise **2**
> **VPR** to go up **1** ▪ to stand up **2** ▪ to rise **2–4, 6** ▪ to get up **3** ▪ to break **4, 5**

VT **A.** 1 *(faire monter)* to raise, to lift; *(soulever)* to lift; **lève la vitre** close the window; **l. une barrière** to raise a barrier; **l. le pont d'un château fort** to raise the drawbridge of a castle; **lève ton verre pour que je puisse te servir** lift your glass so that I can serve you; **levons nos verres à sa réussite** let's raise our glasses to *or* let's drink to his/her success; **je lève mon verre à votre réussite/aux futurs époux** here's to your success/the happy couple; *Théât* **l. le rideau** to raise the curtain; **l. l'ancre** to weigh anchor; *Fig (partir)* to take off, to hit the road, to go; *Fig* **l.**

l'étendard de la révolte to rise up in revolt, to raise the banner of rebellion; *Fig* **l. haut son drapeau** *(défendre publiquement ses opinions)* to nail one's colours to the mast
2 *(diriger vers le haut → partie du corps)* to lift, to raise; **l. la tête** to lift *or* to raise one's head; **en entendant la sonnette, elle leva la tête** she looked up *or* she raised her head when she heard the bell; **l. les yeux** *(de son livre)* to look up; **je n'osais plus l. les yeux** I no longer dared look up; **l. les yeux au ciel** to lift up *or* to raise one's eyes to heaven; **lève les pieds quand tu marches** lift *or* don't drag your feet when you walk; **l. le pied** *(automobiliste)* to drive slowly; **on conseille aux automobilistes de l. le pied ce soir** motorists are advised to drive slowly this evening; **l. la main pour prêter serment** to raise one's hand to take an oath; **l. le doigt** *ou* **la main avant de prendre la parole** to put up *or* to raise one's hand before speaking; **l. la main sur qn** to raise *or* to lift one's hand to sb; **le chien lève la patte** the dog cocks its leg; **l. les bras au ciel** to throw up one's hands; **l. le cœur à qn** to turn sb's stomach; **la seule pensée d'avoir à le toucher me lève le cœur** just the thought of having to touch it makes my stomach turn; **la puanteur qui s'en échappe vous lève le cœur** the stench coming from it is nauseating; **lève** *Fam* **tes fesses** *ou très Fam* **ton cul de là!** shift (yourself)!
3 *(sortir du lit)* **l. qn** to get sb up, to get sb out of bed; **nous levons les pensionnaires à huit heures** we rouse the boarders at eight o'clock
B. 1 *(ramasser → filets de pêche)* to raise; *(→ courrier, impôt)* to collect
2 *(dessiner → carte)* to draw (up); **il faudra l. le plan du domaine** a plan of the estate will have to be drawn up
3 *Culin (viande)* to carve; **l. les filets d'un poisson** to fillet a fish
4 *(faire cesser → blocus, interdiction, embargo)* to lift; *(→ audience, séance)* to close; *(→ scrupules, ambiguïté)* to remove; *(→ punition)* to lift; *(→ obstacle)* to get rid of, to remove; *Mil (→ siège)* to raise; *Jur* **la séance est levée** the court is adjourned; **l. un interdit/une excommunication** to lift an interdict/an excommunication; **la réforme ne lèvera pas toutes les difficultés** the reform will not remove all the difficulties
5 *Bourse* **l. une valeur** to take up a security; **l. des titres** to take delivery of stock; **l. une option** to take up an option
6 *Cartes* to pick up; **l. les cartes** to take *or* to pick up a trick
C. 1 *Chasse* to flush; **l. une compagnie de perdreaux** to flush a covey of partridges
2 *très Fam (séduire)* to pick up, *Br* to pull
3 *Mil (mobiliser)* to raise; **l. des troupes** to raise troops; **le gouvernement a levé deux classes** the government has raised *or* mobilized two contingents
VI **1** *(pousser → blé, avoine)* to come up
2 *Culin* to rise, to prove; **la pâte a levé** the dough has risen *or* proved; **laisser l. la pâte** to let the dough rise *or* prove
▸**se lever** VPR **1** *(monter)* to go up; **je vois une main qui se lève au fond de la classe** I see a hand going up at the back of the class; **tous les yeux** *ou* **regards se levèrent vers elle** all eyes turned towards her; **le rideau se lève sur un salon bourgeois** the curtain rises on a middle-class drawing room
2 *(se mettre debout)* to stand up, to rise; **levez-vous quand le proviseur entre** stand up when the headmaster comes in; **le public se leva pour l'applaudir** the public stood up *or* rose to applaud him/her; **se l. de sa chaise** to get up *or* to rise from one's chair; **ne te lève pas de table!** don't leave the table!; *Fig* **se l. contre** to rise up against; **le peuple s'est levé contre l'oppression** the people rose up against oppression; **il est temps que les hommes de bonne volonté se lèvent** it is time for men of goodwill to stand up and be counted; *Bible* **lève-toi et marche** take up thy bed and walk
3 *(sortir du lit → dormeur)* to get up, *Littéraire* to rise; *(→ malade)* to get out of bed; **il est l'heure de se l.!** time to get up!; **je ne peux pas me l. le matin** I can't get up *or* I can't get out of bed in the morning; **il ne s'est levé que la semaine dernière** *(malade)* he only got out of bed last week; **elle ne se lève plus** she no longer leaves her bed; **se l. avec le soleil** to be up with the lark; *Fig* **pour la prendre en défaut il faut se l. tôt** *ou* **de bonne heure!** you'd have to be on your toes to catch her out!; **pour trouver du bon pain ici, tu peux te l. de bonne heure** you've got your work cut out finding *or* you'll be a long time finding good bread round here; **ils m'ont encore fait l. aux aurores aujourd'hui** they got me up at the crack of dawn again today; **j'ai du mal à le faire se l. aujourd'hui** I'm having trouble getting him out of bed this morning
4 *(apparaître → astre)* to rise; *(→ jour)* to dawn, to break; **le soleil se levait quand nous partîmes** the sun was rising as we left; **au moment où la lune se lève** at the rising of the moon; **le jour se lève** day is dawning *or* breaking
5 *Météo (vent)* to get up; *(orage)* to break; *(brume)* to lift, to clear; **le temps se lève** the sky's clearing (up); **de violents orages se levèrent au cours de la nuit** fierce storms broke during the night; **le vent se lève** the wind's getting up; **si le brouillard se lève** if the fog lifts; **la mer se lève** the sea's getting up *or* getting rough
6 *Littéraire (surgir, naître)* to rise (up); **l'espoir commença à se l. dans tous les cœurs** hope welled up in everyone's heart

---

lève-tard [lɛvtar] NMF INV late riser
lève-tôt [lɛvto] NMF INV early riser, early bird
lève-vitre [lɛvvitr] *(pl* **lève-vitres***)* NM window winder; **l. électrique** electric window
Lévi [levi] NPR *Bible* Levi
levier [ləvje] NM **1** *Tech* lever; **faire l. sur qch** to lever sth up *or* off; **soulever/ouvrir qch avec un l.** to prize *or* to prise *or* to lever sth up/open
2 *(manette)* lever; **l. (de changement) de vitesse** *Br* gear lever, *Am* gearshift; **l. de frein à main** handbrake lever; **l. de commande** control (lever); **être aux leviers de commande** to be at the controls; *Fig* to be in command *or* in the driver's seat *or* at the controls
3 *Fig (moyen de pression)* means of pressure, lever; **la grève peut être un puissant l. politique** strike action can be a powerful political lever
4 *Écon* **effet de l.** leverage, gearing
lévigation [levigasjɔ̃] NF *Chim* levigation
léviger [17] [leviʒe] VT *Chim* to levigate
lévirat [levira] NM *Rel* levirate
lévitation [levitasjɔ̃] NF levitation; **être en l.** to be levitating
lévite [levit] NM *Hist* Levite
Lévitique [levitik] NM *Bible* **le L.** Leviticus
lévodopa [levɔdɔpa] NF *Pharm* levodopa
lévogyre [levɔʒir] ADJ *Chim* levogyrous, levogyrate; **composé l.** levo-compound
levraut [ləvro] NM leveret
lèvre [lɛvr] NF **1** *(de la bouche)* lip; **elle avait le sourire aux lèvres** she had a smile on her lips; **lire sur les lèvres** to lip-read; **l. inférieure/supérieure** lower/upper lip; **être pendu** *ou* **suspendu aux lèvres de qn** to be hanging upon sb's every word; **son nom est sur toutes les lèvres** his/her name is on everybody's lips
2 *(de la vulve)* lip, labium; **les lèvres** the labia; **grandes/petites lèvres** labia majora/minora
3 *Géol* edge, side, rim
4 *Méd (d'une plaie)* lip
5 *Bot* lip, *Spéc* labium
levrette [ləvrɛt] NF **1** *(chien)* greyhound bitch; **l. (d'Italie)** Italian greyhound **2** *très Fam (locution)* **en l.** doggy-style
levretté, -e [ləvrete] ADJ with a greyhound belly
levretter [3] [ləvrɛte] VI to litter
lévrier [levrije] NM *(chien)* greyhound; **l. afghan** Afghan hound; **l. arabe** sloughi, Arabian greyhound; **l. barzoï** borzoi, Russian wolfhound; **l. d'Écosse** *ou* **écossais** deerhound; **l. d'Irlande** *ou* **irlandais** Irish wolfhound; **l. d'Italie** *ou* **italien** Italian greyhound; **l. russe** borzoi, Russian wolfhound
levron, -onne [ləvrɔ̃, -ɔn] NM,F **1** *(petit du lévrier)* young greyhound, sapling **2** *(race de lévrier)* Italian greyhound
lévulose [levyloz] NM *Chim* laevulose
levure [ləvyr] NF yeast; **l. de bière** brewer's yeast, dried yeast; **l. de boulanger** fresh *or* baker's yeast; **l. (chimique)** baking powder
lewisite [lewisit] NF *Chim* lewisite
lexème [lɛksɛm] NM *Ling* lexeme
lexical, -e, -aux, -ales [lɛksikal, -o] ADJ *Ling* lexical
lexicalisation [lɛksikalizasjɔ̃] NF *Ling* lexicalization
lexicalisé, -e [lɛksikalize] ADJ *Ling* lexicalized
lexicaliser [3] [lɛksikalize] *Ling* VT to lexicalize
▸**se lexicaliser** VPR to become lexicalized
lexicographe [lɛksikɔgraf] NMF lexicographer
lexicographie [lɛksikɔgrafi] NF lexicography
lexicographique [lɛksikɔgrafik] ADJ lexicographical
lexicologie [lɛksikɔlɔʒi] NF lexicology
lexicologique [lɛksikɔlɔʒik] ADJ lexicological
lexicologue [lɛksikɔlɔg] NMF lexicologist
lexie [lɛksi] NF *Ling* lexical item *or* unit
lexique [lɛksik] NM **1** *(ouvrage)* glossary, lexicon
2 *(d'une langue)* lexis, vocabulary; *(d'un auteur)* vocabulary
lexis [lɛksis] NF *(en logique)* utterance
lexovien, -enne [lɛksɔvjɛ̃, -ɛn] ADJ of/from Lisieux
□ **Lexovien, -enne** NM,F = inhabitant of or person from Lisieux
Leyde [lɛd] NM Leiden
lez [lɛ] PRÉP by, near
lézard [lezar] NM **1** *Zool* lizard; **l. à collerette** frilled lizard; **l. vert/des murailles** green/wall lizard; **faire le l.** to bask in the sun **2** *(peau)* lizardskin; **ceinture en l.** lizard-skin belt **3** *Fam (difficulté)* **il y a pas de lézards** no problem, no sweat, *Br* no probs
lézarde [lezard] NF crack, crevice
lézarder [3] [lezarde] VI *Fam (au soleil)* to bask in the sun; *(paresser)* to laze about, to lounge (about)
VT *(fissurer)* to crack; **mur lézardé** cracked wall, wall full of cracks
▸**se lézarder** VPR to crack
LFAJ [ɛlɛfaʒi] NF *(abrév* **Ligue française des auberges de jeunesse***)* = French youth hostel association
Lhassa [lasa] NM Lassa, Lhasa
li [li] NM *(mesure chinoise)* li
Lia [lja] NPR *Bible* Leah
liage [ljaʒ] NM *(action de lier)* binding
liais [ljɛ] NM *Constr* hard limestone
liaison [ljɛzɔ̃] NF **1** *(contact)* contact; **être en l. avec qn** to be in contact with sb; **le secrétaire assure la l. entre les divers services** the secretary liaises between the various departments
2 *Tél* contact; **la l. téléphonique n'est pas très bonne** the line is not very good; **nous sommes en l. directe avec notre correspondant** we have our correspondent on the line; **l. radio** radio contact; **l. par satellite** satellite link *or* link-up; *Tél* **l. de télécommunications** telecommunications link
3 *Transp* link; **un train/car assure la l. entre Édimbourg et Glasgow** there is a train/coach service operating between Edinburgh and Glasgow; **toutes les liaisons Paris–Téhéran sont suspendues** all services between Paris and Tehran have been suspended; **l. aérienne/maritime/ferroviaire/fluviale/routière** air/sea/rail/river/road link
4 *(rapport)* connection, link; **il y a un manque de l. dans l'expression de vos idées** you express your ideas in a disjointed fashion; **son départ est sans l. avec la dispute d'hier** his/her departure is in no way linked to yesterday's argument
5 *Littéraire (relation)* relationship; **ils ont une l. d'affaires** they have a business relationship; **avoir une l. (amoureuse) avec qn** to have an affair with sb
6 *Chim* bond; **l. de covalence** covalent bond; **l. hydrogène** hydrogen bond; **l. métallique** metallic bond
7 *Constr* joint
8 *Culin (pour une sauce)* thickening; *(pour farce)* binding
9 *Ordinat* link; **l. logique** logical link; **l. par modem** modem link; **l. spécialisée** dedicated line

10 *Ling* liaison; **faire la l.** to make *or* to sound the liaison

11 *Mus (pour tenir une note)* tie; *(pour lier plusieurs notes)* phrase mark, slur

12 *Jur* **l. de l'instance** = hearing at which submissions are exchanged and after which pleas are inadmissible

13 *TV* **l. ascendante** uplink; **l. descendante** downlink; **l. montante** uplink; **l. vidéo** video link

❑ **en liaison** ADV in touch, in contact; **être/rester en l. (avec qn)** to be/to remain in contact (with sb); **nous resterons en l.** we will stay in touch; **travailler en l. avec qn** to liaise with sb, to work closely with sb; **il travaille en l. avec un marchand d'art à New York** he works in close contact with an art dealer in New York

'Les Liaisons dangereuses' *Laclos, Frears* 'Dangerous Liaisons'

liaisonner [3] [ljɛzɔne] VT *Constr* to bond

liane [ljan] NF *(vigne, lierre)* creeper; *(en forêt équatoriale)* liana

lianescent, -e [ljanɛsɑ̃, -ɑ̃t] ADJ *Bot* creeper-like

liant, -e [ljɑ̃, -ɑ̃t] ADJ sociable; **il n'est pas très l.** he's not very sociable, he doesn't make friends easily

NM **1** *Littéraire (affabilité)* **avoir du l.** to be sociable, to have a sociable nature **2** *Chim & Constr* binder **3** *(souplesse)* flexibility, pliability

liard [ljar] NM **1** *Hist* = coin worth three "deniers", *Br* ≃ farthing **2** *Vieilli (très petite quantité)* **il n'a pas un l. de bon sens** he hasn't an ounce *or* a grain of common sense **3** *Vieilli (sou)* **je n'en donnerais pas deux liards** it isn't worth *Br* a penny *or Am* a red cent

liarder [3] [ljarde] VI *Vieilli* to skimp (**sur** on)

lias [ljas] NM *Géol* Lias

liasique [ljazik] ADJ *Géol* Liassic

liasse [ljas] NF *(de billets)* wad; *(de documents)* bundle

libage [libaʒ] NM *Constr* bastard ashlar

Liban [libɑ̃] NM **le L.** (the) Lebanon; **vivre au L.** to live in (the) Lebanon; **aller au L.** to go to (the) Lebanon

libanais, -e [libanɛ, -ɛz] ADJ Lebanese

❑ **Libanais, -e** NM,F Lebanese (person); **les L.** the Lebanese

libanisation [libanizasjɔ̃] NF Balkanization

libation [libasjɔ̃] NF *Antiq* libation

❑ **libations** NFPL **faire de joyeuses libations** to drink copious amounts (of alcohol)

Libé [libe] NM *Fam Presse* = nickname of the "Libération" newspaper

libeccio [libɛtʃjo] NM libeccio

libelle [libɛl] NM lampoon; **écrire des libelles contre qn** to lampoon sb

libellé [libele] NM *(d'une lettre, d'un acte, d'un contrat)* wording; *Compta (d'une écriture)* particulars; **le l. du chèque est incorrect** the cheque is not made out correctly

libeller [4] [libele] VT **1** *(lettre, acte, contrat)* to word; **le sujet de dissertation était mal libellé** the subject of the essay was not clearly worded

2 *Admin (texte juridique)* to word, to draw up; **libellé comme suit...** worded as follows...

3 *(chèque)* to make out; **libellez votre chèque au nom** *ou* **à l'ordre de...** make your cheque payable to...; **je n'avais pas libellé le chèque** I hadn't put the name of the payee on the cheque; **être libellé au porteur** to be made out to bearer, to be made payable to bearer; *Fin* **libellé en dollars** *(chèque)* made out in dollars; *(cours)* quoted *or* given in dollars

libelliste [libelist] NMF *Vieilli* lampoonist, lampooner

libellule [libelyl] NF *Entom* dragonfly

liber [libɛr] NM *Bot* secondary phloem, liber

Libera [libera] NM INV *Mus & Rel* Libera Me

libérable [liberabl] ADJ **1** *Mil (militaire, contingent)* dischargeable; **permission l.** demob leave **2** *Jur (prisonnier)* eligible for release

libéral, -e, -aux, -ales [liberal, -o] ADJ **1** *(aux idées larges)* liberal, liberal-minded, broad-minded

2 *Écon* free-market *(avant n)*, free-enterprise *(avant n)*; **l'économie libérale** the free-market economy

3 *Hist* liberal

4 *Pol (en Grande-Bretagne, au Canada)* Liberal; *(en France)* favouring the free-market economy

NM,F **1** *Pol (en Grande-Bretagne, au Canada)* Liberal; *(en France)* free-marketeer

2 *(personne tolérante)* broad-minded person

libéralement [liberalmɑ̃] ADV **1** *(généreusement)* liberally, generously **2** *(avec tolérance)* broad-mindedly

libéralisation [liberalizasjɔ̃] NF **1** *Pol* liberalization

2 *Écon* deregulation, easing of restrictions; **l. du commerce** deregulation of trade, easing of trade restrictions; **la l. complète de l'économie** the application of free-market principles throughout the economy; **la l. des télécommunications** the deregulation of the telecommunications market

libéraliser [3] [liberalize] VT **1** *(mœurs, régime)* to liberalize **2** *Écon (commerce)* to deregulate, to ease restrictions on; **l. l'économie** to reduce state intervention in the economy

►**se libéraliser** VPR *(régime)* to become (more) liberal; *(mœurs)* to become freer

libéralisme [liberalism] NM **1** *Pol* liberalism **2** *Écon* free-market economics, free enterprise **3** *(tolérance)* broad-mindedness, liberal-mindedness

libéralité [liberalite] NF **1** *(générosité)* generosity, *Sout* liberality **2** *Jur* gift

❑ **libéralités** NFPL *(dons)* (cash) donations, liberalities; **je ne tiens pas à vivre de vos libéralités** I do not want to live off your generosity *or* good favours; **faire des libéralités à qn** to give liberally *or* freely to sb

libérateur, -trice [liberatœr, -tris] ADJ **1** *(rire, geste)* liberating, *Littéraire* cathartic **2** *Pol* liberating; **l'armée libératrice** the liberating army, the army of liberation

NM,F liberator

libération [liberasjɔ̃] NF **1** *(d'un pays)* liberation; *(d'un prisonnier, d'un otage)* release; *(d'un soldat)* discharge; *Hist* **la L.** the Liberation (of France); **à la L.** when France was liberated

2 *Jur (d'un détenu)* release; **l. anticipée** early release; **l. sous caution** release on bail; **l. conditionnelle** (release on) parole

3 *(émancipation)* liberation; *Fig* **éprouver un sentiment de l.** to feel liberated; **la l. de la femme** women's liberation

4 *Écon & Fin (d'une dette)* payment in full, discharge; *(d'une action, du capital)* paying up; *(d'un débiteur)* discharge, release; *(d'un garant)* discharge; **l. des changes** relaxing of foreign exchange controls; **la l. des échanges commerciaux** the deregulation of trade; **la l. des prix** the deregulation of prices, the removal of price controls; **la l. des loyers** the lifting of rent control

5 *Presse* **L.** = French left-of-centre daily newspaper

6 *Chim, Phys, Méd & Physiol* release; **à l. prolongée** slow-release

libératoire [liberatwar] ADJ **paiement l.** payment in full discharge; **prélèvement l. de 30 pour cent sur les revenus des obligations** 30 percent tax in full discharge on earnings from bonds; **avoir force l.** to be legal tender

libératrice [liberatris] *voir* **libérateur**

libéré, -e [libere] ADJ **1** *(en liberté, émancipé)* liberated **2** *Fin (action)* (fully) paid-up; **non (entièrement) l., partiellement l.** partly paid-up; **un titre de 1000 euros l. de 750 euros** *ou* **l. à 75 pour cent** a 1,000-euro share of which 750 euros are paid up; **l. d'impôt** tax paid

LIBÉRER [18] [libere]

VT to free **1–3** ▪ to release **2, 3, 7, 8** ▪ to relieve **4** ▪ to let go **5** ▪ to vacate **6** ▪ to lift restrictions on **9** ▪ to discharge **11**
VPR to free oneself **1** ▪ to become more liberated **4** ▪ to become vacant **5**

VT **1** *(délivrer)* to free; **quand les Alliés libérèrent Paris** when the Allies liberated Paris; **l. qn de qch** to free sb from sth; **l. qn de ses chaînes** to free sb from his/her chains; **elle n'est pas complètement libérée de l'emprise de la drogue** she's not completely free from drug addiction

2 *(remettre en liberté)* to release, to (set) free; **il ne sera libéré qu'à l'expiration de sa peine** he will not be released until he has served his sentence

3 *(décharger)* **l. qn d'une promesse** to free *or* to release sb from a promise; **libéré de sa dette** free from his debt; **l. qn de la responsabilité légale** to relieve sb of legal liability

4 *(soulager* → *conscience)* to relieve, to salve; **la machine a libéré l'homme des travaux dangereux** the machine has relieved man of dangerous work; **tu me libères d'un gros souci** *ou* **d'un gros poids** you've taken a load off my mind; **l. son cœur** to unburden one's heart

5 *(laisser partir* → *élèves, employés)* to let go; **on nous a libérés avant l'heure** we were allowed to leave *or* they let us go early

6 *(rendre disponible* → *appartement, chambre d'hôtel)* to vacate, to move out of; *(*→ *étagère)* to clear; **je libérerai les lieux le 31 au plus tard** I will vacate the premises on the 31st at the latest; **libérez le passage** clear the way; **je n'arrive même pas à l. une heure pour jouer au tennis** I can't even find a free hour *or* an hour to spare to play tennis; **les postes libérés par les mises à la retraite anticipée** vacancies created by early retirement

7 *(débloquer* → *mécanisme, émotions)* to release; **avant de l. le cran de sûreté du revolver** before releasing the safety catch of the revolver

8 *Chim & Phys (gaz, hormone, énergie, chaleur)* to release

9 *Écon (prix, salaires)* to lift restrictions on, to deregulate

10 *Fin* **l. entièrement une action** to make a share fully paid-up, to pay up a share in full

11 *Mil (conscrit)* to discharge; **le candidat devra être libéré des obligations militaires** the applicant must be released from *or* must have discharged his military service obligations

►**se libérer** VPR **1** *(se délivrer)* to free oneself; **se l. de ses chaînes** to free oneself from one's chains

2 *(se dégager)* **se l. de qch** *(dette)* to redeem sth, to liquidate sth; *(engagement)* to free oneself from sth

3 *(dans un emploi du temps)* **essaie de te l. pour demain** try to make some time tomorrow; **je ne pourrai pas me l. avant 17 h** I won't be able to get away before 5 o'clock

4 *(s'émanciper* → *femmes)* to become more liberated

5 *(emploi, appartement)* to become vacant *or* available; **il y a une place qui s'est libérée au coin de la rue** somebody's just left a parking space at the corner of the street

Liberia [liberja] NM **le L.** Liberia; **vivre au L.** to live in Liberia; **aller au L.** to go to Liberia

libérien, -enne [liberjɛ̃, -ɛn] ADJ Liberian

❑ **Libérien, -enne** NM,F Liberian

libérine [liberin] NF *Chim & Méd* liberine

libériste [liberist] *Sport* ADJ hang-gliding *(avant n)*

NMF hang-glider (pilot)

libero, libéro [libero] NM *Ftbl* sweeper

libéro-ligneux, -euse [liberɔliɲø, -øz] *(mpl* **libéro-ligneux,** *fpl* **libéro-ligneuses)** ADJ *Bot* wood-and-bast

libertaire [libɛrtɛr] ADJ & NMF libertarian, anarchist

liberté [libɛrte] NF **1** *(gén) & Jur* freedom; **rendre la l. à un otage** to release a hostage; **rendre la l. à un oiseau** to set a bird free; **le pays de la l.** the land of the free *or* of freedom; **défenseur de la l.** defender of freedom *or* liberty; **l. sous caution** release on bail; **l. conditionnelle** (release on) parole; **mettre qn en l. conditionnelle** to release sb on parole; **l. individuelle** personal freedom; **l. sur parole** (release on) parole; **mettre qn en l. sur parole** to release sb on parole; **l. provisoire** bail; **mettre qn en l. provisoire** to release sb on bail; **l. surveillée** probation; **mettre qn en l. surveillée** to release sb on probation; **la statue de la L.** the Statue of Liberty

2 *(droit)* right, freedom; **l. d'association/du travail** right of association/to work; **l. du culte/d'opinion/de mouvement** freedom of worship/

of thought/of movement; **libertés civiques** *ou* **du citoyen** civil liberties; **l. civile** civil liberty *(freedom to do anything not forbidden by law)*; **l. d'aller et venir** right of access; **l. de la défense** = right of both parties to proceedings to be heard and to choose their own lawyers; **l. d'entreprise** free enterprise, right to set up a business; **libertés individuelles** individual freedom; **l. de la presse/d'expression** freedom of the press/of speech; **L., Égalité, Fraternité** Liberty, Equality, Fraternity *(motto of the French Revolution and, today, of France)*

3 *(indépendance)* freedom; **l. de jugement/de pensée** freedom of judgement/of thought; **avoir toute l. d'action** to have a free hand *or* complete freedom of action; **on lui laisse trop peu de l.** he's/she's given too little freedom; **avoir toute l. pour décider** to be totally free *or* to have full freedom to decide; **prendre la l. de faire** to take the liberty of doing; **reprendre sa l.** *(sentimentalement)* to regain one's freedom

4 *(temps libre)* free time; **jour de l.** free day, day off; **tous mes moments de l.** all my free time; **je n'ai pas un instant de l.** I haven't got a minute to myself

5 *(désinvolture, irrévérence)* **il prend trop de l. avec nous** he is a bit overfamiliar with us; **il y a une trop grande l. dans la traduction** the translation is not close enough to the original *or* is too free; **l. de langage** overfree use of language

6 *Écon* **l. des prix** freedom from price controls; **instaurer la l. des prix** to end *or* to abolish price controls; **l. du commerce** freedom of trade; **l. d'entreprise** (right of) free enterprise; **l. syndicale** freedom to join a union, union rights

□ **libertés** NFPL **1** *(droits légaux)* liberties, freedom *(UNCOUNT)*; **atteinte aux/défense des libertés** attack on/defence of civil liberties; **les libertés publiques** civil liberties

2 *(privautés)* **prendre** *ou* **se permettre des libertés avec qn** to take liberties with sb; **j'ai pris quelques libertés avec la recette** I took a few liberties with *or* I didn't stick entirely to the recipe

□ **en liberté** ADV free; **être en l.** *(personne)* to be free *or* at large; *(animal)* to be free *or* in the wild; **un parc national où les animaux vivent en l.** a national park where animals roam free; **il laisse ses perruches en l. dans la maison** he leaves his budgerigars free to fly around the house; *Jur* **(re)mettre qn en l.** to release sb, to set sb free

□ **en toute liberté** ADV freely; **vous pouvez vous exprimer en toute l.** you can talk freely; **agir en toute l.** to act quite freely

'La Liberté guidant le peuple' *Delacroix* 'Liberty guiding the People'

libertel [libɛrtɛl] NF *Ordinat* freenet

liberticide [libɛrtisid] ADJ *Littéraire* liberticidal; **lois liberticides** laws that are destroying freedom *or* freedoms

libertin, -e [libɛrtɛ̃, -in] ADJ **1** *Littéraire (personne)* dissolute, dissipated, debauched; *(propos, publication)* licentious **2** *Hist & Rel* libertine, freethinking

NM,F **1** *Littéraire (personne dissolue)* libertine **2** *Hist & Rel* libertine, freethinker

libertinage [libɛrtinaʒ] NM **1** *Littéraire (comportement)* debauchery, dissipation, *Sout* libertinism **2** *Hist & Rel* libertine philosophy, libertinism

Liberty® [libɛrti] NM INV Liberty® print material; **une housse de coussin en L.** a Liberty® cushion cover

liberum veto [liberɔmveto] NM INV *Hist* liberum veto

libidinal, -e, -aux, -ales [libidinal, -o] ADJ *Psy* libidinal

libidineux, -euse [libidinø, -øz] ADJ *(vieillard)* lecherous; *(regard)* lustful, *Sout* libidinous

libido [libido] NF libido; **avoir une forte l.** to have a high libido

libitum [libitɔm] *voir* **ad libitum**

libraire [librɛr] NMF bookseller

libraire-éditeur [librɛreditœr] *(pl* **libraires-éditeurs)** NM publisher and bookseller

librairie [librɛri] NF **1** *(boutique) Br* bookshop, *Am* bookstore; **paraîtra en l. le 3 juin** due out on 3 June, in the bookshops from 3 June; **un livre qu'on ne trouve plus en l.** a book which is no longer on sale; **le rayon l.** the book department; **l. d'art/d'occasion** art/second-hand bookshop **2 la l.** *(commerce)* bookselling; *(profession)* the book trade

librairie-papeterie [librɛripapɛtri] *(pl* **librairies-papeteries)** NF stationer's and bookseller's

libration [librasjɔ̃] NF *Astron* libration

LIBRE [libr]

free **1, 2, 4–6, 8–12** ■ available **2** ■ vacant **2** ■ unattached **3** ■ daring **5** ■ deregulated **6** ■ independent **7** ■ private **7**

ADJ **1** *(gén) & Pol* free; *Hist* **la France l.** Free France; **à la suite du non-lieu, l'accusé s'est retrouvé l.** owing to lack of evidence, the accused found himself a free man again; **si j'ai envie de la voir, je suis bien l.!** if I feel like seeing her, it's up to me *or* that's my affair!; **laisser qn l. d'agir** to leave sb a free hand, to leave sb free to act; **il ne me laisse pas l. d'inviter qui je veux** he doesn't leave me free to invite who *or* whom I please; **il nous laisse libres de partir** he lets us go when we want; **être l. de tout souci** to be free from care, to be carefree; **être l. de ses mouvements** to be free to do what one likes; **l. d'hypothèque** free from mortgage; **l. d'impôt** tax-free; **l. à toi/à elle de refuser** you're/she's free to say no; **j'y vais? – alors là, l. à toi!** shall I go? – well, that's entirely up to you *or* you're (entirely) free to do as you wish!; **être l. comme l'air** to be as free as (the) air

2 *(disponible* → *personne, salle)* free, available; *(*→ *appartement, maison, chambre)* available; *(*→ *place de parking)* free, unoccupied; *(*→ *poste, siège)* vacant, free; *(*→ *table)* free; *(*→ *toilettes)* vacant; *(*→ *passage)* clear; **la ligne n'est pas l.** *(au téléphone)* the line is *Br* engaged *or Am* busy; **la voie est l.** the way is clear; **j'ai trouvé une place l. pour me garer** I found a place to park; **l.** *(sur un taxi)* for hire; **studio à louer, l. de suite** *(annonce)* studio *Br* flat *or Am* apartment to rent, available immediately; **il faut que j'aie la tête** *ou* **l'esprit l. pour prendre une décision** I have to have a clear head before I'm able to make a decision; **être l.** to be free; **le directeur des ventes n'est pas l. en ce moment** the sales manager isn't free *or* available at the moment; **tu as un moment de l.?** have you got a minute (to spare)?; **êtes-vous l. à l'heure du déjeuner?** are you free for lunch?; **j'ai deux après-midi (de) libres par semaine** I've got two afternoons off *or* two free afternoons a week; **le lundi est mon jour (de) l.** Monday is my day off, I have Mondays free; **je n'ai pas eu une minute de l. aujourd'hui** I haven't had a spare minute today

3 *(sentimentalement)* unattached; **je ne suis pas l.** I'm already seeing somebody; **je préfère rester l.** I prefer to remain unattached

4 *(franc)* free, open; **je suis très l. avec elle** I am quite free (and easy) *or* open with her

5 *(désinvolte, inconvenant* → *attitude)* free, daring; **ses remarques un peu libres nous ont choqués** his/her somewhat coarse remarks shocked us; **il se montre un peu trop l. avec ses secrétaires** he is a bit overfamiliar *or* too free with his secretaries

6 *(non réglementé* → *prix, marché)* free, deregulated; **leurs honoraires sont libres** there are no restrictions on their fees; **bibliothèque en l. accès** public library; **l'entrée de l'exposition est l.** entrance to the exhibition is free; **l. circulation** free movement; *UE* **l. circulation des travailleurs** free movement of workers; **l. concurrence** free competition; **par le l. jeu de la concurrence** through free competition; **la l. entreprise** free enterprise

7 *(privé* → *radio, télévision)* independent; *(*→ *école, enseignement)* private *(in France, mostly Catholic)*

8 *(non imposé* → *improvisation, style)* free; **je leur ai donné un sujet l.** I gave them a free choice of subject, I left it up to them to choose the subject; **escalade l.** free climbing; **vers l.** free verse

9 *(non entravé* → *mouvement, membre)* free, unrestrained; **le bandage laisse les doigts libres** the bandage leaves the fingers free; **elle porte les cheveux libres** she wears her hair down *or* loose

10 *(non fidèle* → *adaptation)* free; **dans une traduction un peu l. de Brecht** in a rather free *or* loose translation of Brecht

11 *Chim & Math* free

12 *Tech (engrenage)* free, disengaged

ADV **ça sonne l. ou occupé?** is it ringing or *Br* engaged *or Am* busy?

libre arbitre [librarbitr] NM free will; **le Président a perdu son l. après le scandale** the President lost his freedom of action after the scandal

libre-échange [librеʃɑ̃ʒ] *(pl* **libres-échanges)** NM *Écon* free trade

libre-échangisme [libreʃɑ̃ʒism] NM *Écon* (doctrine of) free trade

libre-échangiste [libreʃɑ̃ʒist] *(pl* **libre-échangistes)** *Écon* ADJ *(politique, économie)* free-trade *(avant n)*; *(idée, personne)* in favour of free trade

NMF free trader

librement [librəmɑ̃] ADV freely

libre opinion [librɔpinjɔ̃] NF *Journ* editorial

libre-pensée [librəpɑ̃se] *(pl* **libres-pensées)** NF freethinking

libre-penseur [librəpɑ̃sœr] *(pl* **libres-penseurs)** NM freethinker

libre-service [librəsɛrvis] *(pl* **libres-services)** NM **1** *(principe)* self-service **2** *(magasin)* self-service *Br* shop *or Am* store; *(cantine)* self-service canteen; *(restaurant)* self-service restaurant; *(station-service)* self-service *Br* petrol *or Am* gas station

□ **en libre-service** ADJ self-service

librettiste [librɛtist] NMF librettist

libretto [librɛto] NM libretto

Libreville [librəvil] NM Libreville

Libye [libi] NF **la L.** Libya; **vivre en L.** to live in Libya; **aller en L.** to go to Libya; **le désert de L.** the Libyan Desert

libyen, -enne [libjɛ̃, -ɛn] ADJ Libyan

□ **Libyen, -enne** NM,F Libyan

lice [lis] NF **1** *Sport (bordure de piste)* line; *(en hippisme)* rail **2** *Hist (palissade)* lists; *(terrain)* tilt-yard **3** *Chasse* bitch; **l. portière** breeding bitch **4** *Tex* = **lisse**

□ **en lice** ADV *aussi Fig* **entrer en l.** to enter the lists; *Fig (intervenir dans une discussion)* to enter the fray; **les deux candidats encore en l.** the two candidates still in the running

licéité [liseite] NF *Jur* licitness, lawfulness

licence [lisɑ̃s] NF **1** *Littéraire (liberté excessive)* licence; *(débauche)* licentiousness; **avoir toute** *ou* **pleine l. de faire qch** to be at liberty *or* quite free to do sth

2 *Littérature* **l. poétique** poetic licence

3 *Univ* (bachelor's) degree; **passer sa l.** to sit *or* to take one's degree exams *or* one's finals; **l. d'économie** degree in economics; **l. de russe/de droit** Russian/law degree; **l. ès lettres** arts degree, *Br* ≃ BA, *Am* ≃ AB; **l. ès sciences** science degree, *Br* ≃ BSc, *Am* ≃ BS

4 *Jur (permis)* licence; *Ordinat (pour l'utilisation d'un logiciel)* registration card; **accorder une l. à qn** to license sb; **l. d'importation/d'exportation** import/export licence; **l. de débit de boissons,** *Can* **l.** *Br* licence for the sale of alcohol, *Am* liquor license; **l. exclusive** exclusive licence; **l. d'exploitation d'un brevet** licence to use a patent; **l. de fabrication** manufacturing licence; *Ordinat* **l. individuelle d'utilisation** single user licence; **l. de pêche** fishing licence; **l. de vente** selling licence

5 *Sport* membership card *(allowing entry into official competitions)*

6 *Can Joual (plaque d'immatriculation) Br* number plate ■, *Am* license plate ■; *(permis de conduire) Br* driving licence ■, *Am* driver's license ■

□ **sous licence** ADJ licensed ADV **fabriqué sous l.** made *or* manufactured under licence

licencié, -e [lisɑ̃sje] ADJ **1** *Univ* graduate *(avant n)*; **il est l.** he's a graduate

2 *Can Joual (établissement)* licensed (to sell alcohol) ■

NM,F **1** *Univ* (university) graduate; **l. ès lettres/ès sciences** arts/science graduate; **l. en droit**

law graduate; **l. en anglais** English graduate, graduate in English

2 *Sport* registered member; **seuls les licenciés bénéficient des tarifs réduits** *(dans le cadre d'un club sportif)* discount for club members only

3 *(chômeur → pour raisons économiques)* laid off *or Br* redundant employee; *(→ pour faute professionnelle)* dismissed employee; **il y a eu quatre licenciés** four employees were laid off *or Br* made redundant, there were four lay-offs *or Br* redundancies

4 *Com* licensed manufacturer

licenciement [lisɑ̃simɑ̃] **NM** *(structurel)* lay-off, *Br* redundancy; *(pour faute professionnelle)* dismissal; **depuis mon l.** since I was laid off *or Br* made redundant; **avis** *ou* **lettre de l.** letter of dismissal; **l. abusif** unfair dismissal; **licenciements boursiers** = redundancies made to improve the stock market valuation of a company; **l. collectif** mass redundancies; **l. (pour raison) économique** redundancy; **l. sans préavis** dismissal without notice; **l. sec** = redundancy without any form of statutory compensation

licencier [9] [lisɑ̃sje] **VT** *(pour raison économique)* to lay off, *Br* to make redundant; *(pour faute)* to dismiss, to fire; **se faire l.** to be made redundant

licencieuse [lisɑ̃sjøz] *voir* **licencieux**

licencieusement [lisɑ̃sjøzmɑ̃] **ADV** licentiously

licencieux, -euse [lisɑ̃sjø, -øz] **ADJ** licentious, lewd

liche [liʃ] **NF** *Ich* leerfish

lichen [likɛn] **NM 1** *Bot* lichen; **l. foliacé/fruticuleux** foliose/fruticose lichen **2** *Méd* **l. (plan)** lichen

licher [3] [liʃe] **VT 1** *Fam Vieilli (boire)* to quaff, to drink▪ **2** *Can Fam (lécher)* to lick▪

lichette [liʃɛt] **NF 1** *Fam (petite quantité)* **une l. de vin/de lait** a (teeny) drop of wine/of milk; **une l. de beurre** a smidgen *or* a spot of butter; **une l. de gâteau** a sliver *or* (tiny) bit of cake **2** *Belg (cordon)* loop, tag

licier [lisje] = **lissier**

licitation [lisitasjɔ̃] **NF** auction *(by the co-owners of an estate)*

licite [lisit] **ADJ** licit, lawful

licitement [lisitmɑ̃] **ADV** licitly, lawfully

liciter [3] [lisite] **VT** to auction *(an estate in co-ownership)*

licol [likɔl] = **licou**

licorne [likɔrn] **NF 1** *Myth* unicorn **2 l. de mer** *(narval)* sea unicorn, narwhal

licou [liku] **NM** halter; **passer le l. à un cheval** to put the halter on a horse

LICRA [likra] **NF** *(abrév* **Ligue internationale contre le racisme et l'antisémitisme**) = anti-racist movement

licteur [liktœr] **NM** *Antiq* lictor

lidar [lidar] **NM** *Tech (abrév* **light detection and ranging**) lidar

lido [lido] **NM** sandbar; **le L. (de Venise)** the Venice Lido; **le L.** *(à Paris)* = famous cabaret on the Champs-Élysées in Paris

Lidocaïne® [lidɔkain] **NF** *Pharm* lidocaine

lie [li] **NF 1** *(dépôt)* dregs, lees; **l. de vin** wine dregs; **il y a de la l. au fond de la bouteille** there's some sediment at the bottom of the bottle; *Fig* **boire la coupe** *ou* **le calice jusqu'à la l.** to drink one's cup of sorrow to the dregs **2** *(rebut)* dregs, rejects; **la l. de la société** the dregs of society

lié, -e [lje] **ADJ 1** *(en relation étroite)* **être (très) l. avec qn** to be (great) friends with sb, to be (very) close to sb; **nous sommes très liés** we are great friends, we are very close **2** *Mus (notes différentes)* slurred; *(note tenue)* tied **3** *Math* bound

Liechtenstein [liʃtɛnʃtajn] **NM le L.** Liechtenstein; **vivre au L.** to live in Liechtenstein; **aller au L.** to go to Liechtenstein

liechtensteinois, -e [liʃtɛnʃtajnwa, -az] **ADJ** from Liechtenstein

▫ **Liechtensteinois, -e NM,F** Liechtensteiner

lied [lid] *(pl* **lieds** *ou* **lieder** [lidər]) **NM** lied; **un récital de lieds** *ou* **de lieder** a lieder recital

lie-de-vin [lidvɛ̃] **ADJ INV** wine-coloured

liégé, -e [ljeʒe] **ADJ** *Pêche* floated with cork, corked

Liège [ljɛʒ] **NM 1** *(ville)* Liege **2 le L.** Liège province

liège [ljɛʒ] **NM** cork; **de** *ou* **en l.** cork; **bouchon de** *ou* **en l.** cork

liégeois, -e [ljeʒwa, -az] **ADJ 1** *(personne)* of/from Liège **2** *Culin* **café/chocolat l.** coffee/chocolate sundae *(topped with whipped cream)*

▫ **Liégeois, -e NM,F** = inhabitant of or person from Liège

lien [ljɛ̃] **NM 1** *(entre des choses)* link, connection; **y a-t-il un l. direct entre ces deux phénomènes?** is there a direct link between these two phenomena?; **l. de cause à effet** causal relationship, relationship of cause and effect

2 *(entre des gens)* link, connection; **nouer des liens d'amitié** to make friends, to become friends; **les liens conjugaux** *ou* **du mariage** marriage bonds *or* ties; **je vous déclare unis par les liens du mariage** = I now pronounce you man and wife; **l. de parenté** family ties; **ils ont un vague l. de parenté** there is some distant family connection between them, they're distantly related; **les liens du sang** blood ties; **l. social** social *or* civic bond; **la crise du l. social** the breakdown of a sense of community in society

3 *(lanière)* tie; **il s'est libéré de ses liens** he freed himself (from his bonds)

4 *Ordinat* link; **l. hypertexte** hypertext link

5 *Jur* **l. contractuel** privity

lier [9] [lje] **VT 1** *(attacher → cheveux, paquet, fagot)* to tie up; **on les lia au poteau** they were tied up to the post

2 *Méd* **l. une veine** to ligate a vein

3 *(logiquement)* to link, to connect; **il faut l. le nouveau paragraphe au reste du texte** the new paragraph must be linked to the rest of the text; **les deux faits ne sont pas liés** the two facts are not connected, there is no connection between the two facts; **informatisation et efficacité sont étroitement liées** computerization and efficiency are closely linked; **tout est lié** everything's interconnected, it all fits together

4 *(enchaîner → gestes)* to link together

5 *(par contrat)* to bind; **votre contrat ne vous lie pas à la société** your contract does not bind you to the company

6 *(associer volontairement)* **l. son sort à qn** to join forces with sb; **l. son sort à qch** to stick with sth for better or worse

7 *(unir par des sentiments)* to bind, to unite; **leur passé commun les lie** they are united by their common past; **l'amitié qui nous lie** the friendship which binds us; **cette maison est liée à mon enfance** this house is linked to my childhood

8 *(commencer)* **l. amitié** to become friends; **l. amitié avec qn** to strike up a friendship with sb; **l. connaissance/conversation avec qn** to strike up an acquaintance/a conversation with sb

9 *Constr* to bind

10 *Culin (sauce)* to thicken; *(farce)* to bind

11 *Ling* to link *(with liaisons)*

12 *Mus (notes)* to slur

▸**se lier VPR se l. (d'amitié)** to become friends; **se l. (d'amitié) avec qn** to strike up a friendship with sb, to become friends with sb; **il se lie facilement** he makes friends easily

lierne [ljɛrn] **NF 1** *Constr* intertie **2** *Archit* lierne

lierre [ljɛr] **NM** *Bot* ivy; **l. terrestre** ground ivy

liesse [ljɛs] **NF** *Littéraire* jubilation, exhilaration; **en l.** jubilant; **une foule en l.** a jubilant crowd

lieu[1], **-s** [ljø] **NM** *Ich* hake; **l. jaune** pollack; **l. noir** coalfish

lieu[2], **-x** [ljø] **NM 1** *(endroit)* place; **ce n'est pas le l. pour une dispute** this is no place *or* this isn't the place to have an argument; **l. de culte** place of worship; **l. de départ** point of departure; *Fin* **l. d'émission** place of issue; **l. de livraison** place of delivery, point of delivery; **l. de mémoire** memorial; *Fig* repository of culture; **l. de naissance** birthplace, place of birth; **l. de paiement** place of payment; **les mendiants se mettent de préférence sur les lieux de passage** beggars prefer busy areas *or* areas where there are lots of people going past; **cette ville n'est qu'un l. de passage** people merely pass through the town; **l. de pèlerinage** place of *or* centre for pilgrimage; **l. de perdition** den of iniquity; **leur l. de promenade habituel** the place where they usually go for a walk; **l. public** public place; **l. de rassemblement** place of assembly, assembly point; **l. de rencontre** meeting place; **l. de rendez-vous** meeting place; **fixons un l. de rendez-vous** let's decide on somewhere to meet *or* on a meeting place; **l. de résidence** (place of) residence; **l. saint** shrine; *Cin* **l. de tournage** location; **sur le l. de travail** in the workplace; **sur votre l. de travail** at your place of work; **l. de vente** point of sale

2 *Gram* **adverbe/complément (circonstanciel) de l.** adverb/complement of place

3 *Géom* **l. géométrique** locus

4 *Ling* **l. commun** commonplace, platitude

5 *(locutions)* **avoir l.** *(entrevue, expérience, spectacle)* to take place; *(accident)* to happen; *(erreur)* to occur; **avoir l. de** *(avoir des raisons de)* to have (good) reason to; **j'ai tout l. de croire que...** I have good *or* every reason to believe that...; **vous n'aurez pas l. de vous plaindre** you won't find any cause *or* any reason for complaint; **tes craintes n'ont pas l. d'être** your fears are groundless *or* unfounded; **il n'y a pas l. de s'affoler** there's no need to panic; **s'il y a l.** if necessary, should the need arise; **il y a tout l. de croire...** there is every reason to believe...; **donner l. à** *(querelle, problèmes)* to cause, to give rise to; **sa mort a donné l. à une enquête** his/her death prompted an investigation; **son retour a donné l. à une réunion de famille** his/her return was the occasion for a family gathering; **tout donne l. de croire que...** everything leads me/us/*etc* *or* there is every reason to believe that...; **son chien lui tient l. d'enfant** his/her dog is a substitute for a child; **ça tiendra l. de champagne!** that will do instead of champagne!; **le canapé tient l. de lit** the settee is used as a bed

▫ **lieux NMPL 1** *(endroit précis)* scene; **les lieux de nos premières amours/de l'accident/du crime** the scene of our first love/of the accident/of the crime; **la police est déjà sur les lieux (du crime)** the police are already at the scene of the crime; **pour être efficace, il faut être sur les lieux 24 heures sur 24** if you want to do things properly, you have to be on the spot 24 hours a day; **rendez-vous immédiatement sur les lieux** go there immediately; **les Lieux saints** the Holy Places

2 *(bâtiments)* premises; **les grévistes occupent les lieux** the strikers are occupying the premises; **quitter** *ou* **vider les lieux** to vacate the premises; **quand nous serons dans les lieux** when we're in occupation *or* in residence; **le propriétaire est dans les lieux** the landlord is on the premises; *Euph* **les lieux d'aisances** the smallest room, *Br* the lavatory, *Am* the bathroom

▫ **au lieu de PRÉP** instead of; **elle aurait dû me remercier, au l. de ça, elle m'en veut** she should have thanked me, instead of which she bears a grudge against me; **au l. de faire qch** instead of doing sth

▫ **au lieu que CONJ** instead of, rather than; **je préfère ranger moi-même mon bureau au l. que tu viennes tout changer de place** I prefer to tidy my desk myself instead of *or* rather than having you changing everything around

▫ **en dernier lieu ADV** finally, lastly; **n'ajoutez le sucre qu'en tout dernier l.** do not add the sugar until the last moment

▫ **en haut lieu ADV** in high places; **ça se décidera en haut l.** the decision will be made at a high level

▫ **en lieu et place de PRÉP** in place of, on behalf of, in lieu of; **le président n'étant pas là, j'ai assisté à l'enterrement en ses l. et place** as the president wasn't available, I attended the funeral on his behalf; **en l. et place d'honoraires/de préavis** in lieu of fees/of notice

▫ **en lieu sûr ADV** in a safe place; **range-le en l. sûr** put it away in a safe place, put it away somewhere safe

▫ **en premier lieu ADV** in the first place, firstly, first of all

▫ **en tous lieux ADV** everywhere; **sa politique est critiquée en tous lieux** his/her policy is under criticism in all quarters *or* everywhere

lieu-dit [ljødi] *(pl* **lieux-dits**) **NM** *(avec maisons)* hamlet; *(sans maisons)* place; **au l. La Folie** at the place called La Folie

lieue [ljø] **NF 1** *(mesure)* league; **l. marine** league

2 *(locutions)* **nous étions à cent lieues de penser que...** it would never have occurred to us that..., we never dreamt that...; **à cent lieues à la ronde** for miles (and miles) around

lieur, -euse [ljœr, -øz] NM,F *Arch (de gerbes, de bottes)* binder

▫ **lieuse** NF *(machine)* (sheaf) binder

Lieut. *(abrév écrite* **Lieutenant**) Lieut

Lieut.-col. *(abrév écrite* **Lieutenant-colonel**) Lieut.-Col

lieutenance [ljøtnɑ̃s] NF *Littéraire* lieutenancy

lieutenant [ljøtnɑ̃] NM 1 *Mil (de l'armée de terre, de la marine)* ≃ lieutenant; *(de l'armée de l'air) Br* ≃ flying officer, *Am* ≃ first lieutenant 2 *(de la marine marchande)* mate; **l. de vaisseau** ≃ lieutenant 3 *Suisse Mil* second lieutenant 4 *(assistant)* lieutenant, second-in-command; **il est entré, flanqué de ses deux lieutenants** he came in flanked by his two henchmen

lieutenant-colonel [ljøtnɑ̃kɔlɔnɛl] *(pl* **lieutenants-colonels**) NM *(de l'armée de terre)* ≃ lieutenant-colonel; *(de l'armée de l'air) Br* ≃ wing commander, *Am* ≃ lieutenant-colonel

lièvre [ljɛvr] NM 1 *Zool* hare; **lever un l.** to start a hare; *Fig* to raise a burning issue, to touch on a sore point; **l. arctique** arctic hare; **l. marin** sea hare; **l. de Patagonie** Patagonian hare, mara; **l. sauteur** spring hare; **l. sifflant** whistling hare, pika; **l. variable** variable *or* blue *or* snowshoe hare 2 *(fourrure)* hareskin 3 *Sport* pacemaker, pacesetter

LIFO [lifo] NM *Com & Compta (abrév* **last in first out**) LIFO

lift [lift] NM *Sport* topspin; **faire un l.** to put topspin on the ball

lifté, -e [lifte] ADJ *Sport* **une balle liftée** a ball with topspin; **elle a un jeu très l.** she plays a heavy topspin game

lifter [3] [lifte] VT 1 *Sport* **l. une balle** to give a ball topspin, to put topspin on a ball 2 *(faire un lifting à)* to perform a facelift on; *Fig (rénover)* to give a facelift to, to facelift

VI *Sport* to put topspin on the ball

liftier, -ère [liftje, -ɛr] NM,F *Br* lift attendant, *Am* elevator attendant

lifting [liftiŋ] NM 1 *(de la peau)* facelift; **se faire faire un l.** to have a facelift 2 *Fam (rénovation → d'une institution, d'un bâtiment)* facelift

ligament [ligamɑ̃] NM *Anat* ligament

ligamentaire [ligamɑ̃tɛr] ADJ *Anat* ligamentous, ligamentary

ligamenteux, -euse [ligamɑ̃tø, -øz] ADJ *Anat* ligamentous, ligamentary

ligand [ligɑ̃] NM *Chim* ligand

ligase [ligaz] NF *Biol & Chim* ligase

ligature [ligatyr] NF 1 *Méd (opération, fil)* ligature, ligation; **l. des trompes (de Fallope)** tubal ligation 2 *Typ* ligature, tied letter 3 *Hort (processus)* tying up; *(attache)* tie

ligaturer [3] [ligatyre] VT 1 *(attacher)* to tie on 2 *Méd* to ligate, to ligature; **se faire l. les trompes** to have one's (Fallopian) tubes tied 3 *Hort* to tie up

lige [liʒ] ADJ 1 *Hist* liege 2 *Sout* **être l'homme l. de qn** to be totally devoted to sb

ligérien, -enne [liʒerjɛ̃, -ɛn] ADJ of/from the Loire

▫ **Ligérien, -enne** NM,F = inhabitant of or person from the Loire

light [lajt] ADJ INV *(plat, préparation)* low-fat; *(boisson)* diet *(avant n)*, low-cal

lighteur [lajtœr] NM *Can Joual (briquet)* lighter■

ligie [liʒi] NF *Zool* sea slater

lignage [liɲaʒ] NM 1 *(ascendance)* lineage; **de haut l.** of noble lineage 2 *Typ* linage, lineage

lignard [liɲar] NM *Fam* 1 *Hist (soldat)* soldier of the line■; **les lignards** the infantry■ 2 *Élec* lineman■, (electric) line technician■ 3 *Journ* penny-a-liner

LIGNE [liɲ]

line **1–3, 5–11, 13, 14, 16** ■ outline **4** ■ figure **4** ■ row **5** ■ range **10** ■ fishing line **12**

NF 1 *(gén) & Géom* line; **soit une l. AB** let there be a line AB; **tracer** *ou* **tirer une l.** to draw a line; **les lignes de la main** the lines of the hand; **l. de cœur/de tête/de vie** heart/head/life line; **l. pointillée/brisée** dotted/broken line; **l. droite** straight line; **une l. droite** *(route)* a straight stretch of road; **la route est en l. droite sur 3 km** the road is straight for 3 km; **avancer en l. droite** to advance in a straight line; *Fam* **une l. de coke** a line of coke

2 *(texte)* line; **le prof m'a donné cent lignes** *(punition)* the teacher gave me a hundred lines; **il est payé à la l.** he is paid by the *or* per line; **elle m'a juste envoyé deux lignes** she just dropped me a line; **je vous envoie ces quelques lignes pour vous donner les dernières nouvelles** this is just a note to give you the latest news; **aller à la l.** to begin a new line *or* a new paragraph; **(allez) à la l.!** new paragraph!; *Presse* **tirer à la l.** to pad (out) an article; *Ordinat* **l. d'impression** print line; *Ordinat & Typ* **l. orpheline** orphan; *Mus* **l. supplémentaire** ledger line; *Ordinat & Typ* **l. veuve** widow

3 *(limite)* line; **tracer les lignes d'un court** to mark out a court; **passer la l. (de l'équateur)** to cross the line; *Can Joual* **passer les lignes** to cross the border; **l. d'arrivée** finishing line; *Sport* **l. de ballon mort** dead-ball line; **l. blanche** white line *(on roads)*; *Sport* **l. de but** goal line; *Naut* **l. de charge** load line; **l. continue** continuous line; *Sport* **lignes de côté** *(au tennis)* tramlines; **l. de démarcation** *(gén)* boundary; *Mil* demarcation line; **l. de départ** starting line; **l. discontinue** *(sur la route)* broken line; **l. d'eau** *Natation* (swimming) lane; *Naut* waterline; *Géol* **l. de faille** fault line; **l. de faîte** watershed, crest line; *Sport* **l. de faute** foul line; *Naut* **l. de flottaison** waterline; **l. de flottaison en charge** Plimsoll line; *Sport* **l. de fond** *(au tennis)* baseline; **l. d'horizon** skyline; **l. jaune** yellow line *(on roads)*; **l. de mire** line of sight; **l. de partage** dividing line; **l. de partage des eaux** watershed; *Sport* **l. de service** *(au tennis)* service line; **l. de tir** line of fire; **l. de touche** touchline; **l. de visée** line of sight

4 *(silhouette → d'un objet)* outline; *(→ d'une personne)* figure; **avoir la l.** to be slim; **je surveille ma l.** I look after *or* watch my figure; **garder la l.** to keep one's figure; **la l. de l'été sera très épurée** this summer's look will be very simple; **la l. élégante d'une voiture** the elegant lines of a car

5 *(rangée)* line, row; **plantés en l.** planted in a line *or* row; **se mettre en l.** to line up, to form a line; *Sport* **la l. d'avants/d'arrières** the forwards/backs; *Mil* **l. d'attaque** line of attack; *Mil* **l. de bataille** line of battle, battle line; **l. de défense** line of defence; **l. de front** front line; **les lignes ennemies** the enemy lines; *Mil & Fig* **être/monter en première l.** to be in/to go to the front line; *Sport* **un première/deuxième/troisième l.** a front-row/second-row/back-row forward

6 *(orientation)* line; *Pol* **l. du parti** party line; **suivre la l., être dans la l.** to follow *or* to toe the party line; **sa décision est dans la droite l. de la politique gouvernementale** his/her decision is completely in line with government policy; **redéfinir sa l. d'action** to adopt a different line *or* course of action; **l. de conduite** line of conduct; **l. directrice** main line; **lignes de force** *(grandes lignes)* dominating *or* guiding principles; *Phys* lines of force; **elle a décrit la situation dans ses grandes lignes** she gave a broad outline of the situation, she outlined the situation

7 *(généalogique)* line; **l. directe/collatérale** direct/collateral line; **descendre en l. directe de** to be directly descended from

8 *Transp* line; **l. aérienne** *(société)* airline (company); *(service)* air service, air link; *(itinéraire)* route; **l. d'autobus** *(service)* bus service; *(itinéraire)* bus route; **lignes de banlieue** suburban lines; **il n'y a que deux lignes de bus qui fonctionnent la nuit** there are only two late-night bus services; **l. de chemin de fer** *Br* railway line, *Am* railroad line; **lignes intérieures** *ou Can* **domestiques** *(aériennes)* domestic flights; **l. maritime** shipping line; **l. de métro** *Br* underground line, *Am* subway line; **l. secondaire** branch line; **les grandes lignes** the main lines; *Rail* **départ grandes lignes** mainline departures

9 *Élec & Tél* line; **la l. est occupée** the line is *Br* engaged *or Am* busy; **la l. est en dérangement** the line is out of order; **la l. a été coupée** I've/we've/*etc* been cut off; *Élec* **l. d'alimentation** feeder; *Tél* **l. commune** party line; *Tél* **l. directe/intérieure/extérieure** direct/internal/outside line; *Élec* **l. à haute tension** high-voltage line; *Ordinat* **l. louée** leased line; **l. ouverte** open line; **l. privée** private line; *Élec* **l. de** *ou* **à retard** delay line; **l. RNIS** ISDN line; **l. spécialisée** dedicated line; **l. télégraphique** telegraph line; **l. téléphonique** telephone line

10 *Com* line, range; **l. pour hommes** range for men; **une nouvelle l. de produits** a new line *or* range of products, a new product line *or* range

11 *TV (d'une image)* line

12 *Pêche* fishing line; **l. de fond** ground *or* ledger line; **l. volante** fly line

13 *Banque* **l. de crédit** line of credit, credit line; **l. de cotation** line of quotation; **l. de découvert** line of credit, credit line; **l. de substitution** backup line

14 *Ordinat* line; **sur l.** on line; **hors l.** off line; **l. de commande** command line; **l. d'état** status line

15 *Belg (raie des cheveux) Br* parting, *Am* part

16 *Can Vieilli (mesure)* line, = 2.3 mm

17 *(locution)* **entrer en l. de compte** to come *or* to be taken into consideration; **le coût doit entrer en l. de compte** the cost has to be taken into account *or* consideration; **le prix n'a pas à entrer en l. de compte** the cost doesn't come into it

▫ **en ligne** ADV 1 *(en rang)* **mettez-vous en l.!** line up!, get into line!; **en l. pour le départ!** line up ready for the start!

2 *Ordinat* on line

3 *Mil* **monter en l.** *(aller à l'assaut)* to advance (for the attack)

4 *Tél* **restez en l.!** hold the line!; **parlez, vous êtes en l.** go ahead, you're through *or* you're connected; **je l'ai en l.** I've got him/her on the line; **il est en l.** he's on another call just now; **elle est en l., vous patientez?** her line's *Br* engaged *or Am* busy, will you hold?

▫ **hors ligne** ADJ *(hors pair)* unrivalled, matchless

▫ **sur toute la ligne** ADV **gagner sur toute la l.** to win hands down; **se tromper sur toute la l.** to be completely mistaken

Allusion

La ligne bleue des Vosges

In his will, the 19th-century statesman Jules Ferry expressed his wish to be buried in his native village of Saint-Dié in the Vosges: "I wish to be laid to rest... facing the blue line of the Vosges, whence rises the sad lament of the defeated to touch my faithful heart." Jules Ferry's allusion was to France's concession of Alsace-Lorraine at the end of the Franco-Prussian war, when the frontier was moved to run across the Vosges. Today, if one says of someone **Il a les yeux fixés sur la ligne bleue des Vosges**, it means that he is on the watch for a potential enemy so as not to be caught unawares. Sometimes, too, the expression is used quite out of context, to describe someone who is gazing absent-mindedly into space. In that case, it simply means "the far blue yonder".

Culture

LA LIGNE DE DÉMARCATION

The armistice signed by Pétain on 22 June 1940 established the "ligne de démarcation" which officially sanctioned German occupation of a part of French territory. Marked in places by barbed wire and mines, it divided France into the occupied zone, north of the Loire, controlled by the Germans, and the unoccupied zone, south of the Loire, which remained under the jurisdiction of the Vichy government. It enabled the Germans to monitor the movement of goods, mail and people (who had to have an *Ausweis* or pass) between the two zones. It ceased to exist on 11 November 1942, when German troops invaded the southern zone.

ligne-bloc [liɲblɔk] *(pl* **lignes-blocs***)* **NF** *Typ* slug

lignée [liɲe] **NF 1** *(descendance)* descendants; **avoir une nombreuse l.** to have many descendants; **le premier/dernier d'une longue l.** the first/last of a long line (of descent)

2 *(extraction, lignage)* stock, lineage; **être de noble l.** to be of noble lineage

3 *(tradition)* line, tradition; **elle s'inscrit dans la l. des romancières féministes** she is in the tradition of feminist novelists

4 *Biol* line, stock; **l. cellulaire** cell line; **l. pure** pure line

ligner [3] [liɲe] **VT** to line

ligneul [liɲœl] **NM** shoemaker's end, wax end

ligneux, -euse [liɲø, -øz] **ADJ** ligneous, woody

lignicole [liɲikɔl] **ADJ** lignicolous

lignification [liɲifikasjɔ̃] **NF** lignification

lignifier [9] [liɲifje] **se lignifier VPR** to lignify

lignine [liɲin] **NF** lignin

lignite [liɲit] **NM** *Mines* brown coal, lignite

lignomètre [liɲɔmɛtr] **NM** *Typ* type scale

ligot [ligo] **NM** bundle of firelighters

ligotage [ligɔtaʒ] **NM** binding, tying up

ligoter [3] [ligɔte] **VT** to bind, to tie up; **ligoté à sa chaise** tied to his chair

ligue [lig] **NF 1** *(morale, de défense)* league, pressure group; **l. antialcoolique** temperance league; **L. des droits de l'homme** League of Human Rights; **la L. nationale contre le cancer** = cancer research charity; **L. pour la protection des oiseaux** = society for the protection of birds, *Br* ≃ RSPB

2 *Hist & Pol* **la (Sainte) L.** the (Holy Catholic) League; **la L. arabe** the Arab League; **L. communiste révolutionnaire** = militant Trotskyist organization

liguer [3] [lige] **VT être ligué contre** to be united against

▸**se liguer VPR se l. contre** to join forces against

ligueur, -euse [ligœr, -øz] **NM,F 1** *Pol* member *(of a league)* **2** *Hist* member of the (Catholic) League

ligule [ligyl] **NF** *Bot* ligula, ligule, strap

ligulé, -e [ligyle] **ADJ** *Bot* ligulate

liguliflore [ligyliflɔr] *Bot* **NF** member of the Liguliflorae family

❑ **liguliflores NFPL** Liguliflorae

ligure [ligyr] = **ligurien**

Ligurie [ligyri] **NF la L.** Liguria

ligurien, -enne [ligyrjɛ̃, -ɛn] **ADJ** Ligurian

❑ **Ligurien, -enne NM,F** Ligurian

ligustrum [ligystrɔm] **NM** *Belg Bot* privet, *Spéc* ligustrum

lilas [lila] **NM** *(arbre)* lilac (tree); *(fleur)* lilac; **l. simple/double** single-/double-bloom lilac

ADJ INV lilac *(avant n)*, lilac-coloured

liliacée [liljase] *Bot* **NF** liliacea, *Spéc* member of the Liliaceae

❑ **liliacées NFPL** Liliaceae

lilial, -e, -aux, -ales [liljal, -o] **ADJ** *Littéraire (qui a la couleur du lis)* lily-white

liliales [liljal], **liliiflores** [liliiflɔr] **NFPL** *Bot* Liliales, Liliiflorae

Lilith [lilit] **NPR** *Myth* Lilith

Lille [lil] **NM** Lille

lilliputien, -enne [lilipysjɛ̃, -ɛn] **ADJ** Lilliputian, tiny

❑ **Lilliputien, -enne NM,F** Lilliputian

lillois, -e [lilwa, -az] **ADJ** of/from Lille

❑ **Lillois, -e NM,F** = inhabitant of or person from Lille

Lilongwe [lilɔ̃gwe] **NM** Lilongwe

Lima [lima] **NM** Lima

limace [limas] **NF 1** *Zool* slug **2** *Fam Péj (personne) Br* slowcoach, *Am* slowpoke; **le bus se traîne comme une l.** the bus is crawling along **3** *Fam (chemise)* shirt▪ **4** *Can Ich* sea snail

limaçon [limasɔ̃] **NM 1** *Zool* snail **2** *Anat* cochlea

limage [limaʒ] **NM** *(d'une clé)* filing; *(d'une rugosité)* filing off *or* away; *(d'une pièce de métal, de bois)* filing down; *(d'un cadenas, d'un barreau)* filing through

limaille [limaj] **NF** filings; **l. de fer** iron filings

liman [limɑ̃] **NM** liman, freshwater lagoon

limande [limɑ̃d] **NF** *Ich* dab; **fausse l.** megrim, scaldfish

limande-sole [limɑ̃dsɔl] *(pl* **limandes-soles***)* **NF** *Ich* lemon sole

limbaire [lɛ̃bɛr] **ADJ** *Bot* limb *(avant n)*

limbe [lɛ̃b] **NM 1** *(d'un cadran)* limb **2** *Astron* limb **3** *Bot* limb, lamina

limbes [lɛ̃b] **NMPL 1** *Rel* limbo; **dans les l.** in limbo

2 *(état vague, incertain)* **être dans les l.** to be in (a state of) limbo; **son projet est encore dans les l.** his/her project is still at the embryonic stage *or* hasn't yet got off the ground

limbique [lɛ̃bik] **ADJ** *Anat (lobe, système)* limbic

Limbourg [lɛ̃bur] **NM le L.** Limburg

lime [lim] **NF 1** *(outil)* file; **l. à ongles** nail file; **l. sourde** dead-smooth file **2** *Bot & Culin* lime **3** *Zool (mollusque)* lima

limé, -e [lime] **ADJ** *(vêtement)* worn, threadbare

limer [3] [lime] **VT 1** *(clé)* to file; *(rugosité)* to file off *or* away; *(pièce de métal, de bois)* to file down; *(cadenas, barreau)* to file through; **le cadenas a été limé** the padlock has been filed through **2** *Vulg (posséder sexuellement)* to hump, to screw, *Br* to shaft

▸**se limer VPR se l. les ongles** to file one's nails

limerick [limrik] **NM** *Littérature* limerick

limes [limɛs] **NM** *Hist* limes, Roman boundary work

limette [limɛt] **NF** *Bot* lime

limettier [limetje] **NM** *Bot* lime (tree)

limeur, -euse [limœr, -øz] **ADJ** filing *(avant n)*

NM,F *(ouvrier)* filer

❑ **limeuse NF** filing machine

limicole [limikɔl] *Zool* **ADJ** limicolous

NM member of the Limicolae family

❑ **limicoles NMPL** Limicolae

limier [limje] **NM 1** *Zool (chien)* bloodhound, sleuth-hound **2** *Fam (policier)* **fin l.** sleuth

liminaire [liminɛr] **ADJ 1** *(discours)* introductory, preliminary; **un discours l.** a keynote speech **2** *Psy* liminal, threshold *(avant n)*

liminal, -e, -aux, -ales [liminal, -o] **ADJ** *Psy* liminal, threshold *(avant n)*

limitable [limitabl] **ADJ** limitable

limitatif, -ive [limitatif, -iv] **ADJ** *(liste)* restrictive, limitative; *(clause)* restrictive; **une liste non limitative** an open-ended list

limitation [limitasjɔ̃] **NF** limitation, restriction; **l. des armements** arms control *or* limitation; **l. des naissances** birth control; **l. des prix** price restrictions *or* controls; *Jur* **l. de responsabilité** limitation of responsibility; **l. des salaires** wage restraint; **l. de vitesse** speed limit *or* restrictions; **ce test se fait sans l. de temps** there is no time limit for the test

limitative [limitativ] *voir* **limitatif**

limite [limit] **NF 1** *(maximum ou minimum)* limit; **l. de temps** time limit; *Fam* **il veut mon article demain dernière l.** he wants my article by tomorrow at the (very) latest; **fixer** *ou* **mettre une l. à qch** to set a limit to sth, to limit sth; **la l. a été fixée à 30 participants** the number of participants has been limited *or* restricted to 30; **entrée gratuite dans la l. des places disponibles** *(à l'entrée d'un spectacle)* free admission subject to availability; **dans la l. des stocks disponibles** while stocks last; **dans les limites du possible** as far as is humanly possible; **nos dépenses sont restées dans les limites du raisonnable** our expenses stayed within reasonable bounds; **dans une certaine l.** up to a point, to a certain extent; **c'est dans la l. de mes moyens** it's within my means; **ma patience a des limites!** there's a limit to my patience!; **il y a des limites!** there are limits!; **sa haine ne connaît pas de limites** his/her hatred knows no bounds; **son égoïsme est sans l.** his/her selfishness knows no bounds; **l. d'âge** age limit; **l. de crédit** credit limit; *Tech* **l. d'élasticité** elastic limit; **l. d'endettement** debt limit

2 *(frontière* → *d'un bois)* border, edge; *(*→ *d'un pays)* boundary, border; **les limites d'un terrain de football** the boundary (lines) of a football pitch; **essaie de jouer dans les limites du court!** try to keep the ball inside the court!

3 *Math* limit

4 *Boxe* **avant la l.** inside *or* within the distance; **tenir jusqu'à la l.** to go the (full) distance

5 *Bourse* limit; **l. de la baisse** limit down; **l. de la hausse** limit up; **l. inférieure** limit down; **l. de position** position limit; **l. supérieure** limit up

ADJ 1 *(maximal)* **âge/vitesse l.** maximum age/speed

2 *Fam (juste)* **j'ai réussi l'examen, mais c'était l.** I passed the exam, but it was a close *or* near thing; **elle est l., ta dissertation** your essay's a borderline case *or* only just this side of acceptable; **je suis un peu l. côté fric** I'm a bit short of funds *or Br* strapped for cash; **question propreté, c'était l.** hygiene-wise, it was a bit iffy *or Br* dodgy

3 *Fam (grivois)* **des plaisanteries un peu l.** jokes bordering on the offensive; **ta remarque était un peu l.** your remark was a bit near the knuckle

❑ **limites NFPL** *(physiques, intellectuelles)* limitations; **je connais mes limites** I know my limitations

❑ **à la limite ADV à la l., on peut toujours dormir dans la voiture** if the worst comes to the worst, we can always sleep in the car; **à la l., je lui prêterais l'argent** if necessary *or* if it came to the crunch, I'd lend him/her the money; **à la l., je préférerais rester ici** I'd almost prefer to stay here

❑ **à la limite de PRÉP c'était à la l. du mauvais goût/de l'insolence** it was verging on bad taste/on impertinence

> *Allusion*
>
> **Au-delà de cette limite votre billet n'est plus valable**
>
> The title of Romain Gary's 1975 novel, this is in fact a sign in the Paris metro on the exit doors. It means: "Your ticket is no longer valid beyond this point". The novel is about a man coming to terms with aging after an easy and pleasant life. People allude to the title when they feel they are no longer wanted, and generally seen as "past it". In English one might say wryly: "I'm past my sell-by date" or "I've had it"; in French one might murmur **Au-delà de cette limite...**

limité, -e [limite] **ADJ 1** *(influence, connaissances)* limited; *(nombre, choix, durée)* limited, restricted; **en temps l.** in a limited amount of time; **d'une importance limitée** of limited *or* minor importance **2** *Fam (personne)* **être l.** to have limited abilities▪, to be of limited ability▪; **il est assez l. en maths** he's rather weak *or* poor at maths **3** *Can* Limited, Ltd; **Desrochers et Cie limitée** Desrochers and Co Ltd

limiter [3] [limite] **VT 1** *(réduire* → *dépenses, nombre)* to limit, to restrict; *(*→ *temps, influence)* to limit; **la vitesse n'est pas limitée** there is no speed limit; *aussi Fig* **essayez de l. les dégâts** try and limit the damage; **je ne connaissais pas vraiment le sujet de l'examen, mais j'ai limité les dégâts** I didn't really know anything about the exam subject but I managed to make something of it; **l. qch à** to limit *or* to restrict sth to; **j'ai limité mon budget à 200 euros par semaine** I've limited *or* restricted my weekly budget to 200 euros

2 *(circonscrire)* to mark the limit of, to delimit; **des haies limitent la propriété** hedges mark out the limits of the estate

▸**se limiter VPR 1** *(emploi réfléchi)* **il ne sait pas se l.** he's incapable of self-restraint; **plus de gâteaux, merci, il faut que je me limite** no more cakes, thanks, I've got to watch what I eat

2 se l. à *(se résumer à)* to be restricted to, to be confined to; **l'exposé s'est limité à l'aspect historique** the talk only dealt with *or* was restricted to the historical aspect; **sa fortune se limite à peu de chose** his/her fortune does not amount to very much

3 se l. à *(se contenter de)* to limit oneself to; **il se limite à faire ce qu'on lui dit** he only does *or* he limits himself to doing what he's told to do

limiteur [limitœr] **NM** limiter

limitrophe [limitrɔf] **ADJ des comtés limitrophes** adjoining *or* neighbouring counties; **nos villages sont limitrophes** our villages lie (just) next to each other; **les pays limitrophes de la Belgique** the countries bordering on Belgium

limivore [limivɔr] **ADJ** *Biol* limivorous

limnée [limne] **NF** *Zool* pond snail, *Spéc* limnaea

limnologie [limnɔlɔʒi] **NF** limnology

limnologique [limnɔlɔʒik] **ADJ** limnological

limnoria [limnɔrja] **NM** *Zool* gribble

limogeage [limɔʒaʒ] **NM** dismissal

limoger [17] [limɔʒe] VT to dismiss; **il s'est fait l.** he was dismissed

Limoges [limɔʒ] NM Limoges *(town in central France famous for its fine porcelain)*

limon [limɔ̃] NM **1** *Géol* silt, alluvium; *Fig Littéraire* **il se croit d'un autre l. que nous** he thinks he is of a different clay from ours; **le l. du vice** the slough of vice **2** *Agr* loam **3** *(d'attelage)* shaft **4** *(d'escalier)* stair stringer, stringboard

limonade [limɔnad] NF (fizzy) lemonade

limonadier, -ère [limɔnadje, -ɛr] NM,F **1** *(cafetier)* cafe owner **2** *(fabricant)* soft drinks manufacturer

limonage [limɔnaʒ] NM *Agr* enriching with loam

limonaire [limɔnɛr] NM *(petit)* barrel organ, hurdy-gurdy; *(grand)* fairground organ

limonène [limɔnɛn] NM *Chim* limonene

limoner [3] [limɔne] VI *Can Fam* **1** *(se plaindre)* to moan, to whinge; *(pleurnicher)* to whinge **2** *(hésiter)* to dither

limoneux, -euse [limɔnø, -øz] ADJ silty, silt-laden

limonier[1] [limɔnje] NM *Vieilli (cheval)* shaft horse

limonier[2] [limɔnje] NM *Bot* sour-lime tree

limonière [limɔnjɛr] NF shafts

limonite [limɔnit] NF *Minér* limonite, brown iron ore

limoselle [limɔzɛl] NF *Bot* mudwort, limosella

limougeaud, -e [limuʒo, -od] ADJ of/from Limoges

❑ **Limougeaud, -e** NM,F = inhabitant of or person from Limoges

limousin, -e[1] [limuzɛ̃, -in] ADJ of/from the Limousin

NM *(dialecte)* Limousin dialect

❑ **Limousin, -e** NM **le L.** the Limousin NM,F = inhabitant of or person from the Limousin

limousinage [limuzinaʒ] NM *Constr* rubble work, rough masonry

limousine[1] [limuzin] ADJ *voir* **limousin**

limousine[2] NF *(automobile)* limousine

Limoux [limu] *voir* **blanquette**

limpide [lɛ̃pid] ADJ **1** *(pur → lac, miroir, regard)* limpid, clear; **pierre d'un bleu l.** limpid *or* clear blue stone **2** *(intelligible → discours, style)* clear, lucid; *(→ affaire)* clear; **leur histoire n'est pas très l.** their story isn't very clear

limpidité [lɛ̃pidite] NF **1** *(d'une eau, d'un regard, d'un diamant)* clearness, *Littéraire* limpidity **2** *(d'un texte)* lucidity; *(d'une affaire)* clarity, clearness

Limpopo [lɛ̃popo] NM **le L.** the Limpopo (river)

limule [limyl] NF *Zool* king crab, horseshoe crab

lin [lɛ̃] NM **1** *Bot* flax; **l. des marais** cotton grass **2** *Tex* linen, flax; **en l.** linen *(avant n)*; **robe en l.** linen dress

linacée [linase] *Bot* NF member of the Linaceae family

❑ **linacées** NFPL Linaceae

linaigrette [linɛgrɛt] NF *Bot* cotton grass

linaire [linɛr] NF *Bot* linaria; **l. cymbalaire** ivy-leaved toadflax; **l. des sables** sand toadflax

linceul [lɛ̃sœl] NM **1** *(suaire)* shroud **2** *Littéraire* **couvert d'un l. de neige** shrouded in snow

linçoir [lɛ̃swar] NM *Constr* trimmer, trimming joist

lindane [lɛ̃dan] NM *Chim* lindane

linéaire [lineɛr] ADJ **1** *Électron, Ling & Math* linear **2** *(simple → discours, exposé)* reductionist, one-dimensional; *(→ récit)* linear; **il a exposé le problème de façon l.** he gave a one-dimensional account of the problem

NM *Com* shelf space; *(étalage)* shelf display; **ce produit n'apparaît pas dans les linéaires de magasins non spécialisés** non-specialist shops do not stock this product

linéairement [lineɛrmɑ̃] ADV *(en ligne droite)* in a straight line; *Math* linearly

linéament [lineamɑ̃] NM **1** *Littéraire* **linéaments** *(du visage)* lineaments, features **2** *(ébauche → d'un discours, d'une réforme)* outline, main points **3** *Géol* lineament

linéarité [linearite] NF linearity

linéature [lineatyr] NF **1** *Phot* ruling **2** *TV* line system, (television) lines

linéique [lineik] ADJ *Phys* per unit length

liner [lajnœr] NM *Naut* liner

linette [linɛt] NF linseed, flax seed

linga [lɛ̃ga], **lingam** [lɛ̃gam] NM linga, lingam

linge [lɛ̃ʒ] NM **1** *(pour l'habillement et la maison)* linen *(UNCOUNT)*; *(lavé)* washing *(UNCOUNT)*; **10 kg de l.** 10 kg of washing; **étendre/repasser le l.** to hang out/to iron the washing; **faire sécher le l.** to dry the washing; **pour un l. plus blanc, employez X** for a whiter wash, use X; **le l. blanc** household linen; **l. de corps** underwear *(UNCOUNT)*, underclothes; **l. de maison** household linen; **l. de table** table linen; **linges d'autel** altar cloth; **du petit l.** small items (of laundry); **du gros l.** big items (of laundry); *Fam* **il ne fréquente que du beau l.** he only mixes in high circles *or* with the upper crust; *Fam* **il y avait du beau l. au vernissage** anyone who was anyone was at the opening

2 *(chiffon)* cloth

3 *Suisse* towel

4 *Can Vieilli (vêtements)* clothing *(UNCOUNT)*; *(vêtement)* garment, article of clothing

lingère [lɛ̃ʒɛr] NF *(d'une institution)* laundry supervisor

lingerie [lɛ̃ʒri] NF **1** *(sous-vêtements)* lingerie *(UNCOUNT)*, women's underwear *(UNCOUNT)*; **l. fine** lingerie **2** *(lieu)* linen room

lingette [lɛ̃ʒɛt] NF *(pour bébés)* babywipe

lingot [lɛ̃go] NM **1** *Fin* ingot; **l. d'or** gold ingot *or* bar; **lingots en or** gold bullion *(UNCOUNT)*; **or en l.** *ou* **en lingots** gold bullion **2** *Typ* space

lingotière [lɛ̃gɔtjɛr] NF *Métal* ingot mould

lingua franca [lingwafrɑ̃ka] NF INV lingua franca

lingual, -e, -aux, -ales [lɛ̃gwal, -o] ADJ lingual

linguatule [lɛ̃gwatyl] NF *Zool* linguatula, tongue worm

lingue [lɛ̃g] NF *Ich* ling

linguette [lɛ̃gɛt] NF sublingual tablet

linguiste [lɛ̃gɥist] NMF linguist

linguistique [lɛ̃gɥistik] ADJ linguistic

NF linguistics *(singulier)*; **l. descriptive** descriptive linguistics

linguistiquement [lɛ̃gɥistikmɑ̃] ADV linguistically

linier, -ère [linje, -ɛr] ADJ flax *(avant n)*

❑ **linière** NF flax field

liniment [linimɑ̃] NM liniment

linkage [linkaʒ] NM *Biol* linkage

links [liŋks] NMPL *Sport* links

Linné [line] NPR Linneus, Linnaeus

linnéen, -enne [lineɛ̃, -ɛn] ADJ *Biol* Linnean, Linnaean

lino [lino] NM *Fam (abrév* **linoléum***)* linoleum■, *Br* lino

linogravure [linɔgravyr] NF linocut

linoléine [linɔlein] NF *Chim* linolein

linoléique [linɔleik] ADJ *Chim* linoleic

linoléum [linɔleɔm] NM linoleum

linon [linɔ̃] NM *Tex* lawn

linotte [linɔt] NF *Orn* linnet

Linotype® [linɔtip] NF *Typ* Linotype®

linotypie [linɔtipi] NF *Typ* Linotype® setting

linotypiste [linɔtipist] NMF *Typ* linotypist

linsang [lɛ̃sɑ̃g] NM *Zool* linsang

linsoir [lɛ̃swar] NM *Constr* trimmer, trimming joist

linteau, -x [lɛ̃to] NM lintel

linters [lintɛrs] NMPL linters

Linux® [linyks] NM *Ordinat* Linux

Linz [lints] NM *Géog* Linz

Lion [ljɔ̃] NM **1** *Géog* **golfe du L.** Gulf of Lions **2** *Astron* Leo **3** *Astrol* Leo; **être L.** to be (a) Leo *or* a Leonian

lion [ljɔ̃] NM *(animal) & Fig* lion; **l. de mer** sea lion; **tourner comme un l. en cage** to pace up and down (like a caged lion)

lionceau, -x [ljɔ̃so] NM (lion) cub

liondent [ljɔ̃dɑ̃] NM *Bot* hawkbit; **l. d'automne** autumn hawkbit; **l. hispide** rough hawkbit

lionne [ljɔn] NF lioness

Lip [lip] NF = former watchmaking company in Besançon which was taken over and run by its workers when it went bankrupt in 1973; the only partially successful attempt to keep the plant going made the workers into national heroes

liparis [liparis] NM **1** *Ich* sea snail **2** *Entom* tussock moth **3** *Bot* liparis

lipase [lipaz] NF *Biol & Chim* lipase

lipémie [lipemi] NF *Méd* lipaemia

lipide [lipid] NM *Biol & Chim* lipid

lipidémie [lipidemi] NF *Méd* lipaemia

lipidique [lipidik] ADJ *Biol & Chim* lipidic

lipizzan [lipidzɑ̃] ADJ Lipizzaner *(avant n)*, Lippizaner *(avant n)*

NM Lipizzaner, Lippizaner

lipoatrophie [lipoatrɔfi] NF *Méd* lipoatrophy; **l. du visage** face-wasting

lipochrome [lipɔkrom] NM *Biol & Chim* lipochrome

lipogenèse [lipɔʒənɛz] NF *Biol* lipogenesis

lipogramme [lipɔgram] NM *Littérature* lipogram

lipoïde [lipɔid] NM *Biol* lipoid

lipoïdique [lipɔidik] ADJ *Biol* lipoid

lipolyse [lipɔliz] NF *Physiol* lipolysis

lipolytique [lipɔlitik] ADJ *Physiol* lipolytic

lipome [lipom] NM *Méd* lipoma

lipophile [lipɔfil] ADJ *Biol* lipophilic

lipophobe [lipɔfɔb] ADJ *Biol* lipophobic

lipoprotéine [lipɔprɔtein] NF *Biol* lipoprotein

liposoluble [lipɔsɔlybl] ADJ *Biol* liposoluble, fat-soluble

liposome [lipɔzom] NM *Biol* liposome

liposuccion [liposyksjɔ̃, liposysjɔ̃] NF liposuction

lipothymie [lipɔtimi] NF *Méd* lipothymia

lipotrope [lipɔtrɔp] ADJ *Biol* lipotropic

lippe [lip] NF **1** *(lèvre inférieure)* lower lip **2** *Fam (locutions)* **faire la** *ou* **sa l.** *(faire la moue)* to pout; *(bouder)* to sulk; **je lui ai demandé de m'aider et il a fait la** *ou* **sa l.** I asked him to help me and he pulled a face

lippée [lipe] NF *Arch* **1** *(bouchée)* mouthful **2** *(repas)* **une franche l.** a good tuck-in at someone else's expense

lippu, -e [lipy] ADJ *(personne, bouche)* thick-lipped; *(lèvres)* thick

liquation [likwasjɔ̃] NF *Métal* liquation

liquéfacteur [likefaktœr] NM liquefier

liquéfaction [likefaksjɔ̃] NF liquefaction

liquéfiable [likefjabl] ADJ liquefiable

liquéfiant, -e [likefjɑ̃, -ɑ̃t] ADJ **1** *Chim & Pétr* liquefying **2** *Fam (épuisant)* exhausting■, *Br* knackering

liquéfier [9] [likefje] VT **1** *Chim, Métal & Pétr* to liquefy; **plomb liquéfié** liquefied lead **2** *Fam (épuiser → personne)* to exhaust■, *Br* to knacker; **cette chaleur m'a liquéfié** this heat has knocked me out

►**se liquéfier** VPR **1** *(plomb, gaz)* to liquefy, to be liquefied **2** *Fam (s'amollir)* to collapse in a heap

liquette [likɛt] NF *Fam (chemise)* shirt■

liqueur [likœr] NF **1** *(boisson)* liqueur; **l. de fruit** fruit liqueur; **bonbon à la l.** liqueur-filled *Br* sweet *or Am* candy; **chocolat à la l.** (chocolate) liqueur **2** *Pharm* solution; **l. de Fehling** Fehling's solution **3** *Can Joual* **l. (douce)** soft drink■; **l. forte** strong drink, hard liquor; **l. gazeuse** *Br* fizzy drink, *Am* soda

liquidable [likidabl] ADJ *Fin* liquidable, that can be liquidated

liquidambar [likidɑ̃bar] NM *Bot* liquidambar

liquidateur, -trice [likidatœr, -tris] ADJ liquidating

NM liquidator; **l. judiciaire** official liquidator; *Bourse* **l. officiel** official assignee

liquidatif, -ive [likidatif, -iv] ADJ **valeur liquidative** market *or* breakup value

liquidation [likidasjɔ̃] NF **1** *(règlement)* settling; **la l. de la crise ministérielle** the settling of the ministerial crisis

2 *Fam (assassinat)* elimination

3 *Bourse* settlement; *(d'une position)* liquidation; **l. en espèces** cash settlement; **l. de fin de mois** end-of-month settlement; **l. de quinzaine** two-weekly *or Br* fortnightly settlement, two-weekly *or Br* fortnightly account

4 *Com (d'un stock)* selling off, clearance; *(d'un commerce)* closing down, *Am* closing out; **l. totale** *(sur panneau)* closing down sale, everything must go

5 *Fin & Jur (d'une société)* liquidation; *(d'un impôt, d'une dette)* settlement, payment; **l. de biens** selling (off) *or* liquidation of assets; **l. des dépens** = taxation of court costs against a party; **l. (par décision) judiciaire** official receivership; **l. forcée** compulsory liquidation; **l. judiciaire** official receivership; **l. volontaire** voluntary liquidation

❑ **en liquidation** ADV *Jur* **être en l.** to have gone into liquidation; **entrer en l.** to go into liquidation; **mettre en l.** to put into liquidation, to

liquidate; **l'entreprise a été mise en l.** the firm was put into liquidation

liquidative [likidativ] *voir* **liquidatif**

liquidatrice [likidatris] *voir* **liquidateur**

liquide [likid] ADJ 1 *(qui coule)* liquid; **le mercure est un métal l.** mercury is a liquid metal; **des aliments liquides** fluids, liquid food *or* foods

2 *(trop fluide)* watery, thin; **soupe trop l.** watery *or* excessively thin soup

3 *Fin (déterminé → créance)* liquid; **dette l.** liquid debt; **peu l.** illiquid

4 *(argent)* **argent l.** cash

5 *Ling* liquid

NM 1 *(substance fluide)* liquid, fluid; **un l. huileux** an oily liquid; **l. correcteur** correction fluid; **l. de freins** brake fluid; **l. de refroidissement** coolant, coolant fluid; **l. vaisselle** washing-up liquid, *Am* dish soap

2 *(aliment)* fluid; **pour le moment, ne lui donnez que des liquides** only give him/her fluids for the moment

3 *Physiol* fluid; **l. amniotique** amniotic fluid; **l. céphalo-rachidien** spinal fluid; **l. organique** organic fluid

4 *(espèces)* cash; **je n'ai pas de l.** I haven't got any cash (on me); **payer en l.** to pay cash

NF *Ling* liquid (consonant)

liquider [3] [likide] VT 1 *Fin & Jur (marchandises, société, biens)* to liquidate; *(succession, compte)* to settle; *(dette)* to settle, to pay off; *Bourse (position)* to liquidate

2 *Com (volontairement → stock)* to sell off, to clear; *(→ commerce)* to close down, *Am* to close out; **on liquide** *(sur la vitrine d'un magasin)* closing down sale

3 *Fam (éliminer → problème)* to get rid of, to scrap; **ça, je ne veux plus en entendre parler, liquidé!** I don't want to hear another word about it, subject closed!

4 *(expédier → travail)* to finish off; *(→ client)* to deal with (quickly); *(→ affaire)* to settle

5 *Fam (nourriture)* to scoff, to guzzle; *(boisson)* to sink, to down

6 *Fam (tuer)* to liquidate, to ice, to bump off

liquidien, -enne [likidjɛ̃, -ɛn] ADJ liquid *(avant n)*

liquidité [likidite] NF *Chim & Fin* liquidity; **l. du portefeuille** portfolio liquidity

❑ **liquidités** NFPL *Fin* liquid assets; **liquidités excédentaires** excess liquidities; **liquidités internationales** international liquidity; **liquidités obligatoires** mandatory liquid assets

liquoreux, -euse [likɔrø, -øz] ADJ syrupy

liquoriste [likɔrist] NMF liqueur seller

lire¹ [lir] NF *(monnaie)* lira

LIRE² [106] [lir] VT 1 *(texte, thermomètre, carte)* to read; **j'ai lu tout Brecht** I've read everything Brecht wrote; **on a lu 'le Grand Meaulnes' en classe** we read 'le Grand Meaulnes' in class; **avez-vous des choses à l. pour le voyage?** have you got something to read for the journey?; **à l. ce mois-ci** this month's selection; **l. attentivement la notice** *(sur l'emballage d'un médicament)* read instructions carefully; **l. un rapport en diagonale** to flick *or* to skim through a report; **il m'a lu ta lettre au téléphone** he read me your letter over the phone; **je l'ai lu dans le magazine** I read (about) it in the magazine; **vous êtes beaucoup lu** many people read your works; **elle a beaucoup lu** she's well read; **en espérant vous l. bientôt** *(dans la correspondance)* hoping to hear from you soon; **lu et approuvé** *(sur un contrat)* read and approved; **allemand lu et parlé** *(dans un curriculum)* fluent German; **il faut l. 50 au lieu de 500** 500 should read 50

2 *(déceler)* to read; **on lisait la déception dans ses yeux** you could read *or* see the disappointment in his/her eyes; **l. les lignes de la main à qn** to read sb's palm; **l. l'avenir dans le marc de café** ≃ to read (the future in the) tea leaves

3 *(interpréter)* to interpret; **on peut l. son rapport de deux façons** his/her report can be interpreted *or* read in two ways; **ils ne lisent pas Malraux de la même manière** their interpretations *or* readings of Malraux differ

4 *Ordinat (disquette)* to read; *(signes)* to sense; *(images)* to scan

USAGE ABSOLU **apprendre à l.** to learn to read; **elle lit bien maintenant** she can read well now; **l. sur les lèvres** to lip-read; *Fig* **l. entre les lignes** to read between the lines

❑ **lire dans** VT IND **l. dans les pensées de qn** to read sb's thoughts *or* mind

▸ **se lire** VPR 1 *(être déchiffré)* to read; **ça se lit facilement** it's easy to read; **ce roman se lit en une soirée** this novel can be read in an evening; **ça se lit comme un roman** it reads like a novel; **l'hébreu se lit de droite à gauche** Hebrew reads *or* you read Hebrew from right to left; **ce genre de fautes se lit couramment** you read this sort of mistake a lot

2 *(apparaître)* to show; **l'inquiétude se lisait sur son visage** anxiety showed on *or* was written all over his/her face

lis [lis] NM 1 *Bot* lily; **l. d'eau** water lily; **l. des vallées** lily of the valley; **un teint de l.** a lily-white complexion 2 *Zool* **l. de mer** sea lily

lisage [lizaʒ] NM *Tex* 1 *(analyse)* reading in, reading off 2 *(machine)* reading-in *or* leasing machine

lisait *etc voir* **lire²**

Lisboète, lisboète [lisbɔɛt] = **lisbonnin, -e**

Lisbonnais, -e, lisbonnais, -e [lisbɔnɛ, -ɛz] = **lisbonnin, -e**

Lisbonne [lisbɔn] NM Lisbon

lisbonnin, -e [lizbɔnɛ̃, -in] ADJ of/from Lisbon

❑ **Lisbonnin, -e** NM,F = person from or inhabitant of Lisbon

lise [liz] NF *(sable mouvant)* quicksand

liserage [lizraʒ], **lisérage** [lizeraʒ] NM ornamental edging

liseré [lizre], **liséré** [lizere] NM edging

liserer [3] [lizre], **lisérer** [18] [lizere] VT to edge, to sew an edging on

liseron [lizrɔ̃] NM bindweed, *Spéc* convolvulus; **l. de mer** sea bindweed

lisette [lizɛt] NF 1 *(petit maquereau)* small mackerel 2 *Littéraire* = gay *or* light-hearted work girl (of popular songs); *Théât* **jouer les Lisettes** to take the witty soubrette parts

liseur, -euse [lizœr, -øz] NM,F reader

❑ **liseuse** NF 1 *(veste)* bed-jacket 2 *(coupe-papier)* (bookmark and) paperknife 3 *(couvre-livre)* dust jacket 4 *(lampe)* reading-light

lisibilité [lizibilite] NF *(d'une écriture)* legibility; *(d'un texte, d'un fichier informatique)* readability

lisible [lizibl] ADJ 1 *(écriture, signe)* legible; *Ordinat* **l. par ordinateur** machine-readable 2 *(roman)* readable

lisiblement [lizibləmɑ̃] ADV legibly

lisier [lizje] NM *Agr* slurry

lisière [lizjɛr] NF 1 *(d'une forêt)* edge 2 *Tex* selvage, selvedge

LISP [lisp] NM *Ordinat (abrév* **list processing***)* LISP

lissage [lisaʒ] NM 1 *Tech (de papier)* glazing; *(d'un cuir)* sleeking; *Tex* smoothing 2 *Écon & Math* smoothing (out) 3 *Offic Méd* facelift 4 *Ordinat* **l. de courbes/des caractères** curve/character smoothing

lisse [lis] ADJ *(planche, peau, pâte)* smooth; *(cheveux, fourrure)* sleek; *(pneu)* bald; **rendre qch l.** to smooth sth (down)

NF 1 *Naut (membrures)* ribband; *(garde-fou)* handrail 2 *Tex* heddle; **métier de haute/basse l.** high-/low-warp loom

lissé [lise] NM *Culin* gloss stage *(in sugar boiling)*

lisser [3] [lise] VT *(barbe, mèche)* to smooth (down); *(nappe, feuille)* to smooth out; *(plumes)* to preen; *Tech (papier)* to glaze; *(cuir)* to sleek; *Tex* to smooth; **le canard lissait sa queue** the duck was preening its tail

▸ **se lisser** VPR **se l. la moustache/les plumes** to preen one's moustache/its feathers; **le canard se lisse la queue** the duck is preening its tail

lisseur, -euse [lisœr, -øz] NM,F *Tex* smoother

NM *Ordinat* **l. de fontes** font smoother

❑ **lisseuse** NF *(machine)* smoothing machine

lissier [lisje] NM *Tex* loom setter

lissoir [liswar] NM *Tech* smoother

listage [listaʒ] NM *Offic* listing; **faire le l. des modèles en stock** to list the models in stock

liste [list] NF 1 *(énumération → de noms, de chiffres)* list; **faire** *ou* **dresser une l.** to make (out) *or* to draw up a list; **tu as la l. des courses (à faire)?** have you got the shopping list?; **j'ai fait la l. des avantages et des inconvénients** I have listed *or* made a list of the pros and cons; **tu n'es pas sur la l.** you're not on the list, your name isn't listed; **la l. des invités** the guest list; **la l. des réclamations s'allonge de jour en jour** the list of complaints is getting longer every day; **l. d'adresses** mailing list, address list; **l. d'attente** waiting list; *Mktg* **l. d'attributs** attribute list; **l. civile** civil list; **l. de clients** customer *or* client list; *Com* **l. de colisage** packing list; **l. de contrôle** checklist; *Com* **l. de diffusion** mailing list; *Ordinat* distribution *or* discussion *or* mailing list; **l. de distribution** distribution list; **l. d'émargement** payroll; **l. d'envoi** mailing list; **l. des exportations** export list; **l. des importations** import list; **l. de mariage** wedding list; **l. de naissance** = list of presents requested by the parents of a newborn baby; **l. noire** blacklist; **elle est sur la l. noire** she has been blacklisted; **l. ouverte/close** open/closed list; *Can Joual* **l. de paie** payroll*; **l. de(s) prix** price list; **l. de publipostage** mailing list; **l. à puces** bulleted list; *Tél* **être sur l. rouge** *Br* to be ex-directory, *Am* to have an unlisted number; **l. des signatures autorisées** authorized signatory list; *Com* **l. des tarifs** price list, tariff

2 *Pol* **l. électorale** electoral roll; **être inscrit sur les listes électorales** to be on the electoral roll; **la l. d'opposition** the list of opposition candidates; **l. commune** joint list (of candidates); **l. bloquée** set list of candidates *(which electors cannot modify)*; **l. panachée** = ballot paper in which a voter votes for candidates from different lists rather than for a list as a whole

3 *Ordinat* list; **l. de fichiers à imprimer** print list, print queue; **l. rapide** draft; **l. de signets** bookmark list

4 *Aviat* **l. de vérification** checklist

5 *(d'un cheval)* star

listeau, -x [listo], **listel** [listɛl] NM 1 *Archit* listel, fillet 2 *(d'une pièce de monnaie)* rim

lister [3] [liste] VT 1 *(mettre en liste)* to list 2 *Ordinat* to list (out)

listéria [listerja] NF *Biol* listeria

listériose [listerjoz] NF *Méd* listeriosis

listing [listiŋ] NM 1 *(gén)* list 2 *Ordinat* printout, listing

liston [listɔ̃] NM *Naut* sheer rail, rubbing strake

LIT *(abrév écrite* **lire italienne***)* L, Lit

lit [li] NM 1 *(meuble)* bed; **l. en pin/en fer** pine/iron bed; *Fam* **un canapé qui fait l.** a sofa bed; **garder le l., rester au l.** to stay *or* to be in bed; **aller au l.** to go to bed; **envoyer/mettre qn au l.** to send/to put sb to bed; **se mettre au l.** to get into bed; **tu es encore au l.?** you're still in bed?; **maintenant, au l.!** come on now, it's bedtime!; **tirer** *ou* **sortir qn du l.** to drag sb out of bed; **je ne te tire** *ou* **ne te sors pas du l., au moins?** I hope I didn't get you out of bed; **faire l. à part** to sleep in separate beds; **le l. est/n'est pas défait** the bed has/hasn't been slept in; **faire le l. de qn** to make sb's bed; **mourir dans son l.** to die in one's bed; **c'est un hôpital de 150 lits** it's a 150-bed hospital; **l. à baldaquin** four-poster (bed); **l. bateau** = bed with curved sides, higher at the ends; **l. de jour** *ou* **de repos** daybed; **l. breton** *ou* **clos** box bed; **l. de camp** camp bed; **le l. conjugal** the marriage bed; **l. d'enfant, petit l.** *Br* cot, *Am* crib; **l. escamotable** foldaway bed; **l. à deux places, grand l.** double bed; **l. à une place** single bed; **l. pliant** folding bed; **l. en portefeuille** *Br* apple-pie bed, *Am* short-sheeted bed; **sur son l. de mort** on his/her deathbed; **sur son l. de douleur** on his/her sickbed; **lits gigognes** stowaway beds; **lits jumeaux** twin beds; **lits superposés** bunk beds, bunks; **faire le l. de qch** to pave the way for sth; **en cédant au chantage, on fait le l. du terrorisme** by giving in to blackmail, you play into the hands of terrorists; *Prov* **comme on fait son l., on se couche** as you make your bed, so you must lie in it

2 *Jur (mariage)* **enfant d'un premier/deuxième l.** child of a first/second marriage

3 *(couche)* bed, layer; **l. de feuilles/mousse** bed of leaves/moss; **posez la viande sur un l. de légumes verts** place the meat on a bed of green vegetables; *Géol* **l. d'argile** layer *or* bed of clay

4 *Géog* bed; **la rivière est sortie de son l.** the river has burst *or* overflowed its banks; **l. majeur** high water *or* bed; **l. mineur** mean water *or* bed

5 *Hist & Jur* **l. de justice** = canopied bed in

which the king would preside over formal sessions of Parliament, and by extension these sessions themselves

6 *Naut* **le l. du courant** *ou* **de marée** the tideway; **le l. du vent** the set of the wind, the wind's eye

7 *Constr* **l. de pose** bearing surface

litanie [litani] **NF** *(longue liste)* **une l. de plaintes** a litany of complaints; **(avec lui, c'est) toujours la même l.!** he never stops moaning!

❑ **litanies NFPL** *Rel* litanies

litas [litɑs] **NM** *(monnaie)* litas

lit-cage [likaʒ] *(pl* **lits-cages***)* **NM** folding *Br* cot *or Am* crib

litchi [litʃi] **NM 1** *(arbre)* lychee, lichee, litchi **2** *(fruit)* lychee, lichee, litchi

liteau, -x [lito] **NM 1** *(sur linge)* coloured stripe **2** *(tasseau)* bracket **3** *(bois débité)* batten

litée [lite] **NF 1** *(groupe d'animaux* → *lions)* pride; *(*→ *loups)* pack **2** *(portée d'une laie)* wild sow's litter

liter [3] [lite] **VT** *(harengs)* to put into layers in a barrel

literie [litri] **NF** bedding

litharge [litarʒ] **NF** *Chim* litharge

lithergol [litɛrgɔl] **NM** *Chim* hybrid propellant, lithergol

lithiase [litjaz] **NF** *Méd* lithiasis

lithiasique [litjazik] **ADJ** lithic

NMF lithiasis sufferer

lithine [litin] **NF** *Chim* lithia

lithiné [litine] **ADJ eau lithinée** lithia water

❑ **lithinés NMPL** lithium salts

lithinifère [litinifɛr] **ADJ** *Chim* containing lithium

lithique [litik] **ADJ** lithic

lithium [litjɔm] **NM** *Chim* lithium

litho [lito] **NF** *Fam (abrév* **lithographie***)* litho

lithobie [litɔbi] **NM** *Entom* lithobius

lithodome [litɔdɔm] **NM** *Zool* lithodomus

lithogenèse [litɔʒənɛz] **NF** *Géol* lithogenesis

lithographe [litɔgraf] **NMF** lithographer

lithographie [litɔgrafi] **NF 1** *(procédé)* lithography **2** *(estampe)* lithograph

lithographier [9] [litɔgrafje] **VT** to lithograph

lithographique [litɔgrafik] **ADJ** lithographic

lithologie [litɔlɔʒi] **NF** lithology

lithologique [litɔlɔʒik] **ADJ** lithological

lithopédion [litɔpedjɔ̃] **NM** *Obst* lithopaedion

lithophage [litɔfaʒ] **ADJ** *Zool (mollusque)* lithophagous

lithophanie [litɔfani] **NF** lithophane

lithopone [litɔpɔn] **NM** lithopone

lithosol [litɔsɔl] **NM** *Géol* lithosol

lithosphère [litɔsfɛr] **NF** *Géol* lithosphere

lithosphérique [litɔsferik] **ADJ** *Géol* lithospheric

lithothamnium [litɔtamnjɔm] **NM** lithothamnion

lithotomie [litɔtɔmi] **NF** *Méd* lithotomy

lithotripsie [litɔtripsi] **NF** *Méd* lithotripsy; **l. extracorporelle** extracorporeal shock wave lithotripsy

lithotripteur [litɔtriptœr], **lithotriteur** [litɔtritœr] **NM** *Méd* lithotripter, lithotrite

lithotritie [litɔtriti] **NF** *Méd* lithotripsy, lithotrity; **l. extracorporelle** extracorporeal shock wave lithotripsy

lithotypographie [litɔtipɔgrafi] **NF** lithotypography

litière [litjɛr] **NF** *(pour animaux, palanquin)* litter; **l. pour chats** cat litter

litigant, -e [litigɑ̃, -ɑ̃t] *Jur* **ADJ** litigant *(avant n)*

NM litigant

litige [litiʒ] **NM 1** *(différend)* dispute; **question en l.** contentious *or* controversial question; **au centre du l.** at the heart of the dispute; **objet de l.** bone of contention **2** *Jur* dispute; **objet** *ou* **point de l.** subject of the action; **être en l.** to be in dispute *or* involved in litigation; **l. commercial** commercial dispute

litigieux, -euse [litiʒjø, -øz] **ADJ** contentious, *Sout* litigious

litisconsorts [litiskɔ̃sɔr] **NMPL** *Jur* co-parties

litispendance [litispɑ̃dɑ̃s] **NF** *Jur* **1** *Vieilli* pendency, lis pendens **2** *(simultanéité)* concurrent proceedings

litorne [litɔrn] **NF** *Orn* fieldfare

litote [litɔt] **NF** understatement, *Spéc* litotes *(UNCOUNT)*; **quand je dis que ce n'est pas fameux, c'est une l.** when I say it's not all that good, that's an understatement

litre [litr] **NM 1** *(unité)* litre **2** *(bouteille)* litre bottle

litron [litrɔ̃] **NM** *Fam* bottle of wine■

littéraire [literɛr] **ADJ** *(style, œuvre, prix)* literary; **il fera des études littéraires** he's going to study literature; **elle est très l.** she's very literary

NMF *(étudiant)* arts student; *(professeur)* arts teacher; *(amateur de lettres)* literary person

littérairement [literɛrmɑ̃] **ADV** in literary terms, literarily

littéral, -e, -aux, -ales [literal, -o] **ADJ** *(transcription, traduction)* literal, word-for-word; *(sens)* literal

littéralement [literalmɑ̃] **ADV** literally; **c'est l. du chantage!** that's sheer blackmail!

littéralité [literalite] **NF** literality

littérarité [literarite] **NF** literariness

littérateur [literatœr] **NM** *Péj* hack (writer)

littérature [literatyr] **NF 1 la l.** *(art, œuvres)* literature; *(activité)* writing; **faire carrière dans la l.** to make a career in writing; **ce qu'il écrit, c'est de la mauvaise l.** he writes badly, he's a bad writer; *Péj* **les discours des politiciens, c'est de la l.** the politicians' speeches are just (a lot of) fine words; **l. de colportage** chapbooks

2 *(documentation)* literature, material; **il y a toute une l. là-dessus** you'll find a lot of material *or* literature on the topic

littoral, -e, -aux, -ales [litɔral, -o] **ADJ** coastal, *Spéc* littoral

NM coastline, *Spéc* littoral

littorine [litɔrin] **NF** *Zool* common periwinkle

Lituanie [litɥani] **NF la L.** Lithuania; **vivre en L.** to live in Lithuania; **aller en L.** to go to Lithuania

lituanien, -enne [litɥanjɛ̃, -ɛn] **ADJ** Lithuanian

NM *(langue)* Lithuanian

❑ **Lituanien, -enne NM,F** Lithuanian

liturgie [lityrʒi] **NF** liturgy

liturgique [lityrʒik] **ADJ** liturgical

liure [ljyr] **NF 1** *(pour charrette)* lashing **2** *Naut* gammoning, frapping

livarde [livard] **NF** *Naut* sprit; **voile à l.** sprit sail

livarot [livaro] **NM** livarot (cheese)

live [lajv] **ADJ INV** live; **spectacle l.** live show

livèche [livɛʃ] **NF** *Bot* lovage

livedo [livedo] **NM** *Méd* livedo

Liverpool [livɛrpul] **NM** Liverpool

livet [livɛ] **NM** *Naut* sheer line; **l. de pont** deck line

livide [livid] **ADJ 1** *(pâle* → *visage, teint)* pallid, sallow; *(*→ *malade, blessé)* whey-faced **2** *Littéraire (d'une couleur plombée)* livid

lividité [lividite] **NF** lividness

living [liviŋ] *(pl* **livings***)*, **living-room** [liviŋrum] *(pl* **living-rooms***)* **NM** living room

Livourne [livurn] **NM** Livorno, Leghorn

livrable [livrabl] **ADJ 1** *(marchandises)* which can be delivered; **les marchandises ne sont pas livrables à domicile** goods cannot be delivered **2** *Bourse* deliverable

livraison [livrɛzɔ̃] **NF 1** *Com (action, marchandises)* delivery; **payer à la l.** to pay cash on delivery; **prendre l. de qch** to take delivery of sth; **faire** *ou* **effectuer une l.** to make a delivery; **l. au comptant immédiate** spot delivery; **l. à domicile** *(sur panneau)* home delivery, door-to-door delivery; **l. franco** free delivery, delivered free; **l. franco à domicile** free home delivery; **l. franco par nos soins** carriage paid; **l. gratuite** *(dans un catalogue)* free delivery, free delivery service; **l. immédiate** immediate delivery; **l. le jour même** same-day delivery; **l. lendemain** next-day delivery; **l. contre remboursement** *Br* cash on delivery, *Am* collect on delivery

2 *Typ* instalment

3 *Bourse* delivery; **l. à terme** future delivery, forward delivery

livre [livr] **NM 1** *(œuvre, partie d'une œuvre)* book; **le l. de la vie** the book of life; **son l. a eu un énorme succès** his/her book was a best-seller; **on s'est rencontrés comme dans les livres, à un bal au château** we met at a ball in the castle, just like in a novel; **elle parlait comme un l.** she talked like a book; **l. audio** audio book; **l. cartonné** hardback (book); **c'est mon l. de chevet** it's a book I read and reread; **l. de classe** school book, textbook; **l. de cuisine** cookbook, *Br* cookery-book; **l. électronique** e-book; **livres pour enfants** children's books; **l. d'exercices** exercise book; **l. de grammaire** grammar book; **l. d'heures** book of hours; **l. d'histoire** history book; **l. d'images** picture book; **l. in-folio** folio (book); **l. de lecture** reading-book; **l. de messe** hymn-book, missal; **l. numérique** e-book; **l. d'occasion** second-hand book; **l. de poche** paperback (book); **l. de prières** prayer book; **l. relié** hardback (book); **l. scolaire** school book, textbook; **l. spécimen** desk copy; **il est pour moi comme un l. ouvert** I can read him like a book

2 **le l.** *(l'édition)* the book trade; **l'industrie du l.** the book industry; **les ouvriers du l.** the print-workers

3 *(registre)* book; *Compta* **l. d'achats** purchase ledger, bought ledger; **l. d'actionnaires** register of shareholders; **l. de bord** logbook; *Compta* **l. de caisse** cash book; *Compta* **l. de commandes** order book; *Compta* **l. de commerce, l. de comptabilité, l. de comptes** (account) book, ledger; *Compta* **l. des créanciers** accounts payable ledger; *Compta* **l. des débiteurs** accounts receivable ledger; *Compta* **l. de dépenses** cash book; *Mktg* **l. d'échantillons** sample book; *Compta* **l. d'échéance** bill book; *Compta* **l. des effets à payer** bills payable ledger; *Compta* **l. des effets à recevoir** bills receivable ledger; *Compta* **l. des entrées** purchase ledger; *Jur* **l. foncier** Land Register; *Compta* **l. fractionnaire** day book, book of prime entry; **l. d'inventaire** balance book; *Compta* **l. des inventaires** stock book; *Compta* **l. journal** day book, journal; **l. d'or** visitors' book; *Ordinat* guestbook; *Compta* **l. de paie** pay ledger; *Compta* **l. de petite caisse** petty cash book; *Compta* **l. des réclamations** claims book; *Compta* **l. des rendus** returns ledger; *Compta* **l. des sorties** sales ledger; *Compta* **l. de trésorerie générale** general cash book; *Compta* **l. des ventes** sales ledger; *Compta* **grand l.** ledger

4 *Pol* **l. blanc** white paper

NF 1 *(unité de poids)* half a kilo, ≃ pound; *Can* pound

2 *Fin* pound; **ça coûte trois livres** it costs three pounds; **l. égyptienne/chypriote** Egyptian/Cypriot pound; *Anciennement* **l. irlandaise** Irish pound, punt; **l. sterling** pound (sterling)

3 *Hist* livre

❑ **à livre ouvert ADV** at sight; **elle lit/traduit le grec à l. ouvert** she can read/translate Greek at sight

'Le Livre de la jungle' *Kipling, Reitherman* 'The Jungle Book'

livre-cassette [livrəkasɛt] *(pl* **livres-cassettes***)* **NM** audio book

livrée [livre] **NF 1** *(de domestique)* livery; **chauffeur en l.** liveried chauffeur **2** *Zool (pelage)* coat; *(plumage)* plumage

livre-jeu [livrəʒø] *(pl* **livres-jeux***)* **NM** activity book

livre-journal [livrəʒurnal] *(pl* **livres-journaux** [-o]*)* **NM** day book

LIVRER [3] [livre]

> **VT** to hand over **1** ■ to inform on **2** ■ to give away, to reveal **3** ■ to deliver **4, 5**
> **VPR** to give oneself up **1, 4** ■ to confide **2** ■ to hold **3** ■ to conduct **3** ■ to be engaged in **3** ■ to abandon oneself to **4**

VT 1 *(abandonner* → *personne, pays, ville)* to hand over; **les traîtres ont livré la ville à l'ennemi** the traitors handed the town over to the enemy; **l. qn à la justice** to deliver *or* to hand over sb to the authorities; **vous le livrez à la mort** you are sending him to his death; **le pays est livré à la corruption** the country has been given over to *or* has sunk into corruption; **son corps fut livré aux flammes** his/her body was committed to the flames; **bateau livré à la tempête** boat at the mercy of the storm; **être livré à soi-même** to be left to oneself *or* to one's own devices

2 *(dénoncer)* to inform on, to denounce; **il a livré son complice à la police** he handed his accomplice over to the police

3 *(révéler)* **l. un secret** to give away *or* to betray a secret; **l'épave du Titanic n'a pas encore livré tous ses secrets** the wreck of the Titanic still hasn't given up *or* yielded all its secrets; **dans**

ses romans, elle livre peu d'elle-même she doesn't reveal much about herself in her novels

4 *Com (article, commande)* to deliver; *(client)* to deliver to; **l. qch à domicile** to deliver sth *(to the customer's home)*; **nous livrons à domicile** *(sur panneau)* we deliver to your door; **livré franco domicile** delivered free; **nous vous livrerons** *ou* **vous serez livré demain** you will receive delivery tomorrow; **l. une usine clés en mains** to hand over a turnkey factory

5 *Fin & Bourse* to deliver; **l. à terme fixe** to deliver at a fixed term; **prime pour l.** seller's option; **vente à l.** sale for delivery

6 *(locutions)* **l. bataille** *ou* **combat (à)** to wage *or* to do battle (with); **l. passage à** to make way for; **la foule s'écarta pour l. passage au ministre** the crowd parted to make way for the minister

▸ **se livrer** VPR **1** *(se rendre)* to give oneself up **(à** to); **se l. à la police** to give oneself up to the police

2 *(faire des confidences)* to confide **(à** in); **elle ne se livre jamais** she never confides in anybody, she never opens up

3 **se l. à** *(faire → enquête)* to hold, to conduct; *(→ recherches, chantage)* to be engaged in; *(→ suppositions)* to make; **se l. à l'étude** to devote oneself to study; **elle s'est livrée à des commentaires désobligeants** she made some rather insulting remarks

4 **se l. à** *(s'abandonner à → débauche)* to abandon oneself to; *(→ sentiment)* to give oneself up to; **une fois seul, je me livrai à ma peine** as soon as I found myself alone, I gave way to my sorrow; **ils se livrent enfin à la joie de se retrouver** they can finally give themselves up to the joy of being together again

5 *Littéraire* **se l. à** *(amant)* to give *or* to offer oneself to

livresque [livʀɛsk] ADJ *(connaissances)* acquired from books; *(esprit, exposé)* bookish; **son savoir n'est que l.** his/her knowledge comes straight out of books

livret [livʀɛ] NM **1** *(carnet)* notebook

2 *Banque* **l. A** = tax-exempt savings account issued by the French National Savings Bank and the Post Office; **l. B** = savings account with no maximum holding; **l. (de caisse) d'épargne** savings book, passbook; **l. de compte** bank book; **l. de dépôt** deposit book, passbook; **l. d'épargne-entreprise** = savings account designed to aid setting up a company; **l. d'épargne logement** *Br* ≃ building society passbook, *Am* ≃ savings and loan association passbook; **l. d'épargne populaire** *(compte)* = special tax-exempt savings account; *(carnet)* savings book, passbook; **l. jeunes** = savings account for young people aged 12–25; **compte sur l.** savings account

3 *Jur* **l. de famille** *ou* **de mariage** family record book *(in which dates of births and deaths are registered)*

4 *Scol* **l. scolaire** school report (book)

5 *Mil* **l. militaire** army *or* military record

6 *Mus* libretto

7 *Suisse* multiplication table

livreur, -euse [livʀœʀ, -øz] NM,F **1** *(qui effectue des livraisons)* deliveryman, *f* deliverywoman **2** *Fin & Bourse* deliverer

lixiviation [liksivjasjɔ̃] NF leaching, lixiviation; **extraire par l.** to leach out

lixivier [9] [liksivje] VT to leach, to lixiviate

Lizard [lizaʀ] NM **le cap L.** the Lizard, Lizard Point

LJM *Com (abrév écrite* **livraison le jour même***)* same-day delivery

Ljubljana [ljubljana] NM Ljubljana

llanos [ljanos] NMPL *Géog* llanos

lm *(abrév écrite* **lumen***)* lm

LMD [ɛlɛmde] ADJ *Univ (abrév* **licence, master, doctorat***)* **système (européen) L.** European Bachelors, Masters, Doctorate system *(aimed at standardizing university qualifications across the EU)*

LMDS [ɛlɛmdeɛs] NM *Tél (abrév* **local multipoint distribution system***)* LMDS

LMNH [ɛlɛmɛnaʃ] NM *Méd (abrév* **lymphome malin non hodgkinien***)* NHML

LNH [ɛlɛnaʃ] NM *Méd (abrév* **lymphome non hodgkinien***)* NHL

LNPA [ɛlɛnpea] NF *Ordinat & Tél (abrév* **ligne numérique à paire asymétrique***)* ADSL

LO [ɛlo] NF *(abrév* **Lutte ouvrière***)* = militant Trotskyist organization

LOA [ɛloa] NF *Com (abrév* **location avec option d'achat***)* lease financing

loader [lodœʀ] NM loader, loading machine

lob [lɔb] NM *Sport* lob; **faire un l.** to hit a lob, to lob; **l. lifté** topspin lob

lobaire [lɔbɛʀ] ADJ lobar

lobby [lɔbi] *(pl* **lobbys** *ou* **lobbies***)* NM lobby, pressure group; **le l. antinucléaire** the antinuclear lobby

lobbying [lɔbiiŋ], **lobbyisme** [lɔbiism] NM lobbying

lobbyist, lobbyiste [lɔbiist] NMF lobbyist

lobbysme [lɔbism] NM lobbying

lobe [lɔb] NM **1** *Anat & Bot* lobe; **l. de l'oreille** earlobe **2** *Archit* foil

lobé, -e [lɔbe] ADJ **1** *Bot* lobed **2** *Archit* foiled

lobectomie [lɔbɛktɔmi] NF *Méd* lobectomy

lobélie [lɔbeli] NF *Bot* lobelia

lober [3] [lɔbe] *Sport* VT to lob
VI to lob

lobotomie [lɔbɔtɔmi] NF lobotomy; **on lui a fait une l.** he's/she's had a lobotomy

lobotomiser [3] [lɔbɔtɔmize] VT to lobotomize; **il a été lobotomisé** he's had a lobotomy

lobulaire [lɔbylɛʀ] ADJ lobular

lobule [lɔbyl] NM lobule

lobulé, -e [lɔbyle] ADJ lobular

lobuleux, -euse [lɔbylø, -øz] ADJ lobular

local, -e, -aux, -ales [lɔkal, -o] ADJ *(anesthésie, élu, radio)* local; *(averses)* localized
NM **1** *(à usage déterminé)* premises; **l. d'habitation** domestic premises; **l. professionnel** premises used for professional purposes; **locaux commerciaux** *ou* **à usage commercial** business premises; **locaux disciplinaires** disciplinary quarters

2 *(sans usage déterminé)* place; **je cherche un l. pour faire une fête** I'm looking for a place to hold a party

3 *Can Tél* extension

▫ **locale** NF *Journ* local news

localement [lɔkalmã] ADV **1** *(à un endroit)* locally **2** *(par endroits)* in places; **demain, le ciel sera l. nuageux** tomorrow there will be patchy cloud *or* it will be cloudy in places

localier [lɔkalje] NM *Journ* local affairs correspondent

localisable [lɔkalizabl] ADJ localizable

localisateur, -trice [lɔkalizatœʀ, -tʀis] *Méd* ADJ *(valeur, symptôme)* localizing
NM *(en radiographie)* localizer, treatment cone

localisation [lɔkalizasjɔ̃] NF **1** *(détection, emplacement)* location; *(d'un appel téléphonique)* tracing **2** *Astron* location, tracking; *(limitation)* localization, confinement **3** *Anat* **l. cérébrale** cerebral localization **4** *Ordinat* **l. de logiciel** software localization

localisatrice [lɔkalizatʀis] *voir* **localisateur**

localisé, -e [lɔkalize] ADJ **1** *(déterminé)* located **2** *(limité)* local, localized; **combats localisés** localized fighting

localiser [3] [lɔkalize] VT **1** *(situer)* to locate; *(appel téléphonique)* to trace; **il a fallu l. la fuite** we had to locate the leak **2** *(limiter)* to confine, to localize **3** *Ordinat* to localize

localité [lɔkalite] NF *(petite)* village; *(moyenne)* small town; **dans toute la l.** throughout the town, all over town

locataire [lɔkatɛʀ] NMF *(d'un appartement, d'une maison)* tenant; *(d'une chambre chez le propriétaire)* lodger; *Jur* **l. (à bail)** lessee

locateur, -euse [lɔkatœʀ, -øz] NM,F *Jur* lessor

locatif, -ive [lɔkatif, -iv] ADJ **1** *(concernant le locataire, la chose louée)* **le marché l.** the property rental market; **réparations locatives** repairs incumbent upon the tenant; **valeur locative** rental value **2** *Suisse (habitation)* to rent, rental *(avant n)*; **immeuble l.** rented apartment building **3** *Ling* **préposition locative** locative preposition
NM **1** *Ling* locative (case) **2** *Suisse (immeuble)* rented apartment building

location [lɔkasjɔ̃] NF **1** *(par le propriétaire → d'un*

logement) renting (out), *esp Br* letting; *(→ matériel, d'appareils)* renting (out), rental, *esp Br* hiring (out); *(→ de costumes, de skis)* rental, *esp Br* hire; *(→ d'un navire, d'un avion)* leasing; **l. de voitures** car rental, *Br* car hire

2 *(par le locataire → d'un logement)* renting; *(→ d'une machine)* renting, *esp Br* hiring; *(→ d'un navire, d'un avion)* leasing; **l. avec option d'achat** lease financing

3 *(logement)* rented accommodation; **désolé, nous n'avons pas de locations** sorry, we have no accommodation for rent; **nous n'avons pas trouvé de l. pour cet été** we haven't found anywhere to rent this summer; **l. meublée** furnished accommodation

4 *(réservation)* booking; **la l. est ouverte un mois à l'avance** booking starts a month in advance; *Cin* **l. en bloc** block booking

5 *(période)* lease; **(contrat de) l. de deux ans** two-year rental *or* lease *or* tenancy agreement

6 *(prix → d'un logement)* rent; *(→ d'un appareil)* rental

7 *(en sociologie)* **l. d'utérus** surrogate motherhood

▫ **en location** ADJ **être en l.** *(locataire)* to be renting; *(appartement)* to be available for rent, to be up for rent; **j'ai un appartement, mais il est en l.** *(déjà loué)* I've got *Br* a flat *or* *Am* an apartment but it is rented out ADV **donner** *ou* **mettre une maison en l.** to rent (out) *or* to let a house; **prendre une maison en l.** to rent a house

location-accession [lɔkasjɔ̃aksɛsjɔ̃] *(pl* **locations-accessions***)* NF mortgage

location-gérance [lɔkasjɔ̃ʒeʀãs] *(pl* **locations-gérances***)* NF *Com* = agreement with a liquidator to manage a company in liquidation

location-vente [lɔkasjɔ̃vãt] *(pl* **locations-ventes***)* NF **1** *(d'un véhicule, d'équipement)* hire purchase; **la voiture est en l.** the car is being bought in instalments *or* on hire purchase; **acheter qch en l.** to buy sth on hire purchase **2** *(d'une maison)* = arrangement by which a tenant may, after a stipulated length of time, purchase the property they are renting

locative [lɔkativ] *voir* **locatif**

loc. cit. *(abrév écrite* **loco citato***)* loc. cit.

loch [lɔk] NM **1** *Géog* loch **2** *Naut* log

loche [lɔʃ] NF **1** *Ich (de rivière)* loach; *(de mer)* rockling **2** *(limace)* slug **3** *très Fam (sein)* tit, boob

locher [3] [lɔʃe] VT *(terme normand) (arbre)* to shake *(to dislodge the fruit)*

lochies [lɔʃi] NFPL *Obst* lochia, cleansings

locked-in syndrome [lɔktinsɛ̃dʀom] NM *Méd* locked-in syndrome

lock-out [lɔkaut] NM INV *Ind* lockout

lock-outer [3] [lɔkaute] VT *Ind* to lock out

locks [lɔks] NFPL *Fam* dreads, dreadlocks▪

loco [lɔko] NF *Fam (abrév* **locomotive***)* loco

locomobile [lɔkɔmɔbil] NF *Hist* transportable steam engine

locomoteur, -trice [lɔkɔmɔtœʀ, -tʀis] ADJ **1** *Tech* locomotive *(avant n)* **2** *Anat* locomotive *(avant n)*, locomotor *(avant n)*; **ataxie locomotrice** locomotor ataxia
NM motor unit

▫ **locomotrice** NF *Rail* electric engine

locomotion [lɔkɔmɔsjɔ̃] NF locomotion

locomotive [lɔkɔmɔtiv] NF **1** *Tech* locomotive, *(railway)* engine **2** *Fam (d'un parti, d'une économie)* pacemaker, pacesetter **3** *Sport* pacemaker, pacesetter

locomotrice [lɔkɔmɔtʀis] *voir* **locomoteur**

locorégional, -e, -aux, -ales [lɔkɔʀeʒjɔnal, -o] ADJ *Méd* locoregional

locotracteur [lɔkɔtʀaktœʀ] NM shunter, *Am* dolly

loculaire [lɔkylɛʀ] ADJ *Bot* locular

loculé, -e [lɔkyle], **loculeux, -euse** [lɔkylø, -øz] ADJ *Bot* loculate, loculated

locus [lɔkys] NM INV *Biol* locus

locuste [lɔkyst] NF locust

locustelle [lɔkystɛl] NF *Orn* **l. tachetée** grasshopper warbler

locuteur, -trice [lɔkytœʀ, -tʀis] NM,F *Ling* speaker; **l. natif** native speaker

locution [lɔkysjɔ̃] NF **1** *(expression)* phrase, locution; **une l. figée** *ou* **toute faite** a set phrase *or* idiom **2** *Gram* phrase; **l. adverbiale/nominale** adverbial/noun phrase

locutrice [lɔkytris] *voir* **locuteur**

loden [lɔdɛn] NM **1** *Tex* loden **2** *(manteau)* loden coat

lods [lo] NMPL *Hist* **l. et ventes** = transfer tax payable to a lord when a tenant's property changed hands outside the direct line of inheritance

lœss [løs] NM loess, löss

lof [lɔf] NM *Naut* windward side; **aller au l.** to luff; **virer l. pour l.** to wear

lofer [3] [lɔfe] VI *Naut* to luff; **lofe!** hard aweather!

lofing-match [lɔfiŋmatʃ] *(pl* **lofing-matchs**) NM *Sport* luffing match

loft [lɔft] NM loft (conversion)

logarithme [lɔgaritm] NM logarithm; **l. népérien ou naturel** natural logarithm

logarithmique [lɔgaritmik] ADJ logarithmic

loge [lɔʒ] NF **1** *(d'artiste)* dressing room; *(de candidats)* exam room; *Belg* **l. foraine** stall
2 *(de concierge, de gardien)* lodge
3 *(de francs-maçons)* lodge; **la Grande L.** the Grand Lodge
4 *Théât* box; **premières/secondes loges** dress/upper circle boxes; *Fig* **être aux premières loges** to have a ringside *or* front seat; **de notre fenêtre, on est aux premières loges pour les défilés** we have a grandstand view of processions from our window
5 *Archit* loggia
6 *Biol & Bot* loculus

logeable [lɔʒabl] ADJ **cet appartement est l., je suppose** I suppose I/we/*etc* could live in this *Br* flat *or Am* apartment; **c'est l. dans le placard** there's room for it in the cupboard

logement [lɔʒmã] NM **1** *(habitation)* accommodation *(UNCOUNT)*; **un l. de trois pièces** *(appartement)* a three-room *Br* flat *or Am* apartment; *(maison)* a three-room house; **chercher un l.** to look for accommodation *or* somewhere to live; **ils ont construit des logements pour leurs employés** they have built accommodation for their employees; **l. locatif** rented accommodation; **logements sociaux** *Br* local authority housing, council housing, *Am* housing projects
2 *Mil (chez l'habitant)* billet; *(sur une base)* (married) quarters
3 *(hébergement)* housing *(UNCOUNT)*; **la crise du l.** the housing shortage
4 *Tech* housing, casing

<hr>

LOGER [17] [lɔʒe]

VT to put up **1** ■ to find accommodation for **2** ■ to accommodate **3** ■ to put **3, 4** ■ to track down **5**	
VI to live **1** ■ to stay **2**	
VPR to find somewhere to live **1** ■ to find somewhere to stay **2** ■ to lodge itself **3** ■ to fit **5**	

VT 1 *(recevoir → ami, visiteur)* to put up; **nous pouvons vous l. pour une nuit ou deux** we can put you up for a night or two; **je suis bien/mal logé** I'm comfortably/badly housed; **être logé, nourri et blanchi** to get board and lodging with laundry (service) included; *Fig* **on est tous logés à la même enseigne** everybody is in the same boat
2 *(trouver un logement pour → gén)* to find accommodation for; *(→ soldats)* to billet; **on a logé le régiment chez l'habitant** the regiment was billeted with the local population
3 *(contenir → personnes)* to accommodate; *(→ choses)* to put; **l'école peut l. cinq cents élèves** the school can accommodate five hundred pupils; **où allons-nous l. tout ça?** where are we going to put all that stuff?; **le placard peut l. trois grosses valises** the cupboard can take *or* hold three big suitcases
4 *(mettre)* to put; **j'ai réussi à l. ton sac entre les deux valises** I managed to put your bag between the two cases; **l. une balle dans la tête à qn** to put a bullet in sb's head; **l. une idée dans la tête à qn** to put an idea into sb's head
5 *Fam (repérer)* to track down

VI 1 *(habiter)* to live; **où logez-vous?** where do you live?; **elle loge chez sa tante/à l'hôtel/rue de la Paix/dans une caravane** she lives with her aunt/in a hotel/on rue de la Paix/in a trailer;

les étudiants logent tous en cité all the students are accommodated at *or* live in halls of residence
2 *(séjourner)* to stay; **pour l'instant je loge chez lui** I'm living *or* staying at his place at the moment; **les touristes logeaient chez l'habitant** the tourists were staying in boarding houses *or* in bed-and-breakfasts; **les soldats logeaient chez l'habitant** the soldiers were billeted with the local population

▶ **se loger** VPR **1** *(à long terme → couple, famille)* to find somewhere to live; **ils se marient dans une semaine et n'ont pas encore trouvé à se l.** they're getting married in a week and they still haven't found anywhere to live
2 *(provisoirement → touriste, étudiant)* to find accommodation *or* somewhere to stay; **étudiant en médecine cherche à se l. pour deux trimestres** medical student seeks lodgings *or* accommodation for two terms; **nous avons trouvé à nous l.** we've found accommodation, we've found somewhere to stay
3 *(pénétrer)* to lodge itself; **un éclat de verre s'était logé dans son œil droit** a splinter of glass had lodged itself in his/her right eye; **mon ballon est allé se l. entre l'antenne de télé et la cheminée** my ball got stuck *or* lodged itself between the television *Br* aerial *or Am* antenna and the chimney; **comment ces idées stupides ont-elles pu se l. dans ton esprit?** where did you get all those stupid ideas from?
4 *(se mettre)* **il s'est logé une balle dans la tête** he put a bullet through his head, he shot himself in the head
5 *Tech* to fit, to be housed

logette [lɔʒɛt] NF **1** *Archit (fenêtre)* oriel window; *(cellule)* cubicle **2** *(à vaches)* byre

logeur, -euse [lɔʒœr, -øz] NM,F landlord, *f* landlady *(of furnished apartments)*

loggia [lɔdʒja] NF loggia

logiciel, -elle [lɔʒisjɛl] ADJ software *(avant n)*
NM software; **ils viennent de sortir un nouveau l.** they've just brought out a new software package; **l. d'application** application *or* software package; **l. auteur** authoring software; **l. de base** systems teaching software; **l. de bureautique** business software; **l. client** client software; **l. de communication** communications package, comms package, communications software; **l. de compression de données** data compression software; **l. de comptabilité** accounts software; **l. de conception assistée par ordinateur** computer-aided design package; **l. contributif** shareware; **l. de conversion** conversion software; **l. de courrier électronique** e-mail software; **l. de décompression** decompression software, decompressor; **l. de dessin** art package, drawing program; **l. du domaine public** public domain software; **l. espion** spyware; **l. d'exploitation** operating system software; **l. de filtrage** filtering software; **l. grapheur** graphics software; **l. graphique** illustration software; **l. intégré** integrated software; **l. de jeux** games program; **l. de lecture de nouvelles** news reader; **l. libre** freeware, open source (software); **l. de mise en page** desktop publishing package; **l. multi-utilisateur** multi-user software; **l. de navigation** browser; **l. de PAO** DTP software; **l. pirate** pirate software; **l. de planification** scheduler; **l. de présentation** presentation software; **l. public** public domain software; **l. de reconnaissance de caractères** OCR software, character recognition software; **l. de reconnaissance vocale** voice recognition software; **l. relationnel** social software; **l. de réseau** network software; **l. de SGBD** DBMS software; **l. social** social software; **l. de système** system software; **l. de système d'exploitation** operating system software; **l. de télémaintenance** remote-access software; **l. de traitement de texte** word-processing software, word-processing software package, WP package; **l. utilisateur** user software; **l. utilitaire** utility program

logicien, -enne [lɔʒisjɛ̃, -ɛn] NM,F logician

logicisme [lɔʒisism] NM logicism

logique [lɔʒik] ADJ **1** *Phil* logical
2 *(cohérent, clair)* sensible, logical; **soyons logiques** let's be logical *or* sensible about this;

tu n'es pas l.! you're being illogical!; **ah oui, c'est l., je n'y avais pas pensé!** ah, that makes sense, I hadn't thought of that!; **ce n'est pas l.** it doesn't make sense; **sois l. avec toi-même, tu veux qu'elle vienne ou pas?** you can't have it both ways, do you want her to come or not?
3 *(normal, compréhensible)* logical, normal, natural; **c'est dans la suite l. des événements** it's part of the normal course of events; **il est tout à fait l. que tu n'aies pas envie de le revoir** it's quite natural that you don't want to see him again; **tu la brimes, elle t'en veut, c'est l.** if you pick on her she'll hold it against you, that's only normal *or* logical
4 *Ordinat* logic

NF **1** *Phil* logic; **l. déductive** deductive reasoning, deduction; **l. floue** fuzzy logic; **l. formelle ou pure** formal logic
2 *(cohérence)* logic; **ton raisonnement manque de l.** your argument isn't very logical *or* consistent; **telle est la l. des fous/des enfants** that's a madman's/a child's logic; **nous sommes entrés dans une l. de guerre** war is inevitable, war is the next logical step; **il n'y a aucune l. là-dedans** none of this makes sense; **c'est dans la l. des choses** it's in the nature of things; **en toute l., voilà ce qui devrait se passer** logically, that's what ought to happen
3 *Ordinat* logic; **l. binaire/booléenne** binary/Boolean logic; **l. câblée** wired logic; **l. à couplage par l'émetteur** emitter-coupled logic, ECL; **l. programmable** field programmable logic array

logiquement [lɔʒikmã] ADV **1** *(avec cohérence)* logically; **procédons l.** let's proceed logically
2 *(normalement)* **l., il devrait bientôt être là** if all goes well *or* unless something goes wrong, he should soon be here

logis [lɔʒi] NM *Littéraire* dwelling, abode; **il n'y avait personne au l.** there was nobody (at) home; **quand Renard rentra au l.** when Reynard the fox returned to his abode

logisticien, -enne [lɔʒistisjɛ̃, -ɛn] NM,F logistician

logistique [lɔʒistik] ADJ **1** *Mil* logistic **2** *(organisationnel)* **les élus locaux apportent un important soutien l. au parti** local councillors make an important contribution to the running of the party
NF logistics *(singulier)*; *Mktg* **l. commerciale** marketing mix

logithèque [lɔʒitɛk] NF software library

logo [lɔgo] NM logo

logographe [lɔgɔgraf] NM *Antiq* logographer

logographie [lɔgɔgrif] NM logograph

logomachie [lɔgɔmaʃi] NF **1** *(discussion)* logomachy, semantic argument **2** *(suite de mots creux)* bombast

logomachique [lɔgɔmaʃik] ADJ **1** *(formel)* logomachic **2** *(creux)* bombastic

logopède [lɔgɔpɛd] = **logopédiste**

logopédie [lɔgɔpedi] NF logopedics *(singulier)*

logopédique [lɔgɔpedik] ADJ *Belg & Suisse* speech therapy *(avant n)*

logopédiste [lɔgɔpedist] NMF *Belg & Suisse* speech therapist

logorrhée [lɔgɔre] NF logorrhoea

logorrhéique [lɔgɔreik] ADJ logorrhoeic

logos [lɔgɔs] NM **1** *Rel* logos, the Word **2** *Phil* logos

logotisé, -e [lɔgɔtize] ADJ *Mktg* branded

logotype [lɔgɔtip] NM logotype

LOI [lwa] NF A. **1** *(règles publiques)* law; **les lois de notre pays** the law of the land; **selon la l. en vigueur** according to the law as it stands; **la l. salique** the Salic law
2 *Jur (décret)* act, law; **la l. Dupont a été votée la nuit dernière** the Dupont Act was passed last night; **la l. (de) 1901** law concerning the setting up of non-profit-making organizations; **nous sommes une association l. de 1901** we're a non-profit-making organization; **l. de 1948** = former law protecting tenants from unreasonable rent increases (rental on properties which still fall under this law is often extremely low); **l. du 28 juillet 1882, défense d'afficher** *(sur un mur)* ≃ billposters will be prosecuted; **l. d'amnistie** amnesty law; **l. anticasseurs** = law

against violence and vandalism during demonstrations; *Com* **l. antitrust** antitrust *or Br* antimonopoly law; **l. d'application immédiate** law with immediate effect; *Journ & TV* **l. de censure** censorship law; **l. de conservation** conservation law; **l. constitutionnelle** *(loi de révision de la constitution)* constitutional amendment; **la l. constitutionnelle** *(la constitution)* the Constitution; **la l. Debré** = law passed in 1959 enabling private schools to receive state subsidies; **l. d'exception** emergency legislation; **la l. Faure** = far-reaching education reform act following the student disturbances of 1968; **l. de finances** Finance Act; **l. fondamentale** fundamental law; **l. d'habilitation** enabling Act; **l. impérative** mandatory law *(any agreement to the contrary notwithstanding)*; **l. Informatique et Libertés** = French law regulating the protection of computer privacy, *Br* ≃ Data Protection Act; **la l. Lang** = book price agreement introduced in 1982; **l. martiale** martial law; **l. ordinaire** ordinary act; **l. d'ordre public** public policy; **l. organique** organic law; **l. d'orientation** = act laying down the basic principles for government action in a given field; **l. de pleins pouvoirs** enabling act; **l. de police** public order act; **l. réelle** = law relating to public security; **l. référendaire** = laws passed by means of a referendum; **l. répressive** criminal law; **la l. Savary** = law of 1984 introducing selective entry to education courses; **lois scélérates** pernicious legislation; **l. au sens formel** *Br* ≃ Act of Parliament, *Am* ≃ Act of Congress; **l. au sens matériel** = general measure issued by a duly constituted authority; **l. supplétive** non-mandatory law *(in the absence of any expressed intention to the contrary)*; *Hist* **la l. du talion** lex talionis; *Fig* **dans ce cas-là, c'est la l. du talion** in that case, it's an eye for an eye (and a tooth for a tooth); **l. uniforme** uniform legislation; **l. de validation** validation law

3 *(légalité)* **la l.** the law; **ça devrait être interdit par la l.!** there ought to be a law against it!; **je suis désolé mais c'est la l.** I'm sorry but that's the law *or* the law's the law; **avoir la l. pour soi** to have the law on one's side; **tomber sous le coup de la l.** to be covered by the law

B. 1 *(devoir)* rule; **les lois de la guerre** the laws of war; **les lois de l'hospitalité/du savoir-vivre** the rules of hospitality/etiquette; **les lois de l'honneur** the code of honour; **se faire une l. de faire qch** to make a point of doing sth; **se faire une l. de réussir** to make a point of succeeding; **elle ne connaît d'autre l. que son plaisir** she obeys only her desire for pleasure

2 *Rel* law; **la l. divine** divine law; **la l. mosaïque** *ou* **de Moïse** the Mosaic Law

C. 1 *(domination)* law, rule; **tenir qn/un pays sous sa l.** to rule sb/a country; **dicter** *ou* **imposer sa l., faire la** *ou* **sa l.** to lay down the law; **c'est elle qui fait la l. ici** she's the one who lays down the law around here; **l'équipe de Bordeaux a dicté** *ou* **imposé sa l. à celle de Marseille** Bordeaux dominated Marseilles

2 *(règles d'un milieu)* **la l. du milieu** the law of the underworld; **c'est la l. de la nature** it's nature's way; **la l. de la jungle/du silence** the law of the jungle/of silence; **dans la cour de récréation c'est la l. du plus fort** it's the law of the jungle in the *Br* playground *or Am* schoolyard

D. *PRINCIPE* law; **la l. de la gravitation universelle** *ou* **de la pesanteur** *ou* **de la chute des corps** the law of gravity; **les lois de Mendel** Mendel's laws; *Hum* **la l. du moindre effort** the line of least resistance; **la l. de l'offre et de la demande** the law of supply and demand; **les lois de la mode** the dictates of fashion; **les lois de la perspective** the laws of perspective; **l. de probabilité** law of probability; **l. des rendements décroissants** law of diminishing returns

> *Culture*
>
> **LA LOI SALIQUE**
>
> This refers to a code of laws of the Salian Franks (a Germanic tribe) which included a provision excluding women from inheriting land. This law was applied from the 16th century in France to prevent women from succeeding to the throne.

loi-cadre [lwakadr] *(pl* **lois-cadres***)* **NF** parent act

LOIN [lwɛ̃] **ADV** 1 *(dans l'espace)* far (away); **ils habitent l.** they live a long way away; **c'est l. l'hôtel?** is the hotel far away?, is it far to the hotel?; **en avion ce n'est pas l.** it's not far by plane; **ils se sont garés un peu plus l.** they parked a bit further on; **le prisonnier s'est échappé mais il n'est pas allé bien l.** the prisoner escaped but he didn't get very far; **il n'y a pas l. entre Paris et Versailles** it's not far from Paris to Versailles; **elle est l. derrière nous** she is far *or* way behind us; **aussi l. (que)** as far (as); **aussi l. que l'œil peut porter** as far as the eye can see; **moins l. (que)** not as *or* so far (as); **plus l. (que)** further *or* farther (than); **voir plus l.** *(dans un texte)* see below; **cette arme porte l.** this weapon has a long range

2 *(dans le temps)* far (away), a long way off; **Noël n'est plus très l.** Christmas isn't very far away now *or* a long way off now; **la guerre, l'Occupation, c'est bien l.!** the war, the Occupation, it all seems a long way off now!; **c'est l. tout ça!** *(dans le passé)* that was a long time ago!, that seems a long way off now!; *(dans le futur)* that's a long way off!

3 *Fig* far; **il y a l. entre ce qu'on dit et ce qu'on fait** there's a big difference between words and deeds; **de là à lui faire confiance, il y a l.** there is a big difference between that and trusting him/her; **d'ici à l'accuser de mensonge, il n'y a pas l.** that's close to calling him/her a liar; **aller l.** to go far; **il est brillant, il ira l.** he's brilliant, he'll go far; **aller un peu** *ou* **trop l.** to go (a bit) too far; **là, tu vas un peu l.** come on now, you're taking things a bit far *or* you're going a bit too far; **tu es allé trop l. dans ta critique** you took your criticism too far; **ça va (très) l. ce que vous dites** that's taking things a bit far; **j'irai plus l. et je dirai que...** I'd go even further and say that...; **étouffons l'affaire, il ne faut pas que ça aille plus l.** let's hush up this business, it mustn't go any further; **une analyse qui ne va pas très l.** an analysis lacking in depth; **il ne va pas aller bien l. sans argent** he won't get very far without any money; **avec 20 euros, on ne va pas l.** you can't get very far on 20 euros; **cette affaire risque de vous mener l.** this affair could land you in serious trouble; **ces quelques preuves ne vont pas nous mener très l.** these few scraps of evidence won't get us very far; **ce conflit peut nous entraîner très l.** this dispute could lead to a very serious situation; **la possession de stupéfiants, ça peut mener l.** possession of drugs can lead to serious trouble; **je trouve que vous poussez un peu l.** I think you're going a bit far; **ils ont poussé les recherches très l.** they took the research as far as possible; **voir l.** to be far-sighted; **elle ne voit pas plus l. que le bout de son nez** she can't see further than the end of her nose; *Prov* **il y a l. de la coupe aux lèvres** there's many a slip 'twixt cup and lip

4 *Suisse (absent)* **il est l.** he's not here

❑ **au loin ADV** in the distance; **le bateau disparut au l.** the boat disappeared into the distance; **on voyait, au l., une rangée de peupliers** a row of poplars could be seen in the far distance *or* far off in the distance

❑ **d'aussi loin que CONJ il lui fit signe d'aussi l. qu'il la vit** he signalled to her as soon as he saw her in the distance; **d'aussi l. que je me souvienne** as far back as I can remember

❑ **de loin ADV** 1 *(depuis une grande distance)* from a long way, from a distance; **je vois mal de l.** I can't see very well from a distance; **la tour se voyait de (très) l.** the tower could be seen from a long way off; **avec sa chevelure rousse, on la reconnaît de l.** you can recognize her from a long way off, thanks to her red hair; **vue de l., cette histoire n'a pas l'air bien grave** from a distance, this business doesn't seem all that serious; **tu verras mieux d'un peu plus l.** you'll see better from a bit further away; **ils sont venus d'assez l. à pied** they came a fair distance *or* quite a long way on foot; **admirer qn de l.** to admire sb at *or* from a distance *or* from afar; **ils sont parents, mais de l.** they are only distantly related; *Fam* **je l'ai vu venir de l.** I saw him coming a mile off

2 *(assez peu)* **il ne s'intéresse que de l. à la politique** he's only slightly interested in politics; **suivre les événements de l.** to follow events from a distance

3 *(de beaucoup)* far and away, by far; **c'est de l. le meilleur cognac** it's far and away *or* it's by far the best brandy; **il est de l. le plus compétent** he's far and away *or* by far the most competent; **je le préfère à ses collègues, et de l.** I much prefer him to his colleagues

❑ **de loin en loin ADV** 1 *(dans l'espace)* at intervals, here and there 2 *(dans le temps)* from time to time, every now and then

❑ **du plus loin que CONJ il lui fit signe du plus l. qu'il l'aperçut** he signalled to him/her as soon as he saw him/her in the distance; **du plus l. qu'il se souvienne** as far back as he can remember

❑ **loin de PRÉP** 1 *(dans l'espace)* a long way *or* far (away) from; **quand je suis l. de toi** when I'm far (away) from you; **pas l. d'ici** not far from *or* quite close to here; **l. de là** far from there; **non l. de** not far from; **c'est assez l. d'ici** it's quite a long way *or* distance from here; **ils vivent l. de l'agitation des villes** they live far away *or* a long way from the bustle of towns

2 *Fig* far from; **elle est l. d'être bête** she is far from stupid; **je suis encore l. d'avoir fini** I'm still far from finished; **je ne suis pas l. de leur dire le fond de ma pensée** it wouldn't take me much to tell them what I think, I have a good mind to tell them what I really think; **je ne suis pas l. de penser que...** I've more or less come to the conclusion that...; **j'étais l. de me douter que...** I never imagined...; **vous êtes l. du sujet** you've gone (way) off the subject; **j'étais l. de la vérité, ça a coûté 300 euros!** I was way out (in my calculations), it cost 300 euros!; **l. de moi l'idée de t'accuser** far be it from me to accuse you; **l. de moi cette idée!** nothing could be further from my mind!; **l. de là** far from it; **je ne vous en veux pas, l. de là** I'm not angry with you, far from it; *Prov* **l. des yeux, l. du cœur** out of sight, out of mind

3 *(dans le temps)* a long way (away); **la Première Guerre mondiale est bien l. de nous maintenant** the First World War is a long way away from us now; **nous ne sommes plus l. de la fin de l'année maintenant** we're not far off the end of the year now

4 *(au lieu de)* **l. de m'aider** far from helping me; **l. de leur en vouloir, il leur en était reconnaissant** far from being angry with them, he was very grateful

❑ **loin que CONJ** *Littéraire* far from; **l. que cette offre lui plût, elle lui fit peur** far from appealing to him/her, this proposal frightened him/her

❑ **pas loin de ADV** *(presque)* nearly, almost; **il n'est pas l. de midi** it's getting on for midday, it's nearly midday; **ça ne fait pas l. de quatre ans qu'ils sont mariés** they've been married nearly four years; **cela ne fait pas l. de trois kilomètres** it's almost *or* nearly three kilometres

lointain, -e [lwɛ̃tɛ̃, -ɛn] **ADJ** 1 *(dans l'espace)* distant, far-off; *(île)* remote; **les lointaines collines sortaient peu à peu de la brume** the distant hills were gradually emerging from the mist; **il était une fois, dans un pays l....** once upon a time, in a far-off *or* distant land...; **un l. son de flûte** the distant *or* far-off sound of a flute

2 *(dans le temps → passé)* distant, far-off; *(→ futur)* distant; **mes souvenirs les plus lointains** my earliest recollections; **aux jours lointains de notre enfance** in the far-off days of our childhood; **dans un l. avenir** in the distant *or* remote future

3 *(indirect → parent, cousin)* remote

4 *(absent → air, sourire)* faraway; **je l'ai trouvée un peu lointaine** *(préoccupée)* she seemed to have something on her mind; *(distraite)* I found her rather vague

5 *(dans la pensée → lien, rapport)* remote, distant; *(→ ressemblance)* vague; **il n'y a qu'un l. rapport entre...** there's only the remotest connection between...

NM 1 *(fond)* **dans le** *ou* **au l.** *(vers l'horizon)* in the distance

2 *Beaux-Arts* **les lointains** the background; **l. vaporeux** sfumato background

lointainement [lwɛ̃tɛnmɑ̃] **ADV** remotely

loi-programme [lwaprɔgram] (*pl* **lois-pro-grammes**) NF (framework) legislation, *Br* ≃ Command Paper

loir [lwar] NM *Zool* dormouse

Loire [lwar] NF **1** (*fleuve*) **la L.** the (River) Loire **2** (*région*) **la L.** the Loire (area) *or* valley; **les châteaux de la L.** the châteaux of the Loire **3** (*département*) **la L.** Loire

Loire-Atlantique [lwaratlãtik] NF **la L.** Loire-Atlantique

Loiret [lwarɛ] NM **le L.** Loiret

Loir-et-Cher [lwareʃɛr] NM **le L.** Loir-et-Cher

loisible [lwazibl] ADJ **il est l. de...** it is permissible to...; **il vous est tout à fait l. de partir** you are totally at liberty *or* quite entitled to go

loisir [lwazir] NM **1** (*temps libre*) spare time, free time, leisure time; **comment occupez-vous vos heures de l.?** what do you do in your spare time?; **avoir beaucoup de loisirs** to have a lot of spare time; **il consacre tous ses loisirs à l'informatique** he spends all his spare time on computers **2** (*possibilité*) **avoir (tout) le l. de** to have the time *or* the opportunity to; **ils ont eu tout le l. de préparer leur réponse** (*la liberté*) they have been left entirely free to prepare their answer; (*le temps*) they've had ample time to prepare their answer; **on ne lui a pas donné** *ou* **laissé le l. de s'expliquer** he/she was not allowed (the opportunity) to explain his/her actions
▫ **loisirs** NMPL (*activités*) leisure (UNCOUNT), spare-time activities; **nous vivons de plus en plus dans une société de loisirs** we live in a society where leisure is taking on more and more importance
▫ **(tout) à loisir** ADV at leisure; **faites-le (tout) à l.** do it at (your) leisure

lokoum [lɔkum] = **loukoum**

lolette [lɔlɛt] NF *Suisse Br* dummy, *Am* pacifier

lolita [lɔlita] NF *Fam* nymphet

lollard [lɔlar] NM *Hist* Lollard

lolo [lolo] NM **1** *Fam* (*lait*) milk ▪ **2** *très Fam* (*sein*) boob, jug

lombago [lɔ̃bago] = **lumbago**

lombaire [lɔ̃bɛr] *Anat* ADJ lumbar
  NF lumbar vertebra

lombalgie [lɔ̃balʒi] NF *Méd* lumbago

lombard, -e [lɔ̃bar, -ard] ADJ Lombardic
  NM (*dialecte*) Lombard dialect
▫ **Lombard, -e** NM,F Lombard

Lombardie [lɔ̃bardi] NF **la L.** Lombardy

lombarthrose [lɔ̃bartroz] NF *Méd* spondylosis lumbalis

lombes [lɔ̃b] NFPL *Anat* lower back, *Spéc* lumbus; **douleur dans les l.** lower back pain

lombo-sacré, -e [lɔ̃bɔsakre] (*mpl* **lombo-sacrés,** *fpl* **lombo-sacrées**) ADJ *Anat* sacrolumbar, lumbo-sacral

lombostat [lɔ̃bɔsta] NM orthopaedic lumbar corset

lombric [lɔ̃brik] NM *Zool* earthworm, *Spéc* lumbricus

Lomé [lɔme] NM Lomé

lompe [lɔ̃p] NM *Ich* lumpfish, lumpsucker

londonien, -enne [lɔ̃dɔnjɛ̃, -ɛn] ADJ of/from London, London (*avant n*); **les bus londoniens** the London buses
▫ **Londonien, -enne** NM,F Londoner

Londres [lɔ̃dr] NM London; **le Grand L.** Greater London

londrès [lɔ̃drɛs] NM *Vieilli* Havana cigar

█ LONG, LONGUE █ [lɔ̃, lɔ̃g]

> | ADJ | long A1–3, 5, B1–3, 5 ▪ thin A4 ▪ long-standing B3 ▪ long-term B4 |
> | NM | in length 1 |

ADJ A. DANS L'ESPACE 1 (*grand*) long; **une longue rangée d'arbres** a long row of trees; **la route traverse de longues plaines** the road crosses open *or* wide plains; **un vieillard l. et maigre le regardait fixement** an old man, tall and thin, was staring at him; **chat/chien à poil l.** long-haired cat/dog; **ils se servent de longs bâtons** they use long sticks; **l'âne a de longues oreilles** donkeys have long ears; **une fille aux longues jambes** a long-legged girl, a girl with long legs; **avoir de longs bras** to have long arms; **c'est l. de sept mètres** it's seven metres long; **tunnel l. de deux kilomètres** two-kilometre long tunnel
  2 *Bot* (*feuille*) elongated; (*tige*) long
  3 (*vêtement*) long; **les jupes seront longues cet hiver** this winter, skirts will be (worn) long; **ton jupon est trop l.**, **il dépasse** your slip's too long, it's showing; **à manches longues** long-sleeved; **elles portaient toujours des manches longues** they always wore long-sleeved clothes *or* long sleeves; **porter des pantalons longs** to wear long trousers; **une robe longue** a full-length *or* long dress
  4 *Culin* thin; **une sauce longue** a thin sauce; **l. drink** long drink
  5 *Cartes* long; **couleur longue** long suit

B. DANS LE TEMPS 1 (*qui dure longtemps*) long; **c'est un travail l. et difficile** it's a long and difficult job; **ils échangèrent un l. baiser** they gave each other a long kiss; **un l. soupir** a long-drawn *or* lengthy sigh; **boire à longs traits** to drink in long gulps *or* draughts; **de longues négociations** protracted *or* long negotiations; **une longue bataille** a long *or* long-drawn-out battle; **je suis fatigué, la journée a été longue** I'm tired, it's been a long day; **que cette attente est longue!** what a long wait!; **je suis restée de longs mois sans nouvelles de lui** I had no word from him for months and months; **ces quelques minutes furent bien longues** those few minutes were very long *or* lasted a long time; **dix jours, c'est l.** ten days is a long time; **obligé d'attendre un l. quart d'heure** kept waiting for a good quarter of an hour; **notre émission de ce soir est plus longue que d'habitude** our programme this evening is longer than usual; **une longue explication** (*détaillée*) a long explanation; (*verbeuse*) a long-winded *or* lengthy explanation; **le film est trop l.** the film is too long *or* is overlong; **vous êtes trop l. dans la dernière partie** you are too long-winded *or* too wordy in the last part; **ne sois pas trop longue ou personne ne t'écoutera jusqu'à la fin** don't take too long *or* don't speak for too long or nobody will listen to you all the way through; **les journées sont plus longues** the days are longer; **les longues soirées d'hiver** the long winter evenings; **arrivé au terme d'une longue vie** (having arrived) at the end of a long life; **un congé de longue durée** a (period of) long leave; **chômage de longue durée** long-term unemployment; **j'ai trouvé le temps l.** the time seemed to go (by) really slowly; **ce voyage/discours est l. comme un jour sans pain** this journey/speech seems to be lasting forever *or* dragging on forever; **une traversée longue de deux mois** a two-month (long) crossing; **une attente longue de trois heures** a three-hour wait; *Can* **à l'année/à la journée longue** all year/day long, throughout the year/day
  2 (*qui tarde → personne*) **je ne serai pas l.** I won't be long; **ce ne sera pas l.** it won't take long; **qu'est-ce que tu es l.!** you're so slow!, you're taking forever!; **il s'en sortira, mais ce sera l.** he'll recover but it'll take a long time *or* it will be a slow process; **ne soyez pas trop l. à me répondre** don't take too long answering me; **je n'ai pas été longue à comprendre qu'elle mentait** it didn't take me long to see that she was lying; **l'eau est longue à bouillir** the water is taking a long time to boil; **il est l. à venir, ce café!** that coffee's a long time coming!; **être l. à réagir** to be slow to react; **la viande de porc est longue à cuire** pork takes a long time to cook
  3 (*qui existe depuis longtemps*) long-standing; **sa longue expérience de journaliste** his/her many years spent *or* his/her long experience as a journalist; **une longue amitié** a long-standing friendship; **un ami de longue date** an old friend, a friend of long standing; **avoir de longs états de service** to have a long service record
  4 (*dans le futur*) **à longue échéance, à l. terme** (*prévision*) long-term; **faire des prévisions à longue échéance** to make long-term forecasts; **ce sera rentable à l. terme** it will be profitable in the long term; **à plus ou moins longue**

échéance sooner or later; **emprunt à l. terme** long-term loan; **quels sont tes projets à l. terme?** what are your long-term plans?
  5 *Ling & Littérature* long; **une voyelle longue** a long vowel; **"a" l.** long "a"

NM 1 (*longueur*) **le terrain a** *ou* **fait 100 mètres de l.** the plot is 100 metres long *or* in length; **une table de deux mètres de l.** a table two metres long; **les plus grands spécimens atteignent huit mètres de l.** the biggest specimens reach up to eight metres in length; **faire une mine** *ou* **une tête de dix pieds de l.** (*par déconvenue*) to pull a long face; (*par mauvaise humeur*) to have *or* to wear a long face
  2 le l. (*vêtements*) long styles; **la mode est au l.** long styles are in fashion
  ADV **1** (*avec des vêtements longs*) **elle s'habille l.** she wears long skirts *or* dresses
  2 (*beaucoup*) **geste/regard qui en dit l.** eloquent gesture/look; **une remarque qui en dit l. sur ses intentions** a remark which says a lot about *or* speaks volumes about his/her intentions; **elle pourrait vous en dire l. sur cette affaire** she could tell you a few things about this business; **demande-le-lui, il en sait l.** ask him, he knows all about it; **j'en sais l. sur cette affaire** I know all about this business; **elle en connaît déjà l. sur la vie** she knows a thing or two about life
▫ **longue** NF **1** *Cartes* long suit; **longue à pique/trèfle** long suit of spades/clubs
  2 *Ling & Littérature* long syllable
  3 *Mus* long note
▫ **à la longue** ADV (*avec le temps*) in the long term *or* run, eventually; **à la longue, tout se sait** everything comes out in the end; **tu oublieras tout ceci à la longue** you'll forget all this eventually
▫ **au long** ADV in full, fully; **elle a écrit le titre au l.** she wrote the title out in full
▫ **au long de** PRÉP **1** (*dans l'espace*) along; **des touristes flânaient au l. des rues** tourists were wandering lazily down *or* along the streets
  2 (*dans le temps*) during; **il s'est aguerri au l. de ces années difficiles** he's become tougher during *or* over these difficult years
▫ **de long en large** ADV back and forth, up and down; **j'ai arpenté le hall de la gare de l. en large** I paced back and forth across *or* I paced up and down the main hall of the station
▫ **de tout son long** ADV **tomber de tout son l.** to fall flat on one's face; **il était étendu de tout son l.** he was stretched out at full length
▫ **en long** ADV lengthwise, lengthways; **fends-les en l.** split them lengthwise *or* down the middle
▫ **en long, en large et en travers, en long et en large** ADV **1** (*examiner*) from every (conceivable) angle; **on a étudié la question en l., en large et en travers** we have studied the question from every (conceivable) angle
  2 (*raconter*) in the minutest detail, at some considerable length
▫ **le long de** PRÉP **1** (*horizontalement*) along; **en marchant le l. de la rivière** walking along the riverbank; **les plaines qui s'étendent le l. du fleuve** the plains which extend along the river
  2 (*verticalement → vers le haut*) up; (→ *vers le bas*) down; **grimper/descendre le l. de la gouttière** to climb up/to climb down the drainpipe
▫ **tout au long** ADV (*en détail*) in detail; **il nous a fait tout au l. le récit de son entretien** he gave us a detailed description of his interview
▫ **tout au long de** PRÉP **1** (*dans l'espace*) all along; **les policiers postés tout au l. du parcours** policemen positioned all along the route
  2 (*dans le temps*) throughout, all through; **il est resté calme tout au l. de la discussion** he remained calm throughout *or* all through the discussion; **tout au l. de l'année** all year long, throughout the year
▫ **tout du long** ADV **1** (*dans l'espace*) **nous avons parcouru la rue tout du l.** we travelled the whole length of the street; **ils ont descendu le fleuve tout du l.** they went all the way down the river, they descended the entire length of the river

2 *(dans le temps)* all along; **il m'a rabâché la même chose tout du l.** he kept on repeating the same thing all along *or* the whole time

❑ **tout le long de** PRÉP **1** *(dans l'espace)* all (the way) along; **il y a des arbres tout le l. de la route** there are trees all (the way) along the road; **nous avons chanté tout le l. du chemin** we sang all the way

2 *(dans le temps)* throughout, all through; **tout le l. du jour/de la nuit** all day/night long, throughout *or* all through the day/night

long. *(abrév écrite* **longitude***)* long

longane [lɔ̃gan] NM longan (fruit)

longanier [lɔ̃ganje] NM longan (tree)

longanimité [lɔ̃ganimite] NF *Littéraire* forbearance

long-courrier [lɔ̃kurje] *(pl* **long-courriers***)* ADJ **1** *Aviat (vol)* long-distance, long-haul; *(avion)* long-haul **2** *Naut* ocean-going

NM **1** *Aviat* long-haul aircraft; **compagnie de l.** long-haul operator; **transport par l.** long-haul (transport) **2** *Naut (navire → marchand)* ocean-going ship *or* freighter; *(→ avec passagers)* ocean liner, oceaner; *(matelot)* foreign-going seaman

longe [lɔ̃ʒ] NF **1** *(demi-échine)* loin; **l. de porc** pork (rear) loin, loin of pork; **l. de veau** loin of veal **2** *(lien → pour attacher)* tether; *(→ pour mener)* lunge

longer [17] [lɔ̃ʒe] VT **1** *(avancer le long de → gén)* to go along, to follow; *(→ mur, côte)* to follow, to hug; **ils ont longé la pinède à pied/en voiture/en canot/à bicyclette** they walked/drove/sailed/cycled along the edge of the pinewood **2** *(border)* to run along, to border; **un bois de hêtres longe la route** a beech wood borders the road; **les voies/câbles qui longent le mur** the rails/cables that run along the wall

longère [lɔ̃ʒɛr] NF longère, = long, low-slung stone farmhouse

longeron [lɔ̃ʒrɔ̃] NM **1** *(en travaux publics)* (longitudinal) girder **2** *Rail (d'un wagon)* (side) frame (member), bar **3** *Aviat (du fuselage)* longeron, longitudinal; *(d'une aile)* spar **4** *Aut* side member *or* rail

longévité [lɔ̃ʒevite] NF **1** *(longue vie → d'une personne, d'une espèce)* longevity; **à quoi attribuez-vous votre l.?** how do you account for your longevity? **2** *(durée de vie)* life expectancy **3** *(d'un produit, des capitaux)* life

longicorne [lɔ̃ʒikɔrn] *Entom* ADJ longicorn

NM longicorn beetle

longiligne [lɔ̃ʒiliɲ] ADJ slender

longitude [lɔ̃ʒityd] NF longitude; **par 30° de l. est/ouest** at longitude 30° east/west; **le bureau des Longitudes** = scientific organization founded in 1795, specializing in astronomy and related fields

longitudinal, -e, -aux, -ales [lɔ̃ʒitydinal, -o] ADJ **1** *(en longueur)* lengthwise, lengthways, *Spéc* longitudinal **2** *Électron* longitudinal; **onde longitudinale** longitudinal wave **3** *Mktg (étude, recherche)* longitudinal, continuous

longitudinalement [lɔ̃ʒitydinalmɑ̃] ADV lengthwise, lengthways, *Spéc* longitudinally

long-jointé, -e [lɔ̃ʒwɛ̃te] *(mpl* **long-jointés,** *fpl* **long-jointées***)* ADJ long-pasterned

long-métrage, long métrage [lɔ̃metraʒ] *(pl* **longs-métrages, longs métrages***)* NM feature- *or* full-length film; **l. d'animation** feature-length cartoon

longotte [lɔ̃gɔt] NF = thick, heavy cotton material

longrine [lɔ̃grin] NF **1** *Constr* longitudinal beam *or* girder *or* member **2** *Rail* longitudinal sleeper

LONGTEMPS [lɔ̃tɑ̃] ADV **1** *(exprimant une durée)* for a long time; **j'ai attendu l. avant d'entrer** I waited for a long time before going in; **a-t-il dû attendre l.?** did he have to wait long?; **ça fait l. que tu attends?** have you been waiting long?; **je n'ai pas attendu l.** I didn't wait long; *Ironique* **tu peux attendre l.** you'll have a long wait; **on a l. pensé que…** it was long thought that…, it was thought for a long time that…; **il faut l. pour…** it takes a long time *or* a while to…; **pas de l.** *ou* **d'ici l.** not for a (long) while *or* long time; **on ne le verra pas d'ici l.** we won't see him for a long time *or* while; **je ne pensais pas le revoir de l.** I didn't expect to see him again for a long time *or* while; **aussi l. que tu veux** as long as you wish; **nous avons attendu assez/très/trop l.** we waited long enough/for ages/too long; **moins l. (que)** for a shorter time (than); **plus l. (que)** longer (than); **mettre** *ou* **prendre l.** to take a while *or* a long time; **elle a mis** *ou* **ça lui a pris l.** she took *or* was a long time (over it); **je n'en ai pas pour l.** I won't be long, it won't take me long; **en as-tu encore pour l.?** are you going to be much longer?; **il n'en a plus pour l.** *(pour finir)* he won't be much longer; *(à vivre)* he won't last much longer, he's not got much longer to live; *Fam* **d'ici à ce qu'il pleuve, il n'y en a pas pour l.!** it won't be long till the rain starts!▪; **avec moi, il ne va pas y en avoir pour l., tu vas voir!** I'll have this sorted out in no time (at all), just you see!; **ça va durer (encore) l.?** *(ton irrité)* is this going to go on for much longer?, have you quite finished?; **il a été absent pendant l.** he was away for a long time; **avant l.** before long; **pas avant l.** not for a long time; **je ne reviendrai pas avant l.** I won't be back for a long time; **il restera ici encore l.** he'll be here for a while *or* for a long time (yet); **l. avant** long *or* a long time before (that), much earlier; **l. après** much later, long after (that), a long time after (that); **ils en reparlèrent l. après** they spoke about it again a long time after

2 *(avec "il y a", "depuis")* **il y a l. (de ça)** ages *or* a long time ago; **il n'y a pas l.** not long ago; **il n'y a pas l. qu'elle est partie** she went not long ago; **il y a l. que** *ou* **cela fait l. que nous sommes amis** we've been friends for a long time (now); **il y a l.** *ou* **cela fait l. que je l'ai lu** it's been a long time since I read it; **il y a l. qu'il est mort** he's long dead, he's been dead for a long time; **il y a l. que j'ai arrêté de fumer** I stopped smoking long *or* ages ago; **il y a** *ou* **cela fait l. que je ne l'ai pas vu** it's a long time *or* ages since I saw him; *Fam* **tiens, il y avait l.!** *(qu'on ne t'avait pas vu)* long time no see!; *(que tu n'avais pas parlé de ça)* here we go again!; **nous ne nous sommes pas vus depuis l.** we haven't seen each other for ages *or* for a long time; **il travaille là depuis l.** he's been working there for ages *or* a long time

longue [lɔ̃g] *voir* **long**

longuement [lɔ̃gmɑ̃] ADV **1** *(longtemps)* for a long time, long; **les jurés ont l. délibéré** the jurors deliberated for a long time; **il a l. insisté pour que je vienne** he kept on insisting that I should come; **il faut l. pétrir la pâte** the dough must be kneaded thoroughly; **parler l. avec qn** to have a (good) long talk with sb

2 *(en détail → expliquer, commenter)* in detail, in depth; *(→ scruter)* at length; **il faudrait analyser plus l. les personnages** the characters should be analysed in greater detail

longuet, -ette [lɔ̃gɛ, -ɛt] ADJ *Fam* a bit long, longish, a bit on the long side; **il est l., ce film!** it's dragging on a bit, this film!

NM breadstick

longueur [lɔ̃gœr] NF **1** *(dimension)* length; **mesure de l.** linear measurement; **unité de l.** unit of length; **un ruban de 10 cm de l.** *ou* **d'une l. de 10 cm** a ribbon 10 cm long *or* in length; **le jardin est tout en l.** the garden is long and narrow; **un visage tout en l.** a long thin face; **quelle est la l. de l'Amazone?** how long is the Amazon?; **j'ai traversé l'île dans toute sa l.** *(à pied)* I walked the whole length of the island; **sa l. peut atteindre 1 m** it can reach 1 m in length

2 *(unité de mesure)* length; **une l. de fil** a length of cotton

3 *(dans une course, en natation)* length; **faire des longueurs** to do lengths; **il l'a emporté d'une l.** he won by a length; **elle a pris deux longueurs d'avance** she's leading by two lengths; *Fig* **avoir une l. d'avance (sur)** to be well ahead (of)

4 *Sport* **saut en l.** long jump

5 *Ordinat* length, size; **l. de bloc/de mot** block/word length; **l. implicite** *(d'un programme)* sizing (estimate)

6 *Opt* **l. optique** optical path

7 *Rad* **l. d'onde** wavelength; *Fig* **être sur la même l. d'onde** to be on the same wavelength

8 *Tech* **l. hors tout** overall length; **l. à la flottaison** length at waterline

9 *(dans le temps)* length; **le film était d'une l.!** the film was incredibly long *or* dragged on forever; **d'une l. désespérante** sickeningly long; **excusez la l. de mon discours** please forgive the length of my speech

10 *(en escalade)* pitch

11 *Typ* **l. de ligne** line width; **l. de page** page length

❑ **longueurs** NFPL overlong passages; **il y a des longueurs dans le film** the film is a little tedious in parts; **il y avait des longueurs** some passages were a little boring

❑ **à longueur de** PRÉP **à l. de semaine/d'année** all week/year long; **il se plaint à l. de temps** he's forever complaining, he complains all the time

longue-vue [lɔ̃gvy] *(pl* **longues-vues***)* NF telescope, field glass

Longwood [lɔ̃gwud] NF = Napoleon I's place of imprisonment on the island of Saint Helena

looch [lɔk] NM *Pharm* soothing emulsion

loofa [lufa] NM **1** *(cucurbitacée)* loofah, sponge cucumber **2** *(éponge)* loofah

look [luk] NM *Fam* **1** *(style)* look, fashion; **le l. des années 80** the 80s look; **t'as le l., coco!** you look great, baby! **2** *(présentation)* image; **le magazine a changé de l.** the magazine has changed its image; **soigner son l.** to cultivate one's image; **avoir un l. d'enfer** to look out of this world

looké, -e [luke] ADJ *Fam* **être l. punk/grunge** to have a punky/grungy look *or* image

looping [lupiŋ] NM *Aviat* loop; **faire des loopings** to loop the loop

lope [lɔp], **lopette** [lɔpɛt] NF *très Fam Péj* **1** *(homme veule)* wimp **2** *(homosexuel)* fairy, *Br* poof, *Am* fag, = offensive term used to refer to a male homosexual

lophophore [lɔfɔfɔr] NM **1** *(oiseau)* lophophore, monaul **2** *(tentacules)* lophophore

lopin [lɔpɛ̃] NM **1** *(parcelle)* **l. (de terre)** patch *or* plot (of land) **2** *Métal (cylindre → grand)* bloom; *(→ petit)* billet

loquace [lɔkas] ADJ talkative, *Sout* loquacious; **tu n'es pas très l. aujourd'hui!** you've not got much to say for yourself today!

loquacité [lɔkasite] NF talkativeness, *Sout* loquacity; **elle a retrouvé sa l. d'autrefois** she's her old talkative self again

loque [lɔk] NF **1** *(haillon)* rag; **ce n'est plus un manteau, c'est une l.!** that's not a coat any more, it's an old rag! **2** *(personne)* **l. (humaine)** wreck; **depuis sa faillite, c'est devenu une l.** since his/her bankruptcy, he's/she's been a complete wreck; **n'être qu'une l.** to be a wreck **3** *Belg (serpillière)* mop

❑ **en loques** ADJ tattered, in tatters; **ses vêtements tombaient en loques** his/her clothes were all in rags *or* tatters

loquedu [lɔkdy] NM *Fam* **1** *(bon à rien)* good-for-nothing, loser, no-hoper, *Br* waster **2** *(individu méprisable)* scumbag, *Br* swine, *Am* stinker

loquet [lɔkɛ] NM latch, catch bolt

loqueteau, -x [lɔkto] NM small catch, hasp

loqueteux, -euse [lɔktø, -øz] ADJ **1** *(personne)* dressed in rags, in tatters **2** *(manteau)* ragged, tattered

NM,F ragamuffin

loran [lɔrɑ̃] NM *(abrév* **Long Range Aid to Navigation***)* loran

lord [lɔr, lɔrd] NM lord; **l. Chancelier** Lord Chancellor

lord-maire [lɔrdmɛr] *(pl* **lords-maires***)* NM Lord Mayor

lordose [lɔrdoz] NF *Méd* lordosis

lordotique [lɔrdɔtik] ADJ *Méd* lordotic

lorette [lɔrɛt] NF *Vieilli* strumpet

lorgner [3] [lɔrɲe] VT **1** *(regarder)* to ogle, to eye; **le type la lorgnait depuis un bon moment** the guy had been eyeing her up *or* ogling her for some time; **le gamin lorgnait les gâteaux** the kid was eyeing the cakes; **l. qn/qch du coin de l'œil** to cast sidelong glances at sb/sth **2** *(convoiter → héritage, poste)* to have one's (beady) eye on

lorgnette [lɔrɲɛt] NF *(lunette)* spyglass; *(jumelles de théâtre)* opera glasses

lorgnon [lɔrɲɔ̃] NM *(à main)* lorgnette, lorgnon; *(à ressort)* pince-nez

lori [lɔri] NM *Orn* lory

loricaire [lɔrikɛr] NM *Ich* loricarian

loriot [lɔrjo] NM *Orn* oriole; **l. jaune** golden oriole

loriquet [lɔrikɛ] NM *Orn* lorikeet

loris [lɔris] NM *Zool* loris

lorrain, -e [lɔrɛ̃, -ɛn] ADJ of/from Lorraine
▪ NM (*dialecte*) Lorraine dialect
□ **Lorrain, -e** NM,F = inhabitant of or person from Lorraine

Lorraine [lɔrɛn] NF **la L.** Lorraine

lorry [lɔri] (*pl* **lorries** *ou* **lorrys**) NM (platelayer's) trolley, lorry

lors [lɔr] **lors de** PRÉP (*pendant*) during; (*au moment de*) at the time of; **l. de la Première Guerre mondiale** during the First World War; **il la rencontra l. d'un déjeuner d'affaires** he met her at a business lunch; **l. du déjeuner** during lunch; **l. de sa mort** at the time of his/her death
□ **lors même que** CONJ *Littéraire* even if, even though; **l. même que nous ferions tous les efforts possibles, nous ne serions pas sûrs d'y parvenir** even if we made every possible effort, we still couldn't be sure of succeeding; **ce sera ainsi, l. même que tu t'y opposerais** that is how it will be, even though you may be opposed to it

lorsque [lɔrsk]

> **lorsqu'** is used before a word beginning with a vowel or h mute.

CONJ **1** (*au moment où*) when; **nous allions partir lorsqu'on a sonné** we were about to leave when the doorbell rang; **il faut agir lorsqu'il est encore temps** we must act while there is still time; **on réglera ce problème l. vous viendrez** we'll sort out this problem when you come **2** (*alors que*) **on a tort de parler lorsqu'il faudrait agir** we shouldn't be talking when we ought to be doing something

losange [lɔzɑ̃ʒ] NM (*forme*) diamond, *Spéc* lozenge; *Géom* rhomb, rhombus; *Hér* lozenge; **en forme de l.** diamond-shaped, rhomboid; **tracez un l.** draw a lozenge

losangé, -e [lɔzɑ̃ʒe] ADJ (*frise*) with a diamond pattern; *Hér* lozengy

Los Angeles [lɔsɑ̃ʒɔlɛs] NM Los Angeles

losangique [lɔzɑ̃ʒik] ADJ diamond-shaped, lozenge-shaped

loser [luzœr] NM *Fam* loser

Lot [lɔt] NM **1** (*rivière*) **le L.** the (River) Lot **2** (*département*) **le L.** the Lot (area)
▪ NPR *Bible* Lot

lot [lo] NM **1** (*prix*) prize; **j'ai gagné un l.!** I've won a prize!; **l. de consolation** consolation prize; *aussi Fig* **gagner le gros l.** to win *or* to hit the jackpot
2 (*part → d'objets*) share; (*→ de terre*) plot, lot; **diviser une propriété en plusieurs lots** to divide an estate into several plots; **à chacun son l. d'infortunes** to each of us his share of misfortunes
3 *Jur* lot; **en lots** lot by lot
4 (*ensemble → de livres*) collection; (*→ de vaisselle, de linge*) set; (*→ de savons, d'éponges*) (special offer) pack; (*→ aux enchères*) lot; *Com* (*de marchandises*) batch; **vendus par lots** (*torchons, couverts*) sold in sets; **j'ai récupéré tout un l. de ferraille** I've picked up a whole lot of scrap iron; **dans le l., il y aura bien quelque chose qui t'intéresse** out of all these things, you're bound to find something interesting; **dans le l., il y aura bien un fort en maths** there must be at least one person who's good at maths among them; **à vendre en un seul l.** for sale as a job lot; **se dégager** *ou* **se détacher du l.** to stand out from the rest; **être au-dessus du l.** to be a cut above the rest; **l. dépareillé** odd lot; **l. d'envoi** consignment; **l. de fabrication numéro 34** series *or* batch number 34
5 *Ordinat* batch; **traitement par lots** batch processing
6 *Littéraire* (*destin*) lot, fate; **tel est notre l. commun** such is our common fate
7 *Bourse* (*d'actions*) parcel
8 *très Fam* (*femme*) **c'est un beau petit l.** she's a real looker *or Br* a nice bit of stuff *or* a bit of all right

lote [lɔt] = **lotte**

loterie [lɔtri] NF **1** (*jeu*) lottery, draw; **l. foraine** fairground lottery; **l. nationale** national lottery

2 (*hasard*) lottery; **le mariage est une l.** marriage is just a game of chance; **c'est une vraie l.!** it's the luck of the draw!

Lot-et-Garonne [lɔtegarɔn] NM **le L.** Lot-et-Garonne

Loth [lɔt] = **Lot**

Lothaire [lɔtɛr] NPR Lothair

loti, -e [lɔti] ADJ **être bien l.** to be well off *or* well provided for; **être mal l.** to be badly off *or* poorly provided for; **tu n'es pas mieux l. que moi** you're no better off than I am; *Fam Ironique* **la voilà bien lotie avec ce type-là!** she really hit the jackpot with that guy!

lotier [lɔtje] NM *Bot* birdsfoot trefoil

lotion [lɔsjɔ̃] NF lotion; **l. après-rasage** aftershave lotion; **l. capillaire** hair lotion; **l. tonique** toning lotion, toner

lotionner [3] [lɔsjɔne] VT (*cuir chevelu*) to rub lotion into; (*épiderme*) to apply lotion to

lotir [32] [lɔtir] VT **1** (*terrain → partager*) to portion off, to divide into plots; (*vendre*) to sell by plots; (*immeubles*) to divide into lots; **on va l. le jardin de l'ancien presbytère** the old vicarage garden is to be divided into plots; **à l.** (*sur panneau*) to be divided up for sale
2 (*attribuer à*) **l. qn de qch** (*immeuble, parcelle*) to allot sth to sb; **le sort l'avait loti d'une timidité maladive** he had the misfortune to be painfully shy

lotissement [lɔtismɑ̃] NM **1** (*terrain → à construire*) building plot, site (*for a housing development*); (*→ construit*) housing development, *Br* (housing) estate **2** (*partage → d'un terrain*) division into lots, parcelling out; (*→ d'immeubles*) dividing into lots

lotisseur, -euse [lɔtisœr, -øz] NM,F property developer

loto [lɔto] NM **1** (*jeu*) lotto; (*boîte*) lotto set **2** **le L.** ≃ the (French state-run) lottery (*similar to the British National Lottery*); **le L. sportif** *Br* ≃ the football pools, *Am* ≃ the soccer sweepstakes

> **Culture**
> **LE LOTO**
> "Loto" is a popular game of chance with large cash prizes. Printed grids ("bulletins") are available at tobacconists or special kiosks. Players mark six numbers on the grid and pay a fee. The twice-weekly prize draw is broadcast on television. "Loto Sportif" is a version of "Loto" in which players bet on the football results.

lotte [lɔt] NF *Ich* (*de rivière*) burbot; **l. (de mer)** monkfish, angler fish

lotus [lɔtys] NM lotus

louable [lwabl] ADJ **1** (*comportement, décision*) praiseworthy, commendable, laudable **2** (*appartement, maison*) rentable, up for rent; **un appartement difficilement l.** an apartment that is difficult to rent

louage [lwaʒ] NM (*cession*) letting; (*jouissance*) renting; **prendre qch à l.** to rent sth; *Jur* **l. de choses** lease of real property; **l. de services** contract of employment, work contract

louange [lwɑ̃ʒ] NF praise; **faire un discours à la l. de qn** to make a speech in praise of sb; *Littéraire* **nous dirons à sa l. que…** to his/her credit, it must be said that…
□ **louanges** NFPL praise; **son interprétation fut saluée par un concert de louanges** his/her performance was praised to the skies; **digne de louanges** (*personne*) praiseworthy; (*action*) praiseworthy, commendable; **chanter** *ou* **célébrer les louanges de qn** to sing sb's praises; **couvrir qn de louanges** to heap praise on sb

louanger [17] [lwɑ̃ʒe] VT *Littéraire* to praise

louangeur, -euse [lwɑ̃ʒœr, -øz] ADJ *Littéraire* laudatory; **paroles louangeuses** words of praise
▪ NM,F *Littéraire* laudator

loubard [lubar] NM *Fam Br* yob, *Am* hood

loucedé [lusde] **en loucedé** ADV *Fam Vieilli* on the quiet

louche[1] [luʃ] ADJ **1** (*douteux → personne*) shifty, shady; (*→ attitude, passé*) shady; (*→ affaire*) shady, sleazy; (*→ endroit*) sleazy; **un individu l.** a shady character; **j'ai repéré son manège l.** I've spotted his/her shady little game; **n'y va pas, c'est l.** don't get involved, there's something fishy about it

2 (*trouble → couleur, lumière*) murky; (*→ liquide*) cloudy
▪ NM **il y a du l. là-dessous!** there's something fishy going on!, I smell a rat!

louche[2] [luʃ] NF **1** (*ustensile*) ladle
2 *très Fam* (*main*) mitt, paw; **serrer la l. à qn** to shake hands with sb

louchébème [luʃebɛm] = **loucherbem**

louchement [luʃmɑ̃] NM squinting (*UNCOUNT*)

loucher [3] [luʃe] VI **1** *Méd* to (have a) squint; **il louche** he has a squint, he's squint-eyed; **l. de l'œil gauche** to have a squint in the left eye **2** (*volontairement*) to go cross-eyed
□ **loucher sur** VT IND *Fam* (*convoiter → personne*) to ogle; (*→ biens*) to have an eye on; **ce type n'arrête pas de l. sur ta sœur** that guy hasn't stopped ogling your sister; **ils louchent tous sur les millions de leur oncle** they all have an eye *or* their (beady) eyes on their uncle's millions

loucherbem [luʃerbɛm] NM **1** *Fam Vieilli* (*boucher*) butcher[*] **2** (*argot*) = type of slang, a variety of "largonji" where "em" is added to the end of the word (eg "boucher" becomes "loucherbem")

loucherie [luʃri] NF squinting (*UNCOUNT*)

louchet [luʃɛ] NM draining spade

loucheur, -euse [luʃœr, -øz] NM,F cross-eyed person[*], person with a squint[*]

louchon [luʃɔ̃] NM *Fam Vieilli* cross-eyed person[*], person with a squint[*]

louer[1] [6] [lwe] VT (*glorifier*) to praise; **louons le Seigneur** praise the Lord; **Dieu soit loué** thank God; **vous pouvez l. Dieu** *ou* **le ciel** *ou* **la providence qu'il n'y ait pas eu d'accident** you can thank God *or* thank your lucky stars there wasn't an accident; **loués soient les philanthropes qui…** praise be to the philanthropists who…; **l. qn de pour qch** to praise sb for sth; **on ne peut que vous l. d'avoir agi ainsi** you deserve nothing but praise for having acted in this way; **on ne peut que l. son dévouement** you cannot but praise his/her dedication
▸ **se louer** VPR (*se féliciter*) **se l. de qch** to be pleased with sth; **je n'ai qu'à me l. de mon choix** I must congratulate myself on my choice; **je n'ai qu'à me l. de votre ponctualité/travail** I have nothing but praise for your punctuality/work; **se l. d'avoir fait qch** to congratulate oneself on having done sth; **je peux me l. d'avoir vu juste** I can congratulate myself for having got it right

louer[2] [6] [lwe] VT **1** (*donner en location → logement*) to rent, *Br* to let (out); (*→ appareil, véhicule*) to rent (out), *Br* to hire (out); (*→ usine*) to lease (out); **l. qch à qn** to rent sth to sb, to rent sth out; **le propriétaire me la loue pour 200 euros** the landlord rents it out to me for 200 euros; **désolé, la maison est déjà louée** sorry, but the house is already let; **ils ont loué leur villa à Julie pour l'été prochain** they've rented their villa to Julie for next summer
2 (*prendre en location → logement*) to rent (à from); (*→ appareil, véhicule*) to rent, *Br* to hire (à from); (*→ usine*) to lease (à from); **on a loué le hall d'exposition à une grosse société** we've leased the exhibition hall from a big firm
3 (*réserver*) to book; **pour ce spectacle, il est conseillé de l. les places à l'avance** advance booking is advisable for this show
4 *Vieilli* (*engager → personne*) to engage; **l. du personnel d'entretien** to engage cleaning staff
USAGE ABSOLU **elle ne loue pas cher** she doesn't ask for very much (by way of) rent; **l'été nous préférons l.** we prefer renting accommodation for our summer holidays; **vous êtes propriétaire? – non, je loue** do you own your house? – no, I rent *or* I'm a tenant; **on peut l. par téléphone** telephone bookings are accepted
□ **à louer** ADJ *Br* to let, *Am* for rent; **chambres à l. à la semaine** (*sur panneau*) rooms *Br* to let *or Am* to rent weekly; **voitures à l.** (*sur panneau*) *Br* cars for hire, *Am* cars for rent
▸ **se louer** VPR **1** (*travailleur*) to hire oneself; **il s'est loué à un fermier pour la moisson** he got hired by a farmer for the harvest
2 (*logement*) to be rented *or Br* let; **cette chambre se louerait aisément** you'd have no

problem letting this room *or* finding somebody to rent this room; **les locaux situés au centre de la capitale se louent à prix d'or** city centre premises are very expensive to rent

3 *(appareil)* to be rented *or Br* hired; **le téléviseur se loue au mois** this TV set is rented *or Br* hired on a monthly basis

loueur, -euse [lwœr, -øz] NM,F *Jur* lessor; *(entreprise)* rental *or Br* hire company; **l. de bateaux/ chevaux/costumes** person who rents (out) *or Br* hires (out) boats/horses/costumes

louf [luf], **loufedingue** [lufdɛ̃g] ADJ *Fam* crazy, nuts; **il est complètement l.!** he's completely nuts *or* off his rocker!

loufiat [lufja] NM *très Fam* waiter ▪

loufoque [lufɔk] ADJ **1** *(fou)* crazy, nuts; **il est devenu un peu l. après la guerre** he went a bit crazy after the war **2** *(invraisemblable → récit, histoire)* weird, bizarre, freaky; **cette histoire est tout à fait l.!** that's a really weird story! **3** *(burlesque)* **un film l.** a zany comedy NMF crank, *Am* screwball

loufoquerie [lufɔkri] NF *(caractère, acte)* eccentricity

lougre [lugr] NM *Naut* lugger

Louis [lwi] NPR **1** *(roi de France)* Louis **2** *(roi de Bavière)* Ludwig

louis [lwi] NM louis d'or

louise [lwiz] NF *Fam* fart; **lâcher une l.** to fart, *Br* to let off, *Am* to lay one

louise-bonne [lwizbɔn] *(pl* **louises-bonnes)** NF louise-bonne pear

Louisiane [lwizjan] NF **la L.** Louisiana; **en L.** in Louisiana

Louis-Philippe [lwifilip] NPR Louis Philippe

loukoum [lukum] NM piece of Turkish delight; **des loukoums** Turkish delight *(UNCOUNT)*

Louksor [luksɔr] = **Louqsor**

loulou[1] [lulu] NM **1** *(chien)* spitz; **l. de Poméranie** Pomeranian (dog) **2** *Fam (voyou) Br* yob, *Am* hood

loulou[2], **-oute** [lulu, -ut] NM,F *Fam* **1** *(en appellatif)* **mon l., ma louloute** (my) darling **2** *(personne)* hoodlum, hooligan; **c'est un drôle de l.!** he's a weird guy!

loup [lu] NM **1** *(mammifère)* wolf; **l. à crinière** maned wolf; **l. doré** Indian jackal; **l. gris d'Amérique** (American) timber wolf; **l. de Magellan** culpeo; **l. de Tasmanie** Tasmanian wolf; *Fig* **faire entrer le l. dans la bergerie** to set the fox to mind the geese; *Fig* **avoir vu le l.** to have lost one's virginity; **il est connu comme le l. blanc** everybody knows him; **à pas de l.** stealthily; *Prov* **les loups ne se mangent pas entre eux** there is honour among thieves; *Prov* **quand on parle du l., on en voit la queue** talk of the devil (and he's sure to appear); **l'homme est un l. pour l'homme** brother will turn upon brother

2 *(personne)* **jeune l.** *(en politique)* young Turk; *(en affaires)* go-getter; **un vieux l. de mer** an old sea-dog *or* salt

3 *Fam (en appellatif)* **mon (petit** *ou* **gros) l.** my (little) darling *or* love *or* sweetheart

4 *(masque)* (eye) mask

5 *Ich* (European) sea bass

6 *Tech (défaut)* flaw

loupage [lupaʒ] NM *Fam* messing up, botching

loup-cervier [luservje] *(pl* **loups-cerviers)** NM **1** *Zool* (European) lynx **2** *(fourrure)* lucern

loupe [lup] NF **1** *Opt* magnifying glass; **observer qch à la l.** to look at sth through a magnifying glass; *Fig* to put sth under a microscope, to scrutinize sth **2** *Méd* wen **3** *Bot* knur; **l. d'érable/ de noyer** burr maple/walnut **4** *Métal Br* bear, *Am* salamander

loupé, -e [lupe] *Fam* ADJ missed▪, failed▪; **l.!** missed!; **mon gâteau est l.!** my cake's a failure!▪, I've made a mess of my cake!; **la soirée a été complètement loupée!** the party was a total flop *or* wash-out!; **la fin du film est complètement loupée** the end of the film is completely botched *or* bungled

NM *Br* boob, *Am* screw-up; **il y a eu quelques loupés au début** we/they/*etc Br* made a few boobs *or Am* screwed up a few times to start with

louper [3] [lupe] *Fam* VT **1** *(examen)* to fail▪, to flunk; *(dessin, discours, tarte)* to botch, to bungle,

to make a botch *or* a mess of; **l. son coup** to bungle it

2 *(laisser échapper → train, personne)* to miss; **je t'ai loupé de cinq minutes** I (just) missed you by five minutes; **dépêche-toi, tu vas me faire l. mon bus!** hurry up! you're going to make me miss my bus!; **l. une occasion** to let an opportunity slip, to pass up an opportunity

3 *(locutions)* **ne pas l. qn** *(le punir)* to sort sb out, to give sb what for; **elle le recommence, il ne la loupera pas!** if she does that again he'll sort her out!; **il n'en loupe pas une!** *(il est gaffeur)* he's always putting his foot in it!

VSI **tu continues comme ça tu vas tout faire l.** if you carry on like that you'll mess everything up *or* make a mess of everything; **ça ne va pas l.** it's bound to happen, it (just) has to happen; **elle lui avait dit que ça ne marcherait pas et ça n'a pas loupé!** she told him/her it wouldn't work and sure enough it didn't!

▶**se louper** VPR **1** *(ne pas se rencontrer)* **on s'est loupés de quelques secondes** we missed each other by (just) a few seconds

2 *(manquer son suicide)* **Dieu merci, elle s'est loupée** she bungled it, thank God; **cette fois, il ne s'est pas loupé** this time he hasn't bungled it; **tu as vu son maquillage? elle ne s'est pas loupée!** have you seen her make-up? she's put it on with a trowel!; **il s'est coupé les cheveux tout seul et il s'est pas loupé!** he cut his own hair and made some job of it!; **je me suis blessé avec l'ouvre-boîte – dis donc, tu ne t'es pas loupé!** I've cut myself on the can opener – you certainly have!

loup-garou [lugaru] *(pl* **loups-garous)** NM **1** *Myth* werewolf **2** *(personnage effrayant)* bogeyman; **si tu n'arrêtes pas, j'appelle le l.** *(à un enfant)* if you don't stop, the bogeyman will come and get you

loupiot, -e[1] [lupjo, -ɔt] NM,F *Fam (enfant)* kid, *Br* nipper

loupiote[2] [lupjɔt] NF *(lampe)* (small) light

loup-marin [lumarɛ̃] *(pl* **loups-marins)** NM *Can* (common) seal

Louqsor [luksɔr] NM Luxor

LOURD, -E [lur, lurd]

ADJ	heavy 1–5, 7–9, 11	deep 1	rich 3
thick 4, 5	sultry 6	strong 7	clumsy 9
high 11	serious 11		
ADV	close 1		

ADJ **1** *(pesant → gén)* heavy; *(→ sommeil)* heavy, deep; **ma valise est trop lourde** my suitcase is too heavy; **gaz plus l. que l'air** heavier-than-air gas; **une démarche lourde** a heavy tread; **d'un pas l.** with a heavy tread *or* step; **le vol l. des corbeaux** the clumsy flight of the crows; **un regard l.** a hard stare; **j'ai la tête lourde/les jambes lourdes** my head feels/my legs feel heavy; **les paupières lourdes de sommeil** eyelids heavy with sleep; **avoir le sommeil l.** to be a heavy *or* deep sleeper

2 *(complexe → artillerie, chirurgie, industrie)* heavy

3 *(indigeste)* heavy, rich; **des repas trop lourds** excessively rich meals

4 *(compact → sol, terre)* heavy, thick; **terrain l. aujourd'hui à Longchamp** the going is heavy today at Longchamp

5 *(chargé)* heavy, thick; **de lourdes tapisseries** thick *or* heavy wall-hangings; **de lourds nuages** thick *or* dense clouds; **l. de** heavy with; **des branches lourdes de fruits** branches heavy with *or* bowed down with fruit; **un ciel l. de nuages** a heavily clouded *or* heavy sky; **son ton est l. de menace** the tone of his/her voice is ominous *or* menacing; **il régnait dans l'assistance un silence l. d'angoisse** people sat there in anxious silence; **un discours l. de sous-entendus** a speech packed *or* loaded with innuendos; **cette décision est lourde de conséquences** this decision will have far-reaching consequences

6 *(accablant → atmosphère, temps)* sultry, oppressive

7 *(entêtant → odeur)* heavy, strong; **le parfum l. des jasmins** the heavy scent of jasmine trees

8 *(sans grâce → bâtiment, façade)* heavy, heavy-looking; **un visage aux traits lourds** a coarse-featured face

9 *(sans finesse → remarque)* clumsy, heavy-handed; *(→ mouvement, style)* heavy, ponderous; **des plaisanteries plutôt lourdes** rather unsubtle jokes; **certains passages sont lourds** some passages are a bit laboured *or* tedious; **avoir l'esprit l.** to be slow(-witted) *or* dull-witted

10 *Fam (agaçant)* **sans vouloir être l., je te rappelle que ça doit être fini dans 15 minutes** I don't want to nag but don't forget that you have to finish in 15 minutes; **t'es l. avec tes questions** you're such a pain with all your questions

11 *(important → chiffres)* high; *(→ horaire, tâche, dépenses)* heavy; *(→ perte)* heavy, serious, severe; *(→ dette)* heavy, serious; *(→ faute)* serious, grave; **notre facture d'électricité a été lourde l'hiver dernier** we had a big electricity bill last winter; **les effectifs des classes sont trop lourds** class sizes are too big; **tu as là une lourde responsabilité** that is a heavy responsibility for you; **l. bilan pour la catastrophe aérienne d'hier** heavy death toll in yesterday's air disaster; **de lourdes accusations pèsent sur le prévenu** the accused faces serious *or* weighty charges; **elle a une lourde hérédité** she's got an unfortunate background

ADV **1** *(chaud)* **il fait très l.** it's very close

2 *Fam (beaucoup)* **tu n'en fais pas l.** you don't exactly kill yourself; **ça ne fait pas l.** it's not much to show for it; **je ne gagne pas l.** I don't exactly make a fortune; **il n'en sait pas l. sur l'histoire de son pays** he doesn't know much about the history of his country ▪

lourdaud, -e [lurdo, -od] ADJ oafish, clumsy NM,F oaf, nitwit

lourde[1] [lurd] ADJ *voir* **lourd**

lourde[2] NF *Fam (porte)* door ▪

lourdement [lurdəmã] ADV **1** *(très)* heavily; **la voiture était l. chargée** the car was heavily laden

2 *(sans souplesse)* heavily; **il tomba l. à terre** he fell heavily to the ground; **marcher l.** to tread heavily, to walk with a heavy step

3 *(beaucoup)* greatly; **tu te trompes l.!** you are greatly mistaken!; **cet investissement grève l. le budget** this investment puts a serious strain on the budget; **insister l. sur qch** to be most emphatic about sth

lourder [3] [lurde] VT *très Fam* **1** *(congédier)* to kick out, to throw out **2** *(importuner)* to piss off; **tu commences à me l. avec tes histoires** you're starting to piss me off with all your nonsense; **ça me lourde de me taper une heure de métro pour y aller** it's a real pain having to spend an hour on the metro to get there

Lourdes [lurd] NM Lourdes *(the most famous place of pilgrimage in France since Bernadette Soubirous claimed to have had visions of the Virgin Mary there in 1858)*

lourdeur [lurdœr] NF **1** *(d'un fardeau, d'une valise)* heaviness; *Fig* **la l. de la tâche m'effraie** the workload frightens me; *Fig* **la l. de l'appareil du parti** the unwieldiness of the party structure

2 *(d'un mouvement)* heaviness, clumsiness; **danser avec l.** to dance heavily *or* clumsily

3 *(douleur)* heavy feeling; **avoir des lourdeurs d'estomac** to feel bloated; **j'ai des lourdeurs dans les jambes** my legs feel heavy

4 *(du temps)* closeness, sultriness

5 *(des formes, des traits)* heaviness; *(d'un bâtiment, d'une architecture)* heaviness, massiveness

6 *(d'un propos, d'un comportement)* bluntness, clumsiness; **l. d'esprit** dullness; **quelle l. dans ses compliments!** his/her compliments are so clumsy!; **il est d'une telle l. d'esprit!** he's such an oaf!

7 *(gravité → d'une peine, d'une punition)* severity; *(→ d'un crime)* gravity; *(→ d'une responsabilité)* weight; **cette guerre égale la précédente par la l. des pertes** this war must rank with the last one in terms of the heavy losses suffered

❑ **lourdeurs** NFPL *(maladresses)* **idées intéressantes mais trop de lourdeurs** interesting ideas, but clumsily expressed

lourdingue [lurdɛ̃g] ADJ *très Fam* **1** *(physiquement)* clumsy▪, awkward▪ **2** *(peu subtil → personne)* dim-witted, *Br* thick; *(→ plaisanterie, réflexion)* pathetic, stupid; *(→ style)* heavy

loure [lur] NF **1** *(instrument)* (Normandy) bagpipe **2** *(danse)* slow dance in 3/4 time

louré [lure] ADJ *Mus* louré, slurred

lourer [3] [lure] VT *Mus* to slur

lousse [lus] ADJ *Can Joual* **1** *(ample)* loose▪; *(sans entraves)* loose, free▪ **2** *(généreux)* generous▪, free with one's money

loustic [lustik] NM *Fam* **1** *(individu louche)* shady character; **c'est un drôle de l.** that guy's pretty fishy **2** *(farceur)* joker, funny guy; **faire le l.** to play the fool, to fool around

loutre [lutr] NF **1** *Zool* otter; **l. géante (du Brésil)** giant otter; **l. de mer** sea otter; **l. de rivière** river otter **2** *(fourrure)* otter skin *or* pelt; **manteau de l.** otter-skin coat

Louvain [luvɛ̃] NM Leuven, Louvain

louvart [luvar] NM *Zool* young wolf

louve [luv] NF **1** *Zool* she-wolf, bitch **2** *(pour pierres de taille)* hoisting-scissors, lewis

louver [3] [luve] VT to lewis

louvet, -ette [luvɛ, -ɛt] ADJ dun

louveteau, -x [luvto] NM **1** *Zool* (wolf) cub **2** *(scout)* cub, Cub Scout

louveter [27] [luvte] VI to whelp

louveterie [luvtri] NF **1** *Arch* wolf-hunting **2** forestry pest control; **lieutenant de l.** forestry pest control officer

louvetier [luvtje] NM **1** *Hist* **Grand L.** master of the wolf-hunt **2** *(fonctionnaire)* forestry pest control officer

louvette [luvɛt] ADJ *voir* **louvet**
▪ NF = member of the Girl Guides aged between 8 and 12, *Br* ≃ Brownie, *Am* ≃ Girl Scout

louvoie *etc voir* **louvoyer**

louvoiement [luvwamɑ̃], **louvoyage** [luvwajaʒ] NM **1** *Naut* tacking **2** *Fig (manœuvre)* subterfuge

louvoyer [13] [luvwaje] VI **1** *Naut* to tack (about) **2** *(biaiser)* to hedge, to equivocate

Louvre [luvr] NM **le (palais du) L.** the Louvre; **le Grand L.** the enlarged "Musée du Louvre" *(including all the new constructions and excavations)*; **l'école du L.** = art school in Paris

---

Culture

LE LOUVRE

This former royal palace became a museum in 1791–1793. It houses one of the richest art collections in the world. The museum was extended in 1989, with the construction of the glass "pyramide du Louvre" in the main courtyard, and again in 1993 when the Richelieu wing, formerly occupied by the Ministry of Finance, was inaugurated.

Louxor [luksɔr] = **Louqsor**

lovelace [lɔvlas] NM *Littéraire* libertine

lover [3] [lɔve] VT *Naut* to coil
▪**se lover** VPR *(serpent)* to coil up; *(personne)* to curl up

low-cost [lokɔst] *(pl inv ou* **low-costs***)* ADJ *(compagnie aérienne)* low-cost, no-frills
▪ NM ou NF low-cost *or* no-frills airline

loxodromie [lɔksɔdrɔmi] NF *Naut* loxodromic curve, rhumb line

loxodromique [lɔksɔdrɔmik] ADJ *Naut (courbe, navigation)* loxodromic; **navigation l.** plane sailing, loxodromics *(singulier)*

loyal, -e, -aux, -ales [lwajal, -o] ADJ **1** *(fidèle)* loyal, faithful, trusty; **un compagnon l.** a loyal *or* faithful companion; **20 ans de bons et loyaux services** 20 years' unstinting devotion **2** *(honnête → personne)* honest, fair; *(→ adversaire)* honest; *(→ combat)* clean; **il a été l. avec moi** he was honest *or* straight with me; **un procédé l.** honest behaviour, upright conduct; **un jeu l.** a fair game; **c'est quelqu'un de parfaitement l. en affaires** he's a scrupulously fair businessman
❑ **à la loyale** ADV **se battre à la loyale** to fight cleanly *or* fairly

loyalement [lwajalmɑ̃] ADV **1** *(fidèlement)* loyally, faithfully; **servir qn l.** to serve sb faithfully; **très l.** with great loyalty, very loyally **2** *(honnêtement → se conduire, agir)* honestly; *(→ se battre)* cleanly

loyalisme [lwajalism] NM **1** *(fidélité)* loyalty **2** *Pol* loyalism, Loyalism

loyaliste [lwajalist] ADJ **1** *(fidèle)* loyal **2** *Hist* loyalist, Loyalist *(in American War of Independence)*
▪ NMF **1** *(fidèle)* loyal supporter **2** *Hist* loyalist, Loyalist *(in American War of Independence)*

loyauté [lwajote] NF **1** *(fidélité)* loyalty, faithfulness **2** *(honnêteté)* honesty, fairness; **elle a répondu en toute l.** she answered completely fairly *or* honestly

loyer [lwaje] NM **1** *(d'un logement)* rent; **une hausse des loyers** a rent rise *or* increase, *Am* a rent hike; **j'ai trois loyers de retard** I'm three months behind with my rent; **devoir trois mois de l.** to owe three months' rent; **donner à l.** to rent (out), *Br* to let (out); **prendre à l.** to rent; *Can* **être à l.** to be a tenant, to be in rented accommodation; *Jur* **l. symbolique** peppercorn rent **2** *Fin* **le l. de l'argent** the interest rate, the price of money

Lozère [lozɛr] NF **la L.** the Lozère

lozérien, -enne [lozerjɛ̃, -ɛn] ADJ of/from the Lozère
❑ **Lozérien, -enne** NM,F = inhabitant of or person from the Lozère

LP [ɛlpe] NM **1** *(abrév* **lycée professionnel***)* vocational high school **2** *(abrév* **Long Playing***)* LP

LPG [ɛlpeʒe] NM *Belg (abrév* **Liquid Petroleum Gas***)* LPG

LPO [ɛlpeo] NF *(abrév* **Ligue pour la protection des oiseaux***)* = society for the protection of birds, *Br* ≃ RSPB

LSD [ɛlɛsde] NM *(abrév* **lysergic acid diethylamide***)* LSD

LSI [ɛlɛsi] NF *Ordinat (abrév* **large scale integration***)* LSI

lu, -e [ly] PP *voir* **lire²**

Luanda [lwɑ̃da] NM Luanda

Lübeck [lybɛk] NM Lübeck

lubie [lybi] NF whim; **c'est sa dernière l.** it's his/her latest whim; **encore une de ses lubies!** another one of his/her crazy ideas!

lubricité [lybrisite] NF *(d'une personne, d'un regard)* lustfulness, lechery; *(d'un propos, d'une conduite)* lewdness

lubrifiant, -e [lybrifjɑ̃, -ɑ̃t] ADJ lubricating
▪ NM lubricant

lubrificateur, -trice [lybrifikatœr, -tris] ADJ lubricating
▪ NM lubricant

lubrification [lybrifikasjɔ̃] NF lubrication

lubrificatrice [lybrifikatris] *voir* **lubrificateur**

lubrifier [9] [lybrifje] VT to lubricate

lubrique [lybrik] ADJ *Littéraire (personne, regard)* lustful, lecherous; *(attitude, propos)* lewd, libidinous

lubriquement [lybrikmɑ̃] ADV lecherously, lewdly

Luc [lyk] NPR *Bible* Luke

lucane [lykan] NM *Entom* stag beetle, *Spéc* lucanid

lucaniste [lykanist], **lucanophile** [lykanɔfil] NMF kite-flyer, kite fan

lucarne [lykarn] NF *(fenêtre)* skylight; **l. faîtière** skylight; **l. pendante** garret window; **l. pignon** dormer (window) **2** *Ftbl* top corner (of the net)

lucernaire [lysɛrnɛr] NF *Zool* stalked jellyfish

Lucerne [lysɛrn] NM Lucerne; **le canton de L.** Lucerne

lucide [lysid] ADJ **1** *(clairvoyant → personne)* lucid, clear-headed; *(→ esprit, raisonnement)* lucid, clear; *(→ critique)* perceptive; **elle est très l. sur elle-même** she's extremely perceptive about herself; **il jette sur la société contemporaine un regard très l.** he casts a very lucid *or* clear eye on contemporary society **2** *(éveillé)* conscious; *(qui a toute sa tête)* lucid

lucidement [lysidmɑ̃] ADV clearly, lucidly

lucidité [lysidite] NF **1** *(clairvoyance → d'une personne)* lucidity, clear-headedness; *(→ de l'esprit, d'un raisonnement)* lucidity, clarity; **avec l.** lucidly; **une critique d'une grande l.** a very perceptive criticism **2** *(possession des facultés)* lucidity; **elle n'a plus toute sa l.** her mind's wandering a bit; **dans ses moments de l.** in his/her lucid moments

Lucifer [lysifɛr] NPR Lucifer

luciférien, -enne [lysiferjɛ̃, -ɛn] ADJ Luciferian
▪ NM,F *Hist* Satanist

luciférine [lysiferin] NF *Biol & Chim* luciferin

lucifuge [lysifyʒ] *Zool* ADJ lucifugous
▪ NM lucifugous termite

lucilie [lysili] NF *Entom* lucilia

lucimètre [lysimɛtr] NM *Opt* lucimeter

luciole [lysjɔl] NF *Zool* firefly, *Am* lightning bug

lucite [lysit] NF *Méd* sun allergy, rash *(caused by exposure to the sun)*

Lucius [lysjys] NPR Lucius

Lucques [lyk] NM *Géog* Lucca

lucratif, -ive [lykratif, -iv] ADJ lucrative, profitable; **un métier l.** a job that pays well, a well-paid job

lucrativement [lykrativmɑ̃] ADV lucratively

lucre [lykr] NM profit, *Sout* lucre; **faire qch par goût du l.** to do sth out of love for money

Lucrèce [lykrɛs] NPR Lucretius; **L. Borgia** Lucrezia Borgia

luddisme [lydism] NM Luddism

luddite [lydit] NM Luddite

ludiciel [lydisjɛl] NM computer game *(software)*

ludion [lydjɔ̃] NM Cartesian diver

ludique [lydik] ADJ *(avant n)*, *Spéc* ludic; **le comportement l. des enfants** children's behaviour at play; **il y a un côté l. dans ses mises en scène** his/her productions have a playful quality to them

ludisme [lydism] NM *Psy* obsessive play

ludo-éducatif, -ive [lydoedykatif, -iv] *(mpl* **ludo-éducatifs**, *fpl* **ludo-éducatives***)* ADJ edutainment *(avant n)*

ludologue [lydɔlɔg] NMF = person who compiles puzzles and brainteasers for newspapers and magazines

ludospace [lydɔspas] NM *Aut* people carrier

ludothécaire [lydɔtekɛr] NMF = person in charge of a toys and games library

ludothèque [lydɔtɛk] NF toys and games library

luette [lɥɛt] NF **1** *Anat* uvula **2** *Can Fam* **se mouiller** *ou* **se rincer la l.** *(prendre un verre)* to wet one's whistle, to have a drink▪; *(se soûler)* to get sloshed *or* drunk▪

lueur [lɥœr] NF **1** *(lumière → de l'âtre, du couchant)* glow; *(→ de la lune, d'une lampe)* light; *(→ d'une lame)* gleam; **une faible l.** a glimmer; **les lueurs rougeoyantes de l'incendie** the reddish glow of the fire; **l. vacillante** flicker; **à la l. d'une bougie** by candlelight; **aux premières lueurs de l'aube** in the first light of dawn; *Fig* **à la l. des derniers événements** in the light of recent events **2** *Fig (éclat)* glint, glimmer; **une l. de colère** a gleam *or* glint of anger; **une l. d'intelligence/d'espoir/de joie** a glimmer of intelligence/of hope/of joy; **une l. mauvaise** a nasty glint

luffa [lyfa] = **loofa**

Lugano [lygano] NM Lugano

luge [lyʒ] NF **1** *(gén)* toboggan, *Br* sledge, *Am* sled; **faire de la l.** to toboggan, *Br* to go sledging, *Am* to go sledding **2** *Sport* **luge 3** *Suisse* = large sledge used to carry loads

lugée [lyʒe] NF *Suisse Fam (échec)* failure▪

luger [17] [lyʒe] VI **1** *(descendre en luge)* to toboggan, *Br* to sledge, *Am* to sled **2** *Suisse (déraper)* to skid **3** *Suisse Fam (échouer)* to fail▪
▪**se luger** VPR *Suisse* **1** *(faire de la luge)* to toboggan, *Br* to go sledging, *Am* to go sledding **2** *Fam (échouer)* to fail▪

lugeur, -euse [lyʒœr, -øz] NM,F **1** *(gén)* tobogganer, *Br* sledger, *Am* sledder **2** *Sport* luger

lugubre [lygybr] ADJ *(personne, mine, pensées)* gloomy, lugubrious; *(endroit, atmosphère, soirée)* gloomy; *(son, cri)* doleful, mournful

lugubrement [lygybrəmɑ̃] ADV lugubriously, gloomily; **les cris des pleureuses retentissaient l.** the cries of the mourners rang out lugubriously

lui¹ [lɥi] PP *voir* **luire**

LUI² [lɥi]

(to) him/her/it A1 ▪ he B1, 2 ▪ it B1, 3 ▪
him B2, 3 ▪ himself B4

PRON **A.** *REPRÉSENTANT LE GENRE MASCULIN OU FÉMININ* **1** *(complément → homme)* (to) him; *(→ femme)* (to) her; *(→ chose, animal)* (to) it; *(→ nouveau-né, animal domestique mâle)* (to) him,

(to) it; (→ *nouveau-née, animal domestique femelle*) (to) her, (to) it; **je l. ai parlé** I spoke to him/her; **je l. ai serré la main** I shook his/her hand; **ils l. ont jeté des pierres** they threw stones at him/her; **il a rencontré Hélène et (il) l. a plu** he met Hélène and she liked him; **pensez-vous que cela puisse l. nuire?** do you think that can harm him/her?; **il entend qu'on l. obéisse** he means to be obeyed; **il le l. a présenté** he introduced him to him/her; **qui le l. a dit?** who told him/her?; **je le l. ai reproché** I reproached him/her for it; **donne-le-l.** give it to him/her; **ça ne l. rapporte rien** he/she isn't getting anything out of it; **il l. est difficile de venir** it's difficult for him/her to come

2 *(se substituant à l'adjectif possessif)* **il l. a serré la main** he shook his/her hand; **le bruit l. donne mal à la tête** the noise gives him/her a headache

B. *REPRÉSENTANT LE GENRE MASCULIN* **1** *(sujet → personne)* he; *(→ chose, animal)* it; *(→ nouveau-né, animal domestique)* he, it; **elle est charmante, mais l. est impossible** she's charming, but he's infuriating; **elle aime le cinéma, l. non** she likes the cinema, he doesn't; **nous travaillons et l., en attendant, il se repose** we're working, and meanwhile, HE'S having a rest; **l. ne voulait pas en entendre parler** HE didn't want to hear anything about it; **Paul et l. sont rentrés ensemble** he and Paul went back together; **il sait de quoi je parle, l.** HE knows what I'm talking about; **mon frère, l., n'est pas venu** as for my brother, he didn't come; **si j'étais l....** if I were him...; **quant à l., il n'était pas là** as for him, he wasn't there; **qui ira avec elle? – l. who'll go with her? – he will; **l.? il ne ferait jamais ça!** him? he'd never do that!; **l. aussi se pose des questions** he is wondering about it too; **il doit suivre un régime: il est malheureux, l. qui est si gourmand!** he has to go on a diet, and loving his food as he does, he's not happy about it!; **l. seul pourrait te le dire** only he could tell you

2 *(avec un présentatif)* **c'est l. qui vous le demande** HE'S asking you; **c'est l. qui nous a présentés** he's the one who introduced us, HE introduced us; **des deux frères, c'est l. que je connais le mieux** of the two brothers I know him *or* it's him I know best; **c'est encore l.?** is it him again?; **c'est tout l.!** that's typical of him!, that's him all over!

3 *(complément → personne)* him; *(→ chose, animal)* it; **en ce moment on ne voit que l.** you see him everywhere at the moment; **elle n'écoute que l.** she will only listen to HIM; **elle ne veut que l. pour avocat** he's the only lawyer she will accept, she won't have any lawyer but him; **on l'a vu, l.** we saw HIM; **l., tout le monde le connaît** everybody knows HIM; **elle est plus jeune que l.** she's younger than him, she's younger than he (is); **j'apprécie Marie plus que l.** *(plus qu'il ne l'apprécie)* I like Marie more than he does *or* than him; *(je préfère Marie)* I like Marie more than him; **avez-vous pensé à l.?** have you thought about him?; **elle ne l. a pas plu, à l.** he didn't like her at all; **cette valise n'est pas à l.?** isn't that his suitcase?, doesn't that suitcase belong to him?; **une amie à l.** a friend of his; **il a réussi à le soulever à l. (tout) seul** he managed to lift it on his own *or* without any help; **à l. seul, il possède la moitié de la ville** he owns half of the town himself; **sans l., tout était perdu** without him *or* if it hadn't been for him, all would have been lost; **je vais chez l.** I'm going to his house; **elle se méfie de l.** she doesn't trust him; **l'enfant n'est pas de l.** the child is not his

4 *(en fonction de pronom réfléchi)* himself; **il est content de l.** he's pleased with himself; **il ne pense qu'à l.** he only thinks of himself

lui-même [lɥimɛm] PRON *(une personne)* himself; *(une chose)* itself; **M. Dupont? – l.** Mr Dupont? – at your service; *(au téléphone)* Mr Dupont? – speaking; **il me l'a dit l.** he told me himself; **il paraissait surpris** he himself seemed surprised; **il se coupe les cheveux l.** he cuts his own hair, he cuts his hair himself; **de l., il a parlé**

du prix he mentioned the price without being prompted *or* asked; **il n'a qu'à venir voir par l.** all he has to do is come and see for himself; **il pensait en l. que...** he thought to himself that...

luire [97] [lɥir] VI **1** *(briller → métal, eau, yeux)* to gleam; *(→ surface mouillée)* to glisten; *(→ bougie, lumignon)* to glimmer; *(→ feu)* to glow; *(→ soleil, étoile)* to shine; **des larmes luisaient dans leurs yeux** their eyes were glistening with tears, tears were glistening in their eyes; **son uniforme luisait d'usure** his/her uniform was shiny with wear

2 *Fig* to shine, to glow; **un faible espoir luit encore** there is still a glimmer of hope; **cette phrase fit l. un espoir dans son cœur** the words brought a glimmer of hope to his/her heart

luisance [lɥizãs] NF *Littéraire* gleam; **l. des cheveux** sheen on the hair

luisant, -e [lɥizã, -ãt] ADJ *(métal)* gleaming; *(soleil, étoile)* shining; *(flamme)* glowing; *(pavé, pelage)* glistening; **il frappait sur l'enclume, le front l. de sueur** he was striking the anvil, his forehead glistening with sweat; **les yeux luisants de colère** with eyes ablaze, with eyes blazing with anger; **un manteau l. d'usure** a coat shiny with wear

▪ NM *(d'une étoffe, d'un meuble)* sheen; *(d'une fourrure)* gloss

luisent *etc voir* **luire**

lulu [lyly] NM *Orn* woodlark

luma [lyma] NM *(en français régional → escargot)* (edible) snail

lumachelle [lymaʃɛl] NF *Minér* lumachel, lumachelle

lumbago [lœbago, lɔ̃bago] NM *Méd* lumbago

lumen [lymɛn] NM *Phys* lumen

lumerotte [lymərɔt] NF *Belg* **1** *(bougie)* candle end **2** *(petite lampe)* small light

lumière [lymjɛr] NF **1** *(naturelle → gén)* light; *(→ du soleil)* sunlight; **dehors, la l. était aveuglante** the sunlight *or* the light was blinding outside; **l'atelier reçoit la l. du nord** the studio faces north; **la l. du jour** daylight; **la l. des étoiles** starlight; **à la l. de la lune/d'une bougie** by moonlight/candlelight; **sans l.** *(pièce)* dark; **revoir la l.** *(recouvrer la vue)* to be able to see again; *(en sortant d'un lieu sombre)* to see daylight again; *(retrouver la liberté)* to be free again; *Fig* **voir** *ou* **apercevoir la l. au bout du tunnel** to see (the) light at the end of the tunnel

2 *(artificielle)* light; **j'ai vu de la l. et je suis entré** I saw a light (on) so I went in; **allumer la l.** to turn *or* to switch on the light; **éteindre la l.** to turn *or* to switch off the light; **il reste une l. allumée** there's still a light on; **les lumières de la ville** the lights of the city, the city lights; **lumières tamisées** soft lighting

3 *(éclaircissement)* light; **jeter une l. nouvelle sur qch** to throw *or* to shed new light on sth; **toute la l. sera faite** we'll get to the bottom of this

4 *(génie)* genius, (shining) light; **une l. de la littérature contemporaine** a shining light of contemporary literature; **cet enfant n'est pas une l.!** that child is hardly a genius *or* a shining light!

5 *Astron & Opt* light; **l. blanche** white light; **l. cendrée** earth-shine; **l. froide** blue light; **l. noire** (ultraviolet) black light; **l. de Wood** (ultraviolet) black light; **l. zodiacale** zodiacal light

6 *Beaux-Arts* light

7 *Rel* **la l. éternelle** *ou* **de Dieu** divine light; *Fig* **cacher la l. sous le boisseau** to hide one's light under a bushel; **que la l. soit!** let there be light!

8 *Tech* *(orifice → dans un instrument)* opening; **l. d'admission/d'échappement** inlet/exhaust port

9 *Can (ampoule électrique)* light bulb; *Can Joual (feu de circulation)* traffic light ▪

10 *Cin & TV* **l. ambiante** ambient light; **l. de base** key light; **l. diffuse** scattered light; **l. naturelle** available light; **l. parasite** spill light, flare

▫ **lumières** NFPL **1** *(connaissances)* insight *(UNCOUNT)*, knowledge *(UNCOUNT)*; **elle a des lumières sur le problème** she has (some) insight into the problem; **j'ai besoin de tes lumières** I need the benefit of your wisdom; *Hist* **les Lumières** the Enlightenment

2 *Aut* lights; **les lumières sont restées allumées toute la nuit** the lights stayed on all night

▫ **à la lumière de** PRÉP *(étant donné)* in (the) light of; **à la l. de ce que tu me dis** in (the) light of what you're telling me

▫ **en lumière** ADV **mettre qch en l.** to bring sth out, to shed light on sth

lumignon [lymiɲɔ̃] NM **1** *(bougie)* candle end **2** *(petite lampe)* small light

luminaire [lyminɛr] NM **1** *(lampe)* light, lamp; **magasin de luminaires** lighting shop **2** *Astrol* luminary **3** *Rel* lighting *(UNCOUNT)*

luminance [lyminãs] NF luminance

luminescence [lyminɛsãs] NF luminescence

luminescent, -e [lyminɛsã, -ãt] ADJ luminescent

lumineuse [lyminøz] *voir* **lumineux**

lumineusement [lyminøzmã] ADV luminously, clearly; **il a très l. exposé les faits** he gave a very lucid presentation of the facts

lumineux, -euse [lyminø, -øz] ADJ **1** *(qui émet de la lumière)* luminous

2 *(baigné de lumière → journée, appartement)* sunny

3 *(éclatant → couleur)* bright, brilliant

4 *(radieux → teint, sourire, regard)* radiant

5 *(lucide → esprit)* **il a une intelligence lumineuse** he has great insight

6 *(clair → exposé)* limpid, crystal clear; **son explication était lumineuse** his/her explanation was crystal clear

7 *(de génie → idée)* brilliant

luminisme [lyminism] NM *Beaux-Arts* luminarism

luministe [lyminist] *Beaux-Arts* ADJ luminarist

▪ NMF luminarist

luminophore [lyminɔfɔr] NM *Électron* luminophore, luminescent material

luminosité [lyminozite] NF **1** *(éclat)* brightness, radiance **2** *(clarté)* luminosity; **le temps de pose dépend de la l.** shutter speed depends on the amount of light available; **la l. est insuffisante pour prendre une photo** there is insufficient light (available) for taking a photo **3** *(d'un écran)* brightness **4** *Astron* luminosity

Lumitype® [lymitip] NF *Typ* Lumitype®

lumme [lym] NM *Orn* black-throated diver

lump [lœp] NM *Ich* lumpfish, lumpsucker

lumpenprolétariat [lœmpɛnprɔletarja] NM lumpenproletariat

lunaire [lynɛr] ADJ **1** *Astron* lunar; **mois l.** lunar month **2** *(qui évoque la lune → paysage)* lunar; **un visage l.** a moonface **3** *Littéraire (chimérique)* **un projet l.** a fanciful *or* an outlandish plan

▪ NF *Bot* honesty, *Spéc* lunaria

lunaison [lynɛzɔ̃] NF lunar month, *Spéc* synodic month, lunation

lunatique [lynatik] ADJ moody, temperamental

▪ NMF temperamental *or* capricious person

lunch [lœ̃ʃ, lœntʃ] *(pl* **lunchs** *ou* **lunches***)* NM cold buffet *(served at lunchtime for special occasions)*

lundi [lœdi] NM Monday; **le l. de Pâques/Pentecôte** Easter/Whit Monday; *voir aussi* **mardi**

lune [lyn] NF **1** *Astron* moon; **la L.** the Moon; **nuit sans l.** moonless night; **pleine/nouvelle l.** full/new moon; **l. de miel** honeymoon; **la l. de miel entre le président et l'Assemblée nationale a été de courte durée** the honeymoon period between the President and the National Assembly didn't last long; **l. rousse** April frost *(at night)*; **être dans la l.** to have one's head in the clouds; **pardon, j'étais dans la l.** sorry, I was miles away *or* my mind was elsewhere; **promettre la l. à qn** to promise sb the moon *or* the earth; **demander** *ou* **vouloir la l.** to ask for the moon;

tomber de la l. to be flabbergasted; *très Fam* **il est con comme la l.** he's *Br* as daft as a brush *or Am* dead from the neck up
2 *Fam (fesses)* behind
3 **vieilles lunes** *(idées dépassées)* old-fashioned *or* outmoded ideas
4 *Arch ou Littéraire (mois)* moon, month
5 *Ich* **l. (de mer)** sunfish, moonfish
6 *(nymphéa)* white water lily
luné, -e [lyne] **ADJ** *Fam* **bien/mal l.** in a good/bad mood; **toujours mal l.** always bad-tempered
lunetier, -ère [lyntje, -ɛr] **ADJ** spectacle *(avant n)*
NM,F 1 *(fabricant) Br* spectacle *or Am* eyeglass manufacturer 2 *(marchand)* optician
lunette [lynɛt] **NF** 1 *Opt* telescope; **l. d'approche** refracting telescope, *Arch* spyglass; **l. astronomique** astronomical telescope; **l. de pointage** sighting telescope; **l. terrestre** terrestrial telescope; **l. de tir** sights telescope
2 *(d'une montre)* bezel
3 *(des toilettes → ouverture)* rim; *(→ siège)* seat
4 *Archit, Beaux-Arts & Constr* lunette
5 *(de guillotine)* lunette
6 *Naut* **l. d'étambot** propeller shaft hole
7 *Tech* **l. fixe/à suivre** steady/follow rest
8 *Aut* **l. (arrière)** rear window
❑ **lunettes NFPL** 1 *(verres correcteurs)* glasses; **une paire de lunettes** a pair of glasses; **porter des lunettes** to wear glasses; **un petit garçon à lunettes** a little boy wearing glasses; **mets des lunettes!** *(regarde mieux)* buy yourself a pair of specs!; **lunettes de vue** *ou* **correctrices** spectacles; **lunettes bifocales** bifocals; **lunettes noires** dark glasses; **lunettes de plongée** swimming goggles; **lunettes de protection** goggles; **lunettes de soleil,** *Belg* **lunettes solaires** sunglasses
2 *(verres protecteurs)* goggles; **lunettes de ski** skiing goggles
lunetté, -e [lynəte] **ADJ** *Fam* wearing glasses■, with glasses on■
lunetterie [lynɛtri] **NF** 1 *(industrie) Br* spectacle *or Am* eyeglass manufacture 2 *(commerce) Br* spectacle *or Am* eyeglass trade
luni-solaire [lynisɔlɛr] *(pl* **luni-solaires***)* **ADJ** lunisolar
lunule [lynyl] **NF** 1 *Anat* half-moon, *Spéc* lunule 2 *Géom* lune
lunure [lynyr] **NF** lunate, crescent-shaped defect in wood
lupanar [lypanar] **NM** *Littéraire* brothel, house of ill repute
lupercales [lypɛrkal] **NFPL** *Antiq* Lupercalia
luperque [lypɛrk] **NM** *Antiq* = member of the priesthood that celebrated Lupercalia
lupin [lypɛ̃] **NM** *Bot* lupin
lupique [lypik] *Méd* **ADJ** 1 *(relatif au lupus)* lupous 2 *(atteint du lupus)* suffering from lupus
NMF lupus patient
lupome [lypom] **NM** *Méd* lupoma
lupulin [lypylɛ̃] **NM** lupulin (powder)
lupuline [lypylin] **NF** 1 = **lupulin** 2 *Bot* medick
lupus [lypys] **NM** *Méd* lupus; **l. vulgaire** lupus vulgaris
lurette [lyrɛt] **NF** *Fam* **il y a belle l.** ages ago; **il y a belle l. qu'elle est partie** *(depuis des années)* she left donkey's years ago *or* ages go; *(depuis des heures)* she left hours ago *or* ages ago
Lurex® [lyrɛks] **NM** Lurex®
luron, -onne [lyrɔ̃, -ɔn] **NM,F** *Fam* **c'est un gai** *ou* **joyeux l.** he's a bit of a lad; **c'est une gaie luronne** she's quite a girl
Lusaka [lysaka] **NM** *Géog* Lusaka
lusciniole [lysinjɔl] **NF** *Orn* **l. à moustaches** moustached warbler
lusin [lyzɛ̃] **NM** *Naut* houseline, marline
Lusitanie [lyzitani] **NF** **la L.** Lusitania
lusitanien, -enne [lyzitanjɛ̃, -ɛn] **ADJ** Lusitanian
❑ **Lusitanien, -enne NM,F** Lusitanian
lusophone [lyzɔfɔn] **ADJ** Portuguese-speaking; **les populations lusophones** Portuguese-speaking populations
NMF Portuguese speaker
lustrage [lystraʒ] **NM** *(d'une poterie)* lustring; *(d'un tissu, d'une peau)* lustring, calendering; *(d'une peinture)* glazing; *(d'une voiture)* polishing
lustral, -e, -aux, -ales [lystral, -o] **ADJ** lustral
lustration [lystrasjɔ̃] **NF** *Rel* lustration
lustre [lystr] **NM** 1 *(lampe → de Venise, en cristal)* chandelier; *(→ simple)* (ceiling) light
2 *(reflet → mat)* glow; *(→ brillant)* shine, polish
3 *Tech (d'une poterie)* lustre; *(d'un tissu, d'une peau)* lustre, calendering; *(d'une peinture)* glaze, gloss; *(du papier)* calendering; *(d'un métal)* polish
4 *Littéraire (prestige)* brilliance, glamour; **sans l.** lacklustre; **rendre** *ou* **redonner du l. à qch** to restore sth to its former glory
5 *Littéraire (cinq ans)* lustrum
❑ **lustres NMPL** **il y a des lustres de ça!** it was ages ago!; **depuis des lustres** for ages
lustré, -e [lystre] **ADJ** 1 *Tech (tissu, peau)* lustred, calendered; *(peinture)* glazed, glossy; *(poterie)* lustred; **poterie lustrée** lustreware 2 *(brillant → pelage)* sleek; *(→ cheveux)* glossy, shiny 3 *(usé)* shiny (with wear)
lustrer [3] [lystre] **VT** 1 *Tech (poterie)* to lustre; *(tissu, peau)* to lustre, to calender; *(peinture)* to glaze 2 *(faire briller → voiture)* to polish; **le chat lustre son pelage** the cat is cleaning its coat; **le temps a lustré la pierre** the stone is shiny (and worn) with age
lustrerie [lystrəri] **NF** *(lampes)* chandeliers; *(commerce, fabrication)* lighting industry
lustrine [lystrin] **NF** 1 *(soie)* lustring 2 *(percaline)* lustre 3 *(coton)* glazed cotton
lut [lyt] **NM** *Tech* lute, luting
lutéal, -e, -aux, -ales [lyteal, -o] **ADJ** *Biol* luteal
Lutèce [lytɛs] **NF** Lutetia
lutécien, -enne [lytesjɛ̃, -ɛn] **ADJ** *Hist & Géol* Lutetian
NM *Géol* Lutetian
❑ **Lutécien, -enne NM,F** *Hist* Lutetian
lutécium [lytesjɔm] **NM** *Chim* lutetium
lutéine [lytein] **NF** *Biol & Chim* lutein
lutéinique [lyteinik] **ADJ** *Biol* luteal
luter [3] [lyte] **VT** *Tech* to lute
lutétien, -enne [lytesjɛ̃, -ɛn] = **lutécien**
luth [lyt] **NM** 1 *Mus* lute; **jeu de l.** lute stop; *Littéraire* **prendre son l.** to start composing (poetry) 2 *Zool* **(tortue) l.** leatherback, leathery turtle
Luther [lytɛr] **NPR** **Martin L.** Martin Luther
luthéranisme [lyteranism] **NM** *Rel* Lutheranism
lutherie [lytri] **NF** 1 *(fabrication)* stringed-instrument manufacture 2 *(commerce)* stringed-instrument trade 3 *(boutique)* stringed-instrument maker's shop *or* workshop
luthérien, -enne [lyterjɛ̃, -ɛn] **ADJ** Lutheran
❑ **Luthérien, -enne NM,F** Lutheran
luthier, -ère [lytje, -ɛr] **NM,F** 1 *(fabricant)* stringed-instrument maker 2 *(marchand)* stringed-instrument dealer
luthiste [lytist] **NMF** lutenist, lute-player
lutin, -e [lytɛ̃, -in] **ADJ** *Littéraire* impish, mischievous
NM 1 *(démon → gén)* elf, goblin, imp; *(→ en Irlande)* leprechaun 2 *Arch (enfant)* (little) imp, (little) devil
lutiner [3] [lytine] **VT** *Littéraire* to fondle
lutraire [lytrɛr] **NF** *Zool* otter shell
lutrin [lytrɛ̃] **NM** 1 *(pupitre)* lectern; *(sur un bureau)* reading *or* book stand; *Mktg (pour un livre)* plinth 2 *(emplacement)* schola cantorum
3 *Belg, Can & Suisse Mus* music stand, lectern
lutte [lyt] **NF** 1 *(affrontement)* struggle, fight, conflict; **des luttes intestines** infighting *(UNCOUNT)*; **la l. est inégale** they are unfairly matched; **se livrer à une l. acharnée** to fight tooth and nail; **une l. d'influence** a fight for domination
2 *Pol* struggle; **la l. pour l'indépendance/pour la liberté** the struggle for independence/for freedom; **la l. menée par les intellectuels/syndicats** the struggle led by the intellectuals/unions; **luttes politiques/religieuses** political/religious struggles; **l. armée** armed struggle; **la l. des classes** the class struggle *or* war; **L. Ouvrière** = militant Trotskyist organization
3 *(efforts → contre un mal)* fight; **l. contre les incendies** firefighting *(UNCOUNT)*; **la l. contre le sida** the fight against AIDS; **la l. contre l'alcoolisme** the fight against alcoholism
4 *(résistance)* struggle; **une l. incessante contre elle-même** an incessant inner struggle; **la l. d'un malade contre la mort** a sick person's struggle for life *or* battle against death; **sa vie n'a été qu'une longue l. contre l'adversité** his/her life was just one long struggle against adversity
5 *(antagonisme)* fight; **la l. entre le bien et le mal** the fight between good and evil
6 *Agr* control *(UNCOUNT)*; **l. biologique** biological (pest) control; **l. génétique** genetic control; **l. intégrée** integrated control, pest management
7 *Biol* **la l. pour la vie** the struggle for survival
8 *Sport* wrestling *(UNCOUNT)*; **faire de la l.** to wrestle; **l. libre/gréco-romaine** all-in/Graeco-Roman wrestling
9 *Zool (accouplement)* mating *(UNCOUNT)*
❑ **de haute lutte, de vive lutte ADV** after a hard fight; **conquérir** *ou* **emporter qch de haute l.** to obtain sth after a hard fight
❑ **en lutte ADJ** **les travailleurs en l. ont défilé hier** the striking workers demonstrated yesterday; **nos camarades en l.** our struggling comrades; **être en l. contre qn** to be at loggerheads with sb
lutter [3] [lyte] **VI** 1 *(se battre)* **l. contre** to fight (against); **l. contre la bêtise** to fight stupidity; **ils luttent contre le gouvernement** they are struggling against *or* fighting the government; **l. contre la mort** to fight for one's life; **l. contre l'alcoolisme** to fight against *or* to combat alcoholism; **l. contre le sommeil** to fight off sleep; **l. pour** to fight for; **ils luttent pour leurs droits** they are fighting for their rights; **toute sa vie, elle a lutté pour que soient reconnus les droits de la femme** she struggled all her life for the recognition of women's rights
2 *(rivaliser)* **ils ont lutté de vitesse** each strove to be faster than the other; **elles luttaient d'adresse** they were trying to outwit each other
3 *Sport* to wrestle (**contre** with)
4 *Zool (bélier)* to mate, *Br* to tup
lutteur, -euse [lytœr, -øz] **NM,F** 1 *Sport* wrestler, *f* female wrestler 2 *(battant)* fighter; **c'est une lutteuse, elle s'en remettra** she's a fighter, she'll get over it
lutz [luts, lyts] **NM** *(en patinage artistique)* lutz
lux [lyks] *(pl inv ou* **luxes***)* **NM** *Phys* lux
luxation [lyksasjɔ̃] **NF** *Méd* dislocation, *Spéc* luxation
luxe [lyks] **NM** 1 *(faste)* luxury, wealth; **vivre dans le l.** to live in (the lap of) luxury; **c'est le (grand) l. ici!** it's the height of luxury *or* it's luxurious in here!; **un l. insolent** a pretentious display of wealth; **l'industrie du l.** the luxury goods industry
2 *(plaisir)* expensive treat, luxury, indulgence; **son seul l. c'est une cigarette après le déjeuner** the only treat he/she allows himself/herself is a cigarette after lunch; **pour une fois tu peux bien te permettre ce l.** for once you can treat yourself to *or* you can afford this luxury; **je ne peux pas m'offrir le l. de partir en vacances** I can't afford the luxury of a holiday; *Fig* **elle ne peut pas s'offrir** *ou* **se payer le l. de dire ce qu'elle pense** she can't afford to speak her mind
3 *(chose déraisonnable)* **la viande, c'est devenu un l.** buying meat has become a luxury; *Fam* **ils ont nettoyé la moquette, ce n'était pas du l.!** they cleaned the carpet, (and) it was about time too!
4 **un l. de** *(beaucoup de)* a host *or* a wealth of; **avec un l. de détails** with a wealth of detail
❑ **de luxe ADJ** 1 *(somptueux)* luxury *(avant n)* 2 *Com (voiture, hôtel)* de luxe, luxury *(avant n)*; *(modèle, édition)* de luxe; *(appartement, boutique)* luxury *(avant n)*
Luxembourg [lyksɑ̃bur] **NM** 1 *(ville)* Luxembourg; **à L.** in (the city of) Luxembourg 2 *(pays)* **le L.** Luxembourg; **vivre au L.** to live in Luxembourg; **aller au L.** to go to Luxembourg
3 *(en Belgique)* **le L.** Luxembourg province 4 *(à Paris)* **le L., les jardins du L.** the Luxembourg Gardens; **le (palais du) L.** the (French) Senate
luxembourgeois, -e [lyksɑ̃burʒwa, -az] **ADJ** of/from Luxembourg
❑ **Luxembourgeois, -e NM,F** = inhabitant of or person from Luxembourg
luxer [3] [lykse] **VT** *Méd* to dislocate, *Spéc* to luxate
►**se luxer VPR** **se l. le genou/l'épaule** to dislocate one's knee/shoulder

luxmètre [lyksmɛtr] **NM** *Opt* luxmeter

luxueuse [lyksyøz] *voir* **luxueux**

luxueusement [lyksyøzmã] **ADV** luxuriously

luxueux, -euse [lyksyø, -øz] **ADJ** luxurious; **un cadre l.** a luxurious environment; **vivre dans un cadre l.** to live in luxurious surroundings; **maison luxueuse** luxurious house

luxure [lyksyr] **NF** *Littéraire* lechery, lust

luxuriance [lyksyrjãs] **NF** *Littéraire* luxuriance; **une l. de couleurs** a luxuriance of colours

luxuriant, -e [lyksyrjã, -ãt] **ADJ** *Littéraire* **1** *(végétation)* luxuriant, lush; *(chevelure)* thick **2** *(imagination)* fertile

luxurieux, -euse [lyksyrjø, -øz] **ADJ** *Littéraire* lascivious, lustful

luzerne [lyzɛrn] **NF** *Bot Br* lucerne, *Am* alfalfa; **l. d'Arabie** spotted medick; **l. naine** bur medick; **l. polymorphe** toothed medick

luzernière [lyzɛrnjɛr] **NF** *Br* lucerne field, *Am* alfalfa field

luzin [lyzɛ̃] **NM** *Naut* houseline, marline

luzule [lyzyl] **NF** *Bot* sweet bent

lx *(abrév écrite* **lux**) lx

lycanthrope [likãtrɔp] **NM** lycanthrope

lycanthropie [likãtrɔpi] **NF** *(métamorphose)* & *Psy* lycanthropy

lycaon [likaɔ̃] **NM** *Zool* wild dog; *(en Afrique)* Cape hunting dog

lycée [lise] **NM 1** *(gén) Br* secondary school, *Am* high school *(providing three years' teaching after the "collège", in preparation for the baccalauréat examination)*; **il se souvient du l. comme de ses meilleures années** he looks back on his schooldays as the best years of his life; **l. d'enseignement général et technologique, l. polyvalent** *Br* secondary school, *Am* high school *(for both general and technical studies)*; **l. professionnel** vocational high school; *Anciennement* **l. d'enseignement professionnel** = former name for a "lycée professionnel"

　2 *Belg (de filles)* girls' *Br* secondary *or Am* high school

lycéen, -enne [liseɛ̃, -ɛn] **NM,F** *Br* ≃ secondary school pupil, *Am* ≃ high school student; **quand j'étais lycéenne** when I was at school; **un groupe de lycéens** a group of school students; **ce groupe attire surtout les lycéens** this group is mainly a success with teenagers

　ADJ school *(avant n)*; **le mouvement l.** the school students' movement

lycène [lisɛn] **NF** *Entom* common blue, *Spéc* lycaena

lycénidé [lisenide] *Entom* **NM** lycaenid, *Spéc* member of the Lycaenidae

□ **lycénidés** **NMPL** lycaenids, *Spéc* Lycaenidae

lychee [litʃi] = **litchi**

lychnis [liknis] **NM** *Bot* lychnis

lycope [likɔp] **NM** *Bot* gypsywort, water horehound

lycopène [likɔpɛn] **NM** *Chem* lycopene

lycoperdon [likɔpɛrdɔ̃] **NM** *Bot* lycoperdon

lycophyte [likɔfit] **NM** lycophyte

lycopode [likɔpɔd] **NM** *Bot* lycopod, lycopodium; **poudre de l.** lycopodium (powder)

lycopodiale [likɔpɔdjal] *Bot* **NF** lycopod, *Spéc* member of the Lycopodiales

□ **lycopodiales** **NFPL** lycopods, *Spéc* Lycopodiales

lycose [likoz] **NF** *Entom* wolf spider

Lycra® [likra] **NM** Lycra®

lyddite [lidit] **NF** lyddite

Lydie [lidi] **NF** *Hist* **la L.** Lydia

lydien, -enne [lidjɛ̃, -ɛn] **ADJ** *Hist* & *Mus* Lydian
　NM,F *Hist* Lydian

lymphadénectomie [lɛ̃fadenɛktɔmi] **NF** *Méd* lymphadenectomy

lymphadénite [lɛ̃fadenit] **NF** *Méd* lymphadenitis

lymphadénopathie [lɛ̃fadenɔpati] **NF** *Méd* lymphadenopathy

lymphangiome [lɛ̃fãʒjom] **NM** *Méd* lymphangioma

lymphangite [lɛ̃fãʒit] **NF** *Méd* lymphangitis

lymphatique [lɛ̃fatik] **ADJ 1** *Biol* lymphatic **2** *(apathique)* sluggish, apathetic, lethargic
　NM lymphatic vessel

lymphe [lɛ̃f] **NF** lymph

lymphoblaste [lɛ̃fɔblast] **NM** *Biol* lymphoblast

lymphocytaire [lɛ̃fɔsitɛr] **ADJ** *Biol* lymphocytic

lymphocyte [lɛ̃fɔsit] **NM** *Biol* lymphocyte; **l. T4** T4-lymphocyte

lymphocytose [lɛ̃fɔsitoz] **NF** *Méd* lymphocytosis

lymphogranulomatose [lɛ̃fɔgranylomatoz] **NF** *Méd* lymphogranulomatosis; **l. bénigne** benign lymphogranulomatosis, sarcoidosis; **l. maligne** Hodgkin's disease

lymphographie [lɛ̃fɔgrafi] **NF** *Méd* lymphography

lymphoïde [lɛ̃fɔid] **ADJ** lymphoid

lymphokine [lɛ̃fɔkin] **NF** *Biol* lymphokine

lymphome [lɛ̃fom] **NM** *Méd* lymphoma; **l. hodgkinien** Hodgkin's lymphoma; **l. malin non hodgkinien** non-Hodgkin's malignant lymphoma; **l. non hodgkinien** non-Hodgkin's lymphoma

lymphopénie [lɛ̃fɔpeni] **NF** *Méd* lymphopenia, lymphocytopenia

lymphopoïèse [lɛ̃fɔpɔjɛz] **NF** *Physiol* lymphopoiesis

lymphoréticulose [lɛ̃fɔretikyloz] **NF** *Méd* **l. bénigne d'inoculation** cat scratch illness *or* fever

lymphosarcome [lɛ̃fɔsarkom] **NM** *Méd* lymphosarcoma

Lynch [lintʃ] **NPR** **loi de L.** lynch-law

lynchage [lɛ̃ʃaʒ] **NM** lynching; **l. médiatique** media lynching

lyncher [3] [lɛ̃ʃe] **VT** to lynch; **se faire l.** to be *or* to get lynched

lyncheur, -euse [lɛ̃ʃœr, -øz] **NM,F** lyncher

lynx [lɛ̃ks] **NM 1** *Zool* lynx **2** *(fourrure)* lynx fur, lucern

Lyon [ljɔ̃] **NM** Lyon, Lyons

lyonnais, -e [ljɔnɛ, -ɛz] **ADJ** of/from Lyon
　NM *(dialecte)* Lyon dialect

□ **Lyonnais, -e** **NM** *Géog* **le L., les monts du L.** the Lyonnais Mountains
　NM,F = inhabitant of or person from Lyon

□ **à la lyonnaise** **ADJ 1** *Culin* (à la) lyonnaise *(cooked with minced onions stewed in butter)* **2** *Tex* printed in the frame

lyophile [ljɔfil] **ADJ** lyophilic

lyophilisat [ljɔfiliza] **NM** freeze-dried *or Spéc* lyophilized product

lyophilisation [ljɔfilizasjɔ̃] **NF** freeze-drying, *Spéc* lyophilization

lyophilisé, -e [ljɔfilize] **ADJ** freeze-dried, *Spéc* lyophilized

lyophiliser [3] [ljɔfilize] **VT** to freeze-dry, *Spéc* to lyophilize

lyre [lir] **NF** *Mus* lyre

lyric [lirik] **NM** *(dans un film, dans un spectacle)* sung part

lyrique [lirik] **ADJ 1** *Littérature (poésie)* lyric; *(inspiration, passion)* lyrical; *Fig* **quand il parle d'argent, il devient l.** he really gets carried away when he talks about money

　2 *Mus* & *Théât* lyric; **art/drame l.** lyric art/drama; **ténor/soprano l.** lyric tenor/soprano; **artiste l.** opera singer
　NM lyric poet

lyriquement [lirikmã] **ADV** lyrically

lyrisme [lirism] **NM** lyricism; **avec l.** lyrically; *Fig* **parler de qch avec l.** to wax lyrical about sth

lys [lis] = **lis**

'**Le Lys dans la vallée**' *Balzac* 'Lily of the Valley'

Lysandre [lizãdr] **NPR** Lysander

lysat [liza] **NM** *Biol* lysate

lyse [liz] **NF** *Biol* lysis

lyser [3] [lize] **VT** *Biol* to lyse

lysergamide [lizɛrgamid], **lysergide** [lizɛrʒid] **NM** LSD, lysergic acid

lysergique [lizɛrʒik] **ADJ** lysergic

lysimaque [lizimak] **NF** *Bot* yellow loosestrife, yellow pimpernel; **l. nummulaire** creeping Jenny

lysine [lizin] **NF** *Biol* & *Chim* **1** *(anticorps)* lysin **2** *(acide aminé)* lysine

lysis [lizis] **NF** *Méd* lysis

Lysol® [lizɔl] **NM** *Pharm* Lysol®

lysosome [lizozɔm] **NM** *Biol* lysosome

lytique [litik] **ADJ** lytic

M¹, m¹ [ɛm] NM INV (lettre) M, m

M² 1 (abrév écrite **million**) M 2 (abrév écrite **masculin**) M 3 (abrév écrite **méga**) M 4 Mil (abrév écrite **Major**) M 5 Naut (abrév écrite **mile (marin)**) nm 6 Anciennement Élec (abrév écrite **maxwell**) Mx

m² 1 (abrév écrite **mètre**) **60 m** 60 m 2 (abrév écrite **milli**) m

M. (abrév écrite **Monsieur**) Mr

m' [m] PRON voir **me**

M° (abrév écrite **métro**) metro

M6 [ɛmsis] NF = private television channel broadcasting mainly entertainment-based programmes and aimed at a younger audience

MA [ɛma] NM Anciennement Scol (abrév **maître auxiliaire**) Br supply or Am substitute teacher

ma [ma] voir **mon**

maar [maar] NM maar

Maastricht [mastriʃt] NM Maastricht; **les accords de M.** the Maastricht agreement; **le traité de M.** the Maastricht Treaty

maboul, -e [mabul] Fam ADJ crazy, bananas NM,F (raving) loony

Mac [mak] NM Ordinat Mac

mac [mak] NM Fam (abrév **maquereau**) pimp, Am mack

macabre [makabr] ADJ (découverte) macabre, gruesome; (spectacle) gruesome, macabre, grisly; (humour) macabre; **un goût pour ce qui est m.** a taste for the macabre

macache [makaʃ] ADV Fam Vieilli **m. (bono)!** no way (José)!, Br nothing doing!

macadam [makadam] NM 1 (matériau, surface) macadam; **m. goudronné** tarmacadam; **route en m.** tarmac road 2 (route) road, roadway, Spéc macadam; Fam **faire le m.** to walk the streets

macadamiser [3] [makadamize] VT to macadamize

Macao [makao] NM Macao, Macau; **vivre à M.** to live in Macao; **aller à M.** to go to Macao

macaque [makak] NM Zool macaque; **m. rhésus** rhesus monkey
NMF Fam (personne laide) pig; **un vieux m.** an old baboon

macareux [makarø] NM Orn puffin

macaron [makarɔ̃] NM 1 Culin macaroon 2 (vignette → officielle) badge; (→ publicitaire) sticker; Journ **m. de presse** press badge 3 Fam (décoration honorifique) rosette■; **il a eu son m.** he got his decoration■ 4 (de cheveux) coil; **porter des macarons** to wear (one's hair in) coils 5 Fam (coup) blow■, biff

macaronée [makarone] NF Littérature macaronic verse

macaroni [makarɔni] NM 1 Culin piece of macaroni; **des macaronis** macaroni; **gratin de macaronis** Br macaroni cheese, Am macaroni and cheese 2 très Fam (Italien) wop, Eyetie, = offensive term used to refer to an Italian

macaronique [makarɔnik] ADJ Littérature macaronic

macassar [makasar] NM **(huile de) m.** macassar (oil); **(bois de) m.** macassar wood

Macau [makao] = **Macao**

Maccabéen, -enne [makabeɛ̃, -ɛn] ADJ Hist Maccabean

Maccabées [makabe] NMPL Hist **les M.** the Maccabees

maccarthysme [makkartism] = **maccartisme**

maccarthyste [makkartist] = **maccartiste**

maccartisme [makkartism] NM Pol & Hist McCarthyism

maccartiste [makkartist] Pol & Hist ADJ McCarthyist, McCarthyite
NMF McCarthyist, McCarthyite

macchabée [makabe] NM Fam (cadavre) stiff

MacDo [makdo] NM Fam McDonalds■

macdonaldisation [makdɔnaldizasjɔ̃] NF McdonaldIzation

macdonaldiser [3] [makdɔnaldize] VT to McdonaldIze

Macédoine [masedwan] NF Géog **la M.** Macedonia; **vivre en M.** to live in Macedonia; **aller en M.** to go to Macedonia

macédoine [masedwan] NF 1 Culin **m. de fruits** fruit salad; **m. de légumes** (diced) mixed vegetables 2 Fam (mélange) mishmash

macédonien, -enne [masedɔnjɛ̃, -ɛn] ADJ Macedonian
NM (langue) Macedonian
❑ **Macédonien, -enne** NM,F Macedonian

macérateur [maseratœr] NM macerator

macération [maserasjɔ̃] NF 1 Culin maceration, steeping 2 Pharm & (en œnologie) maceration 3 Rel (punition) mortification of or mortifying the flesh, Sout maceration

macérer [18] [masere] VI 1 Culin to macerate, to steep; **faire m. le poisson cru dans du jus de citron** macerate or steep the raw fish in lemon juice; **les oranges ont macéré 24 heures** the oranges have been macerating for 24 hours; **la viande doit m. plusieurs jours** the meat should be left to steep or soak for several days
2 Pharm to macerate
3 Fig **m. dans le doute** to be steeped in doubt; Fam **laisse-le m. dans son jus** let him stew in his (own) juice
VT 1 Culin to macerate, to steep
2 Pharm to macerate
3 Rel **m. sa chair** to mortify oneself

maceron [masrɔ̃] NM Bot maceron

Mach [mak] NPR Aviat Mach; **(nombre de) M.** Mach (number); **voler à M. 2** to fly at Mach 2

machaon [makaɔ̃] NM Entom swallowtail (butterfly)

mâche [maʃ] NF corn salad, lamb's lettuce

mâchefer [maʃfɛr] NM 1 (du charbon) clinker, slag 2 (du plomb) (lead) dross

mâchement [maʃmɑ̃] NM chewing, Sout mastication

mâcher [3] [maʃe] VT 1 (aliment, chewing-gum) to chew; (brin d'herbe, tige de fleur) to chew or to nibble (at); (sujet: animal → fourrage) to champ, to chomp; **mâche-le bien** chew it well; **ne fais pas tant de bruit quand tu mâches** don't munch so loudly; Fig **il ne mâche pas ses mots** he doesn't mince his words
2 Fam (tâche) **m. le travail** ou **la besogne à qn** to spoon-feed sb; **faut-il que je te mâche tout le travail?** do I have to show or tell you how to do everything?
3 (déchiqueter → matériau, papier) to chew up; **le papier ressort tout mâché** the paper comes out all crumpled (up) or chewed up
4 Fig Littéraire (ressasser) to chew over, to mull over

machette [maʃɛt] NF machete

mâcheur, -euse [maʃœr, -øz] NM,F chewer

Machiavel [makjavɛl] NPR Machiavelli

machiavel [makjavɛl] NM **c'est un m.** he's a Machiavellian character

machiavélique [makjavelik] ADJ Machiavellian

machiavélisme [makjavelism] NM Machiavellianism

mâchicoulis [maʃikuli] NM machicolation
❑ **à mâchicoulis** ADJ machicolated

machin [maʃɛ̃] NM Fam 1 (chose) thing■, thingy; **c'est quoi, ce m.?** what's this thing?
2 (personne → en s'adressant à la personne) what's-your-name; (homme → en parlant de lui) what's-his-name; (femme → en parlant d'elle) what's-her-name; **M. chouette** what's-his-name, f what's-her-name; **monsieur M.** Mr What's-his-name, what-d'you-call-him; **madame M.** Mrs What's-her-name, what-d'you-call-her; Péj **espèce de vieux m.!** you old fool!

machinal, -e, -aux, -ales [maʃinal, -o] ADJ (geste) involuntary, unconscious; (réaction) automatic, instinctive; (parole) mechanical; **un travail m.** mechanical work; **faire qch de façon machinale** to do sth automatically; **j'emprunte toujours ce chemin-là, c'est m.!** I always go that way, I do it without thinking!

machinalement [maʃinalmɑ̃] ADV 1 (involontairement) automatically, without thinking; **m., il lui rendit son sourire** he smiled back at him/her automatically; **excuse-moi, je l'ai fait m.** sorry, I did it automatically or without thinking 2 (mécaniquement) mechanically, without thinking; **elle fait son travail m.** she does her work mechanically or without thinking

machination [maʃinasjɔ̃] NF plot, conspiracy, machination; **des machinations** plotting (UNCOUNT), machinations

machine [maʃin] NF 1 (appareil) machine, piece of machinery; **l'âge des machines** ou **de la m.** the machine age, the age of the machine; Fam **aller en m.** (vêtement) to be machine-washable■; **m. à additionner, m. à calculer** calculator; (plus grande) adding machine, calculating machine; **m. à adresser** addressing machine; **m. à affranchir** Br franking machine, Am postal meter; **m. agrafeuse** stapling machine, stapler; **m. à aléser** boring machine, fine borer; **m. à battre** threshing machine; **m. de bureau** office machine; **m. à café** coffee machine; Typ **m. à composer** typesetting machine; **m. comptable** accounting machine; **m. à coudre** sewing machine; **m. à écrire** typewriter; **m. à écrire à mémoire** memory typewriter; Aut **m. d'équilibrage des roues** wheel-balancing machine; **m. à fraiser** milling machine; **m. de guerre** Hist engine of war; Fig war machine; **m. infernale** explosive device, Arch infernal machine; **m. interprète de cartes perforées** punch-card reader; **m. à laver** washing machine; **m. à laver séchante** washer-dryer; **m. à laver la vaisselle** dishwasher; Belg **m. à lessiver** washing machine; **m. à plier les documents** paper folding machine; **m. poinçonneuse** (de cartes perforées) punch; **m. à polycopier** duplicating machine; **m. à rayons X** X-ray machine; Tech **m. de rectification** grinding machine; **m. à repasser** steam press; **m. simple/composée** simple/compound machine; **m. à sous** one-armed bandit, Br fruit machine; **m. de traitement de l'information** data processor; **m. à** ou **de traitement de texte** word processor; **m. à tricoter** knitting machine; **m. trieuse** sorter; **m. à vapeur** steam engine; **m. volante** flying machine
2 (véhicule agricole) machine; Fam (moto) machine; **machines agricoles** agricultural machinery
3 (locomotive) locomotive, engine
4 Naut (moteur) engine; **arrêtez** ou **stoppez les machines!** stop all engines!; **chambre** ou **salle des machines** engine room; **faire m. arrière** to go astern; Fig to backtrack

5 *(organisation)* machine, machinery; **le projet a nécessité la mise en place d'une lourde m. administrative** the project meant that a cumbersome administrative framework had to be set up; **les lourdeurs de la m. judiciaire** the cumbersome legal machine; *Pol* **m. du parti** party machine

6 *Théât* machine, piece of theatre machinery; **pièce à machines** play with stage effects

7 *Fig Péj (automate)* machine; **je ne veux pas devenir une m. à écrire des chansons** I don't want to become a song-writing machine; **il n'est qu'une m. à faire de l'argent** he's nothing but a money-making machine

8 *Can Joual (voiture)* car ■, wheels, *Br* motor

9 *Fig Hum* **la m. est usée** *(le corps humain)* the old body is tired

10 *Fam (femme → en s'adressant à elle)* what's-your-name; *(→ en parlant d'elle)* what's-her-name □ **à la machine** ADV *(fait)* **à la m.** *(objets)* machine-made; *(opération)* done by machine; **coudre qch à la m.** to sew sth on the machine, to machine *or* to machine-sew sth; **laver qch à la m.** to machine-wash sth, to wash sth in the machine; **taper qch à la m.** to type sth; **tricoter qch à la m.** to machine-knit sth, to make sth on the knitting machine; **travailler le métal à la m.** to machine metal

machine-outil [maʃinuti] *(pl* **machines-outils)** NF machine tool; **l'industrie de la m.** the machine-tool industry **m. à commande numérique** numerically controlled machine tool

machiner [3] [maʃine] VT *Fam (préparer → complot)* to hatch; *(→ affaire, histoire)* to plot; **ils ont machiné toute l'histoire afin de l'éliminer** they engineered the whole thing to get rid of him/her

machinerie [maʃinri] NF **1** *(machines)* machinery, equipment, plant; **c'est la m. qui coûte le plus cher** most of the money goes on equipment **2** *(salle)* machine room; *Naut* engine room **3** *Théât* machinery

machine-transfert [maʃinträsfɛr] *(pl* **machines-transferts)** NF automated machine tool

machinisme [maʃinism] NM mechanization

machiniste [maʃinist] NMF **1** *Théât* stagehand, scene shifter; **les machinistes** (the) stage staff **2** *Cin & TV* **m. (de plateau)** grip; **m. caméra** dolly operator; **m. de travelling** tracker **3** *Transp (chauffeur)* driver; **faire signe au m.** *(sur panneau)* ≃ request stop **4** *Belg (conducteur de train)* train driver **5** *Ind* machine tool operator

machisme [matʃism] NM *Péj* male chauvinism

machiste [matʃist] *Péj* ADJ male chauvinist *(avant n)*
NM male chauvinist

machmètre [makmɛtr] NM machmeter

macho [matʃo] *Fam Péj* ADJ **1** *(viril)* macho **2** *(phallocrate)* male chauvinist ■ *(avant n)*
NM **1** *(viril)* macho **2** *(phallocrate)* male chauvinist ■

mâchoire [maʃwar] NF **1** *Anat* jaw; **m. inférieure/supérieure** lower/upper jaw; *Fam* **jouer** *ou* **travailler des mâchoires** *(manger avec appétit)* to get stuck in **2** *Zool* jaw; *(d'insectes)* mandible □ **mâchoires** NFPL *(d'un outil)* jaws; *(d'une poulie)* flange; **mâchoires de frein** brake shoes

mâchon [maʃõ] NM *(terme lyonnais) (restaurant)* = restaurant serving light meals; *(repas)* light meal

mâchonnement [maʃɔnmã] NM **1** *(fait de mâcher)* chewing *(UNCOUNT)*; **des mâchonnements bruyants** munching *(UNCOUNT)*, chomping *(UNCOUNT)* **2** *Méd* bruxism

mâchonner [3] [maʃɔne] VT **1** *(mâcher → aliment)* to chew; *(→ brin d'herbe, tige de fleur, crayon)* to chew *or* to nibble (at); *(→ cigare)* to chew (on); *(sujet: âne, cheval)* to munch; **m. son crayon** to chew (the end of) one's pencil; **un âne mâchonnait de la paille** a donkey was munching some straw **2** *Fig (marmonner)* to mumble; **en mâchonnant des injures** mumbling insults

mâchouiller [3] [maʃuje] VT *Fam (aliment)* to chew (away) at ■; *(brin d'herbe, tige de fleur)* to chew *or* to nibble (away) at ■; **arrête de m. des bonbons!** stop chewing sweets all the time!

Machu Picchu [matʃupitʃu] NPR Machu Picchu

mâchure [maʃyr] NF *Tex* flaw

mâchurer[1] [3] [maʃyre] VT **1** *Vieilli (noircir → vêtement, papier)* to blacken, to stain, to daub;

(→ peau, visage) to blacken **2** *Typ* to mackle, to blur

mâchurer[2] [3] [maʃyre] VT *(écraser)* to crush, to squash, to mash; *Tech (partie métallique d'un étau)* to dent, to bruise

macis [masi] NM *Culin* mace

Mackenzie [makenzi] NM *Géog* **le M.** *(fleuve)* the Mackenzie

mackinaw [makina, makino] NM *Can* lumberjack shirt

maclage [maklaʒ] NM mixing, stirring

macle [makl] NF *(de cristaux)* macle

maclé, -e [makle] ADJ macled

macler [3] [makle] VT to mix, to stir

mâcon [makõ] NM Mâcon (wine)

maçon, -onne [masõ, -ɔn] ADJ *Zool* mason *(avant n)*; **guêpe maçonne** mason wasp
NM,F *(franc-maçon)* Mason
NM *Constr (entrepreneur)* builder; *(ouvrier)* Br bricklayer, *Am* mason; *(qui travaille la pierre)* (stone)mason

maçonnage [masɔnaʒ] NM **1** *(travail)* building, bricklaying; *(de pierres)* laying of stones **2** *(ouvrage)* masonry; **le m. est solide** *(les briques)* the brickwork *or* bricklining is good; *(les pierres)* the stonework *or* masonry is good

maçonne [masõn] *voir* **maçon**

maçonner [3] [masɔne] VT **1** *(construire)* to build **2** *(réparer)* to rebuild, to redo the brickwork of **3** *(revêtir → gén)* to line; *(→ avec des briques)* to brickline, to line with bricks; *(→ avec des pierres)* to face with stone **4** *(boucher → gén)* to block up; *(→ avec des briques)* to brick up *or* over; *(→ porte, fenêtre)* to wall up; **ça a été bien maçonné** *(gén)* the masonry's good; *(pierres)* the stonework's good; *(briques)* the brickwork's good

maçonnerie [masɔnri] NF **1** *(ouvrage → en pierres, en moellons)* stonework, masonry; *(→ en briques)* brickwork; **entreprise de m.** building *or* construction firm; **m. à sec** *ou* **en pierres sèches** dry masonry; **m. composite** composite masonry; **m. en blocage** rubblework
2 *(travaux)* **grosse m.** work on the superstructure; **petite m.** interior building work
3 *(franc-maçonnerie)* Freemasonry

maçonnique [masɔnik] ADJ Masonic

macoute [makut] *voir* **tonton**

macque [mak] NF *Tex* brake

macramé [makrame] NM macramé; **en m. macramé** *(avant n)*

macre [makr] NF water chestnut

macreuse[1] [makrøz] NF *Orn* scoter (duck); **m. brune** velvet scoter; **m. noire** common scoter

macreuse[2] [makrøz] NF *Culin* shoulder of beef

macro [makro] NF *Ordinat (abrév* **macro-instruction)** macro

macro- [makro] PRÉF macro-

macrobibliothèque [makrobiblijotɛk] NF macrolibrary

macrobiotique [makrobjɔtik] ADJ macrobiotic
NF macrobiotics *(singulier)*; **la m. exige la cuisson à la vapeur** macrobiotic food must be cooked by steaming

macrocéphale [makrosefal] ADJ macrocephalic, macrocephalous
NMF person suffering from macrocephaly

macrocéphalie [makrosefali] NF macrocephaly

macrochimie [makroʃimi] NF macrochemistry

macroclimat [makroklima] NM macroclimate

macroclimatique [makroklimatik] ADJ macroclimatic

macro-commande [makrokomãd] *(pl* **macro-commandes)** NF *Ordinat* macro (command)

macrocosme [makrokɔsm] NM macrocosm

macrocosmique [makrokɔsmik] ADJ macrocosmic

macrocytaire [makrositɛr] ADJ *Méd* macrocytic

macrocyte [makrosit] NM *Méd* macrocyte

macrocytose [makrositoz] NF *Méd* macrocytosis

macrodéchets [makrodeʃɛ] NMPL = large items of rubbish polluting the sea

macroéconomie [makroekɔnɔmi] NF macroeconomics *(singulier)*

macroéconomique [makroekɔnɔmik] ADJ macroeconomic

macroenvironnement [makroãvirɔnmã] NM *Mktg* macroenvironment

macrofaune [makrofɔn] NF *Écol* macrofauna; **m. du sol** soil macrofauna

macroglobuline [makroglobylin] NF *Physiol* macroglobulin

macroglobulinémie [makroglobylinemi] NF *Méd* macroglobulinaemia

macrographie [makrografi] NF macrograph

macrographique [makrografik] ADJ macrographic

macroinformatique [makroɛ̃fɔrmatik] NF macrocomputing

macro-instruction [makroɛ̃stryksjõ] *(pl* **macro-instructions)** NF *Ordinat* macro(instruction)

macrolangage [makrolãgaʒ] NM *Ordinat* macro language

macrolide [makrolid] NM *Pharm* macrolide

macromarketing [makromarketiŋ] NM macromarketing

macromoléculaire [makromolekylɛr] ADJ *Chim* macromolecular

macromolécule [makromolekyl] NF *Chim* macromolecule

macromutation [makromytasjõ] NF *Biol* macromutation

macron [makrõ] NM *Typ* macron

macronutriment [makronytrimã] NM *Physiol* macronutrient

macro-ordinateur [makroordinatœr] *(pl* **macro-ordinateurs)** NM mainframe

macrophage [makrofaʒ] *Physiol* ADJ macrophagic
NM macrophage

macrophotographie [makrofotografi] NF macrophotography

macrophotographique [makrofotografik] ADJ macrophotographic

macrophysique [makrofizik] NF macrophysics *(singulier)*

macropode [makropod] ADJ **1** *Bot* macropodous **2** *Zool (nageoires)* macropterous; *(pieds)* macropod
NM *Ich* paradise fish

macropodidé [makropodide] NM *Zool* macropod

macroscélide [makroselid] NM *Zool* elephant shrew

macroscopique [makroskopik] ADJ macroscopic

macrosegment [makrosegmã] NM *Mktg* macrosegment

macrosegmentation [makrosegmãtasjõ] NF *Mktg* macrosegmentation

macrosociologie [makrososjoloʒi] NF macrosociology

macrosporange [makrosporãʒ] NM *Bot* macrosporangium

macrospore [makrospor] NF macrospore, megaspore

macrostructure [makrostryktyr] NF macrostructure

macroure [makrur] *Zool* NM macruran, *Spéc* member of the Macrura
□ **macroures** NMPL macrurans, *Spéc* Macrura

macula [makyla] NF *Anat* macula

maculage [makylaʒ] NM **1** *Typ* mackle **2** *Littéraire (fait de salir)* dirtying, soiling; *(salissures)* stains, marks, dirt *(UNCOUNT)*

maculature [makylatyr] NF **1** *Typ (pour l'emballage)* waste sheet; *(feuille tachée)* smudged *or* mackled sheet; *(feuille intercalaire)* interleaf **2** *Littéraire (tache)* stain; *(d'encre)* mackled smudge

macule [makyl] NF **1** *Méd* macula, macule **2** *Typ (pour l'emballage)* waste sheet; *(feuille tachée)* smudged *or* mackled sheet; *(tache)* mackle, smudge; *(feuille intercalaire)* interleaf **3** *Littéraire (tache)* stain, spot

maculer [3] [makyle] VT **1** *Typ* to mackle **2** *Littéraire (tacher)* to dirty, to spatter (**de** with); **maculé de sang** bloodstained; **maculé de boue** spattered with mud; **maculé de taches d'encre** smeared with ink stains

macumba [makumba] NF macumba

Madagascar [madagaskar] NF *Géog* Madagascar; **vivre à M.** to live in Madagascar; **aller à M.** to go to Madagascar; **la République démocratique de M.** the Democratic Republic of Madagascar

Madame [madam] *(pl* **Mesdames** [medam]) NF **1** *(au début d'une lettre)* **M.** Dear Madam; **Chère M.** Dear Madam; **M. la Générale** Dear Madam; **M. le**

Maire Dear Madam, *Sout* Madam; **M. la Vicomtesse** Madam

2 *(sur une enveloppe)* **M. Duval** Mrs Duval; **M. Marie Duval** Mrs Marie Duval; **Mesdames Duval** Mesdames Duval; **Mesdames Duval et Lamiel** Mrs Duval and Mrs Lamiel; **M. la Colonelle Duval** Mrs Duval; **M. la Présidente Duval** Mrs Duval

3 *(terme d'adresse)* Madam; **Mesdames** ladies; **bonjour M.** good morning(, Madam); **bonjour M. Duval** good morning, Mrs Duval; **bonjour Mesdames** good morning(, ladies); **bonjour M. la Marquise** good morning, Madam *or* Ma'am *or* your Ladyship; **bonjour M. le Consul** good morning, Madam; **merci, M.** thank you; **M. la Présidente, je proteste!** Madam Chairman, I must raise an objection!; **Mesdames, vous êtes priées de vous asseoir!** *Br* will the Honourable lady Members please sit down!; **Mesdames, Mesdemoiselles, Messieurs!** Ladies and Gentlemen!; **et voilà, M., une belle laitue fraîche** here you are, Madam, a nice fresh lettuce; **M. désirerait voir les pantalons?** would Madam like to see some trousers?; *Sout ou Hum* **M. est servie** *(au dîner)* dinner is served(, Madam); *(pour le thé)* tea is served(, Madam); **M. a sonné?** you rang, Madam?; **le frère de M. attend en bas** *(à une roturière)* your brother is waiting downstairs, Miss *or Sout* Madam; *(à une femme titrée)* Your Ladyship's brother is waiting downstairs; **vous n'y pensez pas, chère M.!** you can't be serious, my dear lady *or* Madam!; **bonjour M., je voudrais la comptabilité s'il vous plaît** *(au téléphone)* hello, I'd like to speak to someone in the accounts department, please

4 *(en se référant à une tierce personne)* **adressez-vous à M. Duval** go and see Mrs Duval; **Mesdames Martin** the Mrs Martin; **M. veuve Duval** Mrs Duval, widow of Mr Duval; **M. votre mère** your (good) mother; *Sout* **comment va M. votre mère?** how is your mother?; **Monsieur le docteur Duval et M.** *(pour annoncer)* Doctor (Duval) and Mrs Duval; **M. la Générale sera présente** Mrs Duval(, wife of General Duval,) will attend; **M. la Présidente regrette de ne pas pouvoir venir** the chairwoman regrets she is unable to come; **m. la Marquise/la Comtesse de X** the Marchioness/the Countess of X; **M. la Duchesse me prie de vous informer que...** Madam *or* Her Grace asks me to inform you that...; **M. est sortie** Madam is not at home; **c'est le chapeau de M.** it's the lady's hat; **peux-tu prêter un instant ton stylo à M.?** could you lend the lady your pen for a minute?; **M. se plaint que...** *(dit par machine)* the lady *or* this lady is complaining that...; **je voudrais parler à m. la Directrice** *(du magasin)* I would like to speak to the manageress; *(d'un service)* I would like to speak to the manager; *(d'une école)* I would like to speak to the headmistress

5 *Scol* **M., j'ai fini mon addition!** (please) Miss, I've finished my sums!

6 *Fam Ironique* **et en plus, M. exige des excuses!** and so Her Ladyship wants an apology as well, does she?; **alors, M. la spécialiste, qu'en penses-tu?** what does Her Ladyship think, then?

7 *Hist* Madame *(title given to some female members of the French royal family)*

▭

'Madame Bovary' *Flaubert* 'Madame Bovary'

♫

'Madame Butterfly' *Puccini* 'Madame Butterfly'

Tout va très bien, Madame la Marquise

This expression is used ironically. It means "Everything is fine, Madam" and comes from a song by a French jazz band of the 30s and 40s, Ray Ventura et ses Collégiens. The Marquise in question is telling the servants, over the telephone, how everything is going on the estate. They reply with a list of disasters, but after describing each one add "But apart from that, Madam, everything is fine." When people say this today, it means the exact opposite: everything is going disastrously wrong.

madame [madam] *(pl* **madames***)* NF lady; **jouer à la m.** *(femme)* to put on airs; *(enfant)* to play at being grown up

madapolam [madapɔlam] NM madapolam, madapolam, fine calico

Madeleine [madlɛn] NPR *Bible* Magdalen(e)

madeleine [madlɛn] NF **1** *Culin* madeleine; **pour moi, ce fut (comme) la m. de Proust** it brought back (a flood of) old memories **2** *(cépage)* madeleine *(vine ripening early, around St Mary Magdalene's Day, 22 July)*

La madeleine de Proust

A madeleine is a small, individual Madeira cake, sometimes shell-shaped. Marcel Proust's novel *À la recherche du temps perdu* begins with recollections of childhood. When Marcel, the narrator, tastes a madeleine for the first time in many years, he is transported back to Combray, where he lived as a child. Anything that triggers a vivid memory of the past for someone can be spoken of as **la madeleine de Proust**.

madelonnette [madlɔnɛt] NF *Vieilli Rel (religieuse)* Madelonnette (nun); **maison des Madelonnettes** Magdalen asylum

Mademoiselle [madmwazɛl] *(pl* **Mesdemoiselles** [medmwazɛl]*)* NF **1** *(dans une lettre)* **M.** Dear Madam; **Chère M.** Dear Madam

2 *(sur une enveloppe)* **M. Duval** Miss Duval; **M. Anne Duval** Miss Anne Duval; **Mesdemoiselles Duval** the Misses Duval; **Mesdemoiselles Duval et Jonville** Miss Duval and Miss Jonville

3 *(terme d'adresse)* Miss, *Sout ou Hum* Miss, Madam; **Mesdemoiselles** ladies; **bonjour M.** good morning(, Miss); **bonjour Mesdemoiselles** good morning(, ladies); **bonjour M. Duval** good morning, Miss Duval; **bonjour Mesdemoiselles Duval** good morning, (young) ladies; **merci m.** thank you, *Sout* thank you, Miss; *(à une femme qui s'appelle Martin)* thank you, Miss Martin; **et voilà, M., une belle laitue pommée** here you are, Miss, a nice round lettuce; **M., vous attendrez votre tour comme tout le monde!** you'll have to wait your turn like everybody else, young lady!; **Mesdemoiselles, un peu de silence, s'il vous plaît!** *(à des fillettes)* girls, please be quiet!; *(à des jeunes filles)* ladies, would you please be quiet!; **M. désire-t-elle voir nos derniers modèles?** would Madam like to see our latest designs?; *Sout ou Hum* **M. est servie** *(au dîner)* dinner is served(, Miss); *(pour le thé)* tea is served(, Miss); **M. a sonné?** you rang, Miss?; **le frère de M. attend en bas** *(à une roturière)* your brother is waiting downstairs, Miss *or Sout* Madam; *(à une jeune femme titrée)* Your Ladyship's brother is waiting downstairs; **vous n'y pensez pas, chère M.!** you can't be serious, dear *or* young lady!

4 *(en se référant à une tierce personne)* **c'est M. Duval qui s'en occupe** Miss Duval is dealing with it; **M. votre sœur** your good *or* dear sister; *Vieilli Sout* **comment va M. votre cousine?** how is your cousin?; **Monsieur le docteur Duval et M.** *(pour annoncer)* Doctor (Duval) and Miss Duval; **Mesdemoiselles, Messieurs!** Ladies and Gentlemen!; **c'est le chapeau de M.** it's the young lady's hat; **peux-tu prêter un moment ton stylo à M.?** could you lend the young lady your pen for a minute?; **M. est sortie** the young lady is not at home

5 *Scol* **M., j'ai fini mon dessin!** Miss, I've finished my drawing!

6 *Fam Ironique* **et en plus, M. se plaint!** so, Her Ladyship is complaining as well, is she?; **alors, M. la spécialiste, qu'en penses-tu?** what does Her Ladyship think, then?

7 *Hist (titre royal)* Mademoiselle *(title given to some female members of the French royal family)*; *(pour une femme noble non titrée)* Her Ladyship

Madère [madɛr] NM Madeira; **à M.** in Madeira

madère [madɛr] NM *(vin)* Madeira (wine)

madérisation [maderizasjɔ̃] NF maderization

madériser [3] [maderize] **se madériser** VPR to maderize

madicole [madikɔl] ADJ *Écol* = living in rock pools

madone [madɔn] NF **1** *Beaux-Arts* Madonna; **les madones de Raphaël** Raphael's Madonnas; **un visage de m.** a Madonna-like face; **une m. à**

l'enfant a Madonna and Child **2** *(statuette)* Madonna, statue of the Virgin Mary **3** *Rel* **la M.** the Madonna, the Virgin Mary

▭

'Madone à la grenade' *Botticelli* 'The Madonna of the Pomegranate'

madrague [madrag] NF madrague *(used for catching tuna)*

Madras [madras] NM Madras

madras [madras] NM **1** *(étoffe)* madras (cotton) **2** *(foulard)* madras scarf

madrasa [madrasa] NF INV *Scol & Univ* madrasa

madré, -e [madre] ADJ **1** *(bois)* knotty **2** *Littéraire (rusé)* crafty, cunning

□ NM,F *Littéraire* crafty person; **c'est une petite madréel** she's a sly one!; **c'est un vieux m.!** he's a crafty *or* cunning old devil!

madréporaire [madrepɔrɛr] NM stony coral, madrepore, *Spéc* member of the Madreporaria □ **madréporaires** NMPL stony corals, madrepores, *Spéc* Madreporaria

madrépore [madrepɔr] NM madrepore

madréporien, -enne [madrepɔrjɛ̃, -ɛn], **madréporique** [madrepɔrik] ADJ madreporic; **île madréporique** coral island; **plaque madréporique** madreporite

Madrid [madrid] NM Madrid

madrier [madrije] NM (piece of) timber; *(façonné)* thick board *or* plank; *(poutre)* beam

madrigal, -aux [madrigal, -o] NM **1** *Mus & Littérature* madrigal **2** *Littéraire (propos galant)* compliment, gallant remark

madrigaliste [madrigalist] NM,F *(auteur)* madrigal writer, madrigalist

madrilène [madrilɛn] ADJ of/from Madrid □ **Madrilène** NM,F = inhabitant of *or* person from Madrid

madrure [madryr] NF mottle *(in wood)*

maelström [maɛlstrɔm] NM **1** *Géog* maelstrom **2** *Fig (agitation)* maelstrom, whirlpool; **le m. de la vie parisienne** the maelstrom *or* tumult of Parisian life

maërl [maɛrl] NM = sand and seaweed mixture used for fertilizing soil

maestria [maɛstrija] NF (great) skill, mastery, brilliance; **avec m.** masterfully, brilliantly

maestro [maɛstro] NM *Mus* maestro; *Fig* maestro, master

mafé [mafe] NM *Culin (en Afrique francophone)* = meat or fish stew in peanut sauce

maffia [mafja] = **mafia**

maffieux, -euse [mafjø, -øz] = **mafieux**

maffioso [mafjozo] *(pl* **maffiosi** [mafjozi]*)* = **mafioso**

mafflu, -e [mafly] ADJ *Littéraire (personne)* chubby-cheeked, chubby-faced; *(visage)* chubby

mafia [mafja] NF **1** *(en Sicile, aux États-Unis)* **la M.** the Mafia **2** *(bande)* gang; **il s'était formé toute une m. de petits commerçants** the shopkeepers had formed themselves into a real little gang **3** *Péj (groupe fermé)* clique; **le milieu du cinéma est une véritable m.** the cinema world is very cliquey

mafieux, -euse [mafjø, -øz] ADJ **le milieu m.** the Mafia; *Fig* **des méthodes mafieuses** Mafia-like methods

□ NM,F mafioso

mafioso [mafjozo] *(pl* **mafiosi** [mafjozi]*)* NM mafioso; **des mafiosi** mafiosi, mafiosos

magalogue [magalɔg] NM *Presse* magalogue

magané, -e [magane] ADJ *Can Fam* **1** *(usé)* worn out **2** *(fatigué)* done in; *(malade)* run-down

maganer [3] [magane] VT *Can Fam* **1** *(user)* to wear out **2** *(réprimander)* **m. qn** to lay into sb, to bawl sb out

magasin [magazɛ̃] NM **1** *(boutique)* esp *Br* shop, esp *Am* store; **faire** *ou* **courir les magasins** to go round the shops, to go shopping; **elle tient un m. en face de l'église** she has *or* keeps a shop opposite the church; **vous trouverez ça dans n'importe quel m.** you'll find it anywhere; **grand m.** department store; **m. d'alimentation** *Br* food shop, *Am* grocery store; **un petit m. d'alimentation** *Br* a grocer's shop, *Am* a grocery (store); **m. d'ameublement** furniture shop; **m. (d'articles) de sport** *Br* sports shop, *Am* sporting

goods store; **m. de détail** retail shop *or* outlet; **m. détaxé** duty-free shop; **m. de discount** discount store; *Ordinat* **m. électronique** on-line shop; **m. d'exposition** showroom; **m. franchisé** franchise; **m. sous franchise exclusive** tied outlet; *Can Fam* **m. général** general store■; **m. à grande surface** hypermarket; **m. hors taxe** duty-free shop; **m. d'informatique** computer store; **m. de jouets** toy shop; *Mktg* **m. laboratoire** = test-shop used to monitor consumer behaviour; **m. de luxe** luxury goods shop; **m. minimarge** discount store; *Vieilli* **m. de nouveautés** *Br* draper's shop, *Am* dry goods store; **m. à prix unique** *Br* one price shop, *Am* dime store; **m. de proximité** local shop; *Can Fam* **m. à rayons** department store■; **m. à succursales (multiples)** chain *or* multiple store; **m. de tissus** drapery; **m. d'usine** factory shop, factory outlet; **m. de vente au détail** retail shop; **m. de vêtements** *Br* clothes shop, *Am* clothing store; **m. vidéo** video shop

2 (*entrepôt* → *industriel*) warehouse, store, storehouse; (→ *d'une boutique*) storeroom; (→ *d'une unité militaire*) quartermaster's store, magazine; **avoir qch en m.** to have sth in stock; *Mil* **m. d'armes** armoury; *Mil* **m. d'explosifs** explosives store *or* magazine; *Douanes* **magasins généraux** bonded warehouse; **m. à grains** silo; *Mil* **m. à poudre** (powder) magazine

3 *Théât* **m. des accessoires** prop room; *TV* **m. de décors** scene dock

4 *Phot & (d'une arme)* magazine

5 *Ordinat* **m. à papier** (*d'une imprimante*) paper tray

magasinage [magazinaʒ] NM **1** *Com* (*mise en magasin*) warehousing, storing; **frais** *ou* **droits de m.** warehouse *or* storage (charges) **2** *Can* (*courses*) shopping; **faire du m.** to go shopping

magasiner [3] [magazine] *Can* VI to shop; **aller m.** to go shopping; **m. en ligne** to shop on-line
VT to shop around for

magasinier [magazinje] NM (*dans une usine*) storekeeper, storeman; (*dans un entrepôt*) warehouseman

magazine [magazin] NM **1** (*de presse écrite*) magazine; **elle est dans tous les magazines en ce moment** her photo is in all the magazines at the moment; **m. d'actualités** current affairs magazine; **m. d'art de vivre** lifestyle magazine; **m. de bandes dessinées** comic book; **les magazines féminins** women's magazines; **m. inflight** inflight magazine; **m. d'information** news magazine; **m. littéraire** literary magazine *or* review; **le M. littéraire** = French monthly literary magazine; **un m. médical** a medical journal; **m. people** celebrity magazine; **m. à sensation** trashy magazine; **m. de spectacles** listings magazine

2 *Rad & TV* magazine (programme); **m. d'actualités** news programme; **m. culturel** arts programme; *Ordinat* **m. électronique** ezine, e-zine; **m. d'information** current affairs magazine (programme); *TV* **m. télé**, **m. télévisé** magazine programme

magdalénien, -enne [magdalenjɛ̃, -ɛn] ADJ Magdalenian
NM Magdalenian

mage [maʒ] NM **1** *Antiq & Rel* magus **2** *Fig* (*voyant*) seer

Magellan [maʒelɑ̃] NPR Magellan; **le détroit de M.** the Strait of Magellan; *Astron* **Nuages de M.** Magellanic clouds

magenta [maʒɛta] ADJ INV magenta
NM magenta

Maghreb [magrɛb] NM **le M.** the Maghreb

maghrébin, -e [magrebɛ̃, -in] ADJ North African
□ **Maghrébin, -e** NM,F North African

maghzen [magzɛn] NM maghzen, makhzen

magicien, -enne [maʒisjɛ̃, -ɛn] NM,F **1** (*illusionniste*) magician **2** (*sorcier*) magician, wizard;

Circé la magicienne Circe the sorceress **3** *Fig* (*virtuose*) magician; **un m. de** a master of; **vous êtes un m. du dessin/de la cuisine!** your art work/your cooking is magic!

magie [maʒi] NF **1** (*sorcellerie*) magic; **m. blanche/ noire** white/black magic; **comme par m.** as if by magic; *Ironique* **alors, ce bracelet, il a disparu comme par m.?** so this bracelet just disappeared by magic, did it? **2** (*charme*) magic; **la m. du printemps/du verbe** the magic of spring/language

Maginot [maʒino] NPR **la ligne M.** the Maginot Line

magique [maʒik] ADJ **1** (*surnaturel*) magical, magic; (*formule, baguette*) magic; **dites le mot m.** say the magic word **2** (*féerique*) magical, wonderful; **un monde m. les attendait dans la vitrine de Noël** a wonderland was waiting for them in the Christmas window display **3** *Phys* magical

magiquement [maʒikmɑ̃] ADV magically

magister [maʒistɛr] NM **1** *Arch* (*maître d'école*) (village) schoolmaster **2** *Péj* (*pédant*) pedant

magistère [maʒistɛr] NM **1** *Rel* (*dans un ordre*) magister, master; (*autorité*) magisterium **2** *Univ* senior (professional) diploma **3** *Pharm* magistery **4** (*titre*) Grand Master; **le M. de l'Ordre de Malte** the Grand Master of the Order of Malta

magistral, -e, -aux, -ales [maʒistral, -o] ADJ **1** (*remarquable*) brilliant, masterly; (*réussite*) brilliant, resounding; **une œuvre magistrale** a masterpiece, a masterwork

2 (*docte*) authoritative, masterful, *Sout* magisterial; **il prend toujours un ton m.** he always adopts an authoritative tone

3 *Scol* **cours m.** lecture; **enseignement m.** lecturing

4 *Pharm* specific, *Spéc* magistral; **préparation magistrale** = prescribed medication specially made up by the pharmacist for the particular patient

5 (*en intensif*) huge; (*erreur*) colossal, monumental; **une engueulade magistrale** a huge *or* massive row; **une claque magistrale** a great slap; **elle lui a cloué le bec de façon magistrale** she really shut him/her up in style

magistralement [maʒistralmɑ̃] ADV *aussi Hum* brilliantly, magnificently

magistrat [maʒistra] NM

Note that it is no longer considered a mistake to feminize this word in senses 1 and 2 and to say **une magistrate** but some French speakers nonetheless regard this form as unacceptable, especially in France. See also the entry **féminisation**.

1 *Jur* (*qui rend la justice*) judge; (*qui applique la loi*) *Br* public prosecutor, *Am* prosecuting attorney; **m. inspecteur** visiting magistrate; **m. instructeur** investigating judge; **m. à la cour** *Br* public prosecutor, *Am* prosecuting attorney; **m. du parquet** ≃ member of the State Counsel's Office; **m. du siège** judge

2 *Admin & Pol* = any high-ranking civil servant with judicial authority; **m. municipal** *Br* town councillor, *Am* city councillor; **il est le premier m. de France** he is France's supreme judicial officer

3 *Mil* **m. militaire** judge advocate

4 *Antiq* magistrate; **m. éponyme** eponymous magistrate

magistrature [maʒistratyr] NF **1** (*personnes*) **la m.** the judicial authorities; **entrer dans la m.** (*devenir juge*) to be appointed a judge; (*devenir fonctionnaire public*) to be appointed a public prosecutor; *Jur* **la m. assise** the Bench *or* judges; *Jur* **la m. debout** *Br* the (body of) public prosecutors, *Am* the (body of) prosecuting attorneys; **la m. du parquet** ≃ the State Counsel's Office; **la m. du siège** ≃ the Bench, the judges of the ordinary courts; **la m. suprême** the presidency

2 (*fonction*) office; **pendant sa m.** during his/her period in office

magma [magma] NM **1** *Chim & Géol* magma **2** *Fig Péj* (*mélange confus*) jumble; **un m. informe de boue et de pierres** a shapeless heap *or* pile of mud and stones

magmatique [magmatik] ADJ *Géol* magmatic; **chambre** *ou* **réservoir m.** magma chamber

magmatisme [magmatism] NM *Géol* magmatism

magnan [maɲɑ̃] NM *Entom* **1** (*dans le Midi*) silkworm **2** (*en Afrique*) visiting ant

magnanarelle [maɲanarɛl] NF (*dans le Midi*) silkworm breeder, woman who breeds silkworms

magnanerie [maɲanri] NF **1** (*activité*) silkworm breeding **2** (*lieu*) silkworm nursery

magnanier, -ère [maɲanje, -ɛr] NM,F silkworm breeder

magnanime [maɲanim] ADJ magnanimous; **se montrer m.** to show magnanimity, to be magnanimous

magnanimement [maɲanimmɑ̃] ADV magnanimously

magnanimité [maɲanimite] NF magnanimity; **elle a fait preuve de m. à leur égard** she displayed magnanimity *or* she was magnanimous towards them

magnard [maɲar] NM *Fam Presse* editorial ■

magnat [maɲa] NM **1** (*grand patron*) magnate, tycoon; **m. des médias** media mogul *or* magnate *or* tycoon; **m. du pétrole** oil tycoon; **m. de la presse** press baron **2** *Hist* (*de Pologne, de Hongrie*) magnate, grandee

magner [3] [maɲe] se magner VPR *Fam* **se m.** (**le train** *ou* **le popotin**) to get a move on, to get one's skates on, *Am* to get it in gear; *très Fam* **se m. le cul** to move *or* shift one's *Br* arse *or* *Am* ass; *Fam* **fais-les se m. un peu!** tell them to get a move on!

magnésie [maɲezi] NF *Chim* magnesia; (*pour l'escalade*) chalk; *Pharm* **sulfate de m.** Epsom salts

magnésien, -enne [maɲezjɛ̃, -ɛn] ADJ magnesian

magnésiothermie [maɲezjɔtɛrmi] NF *Chim* thermal reduction with magnesium

magnésite [maɲezit] NF *Minér* **1** (*carbonate*) magnesite **2** (*silicate*) meerschaum

magnésium [maɲezjɔm] NM *Chim* magnesium; **éclair de m.** magnesium light *or* flash

magnet [maɲɛt] NM fridge magnet

magnétique [maɲetik] ADJ **1** *Ordinat & Phys* magnetic **2** *Fig* (*regard, personnalité*) magnetic; **exercer un pouvoir m. (sur)** to exert a hypnotic *or* magnetic power (on *or* over); **une attraction m. les poussa l'un vers l'autre** they were irresistibly drawn to each other

magnétiquement [maɲetikmɑ̃] ADV magnetically

magnétisable [maɲetizabl] ADJ **1** *Phys* magnetizable **2** (*personne*) hypnotizable

magnétisant, -e [maɲetizɑ̃, -ɑ̃t] ADJ magnetizing

magnétisation [maɲetizasjɔ̃] NF **1** *Phys* magnetization **2** (*fascination*) fascination, mesmeric effect

magnétiser [3] [maɲetize] VT **1** *Phys* to magnetize **2** (*fasciner*) to mesmerize, to fascinate, to hypnotize; **il sait m. les foules** he hypnotizes audiences, he has a mesmerizing effect on audiences

magnétiseur, -euse [maɲetizœr, -øz] NM,F hypnotist

magnétisme [maɲetism] NM **1** *Phys* magnetism **2** (*fascination, charisme*) magnetism, charisma; **le m. de son sourire** the magnetism of his/her smile, his/her magnetic smile **3** (*fluide*) **m. animal** animal magnetism

magnétite [maɲetit] NF magnetite

magnéto [maɲeto] NM *Fam* **1** (*magnétophone*)

tape recorder, cassette player **2** *(magnétoscope)* Br video, Am VCR
NF *Électron* magneto; **m. à induit fixe** fixed armature magneto
magnétocassette [maɲetɔkasɛt] NM cassette deck *or* recorder
magnétochimie [maɲetɔʃimi] NF magnetochemistry
magnétodynamique [maɲetɔdinamik] ADJ *Électron* fixed-magnet *(avant n)*
NF **m. des fluides** magnetohydrodynamics *(singulier)*
magnétoélectrique [maɲetɔelɛktrik] ADJ magnetoelectric
magnétoencéphalographie [maɲetɔɑ̃sefalɔgrafi] NF *Méd* magnetoencephalography
magnétohydrodynamique [maɲetɔidrɔdinamik] ADJ magnetohydrodynamic
NF magnetohydrodynamics *(singulier)*
magnétomètre [maɲetɔmɛtr] NM magnetometer
magnétométrie [maɲetɔmetri] NF magnetometry
magnétomoteur, -trice [maɲetɔmɔtœr, -tris] ADJ magnetomotive
magnéton [maɲetɔ̃] NM *Phys* magneton
magnéto-optique [maɲetɔɔptik] *(pl* **magnéto-optiques)** ADJ magneto-optical
NF magneto-optics *(singulier)*
magnétopause [maɲetɔpoz] NF magnetopause
magnétophone [maɲetɔfɔn] NM tape recorder; **m. à cassette** cassette recorder; **m. à bande** audio tape recorder; **m. à bobines** reel-to-reel tape recorder; **je l'ai enregistré sur** *ou* **au m.** I've taped *or* tape-recorded it
magnétoscope [maɲetɔskɔp] NM *Br* video, video recorder, *Am* VCR; **enregistrer un film au m.** to video a film, to record a film on video; **m. d'enregistrement** recording deck; **m. de lecture** playback deck; **m. de standard professionnel** video(tape) recorder, VTR; **m. à cassette** video cassette recorder, VCR; **m. à cassette vidéo numérique** digital video(tape) recorder
magnétoscoper [3] [maɲetɔskɔpe] VT to videotape, to video
magnétosphère [maɲetɔsfɛr] NF magnetosphere
magnétostatique [maɲetɔstatik] ADJ magnetostatic
NF magnetostatics *(singulier)*
magnétostriction [maɲetɔstriksjɔ̃] NF *Phys* magnetostriction
magnétron [maɲetrɔ̃] NM magnetron
magnificat [maɲifikat] NM INV Magnificat
magnificence [maɲifisɑ̃s] NF **1** *(faste)* luxuriousness, magnificence, splendour **2** *Littéraire (prodigalité)* munificence, lavishness
magnifier [9] [maɲifje] VT **1** *(célébrer)* to glorify, *Sout* to magnify; **m. le Seigneur** to magnify the Lord **2** *(élever)* to exalt, to idealize
magnifique [maɲifik] ADJ **1** *(très beau → vue, nuit, robe)* magnificent, splendid, superb; **il faisait un temps m.** the weather was gorgeous *or* glorious; **sa sœur est m.** his/her sister is superb *or* gorgeous; **elle était m. dans sa robe de mariée** she looked magnificent *or* wonderful in her wedding dress; **un bébé m.** a beautiful baby **2** *(de grande qualité)* magnificent, excellent, wonderful; **mon boucher a de la viande m.** my butcher has excellent *or* first-rate meat; **elle a une situation m. chez un agent de change** she has a fantastic *or* marvellous job with a stockbroker **3** *(remarquable → découverte, progrès)* remarkable, wonderful; **les magnifiques progrès techniques actuels** the wonderful *or* marvellous technological achievements of our time **4** *(somptueux → appartement, repas)* splendid, magnificent; **la m. salle du trône** the magnificent *or* grandiose throne room **5** *Vieilli (généreux, prodigue → personne)* liberal, munificent; **Laurent le M.** Lorenzo il Magnifico

'Gatsby le Magnifique' Fitzgerald, Clayton 'The Great Gatsby'

magnifiquement [maɲifikmɑ̃] ADV **1** *(somptueusement)* magnificently, lavishly, gorgeously; **m. illustré** lavishly illustrated; **m. vêtu** beautifully dressed
2 *(bien)* superbly; **il se porte m.** he's in great

shape; **la journée avait m. commencé** the day had begun gloriously; **un morceau de musique m. exécuté** a brilliantly performed piece of music
magnitude [maɲityd] NF **1** *Géol* magnitude; **un séisme de m. 5 sur l'échelle de Richter** an earthquake measuring 5 on the Richter scale **2** *Astron* **m. absolue/apparente/photographique** absolute/apparent/photographic magnitude
magnolia [maɲɔlja] NM magnolia (tree)
magnoliacée [maɲɔljase] NF *Bot* NF member of the Magnoliaceae family
❑ **magnoliacées** NFPL Magnoliaceae
magnolier [maɲɔlje] NM magnolia (tree)
magnum [magnɔm] NM magnum *(bottle)*
magot¹ [mago] NM **1** *(singe)* Barbary ape, magot **2** *(figurine orientale)* magot; **les Deux Magots** = famous café on the boulevard Saint-Germain in Paris, a meeting-place for Parisian "café society" after the Second World War
magot² [mago] NM *Fam* **1** *(argent caché)* stash; **où t'as mis le m.?** where've you stashed the loot? **2** *(argent)* loot, pile; **il a amassé** *ou* **il s'est fait un m. en Orient** he made a packet in the Far East; *Hum* **on partage le m.** let's share the loot
magouillage [maguja:ʒ] NM = **magouille**
magouille [maguj] NF *Fam* scheme; **magouilles électorales** vote-rigging; **se livrer à des magouilles** to scheme, to do some wheeling and dealing
magouiller [3] [maguje] *Fam* VT **il magouille quelque chose** he's up to something
VI to scheme, to wheel and deal; **dans la vie, faut m.** you've got to go in for a bit of wheeling and dealing if you want to get through life; **il l'a eu en magouillant** he wangled it; **elle a dû m. pour avoir ce poste** she had to do some scheming to get the job
magouilleur, -euse [magujœr, -øz] *Fam* ADJ scheming
NM,F schemer, wheeler-dealer
magret [magrɛ] NM **m. (de canard)** magret of duck, fillet of duck breast
magyar, -e [magjar] ADJ Magyar
❑ **Magyar, -e** NM,F Magyar
mahaleb [maalɛb] NM *Bot* mahaleb
maharadjah, maharaja [maaradʒa] NM maharajah, maharaja
maharané [maarane], **maharani** [maarani] NF maharani, maharanee
mahatma [maatma] NM mahatma
Mahaut [mao] NPR *Hist* **M. d'Angleterre** the Empress Maud
mahayana [maajana] ADJ **bouddhisme m.** Mahayana (Buddhism)
mahdi [madi] NM *Rel* Mahdi
mahdisme [madism] NM *Rel* Mahdism
mahdiste [madist] *Rel* ADJ Mahdist
NMF Mahdist
mah-jong [maʒɔ̃g] NM mah-jongg, mah-jong
Mahomet [maɔmɛ] NPR Mahomet, Mohammed
mahométan, -e [maɔmetɑ̃, -an] *Vieilli* ADJ Mohammedan
❑ **Mahométan, -e** NM,F Mohammedan
mahométisme [maɔmetism] NM *Vieilli* Mohammedanism
mahonia [maɔnja] NM *Bot* mahonia
mahonne [maɔn] NF *(chaland)* barge
mahous, -ousse [maus] = **maous**
mahratte [marat] NM Maratha, Mahratta
NM *(langue)* Marathi, Mahratti, Mahratta
❑ **Mahratte** NMF Maratha, Mahratta
mai [mɛ] NM **1** *(mois)* May; **le premier m.** *(fête)* May Day; **le huit m.** *(fête)* VE Day; *Prov* **en m., fais ce qu'il te plaît** = in May, you don't need to wear winter clothes any more; **(les événements de) m. 1968** May 1968; *voir aussi* **mars 2** *Hist (arbre)* may *or* maypole tree **3** *Littéraire (jeunesse)* **une jeune fille en son m.** a young girl in the flush of youth

Culture
MAI 68
The events of May 1968 came about when student protests, coupled with widespread industrial unrest, culminated in a general strike and rioting. De Gaulle's government survived the crisis, but the issues raised made the events a turning point in French social history.

maïa [maja] NM spider crab
maiche [mɛʃ] NM *(terme de Louisiane)* = treeless coastal marshland
maie [mɛ] NF **1** *(pour le pain → huche)* bread chest *or* box; *(→ pétrin)* dough *or* kneading trough **2** *(d'un pressoir)* squeezer base
maïeur, -e [majœr] NM,F *Belg* mayor
maïeutique [majøtik] NF maieutics *(singulier)*
MAIF [maif] NF *(abrév* **Mutuelle assurance des instituteurs de France)** = mutual insurance company for primary-school teachers in France
maigre [mɛgr] ADJ **1** *(très mince)* thin; **des bras/jambes maigres** thin arms/legs; **un visage m.** a thin face; **des joues maigres** thin cheeks; **tu deviens trop m.** you're getting too thin; **un homme grand et m.** a tall, thin man; **m. comme un hareng saur** *ou* **un clou** *ou* **un coucou** as thin as a rake; *Can Fam* **m. comme un chicot** *ou* **un manche à balai** as thin as a rake
2 *Culin* **une soupe m.** a clear soup; **du fromage/yaourt m.** low-fat cheese/yoghurt; **viande/poisson m.** lean meat/fish; **régime m.** low-fat diet
3 *Rel* **jour m.** fast day
4 *Agr* poor; **des terres maigres** poor lands; **des pâturages maigres** poor grazing land; **végétation m.** sparse vegetation
5 *(insuffisant → gén)* thin, poor; *(→ ration, repas)* small; *(→ récolte, résultats, revenus)* meagre, poor; *(→ barbe)* straggly, sparse; **ils n'avaient qu'une m. ration à se mettre sous la dent** they had only a small ration to eat; **de maigres averses au printemps contribuent à la pauvreté des récoltes** low rainfall *or* light rain in the springtime contributes to the poor harvests; **un m. feu** a meagre *or* small fire; **un m. filet d'eau** a thin stream of water; **un m. filet de voix** a thin voice; **les bénéfices sont maigres** the profits are low *or* meagre *or* *Péj* paltry; **de maigres économies** (very) small savings; **de maigres ressources** meagre *or* scant resources; **un m. espoir** a slim *or* slight hope; **quelques maigres idées** a few flimsy ideas
6 *Fam (peu)* **8 euros après deux heures de collecte, c'est m.!** 8 euros after collecting for two hours, that's not much!; **c'est un peu m. comme prétexte!** that's a pretty poor excuse!
7 *Typ* roman, light, light-face(d); **caractères maigres** roman type, light-face(d) type
NMF thin person; **c'est une fausse m.** she isn't as thin as she looks
NM **1** *(d'une viande)* lean part
2 *Rel* **faire m.** to go without meat, to eat no meat; **le vendredi, on faisait m.** we never ate meat on Fridays
3 *Typ* roman *or* light-face(d) type
4 *Ich* meagre, maigre
❑ **maigres** NMPL *Géol* shallows
maigréchine [mɛgreʃin] ADJ *Can Fam* scrawny, skinny
maigrelet, -ette [mɛgrəlɛ, -ɛt] *Fam* ADJ (a bit) thin *or* skinny
NM,F skinny *or* thin person
maigrement [mɛgrəmɑ̃] ADV meagrely, poorly; **il est m. payé** he gets meagre wages
Maigret [mɛgrɛ] NPR = the subtle detective hero of many of the novels of the Belgian writer Georges Simenon (1903–1989)
maigreur [mɛgrœr] NF **1** *(minceur excessive)* thinness, leanness; **la m. de son visage/ses joues** the thinness of his/her face/cheeks; **le malade était d'une m. effrayante** the sick man was dreadfully thin **2** *(insuffisance)* thinness, meagreness, scantiness; *(de végétation)* sparseness, scantiness; **la m. de leur ration quotidienne** the scantiness of their daily rations; **la m. du gazon** the sparseness of the grass; **la m. de nos bénéfices/économies** the sparseness *or* meagreness of our profits/savings; **la m. de nos ressources** the scantiness *or* meagreness of our resources
maigrichine [mɛgriʃin] = **maigréchine**
maigrichon, -onne [mɛgriʃɔ̃, -ɔn] *Fam* ADJ skinny; **il est tout m.** he's scrawny; **des jambes maigrichonnes** skinny legs
NM,F skinny person
maigriot, -otte [mɛgrijo, -ɔt] ADJ *Fam* skinny, scrawny
maigrir [32] [mɛgrir] VI to get *or* to grow thinner;

tu n'as pas besoin de m. you don't need to lose (any) weight; **j'ai maigri de dix kilos** I've lost ten kilos; **je veux que vous maigrissiez de 12 kilos avant de commencer le judo** I want you to lose 12 kilos before taking up judo; **elle a beaucoup maigri du visage** her face has got a lot thinner; **produits pour m.** diet *or Br* slimming aids; **faire m. qn** to make sb lose weight; **ces régimes ne (vous) font pas m.** these diets don't help you lose weight; *Fig* **mes économies maigrissent à vue d'œil** my savings are just vanishing *or* disappearing by the minute

VT 1 m. qn *(maladie)* to make sb thin *or* thinner; *(vêtement)* to make sb look thin *or* thinner; **ce costume le maigrit** this suit makes him look thinner **2** *(pièce de bois)* to thin

mail [maj] **NM 1** *(allée)* mall; **sur le m.** along the mall **2** *Hist (jeu)* mall, pall-mall; *(maillet)* mallet **3** *Mil* maul

mail-coach [mɛlkotʃ] *(pl* **mail-coaches** *ou* **mail-coachs***)* **NM** *Hist* four-in-hand, tally-ho coach

mailing [mɛliŋ] **NM 1** *(procédé)* mailing, mail canvassing; **ce sont des clients que nous avons eus par m.** we acquired these customers through a mailshot **2** *(envoi de prospectus)* mailshot; **faire un m.** to do *or* send a mailshot

maillage [majaʒ] **NM 1** *Pêche* meshing **2** *Électron* grid

maillant [majɑ̃] *voir* **filet**

maille [maj] **NF 1** *(d'un filet)* mesh; **filet à mailles fines/larges** close-/wide-mesh(ed) net; *aussi Fig* **passer à travers les mailles du filet** to slip through the net

2 *Couture* stitch; **m. filée** *Br* ladder, *Am* run; **m. à l'endroit/à l'envers** plain/purl stitch; **tricoter une m. à l'endroit, une m. à l'envers** knit one, purl one

3 *(vêtements en maille)* knitwear; **on fait beaucoup de m. cette année** we're selling a lot of knitwear this year; **une robe en m. de coton** a knitted cotton dress; **l'industrie de la m.** the knitwear industry

4 *(d'une chaîne)* link; **j'aime la m. de son bracelet** I like the style of link in his/her bracelet

5 *Électron* mesh

6 *Menuis* **débité sur m.** crosscut

7 *Naut* frame space

8 *(sur le plumage)* speckle

9 *Fam (argent)* cash, *Br* dosh, *Am* bucks

10 *(locution)* **avoir m. à partir avec** to be at odds with; **il a eu m. à partir avec la justice** he's been in trouble *or* he's had a brush with the law

maillé, -e [maje] **ADJ 1** *(réseau)* grid *(avant n)* **2** *(sanglier, perdreau)* speckled **3** *(armure)* (chain) mail *(avant n)*

maillechort [majʃɔr] **NM** nickel *or* German silver

mailler [3] [maje] **VT 1** *(fil)* to net, to mesh **2** *Naut* to shackle **3** *(organiser en réseau)* to network **4** *Suisse (tordre, fausser)* to warp

VI 1 *Pêche* to be netted **2** *Suisse (s'énerver, se mettre en colère)* to get worked up

►**se mailler VPR** *Suisse (se tordre)* **se m. la cheville/le genou** to twist one's ankle/one's knee; *Fig* **se m. de rire** to kill oneself (laughing), to be in stitches

maillet [majɛ] **NM 1** *(marteau)* mallet, maul **2** *Sport (au croquet)* mallet; *(au polo)* polo stick

mailloche [majɔʃ] **NF 1** *Tech (maillet, outil chauffant)* beetle; *(de mouleur)* rake **2** *Mus* bass drumstick

maillon [majɔ̃] **NM 1** *(chaînon)* link; **m. tournant** swivel; *Fig* **n'être qu'un m. de la chaîne** to be just one link in the chain **2** *Naut* shackle **3** *Tex* mail, eye

maillot [majo] **NM 1** *(tee-shirt)* T-shirt, tee shirt; *(pour la danse)* leotard; *(de footballeur, d'équipe)* shirt, jersey; *(de coureur, de rameur)* vest, singlet; **m. (de bain)** *(de femme)* bathing *Br* costume *or Am* suit, *Br* swimming costume; *(d'homme)* (swimming *or* bathing) trunks; **m. une pièce/deux pièces** one-piece/two-piece swimsuit; **m. brassière** tankini; **la nouvelle collection de maillots** the new swimwear collection; **m. de corps** undershirt, *Br* vest, singlet; **le m. jaune** the yellow jersey; *(cycliste)* the leading cyclist in the Tour de France; **être m. jaune** to be the overall leader of the Tour de France; **le m. vert** the green jersey; *(cycliste)* the leading sprinter in the Tour de France

2 *Hist (pour bébé)* swaddling clothes

maillotin[1] [majɔtɛ̃] **NM** *(arme)* war hammer

❑ **Maillotins NMPL** *Hist* = Parisian insurgents protesting against direct taxes in 1382

maillotin[2] [majɔtɛ̃] **NM** *(pressoir à olives)* olive-press

maillure [majyr] **NF 1** *(sur le plumage)* speckle **2** *(sur le bois)* star shaking

MAIN [mɛ̃] **NF 1** *(partie du corps)* hand; **avoir/tenir qch dans la m.** to have/hold sth in one's hand; **donner la m. à qn** to hold sb's hand; *Fig (en français régional) (l'aider)* to give sb a hand; **donne-moi la m.** give me your hand, hold my hand; **les enfants, tenez-vous par** *ou* **donnez-vous la m.** hold hands, children; **ils se donnaient la m., ils se tenaient (par) la m.** they were holding hands; *Fig* **ils peuvent se donner la m.!** they're as bad as each other!; **prendre qn par la m.** to take sb's hand, to take sb by the hand; *Fig* **tendre la m.** *(faire l'aumône)* to hold out one's hand, to beg; **tendre la m. (à qn)** to hold out *or* stretch out one's hand (to sb); *Fig (pour l'aider)* to hold out *or* stretch out a hand (to sb); *Fig* **tendre la m. à qn** *(lui pardonner)* to hold out one's hand to sb (in forgiveness); *Fig* **tenir la m. de qn** to hold sb's hand; **porter la m. à son chapeau** *(pour saluer)* to touch one's hat, to tip one's hat; *Fig* **mettre la m. à la poche** to put one's hand in one's pocket; *Fig* **on ne le voit pas souvent mettre la m. à son portefeuille** you don't often see him putting his hand in his pocket; **lève la m.** *(à l'école)* put your hand up, raise your hand; **levez la m. droite et dites...** raise your right hand and say...; *Fig* **lever la m. sur qn** to raise one's hand to sb; **tu veux ma m. sur la figure?** do you want a slap?, you're asking for a slap!; **les mains en l'air!, haut les mains!** hands up!; **les mains derrière le dos/au-dessus de la tête!** hands behind your back/above your head!; **il m'a arraché le sac des mains** he snatched the bag out of my hands *or* from my hands; **la tasse lui a échappé des mains** the cup slipped *or* fell from his/her hands; **d'une m. assurée/tremblante** with a steady/trembling hand; **faire qch d'une m. habile** *ou* **experte** *ou* **exercée** to do sth skilfully; **travailler de ses mains** to work with one's hands; **ne rien savoir faire de ses mains** to be hopeless with one's hands; **écrire une lettre de sa propre m.** to write a letter in one's own hand; **prendre un plateau à deux mains** to take a tray in both hands; **empoigner** *ou* **prendre qch à pleines mains** to grab sth with both hands; **il prenait des bonbons à pleines mains** he was taking handfuls of sweets; *Mus* **à quatre mains** *(morceau)* for four hands; *(jouer)* four-handed; **mettre la m. sur qch** *(trouver ce que l'on cherchait)* to lay *or* to put one's hand(s) on sth; *(trouver par hasard)* to come across sth, to find sth; **je n'arrive pas à mettre la m. dessus** I can't find it, I can't lay my hands on it; *Hum* **je n'ai que deux mains** I only have one pair of hands; **il y a m.!** *(au football)* handball!

2 *(savoir-faire)* **avoir la m.** to have the knack; **garder** *ou* **s'entretenir la m.** to keep one's hand in; **il avait gardé la m.** he hadn't lost the knack *or* his touch; **se faire la m.** to practise; **perdre la m.** to lose one's touch; *(sportif, musicien)* to be out of practice

3 *Fig (intervention)* hand; **la m. de Dieu/du diable/du destin** the hand of God/of the Devil/of fate; **certains y voient la m. des services secrets** some people believe that the secret service have a hand in it; **reconnaître la m. de qn** to recognize sb's touch; **on reconnaît la m. du maître** this is obviously the work of a master

4 *Vieilli (permission d'épouser)* **demander/obtenir la m. d'une jeune fille** to ask for/to win a young lady's hand (in marriage); **elle m'a refusé sa m.** she refused my offer of marriage; **m'accorderez-vous votre m.?** will you give me your hand (in marriage)?

5 *Cartes* **m. pleine** full house *(at poker)*; **avoir la m.** *(faire la donne)* to deal; *(jouer le premier)* to lead; **céder** *ou* **passer la m.** to pass the deal; *Fig* to step *or* to stand down; *Fig* **passer la m. à son fils** to hand over the reins to one's son; **jouer à la m. chaude** *(en superposant les mains)* = to play a children's game in which hands are placed upon each other in turn, the hand from below coming to the top of the pile

6 *(gant de cuisine)* (oven) glove

7 *(ornement)* **m. de Fatma** hand of Fatima (pendant); **m. de justice** (hand-shaped) sceptre

8 *Couture* **petite m.** apprentice

9 *Typ (quantité)* ≃ quire *(of 25 sheets)*; **papier qui a de la m.** *(tenue)* paper which has bulk *or* substance; **m. de passe** overs

10 *Tex (tenue)* feel; *(apprêt)* finish

11 *Constr (poignée)* handle; **m. courante** handrail

12 *Compta* **m. courante** daybook; **m. courante de caisse** counter cash book; **m. courante de dépenses** paid cash book; **m. courante de justice** *(de commissariat de police)* incident book; **m. courante de recettes** received cash book

13 *Aut* **m. de ressort** dumb iron

14 *Équitation* **mener un cheval en m.** to lead a horse; **le cheval est dans** *ou* **sur la m.** the horse is well in hand; **mettre un cheval sur la m.** to put a horse on the bit; **rendre la m. à un cheval** to give a horse its head; **en arrière de la m.** behind the bit

15 *Écon* **m. invisible** invisible hand

16 *(locutions) Vieilli* **de longue m.** for a long time (past); **à m. levée** *(voter)* by a show of hands; *(dessiner)* freehand; **à mains nues** bare-handed; **combattre à mains nues** to fight bare-handed *or* with one's bare hands; **combat à mains nues** bare-fisted *or* bare-knuckle fight; **grand comme la m.** tiny; **un jardin grand comme la m.** a pocket-handkerchief-sized garden; **mener** *ou* **régenter qch d'une m. de fer** to rule sth with an iron hand; **une m. de fer dans un gant de velours** an iron fist in a velvet glove; **la m. sur le cœur** with one's hand on one's heart, in perfect good faith; **chercher une m. secourable** to look for a helping hand *or* for help; **aucune m. secourable ne se présenta** nobody came forward to help; **de m. de maître** masterfully, brilliantly; **un concerto exécuté de m. de maître** a masterfully performed concerto; **la cérémonie a été organisée de m. de maître** the ceremony was a masterpiece of organization; **le homard a été préparé de m. de maître** the preparation of the lobster was the work of a genius *or* a brilliant chef; **c'est fait de m. de maître** it's a masterpiece; **passer aux mains de...** to pass *or* fall into the hands of...; **la décision est entre les mains du juge** the decision rests with *or* is in the hands of the judge; **le carnet est entre les mains de la police** the notebook is in the hands of the police; **mon avenir est entre vos mains** my future is in your hands; **la décision est entre vos mains** the decision is in your hands *or* is up to you *or* is yours; **être en bonnes mains, être entre de bonnes mains** to be in good hands; **j'ai laissé l'affaire en de bonnes mains** I left the matter in good hands; *Fig* **avoir/garder les mains libres** to have/to keep a free hand; **un téléphone avec fonction mains libres** a mobile phone with hands-free option; **laisser les mains libres à qn** to give sb carte blanche *or* a free hand; *Fig* **j'ai les mains liées** my hands are tied; **arriver/rentrer les mains vides** to turn up/to go home empty-handed; *Fam Fig* **les mains dans les poches** with not a care in the world, free and easy; **pourquoi s'inquiéter? moi j'y vais les mains dans les poches!** why worry? I'm easy about the whole thing!; **gagner haut la m.** to win hands down; **avoir la haute m. sur** to have total *or* absolute control over; **avoir la m. heureuse** to be lucky; **tu as eu la m. heureuse, j'adore les œillets!** you've struck lucky, I love carnations!; **avoir la m. malheureuse** to be unlucky; **avoir la m. légère** *(être clément)* to be lenient; *(en cuisine)* to underseason; **avoir la m. leste** to be quick with one's hands; **avoir la m. lourde** *(être sévère)* to be harsh *or* heavy-handed; *(en cuisine)* to be heavy-handed (with the seasoning); **avoir la m. verte** to have *Br* green fingers *or Am* a green thumb; *Fam* **avoir qn à sa m.** to have sb under one's thumb; **avoir qch sous la m.** to have sth handy *or* within easy reach *or* close at hand; **garder qch sous la m.** to keep sth at *or* to hand; **j'ai ce qu'il me faut sous la m.** I have what I need at *or* to

hand; **en venir aux mains** to come to blows; **faire m. basse sur** *(palais)* to raid, to ransack; *(marchandises, documents)* to get one's hands on; *Hum* **c'est toi qui as fait m. basse sur les chocolats?** are you the one who's been at the chocolates?; **faire qch en sous m.** to do sth in an underhand way; **j'en mettrais ma m. au feu** *ou* **à couper** I'd swear to it; **c'est lui, j'en mettrais ma m. au feu** that's him, I'd stake my life on it; **elle n'y est pas allée de m. morte** *(en frappant ou en insultant quelqu'un)* she didn't pull her punches; *(exagérer)* she overdid it; **attention, la m. me démange!** watch it or you'll get a slap!; **mettre la m. à l'ouvrage** *ou* **à la pâte** to lend a hand; **mettre** *ou* **prêter la m. à** to have a hand *or* to take part in; **des spécialistes ont prêté la m. à la préparation du documentaire** experts had a hand in *or* participated in the making of the documentary; **mettre la dernière m. à qch** to put the finishing touches to sth; **c'est une photo à ne pas mettre entre toutes les mains** this photo mustn't fall into the wrong hands; **ce sont des documents qu'on ne peut pas mettre entre toutes les mains** these documents are not for general distribution; *Fam* **passer la m. dans le dos à qn** to butter sb up; **prendre qn la m. dans le sac** to catch sb red-handed; *Hum* **ah, ah, je te prends la m. dans le sac!** ha! I've caught you at it!; **tu ne trouveras pas de travail si tu ne te prends pas par la m.** you won't find a job unless you get a grip on yourself *or Br* you pull your socks up; **tomber dans les** *ou* **entre les** *ou* **aux mains de** to fall into the hands *or Péj* clutches of; **tomber aux mains de l'ennemi** to fall into enemy hands; **la première chemise qui me tombe sous la m.** the first shirt that comes to hand

ADV *(fabriqué, imprimé)* by hand; **fait/tricoté/cousu m.** hand-made/-knitted/-sewn; **trié m.** hand-picked

❑ **à la main ADV 1** *(artisanalement)* **faire qch à la m.** to do sth by hand; *(fabriquer)* to make sth by hand; **fait à la m.** hand-made

2 écrit à la m. handwritten; **notes écrites à la m.** handwritten notes

3 *(dans les mains)* **avoir** *ou* **tenir qch à la m.** to hold sth in one's hand; **la fourchette à la m.** with one's fork in one's hand, fork in hand; **mourir les armes à la m.** to die on the battlefield

❑ **à main ADJ** *(levier, outil)* hand *(avant n)*, manual

❑ **à main droite ADV** on the right-hand side; **à m. droite, vous avez le lac** the lake is to *or* on your right

❑ **à main gauche ADV** on the left-hand side; **à m. gauche, vous avez l'église** the church is to *or* on your left

❑ **de la main ADV** with one's hand; **faire qch de la m. droite/gauche** to do sth right-handed/left-handed *or* with one's right/left hand; **saluer qn de la m.** *(pour dire bonjour)* to wave (hello) to sb; *(pour dire au revoir)* to wave (goodbye) to sb, to wave sb goodbye; **dire adieu de la m. à qn** to wave goodbye to sb; **de la m., elle me fit signe d'approcher** she waved me over

❑ **de la main à la main ADV** directly, without any middleman; **j'ai payé le plombier de la m. à la m.** I paid the plumber cash in hand

❑ **de la main de PRÉP 1** *(fait par)* by; **une toile de la m. de Warhol** a canvas (painted) by Warhol; **la lettre est de la m. même de Proust** the letter is in Proust's own hand; **la lettre est de votre m.** the letter is in your handwriting

2 *(donné par)* from (the hand of); **elle a reçu son prix de la m. du président** she received her award from the President himself

❑ **de main en main ADV** from hand to hand, from one person to the next; **passer de m. en m.** *(objet)* to pass *or* be passed from hand to hand *or* from person to person; *Fig (maison, entreprise)* to go *or* pass through several hands

❑ **de première main ADJ** *(information)* first-hand; *(érudition, recherche)* original **ADV nous tenons de première m. que...** we have it on reliable authority that...

❑ **de seconde main ADJ** *(information, voiture)* secondhand

❑ **d'une main ADV** *(ouvrir, faire)* with one hand; *(prendre)* with *or* in one hand; **prenant d'une m. la bouteille et de l'autre le tire-bouchon** taking the bottle in one hand and the corkscrew in the other; **donner qch d'une m. et le reprendre de l'autre** to give sth with one hand and take it back with the other

❑ **en main ADJ l'affaire est en m.** the matter is in hand *or* is being dealt with; **le livre est actuellement en m.** *(il est consulté)* the book is being consulted at the moment **ADV avoir** *ou* **tenir qch en m.** to be holding sth; *Fig* **avoir** *ou* **tenir qch (bien) en m.** to have sth well in hand *or* under control; **quand tu auras la voiture bien en m.** when you've got the feel of the car; *Fig* **prendre qch en m.** to take control of *or* over sth; **prendre une affaire/une situation en m.** to take a matter/a situation in hand; **j'ai la situation en m.** I've got the situation in hand *or* under control; *Fig* **reprendre qch en m.** to regain control of *or* over sth; **la société a été reprise en m.** the company was taken over; *Fig* **prendre qn en m.** to take sb in hand; *Fig* **se prendre en m.** to take oneself in hand

❑ **en main propre, en mains propres ADV** *(directement)* personally; **remettre qch à qn en m. propre** *ou* **en mains propres** to deliver sth to sb in person

❑ **la main dans la main ADV** *(en se tenant par la main)* hand in hand; *Fig* together; *Péj* hand in glove

❑ **mains libres ADJ** *Tél* hands-free

'La Main au collet' *Hitchcock* 'To Catch a Thief'

mainate [mɛnat] **NM** *Orn* (hill) mynah bird

main-d'œuvre [mɛ̃dœvr] *(pl* **mains-d'œuvre)** **NF 1** *(travail)* labour; **le prix de la m.** the cost of labour, labour costs; **les enfants fournissaient une m. bon marché** children supplied cheap labour; **industrie de m.** labour-intensive industry **2** *(personnes)* workforce, labour force; **les besoins en m. ont augmenté** manpower requirements have increased; **embaucher de la m.** to take on workers; **réserve** *ou* **réservoir de m.** labour pool *or* reservoir; **m. contractuelle** contract labour; **m. directe** direct labour; **m. étrangère** foreign labour; **m. féminine** female labour; **m. indirecte** indirect labour; **m. occasionnelle** casual labour; **m. peu qualifiée** unskilled labour; **m. productive** productive labour; **m. qualifiée** skilled labour; **il y a une pénurie de m. qualifiée** there is a shortage of skilled labour; **m. spécialisée** semi-skilled labour; **m. syndiquée** organized labour

Maine [mɛn] **NM 1** *Hist (en France)* Maine **2** *Géog (aux États-Unis)* **le M.** Maine; **dans le M.** in Maine

Maine-et-Loire [mɛnelwar] **NM le M.** Maine-et-Loire

main-forte [mɛ̃fɔrt] **NF prêter m. à qn** to give sb a (helping) hand

mainlevée [mɛ̃ləve] **NF 1** *Jur* withdrawal; *(d'une hypothèque)* discharge, cancellation; **m. de la saisie** replevin, restoration of goods taken in distraint **2** *Rel (d'une interdiction)* withdrawal

mainmise [mɛ̃miz] **NF** *(appropriation)* seizure (**sur** of); *(emprise)* grip, hold (**sur** on); **la m. de Hitler sur les Balkans** Hitler's seizure *or* takeover of the Balkans; *Fig* **la m. du gouvernement sur les médias** the government's hold on the media; **la m. d'une seule société sur le marché du logiciel en inquiète plus d'un** many people are worried about a single company having a stranglehold on the software market

mainmortable [mɛ̃mɔrtabl] **ADJ** *Jur* subject to mortmain

mainmorte [mɛ̃mɔrt] **NF** *Hist* mortmain

maint, -e [mɛ̃, mɛ̃t] **ADJ** *Littéraire* many a, a great many; **mainte personne** many a person, a great many people; **maints pays** many a country, a great many countries; **maintes et maintes fois, à maintes reprises, en maintes et maintes occasions** time and time again; **je l'ai mis en garde à maintes reprises** I've warned him many a time *or* time and time again

maintenance [mɛ̃tnɑ̃s] **NF 1** *(de matériel, d'un bien)* upkeep; *(d'un appareil, d'un véhicule)* maintenance, servicing; **m. sur site** on-site maintenance **2** *Mil (moyens)* maintenance unit; *(processus)* maintenance

maintenant [mɛ̃tnɑ̃] **ADV 1** *(à présent)* now; **je me sens mieux m.** I feel better now; **m., on peut y aller** we can go now; **à vous m.** now it's your turn; **il y a m. trois ans que cela dure** this has been going on for three years now; **c'est m. que tu arrives?** what time do you call this?; **l'avion a sûrement décollé m.** the plane must have taken off (by) now; **ils sont sûrement arrivés depuis longtemps m.** they must have arrived a long time ago (now); **il est huit heures, ils ne viendront plus m.** it's eight o'clock, they'll never come now; **m. tu sauras à quoi t'en tenir** now *or* from now on you'll know what to expect; **à partir de m.** from now on *or* onwards; **c'est m. ou jamais** it's now or never; **les jeunes de m.** today's youth, young people today

2 *(cela dit)* now; **je l'ai lu dans le journal, m. si c'est vrai ou faux, je n'en sais rien** I read it in the paper, but *or* now whether or not it's true, I don't know; **vous connaissez mon point de vue, m. faites ce que vous voulez** you know what I think, now (you) do what you want; **m. on va voir si les employés voudront reprendre le travail** the question now is whether the employees will be willing to go back to work

❑ **maintenant que CONJ** now (that); **m. que tu me le dis, je m'en souviens** now (that) you say so *or* tell me, I remember; **m. que Durand est chef du département,...** with Durand now head of department,...

mainteneur [mɛ̃tnœr] **NM 1** *Littéraire (défenseur)* upholder, supporter **2** *Bourse* **m. de marché** market maker

MAINTENIR [40] [mɛ̃tnir]

> **VT** to hold firm **1** ■ to hold back **2** ■ to keep **3, 4** ■ to maintain **4, 5** ■ to uphold **4**
> **VPR** to remain ■ to hold steady

VT 1 *(tenir)* to hold firm *or* in position; **des rivets maintiennent l'assemblage** the structure is held tight *or* together by rivets; **les colonnes maintiennent la voûte** the columns hold up *or* support the vault; **le pantalon est maintenu par une ceinture** the trousers are held *or* kept up by a belt; **couvrez les pots de morceaux d'étamine maintenus par des élastiques** cover the jars with pieces of muslin held in place by rubber bands; **nous sommes maintenus au sol par la pesanteur** the force of gravity is what keeps us on the ground; **les muscles maintiennent le corps en équilibre** muscles ensure that the body retains its balance; **m. qn assis/debout** to keep sb seated/standing; **une sangle la maintenait sur son lit** a strap held her to her bed, she was strapped to her bed; **il a fallu trois hommes pour le m. allongé** three men were needed to keep him down

2 *(empêcher d'avancer → foule)* to hold back; **m. qn à distance** to keep sb at a distance

3 *(garder)* to keep; **m. l'eau à ébullition** keep the water boiling; **m. la température à −5** keep the temperature at −5; **m. au frais** keep in a cool place; **m. qn en vie** to keep sb alive; **m. les yeux fermés** to keep one's eyes shut; **m. la tête sous l'eau** to keep one's head under water; **maintenez les jambes en l'air le plus longtemps possible** keep your legs up as long as possible; **m. un membre dans une attelle** to keep a limb strapped up

4 *(conserver → statu quo, tradition)* to maintain, to uphold; *(→ prix)* to keep in check, to hold steady; *(→ loi)* to uphold; *(→ paix, discipline)* to maintain, to keep; *(→ décision)* to abide by; **m. une entreprise en activité** to keep a company operating; **des traditions qui maintiennent les clivages sociaux** traditions which sustain *or* perpetuate divisions in society; **les ordres sont maintenus** the original orders remain unchanged; **m. l'ordre** to keep order; **punitions maintenues!** punishments upheld!; **m. sa candidature** *(pour un emploi)* to maintain one's application; *Pol* to continue to stand; **m. qn dans ses fonctions** to maintain *or* keep sb in office; **m. sa position** to maintain one's position; **nos programmes sont maintenus malgré la grève** the normal programmes will be shown despite the strike

mai–mai

5 *(continuer à dire)* to maintain; **il dit que tu as tort et il le maintient** he says you're wrong and he's standing by it; **je maintiens que c'est possible** I maintain that it's possible; **m. une accusation** to stand by *or* to maintain an accusation; **l'accusée a maintenu sa version des faits** the defendant stuck to *or* maintained her story

▸**se maintenir** VPR to remain; *(prix, monnaie, taux de change, cours de la Bourse)* to remain steady, to hold up *or* steady; **la monarchie se maintient encore dans quelques pays** monarchy lives on *or* survives in a few countries; **le beau temps se maintiendra** the weather will stay *or* remain fine; **la livre se maintient à 1,50 euros** the pound is remaining steady at 1.50 euros; **la livre se maintient par rapport au dollar** the pound is holding its own against the dollar; *Bourse* **ces actions se maintiennent à 6,55 euros** these shares remain firm at 6.55 euros; **le niveau des commandes se maintient** orders are holding up *or* steady; *Pol* **il se maintient au second tour** he's decided to stand again in the second round; **pourra-t-elle se m. dans les dix premiers?** will she be able to remain in the top ten?; **se m. à flot** *(dans l'eau)* to stay afloat; *(dans son travail)* to keep one's head above water; **se m. en équilibre** to keep one's balance; **se m. en bonne santé** to stay in good health; *Fam* **comment ça va? – on *ou* ça se maintient** how's everything going? – so-so *or* not so bad *or* bearing up

maintien [mɛ̃tjɛ̃] NM **1** *(conservation)* maintenance, upholding; *(de la loi, d'un principe)* upholding; *(de la discipline)* maintenance, keeping; **comment garantir le m. du libre-échange?** how is it possible to uphold *or* to preserve free trade?; **le m. du pouvoir d'achat des salariés doit être une priorité** maintaining wage-earners' purchasing power must be a priority; *Jur* **m. dans les lieux** right of tenancy; **le m. de l'ordre** the maintenance of law and order; **assurer le m. de l'ordre** to maintain law and order; **m. de la paix** peacekeeping; **force de m. de la paix** peacekeeping force; **assurer le m. de la paix** to keep the peace; *Ordinat* **m. majuscule** caps lock

2 *(port)* bearing, deportment; **cours/professeur de m.** lesson in/teacher of deportment

3 *(soutien)* support; **ce soutien-gorge assure un bon m.** this bra gives good support

maintient *etc voir* **maintenir**

maïolique [majɔlik] NF *Cér* majolica

maïoral, -e, -aux, -ales [majɔral, -o] ADJ *Belg* mayoral

maïorat [majɔra] NM *Belg* office of mayor

maire [mɛr] NM *(d'une commune, d'un arrondissement)* ≃ mayor; *(d'une grande ville)* *Br* ≃ (lord) mayor, *Am* ≃ mayor, *Scot* ≃ provost; **monsieur/madame le m.** the Mayor, His/Her Worship (the Mayor); *(en s'adressant à lui/elle)* Your Worship; *Hum* **passer devant monsieur le m.** to tie the knot, to get hitched; **m. adjoint** deputy mayor

> *Culture*
> **MAIRE**
> In France, the mayor has obligations not only to the community but also to national government. He or she is responsible for promulgating national law as well as supervising the local police and officiating at civic occasions. Mayors are elected by the "conseil municipal" (and thus indirectly by the town's residents).

mairesse [merɛs] NF **1** *(femme maire)* (lady) mayor **2** *(épouse du maire)* mayoress

mairie [meri] NF **1** *(fonction)* office of mayor, *Sout* mayoralty; **il brigue la m. de Paris** he's running for the office of Mayor of Paris; **la m. l'occupe beaucoup** his/her duties as Mayor/Mayoress keep him/her very busy

2 *(administration → gén)* town council; *(→ d'une grande ville)* city council; **organisé par la m. de Lyon** sponsored by Lyons city council; **la m. a organisé un voyage pour les personnes âgées de la ville** *Br* the council *or Am* city hall has organized a trip for the town's senior citizens; **c'est la responsabilité de la m.** it's the council's responsibility; **m. d'arrondissement** *(de Paris, Lyon ou Marseille)* district council

3 *(édifice)* town hall; **demandez une attestation à la m.** you must apply to the town hall for a certificate; **m. de quartier** *(de Paris, Lyon ou Marseille)* local town hall; **m. du village** village *or* town hall

> *Culture*
> **MAIRIE**
> Also called the "hôtel de ville", this is the centre of municipal government. The "mairie" serves as a vital information source for town residents. People go there to ask about taxes, to get married in a civil ceremony, to enrol in certain community-sponsored classes, etc.

mais [mɛ] CONJ **1** *(servant à opposer deux termes)* **finalement je n'en veux pas un m. deux** actually, I want two not one; **ce n'est pas bleu, m. vert** it's not blue, it's green; **non, ce n'est pas 123 m. 124** no, it's not 123, it's (actually) 124

2 *(introduisant une objection, une restriction, une précision)* but; **une famille riche m. honnête** a rich but honest family; **m. pourtant vous connaissez le dossier?** but you are familiar with the case, aren't you?; **oui, m....** yes, but...; **m. ce n'est pas du tout ce que j'ai dit!** (but) that's not what I said at all!; **j'aime bien cette jupe m. je la préfère en vert** I like that skirt but I prefer it in green; **ces chaussures sont jolies m. trop chères** these shoes are nice, but they're too expensive; **c'est sûr qu'il viendra, m. il ne sait pas quand** he's definitely coming, but he doesn't know when; **j'ai trouvé le même, m. moins cher** I found the same thing, only *or* but cheaper

3 *(introduisant une transition)* **m. revenons à notre sujet** but let's get back to the point; **m. Fred, tu l'as vu ou non?** (and) what about Fred, did you see him or not?; **m. dis-moi, ton frère, il ne pourrait pas m'aider?** I was thinking, couldn't your brother help me?; **m. alors, vous ne partez plus?** so you're not going any more?; **m. qu'avez-vous donc?** whatever's the matter?; **m. j'y pense, je ne l'ai pas encore appelé!** I've just thought, I haven't rung him yet!

4 *(renforçant des adverbes)* **m. oui!** oh yes!, of course!, *Am* sure!; **m. non!** oh no!, not at all!, of course not!; **vous êtes d'accord? – m. oui, tout à fait** do you agree? – yes, absolutely; **m. oui, ça ira comme ça** yes, that will do; **tu pleures? – m. non, m. non...** are you crying? – no, no, it's all right...; **tu as peur? – m. non!** are you scared? – of course not!; **tu m'aimes? – m. bien sûr que je t'aime!** do you love me? – of course I love you!; **vous venez aussi? – m. bien sûr!** are you coming as well? – of course (I am/we are)!; **tu m'accompagneras à la gare? – m. certainement** will you come with me to the station? – of course (I will); **nous allons à Venise, m. aussi à Florence et à Sienne** we're going to Venice, and to Florence and Siena too; **nous exportons en Allemagne, m. aussi en Suède et aux Pays-Bas** we export to Germany, but also to Sweden and the Netherlands; **c'est joli, m. encore trop cher** it's nice, but it's still too expensive; **il est génial, m. même ses plus proches amis ont du mal à le supporter** he's great, but even his closest friends find it hard to put up with him; **...m. bon, il ne veut rien entendre** ...but he just won't listen; **m. enfin!** well really!; **m. enfin je te l'avais bien dit!** I TOLD you!; **je sais, m. enfin, qu'est-ce qu'on peut dire dans ces cas-là?** I know, but (after all) what can you say in a situation like that?; **elle ne fait rien de la journée, m. vraiment rien** she does nothing all day, absolutely nothing

5 *(employé exclamativement → avec une valeur intensive)* **cet enfant est nerveux, m. nerveux!** that child is highly-strung, and I mean highly-strung!; **j'ai faim, m. faim!** I'm SO hungry!; **il a pleuré, m. pleuré!** he cried, how he cried!; **c'était une fête, m. une fête!** what a party that was!, that was a real party!

6 *(exprimant l'indignation, l'impatience)* **non m. des fois!** (but) really!; **non m. ça ne va pas!** you're/he's/*etc* mad!; **m. vous êtes fou!** you're mad!; **non m. pour qui tu me prends?** who do you take me for anyway?; **m. dis donc, tu n'as pas honte?** well really, aren't you ashamed of yourself?; **m. enfin, en voilà une manière de traiter les gens!** well *or* I must say, that's a fine way to treat people!; **non m. tu plaisantes?** you can't be serious!, you must be joking!; **m. puisque je te le dis!** it's true I tell you!; **m. écoute-moi un peu!** will you just listen to me a minute!; *Fam* **m. tu vas te taire, bon sang!** for God's sake, will you shut up!; **m. c'est pas un peu fini ce vacarme?** have you quite finished making that racket?; **m. ça suffit maintenant!** that's enough now!; **m. je vais me fâcher, moi!** I'm not going to put up with this!

7 *(exprimant la surprise)* **m. tu saignes!** you're bleeding!; **m. c'est Paul!** hey, it's Paul!; **m. dis donc, tu es là, toi?** what (on earth) are you doing here?

ADV *Littéraire* **n'en pouvoir m.** to be helpless

NM but; **il n'y a pas de m. (qui tienne), j'ai dit au lit!** no buts about it, I said bed!; **il y a un m.** there's one snag, there's a but; **je vais t'aider, cependant il y a un m.** I'll help you, but on one condition; **je ne veux pas de si ni de m.** I don't want any ifs and buts

maïs [mais] NM *Bot Br* maize, *Am* corn; *Culin* sweetcorn; **m. en épi** corn on the cob

maïserie [maisri] NF **1** *(usine)* corn mill **2** *(activité)* corn processing

MAISON [mɛzɔ̃]

> NF house **A1, 2, B3, C2, D** ■ home **A2** ■ family **B1** ■ household **B2, 4** ■ firm **C1**
> ADJ INV home-made **1** ■ in-house **2** ■ first-rate **3**

NF **A. 1** *(bâtiment)* house, *Sout* dwelling; **maisons (d'habitation)** private dwellings; **m. bourgeoise** substantial house *or Sout* residence; **m. de campagne** *(gén)* house *or* home in the country; *(rustique)* (country) cottage; **m. individuelle** *(non attenante)* detached house; **m. de maître** *(en bien propre)* owner-occupied house; *(cossue)* large house; *(en Belgique)* (fine) town house; **m. de poupée** doll's house; **m. préfabriquée** prefabricated house; *Fam* **gros comme une m.** plain for all to see; *Fam* **un mensonge gros comme une m.** a whopping great lie; *Fam* **il te drague, c'est gros comme une m.** he's flirting with you, it's as plain as the nose on your face

2 *(foyer, intérieur)* home, house; **sa m. est toujours propre** his/her house *or* home is always clean; **je l'ai cherché dans toute la m.** I've looked for it all over the house; **il a quitté la m. à 16 ans** he left home when he was 16; *Hum* **entrez donc dans notre humble m.** welcome to our humble abode; **déménager/changer (toute) la m.** to move/to change everything but the kitchen sink; **tenir une m.** to look after a house, to keep house; **les dépenses de la m.** household expenditure; **à la m.** at home; **cet après-midi, je suis à la m.** I'm (at) home this afternoon; **rentre à la m.!** *(locuteur à l'extérieur)* go home!; *(locuteur à l'intérieur)* come *or* get back in!; **j'ai trois enfants qui sont encore à la m.** I've got three children still at home; **tout pour la m.** *(sur la vitrine d'un magasin)* household goods; **chez eux c'est la m. du bon Dieu** they are very hospitable, their door is always open

B. 1 *(famille, groupe)* family; **quelqu'un de la m.** a member of the family; **visiblement, vous n'êtes pas de la m.** you obviously don't work here; **toute la m. est partie pour Noël** the whole family has gone away for Christmas

2 *(personnel)* household; **la m. civile/militaire** the civil/military household; **la m. du président de la République/du roi** the presidential/King's household

3 *(dynastie)* house; **la m. des Tudor** the House of Tudor; **être le descendant d'une grande m.** to be of noble birth

4 *(lieu de travail → d'un domestique)* household *(where a person is employed as a domestic)*; **j'ai fait les meilleures maisons** I've been in service with the best families; **vous avez combien d'années de m.?** how long have you been in service?

C. 1 *Com (entreprise)* firm, company, business; **la réputation de la m.** the firm's good name;

une **m. de renom** a company of high repute; **il a servi la m. pendant 30 ans** he worked with the firm for 30 years; **j'ai 20 ans de m.** I've been with the company for 20 years; **un habitué de la m.** a regular (customer); **la m. ne fait pas crédit** *(sur panneau)* no credit given; **la m. n'accepte pas les chèques** *(sur panneau)* no cheques (accepted); *Banque* **m. d'acceptation** *Br* accepting house, *Am* acceptance house; **m. affilié** affiliated company, *Am* affiliate; **m. de banque** banking house; **m. de commerce** (commercial) firm *or* company; **m. de courtage** brokerage house; **m. de couture** fashion house; **m. de détail** retail company; **m. d'édition** publishing house; **m. d'exportation** export firm; **m. de gros** wholesale company; **m. d'importation** import firm; **m. d'import-export** import-export firm *or* company *or* business; **m. mère** parent *or Br* mother company; **M. de la presse** newsagent's; **m. de prêt** loan office *or* company; **m. de rabais** discount store; **m. à succursales multiples** chain store; *Bourse* **m. de titres** securities company; **m. de vente par correspondance** mail-order company

2 *Rel* **la m. de Dieu** *ou* **du Seigneur** the house of God, the Lord's house; **m. mère** mother house; **m. religieuse** convent

3 *(lieu spécialisé)* **m. d'arrêt** remand centre; **m. centrale** (long-stay) prison; **m. centrale (de force)** prison, *Am* State penitentiary; *Vieilli* **m. close** brothel; **m. de convalescence** convalescent home; *Hist* **m. de correction** reformatory, *Br* remand home, borstal; **m. de la culture** ≃ arts *or* cultural centre; **m. d'éducation surveillée** reformatory, *Br* approved school; **m. d'enfants** (residential) holiday centre for children, *Am* camp; **m. familiale** *Br* holiday home, *Am* vacation home *(for low-income families)*; *Péj* **m. de fous** madhouse; **m. d'habitation** dwelling house; **m. de jeu** gambling *or* gaming house; **m. des jeunes et de la culture** ≃ youth and community centre; **la m. du marin** the Seamen's hostel; **m. maternelle** family home; **m. de passe** sleazy hotel *(used by prostitutes)*; **m. du peuple** ≃ trade union and community centre; **la M. de la radio** = Parisian headquarters and studios of French public radio, *Br* ≃ Broadcasting House; *Hist* **m. de redressement** reformatory, *Br* remand home, borstal; **m. de rendez-vous** lovenest; **m. de repos** rest *or* convalescent home; **m. de retraite** old people's home, retirement home; **m. de santé** nursing home; **la m. du soldat** the Servicemen's hostel; *Vieilli* **m. de tolérance** brothel

D. *Astrol* house, mansion

E. *Agr & Hort* **m. à champignon** mushroom farm

ADJ INV 1 *(fabrication)* home-made; **tous nos desserts sont (faits) m.** all our desserts are home-made; **spécialité m.** speciality of the house

2 *(employé)* in-house; **nous avons nos traducteurs m.** we have our own translators in-house; **ingénieur m.** self-taught engineer; **syndicat m.** company union

3 *Fam (en intensif)* first-rate, top-notch; **une engueulade/raclée m.** an almighty ticking-off/ thrashing

---

'Maison de poupée' *Ibsen* 'A Doll's House'

Maison-Blanche [mɛzɔ̃blɑ̃ʃ] NF **la M.** the White House

maisonnée [mɛzɔne] NF household; **son cri réveilla toute la m.** his/her scream woke up the whole household *or* everyone in the house

maisonnette [mɛzɔnɛt] NF small house; *(à la campagne)* cottage

maistrance [mɛstrɑ̃s] NF **la m.** the (ship's) petty officers

---

MAÎTRE, MAÎTRESSE [mɛtr, mɛtrɛs]

ADJ	main 1, 2 ■ master 4
NM,F	master 1 ■ mistress 1 ■ teacher 2
NM	master 1–5
NF	mistress

ADJ 1 *(après le nom)* *(essentiel)* main, central, major; **l'idée maîtresse du texte** the main theme *or* central idea in the text; **sa qualité maîtresse est le sang-froid** a cool head is his/ her outstanding *or* chief quality

2 *(après le nom)* *(le plus important)* main; **branche maîtresse** largest *or* main branch; *Cartes & Fig* **carte maîtresse** trump card; **cheville maîtresse** kingpin; **poutre maîtresse** *(en bois)* main beam; *(en fer)* main girder

3 *(avant le nom)* **le m. mot** the key word; **maîtresse femme** powerful woman

4 *(dans des noms de métiers)* master; **m. boulanger/forgeron** master baker/blacksmith; **m. charpentier** master carpenter; **m. compagnon** ≃ master craftsman; **m. coq** *ou* **queux** chef; **m. de forges** ironmaster; **m. maçon** master builder *or* mason; **m. sonneur** head *or* chief bellringer

NM,F 1 *(personne qui contrôle)* master, *f* mistress; **maîtres et esclaves** masters and slaves; **ce chien n'obéit qu'à sa maîtresse** this dog only obeys his mistress; **être m. chez soi** to be master in one's own house; **ils sont maintenant installés en maîtres chez nous** they now rule the roost in our own house; **agir en m.** to behave as though one were master; **être/rester m. de soi** to be/remain self-possessed, to be/remain in control of one's emotions; **il faut rester m. de soi** you must keep your self-control; **il n'était plus m. de lui-même** he lost control (of himself); **rester m. de ses émotions** to keep one's emotions under control; **être m. d'une situation/de son véhicule** to be in control of a situation/of one's vehicle; **le conducteur n'était plus m. de son véhicule** the driver (had) lost control of the car; **les maîtres du monde** the world's rulers; **un dictateur fou qui veut devenir le m. du monde** a mad dictator who wants to take over *or* rule the world; **se rendre m. de** *(d'un pays)* to take *or* seize control of; *(d'une personne)* to make oneself master of; *(d'un incendie)* to get under control; **à la maison, c'est lui le m.** he's (the) boss at home; **en fait, c'est elle qui est le m. ici** in fact, she's (the) boss around here; **être son (propre) m.** to be one's own master *or* boss; **il est son propre m.** he's his own man; **elle est son propre m.** she's her own woman; **être** *ou* **rester m. de faire qch** to be free to do sth; **m. jacques** factotum; **le m. de ces lieux** *ou* **de céans** the master of the house; *Littéraire* **il vous faut prendre congé du m. de ces lieux** it's time to bid your host farewell; **m. de maison** host; **pourrais-je parler au m. de maison?** could I speak to the man *or* the master of the house?; **maîtresse de maison** lady of the house, hostess; **pourrais-je parler à la maîtresse de maison?** could I speak to the lady of the house?; *Prov* **les bons maîtres font les bons valets** a good master makes a good servant; *Prov* **tel m., tel valet** like master, like man

2 *(professeur)* **m. (d'école)**, **maîtresse (d'école)** teacher, schoolteacher; **elle fait très maîtresse d'école** she's very schoolmarmish; **Maîtresse, j'ai trouvé!** *Br* Miss *or Am* teacher, I've found the answer!; **m. d'internat** house *Br* master *or Am* director *(responsible for boarders after school)*; **m./maîtresse de ballet** ballet teacher, *Br* ballet master/mistress; **m. de musique** music teacher

NM 1 *(dans des noms de fonctions)* **grand m. (de l'ordre)** grand master; **grand m. de l'Université** *Br* ≃ Secretary of State for Education, *Am* ≃ Secretary of Education; **m. d'armes** fencing master; *Anciennement* **m. auxiliaire** *Br* supply *or Am* substitute teacher; **m. de cérémonie** master of ceremonies; **m. de chapelle** choirmaster;

m. de conférences *Br* ≃ senior lecturer, *Am* ≃ assistant professor; *Belg* **m. de conférences** *ou* **de conférence** ≃ part-time lecturer; **m. d'équipage** *Chasse* master of the hunt; *Hist & Naut* boatswain; **m. de manège** *(directeur)* riding school director; *(moniteur)* riding instructor; **m. d'ouvrage** *(particulier)* client *(of an architect)*; *(organisme public)* contracting authority; **m. de pêche** trawler master; **m. de recherches** research director; **m. des requêtes** ≃ government *Br* counsel *or Am* attorney; *Ordinat* **m. de postes** postmaster

2 *(expert)* master; **être passé m. dans l'art de** to be a past master in the art of; **elle est passée m. dans l'art de tromper son monde** she is a past master in the art of misleading people

3 *Beaux-Arts, Littérature & Phil* master; **les grands maîtres de la peinture flamande** the great masters of Flemish painting; **les grands maîtres de la musique** the great composers; **dans le style des maîtres de l'écriture classique** in the classical style; **le m. de Moulins/Madrid** the Master of Moulins/Madrid; *Fig* **trouver son m.** to meet one's master *or* more than one's match; **m. à penser** mentor, guru; **petit m.** *(artiste)* minor artist; *Péj (écrivain)* second-rate writer

4 *Rel* **le m. de l'Univers** *ou* **du monde** the Master of the Universe; *Fig* **se croire le m. du monde** to feel invincible

5 *Cartes* **être m. à carreau** to hold the master *or* best diamond

6 *(titre)* **M. Suzanne Thieu** Mrs/Miss Suzanne Thieu; **M. Dulles, avocat à la cour** ≃ Mr Dulles *Br* QC *or Am* member of the Bar; **cher M., à vous!** *(à un artiste)* Maestro, please!; *Hum* **M. Chat/Renard** Mister Cat/Fox

7 *Naut Br* ≃ chief petty officer, *Am* ≃ petty officer first class; **m. principal** *Br* ≃ fleet chief petty officer, *Am* ≃ master chief petty officer; **premier m.** *Br* ≃ chief petty officer, *Am* ≃ petty officer first class; **second m.** *Br* ≃ petty officer, *Am* ≃ petty officer second class; **être le seul m. à bord** to be sole master on board; *Fig* to be free to choose, to be free to do whatever one wants; *Fig* **c'est toi le seul m. à bord** you're the boss, you're in charge

8 *Zool* **m. de la brousse** *(serpent)* bushmaster
❑ **maîtresse** NF *(d'un homme)* mistress; **devenir la maîtresse de qn** to become sb's mistress
❑ **de maître** ADJ **1** *(qui appartient à un riche particulier)* **chauffeur de m.** (personal) chauffeur; **voiture de m.** expensive car

2 *(exécuté par un grand artiste)* **un tableau** *ou* **une toile de m.** an old master; *Fig* **un coup de m.** a masterstroke; **pour un coup d'essai, c'est un coup de m.** for a first attempt, it was brilliant
❑ **maître chanteur** NM **1** *(qui menace)* blackmailer

2 *Mus* Meistersinger, mastersinger
❑ **maître couple** NM **1** *(de navire)* main frame

2 *Phys* frontal area
❑ **maître d'hôtel** NM *(dans un restaurant)* maître (d'hôtel), head waiter, *Am* maître d'; *(chez un particulier)* butler; *Naut* chief steward ADJ *Culin* **beurre m. d'hôtel** parsley butter, maître d'hôtel butter; **pommes de terre à la m. d'hôtel** maître d'hôtel potatoes
❑ **maître d'œuvre** NM **1** *Constr* main contractor

2 *Fig* **ce volume a eu Diderot lui-même pour m. d'œuvre** Diderot himself took overall responsibility for the compilation of this volume; **le Premier ministre est le m. d'œuvre de l'accord signé hier** the Prime Minister was the architect of the agreement that was signed yesterday

---

maître-à-danser [mɛtradɑ̃se] *(pl* **maîtres-à-danser)** NM *Math* (pair of) callipers
maître-assistant, -e [mɛtrasistɑ̃, -ɑ̃t] *(mpl* **maîtres-assistants,** *fpl* **maîtres-assistantes)** NM,F *Anciennement Br* ≃ (senior) lecturer, *Am* ≃ assistant professor
maître-autel [mɛtrotɛl] *(pl* **maîtres-autels)** NM high altar
maître-chien [mɛtrəʃjɛ̃] *(pl* **maîtres-chiens)** NM dog trainer *or* handler

maître-couple [mɛtrkupl] (pl **maîtres-couples**) NM **1** (de navire) main frame **2** Phys frontal area

maître-cylindre [mɛtrɔsilɛ̃dr] (pl **maîtres-cylindres**) NMAut master cylinder

maître de conf' [mɛt(r)dəkɔ̃f] (pl **maîtres de conf'**) NM Fam Univ Br ≃ senior lecturer ■, Am ≃ assistant professor ■

maître-nageur [mɛtrənaʒœr] (pl **maîtres-nageurs**) NM swimming teacher or instructor; **m. sauveteur** lifeguard

maître-penseur [mɛtrpɑ̃sœr] (pl **maîtres-penseurs**) NM mentor, guru

maîtresse [mɛtrɛs] voir **maître**

maîtrisable [metrizabl] ADJ **1** (que l'on peut dominer → sentiment, douleur) controllable **2** (que l'on peut apprendre) **ces nouvelles techniques sont facilement maîtrisables** these new techniques are easy to master

maîtrise [metriz] NF **1** (contrôle) mastery, control; **avoir la m. des mers** to have complete mastery of the sea; **sa m. du japonais est étonnante** he/she has an amazing command of Japanese; **avoir la m. d'un art** to have mastered an art; **elle exécuta le morceau avec une grande m.** she performed the piece masterfully or with great skill; **m. de la colère** anger management; **m. de soi** self-control, self-possession

2 (dans une entreprise) supervisory staff

3 Univ ≃ master's degree; **elle a une m. de géographie** she has a master's (degree) or an MA in geography, Am she mastered in geography

4 Rel (chœur) choir; (école) choir school

> **Culture**
> **MAÎTRISE**
> The "maîtrise" is a one-year degree course taken at "deuxième cycle", or postgraduate, level, after the "licence". To obtain the degree, students must attend seminars and submit several short essays throughout the year as well as a "mémoire" or dissertation at the end of the year.

---

maîtriser [3] [metrize] VT **1** (personne) to overpower; (adversaire) to get the better of; (élèves, animal) to control; **le chien avait la rage, il n'y avait pas moyen de le m.** the dog had rabies, there was no controlling it; **il a fallu trois hommes pour le m.** three men were needed to bring him under control or to overpower him; **c'est un adversaire difficile, mais je le maîtriserai** he's a tough opponent, but I'll get the better of him

2 (danger, situation) to bring under control; (flammes, opposition) to subdue; (incendie, épidémie) to control, to get under control; (sentiment) to master, to control; (passion, impatience) to control, to curb, to contain; (peur) to master, to overcome; **l'incendie a été rapidement maîtrisé** the fire was quickly brought under control; **ils maîtrisent maintenant la situation** they now have the situation (well) in hand or under control; **il était trop bouleversé pour m. ses larmes** he was too overcome to hold back his tears; **je réussis à m. ma colère** I managed to contain my anger; **m. ses nerfs** to control or contain one's temper

3 (technique, savoir) to master; **m. son sujet** to master one's subject; **il ne maîtrise pas la langue** he hasn't mastered the language; **elle maîtrise bien les déclinaisons latines** she has a good mastery or grasp of Latin declensions

▸**se maîtriser** VPR to control oneself; **ne pas savoir se m.** to have no self-control; **je sais que tu as du chagrin, mais il faut te m.** I know you're upset, but you must get a grip on yourself; **sous l'influence de l'alcool, on n'arrive plus à se m.** under the influence of alcohol, one loses (all) control

Maïzena® [maizena] NF Br cornflour, Am cornstarch

majesté [maʒɛste] NF **1** (grandeur) majesty, grandeur; (de port) majesty, dignity, stateliness; **le mont Fuji se dressait devant nous dans toute sa m.** Mount Fuji stood before us in all its majesty; **m. divine/royale** divine/royal majesty

2 (titre) **M.** Majesty; **Sa M. (le Roi)** His Majesty (the King); **Sa M. (la Reine)** Her Majesty (the Queen); **Sa Très Gracieuse M., la reine Élisabeth** Her Most Gracious Majesty, Queen Elizabeth; **Leurs Majestés veulent-elles bien me suivre?** will Their Majesties kindly follow me?; Hist **Sa M. Catholique** His (Catholic) Majesty; Hist **Sa M. Très Chrétienne** His Majesty (the King of France)

▫ **en majesté** ADJ Beaux-Arts (Christ, saint, Vierge) in majesty, enthroned

---

> **'Sa Majesté des Mouches'** Golding, Brook 'Lord of the Flies'

---

majestueuse [maʒɛstɥøz] voir **majestueux**

majestueusement [maʒɛstɥøzmɑ̃] ADV majestically

majestueux, -euse [maʒɛstɥø, -øz] ADJ majestic, stately; (silhouette) majestic, imposing; **il avait en toute circonstance un port m.** his bearing was at all times majestic or noble or regal; **le paon est un oiseau m.** peacocks are majestic birds; **un palais m.** a stately palace

Majeur [maʒœr] voir **lac**

majeur, -e [maʒœr] ADJ **1** (le plus important) major, greatest; **une des réalisations majeures de notre siècle** one of our century's major or greatest or main achievements; **le bonheur de mon fils est mon souci m.** my son's happiness is my major or principal concern; **la raison majeure de qch** the main or chief reason for sth; **être absent pour raison majeure** to be unavoidably absent; **la majeure partie de son temps/énergie** the major part of his/her time/energy; **la majeure partie des gens** the majority of people, most people

2 (grave) major; **y a-t-il un obstacle m. à sa venue?** is there any major reason why he/she shouldn't come?

3 (adulte) **être m.** to be of age; **tu auras une voiture quand tu seras m.** you'll have a car when you come of age or Sout when you reach your majority; Fig **il est m., il sait ce qu'il fait** he's old enough or grown up, he knows what he's doing; Fam **je n'ai pas besoin de tes conseils, je suis m. (et vacciné)** I don't want any of your advice, I'm old enough to look after myself now

4 Cartes (couleur) major; **tierce/quarte majeure** tierce/quart major

5 Mus major; **concerto en la m.** concerto in A major; **gamme majeure** major scale; **le mode m.** the major key or mode

6 Rel **causes majeures** causae majores

NM **1** (doigt) middle finger

2 Ling major term

3 Mus major key or mode

4 Jur **m. incapable** mentally incompetent person; **m. protégé** protected person of full age

▫ **majeure** NF **1** Cartes major suit

2 Ling major premise

▫ **en majeure partie** ADV for the most (part); **son œuvre est en majeure partie hermétique** the major part or the bulk of his/her work is abstruse

majolique [maʒɔlik] NF majolica

major [maʒɔr] ADJ (supérieur par le rang) chief (avant n), head (avant n)

NM **1** (dans la marine) ≃ warrant officer; Hist **m. de vaisseau** commander

2 (dans l'armée de l'air) Br ≃ warrant officer, Am ≃ master sergeant

3 (dans l'armée de terre) Br ≃ warrant officer first class, Am ≃ chief warrant officer 4–5; **m. du camp** camp commandant; (médecin) **m.** medical officer; **m. général** chief of staff (of a commander-in-chief in the field)

4 Belg, Can & Suisse Mil ≃ major

5 Univ top student (in the final examination at a "grande école"); **être m. de promotion** = to be top of one's year; **elle était le m. de la promotion de 58** she came out first in her year in 1958

6 Suisse **m. de table** master of ceremonies

NF **1** (société) major (company)

2 (dans l'industrie de la musique) major music conglomerate

3 Cin **les majors** the Majors

majoral, -aux [maʒɔral, -o] NM **1** (berger) chief herdsman **2** (du félibrige) member of a "félibrige" committee

majorant [maʒɔrɑ̃] NM Math upper bound

majorat [maʒɔra] NM Hist entailed property, estate in tail

majoration [maʒɔrasjɔ̃] NF **1** (hausse → de prix) rise, increase (**de** in); (pour plus de bénéfices) markup; (→ d'une facture) surcharge, additional charge (**de** on); **procéder à une m. des prix** to increase prices; **ils demandent une m. de leurs salaires** they're asking for a wage increase; **m. fiscale, m. d'impôts** surcharge on taxes; **m. pour retard de paiement** additional charge or surcharge for late payment

2 (surestimation) overestimation

majordome [maʒɔrdɔm] NM majordomo

majorer [3] [maʒɔre] VT **1** (augmenter → prix) to increase, to raise (**de** by); (pour faire plus de bénéfices) to mark up; (→ facture) to put a surcharge or an additional charge on; **les allocations familiales seront majorées de 15 pour cent** family credit is to be increased by 15 percent; **tous les impôts impayés avant la fin du mois seront majorés de 5 pour cent** there will be a 5 percent surcharge or penalty charge on all taxes not paid by the end of the month; **m. une facture de 10 pour cent** to put a surcharge of 10 percent on an invoice, to increase an invoice by 10 percent

2 (surestimer) to overestimate; (donner trop d'importance à) to overstate, to play up; **il majore son apport personnel dans cette affaire** he is playing up his part in this affair

3 Math (suite) to majorize; (sous-ensemble) to contain

majorette [maʒɔrɛt] NF (drum) majorette

majoritaire [maʒɔritɛr] ADJ **1** (plus nombreux) majority (avant n); **être m.** to be in the majority; **les femmes sont majoritaires dans l'enseignement** women outnumber men or are in the majority in the teaching profession; **vote/parti m.** majority vote/party; **quel est le parti m. au Parlement?** which party has the majority or which is the majority party in Parliament?; **coton m.** (sur l'étiquette d'un vêtement) cotton-rich

2 Écon & Bourse (actionnaire, participation) majority (avant n); **se rendre m.** to acquire a majority interest or shareholding; **il a une participation m. dans la société** he has a majority interest or shareholding in the company

NMF member of a majority group; Bourse majority shareholder; **voter avec les majoritaires** to vote with the majority

majoritairement [maʒɔritɛrmɑ̃] ADV in the majority

majorité [maʒɔrite] NF **1** (le plus grand nombre) majority; **la m. de** the majority of, most; **la m. des personnes interrogées...** the majority of (the) people or most (of the) people questioned...; **la m. des spectateurs était choqués par la pièce** the majority of or most spectators were shocked by the play; **décision prise à la m. (des voix)** decision taken by a majority, majority decision; **dans la m. des cas** in most cases; **nous sommes une m. à vouloir combattre ce fléau** the or a majority of us want to fight against this scourge; **la m. silencieuse** the silent majority; Mktg **m. conservatrice/innovatrice** late/early majority; Mktg **m. précoce/tardive** early/late majority

2 Pol (à l'issue d'élection) majority; **avoir la m.** to have the majority; **remporter la m. des suffrages** to win a or the majority of the votes, to win a majority; **élu avec dix voix de m.** elected by a majority of ten; **ils ont gagné avec une faible/une écrasante m.** they won by a narrow/an overwhelming margin; **m. absolue/simple ou relative** absolute/relative majority; **être élu à la m. absolue** to be elected with an absolute majority; **m. qualifiée** qualified majority

3 Parl (parti) majority party; **la m.** (parti) the majority, the party in power, the governing party; **m. gouvernementale** parliamentary majority; **être dans la m.** to be a member of the majority party

4 (âge légal) majority; **atteindre sa m.** to come of age, Sout to reach one's majority; **à ta m.** (dans l'avenir) when you come of age; (dans le passé) when you came of age; **m. civile** (attainment of) voting age; **m. légale** (minimum) voting age; **m. pénale** legal majority

▫ **en majorité** ADJ in the majority; **nous sommes en m.** we are in the majority ADV **les**

citoyens pensent en m. que... the majority of citizens *or* most citizens think that...

Majorque [maʒɔrk] **NF** Majorca; **vivre à M.** to live in Majorca; **aller à M.** to go to Majorca

majorquin, -e [maʒɔrkɛ̃, -in] **ADJ** Majorcan
▫ **Majorquin, -e NM,F** Majorcan

majuscule [maʒyskyl] **ADJ 1** *(gén)* capital; **B m.** capital B **2** *Typ* upper-case; **les lettres majuscules** upper-case letters
NF 1 *(gén)* capital, block letter; **majuscules d'imprimerie** block letters, block capitals; **écrivez votre nom en majuscules** write your name in capitals, print your name (in block letters); **mettez une m. à Rome** write Rome with a capital, *Sout* capitalize Rome **2** *Typ* upper case, upper-case letter

majuscule-clic [maʒyskylklik] (*pl* **majuscules-clics**) **NM** *Ordinat* shift-click

majuscule-glisser [maʒyskylglise] (*pl* **majuscules-glisser**) **NM** *Ordinat* shift-drag

makaire [makɛr] **NM** *Ich* marlin

makhzen [makzɛn] **NM** makhzen, maghzen

maki [maki] **NM** *Zool* ring-tailed lemur

makila [makila] **NM** *(terme basque)* = type of metal-tipped cane

making of [mɛkiŋɔv] **NM** *Cin* = "making of" feature, film, video etc

MAL, Mal[1] [mal] **NF** *(abrév* **maison d'animation et des loisirs**) ≃ cultural centre

Mal[2] *Mil (abrév écrite* **maréchal**) marshal

MAL[1] [mal] (*pl* **maux** [mo])

pain **1, 4** ■ illness **2** ■ sickness **2** ■ harm **3** ■ ill **5** ■ evil **5, 7** ■ trouble **6** ■ difficulty **6**

NM 1 *(souffrance physique)* pain; **m. de dents** toothache; **m. de dos** backache; **m. de gorge** sore throat; **m. de tête** headache; **maux de tête** headaches; **maux d'estomac** stomach pains; **contre les maux d'estomac** for stomach pain; **avoir des** *ou* **souffrir de maux de tête/ventre** to get *or* suffer from headaches/stomach aches; **où as-tu m.?** where does it hurt?, where is the pain?; **j'ai m. là** it hurts *or* it's painful here; **j'ai m. aux dents** I've got *Br* toothache *or Am* a toothache; **j'ai m. aux oreilles** I've got *Br* earache *or Am* an earache; **j'ai m. à la tête** I've got a headache; **avoir m. à la cheville/à la gorge/au pied** to have a sore ankle/throat/foot; **avoir m. au dos** to have backache *or* a sore back; **il a m. au ventre** he has a stomach ache; **j'ai m. au bras** I have a sore arm, my arm hurts *or* aches; *Fam* **avoir m. aux cheveux** to have a hangover[■]; **faire (du) m. à** to hurt; **sa chaussure lui fait m.** his/her shoe is hurting him/her; **le dentiste ne te fera pas (de) m.** the dentist won't hurt you; **la piqûre ne vous fera pas m.** the injection won't hurt (you); **ça vous fait encore m.?** does it still hurt?, is it still hurting you?; **mon genou me fait m.** my knee hurts; **aïe, ça fait m.!** ouch, it *or* that hurts!; **se faire m.** to hurt oneself; **je me suis fait m. à la main** I've hurt my hand; *Fam* **ça te ferait m. de t'excuser?** it wouldn't hurt you to apologize!; *Fam* **tu vas lui prêter ta robe? – ça me ferait m.** are you going to lend her your dress? – no way *or* not on your life!; *très Fam* **ça me ferait m. aux seins!** it would kill me!; *Fam Fig* **un spectacle qui fait m. (au cœur** *ou* **au ventre)** a painful sight; *Fam* **ça me ferait m. au ventre!** it would make me sick!; *Fam* **ça fait m. au ventre de voir des choses pareilles!** it makes you sick *or* it's sickening to see things like that!; *Fam Fig* **ça va faire m.!** we're in for it now!; *Fam* **attention, c'est à moi de jouer, ça va faire m.!** watch out, it's my turn, this is going to be something!; **il n'y a pas de m.!** *(après un heurt)* no broken bones!; *(après une erreur)* no harm done!; **mettre qn à m.** *ou* **à m. qn** to manhandle *or* to maltreat sb

2 *(maladie, malaise)* illness, sickness; *Fam* **tu vas attraper** *ou* **prendre du m.** watch you don't get a cold; *Arch* **le m. français** *ou* **napolitain** syphilis; **m. de l'air** airsickness; **avoir le m. de l'air** to be airsick; **m. blanc** whitlow; **m. de Bright** Bright's disease; **avoir m. au foie** to feel liverish; **m. de mer** seasickness; **avoir le m. de mer** *(en général)* to suffer from seasickness; *(au cours d'un voyage)* to be seasick; **m. des montagnes** altitude sickness; **m. du pays** homesickness; **avoir le m. du pays** to be homesick; **m. de Pott** Pott's disease; **m. des rayons** radiation sickness; **m. de la route** carsickness; **m. des transports** travel sickness

3 *(dommage, tort)* harm; **s'en tirer sans aucun m.** to escape uninjured *or* unhurt *or* unscathed; **le m. est fait** the damage is done (now); **faire du m.** to do harm; **faire du m. à qn** to do sb harm, to harm sb; **bois du lait, ça ne peut pas te faire de m.** drink some milk, it can't do you any harm; *Fam* **allez, un p'tit coup de gnôle, ça n'a jamais fait de m. à personne!** go on, a little tipple never did anyone any harm!; **ne bougez pas et aucun m. ne vous sera fait** don't move and nobody will get hurt; **faire du m. à qch** to do harm to sth, to harm *or* to damage sth; **les insecticides font-ils plus de m. que de bien?** do insecticides do more harm than good?; **vouloir du m. à qn** to wish sb ill *or* harm; **je ne leur veux aucun m.** I don't wish (to cause) them *or* I don't mean them any harm; **il n'y a pas de m. à demander** there's no harm in asking; **il n'y a pas de m. à cela** there's no harm in that; **quel m. y a-t-il à cela?** what harm can that do?, what harm is there in it?; **et si j'en ai envie, où est le m.?** and if that's what I feel like doing, what harm is there in that?; **dire du m. de qn** to gossip about sb, to speak ill of sb; **parler en m. de qn** to speak ill of sb; **penser du m. de qn** to think badly of sb; **m. lui en a pris** he's/she's had cause to regret it; **ne le provoquez pas ouvertement, m. vous en prendrait** don't provoke him or you'll live to regret it; **mettre qch à m.** to damage sth; *Fig Vieilli* **il avait mis à m. toutes les servantes** he had ravished all the maidservants

4 *(douleur morale)* pain; **faire (du) m. à qn** to hurt sb, to make sb suffer; **quand j'y repense, ça me fait du** *ou* **ça fait m.** it hurts to think about it; **n'essaie pas de la revoir, ça te ferait du m.** don't try to see her again, it'll only cause you pain *or* upset you

5 *(affliction, inconvénient)* ill, evil; **c'est un m. nécessaire** it's a necessary evil; **souffrir de trois grands maux** to suffer from three great evils; **les maux dont souffre leur génération** the ills that plague their generation; *Littéraire* **le m. du siècle** world-weariness, Romantic melancholy; **la dépression est le nouveau m. du siècle** depression is the new scourge of the century; **m. de vivre** weariness with life; **avoir le m. de vivre** to be tired of life; *Prov* **entre deux maux, il faut choisir le moindre** always choose the lesser of two evils

6 *(difficulté, tracas)* trouble *(UNCOUNT)*, difficulty *(UNCOUNT)*; **avoir du m. à faire qch** to have difficulty (in) *or* trouble doing sth; **avoir le plus grand m. à faire qch** to have the utmost *or* a great deal of difficulty doing sth; **avoir de plus en plus de m. à faire qch** to find it harder and harder to do sth; **j'ai eu beaucoup de m. à te contacter** I've had a lot of trouble getting in touch with you; **j'ai du m. à le comprendre** *(gén)* I have trouble *or* difficulty understanding him; *(je l'entends mal)* I'm having trouble *or* difficulty hearing him properly; **j'ai de plus en plus de m. à me souvenir des noms** I'm finding it harder and harder to remember names; **non sans m.** not without difficulty; **donner du m. à qn** to give sb trouble; **se donner du m. pour faire qch** to go to a lot of trouble to do sth, to take pains to do sth; **je me suis vraiment donné du m. pour que la soirée soit réussie** I really went to a lot of trouble *or* I took great pains to make the party a success; **je me suis donné beaucoup de m. pour faire cette traduction** I worked really hard on this translation; **il a réussi sans se donner de m.** he succeeded without much trouble; *Ironique* **tu ne t'es pas donné trop de m., à ce que je vois!** I see you didn't exactly take a lot of trouble over it!; **ne vous donnez pas tant de m. pour moi** please don't go to all this trouble on my behalf; **ils s'étaient pourtant donné du m. pour dissimuler leurs traces** and yet they had gone to great lengths to cover their tracks; **on n'a rien sans m.** you don't get anything easily

7 *(par opposition au bien)* **le m.** evil; **le bien et le m.** right and wrong, good and evil; **il n'a jamais fait le m.** he has never committed any evil act *or* done any evil; *Rel* **faire le m.** to do evil; **faire le m. pour le m.** to commit evil for evil's sake; **rendre le m. pour le m.** to give as good as one gets, to answer evil by evil; **voir le m. partout** to see the bad side of everything; **il ne pense pas à m.** he doesn't mean any harm, he means well; **il a changé en m.** he has changed for the worse

MAL[2] [mal]

ADV wrong **1** ■ unwell **2** ■ badly **3–6** ■ not properly **4** ■ uncomfortably **7**
ADJ INV wrong **1** ■ unwell **2** ■ bad **3** ■ mad **4**

ADV 1 *(désagréablement)* wrong; **tout va m.** everything's going wrong; **ça commence m., c'est m. parti** things are off to a bad start; **il a m. fini** *(délinquant)* he came to a bad end; **ça va finir m.** *ou* **m. finir** *(gén)* it'll end in disaster; *(à des enfants turbulents)* it'll all end in tears; **leur histoire a m. fini** their story had a sad *or* an unhappy ending; **ça tombe m.** *(au mauvais moment)* it comes at a bad time; **il sera là aussi, ça tombe m.** he'll be there too, which is unfortunate; **tu tombes m.** you've come at a bad time

2 *(en mauvaise santé)* **aller m., se porter m.** to be ill *or* unwell, to be in poor health; **il est** *ou* **il va très m.** he's in a very bad way; **comment va-t-elle? – m.** how is she? – not (very) well at all *or* (very) ill

3 *(défavorablement)* badly; **prendre m. qch, m. prendre qch** to take sth badly, to take exception to sth; **elle a très m. pris que je lui donne des conseils** she reacted badly *or* she took exception to my giving her advice; **il prend tout m.** he takes exception to everything; **ne le prends pas m., mais...** I hope you won't be offended, but..., don't take it the wrong way, but...; *Fam* **être/se mettre m. avec qn** to be/to get on the wrong side of sb

4 *(de façon incompétente ou imparfaite)* badly, not properly; **la porte est m. fermée** the door is not closed properly; **ils se plaignent d'avoir été m. accueillis** they complain that they weren't looked after properly; **c'est m. fait** it's not been done properly; **c'est du travail m. fait** it's a shoddy piece of work; **être m. fait (de sa personne)** to be misshapen; **elle n'est pas m. faite** she's got quite a good figure; **vous ne feriez peut-être pas m. de...** it wouldn't be a bad thing (if you were) to..., it might not be a bad idea to...; **cette veste lui va m.** this jacket doesn't suit him/her; **le vert me va m.** green doesn't suit me; **ça lui va m. de donner des conseils** he's/she's hardly in a position to hand out advice; **je le connais m.** I don't know him very well; **s'ils croient que je vais me laisser faire, ils me connaissent m.!** if they think I'm going to take it lying down, they don't know me very well!; **m. comprendre** to misunderstand; **je comprends m. ce que tu me dis** *(je ne t'entends pas bien)* I can't make out what you're saying; *(je ne te suis pas)* I don't really understand what you're saying; **m. interpréter qch** to misinterpret sth, to misconstrue sth; **je dors m.** I have trouble sleeping; **il mange m.** *(salement)* he's a messy eater; *(trop peu)* he doesn't eat enough; *(mal équilibré)* he doesn't eat well; **qu'est-ce qu'on mange m. ici!** the food's really bad here!; **il parle m.** he can't talk properly; **elle parle m. l'allemand** her German isn't very good; **elle chante m.** she's a bad singer; **tu te tiens m.** *(tu es voûté)* you've got poor posture; *(à table)* you don't have any table manners; **elle a m. vécu sa grossesse** she had a bad time with her pregnancy; **cette lampe éclaire m.** this lamp doesn't give much light; **on voit m. d'ici** you can't see (very) well *or* properly from here; *Fig* **on voit m. comment...** it's difficult *or* not easy to see how...; *Fam* **je me vois m. en bermuda/avec un mari comme le sien!** I just can't really see myself in a pair of Bermuda shorts/with a husband like hers!; *Fam* **elle se voyait m. allant**

lui réclamer l'argent she couldn't quite imagine going to ask him/her for the money; **s'y prendre m.** to go about it the wrong way; **je m'y prends m.** I'm not going about this the right way; **donne l'aiguille, tu t'y prends horriblement m.** hand me the needle, you're getting in a terrible mess; **tu t'y es m. pris pour assembler la bibliothèque** you've gone the wrong way about assembling the bookcase; **s'y prendre m. avec qn** to handle sb the wrong way; **elle s'y prend m. avec les enfants** she's not very good with children; **m. choisir** to make the wrong choice, to choose wrongly; **tu as m. choisi ton jour pour te plaindre** you've chosen the wrong day to complain; **m. dessiné** badly drawn; **il a été m. élevé** he was brought up or raised badly; **m. élevé** bad-mannered, impolite; **m. habillé** badly dressed, poorly dressed; **m. vu** *(peu aimé)* poorly thought of

5 *(insuffisamment)* badly, poorly; **vivre m.** to have trouble making ends meet; **m. approvisionné** poorly stocked; **être m. nourri** *(trop peu)* to be underfed or undernourished; *(avec de la mauvaise nourriture)* to be badly fed; **m. payé** badly or poorly paid

6 *(malhonnêtement → agir)* badly; **vous avez m. agi** you did wrong, you acted badly; **m. tourner** *(situation)* to turn sour; *(dispute)* to turn ugly; *(personne)* to go to the dogs; **à 16 ans, il a commencé à m. tourner** when he was 16, he started going off the rails

7 *(inconfortablement)* uncomfortably; **être m. assis** to be uncomfortably seated or uncomfortable; **on dort m. dans ton canapé-lit** your sofa bed isn't very comfortable

8 *(locutions) Fam* **ça la fiche m.** it looks pretty bad; *très Fam* **ça la fout m.** it looks bloody awful; *Fam* **si je n'y vais pas, ça la fiche m.** if I don't go, it looks really bad

ADJ INV 1 *(immoral)* wrong; **c'est m. de tricher** it's wrong to cheat; **c'est très m. de faire ça** *(en parlant à un enfant)* it's very naughty to do that; **je n'ai rien dit/fait de m.** I haven't said/done anything wrong

2 *(malade)* ill, unwell, not well; **il est très m.** he's in a (very) bad way; **se sentir m.** to feel unwell; **se trouver m.** *(s'évanouir)* to faint, to pass out, *Sout* to swoon

3 *(peu satisfaisant)* **ça n'était pas si m.** it wasn't that bad; **ce n'était pas m. du tout** it wasn't at all bad; *Fam* **elle n'est pas m.** *(plutôt jolie)* she's quite good-looking; **qu'est-ce que tu penses de ce pull? – pas m.** what do you think of this sweater? – it's not bad or it's OK

4 *Fam (fou)* mad, crazy

❑ **au plus mal** ADJ **1** *(très malade)* very sick, desperately ill, critical

2 *(fâché)* **être au plus m. avec qn** to be at loggerheads with sb; **ils sont au plus m. (l'un avec l'autre)** they're at loggerheads (with each other)

❑ **de mal en pis** ADV from bad to worse

❑ **en mal de** PRÉP **être en m. de qch** to be yearning or desperate for sth, to be badly in need of sth; **être en m. d'affection** to be longing or yearning for love; **être en m. d'inspiration** to be short of or lacking inspiration; **je ne me laisserai pas calomnier par des journalistes en m. de copie** I'm not going to be slandered by journalists with nothing better to write about or short of copy; **une femme en m. d'enfants** a woman desperate for children or to have children

❑ **mal à l'aise** ADJ uncomfortable, ill at ease; **m. à l'aise dans ses vêtements usés** feeling uncomfortable in his/her shabby clothes; **je suis m. à l'aise devant elle** I feel ill at ease with her

❑ **mal à propos** ADV at the wrong time; **ils sont arrivés m. à propos** they timed their arrival badly, they arrived at the wrong moment; **faire une intervention m. à propos** to speak out of turn

❑ **mal portant, -e** ADJ unwell, in poor health; **elle a toujours été m. portante** she's never been very healthy

mal³, -e [mal] ADJ *Littéraire* **1** *(inopportun)* ill-timed, untimely **2** *(locution)* **à la male heure** *(à l'heure de la mort)* upon the hour of death

MAL- [mal] PRÉF

Mal- is an adverb of Latin origin often used as a prefix, always with a NEGATIVE connotation, but in several different ways.

● This prefix can be added to an adjective (without a hyphen) to form its opposite. The English translation sometimes includes an equivalent prefix such as un- or dis-, eg:
malpropre unclean; **malpoli(e)** rude, impolite; **malhonnête** dishonest; **maladroit(e)** clumsy; **malintentionné(e)** spiteful

● **Mal-** can precede a past participle to create a noun. The hyphen is sometimes optional, eg:
les mal-logés the badly housed, the poorly housed

● A number of words prefixed with **mal-** have recently become very popular in the media. Some of them, like **mal-être**, were actually old words which have enjoyed a new lease of life with a different meaning. They are based on nouns, eg:
le mal-être des adolescents teenage angst; **le mal-vivre des cités** the poor living conditions on council estates; **le mal-parler** sloppy language
In the same vein, the word **malbouffe** was coined in the 90s and has since been widely used to refer to junk food and poor diet.

● **Mal-** is also a prefix used in the area of social work and disability to refer to certain things in a euphemistic way, eg:
les malvoyants the partially sighted; **les mal-entendants** the hearing-impaired

Malabar [malabar] NM **la côte de M.** the Malabar Coast

malabar [malabar] NM *Fam (colosse)* hulk

Malabo [malabo] NF Malabo

malabsorption [malapsɔrpsjɔ̃] NF *Méd* malabsorption

Malacca [malaka] NF **(la presqu'île de) M.** the Malay Peninsula; **le détroit de M.** the Strait of Malacca

Malachie [malaʃi, malaki] NPR *Bible* Malachi

malachite [malakit] NF malachite

malacologie [malakɔlɔʒi] NF malacology

malacoptérygien, -enne [malakɔpteriʒjɛ̃, -ɛn] *Ich* ADJ malacopterygian

NM malacopterygian, *Spéc* member of the Malacopterygii

❑ **malacoptérygiens** NMPL malacopterygians, *Spéc* Malacopterygii

malacostracé [malakɔstrase] *Zool* NM malacostracan

❑ **malacostracés** NMPL malacostracans, *Spéc* Malacostraca

malade [malad] ADJ **1** *(souffrant)* ill, sick, unwell; **une personne m.** a sick person; **un enfant toujours m.** a sickly child; **gravement m.** gravely or seriously ill; **m. de la fièvre typhoïde** ill with typhoid; **se sentir m.** to feel ill or unwell; **se sentir un peu m.** to feel off-colour; **tomber m.** to fall ill; *Belg* **il fait m.** *(lourd)* the weather is close; **se faire porter m.** to call in or to report sick; **être m.** *très Fam* **à crever** ou *Fam* **comme un chien** ou *Fam* **comme une bête** *(souffrir)* to be incredibly ill or at death's door; *(vomir)* to be sick as a dog or violently ill; **j'étais là, m. à crever, et ils s'en fichaient** there I was, dying, and they didn't give a damn

2 *(atteint d'une lésion)* bad, diseased; **avoir une dent m.** to have a bad or rotten tooth; **avoir une jambe m.** to have a bad or *Br* gammy leg; **avoir le cœur m.**, **être m. du cœur** to have a heart condition, to have heart trouble; **j'ai les intestins malades, je suis m. des intestins** I have trouble with my intestines; **une vigne m.** a diseased vine; **cette année, les pommiers sont malades** the apple trees have got a disease this year

3 *(nauséeux)* sick; **je suis m. en bateau/voiture/avion** I suffer from seasickness/carsickness/airsickness; **rendre qn m.** to make sb sick or ill

4 *(dément)* (mentally) ill or sick; **avoir l'esprit m.** to be mentally ill

5 *(en mauvais état)* decrepit, dilapidated; *(industrie)* ailing; **la vieille maison est bien m.** the old house is rather decrepit or is in rather a sorry state; **des jouets/livres plutôt malades** toys/

books in a rather dilapidated condition; **nous avons une économie m.** our economy is sick or shaky or ailing

6 *(affecté moralement)* ill, sick; **m. de jalousie** sick with jealousy, horribly jealous; **m. de peur** sick with fear; **m. d'inquiétude** sick or ill with worry; **ça me rend m. de la voir si démunie** it makes me ill to see her so penniless; **et pourtant, c'est elle qui a eu le poste – tais-toi, ça me rend** ou **j'en suis m.!** all the same, she's the one who got the job – don't, it makes me sick!; **quand j'ai su qu'il n'y avait plus de place, j'en étais m.** when I heard there were no seats left, I could have cried

7 *Fam (déraisonnable)* mad ▪, crazy; **t'es pas un peu m.?** are you right in the head?, are you off your rocker?; **ne hurle pas comme ça, tu es m. ou quoi?** stop yelling like that, are you off your head?; **du whisky avec de la vodka, il est m., celui-là!** whisky mixed with vodka, that guy's sick or out of his mind!; **ils veulent en plus qu'on paie la TVA, ils sont malades!** and what's more they want us to pay VAT, they're off their heads or they're crazy!

NMF **1** *(patient → gén)* sick person, sick man, *f* woman; *(→ d'un hôpital, d'un médecin)* patient; *(sujet atteint)* sufferer; **un grand m.** a seriously ill person; **les grands malades** the seriously ill; **les malades en phase terminale** terminal patients; **dans les cas aigus, le m. ressent une vive douleur** in acute cases, the sufferer feels a sharp pain; **faire le m.** to pretend to be ill, to malinger; **c'est un m. imaginaire** he's a hypochondriac

2 *(dément)* **m. (mental)** mentally ill or sick person; *(d'un hôpital)* a mental patient; **l'accusé est un m.** the defendant is a sick man or *Péj* has a sick mind or *Jur* is mentally ill

3 *Fam (fou)* maniac, headcase, *Br* nutter, *Am* screwball; **comme un m.** *(travailler, courir, pousser)* like mad or crazy; **on a bossé comme des malades pour finir à temps** we worked like mad or crazy to finish on time; **il conduit comme un m.** he drives like a maniac; **il a flippé comme un m.** he totally flipped or freaked out; **c'est un m., ce mec!** that guy isn't right in the head!

4 *Fam (fanatique)* nut, freak; **un m. de la vitesse** a speed fiend or freak; **ce sont des malades du golf** they're golf-crazy

═══════════ ❧ ═══════════

'Le Malade imaginaire' *Molière* 'The Hypochondriac' or 'The Imaginary Invalid'

┌─────────────────────────────────────┐
Allusion

Un malade imaginaire
This phrase ("an imaginary invalid") comes from Molière's comedy *Le Malade imaginaire* about a grumpy hypochondriac with thousands of imaginary ailments. His servant Toinette decides to teach him a lesson by disguising herself as a doctor and playing tricks on him. Molière pinpointed the fixations of the hypochondriac so accurately that the play's title has become a familiar everyday phrase.
└─────────────────────────────────────┘

maladie [maladi] NF **1** *(mauvaise santé)* illness, ill health, sickness; **il n'a jamais pu réintégrer son service à cause de la m.** due to ill health, he never went back to his job

2 *Méd & Vét (mal spécifique)* illness, disease; **attraper une m.** to catch a disease; **une petite m.** an ailment, a minor illness; **une m. bénigne** a minor illness; **une m. grave** a serious illness; **il est mort des suites d'une longue m.** he died after a long illness; **il est venu me consulter, se plaignant d'une vague m.** he came to see me complaining of a vague illness; **quelle est l'évolution probable de cette m.?** how is this illness likely to develop?; *Fam* **cet hiver, le petit nous a fait toutes les maladies** this winter our little one's had all the diseases under the sun; **la m. peut avoir des suites** there may be complications; **la m. qui l'a emportée** her last or fatal illness; **fermé pour cause de m.** *(sur la vitrine d'un magasin)* closed due to illness; *Fam* **être en congé m.** ou **en m.** to be on sick leave or off sick; **elle est toujours en m.** she's always off

sick; *Fam* **je vais me mettre en m.** I'm going to take some sick leave *or* time off sick; **être en longue m.** to be on indefinite sick leave; **la m. d'Addison** Addison's disease; **la m. d'Alzheimer** Alzheimer's disease; **la m. de Basedow** Graves' *or* Basedow's disease; **la m. bleue** cyanosis, blue disease; **la m. bronzée (d'Addison)** Addison's disease; **m. de carence** deficiency disease; **la m. du charbon** anthrax; **m. chronique** chronic illness *or* condition; **m. de cœur** heart complaint *or* disease; **m. contagieuse** contagious disease; **la m. de Creutzfeldt-Jakob** Creutzfeldt-Jakob disease; **la m. de Crohn** Crohn's disease; **m. de foie** liver complaint *or* disease; **la m. de Gilles de la Tourette** Tourette's syndrome; **m. héréditaire** hereditary disease; **la m. de Hodgkin** Hodgkin's disease; **la m. de Horton** Horton's disease; **m. infantile** childhood illness, infantile disorder; **m. infectieuse** infectious disease; **maladies infectieuses émergentes** emerging infectious diseases, EID; **la m. du légionnaire** legionnaire's disease; **la m. de Lyme** Lyme disease; **m. mentale** mental illness *or* disorder; **m. mortelle** fatal disease *or* illness; **m. orpheline** orphan disease *or* illness; **la m. de Parkinson** Parkinson's disease; **m. de peau** skin disease; **m. péduculaire** phthiriasis; **m. professionnelle** occupational *or* industrial disease; **la m. de Raynaud** Raynaud's disease; **la m. de Sanfilippo** Sanfilippo's syndrome; **m. sexuellement transmissible** sexually transmitted disease; **m. du sommeil** sleeping sickness; **la m. de Still** Still's disease; **m. vasculaire** vascular disease; **m. vénérienne** venereal disease, VD; *Fam Hum* **c'est une bonne m.!** that's no bad thing!, that's a good sign!

3 *Bot* disease; **les pruniers ont tous eu la m.** all the plum trees got diseased *or* the disease; **m. de l'encre** ink disease

4 *Vét (des chiens)* (canine) distemper; **m. de Carré** (canine) distemper; **m. du dépérissement chronique** chronic wasting disease, CWD; **la m. de la vache folle** mad cow disease

5 *Fig (obsession)* obsession; **la peur du noir peut devenir une m.** fear of the dark can turn into a phobia; *Hum* **elle a encore rangé tous mes journaux, c'est une m. chez elle!** she's tidied up all my papers again, it's an obsession with her!; *Hum* **j'adore le fromage, c'est une véritable m.!** I love cheese, I just can't get enough of it!; *Fam* **c'est quoi, cette m. de toujours tout critiquer?** what's with this mania for *or* obsession with criticizing everything?; *Fam* **en faire une m.** to make a song and dance about it; **il n'y a pas de quoi en faire une m.!** no need to make a song and dance about it *or* to throw a fit!

maladif, -ive [maladif, -iv] **ADJ 1** *(personne)* puny, sickly; *(teint)* sickly-looking, unhealthy; *(constitution)* weak; **il a toujours un air m.** he always looks rather unhealthy *or* ill; **elle était d'une pâleur maladive** she was unhealthily pale

2 *(compulsif)* obsessive, pathological; **d'une sensibilité maladive** acutely sensitive; **d'une jalousie maladive** pathologically *or* obsessively jealous; **d'une curiosité maladive** obsessively inquisitive; **elle est d'une inquiétude maladive** she's a pathological *or* an obsessive worrier; **il adore les jeux d'argent, c'est m.** he's a compulsive gambler *or* he can't stop gambling, it's like a disease (with him)

maladivement [maladivmɑ̃] **ADV** *(à l'excès)* pathologically, morbidly; *(inquiet, ordonné)* obsessively; **être m. timide** to be excessively shy

maladrerie [maladrəri] **NF** *Hist* lazar house, lazaretto

maladresse [maladrɛs] **NF 1** *(manque de dextérité)* clumsiness, awkwardness; **ne le laisse pas porter les verres, il est d'une telle m.!** don't let him carry the glasses, he's so clumsy!

2 *(manque de tact)* clumsiness, tactlessness; **la m. de son intervention peut compromettre toute la campagne** the whole campaign may be jeopardized because of his/her tactless initiative; **quelle m. de lui avoir dit que tu n'aimais pas sa robe!** how tactless of you to tell her that you didn't like her dress!

3 *(manque d'assurance)* awkwardness; **en société, il est d'une grande m.** he's very awkward *or* gauche in company

4 *(remarque, acte)* blunder, gaffe, *Sout* faux pas; **ses maladresses étaient devenues légendaires** *(remarques)* he'd/she'd become famous for his/her tactless remarks *or* for (always) saying the wrong thing; *(actes)* he'd/she'd become famous for his/her blunders; **le but a été marqué sur une m. de la défense** the goal was the result of a blunder *or* slip-up by the defence

5 *Scol* **bon devoir, mais des maladresses** good work if somewhat awkward in places; **il y a quelques maladresses de style** there are a few awkward *or* clumsy turns of phrase

maladroit, -e [maladrwa, -at] **ADJ 1** *(manquant de dextérité)* clumsy, awkward **2** *(manquant de savoir-faire)* clumsy, inept; *(manquant d'assurance)* clumsy, awkward, gauche; *(manquant de tact)* clumsy, tactless, heavy-handed; **une initiative maladroite** a clumsy *or* bungling initiative

NM,F 1 *(de ses mains)* clumsy person; **attention, m., tu as failli lâcher la tasse!** look out, butter-fingers, you nearly dropped the cup! **2** *(gaffeur)* blunderer, blundering fool; *(incompétent)* blithering idiot

maladroitement [maladrwatmɑ̃] **ADV 1** *(sans adresse)* clumsily, awkwardly; **ils s'y sont pris m.** they set about it the wrong way **2** *(sans tact)* clumsily, tactlessly, heavy-handedly

Malaga [malaga] **NM** Malaga

malaga [malaga] **NM 1** *(vin)* Malaga (wine) **2** *(raisin)* Malaga grape

mal-aimé, -e [maleme] *(mpl* **mal-aimés,** *fpl* **mal-aimées) NM,F** outcast; **c'est le m. de la famille** he's the unpopular one in the family; **il a été le m. de cette génération de réalisateurs** he was the forsaken member of that generation of (film) directors; **les mal-aimés de la société** social outcasts

malaire [malɛr] *Anat* **ADJ** malar; **os m.** malar bone, cheekbone

NM malar bone, cheekbone

malais, -e[1] [malɛ, -ɛz] **ADJ** Malay, Malayan, Malaysian; **la presqu'île Malaise** the Malay Peninsula

NM *(langue)* Malay

❑ **Malais, -e NM,F** Malay, Malayan, Malaysian

malaise[2] [malɛz] **NM 1** *(indisposition)* (sudden) weakness, faintness, *Sout* malaise; *(évanouissement)* fainting fit, blackout; *(étourdissement)* dizzy spell; **avoir un m., être pris d'un m.** to feel weak/faint/dizzy

2 *(désarroi, angoisse)* uneasiness *(UNCOUNT)*, anxiety *(UNCOUNT)*, disquiet *(UNCOUNT)*; **ce genre de film provoquait toujours chez elle un m. profond** this sort of film always disturbed her deeply

3 *(mécontentement)* discontent, anger; **il y a un m. croissant chez les viticulteurs** there's mounting tension *or* discontent among wine growers; **m. social** social unrest

4 *(gêne)* unease, awkwardness; **la remarque a créé un m.** the remark caused a moment of unease *or* embarrassment

5 *Fam (problème)* **il y a comme un m.** there's a bit of a snag *or* a hitch

malaisé, -e [maleze] **ADJ** difficult, hard, arduous; **il sera m. de lui apprendre la vérité** telling him/her the truth will be no easy matter; **certains auteurs sont d'une traduction malaisée** certain authors are difficult to translate

malaisément [malezemɑ̃] **ADV** with difficulty

Malaisie [malɛzi] **NF** *Géog* **la M.** Malaya; **vivre en M.** to live in Malaya; **aller en M.** to go to Malaya

malaisien, -enne [malɛzjɛ̃, -ɛn] **ADJ** Malay, Malayan, Malaysian

❑ **Malaisien, -enne NM,F** Malay, Malayan, Malaysian

malandre [malɑ̃dr] **NF 1** *Constr* rotten knot, defect **2** *Vét* malanders, mallenders

malandrin [malɑ̃drɛ̃] **NM** *Littéraire (voleur)* robber, thief; *(bandit de grand chemin)* highwayman; **une bande de malandrins** a band of miscreants

malappris, -e [malapri, -iz] *Vieilli* **NM,F** boor, lout; **eh bien, jeune m., allez-vous me laisser passer?** well, you ill-bred young lout, are you going to let me past or not?; **cette petite malapprise me tirait la langue!** that rude little minx stuck her tongue out at me!

ADJ boorish, loutish, ill-mannered

malard [malar] **NM** drake

malaria [malarja] **NF** *Méd* malaria

malart [malar] = **malard**

Malassis [malasi] **NMPL la Coopérative des M.** = group of painters founded in 1970 (Henri Cuéco, Lucien Fleury, Jean-Claude Latil, Michel Parré and Gérard Tisserand)

malavenant, -e [malavənɑ̃, -ɑ̃t] *Can* **ADJ** *(désagréable)* unpleasant; *(hargneux)* grumpy; *(peu serviable)* disobliging

NM,F *(personne désagréable)* unpleasant person; *(personne hargneuse)* grump, grumpy person; *(personne peu serviable)* disobliging person

malavisé, -e [malavize] **ADJ** unwise, ill-advised, misguided; **être m. de faire qch** to be ill-advised *or* unwise to do sth; **tu as été m. de ne pas venir** it was unwise of you *or* you were ill-advised not to come

Malawi [malawi] **NM** *Géog* **1** *(État)* **le M.** Malawi; **vivre au M.** to live in Malawi; **aller au M.** to go to Malawi **2** *voir* **lac**

malawite [malawit] **ADJ** Malawian

❑ **Malawite NMF** Malawian

malaxage [malaksaʒ] **NM** *(d'une pâte)* kneading; *(d'un mélange)* mixing; *(de beurre)* creaming

malaxer [3] [malakse] **VT 1** *(mélanger)* to mix, to blend; *(pétrir → pâte)* to knead; *(→ beurre)* to cream; **m. le beurre pour le ramollir** work the butter until soft **2** *(masser)* to massage; **elle me malaxait vigoureusement l'épaule** she was giving my shoulder a vigorous massage

malaxeur [malaksœr] **NM** *(gén)* mixer, mixing machine; *(de béton)* cement mixer; *(de beurre)* butter creamer; *(de sucre)* mixer, agitator

malayalam [malajalam] **NM** *(langue)* Malayalam

malayo-polynésien, -enne [malɛjopɔlinezjɛ̃, -ɛn] *(mpl* **malayo-polynésiens,** *fpl* **malayo-polynésiennes) ADJ** Malayo-Polynesian

NM *(langue)* Austronesian

Malaysia [malɛzja] **NF la M.** Malaysia; **la M. occidentale** Malaya

mal-baisée [malbeze] *(pl* **mal-baisées) NF** *Vulg* **c'est une m.** she needs a good fuck

malbâti, -e [malbati] **ADJ** misshapen, ill-proportioned

NM,F misshapen person

malbec [malbɛk] **NM** *(cépage)* Malbec

malbouffe [malbuf] **NF** *Fam* unhealthy eating

malchance [malʃɑ̃s] **NF 1** *(manque de chance)* bad luck, misfortune; **il a eu la m. de...** he was unlucky *or* unfortunate enough to..., he had the misfortune to...; **jouer de m.** to be dogged by ill fortune

2 *(mésaventure)* mishap, misfortune; **une série de malchances** a run of bad luck, a series of mishaps *or* misfortunes

❑ **par malchance ADV** unfortunately, as ill luck would have it; **par m., ils sont passés à Paris quand j'étais absent** unfortunately *or* as ill luck would have it, they came to Paris when I was away

malchanceux, -euse [malʃɑ̃sø, -øz] **ADJ** unlucky, luckless; **spéculateurs m.** unlucky *or* luckless *or* hapless speculators; **il a toujours été m.** he's never had any luck; **être m. au jeu/en amour** to be unlucky at gambling/in love

NM,F unlucky person, unlucky man, *f* woman

malcommode [malkɔmɔd] **ADJ 1** *(appareil)* impractical; *(fauteuil, position)* uncomfortable; *(horaire, système)* inconvenient, awkward **2** *Can (personne → indiscipliné)* unruly; *(→ hargneux)* cantankerous

Maldives [maldiv] **NFPL** *Géog* **les (îles) M.** the Maldive Islands, the Maldives; **vivre aux M.** to live in the Maldives; **aller aux M.** to go to the Maldives

maldonne [maldɔn] **NF 1** *Cartes* misdeal; **tu as fait m.** you misdealt **2** *Fam* **il y a m.** something's gone wrong somewhere

male [mal] *voir* **mal**[3]

Malé [male] **NM** Malé

mâle [mal] **ADJ 1** *Biol, Zool & Bot* male; **le sexe m.** the male sex; **m. alpha** alpha male

2 *(viril)* virile, masculine, manly; **son beau visage m.** his handsome, manly face; **avec une**

m. assurance with robust confidence; **une belle voix m.** a fine manly voice

3 *Tech* male; **vis/connexion m.** male screw/connection; **pièce m.** male component; **prise m.** plug

4 *Zool (avec des noms d'animaux)* male; *(oiseau)* cock; **antilope m.** male antelope; **canard m.** drake; **chat m.** tom, tomcat; **cygne m.** male swan, cob; **éléphant m.** bull elephant; **hamster m.** male hamster; **hérisson m.** male hedgehog; **lapin m.** buck rabbit; **loup m.** male wolf, he-wolf; **ours m.** male bear, he-bear; **pigeon m.** cock pigeon; **renard m.** dog fox

NM male; **le m. de l'espèce** the male of the species; **est-ce un m. ou une femelle?** is it a he or a she?; **le jars est le m. de l'oie** a gander is a male goose; **la tigresse est à la recherche d'un m.** the tigress is looking for a mate; *Fam Hum* **quel m.!** what a man!; **un beau m.** *(animal)* a beautiful male specimen; *Hum (homme)* a real he-man; *Jur* **hériter par les mâles** to inherit through the male line

malédiction [malediksjɔ̃] NF **1** *(imprécation)* curse, *Sout* malediction; **donner sa m. à qn** to call down a curse upon sb, to curse sb; **que la m. te poursuive!** a curse on you *or* on your head!; **cette m. poursuivra la famille pendant trois générations** this curse will hang over the family for three generations; **une m. pèse sur elle** she is under a curse, a curse is hanging over her

2 *(malheur)* malediction; **encourir la m. divine** to incur the wrath of God; **comme si le sort les poursuivait de sa m.** as if fate had cast her evil eye on them

EXCLAM *Hum* curses!, curse *or* damn it!; **m., le revoilà!** curses, here he comes again!

maléfice [malefis] NM evil spell *or* charm; **jeter un m. sur qn** to cast an evil spell on sb; **écarter un m.** to ward off an evil spell

maléficié, -e [malefisje] ADJ *Arch & Littéraire* bewitched, under a spell

maléfique [malefik] ADJ *Littéraire (charme, signe, personne)* evil, malevolent; *(émanation, influence)* evil, cursed; *(étoile, planète)* unlucky; **les puissances maléfiques** the forces of evil

maléique [maleik] ADJ *Chim* maleic

malékisme [malekism] NM *Rel* Malikism

malencontreuse [malɑ̃kɔ̃trøz] *voir* **malencontreux**

malencontreusement [malɑ̃kɔ̃trøzmɑ̃] ADV ill-advisedly; **ayant m. gardé ses lettres** having ill-advisedly kept *or* having been ill-advised enough to have kept his/her letters

malencontreux, -euse [malɑ̃kɔ̃trø, -øz] ADJ *(fâcheux → retard, tentative, visite)* ill-timed, inopportune; *(→ remarque)* unfortunate, untoward; *(mal choisi → parole)* inopportune, ill-advised, unfortunate; **un m. incident diplomatique** an unfortunate diplomatic incident; **par un hasard m.** by a stroke of ill luck

malengueulé, -e [malɑ̃gøle] *Can Fam* ADJ vulgar▪, uncouth▪

NM,F vulgar *or* uncouth person▪

mal-en-point [malɑ̃pwɛ̃] ADJ INV *(en mauvais état → de santé)* in a bad way, *Br* poorly; *(→ financier)* badly off; *(en mauvaise situation)* in a bad *or* poor way; **je l'ai trouvé m.** I found him very much out of sorts; **le candidat est m.** the candidate is in a bad position *or* is badly placed; **l'industrie textile est m.** the textile industry is in a bad way *or* a sorry state

malentendant, -e [malɑ̃tɑ̃dɑ̃, -ɑ̃t] ADJ hearing-impaired

NM,F hearing-impaired person; **les malentendants** the hearing-impaired

malentendu [malɑ̃tɑ̃dy] NM misunderstanding, *Sout* malentendu; **je répète pour qu'il n'y ait pas de m.** I'll say it again so there's no misunderstanding; **attends, je crois qu'il y a un m. (entre nous)** wait, I think we're at cross purposes; **un m. diplomatique** a diplomatic misunderstanding

mal-en-train [malɑ̃trɛ̃] ADJ INV *Can* unwell, *Br* poorly; **avoir l'air m.** to look unwell *or Br* poorly

mal-être [malɛtr] NM INV malaise

Malevitch [malevitʃ] NPR Malevich

malfaçon [malfasɔ̃] NF defect; **la construction présente de nombreuses malfaçons** there are many defects in the building

malfaisance [malfəzɑ̃s] NF *Littéraire* maleficence, evil-mindedness

malfaisant, -e [malfəzɑ̃, -ɑ̃t] ADJ **1** *(qui cherche à nuire)* evil, wicked; **un homme m.** an evil man **2** *(néfaste, pernicieux)* evil, pernicious, noxious; *(influence)* evil, harmful; **on dit que cette pierre a un pouvoir m.** this stone is said to have evil powers; **des idées malfaisantes** pernicious ideas

malfaiteur [malfɛtœr] NM criminal

mal famé, -e, *(mpl* **mal famés,** *fpl* **mal famées)**

malfamé, -e [malfame] ADJ disreputable; **des lieux mal famés** places of ill repute

malformation [malfɔrmasjɔ̃] NF *Biol & Méd* malformation, abnormality; **m. (congénitale)** (congenital) malformation

malfrat [malfra] NM *Fam* gangster, crook, hoodlum

malgache [malgaʃ] ADJ Madagascan, Malagasy

NM *(langue)* Madagascan, Malagasy

❑ **Malgache** NMF Madagascan, Malagasy; **les Malgaches** the Madagascans, the Malagasy *or* Malagasies

malgracieux, -euse [malgrasjø, -øz] ADJ **1** *Vieilli (qui manque de politesse)* ungracious, churlish, rude **2** *Littéraire (qui manque d'élégance)* inelegant, ungainly, clumsy

malgré [malgre] PRÉP in spite of, despite; **il est sorti m. la pluie** he went out in spite of *or* despite the rain; **il a pénétré dans l'enceinte m. les ordres** he entered the area against orders; **m. tous les avis contraires, il a essayé à nouveau** in spite of *or* despite all advice to the contrary, he tried again; **m. sa fortune, il n'a jamais été heureux** for all his wealth, he's never been happy; **m. soi** *(involontairement)* unwillingly, in spite of oneself; *(à contrecœur)* reluctantly, against one's better judgment; *(forcé)* against one's will; **il a laissé voir m. lui à quel point il était gêné** he revealed in spite of himself *or* he unwillingly revealed how embarrassed he was; **j'ai consenti, bien m. moi** I agreed, very reluctantly *or* much against my better judgment; **on l'a conduit m. lui au poste de police le plus proche** they took him against his will *or* by force to the nearest police station; **c'est tout à fait m. lui qu'il a dû quitter son pays natal** he left his native country entirely against his will

❑ **malgré que** CONJ **1** *Fam (bien que)* although, despite the fact that; **m. qu'il fasse froid** despite the fact that *or* although it's cold

2 *(locution) Littéraire* **m. que j'en aie/qu'il en ait/***etc* however reluctantly

❑ **malgré tout** ADV **1** *(en dépit des obstacles)* in spite of *or* despite everything; **je réussirai m. tout** I'll succeed in spite of everything; **m. tout, ils ont réuni la somme nécessaire** despite everything, they raised the required amount

2 *(pourtant)* all the same, even so; **c'était m. tout un grand champion** all the same, he was a great champion; **il faut dire une chose m. tout...** even so, one thing has to be said...; **c'est convaincant mais m. tout je n'y crois pas** it's convincing but all the same *or* nevertheless *or* even so, I don't believe it

malhabile [malabil] ADJ **1** *(maladroit)* clumsy; **elle est m. de ses doigts** she's all fingers and thumbs **2** *Littéraire (inapte)* **il a toujours été m. à marchander** he's always lacked skill *or* been bad at haggling

malhabilement [malabilmɑ̃] ADV clumsily, awkwardly

MALHEUR [malœr]

misfortune **1, 2** ▪ accident **1** ▪ sorrow **3** ▪ trouble **4**

NM **1** *(incident)* misfortune; *(accident)* accident; **un grand m.** a (great) tragedy *or* catastrophe; **le pays a eu** *ou* **connu beaucoup de malheurs à cette époque** the country experienced great misfortune *or* hardship at that time; **ils ont eu des malheurs** they have been through difficult times; *Ironique* **eh bien, tu en as des malheurs!** oh dear, it's not your day, is it?; **depuis quelques années, il ne m'arrive que des malheurs** for some years now I've had nothing but misfortune; **il a dû lui arriver m.** something (terrible) must have happened to him/her; **si jamais il lui arrive (un) m.** if (ever) anything happens to him/her; **en cas de m.** if anything awful should happen; **quel m.!** what a tragedy!; **un petit m.** a (slight) mishap; *Hum* **il n'arrête pas de me raconter ses petits malheurs** he's forever telling me (about) all his petty cares and woes; *Fam* **ne le laissez pas rentrer ou je fais un m.** don't let him in or I won't be responsible for my actions; **elle passait en première partie, et c'est elle qui a fait un m.** she was only the supporting act, but it was she who brought the house down; **cette chanson a fait un m. en son temps** that song was a huge success in its day; **son bouquin a fait un m. en librairie** his/her book was a runaway success in the bookshops; **sa nouvelle pièce fait un m.** his/her latest play is a big hit; **les rollers font un m. en France** rollerblades are all the rage in France; **je verrouille la grille quand les enfants sont dans le jardin, un m. est si vite arrivé!** I lock the gate when the children are in the garden, you can't be too careful!; **pose cette tasse, un m. est si vite arrivé!** put that cup down before there's an accident!; *Fam* **je crois qu'on va déménager à Londres – parle pas de m.!** I think we're moving to London – God forbid *or* Lord save us!; **ils veulent tous venir chez toi – parle pas de m.!** they all want to come to your place – oh please no!; *Prov* **un m. ne vient** *ou* **n'arrive jamais seul** it never rains but it pours; **et maintenant, j'apprends qu'il est malade, un m. ne vient jamais seul!** and now I hear he's ill, if it's not one thing (then) it's another!

2 *(malchance)* **le m.** misfortune, bad luck; **le m. a voulu que...** as bad luck would have it...; **le m., c'est que...** the unfortunate thing is that...; **avoir le m. de** to be unfortunate enough to, to have the misfortune to; **ceux qui ont le m. de le connaître** those who are unfortunate *or* unlucky enough to know him; **j'ai eu le m. de perdre mon père jeune** I had the *or* it was my misfortune to lose my father when I was young; **j'ai eu le m. de lui dire que je n'étais pas d'accord avec lui** I made the mistake of telling him that I didn't agree with him; **j'ai eu le m. de lui dire de se taire!** I was foolish enough to ask him/her *or* I made the mistake of asking him/her to be quiet!; **une vie marquée par le m.** a life of misfortune *or* sorrow; **être dans le m.** to suffer misfortunes *or* hard times; **il est resté très digne dans le m.** he remained very dignified in (his) adversity; **montrer du courage dans le m.** to show courage in the face of adversity *or* hardship; **faire l'expérience du m.** to taste misfortune; **porter m. à qn** to bring sb bad luck; **arrête, ça porte m.!** stop, it brings bad luck!; **je l'ai bien connu, pour mon m.** I knew him well, more's the pity; **pour son m., il était l'aîné de six enfants** unfortunately for him, he was the oldest of six; **je joue de m. en ce moment** I'm dogged by *or* I've got a run of bad luck at the moment; *Prov* **c'est dans le m. qu'on connaît ses vrais amis** a friend in need is a friend indeed

3 *(désespoir)* **faire le m. de qn** to cause sb unhappiness, to bring sorrow to sb; **elle avait rencontré l'homme qui allait faire son m.** she'd met the man who was to be the curse *or* bane of her life; *Prov* **le m. des uns fait le bonheur des autres** one man's joy is another man's sorrow

4 *(inconvénient)* trouble, problem; **le m., c'est que j'ai perdu l'adresse** unfortunately *or* the trouble is I've lost the address; **son mari ne l'a jamais crue, c'est là le m.!** her husband never believed her, there's the tragedy (of it)!; **sans permis de travail, pas de possibilité d'emploi, c'est ça le m.** without a work permit you can't get a job, that's the snag *or* the problem; **quel m. que je ne l'aie pas su!** what a pity *or* shame I didn't know (about it)

EXCLAM damn!; **m., mon lait qui se sauve!** oh, damn, the milk's boiling over!; **m. à** woe betide; **m. à toi et à toute ta descendance!** a curse on you and all your family!; *Bible* **m. à l'homme par qui le scandale arrive** woe to that man by whom the offence cometh; **m. aux vaincus!** vae victis!, woe to the vanquished!

▫ **de malheur** ADJ *Fam Hum* accursed, wretched; **je ne remonterais plus sur ce vélo de m.** I'll never ride that wretched *or* accursed bike again

▫ **par malheur** ADV unfortunately; **par m., j'ai laissé la porte ouverte** unfortunately, I left the door open; **par m., son fils est né avec la même maladie** sadly, his/her son was born with the same disease

malheureuse [malœrøz] *voir* **malheureux**

malheureusement [malœrøzmɑ̃] ADV unfortunately; **je ne retrouve m. pas mon agenda** unfortunately, I can't lay my hands on my diary, I'm afraid I can't lay my hands on my diary; **m. pour toi, il ne reste plus de petites tailles** you're out of luck, there are no small sizes left; **m., elle est morte le lendemain** sadly, she died the next day

malheureux, -euse [malœrø, -øz] ADJ **1** *(peiné)* unhappy, miserable, wretched; *(expression, air, regard)* unhappy, sad, miserable; **il est m. s'il ne peut pas sortir** he's miserable *or* unhappy when he can't go out; **je suis m. de ne pouvoir l'aider** I feel sad *or* wretched at not being able to help him/her; **leur air m. en disait long** their unhappy *or* miserable faces spoke volumes; **rendre qn m.** to make sb miserable *or* unhappy; **il l'a rendue malheureuse toute sa vie** he made her life a misery, he caused her lifelong unhappiness; **n'y pense plus, tu ne fais que te rendre m.** don't think about it any more, you're only making yourself miserable; **m. en ménage** unhappily married; **être m. comme une pierre** *ou* **les pierres** to be dreadfully unhappy

2 *(tragique → enfance)* unhappy; *(→ destin)* cruel; **sans le savoir, nous entrions dans une époque malheureuse** without knowing it, we were entering an unhappy period

3 *(malchanceux)* unfortunate, unlucky; **les candidats m. recevront une montre digitale** the unlucky contestants will receive a digital watch; **le candidat m. verra ses frais de déplacement remboursés** the unsuccessful candidate will have his travel expenses paid; **il est m. au jeu/en amour** he has no luck with gambling/women; **avoir la main malheureuse** to be unlucky; **des amours malheureuses** unhappy love affairs; **les m. réfugiés/sinistrés** the unfortunate *or* hapless refugees/victims; **la malheureuse femme ne savait rien de la catastrophe** nobody had told the poor *or* unfortunate *or* wretched woman about the catastrophe

4 *(infructueux → initiative, effort)* thwarted; *(→ amour)* unrequited; *(malencontreux → tentative)* unfortunate, ill-fated; *(→ conséquences)* unfortunate, unhappy; *(→ incident)* unfortunate; **son intervention a eu des suites malheureuses** his/her action had some unfortunate *or* unhappy consequences; **oublions tout de ce m. incident** *ou* **de cet incident m.** let's forget this unfortunate incident; **par un m. hasard** by an unfortunate coincidence, as bad luck would have it

5 *(regrettable → geste, mot)* unfortunate; **parler de suicide devant elle, le mot était m.** it was rather clumsy *or* unfortunate to talk about suicide in front of her

6 *(avant le nom) (insignifiant)* **pleurer ainsi pour un m. parapluie perdu/une malheureuse piqûre!** all these tears for a stupid lost umbrella/a tiny little injection!; **ne nous battons pas pour quelques m. cents** let's not fight over a few measly cents; **sur le plat, il n'y avait qu'un m. poulet et deux poireaux** on the dish there was just a pathetic-looking chicken and a couple of leeks

7 *(dans des tournures impersonnelles)* **il est m. que vous ne l'ayez pas rencontré** it's unfortunate *or* a pity *or* a shame you didn't meet him; **il est m. que le gouvernement n'ait pas compris cet appel** it is to be regretted that the Government didn't hear that plea; **ce serait m. de ne pas en profiter** it would be a pity *or* shame not to take advantage of it; **c'est m. à dire, mais c'est la vérité** it's an awful thing to say, but it's the truth; **c'est m. à dire, mais je m'ennuie** I hate to say so, but I'm bored; *Fam* **si c'est pas m. (de voir/d'entendre ça)!** it's a (crying) shame (to see/to hear that)!; **c'est bien m. pour vous!** it's hard for you!; *Fam* **ce n'est pas m.!** about time too!, not a moment too soon!

NM,F **1** *(indigent)* poor *or* needy man, *f* woman; **secourir les m.** to help the poor *or* the needy *or* those in need

2 *(personne pitoyable)* unfortunate *or* wretched man, *f* woman; **il est bien seul maintenant, le m.** he's very much on his own now, the poor devil; **le m. ne comprenait rien à ce qui se passait** the poor wretch *or* soul didn't understand anything that was going on; **faire un m.** *(attrister quelqu'un)* to make someone unhappy; **vous allez faire des m. avec votre nouvelle taxe** you'll make some people (very) unhappy with your new tax; **elle a fait plus d'un m. quand elle s'est mariée** she made more than one man unhappy *or* broke quite a few hearts when she got married; **attention, petit m.!** careful, you wretched boy *or* little wretch!; **qu'as-tu dit là, m.!** honestly, what a thing to say!; **m.! qu'avez-vous fait?** you wretch! what have you done?

malhonnête [malɔnɛt] ADJ **1** *(sans scrupules)* dishonest, crooked; **des procédés malhonnêtes** underhand *or* dishonest methods; **c'est m. de sa part** it's dishonest of him/her **2** *Suisse ou Vieilli (impoli)* rude, impolite **3** *Vieilli (indécent → geste)* indecent; *(→ suggestion)* improper

NMF **1** *(personne sans scrupules)* cheat, crook **2** *Suisse (personne impolie)* rude person

malhonnêtement [malɔnɛtmɑ̃] ADV **1** *(sans probité)* dishonestly **2** *Vieilli (impoliment)* rudely

malhonnêteté [malɔnɛtte] NF **1** *(manque de probité)* dishonesty, crookedness; **la m. de ses procédés** the underhandedness *or* the dishonesty of his/her methods; **m. intellectuelle** intellectual dishonesty **2** *Vieilli (manque de politesse)* rudeness, impoliteness; *(remarque impolie)* rude remark; **il m'a dit une m.** he said something rude to me

Mali [mali] NM *Géog* **le M.** Mali; **vivre au M.** to live in Mali; **aller au M.** to go to Mali

mali [mali] NM *Belg* deficit

malice [malis] NF **1** *(espièglerie)* mischievousness, impishness, prankishness; **il a de la m., ce petit-là!** he's a mischievous *or* cheeky little thing, that one!; **un regard plein** *ou* **pétillant de m.** an impish *or* a mischievous look

2 *Vieilli (méchanceté)* malice, spitefulness; **ne pas entendre m. à qch** *(ne voir rien de mal à quelque chose)* to see no harm in sth; *(ne pas avoir l'intention de faire du mal)* to mean no harm by sth; **je suis sûre qu'elle n'y entendait pas m.** I'm sure she didn't mean any harm (by it); **il n'y a vu aucune m. de leur part** he didn't think they meant anything by it

▫ **à malices** ADJ **sac/boîte à malices** bag/box of tricks

▫ **sans malice** ADJ guileless, innocent ADV **je me suis moqué de lui, mais c'était sans m.** I made fun of him but it wasn't serious

malicieuse [malisjøz] *voir* **malicieux**

malicieusement [malisjøzmɑ̃] ADV mischievously, impishly

malicieux, -euse [malisjø, -øz] ADJ **1** *(espiègle)* mischievous, impish; **elle a la repartie malicieuse** she's never at a loss for a smart answer **2** *Vieilli (méchant)* malicious

malien, -enne [maljɛ̃, -ɛn] ADJ Malian

▫ **Malien, -enne** NM,F Malian

maligne [maliɲ] *voir* **malin**

malignement [maliɲmɑ̃] ADV *(avec méchanceté)* spitefully; *(par méchanceté)* out of spite

malignité [maliɲite] NF **1** *(d'une action, d'une personne)* malice, spitefulness, spite; *(du sort)* cruelty; **la m. de cette remarque n'échappa à personne** the spitefulness of the remark wasn't lost on anyone **2** *Méd* malignancy

malikisme [malikism] = **malékisme**

malin, -igne *ou Fam* **-ine** [malɛ̃, -iɲ, -in] ADJ **1** *(rusé)* cunning, crafty, shrewd; **elle avait un petit air m.** she had a wily *or* cunning look about her; **être m. comme un singe** to be as cunning as a fox; **à trois ans, il était déjà m. comme un singe** at three years of age he was already an artful little monkey; **jouer au plus m. avec qn** to try and outsmart *or* outwit sb

2 *(intelligent)* bright, clever, *esp Am* smart; **elle est très maligne** she's very smart *or* bright; **il est plus m. que ça** he knows better; *Fam* **elle n'est pas bien maligne** she's not very clever *or* not all that bright; **tu te crois m.?** do you think you're clever?; **tu te crois m. d'avoir copié sur les autres?** so you think cribbing from the others was a clever thing to do?; *Ironique* **c'est m.!** very clever!; **ce n'était pas très m. (de ta part)** that wasn't very bright, was it?; **c'est pas bien m.!** that's dead easy!, that's simple!; **alors, 224 multiplié par 2, ce n'est pourtant pas bien m.!** so, 224 times 2, that's not so hard *or* that's not taxing your brain too much, is it?; **bien m. qui comprendra** it'll take a genius to understand that

3 *Méd (tumeur)* malignant

4 *(malveillant → plaisir)* malicious; *Arch (→ influence)* malignant, evil; **elle mettait une joie maligne à me poser les questions les plus difficiles** she would take a perverse pleasure in asking me the most difficult questions; **éprouver un m. plaisir à faire qch** to experience (a) malicious pleasure in doing sth

5 *Can (méchant, irascible)* irritable, bad-tempered; **un chien m.** a vicious dog

NM,F clever person; **c'est un m., il trouvera bien une solution** he's a bright spark, he'll find a way; *Fam Ironique* **gros m., va!** very clever!; *Fam Ironique* **alors, gros m., montre-nous ce que tu sais faire** OK, wise guy, show us what you can do; **un petit m.** a crafty one, a smart aleck, *Br* a clever dick; *Fam* **c'est une petite maligne** she's a sly one, she's a little imp; *Ironique* **les petits malins qui doublent sur une ligne blanche** the smart alecks *or Br* clever dicks who overtake on a solid white line; **la petite maligne avait tout prévu** the crafty little so-and-so had thought of everything; **faire le m.** to show off, to try to be smart; **arrêtez de faire les malins!** stop messing about!; **fais pas le m. avec moi** don't (you) get smart with me; *Prov* **à m., m. et demi** = there's always somebody cleverer than you somewhere

▫ **Malin** NM **le M.** the Devil, the Evil One

maline *Fam* = **maligne**

malines [malin] NF *(dentelle)* Malines, Mechlin

malingre [malɛ̃gr] ADJ puny, sickly, frail; **son corps m.** his/her puny *or* frail body

malinois [malinwa] NM Belgian sheepdog

malintentionné, -e [malɛ̃tɑ̃sjɔne] ADJ nasty, spiteful; **des propos malintentionnés** malicious *or* spiteful remarks; **être m. à l'égard de** *ou* **envers qn** to be ill-disposed towards sb

malique [malik] ADJ *Chim* malic

mal-jugé [malʒyʒe] *(pl* **mal-jugés***)* NM *Jur* miscarriage of justice

malle [mal] NF **1** *(valise)* trunk; **faire sa m.** *ou* **ses malles** to pack one's bags; *Fam* **se faire la m.** *(partir)* to beat it, *Br* to clear off, *Am* to book it; *(se détacher)* to fall off▪; *Fam* **allez, on se fait la m.!** come on, let's get out of here!

2 *Vieilli Aut Br* boot, *Am* trunk; **m. arrière** luggage compartment, load area

3 *Hist (voiture de la poste)* mail coach; **la M. des Indes** the Indian Mail; *Can Fam* **mettre une lettre à la m.** to mail a letter▪, *Br* to post a letter▪

4 *Belg Transp* **la M. d'Anvers** the Antwerp ferry

malléabilisation [maleabilizasjɔ̃] NF malleabilizing

malléabiliser [3] [maleabilize] VT to malleabilize

malléabilité [maleabilite] NF **1** *(souplesse)* flexibility, malleability, pliability **2** *Métal* malleability

malléable [maleabl] ADJ **1** *(cire)* soft; *(caractère, personnalité)* easily influenced *or* swayed; **elle n'est pas très m.** she's rather rigid *or* inflexible **2** *Métal* malleable

malle-cabine [malkabin] *(pl* **malles-cabine***)* NF cabin trunk

malléolaire [maleɔlɛr] ADJ *Anat* malleolar

malléole [maleɔl] NF *Anat* malleolus

malle-poste [malpɔst] *(pl* **malles-poste***)* NF *Hist* mailcoach

maller [3] [male] VT *Can Joual* to mail▪, *Br* to post

mallette [malɛt] NF **1** *(valise)* suitcase; *(porte-documents)* attaché case, briefcase; *(trousse à outils)* toolbox; **une m. en osier** a wicker (picnic) basket **2** *Belg (musette d'ouvrier)* (canvas) haversack; *(sacoche)* bag; *(cartable d'écolier)* satchel

mal-logé, -e [malloʒe] *(mpl* **mal-logés,** *fpl* **mal-logées)* NM,F person living in bad housing; **les mal-logés** the badly *or* poorly housed

mallophage [mallofaʒ] *Entom* NM mallophagan, *Spéc* member of the Mallophaga
  □ **mallophages** NMPL mallophagans, *Spéc* Mallophaga

malm [malm] NM *Géol* malm

malmener [19] [malməne] VT **1** *(brutaliser)* to manhandle, to treat roughly; **arrête de m. cet enfant** stop being so rough with that child
  2 *(objet)* to handle *or* treat roughly; *(matériel, véhicule)* to mistreat; **m. la grammaire** to misuse grammar, to make grammatical mistakes
  3 *Fig (traiter sévèrement)* to bully, to push around; **un metteur en scène réputé pour m. ses acteurs** a director renowned for giving actors a rough *or* hard time; **malmené par la presse** mauled by the press; **malmené par la critique** panned by the critics
  4 *Sport* **m. un adversaire** to give an opponent a hard time, to maul an opponent

malmignatte [malmiɲat] NF *Entom* malmignatte

malnutri, -e [malnytri] ADJ malnourished
  NM,F person suffering from malnutrition

malnutrition [malnytrisjɔ̃] NF malnutrition

malodorant, -e [malɔdɔrɑ̃, -ɑ̃t] ADJ foul-smelling, smelly, *Sout* malodorous

malonique [malɔnik] ADJ *Chim* malonic

malotru, -e [malɔtry] NM,F boor, lout, oaf

malouin, -e [malwɛ̃, -in] ADJ of/from Saint-Malo
  □ **Malouin, -e** NM,F = inhabitant of or person from Saint-Malo

Malouines [malwin] NFPL **les (îles) M.** the Falkland Islands, the Falklands, the Malvinas; **vivre aux M.** to live in the Falkland Islands; **aller aux M.** to go to the Falkland Islands; **un habitant des M.** a Falkland Islander

mal-pensant [malpɑ̃sɑ̃] *(pl* **mal-pensants)** NM dissenter

malpighie [malpigi] NF *Bot* malpighia

malpoli, -e [malpɔli] *Fam* ADJ rude", impolite", bad-mannered"; **c'est m.!** that's rude!
  NM,F lout, boor; **petit m.!** you rude (little) boy!; **petite malpolie!** you rude (little) girl!

malposition [malpozisjɔ̃] NF malposition; **lorsqu'il y a m. dentaire** *ou* **de la dent** when the tooth comes through the wrong way

malpropre [malprɔpr] ADJ **1** *(crasseux)* dirty, filthy, unclean; *(apparence)* slovenly, untidy; **des mains malpropres** dirty *or* grubby hands
  2 *(mal fait → ouvrage, tâche)* shoddy, sloppily done; **cette serrure, c'est du travail m.** that lock is a shoddy piece of work
  3 *(inconvenant, impudique)* dirty, filthy, smutty
  4 *(malhonnête)* obnoxious, dishonest, unsavoury
  NMF filthy swine; **se faire traiter comme un m.** to be treated like dirt; **se faire chasser** *ou* **renvoyer comme un m.** to be sent packing

malproprement [malprɔprəmɑ̃] ADV *(manger)* messily; *(travailler)* shoddily, sloppily; *(agir)* vilely, sordidly

malpropreté [malprɔprəte] NF **1** *(aspect sale)* dirtiness, filthiness, uncleanliness **2** *Fig (acte malhonnête)* low *or* dirty *or* filthy trick **3** *Fig (propos indécent)* dirty *or* smutty remark; **dire des malpropretés** to talk smut; **où as-tu appris ces malpropretés?** where did you learn such filthy *or* disgusting language?

malsain, -e [malsɛ̃, -ɛn] ADJ **1** *(nuisible à la santé)* unhealthy; **climat m.** unhealthy climate; **nourriture malsaine** unhealthy *or* unwholesome food
  2 *Fig (qui va mal → industrie)* ailing
  3 *Fig (pervers → personne)* unwholesome; *(→ ambiance, curiosité, esprit)* unhealthy; *(→ littérature)* unwholesome; **une insistance malsaine** an unhealthy *or* a morbid insistence; **ils ont des rapports malsains** they have an unhealthy relationship; **c'est m. de laisser les enfants voir de tels films** it's unhealthy *or* dangerous to let children watch films like that
  4 *Fam (dangereux)* **c'est plutôt m. par ici** it's a bit rough *or Br* dodgy around here; **je sentais que ça allait devenir m.** I could sense things would soon turn nasty; **un quartier m.** a rough *or* tough area

malséant, -e [malseɑ̃, -ɑ̃t] ADJ *Littéraire (contraire aux conventions)* unseemly, improper, indecorous; *(contraire à la décence)* indecent, improper; **il serait m. que tu m'accompagnes** it would be quite unseemly *or* unbecoming for you to accompany me

malsonnant, -e [malsɔnɑ̃, -ɑ̃t] ADJ *Littéraire (inconvenant)* offensive; *Hum* **après un échange de propos malsonnants** after exchanging a few uncomplimentary remarks

malstrom [malstrɔm] = **maelström**

malt [malt] NM malt; **m. vert** green malt

maltage [maltaʒ] NM malting

maltais, -e [maltɛ, -ɛz] ADJ Maltese
  NM **1** *(langue)* Maltese **2** *(chien)* Maltese (dog)
  □ **Maltais, -e** NM,F Maltese; **les M.** the Maltese
  □ **maltaise** NF Maltese (blood orange)

maltase [maltaz] NM *Chim* maltase

Malte [malt] NM *Géog* **(l'île de) M.** Malta; **vivre à M.** to live in Malta; **aller à M.** to go to Malta

malter [3] [malte] VT to malt; **lait malté** malted milk

malterie [maltəri] NF **1** *(usine)* maltings **2** *(processus)* malting

malteur [maltœr] NM maltster, maltman

malthusianisme [maltyzjanism] NM Malthusianism

malthusien, -enne [maltyzjɛ̃, -ɛn] ADJ Malthusian
  NM,F Malthusian

maltose [maltoz] NM *Chim* maltose

maltôte [maltot] NF *Hist* **1** *(impôt)* = tax on goods levied by Philip the Fair **2** *(collecteurs d'impôt)* tax collectors

maltraitance [maltrɛtɑ̃s] NF *(physical)* abuse

maltraitant, -e [maltrɛtɑ̃, -ɑ̃t] ADJ abusive; **des parents maltraitants** abusive parents

maltraiter [4] [maltrete] VT **1** *(brutaliser)* to ill-treat, to mistreat, to maltreat; *(verbalement)* to attack; **les otages n'ont pas été maltraités par leurs ravisseurs** the hostages were not mistreated by their kidnappers; **m. sa femme/ses enfants** to batter one's wife/one's children
  2 *Fig (malmener)* to misuse; **les accords internationaux sont bien maltraités** international agreements are being ignored *or* trampled on; **la pièce a été maltraitée par la critique** the play was mauled by the critics

malus [malys] NM *Assur* surcharge, extra premium

malvacée [malvase] *Bot* NF member of the Malvaceae family
  □ **malvacées** NFPL Malvaceae

malveillance [malvɛjɑ̃s] NF **1** *(méchanceté)* malevolence, spite, malice; **avec m.** malevolently, spitefully, maliciously; **par pure m.** out of sheer spite *or* malice; **ne voyez là aucune m. de ma part** please do not think there is any ill will on my part; **c'était sans m. de sa part** he/she meant no ill
  2 *(intention criminelle)* criminal intent; **un incident dû à la m.** a malicious incident; **d'après la police, l'incendie serait le fait de la m.** according to the police, the fire was started with malicious intent

malveillant, -e [malvɛjɑ̃, -ɑ̃t] ADJ *(personne, propos)* malicious, spiteful; *(sourire)* malevolent, malicious; **l'intention malveillante a été prouvée** malicious intent has been proved
  NM,F malicious *or* malevolent person

malvenu, -e [malvəny] ADJ **1** *(inopportun)* untimely, inopportune; **votre remarque était malvenue** your remark was untimely
  2 *Littéraire* **être m. à** *ou* **de faire qch** to be in no position to do sth; **il serait m. à** *ou* **de se plaindre** he's hardly in a position to complain; **il serait tout à fait m. de le critiquer** it would be quite inappropriate to criticize him
  3 *(mal formé → arbre, enfant)* underdeveloped, malformed

malversation [malvɛrsasjɔ̃] NF embezzlement *(UNCOUNT)*; **il est coupable de malversations** he is guilty of embezzlement *or* misappropriation of funds

mal-vivre [malvivr] NM INV miserable existence

malvoisie [malvwazi] NF **1** *(vin)* malmsey **2** *(cépage)* malvasia, malmsey grape

malvoyant, -e [malvwajɑ̃, -ɑ̃t] ADJ partially sighted
  NM,F partially sighted person; **les malvoyants** the partially sighted

malware [malwɛr] NM *Ordinat* malware

maman [mamɑ̃] NF **1** *(terme d'appellation) Br* mum, mummy, *Am* mom **2** *(mère) Br* mum, *Am* mom; **toutes les mamans sont invitées** all the mothers *or Br* mums *or Am* moms are invited; **la plus belle récompense d'une m.** the finest reward a mother could ask for

'La Maman et la putain' *Eustache* 'The Mother and the Whore'

mamba [mɑ̃ba] NM *Zool* mamba; **m. noir/vert** black/green mamba

mambo [mɑ̃bo] NM mambo

mamelle [mamɛl] NF **1** *Vieilli (sein)* breast; *Littéraire* **un enfant à la m.** a suckling (child) **2** *(de vache)* udder; *(de chienne, de truie)* teat, dug **3** *(du sabot d'un cheval)* side walls

mamelon [mamlɔ̃] NM **1** *Anat & Zool (d'une femme)* nipple **2** *(colline)* hillock, hummock, *Spéc* mamelon **3** *(d'un gond)* gudgeon

mamelonnaire [mamlɔnɛr] ADJ *Anat & Zool* mamillary

mamelonné, -e [mamlɔne] ADJ **1** *Anat, Zool & Méd Br* mamillated, *Am* mammillated **2** *Géog* hummocky

mamelouk [mamluk] NM *Hist* Mameluke

mamelu, -e [mamly] ADJ *Arch* busty

mameluk [mamluk] = **mamelouk**

m'amie, mamie[1] [mami] NF *Arch (mon amie)* my beloved

mamie[2] [mami] NF *Fam* **1** *(grand-mère)* granny, gran **2** *(vieille dame)* old lady"

mamillaire [mamilɛr] ADJ mamillary; **corps** *ou* **tubercules mamillaires** mamillary bodies
  NF *Bot* nipple cactus

mammaire [mamɛr] ADJ mammary

mammalien, -enne [mamaljɛ̃, -ɛn] ADJ mammalian

mammalogie [mamalɔʒi] NF mammalogy

mammectomie [mamɛktɔmi] NF *Méd* mastectomy

mammifère [mamifɛr] NM mammal; **les grands mammifères** the higher mammals

mammite [mamit] NF mastitis

mammographie [mamɔgrafi] NF *Méd* **1** *(cliché)* mammogram, mammograph **2** *(technique)* mammography

Mammon [mamɔ̃] NM Mammon

mammoplastie [mamɔplasti] NF mammoplasty, mammaplasty

mammouth [mamut] NM mammoth

mammy [mami] = **mamie[2]**

mamours [mamur] NMPL *Fam* cuddle; **faire des m. à qn** to cuddle sb; **se faire des m.** to cuddle

mam'selle [mamzɛl] NF *Fam* Miss; **alors, ma petite m., ça va?** and how's my little Miss?

mamy [mami] = **mamie[2]**

mam'zelle [mamzɛl] = **mam'selle**

MAN [ɛmaɛn] NMF *Can Pol (abrév* **Membre de l'Assemblée Nationale)** MNA

Man [man] *voir* **île**

man [mɑ̃] NM cockchafer grub

mana [mana] NM *(force surnaturelle)* mana

manade [manad] NF = herd of horses or bulls in the Camargue

management [manadʒmɛnt] NM *Com & Sport* management; **m. des ressources humaines**

human resources management; **m. de transition** transition management
manager[1] [17] [manadʒe] **VT** *Com & Sport* to manage
manager[2] [manadʒœr] **NM** *Com & Sport* manager
managérial, -e, -aux, -ales [manadʒerjal, -o] **ADJ** managerial
Managua [managwa] **NM** *Géog* Managua
Manama [manama] **NM** *Géog* Manama
manant [manɑ̃] **NM** **1** *Hist (villageois)* villager; *(paysan)* peasant, villein **2** *Littéraire (mufle)* churl, boor
manceau, -elle[1] [mɑ̃so, -ɛl] **ADJ** of/from Le Mans
❑ **Manceau, -elle NM,F** = inhabitant of or person from Le Mans
mancelle[2] [mɑ̃sɛl] **NF** tug strap
mancenille [mɑ̃snij] **NF** *Bot* manchineel apple
mancenillier [mɑ̃snije] **NM** *Bot* manchineel (tree)
manchabalisme, manchaballisme [mɑ̃ʃabalism] **NM** *Belg Fam Arg scol* crawling, sucking up
Manche [mɑ̃ʃ] **NF** **1** *(mer)* **la M.** the (English) Channel **2** *(région d'Espagne)* **la M.** La Mancha **3** *(département)* **la M.** the Manche
manche[1] [mɑ̃ʃ] **NM** **1** *(d'outil)* handle; *(de poignard)* handle, haft; *(de club de golf)* shaft; *(de fouet)* stock; **à m. court** short-handled; **à m. long** long-handled; **couteau à m. d'ivoire** ivory-handled knife, knife with an ivory handle; **m. de pioche** pickaxe handle *or* shaft; **m. de** *ou* **à balai** broomstick; *Fam* **être** *ou* **se mettre du côté du m.** to side with the winner; *Prov* **il ne faut jamais jeter le m. après la cognée** never say die
2 *Fam (personne maladroite)* clumsy oaf, *Br* cack-handed idiot, *Am* klutz; *(personne incapable)* useless idiot, *Br* pillock, *Am* dork; **s'y prendre comme un m.** to make a right mess of things; **tu t'y prends comme un m.** you're making a right mess of it; **pour l'organisation du dîner, vous vous êtes débrouillés** *ou* **vous vous y êtes pris comme des manches** you made a right mess of organizing the dinner; **avec les femmes, il s'y prend comme un m.** he's absolutely useless with women; **il conduit/danse comme un m.** he's a lousy *or* hopeless driver/dancer
3 *très Fam (obstacle)* **tomber sur un m.** to come up against a snag
4 *Fam Aviat & Ordinat* **m. à balai** joystick
5 *Culin (de côtelette, de gigot)* bone; **m. à gigot** leg of mutton holder
6 *Mus (de violon, de guitare)* neck
ADJ *Fam (maladroit)* ham-fisted, *Br* cack-handed
manche[2] [mɑ̃ʃ] **NF** **1** *(de vêtement)* sleeve; **sans manches** sleeveless; **à manches courtes/longues** short-/long-sleeved; **être en manches de chemise** to be in one's shirt-sleeves; **relever** *ou* **retrousser ses manches** to roll up one's sleeves; *Fig* to roll up one's sleeves, to get down to work; *Fam Fig* **avoir qn dans sa m.** to have sb in one's pocket; **il a le conseil municipal dans sa m.** he's well in with the local council; **m. bouffante/trois-quarts** puff/three-quarter sleeve; **m. gigot/raglan** leg-of-mutton/raglan sleeve; **m. ballon** puff sleeve; **m. chauve-souris** batwing sleeve; **manches kimono** kimono sleeves
2 *(conduit → de ballon)* neck; **m. à air** *Aviat* windsock; *Naut* windsail; **m. à charbon** coal chute; **m. à ordures** *Br* rubbish chute, *Am* garbage shoot; **m. à vent** windsock
3 *Géog* channel, straits
4 *(dans un jeu)* round; *(au bridge)* game; *Sport (gén)* leg; *(au tennis)* set; *Fig* **gagner la première m.** to win the first round; *Fig* **une négociation en plusieurs manches** a multiround negotiation
5 *Fam (locution)* **faire la m.** *(mendiant)* to beg■; *(musicien, mime)* to perform in the streets■, *Br* to busk
manche-à-balle [mɑ̃ʃabal] *(pl* **manche-à-balles***)* *Belg Fam Arg scol* **ADJ** crawling, bootlicking
NM crawler, bootlicker
manchego [mɑ̃tʃego] **NM** *(fromage)* manchego
mancheron [mɑ̃ʃrɔ̃] **NM** **1** *(courte manche)* short sleeve **2** *Agr* handle *(of plough)*
Manchester [mɑ̃tʃɛstɛr] **NM** Manchester
manchette [mɑ̃ʃɛt] **NF** **1** *(rabat de manche → décoratif)* cuff; *(→ de protection)* oversleeve **2** *Presse* (front-page) headline; **la nouvelle a fait la m. de tous les journaux** the news made the headlines *or* the story was headline news in all the papers **3** *Typ (note)* side note **4** *Sport* forearm smash; *Escrime* slash on the sword wrist; *(au volley-ball)* dig **5** *Constr* **m. de garantie** watertight sleeve *or* collar
manchon [mɑ̃ʃɔ̃] **NM** **1** *(fourreau pour les mains)* muff; *(guêtre)* gaiter **2** *Tech (de protection)* sleeve, casing; *(pour axe, arbre)* sleeve; *(de palier)* bush(ing); *(pour pivot)* socket; **m. d'accouplement** coupling sleeve; *Aut & Tech* **m. d'embrayage** clutch; **m. à gaz** *ou* **à incandescence** incandescent mantle **3** *Culin* **manchons de canard** duck drumsticks **4** *Chasse* **faire m.** *(lièvre)* to cartwheel
manchot, -e [mɑ̃ʃo, -ɔt] **ADJ** *(d'un bras)* one-armed; *(d'une main)* one-handed; *(des deux bras)* armless, with no arms; *(des deux mains)* with no hands; *Fam* **il n'est pas m.** *(il est habile de ses mains)* he's clever with his hands; *(il est efficace)* he knows how to go about things; *(il peut le faire lui-même)* he's got hands, hasn't he?
NM,F *(d'un bras)* one-armed person; *(d'une main)* one-handed person; *(des deux bras)* armless person, person with no arms; *(des deux mains)* person with no hands
NM *Orn* penguin; **m. empereur** emperor penguin
manchou, -e [mɑ̃dʃu] = **mandchou**
mancie [mɑ̃si] **NF** divination, divining
mandala [mɑ̃dala] **NM** mandala
Mandalay [mɑ̃dalɛ] **NM** Mandalay
mandale [mɑ̃dal] **NF** *Fam* clout, slap■; **filer une m. à qn** to clout *or* slap sb; **tu veux une m.?** do you want a clip round the ear?
mandant, -e [mɑ̃dɑ̃, -ɑ̃t] **NM,F** **1** *Jur* principal **2** *Pol (gén)* voter; *(d'un député)* constituent
mandarin [mɑ̃darɛ̃] **NM** **1** *Hist* mandarin **2** *Fig Péj (personnage influent)* mandarin **3** *Orn* mandarin duck **4** *(langue)* Mandarin Chinese
mandarinal, -e, -aux, -ales [mɑ̃darinal, -o] **ADJ** mandarin *(avant n)*, mandarinic
mandarinat [mɑ̃darina] **NM** **1** *Hist* mandarinate **2** *Fig Péj (élite)* **le m. littéraire/politique** the literary/political establishment
mandarine [mɑ̃darin] **NF** **1** *(fruit)* mandarin (orange) **2** *TV & Cin (éclairage)* redhead
mandarinier [mɑ̃darinje] **NM** mandarin tree
mandat [mɑ̃da] **NM** **1** *Jur (procuration)* power of attorney, proxy; *(ordre)* warrant; **donner m. à qn (pour faire qch)** to give sb power of attorney (to do sth); **choisissez une personne à qui donner votre m.** choose a proxy; **m. d'action** receiving order (in bankruptcy); **m. d'amener** = warrant for a suspect or witness; **m. d'arrêt** (arrest) warrant; **un m. d'arrêt à l'encontre de...** a warrant for the arrest of...; **m. de comparution** summons *(singulier)*; **m. de contrôle** watching brief; **m. de dépôt** committal (order); **placer qn sous m. de dépôt** to commit sb; **m. d'expulsion** eviction order; **m. de justice** (police) warrant; **m. de perquisition** search warrant
2 *Pol (fonction)* mandate; *(durée)* term of office; **m. de député** member's (electoral) mandate; **m. politique** political mandate; **m. présidentiel** president's *or* presidential term of office; **l'homme à qui vous avez donné votre m.** the man you have elected; **tel est mon m.** that is what I was elected to do; **ces prérogatives n'entrent pas dans son m.** he/she does not have a mandate to exercise these prerogatives; **solliciter le renouvellement de son m.** to seek re-election; **elle a rempli son m.** *(gén)* she's done what she was asked to do; *Pol* she's fulfilled her mandate
3 *Fin* **m. (de paiement)** order to pay; **m. poste** *ou* **postal** *Br* postal order, *Am* money order; **m. international** *ou* **sur l'étranger** international money order; **m. télégraphique** telegraphic money order; **m. du Trésor** Treasury warrant; **m. de virement** transfer order
4 *(autorité)* mandate; **m. international** international mandate; **les pays sous m. (international)** mandated countries, mandates
mandataire [mɑ̃datɛr] **NMF** **1** *Jur* attorney, proxy; **constituer un m.** to appoint a proxy **2** *Pol* representative **3** *Com* authorized agent; **m. général** general agent; **m. aux Halles** sales agent *(at a wholesale market)*
NM *Ordinat* proxy
mandataire-liquidateur [mɑ̃datɛrlikidatœr] *(pl* **mandataires-liquidateurs***)* **NM** official receiver
mandat-carte [mɑ̃dakart] *(pl* **mandats-cartes***)* **NM** *Br* postal order, *Am* money order
mandat-contributions [mɑ̃dakɔ̃tribysjɔ̃] *(pl* **mandats-contributions***)* **NM** *Br* postal order, *Am* money order *(for payment of income tax)*
mandatement [mɑ̃datmɑ̃] **NM** **1** *Jur* appointment, commissioning; **m. d'office** establishment of a commission **2** *Fin* order to pay
mandater [3] [mɑ̃date] **VT** **1** *(députer)* to appoint, to commission **2** *Pol* **m. qn** to elect sb, to give sb a mandate; **m. des délégués pour un congrès** to mandate delegates to a conference **3** *Fin* to pay by *Br* postal order *or Am* money order
mandat-lettre [mɑ̃dalɛtr] *(pl* **mandats-lettres***)* **NM** *Br* postal order, *Am* money order *(with space for a short message)*
mandature [mɑ̃datyr] **NF** term of office
mandchou, -e [mɑ̃dʃu] **ADJ** Manchu, Manchurian
NM *(langue)* Manchu
❑ **Mandchou, -e NM,F** Manchu; **les Mandchous** the Manchus *or* Manchu
Mandchourie [mɑ̃dʃuri] **NF** **la M.** Manchuria
mandé [mɑ̃de] **NM** *(langue)* Mande
mandéen, -enne [mɑ̃deɛ̃, -ɛn] **ADJ** Mandaean, Mandean
❑ **Mandéen, -enne NM,F** Mandaean, Mandean
mandéisme [mɑ̃deism] **NM** Mandaeism, Mandeism
mandement [mɑ̃dmɑ̃] **NM** **1** *Hist* command, mandate, order **2** *Rel* pastoral (letter)
mander [3] [mɑ̃de] **VT** *Vieilli & Littéraire* **1** *(faire venir)* to send for **2** *(ordonner)* **m. à qn de faire qch** to instruct sb to do sth **3** *(informer)* **m. une nouvelle à qn** to convey news to sb
mandibulaire [mɑ̃dibylɛr] **ADJ** *Anat & Zool* mandibular
mandibulate [mɑ̃dibylat] **NM** *Anat & Zool* mandibulate
mandibule [mɑ̃dibyl] **NF** *Anat & Zool* mandible
❑ **mandibules NFPL** *Fam* **jouer des mandibules** to munch away
mandingue [mɑ̃dɛ̃g] **ADJ** Mandingo
NMF Mandingo
NM *Ling* Mandingo
mandoline [mɑ̃dɔlin] **NF** **1** *Mus* mandolin, mandoline **2** *(hachoir)* (vegetable) slicer, mandolin, mandoline
mandoliniste [mɑ̃dɔlinist] **NMF** mandolin player, mandolinist
mandore [mɑ̃dɔr] **NF** *Mus* mandola, mandora
mandorle [mɑ̃dɔrl] **NF** *Beaux-Arts* mandorla
mandragore [mɑ̃dragɔr] **NF** mandrake, mandragora
mandrill [mɑ̃dril] **NM** *Zool* mandrill (ape)
mandrin [mɑ̃drɛ̃] **NM** **1** *(pour soutenir → sur un tour)* mandril, mandrel; *(→ sur une machine-outil)* chuck; **m. à griffes/mâchoires** claw/jaw chuck **2** *(pour percer)* punch; *(pour agrandir des trous)* drift **3** *(en papeterie)* mandrel, core
mandrinage [mɑ̃drinaʒ] **NM** **1** *(sur un tour)* chucking **2** *(de trous)* drifting
mandriner [3] [mɑ̃drine] **VT** **1** *(sur un tour)* to chuck **2** *(trous)* to drift
manducation [mɑ̃dykasjɔ̃] **NF** mastication
manécanterie [manekɑ̃tri] **NF** *Vieilli* parish choir school
manège [manɛʒ] **NM** **1** *Équitation (salle)* manege; *(école)* riding school, manege; *(exercices)* riding exercises, manege work; **faire du m.** to do riding exercises *or* manege work; **heures de m.** = hours spent riding in a manege
2 *(attraction)* **m. (de chevaux de bois)** merry-go-round, roundabout; **la foire a installé ses manèges** the funfair has set up its attractions *or* machines *or* shows
3 *Fig (manigances)* (little) game; **tu copies sur ton frère, j'ai bien vu ton (petit) m.** you've been cribbing from your brother's work, I've seen what you're up to *or* I'm on to your little game; **j'observai quelques instants ce m.** I watched these goings-on for a few minutes; **je ne comprenais rien à leur m.** I couldn't figure out what they were up to
4 *(en danse)* manège

man–man

5 *Agr* **m. de traite** rotary milking platform *or* parlour, rotolactor
6 *(piste de cirque)* ring

'Le Manège enchanté' 'The Magic Roundabout'

mânes [man] **NMPL 1** *Antiq* manes **2** *Littéraire* spirits; **les m. de nos ancêtres** the spirits of our ancestors
maneton [mantɔ̃] **NM** crankpin
manette [manɛt] **NF** (hand) lever, (operating) handle; *Aviat* **m. des gaz** throttle (control *or* lever); **m. de jeux** joystick; *Fam* **à fond les manettes** at full speed ■, *Br* like the clappers, *Am* like sixty
manga [mɑ̃ga] **NM** manga
manganate [mɑ̃ganat] **NM** *Chim* manganate
manganèse [mɑ̃ganɛz] **NM** *Chim* manganese
manganeux [mɑ̃ganø] **ADJ M** *Chim* manganous
Manganine® [mɑ̃ganin] **NF** *Métal* Manganin®
manganique [mɑ̃ganik] **ADJ** *Chim* manganic
manganite [mɑ̃ganit] *Chim* **NM** manganite (salt)
NF manganite (hydroxide)
mangeable [mɑ̃ʒabl] **ADJ 1** *(comestible)* edible **2** *(médiocre)* (just about) edible *or* eatable; **c'est bon? – c'est m.** is it good? – it's edible
mangeaille [mɑ̃ʒaj] **NF 1** *Vieilli (pâtée d'animaux → gén)* feed; *(→ pour cochons)* (pig) swill **2** *Péj (nourriture)* food; **la vue de toute cette m. me soulevait le cœur** the sight of that mound of awful food made me feel sick
mange-disque [mɑ̃ʒdisk] *(pl* **mange-disques***)* **NM** slotfed record player
mange-mil [mɑ̃ʒmil] **NM INV** *Orn* red-tailed quelea
mangeoire [mɑ̃ʒwar] **NF** *(pour le bétail)* trough, manger; *(pour les animaux de basse-cour)* trough; *(pour des oiseaux en cage)* feeding dish
mangeotter [3] [mɑ̃ʒɔte] *Fam* **VI** to nibble *or* to pick *or* to peck (at one's food), to play with one's food
VT to pick *or* to nibble at
manger[1] [mɑ̃ʒe] **NM** food, meal; **je ne pourrai pas rentrer avant m.** I won't be able to get back before lunch/dinner/*etc*; **à prendre après m.** *(sur étiquette)* to be taken after meals; **je suis en train de lui faire son m.** I'm getting his/her food ready (for him/her); **on peut apporter son m.** customers *or* patrons are allowed to consume their own food on the premises
manger[2] [17] [mɑ̃ʒe] **VT 1** *(pour s'alimenter)* to eat; **m. un sandwich** to eat a sandwich; *(au lieu d'un repas)* to have a sandwich; **m. un morceau** to have a bite to eat; **m. du poisson** to eat fish; **je ne mange pas de poisson** I don't eat fish; **elle mange de tout** she'll eat anything, she's not a fussy eater; **elle a tout mangé** she's eaten it all up; **mange ta soupe** eat (up) *or* drink (up) your soup; **qu'est-ce qu'on mange?** what are we having to eat?, what's for lunch/dinner/*etc*?; **qu'est-ce que vous avez mangé aujourd'hui à la cantine, les enfants?** what did you have (to eat) for dinner at school today, children?; *Hum* **on en mangerait!** it looks good enough to eat!; **faire m. qch à qn** to give sb sth to eat; *Fam Fig* **on s'est fait m. par les moustiques** we were bitten to death *or* eaten alive by mosquitoes; *Fam* **m. de la vache enragée** to have a hard time of it; **il a mangé de la vache enragée dans les années 60** he had a lean *or* hard time of it in the 60s; *Fam* **il a mangé du lion aujourd'hui** he's full of beans today; *Can Fam* **m. des bêtises** *(se faire insulter)* to take abuse ■; *(se faire réprimander)* to get told off ■; *Can Fam* **m. de la misère** *(vivre misérablement)* to lead a hand-to-mouth existence ■, to live in dire poverty ■; *(avoir une vie difficile)* to have a hard time of it; **il ne mange pas de ce pain-là** he doesn't go in for that sort of thing, that's not his cup of tea; *Fam* **il peut me m. la soupe sur la tête** *(il est beaucoup plus grand)* he's a head taller than me ■; *(il est bien meilleur)* he's miles better than me; *Fam* **m. la laine sur le dos à qn** to sponge shamelessly off sb; *Fam* **m. les pissenlits par la racine** to be pushing up (the) daisies; **m. son pain blanc le premier** to have it easy for a while; **m. son pain noir le premier** to get the worst part over with first; *Fam* **m. du curé** to be violently anticlerical ■; **dis-moi ce que tu manges, je te dirai qui tu es** tell me what you eat and I'll tell you who you are, you are what you eat
2 *Fig* to eat; **elle le mangeait des yeux** *(personne)* she (just) couldn't take her eyes off him; *(objet)* she gazed longingly at it; **m. qn de baisers** to smother sb with kisses; **il est mignon, on le mangerait!** he's so cute I could eat him (all up)!; *Hum* **elle ne va pas te m.!** she's not going to eat *or* to bite you!
3 *(ronger)* **m. ses ongles** to bite one's nails; **des couvertures mangées aux mites** *ou* **par les mites** moth-eaten blankets; **une statue mangée par l'air marin** a statue eaten away by the sea air; **la rouille mange l'acier** rust eats into steel
4 *(prendre toute la place dans)* **le canapé mange tout le salon** the settee takes up *or* eats up all the space in the lounge; **tes cheveux te mangent la figure** your hair is hiding your face; **elle avait de grands yeux qui lui mangeaient le visage** her eyes seemed to take up her whole face; **une horrible cicatrice lui mangeait tout le front** his/her forehead had a horrible scar running across it
5 *(négliger)* **m. ses mots** *ou* **la moitié des mots** to swallow one's words, to mumble, to mutter; **m. la commission/la consigne** to forget the message/one's orders; *Belg* **m. sa parole** to break one's promise, to fail to keep one's word
6 *(dépenser)* to get through; **m. son capital** to eat up one's capital; **peu à peu, j'ai mangé mes économies** I gradually ran through my savings; **la chaudière mange un stère de bois tous les cinq jours** the boiler gets through *or* eats up *or* consumes a cubic metre of wood every five days; **l'imprimante mange du papier** the printer is heavy on paper; **m. son blé en herbe** to spend one's money even before one gets it; *Fam* **ça ne mange pas de pain** it doesn't cost anything; **on peut toujours essayer, ça ne mange pas de pain** we can always have a go, it won't cost us anything
VI 1 *(s'alimenter)* to eat; **m. dans une assiette** to eat off a plate; **il ne sait pas m. avec une fourchette/des baguettes** he doesn't know how to eat with a fork/with chopsticks; **apprends-lui à m. correctement à table** teach him/her some (proper) table manners; **il a bien mangé** *(en quantité ou en qualité)* he's eaten well; **nous avons bien mangé** we had a very good meal; **j'ai mal mangé** *(insuffisamment)* I didn't eat enough, I didn't have enough to eat; *(de la mauvaise qualité)* I didn't have a very good meal; **il faut m. léger** you should eat light meals; **m. à sa faim** to eat one's fill; **nous ne mangions pas tous les jours à notre faim** we didn't always have enough food *or* enough to eat; **le bébé/chat mange toutes les trois heures** the baby/cat has to be fed once every three hours; **faire m. qn** to feed sb; *Fam* **m. comme un cochon** to eat like a pig; *Fam* **m. comme quatre** *ou* **comme un ogre** *ou* **comme un chancre** to eat like a horse; **m. comme un moineau** *ou* **comme un oiseau** to eat like a sparrow; **m. à s'en faire péter la sous-ventrière** to eat till one is fit to burst; **m. du bout des dents** to pick at one's food; *Fig* **il lui mange dans (le creux de) la main** he eats out of his/her hand; **m. sur le pouce** to have a snack, to grab a bite to eat; *Péj* **il mange à tous les râteliers** he's got a finger in every pie; **ce journaliste politique mange à tous les râteliers** this political journalist jumps on every passing bandwagon; *Hum* **c'est tellement propre chez elle qu'on mangerait par terre** her house is so clean you could eat off the floor; **il faut m. pour vivre et non pas vivre pour m.** one must eat to live and not live to eat
2 *(participer à un repas)* to eat; **venez m.!** *(à table!)* come and get it!; **venez m. demain soir** come to dinner tomorrow evening; **vous mangerez bien avec nous?** won't you (have something to) eat with us?; **ils m'ont demandé de rester m.** they asked me to stay for a meal; **j'ai mangé avec eux** I had a meal *or* I ate with them; **inviter qn à m.** *(chez soi)* to ask sb round for a meal; *(au restaurant)* to ask sb out for a meal; *Fam* **on a eu les Michaud à m.** we had the Michauds round for a meal; **m. à la carte** to eat à la carte *or* from the à la carte menu; **m. dehors** *(en plein air)* to eat outside; *(ailleurs que chez soi)* to eat out, to go out for a meal; **m. au restaurant** to eat out; **m. chez soi** to eat in *or* at home; **c'est un restaurant simple mais on y mange bien** it's an unpretentious restaurant, but the food is good
3 *(comme locution nominale)* **je veux à m.** I want something to eat; **as-tu eu assez à m.?** have you had enough to eat?; **les pays qui n'ont pas assez à m.** the countries where people don't have enough food *or* enough to eat; **donner à m. à qn** to feed sb, to give sb something to eat; **donner à m. à un animal/bébé** to feed an animal/a baby; **faire à m. à qn** to make something to eat for sb; **que veux-tu que je fasse à m. ce soir?** what would you like me to make for dinner (tonight)?
▸**se manger VPR 1** *(emploi passif)* to be eaten; **ça se mange avec de la mayonnaise** you eat it *or* it is served with mayonnaise; **les huîtres se mangent crues** oysters are eaten raw; **cette partie ne se mange pas** you don't eat that part, that part shouldn't be eaten *or* isn't edible
2 *Fam (se disputer)* to have a set-to; **ils se mangent entre eux** they're at each other's throats, they're squabbling among themselves; **se m. le nez** to quarrel; **toujours à se m. le nez, ces deux-là!** these two are always at each other's throats!
3 *Fam* **se m. qch** *(percuter)* to go head-first into sth
mange-tout [mɑ̃ʒtu] **NM INV 1** *Bot (haricot) Br* runner bean, *Am* string bean; *(petit pois) Br* mangetout, sugar pea, *Am* snow pea **2** *Vieilli (gaspilleur)* squanderer, wastrel
mangeur, -euse [mɑ̃ʒœr, -øz] **NM,F** eater; **c'est un gros m.** he's a big eater, he eats a lot; **les Asiatiques sont de gros mangeurs de riz** people from Asia eat a lot of rice *or* are big rice-eaters; **mangeurs d'hommes** cannibals, man-eating savages; **tigre/requin m. d'hommes** man-eating tiger/shark; *Fam* **mangeuse d'hommes** man-eater; **attention, c'est une mangeuse d'hommes** watch out, she's a man-eater *or* she eats men for breakfast; *Can Fam* **m. de curés** *ou* **de soutanes** = violently anti-clerical person; *Can Fam Péj* **m./mangeuse de balustrades** Holy Joe, *f* Mary

'Les Mangeurs de pomme de terre' *Van Gogh* 'The Potato Eaters'

mangeure [mɑ̃ʒyr] **NF** *Vieilli* eaten part; *Chasse* **faire ses mangeures** *(sanglier)* to feed
mangeuse [mɑ̃ʒøz] *voir* **mangeur**
mangle [mɑ̃gl] **NF** mangrove fruit
manglier [mɑ̃glije] **NM** mangrove (tree)
mangonneau, -x [mɑ̃gɔno] **NM** *Hist* mangonel
mangoustan [mɑ̃gustɑ̃] **NM** mangosteen (fruit)
mangoustanier [mɑ̃gustanje] **NM** mangosteen (tree)
mangouste [mɑ̃gust] **NF 1** *Zool* mongoose; **m. ichneumon** Egyptian mongoose **2** *(fruit)* mangosteen
mangrove [mɑ̃grɔv] **NF** mangrove swamp
mangue [mɑ̃g] **NM** *Zool* mangue
NF *Bot* mango
manguier [mɑ̃gje] **NM** mango (tree)
maniabilité [manjabilite] **NF 1** *(d'un outil)* manageability, practicability; *(d'une voiture)* handling ability, manoeuvrability; *(d'un avion)* manoeuvrability; *(d'un logiciel)* user-friendliness; **une caméra d'une grande m.** a camera which is very easy to handle; **critiqué par les consommateurs pour son manque de m.** criticized by consumers for its unwieldiness
2 *(plasticité → de l'argile)* plasticity; *(→ du béton)* workability
maniable [manjabl] **ADJ 1** *(facile à utiliser → outil)* handy, easy to use, easy to handle; *(facile à travailler → cuir)* easy to work
2 *(manœuvrable → voiture)* easy to drive; *(→ avion)* easy to control, easy to manoeuvre; *(→ tondeuse)* easy to handle, easy to manoeuvre
3 *Naut* **temps m.** fine weather; **vent m.** moderate wind
4 *(docile)* tractable, malleable
5 *(matière plastique)* plastic; *(béton)* workable; **l'argile est une matière m.** clay is an easily moulded material
maniaco-dépressif, -ive [manjakɔdeprɛsif, -iv]

(*mpl* **maniaco-dépressifs**, *fpl* **maniaco-dépressives**) ADJ manic-depressive; **psychose maniaco-dépressive** manic depression
NM,F manic-depressive

maniaque [manjak] ADJ **1** *(obsessionnel)* fussy, fastidious; **il range ses livres avec un soin m.** he's obsessively *or* fanatically tidy about his books
2 *(exigeant)* fussy; **elle est si m. pour les chaussures qu'elle les fait faire sur mesure** she's so particular *or* fussy when it comes to shoes that she has them made to measure
3 *Psy* manic; **état m.** mania
NMF **1** *(personne → trop difficile)* fussy person; *(→ qui a une idée fixe)* fanatic; **c'est un m. de l'hygiène/de l'ordre** he's fanatical about *or* obsessed with hygiene/tidiness; **mon médecin est un m. des antibiotiques** my doctor prescribes antibiotics for everything; **enfin, un logiciel pour les maniaques de l'orthographe/des mots croisés!** at last, a software package for spelling/crossword buffs!
2 *(dément)* maniac; **m. sexuel** sexual pervert, sex maniac

maniaquerie [manjakri] NF fussiness; **son exactitude frôle la m.** there's something almost obsessive about his/her punctuality

manichéen, -enne [manikeɛ̃, -ɛn] ADJ **1** *Rel* Manichean **2** *Fig* **il est très m.** he sees everything in very black-and-white terms
NM,F Manichean

manichéisme [manikeism] NM **1** *Rel* Manicheism **2** *Fig* rigid *or* uncompromising approach to things; **faire du m.** to see things in black and white

manichordion [manikɔrdjɔ̃] NM *Mus* manichord, manichordion

manicle [manikl] NF *(pour la cuisine)* oven glove; *Tech* protective glove

manicorde [manikɔrd] NM *Mus* manichord, manichordion

manie [mani] NF **1** *(habitude)* odd habit; *(idée fixe)* obsession, quirk; **avoir la m. de la propreté** to be obsessively clean *or* a stickler for cleanliness; **il a la m. de fermer toutes les portes** he has a habit of always closing doors; **chacun a ses petites manies** everyone has their own peculiar ways *or* little quirks; **il a des manies de vieille fille** he's a real old woman; **c'est une m. chez elle de dire du mal des autres** it's become a habit with her to run other people down; **c'est une m., chez toi!** it's an obsession with you!; **c'est ta nouvelle m., de fumer la pipe?** is that your latest fad *or* craze, smoking a pipe?; **ça tourne à la m.** it's getting to be a fixation *or* an obsession
2 *Psy* mania

maniement [manimɑ̃] NM **1** *(manipulation)* handling, operating; **nous cherchons à simplifier le m. de nos appareils** we're trying to make our equipment easier to handle *or* to operate; **montre-lui le m. de la télécommande** show him/her how to use *or* to work the remote control; *Fig* **le m. de la langue lui a toujours paru facile** he's/she's always found it easy to speak the language *or* had an easy command of the language; **quand vous aurez compris le m. des concepts, nous passerons à la pratique** when you've grasped the ideas, we'll start putting them into practice; *Fig* **rompu au m. des affaires/des foules** used to handling business/manipulating crowds; **à l'armée ils sont initiés au m. des armes** in the army they learn how to use a gun; *Mil* **m. d'armes** (arms) drill
2 *(des animaux de boucherie)* points (in fatstock)

manier [9] [manje] VT **1** *(manipuler → objet, somme)* to handle; **vers dix mois, il commencera à vouloir m. les objets** at ten months, he'll want to start handling *or* manipulating objects; **je n'aime pas la façon dont tu manies ce couteau** I don't like the way you're wielding *or* using that knife; **facile/difficile à m.** easy/difficult to handle; **la charrue est moins facile à m. que tu ne le crois** the plough isn't as easy to handle as you think; **m. qch avec délicatesse** to handle sth gently; **m. de grosses sommes** to handle large sums (of money); **elle manie des valeurs en tous genres** she deals with *or* handles all types of securities
2 *(diriger, contrôler → hommes, cheval)* to handle, to manage; *(→ avion)* to control, to manoeuvre; **m. les avirons** to ply *or* pull the oars
3 *(utiliser)* to use, to operate; **avez-vous déjà manié un télescope/micro?** have you ever used a telescope/microphone?; **une imprimante portative très facile à m.** an easy-to-use portable printer; **elle sait m. la caméra** she's good with a cine camera; **il savait m. la plume** he was a fine writer; **il sait m. l'ironie** he knows how *or* when to use irony; **quelle maîtrise dans l'art de m. le sarcasme!** what a masterful use of sarcasm!
4 *(modeler → pâte)* to knead; *(→ argile)* to handle, to fashion
5 *Arch (tissu)* to feel
►**se manier** VPR *Fam* to get a move on, to get one's skates on

maniéré, -e [manjere] ADJ **1** *(personne)* affected; **elle est tellement maniérée dans sa façon de parler!** she has such an affected way of speaking! **2** *Beaux-Arts & Littérature (style)* mannered

manière [manjɛr] NF **1** *(façon, méthode)* way, manner; **d'une m. ridicule** in a ridiculous manner, ridiculously; **d'une m. bizarre** in a strange manner, strangely; **d'une m. assez particulière** in a rather unusual way *or* manner; **de m. habile** skilfully; **il y a différentes manières d'accommoder le riz** there are many ways of preparing rice; **quelle est la meilleure m. d'aborder le sujet?** what's the best way of approaching the subject?; **nous ne faisons pas les choses de la même m.** we don't do things (in) the same way; **sa m. de s'habiller, la m. dont elle s'habille** the way she dresses, her way of dressing; **la m. qu'elle a de regarder les gens par en dessous** the furtive way she has of looking at people; **de quelque m. qu'on s'y prenne, on obtient toujours le même résultat** however you go about it you always get the same result; **user de** *ou* **employer la m. forte** to use strong-arm tactics; **m. de voir** *ou* **de penser** way of looking at things; **c'est une m. de parler** it's just a manner of speaking; **il y a m. et m.** there are ways and ways; **il fallait bien que je lui dise la vérité – oui mais il y a m. et m.** I had to tell him/her the truth – yes, but there are ways and ways (of doing it)
2 *Gram* manner; **adjectif/adverbe de m.** adjective/adverb of manner
3 *(savoir-faire)* **je comprends qu'il t'ait critiqué, mais il y a la m.** I can understand him criticizing you, but there are ways of doing these things; **il faut avoir la m.** you've got to have the knack; **refusez, mais mettez-y la m.** say no, but do it with tact; **les histoires qu'il raconte ne sont pas très drôles, mais il a la m.** the stories he tells aren't particularly funny, but it's the way he tells them; *Fam* **avec les gosses, il a la m.** he's got a way *or* he's good with kids
4 *(style)* way, style; **elle ne se plaindra pas, ce n'est pas dans sa m.** she won't complain, it's not her way *or* style; **c'est ma m. d'être** that's the way I am; **sa m. de marcher/s'habiller** his/her way of walking/dressing, the way he/she walks/dresses; **il a une drôle de m. de recevoir les gens** he has a funny way of welcoming people
5 *Beaux-Arts & Cin* manner, style; **un tableau dans la m. de Watteau** a painting in the manner *or* style of Watteau; **un Truffaut première/dernière m.** an early/late Truffaut; *Beaux-Arts* **m. noire** mezzotint
6 une m. de *(une sorte de)* a *or* some sort of, a *or* some kind of; **derrière la maison, il y a une m. de pergola** there is a kind of pergola behind the house; **c'est une m. de poème épique** it's a sort of (an) epic *or* an epic of sorts; **le silence est parfois une m. de mensonge** silence is sometimes a way of lying
❑ **manières** NFPL *(façons de se comporter)* manners; **belles manières** social graces; **bonnes manières** (good) manners; **je vais t'apprendre les bonnes manières, moi!** I'll teach you to be polite *or* to behave yourself!; **mauvaises manières** bad manners; *Péj* **qu'est-ce que c'est que ces** *ou* **en voilà des manières!** what a way to behave!; **faire des manières** *(être poseur)* to put on airs and graces; *(se faire prier)* to stand on ceremony, to make a fuss; *Péj* **cesse de faire des manières et prends un chocolat** stop pussyfooting around and have a chocolate; **sans manières** without (a) fuss; **elle a pris l'argent sans (faire de) manières** she took the money without any fuss, she made no bones about taking the money; **venez dîner ce soir, mais vous savez, ce sera sans manières** come and have dinner tonight, but you know, it'll only be a simple meal
❑ **à la manière** ADV **à la m. paysanne** in the peasant way *or* manner
❑ **à la manière de** PRÉP **1** *(dans le style de)* in the manner *or* style of; **un tableau à la m. de Degas** a painting after (the manner of) Degas; **une chanson à la m. de Cole Porter** a song à la Cole Porter; **une profonde révérence à la m. d'un acteur** a deep bow like an actor's; **sauce tomate à la m. de tante Flo** tomato sauce like Auntie Flo used to make it
2 *(comme nom) Beaux-Arts & Littérature* **un à la m. de** a pastiche
❑ **à ma/sa/*etc* manière** ADV in my/his/her/*etc* (own) way; **elle dit qu'elle l'aime à sa m.** she says she loves him/her in her own way; **laissez-moi faire à ma m.** let me do it my (own) way
❑ **de cette manière** ADV (in) this *or* that way; **je conserve tous les reçus, de cette m. je sais combien j'ai dépensé** I keep all the receipts, that way I know how much I've spent
❑ **de la belle manière, de la bonne manière** ADV *Ironique* properly, well and truly; **il s'est fait expulser de la bonne m.!** he was thrown out good and proper!
❑ **de la manière que** CONJ as; **tout s'est passé de la m. que l'on avait prévu** everything turned out as planned
❑ **de la même manière** ADV in the same way
❑ **de manière à** CONJ so as to, so that, in order to; **j'ai écrit aux parents de m. à les rassurer** I wrote to father and mother in order to reassure them
❑ **de manière (à ce) que** CONJ *(pour que)* so (that); **laisse la porte ouverte, de m. que les gens puissent entrer** leave the door open so people can come in
❑ **de manière générale** ADV **1** *(globalement)* on the whole; **de m. générale, il réussit plutôt bien** he does quite well on the whole
2 *(le plus souvent)* generally, as a general rule; **de m. générale, je ne bois pas de vin** as a general rule, I don't drink wine
❑ **de manière que** CONJ *(ce qui fait que)* in such a way that; **tu dis cela de m. que tu déplais à tout le monde** the way you say that upsets everybody
❑ **de telle manière que** CONJ in such a way that; **rabattez le pan A de telle m. qu'il se pose sur la figure B** fold over flap A so that it rests on figure B
❑ **de toute manière, de toutes les manières** ADV anyway, in any case *or* event, at any rate; **de toute m., tu as tort** in any case, you're wrong; **de toutes les manières, la promenade lui aura fait du bien** at any rate *or* anyway, the walk will have done him/her good
❑ **d'une certaine manière** ADV in a way; **j'étais d'une certaine m. prisonnière** I was what you might call a prisoner; **d'une certaine m., je suis content que ce soit fini** in a way, I'm glad it's over
❑ **d'une manière générale** = **de manière générale**
❑ **d'une manière ou d'une autre** ADV somehow (or other), one way or another; **d'une m. ou d'une autre il devra accepter** he's going to have to agree one way or another; **avertie ou pas, d'une m. ou d'une autre elle va s'inquiéter** whether she's told about it or not she's going to worry
❑ **en aucune manière** ADV in no way, on no account, under no circumstances; **est-ce de sa faute? – en aucune m.** is it his/her fault? – no, not in the slightest *or* least; **avez-vous eu connaissance des documents? – en aucune m.** did you get to see the documents? – no, not at all *or* no, I didn't at all
❑ **en manière de** PRÉP by way of; **elle n'était pas mon genre, se dit-il en m. de consolation** she wasn't my type, he told himself by way of consolation; **une boîte en carton en m. d'abri** a cardboard box by way of a shelter

man-man

❏ **en quelque manière** ADV in a way, as it were; **elle était en quelque m. ma fille** she was like a daughter to me
❏ **par manière de = en manière de**
maniérer [8] [manjere] VT *Beaux-Arts & Littérature* **m. son style** to introduce mannerisms into one's style
maniérisme [manjerism] NM **1** *(comportement)* affectation, *Sout* mannerism **2** *Beaux-Arts & Littérature* mannerism, Mannerism
maniériste [manjerist] ADJ mannerist, Mannerist
NMF mannerist, Mannerist
manieur, -euse [manjœr, -øz] NM,F **m. d'argent** businessman; **manieuse d'argent** businesswoman; **c'est un m. d'hommes** he's a leader of men *or* a born leader
manif [manif] NF *Fam (abrév* **manifestation***)* demo; **une m. lycéenne/étudiante** a student demo
manifestant, -e [manifɛstɑ̃, -ɑ̃t] NM,F demonstrator
manifestation [manifɛstasjɔ̃] NF **1** *Pol* demonstration; **une m. contre le nucléaire** an anti-nuclear demonstration; **participer** *ou* **prendre part à une m.** to take part in a demonstration
2 *(marque)* expression; **des manifestations de joie** expressions of joy; **il n'y a eu aucune m. de mécontentement** nobody expressed any dissatisfaction; **sa pièce est la m. d'un grand trouble intérieur** his/her play is the expression of *or* expresses a deep-seated malaise
3 *(événement)* event; **m. artistique/culturelle/sportive** artistic/cultural/sporting event; **parmi les manifestations musicales de l'été** among the summer's music events *or* musical attractions
4 *Méd* sign, symptom; **les manifestations précoces de la maladie** early symptoms of the disease
5 *Rel* revelation
manifeste[1] [manifɛst] ADJ *(évident)* obvious, evident, *Sout* manifest; **n'est-ce pas une preuve m. de son innocence?** isn't it clear proof of his/her innocence?; **tel était son désir, rendu m. dans son testament** such was his/her wish, as manifested in his/her will; **il est m. que ses études ne l'intéressent pas** it's obvious that he/she isn't interested in his/her studies; **il est d'une incompétence m.** he is obviously *or* manifestly incompetent; **une erreur m.** an obvious error
manifeste[2] [manifɛst] NM **1** *Littérature & Pol* manifesto **2** *Aviat* manifest; *Naut* (ship's) manifest; **m. de douane** customs manifest; **m. d'entrée** inward manifest; **m. de fret** freight manifest; **m. de sortie** outward manifest

'Le Manifeste du parti communiste' *Marx & Engels* 'The Communist Manifesto'

manifestement [manifɛstəmɑ̃] ADV evidently, obviously, plainly; **il n'a m. pas envie de venir avec nous** he clearly *or* plainly doesn't feel like coming with us; **m., elle nous a menti** she has plainly been lying to us
manifester [3] [manifɛste] VT **1** *(exprimer)* to express, to show; **m. son étonnement** to express one's surprise; **m. son mécontentement à qn** to indicate *or* to express one's dissatisfaction to sb; **je lui manifeste mon amour tous les jours** I show my love for him/her every day; **écrivez-leur pour leur m. notre sympathie** write to them to express our sympathy; **m. sa volonté** to make one's wishes clear; **nous vous avons toujours manifesté notre volonté de vous aider** we have always indicated *or* expressed our desire to help you; **m. son soutien à qn** to assure sb of one's support; **m. un désir** to express *or* to indicate a wish; **a-t-elle manifesté le désir d'être enterrée près de son mari?** was it her wish that she should be buried near her husband?
2 *(révéler)* to show, to demonstrate; **rien ne manifestait son désespoir intérieur** nothing indicated his/her inner despair; **sans m. la moindre irritation/admiration** without the slightest show of anger/admiration
VI to demonstrate; **m. contre qch** to demonstrate against sth
▸**se manifester** VPR **1** *(personne)* to come forward; *Rel* to become manifest; **aucun témoin ne s'est manifesté** no witnesses came forward;

que le gagnant se manifeste, s'il vous plaît! would the (lucky) winner step forward *or* come forward please!; **bon élève, mais devrait se m. plus/moins souvent en classe** good student, but should contribute more/be quieter in class; **le livreur ne s'est pas manifesté** the delivery man didn't show (up) *or* turn up; **ça fait très longtemps qu'il ne s'est pas manifesté** he hasn't been in touch for ages, I/we/*etc* haven't heard from him for ages; **je n'ai pas osé me m.** I didn't dare (to) show myself
2 *(sentiment)* to show (**par** in); *(phénomène)* to appear (**par** in); **sa joie de vivre se manifeste dans toutes ses toiles** his/her joie de vivre is expressed *or* expresses itself in every one of his/her paintings; **de petites plaques rouges se manifestent vers le troisième jour** small red spots come up *or* appear around the third day
manifold [manifɔld] NM **1** *(carnet)* duplicate book **2** *Tech* manifold
manigance [manigɑ̃s] NF *(souvent au pl)* scheme, trick; **manigances** scheming (UNCOUNT), schemes; **à cause des manigances internes au conseil d'administration** on account of internal machinations at board level; **victime de toutes sortes de manigances** victim of all kinds of scheming
manigancer [16] [manigɑ̃se] VT to scheme, to plot; **m. une évasion** to plot *or* to engineer an escape; **l'affaire a été manigancée pour déshonorer le ministre** the whole affair was set up to discredit the minister; **qu'est-ce qu'ils manigancent?** what's their (little) game?, what are they up to?; **je me demande ce que les enfants sont en train de m.** I wonder what the children are up to; **toujours en train de m. quelque chose** always up to some little game; **je ne sais pas ce que je vais pouvoir m. pour ne pas le rencontrer** I don't know what I'll be able to come up with to avoid meeting him
maniganceur, -euse [manigɑ̃sœr, -øz] *Can Fam* ADJ scheming ▪
NM,F schemer ▪
maniguette [manigɛt] NF *Bot* malaguetta pepper, grains of Paradise
Manille [manij] NM Manila
manille[1] [manij] NM **1** *(cigare)* Manila (cigar) **2** *(chapeau)* Manila hat
manille[2] [manij] NF *Tech* shackle, clevis; *Naut* shackle; **m. d'assemblage** connecting shackle; **m. lyre** harp shackle; **m. à vis** screw shackle
manille[3] [manij] NF *(jeu)* manille (French card game); *(carte)* ten
manillon [manijɔ̃] NM *Cartes* ace
manioc [manjɔk] NM manioc, cassava; **farine de m.** cassava
manip, manipe [manip] NF *Fam* **1** *(coup monté)* frame-up **2** *Scol* practical ▪, experiment ▪ **3** *(manipulation)* manipulation ▪
manipulable [manipylabl] ADJ manipulable, manipulatable
manipulateur, -trice [manipylatœr, -tris] NM,F **1** *(opérateur)* technician; *(de machine)* operator; *(d'argent, de biens)* handler; **m. de laboratoire** laboratory technician; **m. radio(graphe)** X-ray technician *or* assistant
2 *Péj* manipulator; **le comité est la proie de manipulateurs** the committee has fallen prey to a group of manipulators
3 *(prestidigitateur)* conjurer, conjuror
NM **1** *Tech* **m. à distance** remote-control manipulator
2 *Tél* sending *or* signalling key; **m. automatique** automatic key
manipulation [manipylasjɔ̃] NF **1** *(maniement)* handling; **montre-lui la m. de la télécommande** show him/her how to use *or* to work the remote control; *Fig* **s'exercer à la m. des concepts mathématiques** to learn to handle *or* to manipulate mathematical concepts
2 *Scol & (en sciences)* experiment, piece of practical work; **cahier de manipulations** experiments notebook; **m. génétique, manipulations génétiques** genetic engineering (UNCOUNT)
3 *Méd* manipulation; **m. vertébrale** (vertebral) manipulation; **un ostéopathe m'a fait des manipulations** an osteopath manipulated my spine
4 *(en prestidigitation)* conjuring trick

5 *Péj (intervention)* interference, manipulation; **manipulations électorales** *(coup monté)* vote rigging; **le nouvel organisme risque d'être victime des pires manipulations** the new organization risks falling victim to the worst kinds of manipulation; **nous craignons la m. des statistiques de l'emploi** we are afraid the employment figures might be interfered with *or* massaged; **à travers son journal, il orchestre la m. de l'opinion publique** he manipulates public opinion through his newspaper
6 *Ordinat* manipulation; **m. de colonnes** column handling; **m. de documents** document handling; **m. de données** data manipulation
7 *Fin* **m. monétaire** currency manipulation
manipulatrice [manipylatris] *voir* **manipulateur**
manipule [manipyl] NM *Antiq & Rel* maniple
manipuler [3] [manipyle] VT **1** *(manier → objet, somme)* to handle; *(→ outil compliqué)* to manipulate; **vers dix mois, il commencera à vouloir m. les objets** at about ten months, he'll want to start handling *or* manipulating objects; **habitué à m. les produits toxiques** used to handling *or* manipulating toxic substances; **m. de grosses sommes** to handle large sums of money
2 *Péj (influencer → personne, électeurs)* to manipulate; *(→ scrutin)* to rig; *(→ statistiques)* to massage; *(→ comptes)* to fiddle; **l'opinion publique est plus difficile à m. qu'ils ne le croient** public opinion is not as easily swayed *or* manipulated as they think; **il a prétendu que la police l'avait manipulé** he claimed that the police had manipulated him; **elle s'est fait complètement m. par ce type** she allowed the guy to twist her around his little finger
3 *Ordinat* to manipulate
manique [manik] NF *(pour la cuisine)* oven glove; *Tech* protective glove
Manitoba [manitɔba] NM **le M.** Manitoba
manitou [manitu] NM **1** *(chez les Algonquins)* manitu, manitou **2** *Fam Fig* **(grand) m.** big shot *or* chief; **les grands manitous du pétrole** oil magnates ▪ *or* tycoons ▪; **c'est un grand m. de la finance** he's a big shot in finance
manivelle [manivɛl] NF **1** *Tech* crank; *(pour un moteur)* crank (handle); *Aut* starting handle; *(de lève-glace)* window winder; **j'ai dû donner plusieurs tours de m.** I had to turn the handle a few times; **démarrer à la m.** to crank (up) the engine; **bras/course de m.** crank arm/throw; **m. de mise en marche** starting handle
2 *(de pédalier)* pedal crank
3 *Cin (sur les anciennes caméras)* winding handle; *Fig* **dès le premier tour de m.** as soon as shooting started
manne[1] [man] NF **1** *Bible* manna **2** *Fig (aubaine)* godsend, manna; **comme la m. céleste** like manna from heaven **3** *Can Entom* mayfly, dayfly **4** *(éphémères)* **m. des poissons** *ou* **des pêcheurs** mayfly swarms **5** *Bot* manna
manne[2] [man] NF *(panier)* (large) wicker basket; **m. d'enfant** wicker cradle, Moses basket
mannequin[1] [manke̍] NM

Note that it is no longer considered a mistake to feminize this word in sense 1 and to say **une mannequin** but some French speakers nonetheless regard this form as unacceptable, especially in France. See also the entry **féminisation**.

1 *(personne)* model; **m. de charme** glamour model; **m. homme** male model; **elle est m. chez Zoot** she works as a model for Zoot **2** *(de vitrine)* dummy, mannequin; *(de couture)* dummy **3** *Fig Péj (fantoche)* puppet **4** *Beaux-Arts* lay figure

mannequin[2] [manke̍] NM *(panier)* small (two-handled) basket
mannequinat [mankina] NM modelling
mannite [manit] NF *Chim* mannite, mannitol, manna-sugar
mannitol [manitɔl] NM = **mannite**
mannose [manoz] NM *Chim* mannose
manodétendeur [manɔdetɑ̃dœr] NM *Tech* (pressure) reducing valve
manœuvrabilité [manœvrabilite] NF manoeuvrability; **à sa sortie, le véhicule a été acclamé pour sa m.** when it was launched, the vehicle was praised for its easy handling

manœuvrable [manœvrabl] **ADJ** *(maniable)* easy to handle, manoeuvrable; **cette voiture est peu m.** the car is not at all easy to manoeuvre *or* handle

manœuvre[1] [manœvr] **NF 1** *(maniement)* operation, handling; **du sol, elle surveillait la m. de la grue** from the ground, she was checking the handling of the crane *or* how the crane was being operated; **apprendre la m. d'un fusil/d'un télescope** to learn how to handle a rifle/to operate a telescope

2 *(en voiture)* manoeuvre; **m. de stationnement** parking manoeuvre; **faire une m.** to (do a) manoeuvre; **faire une fausse m.** to manoeuvre badly; **j'ai manqué ma m. en essayant de me garer** I messed up my manoeuvre when I was parking

3 *aussi Fig (opération)* **fausse m.** wrong move; *Fig* **faire une fausse m.** to get it wrong; **une fausse m. au clavier et tu risques d'effacer ton document** one simple keying error is enough to erase your document; **la motion a été rejetée après une fausse m. du comité** the motion was thrown out as a result of a wrong move on the part of the committee

4 *Mil (instruction)* drill; *(simulation)* exercise; *(mouvement)* movement; *Vieilli* **les manœuvres, les grandes manœuvres** (army) manoeuvres; **être en manœuvres** *(à petite échelle)* to be on exercise; *(à grande échelle)* to be on manoeuvres; **m. d'encerclement** encircling movement; **m. de repli** (movement of) withdrawal

5 *Naut (action)* manoeuvre; **le bateau a commencé sa m. d'accostage** the ship has started docking

6 *Naut (cordage)* rope; **manœuvres dormantes** standing rigging; **manœuvres courantes** running rigging; **fausses manœuvres** preventer rigging *or* stays

7 *Fig* **laisser à qn une grande liberté de m.** to give sb freedom of action; **vous avez toute liberté de m.** you have a completely free hand, you have complete freedom of action

8 *Fig Péj (machination)* manoeuvre; **manœuvres** scheming *(UNCOUNT)*, manoeuvring *(UNCOUNT)*; **pris de court par les manœuvres de débordement de l'opposition** stopped short by the opposition's outflanking tactics; **la principale victime de ces manœuvres, c'est la démocratie** democracy is the first victim of this political manoeuvring; *Bourse* **manœuvres boursières** stock market manipulation; **manœuvres électorales** electioneering; *Jur* **manœuvres frauduleuses** embezzling

9 *Méd* manipulation; **une m. obstétricale a été réalisée** the baby had to be turned

10 *Astron* manoeuvre

11 *Rail Br* shunting, *Am* switching; **voie de m.** *Br* shunting *or Am* switching track

manœuvre[2] [manœvr] **NM** *(ouvrier)* unskilled worker; *Constr & (en travaux publics)* labourer; **m. agricole** farm labourer *or* hand; **m. qualifié** skilled worker; **m. saisonnier** seasonal worker; **m. spécialisé** skilled worker; **travail de m.** unskilled work

manœuvrer [5] [manœvre] **VT 1** *(faire fonctionner)* to work, to operate; **il ne sait pas m. la machine à café** he doesn't know how to work the coffee machine; **le monte-charge est manœuvré à la main** the hoist is hand-operated

2 *(faire avancer et reculer → véhicule)* to manoeuvre; *Rail (→ wagons à plate-forme)* to shunt, to marshal; **il manœuvre des bateaux dans le port de Cherbourg depuis 20 ans** he's been manoeuvring ships in and out of Cherbourg docks for 20 years

3 *(influencer)* to manipulate; **j'ai été manœuvré!** I've been manipulated!

4 *Pêche* to pull in

USAGE ABSOLU ne manœuvrez jamais sur une route à grande circulation don't manoeuvre *or* do any manoeuvring on a busy road; **il se laisse m. par sa femme** he lets himself be manipulated *or* manoeuvred by his wife

VI 1 *(agir)* to manoeuvre; *Fig* to manoeuvre, to scheme; *Péj* **ils manœuvrent tous pour devenir chef du parti** they're all jockeying for the position of party leader; **bien manœuvré!** clever *or* good move!; **m. dans l'ombre** to work behind the scenes

2 *Mil (s'exercer)* to drill; *(simuler)* to be on manoeuvres; **faites-les m. dans la cour** drill them in the yard; **ils sont partis m. sur la lande** they're off to the moors on manoeuvres; **à l'époque où le contingent manœuvre** at the time (of the year) when the troops are on manoeuvres

manœuvrier, -ère [manœvrije, -ɛr] **ADJ** *(tactique)* skilful

NM,F *(tacticien)* tactician; *(manipulateur)* manoeuvrer; **un fin m. de la politique** a clever political manoeuvrer

NM *Naut* able *or* expert seaman

manographe [manɔgraf] **NM** manograph, recording (pressure) gauge

manoir [manwar] **NM** manor (house), (country) mansion

manomètre [manɔmɛtr] **NM** pressure gauge; *(en forme d'U)* manometer; *Aut* **m. de compression** cylinder compression gauge; *Aut* **m. de pression d'huile** oil pressure gauge

manométrie [manɔmetri] **NF** manometry

manométrique [manɔmetrik] **ADJ** manometric, manometrical

manoque [manɔk] **NF 1** *(de feuilles de tabac)* hand

2 *Naut (pelote)* hank

manostat [manɔsta] **NM** *Tech* manostat

manouche [manuʃ] **ADJ** gypsy *(avant n)*, gipsy *(avant n)*

NMF gypsy, gipsy

manouvrier [manuvrije] **NM** *Hist* seasonal farm worker

manquant, -e [mɑ̃kɑ̃, -ɑ̃t] **ADJ** missing; **la pièce manquante** the missing part; **les deux pages manquantes** the two missing pages; **désolé, ce titre est m. pour le moment** sorry, but we're temporarily out of this book *or* this book's out of stock at the moment; **les soldats manquants à l'appel** the soldiers missing at roll-call

NM,F missing one; **les manquants** *(élèves)* the absent pupils; **nous avons trouvé toutes les factures, les manquantes étaient dans le tiroir** we've found all the invoices, the missing ones were in the drawer

NM *Com* shortfall; **éviter des manquants dans la marchandise** to prevent short delivery; **m. en caisse** cash shortage; **m. en stock** stock shortage

manque[1] [mɑ̃k] **NM 1** *(insuffisance)* **m. de** *(imagination, place, sommeil)* lack of; *(appartements, denrées)* shortage of, scarcity of; *(personnel)* lack of, shortage of; **ce serait un m. de respect** it would be lacking in respect, it would show lack of respect; **par m. de** *(originalité, audace)* for lack of, for want of; *(main-d'œuvre)* through lack *or* shortage of; **être en m. d'affection** to be starved of affection; **souffrir d'un m. affectif** to suffer from a lack of affection; **m. de chance** *ou Fam* **de bol** *ou Fam* **de pot** hard *or* tough luck; *Fam* **m. de bol, j'ai du travail** it's just (my) tough *or* rotten luck that I've got work to do; *Com* **m. à la livraison** short delivery

2 *(absence → d'une personne)* gap; **quand il sera parti, il y aura un m.** his departure will leave a gap

3 *(de drogue)* **être en (état de) m.** to have *or* to feel withdrawal symptoms; *Hum* **la charge de travail a baissé, je suis en (état de) m.** I've got less work to do, I'm suffering from withdrawal symptoms

4 *Écon & Jur* **m. à gagner** loss of (expected) income *or* earnings; **il y aura un m. à gagner de 200 euros** there will be a shortfall of 200 euros; *Compta* **m. de caisse** cash unders

5 *(à la roulette)* manque

6 *Couture & Tex* slipped stitch

❑ **manques NMPL** *(insuffisances)* failings, shortcomings; *(lacunes)* gaps; **avoir conscience de ses manques** to be aware of one's shortcomings *or* failings; **il y a beaucoup de manques dans ce rapport** there's a lot missing from this report

manque[2] [mɑ̃k] **à la manque ADJ** *Fam* useless, pathetic; **qu'est-ce que c'est que cette histoire à la m.?** what kind of a pathetic story is that?

manqué, -e [mɑ̃ke] **ADJ 1** *(non réussi → attentat)* failed; *(→ vie)* wasted; *(→ occasion)* missed, lost; *(→ rendez-vous)* missed; *(→ tentative)* failed, abortive, unsuccessful; *(→ photo, sauce)* spoilt; **je vais essayer de toucher la pomme – m.!** I'll try and hit the apple – missed! **2** *(personne)* **c'est un cuisinier/un médecin m.** he should've been a cook/a doctor

NM *Culin* = almond-flavoured cake

manquement [mɑ̃kmɑ̃] **NM** breach (**à** of); **m. à la discipline** breach of *or* lapse in discipline; **m. à un devoir** dereliction of duty; **m. aux bonnes manières** breach of etiquette; **m. à une règle** breach *or* violation of a rule

MANQUER [3] [mɑ̃ke]

> **VT** to miss **1, 2, 4** ▪ to fail **3** ▪ to spoil **3**
> **VI** to be missing **1** ▪ to be away **1** ▪ to be lacking **3** ▪ to want **5** ▪ to fail **6**

VT 1 *(laisser échapper → balle)* to miss, to fail to catch; *(→ marche, autobus)* to miss; **j'ai manqué le train de trois minutes** I missed the train by three minutes; **l'église est à droite, vous ne pouvez pas la m.** the church is on the right, you can't miss it; *Sport* **m. le but** to miss the goal; *Fig* **m. son but** to fail to reach one's goal; **m. la cible** *Mil* to miss the target; *Fig* to miss one's target, to fail to hit one's target, to shoot wide; **il l'a manquée de peu** *(la cible)* he just missed it; **m. son coup** to miss; *Fig* to miss one's chance; *Fig* **elle s'est moquée de moi mais je ne la manquerai pas!** she made a fool of me but I'll get even with her!; **je n'ai pas vu cet opéra – tu n'as rien manqué/tu as manqué quelque chose!** I didn't see that opera – you didn't miss anything/you really missed something there!; **c'est une émission à ne pas m.** this programme shouldn't be missed *or* is a must; **il ne faut surtout pas m. ça** you really mustn't miss it; **m. une occasion** to miss (out on) an opportunity; *Hum* **tu as manqué une bonne occasion de te taire** why couldn't you have just kept your mouth shut for once?; *Fam* **il n'en manque jamais une!** *(il remarque tout)* he never misses a trick!; *(il est gaffeur)* (you can always) trust him to put his foot in it!

2 *(ne pas rencontrer)* to miss; **vous l'avez manquée de peu** you've just missed her

3 *(ne pas réussir → concours)* to fail; *(→ photo, sauce)* to spoil, to make a mess of; *aussi Hum* **tu as manqué ta vocation** you've missed your vocation; **coup manqué** failure, botch-up; **moi qui croyais lui faire plaisir, c'est vraiment un coup manqué** *ou* **j'ai vraiment manqué mon coup!** and here's me thinking I would make him/her happy, (just) how wrong can you get!

4 *(ne pas aller à)* to miss; **m. un cours** *(volontairement)* to miss *or* to skip a class; *(involontairement)* to miss a class; **j'ai bien envie de m. la gym** I feel like skipping gym; **il a manqué la messe, dimanche?** did he miss Mass on Sunday?

VI 1 *(être absent → fugueur, bouton, argenterie)* to be missing; *(→ employé, élève)* to be away *or* off *or* absent; **le bouton qui manque à ma veste** the button that's missing from my jacket, the missing button on my jacket; **une pièce manque au puzzle** there's a piece missing from the jigsaw puzzle, a piece of the jigsaw puzzle is missing; **j'ai suivi tous les cours et je n'ai pas manqué une seule fois** I attended all the classes and never missed one *or* and I was never absent once; **elle a beaucoup manqué le mois dernier** she was off (school) a lot *or* missed a lot of classes last month; **m. à l'appel** *Mil* to be absent (at roll call); *Fig Hum* to be missing

2 *Ironique (tournure impersonnelle)* **il ne manquait plus qu'elle!** she's all we/I/*etc* need *or* needed!; **il ne manquait plus que ça** that's all we/I/*etc* need; **il ne manquerait plus qu'elle tombe enceinte!** it would be the last straw if she got pregnant!

3 *(être insuffisant)* to be lacking, to be in short supply; **commencer à m.** to begin to run short *or* run out; **quand le pain vint à m., ils descendirent dans la rue** when they ran short of *or* ran out of bread, they took to the streets; **seul le courage a manqué** only courage was lacking; **les occasions de te rendre utile ne manqueront pas** there will be no shortage of opportunities to make yourself useful; **la pluie/le travail,**

ce n'est pas ce qui manque! there's no shortage of rain/work!; *Fam* **il n'y a pas d'eau chaude et ça manque!** there's no hot water and don't we know it!; **le pied m'a manqué** I lost my footing; **le temps m'a manqué** I didn't have enough time, I was short of time; **la place me manque** I don't have enough room; **l'argent leur a toujours manqué** they've always been short of money *or* lacked money; **la force/le courage lui manqua** (his/her) strength/courage failed him/her; *Littéraire* **le cœur lui manqua** his/her heart failed him/her; **les mots me manquent** words fail me, I'm at a loss for words; **la voix me manqua** words failed me; **ce n'est pas l'envie qui m'en manque, mais...** not that I don't want to *or* I'd love to, but...; **les occasions ne manquent pas, ce ne sont pas les occasions qui manquent** there's no lack of opportunity

4 *(tournure impersonnelle)* **il manque une bouteille/un bouton** there's a bottle/a button missing; **il nous manque trois joueurs** *(ils sont absents)* we have three players missing; *(pour jouer)* we're three players short; **il me manque trois euros** I'm three euros short, I need another three euros; **il lui manque un bras** he/she has only one arm, he/she has lost an arm; **il ne manquait plus rien à son bonheur** his/her happiness was complete; **il ne manque pas de gens pour dire que...** there is no lack *or* shortage of people who say that...; **il ne lui manque que la parole** *(animal)* the only thing it can't do is speak; *(machine)* it does everything but talk; *Fig* **il lui manque toujours dix-neuf sous pour faire un franc** *Br* he/she never has two pennies to rub together, *Am* he/she never has a red cent; *Fam* **il lui manque une case** he's/she's got a screw loose

5 *(être pauvre)* to want; **elle a toujours peur de m.** she's always afraid of having to go without

6 *(échouer)* to fail; **ça ne manquera pas** it's sure *or* bound to happen; **j'ai dit qu'elle reviendrait et ça n'a pas manqué** I said she'd come back and sure enough(, she did)!; **je serai là sans m.** I'll be there without fail

▢ **manquer à** VT IND1 *(faillir à)* **m. à son devoir/son honneur** to fail in one's duty/one's honour; **m. à ses devoirs** to neglect one's duties; *Hum* **je manque à tous mes devoirs!** I'm neglecting my duties!; **m. à sa parole/promesse** to fail to keep one's word/promise, to break one's word/promise; **m. à la consigne** to disregard orders; **m. au règlement** to break the rules; **m. aux usages** to defy *or* to flout convention; **m. à ses engagements financiers** to fail to meet one's financial liabilities

2 *(être regretté par)* **elle manque à ses enfants** her children miss her; **il me manque** I miss him; **ma famille me manque** I miss my family; **c'est au parti qu'il manque le plus** it's the party that's missing him most

3 *Littéraire* *(offenser)* to be disrespectful to *or* towards, to behave disrespectfully towards

▢ **manquer de** VT IND1 *(ne pas avoir assez de)* to lack, to be short of; **m. de temps** to be short of time; **m. de courage** to lack courage; **m. de métier/d'expérience** to lack experience; **m. de personnel** to be short-staffed, to be short of staff; **je manque de sommeil** I'm not getting enough sleep; **nous manquons de l'essentiel** we lack *or* we're short of the basics; **ils manquent de tout** they're short of *or* they lack everything; **nous n'avons jamais manqué de rien** we never went short of anything; **ta soupe manque de sel** your soup needs salt; **la chambre manque de lumière** the room doesn't get enough light, the room is lacking in *or* lacks light; **on manque d'air dans la chambre du haut** there's no air in the upstairs bedroom; **on commence à m. d'eau** we're beginning to run out of water; **ils ont fini par m. d'air et mourir** they finally ran out of air and died; **tu ne manques pas d'audace** *ou* **d'air** *ou Fam* **de culot!** you've (certainly) got some nerve!; *Fam* **ça manque de pain!** we're a bit short of bread!; *Fam* **ça manque de musique!** we could do with some music!

2 *(oublier de)* **vous viendrez? – je n'y manquerai pas** will you come? – definitely *or* without fail; **ne manquez pas de me le faire savoir** be sure to let me know, do let me know; **ne manquez pas de nous écrire** be sure to write to us, mind you write to us; **il n'a pas manqué de faire remarquer mon retard** he didn't fail to point out that I was late; **elle ne manquera pas de s'en faire la remarque** she'll be quite sure *or* she's bound to point it out to you

3 *(s'empêcher de)* **on ne peut m. de constater/penser...** one can't help but notice/think...; **personne ne peut m. d'observer...** no one can fail to notice...; **vous ne manquerez pas d'être frappé par cette coïncidence** you're bound to be struck by this coincidence; **tu ne manqueras pas d'être surpris** you're sure *or* bound to be surprised; **il n'a pas manqué d'être étonné** he couldn't help but be surprised; **cela ne pouvait m. d'arriver** it was bound to happen, it had to happen

4 *(faillir)* **elle a manqué (de) se noyer** she nearly *or* almost drowned (herself); **il a manqué (de) ne pas me reconnaître** he nearly failed to *or* nearly didn't recognize me; **tiens-lui le bras, il manque de glisser toutes les deux minutes** hold his arm, he's tripping up every couple of minutes

▸ **se manquer** VPR **1** *(emploi réciproque)* **nous nous sommes manqués à l'aéroport** we missed each other at the airport

2 *(emploi réfléchi)* to fail (in one's suicide attempt); **il s'est manqué pour la troisième fois** that's his third (unsuccessful) suicide attempt; **la deuxième fois, elle ne s'est pas manquée** her second suicide attempt was successful

3 *(tournure impersonnelle)* **il s'en manque de beaucoup** far from it

Mans [mɑ̃] NM **Le M.** Le Mans; **les 24 Heures du M.** the Le Mans 24-hour race
mansarde [mɑ̃sard] NF **1** *(chambre)* garret, attic (room) **2** *Archit* **comble en m.** mansard roof; **fenêtre en m.** dormer window
mansardé, -e [mɑ̃sarde] ADJ *(chambre, étage)* attic *(avant n)*; *(toit)* mansard *(avant n)*; **une pièce mansardée** an attic room, a room with a sloping ceiling
manse [mɑ̃s] NM OU NF *Hist* messuage, small manor
mansion [mɑ̃sjɔ̃] NF *Théât* mansion
mansuétude [mɑ̃sɥetyd] NF *Littéraire* indulgence, goodwill, mansuetude
manta [mɑ̃ta] NF *Ich* manta (ray)
mante [mɑ̃t] NF **1** *Entom* **m. (religieuse** *ou* **prie-Dieu)** (praying) mantis **2** *Fig Hum* **m. religieuse** man-eater **3** *Ich* manta (ray) **4** *(manteau)* mantle
manteau, -x [mɑ̃to] NM **1** *(vêtement de ville)* coat; *(capote)* greatcoat; **m. de fourrure** fur coat; **m. de gabardine** gabardine (coat); **m. impérial** imperial mantle, robe of state; **m. de pluie** raincoat
2 *Fig Littéraire (épaisse couche)* layer, blanket, mantle; **un lourd m. de neige/silence** a heavy mantle of snow/silence
3 *Zool (dos)* back; *(membrane → d'un mollusque)* mantle
4 *Archit* **m. de cheminée** mantelpiece, mantel
5 *Théât* **m. d'Arlequin** proscenium arch
6 *Géol* mantle; **m. neigeux** snow mantle
7 *Hér* mantling, mantle
8 *(locutions)* **sous le m.** unofficially, on the sly; **faire qch sous le m.** to do sth secretly *or Sout* clandestinely; **sous le m. de** under cover of, under the cloak of; **sous le m. de la nuit** under (the) cover of darkness; **sous le m. de la charité, il faisait de la publicité pour sa société** he was advertising for his company, using charity as a pretext
mantelé, -e [mɑ̃tle] ADJ **1** *Hér* mantled **2** *Zool (corbeau)* hooded
▢ **mantelée** NF*Entom* sallow
mantelet [mɑ̃tlɛ] NM **1** *(cape → de femme)* mantelet; *(→ de prélat)* mantelletta **2** *Mil* mantelet **3** *Naut* deadlight
mantelure [mɑ̃tlyr] NF*Zool* back
mantille [mɑ̃tij] NF mantilla *(scarf)*
mantique [mɑ̃tik] NF divination, soothsaying

mantisse [mɑ̃tis] NF*Math* mantissa
Mantoue [mɑ̃tu] NM Mantua
mantra [mɑ̃tra] NM mantra
manualité [manɥalite] NF predominance of the left *or* right hand; *(de la main droite)* dextrality; *(de la main gauche)* sinistrality
manubrium [manybrijɔm] NM*Anat & Zool* manubrium
manucure [manykyr] NMF manicurist
NF manicure; **se faire faire une m.** to have a manicure
manucurer [3] [manykyre] VT to manicure; **se faire m. les mains** to have a manicure
manuel, -elle [manɥɛl] ADJ **1** *(métier, travailleur)* manual; *(outil)* hand-held; **je ne suis pas m. pour deux sous** I'm no good at all with my hands; **corrections manuelles** corrections by hand, manual corrections
2 *(non automatique)* manual; **commande manuelle** hand *or* manual control; **à commande manuelle** manually controlled; *Aviat* **passer en m.** to switch (over) to manual
NM,F **1** *(personne habile de ses mains)* practical person; **c'est une manuelle** she's good with her hands
2 *(travailleur)* manual worker
NM *(mode d'emploi, explications)* manual, handbook; **m. d'histoire/de géographie** history/geography book *or* textbook; **m. scolaire** (school) textbook; **m. de sténographie** shorthand manual; **m. d'entretien** service manual, maintenance manual, workshop manual; **m. d'installation** installation manual; **m. de style** *(dans l'édition)* style book; **m. d'utilisation, m. de l'utilisateur** instruction book *or* manual; *Aviat* **m. de vol** flight manual
manuélin, -e [manɥelɛ̃, -in] ADJ*Archit* Manoeline
manuellement [manɥɛlmɑ̃] ADV manually, by hand; **travailler m.** to work with one's hands; **un dispositif qui fonctionne m.** a manually operated device
manufacturable [manyfaktyrabl] ADJ manufacturable; **ces produits ne sont pas manufacturables dans nos usines** these products cannot be manufactured in our factories
manufacture [manyfaktyr] NF **1** *(atelier)* factory; *Hist* manufactory; **m. de soie/pipes** silk/pipe factory; **la m. des Gobelins** the Gobelins tapestry workshop; **la M. de porcelaine de Sèvres** the Sèvres porcelain factory **2** *(fabrication)* manufacture, manufacturing
manufacturé, -e [manyfaktyre] ADJ manufactured; **produits manufacturés** manufactured goods
manufacturer [3] [manyfaktyre] VT to manufacture
manufacturier, -ère [manyfaktyrje, -ɛr] ADJ manufacturing
NM,F*Arch* industrialist, factory owner
Manufrance [manyfrɑ̃s] NF = former mail-order and manufacturing company in Saint-Étienne partly taken over and run by the local Communist council to avoid closure
manu militari [manymilitari] ADV **1** *(par la violence)* by force; **être expulsé m.** to be forcibly expelled **2** *Jur (par la gendarmerie)* by the forces of law and order
manumission [manymisjɔ̃] NF manumission, freeing
manuscrit, -e [manyskri, -it] ADJ *(lettre)* handwritten; *(page, texte)* manuscript *(avant n)*
NM **1** *(texte écrit à la main)* handwritten text
2 *(texte à publier)* manuscript; **m. dactylographié** manuscript, typescript; **sous forme de m.** in manuscript (form)
3 *(texte ancien)* **m. (ancien)** ancient manuscript; *(sous forme de rouleau)* scroll; **un m. du XIIIème siècle** a 13th-century manuscript; **les manuscrits de la mer Morte** the Dead Sea Scrolls
manutention [manytɑ̃sjɔ̃] NF **1** *(manipulation)* handling **2** *(entrepôt)* warehouse, store house
manutentionnaire [manytɑ̃sjɔnɛr] NMF *(homme)* warehouseman, warehouse worker; *(femme)* warehouse worker; **il est m. dans une fabrique de meubles** he's a packer in a furniture factory
manutentionner [3] [manytɑ̃sjɔne] VT *(déplacer)* to handle; *(emballer)* to pack
manuterge [manytɛrʒ] NM*Rel* manutergium

manzanilla [mãzanija]**NM** manzanilla (wine)

maoïsme [maɔism]**NM** Maoism

maoïste [maɔist]**ADJ** Maoist
NMF Maoist

maori, -e [maɔri]**ADJ** Maori
NM *(langue)* Maori
❏ **Maori, -e NM,F** Maori; **les Maoris** the Maoris *or* Maori

Mao Tsé-toung [maotsetuŋ] **NPR** Mao Tse-tung, Mao Zedong

maous, -ousse [maus] **ADJ** *Fam* ginormous, humongous

Mao Zedong [maodzedɔg] = **Mao Tsé-toung**

mappemonde [mapmɔ̃d] **NF** *(globe)* globe; *(carte)* map of the world *(showing both hemispheres)*; **m. céleste** planisphere

mapping [mapiŋ]**NM** *Mktg* mapping

Maputo [maputo]**NM** Maputo

maqué, -e[1] [make] **ADJ** *Fam* **être m.** *(homme)* to have a partner■; **ils sont maqués** they're an item; **elle est maquée avec lui** she's shacked up with him

maquée[2] [make]**NF** *Belg* cottage cheese

maquer [3] [make] **VT** *Belg (frapper)* to beat up; *Fig (abasourdir)* to stun, to astound
▶**se maquer VPR** *Fam (se marier)* to get hitched *or* spliced, to tie the knot; *(s'établir en couple)* to shack up together; **se m. avec qn** *(se marier)* to get hitched to sb; *(s'établir en couple)* to shack up with sb

maqueraison [makrɛzɔ̃]**NF** mackerel season

maquereau, -x [makro] **NM 1** *Ich* mackerel; **m. espagnol** Spanish mackerel **2** *Fam (souteneur)* pimp, *Am* mack

maquerelle [makrɛl] **NF** *Fam* **(mère) m.** madam *(in brothel)*

maquette [makɛt] **NF 1** *(modèle réduit)* (scale) model; **m. d'avion/de village** model aircraft/ village; **faire des maquettes** to make models **2** *Beaux-Arts (d'une sculpture)* model, maquette; *(d'un dessin)* sketch **3** *Théât (de mise en scène)* model **4** *Typ (de pages)* paste-up, layout; *(d'un livre)* dummy **5** *Ind* mock-up, (full-scale) model

maquettisme [makɛtism]**NM** model making

maquettiste [makɛtist]**NMF 1** *(modéliste)* model maker **2** *Typ* layout artist

maquignon [makiɲɔ̃] **NM 1** *(marchand → de chevaux)* horse trader; *(→ de bestiaux)* cattle trader **2** *Péj (entremetteur)* trickster

maquignonnage [makiɲɔnaʒ] **NM 1** *(vente → de chevaux)* horse trading; *(→ de bétail)* cattle trading **2** *Péj (manœuvre douteuse)* shady dealing, wheeling and dealing

maquignonner [3] [makiɲɔne] **VT 1** *(bétail, cheval)* to deal *or* to trade *or* to traffic in **2** *Péj (manœuvrer)* **ils ont maquignonné cette affaire entre eux** they've cooked this business up between them

maquillage [makijaʒ] **NM 1** *(cosmétiques)* make-up; *(application)* making up, putting on make-up; **elle met beaucoup de soin dans son m.** she takes a lot of care with her make-up **2** *(falsification → d'un passeport, d'un texte)* falsifying, faking; *(→ de photos)* faking; *(→ de preuves, de comptes)* falsifying; *(→ d'un véhicule)* respraying

maquiller [3] [makije] **VT 1** *(visage)* to make up; **être bien/mal maquillé** to be nicely/badly made up; **être trop maquillé** to be wearing too much make-up; **qui vous a maquillé?** who did your make-up?; **elle est allée se faire m. dans un institut de beauté** she went to a beauty parlour to get her make-up done
2 *(falsifier → passeport, texte)* to falsify, to fake; *(→ photos)* to fake; *(→ preuves, comptes)* to falsify; *(→ véhicule)* to respray; **après avoir maquillé la carrosserie** after doing a paint job on the bodywork; **m. un crime en suicide** to make a murder look like a suicide
▶**se maquiller VPR** **se m. (le visage)** to make up (one's face), to put on one's make-up; **se m. les yeux** to put one's eye make-up on; **tu te maquilles déjà à ton âge?** are you using make-up already at your age?; **elle se maquille trop** she uses too much make-up, she puts too much make-up on

maquilleur, -euse [makijœr, -øz]**NM,F** make-up artist; *TV* **passer chez le m.** to have one's make-up done, to go into make-up; *Cin, TV* **elle est**

maquilleuse de studio she works at a studio as a make-up artist

maquis [maki] **NM 1** *Géog* scrub, scrubland, maquis **2** *Hist* **le M.** the Maquis *(French Resistance movement in World War II)*; **prendre le m.** *Hist* to take to the maquis; *Fig* to go underground; **les m. d'Afghanistan** the Afghan freedom fighters **3** *Fig (labyrinthe)* **dans le m. des lois/de la finance internationale** in the jungle of law/of international finance

maquisard [makizar] **NM 1** *Hist* maquis, French Resistance fighter *(in World War II)* **2** *(guérillero)* guerrilla fighter

mara [mara]**NM** *Zool* mara, Patagonian hare

marabout [marabu] **ADJ INV** *Can* bad-tempered, grumpy
NM 1 *(oiseau, plume)* marabou, marabout **2** *(ermite, tombeau)* marabout **3** *(sorcier)* witch-doctor **4** *Can (personne acariâtre)* bad-tempered person

maraboutage [marabutaʒ]**NM** *(en Afrique francophone)* using the evil eye

marabouter [3] [marabute] **VT** *(en Afrique francophone)* to put the evil eye on

maraca [maraka]**NF** maraca

maracudja [marakudʒa] **NM** *Bot (aux Antilles)* passion fruit, maracuja

maraging [maredʒiŋ] **ADJ INV** **acier m.** maraging steel

maraîchage [marɛʃaʒ] **NM** *Br* market gardening, *Am* truck farming *or* gardening

maraîcher, -ère [marɛʃe, -ɛr] **NM,F** *Br* market gardener, *Am* truck farmer
ADJ vegetable *(avant n)*; **produits maraîchers** *Br* market garden produce *(UNCOUNT)*, *Am* truck *(UNCOUNT)*

maraîchin, -e [marɛʃɛ̃, -in]**ADJ** of/from the Marais *(of Poitou or Britanny)*
❏ **Maraîchin, -e NM,F** = inhabitant of or person from the Marais *(of Poitou or Britanny)*

Marais [marɛ] **NM 1** *(quartier)* **le M.** the Marais *(district of Paris)* **2** *Hist* **le M.** the Marais, the Swamp *(moderate party in the French Revolution)* **3** *Géog* **le M. poitevin** = marshland in the southern Vendée region with a network of waterways; **le M. breton** = area of marshland with canals in the north-western Vendée region

---

Culture

LE MARAIS
The Marais district of Paris includes the place des Vosges and the predominantly Jewish quarter around the rue des Rosiers. The large number of "hôtels particuliers" in the Marais, many of them now converted into museums, testifies to the district's aristocratic past in the 17th and 18th centuries, prior to the Revolution. Today it is a fashionable area with many shops, restaurants and bars, and is the main focus of the city's gay community.

---

marais [marɛ] **NM 1** *(terrain recouvert d'eau)* marsh, swamp; **m. maritime** tidal marsh; **m. salant** salt marsh, salina **2** *(région)* marsh, marshland, bog **3** *(terrain consacré à la culture maraîchère)* *Br* market garden, *Am* truck farm **4** *Fig* quagmire **5** *Météo* **m. barométrique** shallow depression

marans [marã] **ADJ INV** **poule m.** = type of hen producing large eggs
NF = type of hen producing large eggs

maranta [marãta]**NM** *Bot* maranta, arrowroot

marante [marãt]**NF** *Bot* maranta, arrowroot

marasme [marasm]**NM 1** *Écon* slump, stagnation; **le m. des affaires** the slump in business; **l'économie des pays d'Asie traverse actuellement une période de m.** Asian economies are currently going through a period of stagnation; **dans le m. économique actuel** in the present economic slump; **nous sommes en plein m.** we're going through a slump, our economy's in the doldrums **2** *Fig (apathie)* listlessness, apathy, depression **3** *Méd* marasmus, cachexia

marasque [marask]**NF** marasca cherry

marasquin [maraskɛ̃]**NM** maraschino; **cerises au m.** maraschino cherries

marathe [marat]**ADJ** Mahratta
NM *(langue)* Marathi, Mahratti
❏ **Marathe NMF** Mahratta

marathon [maratɔ̃] **NM 1** *Sport* marathon; **courir un m.** to run a marathon; **m. de danse** dance marathon **2** *Fig* **m. diplomatique/électoral** diplomatic/electoral marathon **3** *(comme adj inv; avec ou sans trait d'union)* marathon *(avant n)*; **discussion/séance m.** marathon discussion/session

marathonien, -enne [maratɔnjɛ̃, -ɛn]**NM,F** marathon runner

marâtre [marɑtr]**NF 1** *(méchante mère)* unnatural *or* wicked mother **2** *(belle-mère)* stepmother

maraud, -e [maro, -od]**NM,F** *Vieilli* rascal, rapscallion

maraudage [marodaʒ]**NM** pilfering *(of food)*

maraude [marod]**ADJ** *voir* **maraud**
NF *(vol)* pilfering *(of food)*
❏ **en maraude ADJ** **un taxi en m.** a cruising taxi

marauder [3] [marode] **VI 1** *(personne)* to filch *or* to pilfer *(food)*; *(soldat)* to maraud **2** *(taxi)* to cruise

maraudeur, -euse [marodœr, -øz] **NM,F** *(gén)* pilferer; *(soldat)* marauder
ADJ 1 *(renard)* on the prowl; *(oiseau)* thieving **2** *(taxi)* cruising

marave[1] [marav] **NF** *Fam* scuffle, *Br* punch-up, *Am* slugfest

marave[2] [marav]**VT** *Fam* **1** *(battre)* **m. qn** to waste sb's face, *Am* to punch sb out **2** *(tuer)* to kill■, to waste, *Am* to snuff

maravédis [maravedi]**NM** *Hist* maravedi

maraver [3] [marave] = **marave**[2]

marbre [marbr] **NM 1** *Minér* marble; **m. veiné** streaked *or* veined marble; **m. tacheté** mottled marble; **une colonne/un tombeau de m.** a marble pillar/tomb; **un escalier/une statue en m.** a marble staircase/statue; **un mur en faux m.** a marbleized wall; *Fig* **ce n'est pas écrit dans le m.** it's not set in stone, it's not written in (tablets of) stone
2 *(plateau → de cheminée, meuble)* marble top **3** *Beaux-Arts (statue)* marble (statue); *(plaque)* marble plate; **les marbres romains** the Roman marbles
4 *Typ (forme)* bed; *Journ* reserve feature; **mettre sur le m.** *(journal)* to put to bed; *(livre)* to put on the press; *Fam* **avoir du m.** to have copy over; **rester sur le m.** to be excess copy
5 *Tech* surface plate
6 *Sport (au base-ball)* home base, home plate
7 *Can Joual (bille)* marble■
❏ **de marbre ADJ 1** *(insensible)* insensitive; **avoir un cœur de m.** to have a heart of stone; **il resta de m.** he remained impassive; **la mort de sa mère l'a laissé de m.** his mother's death left him cold *or* unmoved
2 *(impassible)* impassive; **un visage de m.** a poker face; **il est resté de m. pendant qu'on lui arrachait ses galons** he remained impassive while they tore off his stripes

marbré, -e [marbre] **ADJ 1** *(tacheté)* marbled, mottled; *(veiné)* veined; **peau marbrée** blotchy skin; **il avait la peau toute marbrée de coups** his skin was all marked with bruises **2** *Tech* marbled; *Constr* marbleized
NM *Ich* striped sea bream

marbrer [3] [marbre]**VT 1** *(papier, tranche de livre)* to marble; *Constr* to marbleize **2** *(peau)* to mottle, to blotch; **jambes/joues marbrées par le froid** legs/cheeks mottled with the cold

marbrerie [marbrəri] **NF 1** *(industrie)* marble industry **2** *(atelier)* marble (mason's) yard **3** *(métier, art)* marble work; **m. funéraire** monumental (marble) masonry

marbreur, -euse [marbrœr, -øz]**NM,F** marbler

marbrier, -ère [marbrije, -ɛr] **ADJ** marble *(avant n)*
NM marbler; **m. (funéraire)** monumental mason
❏ **marbrière NF** marble quarry

marbrure [marbryr] **NF 1** *(aspect marbré)* marbling; *(imitation)* marbleizing, marbling **2** *(de peau)* mottling
❏ **marbrures NFPL** blotches, streaks, veins

Marc [mark] **NPR** *Bible* Mark; *Antiq* **M. Antoine** Mark Antony; *Antiq* **M. Aurèle** Marcus Aurelius

marc[1] [mar]**NM 1** *(résidu de fruit)* marc **2** *(eau-de-vie)* marc (brandy) **3 m. (de café)** coffee grounds *or* dregs; **lire l'avenir dans le m. de café** ≃ to read the future in tea leaves

marc² [mar] NM **1** *(monnaie, poids)* mark; **un m. d'or/d'argent** *(monnaie)* a gold/silver mark; *(poids)* a mark of gold/silver **2** *Jur* **au m. le franc** pro rata, proportionally

marcassin [markasɛ̃] NM young wild boar, squeaker; **cuissot de m.** haunch of wild boar

marcassite [markasit] NF *Minér* marcasite

marcel [marsɛl] NM singlet, *Br* vest

marcescence [marsɛsɑ̃s] NF *Bot* marcescence, withering

marcescent, -e [marsɛsɑ̃, -ɑ̃t] ADJ *Bot* marcescent, withering

marchand, -e [marʃɑ̃, -ɑ̃d] NM,F *(négociant) Br* shopkeeper, *Am* storekeeper; (→ *en vin)* merchant; (→ *de meubles, de chevaux)* dealer; (→ *sur un marché)* stallholder; **m. ambulant** (street) pedlar; **m. de biens** *Br* ≃ estate agent, *Am* ≃ real estate agent; *Péj* **m. de canons** arms dealer; **m. de charbon** coal merchant; **m. de chaussures** *Br* shoe-shop owner, *Am* shoe-store owner; **m. de couleurs** hardware store owner, *Br* ironmonger; **m. au détail** retailer; **m. d'esclaves** slave trader; **m. de fleurs** florist; **m. de frites** *Br* ≃ chip shop man, *Am* ≃ hot-dog stand man; **m. de fromage** cheese merchant; **m. de fruits** fruiterer; **m. en gros** wholesaler, wholesale dealer; *Péj* **m. d'illusions** dealer in false promises; **m. de journaux** *(en boutique)* newsagent; *(en kiosque)* newsstand man, newsvendor; **m. de légumes** *Br* greengrocer, *Am* vegetable seller; **m. de marée** *ou* **de poisson** fishmonger; **m. des quatre-saisons** *Br* costermonger, *Am* fruit and vegetable seller; *Péj* **m. de sommeil** rack-renter, slumlord; *Péj* **m. de soupe** *(restaurateur)* owner of a second-rate restaurant; *Scol* = headmaster who thinks only of making a profit; **m. de tabac** tobacconist; **m. de tableaux** art dealer; **m. de tapis** carpet dealer; *Fig Péj* haggler; *Fig Péj* **des discussions de marchands de tapis** haggling; **m. de vin** wine merchant, vintner; **m. de voitures** car salesman; **le m. de sable est passé** the sandman's coming

ADJ **1** *(valeur, prix)* market *(avant n)*; *(denrée)* marketable; *(qualité)* standard; **un tableau sans aucune valeur marchande** a painting of no saleable *or* marketable value

2 *(rue)* shopping *(avant n)*; *(quartier, ville)* commercial

3 *(marine, navire)* merchant *(avant n)*

marchandage [marʃɑ̃daʒ] NM **1** *(discussion d'un prix)* haggling, bargaining; **faire du m.** to haggle **2** *Péj (tractation)* wheeler-dealing **3** *Jur* subcontracting

marchander [3] [marʃɑ̃de] VT **1** *(discuter le prix de)* to bargain *or* to haggle over; **m. qch avec qn** to haggle *or* bargain with sb over sth; *Fig* **nous ne marchanderons pas le droit des peuples à disposer d'eux-mêmes** the right of peoples to self-determination is not up for discussion *or* negotiation

2 *(au négatif) (lésiner sur)* to spare; **ils n'ont pas marchandé leur effort** they spared no effort; **la presse n'a pas marchandé ses éloges pour sa dernière pièce** the press wasn't sparing of its praise for his/her last play

3 *Jur* to subcontract

VI to haggle, to bargain; **il a acheté un tableau sans m.** he bought a painting without haggling (over its price)

marchandeur, -euse [marʃɑ̃dœr, -øz] NM,F haggler

NM *Jur* subcontractor

marchandisage [marʃɑ̃dizaʒ] NM merchandizing

marchandisation [marʃɑ̃dizasjɔ̃] NF merchandization

marchandise [marʃɑ̃diz] NF **1** *(produit)* commodity; **marchandises** goods, merchandise (UNCOUNT); **marchandises au détail** retail goods; **marchandises en entrepôt** warehoused goods, goods in storage; *Douanes* bonded goods, goods in bond; **marchandises à l'export** export goods; **marchandises en gros** wholesale goods; **marchandises à l'import** import goods; **marchandises en magasin** stock in hand; **marchandises d'origine** = goods of guaranteed origin; **marchandises périssables** perishable goods, perishables; **marchandises de qualité** quality goods; **marchandises en souffrance** unclaimed goods; **marchandises en vrac** bulk goods

2 *(fret, stock)* **la m.** the goods, the merchandise; **la m. sera livrée à Londres** the merchandise will be delivered in London; **on lui a volé toute sa m.** all his/her goods were stolen; **notre boucher a de la bonne m.** our butcher sells good-quality meat; *Fam* **la m. est arrivée à bon port** the stuff got here all right

3 *Fam aussi Fig* **tromper** *ou* **voler qn sur la m.** to swindle sb; *Fig* **vanter** *ou* **étaler** *ou* **faire valoir sa m.** to make the most of oneself; *Hum* **ce n'est pas à moi de vanter la m. mais ma tarte est bonne** my tart is good, though I (do) say so myself; *Péj* **il vend sa m.** he's plugging his own stuff

4 *Fam Hum (organes sexuels masculins)* family jewels, *Br* tackle

marchandiser [3] [marʃɑ̃dize] VT to merchandize

marchandiseur [marʃɑ̃dizœr] NM merchandizer

marchante [marʃɑ̃t] *voir* **aile**

marchantia [marʃɑ̃tja] NF *Bot* marchantia

MARCHE [marʃ]

walking **1** ▪ walk **2, 7** ▪ march **3–5, 13** ▪ pace **6** ▪ running **8–10** ▪ working **9, 10** ▪ step **6, 12**

NF **1** *(activité, sport)* walking; **la m. (à pied)** walking; **la m. en montagne** hillwalking; **m. nordique** Nordic walking; **j'en ai fait de la m. aujourd'hui!** I've done quite a bit of walking today!; **elle fait de la m.** *(comme sport)* she goes walking; **aimer la m.** to be fond of walking; **poursuivre sa m.** to keep (on) *or* to carry on walking, to walk on; **la frontière n'est qu'à une heure de m.** the border is only an hour's walk away

2 *(promenade)* walk; **nous avons fait une m. de huit kilomètres** we did an eight-kilometre walk; *Can* **prendre une m.** to go for a walk

3 *(défilé)* march; **m. pour la libération d'un prisonnier politique** march for the release of a political prisoner; **m. silencieuse/de protestation** silent/protest march; **m. pour la paix** peace march; **ouvrir la m.** to lead the way; **fermer la m.** to bring up the rear

4 *Mus* march; **m. nuptiale/funèbre/militaire** wedding/funeral/military march

5 *Mil* march; **colonne en m.** column on the march; **ordre(s) de m.** marching orders; **en avant, m.!** forward, march!; **faire m. sur une citadelle** to march on *or* upon a citadel; **m. forcée** forced march; *Hist* **la Longue M.** the Long March; *Hist* **la M. sur Rome** the March on Rome

6 *(allure)* pace, step; **il régla sa m. sur celle de l'enfant** he adjusted his pace to the child's; **ralentir sa m.** to slow (down) one's pace; **accélérer sa m.** to increase *or* to step up one's pace

7 *(démarche)* walk, gait; **sa m. gracieuse** her graceful gait

8 *(déplacement* → *d'un train, d'une voiture)* running; (→ *de bateaux)* sailing, running; (→ *d'une étoile)* course; **dans le sens de la m.** *(dans un train)* facing the engine; *(dans un bus)* facing forward; **dans le sens contraire de la m.** *(dans un train)* (with one's) back to the engine; *(dans un bus)* facing backwards; *Aut* **m. avant/arrière** forward/reverse gear; **entrer/sortir en m. arrière** to reverse in/out, to back in/out; **faire m. arrière** *(conducteur)* to reverse, to back up; *Fig* to backpedal, to backtrack; **en voyant le prix, j'ai fait m. arrière** when I saw the price I backed out of buying it; *Cin & TV* **m. arrière** reverse motion

9 *(fonctionnement* → *d'une machine)* running, working; **m., arrêt** on, off; **en (bon) état de m.** in (good) working order; **être en m.** *(machine)* to be running; *(fourneau)* to be in blast; **régler la m. d'une pendule** to adjust the movement of a clock; **ne pas ouvrir pendant la m.** do not open while the machine is running

10 *(d'une entreprise, d'un service)* running, working, functioning; **pour assurer la bonne m. de notre coopérative** to ensure the smooth running of our co-op; **la privatisation est-elle un obstacle à la bonne m. de l'entreprise?** is privatization an obstacle to the proper working *or* functioning of the company?

11 *(progression)* **la m. du temps** the passing *or Sout* march of time; **la m. de l'histoire** the course of history; **la m. des événements** the course *or Sout* march of events; **la révolution est en m.** revolution is on the march *or* move

12 *(degré* → *d'un escalier)* step, stair; (→ *d'un marchepied)* step; (→ *d'un métier à tisser)* treadle; (→ *d'un orgue)* pedal; **la première/dernière m.** *(en montant)* the bottom/top step; *(en descendant)* the top/bottom step; **descendre/monter les marches** to go down/up the stairs; **attention à la m.** *(sur panneau)* mind the step; *Archit* **m. dansante** winder

13 *Hist (frontière)* march

14 m. à suivre *(instructions)* directions (for use); *(pour des formalités)* procedure, form

15 *Bourse* **m. aléatoire** random walk

❑ **en marche** ADV **monter/descendre d'un train en m.** to get on/off a moving train; **je suis descendu du bus en m.** I got off the bus while it was still moving; **mettre en m.** *(moteur, véhicule)* to start (up); *(appareil)* to switch *or* to turn on; **se mettre en m.** *(machine)* to start; **le four se mettra automatiquement en m. dans une heure** the oven will turn *or* switch itself on automatically in an hour ADJ moving, in motion; **navire en m.** ship under way

marché¹ [marʃe] NM **1** *(lieu de vente)* market; **aller au m.** to go to the market; **je l'ai acheté au m.** I bought it at the market; **faire son m.** to go (grocery) shopping; **faire les marchés** *(commerçant)* to go round *or* to do the markets; **jour de m.** market day; **m. aux fleurs/à la volaille** flower/poultry market; **m. aux poissons/bestiaux** fish/cattle market; **m. aux puces** flea market; **m. couvert** covered market; **m. en plein air** open-air market; **m. d'intérêt national** wholesale market for agricultural produce

2 *Com & Écon* market; **m. des matières premières/du sucre/du café** raw materials/sugar/coffee market; **m. du travail** labour market; **m. extérieur/intérieur** foreign/home market, overseas/domestic market; **mettre qch sur le m.** to put sth on the market; **mettre** *ou* **lancer un nouveau produit sur le m.** to put *or* to launch a new product on the market; **retirer qch du m.** to take sth off the market; **conquérir un m.** to break into a market; **arriver sur le m.** to come onto the market; **le vaccin n'est pas encore sur le m.** the vaccine is not yet (available) on the market; **il n'y a pas de m. pour ce type d'habitation** there is no market for this type of housing; **ils ont ouvert leur m. aux produits japonais** they've opened their markets to Japanese products; **le Grand M. (européen)** the European Market; **étude/économie de m.** market research/economy; **m. d'acheteurs** buyers' market; **m. à la baisse** buyers' market; **m. des besoins** need market; **m. captif** captive market; **m. cible** target market; **le M. commun** the Common Market; **m. de concurrence** competitive marketplace; **m. des consommateurs** *ou* **de la consommation** consumer market; **m. effectif** available market; **m. d'équipement** capital goods market; **m. de l'escompte** discount market; **m. à l'export** *ou* **à l'exportation** export market; **m. extérieur** foreign *or* overseas market; **m. générique** generic market; **m. global** global market; **m. grand public** consumer market, mass market; **m. gris** grey market; **m. industriel** industrial market; **m. intérieur** home *or* domestic market; **m. des intermédiaires** middleman's market; **m. libre** free market; **m. de masse** mass market; **m. mondial** world market; **m. monopolistique** monopoly market; **m. national** national market, home market; **m. noir** black market; **faire du m. noir** to buy and sell on the black market; **m. officiel** official market; **m. d'outre-mer** overseas market; **m. parallèle** parallel market, black market; **m. porteur** growth market; **m. primaire** primary market; **m. principal** core market; **m. de référence** core market; **m. de renouvellement** repurchase market; **m. de revente** second-hand market; **m. secondaire** secondary market; *Mktg* **m. témoin** control market, test market; *Mktg* **m. test** test

market; **le M. unique (européen)** the Single (European) Market; *Mktg* **m. utile** addressable market; **m. vendeur** sellers' market; **m. visé** target market

3 *Bourse & Fin* market; **m. des actions** stock market; **m. de l'argent** money market; **m. boursier** stock market; **m. cambiste** foreign exchange market; **m. des capitaux** capital market; **m. des changes** foreign exchange market; **m. au comptant** spot market; **m. de cotation** securities market; **m. en coulisse** outside market; **m. du crédit** credit market; **m. dérivé** derivatives market; **m. des devises (étrangères)** foreign exchange market; **m. du disponible** spot market; **m. électronique privé** ECN, electronic communications network; **m. de l'eurodevise** *ou* **des eurodevises** euromarket; **m. financier** capital *or* financial market; **m. de gré à gré entre banques** interbank wholesale market; **m. à la hausse, m. haussier** sellers' market; **m. hors cote** unlisted securities market, *Am* over-the-counter market; **m. hypothécaire** mortgage market; **m. interbancaire** interbank market; **m. monétaire** money market; **m. du neuf** primary market; **m. obligataire** bond market; **m. à** *ou* **des options** options market; **m. des prêts** loan market; **m. à primes** options market; **m. réglementé** regulated market; **m. secondaire** off-exchange market, OFEX; **m. à terme** futures market; **m. des titres** stock market; **m. des valeurs mobilières** share market

4 *(accord)* deal, bargain; *(plus officiel)* contract; **faire** *ou* **passer un m. (avec qn)** to strike a deal *or* bargain (with sb), to clinch a deal (with sb); **conclure un m. (avec qn)** to make a deal (with sb); **m. conclu!** it's a deal!, that's settled!; **c'est un m. de dupes** it's a con; **mettre le m. en main à qn** to force sb to take it or leave it

5 *Fam (locution)* **par-dessus le m.** into the bargain, what's more; **il est jeune, intelligent et beau par-dessus le m.** he's young, intelligent and handsome into the bargain; **et il se plaint, par-dessus le m.!** and, what's more, he's complaining!

▫ **à bon marché** ADV cheaply; **fabriqué à bon m.** cheaply made; **je l'ai eu à bon m.** I got it cheap

▫ **bon marché** ADJ cheap, inexpensive ADV **faire bon m. de qch** to treat sth lightly; **faire bon m. de sa vie** to hold one's life cheap; **il a fait bon m. de mes conseils** he took no notice of my advice

▫ **meilleur marché** ADJ INV cheaper; **je l'ai eu meilleur m. à Paris** I got it cheaper in Paris

marché[2] [marʃe] NM *(au basket-ball)* travelling

marchéage [marʃeaʒ] NM *Mktg* marketing mix *or* spectrum; **m. de distribution** retailing mix

marchéisation [marʃeizasjɔ̃] NF marketization

marchepied [marʃəpje] NM **1** *(d'un train)* step, steps; *(d'un camion)* footboard; *(d'une voiture)* running board; **m. amovible** retractable step **2** *Fig (tremplin)* stepping stone; **ce petit rôle lui a servi de m. pour devenir célèbre** this small role put him/her on the road to fame **3** *(estrade)* dais; *(banc)* footstool; *(escabeau)* pair of steps **4** *(sur une berge)* footpath

MARCHER [3] [marʃe]

> to walk **1** ▪ to march **2** ▪ to step **3** ▪ to work **4, 5** ▪ to run **4** ▪ to be working out **5** ▪ to go along with things **8** ▪ to fall for it **9**

VI **1** *(se déplacer à pied)* to walk; **m. sans but** to walk aimlessly; **m. tranquillement** to amble along; **descendre une avenue en marchant lentement/rapidement** to stroll/to hurry down an avenue; **m. à grands pas** *ou* **à grandes enjambées** to stride (along); **m. à petits pas** to take small steps; **m. à quatre pattes** to walk on all fours; **m. à reculons** to walk backwards; **m. de long en large (dans une salle)** to walk up and down (a room); **m. sur la pointe des pieds** to walk on tiptoe; **m. sur les mains** to walk on one's hands; **boiter en marchant** to walk with a limp; **il a une drôle de façon de m.** he has a funny walk; **m. sur les traces de qn** to follow in sb's footsteps; *Fig* **m. vers le succès** to be on the road to success; *Fig* **un peuple qui marche vers la liberté** a people marching *or* on the march towards liberty *or* freedom; *Fig* **l'État marche à la ruine** the State is heading for ruin; **m. droit** to walk straight *or* in a straight line; *Fig* to toe the line; **m. sur des œufs** *(marcher avec précaution)* to walk gingerly; *(devoir être prudent)* to tread carefully; *Fam* **c'est marche ou crève!** it's do or die!, it's sink or swim!

2 *Mil* to march; **m. au pas** to march in step; **m. au combat** to march into battle; **m. sur une ville/sur l'ennemi** to march on a city/against the enemy

3 *(poser le pied)* **m. sur** to step *or* to tread on; **m. dans** *(flaque, saleté)* to step *or* to tread in; **ne marche pas sur les fleurs!** keep off the flowers!, don't walk on the flowers!; **tu marches sur tes lacets** you're treading on your laces; **m. sur les pieds à qn** to tread *or* to stand *or* to step on sb's feet; *Fig* **il ne faut pas se laisser m. sur les pieds** you shouldn't let people walk all over you

4 *(fonctionner → machine)* to work, to function; *(→ moteur)* to run; **m. au gaz** to work on gas; **m. à l'électricité** to work *or* to run on electricity; **le jouet marche à piles** the toy is battery-operated; **comment ça marche?** how does it work?; **ma montre ne marche plus** my watch isn't working *or* going; *Fam* **les trains ne marchent pas aujourd'hui** the trains aren't running today▪; **faire m.** *(machine)* to work, to operate; **tu sais faire m. la machine à laver?** do you know how to work the washing machine?

5 *(donner de bons résultats → manœuvre, ruse)* to come off, to work; *(→ projet, essai)* to be working (out), to work; *(→ activité, travail)* to be going well; **ses études marchent bien/mal** he's/she's doing well/not doing very well at college; *Fam* **elle marche bien en chimie/au tennis** she's doing well in chemistry/at tennis; *Fam* **un jeune athlète qui marche très fort** an up-and-coming young athlete; **la répétition a bien/mal marché** the rehearsal went well/badly; **les affaires marchent mal/très bien** business is slack/is going well; **ça fait m. les affaires** *ou* **le commerce** it's good for business *or* for trade; **rien ne marche** nothing's going right; **tout a très bien marché jusqu'ici** everything's gone very well until now; **ne t'inquiète pas, ça va m.** don't worry, it'll be OK; **et le travail, ça marche?** how's work (going)?; **ça marche pour mardi?** is it OK for Tuesday?; **ça marche comme ça?** *(arrangement, rendez-vous)* is that OK with you?; **ça marche pour ce soir? – ça marche!** is it OK for this evening *or* are we on for this evening? – definitely *or* sure!; **on partage les bénéfices 50/50, ça marche?** we'll share the profits 50/50, (is that) agreed *or* OK?; **si ça marche, je monterai une exposition** if it works out, I'll organize an exhibition; **leur couple/commerce n'a pas marché** their relationship/business didn't work out; **ça a l'air de bien m. entre eux** they seem to be getting on fine together, things seem to be going well between them

6 *Fam (en voiture)* **on a bien marché jusqu'à ce qu'un pneu éclate** we were doing well *or* making good time until we had a burst tyre; **en marchant bien, tu seras à Bruxelles ce soir** if you keep your speed up you'll be in Brussels by tonight; **tu marches à combien, là?** what are you doing *or* what speed are you doing at the moment?

7 *(au restaurant)* **faites m. deux œufs au plat!** two fried eggs!; **ça marche!** coming up!

8 *Fam (s'engager, accepter)* to go along with things; **tu marches avec nous?** can we count you in?; **OK, je marche!** OK, count me in!; **je ne marche pas!** nothing doing!, count me out!; **elle ne marchera jamais** she'll never agree; **m. dans une affaire** to get mixed up *or* involved in a scheme; **m. dans la combine** to get involved

9 *Fam (croire naïvement)* to fall for it, to swallow it; **elle a marché** she fell for it, she swallowed it; *Hum* **je lui ai dit que ma tante était malade et il n'a pas marché, il a couru** I told him that my aunt was ill and he bought the whole story *or* and he swallowed it hook, line and sinker; **faire m. qn** *(le taquiner)* to pull sb's leg, *Br* to wind sb up; *(le berner)* to take sb for a ride, to lead sb up the garden path; **ce n'est pas vrai, tu me fais m.?** are you pulling my leg?, *Br* are you having me on?

10 *(au basket-ball)* to travel

Marches [marʃ] NFPL *Géog* **les M.** the Marches

marchette [marʃɛt] NF *Can (chariot d'enfant)* baby-walker; *(support de marche)* walking frame, Zimmer® frame

marcheur, -euse [marʃœr, -øz] ADJ **1** *Orn* **oiseaux marcheurs** flightless birds **2 navire bon m.** fast ship

NM,F **1** *(gén) & Sport* walker; **c'est un bon m.** he's a good walker; **les marcheurs de Strasbourg–Paris arrivent cette nuit** the participants in the Strasbourg–Paris walk will be arriving tonight **2** *(manifestant)* marcher; **m. de la paix** peace marcher

▫ **marcheuse** NF *Théât* walk-on

marcionisme [marsjɔnism] NM Marcionitism

marconi [markɔni] ADJ INV *Naut* Marconi *(avant n)*

marcophilie [markɔfili] NF **la m.** collecting postmarks

marcottage [markɔtaʒ] NM layering; **m. aérien** air layering

marcotte [markɔt] NF layer

marcotter [3] [markɔte] VT to layer

mardi [mardi] NM Tuesday; **Nice, le m. 10 août** Nice, *Br* Tuesday 10 August *or Am* Tuesday August 10th; **je suis né un m. 18 avril** I was born on *Br* Tuesday 18 April *or Am* Tuesday April 18th; **nous sommes m. aujourd'hui** today's Tuesday; **je reviendrai m.** I'll be back on Tuesday; **je suis revenu m.** I came back on Tuesday; **m. dernier/prochain** last/next Tuesday; **ce m., m. qui vient** this (coming) Tuesday, Tuesday next, next Tuesday; **m. en huit** a week on Tuesday, Tuesday week; **m. en quinze** *Br* a fortnight on Tuesday, *Am* two weeks from Tuesday; **il y aura huit jours m.** a week on Tuesday; **tous les mardis** every Tuesday, on Tuesdays; **l'autre m.** *(dans le passé)* (the) Tuesday before last; *(dans l'avenir)* Tuesday after this; **le premier/dernier m. du mois** the first/last Tuesday of the month; **tous les deuxièmes mardis du mois** every second Tuesday in the month; **un m. sur deux** every other *or* every second Tuesday; **m. matin/après-midi** Tuesday morning/afternoon; **m. midi** Tuesday lunchtime, Tuesday (at) noon; **m. soir** Tuesday evening *or* night; **m. dans la nuit** Tuesday (during the) night; **dans la nuit de m. à mercredi** Tuesday night; **la séance/le marché du m.** the Tuesday session/market; **M. gras** *Rel* Shrove Tuesday; *(carnaval)* Mardi Gras; *Fam* **ce n'est pas M. gras, aujourd'hui!** what do you think this is, a carnival or something?

> *Culture*
> **MARDI GRAS**
> This is a very popular festival, falling on the eve of Ash Wednesday, at the end of the carnival. On this day, crêpes are prepared and eaten, and children dress up at school.

mare [mar] NF **1** *(pièce d'eau)* pond; **m. aux canards** duck pond **2** *(de sang, d'essence)* pool

marécage [marekaʒ] NM **1** *Géog* marsh, bog; *(dans un pays chaud)* swamp; *(terres marécageuses)* marshland **2** *Fig Littéraire* **les marécages de la politique** the quagmire of politics

marécageux, -euse [marekaʒø, -øz] ADJ **1** *(région)* marshy, boggy; *(dans un pays chaud)* swampy **2** *(plante)* marsh *(avant n)*

maréchal, -aux [mareʃal, -o] NM **1** *Mil (en France)* marshal; *(en Grande-Bretagne)* field marshal; *(aux États-Unis)* five star general, general of the army; **M. de France** Marshal of France; **m. des logis** sergeant; **m. des logis-chef** *Br* ≃ staff sergeant, *Am* ≃ top sergeant **2** *Hist & Mil* marshal *(in a royal household)*

maréchalat [mareʃala] NM marshalcy, marshalship; **atteindre le m.** to reach the rank of marshal

maréchale [mareʃal] NF **1** *Mil* (field) marshal's wife **2** *Mines* forge coal

maréchalerie [mareʃalri] NF **1** *(métier)* blacksmith's trade, smithery, *Br Spéc* farriery **2** *(atelier)* blacksmith's (shop), smithy, *Br Spéc* farriery

maréchal-ferrant [mareʃalferɑ̃] *(pl* **maréchaux-ferrants***)* NM blacksmith, *Br Spéc* farrier

maréchaussée [mareʃose] NF **1** *Hist* mounted police *or Br* constabulary **2** *Fam Hum* **la m.** the police▪, *Br* the boys in blue, the constabulary

marée [mare] NF **1** *Géog* tide; **(à) m. haute/basse** (at) high/low tide; **changement de m.** turn *or* turning of the tide; **horaire des marées** tide tables; **grande/faible m.** spring/neap tide; **m. montante** flowing *or* flood tide; **m. descendante** ebb tide; **lorsque la m. monte/descend** when the tide is rising/ebbing, when the tide comes in/goes out; **m. d'équinoxe** equinoctial tide; **m. de morte-eau** *ou* **de quadrature** neap tide; *École* **m. noire** oil slick; *Fig* **une m. humaine** a flood of people; *Can Fig* **manquer la m.** to be left on the shelf, to stay unmarried

2 *(poissons, crustacés etc)* (fresh) seafood; **arriver comme m. en carême** to come as surely as night follows day

marégraphe [maregraf] NM tide gauge

marelle [marɛl] NF *(jeu)* hopscotch; *(figure)* (set of) hopscotch squares; **jouer à la m.** to play hopscotch

marémoteur, -trice [maremɔtœr, -tris] ADJ tidal; **usine marémotrice** tidal power station

marengo [marɛ̃go] ADJ INV *Culin voir* **veau**

NM *Tex* = black cloth flecked with white

marennes [marɛn] NF (Marennes) oyster

mareyage [marɛjaʒ] NM fish trade

mareyeur, -euse [marɛjœr, -øz] NM,F fish and seafood wholesaler

margaille [margaj] NF *Belg Fam* **1** *(rixe)* fight■, *Br* ruck **2** *(tapage)* row

margarine [margarin] NF margarine

margauder [3] [margɔde] VI *(caille)* to call

margaux [margo] NM *(vin)* Margaux

margay [margɛ] NM *Zool* margay

marge [marʒ] NF **1** *(espace blanc)* margin; **laisser une grande/petite m.** to leave a wide/narrow margin; **laissez une m. de trois centimètres** leave a margin of three centimetres; **écrire qch dans la m.** to write sth in the margin; **m. de droite/gauche** right-/left-hand margin, right/left margin; **m. extérieure** outside margin; **m. de fond/gouttière** inner/gutter margin; **m. du haut** *ou* **supérieure** top margin; **m. inférieure** *ou* **du bas** bottom margin; **m. intérieure** back *or* inside *or* inner margin; **m. de pied** tail; **m. de reliure** inside margin; **m. de tête** head *or* top margin

2 *Fig (liberté d'action)* leeway; **avoir de la m.** to have some leeway; *(temps)* to have time to spare; **je vous donne deux mètres de tissu/deux mois, comme ça, vous avez de la m.** I'll give you two metres of cloth/two months, that'll be more than enough; **laisser à qn une m. de liberté** to give sb some latitude *or* leeway; **prévoir une m. d'erreur de 40 centimètres/de dix euros** to allow for a margin of error of 40 centimetres/of ten euros; **m. de manœuvre** room for manoeuvre; **m. de sécurité** safety margin; **il a neuf minutes d'avance sur ses poursuivants, c'est une m. (de sécurité) confortable** he has a nine-minute lead over his pursuers, that's a comfortable (safety) margin; **m. de tolérance** (range of) tolerance

3 *Com* margin; **avoir une faible/forte m.** to have a low/high (profit) margin; **nous faisons 30 pour cent de m. sur ce produit** we make a 30 percent margin on this product; **m. avant impôt** pre-tax margin; **m. arrière** refund *(given to distributors at end of financial year)*; **m. bénéficiaire** profit margin; **m. brute** gross margin; **m. brute d'autofinancement** gross cashflow; **m. commerciale brute** gross profit margin; **m. commerciale nette** net profit margin; *Compta* **m. sur coûts variables** contribution; **m. de crédit** credit margin; **m. du détaillant** retailer margin; **m. du distributeur** distributor's margin; **m. de flottement, m. de fluctuation** fluctuation band, fluctuation margin; **m. du grossiste** wholesaler margin; **m. de l'importateur** importer's margin; **m. avant impôt** pre-tax margin; **m. initiale** initial margin; **m. nette** net margin; **m. nette d'exploitation** operating margin; **m. de profit** profit margin; **m. sectorielle** segment margin; **m. supplémentaire** additional margin

4 *Bourse* **appel de m.** margin call

5 *Géog* **m. continentale** continental margin

□ **en marge** ADJ *(original)* fringe *(avant n)*; **un artiste en m.** an unconventional *or* a fringe artist; **annotations** *ou* **notes en m.** notes in the margin, *Sout* marginalia ADV **1** *(d'une feuille de papier)* in the margin; **faites vos annotations en m.** write your notes in the margin **2** *(à l'écart)* **vivre en m.** to live on the fringe *or* fringes (of society); **il est toujours resté en m.** he's always been a loner; **elle a fait une carrière en m.** she made an unconventional career for herself

□ **en marge de** PRÉP **vivre en m. de la société** to live on the fringe *or* margin *or* edge of society; **les événements en m. de l'histoire** footnotes to history, marginal events in history; **beaucoup d'accords sont signés en m. des négociations officielles** a lot of agreements are signed outside of the official negotiating sessions; **il y a une grande exposition de photos en m. du festival** there's a big exhibition of photographs as a fringe event; **en m. de ses activités de professeur, il aidait les enfants handicapés** in addition to his work as a teacher, he helped handicapped children; *Univ* **activité en m. des études** extra-curricular activity

margelle [marʒɛl] NF *(d'une fontaine)* edge, *Br* kerb, *Am* curb

marger [17] [marʒe] VT **1** *Typ* to feed in, to lay on **2** *(machine à écrire)* to set the margins of **3** *Ordinat* **m. une page** to set the page margins

VI to set the margin/margins; **m. à droite/à gauche** to set the right/left margin

margeur, -euse [marʒœr, -øz] NM,F *(ouvrier)* layer-on

NM **1** *Typ* (paper) feed **2** *(sur une machine à écrire)* margin setter

marginal, -e, -aux, -ales [marʒinal, -o] ADJ **1** *(secondaire → problème, rôle)* marginal, minor, peripheral; **ce problème n'a qu'une importance marginale** this problem is of only marginal importance

2 *(à part → personne, mode de vie)* on the fringes of society; **groupe m.** *Pol* fringe group; *(en sociologie)* marginal group; **avec la crise, leur existence est de plus en plus marginale** the economic crisis is pushing them further and further out to the margins *or* fringes of society

3 *Écon* marginal

4 *(annotation)* marginal; **notes marginales** marginal notes, *Sout* marginalia

5 *Géog (récif)* fringing

NM,F dropout; **les marginaux** the fringe elements of society; **ça a toujours été un m.** he's always been a bit of a dropout; **les marginaux de l'expressionnisme** people on the outer fringes of the expressionist movement

marginalement [marʒinalmɑ̃] ADV **vivre m.** to live on the fringe *or* margin of society; **ils ont choisi de vivre m.** they've chosen to opt out (of society)

marginalisation [marʒinalizasjɔ̃] NF marginalization; **la crise économique a favorisé la m. de certaines couches sociales** the economic crisis has led to the marginalization of certain groups in society; **la pauvreté est un facteur de m.** poverty is one of the causes of marginalization

marginaliser [3] [marʒinalize] VT to marginalize; **la toxicomanie a marginalisé une partie de la jeunesse** drug addiction has marginalized a large number of young people; **la tendance radicale du parti a été marginalisée** the radical tendency in the party has been marginalized

▸**se marginaliser** VPR **1** *(volontairement)* to opt out; **elle a choisi de se m.** she has chosen to live outside the mainstream of society

2 *(involontairement)* **il se marginalise de plus en plus depuis son licenciement** he's been feeling increasingly isolated since he was made redundant

3 *(rôle, fonction)* to become marginalized *or* irrelevant; **le rôle du parti s'est marginalisé** the party no longer plays a central role

marginalisme [marʒinalism] NM *Écon* marginal utility

marginaliste [marʒinalist] *Écon* ADJ marginalist

NMF marginalist

marginalité [marʒinalite] NF **1** *(d'un problème, d'un rôle)* minor importance, insignificance, marginality **2** *(d'une personne)* nonconformism; **vivre** *ou* **être dans la m.** to live on the fringe *or* fringes of society; **ils ont préféré vivre dans la m.** they preferred to opt out

marginer [3] [marʒine] VT to write notes in the margin of

margis [marʒi] NM *Fam Arg mil* sarge

margoter, margotter [3] [margɔte] VI *(caille)* to call

margouillat [marguja] NM *Zool* (West African) grey lizard, agama

margouillis [marguji] NM *Fam Vieilli* **1** *(gâchis)* mess■ **2** *(boue)* mud■

margoulette [margulɛt] NF **1** *Fam (bouche)* mouth■, *Br* gob; **casser la m. à qn** to smash sb's face in, to rearrange sb's features; **se casser la m.** to fall flat on one's face **2** *Can (pomme d'Adam)* Adam's apple

margoulin [margulɛ̃] NM *Fam Péj* **1** *(escroc)* crook, swindler **2** *(incompétent)* prat, *Br* pillock, *Am* dork **3** *Bourse* petty speculator■

margousier [marguzje] NM *Bot* margosa

margrave [margrav] *Hist* NM margrave

NF margravine

margraviat [margravja] NM *Hist* margraviate

Marguerite [margərit] NPR **M. d'Anjou** Margaret of Anjou; **M. de Navarre** Margaret of Navarre

marguerite [margərit] NF **1** *Bot* daisy; **grande m.** oxeye daisy, marguerite; **m. dorée** corn marigold **2** *Typ* daisy wheel

marguillier [margije] NM *Hist* churchwarden

mari [mari] NM husband; *Fam* **son petit m.** her hubby

mariable [marjabl] ADJ marriageable

mariachi [marjatʃi] NM mariachi

mariage [marjaʒ] NM **1** *(union)* marriage; *(état)* marriage, matrimony; **proposer le m. à qn** to propose (marriage) to sb; **il m'avait promis le m.** he had promised to marry me; **donner sa fille en m.** to give one's daughter in marriage; **je ne pense pas encore au m.** I'm not thinking about getting married yet; **elle a fait un mauvais m.** she made a bad marriage; **faire un m. d'amour** to marry for love, to make a love match; **faire un m. d'argent** *ou* **d'intérêt** to marry for money; **m. arrangé** arranged marriage; **m. blanc** unconsummated marriage, marriage in name only; **faire un m. blanc** to enter into a marriage of convenience *(primarily in order to acquire nationality)*; **m. de convenance** *ou* **de raison** marriage of convenience; **m. forcé** *ou Can Vieilli* **obligé** forced marriage; **m. homosexuel** gay marriage; **m. mixte** mixed marriage; **enfants (nés) d'un premier m.** children from a first marriage; **enfants nés hors du m.** children born out of wedlock

2 *(vie commune)* married life, *Sout* matrimony; **les premiers temps du m.** early married life; **leur première année de m.** their first year of married life *or* marriage; **le m. ne lui a pas réussi** marriage *or* married life didn't suit him/her

3 *(cérémonie)* wedding; *(cortège)* wedding procession; **m. en blanc** white wedding; **m. civil** civil wedding; *Can* **m. forcé, m. obligé** shotgun wedding; *Jur* **m. putatif** putative marriage; **m. religieux** church wedding; **de m.** wedding *(avant n)*; **anniversaire de m.** wedding anniversary; **ils ont fêté leurs 25 ans de m.** they celebrated their 25th wedding anniversary *or* their silver wedding

4 *Fig (d'arômes, de saveurs)* blend, mixture; *(de couleurs)* combination; *(d'associations, d'organisations)* merging; **cette fille, c'est le m. de l'intelligence et de la beauté** this girl is a combination of *or* combines intelligence and beauty; *Fam* **c'est le m. de la carpe et du lapin** they make strange bedfellows

5 *Cartes* king and queen *(of a suit)*; *(au bésigue)* marriage

6 *Tex* (accidental) slub

'Le Mariage de Figaro' *Beaumarchais* 'The Marriage of Figaro'

Culture

MARIAGE

In France, a civil ceremony (which takes place at the "mairie") is required of all couples wishing to marry, though some choose to have a church wedding as well. The traditional wedding involves a long and sumptuous meal at which the wedding cake, a "pièce montée", is served.

marial, -e, -als *ou* **-aux, -ales** [marjal, -o] ADJ Marian *(avant n)*

marianiste [marjanist] NM Marianist

Marianne [marjan] NF *(figure)* Marianne *(personification of the French Republic)*

MARIANNE

Marianne is the personification of the French Republic; there is a bust of her in every town hall in France, and her portrait appears on French stamps as well as on certain coins. Her face has changed over the years, but she can always be recognized by the "bonnet phrygien" she wears. Every ten years, France's mayors choose a well-known Frenchwoman to be "the face of Marianne", a model for the icon of the French Republic. Famous women on whom this honour has been conferred include Brigitte Bardot and Catherine Deneuve.

Marie [mari] NPR **1** *Rel* Mary; **la Vierge M.** the Virgin Mary **2** *Hist* **M. Stuart** Mary Queen of Scots, Mary Stuart; **M. de Médicis** Maria de Medici

marié, -e [marje] ADJ married; **non m.** unmarried, single; **il est m. avec Maud** he's married to Maud; **je suis m. depuis trois ans** I've been married for three years; *Fam* **on n'est pas mariés, dis donc!** just a minute, you're not my mother!

  NM **le (jeune) m.** the groom, the bridegroom; **le futur m.** the bridegroom-to-be

  ❑ **mariée** NF **la (jeune) mariée** the bride; **la future mariée** the bride-to-be; **une robe de mariée** a wedding dress; **la robe/le bouquet de la mariée** the bride's dress/bouquet; *Fig* **tu te plains que la mariée est trop belle!** you don't know how lucky you are!

  ❑ **mariés** NMPL **les mariés** *(le jour de la cérémonie)* the bride and groom *or* bridegroom; **les futurs mariés** the bride and groom-to-be; **les jeunes mariés** the newly-weds; **féliciter les mariés** to congratulate the bride and groom *or* the married couple

'La Mariée était en noir' *Truffaut* 'The Bride Wore Black'

Marie-Antoinette [mariãtwanɛt] NPR Marie Antoinette

Marie-Chantal [mariʃãtal] NF INV *Fam Br* ≃ Sloane (Ranger), *Am* ≃ preppy

Marie-couche-toi-là [marikuʃtwala] NF INV *Fam* trollop, slut

marie-jeanne [mariʒan] NF INV *Fam Arg drogue (cannabis)* Mary Jane, pot

marie-louise [marilwiz] *(pl* **maries-louises)** NF **1** *(passe-partout)* inner frame **2** *(encadrement)* harmonized border

Marie-Madeleine [marimadlɛn] NPR *Bible* Mary Magdalene

marier [9] [marje] VT **1** *(unir)* to marry, *Littéraire* to wed; **le maire/le prêtre les a mariés hier** the mayor/the priest married them yesterday

  2 *(donner en mariage)* to marry; **ils marièrent leur fille à un médecin** they married their daughter to a doctor; **elle a encore un fils/une fille à m.** she still has a son/a daughter to marry off; **elle est bonne à m.** she's of marriageable age

  3 *(parfums, couleurs)* to blend, to combine, *Sout* to marry; *(styles, sons)* to harmonize, to combine, *Sout* to marry; *(vêtements, styles de meubles)* to harmonize; **il marie l'égoïsme à la plus parfaite indifférence** he is a combination of selfishness and total indifference

  4 *Belg (épouser)* to marry

  5 *Naut (cordages)* to hold together

  ▸**se marier** VPR **1** *(personnes)* to get married, to marry, *Littéraire* to wed; **se m. à** *ou* **avec qn** to marry sb, to get married to sb; **il veut se m. à l'église** he wants to have a church wedding *or* to get married in church

  2 *(couleurs, arômes, styles)* to go together; **ça se marie bien avec le vert** it goes nicely with the green

marie-salope [marisalɔp] *(pl* **maries-salopes)** NF **1** *(péniche)* hopper (barge); *(drague)* dredger **2** *très Fam (souillon)* slut

Marie-Thérèse [mariterɛz] NPR **M. d'Autriche** Maria Theresa of Austria

marieur, -euse [marjœr, -øz] NM,F *Fam* matchmaker

Marignan [mariɲã] NM **la bataille de M.** = famous victory of Francis I at Marignano in Italy over the Swiss Holy League in 1515

Marigny [mariɲi] NM **l'hôtel M.** = a house attached to the French President's office where foreign dignitaries are accommodated and press conferences held

marigot [marigo] NM **1** *(bras de fleuve)* side channel, backwater, marigot **2** *(région inondable)* flood lands

marihuana [marirwana], **marijuana** [mariʒɥana] NF marijuana

marimba [marimba] NM *Mus* marimba

marin, -e [marɛ̃, -in] ADJ **1** *(air, courant, sel)* sea *(avant n)*; *(animal, carte)* marine *(avant n)*, sea *(avant n)*; *(plante, vie)* marine *(avant n)*; **paysage m.** seascape; **navire m.** seaworthy ship; **monstres marins** sea monsters

  2 *Pétr* offshore *(avant n)*

  NM **1** *(gén)* seaman, seafarer; **un peuple de marins** a seafaring nation; **ses qualités de m. ne sont plus à démontrer** he's an accomplished seaman

  2 *Mil & Naut* seaman, sailor; **costume/béret de m.** sailor suit/hat; **simple m.** able *or* able-bodied seaman; **marins marchands** *ou* **du commerce** merchant seamen; **m. pêcheur** (deep-sea) fisherman; *Hum* **m. d'eau douce** Sunday sailor

  3 *Météo* marin, sea wind *(from the south-east coast of France)*

marina [marina] NF marina

marinade [marinad] NF **1** *(saumure)* pickle; *(mélange aromatique)* marinade; **viande en m.** marinated *or* marinaded meat **2** *Can* pickle; **marinades** pickles

marinage [marinaʒ] NM marinating

marine [marin] ADJ F *voir* **marin**

  ADJ INV *(bleu marine)* navy (blue)

  NF **1** *Naut* navy; **la M. nationale** the (French) Navy; **m. marchande** merchant navy *or* marine; **m. de plaisance** yachting; **m. à vapeur** steamers, steamships; **m. à voile** sailing ships

  2 *Mil* **m. (de guerre)** navy; **le musée de la M.** = the Paris Naval Museum, in the Palais de Chaillot

  3 *(navigation)* seamanship; **terme de m.** nautical term

  4 *Beaux-Arts* seascape

  NM **1** *(fusilier marin → britannique)* Royal Marine; *(→ des États-Unis)* (US) Marine; **les Marines** *Br* the Royal Marines, *Am* the US Marine Corps, the Marines

  2 *(couleur)* navy (blue)

mariner [3] [marine] VT *(pour assaisonner)* to marinate, to marinade; *(dans une saumure)* to pickle, to souse; **des harengs marinés** pickled herrings

  VI **1** *Culin* to marinate; **laissez la viande m.** *ou* **faites m. la viande pendant plusieurs heures** allow the meat to marinate for several hours

  2 *Fam (personne)* to wait■, to hang around *or* *Br* about; **il marine en prison** he's rotting in prison; **laisse-la m.!** let her stew for a while!; **ne nous fais pas m.!** don't keep us hanging around!; **il m'a fait m. pendant deux heures** he kept me hanging around for two hours

maringouin [marɛ̃gwɛ̃] NM *Can* mosquito; **m. domestique** northern house mosquito

marinier [marinje] NM **1** *(batelier)* *Br* bargee, *Am* bargeman **2** *Arch (marin)* mariner

marinière [marinjɛr] NF **1** *(blouse)* sailor blouse; *(maillot rayé)* (white and navy blue) striped jersey **2** *Culin* **sauce m.** white wine sauce; **(à la) m.** in a white wine sauce

marinisme [marinism] NM *Littérature* Marinism

mariole, mariolle [marjɔl] *Fam* ADJ *(astucieux)* smart, clever■

  NM smart aleck, *Br* clever dick, *Am* wise guy; **faire le m.** to act smart; **fais pas le m. sur ta moto/avec ce revolver** don't try and be clever on that bike/with that gun

mariologie [marjɔlɔʒi] NF Mariology

marionnette [marjɔnɛt] NF **1** *(poupée)* **m. (à fils)** puppet, marionette; **m. (à gaine)** (hand *or*

glove) puppet; **spectacle/théâtre de marionnettes** puppet show/theatre; **on va aux marionnettes** we're going to the puppet show; *Fam* **faire les marionnettes** = to move one's hands and sing in order to amuse a young child **2** *Péj (personne)* puppet

marionnettiste [marjɔnɛtist] NMF puppeteer

marisque [marisk] NF *Méd* marisca, haemorrhoidal tumour

mariste [marist] ADJ Marist

  NM Marist

marital, -e, -aux, -ales [marital, -o] ADJ *Jur* **1** *(relatif au mari)* marital; **l'autorisation maritale** the husband's authorization; **les biens maritaux** the husband's possessions **2** *(relatif à l'union libre)* **au cours de leur vie maritale** while they lived together (as man and wife)

maritalement [maritalmã] ADV **vivre m.** to live as husband and wife; **vivre m. avec qn** to cohabit with sb

maritime [maritim] ADJ **1** *(du bord de mer → village)* coastal, seaside *(avant n)*, *Am* seaboard *(avant n)*; **province m.** maritime *or* coastal province; *Admin* **région m.** coastal area; **ville m.** seaside town

  2 *(naval → hôpital, entrepôt)* naval; *(→ commerce)* seaborne, maritime; **puissance m.** maritime *or* sea power

  3 *Jur (législation, droit)* maritime, shipping *(avant n)*; *(agent)* shipping *(avant n)*; *(assurance)* marine *(avant n)*

maritorne [maritɔrn] NF *Littéraire* sloven, slattern

Marius [marjys] NPR = a play by Marcel Pagnol (1928), strongly evocative of the traditions of Marseille

marivaudage [marivodaʒ] NM *Littéraire* light-hearted banter

marivauder [3] [marivode] VI *Littéraire* to banter, to exchange gallantries

marjolaine [marʒɔlɛn] NF *Bot* marjoram

mark [mark] NM *Anciennement Fin* mark

marketing [marketiŋ] NM marketing; **faire du m.** *(étudier)* to do marketing; *(avoir pour profession)* to be in marketing; **m. par affinité** affinity marketing; **m. "à la carte"** customized *or* tailored marketing; **m. après-vente** after-sales marketing; **m. ciblé** niche marketing, target marketing; **m. commercial** trade marketing; **m. concentré** concentrated marketing; **m. de contact** direct marketing; **m. défensif** defensive marketing; **m. différencié** *ou* **de différenciation** differentiated marketing; **m. direct** direct marketing; **m. écologique** green marketing; **m. électronique** on-line marketing, e-marketing; **m. expansionniste** rollout marketing; **m. d'expérience** experiential marketing; **m. global** global marketing; **m. de grande consommation** mass marketing; **m. guérilla** *ou* **guérilla m.** guerrilla marketing; **m. hors-média** below-the-line marketing; **m. indifférencié** undifferentiated marketing; **m. industriel** industrial marketing; **m. interactif** interactive marketing; **m. international** global marketing; **m. interne** internal marketing; **m. de masse** mass marketing; **m. sur mesure** customized marketing; **m. mix** marketing mix; **m. multinational** multinational marketing; **m. non commercial** non-business marketing; **m. non lucratif** not-for-profit marketing; **m. de nouveaux produits** new product marketing; **m. one to one** one-to-one marketing; **m. opérationnel** operational marketing; **m. de la permission** permission marketing; **m. de relance** remarketing; **m. relationnel** relationship marketing; **m. de réseau** multi-level marketing; **m. sélectif** selective marketing; **m. de stimulation** stimulation *or* incentive marketing; **m. stratégique** strategic marketing; **m. téléphonique** telemarketing; **m. terrain** grass-roots marketing; **m. de la valeur** value marketing; **m. vert** green marketing; **m. viral** viral marketing

markhor [markɔr] NM *Zool* markhor

marli [marli] NM *(d'un plat, d'une assiette)* inner rim

marlin [marlɛ̃] NM *Ich* spearfish

marlot [marlo] NM *Can Fam* good-for-nothing

marlou [marlu] NM *Fam* **1** *(voyou)* hoodlum **2** *(souteneur)* pimp, *Am* mack

marmaille [marmaj] NF *Fam Péj* brood, kids; **elle est venue avec toute sa m.** she came with her whole brood

marmelade [marməlad] NF *Culin* compote; **m. de fraises** strawberry compote; **m. d'oranges** (orange) marmalade; **m. de pommes** stewed apple *or* apples, apple compote; *(pour viande)* apple sauce

▫ **en marmelade** ADJ 1 *Culin* stewed; *(trop cuit, écrasé)* mushy 2 *Fam (en piteux état)* **j'ai les pieds en m.** my feet are absolutely killing me; **elle avait le visage en m.** her face was all smashed up; **mettre qn en m.** to reduce sb to a pulp

marmenteau, -x [marmãto] *Jur* ADJ **arbre m. =** full-grown ornamental tree forming part of the amenities of an estate and not to be cut down

NM = full-grown ornamental tree forming part of the amenities of an estate and not to be cut down

marmite [marmit] NF 1 *Culin (contenant)* pot, cooking pot; *(contenu)* pot, potful; **m. norvégienne** haybox 2 *Phys* **m. de Papin** Papin's digester 3 *Géol* **m. torrentielle** *ou* **de géants** pothole

marmitée [marmite] NF *(contenu)* pot, potful

marmiton [marmitɔ̃] NM young kitchen hand

marmonnement [marmɔnmã] NM mumbling, muttering

marmonner [3] [marmɔne] VI to mumble, to mutter; **la vieille femme marmonnait dans son coin** the old woman was muttering (away) to herself

VT to mumble, to mutter; **qu'est-ce que tu marmonnes encore?** what's that you're muttering *or* mumbling (now)?

marmoréen, -enne [marmɔreɛ̃, -ɛn] ADJ 1 *Géol* marmoreal, marmorean 2 *Littéraire* marmoreal, marble *(avant n)*

marmot [marmo] NM *Fam* (little) kid, *Br* nipper

marmotte [marmɔt] NF 1 *Zool* marmot; **m. d'Amérique** *ou* **du Canada, m. commune** woodchuck; *Fig* **tu es une vraie m.!** you're a *Br* real *or Am* regular dormouse! 2 *(fourrure)* marmot; **de** *ou* **en m.** marmot *(avant n)* 3 *Bot* (marmotte) cherry

marmottement [marmɔtmã] NM mumbling, muttering

marmotter [3] [marmɔte] VI to mutter, to mumble

VT to mutter, to mumble

marmouset [marmuzɛ] NM 1 *Archit* grotesque (figure), (small) gargoyle 2 *(chenet)* carved fire dog 3 *Zool* marmoset

▫ **marmousets** NMPL *Hist* = name by which the Duke of Burgundy and the Duke of Berry referred to the former advisers of Charles V

marnage[1] [marnaʒ] NM *Agr* marling

marnage[2] [marnaʒ] NM *(d'un plan d'eau)* tidal range

Marne [marn] NF 1 *(rivière)* **la M.** the (River) Marne; **la bataille de la M.** the Battle of the Marne 2 *(département)* **la M.** the Marne

---

Culture

LA BATAILLE DE LA MARNE

This was the successful campaign led by Joffre against the advancing German forces in September 1914, famous for the **taxis de la Marne** (see entry **taxi**), the Paris taxis requisitioned to take troops to the front line.

---

marne [marn] NF marl

marner [3] [marne] VT *Agr* to marl

VI 1 *Fam (personne)* to slog, to sweat blood; **j'ai marné toute ma vie** I've sweated blood all my life; **il nous fait m.** he keeps us hard at it *or* slaving away 2 *(mer)* to rise

marneur [marnœr] NM *Agr* marl spreader

marneux, -euse [marnø, -øz] ADJ marly

marnière [marnjɛr] NF marl pit

Maroc [marɔk] NM *Géog* **le M.** Morocco; **vivre au M.** to live in Morocco; **aller au M.** to go to Morocco

marocain, -e [marɔkɛ̃, -ɛn] ADJ Moroccan

NM *(langue)* Moroccan (Arabic)

▫ **Marocain, -e** NM,F Moroccan

maroilles [marwal] NM Maroilles cheese *(soft cheese made from cow's milk)*

marollien [marɔljɛ̃] NM *Ling* = slang spoken in the suburbs of Brussels, a hybrid of French and Flemish

maronite [marɔnit] NMF Maronite

ADJ Maronite

---

maronner [3] [marɔne] VI *Fam* 1 *(maugréer)* to grumble, to grouch; *(être en colère)* to be fuming; **ne la fais pas m.** don't get her back up 2 *(attendre)* to hang about *or* around; **il nous fait toujours m.** he always keeps us hanging about *or* around waiting

maroquin [marɔkɛ̃] NM 1 *(peau)* morocco 2 *Fam (ministère)* minister's portfolio■

maroquinage [marɔkinaʒ] NM tanning *(of a skin into morocco leather)*

maroquiner [3] [marɔkine] VT to tan *(into morocco leather)*

maroquinerie [marɔkinri] NF 1 *(commerce)* leather trade; *(industrie)* leather craft; *(magasin)* leather (goods) *Br* shop *or Am* store 2 *(articles)* (small) leather goods 3 *(atelier)* tannery; *(tannage)* tanning

maroquinier, -ère [marɔkinje, -ɛr] ADJ **ouvrier m.** leather worker; **marchand m.** leather merchant

NM,F *(ouvrier)* tanner; *(artisan)* leather craftsman; **je l'ai acheté chez un m.** I bought it from a leather (goods) *Br* shop *or Am* store

marotte [marɔt] NF 1 *Fam (passe-temps)* pet hobby; *(manie)* fad, craze; **c'est sa m.** it's his/her pet hobby *or* thing; **il a la m. des mots croisés** crosswords are his pet hobby; **c'est devenu une m.** it's become an obsession 2 *(sceptre)* fool's bauble 3 *(de coiffeur, de modiste)* dummy head

marouette [marwɛt] NF *Orn* crake, rail; **m. de la Caroline** sora rail; **m. ponctuée** spotted crake; **m. poussin** little crake

maroufle [marufl] NF *Beaux-Arts* strong paste *(used for backing)*

maroufler [3] [marufle] VT *Beaux-Arts* to back; **une toile marouflée** a backed picture

maroute [marut] NF *Bot* stinking camomile

marquage [markaʒ] NM 1 *Sport* marking 2 *(de linge)* marking; *(d'animaux)* marking, branding; *Aut* **m. au sol** road markings; **m. en zig-zag** zig-zag marking 3 *(de marchandises)* marking; *Com* branding, labelling 4 *Phys* **m. radioactif** radioactive labelling *or* tracing

marquant, -e [markã, -ãt] ADJ 1 *(personne)* prominent, outstanding; **les personnalités marquantes de ce siècle** this century's most influential figures 2 *(détail, trait)* striking; *(fait, épisode)* significant; **un événement particulièrement m.** an event of particular *or* outstanding importance; *Littérature* **passages marquants** highlights, purple passages

---

MARQUE [mark]

mark 1–3, 5 ■ marker 2, 9, 12 ■ make 4 ■ brand 4 ■ hallmark 5 ■ score 6, 7	

NF 1 *(trace)* mark; *(cicatrice)* mark, scar; **marques de coups** marks of blows; **on voit encore la m. du coup qu'elle a reçu** you can still see where she was hit; **marques de doigts** *(sales)* fingermarks; *(empreintes)* fingerprints; **les marques de la vieillesse** marks *or* traces of old age; **les roues avaient laissé des marques sur le sable** the wheels had left marks in the sand; **les brûlures n'ont laissé aucune m. sur son bras** the burns left no marks *or* scars on his/her arm; **il y avait encore la m. de son corps dans l'herbe** the imprint of his/her body in the grass was still there; **faire une m. au couteau sur qch** to make a mark with a knife *or* a knife mark on sth, to mark sth with a knife; **le cintre a fait une m. sur ce vêtement** the coat-hanger has left a mark on this garment

2 *(signet)* marker, bookmark; *(trait)* mark; **m. au crayon/à la craie** pencil/chalk mark; *Com* **marques d'expédition** shipping marks; **m. de garantie** certification mark; **m. de service** mark of quality, quality guarantee *(on range of services offered by company or manufacturer)*

3 *Fig (preuve)* mark; **comme m. d'amitié/d'estime/de confiance** as a token of friendship/esteem/trust; **c'est là la m. d'une grande générosité** that's the sign *or* mark of real generosity

4 *Com (de produits manufacturés)* make, brand; *(de produits alimentaires et chimiques)* brand; *(de voitures)* make, marque; *(sur l'article)* trademark;

(nom du fabricant) logo; **voiture de m. française** French-made *or* French-built car; **j'ai eu des voitures de trois marques différentes** I've had three different makes of car; **grande m.** famous make, well-known brand; *(dans la mode)* designer label; **les grandes marques d'électroménager** the main brands of electrical appliance(s); **c'est une grande m. de cigarettes/de voitures** *(célèbre)* it's a well-known brand of cigarette/make of car; *(de luxe)* it's a brand of luxury cigarette/a make of luxury car; **produits de grande m.** top brand *or* name products; **m. d'appel** loss leader brand; **m. clé** key brand; **m. collective** label; **m. commerciale, m. de commerce** trademark, brand (name); **m. déposée** registered trademark; **m. de détaillant** retailer brand; **m. de distributeur** distributor's brand name, own brand; **m. dominante** dominant brand; **m. économique** economy brand; **m. d'enseigne** retailer brand, shop's own brand; **m. de fabricant** manufacturer's brand (name); **m. de fabrique** trademark, brand (name); **m. générale** family brand; **m. générique** generic brand; **m. globale** global brand; **m. grand public** consumer brand; **m. de magasin** store brand; **m. milieu de gamme** middle brand, middle-of-the-range brand; **m. multiple** multibrand; **m. ombrelle** umbrella brand; **m. d'origine** origin of goods label; **m. de tête** brand leader

5 *(identification → sur bijoux)* hallmark; *(→ sur meubles)* stamp, mark; *(→ sur animaux)* brand; *Vét* **m. de l'inspection vétérinaire** Health Officer's inspection stamp; **un produit qui porte la m. de la douane** goods that have been stamped at customs; *Fig* **il a dessiné ces jardins, il est facile de reconnaître sa m.** he designed these gardens, it's easy to recognize his style; *Fig* **porter la m. du génie** to bear the stamp *or* the hallmark of genius; *Fig* **on reconnaît la m. du génie** that's the hallmark *or* stamp of genius; *Hist* **d'infamie** brand *(on prostitutes)*

6 *(dans un jeu → jeton)* chip; *(→ décompte)* score; **tenir la m.** to keep (the) score

7 *Sport (score)* score; **mener à la m.** to be ahead, to be in the lead

8 *Sport (au rugby)* **m.!** mark!

9 *Ling* marker; **en français, le e est souvent la m. du féminin** in French the letter e often indicates that the word is in the feminine form; **porter la m. du féminin/pluriel** to be in the feminine/plural form

10 *Typ* **m. d'imprimeur** printer's colophon

11 *Naut* **la m. de l'amiral** the admiral's flag

12 *Ordinat* marker, flag, tag; **m. d'insertion** insertion marker; **m. de paragraphe** paragraph mark

▫ **marques** NFPL *Sport* **prendre ses marques** *(coureur)* to take one's marks; *(sauteur)* to pace out one's run up; *Fig* **chercher ses marques** to try to find one's bearings; **à vos marques! prêts! partez!** on your marks! get set! go!, ready! steady! go!

▫ **de marque** ADJ *(produit)* branded; *(hôte)* distinguished; **articles de m.** branded goods; **produits de m. courante** well-known branded goods; **personnage de m.** VIP

---

marqué, -e [marke] ADJ 1 *(visible → différence)* marked, distinct; *(→ préférence)* marked, obvious; *(→ accent)* marked, broad, strong; *(→ traits)* pronounced; **il a le visage très m.** *(par des blessures)* his face is covered with scars; *(par la maladie)* illness has left its mark on his face; **visage m. par la petite vérole** pockmarked face; **visage m. par l'âge** face lined with age; **robe à la taille marquée** dress fitted at the waist

2 *Fig (impressionné)* **j'ai été très m. par ce film** the film made a strong impression on me; **il est m. à vie par cette expérience** he has been marked for life by the experience

3 *Fig (engagé)* **il est très m. politiquement** politically he is very committed

4 *(écrit)* **il n'y a rien (de) m. dessus** there's nothing marked *or* written on it; **il est m. qu'il faut une pièce d'identité** it says that some form of identification is required; **qu'est-ce qui est m.** *ou* **qu'est-ce qu'il y a de m. sur l'enveloppe?**

what does it say on the envelope?, what's written on the envelope?

marque-page [markpaʒ] NM INV bookmark

marquer [3] [marke] VT **1** *(montrer)* to mark; **m. la limite de qch** to mark sth (off), to mark the limit of sth; **les lignes bleues marquent les frontières** the blue lines show *or* indicate where the border is; **l'horloge marque trois heures** the clock shows *or* says three o'clock; **la balance marque 3 kg** the scales register *or* read 3 kg; **le thermomètre marque 40°C** the thermometer shows *or* registers 40°C

2 *(signaler → passage d'un texte)* to mark; *(→ bétail)* to brand, to mark; *(→ arbre)* to blaze; *(→ linge)* to label, to tag; **marque-le à ton nom** mark it with your name; **marquez-le d'un tiret/d'une flèche/d'une croix** mark it with a dash/an arrow/a cross; **m. sa page** *(avec un signet)* to mark one's place (with a bookmark); *(en cornant la page)* to turn down the corner of one's page; **m. au fer rouge** to brand; *Fig* **cet événement a marqué la fin de son adolescence** this event marked the end of his/her adolescence; *Fig* **ce jour est à m. d'une pierre blanche** this will go down as a red-letter day

3 *(témoigner de)* to mark, to show; **pour m. sa confiance** as a token *or* mark of his/her trust

4 *(événement, date)* to mark; **de nombreuses manifestations ont marqué le bicentenaire** a number of events marked *or* commemorated the bicentenary; *Fam* **m. le coup** *(fêter quelque chose)* to mark the occasion▪; *(réagir)* to react▪

5 *(prendre en note)* to write *or* to take *or* to note (down); *(tracer)* to mark, to write; **marquez votre nom en haut à gauche** write your name in the top left-hand corner; **tu l'as marqué?** have you made a note of it?; **marqué à l'encre/à la craie/au crayon sur le mur** marked in ink/chalk/pencil on the wall, inked/chalked/pencilled on the wall; **m. les prix** to mark prices

6 *(sujet: difficulté, épreuve)* to mark; **le chagrin a marqué son visage** his/her face is lined *or* furrowed with sorrow; **la guerre l'a beaucoup marqué** the war certainly left its mark on him *or* left a deep impression on him; **ces années de pauvreté l'ont marquée (à jamais)** those years of poverty have left their (indelible) mark on her; **cette expérience l'a marqué à vie** he was scarred for life by this experience; **le choc a marqué la carrosserie** the bodywork was marked *or* damaged in the collision

7 *(impressionner)* to mark, to affect, to make an impression on; **ça m'a beaucoup marqué** it made a big *or* lasting impression on me; **il a profondément marqué les musiciens de son époque** he made a deep impression on the musicians of the period; **c'est un film qui ne m'a pas marqué** I wasn't very struck by the film

8 *Sport & (dans un jeu)* **m. un point/but** to score a point/goal; **m. 30 points** to score 30 (points); **ne m. aucun point** to fail to score (a single point); **m. les points** to note *or* to keep the score; *Fig* **l'argument est judicieux, vous marquez un point** the argument is valid, that's one to you *or* you've scored a point; **m. un joueur** to mark a player

9 *(rythmer)* **il marquait la cadence du pied** he beat time with his foot; *Mus* **m. la mesure** to keep the beat; **m. un temps d'arrêt** to pause *(for a moment)*; **m. le pas** to mark time; *Fig* **la réforme marque le pas** the reform is dragging its feet

10 *Couture* **manteau qui marque bien la taille** coat that shows off the figure; **les robes, cet été, marqueront la taille** this summer's dresses will emphasize the waistline

11 *Can Fam* **m. un achat** to charge a purchase (to one's account)▪, to have a purchase put on one's tab; **elle fait m. et paie pour tout à la fin du mois** she charges everything to her account and pays for it all at the end of the month

12 *Ordinat* to mark, to flag, to tag

13 *Com (article, produit)* to brand, to label

VI **1** *(événement)* to stand out; *(personne)* to make one's mark; **les grands hommes qui ont marqué dans l'histoire** the great men who have left their mark on history; **sa mort a marqué dans ma vie** his/her death had a great effect *or* impact on my life

2 *(crayon, objet)* **ce feutre ne marque plus** this felt-tip pen doesn't write any more; **attention, ça marque!** careful, it'll leave a mark!; **le verre a marqué sur la table** the glass left a mark on the table, the glass marked the table

3 *Sport* to score

marqueté, -e [markəte] ADJ *(meuble)* inlaid

marqueter [27] [markəte] VT **1** *(bois)* to inlay **2** *Littéraire (tacheter)* to speckle, to dot

marqueterie [markɛtri] NF **1** *(décoration)* marquetry, inlay; **un panneau en m.** a marquetry panel; **un guéridon en m.** an inlaid pedestal table; **bois de m.** marquetry wood; *Fig* **une m. de tendances politiques** a *Br* hotchpotch *or Am* hodgepodge of different political tendencies **2** *(métier)* marquetry

marqueteur, -euse [markətœr, -øz] NM,F inlayer

marqueur, -euse [markœr, -øz] NM,F **1** *(de documents)* stamper; *(de bétail)* brander

2 *(qui compte les points)* scorekeeper, scorer; *(qui gagne les points)* scorer; **m. automatique** *(au bridge)* scoreboard

NM **1** *(gros feutre)* marker (pen); *(surligneur)* highlighter; **la phrase indiquée au m.** the highlighted sentence

2 *Biol, Ling & Méd* marker

3 *Nucl* tracer

4 *Ordinat* marker, flag; **m. de fin de texte** end of text marker

❑ **marqueuse** NF *Com* marking *or* stamping machine

marquis [marki] NM marquess, marquis; **merci, Monsieur le M.** thank you, your Lordship

marquisat [markiza] NM *(rang, fief)* marquessate, marquisate

marquise [markiz] NF **1** *(titre → gén)* marchioness, *(→ en France)* marquise; **merci, Madame la M.** thank you, your Ladyship; **elle est maintenant m.** she's now a marchioness **2** *(abri de toile)* awning; *(auvent vitré)* (glass) canopy; *(de gare)* glass roof **3** *(bijou)* marquise ring **4** *Culin* **m. glacée** iced marquise **5** *(chaise)* marquise

Marquises [markiz] NFPL **les (îles) M.** the Marquesas Islands; **aux (îles) M.** in the Marquesas Islands

marquoir [markwar] NM *Couture* (tailor's) marking tool

marraine [marɛn] NF **1** *Rel* godmother **2** *(d'un bateau)* christener, namer; **elle fut choisie comme m. du bateau** she was chosen to launch *or* to name the ship **3** *(d'un nouveau membre)* sponsor; **m. de guerre** soldier's wartime penfriend *or* penpal

Marrakech [marakɛʃ] NM Marrakech, Marrakesh

marrane [maran] NM Marrano

marrant, -e [marɑ̃, -ɑ̃t] *Fam* ADJ **1** *(drôle)* funny▪; **il est (trop) m.!** he's a hoot *or* scream!; **elle n'est pas marrante, sa femme** his wife is no fun!; **je ne veux pas y aller – t'es pas m.!** I don't want to go – you're no fun!; **vous êtes marrants, je n'ai pas que ça à faire!** come on, I've got other things to do, you know!

2 *(bizarre)* funny▪, odd▪, strange▪; **c'est m. qu'elle ne soit pas encore là** funny (that) she hasn't arrived yet

NM,F joker, funny guy, *f* girl; **être un m.** to be fun, to be a laugh *or* a riot; **c'est un m., celui-là** that guy's a scream, that guy's hilarious; **son père, c'est pas un m.** his dad's not much fun *or* not much of a laugh; **le nouveau directeur, c'est vraiment pas un m.** the new manager doesn't fool around; **c'est un petit m. qui se croit tout permis** he's a little joker who thinks he can do as he likes

marre [mar] ADV *Fam* **en avoir m. (de)** to be fed up (with) *or* hacked off (with); **en avoir m. de faire qch** to be fed up *or* sick and tired of doing sth; **il en a m. de ses études** he's fed up with *or* sick and tired of studying; **je commence à en avoir plus que m. de tes mensonges** I've just about had enough of your lies, I'm sick and tired of your lies; **j'en ai m. de venir à pied tous les jours** I'm fed up with *or* I'm sick of walking here every day; **j'en ai m. que ce soit toujours moi qui fasse les courses** I'm fed up with always having to do the shopping; **j'en ai m.!** I've had enough!; **il y en a m. (de)** that's enough (of); **il y en a m. de te voir ne rien faire** I'm sick (and tired) of seeing you lie around doing nothing; *Vieilli* **c'est m.!** that's enough!, that'll do!; *Vieilli* **allez, c'est m., on se tire!** come on, that's enough, let's clear off!

marrer [3] [mare] *Fam* VI **faire m. qn** to make sb laugh▪; **tu me fais m. avec tes histoires de télépathie!** you make me laugh with all your telepathy nonsense!; *aussi Ironique* **me fais pas m.** don't make me laugh

►**se marrer** VPR to have a (good) laugh; **on s'est drôlement marrés hier soir** we really had a good laugh *or* a great time last night; **elle ne doit pas se m. tous les jours avec ce type-là** she can't have much fun with that guy; *Ironique* **quand elle me dit qu'elle va chercher du boulot, je me marre** when she tells me she's going to look for a job, I have to laugh; *Ironique* **alors là, je me marre!** that's a laugh!, don't make me laugh!; *Ironique* **qu'est-ce qu'on se marre!** this is great fun, not! *or* I don't think!

marri, -e [mari] ADJ *Arch (contrarié, fâché)* **être (fort) m.** to be (most) aggrieved; **si je vous ai blessé, j'en suis bien m.** I would be most grieved *or* distressed to think that I had hurt you

marron[1] [marɔ̃] NM **1** *Bot* chestnut; **m. d'Inde** horse chestnut, *Fam* conker; **marrons chauds** roast *or* roasted chestnuts; **marrons glacés** marrons glacés, crystallized *or* candied chestnuts; **crème de m.** chestnut purée; *Fig* **tirer les marrons du feu** to do all the dirty work

2 *(couleur)* brown; **j'aime le m.** I like brown

3 *Fam (coup)* belt, wallop; **flanquer** *ou* **coller un m. à qn** to belt *or* wallop sb one; **il s'est pris de ces marrons!** he got a real thumping *or* walloping!

ADJ INV *(brun)* brown; **m. clair** light brown

ADJ *Fam (dupé)* **être m.** *(avoir été dupé)* to have been taken in *or* for a ride, *Am* to have been rooked; **faire qn m.** to take sb in *or* for a ride, *Am* to rook sb; **zut, voilà le contrôleur, on est marrons!** *(on est coincés)* oh, no, we've had it now, here comes the ticket collector!

marron[2], **-onne** [marɔ̃, -ɔn] ADJ *(malhonnête)* crooked; **amateurisme m.** shamateurism; **avocat m.** crooked lawyer; **esclave m.** escaped slave; **médecin m.** quack

marronnier [marɔnje] NM chestnut tree; **m. d'Inde** horse chestnut (tree)

marrube [maryb] NM *Bot* marrubium, hoarhound

Mars [mars] NF *Astron* Mars

NPR *Myth* Mars

mars [mars] NM **1** *(mois)* March; **en m.** in March; **au mois de m.** in (the month of) March; **nous y allons tous les ans en m.** *ou* **au mois de m.** we go there every (year in) March; **au début du mois de m., (au) début m.** at the beginning of March, in early March; **au milieu du mois de m., à la mi-m.** in the middle of March, in mid-March; **à la fin du mois de m., (à la) fin m.** at the end of March, in late March; **en m. dernier/prochain** last/next March; **Nice, le 5 m. 2007** Nice, 5 March 2007; **la commande vous a été livrée le 31 m.** your order was delivered on 31 March; **j'attendrai jusqu'au (lundi) 4 m.** I'll wait until (Monday) 4 March; *Fig* **arriver comme m. en carême** to come as surely as night follows day

2 *Entom* **grand m. (changeant)** purple emperor; **petit m. (changeant)** lesser purple emperor; **petit m. oriental** Freyer's purple emperor

marsala [marsala] NM Marsala

marsault [marso] NM goat willow

marseillais, -e [marsɛjɛ, -ɛz] ADJ of/from Marseilles; **histoire marseillaise** tall story

❑ **Marseillais, -e** NM,F = inhabitant of or person from Marseilles

❑ **Marseillaise** NF *Mus* **la Marseillaise** the Marseillaise *(the French national anthem)*

> *Culture*
>
> **LA MARSEILLAISE**
>
> The French national anthem, most probably written by Rouget de Lisle, was sung for the first time in 1792 by a group of revolutionaries as they arrived in Paris from Marseilles. It became the national anthem in 1795.

Marseille [marsɛj] NM Marseilles, Marseille; **tu ne serais pas de M. par hasard?** you're a great one for telling tall stories, aren't you!

Marshall [marʃal] NPR *voir* **île**

mar–mas

marshmallow [marʃmalo] NM *Bot* marshmallow

marsouin [marswɛ̃] NM **1** *Zool* porpoise **2** *Fam Arg mil* Marine▪ **3** *Can Fam (malin)* rascal▪

marsupial, -e, -aux, -ales [marsypjal, -o] ADJ marsupial
▫ NM marsupial

marsupium [marsypjɔm] NM *Zool* marsupium

martagon [martagɔ̃] NM *Bot* martagon (lily)

marte [mart] = **martre**

marteau, -x [marto] NM **1** *(maillet)* hammer; **coup de m.** blow with a hammer; **enfoncer un clou à coups de m.** to hammer a nail home *or* in; **travailler le fer au m.** to work iron with a hammer; *Fig* **être entre le m. et l'enclume** to be stuck in the middle; **le m. du commissaire-priseur** the auctioneer's hammer *or* gavel; **m. à panne fendue** claw hammer; **m. piqueur** *ou* **pneumatique** pneumatic drill; **m. perforateur** hammer drill
  2 *(pièce → d'une horloge)* striker, hammer; *(→ d'une porte)* knocker, hammer; *(→ dans un piano)* hammer
  3 *Anat* hammer, *Spéc* malleus
  4 *Sport* hammer
  5 *(poisson)* hammerhead shark
  6 *(pour les arbres)* **m. forestier** blazer, marking hammer *or* hatchet
  7 *Métal* **m. à emboutir** embossing hammer; **m. à main** hand sledge; **m. à frapper devant** aboutsledge
  8 *Suisse & (en français régional) (molaire)* molar
  ADJ *Fam (fou)* nuts, crazy, *Br* bonkers; **être m.** to be not all there, to have a screw *or Br* a slate loose
▫ **marteaux** NMPL *(en danse)* Cossack dance steps *(in squatting position)*

🎵

'Le Marteau sans maître' *Boulez* 'The Hammer Without a Master'

marteau-pilon [martopilɔ̃] *(pl* **marteaux-pilons)** NM power *or* drop hammer

marteau-piolet [martopjɔlɛ] *(pl* **marteaux-piolets)** NM piton hammer

martel [martɛl] NM **se mettre m. en tête** to be worried sick; **ne te mets pas m. en tête pour si peu** don't get worked up about such a small thing

martelage [martəlaʒ] NM **1** *Métal* hammering; **faire disparaître une bosse par m.** to hammer out a bump **2** *(des arbres)* blazing

martelé, -e [martəle] ADJ **1** *Métal (travaillé au marteau)* hammered; **argent m.** beaten silver **2** **paroles martelées** hammered-out words

martèlement [martɛlmɑ̃] NM *(bruit → d'un marteau)* hammering; *(→ de pas, de bottes)* pounding; **j'entends le m. de la pluie sur le toit de zinc** I can hear the rain beating on the zinc roof

marteler [25] [martəle] VT **1** *Métal* to hammer; **m. à froid** to cold-hammer
  2 *Fig (frapper)* to hammer (at), to pound (at); **il martelait la table de ses poings** he was hammering with *or* banging his fists on the table; **martelant le lutrin au rythme de chaque phrase** striking *or* thumping the lectern with each sentence; **la douleur martelait ma tempe** the pain was hammering away at my temple; **la douleur lui martelait la tête** his/her head was throbbing with pain
  3 *Fig (scander)* to hammer out; **m. ses mots** to hammer out one's words

marteleur [martəlœr] NM hammerman

martensite [martɛ̃zit] NF *Métal* martensite

martensitique [martɛ̃zitik] ADJ *Métal* martensitic

Marthe [mart] NPR *Bible* Martha

martial, -e, -aux, -ales [marsjal, -o] ADJ **1** *Littéraire (guerrier)* martial, warlike; **un discours m.** a warlike speech
  2 *Sport* **arts martiaux** martial arts
  3 *(résolu, décidé)* resolute, determined; **une démarche/voix martiale** a firm tread/voice
  4 *Jur* **cour martiale** court martial; **passer devant la cour martiale pour haute trahison** to be court-martialled for high treason; **loi martiale** martial law; **code m.** articles of war
  5 *Méd (relatif au fer)* iron *(avant n)*; **carence martiale** iron deficiency

martien, -enne [marsjɛ̃, -ɛn] ADJ Martian
▫ **Martien, -enne** NM,F Martian; **j'ai l'impression de parler à des Martiens** I might as well be talking to Martians

martin [martɛ̃] NM *Orn* mynah bird

martin-chasseur [martɛ̃ʃasœr] *(pl* **martins-chasseurs)** NM *Orn* wood kingfisher

martinet¹ [martinɛ] NM **1** *(fouet)* strap, cat-o'-nine-tails; **avoir six coups de m.** to get six of the strap *or* of the best **2** *Métal (small)* drop hammer

martinet² [martinɛ] NM *Orn* swift; **m. alpin** Alpine swift; **m. des maisons** house swift; **m. noir** swift; **m. pâle** pallid swift

martingale [martɛ̃gal] NF **1** *(ceinture)* half belt **2** *Équitation (sangle)* martingale **3** *(au jeu → façon de jouer)* doubling-up; ≃ martingale; *(→ combinaison)* winning formula

martini [martini] NM martini
▫ **Martini®** NM Martini®

martiniquais, -e [martinikɛ, -ɛz] ADJ Martinican
▫ **Martiniquais, -e** NM,F Martinican

Martinique [martinik] NF *Géog* **la M.** Martinique; **vivre en M.** to live in Martinique; **aller en M.** to go to Martinique

martinisme [martinism] NM *Rel* Martinism

martin-pêcheur [martɛ̃peʃœr] *(pl* **martins-pêcheurs)** NM *Orn* kingfisher

martre [martr] NF **1** *Zool* marten; **m. d'Amérique** American marten; **m. du Canada** mink **2** *(fourrure)* sable

martyr, -e [martir] ADJ martyred; **un peuple m.** a martyred people; **les enfants martyrs** battered children
  NM,F **1** *(personne qui se sacrifie)* martyr; **les martyrs chrétiens** the Christian martyrs; **les martyrs de la Résistance** the martyrs of the Resistance
  2 *Hum* martyr; **arrête de jouer les martyrs** *ou* **de prendre des airs de m.** stop being a *or* playing the martyr!

martyre NM **1** *(supplice)* martyrdom; **le martyre des premiers chrétiens** the martyrdom of the early Christians; *Fig* **mettre qn au martyre** to torture sb
  2 *Fig (épreuve)* torture, martyrdom; *(douleur)* agony; **toute sa vie fut un martyre** his/her life was sheer misery from beginning to end; **souffrir le martyre** to be in agony; **cette visite a été un véritable martyre!** that visit was sheer torture!

martyriser [3] [martirize] VT **1** *(supplicier → gén)* to martyrize; *Rel* to martyr **2** *Fig (maltraiter → animal)* to ill-treat, to torture; *(→ enfant)* to beat, to batter; *(→ collègue, élève)* to bully; **on n'imagine pas le nombre d'enfants qui se font m. à l'école** you'd be amazed how many children are bullied at school

martyrium [martirjɔm] NM *Rel* martyry, shrine

martyrologe [martirɔlɔʒ] NM martyrology; *Fig* **le m. de la Résistance** the list of the martyrs of the Resistance

maruche [maryʃ] NF *Can (en acadien)* small pond

marxien, -enne [marksjɛ̃, -ɛn] ADJ Marxian

marxisant, -e [marksizɑ̃, -ɑ̃t] ADJ Marxist-influenced

marxisme [marksism] NM Marxism

marxisme-léninisme [marksismleninism] NM Marxism-Leninism

marxiste [marksist] ADJ Marxist
  NMF Marxist

marxiste-léniniste [marksistleninist] *(pl* **marxistes-léninistes)** ADJ Marxist-Leninist
  NMF Marxist-Leninist

marxologue [marksɔlɔg] NMF Marxologist

Maryland [marilɑ̃d] NM *Géog* **le M.** Maryland; **dans le M.** in Maryland

maryland [marilɑ̃d] NM Maryland (tobacco)

MAS [mas] NF *(abrév* **Maison d'accueil spécialisée)** = nursing home for severely disabled people

mas [ma(s)] NM = traditional country house or farm in Provence

mascara [maskara] NM mascara; **(se) mettre du m.** to put mascara on

mascarade [maskarad] NF **1** *(bal)* masked ball, masquerade; *Hist (danse)* masquerade **2** *Péj (accoutrement)* **qu'est-ce que c'est que cette m.?** what on earth is that outfit you're wearing? **3** *Fig (simulacre)* farce, mockery; **le candidat ayant déjà été choisi, l'entrevue ne fut qu'une m.** the candidate had already been selected so the interview was a complete farce *or* charade

mascaret [maskarɛ] NM **1** *(vague)* (tidal) bore, mascaret **2** *(raz de marée)* tidal wave

mascaron [maskarɔ̃] NM *Beaux-Arts* grotesque mask, *Spéc* mascaron

mascarpone [maskarpɔn] NM *(fromage)* mascarpone

Mascate [maskat] NM *Géog* Muscat

mascotte [maskɔt] NF mascot

masculin, -e [maskylɛ̃, -in] ADJ **1** *(propre à l'homme)* male; *(qui a les caractères de l'homme → trait, orgueil)* masculine; *(→ femme)* masculine, mannish; **le sexe m.** the male sex; **la mode masculine** men's fashion; **un métier m.** a male profession; **une voix masculine** *(d'homme)* a male *or* man's voice; *(de femme)* a masculine voice; **c'est bien un préjugé m.!** that's a typical male prejudice!; **elle a une allure masculine** she looks quite masculine
  2 *(composé d'hommes)* **une équipe masculine** a men's team; **main-d'œuvre masculine** male workers
  3 *Ling* masculine; **nom m.** masculine noun
  NM *Ling* masculine; **au m.** in the masculine; **ce mot est du m.** this word is masculine; **ces mots sont des masculins** these words are masculine

masculinisation [maskylinizasjɔ̃] NF **1** *Méd* masculinization **2** **la m. d'une profession** the increase in the number of men in a profession

masculiniser [3] [maskylinize] VT **1** **m. qn** *(vêtement, coupe)* to make sb look masculine; **m. une profession** to increase the number of men in a profession, to attract more and more men to a profession **2** *Biol* to produce male characteristics in, to masculinize
  ▸ **se masculiniser** VPR *(profession)* to attract more and more men; *(population)* to become predominantly male

masculinité [maskylinite] NF **1** *(comportement)* masculinity, virility, manliness **2** *(dans des statistiques)* **taux de m.** sex ratio

maser [mazɛr] NM *Phys* maser

maskinongé [maskinɔ̃ʒe] NM *Ich* muskellunge

maso [mazo] *Fam (abrév* **masochiste)** ADJ masochistic▪; **t'es m. ou quoi?** you're a real glutton for punishment; **je ne vais pas lui dire la vérité tout de suite, je ne suis pas m.** I won't tell him/her the truth right away, I'm not a masochist; **t'es complètement m. d'avoir accepté!** you must be a masochist *or* a glutton for punishment if you agreed!
  NMF masochist▪; **c'est un m.** he's a glutton for punishment *or* a masochist

masochisme [mazɔʃism] NM masochism

masochiste [mazɔʃist] ADJ masochist, masochistic
  NMF masochist

masquage [maskaʒ] NM *(gén)* & *Ordinat & Phot* masking

masque [mask] NM **1** *(déguisement, protection)* mask; **l'homme au m. de fer** the man in the iron mask; **m. de carnaval** *ou* **de Mardi gras** (carnival) mask; **m. funéraire** *ou* **mortuaire** death mask; **m. d'escrime/de plongée** fencing/diving mask; **m. d'anesthésie/à oxygène/stérile** anaesthetic/oxygen/sterile mask; **m. de chirurgien** operating *or* surgeon's mask; **m. de soudeur** welding mask; **m. à gaz** gas mask
  2 *(pour la peau)* **m. (de beauté)** face pack *or* mask; **m. à l'argile** mudpack
  3 *Méd* **m. de grossesse** (pregnancy) chloasma
  4 *Fig (apparence)* mask, front; **son visage était un m. impénétrable** his/her face was an impenetrable mask; **sous ce m. jovial, elle cache son amertume** under that jovial facade *or* appearance, she conceals her bitterness; **sous le m. de la vertu** under the mask of *or* in the guise of virtue; **sa bonté n'est qu'un m.** his/her kindness is just a front *or* is only skin-deep; **lever** *ou* **tomber le m., jeter (bas) son m.** to unmask oneself, to show one's true colours, to take off one's mask
  5 *Littéraire (personne masquée)* mask

6 *Mus & Théât* mask, masque; **parler** *ou* **chanter dans le m.** to pitch one's voice forward
7 *(en acoustique)* **effet de m.** (audio) masking
8 *Électron, Typ & Phot* mask
9 *Zool* mask
10 *Ordinat* mask; **m. d'écran** screen mask; **m. d'entrée, m. de saisie** input mask

masqué, -e [maske] ADJ **1** *(voleur)* masked, wearing a mask; *(acteur)* wearing a mask, in a mask **2** *(virage)* blind **3** *Mil* **tir m.** hidden *or* concealed fire

masquer [3] [maske] VT **1** *(dissimuler → obstacle, ouverture)* to mask, to conceal; *(→ lumière)* to shade, to screen (off), to obscure; *(→ difficulté, intentions, sentiments)* to hide, to conceal, to disguise; *(→ saveur, goût)* to mask, to disguise, to hide; *Naut (navire)* to darken; **le mur masque la vue** the wall blocks out *or* masks the view; **la colline masquait les chars ennemis** the enemy tanks were hidden *or* concealed by the hill; **la cuisine est masquée par** *ou* **avec un paravent** the kitchen is hidden behind a partition *or* is partitioned off; **son arrogance lui servait à m. sa lâcheté** he/she hid *or* concealed his/her cowardice under a mask of arrogance; *Mil* **m. une batterie** to conceal *or* hide a battery; *Naut* **naviguer à feux masqués** to sail without lights
2 *(déguiser → enfant)* to put a mask on
VI *Naut* to back the sails
▸**se masquer** VPR **1** *(se déguiser)* to put a mask on, to put on a mask
2 *(ignorer)* **se m. qch** to ignore sth; **ne nous masquons pas les difficultés** let us not blind ourselves to *or* ignore the difficulties

Massachusetts [masaʃysɛts] NM *Géog* **le M.** Massachusetts; **dans le M.** in Massachusetts

massacrante [masakrɑ̃t] ADJ F *Fam* **être d'une humeur m.** to be in a foul *or* vile mood

massacre [masakr] NM **1** *(tuerie)* massacre, slaughter; **envoyer des troupes au m.** to send troops to the slaughter; *Bible* **le m. des Innocents** the Massacre of the Innocents
2 *Fam (d'un adversaire)* massacre, slaughter; **5 à 0, c'est un m.!** 5 nil, it's a massacre!; **il a fait un m. dans le tournoi** he massacred *or* slaughtered *or* made mincemeat of all his opponents in the tournament
3 *Fam (travail mal fait)* **c'est du** *ou* **un m.** *(gâchis)* it's a mess; *(bâclage)* it's a botch-up *or Am* botch; **quel m., son 'Phèdre'!** she's managed to murder 'Phèdre'; **regarde comment il m'a coupé les cheveux, c'est un vrai m.!** look at the mess he's made of my hair!; **attention en découpant le gâteau, quel m.!** watch how you cut the cake, you're making a pig's ear *or* a real mess of it!
4 *Fam (succès)* **faire un m.** to be a runaway success, to be a smash (hit); **elle fait actuellement un m. sur la scène de la Lanterne** she's currently bringing the house down at the Lanterne theatre; **une chanson qui a fait un m. à sa sortie** a song which was a smash (hit) when it first came out
5 *Chasse (trophée)* stag's antlers *or* attire
6 *Hér* harts attired *or* caboched

massacrer [3] [masakre] VT **1** *(tuer → animal, personne)* to slaughter, to massacre, to butcher; **les terroristes ont massacré les otages** the terrorists butchered the hostages; **ils vont se faire m. s'ils restent là!** they're going to be slaughtered if they stay there!
2 *Fam (vaincre facilement → adversaire)* to make mincemeat of, to massacre, to slaughter; **je l'ai massacré au tennis** I slaughtered *or* demolished him at tennis; **notre équipe s'est fait m.** our team was massacred; **jouer aux échecs avec lui? tu vas te faire m.!** you're going to play chess with him? he'll wipe the floor with you!
3 *Fam (critiquer)* to pan, *Br* to slate; **la pièce s'est fait m.** the play got torn to pieces *or Br* slated; **ils l'ont massacré dans les journaux** they made mincemeat out of him *or* tore him to pieces in the papers; **lors du débat, il s'est vraiment fait m. par son interlocuteur** he was really savaged by his opponent in the debate
4 *Fam (gâcher → concerto, pièce de théâtre)* to murder, to make a mess of; *(→ langue)* to murder; *(→ vêtements)* to ruin; **écoute-le m. la langue française** listen to him massacring *or* murdering the French language
5 *Fam (bâcler → travail)* to make a mess *or* hash of, to botch (up), to make a pig's ear (out) of

massacreur, -euse [masakrœr, -øz] NM,F **1** *(tueur)* slaughterer, butcher **2** *Fam (mauvais exécutant → d'un concerto, d'une pièce)* murderer; *(bâcleur)* botcher, bungler

massage [masaʒ] NM massage; **faire un m. à qn** to massage sb, to give sb a massage; *Méd* **m. cardiaque** cardiac *or* heart massage; **m. indien du crâne** Indian head massage; **m. thaïlandais** Thai massage

massaliote [masaljɔt] ADJ of/from Ancient Marseilles
NMF = inhabitant of or person from Ancient Marseilles

masse[1] [mas] NF **1** *(bloc informe)* mass; **m. de cheveux/terre** mass of hair/earth; **m. de nuages** bank of clouds; **m. d'eau** body of water; *(en mouvement)* mass of water; *Météo* **m. d'air** mass of air; **il vit une m. sombre sur le sol** he saw a dark mass *or* a great dark shape on the ground; **sculpté** *ou* **taillé dans la m.** carved from the block; *Fam* **un grand type taillé dans la m.** a big, heavily-built sort of chap; **s'abattre** *ou* **s'écrouler** *ou* **s'affaisser comme une m.** to collapse *or* to slump heavily
2 *Fam (grande quantité)* **une m. de** *(objets)* heaps *or* masses of; *(gens)* crowds *or* masses of; **il y avait des masses de livres** there were masses (and masses) of books; **il (n')y en a pas des masses** *(objets)* there aren't masses of them; *(sucre, farine)* there isn't masses (of it); **pas des masses** *(se rapportant à un indénombrable)* not that much; *(se rapportant à un dénombrable)* not that many; **des amis, il n'en a pas des masses** he hasn't got that many friends; **vous vous êtes bien amusés? – pas des masses!** did you have fun? – not that much!
3 *Com (grosse quantité)* stock; *(douze grosses)* great gross
4 *(groupe social)* **la m.** the masses; **communication/culture de m.** mass communication/culture; **les masses (populaires)** the mass (of ordinary people); **les masses laborieuses** the toiling masses
5 *(ensemble)* body, bulk; *(majorité)* majority; *Ordinat (d'informations)* bulk; **la grande m. des étudiants ne se sent pas concernée** the great majority of the students don't feel concerned; **la m. des connaissances** the total sum of knowledge
6 *Écon & Fin* fund, stock; **la m. des créanciers/obligataires** the body of creditors/bondholders; **m. active** assets; **m. monétaire** money supply; **m. passive** liabilities; **m. salariale** wage bill; **il faut établir la m. d'équipement dans le budget de cette année** we have to establish the total amount of (money allowed for) capital goods in this year's budget
7 *Mil (allocation)* fund; **m. d'habillement** clothing fund
8 *Électron Br* earth, *Am* ground; **mettre à la m.** *Br* to earth, *Am* to ground; **mise à la m.** *Br* earthing, *Am* grounding
9 *Chim & Phys* mass; **le kilogramme est l'unité de m.** the kilogram is the unit of mass; **m. atomique/moléculaire** atomic/molecular mass; **m. critique** critical mass; **m. volumique** relative density
▫ **à la masse** *Fam* **être à la m.** to be rather slow on the uptake
▫ **en masse** ADJ *(licenciements, production)* mass *(avant n)* ADV **1** *(en grande quantité)* **produire** *ou* **fabriquer en m.** to mass-produce; **la population a approuvé en m. le projet de réforme** the reform bill gained massive support; **arriver en m.** *(lettres, personnes)* to pour in; **se déplacer en m.** to go in a body *or* en masse; **arrivée en m. des estivants sur les plages** *(titre dans un journal)* holidaymakers invade the beaches *or* take to the beaches in droves; **les villageois se préparent à une arrivée en m. des touristes** villagers are bracing themselves for a tourist invasion; *Fam* **avoir des bijoux en m.** to have stacks *or* masses *or* loads of jewellery **2** *Com (en bloc)* in bulk

masse[2] [mas] NF **1** *(outil)* sledgehammer, beetle; **m. en bois** beetle
2 *(d'huissier)* (ceremonial) mace; *Mil* **m. d'armes** mace
3 *(de queue de billard)* butt
4 *(dans un jeu)* stake
5 *Fam Fig* **coup de m.** (very) nasty shock; **ça a été le coup de m.** it came as a (very) nasty shock

massé [mase] NM massé (shot); **faire un m.** to play a massé shot

masselotte [maslɔt] NF **1** *(sur pièce de fonderie)* sprue **2** *(dans un mécanisme)* bob weight

massepain [maspɛ̃] NM marzipan

masser[1] [3] [mase] VT **1** *(réunir → enfants)* to gather *or* to bring together; *(→ soldats)* to mass; *(→ livres, pièces)* to put together **2** *Beaux-Arts* to group, to arrange into groups **3** *(au billard)* **m. une bille** to play a massé shot
▸**se masser** VPR to gather, to assemble, to mass; **les enfants se massèrent dans la cour de l'école** the children assembled *or* gathered in the *Br* school playground *or Am* schoolyard; **les manifestants se massèrent devant l'hôtel de ville** the demonstrators massed *or* gathered in front of the town hall

masser[2] [3] [mase] VT *(membre, muscle)* to massage; **m. qn** to massage sb, to give sb a massage; **se faire m.** to be massaged, to have a massage; **masse-moi le bras** rub *or* massage my arm
▸**se masser** VPR **se m. le genou/le bras** to massage one's knee/one's arm; **elle se masse les tempes quand elle a mal à la tête** she rubs her temples when she has a headache

masséter [masetɛr] *Anat* ADJ M **muscle m.** masseter muscle
NM masseter

massette [masɛt] NF **1** *(outil)* two-handed hammer **2** *Bot* bulrush, reed mace

masseur, -euse [masœr, -øz] NM,F masseur, *f* masseuse
NM *(appareil)* (vibro)massager

masseur-kinésithérapeute, masseuse-kinésithérapeute [masœrkineziterapøt, masøzkineziterapøt] *(mpl* **masseurs-kinésithérapeutes,** *fpl* **masseuses-kinésithérapeutes)** NM,F *Br* physiotherapist, *Am* physical therapist

massicot[1] [masiko] NM *(d'imprimeur)* guillotine; *(pour papier peint)* trimmer

massicot[2] [masiko] NM *Chim* massicot

massicotage [masikɔtaʒ] NM *(de papier)* guillotining; *(de papier peint)* trimming

massicoter [3] [masikɔte] VT *(papier)* to guillotine; *(papier peint)* to trim

massier[1], **-ère** [masje, -ɛr] NM,F = art student in charge of the kitty for buying materials

massier[2] [masje] NM *Hist (huissier)* macebearer

massif, -ive [masif, -iv] ADJ **1** *Menuis & (en joaillerie)* solid; **argent/or m.** solid silver/gold; **armoire en acajou m.** solid mahogany wardrobe
2 *(épais)* massive, heavy-looking, bulky; **une bâtisse au fronton m.** a building with a massive pediment; **sa silhouette massive** his/her huge frame
3 *Fig (en grand nombre)* mass *(avant n)*, massive; *(en grande quantité)* massive, huge; **des migrations massives vers le Nouveau Monde** mass migrations to the New World; **un apport m. d'argent liquide** a massive cash injection; **une réponse massive de nos lecteurs** an overwhelming response from our readers
4 *Mines* compact, massive
5 *Ling* uncountable
NM **1** *Géog & Géol* **m. (montagneux)** mountainous mass, massif; **m. ancien** primary *or* Caledonian massif; **le M. central** the Massif Central; **le M. éthiopien** the Ethiopian Hills; **le m. du Hoggar** the Hoggar Mountains
2 *Hort* **m. (de fleurs)** flowerbed; **un m. de roses** a rosebed, a bed of roses; **m. d'arbustes** clump of bushes; **les rhododendrons font de jolis massifs** rhododendrons look nice planted together in groups
3 *Constr* underpin, foundation
4 *(panneaux publicitaires)* composite site
5 *Mines* pillar

massification [masifikasjɔ̃] NF **la m. de la culture/des études** making culture/studying accessible to the masses

massifier [9] [masifje] VT to make accessible to the masses

massique [masik] ADJ **1** *Phys* mass *(avant n)* **2** *Tech* **puissance m.** power-to-weight ratio, power-weight ratio

massive [masiv] *voir* **massif**

massivement [masivmɑ̃] ADV *(en grand nombre)* massively, en masse; **ils ont voté m. pour le nouveau candidat** they voted overwhelmingly for the new candidate; **les Français ont voté m.** the French turned out in large numbers to vote

massivité [masivite] NF massiveness

mass media, mass-média(s) [masmedja] NMPL mass media

massorah [masɔra], **massore** [masɔr] NF *Rel* Masora, Masorah

massorète [masɔrɛt] NM *Rel* Masorete, Masorite

massue [masy] NF **1** *(gourdin)* club; *(à pointes)* mace; **un coup de m.** a blow with a club; *Fig (événement imprévu)* staggering blow, bolt from the blue; *(prix excessif)* rip-off **2** *(comme adj)* **un argument m.** a sledgehammer argument **3** *Zool* **m. antennaire** capitate end of the antenna

mastaba [mastaba] NM *Archéol* mastaba, mastabah

mastaire [mastɛr] NM *Univ* post-graduate qualification

mastard [mastar] NM *Fam* hulk

mastectomie [mastɛktɔmi] NF *Méd* mastectomy

master [mastɛr] NM *Univ* ≃ masters (degree), two-year postgraduate qualification

mastère [mastɛr] NM *Univ (d'ingénieur)* DEng; *(de commerce)* MBA

mastic [mastik] ADJ INV putty-coloured
NM **1** *Constr* mastic; *(pour vitrier)* putty; *(pour menuisier)* filler; **m. de colmatage** filler paste **2** *(en travaux publics)* **m. d'asphalte** asphalt mastic **3** *Typ* transposition; **faire un m.** to (accidentally) transpose characters **4** *Bot* mastic **5** *(d'arboriculteur)* **m. à greffer** grafting wax

masticage [mastikaʒ] NM *Constr (d'une vitre)* puttying; *(d'une lézarde, d'une cavité)* filling

masticateur, -trice [mastikatœr, -tris] ADJ masticatory
NM *(ustensile)* masticator

mastication [mastikasjɔ̃] NF **1** *(d'aliments)* chewing, *Spéc* mastication **2** *Tech* mastication

masticatoire [mastikatwar] *Méd* ADJ masticatory
NM masticatory

masticatrice [mastikatris] *voir* **masticateur**

mastiff [mastif] NM (bull) mastiff

mastiquer[1] [3] [mastike] VT *(pain, viande)* to chew, *Spéc* to masticate

mastiquer[2] [3] [mastike] VT *(joindre → lézarde, cavité)* to fill (in); *(→ vitre)* to putty; **couteau à m.** putty knife

mastite [mastit] NF *Méd* mastitis

mastoc [mastɔk] ADJ INV *Fam* **1** *(lourd → personne)* hefty; *(→ objet)* bulky; *(→ construction)* cumbersome **2** *Belg (fou → personne)* crazy, nuts

mastocyte [mastɔsit] NM *Physiol* mast cell, mastocyte

mastodonte [mastɔdɔ̃t] NM **1** *Zool* mastodon **2** *Fam (personne)* colossus, enormous man, *f* woman; **c'est un m.** he's/she's built like the side of a house **3** *Fam (objet)* hulking great thing; *(camion) Br* juggernaut■, *Am* tractor-trailer■

mastodynie [mastɔdini] NF *Méd* mastodynia

mastoïde [mastɔid] ADJ *Anat* mastoid

mastoïdien, -enne [mastɔidjɛ̃, -ɛn] ADJ *Anat* mastoid

mastoïdite [mastɔidit] NF *Méd* mastoiditis

mastologie [mastɔlɔʒi] NF *Méd* mastology

mastopathie [mastɔpati] NF *Méd* mastopathy

mastroquet [mastrɔkɛ] NM *Fam Vieilli* **1** *(cafetier)* bar owner, *Br* publican **2** *(bistro)* bar, *Br* pub

masturbation [mastyrbasjɔ̃] NF masturbation; **c'est de la m. intellectuelle** it's intellectual self-indulgence *or* masturbation

masturbatoire [mastyrbatwar] ADJ masturbatory

masturber [3] [mastyrbe] VT to masturbate
▸**se masturber** VPR **1** *(emploi réfléchi)* to masturbate **2** *(emploi réciproque)* to masturbate each other

m'as-tu-vu [matyvy] ADJ INV showy, flashy; **leur maison est très m.** their house is very showy; **qu'est-ce qu'elle est m.!** what a show-off she is!
NMF INV show-off; **faire le** *ou* **son m.** to show off

masure [mɑzyr] NF shack, hovel

mat, -e [mat] ADJ **1** *(couleur)* dull, matt; *(surface)* unpolished; *(peinture)* matt; *Phot* matt **2** *(teint)* olive **3** *(son)* **un son m.** a thud, a dull sound
▫ **mat** NM **1** *Échecs* checkmate, mate; **être sous le m.** to be under the threat of checkmate *or* mate **2** *Tex* mat ADJ INV *Échecs* checkmated, mated; **le roi est m.** the king is checkmated *or* in checkmate; **tu es m.** (you're) checkmate; **faire m. en trois coups** to mate *or* checkmate in three; **il m'a fait m. en trois coups** he mated *or* checkmated me in three moves

mat' [mat] NM *Fam* morning■; **deux/trois heures du m.** two/three a.m. *or* in the morning

mât [mɑ] NM **1** *(poteau)* pole, post; *(en camping)* pole; **m. de cocagne** greasy pole
2 *(hampe)* flagpole
3 *Tech* **m. de charge** cargo beam, derrick; **m. de levage** lift mast; *Pétr* **m. de forage** drilling mast
4 *Naut* mast; **m. d'artimon** mizzen, mizzen-mast; **m. de beaupré** bowsprit; **m. de charge** cargo boom, derrick; **m. de hune** topmast; **m. de misaine** foremast; **grand m.** main mast; **navire à trois mâts** three-masted ship, three-master
5 *Rail* **m. (de signal)** signal post

matabiche [matabiʃ] NM *(en Afrique francophone)* bribe

mataché, -e [mataʃe] ADJ *Can (animal, pelage)* spotted

matacher [3] [mataʃe], **matachier** [9] [mataʃje] *Can* VT *(corps, figure)* to paint
▫ **se matacher** VPR to paint one's face and body

matador [matadɔr] NM matador

mataf [mataf] NM *Fam (matelot)* tar, sailor■

matage [mataʒ] NM **1** *(d'une dorure)* matting **2** *(d'une soudure)* caulking

matamore [matamɔr] NM braggart; **il joue les matamores** he's nothing but a braggart

match [matʃ] *(pl* **matchs** *ou* **matches**) NM match, *Am* game; **disputer un m.** to play a match; **on fait un m.?** shall we have *or* play a match?; **m. de boxe** boxing match; **m. de tennis** tennis match, game of tennis; **m. aller/retour** first/second leg (match); **m. amical** friendly (match); **m. de barrage** play-off, decider; **m. de championnat** league match; **m. d'improvisation** = live improvisation contest between two teams, the winning team being decided by the audience; **m. nul** draw; **faire m. nul** to draw, *Am* to tie; **ils ont fait m. nul** they drew *or Am* tied, the match ended in a draw *or Am* tie; **m. de sélection** trial

matchiche [matʃiʃ] NF maxixe

match-play [matʃplɛ] *(pl* **match-plays**) NM *(au golf)* match-play

maté [mate] NM **1** *Bot* maté (tree) **2** *(boisson)* maté

matefaim [matfɛ̃] NM *Culin* = type of thick pancake, a speciality of the Lyons area

matelas [matla] NM **1** *(d'un lit)* mattress; **m. à ressorts/de laine** spring/wool mattress; **m. de mousse** foam-rubber mattress; **m. pneumatique** air mattress **2** *(couche → de feuilles mortes, de neige)* layer, carpet; *Fam* **un m. de billets de banque** *(liasse)* a wad *or* roll of *Br* banknotes *or Am* bills; *(fortune)* a pile (of money) **3** *Constr* **m. d'air** air space **4** *Ind* sandwich

matelassage [matlasaʒ] NM **1** *(d'un fauteuil)* padding **2** *Couture (doublage)* lining; *(rembourrage)* quilting, padding **3** *Tex (avec du matelassé)* covering with quilted material

matelassé, -e [matlase] ADJ **1** *(fauteuil)* padded; **enveloppe matelassée** padded envelope, Jiffy bag® **2** *Couture (doublé)* lined; *(rembourré)* quilted, padded **3** *Tex (avec du matelassé)* covered with quilted material
NM quilted material; **du m. de soie** quilted silk

matelasser [3] [matlase] VT **1** *(fauteuil)* to pad; *(meuble)* to upholster **2** *Couture (doubler)* to line; *(rembourrer)* to quilt; **matelassé de soie** silk-lined **3** *Tex (recouvrir de matelassé)* to cover with quilted material

matelassier, -ère [matlasje, -ɛr] NM,F mattress maker

matelassure [matlasyr] NF padding, mattress filling

matelot [matlo] NM **1** *(de la marine → marchande)* sailor, seaman; *(→ militaire)* sailor; **servir comme simple m.** to sail before the mast; **m. de (breveté) première/deuxième/troisième classe** leading/able/ordinary seaman; **m. breveté** *Br* able rating, *Am* seaman apprentice; **m. de pont** deck hand **2** *(bâtiment)* ship, vessel; **m. d'avant/d'arrière** ship ahead/astern

matelotage [matlɔtaʒ] NM **1** *(solde)* sailor's pay **2** *(travaux, connaissances)* seamanship

matelote [matlɔt] NF **1** *Culin* matelote, fish stew *(with wine, onion and mushroom sauce)*; **m. d'anguilles** stewed eels *(in red wine sauce)*; **sauce m.** red wine and onion sauce **2** *(danse)* (sailor's) hornpipe

mater[1] [3] [mate] VT **1** *Échecs* to mate, to checkmate
2 *Fig (dompter → personne, peuple)* to bring to heel; *(→ révolte)* to quell, to curb, to put down; **m. l'orgueil de qn** to humble sb, to crush sb's pride; *Fam* **petit morveux, je vais te m., moi!** you little swine, I'll show you who's boss!
USAGE ABSOLU *Échecs* to mate, to checkmate; **m. en six coups** to mate *or* checkmate in six moves

mater[2] [3] [mate] VT **1** *(dépolir)* to matt
2 *Métal* to caulk

mater[3] [3] [mate] *Fam* VT **1** *(vérifier)* to check out; **mate un peu si le prof arrive** keep your eyes peeled, see if the teacher's coming
2 *(regarder avec convoitise)* to ogle, to eye up; **mate un peu la gonzesse!** just take a look at *or* get an eyeful of that chick!; **mate-moi ça!** check it out!, *Br* get a load of that!; **t'as fini de le m.?** have you quite finished checking him out?; **qu'est-ce qu'on s'est fait m. à la plage!** we got eyed up so much at the beach!
VI to eye up *or* ogle (the) women/men; **qu'est-ce que ça mate, ici!** all these men/women eyeing us up!

mater[4] [matɛr] NF *Fam* old lady, *Br* old dear *(mother)*

mâter [3] [mɑte] VT **1** *Naut (pourvoir de mâts)* to mast **2** *Can (dresser)* to set upright
▸**se mâter** VPR *Can (animal)* to rear up (on its hind legs); *Fig Vieilli (personne)* to lose one's temper, to get one's dander up

mâtereau, -x [mɑtro] NM *Naut* small mast, hand mast

matérialisation [materjalizasjɔ̃] NF **1** *(réalisation)* materialization; **c'est la m. de tous mes rêves** it's a dream come true for me **2** *Phys* **m. de l'énergie** mass-energy conversion **3** *(dans le spiritisme)* materialization

matérialisé, -e [materjalize] ADJ *Admin* **voie matérialisée** = section of road delimited by a white line; **voie non matérialisée pendant 1 km** *(sur panneau)* no markings *or* roadmarkings for 1 km

matérialiser [3] [materjalize] VT **1** *(concrétiser)* to materialize; **m. un projet** to carry out *or* to execute a plan **2** *(indiquer)* to mark out, to indicate; **le poteau matérialise la frontière** the pole marks where the border is **3** *(symboliser)* to symbolize, to embody
▸**se matérialiser** VPR to materialize; *Hum* **le serveur se matérialisa enfin** the waiter eventually materialized

matérialisme [materjalism] NM materialism; **m. dialectique/historique** dialectical/historical materialism

matérialiste [materjalist] ADJ **1** *Phil* materialist **2** *(esprit, civilisation)* materialistic
NMF materialist

matérialité [materjalite] NF **1** *(caractère de ce qui est réel, matériel)* materiality; *Jur* **la m. d'un fait** the material circumstances, the materiality of a fact **2** *(matérialisme)* materialism

matériau, -x [materjo] NM *(substance)* material; **m. composite** composite
▫ **matériaux** NMPL **1** *Constr* material, materials; **matériaux de construction** building *or* construction material(s) **2** *Fig (éléments)* components, elements; **rassembler des matériaux pour une enquête** to assemble (some) material for a survey

matériel, -elle [materjɛl] ADJ **1** *(réel → preuve)* material; **c'est une impossibilité matérielle** it's a literal impossibility; **je n'ai pas le temps m. de faire l'aller et retour** I simply don't have the time to go there and back; **il n'a pas le pouvoir m. de le faire** he doesn't have the means to do it
2 *(pécuniaire, pratique → difficulté, aide)* material; **nos besoins matériels** our material

mas–mat

needs; **sur le plan m., il n'a pas à se plaindre** from a material point of view, he has no grounds for complaint; **l'organisation matérielle de la fête a posé de gros problèmes** the practical organization of the party posed great problems

3 (physique) material; **être dans l'impossibilité matérielle de bouger** to find it physically impossible to move; **pour mon confort m.** for my material well-being; **les plaisirs matériels** material pleasures

4 (matérialiste → esprit, civilisation) material

5 Phil (être, univers) physical, material

6 Math & Tech (point) material, physical

NM **1** (équipement, machines) equipment; **m. agricole** agricultural equipment; **m. de bureau** office equipment; **m. de camping** camping equipment or gear; **m. d'enregistrement** recording equipment; **m. d'exploitation** working plant; **m. ferroviaire** Br railway or Am railroad equipment; **m. hi-fi** hi-fi equipment; **m. industriel** industrial equipment; **m. à longévité élevée** long-life equipment; **m. lourd** heavy equipment; **m. de pêche** fishing tackle or gear; **m. de peinture** painting equipment or gear; Rail **m. roulant** rolling stock

2 (documentation) material; **m. d'archives** archive material; **m. pédagogique** teaching materials; Mktg **m. de PLV** point-of-sale material; Mktg **m. de présentation** display material; **m. de promotion** promotional material; **m. publicitaire** advertising material; **m. scolaire** school materials

3 Mil **m. de guerre** weaponry, matériel; **arme ou service du m.** Ordnance Corps

4 Écon **le m. humain** the workforce, human material

5 Biol & Psy material

6 Ordinat hardware; **m. de composition** film-setting hardware; **m. informatique** computer hardware

7 Beaux-Arts material

8 Can Joual (tissu) material, cloth

◻ **matérielle** NF Fam Hum wherewithal■, (daily) sustenance■; **assurer la matérielle** to make a living■

matériellement [materjɛlmɑ̃] ADV **1** (concrètement) materially; **il m'est m. impossible de le faire** it's physically impossible for me to do it; **je ne peux m. pas accepter un travail à temps complet** it is physically impossible for me to take on a full-time job; **je n'ai m. pas le temps de venir te voir** I simply don't have time to come and see you; **une tâche m. impossible à effectuer** a physically impossible task

2 (financièrement) materially, financially; **des familles m. défavorisées** families with financial difficulties

maternage [matɛrnaʒ] NM mothering

maternel, -elle [matɛrnɛl] ADJ **1** (propre à la mère → autorité, instinct) maternal, motherly; (→ soins, gestes) motherly; **il craignait la colère maternelle** he feared his mother's anger; **elle est très maternelle avec ses collègues** she acts in a very maternal or motherly way towards her colleagues

2 (qui vient de la mère) maternal; **grand-mère maternelle** maternal grandmother; **du côté m.** on the mother's or maternal side; **il y a de l'asthme dans ma famille du côté m.** there is asthma on my mother's side of the family

◻ **maternelle** NF **1** (école) nursery school, kindergarten, Br infant school

2 Fam (mère) old lady, Br old dear

maternellement [matɛrnɛlmɑ̃] ADV maternally; **elle s'occupait de lui m.** she cared for him like a mother or in a motherly fashion

materner [3] [matɛrne] VT to mother; **tu ne vas pas m. ton fils jusqu'à 30 ans, non?** you're not going to mollycoddle or baby your son until

he's 30, are you?; **il aime se faire m.** he likes to be mothered or mollycoddled

maternisé [matɛrnize] ADJ M voir lait

materniser [3] [matɛrnize] VT to make suitable for infants

maternité [matɛrnite] NF **1** (clinique) maternity hospital or home; (service) maternity ward **2** (fait d'être mère) motherhood; **ça te va bien, la m.!** being a mother suits you! **3** (grossesse) pregnancy; **un corps déformé par des maternités successives** a body misshapen by successive pregnancies **4** Jur maternity; **action en recherche de m. naturelle** maternity suit **5** Beaux-Arts mother and child

mateur, -euse [matœr, -øz] NM,F Fam ogler; **c'est un sacré m.** he's always eyeing up women

math [mat] NF = **maths**

mathématicien, -enne [matematisjɛ̃, -ɛn] NM,F mathematician

mathématique [matematik] ADJ **1** Math mathematical **2** Fig (précis, exact) mathematical; (esprit) logical; **organisé avec une précision m.** organized with mathematical precision **3** Fig (inévitable) inevitable; **elle était sûre de perdre, c'était m.** she was sure to lose, it was Br a dead cert or Am a surefire thing

NF mathematics (singulier)

mathématiquement [matematikmɑ̃] ADV **1** Math mathematically

2 Fig (objectivement) mathematically, absolutely; **c'est m. impossible** it's mathematically or utterly impossible; **je vais te prouver m. qu'il fallait voter à gauche** I'm going to prove to you mathematically or scientifically that you should have voted for the left

3 Fig (inévitablement) inevitably; **m., il devait perdre** he was bound to lose

mathématiques [matematik] NFPL mathematics (singulier); **m. appliquées/pures** applied/pure mathematics; **M. supérieures/spéciales** = first/second year of a two-year science course preparing for entrance to the "Grandes Écoles"

mathématisation [matematizasjɔ̃] NF mathematization

mathématiser [3] [matematize] VT to mathematicize, to mathematize

matheux, -euse [matø, -øz] NM,F Fam **1** (gén) c'est un m. he's a whizz at Br maths or Am math; **demandez à Jeanne, c'est elle, la matheuse** ask Jeanne, she's the Br maths or Am math whizz **2** (étudiant) Br maths or Am math student

Mathias [matjas] NPR Bible Matthias

Mathilde [matild] NPR Hist **M. d'Angleterre** the Empress Maud

maths [mat] NFPL Fam Br maths, Am math; **fort en m.** good at Br maths or Am math; **m. sup/spé** = first/second year of a two-year science course preparing for entrance to the "Grandes Écoles"

mathurin [matyrɛ̃] NM **1** Rel Mathurin **2** Fam Vieilli (matelot) Jack Tar

Mathusalem [matyzalɛm] NPR Bible Methuselah; Fam **ça date de M.** it's out of the ark, it's as old as the hills; Fam **vieux comme M.** as old as Methuselah

mathusalem [matyzalɛm] NM (bouteille) Methuselah

MATIÈRE [matjɛr]

matter **1, 2, 4, 5** ■ material **1, 3** ■ subject **3, 5** ■ medium **6**

NF **1** (substance) matter, material; Typ matter; **c'est en quelle m.?** what's it made of?; Nucl **m. fissile/nucléaire** fissile/nuclear material; **matières (fécales)** faeces; **m. plastique, matières plastiques** plastic, plastics; **sachet en m. plastique** plastic bag; **m. première, matières premières** raw material or materials; **m. synthétique** synthetic material

2 Biol, Chim, Phil & Phys **la m.** matter; **m. organique/inorganique** organic/inorganic matter; **m. inanimée/vivante** inanimate/living matter; **m. grasse, matières grasses** fat; **60 pour cent de matières grasses** 60 percent fat content; **sans matières grasses** fat-free, non-fat; Fam **m. grise** grey matter; **fais travailler ta m. grise!** use your brains or head!; **elle a de la m. grise**

she's not lacking in grey matter; Astron **m. noire ou sombre** dark matter

3 Fig (contenu → d'un discours, d'un ouvrage) material, subject matter; (→ de conversation) subject, topic, theme; **je n'avais pas assez de m. pour en faire un livre** I didn't have enough material to write a book; **entrer en m.** to tackle a subject; **une entrée en m.** an introduction, a lead-in

4 Fig (motif, prétexte) matter; **donner m. à qch** to give cause for sth; **il n'y a pas là m. à rire ou plaisanter** this is no laughing matter; **il y a m. à discussion** there are a lot of things to be said about that; **cela donne m. à réfléchir** ou **à réflexion** this is a matter for serious thought, this matter requires some serious thinking; **y a-t-il là m. à dispute/procès?** is this business worth fighting over/going to court for?; Jur **m. à litige** issuable matter; Jur **m. d'une accusation** substance of a charge, Spéc gravamen; **m. d'un crime** criminal matter; **matières sommaires** summary matter

5 Fig (domaine) matter, subject; Scol subject; **je suis incompétent en la m.** I'm ignorant on the subject; **il est mauvais/bon juge en la m.** he's a bad/good judge of this subject; **en m. philosophique/historique** in the matter of philosophy/history, as regards philosophy/history; **le latin est ma m. préférée** Latin is my favourite subject; **les matières à l'écrit/à l'oral** the subjects for the written/oral examination

6 Beaux-Arts medium

7 Fin **m. imposable** taxable income

◻ **en matière de** PRÉP as regards; **en m. de cuisine** as far as cooking is concerned, as regards cooking

matiérisme [matjerism] NM Beaux-Arts matierism

matiériste [matjerist] Beaux-Arts ADJ matieristic
NMF matierist

MATIF, Matif [matif] NM **1** Bourse (abrév **Marché à terme international de France**) = body regulating activities on the French stock exchange **2** Fin (abrév **Marché à terme des instruments financiers**) financial futures market; Br ≃ LIFFE, Am ≃ CBOE

matifiant, -e [matifjɑ̃, -ɑ̃t] ADJ (produit cosmétique) shine-control (avant n), mattifying

Matignon [matiɲɔ̃] NM (l'hôtel) **M.** = building in Paris which houses the offices of the Prime Minister; **les accords (de) M.** the Matignon Agreements; Hum **le locataire de M.** the (French) Prime Minister; **M. a décidé que...** the Prime Minister's office has decided that...

matin [matɛ̃] NM **1** (lever du jour) morning; **de bon ou grand m., le m. de bonne heure** in the early morning, early in the morning; **partir au petit m.** to leave early in the morning; **rentrer au petit m.** to come home in the early or small hours; **du m. au soir** all day long, from morning till night; **l'étoile/la rosée du m.** the morning star/dew

2 (matinée) morning; **ce m., Can à m.** this

mat-mat

morning; **par un m. d'été/de juillet** one summer/July morning; *Fam* **un beau m., un de ces (quatre) matins** one fine day, one of these (fine) days; **le m. du 8, le 8 au m.** on the morning of the 8th; **il est trois heures du m.** it's three a.m. *or* 3 (o'clock) in the morning; **je suis du m.** *(actif le matin)* I'm an early riser; *(de service le matin)* I'm on *or* I do the morning shift, I'm on mornings; **il travaille le m.** he works mornings *or* in the morning; **elle travaille seulement le m.** she only works mornings, she only works in the morning; **le docteur visite le m.** the doctor does his house-calls in the morning; **à prendre m., midi et soir** to be taken three times a day

3 *Littéraire* **le m. de la vie** the dawn of life; **au m. de sa vie** in the morning of his/her life

ADV 1 *Littéraire (de bonne heure)* early in the morning, in the early hours (of the morning); **se lever très m.** to get up very early

2 *(durant la matinée)* **demain/hier m.** tomorrow/yesterday morning; **tous les dimanches m.** every Sunday morning

ADJ *Can* = **matinal 1**

mâtin, -e [mɑtɛ̃, -in] NM,F *Fam Vieilli* imp, monkey; **le m., il a filé!** the little devil *or* rascal has taken off!; **ah, la mâtine!** oh, the cheeky little hussy!

NM *(chien)* mastiff, guard dog

EXCLAM *Fam Vieilli* by Jove!, great Scott!; **m., la belle fille!** by Jove, what a lovely girl!

matinal, -e, -aux, -ales [matinal, -o] ADJ 1 *(du matin)* morning *(avant n)*; **promenade/brise matinale** morning walk/breeze 2 *(du petit matin)* **heure matinale** early hour 3 *(personne)* **être m.** to be an early riser; **je suis assez m.** I'm quite an early riser; **vous êtes bien m. aujourd'hui** you're up early today

mâtiné, -e [mɑtine] ADJ crossbred; *Fig* **m. de qch** mixed with sth; **c'est un berger allemand m. de lévrier** it's an Alsatian crossed with a greyhound, it's a cross between an Alsatian and a greyhound; *Fig* **un français m. d'italien** French peppered with Italian words; *Fig* **il parle un français m. d'anglais** his French is full of anglicisms; *Fig* **un humour m. d'une touche de mépris** humour tinged with scorn

matinée [matine] NF 1 *(matin)* morning; **je vous verrai demain dans la m.** I'll see you sometime tomorrow morning; **en début/fin de m.** at the beginning/end of the morning; **j'ai travaillé toute la m.** I've worked all morning; **j'ai passé toute ma m. à l'attendre/au lit** I spent the whole morning waiting for him/her/in bed; **je ne l'ai pas vu de toute la m.** I haven't seen him all morning; **une m. de lecture** a morning (spent) reading; **par une belle m. de printemps/de juillet** on a fine spring/July morning

2 *Théât & Cin* matinee; **y a-t-il une séance en m.?** is there an afternoon *or* matinee performance?; **on joue ce film en m.** the film is showing as a matinée

3 *Bourse* **m. de Bourse** morning session

mâtiner [3] [mɑtine] VT to cross

matines [matin] NFPL matins, mattins

matineux, -euse [matinø, -øz] *Vieilli ou Littéraire* ADJ **être m.** to be an early riser

NM,F early riser

matinier, -ère [matinje, -ɛr] ADJ *Vieilli* matinal; **l'étoile matinière** the morning star

matir [32] [matir] VT to matt, to dull

matité [matite] NF 1 *(aspect mat → gén)* matt look; *(→ d'une peinture)* matt finish 2 *(d'un son)* dullness 3 *Méd* flatness

Mato Grosso [matogrɔso] NM **le M.** the Mato Grosso

matoir [matwar] NM matting tool

matois, -e [matwa, -az] *Littéraire* ADJ sly, cunning, wily

NM,F cunning person; **c'est un fin m.** he's a cunning old fox

maton¹ [matɔ̃] NM *Belg (lait caillé)* curdled milk

maton², -onne [matɔ̃, -ɔn] NM,F *Fam Arg crime (gardien de prison)* screw, *Am* hack, bull

matorral, -als [matɔral] NM matorral, heathland

matos [matos] NM *Fam* gear, stuff; **ils ont un sacré m.** they've got loads of gear

matou [matu] NM *Fam* tom, tomcat; *Can Fig (individu lubrique)* sex fiend *or* maniac

Matra [matra] NF = electrical engineering and armaments manufacturing group

matraquage [matrakaʒ] NM 1 *(dans une bagarre)* bludgeoning, clubbing; *(dans une manifestation) Br* truncheoning, *Am* clubbing 2 *Fam (propagande)* **m. publicitaire** hype; **le m. d'un disque** the plugging of a record; **tu as vu le m. qu'ils font pour le bouquin/le concert?** have you seen all the hype about the book/the concert?

matraque [matrak] NF 1 *(de police) Br* truncheon, *Am* billy club, night stick; **il a reçu un coup de m.** he was hit with a *Br* truncheon *or Am* billy club; *Fam Fig* **100 euros, c'est le coup de m.!** 100 euros, that's a bit steep! 2 *(de voyou)* club, *Br* cosh; **tué à coups de m.** bludgeoned *or* clubbed to death

matraquer [3] [matrake] VT 1 *(frapper → sujet: malfaiteur)* to bludgeon, to club; *(→ sujet: agent de police) Br* to truncheon, *Am* to club; **les manifestants se sont fait m. par la police** the demonstrators were beaten by the police

2 *Fam Fig (auditeur, consommateur)* to bombard; *(disque, chanson)* to plug, to hype

3 *Fam Fig* **m. le client** to rip off *or* fleece the customer; **on se fait m. dans ce restaurant!** they really rip you off *or Am* soak you in this restaurant!

matraqueur, -euse [matrakœr, -øz] NM,F *(agresseur)* mugger

matras [matrɑ] NM *Chim* matrass, bolt-head

matriarcal, -e, -aux, -ales [matrijarkal, -o] ADJ matriarchal

matriarcat [matrijarka] NM matriarchy

matriçage [matrisaʒ] NM die forging, drop forging

matriçai *etc voir* **matricer**

matricaire [matrikɛr] NF *Bot* feverfew; **m. odorante** pineapple weed

matrice [matris] NF 1 *(moule → gén)* mould, die, *Spéc* matrix; *(→ d'un caractère d'imprimerie)* mat, matrix; **m. d'un disque/d'une bande** matrix record/tape; **coulé en m.** die-cast

2 *Math* matrix; **m. carrée** square matrix; *Mktg* **m. BCG** Boston matrix; *Mktg* **m. croissance-part de marché** growth-share matrix

3 *Ordinat* matrix; *(de données)* array; **m. active/passive** active/passive matrix; **m. d'aiguilles** dot matrix; **m. de vérité** truth table

4 *Admin* **m. du rôle des contributions** original list of taxpayers; **m. cadastrale** cadastre

5 *Vieilli (utérus)* womb

6 *Métal (d'un alliage)* matrix

matricer [16] [matrise] VT to die forge, to drop forge

matricide [matrisid] NMF *(personne)* matricide

NM *Littéraire (crime)* matricide

matriciel, -elle [matrisjɛl] ADJ 1 *Admin* tax-assessment *(avant n)*; **loyer m.** *Br* rateable value, *Am* assessment of rent *(used to calculate taxes)* 2 *Math* **calcul m.** matrix calculation; **algèbre matricielle** matrix algebra 3 *Ordinat (écran)* dot matrix *(avant n)*

❑ **matricielle** NF *Ordinat* dot matrix

matriclan [matriklɑ̃] NM matriclan, matrilineal clan

matriçons *voir* **matricer**

matricule [matrikyl] ADJ reference *(avant n)*; **numéro m.** reference number

NM 1 *Admin* reference number 2 *Mil* roll number; *Fam* **sois là à l'heure ou gare à ton m.!** be there on time or you'll be in for it!

NF 1 *Admin* register; *(de prison, d'hôpital)* roll, register, list; *Mil* (regimental) roll; *(immatriculation)* registration 2 *(extrait)* registration certificate

matrilignage [matriliɲaʒ] NM matriliny

matrilinéaire [matrilineɛr] ADJ matrilinear

matrilocal, -e, -aux, -ales [matrilɔkal, -o] ADJ matrilocal

matrimonial, -e, -aux, -ales [matrimɔnjal, -o] ADJ matrimonial

matriochka [matriɔʃka] NF *(poupée)* matryoshka, Russian doll; *(série de poupées)* set of matryoshki *or* Russian dolls

matrone [matrɔn] NF 1 *(femme → respectable)* staid *or* upright woman, matron; *(→ corpulente)* stout *or* portly woman 2 *Antiq* matron 3 *Can (gardienne de prison) Br* prison officer, *Am* prison guard

matronyme [matrɔnim] NM matronymic, metronymic

matte [mat] NF *Métal* matte, coarse metal

Matthias [matjas] NPR *Bible* Matthias

Matthieu [matjø] NPR *Bible* Matthew

matthiole [matjɔl] NF *Bot* mathiola, matthiola, stock

maturation [matyrasjɔ̃] NF 1 *Bot* maturation; *Fig* **son talent est arrivé à m.** his/her talent has reached its peak 2 *Méd* maturation; **m. sexuelle** sexual maturation 3 *(du fromage)* ripening, maturing 4 *Agr* maturation, ripening 5 *Métal* age-hardening

mature [matyr] ADJ 1 *Ich* ripe 2 *(développé)* mature

mâture [mɑtyr] NF *Naut* 1 *(mâts)* masts; **dans la m.** aloft; **pièces de m.** timber for masts 2 *(atelier)* mast house

maturité [matyrite] NF 1 *(d'un fruit)* ripeness; *Fig (de personne, d'animal, de pensée)* maturity; *(du marché)* maturity; **venir** *ou* **parvenir à m.** to become ripe, to ripen; *Fig* to become mature, to reach maturity; **manquer de m.** to be immature; **cette jeune femme ne manque pas de m.** that young woman is very mature; **attendons qu'elle ait une plus grande m. d'esprit** *ou* **de jugement** let's wait until she's more intellectually mature

2 *(âge)* prime (of life); **l'artiste fut frappée en pleine m.** the artist was struck down at the height of her powers *or* of her creative genius

3 *Suisse (baccalauréat)* school-leaving diploma *(from a "gymnase", granting admission to university)*

matutinal, -e, -aux, -ales [matytinal, -o] ADJ *Littéraire* morning *(avant n)*

maubèche [mobɛʃ] NF *Orn* sandpiper

maudire [104] [modir] VT 1 *Rel* to damn 2 *(vouer à la calamité)* to curse; **m. le destin** to curse fate; **je maudis le jour où je l'ai rencontré** I curse the day (when) I met him; **tu vas finir par te faire m.** you're going to make yourself very unpopular

maudit, -e [modi, -it] ADJ 1 *(damné)* cursed; **sois m.!** curse you! *Littéraire* **m./maudite soit** a curse *or* plague on; *Littéraire* **m. sois-tu!** a curse on you!

2 *(mal considéré)* accursed; **c'est un livre m.** the book has been censured; **peintre m.** accursed painter; **poète m.** damned *or* cursed poet

3 *(avant le nom) Fam (dans des exclamations)* cursed, blasted, damned; **encore ce m. temps!** this damn weather again!; **maudite bagnole!** blasted *or Am* goddamn car!

4 *Can très Fam (très)* **c'est une maudite belle fille!** she's a damn good-looking girl!, she's one hell of a good-looking girl!

NM *Rel* **le M.** Satan, the Fallen One; **les maudits** the Damned

EXCLAM *Can très Fam* shit!, *Br* bloody hell!

❑ **en maudit** ADV 1 *Can très Fam (en colère)* in a foul temper

2 *(en intensif)* **c'est un beau film en m.** it's a damn *or Br* bloody good film; **il court vite en m.** he's a damn *or Br* bloody fast runner

'M le Maudit' *Lang* 'M'

mauditement [moditmɑ̃] ADV *Can Fam* damn, *Br* bloody; **m. cher** damn *or Br* bloody expensive

maugréer [15] [mogree] VI to grumble; **m. contre qch** to grumble about sth

maul [mol] NM *(au rugby)* maul

maurandia [morɑ̃dja] NF *Bot* maurandia

maure [mɔr] ADJ Moorish

❑ **Maure** NM Moor; **les Maures** the Moors

mauresque [mɔrɛsk] ADJ Moorish

NF 1 *(motif)* moresque, Moresque 2 *(boisson)* = pastis with barley water and water

❑ **Mauresque** NF Moorish woman

Maurice [moris] NF *Géog* **l'île M.** Mauritius; **vivre à l'île M.** to live in Mauritius; **aller à l'île M.** to go to Mauritius

mauricien, -enne [morisjɛ̃, -ɛn] ADJ Mauritian

❑ **Mauricien, -enne** NM,F Mauritian

mauriste [morist] NM *Rel* Maurist

Mauritanie [moritani] NF *Géog* **la M.** Mauritania; **vivre en M.** to live in Mauritania; **aller en M.** to go to Mauritania

mauritanien, -enne [mɔritanjɛ̃, -ɛn] ADJ Mauritanian

❑ **Mauritanien, -enne** NM,F Mauritanian

mauser [mozɛr] NM Mauser

mausolée [mozɔle] NM mausoleum

maussade [mosad] ADJ **1** (*de mauvaise humeur*) glum, sullen; **elle l'accueillit d'un air m.** she greeted him/her sullenly **2** (*triste → temps*) gloomy, dismal

maussaderie [mosadri] NF *Littéraire* moroseness, glumness

MAUVAIS, -E [movɛ, -ɛz]

> ADJ bad A, B, C2, D1, 3, 4 ■ poor A1, 3 ■ wrong A2, C1, 2 ■ unpleasant B1, D2 ■ nasty B1, D1, 2 ■ inconvenient C2
> NM,F bad person
> NM bad
> ADV bad 1

ADJ **A.** *EN QUALITÉ* **1** (*médiocre*) bad, poor; **son deuxième roman est plus/moins m. que le premier** his/her second novel is worse than his/her first/is not as bad as his/her first; **en m. état** in bad or poor condition; **un produit de mauvaise qualité** a poor quality product; **du m. travail** bad or poor or shoddy work; **la récolte a été mauvaise cette année** it was a bad or poor harvest this year; **la route est mauvaise** the road is bad or in a bad state; **j'ai une mauvaise vue** ou **de m. yeux** I've got bad eyesight; **il s'exprimait dans un m. français** he spoke in bad French; **elle a fait une mauvaise performance** she turned in a bad or poor performance; **après l'entracte, la pièce devient franchement mauvaise** after the interval, the play gets really bad; **de m. résultats** (*dans une entreprise*) poor results; (*à un examen*) bad or poor or low grades; **ce n'est pas un m. conseil qu'il t'a donné là** that's not a bad piece of advice he's just given you; **m. goût** (*d'une image, d'une personne, d'une idée*) bad taste; **c'est de m. goût** it's in bad taste; **il porte toujours des cravates de m. goût** he always wears such tasteless ties; **elle a très m. goût** she has very bad or poor taste

2 (*défectueux*) bad, wrong, faulty; **la ligne est mauvaise** (*téléphone*) the line is bad; *Sport* **la balle est mauvaise** the ball is out; *Sport* **le service est m.** it's a bad or faulty serve

3 (*incompétent*) bad, poor; **un m. mari** a bad husband; **va à la réunion si tu ne veux pas être traité de m. syndicaliste** go to the meeting unless you want to be called a bad union member; **il a été m. à la télévision hier** he was bad on TV yesterday; **je suis mauvaise en économie** I'm bad or poor at economics

B. *DÉSAGRÉABLE* **1** (*odeur, goût*) bad, unpleasant, nasty; **prends ton sirop – c'est m.!** take your cough mixture – it's nasty!; **je n'irai plus dans ce restaurant, c'était trop m.** I won't go to that restaurant again, it was too awful; **il n'est pas si m. que ça, ton café** your coffee isn't that bad; **le poisson a une mauvaise odeur** the fish smells bad; **les mauvaises odeurs** bad or unpleasant smells; **elle a mauvaise haleine** she has bad breath; **m. goût** (*de la nourriture, d'un médicament*) bad or nasty or unpleasant taste; **jette ça, c'est m.** (*pourri*) throw that away, it's gone bad; **enlève ce qui est m.** (*dans un fruit*) take off the bad bits

2 (*éprouvant*) bad; **passer un m. hiver** to have a bad winter; **j'ai eu une mauvaise expérience du ski** I had a bad experience skiing; **le temps** bad weather; *Fam* **la trouver** ou **l'avoir mauvaise** to be hacked off or bummed; **tirer qn d'un m. pas** to get sb out of a fix

3 (*défavorable*) bad; **les prévisions pour l'an prochain sont mauvaises** the forecasts for next year are bad; **je vous apporte de mauvaises nouvelles** I've got some bad news for you; **mauvaise nouvelle, elle ne vient plus** bad news, she's not coming any more; **mauvaise affaire** bad deal; **tu as fait une mauvaise affaire** you've got a bad deal (there); **faire de mauvaises affaires** to get some bad deals

C. *NON CONFORME* **1** (*erroné, inapproprié*)

wrong; **l'arbre pousse du m. côté de la barrière** the tree is growing on the wrong side of the fence; **fais demi-tour, on est sur la mauvaise route** turn round, we're on the wrong road; **tu vas dans la mauvaise direction** you're going the wrong way; **prendre qch dans le m. sens** to take sth the wrong way; *Fig* **faire un m. calcul** to miscalculate

2 (*inopportun*) bad, inconvenient, wrong; **j'ai téléphoné à un m. moment** I called at a bad or an inconvenient time; **tu as choisi le m. jour pour me parler d'argent** you've picked the wrong day to talk to me about money; **il ne serait pas m. de la prévenir** it wouldn't be a bad idea to warn her

D. *NÉFASTE* **1** (*dangereux*) bad, nasty; **une mauvaise égratignure** a nasty scratch; **un m. rhume** a bad or nasty cold; **hospitalisé pour une mauvaise bronchite** in hospital with a nasty or severe case of bronchitis; **elle est retombée dans une mauvaise position et s'est tordu la cheville** she landed badly and sprained her ankle; **c'est m. pour les poumons/plantes** it's bad for your lungs/for the plants; **ne bois pas l'eau, elle est mauvaise** don't drink the water, it's unsafe or not safe; **je trouve m. que les enfants regardent trop la télévision** I think it's bad or harmful for children to watch too much television

2 (*malveillant*) nasty, unpleasant; **un rire/sourire m.** a nasty laugh/smile; **m. coup** (*de poing*) nasty blow or punch; (*de pied*) nasty kick; **n'y va pas, tu risques de prendre un m. coup** ou **des m. coups** don't go, you might get hurt; **faire un m. coup** to get up to no good; **faire un m. coup à qn** to play a dirty trick on sb; **avoir l'air m.** to look nasty; **si on la contrarie, elle devient mauvaise** when people annoy her, she gets vicious or turns nasty; **en fait, ce n'est pas un m. homme/une mauvaise femme** he/she means no harm(, really)

3 (*immoral*) bad; **de mauvaises influences** bad influences; **avoir de m. instincts** to have bad or base instincts; **une mauvaise conduite** bad behaviour

4 (*funeste*) bad; **c'est (un) m. signe** it's a bad sign; **m. présage** bad or ill omen

NM,F (*personne méchante*) bad person; **oh, le m./la mauvaise!** (*à un enfant*) you naughty boy/girl!

NM (*ce qui est critiquable*) **il n'y a pas que du m. dans ce qu'il a fait** what he did wasn't all bad; **il y a du bon et du m. dans leur proposition** there are some good points and some bad points in their proposal

ADV **1** *Météo* **il fait m.** the weather's bad or nasty **2** (*suivi d'un infinitif*) **il fait m. être/avoir...** it's not a good idea to be/to have...; **à cette époque-là, il faisait m. être juif** it was hard to be Jewish in those days

mauve [mov] ADJ mauve
NM mauve
NF *Bot* mallow; **grande m.** common mallow; **petite m., m. négligée** dwarf mallow; **m. musquée** musk mallow

mauvéine [movein] NF *Chim* mauveine

mauviette [movjɛt] NF **1** *Fam* (*gringalet*) weakling; (*lâche*) sissy, wimp; **t'es un homme ou t'es une m.?** are you a man or a mouse? **2** *Orn* lark

mauvis [movi] *Orn* redwing

maux [mo] *voir* **mal¹**

MAV [ɛmave] NM *Mktg* (*abrév* **marketing après-vente**) after-sales marketing

max [maks] NM *Fam* (*abrév* **maximum**) **1** (*peine*) maximum sentence■; **il a écopé du m.** he got the maximum sentence or *Am* rap, *Br* copped the full whack

2 (*locution*) **un m.** loads, lots; **ça va te coûter un m.** it's going to cost you a packet or *Br* a bomb; **on s'est éclaté un m.** we had a really fantastic time; **il débloque un m.** he's totally off his rocker; **il en a rajouté un m.** he went completely overboard; **assurer un m.** to do brilliantly; **sur scène ils assurent un m.** they really rock on stage; **un m. de fric** loads of money; **un m. de monde/de voitures** stacks or a ton of people/cars

max. (*abrév écrite* **maximum**) max

maxi [maksi] ADJ INV **1** (*long*) maxi; **un manteau m.** a maxi coat; **un m. 45 tours** a twelve-inch single

2 *Fam* (*maximum*) **vitesse m.** top or full speed■

NM *Couture* maxi; **le m. revient à la mode** maxis are back in fashion; **la mode du m.** the maxi fashion

ADV *Fam* (*au maximum*) max, tops; **on sera vingt m.** there'll be twenty of us max or tops; **ça prendra deux heures m.** it'll take two hours max or tops

MAXI- [maksi] PRÉF

● This prefix conveys the idea of LARGENESS. It is used before a noun, mostly in the language of fashion and advertising where it often contrasts with **mini-**. As far as spelling is concerned, there seems to be some hesitation as to the use of the hyphen, eg:
> **une maxi(-)jupe** a maxi skirt; **un maxi tee-shirt** a baggy or an oversized T-shirt; **un maxi(-)écran** a giant screen

● **Maxi-** can also refer to something large in terms of volume or importance, and is even used, in colloquial French, as an INTENSIFIER in the same vein as **super-** or **méga-** (see entries), eg:
> **une maxi dose de café** a mega dose of coffee; **maxi promo sur toute la gamme!** prices slashed across the whole range!

maxidiscompte [maksidiskɔ̃t] NM *Com* hard discount

maxillaire [maksilɛr] *Anat* ADJ maxillary; **os m.** jawbone, *Spéc* maxilla
NM jaw, jawbone, *Spéc* maxilla; **les maxillaires** the maxillae; **m. supérieur/inférieur** upper/lower jaw

maxille [maksil] NF *Zool* maxilla; **les maxilles** the maxillae

maxillipède [maksilipɛd] NM maxilliped

maxillo-facial, -e, -aux, -ales [maksilɔfasjal, -o] ADJ maxillofacial

maxima [maksima] *voir* **maximum**

maximal, -e, -aux, -ales [maksimal, -o] ADJ **1** (*le plus grand*) maximal, maximum (*avant n*); **pour un confort m.** for maximum comfort; **à la vitesse maximale** at top speed; **vitesse maximale autorisée: 60 km/h** speed limit: 60 kmph; **température maximale** highest or maximum temperature **2** *Math* maximal

maximalisation [maksimalizasjɔ̃] NF maximation, maximization; **m. du profit** profit optimization

maximaliser [3] [maksimalize] VT to maximize

maximalisme [maksimalism] NM maximalism

maximaliste [maksimalist] ADJ maximalist
NMF maximalist

maxime [maksim] NF maxim

maximisation [maksimizasjɔ̃] = **maximalisation**

maximiser [3] [maksimize] = **maximaliser**

maximum [maksimɔm] (*pl* **maximums** *ou* **maxima** [-ma]) ADJ maximum; **pressions maxima** maximum pressures; **vitesse m.** maximum or top speed; **des rendements maximums** maximum or top production figures

NM **1** (*le plus haut degré*) maximum; **le m. saisonnier** the maximum temperature for the season; **en rentrant, on a mis le chauffage au m.** when we got home, we turned the heating on full; **le thermostat est réglé sur le m.** the thermostat is on the highest setting; **la crue était à son m.** the river had risen to its highest level or was in full spate; **faire le m. (pour faire qch)** to do one's utmost or one's best (to do sth); **nous ferons le m. le premier jour** we'll do as much as we can on the first day; **je ferai le m. pour finir dans les temps** I'll do my utmost or I'll do all I can to finish on time

2 *Fam* (*en intensif*) **un m.** (*beaucoup*) loads; **un m. de** an enormous amount of; **un m. de gens** (*le plus possible*) as many people as possible■; (*énormément*) loads of people; **on a eu un m. d'ennuis** everything went wrong; **il y a eu un m. de visiteurs le premier jour** we/they/*etc* had an enormous number of visitors the first day; **pour ça, il faut un m. d'organisation** that sort of thing needs a huge amount of or needs loads of organization; **je voudrais un m. de silence**

pendant le film I want total silence during the film; **on s'est amusés un m.** we had a really great time; **on en fera un m. le premier jour** we'll do as much work as we can on the first day; **ça rendra un m. sur papier brillant** it will come up great on gloss paper

3 *(peine)* **le m.** the maximum sentence; **il a eu le m.** he got the maximum sentence

ADV at the most *or* maximum; **il fait 3°C m.** the temperature is 3°C at the most *or* at the maximum

◽ **au maximum** ADV **1** *(au plus)* at the most *or* maximum; **deux jours au m.** two days at the most; **au grand m.** at the very most

2 *(le plus possible)* **un espace utilisé au m.** an area used to full advantage; **je nettoie au m., mais c'est quand même sale** I do as much cleaning as possible but it's still dirty; **porter la production au m.** to increase production to a maximum, to maximize production

maxwell [makswɛl] NM *Anciennement Phys* maxwell

May [me] NM *Beaux-Arts & Hist* = name given to the religious paintings commissioned for Notre-Dame Cathedral, presented on 1 May every year from 1630 to 1707

maya¹ [maja] ADJ Maya, Mayan

NM *(langue)* Maya, Mayan

◽ **Maya** NMF Maya, Mayan; **les Mayas** the Maya *or* Mayas, the Mayans

maya² [maja] NF *Rel* maya

mayen [majɛ̃] NM *Suisse* = Alpine pasture in the Valais canton for spring and autumn grazing

Mayence [majɑ̃s] NM Mainz

Mayenne [majɛn] NF **1** *(département)* **la M.** the Mayenne **2** *(ville)* Mayenne

mayeur, -e [majœr] = **maïeur**

mayonnaise [majɔnɛz] NF *Culin* mayonnaise; **crabe à la m.** crab in mayonnaise; **œufs m.** egg mayonnaise; **la m. ne prend pas** the mayonnaise won't set; *Fam Fig* **la m. n'a pas pris** it didn't work■; **la m. a pris** it worked■; *Fam* **la m. ne prend pas entre eux** they don't see eye to eye; *Fam Fig* **faire monter la m.** to stir things up

mayoral, -e, -aux, -ales [majɔral, -o] = **maïoral**

mayorat [majɔra] = **maïorat**

Mayotte [majɔt] NF Mayotte Island

mazagran [mazagrɑ̃] NM = glazed earthenware cup for drinking coffee

mazama [mazama] NM *Zool* brocket

mazarinade [mazarinad] NF *Hist* lampoon on Cardinal Mazarin

Mazarine [mazarin] NF **la bibliothèque M.** = public library in Paris

mazdéen, -enne [mazdeɛ̃, -ɛn] ADJ *Rel* Mazdean

mazdéisme [mazdeism] NM *Rel* Mazdaism

mazéage [mazeaʒ] NM *Métal* refining

mazer [3] [maze] VT *Métal* to refine

mazette [mazɛt] EXCLAM *Vieilli Hum* my (word)!; **m., la belle voiture!** my, what a beautiful car!; **m., un vison, quelle élégance!** my, a mink coat, how elegant!

mazot [mazo] NM *Suisse* **1** *(dans le canton du Valais → agricole)* = small stone building used as a house by seasonal vineyard workers from the mountains **2** *(résidence secondaire)* = traditional wooden building in the mountains of the Valais canton, now often used as a holiday home

mazout [mazut] NM (fuel) oil; **chauffage central au m.** oil-fired central heating

mazouter [3] [mazute] VT to pollute (with oil); **plages mazoutées** oil-polluted beaches, beaches polluted with oil; **oiseaux mazoutés** oil-stricken birds

VI to refuel

mazurka [mazyrka] NF mazurka

Mb *Ordinat* (*abrév écrite* **mégabit**) Mb

MBA¹ [ɛmbea] NF *Compta* (*abrév* **marge brute d'autofinancement**) cashflow, funds generated by operations

MBA² [ɛmbea] NM (*abrév* **Master of Business Administration**) MBA

Mbabane [mbabane] NM *Géog* Mbabane

Mbps *Ordinat* (*abrév écrite* **mégabits par seconde**) mbps

MCAC [ɛmseasə] NM (*abrév* **Marché commun d'Amérique centrale**) CACM

MCCA [ɛmsesea] NM (*abrév* **Marché commun centraméricain**) CACM

McDo [makdo] NM *Fam* McDonalds■

MCJ [ɛmseʒi] NF (*abrév* **maladie de Creutzfeldt-Jakob**) CJD

McLuhanisme [maklyanism] NM McLuhanism

m-commerce [ɛmkɔmɛrs] NM m-commerce

MDD [ɛmdede] NF *Com* (*abrév* **marque de distributeur**) distributor's brand name, own brand

MDR *Ordinat & Tél* (*abrév écrite* **mort de rire**) LOL

Mᵉ (*abrév écrite* **Maître**) = title for lawyers

me [mə]

PRON **1** *(avec un verbe pronominal)* myself; **je me suis fait mal** I've hurt myself; **je me suis évanoui** I fainted; **je ne m'en souviens plus** I don't remember any more; **je me disais que...** I thought to myself...

2 *(objet direct)* me; **il me connaît** he knows me; **il est venu me chercher** he came to fetch me; **il me regarde sans me voir** he looks right through me; **ça me regarde** that's my business; **me voici** here I am

3 *(objet indirect)* (to) me; **il m'a écrit** he wrote to me; **il me l'a donné** he gave it (to) me, he gave me it; **donnez-m'en** give me some; **ton idée me plaît** I like your idea; **ton amitié m'est précieuse** your friendship is precious *or* means a lot to me; **ça me soulève le cœur** it makes me sick; **il m'a fait lire ce livre** he made me read this book; *Fam* **il me court après depuis un certain temps** he's been chasing me for some time

4 *Fam (emploi expressif)* **tu veux bien m'éteindre la lumière?** would you switch off the light (for me)?; **va me fermer cette porte** shut that door, will you?; **va me faire tes devoirs** go and get that homework done; **qu'est-ce qu'ils m'ont encore fait comme bêtises?** what kind of stupid tricks have they got up to now?; **où est-ce que tu m'as mis le sucre?** now where have you hidden the sugar?

MÉ- [me] PRÉF

When added to verbs, nouns or adjectives, the prefix **mé-** has a generally NEGATIVE connotation – it expresses the opposite of what the verb, noun or adjective represents. It is often translated by an equivalent prefix, either *mis-* or *dis-*, eg:

méconnaître to misjudge, to misunderstand; **mécontent(e)** displeased; **médire de quelqu'un** to speak ill of somebody; **se méfier de quelqu'un** to distrust somebody; **par mégarde** inadvertently; **se méprendre** to be mistaken; **mépriser** to despise; **une mésaventure** a misadventure, a misfortune

mea culpa [meakylpa] NM INV **1** *Rel* mea culpa; **faire** *ou* **dire son m.** to say one's mea culpa

2 *Fig* **ils ont fait leur m.** they acknowledged responsibility, they admitted it was their fault; **le journal a publié hier un m. en première page** yesterday the paper published a front page apology

EXCLAM *Hum* it's my fault!, mea culpa!; **m.! c'est moi le responsable** it's my fault!, I'm to blame!

méandre [meɑ̃dr] NM *Archit & Géog* meander; *(de route)* bend; **le fleuve fait des méandres** the river meanders *or* twists and turns; *Fig* **perdu dans les méandres de sa propre stratégie** lost in the twists and turns of his own strategy; **l'affaire s'enlisait dans les méandres de la procédure** the case was getting bogged down in a morass *or* maze of legalities; **les méandres de sa pensée** the twists and turns of his/her thoughts; **se perdre dans les méandres d'un raisonnement** to get lost in the intricacies of an argument

méandrine [meɑ̃drin] NF *Zool* meandrina

méat [mea] NM **1** *Anat* meatus; **m. urinaire** urinary meatus **2** *Bot* lacuna

mec [mɛk] NM *Fam* **1** *(homme)* guy, *Br* bloke; **un beau m.** a good-looking guy; **c'est un drôle de m.** he's a strange guy; **pauvre m., va!** you creep!; **écoute, petit m.!** listen, (you little) punk!; *Hum* **ça, c'est un vrai m.!** there's a real man for you!; **salut les mecs!** hi, guys!; **hé, les mecs!** hey, you guys!; **t'en fais pas, m.!** don't worry about it, pal *or* man

2 *(petit ami)* boyfriend■, man, *Br* bloke; **elle est venue sans son m.** she came without her man

meca [mɔka] NF *Fam* drugs■, stuff, *Br* gear

mécanicien, -enne [mekanisjɛ̃, -ɛn] NM,F **1** *(monteur, réparateur)* mechanic; *Naut* engineer; *Aviat* **m. (de bord)** *ou* **navigant** (flight) engineer; **ouvrier m.** mechanic **2** *(physicien)* mechanical engineer **3** *Rail Br* engine driver, *Am* engineer

◽ **mécanicienne** NF *Couture* machinist

mécanicien-dentiste [mekanisjɛ̃dɑ̃tist] (*pl* **mécaniciens-dentistes**) NM dental technician

mécanique [mekanik] ADJ **1** *(de la mécanique)* mechanical

2 *(non manuel → tapis, tissage)* machine-made; *(→ abattage, remblayage)* mechanical, machine *(avant n)*; **repassage m.** machine ironing

3 *(non électrique, non électronique → commande)* mechanical; *(→ jouet)* clockwork; *(→ montre)* wind-up

4 *(non chimique)* **moyens mécaniques de contraception** barrier methods of contraception **5** *(du moteur)* engine *(avant n)*; **nous avons eu un incident m.** *ou* **des ennuis mécaniques** we had engine trouble

6 *(machinal)* mechanical; **je n'aime pas faire mon travail de façon m.** I don't like working like a robot *or* machine; **c'est un travail très m.** it's very mechanical work; **gestes mécaniques** mechanical gestures

7 *Mines & Minér* mechanical

NF **1** *(science)* mechanics *(singulier)*; *Ind & Tech* mechanical engineering; **m. quantique/relativiste** quantum/relativistic mechanics; **m. des fluides** fluid mechanics; **m. ondulatoire** wave mechanics

2 *Aut* car mechanics *(singulier)*; **il aurait voulu faire de la m.** he'd have liked to have been a (car) mechanic

3 *(machine)* piece of machinery; *(dispositif)* mechanism; *(d'une imprimante laser)* engine; **marcher** *ou* **tourner comme une m. bien huilée** to work like a well-oiled machine; **une belle m.** *(moto, voiture)* a fine piece of engineering

mécaniquement [mekanikmɑ̃] ADV mechanically

mécanisation [mekanizasjɔ̃] NF mechanization; **l'ère de la m.** the machine age

mécaniser [3] [mekanize] VT to mechanize; **ces tâches ont été mécanisées** these jobs have been mechanized *or* are now done by machine

mécanisme [mekanism] NM **1** *(processus)* mechanism; *(dispositif)* mechanism, device; **le m. de la violence** the mechanism of violence; **le m. du corps humain** the human mechanism; **elle étudie le m.** *ou* **les mécanismes de la finance** she's studying the workings of finance; **m. administratif** administrative machinery; **m. bancaire** banking mechanism; **grâce à des mécanismes bancaires spécifiques** thanks to specific banking mechanisms; **m. budgétaire** budgetary mechanism; *UE* **m. de change** Exchange Rate Mechanism; *UE* **m. de change européen** European Exchange Rate Mechanism; *Psy* **mécanismes de défense** defence mechanisms; **mécanismes économiques** economic machinery; **m. de l'escompte** discount mechanism; **le m. de la fraude fiscale** the mechanism of tax evasion; **m. du marché** market mechanism; **m. de l'offre et de la demande** supply and demand mechanism; **m. des prix** price mechanism; *UE* **m. des taux de change** Exchange Rate Mechanism

2 *Tech (d'une serrure, d'une horloge)* mechanism; *(d'un fusil)* mechanism, workings; *Aut* **m. d'avance automatique** automatic advance mechanism; *Aut* **m. d'avance centrifuge** centrifugal advance mechanism; *Aut* **m. de bascule-ment** tipping gear; *Aut* **m. de direction** steering gear

3 *Phil* mechanism; *(de la pensée, de la parole)* mechanics

mécaniste [mekanist] *Phil* **ADJ** mechanistic **NMF** mechanist

mécano [mekano] **NM** *Fam* **1** *Aut* mechanic■ **2** *Rail Br* engine driver■, *Am* engineer■

🎬

'Le Mécano de la "General"' *Keaton* 'The General'

mécanographe [mekanɔgraf] **NMF** punch card (machine) operator

mécanographie [mekanɔgrafi] **NF 1** *(procédé)* data processing *(with punch card machines)* **2** *(service)* data processing department

mécanographique [mekanɔgrafik] **ADJ** **service m.** (mechanical) data processing department, punch card department; **fiche m.** punch *or* punched card

mécanorécepteur [mekanɔresɛptœr] **NM** mecanoreceptor

mécanothérapie [mekanɔterapi] **NF** mecanotherapy

Mec Art, Mec'Art [mɛkart] **NM** *Beaux-Arts (abrév* **Mechanical Art)** Mec Art

mécatronique [mekatrɔnik] *Ind* **ADJ** mechatronic **NF** mechatronics *(singulier)*

Meccano® [mekano] **NM** Meccano® (set)

mécénat [mesena] **NM** *(par une personne)* patronage, sponsorship; *(par une société)* sponsorship; **le m. d'entreprise** corporate sponsorship

Mécène [mesɛn] **NPR** *Antiq* Maecenas

mécène [mesɛn] **NM** *(personne)* patron, sponsor; *(société)* sponsor

méchage [meʃaʒ] **NM 1** *Méd (pour coaguler)* packing; *(pour drainer)* gauze drainage **2** *(en œnologie)* matching

méchamment [meʃamã] **ADV 1** *(avec cruauté)* nastily, spitefully, wickedly; **il ne l'a pas fait m.** he didn't do it nastily **2** *Fam (très, beaucoup)* really■, *Br* dead, *Am* real; **être m. déçu/embêté** to be *Br* dead *or* *Am* real disappointed/annoyed; **il est rentré m. bronzé** he came back with a fantastic tan; **ça a m. cartonné hier au bar** there was one hell of a punch-up in the bar yesterday

méchanceté [meʃãste] **NF 1** *(volonté de nuire)* spite, malice, nastiness; **par pure m.** out of sheer spite; **soit dit sans m., elle n'est pas futée** without wishing to be unkind, she's not very bright
2 *(caractère méchant)* maliciousness, nastiness, spitefulness; **la m. se lit dans son regard** you can see the malice in his/her eyes
3 *(acte, propos)* spiteful *or* nasty action/remark; **dire des méchancetés à qn** to say nasty *or* horrible things to sb; **faire des méchancetés à qn** to be nasty *or* horrible to sb; **c'était la pire m. qu'il pouvait faire** it was the nastiest *or* meanest thing he could have done

méchant, -e [meʃã, -ãt] **ADJ 1** *(cruel → animal)* nasty, vicious; *(→ personne)* wicked; *(haineux)* nasty, spiteful, wicked; *(remarque)* spiteful, nasty, malicious; **un regard m.** a nasty *or* wicked look; **il n'est pas m.** *(pas malveillant)* there's no harm in him, he's harmless; *(pas dangereux)* he won't do you any harm; **en fait, ce n'est pas une méchante femme** she means no harm *or* she's not that bad, really; **je ne voudrais pas être m., mais vous avez une sale tête aujourd'hui!** I don't want to be nasty, but you look dreadful today!
2 *(très désagréable)* horrible, horrid, nasty; **ne sois pas si m. avec moi** don't be so nasty *or* horrible to me; **de fort méchante humeur** in a (really) foul mood; **il s'est mis sur le dos une méchante affaire ou querelle** he's got himself into some nasty business
3 *(enfant)* naughty, bad; **la dame me dira si vous avez été méchants** the lady will tell me if you've been naughty
4 *(grave)* nasty, very bad; **c'est une méchante plaie qui risque de s'infecter** it's a nasty gash which may become infected; **il a attrapé une méchante grippe** he caught a nasty dose of flu; *Fam* **ça n'était pas bien m., finalement, cette piqûre/ce permis?** the injection/driving test wasn't that bad after all, was it?
5 *(avant le nom) Fam (formidable)* amazing,

terrific, great; **il y avait une méchante ambiance** there was a great atmosphere; **ce tube a eu un m. succès** that record was a huge hit; **j'avais une méchante envie de dormir/lui casser la figure** I had an incredible urge to sleep/to smash his face in
6 *(avant le nom) (pitoyable)* pathetic, wretched, miserable; **elle essayait de vendre deux ou trois méchantes salades** she was trying to sell a couple of pathetic-looking lettuces
7 *Can Fam (mauvais)* foul, awful; **la soupe n'est pas méchante** the soup isn't bad at all■, *Br* the soup isn't half bad; **il fait m.** the weather's lousy
8 *Can Fam (incorrect)* wrong■; **le m. numéro** the wrong number
    NM,F 1 *(en langage enfantin)* naughty child; **la poupée, c'est une méchante!** naughty dolly!; **faire le m.** to turn nasty
    2 *(dans un film, dans un livre)* bad guy, baddy
    3 *Can Fam* **faire sortir le m.** *(se défouler)* to let it all out

mèche [mɛʃ] **NF 1** *(de cheveux)* lock; **se faire (faire) des mèches** to have highlights *or* streaks put in; **mèches folles** wispy curls; **une m. rebelle** a wayward strand of hair; **une m. dans les yeux** (a strand of) hair in his/her eyes
2 *(pour lampe, bougie, explosifs, feu d'artifice)* wick; *(pour canon)* match; *(de mine)* fuse; **m. lente** ou **de sûreté** safety fuse; *Fam* **découvrir** ou **éventer la m.** to uncover the plot■
3 *Tech (de perceuse)* bit; **m. torse** twist drill; **m. torsadée** auger bit
4 *(de câble etc)* core, heart; *(de fouet)* lash; *Élec* **charbon à m.** cored carbon
5 *Menuis* auger, gimlet; **m. anglaise** ou **à trois pointes** centre bit; **m. hélicoïdale** twist bit, twist drill
6 *Méd (pour coaguler)* pack; *(pour drainer)* (gauze) wick
7 *Naut* **m. de gouvernail** stock
8 *Tex* **m. de préparation** roving
9 *Fam (locutions)* **être de m. avec qn** to be in league *or* in cahoots with sb; **ils sont de m. avec les dignitaires du coin** they're hand in glove with the local dignitaries; **ils étaient de m.** they were in it together; **il n'y a pas m.** no way, no chance; *Can* **il y a une m.** ages ago, a long time ago■; *Can* **à une m. de** far away from■, quite a distance from■

mécher [18] [meʃe] **VT 1** *Méd (pour coaguler)* to pack (with gauze); *(pour drainer)* to drain (with a wick) **2** *(en œnologie)* to match

mécheux, -euse [meʃø, -øz] **ADJ** *Tex* wispy

méchoui [meʃwi] **NM** *(repas)* barbecue *(of a whole sheep roasted on a spit)*; *(fête)* barbecue (party)

mechta [meʃta] **NF** hamlet

Mecklembourg [mɛklãbur] **NM** *Anciennement* Mecklenburg

Mecklembourg-Poméranie-Occidentale [mɛklãburpɔmeraniɔksidãtal] **NM** Mecklenburg-West Pomerania

mécompte [mekɔ̃t] **NM 1** *Littéraire (désillusion)* disappointment, disillusion **2** *Vieilli (erreur)* miscalculation, error

méconduire [98] [mekɔ̃dɥir] **se méconduire VPR** *Belg* to misbehave

méconduite [mekɔ̃dɥit] **NF** *Belg* misbehaviour

méconium [mekɔnjɔm] **NM** *Méd* meconium

méconnais etc voir **méconnaître**

méconnaissable [mekɔnɛsabl] **ADJ** *(à peine reconnaissable)* hardly recognizable; *(non reconnaissable)* unrecognizable; **sans sa barbe il est m.** you wouldn't recognize him without his beard; **dix ans après, elle était m.** ten years later she had changed beyond recognition

méconnaissait etc voir **méconnaître**

méconnaissance [mekɔnɛsɑ̃s] **NF 1** *(ignorance)* ignorance, lack of knowledge; **il a fait preuve d'une totale m. du sujet** he displayed a complete lack of knowledge of the subject; **sa m. de la psychologie est inquiétante** his/her ignorance of psychology is worrying; **par m. des faits** through ignorance of the facts, through not being acquainted with the facts; **la m. du règlement vous exposerait à des poursuites** ignorance of the regulations may render you liable to prosecution

2 *(incompréhension)* lack of comprehension *or* understanding; **nous déplorons de la part de l'auteur une grande m. de ce que fut la Rome antique** it is regrettable that the author utterly fails to comprehend ancient Rome
3 *(refus de reconnaître comme valable → d'un droit, d'une loi)* disregard

méconnaître [91] [mekɔnɛtr] **VT** *Littéraire* **1** *(ignorer)* to be unaware of; **nous ne méconnaissons pas que ce (ne) soit rare** we're not unaware of the fact that it is unusual
2 *(ne pas reconnaître)* to fail to recognize; **sans vouloir m. ce qu'ils ont fait pour nous** while not wishing to minimize *or* to underestimate what they have done for us; **il était méconnu de ses contemporains** he went unrecognized by his contemporaries
3 *(mal comprendre)* to fail to understand; *(personne)* to misunderstand, to misjudge; **c'est m. le milieu universitaire!** you're/he's/etc misjudging the academic world!; **c'est le m. que de le croire chauvin** if you think he's chauvinistic, you don't really know him
4 *(négliger → devoir)* to disregard

méconnu, -e [mekɔny] **ADJ** *(incompris)* unappreciated, unrecognized; *(peu connu)* obscure; **un coin m. mais très joli de la Bretagne** a little-known but very pretty part of Brittany; **rester m.** *(non apprécié)* to go unrecognized, to remain unappreciated; *(sans gloire)* to remain unknown; **malgré son grand talent, il est mort pauvre et m.** in spite of his great talent he died penniless and in obscurity; **mes mérites sont méconnus** my merits have never been acknowledged

méconnut etc voir **méconnaître**

mécontent, -e [mekɔ̃tã, -ãt] **ADJ 1** *(insatisfait)* displeased (**de** with); **elle est très mécontente du travail du plombier** she is very dissatisfied with the plumber's work; **elle est toujours mécontente de quelque chose** she's always annoyed *or* disgruntled about something; **je ne suis pas mécontente de mes résultats** I am not altogether dissatisfied *or* unhappy with my results; **je ne suis pas m. de mon sort** I am not discontented with my lot; **nous ne sommes pas mécontents que tout soit terminé** we are not sorry that it's all over
2 *(fâché)* annoyed; **il s'est montré très m. de ma décision** he was very annoyed at my decision; **les enfants, je suis très m.!** children, I am extremely *or* very annoyed!; **être m. que...** to be annoyed that...
    NM,F 1 *(gén)* complainer, grumbler, moaner
    2 *Pol* **les mécontents** the discontented, the disgruntled; **cette politique va faire des mécontents** this measure is going to displease quite a few people

mécontentement [mekɔ̃tãtmã] **NM 1** *(agitation sociale)* discontent, unrest; **il y a un m. croissant chez les étudiants** there is growing discontent *or* unrest amongst students; **cela risque de provoquer le m. des agriculteurs** that might anger the farmers; **c'est un sujet de m.** it's a source of discontent *or* dissatisfaction; **m. populaire** popular unrest
2 *(agacement)* annoyance; **à mon grand m.** to my great annoyance; **marquer** ou **exprimer son m.** to show *or* express one's annoyance *or* displeasure

mécontenter [3] [mekɔ̃tãte] **VT** *(déplaire à)* to fail to please, to displease; *(irriter)* to annoy, to irritate; **la réforme risque de m. les milieux d'affaires** the reform might anger business circles

mécoptère [mekɔptɛr] *Entom* **NM** mecopteran
   ❏ **mécoptères** **NMPL** Mecoptera

Mecque [mɛk] **NF 1** *Géog* **La M.** Mecca **2** *Fig* **la M. des surfeurs** a mecca for surfers

mécréance [mekreãs] **NF** *Littéraire* **1** *(foi en une autre religion)* misbelief, heterodoxy **2** *(irréligion)* unbelief

mécréant, -e [mekreã, -ãt] *Littéraire* **ADJ** infidel, unbelieving
    NM,F infidel, miscreant

mecton [mɛktɔ̃] **NM** *Fam* guy, *Br* bloke

MÉDAF [medaf] **NM** *Fin (abrév* **modèle d'évaluation des actifs)** CAPM

médaille [medaj] **NF 1** *(pour célébrer, récompenser)* medal; **m. d'argent/de bronze** silver/bronze

medal; **m. d'or** gold medal; **être m. d'or** *(sportif)* to be a gold medallist, to be a gold medal winner; **détenir la m. du 60 mètres** to hold the medal for the 60 metres; *Fam Hum* **t'as gagné une m. en chocolat!** you'll get a gold star for this!; **m. d'honneur** = medal for honourable service in a profession; **m. du travail** medal for long service; *Prov* **toute m. a son revers** every rose has its thorn

2 *(pour identifier)* (official) badge; *(de chat, de chien)* (identity) disc *or* tag

3 *(bijou)* pendant; **une m. de la Vierge** a medal of the Virgin Mary; **m. pieuse** holy medal

médaillé, -e [medaje] **ADJ** *(soldat)* decorated; *Sport* medal-holding *(avant n)*; **un camembert m.** an award-winning camembert

  NM,F 1 *Admin & Mil* medal-holder; **les médaillés du travail** holders of long-service medals **2** *Sport* medallist; **les médaillés olympiques** the Olympic medallists

médailler [3] [medaje] **VT** to award a medal to

médailleur [medajœr] **NM** medalmaker, medallist

médaillier [medaje] **NM 1** *(collection)* medal collection **2** *(meuble)* medal cabinet

médaillon [medajɔ̃] **NM 1** *(bijou)* locket **2** *Culin* medallion **3** *(élément décoratif)* medallion **4** *TV, Cin & Journ* inset

medal play [medəlplɛ] *(pl* **medal plays)** **NM** *Golf* medal play

mède [mɛd] **ADJ** Median, Medic
  NMF Mede

médecin [medsɛ̃] **NM**

> Note that it is no longer considered a mistake to feminize this word and to say **une médecin** but some French speakers nonetheless regard this form as unacceptable, especially in France. See also the entry **féminisation**.

1 *(docteur)* doctor, physician; **aller chez le m.** to go to the doctor('s); **une femme m.** a woman doctor; **m. agréé** = doctor whose fees are partially reimbursed by the social security system; **m. des armées** army medical officer; **m. de bord** ship's doctor; **m. de campagne** country doctor; **m. consultant** consultant; **m. conventionné** = doctor who meets the French social security criteria, *Br* ≃ NHS doctor; **m. de famille** family doctor; **m. généraliste** *Br* general practitioner, GP, *Am* family doctor or physician; **m. des hôpitaux** hospital doctor; **m. hypnotiseur** hypnotherapist; **m. légiste** forensic expert *or* scientist, *Am* medical examiner; **m. aux pieds nus** barefoot doctor; **m. de quartier** local doctor; **m. spécialiste** specialist (physician); **m. traitant** attending physician; **qui est votre m. (traitant)?** who is your (regular) doctor?; **m. du travail** *(dans le privé)* company doctor; *(dans le secteur public)* health or *Br* medical officer; **Médecins du monde, Médecins sans frontières** = organizations providing medical aid to victims of war and disasters, especially in the Third World

2 *Fig Littéraire* **m. de l'âme** *ou* **des âmes** *(confesseur)* confessor

'**Le Médecin malgré lui'** *Molière* 'A Doctor in spite of himself' *or* 'The Reluctant Doctor'

'**Le Médecin de campagne'** *Balzac* 'The Country Doctor'

médecin-chef [medsɛ̃ʃɛf] *(pl* **médecins-chefs)** **NM** ≃ senior consultant

médecin-conseil [medsɛ̃kɔ̃sɛj] *(pl* **médecins-conseils)** **NM** medical consultant *(who checks the validity of claims)*

médecin-dentiste [medsɛ̃dãtist] *(pl* **médecins-dentistes)** **NM** *Suisse* dentist

médecine [medsin] **NF 1** *(gén)* medicine; **exercer la m.** to practise medicine; **ce n'est plus du ressort de la m.** it's no longer a medical matter; **docteur en m.** doctor of medicine, MD; **médecines alternatives, médecines douces** alternative medicine; **m. générale** general practice; **m. par les herbes** herbalism; **m. homéopathique** homeopathic medicine, homeopathy; **m. interne** internal medicine; **m. légale** forensic

medicine; **m. opératoire** surgery; **médecines parallèles** alternative medicine; **m. préventive** preventive *or* preventative medicine; **m. sportive** sports medicine; **m. traditionnelle** traditional medicine; **m. du travail** industrial *or* occupational medicine; **m. d'urgence** emergency medicine; **m. de ville** community medicine

2 *Univ* medicine, medical studies; **étudiant en m.** medical student; **il fait (sa) m., il est en m.** he's studying medicine, he's a medical student; **elle est en troisième année de m.** she's in her third year at medical school, she's a third-year medical student; **elle a fini sa m. en 1980** she qualified (as a doctor) in 1980

3 *Arch (remède)* medicine, remedy

médecine-ball [medsinbol] *(pl* **médecine-balls)** **NM** medicine ball

Médée [mede] **NPR** *Myth* Medea

Medef [medɛf] **NM** *(abrév* **Mouvement des Entreprises de France)** French employers' association, *Br* ≃ CBI

medersa [medɛrsa] **NF INV** madrasa

média [medja] **NM 1** medium; **les médias** the media; **la télévision est un m. privilégié** television is the most efficient medium; **faire campagne dans tous les médias** to carry out a media-wide advertising campaign; **médias électroniques** electronic media; **m. de masse** mass media; **médias numériques** digital media; **médias numériques interactifs** interactive digital media; **m. planner** media planner; **m. planning** media planning; **m. publicitaire** advertising media; **médias de télécommunication** telecommunications media; **les nouveaux médias** new media

médiacratie [medjakrasi] **NF** mediacracy

médiale [medjal] **NF** median

médialogie [medjalɔʒi] **NF** media research

médian, -e [medjã, -an] **ADJ 1** *Géom* median **2** *Ling* medial
  ❏ **médiane NF 1** *(en statistique)* median **2** *Ling* mid vowel

médianoche [medjanɔʃ] **NM** *Arch ou Littéraire* midnight meal

médiante [medjãt] **NF** *Mus* mediant

médiaplaneur, médiaplanneur [medjaplanœr] **NM** media planner

médiaplanning [medjaplaniŋ] **NM** media planning

médiastin [medjastɛ̃] **NM** *Anat* mediastinum

médiastinite [medjastinit] **NF** *Méd* mediastinitis

médiat, -e [medja, -at] **ADJ** mediate

médiateur, -trice [medjatœr, -tris] **ADJ** mediating, mediatory; **commission médiatrice** arbitration commission *or* board
  NM,F intermediary, go-between, mediator; **servir de m.** to act as a go-between; **le président sert de m. entre les deux factions** the president is mediating *or* arbitrating between the two factions
  NM 1 *Ind* arbitrator, mediator **2** *Admin & Pol* mediator, ombudsman; **le M. européen** the European Ombudsman; **le M. (de la République)** *Br* ≃ the Parliamentary Commissioner, ≃ the Ombudsman **3** *Physiol* **m. chimique** neurotransmitter
  ❏ **médiatrice NF** *Géom* midperpendicular

médiathèque [medjatɛk] **NF** media library

médiation [medjasjɔ̃] **NF 1** *(entremise)* & *Pol* mediation; *Ind* arbitration; **il a fallu la m. de l'évêque** the bishop had to mediate; **j'offre ma m.** I volunteer to act as a go-between *or* as an intermediary **2** *Physiol* neurotransmission

médiatique [medjatik] **ADJ** media *(avant n)*; **un événement m.** a media *or Péj* a media-staged event; **c'est un sport très m.** it's a sport well suited to the media; **il est très m.** *(il passe bien à la télévision)* he comes over well on television; *(il exploite les médias)* he uses the media very successfully; **d'un intérêt m.** newsworthy
  NF communications, communication technology

médiatisation [medjatizasjɔ̃] **NF 1** *Rad & TV (popularisation)* media coverage; **la m. d'un événement** the media coverage or attention given to an event; **on assiste à une m. croissante de la production littéraire** literary works are getting more and more media exposure; **nous**

déplorons la m. de la politique it's a shame to see politics being turned into a media event **2** *Pol* mediatization

médiatisé, -e [medjatize] **ADJ** **il est très m.** he's got a high media profile

médiatiser [3] [medjatize] **VT 1** *Rad & TV (populariser)* to popularize through the (mass) media; *(événement)* to give media coverage to; **m. les élections/la guerre** to turn elections/the war into a media event **2** *Pol* to mediatize

médiator [medjatɔr] **NM** *Mus* plectrum

médiatrice [medjatris] *voir* **médiateur**

médical, -e, -aux, -ales [medikal, -o] **ADJ** medical

médicalement [medikalmã] **ADV** medically; **m., il est guéri** medically speaking, he's cured

médicalisation [medikalizasjɔ̃] **NF 1** *(d'une région)* **la m. des pays pauvres** the provision of health care to poor countries **2** *(d'un état, d'une pathologie)* medicalization; **la m. croissante de la grossesse** the increasing reliance on medical intervention during pregnancy

médicalisé, -e [medikalize] **ADJ** medicalized; **accouchement m.** medicalized childbirth; **maison de retraite médicalisée** nursing home *(providing medical care)*

médicaliser [3] [medikalize] **VT 1** *(région, pays)* to provide with health care **2** *(maternité, vieillesse)* to medicalize, to increase medical intervention in

médicament [medikamã] **NM** medicine, drug; **prends tes médicaments** take your medicine; **est-ce que vous prenez des médicaments?** are you on any kind of medication?; **m. de confort** = pharmaceutical product not considered to be essential and not fully reimbursed by the French social security system; **m. délivré sans ordonnance, m. en vente libre** medicine issued without a prescription, over-the-counter drug; **m. homéopathique** homeopathic drug; **m. en vente sur ordonnance** drug available on prescription, prescription drug; **m. préventif** *ou* **prophylactique** preventive; **m. tétanique** tetanic drug

médicamenteux, -euse [medikamãtø, -øz] **ADJ** medicinal

médicastre [medikastr] **NM** *Hum Péj* quack (doctor), charlatan

médication [medikasjɔ̃] **NF** medication, (medicinal) treatment

médicinal, -e, -aux, -ales [medisinal, -o] **ADJ** medicinal

medicine-ball [medisinbol] *(pl* **medicine-balls)** **NM** medicine ball

médicinier [medisinje] **NM** *Bot* oil tree

Médicis [medisis] **NPR** *Hist* Medici; **Catherine de M.** Catherine de' Medici; **les M.** the Medicis
  NM *Littérature* **le prix M.** = French literary prize

médico-chirurgical, -e, -aux, -ales [medikɔʃiryrʒikal, -o] **ADJ** medico-surgical

médico-éducatif, -ive [medikoedykatif] *(mpl* **médico-éducatifs,** *fpl* **médico-éducatives)** **ADJ** **institut m.** special needs school

médico-légal, -e [medikɔlegal, -o] *(mpl* **médico-légaux,** *fpl* **médico-légales)** **ADJ** forensic, medico-legal; **institut m.** institute of forensic medicine

médico-pédagogique [medikɔpedagɔʒik] *(pl* **médico-pédagogiques)** **ADJ** **institut m.** special school *(for children with special needs or learning disabilities who are under 14)*

médico-professionnel, -elle [medikɔprɔfɛsjɔnɛl] *(mpl* **médico-professionnels,** *fpl* **médico-professionnelles)** **ADJ** **institut m.** = social education workshop for young people with learning disabilities

médico-psychologique [medikɔpsikɔlɔʒik] *(pl* **médico-psychologiques)** **ADJ** medico-psychological

médico-social, -e [medikɔsɔsjal, -o] (*mpl* **médico-sociaux,** *fpl* **médico-sociales**) ADJ medico-social; **centre m.** health centre; **équipe médico-sociale** health and social services team; **services médico-sociaux** health and social services network

médico-sportif, -ive [medikɔsportif, -iv] (*mpl* **médico-sportifs,** *fpl* **médico-sportives**) ADJ **recherche médico-sportive** research in sports medicine; **institut m.** institute for sports medicine

médiéval, -e, -aux, -ales [medjeval, -o] ADJ medieval; **l'époque médiévale** the medieval period, the Middle Ages

médiévisme [medjevism] NM medieval studies

médiéviste [medjevist] NMF medievalist

médina [medina] NF medina

Médine [medin] NM Medina

médiocratie [medjɔkrasi] NF mediocracy

médiocre [medjɔkr] ADJ 1 (*rendement, efficacité, qualité etc*) mediocre, poor; **cette année les rendements en blé ont été médiocres** wheat production has been mediocre *or* poor this year; **elle est m. en mathématiques** she's pretty mediocre at mathematics; **temps m. sur toute la France** poor weather throughout France

2 (*quelconque*) second-rate, mediocre; **il a fait une carrière m.** his career has been unsuccessful; **je refuse de mener une vie m.** I refuse to live a life of mediocrity

3 (*avant le nom*) (*piètre*) poor; **un livre de m. intérêt** a book of little interest

NMF (*personne*) nonentity; **dans cette classe, il n'y a que des médiocres** there are only mediocrities in this class

NM (*médiocrité*) mediocrity; **se complaire dans le m.** to revel in mediocrity

médiocrement [medjɔkrəmɑ̃] ADV indifferently, poorly; **un enfant m. doué pour les langues** a child with no great gift for languages; **m. satisfait, il décida de recommencer** not very satisfied, he decided to start again; **j'ai répondu assez m. à l'examen oral** my answers in the oral exam were rather poor; **elle chante très m.** she's a very mediocre singer; **la station n'est que m. équipée** the resort's facilities are below average

médiocrité [medjɔkrite] NF 1 (*en qualité*) mediocrity, poor quality; (*en quantité*) inadequacy; **ce genre de spectacle ne souffre pas la m.** this type of show will not allow for *or* admit mediocrity 2 (*personne*) nonentity

médiologie [medjɔlɔʒi] NF mediology

médique [medik] ADJ Median, Medic

médire [103] [medir] **médire de** VT IND (*critiquer*) to speak ill of, to run down; (*calomnier*) to spread scandal about, to malign

USAGE ABSOLU **arrête de m.!** stop criticizing!

médisance [medizɑ̃s] NF 1 (*dénigrement*) gossip, scandalmongering; **c'est de la m.!** that's slander!; **victime de la m.** victim of (malicious) gossip; **les gens qui se livrent à la m.** scandalmongers 2 (*propos*) gossip; **les médisances de ses collègues lui ont fait du tort** his/her colleagues' (malicious) gossip has damaged his/her good name

médisant, -e [medizɑ̃, -ɑ̃t] ADJ slanderous; (*personne*) scandalmongering; **qu'est-ce que tu peux être m.!** what a scandalmonger you are!; **sans vouloir être m., je dois dire que je le trouve un peu naïf** no malice intended, but I have to say that I find him a bit naïve

NM,F (*auteur de ragots*) gossip, gossipmonger; (*auteur de diffamation*) slanderer

médisez *etc voir* **médire**

médit [medi] PP *voir* **médire**

méditatif, -ive [meditatif, -iv] ADJ meditative, contemplative, thoughtful; **il avait un air m.** he appeared to be deep in thought

NM,F thinker

méditation [meditasjɔ̃] NF 1 *Psy & Rel* meditation; **m. transcendantale** transcendental meditation 2 (*réflexion*) meditation, thought; **plongé dans la m.** lost in thought; **le fruit de mes méditations** the fruit of my meditation *or* meditations

□ **Méditations** NFPL *Littérature & Phil* Meditation, Meditations

méditative [meditativ] *voir* **méditatif**

méditer [3] [medite] VT 1 (*réfléchir à*) to reflect on *or* upon, to ponder (upon); **elle veut encore m. sa décision** she wants to think some more about her decision; **m. une vengeance** to contemplate vengeance

2 (*projeter*) to plan; **qu'est-ce qu'ils méditent encore?** what are they planning now?; **m. de faire qch** to be contemplating doing sth

VI to meditate; **m. sur** to meditate on, to think about

Méditerranée [mediterane] NF **la (mer) M.** the Mediterranean (Sea); **en M.** in the Mediterranean; **une croisière sur la M.** a Mediterranean cruise

méditerranéen, -enne [mediteraneɛ̃, -ɛn] ADJ Mediterranean

□ **Méditerranéen, -enne** NM,F 1 (*de la Méditerranée*) Mediterranean, Southern European (*from the Mediterranean area*) 2 (*en France*) Southerner

médium [medjɔm] NMF (*spirite*) medium

NM 1 *Mus* middle register 2 (*support*) medium 3 (*liant*) medium, vehicle

médiumnique [medjɔmnik] ADJ **facultés médiumniques** powers of a medium

médiumnité [medjɔmnite] NF mediumism

médius [medjys] NM middle finger

médoc[1] [medɔk] NM Médoc (wine)

médoc[2] [medɔk] NM *Fam* medicine■, meds

Médor [medɔr] NM = typical name for a dog

médulla [medyla] NF *Anat* medulla

médullaire [medylɛr] ADJ *Anat* medullary

médulleux, -euse [medylø, -øz] ADJ *Anat* medullated, medullary

médullosurrénale [medylɔsyrenal] *Anat* ADJ F adrenal medullar

NF adrenal medulla

Méduse [medyz] NPR *Myth* Medusa

méduse [medyz] NF jellyfish, *Spéc* medusa

médusé, -e [medyze] ADJ stunned, dumbfounded, stupefied; **d'un air m.** in stupefaction; **j'en suis restée médusée** I was stunned *or* dumbfounded by it

méduser [3] [medyze] VT to astound, to stun, to stupefy; **sa réponse m'a médusé** his/her reply stunned me

meeting [mitiŋ] NM (public) meeting; **m. aérien** air show; **m. d'athlétisme** athletics *Br* meeting *or Am* meet

méfait [mefɛ] NM (*mauvaise action*) misdeed, wrong, wrongdoing; (*délit*) offence; *Jur* misdemeanour

□ **méfaits** NMPL (*ravages*) **les méfaits du temps/de la guerre** the ravages of time/war; **les méfaits du laxisme parental** the damaging effects of a lack of parental discipline; **les méfaits de l'alcoolisme** the ill effects of *or* the damage done by alcoholism; **les méfaits de la télévision** the harm caused by television

méfiance [mefjɑ̃s] NF (*manque de confiance*) distrust; (*suspicion*) mistrust, suspicion; **avoir de la m. envers qn** to distrust sb; (*avoir de la suspicion*) to mistrust sb, to be suspicious of sb; **avoir de la m. envers tout ce qui est nouveau** to be distrustful of *or* to be wary of *or* to distrust anything new; **sa m. envers les étrangers** his/her distrust of foreigners; **éveiller la m. de qn** to make sb suspicious; **il renifla le paquet avec m.** he warily sniffed the parcel; **elle est sans m.** she has a trusting nature; **m.!** be careful!, be on your guard!; *Prov* **m. est mère de sûreté** better safe than sorry

méfiant, -e [mefjɑ̃, -ɑ̃t] ADJ (*n'ayant pas confiance*) distrustful; (*suspicieux*) mistrustful, suspicious; **m. de nature** naturally distrustful; **il n'est pas assez m.** he is too unsuspecting *or* trusting; **être m. envers qch** to be sceptical of sth; **on n'est jamais assez m.** you can never be too careful

NM,F doubter, suspicious *or* doubting person

méfier [9] [mefje] **se méfier** VPR 1 (*faire attention*) to be careful *or* wary; **il ne se méfiait pas** he was not on his guard; **on ne se méfie jamais assez** you can't be too careful; **méfie-toi!** be careful!, watch out!, be on your guard!

2 **se m. de qn** to distrust sb; (*avoir de la suspicion*) to mistrust sb, to be suspicious of sb; **se m. de qch** to be wary of sth, to be on one's

guard against sth; **il se méfie même de ses proches** he is even suspicious of *or* he even mistrusts his own family; **méfie-toi de lui/de son air doux** don't trust him/his mild manners; **méfiez-vous des pickpockets** beware of pickpockets; **méfiez-vous des contrefaçons** beware of forgeries; **il faut se m. des apparences** you shouldn't trust appearances; **il aurait dû se m. davantage des derniers tournants** he should have been more careful on the last bends; *Fam* **méfiez-vous qu'ils ne se sauvent pas** watch out *or* mind they don't run away

méforme [mefɔrm] NF unfitness, lack of fitness; **après quelques jours de m.** after a few days off form

MEG [ɛməʒe] NM *Méd* (*abrév* **magnétoencéphalographie**) MEG

méga [mega] NM *Fam Ordinat* megabyte■, meg

MÉGA- [mega] PRÉF

This prefix of scientific origin has come to prominence with the advent of mass computing and its *megabytes* (**mégaoctets**) and *megaflops* (**mégaflops**). It has since passed into colloquial language as an INTENSIFIER:

méga-promo sur toute la gamme! prices slashed across the whole range!; **on a fait une méga-teuf** we had a massive party; **ce film, c'est le méga délire!** this film is absolutely brilliant!; **c'est méga cool!** wicked!

As far as spelling is concerned, there seems to be some hesitation as to the use of the hyphen.

It is worth noting that, in colloquial computing speak, **mégaoctet** or **mégabit** are often abbreviated to just **méga** (*meg* in English), eg:

100 mégas d'espace Web perso 100 megs of personal Web space; **accès ADSL jusqu'à 8 mégas** broadband access up to 8 megs

mégabase [megabaz] NF *Ordinat* mega, mega- 2 *Fam* (*en intensif*) very large database

mégabit [megabit] NM *Ordinat* megabit; **mégabits par seconde** megabits per second

mégacaryocyte [megakarjɔsit] NM *Biol* megakaryocyte

mégacéros [megaserɔs] NM *Zool* megaloceros, megaceros, Irish elk

mégacôlon [megakolɔ̃] NM *Méd* megacolon

mégacycle [megasikl] NM megacycle

mégaflop [megaflɔp] NM *Ordinat* megaflop

mégahertz [megaɛrts] NM megahertz

mégajoule [megaʒul] NM megajoule

mégalérythème [megaleritɛm] NM *Méd* **m. épidémique** erythema infectiosum

mégalithe [megalit] NM megalith

mégalithique [megalitik] ADJ megalithic

mégalithisme [megalitism] NM megalithism

mégalo [megalo] *Fam* ADJ megalomaniac■, power-mad; **il est complètement m.** he thinks he's God; **tu n'es pas un peu m.?** don't you think you're aiming a bit high?

NMF megalomaniac■, power maniac, control freak

mégaloblaste [megalɔblast] NM *Physiol* megaloblast

mégaloblastique [megalɔblastik] ADJ *Physiol* megaloblastic

mégalocéros [megalɔserɔs] NM *Zool* megaloceros, megaceros, Irish elk

mégalocyte [megalɔsit] NM *Physiol* megalocyte

mégalomane [megalɔman] ADJ megalomaniac

NMF megalomaniac

mégalomaniaque [megalɔmanjak] ADJ megalomaniac

mégalomanie [megalɔmani] NF megalomania

mégalopole [megalɔpɔl], **mégalopolis** [megalɔpolis] NF megalopolis

mégaloptère [megalɔptɛr] *Entom* NM megalopteran

□ **mégaloptères** NMPL Megaloptera

méga-octet [megaɔktɛ] (*pl* **méga-octets**) NM *Ordinat* megabyte

mégaphone [megafɔn] NM megaphone, *Br* loudhailer, *Am* bullhorn

mégapode [megapɔd] NM *Orn* megapode

mégapole [megapɔl] NF megalopolis

mégaptère [megaptɛr] *Zool* NM humpback (whale)

□ **mégaptères** NMPL Megaptera

med-meg

meg–mel

mégarde [megard] **par mégarde** ADV *(par inattention)* inadvertently, by accident, accidentally; *(par erreur)* by mistake, inadvertently; *(sans le vouloir)* unintentionally, inadvertently, accidentally

mégaron [megarɔn] NM *Antiq* megaron

mégathérium [megaterjɔm] NM megatherium

mégatonne [megatɔn] NF megaton

mégawatt [megawat] NM megawatt

Mégère [meʒɛr] NPR *Myth* Megaera

mégère [meʒɛr] NF shrew, harridan

═══════ 🕮 ═══════

'**La Mégère apprivoisée**' *Shakespeare* 'The Taming of the Shrew'

mégir [32] [meʒir] VT to taw

mégis [meʒi] ADJ M **cuir m.** tawed leather, white leather
◻ NM alum steep

mégisser [3] [meʒise] VT to taw

mégisserie [meʒisri] NF 1 *(commerce)* tawing 2 *(usine)* tawery; *(peaux)* (tawed) skins

mégissier [meʒisje] NM tawer

mégohm [megom] NM megohm

mégot [mego] NM *(de cigarette)* cigarette butt *or* end; *(de cigare)* cigar butt

mégotage [megotaʒ] NM *Fam* skimping, scrimping (and saving); **pas de m. sur la qualité** no skimping on the quality; **avec lui, c'était des mégotages sur tout** he was always scrimping and saving *or* always pinching and scraping

mégoter [3] [megote] VI *Fam* to skimp, to scrimp; **on ne va pas m. pour quelques euros** let's not quibble about a few euros; **arrête de m., achète du vrai Champagne!** don't be stingy, buy real champagne!; **m. sur qch** to skimp *or* to scrimp on sth; **les organisateurs ont mégoté sur tout** the organizers have skimped on everything; **il a pas mégoté sur le piment** he didn't skimp on the chilli

méharée [meare] NF mehari journey, ride on a mehari

méhari [meari] *(pl* **méharis** *ou* **méhara** [-ra]) NM racing camel *or* dromedary, mehari

méhariste [mearist] NMF dromedary rider
◻ NM = mounted soldier of the French Camel Corps in North Africa

meï, mei [mɛj] NF *Belg Fam Br* bird, *Am* chick

meilleur, -e [mɛjœr] ADJ 1 *(comparatif)* better; **elle est meilleure que lui** she is better than him *or* than he is; **il est m. en anglais qu'en allemand** he is better at English than German; **il est m. père que mari** he is a better father than he is a husband; **il est m. danseur que coureur** he is a better dancer than he is a runner, he is better at dancing than running; **je ne connais rien de m.** I don't know anything better; **il n'y a rien de m., il n'y a pas m.** there's nothing to beat it, there's nothing better; **c'est m. avec de la crème** it's better *or* it tastes better with cream; **c'est m. marché** it's cheaper; **meilleure santé!** get well soon!; *Suisse* **avoir m. temps de faire qch** to be better off doing sth; **t'as m. temps de te taire** you'd be better off keeping quiet

2 *(superlatif)* **le m. élève** *(de tous)* the best pupil; *(de deux)* the better pupil; **son m. ami** his/her best friend; **c'est le m. des maris** he's the best husband in the world; **nous sommes les meilleurs amis du monde** we're the best of friends; **avec la meilleure volonté** with the best will in the world; **dans le m. des mondes** in the best of all possible worlds; **meilleurs vœux** best wishes; **meilleurs vœux de prompt rétablissement** get well soon; **m. souvenir de Cannes** *(sur une carte postale)* greetings from Cannes; *(en fin de lettre)* best wishes from Cannes; **information prise aux meilleures sources** information from the most reliable sources; **il appartient au m. monde** he moves in the best circles

◻ NM,F **le m.** *(de tous)* the best; *(des deux)* the better; **seuls les meilleurs participeront à la compétition** only the best (players) will take part in the competition; **que le m. gagne!** may the best man win!

◻ NM **le m.** *(de tous)* the best; *(des deux)* the better; **garder le m. pour la fin** to save the best till last; **mange-le, c'est le m.** eat it, it's the best part; **il a donné** *ou* **il y a mis le m. de lui-même** he gave his all, he gave of his best; **elle lui a consacré le m. de sa vie** she gave him/her the best years of her life; **et le m. de l'histoire, c'est que c'est lui qui m'avait invité** and the best part of it is that he's the one who'd invited me; **pour le m. et pour le pire** for better or for worse; *Sport* **prendre le m. sur son adversaire** to get the better of one's opponent

◻ ADV **il fait m. aujourd'hui** the weather's *or* it's better today; **il fait m. dans la chambre** *(plus chaud)* it's warmer in the bedroom; *(plus frais)* it's cooler in the bedroom

◻ **meilleure** NF *Fam* **tu ne connais pas la meilleure** *(fin de l'histoire)* you haven't heard the best bit yet; *(histoire)* wait until I tell you this one; **ça alors, c'est la meilleure (de l'année)!** that's the best (one) I've heard in a long time!; **ça c'est la meilleure!** that just tops it all!; **j'en passe, et des meilleures** and I could go on

═══════ 📖 ═══════

'**Le Meilleur des mondes**' *Huxley* 'Brave New World'

┌─────────────┐
│ *Allusion* │
└─────────────┘

Le meilleur des mondes possibles

In Voltaire's *Candide, ou l'optimisme*, Candide has a tutor, Pangloss, who constantly quotes the German philosopher Leibnitz and his fatalistic views. Distorting the doctrine of Optimism, Pangloss greets all the miseries of human life – atrocities, injustice, disasters – with the comment **Tout est pour le mieux dans le meilleur des mondes possibles** ("All is for the best in the best of all possible worlds"). To accept this idea – that all was part of a divinely ordained master plan – seemed to Voltaire to be wilful stupidity. The modern usage is almost always ironic. If one questions the value of something that others seem to accept uncritically, one can allude to **Le meilleur des mondes possibles**.

méiose [mejoz] NF *Biol* meiosis

méiotique [mejotik] ADJ *Biol* meiotic

meistre [mɛstr] = **mestre**

meitnérium [majtnɛrjɔm] NM *Chim* meitnerium

méjuger [17] [meʒyʒe] *Littéraire* VT to misjudge
◻ **méjuger de** VT IND to underestimate, to underrate
▶ **se méjuger** VPR to underestimate oneself

Meknès [mɛknɛs] NM Meknes

Mékong [mekɔ̃g] NM **le M.** the Mekong

mél [mel], **mel** [mɛl] NM *(adresse électronique)* e-mail address; *(courrier électronique)* e-mail

melæna [melena] NM *Méd* melaena

mélamine [melamin] NF melamine

mélaminé, -e [melamine] ADJ melamine
◻ NM melamine

mélampyre [melɑ̃pir] NM *Bot* melampyrum, cow-wheat

mélancolie [melɑ̃kɔli] NF 1 *(tristesse)* melancholy; **j'y pense avec m.** I feel melancholy when I think about it; **avoir un accès de m.** to be feeling a bit melancholy; **ne pas engendrer la m.** to be great fun 2 *Psy & Arch* melancholia

mélancolique [melɑ̃kɔlik] ADJ 1 *(triste, désenchanté)* melancholy 2 *Psy* melancholic
◻ NMF melancholic

mélancoliquement [melɑ̃kɔlikmɑ̃] ADV melancholically

Mélanésie [melanezi] NF **la M.** Melanesia

mélanésien, -enne [melanezjɛ̃, -ɛn] ADJ Melanesian
◻ NM *(langue)* Melanesian
◻ **Mélanésien, -enne** NM,F Melanesian

mélange [melɑ̃ʒ] NM 1 *(processus)* mixing; *(de thés, de parfums, de tabacs)* blending

2 *(résultat)* mixture; *(de thés, de parfums, de tabacs)* blend; **battre les œufs et le sucre jusqu'à ce que le m. blanchisse** beat the eggs and the sugar till the mixture turns pale; **c'est un m. de plusieurs thés/parfums** it's a blend of several teas/perfumes; **ma famille et mes collègues, ça donne un curieux m.!** my family and my colleagues, that makes for a strange mixture!; **un m. de fermeté et de gentillesse** a mixture of strictness and kindness; **attention aux mélanges (d'alcools)** don't mix your drinks; **pas de whisky après le vin, je ne fais pas de mélanges** no whisky after my wine, I don't mix my drinks; **du café et du jaune d'œuf, quel horrible m.!** coffee and egg yolk, what a disgusting mixture!

3 *Aut* mixture; **m. détonant/pauvre/riche** explosive/poor/rich mixture; **m. air/carburant** air/fuel mixture; **m. carburé** explosive mixture; **m. gazeux** gas mixture

4 *(en acoustique)* mixing

5 *Chim* **m. racémique** racemate

◻ **mélanges** NMPL *Littérature (gén)* miscellany; *(en hommage)* festschrift

◻ **sans mélange** ADJ *(joie)* unalloyed; *(admiration)* unmitigated

mélangé, -e [melɑ̃ʒe] ADJ *(auditoire, population)* mixed; *(coton, laine)* mixed; **c'est un coton m.** it's a cotton mixture

mélanger [17] [melɑ̃ʒe] VT 1 *(remuer → cartes)* to shuffle; *(→ salade)* to toss; **ajoutez le lait et mélangez** add the milk and mix (well); **m. le citron à la crème** to mix the lemon (in) with the cream

2 *(mettre ensemble)* to mix; *(thés, vins, tabacs)* to blend; *(idées, documents)* to mix up; **m. des couleurs** to blend colours; **ils ne veulent pas m. les filles et les garçons** they want to keep boys and girls separate; **mélangez les œillets rouges avec les blancs** mix the red carnations with the white ones

3 *(confondre)* to mix up; **ne mélange pas tout** don't get everything (all) mixed *or* jumbled *or* muddled up; **on a un peu trop mélangé les genres** it's a mixture of too many different styles; *Fig Hum* **il ne faut pas m. les torchons et les serviettes** (don't get them mixed up,) they're in a different class

▶ **se mélanger** VPR 1 *(se fondre)* **se m. avec** to mix with; **l'eau et l'huile ne se mélangent pas bien** water and oil don't mix well; **les nouveaux venus ne se mélangent pas avec les habitués du club** the newcomers don't mix *or* socialize with the regular club members

2 *(devenir indistinct)* to get mixed up; **mes souvenirs se mélangent après tant d'années** my memories are getting confused *or* muddled after so many years; **tout se mélange dans ma tête** I'm getting all mixed *or* muddled up

3 *Fam* **se m. les pédales** *ou* **les pinceaux (dans qch)** to get (oneself) into a muddle (with sth), to get (sth) muddled up

4 *Fam Hum (avoir des rapports sexuels)* to exchange bodily fluids

mélangeur [melɑ̃ʒœr] NM 1 *(robinet) Br* mixer tap, *Am* mixing faucet 2 *(de son)* mixer 3 *TV & Cin* **m. d'images** vision mixer; **m. numérique** digital mixer; **m. de postproduction** postproduction mixer; **m. (de production)** production mixer *or* switcher; **m. de signaux** mixer; **m. de son** dubbing *or* sound mixer; **m. vidéo** vision mixer 4 *Métal* mixer

mélanine [melanin] NF *Physiol* melanin

mélanique [melanik] ADJ *Chim* melanic

mélanisme [melanism] NM *Méd* melanism

mélanocyte [melanɔsit] NM *Biol* melanocyte

mélanoderme [melanɔdɛrm] ADJ *Méd* melanodermic

mélanodermie [melanɔdɛrmi] NF *Méd* melanoderma

mélanome [melanom] NM *Méd* melanoma

mélanose [melanoz] NF *Méd* melanosis, black degeneration

mêlant, -e [mɛlɑ̃, -ɑ̃t] ADJ *Can* **c'est pas m.** there's no doubt about it

mélasse [melas] NF 1 *(sirop)* molasses *(singulier)*, *Br* treacle 2 *Fam (brouillard)* pea-souper; *Fig* **être dans la m.** *(avoir des ennuis)* to be in a jam *or* a fix *or* a pickle; *(être sans argent)* to be hard up

mélatonine [melatɔnin] NF *Physiol* melatonin

Melba [mɛlba] ADJ INV **pêche/poire M.** peach/pear Melba

Melbourne [mɛlburn] NM Melbourne

Melchior [mɛlkjɔr] NPR Melchior

melchite [mɛlkit] *Rel* ADJ Melchite
◻ NMF Melchite

meldois, -e [mɛldwa, -az] ADJ of/from Meaux
◻ **Meldois, -e** NM,F = person from *or* inhabitant of Meaux

mêlé, -e [mele] ADJ **1** *(mélangée)* mixed (**de** with); **du vin m. d'eau** wine mixed with water; **une société mêlée** a mixed society; **des sentiments (très) mêlés** (very) mixed feelings; **un chagrin m. de pitié** sorrow mixed or mingled with pity

2 *(emmêlé)* **dans cette histoire, la politique et le crime sont très mêlés** politics and crime are closely linked in this business; **tout est m. dans son suicide: la drogue, sa célébrité déclinante...** everything played a part in his/her suicide: drugs, his/her declining fame...

3 *Can (désorienté)* disoriented; *(embrouillé)* mixed-up; **être m. dans ses papiers** to be confused or mixed-up

❑ **mêlée** NF **1** *(combat)* fray, melee; *Fig* **être au-dessus de la mêlée** to be above the fray; *Fig* **rester au-dessus de la mêlée** to stay above the fray, to remain aloof; *Fig* **entrer dans la mêlée** to join or enter the fray; **elle reste à l'écart de la mêlée politique** she keeps out of the hurly-burly of politics

2 *(bousculade)* scuffle, free-for-all; *(désordre)* commotion, confusion; **j'ai perdu mon parapluie dans la mêlée** I lost my umbrella in the general confusion; **il y a eu une mêlée générale** there was a general free-for-all

3 *(au rugby)* scrum, scrummage; **effondrer/tourner la mêlée** to collapse/to wheel the scrum; **mêlée ouverte** *(gén)* loose scrum; *(balle par terre)* ruck; *(balle en main)* maul

méléagrine [meleagrin] NF *Zool* pearl oyster

mêlé-cass, mêlé-casse [melekas] NM INV *très Fam (boisson)* = brandy with crème de cassis **2 voix de m.** hoarse voice■

mêlé-cassis [melekasis] NM INV brandy with crème de cassis

méléna [melena] = **melæna**

mêler [4] [mele] VT **1** *(mélanger)* to mix (**à** or **avec** with); **m. deux races de chien** to cross two breeds of dog; **je n'aime pas m. les styles de mobilier** I don't like mixing different styles of furniture; **nous mêlions nos souvenirs** we'd share our memories; **des fleurs variées mêlaient leurs parfums** the scents of various flowers were mingling in the air

2 *(allier → sujet: personne)* to combine; *(sujet: chose)* to be a mixture or combination of; **elle mêle la rigueur à la fantaisie** she combines or mixes seriousness with light-heartedness; **son sourire mêlait la fausseté et la veulerie** his/her smile was a mixture of falseness and cowardly indecision

3 *(embrouiller → documents, papiers)* to mix or to muddle or to jumble up; *(→ cartes, dominos)* to shuffle; **j'ai mêlé tous les dossiers** I've got all the files mixed up

4 *(impliquer)* **m. qn à** to involve sb in, to get sb involved in; **m. qn à la conversation** to bring sb into the conversation; **ne me mêle pas à tes mensonges** don't involve me in your lies; **être mêlé à un scandale** to be involved in or linked with a scandal

▶ **se mêler** VPR **1** *(se mélanger)* to mix, to mingle; *(sons, parfums)* to blend; **les styles se mêlent harmonieusement** the styles blend well together

2 se m. à ou **avec** *(s'unir)* to mix or to mingle with; **ses cris se mêlèrent au bruit de la foule** his/her shouts mingled with the noise of the crowd; **se m. à la foule** to mingle with or blend into the crowd

3 se m. à *(participer à)* to take part in, to join in; **se m. à la conversation** to take part or to join in the conversation; **se m. à un cortège/une manifestation** to take part in a procession/a demonstration

4 se m. de *(de manière inopportune)* to interfere or to meddle in, to get mixed up in; **se m. des affaires d'autrui** to meddle or to interfere in other people's business; **elle se mêle de ce qui ne la regarde pas** she is interfering in things that are no concern of hers; **mêlez-vous de ce qui vous regarde** mind your own business; **de quoi se mêle-t-il?** what business is it of his?; *Fam* **de quoi je me mêle?** mind your own business!; **si le mauvais temps s'en mêle, la récolte est perdue** if the weather decides to turn nasty, the crop will be ruined; **il se mêle de tout** he is very nosy; *Péj* **il se mêle de poésie maintenant!** so he's started dabbling in poetry now, has he?;

elle se mêle de me dire ce que j'ai à faire she seems to think she can tell me what I should do

mêle-tout [mɛltu] NMF INV *Belg Fam* busybody, *Br* nosey parker

mélèze [melɛz] NM larch

melia [melja] NM *Bot* margosa

méliacée [meljase] *Bot* NF member of the Meliaceae family

❑ **méliacées** NFPL Meliaceae

mélilot [melilo] NM *Bot* melilot; **m. blanc** white melilot; **m. élevé** tall melilot; **m. d'Inde** small melilot; **m. officinal** ribbed melilot

méli-mélo [melimelo] *(pl* **mélis-mélos***)* NM *(d'objets)* mess, jumble; *(d'idées, de dates)* mishmash, *Br* hotchpotch, *Am* hodgepodge; **ils ont fait un m. incroyable avec les réservations** they made a real mess of the reservations; **quel m.!** what a mess!

mélinite [melinit] NF melinite

mélioratif, -ive [meljɔratif, -iv] ADJ meliorative NM meliorative

méliphagidé [melifaʒide] NM *Orn* honeyeater

mélique [melik] ADJ *Littérature* melic

mélisse [melis] NF *Bot* (lemon) balm

mélitococcie [melitɔkɔksi] NF *Méd* Malta fever, undulant fever

mélitte [melit] NF *Bot* melittis

melkite [mɛlkit] *Rel* ADJ Melchite NMF Melchite

mellah [mela] NM *Hist (dans les villes marocaines)* Jewish area

mellifère [mɛlifɛr] ADJ **1** *(plante)* melliferous, honey-yielding **2** *(insecte)* mellific, honey-making

mellification [mɛlifikasjɔ̃] NF mellification, honey-making

mellifique [mɛlifik] ADJ mellific, honey-making

mellifluu, -e [mɛlifly] ADJ *Littéraire* mellifluous, honeyed

mellite [mɛlit] NM *Pharm* honey preparation

mélo [melo] *Fam* ADJ *(qui tient du mélodrame)* melodramatic■, over-the-top, *Br* OTT; *(qui donne dans la sensiblerie)* sentimental■, mushy, *Am* schmaltzy NM melodrama■; **nous sommes en plein m.!** this is melodramatic or blood-and-thunder stuff!

mélodie [melodi] NF **1** *(air de musique)* melody, tune; *(en composition)* melody, song **2** *Fig (d'une langue)* melodiousness; **la m. des vers de Lamartine** the melodic quality of Lamartine's verse

'**La Mélodie du bonheur**' *Wise* 'The Sound of Music'

mélodieuse [melodjøz] *voir* **mélodieux**

mélodieusement [melodjøzmɑ̃] ADV melodiously, tunefully

mélodieux, -euse [melodjø, -øz] ADJ *(son)* melodious; *(air)* tuneful; *(voix)* melodious, musical; **une musique mélodieuse** a tuneful (piece of) music; **de sa voix mélodieuse** in his/her melodious or musical voice

mélodique [melodik] ADJ melodic

mélodiste [melodist] NMF melodist

mélodramatique [melodramatik] ADJ melodramatic

mélodrame [melodram] NM melodrama; **nous sommes en plein m.!** this is like (something out of) a melodrama!

méloé [meloe] NM *Entom* meloe, meloid (beetle)

mélomane [meloman] ADJ music-loving; **êtes-vous m.?** do you like music?, are you musical? NMF music lover

mélomanie [melomani] NF love of music, *Spéc* melomania

melon [məlɔ̃] NM **1** *Bot* melon; **m. d'eau** watermelon; **m. d'Espagne** honeydew melon **2** *(chapeau) Br* bowler (hat), *Am* derby **3** *Fam (Maghrébin)* = offensive term used to refer to a North African Arab

mélongène [melɔ̃ʒɛn], **mélongine** [melɔ̃ʒin] NF *Vieilli Br* aubergine, *Am* eggplant

melonnière [məlɔnjɛr] NF *Hort* melon bed or patch

mélopée [melope] NF **1** *(mélodie)* lament, threnody **2** *Antiq* melopoeia

mélophage [melofaʒ] NM sheep ked or tick

méloplastie [meloplasti] NF *Méd* meloplasty

Melpomène [mɛlpomɛn] NPR *Myth* Melpomene

melting-pot [mɛltiŋpɔt] *(pl* **melting-pots***)* NM melting pot

MEM [mɛm] NF *Ordinat (abrév* **mémoire morte***)* ROM

membranaire [mɑ̃branɛr] ADJ membranaceous, membranous

membrane [mɑ̃bran] NF **1** *Biol* membrane; *Méd* **fausse m.** false membrane; **m. cellulaire** cell or plasma membrane **2** *Mus* membrane, skin **3** *Tél* diaphragm **4** *(en travaux publics)* **m. d'étanchéité** sealing membrane or blanket

membraneux, -euse [mɑ̃branø, -øz] ADJ membranous

membre [mɑ̃br] NM **1** *Anat* limb; **m. inférieur/supérieur** lower/upper limb; **m. (viril)** (male) member; *Méd* **m. fantôme** phantom limb **2** *Zool* limb; **m. antérieur** foreleg, fore limb; **m. postérieur** back leg, rear limb

3 *(adhérent)* member; **m. d'un comité** committee member; **m. du conseil d'administration** member of the board, board member; **être m. d'un syndicat** to belong to or to be a member of a union; **devenir m. d'une association** to join an association; **envoyer une lettre à tous les membres** to send a letter to (all) the members or to the entire membership; **elle a été élue m. de l'Académie** she was elected to the Academy; **ils le considèrent comme un m. de la famille** they treat him as one of the family; **tous les membres de la famille** the whole family; *Can* **M. de l'Assemblée Nationale** Member of the National Assembly; **les États membres** the member states; **les pays membres** the member countries; **m. bienfaiteur** supporter; *Bourse* **m. de compensation** clearing member; **m. fondateur** founder, founding member; **m. honoraire** honorary member; **m. du Parlement** member of Parliament; **m. du Parlement européen** Member of the European Parliament, MEP, Euro-MP; **m. du parti** party member; **m. permanent** permanent member; **m. perpétuel** life member; **m. suppléant** deputy member

4 *Math* member; **premier/second m. d'une équation** left-hand/right-hand member of an equation

5 *Gram* **m. de phrase** member or clause of a sentence

6 *Archit & Géol* member

7 *Naut* timber, rib

membré, -e [mɑ̃bre] ADJ *Littéraire* **bien m.** strong-limbed; **mal m.** weak-limbed; *Fam Hum* **être bien/mal m.** *(homme)* to be/not to be well-hung

membron [mɑ̃brɔ̃] NM *Constr* hip moulding

membru, -e [mɑ̃bry] ADJ *Littéraire* big-limbed, big-boned

membrure [mɑ̃bryr] NF **1** *(d'un corps humain)* limbs; **homme à forte m.** strong-limbed or powerfully built man **2** *Constr* member; *Menuis* frame **3** *Naut (en bois)* rib; *(en métal)* frame

MÊME [mɛm]

ADJ	same **1, 2** ■ very **3** ■ myself/yourself/etc **4**
PRON INDÉFINI same
ADV even

ADJ INDÉFINI 1 *(avant le nom) (identique, semblable)* same; **elles sont nées le m. jour** they were born on the same day; **ils fréquentent le m. club** they go to the same club; **nous avons été confrontés à des problèmes de m. nature** we came up against the same kind of problem; **mettre deux choses sur le m. plan** to put two things on the same level; **tous rassemblés en un m. lieu** all gathered in the same place; **en m. temps** at the same time

2 *(en corrélation avec "que")* **il a le m. âge que moi** he's the same age as me; **j'utilise le m. parfum que toi** I use the same perfume as you (do); **j'ai la m. voiture qu'elle** I have the same car as her or as she does

3 *(après le nom) (servant à souligner)* **elle est la bonté m.** she is kindness itself; **ce sont ses paroles mêmes** those are his/her very words; **ils sont repartis le soir m.** they left that very evening; **je l'ai fait le jour m.** I did it that (very)

same day; **aujourd'hui m.** this very day; **il habite ici m.** he lives in this very place/house; **la dernière version, celle-là m. qui est arrivée hier** the latest version, the one which arrived yesterday; **c'est le titre m. que vous avez à traduire** it's the title itself *or* the actual title that you have to translate; **c'est cela m. que je cherchais** it's the very thing I was looking for; **c'est cela m.** *(c'est exact)* that's it exactly

4 moi-m. myself; **toi-m.** yourself; **lui-m.** himself/itself; **elle-m.** herself/itself; **soi-m.** oneself; **nous-mêmes** ourselves; **vous-mêmes** yourselves; **eux-/elles-mêmes** themselves; **moi-m., quand j'y pense, j'en ai des frissons** I get shivers myself when I think about it; **par toi-m.** by yourself; **j'ai dû y aller car elle-m. ne peut plus se déplacer** I had to go because she can't get about herself any more; **il l'a fait lui-m.** he did it himself; **faire qch de soi-m.** to do sth of one's own accord; **c'est lui-m. qui me l'a dit, il me l'a dit lui-m.** he told me himself; **je l'ai trouvée pareille à elle-m.** I found she hadn't changed, I found her the same as ever; **rester/être égal à soi-m.** to remain/be true to form; **égale à elle-m., elle est restée très calme** typically *or* true to form, she remained calm; **la chose n'est pas mauvaise en elle-m.** the thing is not bad in itself *or* per se; **je pensais en moi-m. que...** I was thinking to myself that...; **menteur! – toi-m.!** liar! – liar yourself!

PRON INDÉFINI le m. the same; **elle est toujours la m.** she's still the same; **ce sont toujours les mêmes qui gagnent** it's always the same ones who win; **depuis quelque temps, leurs rapports ne sont plus les mêmes** for some time their relationship has not been the same; **mes intérêts ne sont pas les mêmes que les vôtres** my interests are not the same as yours; *Hum* **on prend les mêmes et on recommence** it's the same mixture as before; *Hum* **les mêmes, trois heures plus tard** same scene, three hours later; **cela** *ou* **ça revient (strictement) au m.** it comes to *or* amounts to (exactly) the same thing

ADV even; **m. les savants** *ou* **les savants m. peuvent se tromper** even scientists can make mistakes; **m. Paul est d'accord** even Paul agrees; **j'ai écrit, j'ai téléphoné, et j'ai m. envoyé un télégramme** I wrote, I phoned and I even sent a telegram; **je le pense et m. j'en suis sûr** I think so, in fact I'm sure of it; **elle ne va m. plus au cinéma** she doesn't even go to the cinema any more; **je n'ai pas m.** *ou* **je n'ai m. pas le prix de mon voyage** I haven't even enough to pay my fare; **je ne sais m. pas l'heure qu'il est** I don't even know what time it is; **t'a-t-elle remercié? – m. pas!** did she thank you? – not even (that)!; **il y va m. quand il pleut** he goes (there) even when it rains; **il a toujours rêvé de faire ce métier, m. lorsqu'il était enfant** he always dreamed of doing this job, even when he was a child

❑ **à même PRÉP dormir à m. le sol** to sleep on the floor; **être couché à m. le sable** to be lying on the bare sand; **boire à m. la bouteille** to drink straight from the bottle; **je ne supporte pas la laine à m. la peau** I can't stand wool next to my skin; **des marches taillées à m. le roc** steps hewn out of the rock

❑ **à même de PRÉP** able to, in a position to; **être à m. de faire qch** to be able *or* in a position to do sth; **elle est à m. de vous aider** she can help you; **il n'est pas à m. de faire le voyage** he's not up to making the journey; **nous ne sommes pas à m. de satisfaire votre commande** we are not able to meet your order; **je serai bientôt à m. de vous en dire plus** I shall soon be able to tell you more

❑ **de même ADV 1** *(pareillement)* **faire de m.** to do likewise *or* the same, to follow suit; **la France a privatisé ses banques et la Grande-Bretagne a fait de m.** France has privatized its banks and Great Britain has followed suit; **il est parti avant la fin, moi de m.** he left before the end, and so did I; **je vous souhaite le bonsoir – moi de m.** I wish you goodnight – likewise; **Joyeux Noël – vous de m.** Merry Christmas – same to you; **il en est de m. des autres** it's the same for the others, the same is true *or* holds good for the others; **il en va de m. pour vous** the same is true for you

2 *Can (comme cela)* like this, (in) this way; **place tes mains de m. et pousse** place your hands like this and push; **quel dommage, cet accident, une belle fille de m.!** what a tragic accident, a lovely girl like that!; **qui croirait une histoire de m.?** who could believe such a story *or* a story like that?

❑ **de même que CONJ** just as; **de m. que qn** just like sb; **de m. que qch** just like sth; *(aussi bien que)* as well as sth; **il a refusé de travailler pour eux, de m. qu'il avait refusé de le faire pour moi** he refused to work for them, just as *or* just like he had refused to for me; **je déteste la Bretagne de m. que la Normandie** I hate Brittany just as much as Normandy

❑ **même que CONJ** *Fam* so much so that▪; **elle roulait très vite, m. que la voiture a failli déraper** she was driving so fast that the car nearly skidded; **il va venir, m. qu'il me l'a promis!** he'll come, what's more he promised me he would!; **m. que je te l'avais déjà dit!** but I already TOLD you!

❑ **même si CONJ** even if; **m. si je le savais** even if I knew; **m. s'il me le demandait, je n'accepterais pas** even if he asked me, I wouldn't accept; **m. si je (le) voulais, je ne pourrais pas** even if I wanted to, I couldn't; **m. s'il pleut** even if it rains; **ne dis rien, m. si l'occasion se présente** don't say anything, even if the opportunity arises

mémé [meme] *Fam* **NF 1** *(en appellatif) (grand-mère)* grandma, granny, *Br* gran **2** *(vieille dame)* old dear; **une petite m.** an old dear **3** *Péj* old woman▪

ADJ INV *Péj* dowdy, frumpy, grannyish; **elle fait très m. avec cette coiffure** that hairstyle makes her look so dowdy; **elle fait m., ta robe!** that dress makes you look like an old granny!, you look like an old frump in that dress!

mêmement [mɛmmɑ̃] **ADV** *Vieilli* equally, likewise

mémento [memɛ̃to] **NM 1** *(agenda)* diary **2** *Scol* revision notes; **m. d'histoire** history revision notes **3** *Rel* memento

mémèrage [memɛraʒ] **NM** *Can Fam* gossip▪

mémère [memɛr] *Fam* **NF 1** *(en appellatif) (grand-mère)* grandma, granny, *Br* gran

2 *Péj (femme d'un certain âge)* old biddy, *Br* old dear; **une grosse m.** a fat old bag; *Hum* **le petit chien-chien à sa m.** mummy's little doggie-woggie

ADJ *Péj (style, vêtements)* dowdy, frumpy, grannyish; **faire m.** *(style, femme, vêtements)* to look dowdy *or* frumpy; **ça fait m. chez elle** her house is like an old granny's house; **tu fais m. avec cette robe!** that dress makes you look dowdy *or* frumpy; **il fait m., ton chemisier** that blouse makes you look dowdy *or* frumpy; **qu'est-ce qu'elle est m., cette fille!** she looks so dowdy, that girl!; **si seulement elle portait des robes un peu moins mémères** if only she wore slightly less dowdy dresses

mémérer [18] [memere] **VI** *Can Fam* to gossip▪

mémo [memo] **NM 1** *(carnet)* memo pad, note book, notepad **2** *(note de service)* memo

mémoire[1] [memwar] **NF 1** *(faculté)* memory; **avoir (une) mauvaise m.** to have a poor *or* bad memory; **avoir (une) bonne m.** to have a good memory; **si j'ai bonne m.** if I remember correctly; **si ma m. ne me trompe pas** if my memory serves me right, if I remember correctly; **avoir la m. des noms/dates** to have a good memory for names/dates; *Fam* **avoir une m. d'éléphant** to have a memory like an elephant; **perdre la m.** to lose one's memory; **il n'a plus de m.** he's lost his memory; **il n'a pas de m.** he's got a bad memory; **je n'ai aucune m.!** I can never remember anything!; **tu as la m. courte!** you've got a short memory!; **fais un effort de m.** try hard to remember, search (your memory) hard; **rappeler qch à la m. de qn, remettre qch en m. à qn** to remind sb of sth; **se remettre qch en m.** to recall sth; **je n'ai plus son nom en m.** his/her name has slipped my memory, his/her name escapes me; **une vieille expression me revint** *ou* **remonta à la m.** an old saying came (back) to me; **son nom est resté dans toutes les mémoires** his/her name is remembered by everyone; **ce détail est resté à jamais** *ou* **s'est gravé dans ma m.** this detail has stayed with me ever since *or* has forever remained engraved in my memory; **réciter qch de m.** to recite sth from memory; **la m. collective** collective memory

2 *(souvenir)* memory; **honorer la m. de qn** to honour the memory of sb; **fidèle à la m. de sa femme** faithful to his wife's memory; **faire un travail de m.** = to come to terms with atrocities committed by one's country in the past and accept one's share of collective responsibility; **nous avons un devoir de m. envers les victimes de l'Holocauste** we must remember the victims of the Holocaust and make sure such atrocities never happen again; **en ces temps de triste m.** in those days of bitter memory; **de sinistre m.** *(personne, événement, lieu)* notorious, infamous; *(date, jour)* dark, tragic; **un règne de joyeuse m.** a fondly-remembered reign

3 *Ordinat* memory, storage; **m. de 40 mégaoctets** 40-megabyte memory; **une m. de 15 caractères** a 15-character memory; **m. centrale** *ou* **principale** main memory *or* storage; **mettre un dossier en m.** to write a file to memory; **m. à accès direct** direct access storage; **m. auxiliaire** auxiliary *or* secondary storage; **m. bloc-notes** scratchpad memory; **m. à bulles** bubble memory; **m. cache** cache memory; **mettre en m. cache** to cache; **m. conventionnelle** conventional memory; **m. disponible** available memory; **m. à disque** disk memory, RAM disk; **m. écran** screen memory; **m. étendue** extended memory; **m. expansée** expanded memory; **m. externe** external memory; **m. haute** high memory; **avoir chargé en m. haute** to have memory loaded high; **m. d'images** picture memory; **m. intermédiaire** buffer memory; **m. de masse** mass storage; **m. morte** read-only memory; **m. morte masquée** masked ROM; **m. non effaçable** non-erasable memory; **m. paginée** expanded memory; **m. permanente** permanent memory; **m. RAM dynamique** dynamic RAM; **m. de stockage** mass memory; **m. tampon** buffer (storage); **m. tampon de données** data buffer; **m. tampon d'imprimante** *ou* **pour imprimante** printer buffer; **m. tampon de sortie** output buffer; **m. tampon de texte** text buffer; **m. vidéo** video memory; **m. virtuelle** virtual memory; **m. vive** random access memory; **m. vive dynamique** DRAM, dynamic random access memory; **m. vive statique** SRAM, static RAM, static random access memory; **m. volatile** volatile memory

❑ **à la mémoire de PRÉP** in memory of, to the memory of; **à la m. du comique disparu** in memory of the late comedian; **faire qch à la m. de qn** to do sth in memory of sb

❑ **de mémoire ADV** from memory

❑ **de mémoire de PRÉP de m. de sportif** in all my/his/*etc* years as a sportsman; **de m. d'homme** in living memory; **de m. de pêcheur, je n'avais jamais vu de si gros poisson** in all my years as an angler, I've never seen such a big fish

❑ **en mémoire de = à la mémoire de**

❑ **pour mémoire ADV** *Com & Fig* for the record; **je signale, pour m., que...** I might mention, for the record, that...; **je vous signale pour m. que...** I would remind you that...

mémoire[2] [memwar] **NM 1** *(rapport)* report, paper **2** *Univ* thesis, dissertation; **m. de maîtrise** ≃ MA thesis *or* dissertation **3** *Jur* statement of case **4** *Com & Fin* bill, statement (of account)

❑ **Mémoires NMPL** memoirs; **écrire ses Mémoires** to write one's memoirs

'Mémoires d'outre-tombe' *Chateaubriand*
'Memoirs from Beyond the Tomb'

'Mémoires d'une jeune fille rangée' *de Beauvoir*
'Memoirs of a Dutiful Daughter'

mémomarque [memɔmark] **NF** *Mktg* brand name recall

mémorable [memɔrabl] **ADJ** memorable; **ce fut une soirée m.** it was a memorable evening

mémorandum [memɔrɑ̃dɔm] NM **1** *(note)* memorandum; *Naut* **m. de combat** battle orders **2** *(carnet)* notebook

mémorial, -aux [memɔrjal, -o] NM **1** *(texte)* memoir; *Pol* memorial **2** *(monument)* memorial ❏ **Mémorial** NM *(Mémoires)* memoirs

mémorialiste [memɔrjalist] NMF memorialist

mémoriel, -elle [memɔrjɛl] ADJ *Ordinat & Psy* memory *(avant n)*

mémorisable [memɔrizabl] ADJ *Ordinat* storable

mémorisation [memɔrizasjɔ̃] NF **1** *(processus)* memorization; *Mktg* recall; *Mktg* **m. un jour après** day-after recall; *Mktg* **m. de la marque** brand name recall **2** *Ordinat* storage, writing to memory

mémoriser [3] [memɔrize] VT **1** *(apprendre par cœur)* to memorize; **il a mémorisé les conjugaisons** he has learnt the verb tables by heart **2** *Ordinat* to store, to write to memory

Memphis [mɛmfis] NM Memphis

menaçant, -e [mənasɑ̃, -ɑ̃t] ADJ **1** *(comminatoire → personne, geste, ton)* menacing, threatening; **une foule menaçante** a threatening crowd; **de façon menaçante** threateningly; **d'un ton m.** menacingly **2** *(inquiétant → signe, silence, nuage)* menacing, threatening, ominous; *(ciel)* threatening; **il y a quelque chose de très m. dans son regard** there's a threatening look in his eyes; **le temps est m.** the weather's looking ominous

menace [mənas] NF **1** *(source de danger)* threat; **une m. pour l'ordre public** a danger or threat to law and order; **m. de tempête/d'épidémie** threat of a storm/an epidemic **2** *(acte, parole)* threat; *Jur* **menaces** intimidation; **comment, des menaces maintenant!** so it's threats now, is it?; **des menaces en l'air** idle threats; **mettre ses menaces à exécution** to carry out one's threats; **des menaces de mort** death threats; **la victime avait reçu des menaces de mort** the victim had been threatened with death or had received death threats; **ils ont même essayé la m.** they even tried threats; **sous la m.** under duress; **il a signé sous la m.** he signed under duress; **sous la m. de** under (the) threat of; **sous la m. de la torture** under (the) threat of torture; **sous la m. d'une arme** at gunpoint; **sous la m. de sanctions** under threat of sanctions; **un geste de m.** a threatening or menacing gesture; **ton lourd ou plein de m.** tone heavy or fraught with menace; *Littéraire* **un ciel lourd de m.** a sky heavy with foreboding

menacé, -e [mənase] ADJ threatened, under threat, endangered; **le groupe le plus m.** the group under the heaviest threat; **ses jours sont menacés** his/her life is in danger; **espèce menacée** endangered species

menacer [16] [mənase] VT **1** *(mettre en danger)* to threaten, to menace; **un danger mortel le menace** he's in mortal danger; **rien ne la menace** she's in no danger; **l'apoplexie le menace** he's in danger of having a stroke; **une nouvelle crise nous menace** a new crisis is threatening us or looming; **les fluctuations du dollar menacent notre système monétaire** fluctuations in the dollar are a threat to our monetary system; **se faire m.** to be threatened **2** *(pour impressionner, contraindre)* to threaten (**de** with); **m. qn du doigt/poing** to shake one's finger/fist at sb; **m. qn d'un procès** to threaten sb with legal proceedings; **m. qn de mort** to threaten to kill sb; **il est menacé de mort** he's being threatened with death **3** *(location)* **le pont menace ruine** the bridge is in (imminent) danger of collapsing

VI *(crise)* to threaten; *(tempête, orage, révolution)* to be brewing; **l'orage menace** there's a storm brewing; **la pluie menace** it's threatening to rain, it looks like rain

❏ **menacer de** VT IND **m. de faire qch** to threaten to do sth; **elle menace d'annuler le concert si ses exigences ne sont pas satisfaites** she's threatening to cancel the concert if her demands aren't met; **le procès menace d'être long** the trial threatens to be lengthy; **le conflit menace de s'étendre** there is a (real) danger of the conflict spreading; **le mur menace de s'écrouler** the wall is in danger of collapsing; **cette étagère menace de tomber** that shelf

looks like it will fall; **l'orage menace d'éclater avant la fin de la soirée** the storm looks like it will break before the end of the evening

ménade [menad] NF *Myth* maenad, bacchante

ménage [menaʒ] NM **1** *(couple)* couple; *(en sociologie)* household; **être heureux en m.** to be happily married; **leur m. marche mal** their marriage isn't going very well; **faire bon/mauvais m. avec qn** to get on well/badly with sb; **ils se sont mis en m.** they've moved in together; **ils sont en m.** they live together; **monter son m.** to set up house; **un m. sans enfants** a childless couple; **m. à trois** ménage à trois; *Jur* **m. de fait** cohabitation, cohabiting

2 *(économie domestique)* housekeeping; **les soucis du m.** domestic worries; **avoir la charge des soins du m.** to be in charge of the housekeeping; **tenir le m. (de qn)** to keep house (for sb)

3 *(nettoyage)* housework, cleaning; **faire le m.** to do the housework, *Am* to clean house; **faire le m. en grand** ou **à fond** to clean the house from top to bottom; **faire le m. dans une armoire** to clean out a wardrobe; **faire le m. dans un bureau** to tidy an office; **le m. est mal fait** the housework or cleaning hasn't been done properly; **demain, je fais du/mon m.** tomorrow I'm going to do some/my housework; *Fig* **le directeur a fait le (grand) m. dans son service** the manager has shaken up or spring-cleaned his department; **faire des ménages** to clean for people, to go out cleaning

4 *(meubles)* *Vieilli* **monter son m.** to furnish one's house; *Vieilli* **m. de poupée** set of doll's furniture; *Can* **avoir du beau m.** to have nice furniture

❏ **de ménage** ADJ *Vieilli* **1** *(fabriqué à la maison)* homemade; **pain de m.** homemade bread; **chocolat de m.** cooking chocolate

2 *(pour l'entretien)* household *(avant n)*, cleaning *(avant n)*; **savon de m.** household soap

ménagé, -e [menaʒe] ADJ *Chim* **oxydation ménagée** controlled oxydation

ménagement [menaʒmɑ̃] NM care, caution, circumspection; *(tact)* thoughtfulness, consideration, *Sout* solicitude

❏ **avec ménagement** ADV carefully, cautiously; *(avec tact)* tactfully, gently; **traite ma voiture avec m.** treat my car with care, take (good) care of my car; **traiter qn avec le plus grand m.** to treat sb with great consideration

❏ **sans ménagement** ADV *(annoncer)* bluntly; *(éconduire, traiter)* unceremoniously

ménager¹ [17] [menaʒe] VT **1** *(économiser)* to be sparing with; **m. son argent** to be sparing with one's money; **le pays doit m. ses maigres ressources** the country has to husband its meagre resources; **sans m. ses efforts** ou **sa peine** tirelessly; **elle ne ménage pas ses efforts** ou **sa peine** she spares no effort; **m. ses forces** to conserve one's strength; **sans m. ses paroles** without mincing one's words; **la critique n'a pas ménagé ses louanges à l'artiste** the critics lavished praise on the artist

2 *(traiter avec soin)* to treat or to handle carefully; *(personne)* to treat tactfully or with consideration; **m. sa santé** to take care of one's health; **je prends l'ascenseur pour m. mes vieilles jambes** I take the *Br* lift or *Am* elevator to spare my old legs; **ménage ton foie, ne bois pas d'alcool** take care of or look after your liver, don't drink alcohol; **ménagez-le, il a le cœur malade** treat him gently, he has a weak heart; **m. son cheval** not to tire one's horse

3 *(respecter)* to spare; **ménage sa susceptibilité** humour him/her; **ménage sa fierté** spare his/her pride; **ménage mes sentiments** spare my feelings; *Fig* **m. la chèvre et le chou** to sit on the fence, to run with the hare and hunt with the hounds

4 *(arranger → passage, escalier)* to put in; *(→ entretien, rencontre)* to organize, to arrange; **m. une sortie** to provide an exit; **j'ai ménagé un espace pour planter des légumes** I've left some space for growing vegetables; **nous avons ménagé une ouverture pour accéder directement au garage** we knocked a door through to the garage; **pourriez-vous me m. une entrevue avec le directeur?** could you set up or arrange

a meeting for me with the manager?; **m. une surprise à qn** to prepare a surprise for sb

▶**se ménager** VPR **1** *(prendre soin de soi)* to save oneself; **elle ne se ménage pas assez** she drives herself too hard; **ménage-toi** take it easy, don't overdo it; **elle se ménage pour le troisième set** she's saving herself or conserving her energy for the third set

2 se m. qch *(se réserver qch)* to set sth aside for oneself; **se m. une sortie** to provide oneself with a way out; **se m. des temps de repos dans la journée** to set aside rest periods for oneself during the day

ménager², -ère [menaʒe, -ɛr] ADJ **1** *(de la maison)* domestic *(avant n)*, household *(avant n)*; **enseignement m.** domestic science; **équipement m.** domestic or household appliances **2** *Littéraire* **être m. de son temps** to be economical or sparing with one's time **3** *Can (économe)* thrifty, careful (with money)

NM *Com* **le gros/petit m.** major/small household appliances

❏ **ménagère** NF **1** *(femme)* housewife; **elle est bonne ménagère** she's a good housekeeper **2** *(couverts)* canteen (of cutlery); **une ménagère en argent** a canteen of silver cutlery

ménagerie [menaʒri] NF menagerie; *Fig* **c'est une vraie m. ici!** it's like a zoo in here!

ménagiste [menaʒist] NMF household or domestic appliances retailer

ménapien, -enne [menapjɛ̃, -ɛn] *Belg Beaux-Arts* ADJ primitive Flemish

❏ **Ménapien, -enne** NM,F primitive Flemish painter

ménarche [menarʃ] NM *Physiol* menarche

menchevique, menchevik [mɛnʃevik] ADJ Menshevik *(avant n)*

NMF Menshevik

Mendel [mɛndɛl] *voir* **loi**

mendélévium [mɑ̃delevjɔm] NM *Chim* mendelevium

mendélien, -enne [mɛ̃deljɛ̃, -ɛn] ADJ Mendelian

mendélisme [mɛ̃delism] NM Mendelianism, Mendelism

mendiant, -e [mɑ̃djɑ̃, -ɑ̃t] NM,F *(clochard)* beggar; **les rues étaient pleines de petits mendiants** the streets were full of children begging

NM *Culin* = almond, fig, hazelnut and raisin biscuit

ADJ M *Rel* mendicant

mendicité [mɑ̃disite] NF **1** *(action)* begging; **vivre de m.** to beg for a living **2** *(état)* beggary, *Sout* mendicity, mendicancy; **être réduit à la m.** to be reduced to begging

mendier [9] [mɑ̃dje] VI to beg; **il mendie pour survivre** he gets by by begging

VT *(argent, sourire)* to beg for; **m. des votes** to canvass for votes

mendigot, -e [mɑ̃digo, -ɔt] NM,F *très Fam Vieilli* beggar■, *Am* panhandler

mendigoter [3] [mɑ̃digɔte] *très Fam Vieilli* VI to bum, *Am* to panhandle

VT to bum

mendole [mɑ̃dɔl] NF *Ich* blotched picarel

mené [mɔne] NM *Can* = small fish used as bait

meneau, -x [mɔno] NM *(horizontal)* transom; *(vertical)* mullion; **fenêtre à meneaux** mullioned window

menée [mɔne] NF **1** *Chasse* (stag's) track **2** *Suisse (congère)* snowdrift

menées [mɔne] NFPL *(intrigues)* intrigues, machinations; **des m. subversives** subversive activities; **les m. de l'opposition** the opposition's intrigues or scheming; **déjouer les m. de qn** to thwart or outwit sb

Ménélas [menelas] NPR *Myth* Menelas

MENER [19] [mɔne]

| VT to take **1, 2** ■ to lead **1–6** ■ to run **4** ■ to conduct **4** |
| VI to be in the lead |

VT **1** *(conduire → personne)* to take, to lead (**à** to); **m. qn à sa chambre** to take or show sb to his/her room; **comment mènes-tu tes enfants à l'école?** how do you take your children to school?; *Fig* **elle mènera son club à la victoire** she'll lead her club to victory; **son inconscience le mène au désastre** his thoughtlessness is

leading him to disaster; **cette petite somme ne te mènera pas bien loin** that won't get you very far; **un million de réparations, ça nous mène déjà assez loin** one million euros worth of repairs? that'll do nicely to be getting on with; *Fam* **un feu rouge grillé, ça va vous m. loin!** you went through the lights, that'll cost you!

2 (*sujet: escalier, passage, route*) to take, to lead; **le bus te mènera jusqu'à l'hôtel** the bus will take you (right) to the hotel

3 (*être à la tête de* → *cortège, course*) to lead; **le champion mène le peloton** the champion is leading the pack; **m. le deuil** to lead the funeral procession

4 (*diriger* → *groupe, équipe*) to lead; (→ *combat, négociation*) to carry on; (→ *affaire, projet*) to run, to manage; (→ *enquête*) to conduct, to lead; (→ *campagne*) to conduct; (→ *débat*) to lead, to chair; **m. la danse** *ou* **le bal** to lead the dance; *Fig* to call the tune; **m. le jeu** *Sport* to be in the lead; *Fig* to have the upper hand, to call the tune; **m. qch à bien** *ou* **à terme** *ou* **à bonne fin** (*finir*) to see sth through successfully; **je mènerai les fouilles à terme** *ou* **à bonne fin** I'll see the dig through to the end; **sauras-tu m. à bien cette entrevue?** will you be able to get through this interview?; **m. de front plusieurs projets** to run *or* manage several projects at once

5 (*vie*) to lead; **m. joyeuse vie** to lead a merry life; **m. une vie triste** to lead a sad life; **m. la vie dure à qn** to give sb a hard time; **laissez-la m. sa vie** let her live her life

6 (*contrôler*) **il se laisse trop facilement m.** he's too easily led; *Fig* **m. qn par le bout du nez** to lead sb by the nose; **se laisser m. par le bout du nez** to let oneself be led

7 *Math* to draw

8 *Tech* to drive

9 (*locution*) **il n'en menait pas large avant la publication des résultats** his heart was in his boots before the results were released

USAGE ABSOLU (*conduire*) **le chemin qui mène à la ville** the road that leads to the town; **cette porte mène à la cave** this door leads to the cellar; **la ligne n° 1 mène à Neuilly** line No. 1 takes you *or* goes to Neuilly; **la deuxième année mène au dessin industriel** after the second year, you go on to technical drawing; *Fig* **cela ne mène à rien** this is getting us nowhere

VI to (be in the) lead; **l'équipe locale mène par 3 buts à 0** the local team is leading by 3 goals to 0; **le skieur italien mène avec 15 secondes d'avance sur le Suisse** the Italian skier has a 15-second lead *or* advantage over the Swiss; **de combien on mène?** what's our lead?

ménestrel [menɛstrɛl] **NM** minstrel

ménétrier [menetrije] **NM 1** *Arch* (*violoneux*) fiddler **2** *Hist* musician

meneur, -euse [mənœr, -øz] **NM,F 1** (*dirigeant*) leader; **c'est un m. d'hommes** he's a born leader (of men); **m. de jeu** *Sport* play maker; *TV & Rad* quiz master, question-master; **meneuse de revue** chorus-line leader; *Can Sport* **meneuse de claque** cheerleader **2** *Péj* (*agitateur*) ringleader, leader, agitator

menhaden [mɛnadɛn] **NM** *Ich* menhaden

menhir [mɛnir] **NM** menhir

Ménilmontant [menilmɔ̃tɑ̃] **NM** = densely-populated and picturesque working-class district of Paris, in the 20th arrondissement

menin, -e [mənɛ̃, -in] **NM,F** *Hist* = young nobleman or noblewoman serving as companion to a Spanish prince or princess of the blood

'Les Menines' Velázquez 'Las Meninas'

méninge [menɛ̃ʒ] **NF** *Anat* meninx; **méninges** meninges
  ❏ **méninges** **NFPL** *Fam* brains; **il ne se fatigue pas** *ou* **ne se creuse pas les méninges!** he's in no danger of wearing his brain out!; **se remuer les méninges** to rack *or* *Am* cudgel one's brains; **fais travailler tes méninges** use your brains

méningé, -e [menɛ̃ʒe] **ADJ** meningeal

méningiome [menɛ̃ʒjom] **NM** *Méd* meningioma

méningite [menɛ̃ʒit] **NF** *Méd* meningitis; *Hum* **il ne risque pas la** *ou* **d'attraper une m.!** no danger of him wearing his brain out!

méningitique [menɛ̃ʒitik] **ADJ** *Méd* meningitic

méningocoque [menɛ̃gɔkɔk] **NM** *Méd* meningococcus

méningo-encéphalite [menɛ̃gɔɑ̃sefalit] (*pl* **méningo-encéphalites**) **NF** *Méd* meningoencephalitis

méniscal, -e, -aux, -ales [meniskal, -o] **ADJ** *Anat* meniscal

méniscite [menisit] **NF** meniscitis

méniscographie [meniskografi] **NF** *Méd* meniscography

ménisque [menisk] **NM** *Anat, Opt & Phys* meniscus

mennonite [menɔnit] **NMF** *Rel* Mennonite

ménologe [menɔlɔʒ] **NM** *Rel* menology, martyrology

ménopause [menɔpoz] **NF** menopause; *Fam* **faire sa m.** to go through the menopause∎

ménopausée [menɔpoze] **ADJ F** **une femme m.** a post-menopausal woman

ménopausique [menɔpozik] **ADJ** menopausal, menopausic

menora [menɔra] **NF** menorah

ménorragie [menɔraʒi] **NF** *Méd* menorrhagia

ménorragique [menɔraʒik] **ADJ** *Méd* menorrhagic

ménorrhée [menɔre] **NF** *Méd* menorrhoea

menotte [mənɔt] **NF** (*main*) tiny (little) hand
  ❏ **menottes** **NFPL** handcuffs; **passer les menottes à qn** to handcuff sb; **menottes aux poignets** handcuffed, in handcuffs

menotter [3] [mənɔte] **VT** to handcuff

mense [mɑ̃s] **NF** *Hist* revenue, income

mens *etc voir* **mentir**

mensonge [mɑ̃sɔ̃ʒ] **NM 1** (*action*) **le m.** lying, untruthfulness; **détester le m.** to hate lying *or* lies; **vivre dans le m.** to live a lie

2 (*propos*) lie; **faire** *ou* **dire un m.** to tell a lie; **dire des mensonges** to tell lies; **un m. par omission** a lie of omission; **elle n'a raconté que des mensonges** she just told a pack of lies; *Fam* **c'est vrai, ce m.?** are you having me on?; **petit m., pieux m.** white lie; **gros m.** downright lie

3 *Littéraire* (*illusion*) illusion, lie; **ma vie était un m.** I was living a lie, my life was a lie

mensonger, -ère [mɑ̃sɔ̃ʒe, -ɛr] **ADJ** untruthful, *Sout* mendacious; (*promesse*) false, empty; (*publicité*) misleading; **des déclarations mensongères** untruthful statements

mensongèrement [mɑ̃sɔ̃ʒɛrmɑ̃] **ADV** deceitfully, falsely, untruthfully

menstruation [mɑ̃stryasjɔ̃] *Physiol* **NF** menstruation, menstruating
  ❏ **menstruations** **NFPL** menses

menstruel, -elle [mɑ̃stryɛl] **ADJ** menstrual

menstrues [mɑ̃stry] **NFPL** *Vieilli* menses

mensualisation [mɑ̃sɥalizasjɔ̃] **NF** (*des salaires, des impôts, du personnel*) monthly payment; **pour vos règlements, pensez à la m.** don't forget that you can pay in monthly instalments

mensualiser [3] [mɑ̃sɥalize] **VT** to pay on a monthly basis; **être mensualisé** (*pour les impôts*) = to pay one's income tax in advance monthly instalments, the amount paid being an estimation based on previous years; (*pour un salaire*) to be paid monthly; **l'impôt est mensualisé** income tax is paid monthly; **je me suis fait m. pour tout** I pay everything monthly *or* on a monthly basis

mensualité [mɑ̃sɥalite] **NF 1** (*somme perçue*) monthly payment; (*somme versée*) monthly instalment; **m. de remboursement** monthly repayment **2** (*salaire*) monthly salary
  ❏ **par mensualités** **ADV** monthly, on a monthly basis; **payer par mensualités** to pay by monthly instalments

mensuel, -elle [mɑ̃sɥɛl] **ADJ** monthly
  NM,F worker paid by the month
  NM *Journ* monthly (magazine)

mensuellement [mɑ̃sɥɛlmɑ̃] **ADV** monthly, every month

mensuration [mɑ̃syrasjɔ̃] **NF** measurement, mensuration
  ❏ **mensurations** **NFPL** measurements; **prendre les mensurations de qn** to take sb's measurements; **elle a des mensurations à faire rêver** her vital statistics are out of this world; *Jur*

mensurations judiciaires height and weight (as shown on one's criminal record)

-MENT [mɑ̃] **SUFF**
This suffix appears in many adverbs formed from an adjective. Whatever its connotations, *-ly* is usually the corresponding suffix in English.
- In most cases, they are adverbs of MANNER, equivalent in meaning to "in a ... manner" where "..." is the adjective on which the adverb is based, eg:
  simplement simply; **gentiment** kindly; **rapidement** quickly, rapidly; **bêtement** foolishly, stupidly; **il mange salement** he's a messy eater
- Some adverbs ending in **-ment** are adverbs of INTENSITY, some of which can be colloquial, eg:
  énormément enormously, a great deal; **extrêmement** extremely; **légèrement** slightly; **totalement** totally; **drôlement** awfully; **vachement** really; **sacrément** damn, bloody
- A number of adverbs ending in **-ment** are equivalent to "FROM A ... POINT OF VIEW", where "..." is the adjective used as a basis, eg:
  économiquement economically; **politiquement** politically; **moralement** morally

mental, -e, -aux, -ales [mɑ̃tal, -o] **ADJ** mental
  NM **le m.** the mind, the mental state; **un m. d'acier** a positive mental attitude

mentalement [mɑ̃talmɑ̃] **ADV** mentally; **calcule-le m.** work it out *or* calculate it in your head; **j'ai préparé m. ce que j'allais lui répondre** I prepared in my head the answer I was going to give him/her

mentalisation [mɑ̃talizasjɔ̃] **NF** *Psy* mentalization

mentalisme [mɑ̃talism] **NM** mentalism

mentalité [mɑ̃talite] **NF** mentality; **avoir une m. de petit bourgeois** to have a lower middle-class mentality; **avoir une sale m.** to have a nasty mind; **faire changer les mentalités** to change people's mentality *or* the way people think; **les mentalités ne sont plus les mêmes** (people's) attitudes are different nowadays; **quelle (sale) m. dans ce bureau!** what an atmosphere *or* a nasty atmosphere there is in this office!; **quelle sale m.!** what an unpleasant character!; *Ironique* **belle** *ou* **jolie m.!** that's a nice attitude!; **l'histoire des mentalités** the history of mentalities

menterie [mɑ̃tri] **NF** *Fam Vieilli ou Can* lie∎, fib∎

menteur, -euse [mɑ̃tœr, -øz] **ADJ** (*personne*) untruthful, lying; (*discours, compliments*) deceitful; **enfant, il était très m.** he used to tell lies all the time when he was a child
  NM,F liar; *Fam* **sale m.!** you fibber!
  NM (*jeu*) **jouer au m.** to play cheat
  ❏ **menteuse** **NF** *Fam* (*langue*) tongue∎

menthe [mɑ̃t] **NF 1** *Bot* mint; **m. aquatique** water mint; **m. poivrée** peppermint; **m. verte** spearmint

2 (*tisane*) mint tea; **je prendrai une verveine-m.** I'll have verbena and mint tea

3 (*sirop*) **m. à l'eau** peppermint cordial; **boire** *ou* **prendre une m. à l'eau** to drink a glass of peppermint cordial

4 (*essence*) peppermint; **parfumé à la m.** mint-flavoured; **dentifrice à la m.** mint *or* mint-flavoured toothpaste; **bonbons à la m.** mints, peppermints; **pastilles de m.** mints, peppermints

menthol [mɑ̃tɔl] **NM** menthol; **bonbons/cigarettes au m.** menthol(ated) sweets/cigarettes

mentholé, -e [mɑ̃tɔle] **ADJ** mentholated, menthol (*avant n*)

mention [mɑ̃sjɔ̃] **NF 1** (*référence*) mention; **faire m. de qch** to refer to *or* to mention sth; **on ne fait pas m. de votre nom** there's no mention of your name

2 (*texte*) note, comment; **apposez votre signature précédée de la m. manuscrite "lu et approuvé"** append your signature after adding in handwriting "read and approved"; **l'enveloppe portait la m. "urgent"** the word "urgent" appeared *or* was written on the envelope; **mentions obligatoires** (*sur formulaire*) essential information; *Jur* **m. au dossier** official record

3 *Scol & Univ* distinction; **être reçu avec m.** to pass with distinction; **être reçu sans m.** to get an ordinary pass; **décrocher une m.** to pass with

men-men

distinction; **m. très bien** *Br* ≃ first class honours, *Am* ≃ grade A; **m. bien** *Br* ≃ upper second class honours, *Am* ≃ grade B; **m. assez bien** *Br* ≃ lower second-class honours, *Am* ≃ grade C; **m. passable** = minimum pass grade; **m. honorable** = first level of distinction for a PhD; **m. très honorable** = second level of distinction for a PhD; **m. très honorable avec les félicitations du jury** = highest level of distinction for a PhD

4 *Cin* **m. spéciale** special mention

5 *(dans l'édition)* **m. de réserve** copyright notice

mentionner [3] [mɑ̃sjɔne] VT to mention; **le nom du traducteur n'est pas mentionné** the translator's name does not appear; **l'article ne mentionne même pas sa dernière découverte** the article doesn't even mention his/her latest discovery; **le service mentionné ci-dessus** the above-mentioned department, the department mentioned above; *TV & Cin* **m. au générique** to acknowledge *or* feature in the credits

mentir [37] [mɑ̃tir] VI *(gén)* to lie; *(une fois)* to tell a lie; *(plusieurs fois)* to tell lies; **m. à qn** to lie to sb, to tell sb a lie/lies; **elle ment à son mari** she is deceiving her husband; **tu mens (effrontément)!** you're lying (shamelessly)!, you're a (barefaced) liar!; **j'ai prédit que tu allais gagner, ne me fais pas m.** I said you'd win, don't prove me wrong *or* don't make a liar out of me; **et je ne mens pas!** and that's the truth!; **sans m.!** honestly!; **sans m., elle me l'a dit quinze fois** without a word of a lie, she told me fifteen times; **m. par omission** to lie by omission; *Fam* **elle ment comme elle respire** *ou* **comme un arracheur de dents** she lies through her teeth; **si je mens je vais en enfer** cross my heart and hope to die; **faire m. le proverbe** to give the lie to the proverb

❑ **mentir à** VT IND *Littéraire (manquer à)* to belie; **m. à sa réputation** not to live up to one's reputation; **pour ne pas m. à son image** so as not to belie *or* to betray his/her image

▸**se mentir** VPR **1** *(emploi réfléchi)* **se m. à soi-même** to fool oneself **2** *(emploi réciproque)* to lie to each other, to tell each other lies

menton [mɑ̃tɔ̃] NM chin; **m. en galoche/pointu/rond** protruding/pointed/round chin; **avoir un m. volontaire** to have a firm *or* determined chin

mentonnet [mɑ̃tɔnɛ] NM *Rail* flange

mentonnier, -ère[1] [mɑ̃tɔnje, -ɛr] ADJ of the chin

mentonnière[2] [mɑ̃tɔnjɛr] NF **1** *(d'un chapeau)* chin strap; *(d'un casque)* chin piece **2** *Méd* chin bandage **3** *Mus* chin rest

Mentor [mɑ̃tɔr] NPR *Myth* Mentor

mentor [mɑ̃tɔr] NM **1** *Littéraire* mentor **2** *Can (guide)* mentor

mentorat [mɑ̃tɔra] NM *Can (aide)* mentoring

mentoré, -e [mɑ̃tɔre] NMF *Can (personne aidée)* mentee

menu[1] [məny] NM **1** *(liste, carte)* menu; **composer son m.** to plan one's meal; **qu'y a-t-il au m. aujourd'hui?** what's on the menu today?; *Fig* what's on the agenda for today?

2 *(repas)* set meal; **deux menus à 20 euros** two 20-euro menus *or* set meals; **le m. touristique** the set menu; **le m. gastronomique** the gourmet menu; **m. enfant** children's menu; **m. table d'hôte** table d'hôte menu; **m. à prix fixe** set menu, fixed-price menu

3 *Ordinat* menu; **contrôlé par m.** *ou* **menus** menu-driven; **m. primaire/secondaire/principal** primary/secondary/main menu; **m. d'aide** help menu; **m. de césure** hyphenation menu; **m. déroulant** pull-down menu; **m. fichier** file menu; **m. flottant** tear-off menu; **m. hiérarchique** hierarchical menu; **m. d'impression** print menu; **m. local** pop-up menu, pop-up; **m. pomme** Apple menu; **menus en cascade** pull-down menus, cascading menus

menu[2], **-e** [məny] ADJ **1** *(attaches, silhouette)* slim, slender; *(voix)* small, thin; *(écriture)* small, tiny; *(enfant)* tiny; *(femme)* petite; **l'enfant était très m. pour son âge** the child was tiny for his age; **à pas menus** with minute *or* tiny steps

2 *(avant le nom) (petit)* small, tiny; **elle coupa le jambon en menus morceaux** she cut the ham into tiny pieces

3 *(avant le nom) (négligeable)* small; **il fait les menus travaux** he does odd jobs; **menues dépenses** out-of-pocket expenses; **menus frais** minor expenses; **de la menue monnaie** small change; **m. fretin** *Ich* fry; *Fig* small fry; **m. gibier** small game; **les menus plaisirs** life's little pleasures; *Hist* **les Menus Plaisirs** the royal entertainment *(at the French Court)*; **voici un peu d'argent pour tes menus plaisirs** here's a little pin money

❑ **menu** ADV *(couper, hacher)* thoroughly, finely; **écrire m.** to write small

❑ **par le menu** ADV *(raconter)* in detail; *(vérifier)* thoroughly; **il m'a raconté ses aventures par le m.** he told me about his adventures in great detail

menu-carte [mənykart] *(pl* **menus-cartes***)* NM set menu

menuet [mənɥɛ] NM minuet

menuise [mənɥiz] NF **1** *Ich* sprat **2** *Mil* dust shot **3** *Menuis* small logs

menuiser [3] [mənɥize] VT *(découper)* to cut down; *(amincir)* to plane down

menuiserie [mənɥizri] NF **1** *(activité)* joinery; **m. métallique** metal joinery **2** *(atelier)* (joiner's) workshop **3** *(boiseries)* woodwork

menuisier, -ère [mənɥizje, -ɛr] NM,F joiner

ménure [menyr] NM *Orn* menura, lyre bird

ményanthe [menjɑ̃t] NM *Bot* menyanth

Méphistophélès [mefistɔfelɛs] NPR Mephistopheles

méphistophélique [mefistɔfelik] ADJ Mephistophelian, Mephistophelean

méphitique [mefitik] ADJ noxious, mephitic, mephitical

méphitisme [mefitism] NM mephitis

méplat, -e [mepla, -at] ADJ flat; **bois m.** (wood in) planks

NM **1** *(pièce méplate)* flat surface; *(de rocher)* ledge; *Beaux-Arts* plane **2** *(partie du corps)* **un visage aux méplats accusés** a finely-chiselled face

méprendre [79] [meprɑ̃dr] **se méprendre** VPR to make a mistake, to be mistaken (**sur** *ou* **quant à** about); **vous vous méprenez** you are mistaken; **je me suis mépris sur ses intentions réelles** I was mistaken about *or* I misunderstood his/her real intentions; **se m. sur qn** to misjudge sb; **on dirait de la soie, c'est à s'y m.** it feels just like silk; **on dirait ta sœur, c'est à s'y m.** she looks just like your sister; **il imitait le maître à s'y m.** he could give a lifelike imitation of the master

mépris [mepri] NM contempt, disdain, scorn; **avoir** *ou* **éprouver du m. pour** to be filled with contempt for, to despise; **paroles/regard de m.** contemptuous words/look; **avec m.** scornfully, contemptuously; **avoir** *ou* **tenir qn en m.** to hold sb in contempt; **le m. de** *(convenances, tradition)* contempt for, lack of regard for; **avoir le m. de l'argent/des conventions** to scorn *or* despise money/convention; **il a le m. de la parole donnée** he does not feel bound by a promise

❑ **au mépris de** PRÉP with no regard for, regardless of; **au m. du danger/du règlement** regardless of the danger/the rules; **au m. des convenances** spurning convention

'Le Mépris' *Godard* 'Contempt'

méprisable [meprizabl] ADJ contemptible, despicable; **un être totalement m.** a creature beneath contempt

méprisant, -e [meprizɑ̃, -ɑ̃t] ADJ contemptuous, disdainful, scornful; **se montrer très m. envers qn** to pour scorn on sb, to be very contemptuous towards sb

méprise [mepriz] NF mistake, error; **commettre une m.** to make a mistake; **victime d'une m.** victim of a misunderstanding; **il y a m. sur le destinataire** it has been delivered to the wrong person

❑ **par méprise** ADV by mistake

mépriser [3] [meprize] VT **1** *(dédaigner)* to look down on, to despise, to scorn; **je le méprise d'être si lâche** I despise him for being such a coward; **elle méprise l'argent** she thinks nothing of *or* scorns money **2** *(braver* → *conventions, règlement)* to disregard, to defy; *(*→ *mort, danger)* to defy; *(*→ *conseil, offre)* to disregard

méprobamate [meprɔbamat] NM *Pharm* meprobamate

mer [mɛr] NF **1** *Géog* sea; **mettre un canot à la m.** *(d'un navire)* to lower *or* to launch a boat; *(de la terre)* to get out a boat; **jeter qch à la m.** *(d'un navire)* to throw sth overboard; *(de la terre)* to throw sth into the sea; **un homme à la m.!** man overboard!; **de l'autre côté de la m.** over the sea; **ils sont partis en m.** they've gone out to sea; **perdus en m.** lost at sea; **en haute** *ou* **pleine m.** (out) at sea; **sous/sur la m.** under/on the sea; **vers la m.** seawards, towards the sea; **voyager par m.** to travel by sea; **par (la) m., c'est à un jour d'ici** it's a day's trip from here by sea; **prendre la m.** to put out to sea; **ce capitaine/navire n'a pas pris la m. depuis 20 ans** this captain/boat hasn't been to sea for 20 years; **état de la m.** sea conditions; **m. calme/belle/peu agitée** calm/smooth/moderate sea; **m. très grosse, grosse m.** very heavy *or* stormy sea; **par grosse m.** when the sea is heavy; **m. agitée devenant forte** sea moderate becoming heavy; **la m. est mauvaise** the sea is rough; **m. d'huile** sea as calm as a millpond; **m. intérieure** inland sea; **m. territoriale** territorial waters; **droit de la m.** maritime law; **coup de m.** heavy swell; **essuyer un coup de m.** to be struck by a heavy sea; *Fam* **ce n'est pas la m. à boire** it's not that hard, it's no big deal; **la m. Adriatique** the Adriatic Sea; **la m. des Antilles** the Caribbean Sea; **la m. d'Arafura** the Arafura Sea; **la m. d'Aral** the Aral Sea; **la m. d'Azov** the Sea of Azov; **la m. Baltique** the Baltic Sea; **la m. de Barents** the Barents Sea; **la m. de Beaufort** the Beaufort Sea; **la m. de Béring** the Bering Sea; **la m. Blanche** the White Sea; **la m. Caraïbe** *or* **des Caraïbes** the Caribbean Sea; **la m. Caspienne** the Caspian Sea; **la m. de Célèbes** the Celebes Sea; **la m. de Chine** the China Sea; **la m. de Corail** the Coral Sea; **la m. Égée** the Aegean Sea; **la m. de Galilée** the Sea of Galilee; **la m. du Groenland** the Greenland Sea; **la m. Intérieure** the Inland Sea; **la m. Ionienne** the Ionian Sea; **la m. d'Irlande** the Irish Sea; **la m. Jaune** the Yellow Sea; **la m. de Kara** the Kara Sea; **la m. des Laptev** the Laptev Sea; **la m. de Marmara** the Sea of Marmara; **la m. Méditerranée** the Mediterranean Sea; **la m. Morte** the Dead Sea; **la m. Noire** the Black Sea; **la m. du Nord** the North Sea; **la m. de Norvège** the Norwegian Sea; **la m. d'Oman** the Arabian Sea; **la m. d'Okhotsk** the Okhotsk Sea; **la m. de Ross** the Ross Sea; **la m. Rouge** the Red Sea; **la m. des Sargasses** the Sargasso Sea; **la m. de Sibérie orientale** the East Siberian Sea; **la m. de Tasman** the Tasman Sea; **la m. de Tchouktches** the Chukchi Sea; **la m. de Timor** the Timor Sea; **la m. de la Tranquillité** the Sea of Tranquillity; **la m. Tyrrhénienne** the Tyrrhenian Sea; **la m. des Wadden** the Waddenzee; **la m. de Weddell** the Weddell Sea

2 *(marée)* tide; **à quelle heure la m. sera-t-elle haute/basse?** what time is high/low tide?

3 *(région côtière)* seaside; **à la m.** at *or* by the seaside; **aller à la m.** to go to the seaside; **au bord de la m.** at *or* by the seaside, by the sea; **les paysages de m.** coastal landscapes

4 *Fig (grande étendue)* **une m. de sang** a sea *or* lake of blood; **m. de glace** glacier; **m. de sable** ocean of sand, sand sea

5 *Astron* mare

mer-air [mɛrɛr] ADJ INV *Mil* **missile m.** sea-to-air missile

mercanti [mɛrkɑ̃ti] NM *Péj* shark, profiteer

mercantile [mɛrkɑ̃til] ADJ **1** *Péj (intéressé)* mercenary, self-seeking, venal **2** *(commercial)* mercantile

mercantilisme [mɛrkɑ̃tilism] NM **1** *Littéraire (attitude)* mercenary *or* self-seeking attitude **2** *Écon (théorie)* mercantilism; *(système)* mercantile system

mercantiliste [mɛrkɑ̃tilist] ADJ mercantilist

NMF mercantilist

mercaphonie [mɛrkafɔni] NF *Mktg* telemarketing, telephone marketing

mercaptan [mɛrkaptɑ̃] NM *Chim* mercaptan

mercaptide [mɛrkaptid] NM *Chim* mercaptide

mercaticien, -enne [mɛrkatisjɛ̃, -ɛn] NM,F marketing expert

mercatique [mɛrkatik] NF marketing

mercenaire [mɛrsənɛr] ADJ *Littéraire (troupe)* mercenary; *(travail)* paid
NM mercenary

mercerie [mɛrsəri] NF **1** *(magasin) Br* haberdasher's shop, *Am* notions store **2** *(industrie, articles) Br* haberdashery, *Am* notions; **des articles de m.** sewing materials

mercerisage [mɛrsərizaʒ] NM mercerization

merceriser [3] [mɛrsərize] VT to mercerize; **coton mercerisé** mercerized cotton

merchandisage [mɛrʃɑ̃dizaʒ], **merchandising** [mɛrʃɑ̃dajziŋ] NM merchandizing

merci [mɛrsi] NM thank you; **dites-lui un grand m. pour son aide** give him/her a big thank you *or* all our thanks for his/her help
EXCLAM thank you, thanks; **m. de votre cadeau/amabilité** thank you *or* thanks for your present/kindness; **m. de** *ou* **pour votre offre** thank you for your offer; **m. d'avoir répondu aussi vite** thank you for replying so promptly; **dire m.** to say thank you *or* thanks; **as-tu dit m. à la dame?** did you thank the lady *or* say thank you to the lady?; **m. bien, m. beaucoup** thank you very much, thanks a lot; **m. (beaucoup) d'être venu** thanks (a lot) for coming; *Ironique* **m'excuser? m. bien, après ce qu'il m'a fait!** apologize? no way *or* no thanks, not after what he did to me!; **m. mille fois** thank you so much *or* very much; **mille mercis pour votre invitation** thank you so much *or* many thanks for your invitation; **voulez-vous du fromage? – (non) m., je n'ai pas faim** would you like some cheese? – no thank you *or* thanks, I'm not hungry; **un café? – m., volontiers** would you like a coffee? – (yes,) thanks, I'd love one; *Fam* **m., très peu pour moi!** thanks but no thanks!; *Ironique* **m. du compliment!** thanks for the compliment!; *Fam* **m. qui? m. mon chien!** don't bother to say thank you!; **m. de fermer la porte** *(écriteau dans un magasin)* please shut the door
NF *Littéraire* mercy; **demander m.** to ask for mercy
▫ **à la merci de** PRÉP at the mercy of; **tenir qn à sa m.** to have sb at one's mercy *or* in one's power
▫ **sans merci** ADJ merciless, pitiless, ruthless; **une lutte sans m.** a merciless struggle ADV mercilessly, pitilessly, ruthlessly

mercier, -ère [mɛrsje, -ɛr] NM,F *Br* haberdasher, *Am* notions dealer

Mercosur [mɛrkosyr] NM *Écon (abrév* **Marché commun du cône sud***)* Mercosur

mercredi [mɛrkrədi] NM Wednesday; **m. des Cendres** Ash Wednesday; *voir aussi* **mardi**
EXCLAM *Euph* sugar!

Mercure [mɛrkyr] NF *Astron* Mercury
NPR *Myth* Mercury

mercure [mɛrkyr] NM *Chim* mercury

mercureux [mɛrkyrø] ADJ M *Chim* mercurous

mercurey [mɛrkyrɛ] NM Mercurey (wine)

mercuriale[1] [mɛrkyrjal] NF *Littéraire (accusation)* remonstrance, admonition

mercuriale[2] [mɛrkyrjal] NF *Bourse* market price list, commodity price list

mercuriale[3] [mɛrkyrjal] NF *Bot* mercury

mercuriel, -elle [mɛrkyrjɛl] ADJ *Chim* mercurial

mercurique [mɛrkyrik] ADJ *Chim* mercuric

Mercurochrome® [mɛrkyrɔkrɔm] NM Mercurochrome®

merde [mɛrd] *très Fam* NF **1** *(excrément)* shit, crap; **une m. de chien** a dog turd; **tu as de la m. sous tes pompes** you've got shit on your shoes; *Fig* **traîner qn dans la m.** to drag sb's name through the mud; *Fig* **il a de la m. dans les yeux** he never sees a thing, he can't see what's going on right in front of him; **il ne se prend pas pour une** *ou* **pour de la m.** *Br* he thinks the sun shines out of his arse, *Am* he thinks he's God's gift to the world
2 *(chose de mauvaise qualité)* shit, crap; **c'est une m., cet ordinateur** this computer's (a load of) shit; **une m. à 10 euros** some cheap rubbish costing 10 euros; **ce film/bouquin est une vraie m.** this film/book is a load of crap; **de la m.** (a load of) shit; **c'est de la m., ce rasoir!** this razor's (a load of) shit!; **de m.** shitty; **ce temps de m.** this shitty weather; **un boulot/un quartier de m.** a shit *or* shitty job/area; **tu vas éteindre ta radio de m., oui?** will you turn that *Br* bloody *or Am* goddamn radio off!
3 *(désordre) Br* bloody *or Am* godawful mess; **foutre** *ou* **semer la m.** to create havoc; **chaque fois que ce gosse est dans ma classe, il fout la** *ou* **sa m.** whenever that kid is in my classroom, it's total chaos; **c'est la m. dans le pays en ce moment** the country's a *Br* bloody *or Am* goddamn mess *or* shambles at the moment; **c'est la m. pour circuler dans Paris en ce moment** driving in Paris is *Br* bloody *or Am* goddamn chaos at the moment
4 *(ennuis)* **c'est la m.!** it's hell!; **être dans la m. (jusqu'au cou)** to be (right) in the shit, to be up shit creek (without a paddle); **mettre** *ou* **foutre qn dans la m.** to drop sb in the shit
5 *(mésaventure)* shitty mess; **il m'arrive encore une m.** I've got another *Br* bloody *or Am* goddamn problem; **et si il nous arrivait une m.?** what if we ended up in the shit?; **je me suis fait piquer ma bagnole, quelle m.!** I've had my car pinched, what a shitty thing to happen!
EXCLAM shit!; **m. alors!** oh shit!; **et m., j'en ai marre!** to hell with it *or Br* sod it, I've had enough!; *Fig* **dire m. à qn** to tell sb to piss off *or Br* bugger off; **(je te dis) m.!** *(ton agressif)* to hell with you!; *(pour souhaiter bonne chance)* break a leg!; **alors, tu viens, oui ou m.?** are you coming or not, for Christ's sake?; **avoir un œil qui dit m. à l'autre** to have a squint■

merder [3] [mɛrde] *très Fam* VI to screw up, *Br* to cock up; **mon imprimante merde depuis trois jours** my printer's been on the blink for the last three days; **j'ai complètement merdé en littérature anglaise** I completely screwed up the English Lit paper; **j'ai envie de partir en vacances, mais j'ai l'impression que ça va m.** I want to go on holiday, but I've a feeling things are going to get screwed up; **il a fait m. l'affaire en racontant ce qu'il savait** he managed to screw up the whole thing by telling them what he knew; **ça merde entre eux** things between them are really screwed up
VT *(rater)* to screw up, *Br* to cock up; **il a merdé son examen** he made a complete *Br* balls-up *or Am* ball-up of his exam

merdeux, -euse [mɛrdø, -øz] *très Fam* ADJ *(coupable)* shitty, crappy; **se sentir m.** to feel shit *or* shitty
NM,F **1** *(personne méprisable)* shit **2** *(enfant)* little shit; **un m. de 14 ans** a 14-year old brat

merdier [mɛrdje] NM *très Fam* **1** *(désordre)* pigsty; **range un peu tes affaires, c'est le m. ici** it's like a pigsty in here, tidy up your things **2** *(situation confuse)* **être dans le m.** to be in the shit; **on s'est retrouvé dans un beau m. après son départ** we were in one hell of a mess after he/she left

merdique [mɛrdik] ADJ *très Fam* shit, shitty, crappy; **leur voiture est complètement m.** their car's a pile of crap

merdouille [mɛrduj] NF *Fam* **1** *(situation déplaisante)* mess■; **être dans la m.** to be in the shit **2** *(chose sans valeur)* **de la m.** (a load of) shit

merdouiller [3] [mɛrduje], **merdoyer** [13] [mɛrdwaje] VI *très Fam* to screw up, *Br* to cock up; **j'ai complètement merdouillé à l'oral** I made *Br* a right cock-up *or Am* a real screw-up of the oral

mère [mɛr] NF **1** *(génitrice)* mother; **elle est m. de cinq enfants** she is a mother of five; **c'est une m. pour lui** she's like a mother to him; **frères/sœurs par la m.** half-brothers/half-sisters on the mother's side; **il l'a rendue m. au bout de dix ans de mariage** he gave her a child after ten years of marriage; **ne touche pas les chiots, la m. est agressive** don't touch the pups, the mother can be aggressive; **veau élevé sous la m.** calf nourished on its mother's milk; **m. adoptive** adoptive mother; **m. biologique** biological mother; **m. célibataire** unmarried mother; **m. de famille** mother; **elle est m. de famille** she is a wife and mother; **m. nourricière** foster mother; **m. porteuse** *ou* **de substitution** surrogate mother; *aussi Fig* **m. poule** mother hen
2 *Fam (madame)* **la m. Vorel** old mother Vorel; **alors la petite m., on a calé?** stalled, have you, *Br* missus *or Am* ma'am?
3 *très Fam (insulte)* **ta m.!** fuck off!, *Br* piss off!; *Vulg* **enculé de ta m.!** you fucking prick!; *Vulg* **niquer sa m. à qn** to kick sb's fucking head in, *Am* to punch sb out; **flipper sa m.** to be scared shitless
4 *Rel* Mother; **m. Élisabeth** Mother Elizabeth; **oui, ma m.** yes, Mother; **la m. supérieure** the Mother Superior
5 *Littéraire (origine)* mother; **m. patrie** mother country; **la Grèce, m. de la démocratie** Greece, mother of democracy
6 *Chim* **m. de vinaigre** mother of vinegar
7 *Tech* mould
8 *(comme adj) Ordinat* **carte m.** motherboard; *Biol* **cellule m.** mother cell; *Ordinat* **disque m.** (positive) matrix; *Com* **maison m.** headquarters, head office; *Com* **société m.** parent company
ADJ F *(avant le nom)* **m. goutte** *(huile)* first pressing; *(vin)* bottoms *(wine from the mother)*

'Mère Courage et ses enfants' *Brecht* 'Mother Courage and Her Children'

'Ma Mère l'Oye' *Ravel* 'Mother Goose'

mère-grand [mɛrgrɑ̃] *(pl* **mères-grand***)* NF *Vieilli* grandmother

mérens [merɛ̃s] NM = breed of pony originating from the Ariège region of France

merguez [mɛrgɛz] NF merguez *(spicy North African sausage)*

Culture
MERGUEZ
This spicy sausage is typically sold barbecued at outdoor events, and is often associated with the relaxed family atmosphere at popular sporting events and political rallies.

mergule [mɛrgyl] NM *Orn* **m. nain** little auk, *Am* dovekie

méridien, -enne [meridjɛ̃, -ɛn] ADJ **1** *Littéraire (de midi)* meridian; **l'heure méridienne** noon, midday; **chaleur méridienne** midday heat; **ombre méridienne** shadow at noon
2 *Astron* meridian; **cercle m., lunette méridienne** meridian circle
NM **1** *Astron & Météo* meridian; **m. international** *ou* **origine** prime *or* Greenwich meridian; **m. céleste/magnétique/terrestre** celestial/magnetic/terrestrial meridian
2 *Méd* meridian
▫ **méridienne** NF **1** *Math* meridian (section); *Géog* meridian line; *Géol* triangulation line
2 *Littéraire (sieste)* siesta
3 *(lit)* chaise longue

méridional, -e, -aux, -ales [meridjɔnal, -o] ADJ **1** *(du Sud)* southern, *Sout* meridional **2** *(du sud de la France)* of/from the South of France
NM,F **1** *(du Sud)* Southerner **2** *(du sud de la France)* = inhabitant of or person from the South of France; **les méridionaux** Southern French people

meringue [mərɛ̃g] NF meringue

meringuer [3] [mərɛ̃ge] VT to cover with meringue; **tarte au citron meringuée** lemon meringue pie

mérinos [merinos] NM **1** *Zool* merino **2** *Tex* **(laine) m.** merino wool **3** *Fam Hum* **laisser pisser le m.** to let things take their course■

merise [məriz] NF wild cherry, merise

merisier [mərizje] NM **1** *(arbre)* wild cherry (tree)
2 *(bois)* cherry (wood)

mérisme [merism] NM distinctive feature

méristème [meristɛm] NM *Bot* meristem

méritant, -e [meritɑ̃, -ɑ̃t] ADJ worthy, deserving; **peu m.** undeserving; **les élèves les plus méritants ont été récompensés** the most deserving pupils were given a reward

mérite [merit] NM **1** *(vertu)* merit, worth; **gens de m.** people of merit; **avoir du m.** to be deserving of *or* to deserve praise; **il a bien du m.!** you have to take your hat off to him!; **tu as du m. de t'occuper d'eux** it is greatly to your credit that you take such care of them; **je n'ai aucun m.** I deserve no credit, I can't take any credit (for it)
2 *(gloire)* credit; **s'attribuer le m. de qch** to take the credit for sth; **tout le m. de l'affaire**

vous revient all the credit for the deal is yours, you deserve all the credit for the deal; **tu n'as même pas le m. de l'avoir fait tout seul** you can't even take credit for doing it yourself

3 *(qualité)* merit; **j'ai pu juger les mérites de son manuel** I have been able to assess the merits *or* quality of his/her handbook; **sa déclaration a au moins le m. d'être brève** his/her statement at least has the merit of being brief; **selon ses mérites** according to his/her merits; **par ordre de m.** in order of merit; **au seul m.** on merit alone

mériter [3] [merite] **VT 1** *(sujet: personne)* to deserve, *Sout* to merit; **il ne méritait pas pareille punition** he didn't deserve such punishment; **tu mérites une fessée** you deserve to be spanked; **tu mérites qu'on te fasse la même chose** you deserve to have the same thing happen to you; **tu l'as bien mérité!** it serves you right!, you got what you deserve!; **il n'a que ce qu'il mérite!** he's got what he deserves, it serves him right; **ils ne méritent pas qu'on s'intéresse à eux** they are not worth bothering with; **tu mériterais que je te laisse là tout seul** it would serve you right if I left you there on your own; **un repos bien mérité** a well-deserved rest; **son renvoi, il l'a bien mérité** he fully deserved to be fired

2 *(sujet: objet, idée)* to be worth, to deserve, *Sout* to merit; **une exposition qui mérite d'être vue** an exhibition worth seeing *or* which deserves to be seen; **la proposition mérite réflexion** the proposal is worth thinking about

3 *(valoir)* **voilà ce qui lui a mérité cette renommée** this is what earned him/her this fame
▫ **mériter de VT IND avoir bien mérité de la patrie** to have served one's country well
►**se mériter VPR 1** *(ne pas être donné)* **un cadeau pareil, ça se mérite** you have to do something special to get a present like that
2 *Can (recevoir)* **se m. un prix/une récompense** to be awarded *or* to receive a prize/a reward

méritocratie [meritɔkrasi] **NF** meritocracy
méritoire [meritwar] **ADJ** commendable, praiseworthy, *Sout* meritorious
merl [mɛrl] = **maërl**
merlan [mɛrlɑ̃] **NM 1** *Ich* whiting; **m. bleu** blue whiting, (Southern) poutassou; *Fam* **faire des yeux de m. frit à qn, regarder qn avec des yeux de m. frit** *(sans comprendre)* to gaze blankly at sb▪, to gape at sb▪; *(amoureusement)* to make sheep's eyes at sb **2** *Fam Vieilli (coiffeur)* barber▪, hairdresser▪ **3** *Culin Br* topside, *Am* top round
merle [mɛrl] **NM 1** *Orn* **m. (noir)** blackbird; **m. américain** (American) robin; **m. bleu** blue rock thrush; **m. d'eau** dipper; **m. migrateur** American robin; **m. à plastron** ou **à collier** ring ouzel; **m. de roche** rock thrush **2** *Ich (poisson)* ballan wrasse **3** *(individu désagréable)* **un vilain m., ton propriétaire!** what a nasty piece of work that landlord of yours is!
▫ **merle blanc NM 1** *Orn* white crow **2** *(personne)* rare bird, exceptional person; **chercher le m. blanc** to ask for the moon **3** *(objet)* rarity
merlette [mɛrlɛt] **NF** *Orn* hen blackbird
Merlin [mɛrlɛ̃] **NPR M. l'Enchanteur** Merlin the Wizard
merlin [mɛrlɛ̃] **NM 1** *Naut* marline **2** *(pour fendre le bois)* (clearing) axe; *(pour assommer le bétail)* poleaxe
merlon [mɛrlɔ̃] **NM** *(d'une fortification)* merlon; *(dans une poudrerie)* earthwork
merlot [mɛrlo] **NM 1** *(cépage)* Merlot **2** *Can Fam (vaurien)* good-for-nothing▪
merlu [mɛrly] **NM** hake
merluche [mɛrlyʃ] **NF 1** *Ich* hake **2** *Com & Culin* dried (unsalted) cod, stockfish
mer-mer [mɛrmɛr] **ADJ INV** *Mil* **missile m.** sea-to-sea missile
mérou [meru] **NM** *Ich* grouper; **m. des Basques** stone bass *or* brass, wreck fish
mérovingien, -enne [merɔvɛ̃ʒjɛ̃, -ɛn] **ADJ** Merovingian *(dynasty of Frankish kings, 481–751)*
▫ **Mérovingien, -enne NM,F** Merovingian
merrain [mɛrɛ̃] **NM 1** *(bois de tonnellerie)* cask wood, stave wood **2** *Zool (d'un cerf)* beam
mer-sol [mɛrsɔl] **ADJ INV** *Mil* **missile m.** sea-to-ground missile

mérule [meryl] **NM** OU **NF** merulius, house fungus
merveille [mɛrvɛj] **NF 1** *(chose remarquable)* marvel, wonder, treasure; **cette liqueur est une m.** this liqueur is amazing; **ce bracelet est une m.** this bracelet is marvellous; **ma couturière est une m.** my seamstress is a treasure; **sa fille est une m. d'ingéniosité** a marvel of ingenuity; **les merveilles de la technologie** the marvels *or* wonders of technology; **sa fille est une m. de patience** his/her daughter has the patience of a saint; **c'est m. que vous soyez à l'heure** it's a wonder that you're on time; **dire m. de qn** to heap praise upon sb; **faire des merveilles, faire m.** to work wonders
2 *Culin* ≃ type of sweet fritter
▫ **à merveille ADV** wonderfully, marvellously; **ils s'entendent à m.** they get on marvellously (well) *or* like a house on fire; **se porter à m.** to be in perfect health; **la soprano chantait à m.** the soprano sang marvellously; **ce travail lui convient à m.** this job suits him/her down to the ground; **ce chèque tombe à m.** this cheque couldn't have come at a better time; **elle s'y est adaptée à m.** she took to it like a duck to water
merveilleuse [mɛrvɛjøz] *voir* **merveilleux**
merveilleusement [mɛrvɛjøzmɑ̃] **ADV** wonderfully, marvellously; **il fait m. beau** it's marvellous *or* wonderful weather, the weather's marvellous *or* wonderful; **aller m. bien** to be wonderfully well, to be in excellent health; **elle a m. réussi son examen** she passed her exam with excellent results
merveilleux, -euse [mɛrvɛjø, -øz] **ADJ 1** *(formidable)* wonderful, marvellous, amazing
2 *(qui surprend)* marvellous, amazing; **un travail m. de délicatesse** a marvellously fine piece of work; **c'est m. ce qu'il a changé** it's marvellous how he's changed
3 *(après le nom) (fantastique)* magic; **une histoire merveilleuse** a wondrous tale; **la lampe merveilleuse** the magic lamp
NM 1 *(surnaturel)* **le m.** the supernatural *or* marvellous; *Cin & Littérature* **l'emploi du m.** the use of the fantastic element
2 *(caractère extraordinaire)* **le m. de l'histoire, c'est qu'il est vivant** the amazing thing about the whole story is that he's still alive
3 *Belg Culin* ≃ meringue coated with chocolate and cream
▫ **merveilleuse NF** *Hist* merveilleuse, fine lady
mérycisme [merisism] **NM** *Méd* merycism
mes [me] *voir* **mon**
mesa [meza] **NF** *Géog* mesa
mésadapté, -e [mezadapte] *Can* **ADJ** *(enfant)* with special needs, maladjusted
NM,F *(adulte)* person with social difficulties; *(enfant)* child with special needs, maladjusted child
mésaise [mezɛz] **NM** *Vieilli* malaise
mésalliance [mezaljɑ̃s] **NF** misalliance, mismatch; **faire une m.** to marry beneath oneself *or* one's station
mésallier [9] [mezalje] **se mésallier VPR** to marry beneath oneself *or* one's station
mésange [mezɑ̃ʒ] **NF** tit, titmouse; **m. bleue** blue tit; **m. boréale** willow tit; **m. charbonnière** great tit; **m. huppée** crested tit; **m. à moustaches** bearded tit; **m. noire** coal tit; **m. rémiz** penduline tit
mésangeai [mezɑ̃ʒe] **NM** *Orn* **m. imitateur** ou **de malheur** Siberian jay; **m. du Canada** gray jay, *Am* camp robber
mésangette [mezɑ̃ʒɛt] **NF** bird trap
mésaventure [mezavɑ̃tyr] **NF** misadventure, misfortune, mishap
mésaxonien [mezaksɔnjɛ̃] *Zool* **ADJ M** imparidigitate
NM imparidigitate animal
mescal [mɛskal] **NM** mescal
mescaline [mɛskalin] **NF** mescalin, mescaline
mesclun [mɛsklœ̃] **NM** mixed green salad
Mesdames [medam] *voir* **Madame**
Mesdemoiselles [medmwazɛl] *voir* **Mademoiselle**
mésembryanthème [mezɑ̃briɑ̃tɛm] **NM** *Bot* mesembryanthemum
mésencéphale [mezɑ̃sefal] **NM** *Anat* midbrain, mesencephalon

mésenchyme [mezɑ̃ʃim] **NM** *Biol* mesenchyma, mesenchyme
mésentente [mezɑ̃tɑ̃t] **NF** disagreement, difference of opinion; **oublions notre m. passée** let's forget our past disagreements
mésentère [mezɑ̃tɛr] **NM** *Anat* mesentery
mésentérique [mezɑ̃terik] **ADJ** mesenteric
mésestimation [mezɛstimasjɔ̃] **NF** *Littéraire (mépris)* lack of respect, low esteem *or* regard; *(fait de sous-estimer)* underestimation, underrating
mésestime [mezɛstim] **NF** *Littéraire* lack of respect, low esteem *or* regard; **tenir qn en m.** to hold sb in low esteem, to have little regard for sb
mésestimer [3] [mezɛstime] **VT** *Littéraire (mépriser)* to have a low opinion of; *(sous-estimer)* to underestimate, to underrate
mésinformer [3] [mezɛ̃fɔrme] **VT** to misinform
mésintelligence [mezɛ̃teliʒɑ̃s] **NF** *Littéraire* disagreement, lack of (mutual) understanding, discord
mesmérien, -enne [mɛsmerjɛ̃, -ɛn] **ADJ** mesmerian, mesmeric
NM,F mesmerist, mesmerite
mesmérisme [mɛsmerism] **NM** mesmerism
méso-américain, -e [mezoamerikɛ̃, -ɛn] **ADJ** Central American
mésoblaste [mezɔblast] **NM** *Biol* mesoblast
mésoblastique [mezɔblastik] **ADJ** *Biol* mesoblastic
mésocarpe [mezɔkarp] **NM** *Bot* mesocarp
mésoderme [mezɔdɛrm] **NM** *Biol* mesoblast
mésodermique [mezɔdɛrmik] **ADJ** *Biol* mesoblastic
mésoéconomie [mezoekɔnɔmi] **NF** intermediate scale economics *(singulier)*
mésolithique [mezɔlitik] *Géol* **ADJ** Mesolithic
NM le m. the Mesolithic (age)
mésomère [mezɔmɛr] **ADJ** *Chim* mesomeric
mésomérie [mezɔmeri] **NF** *Chim* mesomerism
mésomorphe [mezɔmɔrf] **ADJ** *Phys* mesomorphic
méson [mezɔ̃] **NM** *Phys* meson; **m. mu** mu meson, muon; **m. pi** pi meson, pion; **m. K** K meson, kaon
mésopause [mezɔpoz] **NF** mesopause
Mésopotamie [mezɔpɔtami] **NF la M.** Mesopotamia
mésopotamien, -enne [mezɔpɔtamjɛ̃, -ɛn] **ADJ** Mesopotamian
▫ **Mésopotamien, -enne NM,F** Mesopotamian
mésosphère [mezɔsfɛr] **NF** mesosphere
mésothérapie [mezoterapi] **NF** mesotherapy, = treatment of cellulite, circulation problems, rheumatism etc involving the use of tiny needles
mésothorax [mezɔtɔraks] **NM** *Zool* mesothorax
mésozoaire [mezɔzɔɛr] **NM** mesozoan
mésozoïque [mezɔzɔik] *Géol* **ADJ** Mesozoic
NM Mesozoic
mesquin, -e [mɛskɛ̃, -in] **ADJ 1** *(médiocre)* mean, petty; **des préoccupations mesquines** petty concerns; **laissons cela aux esprits mesquins** let's not waste our time on such petty concerns
2 *(parcimonieux)* mean, stingy, niggardly; **une portion mesquine** a stingy portion; **des économies mesquines** penny-pinching
mesquinement [mɛskinmɑ̃] **ADV 1** *(selon des vues étroites)* pettily, small-mindedly **2** *(avec parcimonie)* meanly, stingily
mesquinerie [mɛskinri] **NF 1** *(étroitesse d'esprit)* meanness, petty-mindedness, pettiness **2** *(parcimonie)* meanness, stinginess; **connu pour sa m.** renowned for his stinginess
mess [mɛs] **NM** mess; **le m. des officiers** the officers' mess
message [mesaʒ] **NM 1** *(information)* message; **prendre un m.** to take a message; **faire parvenir un m. à qn** to send a message to sb; **veuillez laisser un m. après le signal sonore** *(sur répondeur)* please leave a message after the tone; **m. chiffré** message in cipher; **m. codé** coded message; **m. de détresse** distress message; **m. enregistré** recorded message; *Ordinat* **m. instantané** instant message; *Mktg* **m. principal** core message; **m. publicitaire** advertisement; *Tél* **m. téléphoné** *Br* ≃ Telemessage®, *Am* ≃ telegram *(delivered on the telephone)*; **m. téléphonique** telephone message; **m. télex** telex *(message)*; *Tél* **m. texte** text message; **envoyer un m. texte à qn** to text sb, to text-message sb

2 *(déclaration)* speech; **un m. de bienvenue** a message of welcome

3 *(pensée)* message; **le m. de l'Évangile** the message of the Gospel

4 *Biol* **m. génétique** genetic information *or* code; **m. nerveux** nerve impulse *or* message

5 *Ordinat* **m. d'accueil** welcome message; **m. d'aide** help message; **m. d'alerte** warning message, alert box; **m. d'attente (du système)** (system) prompt; **m. électronique** e-mail; **envoyer un m. électronique à qn** to e-mail sb; **m. d'erreur** error message; **m. d'invite** *(du système)* prompt; **m. guide-opérateur** prompt

❏ **à message** ADJ with a message; **un livre/une chanson à m.** a book/a song with a message

message-guide [mesaʒgid] *(pl* **messages-guide)** NM *Ordinat* prompt

messager, -ère [mesaʒe, -ɛr] NM,F **1** *(personne qui transmet)* messenger; **m. de malheur** bearer of bad news; **je me ferai votre m. auprès de lui** I'll speak to him on your behalf **2** *Littéraire (annonciateur)* **m. de bonheur** harbinger of happiness

NM **1** *Hist* messenger; *Myth* **Mercure, le m. des dieux** Mercury, the messenger of the gods **2** *Orn* carrier pigeon **3** *(de colis, de cargaison)* courier

messagerie [mesaʒri] NF *Ordinat & Tél* **m. de dialogue en direct** chat; **m. électronique** e-mail; **m. instantanée** instant messaging; **m. vocale** voice mail; **les messageries télématiques videotex** messaging services; **les messageries roses** = interactive Minitel® services enabling individuals seeking companionship to make contact

❏ **messageries** NFPL parcels service; **messageries aériennes** air freight company; **messageries de presse** newspaper distributing service; **messageries maritimes** shipping line; **bureau de(s) messageries** *Naut* shipping office; *Rail* parcel(s) office; *Hist* stagecoach office

messe [mɛs] NF **1** *Rel* Mass; **aller à la m.** to go to Mass; **célébrer** *ou* **dire la m.** to celebrate *or* say Mass; **faire dire une m. pour qn** to have a Mass said for sb; **des messes ont été dites pour la paix dans le monde** Masses were held for world peace; *Fig* **la m. est dite** the die is cast; **m. basse** Low Mass; *Fig* **faire** *ou* **dire des messes basses** to whisper; *Fig* **pas de messes basses, s'il vous plaît!** no whispering, please!; **m. de minuit** midnight Mass; **m. des morts** *ou* **de requiem** Mass for the dead, Requiem; **m. noire** black mass; *Can* **il y a du monde à la m.!** the place is jam-packed!

2 *Mus* mass; **m. concertante** (oratorio-style) mass; **m. en si mineur** mass in B minor

messéance [meseãs] NF *Arch ou Littéraire (inconvenance → d'une conduite)* unseemliness, impropriety

messéant, -e [meseã, -ãt] ADJ *Arch ou Littéraire* **1** *(peu seyant)* unbecoming (**à** to) **2** *(inconvenant → tenue, conduite, langage)* unseemly, improper

Messeigneurs [mesɛɲœr] *voir* **Monseigneur**

messeoir [67] [meswar] **messeoir à** VT IND *Littéraire* **1** to be unbecoming to, to ill befit; **cela messied à votre âge** that doesn't become you at your age **2** *(tournure impersonnelle)* **il ne messied pas parfois d'avoir un esprit critique** there are times when it behoves one to have a critical mind

messer [mese] NM *Vieilli ou Hum* my lord

messianique [mesjanik] ADJ messianic

messianisme [mesjanism] NM messianism

messidor [mesidɔr] NM = 10th month of the French Revolutionary calendar, from 19 or 20 June to 18 or 19 July

messie [mesi] NM messiah; **le M.** the Messiah; *Fig* **attendre qn comme le M.** to wait eagerly for sb; *Can* **attendre le M.** *(attendre un enfant)* to be expecting a child; *(attendre l'impossible)* to expect the impossible

♩

'Le Messie' *Haendel* 'Messiah'

messied *etc voir* **messeoir**

messier [mesje] NM *Hist* official crop watcher *(before the harvesting season)*

Messieurs [mesjø] *voir* **Monsieur**

messieurs [mesjø] *voir* **monsieur**

---

messin, -e [mesɛ̃, -in] ADJ of/from Metz

❏ **Messin, -e** NM,F = inhabitant of or person from Metz

Messine [mɛsin] NM Messina

messire [mesir] NM *Hist* my lord; **m. Thomas** my lord Thomas

mestrance [mɛstrãs] = **maistrance**

mestre [mɛstr] NM **1** *Mil* **m. de camp** colonel **2** *Naut* **(arbre de) m.** mainmast; **voile de m.** mainsail

mesurable [məzyrabl] ADJ measurable

mesurage [məzyraʒ] NM measurement, measuring

MESURE [məzyr]

measurement **1, 2, 4** ▪ measure **2, 3, 6, 7, 11, 13** ▪ moderation **5** ▪ step **7** ▪ extent **8** ▪ time **9** ▪ bar **9** ▪ metre **10**

NF **1** *(évaluation d'une dimension)* measuring (UNCOUNT), measurement; *(résultat)* measurement; **prendre les mesures de qch** to take the measurements of sth; **la m. de la productivité a été améliorée grâce à de nouvelles techniques** productivity measurement has been improved thanks to new techniques; *Mktg* **m. d'audience** audience measurement; *Mktg* **m. d'impact** impact measurement; *Mktg* **m. de satisfaction de la clientèle** customer satisfaction measurement

2 *(valeur)* measure, measurement; **unité de m.** unit of measurement; **m. de surface/longueur** measure of surface area/of length; **m. de volume** cubic measure; **l'homme est la m. de toute chose** man is the measure of all things; *Fig* **sans commune m.** unrivalled; *Fig* **il n'y a pas commune m. entre ces deux vins** there is no comparison between the two wines

3 *(récipient)* measure; **verser une m. de vin à qn** to pour sb out a measure of wine; **de vieilles mesures en étain** old pewter measures; **m. de capacité** *(pour liquides)* (liquid) measure; *(pour le grain, les haricots)* (dry) measure; *Com* **faire bonne m.** to give good measure; **il m'a donné deux pommes pour faire bonne m.** he gave me two apples for good measure; *Hum* **et pour faire bonne m., j'ai perdu ma clef** and to cap it all, I've lost my key; **la m. est (à son) comble** enough's enough

4 *Couture* measurement; **prendre les mesures d'un client** to take a customer's measurements

5 *(retenue)* moderation; **manquer de m.** to be excessive, to lack moderation; **garder une juste m.** to keep a sense of moderation; **rester dans la juste m.** to keep within bounds; **avoir le sens de la m.** to have a sense of moderation; **passer** *ou* **dépasser la m.** to overstep the mark, to go too far; **tu passes** *ou* **dépasses la m.** you're going too far; **leur cynisme passe la m.** they're excessively cynical; **oublier toute m.** to fling aside all restraint, to lose all sense of moderation *or* proportion; **dépenser avec/sans m.** to spend with/without moderation; **ambition sans m.** unbounded *or* limitless ambition; **un homme plein de m.** a man with a sense of moderation

6 *(qualité)* measure; *Fig* **donner toute sa m.** to show what one is capable of; **il ne donne (toute) sa m. que dans la dernière scène** he only displays the full measure of his talent *or* only shows what he's capable of in the last scene; **prendre la m. d'un adversaire** to size up an opponent

7 *Admin, Jur & Pol* measure, step; **prendre des mesures** to take measures *or* steps *or* action; **prendre des mesures contre qch** to take action against sth; **prendre des mesures pour faire qch/pour que...** to take measures *or* steps to do sth/so that...; **j'ai pris mes mesures pour que les enfants soient gardés** I've made arrangements for the children to be looked after; **m. conservatoire** protective measure; **mesures déflationnistes** deflationary measures; **m. économique** economic measure; **mesures d'exécution sur les véhicules terrestres à moteur** = seizure of motorized vehicle; **m. exécutoire** binding measure; **m. incitative** initiative; **mesures incitatives visant à encourager les naissances** initiatives designed

---

to encourage families to have more children; *Jur* **m. d'instruction** investigative measure; **m. préventive** preventative measure *or* step; **mesures protectionnistes** protectionist measures; **mesures provisoires** temporary measures; **m. de rétorsion** retaliatory measure, reprisal; **m. de sécurité** safety measure; **m. de sûreté** security measure, preventive measure; **m. d'urgence** emergency measure; **par m. d'hygiène** in the interest of hygiene; **par m. de salubrité** as a health measure; **par m. de sécurité** as a safety precaution; **par m. d'économie** as a cost-saving measure, for reasons of economy

8 *(degré)* extent; **son attitude donne la m. de son cynisme** his/her behaviour shows just how cynical he/she really is; **prendre la (juste) m. de qch** to understand the full extent of sth; **être en m. de** to be able *or* in a position to; **elle n'est pas en m. de te payer** she's not in a position to *or* she can't pay you; **dans la m. de mes possibilités** insofar as I am able; **dans la m. du possible** as far as possible; **je vous aiderai dans la m. de mes forces** *ou* **du possible** I'll help you to the best of my ability *or* as much as I can *or* as best I can; **ces dépenses ne sont pas dans la m. de mes moyens** this expenditure is beyond my means; **dans la m. où cela peut lui être agréable** insofar as *or* inasmuch as he/she might enjoy it; **dans une certaine m.** to some *or* a certain extent; **dans quelle m.?** to what extent *or* degree?

9 *Mus (rythme)* time, tempo; *(division)* bar; **battre la m.** to beat time; **être en m.** to be in time; **en m., s'il vous plaît!** (keep in) time, please!; **m. composée/simple** compound/simple time; **m. à quatre temps** four-four time *or* measure, common time *or* measure

10 *Littérature* metre

11 *Géom* measure

12 *Équitation* gait

13 *Escrime* measure, reach

❏ **à la mesure de** PRÉP worthy of; **être à la m. de qn/qch** to measure up to sb/sth; **des aspirations qui ne sont pas à la m. de l'homme** aspirations which are beyond the scope of human achievement; *Sport & Fig* **trouver un adversaire à sa m.** to meet one's match; **elle a un adversaire à sa m.** she's got an opponent worthy of her *or* who is a match for her

❏ **à mesure** ADV as one goes along

❏ **à mesure que** CONJ as; **à m. que le temps passe** as time goes by

❏ **dans une large mesure** ADV to a great *or* large extent

❏ **sur mesure** ADJ **1** *Couture* made-to-measure; **fabriquer des vêtements sur m.** to make clothes to measure; **fait sur m.** custom-made; **costume (fait) sur m.** made-to-measure suit; **mousse sur m.** foam cut to size; **j'ai trouvé un travail sur m.** I've found the ideal job (for me); **le producteur lui a trouvé un rôle sur m.** the producer found him/her a role that was tailor-made for him/her

2 *(comme nom)* **c'est du sur m.** *Couture* it's made to measure; *Fig* it fits the bill

---

mesuré, -e [məzyre] ADJ **1** *(lent)* measured; **à pas mesurés** at a measured pace **2** *(modéré)* steady, moderate; *(langage, personne)* moderate, restrained; **il emploie toujours un ton m.** he never raises his voice

mesurer [3] [məzyre] VT **1** *(déterminer la dimension ou le volume de)* to measure; *(tissu)* to measure off *or* out; **m. qch en hauteur/largeur** to measure the height/width of sth; **m. qch en biais** to measure sth diagonally; **je vais vous en m. le double** I'll measure out twice as much for you; **m. qn** to take sb's measurements, to measure sb (up); **je vais te m. pour voir si tu as grandi** I'm going to measure you to see if you've grown

2 *(difficulté, qualité)* to assess; **il ne mesure pas sa force** *ou* **ses forces** he doesn't know his own strength; **m. ses paroles** to be careful what one says; **mesure-t-elle la portée de ses paroles?** is she aware of the consequences of what she's saying?; **il n'a pas entièrement mesuré les risques** he didn't fully consider *or* assess the risks;

on mesure le travail au résultat the work is measured by results; **m. qn du regard** to look sb up and down, to size sb up

3 *(limiter)* to limit; **m. la nourriture à qn** to ration sb's food; **m. l'argent à qn** to ration out money to sb; **on nous mesure les crédits** our funds are limited; **il ne mesure pas sa peine** he doesn't spare his efforts; **et pourtant, je mesure mes mots** and I'm choosing my words carefully; **le temps vous sera mesuré pour cette épreuve** you will have a limited amount of time for this test

4 *(adapter)* **m. qch à** to adapt sth to; **m. le châtiment à l'offense** to make the punishment fit the crime; **je mesure mes dépenses à mes revenus** I gear my expenditure to my income

vi to measure; **combien mesures-tu?** how tall are you?; **il mesure presque deux mètres** he's almost two metres tall; **le sapin ne mesure que deux mètres** the fir tree is only two metres high; **la cuisine mesure deux mètres sur trois** the kitchen is *or* measures two metres by three

▸**se mesurer** VPR **1** *(emploi réciproque)* **se m. des yeux** *ou* **du regard** to size each other up, to look each other up and down

2 se m. à *(lutter avec)* to have a confrontation with, to pit oneself against; **je n'ai pas envie de me m. à lui** I don't feel like tackling him

mesurette [məzyrɛt] NF **1** *(cuillère)* measuring spoon **2** *Fam Péj (petite réforme)* petty reform ■

mesureur [məzyrœr] NM **1** *(agent)* measurer **2** *(instrument)* gauge, measure; **m. de distance** distance gauge; **m. de pression** pressure gauge

ADJ M **verre m.** measuring cup *or* jug

mésusage [mezyzaʒ] NM *Littéraire* misuse

mésuser [3] [mezyze] **mésuser de** VT IND *Littéraire* to misuse; **m. de son talent** to misuse one's talent; **m. de son pouvoir** to abuse one's power

met *etc voir* **mettre**

meta [meta] NF white orb-web spider, *Spéc* Meta segmentata

Méta® [meta] NM *Tech* Meta

métabisulfite [metabisylfit] NM *Chim* metabisulphite; **m. de sodium** *ou* **de soude** sodium metabisulphite

métabole [metabɔl] ADJ *Physiol* metabolic

métabolique [metabɔlik] ADJ *Physiol (du métabolisme)* metabolic

métaboliser [3] [metabɔlize] VT *Physiol* to metabolize

métabolisme [metabɔlism] NM *Physiol* metabolism

métabolite [metabɔlit] NM *Physiol* metabolite

métabotropique [metabɔtrɔpik] ADJ *Physiol* metabotropic

métacarpe [metakarp] NM *Anat* metacarpus

métacarpien, -enne [metakarpjɛ̃, -ɛn] *Anat* ADJ metacarpal

NM metacarpal

métacentre [metasɑ̃tr] NM metacentre

métacentrique [metasɑ̃trik] ADJ *Biol & Naut* metacentric

métacognition [metakɔgnisjɔ̃] NF *Psy* metacognition

métaconnaissance [metakɔnɛsɑ̃s] NF metaknowledge

métagalaxie [metagalaksi] NF *Astron* metagalaxy

métagenèse [metaʒɔnɛz] NF *Biol* metagenesis

métairie [metɛri] NF sharecropping farm, metairie

métal, -aux [metal, -o] NM **1** *Métal & Chim* metal; **m. anglais/blanc** Britannia/white metal; **m. en barres/lingots** metal in bars/ingots; **m. déployé/en feuilles** expanded/sheet metal; **m. précieux** precious *or* noble metal; **le m. jaune** gold; **m. de transition** transition metal; **m. antifriction** Babbit metal, bearing metal; **métaux lourds** heavy metals; **métaux vils** base metals

2 *Littéraire (caractère)* metal; **il est fait d'un m. pur** he's made of fine stuff

3 *Fin & Hér* metal

métalangage [metalɑ̃gaʒ] NM metalanguage

métalangue [metalɑ̃g] NF metalanguage

métal-carbonyle [metalkarbɔnil] *(pl* **métaux-carbonyles** [metokarbɔnil]*)* NM *Chim* metal-carbonyl

métaldéhyde [metaldeid] NM *Chim* metaldehyde

métalinguistique [metalɛ̃ɡɥistik] ADJ metalinguistic

métallerie [metalri] NF structural metalwork

métallier, -ère [metalje, -ɛr] NM,F **1** *Métal* ironworker, metalworker **2** *(serrurier)* locksmith

métallifère [metalifɛr] ADJ metal-bearing, metalliferous

métallique [metalik] ADJ **1** *(en métal)* metal *(avant n)*; **câble m.** wire rope **2** *(semblable au métal)* metallic, steel *(avant n)*, steely; **un bruit/une voix m.** a metallic noise/voice; **rendre un son m.** to clang, to clank; **bleu m.** steel *or* steely blue **3** *Fin* **réserve m.** bullion reserve

métallisation [metalizasjɔ̃] NF plating, metalplating, metallization

métallisé, -e [metalize] ADJ *(couleur, finition)* metallic; *(papier)* metallized; **voiture bleu m.** metallic blue car

métalliser [3] [metalize] VT to metallize

métalliseur, -euse [metalizœr, -øz] ADJ M metal-spraying *(avant n)*

NM,F *(ouvrier)* metal sprayer

métallo [metalo] NM *Fam (ouvrier)* metalworker ■; *(dans une aciérie)* steelworker ■

métallochromie [metalɔkrɔmi] NF metallochromy

métallogénie [metalɔʒeni] NF metallogeny

métallographie [metalɔgrafi] NF metallography

métallographique [metalɔgrafik] ADJ metallographic

métalloïde [metalɔid] NM *Vieilli Chim* metalloid

métallophone [metalɔfɔn] NM *Mus* metallophone

métalloplastique [metalɔplastik] ADJ copper asbestos *(avant n)*

métalloprotéine [metalɔprɔtein] NF metalloprotein

métallurgie [metalyrʒi] NF metallurgy

métallurgique [metalyrʒik] ADJ *(procédé)* metallurgical; *(atelier → gén)* metalworking *(avant n)*; *(→ dans une aciérie)* steelworking *(avant n)*

métallurgiste [metalyrʒist] NM **1** *(ouvrier)* metalworker; *(dans une aciérie)* steelworker **2** *(industriel, expert)* metallurgist

métalogique [metalɔʒik] ADJ metalogic, metalogical

NF metalogic

métamathématique [metamatematik] ADJ metamathematical

NF metamathematics *(singulier)*

métamère [metamɛr] ADJ *Chim* metameric

NM *Zool* metamere

métamérie [metameri] NF *Biol & Chim* metamerism, metamery

métamérique [metamerik] ADJ *Biol* metameric

métamérisé, -e [metamerize] ADJ *Biol* metameric

métamorphique [metamɔrfik] ADJ metamorphic, metamorphous

métamorphiser [3] [metamɔrfize] VT to metamorphose

métamorphisme [metamɔrfism] NM metamorphism

métamorphosable [metamɔrfozabl] ADJ metamorphosable

métamorphose [metamɔrfoz] NF **1** *Biol & Myth* metamorphosis **2** *Fig (transformation)* metamorphosis, transformation

═══════📖═══════

'La Métamorphose' *Kafka* 'Metamorphosis'

métamorphoser [3] [metamɔrfoze] VT **1** *Myth* **m. qn en** to change *or* to turn sb into **2** *Fig (transformer)* to transform, to change; **ses vacances l'ont métamorphosé** his holiday has really changed him

▸**se métamorphoser** VPR **1** *Myth* **se m. en** to turn into, to be metamorphosed into **2** *Fig (se transformer)* to change, to transform; **en 20 ans, la télévision s'est métamorphosée** television has undergone a transformation over the last 20 years

métamoteur [metamɔtœr] NM *Ordinat* **m. (de recherche)** metasearch engine

métamyélocyte [metamjelɔsit] NM *Biol* metamyelocyte

métaphase [metafaz] NF *Biol* metaphase

métaphore [metafɔr] NF metaphor; **parler par métaphores** to speak in metaphors; **m. filée** extended metaphor

métaphorique [metafɔrik] ADJ metaphoric, metaphorical, figurative

métaphoriquement [metafɔrikmɑ̃] ADV metaphorically, figuratively

métaphosphorique [metafɔsfɔrik] ADJ metaphosphoric

métaphyse [metafiz] NF *Anat* metaphysis

métaphysicien, -enne [metafizisjɛ̃, -ɛn] NM,F metaphysician, metaphysicist

métaphysique [metafizik] ADJ **1** *Beaux-Arts & Phil* metaphysical **2** *(spéculatif)* metaphysical, abstruse, abstract

NF **1** *Phil* metaphysics *(singulier)*; *(système de pensée)* metaphysic; **la m. kantienne** the Kantian metaphysic **2** *(spéculations)* abstractness, abstruseness; *Fam* **il ne s'embarrasse pas de m.** he doesn't let anything get in his way

métaphysiquement [metafizikmɑ̃] ADV metaphysically

métaplasie [metaplazi] NF *Méd* metaplasia

métapsychique [metapsiʃik] *Vieilli* ADJ psychic

NF parapsychology

métapsychologie [metapsikɔlɔʒi] NF metapsychology

métastable [metastabl] ADJ *Chim & Phys* metastable

métastase [metastaz] NF *Méd* metastasis; **former des métastases** to metastasize

métastaser [3] [metastaze] VI *Méd* to metastatize

métastatique [metastatik] ADJ *Méd* metastatic

métatarse [metatars] NM *Anat* metatarsus

métatarsien, -enne [metatarsjɛ̃, -ɛn] *Anat* ADJ metatarsal

NM metatarsal

métathéorie [metateɔri] NF metatheory

métathérien [metaterjɛ̃] NM *Zool* metatherian

métathèse [metatɛz] NF metathesis

métathorax [metatɔraks] NM metathorax

métayage [metɛjaʒ] NM sharecropping

métayer, -ère [meteje, -ɛr] NM,F sharecropper, sharecropping tenant

métazoaire [metazɔɛr] *Zool* NM metazoan

❑ **métazoaires** NMPL Metazoa

méteil [metɛj] NM *Agr* (mixed crop of) wheat and rye

métempsycose [metɑ̃psikoz] NF metempsychosis

métencéphale [metɑ̃sefal] NM *Anat* metencephalon

météo [meteo] ADJ INV weather *(avant n)*, meteorological; **bulletin m.** weather report; **prévisions m.** (weather) forecast; **station m.** meteorological *or* weather station; **frégate** *ou* **navire m.** weather ship

NF *(service)* Br Met Office, Am Weather Bureau; *(temps prévu)* weather forecast; **la m. a dit que...** the weather forecast said...; **Monsieur M.** the weatherman

météore [meteɔr] NM **1** *Astron* meteor **2** *Fig* nine days' wonder; **un m. dans le monde de l'art** a flash in the pan *or* nine days' wonder in the art world

Météores [meteɔr] NMPL **les M.** the Meteori

météorique [meteɔrik] ADJ **1** *Astron* meteoric **2** *(éphémère)* meteoric, short-lived, fleeting

météorisation [meteɔrizasjɔ̃] NF **1** *Vét* bloat **2** *Géol* atmospheric alteration *(of rocks)*

météoriser [3] [meteɔrize] VI to become flatulent *or* distended

météorisme [meteɔrism] NM flatulence, *Spéc* meteorism tympanites

météorite [meteɔrit] NF **1** *(météoroïde)* meteoroid **2** *(aérolithe)* meteorite

météoritique [meteɔritik] ADJ meteoritic, meteoritical

météorologie [meteɔrɔlɔʒi] NF **1** *(science)* meteorology **2** *(organisme)* Br Met Office, Am Weather Bureau

météorologique [meteɔrɔlɔʒik] ADJ meteorological, weather *(avant n)*

météorologiste [meteɔrɔlɔʒist], **météorologue** [meteɔrɔlɔg] NMF meteorologist

métèque [metɛk] NM *Hist* metic

NMF *Fam* = offensive term used to refer to any dark-skinned foreigner living in France, especially one from the Mediterranean

méthacrylate [metakrilat] NM *Chim* methacrylate

méthacrylique [metakrilik] ADJ *Chim* methacrylic

méthadone [metadɔn] NF *Pharm* methadone

méthamphétamine [metãfetamin] NF *Pharm* methamphetamine

méthanal, -als [metanal] NM *Chim* methanal

méthane [metan] NM *Chim* methane (gas)

méthanier [metanje] NM methane tanker *or* carrier

méthaniser [3] [metanize] VT *Chim* to methanize, to convert into methane

méthanoïque [metanɔik] ADJ *Chim* **acide m.** methanoic acid

méthanol [metanɔl] NM *Chim* methanol

méthémoglobine [metemɔglɔbin] NF *Biol* methaemoglobin

méthémoglobinémie [metemɔglɔbinemi] NF *Méd* methaemoglobinaemia

méthionine [metjɔnin] NF *Biol & Chim* methionine

méthode [metɔd] NF **1** *(façon de procéder)* method; *Tech* method, technique; **c'est une bonne m. pour apprendre l'anglais** it's a good way of learning English; **j'ai ma m. pour le convaincre** I have my own way of convincing him; **c'est quoi ta m. pour rester aussi mince?** how do you manage to stay so slim?; **je vais changer de m.** I'm going to change my methods; **une m. de rangement** a method for storing things away; **leur m. de vinification** their wine-making techniques; *Compta* **m. d'achat** purchase method; *Scol* **m. active** activity method, activity-based learning approach; *Compta* **m. d'amortissement dégressif** declining balance method; *Compta* **m. d'amortissement linéaire** straight-line depreciation method; **m. d'analyse statistique** method of statistical analysis; *Mktg* **m. de la boule de neige** referral system; **m. du chemin critique** critical path method; *UE* **m. communautaire** Community method; *Compta* **m. des coûts marginaux** cost pricing; *Compta* **m. du coût de revient complet** full costing, full cost accounting (method); *Compta* **m. des coûts standards** standard cost accounting, standard costing; *Compta* **m. des coûts variables** direct costing; *Mktg* **m. d'échantillonnage** sampling method; *Compta* **m. par** *ou* **à échelles** daily balance interest calculation; **m. de financement** funding method; **m. de gestion** management technique; *Scol* **m. globale** = method of teaching children literacy that emphasizes word recognition and reading for meaning, ≃ whole language approach; *Méd* **m. d'Heimlich** Heimlich manoeuvre; *Compta* **m. linéaire** straight-line method; *Scol* **m. mixte** = method of teaching children literacy that combines phonics and meaning-based techniques; *Mktg* **m. non probabiliste** non-probability method; **méthodes et organisation** organization and methods; *Mktg* **m. probabiliste** probability method; *Compta* **m. prospective** projected benefit valuation method; *Mktg* **m. des quotas** quota sampling method; *Mktg* **m. de sélection** selection method; *Scol* **m. semi-globale** = method of teaching children literacy that combines phonics and meaning-based techniques; *Mktg* **m. de sondage** polling method; *Cin* **m. Stanislavski** Method acting; *Scol* **m. syllabique** phonics method; **m. de travail** method, modus operandi; *Mktg* **m. de vente** sales *or* selling technique

2 *(organisation)* method; **vous manquez de m.** you lack method, you aren't methodical enough; **avec m.** methodically; **sans m.** unmethodically

3 *Fam (astuce)* **faut avoir la m.** you've got to have the knack; **tu as vraiment la m. avec les enfants!** you really have a way with *or* know how to handle children!; **lui, il a trouvé la m.!** he's got the hang of it!

4 *(manuel)* **m. d'anglais** English course book; **m. d'apprentissage** course book; **m. de lecture** primer; **m. de solfège** music handbook *or* manual; **m. de piano** piano tutor; **m. de relaxation** (book of) relaxation techniques

méthodique [metɔdik] ADJ methodical; **de façon m.** methodically

méthodiquement [metɔdikmã] ADV methodically

méthodisme [metɔdism] NM Methodism

méthodiste [metɔdist] ADJ Methodist
    NMF Methodist

méthodologie [metɔdɔlɔʒi] NF methodology

méthodologique [metɔdɔlɔʒik] ADJ methodological

méthylacrylique [metilakrilik] ADJ methacrylic, methylacrylic

méthylal [metilal] NM *Chim* methylal

méthylation [metilasjɔ̃] NF *Chim* methylation

méthyle [metil] NM *Chim* methyl

méthylène [metilɛn] NM *Chim* methylene; *Com* methyl alcohol

méthyler [3] [metile] VT *Chim* to methylate

méthylique [metilik] ADJ *Chim* methyl *(avant n)*

méthylorange [metilɔrãʒ] NM *Chim* methyl orange

métical, -als [metikal] NM *(monnaie)* metical

méticuleuse [metikyløz] *voir* **méticuleux**

méticuleusement [metikyløzmã] ADV meticulously

méticuleux, -euse [metikylø, -øz] ADJ **1** *(minutieux → personne)* meticulous; *(→ enquête)* probing, searching; **un élève m.** a meticulous pupil **2** *(scrupuleux)* meticulous, scrupulous; **d'une propreté méticuleuse** spotlessly *or* scrupulously clean

méticulosité [metikylozite] NF *Littéraire* meticulousness

métier [metje] NM **1** *(profession)* trade; **mon m.** my job *or* occupation *or* trade; **le m. de banquier** the banking profession, banking; **les métiers manuels** the manual trades; **les métiers d'art** (arts and) crafts; **les métiers de bouche** the food and catering trade; **quel est votre m.?** what do you do (for a living)?, what's your job?; **faire** *ou* **exercer le m. de chimiste** to work as a chemist; **j'ai fait tous les métiers** I've done every sort of job there is; **qu'est-ce que tu feras comme m. plus tard?** what do you want to be when you grow up?; **exercer son m. en travailleur indépendant** to work freelance; **j'exerce le m. de journaliste** I'm a journalist (by profession); **je n'ai pas la possibilité d'exercer mon m. ici** I can't do my job here; **changer de m.** to change career; **elle a un bon m.** she has a good job; **études qui ne mènent à aucun m.** course with no job prospects; **la soudure ne tiendra pas, et je connais mon m.!** the welding won't hold, and I know what I'm talking about!; **apprendre son m. à qn** to teach sb one's trade; **ce n'est pas toi qui vas m'apprendre mon m.!** don't teach me my business!, I know what I'm doing!; **le m. de mère** a mother's job; **le m. de roi est chose difficile** being a king is not easy *or* no easy job; *Fam* **quel m.!** what a life!; **quel m. de fou!** you don't have to be crazy to do this job but it helps!; *Euph* **le plus vieux m. du monde** the oldest profession in the world; *Littéraire* **faire m. et marchandise de mensonges** to deal in lies; **il n'y a pas de sot m.(, il n'y a que de sottes gens)** there's no such thing as a worthless trade; **chacun son m. (et les vaches seront bien gardées)** you do your job and I'll do mine

2 *(expérience)* skill, experience; **avoir du m.** to have job experience; **elle manque encore un peu de m.** she still lacks experience; **c'est le m. qui rentre** it shows you're learning

3 *(machine)* **m. à filer/tricoter** spinning/knitting machine; **m. à broder** embroidery frame, tambour frame; **m. à tisser** loom; **m. à tisser mécanique** power loom; **m. à tapisserie** tapestry frame *or* loom; *Fig* **avoir qch sur le m.** to have sth lined up; **trois articles sur le m.** three articles in progress *or* on the stocks; *Fig* **qu'est-ce que tu as sur le m. en ce moment?** what are you working on at the moment?

□ **de métier** ADJ *(homme, femme, armée)* professional; *(argot)* technical; *(technique)* of the trade ADV **avoir 15 ans de m.** to have been in the job *or* business for 15 years

□ **de son métier** ADV by trade; **être boulanger de son m.** to be a baker by trade; **être journaliste de son m.** to be a journalist by profession

□ **du métier** ADJ of the trade; **les gens du m.** people in the trade *or* in the business; **quand on est du m.** *(membre de la profession)* when you're in the business; *(expert)* when you're an expert at the job; **demander à quelqu'un du m.** ask a professional *or* an expert

métis, -isse [metis] ADJ **1** *(personne)* of mixed race; **un enfant m.** a mixed-race child **2** *Zool*

crossbred, hybrid, cross; *(chien)* crossbred **3** *Bot* hybrid

    NM,F **1** *(personne)* person of mixed race; **les M.** = aboriginal ethnic group in Canada **2** *Zool* crossbreed, hybrid, cross; *(chien)* crossbreed **3** *Bot* hybrid
    NM *Tex* (heavy) linen-cotton mixture

Culture

LES MÉTIS

In New France (see box at **Nouvelle-France**), a group of fur-trader settlers of European origin (known as "coureurs de bois") traded regularly with aboriginal communities, and often married aboriginal women. By the mid-19th century, a large group of their descendants (now known as the "Métis") lived in the Western Prairies of Canada, where they pursued a semi-aboriginal lifestyle. They spoke French and were, by and large, Catholics. The "Métis" came into conflict with British Canadians in a dispute over lands west of Ontario. Under the leadership of Louis Riel, they sought admission to the Canadian Confederation as a distinct group. The violence that resulted from British-Canadian opposition to this move led to the trial and hanging of Louis Riel in 1885, and the crushing of the "Métis" aspirations. Louis Riel has now been recognized as a national hero, and the "Métis" as one of the peoples protected by federal aboriginal laws.

---

métissage [metisaʒ] NM **1** *Biol (de personnes)* interbreeding; *(d'animaux)* crossbreeding, hybridization; *(de plantes)* hybridization **2** *(en sociologie)* intermarrying; *Fig* **le m. culturel** multiculturalism; **le m. de la salsa et du rock** the fusion of salsa and rock music

métisser [3] [metise] VT *Zool* to cross, to crossbreed; *Bot* to hybridize; **une population très métissée** a highly intermixed population; **musique métissée** crossover *or* fusion music

métiver [3] [metive] VT *Can (en acadien)* to harvest with a scythe, to scythe

métives [metiv] NFPL *Can (en acadien)* harvest

métonymie [metɔnimi] NF *Ling* metonymy

métonymique [metɔnimik] ADJ *Ling* metonymic

métope [metɔp] NF *Archit* metope

métrage [metraʒ] NM **1** *(prise de mesures)* measurement; *Constr* quantity surveying

2 *(longueur)* length; *Couture* length, yardage; **grand/petit m.** *(tissu)* cut lengthways/crossways; **vous le voulez en quel m.?** what width would you like?; **quel m. faut-il pour un manteau?** how many yards are needed to make a coat?

3 *Cin* footage, length; **long m.** feature(-length) film; **moyen m.** medium-length film; **court m.** short (film)

mètre[1] [mɛtr] NM **1** *(unité)* metre; **m. carré/cube** square/cubic metre; **m. par seconde** metre per second; **m. étalon** standard metre; **m. linéaire** linear metre **2** *Sport* **le 400 mètres** the 400 metres, the 400-metre race; **il court le 100 mètres en dix secondes** he runs the 100 metres in ten seconds **3** *(instrument)* (metre) rule; **m. pliant** folding rule; **m. à ruban** tape measure, measuring tape

mètre[2] [mɛtr] NM *Littérature* metre

métré [metre] NM **1** *(mesure)* measurement **2** *Constr (devis)* bill *or* schedule of quantities

métrer [8] [metre] VT **1** *(mesurer)* to measure *(in metres)* **2** *Constr* to survey, to do a quantity survey of

métreur, -euse [metrœr, -øz] NM **m. (vérificateur)** quantity surveyor

□ **métreuse** NF *Cin* footage (number) meter

métricien, -enne [metrisjɛ̃, -ɛn] NM,F *Littérature* metrician, metrist

métrique[1] [metrik] *Math* ADJ metric; **adopter le système m.** to adopt the metric system
    NF metric

métrique[2] [metrik] *Littérature* ADJ metrical
    NF prosody, metrics *(singulier)*

métrisation [metrizasjɔ̃] NF metrication

métrite [metrit] NF *Méd* metritis

métro [metro] NM *Br* underground, *Am* subway; **le m. parisien/de Montréal** the Paris/Montreal metro; **le m. londonien** *ou* **de Londres** the London underground (system), *Fam* the tube; **le**

premier m. the first *or* milk train; **le dernier m.** the last train; **m. aérien** elevated *or* overhead railway; **au m. Charonne** at Charonne metro (station); **prendre le m.** to take the *Br* underground *or Am* subway; **je préfère y aller en m.** I'd rather go by *Br* underground *or Am* subway; *Fam Fig* **elle a toujours un m. de retard** she's always the last one to know what's going on; *Fam* **m., boulot, dodo** the daily grind, the nine-to-five routine; **depuis que j'habite à Paris, ma vie c'est vraiment m., boulot, dodo** life has become very humdrum *or* routine since I moved to Paris

métrologie [metrɔlɔʒi] NF metrology

métrologique [metrɔlɔʒik] ADJ metrological

métrologiste [metrɔlɔʒist] NMF metrologist

métronome [metrɔnɔm] NM metronome; **avec la régularité d'un m.** like clockwork, (as) regular as clockwork

métropole [metrɔpɔl] NF **1** *(ville)* metropolis **2** *Admin* mother country; **les Français de la m.** the metropolitan French; **sorties m.** *(panneau dans un aéroport)* domestic arrivals **3** *Rel* metropolis

métropolitain, -e [metrɔpɔlitɛ̃, -ɛn] ADJ *Admin & Rel* metropolitan; *(église)* archiepiscopal; **troupes métropolitaines** home troops

NM **1** *Vieilli (métro) Br* underground (railway), *Am* subway **2** *Rel* metropolitan (primate)

métropolite [metrɔpɔlit] NM *Rel* metropolitan

métrorragie [metrɔraʒi] NF *Méd* metrorrhagia

métrosexuel, -elle [metrɔsɛksɥɛl] ADJ metrosexual

NM metrosexual

mets [mɛ] NM *(aliment)* dish; **des m. de grande qualité** gourmet fare

mettable [mɛtabl] ADJ **1** *(vêtement)* wearable; **la veste est encore m.** the jacket's still wearable; **je n'ai plus rien de m.** I don't have anything decent left to wear **2** *Vulg (personne)* fuckable, *Br* shaggable

metteur [mɛtœr] NM

> Note that it is no longer considered a mistake to feminize this word and to say **une metteur en scène/en page/etc** or even **une metteuse en scène/en page/etc** but some French speakers nonetheless regard these forms as unacceptable, especially in France. See also the entry **féminisation**.

Cin & Théât **m. en scène** director; *Tech* **m. au point** adjuster, setter; **m. en œuvre** *(en joaillerie)* setter; *Rad* **m. en ondes** producer; *Typ* **m. en pages** layout artist

METTRE [84] [mɛtr]

> VT to put **1, 2, 6, 11** ■ to lay **2** ■ to set **4** ■ to put on **7** ■ to wear **7** ■ to turn on **8** ■ to put in **9** ■ to take **10** ■ to give **13**
> VI to set sail
> VPR to go **1–3** ■ to get **4** ■ to put on **5, 7** ■ to wear **5, 7** ■ to start **12**

VT **1** *(placer)* to put; **m. des verres dans un placard** to put glasses (away) in a cupboard; **m. la main sur le bras de qn** to lay *or* to put one's hand on sb's arm; **m. l'amour avant l'argent** to put *or* to place love before money; **m. qn parmi les grands** to rate *or* to rank sb among the greats; **m. sa confiance/tout son espoir en** to put one's trust/all one's hopes in; **m. la confusion dans un service** to throw a department into confusion; **j'avais mis beaucoup de moi-même dans le projet** I'd put a lot into *or* invested a lot in the project; **elle a mis son talent au service des défavorisés** she used her talent to help the underprivileged; **ne mets pas les coudes sur la table!** don't put your elbows on the table!; **il a mis de la boue sur le tapis** he's got mud on the carpet; **m. une pièce à l'affiche** to bill a play; **m. une lettre à la poste** to post a letter; **m. un enfant au lit** to put a child to bed; **m. le ballon au fond des filets** to put the ball in the back of the net; **on l'a mise à un poste clé** she was put in *or* appointed to a key position; **on m'a mis au standard** they put me on the switchboard; **je n'ai pas pu la m. à l'école du quartier** I couldn't get her into the local school; **m. qn dans l'avion/le train** to put sb on the plane/the train; **m. ses enfants dans le privé** to send one's children to a private school; **m. un enfant en pension** to put a child in a *or* to send a child to boarding school; **m. qn en prison** to put sb in prison; **m. qn au cachot** to put sb behind bars; **m. 20 euros sur un cheval** to put *or* to lay 20 euros on a horse; **m. de l'argent sur son compte** to put *or* to pay some money into one's account; *Fam* **m. qn en boîte** to pull sb's leg

2 *(poser horizontalement)* to lay, to put; **mets les cartes face dessous** lay *or* put *or* place the cards face down; **il mit le tapis par terre** he laid *or* put the carpet down on the floor; **il a mis le pied sur une peau de banane** he stepped on a banana skin; **m. le tissu sur le patron** to lay the material on the pattern; **m. qch à plat** to lay sth down flat; **il mit le dossier devant moi** he set *or* laid the file down in front of me

3 *(disposer)* **m. le loquet** to put the latch down; *Fam* **mets le store** *(tire-le)* pull the blind (down)

4 *(ajuster)* to set; **m. qch droit** to set sth straight; **m. une pendule à l'heure** to set a clock to the right time; **mets le magnétoscope sur la deuxième chaîne** set the *Br* video *or Am* VCR on channel two; **mets la sonnerie à 20 h** set the alarm for 8 p.m.

5 *(établir → dans un état, une situation)* **m. un étang à sec** to drain a pond; **m. le nom au pluriel** to put the noun into the plural; **mettez les verbes à l'infinitif** put the verbs into the infinitive; **m. qn à l'amende** to fine sb, to impose a fine on sb; **m. qn au régime** to put sb on a diet; **m. qn au travail** to set sb to work, to get sb working; **m. qn au désespoir** to cause sb to despair; **m. qn dans la confidence** to let sb in on *or* into the secret; **m. qn dans l'embarras** *(perplexité)* to put sb in a predicament; *(pauvreté)* to put sb in financial difficulty; **m. qn dans l'obligation de faire qch** to oblige sb to do sth; **m. qn dans une situation délicate** to put sb in an awkward position; **m. une maison en vente** to put a house up for sale; **m. du vin en bouteilles** to put wine into bottles, to bottle wine; **mis en bouteille au château** *(sur une bouteille de vin)* chateau-bottled; **m. des fruits en bocaux** to put fruit into jars, to bottle fruit; *Jur* **m. qn en examen** to indict sb; **m. qch en œuvre** to implement sth; **m. une plante en pot** to pot a plant; **m. une plante en terre** to put a plant into the soil; **m. qch en miettes** to smash sth to bits; **m. un poème en musique** to set a poem to music; **il a fallu m. le texte en espagnol** the text had to be put into Spanish; *Typ* **m. qch en page** to make sth up; **m. qch en vigueur** to bring sth into force *or* operation; **m. qch à cuire** to put sth on to cook; **m. qch à réchauffer** to heat sth up (again); **m. de l'eau à chauffer** to put some water on to heat (up); **m. du linge à sécher** *(dans la maison)* to put *or* to hang clothes up to dry; *(à l'extérieur)* to put *or* to hang clothes out *or* up to dry; **mets les chaussettes à sécher** *(dans la maison)* put *or* hang the socks up to dry; *(à l'extérieur)* put *or* hang the socks out to dry; **m. des fleurs à sécher** to leave flowers to dry, to dry flowers; **m. qch à tremper** to put sth to soak, to soak sth; **m. qn sous tranquillisants** to put sb on tranquillizers

6 *(fixer, ajouter)* to put; **m. une pièce à un pantalon** to put a patch on *or* to patch a pair of trousers; **m. un bouton à sa veste** to sew a button on one's jacket; **il faut lui m. des piles** you have to put batteries in it; **j'ai fait m. de nouveaux verres à mes lunettes** I had new lenses put in my glasses

7 *(se vêtir, se coiffer, se chausser de)* to put on; *(porter régulièrement)* to wear; **m. son manteau/une robe** to put on one's coat/a dress; **m. du fond de teint/du parfum** to put on some foundation/some perfume; **j'ai du mal à m. mes souliers** I find it difficult to get my shoes on; **mets tes skis/ta casquette** put your skis/your cap on; **mets une barrette** put a (hair) slide in; **tu devrais m. une ceinture avec cette robe** you should wear a belt with that dress; **je n'ai plus rien à m.** I've nothing to wear; **je lui ai mis son manteau** I put his/her coat on (for him/her); **n'oubliez pas de m. un collier anti-puce à votre chien** don't forget to put a flea collar on your dog

8 *(faire fonctionner → appareil)* to turn *or* to put *or* to switch on; **m. le chauffage** to put *or* to switch *or* to turn the heating on; **m. un disque** to put a record on; **mets de la musique** put some music on, play some music; **m. la radio plus fort** to turn up the radio; *Fam* **mets les sports/la première chaîne** put on the sport channel/channel one

9 *(installer)* to put in, to install; **faire m. l'électricité** to have electricity put in; **faire m. le chauffage central** to have central heating put in *or* installed; **faire m. l'eau et le gaz** to have water and gas put in; **m. la table** *ou* **le couvert** to lay *or* set the table; **m. des rideaux aux fenêtres** to put curtains at the windows, to put up curtains; **m. des étagères** to put up shelves; **m. du papier peint/de la moquette dans une pièce** to wallpaper/to carpet a room; **nous avons mis du gazon dans le jardin** we turfed the garden; **ça mettra de la couleur dans la pièce** it will give the room a bit of colour

10 *(consacrer → temps)* to take; **m. du temps à faire qch** to take time to do sth; **il a mis trois heures à faire ses devoirs** he took three hours to do *or* he spent three hours over his homework; **elle a mis trois mois à me répondre** she took three months *or* it took her three months to answer me; **combien de temps met-on pour y aller?** how long does it take to get there?; **nous y mettrons le temps/le prix qu'il faudra** we'll spend as much time/money as we have to; *Fam* **tu as mis le temps!** you took your time about it!, you took long enough!; **tu en a mis du temps pour te décider!** you took some time to make up your mind!; **m. de l'argent dans une voiture** to put money in *or* into a car; **m. de l'argent sur un cheval** to put money on a horse, to back a horse; **m. 500 euros dans qch** to spend 500 euros on sth; **m. 10 000 euros dans une affaire** to sink 10,000 euros into a business venture; **je serais prêt à m. tout ce que j'ai dans cette entreprise** I'd be willing to put everything I have into this venture; **m. toute son énergie/tout son enthousiasme à faire qch** to put all one's energy/enthusiasm into doing sth; **j'y mettrai tous mes soins** I'll give it my full attention; **nous avons mis trois kilomètres entre nous et nos poursuivants** we put three kilometres between us and our pursuers

11 *(écrire)* to put; **que faut-il m. dans les cases de droite?** what do you have to put *or* write in the right-hand boxes?; **ne mets rien dans le cadre B** don't write anything in box B; **on met un accent sur le "e"** "e" takes an accent; **on met deux m à "pomme"** "pomme" has two m's; *Fam* **mets qu'il a refusé de signer** write *or* put down that he refused to sign; **tu veux lui m. un petit mot?** *(sur la carte, lettre)* do you want to write him/her a little note?; **je ne sais pas quoi m. sur la carte de vœux** I don't know what to put *or* to write on the (greetings) card; **tu n'as qu'à m. que je le remercie** *(dans une lettre)* tell him thanks, give him my thanks; **qu'est-ce qu'elle met, dans sa lettre?** what does she say in her letter?; **je t'ai mis sur la liste des invités** I've put you on the guest list

12 *(supposer)* **mettons** (let's) say; **et mettons que tu gagnes?** suppose *or* let's say you win?; **il faut, mettons, deux mètres de tissu** we need, (let's) say *or* shall we say, two metres of material; **mettons que ça fasse 50 euros** (let's) call it *or* say 50 euros; **mettons que j'ai mal compris!** *(acceptation)* let's just say I got it wrong!; **mettez que je n'ai rien dit** pretend I didn't say anything

13 (*donner*) to give; **vous me mettrez trois douzaines d'huîtres** give me *or* let me have three dozen oysters; **je vous mets un peu plus de la livre** I've put in a bit more than a pound; **le prof m'a mis 18** ≃ the teacher gave me an A

14 *Fam* (*infliger*) **qu'est-ce qu'il m'a mis au ping-pong!** he really hammered me at table tennis!; **on leur a mis cinq buts en première mi-temps** we hammered in five goals against them in the first half; **m. son poing dans la figure de qn** to punch sb's face, to give sb a punch in the face; **je lui ai mis une bonne claque** I gave *or* landed him/her a good slap; **qu'est-ce que son père va lui m.!** his/her father is really going to give it to him/her!

15 *Vulg* (*posséder sexuellement*) to fuck, to screw, *Br* to shag; **se faire m.** to get fucked *or* laid; **va te faire m.!** up yours!, fuck off!

16 *Naut* **m. une voile au vent** to hoist *or* set a sail

17 (*locutions*) **m. les bouts** ou **les voiles** to make tracks, to hit the road; *très Fam* **on les met!** let's get out of here!

VI *Naut* **m. à la voile** to set sail

▶**se mettre VPR 1** (*dans une position, un endroit* → *chose*) to go; **où se mettent les tasses?** where do the cups go?; **les pieds, ça ne se met pas sur la table!** tables aren't made to put your feet on!

2 (*aller* → *vêtement*) to go; **le noir se met avec tout** black goes with everything

3 (*s'installer, s'établir* → *dans une position*) **se m. derrière un arbre** to go *or* get behind a tree; **se m. contre un mur** to stand *or* lean against a wall; **se m. devant qn** (*debout*) to stand in front of sb; (*assis*) to sit in front of sb; **se m. au lit** to get into bed; **se m. à table** to sit down at the table; **se m. au soleil/à l'ombre** to sit in the sunshine/shade; **se m. debout** to stand up; **se m. sur le dos/ventre** to lie (down) on one's back/stomach; **mets-toi sur cette chaise** sit on that chair; **mets-toi près de la fenêtre** (*debout*) stand near the window; (*assis*) sit near the window; **mettez-vous près du feu** sit (down) by the fire; **mettez-vous en cercle** arrange yourselves into *or* form a circle; **mettez-vous autour de grand-mère pour la photo** gather round grandmother for the photo; **mets-toi là et ne bouge plus** stand/sit there and don't move; **il est allé se m. au piano** he went and sat down at the piano; **je me mets dehors pour travailler** I go outside to work; **mettez-vous dans la position du lotus** get into the lotus position; *Belg* **mettez-vous!** take a seat!, sit down!; *Fig* **je ne savais plus où me m.** I didn't know where to put myself; **les mites se sont mises dans mon châle** the moths have got in my shawl; **se m. entre les mains d'un spécialiste** to place oneself in the hands of a specialist

4 (*entrer* → *dans un état, une situation*) **ne te mets pas dans un tel état!** don't get (yourself) into such a state!; **se m. en rage** to get into a rage; **il s'est mis dans une position difficile** he's got *or* put himself in a difficult situation

5 (*s'habiller*) **se m. en** to put on; **se m. en pantalon** to put on a pair of trousers; **se m. en civil** to dress in civilian clothes; **se m. en uniforme** to put on one's uniform; **elle se met toujours en jupe** she always wears a skirt; **elle ne se met jamais en pantalon/en rouge** she never wears trousers/red

6 (*s'unir*) **se m. avec qn** (*pour un jeu*) to team up with sb; (*dans une discussion*) to side with sb; *Fam* (*pour vivre*) to move in with sb; **se m. avec qn pour faire qch** to join forces with sb to do sth; **on a dû se m.** ou **s'y m. à trois pour bouger l'armoire** it took three of us to move the wardrobe; **on s'est tous mis ensemble pour acheter le cadeau** we all clubbed together to buy the present; **on s'est mis par équipes de six** we split up into *or* we formed teams of six (people)

7 *Vulg* **son contrat, il peut se le m. quelque part!** he can shove his contract up his *Br* arse *or Am* ass!

8 *Fam* **s'en m. jusque-là** to stuff oneself *or* one's

face; **qu'est-ce qu'on s'est mis!** we really stuffed ourselves *or* our faces!

9 *Fam* **qu'est-ce qu'ils se sont mis!** (*dans une bagarre*) they really laid into each other!, they were going at it hammer and tongs!

10 **se m. qch** to put sth on; **se m. une belle robe/du parfum** to put on a nice dress/some perfume; **se m. un nœud dans les cheveux** to put a bow in one's hair; **se m. du vernis à ongles** to put on nail varnish, to paint *or* varnish one's nails; **je n'ai rien à me m.!** I haven't got anything to wear *or* to put on!; **se m. de la crème sur les mains** to put some cream on one's hands; **je me suis mis de la peinture dans les cheveux/de la confiture sur les doigts** I've got paint in my hair/jam on my fingers; **se m. nu** to undress, to strip off

11 (*pour indiquer une évolution*) **quand le feu se met au rouge** when the lights turn *or* go red; **le temps se met au beau** it's getting sunny; **le temps se met au froid/à la pluie** it's getting *or* turning cold/starting to rain; *Fam* **ça se met à la neige** it looks like snow

12 **se m. à faire qch** (*commencer*) to start doing sth; **se m. à rire/chanter/pleurer** to begin *or* start to laugh/sing/cry, to start laughing/singing/crying; **il s'est mis à boire après le dessert** he started drinking after dessert; **c'est quand sa femme est morte qu'il s'est mis à boire** he started drinking *or* took to drink after his wife died; **se m. au régime** to put oneself on a diet, to go on a diet; **se m. au judo** to take up judo; **se m. à l'allemand** to start (learning) German; **se m. à l'ouvrage** ou **au travail** to set to work, to get down to work; **voilà qu'il se met à pleuvoir!** now it's started to rain *or* raining!; **s'y m.** (*au travail*) to get down to it; (*à une activité nouvelle*) to have a try; **si tu veux avoir l'examen, il faut que tu t'y mettes sérieusement!** if you want to pass the exam, you've really got to get down to some work!; **je n'ai jamais fait de piano, mais j'ai bien envie de m'y m.** I've never played the piano, but I'd quite like to have a try; *Fam* **si tu t'y mets aussi, je renonce!** if you join in as well, I give up!; *Fam* **elle est insupportable quand elle s'y met** she's unbearable once she gets started *or* going; *Fam* **si le (mauvais) temps s'y met, il faut annuler la kermesse** if the weather decides to turn bad, we'd better cancel the fête

Metz [mɛ(t)s] NM Metz

meublant, -e [mœblã, -ãt] ADJ *voir* **meuble** NM **2**

meuble [mœbl] ADJ **1** *Agr & Hort* loose, light

2 *Géol* crumbly, friable; **formation m.** crumb

3 *Jur* **biens meubles** movables, movable assets, personal estate

NM **1** (*élément du mobilier*) **un m.** a piece of furniture; **des meubles** furniture; **les meubles du salon** the furniture in the living room; **être dans ses meubles** to have a place of one's own; **êtes-vous dans vos meubles ici?** do you own the furniture here?; **quelques pauvres meubles** a few sticks of furniture; **m. de rangement** cupboard; **je manque de meubles de rangement** I don't have much storage space; **m. d'angle** corner unit; **meubles de bureau** office furniture; **des meubles de salon** living room furniture; **des meubles de style** period furniture; **m. urbain** street furniture; *Fam* **faire partie des meubles** to be part of the furniture

2 *Jur* movable; **en fait de meubles, possession vaut titre** (as far as goods and chattels are concerned) possession amounts to title; **meubles corporels** tangible assets *or* movables; **meubles à demeure** fixtures; **meubles incorporels** intangible assets *or* movables; **les meubles meublants** (household) furniture, movables

3 *Hér* charge

meublé, -e [mœble] ADJ furnished; **une maison meublée/non meublée** a furnished/an unfurnished house

NM (*une pièce*) furnished room; (*plusieurs pièces*) furnished *Br* flat *or Am* apartment; **habiter** ou **vivre en m.** to live in furnished accommodation

meubler [5] [mœble] VT **1** (*garnir de meubles*) to furnish; **ils ont meublé leur maison en Louis**

XIII they furnished their home in the Louis XIII style; **ils sont entièrement meublés en chêne** all their furniture is oak; **comment vas-tu m. la cuisine?** what sort of furniture are you going to put in the kitchen?; **une cellule meublée d'un lit et d'une table** a cell furnished with a bed and a table

2 (*remplir*) to fill; **m. le silence/sa solitude** to fill the silence/one's solitude; **pour m. la conversation** to stop the conversation from flagging, for the sake of conversation; **m. ses soirées en lisant** to spend one's evenings reading

▶**se meubler VPR** to buy (some) furniture; **alors, on se meuble?** so, you're furnishing the place, are you?; **meublez-vous chez Caudin** buy your furniture at Caudin's

meuf [mœf] NF *Fam* (*verlan de* **femme**) **1** (*fille*) chick, woman, *Br* bird **2** (*compagne*) girlfriend■, woman, *Br* bird

meuglement [møgləmã] NM **un m.** a moo; **le m. des vaches** the mooing of the cows; **des meuglements** mooing

meugler [5] [møgle] VI to moo

meuh [mø] NM moo; **faire m.** to moo

meulage [mølaʒ] NM grinding

meule [møl] NF **1** *Agr* stack, rick; **mettre en meules** to stack, to rick; **m. de foin** hayrick, haystack; **m. de paille** stack of straw

2 *Hort* **m. à champignons** mushroom bed

3 *Tech* (*grinding*) wheel; **m. à aiguiser** ou **affûter** grindstone; **m. à polir/à rectifier** polishing/trueing wheel

4 *Culin* **une m. de fromage** a (whole) cheese

5 (*d'un moulin*) millstone

6 *Suisse Fam* (*chose, personne fastidieuse*) bore, drag; **faire la m.** ou **des meules à qn** to hassle sb

7 *Fam* (*mobylette®*) moped

▫ **meules** NFPL *Fam* (*postérieur*) butt, *Br* bum, *Am* fanny

meuler [5] [møle] VT (*pour aiguiser*) to grind; (*pour éliminer*) to grind down; **machine/roue à m.** grinding machine/wheel

meulette [mølɛt] NF *Agr* (*de foin, de paille*) small stack *or* rick; (*de maïs*) stook, shock; **m. de foin** haycock; **mettre les gerbes en meulettes** to stook *or* shock the sheaves

meulière [møljɛr] ADJ F **pierre m.** millstone (grit)

NF **1** (*carrière*) millstone quarry **2** (*pierre*) millstone grit

meulon [mølɔ̃] NM *Agr* (*de foin, de paille*) small stack *or* rick

meunerie [mønri] NF **1** (*activité*) (flour) milling **2** (*commerce*) flour *or* milling trade **3** (*usine*) flour works (*singulier*)

meunier, -ère [mønje, -ɛr] ADJ flour-milling (*avant n*), milling (*avant n*)

NM **1** (*artisan*) miller; **échelle** ou **escalier de m.** narrow flight of steps **2** *Ich* miller's thumb, bullhead **3** *Entom* cockroach **4** *Orn* (*martin-pêcheur*) kingfisher

▫ **meunière** NF **1** (*épouse du meunier*) miller's wife **2** *Culin* **sole (à la) meunière** sole meunière (*coated with flour and fried in butter*)

meurette [mørɛt] NF *Culin* red wine sauce

meuron [mørɔ̃] NM *Suisse Bot* mulberry

meursault [mørso] NM Meursault (wine)

meurt *etc voir* **mourir**

Meurthe-et-Moselle [mœrtəmɔzɛl] NF **la M.** Meurthe-et-Moselle

meurtre [mœrtr] NM murder; **crier au m.** to scream blue murder; **m. avec préméditation** premeditated murder, *Am* ≃ first-degree murder; **m. sans préméditation** murder, *Am* ≃ second-degree murder

'**Meurtre dans un jardin anglais**' Greenaway 'The Draughtsman's Contract'

'**Petits meurtres entre amis**' Boyle 'Shallow Grave'

meurtri, -e [mœrtri] ADJ (*bras, fruit*) bruised; **visage m.** bruised *or* battered face; (*par la fatigue*) ravaged face; **être tout m.** to be black and blue all over; **il avait les mains meurtries par le froid** his hands were blue with cold; *Fig*

m. par l'indifférence de son fils wounded by his son's indifference; *Fig* **elle est sortie très meurtrie de cette expérience** she was bruised by the experience, it was a very bruising experience for her

meurtrier, -ère [mœrtrije, -ɛr] ADJ **1** *(qui tue → engin, lame)* deadly, lethal; *(→ guerre, attentat)* murderous; *(→ avalanche)* deadly, fatal; *(→ route)* lethal, murderous; *(→ folie, passion)* murderous; *(→ épidémie)* deadly; **une chasse à l'homme meurtrière** a bloody *or* murderous manhunt; **humour m.** lethal *or* devastating humour; **le lundi de Pâques est souvent m.** there are often a lot of deaths on the road on Easter Monday
  2 *Arch (personne)* murderous, guilty of murder
▸ NM,F murderer, *f* murderess
❑ **meurtrière** NF *Archit* (arrow) loophole

meurtrir [32] [mœrtrir] VT **1** *(contusionner)* to bruise **2** *Fig Littéraire* to hurt, to wound **3** *(poire, fleur)* to bruise

meurtrissure [mœrtrisyr] NF **1** *(contusion)* bruise **2** *Fig Littéraire* scar, wound; **les meurtrissures du cœur** sorrows of the heart **3** *(tache)* bruise; **des poires pleines de meurtrissures** pears covered in bruises

Meuse [møz] NF **la M.** the Meuse

meut *etc voir* **mouvoir**

meute [møt] NF *(de chiens)* pack; *Fig (de gens)* mob, crowd; **lancer la m.** to loose the pack *or* hounds; **la m. des créanciers** the mob of creditors; **une m. de paparazzi** a crowd *or* mob of paparazzi

meuvent *etc voir* **mouvoir**

MEV [mɛv] NF *Ordinat (abrév* **mémoire vive**) RAM

MeV *(abrév écrite* **méga-électronvolts**) MeV

mévente [mevɑ̃t] NF **1** *(baisse des ventes)* slump (in sales), slack period; **c'est une période de m. dans l'immobilier** the property market is experiencing a slump **2** *(vente à perte)* selling at a loss

mexicain, -e [mɛksikɛ̃, -ɛn] ADJ Mexican
❑ **Mexicain, -e** NM,F Mexican

Mexico [mɛksiko] NM Mexico City

Mexique [mɛksik] NM **le M.** Mexico; **vivre au M.** to live in Mexico; **aller au M.** to go to Mexico; **le golfe du M.** the Gulf of Mexico

mey [mɛj] = **meï**

mézail [mezaj] NM *Hist* mesail, vizor

mezcal [mɛzkal] NM mescal

mézigue [mezig] PRON *Fam* yours truly, *Br* muggins (here); **et qui est-ce qui va casquer? c'est m.!** and who's going to pay? yours truly *or Br* muggins here!

mezzanine [mɛdzanin] NF **1** *Archit (entresol)* mezzanine; *(fenêtre)* mezzanine window **2** *Théât (corbeille)* dress circle

mezza voce [mɛdzavɔtʃe] ADV mezza voce, in a low tone *or* voice

mezze [mɛdze] NMPL *Culin* meze

mezzo-soprano [mɛdzosoprano] *(pl* **mezzo-sopranos**) NM *(voix)* mezzo-soprano
▸ NF *(cantatrice)* mezzo-soprano

mezzotinto [mɛdzotinto] NM INV mezzotint

MF¹ [ɛmɛf] NF *Rad (abrév* **modulation de fréquence**) FM

MF² *Anciennement* **1** *(abrév écrite* **mark finlandais**) Mk, Fmk **2** *(abrév écrite* **million de francs**) a million francs, one million francs; **10 MF** 10 million francs

Mflops *Ordinat (abrév écrite* **mégaflops**) Mflop

mg *(abrév écrite* **milligramme**) mg

Mgr. *Rel (abrév écrite* **Monseigneur**) Mgr

MHD [ɛmaʃde] NF *Phys (abrév* **magnétohydrodynamique**) MHD

MHz *(abrév écrite* **megahertz**) MHz

mi [mi] NM INV **1** *(note)* E; *(chanté)* mi, me **2** *(d'un violon)* first string, E string

MI- [mi] PRÉF
This particle suggesting an INTERMEDIARY STATE is a very productive one, with several grammatical functions.
● It can be combined with adjectives to form a new adjectival expression, eg:
  des cheveux mi-longs shoulder-length hair; **les yeux mi-clos** with eyes half-closed
The adjective in **mi-** is often part of a succession of two such words, ie **mi-..., mi-...**, in combination

with adjectives or nouns. The English equivalent can be *half-..., half-...*, but sometimes it is necessary to use a different turn of phrase, eg:
  il la regardait, mi-amusé, mi-intrigué he was looking at her half-amused, half-puzzled; **une créature mi-homme, mi-bête** a creature that is half-man, half-beast; **un sourire mi-figue, mi-raisin** a quizzical smile
● The prefix **mi-** can be attached to a noun and preceded by **à** or **jusqu'à**, thus forming an adverbial expression, usually relating to DISTANCE or LEVEL. The translation often includes the word *halfway*, eg:
  à mi-chemin halfway; **à mi-course** halfway through the race; **à mi-pente** halfway up/down the hill; **à mi-parcours** halfway along (the route); **elle avait de l'eau jusqu'à mi-jambe** the water came halfway up her legs
● When joined to a noun, **mi-** can be used to form feminine nouns relating to TIME, eg:
  la première mi-temps the first half (of the game); **à la mi-juillet** mid-July

miam [mjam], **miam-miam** [mjamjam] EXCLAM *Fam* yum-yum!; **m.-miam, ça a l'air bon** that looks yummy

Miami [mjami] NM Miami

miaou [mjau] NM miaow; **faire m.** to miaow

miasmatique [mjasmatik] ADJ *Littéraire* miasmatic

miasme [mjasm] NM *Littéraire* miasma; **des miasmes** miasmas, miasmata

miaulement [mjolmɑ̃] NM miaowing, mewing; **on entendait de terribles miaulements dans la cour** some cats were making a dreadful noise in the courtyard

miauler [3] [mjole] VI to miaow, to mew

miauleur, -euse [mjolœr, -øz] ADJ miaowing, mewing

mi-bas [miba] NM INV *(en laine)* knee-high *or* knee-length sock; *(en voile)* popsock

mi-bois [mibwa] **à mi-bois** ADJ *Menuis* **assemblage** *ou* **enture à m.** half-lap joint

mica [mika] NM **1** *(roche)* mica **2** *(vitre)* Muscovy glass

micacé, -e [mikase] ADJ micaceous

mi-carême [mikarɛm] *(pl* **mi-carêmes**) NF **à la m.** on the third Thursday of Lent

micaschiste [mikaʃist] NM mica schist

micellaire [misɛlɛr] ADJ *Chim* micellar

micelle [misɛl] NF *Chim* micella, micelle

miche [miʃ] NF **1** *(pain)* round loaf **2** *Belg & Suisse (petit pain)* (bread) roll
❑ **miches** NFPL *Fam (fesses)* butt, *Br* bum, *Am* fanny; *(seins)* knockers, boobs; **avoir les miches à zéro** to be scared stiff; **vire tes miches** move yourself, move your backside; **gare à tes miches** mind yourself

Michée [miʃe] NPR *Bible* Micah

Michel-Ange [mikelɑ̃ʒ] NPR Michelangelo

micheline [miʃlin] NF railcar

mi-chemin [miʃmɛ̃] **à mi-chemin** ADV halfway, midway; **s'arrêter à m.** to stop halfway; **nous sommes à m.** we're halfway there
❑ **à mi-chemin de** PRÉP halfway to; **à m. de Lyon** halfway to Lyons; **à m. de l'église et de l'école** halfway *or* midway between the church and the school

micheton [miʃtɔ̃] NM *Fam Arg crime esp Br* punter, *Am* john; **elle s'est fait cinq michetons dans la soirée** she turned five tricks that evening

michetonner [3] [miʃtɔne] VI *Fam Arg crime* to turn the occasional trick

Michigan [miʃigɑ̃] NM *Géog* **le M.** Michigan; **au M.** in Michigan; **le lac M.** Lake Michigan

Mickey [mike] NPR Mickey Mouse

mickey [mikɛ] NM *Fam* nobody■, nonentity■

mi-clos, -e [miklo, -kloz] ADJ half-closed

micmac [mikmak] NM *Fam* **1** *(affaire suspecte)* funny *or* fishy business, strange carry-on; **des micmacs financiers** financial wheeler-dealing **2** *(complications)* muddle, shambles; **ça a été tout un m. pour pouvoir entrer** trying to get in was a real performance **3** *Can Fam (désordre)* mess■; **as-tu nettoyé le m. dans ta chambre?** have you cleaned up the mess in your room?

micocoulier [mikokulje] NM nettle tree

micoquien, -enne [mikɔkjɛ̃, -ɛn] ADJ Micoquian
▸ NM Micoquian

mi-corps [mikɔr] **à mi-corps** ADV *(à partir du bas)* up to the waist; *(à partir du haut)* down to the waist; **portrait à m.** half-length portrait; **l'eau nous arrivait à m.** the water came up to our waists

mi-côte [mikot] **à mi-côte** ADV *(en partant du bas)* halfway up the hill; *(en partant du haut)* halfway down the hill

micouenne [mikwan] NF *Can* wooden ladle

mi-course [mikurs] **à mi-course** ADV halfway through the race, at the halfway mark

micro [mikro] NM **1** *(microphone)* mike; *(tenu à la main)* baton *or* stick mike; **parler dans le m.** to speak into the mike; **m. bidirectionnel** bidirectional mike; **m. caché** concealed mike; **m. canon** rifle *or* gun mike; **m. cardioïde** cardioid mike; **m. sur casque** headphone talkback; **m. à condensateur** condenser mike; **m. directionnel** directional mike; **m. électro-dynamique** dynamic mike; **m. électrostatique** condenser mike; **m. sur girafe** boom mike; **m. sur perche** boom mike; **m. sur pied** stand mike; **m. portatif** hand mike; **m. à ruban** ribbon mike; **m. sans fil** radio mike; **m. suspendu** hung *or* hanging *or* slung mike; **m. de table** desk mike
  2 *Fam (micro-ordinateur)* PC■
▸ NF *Fam* microcomputing■

micro- [mikro] PRÉF micro-

microalvéole [mikroalveɔl] NF *(sur disque compact)* pit

microampère [mikroɑ̃pɛr] NM microampere

microanalyse [mikroanaliz] NF microanalysis

microbalance [mikrobalɑ̃s] NF microbalance

microbe [mikrob] NM **1** *Biol* germ, *Spéc* microbe; **attraper un m.** to catch a bug **2** *Fam (personne)* shrimp, (little) runt *or* pipsqueak

microbicide [mikrobisid] *Vieilli* ADJ bactericidal, germ-killing
▸ NM bactericide, germ-killer

microbien, -enne [mikrobjɛ̃, -ɛn] ADJ *Biol (relatif aux microbes)* microbial, microbic; *(causé par les microbes)* bacterial

microbille [mikrobij] NF **1** *Métal* micronized shot (particle) **2** *(de pigment)* micronized pigment particle

microbiologie [mikrobjɔlɔʒi] NF microbiology

microbiologique [mikrobjɔlɔʒik] ADJ microbiological

microbiologiste [mikrobjɔlɔʒist] NMF microbiologist

microbouturage [mikrobutyraʒ] NM *Biol* micropropagation

microbrasserie [mikrobrasri] NF *Can (brasserie artisanale)* microbrewery; *(établissement où l'on consomme de la bière)* = pub attached to a microbrewery

microbus [mikrobys] NM minibus

microcalorimètre [mikrokalorimɛtr] NM microcalorimeter

microcalorimétrie [mikrokalorimetri] NF microcalorimetry

microcassette [mikrokasɛt] NF microcassette

microcéphale [mikrosefal] ADJ microcephalic
▸ NMF microcephalic

microcéphalie [mikrosefali] NF microcephaly

microchimie [mikroʃimi] NF microchemistry

microchirurgie [mikroʃiryrʒi] NF microsurgery

microcircuit [mikrosirkɥi] NM *Ordinat* microcircuit; **microcircuits** microcircuitry

microclimat [mikroklima] NM microclimate

microcline [mikroklin] NM *Minér* microcline

micrococcus [mikrokɔkys] NM *Biol* micrococcus

microcode [mikrokod] NM microcode

microcopie [mikrokɔpi] NF microcopy

microcoque [mikrokɔk] NM *Biol* micrococcus

microcosme [mikrokɔsm] NM microcosm

microcosmique [mikrokɔsmik] ADJ microcosmic

microcoupure [mikrokupyr] NF *Électron* power blip

micro-cravate [mikrokravat] *(pl* **micros-cravates**) NM lapel mike

microcrédit [mikrokredi] NM *Fin* microcredit

microcristal, -aux [mikrokristal, -o] NM microcrystal

microcuvette [mikrokyvɛt] NF *(sur disque compact)* pit

microcyte [mikrosit] NF *Physiol* microcyte

microcytose [mikrositoz] NF *Méd* microcytosis

microdisquette [mikrodiskɛt] NF *Ordinat* micro-floppy

microdissection [mikrodisɛksjɔ̃] NF *Biol* microdissection

microdrome [mikrodrom] NM *Mil* micro air vehicle, MAV

microéconomie [mikroekonomi] NF microeconomics *(singulier)*

microéconomique [mikroekonomik] ADJ microeconomic

microécosystème [mikroekosistɛm] NM microhabitat

microédition [mikroedisjɔ̃] NF desktop publishing

microélectronique [mikroelɛktronik] ADJ microelectronic
NF microelectronics *(singulier)*

micro-émetteur [mikroemɛtœr] *(pl* **micros-émetteurs***)* NM radio mike

microentreprise [mikroɑ̃trəpriz] NF microenterprise, microbusiness

micro-État [mikroeta] *(pl* **micro-États***)* NM *Pol* statelet, microstate

microfaune [mikrofon] NF *Écol* microfauna

microfibre [mikrofibr] NF microfibre

microfiche [mikrofiʃ] NF microfiche

microfilament [mikrofilamɑ̃] NM *Biol* microfilament

microfilm [mikrofilm] NM microfilm

microfilmer [3] [mikrofilme] VT to microfilm

microfinance [mikrofinɑ̃s] NF microfinance

microflore [mikroflor] NF *Biol* microflora

microforme [mikroform] NF microform

microfossile [mikrofosil] NM microfossil

microfractographie [mikrofraktografi] NF *Tech* microfractography

microglobuline [mikroglobylin] NF *Biol* microglobulin

micrographie [mikrografi] NF **1** *(science)* micrography **2** *(photographie)* micrograph **3** *Métal* microstructural microscopy

micrographique [mikrografik] ADJ micrographic

microgravité [mikrogravite] NF microgravity

microgrenu, -e [mikrogrəny] ADJ *Géol* microgranular

microhabitat [mikroabita] NM microhabitat

micro-informatique [mikroɛ̃formatik] *(pl* **micro-informatiques***)* NF microcomputing

micro-intervalle [mikroɛ̃tɛrval] *(pl* **micro-intervalles***)* NM *Mus* microinterval

micro-irrigation [mikroirigasjɔ̃] *(pl* **micro-irrigations***)* NF microirrigation

microlinguistique [mikrolɛ̃ɡɥistik] NF microlinguistics *(singulier)*

microlite [mikrolit] NM *Minér* microcrystal, microlite

microlithe [mikrolit] NM *Archéol* microlith

micromanipulation [mikromanipylasjɔ̃] NF *Tech* micromanipulation

micromarketing [mikromarketiŋ] NM micromarketing

micromécanique [mikromekanik] NF micromechanics *(singulier)*

micrométéorite [mikrometeorit] NF micrometeorite

micrométéorologie [mikrometeorolɔʒi] NF micrometeorology

micromètre [mikromɛtr] NM **1** *(instrument)* micrometer **2** *(unité)* micrometre

micrométrie [mikrometri] NF micrometry

micrométrique [mikrometrik] ADJ micrometric, micrometrical

micromodule [mikromodyl] NM micromodule

micromutation [mikromytasjɔ̃] NF *Biol* micromutation

micron [mikrɔ̃] NM micron

Micronésie [mikronezi] NF *Géog* **la M.** Micronesia; **vivre en M.** to live in Micronesia; **aller en M.** to go to Micronesia

micronésien, -enne [mikronezjɛ̃, -ɛn] ADJ Micronesian
□ **Micronésien, -enne NM,F** Micronesian

micronisation [mikronizasjɔ̃] NF **1** *Ordinat* downsizing **2** *Phys* micronization

microniser [3] [mikronize] VT **1** *Ordinat* to downsize **2** *Phys* to micronize

micronutriment [mikronytrimɑ̃] NM *Physiol* micronutrient

micro-ondable [mikroɔ̃dabl] *(pl* **micro-ondables***)* ADJ microwaveable

micro-onde [mikroɔ̃d] *(pl* **micro-ondes***)* NF microwave
□ **micro-ondes NM INV** microwave (oven); **faites dégeler au micro-ondes** defrost in the microwave; **faire cuire qch au micro-ondes** to cook sth in the microwave, to microwave sth

micro-ordinateur [mikroordinatœr] *(pl* **micro-ordinateurs***)* NM microcomputer; **m. de bureau** desktop computer; **m. portable** laptop (computer)

micro-organisme [mikroorganism] *(pl* **micro-organismes***)* NM *Biol* microorganism

micro-paiement [mikropɛmɑ̃] *(pl* **micro-paiements***)* NM *Ordinat* micropayment

micropaléontologie [mikropaleɔ̃tolɔʒi] NF micropaleontology

micropesanteur [mikropəzɑ̃tœr] NF microgravity

microphage [mikrofaʒ] NM *Biol* microphage

microphone [mikrofon] NM microphone; **m. à condensateur** condenser microphone; **m. sur girafe** sound-boom microphone; **m. sur pied** stand microphone

microphonique [mikrofonik] ADJ microphonic

microphotographie [mikrofotografi] NF **1** *(technique)* microphotography **2** *(image)* microphotograph

microphotographique [mikrofotografik] ADJ microphotographic, photomicrographic

microphysique [mikrofizik] NF microphysics *(singulier)*

micropilule [mikropilyl] NF minipill

microplaquette [mikroplakɛt] NF *Électron* chip

micropodiforme [mikropodiform] *Orn* NM member of the order of Micropodiformes
□ **micropodiformes NMPL** Micropodiformes

microprocesseur [mikroprosesœr] NM *Ordinat* microprocessor; **m. en tranches** bit slice microprocessor

microprogrammation [mikroprogramasjɔ̃] NF *Ordinat* microprogramming

microprogramme [mikroprogram] NM *Ordinat* microprogram, firmware

micropropagation [mikropropagasjɔ̃] NF *Biol* micropropagation

micropsie [mikropsi] NF *Méd* micropsia, micropsy

micropyle [mikropil] NM *Biol & Bot* micropyle

microsatellite [mikrosatelit] NM microsatellite

microscope [mikroskop] NM microscope; **visible au m.** visible under the microscope; **étudier qch au m.** to examine sth under or through a microscope; *Fig* to put sth under the microscope; **m. à effet tunnel** tunnel effect microscope; **m. électronique** electron microscope; **m. électronique à balayage** scanning electron microscope; **m. optique** optical or light microscope

microscopie [mikroskopi] NF microscopy

microscopique [mikroskopik] ADJ microscopic; *Fig (petit)* microscopic, tiny, minute

microsegment [mikrosɛɡmɑ̃] NM *Mktg* microsegment

microsegmentation [mikrosɛɡmɑ̃tasjɔ̃] NF *Mktg* microsegmentation

microséisme [mikroseism] NM microseism

microserveur [mikrosɛrvœr] NM *Ordinat* microserver

microsillon [mikrosijɔ̃] NM *(sillon)* microgroove; **(disque) m.** record

microsite [mikrosit] NM *Ordinat* microsite

microsociologie [mikrososjolɔʒi] NF microsociology

microsociologique [mikrososjolɔʒik] ADJ microsociological

microsome [mikrosom] NF *Biol* microsome

microsonde [mikrosɔ̃d] NF microprobe

microsporange [mikrospɔrɑʒ] NM *Bot* microsporange, microsporangium

microspore [mikrospɔr] NF *Bot* microspore

microstation [mikrostasjɔ̃] NF **m. (terrienne)** VSAT

microstructure [mikrostryktyr] NF microstructure

microtechnique [mikrotɛknik] NF microtechnology

microtome [mikrotom] NM *Biol* microtome

microtracteur [mikrotraktœr] NM microtractor

microtraumatisme [mikrotromatism] NM *Méd* microtraumatism

micro-trottoir [mikrotrotwar] *(pl* **micros-trottoirs***)* NM street interview, *Br Fam* vox pop

microtubule [mikrotybyl] NM *Biol* microtubule

microvillosité [mikrovilozite] NF *Anat* microvillus

microvoiture [mikrovwatyr] NF microcar

miction [miksjɔ̃] NF urination, *Spéc* micturition

Midas [midas] NPR Midas

MidCAC [midkak] NM *Bourse* **le M., l'indice M.** = Paris stock exchange index comprising 100 medium-range shares, ≃ MidCap

middle jazz [midœldʒaz] NM INV mainstream (jazz)

middlemaat [midəlmat] NM *Belg (juste milieu)* mainstream, middle ground; *Péj (médiocrité)* mediocrity, second-rateness

middlematig [midəlmatig] ADJ INV *Belg (intermédiaire)* middle-of-the-road; *Péj (indécis → personne)* dithering, indecisive

MIDEM, Midem [midɛm] NM *(abrév* **Marché international du disque et de l'édition musicale***)* = trade fair for the music industry which takes place annually in Cannes

MIDI [midi] NM *(abrév* **musical instrument digital interface***)* MIDI

midi¹ [midi] NM **1** *(milieu du jour)* midday, lunchtime, noon; **en plein m.** at the height of noon; **qu'est-ce que tu fais, ce m.?** what are you doing at lunchtime or for lunch?; **je m'arrête à m.** I stop at lunchtime; *(pour déjeuner)* I stop for lunch; **je joue au squash à m.** *(pendant la pause)* I play squash at lunchtime; **tous les midis** every day at lunchtime, every lunchtime; **il mange des pâtes tous les midis** he has pasta for lunch every day; *Fig* **voir m. à sa porte** to be wrapped up in oneself
2 *(heure)* midday, twelve (o'clock), (twelve) noon; **il est m.** it's midday, it's twelve (noon); **il est m. passé** it's after twelve, it's past midday; **m. et demi** half-past twelve; **m. et quart** a quarter past twelve; **m. moins vingt** twenty to twelve; **entre m. et deux (heures)** between twelve and two, during lunch or lunchtime; **fermé de m. à 14 h** closed from 12 to 2 p.m.; **vers m.** round (about) twelve or midday; **sur le coup de m.** on the stroke of twelve
3 *(sud)* south; **exposé au m.** south-facing, facing south
4 *Littéraire (milieu)* **au m. de sa vie** in the middle of his/her life
□ **Midi NM** *(région du sud)* South; **le M. (de la France)** the South of France; **du M.** Southern, southern; **le climat du M.** the Southern climate; **l'accent du M.** southern (French) accent
□ **de midi** ADJ *(repas, informations)* midday *(avant n)*; **la pause de m.** the lunch break

midi² [midi] ADJ INV *(de taille moyenne)* **chaîne m.** midi system

midinette [midinɛt] NF **1** *Fam Vieilli (cousette)* dressmaker's apprentice, seamstress **2** *Péj (jeune fille)* starry-eyed girl; **des amours de m.** the loves of some starry-eyed young girl; **des lectures de m.** slushy novels

Midi-Pyrénées [midipirene] NM Midi-Pyrénées

mi-distance [midistɑ̃s] **à mi-distance** ADV halfway, midway
□ **à mi-distance de PRÉP** halfway or midway between; **nous sommes à m. de notre but** we are halfway to our goal

midrash [midraʃ] NM *Rel* Midrash

midship [midʃip] NM *Fam Naut* middy

Midwest [midwɛst] NM **le M.** the Midwest

mie¹ [mi] NF *(de pain)* white or soft or doughy part; **mettez de la m. de pain à tremper** soak some bread, having removed the crusts
□ **à la mie de pain** ADJ *Fam Vieilli (minable)* pathetic, crummy; **un petit truand à la m. de pain** a small-time crook, *Am* a two-bit crook

mie² [mi] NF *Arch & Littéraire (femme)* truelove, ladylove; **ma m.** my beloved; **venez, ma m.** come, fair damsel

miel [mjɛl] NM **1** *(d'abeilles)* honey; **m. liquide/solide/rosat** clear/set/rose honey; **m. d'acacia** acacia honey **2** *(locutions)* **faire son m. de qch** to make capital out of sth; **il est (tout sucre) tout m.** he's a sweet talker
EXCLAM *Fam Euph* sugar!
□ **au miel** ADJ honey *(avant n)*, honey-flavoured

miellat [mjela] NM honeydew *(secreted by insects)*

miellé, -e [mjele] ADJ *Littéraire (parfum)* honeyed; *(boisson)* tasting of honey; **du thé m.** honey-sweetened tea; **la couleur miellée de ses cheveux** the golden colour of his/her hair
❑ **miellée** NF *Bot* honeydew *(exuded by plants)*

mielleuse [mjɛløz] *voir* **mielleux**

mielleusement [mjɛløzmɑ̃] ADV smarmily; **sourire m.** to give a sweet, sugary smile; **il s'exprime m.** he's a sweet talker

mielleux, -euse [mjɛlø, -øz] ADJ **1** *Péj (doucereux)* sickly sweet; *(personne)* sugary; **un sourire m.** a saccharine smile; **d'un ton m.** in a syrupy voice; **un discours m.** a speech oozing with insincerity **2** *(relatif au miel)* honey *(avant n)*, honey-like

mien, mienne [mjɛ̃, mjɛn] *(mpl* **miens,** *fpl* **miennes)** ADJ *Littéraire* **c'est un principe que j'ai fait m. depuis longtemps** it has long been a principle of mine; **j'ai fait m. ce mot d'ordre** I've adopted this slogan as my own; **je fais miennes les félicitations qu'il vous adresse** I join (with) him in congratulating you; **une mienne cousine** a cousin of mine
❑ **le mien, la mienne** *(mpl* **les miens,** *fpl* **les miennes)** PRON mine; **je te prête le m.** you can borrow mine; **vous avez entendu son point de vue; voici le m.** you've heard his/her point of view; here is mine; **puis-je prendre ta voiture? la mienne est au garage** may I take your car? mine is at the garage; **je suis parti avec une valise qui n'était pas la mienne** I left with a suitcase that wasn't mine *or* that didn't belong to me; **il ressemble au m.** it looks like mine; **je veux bien te donner du m.** please have some of mine; **tes enfants sont plus âgés que les miens** your children are older than mine (are); **ce parapluie n'est pas le m.** this is not my umbrella, this umbrella is not mine; **vos préoccupations sont aussi les miennes** I share your anxieties; **ton jour/ton prix sera le m.** name the day/your price; **les deux miens** my two, both of mine; *(en insistant)* my own two; **je lui ai laissé deux des miens** I gave him/her two of mine; *très Fam* **le m. de bébé est plus intelligent** my baby is more intelligent▪; *Fam* **à la mienne!** *(en buvant)* here's to me!
NM **j'y mets du m.** *(en faisant des efforts)* I'm making an effort; *(en étant compréhensif)* I'm trying to be understanding; *Fam* **j'ai encore fait des miennes!** I've (gone and) done it again!
❑ **les miens** NMPL *(ma famille)* my family, *Am* my folks; *(mes partisans)* my followers; *(mes coéquipiers)* my team-mates

miette [mjɛt] NF **1** *(d'aliment)* crumb; **une m. de pain** a crumb of bread; **des miettes de pain** breadcrumbs; **des miettes de crabe/de thon** crab/tuna flakes
2 *(petite quantité)* **pas une m. de** not a shred of; **tu n'en auras pas une m.!** you're not getting any of it!; **ils n'en ont pas laissé une m.** they didn't leave a crumb, they ate the lot; **elle n'a pas perdu une m. de la conversation** not one scrap of the conversation escaped her *or* passed her by; **une m. de** a little bit of; **du gâteau? – j'en prendrai une m.** some cake? – I'll have just a tiny bit
3 *Belg (locution)* **une m.** a bit, a little
❑ **miettes** NFPL **1** *(restes)* leftovers, crumbs, scraps; **après le partage, ma cousine n'a eu que des miettes** my cousin had to make do with what little was left over after the inheritance was shared out
2 *(morceaux)* piece, fragment, bit; **mettre** *ou* **réduire qch en miettes** *(objet)* to smash sth to pieces *or* bits *or* smithereens; **sa voiture est en miettes** his/her car's a wreck; **son rêve est en miettes** his/her dream is in shreds *or* tatters

MIEUX [mjø]

ADV	better **A, B, C** ■ best **B**
ADJ	better **1–3**
NM	improvement **1** ■ best **2**

ADV **A.** *COMPARATIF DE "BIEN"* **1** *(d'une manière plus satisfaisante)* better; **tout va m.** things are better (now); **elle va m.** she's better; **il travaille m. depuis quelque temps** he's been working better for some time *or* a while now; **cette jupe te va m.** *(d'aspect)* that skirt suits you better; *(de taille)* that skirt fits you better; **le vert me va m.** green suits me better; **qui dit m.?** *(aux enchères)* any advance (on that)?, any more bids?; *Fig* who can top that?; **repassez demain, je ne peux pas vous dire m.** come again tomorrow, that's the best *or* all I can tell you; **je m'y prends m. depuis** I'm handling it better now, I've got better at it since; **il s'y prend m. avec lui maintenant** he deals with *or* handles him better now; **m. prendre qch** to take sth better; **cette fois-ci, elle a m. pris la plaisanterie** this time she took the joke better; **m. payé** better paid; **m. assis** *(plus confortablement)* sitting more comfortably; *(au spectacle)* in a better seat; **un peu m.** a little *or* a bit better; **beaucoup** *ou* **bien m.** a lot *or* much better; **vraiment m.** much better; **depuis un mois, elle va vraiment m.** she's been feeling much better for the past month; **se sentir m.** to feel better; **moins je le vois, m. je me porte!** the less I see of him, the better I feel!; **plus je le lis, m. je le comprends** the more I read it, the better I understand it; **il parle italien m. que je ne pensais** he speaks Italian better than I thought; **il ne lit pas m. qu'il ne parle** he doesn't read any better than he speaks
2 *(conformément à la raison, à la morale)* better; **il se comporte m.** he's behaving better; **pas m.** no better; **son frère ne fait que des bêtises, et elle ce n'est pas m.** her brother is always misbehaving and she's no better; **il ferait m. de travailler/de se taire** he'd do better to work/to keep quiet; **il pourrait m. faire** he could do better; **on ne peut pas m. dire** you can't say better *or* fairer than that
B. *SUPERLATIF DE "BIEN"* **le m.** *(de deux)* the better; *(de plusieurs)* the best; **c'est le mannequin le m. payé** *(des deux)* she's the better-paid model; *(de plusieurs)* she's the best-paid model; **voilà ce qui me convient le m.** this is what suits me best; **des deux, qui est la m.?** who's the better of the two?; **la m. de toutes** the best of them all; **le m. qu'il peut** the best he can; **le m. possible** as well as possible; **j'ai classé les dossiers le m. possible** I filed everything as best I could; **le m. du monde** beautifully; **il parlait, oh, le m. du monde!** he spoke, oh, so beautifully!; **s'entendre le m. du monde avec qn** to be on the best of terms with sb
C. *EMPLOI NOMINAL* better; **c'est pas mal, mais il y a m.** it's not bad, but there's better; **en attendant/espérant m.** while waiting/hoping for better (things); **il s'attendait à m., il attendait m.** he was expecting (something) better; **faute de m., je m'en contenterai** since there's nothing better, I'll make do with it; **c'est sa mère en m.** she's like her mother, only better-looking; **changer en m.** to take a turn for *or* to change for the better
ADJ **1** *(plus satisfaisant)* better; **voilà, c'est déjà beaucoup m.!** there, it's already much *or* a lot better!; **se taire est beaucoup m.** it's much better not to say anything; **on ne se voit plus, c'est m. ainsi** we don't see each other any more, it's better that way; **ça ne vous semble pas m. comme ça?** don't you think it's better that way?; **c'était m. que jamais** it was better than ever; **c'est m. que rien** it's better than nothing; **le dernier modèle est m. que le précédent** the latest model is better than *or* is an improvement on the previous one
2 *(du point de vue de la santé, du bien-être)* better; **il est m.** he's better; **on sent qu'il est m. dans sa peau** you can tell he's feeling better about himself; **tu seras m. en pantalon** you'd be better in trousers; **on est m. dans ce fauteuil** this armchair is more comfortable
3 *(plus beau)* better; **elle est m. avec les cheveux courts** she looks better with short hair; **prends cette robe, elle est m. que l'autre** take this dress, it's better than the other (one); **elle est m. que sa sœur** she's better-looking than her sister
NM **1** *(amélioration)* improvement; **il y a du m.** things have got better, there's some improvement; **il y a un m.** there is an improvement; **la situation connaît un léger m.** the situation has improved slightly, there's been a slight improvement in the situation
2 *(ce qui est préférable)* **le m. est de ne pas y aller** it's best not to go; **le m., c'est de partir un peu plus tôt** it's best to leave a bit earlier; **faire de son m.** to do one's (level) best; **il a fait de son m.** he did his best; *Prov* **le m. est l'ennemi du bien** the best is the enemy of the good
❑ **à qui mieux mieux** ADV **les enfants répondaient à qui m. m.** the children were trying to outdo each other in answering
❑ **au mieux** ADV **faire au m.** to do whatever's best, to act for the best; **ils sont au m. (l'un avec l'autre)** they're on very good terms; **en mettant les choses au m.** at best; **vous l'aurez lundi, en mettant les choses au m.** you'll get it on Monday at the very earliest; **au m. de sa forme** on top form, in prime condition; **j'ai agi au m. de vos intérêts** I acted in your best interest; *Bourse* **acheter/vendre au m.** to buy/sell at the best price
❑ **de mieux** ADJ **1** *(de plus satisfaisant)* **c'est ce que nous avons de m.** it's the best we have; **si tu n'as rien de m. à faire, viens avec moi** if you've got nothing better to do, come with me
2 *(de plus)* **j'ai mis 30 euros de m.** I added an extra 30 euros
❑ **de mieux en mieux** ADV better and better; **elle joue de m. en m.** she plays better and better; *Ironique* **et maintenant, de m. en m., j'ai perdu mes clefs!** and now, to cap it all, I've lost my keys!; *Ironique* **de m. en m.!** it gets better!
❑ **des mieux** ADV **j'ai un ami qui est des m. placé** *ou* **placés au ministère** I have a friend who's high up in the ministry; *Arch ou Littéraire* **il chante des m.** he sings extremely well
❑ **on ne peut mieux** ADV extremely well; **il s'exprime on ne peut m.** he expresses himself extremely well; **le stage va on ne peut m.** the course couldn't be going better
❑ **pour le mieux** ADV for the best; **tout va pour le m.** everything is for the best; **faire pour le m.** to act for the best
❑ **qui mieux est** ADV even better, better still

mieux-disant [mjødizɑ̃] *(pl* **mieux-disants)** NM elite

mieux-être [mjøzɛtr] NM INV better quality of life

mieux-vivre [mjøvivr] NM INV better *or* higher standard of living; **la lutte pour le m.** the struggle for a better *or* higher standard of living

mièvre [mjɛvr] ADJ *Péj* **1** *(fade)* insipid, vapid, bland; *(sentimental)* mawkish, syrupy; **un roman m.** a mawkish novel **2** *(maniéré)* mawkish, precious; **avec une grâce un peu m.** demurely; **sa façon un peu m. de dire bonjour** his/her slightly simpering *or Br* twee way of saying hello **3** *(joli sans vrai talent → dessin)* pretty-pretty, flowery

mièvrement [mjɛvrəmɑ̃] ADV *Péj* **1** *(fadement)* insipidly, vapidly, blandly **2** *(sentimentalement)* mawkishly, in a syrupy *or* sickly-sweet manner **3** *(joliment)* in a pretty-pretty way

mièvrerie [mjɛvrəri] NF *Péj* **1** *(fadeur)* insipidness; *(sentimentalité)* mawkishness; *(caractère maniéré)* sickly affectation; *(joliesse)* floweriness, insipid prettiness **2** *(acte)* mawkish behaviour *(UNCOUNT)*; *(propos)* mawkish *or Br* twee remark; **ces mièvreries qu'on nous sert à la télé** these stupid programmes *or* the pap they show on TV

mi-fer [mifɛr] **à mi-fer** ADJ *Métal* **assemblage** *ou* **enture à m.** half-lap joint

mi-fin, -e [mifɛ̃, -fin] *(mpl* **mi-fins,** *fpl* **mi-fines)** ADJ *Com* medium

migmatite [migmatit] NF *Géol* migmatite

mignard, -e [miɲar, -ard] ADJ *Littéraire (gracieux)* dainty; *Péj (affecté)* affected

mignardise [miɲardiz] NF **1** *Littéraire (grâce)* daintiness; *Péj (affectation)* affectedness **2** *Bot* **(œillet) m.** garden pink

mignon, -onne [miɲɔ̃, -ɔn] ADJ **1** *(joli → enfant, chiot)* sweet, cute; *(→ femme)* pretty; **il est si m. avec ses fossettes** he's got the cutest dimples; **elle est plus mignonne avec les cheveux courts** she's prettier with short hair; **il est m., ton appartement** you've got a lovely little *Br* flat *or Am* apartment; **c'est m. comme tout chez eux** they have a delightful *or* charming home;

Fam **c'est m. tout plein à cet âge-là** children are as cute as anything at that age; *Fam* **un mec super m.** a great-looking guy

2 *Fam (gentil)* sweet■, nice■, lovely■; **il m'a apporté des fleurs, c'était m. comme tout** he brought me flowers, it was so sweet of him; **allez, sois mignonne, va te coucher** come on, be a darling *or* sweetie and go to bed

NM,F *Fam (terme d'affection)* darling, sweetie; **ma mignonne** darling, sweetie

NM *Hist* minion, favourite

> *Allusion*
>
> **Mignonne, allons voir si la rose**
>
> This is the first line of a sonnet by Ronsard, from *Les Amours* (1552), dedicated to Cassandre. In the poem, the poet turns to the theme beloved of antiquity, *carpe diem* (ie "seize the day, enjoy the present"), and celebrates his lady as the inspiration for Platonic love. In this line, the poet invites his "darling" to come with him into the garden to look at a rose, to see how it has changed since the previous day. Today people use the expression jokingly, substituting words for **la rose**, when they propose doing something with a friend.

mignonnet, -ette [miɲɔnɛ, -ɛt] **ADJ** pretty-pretty

❑ **mignonnette NF 1** *Bot (réséda)* mignonette; *(saxifrage)* London pride; *(œillet mignardise)* garden pink; *(chicorée sauvage)* wild chicory **2** *(poivre)* coarse-ground pepper **3** *(gravillon)* small gravel **4** *(bouteille miniature)* miniature (bottle) **5** *Tex* mignonette lace

mignoter [3] [miɲɔte] **VT** *Fam Vieilli (dorloter)* to pamper

migraine [migrɛn] **NF** *(mal de tête)* bad headache; *Méd* migraine; **avoir la m.** to have a bad headache; **avoir des migraines** to get bad headaches/migraines; *Fig* **ces formulaires à remplir, c'est à vous donner la m.** filling in these forms is a real headache; **m. ophtalmique** headache caused by eyestrain

migraineux, -euse [migrɛnø, -øz] *Méd* **ADJ** migrainous

NM,F migraine sufferer

migrant, -e [migrɑ̃, -ɑ̃t] **ADJ** migrant *(avant n)*

NM,F migrant; **m. économique** economic refugee; **m. en situation irrégulière** irregular migrant

migrateur, -trice [migratœr, -tris] **ADJ** *Biol & Zool* migratory

NM *(oiseau)* migrator, migrant

migration [migrasjɔ̃] **NF 1** *(des oiseaux, des travailleurs)* migration; *Fig* **les grandes migrations estivales vont commencer** the mass summer migrations are about to begin; **m. forcée** forced migration **2** *Chim & Géol* migration

migratoire [migratwar] **ADJ** migratory

migratrice [migratris] *voir* **migrateur**

migrer [3] [migre] **VI** to migrate (**vers** to); *Ordinat* **faire m.** to transmit

mihrab [mirab] **NM** mihrab

mi-jambe [miʒɑ̃b] **à mi-jambe ADV** *(à partir du bas)* up to the knees; *(à partir du haut)* down to the knees; **on était dans la neige à m.** we were knee-deep in snow

mijaurée [miʒɔre] **NF** *(pimbêche)* (stuck-up) little madam; **faire la m.** to put on airs

mijoter [3] [miʒɔte] **VT 1** *Culin (faire cuire)* to simmer; *(préparer avec soin)* to cook up; **bœuf mijoté** beef stew; **m. des petits plats** to spend time preparing delicious meals; **elle mijote avec amour de bons petits plats à son mari** she lovingly prepares wonderful meals for her husband

2 *Fam (coup, plan)* to plot■, to cook up; **qu'est-ce que tu mijotes?** what are you up to?; **elle mijote quelque chose** she's got something up her sleeve; **ils ont mijoté ça entre eux** they cooked it up between them

VI 1 *Culin* to simmer, to stew gently; **continuez à faire** *ou* **laissez m. jusqu'à ce que la viande soit cuite** (allow to) simmer until the meat is cooked

2 *Fam Fig* **laisse-la m. dans son coin** *ou* **jus** leave her a while to stew in her own juice

▸**se mijoter VPR** *Fam (coup, plan)* to be cooking *or* brewing, to be afoot

mijoteuse [miʒɔtøz] **NF** slow cooker

❑ **mijoteuse ADJ F plaque m.** simmering plate

mi-journée [miʒurne] **NF les informations de la m.** the lunchtime news

mikado [mikado] **NM 1** *(titre)* mikado **2** *(jeu)* mikado, spillikins *(singulier)*

mil[1] [mil] **ADJ INV** *(mille)* thousand *(used only in writing out AD dates)*; **l'an m. neuf cent quatre-vingt-dix** (the year) nineteen hundred and ninety

mil[2] [mil] **NM** *(céréale)* millet; **petit m.** pearl millet

Milan [milɑ̃] **NM** Milan

milan [milɑ̃] **NM** *Orn* kite; **m. noir** black kite; **m. royal** red kite

milanais, -e [milanɛ, -ɛz] **ADJ** Milanese

❑ **Milanais, -e NM,F** Milanese; **les M.** the Milanese

mildiou [mildju] **NM** *(gén)* mildew; *(de la pomme de terre)* potato blight; *(de la vigne)* brown rot

mildiousé, -e [mildjuze] **ADJ** mildewy, mildewed

mile [majl] **NM** (statute) mile

miler [majlœr] **NM** *(athlète, cheval)* miler

miliaire [miljɛr] *Méd* **ADJ** miliary

NF prickly heat, *Spéc* miliaria

milice [milis] **NF 1** *Hist* militia **2** *(organisation paramilitaire)* militia; **m. privée** private militia **3** *Belg (service militaire)* military service; **la m.** *(armée)* the army

milicien, -enne [milisjɛ̃, -ɛn] **NM,F** militiaman, *f* militia woman

NM *Belg Br* conscript, *Am* draftee

milieu, -x [miljø] **NM 1** *(dans l'espace)* middle, centre; **une nappe déchirée/décorée en son m.** a tablecloth torn/decorated in the middle; **sciez-la par le** *ou* **en son m.** saw it through *or* down the middle; **la table du m.** the middle table; **celui du m.** the one in the middle, the middle one

2 *(dans le temps)* middle; **l'incendie s'est déclaré vers le m. de la nuit** the fire broke out in the middle of the night; **en m. de trimestre** in mid-term; **il est entré en plein m. d'une discussion** he came in right in the middle of a discussion

3 *(moyen terme)* middle way *or* course; **il n'y a pas de m. entre ces deux solutions** there's no (way to) compromise between these two solutions; **le juste m.** the happy medium; **il faut trouver un juste m.** we have to find a happy medium; **tenir le m. entre... et...** to steer a middle course between... and...

4 *(entourage)* environment, milieu; **l'influence du m. familial** *ou* **d'origine sur la réussite scolaire** the influence of the home background *or* environment on achievement at school; **m. socioculturel** (social) background; **des gens de tous les milieux** people from all walks of life *or* backgrounds; **dans mon m. professionnel** *(parmi mes collègues)* amongst the people I work with; **c'est un m. très snob** it's a very snobbish environment; **les milieux scientifiques** scientific circles; **les milieux bien informés** well-informed circles; **dans les milieux financiers** in financial circles; **se sentir/ne pas se sentir dans son m.** to feel at home/out of place; **je n'appartiens pas à leur m., je ne suis pas de leur m.** I don't belong to *or* I'm not part of their set *or* circle, I don't move in their circles; **en m. ouvert** *(éducation, réhabilitation)* in the community

5 *Biol (environnement)* environment, habitat; **dans un m. acide** in an acid medium; **m. de culture** culture medium; **m. intérieur** internal environment; **m. naturel** natural habitat; **en m. stérile** in a sterile environment

6 *Phys* medium

7 *Ind & (en sciences)* **en m. réel** in the field

8 *(pègre)* **le m.** the underworld

9 *Math* midpoint, midrange

❑ **au beau milieu de PRÉP** right in the middle of

❑ **au (beau) milieu ADV** (right) in the middle, (right) in the centre; **et là, au m., il y avait un puits** and there, right in the middle, was a well

❑ **au milieu de PRÉP 1** *(dans l'espace)* in the middle of, in the centre of; **au m. de la pièce** in the middle *or* centre of the room; **au m. du courant** in midstream

2 *(dans le temps)* in the middle of; **au m. de la journée/nuit** in the middle of the day/night; **au m. du mois** in the middle of the month; **au m. de l'hiver/l'été** in midwinter/midsummer; **au m. du mois de mars** in mid-March; **au m. du trimestre** in mid-term; *Pol* **au m. de son mandat** in mid-term; **vers le m. du mois** about the middle of the month; **elle est partie au m. de mon cours** she left in the middle of *or* halfway through my lesson; **nous en sommes au m. de l'enquête** we've now got to the halfway mark in the survey

3 *(parmi)* amongst, in the midst of, surrounded by; **mourir au m. des siens** to die amongst *or* surrounded by one's loved ones; **au m. de la foule** in the middle *or* in the midst of the crowd; **il quitta la scène au m. des huées** he was booed off the stage

❑ **milieu de terrain NM** *Sport (zone)* midfield (area); *(joueur)* midfield player

militaire [militɛr] **ADJ** *(gén)* military; *(de l'armée de terre)* army *(avant n)*, service *(avant n)*; *(de l'armée de l'air, de la marine)* service *(avant n)*; **tous les personnels militaires** all service personnel; **avoir la fibre m.** to be a born soldier; **allure m.** military *or* soldierly bearing

NM *(soldat → gén)* soldier; *(→ de l'armée de terre)* soldier, serviceman; *(→ de l'armée de l'air, de la marine)* serviceman; **c'est un ancien m.** he's an ex-serviceman; **m. du contingent** national serviceman; **m. de carrière** professional soldier; **les militaires** the military, the armed forces, the services

militairement [militɛrmɑ̃] **ADV saluer m.** to salute in military fashion; **les bases ennemies sont occupées m.** the enemy bases are occupied by the military; **il nous faut intervenir m.** we have to resort to military intervention

militance [militɑ̃s] **NF** militancy

militant, -e [militɑ̃, -ɑ̃t] **ADJ** militant

NM,F militant, activist; **les militants de base sont d'accord** the grassroots militants agree; **m. syndical** trade union militant *or* activist

militantisme [militɑ̃tism] **NM** militancy, militantism

militarisation [militarizasjɔ̃] **NF** militarization

militariser [3] [militarize] **VT** to militarize

militarisme [militarism] **NM** militarism

militariste [militarist] **ADJ** militaristic

NMF militarist

militaro-industriel, -elle [militarɔɛ̃dystrijɛl] *(mpl* **militaro-industriels**, *fpl* **militaro-industrielles) ADJ complexe m.** military-industrial complex

militer [3] [milite] **VI 1** *(agir en militant)* to be a militant *or* an activist; **m. au** *ou* **dans le parti socialiste** to be a socialist party activist; **m. pour/contre qch** to fight for/against sth

2 *Fig (plaider)* to militate; **ces témoignages ne militent pas en votre faveur** this evidence goes *or* militates against you; **les derniers bilans militent en faveur d'une refonte de la société** the latest balance sheets are a good argument *or* make a good case for restructuring the company

milk-shake [milkʃɛk] *(pl* **milk-shakes) NM** milkshake; **m. à la banane** banana milkshake

millage [milaʒ] **NM** *Can* mileage

millas [mijas] **NM** *Culin (dans le sud-ouest de la France)* = fried or toasted cornflour-based snack

mille[1] [mil] **ADJ INV 1** *(dix fois cent)* a *or* one thousand; **m. hommes** a thousand men, one thousand men; **m. un** a thousand and one, one thousand and one; **dix/cent m.** ten/a hundred thousand; **m. fois trois égale trois m.** one thousand times three is three thousand; **en l'an m. cinquante** in the year one thousand and fifty; **l'an m. neuf cent avant J.-C.** (the year) nineteen hundred BC; **c'est à m. kilomètres d'ici** it's a thousand kilometres from here

2 *(beaucoup de → exemples, raisons)* countless, numerous, many; **je vous l'ai dit m. fois** I've told you a thousand times, I've told you time and time again; **vous avez m. fois raison** you are so right; **c'est m. fois trop grand** it's miles too big; **ton énigme est m. fois trop compliquée pour moi** your riddle is far too difficult for me; **m. baisers** lots *or* tons of kisses; **m. mercis, merci m. fois** many thanks; **m. excuses** *ou* **pardons si je t'ai blessé** I'm dreadfully sorry if I've hurt you; **voilà un exemple**

entre m. here's just one of the countless examples I could choose, here's an example taken at random; **en m. morceaux** in pieces; **il y a m. et une manières de réussir sa vie** there are thousands of ways *or* a thousand and one ways of being successful in life; **endurer** *ou* **souffrir m. morts** to go through agonies; **(m. milliards de) m. sabords!** ≃ shiver me timbers!

NM INV 1 (*nombre*) a *or* one thousand; **ils sont morts par centaines de m.** they died in (their) hundreds of thousands; **il y a une chance sur m. que ça marche** there's a one-in-a-thousand chance that it'll work; **vingt pour m. des femmes** twenty women out of *or* in every thousand; **les chances de guérison sont de dix pour m.** there's a one in a hundred chance of a cure; **un taux de natalité de 5 pour m.** a birthrate of 0.5 percent; *Com* **un m. d'épingles** one thousand pins; *Com* **acheter/vendre au m.** to buy/to sell by the thousand; **par m. de briques vendu(es)** per thousand bricks sold, for every thousand bricks sold; *Com* **le disque en est à son cinquantième m.** the record has sold fifty thousand copies; *Fam* **je te le donne en m.!** I bet you'll never guess!; *Fam* **des m. et des cents** loads of money; **il ne gagne pas des m. et des cents** he doesn't exactly earn a fortune

2 (*centre d'une cible*) bull's eye; *Fam* **mettre** *ou* **taper (en plein) dans le m.** to hit the bull's-eye■; *Fig* to score a bull's-eye, to be bang on target

'Les Mille et une nuits' 'Arabian Nights' *or* 'The Thousand and One Nights'

mille² [mil] **NM 1** *Naut* **m. (marin** *ou* **nautique)** nautical mile

2 *Can Anciennement* **m. (anglais)** (*statute*) mile
3 *Hist* **le m. romain** the Roman mile

mille-feuille [milfœj] (*pl* **mille-feuilles**) **NF** *Bot* yarrow, milfoil

NM *Culin* millefeuille, *Am* napoleon

millefiori [milfjori] **NM INV** (*objet*) piece of millefiori glassware; (*verre*) millefiori (glass)

mille-fleurs [milflœr] **NF INV** millefleurs

millénaire [milenɛr] **ADJ** thousand-year-old; **un arbre m.** a thousand-year-old tree; **des traditions (plusieurs fois) millénaires** age-old *or* time-honoured traditions; **cette superstition est plusieurs fois m.** the superstition has existed for several thousands of years

NM 1 (*période*) millennium; **au cours du troisième m. avant Jésus-Christ** in the third millennium BC; **dater du premier m. av. J.-C.** to date from the first millennium BC; **cette tradition est vieille d'au moins un m.** the tradition has existed for at least a thousand years

2 (*anniversaire*) millennium, thousandth anniversary; **l'année du m. capétien** the millennium of the foundation of the Capetian dynasty

millénarisme [milenarism] **NM** millenarianism

millénariste [milenarist] **ADJ** millenarian

NMF millenarian

millenium [milenjɔm] **NM** *Rel* millennium

mille-pattes [milpat] **NM INV** *Entom* millipede, centipede

millepertuis [milpɛrtɥi] **NM** *Bot* St John's wort

millépore [milepɔr] **NM** *Zool* millepore

milleraies [milrɛ] **NM INV** needlecord

ADJ INV velours m. needlecord

millerandage [milrɑ̃daʒ] **NM** *Agr* millerandage

millerandé, -e [milrɑ̃de] **ADJ** *Agr* affected by millerandage

millésime [milezim] **NM 1** (*date*) date, year; **une pièce au m. de 1962** a coin dated 1962 **2** (*en œnologie → date de récolte*) year, vintage; **le m. 1976 est l'un des meilleurs** the 1976 vintage is among the best; **il ne boit que de grands millésimes** he only drinks vintage wine

millésimé, -e [milezime] **ADJ 1** (*vin*) vintage (*avant n*); **un bourgogne m. 1970** a 1970 (vintage) Burgundy; **une bouteille millésimée 1880** a bottle dated 1880 **2** (*pièce*) dated

millésimer [milezime] **VT** to date, to put a date on

millet [mijɛ] **NM** millet; **(grains de) m.** birdseed, canary seed

milliaire [miljɛr] **ADJ** *Antiq* milliary; **borne** *ou* **pierre m.** milliary (column)

milliampère [miljɑ̃pɛr] **NM** milliamp, milliampere

milliampèremètre [miljɑ̃pɛrmɛtr] **NM** milliammeter

milliard [miljar] **NM** billion, *Br Vieilli* thousand million; **cela a coûté deux milliards (d'euros)** it cost two billion (euros); **des milliards de globules rouges** billions of red corpuscles

milliardaire [miljardɛr] **ADJ sa famille est plusieurs fois m.** his/her family is worth billions

NMF billionaire

milliardième [miljardjɛm] **ADJ** billionth, *Br Vieilli* thousand millionth

NMF 1 (*personne*) billionth, *Br Vieilli* thousand millionth **2** (*objet*) billionth (one), *Br Vieilli* thousand millionth (one)

NM (*partie*) billionth, *Br Vieilli* thousand millionth

milliasse [mijas] **NF** *Culin* (*dans le sud-ouest de la France*) = fried or toasted cornflour-based snack

millibar [milibar] **NM** *Météo* millibar

millième [miljɛm] **ADJ** thousandth

NMF 1 (*personne*) thousandth **2** (*objet*) thousandth (one)

NM (*partie*) thousandth; **elle ne connaît pas le m. de mes sentiments** she can't begin to have an idea of my feelings; **il ne fournit pas le m. du travail nécessaire** he isn't doing a fraction of the work that has to be done

NF *Théât* thousandth performance; *voir aussi* **cinquième**

millièmement [miljɛmmɑ̃] **ADV** in the thousandth place

millier [milje] **NM** thousand; **un m. de badges/livres ont été vendus** a thousand badges/books have been sold; **des milliers de** thousands of ❑ **par milliers ADV** (*arriver*) in their thousands; (*envoyer, commander*) by the thousand; **des ballons ont été lâchés par milliers** thousands (upon thousands) of balloons have been released

milligramme [miligram] **NM** milligram, milligramme

millilitre [mililitr] **NM** millilitre

millimètre [milimɛtr] **NM** millimetre

millimétré, -e [milimetre], **millimétrique** [milimetrik] **ADJ** millimetric; **échelle millimétrée** millimetre scale

million [miljɔ̃] **NM 1** (*quantité*) million; **un m. de personnes** a *or* one million people; **quatre millions d'hommes** four million men; **des millions de** millions of; *Fig* **il n'y en a pas des millions à s'appeler comme ça** there can't be too many people with a name like that

2 (*somme*) **il a joué et perdu dix millions d'euros** he gambled away ten million euros; *Anciennement Fam* **la maison vaut 35 millions** (*de centimes*) the house is worth 350,000 francs; *Anciennement Fam* **un m. cinq** (*de centimes*) 15,000 francs; (*de francs*) 1.5 million francs

millionième [miljɔnjɛm] **ADJ** millionth

NMF 1 (*personne*) millionth **2** (*objet*) millionth (one)

NM (*partie*) millionth

millionnaire [miljɔnɛr] **ADJ** millionaire; **être/devenir m.** to be/to become a millionaire; **elle est plusieurs fois m. (en dollars)** she's a (dollar) millionaire *or* millionairess several times over

NMF millionaire, *f* millionairess; **le loto a fait deux millionnaires cette semaine** the lottery has made two people into millionaires this week

milliseconde [milisəgɔ̃d] **NF** millisecond

millivolt [milivɔlt] **NM** millivolt

millivoltmètre [milivɔltmɛtr] **NM** millivoltmeter

milliwatt [miliwat] **NM** milliwatt

Milo [milo] **NPR la Vénus de M.** the Venus de Milo

mi-long, mi-longue [milɔ̃, milɔ̃g] (*mpl* **mi-longs**, *fpl* **mi-longues**) **ADJ** (*jupe*) half-length; (*cheveux*) shoulder-length

milonga [milɔ̃ga] **NF** *Mus* milonga

milord [milɔr] **NM 1** (*en appellation*) lord; **après vous, m.** after you, my lord **2** *Fam Vieilli* (*homme riche*) toff; **donnant des ordres à tout le monde comme un m.** ordering everyone about as if he was God **3** (*véhicule*) victoria

milouin [milwɛ̃] **NM** *Orn* pochard

mi-lourd [milur] (*pl* **mi-lourds**) *Boxe* **ADJ M** light heavyweight (*avant n*)

NM light heavyweight

MIME [mim] **NM** *Ordinat* (*abrév* **Multipurpose Internet Mail Extensions**) MIME

mime [mim] **NMF 1** (*artiste*) mime (artist) **2** (*imitateur*) mimic

NM 1 (*art*) mime; **faire du m.** to be a mime (artist); **un spectacle de m.** a mime show **2** (*action de mimer*) miming (UNCOUNT)

mimer [3] [mime] **VT 1** *Théât* to mime; **le jeu consiste à m. des titres de films** the idea of the game is to mime film titles **2** (*imiter*) to mimic

mimésis [mimesis] **NF** *Beaux-Arts & Littérature* mimesis

mimétique [mimetik] **ADJ** *Biol, Beaux-Arts & Littérature* mimetic

mimétisme [mimetism] **NM 1** *Biol* mimetism, mimesis **2** (*imitation*) mimicry, mimicking; **le nouveau-né sourit à sa mère par m.** a new-born baby mimics its mother's smile; **par m., elle a fini par faire aussi de la peinture** taking the attitude that if you can't beat them, join them, she ended up doing painting too

mimi [mimi] **ADJ INV** *Fam* (*mignon*) lovely■, sweet■, cute

NM 1 (*en langage enfantin → chat*) pussy (cat) **2** *Fam* (*bisou*) kiss■; (*caresse*) cuddle■, hug■; **fais m. à ta sœur** give your sister a kiss; **faire un gros m. à qn** to give sb a big kiss; **elle adore faire des mimis à son petit frère** she loves cuddling her little brother

3 *Fam* (*terme d'affection*) darling, sweetie, honey; **qu'est-ce qui ne va pas, mon m.?** what's wrong, sweetie-pie?

4 (*grimace*) facial expression

5 *très Fam* (*sexe de la femme*) pussy, *Br* fanny

Mimi Pinson [mimipɛ̃sɔ̃] **NPR** = heroine of a story by Alfred de Musset, the archetype of the Parisian "grisette"

mimique [mimik] **ADJ langage m.** sign language

NF 1 (*gestuelle*) gesture; **il fit une m. de désespoir** he made a despairing gesture **2** (*grimace*) facial expression; **il a fait une curieuse m.** he made a strange face

Mimivirus [mimivirys] **NM** *Biol* Mimivirus, mimivirus

mimodrame [mimɔdram] **NM** dumb show

mimolette [mimɔlɛt] **NF** Mimolette (cheese)

mi-mollet [mimɔlɛ] **à mi-mollet ADV** (*à partir du bas*) up to the calf; (*à partir du haut*) down to the calf; **bottes à m.** calf-length boots; **robe à m.** calf-length dress

mimologie [mimɔlɔʒi] **NF** (*art of*) mimicry, imitation

mimosa [mimɔza] **NM 1** *Bot* mimosa **2** *Culin* **œuf m.** egg mayonnaise (*topped with crumbled yolk*)

mimosacée [mimɔzase], **mimosoïdée** [mimɔzoide] *Bot* **NF** member of the Mimosaceae ❑ **mimosacées NFPL** Mimosaceae

mi-moyen [mimwajɛ̃] (*pl* **mi-moyens**) *Boxe* **ADJ M** welterweight (*avant n*)

NM welterweight

mimule [mimyl] **NM** *Bot* **m. musqué** musk (monkeyflower); **m. tacheté** monkeyflower

MIN [min] **NM** (*abrév* **marché d'intérêt national**) = wholesale market for agricultural produce

min (*abrév écrite* **minute**) min

min. (*abrév écrite* **minimum**) min

minable [minabl] *Fam* **ADJ 1** (*pauvre → logement*) shabby, grotty

2 (*mesquin*) **une petite vengeance m.** petty revenge; **c'est m., ce que tu lui as fait** that was a rotten trick you played on him/her

3 (*insuffisant → salaire, repas*) pathetic, lousy

4 (*sans envergure*) small-time, third-rate; **un escroc m.** a small-time crook

NMF loser, no-hoper, dead loss; **tu n'es qu'un m.!** you're so pathetic!; **pauvre m., va!** you pathetic loser!; **quelle bande de minables!** what a pathetic *or* useless bunch!

minablement [minabləmɑ̃] **ADV** *Fam* **1** (*pauvrement*) shabbily **2** (*lamentablement*) pathetically, hopelessly; **ils ont échoué m.** they failed miserably

minage [minaʒ] **NM** *Mines & (en travaux publics)* mining

minahouet [minawɛ] **NM** *Naut* serving-board

minaret [minarɛ] **NM** minaret

mil-min

minauder [3] [minode] vi to mince, to simper; **elle répondait aux questions en minaudant** she answered the questions with a simper; **arrête de m.!** don't be such a poser!

minauderie [minodri] NF **1** *(préciosité)* (show of) affectation **2** *(acte, propos)* affectation; **minauderies** simpering

minaudier, -ère [minodje, -ɛr] ADJ affected, simpering, mincing

Minaudière® [minodjɛr] NF make-up box *(carried in the hand)*

minbar [minbar] NM mimbar

mince [mɛ̃s] ADJ **1** *(sans épaisseur)* thin; **une m. couche de vernis** a thin layer of varnish; **une m. tranche de bacon** a sliver *or* a thin slice of bacon; **des lèvres minces** thin lips; **un m. filet d'eau** a thin trickle of water; **m. comme une feuille de papier à cigarette** paper-thin, wafer-thin

2 *(personne → svelte)* slim, slender; **être m.** to be slim *or* slender; **m. comme un fil** as thin as a rake

3 *Fig (négligeable)* slim, slender; **de minces bénéfices** slender profits; **les preuves sont bien minces** the evidence is rather slim; **mes connaissances dans ce domaine sont trop minces** I know too little about this field, my knowledge in this field is too scanty; **ce n'est pas une m. affaire** this is no small affair; **ce n'est pas une m. responsabilité** it's no small responsibility; **un demi-chapitre sur la Révolution, c'est un peu m.** half a chapter on the French Revolution is a bit feeble; **une livre de viande pour quatre, c'est un peu m.** a pound of meat for four, that's cutting it a bit fine; **c'est un peu m. comme excuse!** it's a bit of a poor excuse!

ADV thinly

EXCLAM *Fam (pour exprimer l'exaspération)* blast!; *(pour exprimer la surprise)* wow!, *Br* blimey!, *Am* gee (whiz)!; **m. alors, qui l'aurait cru!** wow *or Br* blimey *or Am* gee (whiz), who'd have thought it!

minceur [mɛ̃sœr] NF **1** *(finesse)* slimness, thinness **2** *(sveltesse)* slimness, slenderness **3** *Fig (insuffisance)* weakness, feebleness; **la m. d'un argument** the weakness *or* flimsiness of an argument; **étant donné la m. de mes revenus** since my income is so small

mincir [32] [mɛ̃sir] vi *(personne)* to get slimmer *or* thinner; **elle essaie de m.** she's trying to lose weight

VT *(sujet: vêtement, couleur)* **cette robe te mincit** that dress makes you look slimmer

mindel [mindɛl] NM *Géol* Mindel

mine¹ [min] NF **1** *(apparence)* appearance, exterior; **sous sa m. respectable** under his/her respectable exterior; **elle fit m. de raccrocher, puis se ravisa** she made as if to hang up, then changed her mind; **ne fais pas m. de ne pas comprendre** don't act as if *or* pretend you don't understand; *Fam* **m. de rien, ça finit par coûter cher** it may not seem much but in the end it all adds up; **m. de rien, elle était furieuse** although *or* though she didn't show it, she was furious; **il est 4 heures du matin, m. de rien** it's hard to believe *or* you wouldn't think it, but it's four in the morning; **m. de rien, l'affaire progresse** the work is progressing, though you wouldn't think so to look at it; **m. de rien, essaie de vérifier** try to check on it without letting on (what you're up to)

2 *(teint)* **avoir bonne m.** to look well; **il a mauvaise m.** he doesn't look very well; *Fig Ironique* **tu as bonne m., avec ta veste à l'envers!** you look great with your jacket on inside out!; *Fig Ironique* **nous avons bonne m. maintenant!** we look really good now, don't we!; **avoir une m. superbe** *ou* **resplendissante** to be the (very) picture of health; *Fam* **avoir une sale m.** to look dreadful *or* awful; *Fam* **avoir une petite m.** to look out of sorts *or* off-colour; *Fam* **avoir une m. de papier mâché** *ou* **de déterré** to look like death warmed up; **je lui trouve meilleure m.** I think he/she looks better *or* in better health

3 *(visage, contenance)* look, countenance; **m. boudeuse** sulky expression; **il ne faut pas vous fier à sa m. de petite fille sage** don't trust that butter-wouldn't-melt-in-my-mouth expression

---

of hers; **avoir une m. réjouie** to beam, to be beaming; **faire grise** *ou* **triste** *ou* **piètre m.** to look chastened; **faire grise** *ou* **triste** *ou* **piètre m.** to make *or Br* to pull a long face; **ne fais pas cette m.!** don't look so downhearted!; **faire bonne m. à qn** to greet sb warmly; **faire mauvaise m. à qn** to be cool with sb; **juger les gens sur la m.** to judge people by *or* on appearances

❑ **mines** NFPL *(manières → de bébé)* gestures, expressions; **faire des mines** to simper; **il m'énerve à toujours faire des mines** he irritates me, always simpering around; **elles font des mines devant le miroir** they're making faces in the mirror

mine² [min] NF **1** *Géol* deposit; *(installations → de surface)* pithead; *(→ en sous-sol)* pit; *(gisement)* mine; **travailler à la m.** to work in the mine, to be a miner; **mon fils n'ira pas à la m.** my son isn't going down the mine *or* pit; **m. de charbon** *ou* **de houille** coal mine; **m. à ciel ouvert** opencast mine; *aussi Fig* **une m. d'or** a gold mine

2 *Fig (source importante)* **une m. de** a mine *or* source of; **une m. de renseignements** a mine of information

3 *(d'un crayon)* lead; **crayon à m. grasse/dure** soft/hard pencil; **m. de plomb** graphite *or* black lead

4 *Mil (galerie)* mine, gallery, sap; *(explosif)* mine; **poser** *ou* **mouiller une m.** to lay a mine; **faire jouer une m.** to fire a blast *or* a mine; **m. aérienne/sous-marine/terrestre** aerial/submarine/land mine; **m. télécommandée** radio-controlled mine

5 *(explosif)* **coup de m.** blast; **attention, coups de m.!** *(sur panneau)* danger, blasting; **ouvrir une roche à coups de m.** to blast a rock; **exploitation à la m.** blasting

❑ **mines** NFPL **1** *Géog* mining area, mines; *Écon* mining industry

2 *Admin* **les Mines** = government department responsible for supervising all construction projects involving tunnelling; **École des Mines, les Mines** = "grande école" of engineering studies; **service des Mines** = government department which verifies the roadworthiness of cars

miner [3] [mine] VT **1** *(terrain)* to mine; **danger! zone minée** *(sur panneau)* beware of mines

2 *(ronger)* to undermine, to erode, to eat away (at) *or* into; **l'humidité a miné les fondations** the damp has eaten into the foundations

3 *Fig (affaiblir)* to undermine, to sap; **l'opposition cherche à m. les efforts du gouvernement** the opposition is trying to undermine the government's work; **ces ennuis la minent** these problems are wearing her down; **m. les forces/la santé de qn** to sap sb's strength/health; **la froideur de son accueil m'a miné le moral** the cold reception he/she gave me sapped my spirits; **miné par le chagrin** consumed with *or* worn down by grief

minerai [minrɛ] NM ore; **m. de fer/d'uranium** iron/uranium ore; **m. marchand** *ou* **net** pure ore; **m. riche/pauvre** high-grade/low-grade ore; **m. brut** crude ore; **m. métallique** metalliferous *or* metal-bearing ore

minéral, -e, -aux, -ales [mineral, -o] ADJ mineral *(avant n)*
NM mineral

minéralier [mineralje] NM ore carrier

minéralier-pétrolier [mineraljepetrɔlje] *(pl* **minéraliers-pétroliers)** NM ore-oil carrier

minéralisateur, -trice [mineralizatœr, -tris] ADJ mineralizing
NM mineralizer

minéralisation [mineralizasjɔ̃] NF mineralization

minéralisatrice [mineralizatris] *voir* **minéralisateur**

minéralisé, -e [mineralize] ADJ mineralized; **eau faiblement minéralisée** water with a low mineral content

minéraliser [3] [mineralize] VT *(métal, eau)* to mineralize

minéralocorticoïde [mineralokɔrtikɔid] *Méd* ADJ mineralocorticoid
NM mineralocorticoid

minéralogie [mineralɔʒi] NF mineralogy

minéralogique [mineralɔʒik] ADJ **1** *Géol* mineralogical **2** *Aut* **numéro m.** *Br* registration *or Am* license number

---

minéralogiste [mineralɔʒist] NMF mineralogist

minéralurgie [mineralyrʒi] NF ore processing

minerval, -als [minɛrval] NM *Belg (pension)* pension; *(frais d'inscription)* school tuition fees

Minerve [minɛrv] NPR *Myth* Minerva

minerve [minɛrv] NF *Méd* neck brace, (surgical) collar

minervois [minɛrvwa] NM Minervois (wine)

minestrone [minɛstrɔn] NM minestrone

minet, -ette [minɛ, -ɛt] NM,F *Fam* **1** *(jeune garçon)* trendy young guy, pretty boy; *(jeune femme)* babe, trendy young chick **2** *(chat)* puss, pussy (cat) **3** *(terme d'affection)* sweetie, honey; **mon m., ma minette** sweetie, honey

❑ **minette** NF **1** *Mines* minette **2** *Bot* black medick **3** *très Fam (sexe de la femme)* pussy, snatch; **faire minette (à qn)** to go down (on sb), to give (sb) head

mineur, -e [minœr] ADJ **1** *(secondaire)* minor; **d'un intérêt m.** of minor interest

2 *Jur* below the age of criminal responsibility; **enfants mineurs** under-age children, minors; **être m.** to be under-age *or* a minor

3 *Mus* minor; **concerto en sol m.** concerto in G minor; **accord parfait m.** minor chord

4 *Hist & Rel* **un frère m.** a Friar Minor, a Franciscan

5 *Cartes* **couleur mineure** minor suit

6 *Ling* minor

NM,F *Jur* minor; **interdit aux mineurs** *(film)* adults only; **cet établissement est interdit aux mineurs** these premises are banned to persons under 18; **délinquant m.** juvenile offender; **détournement** *ou* **enlèvement de m.** abduction

NM **1** *(ouvrier)* miner, mineworker; **famille de mineurs** mining family; **grève/maladie des mineurs** miners' strike/disease; *Tech* **m. continu** continuous miner; **m. de fond** underground worker; **m. de houille** coalminer, *Br* collier

2 *Mil* sapper, miner

3 *Mus* **en m.** in the minor mode *or* key

4 *Ling* minor term

❑ **mineure** NF *Ling* minor premise

mini [mini] ADJ INV **la mode m.** the mini-length *or* thigh-length fashion; **la mode m. est de retour** the mini is back (in fashion)

ADV **s'habiller m.** to wear miniskirts

NM **1** *(mode courte)* mini; **le m. est de retour** minis *or* miniskirts are back **2** *Fam Ordinat* mini, minicomputer■

mini- [mini] PRÉF mini-, small; **mini-sondage** snap poll

miniature [minjatyr] ADJ miniature; **un train m.** a model *or* miniature train

NF **1** *(modèle réduit)* small-scale replica *or* model **2** *Beaux-Arts* miniature; **peintre de miniatures** miniature painter, miniaturist

❑ **en miniature** ADJ miniature *(avant n)*; **c'est un jardin en m.** it's a model *or* miniature garden

miniaturé, -e [minjatyre] ADJ *(manuscrit)* illuminated; *(portrait)* miniature

miniaturisation [minjatyrizasjɔ̃] NF miniaturization

miniaturiser [3] [minjatyrize] VT to miniaturize

▶**se miniaturiser** VPR to become miniaturized; **la hi-fi se miniaturise** sound systems are getting much smaller

miniaturiste [minjatyrist] ADJ **un peintre m.** a miniaturist
NMF miniaturist

minibar [minibar] NM **1** *(dans le train)* trolley; **un service de m. est assuré dans ce train** there is a trolley service on the train **2** *(à l'hôtel)* minibar

minibus [minibys], **minicar** [minikar] NM minibus

minicassette [minikasɛt] NF (small) cassette
NM (small) cassette recorder

minichaîne [miniʃɛn] NF mini (stereo) system

MiniDisc® [minidisk] NM MiniDisc®

minidisque [minidisk] NM MiniDisc®

mini-disquette [minidiskɛt] *(pl* **mini-disquettes)** NF minidisk, mini-floppy

mini-écouteur [miniekutœr] *(pl* **mini-écouteurs)** NM earbud, in-ear headphone

minier, -ère [minje, -ɛr] ADJ mining *(avant n)*

❑ **minière** NF *Arch* **1** *(exploitation)* opencast mining company **2** *(tourbière)* peat bog

mini-feuilleton [minifœjtɔ̃] *(pl* **mini-feuilletons)** NM *TV* mini-series

minigolf [minigɔlf] NM crazy golf, miniature golf

minijupe [miniʒyp] NF miniskirt

minima [minima] *voir* **minimum**

mini-major [minimaʒɔr] *(pl* **mini-majors**) NM *Cin* mini-major

minimal, -e, -aux, -ales [minimal, -o] ADJ **1** *(seuil, peine)* minimum *(avant n); (art)* minimal; **température minimale** minimal *or* minimum temperature **2** *Math* minimal

minimalisation [minimalizasjɔ̃] NF minimalization

minimaliser [3] [minimalize] VT to minimize

minimalisme [minimalism] NM minimalism

minimaliste [minimalist] ADJ minimalist ▪ NM minimalist

minime [minim] ADJ *(faible)* minimal, minor; *(rôle)* minor; *(perte)* trivial; *(valeur)* trifling; **l'intrigue n'a qu'une importance m.** the plot is of only minor importance; **la différence est m.** the difference is negligible ▪ NMF *Sport* (school) Junior ▪ NM *Rel* Minim

minimessage [minimesaʒ] NM *Tél* text message; **envoyer un m. à qn** to text sb, to send sb a text message

minimex [minimɛks] NM *Belg (abrév* **minimum de moyens d'existence)** *Br* ≃ income support, *Am* ≃ welfare

minimexé, -e [minimekse] NM,F *Belg* ≃ person on *Br* income support *or Am* welfare

minimisation [minimizasjɔ̃] NF minimization, minimizing; **m. des pertes** mitigation of damages

minimiser [3] [minimize] VT **1** *(rôle)* to minimize, to play down; *(risque)* to minimize, to cut down; **sans vouloir m. sa contribution** without wishing to minimize *or* play down his/her contribution **2** *Math* to minimize

minimum [minimɔm] *(pl* **minimums** *ou* **minima** [-ma]) ADJ minimum; **poids/service m.** minimum weight/service; *Électron* **charge m.** base *or* minimum load; **mise de fonds m.** minimum stake; **prix m.** minimum *or* bottom price; *(aux enchères)* reserve price ▪ NM **1** *(le plus bas degré)* minimum; **températures proches du m. saisonnier** temperatures approaching the minimum *or* the lowest recorded for the season; **dépenser le m.** to spend as little as possible; **réduire les frais au m.** to reduce expenses to a minimum; **mets le chauffage au m.** turn the heating down as low as it will go; **réduisez la flamme au m.** turn the flame down as far as it will go; **j'ai réduit les matières grasses au m.** I've cut down on fat as much as possible, I've cut fat down to a minimum; **la rivière était à son m.** the river was at its lowest level; **avoir le m. vital** *(financier)* to be on subsistence level, to earn the minimum living wage; **ils n'ont même pas le m. vital** they don't even have the bare minimum, they're living below the breadline

2 *Jur (peine la plus faible)* **le m.** the minimum sentence

3 *(petite quantité)* **un m. (de)** a minimum (of); **un m. de temps** a minimum amount of time; **en un m. de temps** in as short a time as possible; *Fam* **je n'y resterai que le m. de temps** I'll make it as brief as I can; **avec un m. d'efforts** with a minimum of effort; **s'il avait un m. de bon sens/ d'honnêteté** if he had an ounce of common sense/of decency; **nous exigeons un m. de garanties** we demand the minimum guarantees; **tu as vraiment fait un m.!** you really have done just the bare minimum!; **c'est vraiment le m. que tu puisses faire pour elle** it's the least you can do for her; **trois mois, c'est un m. pour s'habituer au climat** three months is the minimum it takes *or* it takes at least three months to get used to the climate

4 *Fin & Admin* **m. imposable** tax threshold; **m. vieillesse** basic state pension; **les minima sociaux** = basic income support

5 *Math* **m. relatif** constraint minimum

6 *Écol* **loi du m.** law of the minimum ▪ ADV minimum; **il fait 3°C m.** the minimum temperature is 3°C

❑ **au minimum** ADV *(au moins)* at the least; **deux jours au m.** at least two days, a minimum of two days; **au m. cinq ans d'expérience** at least five

years' experience, a minimum of five years' experience

mini-ordinateur [miniɔrdinatœr] *(pl* **mini-ordinateurs)** NM minicomputer

minipilule [minipilyl] NF minipill

minisatellite [minisatelit] NM minisatellite

mini-séjour [miniseʒur] *(pl* **mini-séjours)** NM mini-break, short break

mini-série [miniseri] *(pl* **mini-séries)** NF *TV* mini-series

mini-slip [minislip] *(pl* **mini-slips)** NM tanga

ministère [ministɛr] NM **1** *Pol (charge) Br* ministry, *Am* administration; **elle a refusé le m. qu'on lui proposait** she turned down the government position she was offered; **sous le m. de M. Thiers** when M. Thiers was (the) minister, under M. Thiers' *Br* ministry *or Am* secretaryship

2 *(cabinet)* government, ministry; **former un m.** to form a government; **entrer au m.** to take over as a minister, *Am* to take a position in the administration

3 *(bâtiment) Br* ministry, *Am* department (offices); *(département) Br* ministry, *Am* department; **m. des Affaires étrangères** Ministry of Foreign Affairs, *Br* ≃ Foreign and Commonwealth Office, *Am* ≃ State Department; **m. de l'Agriculture** Ministry *or* Department of Agriculture; **m. du Commerce** Ministry of Trade, *Br* ≃ Department for Trade and Industry, *Am* ≃ Department of Commerce; **m. de la Culture** Ministry of Culture, Ministry for the Arts; **m. de la Défense** *Br* ≃ Ministry of Defence, *Am* ≃ Department of Defense; **m. de l'Économie et des Finances** Ministry of Finance, *Br* ≃ HM Treasury, *Am* ≃ Treasury Department; **m. de l'Éducation nationale** ≃ Department of Education; **m. de l'Environnement** Ministry of the Environment, *Br* ≃ Department for Environment, Food and Rural Affairs, *Am* ≃ Department of the Environment; **m. de l'Intérieur** Ministry of the Interior, *Br* ≃ Home Office, *Am* ≃ Department of the Interior; **m. de la Justice** Department of Justice; **m. des Relations extérieures** Ministry of Foreign Affairs, *Br* ≃ Foreign and Commonwealth Office, *Am* ≃ State Department; **m. de la Santé et de la Sécurité Sociale** *Br* ≃ Department for Work and Pensions, *Am* ≃ Department of Health and Human Services; **m. du Travail** Ministry for Employment, *Br* ≃ Department for Education and Skills, *Am* ≃ Department of Labor

4 *Jur* **l'accusé a droit au m. d'un avocat** the accused has the right to counsel *or Am* a lawyer; **par m. d'huissier** served by a bailiff; **m. public** public prosecutor's department, *Br* ≃ Crown Prosecution Service, *Am* ≃ District Attorney's office

5 *Rel* ministry; **exercer un m.** to serve as minister, to perform one's ministry

6 *Arch ou Littéraire (entremise)* agency; **proposer son m.** to offer to act as a mediator; **user du m. de qn** to make use of sb's services

ministériel, -elle [ministerjɛl] ADJ **1** *(émanant d'un ministre) Br* ministerial, *Am* departmental **2** *(concernant le gouvernement)* cabinet *(avant n), Br* ministerial

ministrable [ministrabl] ADJ in line for a government *or Br* ministerial position; **elle est m.** she's a likely candidate for *Br* a ministerial post *or Am* a post in the administration ▪ NMF potential secretary of state, *Br* ministerial hopeful

ministre [ministr] NM

Note that it is no longer considered a mistake to feminize this word and to say **une ministre** but some French speakers nonetheless regard this form as unacceptable, especially in France. See also the entry **féminisation**.

1 *Pol Br* minister, *Am* secretary; **m. d'État** secretary of state, *Br* minister; **m. sans portefeuille** minister without portfolio; **m. des Affaires étrangères** Minister of Foreign Affairs, *Br* ≃ Foreign Secretary, *Am* ≃ Secretary of State; **m. de l'Agriculture** Agriculture Minister, Minister for Agriculture; **m. du Commerce** *Br* ≃ Secretary of State for Trade and Industry, *Am* ≃ Secretary of Commerce; **m. de la Culture** Minister for the Arts; **m. de la Culture et de la**

Communication Minister of Culture and Communication; **m. de la Défense (nationale)** ≃ Secretary of State for Defence, Minister of Defence; **m. de l'Économie et des Finances** Finance Minister, *Br* ≃ Chancellor of the Exchequer, *Am* ≃ Secretary of the Treasury; **m. de l'Éducation nationale** ≃ Secretary of State for Education; **m. de l'Environnement** *Br* ≃ Secretary of State for Environment, Food and Rural Affairs, *Am* ≃ Secretary of the Environment; **m. de l'Intérieur** Minister of the Interior, *Br* ≃ Home Secretary, *Am* ≃ Secretary of the Interior; **m. de la Justice** Minister of Justice, *Br* ≃ Lord (High) Chancellor, *Am* ≃ Attorney General; **m. des Relations extérieures** Minister of Foreign Affairs, *Br* ≃ Foreign Secretary, *Am* ≃ Secretary of State; **m. de la Santé et de la Sécurité Sociale** *Br* ≃ Secretary of State for Social Security, *Am* ≃ Secretary for Health and Human Services; **m. des Transports** *Br* ≃ Secretary of State for Transport, *Am* ≃ Transportation Secretary; **m. du Travail** *Br* ≃ Secretary of State for Education and Skills, *Am* ≃ Labor Secretary

2 *(ambassadeur)* **m. plénipotentiaire (auprès de)** minister plenipotentiary (to)

3 *Rel (pasteur)* **m. du culte** minister

4 *Arch ou Littéraire (de Dieu, d'un prince)* servant, agent

Minitel® [minitɛl] NM viewdata service, *Br* ≃ Prestel®, *Am* ≃ Minitel®; **sur M.** on viewdata, *Br* ≃ on Prestel®, *Am* ≃ on Minitel®; **M. rose** erotic viewdata service

---

| **Culture** |

MINITEL®

The domestic viewdata service run by France Télécom has become a familiar part of French life. The basic monitor and keyboard are given free of charge, and the subscriber is charged for the services used on his or her ordinary telephone bill. The subscriber dials a four-figure number (typically 3615); a code word then gives access to the particular service required. Some Minitel® services are purely informative (the weather, road conditions, news etc); others are interactive (enabling users to carry out bank transactions, book tickets for travel, register for and obtain the results of nationwide examinations, for example). Minitel® also serves as an electronic telephone directory. Nowadays the services offered by Minitel® are increasingly available on the Internet.

---

minitéliste [minitelist] NMF Minitel® user

mini-tour [minitur] *(pl* **mini-tours)** NF *Ordinat* mini tower

minium [minjɔm] NM **1** *Chim* red lead, minium **2** *(peinture)* red lead paint

minivague [minivag] NF light perm

Minneapolis [mineapolis] NM Minneapolis

minnesang [minəsãg] NM *Littérature* Minnesang

minnesänger [minəsɛngɛr] NM INV *Littérature* Minnesinger

Minnesota [minezɔta] NM *Géog* **le M.** Minnesota; **au M.** in Minnesota

Minnie [mini] NPR Minnie Mouse

minoen, -enne [minɔɛ̃, -ɛn] ADJ Minoan ▪ NM Minoan period

minois [minwa] NM pretty little face

minorant, -e [minɔrã, -ãt] *Math* ADJ minorant ▪ NM *(d'un ensemble)* lower bound; *(d'une série)* minorant series

minoratif, -ive [minɔratif, -iv] ADJ *Littéraire* minimizing

minoration [minɔrasjɔ̃] NF **1** *(baisse)* reduction, cut; **une m. de cinq pour cent du tarif de base** a five percent cut in the basic rate; **procéder à une m. des loyers** to reduce *or* to lower rents **2** *(minimisation)* minimizing

minoratif, -ive [minɔrativ] *voir* **minoratif**

minorer [3] [minɔre] VT **1** *(baisser)* to reduce, to cut, to mark down; **m. les prix de deux pour cent** to cut prices by two percent **2** *(minimiser)* to minimize, to downplay the importance of

minoritaire [minɔritɛr] ADJ **1** *(moins nombreux)* minority *(avant n)*; **parti m.** minority party; **ils sont minoritaires à l'Assemblée** they are in the minority in the Assembly; **les femmes sont**

minoritaires dans cette profession women are a minority in this profession; **très minoritaires** very much in the minority **2** *(non reconnu)* minority *(avant n)*; **opinion m.** minority opinion

NMF member of a minority (group); *Bourse* minority shareholder; **les minoritaires** the minority

minorité [minɔrite] NF **1** *(le plus petit nombre)* minority; **une m. de** a minority of; **dans une m. de cas** in a minority of cases

2 *(groupe)* minority (group); **m. ethnique** ethnic minority; **m. nationale** national minority; **m. agissante** active minority

3 *(âge légal)* minority; *Jur* nonage; **pendant sa m.** before he/she came of age, while he/she was under age; **m. pénale** nonage

4 *Écon* **m. de blocage** blocking minority

❑ **en minorité** ADJ in a *or* the minority; **nous sommes en m.** we're in a minority ADV **mettre le gouvernement en m.** to defeat the government; **la gauche a été mise en m. lors des dernières élections** the left became the minority party at the last elections

Minorque [minɔrk] NF Minorca; **à M.** in Minorca

minorquin, -e [minɔrkɛ̃, -in] ADJ Minorcan

❑ **Minorquin, -e** NM,F Minorcan

Minos [minɔs] NPR *Myth* Minos

minot [mino] NM **1** *Naut* boomkin **2** *Fam (dans le sud-est de la France* → *gamin)* kid, brat **3** *Can Vieilli (mesure de capacité des grains)* ≃ bushel

Minotaure [minɔtɔr] NM *Myth* **le M.** the Minotaur

minoterie [minɔtri] NF **1** *(lieu)* flourmill **2** *(activité)* flour-milling

minotier [minɔtje] NM miller, (flour) millowner

minou [minu] NM **1** *Fam (chat)* pussy, pussy cat; **m.! m.! m.!** puss! puss!, kitty! kitty! **2** *Fam (chéri)* darling, sweetie, honey **3** *très Fam (sexe de la femme)* pussy, *Br* fanny **4** *Can (bourgeon de saule)* pussy willow **5** *Can (boule de poussière)* piece of fluff, *Am* dustball, dust bunny

minouche [minuʃ] NF *Can (en langage enfantin)* cuddle

minoucher [3] [minuʃe] VT *Can (en langage enfantin)* to cuddle; *Fam Fig (flatter)* to soft-soap

minoune [minun] NF *Can (en langage enfantin* → *chatte)* pussy cat; *(terme d'affection)* darling, sweetie, honey

minque [mɛ̃k] NF *Belg* = covered fish market

Minsk [minsk] NM Minsk

minuit [minɥi] NM **1** *(milieu de la nuit)* midnight

2 *(heure)* midnight, twelve midnight, twelve o'clock (at night); **il est m.** it's twelve (midnight), it's midnight; **il est m. passé** it's after *or* past midnight; **m. et demi** half-past twelve at night; **m. et quart** a quarter *Br* past *or Am* after twelve *or* midnight; **m. moins vingt** twenty to twelve *or* to midnight; **à m.** at midnight, at twelve o'clock (at night); **vers m., vers les m.** about twelve *or* midnight; **sur le coup de m.** on the stroke of twelve *or* of midnight; *Hum* **m., l'heure du crime!** midnight, the witching hour!

❑ **de minuit** ADJ midnight *(avant n)*

MINUK [minyk] NF *(abrév* **Mission d'administration intérimaire des Nations Unies au Kosovo***)* UNMIK

minus [minys] NM *Fam* **1** *(nabot)* midget, shortie, runt **2** *(incapable)* loser

minuscule [minyskyl] ADJ **1** *(très petit)* minute, minuscule, tiny; **des bestioles minuscules** tiny *or* microscopic creatures; **elle est m. à côté de lui** she's minute *or* tiny compared with him **2 un b m.** a small *or Typ* lower-case b; **lettre** *ou* **caractère m.** small *or Typ* lower-case letter

NF small letter; *Typ* lower-case letter; **écrire en minuscules** to write in small *or Typ* lower-case letters

minus habens [minysabɛ̃s] NMF INV *Péj* halfwit

minutage [minytaʒ] NM timing

minutaire [minytɛr] ADJ *Jur* in draft

minute [minyt] NF **1** *(mesure du temps)* minute; **une m. de silence** a minute's silence, a minute of silence; **une m. plus tard et vous la ratiez** a couple of minutes later and you would have missed her; **les minutes passent vite** time flies; **les minutes sont longues** time drags by; **chaque m. compte** every minute counts; **il n'y a pas une m. à perdre** there's not a minute to lose; **à la m. près** on the dot, right on time; *Fam* **on n'est pas à la m. près** *ou* **à la m.!** there's no hurry!; **à deux minutes (de voiture/de marche) de chez moi** two minutes(' drive/walk) from my house

2 *(moment)* minute, moment; **revenez dans une petite m.** come back in a minute *or* moment (or two); **il y a une m.** *ou* **il n'y a pas même une m., tu disais tout le contraire** just a minute *or* moment ago, you were saying the very opposite; **il est parti il y a deux minutes** he left a couple of minutes ago; **de m. en m.** by the minute; **ne pas avoir une m. de répit** not to have a moment's *or* minute's rest; **ne pas avoir une m. à soi** not to have a minute *or* a moment to oneself; **as-tu une m.? j'ai à te parler** do you have a minute? I have to talk to you; **la m. de vérité** the moment of truth

3 *(comme adj inv) (instantané)* **nettoyage m.** same-day cleaning; **talon m.** on-the-spot shoe repair, *Br* heel bar; **clés m.** key bar; **steak m.** minute steak; **repas m.** convenience meal

4 *Géom* minute

5 *Jur (d'un document)* original; *(de contrat)* minute, draft; *(d'acte, de jugement)* record; **les minutes** *(d'une réunion)* minutes

EXCLAM *Fam* wait a minute *or* moment!; **m., je n'ai pas dit ça!** hang on *or* wait a minute, I never said that!; **m., papillon!** hold your horses!, not so fast!

❑ **à la minute** ADV **1** *(il y a un instant)* a moment ago; **elle est sortie à la m.** she's just this minute gone out

2 *(sans attendre)* this minute *or* instant; **faire qch à la m.** to do sth at a minute's *or* a moment's notice; **je veux que ce soit fait à la m.** I want it done this instant

3 *(toutes les 60 secondes)* per minute; **45 tours à la m.** 45 revolutions a *or* per minute

❑ **d'une minute à l'autre** ADV any time; **il sera là d'une m. à l'autre** he'll be here any minute (now), he won't be a minute; **les choses peuvent changer d'une m. à l'autre** things may change at any moment

minuter [3] [minyte] VT **1** *(spectacle, cuisson)* to time; **sa journée de travail est soigneusement minutée** he/she works to a very tight *or* strict schedule **2** *(accord)* to draw up, to draft; *(acte, jugement)* to record, to enter

minuterie [minytri] NF **1** *Élec* time switch, timer; **il y a une m. dans l'escalier** the stair light is on a time switch **2** *(d'une horloge)* motion work; *(d'un compteur)* counter mechanism

minuteur [minytœr] NM timer

minutie [minysi] NF **1** *(application)* meticulousness, thoroughness; **remarquez la m. des broderies sur ce tissu** notice the intricacy of the embroidery on this material; **avec m.** *(travailler)* meticulously, carefully; *(examiner)* in minute detail, thoroughly **2** *Vieilli (détail)* minute detail; **minuties** trifles, petty details, *Sout* minutiae

minutier [minytje] NM *Jur* (lawyer's) minute book; **m. central** = archives for ancient records, *Br* ≃ Public Records Office

minutieuse [minysjøz] *voir* **minutieux**

minutieusement [minysjøzmɑ̃] ADV **1** *(avec précision)* meticulously, carefully **2** *(en détail)* in minute detail

minutieux, -euse [minysjø, -øz] ADJ **1** *(personne)* meticulous, thorough; **déjà enfant, il était très m.** even as a child, he used to do everything very meticulously **2** *(travail)* meticulous, detailed, thorough; *(dessin, sculpture)* detailed; **enquête/recherche minutieuse** thorough investigation/research; **la broderie est un travail très m.** embroidery demands close work *or* attention to detail

miocène [mjɔsɛn] ADJ Miocene

NM **le m.** the Miocene (period)

mioche [mjɔʃ] NMF *Fam* kid, *Br* nipper

mi-parti, -e [miparti] *(mpl* **mi-partis,** *fpl* **mi-parties***)* ADJ **1** *(à moitié)* **m.... m....** half... half...; **robe mi-partie de blanc et de noir** dress half black and half white **2** *Hér* party per pale **3** *Hist* **chambres mi-parties** = parliamentary tribunals set up under the Edict of Nantes and comprising an equal number of Catholic and Protestant judges

mi-pente [mipɑ̃t] **à mi-pente** ADV halfway up/down the hill

MIPS [mips] NM *Ordinat (abrév* **million d'instructions par seconde***)* MIPS

MIP-TV [mipteve] NF *(abrév* **marché international des programmes de télévision***)* = trade fair for the television industry which takes place annually in Cannes

mir [mir] NM *Hist* mir

mirabelle [mirabɛl] NF *(fruit)* mirabelle (plum); *(liqueur)* mirabelle *(plum brandy)*

mirabellier [mirabelje] NM mirabelle plum tree

mirabilis [mirabilis] NM *Bot* four o'clock, marvel of Peru

miracidium [mirasidjɔm] NM *Zool* miracidium

miracle [mirakl] NM **1** *(intervention divine)* miracle; **sa guérison tient du m.** his/her recovery is (nothing short of) a miracle

2 *(surprise)* miracle, marvel; **et le m. se produisit, l'enfant parla enfin** and the miracle happened, the child at last spoke; **c'est (un) m. que...** + *subjonctif* it's a miracle *or* a wonder that...; **faire des miracles** to work miracles *or* wonders; **le m. de l'amour** the miracle *or* wonder of love; **les miracles de la science** the wonders *or* marvels of science; **m. économique** economic miracle; **le m. industriel allemand** the German industrial miracle; **un m. d'architecture** a marvel *or* miracle of architecture; **le deuxième mouvement est un m. de délicatesse** the second movement is wonderfully delicate

3 *Théât* miracle play

4 *(comme adj; avec ou sans trait d'union)* miracle *(avant n)*, wonder *(avant n)*; **médicament m.** miracle *or* wonder drug; **une crème m. contre la cellulite** a cream that works miracles *or* wonders on cellulite; **la solution-m. à vos problèmes de rangement** the miracle solution to your storage problems; **je ne crois pas aux solutions-m.** I don't believe in miracle cures

❑ **par miracle** ADV by a *or* some miracle, miraculously; **échapper à qch par m.** to have a miraculous escape from sth; **comme par m.** as if by a *or* some miracle; **mais par m., j'avais pensé à fermer le gaz** but, miraculously *or* amazingly enough, I'd remembered to turn off the gas

miraculé, -e [mirakyle] ADJ *(d'une maladie)* miraculously cured; *(d'un accident)* miraculously saved

NM,F **1** *Rel* **c'est un m. de Lourdes** he was miraculously cured at Lourdes **2** *(survivant)* miraculous survivor; **une des rares miraculées du tremblement de terre** one of the few (people) who miraculously survived the earthquake; **c'est un m.** he's lucky to be alive

miraculeuse [mirakyløz] *voir* **miraculeux**

miraculeusement [mirakyløzmɑ̃] ADV miraculously, (as if) by a *or* some miracle

miraculeux, -euse [mirakylø, -øz] ADJ **1** *(qui tient du miracle)* miraculous, miracle *(avant n)*; **cela n'a rien de m.!** there's nothing miraculous *or* special about it! **2** *(très opportun)* miraculous, wonderful **3** *(prodigieux)* miraculous, miracle *(avant n)*; **produit/sauvetage m.** miracle product/rescue

mirador [miradɔr] NM **1** *Archit* mirador **2** *Mil* watchtower, mirador

mirage [miraʒ] NM **1** *(illusion optique)* mirage **2** *(chimère)* mirage, delusion; **je m'étais laissé prendre au m. de l'amour** I had fallen for the illusion of perfect love **3** *(d'un œuf)* candling

miraud [miro] = **miro**

mirbane [mirban] NF **essence de m.** oil of mirbane, nitrobenzene

mire [mir] NF **1** *(de fusil)* **cran de m.** backsight (notch); **point de m.** aim, target; *Fig* **pendant les Jeux, la ville sera le point de m. du monde entier** the eyes of the world will be on the city during the Games **2** *(d'un téléviseur)* **m. (de réglage)** test card, *Spéc* test pattern **3** *Tech (pour niveler)* levelling rod *or* staff; *(piquet)* (surveyor's) ranging pole; **m. parlante** target rod

mire-œuf [mirœf], **mire-œufs** [mirø] *(pl* **mire-œufs***)* NM candling light

mirepoix [mirpwa] NF *Culin* mirepoix

mirer [3] [mire] VT **1** *(œuf)* to candle

2 *Littéraire (voir se refléter)* **le saule mire ses branches dans la rivière** the willow branches are reflected *or* mirrored in the river

3 *Arch (regarder)* to watch; *(viser)* to aim at, to take aim at

▸**se mirer** VPR *Littéraire* **1** *(se regarder)* to gaze at oneself

2 *(se refléter)* to be mirrored *or* reflected; **les saules se miraient dans le lac** the willows were mirrored *or* reflected in the lake

mirettes [mirɛt] NFPL *Fam* eyes■, peepers, *Am* baby blues; **on s'en est pris plein les m.** we feasted our eyes on it

mireur, -euse [mirœr, -øz] NM,F candler

mirifique [mirifik] ADJ *Hum* fabulous, amazing, staggering

mirliflor, mirliflore [mirliflɔr] NM *Hum Vieilli* dandy, fop

mirliton [mirlitɔ̃] NM **1** *Mus* kazoo, mirliton; **une musique de m.** second-rate music; **des vers de m.** doggerel, bad verse **2** *Mil* shako

mirmidon [mirmidɔ̃] NM *Vieilli* whippersnapper, pipsqueak, little runt

mirmillon [mirmijɔ̃] NM *Antiq* myrmillo

miro [miro] *Fam* ADJ *(myope)* short-sighted■; **sans mes lunettes, je suis complètement m.** I'm as blind as a bat without my glasses

NMF short-sighted person■

mirobolant, -e [mirɔbɔlɑ̃, -ɑ̃t] ADJ *Fam (mirifique)* fabulous, stupendous, amazing; **carrière mirobolante** glittering career; **il touche un salaire m.** he earns an absolute fortune; **des promesses mirobolantes** extraordinary *or* grandiose promises

miroir [mirwar] NM **1** *(verre réflecteur)* mirror; **m. déformant/grossissant** distorting/magnifying mirror; **m. à main/à barbe** hand/shaving mirror; **m. (pliant) à trois faces** triple mirror; **m. aux alouettes** *Chasse* decoy; *Fig* trap for the unwary; *Aut* **m. de courtoisie** vanity mirror

2 *Littéraire (surface unie)* mirror-like surface; **le m. des eaux** the mirror-like surface of the water

3 *Littéraire (image, reflet)* mirror, reflection; **les yeux sont le m. de l'âme** the eyes are the windows of the soul

4 *Méd* **m. frontal** head mirror

5 *Hort* **m. d'eau** ornamental lake

6 *Aviat* **m. d'appontage** landing mirror

7 *Entom (papillon)* silver-spotted skipper moth

8 *Nucl* **m. magnétique** magnetic mirror

9 *Géol* **m. de faille** slickenslide

'De l'autre côté du miroir' *Carroll* 'Through the Looking Glass'

miroitant, -e [mirwatɑ̃, -ɑ̃t] ADJ **1** *(luisant)* glistening, gleaming **2** *(chatoyant)* shimmering

miroité, -e [mirwate] ADJ *(cheval, robe)* dappled

miroitement [mirwatmɑ̃] NM **1** *(lueurs)* glistening, gleaming **2** *(chatoiement)* shimmering

miroiter [3] [mirwate] VI **1** *(luire)* to glisten, to gleam; *(chatoyer)* to shimmer **2** *Fig* **faire m. qch à qn** to (try and) lure sb with the prospect of sth; **on lui a fait m. une augmentation** they dangled the prospect of a *Br* rise *or Am* raise before him/her

miroiterie [mirwatri] NF **1** *(industrie)* mirror industry **2** *(commerce)* mirror trade **3** *(fabrique)* mirror factory

miroitier [mirwatje] NM **1** *(ouvrier)* mirror cutter, silverer **2** *(fabricant)* mirror manufacturer **3** *(vendeur)* mirror dealer

miroton [mirɔtɔ̃], **mironton** [mirɔ̃tɔ̃] NM **(bœuf) m.** = sliced beef and onions stewed in white wine

MIRV [mirv] NM *Nucl* (*abrév* **multiple independently targetable reentry vehicle**) MIRV

Mirza [mirza] NM = typical name for a small dog

Mis (*abrév écrite* **Marquis**) Marquis, Marquess

mis, -e[1] [mi, miz] PP *voir* **mettre**

ADJ **1** *(vêtu)* **bien m.** well dressed, nicely turned out **2** *Équitation (dressé)* **cheval bien/mal m.** well-trained/badly-trained horse

misaine [mizɛn] NF **(voile de) m.** foresail

misandre [mizɑ̃dr] ADJ man-hating, *Sout* misandrous, misandrist

NMF man-hater, *Sout* misandrist

misandrie [mizɑ̃dri] NF hatred of men, *Sout* misandry

misanthrope [mizɑ̃trɔp] ADJ misanthropic

NMF misanthrope, misanthropist

'Le Misanthrope' *Molière* 'The Misanthrope'

misanthropie [mizɑ̃trɔpi] NF misanthropy

misanthropique [mizɑ̃trɔpik] ADJ *Littéraire* misanthropic

miscellanées [misɛlane] NFPL *Littéraire* miscellany, miscellanea

miscibilité [misibilite] NF miscibility

miscible [misibl] ADJ miscible

Mise (*abrév écrite* **Marquise**) Marchioness

mise[2] [miz] ADJ F *voir* **mis**

NF **1** *Cartes & (au jeu)* stake; *(à une vente aux enchères)* bid; **augmenter la m.** to up the stakes; **doubler sa m.** to double one's stake; *Fin* **m. sociale** = capital brought into a business by a partner

2 *(tenue)* attire, dress; **soigner sa m.** to take care over one's appearance; **être simple dans sa m.** to dress simply; **on voit à sa m. qu'elle n'est pas très riche** you can see from the way she dresses *or* the clothes she wears that she's not very rich

3 *Suisse (vente)* auction (sale)

4 *(dans des expressions) Fig* **m. à l'abri** putting in a safe place; **m. à l'affiche** *(d'un film)* screening; *(d'un concert, d'une pièce)* putting on, billing; *Naut* **m. à l'eau** launch; **m. à exécution** carrying out, implementation; **avec m. à exécution immédiate** to be carried out immediately; **m. à feu** *(de fusée etc)* firing; **m. à l'heure** setting (to the right time); **m. à jour** *(réactualisation)* updating, update, bringing up to date; *(résultat)* update, updated version; *Ordinat* upgrading; **m. à mort** *(gén)* putting to death; *(en tauromachie)* execution; *Chasse* kill, *Spéc* mort; *Chasse* **au moment de la m. à mort** at the kill; **m. à neuf** renovation; *Ordinat* **m. à niveau** upgrade; *Scol* **faire une m. à niveau en maths** = to catch up in maths *(after switching to another specialization)*; **m. à pied** *(disciplinaire)* suspension; *(économique)* laying off; **donner trois jours de m. à pied à qn** to give sb three days' suspension, to suspend sb for three days; **m. à la retraite** pensioning off; **m. à la retraite anticipée** early retirement; **m. à sac** *(d'une ville)* sacking; *(d'un appartement)* ransacking; **se livrer à une m. à sac** *(voyous)* to go on a looting spree; **m. à terre** *(de marchandises)* landing; **m. au courant** informing; **m. au monde** birth; **m. au pas** *Équitation* reining in (to a walk); *(d'une personne, de l'économie)* bringing into line; **m. au propre** making a fair copy, tidying up *(of a document)*; *Jur* **m. au rôle** *(d'une affaire)* putting on the *Br* cause list *or Am* docket; **m. au tombeau** entombment; **m. en accusation** indictment; *Fig* **on a assisté à une véritable m. en accusation du président du club** accusations were hurled at the club chairman; **m. en application** implementation; **m. en attente** postponing, shelving; *Ordinat & Tél* hold; *Tél* **m. en attente d'appels** call holding; *Ordinat* **m. en attente des fichiers à imprimer** printer spooling; **m. en bière** placing in the coffin; **assister à la m. en bière** to be present when the body is placed in the coffin; *Cin & Rad* **m. en boîte** editing; *Fam Fig* **être la victime d'une m. en boîte** to have one's leg pulled, *Br* to be the victim of a wind-up; **m. en bouteilles** bottling; **m. en branle** starting up, getting going; **m. en cause** *(d'une personne)* implication; *(d'une idée)* calling into question; *Fin* **m. en circulation** issue; **m. en communication** pooling; **m. en condition** *(du corps)* getting fit; *(de l'esprit)* conditioning; **m. en conserve** canning; *Jur* **m. en délibéré** = adjourning for further consultation of judges; **m. en demeure** injunction, formal notification; *(de paiement)* formal demand; *Com* **m. en dépôt** warehousing; *Jur* **m. en détention provisoire** detention pending trial; **m. en disponibilité** leave of absence; **demander sa** *ou* **une m. en disponibilité** to ask for leave of absence; **m. en doute** putting into doubt, questioning; **m. en eau** *(installation du système)* installation of water; *(ouverture des robinets)* switching on of water; *(remplissage)* filling; **m. en état** *Jur* preparation for hearing; *(d'un engin)* getting into working order; *(d'un local)* renovation; *Jur* **m. en examen** indictment; **m. en exploitation** *(d'une machine)* commissioning; **m. en forme** *(d'un chapeau)* shaping; *Ordinat* formatting; *Typ* imposition; *Sport* fitness training; **m. en gage** pawning, pledging; **m. en garde** warning; **m. en jeu** *(au début) Sport* kick-off; *(au hockey)* bully-off; *(à la touche) Ftbl* throw-in; *(au rugby)* line-out; *Fig* bringing into play; *Jur* **m. en liberté** release; *Jur* **m. en liberté conditionnelle** conditional discharge; *Jur* **m. en liberté provisoire** release on bail; *Ordinat* **m. en ligne** putting on-line; **m. en marche** starting up; *Ordinat* **m. en mémoire** storing *or* saving (in the memory); **m. en mouvement** setting in motion; **m. en musique d'un poème** setting a poem to music; **m. en œuvre** implementation; *Rad* **m. en ondes** production; **m. en orbite** putting into orbit; **depuis sa m. en orbite** since it was put into orbit; **m. en ordre** *(d'un local)* tidying up; *Ordinat (d'un fichier)* sequencing; *(d'un programme)* housekeeping; *Math* ordering; *Fin* **m. en paiement** *(d'un dividende)* payment; *Fin* **m. en pension** borrowing against securities, pledging; *Jur* **m. en péril des mineurs** endangering minors; **m. en place** setting up, organization; *Mktg* **m. en place marketing** marketing implementation; **nous avons dû retarder la m. en place du nouveau système** we have had to postpone setting up the new system; **la m. en place du nouveau réseau demandera plusieurs mois** it will take several months to set up the new system *or* to get the new system up and running; **m. en pratique** carrying out, putting into practice; **m. en question** questioning, challenging; *Ordinat* **m. en relation** *(avec un service)* log-on; *Ordinat* **m. en relief** highlighting; *Ordinat* **m. en réseau** networking; *Typ* **m. en retrait** indent; **m. en retraite** pensioning (off), retirement on a pension; **il y aura 50 mises en retraite** 50 people will be retired; **m. en route** starting up; **m. en séquence** sequencing; **m. en service** putting into service; **sa m. en service ne se fera qu'en septembre** it won't come into service until September; *Fin* **m. en terre** burial; **m. en train** *(d'un projet)* starting up; *Sport* warming up; *(d'une soirée)* breaking the ice; **m. en valeur** *Fin (d'un investissement)* turning to account; *(d'un sol, d'une région)* development; *(de biens)* improvement; *(de qualités)* setting off, enhancement; **m. en vente** (putting up for) sale; *(d'un produit)* bringing onto the market, launching; **m. en vigueur** bringing into force, implementation; *Fin* **m. hors** *(action)* disbursement; *(somme)* sum advanced; **m. hors circuit** *Électron* disconnection; *Tech* disabling; *Fam Fig* **la m. hors circuit du champion** knocking the champion out of the race; **m. hors la loi** outlawing; **m. hors service** placing out of service; **m. hors tension** power-down; *Jur* **m. sous séquestre** sequestration; *Jur* **m. sous scellés** affixing the official seals; **m. sous surveillance** putting under surveillance; **m. sous tension** supplying with electricity; *(d'un ordinateur, d'une turbine)* power-up; **m. sur écoutes** (phone) tapping; **m. sur pied** setting up

❑ **de mise** ADJ appropriate; **si tu y vas, sache que la cravate est de m.** if you go, you'll have to wear a tie, mind; **le tutoiement n'est pas de m.** it's not the done thing to say "tu"; **ta colère n'est plus de m.** your anger is out of place now, there's no point in your being angry any more

❑ **mise à feu** NF *Mil* firing; *Astron* blast-off, launch; *Mines & Tech* firing, ignition

❑ **mise à prix** NF *Br* reserve *or Am* upset price

❑ **mise au point** NF **1** *Opt & Phot* focusing, focussing

2 *Tech* tuning, adjustment; *(d'un moteur)* tuning

3 *Ordinat* trouble-shooting, debugging

4 *Fig* clarification, correction; *(d'un document, d'un rapport)* finalization, finalizing; *(d'un produit)* development; **après cette petite m. au point** now that the record has been set straight; **je voudrais faire une m. au point** I'd like to clarify something

❑ **mise de fonds** NF capital investment; **m. de fonds initiale** *(pour un achat)* initial outlay; *(pour monter une affaire)* initial investment, seed money

❑ **mise en page, mise en pages** NF **1** *Typ (maquette)* page design *or* layout; *(composition)* make-up, making up

2 *Ordinat* editing; **je n'aime pas la m. en page de la revue** I don't like the layout of the magazine

❑ **mise en plis** NF set; **faire une m. en plis à qn** to set sb's hair, to give sb a set; **shampooing et m. en plis** shampoo and set

❑ **mise en scène** NF *Cin & Théât* direction; **c'est elle qui a signé la m. en scène** she was responsible for staging the play; *Fig* **toute cette histoire n'était en fait qu'une vaste m. en scène** the entire story was just one big set-up; *Fig* **son remords n'était que de la m. en scène** his remorse was only an act

miser [3] [mize] VT **1** *(parier)* to stake, to bet (**sur** on); **j'ai misé cinq euros sur le numéro 29** I've staked *or* bet five euros on number 29

2 *Suisse (acheter)* to buy *(at an auction)*; *(vendre)* to put up for auction

❑ **miser sur** VT IND **1** *(cheval)* to bet on, to back; *(numéro)* to bet on; *Fig* **m. sur les deux tableaux** to back both horses, to hedge one's bets; *Bourse* **m. sur une hausse/une baisse** to speculate on a rising/falling market

2 *(compter sur → quelque chose)* to bank *or* to count on; *(→ quelqu'un)* to count on; **elle mise sur le succès de son livre pour s'acheter une maison** she's banking on the success of her book to be able to buy a house; **il vaut mieux ne pas m. sur lui** we'd better not count on him

misérabilisme [mizerabilism] NM *Cin & Littérature* miserabilism

misérabiliste [mizerabilist] *Cin & Littérature* ADJ miserabilist

NMF miserabilist

misérable [mizerabl] ADJ **1** *(après le nom) (sans ressources)* impoverished, poverty-stricken, poor; **quartier m.** poor *or* poverty-stricken district; **tout le pays est m.** the whole country is wretchedly *or* miserably poor

2 *(pitoyable)* pitiful, miserable, wretched; **une cabane m.** a wretched little shack; **elle me fit le récit de sa m. existence** she told me the tale of her wretched life

3 *(insignifiant)* miserable, paltry; **elles se disputent pour un m. vase** they're arguing over a stupid vase; **travailler pour un salaire m.** to work for a pittance; **pour la m. somme de dix euros** for a paltry ten euros

4 *Littéraire (méprisable)* despicable, mean

NMF **1** *Sout ou Hum (malheureux)* **m., qu'as-tu fait là!** what have you done, you wretch!

2 *Littéraire (miséreux)* pauper, wretch

3 *Littéraire (canaille)* (vile) rascal *or* scoundrel

'Les Misérables' *Hugo* 'Les Misérables'

misérablement [mizerabləmɑ̃] ADV **1** *(pauvrement)* in poverty, wretchedly **2** *(lamentablement)* pitifully, miserably, wretchedly

misère [mizɛr] NF **1** *(indigence)* poverty, *Sout* destitution; **être dans la m.** to be destitute *or* poverty-stricken; **ils sont dans une m. noire** they have nothing, they are quite destitute; **vivre dans la m.** to live in poverty; **tomber dans la m.** to become destitute; **m. dorée** splendid poverty; **réduire qn à la m.** to reduce sb to poverty; *Hum* **il se jeta sur la nourriture comme la m. sur le monde** he went at the food like a starving man *or* like a wolf on its prey; *Can Fam* **avoir de la m. à faire qch** to have trouble doing sth▪; *Can Fam* **faire de la m. à qn** to give sb a hard time, to make sb's life a misery▪

2 *Fig* poverty; **il y avait une grande m. culturelle pendant la dictature** there was great cultural poverty under the dictatorship; **m. sexuelle** sexual deprivation *or* misery

3 *(malheur)* **c'est une m. de les voir se séparer** it's pitiful *or* it's a shame to see them break up

4 *(somme dérisoire)* pittance; **gagner une m.** to earn a pittance; **je l'ai eu pour une m.** I got *or* bought it for next to nothing; **dix euros? une m.!** ten euros? a mere nothing!

5 *Méd* **m. physiologique** (serious) malnutrition

6 *Cartes* misère

7 *Bot* tradescantia

8 *Belg (locution)* **chercher m. à qn** to try to pick a quarrel with sb

EXCLAM oh Lord!; *Hum* **m. de moi!** woe is me!

❑ **misères** NFPL *Fam* **des misères** *(broutilles)* trifles, minor irritations▪; *(ennuis de santé)* aches and pains; **les petites misères de la vie conjugale** *(ennuis)* the little upsets of married life; **faire des misères à qn** to torment sb▪; **ne fais pas de misères à ce chien!** stop tormenting that dog!; **raconte-moi tes misères** tell me all your woes; **il t'arrive des misères?** what's the matter, then?; **il te fait des misères?** has he been horrible to you?

❑ **de misère** ADJ **un salaire de m.** a starvation wage, a pittance; **un lit de m.** a sick bed; *Littéraire* **vallée de m.** vale of woe, vale of tears

miserere NM INV [mizerere] miserere

miséréré NM = **miserere**

miséreux, -euse [mizerø, -øz] ADJ *Vieilli (pauvre)* poverty-stricken, destitute

NM,F poor person, pauper; **aider** *ou* **secourir les m.** to help the poor

miséricorde [mizerikɔrd] NF *Littéraire* **1** *(pitié)* mercy, forgiveness; **implorer m.** to beg *or* to cry for mercy; **m. divine** divine mercy; *Vieilli ou Hum* **m.!** heaven help us!, mercy on us! **2** *(siège)* misericord, misericorde

miséricordieux, -euse [mizerikɔrdjø, -øz] ADJ *Littéraire* merciful, forgiving; **être m. envers qn** to show mercy towards sb; **soyez m.** have mercy

misogyne [mizɔʒin] ADJ misogynous, misogynistic

NMF misogynist, woman-hater

misogynie [mizɔʒini] NF misogyny

misonéisme [mizɔneism] NM misoneism

misonéiste [mizɔneist] ADJ misoneistic

NMF misoneist

mispickel [mispikɛl] NM *Minér* mispickel, arsenical pyrites

miss [mis] *(pl inv ou* **misses** [mis]*)* NF **1** *Vieilli (gouvernante)* governess **2** *Fam Hum* **ça va, la m.?** how's things, beauty?; **et comment va m. Martin?** and how is Miss Martin?; *(en s'adressant directement à la personne)* and how are we today, Miss Martin?

❑ **Miss** NF INV *(reine de beauté)* beauty queen; **M. Japon/Monde** Miss Japan/World

missel [misɛl] NM missal

missi dominici [misidɔminisi] NMPL *Hist* missi dominici

missile [misil] NM missile; **m. air-air** air-to-air missile; **m. antiaérien** antiaircraft missile; **m. antibalistique** antiballistic missile; **m. antichar** antitank missile; **m. antimissile** antimissile missile; **m. anti-sous-marins** anti-submarine missile; **m. balistique** ballistic missile; **m. balistique de moyenne portée** intermediate-range ballistic missile; **m. balistique de portée intermédiaire** intermediate-range ballistic missile; **m. de courte portée** short-range missile; **m. de croisière** cruise missile; **m. guidé** guided *or* smart missile; **m. intercontinental** intercontinental missile; **m. de longue portée** long-range missile; **m. Pershing** Pershing missile; **m. sol-sol** ground-to-ground missile; **m. stratégique** strategic missile; **m. tactique** tactical missile; **m. téléguidé** guided *or* smart missile; **m. à tête chercheuse à infrarouge** heat-seeking missile

missilier [misilje] NM missile-operating personnel, missileman

mission [misjɔ̃] NF **1** *(charge)* mission, assignment; *(dans le cadre d'une entreprise)* assignment; *(dossier)* brief; **au cours de votre m. à Boston** while you are/were working in Boston; **envoyer qn en m. aux États-Unis** to send sb to the United States; **recevoir pour m. de faire qch** to be commissioned to do sth; **j'ai pour m. de...** my job *or* task is to...; **être en m.** to be on an assignment; **ministre en m. spéciale à Paris** minister on a special mission to Paris; **m. vous avait été confiée de faire...** you were given the job of doing..., *Sout* you were assigned the task of doing...; *Hum* **viens ici, j'ai une m. à te confier** *(à un enfant)* come here, I have a special job for you; **m. de bons offices** goodwill mission; *Mil* **m. de reconnaissance** reconnaissance mission; **être en m. de reconnaissance** to be on reconnaissance duty; **m. accomplie** mission accomplished; **m. d'activité** *ou* **d'entreprise** business mission

2 *(devoir)* mission, task; **la m. civilisatrice de l'école** the civilizing mission of schools; **la m. de notre organisation est de défendre les droits de l'homme** our organization's mission is to defend human rights; **la m. du journaliste est d'informer** a journalist's task is to inform; **il s'était donné pour m. de sauver les enfants** he had taken it upon himself to save the children

3 *(groupe)* mission; **m. commerciale** business assignment; *(gouvernementale)* trade mission; **m. diplomatique** diplomatic mission; **m. scientifique** scientific mission; **partir en m. au pôle Nord** to go on an expedition to the North Pole

4 *Rel (organisation)* mission; **missions étrangères** foreign missions; *(lieu)* mission (station); **il y a un hôpital dans la m.** there's a hospital at the mission; **la M. de France** = Catholic evangelical organization

missionnaire [misjɔnɛr] ADJ missionary *(avant n)*; **la vocation m.** the vocation of a missionary

NMF missionary

Mississippi [misisipi] NM *Géog* **1** *(fleuve)* **le M.** the Mississippi (River) **2** *(État)* **le M.** Mississippi; **au M.** in Mississippi

missive [misiv] ADJ F missive *(avant n)*

NF *Littéraire* missive

Missolonghi [misɔlɔ̃gi] NM Missolonghi

Missouri [misuri] NM *Géog* **le M.** Missouri; **dans le M.** in Missouri

mistelle [mistɛl] NF = unfermented grape juice blended with alcohol

mistigri [mistigri] NM **1** *Fam (chat)* puss **2** *Cartes* jack *or Br* knave of clubs

miston, -onne [mistɔ̃, -ɔn] NM,F *Fam Vieilli (gamin)* kid

mistoufle [mistufl] NF *très Fam Vieilli* **1** *(misère)* **être dans la m.** to be down at heel **2** *(méchanceté)* **faire des mistoufles à qn** to play dirty tricks on sb

Mistra [mistra] NM Mistra

mistral, -als [mistral] NM mistral

mit *etc voir* **mettre**

mita [mita] NF *Hist* mita

mitage [mitaʒ] NM = increase in the number of houses in a rural area

mitaine [mitɛn] NF fingerless glove; *Can & Suisse (moufle)* mitten

mitan [mitɑ̃] NM *Vieilli* **1** *(centre)* middle, centre **2** *Fam Arg crime* **le m.** the underworld, gangland

mitard [mitar] NM *Fam Arg crime (cachot)* disciplinary cell▪, cooler; **être au m.** to be in solitary *or* in the cooler; **se retrouver au m.** to end up in solitary *or* in the cooler

mite [mit] NF **1** *(papillon)* (clothes) moth; **rongé par les** *ou* **aux mites** moth-eaten **2** *(ciron)* **m. du fromage** cheese-mite

mité, -e [mite] ADJ moth-eaten

mi-temps [mitɑ̃] NF INV *Sport* **1** *(moitié)* half; **la première/seconde m.** the first/second half; *Hum* **la troisième m.** the post-match celebrations

2 *(pause)* half-time; **le score est de zéro à zéro à la m.** the half-time score is nil-nil; **siffler la m.** to blow the whistle for half-time

NM INV part-time job; **chercher un m.** to look for a part-time job; **faire un m.** to work part-time; *Scol* **m. pédagogique** part-time teaching position

❑ **à mi-temps** ADJ part-time; **travailleur à m.** part-timer, part-time worker ADV **travailler** *ou* **être à m.** to work part-time; **elle travaille à m. comme serveuse** she's a part-time waitress

miter [3] [mite] **se miter** VPR to become moth-eaten

miteux, -euse [mitø, -øz] *Fam* ADJ **1** *(costume, chambre, hôtel)* shabby, grotty; *(personne)* seedy-looking, shabby, down-at-heel **2** *(situation, salaire)* pathetic; *(escroc)* small-time

NM,F *(incapable)* nonentity, loser, *Br* no-hoper; *(indigent)* bum, *Br* dosser

Mithra [mitra] NPR *Myth* Mithra

mithriacisme [mitrijasism], **mithraïsme** [mitraism] NM Mithraism

mithriaque [mitriak] ADJ Mithraic

Mithridate [mitridat] NPR Mithridates

mithridatisation [mitridatizasjɔ̃] NF *Méd* mithridatism, immunity to poison

mithridatiser [3] [mitridatize] **VT** *Littéraire* to mithridatize

mithridatisme [mitridatism] **NM** *Méd* mithridatism, immunity to poison

mitigation [mitigasjɔ̃] **NF** mitigation; **la m. d'une peine** the mitigation of a sentence

mitigé, -e [mitiʒe] **ADJ 1** *(modéré)* mixed; **des critiques mitigées** mixed reviews; **manifester un enthousiasme m.** to be reserved in one's enthusiasm; **j'avais des sentiments mitigés à son égard** I had mixed feelings about him/her; **le public était assez m.** the public was quite mixed in its reaction; **morale mitigée** lax morals; *Jur* **peine mitigée** reduced sentence **2 m. de** *(mêlé de)* mitigated or qualified by; **des éloges mitigés de critiques** praise qualified by criticism

mitiger [17] [mitiʒe] **VT** *Vieilli* to mitigate; *(peine)* to reduce, to mitigate; *(règlement, loi)* to relax; **m. qch de** to mix or to temper sth with; **ayant mitigé ses critiques de quelques compliments** having tempered his/her criticism with a few words of praise

mitigeur [mitiʒœr] **NM** mixer tap, *Am* mixing faucet; **m. de douche** shower mixer

mitochondrie [mitokɔ̃dri] **NF** *Biol* mitochondrion

mitonner [3] [mitɔne] **VT 1** *Culin* to simmer, to slow-cook; **bœuf mitonné** stewed beef, beef stew; **je vous ai mitonné une petite recette à moi** I've cooked you one of my tasty little recipes **2** *Fig (coup, plan)* to plot, to cook up; **j'ai bien mitonné ma vengeance** I carefully plotted my revenge **3** *Littéraire* **m. qn** to cosset or to pamper sb **VI** *Culin* to simmer, to stew gently; **laissez m. la viande** leave the meat to simmer

mitonneur [mitɔnœr] **NM** *Culin* slow cooker

mitose [mitoz] **NF** *Biol* mitosis

mitotique [mitotik] **ADJ** *Biol* mitotic

mitoyen, -enne [mitwajɛ̃, -ɛn] **ADJ 1** *(commun)* common, shared; **puits m. entre les deux maisons** well shared by or common to the two houses; **cloison mitoyenne** dividing wall *(between two rooms)* **2** *(jouxtant)* bordering, neighbouring; **les champs sont mitoyens** the fields are adjacent to each other; **le jardin m. du nôtre** the garden (immediately) next to ours, the neighbouring garden (to ours); **deux maisons mitoyennes** semi-detached houses; **une rue de maisons mitoyennes** a street of terrace or terraced houses **3** *(en copropriété)* commonly owned, jointly owned; **mur m.** party wall

mitoyenneté [mitwajɛnte] **NF 1** *(copropriété)* common or joint ownership **2** *(contiguïté)* adjacency

mitraillade [mitrajad] **NF** volley of shots

mitraillage [mitrajaʒ] **NM** machinegunning

mitraille [mitraj] **NF 1** *Mil* grapeshot; *(décharge)* volley of shots **2** *Métal* scrap metal or iron **3** *Fam (petite monnaie)* small or loose change■, *Br* coppers

mitrailler [3] [mitraje] **VT 1** *Mil* to machinegun **2** *Fam (photographier)* to snap (away) at; **se faire m. par les photographes** to be besieged by photographers **3** *Fig (assaillir)* **m. qn de questions** to fire questions at sb, to bombard sb with questions **4** *Métal* to scrap

mitraillette [mitrajɛt] **NF** submachine-gun, machine pistol

mitrailleur [mitrajœr] **NM** machine-gunner; **m. d'avion** air-gunner; *Mil & Aviat* **m. arrière** rear gunner

mitrailleuse [mitrajøz] **NF** machine gun; **m. d'avion** *ou* **d'aviation** aircraft machine gun; **m. légère/lourde** light/heavy machine gun; **m. de tourelle** mounted (turret) machine gun

mitral, -e, -aux, -ales [mitral, -o] **ADJ** mitral

mitre [mitr] **NF 1** *Rel* mitre; **recevoir la m.** to be mitred **2** *Constr (chimney)* cowl

mitré, -e [mitre] **ADJ** mitred

mitron [mitrɔ̃] **NM 1** *(garçon pâtissier)* pastry cook's apprentice or boy; *(garçon boulanger)* baker's apprentice or boy **2** *Constr* chimney cowl seating or head

mi-voix [mivwa] **à mi-voix** **ADV** in a low or hushed voice, in hushed tones; **chanter à m.** to sing

softly; **parler à m.** to speak quietly or in a low voice

mix [miks] **NM** *Mktg (marchéage)* mix; **m. média** media mix; **m. de produits** product mix

mixage [miksaʒ] **NM** *Rad, TV & Mus* mixing; **m. final** master soundtrack; **m. d'images** vision mixing; **m. magnétique final** master soundtrack; **m. sonore** sound mixing

mixer¹ [3] [mikse] **VT 1** *Culin (à la main)* to mix; *(au mixer)* to blend, to liquidize **2** *Mus* to mix

mixer², mixeur [miksœr] **NM** blender, liquidizer

mixité [miksite] **NF 1** *(gén)* mixed nature **2** *Scol* coeducation, coeducational system

mixte [mikst] **ADJ 1** *(des deux sexes)* mixed; *Scol* **classe m.** mixed class; *Sport* **double m.** mixed doubles; **école m.** mixed or coeducational school; **équipe m.** mixed team **2** *(de nature double)* mixed; *Jur* **action m.** mixed action; **billet m.** combined rail and road ticket; **commission m.** joint commission; **train m.** composite train *(goods and passengers)* **3** *(à double usage)* **cuisinière m.** combined gas and electric *Br* cooker or *Am* stove; **race bovine m.** milk-producing and meat-producing cattle breed **NM** *Sport* mixed doubles match

mixtion [mikstjɔ̃] **NF** *Chim & Pharm (action)* blending, compounding; *(médicament)* mixture

mixture [mikstyr] **NF 1** *Chim & Pharm* mixture **2** *(boisson, nourriture)* mixture, concoction; **on nous a servi une m. infâme** they served us a vile concoction

mizuna [mizuna] **NM** *Bot & Culin* mizuna

MJC [ɛmʒise] **NF** *(abrév* **maison des jeunes et de la culture)** community centre

MJPEG [ɛmʒipɛg] **NM** *Ordinat (abrév* **Moving Joint Photographic Expert Group)** MJPEG

ml *(abrév écrite* **millilitre)** ml

MLF [ɛmɛlɛf] **NM** *(abrév* **Mouvement de libération de la femme)** = women's movement, *Am* ≃ NOW

Mlle *(abrév écrite* **Mademoiselle)** Miss

Mlles *(abrév écrite* **Mesdemoiselles)** Misses

mm *(abrév écrite* **millimètre(s))** mm

MM. *(abrév écrite* **Messieurs)** Messrs

Mme *(abrév écrite* **Madame)** *(femme mariée)* Mrs; *(femme mariée ou célibataire)* Ms

Mmes *(abrév écrite* **Mesdames)** Ladies

MMPI [ɛmɛmpei] **NM** *Psy (abrév* **Minnesota multiphasic personality inventory)** MMPI

MMS [ɛmɛmɛs] **NM** *Tél (abrév* **multimedia message service)** MMS

mnémonique [mnemonik] **ADJ** mnemonic; **procédé** *ou* **moyen m.** mnemonic

mnémotechnie [mnemɔtɛkni] **NF** mnemonics *(singulier)*

mnémotechnique [mnemɔtɛknik] **ADJ** mnemonic; **formule m.** mnemonic **NF** mnemonics *(singulier)*

mnésique [mnezik] **ADJ** mnemonic

MNR [ɛmɛnɛr] **NM** *(abrév* **Mouvement National Républicain)** = right-wing French political party

MNS [ɛmɛnɛs] **NM** *(abrév* **maître nageur sauveteur)** lifeguard

Mo [ɛmo] **NM** *Ordinat (abrév* **mégaoctet)** MB, Mb

moa [moa] **NM** moa

moabite [moabit] *Bible* **ADJ** Moabite **NMF** Moabite

mob¹ [mɔb] **NF** *Fam (Mobylette®)* moped

mob² [mɔb] **NF** *Suisse Hist* = mobilization of the Swiss reserve army during the First and Second World Wars

mobile [mɔbil] **ADJ 1** *(qui se déplace → pont, cible)* moving; *(→ main-d'œuvre, population, personne âgée)* mobile; *(→ organe, cartilage)* mobile, having freedom of movement; *(→ panneau)* sliding; *(amovible)* movable, removable; *(feuillets)* loose; **trois étagères mobiles et deux fixes** three movable or removable shelves and two fixed ones; **carnet à feuilles mobiles** loose-leaf notepad; **le boxeur est très m.** the boxer is very nimble or quick on his feet; *Tech* **organes mobiles** sliding or working or moving parts **2** *Mil (unité)* mobile **3** *(changeant)* mobile; *Vieilli (humeur)* changeable; **un visage m.** a lively or animated face **4** *Typ (à valeur non fixe)* **caractère m.** movable character

NM 1 *(de sculpteur, pour enfant) & Beaux-Arts* mobile; *Mktg* **m. publicitaire** advertising mobile **2** *Phys* moving object **3** *(motif)* motive; **le m. d'un crime** the motive for a crime; **quel m. l'a poussé à agir ainsi?** what motivated or prompted him to act this way?; *Mktg* **m. d'achat** buying inducement, purchasing motivator; **4** *(téléphone portable) Br* mobile (phone), *Am* cellphone

mobile home [mɔbilom] *(pl* **mobile homes)** **NM** mobile home

mobilier, -ère [mɔbilje, -ɛr] **ADJ** *Jur (propriété)* personal, movable; *(titre)* transferable; **biens mobiliers** personal property *(UNCOUNT)*; **effets mobiliers** chattels **NM** *(d'une habitation)* furniture, furnishings; **du m. Louis XIII/Renaissance** Louis XIII/Renaissance (style) furniture; **le m. de la salle à manger** the dining room furniture; **M. national** = state-owned furniture (in France) **2** *(pour un usage particulier)* **m. de bureau/jardin** office/garden furniture; **m. scolaire** school furniture or furnishings; **m. de présentation** display stands **3** *Jur* movable property, movables **4 m. urbain** street fittings, street furniture

mobilisable [mɔbilizabl] **ADJ 1** *Mil* liable to be called up, mobilizable; **les jeunes de moins de 18 ans ne sont pas mobilisables** young people under 18 are not eligible for call-up **2** *(disponible)* available **3** *Fin (capital)* realizable; *(actif, biens immobiliers)* mobilizable

mobilisateur, -trice [mɔbilizatœr, -tris] **ADJ** mobilizing; **un slogan m.**, **c'est un thème très m. en ce moment** it's an issue which is stirring a lot of people into action at the moment

mobilisation [mɔbilizasjɔ̃] **NF 1** *Mil (action)* mobilization, mobilizing, calling up; *(état)* mobilization; **m. générale/partielle** general/partial mobilization; **ordre de m. générale** general mobilization order **2** *(d'une force politique)* mobilization; *(d'énergie, de volonté)* mobilization, summoning up; **il appelle à la m. de tous les syndicats** he is calling on all the unions to mobilize; **les syndicats comptent beaucoup sur la m. des enseignants contre ce projet de réforme** the unions are relying heavily on the teachers to rally against this proposed reform **3** *Fin (de capital)* realization; *(d'actif, de biens immobiliers)* mobilization; *(de fonds)* raising **4** *Méd & Physiol* mobilization

mobilisatrice [mɔbilizatris] *voir* **mobilisateur**

mobiliser [3] [mɔbilize] **VT 1** *Mil (population)* to call up, to mobilize; *(armée)* to mobilize; *(réserviste)* to call up; *Fig Hum* **nous fûmes tous mobilisés pour l'aider à déménager** we were all marshalled or mobilized into helping him/her move; *Fig* **toute la famille fut mobilisée pour préparer la fête** the whole family was put to work to organize the party **2** *(syndicalistes, consommateurs, moyens techniques)* to mobilize; *(volontés)* to mobilize, to summon up; **m. toute son énergie** to summon up all one's energy; **m. qn pour faire qch** to mobilize sb into doing sth; **m. l'opinion en faveur des réfugiés politiques** to rally public opinion for the cause of the political refugees; **m. les forces vives d'une nation** to call upon the full resources of a nation **3** *Fin (capital)* to realize; *(actif, biens immobiliers)* to mobilize; *(fonds)* to raise **4** *Méd & Physiol (membre, articulation)* to mobilize

►se mobiliser VPR to mobilize **(contre/en faveur de** against/in support of); **tout le village s'est mobilisé contre le projet** the whole village rose up in arms against the plan or mobilized to fight the plan

mobilisme [mɔbilism] **NM 1** *Phil* doctrine of constant flux **2** *Géol* theory of continental drift

mobilité [mɔbilite] **NF 1** *(dans l'espace → d'une personne, d'une population)* mobility; *(dans le travail)* willingness to move or relocate; *(des organes)* freedom of movement **2** *(expression → d'un regard)* expressiveness; *Fig (de caractère, d'humeur)* changeability **3** *(dans une hiérarchie)* mobility; **m. interne** internal mobility; **m.**

mit-mob

professionnelle professional mobility; **m. sociale** social mobility **4** *Électron & Mil* mobility

moblot [mɔblo] **NM** *Fam Hist* = nineteenth-century militiaman

Mobutu [mɔbutu] *voir* **lac**

Mobylette® [mɔbilɛt] **NF** Mobylette®, moped; **faire de la M.** to ride a moped; **elle y va en** *ou* **à M.** she goes there on her moped

mocassin [mɔkasɛ̃] **NM 1** *(chaussure)* moccasin **2** *(serpent)* (water) moccasin

mocauque [mɔkok] **NM** *Can (en acadien → terrain marécageux)* marsh; *(→ canneberge)* cranberry *(that grows in marshland)*

mochard, -e [mɔʃar, -ard] **ADJ** *Fam* quite ugly▪

moche [mɔʃ] **ADJ** *Fam* **1** *(laid → personne)* ugly▪; *(→ objet, vêtement)* ugly▪, awful, horrible; **qu'est-ce qu'elle est m. aujourd'hui!** she looks a real sight today!; **t'as vu ses chaussures? ce qu'elles sont moches!** have you seen his/her shoes? they're hideous *or* awful!

2 *(moralement répréhensible)* lousy, rotten; **c'est m., ce qu'elle lui a fait** it was rotten, what she did to him/her

3 *(regrettable)* rotten; **c'est m., ce qui lui est arrivé** it was rotten *or* terrible what happened to him/her; **c'est trop m. de mourir à 20 ans** it's terrible to die at 20

4 *(pénible)* **tu ne peux pas prendre de congé? c'est m., dis donc!** can't you take any time off? that's terrible!; **c'est m. qu'il pleuve aujourd'hui!** it's a real drag *or* pain that it had to rain today!

mocheté [mɔʃte] **NF** *Fam* **1** *(laideur)* ugliness▪; **c'est d'une m.!** what an eyesore!, it's absolutely hideous!; **la mode de cet été est d'une m.!** this summer's fashions are hideous! **2** *(personne laide)* moose, horror, *Br* minger; *(objet)* eyesore; **c'est une vraie m.!** she's as ugly as sin!; **quelle m., cette lampe!** that lamp's such an eyesore *or* absolutely hideous!

moco [mɔko] **NM** *Fam* **1** *(marin toulonnais)* sailor from Toulon▪ **2** *(Provençal)* Provençal▪

M-octet *Ordinat (abrév écrite* **mégaoctet**) MB, Mb

mod [mɔd] **NM** *Ordinat* mod

modal, -e, -aux, -ales [mɔdal, -o] **ADJ** *Ling & Mus* modal

NM *Ling* modal (auxiliary)

modalisation [mɔdalizasjɔ̃] **NF** *Ling* modalization

modalité [mɔdalite] **NF 1** *(façon)* mode, method; *(d'application d'une loi)* mode; *Jur* **modalités** (restrictive) clauses; *Scol* **modalités de contrôle** methods of assessment; **modalités de financement** financing terms *or* conditions; **modalités de paiement** *(conditions)* conditions *or* terms of payment; *(liquide, chèque etc)* methods of payment; **modalités de remboursement** terms of repayment

2 *(circonstances)* **les modalités de l'accord** the terms of the agreement; *Jur* **modalités d'application d'un décret** modes of enforcement of a ruling; *Écon* **modalités d'une émission** terms and conditions of an issue; **modalités d'intervention** procedure; **les modalités de notre collaboration** the details of exactly how we intend to work together

3 *Ling, Mus & Phil* modality; **adverbe de m.** modal adverb

moddeur [mɔdœr] **NM** *Ordinat* modder

modding [mɔdiŋ] **NM** *Ordinat* modding

mode¹ [mɔd] **NF 1** *(vêtements)* **la m.** fashion; **la m. (de) printemps/(d')hiver** the spring/winter fashion; **la m. courte/longue** the (fashion for) high/low hemlines; **la m. est aux couleurs pastel** pastels are in (fashion); **la m. des pantalons pattes d'éléphant est revenue** flares are back (in fashion); **c'est la m. des bas résille** fishnet stockings are in fashion *or* in vogue; **c'est la dernière** *ou* **c'est la grande m.** it's the latest fashion; **passer de m.** to go out of fashion; **c'est passé de m.** it's out of fashion, it's no longer fashionable; **ceux qui font la m.** trendsetters, fashionsetters; **lancer une m.** to set a fashion *or* a trend; **il a lancé la m. de la fausse fourrure** he launched the fashion for imitation fur; **suivre la m.** to follow fashion

2 *(activité)* **la m.** *(gén)* the fashion industry *or* business; *(stylisme)* fashion designing; **un professionnel de la m.** a fashion professional; **journal de m.** fashion magazine

3 *(goût du jour)* fashion; **c'était la m. de faire du jogging** jogging was all the rage then; **ce n'est plus la m. de se marier** marriage is outdated *or* has gone out of fashion; **la m. des années quatre-vingt-dix** the style of the nineties

4 *Vieilli (coutume)* custom, fashion; **c'était l'ancienne m.!** those were the days!

5 *Arch* **modes** *(vêtements)* fashions; **gravures de modes** fashion plates; **magasin de modes** milliner's shop

ADJ INV *(coloris, coupe)* fashion *(avant n)*, fashionable; **c'est très m.** it's very fashionable, it's very much in fashion; **il ne porte que des choses très m.** he only wears things that are the height of fashion

❑ **à la mode ADJ** *(vêtement)* fashionable, in fashion; *(personne, sport)* fashionable; *(chanson)* (currently) popular; **être à la m.** *(vêtement, objet)* to be in fashion *or* in vogue; **ce n'est plus à la m.** it's out of fashion; **dans un café à la m.** in a fashionable café; **ce sont des gens à la m.** they're very fashionable **ADV se mettre à la m.** to follow the latest fashion; **revenir à la m.** to come back into fashion

❑ **à la mode de PRÉP 1** *(suivant l'usage de)* in the fashion of; **elle cuisine à la m. de Provence** she cooks in the Provençal fashion; **je les fais toujours à la m. de chez nous** I always do them like we do at home

2 *(locutions)* **cousin à la m. de Bretagne** distant cousin, first cousin once removed; **neveu/oncle à la m. de Bretagne** nephew/uncle six times removed

mode² [mɔd] **NM 1 m. de** *(méthode)* mode *or* method of; *(manière personnelle)* way of; **m. d'action** form *or* mode of action; **on ne connaît pas le m. d'action de cette substance** we don't know how this substance works; *Compta* **m. d'amortissement linéaire** straight-line depreciation method; **m. de classement** filing system; **m. de codification** coding method; **m. de cuisson** cooking instructions; **m. d'emploi** directions *or* instructions for use; **m. d'existence** way of living; **m. d'expédition** method of delivery; **m. d'expression** means of expression; **m. de fonctionnement** method of operation; **m. de gestion** management method *or* style; *Compta* **m. linéaire** straight-line method; **m. opératoire** modus operandi; **m. de paiement** mode *or* method of payment; **m. de pensée** way of thinking; **m. de production** mode of production; **m. de règlement** mode *or* method of payment; **m. de scrutin** voting system; **m. de transport** method of transport; **m. de vie** *(gén)* lifestyle, way of life; *(en sociologie)* pattern of living

2 *Ling* mood, mode

3 *Ordinat* mode; **m. d'accès** access mode; **m. ajout** append mode; **m. autonome** off-line mode; **m. brouillon** draft mode; **m. canal** channel mode; **m. connecté** on-line mode; **m. continu** continuous mode; **m. conversationnel** *(d'un modem)* conversation mode; **m. dialogue** *(d'un modem)* dialogue mode; **m. différé** delayed mode, non real-time mode; **m. édition** edit mode; **m. en ligne** on-line mode; **m. esclave** slave mode; **m. graphique** graphics mode; **m. hors ligne** off-line mode; **m. d'impression rapide** draft mode; **m. d'insertion** insert mode; **m. lecture seule** read-only mode; **m. local** off-line mode; **m. maître** master mode; **m. multitâche** multitasking mode; **m. paysage** landscape mode; **en m. point** *(image)* bitmapped, bitmap; **m. portrait** portrait mode; **m. problème** *ou* **programme** problem mode; **m. rapide** draft mode; **m. réponse** *(d'un modem)* draft mode; **m. de superposition** overwrite mode; **m. superviseur** supervisor mode; **m. survol** browser mode; **m. télétraitement** remote mode; **m. texte** text mode; **m. de transmission** data communication mode; **m. utilisateur** user mode

4 *Math, Mus & Phil* mode

5 *Typ* **m. à la française** portrait mode; **m. à l'italienne** landscape mode

6 *Aut* **m. de conduite hiver** winter driving mode; **m. de sélecteur de vitesses** gear selector; **m. dégradé** limp-home mode

modelage [mɔdəlaʒ] **NM 1** *(action)* modelling; *Métal* moulding **2** *(objet)* sculpture

modelé [mɔdəle] **NM 1** *(sur tableau)* relief; *(d'une sculpture, d'un buste)* contours, curves **2** *Géog* (surface) relief

modèle [mɔdɛl] **NM 1** *(référence à reproduire → gén)* model; *(→ de tricot, de couture)* pattern; **prendre m. sur qch** to use sth as a model; **construire qch sur le m. de** to build sth on the model of; *Beaux-Arts* **dessiner d'après un m.** to draw from life; **j'ai pris ton pull comme m.** I used your sweater as a pattern; **m. de lettre** standard letter; **m. de signature** specimen signature

2 *Scol (corrigé)* model answer; **résumez le texte en vous aidant du m.** summarize this text along the same lines

3 *(bon exemple)* model, example; **elle est un m. pour moi** she's my role model; **prendre qn pour m.** to model oneself on sb; **servir de m. à qn** to serve as a model for sb, to be a model to sb; **c'est le m. du parfait employé** he's a model employee; *Fam* **ta sœur, c'est pas un m.!** your sister is no example to follow!; **c'est un m. de discrétion** he's/she's a model of discretion; **c'est un m. du genre** it's a perfect example of its type; **un m. de vertu** a paragon of virtue; **le m. américain/japonais** the American/Japanese model

4 *Com (prototype, version → gén)* model; *(→ vêtement)* model, style, design; **grand/petit m.** large-scale/small-scale model; *Aut* **m. sport/deux portes** sports/two-door model; **une voiture dernier m.** a car of the latest design; **c'est un ancien m.** it's an old model; **ce m. existe aussi en rouge** this model also comes in *or* is also available in red; **il y a de beaux modèles dans sa collection d'hiver** there are some fine designs in his/her winter collection; **vous avez ce m. en 38?** do you have this one in a 38?; **m. de démonstration** demonstration model; **m. déposé** registered design; *Tech* **m. de fabrique** factory prototype; **m. familial** family model; **des machines bâties sur le même m.** machines built to one pattern *or* along the same lines

5 *(maquette)* model; **m. réduit** scale model; **m. réduit d'avion** model aeroplane; **un m. au 1/10** a 1 to 10 (scale) model

6 *Beaux-Arts (personne qui pose)* model; **servir de m. à un artiste** to sit *or* to model for an artist

7 *Ordinat* model; **m. client-serveur** client-server model

8 *Ling* pattern

9 *Com & Math (représentation schématique)* model; **m. du chemin critique** critical path model; **m. de décision** *ou* **décisionnel** decision model; **m. de décision en arborescence** decision-tree model; **m. déterministe** decision model; **m. économique** economic model; **m. d'entreprise** corporate model; **m. d'évaluation des actifs** capital asset pricing model; **m. mathématique** mathematical model; **m. de prévision des ventes** sales forecast model; **m. de prise de décision** *ou* **décisions** decision-making model; **m. de relations réciproques** reciprocal relationships model

10 *Géog & Météo* model; **m. climatique** climatic model; **m. météorologique** meteorological model

11 *Métal* pattern

ADJ 1 *(parfait)* model *(avant n)*; **il a eu un comportement m.** he was a model of good behaviour

2 *(qui sert de référence)* **ferme/prison m.** model farm/prison

modeler [25] [mɔdle] **VT 1** *(argile)* to model, to shape, to mould; *(figurine)* to model, to mould, to fashion; **m. des animaux en terre** to mould *or* to model animals in clay; **l'eau/l'érosion a modelé le relief de la côte** water/erosion has shaped the coastline; **les glaciers ont modelé le paysage** the glaciers moulded the landscape

2 *Fig (idées, caractère, opinion publique)* to shape, to mould; **m. sa conduite sur qn** *ou* **celle de qn** to model one's behaviour on sb *or* sb's

▸**se modeler VPR se m. sur** to model oneself on

modeleur, -euse [mɔdlœr, -øz] **NM,F 1** *Beaux-Arts* modeller **2** *Métal* pattern-maker

modélisation [mɔdelizasjɔ̃] **NF** modelling

modéliser [3] [mɔdelize] **VT** to model

modélisme [mɔdelism] **NM** scale model making

modéliste [mɔdelist] **NMF 1** *(de maquettes)* model maker **2** *Couture* (dress) designer

modem [mɔdɛm] **NM** *Ordinat* modem; **envoyer qch à qn par m.** to modem sth to sb, to send sth to sb by modem; **m. courte distance** limited distance modem; **m. externe** external modem; **m. fax** fax modem; **m. interne** internal modem; **m. longue distance** long-haul modem; **m. nul** null modem; **m. Numéris** ISDN modem; **m. réseau commuté** dial-up modem; **m. RNIS** ISDN modem

modem-câble [mɔdɛmkabl] *(pl* **modems-câbles)** **NM** *Ordinat* cable modem

modénature [mɔdenatyr] **NF** *Archit* modenature

Modène [mɔdɛn] **NM** Modena

modérateur, -trice [mɔderatœr, -tris] **ADJ 1** *(élément, présence)* moderating, restraining **2** *Physiol (nerf, substance)* moderating

     NM,F mediator, moderator; **jouer un rôle de m.** to have a moderating influence

     NM 1 *Tech* regulator, moderator **2** *Nucl & Rel* moderator **3** *(dans un forum Internet)* regulator

modération [mɔderasjɔ̃] **NF 1** *(mesure)* moderation, restraint; **avec m.** *(boire, manger, utiliser)* in moderation; *(agir)* moderately, with moderation; **une réponse pleine de m.** a very restrained answer **2** *(réduction → de dépenses)* reduction, reducing; *(atténuation → d'un sentiment)* restraint, restraining **3** *Jur* **m. de droit** ≃ tax concession **4** *Nucl* moderation

moderato [mɔderato] *Mus* **ADV** moderato

     NM moderato

modératrice [mɔderatris] *voir* **modérateur**

modéré, -e [mɔdere] **ADJ 1** *(prix)* moderate, reasonable; *(vent, température)* moderate; *(enthousiasme, intérêt, succès)* moderate, reasonable; *Météo* **mer modérée à belle** sea moderate to good

     2 *(mesuré, raisonnable)* moderate; *(plein de retenue)* moderate, restrained; **être m. dans ses propos** to be moderate in what one says

     3 *Pol* moderate

     NM,F *Pol* moderate; **les modérés** the moderates

modérément [mɔderemɑ̃] **ADV 1** *(sans excès)* in moderation

     2 *(relativement)* moderately, relatively; **je ne suis que m. surpris** I'm only moderately surprised, I'm not really all that surprised; *Ironique* **j'ai m. apprécié sa remarque** I didn't much appreciate his/her remark; *Ironique* **j'apprécie m. qu'on mette le nez dans mes affaires** I'm not very keen on people sticking their noses into my business

modérer [18] [mɔdere] **VT** *(ardeur, enthousiasme, impatience, dépenses)* to moderate, to restrain, to curb; *(vitesse)* to reduce; *(exigences)* to moderate, to restrain; **elle voulait un gros salaire mais elle a dû m. ses prétentions** she wanted a high salary but she had to set her sights a bit lower; **modérez vos propos!** please tone down *or* moderate your language!; *Hum* **modère tes ardeurs!** control yourself!

     ►**se modérer VPR 1** *(se contenir)* to restrain oneself; **elle n'a jamais su se m.** she's never been able to restrain herself

     2 *(se calmer)* to calm down; **je t'en prie, modère-toi!** please calm down *or* control yourself!

modern dance [mɔdɛrndɑ̃s] *(pl* **modern dances)** **NF** modern dance

moderne [mɔdɛrn] **ADJ 1** *(actuel, récent → mobilier, bâtiment, technique, théorie)* modern; **les temps modernes, l'époque m.** modern times; **le mode de vie m.** modern living, today's way of life

     2 *(progressiste → artiste, opinions, théoricien)* modern, progressive; **la femme m. travaille** the modern woman goes out to work; **c'est une grand-mère très m.** she's a very modern *or* up-to-date grandmother; **il faut être m.** you've got to be modern

     3 *Beaux-Arts* modern, contemporary; *Archit* **mouvement m.** international style

     4 *Scol (maths)* modern, new; *(études, histoire)* modern, contemporary

     5 *Ling (langue, sens)* modern; **grec m.** Modern Greek

     NM 1 *Beaux-Arts* modern artist; *Littérature* modern writer

2 le m. *(genre)* modern style; *(mobilier)* modern furniture; **je préférerais du m. pour la cuisine** I'd prefer modern furniture in the kitchen; **nous avons tout meublé en m.** all our furniture is modern; **mélanger le m. et l'ancien** to mix old and new

modernisateur, -trice [mɔdɛrnizatœr, -tris] **ADJ** *(tendance, réforme)* modernizing

     NM,F modernizer

modernisation [mɔdɛrnizasjɔ̃] **NF** modernization, modernizing, updating; **un effort de m. de l'enseignement** an attempt to modernize education

modernisatrice [mɔdɛrnizatris] *voir* **modernisateur**

moderniser [3] [mɔdɛrnize] **VT** to modernize, to bring up to date

     ►**se moderniser VPR** to modernize

modernisme [mɔdɛrnism] **NM** modernism

moderniste [mɔdɛrnist] **ADJ** modernist

     NMF modernist

modernité [mɔdɛrnite] **NF** modernity

modern style [mɔdɛrnstil] **ADJ INV** modern style *(avant n)*, art nouveau *(avant n)*; **une glace m.** an art nouveau mirror

     NM INV modern style, art nouveau

modeste [mɔdɛst] **ADJ 1** *(logement)* modest; *(revenu)* modest, small; *(goût, train de vie)* modest, unpretentious; *(tenue)* modest, simple; **une pièce aux dimensions modestes** a small room, a room of modest dimensions; **tu es trop m. dans tes prétentions** you're not asking for enough money

     2 *(milieu)* modest, humble; **être d'origine très m.** to come from a very modest *or* humble background

     3 *(avant le nom) (modique)* modest, humble, small; **ce n'est qu'un m. présent** it's only a very modest *or* small gift, it's just a little something; **je ne suis qu'un m. commerçant** I'm only a shopkeeper

     4 *(sans vanité)* modest; **c'était facile – tu es trop m.** it was easy – you're (being) too modest **5** *Vieilli (pudique → air, jeune fille)* modest; **une attitude m. était exigée des jeunes filles** a modest demeanour was expected from the young ladies

     NMF faire le/la m. to put on a show of modesty; **allons, ne fais pas la** *ou* **ta m.!** come on, don't be (so) modest!; **elle joue les modestes** she's acting modest

modestement [mɔdɛstəmɑ̃] **ADV 1** *(simplement)* modestly, simply; **être m. logé** to live in modest surroundings; **ils vivent très m.** they live very modestly, they lead a very simple life **2** *(sans vanité)* modestly; **il m'a m. demandé si je connaissais ses œuvres** he modestly asked me if I was familiar with his work **3** *Vieilli (avec réserve)* modestly, unassumingly; *(avec pudeur)* modestly

modestie [mɔdɛsti] **NF 1** *(humilité)* modesty; **faire preuve de m.** to be modest; **il a su garder une grande m.** he remained extremely modest; **ce n'est pas la m. qui l'étouffe!** you can't say he's/she's overmodest!; **en toute m.** in all modesty; **fausse m.** false modesty; *Ironique* **allons, pas de fausse m.!** come on, don't be so modest!

     2 *Vieilli (réserve)* modesty, self-effacement; *(pudeur)* modesty

     3 *(d'exigences, d'ambitions, de revenus)* modesty

     4 *Vieilli (ajouté à un décolleté)* modesty (piece *or* lace)

modeux, -euse [mɔdø, -øz] **NM,F** *Fam* fashionista

modicité [mɔdisite] **NF** *(de prix, de rémunération)* smallness; **malgré la m. du loyer** despite the low rent; **la m. de leur salaire ne leur permet pas de partir en vacances** they can't go on holiday because they earn so little

modifiable [mɔdifjabl] **ADJ** modifiable; **après cela, le texte ne sera plus m.** after that, the text cannot be amended

modificateur, -trice [mɔdifikatœr, -tris] **ADJ** modifying, modificatory

     NM *Biol, Gram & Ordinat* modifier

modificatif, -ive [mɔdifikatif, -iv] **ADJ** modifying

modification [mɔdifikasjɔ̃] **NF 1** *(processus)* modification, modifying, changing; *(altération)* modification, alteration, change; *(à une loi, un*

contrat) amendment; **apporter** *ou* **faire une m. à qch** to make an alteration to sth, to modify sth; **apporter une m. à la loi** to change the law

     2 *Ordinat* alteration, modification; **m. d'adresse** address modification; **m. de configuration binaire** bit handling

modificative [mɔdifikativ] *voir* **modificatif**

modificatrice [mɔdifikatris] *voir* **modificateur**

modifier [9] [mɔdifje] **VT 1** *(transformer → politique, texte)* to modify, to change, to alter; *(→ vêtement)* to alter; *(→ loi)* to amend, to change; **j'ai modifié la disposition des meubles** I've moved *or* changed the furniture around; *Naut* **m. la route** to alter course

     2 *Gram* to modify

     3 *Ordinat* to alter, to modify; **m. la configuration de qch** to reconfigure sth

     ►**se modifier VPR** to change, to alter, to be modified

modillon [mɔdijɔ̃] **NM** *Archit* modillion

modique [mɔdik] **ADJ** *(peu élevé → prix, rémunération)* modest, small; **et pour la m. somme de 20 euros, mesdames, je vous donne deux couvertures!** and for the modest sum of 20 euros, ladies, I'll give you two blankets!; *Ironique* **sa voiture a coûté la m. somme de 20 000 euros** his/her car cost a cool 20,000 euros

modiquement [mɔdikmɑ̃] **ADV** *(rétribuer)* poorly, modestly, meagrely

modiste [mɔdist] **NMF 1** *(fabricant ou vendeur de chapeaux)* milliner **2** *Can Vieilli (couturière)* seamstress, dressmaker

modulable [mɔdylabl] **ADJ** *(équipement, installation)* modular, flexible; *(horaires, tarif)* flexible; *(chauffage, éclairage)* adjustable; **bibliothèque composée d'éléments modulables** bookshelves made of versatile *or* modular units

modulaire [mɔdyler] **ADJ** modular

modulant, -e [mɔdylɑ̃, -ɑ̃t] **ADJ** *Mus* modulatory

modulateur, -trice [mɔdylatœr, -tris] **ADJ** modulating *(avant n)*; **lampe modulatrice** modulator lamp

     NM *Ordinat & Tél* modulator; **m. de fréquence** converter

modulation [mɔdylasjɔ̃] **NF 1** *(tonalité → de la voix)* modulation; *Mus & (en acoustique)* modulation

     2 *Électron, Ordinat, Rad & Tél* modulation; **m. d'amplitude/de fréquence** amplitude/frequency modulation; **poste à m. de fréquence** frequency modulation *or* FM (radio) set; **m. par déplacement de fréquence/phase** frequency/phase shift keying; **m. par impulsions et codage** pulse code modulation; **rapidité/taux de m.** modulation rate/factor

     3 *Fig (nuance)* modulation, variation

     4 *Fig (ajustement)* adjustment; **m. annuelle du temps de travail** annual adjustment of working hours

     5 *Archit* building-block *or* modular principle

     6 *Ling* modulation

modulatrice [mɔdylatris] *voir* **modulateur**

module [mɔdyl] **NM 1** *(élément → gén)* module, unit; *Archit & Constr* module; **les modules de la bibliothèque** the units that make up the bookshelves; **m. (d'enseignement)** module; **m. solaire** solar panel; *Astron* **m. lunaire/de commande** lunar/command module

     2 *Math & Phys* modulus; *Tech* **m. d'élasticité** modulus of elasticity; *Tech* **m. de rupture** modulus of rupture

     3 *Ordinat* module; **m. d'aide** help module; **m. binaire** binary deck; **m. chargeable** load module; **m. exécutable** run module; **m. d'extension** plug-in; **m. maître** master module

moduler [3] [mɔdyle] **VT 1** *Tech* to modulate **2** *(adapter)* to adjust **(en fonction de** in relation to); **m. des paiements** to adjust the rate of payment **3** *(nuancer)* to vary; *(voix)* to inflect, to modulate

     VI *Mus* to modulate

modulo [mɔdylo] *Math* **ADJ INV** modulo

     NM modulus (divisor)

Modulor® [mɔdylɔr] **NM** *Archit* Modulor®

modus vivendi [mɔdysvivɛ̃di] **NM INV** modus vivendi; **trouver un m. avec** to come to a working arrangement with

moé [mwe] **PRON** *Can Fam* me

mod-moe

moelle [mwal] **NF 1** *Anat* marrow, *Spéc* medulla; **m. épinière** spinal cord; **m. osseuse/jaune/rouge** bone/yellow/red marrow; *Fig* **jusqu'à la m.** to the core; **être gelé** *ou* **transi jusqu'à la m. des os** to be frozen to the marrow *or* to the bone **2** *Culin* (bone) marrow **3** *Bot* pith

Allusion

La substantifique moelle

In the prologue to *Gargantua* (1535), Rabelais uses this famous metaphor. He is speaking of how his reader can best grasp the text and understand it fully. **Rompre l'os et sucer la substantifique moelle** means "Crack open the bone and suck out the substantific marrow". The adjective was coined by Rabelais to mean the true inner philosophical message as opposed to the superficial appearance. Today, the phrase **la substantifique moelle** means "the true substance", as opposed to mere superficiality. This is one of the expressions forever linked with Rabelais' name. It is often used to encourage people to "dig deeper" and look beyond the outward appearance of things.

moelleuse [mwaløz] *voir* **moelleux**

moelleusement [mwaløzmɑ̃] **ADV** *(s'installer)* comfortably, snugly, luxuriously; **s'enfoncer m. dans un coussin de plumes** to snuggle down into a feather cushion; **être m. installé dans un fauteuil/sous une couette** to be snuggled up in an armchair/under a quilt

moelleux, -euse [mwalø, -øz] **ADJ 1** *(au toucher)* soft; **des coussins m.** soft *or* comfortable cushions

2 *(à la vue, à l'ouïe)* mellow, warm; **une voix moelleuse** a mellow voice

3 *(au palais → vin)* mellow, well-rounded; *(→ viande)* tender; *(→ gâteau)* moist; *(→ fromage)* smooth

4 *Littéraire (gracieux)* soft; **une courbe moelleuse** a soft *or* gentle *or* graceful curve

NM softness, mellowness; *(d'un vin)* mellowness; **un vin qui a du m.** a mellow *or* smooth wine

moellon [mwalɔ̃] **NM** *Constr* rubble, rubble-stone, moellon; **construction en moellons** rubble work; **m. d'appareil** ashlar; **m. brut** quarry stone

moere, moëre [mwɛr, mur] **NF** *Géog* polder

mœurs [mœr, mœrs] **NFPL 1** *(comportement social)* customs, habits, *Sout* mores; *(d'animaux)* habits; **les m. politiques** political practice; **c'est entré dans les m.** it's become part of everyday life; **les m. de notre temps** the social mores of our time; **autres temps, autres m.** times have changed

2 *(comportement personnel)* manners, ways; **elle a des m. vraiment bizarres** she behaves in a really odd way; **quelles drôles de m.!** what a strange way to behave!

3 *(style de vie)* lifestyle; **avoir des m. simples** to have a simple lifestyle *or* way of life, to lead a simple life

4 *(principes moraux)* morals, moral standards; **avoir des m. très strictes** to have very strict moral standards *or* morals; **avoir des m. dissolues** to lead a dissolute life, to have loose morals; *Euph* **des m. particulières** particular tastes; **une femme de m. légères** a woman of easy virtue; **les bonnes m.** morality; **c'est contraire aux bonnes m.** it goes against accepted standards of behaviour; *Arch* **avoir des m.** to be of good moral character; *Fam* **la police/brigade des m., les M.** ≃ the vice squad

5 *Zool* habits

❑ **de mœurs ADJ 1** *(sexuel)* **affaire de m.** sex case

2 *Littérature* **comédie/roman de m.** comedy/novel of manners

mofette[1] [mɔfɛt] **NF** *Géol* mofette

mofette[2] [mɔfɛt] **NF** *Zool* skunk

moflé, -e, mofflé, -e [mɔfle] **NM,F** *Belg Fam* failed (exam) candidate▪

mofler [3], **moffler** [3] [mɔfle] **VT** *Belg Fam* **j'ai été moflé** I failed my exam▪

mofleur, moffleur [mɔflœr] **NM** *Belg Fam* = teacher who fails a lot of students

Mogadiscio [mɔgadiʃjo] **NM** Mogadishu, Mogadiscio

mogette [mɔʒɛt] **NF** = type of bean from the Vendée area

moghol, -e [mɔgɔl] **ADJ** Mogul

❑ **Moghol, -e NM,F** Mogul; **les Grands Moghols** the Great Moguls

mohair [mɔɛr] **NM** mohair; **un pull en m.** a mohair sweater

Mohican [mɔikɑ̃] **NM** Mohican; **les Mohicans** the Mohicans, the Mohican

moho [mɔɔ] **NM** *Géol* Moho

moi [mwa] **PRON 1** *(sujet)* **qui est là? – m.** who's there? – me; **je l'ai vue hier – m. aussi** I saw her yesterday – so did I *or* me too; **elle est invitée, et m. aussi** she's invited, and so am I; **je n'en sais rien – m. non plus** I have no idea – neither do I *or* me neither; **m. parti, il ne restera personne** when I'm gone, there'll be nobody left; **m.? je n'ai rien dit!** me? I didn't say a word!; **m., je n'y comprends rien!** I don't understand a thing (about it)!; **m. m'sieur, m. m'sieur, je connais la réponse!** me sir, me sir, I know the answer!; **m., quand je serai grand...** when I grow up...; **m. qui vous parle, je l'ai vu de mes propres yeux** I'm telling you, I saw him with my very own eyes; **et vous voulez que m., j'y aille?** you want ME to go?; **et m. qui te faisais confiance!** and to think (that) I trusted you!; **il faisait nuit, et m. qui ne savais pas où aller!** it was dark, and there was me, not knowing where to go!; **les enfants et m., nous rentrons** the children and I are going back; **m. seul possède la clef** I'm the only one with the key; *Fam* **m., les femmes, c'est fini!** I've had my fill of women!, I'm finished with women!

2 *(avec un présentatif)* **c'est m. qui lui ai dit de venir** I was the one who *or* it was me who told him/her to come; **salut, c'est m.!** hi, it's me!; **c'est m. qui te le dis!** I'm telling you!; **je vous remercie – non, c'est m.** thank you – thank YOU

3 *(complément)* **dites-m.** tell me; **donne-le-m.** give it to me; **attendez-m.!** wait (for me)!; **et m.? vous m'oubliez?** what about me? have you forgotten me?; **vous me soupçonnez, m.?** you suspect ME?; **il nous a invités, ma femme et m.** he invited both my wife and me

4 *(avec une préposition)* **avec/pour/sans m.** with/for/without me; **ce livre est à m.** this book is mine *or* belongs to me; **c'est à m. qu'il a confié cette tâche** he gave ME this task, it was me he gave this task to; **c'est à m. qu'il l'a donné** he gave it to ME; **c'est à m. qu'il a fait cette confidence** he confided this to ME; **qu'est-ce que ça peut me faire, à m.?** what difference does that make to ME?; **il me l'a dit, à m.** he told ME; **une chambre à m. tout seul** a room of my own; *Fam* **un ami à m.** a friend of mine▪; **à m.!** *(au secours)* help!; *(de jouer)* it's my turn!; *(d'essayer)* let me have a go!; **parlez-lui de m.** mention my name to him/her; **ça ne vient pas de m.** it isn't from me; **une lettre de m.** one of my letters; **ces vers ne sont pas de m.** these verses are not mine; **c'est de m., cette lettre?** is this letter from me?, is this letter one of mine?, is this one of my letters?; **c'est en m.** it's in me; **c'est pour m.** it's for me; *(je vais payer l'addition)* I'll get this; **comptez sur m.** you can count on me; **ne soyez pas si désagréable envers m.** don't be so unkind to me

5 *(dans les comparaisons)* **il est plus âgé que m.** he is older than me *or* than I am; **tu as d'aussi bonnes raisons que m.** you have just as good reasons as me *or* as I have

6 *(en fonction de pronom réfléchi)* myself; **je suis contente de m.** I'm pleased with myself; **je devrais penser un peu plus à m.** I ought to think of myself a bit more

7 *(emploi expressif)* **regardez-m. ça!** just look at that!; **rangez-m. ça tout de suite!** put that away right now!; **sors-m. ce chien de là!** get that dog out of here!

NM *Phil* **le m.** the self; *Psy* the ego; **la psychanalyse nous aide à découvrir notre vrai m.** psychoanalysis helps us discover our true selves; *Psy* **le m. idéal** the ego ideal

moie [mwa] **NF** *Géol* soft vein *or* lode

moignon [mwaɲɔ̃] **NM** stump *(of a limb)*

moi-même [mwamɛm] **PRON** myself; **j'ai m. vérifié** I checked it myself; **mon épouse et m.** my wife and I; **je préfère vérifier par m.** I prefer to check for myself; **j'y suis allé de m.** I went there on my own initiative; **c'est m.** *(au téléphone) Br* speaking, *Am* this is he/she

moindre [mwɛ̃dr] **ADJ 1** *(comparatif) (perte)* lesser, smaller; *(qualité)* lower, poorer; *(quantité)* smaller; *(prix)* lower; **de m. gravité** less serious; **de m. importance** less important, of lesser importance; **son talent est bien m.** he's/she's far less gifted; **c'est un m. mal** it's the lesser evil; **c'est couvert par l'assurance, ce qui est un m. mal** it's covered by the insurance, so things aren't as bad as they might have been; **de deux maux, il faut choisir le m.** you have to choose the lesser of two evils

2 *(superlatif)* **le/la m.** *(de deux)* the lesser; *(de trois ou plus)* the least, the slightest; **le m. mouvement/danger** the slightest movement/danger; **pas la m. chance** not the slightest *or* remotest chance; **il n'y a pas le m. espoir de les retrouver vivants** there isn't the slightest hope of finding them alive; **je ne lui ai pas fait le m. reproche** I didn't reproach him/her in the slightest *or* in the least; **il n'a pas fait la m. remarque** he didn't say a single word; **je n'en ai pas la m. idée** I haven't got the slightest *or* faintest *or* remotest idea; **jusqu'au m. détail** down to the last *or* smallest detail; **c'est la m. des choses** it's the least I/he/*etc* can do; **dis merci, c'est la m. des choses!** you could at least say thank you!; **ce serait la m. des politesses** it would be only common courtesy; **un expert, et non des moindres** no mean expert; **c'est une pianiste, et non des moindres!** she's a pianist, and a good one at that!; **c'est là son m. défaut** that's the least of his/her faults; **au m. reproche, il se met à pleurer** he bursts into tears at the slightest reproach

3 *Suisse Fam (malade)* ill▪; **se sentir m.** to feel ill

4 *Suisse Fam* **la m.** a bit▪, a little▪; **parlons la m. de vous** let's talk a bit about you

moindrement [mwɛ̃drəmɑ̃] **ADV** *Littéraire ou Can* **il n'était pas le m. gêné** he wasn't embarrassed in the least *or* in the slightest; **sans être le m. intéressé** without being in the least bit interested

moine [mwan] **NM 1** *Rel* monk, friar; **m. cistercien** Cistercian monk **2** *Zool* Mediterranean (monk) seal **3** *Orn (vautour)* black *or* cinereous vulture; *(macareux)* puffin **4** *Arch (bassinoire)* bed warmer **5** *Can (toupie)* (spinning) top **6** *Can Vulg (pénis)* prick, dick

moineau, -x [mwano] **NM 1** *Orn* sparrow; **m. domestique** house sparrow; **m. friquet** tree sparrow; **m. soulcie** rock sparrow; *Fam* **avoir une cervelle** *ou* **tête de m.** to be bird-brained *or* scatterbrained **2** *Fam (individu)* bird, customer, fellow; **c'est un drôle de m.!** he's an odd *Br* fish *or Am* bird!

moinerie [mwanri] **NF** *Vieilli Péj* **1** *(ensemble des moines)* monastery **2** *(esprit monastique)* monkery

moine-soldat [mwansɔlda] *(pl* **moines-soldats***)* **NM** militant, crusader

moinillon [mwanijɔ̃] **NM** *(jeune moine)* young monk

MOINS [mwɛ̃]

ADV less **A** ▪ least **B**
PRÉP less **1** ▪ minus **1, 3** ▪ to **2**
NM minus sign

ADV A. *COMPARATIF D'INFÉRIORITÉ* **1** *(avec un adjectif, un adverbe)* less; **cinq fois m. cher** five times less expensive; **deux fois m. cher** half as expensive, twice as cheap; **les fraises sont m. sucrées** the strawberries are less sweet *or* aren't as sweet; **elle voit m. bien depuis l'opération** her sight hasn't been as good since the operation; **en m. rapide** but not so *or* as fast; **c'est Venise en m. ensoleillé** it's like Venice minus *or* without the sunshine; **c'est m. bien que l'an dernier** it's not as good as last year; **c'est le même appartement, en m. bien/grand** it's the same *Br* flat *or Am* apartment, only not as nice/big; **il est bien m. beau maintenant** he's much less *or* not as handsome now; **beaucoup/un peu m.** a lot/a little less; **il est m. riche qu'eux** he is not as rich as they are; **je suis m. enthousiaste que toi** I'm less enthusiastic than you, I'm

not as enthusiastic as you; **c'est elle la m. intelligente des deux** she's the less intelligent of the two; **un peu m. beau que...** a bit less handsome than..., not quite as handsome as...; **il est m. timide que réservé** he's not so much shy as reserved; **il n'en est pas m. vrai que...** it is nonetheless true that...; **non m. charmante que...** just as charming as..., no less charming than...; **je suis non m. choqué qu'on ait utilisé mon adresse** I'm just as much shocked by the fact that my address was used; **nous sommes m. que convaincus** we're less than (totally) convinced

2 *(avec un verbe)* less, not... so *or* as much; **je souffre m.** I'm not in so much *or* I'm in less pain; **parle m.!** don't speak so much!; **tu devrais demander m.** you shouldn't ask for so much; **m. tu parles, mieux ça vaut** the less you speak, the better; **j'y pense m. que tu ne le crois** I think about it less than you think; **il travaille m. que sa sœur** he works less than his sister

B. *SUPERLATIF D'INFÉRIORITÉ* **1** *(avec un adjectif, un adverbe)* **c'est lui le m. riche des trois** he's the least wealthy of the three; **c'est le sommet le m. élevé** it's the lowest peak; **c'est le modèle le m. cher qu'on puisse trouver** it's the least expensive (that) you can find; **le m. possible** as little as possible; **il travaille le m. possible** he works as little as possible; **tremper le tissu le m. souvent possible** soak the material as little as possible; **c'est lui qui habite le m. loin** he lives the least far away *or* the nearest; **je ne suis pas le m. du monde surpris** I'm not at all *or* not in the least bit surprised; **je vous dérange? – mais non, pas le m. du monde** am I disturbing you? – of course not *or* not in the slightest

2 *(avec un verbe)* **le m.** (the) least; **c'est le dernier-né qui crie le m.** the youngest is the one who cries (the) least; **c'est ce qui coûte/rapporte le m.** this is the least expensive/makes the least profit; **le m. qu'on puisse faire, c'est de les inviter** the least we could do is invite them; **le m. que l'on puisse dire, c'est qu'il manque de talent** the least one can say is that he lacks talent; **c'est le m. qu'on puisse dire!** that's the least you can say!

PRÉP 1 *(en soustrayant)* minus, less; **dix m. huit font deux** ten minus *or* less eight makes two; **on est seize: m. les enfants, ça fait douze** there are sixteen of us, twelve not counting the children

2 *(indiquant l'heure)* to; **il est m. vingt** it's twenty to; **il est trois heures m. le quart** it's quarter *or* a quarter to three; *Fam* **il était m. une** *ou* **cinq** that was a close call *or* shave; **il était m. une que je ne puisse pas y aller** I was within an ace of not being able to go

3 *(introduisant un nombre négatif)* minus; **m. 50 plus m. 6 égalent m. 56** minus 50 plus minus 6 is *or* makes minus 56; **il fait m. 25** it's 25 below *or* minus 25; **plonger à m. 300 m** to dive to a depth of 300 m

NM minus, minus sign; **mets un m. avant le chiffre 4** put a minus sign in front of the figure 4

❑ **à moins ADV j'étais terrifié – on le serait à m.!** I was terrified – and lesser things have frightened me!

❑ **à moins de PRÉP 1** *(excepté)* **à m. d'un miracle** short of *or* barring a miracle; **à m. d'une éclaircie** unless the clouds break; **nous n'arriverons pas à temps, à m. de partir demain** we won't get there on time unless we leave tomorrow

2 *(pour moins de)* for less than; **vous n'en trouverez pas à m. de 30 euros** you won't find any for under *or* for less than 30 euros

3 *(dans le temps, l'espace)* **il habite à m. de dix minutes/500 m d'ici** he lives less than ten minutes/500 m from here

❑ **à moins que CONJ** unless; **j'irai au tribunal à m. qu'il ne me rembourse** I'll go to court unless he pays me back; **à m. que vous ne vouliez le faire vous-même** unless you wanted to do it yourself

❑ **au moins ADV 1** *(en tout cas)* at least; **dis-moi ce qui t'est arrivé, au m.!** at least tell me what happened to you!; **embrasse au m. ta mère** at least kiss your mother; **il va partir, (tout) au m. c'est ce qu'il dit** he's leaving, at least that's what he says

2 *(au minimum)* at least; **il y a au m. 20 personnes qui attendent** there are at least 20 people waiting; **ça fait au m. un mois qu'on ne l'a pas vu** we haven't seen him for at least a month

❑ **de moins ADV il y a dix euros de m. dans le tiroir** there are ten euros missing from the drawer; **je me sens dix ans de m.** I feel ten years younger; **j'ai un an de m. qu'elle** I'm a year younger than her; **j'ai une tête de m. qu'elle** I'm shorter than her by a head

❑ **de moins en moins ADV** less and less; **nous nous voyons de m. en m.** we see less and less of each other *or* each other less and less; **de m. en m. souvent** less and less often

❑ **de moins en moins de DÉT** *(suivi d'un nom comptable)* fewer and fewer; *(suivi d'un nom non comptable)* less and less; **de m. en m. de gens** fewer and fewer people; **il y a de m. en m. de demande pour ce produit** there is less and less demand for this product; **elle a de m. en m. de fièvre** her temperature is falling

❑ **des moins ADV un accueil des m. chaleureux** a less than warm welcome; **vos amis sont des m. discrets** your friends aren't the most discreet of people

❑ **du moins ADV** at least; **il lui devait de l'argent, du m. c'est ce que je croyais** he owed him/her money, at least that's what I thought; **ils devaient venir samedi, c'est du m. ce qu'ils nous avaient dit** they were supposed to come on Saturday, at least that's what they told us

❑ **en moins ADV il y a une chaise en m.** there's one chair missing, we're one chair short

❑ **en moins de PRÉP** in less than; **en m. d'une heure** in less than an hour, in under an hour; **en m. de temps qu'il n'en faut pour le dire** before you can say Jack Robinson; **en m. de rien** in no time at all; **on a remis à neuf l'appartement en m. de rien** we made the flat look like new in no time at all; *Fam* **en m. de deux** in a jiffy, in two ticks

❑ **moins de DÉT 1** *(comparatif) (avec un nom comptable)* fewer; *(avec un nom non comptable)* less; **un peu m. de bruit!** a little less noise!; **donnez-lui m. de travail** give him/her less work; **ils étaient m. de cent** there were fewer than a hundred of them; **m. de beurre** less butter; **m. de bouteilles** fewer *or* not so many bottles; **je l'ai payé un peu m. de 20 euros** I paid just under *or* a little less than 20 euros for it; **il a m. de 18 ans** he's under 18; **les m. de 18 ans** the under-18s; **il ne me faudra pas m. de trois heures pour tout faire** I'll need at the very least three hours to do everything; **il y avait m. d'enfants que d'habitude** there were fewer children than usual; **il a m. de patience que son frère** he's less patient than his brother

2 *(superlatif)* **le m. de** *(avec un nom comptable)* the fewest; *(avec un nom non comptable)* the least; **c'est lui qui fait le m. de bruit** he makes the least noise; **c'est ce qui consomme le m. d'énergie** it uses the least amount of energy; **c'est à la montagne qu'il y a le m. de monde** it's in the mountains where you find the least number of people; **c'est avec cette voiture que j'ai eu le m. de pannes** this is the car I've had the fewest breakdowns in

❑ **moins... moins ADV** the less... the less; **m. il travaillera, m. il aura de chances de réussir à son examen** the less he works, the less chance he'll have of passing his exam; **m. on mange, m. on grossit** the less you eat, the less weight you put on

❑ **moins... plus ADV** the less... the more; **m. tu dors, plus tu seras énervé** the less you sleep, the more on edge you'll be

❑ **moins que rien ADV** next to nothing; **il m'a fait payer 15 euros, c'est m. que rien** he charged me 15 euros, which is next to nothing

NMF INV nobody; **c'est un/une m. que rien** he's/she's a nobody; **des m. que rien** a useless bunch (of individuals)

❑ **on ne peut moins ADV elle est on ne peut m. honnête** she's totally dishonest; **c'est on ne peut m. loin!** it couldn't be nearer!; **c'est on ne peut m. compliqué!** it couldn't be less complicated!

❑ **pour le moins ADV** at the very least, to say the least; **il y a pour le m. une heure d'attente** there's an hour's wait at the very least; **c'est pour le m. étonnant** it's surprising, to say the least

---

moins-disant [mwɛ̃dizɑ̃] *(pl* **moins-disants***)* **NM** lowest bidder

moins-perçu [mwɛ̃pɛrsy] *(pl* **moins-perçus***)* **NM** amount due

moins-value [mwɛ̃valy] *(pl* **moins-values***)* **NF 1** *(dépréciation)* depreciation, capital loss **2** *(déficit du fisc)* (tax) deficit, shortfall

moirage [mwaraʒ] **NM 1** *(effet)* watered effect *or* finish **2** *(technique)* watering **3** *(sur une image)* cross-hatching **4** *(sur un disque)* moiré (effect)

moire [mwar] **NF 1** *(tissu)* moire, watered fabric; **m. de soie** watered *or* shot silk **2** *Littéraire (irisation)* iridescence, irisation

moiré, -e [mware] **ADJ 1** *Tex* moiré, watered **2** *Littéraire (irisé)* iridescent, irisated, moiré **3** *Menuis* moiré

NM 1 *Tex* moiré, watered effect *or* finish **2** *Littéraire (irisation)* iridescence, irisation **3** *Métal* **m. métallique** etching

moirer [3] [mware] **VT 1** *(tissu)* to moiré, to water **2** *(métal, papier)* to moiré **3** *Littéraire (iriser)* to make iridescent, to irisate; **un rayon de lune moirait la surface du lac** a ray of moonlight made the surface of the lake shimmer *or* glimmer

moirure [mwaryr] **NF** *Littéraire (irisation)* iridescence, irisation

❑ **moirures NFPL** *Tex* moiré (effect), watered effect *or* finish; *Métal* moiré (effect)

mois [mwa] **NM 1** *(division du calendrier)* month; **le m. de mai/décembre** the month of May/December; **au m. de mars** in (the month of) March; **au début/à la fin du m. d'avril** in early/late April; **au milieu du m. d'août** in mid-August *or* the middle of August; **les m. en r** months with an r in them; *Com* **le 15 de ce** *ou* **du m.** the 15th of this month, *Br* the 15th inst *or* instant; **m. commercial** thirty days (month); *Bourse* **m. d'échéance** trading month; *Jur* **m. légal** thirty days (month); **le m. de Marie** the month of Mary *or* May

2 *(durée)* month; **tous les m.** every *or* each month, monthly; **le comité se réunit tous les m.** the committee meets on a monthly basis; **dans un m.** in a month, in a month's time; **pendant mes m. de grossesse/d'apprentissage** during the months when I was pregnant/serving my apprenticeship; **un m. de préavis** a month's notice; **un m. de vacances/salaire** a month's holiday/wages

3 *(salaire)* monthly wage *or* salary *or* pay; *(versement)* monthly instalment; **je vous dois trois m.** *(de salaire)* I owe you three months' wages; *(de loyer)* I owe you three months' rent; **toucher son m.** to receive one's (monthly) salary; **m. double, treizième m.** = extra month's salary paid as an annual bonus

❑ **au mois ADV** by the month, monthly, on a monthly basis; **les intérêts sont calculés au m.** interest is worked out on a monthly basis; **louer qch au m.** to hire sth by the month

❑ **du mois ADJ avez-vous le numéro du m.?** do you have this month's issue?

moise [mwaz] **NF** *Constr* binding piece, tie

Moïse [mɔiz] **NPR** *Bible* Moses

moïse [mɔiz] **NM** Moses basket

moiser [3] [mwaze] **VT** *Constr* to tie, to bind

moisi, -e [mwazi] **ADJ** *(papier, tissu)* mildewy, mouldy; *(fruit, pain)* mouldy; *(logement)* mildewy, fusty

NM *(moisissure)* mildew, mould; **odeur de m.** musty *or* fusty smell; **avoir un goût de m.** to taste mouldy *or* musty; **ça sent le m.** it smells musty; *Fam Fig* I can smell trouble

moisir [32] [mwazir] **VT** to make (go) mouldy

VI 1 *(pourrir)* to go mouldy; *(mur, livre)* to go mildewed; **le pain a moisi** the bread's gone mouldy **2** *Fam (s'éterniser)* to rot; **je ne vais pas m. ici jusqu'à la fin de mes jours!** I'm not going to stay and rot here forever!; **on ne va pas**

m. ici! *(partons!)* let's not hang about here!; **m. en prison** to rot in prison

moisissure [mwazisyr] NF **1** *(champignon)* mould, mildew; *(tache)* patch of mould; **moisissures** mouldy bits, mould *(UNCOUNT)*; **une forte odeur de m.** a strong musty smell **2** *Fig Littéraire* rottenness, rankness

moissine [mwasin] NF = bunch of grapes with the stem attached

moisson [mwasɔ̃] NF **1** *Agr (récolte, époque)* harvest; **faire la m.** *ou* **les moissons** to harvest (the crops); **engranger** *ou* **rentrer la m.** to bring in the harvest *(grande quantité)* **une m. de** an abundance *or* a wealth of; **lis son livre si tu veux faire une bonne m. de clichés** if it's clichés you want, just read his/her book

moissonnage [mwasɔnaʒ] NM harvesting

moissonner [3] [mwasɔne] VT **1** *Agr* to harvest, to reap; *(champ)* to reap; *(récoltes)* to harvest, to gather (in); **m. les blés** to harvest the corn
2 *Fig (recueillir → informations, documents)* to amass; **m. des renseignements** to collect *or* to gather information
3 *Fig (remporter → prix)* to carry off; **les Danois ont moissonné tous les Oscars** the Danes *or* Denmark carried off all the Oscars
4 *Littéraire (décimer)* to decimate; **la guerre a moissonné toute leur génération** the war decimated their entire generation; **être moissonné dans la fleur de l'âge** to be cut off in the prime of life *or* in one's prime

moissonneur, -euse [mwasɔnœr, -øz] NM,F harvester, reaper
□ **moissonneuse** NF **1** *(machine)* harvester **2** *Entom* harvesting ant

moissonneuse-batteuse [mwasɔnøzbatøz] *(pl* **moissonneuses-batteuses)** NF combine (harvester)

moissonneuse-lieuse [mwasɔnøzljøz] *(pl* **moissonneuses-lieuses)** NF reaper, reaper-binder, self-binder

moite [mwat] ADJ *(air)* muggy, clammy; *(chaleur)* moist; *(mains)* sticky, sweaty; *(front)* damp, sweaty; **une journée m. et oppressante** a muggy, stifling day

moite-moite [mwatmwat] ADV fifty-fifty, half-and-half

moiteur [mwatœr] NF *(sueur)* stickiness, sweatiness; *(humidité)* dampness, moistness; *(de l'air)* mugginess

moitié [mwatje] NF **1** *(part)* half; **une m. de** *ou* **la m. d'un poulet** half a chicken; **la m. des élèves** half (of) the pupils; **la m. de ses revenus est consacrée** *ou* **sont consacrés à sa maison** half (of) his/her income is spent on his/her house; **quelle est la m. de douze?** what's half of twelve?; **arrivé à la m. du livre** halfway through the book; **nous ferons la m. du trajet** *ou* **chemin ensemble** we'll do half the journey together; **partager qch en deux moitiés** to divide sth in half *or* into (two) halves, to halve sth
2 *(comme modificateur)* half; **m. riant, m. pleurant** half laughing, half crying; **je suis m. français, m. canadien** I'm half French, half Canadian; **m. déçu, m. soulagé** half disappointed, half relieved; **j'ai acheté m. plus de champignons/de lait** I bought half as many mushrooms/much milk again; **il mange m. moins que moi** he eats half as much as me; **m. moins gros/cher** 50 percent smaller/cheaper; **m. moins de monde** 50 percent fewer people; **c'est m. moins gros que l'autre** it's half the size of the other one; **ça m'a coûté m. moins cher** it cost me half the price; **il n'est pas m. aussi méchant qu'on le dit** he's not half as nasty as people say
3 *Fam Hum (épouse)* **sa/ma (tendre) m.** his/my better half; **sa tendre m. l'attend chez lui** his better half is waiting for him at home
□ **à moitié** ADV half; **à m. mort/cuit/nu/endormi** half-dead/-cooked/-naked/-asleep; **il l'a à m. assommé** he half *or* almost knocked him out; **la bouteille était à m. pleine/vide** the bottle was half-full/-empty; **je ne suis qu'à m. surpris** I'm not completely surprised; **faire les choses à m.** to do things by halves; **le travail n'est fait qu'à m.** only half the work's been done, the work's only half done; **vendre à m. prix** to sell (at) half-price

□ **à moitié chemin** ADV halfway; **j'irai avec toi jusqu'à m. chemin** I'll go halfway with you; *Fig* **elle s'est arrêtée à m. chemin dans ses études** she dropped out halfway through her course
□ **de moitié** ADV by half; **réduire qch de m.** to reduce sth by half, to halve sth; **l'inflation a diminué de m.** inflation has been halved *or* cut by half; **ils s'étaient mis de m. (dans l'affaire)** they'd gone halves *or* fifty-fifty (in the business)
□ **par la moitié** ADV through *or* down the middle
□ **par moitié** ADV in two, in half
□ **pour moitié** ADV partly; **il est pour m. responsable** he is equally *or* just as much to blame, half the responsibility is his; **tu es pour m. dans son échec** you're half *or* partly responsible for his/her failure

moitié-moitié [mwatjemwatje] ADV **1** *(à parts égales)* half-and-half; **faire m.** *(dans une affaire)* to go halves *or* fifty-fifty; *(au restaurant)* to go halves, to split the bill; **ça devrait faire à peu près m.** that should be us just about even **2** *Fam (ni bien ni mal)* so-so; **elle est contente? – m.** is she pleased? – so-so

moitir [32] [mwatir] VT *Vieilli* to dampen, to moisten

mojette [mɔʒɛt] = **mogette**

mojito [mojito] NM *(cocktail)* mojito

moka [mɔka] NM **1** *(gâteau)* mocha cake, coffee cream cake **2** *(café)* mocha (coffee)

mol [mɔl] *voir* **mou**

molaire¹ [mɔlɛr] NF *(dent)* molar

molaire² [mɔlɛr] ADJ *Chim* molar

môlaire [molɛr] ADJ *Méd* molar

molal, -e [mɔlal] ADJ *Chim* molal

molalité [mɔlalite] NF *Chim* molality

molarité [mɔlarite] NF *Chim* molarity

molasse [mɔlas] NF molasse

moldave [mɔldav] ADJ Moldavian
□ **Moldave** NMF Moldavian

Moldavie [mɔldavi] NF **la M.** Moldavia; **en M.** in Moldavia

Moldova [mɔldɔva] NF **la M.** Moldova; **vivre dans la république de M.** to live in the Republic of Moldova; **aller en M.** to go to Moldova

mole [mɔl] NF *Chim* mole

môle [mol] NM **1** *(jetée)* mole, (stone) jetty *or* breakwater **2** *Géol* horst
NF **1** *Ich* sunfish **2** *Méd* mole; **m. hydatiforme** hydatidiform *or* hydatid mole

moléculaire [mɔlekylɛr] ADJ molecular

molécule [mɔlekyl] NF molecule

molécule-gramme [mɔlekylgram] *(pl* **molécules-grammes)** NF gram-molecule

molène [mɔlɛn] NF *Bot* mullein

moleskine [mɔleskin] NF **1** *Tex* moleskin **2** *(imitation cuir)* imitation leather

molester [3] [mɔlɛste] VT to maul, to manhandle, to molest; **la police a molesté les manifestants** the demonstrators were manhandled by the police; **plusieurs journalistes se sont fait m. par les forces de l'ordre** several journalists were manhandled by the police

moletage [mɔltaʒ] NM milling, knurling

moleter [27] [mɔlte] VT to mill, to knurl

molette [mɔlɛt] NF **1** *(pièce cylindrée)* toothed wheel; **m. de réglage** control knob **2** *(dans un briquet)* wheel **3** *(de verrier)* cutting wheel **4** *Menuis (roulette)* beading roller; *(fraise)* (beading) reamer **5** *(d'un éperon)* rowel **6** *(de jumelles)* focus wheel

Molière [mɔljɛr] NPR Molière; **les Molières** = French theatre awards

moliéresque [mɔljerɛsk] ADJ Molieresque; **une satire sociale toute m.** a social satire worthy of *or* in the style of Molière

molinisme [mɔlinism] NM *Rel* Molinism

moliniste [mɔlinist] *Rel* ADJ Molinist
NMF Molinist

molinosisme [mɔlinozism] NM *Rel* Molinism, quietism

molinosiste [mɔlinozist] NMF *Rel* Molinist, quietist

Molise [mɔliz] NM *Géog* **le M.** Molise

mollachu, -e [mɔlaʃy] *Suisse* ADJ slow■, sluggish■
NMF lazy so-and-so

mollah [mɔla] NM mullah, mollah

mollard [mɔlar] NM *très Fam* gob, *Br* gob of spit

mollarder [3] [mɔlarde] VI *très Fam* to spit■, *Br* to gob

mollasse [mɔlas] ADJ **1** *Fam (apathique)* drippy, wimpish, *Br* wet; *(moralement)* spineless; **qu'il est m.!** he's such a drip! **2** *(flasque)* flabby, flaccid, limp; **une poignée de main m.** a limp handshake
NMF *Fam* wimp, drip

mollasserie [mɔlasri] NF *Fam* feebleness■; **il est d'une m. décourageante!** he's such a wimp!

mollasson, -onne [mɔlasɔ̃, -ɔn] *Fam* ADJ slow■, sluggish■
NM,F lazy so-and-so

molle [mɔl] *voir* **mou**

mollé [mɔle] NM mastic tree

mollement [mɔlmɑ̃] ADV **1** *(sans énergie)* listlessly, limply; **il m'a serré m. la main** he gave me a limp handshake; **m. allongé sur un divan** lying languidly *or* limply on a sofa; **les barques se balançaient m. sur l'eau** the small boats were bobbing gently on the water; *Littéraire* **les collines descendent m. jusqu'à la plaine** the hills slope gently down to the plain
2 *(sans conviction)* feebly, weakly; **elle protesta m.** she protested feebly, she made a feeble protest

mollesse [mɔlɛs] NF **1** *(d'une substance, d'un objet)* softness; *(des chairs)* flabbiness; *(d'une poignée de main)* limpness
2 *(d'un relief)* soft shape; *Péj* **la m. de ses traits** the flabbiness *or* shapelessness of his/her features; *Péj* **la m. d'un dessin** the lifelessness of a drawing
3 *(apathie)* feebleness, weakness; **c'est la m. des parents/de l'opposition qui est en cause** parental laxness/the opposition's spinelessness is to blame; **devant la m. de ces protestations** faced with such feeble protests

mollet¹ [mɔlɛ] NM *Anat* calf; *Fam* **avoir des mollets de coq** to have legs like matchsticks, to have spindly legs

mollet², **-ette** [mɔlɛ, -ɛt] ADJ *Littéraire (moelleux)* soft; *(œuf)* soft-boiled; **pain m.** (soft) bread roll

molletière [mɔltjɛr] ADJ F *voir* **bande**
NF puttee

molleton [mɔltɔ̃] NM **1** *(tissu → en coton)* flannelette; *(→ en laine)* flannel **2** *(sous-nappe)* table-felt

molletonné, -e [mɔltɔne] ADJ *(garni)* covered with fleece; *(doublé)* fleece-lined

molletonner [3] [mɔltɔne] VT *(garnir)* to cover with fleece; *(doubler)* to line with fleece

molletonneux, -euse [mɔltɔnø, -øz] ADJ fleecy, fleece *(avant n)*; **étoffe molletonneuse** napped cloth

mollette [mɔlɛt] *voir* **mollet**²

mollir [32] [mɔlir] VI **1** *(chanceler)* **j'ai senti mes jambes m.** I felt my legs give way (under me); **le sol mollissait sous mes pieds** the ground was giving way beneath my feet
2 *(vent)* to drop, *Sout* to abate
3 *(courage, volonté)* to flag; *(forces)* to diminish; **sa détermination mollissait** his/her determination began to flag *or* to wane
VT **1** *Naut (cordage)* to slacken; *(barre)* to ease
2 *Pêche (ligne)* to let out

mollisol [mɔlisɔl] NM mollisol

mollo [mɔlo] ADV *Fam* easy; **y aller m.** to take it easy; **vas-y m. sur cette route!** take it easy on that road!; **m. avec le chocolat!** go easy on the chocolate!

molluscum [mɔlyskɔm] NM *Méd* molluscum

mollusque [mɔlysk] NM **1** *Zool* mollusc **2** *Fam (personne)* drip, wimp

Moloch [mɔlɔk] NPR *Bible* Moloch

moloch [mɔlɔk] NM *Zool* moloch, thorny devil

molosse [mɔlɔs] NM **1** *(chien)* watchdog **2** *(chauve-souris)* free-tailed bat

molossoïde [mɔlɔsɔid] ADJ molossoid
NM molossoid

Molotov [mɔlɔtɔv] NPR **cocktail M.** Molotov cocktail

Moluques [mɔlyk] NFPL **les M.** the Moluccas

molure [mɔlyr] NM *Zool* Indian python

moly [mɔli] NM *Myth* moly

molybdate [mɔlibdat] NM *Chim* molybdate

molybdène [mɔlibdɛn] NM *Chim* molybdenum

molybdénite [mɔlibdenit] NF *Minér* molybdenite

Mombasa [mɔ̃basa] NM Mombasa

mombin [mɔ̃bɛ̃] NM *Bot* *(rouge)* purple mombin, Spanish plum; *(jaune)* yellow mombin, hog plum

môme [mom] *Fam* NMF *(enfant)* kid; **sale m.!** you little brat!

NF *Vieilli (fille)* chick, *Br* bird; *(compagne)* girlfriend■, *Br* bird

ADJ **quand j'étais (tout) m.** when I was (just) a kid

moment [mɔmɑ̃] NM **1** *(laps de temps)* moment, while; **restez avec moi un m.** stay with me a moment *or* a while; **laisse-moi un m. pour réfléchir** give me a moment to think it over; **il y a un (bon) m. que j'attends** I've been waiting for (quite) a while; **pendant un bon m.** for quite some time; **j'en ai pour un (petit) m.** I'll be a (little) while

2 *(instant)* moment, minute; **c'est l'affaire d'un m.** it'll only take a minute *or* moment; **attends-moi, je n'en ai que pour un m.** wait for me, I'll be finished in a minute *or* moment; **je n'ai pas un m. à moi** I don't have a minute *or* moment to myself; **dans un m. de colère** in a moment of anger; **il eut un m. d'hésitation** he hesitated for a moment; **(attends) un m.!** just (wait) a moment!

3 *(période)* moment, time; **attendre le dernier m.** to wait till the last minute; **nous avons passé** *ou* **eu de bons moments** we had some good times; **elle a ses bons et ses mauvais moments** she has her off days; **c'est un mauvais m. à passer** it's just a difficult spell *or Br* a bad patch; **il avait connu des moments d'ivresse avec elle** he had had some blissful moments with her; **les grands moments de l'histoire** the great moments of history; **les derniers moments de sa vie** the last moments of his/her life; **il l'a assistée jusqu'aux derniers moments** he was by her side until the end; **à mes moments perdus** in my spare time; **à quel m. de l'année/la semaine?** at what time of the year/the week?; **à quel m. de l'histoire/sa vie?** at what stage of *or* point in the story/his/her life?; **dans ces moments-là, on ne réfléchit pas** at times like that you don't think

4 *(occasion)* moment, opportunity; **à quel m.?** when?; **choisis un autre m. pour lui parler** choose another time to speak to him/her; **c'est le m. d'intervenir** now's the time to speak up; *Ironique* **c'est bien le m.!** what a time to pick!; **c'est le m. ou jamais** it's now or never; **c'est le m. ou jamais de lui demander** ask him/her, it's now or never; **c'est le m. ou jamais de lui dire ce que tu penses** now's the time (if ever there was one) to tell him/her what you think; **à quel m. voulez-vous venir?** (at) what time would you like to come?; **le m. venu** when the time comes; **le m. venu, il ne sut plus quoi dire** when the time came, he was at a loss for words; **attendre le m. opportun** to wait for an opportune moment *or* the right moment; **arriver au bon m.** to come at the right time; *Ironique* **il arrive toujours au bon m., celui-là!** he really picks his moments!; **au mauvais m.** at the wrong time; **le m. crucial du film/match** the crucial point in the film/match

5 *(temps présent)* **c'est le disque/la star du m.** it's the record/she's the star of the moment

6 *Phys* momentum; **m. électrique** electric moment; **m. cinétique** kinetic moment; **m. magnétique** magnetic moment

▫ **à aucun moment** ADV at no time; **à aucun m. il ne s'est plaint** at no time *or* point did he complain

▫ **à ce moment-là** ADV **1** *(dans le temps)* at that time, then

2 *Fig (dans ce cas)* in that case, if that's so; **à ce m.-là, tu aurais dû me le dire!** in that case *or* if that was the case, you should have told me!

▫ **à tout moment** ADV **1** *(n'importe quand)* (at) any time *or* moment; **il peut téléphoner à tout m.** I/we/*etc* can expect a call from him any time now

2 *(sans cesse)* constantly, all the time; **elle s'interrompait à tout m.** she was constantly stopping, she kept stopping

▫ **au moment de** PRÉP **au m. de son départ** when he/she was leaving; **au m. de partir** just as I/he/*etc* was leaving *or* was about to leave; **au m. de mon divorce** when I was getting divorced,

at the time of my divorce; **au m. de sa naissance/de l'accident** at the time of his/her birth/of the accident; **il me l'a dit au m. de mourir** he told me as he died

▫ **au moment où** CONJ as, when; **au m. où il allait démissionner** as he was about to resign; **juste au m. où le téléphone a sonné** just when *or* as the phone rang

▫ **à un moment donné** ADV at a certain point; **à un m. donné, il a refusé** at one point he refused

▫ **dès le moment où** CONJ **1** *(dans le temps)* from the time *or* moment that, as soon as

2 *(dans un raisonnement)* as soon as, once; **dès le m. où on accepte l'idée d'immortalité** once you accept the idea of immortality

▫ **du moment** ADJ **l'homme du m.** the man of the moment; **le succès/l'idole du m.** the current hit/idol; **des sujets du m.** one of the issues of the day

▫ **du moment que** CONJ *(puisque)* since; **du m. qu'il a signé, tu es garanti** seeing that *or* since he's signed, you're safe; *Fam* **du m. que je te le dis!** you can take my word for it!

▫ **d'un moment à l'autre** ADV *(très prochainement)* any moment *or* minute *or* time now; **il peut téléphoner d'un m. à l'autre** he may phone any minute now

▫ **en ce moment** ADV at the moment, just now

▫ **en un moment** ADV in a moment

▫ **par moments** ADV at times, every now and then, every so often

▫ **pour le moment** ADV for the moment, for the time being; **c'est assez pour le m., repose-toi un peu** that's enough for the time being, have a rest now

▫ **sur le moment** ADV at the time; **sur le m., ça n'a pas fait mal** it didn't hurt at the time

momentané, -e [mɔmɑ̃tane] ADJ momentary, brief; **il y aura des pannes d'électricité momentanées** there will be temporary *or* brief power cuts; **sa passion n'a été que momentanée** his/her passion was only short-lived

momentanément [mɔmɑ̃tanemɑ̃] ADV **1** *(en ce moment)* for the time being, for the moment; **il est m. absent** he's temporarily absent, he's absent for the moment **2** *(provisoirement)* momentarily, for a short while; **les émissions sont m. interrompues** we will be temporarily off the air

momerie [mɔmri] NF *Littéraire & Vieilli* mummery; *(pratique insincère)* insincerity

mômerie [mɔmri] NF *(gén pl) Fam* childishness■, childish behaviour■

momie [mɔmi] NF **1** *Archéol* mummy **2** *(personne très maigre)* skeleton

momification [mɔmifikasjɔ̃] NF mummification

momifier [9] [mɔmifje] VT to mummify

▶ **se momifier** VPR *(personne)* to become mummified; *Fig (esprit)* to become fossilized

momordique [mɔmɔrdik] NF *Bot* balsam apple

mon, ma, mes [mɔ̃, ma, me]

> **ma** becomes **mon** before a word beginning with a vowel or h mute.

ADJ POSSESSIF **1** *(indiquant la possession)* my; **m. ami/amie** my friend; **m. meilleur ami/ma meilleure amie** my best friend; *Littéraire* **m. père et ma mère, mes père et mère** my father and mother; **mes frères et sœurs** my brothers and sisters; **un de mes amis** a friend of mine, one of my friends; **un professeur de mes amis** a teacher friend of mine; **j'ai mis m. chapeau et mes gants** I put on my hat and (my) gloves; *Fam* **j'aurai ma chambre à moi** I'll have my own room■

2 *(dans des appellatifs)* **m. cher Pierre** my dear Pierre; **m. Père** Father; **m. capitaine** Captain; **(oh) m. Dieu!** (oh) my God!; *Sout* **m. oncle, je vous écris pour demander…** I'm writing to you, uncle, to ask you…; **viens, m. enfant** come here, child; *Fam* **alors là, ma grande, c'est ton problème!** well that, my dear, is your problem!; *Fam* **mais m. pauvre vieux, vous n'y arriverez jamais!** you'll never manage it, old chap!

3 *(emploi expressif)* **j'ai m. vendredi** I've got Friday off; *Fam* **je gagne mes 1000 euros par mois** I earn 1,000 euros a month■; *Fam* **m. imbécile de frère** my idiot of a brother; *Fam* **m.**

artiste de mari my husband, the artist■; *Fam* **alors, tu veux le rencontrer, m. artiste?** do you want to meet this artist of mine, then?; *Fam* **mais ma Jacqueline, elle n'était pas du tout d'accord!** but our Jacqueline wasn't going along with that!; *Fam* **et voilà m. Simon qui se met à rouspéter** then old Simon starts grumbling; **m. bonhomme n'était pas du tout content!** I don't mind telling you (that) the fellow wasn't at all pleased!; *très Fam* **ah ben, m. salaud** *ou* **cochon!** lucky bastard!

monacal, -e, -aux, -ales [mɔnakal, -o] ADJ monastic, *Sout* monachal

monachisme [mɔnaʃism] NM monasticism, *Sout* monachism

Monaco [mɔnako] NM *Géog* **(la principauté de) M.** (the principality of) Monaco; **vivre à M.** to live in Monaco; **aller à M.** to go to Monaco

monaco [mɔnako] NM = cocktail consisting of beer, grenadine and lemonade

monade [mɔnad] NF monad

monadelphe [mɔnadɛlf] ADJ *Bot* monadelphous

monadisme [mɔnadism] NM *Phil* monadism

monadologie [mɔnadɔlɔʒi] NF *Phil* monadology

monandre [mɔnɑ̃dr] ADJ *Bot* monandrous

monarchie [mɔnarʃi] NF monarchy; **la m. absolue/constitutionnelle/parlementaire** absolute/constitutional/parliamentary monarchy; **la m. de droit divin** monarchy by divine right; **la m. de Juillet** the July Monarchy

> *Culture*
>
> **LA MONARCHIE DE JUILLET**
> This refers to the eighteen-year reign, from 1830 to 1848, of the "citizen king" Louis-Philippe of Orléans, after the abdication of the Bourbon king Charles X. This was France's first, and last, constitutional monarchy, and saw the rise in influence of the bourgeoisie at the expense of the nobility. It was overthrown by the 1848 Revolution.

monarchien [mɔnarʃjɛ̃] NM *Hist* = member of the "Assemblée nationale" during the French Revolution who favoured an English-style monarchy

monarchique [mɔnarʃik] ADJ monarchic, monarchical, monarchial

monarchisme [mɔnarʃism] NM monarchism

monarchiste [mɔnarʃist] ADJ monarchist, monarchistic

NMF monarchist

monarque [mɔnark] NM monarch

monastère [mɔnastɛr] NM *(de moines)* monastery; *(de religieuses)* convent

monastique [mɔnastik] ADJ monastic

monaural, -e, -aux, -ales [mɔnɔral, -o] ADJ monaural

monazite [mɔnazit] NF *Minér* monazite

monbazillac [mɔ̃bazijak] NM Monbazillac (wine)

monceau, -x [mɔ̃so] NM *(amas)* heap, pile; **un m. de pierres** a pile of stones; **des monceaux de livres** piles *or* stacks of books; *Fig* **des monceaux d'erreurs** masses of mistakes

mondain, -e [mɔ̃dɛ̃, -ɛn] ADJ **1** *(de la haute société)* society *(avant n)*; **avoir des relations mondaines** to have friends in society *or* high circles; **il mène une vie très mondaine** he moves in society circles; **carnet m., rubrique mondaine** society *or* gossip column; **photographe m.** society photographer; **soirée mondaine** society *or* high-society evening

2 *(qui aime les mondanités)* **elle est très mondaine** she likes moving in fashionable circles *or* society, she's a great socialite

3 *Rel* worldly; *Phil* mundane

4 *Jur* **la brigade mondaine** ≃ the vice squad

NM,F socialite, society person

▫ **la Mondaine** NF *Fam* ≃ the vice squad■

mondanité [mɔ̃danite] NF **1** *(style)* society life **2** *Rel* worldliness

▫ **mondanités** NFPL **1** *(réunions)* fashionable gatherings; *(politesses)* social chitchat (UN-COUNT), polite conversation (UNCOUNT); **il aime les mondanités** he likes society life **2** *Presse* society news (UNCOUNT), gossip column

monde [mɔ̃d] NM **1** *(univers)* world; **parcourir** *ou* **courir le m. (à la recherche de)** to travel the

world (in search of); **le m. entier** the whole world; **dans le m. entier** all over the world; **il est connu dans le m. entier** he's known worldwide *or* the world over; **venir au m.** to come into the world; **mettre un enfant au m.** to bring a child into the world; **elle n'était pas de ce m.** she was not of this world; **il n'est plus de ce m.** he's no longer with us, he's gone to the next world; **il est encore de ce m.** he is still with us, he is still alive; **en ce bas m.** here on earth, here below; **l'autre m.** the next world; **elle est dans son m.** she's in her own little world; **elle s'est créé un petit m. à elle** she's created her own little world for herself; **le m. est petit!** it's a small world!; **depuis que le m. est m.** since the beginning of time, since time began; **c'est le m. renversé** *ou* **à l'envers!** what's the world coming to?

2 *(humanité)* world; **le m. entier attend cet événement** the whole world is awaiting this event; **il faut de tout pour faire un m.** it takes all sorts (to make a world); **ainsi va le m.** it's the way of the world; **refaire le m.** to put the world to rights

3 *(pour intensifier)* **il y a un m. entre l'agneau importé et l'agneau de notre région** there's a world of difference between imported lamb and our local lamb; **le plus célèbre au** *ou* **du m.** the most famous in the world; **les meilleurs amis du m.** the best friends in the world; **c'est la meilleure équipe au m.** it's the best team in the world; **c'est la femme la plus charmante du m.** she's the most charming woman you could wish to meet; **le plus simplement/gentiment du m.** in the simplest/kindest possible way; **c'est ce que j'aime/je veux le plus au m.** it's what I love/want most in the world; **je vous dérange? – pas le moins du m.!** am I interrupting? – not in the least!; **je ne m'ennuie pas le moins du m.** I'm not in the least bit bored; **ils s'entendent le mieux du m.** they get on famously; **tout s'est déroulé le mieux du m.** everything went off very smoothly; **rien au m. ne pourrait me faire partir** nothing in the world would make me leave; **pour rien au m.** not for anything, not for the world; **nul** *ou* **personne au m.** nobody in the world; **on m'a dit tout le bien du m. de ce nouveau shampooing** I've been told the most wonderful things about this new shampoo

4 *(communauté)* world; **le m. des affaires** the business world; **le m. de la finance** the world of finance, the financial world; **le m. du spectacle** (the world of) show business; **le m. chrétien/musulman** the Christian/Muslim world; **le m. capitaliste/communiste** the capitalist/communist world; **le m. libre** the Free World; **le m. animal/végétal** the animal/plant world

5 *(gens)* people; **il y a du m.?** *(en entrant chez quelqu'un)* is there anybody home *or* there?; **il y a un m. fou, c'est noir de m.** the place is swarming *or* alive with people; **il y a trop de m.** it's too crowded, there are too many people; *Fam* **il y a plein de m. à la foire** there are loads of people at the fair; **il n'y avait pas grand m. au spectacle** there weren't many people at the show; **je viens de m'installer, je ne connais pas encore beaucoup de m.** I've just settled in, I don't know (very) many people yet; **tu attends du m.?** are you expecting people *or* company?; **il ne voit plus beaucoup de m.** he doesn't socialize very much any more; *Fam* **j'ai du m. à dîner** I've got people coming for dinner; **ne t'en fais pas, je connais mon m.!** don't worry, I know who I'm dealing with!; **grand-mère aime bien avoir tout son petit m. autour d'elle** grandmother likes to have all her family *or Hum* brood around her; **c'est qu'il faut s'en occuper de tout ce petit m.!** *(enfants)* all that little lot takes some looking after!; **comment va tout votre petit m.?** how is your *or* the family?; *Can* **le grand m.** the grownups, the adults; *Fam Hum* **il y a du m. au balcon!** she's well-endowed!; *Fam* **tu te moques** *ou* **te fiches du m.!** you've got a nerve *or* a cheek!; *Fam* **ils se fichent vraiment du m.!** they really must think we're stupid!■

6 *(société)* world; *(groupe social)* circle, set; **se retirer du m.** to withdraw from society; **les plaisirs du m.** worldly pleasures; *Rel* **le m.** the world; **elle n'appartient pas à notre m.** she's not one of us, she doesn't belong to our circle; **ils ne sont pas du même m.** they don't move in the same circles; **le m., le beau m., le grand m.** *(classes élevées)* high society; **aller dans le m.** to mix in society; **ses premiers pas dans le m.** his/her introduction to (high) society; **fréquenter le beau** *ou* **le grand m.** to mix with high society *or* in society; **on n'est pas dans le grand m. ici!** this isn't Buckingham Palace!; **femme du m.** socialite; **homme du m.** man-about-town; **gens du m.** socialites, society people; *Ironique* **embarquez-moi tout ce joli m. dans le panier à salade** throw this bunch *or* crew into the back of the van

7 *(domaine)* world, realm; **le m. de l'imaginaire** the realm of imagination; **le m. du rêve** the world *or* realm of dreams; *Littéraire* **le m. du silence** the silent world (under the sea)

8 *Arch (domestiques)* servants, men, hands

9 *Presse* **Le M.** = French daily broadsheet newspaper, whose political leanings are left-of-centre

10 *Fam (locutions)* **c'est un m.!** that beats everything!, well I never!; **pourquoi ne ranges-tu jamais tes affaires, c'est un m. tout de même!** why in the world *or* why oh why don't you ever put your things away?; **se faire (tout) un m. de qch** to get worked up about sth; **il se fait tout un m. de rencontrer son beau père** he's making a big thing about meeting his father-in-law; **ne te fais pas un m. d'un rien** don't make a mountain out of a molehill

❑ **tout le monde** PRON everybody, everyone; **tout le m. est là?** is everybody here?; **tout le m. n'est pas arrivé** not everybody's here (yet); **tout le m. sait cela** everybody *or* the whole world knows that; **tout le m. ne peut pas le faire!** not everybody can do that!

Allusion

Tout le monde il est beau, tout le monde il est gentil

This was the title of a film by Jean Yanne (1972) which made fun of contemporary society, progressive and "liberated" as it then was. The translation is "Everyone's gorgeous, everyone's great", and the idea is that one would have to be extremely optimistic and naïve to really think so. The expression is used in two ways: firstly, as above, as a warning about human nature; secondly, to reprimand someone who is being too judgemental and harsh about his fellow man, in which case one might say **Te fâche pas! Tout le monde il est beau...**, ie "Calm down! Everyone's gorgeous, everyone's great."

monder [3] [mɔ̃de] VT **1** *(noisettes)* to hull; *(amandes)* to blanch **2** *(arbres)* to prune, to crop

mondial, -e, -aux, -ales [mɔ̃djal, -o] ADJ worldwide, global, world *(avant n)*; **production mondiale de blé** world wheat production; **une crise à l'échelle mondiale** a worldwide crisis, a crisis on a world scale; **une vedette de renommée mondiale** a world-famous star; **leur réseau de distribution m. est leur atout principal** their worldwide distribution network is their main asset

NM *Ftbl* **le M.** the World Cup

mondialement [mɔ̃djalmɑ̃] ADV throughout *or* all over the world; **m. renommé** famous all over the world, world-famous

mondialisation [mɔ̃djalizasjɔ̃] NF globalization; **on assiste à la m. de la reprise économique** a worldwide economic revival is taking place; **la m. libérale** liberal globalization

mondialiser [3] [mɔ̃djalize] VT to globalize

▸**se mondialiser** VPR to become globalized; **la crise s'est rapidement mondialisée** the crisis has rapidly taken on an international dimension

mondialisme [mɔ̃djalism] NM internationalism

mondialiste [mɔ̃djalist] ADJ internationalist

NMF internationalist

mondovision [mɔ̃dɔvizjɔ̃] NF worldwide satellite broadcasting; **en m.** broadcast all over the world by satellite

monégasque [mɔnegask] ADJ Monegasque, Monacan

❑ **Monégasque** NMF Monegasque, Monacan

Monel® [mɔnɛl] NM Monel metal®

monème [mɔnɛm] NM *Ling* moneme

MONEP [mɔnɛp] NM *Bourse (abrév* **marché des options négociables à Paris)** MONEP *(Paris traded options exchange)*, *Br* ≃ LIFFE, *Am* ≃ CBOE

monère [mɔnɛr] NF *Biol* moneron

monergol [mɔnɛrgɔl] NM monopropellant

monétaire [mɔnetɛr] ADJ monetary; **marché/masse m.** money market/supply; **politique/système/unité m.** monetary policy/system/unit

monétarisation [mɔnetarizasjɔ̃] NF monetarization

monétarisme [mɔnetarism] NM monetarism

monétariste [mɔnetarist] ADJ monetarist

NMF monetarist

Monétique® [mɔnetik] NF electronic banking, e-banking

monétisation [mɔnetizasjɔ̃] NF monetization

monétiser [3] [mɔnetize] VT to monetize

mongol, -e [mɔ̃gɔl] ADJ **1** *(de Mongolie)* Mongol, Mongolian **2** *très Fam Péj* moronic

NM *(langue)* Mongolian

❑ **Mongol, -e** NM,F **1** *(de Mongolie)* Mongol, Mongolian **2** *très Fam Péj* moron

Mongolie [mɔ̃gɔli] NF **la M.** Mongolia; **vivre en M.** to live in Mongolia; **aller en M.** to go to Mongolia; *Anciennement* **la M.-Extérieure** Outer Mongolia; **la M.-Intérieure** Inner Mongolia

mongolien, -enne [mɔ̃gɔljɛ̃, -ɛn] *Méd* ADJ **être m.** to have Down's syndrome

NM,F = person with Down's syndrome

mongolique [mɔ̃gɔlik] ADJ Mongolic, Mongolian

mongolisme [mɔ̃gɔlism] NM Down's syndrome

mongoloïde [mɔ̃gɔlɔid] ADJ **1** *(de type mongol)* Mongoloid **2** *Méd (individu)* affected by Down's syndrome; **être m.** to have Down's syndrome

monial, -e, -aux, -ales [mɔnjal, -o] *Arch* = **monacal**

moniale [mɔnjal] ADJ F *voir* **monial**

NF (enclosed) nun

monilie [mɔnili], **monilia** [mɔnilja] NM *Bot* monilia

moniliose [mɔniljoz] NF *Bot* monilia disease, brown rot

monisme [mɔnism] NM *Phil* monism

moniste [mɔnist] *Phil* ADJ monistic

NMF monist

moniteur, -trice [mɔnitœr, -tris] NM,F *Sport* instructor, *f* instructress; *(de colonie de vacances)* (group) supervisor *or* leader, *Am* (camp) counselor; **m. d'atelier** workshop leader *or* instructor; **m. d'auto-école** driving instructor; **m. de ski** ski instructor

NM **1** *Ordinat (écran)* display unit; *(dispositif matériel ou logiciel)* monitor; **m. basse radiation** low-radiation monitor; **m. couleur** RGB *or* colour monitor; **m. à cristaux liquides** liquid crystal monitor; **m. à écran plat** flat screen monitor; **m. pleine page** A4 monitor; **m. SVGA** SVGA monitor; **m. à tube cathodique** cathode ray tube monitor; **m. vidéo** video monitor

2 *Méd* monitor; **m. cardiaque** cardiac *or* heart monitor

3 *Belg* **M. (belge)** = Belgian government publication, *Br* ≃ Hansard, *Am* ≃ Federal Register

monition [mɔnisjɔ̃] NF *Rel* monition

monitoire [mɔnitwar] *Rel* ADJ monitory

NM monitory letter, monitory

monitor [mɔnitɔr] NM **1** *Mil* monitor **2** *Mines* monitor

monitorage [mɔnitɔraʒ] = **monitoring**

monitorat [mɔnitɔra] NM *(enseignement)* instruction; *(de colonie de vacances)* group leading, *Am* camp counseling; *(fonction)* instructorship; *(période de formation)* training to be an instructor; **m. sportif** sports instruction

monitoring [mɔnitɔriŋ] NM monitoring; **elle est sous m.** she's been placed on a monitor

monitrice [mɔnitris] *voir* **moniteur**

monnaie [mɔnɛ] *etc voir* **monnayer**

NF **1** *Écon & Fin (d'un pays)* currency; **frapper la m., battre m.** to coin *or* mint money; **m. d'argent/de nickel/d'or** silver/nickel/gold coin; **les monnaies étrangères** foreign currencies; **la m. allemande** *(gén)* the German currency; **le yen est la m. du Japon** the yen is Japan's (unit of) currency *or* monetary unit; *Fin* **m. d'appoint** fractional money; **m. d'argent** silver money; **m. bancaire, m. de banque** bank money; **m. bloquée** blocked currency; **m. circulante** active money, money in circulation; *UE* **m. commune**

common currency; **m. de compte** account *or* near money; **m. de compte (convertible)** (convertible) money of account; **m. courante** legal currency; *Fig* **c'est m. courante** it's common practice, it's a common *or* an everyday occurrence; **m. décimale** decimal currency *or* coinage; **m. dirigée** managed *or* controlled currency; **m. divisionnaire** fractional currency; *Fig* **m. d'échange** bargaining counter; **m. électronique** electronic money, e-money, e-cash; **m. étrangère** foreign currency; **m. faible** soft currency; **m. fiduciaire** fiduciary money *or* issue, paper money, *Am* fiat money; **m. flottante** floating currency; **m. forte** hard currency; **m. légale** legal tender; **m. de marchandise** commodity money; **m. métallique** metal money; **m. non convertible** blocked currency; **m. d'or** gold currency; **m. de papier** paper money; **m. de réserve** reserve currency; **m. scripturale** bank money; *Fam* **m. de singe** Monopoly money; *Fam* **payer qn en m. de singe** to fob sb off; **m. unique** single currency; **m. verte** green currency; **fausse m.** counterfeit *or* false money

2 *(appoint)* change; **faire de la m.** to get (some) change; **faire de la m. à qn** to give sb some change; **faire la m. de 50 euros** to get change for 50 euros, to change a 50-euro note; **je vais te faire** *ou* **te donner la m. de 20 euros** I'll change 20 euros for you, I'll give you change for 20 euros; **vous auriez de la m. pour le parcmètre?** do you have some change for the parking meter?; **vous auriez la m. de 20 euros?** could you give me change for a 20-euro note?, could you change a 20-euro note for me?; **rendre la m. à qn** to give sb change; **il m'a rendu la m. sur 10 euros** he gave me the change out of *or* from 10 euros; **m. d'appoint** (correct) change; **menue/petite m.** small/loose change; *Fam* **et par ici la m.!** let's be having your money!; *Fam* **allez, envoyez la m.!** come on, get the pennies out *or* cough up!; *Fig* **je lui rendrai la m. de sa pièce!** I'll give him/her a taste of his/her own medicine!

3 *(argent)* cash, *Br* dosh, *Am* bucks

monnaie-du-pape [mɔnɛdypap] *(pl* **monnaies-du-pape)** NF *Bot* honesty

monnayable [mɔnɛjabl] ADJ convertible into money; **ton expérience est m.** you could make money out of your experience

monnayage [mɔnɛjaʒ] NM minting, coining

monnayer [11] [mɔnɛje] VT **1** *(convertir en monnaie)* to mint; **m. de l'argent/du nickel** to mint silver/nickel (coins)

2 *(vendre)* to sell, to make money out of; **m. son expérience/savoir-faire** to cash in on one's experience/know-how; **il refusa de m. son silence** he refused to sell his silence

3 *(échanger)* to exchange; **il a monnayé ses services contre une lettre d'introduction** he asked for a letter of introduction in exchange for his services

▸ **se monnayer** VPR **tu devrais savoir que le talent se monnaie** you ought to know there's money to be made out of talent; **ici tout se monnaie** money can buy (you) anything here, everything here has its price

monnayeur [mɔnɛjœr] NM **1** *(pour faire la monnaie)* change machine; *(pour payer)* coin box **2** *(ouvrier)* coiner, minter

mono [mɔno] *Fam* ADJ INV *(disque)* mono
NF INV mono; **en m.** in mono
NMF **1** *Sport* instructor■, *f* instructress■ **2** *(de colonie de vacances)* (group) supervisor■ *or* leader■, *Am* (camp) counselor■
NM monoski■

mono- [mɔno] PRÉF mono-, single

monoacide [mɔnoasid] NM *Chim* monoacid

monoamine [mɔnoamin] NF *Chim* monoamine

monoamine-oxydase [mɔnoaminɔksidaz] *(pl* **monoamines-oxydases)** NF *Chim* monoamine oxidase

monoatomique [mɔnoatɔmik] ADJ *Chim* monatomic

monobase [mɔnobaz] NF *Chim* monobase

monobasique [mɔnobazik] ADJ *Chim* monobasic

monobloc [mɔnoblɔk] ADJ *(fusil)* cast en bloc, solid; *(cylindre, moteur, roue)* monobloc

monocaméral, -e, -aux, -ales [mɔnokameral, -o] ADJ *Pol* unicameral

---

monocaméralisme [mɔnokameralism], **mono-caméristine** [mɔnokamerism] NM *Pol* unicameralism

monocaténaire [mɔnokatenɛr] ADJ *Biol & Chim* single-stranded

monochromateur [mɔnokromatœr] NM *Phys* monochromator

monochromatique [mɔnokromatik] ADJ *Phys* monochromatic

monochrome [mɔnokrom] ADJ monochrome

monochromie [mɔnokromi] NF monochromaticity

monocinétique [mɔnosinetik] ADJ monokinetic

monocle [mɔnokl] NM (single) eyeglass, monocle

monoclinal, -e, -aux, -ales [mɔnoklinal, -o] *Géol* ADJ monoclinal
NM monocline

monoclinique [mɔnoklinik] ADJ *Chim & Géol* monoclinic

monoclonal, -e, -aux, -ales [mɔnoklonal, -o] ADJ *Biol* monoclonal; **anticorps m.** monoclonal antibody

monocolore [mɔnokɔlɔr] ADJ **1** *(d'une couleur)* one-colour **2** *Pol* one-party

monocoque [mɔnokɔk] ADJ *Aviat, Naut & Aut* monocoque; **avion m.** monocoque; **bateau m.** monohull; **carrosserie m.** *(de voiture)* monocoque body
NM *Naut* monohull
NF *Aut* monocoque

monocorde [mɔnokɔrd] ADJ **1** *Mus (instrument)* single-stringed **2** *(son, ton, voix)* monotonous, droning; **parler d'un ton m.** to speak in a monotone
NM monochord

monocorps [mɔnokɔr] *Aut* ADJ monobox
NM monobox

monocotylédone [mɔnokɔtiledɔn] *Bot* NF monocotyledon
ADJ monocotyledonous

❏ **monocotylédones** NFPL Monocotyledoneae

monocratie [mɔnokrasi] NF monocracy

monocristal, -aux [mɔnokristal, -o] NM monocrystal

monocristallin, -e [mɔnokristalɛ̃, -in] ADJ monocrystalline

monoculaire [mɔnokylɛr] ADJ monocular; **cécité m.** blindness in one eye

monoculture [mɔnokyltyr] NF monoculture; **une région de m.** a monoculture area

monocycle [mɔnosikl] NM unicycle

monocyclique [mɔnosiklik] ADJ *Chim & Zool* monocyclic

monocylindre [mɔnosilɛ̃dr] ADJ single-cylinder *(avant n)*
NM single-cylinder engine

monocylindrique [mɔnosilɛ̃drik] ADJ single-cylinder *(avant n)*

monocyte [mɔnosit] NM *Biol* monocyte; *Méd* **angine à monocytes** *Br* glandular fever, *Am* mononucleosis

monodactyle [mɔnodaktil] ADJ *Zool* monodactylous

monodépartemental, -e, -aux, -ales [mɔnodepartəmɑ̃tal, -o] ADJ *Admin & Jur (région)* = comprising a single ''département''

monodie [mɔnodi] NF *Mus* monody

monodique [mɔnodik] ADJ *Mus* monodic

monœcie [mɔnesi] NF *Bot* monoecism

monœcique [mɔnesik] ADJ *Bot* monoecious

monoéthylèneglycol [mɔnoetilɛnglikɔl] NM *Chim* monoethylene glycol

monofilament [mɔnofilamɑ̃] NM monofilament

monogame [mɔnogam] ADJ monogamous
NMF monogamist

monogamie [mɔnogami] NF monogamy

monogamique [mɔnogamik] ADJ monogamous

monogénique [mɔnoʒenik] ADJ **1** *Biol* monogenic, monogenetic **2** *Géol* monogenetic

monogénisme [mɔnoʒenism] NM *Biol* monogenesis

monogrammatique [mɔnogramatik] ADJ monogrammatic

monogramme [mɔnogram] NM monogram; **marquer qch d'un m.** to monogram sth

monogrammé, -e [mɔnograme] ADJ *(chemise)* monogrammed

monographie [mɔnografi] NF monograph

---

monographique [mɔnografik] ADJ monographic, monographical

monogyne [mɔnoʒin] ADJ *Bot* monogynous

monogynie [mɔnoʒini] NF *Bot* monogyny

monohybride [mɔnoibrid] NM *Biol* monohybride

monohydrate [mɔnoidrat] NM *Chim* monohydrate

monoï [mɔnoj] NM INV Monoi, = scented coconut oil

monoïdéisme [mɔnoideism] NM monoideism, monomania

mono-insaturé, -e [mɔnoɛ̃satyre] *(mpl* **mono-insaturés,** *fpl* **mono-insaturées)** ADJ *(lipide)* mono-unsaturated

monoïque [mɔnoik] ADJ *Bot* monoecious

monokini [mɔnokini] NM monokini, topless swimsuit; **faire du m.** to wear a monokini, to go topless; **m. interdit** *(sur panneau)* no topless bathing

monolingue [mɔnolɛ̃g] ADJ monolingual
NMF monoglot; **les monolingues** people who speak only one language, monoglots

monolinguisme [mɔnolɛ̃gɥism] NM monolingualism

monolithe [mɔnolit] ADJ *Géol* monolithic
NM *Géol & Fig* monolith

monolithique [mɔnolitik] ADJ *Géol & Fig* monolithic

monolithisme [mɔnolitism] NM monolithic state

monologue [mɔnolɔg] NM **1** *(discours)* monologue; *Théât* monologue, soliloquy; **il s'est lancé dans un long m. sur le respect d'autrui** he launched into a long monologue on the need to respect others **2** *Littérature* **m. intérieur** stream of consciousness, interior monologue

'**Monologues du vagin**' Ensler 'The Vagina Monologues'

monologuer [3] [mɔnolɔge] VI *(monopoliser la parole)* to carry on a monologue; *Théât* to soliloquize; **il monologue des heures durant** *(en public)* he can go on (talking) for hours; *(tout seul)* he talks to himself for hours

monomane [mɔnoman] *Psy* ADJ monomaniac *(avant n)*
NMF monomaniac

monomaniaque [mɔnomanjak] *Psy* ADJ monomaniac *(avant n)*
NMF monomaniac

monomanie [mɔnomani] NF *Psy* monomania

monôme [mɔnom] NM **1** *Math* monomial **2** *Fam Arg scol* ≃ students' rag procession

monomère [mɔnomɛr] *Chim* ADJ monomeric
NM monomer

monométallisme [mɔnometalism] NM *Fin* monometallism

monométalliste [mɔnometalist] ADJ *Fin* monometallic

monomètre [mɔnomɛtr] *Littérature* ADJ monometric, monometrical
NM monometer

monomorphe [mɔnomɔrf] ADJ *Biol* monomorphic

monomorphisme [mɔnomɔrfism] NM *Biol* monomorphism

monomoteur [mɔnomotœr] ADJ M single-engine *(avant n)*, single-engined
NM single-engine *or* single-engined aircraft

mononucléaire [mɔnonykleɛr] *Biol* ADJ mononuclear
NM monocyte, mononuclear leucocyte

mononucléé, -e [mɔnonyklee] ADJ *Biol* mononuclear

mononucléose [mɔnonykleoz] NF *Méd* mononucleosis; **m. infectieuse** *Br* glandular fever, *Spéc* mononucleosis, *Am* mononucleosis

monoparental, -e, -aux, -ales [mɔnoparɑ̃tal, -o] ADJ single-parent *(avant n)*

monoparentalité [mɔnoparɑ̃talite] NF single parenthood

monopartisme [mɔnopartism] NM single-partyism

monophasé, -e [mɔnofaze] ADJ single-phase, monophase
NM single-phase (current)

monophonie [mɔnofoni] NF monophony

monophonique [mɔnofonik] ADJ *Mus* monophonic; *(système électroacoustique)* monophonic, monaural

monophtongue [mɔnɔftɔ̃g] NF *Ling* monophthong

monophylétique [mɔnɔfiletik] ADJ *Biol* monophyletic

monophysisme [mɔnɔfizism] NM *Rel* Monophysitism

monophysite [mɔnɔfizit] *Rel* ADJ Monophysite NMF Monophysite

monoplace [mɔnɔplas] ADJ one-seater (*avant n*), single-seater (*avant n*) NM one-seater *or* single-seater (vehicle) NF single-seater racing car

monoplan [mɔnɔplɑ̃] NM monoplane

monoplégie [mɔnɔpleʒi] NF monoplegia

monopode [mɔnɔpɔd] NM *Phot* unipod

monopole [mɔnɔpɔl] NM **1** *Écon* monopoly; **avoir le m. de qch** to have a monopoly on sth; **exercer un m. sur un secteur** to monopolize a sector; **m. d'achat** buyer's monopoly; **m. de droit** legal monopoly; **m. d'embauche** closed shop; **m. d'émission** issuing monopoly; **m. d'État** state monopoly; **m. d'exploitation** operating monopoly; **m. de fabrication** manufacturing monopoly; **m. de fait** monopoly; **m. des prix** price monopoly; **m. de vente** sales monopoly **2** *Fig* monopoly; **vous pensez avoir le m. de la vérité?** do you think you have a monopoly on the truth?

monopoleur, -euse [mɔnɔpɔlœr, -øz] ADJ monopolist NM,F monopolist

monopolisateur, -trice [mɔnɔpɔlizatœr, -tris] NM,F monopolizer

monopolisation [mɔnɔpɔlizasjɔ̃] NF monopolization

monopolisatrice [mɔnɔpɔlizatris] *voir* **monopolisateur**

monopoliser [3] [mɔnɔpɔlize] VT *Écon* to monopolize, to have a monopoly on; *Fig* to monopolize; **m. l'antenne** (*sujet: parti politique, groupe de pression etc*) to rule *or* to monopolize the airwaves; **il a monopolisé l'antenne pendant la majeure partie du débat** he dominated the discussion for most of the programme; **m. la parole** not to let anyone else speak, to monopolize the conversation; **m. le téléphone/la salle de bains** to hog the phone/the bathroom; **ne monopolisez pas notre jeune amie** don't keep our young friend to yourself

monopoliste [mɔnɔpɔlist] ADJ monopolist

monopolistique [mɔnɔpɔlistik] ADJ monopolistic

Monopoly® [mɔnɔpɔli] NM Monopoly®

monoposte [mɔnɔpɔst] NM *Ordinat* stand-alone

monoprocesseur [mɔnɔprɔsesœr] ADJ M *Ordinat* single-processor (*avant n*) NM single (central processing) unit

monoprogrammation [mɔnɔprɔgramasjɔ̃] NF monoprogramming

monopsone [mɔnɔpson] NM *Écon* monopsony

monoptère [mɔnɔptɛr] ADJ monopteral NM monopteron

monorail [mɔnɔraj] ADJ monorail (*avant n*) NM monorail

monorime [mɔnɔrim] ADJ monorhyme

monosaccharide [mɔnɔsakarid] NM *Chim* monosaccharide

monosémie [mɔnɔsemi] NF *Ling* monosemy

monosémique [mɔnɔsemik] ADJ *Ling* monosemic

monosépale [mɔnɔsepal] ADJ *Bot* monosepalous

monoski [mɔnɔski] NM (*planche*) monoski; (*activité*) monoskiing; **faire du m.** to monoski; **m. nautique** (*planche*) wakeboard; (*activité*) wakeboarding; **faire du m. nautique** to wakeboard

monosoc [mɔnɔsɔk] NM single plough

monospace [mɔnɔspas] NM people carrier, people mover

monosperme [mɔnɔspɛrm] ADJ *Bot* monospermous, monospermal

monostable [mɔnɔstabl] ADJ *Électron* monostable

monostyle [mɔnɔstil] ADJ *Archit* (*colonne*) single-shafted

monosyllabe [mɔnɔsilab] *Ling* ADJ monosyllabic NM monosyllable

monosyllabique [mɔnɔsilabik] ADJ *Ling* monosyllabic

mono-tâche [mɔnɔtaʃ] ADJ INV *Ordinat* single-tasking (*avant n*)

monothéisme [mɔnɔteism] NM monotheism

monothéiste [mɔnɔteist] ADJ monotheistic, monotheist (*avant n*) NMF monotheist

monotone [mɔnɔtɔn] ADJ **1** (*voix, bruit*) monotonous; **le tic-tac m. de la pendule** the monotonous ticking of the clock **2** (*discours, style*) monotonous, dull; **une déclamation m.** a dull *or* droning declamation **3** (*vie*) monotonous, dreary, humdrum; (*paysage*) monotonous, dreary **4** *Math* monotonic

monotonie [mɔnɔtɔni] NF monotony, dullness, dreariness; **rompre la m.** to break the monotony

monotrace [mɔnɔtras] ADJ single-track

monotrème [mɔnɔtrɛm] *Zool* NM monotreme
□ **monotrèmes** NMPL Monotremata, monotremes

monotrope [mɔnɔtrɔp] NM monotropa

Monotype® [mɔnɔtip] NF *Typ* Monotype®

monotype [mɔnɔtip] NM **1** *Naut* one-design sailing boat; **course de monotypes** race between boats of the same class **2** *Beaux-Arts* monotype, monoprint **3** *Biol* monotype ADJ *Bot & Zool* monotypic

monovalence [mɔnɔvalɑ̃s] NF *Chim* monovalence, monovalency

monovalent, -e [mɔnɔvalɑ̃, -ɑ̃t] ADJ *Chim* monovalent

monoxyde [mɔnɔksid] NM *Chim* monoxide; **m. de carbone** carbon monoxide

monoxyle [mɔnɔksil] ADJ monoxylous

monozygote [mɔnɔzigɔt] *Biol* ADJ monozygous, monozygotic NMF monozygote

Monrovia [mɔ̃rɔvja] NF Monrovia

Monseigneur [mɔ̃sɛɲœr] (*pl* **Messeigneurs** [mesɛɲœr]) NM **1** (*terme d'adresse → archevêque, duc*) Your Grace; (*→ évêque*) My Lord (Bishop); (*→ cardinal*) Your Eminence; (*→ prince*) Your Royal Highness **2** (*titre → archevêque, duc*) His Grace; (*→ évêque*) His Lordship; (*→ cardinal*) His Eminence (Cardinal); (*→ prince*) His Royal Highness; **M. l'évêque de...** the Lord Bishop of... **3** *Hist* Monseigneur (*the heir to the throne of France*)

Monsieur [mɔ̃sjø] (*pl* **Messieurs** [mesjø]) NM **1** (*dans une lettre*) **M.** Dear Sir, *Sout* Sir; **Cher M. Duval** Dear Mr Duval; **M. et cher Confrère, M. et cher Collègue** (*qui s'appelle Martin*) Dear Mr Martin; **Messieurs** Dear Sirs; **M. le Maire** Dear Sir; **M. le Vicomte** My Lord **2** (*sur une enveloppe*) **M. Duval** Mr Duval; **M. Robert Marceau** Mr Robert Marceau, *Sout* R. Marceau Esq; **Messieurs Thon et Lamiel** Messrs Thon and Lamiel; **Messieurs Marceau et Cie** Messrs Marceau and Co **3** (*terme d'adresse*) **bonjour M.!** good morning!; **bonjour M. Leroy!** good morning, Mr Leroy!; **bonjour M. le Ministre!** good morning, Sir!; **bonjour M. le Consul!** good morning, Sir *or* Your Excellency!; **bonjour M. le Marquis!** good morning, Your Lordship!; **bonjour M. le Duc!** good morning, Your Grace!; **bonjour Messieurs** good morning(, gentlemen); **bonjour Messieurs Duval!** good morning, gentlemen!; *Fam* **(bonjour) Messieurs Dames!** morning, all *or* everybody!; *Vieilli ou Hum* **M. Robert** (*à un petit garçon*) Master Robert; **M. le Président, M. le Premier ministre?** (*au chef de l'État*) Sir *or Am* Mr President, what about inflation?; (*au directeur*) Sir *or* Mr Chairman, what about inflation?; *Br* **Messieurs les députés, vous êtes priés de vous asseoir!** will the Honourable Members please be seated!; **Mesdames, Mesdemoiselles, Messieurs!** Ladies and Gentlemen!; **Messieurs, un peu de silence, s'il vous plaît!** (*à des garçonnets*) boys, please be quiet!; (*à des jeunes gens*) gentlemen, would you please be quiet!; **et voilà, M., une laitue bien fraîche!** here you are, Sir, a nice fresh lettuce!; **M. désirerait voir les pantalons?** would you like to see the trousers, Sir?; *Sout ou Hum* **M. est servi** (*au dîner*) dinner is served(, Sir); (*pour le thé*) tea is served(, Sir); **M. a sonné?** you rang, Sir?; **le frère de M. attend en bas** (*à un roturier*) your brother is waiting downstairs; (*à un homme titré*) Your Lordship's brother is waiting downstairs; **que prendront ces messieurs?** what will you have, gentlemen?; **vous n'y pensez pas, cher** *ou* **mon bon** *ou* **mon pauvre M.!** my dear Sir, you can't be serious!; **peux-tu prêter un instant ton stylo à M.?** could you lend the gentleman your pen for a minute?; **bonjour M., je voudrais parler à quelqu'un de la comptabilité, s'il vous plaît** (*au téléphone*) hello, I'd like to speak to somebody in the accounts department, please **4** (*en se référant à une tierce personne*) **adressez-vous à M. Duval** apply to Mr Duval; **M. votre père** your father; **le docteur Duval et M.** (*pour annoncer*) Doctor Duval and Mr Duval; **M. le Président regrette de ne pas pouvoir venir** (*chef de l'État*) the President regrets he is unable to come; (*directeur*) the Chairman *or* Mr X regrets he is unable to come; **je voudrais parler à m. le Directeur** (*d'un magasin, d'un service*) I would like to speak to the manager; (*d'une école*) I would like to speak to the *Br* headmaster *or Am* principal; **M. le Marquis est arrivé** His Lordship has arrived; **M. le Duc est arrivé** His Grace has arrived; **M. se plaint que...** (*dit par vendeur*) the gentleman *or* this gentleman is complaining that...; **c'est le chapeau de M.** it's the gentleman's hat; **M. est sorti** His Lordship is not at home **5** *Scol* **M., j'ai fini mon addition!** (please) Sir, I've finished my sum! **6** *Fam* (*en appellatif*) **alors, M. le frimeur, tu es satisfait?** so, are you pleased with yourself, Mr Big Shot?; **et en plus, M. exige des excuses!** His Lordship wants an apology as well, does he? **7** *Hist* Monsieur (*title given to the King of France's younger brother*) **8** (*locutions*) **il a été nommé M. sécurité routière** he was made road safety czar; **M. Tout-le-Monde** the man in the street, *Hum Br* Joe Public, *Am* Joe Blow; **m. je-sais-tout** Mr Know-all, Mr Know-it-all; **il va encore nous jouer son m. je-sais-tout** here he goes again, the know-all *or* know-it-all

monsieur [məsjø] (*pl* **messieurs** [mesjø]) NM man, gentleman; **un m. vous a demandé** a man *or* a gentleman's been asking for you; **le jeune m. prendra-t-il une orangeade?** will the young gentleman have an orange juice?; *Péj* **il se prend pour un m.** he thinks he's a gentleman; **c'est un vilain m.** he's a wicked man

monsignor [mɔ̃siɲɔr], **monsignore** [mɔ̃siɲɔre] NM *Rel* Monsignor

monstera [mɔ̃stera] NM *Bot* (Swiss) cheese plant, *Spéc* monstera

monstrance [mɔ̃strɑ̃s] NF *Rel* monstrance

monstre [mɔ̃str] NM **1** *Biol, Myth & Zool* monster; **le m. du Loch Ness** the Loch Ness Monster; **les monstres marins** the monsters of the deep; *Fig* **m. sacré** superstar; **James Dean était un m. sacré du cinéma hollywoodien** James Dean was a Hollywood screen idol **2** (*chose énorme*) monster; **son camion est un vrai m.!** his lorry is an absolute monster! **3** (*personne laide*) monster, monstrously ugly *or* hideous person; (*brute*) monster, brute; **un m. d'ingratitude/d'égoïsme** an ungrateful/a selfish brute **4** *Fam* (*enfant insupportable*) monster, little terror, *Br* perisher; **sortez d'ici, petits monstres!** out of here, you little monsters! ADJ *Fam* (*erreur, difficulté, déficit*) monstrous, enormous, colossal; (*rassemblement*) monstrous, mammoth; (*répercussions, succès, effet*) tremendous, enormous; (*soldes*) gigantic, huge, colossal; **ça a eu un effet m. sur le public** it had an enormous *or* a tremendous effect on the audience; **il y a une queue m. chez le boucher** there's a huge *or* massive queue at the butcher's; **j'ai un boulot m.!** I've got loads *or* tons *or* piles of work to do!; **il a un culot m.!** he's got a damned nerve *or Br* a bloody cheek!

monstrueuse [mɔ̃stryøz] *voir* **monstrueux**

monstrueusement [mɔ̃stryøzmɑ̃] ADV (*laid*) monstrously, hideously; (*intelligent*) prodigiously, stupendously

monstrueux, -euse [mɔ̃stryø, -øz] ADJ **1** (*difforme*) monstrous, deformed; **un être m.**, **une créature monstrueuse** a freak **2** (*laid*) monstrous, hideous, ghastly **3** (*abject, cruel*) monstrous, wicked, vile; **il fut assez m. pour trahir un ami** he was wicked enough to betray a friend; **elle est d'un égoïsme m.** she is a selfish monster; **un crime m.** a heinous *or* monstrous crime

4 Fam (très grave) monstrous, dreadful, ghastly; **une erreur monstrueuse** an awful or a dreadful mistake

monstruosité [mɔ̃stryozite] NF **1** (difformité) deformity **2** (acte, crime) monstrosity; **commettre/dire des monstruosités** to do/to say the most terrible things

mont [mɔ̃] NM **1** Géog mountain; Littéraire mount; **m. sous-marin** seamount; **aller par monts et par vaux** to wander up hill and down dale; Fig **il est toujours par monts et par vaux** he's always on the move; Fig **promettre monts et merveilles à qn** to promise sb the earth or the moon; **les monts Appalaches** the Appalachian Mountains; **le m. Ararat** Mount Ararat; **le m. Athos** Mount Athos; **le m. Aventin** the Aventine Hill; **les monts Balkans** the Balkan Mountains, the Stara Planina; **le m. Blanc** Mont Blanc; **le m. Cameroun** Mount Cameroon; **les monts Cantabriques** the Cantabrian Mountains; **le m. Capitolin** the Capitoline Hill; **le m. Carmel** Mount Carmel; **le m. Cassin** Monte Cassino; **le m. Cervin** the Matterhorn; **le m. Erebus** Mount Erebus; **le m. Etna** Mount Etna; **le m. Everest** Mount Everest; **le m. Fuji-Yama** Mount Fuji; **le m. Kenya** Mount Kenya; **les monts Mackenzie** the Mackenzie Mountains; **le m. McKinley** Mount McKinley; **le m. des Oliviers** the Mount of Olives; **le m. Olympe** Mount Olympus; **le m. Palatin** the Palatine Hill; **le m. Parnasse** Mount Parnassus; **les monts du Pinde** the Pindus Mountains; **le m. Quirinal** Mount Quirinal; **les monts Rhodope** the Rhodope Mountains; **le m. Sinaï** Mount Sinai; **le m. Saint Helens** Mount St Helens; **les monts Transantarctiques** the Transantarctic Mountains; **le m. Vésuve** Mount Vesuvius; **le m. Whitney** Mount Whitney; **les monts du Zagros** the Zagros Mountains

2 (de la main) mount
3 Anat **le m. de Vénus** mons veneris

montage [mɔ̃taʒ] NM **1** (assemblage → d'un meuble, d'un kit) assembly, assemblage; (→ d'une tente) pitching, putting up; (→ de porte) hanging; (→ d'un vêtement) assembling, sewing together; (→ d'un col) setting in; (→ de bijou) setting, mounting; Typ (page) make-up, pasting up; Tech **m. serré** push fit; Tech **m. à la presse** press fit

2 (installation → d'un appareil) installing, fixing; (→ d'une pierre précieuse) mounting, setting; (→ de pneus) fitting
3 Fin **m. de crédit** credit or loan arrangement; **m. financier** financial arrangement; **le m. financier a été difficile** it wasn't easy getting the money together; **le m. financier du projet sera le suivant** money for the project will be provided as follows
4 Cin & (dans l'audiovisuel → processus) editing; (→ avec effets spéciaux) montage; (→ résultat) montage; **m. réalisé par X** (d'un film) film editing by X; (du son) sound editing by X; **couper qch au m.** to edit sth out; **la réplique a été coupée au m.** the line was edited out; **premier m.** rough cut; **m. alterné** (processus) cross-cutting; (résultat) cross-cut; **m. audiovisuel** sound slide show; **m. bout à bout** rough cut; **m. en continuité** continuity editing; **m. définitif** final cut; **m. discontinu** discontinuity editing; **m. fin** fine cut; **m. linéaire** linear editing; **m. négatif** negative cutting; **m. non linéaire** non-linear editing; **m. off-line** offline editing; **m. on-line** online editing; **m. original** edited master; **m. en parallèle** parallel editing; **m. de postproduction** postproduction editing; **m. à la prise de vues** direct camera editing; Cin, Rad & TV **m. sonore** sound editing; (avec truquage) sound montage; **m. sonorisé** sound slide show; **m. synchrone** sync editing; **m. vidéo** video(tape) editing, tape editing; **m. virtuel** virtual editing; Cin **salle de m.** cutting room; Cin **film de m.** film montage
5 Phot mounting; (image truquée) montage; **faire du m. de diapositives** to mount slides; **m. de photos** photomontage
6 Élec & Électron wiring, connecting, connection; **m. compensateur/en pont** flywheel/bridge circuit; **m. en parallèle/série** connection in parallel/in series; **m. symétrique** push-pull circuit
7 Mines overhand, overhand stope

8 (de matériaux de construction) taking up, carrying up

montagnard, -e [mɔ̃taɲar, -ard] ADJ mountain (avant n), highland (avant n)

NM,F mountain dweller; **les montagnards** mountain people
◻ **Montagnard** NM Hist **les Montagnards** the Montagnards, the members of the Mountain

LES MONTAGNARDS

This term refers to a political movement which sought to give national reality to the French Revolution. Successfully rallying the support of the people, the sans-culottes, the Paris Commune and the Jacobins, they became the sole leaders after eliminating the Girondists. They created the Committee of Public Safety, later the chief organ of the government, and the Revolutionary Tribunal in 1793. Leading members included Danton, Marat and Robespierre. "Les Montagnards" is also used to refer to one of the two assemblies under the Third Republic, claiming to be heir to the Jacobin tradition of a strong centralized regime.

montagne [mɔ̃taɲ] NF **1** (mont) mountain; **les montagnes d'Écosse** the Highlands of Scotland; **les montagnes d'Europe** the European (mountain) ranges; **les montagnes Rocheuses** the Rocky Mountains, the Rockies; Fig **déplacer ou soulever des montagnes** to move heaven and earth; **(se) faire une m. de qch** to make a great song and dance about sth; **(se) faire une m. de rien** ou **d'un rien** to make a mountain out of a molehill; **gros comme une m.** (mensonge) huge, colossal; (canular) mammoth (avant n); **c'est la m. qui accouche d'une souris!** what a lot of fuss about nothing!; Prov **il n'y a que les montagnes qui ne se rencontrent pas** there are none so distant that fate cannot bring together; Prov **si la m. ne va pas à Mahomet, Mahomet ira à la m.** if the mountain will not come to Mohammed, Mohammed must go to the mountain **2** (région) **la m.** the mountains; (en Écosse) the highlands; **à la m.** ou **en m.** in the mountains; **de m.** mountain (avant n); **faire de la m.** to go mountaineering; **la basse/haute/moyenne m.** the low mountains/high mountains/uplands; **de basse m.** low-mountain (avant n); **de haute m.** high-mountain (avant n); **de moyenne m.** upland (avant n); **en basse m.** in the foothills; **en haute m.** high in the mountains; **en moyenne m.** in the uplands; **ce n'est que de la m. à vaches** it's only hills
3 (grosse quantité) **une m. de** lots or mountains or a mountain of; **une m. de détritus/spaghettis** a mountain of refuse/spaghetti; **une m. de repassage** a huge pile of ironing; **m. de blé/beurre** wheat/butter mountain
4 **montagnes russes** (attraction foraine) rollercoaster, Br big dipper; **moi, en ce moment, c'est les montagnes russes** (moral, santé) I'm a bit up and down at the moment
5 Hist **la M.** the Mountain

La montagne qui accouche d'une souris

This phrase was popularized by La Fontaine's fable La montagne qui accouche and other seventeenth-century French writers. Meaning literally "The mountain that brings forth a mouse", this expression is used allusively in sarcastic remarks about an undertaking that has been hyped up in advance but which does not live up to the grand claims made for it. It is similar in meaning to the English expression "to be a damp squib".

montagneux, -euse [mɔ̃taɲø, -øz] ADJ mountainous

montaison [mɔ̃tɛzɔ̃] NF **1** (du saumon) = season during which salmon migrate up-river from the sea **2** Agr going to seed

montalbanais, -e [mɔ̃talbanɛ, -ɛz] ADJ of/from Montauban
◻ **Montalbanais, -e** NM,F = inhabitant of or person from Montauban

Montana [mɔ̃tana] NM Géog **le M.** Montana; **dans le M.** in Montana

montanisme [mɔ̃tanism] NM Rel Montanism

montaniste [mɔ̃tanist] Rel ADJ Montanist
NMF Montanist

montant, -e [mɔ̃tɑ̃, -ɑ̃t] ADJ **1** (qui grimpe → sentier) rising, uphill; **la génération montante** the rising generation; Rail **train/quai m.** up train/platform
2 Naut upstream (avant n); Transp up (avant n); Mines **taille montante** raise stope; **tranche montante** rise cut
3 (col) high; (corsage) high-necked, high-neckline (avant n); **chaussures montantes** ankle boot
4 Mil voir **garde**
NM **1** (d'une échelle, d'un châssis) upright; (d'une tente) pole; (d'une porte, d'une fenêtre) jamb; (d'un portail, d'un lit) post; Sport **m. (de but)** (goal)post; Aut **m. de pare-brise** screen pillar, windscreen pillar, A-pillar; Aut **m. de porte** door pillar, B-pillar
2 Mines prop
3 Équitation cheek piece
4 Fin amount, sum, total; **écrivez le m. en toutes lettres** write out the sum in full; **le m. du découvert** the amount of the overdraft, the total overdraft; **quel est le m. du chèque/de la facture?** how much is the cheque/invoice for?; **chèque/facture d'un m. de 500 euros** cheque/invoice for 500 euros; **un cadeau d'un m. total de 150 euros** a present worth 150 euros; **cinq versements d'un m. de 100 euros** five payments of 100 euros (each); **le m. total des réparations s'élève à...**, **les réparations s'élèvent à un m. total de...** the total cost of the repairs adds up to...; **j'ignore le m. de mes dettes** I don't know what my debts amount to; **m. brut** gross amount; UE **montants compensatoires (monétaires)** (compensatory) subsidies, (monetary) compensatory amounts; **m. exonéré de TVA** VAT exempt amount; **m. forfaitaire** lump sum; **m. maximum/minimum** maximum/minimum (amount); **m. net** net total; **m. prévisionnel des ventes** forecast sales level; **m. à régler** (sur une facture) amount due; Compta **m. à reporter** amount brought forward; **m. du retour net** net return; **m. total** total (amount)
5 Culin spiciness, tang
6 (en œnologie) **vin qui a du m.** wine with a strong bouquet

montbéliarde [mɔ̃beljard] ADJ F **race m.** Montbéliarde breed
NF Montbéliarde cow (a breed from the Jura Mountains)

mont-blanc [mɔ̃blɑ̃] (pl **monts-blancs**) NM = chestnut cream dessert

mont-de-piété [mɔ̃dpjete] (pl **monts-de-piété**) NM (state-owned) pawnshop; **mettre qch au m.** to pawn sth; **retirer** ou **dégager qch du m.** to recover sth from the pawnshop

mont-d'or [mɔ̃dɔr] (pl **monts-d'or**) NM Mont d'Or (cheese)

monte [mɔ̃t] NF **1** Équitation (technique) horsemanship **2** (participation à une course) mounting; **j'ai eu trois montes dans la journée** I had three mounts today; **partants et montes probables** probable runners and riders **3** Vét (accouplement) covering; (époque de l'accouplement) breeding or mating season; **mener une jument à la m.** to take a mare to be covered

monté, -e [mɔ̃te] ADJ **1** (pourvu) provided, equipped; **être bien/mal m. (en qch)** to be well/badly equipped (with sth); **elle est bien montée en vaisselle** she's got plenty of crockery; Fam Ironique **tu es bien montée avec un pareil mari!** you've married a good or Br a right one here!
2 (à cheval → police, troupes) mounted
3 (bijou) set, mounted; **m. sur or** gold-mounted; **médaille montée en pendentif** medal mounted as a pendant; **photographies non montées** unmounted photographs
4 Fam (irrité) **être m. contre qn** to be angry with sb■; **les ouvriers sont très montés** the workers are up in arms; **elle est très montée, ne lui en**

'La Montagne magique' Mann 'The Magic Mountain'

parle pas aujourd'hui she's pretty wound up, don't talk to her about it today

5 *Couture* made-up; **manche montée** made-up *or* fitted sleeve

6 *(plante)* seeded, gone to seed, bolted

7 *Culin* **œufs montés en neige** beaten egg whites

8 *Fam* **être bien m.** to be well hung; *très Fam* **être m. comme un âne** *ou* **un bourricot** *ou* **un taureau** to be hung like a horse *or* a donkey

▫ **montée** NF **1** *(pente)* climb, uphill *or* upward slope; **en haut de la montée** at the top of the hill; **méfiez-vous, la montée est raide!** watch out, it's quite a steep climb!

2 *(ascension)* climb; *(d'un avion)* ascent; **la montée jusqu'au chalet** the climb up *or Sout* the ascent to the chalet; **la montée des escaliers lui fut très pénible** he/she climbed *or* struggled up the stairs with great difficulty; **pendant la montée du col** as he was/we were/*etc* going uphill; *Aut & Aviat* **essai de montée** climbing test; *Aviat* **vitesse en montée** climbing speed; *Aut & Rail* speed on a gradient

3 *(élévation → d'une fusée, d'un dirigeable)* ascent; *(→ de la sève)* rise; **la montée des eaux** the rise in the water level

4 *(augmentation → de violence)* rise; *(→ de mécontentement, du nationalisme)* rise, increase, growth; **la montée des prix/températures** the rise in prices/temperatures; **face à la montée en flèche des prix du pétrole** faced with rocketing *or* soaring oil prices; **devant la montée de la violence/du racisme** faced with the rising tide of violence/racism

5 *(accession)* rise, *Sout* ascension; **sa montée au pouvoir** his/her rise to power

6 *Archit* height

7 *Physiol* **montée de lait** onset of lactation

Monte-Carlo [mɔ̃tekarlo] NM Monte Carlo

monte-charge [mɔ̃tʃarʒ] *(pl* **inv** *ou* **monte-charges)** NM hoist, *Br* goods lift, *Am* freight elevator

montée [mɔ̃te] *voir* **monté**

monte-en-l'air [mɔ̃tɑ̃lɛr] NM INV cat burglar

Montego Bay [mɔ̃tegobɛ] NM Montego Bay

monténégrin, -e [mɔ̃tenegrɛ̃, -in] ADJ Montenegrin

▫ **Monténégrin, -e** NM,F Montenegrin

Monténégro [mɔ̃tenegro] NM **le M.** Montenegro; **vivre au M.** to live in Montenegro; **aller au M.** to go to Montenegro

monte-plat, monte-plats [mɔ̃tpla] *(pl* **monte-plats)** NM dumb-waiter, *Br* service lift

MONTER [3] [mɔ̃te]

> **VI** to go up **1, 4, 6** ▪ to climb **1** ▪ to rise **1, 4, 6, 8** ▪ to get on, to board **2** ▪ to increase **4**
> **VT** to go up **1** ▪ to take up **2** ▪ to put up **3, 4, 6** ▪ to turn up **4** ▪ to assemble **6** ▪ to set up **6, 9, 10** ▪ to mount **7, 8, 12** ▪ to fit **7, 13** ▪ to organize **9**
> **VPR** to be ridden **2** ▪ to wind oneself up **3**

VI *(aux être)* **1** *(personne, animal → vu d'en bas)* to go up; *(→ vu d'en haut)* to come up; *(avion)* to climb; *(soleil)* to rise; *(oiseau)* to soar, to fly up; *(drapeau)* to go up; *(rideau de théâtre, air, fumée)* to go up, to rise; *(chemin)* to go up, to rise, to climb; **m. en courant/en rampant** to run/crawl up; **m. se coucher** to go (up) to bed; **m. au grenier** to go up to *or* into the attic; **m. à** *ou* **sur un arbre/une échelle** to climb (up) (into) a tree/ (on to) a ladder; **m. sur une chaise** to stand *or* to get on a chair; **m. dans sa chambre** to go up to one's room; **m. chez qn** to go up to sb's place; **elle ne monte jamais ici** she never comes up here; **monte par l'ascenseur** go up in *or* use the lift; **Anna est arrivée? faites-la m.** Anna's here? tell her to come up; **la voiture est montée sur le trottoir** the car went up on *or* mounted the pavement; **le cortège est monté jusqu'en haut de la colline** the procession went *or* climbed to the top of the hill; **le premier de cordée continuait à m.** the leader continued to climb *or* continued the ascent; **es-tu déjà montée au dernier étage de la tour Eiffel?** have you ever been up to the top of the Eiffel Tower?; **le soir, le brouillard monte** the mist rises in the evening; **m. en pente douce** to climb gently (upwards); **m. en pente raide** to climb steeply *or* sharply; **ça monte trop, passe en première** it's too steep, change down into first; *Naut* **faire m. tous les hommes** to order all hands on deck; **m. de** *(sujet: odeur, bruit)* to rise (up) from, to come from; **une odeur de moisi/brûlé monte de la cave** there's a musty smell/a smell of burning coming (up) from the cellar; **des clameurs montèrent de la place** a clamour rose up from the square

2 *(dans un moyen de transport)* **m. dans** *(avion, train)* to get on *or* onto, to board; *(bus)* to get on, to board; *(voiture)* to get into; **tous les jours quand je monte dans le train** every day as I get on *or* as I board the train; **où êtes-vous monté?** where did you get on?; **elle monte à Versailles** *(dans le train)* she gets on at Versailles (station); **m. en voiture** to get into a car; **faire m. qn (en voiture) avec soi** to give sb a lift; **tu montes (avec moi)?** *(dans ma voiture)* are you coming with me (in my car)?; **m. sur un** *ou* **à bord d'un bateau** to board a ship; **est-ce que tout le monde est monté à bord?** is everybody aboard *or* on board?; **m. sur un cheval** to get on *or* to mount a horse; **m. sur une bicyclette** to get on a bicycle; **ça fait longtemps que je ne suis pas monté sur une bicyclette** it's a long time since I've been on a bicycle; **m. à cheval** to ride, to go riding; **elle monte régulièrement à Vincennes** she rides regularly in Vincennes; **m. à bicyclette** to ride a bicycle

3 *(apparaître après une émotion)* **les larmes lui sont montées aux yeux** tears welled up in his/her eyes, his/her eyes filled with tears; **ça m'a fait m. les larmes aux yeux** it brought tears to my eyes; **le rouge lui est monté aux joues** the colour rose to his/her cheeks; **le sang lui monta au visage** the blood rushed to his/her face

4 *(s'élever → température)* to rise, to go up; *(→ soleil, ballon, fièvre)* to rise; *(→ prix, taux)* to rise, to go up, to increase; *(→ action, rivière)* to rise; *(→ mer, marée)* to come in; *(→ anxiété, mécontentement)* to grow, to increase; **dès dix heures du matin, la chaleur commence à m.** it starts getting hot around ten in the morning; **faire m.** *(tension, peur)* to increase; **faire m. les prix** *(surenchère)* to send *or* to put prices up; *(marchand)* to put up *or* to increase prices; **empêcher les prix de m.** to keep prices down; **les loyers ont monté de 25 pour cent** rents have gone up *or* increased by 25 percent; *Fam* **les travaux de plomberie, ça monte vite** a plumber's bill soon mounts up▪; **le mercure monte dans le thermomètre** the mercury is rising in the thermometer; *Fam* **le thermomètre monte** it's *or* the weather's getting warmer▪; **le lait monte** *(il bout)* the milk is boiling; *(chez une femme qui allaite)* lactation has started; **attendez que l'écume monte à la surface de la confiture** wait for the scum to come *or* to rise (up) to the top of the jam; **prends de grosses aiguilles, ton pull montera plus vite** your sweater will knit up more quickly if you use big needles; *Culin* **faire m. des blancs en neige** to whisk up egg whites; **le soufflé a bien monté/n'a pas monté** the soufflé rose beautifully/didn't rise; **le ton montait** *(de colère)* voices were being raised, the discussion was becoming heated; *(d'animation)* the noise level was rising

5 *(atteindre un certain niveau)* **la cloison ne monte pas assez haut** the partition isn't high enough; **m. à** *ou* **jusqu'à** *(sujet: eau, vêtement, chaussures)* to come up to; **son plâtre monte jusqu'au genou** his leg is in a plaster cast up to the knee; **les pistes de ski montent jusqu'à 3000 m** the ski runs go up to *or* as high as 3,000 m; **la rue va en montant** the street climbs; **la fièvre est montée à 40°C** his/her temperature has gone up to *or* reached 40°C; *Fam* **je peux m. jusqu'à 200 km/h** I can do up to 200 km/h; **le pain est monté à trois euros** bread has gone up to three euros; **l'hectare de vigne peut m. jusqu'à 5000 euros** one hectare of vineyard can cost up to *or* fetch as much as 5,000 euros

6 *Mus (voix)* to go up, to rise; **il peut m. jusqu'au si** he can go *or* sing up to B

7 *(pour attaquer) Naut* **m. à l'abordage** to board; *Mil* **m. à l'attaque** *ou* **à l'assaut** to go into the attack; **m. à l'assaut de** to launch an attack on; **m. au front** *ou* **en ligne** to go into action, to go up to the front (line); **m. au filet** *(au tennis, au volley-ball)* to go up to the net

8 *(dans une hiérarchie)* to rise; **m. en grade** to be promoted; **un chanteur qui monte** an up-and-coming singer; **la génération qui monte** *(dans le temps)* the rising *or* new generation

9 *(aller vers le nord)* **je monte à Paris demain** I'm going (up) to Paris tomorrow; **quand vous monterez à Paris, venez coucher à la maison** when you come (up) to Paris, come and stay with us; **prendre le train qui monte à Bordeaux** to take the train (up) to Bordeaux; **il a dû m. à Lyon pour trouver du travail** he had to move (up) to Lyons in order to find work

10 *(pousser)* to go to seed, to bolt; **les salades sont montées** the lettuces have gone to seed *or* have bolted

11 *Cartes* **m. sur le valet de trèfle** to play a club higher than the jack

VT *(aux avoir)* **1** *(gravir)* to go up; *(colline, escalier)* to go/come up, to climb (up); **m. l'escalier** to go *or* to climb up the stairs, to go upstairs; **m. une marche** to go up a *or* one step; **m. les marches** to go up *or* to climb the steps; **m. la rue en courant** to run up the street; **la voiture a du mal à m. la côte** the car has difficulty getting up the hill; *Mus* **m. la gamme** to go up *or* to climb the scale

2 *(porter en haut → bagages, colis)* to take *or* to carry up; **m. du vin de la cave** to fetch *or* to bring wine up from the cellar; **monte-moi mes lunettes** bring my glasses up for me; **je lui ai monté son journal** I took the newspaper up to him/her; **peut-on se faire m. le repas dans les chambres?** is it possible to have meals brought up to the room?

3 *(mettre plus haut)* **monte l'étagère d'un cran** put the shelf up a notch; **monte un peu le tableau** put the picture up a bit; **monte la vitre, j'ai froid** wind up the (car) window, I'm cold

4 *(augmenter → son)* to turn up; *(→ prix)* to put up; *Fam* **monte la télé** turn the TV up; **l'hôtel a monté ses prix** the hotel has put up its prices; *Beaux-Arts* **m. une couleur** to heighten a colour

5 *(mettre en colère)* **m. (la tête à) qn contre qn** to set sb against sb; **ils ont monté les ouvriers contre la direction** they've turned the workers against the management

6 *(assembler → kit)* to assemble, to put together; *(→ tente)* to pitch, to put up; *(→ abri)* to rig up; *(→ appareil, machine)* to set up, to erect; *(→ porte)* to hang; *Élec* to connect up, to wire (up); **les voitures sont montées à l'usine de Flins** the cars are assembled at the Flins plant; **m. un métier à tisser** to set up a loom, *Spéc* to warp the yarn; *Typ* **m. une page** to make up *or* to paste up *or* to lay out a page; *Élec* **m. en parallèle/série** to connect in parallel/series

7 *(fixer → radiateur)* to fit, to mount; *(→ pneu)* to fit (on); *(→ store)* to put up, to mount; *(→ photo)* to mount; **m. une gravure** *(sur une marie-louise)* to mount an engraving; *(dans un cadre)* to frame an engraving; **il a monté un moteur plus puissant sur sa voiture** he has put a more powerful engine into his car

8 *(bijou)* to mount, to set; **rubis monté sur or** ruby set *or* mounted in gold

9 *(organiser → gén)* to organize; *(→ pièce, spectacle)* to put on, to stage, to produce; *(→ canular)* to think up; *(→ machination)* to set up; **m. une entreprise** to set up a business; **m. un magasin** to set up *or* to open a shop; **l'institut monte une expédition océanographique** the institute is organizing an ocean-survey expedition; **m. un atelier de poterie** to set up a pottery workshop; **il avait monté tout un scénario dans sa tête** he'd thought up some weird and wonderful scheme; **m. un complot** to hatch a plot; **m. un coup** to plan a job; *Fam* **m. le coup à qn** to take sb in, to take sb for a ride

10 *(pourvoir → bibliothèque, collection, cave)* to set up; **m. son ménage** *ou* **sa maison** to set up house; *Équitation* **m. un cavalier** to horse *or* to mount a rider

11 *Équitation* **m. un cheval** to ride a horse
12 *Cin (bobine)* to mount; *(film)* to edit
13 *Couture* to fit (on); **m. une manche** to sew on *or* to attach a sleeve; **le pantalon est prêt à être monté** the trousers are ready to assemble *or* to be made up; **le devant est monté n'importe comment** the front's been sewn together any old how
14 *Tricot* **m. les mailles** to cast on (the stitches)
15 *Culin* **m. des blancs en neige** to beat egg whites; **m. une mayonnaise** to make some mayonnaise
16 *Vét & Zool* to cover, to serve
17 *Naut* to crew; **m. un gréement** to rig a ship
18 *Pêche* to assemble
►**se monter** **VPR 1** *(s'assembler)* **cette bibliothèque se monte facilement** these bookshelves are easy to assemble
2 *(d'un cheval)* to be ridden; **Flicka se monte facilement** Flicka is easy to ride
3 *Fam (s'énerver)* to wind oneself up (to a pitch)
4 se m. à *(coût, dépenses)* to come *or* to amount *or* to add up to; **les frais se montent à des milliers d'euros** the expenses amount to thousands of euros; **la facture se monte à 1000 euros** the bill amounts *or* comes to 1,000 euros; **à combien se monte tout cela?** how much does all this come to *or* add up to *or* amount to?
5 se m. en to equip *or* to provide oneself with; **se m. en linge/vaisselle** to build up one's supplies of linen/crockery; **se m. en vins** to stock (up) one's cellar

monte-sac, monte-sacs [mɔ̃tsak] *(pl* **monte-sacs)** **NM** sack hoist, lift
montesquieu [mɔ̃tɛskjø] **NM** *Anciennement Fam (billet de 200 francs)* 200-franc note■
monteur, -euse [mɔ̃tœr, -øz] **NM,F 1** *Ind & Tech* fitter **2** *Cin* editor; **m. négatif** negative cutter; **m. son** sound editor **3** *(de bijoux)* setter
Montevideo [mɔ̃tevideo] **NM** Montevideo
montgolfière [mɔ̃gɔlfjɛr] **NF** hot-air balloon, montgolfier (balloon)
monticole [mɔ̃tikɔl] **ADJ** mountain *(avant n)*
monticule [mɔ̃tikyl] **NM 1** *(colline)* hillock, mound, *Sout* monticule **2** *(tas)* heap, mound; **un m. de pierres** a heap *or* pile of stones **3** *Sport (au base-ball)* pitcher's mound
montjoie [mɔ̃ʒwa] **NF** *Anciennement* = pile of stones to mark the way or to indicate the location of an important event
montmartrois, -e [mɔ̃martrwa, -az] **ADJ** of/from Montmartre
❑ **Montmartrois, -e** **NM,F** = inhabitant of or person from Montmartre
montmorency [mɔ̃mɔrɑ̃si] **NF INV** morello cherry
montmorillonite [mɔ̃mɔrijɔnit] **NF** *Minér* montmorillonite
montoir [mɔ̃twar] **NM** *Équitation (de cheval)* mounting block; **(côté du) m.** near side *(of a horse)*; **côté hors (du) m.** off side
montois, -e [mɔ̃twa, -az] **ADJ** of/from Mont-de-Marsan
❑ **Montois, -e** **NM,F** = inhabitant of or person from Mont-de-Marsan
Montparnasse [mɔ̃parnas] **NM** Montparnasse

Culture

MONTPARNASSE

This area of Paris was famous between the wars for its bohemian society, which included the "lost generation" of American writers. It is now well known for its lively nightlife and the commercial centre surrounding the 200m high Tour Montparnasse.

montpelliérain, -e [mɔ̃pɛljerɛ̃, -ɛn] **ADJ** of/from Montpellier
❑ **Montpelliérain, -e** **NM,F** = inhabitant of or person from Montpellier
montrable [mɔ̃trabl] **ADJ** *(objet)* exhibitable; *(spectacle)* fit to be seen; **est-ce m. à des enfants?** is it suitable for viewing by children?
montrachet [mɔ̃raʃɛ] **NM** *(vin)* Montrachet
montre [mɔ̃tr] **NF 1** *(instrument)* watch; **il est onze heures à ma m.** it's eleven o'clock by my watch; **il a mis une heure m. en main** it took him *or* he took exactly one hour (by the clock); **jouer la m.** to play for time; **m. antichoc** shockproof watch; **m. digitale** digital watch; **m. étanche** waterproof watch; **m. de gousset** fob *or* pocket watch; **m. de plongée** diver's watch; **m. de précision** precision watch; **m. à quartz** quartz watch
2 *(preuve)* **faire m. de prudence** to show caution, to behave cautiously; **faire m. d'audace** to show *or* to display one's boldness; **je fis m. d'audace et la pris dans mes bras** I made so bold as to take her in my arms; *Littéraire* **faire qch pour la m.** to do sth merely for show
3 *(vitrine)* shop window, display window; *(dans un meuble)* showcase; **mettre qch en m.** to put sth in the window *or* on show *or* on display
Montréal [mɔ̃real] **NM** Montreal, Montréal
montréalais, -e [mɔ̃realɛ, -ɛz] **ADJ** of/from Montreal
❑ **Montréalais, -e** **NM,F** Montrealer
montre-bracelet [mɔ̃trəbraslɛ] *(pl* **montres-bracelets)** **NF** wristwatch
montrer [3] [mɔ̃tre] **VT 1** *(gén)* to show; *(passeport, ticket)* to show, to produce; *(document secret)* to show, to disclose; *(spectacle, œuvre)* to show, to exhibit; **m. qch à qn** to show sth to sb, to show sb sth; **m. la ville à qn** to show sb round the town; **il m'a montré son usine** he showed me (round) his factory; **montrez-moi votre bras** let me see *or* show me your arm; **il faudrait que tu montres ta fille/cette vilaine blessure à un médecin** you should let a doctor have a look at *or* see your daughter/that nasty wound; **peux-tu me m. comment ça marche?** can you show me how it works?; **les toiles ne sont pas encore prêtes à être montrées** the paintings aren't ready to go on show yet; **il a réussi à ne pas m. qu'il était au courant** he managed not to show that he knew about it; **m. le poing à qn** to shake one's fist at sb; *Fig* **m. patte blanche** to produce one's credentials; *aussi Fig* **m. ses cartes** to show one's hand
2 *(exhiber → partie du corps)* to show; *(→ bijou, richesse, talent)* to show off, to parade, to flaunt; **une robe décolletée qui montre les épaules** a low-cut dress which leaves the shoulders bare *or* which exposes the shoulders; **elle montrait ses charmes** she was displaying her charms *or* leaving nothing to the imagination; **tu n'as pas besoin de m. ta science!** no need to show off your knowledge!; **elle a montré ce qu'elle savait faire** she showed what she was capable of
3 *(faire preuve de → courage, impatience, détermination)* to show, to display; *(laisser apparaître → émotion)* to show; **pour m. sa bonne volonté** to show one's goodwill; **j'essayais de ne pas trop m. ma déception/surprise** I tried not to show my disappointment/surprise too much; **il a montré un grand courage** he showed *or* displayed great courage
4 *(signaler)* to point out, to show; **m. la sortie** *(de la tête)* to nod towards the exit; *(du doigt)* to point to the exit; *(de la main)* to gesture towards the exit; **montre-moi de qui tu parles** show me who you mean; **m. la porte à qn** to show sb the door; *aussi Fig* **m. le chemin à qn** to show sb the way; **m. la voie** *ou* **le chemin** to lead *or* to show the way; **m. l'exemple** to set an example, to give the lead; **m. qn du doigt** to point at sb; *Fig* to point the finger of shame at sb; **m. qch du doigt** to point sth out, to point to *or* at sth; *Fig* to point the finger at sth; **il s'est fait m. du doigt dans le village** everyone in the village is pointing at him
5 *(marquer → sujet: aiguille, curseur, cadran)* to show, to point to; *(→ sujet: écran)* to show, to display; **l'astérisque montre la somme restant à payer** the asterisk shows *or* indicates the sum outstanding
6 *(prouver)* to show, to prove; **comme le montrent ces statistiques** as these statistics show; **ce qui montre bien qu'il était coupable** which goes to show *or* which shows *or* which proves that he was guilty; *Fam* **ça montre bien que...** it (just) goes to show that...; **cela te montre qu'il faut être prudent** that (just) shows that you have to be careful
7 *(évoquer)* to show, to depict; **la vie des galériens, si bien montrée dans son roman** the lives of the galley slaves, so clearly depicted in his/her novel
8 *(enseigner → technique, procédé)* to show, to demonstrate; *(→ recette, jeu)* to demonstrate; **m. comment faire qch** to show how to do sth; **la brochure montre comment s'en servir** the booklet explains *or* shows how to use it; **il m'a montré une nouvelle danse** he showed me a new dance, he demonstrated a new dance step for me
►**se montrer** **VPR 1** *(se présenter)* to show oneself, to appear (in public); **je ne peux pas me m. dans cet état!** I can't let people see me like this!; **il n'ose plus se m.** he doesn't dare show himself *or* his face; **montrez-vous!** (come out and) show yourself!; **le voilà, ne te montre pas!** here he is, stay out of sight!; **elle ne s'est même pas montrée au mariage de sa fille** she never even showed up *or* showed her face *or* turned up at her daughter's wedding; **se m. à son avantage** to show oneself in a good light *or* to advantage
2 *(s'afficher)* to appear *or* to be seen (in public); **elle se montrait beaucoup dans les milieux politiques** she was often seen in political circles; **il adore se m.** he loves to be seen (in public); **il se montre partout à son bras** he parades everywhere with him/her on his arm
3 *(se révéler)* **se m. d'un grand égoïsme** to display great selfishness; **ce soir-là, il s'est montré odieux/charmant** he was obnoxious/charming that evening; **elle s'est montrée très gentille/courageuse** she was very kind/courageous, she showed great kindness/courage; **montre-toi un homme, mon fils!** show them you're a man, my son!; **finalement, elle s'est montrée digne/indigne de ma confiance** she eventually proved (to be) worthy/unworthy of my trust; **il s'est montré incapable de faire face à la situation** he proved (to be) *or* he was incapable of facing up to the situation; **la réconciliation s'est montrée impossible/inutile** reconciliation proved (to be) impossible/futile
montreur, -euse [mɔ̃trœr, -øz] **NM,F** **m. de marionnettes** puppeteer; **m. d'ours** bearkeeper
Mont-Saint-Michel [mɔ̃sɛ̃miʃɛl] **NM** **le M.** Mont-Saint-Michel; **au M.** at Mont-Saint-Michel
Montserrat [mɔ̃sera] **NM** Montserrat
montueux, -euse [mɔ̃tɥø, -øz] **ADJ** *Littéraire* hilly; **des paysages m.** hilly *or* rolling countryside
monture [mɔ̃tyr] **NF 1** *(d'une pierre précieuse)* setting; *(de lunettes)* frame; **des lunettes à m. d'écaille/de plastique** horn-/plastic-rimmed glasses; **des lunettes sans m.** rimless glasses **2** *(d'un vase, d'un miroir)* mounting **3** *Équitation* mount; *Prov* **qui veut voyager loin ménage sa m.** slow and steady wins the race **4** *Mil (d'un fusil)* stock; *(d'une épée)* guard **5** *Pêche* tackle
monument [mɔnymɑ̃] **NM 1** *(stèle, statue)* monument; **élever un m. à la mémoire de qn** to erect a monument in memory of *or* to the memory of sb; **m. funéraire** (funerary) monument; **m. aux morts** war memorial
2 *(édifice)* monument, building; **m. historique** historic monument *or* building; **être classé m. historique** to be a listed building; **m. public** civic building; **le musée des Monuments français** = museum of French monuments in the Palais de Chaillot in Paris
3 *Littéraire (travail admirable)* monument, masterpiece; **elle a écrit un m.** she's written a monumental work
4 *Fam Fig* **cette armoire est un m.** this cupboard's enormous; **ce type est un m. de naïveté/lâcheté** that guy is the ultimate dupe/coward
monumental, -e, -aux, -ales [mɔnymɑ̃tal, -o] **ADJ 1** **plan m. de la ville** *(plan touristique)* city map showing buildings of interest **2** *(grandiose)* monumental, incredible; **une œuvre monumentale** a monumental piece of work **3** *Fam (canular, erreur)* monumental, phenomenal, mammoth *(avant n)*; **d'une stupidité monumentale** monumentally *or* astoundingly stupid **4** *Archit* monumental
monumentalité [mɔnymɑ̃talite] **NF** monumental character, monumentality
mooniste [munist] **NMF** *(membre de la secte Moon)* Moonie
mop [mɔp] **NF** *Belg & Can Joual* mop; *Fig (personne molle)* wimp, pushover
moppe [mɔp] *Can Joual* = **mop**

mopper [3] [mɔpe] VT *Belg & Can Joual* to mop
mops *Ordinat (abrév écrite* **mégaoctets par seconde***)* MBps, Mbps
moque [mɔk] NF **1** *Naut* cringle **2** *Suisse Fam (morve)* snot
moquer [3] [mɔke] VT *Littéraire* to mock (at)
►**se moquer** VPR **1** *Littéraire* to jest; **vous vous moquez!** you jest!
2 se m. de *(railler)* to laugh at, to mock (at), to make fun of; **les gens vont se m. d'elle** people will laugh (at her)
3 se m. de *(ignorer → danger, conseil)* to disregard, to ignore
4 se m. de *(être indifférent à)* not to care about; **je me/il se moque de tout ça** I/he couldn't care less about all that; **je me moque de ce que les gens pensent** I couldn't care less what people think; **je me moque de travailler le dimanche** I don't mind having to work on Sundays; **je me moque que tu sois mécontent** I don't care if you're not pleased; **elle s'en moque pas mal** she couldn't care less; *Fam* **il se moque du tiers comme du quart** he doesn't care *or* give a damn about anybody or anything; *Fam* **je m'en moque comme de l'an quarante** *ou* **comme de ma première chemise** I don't give a damn, I don't care two hoots *or* a tinker's cuss
5 se m. de *(duper)* to dupe, to deceive, to trick; **il s'est moqué de toi** he's pulled a fast one on you; **on s'est moqué de toi** you've been taken for a ride; *Fam* **elle ne s'est pas moquée de toi!** *(repas, réception)* she did you proud (there)!; *(cadeau)* she didn't skimp on your present!; *Fam* **ce type se moque du monde!** that guy's got a real nerve!; **vous vous moquez** *ou* **c'est se m. du monde!** you've got a nerve!
moquerie [mɔkri] NF mockery *(UNCOUNT)*, jeering *(UNCOUNT)*; **leurs moqueries continuelles** their constant mockery *or* jeering *or* ridicule; **il était en butte à des moqueries continuelles** he was always being mocked *or* made fun of
moquette [mɔkɛt] NF (wall-to-wall) carpet, *Br* (fitted) carpet; *Tex* moquette; **faire poser de la** *ou* **une m.** to have a (wall-to-wall) carpet laid
moquetter [4] [mɔkete] VT to carpet, *Br* to lay a (fitted) carpet in; **l'entrée est moquettée** the hall is carpeted *or Br* has a (fitted) carpet
moqueur, -euse [mɔkœr, -øz] ADJ **1** *(remarque, rires)* mocking; **d'un ton m.** mockingly, derisively; **d'un air m.** mockingly **2** *(personne)* given to mockery; **elle est très moqueuse** she likes to make fun of people
NM,F mocker; **les moqueurs** mocking *or* jeering people
NM *Orn* mockingbird
moracée [mɔrase] *Bot* NF member of the Moraceae family
❑ **moracées** NFPL Moraceae
moraille [mɔrɑj] NF *(de vétérinaire)* barnacles
❑ **morailles** NFPL *(de verrier)* tongs
moraillon [mɔrɑjɔ̃] NM hasp
moraine [mɔrɛn] NF *Géog* moraine; **m. frontale/latérale/médiane** terminal/lateral/medial moraine; **m. de fond** ground moraine
morainique [mɔrɛnik] ADJ *Géog* morainal, morainic
moral, -e, -aux, -ales [mɔral, -o] ADJ **1** *(éthique → conscience, jugement)* moral; **il n'a aucun sens m.** he has no moral sense *or* no sense of morality; **je me sens dans l'obligation morale de l'aider** I feel morally obliged to *or* I feel I have a moral obligation to help him/her; **prendre l'engagement m. de faire qch** to be morally committed to do sth
2 *(édifiant → auteur, conte, réflexion)* moral; **la fin de la pièce n'est pas très morale!** the end of the play is rather immoral!
3 *(spirituel → douleur)* mental; *(→ soutien, victoire, résistance)* moral; **elle a une grande force morale** she has great moral strength *or* fibre; **avoir la certitude morale que...** to have the moral certainty that...
NM morale, spirits; **toutes ces épreuves n'ont pas affecté son m.** all these ordeals failed to shake her morale; **comment va le m.?** are you in good spirits?; **son m. est bas** his/her spirits are low, he's/she's in low spirits; **avoir le m., avoir bon m.** to be in good *or* high spirits; *Fam* **tu vas t'occuper de ses cinq enfants? dis-donc, tu as le m.!** so you're going to look after his/her five children? well, (I'd) rather you than me!; **il n'a pas le m. en ce moment** he's a bit depressed *or* he's in the doldrums at the moment; **allez, il faut garder le m.!** come on, keep your chin *or* spirits up!; **remonter le m. à qn** *(consoler)* to raise sb's spirits, to give sb's morale a boost; *(égayer)* to cheer sb up; **retrouver le m.** to perk up; **avoir un m. d'acier** to be a tower of strength; **avoir le m. au beau fixe** to be in fine spirits; *Fam* **avoir le m. à zéro** to feel down in the dumps; **au physique comme au m., elle nous bat tous!** physically as well as mentally, she's in better shape than all of us!; **c'est bon pour le m.** it's good for morale; *Écon* **m. des ménages** consumer morale
❑ **morale** NF **1** *(règles → de la société)* moral code *or* standards, morality; *(→ d'une religion)* moral code, ethic; *(→ personnelles)* morals, ethics; **contraire/conforme à la morale** immoral/moral; **ce n'est pas conforme à la morale** it's immoral; **la morale veut qu'on le fasse** morality dictates that we should do it; *Fam* **il a une morale plutôt élastique** his morality is rather flexible; **faire la morale à qn, faire une leçon de morale à qn** to lecture sb, to preach at sb
2 *Phil* moral philosophy, ethics *(singulier)*
3 *(d'une fable, d'une histoire)* moral
moralement [mɔralmɑ̃] ADV **1** *(du point de vue de la morale)* morally; **je me sens m. obligé de...** I feel duty-bound *or* morally bound to...; **être m. responsable de...** to be morally responsible for...; **m., tu ne peux pas lui faire ça** morally speaking *or* morally, you can't do that to him/her; **m., il est peu recommandable** his morals are questionable
2 *(sur le plan psychique)* **m., elle va mieux** she's in better spirits
moralisant, -e [mɔralizɑ̃, -ɑ̃t] ADJ moralizing, moralistic
moralisateur, -trice [mɔralizatœr, -tris] ADJ **1** *(personne, propos)* moralizing, moralistic; **parler à qn sur un ton m.** to speak to sb sanctimoniously **2** *(histoire, principes)* edifying
NM,F moralizer
moralisation [mɔralizasjɔ̃] NF moralization
moralisatrice [mɔralizatris] *voir* **moralisateur**
moraliser [3] [mɔralize] VT **1** *(rendre conforme à la morale)* to moralize **2** *(réprimander)* to lecture
VI *(prêcher)* to moralize, to preach
moralisme [mɔralism] NM moralism
moraliste [mɔralist] ADJ moralistic
NMF moralist
moralité [mɔralite] NF **1** *(éthique)* morality, ethics *(singulier)*; **d'une haute m.** highly moral *or* ethical; **d'une m. douteuse** of questionable morals; **être d'une m. irréprochable** to have impeccable moral standards; **quelqu'un d'une m. au-dessus de tout soupçon** someone with high/impeccable moral standards
2 *(comportement)* morals, moral standing *or* standards; **certificat de m.** character reference
3 *(conclusion)* **m., il faut toujours...** and the moral (of the story) is, you must always...; *Fam* **m., on ne l'a plus revu** and the result was, we never saw him again
4 *Hist & Théât* morality play
morasse [mɔras] NF *Presse* final proof
moratoire [mɔratwar] ADJ moratory; *(paiement)* delayed by agreement; **intérêts moratoires** interest on overdue payments, moratorial interest
NM moratorium
moratorium [mɔratɔrjɔm] NM *Jur* moratorium
morave [mɔrav] ADJ Moravian
❑ **Morave** NMF Moravian
Moravie [mɔravi] NF **la M.** Moravia
morbac, morbaque [mɔrbak] NM **1** *très Fam (pou du pubis)* crab **2** *Fam (enfant)* kid
morbide [mɔrbid] ADJ **1** *(malsain)* morbid, unhealthy **2** *Méd* morbid
morbidesse [mɔrbidɛs] NF **1** *Littéraire (langueur)* languor, languidness **2** *Beaux-Arts* morbidezza
morbidité [mɔrbidite] NF **1** *Littéraire (d'une obsession)* morbidity, morbidness, unhealthiness **2** *Méd & (en sociologie)* morbidity rate
morbier [mɔrbje] NM **1** *(fromage)* Morbier (cheese) **2** *Suisse (horloge)* grandfather clock
Morbihan [mɔrbiɑ̃] NM **le M.** Morbihan
morbilleux, -euse [mɔrbijø, -øz] ADJ *Méd* pertaining to measles, *Spéc* morbillous
morbleu [mɔrblø] EXCLAM *Arch* zounds!, ye gods!
morce [mɔrs] NF *Suisse* mouthful; **manger une m.** to have a bite to eat
morceau, -x [mɔrso] NM **1** *(de nourriture)* piece, bit; *(de viande)* cut, piece; **m. de sucre** lump of sugar, sugar lump; **sucre en morceaux** lump sugar; **m. de choix** choice morsel, *Br* titbit, *Am* tidbit; **bas morceaux** *(de viande)* cheap(er) cuts; **aimer les bons morceaux** to like good things (to eat); **je vous le donne dans quel m.?** which cut would you like?; *Can* **m. des dames** *Br* parson's nose, *Am* pope's nose; **c'est un m. de roi** *ou* **digne d'un roi** it's fit for a king; *Fam Fig* **c'est le gros m.** *(examen, matière)* this is the big one; **tu reprendras bien un petit m.!** come on, have another bit *or* piece!; *Fam* **si on allait manger un m.?** how about going for a bite to eat?; *Fam Fig* **cracher** *ou* **lâcher** *ou* **casser** *ou* **manger le m.** to spill the beans; *Fam Fig* **casser le m. à qn** to give sb a piece of one's mind; *Fam Fig* **emporter** *ou* **enlever le m.** to get one's own way■
2 *(de bois, de métal → petit)* piece, bit; *(→ gros)* lump, chunk; *(de papier, de verre)* piece; *(d'étoffe, de câble → gén)* piece; *(→ mesuré)* length; **il y a des petits morceaux de bouchon dans mon verre** I've got little bits *or* pieces of cork in my glass; **assembler les morceaux de qch** to piece sth together; **en morceaux** in bits *or* pieces; **mettre en morceaux** *(papier, étoffe)* to tear up; *(jouet)* to pull to pieces *or* bits; **tomber en morceaux** to fall apart, to fall to pieces
3 *(extrait)* passage, extract, excerpt; **m. d'anthologie** anthology piece; **cette scène est un véritable m. d'anthologie** it's a truly memorable scene; **m. de bravoure** purple passage; **(recueil de) morceaux choisis** (collection of) selected passages *or* extracts
4 *Mus (fragment)* passage; *(œuvre)* piece; **joue-moi un m. de piano** play something on the piano for me; **m. pour trombone** piece for trombone; **m. de concours** competition piece
5 *Fam (personne)* **un beau m.** a babe, a knockout; **c'est un sacré m., leur fils!** *(il est gros)* their son is a big bruiser!; *(il est musclé)* their son is a real hunk!; *(il est insupportable)* their son is a real pain!
morcelable [mɔrsəlabl] ADJ divisible, dividable; **non m.** indivisible, not to be divided (up)
morceler [24] [mɔrsəle] VT **1** *(partager)* to parcel out; *(démembrer)* to divide (up), to break up **2** *Mil* to split up
morcellement [mɔrsɛlmɑ̃] NM **1** *(d'un terrain)* dividing (up); *(d'un héritage)* parcelling (out) **2** *Mil* splitting (up)
morcellera *etc voir* **morceler**
mordache [mɔrdaʃ] NF *Suisse Fam* **avoir la m.** to have the gift of the gab
mordacité [mɔrdasite] NF *Littéraire* mordancy; **elle est réputée pour la m. de son ironie** she's renowned for her biting irony *or* caustic wit
mordançage [mɔrdɑ̃saʒ] NM *Tech & Tex* mordanting
mordancer [16] [mɔrdɑ̃se] VT *Tech & Tex* to mordant
mordant, -e [mɔrdɑ̃, -ɑ̃t] ADJ **1** *(caustique)* biting, caustic, scathing
2 *(froid)* biting, bitter
NM **1** *(dynamisme → d'une personne)* drive, spirit, punch; *(→ d'un style, d'une publicité)* punch, bite; *(→ de troupes, d'équipe)* keenness; **une campagne qui a du m.** a campaign which really packs a punch; **l'équipe a perdu de son m.** the team has lost its punch
2 *(d'une lame, d'une lime)* bite
3 *(en gravure, teinture, dorure)* mordant
4 *Mus* mordent
mordée [mɔrde] NF *Can* bite; **prendre une m. dans qch** to take a bite out of sth, to bite sth
mordicant, -e [mɔrdikɑ̃, -ɑ̃t] ADJ *Vieilli* stinging
mordicus [mɔrdikys] ADV *Fam* stubbornly, doggedly; **il soutient m. que c'est vrai** he absolutely insists that it's true
mordieu [mɔrdjø] EXCLAM *Arch* death!, zounds!
mordillage [mɔrdijaʒ], **mordillement** [mɔrdijmɑ̃] NM nibbling
mordiller [3] [mɔrdije] VT to nibble *or* to chew (at)

mordoré, -e [mɔrdɔre] ADJ golden brown, bronze
mordorer [3] [mɔrdɔre] VT *Littéraire* to bronze
mordorure [mɔrdɔryr] NF *Littéraire* golden brown, bronze
mordre [76] [mɔrdr] VT **1** *(sujet: animal, personne)* to bite; **m. un fruit** to bite into a piece of fruit; **m. qn au bras** to bite sb's arm, to bite sb on the arm; **m. qn jusqu'au sang** to bite sb and draw blood; **se faire m.** to get bitten; **elle s'est fait m. par un rat** she was bitten by a rat; **il s'est fait m. à la main** he was bitten on the hand; *Hum* **prends la serpillière, elle ne mord pas** *ou* **elle ne te mordra pas!** take the mop, it won't bite (you)!; *Fig* **m. la poussière** to bite the dust; *Fig* **faire m. la poussière à qn** to make sb bite the dust
2 *(sujet: scie, vis)* to bite into; *(sujet: acide)* to eat into; *(sujet: pneus cloutés)* to grip; *(sujet: ancre)* to grip, to bite; *(sujet: froid)* to bite; **le froid lui mordait les doigts** the cold was nipping *or* biting his/her fingers; **l'angoisse me mord le cœur** I'm gnawed by anxiety
3 *(empiéter sur)* **m. la ligne** *(au saut en longueur)* to cross the (take-off) board; *(sur la route)* to cross the white line
4 *Beaux-Arts* **m. une planche** to etch a plate
USAGE ABSOLU **il ne va pas m., ton chien?** your dog won't bite, will he?
VI **1** *Pêche* to bite; **ça mord?** are the fish biting?; **ça ne mord pas beaucoup par ici** the fish aren't biting *or* rising much around here; *aussi Fig* **m. (à l'appât** *ou* **à l'hameçon)** to rise (to the bait), to bite; *Fam Fig* **il** *ou* **ça n'a pas mordu** he wasn't taken in, he didn't fall for it
2 *Tech* to mesh
3 *(gravure)* to bite; *(teinture)* to take
4 *(accrocher)* to bite; **lime/vis qui mord** file/screw that bites *or* has a good bite; **l'ancre ne mord pas** the anchor won't hold *or* grip
❑ **mordre à** VT IND *Fam* **1** *(prendre goût à)* to take to, to fall for, to be hooked by
2 *(être trompé par)* to be taken in by, to fall for
❑ **mordre dans** VT IND to bite into
❑ **mordre sur** VT IND *(ligne, marge)* to go *or* to cross over; *(économies)* to make a dent in, to eat into; *(période)* to overlap; **le stage mordra sur la deuxième semaine de mars** the course will go over into the second week in March; **la route mord sur mon terrain** the road encroaches on my land; *Sport* **m. sur la ligne** *(au tennis)* to have one's foot (just) over the line
▶**se mordre** VPR to bite oneself; *aussi Fig* **se m. la langue** to bite one's tongue; **se m. les lèvres pour ne pas rire/pour ne pas hurler** to bite one's lip so as not to laugh/scream; *Fig* **je m'en suis mordu les doigts** I could have kicked myself; *Fig* **il va s'en m. les doigts** he'll be sorry he did it, he'll live to regret it; **se m. la queue** to chase one's tail; *Fig* to go round in circles
mordu, -e [mɔrdy] ADJ **1** *Fam (passionné)* **il est m. de jazz** he's mad *or* crazy about jazz **2** *Fam (amoureux)* madly in love, completely smitten **3** *Sport* **saut m.** no jump
NM,F *Fam (passionné)* fan, addict; **un m. de cinéma/d'opéra** a film/an opera buff; **un m. de football** a football fan; **les mordus du tennis/de Chaplin** tennis/Chaplin fans; **les mordus de la télé** TV addicts
more [mɔr] = **maure**
moreau, -elle[1], **-aux, -elles,** [mɔro, -ɛl] ADJ black
NM black horse
morelle[2] [mɔrɛl] NF *Bot* nightshade
morène [mɔrɛn] NF *Bot* hydrocharis, frogbit
moresque [mɔrɛsk] = **mauresque** ADJ
morfal, -e, -als, -ales [mɔrfal] NM,F *Fam Br* pig, gannet, *Am* hog
morfil [mɔrfil] NM = excess metal left on the tool after sharpening
morfler [3] [mɔrfle] *Fam* VT **1** *(recevoir)* to get■; **il a morflé une claque dans la tronche** he got a slap in the face **2** *(se voir infliger une peine de)* to get■, to cop
VI **1** *(être abîmé)* to get smashed up; *(être blessé)* to get injured■ **2** *(être puni, pâtir)* to catch it, *Br* to cop it
morfondre [75] [mɔrfɔ̃dr] **se morfondre** VPR **1** *(languir)* to mope; **il se morfondait en attendant les résultats du test** he waited anxiously *or* fretfully for the results of the test **2** *Can (s'épuiser)* to wear oneself out
morfondu, -e [mɔrfɔ̃dy] ADJ *Littéraire* gloomy, dejected
morganatique [mɔrganatik] ADJ morganatic
morganatiquement [mɔrganatikmɑ̃] ADV morganatically
morganite [mɔrganit] NF *Minér* morganite
morgeline [mɔrʒəlin] NF *Bot* common chickweed
morgon [mɔrgɔ̃] NM Morgon (wine)
morgue[1] [mɔrg] NF *(établissement)* morgue; *(dans un hôpital) Br* mortuary, *Am* morgue
morgue[2] [mɔrg] NF *(arrogance)* arrogance, haughtiness, disdainfulness
morguer [3] [mɔrge] VT *Arch* to disdain; **m. le destin** to snap one's fingers at fate
moribond, -e [mɔribɔ̃, -ɔ̃d] ADJ dying, *Sout* moribund
NM,F dying person; **les moribonds** the dying
moricaud, -e [mɔriko, -od] *Fam Péj* ADJ dark-skinned■, swarthy■
NM,F **1** *(personne de race noire)* darkie, nigger, *Br* wog, = racist term used to refer to a black person **2** *(personne à la peau foncée)* dark-skinned *or* swarthy person■
morigéner [18] [mɔriʒene] VT to chide, to rebuke, to upbraid
morille [mɔrij] NF morel
morillon [mɔrijɔ̃] NM **1** *(raisin)* small black grape **2** *Orn* tufted duck **3** *(émeraude)* small rough emerald
moringa [mɔrɛ̃ga] NM *Bot* Moringa
morio [mɔrjo] NM *Entom* Camberwell beauty
morion [mɔrjɔ̃] NM *Hist* morion
morisque [mɔrisk] *Hist* ADJ Mudejar
NMF Mudejar
morlingue [mɔrlɛ̃g] NM *Fam* **1** *(porte-monnaie) Br* purse■, *Am* change purse■ **2** *(portefeuille) Br* wallet■, *Am* billfold■
mormon, -e [mɔrmɔ̃, -ɔn] ADJ Mormon
❑ **Mormon, -e** NM,F Mormon
mormonisme [mɔrmɔnism] NM Mormonism
morna [mɔrna] NF *Mus* morna
morne [mɔrn] ADJ **1** *(triste → personne, regard)* glum, gloomy; *(→ silence)* gloomy; **elle restait m. et silencieuse** she remained glumly silent **2** *(monotone → discussion)* dull; *(→ paysage)* bleak, drab, dreary; **d'un ton m.** in a dreary voice **3** *(maussade → climat)* dull, dreary, dismal; **une journée m.** a dreary day **4** *(terne → couleur, style)* dull
NM *(aux Antilles)* mound, hill
morné, -e [mɔrne] ADJ **1** *(lance)* blunted, harmless **2** *Hér* disarmed, morné
mornifle [mɔrnifl] NF *Fam Vieilli* **1** *(argent)* bread, *Br* dosh, *Am* bucks **2** *(gifle)* slap■, cuff
Moroni [mɔrɔni] NM Moroni
morose [mɔroz] ADJ **1** *(individu, air, humeur, vie)* glum, morose; *(temps, année)* miserable **2** *(économie)* sluggish, slack; **la Bourse était m. ce matin** trading on the Stock Exchange was sluggish this morning
morosité [mɔrozite] NF **1** *(d'une personne)* glumness, sullenness, moroseness; *(d'un climat)* miserableness; *(d'un paysage)* gloominess; **la m. de son humeur** his/her glumness *or* sullenness *or* moroseness **2** *(d'un marché)* slackness, sluggishness
Morphée [mɔrfe] NPR *Myth* Morpheus; *Fig* **dans les bras de M.** in the arms of Morpheus
morphème [mɔrfɛm] NM *Ling* morpheme
morphine [mɔrfin] NF *Pharm* morphine, morphia
morphing [mɔrfiŋ] NM *Cin* morphing
morphinique [mɔrfinik] ADJ *Pharm* morphinic
morphinisme [mɔrfinism] NM *Méd* morphinism
morphinomane [mɔrfinɔman] *Méd* ADJ addicted to morphine
NMF morphine addict, *Spéc* morphinomaniac
morphinomanie [mɔrfinɔmani] NF *Méd* morphine addiction, *Spéc* morphinism
morphisme [mɔrfism] NM *Biol* homomorphism
morphogène [mɔrfɔʒɛn] ADJ *Biol* morphogenic, morphogenetic
morphogenèse [mɔrfɔʒənɛz] NF *Biol* morphogenesis
morphogénétique [mɔrfɔʒenetik] ADJ *Biol* morphogenetic, morphogenic
morphologie [mɔrfɔlɔʒi] NF *Biol* morphology
morphologique [mɔrfɔlɔʒik] ADJ *Biol* morphological
morphologiquement [mɔrfɔlɔʒikmɑ̃] ADV *Biol* morphologically
morphologue [mɔrfɔlɔg] NMF *Biol* morphologist
morphométrie [mɔrfɔmetri] NF *Biol* morphometry
morphopsychologie [mɔrfɔpsikɔlɔʒi] NF *Psy* morphopsychology
morphose [mɔrfoz] NF *Biol* morphosis
morpion [mɔrpjɔ̃] NM **1** *Fam Péj (enfant)* brat **2** *Fam (pou du pubis)* crab **3** *(jeu) Br* ≃ noughts and crosses, *Am* ≃ tic-tac-toe
mors [mɔr] NM **1** *(d'un cheval)* bit; **m. de bride** curb bit; **m. de filet** snaffle; **prendre le m. aux dents** *(sujet: cheval)* to take the bit in its teeth; *Fig* to take the bit between one's teeth, to swing into action **2** *(d'un étau)* jaw, chop; *(d'une pince)* jaw, pincer **3** *(d'un livre)* joint, groove **4** *Bot* **m. du diable** devil's bit scabious
morse[1] [mɔrs] NM *Zool* walrus
morse[2] [mɔrs] NM *(code)* Morse (code); **en m.** in Morse (code)
morsure [mɔrsyr] NF **1** *(d'un animal)* bite; **une m. de chien** a dog bite; **une m. de serpent** a snakebite **2** *Beaux-Arts (de l'acide)* biting **3** *Fig (de la jalousie, du remords)* pang; **les morsures du froid** the biting cold
mort, -e [mɔr, mɔrt] PP *voir* **mourir**
ADJ **1** *(décédé → personne)* dead; **il est m.** he's dead; **il est m. hier** he died yesterday; **elle est morte depuis longtemps** she died a long time ago, she's been dead (for) a long time; **il est m. dans un accident de voiture** he died *or* was killed in a car crash; **elle était comme morte** she looked as if she were dead; **si tu fais un geste, tu es un homme m.** one move and you're a dead man; **laisser qn pour m.** to leave sb for dead; *aussi Fig* **m. et enterré, m. et bien m.** dead and buried, dead and gone, long dead; **m. sur le champ de bataille** *ou* **au champ d'honneur** killed in action; **m. pour la France** killed in action *(annotation on a French death certificate, giving certain entitlements to the relatives of the dead person)*; **m. ou vif** dead or alive; **être plus m. que vif** *(à demi mort)* to be more dead than alive; *(très effrayé)* to be half-dead with fright; *Prov* **morte la bête, m. le venin** = a dead enemy is no longer a threat
2 *(arbre, cellule, dent)* dead; **des branches mortes** dead branches
3 *(en intensif)* **m. de peur/d'inquiétude/de froid** frightened/worried/freezing to death; **il était m. de fatigue** he was dead tired; **être m. de rire** to be killing oneself (laughing)
4 *(passé → amour, désir)* dead; *(→ espoir)* dead, buried, long gone
5 *(inerte → regard)* lifeless, dull; *(→ quartier, bistrot)* dead; *(→ eau)* stagnant; *Fam* **c'est m. par ici le dimanche** it's dead around here on Sundays
6 *Mil* **balle morte** spent bullet
7 *Sport* **ballon m.** dead ball
8 *Fam (hors d'usage → appareil, voiture)* dead, finished; **mon sac est m.** my bag's had it
9 *Fam (épuisé)* **je suis m.!** I'm dead!; **mes jambes sont mortes!** my legs are killing me!
10 *Géog* **la mer Morte** the Dead Sea
NM,F **1** *(personne)* dead person; **les morts** the dead; **le nombre des morts sur la route** the number of deaths on the roads; **l'épidémie n'a pas fait de morts** no one died in the epidemic; **les émeutes ont fait trois cents morts** three hundred people died *or* were killed in the rioting; **l'accident a fait trois morts** the accident claimed three lives, three people died *or* were killed in the accident; **c'est une morte en sursis** she's living on borrowed time; **c'est un m. vivant** *(mourant)* he's at death's door; **les morts vivants** the living dead; **jour** *ou* **fête des morts** All Souls' Day; **messe/prière des morts** mass/prayer for the dead; **faire le m.** to pretend to be dead, to play dead; *Fam Fig* **tu as intérêt à faire le m.** you'd better lie low; *Fam Fig* **je lui ai écrit il y a trois semaines, mais depuis, il fait le m.** I wrote to him three weeks ago, but since then he's been as silent as the grave *or* I haven't heard a thing; *Presse* **principe** *ou* **règle du m. kilométrique** = rule whereby important events occurring in one's home country – particularly those involving deaths – will take journalistic precedence over events occurring elsewhere

2 *(dans un jeu)* dummy; **faire le m.** to be dummy; **je suis le m.** I'm dummy

❏ **mort** NF **1** *(décès)* death; **la m.** death; **à la m. de son père** on his/her father's death; **envoyer qn à la m.** to send sb to his/her death; **frôler la m.** to have a brush with death; **il a vu la m. de près** he saw death staring him in the face; **se donner la m.** to commit suicide, to take one's own life; **trouver la m.** to meet one's death, to die; **trouver la m. dans un accident** to die in an accident; **les émeutes ont entraîné la m. de trente personnes** the riots led to the death *or* deaths of thirty people; **il y a eu m. d'homme** *(une victime)* somebody was killed; *(plusieurs victimes)* lives were lost; **il n'y a pas eu m. d'homme** nobody was killed, there was no loss of life; *(mourir d'une)* **m. subite/lente** (to die a) sudden/slow death; **périr de m. violente** to die a violent death; **il a eu une m. douce** he died painlessly; *Littéraire* **la petite m.** (the moment of) climax; **avoir la m. dans l'âme** to have a heavy heart; **je partis la m. dans l'âme** I left with a heavy heart; **souffrir m. et passion** to suffer agonies; *Fam* **vous allez attraper la m.!** you'll catch your death (of cold)!; *Fam* **c'est pas la m. (du petit cheval)!** it's not the end of the world!; *Fam* **son cours, c'est vraiment la m.!** his/her class is deadly boring!; **la foule scandait "à m., à m.!"** the crowd was chanting "kill, kill!" *or* "kill him, kill him!"; **m. aux traîtres!, m. les traîtres!** death to the traitors!; *Fam* **m. aux vaches!** down with the cops!; **m. cérébrale** *ou* **clinique** brain death; **m. accidentelle** *(gén)* accidental death; **m. naturelle** natural death; *Jur* death from natural causes; **il est m. de m. naturelle** he died from natural causes; **m. subite du nourrisson** cot death, *Spéc* sudden infant death syndrome, SIDS; *Sport* **m. subite** *(au football)* sudden death

2 *(économique)* end, death; **c'est la m. des cinémas de quartier** it's the end of local cinemas; **le monopole est la m. de l'industrie** monopoly means the end *or* is the ruin of industry

3 *Bot* **m. aux loups** wolfsbane; **m. aux poules** henbane

❏ **à mort** ADJ *(lutte, combat)* to the death ADV **1** *Fam (en intensif)* **haïr qn à m.** to hate sb's guts, to loathe and detest sb; **en vouloir à m. à qn** to have a huge grudge against sb; **je lui en veux à m.** I hate his/her guts; **je lui en veux à m. d'avoir dit ça** I'll never forgive him/her for saying that; **j'ai freiné à m.** I braked like hell, I slammed on the brakes; **ils sont brouillés** *ou* **fâchés à m.** they're enemies for life; *très Fam* **déconner à m.** to talk complete crap *or Br* bollocks; *Vulg* **bander à m.** to have a raging hard-on **2** *(mortellement)* **blesser qn à m.** to mortally wound sb; **frapper qn à m.** to strike sb dead; **mettre qn à m.** to put sb to death; **mettre un animal à m.** to kill an animal

❏ **de mort** ADJ *(silence, pâleur)* deathly, death-like; **être en danger** *ou* **péril de m.** to be in mortal danger; **menace/pulsion de m.** death threat/wish

❏ **jusqu'à ce que mort s'ensuive** ADV *Vieilli Jur* until he/she be dead; *Hum* to the bitter end

❏ **jusqu'à la mort** ADV to the death; *Fig* to the bitter end; **je m'en souviendrai jusqu'à la m.** I'll remember it until my dying day

📽 *'La Mort aux trousses'* Hitchcock 'North by Northwest'

📖 *'La Mort dans l'âme'* Sartre 'Iron in the Soul'

📖 *'La Mort heureuse'* Camus 'A Happy Death'

📖 *'Mort à crédit'* Céline 'Death on the Instalment Plan'

📖 *'Mort à Venise'* Mann, Visconti 'Death in Venice'

📖 *'Une Mort très douce'* de Beauvoir 'A Very Easy Death'

mortadelle [mɔrtadɛl] NF mortadella

mortaisage [mɔrtɛzaʒ] NM mortising

mortaise [mɔrtɛz] NF **1** *Menuis* mortise, mortice **2** *(de clavette)* keyway; *(de serrure)* mortise **3** *Naut* sheave slot, mortise

mortaiser [4] [mɔrtɛze] VT **1** *Menuis* to mortise, to mortice **2** *Tech* to slot

mortaiseuse [mɔrtɛzøz] NF *Tech* slotting machine

mortalité [mɔrtalite] NF **1** *(gén)* mortality; *(dans des statistiques)* death rate, mortality (rate); **m. infantile** child *or* infant mortality **2** *Arch (condition mortelle)* mortal nature

mort-aux-rats [mɔrora] NF INV rat poison

mort-bois [mɔrbwa] *(pl* **morts-bois***)* NM underwood, brushwood

morte-eau [mɔrto] *(pl* **mortes-eaux** [mɔrtəzo]*)* NF neap tide, neap

mortel, -elle [mɔrtɛl] ADJ **1** *(qui tue → accident, maladie)* fatal; *(→ dose, poison)* deadly, lethal; *(→ coup, blessure)* fatal, lethal, *Sout* mortal; *(→ champignon)* poisonous, deadly; *(péché)* deadly; **il a fait une chute mortelle** he had a fatal fall; *Fig* **c'est un coup m. porté à notre petite communauté** this is a death-blow for our small community; *Fam Fig* **son revers est m.!** his/her backhand is lethal!; *Fam Fig* **tu as raté l'examen, mais ça n'est pas m.!** you've failed the exam, but it's not the end of the world!

2 *(acharné → ennemi)* mortal, deadly; *(→ haine)* deadly

3 *(qui rappelle la mort → pâleur, silence)* deathly

4 *(qui n'est pas éternel)* mortal

5 *Fam (ennuyeux)* deadly dull, deadly boring; **d'un ennui m.** deadly dull, dead boring

6 *Fam (excellent)* wicked, *Br* fab, *Am* awesome

7 *Fam (très mauvais)* hellish, *Am* gnarly

NM,F *(être humain)* mortal

ADV *Fam* **on s'est éclatés m.!** we had a blast!; *très Fam* **on s'est fait chier m.** we were bored shitless

EXCLAM wicked!, *Br* fab!, *Am* awesome!

mortellement [mɔrtɛlmã] ADV **1** *(à mort)* **m. pâle** deathly pale; **être m. blessé** to be fatally *or Sout* mortally wounded **2** *(en intensif)* **s'ennuyer m.** to be bored to death, to be bored rigid; **le film est m. ennuyeux** the film is deadly boring; **tu l'as m. offensé** you've mortally offended him

morte-saison [mɔrtsɛzõ] *(pl* **mortes-saisons***)* NF slack *or* off season; **à la m.** in the off season

mort-gage [mɔrgaʒ] *(pl* **morts-gages***)* NM *Anciennement Jur* chattel mortgage

mortibus [mɔrtibys] ADJ *Fam* dead∎

mortier [mɔrtje] NM **1** *(récipient)* mortar **2** *Mil* mortar; **tirs de m.** mortar fire; **attaque au m.** mortar attack **3** *Constr* mortar; **m. bâtard/gras/maigre** gauged/fat/lean mortar; **m. liquide** *ou* **clair** grout, grouting; **planche à m.** mortarboard **4** *(bonnet)* judge's cap *(worn by certain judges in France)*

mortifère [mɔrtifɛr] ADJ **1** *(mortel)* mortiferous, death-dealing **2** *Hum (très ennuyeux)* deadly (boring)

mortifiant, -e [mɔrtifjã, -ãt] ADJ mortifying, humiliating

mortification [mɔrtifikasjõ] NF **1** *Rel* mortification **2** *(humiliation)* mortification, humiliation **3** *Culin (faisandage)* hanging *(of game meat)* **4** *Méd* mortification

mortifié, -e [mɔrtifje] ADJ mortified

mortifier [9] [mɔrtifje] VT **1** *Rel* to mortify **2** *(humilier)* to mortify, to humiliate; **elle en a été mortifiée** she was mortified **3** *Culin (faisander)* to (leave to) hang **4** *Méd* to mortify

▶ **se mortifier** VPR to mortify oneself

mortinatalité [mɔrtinatalite] NF stillbirth rate

mort-né, -e [mɔrne] *(mpl* **mort-nés***, fpl* **mort-nées***)* ADJ *aussi Fig* stillborn

NM,F stillborn baby

mortuaire [mɔrtɥɛr] ADJ **1** *(rituel)* mortuary *(avant n)*, funeral *(avant n)*; *(cérémonie, couronne)* funeral *(avant n)*; **chambre m.** death chamber; **drap m.** pall **2** *Admin* **acte m.** death certificate; **registre m.** register of deaths

NF *Belg (maison)* house of the deceased; *(chambre mortuaire)* death chamber

mort-vivant, morte-vivante [mɔrvivã, -ãt] *(mpl* **morts-vivants***, fpl* **mortes-vivantes***)* NM,F member of the living *or* walking dead; **les morts-vivants** the living *or* walking dead

morue [mɔry] NF **1** *Culin & Ich* cod; **m. fraîche** fresh cod; **m. noire** haddock; **m. (verte)** undried salt cod **2** *très Fam (prostituée)* whore, hooker **3** *très Fam (femme)* tart, *Br* slapper

morula [mɔryla] NF *Biol* morula

morutier, -ère [mɔrytje, -ɛr] ADJ cod-fishing *(avant n)*

NM **1** *(navire)* cod-fishing boat **2** *(marin)* cod-fisherman

morvandeau, -elle, -aux, -elles [mɔrvãdo, -ɛl], **morvandiau, -x** [mɔrvãdjo] ADJ of/from the Morvan region

❏ **Morvandeau, -elle** NM,F, **Morvandiau** NMF = person from *or* inhabitant of the Morvan region

morve [mɔrv] NF **1** *(mucus)* nasal mucus **2** *Vét* glanders *(singulier)*

morveux, -euse [mɔrvø, -øz] ADJ **1** *(sale)* snotty-nosed; *(nez)* runny; *Prov* **qui se sent m., qu'il se mouche** if the cap fits, wear it **2** *Vét* glandered

NM,F *Fam* **1** *(enfant)* (snotty-nosed) little kid **2** *(jeune prétentieux)* snotty *or* snotty-nosed little upstart

MOS [ɛmoɛs] NM *(abrév* **métal oxyde semiconducteur***)* MOS; **M. à canal N** NMOS; **M. à canal P** PMOS; **M. complémentaire** complementary MOS

mosaïquage [mɔzaikaʒ] NM *TV* pixellization

mosaïque[1] [mɔzaik] NF **1** *Beaux-Arts* mosaic; **sol en m.** mosaic floor **2** *Fig (mélange → de couleurs)* patchwork, mosaic; *(→ de cultures)* mixture, mosaic; *(→ de populations)* medley; *Ordinat* **afficher en m.** *(fenêtres)* to tile **3** *Bot* mosaic *(disease)* **4** *Biol & Géol* mosaic

mosaïque[2] [mɔzaik] ADJ *Rel* Mosaic

mosaïquer [3] [mɔzaike] VT *(image télévisée)* to distort *(so as to render unrecognizable)*, to pixelize

mosaïsme [mɔzaism] NM *Rel* Mosaism

mosaïste [mɔzaist] NMF mosaicist

mosan, -e [mɔzã, -an] ADJ **art m.** Mosan art

moscatelle [mɔskatɛl] NF *Bot* moschatel

Moscou [mɔsku] NM Moscow

moscovite [mɔskɔvit] ADJ Muscovite

❏ **Moscovite** NMF Muscovite

mosellan, -e [mɔzelã, -an] ADJ of/from Moselle

❏ **Mosellan, -e** NM,F = inhabitant of *or* person from Moselle

Moselle [mɔzɛl] NF **1** *(fleuve)* **la M.** the (River) Moselle **2** *(département)* **la M.** Moselle **3** *(vin)* Moselle (wine)

mosette [mɔzɛt] NF mozetta, mozzetta

mosquée [mɔske] NF mosque

Mossoul [mɔsul] NM Mosul

mot [mo] NM **1** *Ling* word; **un m. à la mode** a buzzword; **"orgueilleux", c'est bien le m.** "arrogant" is the (right) word; **"riche" n'est pas vraiment le m.** "rich" isn't exactly the word I would use; *Euph* **le m. de Cambronne** *ou* **de cinq lettres** the word "merde"; **m. clé** keyword; **m. composé** compound (word); **m. d'emprunt** loanword; **le m. juste** the right *or* appropriate word; **m. de passe** password; **m. vedette** headword; **gros m.** swearword; **ne dis pas de gros mots!** don't swear!; *Belg Péj* **m. à soixante-quinze** *ou* **septante-cinq centimes, m. à un franc soixante-cinq** *ou* **septante-cinq centimes, m. à deux/trois/etc francs soixante-cinq** *ou* **septante-cinq centimes** interminably long word

2 *Ordinat* **m. d'appel** call word; **m. binaire** binary word; **m. d'état** status word; **m. de 6 bits** 6-bit byte; **m. machine** computer word; **m. mémoire** storage *or* memory word

3 *(parole)* word; **il n'a pas dit un m. de toute la soirée** he didn't say a (single) word the entire evening; **dire un m. à qn** to have a word with sb; **pourriez-vous nous dire un m. sur ce problème?** could you say a word (or two) *or* a few words about this problem for us?; **il n'a pas dit un seul m. en ta faveur** he didn't put in a single good word for you; **qui ne dit m. consent** silence is tantamount to consent; **dire deux mots à qn** to have a word with sb; **dire un m. de travers** to say something wrong, to put a foot wrong; **j'ai dit un m. de travers?** have I said something wrong?; **il n'a jamais un m. plus haut**

que l'autre he never raises his voice; **je vais lui en toucher** *ou* **je lui en toucherai un m.** I'll have a word with him/her about it; **pas un m.!** don't say a word!; **pas un m. à qui que ce soit!** not a word to anybody!; **les mots manquent** words are not enough; **les mots manquent pour décrire la beauté de ce matin-là** there are no words to describe *or* words cannot describe the beauty of that particular morning; **les mots me manquent** words fail me; **les mots me manquent pour vous remercier** I'm at a loss for words to express my gratitude; **trouver les mots** to find the (right) words; **je ne trouve pas les mots (pour le dire)** I cannot find the words (to say it); **chercher ses mots** to try to find *or* to search for the right words; **manger** *ou* **avaler ses mots** to mumble; **je ne pouvais pas placer un m.** I couldn't get a word in edgeways; **ce ne sont que des mots!** words, words, words!, all that's just talk!; **à ces mots** at these words; **sur ces mots** with these words; **sur ces mots, il nous quitta** with these words *or* so saying, he left us; **le m. de l'énigme** the key to the mystery *or* puzzle; **m. d'ordre** slogan; *Mil* watchword; **m. d'ordre de grève** call for strike action; **c'est mon dernier m.** it's my last *or* final offer; **avoir le dernier m.** to have the last word; **"voleur", c'est un bien grand m.** "thief", that would be putting it a bit too strongly *or* going a bit too far; **"l'amour", le grand m. est lancé** "love", that's the word we've been waiting for; **avec toi, c'est tout de suite** *ou* **toujours les grands mots** you're always exaggerating; **mots doux** words of love, sweet nothings; **avoir des mots (avec qn)** to have words (with sb); **on a eu des mots** we had words *or* a row; **avoir son m. à dire** to have a *or* one's say; **moi aussi, j'ai mon m. à dire là-dessus** I've got a say in the matter as well; **il faut toujours qu'elle ait son m. à dire** she always has to have her say (in the matter); **tu n'as qu'un m. à dire** just say the word, you just have to say the word; **avoir toujours le m. pour rire** to be a (great) laugh *or* joker; **pas le premier** *ou* **un traître m. de** not a single word of; **je ne sais pas un (traître) m. de russe** I don't know a word of Russian; **prendre qn au m.** to take sb at his/her word; **se donner** *ou* **se passer le m.** to pass the word around; **tout le monde s'était donné le m.** word had been passed around

4 *(parole mémorable)* saying; **m. d'esprit, bon m.** witticism, witty remark; **m. d'auteur** (author's) witty remark; **m. d'enfant** child's remark; **m. de la fin** concluding message, closing words; **mots célèbres** famous sayings *or* quotes

5 *(message écrit)* note, word; **il m'a laissé un m. sur mon bureau** he left a note on my desk; **ce petit m. pour vous dire que je suis bien arrivé** just a note to say that I've arrived safely; **écrire un m. à qn** to write sb a note, to drop sb a line; **m. d'absence** note *(explaining absence)*; **m. d'excuse** word of apology; **m. de remerciements** thank-you note

❑ **à mots couverts** ADV in veiled terms; **dire qch à mots couverts** to hint at sth, to say sth in a roundabout manner; **faire comprendre qch à qn à mots couverts** to give sb to understand sth in a roundabout manner

❑ **au bas mot** ADV at least, at the very least

❑ **en d'autres mots** ADV in other words

❑ **en un mot** ADV in a word; **en un m. comme en cent** *ou* **mille** *(en bref)* in a nutshell, to cut a long story short; *(sans détour)* without beating about the bush

❑ **mot à mot** ADV *(littéralement)* word for word; *(comme nom)* **faire du m. à m., traduire m. à m.** to translate word for word

❑ **mot pour mot** ADV word for word; **répéter qch m. pour m.** to repeat sth word for word *or* verbatim; **c'est ce qu'elle a dit, m. pour m.** those were her very words, that's what she said, word for word

❑ **sans mot dire** ADV without (uttering) a word

'Les Mots' *Sartre* 'Words'

motard, -e [mɔtar, -ard] NM,F *Fam* motorcyclist■, biker

NM 1 *(policier)* motorcycle policeman; **voiture escortée de motards** car with a motorcycle escort 2 *Mil* ≃ dispatch rider

mot-clé, mot-clef [mokle] *(pl* **mots-clés, mots-clefs**) NM key word

motel [mɔtɛl] NM motel

motelier, -ère [mɔtɛlje, -ɛr] NM,F *(propriétaire)* motel owner; *(gérant)* motel manager

motelle [mɔtɛl] NF *Ich* rockling

motet [mɔtɛ] NM *Mus* motet

moteur, -trice [mɔtœr, -tris] ADJ 1 *Tech (force)* driving; **voiture à quatre roues motrices** four-wheel drive car; **roue motrice** driving wheel; **temps m.** power stroke; **unité motrice** power pack *or* unit

2 *Anat (nerf, neurone, muscle)* motor *(avant n)*

NM 1 *Tech* motor, engine; **m. ACT** ohc engine; **m. à allumage par bougie** spark-ignition engine; **m. à allumage commandé** internal combustion engine; **m. à allumage par compression** compression-ignition engine; **m. alternatif à combustion interne** internal combustion (reciprocating) engine; **m. d'avion** aero-engine; **m. carré** square engine; **m. à combustion** combustion engine; **m. à combustion interne** internal combustion engine; **m. à cylindres à plat** boxer engine; **m. à deux temps** two-stroke engine; **m. Diesel** diesel engine; **m. électrique** electric motor; **m. à essence** petrol engine; **m. à explosion** internal combustion engine; **m. à gaz** gas engine; **m. à hélice** propeller engine; **m. hydrogène** hydrogen engine; **m. à injection** fuel injection engine; **m. "lean burn"** lean-burn engine; **m. en ligne** in-line engine; **m. multicylindre** multi-cylinder engine; **m. multisoupape** multi-valve engine; **m. pas à pas** stepper motor; **m. à pistons** piston engine; **m. à piston rotatif** rotary piston engine; **m. à plat** flat engine; **m. polycarburant** multi-fuel engine; **m. polycylindre** multi-cylinder engine; **m. à quatre temps** four-stroke engine; **m. à réaction** jet engine; **m. à refroidissement par air** air-cooled engine; **m. rénové** reconditioned engine, recon; **m. seize soupapes** sixteen-valve engine; **m. thermique** heat engine; **m. turbocompressé** turbocharged engine; **m. turbo-diesel** turbo-diesel engine; **m. en V** vee engine; **m. V6** V6 (engine); **m. à vapeur** steam engine

2 *Fig (cause)* mainspring, driving force; **être le m. de qch** to be the driving force behind sth; **le m. principal de la pensée hégélienne** the mainspring of Hegelian thought; *Littéraire* **Dieu le souverain m. de la nature** God the sovereign mover of nature

3 *Cin* **m.!** camera!

4 *Ordinat* **m. d'impression** *(d'une imprimante laser)* printer engine; **m. de recherche** search engine

❑ **motrice** NF motor unit

❑ **à moteur** ADJ power-driven, motor *(avant n)*; **bateau à m.** motorboat; **à moteurs multiples, à plusieurs moteurs** *(avion)* multi-engine *(avant n)*, multi-engined

moteur-fusée [mɔtœrfyze] *(pl* **moteurs-fusées**) NM rocket engine

motif [mɔtif] NM 1 *(raison)* reason; **venons-en au m. de votre visite** let's turn to the reason for your visit; **quel m. avez-vous de vous plaindre?** what cause *or* grounds have you for complaint?; **le crime avait-il un m.?** did the crime have a motive?, was there a motive to the crime?; **le m. de mon absence** the reason for my absence; **m. de licenciement** grounds for dismissal; **m. de mécontentement** cause *or* grounds for discontent; **elle n'a aucun m. de mécontentement** she has no reason to be unhappy; **m. de réclamation** reason for claim; **il a agi sans m.** he did it for no reason; **peur/soupçons sans motifs** groundless fear/suspicions

2 *Jur (jugement)* grounds; **m. décisoire** material justification; **m. raisonnable** probable cause; **m. surabondant** superfluous plea

3 *(intention)* motive; **les motifs qui l'animent** his/her motivation *or* motives; *Hum ou Vieilli* **est-ce pour le bon m.?** *(en vue du mariage)* are his intentions honourable?; *Mktg* **m. d'achat** buying *or* purchasing motive

4 *(dessin)* pattern, design; **un m. à petites fleurs** a small flower pattern *or* design; **robe à motifs/à grands motifs** patterned/large-pattern dress; **une veste avec des motifs noirs et blancs** a jacket with a black and white design

5 *Beaux-Arts (élément)* motif; *(sujet)* subject

6 *Mus* motif

7 *Chim* **m. cristallin** crystal structure

motilité [mɔtilite] NF motility, motivity

motion [mɔsjɔ̃] NF motion; **voter une m.** to pass a motion; **la m. a été adoptée** the motion was carried; **m. de censure** vote of no confidence

motivant, -e [mɔtivɑ̃, -ɑ̃t] ADJ *(travail, résultat)* motivating; *(salaire, rémunération)* attractive

motivation [mɔtivasjɔ̃] NF 1 *(justification)* motivation, justification, explanation; *(raison)* motivation, motive, reason; **quelles sont vos motivations?** what motivates you?; **joindre une lettre de m. à votre CV** send a *Br* covering letter *or Am* cover letter with your *Br* CV *or Am* résumé

2 *Ling* = relationship between the signifier and the signified

3 *Com & Mktg* motivation, incentive; **étude de m.** motivation *or* motivational research; **m. d'achat** buying *or* purchasing motive; **m. de consommateur** consumer motivation; **m. par le profit** profit motive

4 *Psy* motivation

motivé, -e [mɔtive] ADJ 1 *(personne)* motivated; **élève très m.** very keen *or* motivated pupil; **le personnel n'est plus m.** the staff isn't motivated any longer

2 *(justifié)* well-founded, justified; **un refus m.** a justifiable refusal; **non m.** unjustified, unwarranted; **sa peur n'est pas motivée** his/her fears are groundless; *Jur* **sentence arbitrale motivée** = award stating the reasons on which it is based; *Jur* **avis m.** counsel's opinion

motiver [3] [mɔtive] VT 1 *(inciter à agir)* to spur on, to motivate; **motivé par l'appât du gain** spurred on by greed; **des crimes motivés par l'argent** crimes motivated by money *or* with money as the motive; **l'ambition les motive** they are motivated by ambition

2 *(causer)* to be the reason for; **qu'est-ce qui a motivé votre retard?** what's the reason for your being late?

3 *(justifier)* to justify, to explain; **m. un refus** to give grounds for a refusal

moto [mɔto] NF motorbike, bike; **faire de la m.** to ride a motorbike; **aller au travail à** *ou* **en m.** to go to work on a motorbike, to ride a motorbike to work; **m. tout terrain** *ou* **verte** trail bike; **m. à carénage intégral** superbike

motoball [motobol] NM motoball

motociste [mɔtɔsist] NM motorbike dealer

motocross [mɔtɔkrɔs] NM motocross, *Br* (motorcycle) scramble

motocrotte [mɔtɔkrɔt] NF *Fam* = motorized scooter with an attachment for cleaning up dog dirt in the street

motoculteur [mɔtɔkyltœr] NM *Agr* (motor) cultivator

motoculture [mɔtɔkyltyr] NF motorized *or* mechanized agriculture

motocycle [mɔtɔsikl] NM motorbicycle

motocyclette [mɔtɔsiklɛt] NF *Vieilli* motorcycle

motocyclisme [mɔtɔsiklism] NM motorcycle racing

motocycliste [mɔtɔsiklist] NMF motorcyclist

motomarine [mɔtɔmarin] NF *Can* jet ski; **faire de la m.** to go jet skiing

motonautique [mɔtɔnotik] ADJ **réunion/sport m.** speedboat event/racing

motonautisme [mɔtɔnotism] NM speedboat *or* motorboat racing

motoneige [mɔtɔnɛʒ] NF *Can* snowmobile, skidoo

motoneigisme [mɔtɔneʒism] NM *Can* snowmobiling

motoneigiste [mɔtɔneʒist] NMF *Can* snowmobiler

motopaver [mɔtɔpavœr] NM *Tech* motopaver

motopompe [mɔtɔpɔ̃p] NF motor pump

motopropulseur, -euse [mɔtɔpropylsœr, -øz] ADJ **groupe m.** power unit

NM power unit

motor-home [mɔtɔrom] *(pl* **motor-homes**) NM motor home

motorisation [mɔtɔrizasjɔ̃] NF 1 *(gén)* motorization 2 *Tech* engine specification

motorisé, -e [mɔtɔrize] ADJ 1 *(agriculture)* motorized; *(troupes)* motorized, mechanized 2 *Fam (personne)* **être m.** to have *Br* transport *or Am* transportation; **tu es m.?** have you got a car?

motoriser [3] [mɔtɔrize] **VT 1** *(mécaniser)* to motorize, to mechanize; **m. l'agriculture** to mechanize agriculture **2** *(doter d'automobiles)* to motorize; **m. un régiment** to motorize a regiment

motoriste [mɔtɔrist] **NMF** *(industriel)* engine manufacturer; *(technicien)* engine technician

motorship [mɔtɔrʃip] **NM** motor ship *or* vessel

motoski [mɔtɔski] **NF** snowmobile, skidoo

mototondeuse [mɔtɔtɔ̃døz] **NF** rider *or Br* ride-on mower

mot-outil [mouti] *(pl* **mots-outils)** **NM** *Ling* form word, link word

motrice [mɔtris] *voir* **moteur**

motricité [mɔtrisite] **NF** *Physiol* motor functions

mots croisés [mokrwaze] **NMPL** crossword (puzzle); **que fais-tu? – je fais des m.** what are you doing? – I'm doing a crossword; **il aime faire des m.** he likes doing crosswords

mots-croisiste [mokrwazist] **NMF** *(pl* **mots-croisistes)** crossword compiler

motte [mɔt] **NF 1** *Agr* **m. (de terre)** clod *or* clump (of earth); **m. de tourbe** (turf of) peat; **m. de gazon** sod **2** *Hort* ball; **plantation en m.** ball planting **3** *Culin* **m. de beurre** slab of butter; **beurre à la m.** butter in blocks **4** *Métal (moule)* boxless *or* flaskless mould **5** *Archéol* motte; *(de château)* mound **6** *Vulg (sexe de la femme)* snatch, pussy; **s'astiquer la m.** to finger oneself, to play with oneself

motter [3] [mɔte] **se motter VPR** *Chasse (animal)* to hide behind clumps of earth

motteux [mɔtø] **NM** wheat ear

motton [mɔtɔ̃] **NM** *Can Fam (de terre)* sod■, lump■; *(de glace, de neige)* lump■, clump■; *(dans une sauce)* lump■; *Fig* **avoir le m.** to be loaded, to have pots of money; **faire le m.** to make a bundle *or Br* a packet; **avoir le m. dans la gorge** to have a lump in one's throat

motu proprio [mɔtyprɔprijo] **ADV** spontaneously, of one's own accord

motus [mɔtys] **EXCLAM** *Fam* **m. (et bouche cousue)!** not a word (to anybody)!, mum's the word!

mot-valise [movaliz] *(pl* **mots-valises)** **NM** *Ling* blend, portmanteau word

mot-vedette [movədɛt] *(pl* **mots-vedettes)** **NM** *Typ* catchword

mou, molle [mu, mɔl]

> **mol** is used before masculine singular nouns beginning with a vowel or h mute.

ADJ 1 *(souple → pâte, cire, terre, fruit)* soft; *(→ fauteuil, matelas)* soft; **les biscuits sont tout mous** the biscuits have gone all soft; **devenir m.** to soften, to go soft; **être m. au toucher** to be soft to the touch **2** *(sans tenue → étoffe, vêtement)* limp; *(→ joues, chair)* flabby; *(→ corde)* slack **3** *(sans vigueur physique → mouvement)* limp, lifeless, feeble; *(→ poignée de main)* limp; *(→ geste)* lifeless, limp; **mon revers est trop m.** my backhand is too weak *or* lacks power; *Fam* **j'ai les jambes toutes molles** my legs feel all weak *or* feel like jelly; *Fam* **je me sens tout m.** I feel washed out; **ce qu'il peut être m.!** God, he's feeble *or* useless!; *Fam* **allez, rame plus vite, c'est m. tout ça!** come on, pull on those oars, let's see some effort! **4** *(estompé → contour)* soft; **bruit m.** muffled noise; **des collines au relief m.** rolling hills **5** *(sans conviction → protestation, excuse, tentative)* feeble, weak; *(→ doigté, style)* lifeless, dull; *(→ élève)* apathetic, lethargic; **il m'a fait de molles excuses** he gave me some lame *or* feeble excuses **6** *(sans force de caractère)* spineless; *Fam* **être m. comme une chiffe** *ou* **une chique** to be a real wimp **7** *(trop tolérant → parents, gouvernement)* lax, soft **8** *Ling* soft **9** *Anat* **parties molles** soft tissue *(UNCOUNT)* **10** *Phys* **rayonnements mous** soft radiation *(UNCOUNT)*

NM,F *Fam* **1** *(moralement)* wimp **2** *(physiquement)* weak *or* feeble individual■

ADV 1 elle joue trop m. she doesn't put enough verve into her playing **2** *Fam Vieilli (doucement)* **y aller m.** to go easy, to take it easy; **vas-y m. avec le piment** go easy on *or* take it easy with the chilli

NM 1 *(jeu)* slack, give, play; **avoir du m.** *(sujet: cordage)* to be slack; *(sujet: vis, charnière)* to be loose, to have a bit of play; **donner du m. à un câble** to give a cable some slack; **donner du m. à un cordage** to slacken a rope; **prendre du m.** *(sujet: corde)* to slacken **2** *(abats)* lights, lungs **3** *Fam (locutions)* **bourrer le m. à qn** to pull the wool over sb's eyes; **rentrer dans le m. à qn** *(agresser)* to go for sb, to lay into sb; **c'est du m.** *(c'est faux)* it's a load of rubbish

mouais [mwɛ] **EXCLAM** *Fam* well, yeah!; **alors, t'as aimé le film? – m., j'ai vu pire** did you like the movie, then? – well, yeah, I've seen worse; **m., ce n'est pas mal** it's all right, I suppose

mouchage [muʃaʒ] **NM 1** *(de nez)* blowing **2** *(de chandelles)* snuffing (out)

moucharabieh [muʃarabje] **NM** moucharaby

mouchard, -e [muʃar, -ard] **NM,F** *Fam Péj* **1** *(à l'école)* snitch, *Br* sneak, tell-tale **2** *(indic)* informer■, *Br* grass, *Am* fink

NM 1 *(enregistreur → d'un avion)* black box, flight recorder; *(→ d'un camion)* tachograph; *(contrôleur)* watchman's clock **2** *Aviat & Mil* spy plane **3** *Ordinat* **m. électronique** cookie **4** *Fam (sur une porte)* Judas(-hole)■, spyhole■

mouchardage [muʃardaʒ] **NM** *Fam (gén)* snitching, *Br* sneaking, telling tales; *(pour la police)* informing■, grassing

moucharder [3] [muʃarde] *Fam Péj* **VT 1** *(sujet: enfant)* to snitch on, *Br* to sneak on, to tell tales on **2** *(sujet: indic)* to squeal on, *Br* to grass on, *Am* to fink on

VI 1 *(enfant)* to snitch, *Br* to sneak, to tell tales; **t'as pas intérêt à m.** you'd better not snitch **2** *(indic)* to squeal, *Br* to grass, *Am* to rat

mouche [muʃ] **NF 1** *Entom* fly; **m. bleue** bluebottle; **m. domestique** housefly; *Can* **m. à feu** firefly; *très Fam* **m. à merde** dung fly; *Can Fig Vulg* **m. à merde** *(personne ennuyeuse)* pest; **m. à miel** honey bee; *Can* **m. noire** black fly; *très Fam* **m. à ordure** dung fly; **m. des sables** sandfly; **m. à scie** sawfly; **m. tsé-tsé** tsetse fly; **m. à viande** blowfly; **m. de la viande** flesh fly; **m. du vinaigre** fruit fly; **il ne ferait pas de mal à une m.** he wouldn't hurt a fly; *Fam* **quelle m. te pique?** what's up *or* wrong with you (all of a sudden)?; *Fam* **tomber comme des mouches** to drop like flies; *Fam* **prendre** *ou Suisse* **piquer la m.** to hit the *Br* roof *or Am* ceiling; **elle prend facilement la m.** she's very touchy; **on aurait entendu une m. voler** you could have heard a pin drop; *Belg* **après moi/toi/***etc***, les mouches** whatever happens, I/you/*etc* don't care; *Prov* **on ne prend** *ou* **n'attrape pas les mouches avec du vinaigre** you don't get anywhere by being unpleasant **2** *Pêche* **m. (artificielle)** (artificial) fly; **m. mouillée** wet fly; **m. à saumon** salmon fly; **pêche à la m.** fly-fishing; **pêche à la m. sèche** dry-fly fishing **3** *(sur la peau)* beauty spot, patch; *(poils)* tuft of hair *(under the lower lip)*, soul patch **4** *(de cible)* bull's-eye; *Escrime* button; **faire m.** to hit the bull's-eye, to score a bull's-eye; *Fig* to hit the nail on the head **5** *Méd* **mouches (volantes)** floaters, *Spéc* muscae volitantes **6** *Arch (tache)* spot, speck; *(sur vêtement)* stain

Allusion
Mouche du coche
This expression comes from La Fontaine's fable *The Stagecoach and the Fly*. In the fable, a stagecoach is being pulled up a steep hill by a team of labouring horses, while a fly buzzes around them. When at last the horses have pulled the coach to the top, the fly claims his share of the credit, saying he egged them on. When some people do all the work while others fuss around self-importantly, one speaks of **La mouche du coche** ("the stagecoach fly"), eg **Il est** *or* **il fait la mouche du coche** ("He's always buzzing around but he doesn't pull his weight").

moucher [3] [muʃe] **VT 1** *(nettoyer)* **m. son nez** to blow one's nose; **m. qn** to blow sb's nose; **je mouche du sang** there's blood on my handkerchief when I blow my nose **2** *Fam (rabrouer)* **m. qn** to put sb in his/her place, to teach sb a lesson; **se faire m.** to be put in one's place **3** *(chandelle)* to snuff (out)

▶ **se moucher VPR** to blow one's nose; *Fam* **elle ne se mouche pas du pied** *ou* **du coude** she thinks she's the cat's whiskers *or* the bee's knees

moucheron [muʃrɔ̃] **NM 1** *Entom* midge **2** *Fam (gamin)* kid

moucheronner [3] [muʃrɔne] **VI** *(poisson)* to jump *or* to rise (for flies)

mouchet [muʃɛ] **NM** *Suisse* small tuft

moucheté, -e [muʃte] **ADJ 1** *(œuf, fourrure, laine)* mottled, flecked; *(tissu)* speckled; *(cheval)* dappled; **rouge m. de blanc** red flecked with white; **mer mouchetée d'écume** foam-flecked sea; **nez m. de taches de rousseur** freckled nose **2** *Escrime* buttoned **3** *Menuis* **bois m.** bird's-eye (grain) wood

moucheter [27] [muʃte] **VT 1** *(couvrir de taches)* to speckle; *(parsemer de taches)* to fleck **2** *Escrime* to button

mouchetis [muʃti] **NM** *Constr Br* pebbledash, *Am* rock dash

mouchette [muʃɛt] **NF 1** *Archit (de fenêtre)* outer fillet, mouchette; *(de larmier)* lip **2** *Menuis (rabot)* beading plane; *(moulure)* beading □ **mouchettes NFPL** *(ciseaux)* (pair of) candle snuffers; *(pour bovins)* ring, barnacle

moucheture [muʃtyr] **NF 1** *(d'un pelage, d'un plumage)* speckling; *(d'un tissu)* flecks, flecking; **une écharpe blanche avec des mouchetures noires** a white scarf with black flecks, a white scarf speckled *or* flecked with black **2** *Agr* leaf stripe **3** *Hér* **m. d'hermine** ermine tail

mouchoir [muʃwar] **NM** handkerchief; **m. en papier** (paper) tissue, *Am* Kleenex®; **m. en tissu** handkerchief; **leur jardin est grand comme un m. de poche** their garden is the size of a pocket handkerchief; **arriver dans un m. de poche** to finish neck and neck

mouchure [muʃyr] **NF** (nasal) mucus

mouclade [muklad] **NF** = mussels in white wine, with shallots and cream

moudjahidin, moudjahidine [mudʒaidin] **NMPL** mujaheddin

moudre [85] [mudr] **VT 1** *(café, poivre)* to grind; *(blé)* to mill, to grind; *Fam* **m. qn de coups** to beat sb to a pulp **2** *Vieilli Mus* **m. un air** to crank out a tune *(on a barrel-organ etc)*

moue [mu] **NF** pout; **m. boudeuse** sulk; **faire une m. de dégoût** to screw one's face up in disgust; **faire une m. de dépit** to pull a face; **faire la m.** to pout

mouette [mwɛt] **NF** *Orn* gull, seagull; **m. mélanocéphale** Mediterranean gull; **m. pygmée** little gull; **m. rieuse** black-headed gull; **m. tridactyle** kittiwake

═══ 🎭 ═══

'La Mouette' Tchekhov 'The Seagull'

moufeter [3] [mufte] = **moufter**

moufette, mouffette [mufɛt] **NF** *Zool* skunk

moufle [mufl] **NF 1** *(gant)* mitt, mitten **2** *(poulie)* pulley block

NM *Tech (four, récipient)* muffle

mouflet, -ette [muflɛ, -ɛt] **NM,F** *Fam* kid, *Br* sprog

mouflon [muflɔ̃] **NM** mouflon, moufflon; **m. d'Amérique** *ou* **du Canada** bighorn (sheep); **m. de Dall** Dall's sheep; **m. à manchettes** Barbary sheep

moufter [3] [mufte] **VI** *(à l'infinitif et au participe passé seulement)* *Fam* **ne pas m.** to keep one's mouth shut, *Br* to keep shtum; **sans m.** without a peep

mouillabilité [mujabilite] **NF** *Tech* wettability

mouillable [mujabl] **ADJ** *Phys* absorbing, absorbent

mouillage [mujaʒ] **NM 1** *(du linge)* dampening **2** *Naut (emplacement)* anchorage, moorings, moorage; *(manœuvre)* anchoring, mooring; *(de bouée)* putting down; **être au m.** to be riding at anchor; **prendre son m.** to anchor **3** *(du vin,*

du lait) watering down **4** *Mil* **m. de mines** mine laying

mouillance [mujɑ̃s] NF *Phys* absorptivity

mouillant, -e [mujɑ̃, -ɑ̃t] ADJ *(gén)* & *Chim* wetting ◾ NM wetting agent

mouillasser [3] [mujase] V IMPERSONNEL *Can* & *(régional en France) Fam* to drizzle◾

mouille [muj] NF **1** *(source)* oozing spring **2** *(dans le lit d'une rivière)* alluvial channel **3** *(d'une cargaison)* wetting, dampening *(of cargo)*

mouillé, -e [muje] ADJ **1** *(surface, vêtement, cheveux)* wet, damp; **je suis tout m.** I'm all wet **2** *(voix)* tearful; *(regard)* tearful, watery; **elle le regarda, les yeux mouillés de larmes** she looked at him with tears in her eyes **3** *Ling* palatalized
◾ NM **ça sent le m.** it smells of damp

mouillement [mujmɑ̃] NM *Ling* palatalization

mouiller [3] [muje] VT **1** *(accidentellement → vêtement, personne)* to wet; **ne mouille pas tes chaussons!** don't get your slippers wet!; *Euph* **il mouille encore son lit** he still wets his or the bed; **se faire m.** *(par la pluie)* to get wet; *Fam* **m. sa chemise** *ou* **son maillot** to slog away
2 *(humecter → doigt, lèvres)* to moisten; *(→ linge)* to dampen
3 *Fam (compromettre)* to drag in; **il a cherché à nous m. dans cette affaire** he tried to drag us into this affair
4 *Can Fam (fêter)* **il va falloir m. ça!** we'll have to have a drink to celebrate!◾, this calls for a celebration!◾
5 *Naut (ancre)* to cast, to drop; *(bouée)* to put down; *Mil (mine)* to lay; *Pêche (ligne)* to cast
6 *Ling* to palatalize
7 *(vin, boisson alcoolisée, lait)* to dilute, to water down
USAGE ABSOLU *Culin* **mouillez avec du vin/du bouillon** moisten with wine/stock
◾ VI **1** *Naut (jeter l'ancre)* to cast or to drop anchor; *(stationner)* to ride or to lie or to be at anchor; **mouillez!** let go (the anchor)!
2 *très Fam (avoir peur)* to wet oneself
3 *Can* & *(régional en France) Fam (pleuvoir)* to rain"; *Can* **m. à siau** *ou* **à verse** *ou* **à boire debout** to rain buckets
4 *Vulg (être excitée sexuellement)* to be wet
❑ **en mouiller** V IMPERSONNEL *Can* **des imbéciles comme lui, il en mouille** there's no shortage of idiots like him around, there are loads of idiots like him around
▸**se mouiller** VPR **1** *(volontairement)* **se m. les cheveux** to wet one's hair
2 *(accidentellement)* to get wet; **se m. les pieds** to get one's feet wet
3 *(yeux)* to fill with tears
4 *Fam (prendre un risque)* to stick one's neck out
5 *Can Fam* **se m. la dalle** *ou* **le gargoton** *ou* **le canayen** to get hammered or *Br* pissed

mouillère [mujɛr] NF *Agr* wet or boggy patch

mouillette [mujɛt] NF *(de pain)* finger of bread *(for dunking)*; *Br* soldier

mouilleur [mujœr] NM **1** *(de timbres)* (stamp) sponge damper **2** *Naut* anchor stopper **3** *Mil* **m. de mines** mine-layer

mouilloir [mujwar] NM (stamp) sponge damper

mouillon [mujɔ̃] NM *Suisse (humidité)* dampness; *(flaque)* puddle

mouillure [mujyr] NF **1** *(marque)* wet mark or patch **2** *Ling* palatalization

mouise [mwiz] NF *Fam (misère)* poverty◾; *(ennuis)* grief, hassle, *Br* aggro; **être dans la m.** *(être dans la misère)* to be hard up or broke or *Br* skint; *(avoir des ennuis)* to be in a hole, *Am* to be behind the eightball; **tirer** *ou* **sortir qn de la m.** to get sb out of a hole

moujik [muʒik] NM muzhik, mujik, moujik

moujingue [muʒɛ̃g] NMF *très Fam* kid

moukère [mukɛr] NF *très Fam (femme maghrébine)* Maghrebi woman◾; *(femme)* female

moulage¹ [mulaʒ] NM **1** *Beaux-Arts (processus)* casting; **m. à la cire perdue** lost wax casting **2** *(reproduction)* cast; **un m. en plâtre/bronze de Beethoven** a plaster/bronze cast of Beethoven **3** *Métal* casting, moulding; **m. en carapace/ châssis** shell/flask moulding; **m. par compression/injection** compression/injection moulding **4** *(d'un fromage)* moulding

moulage² [mulaʒ] NM *(du grain)* grinding, milling

moulait *etc* **1** *voir* **moudre 2** *voir* **mouler**

moulant, -e [mulɑ̃, -ɑ̃t] ADJ close-fitting, tight-fitting, clingy

moule¹ [mul] NM **1** *(récipient, matrice)* mould; **m. à gâteau** *Br* cake or baking tin, *Am* cake or baking pan; **m. à gaufre** *ou* **gaufres** waffle iron; **m. à manqué** *Br* sandwich tin, *Am* deep cake pan; **m. à tarte** *Br* flan case, *Am* pie pan; *Fam* **être coulé dans le même m.** to be cast in the same mould; *Fam* **on n'en fait plus des comme lui, on a cassé le m.** they broke the mould when they made him
2 *Fig (modèle imposé)* mould; **elle rejette le m. de l'école** she rejects the image the school demands of her; **elle rejette le m. de sa famille** she rejects her family's values; **refuser d'entrer dans le m.** to refuse to conform; **être coulé dans le même m.** to be cast in the same mould; **être fait au m.** to be very shapely or perfectly shaped

moule² [mul] NF **1** *(mollusque)* mussel; **moules frites** mussels and *Br* chips or *Am* French fries *(speciality of Belgium and the north of France)*; **moules marinières** moules marinières, mussels in white wine; *Belg* **moules parquées** = mussels served raw
2 *Fam (personne)* drip
3 *Vulg (sexe de la femme)* pussy, snatch
4 *Fam* **avoir de la m.** *(de la chance)* to be lucky◾

moulé, -e [mule] ADJ **1** *(pain)* baked in a *Br* tin or *Am* pan **2** *(écriture)* neat, well-shaped; *(lettre)* printed, copperplate **3** *(statue)* cast, moulded; **statue de plâtre m.** plaster cast **4** *Méd (matières fécales)* well-shaped, consistent

moulée [mule] NF *Can (nourriture pour animaux)* feed, scratch grain

mouler [3] [mule] VT **1** *(former → buste, statue)* to cast; *(→ brique, lingot, fromage)* to mould
2 *(prendre copie de → visage, empreinte)* to take or to make a cast of; **m. qch en plâtre/cire** to take a plaster/wax cast of sth
3 *Fig (adapter)* **m. ses pensées/son mode de vie sur** to mould or to model one's thoughts/ lifestyle on
4 *Fig (serrer → hanches, jambes)* to hug, to fit closely (round); **cette jupe te moule trop** this skirt is too tight or tight-fitting for you; **un pantalon qui moule** close-fitting or tight-fitting or skintight trousers; **ses hanches moulées dans une jupe en cuir** her hips moulded in a leather skirt

moules-frites [mulfrit] NM INV *Belg* **1** *Culin* mussels and *Br* chips or *Am* French fries *(speciality of Belgium and the north of France)* **2** *(restaurant)* = restaurant specializing in mussels and *Br* chips or *Am* French fries

mouleur, -euse [mulœr, -øz] NM,F caster, moulder

moulière [muljɛr] NF mussel bed

moulin [mulɛ̃] NM **1** *(machine, bâtiment)* mill; **m. à eau** water mill; **m. à sucre** sugar (crushing) mill, sugar (cylinder) press; **m. à vent** windmill; *Fig* **se battre contre des moulins à vent** to tilt at windmills; *Fig* **on y entre comme dans un m.** anyone can just walk in; **ce n'est pas un m. ici!** you can't just walk in or breeze in as if you owned the place!; *Fam* **m. à paroles** windbag, chatterbox; **le M. Rouge** = famous cabaret in Paris
2 *(instrument)* **m. à café** coffee grinder; **m. à légumes** vegetable mill; **m. à poivre** pepper-mill; *Rel* **m. à prières** prayer wheel
3 *Fam (moteur)* engine◾
4 *Tex (pour la soie)* thrower; *(pour retordre)* doubling frame, twister
5 m. à bois sawmill; **m. à coudre** sewing machine; **m. à scie** sawmill; *Can* **m. à viande** mincer

'Au Moulin Rouge, la danse' *Toulouse-Lautrec* 'Dancing at the Moulin Rouge'

'Le Moulin de la Galette' *Renoir* 'The Ball at the Moulin de la Galette'

moulinage [mulinaʒ] NM **1** *(d'aliments)* milling **2** *Tex* throwing

moulin-à-vent [mulɛ̃avɑ̃] NM INV Moulin-à-Vent (wine)

mouliner [3] [muline] VT **1** *(aliment)* to mill **2** *Pêche* to reel in **3** *Tex (soie grège)* to throw
◾ VI *Fam (pédaler)* to pedal◾

moulinet [mulinɛ] NM **1** *Pêche* reel **2** *Tech* winch **3** *(mouvement)* **faire des moulinets avec un bâton** to twirl or to whirl a stick around; **faire des moulinets avec une épée** to flourish a sword; **il faisait des moulinets avec ses bras** he was whirling or waving his arms around **4** *(tourniquet)* turnstile **5** *Naut* log reel

Moulinette® [mulinɛt] NF **1** *Culin* (hand-held) vegetable mill, Moulinette®; **passer de la viande à la M.** to put some meat through a/the food mill **2** *Fam Fig* **passer qch à la M.** to make mincemeat of sth; **il est passé à la M.** he got put through the mill

moulinette [mulinɛt] NF *(en alpinisme)* top-rope

moulineur, -euse [mulinœr, -øz], **moulinier, -ère** [mulinje, -ɛr] NM,F *Tex* twister

Mouloud [mulud] NM *Rel* Mulud

moult [mult] ADV *Hum ou Vieilli* **je suis venu m. fois** I came many a time; **avec m. détails** with a profusion of details; **avec m. remerciements** with many thanks

moulu, -e [muly] PP *voir* **moudre**
◾ ADJ **1** *(en poudre)* ground; **café fraîchement m.** freshly ground coffee; or **m.** ormolu **2** *Fam (épuisé)* **m. (de fatigue)** dead beat, all in

mouluration [mulyrasjɔ̃] NF mouldings

moulure [mulyr] NF moulding; **m. creuse/lisse/ ronde** concave/plain/convex moulding

moulurer [3] [mulyre] VT to mould; **profils moulurés** mouldings

moulurière [mulyrjɛr] NF *(machine)* moulder

moulut *etc voir* **moudre**

moumoune [mumun] NF *Can Fam Péj* faggot, *Br* poof, = offensive term used to refer to a homosexual

moumoute [mumut] NF *Fam* **1** *(perruque)* wig◾, rug, *Br* syrup **2** *(veste)* sheepskin jacket◾ or coat◾

mouquère [mukɛr] = **moukère**

mourant, -e [murɑ̃, -ɑ̃t] ADJ **1** *(personne, animal, plante)* dying **2** *(lumière, son)* dying, fading; *(voix)* faint
◾ NM,F dying man, *f* woman; **les mourants** the dying

mourir [42] [murir] VI **1** *(personne, animal, plante)* to die; **il est mort hier** he died yesterday; **il est mort assassiné** he was murdered; **il est mort de vieillesse** he died of old age; **m. empoisonné** to die of poisoning or from poison; **m. d'une crise cardiaque/d'un cancer** to die of a heart attack/ of cancer; **m. de chagrin** to die of grief; **m. de mort naturelle** *ou* **de sa belle mort** to die a natural death; **m. de faim** to die of starvation, to starve to death; **m. de soif/chaleur** to die of thirst/heat; **m. de froid** to freeze to death; **il mourut de ses blessures** he died from his wounds; **m. sous les coups** to be beaten to death; **m. sur le coup** to die instantly; **m. à la tâche** to die in harness; **m. en héros** to die a hero's death or like a hero; **m. avant l'âge** to die before one's time; **je l'aime à en m.** I'm desperately in love with him/her; **faire m. qn** to kill sb; *Hum* **tu me feras m.!** you'll be the death of me yet!; *Fig* **faire m. qn à petit feu** to kill sb slowly; **au moment de m.** in the hour of death; **au moment de m., il a fait venir toute sa famille** just before he died, he sent for his entire family; *Fam* **tu n'en mourras pas!** it won't kill you!; *Fam* **plus débile/macho, tu meurs!** they don't come any more stupid/macho than that!
2 *(disparaître → culture)* to die out; *(→ flamme, bougie)* to die out or down; *(→ bruit)* to die away or down; **les vagues qui viennent m. sur la plage** the waves which break and spend themselves on the beach
3 *Fig (pour intensifier)* **m. de faim** to be starving or famished; **m. de soif** to be dying of thirst, to be parched; **m. de chaleur** to be boiling hot; **m. de froid** to be freezing cold; **m. de peur** to be scared to death; **m. d'ennui, s'ennuyer à m.** to be bored to death or to tears; **m. d'envie de faire qch** to be dying to do sth; **je meurs d'envie de boire un thé** I'm dying for a cup of tea; **vous me faites m. d'impatience** the suspense is killing

me; **j'ai cru m. de rire** I thought I would die laughing, I nearly died laughing; **être à m. de rire** *(sujet: film, roman, personne)* to be hilarious; **la pièce est à m. de rire** the play's hilarious *or* a scream; **elle me fait m. de rire!** she really cracks me up!

v IMPERSONNEL il meurt des milliers d'enfants chaque jour thousands of children die every day ►**se mourir** *VPR Littéraire* **1** *(personne)* to be dying; *Fig* **se m. d'amour pour qn** to pine for sb **2** *(civilisation, coutume)* to die out; *(d'un feu)* to die down; **une tradition qui se meurt** a dying tradition

Mourmansk [murmãsk] *NM* Murmansk

mouroir [murwar] *NM Péj* (old people's) home; **certains foyers pour personnes âgées ne sont que des mouroirs** some homes are just places where old people are left to die

mouron [murɔ̃] *NM* **1** *Bot* **faux m.** scarlet pimpernel; **m. blanc** (common) chickweed; **m. d'eau** water speedwell; **m. des fontaines** water chickweed; **m. des oiseaux** (common) chickweed; **m. rouge** scarlet pimpernel **2** *Fam (locution)* **se faire du m.** to worry oneself sick; **te fais pas de m. pour lui!** don't (you) worry about him!

mourra *etc voir* **mourir**

mourre [mur] *NF* mora, morra

mousmé [musme] *NF* **1** *Littéraire (Japonaise)* young Japanese woman **2** *très Fam (femme)* fancy woman

mousquet [muskɛ] *NM* musket

mousquetaire [muskətɛr] *NM* musketeer; **gants (à la) m.** gauntlets

mousqueterie [muskɛtri] *NF Vieilli* musketry

mousqueton [muskətɔ̃] *NM* **1** *(anneau)* snap hook *or* clasp; *(en alpinisme)* karabiner **2** *Mil* carbine

mousquetonner [3] [muskətɔne] *VT (en alpinisme)* to clip to a karabiner

moussage [musaʒ] *NM Chim* foaming

moussaillon [musajɔ̃] *NM Fam* (young) cabin boy

moussaka [musaka] *NF* moussaka

moussant, -e [musã, -ãt] *ADJ (crème à raser)* lathering; *(shampooing, gel)* foaming; **être très m.** to produce a lot of lather

mousse [mus] *ADJ* **1** *Tex* **collant m.** stretch tights **2** *Chim* **caoutchouc m.** foam rubber **3** *Tech (lame, pointe)* blunt
■ *ADJ INV* **vert m.** moss green
■ *NM* **1** *(apprenti marin)* cabin boy, ship's boy **2** *Can Fam (en appellatif)* darling, sweetheart
■ *NF* **1** *(bulles → de shampooing, de crème à raser)* lather, foam; *(→ d'un bain)* bubbles, foam; *(→ de savon)* suds, lather; *(→ de champagne, de cidre)* bubbles; *(→ de bière)* froth; **m. à raser** shaving foam; **faire de la m.** *(savon, crème à raser)* to lather; *Fam* **se faire de la m.** to worry oneself sick **2** *Culin* mousse; **m. au chocolat** chocolate mousse; **m. de saumon** salmon mousse **3** *Fam (bière)* (glass of) beer ■; **on se boit une m.?** fancy a *Br* pint *or Am* brew? **4** *(dans les matériaux synthétiques)* foam; **m. de Nylon®** stretch nylon; **balle en m.** rubber ball; **m. de platine** platinum sponge **5** *Bot* moss; **couvert de m.** mossy

mousseline [muslin] *NF (de coton)* muslin; *(de soie, de Nylon®, de laine)* chiffon, mousseline; **m. de soie** chiffon; **foulard en m.** muslin *or* chiffon scarf
■ *ADJ INV* **pommes m.** puréed potatoes; **sauce m.** mousseline sauce; **verre m.** mousseline

mousser [3] [muse] *VI* **1** *(champagne, cidre)* to bubble, to sparkle; *(bière)* to froth; *(savon, crème à raser)* to lather; *(détergent, shampooing)* to foam, to lather; **ce savon ne mousse pas beaucoup** this soap doesn't lather very well *or* doesn't give much of a lather; **ce champagne mousse beaucoup** there are a lot of bubbles in this champagne, this champagne is very fizzy; **j'ai une méthode infaillible pour faire m. le chocolat chaud** I have an infallible method for making hot chocolate frothy **2** *Fam Fig* **faire m. qn** *(le mettre en colère)* to wind sb up, to rile sb; *(le mettre en valeur)* to sing sb's praises; **faire m. qch** to sing the praises of sth; **se faire m.** to blow one's own trumpet

mousseron [musrɔ̃] *NM* St George's mushroom

mousseux, -euse [musø, -øz] *ADJ* **1** *(vin, cidre)* sparkling; *(bière, lait)* frothy; *(eau)* frothy; *(sauce, jaunes d'œufs)* (light and) frothy; **un chocolat m.** a cup of frothy hot chocolate **2** *Bot* mossy
■ *NM* sparkling wine

moussoir [muswar] *NM* whisk

mousson [musɔ̃] *NF* monsoon

Moussorgski [musɔrski] *NPR* Mussorgsky

moussu, -e [musy] *ADJ* mossy

moustac [mustak] *NM Zool* moustached monkey

moustache [mustaʃ] *NF* **1** *(d'un homme)* moustache; **porter la m.** *ou* **des moustaches** to have a moustache; **elle a de la m.** she's got a bit of a moustache; **m. en brosse** toothbrush moustache; **m. en croc** handlebar moustache; **m. (à la) gauloise** walrus moustache; **m. en guidon de vélo** handlebar moustache **2** *Zool* whiskers

moustachu, -e [mustaʃy] *ADJ* **un homme m.** a man with a moustache; **il est m.** he's got a moustache
■ *NM* man with a moustache

moustelle [mustɛl] = **motelle**

moustérien, -enne [musterjɛ̃, -ɛn] *Archéol ADJ* Mousterian
■ *NM* Mousterian

moustiquaire [mustikɛr] *NF ou Belg NM (d'un lit)* mosquito net; *(d'une ouverture)* mosquito screen; *(de fenêtre)* screen

Moustique [mustik] *N* **M.**, **l'île M.** Mustique; **à M.** in *or* on Mustique

moustique [mustik] *NM* **1** *Entom* mosquito **2** *Fam (gamin)* kid, mite; *(petite personne)* (little) squirt

moût [mu] *NM (de raisin)* must; *(de bière)* wort

moutard [mutar] *NM Fam* kid

moutarde [mutard] *NF* **1** *Bot* mustard; **graines de m.** mustard seeds **2** *Culin* mustard; **m. à l'ancienne** grain mustard; **m. de Dijon** Dijon mustard; **m. à l'estragon** tarragon mustard; **m. forte** Dijon mustard **3** *Fam (locutions)* **la m. lui est montée au nez** he/she lost his/her temper, he/she saw red; **je sens que la m. me monte au nez** I can feel my temper starting to rise
■ *ADJ INV* **1** *(jaune)* mustard *(avant n)*, mustard-coloured **2** *Mil* **gaz m.** mustard gas

moutardier [mutardje] *NM* **1** *(récipient)* mustard pot **2** *(fabricant)* mustard maker *or* manufacturer; *Fam* **il se croit le premier m. du pape** he thinks he's the cat's pyjamas *or* the bee's knees **3** *(marchand)* mustard seller

moutier [mutje] *NM Vieilli* monastery

mouton, -onne [mutɔ̃, -ɔn] *NM* **1** *(animal)* sheep; **m. de Barbarie** Barbary sheep; **m. bleu** blue sheep; *Fig* **m. à cinq pattes** rare bird; **chercher le m. à cinq pattes** to seek the impossible; *Fig* **le m. noir de la famille** the black sheep of the family; *Fig* **compter les moutons** to count sheep; **ils ont tous suivi comme des moutons** they all followed like sheep; *Fig* **revenons** *ou* **retournons à nos moutons** let's get back to the point **2** *(fourrure, cuir)* sheepskin; **veste en (peau de) m.** sheepskin jacket **3** *Culin* mutton; **côte de m.** mutton chop; **ragoût de m.** mutton stew **4** *Fam (individu)* sheep; **c'est un vrai m. de Panurge** he's easily led, he follows the herd **5** *Métal* drop hammer **6** *(en travaux publics)* pile driver **7** *Fam Arg crime (espion) Br* grass, *Am* fink **8** *Can* **m. noir** *(nuage)* rain cloud
■ *ADJ Fig* sheep-like
□ **moutons** *NMPL (poussière)* bits of fluff, fluff *(UNCOUNT)*; *(nuages)* fleecy *or* fluffy clouds; *(écume sur la mer)* white horses

Les moutons de Panurge

In Rabelais' *Quart Livre* (1552), Panurge wants to take revenge on a merchant called Dindenault. He has the idea of buying a sheep from him, then throwing it in the sea to get the other sheep to follow. The plan works perfectly, and the flock is lost. To call people **des moutons de Panurge** is to allude to them disparagingly as having a herd mentality, like a flock of sheep.

Revenons à nos moutons

In the fifteenth-century *La Farce de maître Pathelin*, a cloth merchant takes his shepherd to court, accusing him of stealing his sheep. In court, the merchant suddenly realizes that the shepherd's lawyer, Maître Pathelin, is the very man who has stolen something from him on an earlier occasion. Forgetting the matter in hand, the merchant starts to complain of the lawyer's dishonesty; but the judge intercedes with **Revenons à ces moutons** ("Let's get back to these sheep"). So when people get sidetracked from the central issue, one can say **Revenons à nos moutons** ("Let's get back to the point").

moutonné, -e [mutone] *ADJ* **1** *(ciel)* flecked *or* dotted with fleecy clouds; **roche moutonnée** roche moutonnée **2** **une tête moutonnée** a curly head of hair

moutonnement [mutɔnmã] *NM (de la mer)* frothing; **m. du ciel** dotting of fleecy clouds in the sky

moutonner [3] [mutɔne] *VI (mer)* to froth, to break into white horses; *(ciel)* to become covered with small fleecy clouds

moutonnerie [mutɔnri] *NF* sheep-like behaviour

moutonneux, -euse [mutɔnø, -øz] *ADJ (mer)* flecked with white horses; *(ciel)* spotted *or* dotted with fleecy clouds

moutonnier, -ère [mutɔnje, -ɛr] *ADJ* **1** *Agr* ovine, sheep *(avant n)* **2** *Fig (trop docile)* sheep-like, easily led

mouture [mutyr] *NF* **1** *(version)* version; **ma première m. était meilleure** my first draft was better **2** *Péj (copie, reprise)* rehash **3** *Agr & Culin (des céréales)* milling, grinding; *(du café)* grinding; **si la m. était plus fine** if it were ground more finely; **vous voulez quelle m.?** how would you like it ground? **4** *Fig Vieilli* **tirer deux moutures d'un sac** to profit twice over from sth

mouv' [muv] *NM Fam (abrév* **mouvement***)* **c'est dans le m.** it's dead hip, it's totally cool

mouvance [muvãs] *NF* **1** *(domaine d'influence)* circle of influence; **dans la m. surréaliste** in surrealist circles; **ils se situent dans la m. socialiste** they belong to the socialist camp **2** *Littéraire (instabilité)* unsettledness, instability; **être en m.** to be in a state of flux **3** *Hist* subtenure

mouvant, -e [muvã, -ãt] *ADJ* **1** *(en mouvement → foule)* moving, surging; *(→ cible)* moving **2** *(instable → surface)* unsteady, moving; *(→ terrain)* unstable **3** *(changeant → situation)* unstable, unsettled

mouvement [muvmã] *NM* **1** *(geste)* movement; **faire un m.** to move; **on ne pouvait pas faire un m.** you couldn't move; **ses mouvements sont mal coordonnés** his/her movements are poorly coordinated; **des mouvements gracieux** graceful movements; **un m. de tête** *(affirmatif)* a nod; *(négatif)* a shake of the head; **répondre d'un m. de tête** *(pour dire non)* to answer with a shake of the head; *(pour dire oui)* to answer with a nod, to nod; **elle me fit signe d'entrer d'un m. de tête** she signalled to me to come/go in; **un léger m. de surprise** a start *or* a movement of surprise; **m. vers l'arrière** backward movement *or* motion; **avoir un m. de recul** to start (back); **avoir un m. de dégoût** to recoil in disgust; **des mouvements pour soulager son mal de dos** exercises to relieve backache; **faire des mouvements de gymnastique** to do some exercises; **il y eut un m. dans la foule à l'arrivée du président** a ripple ran through the crowd when the President arrived; **il y eut un m. de foule** a ripple ran through the crowd; **il y eut un m. de foule, et je perdis mon frère de vue** I lost sight of my brother in the crush; **faire un faux m.** to pull something **2** *(impulsion)* **mon premier m. fut de…** my first impulse was to…; **m. de colère** fit *or* burst of anger; **m. d'humeur** outburst (of temper); *Littéraire* **les mouvements du cœur/de l'âme** the impulses of the heart/of the soul; **avoir un bon m.** to make a nice gesture; **allez! un bon m.!** go on, be generous! **3** *(déplacement → d'un astre, d'un pendule)* movement; *(→ de personnes)* movement; *Phys* motion; **surveiller les mouvements de qn** to

monitor sb's movements; **m. rectiligne/uniforme/perpétuel** rectilinear/uniform/perpetual motion; **m. harmonique simple** simple harmonic motion; *Banque* **mouvements de compte** account transactions; *Admin* **m. de personnel** staff transfer *or* changes; **m. de repli** withdrawal; **amorcer un m. de repli** to start falling back; **m. de retraite** retreat; **m. de tenaille** pincer movement; **mouvements de marchandises** movement of goods; **mouvements de troupes** troop movements; *Aut* **m. de caisse** body roll

4 *(évolution → des prix, des taux)* trend, movement; *(→ du marché, des devises)* fluctuation; *Écon* **m. ascensionnel** upward trend; **m. en baisse/en hausse** downward/upward trend; **m. boursier** stock market movement; *Compta* **m. de caisse** cash transaction; *Écon* **m. des capitaux** movement *or* flow of capital; *Bourse* **m. des cours** price fluctuation; *Fin* **m. des devises** currency fluctuation; *Écon* **m. de fonds** movement *or* flow of capital; *Bourse* **m. des valeurs** share movements; **le m. des idées** the evolution of ideas; **les mouvements de l'opinion publique** the trends *or* changes in public opinion; **m. de la population** demographic changes; *Fam* **être dans le m.** to be with it, to be up to date

5 *Pol (action collective)* movement; **m. clandestin** underground movement; **m. consumériste** consumer movement; **m. de contestation** protest movement; **m. de défense du consommateur** consumer protection movement; **m. de grève** strike (movement); **reconduire un m. de grève** to extend a strike; **lancer un m. de grève/révolte** to instigate a strike/revolt; **m. indépendantiste** independence *or* separatist movement; **M. de libération de la femme** Women's Liberation Movement; **M. National Républicain** = right-wing French political party; **le m. ouvrier** the labour movement; **m. pacifiste** peace movement; **m. de protestation** protest rally; **m. séparatiste** separatist *or* independence movement; **m. social** industrial action; **le m. syndical** the *Br* trade-union *or Am* labor-union movement

6 *(animation → d'un quartier)* bustle, liveliness; *(→ dans un aéroport, un port)* activity, traffic; *Rail* **mouvements des trains** train arrivals and departures; *Rail* **chef de m.** traffic manager; **mouvements des navires** shipping intelligence *(UNCOUNT)*; **eh bien, il y a du m. chez vous!** it's all go at your place!; **il aime le m.** he likes change, he likes to move around, he can't stay in one place

7 *Géog* **mouvements sismiques** seismic movements; **m. de terrain** undulation

8 *(impression de vie → d'une peinture, d'une sculpture)* movement; *(→ d'un vers)* flow, movement; *(→ d'une robe)* drape; *(→ de draperies, d'un cou, de reins)* line, lines; *(→ d'un paysage)* undulations

9 *Mus (rythme)* tempo; *(section d'un morceau)* movement; **m. perpétuel** moto perpetuo, perpetuum mobile; **presser/ralentir le m.** to quicken/to slow the tempo

10 *(mécanisme)* movement; **m. d'horlogerie** movement, mechanism *(of a clock or watch)*

❑ **en mouvement** ADJ *(athlète)* moving, in motion; *(population, troupes)* on the move; **cet enfant est toujours en m.!** that child never stops *or* is always on the go!; **c'est une ville toujours en m.** it's a bustling *or* very lively city; **pièces en m.** *(de machine)* moving parts ADV **mettre un mécanisme en m.** to set a mechanism going *or* in motion; **le balancier se mit en m.** the pendulum started moving; **le cortège se mit en m.** the procession started *or* set off

❑ **sans mouvement** ADJ *(personne)* inert

mouvementé, -e [muvmɑ̃te] ADJ **1** *(débat)* (very) lively, heated, stormy; *(voyage, vie, journée)* eventful; *(match)* (very) lively, eventful; **avec eux, c'est toujours m.** there's never a dull moment with them **2** *(paysage)* rolling, undulating

mouvementer [3] [muvmɑ̃te] VT *(compte bancaire)* to balance

mouver [3] [muve] *Can Joual* VT to move■

VI *(déménager)* to move (house)■

►**se mouver** VPR to move■; **mouve-toi!** get a move on!

mouvoir [54] [muvwar] VT *Littéraire* **1** *(bouger → membre, objet)* to move; **mécanisme mû par un ressort** spring-operated mechanism

2 *(activer → machine)* to drive, to power; **mû par l'électricité** electrically driven, electrically powered; **mû par la vapeur** steam-driven

3 *Fig (pousser)* to move, to prompt; **mû par l'intérêt/le désir/la jalousie** prompted by self-interest/desire/jealousy; **mû par la sympathie** moved by sympathy

►**se mouvoir** VPR *(se déplacer)* to move

Moviola® [mɔvjɔla] NF *Cin* Moviola®

MOX [mɔks] NM *Nucl (abrév* **mixte oxyde**) MOX; **combustible M.** MOX fuel

moxa [mɔksa] NM moxa

moxibustion [mɔksibystjɔ̃] NF moxibustion

moye [mwa] NF *Géol* soft vein *or* lode

moyé, -e [mwaje] ADJ *Géol* with soft veins *or* lodes, soft-veined

MOYEN[1] [mwajɛ̃] NM **1** *(méthode)* way, means; **il n'y a qu'un (seul) m. de s'échapper** there is only one way to escape; **il n'y a pas d'autre m.** there's no other way *or* solution; **le ski, c'est le meilleur m. de se casser une jambe!** there's nothing like skiing if you want to break a leg!; **il y a toujours un m. de se faire de l'argent** there are always ways of getting money; **par quel m. peut-on le contacter?** how can he be contacted?; **il y a m. de la contacter par l'intermédiaire de ses parents** she can be contacted through her parents; **j'emploierai tous les moyens** I'll use whatever means *or* do whatever I have to; **nous avons les moyens de vous faire parler!** we have ways of making you talk!; **je l'aurais empêché, si j'en avais eu les moyens** I would have stopped him, if I'd been able to; **trouver un m. de faire qch** to find a way *or* a means of doing sth; **trouver le m. de faire qch** to discover *or* to find out how to do sth; **il a encore trouvé le m. de se faire dispenser** he's managed to get out of it again; *Ironique* **elle a trouvé le m. de se mettre mal avec tous ses collègues** she's managed to get *or* she's succeeded in getting on bad terms with all her colleagues; **et en plus, tu trouves le m. d'être en retard!** not only that, but you've managed to be late as well!; **trouver m. de faire qch** to manage to do sth; **le chien a encore trouvé m. de s'échapper** the dog's managed to escape again; **m. de défense/d'existence** means of defence/existence; **m. de locomotion** *ou* **de transport** means of *Br* transport *or Am* transportation; **disposes-tu d'un m. de transport?** do you have *Br* transport *or Am* transportation?; **m. d'action** means of action; **m. d'expression** means of expression; **ils n'ont utilisé aucun m. de pression** they didn't apply any pressure; **m. de production** means of production; **m. de subsistance** means of subsistence; **employer** *ou* **utiliser les grands moyens** to take drastic steps; **tous les moyens lui sont bons** he'll/she'll stop at nothing

2 *(pour intensifier)* **il n'y a pas m.** it can't be done, it's impossible; **il n'y a pas m. d'ouvrir la porte!** there's no way of opening the door!, the door won't open!; *Fam* **pas m. de dormir ici!** it's impossible to get any sleep around here!; **il n'y a pas m. de le faire obéir!** he just won't do what *or* as he's told!; **j'ai tout fait pour le convaincre, mais il n'y a pas eu m.** I did everything I could to convince him, but it was impossible *or* but I couldn't budge him; *Fam* **je voulais me reposer, mais non, pas m.!** I wanted to get some rest, but no such luck!; **est-ce qu'il y a m. d'avoir le silence?** can we please have some silence around here?; **y a-t-il m. de le faire?** is there any way it can be done?, is it possible (to do it)?; **y a-t-il m. d'éviter le centre-ville?** is there any way of avoiding the centre of town?; **y aurait-il m. de s'arrêter cinq minutes?** would it be possible to *or* could we stop for five minutes?; **y aurait-il m. d'avoir un vol moins cher/d'avoir un peu de pain avec mon fromage?** is there any chance of a cheaper flight/a bit of bread with my cheese?; *Fam* **y'a m.!** can do!

3 *Gram* **adverbe de m.** adverb of means

4 *Can* **avoir le m., être en m.** to be very well-off

❑ **moyens** NMPL **1** *(financiers)* means; **je n'ai pas les moyens de m'acheter un ordinateur** I haven't got the means to *or* I can't afford to buy a computer; **je n'en ai pas les moyens** I can't afford it; **ils ont les moyens** they're well off, they can afford it; **c'est facile d'être généreux quand on a les moyens!** it's easy to be generous when you're well-off *or* when you can afford to be!; **il a largement les moyens de faire construire** he can well afford to build; **j'ai de tout petits moyens** I have a very small income; **avoir de gros moyens** to be very well-off; **je peux te payer une bière, c'est encore dans mes moyens** I can buy you a beer, I can just about manage that; **c'est au-dessus de mes moyens** it's beyond my means, I can't afford it; **vivre au-dessus de ses moyens** to live beyond one's means; **dans la mesure de mes moyens** to the best *or* to the utmost of my ability, as best I can; **moyens de paiement** means of payment; **moyens liquides** liquid resources

2 *(intellectuels, physiques)* **perdre (tous) ses moyens** to go to pieces; **une fois sur scène, j'ai perdu tous mes moyens** once on the stage, I just went blank *or* to pieces; **faire perdre tous ses moyens à qn** to make sb lose his/her head; **faire qch par ses propres moyens** to do sth on one's own *or* unaided; **je suis venu par mes propres moyens** I made my own way here

3 *(pratiques)* **moyens de production** means of production; **moyens de communication** means of communication; **avec les moyens du bord** with the means at one's disposal; **nous avons fait avec les moyens du bord** we made do with what we had; **il faudra faire avec les moyens du bord** we'll have to manage with what we've got; **si tu veux réussir, il faut t'en donner les moyens** if you want to succeed, you have to equip yourself to do so

❑ **au moyen de** PRÉP by means of, with; **il a calé la table au m. d'un ticket de métro** he wedged the table with a metro ticket

❑ **par tous les moyens** ADV by all possible means; *(même immoraux)* by fair means or foul; **j'ai essayé par tous les moyens** I've tried everything

moyen[2]**, -enne**[1] [mwajɛ̃, -ɛn] ADJ **1** *(assez grand, intermédiaire)* medium; **de dimensions moyennes** medium-sized; **être de taille moyenne** *(chose)* to be medium-sized; *(personne)* to be of average height; **les tailles/pointures moyennes** the medium (clothes) sizes/shoe sizes; **cadres moyens** middle-ranking executives, middle managers; **classes moyennes** middle classes; **m. terme** *Phil* middle term; *(solution)* compromise, middle course; **trouver un m. terme** to find a happy medium; **moyenne saison** *(en tourisme)* shoulder period; **à moyenne échéance** in the medium term

2 *(résultant d'un calcul → prix, consommation, distance)* average; *(→ température)* average, mean

3 *(médiocre → aptitudes, niveau, service)* average; *(→ qualité)* average, medium; **ses notes sont trop moyennes** his/her *Br* marks *or Am* grades are too poor; **il est m. en maths** he's average at maths; **la nourriture était moyenne** the food was average; *Péj* **vin d'une qualité très moyenne** very average wine, wine of a very indifferent quality

4 *(ordinaire)* **le spectateur/lecteur m.** the average spectator/reader; **le Français m.** the average Frenchman

5 *Ling (voyelle)* middle; *Mus* **voix moyenne** middle voice

6 *Géog* **le cours m. du Rhône** the middle course of the Rhône

7 *Astron* **temps solaire m.** mean solar time

Moyen Âge [mwajɛnɑʒ] NM **le M.** the Middle Ages

moyenâgeux, -euse [mwajɛnɑʒø, -øz] ADJ medieval; *Hum* **ils utilisent des techniques moyenâgeuses** they use methods out of the Dark Ages

moyen-courrier [mwajɛ̃kurje] *(pl* **moyen-courriers**) NM medium-haul aeroplane

moyen-métrage, moyen métrage [mwajɛ̃metraʒ] *(pl* **moyens-métrages** *ou* **moyens métrages**) NM *Cin* medium-length movie *or Br* film

moyennant [mwajɛnɑ̃] PRÉP (in return) for; **elle garde ma fille m. 20 euros par jour** she looks after my daughter for 20 euros a day; **m. finance**

for a fee *or* a consideration; **faire qch m. finance** to do sth in return for payment *or* for a consideration; **m. paiement** in exchange for payment, subject to payment; **m. quoi** in return for which; **je l'ai aidé à faire son devoir d'anglais, m. quoi il...** I helped him with his English homework, and in return he...

moyenne² [mwajɛn] **ADJ F** *voir* **moyen²**

NF 1 *(gén)* average; **la m. des précipitations/températures** the average rainfall/temperature; **la m. d'âge des candidats est de 21 ans** the average age of the applicants is 21; **calculer** *ou* **faire la m. de** to work out the average of; **supérieure/inférieure à la m.** above/below average, higher/lower than average; **m. de temps entre deux pannes** mean time between failures, MTBF; *Compta* **m. mobile** moving average; *Compta* **m. pondérée** weighted average; **m. des ventes** sales average

2 *Math* mean, average; **m. arithmétique/géométrique** arithmetic/geometric mean

3 *(vitesse moyenne)* **m. (horaire)** (hourly) average; *Aut* average (speed); **faire une m. de 90 km/h** to average 90 km/h

4 *Scol (absolue) Br* pass mark, *Am* passing grade *(of 50 percent)*; *(relative)* average *(Br* mark *or Am* grade); **notes au-dessus/au-dessous de la m.** *Br* marks *or Am* grades above/under half; **j'ai eu tout juste la m.** *(à un examen)* I just got a pass; **la m. de la classe est (de) 8 sur 20** the average *Br* mark *or Am* grade for the class is 8 out of 20; **j'ai 8/20 de m. en mathématiques** ≃ I averaged 40 percent in maths; **j'ai 13 de m. générale** my average *(Br* mark *or Am* grade) is 13 out of 20; **améliorer sa m. de français** to improve one's average *(Br* mark *or Am* grade) in French

5 *(ensemble)* **la m. des gens** most people, the vast majority of people; **d'une intelligence au-dessus de la m.** of above-average intelligence

❑ **en moyenne ADV** on average; **je m'entraîne en m. quatre heures par jour** I train for an average of four hours a day; **c'est ce que la voiture consomme en m.** that's what the car consumes on average, that's what the car's average consumption is

moyennement [mwajɛnmɑ̃] **ADV** moderately, fairly; *Ironique* **c'est m. drôle** it's not that funny; *Ironique* **il a m. apprécié** he didn't find it very funny; *Ironique* **j'ai m. aimé ce qu'elle a dit** I didn't think much of what she said

moyenner [4] [mwajɛne] **VT** *Fam (locution)* **pas moyen de m.** nothing doing

Moyen-Orient [mwajɛnɔrjɑ̃] **NM** **le M.** the Middle East; **au M.** in the Middle East

moyen-oriental, -e [mwajɛnɔrjɑtal] *(mpl* **moyen-orientaux** [-o], *fpl* **moyen-orientales** [-o]) **ADJ** Middle Eastern

moyette [mwajɛt] **NF** *Agr* shock

moyeu, -x [mwajø] **NM 1** *(d'une roue → de voiture)* (wheel) hub; *(→ de charrue)* nave **2** *(d'une hélice)* boss, hub

mozabite [mɔzabit] **ADJ** Mozabite
❑ **Mozabite NMF** Mozabite

mozambicain, -e [mɔzɑ̃bikɛ̃, -ɛn] **ADJ** Mozambican
❑ **Mozambicain, -e NM,F** Mozambican

Mozambique [mɔzɑ̃bik] **NM** *Géog* **le M.** Mozambique; **vivre au M.** to live in Mozambique; **aller au M.** to go to Mozambique

mozarabe [mɔzarab] **ADJ** Mozarabic
NMF Mozarab

Mozart [mɔzar] **NPR** Mozart

---

mozette [mɔzɛt] **NF** mozetta

---

mozzarella [mɔdzarɛla], **mozzarelle** [mɔdzarɛl] **NF** mozzarella

MP3 [ɛmpetrwa] **NM** *Ordinat* MP3

MPEG [ɛmpɛg] **NM** *Ordinat (abrév* **Moving Pictures Expert Group***)* MPEG

MRAM [ɛmram] **NF** *Ordinat (abrév* **magnetic random access memory***)* MRAM

MRAP [mrap] **NM** *(abrév* **Mouvement contre le racisme, l'antisémitisme et pour la paix***)* = pacifist anti-racist organization

MRBM [ɛmɛrbeɛm] **NM** *(abrév* **medium range ballistic missile***)* MRBM

MRG [ɛmɛrʒe] **NM** *(abrév* **Mouvement des radicaux de gauche***)* = left-wing political grouping of local councillors

MRJC [ɛmɛrʒise] **NM** *(abrév* **Mouvement rural des Jeunesses chrétiennes***)* = Catholic youth movement in rural areas

MRP [ɛmɛrpe] **NM** *(abrév* **Mouvement républicain populaire***)* = centre-right political group influential under the Fourth Republic

ms *(abrév écrite* **manuscrit***)* ms

MSBS [ɛmɛsbeɛs] **NM** *Nucl (abrév* **mer-sol balistique stratégique***)* SLBM

MS-DOS [ɛmɛsdɔs] **NM** *Ordinat (abrév* **Microsoft Disk Operating System***)* MS-DOS

MSF [ɛmɛsɛf] **NM** *(abrév* **Médecins sans frontières***)* = organization providing medical aid to victims of war and disasters, especially in the Third World

MSO [ɛmɛso] **NM** *TV (abrév* **multiple system operator***)* MSO

MST¹ [ɛmɛste] **NF** *(abrév* **maladie sexuellement transmissible***)* STD

MST² [ɛmɛste] **NF** *Univ (abrév* **maîtrise de sciences et techniques***)* = master's degree in science and technology; **M. hôtellerie-restauration** = higher vocational qualification in hotel management and catering

MT *(abrév écrite* **moyenne tension***)* MT

MTS [ɛmteɛs] **NF** *Can (abrév* **maladie transmissible sexuellement***)* STD

m.t.s. *Anciennement (abrév écrite* **mètre, tonne, seconde***)* M.T.S.

mu [my] **NM INV** *(lettre)* mu

mû, -ue¹ [my] **PP** *voir* **mouvoir**

muabilité [mɥabilite] **NF** *Arch & Littéraire* mutability, instability

muable [mɥabl] **ADJ** *Arch & Littéraire* mutable, unstable

muance [mɥɑ̃s] **NF 1** *Mus* mutation **2** *Vieilli (à la puberté)* breaking of the voice

mucilage [mysilaʒ] **NM** mucilage

mucilagineux, -euse [mysilaʒinø, -øz] **ADJ** mucilaginous

mucine [mysin] **NF** *Biol* mucin

mucoïde [mykɔid] **NM** *Chim* mucoid

mucopolysaccharide [mykɔpɔlisakarid] **NM** *Biol & Chim* mucopolysaccharide

mucoprotéine [mykɔprɔtein] **NF** *Biol & Chim* mucoprotein

mucopurulent, -e [mykɔpyrylɑ̃, -ɑ̃t] **ADJ** *Méd* mucopurulent

mucor [mykɔr] **NM** mucor

mucoracées [mykɔrase] **NFPL** *Bot* Mucoraceae

mucosité [mykozite] **NF** mucus

mucoviscidose [mykoviskidoz] **NF** *Méd* cystic fibrosis

mucron [mykrɔ̃] **NM** *Bot* mucro, terminal point

mucus [mykys] **NM** mucus

mudéjar, -e [mydeʒar, mydeχar] **ADJ** mudéjar
NM,F mudéjar

mudra [mudra] **NF** mudra

mue¹ [my] **PP** *voir* **mouvoir**

mue² [my] **NF 1** *Zool (transformation → d'un reptile)* sloughing; *(→ d'un volatile, d'un crustacé)* moulting; *(→ d'un mammifère à poils)* shedding hair, moulting; *(→ d'un mammifère sans poils)* shedding *or* casting (of skin); *(→ d'un cerf)* shedding (of antlers); **serin en m.** moulting canary

2 *Physiol (de la voix)* breaking, changing

3 *(dépouille → d'un reptile)* slough; *(→ d'un volatile)* moulted feathers; *(→ d'un crustacé)* discarded shell; *(→ d'un mammifère à poils)* shed hair; *(→ d'un mammifère sans poils)* shed skin; *(→ d'un cerf)* shed antlers

4 *(époque)* moulting season

---

5 *Fig (métamorphose)* change, transformation

6 *(cage → pour volaille)* (hen) coop; *(pour faucons)* mew

muer [7] [mɥe] **VI 1** *Zool (reptile)* to slough, to moult; *(volatile, crustacé)* to moult; *(mammifère à poils)* to shed hair, to moult; *(mammifère sans poils)* to shed skin, to moult; *(cerf)* to shed (its antlers)

2 *Physiol (voix)* to break, to change; **il mue** his voice is breaking

VT *Littéraire* **m. qch en qch** to change *or* to turn sth into sth; **m. sa tête** *(sujet: cerf)* to shed *or* to cast its antlers

▸ **se muer VPR** *Littéraire* **se m. en** to change *or* to turn into

muesli [mɥɛsli] **NM** muesli

muet, -ette [mɥɛ, -ɛt] **ADJ 1** *(qui ne parle pas)* dumb; **m. de naissance** dumb from birth

2 *Fig (silencieux)* silent, mute, dumb; **le ministre préfère rester m. à ce sujet** the Minister prefers to remain silent on this matter; **m. d'admiration** in mute admiration; **m. de stupeur** dumbfounded; **j'écoutais, m. d'étonnement** I listened, speechless with astonishment, I listened in mute astonishment; **il en resta m. d'étonnement** he was struck dumb with astonishment; **m. de colère** speechless with anger; **alors, tu restes** *ou* **es m.?** well, have you nothing to say for yourself?; **elle est restée muette comme une carpe toute la soirée** she never opened her mouth all evening; **je serai m. comme une tombe** my lips are sealed, I won't breathe a word

3 *(non exprimé → douleur, reproche)* unspoken, mute, silent; **les grandes douleurs sont muettes** great sorrow is often silent

4 *Cin (film, cinéma)* silent; *(rôle, acteur)* non-speaking, walk-on

5 *Ling* mute, silent

6 *(sans indication → touche, carte)* blank; **piano m.** dumb piano, dummy keyboard

NM,F *(personne)* mute, dumb person

NM *Cin* **le m.** the silent *Br* cinema *or Am* movies

❑ **muette NF** *Vieilli Mil* **la grande muette** the standing army

muezzin [mɥedzin] **NM** *Rel* muezzin

muffin [mœfin] **NM** muffin

mufle [myfl] **NM 1** *Zool (d'un ruminant)* muffle; *(d'un félin)* muzzle **2** *Fam Péj (malotru)* boor, lout

muflée [myfle] **NF** *Fam* **prendre une m.** to get wasted *or Br* legless; **il tenait une sacrée m.** he was totally wasted *or Br* legless

muflerie [myfləri] **NF** *Fam* **1** *(caractère)* boorishness, loutishness, churlishness **2** *(action)* boorish behaviour; **lassée de ses mufleries** tired of his boorish behaviour *or* boorishness **3** *(parole)* boorish remark

muflier [myflije] **NM** *Bot* snapdragon, antirrhinum

mufti [myfti] **NM** mufti

muge [myʒ] **NM** *Ich* grey mullet

mugir [32] [myʒir] **VI 1** *(vache)* to moo, to low; *(taureau)* to bellow **2** *Littéraire (vent)* to howl, to roar; *(océan)* to roar, to thunder; *(torrent)* to roar; *(sirène)* to wail

mugissant, -e [myʒisɑ̃, -ɑ̃t] **ADJ 1** *(vache)* mooing, lowing; *(taureau)* bellowing **2** *Littéraire (vent)* howling, roaring; *(flots)* roaring, thundering; *(torrent)* roaring; *(sirène)* wailing

mugissement [myʒismɑ̃] **NM 1** *(d'une vache)* mooing, lowing; *(d'un taureau)* bellowing **2** *Littéraire (du vent)* howling, roaring; *(des flots)* roar, thundering; *(d'un torrent)* roaring; *(d'une sirène)* wailing

muguet [mygɛ] **NM 1** *Bot* lily of the valley **2** *Méd* thrush, *Spéc* candidiasis

---

Muhammad [myamad] **NPR** Mohammed

muid [mɥi] **NM** *(futaille, ancienne mesure)* large barrel; *(pour le vin)* hogshead

mulard, -e [mylar, -ard] **NM,F** = cross between a musk duck and a domestic duck

mulassier, -ère [mylasje, -ɛr] **ADJ** mule breeding

(*avant n*); **jument mulassière** mule-breeding mare

❏ **mulassière** NF mule-breeding mare

mulâtre, -esse [mylatr, mylatrɛs] NM,F mulatto

❏ **mulâtre** ADJ INV mulatto

mule¹ [myl] NF **1** *Zool* mule (*female*) **2** *Fam* (*personne entêtée*) mule **3** *Fam Arg drogue* (*passeur de drogue*) mule

---

Allusion

La mule du pape

This expression is a play on the word "mule" in the sense of "slipper" (see next entry). It is used in reference to a tale published by Alphonse Daudet in *Les Lettres de mon moulin* (*Letters from My Mill*), which features an episode in which an apocryphal Pope's mule is cared for by a man who treats the animal very kindly when the Pope is around but starts tormenting the poor beast as soon as the pontiff's back is turned. After an absence of seven years the man is reunited with the Pope and his mule, whereupon the animal, who recognizes its tormentor, gives him a painful kicking. If someone is compared to **la mule du Pape** ("the Pope's mule") it means that they are unforgiving and determined to get their own back, no matter how long after they have been slighted.

---

mule² [myl] NF (*chausson*) mule; **la m. du pape** the Pope's slipper; **baiser la m. du pape** to kiss the Pope's toe

mule-jenny [mylʒeni] (*pl* **mule-jennys**) NF *Tex* mule, mule-jenny

mulet¹ [mylɛ] NM **1** *Zool* mule (*male*) **2** *Fam* (*voiture*) back-up car ▪

mulet² [mylɛ] NM *Ich* mullet; **m. gris** grey mullet; **m. rouge** red mullet

muleta [mulɛta] NF muleta

muletier, -ère [myltje, -ɛr] ADJ **chemin** *ou* **sentier m.** (mule) track; **équipage m.** mule train

    NM,F muleteer, mule driver

mulette [mylɛt] NF freshwater *or* river mussel, naiad, *Spéc* Unio

mulla, mullah [mula] = mollah

Müller [mylɛr] NPR *Physiol* **canaux de M.** Müller canals

mulon [mylɔ̃] NM mulon, salt heap

mulot [mylo] NM field mouse

muloter [mylote] VI *Chasse* (*sanglier, renard*) to mouse

mulsion [mylsjɔ̃] NF *Agr* (*d'une vache*) milking; (*du lait*) drawing

multiaccès [myltiaksɛ] ADJ INV multi-access

multiangle [myltiɑ̃gl] ADJ *Cin* (*plan, scène*) multiangle

multibras [myltibra] ADJ *Tech* multilink; **une suspension m.** multilink suspension

multicâble [myltikabl] ADJ multicabled

    NM multicabled extraction system

multicanal, -e, -aux, -ales [myltikanal, -o] ADJ multichannel

multicantonal, -e, -aux, -ales [myltikɑ̃tɔnal, -o] ADJ *Suisse* involving many cantons

multicarte [myltikart] ADJ (*voyageur de commerce*) = representing several companies

multicast [myltikast] ADJ multicast

multicasting [myltikastiŋ] NM multicasting

multicellulaire [myltiselylɛr] ADJ multicellular

multicolore [myltikɔlɔr] ADJ multicoloured, many-coloured

multiconfessionnel, -elle [myltikɔ̃fɛsjɔnɛl] ADJ *Rel* multidenominational

multicoque [myltikɔk] ADJ **bateau m.** multihull *or* multihulled boat

    NM multihull

multicouche [myltikuʃ] ADJ (*carton, revêtement*) multilayered; (*circuit imprimé*) multilayer (*avant n*)

multicritère [myltikritɛr] ADJ *Ordinat* **recherche m.** multisearch

multiculturalisme [myltikyltyralism] NM multiculturalism

multiculturaliste [myltikyltyralist] ADJ multiculturalist

    NMF multiculturalist

multiculturel, -elle [myltikyltyrɛl] ADJ multicultural

multidevise [myltidəviz] ADJ *Fin* multicurrency

multidiffusé, -e [myltidifyze] ADJ *TV* broadcast by several networks

multidiffusion [myltidifyzjɔ̃] NF multidiffusion

multidimensionnel, -elle [myltidimɑ̃sjɔnɛl] ADJ multidimensional; *Fig* (*expérience, compétence*) multifaceted

multidirectionnel, -elle [myltidirɛksjɔnɛl] ADJ multidirectional

multidisciplinaire [myltidisiplinɛr] ADJ multidisciplinary

multi-écran [myltiekrɑ̃] (*pl* **multi-écrans**) NM *TV* multiscreen, split screen

multiemploi [myltiɑ̃plwa] NM = holding several jobs at the same time

multiethnique [myltiɛtnik] ADJ multiethnic

multifenêtre [myltifənɛtr] ADJ *Ordinat* multiwindow

multifilaire [myltifilɛr] ADJ (*fil*) multicord (*avant n*), multiple-duct (*avant n*); (*antenne*) multiwire (*avant n*)

multiflore [myltiflɔr] ADJ *Bot* multiflora

multifonction, multifonctions [myltifɔ̃ksjɔ̃] ADJ multifunction (*avant n*), multifunctional

multiforme [myltifɔrm] ADJ (*aspect, créature*) multiform; *Fig* (*question, personnalité*) many-sided, multifaceted

multigrade [myltigrad] ADJ multigrade (*avant n*)

multigraphie [myltigrafi] NF *Typ* multigraphy

multijoueur [myltiʒwœr] ADJ multiplayer

multilatéral, -e, -aux, -ales [myltilateral, -o] ADJ multilateral

multilatéralisme [myltilateralism] NM multilateralism

multilinéaire [myltilineɛr] ADJ multilinear

multilingue [myltilɛ̃g] ADJ multilingual

multilinguisme [myltilɛ̃gɥism] NM multilingualism

multilobé, -e [myltilɔbe] ADJ multilobular, multilobate

multiloculaire [myltilɔkylɛr] ADJ multilocular

multimarque [myltimark] NF multibrand

multimédia [myltimedja] ADJ multimedia (*avant n*) NM **le m.** multimedia

multimètre [myltimɛtr] NM multimeter

multimilliardaire [myltimiljardɛr] ADJ multimillionaire (*avant n*)

    NMF multimillionaire

multimillionnaire [myltimiljɔnɛr] ADJ multimillionaire (*avant n*)

    NMF multimillionaire

multinational, -e, -aux, -ales [myltinasjɔnal, -o] ADJ multinational

❏ **multinationale** NF multinational, multinational company

multinationalisation [myltinasjɔnalizasjɔ̃] NF multinationalization

multinévrite [myltinevrit] NF *Méd* polyneuropathy

multinorme [myltinɔrm] ADJ multistandard, multisystem

multipare [myltipar] ADJ multiparous

    NF multipara

multiparité [myltiparite] NF multiparity

multipartisme [myltipartism] NM multiparty system

multipartite [myltipartit] ADJ multiparty (*avant n*), multipartite

multiphasique [myltifazik] ADJ multiphase (*avant n*)

multiplateforme [myltiplatfɔrm] ADJ *Ordinat* cross-platform (*avant n*)

multiple [myltipl] ADJ **1** (*nombreux* → *exemples, incidents, qualités*) many, numerous; (→ *fractures*) multiple; **à usages multiples** multipurpose; **à de multiples reprises** repeatedly, time and (time) again; *Ordinat* **à accès m.** multi-access

    2 (*divers* → *raisons, intérêts*) many, multiple, *Sout* manifold; **personnalité aux multiples facettes** many-sided *or* multifaceted personality; **femme aux talents multiples** multitalented woman; **les causes sont multiples** the reasons are many *or* *Sout* manifold

    3 (*complexe* → *problème, difficulté*) many-sided, multifaceted, complex

    4 *Bot* (*fleur, fruit*) multiple

    5 *Math* **9 est m. de 3** 9 is a multiple of 3

    NM *Math* multiple; **prenez un m. de 3** choose any multiple of 3; **le plus petit commun m.** the lowest common multiple

multiplet [myltiplɛ] NM **1** *Ordinat* byte **2** *Math, Nucl & Phys* multiplet

multiplex [myltiplɛks] *Rad, Tél & TV* ADJ multiplex (*avant n*)

    NM multiplex; **une émission en m.** a multiplex programme; **m. numérique** digital multiplex

multiplexage [myltiplɛksaʒ] NM *Rad, Tél & TV* multiplexing

multiplexe [myltiplɛks] NM multiplex (cinema)

multiplexer [3] [myltiplɛkse] VT to multiplex

multiplexeur [myltiplɛksœr] NM multiplexer

multipliable [myltiplijabl] ADJ multipliable, multiplicable

multiplicande [myltiplikɑ̃d] NM multiplicand

multiplicateur, -trice [myltiplikatœr, -tris] ADJ multiplying (*avant n*); **engrenage m.** step-up gear

    NM *Math* multiplier; **m. de fréquence** frequency multiplier; *Écon* **m. du commerce extérieur** foreign trade multiplier

multiplicatif, -ive [myltiplikatif, -iv] ADJ multiplicative

multiplication [myltiplikasjɔ̃] NF **1** *Biol, Math & Nucl* multiplication; **m. asexuée** monogenesis; *Fig* **la m. des accidents** the increase in the number of accidents **2** *Rel* **la m. des pains** the miracle of the loaves and fishes **3** *Tech* gear ratio; **grande/petite m.** high/low gear; **m. du levier** leverage

multiplicative [myltiplikativ] *voir* **multiplicatif**

multiplicativement [myltiplikativmɑ̃] ADV multiplicatively

multiplicatrice [myltiplikatris] *voir* **multiplicateur**

multiplicité [myltiplisite] NF multiplicity; **la m. des choix qui nous sont offerts** the (very) many choices open to us

multiplier [10] [myltiplije] VT **1** (*contrôles, expériences, efforts*) to multiply, to increase; **m. les erreurs** to make mistake after mistake; **nous avons multiplié les avertissements** we have issued repeated warnings; **le chef de l'État a multiplié les appels au calme** the Head of State has called repeatedly for calm

    2 *Math* to multiply (**par** by); **2 multiplié par 3** 2 multiplied by 3; *Fig* **la production a été multipliée par trois** output has tripled

    3 *Tech* **m. la vitesse de révolution** to gear up

    ▸**se multiplier** VPR **1** (*attentats, menaces*) to multiply, to increase; **les crimes se multiplient** crime is on the increase

    2 *Biol* (*se reproduire*) to multiply

    3 *Fig* to be everywhere (at once); **je ne peux pas me m.** I can't be everywhere at once

multiplieur [myltiplijœr] NM multiplier

multipoint, multipoints [myltipwɛ̃] ADJ (*serrure*) multipoint (*avant n*)

multipolaire [myltipolɛr] ADJ multipolar

multipostage [myltipostaʒ] NM volume mailing

multiposte [myltipost] ADJ multiple-station (*avant n*)

    NM multiple-station computer

multiprise [myltipriz] NF adapter

multiprocesseur [myltiprɔsesœr] ADJ M multiprocessing (*avant n*)

    NM multiprocessor, multiprocessor system

multiprogrammation [myltiprɔgramasjɔ̃] NF *Ordinat* multiprogramming, multiple programming

multiprogrammé, -e [myltiprɔgrame] ADJ *Ordinat* multiprogrammed

multipropriété [myltiprɔprijete] NF time-share, time-sharing; **investir dans la m.** to invest in a time-share; **acheter une maison en m.** to buy a time-share (house)

multiracial, -e, -aux, -ales [myltirasjal, -o] ADJ multiracial

multirécidiviste [myltiresidivist] *Jur* ADJ reoffending

    NMF persistent *or* habitual offender

multirisque [myltirisk] ADJ *Assur* multiple risk (*avant n*); **assurance m.** comprehensive insurance

multirôle [myltirɔl] ADJ multirole

multisalle, multisalles [myltisal] ADJ INV **complexe m.** *Br* multiplex (cinema), *Am* movie theater complex

NM INV *Br* multiplex (cinema), *Am* movie theater complex

multiservice [myltisɛrvis] **ADJ** multiservice

multisoupapes [myltisupap] **ADJ** multivalve

multistades [myltistad] **ADJ** *Chim* **synthèse m.** multistage synthesis

multistandard [myltistɑ̃dar] **ADJ** multistandard, multisystem

multitâche [myltitaʃ] **ADJ** *Ordinat* multitasking, multitask *(avant n)*

multithérapie [myltiterapi] **NF** *Méd* combination therapy, multitherapy

multitraitement [myltitrɛtmɑ̃] **NM** *Ordinat* multiprocessing

multitube [myltityb] **ADJ** *Mil (canon)* multibarrelled

multitubulaire [myltitybylɛr] **ADJ** *Tech* multitubular

multitude [myltityd] **NF 1** *(grande quantité)* **une m. de** a multitude of, a vast number of; **une m. de gens** hosts *or* crowds *or* swarms of people; **il y avait sur la cheminée une m. de bibelots** the mantelpiece was crowded with ornaments **2** *Littéraire (foule)* **la m.** the multitude, the masses

multiutilisateurs [myltiytilizatœr] **ADJ INV** *Ordinat* multiuser *(avant n)*

multivarié, -e [myltivarje] **ADJ analyse multivariée** multivariate analysis

multivibrateur [myltivibratœr] **NM** *Électron* multivibrator

multivoie [myltivwa] *Tél* **ADJ** multiplex **NM** multiplex

mulud [mulud] = **mouloud**

Mumbai [mumbai] **NM** *Géog* Mumbai, *Anciennement* Bombay

mungo [mungo] **NM** mung bean

Munich [mynik] **NM** Munich

munichois, -e [mynikwa, -az] **ADJ** of/from Munich

□ **Munichois, -e NM,F 1** *(personne)* = inhabitant of or person from Munich **2** *Hist* **les M.** the men of Munich

municipal, -e, -aux, -ales [mynisipal, -o] **ADJ** *(élection, conseil)* local, municipal; *(bibliothèque, parc, théâtre)* public, municipal

□ **municipales NFPL** *Pol* local *or Br* council elections

MUNICIPALES

These are the elections where residents choose the town councils. Electors vote for a list of council members whose leader or "**tête de liste**" will become the mayor, a ceremonial and political post.

municipalisation [mynisipalizasjɔ̃] **NF** municipalization

municipaliser [3] [mynisipalize] **VT** to municipalize

municipalité [mynisipalite] **NF 1** *(communauté)* town, municipality **2** *(représentants)* ≃ *(town)* council; **la m.** voulait faire **un parking** the council wanted to build a car park

municipe [mynisip] **NM** *Antiq* municipium

munificence [mynifisɑ̃s] **NF** *Littéraire* munificence

munificent, -e [mynifisɑ̃, -ɑ̃t] **ADJ** *Littéraire* munificent

munir [32] [mynir] **VT m. qn de** to provide *or* to supply sb with; **les visiteurs furent munis de casques** the visitors were provided *with or* given helmets; **munissez les enfants de vêtements de pluie** kit out the children in rainproof clothing; **munie d'un plan de la ville, elle se mit en route** equipped *or* armed with a map of the town, she set off; **muni de ces quelques conseils** armed with this advice; **muni des sacrements de l'Église** fortified with the rites of the Church; **m. qch de** to equip *or* to fit sth with; **la voiture est munie de phares réglementaires** the car is equipped *or* fitted with regulation headlights

▸**se munir VPR se m. de qch** to take sth; **se m. de vêtements chauds/d'un parapluie** to equip oneself with warm clothes/with an umbrella; **munissez-vous de votre passeport** carry your passport *or* take your passport with you

munitionnaire [mynisjonɛr] **NM 1** *Hist (de vivres, de fourrage)* commissary, supply officer **2** *(fournisseur de munitions)* supplier of munitions

munitions [mynisjɔ̃] **NFPL** ammunition *(UNCOUNT)*, munitions; *Hum* **m. de bouche** provisions

Munster [mœstɛr] **NM** *Géog* le Munster

munster [mœstɛr] **NM** Munster (cheese)

muntjac, muntjak [mœtʒak] **NM** *Zool* muntjac, muntjak, barking deer

muon [myɔ̃] **NM** *Phys* muon

muphti [myfti] = **mufti**

muqarnas [mukarna] **NMPL** *Archit* muqarnas

muqueux, -euse [mykø, -øz] **ADJ** mucous

□ **muqueuse NF** mucous membrane; **m. intestinale** intestinal mucus

mur [myr] **NM 1** *(construction)* wall; **il a passé la journée entière entre quatre murs** he spent the whole day shut up inside; **j'en ai marre de rester entre quatre murs toute la journée** I'm tired of being cooped up all day; **après l'incendie, il ne restait plus que les (quatre) murs** only the four walls were left standing after the fire; **les cambrioleurs n'ont laissé que les (quatre) murs** the burglars took everything but the kitchen sink, the burglars stripped the place bare; **je serai dans mes murs la semaine prochaine** I'll have moved in by next week; **c'est comme si tu parlais à un m.** it's (just) like talking to a brick wall; **se heurter à un m.** to come up against a brick wall; *Fam* **faire le m.** *(soldat, interne)* to go or to jump over the wall; *Fam* **tenir le m.** to bum around all day *(because one is unemployed)*; **les murs ont des oreilles** walls have ears; **gros murs main walls; m. d'appui** parapet; **m. aveugle** blank *or* windowless wall; **le m. de Berlin** the Berlin Wall; **m. de clôture** enclosing wall; *Ordinat* **m. coupe-feu** firewall; **m. d'enceinte** outer *or* surrounding wall; **m. des Fédérés** = wall in the Père-Lachaise cemetery in front of which the last remaining defendants of the Paris Commune were executed in 1871; **le m. d'Hadrien** Hadrian's Wall; **le m. des Lamentations** the Wailing Wall; **m. mitoyen** party wall; **m. portant** *ou* **porteur** loadbearing wall; **m. de refend** partition (wall); **m. de séparation** dividing wall; **m. de soutènement** retaining *or* breast wall

2 *(escarpement)* steep slope; **il y a deux murs redoutables sur la piste noire** there are two very steep slopes on the black run; **m. artificiel** rock-climbing *or* artificial wall; **m. d'escalade** climbing wall

3 *Géol* wall

4 *Mines* footwall; **faux m.** wall rock

5 *Fig (de flammes, de brouillard, de pluie)* wall, sheet; *(de silence)* wall; *(de haine, d'incompréhension)* wall, barrier; **les gendarmes formaient un m. devant les manifestants** the police lined up in front of the demonstrators; **le m. de l'Atlantique** the Wall of the Atlantic

6 *Aviat* **m. thermique** *ou* **de la chaleur** heat barrier; **m. sonique** *ou* **du son** sound barrier; **passer** *ou* **franchir le m. du son** to break the sound barrier

7 *Ftbl* wall

□ **murs NMPL 1** *(remparts)* (city) walls; **l'ennemi est dans nos murs** the enemy is within the gates

2 les murs *(d'un commerce)* the building; **il est à présent dans nos murs** *(en visite → dans notre ville)* he is in town at the moment; *(→ dans nos locaux)* he is on the premises at the moment

□ **mur à mur ADJ** *Can Joual* **tapis m. à m.** wall-to-wall carpeting■, *Br* (fitted) carpet■; *Can Fam* **la salle était pleine m. à m.** the room was jam-packed; *Can Fam* **il est fédéraliste m. à m.** he's an out-and-out federalist *or* a federalist through and through

mûr, -e¹ [myr] **ADJ 1** *(fruit, graine, abcès)* ripe; **trop m.** overripe, too ripe; **pas m.** unripe, not ripe; **le blé va être m.** the wheat is nearly ready for harvesting

2 *(personne)* mature; **elle est très mûre pour onze ans** she is very mature for an eleven-year-old; **cette expérience l'a rendu plus m.** he is more mature as a result of this experience; **pas m.** immature

3 *(prêt → révolte, plan)* ripe, ready; **le pays est**

m. pour la guerre civile the country is ripe for civil war; **sommes-nous mûrs pour le mariage?** are we ready for marriage?; **après mûre réflexion** after careful thought *or* consideration

4 *très Fam (saoul)* smashed

5 *Fam (tissu)* worn■

murage [myraʒ] **NM** *(de porte, fenêtre)* walling up, blocking up

muraille [myraj] **NF 1** *(d'une ville, d'un château, de rocs)* wall; **la Grande M. (de Chine)** the Great Wall of China **2** *Naut (de la coque)* side, dead work

mural, -e, -aux, -ales [myral, -o] **ADJ** wall *(avant n)*; **carte murale** wall map; *Archit* **console murale** wall bracket; **peinture murale** mural; **pendule murale** wall clock

□ **mural, -als NM** *(peinture)* mural

□ **mural, -aux NM** *Com* (display) unit

muralisme [myralism] **NM** muralism

muraliste [myralist] **ADJ** mural *(avant n)* **NMF** muralist

Murcie [myrsi] **NM** Murcia

mûre¹ [myr] **ADJ F** *voir* **mûr**

mûre² **NF** *(fruit)* mulberry; **m. sauvage** blackberry, bramble; **m. de Boysen** boysenberry

mûrement [myrmɑ̃] **ADV** **un projet m. réfléchi** a carefully thought-out plan; **après avoir m. réfléchi** after careful thought *or* consideration

murène [myrɛn] **NF** *Ich* moray (eel)

murénidé [myrenide] *Ich* **NM** Muraena

□ **murénidés NMPL** Muraenidae

murer [3] [myre] **VT 1** *(entourer de murs)* to wall in **2** *(boucher → porte, fenêtre)* to wall up, to block up; **m. une fenêtre avec des briques** to brick up a window **3** *(enfermer → personne, chat)* to wall in *or* up

▸**se murer VPR** to shut oneself away; *Fig* **se m. dans le silence** to retreat *or* to withdraw into silence, to build a wall of silence around oneself

muret¹ [myrɛ] **NM** low (dry-stone) wall

muret² [myrɛ] **NM** *Belg Bot* wallflower, gillyflower

muretin [myrtɛ̃] **NM** low (dry-stone) wall

murette [myrɛt] **NF** low (dry-stone) wall

murex [myrɛks] **NM** *Zool* murex

murge [myrʒ] **NF** *Fam* **prendre une m.** to get wasted *or Br* legless; **il tenait une sacrée m.** he was totally wasted *or Br* legless

murger [17] [myrʒe] **se murger VPR** *Fam (s'enivrer)* to get wasted *or Br* legless

muridé [myride] *Zool* **NM** murid

□ **muridés NMPL** Muridae

mûrier [myrje] **NM** mulberry tree *or* bush; **m. blanc** white mulberry; **m. sauvage** bramble (bush), blackberry bush

murin [myrɛ̃] **NM** *Zool* brown bat

mûrir [32] [myrir] **VI 1** *Bot* to ripen; **faire m.** to ripen

2 *(en œnologie)* to mature, to mellow

3 *(abcès)* to come to a head

4 *Fig (évoluer → pensée, projet)* to mature, to ripen, to develop; *(→ personne)* to mature; **elle a beaucoup mûri** she has greatly matured, she has become much more mature

VT 1 *(fruit)* to ripen

2 *Fig (pensée, projet, sentiment)* to nurture, to nurse; **une année à l'étranger l'a mûri** a year abroad has made him more mature; **laisser m. une idée** to give an idea time to gestate

mûrissage [myrisaʒ] **NM** *Bot* ripening

mûrissant, -e [myrisɑ̃, -ɑ̃t] **ADJ 1** *Bot* ripening **2** *(personne)* of mature years

mûrissement [myrismɑ̃] **NM 1** *Bot* ripening **2** *Fig (d'une pensée, d'un plan)* maturing, development

mûrisserie [myrisri] **NF** ripening depot *or* storehouse

murmel [myrmɛl] **NM** bobac, bobak

murmurant, -e [myrmyrɑ̃, -ɑ̃t] **ADJ** *Littéraire* murmuring; **ruisseau m.** babbling brook

murmure [myrmyr] **NM 1** *(d'une personne)* murmur; *Littéraire (d'une source, de la brise)* murmur, murmuring; *(d'un ruisseau)* babbling **2** *(commentaire)* **un m. de protestation/d'admiration** a murmur of protest/of admiration; **il obtempéra sans un m.** he obeyed without a murmur **3** *Méd* murmur

□ **murmures NMPL** *(plaintes)* murmurs, murmurings

murmurer [3] [myrmyre] VI **1** *(parler à voix basse)* to murmur; **les élèves murmuraient en l'absence du professeur** the pupils were chattering during the teacher's absence

2 *Littéraire (source, brise)* to murmur; *(ruisseau)* to babble

3 *(se plaindre)* **m. (contre)** to mutter *or* to grumble (about); **m. entre ses dents** to mutter **4** *(cancaner)* to say things, to talk

VT *(dire à voix basse)* to murmur; **m. des mots tendres à l'oreille de qn** to whisper sweet nothings in sb's ear; **on murmure que...** there is a rumour (going about) that...; **on murmure qu'il va démissionner** rumour has it or there are rumours that he's going to resign

mûron [myrɔ̃] NM *Bot* wild raspberry

murrhin, -e [myrɛ̃, -in] ADJ *Antiq* murrhine

mur-rideau [myrrido] *(pl* **murs-rideaux)** NM curtain wall

Mururoa [myryrɔa] NM Mururoa Atoll; **à M.** on Mururoa Atoll

mus *voir* **mouvoir**

musacée [myzase] *Bot* NF Musa

❏ **musacées** NFPL Musaceae

musagète [myzaʒɛt] ADJ M *Myth* **Apollon m.** (Apollo) Musagetes

musaraigne [myzarɛɲ] NF *Zool* shrew; **m. commune** common shrew

musard, -e [myzar, -ard] *Vieilli* ADJ dawdling

NM,F dawdler

musarder [3] [myzarde] VI *(flâner)* to wander around; *(ne rien faire)* to lounge around

musardise [myzardiz] NF *Littéraire (flânerie)* wandering around; *(oisiveté)* idling

musc [mysk] NM musk

muscade [myskad] NF **1** *Bot & Culin* nutmeg; **fleur de m.** mace **2** *(d'escamoteur)* vanishing ball **3** *(locution)* **passez m.!** hey presto!

muscadet [myskadɛ] NM Muscadet (wine)

muscadier [myskadje] NM nutmeg tree

muscadin [myskadɛ̃] NM *Hist* muscadin; *Arch (dandy)* dandy, fop

muscadine [myskadin] NF muscadine

muscardin [myskardɛ̃] NM dormouse

muscardine [myskardin] NF muscardine

muscari [myskari] NM *Bot* grape hyacinth

muscarine [myskarin] NF *Chim* muscarine

muscat [myska] ADJ muscat *(avant n)*; **raisin m.** muscat grape, muscatel grape; **vin m.** muscatel (wine)

NM *(fruit)* muscat grape; *(vin)* muscat, muscatel (wine)

muscidé [myside] *Entom* NM member of the Muscidae family

❏ **muscidés** NMPL Muscidae

muscinal, -e, -aux, -ales [mysinal, -o] ADJ *Bot* muscoid

muscinée [mysine] *Bot* NF moss, *Spéc* member of the Musci family

❏ **muscinées** NFPL mosses, *Spéc* Musci

muscle [myskl] NM **1** *Anat* muscle; *Fam* **avoir des muscles** *ou* **du m.** to be muscular; **prendre du m.** to develop one's muscles; *Fam* **être tout en m.** to be all muscle; **muscles lisses/striés** smooth/striped muscle *(UNCOUNT)*; **m. antagoniste** antagonistic muscle; **muscles bijumeaux** biceps muscles; **m. cardiaque** cardiac *or* heart muscle; **m. jumeau** gemellus muscle

2 *(vigueur)* muscle, force, punch

musclé, -e [myskle] ADJ **1** *(corps, personne)* muscular; **il est bien m.** he is very muscular, he has well-developed muscles

2 *Fam (énergique)* powerful■, forceful■; **une campagne électorale musclée** a punchy electoral campaign; **mener une politique musclée contre qch** to take a hard line or a tough stance on sth; **l'intervention musclée de la police** the strong-arm tactics of the police; **un régime m.** a strong-arm regime

3 *(vif → style)* robust, vigorous, powerful; *(→ discours)* forceful, powerful

muscler [3] [myskle] VT **1** *Sport* **m. ses jambes/épaules** to develop one's leg/shoulder muscles **2** *Fig (renforcer)* to strengthen

VI *Fam* **le sport, ça muscle** sport builds up your muscles■

▸**se muscler** VPR to develop (one's) muscles; **se m. les bras** to develop one's arm muscles

muscovite [myskɔvit] NF *Minér* muscovite

muscu [mysky] NF *Fam (abrév* **musculation)** body-building (exercises)■; **faire de la m.** to do body-building■, to pump iron

musculaire [myskylɛr] ADJ muscular, muscle *(avant n)*; **fibre m.** muscle fibre

musculation [myskylasjɔ̃] NF body-building (exercises); **faire de la m.** to do body-building

musculature [myskylatyr] NF musculature, muscles; **il a une belle m.** he has a fine set of muscles

musculeux, -euse [myskylø, -øz] ADJ *(athlète)* muscular, brawny; *(bras)* muscular

musculo-membraneux, -euse [myskylomɑ̃branø, -øz] *(mpl inv, fpl* **musculo-membraneuses)** ADJ *Anat* musculomembranous

muse [myz] NF *(inspiratrice)* muse; **invoquer sa m.** to invoke *or* to call on one's muse

❏ **Muse** NF **1** *Myth* Muse; **les (neuf) Muses** the (nine) Muses **2** *Fig Littéraire* **la M., les Muses** the Muse, the Muses; **taquiner la M.** to dabble in poetry, to court the Muse

muséal, -e, -aux, -ales [myzeal, -o] ADJ *(d'œuvres d'art)* Br gallery *(avant n)*, Am museum *(avant n)*; *(des sciences, des techniques)* museum *(avant n)*; **institution muséale** *(d'œuvres d'art)* Br gallery, Am museum; *(des sciences, des techniques)* museum

museau, -x [myzo] NM **1** *Zool (d'un chien, d'un ours)* muzzle; *(d'un porc)* snout; *(d'une souris)* nose **2** *Fam (figure)* face■, mug; **vilain m.** ugly mug **3** *Culin* **m. (de porc)** Br brawn, Am head-cheese; **m. vinaigrette** = brawn in vinaigrette

musée [myze] NM **1** *(d'œuvres d'art)* Br art gallery, Am museum; *(des sciences, des techniques)* museum; **m. des arts et traditions populaires** folk museum; **le m. de l'homme** the Museum of Mankind; *Hum* **c'est le m. des horreurs!** it's a dump! **2** *(comme adj; avec ou sans trait d'union)* **une ville m.** a historical town

muséifier [9] [myzeifje] VT *Péj (quartier, ville)* to museumify

museler [24] [myzle] VT **1** *(chien)* to muzzle **2** *(presse, opposition)* to muzzle, to gag, to silence

muselet [myzlɛ] NM cork wire, cork wiring

muselière [myzəljɛr] NF muzzle; **mettre une m. à un chien** to muzzle a dog

muselle *etc voir* **museler**

musellement [myzɛlmɑ̃] NM **1** *(d'un chien)* muzzling **2** *(de contestataires, de la presse)* muzzling, gagging, silencing

muséographe [myzeɔgraf] NMF museograph

muséographie [myzeɔgrafi] NF museography

muséographique [myzeɔgrafik] ADJ museographic, museographical

muséologie [myzeɔlɔʒi] NF museology

muséologue [myzeɔlɔg] NMF museologist

muser [3] [myze] VI **1** *Littéraire (se promener)* to dawdle, to saunter; *(ne rien faire)* to dilly-dally **2** *Belg (fredonner)* to hum

muserolle [myzrɔl] NF *Équitation* noseband

musette [myzɛt] ADJ INV **bal m.** dance (with accordion music); **orchestre m.** band (with accordions); **valse m.** waltz (played on the accordion)

NM (popular) accordion music

NF **1** *Mus (hautbois, gavotte)* musette

2 *(d'un cheval)* nosebag

3 *(d'un enfant)* satchel; *(d'un soldat)* haversack; *(d'un ouvrier)* (canvas) haversack; *(d'un chasseur)* game bag

4 *Zool* common shrew

muséum [myzeɔm] NM **m. (d'histoire naturelle)** natural history museum; **le M. national d'histoire naturelle** = the Paris Natural History Museum, in the Jardin des Plantes

musical, -e, -aux, -ales [myzikal, -o] ADJ *(voix, événement)* musical; **critique m.** music critic

musicalement [myzikalmɑ̃] ADV musically

musicalité [myzikalite] NF musicality

Musicassette® [myzikasɛt] NF prerecorded (audio) cassette

music-hall [myzikol] *(pl* **music-halls)** NM *(local)* music hall; **le m.** *(activité)* variety, music hall; **numéro de m.** variety act; **faire du m.** to do variety *or Br* music hall *or Am* vaudeville

musicien, -enne [myzisjɛ̃, -ɛn] ADJ musical

NM,F musician

NM *Mil* bandsman■

❏ **musiciens** NMPL *Fam (haricots)* beans■

musicographe [myzikɔgraf] NMF musicographer

musicographie [myzikɔgrafi] NF musicography

musicographique [myzikɔgrafik] ADJ musicographic

musicologie [myzikɔlɔʒi] NF musicology

musicologique [myzikɔlɔʒik] ADJ musicological

musicologue [myzikɔlɔg] NMF musicologist

musicos [myzikos] NM *Fam* muso

musicothérapie [myzikɔterapi] NF musicotherapy

musique [myzik] NF **1** *(gén)* music; **m. de X** music by X; **je mets de la m.?** shall I put some music on?; **ils dansaient sur** *ou* **de la m. rock** they were dancing to (the sound of) rock music; **mettre des paroles en m.** to set words to music; **texte mis en m.** text set *or* put to music; **faire de la m.** *(personne)* to play (an instrument); *(objet)* to play a tune; **lire la m.** to read music; **étudier/dîner en m.** to study/to have dinner with music playing; **faire de la gymnastique en m.** to do exercises (in time) to music; *Can* **faire face à la m.** to face the music; **la grande m.** classical music; **m. d'ambiance** background music; *TV & Cin* **m. d'archives** stock music; **m. de chambre** chamber music; **m. classique** classical music; **m. concrète** concrete music; **m. contemporaine** contemporary music; **m. enregistrée** taped music; **m. en enregistrement numérique** digital music; **une m. de film** a movie *or Br* film theme; **il a composé beaucoup de musiques de film** he has composed a lot of movie *or Br* film scores; **il veut acheter la m. du film** he wants to buy the soundtrack of the movie *or Br* film; *TV & Cin* **m. de fin** playout music; **m. folk** folk music; **m. folklorique** folk music; **m. de fond** background music; *TV & Cin* **m. de générique** title music, theme tune; *TV & Cin* **m. de générique de fin** playout music; **m. légère** light music; *Ordinat* **m. en ligne** online music; **m. militaire** military music; **m. pop** pop music; **m. religieuse** church music; **m. sacrée** sacred music; **m. de scène** incidental music; *Fam* **ça va, je connais la m.** I've heard it all before; *Fam* **c'est toujours la même m. avec lui!** it's always the same old story with him!; *Fam* **en avant la m.!** let's get started!; **la m. adoucit les mœurs** music has charms to soothe a savage breast

2 *(musiciens)* band; **la m. du régiment** the regimental band; **ils entrent dans le village, m. en tête** they come into the village, led by the band

3 *Belg, Suisse & Can* **m. à bouche** harmonica, mouth organ

'**La Musique aux Tuileries**' *Manet* 'Music in the Tuileries Gardens'

musiquette [myzikɛt] NF **on entendait une m.** we heard a simple little tune

musli [mysli] = **muesli**

musoir [myzwar] NM pier-head, jetty head

musqué, -e [myske] ADJ **1** *(parfum, saveur)* musky **2** *Zool* **bœuf m.** musk ox; **canard m.** Muscovy duck, musk duck; **rat m.** muskrat **3** *Bot* musk *(avant n)*; **4** *Arch (poète, style)* affected

mussif [mysif] ADJ M *or* m. mosaic gold, disulphide of tin

mussipontain, -e [mysipɔ̃tɛ̃, -ɛn] ADJ of/from Pont-à-Mousson

NM,F = inhabitant of or person from Pont-à-Mousson

mussitation [mysitasjɔ̃] NF *Méd* mussitation

must [mœst] NM *Fam* must; **c'est un m.** it's a must; **ce film est un m.** this film is compulsory viewing■ *or* a must

mustang [mystɑ̃g] NM mustang

mustélidé [mystelide] *Zool* NM Mustela

❏ **mustélidés** NMPL Mustelidae

musulman, -e [myzylmɑ̃, -an] ADJ Muslim

NM,F Muslim

mutabilité [mytabilite] NF mutability

mutable [mytabl] ADJ mutable

mutage [mytaʒ] NM mutage

mutagène [mytaʒɛn] ADJ *Biol* **agent m.** mutagen

mutagenèse [mytaʒənɛz] NF *Biol* mutagenesis

mutant, -e [mytɑ̃, -ɑ̃t] ADJ mutant

NM,F mutant

mutase [mytaz] NF*Biol & Chim* mutase

mutateur [mytatœr] NM *(gén)* mutator; *(changeur de fréquence)* frequency changer

mutation [mytasjɔ̃] NF **1** *(d'une entreprise, d'un marché)* change, transformation; **industrie en pleine m.** industry undergoing major change *or* a radical transformation; **le secteur sidérurgique a subi de profondes mutations** the steel industry has undergone extensive change *or* changes
 2 *Admin & Jur* transfer; **il a demandé/obtenu sa m. pour raison de santé** he asked for/obtained a transfer for health reasons; *Douanes* **m. d'entrepôt** transfer of bonded goods *(to another bonded warehouse)*
 3 *Biol* mutation
 4 *Ling* **m. consonantique/vocalique** consonant/vowel shift
 5 *Mus* mutation

mutationnisme [mytasjɔnism] NM mutationism

mutationniste [mytasjɔnist] ADJ mutationist
 NM,F mutationist

mutatis mutandis [mytatismytɑ̃dis] ADV mutatis mutandis

mutazilisme [mytazilism] NM Mutazilism

mutazilite [mytazilit] ADJ Mutazilite
 NMF Mutazilite

muter [3] [myte] VT **1** *Admin* to transfer, to move; **il s'est fait m. en province** he's been transferred to the provinces; **ils l'ont fait m. à l'étranger pour étouffer le scandale** they've arranged for him to be transferred abroad to hush up the scandal **2** *(en œnologie)* to fortify
 VI *Biol* to mutate

mutilant, -e [mytilɑ̃, -ɑ̃t] ADJ mutilating

mutilateur, -trice [mytilatœr, -tris] ADJ mutilative, mutilatory; *Fig (expérience)* crippling
 NM,F *Littéraire* mutilator

mutilation [mytilasjɔ̃] NF **1** *(du corps)* mutilation **2** *(d'une œuvre)* mutilation

mutilatrice [mytilatris] *voir* **mutilateur**

mutilé, -e [mytile] NM,F disabled person; **mutilés de guerre** disabled ex-servicemen; **m. du travail** industrially disabled person

mutiler [3] [mytile] VT **1** *(personne, animal)* to mutilate, to maim; **il a eu la main mutilée dans un accident du travail** his hand was badly injured in an industrial accident **2** *(film, poème)* to mutilate; *(statue, bâtiment)* to mutilate, to deface; *(paysage)* to disfigure
 ▶ **se mutiler** VPR to mutilate oneself

mutille [mytij] NF*Entom* velvet ant

mutin, -e [mytɛ̃, -in] ADJ *Littéraire* **1** *(espiègle → enfant)* impish, mischievous, cheeky; *(→ air)* mischievous **2** *Arch (désobéissant)* disobedient, unruly, unbiddable
 NM rebel, mutineer; *Hist* **les mutins de 1917** = the French soldiers who refused to keep on fighting during World War I, following the disastrous offensive of the "Chemin des Dames", some of whom were executed

mutiné, -e [mytine] ADJ mutinous, rebellious
 NM,F mutineer, rebel

mutiner [3] [mytine] **se mutiner** VPR *(marin, soldat)* to mutiny, to rebel, to revolt **(contre** against); *(employés, élèves, prisonniers)* to rebel, to revolt **(contre** against)

mutinerie [mytinri] NF *(de marins, de soldats)* mutiny, revolt, rebellion; *(d'employés, de prisonniers)* rebellion, revolt

mutique [mytik] ADJ mute

mutisme [mytism] NM **1** *(silence)* silence; **observer un m. absolu** to maintain total silence; **s'enfermer dans un m. complet** to retreat into absolute silence **2** *Méd* muteness, dumbness; *Psy* mutism

mutité [mytite] NF*Méd & Psy* mutism

mutualiser [3] [mytɥalize] VT to share among the members

mutualisme [mytɥalism] NM **1** *Zool* mutualism, symbiosis **2** *Écon* mutualism

mutualiste [mytɥalist] ADJ **1** *Biol* symbiotic, mutualistic
 2 *Écon* mutualistic; **société** *ou* **groupement m.** mutual benefit insurance company, *Br* ≃ friendly society, *Am* ≃ benefit society; **pharmacie m.** = chemist associated with private insurance company, which may offer reduced rates on certain items to members of the company
 NMF mutualist, member of a mutual benefit (insurance) company

mutualité [mytɥalite] NF *(système)* mutual (benefit) insurance company; **la m. française** *(ensemble des sociétés mutualistes)* the French mutual (benefit) insurance system

mutuel, -elle [mytɥɛl] ADJ **1** *(partagé, réciproque)* mutual; **responsabilité mutuelle** mutual responsibility **2** *(sans but lucratif)* mutual; **assurance mutuelle** mutual insurance
 □ **mutuelle** NF mutual (benefit) insurance company, *Br* ≃ friendly society, *Am* ≃ benefit society; **prendre une mutuelle** to take out private insurance

---

Culture

MUTUELLE

A "mutuelle" is a non-profit-making health insurance company which provides insurance complementary to that of the "**Sécurité sociale**". Often these companies are set up for a particular profession: there is a "mutuelle" for students, one for teachers etc.

---

mutuellement [mytɥɛlmɑ̃] ADV one another, each other

mutuelliste [mytɥɛlist] *Belg* ADJ *(entreprise, mouvement)* mutualistic
 NMF mutualist, member of a mutual benefit (insurance) company

mutule [mytyl] NF*Archit* mutule

myalgie [mjalʒi] NF*Méd* myalgia

Myanmar [mjanmar] NM *Géog* **le M.** Myanmar; **vivre au M.** to live in Myanmar; **aller au M.** to go to Myanmar

myasthénie [mjasteni] NF*Méd* myasthenia

myatonie [mjatɔni] NF*Méd* myatonia

mycélien, -enne [miseljɛ̃, -ɛn] ADJ mycelial, mycelian

mycélium [miseljɔm] NM mycelium

Mycènes [misɛn] NF Mycenae

mycénien, -enne [misenjɛ̃, -ɛn] ADJ Mycenaean, Mycenian
 NM *(langue)* Mycenaean, Mycenian
 □ **Mycénien, -enne** NM,F *Hist* Mycenaean, Mycenian

mycétome [misetom] NM*Méd* mycetoma

mycobactérie [mykɔbakteri] NF mycobacterium

mycoderme [mikɔdɛrm] NM mycoderma

mycologie [mikɔlɔʒi] NF mycology

mycologique [mikɔlɔʒik] ADJ mycological

mycologue [mikɔlɔg] NMF mycologist

mycoplasme [mikɔplasm] NM mycoplasma

mycorhize [mikɔriz] NF mycorrhiza

mycose [mikoz] NF*(gén)* fungal infection, thrush *(UNCOUNT)*, *Spéc* mycosis *(UNCOUNT)*; *(aux orteils)* athlete's foot

mycosique [mikɔzik] ADJ mycotic

mycosis [mikɔzis] NM *Méd* **m. fongoïde** mycosis fungoides

mydriase [midrjaz] NF*Méd* mydriasis

mydriatique [midrjatik] *Pharm* ADJ mydriatic
 NM mydriatic

mye [mi] NF *Zool* gaper (shell), old maid, *Am* soft(-shell) clam

myélencéphale [mjelɑ̃sefal] NM *Anat* myelencephalon

myéline [mjelin] NF*Physiol* myelin

myélinisé, -e [mjelinize] ADJ*Physiol* myelinated

myélite [mjelit] NF*Méd* myelitis

myéloblaste [mjelɔblast] NM*Biol* myeloblast

myélocyte [mjelɔsit] NM*Biol* myelocyte

myélogramme [mjelɔgram] NM*Méd* myelogram

myélographie [mjelɔgrafi] NF*Méd* myelography

myéloïde [mjelɔid] ADJ*Anat* myeloid

myélome [mjelom] NM*Méd* myeloma

myélopathie [mjelɔpati] NF*Méd* myelopathy

mygale [migal] NF*Entom* tarantula, *Spéc* mygale; **m. aviculaire** bird spider; **m. maçonne** trapdoor spider

myiase [mijaz] NF*Méd* myiasis

mylonite [milɔnit] NF*Minér* mylonite

myocarde [mjɔkard] NM*Anat* myocardium

myocardiopathie [mjɔkardjɔpati] NF *Méd* myocardiopathy

myocardite [mjɔkardit] NF*Méd* myocarditis

myocastor [mjɔkastɔr] NM *Zool* myopotamus, myocastor

myofibrille [mjɔfibrij] NF*Anat* myofibril

myoglobine [mjɔglɔbin] NF *Biol & Chim* myoglobin

myogramme [mjɔgram] NM*Méd* myogram

myographe [mjɔgraf] NM*Méd* myograph

myographie [mjɔgrafi] NF*Méd* myography

myologie [mjɔlɔʒi] NF*Méd* myology

myome [mjom] NM*Méd* myoma

myomectomie [mjɔmɛktɔmi] NF *Méd* myomectomy

myopathe [mjɔpat] *Méd* ADJ myopathic; **il est m.** he has muscular dystrophy
 NMF = person with muscular dystrophy

myopathie [mjɔpati] NF *Méd* myopathy; *(dystrophie musculaire)* muscular dystrophy

myopathique [mjɔpatik] NF*Méd* myopathic

myope [mjɔp] ADJ *Br* short-sighted, *Am* nearsighted, *Spéc* myopic; *Fam* **m. comme une taupe** (as) blind as a bat
 NMF *Br* short-sighted *or Am* nearsighted person, *Spéc* myope

myopie [mjɔpi] NF*Br* short-sightedness, *Am* nearsightedness, *Spéc* myopia; *Mktg* **m. marketing** marketing myopia

myopotame [mjɔpɔtam] NM *Zool* myopotamus, myocastor

myorelaxant, -e [mjɔrəlaksɑ̃, -ɑ̃t] ADJ muscle-relaxant *(avant n)*, muscle-relaxing
 NM muscle relaxant, muscle-relaxant drug

myosine [mjɔzin] NF*Biol & Chim* myosin

myosis [mjɔzis] NM*Méd* miosis, myosis

myosite [mjɔzit] NF*Méd* myositis

myosotis [mjɔzɔtis] NM *Bot* forget-me-not, *Spéc* myosotis

myostatine [mjɔstatin] NF *Biol & Chim* myostatin

myotique [mjɔtik] ADJ*Opt* miotic

myriade [mirjad] NF myriad; **des myriades d'étoiles** myriads of stars

myriapode [mirjapɔd] *Entom* NM myriapod
 □ **myriapodes** NMPL Myriapoda

myringotomie [mirɛ̃gɔtɔmi] NF *Méd* myringotomy

myriophylle [mirjɔfil] NF*Bot* spiky water milfoil

myrmécologie [mirmekɔlɔʒi] NF *Zool* myrmecology

myrmécologiste [mirmekɔlɔʒist] NMF *Zool* myrmecologist

myrmécophile [mirmekɔfil] *Zool* ADJ myrmecophilous
 NMF myrmecophile

myrmidon [mirmidɔ̃] NM*Littéraire* pipsqueak

myrobalan [mirɔbalɑ̃], **myrobolan** [mirɔbɔlɑ̃] NM *Bot* **1** *(fruit)* myrobalan **2** *(arbre)* **(prunier) m.** myrobalan plum (tree)

myrosine [mirɔzin] NF*Chim* myrosin

myroxyle [mirɔksil], **myroxylon** [mirɔksilɔ̃] NM *Bot* Myroxylon, Myrospermum

myrrhe [mir] NF*myrrh*

myrtacée [mirtase] *Bot* NF Myrtus
 □ **myrtacées** NFPL Myrtaceae

myrte [mirt] NM *Bot* myrtle; **m. des marais** bog myrtle

myrtiforme [mirtifɔrm] ADJ*Anat* myrtiform

myrtille [mirtij] NF blueberry, *Br* bilberry

mysidacé [misidase] *Zool* NM opossum shrimp, *Spéc* member of the Mysidacea family
 □ **mysidacés** NMPL Mysidacea

mystère [mistɛr] NM **1** *(atmosphère)* mystery; **entouré de m.** shrouded *or* cloaked in mystery; *Fam* **où est-elle? – m. et boule de gomme!** where is she? – I haven't (got) a clue!
 2 *(secret)* mystery; **cet homme est un m.** that man's a mystery; **j'ai horreur des mystères** I can't stand enigmas *or* mysteries; **ne fais pas tant de mystères** don't be so mysterious; **je ne vois pas où est le m.** I don't see what's so mysterious about it; **si tu avais travaillé, tu aurais réussi l'examen, il n'y a pas de m.!** if you'd worked, you'd have passed your exam, it's as simple as that!; **ça reste un m.** that remains a mystery; **ce n'est un m. pour personne** it's no secret, it's an open secret; **faire un m. de qch** to make a mystery out of sth; **je n'en fais pas (un) m.** I make no mystery *or* secret of it; **les mystères d'Éleusis** the eleusinian mysteries
 3 *Rel* mystery

mut-mys

4 *Hist & Théât* mystery (play); **m. de la Passion** Passion play

5 *Culin* **M.** = ice cream filled with meringue and coated with crushed almonds

mystérieuse [misterjøz] *voir* **mystérieux**

mystérieusement [misterjøzmã] **ADV** mysteriously

mystérieux, -euse [misterjø, -øz] **ADJ 1** *(inexplicable)* mysterious, strange; **la mystérieuse disparition du dossier** the mysterious disappearance of the file; **un crime m.** a mysterious crime

2 *(surnaturel)* mysterious; **une mystérieuse apparition hante le château** a mysterious apparition haunts the castle

3 *(confidentiel)* secret; **les deux présidents se sont rencontrés dans un endroit resté m.** the two presidents met in a place which has been kept secret

4 *(énigmatique)* mysterious; **un m. personnage se tenait près de la porte** a mysterious character stood near the door

NM le m. the mysterious

mysticète [mistisɛt] *Zool* **NM** mysticete

☐ **mysticètes NMPL** Mysticeti

mysticisme [mistisism] **NM** mysticism

mystifiable [mistifjabl] **ADJ** gullible

mystifiant, -e [mistifjã, -ãt] **ADJ** mystifying, deceiving

mystificateur, -trice [mistifikatœr, -tris] **ADJ une lettre mystificatrice** a hoax letter; **avoir un côté m.** to have a mischievous streak

NM,F hoaxer

mystification [mistifikasjɔ̃] **NF 1** *(canular)* hoax, practical joke **2** *(tromperie)* mystification, deception; **m. collective** mass deception **3** *(imposture)* myth

mystificatrice [mistifikatris] *voir* **mystificateur**

mystifier [9] [mistifje] **VT 1** *(duper, se jouer de)* to fool, to take in **2** *(leurrer)* to fool, to deceive; **mystifiés par la propagande** fooled by propaganda

mystique [mistik] **ADJ** mystic, mystical

NMF mystic

NF *Rel* **la m.** mysticism; *Fig* **la m. de la démocratie/paix** the mystique of democracy/peace

mystiquement [mistikmã] **ADV** mystically

mythe [mit] **NM** myth; **elle fut un m. vivant** she was a legend in her own lifetime, she was a living legend

═══◫═══

'**Le Mythe de Sisyphe**' *Camus* 'The Myth of Sisyphus'

mythifier [9] [mitifje] **VT** to mythicize

mythique [mitik] **ADJ** mythic, mythical

mytho [mito] *Fam* **ADJ il est complètement m.** you can't believe anything *or* a word he says

NMF compulsive liar■

mythologie [mitɔlɔʒi] **NF** mythology

mythologique [mitɔlɔʒik] **ADJ** mythological

mythologue [mitɔlɔg] **NMF** mythologist

mythomane [mitɔman] **ADJ** mythomaniac; **il est un peu m.** he has a tendency to make things up

NMF compulsive liar; *Psy* mythomaniac

mythomaniaque [mitɔmanjak] **ADJ** mythomaniac *(avant n)*

mythomanie [mitɔmani] **NF** compulsive lying; *Psy* mythomania

mytiliculteur, -trice [mitilikyltœr, -tris] **NM,F** mussel farmer

mytiliculture [mitilikyltyr] **NF** mussel farming

mytilotoxine [mitilɔtɔksin] **NF** *Chim* mytilotoxine

myxine [miksin] **NF** *Zool* myxine, hagfish

myxœdémateux, -euse [miksedematø, -øz] *Méd* **ADJ** myxoedematous

NM,F myxoedema sufferer

myxœdème [miksedɛm] **NM** *Méd* myxoedema

myxomatose [miksɔmatoz] **NF** *Vét* myxomatosis

myxome [miksom] **NM** *Biol & Méd* mixoma

myxomycète [miksɔmisɛt] **NM** myxomycete

mzabite [mzabit] **ADJ** Mozabite

☐ **Mzabite NM,F** Mozabite

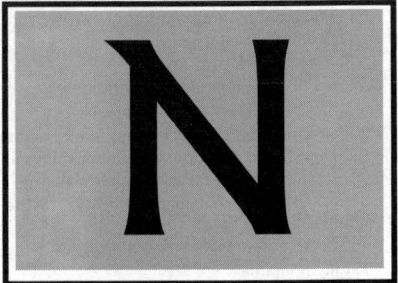

N¹, n¹ [ɛn] NM INV **1** *(lettre)* N, n **2** *Math* n; **à la puissance n** to the power (of) n

N² **1** *(abrév écrite* **newton**) N **2** *(abrév écrite* **nord**) N

n² **1** *(abrév écrite* **numéro**) no. **2** *(abrév écrite* **nano**) n

n' [n] *voir* **ne**

na [na] EXCLAM *Fam* **(et) na!** so there!, and that's that!

nabab [nabab] NM **1** *Fam (homme riche)* nabob **2** *Hist* nabob

nabatéen, -enne [nabateɛ̃, -ɛn] ADJ Nabataean, Nabathaean

NM,F Nabataean, Nabathaean

Nabi [nabi] NM *Beaux-Arts* Nabi; **les Nabis** the Nabis *(group of nineteenth-century painters, including Bonnard and Vuillard, who reacted against impressionism)*

nabi [nabi] ADJ INV *Beaux-Arts* Nabi *(avant n)*
NM *Rel (prophète)* nabi

nable [nabl] NM *Naut* boat drain

nabot, -e [nabo, -ɔt] NM,F *Péj* dwarf, midget

Nabuchodonosor [nabykɔdɔnɔzɔr] NPR Nebuchadnezzar

nabuchodonosor [nabykɔdɔnɔzɔr] NM *(bouteille de champagne)* nebuchadnezzar

nacarat [nakara] *Littéraire* ADJ INV nacarat, orange-red
NM nacarat, orange-red

nacelle [nasɛl] NF **1** *(d'un aérostat)* basket, nacelle, gondola; *(d'un avion)* nacelle, pod; *(d'un landau → détachable)* carrycot; *(→ fixe)* carriage; *(pour un ouvrier)* basket **2** *Littéraire (bateau)* (rowing) wherry **3** *Chim* boat

nacre [nakr] NF **la n.** mother-of-pearl, *Spéc* nacre; **de n.** mother-of-pearl *(avant n)*; **un collier de** *ou* **en n.** a mother-of-pearl necklace

nacré, -e [nakre] ADJ pearly, nacreous

nacrer [3] [nakre] VT **1** *(bijou)* to give a pearly gloss to **2** *Littéraire* to cast a pearly shimmer over

nadir [nadir] NM nadir

nævi [nevi] *pl de* **nævus**

nævo-carcinome [nevokarsinom] *(pl* **nævo-carcinomes**) NM *Méd* malignant melanoma

nævus [nevys] *(pl* **nævi** [-vi]) NM *Méd* naevus; **n. pigmentaire** mole, *Spéc* pigmented naevus

nagaïka [nagaika] NF nagaika

nagari [nagari] NF Nagari

Nagasaki [nagazaki] NM Nagasaki

nage [naʒ] NF **1** *Sport (activité)* swimming; *(style)* stroke; **n. indienne** sidestroke; **n. libre** freestyle; **faire la n. du petit chien** to doggy-paddle; **le 100 mètres quatre nages** the 4 x 100 metres relay

2 *Naut* rowing stroke; **n. à couple** sculling; **n. plate** feathering; **n. en pointe** sweep rowing; **banc de n.** thwart

□ **à la nage** ADV **s'éloigner à la n.** to swim off *or* away; **traverser un lac à la n.** to swim across a lake; **elle gagna la plage à la n.** she swam to the beach

ADJ *Culin* **à la nage** *(cooked in a court-bouillon)*

□ **en nage** ADJ **être en n.** to be dripping with sweat

nageoire [naʒwar] NF **1** *Zool (de poisson)* fin; *(d'otarie, de phoque, de dauphin)* flipper; **nageoires paires/impaires** paired/impaired fins; **n. anale** anal fin; **n. caudale** tail *or* caudal fin; **n. dorsale** dorsal fin; **n. pectorale** pectoral fin; **n. pelvienne** pelvic fin **2** *Aviat (flotteur)* fin

nager [17] [naʒe] VI **1** *Sport* to swim; **n. vers la côte** to swim for the shore; **tu viens n.?** are you coming for a swim?; **il ne sait pas/sait n.** he

can't/can swim; **elle nage très bien** she's a very good swimmer; **n. comme un fer à repasser** to swim like a brick; **n. comme un poisson** to swim like a fish; *Fig* **savoir n.** to know one's way around, to know how to take care of oneself

2 *(flotter → objet)* to float

3 *Fig* **la viande nageait dans la sauce** the meat was swimming in gravy; **il nageait dans son sang** he was bathed in (his own) blood; **n. dans l'opulence** to be rolling in money; **n. dans le bonheur** to be blissfully *or* deliriously happy; **on nageait dans le mystère** we were totally bewildered; *Fam* **tu nages dans ce pantalon!** those trousers are miles too big for you!

4 *Fig Littéraire (vapeurs, nuages, effluves)* to drift

5 *Fam (ne rien comprendre)* to be completely lost, not to have a clue; **il nage complètement en physique** he doesn't have a clue in physics

6 *Naut* to row; **n. à couple** to row double-banked; **n. en arrière** *ou* **à culer** to back water; **n. en pointe** to row single-banked; **n. plat** to feather; **nagez partout!** pull away!

VT **n. le crawl** to swim *or* to do the crawl; **n. la brasse** to swim *or* to do (the) breast-stroke; **n. le 200 mètres** to swim (in) the 200 metres

nageur, -euse [naʒœr, -øz] NM,F **1** *(personne)* swimmer; **être bon/mauvais n.** to be a good/bad swimmer, to swim well/badly; **n. de combat** naval frogman **2** *Naut* rower; **n. de l'avant** bowman; **n. de l'arrière** stroke
ADJ *(animal)* swimming *(avant n)*

naguère [nagɛr] ADV *Littéraire (autrefois)* long ago, formerly; *(il y a peu de temps)* not long ago

nahaïka [naaika] NF nagaika

nahuatl [nawatl] NM Nahuatl

naïade [najad] NF **1** *Myth* naiad; *Littéraire* nymph **2** *Bot & Entom* naiad

naïf, -ïve [naif, -iv] ADJ **1** *(candide → enfant, remarque)* innocent, naive, ingenuous **2** *(trop crédule)* naive, gullible; **ne sois pas si n., il ne te rendra pas l'argent** don't be so naive, he won't give you your money back **3** *Beaux-Arts* naive, primitive

NM,F gullible *or* naive fool; **vous me prenez pour un n.!** what sort of a fool do you take me for?; **jouer les naïfs/les naïves** to act *or* to play the innocent

NM naive *or* primitive painter

nain, -e [nɛ̃, nɛn] ADJ dwarf *(avant n)*; **caniche n.** toy poodle; **poule naine** bantam

NM,F dwarf

NM **1** *(jeu)* **n. jaune** Pope Joan *(card game)* **2** **n. de jardin** garden gnome

□ **naine** NF *Astron* **naine blanche** white dwarf; **naine brune** brown dwarf; **naine rouge** red dwarf

naira [nera] NM *(monnaie)* naira

Nairobi [nɛrɔbi] NM Nairobi

nais *etc voir* **naître**

naissain [nɛsɛ̃] NM *Zool* spat

naissait *etc voir* **naître**

naissance [nɛsɑ̃s] NF **1** *(d'une personne, d'un animal)* birth; **à ta n.** at your birth, when you were born; **donner n. à** to give birth to; **n. multiple** multiple birth; **contrôle** *ou* **limitation** *ou* **régulation des naissances** birth control

2 *(début → d'un sentiment, d'une idée)* birth; *(→ d'un mouvement, d'une démocratie, d'une ère)* birth, dawn; **à la n. du jour** at daybreak; **donner n. à qch** to give birth *or* rise to sth; **prendre n.** *(mouvement)* to arise, to originate; *(idée)* to originate, to be born; *(sentiment)* to arise, to be

born; *Littéraire* **la n. du printemps** the birth of spring; *Littéraire* **la n. du jour** dawn, daybreak, the break of day

3 *(endroit → de langue, d'ongle)* root; *Archit (de pilier, d'arche)* spring; **la n. d'un fleuve** the source of a river; **la n. du cou** the base of the neck; **à la n. des seins** at the top of one's cleavage; **cicatrice à la n. des cheveux** scar just where the hair begins *or* at the hairline

□ **à la naissance** ADV at birth

□ **de naissance** ADV **1** *(congénitalement)* congenitally, from birth; **elle est aveugle de n.** she was born blind, she's been blind from birth; *Fam* **il est bête, c'est de n.!** he was born stupid!; **qu'est-ce que tu es paresseuse! – oui, je sais, chez moi, c'est de n.** you're so lazy! – I know, I was born that way *or* I've been like that since the day I was born

2 *(d'extraction)* **italien de n.** Italian by birth; **être de bonne** *ou* **haute n.** to be of noble birth; **d'obscure n.** of humble birth

'La Naissance de Vénus' Botticelli 'The Birth of Venus'

naissant, -e [nɛsɑ̃, -ɑ̃t] ADJ **1** *(révolte)* incipient; *(sentiment)* growing, budding, *(beauté)* budding, nascent; *(jour)* dawning; **à l'aube naissante** at break of day; **une barbe naissante** the beginnings of a beard; **ses seins naissants** her budding breasts; **il luttait contre cet amour n.** he fought against this growing *or* burgeoning love **2** *Chim (à l'état)* n. nascent **3** *Hér* naissant

naître [92] [nɛtr] VI *(aux être)* **1** *(personne, animal)* to be born; **il naquit/est né en 1880** he was born in 1880; **quand tu es né** when you were born; **je l'ai vu n.** I have known him from birth *or* since he was a baby; **enfant à n.** unborn child; **mon bébé devrait n. en mars** my baby is due in March; **le bébé qui vient de n.** the newborn baby; **une fille lui/leur est née** a girl was born to her/them; **il est né avec un bec-de-lièvre** he was born with a hare-lip; **il est né de parents inconnus** he is of unknown parentage; **il est né de** *ou* **d'une mère hongroise** he was born of a Hungarian mother; **né de parents anglais** born of English parents, of English parentage; **enfant né d'un premier mariage** child born of a first marriage; *Arch & Littéraire* **qui est-elle née?** what was her maiden name?; **elle est née musicienne** she's a born musician, she was born a musician; **je ne suis pas né d'hier** *ou* **de la dernière couvée** *ou* **de la dernière pluie** I wasn't born yesterday; **il est né coiffé** *ou* **sous une bonne étoile** he was born under a lucky star; *Hum* **il n'est pas encore né, celui qui me fera manger des escargots!** the man who can make me eat snails hasn't been born yet!; *Littéraire* **être né l'un pour l'autre** to be made for one another

2 **être né pour** *(être destiné à)* to be born *or* destined *or* meant to; **il était né pour aimer/souffrir** he was born to love/to suffer; **il est né pour être musicien/réussir/diriger** he was born *or* destined to be a musician/to succeed/to be a leader; *Fam* **elle est née pour emmerder le monde** it seems to be her mission in life to get up people's noses

3 *Littéraire* **n. à** *(s'ouvrir à)* to awaken to

4 *(apparaître → sentiment, doute, espoir)* to arise, *Sout* to be born; *(→ peur)* to rise, to arise; *(→ problème)* to crop up *or* to come up; *(→ projet)* to be conceived; *(→ idée)* to originate *(de in)*, to

arise (**de** out of); (→ *communauté, entreprise*) to spring up; (→ *mouvement*) to spring up, to arise; **la légende/l'idée était née** the legend/the idea was born; **une idée naquit dans son esprit** an idea dawned on him/her; **faire n. qch** (*soupçons, sympathie*) to arouse sth; (*doute, espoir*) to give rise to sth; (*sourire*) to raise sth; **son intervention a fait n. une polémique au sein du gouvernement** his/her intervention gave rise to *or* caused much controversy in the government; **n. de** (*provenir de*) to arise *or* to spring from; **cette peur du noir est née du fait qu'enfant il avait été laissé seul** his fear of the dark originates *or* arises from his being left alone as a child; **de là sont nées toutes nos difficultés** that's the cause of all our difficulties; **l'espoir de paix est né de la rencontre des deux présidents** the meeting between the two presidents has given rise to hopes of peace

5 *Littéraire* (*fleur*) to spring *or* to come up; (*jour*) to break, to dawn

6 (*tournure impersonnelle*) **il naît un enfant toutes les secondes** a child is born every second; **il naît plus de filles que de garçons** more girls are being born than boys, there's a higher level of female births than male births; *Fig* **il ne naîtra rien de bon d'une telle alliance** nothing good can come of such a union

naïve [naiv] *voir* **naïf**

naïvement [naivmɑ̃] **ADV 1** (*innocemment*) innocently, naively, ingenuously **2** (*avec crédulité*) naively, gullibly

naïveté [naivte] **NF 1** (*innocence*) innocence, naivety **2** (*crédulité*) naivety, gullibility; **avec n.** naively; **j'ai eu la n. de lui faire confiance** I was naive enough to trust him/her **3** (*remarque*) naive remark

naja [naʒa] **NM** cobra

nambouri [nɑ̃buri] **NM** *Can* (*en acadien*) navel

Namib [namib] *voir* **désert**

Namibie [namibi] **NF** *Géog* **la N.** Namibia; **vivre en N.** to live in Namibia; **aller en N.** to go to Namibia

namibien, -enne [namibjɛ̃, -ɛn] **ADJ** Namibian ❑ **Namibien, -enne** **NM,F** Namibian

Namur [namyr] **NM** *Géog* (*ville*) Namur; **la province de N.** Namur province

namurois, -e [namyrwa, -az] **ADJ** of/from Namur ❑ **Namurois, -e** **NM,F** = inhabitant of or person from Namur

Nana [nana] **NPR** = eponymous heroine of the novel by Émile Zola (1879) who is a symbol both of corrupt sexuality and of the vengeance of the lower class on the upper class

nana [nana] **NF** *Fam* (*femme*) chick, *Br* bird; (*petite amie*) girlfriend■, *Br* bird

nanan [nanɑ̃] **NM** *Fam Vieilli* **c'est du n.!** (*aisé*) it's a piece of cake!, it's a walkover!; (*délicieux*) yummy!

nanane [nanan] **NM** *Can* (*en langage enfantin*) sweetie, *Am* candy

nanar [nanar] **NM** *Fam* **1** (*film*) lousy film, *Am* turkey **2** (*marchandise sans valeur*) junk, trash, garbage

nancéien, -enne [nɑ̃sejɛ̃, -ɛn] **ADJ** of/from Nancy ❑ **Nancéien, -enne** **NM,F** = inhabitant of or person from Nancy

Nancy [nɑ̃si] **NM** Nancy

nandinie [nɑ̃dini] **NF** *Zool* palm civet

nandou [nɑ̃du] **NM** *Orn* nandu, rhea

nandrolone [nɑ̃drɔlɔn] **NF** *Pharm* nandrolone

nanifier [9] [nanifje] **VT** to dwarf

nanisme [nanism] **NM 1** (*d'une personne*) dwarfism **2** (*d'une plante*) nanism

Nanjing [nɑ̃ʒiŋ], **Nankin** [nɑ̃kɛ̃] **NM** Nanking, Nanjing

nankin [nɑ̃kɛ̃] **NM** nankeen

nano- [nano] **PRÉF** nano-

nanoagent [nanoaʒɑ̃] **NM** nanoagent

nanoélectronique [nanoelɛktrik] **NF** *Électron* nanoelectronics (*singulier*)

nanomètre [nanomɛtr] **NM** nanometer

nanophysique [nanofizik] **NF** nanophysics (*singulier*)

nanopublication [nanopyblikasjɔ̃] **NF** nanopublishing

nanorobot [nanorɔbo] **NM** nanobot

nanoscience [nanosjɑ̃s] **NF** nanoscience

nanoseconde [nanosəgɔ̃d] **NF** nanosecond

nanotechnologie [nanotɛknɔlɔʒi] **NF** *Tech* nanotechnology

nanotube [nanotyb] **NM** *Tech* **n. (de carbone)** (carbon) nanotube

nansouk [nɑ̃suk] **NM** nainsook

nantais, -e [nɑ̃tɛ, -ɛz] **ADJ** of/from Nantes ❑ **Nantais, -e** **NM,F** = inhabitant of or person from Nantes

Nantes [nɑ̃t] **NM** Nantes; **l'édit de N.** the Edict of Nantes

L'ÉDIT DE NANTES

Signed in 1598 by Henri IV, the Edict marked the end of the Wars of Religion and guaranteed a number of rights to the Protestant Huguenots, in particular freedom of conscience and the practice of their religion in certain prescribed areas. Its revocation in 1685 by Louis XIV resulted in a brutal repression which caused many Huguenots to emigrate to other European countries.

nanti, -e [nɑ̃ti] **ADJ** (*riche*) affluent, well-to-do, well-off
   NM,F affluent person; **les nantis** the well-to-do

nantir [32] [nɑ̃tir] **VT 1** (*doter*) **n. qn de** to provide sb with; **les fées la nantirent de toutes les qualités** the fairies endowed her with all the qualities; **être bien nanti** to be well off *or* well provided for
   2 *Fin & Jur* (*prêt*) to secure; (*créancier*) to give security to; **n. des valeurs** to deposit shares as security; **entièrement/partiellement nanti** (*créancier*) fully/partly secured
 ▸**se nantir** **VPR** **se n. de** to equip oneself with

nantissement [nɑ̃tismɑ̃] **NM 1** (*objet*) security, pledge **2** (*contrat*) security; **emprunter sur n.** to borrow on security; **déposer des titres en n.** to lodge stock as security; *Bourse* **n. d'actions** lien on shares; **n. de créance** perfected security; *Banque* **n. flottant** *ou* **général** floating charge

nanzouk [nɑ̃zuk] **NM** nainsook

naos [naɔs] **NM** *Archéol* naos

NAP [nap] (*abrév* **Neuilly-Auteuil-Passy**) **ADJ** *Br* ≃ Sloaney, Sloany, *Am* ≃ preppy
   NMF *Br* ≃ Sloane (Ranger), *Am* ≃ preppy type

NAP

Neuilly, Auteuil and Passy are areas in the west of Paris, and are among the wealthiest and most middle-class in the city, although strictly speaking Neuilly is not part of Paris but in the adjoining département Hauts-de-Seine. A "NAP" is typically rich, expensively dressed and politically to the right.

napalm [napalm] **NM** napalm; **bombe au n.** napalm bomb

napée [nape] **NF** *Myth* = nymph of the meadows and copses

napel [napɛl] **NM** *Bot* monkshood, wolfsbane

naphta [nafta] **NM** *Chim* naphtha

naphtalène [naftalɛn] **NM** *Chim* naphthalene, naphthalin

naphtaline [naftalin] **NF** *Chim* (**boules de**) **n.** mothballs; **ça sent la n.** it smells of mothballs; *Fig* it's a bit antiquated; *Can Fig* **sortir qch de la n.** to take sth out of mothballs

naphte [naft] **NM** *Chim* naphtha, mineral oil; **n. de goudron** coal-tar naphtha

naphtol [naftɔl] **NM** *Chim* naphthol

Naples [napl] **NM** Naples

Napoléon [napoleɔ̃] **NPR** Napoleon; **N. Bonaparte** Napoleon Bonaparte

napoléon [napoleɔ̃] **NM** napoleon (*coin*)

napoléonien, -enne [napoleɔnjɛ̃, -ɛn] **ADJ** Napoleonic; **les campagnes napoléoniennes** the Napoleonic Wars

napolitain, -e [napolitɛ̃, -ɛn] **ADJ** Neapolitan
   NM (*dialecte*) Neapolitan
 ❑ **Napolitain, -e** **NM,F** Neapolitan

nappage [napaʒ] **NM** topping

nappe [nap] **NF 1** (*linge*) tablecloth; **mettre/ôter la n.** to lay/to remove the cloth; **n. d'autel** altarcloth
   2 (*couche*) **n. de gaz** layer of gas; **n. de pétrole**

(*souterraine*) layer of oil; (*de marée noire*) oil slick; **n. d'huile** patch of oil; **n. de mazout** oil slick; **n. de brouillard** blanket of fog; **n. d'eau** (*en surface*) stretch *or* expanse *or* sheet of water; (*souterraine*) ground water; **n. de feu** sheet of flames
   3 *Géol* **n. aquifère** aquifer; **n. de charriage** nappe; **n. éruptive** lava flow; **n. phréatique** ground water (table), phreatic layer
   4 *Géom* nappe
   5 *Tex* lap (sheet)
   6 *Tech* **n. d'armature** belt, bracing ply; **n. carcasse** casing ply

napper [3] [nape] **VT 1** *Culin* **n. qch de** to coat sth with; **glace à la vanille nappée de chocolat** vanilla ice cream topped with chocolate *or* with chocolate topping **2** (*recouvrir* → *table*) to cover with a cloth

napperon [naprɔ̃] **NM** (*sous un vase, un bougeoir*) mat; (*sous un plat, un gâteau*) doily; **n. individuel** place mat

naquit *etc voir* **naître**

narcéine [narsein] **NF** *Chim* narceine

Narcisse [narsis] **NPR** *Myth* Narcissus

narcisse [narsis] **NM 1** *Bot* narcissus; **n. des poètes** poet's narcissus; **n. sauvage** *ou* **des prés** daffodil **2** *Littéraire* narcissistic person, narcissist

narcissique [narsisik] **ADJ** narcissistic

narcissisme [narsisism] **NM** narcissism; **tu fais du n.!** you're being narcissistic!

narcoanalyse [narkoanaliz] **NF** *Psy* narcoanalysis

narcodollars [narkodɔlar] **NMPL** narcodollars, drug money

narcolepsie [narkɔlɛpsi] **NF** *Méd* narcolepsy

narcoleptique [narkɔlɛptik] **ADJ** *Méd* narcoleptic

narcose [narkoz] **NF** *Méd* narcosis

narcosynthèse [narkosɛ̃tɛz] **NF** *Psy* narcosynthesis

narcothérapie [narkoterapi] **NF** *Méd* narcotherapy

narcotine [narkɔtin] **NF** *Chim* narcotine

narcotique [narkɔtik] *Pharm* **ADJ** narcotic
   NM narcotic

narcotisme [narkɔtism] **NM** *Méd* narcotism

narcotrafic [narkotrafik] **NM** drug trafficking

narcotrafiquant, -e [narkotrafikɑ̃, -ɑ̃t] **NM,F** drug trafficker

nard [nar] **NM** *Bot & Pharm* nard, spikenard

narghilé [nargile] **NM** nargile, narghile

narguer [3] [narge] **VT 1** (*se moquer de, provoquer*) to taunt, to mock; **il nous nargue avec sa nouvelle voiture** we're not good enough for him now he's got his new car; **ils en ont eu assez de se faire n.** they got fed up with people taunting them **2** (*braver, mépriser*) to scorn, to spurn, to deride

narguilé [nargile] = **narghilé**

narine [narin] **NF** nostril

narquois, -e [narkwa, -az] **ADJ** taunting, mocking

narquoisement [narkwazmɑ̃] **ADV** tauntingly, mockingly

narrateur, -trice [naratœr, -tris] **NM,F** narrator

narratif, -ive [naratif, -iv] **ADJ** narrative

narration [narasjɔ̃] **NF 1** (*exposé*) narrative, narration **2** (*partie du discours*) narration

narrative [narativ] *voir* **narratif**

narratrice [naratris] *voir* **narrateur**

narrer [3] [nare] **VT** *Littéraire* (*conte*) to narrate, to tell; (*événements*) to narrate, to relate

narse [nars] **NF** (*dans le Massif central* → *fondrière*) peat bog; (→ *marécage*) marsh

narthex [nartɛks] **NM** *Archit* narthex

narval, -als [narval] **NM** *Zool* narwhal, narwal

NASA, Nasa [naza] **NF** (*abrév* **National Aeronautics and Space Administration**) NASA, Nasa

nasal, -e, -aux, -ales [nazal, -o] **ADJ** nasal
 ❑ **nasale** **NF** *Ling* nasal

nasalisation [nazalizasjɔ̃] **NF** *Ling* nasalization

nasaliser [3] [nazalize] **VT** *Ling* to nasalize

nasalité [nazalite] **NF** *Ling* nasality

nasard [nazar] **NM** *Mus* nasard

nasarde [nazard] **NF** *Littéraire & Vieilli* flick *or* fillip on the nose

Nasdaq® [nasdak] **NM** *Écon* (*abrév* **National Association of Securities Dealers Automated Quotation**) Nasdaq®

nase¹ [naz] *Fam* **ADJ 1** (*épuisé*) *Br* knackered,

shattered, *Am* bushed, beat **2** *(hors d'usage)* kaput, bust, *Br* clapped-out **3** *(stupide)* thick, dense, *Am* dumb **4** *(de mauvaise qualité)* crap, crappy, lousy

NMF *(personne stupide)* idiot, *Am* jerk; **c'est un n., ce mec** this guy's hopeless, *Br* this guy's bloody useless

NM *(nez)* conk

nase[2] [naz] **NM** *Ich* beaked carp, nose carp

naseau, -x [nazo] **NM** *Zool* nostril; *Fam* **naseaux** *(nez)* hooter

nasillard, -e [nazijar, -ard] **ADJ** *(ton)* nasal; *(radio, haut-parleur)* tinny; **parler d'une voix nasillarde** to talk through one's nose *or* with a (nasal) twang

nasillement [nazijmɑ̃] **NM 1** *(d'une voix)* (nasal) twang; *(d'un haut-parleur)* tinny sound **2** *(d'un canard)* quacking

nasiller [3] [nazije] **VI 1** *(personne)* to speak with a (nasal) twang; *(radio)* to have a tinny sound **2** *(canard)* to quack

nasilleur, -euse [nazijœr, -øz] **NM,F** = person who speaks with a (nasal) twang

nasique [nazik] **NM** *Zool* proboscis monkey

nasitort [nazitɔr] **NM** *Bot* garden cress, golden cress

nasonnement [nazɔnmɑ̃] **NM** *Méd* open rhinolalia, rhinolalia aperta

nasse [nas] **NF 1** *Pêche* (conical) lobster pot **2** *(pour oiseaux)* hoop net **3** *Zool (mollusque)* dog whelk **4** *Fig* **tomber dans la n.** to fall into the trap

Nasser [nasɛr] *voir* **lac**

nastie [nasti] **NF** *Bot* nastic movement

Natal [natal] **NM** *Anciennement* **le N.** Natal

natal, -e, -als, -ales [natal] **ADJ** *(pays, ville)* native; **sa maison natale** the house where he/she was born

nataliste [natalist] **ADJ politique n.** policy to increase the birth rate

natalité [natalite] **NF** birth rate, *Am* natality; **forte/faible n.** high/low birth rate; **courbe de n.** birth-rate curve

natation [natasjɔ̃] **NF** swimming; **club de n.** swimming club; **faire de la n.** to swim; **n. synchronisée** *ou* **artistique** synchronized swimming

natatoire [natatwar] **ADJ** swimming *(avant n)*, *Spéc* natatory

Natel® [natɛl] **NM INV** *Suisse (abrév* **national Telefon***) Br* mobile (phone), *Am* cellphone

Nathan [natɑ̃] **NPR** *Bible* Nathan

natice [natis] **NF** *Zool* natica

natif, -ive [natif, -iv] **ADJ 1** *(originaire)* native; **je suis n. de Paris/Pologne** I was born in Paris/Poland **2** *Littéraire (inné)* native **3** *Métal* native

NM,F native

nation [nasjɔ̃] **NF** nation; **n. commerçante** mercantile nation; **n. la plus favorisée** most favoured nation; **les Nations unies** the United Nations; **n. en voie de développement** developing nation

national, -e, -aux, -ales [nasjɔnal, -o] **ADJ 1** *(de la nation)* national; **équipe nationale de football** national football team; **l'économie nationale** the domestic economy; **funérailles** *ou* **obsèques nationales** state funeral; **la presse nationale en a parlé** the national newspapers *or* the nationals carried stories about it; *Hum* **notre Victor n.** good old Victor (Hugo) **2** *(nationaliste → parti, politique)* nationalist

❑ **nationale NF** *Br* ≃ A road, *Am* ≃ interstate highway

❑ **nationaux NMPL** nationals

nationalisation [nasjɔnalizasjɔ̃] **NF** nationalization

nationalisé, -e [nasjɔnalize] **ADJ** nationalized

nationaliser [3] [nasjɔnalize] **VT** to nationalize

nationalisme [nasjɔnalism] **NM** nationalism

nationaliste [nasjɔnalist] **ADJ** nationalist, nationalistic

NMF nationalist

nationalité [nasjɔnalite] **NF** nationality; **être de n. française/nigériane** to be French/Nigerian; **quelle est sa n., de quelle n. est-il?** what nationality is he?; **les personnes de n. française** people of French nationality, French nationals

national-populisme [nasjɔnalpɔpylism] **NM** national populism

national-socialisme [nasjɔnalsɔsjalism] **NM** National Socialism

national-socialiste [nasjɔnalsɔsjalist] *(pl* **nationaux-socialistes** [nasjɔnosɔsjalist]) **ADJ** National Socialist

NMF National Socialist

native [nativ] *voir* **natif**

nativisme [nativism] **NM** *Phil* nativism

nativiste [nativist] *Phil & Psy* **ADJ** nativistic

NMF nativist

nativité [nativite] **NF 1** *Rel* **la N.** the Nativity **2** *Beaux-Arts* Nativity scene; **une n.** a nativity

'Nativité mystique' *Botticelli* 'Mystic Nativity'

natoufien, -enne [natufjɛ̃, -ɛn] **ADJ** Natufian

NM Natufian

natrémie [natremi] **NF** normal amount of sodium in the blood

natron [natrɔ̃], **natrum** [natrɔm] **NM** *Chim* natron

nattage [nataʒ] **NM 1** *(de cheveux)* braiding, plaiting **2** *(de fils, d'osier)* plaiting, weaving

natte [nat] **NF 1** *(tapis de paille)* (straw *or* rush) mat **2** *(de cheveux) Br* plait, *Am* braid; **porter des nattes** to wear one's hair in *Br* plaits *or Am* braids, to have *Br* plaits *or Am* braids; **porter** *ou* **avoir une n.** to have a *Br* plait *or Am* braid; **n. africaine** French plait

natter [3] [nate] **VT 1** *(cheveux) Br* to plait, *Am* to braid **2** *(fils, osier)* to plait, to weave, to interweave **3** *(mur)* to cover with mats

nattier, -ère [natje, -ɛr] **NM,F** = person who makes straw or rush mats

naturalisation [natyralizasjɔ̃] **NF 1** *Admin, Bot & Ling* naturalization **2** *(empaillage)* stuffing

naturalisé, -e [natyralize] **ADJ** naturalized; **il a été n. américain** he was granted US citizenship

NM,F naturalized person

naturaliser [3] [natyralize] **VT 1** *Admin* to naturalize; **il s'est fait n. français** he was granted French citizenship **2** *Bot & Ling* to naturalize **3** *(empailler)* to stuff

naturalisme [natyralism] **NM** naturalism

naturaliste [natyralist] **ADJ** naturalistic

NMF 1 *Bot & Zool* naturalist **2** *(empailleur)* taxidermist

NATURE [natyr]

> **NF** nature **1–3, 5** ■ country(side) **2** ■ type, sort **4, 5** ■ life **6**
> **ADJ INV** plain **1** ■ natural **2**

NF 1 *(univers naturel)* **la n.** nature; **les lois de la n.** the laws of nature; **à l'état de n.** in the natural state; **la n. fait bien les choses** nature works wonders; **laisser faire** *ou* **agir la n.** to let nature take its course; **je fais plus confiance à la n. qu'à la médecine** I trust nature *or* natural remedies more than medical science; **des formes qui n'existent pas dans la n.** shapes which do not occur in nature; **la n. a horreur du vide** nature abhors a vacuum

2 *(campagne)* **la n.** nature, the country, the countryside; **la n. me manque** I miss the countryside; **une n. luxuriante s'offrit à nos yeux** a luxuriant landscape opened up before us; **elle vit quelque part en pleine n.** she lives somewhere right out in the countryside; **tomber en panne en pleine n.** to break down in the middle of nowhere; **une maison perdue dans la n.** a house out in the wilds; **se promener dans la n.** to go for a walk in the country; *Fig* **disparaître** *ou* **s'évanouir dans la n.** to vanish into thin air; **il n'a pourtant pas disparu dans la n., ce piano!** that piano can't just have walked off *or* vanished!; *Fam* **partir dans la n.** to run into a ditch/a field■; *Fig* **la voiture a fait une embardée et ils se sont retrouvés dans la n.** the car swerved and they ended up in a ditch

3 *(caractère)* nature; **la n. du sol** the nature of the soil; **être d'une n. douce** to have a gentle nature; **ce n'est pas dans sa n.** it's not like him/her, it's not in his/her nature; **ce** *ou* **il n'est pas dans sa n. d'être aussi agressive** it's not like her *or* it's not in her nature to be so aggressive; **c'est dans la n. des choses** it's in the nature of things, that's the way the world is; **il est dans la n. des choses qu'un fils se heurte à son père** it's in the nature of things for a son to clash with his father; **la n. humaine** human nature

4 *(type de personne)* type, sort; **une bonne n.** a good sort; **une heureuse n.** a happy person; **c'est une n. violente** he's/she's a violent sort; **c'est une petite n.** he's/she's a bit feeble

5 *(sorte)* nature, type, sort; **un programme de cette n.** a programme of this kind *or* nature; **les raisonnements de cette n.** this kind of argument, arguments of this kind; **quelle est la n. de la fuite?** what kind of leak is it?

6 *(réalité)* **plus grand que n.** larger than life; *Beaux-Arts* **d'après n.** from life; *Beaux-Arts* **n. morte** still life

ADJ INV 1 *(bœuf, choucroute)* plain, with no trimmings; *(salade, avocat)* plain, with no dressing; *(vin)* still; **riz n.** (plain) boiled rice

2 *Fam (simple)* natural■; **j'aime qu'une fille soit n.** I like a girl to be natural; **les enfants sont n.** children are so natural

❑ **contre nature ADJ** against nature, unnatural; **des sentiments/penchants contre n.** unnatural feelings/leanings; **c'est contre n.** it's not natural, it goes against nature

❑ **de nature ADV** by nature; **il est généreux de n.** he's generous by nature, it's (in) his nature to be generous; **elle est anxieuse de n.** she's the worrying kind *or* anxious type

❑ **de nature à CONJ** likely *or* liable to; **une découverte de n. à révolutionner la science** a discovery likely to revolutionize science; **ce genre de détail n'est pas de n. à les inquiéter** that kind of detail is unlikely to bother them; **je ne suis pas de n. à me laisser faire** I'm not the kind *or* type of person you can push around; **ce discours n'est pas de n. à apaiser les esprits** this speech is hardly going to calm people down

❑ **de toute nature ADJ** of all kinds *or* types; **il y avait des arbustes de toute n.** there were all sorts of shrubs

❑ **en nature ADV** in kind; *aussi Fig* **payer en n.** to pay in kind

❑ **par nature ADV je suis conservateur par n.** I'm naturally conservative, I'm conservative by nature

naturel, -elle [natyrɛl] **ADJ 1** *(du monde physique → phénomène, ressource, frontière)* natural

2 *(physiologique → fonction, processus)* natural, bodily; **les défenses naturelles de l'organisme** the body's natural defences

3 *(inné → disposition, talent)* natural, inborn; *(→ boucles, blondeur)* natural; **il a une grâce naturelle** he is naturally graceful; **ce n'est pas ma couleur naturelle** it's not my natural *or* real hair colour

4 *(sans affectation)* natural; **tu n'as pas l'air n. sur cette photo** you don't look natural in this photograph; **être n.** to be oneself

5 *(normal)* natural; **son inquiétude est tout à fait naturelle** it's only natural that he should be worried; **c'est bien** *ou* **tout n. que je t'aide** it's only natural that I should help you; **je vous remercie – je vous en prie, c'est tout n.!** thank you – please don't mention it, it's the least I could do!; **trouver n. de faire qch** to think nothing of doing sth

6 *(pur → fibre)* pure; *(→ nourriture)* natural; *Com* natural, organic; **soie naturelle** *(sur l'étiquette d'un vêtement)* pure *or* 100% silk

7 *Ling, Mus, Phil & Rel* natural

8 *(illégitime)* natural; **il était le fils n. du roi** he was the natural son of the king

NM 1 *(tempérament)* nature; **elle est d'un n. généreux/peureux/jaloux** she has a generous/timid/jealous nature, she is generous/timid/jealous by nature; **il est d'un n. anxieux** he's the worrying kind, it's (in) his nature to worry; **être d'un bon n.** to be good-natured

2 *(authenticité)* naturalness; **manque de n.** affectation, artificiality; **ce que j'aime chez elle, c'est son n.** what I like about her is she's so natural; **avec n.** naturally; **avec beaucoup de n.** with perfect ease, completely naturally; **elle est mieux au n. qu'à la télévision** she's better in real life than on TV

❑ **au naturel ADJ 1** *Culin* plain; **poires au n.** pears in natural fruit juice

2 *Beaux-Arts* **peindre qch au n.** to paint sth from life

naturellement [natyrɛlmɑ̃] **ADV 1** *(de façon innée)* naturally; **n. timide** naturally shy, shy by nature; **ça lui vient n.** it comes naturally to him/her

2 *(simplement)* naturally, unaffectedly; **c'est le plus n. du monde qu'on nous a reçus** they welcomed us as if it were the most natural thing in the world

3 *(bien sûr)* naturally, of course; **vous viendrez? – n.!** will you be coming? – naturally or of course I will!

4 *Littéraire* frankly, sincerely

naturisme [natyrism] **NM 1** *(nudisme)* naturism; **adepte du n.** naturist, nudist **2** *Méd* naturopathy **3** *Beaux-Arts, Littérature, Phil & Rel* naturalism

naturiste [natyrist] **ADJ 1** *(nudiste)* naturist; **centre n.** nudist colony or camp **2** *Beaux-Arts, Littérature & Phil* naturalist, naturalistic

NMF 1 *(nudiste)* naturist, nudist **2** *Beaux-Arts, Littérature & Phil* naturalist

naturopathe [natyrɔpat] **NMF** naturopath

naturopathie [natyrɔpati], **naturothérapie** [natyrɔterapi] **NF** naturopathy

naucore [nokɔr] **NF** *Entom* naucorid, water creeper

naufrage [nofraʒ] **NM 1** *(d'un navire)* wreck, shipwreck; **faire n.** *(personne)* to be shipwrecked; *(navire)* to be wrecked; **périr dans un n.** to be lost at sea; **lors du n. du Titanic** when the Titanic sank; **le n. du Manureva demeure un mystère** the sinking of the Manureva remains a mystery

2 *Fig (ruine)* ruin, wreckage; *(d'entreprise)* failure; **faire n.** *(entreprise, mariage)* to fail, to collapse; **on a assisté au n. de grandes fortunes pendant la guerre** great fortunes were lost during the war

naufragé, -e [nofraʒe] **ADJ** *(personne → gén)* shipwrecked; *(→ sur une île)* castaway *(avant n)*; *(navire)* wrecked

NM,F *(gén)* shipwreck victim; *(sur une île)* castaway

naufrager [17] [nofraʒe] **VI** *(personne)* to be shipwrecked; *(navire)* to be wrecked

naufrageur, -euse [nofraʒœr, -øz] **NM,F** *aussi Fig* wrecker; **bateau n.** wrecker

naumachie [nomaʃi] **NF** *Antiq* naumachy

naupathie [nopati] **NF** *Méd* seasickness

nauplius [noplijys] **NM** nauplius

nauséabond, -e [nozeabɔ̃, -ɔ̃d] **ADJ 1** *(qui sent mauvais)* putrid, foul, foul-smelling; *(personne, pièce)* foul-smelling **2** *Fig (répugnant)* nauseating, sickening, nauseous

nausée [noze] **NF 1** *(envie de vomir)* nausea; **avoir la n.** to feel sick; **avoir des nausées** *(gén)* to have bouts of sickness; *(femme enceinte)* to have morning sickness; **donner la n. (à)** to nauseate; **à vous donner la n.** *(odeurs, images)* nauseating **2** *Fig (dégoût)* **une telle hypocrisie me donne la n.** such hypocrisy makes me sick; **jusqu'à la n.** ad nauseam

'La Nausée' Sartre 'Nausea'

nauséeux, -euse [nozeø, -øz] **ADJ 1** *(odeur)* nauseating, sickening, repulsive; *(état)* nauseous; **se sentir n.** to feel sick or nauseous **2** *Fig Littéraire (révoltant)* nauseating, sickening, repulsive

Nausicaa [nozikaa] **NPR** *Myth* Nausicaa

nautile [notil] **NM** *Zool* nautilus

nautique [notik] **ADJ** nautical; **carte/géographie n.** nautical map/geography; **le salon n.** ≃ the Boat Show

nautisme [notism] **NM** water sports, aquatics *(singulier)*

nautonier [notɔnje] **NM** *Littéraire* pilot, mariner; **le n. des enfers** the boatman of the underworld

navaja [navaʒa] **NF** navaja

Navajos [navaro] **NMPL les N.** the Navajo(s)

naval, -e, -als, -ales [naval] **ADJ** naval; **architecture navale** naval architecture; **construction navale** shipbuilding (industry)

❑ **Navale NF** *Fam* **faire Navale** ≃ to attend naval college

navalisation [navalizasjɔ̃] **NF** navalization

navarin [navarɛ̃] **NM** navarin *(mutton and vegetable stew)*

navarque [navark] **NM** *Antiq* navarch

Navarre [navar] **NF la N.** Navarre

naveau, -x [navo] **NM** *Can Fam (navet)* turnip ▪; *Fig (crâne chauve)* bald head ▪; *(nigaud)* naive or gormless person ▪

navel [navɛl] **NF** navel orange

navet [navɛ] **NM 1** *Bot* turnip; **n. fourrager** fodder beet **2** *Fam (œuvre)* **c'est un n.** it's (a load of) nonsense or *Br* rubbish; *(film)* it's a lousy movie or *Br* film, *Am* it's a turkey

navette¹ [navɛt] **NF 1** *Aviat & Transp* shuttle; **faire la n. (entre)** to shuttle back and forth or to and fro *(between)*; **un bus fait la n. entre la gare et l'aéroport** there is a shuttle bus *(service)* between the station and the airport; **il fait la n. entre Paris et Marseille** he comes and goes or goes to and fro between Paris and Marseilles; **n. de transfert** transfer bus; **n. gratuite** courtesy bus; **la n. parlementaire** = successive readings of bills by the "Assemblée nationale" and the "Sénat"

2 *(fusée)* **n. (spatiale)** (space) shuttle

3 *Rel* incense holder

4 *Tex* shuttle; *(aiguille → pour filets)* netting or meshing needle; **n. volante** flying shuttle

navette² [navɛt] **NF** *Bot* rape

navetteur, -euse [navɛtœr, -øz] **NM,F** *Belg* commuter

navicert [navisɛr] **NM** navicert

naviculaire [navikylɛr] **ADJ** *Anat* navicular

navicule [navikyl] **NF** *Biol* navicula

navigabilité [navigabilite] **NF 1** *(d'un cours d'eau)* navigability, navigableness **2** **(état de) n.** *Naut* seaworthiness; *Aviat* airworthiness; **en état de n.** *Naut* seaworthy; *Aviat* airworthy

navigable [navigabl] **ADJ** *(cours d'eau)* navigable

navigant, -e [navigɑ̃, -ɑ̃t] **ADJ** *Naut* seafaring; *Aviat* **personnel n.** flight personnel, aircrew, crew

NM,F les navigants *Naut* the crew; *Aviat* the aircrew, the crew

navigateur, -trice [navigatœr, -tris] **NM,F 1** *Naut (voyageur)* sailor, seafarer; *(membre de l'équipage)* navigator; **n. solitaire** single-handed yachtsman **2** *Aviat* navigator, copilot *(in charge of navigation)* **3** *Aut* navigator

NM 1 *(appareil)* navigator; **n. decca** Decca® (navigator) **2** *Ordinat* browser

ADJ M seafaring, seagoing

navigation [navigasjɔ̃] **NF 1** *Naut* navigation, sailing; **la n. est dangereuse ici** sailing is dangerous or it's dangerous to sail around here; **interdit à la n.** *(des gros bateaux)* closed to shipping; *(des petits bateaux)* no sailing or boating; **ouvert à la n.** *(des gros bateaux)* open to shipping; **après un mois de n.** after a month at sea; **n. côtière** coastal navigation; **n. à l'estime** navigation by dead reckoning; **n. extérieure** high seas navigation; **n. fluviale** inland navigation; **n. intérieure** inland navigation; **n. au long cours** deep-sea or ocean navigation; **n. maritime** high seas navigation; **n. de plaisance** yachting, pleasure sailing; **n. à voile** sailing

2 *Aviat* navigation, flying; **n. aérienne** aerial navigation; **n. spatiale** space flight or travel; **n. à vue** contact flying

3 *Ordinat* **n. sur (l')Internet** browsing the Internet, Internet surfing; **n. rapide/sécurisée** rapid/secure browsing

❑ **de navigation ADJ** *(registre)* navigational; *(terme, école)* nautical; *(instrument)* navigation *(avant n)*; **compagnie de n.** *Naut* shipping company; *Aviat* airline company; **permis de n.** ship's passport, sea letter

navigatrice [navigatris] *voir* **navigateur**

naviguer [3] [navige] **VI 1** *Naut* to sail *(vers* to); **le Queen Mary a beaucoup navigué** the Queen Mary did a lot of sailing; **depuis que je navigue** *(plaisancier)* since I first went sailing; *(marin)* since I first went to sea; **n. au compas/à l'estime** to navigate by compass/by dead reckoning

2 *Aviat* to fly; **n. à vue** to use contact flight rules, to fly visually

3 *Ordinat* **n. sur (l')Internet** to surf the Net, to browse the Web

4 *Fig (se déplacer)* to get about; **le dossier a navigué entre les différents responsables du**

projet the file moved around or was passed from project manager to project manager; **savoir n.** to know one's way around

naviplane [naviplan] **NM** hovercraft

navire [navir] **NM** ship, vessel; **n. de charge** freighter, cargo ship; **n. de commerce** merchant ship; **n. de forage** drilling ship; **n. frigorifique** refrigerated vessel; **n. de guerre** warship; **n. de haute mer** ocean-going ship; **n. au long cours** ocean-going ship; **n. marchand** merchant ship; **n. mixte** mixed passenger and cargo ship; **n. de passagers** passenger ship; **n. porte-conteneurs** container ship; **n. à voiles** sailing ship

navire-atelier [naviratəlje] *(pl* **navires-ateliers)** **NM** *Mil* repair ship

navire-citerne [navirsitɛrn] *(pl* **navires-citernes)** **NM** (oil) tanker

navire-école [navirekɔl] *(pl* **navires-écoles)** **NM** training ship

navire-hôpital [navirɔpital] *(pl* **navires-hôpitaux** [navirɔpito]) **NM** hospital ship

navire-jumeau [navirʒymo] *(pl* **navires-jumeaux)** **NM** sister ship

navire-usine [naviryzin] *(pl* **navires-usines)** **NM** factory ship

navrant, -e [navrɑ̃, -ɑ̃t] **ADJ 1** *(attristant → spectacle)* distressing, upsetting; **c'est n. de les voir ainsi se quereller** it's upsetting to see them quarrel like that; **tu es n.!** you're pathetic or hopeless!; **sa bêtise est navrante** he's/she's hopelessly stupid; **un film n. de bêtise** a hopelessly stupid movie or *Br* film **2** *(regrettable)* **c'est n., mais il n'y a rien à faire** it's a terrible shame, but there's nothing we can do

navré, -e [navre] **ADJ** *(personne, expression, ton)* distressed; **être n. de qch** to be very or terribly sorry about sth; **je suis n. de vous l'entendre dire** I'm so sorry to hear you say that; **je suis n. (de l'apprendre)** I'm terribly or very sorry (to hear that); **n. de vous avoir fait attendre** sorry to have kept you waiting

navrement [navrəmɑ̃] **NM** *Littéraire* anguished grief, despair

navrer [3] [navre] **VT** to upset, to distress, to sadden; **la vue d'une telle misère me navre** it distresses me to see such poverty

nay [nɛ] = **ney**

nazaréen, -enne [nazareɛ̃, -ɛn] **ADJ 1** *Géog* Nazarene **2** *Beaux-Arts* **l'école nazaréenne** the Nazarenes

❑ **Nazaréen, -enne NM,F** *Géog* Nazarene; *Rel* **le N.** *(Jésus)* the Nazarene **NM** *Beaux-Arts* Nazarene

Nazareth [nazarɛt] **NM** Nazareth

naze [naz] = **nase**

nazi, -e [nazi] **ADJ** Nazi

NM,F Nazi

nazillon, -onne [nazijɔ̃, -ɔn] **NM,F** *Fam* little Nazi

nazisme [nazism] **NM** Nazism

NB *(abrév écrite* nota bene*)* NB

NBC [ɛnbese] **ADJ** *Mil (abrév* nucléaire, biologique, chimique*)* NBC

nbreuses *(abrév écrite* nombreuses*)* many

nbrx *(abrév écrite* nombreux*)* many

n.c. 1 *(abrév écrite* non communiqué*)* n/a **2** *(abrév écrite* non connu*)* n/a

N.-D. *(abrév écrite* Notre-Dame*)* OL

n.d. 1 *(abrév écrite* non daté*)* nd **2** *(abrév écrite* non disponible*)* n/a

NDA *(abrév écrite* note de l'auteur*)* = author's note

N'Djamena [ndʒamena] **NM** Ndjamena, N'djamena

NDLR *(abrév écrite* note de la rédaction*)* Ed.

NDT *(abrév écrite* note du traducteur*)* translator's note

NE [nə] **ADV A.** *EN CORRÉLATION AVEC UN MOT NÉGATIF* **aucun d'eux ne peut venir** none of them can come; **je ne l'ai dit à personne** I haven't told anyone; **je n'ai vu personne** I saw nobody, I didn't see anybody; **je n'ai rien vu** I saw nothing, I didn't see anything; **nul n'est parfait** nobody's perfect; **ce n'est ni bleu ni vert** it's neither blue nor green; **je n'en parlerai ni à l'un ni à l'autre** I won't speak about it to either of them; **je ne vois guère comment t'aider** I don't really see how I can help you; **le temps n'est**

guère prometteur the weather is not very promising; **il ne répond jamais au téléphone** he never answers the phone; **le téléphone ne marche plus** the telephone doesn't work any more; **ne le dérange pas!** don't disturb him!; **parlez tout bas pour ne pas réveiller le bébé** speak softly so as not to wake the baby; **il ne la voit pas plus dans ce rôle-là que dans l'autre** he can't see *or* imagine her in that role any more than in the other; *Littéraire* **je ne crois point qu'elle veuille l'épouser** I do not believe *or* it is not my belief that she wants to marry him

B. *EN CORRÉLATION AVEC "QUE"* **ils ne font que répéter ce qu'on leur a dit** all they (ever) do is repeat what they've been told; **je ne fais que d'arriver** I've only just arrived; **il n'a pas que des amis** not everybody likes him; **je n'ai pas que cette idée-là** that's not the only idea I have; **il n'y a pas que toi sur terre!** you're not the only person in the world(, you know)!; **tu n'as pas que ta famille, tu as aussi tes amis** you don't just have your family, you have your friends as well; **tu ne sais dire que des mensonges** all you ever do is tell lies; **vous n'avez qu'à lui en parler** all you have to do is speak to him/her (about it); **je n'ai pas d'autre solution que celle-là** I have no other solution but that

C. *EMPLOYÉ SEUL* **1** *(avec une valeur négative)* **je ne puis** I cannot; **il n'ose** he dare not; **il ne cesse de m'appeler** he won't stop calling me; **il n'ose le lui dire** he doesn't dare tell him/her; **je ne sais quoi faire** I don't know what to do; **qui n'agirait ainsi dans de telles circonstances?** who wouldn't do the same in such circumstances?; **quel père n'aiderait son fils?** what father would refuse to help his son?; **beaucoup de choses ont changé depuis que je ne t'ai vu** many *or* a lot of things have changed since I last saw you; **voilà trois jours que je ne l'ai vue** I haven't seen her for three days; **il y a six jours qu'il n'est venu** he hasn't been for six days; **je lui demanderais, si ma timidité ne m'en empêchait** I would ask him/her, if I weren't so shy; **il n'y a rien dans tout cela qui ne soit parfaitement exact** there is nothing in all that which is not perfectly correct; **il n'y a rien qu'il ne fasse pour vous** there's nothing he wouldn't do for you; **je n'avais rien qui ne lui appartînt aussi** I had nothing that didn't also belong to him/her; **prenez garde qu'on ne vous voie** be careful (that) nobody sees you; **que ne le disais-tu plus tôt?** why didn't you say so earlier?, if only you had said so earlier!; **que ne dit-elle ce qu'elle en pense?** why doesn't she say what she thinks (about it)?; **que ne ferais-je pour vous?** what wouldn't I do for you?; *Littéraire* **n'était son grand âge, je l'aurais congédié** had it not been for his advanced age, I would have dismissed him; **n'ayez crainte, je le préviendrai** don't worry, I'll tell him

2 *(avec une valeur explétive)* **je crains qu'elle n'en parle** I'm frightened she'll talk (about it); **je crains qu'il n'accepte** I'm afraid he might say yes; **sa seule crainte, c'était qu'on ne le renvoyât** all he was afraid of *or* his only fear was of being dismissed; **je tremble qu'il ne soit trop tard** I'm afraid it might be too late; **on redoute que l'épidémie ne s'étende** there are fears that the epidemic might spread; **de peur qu'elle ne le voie** for fear she might see him; **évite qu'il ne te rencontre** try to avoid meeting him; **je ne doute pas qu'il ne soit sympathique** I don't doubt (that) he's nice; **peu s'en faut qu'il n'ait réussi** he very nearly succeeded; **à moins qu'il ne vous le dise** unless he tells you; **avant que je ne parte** before I go; **sans que je ne le dise** without me *or* my saying it; **il se porte mieux que je ne croyais** he's better than I'd imagined; **c'est moins efficace que je ne l'espérais** it's not as effective as I'd hoped; **elle est plus douée que vous ne croyez** she's more gifted than you think

---

N-E *(abrév écrite* **Nord-Est***)* NE

né, -e [ne] **PP** *voir* **naître**

ADJ born; **un bébé né prématurément à huit mois** a baby born prematurely at eight months; **né d'une famille bourgeoise** born into a middle-class family; **enfant né d'un premier mariage** child from a first marriage; *Fig* **un film né de la rencontre d'un réalisateur et d'une actrice** a film born of *or* that grew out of a meeting between a director and an actress; **Clara Brown, née Moore** Clara Brown, née Moore; **c'est une musicienne née** she's a born musician, she was born (to be) a musician; **une personne bien née** a person of high birth; **être bien né** to be well born *or* of noble birth

Néandertal [neɑ̃dɛrtal] *voir* **homme**

néandertalien, -enne [neɑ̃dɛrtaljɛ̃, -ɛn] **ADJ** Neanderthal

NM Neanderthal man

néanmoins [neɑ̃mwɛ̃] **ADV** nevertheless, nonetheless; **votre proposition m'intéresse beaucoup; n., je souhaiterais l'examiner plus attentivement** I'm very interested in your proposal; nevertheless, I should like to examine it more carefully; **ce travail est bon, n. vous pouvez mieux faire** this work is good, nevertheless *or* yet you can do better; **je souhaiterais n. qu'il vienne** I would nevertheless *or* nonetheless like him to come; **il est brillant et n. très modeste** he is brilliant but nonetheless *or* nevertheless very modest

néant [neɑ̃] **NM** **1** *(non-être)* nothingness; **une voix sortie du n.** a voice that seemed to come from nowhere **2** *(superficialité)* vacuousness; **dans tous leurs discours, je ne trouve que le n.** I find all their speeches totally vacuous **3** *(manque de valeur)* worthlessness, triviality; **le n. de la gloire** the emptiness of fame **4** *Admin* **enfants: n.** children: none

néanthropien, -enne [neɑ̃trɔpjɛ̃, -ɛn] **ADJ** neoanthropic

NM neoanthropic species

néantiser [3] [neɑ̃tize] **VT** **1** *Phil* to negate, to evacuate **2** *Littéraire (faire disparaître)* to make disappear; *(anéantir)* to annihilate

nebka [nebka] **NF** small dune

Nebraska [nebraska] **NM** *Géog* **le N.** Nebraska; **au N.** in Nebraska

nébuleux, -euse [nebylø, -øz] **ADJ** **1** *(nuageux)* cloudy, clouded; **un ciel n.** a cloudy *or* an overcast sky

2 *Fig (obscur)* obscure, nebulous

▫ **nébuleuse NF** **1** *Astron* nebula; **nébuleuse diffuse/obscure/planétaire** diffuse/dark/planetary nebula

2 *Fig (amas confus)* **leur projet était encore à l'état de nébuleuse** their plan was still pretty vague, they still had only the bare outlines of a plan

3 *(conglomérat)* business conglomerate

nébulisation [nebylizasjɔ̃] **NF** nebulization

nébuliser [3] [nebylize] **VT** to nebulize

nébuliseur [nebylizœr] **NM** nebulizer

nébulosité [nebylozite] **NF** **1** *(nuage)* haze, nebulosity **2** *Météo* cloud cover; **forte n.** heavy cloud cover **3** *Fig Littéraire (imprécision)* haziness, nebulousness

nécessaire [nesesɛr] **ADJ** **1** *(indispensable)* necessary; **un mal n.** a necessary evil; **cela ne sera pas n.** that won't be necessary; **l'opération ne sera pas n.** it will not be necessary to operate; **si (c'est) n.** if necessary, if need be; **je viendrai si c'est vraiment n.** I'll come if it's really necessary; **est-il n. de la mettre** *ou* **qu'elle soit au courant?** does she have *or* need to know?; **il n'est pas n. d'être impoli** there is no need to be rude; **il n'est pas n. de passer par le standard** there is no need *or* it is not necessary to go through the switchboard; **il est n. que vous y alliez en personne** you need to *or* you must go there in person; **ils n'ont pas jugé n. de venir s'excuser** they didn't think *or* consider it necessary to come and apologize; **leur séparation était devenue n.** it had become necessary for them to part; **n. à** *ou* **pour qn/qch** necessary *or* required for sb/sth; **l'eau est n. aux plantes** plants need water; **cette introduction est n. à la compréhension du texte** you have to read this introduction to understand the text

2 *(requis → aptitude)* necessary, requisite; **toutes les qualités nécessaires** all the necessary qualities; **avoir l'argent/le temps/la patience n.** to have the necessary money/time/patience

3 *(logique, inévitable)* necessary, unavoidable, inevitable; **le chômage est-il la conséquence n. de la crise?** is unemployment a necessary consequence of the crisis?

NM **1** *(choses indispensables)* bare necessities; **n'emportez que le strict n.** just take the basic essentials *or* what's absolutely necessary; **il ne fait que le strict n.** he does no more than that which is strictly necessary; **manquer du n.** to lack the necessities *or* basics of life

2 *(démarche requise)* **je vais faire le n.** I'll see to it; **je ferai le n. pour vos réservations** I'll see to your reservations; **ne vous inquiétez pas, j'ai fait le n.** don't worry, I've taken care of things *or* I've done what had to be done; **merci de faire le n. pour qu'on vienne le chercher à l'aéroport** thank you for arranging for him to be met at the airport

3 *(trousse, étui)* **n. à chaussures** shoe-cleaning kit; **n. à couture** needlework basket; **n. à ongles** manicure set; **n. à ouvrage** workbox; **n. de toilette** toilet bag, *Br* sponge bag; **n. de voyage** travel *or Br* overnight bag

4 *Littéraire (serviteur)* servant, domestic, indispensable person

nécessairement [nesesɛrmɑ̃] **ADV** **1** *(inévitablement)* necessarily, unavoidably, inevitably; **n., il devait y avoir collision** the crash was unavoidable **2** *(obligatoirement)* necessarily, *Sout* of necessity; **pas n.** not necessarily; **ce n'est pas n. vrai** it's not necessarily true; **il y a n. une explication à tout cela** there must be an explanation for all this **3** *Ling* necessarily; **condition n. présente** necessary condition

nécessitant, -e [nesesitɑ̃] **ADJ** *Rel* necessitating

nécessité [nesesite] **NF** **1** *(caractère nécessaire)* necessity, need; **être dans la n. de faire qch** to find it necessary to do sth, to have no choice but to do sth; **la n. de dormir/de vaincre** the need to sleep/to win; **elle ne voit pas la n. de se marier** she doesn't see any need to get married; **la crise nous a mis dans la n. de renvoyer la moitié du personnel** the crisis made it necessary for us *or* gave us no choice but to lay off half the staff; **quelle n. y avait-il de le faire?** what need was there to do it?

2 *(chose indispensable)* necessity; **la liberté de la presse est une n.** freedom of the press is essential *or* a necessity; **c'est une n.** it's essential; **c'est une n. absolue de faire bouillir l'eau** it is absolutely necessary *or* essential to boil the water; **faire de n. vertu** to make a virtue out of necessity; *Prov* **n. fait loi** needs must (where the devil drives); **n. faisant loi, il dut vendre le parc** sheer necessity forced him to sell the park

3 *Vieilli (indigence)* destitution, poverty; **être dans la n.** to be in need

4 *Phil* **la n.** necessity

5 *Jur* **état de n.** necessity

▫ **nécessités NFPL** **les nécessités de la vie** the necessities of life; **les nécessités du service** the operational requirements; **des nécessités financières nous obligent à...** we are financially bound to...; **nécessités militaires** military requirements

▫ **de première nécessité ADJ** *(dépenses, fournitures)* basic; *(objets, denrées)* essential; **ne prenez que des objets de première n.** take only what's absolutely necessary

▫ **de toute nécessité ADV vous devez de toute n. réparer le toit** it's absolutely imperative *or* essential that you repair the roof

▫ **par nécessité ADV** of necessity, necessarily, unavoidably; **on dut par n. vendre la moto** there was no choice but to sell the motorbike

nécessiter [3] [nesesite] **VT** to require, to demand; **cela nécessite la présence de toute la famille** it requires the whole family to be present; **cela nécessite que vous veniez** that means you have to come; **ce travail nécessite beaucoup de patience** this job requires a lot of patience; **une telle question nécessite qu'on prenne le temps de réfléchir** such a question requires *or* needs time to be considered

nécessiteux, -euse [nesesitø, -øz] **ADJ** needy, in need; **une famille nécessiteuse** a family in need, a needy family

NM,F needy person; **les n.** the needy

neck [nɛk] **NM** *Géol* neck

nec plus ultra [nɛkplyzyltra] **NM INV** last word,

ultimate; **le n. des cuisines intégrées** the last word in built-in kitchens

nécro [nekro] **NF** *Fam Presse (rubrique)* obits

nécrobie [nekrɔbi] **NF** *Entom* scavenger beetle, *Spéc* necrobia

nécrobiose [nekrɔbjoz] **NF** *Méd* necrobiosis

nécrologe [nekrɔlɔʒ] **NM** necrology, death roll

nécrologie [nekrɔlɔʒi] **NF 1** *(liste)* necrology **2** *(notice biographique)* obituary **3** *(rubrique)* obituary column

nécrologique [nekrɔlɔʒik] **ADJ** obituary *(avant n)*

nécrologue [nekrɔlɔg] **NMF** necrologist, necrographer

nécromancie [nekrɔmɑ̃si] **NF** necromancy

nécromancien, -enne [nekrɔmɑ̃sjɛ̃, -ɛn] **NM,F** necromancer

nécrophage [nekrɔfaʒ] **ADJ** necrophagous

nécrophile [nekrɔfil] **ADJ** necrophiliac *(avant n)*, necrophile *(avant n)*

NMF necrophiliac, necrophile

nécrophilie [nekrɔfili] **NF** necrophilia, necrophilism

nécrophore [nekrɔfɔr] **NM** *Entom* burying beetle

nécropole [nekrɔpɔl] **NF** necropolis

nécropsie [nekrɔpsi] **NF** *Vieilli* necropsy

nécrose [nekroz] **NF 1** *Méd* necrosis **2** *Bot* canker, necrosis

nécroser [3] [nekroze] **VT 1** *Méd* to necrose **2** *Bot* to canker

▸**se nécroser VPR 1** *Méd* to necrose **2** *Bot* to canker

nécrotique [nekrɔtik] **ADJ** *Méd* necrotic

nectaire [nɛktɛr] **NM** *Bot* nectary

nectar [nɛktar] **NM** *(gén)* nectar; **n. de poire/d'abricot** pear/apricot nectar

nectarifère [nɛktarifɛr] **ADJ** nectariferous

nectarine [nɛktarin] **NF** nectarine

nectarivore [nɛktarivɔr] **ADJ** nectarivore

necton [nɛktɔ̃] **NM** *Zool* nekton

née [ne] *voir* **né**

néerlandais, -e [neɛrlɑ̃dɛ, -ɛz] **ADJ** Dutch

NM *(langue)* Dutch

▫ **Néerlandais, -e NM,F** Dutchman, *f* Dutchwoman; **les N.** the Dutch

néerlandophone [neɛrlɑ̃dɔfɔn] **ADJ** Dutch-speaking

NMF Dutch speaker

nef [nɛf] **NF 1** *Archit* nave; **n. centrale** nave; **n. latérale** (side) aisle **2** *Arch ou Littéraire (vaisseau)* vessel, craft

'La Nef des fous' *Bosch* 'The Ship of Fools'

néfaste [nefast] **ADJ 1** *(nuisible)* harmful, noxious; **le gel a été n. aux récoltes** the frost has been disastrous for the crops; **une influence n.** a bad influence **2** *Littéraire (tragique)* ill-fated **3** *Antiq* **jour n.** dies nefasti

Néfertiti [nefɛrtiti] **NPR** Nefertiti

nèfle [nɛfl] **NF 1** *Bot* medlar; **n. du Japon** loquat **2** *Fam (locution)* **des nèfles!** no way!, no chance!

néflier [neflije] **NM** *Bot* medlar (tree); **n. du Japon** loquat (tree)

négateur, -trice [negatœr, -tris] *Littéraire* **ADJ** negative

NM,F decrier, detractor

négatif, -ive [negatif, -iv] **ADJ 1** *(réponse, attitude)* negative **2** *Élec, Ling & Méd* negative **3** *Math* **un nombre n.** a negative *or* minus number

EXCLAM *Fam* nope!

NM *Phot* negative

▫ **négative NF dans la négative** if not; **répondre par la négative** to give a negative answer, to answer in the negative

négation [negasjɔ̃] **NF 1** *(gén) & Phil* negation **2** *Gram* negative (form)

négationnisme [negasjɔnism] **NM** revisionism *(denying that the Holocaust ever happened)*

négationniste [negasjɔnist] **ADJ** revisionist *(denying that the Holocaust ever happened)*

NMF revisionist *(who denies that the Holocaust ever happened)*

négative [negativ] *voir* **négatif**

négativement [negativmɑ̃] **ADV** *(réagir)* negatively; *(répondre)* in the negative

négativisme [negativism] **NM** negativism

négativité [negativite] **NF 1** negativity, negativeness **2** *Élec* negativity

négaton [negatɔ̃] **NM** negaton

négatoscope [negatɔskɔp] **NM** negative viewer, light box

négatrice [negatris] *voir* **négateur**

négligé, -e [negliʒe] **ADJ 1** *(peu soigné → tenue, personne)* sloppy, scruffy, slovenly; *(→ coiffure)* unkempt, untidy; *(→ travail, devoir, style)* slovenly, careless **2** *(délaissé)* neglected

NM 1 *(débraillé, laisser-aller)* scruffiness, slovenly *or* untidy appearance **2** *(robe d'intérieur)* negligee, negligée

négligeable [negliʒabl] **ADJ** *(somme)* trifling; *(détail)* unimportant, trifling; *(différence, quantité, risque)* negligible, insignificant; **son augmentation n'est pas n.** he's/she's been given a quite considerable rise; **un avantage non n.** a not inconsiderable advantage; **une quantité non n. de** a significant quantity of; **elle a une influence non n. sur lui** she has a not inconsiderable influence over him

négligemment [negliʒamɑ̃] **ADV 1** *(sans soin)* negligently, carelessly **2** *(avec nonchalance)* negligently, casually; **un foulard n. noué autour du cou** a scarf casually tied around his/her neck

négligence [negliʒɑ̃s] **NF 1** *(manque de soin)* negligence, carelessness; *(d'un devoir)* neglect; **habillé avec n.** sloppily *or* carelessly dressed; **n. de style** stylistic error, error of style

2 *(manque d'attention)* negligence, neglect; *(oubli)* oversight; **la n. du conducteur** the driver's negligence; **l'accident est dû à une n.** the accident was due to carelessness; **l'erreur est due à une n. de ma secrétaire** the error is due to an oversight on the part of my secretary; **par (pure) n.** through (sheer) carelessness *or* negligence

3 *(nonchalance)* negligence, casualness, nonchalance; **feuilletant son livre avec n.** casually leafing through his/her book; **il me répondit avec n. qu'il viendrait peut-être** he casually *or* nonchalantly replied that he would perhaps come

4 *Jur* **n. coupable** *ou* **criminelle** criminal negligence; **n. grave** gross negligence; **n. professionnelle** professional negligence, malpractice

négligent, -e [negliʒɑ̃, -ɑ̃t] **ADJ 1** *(peu consciencieux)* negligent, careless, neglectful; **vous avez été très n. dans l'exercice de vos fonctions** you have been very negligent in your duty *or* very neglectful of your duties **2** *(nonchalant)* negligent, casual, nonchalant; **d'un geste n., il ramassa le livre** he casually picked up the book

négliger [17] [negliʒe] **VT 1** *(se désintéresser de → études, santé, personne)* to neglect; **si tu négliges ce rhume, il ne fera qu'empirer** if you don't take care of *or* if you neglect that cold, it'll only get worse; **il néglige sa tenue ces derniers temps** he hasn't been taking care of his appearance lately; **ne négligez pas votre devoir de citoyen** don't be neglectful of your duty as a citizen

2 *(dédaigner)* to disregard; *(élément, détail)* to overlook, to disregard; **il ne faut rien n.** you mustn't leave anything to chance; **il ne faut pas n. son offre** don't disregard his/her offer; **en négligeant ses conseils, tu t'exposes à perdre de l'argent** if you disregard *or* ignore his/her advice, you run the risk of losing money

3 *(omettre)* to neglect; **n. de faire qch** to neglect *or* to fail to do sth; **les enquêteurs n'ont rien négligé pour retrouver l'assassin** the police left no stone unturned in their efforts to find the murderer

▸**se négliger VPR 1** *(être mal habillé)* to be careless about *or* to neglect one's appearance **2** *(se désintéresser de sa santé)* to be neglectful of *or* to neglect one's health

négoce [negɔs] **NM 1** *(activité)* business, trade, trading; **faire du n.** to be in trade; **le n. international** international trade *or* trading; **le n. du vin** the wine trade; *Bourse* **n. de titres** share-dealing **2** *(entreprise)* business; **un petit n.** a small business

négociabilité [negɔsjabilite] **NF** negotiability

négociable [negɔsjabl] **ADJ** negotiable; *Fin (bon, traite)* negotiable, transferable, tradeable; **non n.** non-negotiable; **n. en banque** bankable; **n. en Bourse** negotiable on the Stock Exchange

négociant, -e [negɔsjɑ̃, -ɑ̃t] **NM,F 1** *(commerçant)* merchant, trader; **n. exportateur** export merchant; **n. en gros** wholesaler; **n. en vins** wine merchant **2** *(grossiste)* wholesaler **3** *Bourse* trader; **n. courtier** broker-dealer

négociateur, -trice [negɔsjatœr, -tris] **NM,F** *Com & Pol* negotiator

négociation [negɔsjasjɔ̃] **NF 1** *(discussions)* negotiation; **entamer des négociations (sur qch)** to enter into negotiations (on sth); **les deux pays ont engagé des négociations** the two countries have begun negotiations; **être en n.** *(sujet: conditions, contrat, salaire)* to be under negotiation; **être en n. avec qn** to be in negotiation with sb; *UE* **négociations d'adhésion** accession negociations; **négociations collectives** joint negotiations; *(au sein d'une entreprise)* collective bargaining *(UNCOUNT)*; **négociations commerciales** trade negotiations; **négociations commerciales multilatérales** multilateral trade negotiations; **négociations pour la paix** peace negotiations; **négociations précontractuelles** precontractual negotiations; **négociations salariales** wage bargaining *(UNCOUNT)*

2 *Fin & Bourse* negotiation, transaction; **négociations de bloc** block trading *(UNCOUNT)*; **négociations de Bourse** Stock Exchange transactions; **négociations de change** exchange transactions; **négociations au comptant** spot trading *(UNCOUNT)*; **n. à la criée** open-outcry trading; **négociations à prime** options trading *(UNCOUNT)*; **négociations à terme** futures trading *(UNCOUNT)*

négociatrice [negɔsjatris] *voir* **négociateur**

négocié, -e [negɔsje] **ADJ** *(solution)* negotiated

négocier [9] [negɔsje] **VT 1** *Com, Fin & Pol* to negotiate (**avec** with); *Bourse* to trade; **prix à n.** price negotiable **2** *Aut* **n. un virage** to negotiate a bend

VI 1 *(discuter)* to negotiate (**avec** with) **2** *Arch (faire du commerce)* to trade

▸**se négocier VPR l'ancien se négocie à plus de 700 euros le mètre carré** old flats can go for over 700 euros per square metre; **les actions se négocient ce matin à six euros** shares are trading at six euros this morning

négondo [negɔ̃do] **NM** *Bot* box elder

nègre, négresse [nɛgr, negrɛs] **NM,F** Negro, *f* Negress; *(avec une connotation raciste)* nigger, = racist term used to refer to a black person; *Fam* **travailler comme un n.** to work like a slave; **n. blanc** *(à peau claire)* White Negro; **négresse blanche** White Negress; *Hist* **n. marron** maroon

NM 1 *Fam (écrivain)* ghost (writer); **être le n. de qn** to ghost for sb **2** *Culin* **n. en chemise** = chocolate dessert coated with whipped cream

ADJ 1 *Beaux-Arts & Mus* Negro **2** *(personne)* Negro; *(avec une connotation raciste)* nigger, = offensive term used to refer to a black person

▫ **nègre blanc ADJ INV propos n. blanc** double-talk; **une motion n. blanc** a motion that's neither one thing nor the other

négrier, -ère [negrije, -ɛr] **ADJ** slave *(avant n)*; **navire n.** slave ship, slaver

NM 1 *(marchand d'esclaves)* slave trader, slaver **2** *(bateau)* slave ship, slaver **3** *Péj (employeur)* slave-driver

négrille [negrij] **NM** *Vieilli* pygmy

négrillon, -onne [negrijɔ̃, -ɔn] **NM,F** piccaninny, = racist term referring to a black child

négritude [negrityd] **NF** negritude

négro [negro] **NM** Negro, nigger, = offensive term used to refer to a black person

négro-africain, -e [negroafrikɛ̃, -ɛn] *(mpl* **négro-africains**, *fpl* **négro-africaines**) **ADJ** Black African

négroïde [negrɔid] **ADJ** Negroid

NMF Negroid

negro spiritual [negrospiritɥɔl] *(pl* **negro spirituals**) **NM** Negro spiritual

néguentropie [negɑ̃trɔpi] **NF** neguentropy

negundo [negɔ̃do] **NM** *Bot* box elder

négus [negys] **NM** *Hist* Negus

Néhémie [neemi] **NPR** *Bible* Nehemiah

NEI [ɛnəi] **NM** *(abrév* **Nouvel État Indépendant**) newly independent state, NIS

neige [nɛʒ] **NF 1** *Météo* snow; **n. artificielle** artificial snow; *Can* **n. à bonhomme** *ou* **collante**

sticky snow; **les neiges éternelles** permanent snow; *Can* **n. fabriquée** artificial snow; **n. fondue** *(pluie)* sleet; *(boue)* slush; **n. poudreuse** powdery snow; *Ski* **n. pourrie** hazardous *or* crumbly snow; **n. tôlée** crusted snow; *Can* **banc de n.** snow bank, snowdrift

2 *Chim* **n. carbonique** dry ice

3 *Fam Arg drogue (cocaïne)* snow

4 *Culin* **battez les blancs en n.** whisk the whites until they form peaks; **œufs (battus) en n.** stiffly beaten egg whites

❑ **à la neige** ADV *Fam* on a skiing *Br* holiday *or Am* vacation▪; **aller à la n.** to go on a skiing *Br* holiday *or Am* vacation; **j'emmène les enfants à la n.** I'm taking the children skiing▪

❑ **de neige** ADJ **1** *Météo* **chute** *ou* **giboulée de n.** snowfall, fall of snow

2 *Ski* **station de n.** winter sports *or* ski resort

3 *Littéraire (blanc)* snow-white, snowy

neigeasser [3] [nɛʒase] VI *Can* to snow lightly

neigeoter [3] [nɛʒɔte] V IMPERSONNEL *Fam* **il neigeote** it's snowing a little▪

neiger [23] [neʒe] V IMPERSONNEL **il neige** it's snowing

neigeux, -euse [nɛʒø, -øz] ADJ **1** *(cime)* snow-capped, snow-clad; *(toit, pente)* snow-covered **2** *(hiver, temps)* snowy **3** *Fig (barbe, chevelure)* snow-white, snowy; **sa crinière neigeuse** his snowy mane of hair

Neinsager [najnzagɛr] NM INV *Suisse* "no" voter

nélombo, nelumbo [nelɔbo] NM *Bot* nelumbium, nelumbo

nem [nɛm] NM = type of Vietnamese spring roll

némalion [nemaljɔ̃] *Bot* NM nemalion

❑ **némalions** NMPL Nemalionales

némathelminthe [nematɛlmɛ̃t] *Zool* NM nemathelminth

❑ **némathelminthes** NMPL Nemathelminthes

nématique [nematik] ADJ *Phys* nematic

nématoblaste [nematɔblast] NM *Biol* nematoblast, cnidoblast

nématocère [nematɔsɛr] *Entom* NM member of the Nematocera family

❑ **nématocères** NMPL Nematocera

nématocyste [nematɔsist] NM *Biol* nematocyst, cnidocyst

nématode [nematɔd] NM *Zool* roundworm, threadworm, *Spéc* nematode

néméen, -enne [nemeɛ̃, -ɛn] ADJ *Géog & Antiq* Nemean; **jeux Néméens** Nemean Games

némerte [nemɛrt] *Zool* NM OU NF ribbon worm, *Spéc* nemertine, member of the Nemertea *or* Nemertinea family

❑ **némertes** NMPL OU NFPL Nemertea, Nemertinea

némertien [nemɛrsjɛ̃] NM *Zool* nemertine

Némésis [nemezis] NPR *Myth* Nemesis

nemi [nemi] NM *(abrév* **nouvelle échelle métrique de l'intelligence)** = test which evaluates the mental age of children between the ages of three and twelve

némoral, -e, -aux, -ales [nemɔral, -o] ADJ *Littéraire* nemoral, of the woods

néné [nene] NM *Fam (sein)* boob, tit

nénette [nenɛt] NF *Fam* **1** *(femme, fille)* chick, *Br* bird **2** *(petite amie)* girlfriend▪, *Br* bird **3** *(tête)* **se casser la n. (à faire qch)** to go to a lot of bother (to do sth)▪; **tu ne t'es pas trop cassé la n. pour faire ta rédaction** you didn't exactly strain yourself *or* exert yourself over your essay; **te casse pas la n.** don't worry about it▪, don't let it bother you▪

nénies [neni] NFPL *Antiq* neniae, naeniae

nenni [neni] ADV *Arch ou Hum* nay

nénuphar [nenyfar] NM *Bot* waterlily, pond lily; **n. jaune** *ou* **des étangs** yellow waterlily *or* pond lily

néo- [neo] PRÉF neo-

néoblaste [neoblast] NM neoblast

néo-calédonien, -enne [neokaledɔnjɛ̃, -ɛn] *(mpl* **néo-calédoniens,** *fpl* **néo-calédoniennes)** ADJ New Caledonian

❑ **Néo-Calédonien, -enne** NM,F New Caledonian

néocapitalisme [neokapitalism] NM neo-capitalism

néocapitaliste [neokapitalist] ADJ neo-capitalist

NMF neo-capitalist

néoclassicisme [neoklasisism] NM neoclassicism

néoclassique [neoklasik] ADJ neoclassic, neoclassical

néocolonial, -e, -aux, -ales [neokɔlɔnjal, -o] ADJ neocolonial

néocolonialisme [neokɔlɔnjalism] NM neocolonialism

néocolonialiste [neokɔlɔnjalist] ADJ neocolonial, neocolonialist

NMF neocolonialist

néocomien, -enne [neokɔmjɛ̃, -ɛn] *Géol* ADJ Neocomian

NM Neocomian

néocommunisme [neokɔmynism] NM neocommunism

néoconservateur, -trice [neokɔ̃sɛrvatœr, -tris] ADJ neoconservative

NM,F neoconservative

néocortex [neokɔrtɛks] NM neocortex

néodarwinisme [neodarwinism] NM Neo-Darwinism

néodyme [neodim] NM *Chim* neodymium

néofascisme [neofaʃism] NM Neofascism

néofasciste [neofaʃist] ADJ Neofascist

NMF Neofascist

néoformation [neofɔrmasjɔ̃] NF **1** *Biol* neoformation, new growth **2** *Méd* neoplasm

néoformé, -e [neofɔrme] ADJ **1** *Biol* newly grown **2** *Méd* neoplastic

néogène [neoʒɛn] ADJ Neogene

NM Neogene (period)

néo-géo [neoʒeo] NM *Beaux-Arts* neo-geo

néogothique [neogotik] ADJ Neo-Gothic

NM Neo-Gothic (style)

néogrammairien, -enne [neogramɛrjɛ̃, -ɛn] ADJ neogrammarian

NM,F neogrammarian

néogrec, néogrecque [neogrɛk] ADJ **1** *(de la Grèce moderne)* Modern Greek **2** *Beaux-Arts* Neo-Grec

NM *(langue)* Modern Greek

néo-guinéen, -enne [neoginee, -ɛn] *(mpl* **néo-guinéens,** *fpl* **néo-guinéennes)** ADJ New Guinean

❑ **Néo-Guinéen, -enne** NM,F New Guinean

néo-hébridais, -e [neoebride, -ez] *(mpl* inv, *fpl* **néo-hébridaises)** *Anciennement* ADJ from the New Hebrides, Vanuatuan

❑ **Néo-Hébridais, -e** NM,F Vanuatuan

néo-impressionnisme [neoɛ̃presjɔnism] NM Neo-Impressionism

néo-impressionniste [neoɛ̃presjɔnist] *(pl* **néo-impressionnistes)** ADJ Neo-Impressionist

NMF Neo-Impressionist

néokantisme [neokãtism] NM Neo-Kantism, Neo-Kantianism

néo-kitsch ADJ INV neo-kitsch *(avant n)*

NM INV neo-kitsch

néolibéral, -e, -aux, -ales [neoliberal, -o] ADJ neoliberal

NM,F neoliberal

néolibéralisme [neoliberalism] NM neoliberalism

néolithique [neolitik] ADJ Neolithic

NM Neolithic (period)

néolithisation [neolitizasjɔ̃] NF Neolithization

néolocal, -e, -aux, -ales [neolokal, -o] ADJ neolocal

néologie [neolɔʒi] NF neology

néologique [neolɔʒik] ADJ neological

néologisme [neolɔʒism] NM *Ling & Psy* neologism

néoménie [neomeni] NF *Antiq* neomenia

néomercantilisme [neomɛrkãtilism] NM *Écon* neomercantilism

néomortalité [neomɔrtalite] NF neonatal mortality

néomycine [neomisin] NF *Pharm* neomycin

néon [neɔ̃] NM **1** *(gaz)* neon **2** *(éclairage)* neon (lighting); *(lampe)* neon (lamp); *(tube)* neon tube; *(enseigne)* neon sign

néonatal, -e, -als, -ales [neonatal] ADJ neonatal

néonatalogie [neonatalɔʒi] NF neonatology

néonazi, -e [neonazi] ADJ neo-Nazi

NM,F neo-Nazi

néonazisme [neonazism] NM neo-Nazism, neo-Naziism

néophron [neofrɔ̃] NM *Orn* Egyptian vulture

néophyte [neofit] NMF **1** *(nouvel adepte)* novice **2** *Rel* neophyte, novice

néopilina [neopilina] NM *Zool* neopilina

néoplasie [neoplazi] NF *Méd* neoplasm

néoplasique [neoplazik] ADJ neoplastic

néoplasme [neoplasm] NM *Méd* neoplasm

néoplasticisme [neoplastisism] NM *Beaux-Arts* Neo-Plasticism

néoplasticiste [neoplastisist] *Beaux-Arts* ADJ Neo-Plasticist

NMF Neo-Plasticist

néoplatonicien, -enne [neoplatonisjɛ̃, -ɛn] *Phil* ADJ Neoplatonic

NM,F Neoplatonist

néoplatonisme [neoplatonism] NM *Phil* Neoplatonism

néopositivisme [neopozitivism] NM logical positivism

néopositiviste [neopozitivist] ADJ logical positivist

NMF logical positivist

Néoprène® [neoprɛn] NM neoprene

néo-québécois, -e [neokebekwa, -az] *(mpl* inv, *fpl* **néo-québécoises)** ADJ of/from New Quebec

❑ **Néo-Québécois, -e** NM,F New Quebecker

néoréalisme [neorealism] NM *Cin* neorealism

néoréaliste [neorealist] *Cin* ADJ neorealist

NMF neorealist

néoromantique [neoromãtik] *Beaux-Arts* ADJ neoromantic

NMF neoromantic

néoromantisme [neoromãtism] NM *Beaux-Arts* neoromanticism

néorural, -e, -aux, -ales [neoryral, -o] NM,F neorural

néotectonique [neotɛktonik] NF neotectonics *(singulier)*

néotène [neotɛn] NM *Biol* neotenic species

néoténie [neoteni] NF *Biol* neoteny, neoteinia

néoténique [neotenik] ADJ *Biol* neotenic, neoteinic

néothomisme [neotomism] NM *Rel* Neo-Thomism

néottie [neoti] NF *Bot* bird's nest orchid, *Spéc* neottia

néo-zélandais, -e [neozelãde, -ez] *(mpl* inv, *fpl* **néo-zélandaises)** ADJ of/from New Zealand; **agneau n.** New Zealand lamb

❑ **Néo-Zélandais, -e** NM,F New Zealander

Népal [nepal] NM *Géog* **le N.** Nepal; **vivre au N.** live in Nepal; **aller au N.** to go to Nepal

népalais, -e [nepalɛ, -ez] ADJ Nepalese, Nepali

NM *(langue)* Nepali

❑ **Népalais, -e** NM,F Nepalese (person), Nepali; **les N.** the Nepalese, the Nepalis *or* Nepali

nèpe [nɛp] NF *Entom* nepa, water scorpion

népenthès [nepɛ̃tɛs] NM Nepenthes

népérien, -enne [neperjɛ̃, -ɛn] ADJ *(logarithme)* natural, Napierian

nepeta [nepeta] NF *Bot* nepeta

néphélémétrie [nefelemetri] NF *Chim* nephelometry

néphéline [nefelin] NF *Minér* nepheline

néphélion [nefeljɔ̃] NM *Méd* nubecula

néphélométrie [nefelometri] NF *Chim* nephelometry

néphralgie [nefralʒi] NF *Méd* nephralgia

néphralgique [nefralʒik] ADJ *Méd* nephralgic

néphrectomie [nefrɛktomi] NF *Méd* nephrectomy

néphrétique [nefretik] ADJ *Anat* nephritic

néphridie [nefridi] NF nephridium

néphrite [nefrit] NF **1** *Méd* nephritis; **n. chronique** Bright's disease, chronic nephritis **2** *Minér* nephrite

néphrologie [nefrolɔʒi] NF *Méd* nephrology

néphrologique [nefrolɔʒik] ADJ *Méd* nephrological

néphrologue [nefrolɔg] NMF kidney specialist, *Spéc* nephrologist

néphron [nefrɔ̃] NM *Anat* nephron

néphropathie [nefropati] NF *Méd* nephropathy

néphropexie [nefropɛksi] NF *Méd* nephropexy

néphrosclérose [nefroskleroz] NF *Méd* nephrosclerosis

néphrose [nefroz] NF *Méd* nephrosis

népotisme [nepotism] NM nepotism

Neptune [nɛptyn] NPR *Myth* Neptune

neptunisme [nɛptynism] NM *Géol* Neptunism

neptunium [nɛptynjɔm] NM *Chim* neptunium

néré [nere] NM *Bot* nere

Néréide [nereid] NF *Astron* Nereid
□ **Néréides** NFPL *Myth* **les Néréides** the Nereides
néréide [nereid] NF *Zool* nereis
néréis [nereis] NM OU NF *Zool* nereis
nerf [nɛr] NM 1 *Anat* nerve; **n. afférent/efférent** afferent/efferent nerve; **n. moteur/sensitif/mixte** motor/sensor/mixed nerve; **n. gustatif** gustatory nerve
2 *(toujours singulier) (énergie)* **elle manque de n. pour diriger l'entreprise** she hasn't got what it takes to run the company; **son style manque de n.** his/her style is a bit weak; **ça, c'est une voiture qui a du n.!** now that's what I call a responsive car!; **allez, un peu de n. ou du n.!** come on, put some effort into it!; **l'argent est le n. de la guerre** money is the sinews of war
3 *(tendon)* piece of gristle; **une viande pleine de nerfs** a gristly or stringy piece of meat
4 *Vieilli* **un grand athlète tout en n.** a tall, sinewy athlete
5 *(de reliure)* rib; **faux n.** false rib
6 *Mines* horse, rock vein
□ **nerfs** NMPL 1 *(système nerveux)* nerves; *Vieilli* **avoir les nerfs malades** to suffer from nerves; **la pauvre, elle a les nerfs malades** the poor thing's suffering with her nerves; **être malade des nerfs** to suffer from nerves, to have bad nerves; **ses nerfs ont fini par lâcher** he/she eventually cracked; *Fam* **avoir les nerfs à cran ou en boule ou en pelote** to be wound up, to be on edge; **avoir les nerfs à fleur de peau ou à vif** to be a bundle of nerves; **avoir les nerfs solides ou des nerfs d'acier** to have nerves of steel; *Fam* **avoir les nerfs** to be hacked off; **il a ses nerfs en ce moment** he's a bag of nerves or rather on edge at the moment; **avoir les nerfs** to be worked up; **on est tous sur les nerfs depuis ce matin** we've all been on edge since this morning; **il est toujours ou il vit sur les nerfs** he's highly-strung, he lives on his nerves; *Fam* **c'est un paquet ou une boule de nerfs** he's/she's a bundle or a bag of nerves; *Fam* **ne passe pas tes nerfs sur moi** don't take it out on me; *Fam* **porter ou taper sur les nerfs à qn** to get on sb's nerves; **le grincement de la girouette lui portait sur les nerfs** the creaking of the weather vane was grating on his/her nerves; **tu commences à me taper sur les nerfs!** you're starting to get on my nerves or *Br* wick!; *Fam* **foutre les nerfs à qn** to hack sb off, to get sb's back up
2 *Typ* raised bands
□ **nerf de bœuf** NM bludgeon
néritique [neritik] ADJ neritic, relating to the coastal belt; **zone n.** neritic zone
néroli [nerɔli] NM neroli
Néron [nerɔ̃] NPR Nero
néronien, -enne [nerɔnjɛ̃, -ɛn] ADJ Neronian
nerprun [nɛrprœ̃] NM *Bot* buckthorn
nervation [nɛrvasjɔ̃] NF venation, nervation, nervature
nerveuse [nɛrvøz] *voir* **nerveux**
nerveusement [nɛrvøzmɑ̃] ADV 1 *Méd* nervously; **elle est fatiguée n.** she's suffering from nervous exhaustion; **n., ça l'a beaucoup marqué** it really shook (up) his nerves 2 *(de façon agitée)* nervously, restlessly; *(avec impatience)* nervously, impatiently; **rire n.** to laugh nervously
nerveux, -euse [nɛrvø, -øz] ADJ 1 *Anat & Méd (système, maladie)* nervous; *(centre, influx)* nerve *(avant n)*
2 *(énervé → de nature)* nervous, highly-strung; *(→ passagèrement)* nervy, on edge; **tu me rends n.** you're making me nervous; **le café me rend n.** coffee makes me jumpy; **être n. avant une entrevue** to be nervous or on edge before an interview; **tu ne manges pas? – c'est n.!** aren't you eating? – it's my nerves
3 *(toux, rire)* nervous
4 *(mains, corps)* sinewy
5 *(énergique → personne)* dynamic, energetic; *(→ cheval)* spirited, vigorous; *(→ style)* energetic, forceful, vigorous; *(→ voiture)* responsive; *(→ conduite)* dynamic; **une conduite nerveuse** a jerky way of driving
6 *(dur → viande)* gristly, stringy
NM,F nervous or highly-strung person; **c'est un n.** he's very nervous or highly-strung
nervi [nɛrvi] NM *(tueur)* hired killer, hitman; *(homme de main)* henchman, thug

nervin, -e [nɛrvɛ̃, -in] ADJ *Vieilli* nervine
nervosité [nɛrvozite] NF 1 *Méd* nervosity
2 *(excitation → passagère)* nervousness, tension, agitation; *(→ permanente)* nervousness; **la n. du candidat** the candidate's uneasiness; **donner des signes de n.** to show signs of agitation; *Fig* **la n. des marchés financiers** the nervousness or jitteriness of the financial markets
3 *(irritabilité)* irritability, touchiness
4 *(vigueur)* responsiveness; **un moteur d'une grande n.** a highly responsive engine
nervure [nɛrvyr] NF 1 *Bot* vein, nervure 2 *Entom* vein 3 *Aviat & Métal* rib; *Aut* stiffening rib 4 *(de reliure)* rib 5 *Tech* flange; *(de radiateur)* gill 6 *Couture* piping; **nervures** pin tucks 7 *Archit & Constr* rib
nervuré, -e [nɛrvyre] ADJ *(feuille, aile)* veined; *(vêtement)* ribbed
nervurer [3] [nɛrvyre] VT 1 *Bot & Entom* to vein 2 *Aviat & Archit* to rib 3 *Typ* to rib, to band 4 *Tech* to flange 5 *Couture* to pipe
Nescafé® [nɛskafe] NM instant coffee
n'est-ce pas [nɛspa] ADV 1 *(sollicitant l'acquiescement)* **vous viendrez, n.?** you'll come, won't you?; **elle a téléphoné, n.?** she did phone, didn't she?; **nous pouvons compter sur vous, n.?** we can count on you, can't we?; **tu l'as, n.?** you've got it, haven't you?; **vous savez, n., ce qu'il en est** you know what the situation is, don't you?; **n. qu'ils sont mignons?** aren't they cute or sweet?
2 *(emploi expressif)* **la question, n., reste ouverte** the question, of course, remains unanswered; **le problème, n., c'est qu'il est déjà tard** the problem is, you see, that it's already late; *Hum* **lui, n., ne voyage qu'en première classe** he, of course, only ever travels first class
Nestor [nɛstɔr] NPR *Myth* Nestor
nestorianisme [nɛstɔrjanism] NM *Rel* Nestorianism
nestorien, -enne [nɛstɔrjɛ̃, -ɛn] *Rel* ADJ Nestorian
NM,F Nestorian
Net [nɛt] NM **le N.** the Net, the Internet

NET, NETTE [nɛt]

| ADJ | clean, neat 1, 2 ▪ clear 1, 3, 4 ▪ sharp 4, 6 ▪ distinct, definite 5 ▪ net 7 |
| ADV | frankly 2 ▪ net 3 |

ADJ 1 *(propre)* clean, neat; **une chemise pas très nette** a grubby shirt; *Fig* **j'ai la conscience nette** I have a clear conscience, my conscience is clear
2 *(ordonné)* (clean and) tidy, neat (and tidy); **tout est toujours n. chez elle** her house is always so neat and tidy
3 *(pur → peau, vin)* clear; *Littéraire* **n. de** free from; **être n. de tout soupçon** to be above suspicion; **être n. de tout blâme** to be blameless
4 *(bien défini → gén)* clear; *(→ contour)* sharp; *(→ réponse)* plain, straight; **une écriture nette** neat handwriting; **la cassure est nette** the break is clean; **elle a une diction nette** she speaks or articulates clearly; **une réponse nette** a straight answer; **sa position est nette** his/her position is clear-cut; **un refus n.** a flat refusal; **j'ai la nette impression que...** I have the distinct or clear impression that...; **elle a gardé des souvenirs très nets de sa petite enfance** she remembers her childhood quite clearly or vividly
5 *(évident)* distinct, definite; **il a fait de nets progrès** he's made distinct or definite progress; **il y a une nette amélioration** there's a marked improvement; **il fait plus froid ici, c'est très n.** it's noticeably or definitely colder here; **il veut t'épouser, c'est n.!** he wants to marry you, that's obvious!
6 *Phot* sharp; **l'image n'est pas nette** the picture isn't very clear
7 *Com & Fin* net; **n. d'impôt** tax-free; **n. de tout droit** exempt or free from duty; **bénéfice n.** net profit; **revenu n.** net income; **le montant n.** the net amount, the net
8 *Mines* washed, clean
9 *Fam (locution)* **pas n.** *(louche)* shady, *Br* dodgy; *(ivre, drogué)* off one's face, wasted;

wrecked; *(pas complètement sain d'esprit)* not all there, *Br* one sandwich short of a picnic
ADJ INV *Sport* **la balle est n.** (it's a) let
ADV 1 *(brutalement)* **s'arrêter n.** to stop dead; **se casser n.** to break clean through; **être tué n.** to be killed outright; **Fam couper ou casser n. avec qn** to break with sb completely
2 *(sans mentir)* frankly, plainly; *(sans tergiverser)* frankly, bluntly; **refuser (tout) n.** to refuse point-blank or flatly; **je vous le dis tout n.** I'm telling you straight
3 *Com & Fin* net; **je gagne 1000 euros n. par semaine ou 1000 euros par semaine n.** I take home or my take-home pay is 1,000 euros a week
□ **au net** ADV **mettre qch au n.** to make a fair copy of sth; **je ne veux pas lui donner ce que j'ai mis au n.** I don't want to give him/her my fair or clean copy; **après mise au n. (du texte)** after tidying up (the text) NM *Compta* **n. commercial** net profit; **n. financier** *(revenu)* net interest income; *(à payer)* net interest charges; **n. à payer** net payable
netcam [nɛtkam] NF *Ordinat* netcam, webcam
netéconomie [nɛtekɔnɔmi] NF *Écon & Ordinat* Internet economy
netiquette [nɛtikɛt] NF *Ordinat (sur l'Internet)* netiquette
netsuke [nɛtsyke] NM INV netsuke
nette¹ [nɛt] *voir* **net**
nette² [nɛt] NF *Orn* **n. rousse** red-crested pochard
nettement [nɛtmɑ̃] ADV 1 *(distinctement)* clearly, distinctly; **on voit n. la forme du bec** you can clearly see the shape of the beak; **il apparaît n. qu'il est en tort** it's clear that he's in the wrong
2 *(avec franchise)* clearly, frankly, bluntly; **je lui ai dit très n. ce que je pensais de lui** I told him bluntly what I thought of him
3 *(incontestablement)* definitely, markedly; **je travaille n. mieux à la maison qu'ici** I work much better at home than here; **j'aurais n. préféré ne pas y être** I would definitely have preferred not to be there
4 *(beaucoup)* much, distinctly; **ça va n. mieux comme ça** it's a lot or much better like this; **il est n. plus fort que Paul** he's much stronger than Paul
netteté [nɛtte] NF 1 *(propreté)* cleanness, cleanliness 2 *(clarté)* clearness, clarity; **n. des idées** clear thinking 3 *(précision → de l'écriture)* neatness, clearness; *(→ d'une image, d'un contour)* sharpness, clearness; *(→ de souvenir)* clearness, clarity; *(→ de rupture)* cleanness; **offensé par la n. de son refus** offended by the flatness of his/her refusal
nettoie *etc voir* **nettoyer**
nettoiement [netwamɑ̃] NM 1 *(des rues)* cleaning; **service du n.** refuse collection service 2 *Agr* clearing
nettoyage [netwajaʒ] NM 1 *(d'une maison, d'un vêtement)* cleaning; *Fam* **porter sa robe au n.** to take one's dress to the cleaner's; **n. à sec** dry cleaning; *(sur une étiquette)* dry clean only; **entreprise de n.** cleaning firm; **produits de n.** cleaning agents; **(grand) n. de printemps** spring-cleaning; **faire le n. par le vide** to make a clean sweep; **avant de déménager, j'ai fait un n. par le vide** before moving, I had a big clean-out; **se faire faire un n. de peau** to have one's skin cleansed
2 *Fam Fig (d'un quartier, d'une ville)* clean-up; *(par la police)* cleaning or clearing out; **ils ont commencé le n. des rues derrière la gare** they've started cleaning up the area behind the station; **les policiers ont opéré un véritable n. du quartier** the police officers really cleaned out or cleared out the district; *Mil* **opérations de n.** mopping-up operations; *Pol* **n. ethnique** ethnic cleansing
nettoyant, -e [netwajɑ̃, -ɑ̃t] ADJ cleaning *(avant n)*
NM *(gén)* cleaning product; *(détachant)* stain remover
nettoyer [13] [netwaje] VT 1 *(rendre propre → gén)* to clean; *(→ plaie)* to clean, to cleanse; *Naut (pont)* to swab; **n. une maison à fond** to spring-clean a house; **donner un vêtement à n.** to have a garment cleaned, to take a garment to the cleaner's; **n. à sec** to dry-clean; **n. une**

plate-bande (*désherber*) to weed (out) a flower bed; *Fig* **une averse avait nettoyé le ciel** a sudden shower had cleared the sky

2 (*enlever → tache*) to remove

3 *Fam* (*vider*) to clean out; **les cambrioleurs ont tout nettoyé** the burglars cleaned the place out; **je me suis fait n. au poker** I got cleaned out at poker; **et l'héritage? – nettoyé!** what about the inheritance? – all gone!; **en un instant, elle avait nettoyé son assiette** she emptied her plate in a flash; *Mil* **n. les poches de résistance** to mop up

4 *Fam* (*quartier*) to clean up *or* out

5 *Fam* (*épuiser*) to wear out ; **ça suffit pour aujourd'hui, les magasins, je suis nettoyé!** enough shopping for today, I'm worn out!

6 *Fam Arg crime* (*tuer*) to bump off; **les frères Tonini ont été nettoyés** *ou* **se sont fait n.** the Tonini brothers have been bumped off

►**se nettoyer** VPR **1** **se n. les mains** (*gén*) to clean one's hands; (*à l'eau*) to wash one's hands; **se n. les ongles** to clean one's nails

2 (*emploi passif*) **ça se nettoie facilement** it's easy to clean

3 le four se nettoie automatiquement the oven is self-cleaning

nettoyeur, -euse [netwajœr, -øz] ADJ **1** (*d'entretien*) cleaning (*avant n*) **2** *Orn* parasite-eating

NM,F **1** (*employé*) cleaner **2** *Orn* parasite-eater

NM **n. (d'étable)** stable-cleaning machine

Neuchâtel [nøʃatɛl] NM *Géog* (*ville*) Neuchâtel; **le canton de N.** Neuchâtel

neuchâteloise [nøʃatelwaz] NF = Louis XV-style wall clock

neuf¹ [nœf] ADJ INV **1** (*gén*) nine

2 (*dans des séries*) ninth; **page/numéro n.** page/number nine

PRON nine

NM INV **1** (*gén*) nine

2 (*numéro d'ordre*) number nine

3 (*chiffre écrit*) nine

4 *Cartes* nine; *voir aussi* **cinq**

neuf², neuve [nœf, nœv] ADJ **1** (*n'ayant jamais servi*) new; **flambant** *ou* **tout n.** brand-new; **mon appareil photo n'est plus tout n.** my camera is a bit old now; **à l'état n.** as new; (*timbre postal, livre*) in mint condition, unused; **à vendre poussette, état n.** (*dans une annonce*) pushchair for sale, as new *or* hardly used; **comme n.** as good as new

2 (*récemment créé → pays*) new, young; **notre démocratie est encore neuve** democracy is still in its infancy in our country; **une ville neuve** a new town

3 (*original → point de vue, idée*) new, fresh, original; **porter un regard n. sur qn/qch** to take a fresh look at sb/sth; **ce n'est pas un sujet tout n.** it's not a very original topic; **connaissances toutes neuves** newly acquired *or* freshly acquired knowledge; **il est encore (un peu) n. en matière de...** he's still (relatively) new *or* a (relative) newcomer to...

NM **1** (*objets nouveaux*) **faire le n. et l'occasion** to sell new and second-hand goods; **ici, on vend du n. et de l'occasion** here we sell both new and second-hand items; **acheter du n.** (*dans l'immobilier*) to buy new; **meublé de** *ou* **en n.** newly furnished; **vêtu de n.** (dressed) in new clothes; **faire du n. avec du vieux** to recycle things; *Fig* to revamp things; **ce couturier est passé maître dans l'art de faire du n. avec du vieux** this fashion designer has become an expert at creating new variants of old styles

2 (*informations nouvelles*) **tu as du n. pour ton visa?** any news about your visa?, have you heard anything about your visa?; **qu'est-ce qu'il y a de** *ou* **quoi de n.?** what's new?; **rien de n. depuis la dernière fois** nothing new since last time; **il y a du n. dans l'affaire Peters** there are new developments in the Peters case

❑ **à neuf** ADV **un devis pour la remise à n. du local/moteur** an estimate for doing up the premises/overhauling the engine; **remettre qch à n.** to make sth as good as new; (*machine*) to recondition sth, to renovate sth; **j'ai remis** *ou* **refait la maison à n.** I did up the house like new

❑ **coup de neuf** NM **donner un coup de n. à qch** to spruce sth up

neufchâtel [nøʃatɛl] NM = creamy cheese from Neufchâtel-en-Bray

neuf-trois [nœftrwa] NM *Fam* (*département de la Seine-Saint-Denis*) Seine-Saint-Denis

neume [nøm] NM *Mus* neum, neume

neuneu [nønø] *Fam* ADJ daft, *Am* dumb

NMF idiot

neural, -e, -aux, -ales [nøral, -o] ADJ neural; **plaque neurale** neural plate

neurasthénie [nørasteni] NF *Méd & Psy* neurasthenia; *Fam* **faire de la n.** (*de la dépression*) to be depressed

neurasthénique [nørastenik] ADJ *Méd & Psy* neurasthenic; *Vieilli* (*dépressif*) depressed

NMF *Méd & Psy* neurasthenic; *Vieilli* (*dépressif*) depressed person

neurinome [nørinom] NM *Méd* neurinoma

neuro- [nøro] PRÉF neuro-

neurobiochimie [nørobjoʃimi] NF neurochemistry, neurobiochemistry

neurobiologie [nørobjolɔʒi] NF neurobiology

neuroblaste [nøroblast] NM neuroblast

neurochimie [nøroʃimi] NF neurochemistry, neurobiochemistry

neurochimique [nøroʃimik] ADJ neurochemical

neurochirurgical, -e, -aux, -ales [nøroʃiryrʒikal, -o] ADJ neurosurgical

neurochirurgie [nøroʃiryrʒi] NF neurosurgery

neurochirurgien, -enne [nøroʃiryrʒjɛ̃, -ɛn] NM,F neurosurgeon

neurodépresseur [nørodeprɛsœr] *Pharm* ADJ M neurodepressant (*avant n*)

NM neurodepressant

neuroendocrinien, -enne [nøroɑ̃dokrinjɛ̃, -ɛn] ADJ neuroendocrine

neuroendocrinologie [nøroɑ̃dokrinolɔʒi] NF neuroendocrinology

neurofibromatose [nørofibromatoz] NF *Méd* neurofibromatosis

neurohistologie [nøroistolɔʒi] NF neurohistology

neuroleptique [nørolɛptik] ADJ neuroleptic

NM neuroleptic; **être sous neuroleptiques** to be on tranquillizers

neurolinguistique [nørolɛ̃gɥistik] NF neurolinguistics (*singulier*)

neurologie [nørolɔʒi] NF neurology

neurologique [nørolɔʒik] ADJ neurologic, neurological

neurologiste [nørolɔʒist], **neurologue** [nørolɔg] NMF neurologist

neuromarketing [nøromarkɔtiŋ] NM neuromarketing

neuromédiateur [nøromedjatœr] NM neurotransmitter

neuromusculaire [nøromyskylɛr] ADJ neuromuscular

neuronal, -e, -aux, -ales [nørɔnal, -o] ADJ neuronal; **réseau n.** neural net

neurone [nørɔn] NM neuron, neurone

neuronique [nørɔnik] ADJ neuronic

neuropathie [nøropati] NF neuropathy

neuropeptide [nøropɛptid] NM neuropeptide

neurophysiologie [nørofizjolɔʒi] NF neurophysiology

neurophysiologique [nørofizjolɔʒik] ADJ neurophysiologic, neurophysiological

neuroplégique [nøroplɛʒik] ADJ neuroplegic

NM neuroplegic

neuropsychiatre [nøropsikjatr] NMF neuropsychiatrist

neuropsychiatrie [nøropsikjatri] NF neuropsychiatry

neuropsychique [nøropsiʃik] ADJ neuropsychic

neuropsychologie [nøropsikolɔʒi] NF neuropsychology

neuropsychologique [nøropsikolɔʒik] ADJ neuropsychological

neuropsychologue [nøropsikolɔg] NMF neuropsychologist

neuroradiologie [nøroradjolɔʒi] NF neuroradiology

neurosciences [nørosjɑ̃s] NFPL neuroscience

neurosécrétion [nørosekresjɔ̃] NF neurosecretion

neurotomie [nørotɔmi] NF *Méd* neurotomy

neurotonie [nørotɔni] NF neurotonia

neurotonique [nørotɔnik] *Méd* ADJ neurotonic, suffering from neurotonia

NMF = person suffering from neurotonia

neurotoxine [nørotɔksin] NF neurotoxin

neurotoxique [nørotɔksik] ADJ neurotoxic

NM neurotoxic substance

neurotransmetteur [nørotrɑ̃smɛtœr] NM neurotransmitter

neurotransmission [nørotrɑ̃smisjɔ̃] NF neurotransmission

neurotrope [nørotrop] ADJ neurotropic

neurovasculaire [nørovaskylɛr] ADJ neurovascular

neurovégétatif, -ive [nøroveʒetatif, -iv] ADJ *Anat* **système nerveux n.** autonomic nervous system

neurula [nøryla] NF *Biol* neurula

Neustrie [nøstri] NF *Hist* **la N.** Neustria (*former region of Gaul*)

neutralisant, -e [nøtralizɑ̃, -ɑ̃t] ADJ neutralizing

NM *Chim* neutralizing agent

neutralisation [nøtralizasjɔ̃] NF **1** (*gén*) neutralization; *Mil* **tir de n.** neutralizing fire **2** *Tech* **pâte de n.** soap stock

neutraliser [3] [nøtralize] VT **1** (*atténuer*) to tone down; **n. un rouge trop vif en y ajoutant du blanc** to tone down a glaring red by adding white

2 (*annuler*) to neutralize, to cancel out; **le ministre veut n. les mesures prises par son prédécesseur** the minister wants to neutralize the measures taken by his predecessor

3 (*maîtriser*) to overpower, to bring under control; **les agents ont neutralisé le forcené** the police overpowered the maniac

4 (*contrecarrer*) to neutralize, to thwart; **n. un concurrent** to thwart a competitor

5 (*bloquer*) to close; **la voie rapide est neutralisée dans le sens Paris-province** the fast lane is closed to traffic leaving Paris

6 *Pol* (*déclarer neutre*) to neutralize; **n. un État** to neutralize a state

7 *Élec, Ling & Méd* to neutralize

►**se neutraliser** VPR to neutralize; **les deux forces se neutralisent** the two forces cancel each other out

neutralisme [nøtralism] NM neutralism

neutraliste [nøtralist] ADJ neutralist, neutralistic

NMF neutralist

neutralité [nøtralite] NF **1** (*d'une attitude*) neutrality; **observer la n.** to remain neutral; **sortir de sa n.** to take sides; *Pol* to abandon one's neutrality *or* one's neutral position; **violer la n. d'un État** to violate a state's neutrality **2** *Chim & Phys* neutrality **3** *Scol* **n. scolaire** secularity of education

neutre [nøtr] ADJ **1** (*couleur, décor, attitude, pays*) neutral; **d'une voix n.** in a neutral *or* an expressionless voice; **je veux rester n.** I don't want to take sides; **tu ne peux pas rester n.** you can't remain neutral; *Mil* **la zone n.** no-man's-land **2** *Chim, Élec & Phys* neutral **3** *Ling & Entom* neuter

NMF *Pol* **les neutres** the neutral countries

NM **1** *Ling* neuter; **au n.** in the neuter **2** *Élec* neutral (wire) **3** *Can Aut* neutral; **se mettre sur le n.** to go into neutral

neutrino [nøtrino] NM *Phys* neutrino

neutrographie [nøtrografi] NF neutron radiography

neutron [nøtrɔ̃] NM neutron

neutronique [nøtrɔnik] ADJ **1** *Nucl* neutron (*avant n*) **2** *Mil* neutron (bomb) (*avant n*)

neutronographie [nøtronografi] NF neutron radiography

neutropénie [nøtropeni] NF *Méd* neutropenia

neutrophile [nøtrofil] ADJ neutrophil (*avant n*), neutrophile (*avant n*), neutrophilic

NM neutrophil, neutrophile

neuvain [nœvɛ̃] NM *Littérature* nine-line stanza

neuvaine [nœvɛn] NF *Rel* novena

neuve [nœv] *voir* **neuf²**

neuvième [nœvjɛm] ADJ ninth; **le n. art** cartoons

NMF **1** (*personne*) ninth

2 (*objet*) ninth (one)

NM **1** (*partie*) ninth

2 (*étage*) *Br* ninth floor, *Am* tenth floor

3 (*arrondissement de Paris*) ninth (arrondissement)

NF **1** *Anciennement Scol Br* = third year of primary school, *Am* ≃ third grade

2 *Mus* ninth; **la N. (de Beethoven)** Beethoven's Ninth, the Ninth; *voir aussi* **cinquième**

neuvièmement [nœvjɛmmɑ̃] ADV ninthly, in ninth place

Nevada [nevada] **NM** *Géog* **le N.** Nevada; **au N.** in Nevada

ne varietur [nevarjetyr] **ADJ INV** **édition n.** definitive edition

névé [neve] **NM 1** *(dans un glacier)* névé **2** *(plaque)* bank of snow

neveu, -x [nəvø] **NM** nephew; *Fam* **un peu, mon n.!** you bet (your sweet life)!, and how!

'Le Neveu de Rameau' *Diderot* 'Rameau's Nephew'

---

névralgie [nevralʒi] **NF** neuralgia; **avoir une n.** *(un mal de tête)* to have a headache; **avoir des névralgies** to suffer from neuralgia

névralgique [nevralʒik] **ADJ 1** *Méd* neuralgic **2** *Fig voir* **point²**

névraxe [nevraks] **NM** *Anat* central nervous system, cerebrospinal axis

névrilème [nevrilɛm] **NM** *Anat* neurilemma

névrite [nevrit] **NF** *Méd* neuritis

névritique [nevritik] **ADJ** *Méd* neuritic

névroglie [nevrɔgli] **NF** *Anat* neuroglia

névropathe [nevrɔpat] **NMF** *Méd* neuropath

névropathie [nevrɔpati] **NF** *Vieilli Méd* neuropathy

névroptère [nevrɔptɛr] **NM** *Entom* Neuroptera

névrose [nevroz] **NF** *Psy* neurosis; **n. obsessionnelle** obsessive compulsive disorder, OCD; **n. post-traumatique** post-traumatic stress disorder

névrosé, -e [nevroze] **ADJ** neurotic
NM,F neurotic

névrotique [nevrɔtik] **ADJ** neurotic

névrotomie [nevrɔtɔmi] **NF** neurotomy

New Age [njuɛdʒ] **ADJ** New Age *(avant n)*

New Deal [njudil] **NM** *Pol* **le N.** the New Deal

New Delhi [njudeli] **NM** New Delhi

New Hampshire [njuɑ̃pʃœr] **NM** *Géog* **le N.** New Hampshire; **dans le N.** in New Hampshire

New Jersey [njuʒɛrzɛ] **NM** *Géog* **le N.** New Jersey; **dans le N.** in New Jersey

new-look [njuluk] **NM INV 1** *Couture* New Look **2** *(style nouveau)* **le n. publicitaire** the new style of advertising
ADJ INV 1 *Couture* New Look *(avant n)* **2** *(rénové)* new look *(avant n)*

newsgroup [njuzgrup] **NM** *Ordinat* newsgroup

news magazine [njuzmagazin] **NM** *Presse* news magazine, current affairs magazine

newton [njutɔn] **NM** newton

newtonien, -enne [njutɔnjɛ̃, -ɛn] **ADJ** Newtonian

newton-mètre [njutɔnmɛtr] *(pl* **newtons-mètres)** **NM** newton metre

new wave [njuwɛv] **ADJ INV** new wave *(avant n)*
NF INV new wave

New York [nujɔrk] **NM 1** *(ville)* New York (City) **2 l'État de N.** New York State; **dans l'État de N.** in New York State

new-yorkais, -e [nujɔrkɛ, -ɛz] *(mpl inv, fpl* **new-yorkaises)** **ADJ** of/from New York; **les musées n.** the museums in New York
❑ **New-Yorkais, -e NM,F** New Yorker

ney [nɛ] **NM** *Mus* ney

nez [ne] **NM 1** *(partie du corps)* nose; **avoir le n. bouché** to have a stuffed-up *or* blocked nose; **avoir le n. qui coule** to have a runny nose; **avoir le n. qui saigne, saigner du n.** to have a nosebleed; **avoir le n. fin** *(avoir un bon odorat)* to have a good nose *or* a keen sense of smell; **se faire refaire le n.** to have one's nose fixed, to have a nose job; **n. camus** pug nose; **n. en trompette** turned-up nose; **avoir un n. grec** to have a Grecian nose; **avoir un n. en pied de marmite** to have a turned-up nose; **respirer du n.** to breathe through one's nose; **parler du n.** to talk *or* to speak through one's nose

2 *Fig (jugement)* flair, good judgement *(UNCOUNT)*, intuition *(UNCOUNT)*; **avoir du n.** to have good judgement; **elle a du n. pour la qualité des tissus** she's a good judge of fabric, she knows good fabric when she sees it; **il a du n. pour acheter des antiquités** he's got a flair for buying antiques; **avoir le n. fin** *ou* **creux** to be shrewd; **j'ai eu du n.** *ou* **le n. fin** *ou* **le n. creux** my intuition was good; **tu vois, j'ai eu le n. fin de partir avant minuit** you see, I was right to trust my instinct and leave before midnight

3 *(odorat → d'une personne)* sense of smell; *(→ d'un chien)* scent; **avoir du n.** to have a good nose

4 *(en parfumerie → personne)* nose

5 *Aviat* nose; **sur le n.** tilting down

6 *Constr* (tile) nib; **n. de marche** nosing *(of a stair)*

7 *Géog* edge, overhang

8 *Naut* nose, bow; **sur le n.** down by the bows, on the bows

9 *(d'un vin)* nose; **un vin qui a du n.** a wine with a good nose

10 *Tech* shank; *(de moteur)* nosepiece; **n. de broche** spindle shank

11 *Com* **n. de caisse** checkout display

12 *(locutions)* **le n. en l'air** looking upwards; *Fig (sans souci)* without a care in the world; *(en rêvant)* with one's head in the clouds; **partir/se promener le n. au vent** to stroll *or* to dawdle off/along; **il a toujours le n. dans une BD** he's always got his nose buried in a comic; **sans lever le n. de son travail** without looking up from his/her work; **travailler sans lever le n.** to work without a break, to keep one's head down; **montrer (le bout de) son n.** to show one's face, to put in an appearance; **le voisin/soleil n'a pas montré son n. de la semaine** the man next door/sun hasn't come out all week; **fermer/claquer la porte au n. à qn** to shut/to slam the door in sb's face; **raccrocher au n. à qn** to hang up on sb, to put the phone down on sb; **au** *ou* **sous le n. de qn, au n. et à la barbe de qn** under sb's nose; **dérober qch au n. et à la barbe de qn** to steal sth from right under sb's nose; **tu as le n. dessus!, il est sous ton n.!** it's right under your nose!; **le dernier billet m'est passé sous le n.** I just missed the last ticket; **ça m'est passé sous le n.** it slipped through my fingers; **regarder qn sous le n.** to stare at sb; **se trouver n. à n. avec qn** to find oneself face to face with sb; **l'ayant critiquée dans sa rubrique, il eut le désagrément de se trouver n. à n. avec elle** after criticizing her in his column, he had the unpleasant experience of meeting her face to face; *Fam* **ce type, je l'ai dans le n.** I can't stand *or* stomach that guy, *Br* that guy gets right up my nose; **ton n. remue** *ou* **s'allonge!** *(tu mens)* you're lying!, your nose is growing (longer)!; **tu aurais vu le n. qu'il a fait!** you should have seen his face!; **ça se voit comme le n. au milieu de la figure** it's as plain as the nose on your face; **elle est jalouse, ça se voit comme le n. au milieu de la figure** she's jealous, it's written all over her face; **cela te pend au n.** you've got it coming (to you); *Belg* **faire de son n.** to make a fuss; *Fam* **se manger** *ou* **se bouffer le n.** to be at each other's throats; **avoir un verre** *ou* **un coup dans le n.** to be a bit merry *or* tipsy; **elle ne met jamais le n. ici** she never shows her face in here; **je n'ai pas mis le n. dehors de la journée** I didn't set foot outside the door all day; *Fam* **mettre** *ou* **fourrer son n. dans les affaires de qn** to poke *or* to stick one's nose in sb's business; **tu n'as pas intérêt à mettre ton n. dans mes affaires** you'd better keep your (big) nose out of my business; **mettre à qn le n.** *Fam* **dans son caca** *ou très Fam* **dans sa merde** to call sb to order, to pull sb up

❑ **à plein nez ADV ça sent le fromage à plein n.** there's a strong smell of cheese; *Fig* **ça sent l'entourloupe à plein n.** there's some dirty business going on

NF [ɛnɛf] **NF** *(abrév* **Norme française)** = label indicating compliance with official French standards, *Br* ≃ BS, *Am* ≃ US standard

NGV [ɛnʒeve] **NM** *Naut (abrév* **navire à grande vitesse)** = high-speed boat

ni [ni] **CONJ** nor; **je ne peux ni ne veux venir** I can't come and I don't want to either, I can't come, nor do I want to; **il ne veut pas qu'on l'appelle, ni même qu'on lui écrive** he doesn't want anyone to phone him or even to write to him; **elle ne me parle plus, ni même ne me regarde** she doesn't talk to me any more, nor even look at me; **sans argent ni bagages** without money or luggage, with neither money nor luggage; **il est sorti sans pull ni écharpe** he went out without either his jumper or his scarf; **il ne manque pas de charme ni d'aisance** he lacks neither charm nor ease of manner; **il ne mange ni ne boit** he neither eats nor drinks; **je n'ai jamais rien mangé ni bu d'aussi bon** I have never eaten nor drunk anything so good; **ni moi** *(moi non plus)* nor me (either), *Sout* nor I
❑ **ni… ni CONJ** neither… nor; **ni Pierre ni Henri ne sont venus** neither Pierre nor Henri came; **je n'ai ni femme ni enfant ni amis** I have neither wife nor child nor friends; **ni lui ni moi** neither of us; **ni lui ni elle ne sont prêts à céder** neither of them is willing to give way; **je ne veux voir ni lui ni elle** I don't want to see either of them; **ni toi ni moi ne pouvons l'aider** neither you nor I can help him, neither of us can help him; **ni ton père ni toi ne le connaissez** neither your father nor you knows him; **ni l'un ni l'autre** neither of them *or* neither one nor the other; **ni l'un ni l'autre n'est tout à fait innocent** neither (one) of them is completely innocent; **je n'aime ni l'un ni l'autre** I don't like either of them, I like neither of them; **ni d'un côté, ni de l'autre** on neither side, on neither one side nor the other; **ni ici ni ailleurs** neither here nor elsewhere; **il n'a répondu ni oui ni non** he didn't say yes and he didn't say no; **il n'est ni plus sot ni plus paresseux qu'un autre** he's no more silly or lazy than the next man; **c'était comment? – ni bien ni mal** how was it? – OK; **ni fleurs ni couronnes** *(dans faire-part de décès)* no flowers, by request; **ni vu ni connu** without anybody noticing; **et ni vu ni connu, il a empoché les pièces** quick as a flash, he pocketed the coins and nobody was any the wiser; **n'avoir ni dieu ni maître** to serve no master; **ni plus ni moins** neither more nor less

niable [njabl] **ADJ** deniable; **les faits ne sont pas niables** the facts cannot be denied

niacoué, -e [njakwe] **NM,F** *très Fam Br* slant-eye, *Am* gook, = offensive term used to refer to an oriental person

Niagara [njagara] **NM** **les chutes du N.** the Niagara falls

niais, -e [njɛ, njɛz] **ADJ 1** *(sot)* simple, simple-minded, inane; *(sourire)* inane, silly **2** *Orn* **gerfaut n.** nestling gyrfalcon
NM,F simpleton, halfwit; **espèce de grand n.!** you great nincompoop!

niaisage [njɛzaʒ] **NM** *Can* idleness

niaisement [njɛzmɑ̃] **ADV** inanely, stupidly, foolishly; **rire n.** to give a silly laugh, to laugh inanely

niaiser [3] [njɛze] *Can Fam* **VT n. qn** *(faire tourner en bourrique)* to drive sb crazy; *(se moquer de)* *Br* to wind sb up, *Am* to razz sb; *(raconter des histoires à)* to pull sb's leg, *Br* to wind sb up, to have sb on; **faire n. qn** to waste sb's time▪
VI *(hésiter)* to dither; *(ne rien faire)* to loaf about

niaiserie [njɛzri] **NF 1** *(caractère)* simpleness, inanity, foolishness **2** *(parole)* stupid *or* inane remark; **cesse de raconter des niaiseries** stop talking such silly nonsense

niaiseux, -euse [njezø, -øz] *Can Fam* **ADJ** silly▪
NM,F moron, jerk

Niamey [njamɛ] **NM** Niamey

niaouli [njauli] **NM** *Bot* niaouli

niaque [njak] **NF** *Fam* fighting spirit▪, drive▪; **avoir la n., être plein de n.** to have plenty of drive

nib [nib] **ADV** *très Fam* nothing▪; **n. de n.!** nothing at all!▪, *Br* not a sausage!

nibard [nibar] **NM** *très Fam (sein)* tit, knocker

NICAM [nikam] **NM INV** *(abrév* **near instantaneously companded audio multiplex)** NICAM, Nicam

Nicaragua [nikaragwa] **NM** *Géog* **le N.** Nicaragua; **vivre au N.** to live in Nicaragua; **aller au N.** to go to Nicaragua

nicaraguayen, -enne [nikaragwajɛ̃, -ɛn] **ADJ** Nicaraguan
❑ **Nicaraguayen, -enne NM,F** Nicaraguan

niccolite [nikɔlit] **NF** *Minér* niccolite

Nice [nis] **NM** Nice

Nicée [nise] **NF** *Antiq* Nicaea; **le symbole de N.** the Nicene Creed

Nice-Matin [nismatɛ̃] **NM** *Presse* = daily newspaper published in Nice

niche¹ [niʃ] **NF 1** *(renfoncement)* niche, (small) alcove **2** *École* **n. écologique** ecological niche **3** *Mktg* (market) niche **4** *Géog* niche, recess; **n. de**

nivation nivation hollow **5** *(pour chien)* kennel; **à la n.!** into your kennel! **6** *Méd* niche (defect) **7** *Rail* **n. de refuge** refuge hole

niche² [niʃ] NF *Fam (espièglerie)* trick■; **faire des niches à qn** to play pranks on sb

nichée [niʃe] NF **1** *(d'oiseaux)* nest, brood **2** *(de chiots, de chatons)* litter **3** *Fam (enfants)* **il est arrivé avec toute sa n.** he turned up with all his brood

nicher [3] [niʃe] VI **1** *(faire son nid)* to nest (**dans** in)

2 *Fam (habiter)* to crash, *Br* to doss; **elle niche chez moi pour l'instant** she's crashing at my place just now

3 *(couver)* to brood

VT to nestle; **n. sa tête au creux de l'épaule de qn** to nestle one's head on *or* against sb's shoulder

▶**se nicher** VPR **1** *(faire son nid)* to nest

2 *(se blottir)* to nestle; **niché dans un fauteuil** curled up in an armchair; **je rêve d'un petit chalet niché dans la montagne** I dream of a little chalet nestling among the mountains

3 *Fam (se cacher)* **où est-elle allée se n.?** where's she hiding herself?; **où ce chat a-t-il bien pu se n.?** where's the cat got to?; **pourquoi es-tu allé te n. dans ce trou perdu?** why did you have to go and park yourself in the back of beyond?; **où l'amour-propre va-t-il se n.?** pride is found in the strangest places!

nichet [niʃɛ] NM nest egg

nichoir [niʃwar] NM nest-box

nichon [niʃɔ̃] NM *très Fam* boob, tit

nickel [nikɛl] NM nickel

ADJ INV *Fam* **1** *(très propre)* spotless■, gleaming; **c'est n. chez toi!** your house is so spotless! **2** *(parfait)* perfect■, just the thing, *Br* spot-on; **c'est n., comme appareil, pour se mettre à la photo** it's the perfect camera for someone just taking up photography; **ça s'est super bien passé, l'organisation et l'ambiance étaient n.!** it went really well, it was brilliantly organized and the atmosphere was perfect *or Br* spot-on!

ADV *Fam (très bien)* **faire qch n. (chrome)** to do sth really well■

nickelage [niklaʒ] NM nickel-plating, nickelling

nickelé, -e [nikle] ADJ nickel-plated, nickelled; *Fam Vieilli* **avoir les pieds nickelés** *(être trop paresseux pour marcher)* to be too lazy to walk anywhere■; *(avoir de la chance)* to be lucky■ *or Br* jammy

nickeler [24] [nikle] VT to plate with nickel, to nickel

nickéline [nikelin] NF *Minér* niccolite

nicnac [niknak] NM *Belg* = small biscuit

Nicodème [nikɔdɛm] NPR Nicodemus

nicodème [nikɔdɛm] NM *Littéraire & Vieilli* simpleton

niçois, -e [niswa, -az] ADJ of/from Nice

NM *Ling* Nice dialect

□ **Niçois, -e** NM,F = inhabitant of or person from Nice

□ **à la niçoise** ADJ *Culin* à la niçoise *(with tomatoes and garlic)*

nicol [nikɔl] NM *Opt* Nicol (prism)

nicolaïsme [nikɔlaism] NM *Rel* **1** *(au Iᵉʳ siècle)* Nicolaitanism **2** *(mariage des prêtres)* marriage of priests

nicolaïte [nikɔlait] NM *Rel* Nicolaitan

Nicomaque [nikɔmak] NPR *Antiq* Nicomachus

Nicosie [nikɔzi] NM Nicosia

nicotinamide [nikɔtinamid] NM *Biol & Chim* nicotinamide

nicotine [nikɔtin] NF nicotine

nicotinique [nikɔtinik] ADJ nicotinic

nicotinisme [nikɔtinism] NM *Méd* nicotinism

nictation [niktasjɔ̃] NF nictation, nictitation

nictitant, -e [niktitɑ̃, -ɑ̃t] ADJ *Zool* nictitating

nictitation [niktitasjɔ̃] NF nictation, nictitation

nid [ni] NM **1** *(d'oiseau, de guêpes)* nest; **n. d'aigle** eyrie, eagle's nest; *Fig* eyrie

2 *Fig (habitation)* (little) nest; **n. d'amour** love nest; **un (petit) n. douillet** a cosy little nest; **trouver le n. vide** to find (that) the bird has flown; **faire son n.** to nest

3 *(concentration)* nest; **n. de brigands** den of thieves; **un n. d'espions** a spy hideout, a den of spies; **n. de mitrailleuses** machinegun nest; **n. à poussière** dust trap; **n. à rats** slum, hovel; **n. de**

résistance pocket of resistance; **un n. de vipères** a vipers' nest

□ **nid d'ange** *Br* baby's sleeping bag, *Am* bunting bag

□ **nids d'hirondelle** NMPL *Culin* bird's nest

nida [nida] NM *Tech (abrév* **nid-d'abeilles**) honeycomb

nidation [nidasjɔ̃] NF *Biol* nidation

nid-d'abeilles [nidabɛj] *(pl* **nids-d'abeilles**) NM **1** *(tissu)* waffle; *(point de broderie)* smocking; **une robe à n.** a smocked dress **2** *Aut* **radiateur à n.** honeycomb (radiator) **3** *Tech (matériau)* honeycomb **4** *Géol* honeycomb (weathering)

nid-de-pie [nidpi] *(pl* **nids-de-pie**) NM **1** *Mil* lodgement **2** *Naut* crow's nest

nid-de-poule [nidpul] *(pl* **nids-de-poule**) NM pothole

nid-d'oiseau [nidwazo] *(pl* **nids-d'oiseau**) NM *Bot* bird's-nest orchid

nidicole [nidikɔl] ADJ *Orn (oisillon)* nest-reared, *Spéc* nidicolous

nidification [nidifikasjɔ̃] NF nest building, nidification

nidifier [9] [nidifje] VI to nest

nidifuge [nidifyʒ] ADJ *Orn (oisillon)* nest-fleeing, *Spéc* nidifugous

Nidwald [nidvalt] NM *Géog* **le demi-canton de N.** Nidwalden demicanton

niébé [njebe] NM *Bot* cowpea

nièce [njɛs] NF niece

niellage [njɛlaʒ] NM niello work

nielle¹ [njɛl] NF **1** *(plante)* corncockle **2** *(maladie)* **n. des blés** blight, smut

nielle² [njɛl] NM *(incrustation)* niello

nieller¹ [4] [njele] VT *Agr* to blight, to smut

nieller² [4] [njele] VT *(incruster)* to niello

nielleur [njɛlœr] NM niellist, niello-worker

niellure¹ [njelyr] NF *Beaux-Arts* niello work

niellure² [njelyr] NF *Agr* blight, smut

nième, nⁱᵉᵐᵉ [ɛnjɛm] ADJ *Math* nth; **la puissance nⁱᵉᵐᵉ** the nth power

nier [9] [nje] VT **1** *(démentir)* to deny; **je nie l'avoir vue** I deny having seen her; **il nie l'avoir tuée** he denies that he killed her, he denies killing her; **elle nie être coupable** she denies that she's guilty; **je nierai tout en bloc** I'll deny it all outright; **cela, on ne peut le n.** that cannot be denied; **je ne nie pas que j'ai parfois tort** I don't deny that I'm sometimes wrong; **on ne peut pas n. que…** there's no denying *or* one can't deny *or* it's undeniable that…

2 *(rejeter, refuser)* to deny; **n. sa signature** to deny *or* to repudiate one's (own) signature

VI **il continue de n.** he continues to deny it; **l'accusé nie** the accused denies the charge

niet [njɛt] EXCLAM no way!, not a chance!

nietzschéen, -enne [nitʃeɛ̃, -ɛn] *Phil* ADJ Nietzschean

NM,F Nietzschean

Nièvre [njɛvr] NF **la N.** Nièvre

nife [nife] NM *Vieilli Géol* = inner core of the Earth

nigaud, -e [nigo, -od] ADJ simple, stupid

NM,F idiot, halfwit; **gros n.!** you great *or* big idiot!; **quel n.!** what an idiot!

nigauderie [nigodri] NF simpleness, simplemindedness, stupidity

nigelle [niʒɛl] NF *Bot* nigella, love-in-a-mist

Niger [niʒɛr] NM *Géog* **1** *(fleuve)* **le N.** the River Niger **2** *(État)* **le N.** Niger; **vivre au N.** to live in Niger; **aller au N.** to go to Niger

Nigeria [niʒɛrja] NM *Géog* **le N.** Nigeria; **vivre au N.** to live in Nigeria; **aller au N.** to go to Nigeria

nigérian, -e [niʒerjɑ̃, -an] ADJ Nigerian

□ **Nigérian, -e** NM,F Nigerian

nigérien, -enne [niʒerjɛ̃, -ɛn] ADJ Nigerien

□ **Nigérien, -enne** NM,F Nigerien

nigéro-congolais, -e [niʒerɔkɔ̃gɔlɛ, -ɛz] *(mpl inv, fpl* **nigéro-congolaises**) ADJ Niger-Congo *(avant n)*

night-club [najtklœb] *(pl* **night-clubs**) NM nightclub

nihilisme [niilism] NM nihilism

nihiliste [niilist] ADJ nihilist, nihilistic

NMF nihilist

Nijinski [niʒinski] NPR Nijinsky

Nikê [nikɛ] NPR *Myth* Nike

Nil [nil] NM **le N.** the Nile; **le N. Blanc** the White Nile; **le N. Bleu** the Blue Nile

nilgaut [nilgo] NM *Zool* nilgai

nille [nij] NF loose handle

nilles [nij] NFPL *Suisse* knuckles

nilo-saharien, -enne [nilɔsaarjɛ̃, -ɛn] *(mpl* **nilo-sahariens**, *fpl* **nilo-sahariennes**) ADJ *Ling* Nilo-Saharan

nilotique [nilɔtik] ADJ *Ling* of the Nile, Nilotic

nimbe [nɛ̃b] NM **1** *Beaux-Arts & Rel* nimbus, aureole *(round the head)* **2** *Littéraire* halo, nimbus

nimber [3] [nɛ̃be] VT **1** *Beaux-Arts & Rel* to aureole, to halo **2** *Littéraire* **des nuages nimbés d'une lumière argentée** clouds wreathed in silvery light

nimbo-stratus [nɛ̃bostratys] NM INV *Météo* nimbostratus

nimbus [nɛ̃bys] NM INV *Météo* nimbus

Nimègue [nimɛg] NM Nijmegen

Nîmes [nim] NF Nîmes

nîmois, -e [nimwa, -az] ADJ of/from Nîmes

□ **Nîmois, -e** NM,F = inhabitant of or person from Nîmes

n'importe [nɛ̃pɔrt] ADV **1** *(indique l'indétermination)* **quel pull mets-tu? – n.** which sweater are you going to wear? – any of them

2 *(introduit une opposition)* **son roman est très discuté, n., il a du succès** his/her novel is highly controversial, but it's successful all the same

□ **n'importe comment** ADV **1** *(sans soin)* any old how; **il m'a coupé les cheveux n. comment** he cut my hair anyhow *or* any old how

2 *(de toute façon)* anyhow, anyway; **n. comment, il est trop tard pour l'appeler** anyhow *or* anyway, it's too late to call him

□ **n'importe lequel, n'importe laquelle** PRON INDÉFINI any; **n. lequel d'entre eux** any (one) of them; **tu veux le rouge ou le vert? – n. lequel** do you want the red one or the green one? – either *or* I don't mind

□ **n'importe où** ADV anywhere; **ne laisse pas traîner tes affaires n. où** don't just leave your things anywhere

□ **n'importe quand** ADV whenever you/we/*etc* like

□ **n'importe quel, n'importe quelle** ADJ INDÉFINI any; **n. quel débutant sait ça** any beginner knows that

□ **n'importe qui** PRON INDÉFINI anybody, anyone; *Fam* **ce n'est pas n. qui!** he/she is not just anybody!; **ne parle pas à n. qui** don't talk to just anybody; **demande à n. qui dans la rue** ask the first person you meet in the street

□ **n'importe quoi** PRON INDÉFINI anything; **il ferait n. quoi pour obtenir le rôle** he'd do anything *or* he would go to any lengths to get the part; **tu dis vraiment n. quoi!** you're talking absolute nonsense!; *Fam* **c'est un bon investissement – n. quoi!** that's a good investment – don't talk nonsense *or esp Br* rubbish!; **3000 euros, ce n'est pas n. quoi!** 3,000 euros is not to be sneezed at!; **une table Louis XIII d'époque, ce n'est pas n. quoi** a genuine Louis XIII table is no ordinary table

ninas [ninas] NM INV (French) cigar

Ninive [niniv] NM Nineveh

niobium [njɔbjɔm] NM *Chim* niobium

niochon, -onne [njɔʃɔ̃, -ɔn] *Can Fam* ADJ *Péj (niais)* dopey, gormless

NM,F **1** *Péj (personne niaise)* dope, fool■ **2** *Vieilli (dernier-né)* last-born (child)■ *(in a large family)*

niolo [njɔlɔ] NM Niolo *(Corsican cheese)*

NIP [nip] NM *Can Banque (abrév* **numéro d'identification personnel**) ≃ PIN (number)

nippe [nip] *Fam* NF *(vêtement)* **je n'ai plus une n. à me mettre** I've got nothing to wear■

□ **nippes** NFPL *(habits usagés)* gear (UNCOUNT), *Br* clobber (UNCOUNT)

nipper [3] [nipe] *Fam* VT to rig out, to dress up■; **elle est drôlement bien nippée ce soir!** she's dressed to the nines tonight!

▶**se nipper** VPR to get dressed■; **il sait pas se n.** he's got no dress sense■

nippon, -e *ou* **-onne** [nipɔ̃, -ɔn] ADJ Japanese

□ **Nippon, -e** *ou* **-onne** NM,F Japanese; **les Nippons** the Japanese

nique [nik] NF **faire la n. à qn** *(faire un geste de bravade, de mépris à)* to thumb one's nose at sb;

(se moquer de) to poke fun *or* to gibe at sb; **ils se sont échappés en faisant la n. aux gardiens** they escaped, making fun of the guards as they went

niquer [3] [nike] **VT 1** *Vulg (posséder sexuellement)* to fuck, to screw; **va te faire n.!, nique ta mère!** fuck off!, go and fuck yourself!

2 *très Fam (duper)* to shaft, to screw; **se faire n.** to get shafted; **c'est un faux, tu t'es fait n.!** it's a fake, you've been shafted *or* screwed!

3 *très Fam (attraper)* to nab, to collar; **il s'est fait n. par les contrôleurs** he got nabbed *or* collared by the ticket collectors

4 *très Fam (endommager)* to bust, *Br* to knacker, to bugger; **il m'a niqué ma mob** he's bust *or Br* knackered *or* buggered my moped; **je vais lui n. sa gueule!** I'm going to waste his/her fucking face!; **n. sa mère à qn** to waste sb's face, *Br* to punch sb's lights out, *Am* to punch sb out

VI *Vulg* to fuck, to screw

niquet [nikɛ] **NM** *Belg Fam* snooze, nap■

nirvana [nirvana] **NM** nirvana

nissart [nisar] **NM** = dialect of langue d'oc spoken in the area around Nice

nitrant, -e [nitrɑ̃, -ɑ̃t] **ADJ** nitrifying

nitratation [nitratasjɔ̃] **NF** nitrification

nitrate [nitrat] **NM** nitrate; **n. de potassium** nitre

nitrater [3] [nitrate] **VT** to nitrate

nitration [nitrasjɔ̃] **NF** nitration

nitre [nitr] **NM** *Vieilli Chim* nitre, saltpetre

nitré, -e [nitre] **ADJ** nitrated; **composé n.** nitro-compound

nitrer [3] [nitre] **VT** to nitrate

nitreux, -euse [nitrø, -øz] **ADJ** nitrous

nitrière [nitrijɛr] **NF** nitrebed, saltpetrebed

nitrifiant, -e [nitrifjɑ̃, -ɑ̃t] **ADJ** nitrifying

nitrification [nitrifikasjɔ̃] **NF** nitrification

nitrifier [9] [nitrifje] **VT** to nitrify

►**se nitrifier VPR** to nitrify

nitrile [nitril] **NM** nitrile

nitrique [nitrik] **ADJ** nitric

nitrite [nitrit] **NM** nitrite

nitrobacter [nitrobaktɛr] **NM** nitrobacter

nitrobactérie [nitrobakteri] **NF** nitrobacterium

nitrobenzène [nitrobɛ̃zɛn] **NM** nitrobenzene

nitrocellulose [nitroselyloz] **NF** nitrocellulose

nitrogénase [nitroʒenaz] **NF** *Chim* nitrogenase

nitrogène [nitroʒɛn] **NM** *Vieilli* nitrogen

nitroglycérine [nitrogliserin] **NF** nitroglycerin, nitroglycerine

nitrométhane [nitrometan] **NF** *Chim* nitromethane

nitrophénol [nitrofenɔl] **NM** *Chim* nitrophenol

nitrosation [nitrozasjɔ̃] **NF** nitrosation

nitrosé, -e [nitroze] **ADJ** nitroso

nitrosomonas [nitrozɔmɔnas] **NM** nitrosomonas

nitrosyle [nitrozil] **NM** nitrosyl

nitruration [nitryrasjɔ̃] **NF** *Métal* nitriding

nitrure [nitryr] **NM** nitride; **n. de fer** iron nitride

nitrurer [3] [nitryre] **VT** *Métal* to nitride

nitryle [nitril] **NM** *Chim* nitroxyl, nitryl

nival, -e, -aux, -ales [nival, -o] **ADJ** *Géog* nival

niveau, -x [nivo] **NM 1** *(hauteur)* level; **n. de l'eau** water level; **n. d'eau/d'huile** water/oil level; **vérifie les niveaux d'eau et d'huile** check the oil and water levels; **n. des basses/hautes eaux** low-water/high-water mark; **le liquide a atteint le n. de la flèche** the liquid has risen to *or* has reached the level of the pointer; **la Saône n'avait jamais atteint un n. aussi haut** the Saône had never reached such a high level *or* had never been so high; **les deux cadres ne sont pas au même n.** the two frames are not level (with each other); **fixer les étagères au même n. que la cheminée** put up the shelves level with *or* on the same level as the mantelpiece

2 *(étage)* level, storey; **un parking à trois niveaux** a *Br* car park *or Am* parking lot on three levels; **un immeuble à dix niveaux** a ten-storey building; **le supermarché se trouve au troisième n.** the supermarket is on the third level; **n. arrivée** *(d'un aéroport)* arrivals level; **n. départ** *(d'un aéroport)* departures level

3 *(degré)* level; **maintenir les prix à un n. élevé** to maintain prices at a high level; **la production atteint son plus haut n.** production is reaching its peak; **la production n'avait jamais atteint un n. aussi haut** production had never reached such a high level *or* had never been so high; **la natalité n'est jamais tombée à un n. aussi bas** the birth-rate is at an all-time low *or* at its lowest level ever; **la décision a été prise au plus haut n.** the decision was made at the highest level; **au plus haut n. de la hiérarchie** at the highest level of the hierarchy, at the very top; *Fig* **au plus bas n. de l'échelle** at the very bottom of the ladder; **les salaires augmentent régulièrement à tous les niveaux** there are regular salary increases for all grades *or* at all levels; **n. social** social level; **ils sont d'un n. social différent** they are from different social backgrounds; **n. des besoins** need level; **n. d'entrée** *(à un poste)* entry level; *Ling* **n. de langue** register; **n. d'occupation** *(d'un hôtel)* occupancy level; **n. de prix** price level; **n. des stocks** inventory *or* stock level

4 *(étape)* level, stage; **méthode d'apprentissage à plusieurs niveaux** learning method in several stages *or* steps

5 *(qualité)* level, standard; **n. scolaire** academic standard; **son n. scolaire est-il bon?** is he/she doing well at school?; **un n. d'enseignement élevé** a high academic standard; **quel est son n. en anglais?** what is his/her standard in English?; **j'ai un bon n./un n. moyen en russe** I'm good/average at Russian; **les élèves sont tous du même n.** the pupils are all on a par *or* on the same level; **avoir le n. (requis)** to be up to standard; **vous n'avez pas le n. requis** you don't have the required standard; **je ne peux pas nager avec toi, je suis loin d'avoir ton n.** I can't swim with you, I'm not up to your standard; **évaluer le n. des candidats** to evaluate the candidates' level of ability; **nous recherchons un candidat n. baccalauréat/maîtrise** we are looking for a candidate of baccalauréat/master's degree standard; **n. de vie** standard of living

6 *Constr* **n. de pente** graduated plumb level

7 *Géog* level; **n. de la mer** sea level; **n. de base** base-level; **n. hydrostatique** piezometric surface

8 *Mines* level, drift; *(galerie)* gallery, flat slope

9 *Pétr* level

10 *Phys* level; **n. (d'énergie)** energy level

11 *Tél* **n. d'un signal** signal level

12 *(instrument)* level (tube); **n. d'eau** water level; **n. à bulle (d'air)** spirit level; **n. à lunette** dumpy level; **n. de maçon** plumb level; **n. à plomb** vertical *or* plumb level

13 *Ordinat* **n. d'accès** *(dans un réseau)* access level; **n. de gris** grey scale; **n. de sécurité** security level

14 *Bourse* **n. de cours des actions** stock price level; **n. de dépôt requis** margin requirement

❑ **au niveau ADJ** up to standard, of the required level; **dans deux mois, vous serez au n.** in two months' time, you'll have caught up **ADV 1 se mettre au n.** to catch up **2 au n. régional/local** at regional/local level; *Fam* **au n. matériel** on the financial front, financewise, where finance is concerned; *Fam* **au n. sentimental** as far as one's love life is concerned

❑ **au niveau de PRÉP 1** *(dans l'espace)* **au n. de la mer** at sea level; **l'eau lui arrivait au n. du genou** the water came up to his/her knees; **je ressens une douleur au n. de la hanche** I've got a pain in my hip; **au n. du carrefour, vous tournez à droite** when you come to the crossroads, turn right; **j'habite à peu près au n. de l'église** I live by the church

2 *(dans une hiérarchie)* on a par with, at the level of; **cet élève n'est pas au n. de sa classe** this pupil is not on a par with the rest of his class; **ce problème sera traité au n. du syndicat** this problem will be dealt with at union level

3 *aussi Fig* **se mettre au n. de qn** to come down to sb's level

❑ **de niveau ADJ** level; **un sol de n.** a level floor; **mettre qch de n.** to make sth level; **les deux terrains ne sont pas de n.** the two plots of land are not level (with each other); **la terrasse est de n. avec le salon** the terrace is (on a) level with *or* on the same level as the lounge

nivelage [nivlaʒ] **NM** equalizing, levelling (out); **n. par le bas** levelling down

niveler [24] [nivle] **VT 1** *(aplanir)* to level (off); **n. un terrain en pente** to level off a sloping piece of ground; **nivelé par l'érosion** worn (away) by erosion **2** *Fig (égaliser)* to level (off), to even out; **leur but est de n. les revenus des Français** their aim is to reduce salary differentials in France; **n. par le bas** *ou* **au plus bas** to level down; **n. par le haut** *ou* **au plus haut** to level up **3** *Tech* to (measure with a spirit) level

nivelette [nivlɛt] **NF** boning rod

niveleur, -euse [nivlœr, -øz] **NM,F** leveller

NM *Hist* Leveller

❑ **niveleuse NF** *Constr* grader, motor grader

nivelle *etc voir* **niveler**

nivellement [nivɛlmɑ̃] **NM 1** *(aplanissement)* evening out, levelling (out) *or* off **2** *Géog* (erosion) denudation **3** *Fig (égalisation)* equalizing, levelling; **le n. des revenus** income redistribution; **n. par le bas** levelling down **4** *Géol* levelling; **n. géodésique** geodetic levelling

nivéole [niveɔl] **NF** *Bot* snowflake

Nivernais [nivɛrnɛ] **NM le N.** the Nivernais, the region around Nevers

nivernais, -e [nivɛrnɛ, -ɛz] **ADJ** of/from Nevers

❑ **Nivernais, -e NM,F** = inhabitant of or person from Nevers

niverolle [nivərɔl] **NF** *Orn* **n. des Alpes** snow finch

nivicole [nivikɔl] **ADJ** *Écol (animal)* living in snow-covered areas; *(plante)* growing in snow-covered areas

nivo-glaciaire [nivɔglasjɛr] *(pl* **nivo-glaciaires***)* **ADJ** *voir* **régime**

nivologie [nivɔlɔʒi] **NF 1** *(conditions)* snow conditions **2** *(recherche)* snow research, *Spéc* nivology

nivo-pluvial, -e, -aux, -ales [nivɔplyvjal, -o] *voir* **régime**

nivôse [nivoz] **NM** = 4th month of the French Revolutionary calendar (from 21 December to 20 January)

nixe [niks] **NF** *Myth* nixie

nizeré [nizre] **NM** essence of white roses

NL *(abrév écrite* **nouvelle lune***)* new moon

NN *(abrév écrite* **nouvelle norme***)* = revised standard of hotel classification

N-N-E *(abrév écrite* **Nord-Nord-Est***)* NNE

N-N-O *(abrév écrite* **Nord-Nord-Ouest***)* NNW

NNTP [ɛnɛntepe] **NM** *Ordinat (abrév* **Network News Transfer Protocol***)* NNTP

nô [no] **NM INV** *Théât* no, noh

no., n° *(abrév écrite* **numéro***)* no.

N-O *(abrév écrite* **Nord-Ouest***)* NW

Nobel [nɔbɛl] **NM le N. de la paix** *(prix)* the Nobel peace prize; *(personne)* the winner of the Nobel peace prize

nobélisable [nɔbelizabl] **ADJ** *(chercheur, écrivain)* potential Nobel prize-winning

NMF potential Nobel prize-winner

nobéliser [3] [nɔbelize] **VT** *(décerner un prix Nobel à)* to award the Nobel prize to

nobélium [nɔbeljɔm] **NM** *Chim* nobelium

nobiliaire [nɔbiljɛr] **ADJ** nobiliary; **particule n.** nobiliary particle; **titre n.** title

NM peerage list

noblaillon, -onne [nɔblajɔ̃, -ɔn] **NM,F** *Péj* petty nobleman, *f* petty noblewoman

noble [nɔbl] **ADJ 1** *(de haute naissance)* noble **2** *Fig* noble; **un geste n.** a noble deed; **le n. art** the noble art **3** *(en œnologie)* noble, of noble vintage **4** *Métal & Phys* noble; **un gaz n.** a noble gas

NMF noble, nobleman, *f* noblewoman; **les nobles** the nobility

NM *Hist* noble (coin)

noblement [nɔbləmɑ̃] **ADV** nobly

noblesse [nɔblɛs] **NF 1** *(condition sociale)* nobleness, nobility; **famille de n. récente** recently ennobled family; *Hist* **n. de robe** *ou* **d'office** = nobility acquired after having fulfilled specific judicatory duties; **n. d'épée** old nobility; **n. héréditaire** hereditary peerage; **n. terrienne** landed gentry; **la haute n.** the nobility; **la petite n.** the gentry; **n. oblige** (it's a case of) noblesse oblige

2 *(générosité)* nobleness, nobility; **par n. de cœur/d'esprit** through the nobleness of his/her heart/spirit

3 *(majesté)* nobleness, majesty, grandness; **la n. de son style** his/her noble *or* majestic style

'**Noblesse oblige'** *Hamer* 'Kind Hearts and Coronets'

nobliau, -x [nɔblijo] NM *Péj* petty nobleman

noblion [nɔblijɔ̃] NM *Belg Péj* petty nobleman

noce [nɔs] NF **1** *(cérémonie)* wedding; *(fête)* wedding festivities; **être de la n.**, **être invité à la n.** to be invited to the wedding; *Fam* **demain, on est de n.** we've got a wedding tomorrow; **noces et banquets** *(dans une petite annonce)* weddings and all special occasions (catered for); *Fam* **elle n'avait jamais été à pareille n.** she had the time of her life; *Fam* **on n'était pas à la n.** it was no picnic; *Fam* **faire la n.** to live it up; *Fam* **être à la n.** to have the time of one's life, to have a whale of a time

2 *(ensemble des invités)* wedding party; **photographier une n. sur les marches de l'église** to photograph a wedding party on the church steps; **regarder passer la n.** to watch the wedding procession go by

❑ **noces** NFPL wedding; **le jour des noces** the wedding day; **le jour de ses noces** his/her wedding day; **elle l'a épousée en troisièmes noces** he was her third husband; **noces d'argent/d'or/de diamant** silver/golden/diamond wedding (anniversary); *Bible* **les noces de Cana** the marriage at Cana

❑ **de noces** ADJ wedding *(avant n)*; **nuit de noces** wedding night; **repas de noces** wedding breakfast

'**Les Noces de Cana'** *Véronèse* 'The Marriage at Cana'

🎵

'**Les Noces de Figaro'** *Mozart* 'The Marriage of Figaro'

'**Noces'** *Camus* 'Nuptials'

nocebo [nɔsebo] ADJ *Méd* **effet n.** nocebo effect

noceur, -euse [nɔsœr, -øz] *Fam* ADJ **ils sont très noceurs** they like to party, they like to live it up

NM,F reveller, *Am* partyer

nocher [nɔʃe] NM *Littéraire* pilot; **le n. des Enfers** Charon the ferryman

nociceptif, -ive [nɔsiseptif, -iv] ADJ *Physiol* nociceptive

nociception [nɔsisepsjɔ̃] NF *Physiol* nociception

nociceptive [nɔsiseptiv] *voir* **nociceptif**

nocif, -ive [nɔsif, -iv] ADJ noxious, harmful

nocivité [nɔsivite] NF noxiousness, harmfulness

noctambule [nɔktɑ̃byl] NMF night owl

noctambulisme [nɔktɑ̃bylism] NM night life

noctiluque [nɔktilyk] *Zool* ADJ noctilucent

NF noctiluca

noctuelle [nɔktɥɛl] NF *Entom* owlet moth, *Spéc* noctuid, noctua

noctuidé [nɔktɥide] *Entom* NM noctuid

❑ **noctuidés** NMPL Noctuidae

noctule [nɔktyl] NF *Zool* noctule

nocturne [nɔktyrn] ADJ **1** *(gén)* nocturnal, night *(avant n)*; *(attaque, visite)* night *(avant n)*; **évasion n.** escape by night; **vision n.** night vision

2 *Bot & Zool* nocturnal

3 *Opt* scotopic

NM **1** *Mus* nocturne

2 *Rel* nocturn

3 *Orn (rapace)* nocturnal bird (of prey)

NF **1** *Sport* evening *Br* fixture *or Am* meet; **jouer en n.** to play an evening *Br* fixture *or Am* meet; **match disputé en n.** evening game

2 *Com* late-night opening; **le magasin fait n.** *ou* **ouvre en n. le jeudi** the shop stays open late on Thursdays; **n. le mardi** *(sur panneau ou vitrine)* late-night opening: Tuesday

nocuité [nɔkɥite] NF noxiousness

nodal, -e, -aux, -ales [nɔdal, -o] ADJ *Sout* crucial

2 *Bot & Anat* nodal **3** *(point, ligne)* nodal

NM *TV* master control room

nodosité [nɔdozite] NF *Bot & Méd (nodule)* node, nodule; *(état)* nodosity

nodulaire [nɔdylɛr] ADJ nodular

nodule [nɔdyl] NM **1** *Méd* nodule, node **2** *Géol* nodule

---

noduleux, -euse [nɔdylø, -øz] ADJ nodulous

Noé [nɔe] NPR Noah

Noël [nɔɛl] NM **1** *(fête)* Christmas; **à N.** at Christmas (time); **la nuit** *ou* **la veille de N.** Christmas Eve; **le jour de N.** Christmas Day; **le lendemain de N.** *Br* Boxing Day, *Am* the day after Christmas; **joyeux N.!** Merry Christmas!

2 *(période)* Christmas time; **passer N. en famille** to spend Christmas with the family; *Prov* **N. au balcon, Pâques au tison** = a warm Christmas means a cold Easter

NF **la N.** *(fête)* Christmas; *(période)* Christmas time

noël [nɔɛl] NM **1** *(chanson)* (Christmas) carol **2** *Fam (cadeau)* **(petit) n.** Christmas present■

noème [nɔɛm] NM *Phil* noema

noèse [nɔɛz] NF *Phil* noesis

noétique [nɔetik] ADJ *Phil* noetic

nœud [nø] NM **1** *(lien)* knot; **faire un n.** to tie *or* to make a knot; **faire un n. à ses lacets** to do up *or* to tie (up) one's shoelaces; **fais un n. à ton mouchoir** tie a knot in your handkerchief; **faire un n. de cravate** to knot *or* to tie a tie; **tu as des nœuds dans les cheveux** your hair is (all) tangled, you've got lots of knots *or* tangles in your hair; **n. de cabestan** clove hitch; **n. de chaise** bowline (knot); **n. de chaise double** bowline with a bight, French bowline; **n. de chaise simple** bowline (knot); **n. coulant** *(pour serrer)* slipknot, running knot; *(pour étrangler)* noose; **faire un n. coulant à une corde** to make a noose in a rope; **n. d'écoute** sheet bend; *Tech* **n. de grappin** fisherman's bend; **n. en huit** figure of eight; **n. plat** reef knot; *Tech* **n. de vache** carrick bend; **couper** *ou* **trancher le n. gordien** to cut the Gordian knot; *Fig* **avoir un n. dans l'estomac** to have a knot in one's stomach; *Fig* **avoir un n. dans la gorge** to have a lump in one's throat

2 *(étoffe nouée)* bow; **porter un n. noir dans les cheveux** to wear a black bow *or* ribbon in one's hair; **n. papillon,** *Fam* **n. pap** bow tie

3 *(ornement)* bow; **n. de diamants/d'émeraudes** diamond/emerald bow

4 *Naut (vitesse)* knot

5 *Fig (point crucial)* crux; **le n. du problème** the crux *or* heart of the problem; *Théât* **le n. d'une pièce** the crux *or* knot of a play

6 *Anat* node; **n. lymphatique** lymph node; **n. sinusal** sino-atrial node; **n. vital** vital centre

7 *Bot (bifurcation)* node; *(dans le bois)* knot

8 *(de serpent)* coil; **n. de vipères** *aussi Fig* nest of vipers

9 *Astron* **n. ascendant/descendant** ascending/descending node

10 *Élec* **n. de courant** *ou* **tension** (current) node

11 *Ordinat, Ling, Math & Phys* node

12 *Mil* **n. d'épaules** shoulder knot

13 *(en travaux publics)* **n. ferroviaire** rail junction; **n. routier** interchange

14 *Vulg (pénis)* cock, dick; **à la mords-moi le n.** lousy, crappy

📖

'**Le Nœud de vipères'** *Mauriac* 'Vipers' Tangle'

noie *etc voir* **noyer**²

noir, -e [nwar] ADJ **1** *(gén)* black; **n. comme de l'ébène** jet-black, ebony; **n. comme un corbeau** *ou* **du charbon** (as) black as soot, pitch-black; **n. de jais** jet-black; **n. de suie** black with soot; *Fig* **n. de monde** teeming with people

2 *(très sombre → gén)* black, dark; *(→ cheveux, yeux, lunettes)* dark; **un ciel n.** a dark *or* leaden sky; **dans les rues noires** in the pitch-black *or* pitch-dark streets; *Fam* **elle est revenue noire d'Italie** *(bronzée)* she was black when she came back from Italy

3 *(plongé dans l'obscurité → nuit, cellule)* dark

4 *(sale)* black, dirty, grimy; **avoir les ongles noirs** to have dirty fingernails; **être n. comme du charbon** to be as black as soot; **être n. de crasse** to be black with grime

5 *Fig (maléfique)* black; *Littéraire (crime)* heinous, foul; **lancer un regard n. à qn** to shoot sb a black look; **il m'a regardé d'un œil n.** he gave me a black look; **de noirs desseins** dark intentions

6 *(pessimiste)* black, gloomy, sombre; **faire** *ou*

---

peindre un tableau très n. de la situation to paint a very black *or* gloomy picture of the situation; **le lundi/jeudi n.** Black Monday/Thursday; **rien n'est jamais tout blanc ou tout n.** nothing is completely black and white

7 *(extrême)* **saisi d'une colère noire** livid with rage; **être d'une humeur noire** to be in a black *or* foul mood; **être dans une misère noire** to live in abject poverty

8 *(en anthropologie)* black; **le problème n. aux États-Unis** the race problem in the United States

9 *(illégal)* **travail n.** moonlighting

10 *Fam (ivre)* plastered, smashed, wasted

11 *Géog* **la mer Noire** the Black Sea

❑ **Noir, -e** NM,F Black, black man, *f* woman; **les Noirs** (the) Blacks; **N. américain** African American

NM **1** *(couleur)* black; *Chim* **n. animal** animal black; **n. d'acétylène** acetylene black; **n. d'aniline** aniline black; **n. de carbone** carbon black; **n. de Chine** Indian ink; *Am* India ink; **n. de fumée** carbon black; **n. d'ivoire** ivory black; **n. de platine** platinum black; **d'un n. d'ébène** jet-black, ebony-black; **être vêtu de n., être en n.** to be dressed (all) in black; **se mettre du n. aux yeux** to put on eyeliner; **le n. et blanc** *Cin & Phot* black and white photography; *TV* black and white transmissions; *Fig* **c'était écrit n. sur blanc** it was there in black and white

2 *(saleté)* dirt, grime; **nettoie le n. sous tes ongles** clean the dirt from under your fingernails; **tu as du n. sur la joue** you've got a black mark on your cheek

3 *(obscurité)* darkness; **dans le n.** in the dark, in darkness; **avoir peur du n.** *ou* **dans le n.** to be afraid *or* scared of the dark; *Fig* **être dans le n. le plus complet** to be totally in the dark

4 *(dans un jeu)* black; **le n. est sorti** black came up; **les noirs jouent et font mat en trois coups** black to play and mate in three

5 *(technique)* **n. au blanc** *Typ* reverse printing; *Ordinat* reverse video; *Typ* **n. au gris** black-on-tone, BOT

6 *Fam (café)* (black) coffee■; **un petit n., s'il vous plaît** a cup of black coffee, please

7 *Agr* smut

8 *Métal* facing, blacking

9 *Mil (d'une cible)* bull's-eye

ADV dark; **il fait n. de bonne heure** it's getting dark early; **il fait n. comme dans un four** *ou* **tunnel ici** it's pitch-dark *or* pitch-black in here

❑ **noire** NF *Mus Br* crotchet, *Am* quarter note

❑ **au noir** ADJ **travail au n.** moonlighting ADV **1** *(illégalement)* **je l'ai eu au n.** I got it on the black market; **travailler au n.** to moonlight; **acheter/vendre au n.** to buy/sell on the black market **2** *(locution)* **pousser qch au n.** to paint a black picture of sth

❑ **en noir** ADJ *Belg* **travail en n.** moonlighting ADV **1** *(colorié, teint)* black; **habillé en n.** dressed in black, wearing black **2** *Fig* **voir tout en n.** to look on the dark side of things **3** *Belg* **travailler en n.** to moonlight; **acheter/vendre en n.** to buy/sell on the black market

noirâtre [nwarɑtr] ADJ blackish

noiraud, -e [nwaro, -od] ADJ dark, dark-skinned, swarthy

NM,F dark *or* swarthy person

noirceur [nwarsœr] NF **1** *(couleur noire)* blackness, darkness **2** *Littéraire (d'un acte, d'un dessein)* blackness, wickedness; *(d'un crime)* heinousness, foulness **3** *Littéraire (acte)* black *or* evil *or* wicked deed **4** *Can (obscurité)* dark, darkness; **dans la n.** in the dark *or* darkness; **avoir peur dans la n.** to be afraid of the dark; **la Grande N.** = period of authoritarian policies under the Premier of Quebec Maurice Duplessis

noircir [32] [nwarsir] VT **1** *(rendre noir)* to blacken; **noirci par le charbon** blackened with coal; **les parois noircies par la crasse** walls black with dirt *or* grime; *Fam* **n. du papier** to write pages and pages *or* page after page■; **tout ce qu'il est capable de faire, c'est n. du papier** the only thing he's good at is putting ink on paper

2 *Fig (dramatiser)* **n. la situation** *ou* **le tableau** to make the situation out to be darker *or* blacker than it is

3 *Fig (dénigrer)* **n. la réputation de qn, n. qn** to blacken sb's reputation

VI to go black, to darken; *(légumes, fruits)* to go black; **le ciel noircit à l'horizon** the sky is darkening on the horizon

▶**se noircir VPR 1** *(se dénigrer)* to denigrate oneself

2 *(se grimer)* **se n. le visage** to blacken one's face; *Théât* to black up

3 *(s'assombrir)* to darken; **notre avenir se noircit** our future is looking blacker

4 *Fam (s'enivrer)* to get plastered *or* smashed *or* wasted

noircissement [nwarsismɑ̃] **NM 1** *(gén)* blackening, darkening **2** *Métal* facing, blacking

noircissure [nwarsisyr] **NF** black stain

noise [nwaz] **NF** *Littéraire* **chercher n.** *ou* **des noises à qn** to try to pick a quarrel with sb

noiseraie [nwazrɛ] **NF 1** *(de noisetiers)* hazelnut plantation **2** *(de noyers)* walnut plantation

noisetier [nwaztje] **NM** *(plante)* hazel, hazelnut tree; *(bois)* hazel (wood)

noisette [nwazɛt] **NF 1** *Bot* hazelnut

2 *(petite portion)* **une n. de beurre** a knob of butter; **une n. de pommade** a small dab of ointment; **une n. de gel** a small amount of gel

3 *Culin* **n. d'agneau** noisette of lamb; **beurre à la n.** brown butter

4 *(café)* = small coffee with a drop of milk

ADJ INV hazel; *Culin* **beurre n.** brown butter

❑ **noisettes NFPL** *très Fam (testicules)* balls, *Br* bollocks

noix [nwa] **NF 1** *Bot* walnut; **n. du Brésil** Brazil nut; **n. de cajou** cashew (nut); **n. de coco** coconut; **n. de kola** cola nut; **n. de macadamia** macadamia nut; **n. (de) muscade** nutmeg; **n. de pécan** pecan (nut); **n. de Queensland** macadamia nut; *Fam* **des n.!** tripe!, hogwash!

2 *Culin* **n. de bœuf, n. de côtelette, n. de gigot** pope's eye; **n. de veau** cushion of veal

3 *(petite quantité)* **une n. de beurre** a knob of butter

4 *Fam (imbécile)* nut; **quelle n., ce type!** he's such a nitwit!

5 *Fam (camarade)* **salut, vieille n.!** hi, buddy *or Br* old chap!

6 *Tech (poulie)* sprocket (pulley)

7 *Menuis (rainure)* half-round groove

8 *Can (écrou)* nut

❑ **à la noix, à la noix de coco ADJ** *Fam* lousy, crummy; **des excuses à la n.** *ou* **à la n. de coco** lousy excuses; **toi et tes idées à la n.** *ou* **à la n. de coco!** you and your lousy ideas!

noli-me-tangere [nɔlimetɑ̃ʒere] **NM INV** *Bot* balsam, *Br* busy Lizzie

nolisement [nɔlizmɑ̃] **NM** chartering

noliser [3] [nɔlize] **VT** to charter

nom [nɔ̃] **NM 1** *(patronyme)* name; *(prénom)* first name, *Am* given name; **un homme du n. de Pierre** a man by the name of Pierre; **n.... prénom...** *(sur formulaire)* surname... first name...; **n. et prénoms** full name; **vos n., prénoms et adresse** your full name and address; **elle porte le n. de sa mère** *(prénom)* she was named after her mother; *(patronyme)* she has *or* uses her mother's surname; **tu porteras le n. de ton mari?** will you take your husband's name?; **Nokia, c'est un n. que tout le monde connaît** Nokia is a household name; **quelqu'un du n. de** *ou* **qui a pour n. Kregg vous demande** someone called Kregg *or* someone by the name of Kregg is asking for you; **je n'arrive pas à mettre un n. sur son visage** I can't put a name to his/her face; **je la connais de n.** I (only) know her by name; **je ne te dirai pas son n.** I won't tell you who he/she is, I won't tell you his/her name; **quelqu'un dont je tairai le n.** someone who shall remain nameless; **j'écris sous le n. de Kim Lewis** I write under the name of Kim Lewis; **on le connaissait sous le n. de Leduc** he went by *or* was known by the name of Leduc; **sous un faux n.** under a false *or* an assumed name; **voyager sous un faux n.** to travel under a false name *or* an alias; **il veut laisser un n. dans l'histoire** he wants his name to go down in history; **un grand n. de la musique** one of the great names of music; **les grands noms du champagne** the most famous champagne producers; **Louis, onzième du n.** Louis, the eleventh of that name; **en mon/ton n.** in my/your name, on my/your behalf; **parler en son n.** to speak for oneself; **parle-lui en mon n.** speak to him/her on my behalf *or* for me; **n. à particule** *ou Fam* **à rallonges** *ou* **à tiroirs** *ou* **à courants d'air** aristocratic surname, ≃ double-barrelled name; **un n. à coucher dehors** a mouthful; **il a un n. à coucher dehors** his name's a real mouthful; **n. de baptême,** *Fam* **petit n.** Christian *or* first name, *Am* given name; **n. de code** code name; **n. d'emprunt** assumed name; *Bourse* nominee name; **n. de famille** surname; **n. de guerre** nom de guerre, alias; **n. de jeune fille** maiden name; *Fam* **n. d'oiseau** insult▪; **traiter** *ou* **appeler qn de tous les noms** to call sb all the names under the sun; **je lui ai donné tous les noms d'oiseaux** I called him/her every name under the sun; **n. patronymique** patronymic (name); **n. de plume** nom de plume, pen name; **n. de scène** *ou* **de théâtre** stage name; **faire un n. à qn** to help make a name for sb; **se faire un n.** to make a name for oneself; *Bible* **que ton n. soit sanctifié** hallowed be thy name

2 *(appellation → d'une rue, d'un animal, d'un objet, d'une fonction)* name; **comme son n. l'indique** as its name indicates; **cet arbre porte le n. de peuplier** this tree is called a poplar; **il n'est roi que de n.** he is king in name only; **d'empereur, il ne lui manquait que le n.** he was emperor in all but name; **cruauté/douleur sans n.** unspeakable cruelty/pain; **c'est une attitude qui n'a pas de n.!** this is an unspeakable attitude!; **une censure qui ne dit pas son n.** hidden *or* disguised censorship; **c'est du racisme qui n'ose pas dire son n.** it's racism by any other name; **appeler** *ou* **nommer les choses par leur n.** to call a spade a spade, to be blunt; **n. scientifique/vulgaire** *(d'une plante)* scientific/common name; *Ordinat* **n. de champ** field name; **n. commercial** trade name; *Com* **n. déposé** registered trademark; *Ordinat* **n. de domaine** domain name; *Mktg* **n. de famille global** blanket family name; *Ordinat* **n. de fichier** file name; *Mktg* **n. générique** generic name; **n. de lieu** place name; **n. de marque** brand name; *Ordinat* **n. de l'utilisateur** username

3 *Gram & Ling* noun; **n. de chose** concrete noun; **n. commun** common noun; **n. composé** compound (noun); **n. comptable** countable noun; **n. numéral** *ou* **de nombre** numeral; **n. propre** proper noun *or* name

EXCLAM *Fam* **n. de n.!, n. d'un petit bonhomme!, n. d'une pipe!** for goodness' sake!, *Br* blimey!, *Am* gee (whiz)!; **n. d'un chien!** hell!; **n. de Dieu!** for Christ's sake!, Christ (Almighty)!; **n. de Dieu, les voilà!** *Br* bloody hell *or Am* goddamn, here they come!; **je t'avais pourtant dit de ne pas y toucher, n. de Dieu!** for Christ's sake, I did tell you not to touch it!; **n. de n., les voilà!** heck, here they come!; **mais n. de n., qu'est-ce que tu as dans la tête!** for goodness' sake, birdbrain!

❑ **au nom de PRÉP** in the name of; **faire une proposition au n. de qn** to make a proposal for sb *or* on behalf of sb; **faire qch au n. de l'amitié/la justice** to do sth in the name of friendship/justice; **au n. de la loi, je vous arrête** I arrest you in the name of the law; **au n. de notre longue amitié** for the sake of our long friendship; **au n. de toute l'équipe** on behalf of the whole team; **au n. du ciel!** in heaven's name!; **au n. du Père, du Fils et du Saint-Esprit** in the name of the Father, the Son and the Holy Ghost

'Le Nom de la rose' *Eco, Annaud* 'The Name of the Rose'

nomade [nɔmad] **ADJ 1** *(peuple)* nomad *(avant n)*, nomadic **2** *Zool* migratory

NMF nomad; *Jur (gitan)* traveller; *Comput & Tél* road warrior

NF *Entom* Nomada

nomadiser [3] [nɔmadize] **VI** to live as nomads

nomadisme [nɔmadism] **NM** nomadism

no man's land [nomanslɑ̃d] **NM INV** *Fig & Mil* no-man's-land

nombrable [nɔ̃brabl] **ADJ** countable, numerable

nombre [nɔ̃br] **NM 1** *Math (gén)* number; *(de 0 à 9)* number, figure; **un n. de trois chiffres** a three-digit *or* three-figure number; **le n. zéro** the number zero; **n. complexe** complex number; **n. décimal** decimal (number); **n. entier** whole number, integer; **n. naturel** natural number; **n. parfait** perfect number; **n. premier** prime (number); **n. rationnel** rational number; **n. réel** real number; **grands nombres** large numbers

2 *(quantité)* number; **inférieur/supérieur en n.** inferior/superior in number *or* numbers; **nous sommes en n. suffisant** there are enough of us; *(dans une réunion)* we have a quorum; **les exemplaires sont en n. limité** there's a limited number of copies; **les voitures/manifestants convergeaient en très grand n. vers le centre de la ville** the cars/demonstrators were converging in huge numbers on the town centre; *Littéraire* **en n. écrasant** by an overwhelming majority; **un n. de** a number of; **un bon n. de** a good many; **je te l'ai déjà dit (un) bon n. de fois** I've already told you several times; **un grand n. de** a lot of, a great number of, a great many; **elle avait un grand n. d'invités** she had a great number of guests; **un grand/petit n. d'entre nous** many/a few of us; **le plus grand n. d'entre eux a accepté** the majority of them accepted; **un certain n. de** a (certain) number of; **il y a eu un certain n. de gens** there was a (fair) number of people; *Typ* **n. de caractères** character count; *Presse* **n. de lecteurs** readership; **n. de mots** word count, number of words; *Typ* **n. de pages** extent

3 *(masse)* numbers; **vaincre par le n.** to win by sheer weight *or* force of numbers; **venir en n.** to come in large *or* great numbers; **dans le n., il y en aura bien un pour te raccompagner** there's bound to be one of them who will take you home; **sur le n.** among *or* out of (all) those; **ils finirent par succomber sous le n. des assaillants** they were finally overcome by the sheer number of their attackers; **tu subiras la loi du n.** you'll be overwhelmed by sheer weight of numbers; **tous ceux-là n'ont été invités que pour faire n.** those people over there have just been invited to make up the numbers

4 *Astron, Biol & Phys* number; **n. atomique** atomic number; **n. d'Avogadro** Avogadro's number; **n. chromosomique** chromosome number; **n. d'onde** wave number; **n. d'or** golden section *or* mean

5 *Gram* number

❑ **Nombres NMPL** *Bible* **le livre des Nombres** (the Book of) Numbers

❑ **au nombre de PRÉP les invités sont au n. de cent** there are a hundred guests; **ils sont au n. de huit** there are eight of them; **être au n. des élus** to be one of *or* among the elect; *Sout* **mettre** *ou* **compter qn au n. de ses intimes** to number sb among one's friends; **tu peux me compter au n. des participants** you can count me among the participants, you can count me in

❑ **du nombre de PRÉP** amongst; **étiez-vous du n. des invités?** were you amongst *or* one of those invited?

❑ **sans nombre ADJ** countless, innumerable; *(foule)* huge, vast

nombrer [3] [nɔ̃bre] **VT** *Littéraire* to count (up), to enumerate

nombreux, -euse [nɔ̃brø, -øz] **ADJ 1** *(comportant beaucoup d'éléments → famille, armée, groupe)* large; **une foule nombreuse** a large *or* huge crowd; **avoir une nombreuse descendance** to have many descendants

2 *(en grand nombre)* many, numerous; **avoir de n. clients** to have a great number of *or* many *or* numerous customers; **ils sont trop n.** there are too many of them; **ils étaient peu n.** there weren't many of them; **les étudiants sont plus n. qu'avant** there are more students than before; **les fumeurs sont de moins en moins n.** there are fewer and fewer smokers, the number of smokers is decreasing; **vous avez été n. à nous écrire** many of you have written to us; **n. sont ceux qui croient que...** many people believe that...; **venir (très) n.** to come in (very) large numbers; **nous espérons que vous viendrez n.** we hope that a large number of you will come; **venez n.!** all (are) welcome!, everyone (is) welcome!

3 *Littérature (style, prose)* harmonious, rhythmical, well-balanced

nombril [nɔ̃bril] NM 1 *Anat* navel; **une chemise ouverte jusqu'au n.** a shirt open to the waist 2 *Bot* hilum 3 *Fam (locutions)* **il se prend pour le n. du monde** he thinks he's the centre of the universe; **il aime bien se contempler** *ou* **se regarder le n.** he's very self-obsessed■, he spends a lot of time contemplating his navel; *Can* **ne pas avoir le n. sec** to be (still) wet behind the ears

nombrilisme [nɔ̃brilism] NM navel-gazing, self-obsession; **faire du n.** to contemplate one's navel

nome [nom] NM 1 *Hist* nome 2 *(en Grèce)* nomarchy, nome

nomenclateur, -trice [nɔmɑ̃klatœr, -tris] NM,F nomenclator

NM *Littéraire* classified list

nomenclature [nɔmɑ̃klatyr] NF 1 *(ensemble de termes techniques)* nomenclature 2 *(liste → gén)* list; *(→ d'un dictionnaire)* word list; *(→ d'une voiture etc)* parts list; *(→ de soins)* itemization of medical expenses *(with a view to obtaining reimbursement from the "Sécurité sociale")*; **n. douanière** *ou* **générale des produits** customs nomenclature

nomenklatura [nɔmɛnklatura, nɔmɑ̃klatura] NF 1 *Pol* nomenklatura 2 *(élite)* elite; **faire partie de la n.** to be part of the Establishment

nominal, -e, -aux, -ales [nɔminal, -o] ADJ 1 *(sans vrai pouvoir)* nominal; **il n'est que le chef n.** he's just the nominal leader, he's the leader in name only; **j'assume les fonctions purement nominales de recteur** I'm the rector in title only

2 *(par le nom)* of names, *Sout* nominal; **appel n.** roll call; **citation nominale** mention by name; **contrôle n.** name check; **liste nominale** list of names, name list

3 *Gram* nominal; *(en grammaire transformationnelle)* noun *(avant n)*

4 *Bourse, Écon & Fin* **salaire n.** nominal wage *or* salary; **valeur nominale** *(d'une obligation)* par value; *(d'une action)* face *or* nominal value

5 *Ind* rated; **vitesse nominale** rated speed

6 *Astron* nominal

NM *(d'une action)* nominal value; *(d'une obligation)* par value

nominalement [nɔminalmɑ̃] ADV 1 *(sans vrai pouvoir)* nominally, formally; **il dirige n. l'entreprise** he's the nominal head of the business, he's the head of the business in name only 2 *(par le nom)* by name; **être désigné n.** to be mentioned by name 3 *Gram (comme un nom)* nominally, as a noun; **un adverbe employé n.** the substantive *or* nominal use of an adverb

nominalisation [nɔminalizasjɔ̃] NF nominalization

nominaliser [3] [nɔminalize] VT to nominalize

nominalisme [nɔminalism] NM nominalism

nominaliste [nɔminalist] ADJ nominalistic

NM nominalist

nominatif, -ive [nɔminatif, -iv] ADJ 1 *(contenant les noms)* **liste nominative** list of names

2 *Bourse (liste)* nominal; *(titres, actions)* registered

3 *(ticket, carte)* non-transferable; **votre carte bancaire est nominative** *(inscription sur carte)* this banker's card may be used only by the authorized signatory *or* by the person whose name it bears; **les places de concert ne sont pas nominatives** the seats for the concert are transferable

NM 1 *Gram* nominative (case); **au n.** in the nominative (case)

2 *Bourse* **dividende au n.** dividend on registered securities

nomination [nɔminasjɔ̃] NF 1 *(à un poste)* appointment, nomination (**à** to); **attendre sa n.** to expect to be appointed; **elle a obtenu** *ou* **reçu sa n. au poste de directrice** she was appointed (to the post of) manager 2 *(pour un prix, une récompense)* nomination (**à** for); **ce film a trois nominations aux Césars** this film has received three César nominations 3 *Ling & Phil* naming

nominative [nɔminativ] *voir* **nominatif**

nominativement [nɔminativmɑ̃] ADV by name

nominer [3] [nɔmine] VT to nominate; **elle a été nominée pour le César de la meilleure actrice** she's been nominated for the César for best actress

nommage [nɔmaʒ] NM *Ordinat (de site Internet)* designation

nommé, -e [nɔme] ADJ *(appelé)* named; **deux enfants, nommés Victor et Marie** two children, named *or* called Victor and Marie

NM,F **le n. Antoine** the man named *or* called Antoine; **la nommée Chantal** the woman named *or* called Chantal; **le n. Georges Aland est accusé de...** Georges Aland is accused of...; **elle fréquente un n. Paul** she's going out with a man called Paul; **un n. Bertrand a appelé** someone named *or* called Bertrand rang; **Prudence, la bien nommée** the aptly named Prudence; **Mme Douce, la mal nommée** the somewhat inappropriately named Mme Douce

▫ **à jour nommé** ADV *Vieilli* on the appointed day

▫ **à point nommé** ADV *(au bon moment)* (just) at the right moment *or* time; *(au moment prévu)* at the appointed time

nommément [nɔmemɑ̃] ADV 1 *(par le nom → citer, féliciter, accuser)* by name; **il est n. mis en cause** he, in particular, is implicated; **les trois candidats, n. Francis, Anne et Robert** the three candidates, namely Francis, Anne and Robert; **ces deux éléments, n. le cuivre et le zinc** these two elements, namely copper and zinc

2 *(spécialement)* especially, notably, in particular

nommer [3] [nɔme] VT 1 *(citer)* to name, to list; **ils refusent de n. leurs complices** they refuse to name their accomplices; **un homme que je ne nommerai pas** a man who shall remain nameless *or* whom I won't (mention by) name; **ceux qui sont responsables, pour ne pas les n., devront payer** those who are responsible, and who shall remain nameless, will have to pay; *Ironique* **c'est la faute de Nina, pour ne pas la n.** without mentioning any names *or* naming no names, it's Nina's fault

2 *(prénommer)* to name, to call; **ils la nommèrent Aurore** they named her Aurore

3 *(dénommer)* to name, to call, to term; **la chaîne a été nommée TV+** they named *or* called the channel TV+; **ce sentiment que l'on nomme l'amour** that feeling we call love *or* we know as love; **on nomme aumôniers les prêtres attachés à un régiment** priests attached to a regiment are called chaplains

4 *(désigner à une fonction)* to appoint (**à** to); *Mil (officier)* to commission; **n. des experts** to appoint experts; **n. qn directeur** to appoint sb manager; **qui a été nommé directeur?** who was appointed (as) manager?; **elle a été nommée responsable des ventes** she was appointed sales director; **n. qn son héritier** to appoint sb as one's heir; **être nommé à Paris** to be appointed to a post in Paris; **être nommé au grade supérieur** to be promoted

▸**se nommer** VPR 1 *(s'identifier)* to give one's name; *(se présenter)* to introduce oneself; **elle ne s'est même pas nommée** she didn't even introduce herself *or* say who she was

2 *(s'appeler)* to be called *or* named; **elle se nomme Bianca** her name is Bianca, she's called Bianca; **comment se nomme-t-il?** what's his name?, what's he called?

nomogramme [nɔmɔgram] NM nomogram, nomograph

nomographie [nɔmɔgrafi] NF nomography

nomothète [nɔmɔtɛt] NM *Antiq* nomothete, lawgiver

non [nɔ̃] ADV 1 *(en réponse négative)* no; **veux-tu venir? – n.** do you want to come? – no; **n. merci!** no, thank you!; **mais n.!** no!, absolutely not!; **mais n., voyons!** no, of course not!; **mais bien sûr que n.!** of course not!; **certes n.!** most definitely not!; **ma foi n.!** my goodness me, no!; **tu es content? – ma foi n.!** are you happy? – certainly not *or* far from it!; **ah ça n.!** definitely not!; **ah n. alors!** oh no!; **oh que n.!** definitely not!, certainly not!; *Vieilli Hum* **dame n.!, mon Dieu n.!, que n.!** certainly not!, definitely not!; **n., n. et n.!** no, no and no again!; **alors, ton augmentation? – c'est n.** what about your pay rise? – I didn't get it

2 *(pour annoncer ou renforcer la négation)* no; **n., je ne veux pas y aller** no, I don't want to go there; **n., il n'en est pas question** no, it's out of the question

3 *(dans un tour elliptique)* **il part demain, moi n.** he's leaving tomorrow, I'm not; **je me demande si je dois recommencer ou n.** I wonder whether I should start again or not; **que tu le veuilles ou n.** whether you like it or not; **venez-vous ou n.?** are you coming or not?; **n., je vous en prie!** please don't!

4 *(comme complément du verbe)* **il me semble que n.** I think not, I don't think so; **je pense que n.** I don't think so, I think not; **je dis que n.** I say no; **il m'a demandé si c'était possible, je lui ai dit que n.** he asked me if it was possible, I told him it wasn't; **il a fait signe que n.** *(de la main)* he made a gesture of refusal; *(de la tête)* he shook his head; **il voulait traverser la rue, mais sa mère lui fit signe que n.** he was about to cross the road, but his mother signalled to him not to; **il paraît que n.** it would seem not, apparently not; **il a répondu n.** he answered no; **faire n. de la tête** to shake one's head

5 *(en corrélation avec "pas")* **n. pas** not; **il l'a fait par gentillesse et n. (pas) par intérêt** he did it out of kindness and not out of self-interest; **je parle de Gide et n. (pas) de Malraux** I'm talking about Gide *or* it's Gide I'm talking about, not Malraux; **elle a été élevée n. (pas) par ses parents mais par ses grands-parents** she was brought up by her grandparents, not by her parents; **n. (pas) pour moi, mais pour lui** not for me, but for him; *Littéraire* **n. pas!** not so!, not at all!

6 *(en corrélation avec "plus")* **je m'adresse à vous n. plus en tant que ministre mais en tant que citoyen** I'm speaking to you not as a Minister but as a fellow citizen; **nous sommes aujourd'hui n. plus concurrents mais partenaires** today we are no longer competitors but partners; **le problème est cette fois n. plus d'ordre économique mais social** the problem is now not economic but social; **je n'irai pas – moi n. plus** I'm not going – neither *or* nor am I

7 *(n'est-ce pas)* **il devait prendre une semaine de vacances, n.?** he was supposed to take a week's holiday, wasn't he?; **il n'est plus tout jeune, n.?** he's not that young any more, is he?; **c'est anormal, n.?** that's not normal, is it?; **c'est dégoûtant, n., tu ne trouves pas?** it's disgusting, isn't it?; **j'ai le droit de dire ce que je pense, n.?** I am entitled to say what I think, aren't I *or Sout* am I not?

8 *(emploi expressif)* **n.!** never!, no!; **n.! pas possible!** no *or* never! I don't believe it!; **il est parti – n.!** he has left – really?; **n. mais (des fois)!** honestly!, I ask you!; **n. mais celui-là, pour qui il se prend?** who on earth does he think he is?; *Belg* **n. peut-être!** you bet!

9 *(devant un nom, un adjectif, un participe, un adverbe)* **la n.-observation du règlement** failure to comply with the regulations; **n. coupable** not guilty; **il faut que ce soit toi qui lui parles et n. l'inverse** it's you who have to talk to him/her and not the other way round; **un débiteur n. solvable** an insolvent debtor; **un bagage n. réclamé** an unclaimed piece of luggage; **tickets n. numérotés** unnumbered tickets *or* seats; **il a bénéficié d'une aide n. négligeable** he received not insubstantial help; **n. content de conduire sans permis, l'individu était ivre** not content with driving without a licence, the man was also drunk; **n. loin de la ville** not far from the town; **n. sans raison** not without reason; *Math* **analyse** *ou* **mathématique n. standard** non-standard analysis

NM INV 1 *(réponse)* no; **elle m'a opposé un n. catégorique** she flatly refused, she gave me a categorical no; **les n. de la majorité** the noes of the majority

2 *Ordinat & Math* not

▫ **non que, non pas que** CONJ not that; **n. que je ne vous plaigne** not that I don't pity you; **je tiens à cette bague, n. qu'elle ait de la valeur, mais pour son originalité** I'm fond of this ring, not that it's of any great value, I just think it's unusual; **il vit pauvrement, n. (pas) qu'il manque d'argent, mais...** he lives modestly, not that he doesn't have any money, but...; **n. (pas) que je m'en méfie, mais...** it's not that I don't trust him, but...

NON- [nɔ̃] **PRÉF**

Non- is a very productive prefix in French. It conveys an idea of OPPOSITION, and can be added to adjectives or nouns.

In the first case, the general rule is not to use a hyphen, although some adjectives starting with **non-** have become so lexicalized that they appear in dictionaries in hyphenated form. Nouns starting with **non-** normally carry a hyphen.

Besides well-established nouns occurring in dictionaries, recent usage has also created countless words with **non-**, mostly belonging to the field of philosophy or social affairs and carrying a distinctly euphemistic tone.

In many instances, the same prefix can be used in English, but sometimes the translator will need to paraphrase slightly, eg:

il a été déclaré non coupable he was found not guilty; **une boisson non(-)alcoolisée** a non-alcoholic drink; **les pays non-alignés** nonaligned countries; **un pacte de non-agression** a non-aggression pact; **les non-fumeurs** non-smokers; **un état de non-droit** a situation in which law and order have broken down; **le non-respect de la loi** failure to observe the law; **le non-bonheur** unhappiness; **la non-liberté d'expression** lack of freedom of speech

non-acceptation [nɔ̃naksɛptasjɔ̃] **NF** *Banque (d'une lettre de change)* non-acceptance

non-accompli, -e [nɔ̃nakɔ̃pli] (*mpl* **non-accomplis,** *fpl* **non-accomplies**) **Ling ADJ** imperfective
NM imperfective

non-accomplissement [nɔ̃nakɔ̃plismã] **NM** *(d'un contrat)* non-fulfilment

non-activité [nɔ̃naktivite] **NF** *Mil* inactivity; **être en n.** to be temporarily off duty; *Admin* **mettre en n.** *(employé)* to suspend; *Mil (officier)* to put on half-pay; **mise en n.** *(d'un employé)* suspension; *Mil (d'un officier)* putting on half-pay

non-affilié, -e [nɔ̃nafilje] (*mpl* **non-affiliés,** *fpl* **non-affiliées**) **ADJ** non-affiliated

nonagénaire [nɔ̃naʒenɛr] **ADJ** nonagenarian; **être n.** to be in one's nineties
NMF person in his/her nineties; **un sémillant n.** a dashing ninety-year-old

non-agression [nɔ̃nagrɛsjɔ̃] **NF** non-aggression

non-alcoolisé, -e [nɔ̃nalkɔlize] (*mpl* **non-alcoolisés,** *fpl* **non-alcoolisées**) **ADJ** non-alcoholic

non-aligné, -e [nɔ̃naliɲe] (*mpl* **non-alignés,** *fpl* **non-alignées**) **ADJ** non-aligned
NM,F non-aligned country

non-alignement [nɔ̃naliɲmã] **NM** non-alignment

non-animé [nɔ̃nanime] (*mpl* **non-animés,** *fpl* **non-animées**) *Ling* **ADJ** inanimate
NM inanimate noun

nonantaine [nɔ̃nɑ̃tɛn] **NF** *Belg & Suisse* **1** *(quantité)* **une n.** around *or* about ninety, ninety or so; **une n. de voitures** around *or* about ninety cars; **elle a une n. d'années** she's around *or* about ninety (years old) **2** *(âge)* **avoir la n.** to be around *or* about ninety; **quand on arrive à** *ou* **atteint la n.** when you hit ninety

nonante [nɔ̃nɑ̃t] *Belg & Suisse* **ADJ 1** *(gén)* ninety **2** *(dans des séries)* ninetieth; **page/numéro n.** page/number ninety
PRON ninety
NM INV 1 *(gén)* ninety **2** *(numéro d'ordre)* number ninety **3** *(chiffre écrit)* ninety; *voir aussi* **cinquante**

nonantième [nɔ̃nɑ̃tjɛm] *Belg & Suisse* **ADJ** ninetieth
NMF 1 *(personne)* ninetieth **2** *(objet)* ninetieth (one)
NM 1 *(partie)* ninetieth **2** *(étage)* Br ninetieth floor, Am ninety-first floor; *voir aussi* **cinquième**

nonantièmement [nɔ̃nɑ̃tjɛmmã] **ADV** *Belg & Suisse* in ninetieth place

non-assistance [nɔ̃nasistɑ̃s] **NF** *Jur* **n. à personne en danger** failure to assist a person in danger

non-autorisé, -e [nɔ̃nɔtɔrize] (*mpl* **non-autorisés,** *fpl* **non-autorisées**) **ADJ** *Ordinat (nom de fichier etc)* illegal

non-belligérance [nɔ̃beliʒerɑ̃s] **NF** non-belligerence

non-belligérant, -e [nɔ̃beliʒerɑ̃, -ɑ̃t] (*mpl* **non-belligérants,** *fpl* **non-belligérantes**) **ADJ** non-belligerent
NM,F non-belligerent

nonce [nɔ̃s] **NM** nuncio; **n. apostolique** papal nuncio

non-cessible [nɔ̃sesibl] (*pl* **non-cessibles**) **ADJ** *(billet)* not transferable

nonchalamment [nɔ̃ʃalamã] **ADV** *(avec insouciance)* nonchalantly; *(lentement)* listlessly

nonchalance [nɔ̃ʃalɑ̃s] **NF** *(insouciance)* nonchalance; *(lenteur)* listlessness; **avec n.** *(avec insouciance)* nonchalantly; *(lentement)* listlessly

nonchalant, -e [nɔ̃ʃalɑ̃, -ɑ̃t] **ADJ** *(insouciant)* nonchalant; *(lent)* listless; *Littéraire* **n. du terme où finiront mes jours** indifferent as to when my days may end

nonciature [nɔ̃sjatyr] **NF 1** *(charge d'un nonce)* nunciature **2** *(résidence)* nuncio's residence

non-combattant, -e [nɔ̃kɔ̃batɑ̃, -ɑ̃t] (*mpl* **non-combattants,** *fpl* **non-combattantes**) **ADJ** non-combatant
NM,F non-combatant

non-comparant, -e [nɔ̃kɔ̃parɑ̃, -ɑ̃t] (*mpl* **non-comparants,** *fpl* **non-comparantes**) **NM,F** defaulter *(in court)*

non-comparution [nɔ̃kɔ̃parysjɔ̃] **NF** non-appearance *or* defaulting *(in court)*

non-compensé, -e [nɔ̃kɔ̃pɑ̃se] (*mpl* **non-compensés,** *fpl* **non-compensées**) **ADJ** *Banque (chèque)* uncleared

non-comptable [nɔ̃kɔ̃tabl] (*pl* **non-comptables**) **ADJ** uncountable
NM mass *or* uncountable noun

non-conciliation [nɔ̃kɔ̃siljasjɔ̃] **NF** *Jur* irretrievable breakdown

non-concurrence [nɔ̃kɔ̃kyrɑ̃s] **NF** *Jur* **clause de n.** restraint of trade clause

non-conformisme [nɔ̃kɔ̃fɔrmism] **NM 1** *(originalité)* nonconformism **2** *Rel* Nonconformism

non-conformiste [nɔ̃kɔ̃fɔrmist] (*pl* **non-conformistes**) **ADJ 1** *(original)* nonconformist **2** *Rel* Nonconformist
NMF 1 *(original)* nonconformist **2** *Rel* Nonconformist

non-conformité [nɔ̃kɔ̃fɔrmite] **NF** nonconformity

non-connecté, -e [nɔ̃kɔnɛkte] (*mpl* **non-connectés,** *fpl* **non-connectées**) **ADJ** *Ordinat* off-line

non-consigné, -e [nɔ̃kɔ̃siɲe] (*mpl* **non-consignés,** *fpl* **non-consignées**) **ADJ** non-returnable

non-contradiction [nɔ̃kɔ̃tradiksjɔ̃] **NF** non-contradiction

non-coté, -e [nɔ̃kɔte] (*mpl* **non-cotés,** *fpl* **non-cotées**) **ADJ** *Bourse* unquoted

non-croyant, -e [nɔ̃krwajɑ̃, -ɑ̃t] (*mpl* **non-croyants,** *fpl* **non-croyantes**) **ADJ** unbelieving
NM,F non-believer

non-cumul [nɔ̃kymyl] **NM** *Jur* **n. des peines** concurrence of sentences; *Pol* **il faut renforcer les règles de n. des mandats** the laws prohibiting politicians from holding more than one post at a time need to be reinforced

non-dénonciation [nɔ̃denɔ̃sjasjɔ̃] **NF** *Jur* = failure to report a crime

non-destructif, -ive [nɔ̃dɛstryktif, -iv] (*mpl* **non-destructifs,** *fpl* **non-destructives**) **ADJ** non-destructive; **contrôle n.** non-destructive testing

non-directif, -ive [nɔ̃dirɛktif, -iv] (*mpl* **non-directifs,** *fpl* **non-directives**) **ADJ** nondirective

non-directivisme [nɔ̃dirɛktivism] **NM** *Psy* nondirective therapy

non-directivité [nɔ̃dirɛktivite] **NF** *(méthode)* nondirective method; *(attitude)* nondirective attitude

non-discrimination [nɔ̃diskriminasjɔ̃] **NF** non-discrimination

non-dissémination [nɔ̃diseminasjɔ̃] **NF** non-proliferation

non-dit [nɔ̃di] (*pl* **non-dits**) **NM** **le n.** the unsaid; **il y avait trop de n. dans notre famille** too much was left unsaid in our family; **un film riche en non-dits** a film full of meaningful silences

non-droit [nɔ̃drwa] **NM** **zone de n.** area in which law and order have broken down; **état de n.** situation in which law and order have broken down

none [nɔn] **NF 1** *Antiq (heure)* ninth hour; *(partie du jour)* = part of the day beginning at three in the afternoon **2** *Rel (office de 15 heures)* nones
□ **nones NFPL** *Antiq (jour)* Nones

non-écrit [nɔnekri] (*pl* **non-écrits**) **NM** *Jur* unwritten clause

non-encaissé, -e [nɔnɑ̃kese] (*mpl* **non-encaissés,** *fpl* **non-encaissées**) **ADJ** *(chèque)* uncashed

non-engagé, -e [nɔnɑ̃gaʒe] (*mpl* **non-engagés,** *fpl* **non-engagées**) **ADJ** *(personne)* neutral; *(nation)* non-aligned
NM,F *(personne)* neutral person; *(nation)* non-aligned country

non-engagement [nɔnɑ̃gaʒmã] **NM** *(d'une personne)* neutrality, non-commitment; *(d'une nation)* non-alignment

non-être [nɔnɛtr] **NM INV** nonbeing

non-euclidien, -enne [nɔnøklidjɛ̃, -ɛn] (*mpl* **non-euclidiens,** *fpl* **non-euclidiennes**) **ADJ** *Géom* non-Euclidean

non-événement, non-évènement [nɔnevɛnmã] (*pl* **non-événements** *ou* **non-évènements**) **NM** non-event

non-exécution [nɔnɛgzekysjɔ̃] **NF** *(d'un contrat)* non-fulfilment

non-existant, -e [nɔnɛgzistɑ̃, -ɑ̃t] (*mpl* **non-existants,** *fpl* **non-existantes**) **ADJ** non-existent

non-existence [nɔnɛgzistɑ̃s] **NF** non-existence

non-ferreux [nɔ̃ferø] **NM INV** *Métal & Minér* non-ferrous metal

non-figuratif, -ive [nɔ̃figyratif, -iv] (*mpl* **non-figuratifs,** *fpl* **non-figuratives**) *Beaux-Arts* **ADJ** non-figurative
NM,F non-figurative artist, abstractionist

non-figuration [nɔ̃figyrasjɔ̃] **NF** *Beaux-Arts* non-figurative art, abstract art

non-figurative [nɔ̃figyrativ] *voir* **non-figuratif**

non-formaté, -e [nɔ̃fɔrmate] (*mpl* **non-formatés,** *fpl* **non-formatées**) **ADJ** *Ordinat* unformatted

non-fumeur, -euse [nɔ̃fymœr, -øz] (*mpl* **non-fumeurs,** *fpl* **non-fumeuses**) **ADJ** non-smoking
NM,F non-smoker; **compartiment non-fumeurs** non-smoking *or* no-smoking compartment

non-gage [nɔ̃gaʒ] **NM** *Aut* **certificat de n.** certificate of ownership

nonidi [nɔnidi] **NM** *Hist* = ninth day of a ten-day period in the Republican calendar

non-immixition [nɔnimiksjɔ̃] **NF** *Jur* non-assumption

non-imputabilité [nɔnɛ̃pytabilite] **NF** *Jur* non-imputability

non-ingérence [nɔnɛ̃ʒerɑ̃s] **NF** *(par une personne)* non-interference; *(par une nation)* non-interference, non-intervention

non-initialisé, -e [nɔninisjalize, nɔ̃inisjalize] (*mpl* **non-initialisés,** *fpl* **non-initialisées**) **ADJ** *Ordinat* uninitialized

non-initié, -e [nɔninisje] (*mpl* **non-initiés,** *fpl* **non-initiées**) **ADJ** uninitiated; **ce texte sera difficile pour le lecteur n.** this text will be difficult for the lay reader
NM,F **pour les non-initiés** for the layman *or* layperson

non-inscrit, -e [nɔnɛskri, -it] (*mpl* **non-inscrits,** *fpl* **non-inscrites**) **ADJ** independent, non-party
NM,F independent member of parliament

non-intervention [nɔnɛ̃tɛrvɑ̃sjɔ̃] **NF** non-intervention; **une politique de n.** a non-interventionist policy

non-interventionniste [nɔnɛ̃tɛrvɑ̃sjɔnist] (*pl* **non-interventionnistes**) **ADJ** non-interventionist
NMF non-interventionist

non-jouissance [nɔ̃ʒwisɑ̃s] **NF** non-enjoyment

non-justifié, -e [nɔ̃ʒystifje] (*mpl* **non-justifiés,** *fpl* **non-justifiées**) **ADJ** *Typ* unjustified, non-justified; **n. à droite** ragged right; **n. à gauche** ragged left

non-lieu [nɔ̃ljø] (*pl* **non-lieux**) **NM** *Jur* **(ordonnance** *ou* **arrêt de) n.** no grounds for prosecution; **bénéficier d'un n.** to be discharged through lack of evidence; **il a bénéficié d'un n.** charges against him were dropped for lack of evidence; **rendre une ordonnance de n.** to dismiss a case for lack of evidence

non-livraison [nɔ̃livrɛzɔ̃] **NF** *Com* non-delivery

non marchand, -e [nɔ̃marʃɑ̃, -ɑ̃d] (*mpl* **non marchands,** *fpl* **non marchandes**) **ADJ** *Écon* non-market

non-membre [nɔ̃mɑ̃br] (*pl* **non-membres**) **NM** non-member

non-métal [nɔ̃metal] (*pl* **non-métaux** [nɔ̃meto]) **NM** non-metal

non-modifiable [nɔ̃mɔdifjabl] (*pl* **non-modifiables**) **ADJ** (*billet*) not alterable

non-moi [nɔ̃mwa] **NM INV** non-ego

nonne [nɔn] **NF** *Vieilli* nun

non-négociable [nɔ̃negɔsjabl] (*pl* **non-négociables**) **ADJ** non-negotiable

nonnette [nɔnɛt] **NF 1** *Vieilli & Rel* young nun **2** *Orn* **n. (cendrée)** marsh tit **3** *Culin* iced gingerbread (*biscuit*)

nono, -ote [nɔno, -ɔt] **NM,F** *Can Fam* idiot, jerk

nonobstant [nɔnɔpstɑ̃] **PRÉP** *Jur ou Hum* notwithstanding, despite; **nous irons n. le mauvais temps** we'll go in spite of the bad weather; **ce n.** this notwithstanding

nonote [nɔnɔt] *voir* **nono**

non-paiement [nɔ̃pɛmɑ̃] **NM** *Jur* non-payment, failure to pay

nonpareil, -eille [nɔ̃parɛj] **ADJ** *Vieilli* peerless

non-partant [nɔ̃partɑ̃] (*pl* **non-partants**) **NM** (*cheval*) non-starter

non-participant, -e [nɔ̃partisipɑ̃, -ɑ̃t] (*mpl* **non-participants,** *fpl* **non-participantes**) **NM,F** non-participant

non-participation [nɔ̃partisipasjɔ̃] **NF** non-participation

non-polluant, -e [nɔ̃pɔlɥɑ̃, -ɑ̃t] (*mpl* **non-polluants,** *fpl* **non-polluantes**) **ADJ** non-polluting

non-prolifération [nɔ̃prɔliferasjɔ̃] **NF** non-proliferation

non-réception [nɔ̃resɛpsjɔ̃] **NF** *Com* non-delivery

non-recevabilité [nɔ̃rəsəvabilite] **NF** *Jur* (*d'un témoignage*) inadmissibility

non-recevoir [nɔ̃rəsəvwar] *voir* **fin**

non-récupérable [nɔ̃rekyperabl] (*pl* **non-récupérables**) **ADJ** *Ordinat* non-recoverable

non-remboursable [nɔ̃rɑ̃bursabl] (*pl* **non-remboursables**) **ADJ** non-refundable

non-réponse [nɔ̃repɔ̃s] (*pl* **non-réponses**) **NF** non-answer

non-représentation [nɔ̃rəprezɑ̃tasjɔ̃] **NF** *Jur* **n. d'enfant** non-restitution of a child (to its custodian), non-compliance with a custodianship order

non-résident [nɔ̃rezidɑ̃] (*pl* **non-résidents**) **NM** foreign national, non-resident

non-résiliation [nɔ̃reziljasjɔ̃] **NF** (*d'un bail, d'un contrat*) (*en cours*) non-cancellation; (*arrivant à expiration*) non-termination

non-respect [nɔ̃rɛspɛ] **NM** failure to respect; (*d'une loi*) failure to observe

non-responsabilité [nɔ̃rɛspɔ̃sabilite] **NF** non-liability

non-retour [nɔ̃rətur] **NM** **point de n.** point of no return

non-rétroactivité [nɔ̃retroaktivite] **NF** non-retro-activity

non-salarié, -e [nɔ̃salarje] (*mpl* **non-salariés,** *fpl* **non-salariées**) **ADJ** unsalaried

     NM,F self-employed person; **les non-salariés** the self-employed

non-sens [nɔ̃sɑ̃s] **NM INV 1** (*absurdité*) nonsense; **cette situation est un n.** this situation is nonsensical *or* a nonsense **2** *Ling* meaningless word/phrase (*in a translation*)

non-souscrit, -e [nɔ̃suskri, -it] (*mpl* **non-souscrits,** *fpl* **non-souscrites**) **ADJ** *Fin & Bourse* (*action, émission*) undersubscribed

non-spécialiste [nɔ̃spesjalist] (*pl* **non-spécialistes**) **ADJ** non-specialized

     NMF non-specialist

non-stop [nɔnstɔp] **ADJ INV** non-stop

     ADV non-stop

     NF INV *Sport* pre-race downhill run

non-suspendu [nɔ̃syspɑ̃dy] (*pl* **non-suspendus**)

     ADJ M *Aut* (*freins*) outboard

non-synchrone [nɔ̃sɛ̃kron] (*pl* **non-synchrones**) **ADJ** *Cin & TV* non-synchronous

non-syndiqué, -e [nɔ̃sɛ̃dike] (*mpl* **non-syndiqués,** *fpl* **non-syndiquées**) **ADJ** non-union, non-unionized

     NM,F non-union *or* non-unionized worker

non-tissé, -e [nɔ̃tise] (*pl* **non-tissés**) **NM** non-woven fabric

non-titulaire [nɔ̃titylɛr] (*pl* **non-titulaires**) **NMF** non-tenured member of staff

nonupler [3] [nɔnyple] **VT** to multiply by nine

non-usage [nɔnyzaʒ] **NM 1** (*gén*) non-use **2** *Jur* non-usage

non-valeur [nɔ̃valœr] (*pl* **non-valeurs**) **NF 1** *Péj* (*chose*) valueless thing; (*personne*) nonentity **2** *Jur* (*état*) unproductiveness; (*bien*) unproductive asset; **terres en n.** unproductive land (*UNCOUNT*) **3** *Fin* (*créance*) bad debt; *Bourse* worthless security

non-vérifié, -e [nɔ̃verifje] (*mpl* **non-vérifiés,** *fpl* **non-vérifiées**) **ADJ** *Compta* unaudited

non-viabilité [nɔ̃vjabilite] **NF** *Méd* non-viability

non-viable [nɔ̃vjabl] (*pl* **non-viables**) **ADJ 1** *Méd* nonviable **2** *Fig* unfeasible; **c'est un projet n.** the project isn't viable

non-violence [nɔ̃vjɔlɑ̃s] **NF** non-violence

non-violent, -e [nɔ̃vjɔlɑ̃, -ɑ̃t] (*mpl* **non-violents,** *fpl* **non-violentes**) **ADJ** non-violent

     NM,F non-violent protester

non-voyant, -e [nɔ̃vwajɑ̃, -ɑ̃t] (*mpl* **non-voyants,** *fpl* **non-voyantes**) **NM,F** unsighted person, visually impaired person; **les non-voyants** the unsighted, the visually impaired

nopal, -als [nɔpal] **NM** *Bot* nopal, prickly pear

noquette [nɔkɛt] **NF** *Belg* **une n. de beurre** a knob of butter

noradrénaline [noradrenalin] **NF** *Biol & Chim* noradrenalin, noradrenaline

noraf [nɔraf] **NM** *Fam* = offensive term used to refer to a North African Arab

nord [nɔr] **NM INV 1** (*point cardinal*) north; **au n.** in the north; **où est le n.?** which way is north?; **la partie la plus au n. de l'île** the northernmost part of the island; **le vent vient du n.** it's a north *or* northerly wind, the wind is coming from the north; **un vent du n.** a northerly wind; **le vent du n.** the north wind; **aller au** *ou* **vers le n.** to go north *or* northwards; **les trains qui vont vers le n.** trains going north, northbound trains; **rouler vers le n.** to drive north *or* northwards; **aller droit vers le n.** to head due north; **la cuisine est plein n.** *ou* **exposée au n.** the kitchen faces due north; **n. géographique** true *or* geographic north; **n. magnétique** magnetic north; *Fam* **perdre le n.** to go crazy, to lose it

     2 (*partie d'un pays, d'un continent*) north, northern area *or* regions; (*partie d'une ville*) north; **le n. de l'Italie** northern Italy, the north of Italy; **dans le n. de l'Espagne** in northern Spain, in the north of Spain; **elle habite dans le n.** she lives in the north; **il habite dans le n. de Paris** he lives in the north of Paris; **elle est du n.** she's from the north; **les gens du n.** people who live in the north

     ❑ **nord ADJ INV** North **NM 1** *Géog* **le N.** the North; **le grand N.** the Far North; **la mer du N.** the North Sea **2** (*département*) **le N.** Nord

     ❑ **au nord de PRÉP** (to the) north of; **il habite au n. de Paris** he lives to the north of Paris

nordaf [nɔrdaf] **NM** *Fam* = offensive term used to refer to a North African Arab

nord-africain, -e [nɔrafrikɛ̃, -ɛn] (*mpl* **nord-africains,** *fpl* **nord-africaines**) **ADJ** North African

     ❑ **Nord-Africain, -e NM,F** North African

nord-américain, -e [nɔramerikɛ̃, -ɛn] (*mpl* **nord-américains,** *fpl* **nord-américaines**) **ADJ** North American

     ❑ **Nord-Américain, -e NM,F** North American

nord-coréen, -enne [nɔrkɔreɛ̃, -ɛn] (*mpl* **nord-coréens,** *fpl* **nord-coréennes**) **ADJ** North Korean

     ❑ **Nord-Coréen, -enne NM,F** North Korean

nordé [nɔrde] **NM** north-east wind

nord-est [nɔrɛst] **NM INV** north-east

     ADJ INV north-east (*avant n*)

nordet [nɔrdɛ] = **nordé**

nordicité [nɔrdisite] **NF** *Can* northerliness, nordicity

nordique [nɔrdik] **ADJ** (*pays, peuple*) Nordic; (*langue*) Nordic, Scandinavian

     NM (*langue*) Norse

     ❑ **Nordique NMF** Nordic

nordir [32] [nɔrdir] **VI** *Naut* to veer north *or* northward

nordiste [nɔrdist] **ADJ 1** (*en France*) of/from the Nord département **2** (*en France*) of/from the Nord-Pas-de-Calais region **3** (*du Nord des États-Unis*) Northern, Yankee **4** *Am Hist* (*pendant la guerre de Sécession*) Northern, Yankee

     ❑ **Nordiste NMF 1** (*en France*) = inhabitant of or person from the Nord département **2** (*en France*) = inhabitant of or person from the Nord-Pas-de-Calais region **3** (*du Nord des États-Unis*) Northerner, Yankee **4** *Am Hist* (*pendant la guerre de Sécession*) Northerner, Yankee

nord-nord-est [nɔrnɔrɛst] **NM INV** north-north-east

     ADJ INV north-north-east (*avant n*)

nord-nord-ouest [nɔrnɔrwɛst] **NM INV** north-north-west

     ADJ INV north-north-west (*avant n*)

nord-ouest [nɔrwɛst] **NM INV** north-west

     ADJ INV north-west (*avant n*)

Nord-Pas-de-Calais [nɔrpadkalɛ] **NM le N.** Nord-Pas-de-Calais

nord-vietnamien, -enne [nɔrvjɛtnamjɛ̃, -ɛn] (*mpl* **nord-vietnamiens,** *fpl* **nord-vietnamiennes**) **ADJ** North Vietnamese

     ❑ **Nord-Vietnamien, -enne NM,F** North Vietnamese

NOREX [nɔrɛks] **NM** *Com* = source of information on standards and rules governing goods for export

noria [nɔrja] **NF 1** (*machine hydraulique*) bucket elevator, noria **2** *Fig* (*série de véhicules*) endless stream; **une n. de journalistes** a bunch of journalists

normal, -e, -aux, -ales [nɔrmal, -o] **ADJ 1** (*ordinaire* → *vie, personne*) normal; (→ *taille, poids*) normal, standard; (→ *accouchement, procédure*) normal, straightforward; **la situation est redevenue normale** the situation is back to normal; **tu trouves ça n., toi?** do you think that's all right *or* OK?; **la lampe ne s'allume pas, ce n'est pas n.** the light isn't coming on, there's something wrong (with it); **il n'est pas rentré, ce n'est pas n.** he's not back yet, something must have happened (to him); **vitesse normale** normal *or* *Spéc* rated speed

     2 (*habituel*) normal, usual; **elle n'était pas dans son état n.** she wasn't her normal self; **ce n'était pas sa voix normale** that wasn't his/her usual voice; **c'est le prix n.** that's the usual *or* standard price; **en temps n.** in normal circumstances, normally

     3 (*compréhensible*) normal, natural; **c'est n. de lui demander conseil** it's natural to ask him/her for advice; **c'est tout à fait n. que la jeunesse se rebelle** it's only normal *or* natural for young people to rebel; **mais c'est bien n., voyons** it's only natural, don't worry about it; *Fam* **c'est pas n.!** it's not on!

     4 *Fam* (*mentalement*) normal; **elle n'est pas très normale, celle-là!** she's not quite normal!

     5 *Chim* normal; **solution** *ou* **liqueur normale** normal solution

     6 *Géol & Géom* normal

     7 *Typ* roman

     ❑ **normale NF 1** (*situation*) normal (situation); **un retour à la normale** a return to normal **2** *Géom* normal; **normale à une courbe/surface** line normal *or* perpendicular to a curve/surface **3** *Météo* normal; **température au-dessous de la normale (saisonnière)** temperature below the (seasonal) average **4** (*moyenne*) average; **intelligence supérieure à la normale** above average intelligence **5** *Scol* **Normale (Sup)** = "grande école" for teacher-training **6** *Golf* par **7** *Belg* (*essence*) *Br* ≃ two-star petrol, *Am* ≃ regular

normalement [nɔrmalmɑ̃] **ADV 1** (*de façon ordinaire*) normally; **il est n. constitué** he's of normal constitution, *Euph* he's (a man of) flesh and blood

     2 (*sauf changement*) if all goes well; **n., nous partirons en juin** if all goes well, we'll be leaving in June; **n., elle devrait être arrivée** she should be here by now

3 *(habituellement)* normally, usually, generally; **n., elle rentre à trois heures** she normally *or* generally comes home at three (o'clock)

normalien, -enne [nɔrmaljɛ̃, -ɛn] **NM,F 1** *(de l'École normale)* student at an "École normale"; *(ancien de l'École normale)* graduate of an "École normale" **2** *(de l'École normale supérieure)* student at the "École normale supérieure"; *(ancien de l'École normale supérieure)* graduate of the "École normale supérieure"

normalisateur, -trice [nɔrmalizatœr, -tris] **ADJ** standardizing

NM,F standardizer

normalisation [nɔrmalizasjɔ̃] **NF 1** *(d'un produit)* standardization **2** *(d'une situation)* normalization; **jusqu'à la n. de la situation** until the situation becomes normal

normalisatrice [nɔrmalizatris] *voir* **normalisateur**

normalisé, -e [nɔrmalize] **ADJ** standardized

normaliser [3] [nɔrmalize] **VT 1** *(produit)* to standardize **2** *(rapport, situation)* to normalize

▶**se normaliser VPR** to return to normal

normalité [nɔrmalite] **NF** normality, *Am* normalcy

normand, -e [nɔrmɑ̃, -ɑ̃d] **ADJ 1** *(de Normandie)* Normandy *(avant n)*; **je suis n.** I'm from Normandy

2 *Hist* Norman

3 *Ling* Norman French

4 *(viking)* Norse

NM *(langue)* Norman French

❑ **Normand, -e NM,F 1** *(en France)* Norman; **les Normans** the Normans

2 *(Viking)* Norseman, *f* Norsewoman; **les Normands** the Norsemen, the Vikings

❑ **à la normande ADJ** *Culin* = prepared using cream and apples or cider

Normandie [nɔrmɑ̃di] **NF la N.** Normandy

normatif, -ive [nɔrmatif, -iv] **ADJ** normative

normativité [nɔrmativite] **NF** normativeness

norme [nɔrm] **NF 1** *Ind* norm, standard; **n. de production** production norm; **n. de productivité** productivity norm; **produit conforme aux normes de fabrication** product conforming to manufacturing standards; **jouet conforme aux normes de sécurité** toy which conforms to safety standards; **n. française (homologuée)** French standard (of manufacturing), *Br* ≃ British Standard, *Am* ≃ US Standard; **normes européennes** European standards; **normes d'application obligatoires/volontaires** compulsory/voluntary standards; **normes publicitaires** advertising standards; **n. technique** technical standard; **n. de travail** work standard; *Ordinat* **n. USB** USB

2 *(règle)* **la n.** the norm, the rule; **rester dans la n.** to keep within the norm; **échapper à la n.** to be an exception

3 *Ling* **la n.** the norm

4 *Math* norm

normé, -e [nɔrme] **ADJ** *Math* normed

normographe [nɔrmɔgraf] **NM** stencil

norois[1] [nɔrwa] **NM** *(vent)* northwester

norois[2], **-e** [nɔrwa, -az] *Ling* **ADJ** Norse

NM Norse

noroît [nɔrwa] = **norois**[1]

norovirus [nɔrovirys] **NM** *Méd* norovirus

norrois, -e [nɔrwa, -az] = **norois**[2]

Norvège [nɔrvɛʒ] **NF** *Géog* **la N.** Norway; **vivre en N.** to live in Norway; **aller en N.** to go to Norway

norvégien, -enne [nɔrveʒjɛ̃, -ɛn] **ADJ** Norwegian

NM *(langue)* Norwegian

❑ **Norvégien, -enne NM,F** Norwegian

❑ **norvégienne NF** Norway yawl

nos [no] *voir* **notre**

nosémose [nozemoz] **NF** *Zool* nosemosis

nosocomial, -e, -aux, -ales [nozokɔmjal, -o] **ADJ** *Méd (maladie, infection)* nosocomial

nosographie [nɔzɔgrafi] **NF** *Méd* nosography

nosologie [nɔzɔlɔʒi] **NF** *Méd* nosology

nosologique [nɔzɔlɔʒik] **ADJ** *Méd* nosological

nosologiste [nɔzɔlɔʒist] **NMF** *Méd* nosologist

nosophobie [nɔzɔfɔbi] **NF** nosophobia

nostalgie [nɔstalʒi] **NF 1** *(regret)* nostalgia; **la n. des années soixante** sixties nostalgia, nostalgia for the sixties; **penser à qch avec n.** to think of sth nostalgically *or* with nostalgia; **avoir la n. de** to feel nostalgic about; **j'ai la n. de ces temps-là** I look back on that time with nostalgia, I feel nostalgia for that time **2** *(mal du pays)* homesickness; **avoir la n. du pays** to be homesick

nostalgique [nɔstalʒik] **ADJ** nostalgic; **que ces chansons sont nostalgiques!** these songs do take you back *or* are full of nostalgia!

NMF nostalgic person; **les nostalgiques des années 60** people who pine for the 60s, people who are nostalgic for the 60s

nostoc [nɔstɔk] **NM** *Bot* nostoc, star-jelly

Nostradamus [nɔstradamys] **NPR** Nostradamus

nota bene [nɔtabene], **nota** [nɔta] **NM INV** nota bene

notabilité [nɔtabilite] **NF** notable, worthy; **toutes les notabilités locales étaient là** all the local notables *or* worthies were there

notable [nɔtabl] **ADJ** *(fait)* notable; *(différence)* appreciable, noticeable

NM notable, worthy; **tous les notables de la ville** all the town notables *or* worthies

notablement [nɔtabləmɑ̃] **ADV** notably, considerably

notaire [nɔtɛr]

> Note that it is no longer considered a mistake to feminize this word and to say **une notaire** but some French speakers nonetheless regard this form as unacceptable, especially in France. See also the entry **féminisation**.

NM *(qui reçoit actes et contrats)* notary (public), lawyer; *(qui surveille les transactions immobilières)* lawyer, *Br* solicitor

notamment [nɔtamɑ̃] **ADV** especially, in particular, notably; **il y a certains avantages, n. un abattement fiscal** there are some advantages, notably tax deductions

notarial, -e, -aux, -ales [nɔtarjal, -o] **ADJ** notarial, legal

notariat [nɔtarja] **NM le n.** *(fonction)* the legal profession; *(corporation)* lawyers; **son père la destinait au n.** her father wanted her to become a lawyer

notarié, -e [nɔtarje] **ADJ** legally drawn up, authentic; **acte n.** notarized deed

notateur, -trice [nɔtatœr, -tris] **NM,F** specialist in dance notation

notation [nɔtasjɔ̃] **NF 1** *(remarque)* note

2 *Chim, Ling, Math & Mus* notation; **la n. phonétique** phonetic symbols

3 *Scol* **la n. d'un devoir** correcting *or Br* marking *or Am* grading homework

4 *Ordinat* **n. hexadécimale** hex *or* hexadecimal code

5 *(gén) & Fin & Bourse* rating; **n. du personnel** *Admin* personnel *or* merit rating; *Mil* personnel rating; *Bourse* **n. AA** double-A rating; *Bourse* **n. AAA** triple-A rating

notatrice [nɔtatris] *voir* **notateur**

note [nɔt] **NF 1** *Mus (son)* note; *(touche)* key; **sais-tu lire les notes?** can you read music?; **dans la n.** in tune *or* key; *aussi Fig* **être dans la n.** to hit just the right note; **donner la n.** *Mus* to give the keynote; *Fig* to give the lead; **fausse n.** *Mus* wrong note; *Fig* false note; *Mus* **faire une fausse n.** *(pianiste)* to hit a wrong note *or* key; *(violoniste)* to play a wrong note; *(chanteur)* to sing a wrong note; *Fig* **la cérémonie s'est déroulée sans (une) fausse n.** the ceremony went (off) without a hitch; **la n. juste** the right note

2 *(annotation)* note; **prendre des notes** to take *or* to make notes; **prendre quelques notes rapides** to jot down a few notes; **voilà les notes rapides que j'ai prises** here are the notes I jotted down; *Jur* **notes d'audience** court notes; **prendre qch en n., prendre n. de qch** to make a note of sth, to note sth down; **prendre bonne n. de qch** to take due *or* good note of sth; **n. de l'auteur** author's note; **n. explicative** explanatory note; **n. de** *ou* **en bas de page** footnote; **n. de l'éditeur** editor's note; *Ordinat* **n. de fin de document** endnote; **n. marginale** marginal note; **n. de la rédaction** editor's note; **n. de renvoi** cross-reference; **n. du traducteur** translator's note

3 *(communication)* **n. diplomatique/officielle** diplomatic/official note; **n. d'information** *ou* **de service** memo, memorandum; *Douanes* **n. de détail** details, description *(of parcel)*

4 *Scol Br* mark, *Am* grade; **notes trimestrielles** (end-of-term) report; **avoir la meilleure n.** to get the best *or* highest *or* top *Br* mark *or Am* grade; *Fam* **je ne peux pas mettre de n. à un pareil torchon!** I can't *Br* mark rubbish *or Am* grade garbage like this!; **carnet** *ou* **relevé de notes** school report

5 *(nuance)* note, touch, hint; **une n. d'originalité** a touch *or* note of originality; **avec une n. de tristesse dans la voix** with a note *or* hint of sadness in his/her voice; **apporter une n. personnelle à qch** to give sth a personal touch; **mettre une n. de gaieté dans une pièce** to lend a cheerful note to a room; **finir sur une n. positive** to end on a positive note

6 *(facture)* bill, *Am* check; **n. de téléphone** phone bill; **n. de restaurant** restaurant bill; **la n., s'il vous plaît!** may I have the bill, please?; **mettez-le sur ma n.** charge it to my account, put it on my bill; **régler la n.** to pay the bill; *Com* **n. d'avis** advice note; **n. d'avoir** credit note; **n. de commission** commission note, fee note; **n. de crédit** credit note; **n. de débit** debit note; **n. de frais** expense account; *(présentée après coup)* expenses claim form; **présenter sa n. de frais** to claim for expenses; **mettre qch sur sa n. de frais** to put sth on one's expense account; *Com* **n. de fret** freight note; **n. d'honoraires** invoice *(for work done by self-employed person)*; **n. de rappel** reminder

7 *(d'un parfum)* note

❑ **notes NFPL** *(précis)* study notes *(for works of literature)*

noté, -e [nɔte] **ADJ 1 être bien/mal n.** *(élève, employé)* to have a good/bad record; *(devoir)* to have received a good/poor *Br* mark *or Am* grade

2 *Bourse* **n. AA/AAA** double-A/triple-A rated

notebook [nɔtbuk] **NM** *Ordinat* notebook

noter [3] [nɔte] **VT 1** *(prendre en note)* to note *or* to write (down); **je note votre nom** I'll make a note of *or* I'll write down your name; **j'ai noté une mélodie** I noted *or* jotted (down) a tune; **veuillez n. notre nouvelle adresse** please note *or* make a note of our new address; **je vais le n. définitivement sur mon agenda** I'll make a permanent note of it in my diary; **notez que chaque enfant doit apporter un vêtement chaud** please note that every child must bring something warm to wear; **n. une commande** to log *or* to note an order

2 *(faire ressortir → gén)* to mark; *(→ en cochant)* to tick; *(→ en surlignant)* to highlight; **n. qch d'une croix** to put a cross next to sth

3 *(remarquer)* to note, to notice; **j'ai noté une erreur dans votre article** I noticed a mistake in your article; **notez que je ne dis rien** please note that I'm making no comment; **il est à n. que...** it should be noted *or* borne in mind that...; **à n.: les bus ne circulent pas le dimanche** note: there are no buses on Sundays; **très bien, chef, c'est noté** OK, boss, I've got it; *Fam* **je ne veux pas que tu recommences, c'est noté?** I don't want you to do it again, do you understand *or* have you got that *or* is that clear?; **notez bien cela** take good note of this, note this well; **notez bien, il a fait des progrès** mind you, he's improved; *Fam* **note bien, je m'en fiche** to tell you the truth, I couldn't care less; **note bien que je pourrais faire autrement** I could always do something else, you know

4 *(évaluer) Br* to mark, *Am* to grade; *Scol (élève) Br* to give a mark to, *Am* to grade; *(devoir, examen) Br* to mark, *Am* to grade

USAGE ABSOLU 1 *(prendre en note)* **vas-y, je note** go ahead, I've got something to write with; *Fam* **très bien, chef, je note** OK, boss, I've got it

2 *Scol (évaluer)* **n. sur 20** to *Br* mark *or Am* grade out of 20; **elle note généreusement/sévèrement** she gives high/low *Br* marks *or Am* grades

notice [nɔtis] **NF 1** *(résumé)* note; **n. bibliographique** bibliographical details; **n. biographique** biographical note; **n. nécrologique** obituary (notice); **n. publicitaire** *(brochure)* advertising brochure; *(annonce)* advertisement

2 *(instructions)* instruction book *or* booklet, handbook, manual; **n. du constructeur** manufacturer's instructions; **n. explicative** *ou* **d'emploi** directions for use; **n. de fonctionnement** instructions; **n. technique** technical specifications *or* instructions; **as-tu lu la n.?** have you read the instructions?

3 *(préface de livre)* note

notificatif, -ive [nɔtifikatif, -iv] ADJ notifying *(avant n)*

notification [nɔtifikasjɔ̃] NF **1** *(avis)* notification; **donner à qn n. de qch** to give sb notification of sth, to notify sb of sth; **recevoir n. de qch** to receive notification *or* to be notified of sth; **après que n. eut été faite du résultat aux intéressés** after the interested parties had been notified of *or* had received notification of the result **2** *Jur* **n. du protêt** noting and *or* of protest

notificative [nɔtifikativ] *voir* **notificatif**

notifier [9] [nɔtifje] VT *(apprendre)* **n. qch à qn** to notify sb of sth; **on vient de lui n. son renvoi** he's/she's just received notice of his/her dismissal, he's/she's just been notified of his/her dismissal; **en plus, il lui a fait n. son renvoi par sa secrétaire** on top of that, he got his secretary to tell him/her he'd/she'd been sacked; **n. une assignation à qn** to serve a writ on sb; *Jur* **n. son consentement à qn** to signify one's consent to sb; **on lui notifia qu'il aurait à déménager dans les vingt-quatre heures** he received notice to quit within twenty-four hours

USAGE ABSOLU **veuillez n. par courrier** please inform us in writing

notion [nosjɔ̃] NF *(idée)* notion; **il n'a ni la n. du bien ni celle du mal** he has no notion of either good or evil; **perdre la n. du temps** to lose all sense of time, to lose track of time; **perdre la n. de la réalité** to lose all sense of reality; **je n'en ai pas la moindre n.** I haven't (got) the faintest *or* slightest idea

❑ **notions** NFPL **1** *(rudiments)* **notions de base** fundamentals, basic knowledge; **avoir des notions de chimie/russe** to know the basics of chemistry/Russian; **il a quelques notions de physique** he has some knowledge of physics; **anglais: notions** *(sur un CV)* basic knowledge of English

2 *(comme titre d'ouvrage)* primer; **notions de géométrie** geometry primer

notionnel, -elle [nosjɔnɛl] ADJ notional

notochorde, notocorde [nɔtɔkɔrd] NM *Zool* notochord

notoire [nɔtwar] ADJ recognized; *Péj* notorious; *(fait)* well-known; **son sens politique est n.** his/her political acumen is acknowledged by all, he's/she's famous for his/her political acumen; **le fait est n.** it's an acknowledged *or* accepted fact; **un criminel n.** a notorious criminal; **être d'une avarice n.** to be notoriously miserly

notoirement [nɔtwarmɑ̃] ADV manifestly, *Péj* notoriously; **fait n. faux** manifestly false fact; **un malfrat n. connu** a notorious gangster; **ses ressources sont n. insuffisantes** it's widely known that he/she has limited means

notonecte [nɔtɔnɛkt] NF *Entom* water boatman

notoriété [nɔtɔrjete] NF **1** *(renommée)* fame, renown; **sa thèse lui a valu une grande n.** *ou* **a fait sa n.** his/her thesis made him/her famous; **cela lui a valu une certaine n.** that brought *or* earned him/her a certain reputation; **il est de n. publique que...** it's public *or* common knowledge that...

2 *Mktg* awareness; **n. assistée** aided recall; **n. de la marque** brand awareness; **n. du produit** product awareness; **n. publicitaire** advertising awareness; **n. spontanée** spontaneous recall

3 *(personne célèbre)* celebrity, famous person; **à vingt ans, c'était déjà une n.** he/she was already famous at (the age of) twenty

4 *Jur* **acte de n.** sworn affidavit

notorycte [nɔtɔrikt] NM *Zool* marsupial mole

nototrème [nɔtɔtrɛm] NM *Zool* marsupial frog

notre [nɔtr] *(pl* **nos** [no]) ADJ POSSESSIF **1** *(indiquant la possession)* our; **n. ami/amie** our friend; **nos enfants** our children; **n. père et n. mère,** *Littéraire* **nos père et mère** our father and mother; **ils ont mis nos chapeaux et nos gants** they put on our hats and (our) gloves; **nous avons pris n. sac** *(il n'y a qu'un sac)* we took our bag; *(chacun a son sac)* we took our bags; **un de nos amis** a friend of ours, one of our friends; **n. société** our society; *Fam* **nous aurons n. chambre à nous** *(il y a une chambre)* we will have our own room▪; *Fam* **nous avons n. vendredi** we've got Friday off▪

2 *Rel* **N. Père** Our Father; **le N. Père** the Lord's Prayer

3 *(se rapportant au "nous" de majesté ou de modestie)* **car tel est n. bon plaisir** for such is our pleasure; **dans n. second chapitre** in the second chapter; **n. thèse couvre trois décennies** this thesis covers a thirty-year period

4 *(emploi expressif)* our; **comment se porte n. petit malade?** how's our little invalid, then?; **c'est lui, c'est n. homme!** that's him, that's the man we're after *or* that's our man!; *Fam* **n. imbécile de frère** our idiot of a brother; *Fam* **nos artistes de maris** our artist husbands; **nous retrouvons n. héros dix ans plus tard...** we meet our hero again ten years later...

nôtre [notr] ADJ *Littéraire* ours; **un n. cousin** a cousin of ours; **l'objectif que je considère comme n.** the aim which I consider to be ours; **ces espoirs qui furent nôtres** these hopes which were ours; **nous ferons nôtres ses principes** we shall adopt these principles of his/hers; **nous faisons nôtres les félicitations qu'ils vous adressent** we join them in congratulating you

PRON POSSESSIF **le n./la n./les nôtres** ours; **cette valise n'est pas la n.** this isn't our case, this case isn't ours; **un sort tel que le n.** a fate such as ours; **il ressemble au n.** it looks like ours; **nous voulons bien te donner du n.** you can have some of ours; **amenez vos enfants, les nôtres ont le même âge** bring your children, ours are the same age; **vous avez vos problèmes, et nous les nôtres** you have your problems, we have ours; **nous n'en avons pas besoin, nous avons le n.** we don't need it, we've got our own; **cette histoire qui est la n.** this story which is ours; **les deux nôtres** our two, the two of ours, both of ours; *(en insistant)* our own two

NM **les nôtres** *(notre famille)* our family, *Am* our folks; *(nos partisans)* our followers; *(nos coéquipiers)* our team-mates; **c'est un des nôtres** he's one of us; **est-il des nôtres?** *(de notre côté)* is he one of us?; **serez-vous des nôtres demain soir?** will you be joining us tomorrow evening?; **vous n'étiez pas des nôtres pour le réveillon de Noël?** weren't you at our Christmas Eve party?; **il faut y mettre du n.** we must do our bit, we should make an effort; **à la (bonne) n.!** cheers!

Notre-Dame [nɔtrədam] NF *Rel (titre)* Our Lady; *(église)* **N. des Fleurs/de la Passion** Our Lady of the Flowers/Passion; **N. de Paris** *(cathédrale)* Notre Dame; **la fête de N.** the feast of the Assumption

'Notre-Dame de Paris' *Hugo* 'The Hunchback of Notre Dame'

'Notre-Dame des Fleurs' *Genet* 'Our Lady of the Flowers'

notule [nɔtyl] NF (brief) note

nouage [nwaʒ] NM *Tex* knotting, binding

nouaison [nwɛzɔ̃] NF *Bot* setting

Nouakchott [nwakʃɔt] NM Nouakchott

nouba [nuba] NF **1** *Fam (fête)* **faire la n.** to party, to have a wild time **2** *(musique)* (Algerian) military band

nouc [nuk], **noucle** [nukl] NM *Can (en acadien) (nœud)* knot

noucler [3] [nukle] VT *Can (en acadien) (lacets)* to tie, to knot

noue[1] [nu] NF *(terre grasse)* marshy meadow, water meadow

noue[2] [nu] NF *Constr (arête)* valley *(of roof)*; *(bande de plomb ou zinc)* flashing; **pièce de n.** valley tile

noué, -e [nwe] ADJ **avoir la gorge nouée** to have a lump in one's throat; **avoir l'estomac n.** to have a knot in one's stomach

nouer [6] [nwe] VT **1** *(attacher ensemble → lacets, cordes)* to tie *or* to knot (together); **elle noua ses bras autour de mon cou** she wrapped her arms round my neck

2 *(faire un nœud à)* to tie (up), to knot; **n. qch serré** to knot sth tightly, to make a tight knot in sth; **n. sa cravate** to knot one's tie; **laisse-moi n. ta cravate** let me knot your tie; **n. son tablier** to tie one's apron; **j'ai noué le bouquet avec de la ficelle** I tied the bouquet together with string; **il a noué le foulard autour de sa taille** he tied the scarf around his waist; **n. ses cheveux** to tie up one's hair; **elle noua ses cheveux avec un ruban** she tied her hair back *or* up with a ribbon; *Fig* **elle a les articulations nouées par le rhumatisme** her joints are gnarled with rheumatism; *Fig* **la peur lui nouait la gorge/les entrailles** his/her throat/stomach tightened with fear

3 *(établir)* **n. des relations avec qn** to enter into a relationship with sb; **n. conversation avec qn** to enter into conversation with sb; **n. une intrigue** to hatch a plot

4 *Tex* to splice *or* to knot (together)

VI *Bot* to set

▸**se nouer** VPR **1** *(emploi réfléchi)* **se n. les cheveux** to tie up one's hair

2 *(emploi passif) (ceinture)* to fasten, to do up; **les cheveux se nouent d'abord sur la nuque** first tie your hair back at the neck

3 *(s'entrelacer)* to intertwine; **ses mains se nouèrent comme pour prier** his/her hands joined *or* came together as if to pray; **nos doigts se nouèrent** our fingers intertwined

4 *(s'instaurer)* to develop, to build up; **une complicité se noue entre l'acteur et le public** a feeling of complicity builds up *or* develops between the actor and the audience; **c'est à cet âge que beaucoup d'amitiés se nouent** it's at that age that a lot of friendships are made

5 *(prendre forme → intrigue)* to take shape; **l'action ne se noue que dans le dernier chapitre** only in the last chapter does the plot come to a head *or* climax

nouet [nwɛ] NM *Vieilli* = muslin sachet used for infusions

noueux, -euse [nwø, -øz] ADJ **1** *(tronc, bois)* knotty, gnarled **2** *(doigt, mains, tronc d'arbre)* gnarled; **un vieux paysan n.** a wizened old farmer

nougat [nuga] NM **1** *Culin* nougat **2** *Fam (locutions)* **c'est du n.!** it's a cinch!, it's as easy as pie!; **c'est pas du n.!** it's not as easy as it looks!

❑ **nougats** NMPL *Fam (pieds)* feet▪, *Br* plates, *Am* dogs

nougatine [nugatin] NF nougatine

nouille [nuj] ADJ INV **1** *Fam (niais)* dumb, dopey; **le premier acte est complètement n.** the first act is a load of *Br* tripe *or Am* garbage

2 *Beaux-Arts* Art Nouveau *(avant n)*

NF **1** *Culin* noodle

2 *Fam (nigaud)* dimwit, dumbo; *(mollasson)* drip, wimp

3 *très Fam (pénis)* dick, *Br* knob, *Am* schlong; **égoutter la n.** to *Br* have *or Am* take a piss, *Br* to have a slash *or* a leak

❑ **nouilles** NFPL noodles; *Fam (pâtes en général)* pasta▪ *(UNCOUNT)*

noulet [nulɛ] NM *Constr (canal)* valley gutter

Nouméa [numea] NM Nouméa

nouménal, -e, -aux, -ales [numenal, -o] ADJ noumenal

noumène [numɛn] NM noumenon

nounou [nunu] NF *Fam* nanny; **jouer les nounous avec qn** to mollycoddle *or* to nursemaid sb

nounoune [nunun] *Can Fam* ADJ dumb, silly▪

NF twit, dimwit

nounours [nunurs] NM *Fam* teddy (bear)▪

Noureïev [nurejɛf] NPR **Rudolph N.** Rudolph Nureyev

nourrain [nurɛ̃] NM **1** *(poisson)* fry, young fish **2** *(porc)* young pig

nourri, -e [nuri] PP *voir* **nourrir**

ADJ **1** *(dense → fusillade)* sustained, heavy **2** *(ininterrompu → applaudissements)* prolonged, sustained **3** *(riche → style)* rich, full; *(ligne en dessin)* broad, firm; **discussion nourrie** heated debate, lively discussion

nourrice [nuris] NF **1** *(qui allaite)* wet nurse **2** *(qui garde) Br* childminder, *Am* nurse, nursemaid; **mettre un enfant en n.** to leave a child with a childminder; **n. agréée** registered childminder; *Vieilli* **n. sèche** dry nurse **3** *Aut (bidon)* spare can; *(réservoir)* service tank **4** *(morceau de bœuf)* (beef) stewing shank **5** *Entom* nurse (bee)

nourricier, -ère [nurisje, -ɛr] ADJ **1** *Littéraire (qui nourrit)* **notre terre nourricière** mother Earth **2** *Anat* nutrient *(avant n)* **3** *Bot* nutritive

nourrir [32] [nurir] VT **1** *(alimenter)* to feed, *Sout* to

nourish; **n. sa famille** to provide for *or* to feed one's family; **n. qn (de** *ou* **avec qch)** to feed sb (on sth); **n. un bébé au sein/au biberon/à la cuillère** to breastfeed/to bottle-feed/to spoon-feed a baby; **n. un bébé aux petits pots** to feed a baby (on) *or* to give a baby prepared baby-foods; **poulet nourri au grain** corn-fed chicken; **elle est difficile et j'ai du mal à la n.** she's fussy about her food and I have trouble getting her to eat; **être bien nourri** to be well-fed; **être mal nourri** *(sous-alimenté)* to be undernourished; **les enfants sont bien nourris à la cantine** the children get good school dinners

2 *(sujet: crème, lotion → peau, visage, cuir)* to nourish; *(feu)* to feed

3 *(faire subsister)* to feed; **j'ai trois enfants à n.** I've got three mouths to feed; **la Brie nourrit la capitale** the Brie area provides the capital with food; **la chanson/sculpture ne nourrit pas son homme** you can't live off singing/sculpture alone; **le métier est dangereux, mais il nourrit son homme** it's a dangerous job, but it brings in the money *or* it pays well

4 *Fig* **l'art contemporain ne me nourrit pas** I don't get anything out of modern art; **des lectures qui nourrissent l'esprit** reading that improves the mind; **on lui a nourri l'esprit d'idées reçues** his/her mind's been filled with clichés; **j'avais l'esprit nourri de Goethe** I was brought up on Goethe; **un roman nourri des souffrances de l'auteur** a novel inspired by the author's own suffering; **les lettres qu'elle lui envoyait nourrissaient sa passion** the letters she sent him/her sustained his/her passion; *Mus* **n. le son** to give fullness *or* body to the tone

5 *Littéraire (pensée)* to entertain; *(illusion, rancœur, haine)* to harbour, to nurse, *Sout* to nourish; *(espoir)* to entertain, to cherish; *(projet)* to nurse; **il nourrit une vive rancœur contre elle** he harbours a feeling of great resentment towards her; **je nourris de grands espoirs** I have high hopes; **je nourris l'espoir de le revoir** I cherish the hope of seeing him again; **elle nourrissait déjà des projets ambitieux** she was already turning over some ambitious projects in her mind; **n. des doutes au sujet de** to entertain doubts *or* to be doubtful about

USAGE ABSOLU **le lait nourrit (bien)** milk is nourishing

►**se nourrir** VPR **1** *(s'alimenter)* to feed (oneself); *(manger)* to eat; **il est trop petit pour se n. tout seul** he's too young to feed himself; **il se nourrit mal** he doesn't eat properly; **il faut bien se n.** a man has to eat; **il refuse de se n.** he won't eat; **se n. de lait/fruits** to live on milk/fruit; **elle ne se nourrit que de bananes** she only eats bananas; **les koalas se nourrissent de feuilles d'eucalyptus** koalas feed on *or* eat eucalyptus leaves; **il gagne juste de quoi se n.** he earns just enough to live on; **chasser pour se n.** to hunt for one's food

2 *Fig* **se n. d'illusions** to revel in illusions; **se n. de bandes dessinées** to read nothing but comics

nourrissage [nurisaʒ] NM rearing, feeding

nourrissant, -e [nurisɑ̃, -ɑ̃t] ADJ nourishing, nutritious; **crème nourrissante** nourishing cream; **le dessert était un peu trop n.** the dessert was a bit too rich

nourrisseur [nurisœr] NM **1** *(éleveur → de bétail)* stock breeder; *(→ de vaches)* dairyman **2** *(appareil)* feeder

nourrisson [nurisɔ̃] NM **1** *(bébé)* baby, infant; **quand tu n'étais encore qu'un n.** when you were still a tiny baby; **consultation de nourrissons** baby clinic **2** *Arch (bébé au sein)* nursling, suckling

nourriture [nurityr] NF **1** *(alimentation)* food; **donner à qn une n. saine** to provide sb with a healthy diet; **le maïs sert à la n. du bétail** maize is used as a foodstuff for cattle *or* used as cattle-feed

2 **la n.** *(aliments)* food; **mon salaire sert à payer la n.** my wages go towards the food bill; **elle n'absorbe plus aucune n.** she isn't eating any food any more; **il refuse toute n. depuis trois jours** he has been refusing food *or* refusing to eat for three days; **priver qn de n.** to starve sb, to deprive sb of food

3 *(aliment)* food; **le lait est une n. riche en calcium** milk is a food rich in calcium

4 *Littéraire (de l'esprit, du cœur)* nourishment; **c'est bon pour leur n. intellectuelle** it will stimulate their minds

5 *(du cuir)* tawing paste

'Les Nourritures terrestres' *Gide* 'Fruits of the Earth'

---

nous [nu] PRON **1** *(sujet ou attribut d'un verbe)* we; **toi et moi, n. comprenons** you and I understand; **elle et moi, n. partons** she and I are leaving; **c'est n. qui déciderons** we are the ones who'll decide; **c'est n. qui sommes fautifs** we are to blame, it is us *or Sout* we who are to blame; **n., n. restons** *ou Fam* **on reste là** we are staying here; *Fam* **n. sommes allés au restaurant avec mon mari** *(lui et moi)* me and my husband went to the restaurant; *Fam* **n. deux, on s'aimera toujours** the two of us will always love each other; **partons, rien que n. trois** let's leave, just us three *or* the three of us; **coucou, c'est n.!** hello, it's us!; **n. autres médecins pensons que…** we doctors think that…; *Can* **n. autres, on va faire une promenade** WE'RE going for a walk; *Presse* **N. Deux** = French weekly women's magazine

2 *(complément d'un verbe ou d'une préposition)* us; **il ne n. connaît pas** he doesn't know us; **il n. a serré la main** he shook our hands; **les enfants n. ont jeté des pierres** the children threw stones at us; **elle n. en a parlé** she spoke to us about it; **lisez-le-n.** read it to us; **et n., tu n. oublies?** and what about us, have you forgotten us?; **elle n'aime que n. deux** she only loves us two *or* the two of us; **c'est à n. deux qu'il l'a demandé** he asked the two of us *or* (the) both of us; **à n. six, on a fini la paella** between the six of us, we finished the paella; **à n. deux!** *(sur un ton menaçant)* I want a word with you!; **c'est de la part de n. tous** it's from us all; **un ami à n.** a friend of ours; **notre voilier à n.** our (own) yacht; **ces anoraks ne sont pas à n.** these anoraks aren't ours *or* don't belong to us; **chez n.** *(dans notre foyer)* at home, in our house; *(dans notre pays)* at *or* back home; **il était avec n.** he was with us; **entre n.** between us; **pas de politesses entre n.** no need for formality between us; **entre n. (soit dit), elle ment** between us *or* between you and me, she's lying; *Arch* **ce que c'est que de n.!** alas, we are but mere mortals!

3 *(sujet ou complément, représentant un seul locuteur)* we; **dans notre thèse, n. traitons le problème sous deux aspects** in our thesis, we deal with the problem in two ways; **alors, comment allons-n. ce matin?** *(à un malade, un enfant)* and how are we this morning?; **bon, à n. maintenant** so, we can have a talk now; **alors, à n., qu'est-ce qu'il n. fallait?** *(chez un commerçant)* now, what can I do for you?

PRON **1** *(emploi réfléchi)* **n. n. réchauffons** we are warming ourselves; **n. n. sommes versé du vin** we poured ourselves some wine; **n. n. amusons beaucoup** we're having a great time, we're really enjoying ourselves

2 *(emploi réciproque)* each other; **n. n. aimons** we love each other; **n. n. battions avec l'ennemi** we were fighting the enemy

NM **le n. de majesté** the royal we

nous-même [numɛm] PRON *(après "nous" de majesté, de modestie)* ourself

nous-mêmes [numɛm] PRON ourselves; **nous l'avons fait n.** we did it ourselves; **nous y sommes allés de n.** we went there on our own initiative; **vérifions par n.** let's check for ourselves

nouure [nuyr] NF **1** *Bot* setting **2** *Méd* rachitic rosary

NOUVEAU, -ELLE, -AUX, -ELLES [nuvo, -ɛl]

ADJ new **1–6** ■ latest **2** ■ further **3** ■ another **3** ■ novel **4**
NM,F new person
NM new

nouvel is used before masculine singular nouns beginning with a vowel or h mute.

ADJ **1** *(récent → appareil, modèle)* new; *(→ pays)* new, young; **il est n., ce manteau?** is this coat new?; **notre démocratie est encore nouvelle** democracy is still in its infancy in our country; **je suis n. dans le métier** I'm new to this business; **il est encore (un peu) n. en politique** he's still (a bit of) a newcomer to politics; **c'est tout n., ça vient de sortir** *(livre)* it's hot off the press; *(appareil)* it's brand-new, it's just come out; *Fig* **c'est n., ça vient de sortir** that's a new one on me; *Fam* **tu sais ce que c'est, tout n. tout beau, ça lui passera** you know what it's like, it's all new and exciting at first, but he'll/she'll get over it; **la nouvelle génération** the new *or* rising generation; **les nouveaux arrivants** the newcomers; **nouvelle économie** new economy; **les nouveaux mariés** the newlyweds, the newly married couple; **les nouveaux pauvres** the new poor; **les nouveaux pères** modern fathers; **mots nouveaux** new words; *Pol* **nouvel État indépendant** newly independent state; **n. pays industrialisé** newly industrialized country; **n. riche** nouveau riche; *Mktg* **nouvel utilisateur** first-time user; *Méd* **n. variant de la maladie de Creutzfeldt-Jakob** new variant CJD; **n. venu/nouvelle venue** newcomer; *Cin* **nouvelle version** remake; **faire une nouvelle version de** to do a remake of; *Fin* **nouvelle émission** *(d'actions)* new issue; *Fin* **nouveaux emprunts** new borrowings; *Mktg* **n. et amélioré** *(sur emballage)* new improved

2 *(dernier en date)* new, latest; **la nouvelle mode** the latest fashion; **ce nouvel attentat a fait 52 morts** this latest bomb attack leaves 52 dead; **elle se prend pour la nouvelle Marilyn Monroe** she thinks she's another *or* the new Marilyn Monroe; **nouvelle technologie** new technology; **nouvelles technologies de l'information** new information technologies; **techniques nouvelles** new *or* up-to-date techniques; **nouveaux élus** *(députés)* new *or* newly elected deputies; **herbe nouvelle** young grass; **carottes nouvelles** spring carrots; **pommes de terre nouvelles** new potatoes; **oignons nouveaux** spring onions; **le beaujolais n.** the new Beaujolais *or* Beaujolais nouveau; **nouvel an, nouvelle année** New Year; **passer le nouvel an chez des amis** to spend New Year's Eve at friends'; **le N. Monde** the New World; **le N. Testament** the New Testament

3 *(autre)* further, new; **une nouvelle raison/hausse des prix** a further *or* an additional *or* another reason/price rise; **se faire de nouveaux amis** to make new friends; **faire de nouveaux efforts** to make fresh efforts; **faire à qn un n. procès** to retry sb; **écrire un n. chapitre** to write another chapter; **de nouvelles négociations sont prévues** further negotiations are scheduled to take place; **le bail est reconduit pour une nouvelle période de trois ans** the lease is renewed for a further three years *or* another three-year period; **une nouvelle fois, je tiens à vous remercier** let me thank you once more *or* again; **il met tous les jours une nouvelle chemise** he wears a clean *or* different shirt every day

4 *(original → découverte, idée)* new, novel, original; **un esprit/un son n. est né** a new spirit/sound is born; **une conception nouvelle** a novel *or* fresh approach; **porter un regard n. sur qn/qch** to take a fresh look at sb/sth; **elle est mécontente – ce n'est pas n.!** she's not happy – nothing new about that!

5 *(inhabituel)* new; **ce dossier est n. pour moi** this case is new to me, I'm new to this case

6 *(novateur)* **nouvelle critique** new criticism; **nouvelle cuisine** nouvelle cuisine; *Presse* **le Nouvel Économiste** = French weekly economic newspaper; *Beaux-Arts* **la nouvelle objectivité** New Objectivity, Neue Sachlichkeit; *Presse* **le Nouvel Observateur,** *Fam* **le Nouvel Obs** = French weekly news magazine; **les Nouveaux philosophes** = group of left-wing, post-Marxist thinkers, including André Glucksmann and Bernard-Henri Lévy, who came to prominence in the late 1970s; *Beaux-Arts* **le n. réalisme** New Realism; **n. roman** nouveau roman, new novel *(term applied to the work, mainly in the 1950s*

and 1960s, of a number of novelists who rejected the assumptions of the traditional novel); *Beaux-Arts* **nouvelle subjectivité** New Subjectivity

NM,F *(élève)* new boy, *f* new girl; *(adulte)* new man, *f* new woman

NM **qu'est-ce qu'il y a de n.?** what's new?; **rien de n. depuis la dernière fois** nothing new *or* special since last time; **il n'y a rien de n. sous le soleil** there's nothing new under the sun; **il y a quelqu'un de n. au bureau** there's someone new in the office; **il y a eu du n. dans l'affaire Perron** there are new developments in the Perron case; **j'ai du n. au sujet de...** I've got news about...; **tu as du n. pour ton billet d'avion?** have you heard anything more about your plane ticket?

□ **à nouveau** ADV **1** *(de façon différente)* anew, afresh; **faites le plan à n.** redraft the plan, draft the plan again; **recommence à n.** start anew *or* afresh

2 *(encore)* (once) again, once more; **on entend-dit à n. le même bruit** we heard the same noise (once) again

3 *Banque* **porter à n.** to carry forward

□ **de nouveau** ADV again, once again, once more; **tu as fait de n. la même bêtise** you've made the same mistake again; **la terre a de n. tremblé en Californie** there has been another earthquake in California

□ **Nouvelle Vague** NF *Cin* New Wave, Nouvelle Vague

□ **nouvelle vague** NF **la nouvelle vague des ordinateurs** the new generation of computers **ADJ INV** new-generation *(avant n)*; **les imprimantes nouvelle vague** new-generation printers

'La Symphonie du Nouveau Monde' *Dvořák* 'New World Symphony' *or* 'From the New World'

LA NOUVELLE VAGUE

This expression refers to a group of French filmmakers, including François Truffaut and Jean-Luc Godard, who broke away from conventional style and methods in the late 1950s and produced some of the most influential films of the period, using simple techniques and everyday settings.

Allusion

C'est nouveau, ça vient de sortir

This was a catchphrase of the comedian Coluche, whose sketches included comments on the news. It means "It's new, it's just come out". People say this when they suddenly hear about something new. When new regulations come into force without notice, the person announcing the change might say this, meaning "It's just been announced", while a person learning about the change might also say it, meaning "That's a new one on me".

Nouveau-Brunswick [nuvobrœsvik] NM **le N.** New Brunswick

Nouveau-Mexique [nuvomɛksik] NM *Géog* **le N.** New Mexico; **au N.** in New Mexico

nouveau-né, -e [nuvone] *(mpl* **nouveau-nés,** *fpl* **nouveau-nées)** ADJ newborn; **une fille nouveau-née** a newborn baby girl

NM,F 1 *(bébé)* newborn (baby) **2** *(appareil, technique)* new arrival; **un n. dans la gamme des ordinateurs portables** a new addition to the family of portable computers

Nouveau-Québec [nuvokebɛk] NM **le N.** New Quebec; **au N.** in New Quebec

nouveauté [nuvote] NF **1** *(chose nouvelle)* novelty, new thing; *(produit)* new product, innovation; *(livre)* new publication; *(invention)* new invention; **les nouveautés discographiques/littéraires** new releases/books; **vous trouverez ce disque/livre au rayon des nouveautés** you'll find that record in the new releases rack/that book on the new titles shelf; **tu fais de la musculation, c'est une n.!** you've taken up bodybuilding, that's new!; **le racisme a toujours**

existé, ce n'est pas une n. racism has always existed, there's nothing new *or* recent about it

2 *(originalité)* novelty, newness; **recherche constante de la n.** constant search for something new *or* for novelty; **l'exposition a l'attrait de la n.** the exhibition has novelty appeal

3 *Couture* fashion; **le commerce/l'industrie de la n.** the fashion trade/industry; **nouveautés de printemps** new spring fashions; *Vieilli* **magasin de nouveautés** draper's shop, *Am* dry goods store

nouvel [nuvɛl] *voir* **nouveau**

nouvelle [nuvɛl] ADJ F *voir* **nouveau**

NF 1 *(information)* news *(UNCOUNT)*, piece of news; **c'est une n. intéressante** that's an interesting piece of news, that's interesting news; **j'ai une bonne/mauvaise n. pour toi** I have (some) good/bad news for you; **voici une excellente n.!** this is good news!; **une n. plutôt décevante** a rather disappointing piece of news; **tu ne connais pas la n.?** elle est renvoyée haven't you heard (the news)? she's been fired; **la n. de sa mort** the news of his/her death; **fausse n.** false report; **répandre des fausses nouvelles** to spread false rumours; **première n.!** that's news to me!

2 *Littérature* short story, novella

□ **nouvelles** NFPL **1** *(renseignements)* news *(UNCOUNT)*; **je n'ai pas eu de ses nouvelles depuis** I haven't had any news from him/her *or* heard from him/her since; **donne vite de tes nouvelles** write soon; **Paul m'a demandé de tes nouvelles** Paul was asking after you; **prendre des nouvelles de qn** to ask after sb; **j'ai eu des nouvelles de Pierre** *(par lui-même)* I've had news from *or* I've heard from Pierre; *(par quelqu'un d'autre)* I've had news about *or* of Pierre; **j'ai eu de tes nouvelles par ta sœur** your sister told me how you were getting on; **on n'eut plus jamais de leurs nouvelles** they were never heard of again; **je suis sans nouvelles de lui** *(directement)* I've had no news from him, I've not heard from him; *(indirectement)* I've had no news of *or* about him; **on est sans nouvelles des trois alpinistes** there's been no news of the three climbers; **aller aux nouvelles** to go and find out what's (been) happening; **je venais aux nouvelles** I just wanted to find out what's been happening; **les nouvelles vont vite** news travels fast; **aux dernières nouvelles, il était à Lima** he was last heard of in Lima; *Fam* **goûte-moi cette mousse, tu m'en diras des nouvelles** have a taste of this mousse, I think you'll like it; *Fam* **tu ferais mieux de signer, ou tu auras de mes nouvelles!** you'd better sign, or else!; *Prov* **pas de nouvelles, bonnes nouvelles** no news is good news

2 *Rad & TV* news *(UNCOUNT)*; **les dernières nouvelles** the latest news; **à quelle heure sont les nouvelles?** when's the news on?

Nouvelle-Angleterre [nuvɛlɑ̃glətɛr] NF *Géog* **la N.** New England

Nouvelle-Bretagne [nuvɛlbrətaɲ] NF *Géog* **la N.** New Britain

Nouvelle-Calédonie [nuvɛlkaledɔni] NF *Géog* **la N.** New Caledonia

Nouvelle-Castille [nuvɛlkastij] NF *Géog* **la N.** New Castile

Nouvelle-Écosse [nuvɛlekɔs] NF *Géog* **la N.** Nova Scotia

Nouvelle-France [nuvɛlfrɑ̃s] NF *Hist* **la N.** New France

NOUVELLE-FRANCE

The origin of the French colony of New France can be traced to the foundation of Port-Royal, on the Atlantic coast (Acadia), in 1604, and of Quebec in 1608. By 1665, Louis XIV had sent over 1,000 young women, who were dubbed "les Filles du Roy". The handful of French settlers and soldiers who chose to stay were then able to produce a truly native population of European extraction, "les Canadiens". New France ceased to exist in 1763 when France ceded Canada to England in the Treaty of Paris.

Nouvelle-Galles du Sud [nuvɛlgaldysyd] NF *Géog* **la N.** New South Wales

Nouvelle-Guinée [nuvɛlgine] NF *Géog* **la N.** New Guinea

Nouvelle-Irlande [nuvɛlirlɑ̃d] NF *Géog* **la N.** New Ireland

nouvellement [nuvɛlmɑ̃] ADV newly, recently, freshly; **n. élu/nommé** newly elected/appointed; **n. arrivé dans cette ville, il ne savait où aller** being a newcomer to the city, he didn't know where to go

Nouvelle-Orléans [nuvɛlɔrleɑ̃] NF *Géog* **La N.** New Orleans

Nouvelles-Hébrides [nuvɛlzebrid] NFPL *Anciennement* **les N.** the New Hebrides

Nouvelle-Zélande [nuvɛlzelɑ̃d] NF *Géog* **la N.** New Zealand; **vivre en N.** to live in New Zealand; **aller en N.** to go to New Zealand

Nouvelle-Zemble [nuvɛlzɑ̃bl] NF *Géog* **la N.** Novaya Zemlya

nouvelliste [nuvelist] NMF short story writer

nova [nɔva] NF nova

novateur, -trice [nɔvatœr, -tris] ADJ innovative **NM,F** innovator

novation [nɔvasjɔ̃] NF **1** *(gén)* innovation, innovating **2** *Jur* novation, substitution; **n. de créance** substitution of debt; **accord de n.** novation agreement

novatoire [nɔvatwar] ADJ **acte n.** deed of novation

novatrice [nɔvatris] *voir* **novateur**

novélisation [nɔvelizasjɔ̃] NF novelization

novembre [nɔvɑ̃br] NM November; **le premier n.** (on) the first of November, (on) November the first; **le onze n.** *(fête)* *Br* Armistice Day, *Am* Veterans Day; *voir aussi* **mars**

nover [3] [nɔve] VT to novate; *Jur* **n. une créance** to carry out a novation of a debt

novice [nɔvis] ADJ inexperienced, green; **être n. dans** *ou* **en qch** to be inexperienced in *or* a novice at sth

NMF 1 *(débutant)* novice, beginner **2** *Rel* novice **NM** *Naut* junior seaman

noviciat [nɔvisja] NM **1** *Rel* *(période, lieu)* noviciate **2** *Littéraire* *(apprentissage)* probation, trial period

novlangue [nɔvlɑ̃g] NF Newspeak

Novocaïne® [nɔvɔkain] NF *Pharm* Novocaine®

Novossibirsk [nɔvɔsibirsk] NM Novosibirsk

noyade [nwajad] NF **1** *(fait de se noyer)* drowning *(UNCOUNT)*; **une cause fréquente de n.** a common cause of (death by) drowning; **sauver qn de la n.** to save sb from drowning **2** *(accident)* drowning; **être témoin d'une n.** to witness a drowning; **il y a eu beaucoup de noyades ici l'été dernier** many people (were) drowned here last summer **3** *Hist* execution by drowning

noyau, -x [nwajo] NM **1** *(de fruit)* stone, *Am* pit; **n. de cerise/pêche** cherry/peach stone; **enlever le n. d'un fruit** to pit a fruit, to remove the stone from a fruit; *Bot* **n. reproducteur/végétatif** generative/vegetative nucleus

2 *(centre)* nucleus; **n. familial** family nucleus

3 *(petit groupe)* small group; **un n. d'opposants/d'irréductibles** a small group of opponents/hardliners; **le n. dur** *(d'un parti, de l'actionnariat)* the hard core; **n. de résistance** pocket *or* centre of resistance

4 *Anat, Astron, Biol & Phys* nucleus

5 *Élec, Géol & Nucl* core; *Géol* **n. volcanique** volcanic bomb

6 *Métal* (mould) core

7 *Météo* **n. de condensation/congélation** hygroscopic/freezing nucleus

8 *Chim* nucleus, ring

9 *Constr* newel; **n. de voûte** (central) arch pillar; **escalier à n. plein** winding staircase

10 *Math* kernel

11 *Ordinat* node

noyautage [nwajotaʒ] NM **1** *Pol* infiltration **2** *Métal* core blowing

noyauter [3] [nwajote] VT **1** *Pol* to infiltrate; **le syndicat a été noyauté** the union has been infiltrated **2** *Métal* to blow *or* to make cores

noyauteur [nwajotœr] NM *Métal* core maker

noyé, -e [nwaje] PP *voir* **noyer²**

ADJ 1 *(personne)* drowned; **mourir n.** to drown **2** *(moteur)* flooded

3 *Fig* **les yeux noyés** *ou* **le regard n. de larmes** his/her eyes swimming with *or* full of tears; **elle**

avait les yeux noyés de larmes her eyes were swimming with *or* full of tears; **être n. dans la brume** to be shrouded in mist; **être n. dans la foule** to be lost in the crowd; **après l'invasion, le pays fut n. dans le sang** after the invasion, the country was awash with blood; **la maisonnette est noyée dans la verdure** the cottage is lost in the greenery; **l'essentiel est n. dans les détails** the essentials have been buried *or* lost in a mass of detail; **quelques belles phrases sont noyées dans des développements abscons** some fine phrases are buried under a mass of abstruse argument; **noyée dans la masse, sa voix pouvait passer pour puissante** blended in with the rest, his/her voice could be thought of as powerful; *Fam* **être n.** *(ne rien comprendre)* to be out of one's depth

NM,F drowned person; **les noyés** the drowned; **trois disparus et deux noyés** three missing and two drowned; **on a repêché un n. dans la rivière** a drowned man was fished out of the river

noyer[1] [nwaje] **NM 1** *(arbre)* walnut (tree); **n. (blanc) d'Amérique** hickory **2** *(bois)* walnut

noyer[2] [13] [nwaje] **VT 1** *(personne, animal)* to drown; *(terre, champs)* to swamp; *(moteur, soute, vallée)* to flood; **les polders ont été noyés sous des mètres cubes d'eau** the polders were submerged under several cubic metres of water; **n. une sédition/mutinerie dans le sang** to bloodily suppress a revolt/mutiny; **n. son chagrin (dans l'alcool)** to drown one's sorrows (in drink); *Pêche* **n. le poisson** to play the fish; *Fam Fig* **ne cherche pas à n. le poisson** don't try to confuse the issue; *Prov* **qui veut n. son chien l'accuse de la rage** give a dog a bad name (and hang him)

2 *(mouiller abondamment)* **les larmes noyaient son visage** his/her face was drenched with tears; **les larmes noyaient ses joues** tears poured down his/her cheeks

3 *(faire disparaître)* **une épaisse brume noie la vallée** the valley is shrouded in fog; **le piano est noyé par les violons** the violins are drowning out the piano

4 *Culin (sauce)* to water down, to thin (out) too much; *(vin)* to water down

5 *Menuis* to sink in cement; *(vis)* to countersink; **n. un clou** to drive a nail right in

►**se noyer VPR 1** *(se suicider)* to drown oneself; **elle a essayé de se n.** she tried to drown herself

2 *(accidentellement)* to drown

3 *Fig* **se n. dans** *(se plonger dans)* to bury *or* to absorb oneself in; **quand j'ai des ennuis sentimentaux, je me noie dans le travail** when I have problems with my love life, I throw myself into my work *or* bury myself in work

4 *Fig* **se n. dans** *(s'empêtrer dans)* to get tangled up *or* bogged down *or* trapped in; **tu te noies dans tes contradictions/mensonges** you're getting bogged down in your (own) contradictions/tangled up in your (own) lies; **vous vous noyez dans des considérations hors sujet** you're getting tangled up in *or* lost in a series of side issues; *Hum* **se n. dans un verre d'eau** to make a mountain out of a molehill

NPF [ɛnpeɛf] **NF** *(abrév* **nation plus favorisée***)* MFN

NPI [ɛnpei] **NM** *(abrév* **nouveau pays industrialisé***)* NIC

NMPL *(abrév* **nouveaux pays industrialisés***)* NICs

N/Réf *(abrév écrite* **Notre référence***)* our ref

NRF [ɛnɛrɛf] **NF** *(abrév* **Nouvelle Revue française***)* **1** *(revue)* = literary review **2** *(mouvement)* = literary movement

NRJ [ɛnɛrʒi] **NF** = the largest and most successful of the independent French radio stations

N.-S. *(abrév écrite* **Notre-Seigneur***)* Our Lord

N.-S. J.-C. *(abrév écrite* **Notre-Seigneur Jésus-Christ***)* = Our Lord Jesus Christ

NSP *(abrév écrite* **Notre Saint Père***)* = Our Holy Father

NT *Rel (abrév écrite* **Nouveau Testament***)* NT

NTI [ɛntei] **NFPL** *(abrév* **nouvelles technologies de l'information***)* NIT

NTSC [ɛnteɛsse] **NM** *(abrév* **National television system committee***)* NTSC

nu, -e[1] [ny] **ADJ 1** *(sans habits → personne)* naked, nude; **une femme nue** a naked *or* nude woman; **être nu** to be naked *or* in the nude; **il était nu jusqu'à la ceinture** he was stripped to the waist; **être tout nu** to be stark naked; **ne te promène pas tout nu devant la fenêtre** don't walk about in front of the window with nothing on; **se baigner tout nu** to bathe in the nude; **une plage où l'on peut se baigner (tout) nu** a beach where nude bathing is allowed; **se mettre (tout) nu** to take off all one's clothes, to strip naked; **être à demi nu** *ou* **à moitié nu** to be half-naked; **poser nu pour un photographe** to pose in the nude for a photographer; **revue nue** nude show; **être nu comme un ver** *ou* **la main** to be stark naked

2 *(découvert → partie du corps)* bare; **avoir les bras nus/fesses nues** to be bare-armed/bare-bottomed; **avoir le crâne nu** to be bald-headed; **se promener les jambes nues** to walk about barelegged *or* with bare legs; **être pieds nus** to be barefoot *or* barefooted; **marcher pieds nus** to walk barefoot *or* barefooted; **n'y va pas pieds nus** don't go there with bare feet; **avoir les seins nus** to be topless, to have bare breasts; **se baigner seins nus** to bathe topless; **la tête nue** bareheaded, without a hat on; **il travaillait torse nu** he was working without a shirt on; **mettez-vous torse nu** strip to the waist; **visible à l'œil nu** visible to the naked eye; **ça ne se voit pas/ça se voit à l'œil nu** you can't/you can see it with the naked eye; *Fig* **il est jaloux, ça se voit à l'œil nu** he's jealous, it's plain for all to see

3 *Fig (dégarni → sabre)* naked; *(→ paysage)* bare, empty; *(→ mur, pièce, arbre)* bare; *(→ style)* plain, unadorned; **la vérité (toute) nue** the plain *or* naked truth; *Élec* **fil nu** bare wire

4 *Bot (grain, graine)* naked

NM 1 *Beaux-Arts (personne, œuvre)* nude; **le nu** *(genre)* the nude; **une photo de nu** a nude photo

2 *Constr* **nu de mur** plain of a wall

3 *(lettre)* nu

▫ **à nu ADJ** bare; **le fil est à nu** *(accidentellement)* the wire is bare; *(exprès)* the wire has been stripped; **mon âme était à nu** my soul had been laid bare **ADV mettre à nu** to expose; **mettre un fil électrique à nu** to strip a wire; **mettre son cœur à nu** to bare one's soul; **mettre à nu la corruption de la société** to lay bare *or* to expose corruption in society; *Vieilli Équitation* **monter un cheval à nu** to ride (a horse) bareback

'Nu descendant un escalier' *Duchamp* 'Nude Descending a Staircase'

nuage [nɥaʒ] **NM 1** *Météo* cloud; **ciel chargé de nuages** cloudy *or* overcast sky; **n. de fumée/poussière** cloud of smoke/dust; **n. radioactif** radioactive cloud; **n. de sauterelles** cloud of locusts; **n. toxique** toxic cloud; **n. de chaleur** heat haze; **n. d'orage** storm cloud

2 *Fig (menace, inquiétude)* cloud; **il y a de gros nuages à l'horizon économique de 2007** the economic outlook for 2007 is very gloomy *or* bleak; **un n. passa dans ses yeux/sur son visage** his/her eyes/face clouded over; **un n. de tristesse assombrissait son front** his/her face was clouded with sadness

3 *Fig (rêverie)* **être dans les nuages** to have one's head in the clouds, to be daydreaming; **encore dans les nuages?** are you dreaming again?; **être sur un** *ou* **son petit n.** to be on cloud nine

4 *Fig (masse légère)* **un n. de tulle** a mass *or* swathe of tulle

5 *Fig (petite quantité)* **un n. de lait** a drop of milk

6 *(en joaillerie)* cloud

7 *Can (foulard)* = long scarf, designed to cover the entire face

8 *Math* **n. de points** scatter of points

9 *Phys* **n. (électronique)** electron cloud

▫ **sans nuages ADJ 1** *Météo* cloudless; **sous un ciel sans nuages** under cloudless blue skies

2 *Fig (amitié)* untroubled, perfect; *(bonheur)* unclouded, perfect; **vivre sous un ciel sans nuages** to live in unclouded happiness

nuageux, -euse [nɥaʒø, -øz] **ADJ 1** *Météo (temps)* cloudy; **ciel n.** cloudy *or* overcast sky; **ciel devenant n.** increasing cloud; **masse nuageuse** cloudbank; **système n.** cloud system; **zone nuageuse** area of cloud **2** *Fig (confus → esprit, idée)* hazy, nebulous, obscure

nuance [nɥɑ̃s] **NF 1** *(différence → de couleur)* shade, hue; *(→ de son)* nuance; **des nuances de bleu** shades of blue; **n. de sens** shade of meaning, nuance; **il y a une n. entre indifférence et lâcheté** there's a (slight) difference between indifference and cowardice; **je ne saisis pas la n.** I don't quite see the difference; **j'ai dit "peut-être", pas "oui", n.!** I said "perhaps", not "yes", there's a slight difference!

2 *(subtilité)* nuance, subtlety; **toutes les nuances de sa pensée** the many subtleties *or* all the finer aspects of his/her thinking; **personne/personnage tout en nuances** very subtle person/character; **il joue du piano sans nuances/avec n.** his piano-playing lacks subtlety/displays a good sense of musical shading

3 *(trace légère)* touch, tinge; **une n. de regret** a touch of regret; **une n. de mépris** a touch *or* hint *or* suggestion of contempt; **il y avait une n. d'amertume dans sa voix** there was a touch *or* hint of bitterness in his/her voice

4 *Métal* grade, type

nuancé, -e [nɥɑ̃se] **ADJ** *(couleur, ton)* subtle; *Fig (discours, propos, attitude)* full of nuances; **ses réponses sont toujours très nuancées** he always qualifies his answers a lot

nuancer [16] [nɥɑ̃se] **VT 1** *(couleur)* to shade; *(mélanger)* to blend (**de** with); *(musique)* to nuance; *Mus* **n. son jeu** to introduce light and shade into one's playing **2** *(critique, jugement)* to nuance, to qualify; **cette opinion/déclaration demande à être nuancée** this opinion/statement needs to be qualified **3** *Tex* to grade, to tone

nuancier [nɥɑ̃sje] **NM** colour chart; *Com* sample card *or* chart; *Aut* graduated tint shadeband

Nubie [nybi] **NF la N.** Nubia

nubien, -enne [nybjɛ̃, -ɛn] **ADJ** Nubian

NM,F Nubian

nubile [nybil] **ADJ** nubile; **l'âge n.** ≃ the age of consent

nubilité [nybilite] **NF** nubility

nubuck [nybyk] **NM** nubuck

nucal, -e, -aux, -ales [nykal, -o] **ADJ** *Anat* nuchal

nucelle [nysɛl] **NM** *Bot* nucellus

nucléaire [nykleɛr] **ADJ** *Biol, Mil & Phys* nuclear; **particule n.** elementary particle

NM le n. *(énergie)* nuclear power *or* energy; *(industrie)* the nuclear industry

nucléarisation [nyklearizasjɔ̃] **NF** *Ind* = introduction of nuclear power to replace conventional energy sources; *Mil* nuclearization

nucléariser [3] [nyklearize] **VT** *Ind* to supply with nuclear power; *Mil* to supply with nuclear weapons, to nuclearize

►**se nucléariser VPR** to go nuclear

nucléase [nykleaz] **NF** *Biol* nuclease

nucléé, -e [nyklee] **ADJ** *Biol* nucleate, nucleated

nucléide [nykleid] **NM** *Biol* nuclide

nucléine [nyklein] **NF** *Biol* nuclein

nucléique [nykleik] **ADJ acide n.** nucleic acid

nucléolaire [nykleɔlɛr] **ADJ** *Biol* nucleolar

nucléole [nykleɔl] **NM** *Biol* nucleolus

nucléolyse [nykleɔliz] **NF** nucleolysis

nucléon [nykleɔ̃] **NM** nucleon

nucléonique [nykleɔnik] **ADJ** nucleonic

NF nucleonics *(singulier)*

nucléophile [nykleɔfil] *Chim* **ADJ** nucleophilic

NM nucleophile

nucléoplasme [nykleɔplasm] **NM** nucleoplasm

nucléoprotéide [nykleɔprɔteid] **NF** *Biol & Chim* nucleoprotein

nucléoprotéine [nykleɔprɔtein] **NF** *Biol & Chim* nucleoprotein

nucléoside [nykleozid] **NM** *Biol & Chim* nucleoside

nucléosynthèse [nykleɔsɛ̃tɛz] **NF** *Astron* nucleosynthesis

nucléotide [nykleɔtid] **NM** *Biol & Chim* nucleotide

nucléus, nucleus [nykleys] **NM 1** *Archéol* nucleus **2** *Anat* **n. pulposus** nucleus pulposus **3** *(d'une perle)* nucleus

nuclide [nyklid] **NM** nuclide

nudibranche [nydibrɑ̃ʃ] *Zool* **NM** sea slug, *Spéc*

nudibranch, member of the Nudibranchia or Nudibranchiata family
❏ **nudibranches** NMPL Nudibranchia, Nudibranchiata

nudisme [nydism] NM nudism, naturism; **pratiquer le n., faire du n.** to practise nudism

nudiste [nydist] ADJ nudist *(avant n)*
NMF nudist; **camp de nudistes** nudist camp; **plage/village de nudistes** nudist beach/village

nudité [nydite] NF **1** *(d'une personne)* nakedness, nudity; *Fig* **sa mesquinerie se révélait enfin dans toute sa n.** his/her pettiness was at last revealed for what it was; *Fig* **l'horreur étalée dans toute sa n.** the horror displayed in all its starkness; *Fig* **ses crimes furent étalés dans toute leur n.** his/her crimes were exposed for all to see
2 *(d'un lieu)* bareness; **la n. d'une cellule monacale** the starkness or bareness of a monk's cell; **la n. des murs rend la pièce glaciale** the bare walls make the room feel very cold
3 *Beaux-Arts* nude

nue¹ [ny] ADJ F *voir* **nu**

nue² NF *Arch & Littéraire* high cloud(s); **les nues** the skies; **l'oiseau fendait les nues** the bird was cleaving its way through the skies; *Fig* **porter qn/qch aux nues** to laud or to praise sb/sth to the skies; *Littéraire* **se perdre dans les nues** to have one's head (completely) in the clouds, to be lost in the clouds or in daydreams; *Fig* **tomber des nues** to be flabbergasted, to be thunderstruck

nué, -e¹ [nɥe] ADJ *Vieilli* many-hued

nuée² [nɥe] NF **1** *Littéraire* thick cloud; **n. d'orage** storm cloud, thundercloud **2** *Géol* **n. ardente** nuée ardente **3** *(multitude)* horde, host; **une n. de paparazzi/d'admirateurs** a horde of paparazzi/admirers; **n. d'insectes** horde or swarm of insects; **comme une n. de sauterelles** like a plague of locusts **4** *(en joaillerie)* cloud

nuement [nymɑ̃] ADV *Littéraire* frankly, without embellishment

nue-propriété [nyprɔprijete] *(pl* **nues-propriétés)** NF bare ownership

nuer [7] [nɥe] VT *Littéraire (couleurs)* to graduate

nuire [97] [nɥiʁ] **nuire à** VT IND *(être néfaste pour)* **n. à qn** to harm or to injure sb; **ça ne peut que te n.** it can only do you harm; **ils cherchent à nous n. par une publicité mensongère** they're trying to damage our reputation with misleading publicity; **n. à qch** to be harmful to or to damage or to harm sth; **n. aux intérêts de qn** to prejudice or to harm or to damage sb's interests; **le tabac nuit à la santé** smoking damages your health; **ne fais rien qui puisse n. à ta carrière** don't do anything that might damage or harm your career; **cela a nui à l'équilibre de leur couple** their relationship suffered from it; **les grèves nuisent à la reprise économique** strikes are a threat to economic recovery; **mettre qn hors d'état de n.** *(en lieu sûr)* to put sb out of harm's way
▸ **se nuire** VPR to do oneself harm; **tu te nuis à toi-même en faisant cela** you're only hurting yourself by doing that

nuisance [nɥizɑ̃s] NF (environmental) nuisance; **n. acoustique** noise pollution; **n. chimique** chemical pollution

nuisette [nɥizɛt] NF short or baby-doll nightgown

nuisibilité [nɥizibilite] NF harmfulness

nuisible [nɥizibl] ADJ harmful (à to); **gaz/fumées nuisibles** noxious gases/fumes; **des individus nuisibles à la société** individuals harmful to society; **animaux nuisibles** pests; **plantes nuisibles** noxious plants
❏ **nuisibles** NMPL *Zool* vermin, pests

nuisons *etc voir* **nuire**

nuit [nɥi] NF **1** *(obscurité)* night *(UNCOUNT)*, dark, darkness; **il fait n.** it's dark; **il fait n. noire** it's pitch-dark or pitch-black; **il commence à faire n.** it's getting dark; **la n. tombe** it's getting dark, night is falling; **l'hiver, la n. tombe plus tôt** it gets dark earlier in winter; **rentrer avant la n.** to get back before nightfall or dark; **à la n. tombante, à la tombée de la n.** at nightfall, at dusk; **une fois la n. tombée, à n. tombée, à la n. tombée** after dark; **remonter à la n. des temps** to go back to the dawn of time; **se perdre dans la n. des temps** to be lost in the mists of time;

Littéraire **la n. de l'ignorance** the darkness of ignorance; *Littéraire* **dans la n. de son passé** in the mists of his/her past; *Littéraire* **entrer dans la n. éternelle** ou **la n. du tombeau** to descend into the darkness of the grave; *Littéraire* **l'homme ne sait rien, il est dans la n.** man knows nothing, he struggles in the dark; **c'est le jour et la n.!** it's like night and day!
2 *(intervalle entre le coucher et le lever du soleil)* night, night-time; **une n. étoilée** a starry night; **je dors la n.** I sleep at or during the night; **son état a empiré pendant la n.** his/her condition worsened during the night; **faire sa n.** to sleep through the night; **le bébé fait ses nuits** the baby sleeps through the night; **bonne n.!** goodnight!; **passer une bonne n.** *(sujet: malade)* to have a comfortable night; **as-tu passé une bonne n.?** did you have a good night?; **passer la n. à l'hôtel** to spend or stay the night at a hotel; **il ne passera pas la n.** he won't last the night; **une n. de marche/repos/travail** a night's walk/rest/work; **une n. d'extase/de désespoir** a night of ecstasy/despair; **une n. d'insomnie** a sleepless night; **une n. de sommeil ininterrompu** a night of unbroken sleep; *Prov* **la n. porte conseil** = it would be best to sleep on it
3 *(dans des expressions de temps)* **la n. dernière** last night; **cette n.** *(d'aujourd'hui)* tonight; *(passée)* last night; **que s'est-il passé cette n.?** what happened last night?; **nous partons cette n.** we're leaving tonight; **des nuits entières** nights on end; **en pleine n.** in the middle of the night; **en une n.** *(pendant la nuit)* in one night; *(vite)* overnight; **il y a deux nuits** the night before last; **il y a trois nuits** three nights ago; **l'émission passe tard la n.** the programme is on late at night, it's a late-night programme; **ne sors pas seul la n.** don't go out alone at night; **la n. de mardi/vendredi** Tuesday/Friday night; **dans la n. de mardi à mercredi** during Tuesday night, during the night of Tuesday to Wednesday; **la n. où ils ont disparu** the night (that) they disappeared; **la n. où on l'a appelé, il était introuvable!** the (one) night we called him, he was nowhere to be found!; **la n. précédente** ou **d'avant** the previous night, the night before; **la n. suivante** ou **d'après** the next night, the night after; **l'autre n.** the other night; **n. et jour, de n. comme de jour** night and day; **stationnement interdit n. et jour** *(sur panneau)* no parking day or night; **toute la n.** all night (long), through the night; **toutes les nuits** nightly, every night; *Prov* **la n., tous les chats sont gris** all cats are grey in the dark
4 *(dans des noms de dates)* **la n. de cristal** kristallnacht; **la n. des longs couteaux** the Night of the Long Knives; **la n. de Noël** Christmas night; **la n. de la Saint-Jean** Midsummer Night; **la n. de la Saint-Sylvestre** New Year's Eve (night)
5 *(nuitée)* **n. d'hôtel** *(dans l'hôtellerie)* bed-night; **payer une n. d'hôtel** to pay for a night at a hotel; **payer sa n.** to pay for the night; **c'est combien la n.?** how much is it for one night?; **c'est 300 euros la n.** it's 300 euros a night; **la chambre est à 130 euros la n.** rooms are 130 euros a night
❏ **de nuit** ADJ **1** *Zool* **animaux/oiseaux de n.** nocturnal animals/birds **2** *(pharmacie)* night *(avant n)*, all-night *(avant n)*, twenty-four hour *(avant n)* **3** *(qui a lieu ou qui sert la nuit)* night *(avant n)*; **garde/vol de n.** night watch/flight; **train/bateau/voyage de n.** night train/boat or ferry/journey; **conduite de n.** night-driving, driving at night; **être de n.** to work night shifts, to be on nights; **aujourd'hui, je suis de n. à l'hôpital** I'm on night-duty at the hospital tonight; **vêtements de n.** nightwear ADV **travailler de n.** to work nights or the night shift or at night; **conduire de n.** to drive at or by night; **voyager de n.** to travel by night or at night; **nous arriverons plus vite en faisant la route de n.** we'll arrive earlier if we drive at night
❏ **nuit américaine** NF *Cin* day for night; **tourné en n. américaine** shot in day for night
❏ **nuit blanche** NF sleepless night; **passer une n. blanche** *(par insomnie)* to spend a sleepless night; *(volontairement)* to stay up all night
❏ **nuit bleue** NF night of bomb attacks

'**La Nuit américaine**' *Truffaut* 'Day for Night'

'**Nuit et brouillard**' *Resnais* 'Night and Fog'

'**La Nuit étoilée**' *Van Gogh* 'Starry Night'

'**Les Nuits fauves**' *Collard* 'Savage Nights'

'**Ma Nuit chez Maud**' *Rohmer* 'My Night at Maud's'

'**Une Nuit à l'opéra**' *Wood* 'A Night at the Opera'

'**Les Nuits de la pleine lune**' *Rohmer* 'Full Moon in Paris'

'**La Nuit des rois**' *Shakespeare* 'Twelfth Night'

'**La Nuit du chasseur**' *Laughton* 'The Night of the Hunter'

'**Une nuit sur le mont Chauve**' *Moussorgski* 'A Night on Bald Mountain'

nuitamment [nɥitamɑ̃] ADV *Littéraire ou Hum* at or by night

nuitée [nɥite] NF overnight stay; **le gérant de l'hôtel nous a facturé deux nuitées** the hotel manager charged us for two nights

nu-jambes [nyʒɑ̃b] ADV barelegged

nul¹, **nulle**¹ [nyl] ADJ **1** *(inexistant)* nil, non-existent; **les bénéfices sont presque nuls** the profits are almost non-existent or nil or zero; **nos chances de gagner sont nulles** we stand (absolutely) no chance of winning, our chances of winning are nil; **le solde est n.** the balance is nil
2 *Fam (très mauvais → gén)* crap, garbage, *Br* rubbish; *(→ personne)* useless, hopeless, clueless; **leur dernière chanson est nulle** their latest song is crap; **être n. en maths** to be hopeless or useless at maths; **c'est vraiment n. de dire une chose pareille** that's a really crap thing to say; **t'es n.!** *(mauvais)* you're useless!; *(méchant)* you're pathetic!; *Vulg* **c'est n. à chier!** it's fucking awful!
3 *Math* null; **ensemble n.** null or empty set; **matrice nulle** null matrix
4 *Jur* null; **n. et non avenu** invalid, null and void; **rendre n.** to nullify, to annul; **bulletin n.** *(d'élection)* spoilt (ballot) paper
5 *Sport* nil; **le score est n.** *(en fin de match)* the game is drawn, the result is a draw; *(à la mi-temps)* neither team has scored yet, the game so far is drawn; **score n., zéro (à) zéro** *(en fin de match)* match drawn nil-nil; *(à la mi-temps)* score nil-nil
NM,F *Fam* useless idiot, *Br* prat; **quel n., ce mec!** what a useless idiot or *Br* prat!

nul², **nulle**² [nyl] ADJ INDÉFINI *(avant le nom)* no, not any; **tu ne peux faire confiance à n. autre que lui** you can trust nobody but him, he's the only one you can trust; **n. autre que lui n'aurait pu y parvenir** nobody (else) but he could have done it; **à n. autre pareil, à nulle autre pareille** peerless, unrivalled; **je n'éprouve n. ressentiment** I don't feel at all resentful, I don't feel any resentment; **elle n'a nulle envie de me voir** she has no desire (whatsoever) to see me; **il partit sans nulle envie de revenir** he left with no desire to return; **sans n. doute** undoubtedly, without any doubt; **il n. doute qu'il tiendra sa promesse** there is no doubt that he will keep his promise
PRON INDÉFINI no one, nobody; **n. n'aurait mieux su analyser la situation** no one could have analysed the situation better; **n. mieux que lui n'aurait su analyser la situation** no one could have analysed the situation better than him; **n. n'est venu** no one or nobody came; **n. ne peut le nier** no one can deny it; **n. n'est**

nud-nul

parfait nobody's perfect; **n. n'est censé ignorer la loi** ignorance of the law is no defence; *Prov* **n. n'est prophète en son pays** no man is a prophet in his own country

▫ **nulle part** ADV nowhere; **on ne l'a trouvé nulle part** he was nowhere to be found; **nulle part la nature n'est plus belle** nowhere is nature more beautiful; **je ne les vois nulle part** I can't see them anywhere; **le texte ne mentionne nulle part ce détail** this detail is not mentioned anywhere in the text; **il n'a nulle part où aller** he has nowhere to go; **nulle part ailleurs** nowhere else

nullard, -e [nylar, -ard] *Fam* ADJ thick, *Am* dumb
NM,F useless idiot, *Br* prat

nulle [nyl] *voir* **nul**[1,2]

nullement [nylmɑ̃] ADV *Littéraire* not at all, not in the least; **elle n'avait n. honte de ce qu'elle avait fait** she wasn't in the least ashamed of what she'd done; **je n'ai n. l'intention d'y aller** I haven't the slightest *or* least intention of going; **ça vous gêne que je fume? – n.** do you mind my smoking? – not at all *or* not in the least

nullipare [nylipar] ADJ nulliparous
NF nullipara

nullissime [nylisim] ADJ *Fam* totally useless, pathetic

nullité [nylite] NF **1** *(manque de valeur)* incompetence, uselessness; *(de remarque, plaisanterie)* crassness; **cette fille est d'une n. totale** this girl's totally useless *or* incompetent; **ce film est d'une parfaite n.** this film is really terrible
2 *(personne)* useless idiot, *Br* prat; **c'est une n.** he's/she's completely useless
3 *Jur* nullity; **action en n.** action for (a) voidance of contract; **frapper une clause de n.** to render a clause void; **s'agissant du mariage, la bigamie est cause de n.** bigamy is grounds for the annulment of a marriage

nullos [nylos] *Fam* ADJ hopeless, clueless
NMF useless idiot, *Br* prat

numbat [numba] NM *Zool* numbat

nûment [nymɑ̃] ADV *Littéraire* frankly, without embellishment

numéraire [nymerɛr] ADJ **espèces numéraires** legal tender *(UNCOUNT)*, legal currency *(UNCOUNT)*; **valeur n.** face value
NM specie, cash; **payer en n.** to pay in specie, to pay cash; **n. fictif** paper money

numéral, -e, -aux, -ales [nymeral, -o] ADJ numeral
NM numeral

numérateur [nymeratœr] NM numerator

numération [nymerasjɔ̃] NF **1** *(dénombrement)* numeration, numbering *(UNCOUNT)*; *(signes)* notation; **n. décimale/binaire** decimal/binary notation **2** *Méd* **n. globulaire** blood count; **n. et formule sanguine** full blood count

numérique [nymerik] ADJ **1** *(gén)* numerical; **dans l'ordre n.** in numerical order **2** *Math* numerical **3** *Ordinat (ordinateur, donnée)* digital; **balance à affichage n.** digital scales; **enregistrement/disque n.** digital recording/record
NM *Ordinat* **le n.** digital technology; *TV* **n. hertzien** *ou* **n. terrestre** digital terrestrial (broadcasting)

numériquement [nymerikmɑ̃] ADV **1** *(en nombre)* numerically **2** *Ordinat* digitally

numérisation [nymerizasjɔ̃] NF digitization; **n. en lots** batch capture

numérisé, -e [nymerize] ADJ digitized

numériser [3] [nymerize] VT to digitize

numériseur [nymerizœr] NM digitizer; **n. d'image** image digitizer

numéro [nymero] NM **1** *(nombre)* number; *Naut* **n. du navire/de voilure** ship's/class number; **n. d'appel** *(dans une file d'attente)* number; *Phys* **n. atomique** proton number; **n. d'attente** *(dans une file d'attente)* number; **prenez un n. d'attente** please take a ticket and wait for your number to be called; *Cin* **numéros de bord** edge numbers; **n. de chambre** room number; *Aut* **n. de châssis** chassis *or* commission number; *Banque* **n. de chèque** cheque number; *Com* **n. de commande** order number; *Journ* **n. de commission paritaire** publication registration number; *Banque* **n. de compte** account number; **n. d'enregistrement** booking number; **n.**

de fabrication serial number; *Can* **n. d'identification personnel** PIN (number), personal identification number; *Banque* **n. d'identité bancaire** bank sort code; *Aut* **n. d'immatriculation** *Br* registration number, *Am* license number; *Ordinat* **n. Internet** Internet number; *Ordinat* **n. IP** IP number; *Ordinat* **n. de licence** registration number; **n. matricule** number; **n. d'ordre** *(dans une file d'attente)* number; **n. de page** page number; *Typ* folio; *Typ* **n. de Pantone®** Pantone® number; *Suisse* **n. postal** *Br* postcode, *Am* zip code; **n. de référence** reference number; **n. de sécurité sociale** social security number; **n. de série** serial number; **n. de sociétaire** *(d'une assurance)* insurance *or* policy number; **n. de vol** flight number

2 *Tél* **n. (de téléphone** *ou* **d'appel)** (telephone) number; **n. d'appel gratuit** *Br* ≃ 0800 number, Freefone® number, *Am* ≃ toll-free number, 800 number; **n. azur** = telephone number for a call charged at the local rate irrespective of the actual distance covered; **n. de fax** fax number; **n. de poste** extension number; **n. d'urgence** emergency number; **n. vert** *Br* ≃ 0800 number, Freefone® number, *Am* ≃ toll-free number, 800 number; **donne-moi ton n.** give me your number; **refais le n.** dial (the number) again; **j'ai changé de n.** my number has changed; **faire un faux n.** to dial a wrong number; **il n'y a pas d'abonné au n. que vous avez demandé** ≃ the number you have dialled has not been recognized

3 *(habitation, place)* number; **j'habite au n. 10** I live at number 10; **j'habite rue Froment – à quel n.?** I live in the rue Froment – what number?; **j'ai le n. 3B, où dois-je m'asseoir?** I've got (ticket) number 3B, where should I sit?

4 *(exemplaire)* issue, number (**sur** on *or* about); *(d'une émission)* edition; **n. du jour/de la semaine/du mois, dernier n.** current issue *or* number; **ancien n., n. déjà paru** back issue *or* number; **n. spécial** special issue; *Presse* **n. zéro** zero edition; **deux numéros en un** double issue; **acheter un magazine au n.** to buy a magazine as it appears; **il faudra chercher dans de vieux numéros** we'll have to look through some back issues; **j'ai tous les numéros depuis la parution** I've got every issue *or* copy that's ever been published

5 *Mus* number; *(dans un spectacle)* act, turn; **n. de cirque** circus act; **il fait le n. le plus important du spectacle** he's top of the bill; **elle a fait son n. habituel** she went into her usual routine; *Fam* **il aime faire son petit n.** he likes doing his little act; *Fam* **il lui a fait un n. de charme terrible** he really turned on the charm with him/her

6 *(dans un jeu → nombre)* number; **un n. gagnant** a winning number; **n. complémentaire** = extra number in Loto, used as a joker; **tirer le bon/mauvais n.** to draw a lucky/an unlucky number; *Fig* **lui, il a tiré le bon n.!** he's really struck it lucky!; *Fam Fig* **avoir tiré le bon n.** *(conjoint idéal)* to have found Mr/Miss Right

7 *(personne)* **n'être qu'un n.** to be just a number; **le n. un/deux Russe** the Russian number one/two; **le n. un/deux du parti** the number one/two in the party; **le n. un du tennis** the top tennis player; **le n. deux de l'automobile** the second-ranked car manufacturer; *Fam* **quel n.!** *(hurluberlu)* what a character!; *Fam* **c'est un drôle de n.!** he's/she's a strange character!, *Br* he's/she's a right one!

8 *(comme adj; après le nom)* **le lot n. 12** lot 12; **la chambre n. 20** room (number) 20

9 *Opt* number

10 *Tex* count of yarn

numérologie [nymerɔlɔʒi] NF numerology

numérologue [nymerɔlɔg] NMF numerologist

numérotage [nymerɔtaʒ] NM **1** *(attribution d'un numéro)* numbering; *Typ* **n. de pages** page numbering, pagination **2** *Tex* (yarn) counting

numérotation [nymerɔtasjɔ̃] NF **1** *(attribution d'un numéro)* numbering; **la n. des pages** pagination, page numbering; *Ordinat* **n. alphanumérique** alphanumeric numbering; *Ordinat* **n. décimale** decimal numbering **2** *Tél* dialling; **n. abrégée** speed dial; **n. groupée** group dialling

numéroter [3] [nymerɔte] VT to number; **n. les**

pages d'un livre to paginate a book, to number the pages of a book; **les places ne sont pas numérotées** the seats aren't numbered; *Mil* **numérotez-vous (à partir de la droite)!** (from the right) number!; *Fam Hum* **tu peux n. tes abattis!** get ready, you're in for it!
VI *Tél* to dial

numéroteur [nymerɔtœr] NM numbering device

numerus clausus [nymerysklozys] NM INV numerus clausus

numide [nymid] ADJ Numidian
▫ **Numide** NMF Numidian

Numidie [nymidi] NF **la N.** Numidia

numismate [nymismat] NMF numismatist, numismatologist

numismatique [nymismatik] NF numismatics *(singulier)*, numismatology
ADJ numismatic

nummulaire [nymylɛr] NF *Bot* moneywort, creeping Jenny

nunatak [nynatak] NM nunatak

Nunavut [nunavut] NM **le N.** Nunavut

nunchaku [nunʃaku] NM nunchaku

nunuche [nynyʃ] *Fam* ADJ *Br* daft, *Am* dumb
NF dope, halfwit

nuoc-mâm [nɥɔkmam] NM INV *Culin* nuoc mam

nu-pieds [nypje] ADV barefoot
NMPL sandals

nu-propriétaire, nue-propriétaire [nyprɔprietɛr] *(mpl* **nus-propriétaires,** *fpl* **nues-propriétaires)** NM,F bare owner

nuptial, -e, -aux, -ales [nypsjal, -o] ADJ **1** *(de mariage)* wedding *(avant n)*; *(chambre, cortège)* bridal *(avant n)*; **robe nuptiale** wedding dress, bridal gown **2** *Zool* nuptial

nuptialité [nypsjalite] NF marriage rate, nuptiality

nuque [nyk] NF nape (of the neck); **une coiffure qui dégage la n.** a hairstyle that is short at the back; **saisir qn par la n.** to grab sb by the scruff of the neck

nuraghe [nurage] *(pl* **nuraghes** *ou* **nuraghi)** NM nuraghe, nurhag

nuragique [nuraʒik] ADJ nuraghic

Nuremberg [nyrɛ̃bɛr] NM Nuremberg

nursage [nyrsaʒ] = **nursing**

nurse [nœrs] NF *Vieilli* nanny, governess

nursery [nœrsəri] *(pl* **nurserys** *ou* **nurseries)** NF nursery

nursing [nœrsiŋ] NM *Méd* nursing

nu-tête [nytɛt] ADV bareheaded

nutraceutique [nytrasøtik] ADJ nutraceutical

nutriment [nytrimɑ̃] NM nutriment

nutritif, -ive [nytritif, -iv] ADJ **1** *(nourrissant →* *aliment)* nourishing, nutritious; **substance nutritive** nutrient **2** *(relatif à la nutrition)* nutritive, nutritional; **valeur nutritive** nutritional value

nutrition [nytrisjɔ̃] NF **1** *Physiol* nutrition, feeding; **maladies de la n.** nutritional diseases; **spécialiste de la n.** dietary expert; **une mauvaise n.** a bad *or* an unbalanced diet **2** *Bot* nutrition

nutritionnel, -elle [nytrisjɔnɛl] ADJ nutritional, food *(avant n)*; **composition nutritionnelle du lait** nutritional value of milk

nutritionniste [nytrisjɔnist] NMF nutritionist, dietary expert

nutritive [nytritiv] *voir* **nutritif**

nuvite [nyvit] NM *Can* streaker

NVOD [ɛnveode] NM *(abrév* **near video-on-demand)** NVOD

nyala [njala] NM *Zool* nyala

Nyassaland [njasalɑ̃d] NM *Anciennement* **le N.** Nyasaland

nyctaginacée [niktaʒinase] *Bot* NF member of the Nyctaginaceae family
▫ **nyctaginacées** NFPL Nyctaginaceae

nyctalope [niktalɔp] ADJ **1** *Zool* **la chouette est un oiseau n.** the owl has good nocturnal vision **2** *(personne)* having good night vision
NMF **1** *Zool* = animal or bird with good nocturnal vision **2** *(personne)* having good night vision

nyctalopie [niktalɔpi] NF **1** *Zool* good nocturnal vision **2** *Méd* day-blindness, *Spéc* hemeralopia

nycthéméral, -e, -aux, -ales [niktemeral, -o] ADJ nychthemeral

nycthémère [niktemɛr] NM nychthemeron

Nylon® [nilɔ̃] **NM** nylon; **en** *ou* **de N.** nylon; **des bas N.** nylon stockings, nylons

nymphal, -e, -als *ou* **-aux, -ales** [nɛ̃fal, -o] **ADJ** nymphal

nymphalidé [nɛ̃falide] *Entom* **NM** nymphalid, *Spéc* member of the Nymphalidae family
  □ **nymphalidés NMPL** Nymphalidae

nymphe [nɛ̃f] **NF 1** *Myth* nymph; **elle avait un corps de n.** she was nymph-like *or* sylph-like **2** *Entom* nymph **3** *Anat* labia minora, nympha

nymphéa [nɛ̃fea] **NM** *Bot* white water lily

'Les Nymphéas' *Monet* 'Water Lilies'

nymphéacée [nɛ̃fease] *Bot* **NF** member of the Nymphaeaceae family
  □ **nymphéacées NFPL** Nymphaeaceae

nymphée [nɛ̃fe] **NM 1** *Antiq* nymphaeum **2** *(dans un jardin)* grotto

nymphette [nɛ̃fɛt] **NF** nymphet

nympho [nɛ̃fo] **ADJ** *Fam* nympho

nymphomane [nɛ̃fɔman] **ADJ F** nymphomaniac *(avant n)*
  NF nymphomaniac

nymphomanie [nɛ̃fɔmani] **NF** nymphomania

nymphose [nɛ̃foz] **NF** *Entom* nymph stage

nystagmus [nistagmys] **NM** nystagmus

nystatine [nistatin] **NF** *Pharm* nystatin

O¹, o [o] NM INV *(lettre)* O, o
O² [o] *(abrév écrite* **Ouest***)* W
ô [o] EXCLAM *Littéraire* oh!, O!

-O [o] SUFF

The suffix **-o** is widely used in French slang as a way to ABBREVIATE WORDS.

It is not to be confused with the final **-o** of a truncated word which already contains an o (**biologique** → **bio**; **écologique** → **écolo**; **catholique** → **catho**; **information** → **info**; **interrogation** → **interro**; **personnel** → **perso**; **homosexuel** → **homo**), although in both cases the register is colloquial, eg:

alcoolo (from *alcoolique*) alkie; **apéro** (from *apéritif*) aperitif, drink; **facho** (from *fasciste*) fascist; **gaucho** (from *gauchiste*) lefty; **intello** (from *intellectuel*) intellectual, egghead; **proprio** (from *propriétaire*) landlord, landlady; **romano** (from *romanichel*) gippo

Even first names can be abbreviated in this way, eg:

Frédéric → **Frédo**; Madeleine → **Mado**

Note that the radical is sometimes altered when the truncation occurs, eg:

clochard → **clodo**; **directeur** → **dirlo**; **travesti** → **travelo**; **hôpital** → **hosto**

OAA [oɑɑ] NF *(abrév* **Organisation des Nations unies pour l'alimentation et l'agriculture***)* FAO
OACI [oɑsei] NF *(abrév* **Organisation de l'aviation civile internationale***)* ICAO
oaristys [ɔaristis] NF *Littéraire (badinage)* love-making; *(idylle)* romance
OAS [oɑɛs] NF *Hist (abrév* **Organisation armée secrète***)* OAS *(French terrorist organization which opposed Algerian independence in the 1960s)*
oasien, -enne [ɔazjɛ̃, -ɛn] ADJ oasis *(avant n)*
  NM,F oasis dweller
oasis [ɔazis] NF oasis; *Fig* haven, oasis; **une o. de paix** an oasis of peace
OAT [oɑte] NF *Fin (abrév* **obligation assimilable du Trésor***)* = French government bond
obédience [ɔbedjɑ̃s] NF 1 *(adhésion)* allegiance; **pays d'o. socialiste** socialist *or* socialist-run countries; **des communistes d'o. trotskiste** Communists of the Trotskyist tendency 2 *Rel* obedience; **musulman de stricte o.** devout Muslim; **o. religieuse** religious persuasion
obéir [32] [ɔbeir] USAGE ABSOLU 1 *(se soumettre)* **refuser d'o.** to refuse to obey; **elle a fini par o.** she finally did as she was told; **vas-tu o.?** will you do as you're told!
  2 *(répondre)* **le moteur obéit bien** the engine responds well; **soudain, les freins ont cessé d'o.** all of a sudden, the brakes stopped responding
  ❏ **obéir à** VT IND 1 *(se soumettre à)* **o. à qn/qch** to obey sb/sth; **o. à qn au doigt et à l'œil** to be at sb's beck and call; **savoir se faire o. de qn** to command *or* to compel obedience from sb; **il a fini par se faire o.** he was finally obeyed; **c'était un professeur très obéi de ses élèves** as a teacher, he commanded (great) obedience from his pupils; **o. à un ordre** to comply with *or* to obey an order; **o. à un règlement/une loi** to obey a rule/a law, to abide by a rule/a law
  2 *(être régi par)* **o. à qch** to submit to *or* to obey sth; **o. à la force/une contrainte** to yield to force/a constraint; **o. à une théorie/un principe** to obey *or* to follow a theory/a principle; **le marché obéit à la loi de l'offre et de la demande** the market is governed by *or* follows the law of supply and demand; **o. à une impulsion** to follow an impulse; **o. à son instinct** to follow *or* to obey one's instinct; **obéissant à une soif de vengeance** moved *or* prompted by a thirst for revenge; **o. à sa bonté naturelle/à la raison** to be prompted by one's natural kindness/by reason; **o. à sa conscience** to follow the dictates of *or* to obey one's conscience
  3 *(réagir à* → *sujet: mécanisme)* **o. à qch** to respond to sth; *Naut* **o. à la barre** to answer the helm; *Aviat* **o. aux commandes** to respond to the controls
obéissance [ɔbeisɑ̃s] NF 1 *(action d'obéir)* obedience, submission (**à** to); **jurer o. au roi** to swear allegiance to the king; **devoir o. à qn** to owe sb obedience *or* allegiance; **on exige d'eux une o. aveugle** they are expected to be blindly obedient; **o. à une règle** adherence to a rule
  2 *(discipline)* obedience; **les professeurs se plaignent du manque d'o. des élèves** the teachers complain of the pupils' disobedience; **refus d'o.** insubordination
  3 *Rel* obedience
obéissant, -e [ɔbeisɑ̃, -ɑ̃t] ADJ obedient; **être** *ou* **se montrer o. envers qn** to be obedient to *or* towards sb
obel, obèle [ɔbɛl] NM *Typ* obelus, obelisk; **marquer un passage d'un obèle** to obelize a passage
obélisque [ɔbelisk] NM obelisk
Oberland Bernois [ɔbɛrlɑ̃dbɛrnwa] NM **l'O.** the Bernese Alps
Oberammergau [ɔberamɛrgo] NM Oberammergau
obérer [18] [ɔbere] VT 1 *(accabler financièrement)* to be a burden on, to weigh down; **la facture pétrolière obère le budget de l'État** the oil bill is a burden on the country's budget; **très** *ou* **fort obéré** heavily burdened with debt, deeply in debt, debt-ridden 2 *(compromettre)* to compromise; **cette décision obère l'avenir** this decision compromises the future
obèse [ɔbɛz] ADJ obese
  NMF obese person
obésité [ɔbezite] NF obesity, obeseness; **o. morbide** morbid obesity
obi [ɔbi] NF obi
obier [ɔbje] NM *Bot* guelder rose
obit [ɔbit] NM *Rel* obit
obituaire [ɔbityɛr] *Rel* ADJ **registre o.** obituary list
  NM obit book
objectal, -e, -aux, -ales [ɔbʒɛktal, -o] ADJ *Psy* object *(avant n)*
objecter [4] [ɔbʒɛkte] VT 1 *(opposer* → *un argument)* **o. qch à qn** to put sth forward as an argument against sb; **o. des arguments à une théorie** to put forward arguments against a theory; **n'avoir rien à o. à qch** to have no objection to sth; **il n'a rien eu à o. à ce que j'ai dit** he raised no objections to what I said; **que peut-on lui o.?** what arguments can we put forward against him/her?; **on nous objectera le coût trop élevé de l'opération** they will object to the high cost of the operation; **o. que...** to object that...; **on vous objectera que...** they will object that...
  2 *(prétexter)* **on lui objecta sa jeunesse** they took exception to his/her youth, his/her youth counted *or* was held against him/her; **il objecta son incompétence pour se débarrasser de la corvée** he pleaded incompetence to get out of doing the chore; **ils peuvent m'o. que je suis trop jeune** they may object that I am too young
objecteur [ɔbʒɛktœr] NM **o. de conscience** conscientious objector
objectif, -ive [ɔbʒɛktif, -iv] ADJ 1 *(impartial)* objective, unbiased; **un témoin o.** an unbiased witness
  2 *(concret, observable)* objective; **la fièvre est un signe o. de maladie** fever is an objective symptom of disease
  3 *Gram & Phil* objective
  NM 1 *(but à atteindre)* objective, goal, aim; *Com (de croissance, de production)* target; **se fixer/atteindre un o.** to set oneself/to reach an objective; **o. de chiffre d'affaires** sales target; **o. marketing** marketing goal; **o. de production** production target; **o. de profit** profit target; **o. publicitaire** advertising goal; **o. de vente** sales target; **o. lointain/à terme** long-term/short-term objective
  2 *Mil (cible)* target, objective
  3 *Opt & Phot* lens, objective; *(de microscope)* object glass, objective; **braquer son o. sur qch** to train one's camera on sth; **fixer l'o.** to look into the camera; *Phot* **régler l'o.** to adjust the focus; **elle est très naturelle devant l'o.** she's very natural in front of a camera; *TV & Cin* **à courte focale** short-focus lens; *TV & Cin* **o. à distance focale variable** zoom lens; *Phot* **o. fish-eye** fish-eye lens; *TV & Cin* **o. à focale fixe** prime lens; *Phot* **o. grand angle** wide-angle lens; *Phot* **o. normal** normal angle lens; *Phot* **o. ultra grand angle** fish-eye lens; *Phot* **o. zoom** zoom lens
objection [ɔbʒɛksjɔ̃] NF 1 *(gén)* objection; **faire** *ou* **soulever** *ou* **formuler une o. (à qch)** to make *or* to raise an objection (to sth); **tu as** *ou* **tu vois une o.?** do you have any objection?; **je ne vois pas d'o. à continuer le débat/à ce que vous partiez** I have no objection to our continuing the debate/to your leaving; **on me fit l'o. que...** they objected *or* argued that...; **o. de conscience** conscientious objection
  2 *Jur* **o.!** objection!; **o. accordée/refusée** objection sustained/overruled
objectivation [ɔbʒɛktivasjɔ̃] NF objectivization
objective [ɔbʒɛktiv] *voir* **objectif**
objectivement [ɔbʒɛktivmɑ̃] ADV objectively; **vous n'avez pas rendu compte des faits o.** you didn't report the facts objectively, you didn't give an objective account of the facts; **o., qu'est-ce que vous en pensez?** objectively, what do you think of it?
objectiver [3] [ɔbʒɛktive] VT 1 *Psy* to objectify, to objectivize 2 *(sentiment, idée)* to verbalize
objectivisme [ɔbʒɛktivism] NM objectivism
objectiviste [ɔbʒɛktivist] ADJ objectivist, objectivistic
  NMF objectivist
objectivité [ɔbʒɛktivite] NF objectivity; **l'o. d'un rapport/journaliste** the objectivity of a report/journalist, a report's/journalist's objectivity; **manque d'o.** lack of objectivity; **en toute o.** (quite) objectively
objet [ɔbʒɛ] NM 1 *(chose)* object, item; **traiter qn comme un o.** to treat sb like an object *or* a thing; **je ne suis pas un o. dont on dispose** I refuse to be treated like an object; **o. d'art** objet d'art, art object; **o. de luxe** luxury item; **objets personnels** personal belongings *or* effects; **o. sexuel** sex object; **objets de toilette** toiletries; **objets trouvés** lost property *(UNCOUNT)*; **o. volant non identifié** unidentified flying object; **c'est un homme-o.** he's a sex object
  2 *(thème)* subject; **l'o. de leurs discussions était toujours la politique** politics was always the subject of their discussions; **quel est l'o. de la thermodynamique?** what does thermodynamics cover?; **o. (construit)** construct; **o.**

o-obj

mathématique mathematical construct; *Com* **o.: confirmation de demande** *(dans une lettre)* re: confirmation of order; **ceci sera l'o. d'une conférence** there will be a conference on this subject

3 *(personne)* object; *(raison)* cause; **o. de convoitise** object of envy; **o. de pitié/haine** object of pity/hatred; **l'o. de sa haine** the object of his/her hatred; **l'o. de sa curiosité/passion** the object of his/her curiosity/passion; **l'o. de toute cette agitation** the object *or* cause of all this excitement; **l'o. de mes pensées entra soudain** the object of my thoughts suddenly came in

4 *(but)* object, purpose, aim; **mon o. est de** *ou* **j'ai pour o. de vous convaincre** my purpose *or* goal is to convince you; **l'o. de l'émission est de divertir** the purpose *or* aim *or* object of the programme is to entertain; **exposer l'o. de sa visite** to explain the purpose of *or* reason for one's visit; **ma visite a pour o. de...** the object of my visit is to...; **le congrès a rempli son o., qui était d'informer** the congress has achieved its aim *or* purpose, which was to inform; **cet appareil/cette nouvelle mesure remplit tout à fait son o.** the device/the new measure does exactly what it's supposed to; **faire** *ou* **être l'o. de soins particuliers** to receive *or* to be given special care; **les enfants sont l'o. de nombreux soins** children receive a lot of care; **faire l'o. d'une fouille corporelle** to be subjected to a body search; **faire l'o. d'attaques répétées** to be the victim of repeated attacks; **faire l'o. de controverses** to be a controversial subject; **faire l'o. de vives critiques** to be the object *or* target of sharp criticism; **votre requête fera l'o. de toute notre attention** your request will receive our full attention; **l'ancien ministre fait actuellement l'o. d'une enquête** the former minister is currently being investigated; **cela fera l'o. d'une recherche approfondie** this will be the subject of a thorough investigation

5 *Gram* object; **o. direct/indirect** direct/indirect object

6 *Psy* **o. partiel** part object; **o. total** whole object

7 *Phil* object

8 *Jur* matter; **l'o. du litige** the matter at issue; **l'o. de la plainte** the matter of the complaint; **l'o. d'un contrat** the subject matter of a contract; **l'o. désigné dans le contrat** the object of the contract

9 *Ordinat* object

❑ **sans objet** ADJ **1** *(sans but)* aimless, pointless; **des rêveries sans o.** aimless daydreaming

2 *(non justifié)* unjustified, groundless, unfounded; **votre démarche est désormais sans o.** you are no longer justified in taking this step; **ces arguments sont maintenant sans o.** these arguments no longer apply *or* are no longer applicable

objurgations [ɔbʒyrgasjɔ̃] NFPL *Littéraire* **1** *(reproches)* objurgations, castigations **2** *(prières)* entreaties, pleas

oblat, -e [ɔbla, -at] NM,F *Rel* oblate

oblatif, -ive [ɔblatif, -iv] ADJ *Psy* oblative

oblation [ɔblasjɔ̃] NF *Rel* oblation, offering

oblative [ɔblativ] *voir* **oblatif**

oblats [ɔbla] NMPL *Rel* **1** *(pain et vin)* Sacrament **2** *(dons)* oblations

obligataire [ɔbligatɛr] ADJ bonded, debenture *(avant n)*; **dette o.** bonded *or* debenture debt; **emprunt/créancier o.** bonded loan/creditor

NMF debenture holder, bondholder

NM debenture bond

obligation [ɔbligasjɔ̃] NF **1** *(contrainte)* obligation; **la vie communautaire crée certaines obligations** communal life creates certain obligations; **vous pouvez contribuer, mais il n'y a pas d'o.** *ou* **ce n'est pas une o.** you can give money if you wish, but you don't have to *or* there's no obligation; **je suis** *ou* **je me vois dans l'o. de vous expulser** I'm obliged *or* forced to evict you; **je me vois dans l'o. de me taire** I find myself obliged to keep silent; **je me sens dans l'o. de vous avertir** I feel obliged to warn you; **avoir l'o. de faire qch** to be under an obligation to do sth, to be obliged to do sth; **faire o. à qn de** to oblige *or* to require sb to; **la loi vous fait o. de vous présenter en personne** the law requires you to appear in person; **sans o. de votre part** without any obligation (on your part); **sans o. d'achat** *(dans un jeu ou un concours)* no purchase necessary; **o. de réserve** duty of confidentiality

2 *(devoir)* obligation, duty, commitment; **mes obligations de président de la société** my duties as the chairman of the company; **remplir ses obligations** to meet one's obligations; **tu manques à toutes tes obligations** you're not facing up to any of your responsibilities; **avoir/se sentir des obligations envers qn** to be/to feel under an obligation to sb; **obligations familiales** family obligations *or* commitments; **obligations militaires** military obligations *or* duties; **être dégagé des obligations militaires** to have done one's military service; **l'o. scolaire** compulsory education

3 *Jur* obligation; **o. alimentaire** alimony, *Br* maintenance (order); **o. alternative** alternative obligation; **contracter une o. irrévocable** to enter into a binding agreement; **contracter une o. envers qn** to enter into an agreement with sb; **faire honneur à ses obligations** to fulfil one's obligations, to carry out one's duties; **o. civile** civil obligation; **o. conditionnelle** conditional obligation; **o. de conseil** duty to advise; **o. contractuelle** privity of contract; **o. à la dette** obligation to cover a debt; **o. déterminée** determinate obligation; **o. de discrétion professionnelle** duty of professional discretion; **o. divisible** divisible obligation; **o. indéterminée** indeterminate obligation; **o. indivisible** indivisible obligation; **o. d'information** disclosure requirement *or* obligation **o. irrévocable** binding agreement; **contracter une o. irrévocable** to enter into a binding agreement; **o. de moyens** best-efforts obligation; **o. naturelle** natural obligation, moral obligation; **o. de prudence et de diligence** duty of care; **o. réelle** obligation in rem; **o. de résultat** = obligation to achieve a particular result; **o. de sécurité** = guarantee against physical harm; **o. solidaire** joint and several obligation; **o. in solidum** joint and several liability

4 *Bourse & Fin* bond, debenture; **obligations** bonds, loan stock *or* notes; **o. portant un intérêt de 6 pour cent** bond bearing interest at 6 percent; **o. amortissable** redeemable bond; **o. assimilable du Trésor** = French government bond; **o. avec bon de souscription d'actions** bond with share warrant attached; **o. cautionnée** guaranteed bond; **o. chirographaire** simple debenture; **o. convertible** convertible bond; **o. convertible en actions** convertible bond, convertible; **o. à coupon partagé** split coupon bond; **o. à coupon zéro** zero coupon bond; **o. échangeable** convertible bond; **o. échue** matured bond; **o. émise au pair** par bond; **o. d'entreprise** bond, *Br* debenture (stock); **o. d'État** (government) bond; **o. garantie** guaranteed bond; **o. hypothécaire** mortgage bond; **o. indexée** indexed *or* index-linked bond; **o. à intérêt variable** floating-rate bond; **obligations longues** long-dated securities, longs; **o. à lots** prize bond, lottery bond; **o. multimarchés** global bond; **o. négociable** marketable bond; **o. nominative** registered bond; **o. non amortissable** irredeemable bond; **o. non garantie** unsecured bond; **o. or** gold bond; **o. au porteur** bearer bond; **o. de premier ordre, o. à prime** prime bond; **o. privilégiée** preference *or* preferment bond; **o. remboursable** redeemable bond; **o. à revenu fixe** fixed-rate bond; **o. à revenu variable** floating-rate bond; *Fam* **o. Samouraï** Samurai bond; **o. de société** corporate bond; **o. à taux progressif** step-up bond; **o. à taux variable** variable-income bond, floating-rate bond; **o. transférable, o. transmissible** transferable bond

5 *Littéraire (gratitude)* obligation

6 *Rel* **fête d'o.** holy day of obligation

obligatoire [ɔbligatwar] ADJ **1** *(exigé, imposé)* compulsory, obligatory; **lectures/exercices obligatoires** compulsory texts/exercises; **(le port de) la ceinture de sécurité est o.** the wearing of seat belts is compulsory; **le vaccin est o. pour entrer à la maternelle** children must be vaccinated before being admitted to *Br* infant school *or Am* nursery school; **l'école est gratuite et o.** education is free and compulsory; **tenue de soirée o.** *(sur un carton d'invitation)* formal dress required

2 *Fam (inéluctable)* **un jour ou l'autre ils en viendront aux mains, c'est o.** one of these days, they're bound to come to blows

obligatoirement [ɔbligatwarmɑ̃] ADV **1** *(par nécessité)* **vous devez o. montrer votre passeport** you are required to show your passport; **il doit o. avoir la licence pour s'inscrire** he must have a degree to enrol; **nous devons o. fermer les portes à huit heures** we're obliged *or* required to close the doors at eight o'clock; **est-ce qu'il faut porter une robe habillée? – pas o.** do you have to wear an evening dress? – not necessarily

2 *Fam (immanquablement)* inevitably▪; **il va o. tout aller lui répéter** he's bound to go and tell him/her everything▪; **alors, o., il a pensé qu'on lui cachait des choses** so he inevitably thought we were hiding things from him

obligé, -e [ɔbliʒe] ADJ **1** *(contraint)* obliged, compelled (**de faire qch** to do sth); **tu y es allé? – (bien) o.!** did you go? – I had to! *or* I didn't have a choice!; **irez-vous? – bien o.!** are you going? – I have to *or* I don't have any choice, do I?; *Can Vieilli* **se marier o.** to have a shotgun wedding

2 *(nécessaire → conséquence)* necessary; **c'est un passage o.** it's something that has to be done

3 *Fam (inévitable)* **c'était o.!** it was bound to happen!▪; **c'est o. qu'il rate son examen** he's bound to fail his exam

4 *Sout (reconnaissant)* obliged, grateful (**de** for); **je vous serais o. de...** I would be much obliged if you would...

5 *Jur* **être o. envers un créancier** to be under an obligation to a creditor

6 *Mus* obbligato, obligato; **récitatif o.** recitative obbligato

NM,F *Jur* obligee; **je suis votre o. en cette affaire** I'm obliged to you in this matter

obligeamment [ɔbliʒamɑ̃] ADV obligingly; **elle distribuait les bonnes notes un peu trop o.** she was a little too free with high *Br* marks *or Am* grades

obligeance [ɔbliʒɑ̃s] NF **veuillez avoir l'o. de me répondre rapidement** please be so kind as to *or* be kind enough to reply as quickly as possible; **un jeune homme d'une extrême o.** an extremely obliging young man

obligeant, -e [ɔbliʒɑ̃, -ɑ̃t] ADJ obliging, kind; **il n'a eu que des propos obligeants à ton égard** he only had kind words for you; **des remarques peu obligeantes** rather unkind remarks

obliger [17] [ɔbliʒe] VT **1** *(mettre dans la nécessité de)* to oblige, to force; **o. qn à faire qch** to force sb to do sth; **ne m'oblige pas à te punir** don't force me to *or* don't make me punish you; **ce travail m'oblige à me lever à cinq heures tous les matins** this job means I have to get up at five o'clock every morning; **cela m'oblige à changer de train** it means I have to change trains; **une force intérieure l'obligeait à tuer** an inner force compelled him to kill; **son état de santé l'oblige à de longs moments de repos** the state of his/her health means he/she has to rest for long periods; **le devoir/l'honneur m'oblige à révéler mes sources** I'm duty-bound/honour-bound to reveal my sources; **rien ne t'y oblige** you don't have to, nobody's forcing you; **on ne t'y oblige pas** nobody's forcing you; **personne ne t'oblige à aller travailler à l'étranger** nobody's forcing you to go and work abroad; **être obligé de faire qch** to be forced to do sth, to have to do sth; **je suis bien obligé de suivre** I have no option *or* choice but to follow; **ne te sens pas obligé de le faire** don't feel obliged *or* compelled to do it, don't feel you have to do it; **se croire obligé de faire qch** to feel obliged to do sth; *Ironique* **ne te crois pas obligé de tout boire!** don't feel obliged to drink it all!

2 *(contraindre moralement ou juridiquement)* **la loi oblige les candidats à se soumettre à un test** applicants are legally required to take a test; **la loi m'y oblige** I'm required to by law, the law requires me to; **votre signature vous oblige** your signature is legally binding

3 *Sout (faire plaisir à)* to oblige; **vous m'obligeriez en venant** *ou* **si vous veniez** you would oblige me by coming, I would be obliged if you

came; **nous vous sommes très obligés de votre soutien** we are very grateful to you for your support; **je vous serais obligé de bien vouloir m'expédier les articles avant le 31 mai** I would be (greatly) obliged if you would kindly send the items before 31 May

USAGE ABSOLU **j'ai mis une cravate, réunion oblige** I had to wear a tie, what with the meeting and all

▶**s'obliger** VPR **1 s'o. à** *(se forcer à)* to force oneself to; **je m'obligeai à rester poli** I made a great effort *or* forced myself to remain polite; **elle s'oblige à marcher un peu** *ou* **à un peu de marche chaque jour** she forces herself to *or* she makes herself walk a little every day

2 s'o. à *(s'engager à)* to commit oneself to; **par ce contrat, je m'oblige à évacuer les lieux avant le 21** in this contract, I commit myself to leaving *or* I undertake to leave the premises by the 21st

oblique [ɔblik] ADJ **1** *(ligne)* oblique; *(pluie, rayon)* slanting; *(regard)* sidelong; *Fig* **manœuvre o.** *(malhonnête)* underhand move **2** *Ling* **cas o.** oblique case **3** *Jur* indirect **4** *Anat* **muscle o.** oblique muscle

NM *Anat* oblique (muscle)

NF *Géom* oblique (line)

▢ **en oblique** ADV diagonally

obliquement [ɔblikmɑ̃] ADV **1** *(de biais)* obliquely, diagonally, at an angle; **regarder qn o.** to look sideways *or* sidelong at sb **2** *Fig (hypocritement)* obliquely; **il agit toujours o.** he never acts openly

obliquer [3] [ɔblike] VI to turn *or* to veer off; **la voiture obliqua dans une ruelle étroite** the car swerved (off) into a narrow alley; **la route oblique à gauche** the road veers left; **obliquez à gauche/à droite!** bear left/right!

obliquité [ɔblikɥite] NF **1** *Math* obliquity, obliqueness **2** *Astron* **o. de l'écliptique** obliquity of the ecliptic

oblitérateur, -trice [ɔbliteratœr, -tris] ADJ cancelling *(avant n)*

NM cancelling machine; *(pour timbres)* franker

oblitération [ɔbliterasjɔ̃] NF **1** *(apposition d'une marque)* cancellation; *(marque → sur un timbre)* postmark; *(→ sur un ticket)* stamp; **o. premier jour** first-day cover; **cachet d'o.** postmark **2** *Littéraire (altération)* fading **3** *Méd* obturation

oblitératrice [ɔbliteratris] *voir* **oblitérateur**

oblitérer [18] [ɔblitere] VT **1** *(timbre)* to postmark, to cancel; **la lettre n'a pas été oblitérée** the letter hasn't been postmarked; **timbre oblitéré** used stamp **2** *Littéraire (effacer)* to obliterate, to erase, to efface **3** *Méd* to obturate

▶**s'oblitérer** VPR *Littéraire* **peu à peu, le passé s'oblitérait dans sa mémoire** little by little, every trace of the past disappeared from his/her memory

oblong, -ongue [ɔblɔ̃, -ɔ̃g] ADJ **1** *Géom* oblong; *Typ* **format o.** oblong format **2** *(visage, pelouse)* oblong, oval; **un coquillage de forme oblongue** an oblong shell

obnubilation [ɔbnybilasjɔ̃] NF **1** *Littéraire (obsession)* obsession **2** *Psy* obnubilation

obnubilé, -e [ɔbnybile] ADJ **1** *Littéraire (obsédé)* obsessed **2** *Psy* obnubilated

obnubiler [3] [ɔbnybile] VT **1** *(obséder)* to obsess; **être obnubilé par une idée** to be obsessed by an idea; **ça l'obnubile** he's/she's obsessed by it **2** *Fig (obscurcir)* to cloud, to obnubilate

obole [ɔbɔl] NF **1** *(somme d'argent)* (small) contribution *or* donation; *(dans la Bible)* widow's mite; **chacun apporte** *ou* **verse son o.** each person is making a contribution; *Littéraire* **il ne m'a pas fait l'o. d'un sourire** he didn't deign to smile at me **2** *Hist (monnaie → grecque)* obol; *(→ française)* obole

obombrer [3] [ɔbɔ̃bre] VT *Littéraire* **1** *(couvrir d'ombre)* to shadow **2** *(mémoire, souvenir etc)* to cloud

OBSA [ɔpsa] NF *Fin (abrév* **obligation avec bon de souscription d'actions***)* bond with share warrant attached

obscène [ɔpsɛn] ADJ *(licencieux)* obscene, lewd; *(livre, langage)* obscene

obscénité [ɔpsenite] NF **1** *(caractère licencieux)* obscenity, lewdness; *(d'un livre, du langage)* obscenity **2** *(parole, geste)* obscenity; **raconter** *ou* **dire des obscénités** to utter obscenities, to make obscene remarks

obscur, -e [ɔpskyr] ADJ **1** *(sombre)* dark; **une nuit obscure** a pitch-black night; *Fig* **des forces obscures dominaient leur planète** obscure forces *or* forces of darkness ruled their planet

2 *(incompréhensible)* obscure, abstruse; **sa poésie est obscure sauf pour quelques initiés** his/her poetry is obscure to all but a few initiates; **pour quelque raison obscure** for some obscure reason

3 *(indéfini)* obscure, vague, indefinite; *(impression)* vague; **un o. sentiment de pitié l'envahissait** he/she was overcome by a vague *or* indefinable feeling of pity; **un o. pressentiment** a vague premonition

4 *(peu connu)* obscure; **références à d'obscurs auteurs** *ou* **des auteurs obscurs du XIXème siècle** references to obscure nineteenth-century writers

5 *(humble → naissance)* lowly, humble; **une vie obscure** a modest existence

obscurantisme [ɔpskyrɑ̃tism] NM obscurantism

obscurantiste [ɔpskyrɑ̃tist] ADJ obscurantist

NMF obscurantist

obscurcir [32] [ɔpskyrsir] VT **1** *(priver de lumière)* to darken, to make dark; **yeux obscurcis par les larmes** eyes misty *or* dim with tears; **une grande tenture obscurcissait la pièce** a large hanging made the room dark *or* darkened the room; **de gros nuages vinrent o. le ciel** large clouds darkened the sky

2 *(rendre confus → discours, raisonnement)* to make obscure; **le jugement obscurci par l'alcool** his/her judgement clouded *or* obscured *or* confused by drink

▶**s'obscurcir** VPR **1** *(ciel)* to darken; *(pièce, paysage)* to darken, to grow dark; *(vue)* to grow dim; **soudain, tout s'obscurcit et je m'évanouis** suddenly everything went dark *or* black and I fainted; *Fig* **son esprit s'obscurcit avec la maladie** the illness is dulling his/her mind; **son visage s'obscurcit à ces mots** at these words, his/her face clouded (over) *or* darkened; **son regard s'obscurcit** his/her face clouded over *or* darkened

2 *(se compliquer)* to become (more) obscure; **le mystère s'obscurcit** the plot thickens; **dans le dernier chapitre, son message s'obscurcit** in the last chapter, his/her meaning becomes obscure

obscurcissement [ɔpskyrsismɑ̃] NM **1** *(d'un lieu)* darkening **2** *(de l'esprit)* obscuring, clouding over; *(de la vue)* dimming; **l'o. progressif de ses facultés** the gradual weakening *or* loss of his/her faculties

obscurément [ɔpskyremɑ̃] ADV **1** *(vaguement)* obscurely, vaguely, dimly; **je me souviens o. d'une scène** I vaguely remember a scene; **nous sentions o. que...** we had a vague *or* an obscure feeling that... **2** *(de façon inconnue)* **mourir o.** to die in obscurity

obscurité [ɔpskyrite] NF **1** *(manque d'éclairage)* dark, darkness; **avoir peur de l'o.** to be afraid of the dark; **dans l'o.** in darkness, in the dark; **être plongé dans l'o.** to be plunged into darkness; **dans l'o., on voyait luire les yeux du chat** you could see the cat's eyes glowing in the dark; **faire l'o. dans une salle** to make a room dark, to darken a room; **soudain, l'o. se fit dans la chambre** it suddenly became *or* went dark in the room

2 *(caractère complexe)* obscurity, *Sout* abstruseness

3 *(remarque, expression)* obscure *or* abstruse remark; **langage/projet de loi plein d'obscurités** language/bill full of obscurities

4 *Littéraire (anonymat)* **vivre/tomber dans l'o.** to live in/to fall into obscurity; **sortir de l'o.** to emerge from obscurity

obsécration [ɔpsekrasjɔ̃] NF *Rel* obsecration, supplication

obsédant, -e [ɔpsedɑ̃, -ɑ̃t] ADJ *(souvenir, musique)* haunting, obsessive; *(besoin, pensée)* obsessive

obsédé, -e [ɔpsede] ADJ *(gén)* obsessed; *(sexuel)* (sexually) obsessed; **être o. par qch** to be obsessed by *or* with sth; **o. par la pensée de la mort** obsessed *or* gripped with the idea of death

NM,F **1** *(victime d'obsessions)* obsessive; **o. sexuel** sex maniac

2 *Fam (fanatique)* fanatic; **c'est un o. de la moto** he's a motorbike fanatic *or* fiend; **les obsédés de la vitesse** *Br* speed merchants, *Am* speed fiends; **les obsédés de l'hygiène** hygiene freaks

obséder [18] [ɔpsede] VT **1** *(sujet: image, peur)* to haunt, to obsess; **son souvenir m'obsède** I'm obsessed by the memory of him/her; **le cauchemar de l'autre nuit ne cesse de m'o.** I can't stop thinking about the nightmare I had the other night; **c'est un problème, mais ne te laisse pas o.** it's a problem, but don't become obsessed by it *or* don't let it become an obsession

2 *Littéraire (sujet: personne)* to importune, to bother

obsèques [ɔpsɛk] NFPL funeral; **faire à qn des o. nationales** to hold a state funeral for sb

obséquieuse [ɔpsekjøz] *voir* **obséquieux**

obséquieusement [ɔpsekjøzmɑ̃] ADV obsequiously

obséquieux, -euse [ɔpsekjø, -øz] ADJ obsequious; **être o. avec qn** to be obsequious to *or* towards sb

obséquiosité [ɔpsekjozite] NF obsequiousness

observable [ɔpsɛrvabl] ADJ observable; **le phénomène est o. à l'œil nu** the phenomenon can be observed with the naked eye; **un fait o. uniquement dans certaines couches de la population** a phenomenon that can be observed only in certain segments of the population

observance [ɔpsɛrvɑ̃s] NF *(d'un rite, d'une loi)* observance; **franciscain de stricte o.** Franciscan of strict observance; **bénédictin d'ancienne o.** Benedictine of the old school; **communiste de stricte o.** hardline communist

observateur, -trice [ɔpsɛrvatœr, -tris] ADJ *(perspicace)* observant; **avoir un esprit très o.** to be very observant *or* perceptive; **rien n'échappe à l'œil o. du peintre** nothing can escape the painter's perceptive eye

NM,F **1** *(témoin)* observer; **un o. critique de la vie politique** a critical observer of political life; **tous les observateurs s'accordent à trouver le président fatigué** (all) observers agree that the president looks tired

2 *Pol* observer; **un o. de l'ONU** a UN observer

3 *Mil* spotter

observation [ɔpsɛrvasjɔ̃] NF **1** *(remarque)* observation, remark, comment; **faire des observations** to make observations *or* remarks *or* comments; **avez-vous des observations à faire sur ce premier cours?** do you have any comments to make about this first class?; **si je puis me permettre une o.** if I may make an observation *or* say something; **la réponse du ministre appelle plusieurs observations** the minister's answer calls for some comment *or* several observations; **notez vos observations dans la marge** note down your observations *or* comments in the margin

2 *(critique)* (piece of) criticism, critical remark; **je te prie de garder tes observations pour toi** please keep your remarks to yourself; **ma secrétaire est toujours en retard et je lui en ai fait l'o.** my secretary's always late and I've had a word with her about it; **faire des observations** to make *or* pass remarks; **il faisait toujours des observations à ses élèves** he was always finding fault with his pupils; **j'ai horreur qu'on me fasse des observations** I hate people criticizing me *or* making remarks to me; **à la moindre o. de ma part, elle se met en colère** the slightest remark from me and she gets angry, she gets angry if I make the slightest remark; **à la première o., vous sortez!** *(à un élève)* if I have to say one (more) word to you, you're out!

3 *(investigation, exposé → scientifique)* observation; **procéder à des observations météorologiques** to conduct meteorological observations; **observations par satellite** satellite observations

4 *(compte-rendu)* observation; **j'ai lu vos observations sur la danse des abeilles** I read your account of *or* observations on the dance of the bees

obl-obs

5 *(méthode d'étude)* observation, observing; **l'o. de la nature/d'une réaction chimique** observing nature/a chemical reaction; **avoir l'esprit d'o.** to be observant; *Mktg* **o. en situation** personal observation

6 *Mil* observation; **o. aérienne/terrestre** aerial/ground observation; *Mil, Naut & Pêche* **o. sous-marine** underwater observation

7 *(observance)* observance, observing, keeping

8 *Méd (description)* notes; *(surveillance)* observation; **mettre un malade en o.** to put a patient under observation; **être/rester en o.** to be/to remain under observation

❑ **d'observation** ADJ 1 *Aviat, Astron & Mil* observation *(avant n)*; **avion d'o.** spotter plane

2 *(scientifique)* **techniques/erreur d'o.** observation techniques/error

3 *Sport* **un set d'o.** a probing *or* tactical set; **un round d'o.** a sizing-up round

observatoire [ɔpsɛrvatwar] NM 1 *Astron & Météo* observatory 2 *Mil & Fig* observation *or* lookout post 3 *Écon* **O. français des conjonctures économiques** = economic research institute; **o. du livre** = body in charge of monitoring book prices; **o. des prix** price-monitoring watchdog

observatrice [ɔpsɛrvatris] *voir* **observateur**

observer [3] [ɔpsɛrve] VT 1 *(examiner → gén)* to observe, to examine; *(→ scientifiquement)* to observe; **o. qch à la loupe** to examine sth under a magnifying glass; **elle adore o. les gens dans le métro** she loves watching people *or* she loves to people-watch in the metro; **il passait des heures à o. les oiseaux** he spent hours bird-watching

2 *(surveiller)* to watch, to keep a watch *or* an eye on; **attention, on nous observe** careful, we're being watched; **se sentir observé** to feel one is being watched; **o. qn avec attention/du coin de l'œil** to watch sb attentively/out of the corner of one's eye; **il était chargé d'o. le prisonnier** his job was to watch over the prisoner; **elle observait avec curiosité les nouveaux arrivants** she watched the newcomers with curiosity

3 *(respecter → trêve)* to observe; *(→ accord)* to observe, to respect, to abide by; *(→ règlement)* to observe, to keep (to), to comply with; **o. une minute de silence** to observe a minute's silence; **o. le sabbat** to observe *or* to keep the Sabbath; **o. le code de la route** to observe *or* to follow the Highway Code; **faire o. la loi** to enforce (obedience to) the law

4 *(conserver)* **o. une attitude digne** to maintain *or* to keep a dignified attitude; **o. la plus stricte neutralité** to observe *or* to maintain the strictest neutrality

5 *(constater)* to observe, to notice, to note; **nous observons un retour à...** we are seeing *or* witnessing a return to...; **on observe un changement d'attitude chez les jeunes** there is a noticeable change in attitude amongst young people; **on observe une tache noire dans le poumon droit** a dark patch can be seen in the right lung; **faire o. qch à qn** to draw sb's attention to sth, to point sth out to sb; **je te ferai o. que tu t'es trompé** let me point out that you were wrong; **j'observe que cela n'a pas encore été fait** I see that this has not yet been done

6 *(dire)* to observe, to remark; **"tu ne portes plus d'alliance", observa-t-il** "you're not wearing a wedding ring any more," he observed *or* remarked

7 *Naut* to work an observation on; **o. le soleil** to take the sun, to take a sight at the sun

USAGE ABSOLU **c'est comme ça qu'il apprend, en observant** that's how he learns, by watching; **je ne critique pas, je ne fais qu'o.** this isn't a criticism, just an observation

▸**s'observer** VPR 1 *(emploi réfléchi)* to keep a check on oneself

2 *(emploi réciproque)* to observe *or* to watch each other; **elles s'observèrent pendant longtemps** they observed *or* examined each other for some time

3 *(emploi passif)* to be seen *or* observed; **ce phénomène s'observe surtout par temps sec** this phenomenon is mainly seen *or* encountered in dry weather; **ce phénomène ne s'observe que dans les pays tropicaux** this phenomenon can be seen only in tropical countries

obsession [ɔpsesjɔ̃] NF 1 *(hantise)* obsession; **beaucoup de femmes ont l'o. de grossir** many women are obsessed with the idea of putting on weight; **il croit qu'on veut le tuer, c'est devenu une o.** he believes people want to kill him, it's become a real obsession (with him)

2 *(idée fixe)* obsession; **il ne faut pas en faire une o.** it shouldn't become an obsession; **ça tourne à l'o.** it's becoming an obsession; **c'est une o. chez lui!** it's a real obsession with him!; **mais c'est une o.** *ou* **de l'o.!** you're/he's/*etc* obsessed (with the idea)!

obsessionnel, -elle [ɔpsesjɔnɛl] ADJ 1 *(répétitif)* obsessive, obsessional 2 *Psy (comportement)* obsessive; *(névrose)* obsessional; **de manière obsessionnelle** obsessively

NM,F obsessive

obsidienne [ɔpsidjɛn] NF obsidian

obsidional, -e, -ales, -aux [ɔpsidjɔnal, -o] ADJ obsidional; **fièvre obsidionale** mass psychosis of the besieged; *Psy* **délire o.** persecution complex

obsolescence [ɔpsɔlɛsɑ̃s] NF obsolescence; **le taux d'o. des ordinateurs est très élevé** the obsolescence rate of computers is very high, computers very quickly become obsolete; **o. calculée** *ou* **planifiée** *ou* **prévue** built-in *or* planned obsolescence

obsolescent, -e [ɔpsɔlɛsɑ̃, -ɑ̃t] ADJ obsolescent

obsolète [ɔpsɔlɛt] ADJ obsolete

obstacle [ɔpstakl] NM 1 *(objet bloquant le passage)* obstacle; **des troncs ont fait o. à l'écoulement normal du ruisseau** tree trunks have blocked *or* obstructed the normal flow of the stream; **l'immeuble d'en face fait o. au soleil** the building opposite blocks (out) *or* obstructs the sun

2 *Sport* hurdle; *Équitation* fence; **tourner l'o.** *(sujet: cheval)* to run out (at the fence); *Fig* to get round the problem

3 *Fig (difficulté)* obstacle, difficulty, problem; **il y a un gros o.** there's a big problem; **le plus gros o. a été le directeur régional** the main obstacle was the area manager; **buter sur** *ou* **se heurter à un o.** to come up against an obstacle; **être un** *ou* **faire o. à** to be an obstacle to, to hinder, to impede; **la cécité n'est pas un o. à une carrière dans l'enseignement** being blind is no obstacle *or* impediment to a teaching career; **plus rien ne fait o. à notre amour** nothing stands in the way of our love any longer; **plus rien ne faisait o. à mon départ** *ou* **à ce que je parte** there was no longer any reason for me not to go; **plus rien ne fait o. à ce que vous l'épousiez** there's no longer any reason why you shouldn't marry her; **je n'y vois pas d'o.** I don't see any difficulty *or* problem (about it); **mettre un o. aux ambitions de qn** to put an obstacle in the way of sb's ambitions

obstétrical, -e, -aux, -ales [ɔpstetrikal, -o] ADJ obstetric, obstetrical

obstétricien, -enne [ɔpstetrisjɛ̃, -ɛn] NM,F obstetrician

obstétrique [ɔpstetrik] NF obstetrics *(singulier)*

obstination [ɔpstinasjɔ̃] NF 1 *(persévérance)* persistence, perseverance; **à force d'o., elle y est arrivée** she succeeded through strength of purpose 2 *(entêtement)* obstinacy, obstinateness, stubbornness

obstiné, -e [ɔpstine] ADJ 1 *(entêté)* obstinate, stubborn; *(persévérant)* persevering, determined

2 *(incessant)* persistent, relentless; **pluie obstinée** relentless rain; **toux obstinée** persistent cough

3 *(assidu)* obstinate; *(résistance, efforts)* stubborn, dogged; *(refus, silence)* stubborn; **un travail o.** unyielding *or* obstinate work

4 *Mus* **basse obstinée** basso ostinato

NM,F **c'est un o.** *(qui persévère)* he's very determined; *(qui s'entête)* he's very stubborn *or* obstinate

obstinément [ɔpstinemɑ̃] ADV 1 *(avec entêtement)* obstinately, stubbornly; *(refuser, répondre)* stubbornly; **l'enfant tenait o. à rester avec sa mère** the child was stubbornly determined to stay with his/her mother 2 *(avec persévérance)* perseveringly, persistently; *(travailler, avancer)* determinedly, doggedly

obstiner [3] [ɔpstine] **s'obstiner** VPR to persist, to insist; **ne t'obstine pas, abandonne le projet** don't be obstinate, give the project up; **on ne cesse de te dire d'arrêter, mais toi, tu t'obstines** we keep telling you to stop, but you won't listen; **s'o. à faire qch** *(continuer)* to persist in doing sth; *(vouloir)* to be set *or Sout* bent on doing sth; **elle s'obstine à vouloir partir** she persists in wanting to leave *or* insists on leaving; **il s'obstinait à ne rien dire** he obstinately *or* stubbornly refused to talk; **s'o. dans son silence** to remain stubbornly *or* obstinately silent; **s'o. dans ses idées/convictions** to cling stubbornly *or* doggedly to one's ideas/convictions; **pourquoi t'o. dans l'idée qu'il va te quitter?** why do you persist in thinking that he's going to leave you?; **la vague de froid semble s'o. sur toute l'Europe** the cold spell seems to have set in all over Europe

obstruant, -e [ɔpstryɑ̃, -ɑ̃t] ADJ *Méd* obstruent

obstructif, -ive [ɔpstryktif, -iv] ADJ *Méd (tumeur)* obstruent; *(maladie)* obstructive

obstruction [ɔpstryksjɔ̃] NF 1 *(obstacle)* obstruction, blockage; *(blocage)* obstruction, obstructing, blocking; **faire o. à** to block, to obstruct; **o. à la voie publique** obstruction 2 *(action délibérée)* **faire de l'o.** *(gén)* to be obstructive; *Pol* to obstruct (legislation); *Ftbl* to obstruct 3 *Méd* obstruction

obstructionnisme [ɔpstryksjɔnism] NM obstructionism

obstructionniste [ɔpstryksjɔnist] ADJ obstructionist

NMF obstructionist

obstructive [ɔpstryktiv] *voir* **obstructif**

obstruer [7] [ɔpstrye] VT 1 *(passage)* to obstruct, to block; *(tuyau)* to block; **les feuilles mortes obstruent la gouttière** dead leaves have blocked the drainpipe; **le corridor était obstrué par des piles de livres** the corridor was blocked *or* obstructed by piles of books; **une tour obstrue maintenant la vue** now a tower blocks (out) the view

2 *Méd* to obstruct; **il a des artères obstruées** he has blocked arteries

▸**s'obstruer** VPR to become blocked *or* obstructed

obtempérer [18] [ɔptɑ̃pere] USAGE ABSOLU **le soldat s'empressa d'o.** the soldier hurriedly obeyed; *Jur* **refus d'o.** obstruction

❑ **obtempérer à** VT IND 1 *(se soumettre à)* to comply with; **le ministre a obtempéré à l'avis du président** the minister complied with the president's opinion; **o. à un ordre** to obey an order 2 *Jur* to obey; **o. à une sommation** to obey a summons

obtenir [40] [ɔptənir] VT 1 *(acquérir → baccalauréat, licence, note, point)* to obtain, to get; *(→ prix, nomination)* to receive, to win, to get; *(→ consentement)* to get, to win; *(→ prêt, promesse)* to secure, to obtain, to get; *(→ accord)* to reach, to obtain, to get; **essayer d'o. une amélioration** to try to bring about an improvement; **o. la garde d'un enfant** to get *or* to win custody of a child; **o. le droit de vote** to win the right to vote, to get the vote; **le numéro de trapèze obtient toujours un grand succès** the trapeze act is always a big success; **o. qch de qn** to obtain *or* to get sth from sb; **o. de qn une permission** to obtain *or* to get permission from sb; **n'espère plus rien o. de moi** don't expect (to get) anything else from me; **j'ai obtenu d'elle qu'elle vérifie tout** I got her to agree to check everything

2 *(procurer)* **o. qch à qn** to obtain *or* to get *or Sout* to procure sth for sb; **elle lui a obtenu une augmentation** she got him/her a raise; **je nous ai obtenu trois places** I got us three seats; **c'est lui qui m'a fait o. ces renseignements** he's the one who got (hold of) *or* obtained the information for me

3 *(arriver à → résultat)* to obtain, to get, to achieve; *(→ effet, succès)* to achieve; **les résultats obtenus par l'équipe nationale** the national team's results; **o. un précipité** to obtain a precipitate; **si on mélange ces deux substances, qu'obtient-on?** what do you get if you

mix these two substances?; fouettez jusqu'à o. une crème onctueuse whip into a smooth cream; ils ont fini par o. la libération des otages they finally secured the release of the hostages; j'ai travaillé sur ce dossier pendant trois mois et qu'ai-je obtenu? – rien! I've worked on this case for three months and what have I got to show for it *or* what have I achieved? – nothing!; en divisant par deux, on obtient 24 if you divide by two, you get 24; cette technique lui permet d'o. un son très pur this technique allows him/her to achieve great purity of sound; j'ai obtenu qu'elle revienne I arranged for her to come back; j'ai enfin obtenu qu'elle mette ses gants pour sortir I eventually got her to wear her gloves to go out

4 *Tél* o. un numéro to obtain a number

❑ obtenir de VT IND il a obtenu de repousser le rendez-vous he managed to get the meeting postponed; j'ai obtenu de le voir I obtained *or* got permission to see him

►s'obtenir VPR le résultat demandé s'obtient en multipliant 3 par 5 to arrive at *or* to reach the required result, multiply 3 by 5

obtention [ɔptɑ̃sjɔ̃] NF 1 *(acquisition)* obtaining, getting; depuis l'o. de son diplôme since obtaining his/her diploma, since he/she got his/her diploma; pour l'o. de qch (in order) to obtain sth

2 *(production)* creation, production; l'o. d'une nouvelle variété de poire the creation of a new variety of pear; l'o. d'un nouveau vaccin the production of a new vaccine; ajoutez du blanc jusqu'à o. de la couleur désirée add white until the desired colour is obtained

obtenu, -e [ɔptəny] PP *voir* obtenir

obtient *etc voir* obtenir

obturateur, -trice [ɔptyratœr, -tris] ADJ 1 *Tech* obturating *(avant n)*, shutting *(avant n)*

2 *Anat* obturator *(avant n)*; artère obturatrice obturator artery; muscle o. obturator muscle

NM 1 *Phot* shutter; armer/déclencher l'o. to set/to release the shutter; o. focal focal-plane shutter; o. d'objectif/à rideau between-lens/roller-blind shutter; o. de plaque focal-plane shutter; o. au diaphragme diaphragm shutter

2 *Mil* obturator, gas-check

3 *Pétr* (blow-out) preventer

4 *(en plomberie)* shut-off

5 *Anat & Méd (d'une ouverture)* obturator

6 *Aut* throttle; o. de bloc core plug; o. papillon throttle valve

obturation [ɔptyrasjɔ̃] NF 1 *Tech* sealing, stopping up 2 *Méd* l'o. d'une dent the filling of a tooth 3 *Mil* obturation

obturatrice [ɔptyratris] *voir* obturateur

obturer [3] [ɔptyre] VT 1 *Tech (boucher)* to seal, to stop up 2 *Méd* to fill

obtus, -e [ɔpty, -yz] ADJ 1 *Math* obtuse 2 *Fig (borné)* obtuse, dull, slow-witted; ne sois pas o. don't be obtuse

obtusangle [ɔptyzɑ̃gl] ADJ *Géom* obtuse-angled

obtusion [ɔptyzjɔ̃] NF obtuseness

obus [ɔby] NM 1 *Mil* shell; o. à mitraille *ou* à balles shrapnel (shell); o. à mortier/à gaz/fumigène mortar/gas/smoke shell; o. traçant tracer shell

2 *(comme adj)* homme o./femme o. human cannonball

obusier [ɔbyzje] NM howitzer; o. de campagne field howitzer

obvenir [40] [ɔbvənir] VI *Vieilli Jur* o. à qn to revert to sb by escheat

obvie [ɔbvi] ADJ obvious

obvier [19] [ɔbvje] obvier à VT IND *Littéraire (parer à)* to obviate, to ward off; o. à un danger/un accident to forestall a danger/an accident

Obwald [ɔbvalt] NM *Géog* le demi-canton d'O. Obwalden demicanton

OC *Rad (abrév écrite* ondes courtes) SW

oc [ɔk] *voir* langue

OCA [osea] NF *Bourse & Fin (abrév* obligation convertible en actions) convertible bond, convertible

ocarina [ɔkarina] NM *Mus* ocarina

occase [ɔkaz] *Fam* NF 1 *(circonstance favorable)* opportunity■, chance■

2 *(affaire)* steal, *Br* snip; profites-en, c'est une o.! make the most of it, it's a real snip!

3 *(article de seconde main)* second-hand item■; elle est neuve, ta voiture? – non, c'est une o. is your car new? – no, it's second-hand

4 *(moment)* moment■; à la première o. asap, as soon as possible■; j'attends la bonne o. I'm waiting for the right moment

❑ d'occase ADV *Fam* second-hand■; je l'ai acheté d'o. I bought it second-hand

occasion [ɔkazjɔ̃] NF 1 *(circonstance favorable)* opportunity, chance; si l'o. se présente if the opportunity arises, *Sout* should the opportunity arise; l'o. ne se représentera pas there won't be another chance like that again; laisser passer l'o. to let the opportunity slip (by); saisir l'o. (au vol), sauter sur l'o. to seize the opportunity, to jump at the chance; profiter de l'o. pour faire qch to take the opportunity to do sth; à la première o. at the first *or* earliest opportunity; je le lui dirai à la première o. I'll tell him/her as soon as I get a chance; ça te donnera l'o. de la rencontrer it'll give you the opportunity *or* the chance to meet her; avoir l'o. de faire qch to have the opportunity *or* chance of doing *or* to do sth; je n'ai jamais eu l'o. de me plaindre de lui I've never had cause to complain about him; ne manque pas l'o. de le lui dire don't miss your chance of telling him/her; il ne perd jamais une o. d'être désagréable/de se faire remarquer he never misses an opportunity to be unpleasant/to get himself noticed; *Fam* il a manqué *ou* perdu *ou* raté une belle o. de se taire he could have kept his mouth shut; *Fam* c'est l'o. ou jamais de le faire now's the time to do it■; *Fam* c'était l'o. ou jamais de changer de boulot! if ever there was a time to change jobs, it was then!; *Prov* l'o. fait le larron opportunity makes a thief; *Mktg* o. d'entendre opportunity to hear; *Fin* o. de profit profit opportunity; *Mktg* o. de voir opportunity to see

2 *(moment)* occasion; à deux occasions twice; à trois/quatre occasions three/four times; en toute o. on every occasion; en plusieurs/maintes occasions several/many times, on several/many occasions; à cette o. at that point, on that occasion; en pareille o. in circumstances like these, in similar circumstances; dans les grandes occasions on big *or* important *or* special occasions; pour les grandes occasions for special occasions; être l'o. de qch to be the occasion of sth; sa mort a été l'o. de changements importants significant changes took place after his/her death; ces retrouvailles furent l'o. de grandes réjouissances there were great festivities to celebrate this reunion; ce sera l'o. de faire la fête that will be a good excuse for a party

3 *(article de seconde main)* second-hand *or* used article; acheter qch d'o. to buy sth second-hand; elle est neuve, ta voiture? – non, c'est une o. is your car new? – no, it's second-hand; l'o. the second-hand trade; l'o. se vend bien there's a brisk trade in second-hand goods; le marché de l'o. the second-hand market

4 *(bonne affaire)* bargain; à *ou* pour ce prix-là, c'est une o.! it's a (real) bargain at that price!

❑ à l'occasion ADV 1 *(un de ces jours)* one of these days

2 *(éventuellement)* should the opportunity arise; à l'o., passez nous voir drop by some time *or* if you get the chance

3 *(de temps en temps)* on occasion; elle peut être très virulente à l'o. she can be very harsh on occasion

❑ à l'occasion de PRÉP on the occasion of, upon; à l'o. de sa venue upon his/her arrival; à l'o. de votre départ à la retraite on the occasion of your retirement; je l'ai rencontré à l'o. d'un concert I met him at a concert; je m'en suis rendu compte à l'o. d'une visite de routine I realized it during a routine visit

❑ d'occasion ADJ 1 *(non neuf)* second-hand; voiture d'o. second-hand *or* used car

2 *(improvisé)* des amours d'o. chance *or* casual (love) affairs

ADV *(acheter, vendre)* second-hand; j'ai fini par le trouver d'o. in the end, I found a second-hand one

❑ pour l'occasion ADV for the occasion

occasionnalisme [ɔkazjɔnalism] NM *Phil* occasionalism

occasionnel, -elle [ɔkazjɔnɛl] ADJ 1 *(irrégulier)* casual, occasional; *(aide)* casual; je vais parfois au restaurant, mais cela reste très o. I sometimes eat out, but only very occasionally; *Fam* je ne trouve que des (petits) boulots occasionnels I can only get casual work; les touristes forment une clientèle occasionnelle tourists are occasional *or* casual customers

2 *(fortuit)* chance *(avant n)*; rencontre occasionnelle chance meeting

3 *Phil* cause occasionnelle occasional cause

occasionnellement [ɔkazjɔnɛlmɑ̃] ADV occasionally, every now and then, from time to time

occasionner [3] [ɔkazjɔne] VT *(causer)* to cause, to bring about, *Sout* to occasion; le verglas sur les routes a occasionné bon nombre d'accidents icy roads have caused numerous accidents; des lésions occasionnées par le gel injuries caused by frostbite; un déménagement occasionne de nombreux frais moving house is a costly business; o. des ennuis à qn to cause trouble for sb, to get sb into trouble

occident [ɔksidɑ̃] NM 1 *Géog* west 2 *Pol* l'O. the West, *Sout* the Occident

occidental, -e, -aux, -ales [ɔksidɑ̃tal, -o] ADJ 1 *Géog* west *(avant n)*, western; côte occidentale west coast; l'Europe occidentale Western Europe

2 *Pol* Western, *Sout* Occidental; les pays occidentaux, le monde o. Western countries, the West

❑ Occidental, -e NM,F *Pol* Westerner, *Sout* Occidental

❑ à l'occidentale ADV vivre à l'occidentale to live like a Westerner; s'habiller à l'occidentale to wear Western-style clothes

occidentalisation [ɔksidɑ̃talizasjɔ̃] NF westernization, *Sout* occidentalization

occidentaliser [3] [ɔksidɑ̃talize] VT to westernize, *Sout* to occidentalize

►s'occidentaliser VPR to become westernized *or Sout* occidentalized

occidentaliste [ɔksidɑ̃talist] *Hist* ADJ occidentalist

NMF occidentalist

occipital, -e, -aux, -ales [ɔksipital, -o] *Anat* ADJ occipital

NM occipital (bone)

occiput [ɔksipyt] NM *Anat* occiput

occire [ɔksir] VT *(à l'infinitif et au participe passé seulement) Arch* to slay

occitan, -e [ɔksitɑ̃, -an] ADJ *(de la région)* of/from Occitanie; *(langue, littérature)* of/from the langue d'oc

NM *(langue)* langue d'oc *(language spoken in parts of southern France)*

❑ Occitan, -e NM,F = inhabitant of or person from Occitanie

> *Culture*
>
> **OCCITAN**
>
> This is the vernacular of the southern regions of France, and the general term given to the various "langue d'oc" dialects. "Occitan" is still very common today, and of the six million people who understand it, two million are able to speak it. It is now officially recognized as being a "langue régionale", and has therefore been included in the curriculum of some secondary schools and universities since 1951.

Occitanie [ɔksitani] NF l'O. = area of Southern France in which the langue d'oc is spoken

occitanisme [ɔksitanism] NM = movement which promotes the Occitan culture and language

occitaniste [ɔksitanist] ADJ = relating to the langue d'oc

NMF 1 *Univ* expert in the langue d'oc 2 *Pol* defender of the langue d'oc

occlure [96] [ɔklyr] VT to occlude; *Littéraire* si la nuit occlut notre œil, c'est afin que nous écoutions plus if darkness veils our sight, it is so that we may listen the more

occlusif, -ive [ɔklyzif, -iv] ADJ occlusive

❑ occlusive NF *Ling* occlusive (consonant)

occlusion [ɔklyzjɔ̃] NF *Chim, Ling & Méd* occlusion; o. intestinale bowel obstruction, *Spéc* ileus; o. des paupières surgical occlusion *or* closure of the eyelids

occlusive [ɔklyziv] *voir* **occlusif**

occultation [ɔkyltasjɔ̃] **NF 1** *Astron* occultation **2** *Rail* occulting *(UNCOUNT)*; **feu à occultations** intermittent *or* occulting light **3** *Littéraire (obscurcissement)* obscuring, concealment, hiding

occulte [ɔkylt] **ADJ 1** *(surnaturel)* occult **2** *(secret)* occult, secret; *(cause)* hidden; *(rôle)* clandestine, covert; **comptabilité o.** secret bookkeeping; **financements occultes** secret *or* mystery funding *(UNCOUNT)*; **fonds** *ou* **réserves occultes** slush funds

occulter [3] [ɔkylte] **VT 1** *Astron & Rail* to occult; *(signal lumineux)* to block out, *Spéc* to occult **2** *(ville, région)* to black out, to black out TV programmes in **3** *Fig (réalité, problème)* to cover up, to hush up, to gloss over; *(sentiment, émotion)* to deny; **votre récit occulte un détail essentiel** your story glosses over *or* overlooks an essential detail

occultisme [ɔkyltism] **NM** occultism

occultiste [ɔkyltist] **ADJ** occultist

NMF occultist

occupant, -e [ɔkypɑ̃, -ɑ̃t] **ADJ** occupying *(avant n)*; **la puissance occupante** the occupying power

NM,F 1 *(d'un véhicule)* occupant; *(d'un lieu)* occupant, occupier; *(d'un poste)* occupant; **les occupants de la maison** the occupants of the house

2 *Mil* occupier, occupying force; **collaborer avec l'o.** to collaborate with the occupying forces

3 *Jur* **premier o.** first occupant; **o. de bonne foi** bona fide occupier

occupation [ɔkypasjɔ̃] **NF 1** *(professionnelle)* occupation, job; *(de loisirs)* occupation; **avoir de l'o.** to be busy, to have things to do; **la pêche à la ligne, voilà mon o. favorite** angling is my favourite occupation; **o.: sans** *(dans un formulaire)* profession: none; **je n'aime pas qu'il soit** *ou* **reste sans occupations** I don't like seeing him with nothing to do; *Admin* **o. principale** main occupation

2 *(d'un endroit)* occupancy, occupation; *(d'une maison)* possession; **l'o. de l'université par les étudiants** the student sit-in at the university; **o. des lieux** occupancy; **grève avec o. des lieux** sit-down strike, sit-in; **manifestation estudiantine avec o. des locaux** student sit-in

3 *(dans un hôtel)* **o. des chambres/des lits** room/bed occupancy; **o. double** double occupancy; **o. maximale** capacity occupancy

4 *Admin* **o. des sols** land use

5 *Mil* occupation; **les troupes d'o.** the occupying troops

6 *Hist* **l'O.** the (German) Occupation (of France); **la vie sous l'O.** life in occupied France

> *Culture*
>
> **L'OCCUPATION**
>
> This term refers specifically to the military occupation of part of France after the French–German armistice on 22 June 1940, spreading to the whole country in 1942. Under the terms of the armistice, France had to contribute financially to the upkeep of German troops in France and provide labour for German factories. Thousands of French Jews were deported during this period by the Vichy government.

occupationnel, -elle [ɔkypasjɔnɛl] **ADJ** *Méd* occupational

occupé, -e [ɔkype] **ADJ 1** *(non disponible → ligne de téléphone) Br* engaged, *Am* busy; *(→ toilettes) Br* engaged, *Am* occupied; *Fam* **ça sonne o.** *Br* I'm getting the engaged tone, *Am* the line is busy; **ces places sont occupées** these seats are taken; **maison vendue occupée** house sold with sitting tenant

2 *Mil & Pol* occupied

3 *(personne)* busy; **une femme très occupée** a very busy woman; **o. aux préparatifs du départ** busy with the preparations for departure, busy getting ready to leave; **o. à relire le texte** busy rereading the text; **j'ai des journées très occupées** my days are full

occuper [3] [ɔkype] **VT 1** *(donner une activité à)* **o. qn** to keep sb busy *or* occupied; **cela l'occupe beaucoup** it takes up a lot of his/her time; **les enfants m'occupent toute la journée** the children keep me busy all day; **on pourrait o. les petits à des jeux de sable** we could keep the little ones busy playing in the sand; **fais un peu de ménage, ça t'occupera!** do a bit of housework, that'll pass *or* fill the time!; **le textile occupait toute la région** the textile industry used to provide work for *or* to employ people throughout the region; **la question qui nous occupe** the matter in hand; **la lecture de ce livre m'a occupé toute la soirée** reading this book took up my entire evening *or* kept me busy all evening; **ces problèmes m'ont occupé pendant un certain temps** these problems have kept me busy *or* kept me occupied *or* given me something to think about for some time; **être occupé à faire qch** to be busy doing sth

2 *(envahir)* to occupy, to take over; **les rebelles occupent tout le Nord** the rebels have occupied the entire northern area; **o. le terrain** *Mil & Fig* to have the field; *Com* to make one's presence felt in the market

3 *(remplir → espace)* to take up, to occupy; **le bar occupe le fond de la pièce/trop de place** the bar stands at the back of the room/takes up too much space; **les livres d'art occupent trois étagères de la bibliothèque** the art books take up *or* occupy *or* fill three shelves of the bookcase; **le magasin n'occupe que le rez-de-chaussée** the shop takes up *or* occupies only the ground floor; **les grévistes occupent les bureaux** the strikers have occupied the offices; **o. le devant de la scène** to be in the foreground

4 *(remplir → temps)* to fill, to occupy; **faire qch pour o. le temps** to do sth to fill *or* occupy the time; **la séance a occupé la matinée** the meeting took up the whole morning, the whole of the morning was taken up by the meeting; **les enfants occupent la majeure partie de mon temps** the children take up the greater part of my time

5 *(consacrer)* to spend; **o. sa journée à faire qch** to spend one's day doing sth; **j'occupe mes loisirs à lire** I spend my free time reading; **à quoi peut-on o. ses dimanches?** what is there to do on Sundays?

6 *(habiter)* to occupy, to live in; **depuis quand occupez-vous cette chambre?** how long have you been living in *or* have you had this room?; **qui occupe la maison d'en face?** who lives in *or* occupies the house opposite?

7 *(détenir → poste, place)* to hold, to occupy; **il occupe un poste important** he holds an important position; **Liverpool occupe la seconde place du championnat** Liverpool are (lying) second in the league table

USAGE ABSOLU ça occupe! it keeps me/him/*etc* busy; *Fam* **la télé, ça occupe** watching TV helps to pass the time■

▸**s'occuper VPR 1** *(passer le temps)* to keep oneself busy *or* occupied, to occupy oneself; **s'o. en lisant** to spend one's time reading; **je m'occupe en faisant du crochet** I keep myself busy by crocheting; **s'o. à faire qch** to be busy doing sth, to be occupied in doing sth; **à quoi s'occupent les citadins au mois d'août?** how do city dwellers spend their time in August?; **il va falloir qu'elle s'occupe** she'll have to find something to keep her occupied; **tu n'as donc pas de quoi t'o.?** haven't you got something to be getting on with?; **on trouve toujours à s'o.** there's always something to do; **je trouverai bien de quoi m'o. en attendant** I'll find something to keep me busy while I'm waiting; *Fam* **c'est juste histoire de m'o.** it's just for something to do■

2 s'o. de *(avoir pour responsabilité ou tâche)* to deal with, to be in charge of, to take care of; **je m'occupe de jeunes délinquants** I'm in charge of young offenders; **qui s'occupe de votre dossier?** who's dealing with *or* handling your file?; **nous allons maintenant nous o. du bilan** we will now turn (our attention) to the balance sheet; **je m'en occupe** I'll see to it, I'll take care of it; **je m'en occuperai plus tard** I'll see to it later; **je m'en occuperai dès demain matin** I'll attend to *or* take care of that first thing in the morning; **t'es-tu occupé des réservations/de ton inscription?** did you see about the reservations/registering for your course?; **je m'occupe de te faire parvenir ton courrier** I'll see about having your mail sent on to you; **cette maison s'occupe surtout d'argenterie** this firm specializes in silverware; *Fam* **occupe-toi de tes affaires** *ou* **oignons** *ou* **de ce qui te regarde** mind your own business; *Fam* **t'occupe!** mind your own business!, keep your nose out!, butt out!

3 s'o. de *(entourer de soins)* to look after, to care for; **s'o. d'un malade** to care for a patient; **s'o. d'un bébé** to look after a baby; **peux-tu t'o. des invités pendant que je me prépare?** would you look after *or* see to the guests while I get ready?; **on s'occupe de vous, Madame?** are you being attended to *or* served, Madam?; **il ne s'occupe pas assez d'elle** he doesn't pay her enough attention

occurrence [ɔkyrɑ̃s] **NF 1** *(cas)* case; **en pareille o., il faut appeler la police** in such a case *or* in such circumstances, the police must be called

2 *Ling* token, occurrence

3 *Rel* occurrence

4 *Ordinat (lors d'une recherche sur l'Internet)* hit

□ **en l'occurrence ADV** as it happens; **il voulait s'en prendre à quelqu'un, en l'o. ce fut moi** he wanted to take it out on somebody, and it happened to be me *or* and as it happened, it was me; **mais, en l'o., tu as tort** but in this case *or* but this time *or* but as it happens, you're wrong

OCDE [osedeə] **NF** *(abrév* **Organisation de coopération et de développement économiques)** OECD

océan [ɔseɑ̃] **NM 1** *Géog* ocean; **l'o. Atlantique/Antarctique/Indien/Pacifique** the Atlantic/Antarctic/Indian/Pacific Ocean; **l'o. (Glacial) Arctique** the Arctic Ocean **2** *Fig* **un o. de tulipes** a sea of tulips; **un o. de larmes** floods of tears; **un o. de couleurs** a sea of colour

□ **Océan NPR** *Myth* Oceanus

océanaute [ɔseanot] **NMF** oceanaut

océane[1] [ɔsean] **ADJ F 1** *Culin (salade, sauce)* seafood *(avant n)* **2** *Littéraire (de l'Océan)* une **brise o.** a sea breeze; *Arch* **la mer o.** the ocean sea, the Atlantic

□ **Océane NF l'O.** *(autoroute)* = the Paris–Nantes motorway

océane[2] **NF** *Bourse & Fin* convertible or exchangeable bond

océanide [ɔseanid] **NF** *Myth* oceanid, ocean nymph

Océanie [ɔseani] **NF l'O.** Oceania, the (central and) South Pacific

océanien, -enne [ɔseanjɛ̃, -ɛn] **ADJ** Oceanian, Oceanic

□ **Océanien, -enne NM,F** Oceanian, South Sea Islander

océanique [ɔseanik] **ADJ** oceanic

océanographe [ɔseanɔgraf] **NMF** oceanographer

océanographie [ɔseanɔgrafi] **NF** oceanography

océanographique [ɔseanɔgrafik] **ADJ** oceanographic

océanologie [ɔseanɔlɔʒi] **NF** oceanology

océanologique [ɔseanɔlɔʒik] **ADJ** oceanological

océanologue [ɔseanɔlɔg] **NMF** oceanologist

ocelle [ɔsɛl] **NM** *Zool* **1** *(œil)* ocellus **2** *(tache)* ocellus, eyespot

ocellé, -e [ɔsele] **ADJ** ocellate, ocellated

ocelot [ɔslo] **NM 1** *(animal)* ocelot **2** *(fourrure)* ocelot (fur)

> **-OCHE** [ɔʃ] **SUFF**
>
> This slang suffix lends a PEJORATIVE or simply HUMOROUS tone to the new word created from an adjective, noun or verb radical. There is not always a slang equivalent for these words in English, eg:
>
> **cantoche** (from *cantine*) canteen; **cinoche** (from *cinéma*) cinema, movies; **fastoche** (from *facile*) dead easy; **pelloche** (from *pellicule*) camera film; **avoir la pétoche** (from *péter*) to be scared stiff; **pistoche** (from *piscine*) (swimming) pool; **téloche** (from *télévision*) TV, telly; **valoche** (from *valise*) suitcase/eye bag

ochlocrate [ɔklɔkrat] **NMF** *Littéraire* ochlocrat

ochlocratie [ɔklɔkrasi] **NF** *Littéraire* ochlocracy, mob rule

ochlocratique [ɔklɔkratik] **ADJ** *Littéraire* ochlocratic

OCR [ɔseɛr] NF (abrév **optical character recognition**) OCR

ocre [ɔkr] NF ochre; **o. jaune** yellow ochre; **o. rouge** ruddle
　ADJ INV ochre
　NM ochre

ocré, -e [ɔkre] ADJ ochry

ocrer [3] [ɔkre] VT to ochre

ocreux, -euse [ɔkrø, -øz] ADJ ochreous

octaèdre [ɔktaɛdr] ADJ octahedral
　NM octahedron

octaédrique [ɔktaedrik] ADJ octahedral

octal, -e, -aux, -ales [ɔktal, -o] ADJ octal

octane [ɔktan] NM octane

octant [ɔktɑ̃] NM Géom & Naut octant

Octave [ɔktav] NPR Octavian

octave [ɔktav] NF Escrime, Mus & Rel octave; **à l'o. inférieure/supérieure** one octave lower/higher; **jouer à l'o.** (plus haut) to play an octave higher; (plus bas) to play an octave lower

octavier [9] [ɔktavje] VI Mus to octave

octet [ɔktɛ] NM 1 Ordinat octet, (eight-bit) byte; **milliard d'octets** gigabyte; **o. de contrôle** check byte 2 Chim octet

octidi [ɔktidi] NM Hist = eighth day of a ten-day period in the Republican calendar

octobre [ɔktɔbr] NM October; voir aussi **mars**

octocoralliaire [ɔktɔkɔraljer] NM Zool octocorallan

octogénaire [ɔktɔʒenɛr] ADJ octogenarian; **être o.** to be in one's eighties
　NMF person in his/her eighties; **un sémillant o.** a dashing eighty-year-old

octogonal, -e, -aux, -ales [ɔktɔgɔnal, -o] ADJ octagonal

octogone [ɔktɔgon] ADJ octagonal
　NM octagon

octopode [ɔktɔpɔd] ADJ octopod
　NM octopod

octostyle [ɔktɔstil] ADJ Archit octastyle

octosyllabe [ɔktɔsilab] ADJ octosyllabic
　NM octosyllable

octosyllabique [ɔktɔsilabik] ADJ octosyllabic

octroi [ɔktrwa] NM 1 (don) granting, bestowing; Com **o. de licence** licensing 2 Hist (taxe, administration) octroi

octroyer [13] [ɔktrwaje] VT (accorder) to grant; **o. qch à qn** (faveur, permission, congé) to grant sb sth; **o. sa grâce à un condamné a mort** to reprieve a condemned man; **le ministère a fait o. une prime aux soldats du contingent** the ministry gave instructions for a bonus to be paid to the conscripts
　▸s'octroyer VPR **s'o. un congé** to take a day off (without permission); **il s'est octroyé un jour de vacances supplémentaire** he gave himself or awarded himself an extra day's holiday; **s'o. le droit de faire qch** to assume the right to do sth

octuor [ɔktɥɔr] NM octet

octuple [ɔktypl] ADJ octuple; (montant) eightfold
　NM octuple

octupler [3] [ɔktyple] VT to octuple

oculaire [ɔkylɛr] ADJ ocular; **hygiène o.** eye care, care of the eyes
　NM Opt ocular, eyepiece; **o. de visée** (d'une caméra) eyepiece

oculariste [ɔkylarist] NMF ocularist

oculiste [ɔkylist] NMF oculist

oculogyre [ɔkylɔʒir] ADJ Anat oculogyric

oculomoteur, -trice [ɔkylɔmɔtœr, -tris] ADJ Anat oculomotor (avant n)

oculus [ɔkylys] NM Archit oculus

ocytocine [ɔsitɔsin] NF Méd oxytocin

ocytocique [ɔsitɔsik] ADJ Méd oxytocic

odalisque [ɔdalisk] NF 1 Hist odalisque
　2 Littéraire (courtisane) courtesan, odalisque

ODE [ɔdeə] NF Mktg (abrév **occasion d'entendre**) opportunity to hear

ode [ɔd] NF ode

odelette [ɔdlɛt] NF short ode

Oder [ɔdɛr] NM **l'O.** the Oder

Odessa [ɔdesa] NM Odessa

odeur [ɔdœr] NF 1 (de nourriture) smell, odour; (de fleur, de parfum) smell, fragrance, scent; **bonne o.** lovely or pleasant smell; **mauvaise o.** bad or unpleasant smell; **une forte o. de brûlé/chocolat venait de la cuisine** a strong smell of burning/chocolate was coming from the kitchen; **il a une drôle d'o., ce poisson** this fish has a funny smell or smells funny; **ce médicament a une mauvaise o.** this medicine smells bad or has a bad smell; **chasser les mauvaises odeurs** to get rid of (nasty or unpleasant) smells; **sans o.** odourless; **ça n'a pas d'o.** it has no smell, it doesn't smell; **o. corporelle** body odour
　2 Rel **mourir en o. de sainteté** to die in the odour of sanctity; Fig **être en o. de sainteté auprès de qn** to be in sb's good books; Fig **ne pas être en o. de sainteté** to be out of favour; **il n'est pas en o. de sainteté dans le parti** he is out of favour in the party

odieuse [ɔdjøz] voir **odieux**

odieusement [ɔdjøzmɑ̃] ADV odiously, hatefully, obnoxiously

odieux, -euse [ɔdjø, -øz] ADJ 1 (atroce → comportement) odious; (→ crime) heinous; **je me dois de répondre à ces odieuses accusations** it's my duty to answer these monstrous charges
　2 (désagréable → personne) hateful, obnoxious; **l'examinateur a été o. avec moi** the examiner was obnoxious or vile to me; **elle a deux enfants o.** she has two unbearable or obnoxious children; **cela m'est o.** I absolutely loathe it

Odin [ɔdɛ̃] NPR Myth Odin

odomètre [ɔdɔmɛtr] NM (pour véhicule) odometer; (pour piéton) pedometer

odonate [ɔdɔnat] Entom NM odonate
　□ odonates NMPL Odonata

odontalgie [ɔdɔ̃talʒi] NF Méd odontalgia

odontalgique [ɔdɔ̃talʒik] ADJ Méd odontalgic

odontocète [ɔdɔ̃tɔsɛt] Zool NM odontocete
　□ odontocètes NMPL Odontocetes

odontogenèse [ɔdɔ̃tɔʒənez], **odontogénie** [ɔdɔ̃tɔʒeni] NF Biol odontogeny

odontoïde [ɔdɔ̃tɔid] ADJ Anat odontoid; **apophyse o.** odontoid process

odontologie [ɔdɔ̃tɔlɔʒi] NF odontology

odontologiste [ɔdɔ̃tɔlɔʒist] NMF odontologist

odontomètre [ɔdɔ̃tɔmɛtr] NM odontometer

odontostomatologie [ɔdɔ̃tɔstɔmatɔlɔʒi] NF dental surgery

odorant, -e [ɔdɔrɑ̃, -ɑ̃t] ADJ 1 (qui a une odeur) odorous 2 (parfumé) fragrant, sweet-smelling; **leur jardin était lumineux et o.** their garden was bright and fragrant

odorat [ɔdɔra] NM (sense of) smell; **avoir l'o. développé** to have a keen sense of smell; **manquer d'o.** to have no sense of smell

odoriférant, -e [ɔdɔriferɑ̃, -ɑ̃t] ADJ Littéraire (parfumé) sweet-smelling, fragrant, odoriferous

ODV [ɔdeve] NF Mktg (abrév **occasion de voir**) opportunity to see

odyssée [ɔdise] NF odyssey; **nous attendions avec impatience le récit de son o.** we were looking forward to hearing the story of his/her epic journey

'L'Odyssée' Homère 'The Odyssey'

'2001: L'Odyssée de l'espace' Clarke, Kubrick '2001: A Space Odyssey'

OEA [ɔəa] NF (abrév **Organisation des États américains**) OAS

OEB [ɔabe] NM (abrév **Office européen des brevets**) EPO

OECE [ɔaseə] NF (abrév **Organisation européenne de coopération économique**) OEEC

œcuménicité [ekymenisite] NF Littéraire ecumenicalism

œcuménique [ekymenik] ADJ ecumenical

œcuménisme [ekymenism] NM ecumenicalism, ecumenicism

œcuméniste [ekymenist] ADJ ecumenic, ecumenical
　NMF ecumenist

œdémateux, -euse [edematø, -øz] ADJ Méd oedematous

œdématié, -e [edematje] ADJ Méd oedematous, oedematic

œdème [edɛm] NM Méd oedema; **o. aigu du poumon** acute pulmonary oedema; **avoir un o. aux poumons** to have pulmonary oedema

œdicnème [ediknɛm] NM Orn **o. (criard)** stone curlew

Œdipe [edip] NPR Myth Oedipus

'Œdipe à Colone' Sophocle 'Oedipus at Colonus'

'Œdipe roi' Sophocle 'Oedipus Rex'

œdipe [edip] NM Oedipus complex

œdipien, -enne [edipjɛ̃, -ɛn] ADJ oedipal, oedipean

œil [œj] (pl sens 1–9, 11, 13 yeux [jø], pl sens 10, 12 œils) NM 1 Anat eye; **j'ai le soleil dans les yeux** the sun's in or I've got the sun in my eyes; **fermer/ouvrir les yeux** to close/to open one's eyes; Fig **fermer les yeux à qn** to be present at sb's death; **j'ai les yeux qui se ferment (tout seuls)** I can't keep my eyes open; **les yeux fermés** with one's eyes closed; **ouvrir un o.** to half-open one's eyes; **ouvrir de grands yeux** to look surprised; **faire ou ouvrir des yeux ronds** to stare wide-eyed; **baisser les yeux** to lower one's eyes or gaze, to look down; **avoir de grands yeux** to have large eyes; **avoir de gros yeux** to have bulbous eyes; **avoir de petits yeux** to have small eyes; Fig to look (all) puffy-eyed or puffy round the eyes; **avoir les yeux verts/marron** to have green/brown eyes; **avoir l'o. humide** to have tearful eyes or a tearful gaze; **aux yeux de biche** doe-eyed; **elle a des yeux de biche** she's got doe-eyes; **avoir les yeux battus** to have (dark) rings or bags under one's eyes; **il n'a qu'un o.** he's one-eyed, he's only got one eye; **je vois mal d'un o.** one of my eyes is weak; **il ne voit plus que d'un o.** he can only see with one eye now; **je l'ai de mes yeux vu, je l'ai vu de mes propres yeux** I saw it with my own eyes; **o. artificiel ou de verre** artificial/glass eye; Biol **o. composé ou à facettes** compound eye; Littéraire **l'o. intérieur** the inner eye; **le mauvais o.** the evil eye; **jeter le mauvais o. à qn** to give sb the evil eye; Fam **mon o.!** my eye!, my foot!; **généreux, mon o.!** generous, my foot!; Fam **attention les yeux!** get an eyeful of that!; **il a une petite amie/une bagnole, attention les yeux!** you should see his girlfriend/car!, his girlfriend/car is an absolute Br cracker or Am crackerjack!; Fam **avoir un o. poché** ou **au beurre noir** to have a black eye or a shiner; **elle avait les yeux qui lui sortaient de la tête** her eyes were popping out of her head; Fam **il/ça me sort par les yeux de la tête** I can't stand him/it; **il faudrait avoir des yeux derrière la tête!** you'd need (to have) eyes in the back of your head!; Hum **avoir un o. qui dit** Fam **zut** ou très Fam **merde à l'autre**, Fam **avoir les yeux qui se croisent les bras, avoir un o. qui joue au billard et l'autre qui compte les points, avoir un o. à Paris et l'autre à Pontoise** to have a squint■, to be cross-eyed■, Br to be bossy-eyed■; Fam **coûter les yeux de la tête** to cost a fortune■ or a bundle or Br a packet; Fam **viens me lire ça, petit, j'ai besoin d'yeux** come and read this for me, son, I need (somebody with) a good pair of eyes; **faire les gros yeux à un enfant** to look sternly or reprovingly at a child; **maman va te faire les gros yeux!** Mummy's going to tell you off!; **faire qch pour les beaux yeux de qn** to do sth for the love of sb; **je ne travaille pas pour les beaux yeux de mon patron!** I don't do this job for the love of it!; Fam **entre quat'z yeux** in private■; Fam **il n'a pas froid aux yeux** he's got plenty of nerve, he's not backward in coming forward; Fam **tu as les yeux plus grands que le ventre** (tu es trop gourmand) your eyes are bigger than your belly or your stomach; (tu as été trop ambitieux) you've bitten off more than you can chew; Can Fam **tomber dans l'o. à qn** to catch sb's eye, to take sb's fancy; Bible **o. pour o.(, dent pour dent)** an eye for an eye (and a tooth for a tooth); Bible **ils ont des yeux et ils ne voient pas** eyes have they, but they see not
　2 (vision) sight, eyesight; **avoir de bons yeux** to have good eyesight; **avoir de mauvais yeux** to have bad or poor eyesight; **avoir des yeux de lynx** to be eagle-eyed; **il a suivait de son o. d'aigle** he was watching her every move like a hawk; **il a des yeux de chat** he can see like a cat

ocr-œil

in the dark; **je n'ai plus mes yeux de vingt ans** I can't see as well as I used to; **s'user** *ou* **s'abîmer les yeux** to ruin one's eyes *or* eyesight; **fatiguer les yeux** to strain one's eyes; **cette lumière me fatigue les yeux** I'm straining my eyes in this light

3 *(regard)* **ne me fais pas ces yeux-là!** don't look *or* stare at me like that!; **les yeux dans les yeux** *(tendrement)* looking into each other's eyes; *(avec franchise)* looking each other straight in the eye; **regarder qn dans les yeux** to look sb in the eye; **regarder qn avec les yeux de l'amour** to look at sb through the eyes of love; **chercher qn des yeux** to look around for sb; **suivre qn des yeux** to follow sb with one's eyes; **jeter les yeux sur qch** to cast a glance at sth; **dès que j'eus jeté les yeux sur lui** as soon as I had set eyes on him; **jeter un o. à** to have a quick look at; **veux-tu y jeter un o. en vitesse?** do you want to have a quick look at it?; **lever les yeux sur qn/qch** to look up at sb/sth; **sans lever les yeux de son livre** without looking up *or* raising his/her eyes from his/her book; **lever les yeux au ciel** *(pour regarder)* to look up at the sky; *(par exaspération)* to raise one's eyes heavenwards; **poser un o. sur** to have a look at; **elle posait sur tout un o. curieux** she was curious about everything; **n'ayant jamais posé les yeux sur de telles splendeurs** never having laid *or* set eyes on such fabulous sights; **devant les yeux de** before (the eyes of); **les clefs sont devant tes yeux** the keys are right in front of you; *Littéraire* **sous les yeux de, sous l'o. de** under the eye *or* gaze of; **sous l'o. amusé/jaloux de son frère** under the amused/jealous gaze of her brother; **sous mes yeux** *(devant moi)* right in front of me; *(effrontément)* before my very eyes; **il l'a volé sous nos yeux** he stole it from under our very eyes; **elle dépérissait sous mes yeux** I could see her wasting away before my very eyes; **j'ai votre dossier sous les yeux** I've got your file right here in front of me *or* before me; **à l'abri des yeux indiscrets** away from prying eyes; **n'avoir d'yeux que pour** to only have eyes for; **il n'avait d'yeux que pour elle** he only had eyes for her

4 *(expression, air)* look; **son o. malicieux/interrogateur** his/her mischievous/inquiring look; **elle est arrivée, l'o. méchant** *ou* **mauvais** she arrived with a nasty look on her face *or* looking like trouble; **il m'a regardé d'un o. noir/furieux** he gave me a black/furious look; **elle se taisait, mais ses yeux parlaient pour elle** she said nothing, but her eyes did the talking; *Fam* **faire de l'o. à qn** *(pour aguicher)* to give sb the eye, to make eyes at sb; *(en signe de connivence)* to wink knowingly at sb; **arrête de faire de l'o. à tous les garçons!** stop giving all the boys the eye!; **faire les yeux doux** *ou* **des yeux de velours à qn** to make sheep's eyes at sb

5 *(vigilance)* **rien n'échappait à l'o. du professeur** nothing escaped the teacher's notice; **avoir l'o.** to be vigilant *or* watchful; **aie l'o.!** be on the lookout!; **elle a l'o. à tout** she keeps an eye on everything; **il faut avoir l'o. à tout avec les enfants** you've got to keep an eye on everything when children are around; **il a l'o. du maître** *(rien ne lui échappe)* he doesn't miss a thing; **avoir l'o. sur qn** to keep an eye *or* a close watch on sb; **être tout yeux** to be all eyes; **ils étaient tout yeux et tout oreilles** they were all eyes and ears; **ouvrir les yeux à qn sur qch** to open sb's eyes to sth; *Fam* **ouvrir l'o. (et le bon)** to keep one's eyes open *or* peeled *or* skinned; **sauter aux yeux,** *Fam* **crever les yeux** to be blindingly *or* glaringly obvious; *Fam* **il n'a pas les yeux en face des trous** *(il est mal réveillé)* he hasn't come to yet, his brain isn't in gear yet; *(il n'est pas observateur)* he's as blind as a bat, he never sees what's going on right in front of him; *Fam* **elle n'a pas les yeux dans sa poche** she keeps her eyes open, she's very observant▪

6 *(état d'esprit, avis)* **voir qch d'un bon/mauvais o.** to look favourably/unfavourably upon sth; **considérer** *ou* **voir qch d'un o. critique** to look critically at sth; **considérer** *ou* **voir qch d'un o. neuf** to look at sth with a fresh eye; **voir les choses du même o. que qn** to see eye to eye with sb; **nous voyons ça du même o.** we see eye to eye (with each other) about it; **nous ne voyons pas du tout les choses de cet o.-là** we don't see things in that light at all; **il voit tout par les yeux de sa femme** he sees everything through his wife's eyes; **il voit avec les yeux de la foi/de l'amour** he sees things through the eyes of a believer/of love; **aux yeux de** in the eyes of; **aux yeux de tous, il passait pour fou** he was regarded by everyone as a madman; **à mes yeux** in my eyes, in my opinion; **ça n'a aucun intérêt à mes yeux** it's of no interest to me; **aux yeux de la loi** in the eyes of the law

7 *Agr & Hort (de pomme de terre)* eye; **o. dormant/poussant** *(bourgeon)* dormant/shooted bud

8 *Zool (d'un papillon, d'une queue de paon)* eyespot; **o. pinéal** pineal organ

9 *(trou → dans une porte)* Judas (hole), spyhole; *(→ au théâtre)* peep hole; *(→ d'une aiguille, d'un marteau)* eye; *(d'une charnière)* (screw-)hole; *Naut (d'un filin)* grommet, eye; *Météo (d'un cyclone)* eye, centre

10 *Typ* face; **o. du caractère** typeface

11 *Tech* **o. magique** magic eye

12 *Mil* fuse hole

❑ **yeux** NMPL **1** *Fam Hum (lunettes)* glasses▪, *Br* specs; **j'ai oublié mes yeux** I've forgotten my specs **2** *Culin (du pain, du gruyère)* hole; **les yeux du bouillon** the fat *(floating on the surface of the stock)*

❑ **à l'œil** ADV *Fam* **1** *(gratis)* (for) free▪, for nothing▪; **j'ai voyagé à l'o.** I travelled for free; **ce soir-là, j'ai chanté à l'o.** that night, I sang for free; **j'ai eu deux tickets à l'o.** I got two tickets gratis *or* (for) free *or* on the house **2** *(locution)* **avoir** *ou* **tenir qn à l'o.** to have one's eye on sb, to keep an eye on sb; **toi, je t'ai à l'o.!** I've got my eye on you!

❑ **coup d'œil** NM **1** *(regard)* look, glance; **elle s'en rendit compte au premier coup d'o.** she noticed straight away *or* immediately *or* at a glance; **donner** *ou* **jeter un (petit) coup d'o. à** to have a quick look *or* glance at; **d'un coup d'o., il embrassa le tableau** he took in the situation at a glance; **avoir le coup d'o.** *(savoir regarder)* to have a good eye; **pour les coquilles, elle a le coup d'o.** she has a good *or* keen eye for misprints; **valoir le coup d'o.** to be (well) worth seeing **2** *(panorama)* view; **de là-haut, le coup d'o. est unique** the view up there is unique

Allusion

T'as de beaux yeux, tu sais

This expression comes from the 1938 Marcel Carné film *Quai des brumes*, with a screenplay by Jacques Prévert, in which a deserter hiding in a French port meets and falls in love with a girl. The stars were Jean Gabin and Michèle Morgan and, in a legendary close-up, he tells her "You know, you've got beautiful eyes". The expression is used today light-heartedly, but still as a real compliment, by rather more ordinary lovers than Jean Gabin.

œil-de-bœuf [œjdəbœf] *(pl* **œils-de-bœuf***)* *Archit* NM *(oculus)* oculus; *(lucarne)* bull's-eye

œil-de-chat [œjdəʃa] *(pl* **œils-de-chat***)* NM *Minér* cat's-eye

œil-de-perdrix [œjdəpɛrdri] *(pl* **œils-de-perdrix***)* NM **1** *Anat* (soft) corn **2** *(du bois)* small knot **3** *(vin)* oeil-de-perdrix, = Swiss rosé wine made from Pinot Noir grapes

œil-de-pie [œjdəpi] *(pl* **œils-de-pie***)* NM *Naut* eyelet

œil-de-tigre [œjdətigr] *(pl* **œils-de-tigre***)* NM tiger-eye, tiger's-eye

œillade [œjad] NF wink; **jeter** *ou* **lancer des œillades à qn** to give sb the (glad) eye; *Hum* **une o. assassine** a provocative wink

œillard [œjar] NM millstone eye

œillère [œjɛr] NF **1** *(de cheval) Br* blinker, *Am* blinder; *Fig* **avoir des œillères** to be blinkered, to have a blinkered attitude; *(être borné)* to be narrow-minded **2** *(coupelle)* eyebath, eyecup

œillet [œjɛ] NM **1** *Bot (plante)* carnation, pink; *(fleur)* carnation; **o. des fleuristes** carnation; **o. d'Inde** French marigold; **o. mignardise** wild pink; **o. de poète** sweet william; **o. des prés** ragged robin **2** *(perforation)* eyelet hole **3** *(anneau → de papier gommé)* reinforcement ring; *(→ de métal)* eyelet, grommet

œilleton [œjtɔ̃] NM **1** *Bot* eye **2** *Opt* eyepiece shade **3** *(d'une porte)* Judas(-hole), spyhole

œilletonnage [œjtɔnaʒ] NM *Hort* **1** *(multiplication)* layering **2** *(enlèvement des bourgeons)* disbudding

œilletonner [3] [œjtɔne] VT *Hort* **1** *(multiplier)* to layer **2** *(débarrasser des bourgeons)* to disbud, to remove the buds from

œillette [œjɛt] NF oil poppy, opium poppy; **huile d'o.** poppy seed oil

œkoumène [ekumɛn] = **écoumène**

œnanthe [enɑ̃t] NF *Bot* oenanthe

œnanthique [enɑ̃tik] ADJ oenanthic

œnilisme [enilism] NM alcoholism *(from drinking wine)*

œnolique [enɔlik] ADJ **acides œnoliques** oenolic acids

œnolisme [enɔlism] NM alcoholism *(from drinking wine)*

œnologie [enɔlɔʒi] NF oenology; **un stage d'o.** a wine-tasting course

œnologique [enɔlɔʒik] ADJ oenological

œnologue [enɔlɔg] NMF oenologist, wine specialist

œnométrie [enɔmetri] NF alcoholometry

œnométrique [enɔmetrik] ADJ alcoholometric

œnothèque [enɔtɛk] NF wine merchant's, vintner's

œnothera [enɔtera] NM *Bot* oenothera, evening primrose

œnothéracée [enɔterase] *Bot* NF member of the Oenotheraceae family

❑ **œnothéracées** NFPL Oenotheraceae

œnothère [enɔtɛr] NM *Bot* oenothera, evening primrose

œrsted [œrstɛd] NM *Phys* oersted

œsophage [ezɔfaʒ] NM *Anat* oesophagus; *Méd* **cancer de l'o.** cancer of the oesophagus

œsophagectomie [ezɔfaʒɛktɔmi] NF *Méd* oesophagectomy

œsophagien, -enne [ezɔfaʒjɛ̃, -ɛn], **œsophagique** [ezɔfaʒik] ADJ *Anat* oesophageal

œsophagite [ezɔfaʒit] NF *Méd* oesophagitis

œsophagoscope [ezɔfagɔskɔp] NM *Méd* oesophagoscope

œsophagoscopie [ezɔfagɔskɔpi] NF *Méd* oesophagoscopy

œstradiol [ɛstradjɔl] NM *Biol & Chim* oestradiol

œstral, -e, -aux, -ales [ɛstral, -o] ADJ *Biol* oestrous

œstre [ɛstr] NM *Entom* gadfly, warble fly

œstrogène [ɛstrɔʒɛn] NM *Biol & Chim* oestrogen

œstrogénique [ɛstrɔgenik] ADJ oestrogenic

œstrone [ɛstrɔn] NF *Physiol* oestrone

œstroprogestatif, -ive [ɛstrɔprɔʒɛstatif, -iv] ADJ oestrogenic and progestogenic

œstrus [ɛstrys] NM *Biol* oestrus

œuf [œf] *(pl* **œufs** [ø]) NM **1** *Culin* egg; **œufs brouillés** scrambled eggs; **o. en chocolat** chocolate egg; **o. (en) cocotte** coddled egg; **o. (à la) coque** boiled egg; *Belg* **o. cuit dur** hard-boiled egg; **o. dur** hard-boiled egg; **o. en gelée** egg in aspic; **o. du jour** new-laid egg; **œufs au lait** ≃ egg custard; **o. mayonnaise** egg mayonnaise; **o. (au) miroir** fried egg; **o. mollet** soft-boiled egg; **œufs à la neige** floating islands; **œufs en neige** beaten egg whites; **o. de Pâques** Easter egg; **o. sur le plat** *ou* **au plat** fried egg; *Fam* **œufs sur le plat** *(seins)* fried eggs; **elle n'a que des œufs sur le plat** she's as flat as a pancake; **o. poché** poached egg; *Fig* **sortir de l'o.** to be still wet behind the ears; *Fig* **écraser** *ou* **étouffer** *ou* **tuer qch dans l'o.** to nip sth in the bud; **c'est comme l'histoire de l'o. et de la poule** it's a chicken and egg situation; **c'est comme l'o. de Christophe Colomb, il fallait y penser** it's easy when you know how; *Prov* **il ne faut pas mettre tous ses œufs dans le même panier** never put all your eggs in one basket

2 *Fam (imbécile)* oaf, blockhead; **tête d'o.!** you nincompoop!

3 *Biol* (egg) cell, egg; *Zool (d'insecte, de poisson)* egg; *(de homard)* berry; *Zool* **o. de durée** *ou* **d'hiver** over-wintering egg; **œufs de lump** lumpfish eggs *or* roe; *Ich* **œufs de poisson** spawn; *Culin* fish roe

4 *Couture* **o. à repriser** darning egg

5 *(télécabine)* cable car

6 Sport egg; faire l'o. to (go into a) tuck; dans la position en o. in or into the tuck position
7 Ordinat o. de Pâques Easter egg
8 Belg (locution) avoir un o. à peler avec qn to have a bone to pick or a score to settle with sb

œufrier [œfrije] NM egg holder (for boiling eggs)

œuvé, -e [œve] ADJ (poisson) hard-roed; (langouste) berried

œuvre[1] [œvr] NM 1 Archit & Constr une construction dans o./hors (d')o. a construction within/without the perimeter; mesure dans/hors o. inside/outside measurement; gros o. carcass, fabric; le gros o. est enfin terminé the main building work is finished at last; second o. finishing (jobs) 2 Beaux-Arts works; son o. gravé et son o. peint his paintings and his etchings 3 (en alchimie) le Grand o. the Great Work, the Magnum Opus

œuvre[2] [œvr] NF 1 (travail) work; o. de longue haleine long-term undertaking; ce tabouret est l'o. d'un artisan this stool is the work of a craftsman; Ftbl le troisième but a été l'o. de Bergova the third goal was the work of Bergova; cette rencontre était son o. (grâce à lui) it was thanks to him that they met; (à cause de lui) it was because of him that they met; elle a fait o. durable/utile she's done a lasting/useful piece of work; la vieillesse a fait son o. old age has done its work; quand le médecin arriva, la mort avait déjà fait son o. by the time the doctor arrived, the patient had already died; mettre qch en o. to bring sth into play; mettre tout en o. pour que to do all in one's power to ensure that; nous avons mis tous les moyens ou tout en o. pour juguler l'incendie we did everything we could to bring the fire under control; elle a mis tout en o. pour être sélectionnée she pulled out all the stops in order to get selected; Littéraire o. de chair carnal knowledge; o. maîtresse magnum opus; mise en o. (en joaillerie) mounting; faire o. de rénovateur to act as a renovator; Vieilli faire o. de ses dix doigts to work with one's hands
2 Beaux-Arts, Littérature, Mus etc work; toute son o. the whole of his/her works; couronné pour l'ensemble de son o. rewarded for his overall achievement; o. d'art work of art; œuvres choisies/complètes de Molière selected/complete works of Molière; o. de jeunesse early work
3 (charité) o. (de bienfaisance) charitable organization; je fais la collecte pour une o. I'm collecting for charity; (bonnes) œuvres charity (UNCOUNT)
❑ œuvres NFPL 1 Rel works, deeds 2 Admin œuvres sociales community service (UNCOUNT) 3 Naut œuvres mortes dead work (UNCOUNT), topsides; Naut œuvres vives quickwork (UNCOUNT); Fig la France, blessée dans ses œuvres vives France, cut to the quick
❑ à l'œuvre ADV at work; être à l'o. to be at work; se mettre à l'o. to get down to or to start work; voir qn à l'o. to see sb at work

œuvrer [5] [œvre] VI to work, to strive; nous voulons la paix, et nous allons o. pour cela we want peace, and we will do our utmost to achieve it

œuvrette [œvrɛt] NF Fam minor work▪

OFCE [oɛfseə] NM (abrév Observatoire français des conjonctures économiques) = economic research institute

off [ɔf] ADJ INV 1 Cin offscreen; voix o. voice off 2 (festival) fringe (avant n)
NM le o. the Fringe festival; dans le o. on the Fringe (festival); au programme du o. on the Fringe (festival programme)

offensant, -e [ɔfɑ̃sɑ̃, -ɑ̃t] ADJ offensive

offense [ɔfɑ̃s] NF 1 (affront) insult; faire o. à to offend, to give offence to; soit dit sans o., tu n'es plus tout jeune non plus no offence intended or meant, but you're not that young either; c'est une o. au bon goût it's an offence or a crime against good taste; Fam il n'y a pas d'o. no offence taken 2 Rel trespass, transgression 3 Jur o. à la cour contempt of court

offensé, -e [ɔfɑ̃se] ADJ offended, insulted; air o. offended or outraged look; elle s'est sentie offensée she felt offended
NM,F offended or injured party

offenser [3] [ɔfɑ̃se] VT 1 (blesser) to offend, to give offence to; je l'ai offensé sans le vouloir I offended him unintentionally; tu l'offenserais en ne l'invitant pas you'd offend him if you didn't invite him; soit dit sans (vouloir) vous o., votre fils n'est pas un ange without wishing to offend you, your son is no angel; sans vouloir t'o., Jean-Pierre, j'ai bien l'impression que... no offence (intended), Jean-Pierre, or I don't wish to offend, Jean-Pierre, but I get the feeling that...; o. la mémoire de qn to offend sb's memory
2 (enfreindre) to violate; o. un principe to fly in the face of a principle; Rel o. Dieu to offend God, to trespass against God
3 Littéraire (bon goût, délicatesse) to offend against; o. les regards to be an eyesore, to offend the eye
►s'offenser VPR (se vexer) to take offence; s'o. de la moindre critique to take exception to the slightest criticism; elle s'est offensée qu'il ait oublié son anniversaire she was offended because he forgot her birthday

offenseur [ɔfɑ̃sœr] NM offender

offensif, -ive [ɔfɑ̃sif, -iv] ADJ offensive; l'équipe a adopté un jeu très o. the team has opted to play an attacking game; arme/guerre offensive offensive weapon/war
❑ offensive NF Mil & Fig offensive; passer à/prendre l'offensive to go on/to take the offensive; mener une offensive to carry out or to conduct an offensive; le club lillois revient à l'offensive contre Bordeaux the Lille team is back on the offensive or is making a fresh attack against Bordeaux; Fig offensive de charme charm offensive; Fig offensive de l'hiver onslaught of winter; Fig offensive du froid sudden cold spell, cold snap; Pol offensive de paix peace offensive

offensivement [ɔfɑ̃sivmɑ̃] ADV 1 Mil offensively 2 Sport jouer o. to play an attacking game

offert, -e [ɔfɛr, -ɛrt] PP voir offrir

offertoire [ɔfɛrtwar] NM offertory

office [ɔfis] NM 1 (gén) & Hist office; dans son o. de gouvernante in her position as governess; le secrétaire n'a pas rempli son o. the secretary didn't carry out his duties; le signal d'alarme n'a pas rempli son o. the alarm didn't (fulfil its) function; la pénicilline a rempli son o. the penicillin did its job; faire o. de président to act as chairman; une robe blanche toute simple a fait o. de robe de mariée a simple white dress served as a wedding gown; qu'est-ce qui peut faire o. de pièce d'identité? what could serve as proof of identity?; pendant le voyage, j'ai dû faire o. de cuisinier I had to act as cook during the trip; o. ministériel ministerial office
2 Rel service; aller à/manquer l'o. to go to/to miss the church service; l'o. divin the Divine Office; l'o. des morts funeral service; o. du soir evening service
3 (agence) agency, bureau; o. de publicité advertising agency; o. du tourisme espagnol Spanish tourist office or bureau; O. européen des brevets European Patent Office; l'O. national des forêts the French Forestry commission, Br ≃ the Forestry Commission, Am ≃ the Forestry Service; O. du commerce extérieur foreign trade office; O. national de la navigation = French national shipping and inland waterways office; Suisse o. de poste post office
4 les Offices (à Florence) the Uffizi
5 Com (dans l'édition) exemplaire d'o. copy sent on sale or return
NM OU Vieilli NF (d'une cuisine) pantry; (d'un hôtel, d'une grande maison) kitchen, kitchens; tous les verres sont rangés dans l'o. all the glasses are stored in the pantry; enfant, je dînais à l'o. as a child, I used to eat with the servants
❑ offices NMPL accepter les bons offices de qn to accept sb's good offices; proposer ses bons offices to offer to act as mediator; grâce aux bons offices de M. Prat/du gouvernement allemand thanks to Mr Prat's good offices/to the good offices of the German government; Fam monsieur bons offices mediator▪
❑ d'office ADV automatically; être mis à la retraite d'o. to be automatically retired; il a été promu d'o. au rang de général he was automatically promoted to (the rank of) general; je vous mets d'o. parmi les altos I'll put you in straight away with the altos; avocat commis d'o. (officially) appointed lawyer

official, -aux [ɔfisjal, -o] NM Rel official principal, official

officialisation [ɔfisjalizasjɔ̃] NF officialization

officialiser [3] [ɔfisjalize] VT to make official, to officialize

officialité [ɔfisjalite] NF officiality

officiant [ɔfisjɑ̃] ADJ M officiating (avant n)
NM officiant

officiel, -elle [ɔfisjɛl] ADJ 1 (public) official; communiqué o. official communiqué; la version officielle est le suicide the official version is suicide; rien de ce que je vous dis là n'est o. everything I'm telling you is unofficial or off the record; il a rendu officielle sa décision de démissionner he made public or he officially announced his decision to resign; congé o. official holiday; milieux officiels official circles; langage ou jargon o. officialese
2 (réglementaire) formal; tenue officielle formal attire; style o. formal style; notre rencontre n'avait aucun caractère o. our meeting took place on an informal or unofficial basis
NM 1 (représentant) official; les officiels du Parti the Party officials
2 Presse l'O. des Spectacles = weekly entertainments listings guide for Paris

officiellement [ɔfisjɛlmɑ̃] ADV officially; je dépose plainte o. I'm making an official complaint; o., il a donné sa démission, mais... officially, he resigned, but...; il a donné sa démission o. he formally resigned

officier[1] [9] [ɔfisje] VI 1 Rel to officiate
2 Fig Hum to preside; qui officie aux fourneaux ce soir? who's in charge or presiding in the kitchen tonight?

officier[2] [ɔfisje] NM 1 Mil officer; o. d'active regular officer; o. de l'armée de terre army officer; o. général Mil general officer; Naut flag officer; o. de liaison liaison officer; o. de marine naval officer; o. d'ordonnance orderly; o. de paix senior police officer; o. de permanence duty officer, officer of the day, Br orderly officer; Naut o. de pont deck officer; o. de port harbour master; o. de réserve reserve officer; o. en second second-in-command; o. de service duty officer; o. subalterne Br junior or Am company officer; o. supérieur field officer
2 (titulaire → d'une fonction, d'une distinction) o. de l'Armée du salut Salvation Army Officer; o. de l'état civil ≃ registrar; o. de la Légion d'honneur Officer of the Legion of Honour; o. ministériel = member of the legal or allied professions; (notaire) notary (public); (huissier) officer of the court; o. de police judiciaire = police officer in the French Criminal Investigation Department; o. de renseignements intelligence officer

officier-marinier [ɔfisjemarinje] (pl officiers-mariniers) NM petty officer

officieuse [ɔfisjøz] voir officieux

officieusement [ɔfisjøzmɑ̃] ADV unofficially, informally

officieux, -euse [ɔfisjø, -øz] ADJ unofficial, informal; à titre o. unofficially

officinal, -e, -aux, -ales [ɔfisinal, -o] ADJ (plante) medicinal; (remède) officinal; préparation officinale patent medicine

officine [ɔfisin] NF 1 Pharm dispensary, pharmacy
2 Fig Péj o. d'espionnage den of spies

off-line [ɔflajn] ADJ INV Ordinat off-line

offrande [ɔfrɑ̃d] NF 1 Rel (don) offering; (cérémonie) offertory; o. votive votive offering 2 (contribution) offering; apporter son ou une o. (à) to make a donation (to); verser une o. à une œuvre to give to a charity

offrant [ɔfrɑ̃] NM bidder; vendre qch au plus o. to sell sth to the highest bidder; on me propose deux emplois et j'ai décidé de dire oui au plus o. I've got two job offers and I've decided to accept the one offering the most money

offre [ɔfr] NF 1 (proposition) offer; (dans un appel d'offres) tender, bid; (dans une vente aux enchères) bid; (action) offering; recevoir/accepter une o. to receive/to accept an offer; ils lui ont

œu–off

fait une o. avantageuse they made him/her a worthwhile offer; **faire une o. à 1000 euros** to make an offer of 1,000 euros; *(aux enchères)* to bid 1,000 euros; **cette o. est valable jusqu'au 31 mai** this offer is valid until 31 May; **o. de base** basic offer; **o. de bon de réduction** coupon offer; **o. d'échantillon gratuit** free sample offer; **o. d'emploi** job offer, offer of employment; **offres d'emploi** *(dans le journal)* situations vacant; **il y a très peu d'offres d'emploi** there are very few job offers *or* openings; **o. d'essai** trial offer; **o. export** export bid; **o. globale** package deal; **o. de lancement** introductory offer; **o. à prix réduit** reduced-price offer; **o. promotionnelle** promotional offer; **o. de remboursement** money-back offer; **offres de service** offer to help; **faire des offres de service à qn** to offer to help sb; *Com* to solicit orders from sb; **o. spéciale** special offer, *Am* special

2 *Écon* supply; **o. excédentaire** excess supply; **o. de monnaie/devises** money/currency supply; **l'o. et la demande** supply and demand; **lorsque l'o. excède la demande, les prix ont tendance à baisser** when supply exceeds demand, prices have a tendency to fall

3 *Fin* **o. de concours** competitive (state) tender; **o. globale** aggregate supply; **o. publique d'achat** takeover bid; **faire** *ou* **lancer une o. publique d'achat (sur)** to make a takeover bid (for); **o. publique d'échange** exchange offer, takeover bid for shares; **o. publique de retrait** public buy-out offer; **o. publique de vente** public offering, public share offer

4 *Jur* **offres réelles** payment into court

offreur, -euse [ɔfrœr, -øz] **NM,F** *Écon* seller

OFFRIR [34] [ɔfrir]

> **VT** to give **1, 2** ▪ to offer **2–4** ▪ to present **1, 4**
> **VPR** to offer oneself **1** ▪ to offer one's services **2** ▪ to give each other **3** ▪ to treat oneself to **5**

VT 1 *(faire cadeau de)* to give; **o. qch en cadeau à qn** to give sb sth as a present; **on lui offrit une médaille** they presented him/her *or* he/she was presented with a medal; **je vous offre un café/un verre?** can I buy you coffee/a drink?; **ils (nous) ont offert le champagne** they treated us to champagne; **pour finir ce journal, nous vous offrons quelques images de la première neige dans Paris** and now to end the news, we bring you some shots of the first snow of the year in Paris; **elle s'est fait o. une voiture pour ses 25 ans** she was given a car for her 25th birthday; **il s'est fait o. un repas au restaurant** he managed to get himself taken out for a meal

2 *(donner → choix, explication, hospitalité)* to give, to offer; **o. une récompense** to offer a reward; **je vous offre une nouvelle chance** I'm giving you a second chance; **o. son assistance** *ou* **son aide à qn** to offer to help sb; **o. à qn la possibilité de faire qch** to offer *or* to give sb the chance of doing sth

3 *(proposer)* to offer; **o. son bras à qn** to offer *or* to lend sb one's arm; **je lui ai montré mon autoradio, il m'en offre 200 euros** I showed him my car radio and he's offering me 200 euros for it; **elle nous a offert sa maison pour l'été** she offered us her house for the summer; **on lui a offert une place de mécanicien** he was offered a job as a mechanic; **o. de faire qch** to offer to do sth

4 *(présenter → spectacle, vue)* to offer, to present; **elle offre l'image du plus profond désespoir** she seems to be in deep despair; **la conversation n'offrait qu'un intérêt limité** the conversation was of only limited interest; **cette solution offre l'avantage d'être équitable** this solution has *or* presents the advantage of being fair; **le sommet offre un panorama de toute beauté** the summit offers *or* affords the most stupendous views; **le vieil homme/le jardin dévasté offrait un piteux spectacle** the old man/the ruined garden was a pathetic sight; **l'histoire en offre plusieurs exemples** history gives *or Sout* affords several examples of it; **o. une résistance acharnée** to put up stiff *or* fierce resistance

USAGE ABSOLU pourriez-vous me faire un paquet-cadeau, c'est pour o. could you gift-wrap it for me, please, it's a present; **c'est pour o.?** shall I gift-wrap it for you?; **c'est moi qui offre** I'll pay; **o. à déjeuner à qn** to offer sb lunch

▸**s'offrir VPR 1** *(sexuellement)* to offer *or* to give oneself; **s'o. aux regards** *(personne)* to expose oneself to the public gaze

2 *(proposer ses services)* to offer one's services; **s'o. comme guide** to offer to act as a guide, to offer oneself *or* one's services as a guide; **il s'est offert pour un emploi de manutentionnaire** he applied for a job as a packer; **s'o. à payer les dégâts** to offer to pay for the damage; **l'article s'offre à orienter le lecteur dans le marché de la hi-fi** the article aims to help the reader find his way in the world of hi-fi

3 *(emploi réciproque)* to give *or* to buy each other; **à Noël, on s'offre des cadeaux** at Christmas, people give each other presents

4 *(se présenter → occasion)* **un seul moyen s'offrait à moi** there was only one course of action open to me; **plein d'enthousiasme pour la journée qui s'offrait à lui** full of enthusiasm for the day that lay ahead of him; **un panorama exceptionnel s'offre au regard** an amazing view meets your eyes

5 *(se faire cadeau de)* to treat oneself to; **s'o. le luxe de manger du caviar** to indulge in the luxury of eating caviar; **et si on s'offrait à boire?** shall we have a drink?; **tu ne peux vraiment pas t'o. une soirée au cinéma?** can you really not afford a night out at the cinema?; **je ne peux pas m'o. une secrétaire** I can't afford (the luxury of) a secretary

offset [ɔfsɛt] *Typ* **ADJ INV** offset
NM INV offset (process)
NF INV offset (printing) machine

offsetiste [ɔfsetist] **NMF** *Typ* lithographic printer

off-shore, offshore [ɔfʃɔr] **ADJ INV** *Banque, Pétr & Sport* offshore; **bateau o.** speedboat, powerboat; **course o.** speedboat *or* powerboat race
NM INV 1 *Pétr* offshore technology **2** *Sport (activité)* powerboat racing; *(bateau)* powerboat; **faire du o.** to go powerboat racing

offusquer [3] [ɔfyske] **VT** to offend, to upset, to hurt
▸**s'offusquer VPR s'o. de** to take offence at, to take umbrage at; **s'o. d'un rien** to be easily offended, to be quick to take offence

oflag [ɔflag] **NM** *Hist* oflag

OFPRA [ɔfpra] **NM** *(abrév* **Office français de protection des réfugiés et des apatrides**) = government department dealing with refugees and stateless persons

ogham [ɔgam] **NM** ogham alphabet

oghamique [ɔgamik] **ADJ** oghamic

ogival, -e, -aux, -ales [ɔʒival, -o] **ADJ** *(structure)* ogive *(avant n)*, ogival; *(art, style)* gothic

ogive [ɔʒiv] **NF 1** *Archit* ogive, diagonal rib **2** *Mil & Nucl* warhead; *(d'une roquette)* nose cone; **o. nucléaire** nuclear warhead **3** *Géom* ogive

OGM [oʒeɛm] **NM** *(abrév* **organisme génétiquement modifié**) GMO

Ogooué [ɔgue] **NM** *Géog* Ogooué, Ogowe

ogre, -esse [ɔgr, ɔgrɛs] **NM,F 1** *(dans les contes)* ogre, *f* ogress **2** *Fam Fig* ogre, *f* ogress, monster

oh [o] **EXCLAM 1** *(pour indiquer → la surprise, l'admiration, l'indignation)* oh!; **oh là là!** my goodness!; **oh là là, qu'est-ce qu'il fait chaud!** my goodness, it's hot!; **oh là là, qu'est-ce qu'on va faire?** oh dear, what are we going to do?; **oh, quelle horreur!** oh, how awful!; **oh oh, est-ce que j'aurais deviné juste?** oho, could I be right?
2 *(pour interpeller)* hey!; **oh là, qu'est-ce que tu fais?** hey, what are you doing?
NM INV ooh!, oh!; **pousser des oh et des ah devant qch** to ooh and aah at sth

ohé [ɔe] **EXCLAM** hey!; **o.! vous, là-bas** hey, you over there!

Ohio [ɔajo] **NM** *Géog* **l'O.** Ohio; **dans l'O.** in Ohio

ohm [om] **NM** *Élec* ohm

ohmique [omik] **ADJ** *Élec* ohmic

ohmmètre [ommɛtr] **NM** *Élec* ohmmeter

OHQ [oaʃky] **NM** *(abrév* **ouvrier hautement qualifié**) skilled worker

OICS [oisɛs] **NM** *(abrév* **Organe international de contrôle des stupéfiants**) **l'O.** the INCB

oïdium [ɔidjɔm] **NM** *Bot* oidium

oie [wa] **NF 1** *Orn* goose; **o. à bec court** pink footed goose; **o. bleue** blue goose; **o. cendrée** greylag goose; **o. d'Égypte** Egyptian goose; **o. des moissons** bean goose; **o. des neiges** snow goose; **o. rieuse** white-fronted goose; **o. de Ross** Ross's goose
2 *(jeu)* **jeu de l'o.** ≃ snakes and ladders
3 *Mil* **pas de l'o.** goosestep; **défiler** *ou* **marcher au pas de l'o.** to goosestep
4 *Péj (personne)* silly goose; **c'est une o. blanche** she's (wide-eyed and) innocent

oigne [waɲ] **NM** *Vulg Br* arsehole, *Am* asshole; **l'avoir dans l'o.** to have been shafted *or* screwed

oignon [ɔɲɔ̃] **NM 1** *Culin* onion; **soupe à l'o.** onion soup; **o. blanc** spring onion; **petits oignons** baby onions; *Fam* **un week-end aux petits oignons** a great *or* first-rate weekend; *Fam* **soigner qn aux petits oignons** to look after sb really well▪; *Fam* **être soigné aux petits oignons** to get the VIP treatment; *Fam* **c'est pas tes oignons!** it's none of your business!; *Fam* **mêle-toi** *ou* **occupe-toi de tes oignons** mind your own business
2 *Hort (bulbe)* bulb; **oignons à fleurs** flowering bulbs
3 *Méd* bunion
4 *(montre)* fob watch, turnip watch
5 *Vulg (anus) Br* arsehole, *Am* asshole; **l'avoir dans l'o.** to have been shafted *or* screwed

oignonade [ɔɲɔnad] **NF** onion stew

oignonière [ɔɲɔnjɛr] **NF** onion bed

oïl [ɔjl] *voir* **langue**

oilpé [walpe] **à oilpé ADV** *Fam (verlan de* **à poil**) stark naked, in the buff, *Br* starkers

oindre [82] [wɛ̃dr] **VT 1** *(enduire)* to rub with oil **2** *Rel* to anoint

oing, oint[1] [wɛ̃] **NM** *Vieilli* grease, lard; **vieux o.** cart grease

oint[2], **-e** [wɛ̃, wɛ̃t] **ADJ** anointed
NM l'o. du Seigneur the Lord's anointed

OIRT [oiɛrte] **NF** *Anciennement (abrév* **organisation internationale de radio-télévision**) = broadcasting organization of Eastern European countries merged in 1993 with the European Broadcasting Union

Oise [waz] **NF 1** *(rivière)* **l'O.** the (River) Oise **2** *(département)* **l'O.** Oise

oiseau, -x [wazo] **NM 1** *Orn* bird; **o. de bas/haut vol** short-winged/long-winged hawk; **o. marin** *ou* **de mer** seabird; **o. migrateur** migratory bird; **o. nocturne** *ou* **de nuit** night bird; **o. de paradis** bird of paradise; **o. de proie** bird of prey; **o. de volière** aviary bird, cage bird; **o. des îles** tropical bird; *Fig* exotic creature; *Fig* **o. de mauvais augure** *ou* **de malheur** bird of ill omen; **o. de passage** bird of passage; *Fig* **ce n'était qu'un o. de passage** he was just a ship that passed in the night; *Fig* **il est parfait pour cet emploi, tu as vraiment déniché l'o. rare** he's perfect for this job, you've found a rare bird there; **elle cherche l'o. rare** *(comme époux)* she's looking for the ideal man; *(comme employé)* she's looking for the ideal employee; **être comme l'o. sur la branche** to be in a very precarious situation; **le petit o. va sortir!** *(photo)* watch the birdie!; *Prov* **petit à petit, l'o. fait son nid** slow and steady wins the race
2 *Fam (individu douteux)* customer; **c'est un drôle d'o.** *ou* **un vilain o.** he's an odd character he's a funny old bird; **quand la police arriva, l'o. s'était envolé** by the time the police arrived the bird had flown
3 *Constr (auge de maçon)* hod
4 *Can Golf* birdie

'Les Oiseaux' *du Maurier, Hitchcock* 'The Birds'

'L'Oiseau de feu' *Stravinski* 'The Firebird'

oiseau-cloche [wazoklɔʃ] *(pl* **oiseaux-cloches**) **NM** *Orn* bellbird

oiseau-lyre [wazolir] *(pl* **oiseaux-lyres**) **NM** *Orn* lyrebird

oiseau-mouche [wazomuʃ] *(pl* **oiseaux-mouches**)

off–ois

NM *Orn* hummingbird; **o. patagon** giant hummingbird

oiseau-serpent [wazosɛrpɑ̃] (*pl* **oiseaux-serpents**) **NM** *Orn* snakebird

oiseau-souris [wazosuri] (*pl* **oiseaux-souris**) **NM** *Orn* mousebird

oiseau-trompette [wazotrɔ̃pɛt] (*pl* **oiseaux-trompettes**) **NM** *Orn* agami, trumpeter

oiseler [24] [wazle] **VI** to catch birds (*with a net or with bird-lime*)

oiselet [wazlɛ] **NM** *Littéraire* small bird

oiseleur [wazlœr] **NM** bird catcher

oiselier, -ère [wazəlje, -ɛr] **NM,F** bird seller

oiselle [wazɛl] **NF** *Littéraire* (*oiseau femelle*) hen bird; *Fam Fig* naive young girl■

oisellerie [wazɛlri] **NF 1** (*boutique*) bird shop **2** (*commerce*) bird selling

oiseux, -euse [wazø, -øz] **ADJ 1** (*futile*) futile; **des occupations oiseuses** futile occupations; **des rêveries oiseuses** daydreaming (*UNCOUNT*) **2** (*qui ne mène à rien*) irrelevant, pointless; (*conversation*) idle; (*explication*) unsatisfactory

oisif, -ive [wazif, -iv] **ADJ 1** (*personne, vie*) idle **2** *Jur* (*biens*) unproductive
    NM,F man of leisure, *f* woman of leisure; **les oisifs** the idle rich

oisillon [wazijɔ̃] **NM** fledgling

oisive [waziv] *voir* **oisif**

oisivement [wazivmɑ̃] **ADV** idly; **vivre o.** to live in idleness

oisiveté [wazivte] **NF** idleness; **vivre dans l'o.** to live in idleness; *Prov* **l'o. est la mère de tous les vices** the devil finds work for idle hands

oison [wazɔ̃] **NM 1** *Orn* gosling **2** *Vieilli* (*personne*) gullible *or* credulous person

OIT [oite] **NF** (*abrév* **Organisation internationale du travail**) ILO

OJD [oʒide] **NM** (*abrév* **Office de justification de la diffusion des supports de publicité**) = advertising industry watchdog

OK [ɔke] **EXCLAM** *Fam* OK, okay; **OK! pour moi c'est bon!** OK, that's fine by me!

Oka [oka] **NM** **fromage d'O.** = cheese made by Trappist monks in Canada

okapi [ɔkapi] **NM** *Zool* okapi

Oklahoma [ɔklaɔma] **NM** *Géog* **l'O.** Oklahoma; **dans l'O.** in Oklahoma

okoumé [ɔkume] **NM** *Bot* gaboon

ola [ɔla] **NF** Mexican wave; **faire la o.** to do a Mexican wave

olé [ɔle] **EXCLAM** olé!

oléacée [ɔlease] *Bot* **NF** member of the Oleaceae family
    □ **oléacées NFPL** Oleaceae

oléagineux, -euse [ɔleaʒinø, -øz] **ADJ** oil-producing, *Spéc* oleaginous; **graines oléagineuses** oilseeds
    NM oil-producing *or Spéc* oleaginous plant

oléastre [ɔleastr] **NM** *Bot* oleaster

oléate [ɔleat] **NM** *Chim* oleate

olécrane [ɔlekrɑn] **NM** *Anat* olecranon

oléfine [ɔlefin] **NF** *Chim* olefine

oléicole [ɔleikɔl] **ADJ** **industrie o.** (*de l'huile d'olive*) olive oil industry; (*de l'huile d'oléagineux*) vegetable oil industry; **terres oléicoles** (*à olives*) olive-growing area; (*à oléagineux*) oil-cropping area

oléiculteur, -trice [ɔleikyltœr, -tris] **NM,F 1** (*cultivateur*) olive grower **2** (*fabricant d'huile* → *d'olive*) olive oil manufacturer; (→ *d'autres oléagineux*) vegetable oil manufacturer

oléiculture [ɔleikyltyr] **NF** (*culture* → *des olives*) olive growing; (→ *des oléagineux*) oil-crop growing

oléifère [ɔleifɛr] **ADJ** oil-producing, *Spéc* oleiferous

oléiforme [ɔleiform] **ADJ** oil-like

oléine [ɔlein] **NF** *Chim* olein

oléique [ɔleik] **ADJ** *Chim* oleic

oléoduc [ɔleɔdyk] **NM** (oil) pipeline

olé olé [ɔleɔle] **ADJ INV** *Fam* **être un peu o.** (*de mœurs légères*) to be a bit loose; (*peu respectueux*) to be a bit too laid back; **elle est très o. depuis qu'elle a divorcé** she's been leading a pretty wild life since her divorce; **cette blague est un peu o.** that joke is a bit risqué■; **il y a quelques scènes o.** some of the scenes are a bit close to the bone *or* risqué *or Br* near the knuckle

oléomètre [ɔleɔmɛtr] **NM** oleometer

oléopneumatique [ɔleɔpnømatik] **ADJ** air/hydraulic

oléoprotéagineux, -euse [ɔleɔprɔteaʒinø, -øz] **ADJ** oilseed (*avant n*)
    NM oil-and-protein seed crop, oilseed (crop)

oléorésine [ɔleɔrezin] **NF** *Bot & Chim* oleoresin

oléum [ɔleɔm] **NM** *Chim* oleum

olfactif, -ive [ɔlfaktif, -iv] **ADJ** *Physiol* olfactory

olfaction [ɔlfaksjɔ̃] **NF** *Physiol* olfaction

olfactive [ɔlfaktiv] *voir* **olfactif**

olibrius [ɔlibrijys] **NM** *Fam Péj* oddball

olifant [ɔlifɑ̃] **NM** *Hist* oliphant

oligarchie [ɔligarʃi] **NF** oligarchy

oligarchique [ɔligarʃik] **ADJ** oligarchic, oligarchical

oligarque [ɔligark] **NM** oligarch

oligiste [ɔliʒist] *Minér* **ADJ** haematite
    NM haematite

oligocène [ɔligɔsɛn] *Géol* **ADJ** Oligocene
    NM Oligocene (period)

oligochète [ɔligɔkɛt] *Zool* **NM** oligochaete, oligochete
    □ **oligochètes NMPL** Oligochaeta

oligoclase [ɔligɔklaz] **NF** *Minér* oligoclase

oligodendrocyte [ɔligɔdɛ̃drɔsit] **NM** *Biol* oligodendrocyte

oligodendroglie [ɔligɔdɑ̃drɔgli] **NF** *Biol* oligodendroglia

oligoélément [ɔligɔelemɑ̃] **NM** trace element

oligomère [ɔligɔmɛr] *Chim* **ADJ** oligomeric
    NM oligomer

oligophrène [ɔligɔfrɛn] *Psy* **ADJ** mentally subnormal
    NMF mentally subnormal person

oligophrénie [ɔligɔfreni] **NF** *Psy* (mental) subnormality; **o. polydystrophique** Sanfilippo's syndrome

oligopole [ɔligɔpɔl] **NM** *Écon* oligopoly

oligopolistique [ɔligɔpɔlistik] **ADJ** *Écon* oligopolistic

oligopsone [ɔligɔpsɔn] **NM** *Écon* oligopsony

oligopsonique [ɔligɔpsɔnik] **ADJ** *Écon* oligopsonistic

oligosaccharide [ɔligɔsakarid] **NM** *Chim* oligosaccharide

oligothérapie [ɔligɔterapi] **NF** *Méd* oligotherapy

oligotrophe [ɔligɔtrɔf] **ADJ** *Écol* oligotrophic

oligurie [ɔligyri] **NF** *Méd* oliguria

oliphant [ɔlifɑ̃] **NM** *Hist* oliphant

olivacé, -e [ɔlivase] **ADJ** olive, olive-coloured

olivaie [ɔlive] **NF** olive grove

olivaison [ɔlivɛzɔ̃] **NF 1** (*récolte*) olive harvest **2** (*saison*) olive season

olivâtre [ɔlivatr] **ADJ** olive-greenish; (*teint*) sallow

olive [ɔliv] **NF 1** *Bot* olive; **o. noire/verte** black/green olive **2** *Élec* switch **3** *Anat* **o. bulbaire** olivary body; **o. cérébelleuse** olivary nucleus **4** *Zool* (*mollusque*) olive (shell) **5** (*bouton*) (olive-shaped) button
    ADJ INV (*couleur*) **(vert) o.** olive, olive-green
    □ **olives NFPL** *Archit* olive *or* bead moulding

oliveraie [ɔlivrɛ] **NF** olive grove

olivet [ɔlivɛ] **NM** Olivet (*cheese*)

olivétain [ɔlivetɛ̃] **NM** *Rel* Olivetan

olivette [ɔlivɛt] **NF 1** (*tomate*) plum tomato **2** (*raisin*) (olive-shaped) grape **3** (*olivaie*) olive plantation *or* grove

Olivier [ɔlivje] **NPR** (*dans la 'Chanson de Roland'*) Oliver (*Roland's companion in the 'Chanson de Roland', the epitome of the faithful friend who counterbalances the other's impetuousness*)
    □ **Oliviers** *voir* **mont**

olivier [ɔlivje] **NM 1** *Bot* olive tree **2** (*bois*) olive (wood)

olivine [ɔlivin] **NF** *Minér* olivine

ollaire [ɔllɛr] **ADJ F pierre o.** pot-stone, steatite

ollé [ɔle] = **olé**

olographe [ɔlɔgraf] **ADJ** *Jur* holograph

OLP [ɔɛlpe] **NF** (*abrév* **Organisation de libération de la Palestine**) PLO

Olympe [ɔlɛ̃p] **NM** *Géog & Myth* **l'O.** Olympus; **les dieux de l'O.** the Olympic deities, the Olympians; **le mont O.** Mount Olympus

olympe [ɔlɛ̃p] **NM** *Littéraire* Olympus

Olympia [ɔlɛ̃pja] **NM** **l'O.** = major Paris entertainment venue

olympiade [ɔlɛ̃pjad] **NF 1** (*événement*) Olympic

Games; **à la dernière o.** during the last Olympics **2** (*quatre ans*) olympiad
    □ **olympiades NFPL les olympiades** the Olympic Games

Olympie [ɔlɛ̃pi] **NF** Olympia

olympien, -enne [ɔlɛ̃pjɛ̃, -ɛn] **ADJ** *Myth & Hum* Olympian; *Fig* **un calme o.** an Olympian calm

Olympio [ɔlɛ̃pjo] **NPR** *Littérature* = Victor Hugo's poetic alter ego in some of his poetry

olympique [ɔlɛ̃pik] **ADJ** Olympic; **stade/piscine o.** Olympic stadium/pool; **les jeux Olympiques** the Olympic Games, the Olympics

olympisme [ɔlɛ̃pism] **NM 1** (*idéal*) Olympic ideal **2** (*organisation*) organization of the Olympic Games

OM [ɔɛm] **NM** *Ftbl* (*abrév* **Olympique de Marseille**) **l'OM** = the Marseilles football team

Oman [ɔman] **NM** *Géog* Oman; **le golfe d'O.** the Gulf of Oman; **le sultanat d'O.** the Sultanate of Oman; **vivre à O.** to live in Oman; **aller à O.** to go to Oman

omanais, -e [ɔmanɛ, -ɛz] **ADJ** Omani
    NM,F Omani

ombelle [ɔ̃bɛl] **NF** *Bot* umbel; **en o.** umbellate

ombellé, -e [ɔ̃bɛle] **ADJ** *Bot* umbellate, umbellated

ombellifère [ɔ̃belifɛr] *Bot* **ADJ** umbelliferous
    NF umbellifer, member of the Umbelliferae
    □ **ombellifères NFPL** Umbelliferae

ombellule [ɔ̃belyl] **NF** *Bot* umbellet, umbellule

ombilic [ɔ̃bilik] **NM 1** *Anat* navel, *Spéc* umbilicus **2** *Bot* (*renflement*) hilum; (*plante*) navelwort **3** *Math* umbilical point **4** *Beaux-Arts* boss, embossment

ombilical, -e, -aux, -ales [ɔ̃bilikal, -o] **ADJ 1** *Anat* umbilical **2** *Astron* **mât o.** umbilical cord

ombiliqué, -e [ɔ̃bilike] **ADJ** umbilicate, umbilicated

omble [ɔ̃bl] **NM** *Ich* **o. (chevalier)** char

ombrage [ɔ̃braʒ] **NM 1** (*ombre*) shade; **ces arbres donnent** *ou* **font un o. agréable à la terrasse** these trees pleasantly shade the terrace **2** (*feuillage*) canopy, foliage **3** *Littéraire* **prendre o. de qch** to take offence *or* umbrage at sth; **porter** *ou* **faire o. à qn** to cause offence to sb, to offend sb **4** *Ordinat* shading

ombragé, -e [ɔ̃braʒe] **ADJ** shady

ombrager [17] [ɔ̃braʒe] **VT 1** to shade **2** *Fig Littéraire* to overshadow

ombrageux, -euse [ɔ̃braʒø, -øz] **ADJ 1** (*susceptible*) touchy, easily offended **2** (*cheval*) skittish, nervous, jumpy

ombre[1] [ɔ̃br] **NM** *Ich* grayling

ombre[2] [ɔ̃br] **NF 1** (*pénombre*) shade; **projeter une o.** to cast a shadow; **dans l'o. des sous-bois** in the shadowy undergrowth; **le gratte-ciel fait de l'o. à tout le quartier** the skyscraper casts a shadow over the whole area *or* leaves the whole area in shadow; **faire de l'o. à qn** to be in sb's light; *Fig* to be in sb's way; **sortir de l'o.** to emerge from the dark *or* darkness *or* shadows; *Fig* (*artiste*) to emerge from obscurity, to come into the public eye; *Fig* **jeter une o. sur la fête** to cast a shadow *or* a gloom over the festivities
    2 (*forme* → *d'une personne, d'un arbre, d'un mur*) shadow; **j'aperçois une o. dans le jardin** I can see a (vague) shadow *or* shadowy shape in the garden; *Hum* **avoir peur de son o.** to be afraid of one's own shadow; **il n'est plus que l'o. de lui-même** he's a shadow of his former self; **avec l'adolescence, une o. est apparue sur sa lèvre supérieure** in adolescence, a thin shadow appeared on his upper lip; *Opt* **o. portée** (projected) shadow; **o. propre** shadow
    3 (*trace* → *de jalousie, de surprise*) hint; (→ *d'un sourire*) hint, shadow; **pas l'o. d'un remords/d'une preuve** not a trace of remorse/shred of evidence; **pas l'o. d'un reproche** not the slightest hint of blame; **sans l'o. d'un doute** without a shadow of a doubt; **cela ne fait pas** *ou* **il n'y a pas l'o. d'un doute** there's not a shadow of a doubt; **il n'a pas l'o. d'un scrupule!** she's totally unscrupulous *or* without scruples!
    4 *Beaux-Arts* shade, shadow; *Fig* **il y a une o. au tableau** there's a fly in the ointment
    5 (*obscurité*) darkness; *Fig* (*anonymat*) obscurity; **ils disparurent dans l'o. de la nuit** they were swallowed up by the darkness; **leurs agissements délictueux se faisaient dans l'o. de la**

nuit their criminal schemes were carried out under cover of darkness

6 *Astron* umbra

▫ **ombres** NFPL **1** *Théât* **ombres chinoises** shadow play; **théâtre d'ombres** shadow theatre; **leurs profils se projetaient sur le mur en ombres chinoises** their profiles were silhouetted on the wall

2 *Antiq* shadows, departed souls; **le royaume des ombres** the netherworld

▫ **à l'ombre** ADV **1** *(à l'abri du soleil)* in the shade; **il fait 30°C à l'o.** it's 30°C in the shade; *Fam* **marche à l'o.!** *(conseil)* keep a low profile!; *(menace)* stay out of my sight!

2 *Fam (en prison)* inside; **mettre qn/être à l'o.** to put sb/to be behind bars *or* inside

▫ **à l'ombre de** PRÉP in the shade of; *Fig Littéraire* under the protection of; **à l'o. des lois** protected by the law; *Fig* **elle a grandi à l'o. de la Tour Eiffel** she grew up in the shadow of *or* within a stone's throw of the Eiffel Tower

▫ **dans l'ombre** ADV **1** *(dans la pénombre)* in the shade; **le jardin/balcon est dans l'o.** the garden/balcony is in the shade

2 *Fig (dans le secret)* **elle a préféré vivre dans l'o.** she chose a life of obscurity; **rester dans l'o.** *(raison)* to remain obscure *or* unclear; *(personne)* to remain unknown; **laisser qch dans l'o.** to keep sth dark; **l'enquête n'a rien laissé dans l'o.** the enquiry left no stone unturned; **travailler dans l'o.** to work behind the scenes; **ceux qui œuvrent dans l'o. pour la paix** those who work behind the scenes to bring about peace; **vivre dans l'o. de qn** to live in sb's shadow

▫ **ombre à paupières** NF eyeshadow

📖

'À l'ombre des jeunes filles en fleur' *Proust* 'Within a Budding Grove'

Allusion

Tirer plus vite que son ombre

This expression comes from the Belgian comic strip character Lucky Luke. Lucky Luke is a cowboy with amazing shooting skills, so much so that he is said to be able to shoot faster than his own shadow ("Il tire plus vite que son ombre"). The phrase can be used when referring to people or things that possess amazing speed, for example **Alonso, l'homme qui conduit plus vite que son ombre** ("Alonso, the man who drives faster than the speed of light"), or when commenting on the fact that people are wasting no time in doing something, such as **le nouveau gouvernement privatise plus vite que son ombre** ("The new government is privatizing things like there's no tomorrow").

---

ombre[3] [ɔ̃br] NF terre d'o. umber

ombré [ɔ̃bre] NM *Ordinat* shading

ombrée [ɔ̃bre] NF ubac

ombrelle [ɔ̃brɛl] NF **1** *(parasol)* parasol **2** *(d'une méduse)* umbrella

ombrer [3] [ɔ̃bre] VT **1** *Beaux-Arts* to shade; **o. un sujet pour le faire ressortir/pour l'intégrer dans l'arrière-plan** to shade out/in a subject **2** *Littéraire (faire de l'ombre à →* sujet: arbre, store*)* to shade; **un grand chapeau ombrait son visage** a large hat shaded his/her face **3** *(assombrir →* sujet: couleur*)* to darken, to shade; **un maquillage violet ombrait ses paupières** he/she was wearing purple eyeshadow

ombrette [ɔ̃brɛt] NF *Orn* umbre, umbrette

ombreux, -euse [ɔ̃brø, -øz] ADJ *Littéraire* shady

Ombrie [ɔ̃bri] NF l'O. Umbria

ombrien, -enne [ɔ̃brijɛ̃, -ɛn] ADJ Umbrian

▫ **Ombrien, -enne** NM,F Umbrian

ombrine [ɔ̃brin] NF *Ich* umbrina

ombudsman [ɔmbydsman] NM ombudsman

OMC [ɔɛmse] NF *(abrév* **Organisation mondiale du commerce)** WTO

OMCI [ɔɛmsei] NF *(abrév* **Organisation de la navigation maritime consultative et intergouvernementale)** IMCO

oméga [ɔmega] NM INV omega

omelette [ɔmlɛt] NF omelette; **o. aux champignons/au fromage/au jambon** mushroom/cheese/ham omelette; **o. aux fines herbes**

omelette with herbs, omelette (aux) fines herbes; **une o. baveuse** a runny omelette; **o. norvégienne** *ou* **surprise** baked Alaska; **o. soufflée** soufflé omelette; *Prov* **on ne fait pas d'o. sans casser des œufs** you can't make an omelette without breaking eggs

omerta [ɔmɛrta] NF code of silence

omettre [84] [ɔmɛtr] VT to omit, to leave out; **sans o. un seul détail** without leaving out a single detail; **n'omets personne sur ta liste** don't miss anyone off your list; **o. de faire qch** to fail *or* to neglect *or* to omit to do sth; **ils ont omis de nous informer** they failed *or* neglected to inform us

OMI [ɔɛmi] NF *(abrév* **Organisation maritime internationale)** IMO

omicron [ɔmikrɔn] NM INV omicron

omis, -e [ɔmi, -iz] PP *voir* omettre

omission [ɔmisjɔ̃] NF **1** *(oubli)* omission; *(oubli)* oversight; **l'o. d'un mot** leaving out *or* omitting a word; **j'ai relevé plusieurs omissions dans la liste** I noticed that several things are missing *or* have been omitted from the list; **péché/mensonge par o.** sin/lie of omission; **pécher/mentir par o.** to sin/lie by omission **2** *Rel* omission **3** *Jur* **o. de porter secours** failure to assist a person in danger

omit *etc voir* **omettre**

OMM [ɔɛmɛm] NF *(abrév* **Organisation météorologique mondiale)** WMO

ommatidie [ɔmatidi] NF *Zool* ommatidium

omnibus [ɔmnibys] NM **1** *Rail Br* slow *or* stopping train, *Am* local (train) **2** *Arch (à chevaux)* horse-drawn omnibus **3** *Arch (bus)* omnibus

ADJ INV **le train est o. entre Melun et Sens** the train calls at all stations between Melun and Sens

omnicolore [ɔmnikɔlɔr] ADJ of all colours

omnidirectif, -ive [ɔmnidirɛktif, -iv] ADJ omnidirectional

omnidirectionnel, -elle [ɔmnidirɛksjɔnɛl] ADJ omnidirectional

omnidirective [ɔmnidirɛktiv] *voir* **omnidirectif**

omnipotence [ɔmnipɔtɑ̃s] NF omnipotence; **l'o. de l'État** the omnipotence of the state

omnipotent, -e [ɔmnipɔtɑ̃, -ɑ̃t] ADJ omnipotent

omnipraticien, -enne [ɔmnipratisjɛ̃, -ɛn] ADJ **médecin o.** general practitioner

NM,F general practitioner

omniprésence [ɔmniprezɑ̃s] NF omnipresence

omniprésent, -e [ɔmniprezɑ̃, -ɑ̃t] ADJ *(souci, souvenir)* omnipresent; *(publicité, pollution)* ubiquitous; **il est o. dans l'usine** he's everywhere (at once) in the factory

omniscience [ɔmnisjɑ̃s] NF omniscience

omniscient, -e [ɔmnisjɑ̃, -ɑ̃t] ADJ omniscient

omnisports [ɔmnispɔr] ADJ INV **rencontre o.** all-round sports event; **salle o.** sports centre; **terrain o.** sports field

omnium[1] [ɔmnjɔm] NM *Vieilli* **1** *Écon* combine; *Bourse* **o. de valeurs** = investment trust **2** *Sport* open; *Courses de chevaux* open handicap

omnium[2] [ɔmnjɔm] NF *Belg Assur* comprehensive insurance

omnivore [ɔmnivɔr] ADJ omnivorous

NM omnivore

omoplate [ɔmɔplat] NF *Anat* shoulder blade, *Spéc* scapula; **il lui avait pointé un fusil entre les omoplates** he'd shoved a gun in his/her back

OMPI [ɔɛmpei] NF *(abrév* **organisation mondiale de la propriété intellectuelle)** WIPO

OMS [ɔɛmɛs] NF *(abrév* **Organisation mondiale de la santé)** WHO

on [ɔ̃]

---

on may be preceded by the article **l'** in formal contexts.

PRON INDÉFINI **1** *(indéterminé)* you, people, *Sout* one; **on lui a retiré son passeport** they took his/her passport away (from him/her), his/her passport was confiscated; **on construit une nouvelle école** a new school is being built; **il y a dix ans, on ne connaissait pas cette maladie** this illness was unknown ten years ago; **on vit de plus en plus vieux en Europe** people in Europe are living longer and longer; **partout où l'on trouve de ces fossiles** wherever these fossils are found

2 *(avec une valeur généralisante)* you, *Sout* one; **souvent, on n'a pas le choix** often you don't

have any choice, often there's no choice; **on n'a pas le droit de fumer ici** you can't smoke in here; **on n'arrive pas à dormir avec cette chaleur** it's impossible to sleep in this heat; **on ne peut prédire la suite des événements** you *or* *Sout* one can't predict the outcome of events; **on ne sait jamais (ce qui peut arriver)** you never know *or* *Sout* one never knows (what could happen); **on n'en sait rien** nobody knows anything about it; **on dirait qu'il va pleuvoir** it looks like rain; **on ne croirait pas qu'il est malade** you wouldn't think he was ill; **on parlait très peu au déjeuner** we didn't talk much over lunch; **on était le sept mars** it was the seventh of March

3 *(les gens)* people, they; **on jasait** people were talking, there was a lot of talk; **on s'était rué sur les derniers billets** there'd been a rush for the last tickets; **on dit que la vie là-bas n'est pas chère** they say that the cost of living over there is cheap; **on dit qu'elle est folle** it's said *or* they say *or* people say that she's mad, she's said to be mad; **on rapporte que...** it is said that...

4 *(désignant un nombre indéterminé de personnes)* they; **en Espagne, on dîne plus tard** in Spain they eat later; **dans ce bureau, on se moque de vos problèmes** they don't care about your problems in this department; **on m'a dit que vous partiez bientôt** I've been told you're leaving soon; **qu'est-ce qu'on en dit chez toi?** what do your folks have to say about it?, what do they have to say about it at your place?

5 *(quelqu'un)* **on frappe à la porte** someone's *or* somebody's (knocking) at the door, there's a knock at the door; **on sonne** there's the (door)bell, there's someone *or* somebody at the door; **on vous a appelé ce matin** somebody called you *or* there was a (phone) call for you this morning; **on m'a volé mon sac** my bag has been stolen, someone's stolen my bag; **est-ce qu'on t'a vu?** did anyone see you?; **est-ce qu'on vous sert, Monsieur?** are you being served, sir?; **est-ce qu'on pourrait me servir, s'il vous plaît?** could somebody serve me, please?

6 *Fam (nous)* we; **on n'a pas grand-chose à dire** we don't have much to say to one another; **nous, on en a marre, on s'en va** we've had enough of this, we're off; **allez viens, on va bien s'amuser** go on, come with us, it'll be great fun; **on était très déçus** we were very disappointed; **on ne s'était jamais séparés** we had never been separated; **on est dix en tout** there are ten of us in all; **on est allés au cinéma avec les parents** we went to the *Br* cinema *or* *Am* movies with our parents

7 *(se substituant à d'autres pronoms personnels)* **dans ce premier chapitre, on a voulu montrer...** in this first chapter, the aim has been to show...; *Fam* **ça va, on a compris!** all right, I've got the message!; *Fam* **il faut qu'on vous le répète?** do I have to repeat myself?; *Fam* **on est bien habillé, aujourd'hui!** we are dressed up today, aren't we?; *Fam* **alors, on ne répond pas au téléphone?** aren't you going to answer the phone?; *Fam* **on croit tout savoir, hein?** (you) think you know everything *or* it all, don't you?; *Fam* **alors les gars, on cherche la bagarre?** are you guys looking for a fight?; **alors, on s'en va comme ça?** are you really leaving just like that?; *Fam* **on a tout ce qu'il faut et on passe son temps à se plaindre!** he/she has got everything and he/she still complains all the time!

8 *(dans des annonces)* **on cherche un vendeur** salesman wanted *or* required; **ici on parle allemand** *(à l'entrée d'un magasin, d'un restaurant, d'un hôtel)* German spoken (here); **on est prié de laisser sa clé à la réception** keys must be left at reception

onagracée [ɔnagrase] *Bot* NF member of the Oenothera

▫ **onagracées** NFPL Oenothera

onagre[1] [ɔnagr] NF *Bot* evening primrose, oenothera

onagre[2] [ɔnagr] NM *Mil & Zool* onager

onanisme [ɔnanism] NM onanism

onc [ɔ̃k] = **oncques**

once¹ [ɔ̃s] NF *(mesure)* ounce; **il n'a pas une o. de bon sens** he doesn't have an ounce of common sense

once² [ɔ̃s] NF *Zool* ounce, snow leopard

onchocercose [ɔ̃kɔsɛrkoz] NF *Méd* onchocerciasis, onchocercosis

oncial, -e, -aux, -ales [ɔ̃sjal, -o] ADJ uncial
□ **onciale** NF uncial characters

oncle [ɔ̃kl] NM uncle; **l'o. Picsou** Scrooge *(in Donald Duck cartoons)*; **o. d'Amérique** rich uncle; **l'O. Sam** Uncle Sam

oncogène [ɔ̃kɔʒɛn] ADJ *Méd* oncogenic

oncogenèse [ɔ̃kɔʒenɛz] NF *Méd* oncogenesis

oncologie [ɔ̃kɔlɔʒi] NF *Méd* oncology

oncologiste [ɔ̃kɔlɔʒist], **oncologue** [ɔ̃kɔlɔg] NMF *Méd* oncologist

oncotique [ɔ̃kɔtik] ADJ *Méd & Physiol* oncotic

oncques [ɔ̃k] ADV *Arch ou Hum* never; **o. ne vit plus remarquable triomphe!** never had there been such an outstanding triumph!

onction [ɔ̃ksjɔ̃] NF 1 *Méd* unction 2 *Littéraire (douceur → attendrissante)* sweetness, gentleness; *Péj (→ hypocrite)* unctuousness, unctuosity 3 *Rel* unction

onctueuse [ɔ̃ktɥøz] *voir* **onctueux**

onctueusement [ɔ̃ktɥøzmɑ̃] ADV smoothly, *Sout* unctuously

onctueux, -euse [ɔ̃ktɥø, -øz] ADJ 1 *(huileux)* smooth, *Sout* unctuous 2 *Culin* creamy; **un fromage o.** a creamy cheese 3 *Littéraire (personne)* smooth, unctuous

onctuosité [ɔ̃ktɥozite] NF 1 *(d'un dessert)* creaminess; *(d'une crème)* smoothness 2 *Tech* lubricating quality, lubricity

ondatra [ɔ̃datra] NM *Zool* muskrat, *Spéc* ondatra

onde [ɔ̃d] NF 1 *Phys* wave; **o. cérébrale** brainwave; **o. de choc** shock wave; **ondes courtes** short wave; **sur ondes courtes** on short wave; **ondes entretenues** continuous waves; **ondes hertziennes** Hertzian waves; **ondes longues, grandes ondes** long wave; **sur grandes ondes** on long wave; **o. lumineuse** light wave; **ondes moyennes** medium wave; **sur ondes moyennes** on medium wave; **o. porteuse** carrier wave; **o. radio(électrique)** radio wave; **ondes très courtes** very high frequency; **ondes ultra-courtes** ultra high frequency; **l'o. verte** device which sets all traffic lights along a one-way system to green if drivers keep to the speed limit indicated; *Fam Fig* **nous ne sommes pas sur la même longueur d'o.** we're not on the same wavelength

2 *Fig (vague)* wave; **une o. de bonheur l'envahit** a wave of happiness washed over him/her 3 *Littéraire* **l'o.** *(l'eau)* the waters, the deep; **l'o. limpide du ruisseau** the clear waters of the stream

4 *Métal* corrugation

□ **ondes** NFPL *Rad* **mettre en ondes** to produce; **sur les ondes** on the air; **passer sur les ondes** *(sujet: émission)* to be broadcast; *(sujet: personne)* to be on air *or* radio

ondé, -e¹ [ɔ̃de] ADJ *Littéraire (cheveux)* wavy; *(soie)* watered

ondée² [ɔ̃de] NF shower *(of rain)*; **temps à ondées** showery weather; *Littéraire* **une brusque o. de tristesse** a sudden pang of sadness

ondemètre [ɔ̃dmɛtr] NM wavemeter

ondin, -e [ɔ̃dɛ̃, -in] NM,F *Myth* water sprite, undine

on-dit [ɔ̃di] NM INV **je ne me soucie guère des o.** I don't care about what people say; **fonder son opinion sur des o.** to base one's opinion on hearsay; **ce ne sont que des o.** it's only hearsay

ondoie *etc voir* **ondoyer**

ondoiement [ɔ̃dwamɑ̃] NM 1 *Littéraire (du blé, des cheveux)* undulation, swaying motion; *(d'un ruisseau)* undulation 2 *Rel* summary baptism

ondoyant, -e [ɔ̃dwajɑ̃, -ɑ̃t] ADJ *Littéraire* 1 *(blé)* undulating, rippling; *(flamme)* dancing, wavering; *(lumière, ruisseau, reflet)* rippling; *(cheveux)* wavy; *(foule, mouvement)* swaying 2 *(personne)* changeable

ondoyer [13] [ɔ̃dwaje] VI *(champ de blé)* to undulate, to ripple; *(flamme)* to dance, to waver; *(lumière, ruisseau, reflet)* to ripple; *(surface de l'eau)* to undulate; *(drapeau)* to wave

VT *Rel* to baptize summarily

ondulant, -e [ɔ̃dylɑ̃, -ɑ̃t] ADJ 1 *(terrain)* undulating; *(route, rivière)* twisting (and turning),

winding; *(chevelure)* flowing; *(façon de marcher)* swaying; **avoir une démarche ondulante** to swing one's hips 2 *Méd (pouls)* irregular

ondulation [ɔ̃dylasjɔ̃] NF 1 *(de l'eau, du terrain)* undulation; **les ondulations de la plaine** the rolling *or* undulating plain

2 *(du corps)* undulation, swaying *(UNCOUNT)*; **les ondulations de la danseuse** the undulations *or* the swaying of the dancer

3 *(des cheveux)* wave; **les ondulations de sa chevelure** his/her wavy hair

4 *Littéraire (d'une ligne, d'une mélodie)* undulation

5 *Électron* ripple

6 *(en travaux publics)* corrugation

7 *TV* **o. de l'image** picture weave

ondulatoire [ɔ̃dylatwar] ADJ 1 *(forme)* undulatory 2 *Phys (mouvement)* undulatory, wave *(avant n)*

ondulé, -e [ɔ̃dyle] ADJ *(sol)* undulating; *(cheveux)* wavy; *(tôle, carton)* corrugated; **route ondulée** switchback road; **trait o.** wavy line

onduler [3] [ɔ̃dyle] VI 1 *(eau, vagues, champs)* to ripple, to undulate; **la foule ondulait sur la place** in the square, the crowd was swaying 2 *(cheveux)* to be wavy 3 *(personne)* to sway; **la danseuse ondulait des hanches** the dancer swayed her hips

VT 1 *Tech (métal, carton)* to corrugate 2 *(friser)* **se faire o. les cheveux** to have one's hair waved *or* permed

onduleur [ɔ̃dylœr] NM *Élec* inverter; *Ordinat* uninterruptible power supply, UPS

onduleux, -euse [ɔ̃dylø, -øz] ADJ *Littéraire* 1 *(houleux → flots)* swelling 2 *(souple)* undulating; **elle avait une démarche onduleuse** her body swayed as she walked 3 *(paysage)* undulating, rolling; *(sentier, rivière)* twisting, winding

one-man-show [wanmanʃo] NM INV one-man show, solo act

onéreux, -euse [ɔnerø, -øz] ADJ costly, expensive; **à titre o.** subject to payment

one-step [wanstɛp] *(pl* **one-steps***)* NM *Anciennement (danse)* one-step

ONF [ɔɛnɛf] NM *(abrév* **Office national des forêts***)* the French Forestry commission, *Br* ≃ the Forestry Commission, *Am* ≃ the Forestry Service

ONG [ɔɛnʒe] NF *(abrév* **organisation non gouvernementale***)* NGO

ongle [ɔ̃gl] NM 1 *Anat (des doigts de la main)* nail, fingernail; *(des orteils)* toenail; **se faire les ongles** *(les couper)* to cut one's nails; *(les vernir)* to do *or* to paint one's nails; *Fig* **connaître** *ou* **savoir qch sur le bout des ongles** to know sth perfectly; **il est français jusqu'au bout des ongles** he's French to his fingertips, he's every inch a Frenchman; *Fig* **avoir les ongles crochus** to be mean; *Fam* **avoir les ongles en deuil** to have dirty nails▪

2 *Zool* claw; *(de rapace)* talon

□ **à ongles** ADJ *(ciseaux, lime, vernis)* nail *(avant n)*

onglé, -e¹ [ɔ̃gle] ADJ *Littéraire* clawed; *(rapace)* taloned

onglée² [ɔ̃gle] NF **j'avais l'o.** the tips of my fingers were numb with cold

onglet [ɔ̃glɛ] NM 1 *(entaille)* thumb index; *(d'un canif)* thumbnail groove, nail nick; **o. à fenêtre** *(d'une fiche)* window tab

2 *Constr* mitred angle; **tailler à** *ou* **en o.** to mitre; **assemblage en o.** mitre joint

3 *Typ (béquet)* tab; *(d'un livre)* guard, stub; **onglets (de remplissage)** (filling-in) guards; **dictionnaire à onglets** thumb-indexed dictionary

4 *Bot* claw, *Spéc* unguis

5 *Math* ungula

6 *Méd* pterygium

7 *Culin* flank; **o. à l'échalote** = long, narrow steak served fried with chopped shallots

onglette [ɔ̃glɛt] NF scorper, graver

onglier [ɔ̃glije] NM 1 *(nécessaire)* manicure set 2 *(ciseaux)* (nail) scissors

onglon [ɔ̃glɔ̃] NM toenail, *Spéc* unguis

onguent [ɔ̃gɑ̃] NM ointment, salve

onguicule [ɔ̃gikyl] NM *Zool (ongle)* small nail; *(griffe)* small claw

onguiculé, -e [ɔ̃gikyle] ADJ *Zool & Bot* unguiculate, unguiculated
NM *Zool* unguiculate
□ **onguiculés** NMPL *Zool* Unguiculata

ongulé, -e [ɔ̃gyle] *Zool* ADJ hoofed, *Spéc* ungulate
NM ungulate
□ **ongulés** NMPL Ungulates

onguligrade [ɔ̃gyligrad] ADJ unguligrade

onirique [ɔnirik] ADJ 1 *Psy* oneiric 2 *Fig* **une vision o.** a dreamlike vision

onirisme [ɔnirism] NM 1 *Psy* hallucinations 2 *Fig* **des dessins à l'o. troublant** drawings with a disturbing dreamlike quality

onirologie [ɔnirɔlɔʒi] NF interpretation of dreams

oniromancie [ɔnirɔmɑ̃si] NF oneiromancy

oniromancien, -enne [ɔnirɔmɑ̃sjɛ̃, -ɛn] ADJ oneiromantic
NM,F oneiromancer

onirothérapie [ɔnirɔterapi] NF *Psy* oneirotherapy

ONISEP [ɔnizɛp] NM *(abrév* **Office national d'information sur les enseignements et les professions***)* = national careers guidance service

ONN [ɔɛnɛn] NM *(abrév* **Office national de la navigation***)* French national shipping and inland waterways office

O-N-O *(abrév écrite* **Ouest-Nord-Ouest***)* WNW

onomasiologie [ɔnɔmazjɔlɔʒi] NF *Ling* onomasiology

onomastique [ɔnɔmastik] *Ling* ADJ onomastic
NF onomastics *(singulier)*

onomatopée [ɔnɔmatɔpe] NF onomatopoeia

onomatopéique [ɔnɔmatɔpeik] ADJ onomatopoeic

onques [ɔ̃k] = **oncques**

on-shore, onshore [ɔnʃɔr] ADJ *Fin (fonds, investissements, société)* onshore

ont [ɔ̃] *voir* **avoir²**

Ontario [ɔ̃tarjo] NM **l'O.** Ontario; **le lac O.** Lake Ontario

ontique [ɔ̃tik] ADJ *Phil* ontal

ontogenèse [ɔ̃tɔʒənɛz] NF *Biol* ontogenesis, ontogeny

ontogénétique [ɔ̃tɔʒenetik] ADJ *Biol* ontogenetic, ontogenic

ontogénie [ɔ̃tɔʒeni] NF *Biol* ontogenesis, ontogeny

ontologie [ɔ̃tɔlɔʒi] NF *Phil* ontology

ontologique [ɔ̃tɔlɔʒik] ADJ *Phil* ontological

ontologisme [ɔ̃tɔlɔʒism] NM *Phil* ontologism

ONU, O.N.U. [ɔny, ɔenyvy] NF *(abrév* **Organisation des Nations unies***)* UN, UNO

ONUDI, Onudi [ɔnydi] NF *(abrév* **Organisation des Nations unies pour le développement industriel***)* UNIDO

onusien, -enne [ɔnyzjɛ̃, -ɛn] ADJ **projet/expert o.** UN project/expert

onychomycose [ɔnikɔmikoz] NF onychomycosis

onychophagie [ɔnikɔfaʒi] NF *Méd* onychophagy

onychophore [ɔnikɔfɔr] *Zool* NM member of the Onychophora family
□ **onychophores** NMPL Onychophora

onyx [ɔniks] NM onyx

onyxis [ɔniksis] NM *Méd* ingrowing toenail, *Spéc* onyxis

onzain [ɔ̃zɛ̃] NM *Littérature* stanza of eleven lines

onze [ɔ̃z] ADJ 1 *(gén)* eleven

2 *(dans des séries)* eleventh; **page/numéro o.** page/number eleven

PRON eleven

NM INV 1 *(gén)* eleven

2 *(numéro d'ordre)* number eleven

3 *(chiffre écrit)* eleven

4 *Ftbl* **le o. tricolore** the French eleven *or* team; *voir aussi* **cinq**

onzième [ɔ̃zjɛm] ADJ eleventh; **les ouvriers de la o. heure** last-minute helpers

NMF 1 *(personne)* eleventh

2 *(objet)* eleventh (one)

NM 1 *(partie)* eleventh

2 *(étage)* *Br* eleventh floor, *Am* twelfth floor

3 *(arrondissement de Paris)* eleventh (arrondissement)

NF 1 *Anciennement Scol Br* = first year of primary school, *Am* ≃ first grade

2 *Mus* eleventh; *voir aussi* **cinquième**

onzièmement [ɔ̃zjɛmmɑ̃] ADV in eleventh place

oocyte [ɔɔsit] NM *Biol* oocyte

oogamie [ɔɔgami] NF *Biol* oogamy

oogone [ɔɔgɔn] NF *Bot* oogonium

oolite, oolithe [ɔɔlit] NF *Géol* oolite

oolithique [ɔɔlitik] ADJ *Géol* oolitic

oophorectomie [ɔɔfɔrɛktɔmi] NF *Méd* oophorectomy

oophorite [ɔɔforit] NF *Méd* oophoritis

oosphère [ɔɔsfɛr] NF *Bot* oosphere

oospore [ɔɔspɔr] NF *Bot* oospore

oothèque [ɔɔtɛk] NF *Entom* ootheca

OP [ope] NM (*abrév* **ouvrier professionnel**) skilled worker

OPA [opea] NF *Fin* (*abrév* **offre publique d'achat**) takeover bid; **lancer une O. (sur)** to make a takeover bid (for); **être l'objet d'une O.** to be the subject of a takeover bid; **O. amicale** friendly takeover bid; **O. hostile** *ou* **inamicale** *ou* **sauvage** hostile takeover bid

opacification [ɔpasifikasjɔ̃] NF opacifying

opacifier [9] [ɔpasifje] VT to opacify, to make opaque
▸**s'opacifier** VPR to opacify

opacimétrie [ɔpasimetri] NF opacimetry

opacité [ɔpasite] NF 1 *Littéraire* (*ombre*) shadow, darkness; (*d'une forêt*) darkness, denseness 2 *Littéraire* (*inintelligibilité*) opaqueness, opacity 3 *Phys* (*d'un corps*) opacity, opaqueness; (*d'un liquide*) cloudiness, *Sout* turbidity 4 *Méd* **o. radiologique** X-ray shadow

opale [ɔpal] NF opal
ADJ **verre o.** opal glass; *Élec* **ampoule o.** pearl bulb

opalescence [ɔpalesɑ̃s] NF *Littéraire* opalescence

opalescent, -e [ɔpalesɑ̃, -ɑ̃t] ADJ *Littéraire* opalescent

opalin, -e [ɔpalɛ̃, -in] ADJ opaline
❏ **opaline** NF opaline

opalisation [ɔpalizasjɔ̃] NF opalization

opaliser [3] [ɔpalize] VT to opalize

opaque [ɔpak] ADJ 1 *Phys* opaque; **verre o.** opaque glass; **collant o.** opaque *Br* tights *or Am* pantihose; **o. aux rayons X** impervious to X-rays 2 (*sombre*) dark, impenetrable; (*forêt*) dark, dense; **dans la nuit o.** in the pitch-dark *or* jet-black night 3 *Fig* (*incompréhensible*) opaque, impenetrable

op art [ɔpart] NM op art

op. cit. (*abrév écrite* **opere citato, opus citatum**) op. cit.

OPCVM [opeseveɛm] NM *Bourse* (*abrév* **organisme de placement collectif en valeurs mobilières**) collective investment fund, *Br* ≃ unit trust, *Am* ≃ mutual fund; **O. actions** ≃ equity-based *Br* unit trust *or Am* mutual fund

OPE [opeə] NF *Fin* (*abrév* **offre publique d'échange**) exchange offer, takeover bid for shares

opéable [opeabl] ADJ likely to be the target of a takeover bid, vulnerable to takeover bids

opéamania [opeamanja] NF *Fam Fin* takeover fever

open [ɔpɛn] ADJ INV (*billet, tournoi*) open
NM *Sport* open; **o. de tennis** open tennis championship *or* tournament

openfield [ɔpɛnfild] NM *Géog* open country

open market [ɔpɛnmarkɛt] NM *Écon & Fin* open market

OPEP, Opep [ɔpɛp] NF (*abrév* **Organisation des pays exportateurs de pétrole**) OPEC

opéra [ɔpera] NM 1 *Mus* (*œuvre*) opera; (*genre*) opera; **nous allons souvent à l'o.** we often go to the opera; **j'aime écouter de l'o.** I love listening to opera; **o. bouffe** comic opera, opera buffa; **o. rock** rock opera 2 (*bâtiment*) opera (house); **l'O. (de Paris)** the Paris Opera House

≈ 𝄞 𝅘𝅥𝅮 ▯

'L'Opéra du gueux' *Gay, Hogarth* 'The Beggar's Opera'

opéra-ballet [ɔperabalɛ] (*pl* **opéras-ballets**) NM opéra ballet

opérable [ɔperabl] ADJ operable; **la malade n'est plus o.** the patient is no longer operable *or* is beyond surgery

opéra-bouffe [ɔperabuf] (*pl* **opéras-bouffes**) NM comic opera, opera buffa

opéra-comique [ɔperakɔmik] (*pl* **opéras-comiques**) NM light opera, opéra comique; **l'O.**

= opera house in Paris also known as "la Salle Tavart"

opérande [ɔperɑ̃d] NM *Math & Ordinat* operand

opérant, -e [ɔperɑ̃, -ɑ̃t] ADJ 1 (*effectif*) effective; **notre action a été opérante** our action proved to be effective 2 *Rel* operating

opérateur, -trice [ɔperatœr, -tris] NM,F 1 *Cin & TV* **o. banc-titre** rostrum cameraman; **o. magnétoscope** videotape operator; **o. de mixage** vision mixer; **o. de prises de vues** cameraman; **o. du son** sound technician; **o. steadicam** steadicam operator; **o. vidéo** video operator; **o. de la vision** video control operator

2 *Tél* (*employé*) (telephone) operator; (*exploitant*) telephone company; **pour l'étranger, il faut passer par l'o.** to phone abroad, you have to go through the operator; *Tél* **o. historique** ILEC, incumbent local exchange carrier; **o. radio** radio operator

3 *Typ* operative, operator; **o. de PAO** DTP operator;

4 *Tech* **o. (sur machine)** (machine) operator; *Com* **o. de transport multimodal** multi-modal operator

5 *Ordinat* operator; **o. de saisie** keyboarder; **o. de comparaison** comparator; **o. booléen** Boolean operator; **o. logique** logical operator; **o. relationnel** relational operator; **o. système** systems operator, SYSOP

6 *Bourse* operator, dealer; **o. à la baisse** operator for a fall, bear; **o. boursier** stock-exchange dealer; **o. en couverture** hedger; **o. sur écran** screen trader; **o. à la hausse** operator for a rise, bull; **o. d'un jour** day trader

7 *Journ* copytaker

NM 1 *Ling & Math* operator

2 *Mines* **o. (minier)** mining operative

opération [ɔperasjɔ̃] NF 1 *Méd* operation; **pratiquer une o.** to carry out surgery *or* an operation; **subir une grave/petite o.** to undergo major/minor surgery, to have a major/minor operation; **une o. (chirurgicale)** surgery, a surgical operation; **o. à chaud/froid** emergency/interval surgery; **o. à cœur ouvert** open-heart surgery

2 *Math* operation; **poser une o.** to do a calculation; *Scol* **connais-tu les quatre opérations?** do you know how to add, subtract, multiply and divide?

3 *Banque & Bourse* operation, transaction; **en la vendant à moitié prix, j'ai encore fait une belle o.!** even selling it at half price, I still got a really good deal!; **en acceptant de la recevoir pour trois semaines, tu n'as pas fait une bonne o.!** it wasn't very smart of you to agree to put her up for three weeks!; **o. à la baisse/hausse** bull/bear transaction; **o. bancaire** *ou* **de banque** bank transaction; **o. blanche** break-even transaction; **o. boursière** *ou* **de Bourse** stock exchange transaction *or* dealing; *Banque* **opérations de caisse** counter transactions; *Compta* **o. en capital** capital transaction; **o. de change** exchange transaction *or* deal; **o. de clearing** clearing transaction; **opérations de clôture** late trading, trading at the finish; **o. commerciale** business operation; **o. comptable** accounting operation; **o. au comptant** (*gén*) cash transaction; *Bourse* spot *or* cash deal; *Compta* **opérations courantes** normal business transactions; *Bourse* **opérations de couverture** hedging; *Bourse* **o. à découvert** short position; *Bourse* **opérations sur écran** screen trading; **o. d'escompte** discount operation; **o. de face à face** back-to-back loan; **o. financière** financial transaction; **opérations fermes** firm transactions; **opérations internationales** international operations; *Bourse* **o. de journée** day trade; *Bourse* **o. jumbo** jumbo trade; *Bourse* **opérations à option** option dealing *or* trading; *Banque* **o. de prêt** loan transaction; *Bourse* **o. à prime** prime deal; *Bourse* **opérations à terme** futures trading

4 (*manœuvre*) operation; **nous faisons appel à lui pour des opérations ponctuelles** we call upon his services when we need a specific job carried out; **o. prix cassés** (*sur la vitrine d'un magasin*) prices slashed; **o. de commando/de sauvetage** commando/rescue operation; *Com* **o. en commun** joint venture; **la police a effectué une o. coup de poing dans le quartier** the police swooped on the area; **o. coup de poing**

sur les chaînes hi-fi (*sur la vitrine d'un magasin*) hi-fi prices slashed; **une o. escargot a perturbé la circulation hier** a *Br* go-slow *or Am* slowdown by drivers disrupted traffic yesterday; **o. de police** police operation; **o. portes ouvertes à l'Université** *Br* open day *or Am* open house at the University

5 (*campagne*) operation, campaign; **o. marketing** marketing campaign; **o. publicitaire** advertising campaign

6 (*démarche*) process; **les opérations de l'esprit** mental processes, the workings of the mind

7 **par l'o. du Saint-Esprit** *Rel* through the workings of the Holy Spirit; *Fig Hum* by magic; *Hum* **crois-tu que tu y arriveras par l'o. du Saint-Esprit?** do you think you'll succeed just waiting for things to happen?

8 (*ensemble de travaux*) process, operation; **les opérations de fabrication de l'acier** steel making processes; **la machine exécute 18 opérations différentes** the machine performs 18 different operations

9 *Ordinat* operation; **o. "si-alors"** if-then operation

opérationnel, -elle [ɔperasjɔnɛl] ADJ 1 (*en activité*) operational; **les nouveaux ateliers ne seront opérationnels que l'année prochaine** the new workshops won't be operational until next year 2 (*fournissant le résultat optimal*) efficient, operative 3 *Mil* operational

opératoire [ɔperatwar] ADJ 1 *Math* operative 2 *Méd* (*chirurgical*) operating (*avant n*), surgical; (*postopératoire*) post-operative; **médecine o.** surgery 3 *Phil* (*concept, modèle*) working

opératrice [ɔperatris] *voir* **opérateur**

operculaire [ɔpɛrkylɛr] ADJ *Bot & Zool* opercular

opercule [ɔpɛrkyl] NM 1 *Bot & Zool* operculum 2 (*dans un emballage*) lid 3 *Naut* **o. de hublot** deadlight

operculé, -e [ɔpɛrkyle] ADJ 1 *Bot & Zool* operculated 2 (*emballage, pot*) with a lid

opéré, -e [ɔpere] NM,F patient (who has undergone surgery); **le chirurgien est passé voir son dernier o.** the surgeon came round to see the last person he operated on; **les grands opérés** (post-operative) intensive care patients; **c'est un grand o.** he's had major surgery

opérer [18] [ɔpere] VT 1 *Méd* (*blessé, malade*) to operate on; **o. qn des amygdales** to take sb's tonsils out; **elle a été opérée de l'appendicite** she was operated on for appendicitis, she had her appendix removed; **on va l'o. d'un kyste au poignet** they're going to remove a cyst from his/her wrist; **il vient juste d'être opéré** he's just had an operation; **se faire o.** to undergo *or* to have surgery; **se faire o. des amygdales** to have one's tonsils taken out; **se faire o. d'une tumeur** to have an operation to remove a tumour

2 (*procéder à* → *modification, réforme, restructuration*) to carry out; (→ *miracle, retour en arrière*) to bring about; (→ *paiement, virement, distinction*) to make; *Chim* (→ *synthèse*) to perform; **tu dois o. un choix** you have to choose *or* to make a choice; **le pays tente d'o. un redressement économique** the country is attempting to bring about an economic recovery

3 *Mil* (*retraite*) to effect

USAGE ABSOLU *Méd* **le chirurgien a opéré toute la matinée** the surgeon was in the operating theatre all morning

VI 1 (*faire effet*) to work; **le médicament a opéré** the medicine worked; **son charisme n'a pas opéré sur moi** his/her charisma had no effect *or* didn't work on me

2 (*intervenir*) to act, to operate; **la police opère souvent la nuit** the police often operate at night; **la façon dont les cambrioleurs ont opéré** the way the burglars went to work; **je ne sais pas comment il opère en de telles circonstances** I don't know how he proceeds in such circumstances

3 *Bourse* **à découvert** to take a short position, to go short

▸**s'opérer** VPR 1 (*emploi passif*) **ce genre de lésion ne s'opère pas** this type of lesion can't be operated on

2 (*avoir lieu*) to take place; **un grand changement s'est opéré depuis ton départ** a major change has taken place since you left; **une**

transformation s'opéra en elle she underwent a transformation

opérette [ɔpeʀɛt] NF operetta; **chanteuse d'o.** operetta singer

◻ **d'opérette** ADJ **le colonel n'est qu'un soldat d'o.** the colonel is just a tin soldier; **une armée d'o.** a caricature of an army

opéron [ɔpeʀɔ̃] NM *Biol* operon

ophicléide [ɔfikleid] NM *Mus* ophicleide

ophidien [ɔfidjɛ̃] NM *Zool* ophidian

◻ **ophidiens** NMPL ophidians, Ophidia

ophioglosse [ɔfjɔglɔs] NM *Bot* ophioglossum

ophiographie [ɔfjɔgʀafi] NF *Zool* ophiography

ophiolâtrie [ɔfjɔlatri] NF ophiolatry

ophiolite [ɔfjɔlit] NF *Géol* ophiolite

ophiolitique [ɔfjɔlitik] ADJ *Géol* ophiolitic

ophiologie [ɔfjɔlɔʒi] NF *Zool* ophiology

ophite [ɔfit] NM ophite, serpentine

ophiure [ɔfjyʀ] *Zool* NM brittle star, *Spéc* ophiuran

◻ **ophiures** NFPL Ophiuroidea

ophiuride [ɔfjyʀid] NM = **ophiure**

OPHLM [ɔpeaʃɛlɛm] NM (*abrév* **Office public d'habitations à loyer modéré**) = main office responsible for the allocation of council housing

ophrys [ɔfʀis] NM *Bot* ophrys; **o. abeille/mouche** bee/fly orchid

ophtalmie [ɔftalmi] NF ophthalmia; **o. des neiges** snow blindness

ophtalmique [ɔftalmik] ADJ ophthalmic

ophtalmo [ɔftalmo] NMF *Fam* (*abrév* **ophtalmologiste**) eye specialist■

ophtalmologie [ɔftalmɔlɔʒi] NF ophthalmology

ophtalmologique [ɔftalmɔlɔʒik] ADJ ophthalmological

ophtalmologiste [ɔftalmɔlɔʒist], **ophtalmologue** [ɔftalmɔlɔg] NMF ophthalmologist, eye specialist

ophtalmomètre [ɔftalmɔmɛtʀ] NM ophthalmometer, keratometer

ophtalmométrie [ɔftalmɔmetri] NF ophthalmometry

ophtalmoscope [ɔftalmɔskɔp] NM ophthalmoscope

ophtalmoscopie [ɔftalmɔskɔpi] NF ophthalmoscopy

opiacé, -e [ɔpjase] ADJ **1** (*qui contient de l'opium*) opiate, opiated **2** (*qui sert d'opium*) opiate, opium-scented
   NM opiate

opilion [ɔpiljɔ̃] *Zool* NM harvest spider

◻ **opilions** NMPL harvest spiders, *Spéc* Opiliones

opimes [ɔpim] ADJ FPL **dépouilles o.** *Antiq* spolia opima; *Fig* rich profit

Opinel® [ɔpinɛl] NM = folding knife used especially for outdoor activities, scouting etc

opiner [3] [ɔpine] VI *Littéraire* **o. sur qch** to express an opinion about sth; **o. pour/contre qch** to come down in favour of/against sth
   VT *Littéraire* **o. que…** to be of the opinion that…

◻ **opiner à** VT IND *Littéraire* to consent to; **elle opina à ce mariage** she gave her assent *or* consent to this marriage

◻ **opiner de** VT IND **o. de la tête** *ou* **du bonnet** *ou* **du chef** to nod one's assent *or* agreement, to nod in agreement

opiniâtre [ɔpinjatʀ] ADJ **1** (*personne*) stubborn, obstinate **2** (*haine, opposition, lutte*) unrelenting, relentless, obstinate; (*résistance*) stubborn, dogged; (*détermination*) dogged **3** (*toux*) persistent

opiniâtrement [ɔpinjatʀəmɑ̃] ADV **1** (*avec entêtement*) stubbornly, obstinately **2** (*avec ténacité*) relentlessly, persistently, doggedly

opiniâtreté [ɔpinjatʀəte] NF *Littéraire* **1** (*entêtement*) stubbornness, obstinacy **2** (*ténacité*) relentlessness, doggedness

opinion [ɔpinjɔ̃] NF **1** (*point de vue*) opinion (**de** of; **sur** about, on); **j'ai mon o. sur lui** I have my own opinion about him; **se faire soi-même une o.** to make up one's own mind; **se faire une o. sur qch** to make up one's mind about sth, to form an opinion about sth; **mon o. est faite** I've made up my mind; **je ne partage pas votre o.** I don't agree with you, I don't share your views; **partager les opinions de qn** to share sb's opinions *or* views, to think the same way as sb; **au dernier moment, elle changea brusquement d'o.** she suddenly changed her mind at the last

minute; **je vais vous donner mon o.** let me tell you what I think; **c'est une affaire d'o.** it's a matter of opinion; **journal d'o.** = political weekly/monthly (with a particular stance); *Journ* **libre o.** editorial; **opinions politiques/subversives** political/subversive views; **l'o. (publique)** public opinion; **informer l'o.** to inform the public; **sans o.** (*dans un sondage*) don't know; **les sans o.** (*sondés*) the don't knows

2 (*jugement*) opinion; **avoir une bonne/mauvaise/haute o. de qn** to have a good/bad/high opinion of sb; **je me moque de l'o. d'autrui** I don't care what others may think

opiomane [ɔpjɔman] NMF opium addict

opiomanie [ɔpjɔmani] NF opium addiction, *Spéc* opiomania

opisthobranche [ɔpistɔbʀɑ̃ʃ] *Zool* ADJ opisthobranchiate

◻ **opisthobranches** NMPL (*mollusques*) Opisthobranchia(ta)

opisthodome [ɔpistɔdɔm] NM *Antiq* opisthodome, opisthodomos

opisthotonos [ɔpistɔtɔnɔs] NM *Méd* opisthotonos

opium [ɔpjɔm] NM opium; *Fig* **la religion est l'o. du peuple** religion is the opium of the people

OPJ [ɔpeʒi] NM (*abrév* **officier de police judiciaire**) = police officer in the French Criminal Investigation Department

oponce [ɔpɔ̃s] NM *Bot* opuntia

opopanax [ɔpɔpanaks] NM *Bot & Pharm* opopanax

opossum [ɔpɔsɔm] NM *Zool* opossum; **o. d'Australie** Australian opossum; **o. de Virginie** American opossum

opothérapie [ɔpɔteʀapi] NF *Méd* opotherapy, organotherapy

oppidum [ɔpidɔm] NM Roman hill-fort

opportun, -e [ɔpɔʀtœ̃, -yn] ADJ opportune, timely; (*moment, jour*) right; **ton arrivée était plus qu'opportune** you came at just the right time; **je vous donnerai ma réponse en temps o.** I'll give you my answer in due course; **il serait o. de prendre une décision** it's time to make a decision; **il lui est apparu o. de partir avant elle** he/she found it appropriate *or* advisable to leave before her

opportunément [ɔpɔʀtynemɑ̃] ADV opportunely; **la police est arrivée o.** the police arrived just at the right time

opportunisme [ɔpɔʀtynism] NM opportunism

opportuniste [ɔpɔʀtynist] ADJ opportunist; (*maladie*) opportunistic
   NMF opportunist

opportunité [ɔpɔʀtynite] NF **1** (*à-propos*) appropriateness; (*d'une arrivée*) timeliness, *Sout* opportuneness; (*d'un projet, d'une décision*) advisability **2** (*occasion*) opportunity; **o. commerciale** market opportunity; **o. marketing** marketing opportunity

◻ **opportunités** NFPL opportunities

opposabilité [ɔpozabilite] NF *Jur* opposability

opposable [ɔpozabl] ADJ opposable (**à** to); **tu ne trouveras pas d'argument o. à ma décision** you won't be able to use any argument against my decision; **rien n'est o. à ses arguments** there is no answer to his/her arguments, nothing can be said against his/her arguments

opposant, -e [ɔpozɑ̃, -ɑ̃t] ADJ **1** (*adverse*) opposing **2** *Jur* opposing **3** *Anat* **muscles opposants** opponens
   NM,F (*adversaire*) opponent (**à** of); *Pol* member of the Opposition; **les opposants au régime** the opponents of the regime; **les opposants à la politique actuelle** those who oppose current policy
   NM *Anat* **les opposants** the opponens; **o. du pouce** opponens pollicis

opposé, -e [ɔpoze] ADJ **1** (*en vis-à-vis*) opposite; **il est arrivé du côté o.** he came from the other *or* opposite side; **sur le mur o.** on the wall facing us

2 (*contraire → sens, direction*) opposite, other; (*→ mouvement, équipe*) opposing; (*→ goût, caractère*) different; (*→ avis*) opposite; (*→ intérêt*) conflicting; **ils ont des tendances tout à fait opposées** they have completely different

tendencies; **je suis d'une opinion opposée (à la vôtre)** I am of a different opinion

3 (*contrastant → couleur, ton*) contrasting

4 *Bot* (*feuille, rameau*) opposite

5 *Géom & Math* (*côté, angle*) opposite; **angles opposés par le sommet** vertically opposite angles

6 (*contre*) **être o. à une mesure** to oppose *or* to be opposed to *or* to be against a measure; **je suis o. à ce qu'une centrale soit construite dans cette région** I'm opposed to *or* I'm against a power station being built in this area

   NM **1** (*direction*) opposite; **quel est l'o. du sud?** what's the opposite of south?

2 (*contraire*) opposite, reverse; **chaque fois que je te dis quelque chose, tu soutiens l'o.!** whenever I say anything, you say the opposite *or* you contradict it!; **il est tout l'o. de sa sœur** he's the exact opposite of his sister; **le deuxième film de ce réalisateur est vraiment l'o. du premier** the director's second film is the complete opposite of *or* is in complete contrast to his first

3 *Math* (*nombre*) opposite number

◻ **à l'opposé** ADV **1** (*dans l'espace*) opposite, on the other side; *Fig* on the other hand; **la gare est à l'o.** the station is in the opposite direction; **vous cherchez l'église? vous allez à l'o.** you want the church? you're going in the wrong direction

2 (*en désaccord*) **il est de droite et je suis tout à l'o.** his views are right-wing but mine are completely the opposite

◻ **à l'opposé de** PRÉP **1** (*dans l'espace*) opposite; **à l'o. de la gare** opposite the station

2 (*en contradiction avec*) unlike, contrary to; **à l'o. de sa mère, elle n'aimait pas la peinture** unlike her mother, she didn't like painting; **mon avis est à l'o. du sien** my opinion is the opposite of his/hers; **à l'o. de ce que nous attendions** contrary to expectation *or* to what we expected; **cela va à l'o. de ce que l'on m'avait promis/de notre politique** that goes against what I was promised/our policy

opposer [3] [ɔpoze] VT **1** (*objecter → argument*) **je n'ai rien à o. à cette objection** I've nothing to say against that objection; **que peut-il t'o.?** what objection can he have to that?, what can he say against that?; **o. des arguments valables à une théorie** to put forward valid arguments against a theory; **il a opposé à ma théorie des raisons intéressantes** he put forward some interesting objections to my theory; **elle m'a opposé qu'elle n'avait pas le temps de s'en occuper** she objected that she didn't have time to take care of it

2 (*mettre en confrontation → adversaires, armées, pays*) to bring into conflict (with each other); **deux guerres ont opposé nos pays** two wars have brought our countries into conflict; **des intérêts divergents les opposeront toujours** opposing interests will always bring them into conflict; **qui peut-on o. au président sortant?** who can we put up against the outgoing president?; **cette course oppose les meilleurs athlètes d'Europe** this race will see Europe's finest athletes competing against each other; **la finale opposera le joueur français au joueur américain** the final will pit the French player against the American; **la finale opposera la France à l'Italie** France will meet Italy *or* come up against Italy in the final; **à l'idéalisme de son père, Renaud opposa une approche plus pragmatique** Renaud countered his father's idealism with a more pragmatic approach; **nous opposerons nos méthodes** we'll test our methods against each other; **o. Mozart à Debussy** to contrast Mozart with Debussy

3 *Phys* **o. une pression de sens contraire** to apply pressure from the opposite direction; **o. une résistance** to resist, to be resistant; *Fig* to put up a resistance; *Fig* **o. une résistance vigoureuse** to put up *or* to offer vigorous resistance

4 (*disposer vis-à-vis*) to set *or* to place opposite each other

▶**s'opposer** VPR **1** s'o. (*être contre*) to object to, to oppose; **quelqu'un s'oppose-t-il à cette nomination?** are there any objections to this appointment?; **nous nous opposons à ce que**

la centrale soit construite we oppose the building of the power station, we are opposed to *or* are against the power station being built; **le règlement/ma religion s'y oppose** it goes against the rules/my religion; **les conditions météo s'opposent à toute navigation aérienne aujourd'hui** weather conditions are making flying inadvisable today; **nous nous opposons à ce qu'il arrête ses études** we are against *or* we are opposed to the idea of him giving up his studies; **je m'oppose à ce que tu reviennes** I'm against *or* opposed to your coming back; **rien ne s'oppose à votre projet** nothing stands in the way of your plan; **rien ne s'oppose à ce que vous fassiez ce que vous souhaitez** there's nothing to stop you doing what you want to

2 s'o. à *(être en désaccord avec)* to oppose; **je m'oppose à lui sur la politique étrangère** I'm against him *or* I oppose him on foreign policy

3 s'o. à *(affronter)* to oppose, to be against; **il s'opposera ce soir au président dans un débat télévisé** he'll face the president tonight in a televised debate; **les meilleurs joueurs d'échecs s'opposent dans ce tournoi** this tournament pits the best chess players against one another, the best chess players come up against each other in this tournament

4 s'o. à *(contraster avec → couleur, notion, mot)* to be the opposite of; **le noir s'oppose au blanc** black is the opposite of white

opposite [ɔpozit] NM *Arch ou Littéraire* opposite, contrary; **il est tout l'o. de son frère** he is the exact opposite of his brother; **il pense tout l'o. de ce qu'il dit** he thinks quite the reverse of what he says

□ **à l'opposite** ADV **leurs maisons sont à l'o.** their houses are opposite (each other)

□ **à l'opposite de** PRÉP **à l'o. de l'église, vous trouverez le monument** you'll see the monument opposite the church

opposition [ɔpozisjɔ̃] NF **1** *(désaccord)* opposition; *(contraste)* contrast, difference; **o. de** *ou* **entre deux styles** clash of *or* between two styles; **couleurs en o.** contrasting colours

2 *(résistance)* opposition; **le ministre a fait** *ou* **mis o. au projet** the minister opposed the plan; **l'o. de la plupart des citoyens à la guerre n'est pas prouvée** it has not been proved that most citizens are opposed to *or* against the war; **nous avons rencontré une forte o.** we encountered strong opposition; **la loi est passée sans o.** the bill went through unopposed; **il fait de l'o. systématique à tout ce qu'on lui propose** he's automatically against everything you suggest

3 *Pol* **l'o.** the Opposition; **les dirigeants/les partis de l'o.** the leaders/the parties of the Opposition

4 *Jur* caveat; **o. sur titre** attachment against securities; **jugement susceptible d'o.** judgment liable to stay of execution; **faire o. à une décision** to appeal against a ruling; **faire o. à un acte** to lodge an objection to a deed; **faire o. à un chèque** to stop a cheque; **faire o. à un mariage** to raise an objection to *or* to enter a caveat to a marriage; **valeurs frappées d'o.** stopped *or* countermanded bonds

5 *Astrol & Astron* opposition; **planète en o.** *Astrol* planet in opposition; *Astron* planet at opposition

6 *Élec & Ling* opposition

□ **en opposition avec** PRÉP against, contrary to, in opposition to; **agir en o. avec ses principes** to act against one's principles; **c'est en o. totale avec les principes qu'il expose dans ses livres** it is in complete contrast to *or* is totally at odds with *or* totally contradicts the principles that he puts forward in his books; **tout cela est en o. totale avec ce que je pense** all that is the complete opposite of what I think; **je me suis trouvée en o. avec elle sur plusieurs points** I found myself at odds *or* at variance with her on several points

□ **par opposition à** PRÉP as opposed to, in contrast with

oppositionnel, -elle [ɔpozisjɔnɛl] ADJ *Pol* oppositional, opposition *(avant n)*

NM,F oppositionist

oppressant, -e [ɔpresɑ̃, -ɑ̃t] ADJ oppressive

oppressé, -e [ɔprese] ADJ oppressed; **avoir la poitrine oppressée, se sentir o.** to feel tight-chested

oppresser [4] [ɔprese] VT **1** *(situation, atmosphère)* to oppress; **l'obscurité/la chaleur m'oppresse** I find the darkness/the heat oppressive; **elle était oppressée par l'angoisse** she was gripped *or* choked with anxiety; **ils sont oppressés par le remords** they are weighed down with remorse **2** *Littéraire (peuple, nation)* to oppress

oppresseur [ɔpresœr] NM oppressor

ADJ M *(régime)* oppressive

oppressif, -ive [ɔpresif, -iv] ADJ oppressive

oppression [ɔpresjɔ̃] NF **1** *(domination)* oppression **2** *(suffocation)* suffocation, oppression; **o. de la poitrine** tightness of the chest, difficulty in breathing

oppressive [ɔpresiv] *voir* **oppressif**

opprimant, -e [ɔprimɑ̃, -ɑ̃t] ADJ oppressive

opprimé, -e [ɔprime] ADJ oppressed; **les peuples opprimés** the oppressed peoples

NM,F oppressed person; **elle prend toujours le parti des opprimés** she always sides with the underdog

opprimer [3] [ɔprime] VT **1** *(asservir)* to oppress **2** *(censurer)* to suppress, to stifle; **o. la presse** to gag the press

opprobre [ɔprɔbr] NM *Littéraire* **1** *(honte)* shame, opprobrium; **jeter l'o. sur qn, accabler** *ou* **couvrir qn d'o.** to heap shame *or* opprobrium on sb; **il est l'o. de sa famille** he's a disgrace to his family **2** *(avilissement)* shame, infamy; **vivre dans l'o.** to live in infamy

OPR [ɔpeɛr] NF *Fin (abrév* **offre publique de retrait)** public buy-out offer

opsonine [ɔpsɔnin] NF *Méd* opsonin

optatif, -ive [ɔptatif, -iv] ADJ optative

NM optative (mode)

opter [3] [ɔpte] VI **o. entre deux choses** to choose between two things

□ **opter pour** VT IND to opt for; **nous devons o. pour la dernière solution** we must opt for the last solution; **vous devez o. pour une de ces deux possibilités** you'll have to choose between these two possibilities; **j'ai opté pour les cheveux courts** I opted for a short haircut; **le prix m'a fait o. pour une plus petite voiture** the price finally made me come down in favour of a smaller car

opticien, -enne [ɔptisjɛ̃, -ɛn] NM,F optician

optimal, -e, -aux, -ales [ɔptimal, -o] ADJ optimal, optimum *(avant n)*; **pour un rendement o.** for optimal results

optimalisation [ɔptimalizasjɔ̃] NF optimization; *Fin* **o. du profit** *ou* **des profits** profit optimization

optimaliser [3] [ɔptimalize] VT to optimize; *Ordinat (matériel, système)* to upgrade

optimisation [ɔptimizasjɔ̃] NF optimization; *Fin* **o. du profit** *ou* **des profits** profit optimization

optimiser [3] [ɔptimize] VT to optimize; *Ordinat (matériel, système)* to upgrade

optimiseur [ɔptimizœr] NM *Ordinat* optimizer

optimisme [ɔptimism] NM optimism; **avec o.** optimistically

optimiste [ɔptimist] ADJ optimistic; **nous ne sommes pas très optimistes quant à la guérison de ce malade** we're not very optimistic about the patient's chances of recovery *or* that the patient will recover

NMF optimist; **c'est un éternel o.** he always looks on the bright side, he's an eternal optimist

optimum [ɔptimɔm] *(pl* **optimums** *ou* **optima** [-a]*)* ADJ optimum *(avant n)*, optimal; **la température o. ne dépasse pas 5 degrés** the optimum temperature does not exceed 5 degrees

NM optimum; **o. écologique** optimum ecological conditions; **o. de peuplement** optimum population

opting-out [ɔptiŋaut] NM *UE* opting out

option [ɔpsjɔ̃] NF **1** *(choix)* option, choice; **je n'ai pas d'autre o.** I have no other alternative *or* choice

2 *Scol* **(matière à) o.** optional subject; **il avait le latin en o. au baccalauréat** he took Latin as an option *or* an optional subject *or* an elective subject for the baccalauréat

3 *Fin & Bourse* **o. d'achat** call option; **o. d'achat d'actions** stock option; **o. sur actions** option on shares; **o. américaine** American-style option; **o. à l'argent** at-the-money option; **o. de change** foreign currency option; **o. sur contrats à terme** futures option; **o. cotée** traded option; **o. au cours** at-the-money option; **o. du double call** of more; **o. d'échange** swap option; **o. européenne** European-style option; **o. sur indice** index option; **o. à la monnaie** at-the-money option; **o. négociable** traded option; **o. sur titre** stock option; **o. de vente** put option

4 *Com & Jur* option; **prendre une o. sur qch** to take (out) an option on sth; **o. d'achat/de vente** option to buy/to sell; *Jur* **o. de nationalité** = possibility of claiming or renouncing French nationality

5 *(accessoire facultatif)* optional extra; **en o.** as an (optional) extra; **le flash est en o.** the flash is optional *or* is an optional extra

6 *Ordinat* **o. d'impression** print option; **o. de menu** menu option; **o. de sauvegarde** save option

7 *Pol* **o. zéro** zero option

optionnel, -elle [ɔpsjɔnɛl] ADJ optional

optique [ɔptik] ADJ **1** *Anat* optic; **nerf o.** optic nerve

2 *Opt* optical

3 *Phys* optic; **angle o.** optic angle

4 *Ordinat* optical

NF **1** *(science)* optics *(singulier)*; **o. électronique** electron optics; **transmettre par o.** to communicate by visual signals

2 *Tech* (set of) lenses; *(d'un projecteur)* optical system

3 *(point de vue)* perspective; **mon o. est différente** I see it from a different angle *or* point of view; **dans cette o.** from this perspective *or* viewpoint; **nous ne travaillons pas dans la même o.** we're working towards different aims; *Mktg* **o. marketing** *ou* **mercatique** marketing orientation; *Mktg* **o. produit** product orientation; *Mktg* **o. publicitaire** advertising approach; *Mktg* **o. vente** sales orientation

□ **d'optique** ADJ optical

optoélectronique [ɔptɔelɛktrɔnik] NF optoelectronics *(singulier)*

optomètre [ɔptɔmɛtr] NM optometer

optométrie [ɔptɔmetri] NF optometry

optométriste [ɔptɔmetrist] NMF optometrist

opt-out [ɔptaut] NM *Pol* opt-out

optronique [ɔptrɔnik] ADJ optronic

NF optronics *(singulier)*

opulence [ɔpylɑ̃s] NF **1** *(richesse)* opulence, affluence; **vivre dans l'o.** to live an opulent life *or* a life of plenty **2** *Littéraire (ampleur)* fullness, ampleness; **l'o. de ses formes** the fullness of her figure

opulent, -e [ɔpylɑ̃, -ɑ̃t] ADJ **1** *(riche)* affluent, wealthy, opulent; *(moisson, pâturage)* abundant **2** *(physiquement → personne)* corpulent; *(→ forme)* generous, full; **une poitrine opulente** an ample *or* full bosom; **son opulente chevelure** his/her luxuriant hair

opuntia [ɔpɔ̃sja] NM *Bot* opuntia

opus [ɔpys] NM opus

opuscule [ɔpyskyl] NM *(petit ouvrage)* opuscule; *(brochure)* brochure

OPV [ɔpeve] NF *Fin (abrév* **offre publique de vente)** public offering, public share offer

OQ [oky] NM *(abrév* **ouvrier qualifié)** skilled worker

or¹ [ɔr] CONJ *(pour introduire une précision)* now; *(pour introduire une opposition)* well; **il faut tenir les délais; or, ce n'est pas toujours possible** deadlines must be met; now this is not always possible; **avant de le lire, je pensais que le livre était bon, or, il ne l'était pas** before reading it, I thought the book was good, well, it wasn't; **je devais y aller, or au dernier moment, j'ai eu un empêchement** I was supposed to go, but then at the last moment something came up; **il n'achète jamais de chocolats, or...** he never buys chocolates, but...; **or..., donc...** now..., therefore...

or² [ɔr] NM **1** *(métal)* gold; **le cours de l'or** the price of gold; **or monnayé/au titre/sans titre** coined/essayed/unessayed gold; **or en barre** gold bullion; *Fam* **ces actions, c'est de l'or en barre** these shares are a rock-solid investment;

or blanc white gold; **l'or blanc** (*les sports d'hiver*) the winter sports bonanza; **or bleu** blue gold, water; **or brut** gold nuggets; **or jaune** yellow gold; **or rouge** red gold; **l'or noir** black gold; **l'or vert** ''green gold'', forest resources; **or massif** solid gold; **la montre est en or massif** the watch is solid gold; **or pur/fin** pure/fine gold; **la valeur or** value in gold, gold exchange value; *Fig* **pour tout l'or du monde** for all the money in the world, for all the tea in China; **parler d'or** to speak with the voice of wisdom
 2 (*couleur*) gold, golden colour
 3 *Jur* **clause or** gold clause
ADJ INV gold (*avant n*), gold-coloured
□ **d'or** ADJ 1 *Minér & (en joaillerie)* gold (*avant n*)
 2 (*doré → cheveux*) golden, gold (*avant n*); (→ *cadre*) gold (*avant n*)
 3 (*locutions*) **un cœur d'or** a heart of gold; *Littéraire* **le siècle d'or** the golden age
□ **en or** ADJ 1 (*fait d'or → bijou*) gold (*avant n*); **une bague en or** a gold ring
 2 (*excellent*) **une mère en or** a wonderful mother; **une affaire en or** (*occasion*) a real bargain; (*entreprise*) a goldmine; **c'est une occasion en or** it's a golden opportunity

'L'Or' *Cendrars* 'Sutter's Gold'

'L'Or du Rhin' *Wagner* 'The Rhine Gold' or 'The Rhinegold'

ORA [ɔɛʀa] NFPL (*abrév* **obligations remboursables en actions**) redeemable bonds
oracle [ɔʀakl] NM *Antiq & Fig* oracle; **rendre un o.** to pronounce an oracle; **l'o. de Delphes** the Delphic oracle; **parler d'un ton d'o.** to speak with assurance
Oradour-sur-Glane [ɔʀaduʀsyʀglan] NM = village near Limoges (site of a notorious massacre by the SS in 1944)
orage [ɔʀaʒ] NM 1 *Météo* storm, thunderstorm; **un temps d'o.** stormy or thundery weather; **par temps d'o.** in stormy weather; **le temps est à l'o.** there's thunder in the air; **il va y avoir un o.** there's a storm brewing, there's going to be a storm; **o. magnétique/de chaleur** magnetic/heat storm; **pluie d'o.** rainstorm
 2 *Fig* (*dispute*) row, argument; **depuis des semaines, je sentais venir l'o.** I'd known for weeks that trouble was brewing; **il y a de l'o. dans l'air** there's trouble brewing; **laisser passer l'o.** to let the storm blow over
 3 *Littéraire* (*déchirement, tourmente*) upheaval, tumult; **les orages de l'amour** the turmoil of love
orageuse [ɔʀaʒøz] *voir* **orageux**
orageusement [ɔʀaʒøzmã] ADV stormily, tempestuously
orageux, -euse [ɔʀaʒø, -øz] ADJ 1 *Météo* (*ciel*) stormy, thundery; (*chaleur, averse*) thundery; **le temps est o.** it's thundery or stormy, the weather's thundery or stormy 2 *Fig* (*tumultueux → jeunesse, séance*) stormy, turbulent; (→ *discussion*) stormy, heated
oraison [ɔʀɛzɔ̃] NF 1 *Rel* (*prière*) prayer; **l'o. dominicale** the Lord's Prayer 2 *Littérature* **o. funèbre** funeral oration
oral, -e, -aux, -ales [ɔʀal, -o] ADJ 1 (*confession, déposition*) verbal, oral; (*message, tradition*) oral; *Scol* (*épreuve*) oral
 2 *Anat & Ling* oral
 NM 1 (*examen → gén*) oral (examination); (→ *à l'université*) oral (examination), *Br* viva (voce); **notes d'o.** oral *Br* marks or *Am* grades; **j'ai raté l'o. de physique** I failed the physics oral
 2 *Scol & Univ* **l'o.** (*l'expression orale*) **il n'est pas très bon à l'o.** his oral work isn't very good
oralement [ɔʀalmã] ADV orally, verbally
oraliser [3] [ɔʀalize] VT to verbalize
oralité [ɔʀalite] NF orality
Oran [ɔʀã] NM Oran
Orange [ɔʀãʒ] NM **l'État libre d'O.** the Orange Free State
orange [ɔʀãʒ] NF orange; **o. amère/douce** bitter/sweet orange; **o. sanguine** blood orange; **une o. pressée** a glass of freshly squeezed orange juice
 NM (*couleur*) orange; **l'o. ne me va pas** orange

doesn't suit me; *Aut* **passer à l'o.** to go through the lights on amber; **le feu était à l'o.** the lights were at amber
 ADJ INV 1 (*coloré*) orange, orange-coloured 2 *Belg Pol* Christian socialist

'Orange mécanique' *Burgess, Kubrick* 'A Clockwork Orange'

orangé, -e [ɔʀãʒe] ADJ orangey, orange-coloured
 NM orangey colour
orangeade [ɔʀãʒad] NF orange drink
orangeat [ɔʀãʒa] NM candied orange peel
oranger [ɔʀãʒe] NM orange tree; **bois d'o.** orange wood
orangeraie [ɔʀãʒʀɛ] NF orange grove
orangerie [ɔʀãʒʀi] NF 1 (*serre*) orangery 2 (*plantation*) orange grove
orangette [ɔʀãʒɛt] NF = unripe Seville orange (*used in confectionery*)
orangisme [ɔʀãʒism] NM *Pol* Orangism
orangiste [ɔʀãʒist] NMF 1 (*en Irlande du Nord*) Orangeman, *f* Orangewoman 2 *Hist* Orangist
 ADJ Orange (*avant n*)
orang-outan, orang-outang [ɔʀãutã] (*pl* **orangs-outans** *ou* **orangs-outangs**) NM *Zool* orang-outang, orang-utan
orant, -e [ɔʀã, -ãt] NM,F praying figure, *Spéc* orant
orateur, -trice [ɔʀatœʀ, -tʀis] NM,F 1 (*rhétoricien*) orator 2 (*gén*) speaker; **c'est un excellent o.** he is an excellent speaker
oratoire[1] [ɔʀatwaʀ] ADJ (*style, talent*) oratorical; **passage o.** oration; **prendre des précautions oratoires** to choose one's words carefully; **l'art o.** (the art of) oratory, public speaking
oratoire[2] [ɔʀatwaʀ] NM 1 (*chapelle*) oratory 2 *Rel* **l'O. de France** the French Oratory; **l'O. d'Italie** the Oratory (of St Philip Neri); **les pères de l'O.** the Oratorian Fathers
oratorien [ɔʀatɔʀjɛ̃] NM Oratorian (father)
oratorio [ɔʀatɔʀjo] NM oratorio
oratrice [ɔʀatʀis] *voir* **orateur**
orbe[1] [ɔʀb] ADJ *Archit* **mur o.** blind wall
orbe[2] [ɔʀb] NM 1 *Astron* orbit 2 *Littéraire* (*globe*) orb, globe, sphere; (*cercle*) circle, coil, ring; **l'o. rouge du soleil** the red orb of the sun
orbiculaire [ɔʀbikylɛʀ] ADJ 1 circular, *Sout* orbicular 2 *Anat & Géol* orbicular
 NM *Anat* orbicularis
orbitaire [ɔʀbitɛʀ] ADJ orbital
orbital, -e, -aux, -ales [ɔʀbital, -o] ADJ *Astron* orbital
 □ **orbitale** NF *Phys* **orbitale atomique** atomic orbital; **orbitale moléculaire** molecular orbital
orbite [ɔʀbit] NF 1 *Anat* (*eye*) socket, *Spéc* orbit; *Fig* **il était tellement en colère que les yeux lui sortaient des orbites** he was so angry that his eyes were popping out (of their sockets)
 2 (*d'un vaisseau spatial, d'un électron*) & *Astron* orbit; **o. géostationnaire** geostationary orbit; **être sur** *ou* **en o.** to be in orbit; **être en o. autour de qch** (*sujet: astre, engin*) to be in orbit round sth, to orbit sth; **satellite en o. autour de la Terre** Earth-orbiting satellite; **le satellite est en o. basse** the satellite is on a low orbit; **mettre en** *ou* **placer sur o.** to put into orbit
 3 *Phys* orbital
 4 *Fig* (*d'une personne, d'un pays*) sphere of influence, orbit
orbitèle [ɔʀbitɛl] NF *Zool* orbitelarian, geometric spider
orbiter [3] [ɔʀbite] VI to orbit; **o. autour de** to orbit (round)
orbiteur [ɔʀbitœʀ] NM orbiter
Orcades [ɔʀkad] NFPL **les O.** the Orkney Islands, the Orkneys; **les O. du Sud** the South Orkney Islands
orcanette, orcanète [ɔʀkanɛt] NF *Bot* alkanet, dyer's bugloss
orchestral, -e, -aux, -ales [ɔʀkɛstʀal, -o] ADJ orchestral, orchestra (*avant n*); **la partition orchestrale** the orchestral or orchestra score
orchestrateur, -trice [ɔʀkɛstʀatœʀ, -tʀis] NM,F orchestrator
orchestration [ɔʀkɛstʀasjɔ̃] NF 1 *Mus* orchestration; **faire une nouvelle o. d'un morceau** to re-orchestrate a piece 2 *Fig* (*organisation*) orchestration, organization

orchestratrice [ɔʀkɛstʀatʀis] *voir* **orchestrateur**
orchestre [ɔʀkɛstʀ] NM 1 *Mus* (*classique*) orchestra; (*de jazz*) band, orchestra; **grand o.** full orchestra; **o. symphonique/de chambre** symphony/chamber orchestra; **o. de cuivres** brass band; **o. philharmonique** philharmonic (orchestra) 2 *Cin & Théât Br* stalls, *Am* orchestra; **nous sommes à l'o.** we have seats in the *Br* stalls or *Am* orchestra 3 *Antiq* orchestra
orchestrer [3] [ɔʀkɛstʀe] VT 1 *Mus* (*composer*) to orchestrate; (*adapter*) to orchestrate, to score 2 *Fig* (*préparer*) to orchestrate, to organize; **une campagne de diffamation orchestrée par plusieurs partis** a dirty tricks campaign orchestrated by several parties
orchidacée [ɔʀkidase] NF member of the Orchidaceae
orchidectomie [ɔʀkidɛktɔmi] NF *Méd* orchidectomy
orchidée [ɔʀkide] NF orchid
orchis [ɔʀkis] NM *Bot* orchis, wild orchid; **o. militaire** military orchid, soldier orchid; **o. à deux feuilles** butterfly orchid; **o. pourpre** purple orchid; **o. pyramidal** pyramidal orchid; **o. taché** spotted orchid
orchite [ɔʀkit] NF *Méd* orchitis
ordalie [ɔʀdali] NF *Hist* ordeal; **o. par l'eau/le feu** ordeal by water/fire
ordalique [ɔʀdalik] ADJ *Psy* (*conduite*) death-defying

'Ordet' *Dreyer* 'The Word'

ordi [ɔʀdi] NM *Fam* computer■, *Br* puter
ordinaire [ɔʀdinɛʀ] ADJ 1 (*habituel → journée*) ordinary, normal; (→ *procédure*) usual, standard, normal; (→ *comportement*) ordinary, usual, customary; *Jur & Pol* (→ *session*) ordinary; **elle parlait avec son arrogance o.** she was talking with her usual or customary arrogance; **en temps o.** usually, normally; **peu** *ou* **pas o.** (*attitude, méthode, journée*) unusual; (*volonté*) unusual, extraordinary; **nous nous sommes couchés à 22 heures, rien que de très o.** we went to bed at 10, nothing unusual about that; **il n'a même pas téléphoné – voilà qui n'est pas o.!** he didn't even phone – that's odd or that's not like him!; **médecin o. du roi** physician in ordinary to the king
 2 (*de tous les jours → habits, vaisselle*) ordinary, everyday (*avant n*); **mets la vaisselle o.**, **ça ira très bien** bring out the ordinary crockery, that'll do just fine
 3 *Com* (*qualité, modèle*) standard; (*produit*) ordinary
 4 (*banal → cuisine, goûts*) ordinary, plain; (→ *gens*) ordinary, common; (→ *spectacle*) ordinary, run-of-the-mill; (→ *conversation*) run-of-the-mill, commonplace; **c'est quelqu'un de très o.** he's/she's a very ordinary person; **elle mène une existence très o.** she leads a very humdrum existence; **elle n'est pas o., ton histoire!** your story is certainly an unusual one!; **voilà une chose qui n'est pas o.!** that's not something you see every day
 5 *Géom* **point o.** regular point
 NM 1 (*norme*) **l'o.** the ordinary; **voilà ce qui fait l'o. de son existence** that's how he/she generally spends his/her time; **sortir de l'o.** to be out of the ordinary, to be unusual; **son mari sort vraiment de l'o.!** her husband is one of a kind!
 2 (*repas habituel*) everyday or ordinary fare; **pour améliorer l'o. des soldats** in order to improve the soldiers' ordinary fare; **une auberge où l'o. est excellent** an inn where the food is excellent; *Hum* **voulez-vous partager notre o.?** will you share our humble repast?
 3 (*essence*) *Br* ≃ two-star petrol, *Am* ≃ regular
 4 *Mus & Rel* ordinary
 5 *Mil* (company) mess
 □ **à l'ordinaire** ADV **plus intéressant qu'à l'o.** more interesting than usual; **comme à l'o., il arriva en retard** as usual, he turned up late
 □ **d'ordinaire** ADV usually, ordinarily, normally; **plus tôt que d'o.** earlier than usual; **une attitude plus franche que d'o.** an unusually honest attitude
ordinairement [ɔʀdinɛʀmã] ADV usually, ordinarily, normally

ordinal, -e, -aux, -ales [ɔrdinal, -o] **ADJ** *(adjectif, nombre)* ordinal
NM 1 *(nombre)* ordinal (number) **2** *(adjectif)* ordinal (adjective)

ordinand [ɔrdinɑ̃] **NM** *Rel* ordinand

ordinant [ɔrdinɑ̃] **NM** *Rel* ordinant, ordainer

ordinariat [ɔrdinarja] **NM** *Belg Univ* tenured *Br* lectureship *or Am* professorship

ordinateur [ɔrdinatœr] **NM 1** *(machine)* computer; **mettre qch sur o.** to computerize sth, to put sth on computer; **la vitesse a été calculée par o.** the speed was calculated by computer *or* computer-calculated; **o. analogique** analogue computer; **o. autonome** stand-alone (computer); **o. bloc-notes** notebook (computer); **o. de bord** *Aut* trip computer; *Naut* shipboard computer; **o. de bureau** desktop computer; **o. central** mainframe (computer); **o. domestique** home computer; **o. dorsal** back-end computer; **o. à écran tactile** touch-screen computer; **o. embarqué** onboard computer; **o. familial** family computer; **o. frontal** front-end computer; **o. de gestion** business computer; **o. hôte** host computer; **o. individuel** home *or* personal computer, PC; **o. multimédia** multimedia computer; **o. numérique** digital computer; **o. personnel** home *or* personal computer, PC; **o. de poche** palmtop (computer); **o. portable** portable computer; **o. portatif** laptop computer; **o. de réseau** network computer; **o. sans clavier** keyboardless computer; **o. serveur** host computer, server; **o. de table** desktop (PC); **o. vectoriel** vector processor
2 *Rel* ordainer, ordinant

ordination [ɔrdinasjɔ̃] **NF 1** *Rel (d'un prêtre)* ordination; *(consécration)* consecration **2** *Math* ordering

ordinogramme [ɔrdinɔgram] **NM** (process) flow chart *or* flow diagram

ordo [ɔrdo] **NM INV** *Rel* ordo

ordonnance [ɔrdɔnɑ̃s] **NF 1** *(disposition)* organization, order, arrangement; **l'o. des mots dans une phrase** the arrangement *or* order of words in a sentence; **l'o. du dîner avait été décidée un mois auparavant** they had decided a month earlier what the order of the meal would be; **je ne veux pas déranger l'o. de vos papiers** I don't want to disturb your papers
2 *Archit* layout, disposition
3 *Méd* prescription; **un médicament vendu sans o.** a drug that can be bought over the counter; **délivré seulement sur o.** available on prescription only
4 *Jur (loi)* ordinance, statutory instrument; *(jugement)* order, ruling; *(de police)* (police) regulation *or* order; **o. d'amnistie** amnesty order; **o. de clôture** closing order; **o. d'incarcération provisoire** interim detention order; **o. d'interdiction temporaire** restraining order; **o. de mise en détention** detention order; **o. de mise sous séquestre** receiving order, sequestration order; **o. de non-informer** = refusal by examining judge to open an investigation; **o. de non-lieu** non-suit; **rendre une o. de non-lieu** to dismiss a case for lack of evidence; **o. pénale** = simplified sentencing for lesser offences where the defendant is not obliged to be present; **o. de prise de corps** writ of capias; **o. de règlement** disposal order; **o. de renvoi** committal for trial; **o. de saisie** writ of execution; **o. de saisie-attribution** garnishee order; **o. de soit-communiqué** = order to proceed with a criminal prosecution; **o. de taxe** = order for the recovery of taxable charges; **o. de transmission (de pièces)** transfer order
5 *Hist* ordinance (law), decree
6 *Fin* **o. de paiement** order to pay, authorization of payment
7 *Mil* orderly; **revolver d'o.** service pistol; **bottes d'o.** standard issue boots; **officier d'o.** aide-de-camp; *Naut* flag lieutenant
NM OU NF *Arch* (military) orderly

ordonnancement [ɔrdɔnɑ̃smɑ̃] **NM 1** *Ind (organisation des phases)* sequencing; *(prévision des délais)* timing, scheduling **2** *Fin* order to pay **3** *Ordinat* scheduling **4 o. juridique** legal system

ordonnancer [16] [ɔrdɔnɑ̃se] **VT 1** *(agencer)* to arrange, to organize; **qui a ordonnancé la cérémonie?** who arranged the ceremony? **2** *Fin (déclarer bon à payer)* to authorize **3** *Ordinat* to schedule

ordonnancier [ɔrdɔnɑ̃sje] **NM** *(de pharmacien)* prescription book *or* register; *(de médecin)* prescription pad

ordonnateur, -trice [ɔrdɔnatœr, -tris] **NM,F 1** *(organisateur)* organizer; **le comité sera l'o. de la cérémonie** the committee will be in charge of *or* will organize the ceremony; **o. des pompes funèbres** funeral director **2** *Fin* = official in charge of overseeing public expenditure

ordonné, -e[1] [ɔrdɔne] **ADJ 1** *(méthodique → personne)* tidy, neat; *(→ esprit)* methodical, systematic **2** *(rangé → chambre)* tidy, neat, orderly **3** *(régulier → existence, mode de vie)* orderly, well-ordered **4** *Math* ordered

ordonnée[2] [ɔrdɔne] **NF** *Math* ordinate

ordonner [3] [ɔrdɔne] **VT 1** *(commander → silence, attaque, enquête)* to order; *Méd (→ traitement, repos)* to prescribe; **ils ont ordonné le secret sur l'affaire** they've ordered that the matter (should) be kept secret; **o. à qn de faire qch** to order *or* to command sb to do sth; **o. à qn de se taire** to tell sb to be quiet; **o. à qn d'entrer/de sortir** to order sb in/out; **je t'ordonne de me le rendre!** I order you to give it back to me!; **qui a ordonné qu'on les fusille?** who gave orders for them to be shot?
2 *(agencer → documents)* to (put in) order; *(→ arguments, idées)* to (put into) order, to arrange; *(→ chambre)* to tidy (up); *Math (→ nombres, suite)* to arrange in order; **o. des nombres du plus petit au plus grand/du plus grand au plus petit** to list numbers in ascending/descending order; **il faut davantage o. votre argumentation** you need to organize your arguments a bit more, you need to get more order into your arguments
3 *Rel* to ordain; **o. qn prêtre** to ordain sb
▸s'ordonner VPR *(faits)* to fall into order *or* place; **les indices s'ordonnaient dans mon esprit** the clues began to fall into place in my mind

ordovicien, -enne [ɔrdɔvisjɛ̃, -ɛn] *Géol* **ADJ** Ordovician
NM l'o. the Ordovician

ORDRE [ɔrdr]

> order **A, B1, 3–4, C** ▪ command **A1** ▪ sequence **B1** ▪ tidiness, neatness **B2** ▪ nature **C4**

NM A. *INSTRUCTION* **1** *(directive, injonction)* order; *Mil* order, command; **c'est un o.!** (and) that's an order!; **donner un o.** *(parent)* to give an order; *(officiel, policier, officier)* to issue *or* to give an order; **donner (l')o. de** to give the order to; **donner à qn l'o. de faire qch** to order sb to do sth, to give sb the order to do sth; **qui a donné l'o. d'attaquer?** who gave the order to attack?, who ordered the attack?; **donner des ordres à qn** to give sb orders; *Fig* to order sb around; **je n'aime pas qu'on me donne des ordres** I don't like being ordered around; **il aime bien donner des ordres** he likes giving orders; **recevoir des ordres** to receive *or* to take orders; **je n'aime pas recevoir d'ordres!** I don't like to be ordered around!; **recevoir l'o. de faire qch** to be ordered *or* to receive the order to do sth; **j'ai reçu l'o. formel de ne pas le déranger** I've been formally instructed not to disturb him; **par** *ou* **sur o. de** by order of, on the orders of; **être sous les ordres de qn** to be under sb's command; **être aux ordres de qn** to take orders from sb; **je ne suis pas à tes ordres!** I'm not at your beck and call!; *Mil* **o. d'appel** *Br* call-up papers, *Am* draft notice; **o. d'exécution** death warrant; **o. de grève** strike call; **o. d'incorporation** draft card; *Mil* **o. de mission** orders (for a mission); *Mil* **o. de route** marching orders; *Mil ou Hum* **à vos ordres!** yes, sir!
2 *Banque & Bourse* **à l'o. de** payable to, to the order of; **chèque à mon o.** cheque made out *or* payable to me; **c'est à quel o.?** who shall I make it payable to?; **o. d'achat** *(gén)* purchase order; *Bourse* buy order; **o. de Bourse** stock exchange order; **o. au comptant** cash order; *Bourse* **o. conditionnel** contingent order; *Bourse* **o. environ** discretionary order; *Bourse* **o. lié** straddle; *Bourse* **o. de négociation** trading order; *Banque* **o. de paiement** payment order; *Banque* **o. permanent** standing order; *Banque* **o. de prélèvement (permanent)** direct debit; *Bourse* **o. à révocation** good-till-cancelled order; *Bourse* **o. stop** stop order, stop loss order; *Bourse* **o. à terme** futures order; *Bourse* **o. tout ou rien** all-or-none order; *Banque* **o. de transfert permanent** banker's order, *Br* standing order; *Bourse* **o. de vente** selling order, order to sell; *Banque* **o. de virement** transfer order; *Banque* **o. de virement automatique, o. de virement bancaire** banker's order, *Br* standing order
3 *Jur* **o. d'exécution** death warrant; **o. de saisie** distraining order

B. *HIÉRARCHIE, AGENCEMENT* **1** *(succession)* order, sequence; **l'o. des mots dans la phrase** the word order in the sentence; **par o. d'arrivée/de grandeur/d'importance** in order of arrival/size/importance; **par o. chronologique/croissant/décroissant** in chronological/ascending/descending order; *Mil* **en o. de bataille/de marche** in battle/marching order; *Mil* **en o. dispersé/serré** in extended/close order; *Belg* **en o. principal** *(principalement)* principally; *Jur* primarily; *Belg* **en o. secondaire** *(secondairement)* secondly; *Jur* secondarily; *Belg* **en o. subsidiaire** *(subsidiairement)* additionally; *Jur* secondarily; *Aut* **o. d'allumage** firing sequence; **noms classés par o. alphabétique** names filed in alphabetical order; **par o. d'apparition à l'écran** in order of appearance; **par o. d'entrée en scène** in order of appearance; *TV* **o. de passage** running order; **par o. de préséance** in order of precedence; *Jur* **o. des héritiers** order of heirs; *Jur* **o. de juridictions** set *or* hierarchy of courts; *Jur* **o. utile** ranking (of creditor); *Jur* **o. de succession** intestate succession
2 *(rangement)* tidiness, neatness; **j'aimerais qu'il y ait un peu plus d'o. dans ta chambre** I'd like to see your room a little tidier; **attends, j'essaie de mettre de l'o. dans mes cartes** wait a minute, I'm trying to tidy up *or* to order my cards; **sans o.** *(maison, personne)* untidy; **la pièce était en o.** the room was tidy; **mettre qch en o.** to put sth in order; **mets tes vêtements en o.** sort out your clothes; **remettre qch en o.** to tidy sth up; **tenir une maison en o.** to keep a house tidy; **avoir de l'o.** *(sens du rangement)* to be tidy; **manquer** *ou* **ne pas avoir d'o.** to be untidy; **manque d'o.** untidiness
3 *(organisation méthodique → de documents)* order; **mettre qch en o., mettre de l'o. dans qch** *(documents, comptabilité)* to set sth in order, to tidy sth up; **mettre de l'o. dans ses idées** to order one's ideas; **mettre ses affaires en o.** *(avant de mourir)* to settle one's affairs, to put one's affairs in order; **il a laissé ses papiers/ses comptes en o. avant de partir** he left his papers/accounts in order before leaving; **remettre de l'o. dans sa vie** to sort out one's life; **mettre bon o. à qch** to sort sth out; **il abuse de vous, vous devez y mettre bon o.** he's taking advantage of you, you must sort that out
4 *(discipline sociale)* **l'o.** order; **faire régner l'o.** to keep *or* to maintain order; **rappeler qn à l'o.** to call sb to order; **se faire rappeler à l'o.** *(dans une assemblée)* to be called to order; *(dans une classe)* to get told off; **la police est chargée du maintien de l'o.** it's the police's job to keep law and order; **l'o. établi** the established order; **l'o. public** public order, law and order; **puis tout est rentré dans l'o.** then order was restored, then everything went back to normal

C. *CLASSIFICATION, DOMAINE* **1** *Rel* order; **l'o. des dominicains/des capucins** the order of Dominicans/Capuchins; **les ordres mineurs/majeurs** the minor/major orders; **les ordres mendiants** the mendicant orders; **les ordres monastiques** the monastic orders; **les saints ordres** the holy orders; **entrer dans les ordres** to take (holy) orders
2 *(confrérie)* **l'o. administratif** the administrative court system; **l'o. des avocats** *Br* ≃ the Bar, *Am* ≃ the Bar Association; **l'o. judiciaire** the

ordinary court system, the non-administrative court system; **l'o. juridique** the legal system; **l'o. des médecins** *Br* ≃ the British Medical Association, *Am* ≃ the American Medical Association; **les ordres de chevalerie** the orders of knighthood; **l'O. d'Orange** the Orange Order; **o. professionnel** professional body; *Hist* **les trois ordres** the three orders

3 *(association honorifique)* **l'O. des Arts et des Lettres** = order for high literary or artistic achievement; **l'O. de la Jarretière** the Order of the Garter; **l'O. national du Mérite** = the French Order of Merit; **l'O. du Mérite agricole** = award for services to farming; **l'O. du Mérite maritime** = award for maritime service; **l'O. des Palmes académiques** = order for high academic achievement

4 *(nature, sorte)* nature, order; **des problèmes d'o. professionnel** problems of a professional nature; **mes raisons sont d'o. différent** my reasons are of a different order; **dans le même o. d'idées** similarly; **dans un autre o. d'idées** in another connection; **du même o.** *(proposition, responsabilités)* similar, of the same nature; **pour un salaire du même o.** for a similar salary; **de l'o. de** in the region *or* order of; **une augmentation de 5 pour cent? – oui, de cet o.** a 5 percent rise? – yes, roughly *or* in that region; **donner un o. de grandeur** to give a rough estimate; **des sommes du même o. de grandeur** sums of the same order, similar sums of money; **c'est dans l'o. des choses** it's in the order *or* nature of things

5 *Archit & Biol* order; **o. attique/dorique/ionique** Attic/Doric/Ionic order

❑ **de dernier ordre** ADJ third-rate

❑ **de premier ordre** ADJ first-rate

❑ **de second ordre** ADJ *(question)* of secondary importance; *(artiste, personnalité)* second-rate

❑ **ordre du jour** NM **1** *(d'un comité)* agenda; *Parl* order of the day; **être à l'o. du jour** to be on the agenda; *Fig* to be in the news; **mettre qch à l'o. du jour** to put *or* to place sth on the agenda

2 *Mil* general orders, order of the day; **cité à l'o. du jour** mentioned in dispatches

ordré, -e [ɔrdre] ADJ *Suisse (ordonné)* tidy, orderly, neat

ordure [ɔrdyr] NF **1** *très Fam (individu méprisable)* scumbag, *Br* rotter, *Am* stinker

2 *Littéraire (fange)* **l'o.** filth, mire; **se vautrer dans l'o.** to wallow in filth

❑ **ordures** NFPL **1** *(déchets)* refuse *(UNCOUNT)*, *Br* rubbish *(UNCOUNT)*, *Am* garbage *(UNCOUNT)*, trash *(UNCOUNT)*; **ramasser les ordures** to collect the *Br* rubbish *or Am* garbage *or* trash; **vider les ordures** to empty (out) the *Br* rubbish *or Am* garbage *or* trash; **jeter** *ou* **mettre qch aux ordures** to throw sth into the *Br* rubbish bin *or Am* garbage can *or* trash can; **c'est bon à mettre aux ordures!** it's fit for the *Br* dustbin *or Am* garbage can *or* trash can!; **mets-le aux ordures** put it in the *Br* dustbin *or Am* garbage can *or* trash can, throw it away; **ordures ménagères** household refuse

2 *(excréments)* dirt *(UNCOUNT)*, filth *(UNCOUNT)*; **faire ses ordures sur le trottoir** *(chien)* to make a mess on the pavement

3 *Fam (obscénités)* obscenities■, filth *(UNCOUNT)*; **elle ne dit que des ordures** she always uses filthy language; **dire/écrire des ordures sur qn** to talk/to write filth about sb

ordurier, -ère [ɔrdyrje, -ɛr] ADJ foul, filthy, obscene

öre, øre [øʀə] NM *(monnaie)* öre, øre

oréade [ɔread] NF *Myth* oread, grotto *or* mountain nymph

orée [ɔre] NF *Littéraire* edge; **à l'o. du bois** on the edge of the wood

Oregon [ɔregɔ̃] NM *Géog* **l'O.** Oregon; **dans l'O.** in Oregon

oreillard, -e [ɔrɛjar, -ard] ADJ long-eared

NM **1** *(chauve-souris)* long-eared bat **2** *(lièvre, âne)* long-eared animal **3** *(d'un fauteuil)* wing

oreille [ɔrɛj] NF **1** *(partie du corps)* ear; **j'ai mal aux oreilles** I've got earache, my ears are hurting; **avoir les oreilles décollées** to have protruding *or* sticking-out ears; **avoir les oreilles en feuille de chou** to have cauliflower ears; **avoir les oreilles qui bourdonnent** *ou* **des bourdonnements d'o.** to have a buzzing in the ears; **chien aux oreilles courtes/longues** short-eared/long-eared dog; **coucher les oreilles** *(d'un cheval)* to set *or* to lay its ears back; **elle n'entend pas de l'o. gauche** she's deaf in the left ear; *Fig* **il ne l'entend pas de cette o.** he won't hear of it; **mettre** *ou* **porter son chapeau sur l'o.** to wear one's hat over one ear; **o. interne/moyenne** inner/middle ear; **o. externe** outer *or* external ear; *Fig Hum* **les oreilles ont dû lui siffler** his/her ears must have been burning; **elle est repartie l'o. basse** she left with her tail between her legs; *Fig* **frotter les oreilles à qn** to box sb's ears; *Fig* **montrer le bout de l'o.** to show (oneself in) one's true colours; **tirer les oreilles à qn** to pull sb's ears; *Fig (réprimander)* to tell sb off; *Fig* **tu vas te faire tirer les oreilles** you'll get told off, you'll get a telling-off; *Fig* **se faire tirer l'o.** to need a lot of persuading; **il ne s'est pas fait tirer l'o. pour accepter** he didn't have to be asked twice *or* to have his arm twisted before saying yes; *Fam* **chauffer** *ou* **échauffer les oreilles à qn** to get on sb's nerves, to annoy sb

2 *(ouïe)* (sense of) hearing; **avoir l'o. fine** to have an acute sense of hearing; **avoir de l'o.** *ou* **l'o. musicale** to have a good ear for music; **avoir l'o. absolue** to have perfect pitch

3 *(pour écouter)* ear; **dresser** *ou* **tendre l'o.** to prick up one's ears; **écouter une conversation d'une o. distraite** to listen to a conversation with only half an ear; **écouter de toutes ses oreilles, être tout oreilles** to be all ears; **ouvrir ses oreilles toutes grandes** to listen very carefully; **ouvrez bien vos oreilles!** listen very carefully!; **venir** *ou* **parvenir aux oreilles de qn** to come to *or* to reach sb's ears; **l'histoire étant parvenue à mes oreilles, je lui téléphonai** when I got wind of the story, I called him/her; **dire** *ou* **souffler qch à l'o. de qn** *ou* **dans le creux de l'o. de qn** to whisper sth in sb's ear; **je n'en crois pas mes oreilles** I can't believe my ears *or* what I'm hearing; *Fam* **ça rentre par une o. et ça sort par l'autre** it goes in one ear and out the other; *Fam* **ce n'est pas tombé dans l'o. d'un sourd!** it hasn't fallen on deaf ears!

4 *Tech (d'une cocotte)* handle; *(d'un écrou)* wing; *(d'une casquette)* earflap; **fauteuil à oreilles** wing chair

5 *Journ* position to right/left of headline

oreille-de-mer [ɔrɛjdəmɛr] *(pl* **oreilles-de-mer***)* NF earshell, *Spéc* haliotis

oreille-de-souris [ɔrɛjdəsuri] *(pl* **oreilles-de-souris***)* NF *Bot* forget-me-not

oreiller [ɔrɛje] NM pillow; **sur l'o.** in bed; **confidences sur l'o.** pillow talk

oreillette [ɔrɛjɛt] NF **1** *Anat* auricle **2** *(d'une casquette)* earflap; **fauteuil à oreillettes** wing chair **3** *(d'un baladeur)* earphone

oreillette-micro [ɔrɛjɛtmikro] *(pl* **oreillettes-micros***)* NF wireless headset

oreillon [ɔrɛjɔ̃] NM **1** *Archéol* ear-piece, cheek-piece **2** *Anat & Zool* tragus **3** *(moitié d'abricot)* apricot half

❑ **oreillons** NMPL *Méd* mumps; **avoir les oreillons** to have (the) mumps

orémus [ɔremys] NM *Rel* **1** *(invitation à prière)* let us pray **2** *Fam Vieilli (prière)* prayer■

Orénoque [ɔrenɔk] NM **l'O.** the Orinoco

oréopithèque [ɔreɔpitɛk] NM Oreopithecus

oréotrague [ɔreɔtrag] NM *Zool* **o. (sauteur)** klipspringer

ores [ɔr] **d'ores et déjà** ADV already

Oreste [ɔrɛst] NPR *Myth* Orestes

orfèvre [ɔrfɛvr] NM **1** *(artisan qui travaille → l'or)* goldsmith; *(→ l'argent)* silversmith **2** *(locution)* **être o. en la matière** to be an expert in the matter

orfévré, -e [ɔrfevre] ADJ worked, wrought

orfèvrerie [ɔrfɛvrəri] NF **1** *(métier → de l'or)* goldsmithing, gold work; *(→ de l'argent)* silversmithing, silver work; **l'o.** *(produits → en or)* gold plate; *(→ en argent)* silver plate **2** *(boutique → d'objets d'or)* goldsmith's *Br* shop *or Am* store; *(→ d'objets d'argent)* silversmith's *Br* shop *or Am* store

orfraie [ɔrfrɛ] NF white-tailed eagle

orfroi [ɔrfrwa] NM orphrey, orfray

organdi [ɔrgɑ̃di] NM organdie; **d'o., en o.** organdie

organe [ɔrgan] NM **1** *Anat* organ; **organes génitaux** *ou* **sexuels** genitals, genitalia; **organes vocaux** *ou* **de la parole** speech *or* vocal organs; *Méd* **o. cible** receptor; **organes des sens** sense organs; *Biol* **o. sécréteur** secretory

2 *(voix)* voice; **avoir un bel o.** to have a fine voice

3 *Tech* part, component; **organes de commande** controls; **organes de transmission** transmission system; *Ordinat* **o. d'entrée** input unit; *Ordinat* **o. périphérique** peripheral device

4 *(institution)* organ; **les organes de l'État** the apparatus of the state; **l'O. international de contrôle des stupéfiants** the International Narcotics Control Board; **o. de presse** newspaper, publication; **les organes de presse** the press

5 *(porte-parole, publication)* mouthpiece, organ; **l'o. officiel du parti** the official organ *or* mouthpiece of the party

6 *(instrument)* medium, vehicle; **o. de publicité** advertising medium

organeau, -x [ɔrgano] NM **1** *(sur un quai)* mooring ring **2** *(sur une ancre)* anchor ring

organelle [ɔrganɛl] NF *Biol* organelle

organicien, -enne [ɔrganisjɛ̃, -ɛn] NM,F organic chemist, organicist

organicisme [ɔrganisism] NM organicism

organiciste [ɔrganisist] ADJ organicist

NMF organicist

organier [ɔrganje] NM organ builder

organigramme [ɔrganigram] NM **1** *(structure)* organization *or* organizational chart, organigram **2** *Ordinat (de programmation)* flow chart *or* diagram; **o. de production** production flow chart

organique [ɔrganik] ADJ organic

organiquement [ɔrganikmɑ̃] ADV organically

organisable [ɔrganizabl] ADJ organizable

organisateur, -trice [ɔrganizatœr, -tris] ADJ *Biol* organizing *(avant n)*

NM,F organizer; *(d'une rencontre sportive)* promoter, organizer; **o. de conférences/de congrès** conference organizer; **o. d'événements** event coordinator *or* organizer; **o. de mariages** wedding planner; **o. de voyages** tour operator

NM *Biol* organizer; **o. nucléolaire** nucleolar organizer

organisateur-conseil [ɔrganizatœrkɔ̃sɛj] *(pl* **organisateurs-conseils***)* NM management consultant

organisation [ɔrganizasjɔ̃] NF **1** *(organisme)* organization; **O. de l'alimentation et l'agriculture** Food and Agriculture Organization; *Hist* **O. de l'armée secrète** Secret Army Organization *(right-wing group opposed to Algerian independence)*; **O. de l'aviation civile internationale** International Civil Aviation Authority; **O. de coopération et de développement économique** Organization for Economic Cooperation and Development; **O. européenne de coopération économique** Organization for European Economic Cooperation; **o. gouvernementale** governmental organization; **o. humanitaire** aid agency; **o. internationale** international organization *or* agency; **O. internationale de normalisation** International Standards Organization; **O. internationale du travail** International Labour Organization; **O. de libération de la Palestine** Palestine Liberation Organization; **O. maritime internationale** International Maritime Organization; **O. mondiale du commerce** World Trade Organization; **O. mondiale de la santé** World Health Organization; **O. des Nations unies** United Nations Organization; **O. des Nations unies pour le développement industriel** United Nations Industrial Development Organization; **O. des Nations unies pour l'éducation, la science et la culture** United Nations Educational, Scientific and Cultural Organization; **O. de la navigation maritime consultative et intergouvernementale** Intergovernmental Maritime Consultative Organization; **o. non gouvernementale** nongovernmental organization; **o. patronale** employers' organization *or* association; **O. des pays exportateurs de pétrole** Organization of Petroleum Exporting Countries; **o. de solidarité** aid organization; **o. de solidarité internationale** international aid organization; **o. syndicale**

trade union; **O. du traité de l'Atlantique Nord** North Atlantic Treaty Organization; **o. de travailleurs** workers' organization; **O. de l'unité africaine** Organization of African Unity

2 *(mise sur pied → d'une fête, d'une réunion, d'un service)* organization; *(→ d'une manifestation)* organization, staging; *(→ d'un attentat)* organization, planning; **l'o. du temps de travail** the organization of working hours; **o. d'événements** event management

3 *(structure → d'un discours, d'une association, d'un système)* organization, structure; *(→ du travail)* organization; *Ordinat* **o. des données** data organization; *Com* **o. scientifique du travail** organization and methods, time and motion studies; **o. hiérarchique** *ou* **verticale** line organization; **o. horizontale** flat organization

4 *(méthode)* organization; **avoir de l'o.** to be organized; **ne pas avoir d'o.** to be disorganized

5 *Biol (du corps humain)* structure

organisationnel, -elle [ɔrganizasjɔnɛl] **ADJ** organizational

organisatrice [ɔrganizatris] *voir* **organisateur**

organisé, -e [ɔrganize] **ADJ 1** *(regroupé → consommateurs, groupe)* organized **2** *(aménagé)* **bien/mal o.** well-/badly-organized **3** *(méthodique → personne)* organized, well-organized, methodical **4** *Biol* **êtres organisés** organisms

organiser [3] [ɔrganize] **VT 1** *(mettre sur pied → gén)* to organize; *Mil (attaque)* to plan

2 *(agencer → association, journée, tâche)* to organize; *(→ temps, emploi du temps)* to organize, to plan; **le service est organisé en plusieurs sections** the department is organized into several divisions; **j'ai organisé mon emploi du temps de façon à pouvoir partir plus tôt** I've organized *or* planned my schedule so that I can leave earlier

▸**s'organiser VPR 1** *(se préparer)* to be planned; **un voyage, ça s'organise longtemps à l'avance** trips have to be organized *or* planned well in advance

2 *(personne)* to get (oneself) organized, to organize oneself; **il suffit de s'o.** all you need is some organization; **la société s'est vite organisée en classes sociales** society rapidly became organized into social classes

organiseur [ɔrganizœr] **NM** *(agenda, logiciel)* organizer; **o. électronique** electronic organizer

organisme [ɔrganism] **NM 1** *Biol (animal, végétal)* organism; *(humain)* body, organism; **les réactions de l'o.** bodily reactions; **c'est mauvais pour l'o.** it's bad for your health *or* for you; **o. génétiquement modifié** genetically modified organism

2 *(organisation)* organization, body; **o. d'aide** aid organization; **o. de charité** charity (organization); **o. de contrôle** *ou* **de surveillance** watchdog; **o. de crédit** credit organization *or* institution; **o. de défense des consommateurs** consumer organization; **o. de gestion** management body; **o. international** international organization; **o. de normalisation** standards committee; *Fin* **o. de placement collectif** collective investment scheme; *Fin* **o. de placement collectif en valeurs mobilières** *Br* ≃ unit trust, *Am* ≃ mutual fund; **o. professionnel** professional body

organiste [ɔrganist] **NMF** organist

organite [ɔrganit] **NM** *Biol* organelle

organochloré, -e [ɔrganɔklɔre] *Chim* **ADJ** organochlorinated

NM organochlorine

organogenèse [ɔrganɔʒənɛz] **NF** *Biol* organogenesis

organoleptique [ɔrganɔlɛptik] **ADJ** organoleptic

organologie [ɔrganɔlɔʒi] **NF** *Mus* organology

organomagnésien, -enne [ɔrganɔmaɲezjɛ̃, -ɛn] *Chim* **ADJ** organomagnesium *(avant n)*

NM organomagnesium compound

organométallique [ɔrganɔmetalik] *Chim* **ADJ** organometallic, metalorganic

NM organometallic *or* metalorganic compound

organophosphoré, -e [ɔrganɔfɔsfɔre] *Chim* **ADJ** organophosphate

NM organophosphate

organsin [ɔrgɑ̃sɛ̃] **NM** organzine (silk)

organsiner [3] [ɔrgɑ̃sine] **VT** to organzine

organza [ɔrgɑ̃za] **NM** organza

orgasme [ɔrgasm] **NM** orgasm

orgasmique [ɔrgasmik], **orgastique** [ɔrgastik] **ADJ** orgasmic

orge [ɔrʒ] **NF** barley

NM barley; **o. mondé/perlé** hulled/pearl barley

orgeat [ɔrʒa] **NM** orgeat

orgelet [ɔrʒəlɛ] **NM** sty, stye

orgiaque [ɔrʒjak] **ADJ** orgiastic

orgie [ɔrʒi] **NF 1** *(débauche)* orgy; **faire une o.** to have an orgy; *Fig* **j'ai fait une o. de foie gras** I gorged myself on foie gras **2** *(abondance)* riot, profusion; **une o. de roses** a profusion of roses; **une o. de bleus et de rouges** a riot of blues and reds; **une o. de lumières** a profusion of light

▫ **orgies NFPL** *Antiq* orgies

orgue [ɔrg] **NM 1** *Mus* organ; **tenir l'o.** to be at the organ; **jouer de l'o.** to play the organ; **o. électrique/électronique/de chœur** electric/electronic/choir organ; **o. de Barbarie** barrel organ; **o. à plein jeu** full organ; **buffet d'o.** organ case; **grand o.** great organ; **point d'o.** pause

2 *Mil* **orgues de Staline** Katyusha

3 *Zool* **o. de mer** organ-pipe coral, tubipore

▫ **orgues NFPL 1** *Mus* organ; **les grandes orgues de la cathédrale** the great organ of the cathedral; *Fig* **faire donner les grandes orgues** to be pompous

2 *Géol* columnar structure *or* structures; **orgues de basalte** basalt columns

orgueil [ɔrgœj] **NM 1** *(fierté)* pride

2 *(amour-propre)* pride; **il a trop d'o. pour faire des excuses** he's too proud *or* he has too much pride to apologize; **c'est de l'o. mal placé** it's just misplaced pride; **gonflé** *ou* **bouffi d'o.** puffed up *or* bursting with pride

3 *(sujet de fierté)* pride; **j'étais l'o. de ma mère** I was my mother's pride and joy; **le "Nautilus", o. de la flotte** the "Nautilus", the pride of the fleet

orgueilleuse [ɔrgœjøz] *voir* **orgueilleux**

orgueilleusement [ɔrgœjøzmɑ̃] **ADV 1** *(avec arrogance)* proudly, arrogantly **2** *(avec fierté)* proudly

orgueilleux, -euse [ɔrgœjø, -øz] **ADJ 1** *(arrogant)* conceited, arrogant **2** *(fier → personne)* proud **3** *Littéraire (majestueux → démarche, navire)* proud

NM,F 1 *(prétentieux)* arrogant *or* conceited person **2** *(fier)* proud person

orgyie [ɔrʒii] **NF** *Entom* tussock moth

orichalque [ɔrikalk] **NM** orichalc, oricalche

oriel [ɔrjɛl] **NM** oriel (window), bay window

orient [ɔrjɑ̃] **NM 1** *(est)* east, orient; **parfum/tapis d'o.** oriental scent/carpet; *Littéraire* **génie à son o.** rising *or* budding genius **2** *Géog* **l'O.** the East *or* Orient; **en O.** in the East **3** *(d'une perle)* orient

4 le Grand O. *(maçonnique)* the Grand Orient

orientable [ɔrjɑ̃tabl] **ADJ 1** *(antenne, rétroviseur)* adjustable **2** *(lampe)* rotating, swivel *(avant n)*

oriental, -e, -aux, -ales [ɔrjɑ̃tal, -o] **ADJ 1** *Géog* eastern, east *(avant n)*; **la plaine orientale** the eastern plain **2** *(de l'Orient → art, cuisine, civilisation)* oriental, eastern; *(langue)* oriental

NM,F Oriental, Easterner

▫ **à l'orientale ADV** in the oriental style

orientalisme [ɔrjɑ̃talism] **NM** orientalism

orientaliste [ɔrjɑ̃talist] **ADJ** orientalist

NMF orientalist

orientateur, trice [ɔrjɑ̃tatœr, -tris] **NM,F** = **orienteur, -trice**

orientation [ɔrjɑ̃tasjɔ̃] **NF 1** *(direction → d'une enquête, de recherches)* direction, orientation; *(→ d'un mouvement)* orientation; *(→ d'une politique)* thrust; **l'o. de notre entreprise doit changer** our firm must adopt a new outlook; **o. stratégique d'une société** corporate strategic orientation; **o. politique** *(d'un journal, d'une personne)* political leanings *or* tendencies; *(d'un parti)* political direction

2 *Scol (conseil → pour des études)* academic counselling; *(→ vers un métier)* careers guidance; *(direction → des études)* course; *(→ du métier)* career; **choisir une o.** to choose a course of study; **o. en fin de cinquième** = determination of future course of studies at the end of one's second year; **o. professionnelle** careers advice *or* guidance

3 *(position → d'un édifice)* direction; **l'o. plein sud de l'appartement est un de ses principaux atouts** one of the *Br* flat's *or Am* apartment's main assets is that it faces due south

4 *(positionnement → d'un faisceau, d'une lampe)* directing; *(→ d'un rétroviseur)* adjustment; *(→ d'une grue, d'une antenne)* positioning; **o. d'un canon** training of a gun; **à o. libre** free-moving, adjustable; *Aut* **o. de la roue** wheel alignment, tracking

5 *(aptitude)* **avoir le sens de l'o.** to have a good sense of direction; **course d'o.** orienteering course; **parcours d'o.** orienteering course; **table d'o.** orientation *or* panoramic table

6 *Astron* attitude

7 *Biol* orientation

8 *Naut* set, trim; **o. des voiles** set *or* trim of the sails

9 *Math* orientation

10 *(tendance)* **o. de la Bourse** stock market trend; *Mktg* **o. clientèle** customer orientation; **o. économique** economic direction; *Mktg* **o. marché** market orientation *or* trend; **o. du marché à la baisse/hausse** downward/upward market trend

orienté, -e [ɔrjɑ̃te] **ADJ 1** *(positionné)* **o. à l'ouest** *(édifice)* facing west, with a western aspect; *(radar)* directed towards the west; **local bien/mal o.** well-/badly-positioned premises

2 *(idéologiquement → discours, journal)* biased, slanted; **analyse orientée à droite** analysis with a right-wing bias

3 *Scol* **élève bien/mal o.** pupil who has taken the right/wrong academic advice

4 *Math* **segment o.** directed segment; **surface orientée** oriented surface

5 *Géog (carte)* orientated

6 *Bourse* **o. à la baisse** *(marché)* bearish, falling; **o. à la hausse** *(marché)* bullish, rising

7 *Ordinat* **o. bloc** block-orientated; **o. ligne** line-orientated; **o. objet** object-orientated; **o. problème** problem-orientated; **o. procédure** procedure-orientated

orientement [ɔrjɑ̃tmɑ̃] **NM** *Naut* bearing

orienter [3] [ɔrjɑ̃te] **VT 1** *(antenne, haut-parleur, spot)* to direct, to turn, to point; *(rétroviseur)* to adjust, to position; *(télescope)* to point, to direct; *(plante)* to position; *(canon, fusil)* to train (**vers** on); **orientez votre tente à l'est** pitch your tent so that it faces east; **o. un faisceau vers qch** to direct a beam towards sth; **oriente ton flash vers le plafond** point *or* turn your flashlight towards the ceiling; **la chambre est orientée plein nord** the bedroom faces due north

2 *(mettre sur une voie)* **o. vers** *(enquête, recherches)* to direct *or* to orientate towards; *(discussion)* to turn round to; *(passant)* to direct to; **il m'a demandé où était la gare mais je l'ai mal orienté** he asked where the station was, but I misdirected him; **on l'a orienté vers un spécialiste** he was referred to a specialist; **j'ai essayé d'o. la conversation sur toi** I tried to bring *or* to steer the conversation round to you; **o. ses études vers qch** to direct one's studies towards sth; **elle a été orientée vers une école technique** she was advised to go to a technical school; *Scol* **on l'a mal/bien orienté** he was given the wrong/right academic advice

3 *(rendre partial → discours)* to give a bias *or* a slant to; **ses cours sont politiquement orientés** his/her lectures are coloured by his/her political convictions

4 *(carte, plan, bâtiment)* to orientate

5 *Math* to orient; **o. une droite** to indicate the direction of a straight line

6 *Naut (voiles)* to trim

▸**s'orienter VPR 1** *(se repérer)* to take one's bearings; **j'ai toujours du mal à m'o.** I've got no sense of direction; **s'o. sur l'étoile polaire** to take one's bearings from the polar star

2 **s'o. vers** *(sujet: enquête, recherches)* to be directed towards; *(sujet: discussion)* to turn round to; *(sujet: parti, entreprise)* to move towards; *(sujet: étudiant)* to turn to; **il s'oriente vers une carrière commerciale** he's got his sights set on a career in sales; **s'o. vers la vente de produits écologiques** to specialize in the sale of environmentally-friendly products

orienteur, -euse [ɔrjɑ̃tœr, -øz] **NM,F 1** *Scol* academic counsellor **2** *(conseiller professionnel)* careers adviser, careers guidance officer

ADJ M officier o. interviewing officer

NM *(instrument)* orientator

orifice [ɔrifis] **NM 1** *(ouverture)* hole, opening;

oriflamme (*d'un puits, d'une galerie*) mouth; *Tech* port **2** *Anat* orifice **3** *Aut* **o. d'admission** intake port, inlet port; **o. d'air** air port; **o. d'alimentation** feed hole; **o. d'arrivée d'essence** petrol port; **o. d'écoulement d'huile** oil drain hole; **o. de remplissage** filling hole; **o. de sortie** outlet port

oriflamme [ɔriflam] **NF 1** (*bannière d'apparat*) banner, standard **2** *Hist* **l'o.** (*de Saint-Denis*) the sacred red banner of (the abbey of) Saint-Denis

origami [ɔrigami] **NM** origami

origan [ɔrigɑ̃] **NM** *Bot & Culin* oregano

originaire [ɔriʒinɛr] **ADJ 1** (*natif*) **être o. de** (*personne*) to be a native of; (*coutume, plat*) to originate from; **ma mère est o. de Paris** my mother was born in or comes from Paris; **il est o. de la Martinique** he's from Martinique; **animal/fruit/plante o. des pays tropicaux** animal/fruit/plant native to tropical countries **2** (*originel*) innate, inherent; (*membre*) original, founding

originairement [ɔriʒinɛrmɑ̃] **ADV** originally, at first

original, -e, -aux, -ales [ɔriʒinal, -o] **ADJ 1** (*nouveau → architecture, idée, système*) original, novel; (*→ cadeau, film, style, personne*) original; **il n'y a rien d'o. dans son dernier roman** there's nothing original in his/her latest novel

2 (*excentrique → personne*) odd, eccentric; **le moins qu'on puisse dire, c'est qu'elle est originale!** she's a bit eccentric, to say the least!

3 (*d'origine → document, manuscrit*) original

NM,F (*excentrique*) eccentric, character

NM 1 (*d'une œuvre*) original; (*d'un document, d'une disquette*) original or master (copy); (*d'un texte*) top copy, original; (*d'un objet, d'un personnage*) original; **copier qch d'après l'o.** to copy sth from the original; **il ne possède que des originaux** he owns only original works of art

2 (*texte à traduire*) original; **je préfère presque la traduction à l'o.** I like the translation almost more than the original

originalement [ɔriʒinalmɑ̃] **ADV** (*de façon nouvelle*) originally, in an original or novel way

originalité [ɔriʒinalite] **NF 1** (*caractère*) originality, novelty; **cet artiste manque d'o.** there is nothing new or original in this artist's work

2 (*extravagance*) eccentricity; **ses originalités la mettaient au ban de notre petite société** her strange or odd ways excluded her from our little group

3 (*nouveauté*) original feature; **cette robe est une des originalités de notre collection** this dress is one of the outstanding features of our collection

origine [ɔriʒin] **NF 1** (*cause première → d'un feu, d'une maladie, d'une querelle*) origin; **si nous remontons à l'o. du scandale** if we go back to the origin of the scandal; **avoir son o. dans, tirer son o. de** to have one's origins in, to originate in; **avoir qch pour o.** to be caused by sth; **la guerre a-t-elle eu pour o. l'assassinat de l'archiduc?** was the archduke's assassination the cause of the war?; **être à l'o. d'un projet de loi** (*personne*) to be behind a bill; **ces erreurs judiciaires ont été à l'o. du projet de loi** these miscarriages of justice were the impetus for the bill; **être à l'o. d'une querelle** (*personne*) to be behind or to be the cause of an argument; (*malentendu*) to be the origin or at the root of an argument; **symptômes d'o. cardiaque** symptoms due to heart problems

2 (*début*) origin, beginning; **les origines de la civilisation** the origins of civilization; **les vêtements, des origines à nos jours** (*dans un livre, dans un musée*) clothes, from their origins to the present day; **dès l'o.** from the (very) beginning, from the outset; **dès l'o., il y eut un malentendu** there was a misunderstanding right from the very start; **le travail du bronze, dès l'o., fut ornemental** bronze-working had a decorative function from its inception

3 (*source → d'un terme*) origin, root; (*d'une tradition*) origin; (*d'un produit manufacturé*) origin; **tirer son o. de qch** to originate from sth, to have its origins in sth; **le mot tire son o. du latin** the word originates or derives from the Latin; **l'o. de cette coutume est...** the custom has its origins in...; **la police connaît l'o. des**

appels the police know who made the calls; **quelle est l'o. de ces pêches?** where are these peaches from?

4 (*d'une personne*) origin; **il ne sait rien de ses origines** he doesn't know anything about his origins or where he comes from; **elle fait remonter ses origines à Louis-Philippe** she traces her origins back to Louis-Philippe; **d'o. modeste** of humble origin or birth; **d'o. espagnole** of Spanish origin; **il a des origines anglaises** he is of English extraction or has English origins; **la colonie devait son o. aux baleiniers** the colony was founded by or owed its origins to whalers

5 *Jur* **o. de propriété** vendor's title

6 *Géom* origin; *Math* **(point) o.** zero point

☐ **à l'origine** **ADV** originally, initially, at the beginning; **à l'o., je voulais écrire une chanson** I started off intending to or originally I wanted to write a song; **à l'o., le projet était bénévole** it was a voluntary project to begin with

☐ **d'origine** **ADJ** (*pays*) of origin; (*couleur, emballage, nom, monnaie*) original; **ma voiture a encore son moteur d'o.** my car has still got its original engine; **vins d'o.** vintage wines

'**De l'origine des espèces**' *Darwin* 'The Origin of Species'

originel, -elle [ɔriʒinɛl] **ADJ 1** (*primitif → innocence*) original **2** *Rel* original **3** (*premier*) original; (*cause*) original, primary; **sens o. d'un mot** original or primary meaning of a word

originellement [ɔriʒinɛlmɑ̃] **ADV** (*dès l'origine*) from the (very) start or beginning, from the outset; (*au début*) originally, at first

orignal, -aux [ɔriɲal, -o] **NM** *Zool* moose

orillon [ɔrijɔ̃] **NM 1** (*d'un récipient*) ear **2** (*d'un bastion*) orillon, orillion

orin [ɔrɛ̃] **NM** *Naut* mooring line

oriole [ɔrjɔl] **NM** *Can Orn* oriole

Orion [ɔrjɔ̃] **NPR** *Myth* Orion

NF *Astron* Orion

oripeaux [ɔripo] **NMPL** *Littéraire* (*vêtements*) tawdry rags

oriya [ɔrija] **NM** (*langue*) Oriya

ORL [ɔɛrɛl] *Méd* **NMF** (*abrév* **oto-rhino-laryngologiste**) ENT specialist

NF (*abrév* **oto-rhino-laryngologie**) ENT

orle [ɔrl] **NM** *Archit & Hér* orle

orléanais, -e [ɔrleanɛ, -ɛz] **ADJ** of/from Orléans

NM *Ling* Orléans dialect

☐ **Orléanais, -e NM,F** = inhabitant of or person from Orléans

orléanisme [ɔrleanism] **NM** *Hist* Orleanism

orléaniste [ɔrleanist] *Hist* **ADJ** Orleanist

NMF Orleanist

Orléans [ɔrleɑ̃] **NM** Orléans

Culture

LES ORLÉANS

This is the name of the family of the claimants to the throne of France, direct descendants of the last French king, Louis-Philippe. The present head of the family is Henri d'Orléans, Comte de Paris.

Orlon® [ɔrlɔ̃] **NM** Orlon®

Orly [ɔrli] **NM** (*aéroport*) Orly (airport)

Orlyval [ɔrlival] **NM** = train which takes passengers from Paris to Orly airport

ormaie [ɔrmɛ] **NF** elm grove

orme [ɔrm] **NM 1** (*arbre*) elm (tree); **o. blanc, o. de(s) montagne(s)** wych elm; **o. champêtre** ou **à petites feuilles** common elm, English elm; **maladie des ormes** Dutch elm disease **2** (*bois*) elm (wood)

ormeau¹, -x [ɔrmo] **NM** *Bot* young elm (tree)

ormeau², -x [ɔrmo] **NM** *Zool* (*mollusque*) earshell, ormer, abalone, *Spéc* haliotis

ormet [ɔrmɛ], **ormier** [ɔrmje] = **ormeau²**

ormille [ɔrmij] **NF 1** (*jeune orme*) elm sapling **2** (*plant*) plantation of young elms

ormoie [ɔrmwa] **NF** elm grove

Ormuz [ɔrmuz] *voir* **Hormuz**

Orne [ɔrn] **NF 1** (*fleuve*) **l'O.** the (River) Orne **2** (*département*) **l'O.** the Orne

orne [ɔrn] **NM** flowering ash (tree)

orné, -e [ɔrne] **ADJ** (*style*) ornate, florid; **lettre ornée** illuminated letter

ornemaniste [ɔrnəmanist] **NMF** ornamenter, ornamentist

ornement [ɔrnəmɑ̃] **NM 1** (*objet*) ornament

2 *Beaux-Arts* embellishment, adornment; **sans o.** plain, unadorned; **architecture surchargée d'ornements** ornate architecture; **plafonds riches en ornements** ceilings rich in ornament or ornamentation

3 *Hér & Mus* ornament

4 *Rel* **ornements sacerdotaux** vestments

☐ **d'ornement** **ADJ** (*plantes, poupée*) ornamental; *Mus* **notes d'o.** grace notes, ornaments

ornemental, -e, -aux, -ales [ɔrnəmatal, -o] **ADJ** (*motif*) ornamental, decorative; (*plante*) ornamental

ornementation [ɔrnəmatasjɔ̃] **NF** ornamentation

ornementer [3] [ɔrnəmate] **VT** to ornament; **o. qch** ou **avec qch** to ornament or to decorate sth with sth

orner [3] [ɔrne] **VT 1** (*décorer → sujet: personne*) to decorate; (*→ sujet: dessin, plante, ruban*) to adorn, to decorate, to embellish; **des bouquets ornaient la table** the table was decorated with bunches of flowers; **o. avec qch** ou **de qch** to decorate with sth; **sa chambre était ornée de trophées de guerre** his/her room was adorned or decorated with war trophies; **o. une robe de dentelle** to trim a dress with lace; **couloir orné de drapeaux** corridor decked out or hung with flags; **sabre orné de joyaux** sword set with jewels

2 (*enjoliver → texte*) to embellish; (*→ vérité*) to adorn, to embellish; *Littéraire* **o. son esprit** to enrich one's mind

orniérage [ɔrnjeraʒ] **NM** rutted surface

ornière [ɔrnjɛr] **NF 1** (*trou*) rut; **une route pleine d'ornières** a rutted road, a road full of potholes **2** *Fig* (*routine*) **suivre l'o.** to be in a rut; **sortir de l'o.** to get out of a rut **3** *Fig* (*impasse*) **tirer qn de l'o.** to help sb out of a difficulty; **sortir de l'o.** to get oneself out of trouble **4** *Rail* groove

ornithischien [ɔrnitiskjɛ̃] *Zool* **NM** Ornithischian

☐ **ornithischiens NMPL** Ornithischia

ornithogale [ɔrnitɔgal] **NM** *Bot* ornithogalum

ornithologie [ɔrnitɔlɔʒi] **NF** ornithology

ornithologique [ɔrnitɔlɔʒik] **ADJ** ornithological

ornithologiste [ɔrnitɔlɔʒist], **ornithologue** [ɔrnitɔlɔg] **NMF** ornithologist

ornithomancie [ɔrnitomɑ̃si] **NF** *Antiq* ornithomancy

ornithophilie [ɔrnitofili] **NF** ornithophily

ornithorynque [ɔrnitɔrɛ̃k] **NM** *Zool* (duck-billed) platypus, *Spéc* ornithorynchus

ornithose [ɔrnitoz] **NF** *Méd & Vét* ornithosis, psittacosis

orobanche [ɔrɔbɑ̃ʃ] **NF** *Bot* broomrape, chokeweed

orobe [ɔrɔb] **NM** *Bot* orobus, bitter vetch

orogène [ɔrɔʒɛn] **NM** *Géol* orogeny

orogenèse [ɔrɔʒənɛz], **orogénie** [ɔrɔʒeni] **NF** *Géol* orogenesis, orogeny

orogénique [ɔrɔʒenik] **ADJ** *Géol* orogenic, orogenetic

orographie [ɔrɔgrafi] **NF** *Géol* orography

orographique [ɔrɔgrafik] **ADJ** *Géol* orographic, orographical

oronge [ɔrɔ̃ʒ] **NF** *Bot* Caesar's mushroom; **o. vineuse** blushing mushroom, blushing amanita; **fausse o.** fly agaric

oropharynx [ɔrɔfarɛ̃ks] **NM** *Anat* oropharynx

orpaillage [ɔrpajaʒ] **NM** gold washing or panning

orpailleur [ɔrpajœr] **NM** gold washer

Orphée [ɔrfe] **NPR** *Myth* Orpheus

orphelin, -e [ɔrfəlɛ̃, -in] **ADJ 1** (*enfant*) orphan (*avant n*), orphaned; **être o. de père** to be fatherless, to have lost one's father; **les enfants orphelins de mère** motherless children; **être o. de père et de mère** to have lost both one's parents, to be an orphan

2 *Typ* **ligne orpheline** orphan

NM,F orphan

☐ **orpheline NF** *Typ* orphan

☐ **orphelines NFPL** *très Fam* (*testicules*) balls, nuts, *Br* bollocks

orphelinat [ɔrfəlina] **NM** (*bâtiment*) orphanage; (*personnes*) orphans

orphéon [ɔrfeɔ̃] **NM 1** (*fanfare*) band **2** (*chœur*

ori-orp

→ *d'hommes*) male choir; (→ *d'enfants*) (mixed) children's choir

orphéoniste [ɔrfeɔnist] NMF **1** (*d'une fanfare*) band member **2** (*chanteur* → *adulte*) male singer *or* chorister; (→ *enfant*) (little) chorister

orphie [ɔrfi] NF *Ich* garfish, needlefish

orphique [ɔrfik] *Antiq* ADJ Orphean, Orphic ◇ NM Orphean

orphisme [ɔrfism] NM **1** *Antiq* Orphism **2** *Beaux-Arts* Orphism = style of avant-garde painting parallel to Cubism and making use of strongly contrasting colours (eg the paintings of Delaunay and Kandinsky)

orpiment [ɔrpimɑ̃] NM *Minér* orpiment

orpin [ɔrpɛ̃] NM **1** *Vieilli Minér* orpiment **2** *Bot* stonecrop

orque [ɔrk] NF *Zool* killer whale

Orsay [ɔrsɛ] NM **le musée d'O.** = art museum in Paris

Culture
LE MUSÉE D'ORSAY
This museum was originally a railway station on the banks of the Seine. The station was converted into a museum in 1985 and houses works of art from the second half of the 19th century and the early 20th century. It is notable in particular for its collections of Impressionist and Symbolist paintings.

ORSEC, Orsec [ɔrsɛk] ADJ (*abrév* **Organisation des secours**) **plan O.** = disaster contingency plan; **plan O.-Rad** = disaster contingency plan in case of nuclear accident

Culture
LE PLAN ORSEC
This scheme is set in motion whenever there is a major disaster in France, such as flooding or forest fires. Under the provisions of the scheme, the "préfet", or chief of police, is empowered to mobilize both public and private resources to deal with a civil emergency.

orseille [ɔrsɛj] NF *Bot* archil, orchil; (*colorant*) dyer's moss

orteil [ɔrtɛj] NM toe; **gros o.** big toe

ORTF [ɔɛrteɛf] NM *Ancien.ement* (*abrév* **Office de radiodiffusion télévision française**) = former French broadcasting corporation

orthèse [ɔrtɛz] NF *Méd* orthosis, brace

orthétique [ɔrtetik] *Méd* ADJ orthotic ◇ NF orthotics (*singulier*)

orthocentre [ɔrtɔsɑ̃tr] NM *Géom* orthocentre

orthochromatique [ɔrtɔkrɔmatik] ADJ orthochromatic

orthoclase [ɔrtɔklaz] NF *Minér* orthoclase

orthodontie [ɔrtɔdɔ̃si] NF orthodontics (*singulier*), dental orthopedics (*singulier*)

orthodontique [ɔrtɔdɔ̃tik] ADJ orthodontic

orthodontiste [ɔrtɔdɔ̃tist] NMF orthodontist

orthodoxe [ɔrtɔdɔks] ADJ **1** *Rel* Orthodox **2** *Fig* (*méthode, pratique*) orthodox; **pas très** *ou* **peu o.** rather unorthodox ◇ NMF **1** *Rel* person of orthodox beliefs; (*de l'Église orthodoxe*) member of the Orthodox church; **les orthodoxes** the Orthodox **2** (*disciple*) **les orthodoxes de...** the orthodox followers of...

orthodoxie [ɔrtɔdɔksi] NF orthodoxy; **l'o. marxiste** marxist orthodoxy

orthodromie [ɔrtɔdrɔmi] NF *Naut & Aviat* great-circle route

orthodromique [ɔrtɔdrɔmik] ADJ *Naut & Aviat* **navigation o.** great-circle navigation

orthoépie [ɔrtɔepi] NF *Ling* orthoepy

orthogenèse [ɔrtɔʒənɛz] NF *Biol* orthogenesis

orthogénie [ɔrtɔʒeni] NF *Méd* birth control

orthogénique [ɔrtɔʒenik] ADJ orthogenic

orthogénisme [ɔrtɔʒenizm] NM *Euph* eugenics (*singulier*)

orthogonal, -e, -aux, -ales [ɔrtɔgɔnal, -o] ADJ orthogonal

orthogonalement [ɔrtɔgɔnalmɑ̃] ADV orthogonally, at right angles

orthogonalité [ɔrtɔgɔnalite] NF orthogonality

orthographe [ɔrtɔgraf] NF (*graphie*) spelling; (*règles*) spelling system, *Spéc* orthography; (*matière*) spelling, *Spéc* orthography; **il y a deux**

orthographes possibles there are two ways of spelling it *or* two possible spellings; **je ne connais pas l'o. de ce mot** I don't know how to spell this word *or* how this word is spelt; **avoir une bonne/mauvaise o.** to be good/bad at spelling

orthographier [9] [ɔrtɔgrafje] VT to spell; **mal/bien orthographié** wrongly/correctly spelt; **savoir o.** to be good at spelling
▸**s'orthographier** VPR **comment s'orthographie votre nom?** how do you spell your name?; **son nom s'orthographie avec deux L** his/her name is spelt with two L's

orthographique [ɔrtɔgrafik] ADJ spelling (*avant n*), orthographic

orthonormé, -e [ɔrtɔnɔrme] ADJ orthonormal

orthopédie [ɔrtɔpedi] NF orthopaedics (*singulier*)

orthopédique [ɔrtɔpedik] ADJ orthopaedic; **chaussures/semelles orthopédiques** orthopaedic shoes/built-up soles

orthopédiste [ɔrtɔpedist] NMF (*médecin*) orthopaedist; (*fabricant*) maker of orthopaedic apparatus ◇ ADJ **chirurgien o.** orthopaedic surgeon

orthophonie [ɔrtɔfɔni] NF **1** *Ling* orthoepy **2** *Méd* speech therapy

orthophonique [ɔrtɔfɔnik] ADJ **1** *Ling* orthoepic **2** *Méd* speech therapy (*avant n*)

orthophoniste [ɔrtɔfɔnist] NMF speech therapist

orthophosphorique [ɔrtɔfɔsfɔrik] ADJ **acide o.** orthophosphoric acid

orthopnée [ɔrtɔpne] NF orthopnoea

orthoptère [ɔrtɔptɛr] *Entom* NM orthopteran, orthopteron
❑ **orthoptères** NMPL Orthoptera

orthoptie [ɔrtɔpsi] NF orthoptics (*singulier*)

orthoptique [ɔrtɔptik] ADJ orthoptic ◇ NF orthoptics (*singulier*)

orthoptiste [ɔrtɔptist] NMF orthoptist

orthorexie [ɔrtɔrɛksi] NF *Méd & Psy* orthorexia

orthorhombique [ɔrtɔrɔ̃bik] ADJ orthorhombic, trimetric

orthoscopique [ɔrtɔskɔpik] ADJ *Phot* orthoscopic

orthose [ɔrtoz] NF *Minér* orthoclase

orthostate [ɔrtɔstat] NM *Archit* orthostat

orthostatique [ɔrtɔstatik] ADJ *Méd* orthostatic

orthostatisme [ɔrtɔstatism] NM *Méd* orthostatism

orthosympathique [ɔrtɔsɛ̃patik] *Anat* ADJ sympathetic ◇ NM sympathetic nervous system

orthotrope [ɔrtɔtrɔp] ADJ **1** *Bot* orthotropous **2** *Constr* orthotropic

ortie [ɔrti] NF *Bot* (stinging) nettle; **o. blanche/ rouge** *ou* **pourpre** white/red dead-nettle; **o. brûlante** stinging nettle

ortolan [ɔrtɔlɑ̃] NM *Orn* ortolan

orvale [ɔrval] NF *Bot* clary

orvet [ɔrvɛ] NM *Zool* slowworm, blindworm

oryctérope [ɔrikterɔp] NM *Zool* aardvark

oryx [ɔriks] NM *Zool* oryx; **o. algazelle** scimitar-horned oryx; **o. beisa** beisa oryx

OS [oɛs] NM (*abrév* **ouvrier spécialisé**) skilled worker

os [ɔs, *pl* o] NM **1** *Anat & Zool* bone; **j'ai de gros/ petits os** I'm big-boned/small-boned; **il s'est coupé jusqu'à l'os** he cut himself (through) to the bone; **os de seiche** cuttlebone; **cuiller en os** bone spoon; *Fam* **jusqu'à l'os** totally▪, completely▪; *Fig* **être gelé/trempé jusqu'aux os** to be frozen to the marrow/soaked to the skin; *Fig* **être pourri jusqu'à l'os** to be thoroughly corrupt; **il ne fera pas de vieux os!** he's not long for this world!; **elle est tellement maigre qu'on lui voit les os** she's a bag of bones; **c'est un sac** *ou* **paquet** *ou* **tas d'os** he's/she's a bag of bones, he's/she's just skin and bones; *très Fam* **il l'a eu dans l'os!** (*il n'a pas réussi*) he got egg on his face!; (*il s'est fait escroquer*) he's been had!
2 *Culin* bone; **viande avec os** meat on the bone; **viande sans os** meat off the bone, boned meat; **poulet sans os** boneless chicken, boned chicken; **os à moelle**, *Belg* **os à la moelle** marrowbone; **acheter du jambon à l'os** to buy ham off the bone; **donner un os à ronger à qn** to give sb sth to keep him/her quiet
3 *Fam* (*problème*) snag, hitch; **il y a un os** there's a snag *or* a hitch; **elle est tombée sur** *ou* **elle a trouvé un os** she hit a snag

-OS [os] SUFF
The suffix **-os** has proved rather productive in French slang, especially in recent decades. It is used mostly to create adjectives and, more rarely, adverbs or nouns, by replacing the last letters of the word, eg:
rapidos (from *rapidement*) quickly; **craignos** (from *craindre*) dodgy, hideous, crap; *nullos* useless (idiot); **calmos!** (from *calme*) chill out!, take it easy!; **matos** (from *matériel*) gear, stuff

Osaka [ɔzaka] NM Osaka

oscabrion [ɔskabrijɔ̃] NM *Zool* (*mollusque*) chiton, coat-of-mail shell

oscar [ɔskar] NM **1** *Cin* Oscar; **elle a reçu l'o. du meilleur second rôle** she won the Oscar for the best supporting role **2** (*récompense*) **l'o. de la meilleure publicité** the award for the best commercial *or Br* advert

oscarisé, -e [ɔskarize] ADJ *Cin* Oscar-winning; **l'acteur o. pour 'Gladiator'** the actor who won an Oscar for 'Gladiator'

oscariser [3] [ɔskarize] VT *Cin* to award an Oscar to

OSCE [oɛssea] NF (*abrév* **Organisation pour la sécurité et la coopération en Europe**) OSCE

oscillaire [ɔsiler] NF oscillaria, oscillatoria

oscillant, -e [ɔsilɑ̃, -ɑ̃t] ADJ **1** (*qui balance*) oscillating **2** (*incertain*) oscillating, fluctuating **3** *Méd* (*fièvre*) oscillating **4** *Élec* (*décharge*) oscillating **5** *Phys* **circuit o.** oscillating circuit

oscillateur [ɔsilatœr] NM oscillator; *Rad* **maître o., o. pilote** master oscillator

oscillation [ɔsilasjɔ̃] NF **1** (*balancement*) swaying, rocking; **les oscillations du téléphérique** the swaying *or* swinging of the cable car
2 *Fig* (*variation*) fluctuation, variation; **les oscillations des taux de change** the fluctuations in the exchange rates; **oscillations des prix** price variations; **oscillations saisonnières** seasonal fluctuations
3 *Élec & Phys* oscillation; **oscillations amorties/entretenues** damped/sustained oscillations
4 *Tech* vibration

oscillatoire [ɔsilatwar] ADJ oscillatory

osciller [3] [ɔsile] VI **1** (*bouger* → *pendule, objet suspendu*) to oscillate, to swing, to sway; (→ *branche, corde*) to sway, to swing; (→ *arbre, statue*) to sway; (→ *aiguille aimantée*) to flicker; (→ *personne, tête, bateau*) to rock; **la brise faisait o. les roseaux** the reeds were swaying in the breeze; **le choc a fait o. les immeubles pendant de longues secondes** the buildings shook for several seconds under the impact of the blast; **le courant d'air fit o. la flamme** the flame was flickering in the draught
2 (*varier*) **o. entre** to vary *or* to fluctuate between; **o. entre deux options** to waver *or* to hesitate between two options
3 *Fin* (*marché*) to fluctuate

oscillogramme [ɔsilɔgram] NM oscillogram

oscillographe [ɔsilɔgraf] NM oscillograph; **o. cathodique** cathode ray tube

oscillomètre [ɔsilɔmɛtr] NM *Méd* oscillometer

oscilloscope [ɔsilɔskɔp] NM oscilloscope

osculateur, -trice [ɔskylatœr, -tris] ADJ osculatory, osculating

oscule [ɔskyl] NM osculum

ose [oz] NM *Chim* ose, monosaccharose; **les oses** the monosaccharoses

osé, -e [oze] ADJ **1** (*audacieux* → *tentative*) bold, daring **2** (*choquant* → *histoire*) risqué, racy **3** (*téméraire* → *personne*) bold, intrepid

oseille [ozɛj] NF **1** *Bot & Culin* sorrel; **à l'o.** with sorrel; **o. aquatique** water dock **2** *Fam* (*argent*) dough, *Br* dosh, *Am* bucks; **avoir de l'o.** to have bags *or* pots of money, to be loaded

'**Prends l'oseille et tire-toi**'*Allen*'Take the Money and Run'

oser [3] [oze] VT **1** (*avoir l'audace de*) **o. faire qch** to dare (to) do sth; **elle n'ose pas parler** she doesn't dare (to) speak, she daren't speak; **je voudrais qu'il vienne mais je n'ose l'espérer** I'd like him to come but I daren't hope *or* I don't

dare hope that he will; **comment oses-tu répondre à ton père!** how dare you answer your father back! **quand quelqu'un osait l'interrompre** if anybody dared or was bold enough to interrupt him/her; *Littéraire* **o. qch** to dare sth

2 *(suggestion, réponse)* to risk; **ils furent trois à o. l'ascension** three of them risked the climb or were bold enough to climb

3 *(dans les tournures de politesse)* **j'ose croire/espérer que...** I trust/hope that...; **si j'ose dire** if I may say so; **si j'ose m'exprimer ainsi** if I may say so, if I may put it that way

4 *Suisse (avoir la permission de)* **est-ce que j'ose entrer?** may I come in?

USAGE ABSOLU **comment oses-tu!** how dare you!; **vous n'oseriez pas!** you wouldn't dare!; **il faut o. dans la vie!** one has to take risks in life!; **si j'osais, je l'inviterais chez moi** if I dared or if I were bold enough, I'd invite him/her over to my place; **il veut me parler? qu'il ose un peu!** he wants to talk to me? just let him dare!; **approchez si vous osez!** come over here if you dare!

oseraie [ozrɛ] NF osier bed, osiery

OSI [oesi] NF *(abrév* **organisation de solidarité internationale***)* international aid organization

oside [ozid] NM *Chim* oside

osier [ozje] NM **1** *Bot* willow, osier; **o. blanc** osier; **o. rouge** purple willow; **brin d'o.** withy **2** *(matériau)* wicker, wickerwork; **chaise en o.** wicker or wickerwork or basketwork chair

osiériculture [ozjerikyltyr] NF osier or willow cultivation

Osiris [oziris] NPR *Myth* Osiris

Oslo [oslo] NM Oslo

osmanli [osmãli] NM *Hist* Osmanli, Ottoman Turkish

osmique [osmik] ADJ osmic

osmiridium [osmiridjom] NM *Chim* osmiridium

osmium [osmjom] NM *Chim* osmium

osmiure [osmjyr] NM *Chim* osmium alloy; **o. d'iridium** iridium osmium alloy

osmolarité [osmolarite] NF *Biol & Chim* osmolarity

osmomètre [osmometr] NM *Biol & Chim* osmometer

osmonde [osmɔ̃d] NF *Bot* osmund, osmunda; **o. royale** royal fern

osmorégulation [osmoregylasjɔ̃] NF *Biol* osmoregulation

osmose [osmoz] NF **1** *Biol & Chim* osmosis; **o. électrique** electro-osmosis; **o. inverse** reverse osmosis **2** *Fig* osmosis; **une o. s'est produite entre les deux civilisations** the two civilisations have merged into one another

osmotique [osmotik] ADJ *Biol & Chim* osmotic

O-S-O *(abrév écrite* **Ouest-Sud-Ouest***)* WSW

osque [osk] ADJ Oscan

❏ **osques** NMPL **les osques** the Oscans

ossature [osatyr] NF **1** *Anat (d'une personne)* frame, skeleton; *(du visage)* bone structure; **d'une o. puissante** powerfully built, of powerful build **2** *Constr (d'un avion, d'un immeuble)* frame, framework, skeleton; *(d'un pont)* main girders; **pont à o. métallique** bridge with a metal frame or framework **3** *(d'un discours)* framework, structure

osséine [osein] NF ossein

osselet [oslɛ] NM **1** *Anat* ossicle; *Zool* knucklebone **2** *(jeu)* jack, knucklebone; **jouer aux osselets** to play jacks **3** *Vét* osselet

ossements [osmã] NMPL remains, bones

ossète [oset] NM *(langue)* Ossetic, Ossete

❏ **Ossète** NMF Osset

osseux, -euse [osø, -øz] ADJ **1** *Anat* bone *(avant n)*, *Spéc* osseous **2** *Méd* **greffe osseuse** bone graft; **maladie osseuse** bone disease **3** *(aux os apparents)* bony **4** *Ich* **poissons o.** bony fish

ossianique [osjanik], **ossianesque** [osjanɛsk] ADJ *Littérature (littéraire, écrit)* Ossianic; *(style)* Ossianesque

ossianisme [osjanism] NM *Littérature* Ossianism

ossification [osifikasjɔ̃] NF ossification

ossifier [9] [osifje] VT **1** *(transformer en os)* to ossify **2** *Fig Littéraire (rendre insensible)* to harden

▸**s'ossifier** VPR **1** *Anat* to ossify **2** *Littéraire (sensibilité)* to harden

osso-buco [osobuko] NM INV *Culin* osso bucco

ossu, -e [osy] ADJ *Littéraire* big-boned

ossuaire [osɥɛr] NM ossuary

OST [oɛste] NF *Com (abrév* **organisation scientifique du travail***)* organization and methods, time and motion studies

ost [ost] NM *Hist (armée)* host; **service d'o.** = duty of military service owed by a vassal to his lord

ostéalgie [ostealʒi] NF *Méd* ostalgia

ostéichtyen [osteiktjɛ̃] *Ich* NM bony fish, *Spéc* member of the Osteichthyes class

❏ **ostéichtyens** NMPL bony fish, *Spéc* Osteichthyes

ostéite [osteit] NF *Méd* osteitis

Ostende [ostãd] NM Ostend

ostensible [ostãsibl] ADJ conspicuous, open, clear; **avec un mépris o. pour les conventions** with open contempt for convention

ostensiblement [ostãsibləmã] ADV conspicuously, openly, clearly; **il manifesta o. son ennui** he made it quite clear that he was bored

ostensif, -ive [ostãsif, -iv] ADJ **1** *Ling & Phil* ostensive **2** *Vieilli* intended to be shown or to be made public

ostensoir [ostãswar] NM monstrance, ostensory

ostentateur, -trice [ostãtatœr, -tris] ADJ *Littéraire* ostentatious

ostentation [ostãtasjɔ̃] NF *(affectation, vanité)* ostentation; **avec o.** with ostentation, ostentatiously; **sans o.** without ostentation, unostentatiously; *Littéraire* **faire o. de qch** to parade sth

ostentatoire [ostãtatwar] ADJ ostentatious

ostentatrice [ostãtatris] *voir* **ostentateur**

ostéoarthrite [osteoartrit] NF *Méd* osteoarthritis

ostéoarthrose [osteoartroz] NF *Méd* osteoarthrosis

ostéoarticulaire [osteoartikylɛr] ADJ *Méd* joint *(avant n)*, *Spéc* osteoarticular; **douleurs ostéoarticulaires** joint pain

ostéoblaste [osteoblast] NM *Biol* osteoblast

ostéochondrite [osteokɔ̃drit] NF, **ostéochondrose** [osteokɔ̃droz] NF *Méd* osteochondritis

ostéoclasie [osteoklazi] NF *Méd* osteoclasis

ostéoclaste [osteoklast] NM *Biol* osteoclast

ostéoclastome [osteoklastom] NM *Méd* osteoclastoma

ostéocyte [osteosit] NM *Biol* osteocyte

ostéogène [osteoʒɛn] ADJ *Biol* osteogenetic, bone-forming

ostéogenèse [osteoʒənɛz] NF, **ostéogénie** [osteoʒeni] NF *Biol* osteogenesis

ostéologie [osteolɔʒi] NF *Anat* osteology

ostéologique [osteolɔʒik] ADJ *Anat* osteological

ostéolyse [osteoliz] NF *Méd* osteolysis

ostéome [osteom] NM *Méd* osteoma

ostéomyélite [osteomjelit] NF *Méd* osteomyelitis

ostéopathe [osteopat] NMF *Méd* osteopath

ostéopathie [osteopati] NF *Méd (traitement)* osteopathy; *(maladie)* bone disease; **o. crânienne** craniosacral therapy

ostéophyte [osteofit] NM *Méd* osteophyte

ostéoplastie [osteoplasti] NF *Méd* osteoplasty

ostéoporose [osteoporoz] NF *Méd* osteoporosis

ostéosarcome [osteosarkom] NM *Méd* osteosarcoma

ostéosynthèse [osteosɛ̃tɛz] NF *Méd* osteosynthesis

ostéotomie [osteotomi] NF *Méd* osteotomy

Ostie [osti] NM *Géog* Ostia

ostination [ostinasjɔ̃] NF *Can Fam* quarrel■, sparring match■

ostinato [ostinato] NM *Mus* ostinato

ostiner [3] [ostine] **s'ostiner** VPR *Can Fam* to quarrel■, to spar■

ostin, -euse [ostinœr, -øz], **ostineux, -euse** [ostinø, -øz] *Can Fam* ADJ quarrelsome■, argumentative■

NM,F quarrelsome or argumentative person■

ostiole [ostjol] NM *Bot* ostiole

ostracé, -e [ostrase] ADJ ostraceous

ostraciser [3] [ostrasize] VT to ostracize

ostracisme [ostrasism] NM **1** *Antiq* ostracism **2** *(exclusion)* ostracism; **être victime d'o.** to be ostracized; **frapper qn d'o.** to ostracize sb

ostracode [ostrakod] *Zool* NM member of the Ostracode subclass

❏ **ostracodes** NMPL Ostracoda

ostracon [ostrakon] *(pl* **ostraca***)* NM *Archéol* ostracon, ostrakon

ostréicole [ostreikol] ADJ *(région)* oyster farming;

(industrie) oyster *(avant n)*; **parc o.** oyster bed; **la région est l'un des plus grands parcs ostréicoles de la France** it is one of the largest oyster-producing regions in France

ostréiculteur, -trice [ostreikyltœr, -tris] NM,F oyster farmer, oysterman, f oysterwoman

ostréiculture [ostreikyltyr] NF oyster farming

ostréidés [ostreide] NMPL *Zool* Ostreidae

ostrogot, -e, ostrogoth, -e [ostrogo, -ot] ADJ Ostrogothic

NM *Fam (homme malappris)* boor; **un drôle d'o.** a funny or a strange customer

❏ **Ostrogot, -e** NM,F Ostrogoth; **les Ostrogots** the Ostrogoths

-OT, -OTTE [o, ot] SUFF

When added to adjectives, this suffix has a DIMINUTIVE function, sometimes with an affectionate overtone, eg:

pâlot(te) peaky, pale; **jeunot(te)** youngish, rather young; **fiérot(te)** proud; **vieillot(te)** old-fashioned

otage [otaʒ] NM hostage; **prendre qn en o.** to take sb hostage

otalgie [otalʒi] NF *Méd* otalgia

OTAN, Otan [otã] NF *(abrév* **Organisation du traité de l'Atlantique Nord***)* NATO

otarie [otari] NF *Zool* sea lion; **o. à fourrure** fur seal

OTASE [otaz] NF *(abrév* **Organisation du traité de l'Asie du Sud-Est***)* SEATO

ôté [ote] PRÉP *Littéraire* with the exception of

ôter [3] [ote] VT **1** *(retirer)* to take off, to remove *(from)*; *(vêtement)* to take off; *(tache)* to remove, to take out; *(assiettes)* to clear away; **ôtez votre veste** take your jacket off; **ô. des épingles d'un chignon** to take hairpins out of or to remove hairpins from a bun; **ôte tes pieds du fauteuil** take or get your feet off the armchair; **ô. son masque** to take off or to remove one's mask; *Fig* to unmask oneself; **ôte-moi d'un doute, tu ne vas pas accepter!** wait a minute, you're not actually going to say yes!; **cela n'ôte rien à sa valeur/à notre amitié** that in no way detracts from its value/from our friendship

2 *(mettre hors de portée)* to take away; **ô. qch à qn** to take sth away from sb; **personne n'a pensé à lui ô. son arme** nobody thought to take his/her weapon (away) from him/her; **ô. un enfant à ses parents** to take a child away from its parents; *Fig* **ô. le pain de la bouche à qn** to take the bread out of sb's mouth

3 *(supprimer)* to remove *(from)*; **un nouveau produit chimique a ôté à l'eau son mauvais goût** a new chemical removed the bad taste from the water; **ô. à qn l'envie de faire qch** to deprive sb of all desire of doing sth; **ô. la vie à qn** to take sb's life; *Fig* **cela m'ôte un poids** that's a weight off my mind; **son attitude m'a ôté mes dernières illusions** his/her attitude rid me of my last illusions; **on ne m'ôtera pas de l'idée que...** I can't help thinking that...; **cela lui a ôté l'appétit** it has taken away his/her appetite; **cela lui a ôté toute sa force** it has drained him/her of all his/her strength

4 *Math* to take away; **20 ôté de 100 égale 80** 20 (taken away) from 100 leaves 80

▸**s'ôter** VPR **1** *(s'enlever)* to come off, to be removed; **ces bottes s'ôtent facilement** these boots are easy to take off

2 **elle ne peut pas s'ô. de l'idée que...** she can't get it out of her head that...; **ôte-toi cette idée de la tête** get that idea out of your head

3 **ôte-toi de là (que je m'y mette)** budge up (for me); **ôtez-vous de là, vous gênez le passage** move, you're in the way; *Fig* **ôte-toi de mon soleil** get out of my way

Othello [otɛlo] NPR Othello

otique [otik] ADJ *Anat* otic

otite [otit] NF *Méd* earache, *Spéc* otitis; **o. externe** otitis externa; **o. interne** otitis interna; **o. moyenne** otitis media; **o. séreuse** glue ear, *Spéc* serous otitis media

OTM [oteɛm] NF *Com (abrév* **opérateur de transport multimodal***)* multi-modal operator

otocyon [otosjɔ̃] NM *Zool* otocyon, bat-eared fox

otocyste [otosist] NM *Zool* otocyst

otolite, otolithe [otolit] NF *Anat* otolite, otolith

otologie [otolɔʒi] NF *Méd* otology

otoplastie [ɔtɔplasti] **NF** *Méd* otoplasty
oto-rhino [ɔtɔrino] (*pl* **oto-rhinos**) **NMF** *Fam* ear, nose and throat specialist
oto-rhino-laryngologie [ɔtɔrinɔlarɛ̃gɔlɔʒi] **NF** otorhinolaryngology
oto-rhino-laryngologiste [ɔtɔrinɔlarɛ̃gɔlɔʒist] (*pl* **oto-rhino-laryngologistes**) **NMF** ear, nose and throat specialist, *Spéc* otorhinolaryngologist
otorragie [ɔtɔraʒi] **NF** *Méd* otorrhagia
otorrhée [ɔtɔre] **NF** *Méd* otorrhoea
otosclérose [ɔtɔskleroz] **NF** *Méd* otosclerosis
otoscope [ɔtɔskɔp] **NM** otoscope, auriscope
otoscopie [ɔtɔskɔpi] **NF** *Méd* otoscopy
otoscopique [ɔtɔskɔpik] **ADJ** *Méd* otoscopic
otospongiose [ɔtɔspɔ̃ʒjoz] **NF** *Méd* otospongiosis
OTSI (*abrév écrite* **Office du tourisme-syndicat d'initiative**) tourist office
Ottawa [ɔtawa] **NM** Ottawa
-otte *voir* **-ot**
ottoman, -e [ɔtɔmɑ̃, -an] **ADJ** Ottoman
NM *Tex* ottoman (*rib*)
❑ **Ottoman, -e NM,F** Ottoman
❑ **ottomane NF** (*siège*) ottoman (*seat*)
ottonien, -enne [ɔtɔnjɛ̃, -ɛn] **ADJ** Ottonian
ou [u] **CONJ 1** (*indiquant une alternative ou une équivalence*) or; **le rouge ou le bleu, peu importe** red or blue, it doesn't matter which; **tu viens ou quoi?** are you coming or not?; **tu peux venir aujourd'hui ou demain** you can come (either) today or tomorrow; **que tu le veuilles ou non** whether you like it or not; **c'est l'un ou l'autre** it's one or the other; **le patronyme ou nom de famille** the patronymic or surname
2 (*indiquant une approximation*) or; **ils étaient cinq ou six** there were five or six of them
3 (*indiquant la conséquence*) or (else); **rends-le moi, ou ça ira très mal** give it back, or (else) there'll be trouble
❑ **ou (bien)... ou (bien) CONJ** either... or; **ou c'est lui ou c'est moi!** it's either him or me!; **ou bien tu viens et tu es aimable, ou bien tu restes chez toi!** either you come along and be nice, or you stay at home!; **ou tu viens, ou tu restes, mais tu arrêtes de te plaindre** you (can) either come or stay, but stop complaining!
où [u] **PRON RELATIF 1** (*dans l'espace*) where; **la maison où j'habite** the house I live in *or* where I live; **le pays où je suis né** the country where I was born; **nous cherchons un village où passer nos vacances** we're looking for a village where we can spend our holidays; **pose-le là où tu l'as trouvé** put it back where you found it; **vous le trouverez là où vous l'avez laissé** you'll find it where you left it; **j'irai où vous voudrez** I'll go where(ever) you wish; **partout où vous irez** everywhere you go; **d'où j'étais, je voyais la cathédrale** from where I was, I could see the cathedral; **le pays d'où je viens** the country which *or* where I come from; **d'où que tu viennes** wherever you come from; **les villes par où nous passerons** the towns which we will go through
2 (*dans le temps*) **le jour où je suis venu** the day (that) I came; **à la seconde où elle est entrée** the second (that) she came in; **à l'époque où...** in the days when...
3 *Fig* **là où je ne vous suis plus, c'est lorsque vous dites...** the bit where I lose track is when you say...; **c'est une spécialité où il excelle** it's a field in which he excels; **dans l'état où elle est** in her state, in the state she is; **au prix où elle est payée, elle refuse de travailler le soir** she refuses to work nights for the money she gets; **au prix où c'est** at that price; **à l'allure où tu vas** (at) the speed you're going; **au point où nous en sommes** (at) the point we've reached
ADV RELATIF 1 (*dans l'espace*) where; **je vais où je veux** I go where *or* wherever I please; **où que vous alliez** wherever you go; **où que vous soyez** wherever you are; **par où que tu passes** whichever route you take, whichever way you go
2 *Fig* **où je ne le comprends pas, c'est lorsque...** where I don't understand him is when...
ADV INTERROGATIF where; **où habite-t-il?** where does he live?; **où vas-tu?** where are you going?; **d'où viens-tu?** where have you come from?; **d'où viens-tu en Angleterre?** whereabouts are you from in England?; **par où voulez-vous passer?** which way do you want to go?, which route do you want to take?; **par où commencer?** where to begin?, where should I begin?; **par où est-il passé?** which way did he go?; **jusqu'où les a-t-il suivis?** how far did he follow them?; **où en êtes-vous?** how far have you got (with it)?; **où voulez-vous en venir?** what point are you trying to make?, what are you trying to say?; **dites-moi vers où il est allé** tell me which direction he went in; **je me demande où je l'ai mis** I wonder where I put it
❑ **d'où CONJ d'où on conclut que...** which leads us *or* one to the conclusion that...; **d'où il suit que...** from which it follows that...; **je ne savais pas qu'il était déjà arrivé, d'où ma surprise** I didn't know that he'd already arrived, which is why I was so surprised; **d'où sa tristesse** hence his/her sadness
OUA [oya] **NF** (*abrév* **Organisation de l'unité africaine**) OAU
ouabaïne [wabain] **NF** *Chim* ouabain
ouache [waʃ] **NF** *Can* bear's den
Ouagadougou [wagadugu] **NM** Ouagadougou
ouah [wa] **ONOMAT o.! o.!** (*chien*) woof! woof!
ouailles [waj] **NFPL** *Littéraire ou Hum* flock
ouais [wɛ] **EXCLAM** *Fam* yeah!; (*sceptique*) oh yeah?
ouakari [wakari] **NM** *Zool* uakari
ouananiche [wananiʃ] **NF** *Can Zool* Atlantic salmon
ouandérou [wɑ̃deru] **NM** *Zool* **1** (*macaque*) lion-tailed macaque, wanderoo **2** (*langur du Sri Lanka*) purple-faced langur, wanderoo
ouaouaron [wawarɔ̃] **NM** *Can Zool* bullfrog
ouate [wat] **NF 1** (*coton*) cotton wool; **o. de cellulose** cellulose fibre **2** *Tex* wadding, padding; **un manteau doublé d'o.** a quilted coat **3** *Fig* **l'o.** *ou* **la o. des nuages** fleecy clouds; **avoir été élevé dans la o.** to have been brought up in cotton wool
ouaté, -e [wate] **ADJ 1** (*doublé*) quilted **2** (*assourdi*) muffled **3** (*douillet*) cocooned
ouater [3] [wate] **VT 1** (*vêtement*) to quilt; (*couverture*) to wad, to pad **2** *Littéraire* (*estomper*) to muffle
ouatine [watin] **NF** quilting (material)
ouatiné, -e [watine] **ADJ** quilted
ouatiner [3] [watine] **VT** to quilt
Oubangui [ubɑ̃gi] **NM** Ubangi
oubli [ubli] **NM 1** (*fait de ne pas se rappeler*) forgetting, neglecting; **l'o. d'un nom sur une liste peut avoir de graves conséquences** leaving a name off a list can have serious consequences; **l'o. d'un accent sur un mot coûte un point** forgetting *or* neglecting to put an accent on a word will lose you one point
2 (*lacune*) omission; **page 45, il y a un o.** there's an omission on page 45; **il y a beaucoup d'oublis dans sa liste** he/she left a lot of items off his/her list, there are a lot of gaps in his/her list; **réparer un o.** to rectify an omission
3 (*trou de mémoire*) oversight, lapse of memory; **ce n'est qu'un o.** it's just an oversight
4 (*isolement*) **l'o.** oblivion; **arracher qch à** *ou* **tirer qch de l'o.** to snatch *or* to rescue sth from oblivion; **tomber dans l'o.** to sink into oblivion
5 (*consolation*) **l'o. viendra avec le temps** time is a great healer
6 *Littéraire* (*indifférence*) **l'o. de soi** selflessness, self-denial; **pratiquer l'o. des injures** to forgive and forget
oublie [ubli] **NF** *Arch* (*gaufre roulée*) wafer
oublié, -e [ublije] **ADJ 1** (*pièce, roman, peintre*) forgotten; **il mourut o. de tous** he died forgotten by all, he died in obscurity **2** (*abandonné*) left, abandoned; **quelques jouets oubliés** a few abandoned toys, toys that were left behind
NM,F abandoned *or* neglected *or* forgotten person
oublier [10] [ublije] **VT 1** (*ne pas se remémorer* → *nom, rue, date*) to forget; **j'ai oublié son nom** I've forgotten his/her name, his/her name has slipped my mind; **n'oublie pas le rendez-vous** don't forget (that) you have an appointment; **mon Dieu, le dentiste, je l'ai oublié!** God, the dentist, I'd forgotten all about him!; **o. son texte** to forget one's lines; **n'oublie pas que c'est son anniversaire** remember *or* don't forget that it's his/her birthday; **o. où/quand/qui...** to forget where/when/who...; **o. de faire qch** to forget to do sth; *Hum* **il a oublié d'être bête** he's not lacking in brains, he's as clever as they come
2 (*ne pas reconnaître* → *mélodie*) to forget; **j'ai oublié son visage** I've forgotten what he/she looks like; **un visage que je n'oublierai jamais** a face I will never forget
3 (*ne plus penser à* → *héros, injure, souci*) to forget (about); **les preneurs de son sont souvent oubliés par les jurys de prix** sound technicians are often ignored by award juries; **j'ai oublié l'heure** I forgot the time; **n'oubliez pas le guide!** don't forget the guide!; **oublions ce malentendu** let's forget (all) about this misunderstanding; **o. le passé** to forget the past; **oublions le passé** let's let bygones be bygones; **n'oublie pas à qui tu parles!** don't (you) forget who you're talking to!; *Fam* **oublie-moi un peu, veux-tu?** get off my back *or* case, will you?; **sortir me fait o. mes soucis** going out helps me to forget my troubles; **se faire o.** to keep a low profile, to stay out of the limelight
4 (*omettre*) to leave out; **je ferai en sorte de l'o. dans mon testament/sur le registre** I'll make sure she's left out of my will/left off the register
5 (*négliger*) to forget (about); **n'oubliez pas les consignes de sûreté préconisées par la gendarmerie** don't forget the safety precautions recommended by the police; **depuis son mariage, il nous oublie** he's been neglecting us *or* he's forgotten (about) us since he got married
6 (*ne pas prendre*) to forget, to leave (behind); **j'ai oublié mes lunettes chez toi** I've left my glasses (behind) at your place; **j'ai oublié la lettre à la maison** I left the letter at home; **o. son colis dans le train** to leave one's parcel on the train
7 (*ne pas mettre*) to forget; **tu as oublié le citron dans la sauce** you forgot to put lemon in the sauce
USAGE ABSOLU to forget; **qu'a-t-elle dit? j'ai oublié** what did she say? I've forgotten; **il boit pour o.** he drinks to forget
►**s'oublier VPR 1** (*emploi passif*) **les langues étrangères s'oublient facilement quand on ne les pratique pas** foreign languages are easily forgotten when you don't use them; **des choses pareilles ne doivent jamais s'o.** things like that must never be forgotten; **une fois acquise, la technique ne s'oublie jamais** once you've learnt the technique, it stays with you forever *or* you'll never forget it; **c'est comme le vélo, ça ne s'oublie pas!** it's like riding a bike, once you learn you never forget; **la politesse s'oublie à présent** politeness is becoming a thing of the past
2 (*s'exclure*) to forget oneself; *Hum* **tu ne t'es pas oublié, à ce que je vois!** I see you've not forgotten yourself!; *Fam* **il ne s'oublie pas** he always looks after himself, he always takes care of number one
3 (*se relâcher*) to forget oneself; **vous vous oubliez, retirez ce que vous venez de dire** you're forgetting yourself, take back what you've just said
4 *Euph* (*animal, enfant*) to have an accident
oubliette [ublijɛt] **NF** (*fosse*) oubliette
❑ **oubliettes NFPL** (*cachot*) dungeon, black hole; *Fig* **le projet est tombé dans les** *ou* **aux oubliettes** the project has been shelved
oublieux, -euse [ublijø, -øz] **ADJ** *Littéraire* forgetful; **o. de ses devoirs** forgetful of one's duty
OUC [oyse] **NF** *Rad* (*abrév* **ondes ultra-courtes**) USW
ouche [uʃ] **NF** *Vieilli* = small enclosed plot of land near farm buildings
oud [ud] **NM INV** *Mus* oud
oudler [udlœr] **NM** *Cartes* = any of the three particularly important cards in the game of "tarot", the 1, the 21 and the excuse card
ouèbe [wɛb] **NM** *Ordinat* **l'o.** the Web
oued [wɛd] **NM** wadi
Ouessant [wɛsɑ̃] **NF** Ushant; **l'île d'O.** the Isle of Ushant
ouest [wɛst] **NM INV 1** (*point cardinal*) west; **à l'o.** in the west; **où est l'o.?** which way is west?; **la partie la plus à l'o. de l'île** the westernmost part

of the island; **le vent vient de l'o.** it's a west *or* westerly wind, the wind is coming from the west; **un vent d'o.** a westerly wind; **le vent d'o.** the west wind; **aller au** *ou* **vers l'o.** to go west *or* westwards; **les trains qui vont vers l'o.** trains going west, westbound trains; **rouler vers l'o.** to drive west *or* westwards; **aller droit vers l'o.** to head due west; **la cuisine est plein o.** *ou* **exposée à l'o.** the kitchen faces due west; **le soleil se couche à l'o.** the sun sets in the west

2 *(partie d'un pays, d'un continent)* west, western area *or* regions; *(partie d'une ville)* west; **l'o. de l'Italie** western Italy, the west of Italy; **dans l'o. de l'Espagne** in western Spain, in the west of Spain; **elle habite dans l'o.** she lives in the west; **il habite dans l'o. de Paris** he lives in the west of Paris; **elle est de l'o.** she's from the west; **les gens de l'o.** people who live in the west

ADJ INV *(gén)* west *(avant n)*, western; *(côte, face)* west; *(banlieue, partie, région)* western; **la façade o. d'un immeuble** the west-facing wall of a building; **la chambre est côté o.** the bedroom faces west; **dans la partie o. de la France** in the West of France, in western France; **suivre la direction o.** to head *or* to go westwards

❑ **Ouest ADJ INV** West **NM** *Géog* **l'O.** the West

❑ **à l'ouest de PRÉP** (to the) west of; **il habite à l'o. de Paris** he lives to the west of Paris

'À l'Ouest, rien de nouveau' *Remarque, Milestone* 'All Quiet on the Western Front'

ouest-allemand, -e [wɛstalmɑ̃, -ɑ̃d] *(mpl* **ouest-allemands,** *fpl* **ouest-allemandes)** *Anciennement* **ADJ** West German

❑ **Ouest-Allemand, -e NM,F** West German

Ouest-France [wɛstfrɑ̃s] **NM** *Presse* = major French daily regional newspaper

ouest-nord-ouest [wɛstnɔrwɛst] **NM INV** west-northwest

ADJ INV west-northwest

ouest-sud-ouest [wɛstsydwɛst] **NM INV** west-southwest

ADJ INV west-southwest

ouf [uf] **EXCLAM** phew!; **je n'ai pas eu le temps de dire o.** I didn't even have time to catch my breath

NM pousser un o. de soulagement to heave a sigh of relief

Ouganda [ugɑ̃da] **NM l'O.** Uganda; **vivre en O.** to live in Uganda; **aller en O.** to go to Uganda

ougandais, -e [ugɑ̃dɛ, -ɛz] **ADJ** Ugandan

❑ **Ougandais, -e NM,F** Ugandan

ougrien, -enne [ugrijɛ̃, -ɛn] *Ling* **ADJ** Ugric

❑ **Ougrien, -enne NM,F** Ugric

ouguiya [ugija] **NM** *(monnaie)* ouguiya

oui [wi] **ADV 1** *(en réponse affirmative)* yes; **viendra-t-il? – o.** will he come? – yes; **tu en veux? – o., s'il te plaît** do you want some? – (yes) please; **tu t'appelles Luc, c'est ça? – o.** your name is Luc, isn't it? – yes; **voulez-vous prendre X pour époux? – o.** do you take X to be your lawful wedded husband? – I do; **Michel! – o., o., voilà, j'arrive!** Michel! – yes *or* all right, I'm coming!; **tu comprends? – o. et non** do you understand? – yes and no *or* I do and I don't; **alors c'est o. ou c'est non?** so is it yes or no?; **mais o.** yes, of course; **o., bien sûr** yes, of course; **il est audacieux – certes o.** he's rather daring – he certainly is; **o. assurément** yes indeed; **c'est vraiment injuste! – ah ça o.!** that's really unfair! – you said it *or* that's for sure!; *Fam* **tu vas déposer une plainte? – ah ça o.!** are you going to lodge a complaint? – you bet I am!; *Fam* **tu vas la laisser faire? – oh que o.!** are you going to let her go ahead? – you bet!; *Mil* **o., mon capitaine!** (yes) sir!; *Naut* **o., mon commandant!** aye aye sir!

2 *(en remplacement d'une proposition)* **il semblerait que o.** it would seem so; **tu vas voter? – je crois que o.** are you going to vote? – (yes) I think so *or* I think I will; **bien sûr que o.** (yes,) of course; **elle n'a dit ni o. ni non** she didn't say either yes or no, she was very noncommittal; **faire o. de la tête** to nod; **faire signe que o., faire o. de la tête** to nod (one's head); **tu les connais? – lui non, mais elle o., très bien** do you know them? – him no, but her yes, very well; **elle vient aussi? si o., je reste** will she be there too? if so *or* if she is I'll stay

3 *(emploi expressif)* **o., je veux bien y aller** yes, I'd really like to go; **o., j'ai entendu!** yes, I heard!; **eh o., c'est bien moi!** yes, it's me alright!; **o., évidemment, elle a un peu raison** of course, she's right in a way; **eh bien o., c'est moi qui le lui ai dit!** yes, I was the one who told him/her!; **je suis déçu, o., vraiment déçu!** I'm disappointed, really disappointed!; **le nucléaire o., mais pas à n'importe quel prix!** yes to nuclear energy, but not at any cost!; **tu viens, o.?** are you coming then?; **tu me le donnes, o. ou non?** are you going to give it to me or not *or* or aren't you?; **tu viens, o. ou non?** are you coming or not?; *très Fam* **tu viens, o. ou merde?** are you coming or not, for Christ's sake?; **tu me réponds, o.?** answer me will you?, will you answer me?; **elle va se dépêcher, o.?** is she going to hurry up or isn't she?; **c'est bientôt fini de crier, o.?** will you stop shouting?, stop shouting, will you!

NM INV je voudrais un o. définitif I'd like a definitive yes; **un o. franc et massif** a solid yes vote; **les o. et les non** the yesses *or* ayes and the noes; **il y a eu cinq o.** *(dans un vote)* there were five votes for *or* five ayes; **le o. de la mariée s'entendit à peine** the bride could barely be heard when she said "I do"; **répondre par o. ou non** to answer yes or no; **pleurer pour un o., pour un non** to cry at the least (little) thing; **ils se disputent pour un o. pour un non** they quarrel over the slightest (little) thing; **il change d'avis pour un o. pour un non** he changes his mind at the drop of a hat

ouï-dire [widir] **NM INV** hearsay; **cette histoire n'est fondée que sur des o.** this story is just based on hearsay

❑ **par ouï-dire ADV** by hearsay, through the grapevine; **j'ai su par o. que...** I've heard tell that..., I've heard through the grapevine that...

ouïe[1] [wi] **NF 1** *Anat* (sense of) hearing; **avoir l'o. fine** to have a keen ear; *Hum* **continue, je suis tout o.** go on, I'm all ears **2** *Ich* gill **3** *Mus* sound hole **4** *Tech (d'un ventilateur)* ear; *Aut* louvre

❑ **ouïes NFPL** *Can Fam* ears■

ouïe[2] [uj] **EXCLAM** ouch!

ouillage [ujaʒ] **NM** ullaging

ouille [uj] = **ouïe**[2]

-OUILLE/-OUILLER [uj, uje] **SUFF**

Although **-ouille** is used to form nouns and **-ouiller** is used to form verbs, they both have the same PEJORATIVE or DIMINUTIVE function. Words featuring these two suffixes are often colloquial in register, eg:

merdouille mess/load of shit; **glandouille** loafing about; **glandouiller** to loaf about; **grattouiller** to itch; **mâchouiller** to chew at; **merdouiller** to screw up, to cock up

ouiller [3] [uje] **VT** to ullage

-ouiller *voir* **-ouille**

ouillère, ouillière [ujɛr] **NF** *Agr* = space between rows of vines (used for other crops)

Oui-Oui [wiwi] **NPR** *(personnage)* Noddy

ouïr [51] [wir] **VT 1** *Littéraire ou Hum* to hear (tell); **j'ai ouï dire que tu avais déménagé** I heard tell that you had moved; **j'ai souvent ouï dire que...** I have often heard it said that...; *Arch ou Hum* **oyez, oyez braves gens** hear ye, good people **2** *Jur* **o. des témoins** to hear witnesses

ouistiti [wistiti] **NM 1** *Zool* marmoset **2** *Fam (personne)* **drôle de o., celui-là!** he's a bit of a weirdo, that one!

oukase [ukaz] = **ukase**

Oulan-Bator [ulanbatɔr] **NM** *Géog* Ulan Bator

ouléma [ulema] = **uléma**

oulipien, -enne [ulipjɛ̃, -ɛn] **ADJ** *Littérature* = of or relating to the "Oulipo" group of writers

Oulipo [ulipo] **NM** *Littérature (abrév* **Ouvroir de Littérature Potentielle) l'O.** = literary group concerned with experimental writing techniques, founded by Raymond Queneau and François Le Lionnais in 1960 and including the writer Georges Perec

oullière [uljɛr] = **ouillère**

oumiak [umjak] **NM** umiak

Ouolof [wɔlɔf] **NMF les Ouolofs** the Wolofs

❑ **ouolof NM** *(langue)* Wolof

Oupeinpo [upɛ̃po] **NM** *Beaux-Arts (abrév* **Ouvroir de Peinture Potentielle) l'O.** = artistic group founded by Jacques Carelman and Thierry Foulc in 1980, with the aim of applying mathematical principles to painting and inventing new art movements

Our [ur] = **Ur**

ouragan [uragɑ̃] **NM 1** *Météo* hurricane; **il est entré comme un o. et s'est mis à hurler** he burst in like a whirlwind and started yelling **2** *Fig (tumulte)* storm, uproar; **son discours provoqua un o. de protestations** his/her speech caused a storm of protest *or* an uproar

Oural [ural] **NM 1** *(fleuve)* **l'O.** the Ural **2** *(montagnes)* **l'O.** the Urals, the Ural mountains; **dans l'O.** in the Urals

ouralien, -enne [uraljɛ̃, -ɛn] **ADJ** Uralic, Uralian

NM *Ling* Uralic

ouralo-altaïque [uralɔaltaik] *(pl* **ouralo-altaïques) ADJ** *Ling* Ural-Altaic

ouraque [urak] **NM** *Anat* urachus

ourdir [32] [urdir] **VT 1** *Littéraire (complot)* to hatch, to weave; *(intrigue)* to weave **2** *Tech (tissage)* to warp; *(vannerie)* to weave

ourdissage [urdisaʒ] **NM** *Tex* warping

ourdisseur, -euse [urdisœr, -øz] **NM,F 1** *Tex* warper **2** *Littéraire (d'un complot)* hatcher

ourdissoir [urdiswar] **NM** *Tex* (weaver's) warp beam

ourdou [urdu] = **urdu**

ourébi [urebi] **NM** *Zool* oribi

ourlé, -e [urle] **ADJ** *Couture* hemmed; **des oreilles délicatement ourlées** delicately shaped ears; **elle a des lèvres bien ourlées** her lips are well-defined

ourler [3] [urle] **VT 1** *Couture* to hem; **o. à jour** to hemstitch **2** *Littéraire (border)* to fringe; **des paupières ourlées de longs cils** eyelids fringed with long eyelashes

ourlet [urlɛ] **NM 1** *Couture* hem; **faire un o. à une jupe** to hem a skirt; **faux o.** false hem; **point d'o.** hemstitch **2** *(repli, rebord → d'un cratère)* edge; *(de l'oreille)* rim, *Spéc* helix **3** *Métal (de feuilles de métal)* lap joint, hem

ourlien, -enne [urljɛ̃, -ɛn] **ADJ** *Méd (fièvre, virus, vaccin etc)* mumps *(avant n)*

Ours [urs] **NM** *Géog* **le Grand Lac de l'O.** Great Bear Lake

ours [urs] **NM 1** *Zool* bear; **o. blanc** polar bear; **o. brun** brown bear; **o. des cavernes** cave bear; **o. des cocotiers** sun bear; **o. à collier** Asiatic *or* Himalayan black bear, moon bear; **o. gris d'Amérique** grizzly bear; **o. de l'Himalaya** Asiatic *or* Himalayan black bear, moon bear; **o. kodiak** Kodiak bear, Alaskan brown bear; **o. lippu** sloth bear; **o. à lunettes** spectacled bear; **o. malais** sun bear; **o. marin** sea bear, fur seal; **o. noir** black bear; **o. polaire** polar bear; **arrête de tourner en rond comme un o. en cage!** stop pacing up and down like a caged animal!

2 *Fam (personne)* **il est un peu o.** he's a bit grumpy *or* gruff; **quel o. mal léché!** grumpy old thing!

3 *(jouet)* **o. (en peluche)** teddy bear

4 *Journ* masthead

5 *Typ* credits page *(where contributors to a book are acknowledged)*

6 *Fam* **avoir ses o.** *(d'une femme)* to have the curse, to have one's period■

ourse [urs] **NF** *Zool* she-bear

❑ **Ourse NF** *Astron* **la Grande O.** *(constellation)* Ursa Major, the Great Bear; *(sept étoiles)* the Plough, *Am* the Big Dipper; **la Petite O.** Ursa Minor, the Little Bear

oursin [ursɛ̃] **NM** *Zool* sea urchin

ourson [ursɔ̃] **NM** (bear) cub

-OUSE, -OUZE [uz] **SUFF**

This is a suffix used in French SLANG to form feminine nouns. It can either be added to a noun or replace its ending. Note the two spelling options in some cases, eg:

bagouse (from *bague*) ring; **partouze, partouse** (from *partie*) orgy; **perlouse, perlouze** (from *perle*) pearl; **piquouse** (from *piqûre*) shot, jab; **tantouze, tantouse** (from *tante*) fairy (male homosexual)

Oussama Ben Laden [usamabɛnladɛn] NPR Osama Bin Laden

oust, ouste [ust] EXCLAM *Fam* out!, scram!; **allez, o., tout le monde dehors!** come on, get a move on, everybody out!

out [awt] ADV **1** *Sport (au tennis, au badminton etc)* out; **la balle est o.** the ball is out **2** *Boxe* out, knocked out
ADJ INV out; **une balle o.** an out ball

outarde [utard] NF *Orn* **1** bustard; **o. barbue** great bustard; **o. canepetière** little bustard; **o. houbara** houbara **2** *(bernache du Canada)* Canada goose

outardeau, -x [utardo] NM *Orn* young bustard

outer [3] [awte] VT *(révéler l'homosexualité de)* to out

outil [uti] NM **1** *(pour travailler)* tool; **cabane/boîte à outils** tool shed/box; **outils de jardinage** garden implements *or* tools; **o. coupant** *ou* **de coupe** *ou* **tranchant** cutting tool; *(pour bords ou bordures)* edging tool
2 *(moyen, aide)* tool; **o. d'aide à la décision** decision-making tool; *Ordinat* **o. auteur** authoring tool; *Ordinat* **o. de création de pages Web** web authoring tool; **o. de gestion** management tool; *Fig* **savoir utiliser l'o. informatique** to know how to use computers; **o. de marketing** marketing tool; *Fig* **les outils mathématiques** mathematical tools; *Ordinat* **o. de navigation sur le Web** web browser; **outils pédagogiques** teaching aids; **o. de production** production tool; **o. de recherche** research tool; *Bourse* **o. de spéculation** trading instrument; **o. de travail** tool, work instrument
3 *Fam Hum (pénis)* tool

outillage [utijaʒ] NM **1** *(ensemble d'outils)* (set of) tools; *(pour un jardinier)* (set of) tools *or* implements **2** *(industrie)* toolmaking *(UNCOUNT)* **3** *(dans une usine)* (machine) tool workshop

outillé, -e [utije] ADJ **être o. pour faire qch** to be properly equipped *or* to have the proper tools to do sth; **être bien o. en qch** to be well equipped with sth; *Fam Hum* **être bien o.** to be well-hung

outiller [3] [utije] VT *(ouvrier)* to supply with tools; *(atelier, usine)* to equip, to fit with tools
▸**s'outiller** VPR *(usine)* to equip itself; *(bricoleur)* to equip oneself with tools; **vous auriez dû mieux vous o.** you should have made sure you were better equipped

outilleur [utijœr] NM toolmaker

outlaw [awtlo] NM outlaw

output [awtput] NM *Écon* output

outrage [utraʒ] NM **1** *(offense)* insult (**à** to); **subir les outrages de qn** to be insulted by sb; **faire o. à l'honneur de qn** to insult sb's honour; **faire o. à la raison** to be an insult to reason; *Euph* **faire subir les derniers outrages à une femme** to violate a woman; **les outrages du temps** *ou* **des ans** the ravages of time
2 *Jur* **o. à agent** insulting behaviour; **o. aux bonnes mœurs** affront to public decency; **o. à magistrat** (criminal) contempt of court; **o. (public) à la pudeur** indecent exposure

outrageant, -e [utraʒɑ̃, -ɑ̃t] ADJ *(proposition, refus)* insulting; *(plaisanterie, propos)* offensive; *(accusation)* outrageous

outrager [17] [utraʒe] VT **1** *(offenser)* to offend, to insult, to abuse; **o. une femme dans son honneur** to insult a woman's honour
2 *Littéraire (porter atteinte à → la vérité)* to violate; *(→ la raison, le bon goût)* to offend against; *Fig* **o. le bon sens** to be an insult to *or* to offend common sense
▸**s'outrager** VPR **parle franchement, personne ne s'outragera de tes propos** speak freely, your remarks will shock *or* outrage no one

outrageuse [utraʒøz] *voir* **outrageux**

outrageusement [utraʒøzmɑ̃] ADV excessively, extravagantly, outrageously

outrageux, -euse [utraʒø, -øz] ADJ *Littéraire* insulting, offensive, outrageous

outrance [utrɑ̃s] NF **1** *(exagération)* excessiveness, extravagance, outrageousness; **l'o. de sa remarque lui ôte toute crédibilité** his/her remark is so outrageous that he/she loses all credibility
2 *(acte)* extravagance; *(parole)* extravagant *or* immoderate language
▫ **à outrance** ADJ **combat à o.** all-out fight; **industrialisation à o.** all-out industrialization
ADV excessively, extravagantly, outrageously

outrancier, -ère [utrɑ̃sje, -ɛr] ADJ excessive, extravagant, extreme; **des propos outranciers** extreme *or* wild remarks

outre[1] [utr] NF **1** *(pour transporter des liquides)* wine skin; *(en peau de chèvre)* goatskin bottle **2** *Zool* **o. de mer** sea squirt

outre[2] [utr] PRÉP *(en plus de)* besides, as well as; **o. le fait que...** besides the fact that...; **o. cette somme** besides *or* in addition to that sum; **o. leur cousin, ils hébergent une amie en ce moment** as well as *or* besides their cousin they have a friend staying at the moment
ADV **passer o. à qch** to disregard sth; **passer o. à une interdiction/une objection** to disregard a ban/an objection; **elle a passé o. malgré l'interdiction** she carried on regardless of *or* she disregarded the ban
▫ **en outre** ADV besides, furthermore, moreover; **j'ai en o. plusieurs remarques à vous faire** I have moreover several things to say to you
▫ **outre mesure** ADV excessively; **je n'ai pas l'intention d'insister o. mesure** I'm not going to push the matter; **le voyage ne l'avait pas fatigué o. mesure** he wasn't overly tired from the journey; **il ne s'est pas inquiété o. mesure** he didn't worry unduly; **je n'y crois pas o. mesure** I don't set much store by it; **ils ne s'aiment pas o. mesure** they're not overly *or* excessively keen on each other
▫ **outre que** CONJ apart from; **o. (le fait) qu'il est riche** apart from the fact that he's rich, apart from *or* besides *or* in addition to being rich; **o. qu'il est très serviable, il est aussi très efficace** apart from being obliging he's also very efficient, not only is he obliging but he's also very efficient

outré, -e [utre] ADJ **1** *Littéraire (exagéré)* excessive, exaggerated, overdone; **des compliments outrés** excessive *or* exaggerated compliments; **comédien dont le jeu est o.** actor who overacts, actor whose acting is overdone **2** *(choqué)* indignant, shocked, outraged

outre-Atlantique [utratlɑ̃tik] ADV across the Atlantic

outrecuidance [utrəkɥidɑ̃s] NF *Littéraire* **1** *(fatuité)* overconfidence, self-importance **2** *(impertinence)* impudence, impertinence

outrecuidant, -e [utrəkɥidɑ̃, -ɑ̃t] ADJ *Littéraire* **1** *(fat, prétentieux)* overconfident, self-important **2** *(impertinent)* arrogant, impudent, impertinent

outre-Jura [utrəʒyra] ADV *Suisse* in France

outre-Manche [utrəmɑ̃ʃ] ADV across the Channel

outremer [utrəmɛr] ADJ INV ultramarine
NM *Minér* lapis lazuli; *(teinte)* ultramarine

outre-mer [utrəmɛr] ADV overseas; **la France d'o.** France's overseas territories and departments; *Admin* **territoires d'o.** overseas territories

outrepassé [utrəpɑse] ADJ *Archit* **arc o.** horseshoe arch

outrepasser [3] [utrəpase] VT *(droit)* to go beyond; *(ordre)* to exceed; *(pouvoirs)* to abuse; **il a outrepassé les ordres** he exceeded his orders

outre-Quiévrain [utrəkjevrɛ̃] ADV *Hum* **1** *Belg* across the border *(referring to France)* **2** *(d'un point de vue français)* across the border *(referring to Belgium)*

outrer [3] [utre] VT **1** *Littéraire (exagérer)* to exaggerate, to magnify; **o. la vérité** to exaggerate *or* to overstate the truth **2** *(révolter)* to outrage

outre-Rhin [utrərɛ̃] ADV across the Rhine

outre-Sarine [utrəsarin] ADV *Suisse* in German-speaking Switzerland

outre-tombe [utrətɔ̃b] **d'outre-tombe** ADJ INV **une voix d'o.** a voice from beyond the grave

outsider [awtsajdœr] NM outsider

ouvala [uvala] NF *Géog* uvala

Ouvéa [uvea] NF Uvea

ouvert, -e [uvɛr, -ɛrt] PP *voir* **ouvrir**
ADJ **1** *(porte, tiroir)* open; **entre, la porte est ouverte** *ou* **c'est o.** come in, the door's open; **grand o., grande ouverte** wide open; **je vis une porte grande ouverte** I saw a door that was wide open; **col de l'Iseran: o.** *(panneau sur la route)* Iseran Pass: open; **un robinet o. peut causer une inondation** a *Br* tap *or Am* faucet that's been left on can cause flooding; **il avait la chemise ouverte** his shirt was open (to the waist) *or* undone; **n'achetez pas de tulipes ouvertes** don't buy tulips that are already open; **elle s'avança la main ouverte** she moved forward with her hand open
2 *(bouche, yeux)* open; **dormir la bouche ouverte** to sleep with one's mouth open; **ne reste pas là la bouche ouverte!** don't just stand there gawping!; **il était dans son lit, les yeux ouverts** he was lying in bed with his eyes open; **garder les yeux (grands) ouverts** to keep one's eyes (wide) open; *Fig* to keep one's eyes peeled, to be on the lookout
3 *(coupé)* cut, open; **elle a eu la lèvre ouverte** her lip was cut; **il gisait là, le ventre o./la gorge ouverte** he lay there with his stomach slashed open/his throat cut; **plaie ouverte** open *or* gaping wound; **il a le crâne/le genou o.** he has a gaping wound in his skull/knee, his skull/knee has been split open
4 *(magasin, bureau, restaurant, maison)* open; **en ville, je n'ai rien trouvé d'o.** in town none of the shops were open; **vous restez o.?** will you stay open?; **o. de 10 heures à 5 heures** open (from) 10 to 5; *Fam* **l'épicier du coin reste o. jusqu'à minuit** the grocer on the corner stays open till midnight; **les jardins sont ouverts au public** the gardens are open to the public; **ils laissent toujours (tout) o.** *(ne ferment pas à clé)* they never lock the house; *(ne ferment pas les fenêtres)* they always leave the windows open; **une voiture ouverte est une tentation pour les voleurs** a car left unlocked *or* open is an invitation to burglars
5 *(qui a commencé)* **la séance est ouverte** I declare the meeting open; **la chasse/la campagne électorale est ouverte depuis ce matin** the hunting season/the election campaign began *or* started this morning; **les paris sont ouverts** *Courses de chevaux* bets are being taken; *Fig* it's anyone's guess
6 *(réceptif)* open; **un visage o.** an open face; **o. (d'esprit)** open-minded; **avoir l'esprit o.** to be open-minded, to have an open mind; **être o. à** to be open to; **nous sommes ouverts aux idées nouvelles** we are open to new ideas
7 *(non caché)* open; **être en guerre ouverte avec qn** to be openly at war with sb; **c'est la guerre ouverte contre les fumeurs** it's open war on smokers; **c'est la lutte ouverte entre eux** it's open warfare between them; **en conflit o. avec ses parents** in open conflict with his/her parents
8 *Ordinat* open; *(système)* open-ended
9 *Math* open; *Géom* wide
10 *Sport (imprévisible)* **un match très o.** a (wide) open game; **un jeu o.** an open game; *Ski* **porte ouverte** open flags; *Golf* **tournoi o.** open tournament, golf open
11 *Ling (syllabe, voyelle)* open
12 *Élec (circuit)* open; *(machine)* uninsulated
13 *Fin* **à capital o.** with an open *or* a fluctuating authorized capital
14 **ville ouverte** open *or* unfortified town; *Naut* **rade ouverte** open roadstead
NM *Math* open set

ouvertement [uvɛrtəmɑ̃] ADV openly

ouverture [uvɛrtyr] NF **1** *(trou)* opening; **une o. dans le mur** an opening *or* a hole in the wall; *Fig* **l'événement représente une véritable o. pour ces pays** this development will open up real opportunities for these countries; *Fig* **avoir une o. avec qn** to have a chance with sb
2 *(action d'ouvrir)* **l'o. des grilles a lieu à midi** the gates are opened *or* unlocked at noon; **pour ne pas faire la queue, j'étais là avant même l'o.** to avoid queuing I was there even before it *or* the doors opened; **o. des portes à 20 heures** doors open at 8; *Com* **les plus belles affaires se font à l'o.** the best bargains are to be had when the shop opens; **o. en nocturne le jeudi** late closing *or* open late on Thursdays; **heures d'o.** opening hours; **jours d'o.** opening days; **nous attendons avec impatience l'o. du tunnel** we can hardly wait for the tunnel to open; **l'o. du coffre se fera devant témoins** the safe will be opened *or* unlocked in front of witnesses
3 *(mise à disposition)* **pour faciliter l'o. d'un**

compte courant to make it easier to open a current account; **l'o. de vos droits ne date que de février dernier** you were not entitled to claim benefit before last February; **o. de crédit** (bank) credit arrangement

4 *(d'une session, d'un festival)* opening; **je tiens le rayon parfumerie depuis le jour de l'o.** I've been in charge of the perfume department since the day we opened; **discours d'o.** opening speech; *Bourse* **à l'o.** at start of trading; *Bourse* **depuis l'o.** since trading began *or* opened (this morning); *Bourse* **cours d'o.** opening price; **heures d'o.** opening hours; *Jur* **o. des débats** opening of proceedings; *Ordinat* **o. de session** log-on

5 *Chasse & Pêche* opening; **demain, on fait l'o. ensemble** tomorrow we're going out together on the first (official) day of the open season

6 *(écartement → d'une voûte)* width, span; *(des branches d'un compas)* spread

7 *Fig Pol* **l'o. vers la gauche/la droite** broadening the base of government to the left/right; **la politique d'o.** consensus politics; **o. d'esprit** open-mindedness

8 *Sport* opening up; *Boxe* opening; **contrôler l'o. des skis** to be in control of the angle of the skis

9 *Cartes & (dans un jeu)* opening; **avoir l'o.** to have the opening move; **avoir l'o. à trèfle** to lead clubs

10 *Mus* overture

11 *Phot* aperture; **o. du diaphragme** f-stop

12 *Aut (des roues)* toe-out; **o. sans clé** keyless entry

13 *Élec* opening, breaking; **o. d'induit** armature gap

14 *Presse* front-page article

15 *Mktg* opening, window of opportunity; **l'o. de nouveaux débouchés** the opening up of new markets

16 *Golf (d'un club)* loft

▫ **ouvertures** NFPL overtures; **faire des ouvertures de paix** to make peace overtures

ouvrabilité [uvrabilite] NF *Constr* workability

ouvrable [uvrabl] ADJ **heures ouvrables** business hours, shop hours; **pendant les heures ouvrables** *Com* during opening hours; *Admin* during office hours; **jour o.** workday, *Br* working day

ouvrage [uvraʒ] NM **1** *(travail)* work; **se mettre à l'o.** to get down to work, to start work; **un o. de longue haleine** a long-term project *or* undertaking

2 *(œuvre)* (piece of) work; **le gros de l'o. a été exécuté par un jeune artiste** the bulk of the work was done by a young artist; *Archit & Constr* **o. d'art** construction works; **ouvrages de maçonnerie** masonry; **menus ouvrages** finishing (jobs); *Fig* **une rencontre qui est l'o. du hasard** a meeting which is due to chance, a chance meeting; *Fig* **l'o. du temps** the work of time

3 *(tricot, broderie)* work; *Vieilli* **o. de dames** needlework

4 *(livre)* book; **un o. de philosophie** a work of philosophy, a philosophy book; **il existe plusieurs ouvrages sur ce problème** there are several books dealing with this problem; **l'o. se compose de trois volumes** the book is in three volumes; **o. de référence** reference work *or* book, work of reference

5 *Métal* hearth

NF *Hum* **c'est de la belle o.!** that's a nice piece of work!

ouvragé, -e [uvraʒe] ADJ *(nappe)* finely embroidered; *(bijou)* finely worked; *(construction)* elaborate, ornate

ouvrager [17] [uvraʒe] VT *(nappe)* to embroider finely; *(métal, bijou)* to work finely

ouvraison [uvrɛzɔ̃] NF *Tex* **1** *(action)* (process of) working **2** *(tissu)* material worked

ouvrant, -e [uvrɑ̃, -ɑ̃t] ADJ opening, moving

NM *Beaux-Arts (d'un triptyque)* panel

ouvré, -e [uvre] ADJ **1** *(bois, fer)* ornate, elaborate, elaborately decorated; *(nappe)* (finely *or* elaborately) embroidered, finely worked **2** *Tech (fer)* wrought; **produits ouvrés et semi-ouvrés** finished and semi-finished products **3** *Admin & Com* **jour o.** workday, *Br* working day

ouvreau, -x [uvro] NM *Tech* working door, charging door

ouvre-boîte, ouvre-boîtes [uvrəbwat] *(pl* **ouvre-boîtes)** NM can opener, *Br* tin opener

ouvre-bouteille, ouvre-bouteilles [uvrəbutɛj] *(pl* **ouvre-bouteilles)** NM bottle opener

ouvre-huître, ouvre-huîtres [uvrɥitr] *(pl* **ouvre-huîtres)** NM oyster knife

ouvrer [3] [uvre] VT **1** *(bois)* to decorate (elaborately); *(linge)* to embroider, to work (finely) **2** *Tex* to open (silk)

ouvreur, -euse [uvrœr, -øz] NM,F **1** *Cartes & (dans un jeu)* opener **2** *Cin & Théât* usher, *f* usherette **3** *Sport* forerunner

▫ **ouvreuse** NF *Tex* opening machine

ouvrez-moi [uvremwa] NM INV *Ordinat* read-me document

ouvrier, -ère [uvrije, -ɛr] ADJ **1** *(quartier, condition)* working-class; **solidarité ouvrière** working-class solidarity; **agitation ouvrière** industrial unrest; **la classe ouvrière** the working class

2 *Entom* **abeille ouvrière** worker bee; **fourmi ouvrière** worker ant

NM,F (manual) worker; **une ouvrière** a (female) worker; **les ouvriers sur le chantier** the workmen on the site; **une famille d'ouvriers** a working-class family; *Fig Littéraire* **il est l'o. de sa fortune** he is a self-made man; *Littéraire* **le grand o., l'éternel o.** God, the great Architect of the universe; **o. qualifié/spécialisé** skilled/semi-skilled worker; **o. agricole** agricultural worker, farm labourer; **o. du bâtiment** builder; **o. à domicile** home worker; **o. à façon** outworker; **o. hautement qualifié** highly-skilled worker; **o. à la journée** day labourer; **o. mécanicien** garage mechanic; **o. non qualifié** unqualified worker *or* labourer; **o. professionnel** skilled worker; **o. qualifié** skilled worker; **o. spécialisé** semi-skilled worker; **o. du textile** mill worker *or* hand; **o. en bois/sur métaux** woodworker/metalworker

▫ **ouvrière** NF *(abeille)* worker (bee); *(fourmi)* worker (ant)

ouvriérisme [uvrijerism] NM *Pol (autogestion)* worker control; *(syndicalisme)* trade unionism

ouvriériste [uvrijerist] ADJ workerist

NMF workerist

OUVRIR [34] [uvrir]

> **VT** to open **1–8, 10–16** ▪ to open up **2, 3, 6, 10** ▪ to unlock **1** ▪ to undo **4** ▪ to begin, to start **5** ▪ to clear **6** ▪ to turn on **8** ▪ to lead **9** ▪ to cut open **10**
> **USAGE ABSOLU** to answer the door **1** ▪ to open **3, 4**
> **VI** to be open **1** ▪ to open **1, 2**

VT **1** *(portail, tiroir, capot de voiture, fenêtre)* to open; *(porte fermée à clé)* to unlock, to open; *(porte verrouillée)* to unbolt, to open; *(loquet)* to unfasten; *(avec une clef)* to unlock; **o. une fenêtre tout grand** to open a window wide; **il ouvrit la porte d'un coup d'épaule** he shouldered the door open, he forced the door (open) with his shoulder; **il ouvrit la porte d'un coup de pied** he kicked the door open; **o. une porte par effraction** to force a door; **o. sa porte à qn** to throw open one's house to sb; *Fig* **o. la porte à qch** to open the door to sth

2 *(bouteille, pot, porte-monnaie)* to open; *(coquillage)* to open (up); *(paquet)* to open, to unwrap; *(enveloppe)* to open, to unseal; **allez, on ouvre une bouteille de champagne!** come on, let's open *or* crack open a bottle of champagne!; **ils ont ouvert le coffre-fort au chalumeau** they used a blowtorch to break open *or* into the safe; **o. un pot de peinture avec un levier** to prise the lid off a pot of paint

3 *(déplier → éventail)* to open; *(→ carte routière)* to open (up), to unfold; *(→ livre)* to open (up); **ouvrez votre manuel page 15** open your books *Br* on *or Am* to page 15; **les fleurs ouvrent leurs corolles au soleil du matin** the flowers open their petals in the morning sun; *Couture* **o. une couture** to iron a seam flat

4 *(desserrer, écarter → compas, paupières)* to open; *(→ rideau)* to open, to draw back; *(→ aile, bras)* to open (out), to spread (out); *(→ mains)* to open (out); *(déboutonner → veste)* to undo, to unfasten; **o. les bras** *(en signe d'affection)* to open one's arms; **o. les yeux** to open one's eyes; **le matin, j'ai du mal à o. les yeux** *(à me réveiller)* I find it difficult to wake up in the morning; **o. l'œil** to open one's eye; *Fig* to keep one's eyes open; **cette rencontre avec lui m'a ouvert les yeux** meeting him was a real eye-opener for me; **o. de grands yeux** *(être surpris)* to be wide-eyed; **ouvrez grands vos yeux** *(soyez attentifs)* keep your eyes peeled; **o. l'esprit à qn** to broaden sb's outlook; *Fam* **l'o.**, *très Fam* **o. sa gueule** *(parler)* to open one's big mouth; *Fam* **il n'a pas ouvert la bouche, il ne l'a pas ouverte** he didn't open his mouth; **tu ferais mieux de ne pas l'o.!** you'd better keep your mouth *or* trap shut!

5 *(commencer → hostilités)* to open, to begin; *(→ campagne, récit, enquête)* to open, to start; *(→ bal, festival, conférence, saison de chasse)* to open; **la scène qui ouvre la pièce** the opening scene of the play; **l'indice qui a ouvert la séance à la Bourse** the opening share prices on the Stock Exchange today; **voici le candidat qui ouvre notre grand concours** here's the first contestant to enter our competition; **o. le bal** to open the ball; *Ordinat* **o. une session** to log in, to log on

6 *(rendre accessible → chemin, voie)* to open (up), to clear; *(→ frontière, filière)* to open; **il ouvrait un sentier au coupe-coupe** he cleared a path with a machete; *Can* **o. un chemin** *(dégager la neige)* to clear snow from a road; *(en coupant des arbres)* to cut down trees to make way for a new road; **des policiers lui ont ouvert un passage parmi ses fans** policemen cleared a way for him/her through the crowd of fans; **o. son pays** *ou* **ses frontières aux réfugiés politiques** to open up one's country *or* to open one's borders to political refugees; **ils refusent d'o. leur marché aux produits européens** they refuse to open up their market to European products; **il faut o. l'université à tous** universities must be open to all; **ce sont des professions que nous voulons o. aux femmes** they are professions that we want to open up to women; **pourquoi ne pas o. cette formation à de jeunes chômeurs?** why not make this form of training available to young unemployed people?; **le diplôme vous ouvre de nombreuses possibilités** the diploma opens up a whole range of possibilities for you

7 *(créer → boutique, cinéma, infrastructure)* to open; *(→ entreprise)* to open, to set up; **o. une nouvelle salle dans un musée** to open a new room in a museum

8 *(faire fonctionner → radiateur, robinet)* to turn on; *(→ circuit électrique)* to open; *Fam* **ouvre la télé** turn *or* switch the TV on; *Fam* **o. l'eau/l'électricité/le gaz** to turn on the water/the electricity/the gas

9 *(être en tête de → défilé, procession)* to lead; **o. la marche** to lead the march, to walk in front; **c'est son nom qui ouvre la liste** his/her name is (the) first on the list

10 *(inciser → corps)* to open (up), to cut open; *(→ panaris)* to lance, to cut open; *Fam* **ils l'ont ouvert de la cheville au genou** they opened up *or* cut open his leg from the ankle to the knee

11 *Sport* **o. le jeu** to open play; **essayez d'o. un peu plus la partie** try to play a more open game; **o. la marque** *ou* **le score** *(gén)* to open the scoring; *Ftbl* to score the first goal; **il vient d'o. la marque pour son équipe** he's just put his team on the board; *Ski* **o. la piste** to open the run

12 *Banque (compte bancaire, portefeuille d'actions)* to open; *(emprunt)* to issue, to float; **o. un crédit à qn** to give sb credit facilities; **o. un droit à qn** *(dans les assurances)* to entitle sb to a claim

13 *Cartes & (dans un jeu)* to open

14 *Naut* **o. une voile** to brace a sail; **o. un port/une baie** to open a port/bay

15 *Élec* to break, to open

16 *Tex* to open

USAGE ABSOLU **1 je suis allé o. chez les Loriot avant qu'ils rentrent de voyage** I went and opened up the Loriots' house before they came back from their trip; **va o.** go and answer the door; **on a sonné, je vais o.** there's someone at

ouv–ouv

the door, I'll go; **c'est moi, ouvre** it's me, open the door *or* let me in; **o. à qn** to open the door to sb, to let sb in; **va leur o.** go and let them in

2 *(écarter)* **ouvrez!** *(en danse)* open up!

3 *(commencer)* to open; **la scène ouvre par un chœur** the scene opens with a chorus; *TV & Cin* **o. en fondu** to fade in; *TV & Cin* **o. par un volet** to wipe on

4 *Cartes* **o. à cœur** to open (the bidding) in hearts; *(commencer le jeu)* to open *or* to lead with a heart

VI 1 *(boutique, restaurant, spectacle)* to (be) open; *Bourse* to open; **le supermarché ouvre de 9 heures à 22 heures** the supermarket is open *or* opens from 9 a.m. to 10 p.m.; **les magasins n'ouvrent pas les jours de fête** the shops don't open *or* aren't open on public holidays; **le musée ouvrira bientôt au public** the museum will soon be open to the public; **la chasse au faisan/la conférence ouvrira en septembre** the pheasant season/the conference will open in September; *Bourse* **o. en baisse/en hausse** to open down/up; *Bourse* **les valeurs pétrolières ont ouvert ferme** oils opened firm

2 *(couvercle, fenêtre, porte)* to open; **le portail ouvre mal** the gate is difficult to open *or* doesn't open properly; **la porte n'ouvre que de l'intérieur** the door can only be opened from the inside, the door only opens from the inside

❑ **ouvrir sur vt IND 1** *(déboucher sur)* to open onto; **le vasistas ouvre sur le parking** the fanlight opens onto *or* looks out over the car park; **nos fenêtres ouvrent sur la piazza** our windows open out onto *or* have a view of the piazza

2 *(commencer par)* to open with; **le colloque ouvrira sur sa communication** his/her paper will open the conference, the conference will open with his/her paper

3 *Sport* **o. sur qn** to pass (the ball) to sb; **o. sur l'aile gauche** to release the ball to the left wing

▶**s'ouvrir VPR 1** *(boîte, valise)* to open; *(chemisier, fermeture)* to come undone; **ça s'ouvre en dévissant** the top unscrews; **le toit s'ouvre en coulissant** the roof slides open; **la tente s'ouvre des deux côtés avec une fermeture à glissière** the tent can be unzipped on both sides; **la fenêtre de ma chambre s'ouvre mal** the window in my room is difficult to open *or* doesn't open properly

2 *(être inauguré)* to open; **la nouvelle ligne Paris–Bordeaux s'ouvrira en décembre** the new Paris to Bordeaux line will open *or* be opened in December

3 *(se couper → personne)* **il s'est ouvert l'arcade sourcilière** he's got a gash above the eye; **je me suis ouvert le pied sur un bout de verre** I've cut my foot (open) on a piece of glass; **s'o. les veines** to slash *or* to cut one's wrists

4 *(se ménager)* **s'o. un chemin à travers la foule** to push one's way through the crowd

5 *(se desserrer, se déplier → bras, fleur, huître, main)* to open; *(→ aile)* to open (out), to spread, to unfold; *(→ bouche, œil, paupière, livre, rideau)* to open; **ces fleurs s'ouvrent quand le soir tombe** these flowers open at nightfall

6 *(se fendre → foule, flots)* to part; *(→ sol)* to open up; *(→ melon)* to open, to split (open); **la cicatrice s'est ouverte** the scar has opened up; **les flots s'ouvrirent** the sea parted; **un gouffre s'ouvrait sous mes pieds** a chasm opened up *or* yawned under my feet

7 *(boîte, valise → accidentellement)* to (come) open

8 *(fenêtre, portail)* to open; **la fenêtre s'ouvrit brusquement** the window flew *or* was flung *or* was thrown open; **la porte s'ouvrit en coup de vent** the door flew open; **la porte s'ouvre sur la pièce/dans le couloir** the door opens into the room/out into the corridor

9 *(s'épancher)* to open up; **sans s'o. entièrement, elle m'a confié que...** without opening up completely to me, she confided that...; **il éprouvait le besoin de s'o.** he felt the need to talk to somebody; **s'o. à qn** to unburden oneself to sb, to confide in sb; **s'o. à qn de qch** to open one's heart to sb about sth, to confide in sb about sth; **elle ne s'en est jamais ouverte à moi** she's

never confided in me *or* she's never opened her heart to me about it; **s'o. de qch** to open up about sth; **il finit par s'o. de ses problèmes** he eventually talked openly *or* opened up about his problems

10 *(débuter → bal, conférence)* **s'o. par** to open *or* to start with

11 *(se présenter → carrière)* to open up; **toutes les carrières de l'informatique s'ouvrent devant lui** all kinds of careers in computing are opening up for him; **un avenir radieux s'ouvrait devant nous** a bright future opened up before us

12 s'o. à *(des idées, des influences)* to open up to; **s'o. à des cultures nouvelles** to become aware of new cultures; **s'o. à la poésie** to become sensitive to poetry; **leur pays s'ouvre peu à peu au commerce extérieur** their country is gradually opening up to foreign trade; **carrières qui s'ouvrent de plus en plus aux femmes** careers that are opening up more and more to women; **s'o. à de nouvelles technologies** to open (up) one's mind to new technologies

ouvroir [uvrwar] **NM** *(dans un couvent)* workroom; *(dans une paroisse)* sewing room

ouzbek [uzbɛk] **ADJ** Uzbek
　NM *(langue)* Uzbek
　❑ **Ouzbek NMF** Uzbek; **les Ouzbeks** the Uzbeks *or* Uzbek

Ouzbékistan [uzbekistã] **NM l'O.** Uzbekistan

-ouze *voir* **-ouse**

ouzo [uzo] **NM** ouzo

ovaire [ɔvɛr] **NM** *Anat* ovary; *Méd* **cancer de l'o.** ovarian cancer; *Méd* **kyste de l'o.** ovarian cyst

ovalaire [ɔvalɛr] **ADJ** *Anat* oval

ovalbumine [ɔvalbymin] **NF** *Biol* ovalbumin

ovale [ɔval] **ADJ** *(en surface)* oval; *(en volume)* egg-shaped, ovoid
　NM 1 *(forme)* oval; **son visage était d'un o. parfait** his/her face was a perfect oval; **en o.** oval **2** *Tex* throwing mill

ovalie [ɔvali] **NF** *Fam* **l'o.** (the world of) rugby■

ovalien, -enne [ɔvaljɛ̃, -ɛn] **ADJ** rugby *(avant n)* ; **le monde o.** the world of rugby

ovalisation [ɔvalizasjɔ̃] **NF** *Tech* ovalization

ovaliser [3] [ɔvalize] **VT** to make oval, to turn into an oval; *Tech* **l'usure ovalise les cylindres** cylinders become ovalized through wear

ovariectomie [ɔvarjɛktɔmi] **NF** *Méd* ovariectomy, oophorectomy

ovarien, -enne [ɔvarjɛ̃, -ɛn] **ADJ** *Anat* ovarian

ovarite [ɔvarit] **NF** *Méd* ovaritis, oophoritis

ovate [ɔvat] **NM** *Hist* ovate

ovation [ɔvasjɔ̃] **NF** ovation; **le public lui a fait une véritable o.** the audience gave him/her a real ovation; **ils se sont tous levés pour lui faire une o.** he/she got a standing ovation

ovationner [3] [ɔvasjɔne] **VT o. qn** to give sb an ovation; **le groupe s'est fait o. pendant dix minutes** the group were given a ten-minute standing ovation

ove [ɔv] **NM** *Archit* ovolo, ovum

ové, -e [ɔve] **ADJ** egg-shaped, ovate

overbooké, -e [ɔvœrbuke] **ADJ** *Fam (personne)* booked-up, busy■ ; **je peux pas te voir cette semaine, je suis complètement o.** I can't see you this week, I've got a really hectic schedule

overdose [ɔvœrdoz] **NF 1** *(surdose)* overdose; **mourir d'une o.** to die of *or* from an overdose **2** *Fam Fig* overdose, OD; **j'ai eu une o. de chocolat à Noël** I overdosed on chocolate at Christmas

overdrive [ɔvœrdrajv] **NM** *Aut* overdrive

ovibos [ɔvibɔs] **NM** *Zool* ovibos, musk ox

Ovide [ɔvid] **NPR** Ovid

ovidés [ɔvide] **NMPL** *Zool & Agr* Ovidae

oviducte [ɔvidykt] **NM** oviduct

ovin, -e [ɔvɛ̃, -in] **ADJ** ovine
　NM ovine, sheep

oviné [ɔvine] **NM** *(mouton)* ovine; *(chèvre)* caprid

ovipare [ɔvipar] **ADJ** egg-laying, *Spéc* oviparous
　NMF egg-laying *or Spéc* oviparous animal

oviparité [ɔviparite] **NF** egg laying, *Spéc* oviparity

ovipositeur [ɔvipozitœr] **NM** *Entom* ovipositor

oviscapte [ɔviskapt] **NM** *Entom* oviscapt

OVNI, Ovni [ɔvni] **NM** *(abrév* **objet volant non identifié)** **1** *(objet volant)* UFO **2** *Fig (personne*

ou objet atypique) **faire figure d'O.** to stand out, to break the mould; **lors de sa sortie, ce roman a fait figure d'O. dans le paysage littéraire de l'époque** when it was first published this novel really stood out from the literature of the time

ovocyte [ɔvɔsit] **NM** *Biol* oocyte

ovogenèse [ɔvɔʒənɛz] **NF** *Biol* oogenesis

ovogonie [ɔvɔgɔni] **NF** *Biol* oogonium

ovoïde [ɔvɔid], **ovoïdal, -e, -aux, -ales** [ɔvɔidal, -o] **ADJ** egg-shaped, *Spéc* ovoid; *Élec* **maillon o.** egg insulator

ovotide [ɔvɔtid] **NM** *Biol* ootid

ovovivipare [ɔvɔvivipar] **ADJ** ovoviviparous
　NMF ovoviviparous animal

ovoviviparité [ɔvɔviviparite] **NF** ovoviviparity

ovulaire [ɔvylɛr] **ADJ** ovular

ovulation [ɔvylasjɔ̃] **NF** ovulation; **pendant la période d'o.** during ovulation

ovulatoire [ɔvylatwar] **ADJ** ovulation *(avant n)*

ovule [ɔvyl] **NM 1** *Physiol* ovum **2** *Bot & Zool* ovule **3** *Pharm* pessary

ovuler [3] [ɔvyle] **VI** to ovulate

oxacide [ɔksasid] **NM** *Chim* oxyacid, oxygen acid

oxalate [ɔksalat] **NM** *Chim* oxalate; **o. de fer** oxalate of iron, ferrous oxalate

oxalidacée [ɔksalidase] *Bot* **NF** member of the Oxalidaceae family
　❑ **oxalidacées NFPL** Oxalidaceae

oxalide [ɔksalid] **NF** *Bot* oxalis, wood sorrel; **o. blanche** sheep's sorrel

oxalique [ɔksalik] **ADJ acide o.** oxalic acid

oxalis [ɔksalis] **NM** *Bot* oxalis, wood sorrel

oxer [ɔksɛr] **NM** *Équitation* oxer

oxford [ɔksfɔrd] **NM** Oxford (cloth); **une chemise en o.** an Oxford shirt
　ADJ flanelle o. Oxford

oxhydrique [ɔksidrik] **ADJ** *Chim* oxyhydrogen *(avant n)*

oxhydryle [ɔksidril] **NM** *Chim* hydroxyl

oxime [ɔksim] **NF** *Chim* oxim(e)

oxo [ɔkso] **NM** *Chim* oxo

oxonium [ɔksɔnjɔm] **NM** *Chim* oxonium

oxyacétylénique [ɔksiasetilenik] **ADJ** oxyacetylene

oxycarboné, -e [ɔksikarbɔne] **ADJ** *Chim* oxycarburetted

oxychlorure [ɔksiklɔryr] **NM** *Biol & Chim* oxychloride

oxycoupage [ɔksikupaʒ] **NM** *Métal* oxygen cutting

oxycrat [ɔksikra] **NM** *Antiq* oxycrate

oxydable [ɔksidabl] **ADJ** liable to rust, oxidizable; **facilement o.** which rusts easily

oxydant, -e [ɔksidã, -ãt] *Chim* **ADJ** oxidizing
　NM oxidant, oxidizer, oxidizing agent

oxydase [ɔksidaz] **NF** *Biol & Chim* oxidase

oxydation [ɔksidasjɔ̃] **NF** *Chim* oxidation, oxidization

oxyde [ɔksid] **NM** *Chim* oxide; **o. d'azote** nitrogen oxide; **o. de carbone** carbon monoxide; **o. métallique** metallic oxide; **o. nitrique** nitric oxide

oxyder [3] [ɔkside] *Chim* **VT** to oxidize
　▶**s'oxyder VPR** to become oxidized

oxydérurgie [ɔksideryrʒi] **NF** oxygen metallurgy

oxydoréductase [ɔksidɔredyktaz] **NF** *Biol & Chim* oxidoreductase

oxydoréduction [ɔksidɔredyksjɔ̃] **NF** *Biol & Chim* oxidation-reduction

oxygénation [ɔksiʒenasjɔ̃] **NF** *Chim* oxygenation

oxygénase [ɔksiʒenaz] **NF** *Chim & Physiol* oxygenase

oxygène [ɔksiʒɛn] **NM 1** *Chim* oxygen **2** *Fig* **j'ai besoin d'o.** I need some fresh air

oxygéné, -e [ɔksiʒene] **ADJ** *Chim* oxygenated; **cheveux oxygénés** peroxide blonde hair, bleached hair

oxygéner [18] [ɔksiʒene] **VT 1** *Chim & Physiol* to oxygenate, to oxygenize **2** *(cheveux)* to bleach, to peroxide
　▶**s'oxygéner VPR** *Fam* to get some fresh air

oxygénothérapie [ɔksiʒenɔterapi] **NF** *Méd* oxygenation

oxyhémoglobine [ɔksiemɔglɔbin] **NF** *Physiol* oxyhaemoglobin

oxylithe [ɔksilit] **NF** oxylith

oxymore [ɔksimɔr], **oxymoron** [ɔksimɔrɔ̃] **NM** oxymoron

oxysulfide [ɔksylfid], **oxysulfure** [ɔksisylfyr] NM *Chim* oxysulphide

oxytocine [ɔksitɔsin] NF *Méd* oxytocic

oxyton [ɔksitɔ̃] NM *Ling* oxytone

oxyure [ɔksjyr] NM pinworm, *Spéc* oxyuris

oxyurose [ɔksjyroz] NF *Méd* oxyuriasis, enterobiasis

oyat [ɔja] NM lyme grass

Ozalid® [ɔzalid] NM *Typ Br* Ozalid®, *Am* blues

ozène [ɔzɛn] NM *Méd* ozaena, ozena

ozonateur [ɔzɔnatœr] NM *Chim* ozonizer

ozonation [ɔzɔnasjɔ̃] NF *Chim* ozonization

ozone [ozon] NM ozone; **couche d'o.** ozone layer; **diminution de l'o.** ozone depletion

ozoné, -e [ozone] ADJ *Chim* ozonized

ozoner [3] [ozone] VT *Chim* to ozonize

ozoneur [ozonœr] NM *Chim* ozonizer

ozonide [ozonid] NM *Chim* ozonide

ozonisation [ozonizasjɔ̃] NF *Chim* ozonization

ozoniser [3] [ozonize] VT *Chim* to ozonize

ozonosphère [ozonosfɛr] NF ozonosphere, ozone layer

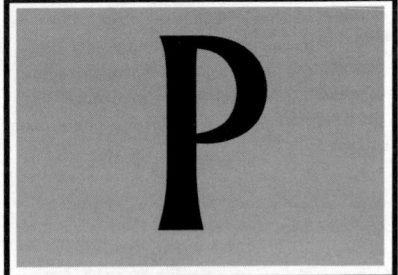

P

P, p¹ [pe] NM INV *(lettre)* P, p; **P comme Pierre** ≃ P for Peter; *Mktg* **les quatre P** *(le marketing mix)* the four Ps

p² **1** *(abrév écrite* **pico**) p **2** *(abrév écrite* **page**) p **3** *Scol (abrév écrite* **passable**) = fair grade (as assessment of schoolwork), ≃ C **4** *(abrév écrite* **pièce**) room; **à louer: 2p** *(dans une annonce)* one-bedroomed *Br* flat *or Am* apartment to let

P. *Rel (abrév écrite* **Père**) F

P2P [pitupi] ADJ *Ordinat (abrév* **peer to peer**) P2P

Pa *Phys (abrév écrite* **pascal**) Pa

PAC, Pac [pak] NF *UE (abrév* **politique agricole commune**) CAP

PACA, Paca [paka] NF *(abrév* **Provence-Alpes-Côte d'Azur**) = region of south-eastern France

paca [paka] NM *Zool* paca

pacage [pakaʒ] NM **1** *(lieu)* pasture, grazing-land; **p. d'été** summer pasture **2** *(action)* grazing; *Jur* **droit de p.** grazing rights

pacager [17] [pakaʒe] VI to graze
  VT to (put out to) graze

pacane [pakan] NF *Bot* pecan (nut)

pacanier [pakanje] NM *Bot* pecan (tree)

pacarana [pakarana] NM *Zool* pacarana

pacemaker [pɛsmekœr] NM (cardiac) pacemaker

pacfung [pakfɔ̃] NM paktong

pacha [paʃa] NM **1** *Hist* pasha **2** *Fam Fig* **mener une vie de p.** to live like a lord■, to live a life of ease■; **tu ne vas pas faire le p. tout le week-end!** don't expect to be waited on hand and foot all weekend! **3** *Naut* skipper

pachalik [paʃalik] NM *Hist* pashalik

pachto [paʃto] NM *(langue)* Pashto

pachtoun, -e [paʃtun] ADJ Pashtun

pachyderme [paʃidɛrm] ADJ pachydermal, pachydermatous
  NM **1** *Zool* pachyderm; **de p.** *(allure, démarche)* elephantine, lumbering; *(grâce)* elephantine **2** *(personne)* (great) elephant

pachydermie [paʃidɛrmi] NF pachydermia

pachyure [pakjyr] NM *Zool* shrew

pacificateur, -trice [pasifikatœr, -tris] ADJ *(réconciliateur)* placatory, pacifying, pacificatory; *Pol* peacemaking
  NM,F pacifier, peacemaker; *Pol* peacemaker

pacification [pasifikasjɔ̃] NF *(gén)* & *Pol* pacification

pacificatrice [pasifikatris] *voir* **pacificateur**

pacifier [9] [pasifje] VT to pacify; **p. les esprits** to pacify people, to calm people down

Pacifique [pasifik] NM **le P.** the Pacific (Ocean)

pacifique [pasifik] ADJ **1** *Pol (pays, gouvernement)* peace-loving **2** *(non militaire)* peaceful, non-military; **exploitation p. de l'atome** harnessing atomic power for peaceful purposes **3** *(débonnaire)* peaceable **4** *(fait dans le calme)* peaceful; **mener une existence p.** to lead a quiet *or* peaceful life
  NMF peace-loving person

pacifiquement [pasifikmɑ̃] ADV **1** *Pol* peacefully, pacifically; **le changement de régime s'est fait p.** the change of regime was achieved by peaceful means **2** *(sans colère)* peaceably, peacefully

pacifisme [pasifism] NM pacifism

pacifiste [pasifist] ADJ pacifist
  NMF pacifist

pack [pak] NM **1** *Sport* pack **2** *Géog* pack ice **3** *Com* pack; **un p. de bière** a pack of beer; **acheter des yaourts en p.** to buy a pack of yoghurts; **acheter de la bière en p. de six** to buy a six-pack (of beer)

package [pakedʒ] NM *(gén)* & *Ordinat* package; **voyage en p.** package holiday

packager [pakadʒœr], **packageur** [pakaʒœr] NM packager

packaging [pakadʒiŋ] NM packaging

pack shot [pakʃɔt] NM *Cin* & *TV* pack shot

pacotille [pakɔtij] NF *(camelote)* cheap junk
  ▭ **de pacotille** ADJ cheap; **des bijoux de p.** baubles, trinkets; *Fig* **un exotisme de p.** bogus exoticism

pacquage [pakaʒ] NM *Pêche* barrelling *(of salt fish)*

pacquer [3] [pake] VT *Pêche* to barrel *(salt fish)*

PACS, Pacs [paks] NM INV *(abrév* **Pacte civil de solidarité**) civil solidarity pact *(bill introduced in the French parliament in 1998 allowing unmarried heterosexual couples and homosexual couples to legally formalize their relationships)*

Culture

LE PACS
The "Pacte civil de solidarité", more commonly known by its acronym "PACS", is a contract which offers legal recognition to adult cohabiting couples, including homosexuals. The law, which does not apply to close blood relatives, allows same-sex or heterosexual couples to register their union formally in a magistrates' court. Passed by the "Assemblée nationale" after more than 120 hours of parliamentary debate, the "PACS" became law in 1999. Although it has the backing of most of the public and more and more people are availing themselves of it, the "PACS" has been criticized for not extending the same rights to non-married couples as it does to married couples.

pacsé, -e [pakse] NM,F = person who has signed a ''Pacs'' contract

pacser [3] [pakse] *Fam* VI = to sign a ''Pacs'' contract, to enter into a civil solidarity pact
  ▶**se pacser** VPR = to sign a ''Pacs'' contract, to enter into a civil solidarity pact

pacson [paksɔ̃] NM *Fam* **1** *(colis)* parcel■, package■ **2** *(somme d'argent)* **toucher le p.** *(dans une affaire)* to make a bundle *or Br* a packet; *(au jeu)* to win a bundle *or Br* a packet

pacte [pakt] NM **1** *(gén)* agreement; **conclure** *ou* **faire** *ou* **sceller un p. (avec qn)** to make an agreement (with sb); **signer un p. avec le diable** to sign a pact with the Devil **2** *Pol* pact, treaty, agreement; **p. de non-agression** non-aggression pact; *UE* **P. de stabilité et de croissance** Stability and Growth Pact; *Hist* **le P. de Varsovie** the Warsaw Pact **3** *Jur* **P. civil de solidarité** civil solidarity pact *(bill introduced in the French parliament in 1998 allowing unmarried heterosexual or homosexual couples to legally formalize their relationships)*; **p. commissoire** = agreement that a contract may be automatically rescinded in the case of in-execution; **p. de famille** family settlement; **p. de préférence** right of first refusal; **p. de quota litis** contingency fee; **p. sur succession future** = agreement relating to a future inheritance

pactiser [3] [paktize] **pactiser avec** VT IND **1** *(conclure un accord avec)* to make a deal *or* pact with; **p. avec l'ennemi** to make a deal *or* pact with the enemy; **p. avec le diable** to make a pact with the devil **2** *(transiger avec)* to collude with, to connive at; **p. avec le crime** to condone crime; **p. avec sa conscience** to stifle one's conscience

pactole [paktɔl] NM **1** *Fig (source de profit)* gold mine; **ce travail est un vrai p.** this type of work is a real gold mine
  2 *(somme)* **elle a touché un joli p. quand son grand-père est mort** she came in to a nice *or* tidy little sum when her grandfather died; **on peut se faire un joli p. dans le pétrole** there are rich pickings to be had in the oil business
  3 *(gros lot)* jackpot

padan, -e [padɑ̃, -an] ADJ *Géog* of the (river) Po; **la plaine padane** the plain of the Po

paddle [padœl] NM *Sport* paddle tennis

paddock [padɔk] NM **1** *(enclos)* paddock **2** *Fam (lit)* bed■, *Br* pit; **se mettre** *ou* **aller au p.** to hit the sack *or* hay

paddy [padi] NM paddy (rice)

padel [padɛl] NM *Sport* paddle tennis

padichah [padiʃa] NM *Hist* padishah

padine [padin] NF *Bot* peacock's tail

padou [padu] NM *Tex* = ribbon made of silk and cotton

padouan, -e [padwɑ̃, -an] ADJ Paduan
  ▭ **Padouan, -e** NM,F = inhabitant of or person from Padua

Padoue [padu] NM Padua

padoue [padu] = **padou**

pæan [peɑ̃] = **péan**

paella [paela] NF paella

PAF [paf] NF *(abrév* **police de l'air et des frontières**) airport and border police
  NM *Rad* & *TV (abrév* **paysage audiovisuel français**) French broadcasting

paf¹ [paf] ADJ INV *Fam* **1** *(ivre)* sloshed, plastered; **il est complètement p.** he's as pissed as a newt **2** *Belg (abasourdi)*, flabbergasted, *Br* gobsmacked
  NM *très Fam (pénis)* dick, *Br* knob

paf² [paf] ONOMAT bam, wham

PAG [peaʒe] NF *Com (abrév* **procédure accélérée générale de dédouanement**) accelerated customs clearance procedure

pagaie [pagɛ] *voir* **pagayer**
  NF *(rame)* paddle

pagaille, pagaïe [pagaj] *Fam* NF **1** *(désordre)* mess, shambles; **il y a une drôle de p., dans ce bureau** this office looks as if a bomb has hit it *or* is a real pigsty; **pour mettre la p., t'es champion** when it comes to making a mess, you're unbeatable; **arrête de mettre la p. dans mes affaires** stop messing up my things
  2 *(confusion)* chaos; **c'est la p. dans les rues de Paris** the streets of Paris are absolute chaos; **semer la p. dans/parmi...** to cause havoc in/among...
  ▭ **en pagaille** ADJ *(maison, chambre)* in a mess; *(affaires, papiers)* all jumbled up, in a mess ADV **1** *(en désordre)* **mettre qch en p.** to mess sth up **2** *(en quantité)* **ils ont de l'argent en p.** they've got loads *or* bags of money, they're rolling in money

paganiser [3] [paganize] VT to paganize

paganisme [paganism] NM paganism

pagaye [pagaj] = **pagaille**

pagayer [11] [pageje] VI to paddle

pagayeur, -euse [pagɛjœr, -øz] NM,F paddler

page¹ [paʒ] NM *Hist* page (boy); **il avait les cheveux coupés à la p.** he had a page-boy haircut

page² [paʒ] = **pageot¹**

page³ [paʒ] NF **1** *(rectangle de papier)* page; **p. blanche** blank page; **arracher les pages** *ou* **feuilles d'un livre** to tear pages *or* leaves out of a book; **ouvrez vos livres à la p. 10** open your books at page 10, open your books and turn to page 10; **en première p. des journaux** on the front page

of the newspapers; faire la première p. des journaux to hit the headlines; suite de l'article en p. 5 (article) continued on page 5; c'est en bas de p. it's at the bottom of the page; une lettre de huit pages an eight-page letter; *Typ* mettre en pages to design, to lay out; p. centrale centre page; *Typ* p. de copyright copyright page; pages financières financial *or Br* City pages; p. de garde flyleaf; *(d'un fax)* cover sheet *or* page; *Tél* les Pages Jaunes the Yellow Pages®; *Typ* p. de titre title page; tourner une p. to turn (over) a page; *Fig* to turn over a new leaf; une p. politique vient d'être tournée avec la mort du sénateur the death of the senator marks the end of a political era; *Fig* tourner la p. to make a fresh start

2 *(extrait)* passage, excerpt; des pages inoubliables unforgettable passages; quelques très belles pages de Proust some very beautiful passages *or* excerpts from Proust; *Rad* et maintenant, une p. musicale and now for some music; *Rad & TV* une p. de publicité a commercial break; pages choisies selected (prose) passages

3 *(épisode)* page, chapter; quelques pages de notre histoire some pages *or* chapters in our history

4 *Ordinat* page; p. d'accueil home page; p. perso, p. personnelle personal home page; p. précédente page up; p. de résultats results page; p. suivante page down; p. web Web page

❑ à la page ADJ *Fam (fashion, people)* with-it; être à la p. to be with it; tu n'es plus à la p. du tout! you're completely out of touch *or* out of it!; il faut te mettre à la p. you're going to have to get with it ADV *(être payé)* by the page

pageau, -x [paʒo] NM *Ich* pandora

page-écran [paʒekrɑ̃] *(pl* pages-écrans) NF *Ordinat* screen page

pagel [paʒɛl] NM *Ich* red sea bream

pageot[1] [paʒo] NM *Fam* bed▪, *Br* pit; se mettre *ou* aller au p. to hit the sack *or* hay

pageot[2] [paʒo] NM *Ich* pandora

pager[1] [paʒœr] NM *Ordinat* pager

pager[2] [17] [paʒe] se pager VPR *Fam* to hit the sack *or* the hay

Pagette® [paʒɛt] NF *Can* pager

pagination [paʒinasjɔ̃] NF 1 *Typ* pagination, page numbering; il y a une erreur de p. the pages have been numbered wrongly 2 *Ordinat* page numbering, paging

paginer [3] [paʒine] VT to paginate, to number the pages of

pagne [paɲ] NM *(en tissu)* loincloth, pagne; *(en rafia)* grass skirt

pagnon [paɲɔ̃] NM *Tex* black broadcloth *(as originally manufactured at Sedan by Pagnon)*

pagnot [paɲo] NM *Fam Vieilli* bed▪, *Br* pit

pagnoter [3] [paɲɔte] se pagnoter VPR *Fam Vieilli (se coucher)* to hit the sack *or* hay

pagode [pagɔd] NF 1 *Archit* pagoda; toit en p. pagoda roof 2 *Couture* (manche) p. pagoda sleeve 3 *(figurine à tête mobile)* mandarin

pagodon [pagɔdɔ̃] NM *Archit* small pagoda

pagre [pagr] NM (common) sea bream, *Br* Couch's sea bream

pagure [pagyr] NM *Zool* hermit crab

pagus [pagys] *(pl* pagus *ou* pagi) NM *Hist* = rural administrative district in France in the Gallo-Roman period up to the late middle ages

pahlavi [palavi] NM *(langue)* Pehlevi, Pahlavi

paie [pɛ] *voir* payer

NF 1 *(salaire)* pay, wages; toucher sa p. to be paid; c'est le jour de p. it's payday 2 *Fam (locution)* ça fait une p. que je ne l'ai pas vu I haven't seen him for ages▪; quand vous êtes-vous rencontrés? – ça fait une p.! when did you meet? – donkey's years ago!

paiement [pɛmɑ̃] NM payment; *(d'un compte)* payment, settlement; faire *ou* effectuer un p. to make a payment; recevoir un p. to receive a payment; contre p. de 100 euros on payment of 100 euros; les paiements par chèques ne sont plus acceptés *(dans un magasin)* cheques are no longer accepted; *aussi Fig* c'est tout ce qu'il a reçu en p. de son travail that's all he got (as payment) for his work; p. par anticipation payment in advance; p. arriéré payment in arrears; p. d'avance payment in advance, advance payment; p. par carte card payment, payment by card; p. par chèque payment by cheque; p. à la commande cash with order; p. (au) comptant cash payment, payment in cash; p. contre documents payment against documents; p. différé deferred payment; à p. différé deferred; p. échelonné staggered payment; p. électronique electronic payment, payment by electronic transfer; p. en espèces payment in cash, cash payment; p. exceptionnel windfall payment; p. de l'indu payment made in error; p. intégral payment in full; p. par intervention payment on behalf of a third party; p. libératoire payment in full discharge from debt; p. en liquide payment in cash, cash payment; p. à la livraison *Br* cash on delivery, *Am* collect on delivery; p. mensuel monthly payment; p. en nature payment in kind; p. partiel part payment; paiements périodiques periodic payments; p. préalable prepayment; p. progressif graduated *or* increasing payments; p. au prorata payment pro rata; *Ordinat* p. sécurisé secure (electronic) transaction; p. en souffrance overdue *or* outstanding payment; p. à tempérament payment by *or* in instalments; p. à terme payment by *or* in instalments

païen, -enne [pajɛ̃, -ɛn] ADJ pagan, heathen

NM,F 1 *(polythéiste)* pagan, heathen 2 *(athée)* atheist, pagan; jurer comme un p. to swear like a trooper

paierie [pɛri] NF local treasury office

paillage [pajaʒ] NM 1 *Hort* (straw) mulching; p. plastique polythene *or* plastic mulching 2 *(d'un siège)* straw (bottom)

paillard, -e [pajar, -ard] ADJ *(personne)* bawdy, coarse; *(chanson)* dirty; *(histoire)* dirty, smutty

NM,F libertine

paillardise [pajardiz] NF 1 *(caractère)* bawdiness, coarseness 2 *(histoire)* dirty *or* smutty story

paillasse[1] [pajas] NF 1 *(matelas grossier)* straw *or* straw-filled mattress 2 *(d'un évier)* drainer, draining board; *(de laboratoire)* (laboratory) bench 3 *Fam (ventre)* stomach▪, belly, guts; trouer la p. à qn to knife sb in the guts

paillasse[2] [pajas] NM clown

paillasson [pajasɔ̃] NM 1 *(d'une entrée)* doormat 2 *Fam Fig (personne)* elle le traite comme un p. she treats him like a doormat; c'est le p. du directeur the manager treats him like a doormat 3 *Hort* (straw) mulch

paillassonnage [pajasɔnaʒ] NM *(d'espalier, de châssis)* mulching (with straw)

paillassonner [3] [pajasɔne] VT *(espalier, châssis)* to mulch (with straw)

paille [paj] NF 1 *(chaume)* straw; p. de blé wheat straw; p. de riz rice straw; *Hum* sur la p. humide des cachots behind bars; *Fam* être/finir sur la p. to be/end up completely broke *or Br* on one's uppers *or Am* without a dime; *Fam* mettre qn sur la p. to ruin sb▪; *Fam* une p.! *(peu de chose)* chickenfeed!, peanuts!

2 *(tige)* piece of straw, straw; *Bible* voir la p. dans l'œil du prochain et ne pas voir la poutre dans le sien to see the mote in one's brother's eye but not the beam in one's own; tirer à la courte p. to draw lots

3 *(pour boire)* (drinking) straw; boire avec une p. to drink through a straw

4 *Tech (défaut)* flaw

5 p. de fer steel wool

ADJ INV straw-coloured

paillé, -e [paje] ADJ 1 *(siège)* straw-bottomed 2 *(métal, pierre précieuse)* flawed 3 *(couleur)* straw-coloured

NM stable litter

paille-en-queue [pajɑ̃kø] *(pl* pailles-en-queue) NM *Orn* tropicbird; p. à bec jaune yellow-billed tropicbird

pailler[1] [paje] NM *(grenier)* straw loft; *(cour)* straw yard; *(meule)* straw stack

pailler[2] [3] [paje] VT 1 *(siège)* to straw-bottom 2 *Hort* to (straw) mulch

paillet [pajɛ] NM *Naut* mat, fender; p. d'abordage *ou* makarov collision mat

pailletage [pajtaʒ] NM *(d'une robe)* spangling

pailleté, -e [pajte] ADJ *(robe)* sequined; *(maquillage)* glittery

pailleter [27] [pajte] VT *(vêtement)* to spangle; *(maquillage, coiffure)* to put glitter on

pailleteur [pajtœr] NM gold washer

paillette [pajɛt] NF 1 *Couture* sequin, spangle; une robe à paillettes a sequined dress 2 *(parcelle → d'or)* speck; *(→ de quartz, de mica)* flake; *(→ de savon)* flake 3 *(d'une pierre précieuse)* flaw

❑ paillettes NFPL 1 *Mil* chaff *(UNCOUNT) (metallic foil)* 2 *(de maquillage)* glitter

pailleux, -euse [pajø, -øz] ADJ 1 *(fumier)* strawy 2 *Métal* flawed

paillis [paji] NM *Agr* mulch

paillon [pajɔ̃] NM 1 *(pour une bouteille)* straw wrapper *or* case 2 *(en joaillerie)* (jeweller's) foil

paillote [pajɔt] NF straw hut

pain [pɛ̃] NM 1 *(substance)* bread; un peu de p. a bit *or* piece of bread; un gros morceau de p. a hunk of bread; gagner son p. to earn one's *or* make a living; mettre qn au p. sec et à l'eau to put sb on dry bread and water; p. azyme unleavened bread; p. bénit consecrated bread; *Fig* c'est p. bénit that's a godsend; *Can Fig* ambitionner sur le p. bénit *(profiter de la bonté de quelqu'un)* to take advantage of someone's good nature; *(exagérer)* to push one's luck, to go too far; p. biologique organic *Br* wholemeal *or Am* wholewheat bread; p. blanc white bread; *Fig* manger son p. blanc le premier to have it easy for a while; p. brioché brioche-like bread; p. complet *Br* wholemeal *or Am* wholewheat bread; p. doré French toast; p. d'épice ≃ gingerbread; p. grillé toast; *Can* p. d'habitant *ou* de famille *ou* du pays homemade bread; p. lavash lavash; p. de mie sandwich bread; p. noir black bread; p. perdu French toast; p. de seigle rye bread; p. de son *Br* wholemeal *or Am* wholewheat bread; gros p. farmhouse bread *(sold by weight)*; notre p. quotidien our daily bread; la maladie, les soucis d'argent, c'était son p. quotidien illness and money worries were his/her daily lot; être bon comme du bon p. to be the salt of the earth; long comme un jour sans p. interminable, endless; avoir du p. sur la planche to have one's work cut out; enlever *ou* retirer *ou* ôter le p. de la bouche à qn to take the bread out of sb's mouth; *Fam* ça mange pas de p. it doesn't cost anything; du p. et des jeux bread and circuses

2 *(individuel → gén)* loaf; *(→ pain long)* baguette, *Br* French stick; *(→ boule)* round loaf (of bread), cob; p. de deux/quatre livres long two-pound/four-pound loaf; *Belg* p. baguette baguette, *Br* French stick; p. bis, *Can* p. de blé entier, p. brun brown loaf, *Br* wholemeal *or Am* wholewheat loaf; p. au chocolat pain au chocolat *(chocolate-filled pastry)*; p. de campagne farmhouse loaf; p. complet *Br* wholemeal *or Am* wholewheat loaf; *Can* p. français baguette, *Br* French stick; p. de Gênes ≃ Genoa cake; *Belg* p. intégral *Br* wholemeal *or Am* wholewheat loaf; p. au lait finger roll *(made with milk)*; p. au levain sourdough loaf; p. de ménage home-made loaf; p. moulé large tin loaf; p. parisien thick French loaf; p. platine, p. à *ou* sur platine large tin loaf; p. aux raisins = circular pastry made from sweetened dough and raisins; p. de seigle rye loaf; p. de son *Br* wholemeal *or Am* wholewheat loaf; p. viennois Vienna loaf; petit p. (bread) roll; *Can Fig* être né pour un petit p. to be destined for the short end of the stick

3 *(préparation)* loaf; p. de poisson fish loaf; p. de courgettes courgette loaf

4 *(bloc)* p. de cire/savon bar of wax/soap; p. à cacheter bar of (sealing) wax; p. de glace block of ice; *Culin* p. de sucre sugarloaf; *Géog* le P. de Sucre Sugarloaf Mountain

5 *Fam (coup)* smack; je lui ai filé un de ces pains! I socked him/her one!

❑ pain brûlé ADJ INV *(tissu, peinture)* dark brown; *(peau)* brown as a berry

pair[1] [pɛr] NM 1 *(noble)* peer

2 *(égal)* peer; être jugé par ses pairs to be judged by one's peers; *Littéraire* traiter qn de p. à compagnon to treat sb as an equal

3 *Bourse* par (value); *Fin* par (rate of exchange); emprunt émis au-dessus du p. loan issued above par

4 *(au jeu)* even numbers; jouer p. to bet on the even numbers

❑ au pair ADJ jeune fille au p. au pair (girl) ADV 1 *(en échange du logement)* travailler *ou* être au p. to work as *or* to be an au pair; elle travaille au p.

en Hollande she works as an au pair in Holland **2** *Fin* at par

❑ **de pair** ADV **aller de p.** to go together, to go hand in hand; **la méchanceté va souvent de p. avec la bêtise** nastiness often goes together *or* hand in hand with stupidity

❑ **hors pair, hors de pair** ADJ unequalled, outstanding; **c'est un traducteur hors p.** as a translator he's second to none *or* in a class of his own; **dans son domaine il est hors de p.** he is unequalled in his field

pair², -e¹ [pɛr] ADJ **1** *(nombre, jour)* even; **jouer un chiffre p.** to bet on an even number; **habiter du côté p.** to live on the even-numbered side of the street; **stationnement les jours pairs seulement** parking on even dates only **2** *Anat (organes)* paired

pairage [pɛraʒ] NM *TV* twinning

paire² [pɛr] NF **1** *(de ciseaux, de chaussures, de chaussettes)* pair; *(de draps)* set; *(de bœufs)* yoke; *(de faisan, de pistolets)* brace; **si tu continues, tu vas recevoir une p. de gifles** if you go on like that, you'll get your face slapped; *Fam* **une belle p. de seins** great breasts, a great rack; *Fam* **une belle p. de fesses** a nice butt *or Br* bum; **vous êtes une belle p. d'hypocrites!** what a pair of hypocrites!; *Fam* **c'est une autre p. de manches** that's a different kettle of fish; *Fam* **se faire la p.** *(s'enfuir)* to take off, to make oneself scarce, *Br* to scarper; *(s'évader)* to break out; *(faire une fugue)* to run away*, Br* to do a bunk; *très Fam* **en glisser une p. à qn** *(posséder sexuellement)* to give sb one, *Br* to slip sb a length **2** *Ling* **p. minimale** minimal pair

pairesse [pɛrɛs] NF **1** *(en Grande-Bretagne)* peeress **2** *(épouse d'un pair)* wife of a peer

pairie [pɛri] NF peerage; **p. à vie** life peerage

pairle [pɛrl] NM *Hér* pall; **en p.** pallwise

paisible [pezibl] ADJ **1** *(doux)* peaceful, quiet; **un homme p.** a quiet man

2 *(serein)* quiet, calm, peaceful; **mener une vie calme et p.** to lead a quiet, peaceful existence; **le bébé dort d'un sommeil p.** the baby is sleeping peacefully

3 *(silencieux)* calm, quiet; **nous habitons un quartier très p.** we live in a very quiet part of town

4 *Jur* **p. possesseur d'un bien** uncontested owner of a piece of property

paisiblement [peziblamɑ̃] ADV **1** *(dormir)* peacefully, quietly **2** *(parler, discuter)* calmly

paissait *etc voir* **paître**

paissance [pɛsɑ̃s] NF free grazing *(on common land)*

paisseau, -x [pɛso] NM *Agr* vine prop

paître [91] [pɛtr] VI *(animaux)* to graze; **faire p. le bétail** to graze the cattle, to put the cattle out to graze; **mener p. les vaches** to take the cows to graze; *Fam* **envoyer qn p.** to tell sb where to go, *Br* to send sb packing

VT **1** *(sujet: animal)* to feed on, to graze (on) **2** *Arch ou Littéraire (bétail)* to feed, to graze

paix [pɛ] NF **1** *Mil & Pol* peace; **demander la p.** to sue for peace; **une menace pour la p. mondiale** a threat to world peace; **pourparlers/offres de p.** peace talks/proposals; **négocier la p.** to negotiate peace; **en temps de p.** in peacetime; **faire la p.** to make peace; **signer/ratifier un traité de p.** to sign/to ratify a peace treaty; **p. armée** armed peace; **p. séparée** separate peace; **la p. des braves** an honourable peace; **p. romaine** Pax Romana; *Prov* **si tu veux la p., prépare la guerre** if you wish for peace, prepare for war

2 *(ordre)* peace; **troubler la p. publique** to disturb public order *or* the peace; **favoriser la p. sociale** to promote social peace

3 *(entente)* peace; **vivre en p. (avec qn)** to live in peace (with sb), to be at peace (with sb); **être en p. avec sa conscience** to have a clear conscience, to be at peace with one's conscience; **faire la p. avec qn** to make one's peace with sb, to make up with sb; **on fait la p.?** let's make up, let's be friends again; **je suis pour la p. des ménages** I'm against stirring things up between couples

4 *(repos)* peace, quiet; **avoir besoin de p. pour se concentrer** to need peace and quiet to concentrate; **j'ai enfin la p. depuis qu'il est parti**

I've at last got some peace and quiet now that he's left; **il ne me laissera pas en p. tant que je ne lui aurai pas tout avoué** he won't give me any peace until I tell him everything; **laisse-moi en p.!** leave me alone!; *Fam* **fiche-moi la p.!** get lost!; *Fam* **je veux qu'on me fiche la p.** I want to be left alone*"* ; *très Fam* **fous-moi la p.!** get the hell out of here!, *Br* sod off!; *Fam* **la p.!** quiet!, shut up!

5 *(sérénité)* peace; **trouver la p. de l'âme** to find inner peace; **la p. du tombeau** the quiet of the grave; **avoir la conscience en p.** to have a clear conscience; **p. à ses cendres** God rest his soul; **qu'il repose en p., p. à son âme** may he *or* his soul rest in peace; **allez en p.** go in peace

6 *(harmonie)* peace, peacefulness; **la p. du soir à la campagne** peaceful evenings in the countryside

pajot [paʒo] = **pageot¹**

Pakistan [pakistɑ̃] NM **le P.** Pakistan; **vivre au P.** to live in Pakistan; **aller au P.** to go to Pakistan

pakistanais, -e [pakistanɛ, -ɛz] ADJ Pakistani

❑ **Pakistanais, -e** NM,F Pakistani

PAL, Pal [pal] ADJ *TV (abrév* **Phase Alternation Line)** PAL

pal, -als [pal] NM **1** *(pieu)* stake, pale; **le supplice du p.** torture by impalement **2** *(plantoir)* planter, dibber

palabre [palabr] NF OU NM *Hist* palaver; **arbre à palabres** *(en Afrique francophone)* palaver tree, village meeting tree

❑ **palabres** NMPL OU NFPL *Péj (discussion oiseuse)* endless talk; **après de longues palabres** after a lengthy discussion; **à ces réunions, ce ne sont que des palabres** these meetings are just talking shops

palabrer [3] [palabre] VI *Péj* to talk endlessly; **vous ne faites que p.** all you ever do is talk

palace [palas] NM luxury hotel; **tu verrais sa maison, c'est un vrai p.** you should see his house, it's palatial *or* luxurious

paladin [paladɛ̃] NM **1** *Hist* paladin **2** *Littéraire (redresseur de torts)* knight in shining armour, righter of wrongs

palafitte [palafit] NM *Archéol* lake dwelling

palais [palɛ] NM **1** *(bâtiment)* palace; **p. des congrès** convention centre; **p. des expositions** exhibition hall; **p. des sports** sports stadium

2 *(monument)* **le P. Brongniart** = the Paris Stock Exchange; **le p. Farnèse** the Farnese Palace; **le p. Garnier** = the (old) Paris opera house; **le p. de l'Institut** = seventeenth-century building on the Left Bank of the Seine housing the tomb of Mazarin, the bibliothèque Mazarine and the Institut de France; **le p. des Papes** = the Papal Palace in Avignon *(the most prestigious venue of the Avignon Festival)*; **le Grand P., le Petit P.** = galleries built for the Exposition universelle in 1900, now used for art exhibitions

3 *Jur* **le P. de justice, le P.** the law courts; **le P. du Luxembourg** = the seat of the French Senate

4 *Anat* palate; **p. dur** hard palate; **p. fendu** cleft palate; **p. mou** soft palate

5 *(organe du goût)* palate; **elle a le p. fin** she has a refined palate; **un goût qui flatte le p.** a flavour that delights the taste buds *or* palate

Palais-Bourbon [palɛburbɔ̃] NM **le P.** the French National Assembly

Palais-Royal [palɛrwajal] NM = palace and gardens built for the cardinal de Richelieu, which later became a popular place of leisure and now houses the Théâtre-Français, the Conseil d'État and the Ministry of Culture

palan [palɑ̃] NM *Tech* hoist; **p. manuel** block and tackle

palanche [palɑ̃ʃ] NF *Tech* yoke

palançon [palɑ̃sɔ̃] NM *Constr* lath *or* stake (in loam work)

palangre [palɑ̃gr] NF *Pêche* long line (and snoods); **p. à cuiller** trolling line; **maître p.** long line

palanque [palɑ̃k] NF *(timber)* stockade

palanquée [palɑ̃ke] NF **1** *Naut* load **2** *Fig (multitude)* **une p. de...** a raft of...

palanquer [3] [palɑ̃ke] VT **1** *(lever avec un palan)* to hoist **2** *(munir de palanques)* to stockade
VI to hoist

palanquin [palɑ̃kɛ̃] NM **1** *(chaise)* palanquin **2** *Naut* reef tackle

palastre [palastr] = **palâtre**

palatal, -e, -aux, -ales [palatal, -o] ADJ **1** *Ling (voyelle)* front; *(consonne)* palatal **2** *Anat* palatal

❑ **palatale** NF *Ling (consonne)* palatal consonant; *(voyelle)* front vowel

palatalisation [palatalizasjɔ̃] NF *Ling* palatalization

palatalisé, -e [palatalize] ADJ *Ling* palatalized

palataliser [3] [palatalize] *Ling* VT to palatalize
▶ **se palataliser** VPR to be palatalized

palatial, -e, -aux, -ales [palasjal, -o] ADJ palatial

Palatin [palatɛ̃] NM **le (mont) P.** the Palatine hill

palatin, -e [palatɛ̃, -in] ADJ **1** *(du palais)* palace *(avant n)* **2** *(du Palatinat)* Palatine *(avant n)* **3** *Anat* palatine, palatal
NM *Hist* Palatine

Palatinat [palatina] NM *Hist* **le P.** the Palatinate

palâtre [palatr] NM *(plaque de serrure)* back plate

pale [pal] NF **1** *(d'une hélice, d'une rame)* blade; *(d'un bateau à aube)* paddle **2** *(vanne)* paddle, sluice(-gate) **3** *Rel* pall

palé, -e [pale] ADJ *Hér* paly

pâle [pal] ADJ **1** *(clair)* pale; *(exsangue)* pale, pallid; **elle est toute p.** she's very pale; **p. de colère** livid with rage; **être p. comme la mort** to be deathly pale; **être p. comme un linge** to be as white as a sheet; *Fam* **être p. des genoux** to be *Br* shattered *or Am* bushed; *Fam Arg mil* **se faire porter p.** to go *or* to report sick*"*

2 *(couleur, lumière)* pale; **la p. lueur de l'aube** the pale light of dawn; **une robe jaune p.** a pale yellow dress

3 *(insipide)* pale, weak; **elle nous a fait un p. sourire** she smiled weakly *or* faintly at us; **son spectacle n'est qu'une p. imitation du livre** his/her show is nothing but a pale *or* poor imitation of the book; **mes aventures semblent bien pâles auprès des vôtres** my adventures pale by comparison with yours; **style p.** *(d'une œuvre littéraire)* colourless style

pale-ale [pɛlɛl] *(pl* **pale-ales)** NF *(bière)* pale ale

paléanthropien, -enne [paleɑ̃trɔpjɛ̃, -ɛn] ADJ palaeoanthropic
NM,F palaeoanthropic man, *f* woman

palée¹ [pale] NF *Constr (pieux)* row of piles; *(palplanches)* sheet piling

palée² [pale] NF *Suisse Ich* = type of whitefish found in Lake Neuchâtel

palefrenier, -ère [palfrənje, -ɛr] NM,F groom; *Arch (d'auberge)* ostler

palefroi [palfrwa] NM *Arch* palfrey

palémon [palemɔ̃] NM *(large)* prawn

paléo- [paleo] PRÉF paleo-

paléoasiatique [paleoazjatik] ADJ *Ling* Paleo-Asiatic

paléoanthropologie [paleoɑ̃trɔpɔlɔʒi] NF palaeoanthropology

paléoanthropologue [paleoɑ̃trɔpɔlɔg] NMF palaeoanthropologist

paléobiogéographie [paleobjoʒeografi] NF paleobiogeography

paléobiologie [paleobjɔlɔʒi] NF paleobiology

paléobotanique [paleobɔtanik] NF paleobotany

paléocène [paleosɛn] ADJ Paleocene
NM Paleocene

paléochrétien, -enne [paleokretjɛ̃, -ɛn] ADJ *Beaux-Arts* early Christian

paléoclimat [paleoklima] NM paleoclimate

paléoclimatologie [paleoklimatɔlɔʒi] NF paleoclimatology

paléoécologie [paleoekɔlɔʒi] NF paleoecology

paléoenvironnement [paleoɑ̃virɔnmɑ̃] NM paleoenvironment

paléogène [paleoʒɛn] ADJ Paleogene
NM **le p.** the Paleogene

paléogéographie [paleoʒeografi] NF paleogeography

paléographe [paleograf] ADJ paleographic
NMF paleographer

paléographie [paleografi] NF paleography

paléographique [paleografik] ADJ paleographic

paléohistologie [paleoistɔlɔʒi] NF paleohistology

paléolithique [paleolitik] ADJ Paleolithic
NM **le p.** the Paleolithic

paléomagnétisme [paleɔmaɲetism] **NM** paleomagnetism

paléontologie [paleɔ̃tɔlɔʒi] **NF** paleontology; **p. humaine/animale** human/animal paleontology

paléontologique [paleɔ̃tɔlɔʒik] **ADJ** paleontological

paléontologiste [paleɔ̃tɔlɔʒist], **paléontologue** [paleɔ̃tɔlɔg] **NMF** paleontologist

paléo-océanographie [paleɔɔseanɔgrafi] **NF** paleo-oceanography

paléorelief [paleɔrəljɛf] **NM** paleorelief

paléosibérien, -enne [paleɔsiberjɛ̃, -ɛn] **ADJ** Ling Paleo-Siberian

paléosol [paleɔsɔl] **NM** paleosol

paléotempérature [paleɔtɑ̃peratyr] **NF** paleotemperature

paléozoïque [paleɔzɔik] **ADJ** Paleozoic
 NM le p. the Paleozoic (era)

Palerme [palɛrm] **NM** Palermo

palermitain, -e [palɛrmitɛ̃, -ɛn] **ADJ** Palermitan
 □ **Palermitain, -e NM,F** Palermitan

paleron [palrɔ̃] **NM** chuck steak

Palestine [palɛstin] **NF la P.** Palestine; **vivre en P.** to live in Palestine; **aller en P.** to go to Palestine

palestinien, -enne [palɛstinjɛ̃, -ɛn] **ADJ** Palestinian
 □ **Palestinien, -enne NM,F** Palestinian

palestre [palɛstr] **NF** Antiq palestra

palet [palɛ] **NM 1** Sport (pour hockey sur glace) puck; (pour curling) stone **2** (à la marelle) quoit

paletot [palto] **NM 1** (pardessus) (short) jacket; Belg Fig **vieux paletots** old guard **2** Fam **tomber sur le p. à qn** (attaquer) to jump on sb, to go for sb; (pour lui parler) to buttonhole sb

palette [palɛt] **NF 1** Beaux-Arts palette; Fig (choix) choice, range; Fig **la p. de Cézanne** Cézanne's palette or range of colours; **proposer toute une p. d'articles** to offer a wide choice or range of articles **2** Culin shoulder **3** (d'une roue à aubes) paddle **4** Tech (pour la manutention) pallet **5** (pour battre le linge) (washerwoman's) beetle **6** Pêche (hook) eye **7** Ordinat **p. graphique** graphics palette; **p. d'outils** tool palette **8** Can (cuillère) wooden spoon (used in cooking maple syrup) **9** Can **p. de chocolat** bar of chocolate

palettisable [paletizabl] **ADJ** Tech that can be palletized

palettisation [paletizasjɔ̃] **NF** Tech palletization

palettiser [3] [paletize] **VT** Tech to palletize

palettiseur [paletizœr] **NM** Tech palletizing machine

palétuvier [paletyvje] **NM** Bot mangrove

pâleur [palœr] **NF 1** (d'une couleur, de la lumière) paleness; (du teint) pallor; **je fus frappé par sa p.** I was surprised to see how pale he/she looked **2** Fig (du style) colourlessness

pali [pali] **NM** (langue) Pali

palicare = palikare

pâlichon, -onne [paliʃɔ̃, -ɔn] **ADJ** Fam a bit pale■, on the pale side■; **ça fait plaisir de voir que tu n'es plus aussi p.** it's nice to see you've got some colour back in your cheeks

palier [palje] **NM 1** (plate-forme) landing; **p. de repos** half-landing **2** (niveau) stage, level; (d'un graphique) plateau; **atteindre un p.** to reach a plateau, to level off; **à partir d'un certain p., le taux change** the rate changes at a certain point **3** Constr level, flat **4** Aviat **voler en p.** to fly level **5** Tech bearing; **p. lisse/à roulement** plain/rolling bearing
 □ **par paliers ADV** in stages, step by step; **la tension monte par paliers** tension is gradually mounting

palière [paljɛr] **ADJ F porte p.** landing door, door opening onto the landing; **marche p.** top step

palikare [palikar] **NM** Hist palikar

palilalie [palilali] **NF** Psy palilalia

palimpseste [palɛ̃psɛst] **NM** palimpsest

palindrome [palɛ̃drom] Ling **ADJ** palindromic
 NM palindrome

palingénésie [palɛ̃ʒenezi] **NF 1** Phil palingenesis **2** Littéraire (retour à la vie, nouvelle vie) palingenesisy

palinodie [palinɔdi] **NF 1** Ling palinode **2** Littéraire (revirement) volte-face

pâlir [32] [palir] **VI 1** (personne) to (turn or go) pale; **p. de froid/peur** to turn pale with cold/fear; **p. de rage/de colère** to become livid with rage/anger; **p. de jalousie/d'envie** to go green

with jealousy/envy; **elle pâlit affreusement** she went ghastly pale; **elle a une voiture/un salaire à faire p.** her car/salary is enough to make anyone green with envy
 2 (couleur, lumière, étoile) to grow dim or pale, to fade; **le soleil a fait p. le tissu du canapé** the sun has faded the couch material
 3 (gloire) to fade (away), to grow faint or fainter, to dim; **mes souvenirs pâlissent avec le temps** my memories are fading (away) with the passage of time
 VT Littéraire to make pale

palis [pali] **NM** (alignement) fence, paling; (pieu) stake, pale; (enclos) enclosure

palissade [palisad] **NF 1** (clôture → de pieux) fence, paling, palisade; (→ de planches) hoarding; (→ d'arbres) hedgerow **2** Mil palisade

palissader [3] [palisade] **VT 1** (clôturer) to fence in, to put a fence round **2** Mil to palisade

palissadique [palisadik] **ADJ** Bot **tissu p.** palisade layer

palissage [palisaʒ] **NM** (opération) training, trellising; (support) trainer, trellis

palissandre [palisɑ̃dr] **NM** rosewood, palissander

pâlissant, -e [palisɑ̃, -ɑ̃t] **ADJ** (lumière) fading, growing or becoming dim

palisser [3] [palise] **VT 1** (plante) to train, to trellis **2** (arbre fruitier) to espalier

palisson [palisɔ̃] **NM** stake

palissonner [3] [palisɔne] **VT** to stake

palissonneur [palisɔnœr] **NM** staker

paliure [paljyr] **NM** Bot Christ's-thorn

palladianisme [paladjanism] **NM** Archit Palladianism

palladien, -enne [paladjɛ̃, -ɛn] **ADJ** Archit Palladian

palladium [paladjɔm] **NM** Chim & Myth palladium; Littéraire **les lois sont le p. de la liberté** the laws are the palladium or the safeguards of liberty

Pallas [palas] **NPR** Pallas

palle [pal] = **pale 3**

palléal, -e, -aux, -ales [paleal, -o] **ADJ** Zool **cavité palléale** mantle cavity

palliatif, -ive [paljatif, -iv] **ADJ** palliative
 NM 1 Méd palliative **2** (expédient) stopgap measure, palliative

pallidum [palidɔm] **NM** Anat globus pallidus

pallier [9] [palje] **VT 1** (manque, erreur, inconvénient) to make up for **2** (difficultés) to overcome; (crise) to resolve **3** Méd (douleur) to palliate
 □ **pallier à VT IND** to make up for

pallium [paljɔm] **NM** Antiq,Rel & Zool pallium

pallot [palo] **NM** très Fam French kiss, Br snog; **rouler un p. à qn** to French kiss sb, Br to snog sb

Palma [palma] **NM P. (de Majorque)** Palma (de Majorca)

palmacée [palmase] Bot **NF** member of the Palmaceae or Palmae
 □ **palmacées NFPL** Palmaceae, Palmae

palmaire [palmɛr] **ADJ** Anat palmar

palmarès [palmarɛs] **NM 1** (liste → de lauréats) prize list, list of prizewinners; (→ de sportifs) winners' list, list of winners; (→ de chansons) charts; **être** ou **figurer au p.** to be among the prizewinners; (de la chanson) to be in the charts; **être premier au p.** to be number one, to top the charts
 2 (succès) **avoir de nombreuses victoires à son p.** to have numerous victories to one's credit; **avoir un beau p.** to have an excellent track record

palmarium [palmarjɔm] **NM** palm house

palmas [palmas] **NFPL** (en danse) clapping

palmatifide [palmatifid] **ADJ** Bot palmatifid

palmatilobé, -e [palmatilɔbe] **ADJ** Bot palmatilobate

palmatiséqué, -e [palmatiseke] **ADJ** Bot palmatisect

palmature [palmatyr] **NF** Méd palmation

palme [palm] **NF 1** Bot (feuille) palm leaf; (palmier) palm tree; **huile/vin de p.** palm oil/wine
 2 (distinction) palm; **la p. du martyre** the crown of martyrdom; **la P. d'Or** = trophy awarded for best film at the Cannes film festival; Hum **pour la goujaterie, c'est lui qui a la p.!** he's a complete boor!; **remporter la p.** (être le meilleur) to win; Ironique to win hands down
 3 Sport flipper

 □ **palmes NFPL palmes (académiques)** = decoration for services to education, the arts or science

palmé, -e [palme] **ADJ 1** Bot palmate; Zool webbed, Spéc palmate **2** Fam Hum (locution) **les avoir palmées** to be bone idle or a complete layabout

palmer¹ [palmɛr] **NM** (instrument) micrometer

palmer² [palmœr] **NM** Pêche palmer

palmeraie [palmərɛ] **NF** palm grove

palmette [palmɛt] **NF 1** Hort palmetto, dwarf fan palm **2** Archit & Beaux-Arts palmette

palmier [palmje] **NM 1** Bot palm (tree); **p. dattier** date palm; **p. de Floride** saw palmetto; **p. à huile** oil palm; **p. nain** dwarf fan palm, palmetto **2** (pâtisserie) palmier (heart-shaped biscuit made of flaky pastry)

palmifide [palmifid] = **palmatifide**

palmipède [palmipɛd] **ADJ** palmiped
 NM palmiped

palmiste [palmist] **NM** Bot cabbage palm

palmitate [palmitat] **NM** Chim palmitate

palmite [palmit] **NM** Bot heart of palm

palmitine [palmitin] **NF** Chim palmitin

palmitique [palmitik] **ADJ M** Chim palmitic

Palm Pilot® [palmpajlɔt] **NM** Ordinat Palm Pilot®

palmure [palmyr] **NF** Zool web

Palmyre [palmir] **NM** Palmyra

palombe [palɔ̃b] **NF** Orn ringdove, wood pigeon

palombière [palɔ̃bjɛr] **NF** Chasse **1** (filet) = net used for catching ringdoves at migration time **2** (cabane) = tree-top hide for ringdove shooting

palomète [palɔmɛt] **NF** Ich plain bonito

palomino [palɔmino] **NM** palomino

palonnier [palɔnje] **NM 1** Aviat rudder (bar) **2** (d'un véhicule) rocking lever; Aut **p. de freinage** compensator **3** (en ski nautique) handle **4** Tech (lifting) beam or leg

palonnière [palɔnjɛr] = **palombière**

palot [palo] **NM** (outil) = narrow spade used for digging worms, shells etc out of the sand

pâlot, -otte [palo, -ɔt] **ADJ** Fam peaky, pale■, on the pale side■; **il est bien p., ton fils!** your boy's very pale or pale-looking!

palotte [palɔt] **ADJ** Can heavy, ungainly

palourde [palurd] **NF** Zool clam, carpet shell (clam)

Palox® [palɔks] **NM** crate

palpable [palpabl] **ADJ 1** (évident) palpable; **des preuves palpables** palpable proof or evidence **2** (concret) tangible; **des avantages palpables** tangible benefits **3** (que l'on peut toucher) palpable

palpation [palpasjɔ̃] **NF** Méd palpation

palpe [palp] **NM** Entom palp, palpus

palpébral, -e, -aux, -ales [palpebral, -o] **ADJ** Anat palpebral

palper [3] [palpe] **VT 1** Méd to palpate **2** (tâter) to feel; **p. un tissu** to finger a fabric **3** Fam (recevoir) **elle a palpé une belle somme** she came into a tidy sum
 USAGE ABSOLU Fam to get one's money■, to collect; **qu'est-ce qu'il a dû p.!** he must have made a mint!

palpeur [palpœr] **NM** sensor

palpitant, -e [palpitɑ̃, -ɑ̃t] **ADJ 1** (passionnant) thrilling, exciting, exhilarating **2** (qui palpite → cœur, pouls) palpitating, fluttering; Fig **p. d'émotion/d'angoisse** quivering or trembling with emotion/anxiety
 NM Fam (cœur) ticker

palpitation [palpitasjɔ̃] **NF 1** (du cœur) pounding; (des artères) throbbing; (des flancs) heaving; (des paupières) fluttering
 2 Littéraire (frémissement) quivering, trembling
 □ **palpitations NFPL** palpitations; **avoir des palpitations** (une fois) to have (an attack of) palpitations; (souvent) to suffer from palpitations; **descends de cette fenêtre, tu me donnes des palpitations!** get down from that window, you'll give me a heart attack!

palpiter [3] [palpite] **VI 1** (artère) to throb; (paupière) to flutter; (flancs) to quiver, to heave; **son cœur palpitait violemment** his/her heart was beating fast or pounding; **sa poitrine palpitait** her bosom was heaving **2** Littéraire (scintiller) to flicker

palplanche [palplɑ̃ʃ] **NF** Tech sheet pile

palsambleu [palsɑ̃blø] **EXCLAM** *Arch* gadzooks!

paltoquet [paltɔkε] **NM** *Fam* **1** *Vieilli (rustre)* boor, peasant **2** *(personne insignifiante)* pipsqueak

palu [paly] **NM** *Fam* malaria ▪

paluche [palyʃ] **NF 1** *Fam* hand▪, paw, mitt **2** *Cin* paluche (camera) *(small, portable video camera handled like a microphone)*

palucher [3] [palyʃe] *très Fam* **VT** to grope, to feel up, to touch up
  ▸**se palucher VPR** to play with oneself, to touch oneself up

palud [paly] **NM** *Vieilli* marsh, swamp

paludarium [palydarjɔm] **NM** amphibian vivarium

palude [palyd] = **palud**

paludéen, -enne [palydeɛ̃, -ɛn] **ADJ 1** *Méd* malarial, paludal **2** *(des marais)* marsh *(avant n)*, paludal

paludier, -ère [palydje, -ɛr] **NM,F** salt-marsh worker

paludine [palydin] **NF** *Zool* paludina

paludique [palydik] **ADJ 1** *Méd* malarial **2** *(des marais)* marsh *(avant n)*, paludal

paludisme [palydism] **NM** *Méd* malaria, paludism

palustre [palystr] **ADJ 1** *Méd* malarial **2** *(des marais)* marsh *(avant n)*, paludal

palynologie [palinɔlɔʒi] **NF** palynology

PAM [pam] **NM** *(abrév* **programme alimentaire mondial***)* WFP

pâmer [3] [pɑme] **se pâmer VPR** *Littéraire ou Hum* to swoon; **se p. d'aise** to be as pleased as Punch, to be tickled pink; **se p. de rire** to be convulsed with laughter; **se p. d'admiration devant** to be in raptures over, to be overcome with admiration for; **se p. devant qn** to swoon over sb; **il se pâme devant les grands de 14 ans** he's overawed by the 14-year-olds

Pamir [pamir] **NM** *Géog* **le P.** the Pamirs

pâmoison [pɑmwazɔ̃] **NF** *Littéraire ou Hum* swoon, fainting fit; **tomber en p. (devant)** to swoon (over)

pampa [pɑ̃pa] **NF** pampas

Pampelune [pɑ̃plyn] **NM** Pamplona

pampero, pampéro [pɑ̃pero] **NM** pampero (wind)

pamphile [pɑ̃fil] **NM** *Entom* sawfly

pamphlet [pɑ̃flɛ] **NM 1** *(écrit satirique)* lampoon, pamphlet **2** *Can Joual (brochure)* pamphlet, booklet

pamphlétaire [pɑ̃fletɛr] **ADJ** *(ton, esprit)* pamphleteering
  NMF lampoonist, pamphleteer

pampille [pɑ̃pij] **NF** pendant

pamplemousse [pɑ̃pləmus] **NM** grapefruit, *Am* pomelo

pamplemoussier [pɑ̃pləmusje] **NM** grapefruit (tree)

pampre [pɑ̃pr] **NM 1** *Bot* vine branch **2** *Beaux-Arts* pampre

Pan [pɑ̃] **NPR** *Myth* Pan

pan¹ [pɑ̃] **ONOMAT** *(gifle)* wham!, whack!; *(coup de feu)* bang!; **et p., le voilà qui entre!** and then, would you believe it, in he comes!; **je vais te faire p. p. (cucul)!** *(langage enfantin)* I'll smack your bottom!

pan² [pɑ̃] **NM 1** *(d'un vêtement)* tail; *(d'une nappe)* fold; **se promener en p. de chemise** to wander about in one's shirt-tails
  2 *Constr* **p. de bois/fer** wood/metal framing; **p. coupé/de verre** canted/plate-glass wall; *Archit* **à pans coupés** canted, with a cut-off corner; **p. de mur** (section of) wall
  3 *(morceau)* section, piece; **un p. de ciel bleu** a patch of blue sky; **un p. de ma vie a disparu avec lui** when he left, he took a piece of my life away with him; **des pans entiers de la société** whole sections or strata of society
  4 *Tech* side, face; **un écrou à six pans** a six-sided nut

panacée [panase] **NF** panacea

panachage [panaʃaʒ] **NM 1** *(mélange)* blend, blending, mixing **2** *Pol* = voting for candidates from different lists rather than for a list as a whole

panache [panaʃ] **NM 1** *(plume)* plume, panache; *Fig* **p. de fumée** plume of smoke **2** *(brio)* panache, style, verve; **avec p.** with great panache; **avoir du p.** to have panache, to show great

verve **3** *Archit (ornement)* panache, (ostrich) feather; *(surface)* pendentive

panaché, -e [panaʃe] **ADJ 1** *(mélangé → sélection, salade)* mixed; *(→ fleurs)* variegated; **un demi p.** a (lager) shandy; **glace panachée** assorted icecream **2** *Pol* **liste panachée** = ballot paper in which a voter votes for candidates from different lists rather than for a list as a whole
  NM (lager) shandy

panacher [3] [panaʃe] **VT 1** *(mélanger)* to blend, to mix **2** *Pol* **p. une liste électorale** = to vote for candidates from different lists rather than for a list as a whole

panachure [panaʃyr] **NF 1** *Littéraire (coloration)* variegation **2** *Hort* variegation

panade [panad] **NF 1** *Culin* bread soup **2** *Fam (locution)* **être dans la p.** to be penniless▪ *or Br* on one's uppers

panafricain, -e [panafrikɛ̃, -ɛn] **ADJ** pan-African

panafricanisme [panafrikanism] **NM** pan-Africanism

panaire [panɛr] **ADJ** panary

panais [panɛ] **NM** parsnip

Panama [panama] **NM 1** *(pays)* **le P.** Panama; **vivre au P.** to live in Panama; **aller au P.** to go to Panama; **le canal de P.** the Panama Canal; **l'isthme de P.** the Isthmus of Panama **2** *(ville)* Panama City; **à P.** in Panama City

panama [panama] **NM** *(chapeau)* Panama (hat)

Paname [panam] **NM** *Fam* = nickname given to Paris

panaméen, -enne [panameɛ̃, -ɛn] **ADJ** Panamanian
  ▫ **Panaméen, -enne NM,F** Panamanian

panaméricain, -e [panamerikɛ̃, -ɛn] **ADJ** pan-American

panaméricanisme [panamerikanism] **NM** pan-Americanism

panamien, -enne [panamjɛ̃, -ɛn] = **panaméen**

panarabe [panarab] **ADJ** pan-Arab

panarabisme [panarabism] **NM** pan-Arabism

panard, -e [panar, -ard] **ADJ** cow-hocked; *Vét* duck-footed
  NM *Fam* **1** *(pied)* foot▪, *Br* plate, *Am* dog; **t'as vu les panards qu'il a?** have you seen the size of his feet? **2** *(plaisir intense)* **quel p.!** great!, terrific!, fantastic!; **ce n'est pas le p.** it's not exactly a load of laughs *or* a barrel of fun; **prendre son p.** *(sexuellement)* to come

panaris [panari] **NM** felon, whitlow

panatela, panatella [panatɛla] **NM** panatella (cigar)

panathénées [panatene] **NFPL** *Antiq* Panathenaea

panavision [panavizjɔ̃] **NF** panavision

panax [panaks] **NM** *Bot* panax (ginseng)

pan-bagnat [pɑ̃baɲa] *(pl* **pans-bagnats***)* **NM** filled roll *(containing tomatoes, onions, green peppers, olives, tuna and anchovies and seasoned with olive oil)*

panca [pɑ̃ka] **NM** punkah; **tireur de p.** punkah boy, punkah wallah

pancartage [pɑ̃kartaʒ] **NM** signposting

pancarte [pɑ̃kart] **NF** *(gén)* sign, notice; *(dans un magasin)* showcard; *(dans une manifestation)* placard; **les manifestants ont levé leurs pancartes** the demonstrators raised their placards

pancetta [pɑ̃tʃeta] **NF** pancetta

panchen-lama [pɑ̃ʃɛnlama] *(pl* **panchen-lamas***)* **NM** Panchen Lama

panchromatique [pɑ̃krɔmatik] **ADJ** *Phot* panchromatic

panchronique [pɑ̃krɔnik] **ADJ** *Ling* panchronic

pancréas [pɑ̃kreas] **NM** *Anat* pancreas

pancréatine [pɑ̃kreatin] **NF** *Pharm* pancreatin

pancréatique [pɑ̃kreatik] **ADJ** *Anat* pancreatic

pancréatite [pɑ̃kreatit] **NF** *Méd* pancreatitis

panda [pɑ̃da] **NM** *Zool* panda; **grand p., p. géant** giant panda; **petit p.** red panda

pandanus [pɑ̃danys] **NM** *Bot* pandanus

pandectes [pɑ̃dɛkt] **NFPL** *Hist* pandects

pandémie [pɑ̃demi] **NF** *Méd* pandemic

pandémique [pɑ̃demik] **ADJ** *Méd* pandemic

pandémonium [pɑ̃demɔnjɔm] **NM** *Littéraire* pandemonium

pandit [pɑ̃dit] **NM** pandit

Pandore [pɑ̃dɔr] **NPR** *Myth* Pandora; **la boîte de P.** Pandora's box

pandore [pɑ̃dɔr] **NM** *Fam Vieilli* cop, *Br* copper

pané, -e [pane] **ADJ** breaded

panégyrique [paneʒirik] **NM** panegyric, eulogy; **faire le p. de qn** to extol sb's virtues, to eulogize sb, *Sout* to panegyreize sb
  ADJ panegyrical

panégyriste [paneʒirist] **NMF** panegyrist

panel [panɛl] **NM 1** *(de spécialistes)* panel
  2 *Mktg (échantillon)* panel, sample group; **p. ad hoc** ad hoc panel; **p. de consommateurs** consumer panel, shopping panel; **p. de détaillants** retail panel; **p. de distributeurs** distributor panel; **p. d'essayeurs de produits** product testing panel; **p. de téléspectateurs** television viewing panel

panéliste [panelist] **NMF** panel member

paner [3] [pane] **VT** to coat with breadcrumbs

panerée [panre] **NF** *Vieilli* basketful

paneterie [pantri, panɛtri] **NF 1** *(pour conserver le pain)* bread store **2** *Hist (office du panetier)* pantler's office, pantry *(in king's household etc)*

panetier [pantje] **NM** *Hist* pantler

panetière [pantjɛr] **NF** bread box

paneton [pantɔ̃] **NM** = basket in which a baker places dough to give it its shape

paneuropéanisme [panørɔpeanism] **NM** pan-Europeanism

paneuropéen, -enne [panørɔpeɛ̃, -ɛn] **ADJ** pan-European

pangermanique [pɑ̃ʒɛrmanik] **ADJ** pan-German, pan-Germanic

pangermanisme [pɑ̃ʒɛrmanism] **NM** pan-Germanism

pangermaniste [pɑ̃ʒɛrmanist] **ADJ** pan-Germanist
  NMF pan-Germanist

Pangloss [pɑ̃glɔs] **NPR** *Littérature* = the tutor and intransigent preacher of the philosophy of optimism in Voltaire's 'Candide' (1759)

pangolin [pɑ̃gɔlɛ̃] **NM** *Zool* pangolin

pangramme [pɑ̃gram] **NM** *Gram* pangram

panhellénique [panelenik] **ADJ** Panhellenic

panhellénisme [panelenism] **NM** Panhellenism

panic [panik] **NM** *Bot* panic grass

panicaut [paniko] **NM** *Bot* **p. champêtre** field eryngo; **p. maritime** sea holly

panicule [panikyl] **NF** panicle

paniculé, -e [panikyle] **ADJ** *Bot* paniculate

panier [panje] **NM 1** *(corbeille)* basket; **p. à bouteilles** bottle case *or* carrier; **p. à couverts** cutlery basket; **p. à diapositives** slide tray; **p. à frites** *Br* chip basket, *Am* French fry basket; **p. à linge** linen basket; **p. de manutention** handling basket; **p. à ouvrage** workbasket; **p. à pain** bread basket; **p. à pique-nique** picnic basket; **p. à provisions** shopping basket; **p. à salade** salad shaker; *Fam (fourgon cellulaire) Br* Black Maria, *Am* paddy wagon; **mettre** *ou* **jeter qch au p.** to throw sth out; **bon à mettre** *ou* **jeter au p.** fit for the *Br* bin *or Am* trash can; **il ne faut pas tous les mettre dans le même p.** you can't lump them all together, they're not all tarred with the same brush; **ils sont tous à mettre dans le même p.** they're all much of a muchness; **être un (véritable) p. percé** *(être dépensier)* to be a (real) spendthrift; *Can Fam (être indiscret)* to be a blabbermouth; *Fam* **mettre la main au p. à qn** to goose sb
  2 *(quantité)* **un (plein) p. de** a basketful of
  3 *Sport* basket; **réussir** *ou* **marquer un p.** to score a basket
  4 *Écon* basket; **p. de la ménagère** shopping basket; **la hausse du beurre se répercute sur le p. de la ménagère** the increase in the price of butter makes a difference to the housekeeping bill; *Bourse* **p. d'actions** basket of shares; **p. de monnaies** *ou* **de devises** basket of currencies; *Écon* **p. moyen** average basket size
  5 *Mktg (présentoir)* dump bin; **p. de présentation en vrac, p. présentoir** dump bin; **p. à la sortie** check-out display; **p. vrac** dump bin
  6 *(nasse)* lobster pot; **c'est un (véritable) p. de crabes** they're always at each other's throats
  7 *(de crinoline)* hoop

panière [panjɛr] **NF** (two-handled) wickerwork basket

panier-repas [panjerəpa] *(pl* **paniers-repas***)* **NM** *Br* packed lunch, *Am* brown bag lunch

panifiable [panifjabl] **ADJ** (céréale) suitable for making bread; **farine p.** bread flour

panification [panifikasjɔ̃] **NF** breadmaking

panifier [9] [panifje] **VT** to make bread from

panini [panini] (pl inv ou **paninis**) **NM** panini

paniquant, -e [panikã, -ãt] **ADJ** frightening, panic-inducing

paniquard [panikar] **NM** Fam Péj scaredy cat, Am fraidy cat

panique [panik] **NF** (terreur) panic; **ne pas céder à la p.** not to panic, not to give way to panic; **il s'est enfui, pris de p.** he fled in panic; **les passagers étaient pris de p.** the passengers were panic-stricken; **il y a eu un mouvement de p.** there was a wave of panic; Fam **c'était la p.!** it was panic stations!; **pas de p.!** don't panic!, there's no need to panic!

ADJ peur p. panic

paniquer [3] [panike] Fam **VT** (angoisser) to panic■, to throw into a panic■; **l'approche des examens le panique** he's starting to panic as the exams get nearer; **elle était complètement paniquée** she was completely panic-stricken, she was in a complete panic

VI to panic■; **elle n'a pas paniqué** she didn't lose her head or didn't panic; **la nouvelle les a fait p.** the news panicked them

▸**se paniquer VPR** to panic■; **ne nous paniquons pas, nous avons tout le temps** let's not panic, we've got plenty of time

panislamique [panislamik] **ADJ** pan-Islamic

panislamisme [panislamism] **NM** pan-Islamism

panjabi [pãdʒabi] **NM** (langue) Punjabi

panka [pãka] = **panca**

panmixie [pãmiksi] **NF** panmixia

panne [pan] **NF 1** (de voiture) breakdown; **vous êtes à l'étranger et soudain c'est la p., que faites-vous?** suppose you're abroad and you suddenly break down, what do you do?; **trouver la p.** to find the problem, to find the cause of the problem; **p. d'électricité** ou **de courant** power cut or failure; **avoir une p. d'essence** to run out of Br petrol or Am gas; **p. de moteur** engine failure; Fam Hum **j'ai eu une p. d'oreiller** I overslept■; **p. de secteur** local mains failure; Fam **il a essayé de me faire le coup de la p.** he tried to pull the old running-out-of-petrol trick on me

2 Ordinat failure, crash; **p. logicielle** software crash; **p. matérielle** hardware crash; **p. du système** system crash

3 Tex panne

4 (d'un cochon) pig's fat or lard

5 (d'un marteau) peen

6 (d'un bâtiment) purlin, purline; **p. intermédiaire** ou **courante** middle purlin

7 Théât bit part

8 Belg (bassin hygiénique) bedpan

9 Belg (tuile) tile

◻ **en panne ADJ** des automobilistes en p. drivers whose cars have broken down; **en p.** out of order; **la machine/voiture est en p.** the machine/car has broken down; **je suis en p.** (automobiliste) I've broken down; Fam Fig **je suis en p. de poivre/d'idées** I've run out of or I'm out of pepper/ideas **ADV mettre un voilier en p.** to heave a sailing ship to; **tomber en p.** (voiture, machine) to break down; (automobiliste) to break down, to have a breakdown; (ordinateur) to crash; Fam **je suis tombé en p. d'essence** ou **sèche** I've run out of petrol

panné, -e [pane] **ADJ** Fam Vieilli broke

panneau, -x [pano] **NM 1** (pancarte) sign; (pour afficher) board; **on a mis un p. à l'entrée de l'usine** they've put up a sign at the factory gate; **p. d'affichage** notice board; Ordinat bulletin board; Ordinat **p. de configuration** control panel; **p. électoral** election billboard or Br hoarding; **p. indicateur** signpost; **p. publicitaire** billboard, Br hoarding; **p. de signalisation** roadsign

2 (plaque) panel; **un p. de contre-plaqué** a piece or panel of plywood; **p. de particules** chipboard, particleboard; **p. solaire** solar panel

3 Beaux-Arts panel

4 Couture panel; **une jupe à trois panneaux** a three-panelled skirt

5 Chasse (game) net; **tomber** ou **donner dans le p.** to fall into the trap

6 Hort (cold) frame

7 Mines distric

8 Naut **p. de cale** hatch cover

panneau-réclame [panoreklam] (pl **panneaux-réclame**) **NM** billboard, Br hoarding

panneauter [3] [panote] Chasse **VT** to poach using nets

VI to poach using nets

panneresse [panrɛs] **NF** Constr stretcher

panneton [pantɔ̃] **NM** bit, web (of a key)

pannicule [panikyl] **NM** Anat panniculus; **p. adipeux** panniculus adiposus

pano [pano] **NM** Fam Cin & TV pan■

panonceau, -x [panɔ̃so] **NM 1** (plaque) plaque, sign; (écriteau) sign; **p. publicitaire** advertisement, Br advert **2** Hist escutcheon

panophtalmie [panɔftalmi] **NF** Méd panophthalmitis

panoplie [panɔpli] **NF 1** (ensemble d'instruments) (complete) set; **la p. du bricoleur** do-it-yourself equipment or kit **2** (déguisement) outfit; **une p. de Zorro/d'infirmière** a Zorro/nurse's outfit **3** Fig (d'arguments) battery; **toute une p. de mesures contre les chauffards** a full array of measures against dangerous drivers **4** Hist (armure complète) panoply

panoptique [panɔptik] **ADJ** panoptic

panorama [panorama] **NM 1** (vue) panorama, view; **après quelques heures de marche, je découvris un splendide p.** after several hours' walking, I came to a place with a splendid view **2** Fig (vue d'ensemble) survey, overview; **pour terminer ce p. de l'actualité musicale** to end this roundup of current musical events **3** Beaux-Arts panorama

panoramique [panoramik] **ADJ** (écran, vue) panoramic; (restaurant) with panoramic views; Rail **wagon** ou **car p.** observation car

NM Cin pan (shot); **faire un p.** to pan; **p. filé** zip pan, whip pan; **p. horizontal** pan shot; **p. de poursuite** following pan; **p. vertical** tilt; **faire un p. horizontal/vertical** to pan/tilt

panoramiquer [panoramike] **VT** TV & Cin to pan; **p. vers le haut/le bas** to pan up/down

panorpe [panɔrp] **NF** Entom scorpion fly

panosse [panɔs] **NF** Suisse mop

panosser [3] [panɔse] **VT** Suisse to mop

panouille [panuj] **NF** Fam **1** (personne stupide) idiot, fool **2** (petit rôle) bit-part

pansage [pãsaʒ] **NM** grooming

panse [pãs] **NF 1** Zool paunch, rumen **2** Fam (d'une personne) paunch, belly; **s'en mettre plein la p., se remplir la p.** to make a pig of oneself, to stuff one's face **3** (d'un vase) belly

pansement [pãsmã] **NM** (action) dressing; (objet) dressing, bandage; **il lui a fait un p. à la jambe** he put a dressing on his/her leg; **elle lui a refait son p.** she changed his/her dressing; **il est couvert de pansements** he's all bandaged up; **p. (adhésif)** Br (sticking) plaster, Elastoplast®, Am Band Aid®; **p. gastrique** (liquide) = milk of magnesia; (poudre) stomach powder; **p. ouatiné** lint

panser [3] [pãse] **VT 1** Méd (personne blessée) to dress the wounds of; (blessure) to dress, to put a dressing on; (membre) to put a dressing on, to bandage; Fig **le temps panse tous les maux** time is a great healer; Fig **p. ses blessures** to lick one's wounds **2** (toiletter → animal) to groom

panslave [pãslav] **ADJ** Pan-Slavic

panslavisme [pãslavism] **NM** Pan-Slavism

panslaviste [pãslavist] **ADJ** Pan-Slavic, Pan-Slav (avant n)

NMF Pan-Slavist

panspermie [pãspɛrmi] **NF** Biol panspermia

pansu, -e [pãsy] **ADJ 1** Fam (ventripotent) paunchy, potbellied **2** (renflé → cruche, bouteille) potbellied

pantacle [pãtakl] **NM** pentacle, pentagram

Pantagruel [pãtagryɛl] **NPR** Littérature = the giant son of Gargantua in Rabelais' novel of that name (1534) and its three sequels (1546–1562)

pantagruélique [pãtagryelik] **ADJ** (appétit) enormous; (repas) gargantuan, pantagruelian

Pantalon [pãtalɔ̃] **NPR** Théât Pantaloon

pantalon [pãtalɔ̃] **NM** (pair of) Br trousers or Am pants; **mon p.** my Br trousers or Am pants; **deux pantalons** two pairs of Br trousers or Am pants; **p. bouffant** (pair of) baggy Br trousers or Am pants; **p. cargo** cargo Br trousers or Am pants; **p. cigarette** Br drainpipe trousers, Am straight-leg pants; **p. de golf** (pair of) plus fours; **p. jazz** jazz pants; **p. multi-poches** combat Br trousers or Am pants; **p. de pyjama** pyjama Br trousers or bottoms or Am pants; **p. de ski** ski pants

pantalon-jupe [pãtalɔ̃ʒyp] (pl **pantalons-jupes**) **NM** (pair of) palazzo pants

pantalonnade [pãtalonad] **NF 1** (hypocrisie) hypocrisy (UNCOUNT), pretence (UNCOUNT); **j'en ai assez de leurs pantalonnades** I've had enough of their hypocrisy **2** Théât (second-rate) farce, slapstick comedy

pante [pãt] **NM** Fam Vieilli sucker, Br mug

pantelant, -e [pãtlã, -ãt] **ADJ 1** (haletant) panting, gasping for breath; Fig **être p. de terreur** to be panting or gasping with terror **2** (palpitant) **chair pantelante** twitching flesh

panteler [24] [pãtle] **VI** Littéraire **1** Vieilli (haleter) to pant **2** (palpiter) to twitch

pantenne [pãtɛn] **en pantenne ADJ** Naut in disorder

panthéisme [pãteism] **NM** pantheism

panthéiste [pãteist] **ADJ** pantheistic

NMF pantheist

panthéon [pãteɔ̃] **NM 1** Antiq & Rel pantheon; **le P.** the Pantheon **2** Fig pantheon, hall of fame; **je le place au p. des accordéonistes** I consider him to be one of the greatest accordion players of all time; **son nom est resté au p. de l'histoire** his/her name went down in history

LE PANTHÉON

Le Panthéon, one of Paris's most distinctive neoclassical monuments, stands on the Montagne Sainte-Geneviève in the 5th arrondissement of the city. When building started in 1764 it was intended to be a church dedicated to Sainte-Geneviève, the patron saint of Paris. However, by the time it was completed, in 1790, the French revolution was in full swing and it was then decided that it would be turned into a mausoleum for the remains of great Frenchmen, although it reverted to its original purpose of being a church during the restoration of the Bourbon monarchy (1815–1830) and during the Second Empire. Among the great figures buried at the Panthéon are Voltaire, Rousseau, Victor Hugo, Émile Zola, Marie Curie and Alexandre Dumas. The Panthéon is also famous for being the place where physicist Léon Foucault conducted his demonstration of the rotation of the Earth with his eponymous pendulum in 1851.

panthère [pãtɛr] **NF 1** Zool leopard; **p. des neiges** snow leopard; **p. noire** panther **2** (fourrure) leopard; **un manteau en (peau de) p.** a leopard-skin coat **3** Pol **les Panthères noires** the Black Panthers **4** Bot voir **amanite**

pantière [pãtjɛr] **NF** net (for catching birds)

pantin [pãtɛ̃] **NM 1** (jouet) jumping jack **2** Fig puppet; **n'être qu'un p. entre les mains de qn** to be sb's puppet

pantographe [pãtograf] **NM** Tech pantograph

pantoire [pãtwar] **NF** Naut pendant

pantois, -e [pãtwa, -az] **ADJ** speechless, dumbstruck; **elle en est restée pantoise** it left her speechless, she was dumbstruck or speechless

pantomètre [pãtomɛtr] **NM** pantometer

pantomime [pãtomim] **NF 1** (jeu de mime) mime; Théât (pièce) mime show **2** Péj (comédie) scene, fuss

pantothénique [pãtotenik] **ADJ** Chim pantothenic

pantouflage [pãtuflaʒ] **NM** Fam = leaving a civil service post to work in the private sector

pantouflard, -e [pãtuflar, -ard] Fam **ADJ** **ils sont très pantouflards** they're real homebodies, they never go out■

NM,F homebody, stay-at-home

pantoufle [pãtufl] **NF** slipper; **p. de vair** (dans Cendrillon) glass slipper; **être en pantoufles** to be in one's slippers

pantoufler [3] [pãtufle] **VI** Fam = to leave a civil service post and work for the private sector

pantoum [pãtum] **NM** Littérature pantoum

pantoute [pɑ̃tut] **ADV** *Can Fam (pas du tout)* absolutely not■, no way; *(jamais de la vie)* never in a million years

panty [pɑ̃ti] (*pl* **panties** [pɑ̃tiz]) **NM** *Vieilli* pantie girdle

panure [panyr] **NF** breadcrumbs *(for coating)*

Panurge [panyrʒ] **NPR** *Littérature* = the faithful companion of Pantagruel, best known for the incident where he throws a sheep into the sea, causing the rest of the flock to follow; *voir* **mouton**

panurgisme [panyrʒism] **NM** *Péj* herd mentality

panzer [pɑ̃dzɛr] **NM** panzer

PAO [peao] **NF** *(abrév* **publication assistée par ordinateur***) Ordinat* DTP

paon [pɑ̃] **NM 1** *Orn* peafowl; **p. (bleu)** peacock; **fier** *ou* **orgueilleux** *ou* **vaniteux comme un p.** (as) proud as a peacock; **faire le p.** to strut (like a peacock) **2** *Entom* **p. de jour** peacock; **p. de nuit** emperor moth

paonne [pan] **NF** *Orn* peahen

paonneau, -x [pano] **NM** *Orn* peachick

PAP [pap] **NM** *(abrév* **prêt d'accession à la propriété***)* = loan for first-time homebuyers

papa [papa] **NM 1** *(père → gén)* dad; *(→ en langage enfantin)* daddy; **jouer au p. et à la maman** to play mummies and daddies

2 *Fam (homme d'un certain âge)* **alors, p., tu traverses?** come on, grandad, get across!

▫ **à la papa** **ADV** *Fam (tranquillement)* leisurely■; **on va faire ça à la p.** we'll take it easy, we'll do it at our own pace

▫ **à papa** **ADJ** *Fam* **c'est un fils/une fille à p.** he's/she's got a rich daddy; **cette école n'est fréquentée que par des fils à p.** only rich kids go to that school

▫ **de papa** **ADJ** *Fam* old-fashioned■

papable [papabl] **ADJ** *Fam* **être p.** to be a likely candidate for the papacy■

papaïne [papain] **NF** *Chim* papaine

papal, -e, -aux, -ales [papal, -o] **ADJ** papal

papamobile [papamɔbil] **NM** popemobile

paparazzi [paparadzi] **NMPL** paparazzi

papas [papas] **NM** *Rel* papas

papauté [papote] **NF** papacy

papaver [papavɛr] **NM** *Bot* papaver

papavéracée [papaverase] *Bot* **NF** member of the poppy family *or Spéc* the Papaveraceae

▫ **papavéracées** **NFPL** poppies, *Spéc* Papaveraceae

papavérine [papaverin] **NF** *Pharm* papaverine

papaye [papaj] **NF** papaya, pawpaw

papayer [papaje] **NM** papaya (tree), pawpaw (tree)

pape [pap] **NM 1** *Rel* pope; **le p. Benoît XVI** Pope Benedict XVI **2** *Fig (chef de file)* high priest, guru **3** *Orn* **p. de la Louisiane** painted bunting

Papeete [papɛt] **NM** Papeete

papelard[1] [paplar] **NM** *Fam* **1** *(bout de papier)* paper■ **2** *Journ* article■, piece; **il a écrit un p. sur la corruption** he wrote a piece on corruption **3** **papelards** *(papiers d'identité)* ID

papelard[2], **-e** [paplar, -ard] **ADJ** *Littéraire (personne)* unctuous; **..., dit-il d'un air p.** ..., he said smoothly

papelardise [paplardiz] **NF** *Littéraire* unctuousness

paperasse [papras] **NF** *Péj* papers, *Br* bumf; **je n'ai pas le temps de remplir toute cette p.** I don't have the time to fill in all these forms; **je passe mon temps à m'occuper de la p.** I spend all my time doing paperwork

paperasserie [paprasri] **NF** *Péj* **1** *(formulaires → gén)* paperwork; *(→ administratifs)* red tape; **toute cette p. va sûrement retarder le projet** all this red tape is bound to delay the project **2** *(amoncellement)* papers

paperassier, -ère [paprasje, -ɛr] *Péj* **ADJ** *(personne)* who loves filling in forms, who loves paperwork

NM,F *Br* penpusher, *Am* pencilpusher

papesse [papɛs] **NF** female pope; **la p. Jeanne** Pope Joan

papet [papɛ] **NM** *Suisse* = Swiss dish made with potatoes, leeks and sausages

papeterie [papɛtri] **NF 1** *(boutique) Br* stationer's (shop), *Am* stationery store **2** *(matériel)* stationery **3** *(usine)* paper mill **4** *(fabrication)* paper manufacturing; *(secteur)* paper industry

papetier, -ère [paptje, -ɛr] **ADJ** paper *(avant n)*, stationery *(avant n)*

NM,F 1 *Com* stationer **2** *Ind* paper-maker

papetier-libraire [paptjelibrɛr] (*pl* **papetiers-libraires**) **NM** *Com* bookseller and stationer

papette [papɛt] **NF** *Suisse* **1** *(bouillie)* baby food **2** *(boue)* mud

papi [papi] **NM** *Fam (grand-père)* granddad

papier [papje] **NM 1** *(matière)* paper; *Fig* **barbouiller** *ou* **noircir du p.** to fill page after page; **toujours à gratter** *ou* **noircir du p.** always scribbling something or other; **sur le p.** on paper; **sur le p., le projet paraît réalisable** on paper, the project seems feasible; **jeter qch sur le p.** to jot sth down; **p. en accordéon** fanfold *or Am* Z-fold paper; **p. d'aluminium**, *Fam* **p. alu** *Br* aluminium *or Am* aluminum foil; **p. d'argent** silver foil *or* paper; **p. d'Arménie** incense paper; **p. avion** airmail paper; *Ordinat* **p. à bandes perforées** perforated paper; **p. bible** bible paper, Oxford India paper; **p. bouffant** bulking paper, featherweight paper; **p. brouillon** rough paper; **p. buvard** blotting paper; **p. cadeau** wrapping paper; **p. carbone** carbon (paper); **p. à cartouche** cartridge paper; **p. à cigarette** cigarette paper; **fin comme du p. à cigarette** *(usé)* like tissue paper; **p. collant** *(adhésif)* adhesive tape; *(gommé)* gummed paper or strip; **p. contact** contact paper; *Ordinat* **p. (en) continu** continuous paper *or* stationery, listing paper; **p. couché** *Ordinat* coated paper; *Beaux-Arts* art paper; **p. crépon** crêpe paper; *très Fam* **p. cul, p. Q** *Br* bog roll, *Am* TP; *Typ* **p. de décharge** set-off sheet, offset sheet; **p. à dessin** drawing paper; **p. d'emballage** (brown) wrapping paper; **p. à en-tête** headed paper *or* notepaper; **p. d'étain** tinfoil; **p. glacé** glazed paper; **sur p. glacé** *(magazine)* glossy; **p. huilé** oilpaper; **p. hygiénique** toilet paper; *Ordinat* **p. d'impression** printer paper; **p. intercalaire** tympan paper; **p. journal** newspaper, newsprint; **p. kraft** brown paper; **p. à lettres** writing paper; **le contrat a été rédigé sur p. libre** the contract was drawn up on a sheet of plain paper; **envoyer une lettre sur p. libre** to apply in writing; *Ordinat* **p. listing** listing paper; **p. mâché** papier-mâché; **p. machine** typing paper; **papier mat** matt art; **p. millimétré** graph paper; **p. ministre** official paper; *Typ* **p. de mise en train** overlay; *Ordinat* **p. multiple** multi-part stationery; **p. à musique** music paper; **p. paraffiné** wax paper; **p. peint** wallpaper; **p. pelure** onion skin (paper); **p. photographique** photographic paper; **p. quadrillé** squared paper; **p. de riz** rice paper; **p. en rouleau** web *or* reel paper; *Can* **p. sablé** sandpaper; **p. sans bois** woodfree paper; **p. de soie** tissue paper; **p. sulfurisé** greaseproof *or Spéc* sulphurized paper; *Ordinat* **p. thermique** *ou* **thermosensible** thermal paper; **p. timbré** stamped paper *(for official use)*; **p. toilette,** *Can* **p. de toilette** toilet paper; **p. torchon** torchon paper; **p. de verre** sandpaper; **p. vélin** vellum *or Br* wove paper

2 *(morceau)* piece of paper; *(page)* sheet of paper, piece of paper; **as-tu un p. et un crayon?** do you have a piece of paper and a pencil?; **son bureau est couvert de papiers** his/her desk is covered in paper(s); **p. de bonbon** *Br* sweet *or Am* candy wrapper; *Beaux-Arts* **p. collé** papier collé; **être dans les petits papiers de qn** to be in sb's good books; **je ne suis plus dans ses petits papiers** I'm no longer in his/her good books

3 *Journ* article, piece; **faire un p. sur** to do a piece *or* an article on

4 *Admin* **papiers** papers; **les papiers du véhicule, s'il vous plaît** may I see your (vehicle) registration papers *or Br* logbook, please?; **les papiers de la vente** the sale documents; **papiers (d'identité)** (identity) papers; **mes papiers sont en règle** my papers are in order; **vos papiers, s'il vous plaît!** can I see your identity papers, please?; **faux papiers** false *or* forged papers

5 *Fin* **p. bancable** bankable paper; **p. de commerce** commercial paper; **p. commercial** commercial bill; **p. commercial de premier ordre** prime bill; **p. sur l'étranger** foreign bill; **p. fait** guaranteed paper, backed bill; **p. financier** *ou* **de crédit** bank credit note; **p. négociable** negotiable paper; **p. à ordre** instrument to order; **p. au porteur** bearer paper; **papiers valeurs** paper securities; **p. à vue** sight paper

▫ **de papier, en papier** **ADJ** paper *(avant n)*; **lanterne en p.** paper lantern

▫ **papiers gras** **NMPL** litter

> *Culture*
>
> **PAPIERS**
>
> All French citizens are required by law to carry a "carte d'identité" (featuring a photograph, address and details of one's physical appearance) at all times. In order to guarantee a cheque, French people are also often required to present some form of identity (whether an identity card, a passport, a residence permit or a driving licence). When voting in elections, French voters must be in possession of a "carte d'électeur" issued by the town hall or "mairie". In the "livret de famille" which is presented to newly married couples at their civil wedding ceremony and is often needed for administrative procedures, details of marriages, divorces and births are recorded. The red tape associated with French bureaucracy is, however, gradually being simplified.

papier-calque [papjekalk] (*pl* **papiers-calque**) **NM** tracing paper

papier-émeri [papjeemri] (*pl* **papiers-émeri**) **NM** emery paper

papier-filtre [papjefiltr] (*pl* **papiers-filtres**) **NM** filter paper

papier-monnaie [papjemɔnɛ] (*pl* **papiers-monnaies**) **NM** paper money

papilionacé, -e [papiljɔnase] *Bot* **ADJ** papilionaceous

▫ **papilionacée** **NF** member of the Papilionaceae

▫ **papilionacées** **NFPL** Papilionaceae

papillaire [papilɛr] **ADJ** *Anat* papillary, papillate

papille [papij] **NF** *Anat* papilla; **papilles gustatives** taste buds; **p. optique** optic disk, blind spot

papilleux, -euse [papijø, -øz] **ADJ** papillose

papillomavirus [papijɔmavirys] **NM** *Méd* papillomavirus, papovavirus

papillome [papilom, papijom] **NM** *Méd* papilloma

papillon [papijɔ̃] **NM 1** *Entom* butterfly; **p. de nuit** moth; *Fig* **papillons noirs** gloomy thoughts; **pour chasser tes papillons noirs** to cheer you up **2** *Fam (contravention)* (parking) ticket■ **3** *(dans un livre)* inset; *(publicité)* leaflet **4** *Fig (esprit volage)* **c'est un (vrai) p.** he's fickle **5** *Tech (écrou)* butterfly *or* wing nut; *(obturateur, clapet)* butterfly valve; *Aut* **p. des gaz** throttle **6** *Natation* **(brasse) p.** butterfly (stroke); **nager le p.** to do the butterfly

papillonnage [papijɔnaʒ] = **papillonnement**

papillonnant, -e [papijɔnɑ̃, -ɑ̃t] **ADJ 1** *(versatile, instable → esprit)* flighty, inattentive **2** *(insecte)* fluttering

papillonnement [papijɔnmɑ̃] **NM 1** *(versatilité, inconstance)* flightiness, inattentiveness **2** *(volettement)* fluttering

papillonner [3] [papijɔne] **VI 1** *(voltiger)* to flit *or* to flutter about; *Fig (d'un lieu à un autre, d'une personne à une autre)* to flit about **2** *(être volage)* to be fickle, to be flighty **3** *(être inattentif)* to be inattentive; **son esprit papillonne** he/she can't keep his/her mind on things

papillonneur, -euse [papijɔnœr, -øz] **NM,F** *Natation* butterfly swimmer

papillotage [papijɔtaʒ] **NM 1** *(des yeux)* blinking; *(d'une lumière, d'un reflet)* flickering, dancing; *(des paupières)* fluttering **2** *Typ* mackling, slurring

papillotant, -e [papijɔtɑ̃, -ɑ̃t] **ADJ 1** *(qui cligne → œil)* blinking; *(→ paupière)* fluttering **2** *(scintillant → lumière, reflet)* flickering, dancing, flashing

papillote [papijɔt] **NF 1** *(bigoudi)* curlpaper; *Fig* **ta dissertation, tu peux en faire des papillotes** your essay isn't worth the paper it's written on **2** *Culin (pour gigot)* frill; **en papillotes** en papillote *(cooked in foil or paper parcels)* **3** *(papier de bonbon) Br* sweet *or Am* candy wrapper; *(bonbon)* = special kind of sweet with bright shiny wrapper available at Christmas

papillotement [papijɔtmɑ̃] **NM 1** *(clignement → des yeux)* blinking; *(→ des paupières)* fluttering

2 *(scintillement → d'une lumière, d'un reflet)* flickering, flashing, dancing **3** *Cin & TV* flicker

papilloter [3] [papijɔte] **VI 1** *(œil)* to blink; *(paupière)* to flicker, to flutter **2** *(lumière, reflet)* to flicker, to flash, to dance

VT *Culin (dans du papier)* to wrap in buttered paper; *(dans de l'aluminium)* to wrap in foil

papin [papɛ̃] **NM** *Belg* poultice

Papineau [papino] **NM** *Can* **ne pas être la tête à P.** to be none too bright

papion [papjɔ̃] *Zool* **NM** baboon

❑ **papions NMPL** Papio

papisme [papism] **NM** papism, popery

papiste [papist] **ADJ** papist

NMF papist

papivore [papivɔr] **NMF** *Fam* bookworm, avid reader

papotage [papɔtaʒ] **NM** *Fam (action)* chattering, *Br* nattering; *(discussion)* chatter, chit-chat, *Br* natter

papoter [3] [papɔte] **VI** *Fam* to chat, *Br* to natter; **j'adore p.** I love a good chat *or Br* natter; **nous avons passé la journée à p.** we spent the day chatting *or Am* shooting the breeze

papou, -e [papu] **ADJ** Papuan

❑ **Papou, -e NM,F** Papuan

Papouasie [papwazi] **NF la P.** Papua

Papouasie-Nouvelle-Guinée [papwazinuvɛlgine] **NF la P.** Papua New Guinea; **vivre en P.** to live in Papua New Guinea; **aller en P.** to go to Papua New Guinea

papouilles [papuj] **NFPL** *Fam* **faire des p. à un bébé** to give a baby a little tickle; **faire des p. à qn** to pet sb; **se faire des p.** to pet (each other)

paprika [paprika] **NM** paprika

papule [papyl] **NF** papule

papuleux, -euse [papylø, -øz] **ADJ** papulous

papy [papi] **NM** *Fam (grand-père)* grandad

papy-boom [papibum] **NM** *Hum* grandpa boom, elderly boom

papyrologie [papirɔlɔʒi] **NF** papyrology

papyrologue [papirɔlɔg] **NMF** papyrologist

papyrus [papirys] **NM** papyrus

paqson [paksɔ̃] = **pacson**

Pâque [pɑk] **NF** *Rel* **la P. (juive)** Passover, Pesach

pâque [pɑk] **NF** *(agneau pascal)* paschal lamb

paquebot [pakbo] **NM** liner

pâquerette [pɑkrɛt] **NF** daisy; *Fam* **voler au ras des pâquerettes** *(conversation, plaisanterie)* to be a bit lowbrow

Pâques [pɑk] **NM** Easter; **à P. ou à la Trinité** never in a month of Sundays; *Fam Vieilli* **faire P. avant les Rameaux,** *Can* **fêter P. avant carême** = to get pregnant before getting married; **l'île de P.** Easter Island

❑ **pâques NFPL joyeuses p.** Happy Easter; **faire ses p.** to take communion (at Easter); **p. fleuries** Palm Sunday

Culture

PÂQUES

In France, Easter is traditionally symbolized not only by eggs but also by bells; according to legend, church bells fly to Rome at Easter. At this time of the year, people offer each other chocolate eggs, bells, fish or hens.

paquet [pakɛ] **NM 1** *(colis)* parcel, package; *(ballot, liasse)* bundle; **faire un p.** to make up a parcel; **faire un p. de vieux journaux** to make up a bundle of old newspapers

2 *Com (marchandise emballée → gén)* packet, pack; *(→ de sucre, de farine)* bag, packet; *(→ de café, de pâtes, de lessive)* packet; *(→ de cigarettes) Br* packet, *Am* pack; **fumer un p. par jour** to smoke *Br* twenty *or Am* a pack a day; **du riz/du café en p.** pre-packed *or* packaged rice/coffee; **p. échantillon** sample pack; **p. économique** economy pack; **p. familial** family-size pack; **p. géant** giant-sized pack; **p. de présentation** presentation pack; **dans un joli p.** prettily gift-wrapped

3 *(valise)* bag; **mets tes paquets là** put your bags down here; **faire ses paquets** to pack one's bags

4 *Fam (quantité importante)* **tout un p. de** a pile *ou* stack of; **il y a un p. d'erreurs dans ce texte** there are a ton of *or* loads of mistakes in this text; *Fig* **mettre le p.** to pull out all the stops, to go all out; **lâcher le p.** to get things off one's chest, to unburden oneself; **toucher le p.** to make a packet *or* mint *or* pile; **il a touché un joli p.** he's made a packet

5 *(masse)* **les manifestants arrivent par petits paquets** the demonstrators are arriving in clusters *or* in small groups; **j'ai reçu un p. de neige sur la tête** a lump of snow fell on my head; **il tombait des paquets d'eau** the rain was coming down in sheets; *Naut* **un p. de mer** a big wave; *Fam* **sa mère est un p. de nerfs** his/her mother's a bundle *or* bag of nerves

6 *Sport* **p. (d'avants)** pack

7 *Ordinat* packet

8 *Bourse (d'actions, de valeurs)* parcel, block

9 *Écon & Fin* **p. fiscal** tax package

paquetage [paktaʒ] **NM** *Mil* kit, pack; **faire son p.** to get one's kit ready

paquet-cadeau [pakɛkado] *(pl* **paquets-cadeaux)** **NM** gift-wrapped purchase; **je vous fais un p.?** shall I gift-wrap it for you?

paqueté, -e [pakte] **ADJ** *Can Fam (ivre) Br* pissed, *Am* bombed

paqueter [24] [pakte] **VT** to parcel up

paqueteur, -euse [paktœr, -øz] **NM,F** packer

paquet-poste [pakɛpɔst] *(pl* **paquets-poste)** **NM** mail parcel

par[1] [par] **NM** *Golf* par

PAR[2] [par]

by **1, 4, 6** ▪ through **1** ▪ on **2** ▪ out of **5** ▪ per **7** ▪ with **8, 9**

PRÉP 1 *(indiquant la direction, le parcours)* by; *(en traversant un lieu)* through; **il est entré p. la porte de derrière** he came in by the back door; **il est arrivé p. la route** he came by road; **sors p. la fenêtre** go out by *or* through the window; **il est arrivé p. la gauche/p. la droite/p. le nord** he arrived from the left/the right/the north; **faut-il passer p. Paris?** do we have to go through *or* via Paris?; **il est passé p. la maison avant de ressortir** he dropped in before going off again; **il allait p. les rues** he was walking through the streets; **la nouvelle s'est répandue p. la ville** the news spread throughout the town

2 *(indiquant la position)* **elle est assise p. terre** she's sitting on the ground; **la neige avait fondu p. endroits** the snow had melted in places; *Naut* **p. 45 de latitude nord** lying at a latitude of 45 north; *Naut* **p. 10 brasses d'eau** in 10 fathoms of water; *Naut* **p. bâbord avant/arrière** on the port bow/stern

3 *(pendant)* **p. un beau jour d'été** on a fine summer's day; **p. une belle matinée de septembre** on a fine morning in September; **p. grand froid/grosse chaleur** in extreme cold/intense heat; **p. le passé** in the past; **p. moments** at times, from time to time; **p. les temps qui courent** these days; **p. deux fois** twice; **p. trois fois** three times, *Littéraire* thrice

4 *(indiquant le moyen, la manière)* by; **prends le couteau p. le manche** take the knife by the handle; **tenir qn p. la taille** to hold sb by the waist; **attraper qn p. les cheveux** to grab sb by the hair; **les lettres sont classées p. ordre d'arrivée** the letters are filed in order of arrival; **envoyer qch p. avion/e-mail** to send sth by airmail/e-mail; **p. air/terre/mer** by air/land/sea; **voyager p. bateau/le train** to travel by boat/train; **voyager p. avion** to travel by plane, to fly; **je l'ai appris p. la radio** I heard it on the radio; **nous sommes arrivés à ce résultat p. une équation** we obtained this result by (means of) an equation; **répondre p. oui ou p. non/p. la négative** to answer yes or no/in the negative; **obtenir qch p. la force/la douceur** to obtain sth by force/through kindness; **je suis avec toi p. la pensée** I'm thinking of you, my thoughts are with you

5 *(indiquant la cause, l'origine)* **faire qch p. habitude/caprice/plaisir/paresse** to do sth out of habit/on a whim/for the pleasure of it/out of laziness; **il n'a pas répondu p. négligence/manque de temps** he didn't answer out of carelessness/because he didn't have the time; **différer p. ses habitudes** to differ in one's habits; **je l'ai rencontré p. hasard** I met him by chance; **je le sais p. expérience** I know it from experience; **fidèle p. devoir** faithful out of duty; **ponctuelle p. habitude** punctual by *or* out of habit; **nous sommes cousins p. ma mère** we're cousins on my mother's side (of the family); **une tante p. alliance** an aunt by marriage

6 *(introduisant le complément d'agent)* by; **les récoltes ont été dévastées p. la grêle** the crops were ruined by the hail; **la maison a été achetée p. des étrangers** the house has been bought by foreigners; **le logiciel est protégé p. un code** the software is protected by *or* with a code; **faire faire qch p. qn** to have sth done by sb; **je l'ai découvert p. son intermédiaire** I discovered it through him/her; **je l'ai appris p. elle** I heard it from her, I learned of it through her; **ils veulent le faire p. eux-mêmes** they want to do it by *or* for themselves; **elles se sont rencontrées p. son intermédiaire** they met through him/her; **les deux appareils sont reliés p. un fil** the two devices are connected by a wire; **le 'Discours de la méthode', p. Descartes** the 'Discourse on Method' by Descartes

7 *(emploi distributif)* **une heure p. jour** one hour a *or* per day; **faire trois repas p. jour** to eat three meals a *or* per day; **100 euros p. personne** 100 euros per person; **une fois p. an** once a year; **un p. un** one by one; **heure p. heure** hour by hour; **mettez-vous deux p. deux** line up in twos; **ils arrivaient p. petits groupes/centaines** they arrived in small groups/in their hundreds

8 *(avec les verbes "commencer" et "finir")* **ça finira p. arriver/p. ressembler à quelque chose** it will end up happening/looking like something; **commence p. travailler** start (off) by working; **il a fini p. avouer** he eventually owned up; **le concert débuta p. une sonate de Mozart** the concert opened with a sonata by Mozart; **notre programme se terminera p. les informations à 23 heures 40** our programmes for the evening will end with the news at 11.40

9 *(suivi d'un verbe)* **il se fatigue p. trop écrire** he tires himself with writing too much; *Littéraire* **l'amour ne cesse de se sauver p. aimer encore mieux ce qu'il aime** love is for ever effecting its own salvation by loving still better the object of its love

❑ **de par PRÉP 1** *(par l'ordre de)* **de p. la loi** according to the law; **de p. le roi** in the name of the king

2 *Littéraire (dans l'espace)* throughout; **de p. le monde** all over *or* throughout the world

3 *(du fait de)* by virtue of; **de p. son éducation, il est tout à fait à l'aise dans ce milieu** by virtue of his upbringing, he is perfectly at ease in this environment

❑ **par-ci par-là ADV 1** *(dans l'espace)* here and there; **des livres traînaient p.-ci p.-là** books were lying around here and there

2 *(dans le temps)* now and then, from time to time, every now and then *or* again

3 *(marquant la répétition)* **avec lui, c'est mon yacht p.-ci, mon avion personnel p.-là** it's my yacht this, my plane that, all the time with him

para [para] **NM** *Fam (gén)* parachutist[■]; *Mil* para

para- [para] **PRÉF 1** *(en marge de)* para- **2** *(qui protège)* para-, anti- **3** *Chim* para-

parabase [parabaz] **NF** *Littérature* parabasis

parabellum [parabɛlɔm] **NM** *Hist* automatic pistol

paraben [parabɛn] **NM** *Chim* paraben

parabiose [parabjoz] **NF** *Biol* parabiosis

parablaste [parablast] **NM** *Biol* parablast

parabole [parabɔl] **NF 1** *Littérature & Rel* parable **2** *Math* parabola **3** *Tél (antenne)* satellite dish, parabolic dish, *Am* dish antenna

parabolique [parabɔlik] **ADJ 1** *Littérature & Rel* parabolic, parabolical **2** *Math* parabolic **3** *(miroir)* parabolic; **radiateur p.** electric fire *(with parabolic reflector)*

paraboliquement [parabɔlikmɑ̃] **ADV** *Littérature & Math* parabolically

paraboloïde [parabɔlɔid] **NM** *Géom* paraboloid

Paracelse [parasɛls] **NPR** Paracelsus

paracentèse [parasɛ̃tɛz] **NF** *Méd* paracentesis

paracétamol [parasetamɔl] **NM** paracetamol; **deux cachets de p.** two paracetamol

parachèvement [paraʃɛvmɑ̃] **NM** (action) completion; (résultat) crowning

parachever [19] [paraʃve] **VT** to complete; **p. un travail** to complete a piece of work; **p. un tableau** to put the finishing touches to a painting

parachimie [paraʃimi] **NF** parachemicals industry, = branch of the chemical industry involving the manufacture of paint, glue, cosmetics and pharmaceutical products

parachronisme [parakrɔnism] **NM** parachronism

parachutage [paraʃytaʒ] **NM 1** (de soldats) parachuting, parachute drop; (de vivres, matériel) parachute drop **2** Fam (d'un candidat) = bringing in a candidate from outside the constituency **3** Fam (dans une entreprise) parachuting in, = bringing an outsider into a firm

parachutal, -e, -aux, -ales [paraʃytal, -o] **ADJ** Zool **vol p.** gliding

parachute [paraʃyt] **NM** parachute; **faire du p.** to go parachuting; Fig **sans p.** without a parachute or a safety-net; **p. ascensionnel** (tracté par véhicule) parascending; (tracté par bateau) parasailing; **p. dorsal** backpack parachute; **p. extracteur** pilot chute; **p. de freinage** parabrake; **p. à rubans** ring slot parachute; **p. à tuyères** ribbon parachute; **p. ventral** lap-pack or chest-pack parachute

parachuter [3] [paraʃyte] **VT 1** Mil & Sport to parachute **2** Fam (candidat) to parachute in **3** Fam (dans une entreprise) **il a été parachuté directeur dans une succursale** he was pitchforked or parachuted into the job of branch manager

parachutisme [paraʃytism] **NM** parachuting; **faire du p.** to go parachuting; **p. ascensionnel** parascending; **p. en chute libre** skydiving

parachutiste [paraʃytist] **NMF 1** Sport parachutist **2** Mil paratrooper; **parachutistes** (corps d'armée) paratroops, paratroopers
■ **ADJ** **troupes parachutistes** paratroops, paratroopers

Paraclet [paraklɛ] **NM** Rel **le P.** the Paraclete

paraclinique [paraklinik] **ADJ** paraclinical

paracommercial, -e, -aux, -ales [parakɔmɛrsjal, -o] **ADJ** relating to parallel trade

paracommercialisme [parakɔmɛrsjalism] **NM** parallel trade

parade [parad] **NF 1** (défilé) parade; **la grande p. du cirque** the grand finale (at the circus); **faire p. de** (connaissances, richesse) to show off, to parade, to display **2** Zool **p. nuptiale** courtship display **3** Boxe (escrime) parry; Escrime parade, parry; Équitation pulling up; Ftbl save **4** (riposte) retort, reply, riposte; **nous devons trouver la p.** we must find a way of counterattacking
□ **de parade** **ADJ 1** (ornemental) ceremonial **2** (feint) **une amabilité de p.** an outward show of friendliness

parade ground [paradgrund] **NM** Belg parade ground

parader [3] [parade] **VI 1** (troupes) to parade **2** Équitation to execute a dressage **3** (personne) to show off, to pose, to strut about

paradeur, -euse [paradœr, -øz] **NM,F** show-off, Br poser, poseur

paradigmatique [paradigmatik] **ADJ** paradigmatic
■ **NF** Ling paradigmatics (singulier)

paradigme [paradigm] **NM** paradigm; **p. économique** economic paradigm

paradis [paradi] **NM 1** Rel paradise, heaven; **ce petit village est un véritable p.** this little village is heaven on earth or paradise; **aller au p.** to go to heaven; **p. fiscal** tax haven; **le P. terrestre** the Garden of Eden or Earthly Paradise; Fig heaven on earth; **le P. Latin** = famous cabaret in Paris **2** Théât **le p.** the (top) gallery, Br the gods

──────────

'Le Paradis perdu' Milton 'Paradise Lost'

──────────

'Le Paradis reconquis' Milton 'Paradise Regained'

Allusion

Le vert paradis des amours enfantines

This comes from a poem, Moesta et errabunda, from Baudelaire's Les Fleurs du mal, in which he evokes the lost world of happy childhood, which the expression now generally suggests. It means literally "the green paradise of our childhood loves".

Allusion

Les paradis artificiels

In a prose poem of 1860 with this title, Baudelaire speaks of how taking drugs can make the user feel he is in paradise. The expression is still used today of a drug-induced state, but the more negative oblivion rather than euphoria is emphasized, eg **De nombreux jeunes en difficulté ont recours aux paradis artificiels** ("Many troubled young people turn to the oblivion of drugs").

---

paradisiaque [paradizjak] **ADJ** heavenly, Sout paradisiacal; **une île p.** a paradise island

paradisier [paradizje] **NM** bird of paradise

parados [parado] **NM** Archit parados

paradoxal, -e, -aux, -ales [paradɔksal, -o] **ADJ 1** (contradictoire) paradoxical; **c'est une situation paradoxale** it's a paradoxical situation; **il a l'esprit p.** he's got a perverse way of looking at things **2** (déconcertant) unexpected, paradoxical; **sa présence parmi eux était paradoxale** it was surprising to find him/her among them **3** Méd paradoxical

paradoxalement [paradɔksalmɑ̃] **ADV** paradoxically

paradoxe [paradɔks] **NM** paradox; Écon **p. de l'épargne** paradox of thrift

parafe [paraf] = **paraphe**

parafer [parafe] = **parapher**

parafeur [parafœr] = **parapheur**

paraffinage [parafinaʒ] **NM** paraffining

paraffine [parafin] **NF** Chim paraffin (wax); **mettre de la p. sur des confitures** to seal jam jars with (paraffin) wax

paraffiner [3] [parafine] **VT** to paraffin

parafiscal, -e, -aux, -ales [parafiskal, -o] **ADJ** (taxe) exceptional, special

parafiscalité [parafiskalite] **NF** indirect taxation, special taxation

paraformaldéhyde [paraformaldeid] **NM** Chim paraformaldehyde

paraforme [parafɔrm] **NM** Chim paraform

parafoudre [parafudr] **NM** lightning conductor

parage [paraʒ] **NM 1** Culin & Méd dressing **2** Vieilli (extraction) **de haut p.** of high lineage, high-born

paragenèse [paraʒənɛz] **NF** Géol paragenesis

parages [paraʒ] **NMPL 1** (environs) area, surroundings; **il habite (quelque part) dans les p.** he lives around here somewhere; **est-ce qu'il est dans les p.?** is he around?; **il est dans les p.** he's around somewhere; **dans les p. de...** in the vicinity of..., near... **2** Naut waters; **les p. du cap Horn** the waters off Cape Horn

paragraphe [paragraf] **NM 1** (passage) paragraph **2** (signe typographique) paragraph (sign), par

paragraphie [paragrafi] **NF** Psy paragraphia

paragrêle [paragrɛl] **NM** anti-hail device
■ **ADJ INV** anti-hail

Paraguay [paragwɛ] **NM** **le P.** Paraguay; **vivre au P.** to live in Paraguay; **aller au P.** to go to Paraguay

paraguayen, -enne [paragwɛjɛ̃, -ɛn] **ADJ** Paraguayan
□ **Paraguayen, -enne** **NM,F** Paraguayan

para-hôtellerie [paraotɛlri] **NF** serviced accommodation industry

parahydrogène [paraidrɔʒɛn] **NM** Chim parahydrogen

parais etc voir **paraître²**

paraison [parɛzɔ̃] **NF** (masse de verre) parison

paraître¹ [parɛtr] **NM** **le p.** appearance, appearances; **l'être et le p.** appearance and reality

paraître² [91] [parɛtr] **VI 1** (se montrer → soleil) to appear, to come out; (→ émotion) to show; (→ personne attendue) to appear, to turn up; (→ dignitaire, prince) to appear, to make a public appearance; (→ acteur) to appear; **il n'a pas paru au bureau depuis huit jours** he hasn't

turned up or appeared at the office for a week now; **laisser p. son émotion** to let one's emotion show

2 (figurer) to appear; **l'usine nous appartient, mais notre logo n'y paraît pas** the factory belongs to us, but our logo isn't (displayed) on it

3 (être publié → livre) to be published, to come out, to appear; **faire p. une petite annonce dans un journal** to put an advertisement in a paper; **à p.** (livre) forthcoming; **vient de p.** just published

4 (sembler) to appear, to seem, to look; **il ne paraît pas très à l'aise dans son costume** he doesn't seem (to be) very comfortable in his suit; **p. plus jeune que l'on n'est** to seem or to look younger than one is; **il paraît moins fatigué qu'hier** he appears to be or looks less tired than yesterday; **il parut céder** he looked as though he was giving in; **paraît-il** apparently; **tu as retrouvé du travail, paraît-il** I hear you've got a new job

5 (se donner en spectacle) to show off; **il cherche toujours à p.** he's always showing off
■ **VT** 75 ans? vous ne les paraissez pas 75 years old? you don't look it
■ **V IMPERSONNEL** ça ne paraît pas (mais...) (ça ne se voit pas) it doesn't look like it (but...); **elle a 50 ans, ça ne paraît pas** she doesn't look 50, does she?; **il n'y paraît pas** it doesn't show; **il n'y paraît pas, mais le plancher est mouillé** it doesn't look like it, but the floor is wet; **dans une semaine il n'y paraîtra plus** in a week it won't show any more; **je tâche de l'aider sans qu'il y paraisse** I try to help him without letting it show; **il me paraît préférable de se décider maintenant** I think it's better or it seems better to make up our minds now; **vous êtes renvoyé? – il paraît** have you been fired? – it looks like it or so it seems; **il paraît que...** I've heard (that)..., it would seem (that)...; **il paraîtrait qu'il a trois enfants** it would seem or appear (that) he's got three children; Fam **paraît que tu vas te marier!** I hear you're getting married!; **à ce qu'il paraît** apparently

paralalie [paralali] **NF** Méd paralalia

paralangage [paralɑ̃gaʒ] **NM** paralanguage

paraldéhyde [paraldeid] **NM** Chim paraldehyde

paralexie [paralɛksi] **NF** Méd paralexia

paralinguistique [paralɛ̃gɥistik] **ADJ** paralinguistic
■ **NF** paralinguistics (singulier)

paralipse [paralips] **NF** Littérature paralipsis, paraleipsis

paralittéraire [paraliterɛr] **ADJ** **les productions paralittéraires** minor literary works

paralittérature [paraliteratyr] **NF** literature with a small "l", minor literary works

parallactique [paralaktik] **ADJ** Astron, Géom & Phot parallactic

parallaxe [paralaks] **NF** Astron, Géom & Phot parallax; **erreur de p.** parallax error; **p. solaire** solar parallax

parallèle [paralɛl] **ADJ 1** Géom, Sport & Ordinat parallel (à to); **les deux droites sont parallèles** the two lines are parallel; **la droite AB est p. à la droite CD** line AB is parallel to line CD

2 (comparable → données, résultats) parallel, comparable, similar; **nous avons eu des carrières parallèles** we had similar careers

3 (non officiel → festival) unofficial, fringe (avant n); (→ marché, transaction) unofficial; (→ police) unofficial, secret; **mener une vie p.** to live a double life

4 Ordinat (port, imprimante, interface) parallel
■ **NM 1** Astron & Géog parallel; **p. de latitude** parallel of latitude

2 (comparaison) parallel; **établir un p. entre deux phénomènes** to draw a parallel between two phenomena

3 Sport parallel turning or skiing
■ **NF** Géom parallel (line)

□ **en parallèle** **ADV 1** (en balance) **mettre deux faits en p.** to draw a parallel between or to compare two facts; **mettre qch en p. avec qch** to compare sth with sth

2 Ordinat (in) parallel

3 Élec in parallel

parallèlement [paralɛlmɑ̃] **ADV 1** Géom **p. à** in a

parallel to 2 *Sport* **skier p.** to do parallel turns **3** *(simultanément)* at the same time; **p. à** at the same time as; **p. à mon cours de danse, je donne aussi un cours de musique** I teach music as well as dance

parallélépipède [paralelepipɛd] NM *Géom* parallelepiped

parallélépipédique [paralelepipedik] ADJ *Géom* parallelepipedal

parallélisme [paralelism] NM **1** *Géom* parallelism **2** *Aut* wheel alignment; **il y a un défaut de p.** there's something wrong with the alignment, the wheels aren't properly aligned **3** *Sport* parallel turning *or* skiing **4** *(concordance)* parallel, concordance; **établir un p. entre deux faits** to draw a parallel between two facts **5** *Jur* **p. des formes** = principle by which the reversal of a decision is subject to the same formalities that were required to make it

parallélogramme [paralelogram] NM **1** *Géom* parallelogram **2** *Aut* **p. de Watt** Watt governor

paralogique [paralɔʒik] ADJ paralogic, paralogical

paralogisme [paralɔʒism] NM paralogism

paralympique [paralɛ̃pik] ADJ Paralympic

paralysant, -e [paraliza, -ãt] ADJ *Méd & Fig* paralysing

paralysé, -e [paralize] ADJ paralysed; **elle a le bras droit p.** her right arm is paralysed; **être p. de peur** to be petrified, to be paralysed with fear; **nous sommes paralysés par l'insuffisance des fonds** we are hamstrung by a lack of funds
NM,F *Méd* paralytic

paralyser [3] [paralize] VT **1** *Méd* to paralyse **2** *(figer, inhiber → gén)* to paralyse; *(→ économie, pays)* to cripple; *(→ circulation)* to bring to a standstill; **la ville est paralysée par la grève** the town is paralysed by the strike; **la fumée paralyse l'action des sauveteurs** the smoke is paralysing rescue work; **ce genre de situation me paralyse** I'm petrified in that kind of situation; **paralysé par le froid** paralysed *or* numb with cold; **paralysé par la peur** petrified, paralysed with fear; **paralysé par le brouillard** fogbound; **paralysé par la neige** snow-bound

paralysie [paralizi] NF **1** *Méd* paralysis; **p. de Bell** Bell's palsy; **p. cérébrale** cerebral palsy; **p. faciale** facial palsy; **p. générale (progressive)** creeping paralysis; **p. du sommeil** common sleep paralysis **2** *(arrêt)* paralysis, paralysation; **la p. de la volonté** paralysis of the will; **la grève a provoqué la p. des transports** the strike has paralysed the transport system

paralytique [paralitik] *Méd* ADJ paralytic
NMF paralytic

paramagnétique [paramaɲetik] ADJ *Phys* paramagnetic

paramagnétisme [paramaɲetism] NM *Phys* paramagnetism

Paramaribo [paramaribo] NM *Géog* Paramaribo

paramécie [paramesi] NF *Zool* paramecium

paramédical, -e, -aux, -ales [paramedikal, -o] ADJ paramedical; **personnel p.** paramedics

paramétrable [parametrabl] ADJ *Ordinat* configurable; **p. par l'utilisateur** user-definable

paramétrage [parametraʒ] NM *Ordinat* configuration

paramètre [parametr] NM **1** *Math* parameter **2** *(élément variable)* parameter, factor **3** *Anat* parametrium **4** *Ordinat* parameter, setting; *(du DOS)* switch

paramétrer [18] [parametre] VT *Ordinat* to configure

paramétrique [parametrik] ADJ parametric, parametrical

paramilitaire [paramiliter] ADJ paramilitary
NMF paramilitary

paramnésie [paramnezi] NF *Méd* paramnesia

paranéoplasique [paraneoplazik] ADJ *Méd* paraneoplastic; **syndrome p.** paraneoplastic syndrome

parangon [parãgɔ̃] NM *Littéraire* paragon; **p. de vertu** paragon of virtue

parangonnage [parãgɔnaʒ] NM *Typ* justification

parangonner [3] [parãgɔne] VT *Typ* to justify

parano [parano] *Fam* ADJ *(abrév* **paranoïaque***)* paranoid■
NMF *(abrév* **paranoïaque***) (personne)* paranoid person■; **c'est un/une p.** he's/she's paranoid

NF *(abrév* **paranoïa***) (maladie)* paranoia■; **tu es en pleine p.!** you're being completely paranoid!■; **arrête ta p.!** stop being paranoid!■

paranoïa [paranɔja] NF paranoia; **tu es en pleine p.!** you're being completely paranoid!■

paranoïaque [paranɔjak] ADJ paranoiac, paranoid
NMF paranoiac

paranoïde [paranɔid] ADJ paranoid

paranormal, -e, -aux, -ales [paranɔrmal, -o] ADJ paranormal
NM **le p.** the paranormal

paranthrope [parãtrɔp] NM paranthropus

parapente [parapãt] NM *(activité)* paragliding; *(parachute)* paraglider; **faire du p.** to go paragliding

parapentiste [parapãtist] NMF paraglider

parapet [parapɛ] NM *Constr* parapet

parapétrolier, -ère [parapetrɔlje, -ɛr] ADJ **industrie/société parapétrolière** oil and gas industry/company

parapharmacie [parafarmasi] NF **1** *(produits)* (non-pharmaceutical) *Br* chemist's *or Am* druggist's merchandise **2** *(magasin)* = *Br* chemist's *or Am* druggist's selling personal hygiene products, ≃ *Am* drugstore

paraphasie [parafazi] NF *Méd* paraphasia

paraphe [paraf] NM **1** *(pour authentifier)* initials; *(pour décorer)* flourish, paraph **2** *Jur ou Sout (signature)* signature

parapher [3] [parafe] VT **1** *(pour authentifier) Br* to initial, *Am* to initialize **2** *Jur ou Sout (signer)* to sign

paraphernal, -e, -aux, -ales [parafɛrnal, -o] ADJ *Jur* **biens paraphernaux** paraphernalia

parapheur [parafœr] NM *(classeur)* signature book

paraphimosis [parafimozis] NM *Méd* paraphimosis

paraphlébite [paraflebit] NF *Méd* periphlebitis

paraphrase [parafraz] NF paraphrase; **faire de la p.** to paraphrase

paraphraser [3] [parafraze] VT to paraphrase; **pour p. Malraux,...** to quote Malraux,...

paraphraseur, -euse [parafrazœr, -øz] NM,F paraphraser

paraphrastique [parafrastik] ADJ paraphrastic

paraphrénie [parafreni] NF *Psy* paraphrenia

paraphyse [parafiz] NF *Bot* paraphysis

paraplégie [parapleʒi] NF *Méd* paraplegia

paraplégique [parapleʒik] *Méd* ADJ paraplegic
NMF paraplegic

parapluie [paraplɥi] NM **1** *(accessoire)* umbrella; **p. de golf** golf umbrella **2** *Pol* **p. nucléaire** *ou* **atomique** nuclear umbrella **3** *Fam (passe-partout)* skeleton key■ *(for spring locks)*

'Les Parapluies de Cherbourg' *Demy* 'The Umbrellas of Cherbourg'

parapode [parapɔd] NM *Zool* parapodium

parapsychique [parapsiʃik] ADJ parapsychological

parapsychologie [parapsikɔlɔʒi] NF parapsychology

parapsychologique [parapsikɔlɔʒik] ADJ parapsychological

parapsychologue [parapsikɔlɔg] NMF parapsychologist

parapublic, -ique [parapyblik] ADJ *(entreprise)* part government-owned

parascève [parasɛv] NF *Rel* **1** *(dans la religion juive)* parasceve **2** *(dans la religion catholique)* parasceve, Good Friday

parasciences [parasjãs] NFPL sciences of the paranormal

parascolaire [paraskɔler] ADJ *(activité)* extracurricular; *(édition, ouvrage)* self-study

parasélène [paraselɛn] NF *Astron* paraselene

parasexualité [parasɛksɥalite] NF *Biol* parasexuality

parasismique [parasismik] = **antisismique**

parasitaire [parazitɛr] ADJ *Biol & Fig* parasitic

parasite [parazit] ADJ **1** *Biol* parasitic, parasitical **2** *Élec* **bruit p.** interference **3** *Fig (superflu)* unnecessary, superfluous
NM **1** *Biol* parasite **2** *(personne)* parasite, scrounger

❏ **parasites** NMPL *Rad, TV & Tél* interference *(UNCOUNT)*, *Br* atmospherics; *Tél* noise, static; **il y a des parasites sur la ligne** the line's bad, there's static on the line

parasiter [3] [parazite] VT **1** *Biol* to live as a parasite on, to be parasitic on, to parasitize; *Fig* **p. la société** to be a parasite on society; *Fam* **je me suis fait p. par un ancien copain** an old friend came around to sponge off me **2** *Rad, TV & Tél* to interfere with, to cause interference on

parasiticide [parazitisid] *Biol* ADJ parasiticidal
NM parasiticide

parasitique [parazitik] ADJ parasitic, parasitical

parasitisme [parazitism] NM **1** *Biol* parasitism **2** *Fig* parasitical behaviour, parasitism **3** *Com* **p. commercial** commercial parasitism

parasitologie [parazitɔlɔʒi] NF *Biol* parasitology

parasitologique [parazitɔlɔʒik] *Méd* parasitological

parasitologue [parazitɔlɔg] NMF *Biol* parasitologist

parasitose [parazitoz] NF *Méd* parasitosis

parasol [parasɔl] NM **1** *(en ville, dans un jardin)* parasol, sunshade; *(pour la plage)* beach umbrella, parasol **2** *Aviat* parasol (wing)

parastatal, -e, -aux, -ales [parastatal, -o] *Belg* ADJ semi-public
NM semi-public organization

parasympathique [parasɛ̃patik] *Méd* ADJ parasympathetic
NM parasympathetic nervous system

parasympatholytique [parasɛ̃patɔlitik] *Méd* ADJ parasympatholytic
NM parasympatholytic

parasympathomimétique [parasɛ̃patɔmimetik] *Méd* ADJ parasympathomimetic
NM parasympathomimetic

parasynthétique [parasɛ̃tetik] *Ling* ADJ parasynthetic; **dérivation p.** parasynthesis
NM parasyntheton

paratactique [parataktik] ADJ *Gram* paratactic

parataxe [parataks] NF *Gram* parataxis

paratexte [paratɛkst] NM *Littérature* title, preface and epigraph *(as opposed to the actual text of a literary work)*

parathormone [paratɔrmɔn] NF *Physiol* parathormone

parathyroïde [paratirɔid] NF *Anat* parathyroid (gland)

parathyroïdien, -enne [paratirɔidjɛ̃, -ɛn] ADJ *Anat* parathyroid

paratonnerre [paratɔnɛr] NM lightning conductor

parâtre [parɑtr] NM **1** *Vieilli (beau-père)* father-in-law **2** *(mauvais père)* bad father

paratyphique [paratifik] ADJ *Méd* paratyphoid

paratyphoïde [paratifɔid] *Méd* ADJ paratyphoid
NF paratyphoid (fever)

paravalanche [paravalɑ̃ʃ] ADJ **mur** *ou* **installation p.** avalanche barrier *or* wall
NM avalanche barrier *or* wall

paravent [paravɑ̃] NM **1** *(écran)* (folding) screen *or* partition **2** *Fig* (smoke)screen, cover; **cette société leur sert de p. pour d'autres activités** the company is a screen *or* front for their other activities

'Les Paravents' *Genet* 'The Screens'

paraxial, -e, -aux, -ales [paraksjal, -o] ADJ *Opt* paraxial

parbleu [parblø] EXCLAM *Vieilli* by Jove!; **je l'ai jeté dehors, p.!** I kicked him out, by Jove!

parc [park] NM **1** *(enclos → à bétail)* pen, enclosure; *(→ à moutons)* fold; *(→ pour bébé)* pen, playpen; **p. à bestiaux** cattle pen; **p. de stationnement** *Br* car park, *Am* parking lot **2** *Pêche* bed; **p. à huîtres** oyster bed **3** *(jardin public)* park; *(domaine privé)* park, grounds; **p. animalier** safari park; **p. aquatique** water park; **p. d'attractions** amusement park; **p. de loisirs** leisure park; **p. national** national park; **le p. national Kruger** Kruger National Park; **le p. national Serengeti** Serengeti National Park; **le p. national du Yosemite** Yosemite National Park; **p. naturel** nature reserve; **le p. des Princes** = large sports stadium in Paris, formerly used for international football and

par-par

rugby matches; **p. régional** regional park; **p. à thème** theme park; **p. zoologique** zoo, zoological gardens

4 *Com* **p. des expositions** exhibition centre; **p. d'activités** *(zone)* business park

5 *(unités d'équipement)* **p. automobile** *(dans une entreprise)* fleet of cars; **le p. automobile français** the total number of cars in France; **notre p. ferroviaire** our (total) rolling stock; **p. immobilier** housing stock; **p. informatique** computer park; **p. d'ordinateurs** computer population, total number of computers in service; **p. technologique** technology park

6 *Ind (entrepôt)* depot; *Can* **p. industriel** industrial *Br* estate *or Am* park

7 **p. éolien, p. d'éoliennes** wind farm

parcage [parkaʒ] NM 1 *(enfermement → d'animaux)* penning in *or* up; *(→ de prisonniers)* confining 2 *Agr (pour fertiliser)* fold-manuring 3 *Aut* parking 4 *Pêche* bedding 5 *Ordinat (de disque dur)* parking; **effectuer le p. d'un disque** to park a disk 6 *Bourse* **p. d'actions** warehousing

parcellaire [parselɛr] ADJ 1 *Admin & Jur* **cadastre** *ou* **plan p.** cadastral survey; **enquête/état p.** division/list of properties *(in plots for compulsory purchase order)* 2 *(fractionné → connaissances, tâche)* fragmented; *Ind* **travail p.** division of labour

NM *Admin & Jur* (detailed survey of) lots

parcellarisation [parselarizasjɔ̃] = **parcellisation**

parcellariser [parselarize] = **parcelliser**

parcelle [parsɛl] NF 1 *Admin* parcel, plot; *(lopin)* plot (of land) 2 *(morceau → d'or)* particle 3 *Fig (petite partie)* **une p. de liberté** a (tiny) bit of freedom; **pas une p. de vérité** not a grain *or* shred of truth; **pas la moindre p. d'intelligence/de vérité** not an ounce of intelligence/truth

parcellisation [parselizasjɔ̃] NF 1 *(gén)* fragmentation, division 2 *Ind* **p. des tâches** division of labour

parcelliser [3] [parselize] VT *(gén)* to fragment, to divide; *(travail)* to break down into individual operations

parce que [parskə] CONJ because; **elle n'est pas venue parce qu'elle se sentait fatiguée** she didn't come because she was feeling tired; **ce n'est pas parce qu'on a eu une dispute que je ne vais plus te parler** just because we've had an argument doesn't mean I'm never going to speak to you again; **il ne répondit rien p. très gêné** he didn't reply because he was so embarrassed; *Fam* **pourquoi pleures-tu? – p.!** why are you crying? – because!; **d'accord, mais c'est bien p. c'est vous!** OK, but only because it's you!

parchemin [parʃəmɛ̃] NM 1 *(peau, document)* parchment 2 *Fam Vieilli (diplôme)* diploma, degree 3 *(titre de noblesse)* title of nobility

parcheminé, -e [parʃəmine] ADJ 1 *(papier)* with a parchment finish 2 *(peau)* wrinkled; *(visage)* wizened

parcheminer [3] [parʃəmine] VT *(papier)* to give a parchment finish to

▸**se parcheminer** VPR *(peau)* to shrivel up, to become shrivelled

parchet [parʃɛ] NM *Suisse* = plot of land for growing vines

parcimonie [parsimɔni] NF parsimony, parsimoniousness

▫ **avec parcimonie** ADV parsimoniously, sparingly; **il distribue les compliments avec p.** he's sparing with his praise

parcimonieuse [parsimɔnjøz] *voir* **parcimonieux**

parcimonieusement [parsimɔnjøzmɑ̃] ADV parsimoniously, sparingly; **distribuer les compliments p.** to be sparing with one's compliments

parcimonieux, -euse [parsimɔnjø, -øz] ADJ parsimonious, sparing

par-ci, par-là [parsiparla] ADV *voir* **par**[2]

parcmètre [parkmɛtr] NM (parking) meter

parcomètre [parkɔmɛtr] NM *Can* (parking) meter

parcotrain [parkɔtrɛ̃] NM train users' *Br* car park *or Am* parking lot

parcourir [45] [parkurir] VT 1 *(distance → gén)* to cover; *(→ en courant)* to run; *(→ en marchant)* to walk; *(→ à cheval, à vélo)* to ride; **la distance à p. par les chevaux** the distance to be run *or* covered by the horses; **il reste deux kilomètres/un long chemin à p.** there are two kilometres/there is a long way to go; **chemin parcouru** distance covered; *Rail* **le prix du kilomètre parcouru** ≃ unit cost per passenger-mile

2 *(pour visiter)* to travel through; *(dans une quête)* to scour, to search (all over); **ils ont parcouru toute l'Amérique** they've travelled the length and breadth of America; **p. les mers** *(marin, bateau)* to sail the seas; **parcourant les montagnes à la recherche d'orchidées** looking for orchids all over the mountains, scouring the mountains for orchids; **je parcourais la ville à la recherche d'un emploi** I was searching all over town for a job

3 *(traverser → sujet: douleur, frisson)* to run through; **un murmure de protestation parcourut la salle** a murmur of protest ran through the room; **le pays est parcouru de canaux** the country has a network of canals

4 *(jeter un coup d'œil à → journal, roman, notes de cours)* to skim *or* to leaf through; *(→ lettre)* to glance at; *(→ document informatique)* to scroll through; **elle parcourut la liste des reçus** she scanned the list of successful students; **elle parcourut la scène du regard** her eyes scanned the scene

5 *Ordinat (document)* to scroll through

parcours [parkur] NM 1 *(trajet → d'une personne)* way, journey; *(→ d'un fleuve)* course; *Transp* route; **elle m'a questionné pendant tout le p.** she asked me questions all the way; **il a effectué le p. en deux heures** he did the trip *or* journey in two hours; **le car fait le p. entre la ville et la côte** the bus runs between the town and the coast; **je fais le p. à pied dans les deux sens** I walk both ways

2 *Fig (évolution personnelle)* career, record, path; **son p. scolaire a été irréprochable** he/she had a faultless school record; **il a eu le p. classique d'un homme d'État français** he had the archetypal training of *or* he followed the usual career path of a French statesman; **après le service militaire, nos p. ont été très différents** after we'd done our national service, we took very different paths

3 *Sport (de golf, de course à pied)* course; *(de course automobile)* circuit; **les chevaux font un p. de 20 kilomètres** the horses run over a distance of 20 kilometres; **p. du combattant** *Mil* assault course; *Fig* obstacle course

4 *Agr* pasture

parcouru, -e [parkury] PP *voir* **parcourir**

pardaf [pardaf] EXCLAM *Belg Fam* crash!

par-dedans [pardədɑ̃] ADV (on the) inside

par-dehors [pardəɔr] ADV (on the) outside

par-delà [pardəla] PRÉP beyond; **p. les mers** over the seas; **p. les siècles** across the centuries

par-derrière [pardɛrjɛr] PRÉP behind, round the back of; **passe p. la maison** go round the back of the house

ADV 1 *(par l'arrière)* from behind, at the rear; **on entre dans la cuisine p.** you get into the kitchen from behind *or* round the back; **ça se boutonne p.** it buttons at the back 2 *Fig (sournoisement)* **il me critique p.** he criticizes me behind my back; **il fait ses coups p.** he operates behind people's backs

par-dessous [pardəsu] PRÉP under, underneath; **passe p. la barrière** go under the fence

ADV underneath; **je suis passé p.** I crept underneath; **prendre qch p.** to get hold of sth underneath

pardessus [pardəsy] NM overcoat

▫ **pardessus** NMPL *Can* overshoes, galoshes

par-dessus [pardəsy] PRÉP 1 *(en franchissant)* over, above; **passe p. la grille** go over the railings

2 *(sur)* **porter un manteau p. sa veste** to wear an overcoat on top of one's jacket

3 *Fig* over; **elle est passée p. le directeur des ventes** she went over the head of the sales manager

ADV *(dans l'espace)* over; **saute p.!** jump over!; **j'ai mis un tee-shirt avec une chemise p.** I wore a T-shirt with a shirt on top *or* with a shirt over it

▫ **par-dessus tout** ADV most of all, above all; **j'aimais p. tout son sourire** what I loved most of all *or* above everything was his/her smile

par-devant [pardəvɑ̃] PRÉP *Admin & Jur* **p. notaire** in the presence of a lawyer *or Br* solicitor, with a lawyer *or Br* solicitor present; **tout a été fait p. notaire** everything was done in the proper legal way

ADV 1 *(passer)* round the front 2 *(ouvertement)* **p. il est toujours d'accord, mais par-derrière il ne fait que critiquer** he always agrees to your face, but does nothing but criticize behind your back

par-devers [pardəvɛr] PRÉP 1 *Jur (en présence de)* before, in the presence of 2 *(en la possession de)* **garder qch p. soi** to keep sth in one's possession *or* to oneself

pardi [pardi] EXCLAM of course!; **je l'ai jeté dehors, p.!** I kicked him out, of course *or* needless to say!

pardieu [pardjø] EXCLAM *Vieilli* by Jove!

pardon [pardɔ̃] NM 1 *(rémission)* forgiveness, *Sout* pardon; **demander p. à qn** to apologize to sb, to ask for sb's forgiveness; **je lui accordai mon p.** I forgave him/her; **pas de p. pour** no mercy for; **demander le p. de ses fautes** to beg mercy for one's sins; **demande p. à la dame** say sorry to *or* apologize to the lady; **p.?** *(pour faire répéter)* sorry?, (I beg your) pardon?; **p., auriez-vous un crayon?** excuse me, do you have a pencil?; **oh, p.!** *(pour s'excuser)* sorry!, excuse me!; *Ironique* (so) sorry!; **ah p., ce n'est pas ce que j'ai dit!** excuse me *or* pardon me, but that's NOT what I said; *Fam* **la mère est déjà désagréable, mais alors la fille, p.!** the mother's bad enough, but the daughter!; *Fam* **qu'est-ce qu'on a bien mangé, alors là, p.!** you should have seen how well we ate, it was something else!; **elle a de ces jambes, p.!** you should see the legs on her!

2 *(en Bretagne)* religious festival

3 *Rel* **le Grand P., le jour du P.** Yom Kippur, the Day of Atonement

pardonnable [pardɔnabl] ADJ excusable, forgivable, pardonable; **à son âge, on est p.!** it's excusable at that age!; **tu es p. d'avoir oublié** you can be forgiven for forgetting; **votre erreur n'est pas p.** your mistake is unforgivable *or* inexcusable; **je ne suis pas p.!** I have no excuse!

pardonner [3] [pardɔne] VT 1 *(oublier → offense)* to forgive, to excuse; *(→ péché)* to forgive, to pardon; **je pardonne les distractions, pas les méchancetés** I can forgive *or* excuse thoughtlessness, but not wickedness; **p. qch à qn** to forgive sb for sth; **allez, je te pardonne tout** all right, I'll let you off (everything); **p. ses péchés à qn** to forgive sb (for) his/her sins; **voilà des paroles qui ne te seront pas pardonnées** you won't be forgiven for saying that; **il ne me pardonne pas d'avoir eu raison** he won't forgive me for having been right; **est-ce que tu me pardonnes?** do you forgive me?, am I forgiven?; **mais vous êtes tout pardonné!** but of course you're forgiven!; **se faire p.** to be forgiven, to win forgiveness; **pour me/te/*etc* faire p.** to make it up; **pour se faire p. son retard** as a way of saying sorry for being late; *Rel* **pardonne-nous nos offenses** forgive us our trespasses

2 *(dans des formules de politesse)* to forgive, to excuse; **pardonnez ma curiosité** *ou* **pardonnez-moi si je suis indiscret mais...** I'm sorry if I'm being *or* excuse me for being nosy, but...; **pardonnez-moi d'insister** excuse me for being so insistent; **pardonnez-moi, mais vous oubliez un détail d'importance** excuse me, but you've forgotten an important point

USAGE ABSOLU to forgive; **apprendre à p.** to learn forgiveness *or* to forgive; **c'est un sport où la méforme ne pardonne pas** in this sport you can't afford to be unfit; **une distraction au volant, ça ne pardonne pas!** one slip in concentration at the wheel is fatal!

▸**se pardonner** VPR 1 *(emploi réfléchi)* **je ne me le pardonnerai jamais** I'll never forgive myself; **je ne me pardonnerai jamais de lui avoir menti** I'll never forgive myself for lying to him/her

2 *(emploi passif)* to be excused *or* forgiven; **une traîtrise ne se pardonne pas** treachery cannot be forgiven

3 *(emploi réciproque)* to forgive one another; **ils se sont pardonné leurs mensonges** they forgave each other's lies

paréage [pareaʒ] = **pariage**

pare-avalanches [paravalɑ̃ʃ] NM INV avalanche barrier *or* wall

pare-balles [parbal] ADJ INV bulletproof
NM INV bullet-shield

pare-brise [parbriz] NM INV *Br* windscreen, *Am* windshield; **p. feuilleté** laminated *Br* windscreen *or Am* windshield

pare-boue [parbu] NM INV mud flap

pare-chocs [parʃɔk] NM INV *Aut* bumper; **p. à absorption d'énergie** energy-absorbing bumper; **nous étions** *ou* **roulions p. contre p.** we were bumper to bumper
NMPL *Fam Hum (seins)* knockers, *Am* hooters

parèdre [parɛdr] *Rel* ADJ lesser, minor
NMF lesser *or* minor divinity

pare-éclats [parekla] NM INV **1** *Menuis* wooden stop **2** *Mil* shellproof screen

pare-étincelles [paretɛ̃sɛl] NM INV **1** *(écran)* sparkguard, fireguard **2** *Rail* spark arrester

pare-feu [parfø] ADJ INV **porte p.** fire door
NM INV **1** *(en forêt)* firebreak **2** *(d'une cheminée)* fireguard **3** *(de pompier)* (helmet) fire-shield **4** *Ordinat* firewall

pare-flammes [parflam] NM INV *Aut* flame arrester

pare-fumée [parfyme] ADJ INV *voir* **écran**
NM INV smoke extractor

parégorique [paregɔrik] ADJ paregoric

pareil, -eille [parɛj] ADJ **1** *(identique)* the same; **leurs bagues sont presque pareilles** their rings are almost identical *or* the same; **il n'y en a pas deux (de) pareils** no two are alike; **vous êtes (bien) tous pareils!** you're all alike *or* the same!; **et lui, qu'est-ce qu'on lui donne? – p., une orange** and what will we give him? – the same (thing), an orange; **comment vas-tu? – toujours p.!** how are you? – same as ever!; **c'est toujours p., personne n'ose se plaindre!** it's always the same, nobody ever dares complain!; **l'an dernier à pareille époque** this time last year; *Fam* **si ça ne te plaît pas, c'est p.** too bad if you don't like it
2 *(similaire)* the same; **tu as vu ses chaussures? – oui, j'en ai de pareilles** have you seen her shoes? – yes, I have a pair just like them; **p. à** the same as, just like; **toujours p. à lui-même** the same as always; *Littéraire* **p. à la rosée** like (the) dew, dew-like; *Fam* **p. que** (the) same as■; **ta jupe est pareille que la mienne** your skirt's the same as mine
3 *(de cette nature)* such (a); **un talent p.** *ou* **un p. talent est très rare** such talent is very rare; **comment peux-tu lire un journal p.?** how can you read such a paper?; **mais je n'ai jamais dit une chose pareille!** but I never said any such thing!; **je n'ai jamais rien vu de p.** I've never seen anything like it; **tu ne vas pas croire une chose pareille!** you're not going to believe something like that!; **on n'avait jamais vu (un) p. scandale!** there'd never been such a scandal!; **qui peut bien téléphoner à une heure pareille?** who could be phoning at this hour *or* time?; **en p. cas** in such a case; **en pareilles circonstances** in such circumstances; **dans de pareils moments, dans des moments pareils** at times like these
NM,F **ne pas avoir son p.** to be second to none; **elle n'a pas sa pareille pour arriver au mauvais moment!** there's nobody quite like her for turning up at the wrong moment!; *Vieilli* **son p./sa pareille** *(personne semblable)* another one like him/her; *(chose semblable)* another one like it; *Vieilli* **impossible de trouver le p.** it's impossible to find another one like it
NM *Fam* **c'est du p. au même** it's six of one and half a dozen of the other, same difference
ADV *Fam* **1** *(pareillement)* the same■; **on a tous fait p.** we all did the same (thing); **je grossis, pourtant je mange p.** I'm putting on weight, but I'm not eating any differently; **on n'a pas dû comprendre p.** we can't have understood the same thing; **ils sont habillés p.** they're dressed the same
2 *Can (quand même)* all the same, nevertheless
3 *Can (exactement)* **p. comme** just like, just the same as; **c'est p. comme si j'étais au ciel!** it's just like being in heaven!
❑ **pareille** NF **rendre la pareille à qn** *(se venger)* to get one's own back on sb, to pay sb back; *(faire preuve de reconnaissance)* to repay sb, to pay sb back; **si on me frappe, je rends la pareille** if anyone hits me I hit them back; *Belg* **(en) dire/faire une pareille** *ou* **de pareilles** to say/do such an outlandish thing
❑ **pareils** NMPL **nos pareils** *(semblables)* our fellow men; *(égaux)* our equals *or* peers; **vous et vos pareils!** you and your kind!
❑ **sans pareil, sans pareille** ADJ *(éclat, beauté, courage)* unrivalled, unequalled; *(talent, habileté)* unparalleled, unequalled; *(artiste, cuisinière)* unequalled, *Sout* peerless; **tu vas voir, la cuisine est sans pareille!** you'll see, the food is unique *or* beyond compare!

pareillement [parɛjmɑ̃] ADV **1** *(de la même manière)* in the same way; **ils s'habillent p.** they dress the same *or* in the same way
2 *(aussi)* equally, likewise; **j'ai été p. surprise** I was equally surprised, I was surprised too; **nous avons été p. heureux de le voir** *(nous deux)* we were both happy to see him; *(nous tous)* we all were happy to see him; **bonne soirée! – et à vous p.!** have a nice evening! – you too!

parélie [pareli] NM parhelion

parement [parmɑ̃] NM **1** *Couture* facing; *(de manche)* cuff **2** *Constr (surface)* facing, face; *(revêtement)* facing, dressing; **p. brut** rough facing **3** *(d'un trottoir) Br* kerbstone, *Am* curbstone **4** *Rel* **p. (d'autel)** (altar) frontal

parementer [3] [parmɑ̃te] VT *Constr* to face

parementure [parmɑ̃tyr] NF *Constr* facing; *Couture (doublure)* lining

parenchymateux, -euse [parɑ̃ʃimatø, -øz] ADJ *Anat & Bot* parenchymatous

parenchyme [parɑ̃ʃim] NM *Anat & Bot* parenchyma

pare-neige [parnɛʒ] NM INV snow fence

parent, -e [parɑ̃, -ɑ̃t] ADJ **1** *(de la même famille)* related; **je suis parente avec eux, nous sommes parents** I'm related to them; **nous sommes parents par ma femme/par alliance** we're related through my wife/by marriage
2 *(analogue)* similar; **ces deux interprétations sont parentes** the two interpretations are similar
3 *Bot, Géol & Zool* parent *(avant n)*
4 *Ling* related, cognate *(avant n)*
NM,F *(personne de la même famille)* relative, relation; **un proche p., un p. proche** a close relative *or* relation; **un lointain p., un p. éloigné** a distant relative *or* relation; **un p. du côté paternel/maternel** a relation on the father's/mother's side; **ce sont des parents en ligne directe/par alliance** they're blood relations/related by marriage; **p. pauvre** poor relation; **c'est le p. pauvre de l'opéra** it's opera's poor relation
NM *(père ou mère)* parent
❑ **parents** NMPL **1** *(père et mère)* parents, father and mother; **la relation parents-enfant** the parent-child relationship; **parents adoptifs** adoptive parents; **parents biologiques** biological parents; **parents collatéraux** collaterals, collateral relatives; **parents d'élèves** (pupils') parents; **association de parents d'élèves** parent-teacher association
2 *Littéraire (aïeux)* **nos parents** our forebears *or* ancestors; **nos premiers parents** *(Adam et Ève)* our first parents

parentage [parɑ̃taʒ] NM *Can* relationship, kinship

parental, -e, -aux, -ales[1] [parɑ̃tal, -o] ADJ parental; **les responsabilités parentales** parental duties

parentales[2] [parɑ̃tal], **parentalies** [parɑ̃tali] NFPL *Antiq* parentalia

parentalité [parɑ̃talite] NF *(gén) & Jur* parenthood

parenté [parɑ̃te] NF **1** *(lien familial)* relationship, kinship; **il n'y a aucune p. entre eux** they're not related in any way; **p. par alliance** relationship by marriage; **p. civile** agnation; **p. directe** blood relationship; **p. naturelle** cognation
2 *(ressemblance)* relationship, connection; **il y avait une p. de caractère entre les deux amis** the two friends had similar temperaments
3 *(famille)* family; **soyez maudits, toi et toute ta p.!** a curse upon you and all your kin!
4 *Ling* relatedness

parentèle [parɑ̃tɛl] NF **1** *Vieilli (parenté)* relationship, kinship **2** *(ensemble de la famille)* (extended) family

parentéral, -e, -aux, -ales [parɑ̃teral, -o] ADJ *Méd* parenteral

parenthèse [parɑ̃tɛz] NF **1** *(signe)* parenthesis, *Br* bracket; **ouvrir/fermer la p.** to open/to close the parentheses *or Br* brackets; *Typ* **p. ouvrante** opening parenthesis *or Br* bracket; **p. fermante** closing parenthesis *or Br* bracket
2 *Fig (digression)* digression, parenthesis; **mais c'est une p.** but that's a digression *or* an aside; **j'ouvre une (brève) p. pour signaler que...** incidentally *or* in parenthesis, we may briefly note that...; **fermons la p.** anyway, enough of that; **cette époque n'a été qu'une p. dans sa vie** that period was only an interlude in his life
3 *Gram* parenthesis, parenthetical clause
❑ **entre parenthèses** ADJ *(mot, phrase)* in parentheses, in *or* between brackets
ADV **1** *(mot, phrase)* **mettre qch entre parenthèses** to put sth in parentheses, to put sth in *or* between brackets; *Fig* **il a dû mettre sa vie privée entre parenthèses** he had to put his private life on hold
2 *Fig (à propos)* incidentally, by the way; **entre parenthèses, elle n'était pas très intelligente** incidentally *or* let it be said in passing, she wasn't very bright
❑ **par parenthèse** ADV *Fig* incidentally, by the way

paréo [pareo] NM *(tahitien)* pareo; *(pour la plage)* sarong

parer[1] [3] [pare] VT **1** *Littéraire (embellir → pièce)* to decorate, to deck out, to adorn; *(→ personne)* to deck out, to adorn; *(vêtir)* to dress; **l'autel paré de lys** the altar bedecked with lilies; **habit richement paré** richly ornamented *or* decorated garment; **elle arriva enfin, parée de fourrures/bijoux** she finally arrived, attired in furs/bedecked in jewels; **elle ne sort que parée de ses plus beaux atours** she only goes out attired in her best finery; **l'espérance pare l'avenir de mille beautés** hope paints the future in glowing colours
2 *(attribuer à)* **p. qn de toutes les vertus** to attribute every virtue to sb, to endow sb with every virtue; **p. qn d'un titre** to grace sb with a title
3 *Naut (préparer → ancre)* to clear; **paré à virer!** (get) ready to tack!; *Fig* **paré? alors on y va!** (are you) ready? then let's go!
4 *Culin (poisson, volaille)* to dress; *(rôti)* to trim
5 *Tech (cuir)* to dress; *(sur le bord)* to pare
6 *Métal* to dress
►**se parer** VPR **1** *(s'habiller avec élégance)* to put one's finery on; **se p. de** *(bijoux, fourrures)* to adorn oneself with; *(titres, honneurs)* to assume; **se p. des plumes du paon** to bask in reflected glory
2 *Can (se préparer)* to get ready

parer[2] [3] [pare] VT **1** *(éviter → coup, danger)* to ward *or* to fend *or* to stave off; *(→ attaque)* to stave off, to parry; *Naut (grain)* to steer clear of; *(abordage)* to fend off; *(cap)* to round; *Boxe & Escrime* to parry
2 *(protéger)* **p. qn contre qch** to shield *or* to protect sb against sth; **je suis paré contre le froid/l'hiver** I'm prepared for the cold/the winter
❑ **parer à** VT IND **1** *(faire face à)* to cope *or* to deal with, to handle; *(prévenir)* to guard against; **pour p. à toute difficulté/à tout retard** in order to guard against any difficulties/delay; **p. à toute éventualité** to prepare for *or* to guard against any contingency; **p. au plus pressé** *(en voyageant, en emménageant)* to deal with basic necessities (first); **je n'ai pu que p. au plus pressé** *(après un incident)* I could only employ stopgap measures; **parons au plus pressé et reconstruisons l'hôpital** first things first, we must rebuild the hospital
2 *(se défendre contre → tir, attaque)* to ward off
►**se parer** VPR **se p. contre** to protect oneself against; **je me suis paré contre les rigueurs de l'hiver** I prepared for the rigours of winter; **se p. contre les incendies** to take precautions against fire

parésie [parezi] NF *Méd* paresis

pare-soleil [parsɔlɛj] NM INV **1** *(de voiture)* sun visor **2** *Phot* lens hood

paresse [parɛs] NF **1** *(fainéantise)* laziness, idleness; **avoir la p. de faire qch** to be too lazy *or*

idle to do sth; **elle est d'une p. incroyable** she's incredibly lazy; **p. intellectuelle** intellectual laziness

2 *(apathie)* indolence, laziness; **elle s'étira avec p.** she stretched indolently

3 *Rel (péché capital)* sloth

4 *Méd* **p. intestinale** sluggishness of the digestive system; **souffrir de p. intestinale** to be slow to digest (one's) food

paresser [4] [parɛse] **VI** to laze (about *or* around); **p. au soleil** to laze in the sun

paresseuse [parɛsøz] *voir* **paresseux**

paresseusement [parɛsøzmɑ̃] **ADV 1** *(avec paresse)* lazily, idly; **elle s'étira p.** she stretched lazily **2** *(avec lenteur)* lazily, idly, sluggishly; **les vagues viennent mourir p. sur la plage** the waves break gently *or* lazily on the beach

paresseux, -euse [parɛsø, -øz] **ADJ 1** *(sans ardeur)* lazy, idle; **c'est un élève très p.** he's a very lazy pupil; **c'est un esprit p.** he's/she's got a lazy mind; **être p. comme un loir** *ou* **une couleuvre** to be *Br* bone-idle *or Am* a goldbricker

2 *(lent)* lazy, slow, indolent; **le cours p. de la rivière** the river's sluggish waters

3 *Méd (digestion)* sluggish

NM,F lazy person; **debout, grand p.!** get up, you lazy thing!

NM *Zool* sloth; **p. à deux doigts** two-toed sloth; **p. à trois doigts** three-toed sloth

paresthésie [parɛstezi] **NF** *Méd* paraesthesia

pareur, -euse [parœr, -øz] **NM,F** finisher, trimmer

❑ **pareuse NF** *Tex* sizing machine

parfaire [109] [parfɛr] **VT 1** *(peaufiner)* to perfect; **il aimerait p. ses connaissances en grec** he would like to perfect his knowledge of Greek; **p. une œuvre** to add the finishing touches to a work **2** *(compléter → opération)* to round off; *(→ somme)* to make up

parfait, -e [parfɛ, -ɛt] **ADJ 1** *(sans défaut → beauté, crime, harmonie, conditions)* perfect; *(→ argumentation, diamant, maquillage)* perfect, flawless; *(→ scolarité, savoir-vivre, personne)* perfect, faultless; **son russe est p.** his/her Russian is perfect *or* flawless, he/she speaks perfect Russian; **il a des manières parfaites** he's got perfect manners; **personne n'est p.** nobody's perfect

2 *Biol* mature; *Bot* perfect; *Math (cercle)* perfect

3 *(en intensif)* perfect, utter; **c'est le p. homme du monde** he's a perfect gentleman; **c'est un p. goujat/idiot** he's an utter boor/fool; **c'est le type même du p. macho!** he's the epitome of the male chauvinist pig!

4 *(complet, total → bonheur, calme, entente)* perfect, complete, total; *(→ ressemblance)* perfect, exact; **elle s'est montrée d'une parfaite délicatesse** she showed exquisite *or* perfect tact; **dans la plus parfaite indifférence** in utter *or* complete *or* total indifference; **être dans l'ignorance la plus parfaite de qch** to be completely ignorant of sth; **nous sommes en p. accord** we're in full *or* perfect agreement

5 *(excellent)* perfect, excellent; **en p. état/parfaite santé** in perfect condition/health; **il a été p.** he was perfect *or* marvellous; **le rôle est p. pour lui** the part is ideal *or* made for him; **10 heures, ça vous va? – c'est p.!** would 10 o'clock suit you? – that's perfect *or* (just) fine!; **p., maintenant passons à autre chose** fine *or* good, now let's go on to something else

NM 1 *(crème glacée)* parfait; **p. au café** coffee parfait

2 *Gram* **le p.** the perfect (tense); **au p.** in the perfect (tense)

parfaitement [parfɛtmɑ̃] **ADV 1** *(très bien)* perfectly, impeccably, faultlessly; **elle parle p. (l')anglais** she speaks English perfectly, she speaks perfect English; **cela m'ira p.** that will suit me perfectly *or* just fine; **ce vin accompagne p. le poisson** this wine is the perfect accompaniment for fish; **j'avais p. entendu!** I heard all right!

2 *(absolument)* perfectly, absolutely, thoroughly; **c'est p. inadmissible/ridicule!** it's quite unacceptable/ridiculous!; **tu as p. le droit de refuser** you are perfectly entitled to refuse; **je comprends p.** I quite understand; **cela lui est p. indifférent** it's a matter of complete indifference to him/her; **il est p. idiot** he's a perfect *or* complete idiot

3 *(oui)* (most) certainly, definitely; **c'est vrai? – p.!** is that true? – it (most) certainly *or* definitely is!; **oui, p., j'y étais** yes indeed, I was there

parfilage [parfilaʒ] **NM** unpicking, unravelling

parfiler [3] [parfile] **VT** to unpick, to unravel; *Littéraire* **on n'a jamais parfilé des riens avec plus de soin et de prétention** never was the spinning of airy nothings taken more seriously

parfois [parfwa] **ADV 1** *(quelquefois)* sometimes; **il venait p. nous voir** he sometimes came to see us **2** *(dans certains cas)* sometimes, at times, occasionally; **ça m'amuse p.** there are times when *or* occasionally I find it funny; **il était là tous les jours, p. seul, p. accompagné** he was there every day, sometimes alone, sometimes *or* other times not

parfondre [75] [parfɔ̃dr] **VT** *Tech* to fuse

parfum [parfœ̃] **NM 1** *(odeur → d'une lotion, d'une fleur)* perfume, scent, fragrance; *(→ d'un mets)* smell, aroma; *(→ d'un vin)* bouquet, aroma; *(→ d'un fruit)* smell; **le p. frais des magnolias** the sweet scent *or* fragrance of the magnolias

2 *Fig* **ce conte a un charmant p. d'autrefois** this tale has a charming aura of times past; **p. de scandale/d'hérésie** whiff of scandal/heresy; **p. d'innocence** flavour of innocence

3 *(cosmétique)* perfume, scent

4 *(goût)* flavour; **tu veux une glace à quel p.?** what flavour ice-cream do you want?; **yaourts sans p. artificiel** yoghurts with no artificial flavouring

❑ **au parfum ADV** *Fam* **être au p.** to be in the know; **mettre qn au p.** to put sb in the picture

parfumé, -e [parfyme] **ADJ 1** *(fleur)* fragrant, sweet-smelling; *(fruit)* sweet-smelling; *(vin, air)* fragrant **2** *(artificiellement → savon, mouchoir)* perfumed, scented; **elle est trop parfumée** *(femme)* she's wearing too much perfume; **glace parfumée au café** coffee-flavoured ice-cream

parfumer [3] [parfyme] **VT 1** *(embaumer)* to perfume; **qu'est-ce qui parfume ainsi la pièce?** where's the lovely smell in this room coming from?; **le gâteau parfume la cuisine** the kitchen smells of cake; **un soupçon de patchouli parfumait son oreiller** her pillow had a faint smell of patchouli

2 *(mettre du parfum sur)* to put *or* to dab perfume on; **être parfumé** *(personne)* to have perfume on, to be wearing perfume; *Fam* **il était parfumé comme une cocotte** he'd doused himself in scent; **se faire p.** *(dans un grand magasin)* to try on perfume

3 *Culin* to flavour (**à** with); **un peu de safran pour p. la sauce** a pinch of saffron to flavour the sauce; **yaourt parfumé à la mangue** mango-flavoured yoghurt

►**se parfumer VPR** *(une fois)* to put on perfume; *(habituellement)* to wear perfume; **parfumez-vous légèrement derrière l'oreille** dab some perfume behind your ear; **je ne me parfume jamais** I never wear *or* use perfume

parfumerie [parfymri] **NF 1** *(magasin)* perfumery, perfume *Br* shop *or Am* store **2** *(usine)* perfume factory, perfumery **3** *(profession)* perfumery, perfume trade *or* industry **4** *(articles)* perfumes (and cosmetics), perfumery

parfumeur, -euse [parfymœr, -øz] **NM,F** perfumer

parfumeur-conseil, parfumeuse-conseil [parfymœrkɔ̃sɛj, parfymøzkɔ̃sɛj] *(mpl* **parfumeurs-conseils,** *fpl* **parfumeuses-conseils) NM,F** cosmetics consultant

parhélie [pareli] **NM** parhelion

pari [pari] **NM 1** *(défi, enjeu)* bet, wager; **faire un p.** to lay a bet, to (have a) bet; **faire un p. avec qn** to make a bet with sb; **c'est un p. que tu fais en l'engageant** you're taking a chance *or* a gamble giving him/her a job; **je suis prêt à faire le p. que…** I'm willing to bet that…; *aussi Fig* **je tiens le p.!** I'll take you up on it!; **perdre un p.** to lose a bet; **cette politique est un p. sur l'avenir** this policy is a gamble on the future

2 *(mise)* bet, stake; **il a gagné son p.** he won his bet; *Fig* **les paris sont ouverts** it's anyone's guess; **p. jumelé** double forecast; **p. mutuel (urbain)** = French betting authority, *Br* ≃ tote, *Am* ≃ pari-mutuel

3 *Phil* **le p. de Pascal** Pascal's wager

paria [parja] **NM 1** *(d'un groupe)* outcast, pariah **2** *(en Inde)* pariah, untouchable

pariade [parjad] **NF** *Orn* **1** *(saison)* pairing season **2** *(accouplement)* pairing **3** *(couple)* pair

pariage [parjaʒ] **NM** *Hist* = agreement to share land ownership and attendant privileges, generally concluded between a religious house and a feudal lord

parian [parjɑ̃] **NM** *Cér* Parian biscuit, Parian

paridé [paride] **NM** member of the Paridae

paridigité, -e [paridiʒite], **paridigitidé, -e** [paridiʒitide] *Zool* **ADJ** artiodactyl

NM Artiodactyl

❑ **paridigités, paridigitidés NMPL** Artiodactyla

parier [9] [parje] **VT 1** *(somme)* to bet, to lay, to stake; *(repas, bouteille)* to bet; **j'ai parié gros sur le trois** I laid *or* put a big bet on number three; **tu as parié combien?** how much did you bet?

2 *(exprimant la certitude)* to bet; **tu crois qu'il a terminé? – je parie que non** do you think he's finished? – I bet he hasn't; **je te parie qu'il ment** I bet you he's lying; **qu'est-ce que tu paries qu'il va refuser?** how much do you bet he'll say no?; **je te parie tout ce que tu veux que…** I bet you anything (you like)…; **elle a refusé, je parie?** I bet she said no; **il y a fort** *ou* **gros à p. que...** the odds are *or* it's odds on that...; **je l'aurais parié!** I knew it!

VI 1 *(faire un pari)* to (lay a) bet; **p. sur un cheval** to bet on *or* to back a horse; *Fam* **tu paries?, on parie?** want to bet?

2 *(être parieur)* to bet; **je ne parie jamais** I'm not a betting man, *f* woman; **p. aux courses** *(de chevaux)* to bet on the horses

pariétaire [parjetɛr] **NF** *Bot* pellitory-of-the-wall

pariétal, -e, -aux, -ales [parjetal, -o] **ADJ 1** *Anat* parietal **2** *Beaux-Arts* **art p.** *(sur parois rocheuses)* rock painting; *(dans grottes)* cave painting

NM parietal bone

parieur, -euse [parjœr, -øz] **NM,F 1** *(qui fait un pari)* better **2** *(qui aime parier)* betting man, *f* woman

parigot, -e [parigo, -ɔt] *Fam* **ADJ** Parisian■

NM,F Parisian■

paripenné, -e [paripene] **ADJ** *Bot* paripinnate

Paris [pari] **NM** Paris; **P.-IV** *(université)* the Sorbonne; **P. XIIIème** *(arrondissement)* XIIIth arrondissement of Paris; **aller à P.** to go to Paris; **j'ai horreur d'aller dans P. le soir** I hate going into Paris in the evening; **je travaille sur P.** I work in Paris; **la banlieue de P.** the Paris suburbs; **dans les environs de P.** in the Paris area; **la mode de P.** Parisian *or* Paris fashion; *Prov* **P. ne s'est pas fait en un jour** Rome wasn't built in a day; **P.(-)Plage** = artificial beach created every summer by the Seine

Culture

PARIS(-)PLAGE

In the summer of 2002, a two-mile stretch of the Right Bank of the Seine (near the Pont-Neuf and Hôtel de Ville) was turned into a beach, complete with white sand, palm trees, sunbeds, parasols and various pools, and was dubbed 'Paris-Plage'. In the few short years since then, Paris-Plage has become a tradition. In addition to lounging on the sunbeds, visitors can take part in various free sporting activities, including pétanque and volleyball, and dance in the old-fashioned dance halls, known as 'les guinguettes'. Paris-Plage is also the setting for numerous concerts held throughout the summer. Originally the name 'Paris Plage' referred to Le Touquet, a seaside town in northern France which was thus nicknamed because of its role as the favourite beach resort of well-to-do Parisians.

Pâris [pɑris] **NPR** *Myth* Paris

paris-brest [paribrɛst] **NM INV** paris-brest *(choux pastry ring filled with praline cream)*

Pariscope [pariskɔp] **NM** *Presse* = weekly entertainments listings guide for Paris

Paris-Dakar [paridakar] **NM le P.** = annual car race crossing the Sahara Desert

parisette [parizɛt] **NF** *Bot* herb Paris

parisianisme [parizjanism] **NM 1** *(attitude)* Paris-centredness; **le p. des médias** the capital-city

mentality of the Paris media **2** *(expression)* Parisian (turn of) phrase **3** *(habitude)* Parisian habit *or* quirk

parisien, -enne [parizjɛ̃, -ɛn] **ADJ 1** *(relatif à Paris, sa région)* Paris *(avant n)*; *(natif de Paris, habitant à Paris)* Parisian; **la banlieue parisienne** the Paris suburbs; **la vie parisienne** life in Paris, Parisian life; **les immeubles parisiens** buildings in Paris **2** *(typique de Paris)* Parisian; **un événement bien p.** a very Parisian occasion

❑ **Parisien, -enne NM,F** Parisian

parisis [parizis] **ADJ INV** *Hist* minted at Paris

Paris-Match [parimatʃ] **NM** *Presse* = French popular weekly magazine

Paris-Normandie [parinɔrmɑ̃di] **NM** *Presse* = daily newspaper published in Rouen

parisyllabique [parisilabik] *Ling* **ADJ** parisyllabic
NM parisyllabic

paritaire [paritɛr] **ADJ** *(commission)* joint *(avant n)*; **représentation p.** parity of representation, equal representation

paritarisme [paritarism] **NM** *Ind* (doctrine of) co-management

parité [parite] **NF 1** *(concordance → entre des rémunérations)* parity, equality; *(→ entre des monnaies, des prix)* parity; *(→ entre des concepts)* comparability; **à p.** at parity, at the money; **p. du change** exchange rate parity; **p. euro-dollar** euro-dollar parity; **p. fixe** fixed parity; **p. hommes-femmes** sexual equality; **il faut faire en sorte d'arriver à une p. hommes-femmes au parlement** a way must be found to ensure that there are an equal number of men and women in parliament; **p. des monnaies** monetary parity; *Bourse* **p. du pouvoir d'achat** purchasing power parity; **p. rampante** crawling peg; **la p. des salaires** equal pay;
2 *Math* parity
3 *Ordinat* parity check

parjure [parʒyr] **ADJ** disloyal, treacherous
NMF *(personne)* disloyal person, traitor, betrayer
NM *(acte)* disloyalty, treachery, betrayal; **commettre un p.** to forswear

parjurer [3] [parʒyre] **se parjurer VPR** *(manquer à son serment)* to break one's word *or* promise

parka [parka] **NM OU NF** parka

Parkérisation® [parkerizasjɔ̃] **NF** Parkerizing

parking [parkiŋ] **NM 1** *(parc de stationnement) Br* car park, *Am* parking lot; **mettre sa voiture au p.** to put one's car in the *Br* car park *or Am* parking lot; **une place de p.** a parking space; **p. couvert** underground *Br* car park *or Am* parking lot **2** *(action de se garer)* **le p. est interdit** parking is prohibited here; **p. payant** *(sur panneau)* pay and display

Parkinson [parkinsɔn] **NPR** *voir* **maladie**

parkinsonien, -enne [parkinsɔnjɛ̃, -ɛn] *Méd* **ADJ** Parkinson's *(avant n)*, parkinsonian
NM,F person with Parkinson's (disease), Parkinson's sufferer

parkinsonisme [parkinsɔnism] **NM** *Méd* parkinsonism

parkour [parkur] **NM** free-running, parkour

parlant, -e [parlɑ̃, -ɑ̃t] **ADJ 1** *(film)* talking *(avant n)*
2 *Fam (bavard)* **il n'est pas très p.** he isn't very talkative▪ *or* hasn't got very much to say (for himself)
3 *(significatif → chiffre, exemple, schéma)* which speaks for itself; **leurs statistiques sont parlantes** their figures speak volumes
4 *(expressif → portrait)* lifelike; *(→ description)* vivid, graphic; *(→ geste, regard)* eloquent, meaningful
NM *Cin* **le p.** talking pictures, the talkies

parlé, -e [parle] **ADJ** *(langue, français, anglais, etc → oral)* spoken; *(→ familier)* colloquial; **ça se dit dans la langue parlée** it's a colloquial term, it's used colloquially
NM *(à l'opéra)* spoken part, dialogue

parlement [parləmɑ̃] **NM 1** *Pol* **le P.** *(en France)* (the French) Parliament; *(en Grande-Bretagne)* (the Houses of) Parliament; **au p.** in Parliament; **P. bicaméral** bicameral *or* two-chamber parliament; **membre du P.** member of Parliament; **le P. européen** the European Parliament; **membre du P. européen** member of the European Parliament, MEP, Euro-MP
2 *Hist (en France)* parliament, parlement *(under the Ancien Régime)*; **P. Court/Croupion/Long** *(en Grande-Bretagne)* Short/Rump/Long Parliament

parlementaire [parləmɑ̃tɛr] **ADJ 1** *(débat, habitude, régime)* parliamentary; **procédure p.** parliamentary procedure **2** *Hist (en Grande-Bretagne)* Parliamentary
NMF 1 *(député)* member of Parliament; *(aux États-Unis)* Congressman, *f* Congresswoman; **p. européen** member of the European Parliament, Euro-MP, MEP **2** *Hist (en Grande-Bretagne)* Parliamentarian **3** *(négociateur)* mediator, negotiator

parlementarisme [parləmɑ̃tarism] **NM** parliamentarianism, parliamentary government

parlementer [3] [parləmɑ̃te] **VI** to negotiate; *Pol* **p. avec** to parley with; **il a dû p. avec l'agent pour qu'il le laisse passer** he had to talk the policeman into letting him through

parler¹ [parle] **NM 1** *(vocabulaire)* speech, way of speaking; **dans le p. de tous les jours** in common parlance
2 *(langue d'une région)* dialect, variety

PARLER² [3] [parle] **VI A.** *FAIRE UN ÉNONCÉ* **1** *(articuler des paroles)* to talk, to speak; **p. du nez** to talk through one's nose; **p. bas** *ou* **à voix basse** to speak softly *or* in a low voice; **p. haut** *ou* **à voix haute** to speak loudly *or* in a loud voice; *Fig* **les syndicats commencent à p. haut** the unions are beginning to make a lot of noise; **elle parle avec un accent** she talks *or* speaks with an accent; **parle plus fort** speak louder *or* up; **parlez moins fort** keep your voice down, don't speak so loud; **elle a une poupée qui parle** she's got a talking doll; **dans ses fables, il fait p. les animaux** in his fables, he makes the animals talk; **p. par gestes** *ou* **signes** to use sign language; **p. avec les mains** to talk with one's hands
2 *(s'exprimer)* to talk, to speak; **vous pouvez p. librement** you can speak *or* talk freely; **parle donc!** speak up!; **ça m'a fait du bien de p.** it's done me good to talk (things over); **je n'ai pas l'habitude de p. en public** I'm not used to speaking in public *or* to public speaking; **le conseiller a parlé le dernier** the councillor spoke last; **il parle mal** *(improprement)* he doesn't talk correctly; **comme tu parles mal!** *(grossièrement)* (mind your) language!; *Ironique* that's a fine way to talk!; **tu n'as qu'à p. pour être servi** just say the word and you'll be served; **mon père parlait peu** my father was a man of few words; **tu parles en nouveaux francs?** are you talking in *or* do you mean new francs?; **il a parlé à la radio** he spoke *or* talked on the radio; **il a fait p. l'adolescent** he drew the adolescent out of himself, he got the adolescent to talk; **les armes ont parlé** weapons were used; **ne laissons pas p. notre haine** let us not yield to hatred; **laisse p. ton cœur** listen to your heart; **p. pour** *ou* **à la place de qn** to speak for sb *or* on sb's behalf; **ne parle pas tout le temps pour moi!** stop answering for me!; *Fig* **sa franchise parle pour lui** his straightforwardness is a point in his favour; *Fam* **parle pour toi!** speak for yourself!; **p. contre/pour** to speak against/for; **il va p. pour la suppression de la peine de mort** he will be speaking against capital punishment; **politiquement/artistiquement parlant** politically/artistically speaking; **p. à qn** *(lui manifester ses sentiments)* to talk to *or* to speak to *or* to have a word with sb; *Fam* **je vais lui p., moi, à ton copain!** I'm going to have a word with that pal of yours!; **parle-moi!** talk *or* speak to me!; **j'aurais aimé te p. la première** I'd have liked to be the first to tell you; **p. à qn** *(s'adresser à)* to talk *or* to speak to sb; **ne parle pas aux gens que tu ne connais pas** don't talk to strangers; **je ne lui ai parlé que brièvement** I only talked to *or* with him/her for a brief moment; **ne me parle pas sur ce ton!** don't talk to me like that!; **c'est à toi que je parle!** it's you I'm talking to!; **je ne leur parle plus** I'm not on speaking terms with them any more, I don't speak to them any more; **le secrétaire général parlera aux travailleurs demain** the general secretary will talk to *or* address the workers tomorrow; **puis-je p. à Virginie?** *(au téléphone)* may *or* could I speak to Virginie?; **vous pouvez p.!** *(message de l'opératrice)* go ahead, caller!; **p. à qn** *(l'émouvoir, le toucher)* to speak *or* to appeal to sb; **sa musique me parle** his/her music speaks to me; **ses tableaux ne me parlent pas** his/her paintings don't appeal to me *or* don't do anything for me; *Fam* **voilà ce qui s'appelle p.!, ça, c'est p.!** well said!; **il sait ce que p. veut dire** he's not stupid; **parlons peu mais parlons bien** let's be brief but to the point
3 *(discuter)* to talk; **les longues soirées d'hiver où l'on parlait autour du feu** the long winter evenings spent talking *or* chatting around the fire; **ne parle pas sans savoir** don't talk about things you don't know about; **p. pour ne rien dire** to talk for the sake of talking; **assez parlé, allons-y!** that's enough chat, let's go!; **p. de qn/qch** to talk *or* to speak about sb/sth; **je sais de quoi je parle** I know what I'm talking about; **je ne sais pas de quoi tu veux p.** I don't know what you mean; **p. de choses et d'autres** to talk about this and that; **tiens, en parlant de vacances, Luc a une villa à louer** hey, talking of holidays, Luc has a villa to let; **je ne veux pas qu'on parle de ça à table!** I won't have that kind of talk at the table!; **ce professeur va venir p. de Proust** this professor will give a talk on Proust; **qui parle d'Europe parle d'axe franco-allemand** you can't talk about Europe without talking about *or* mentioning the special relationship between France and Germany; **il en sera beaucoup parlé dans les jours qui viennent** everybody's going to be talking about it in the next few days
4 *(jaser)* to talk; **les gens commencent à p.!** people are starting to talk!; **tout le monde en parle** everybody's talking about it; **on ne parle que de cela au village** it's the talk of the village; **sa démission a beaucoup fait p. dans l'entreprise** his/her resignation caused quite a stir in the office; **faire p. de soi** to get oneself talked about; *(dans la presse)* to get one's name in the papers
5 *(avouer)* to talk; **ses complices ont parlé** his/her accomplices talked; **faire p. qn** to make sb talk, to get sb to talk; **impossible de le faire p.!** it's impossible to get him to talk!
6 *(être éloquent)* to speak volumes; **les chiffres/faits parlent d'eux-mêmes** the figures/facts speak for themselves
7 *(dans des jeux)* **à qui de p.?** whose bid is it?; **c'est à toi de p.** it's your bid
B. *LOCUTIONS Fam* **tu parles!** *(absolument)* you're telling me!, absolutely!, *Br* too right!; *(absolument pas)* you must be joking!, are you kidding!; **tu parles comme je peux oublier ça!** as if I could ever forget it!; **tu parles si je sais de quoi elle est capable!** you bet I know what she's capable of!; **ça t'a plu? – tu parles!** *(bien sûr)* did you like it? – you bet!; *(pas du tout)* did you like it? – you must be joking!; **ça t'irait, 200 euros? – tu parles (si ça m'irait)!** would 200 euros be OK? – you bet (it would)!; **tu parles que je vais lui rendre!** *(je vais lui rendre)* you bet I'll give it back to him/her!; *(je ne vais pas lui rendre)* there's no way I'm giving it back to him/her!; *Ironique* **tu parles si c'est agréable/intelligent!** that's really nice/clever!; **tu parles si je m'en fiche!** a fat lot I care!; **tu parles si ça m'aide!** much good that is to me!; **la truite pesait au moins 10 kilos! – tu parles!** the trout was at least 10 kilos! – you must be joking! *Br* pull the other one!; **tu parles d'une déception!** talk about a letdown!, it was such a letdown!; **tu parles d'une veine!** what a stroke of luck!; **tu parles d'une cuisinière! elle est pas fichue de faire cuire un œuf** some cook she is, she can't even boil an egg!; **c'est difficile – ne m'en parle pas!** it's difficult – don't tell me *or* you're telling me!; **quel temps! – n'en parlez pas!** what filthy weather! – oh, don't *or* don't even talk about it!; **laisse faire la justice – ah, parlons-en, de leur justice!** let justice take its course – justice indeed *or* some justice!; **sa timidité? parlons-en!** his/her shyness? that's a good one *or* you must be joking!; **la chambre du haut, n'en parlons pas** let's *or* we can forget the upstairs bedroom; **l'échéance d'avril, n'en parlons pas** let's not even talk about *or* mention the April

deadline; **n'en parlons plus** let's not mention it again, let's say no more about it

VT **1** *(langue)* to speak; **il parle plusieurs langues** he speaks *or* he can speak several languages; **elle parle chinois couramment** she's fluent in Chinese, she speaks Chinese fluently; **il parle bien (le) russe** he speaks good Russian; **vous connaissez l'allemand? – je le parle un peu** do you know any German? – I can speak (it) a little; **il ne parle pas un mot de polonais** he doesn't *or* can't speak a word of Polish; **elle parle le langage des sourds-muets** she knows sign language; *Fig* **et pourtant je parle français, non?** ≃ don't you understand plain English?; *Fig* **nous ne parlons pas la même langue** *ou* **le même langage** we don't speak the same language; **p. le langage de la raison** to talk sense; **p. affaires/politique** to talk business/politics

2 *(dire d'une façon naturelle)* to speak, to read out; **parle ton texte, ne le déclame pas** just read out your text, don't recite it

❑ **parler de** VT IND **1** *(mentionner)* **vous ne parlez même pas de Dali dans votre thèse** you don't even mention Dali in your thesis; **le livre parle de la guerre** the book is about *or* deals with the war; **tous les journaux en parlent ce matin** it's (mentioned) in all the newspapers this morning; **ils en ont parlé aux informations** they talked about it on the news; **c'était un excellent acteur, mais on ne parle plus de lui maintenant** he was an excellent actor, but nobody ever talks about *or* mentions him any more; **si elle en parle devant toi, fais comme si tu ne savais rien** if she mentions it in front of you, pretend you don't know anything (about it); **p. (de) religion/(de) littérature** to talk religion/literature; **tu ne vas pas déjà p. de départ!** you're not talking about leaving already, are you?; **je ne l'aime pas, alors ne parlons pas de mariage!** I don't like him, so let there be no talk of marriage!; **p. de faire qch** to talk about *or* of doing sth; **elle parle de déménager** she's talking about *or* of moving house; **ils parlent de réduire les impôts** they're talking about *or* there's talk of cutting taxes; **qui parle de laisser tomber?** who said anything about giving up?; **on parle d'elle comme d'une candidate possible** she's being talked about *or* billed as a possible candidate; **tu en parles comme d'une catastrophe** you make it sound like a catastrophe; **on m'en avait parlé comme d'une femme austère** I'd been told she was *or* she'd been described to me as a stern sort of woman; **n'en parle à personne!** don't mention it to anybody!; **après ça, qu'on ne vienne plus me p. de solidarité** after that, I don't want to hear any more about solidarity; **elle nous a parlé de ses projets** she talked to us about her plans; **parlez-moi un peu de vous/de ce que vous avez ressenti** tell me something about yourself/what you felt; **on m'a beaucoup parlé de vous** I've heard a lot about you; **je cherche un travail, alors, si vous pouviez lui p. de moi...** I'm looking for a job, so if you could put in a good word for me...

2 *Littéraire (rappeler)* to remind of; **tout ici me parle de toi** everything here reminds me of you; **les cals de ses mains parlaient d'une vie laborieuse** the calluses on his hands testified to a life of hard work

❑ **sans parler de** PRÉP to say nothing of, not to mention, let alone; **la misère est inimaginable, sans p. des conditions d'hygiène** the poverty is unimaginable, not to mention the hygiene; **sans p. du fait que...** to say nothing of..., without mentioning the fact that...

►**se parler** VPR **1** *(emploi réciproque)* to talk to one another *or* each other; **il faudrait qu'on se parle tous les deux** I think we two should have a talk; **elles ne se parlent plus** they aren't on speaking terms any more

2 *(emploi réfléchi)* to talk to oneself

3 *(emploi passif)* to be spoken; **le français se parle dans plusieurs pays d'Afrique** French is spoken in several African countries

---

parler-vrai [parlevrɛ] *(pl* **parlers-vrai***)* NM *(gén) & Pol* straight talking *(UNCOUNT)*

parleur, -euse [parlœr, -øz] NM,F talker; **c'est un beau p.** he's a smooth talker

parloir [parlwar] NM **1** *(d'une prison)* visitors' room; *(d'un monastère)* parlour **2** *Belg (salon)* parlour

parlote, parlotte [parlɔt] NF *Fam* chitchat, *Br* natter; **faire la p. (avec qn)** to chat (with sb), to have a chat (with sb)

parlure [parlyr] NF *Can Vieilli ou Littéraire* dialect

Parme [parm] NM Parma

parme [parm] ADJ INV mauve

NM *(couleur)* mauve

parmélie [parmeli] NF *Bot* parmelia

parmentier [parmɑ̃tje] NM *Culin (au bœuf)* ≃ cottage pie; *(avec de la viande blanche)* = dish similar to cottage pie, made with white meat; *(au mouton)* ≃ shepherd's pie

parmesan, -e [parməzɑ̃, -an] ADJ Parmesan

NM *(fromage)* Parmesan (cheese); **spaghettis au p.** spaghetti with Parmesan

❑ **Parmesan, -e** NM,F Parmesan

parmi [parmi] PRÉP among; **p. eux se trouvait un grand homme maigre** there was a tall, thin man among them; **elle erra p. la foule** she wandered in *or* among the crowd; **son nom est réputé p. les scientifiques** his/her name is held in high esteem in *or* by *or* among the scientific community; **il figure p. les meilleurs** he's one of the best, he's among the best; **nous souhaitons vous avoir bientôt p. nous** we hope that you'll soon be with us; **p. tout ce vacarme** in the midst of all this noise; **c'est une solution p. (tant) d'autres** that's one solution; **c'est juste un exemple p. d'autres** it's just one example; **je retiendrai cette solution p. celles qui ont été proposées** I will choose this solution from those which have been suggested

Parnasse [parnas] NM **1** *Géog* **le P.** (Mount) Parnassus **2** *Littérature & Myth* Parnassus

parnassien[1] [parnasjɛ̃] NM *Entom* apollo

parnassien[2]**, -enne** [parnasjɛ̃, -ɛn] ADJ Parnassian

❑ **Parnassien, -enne** NM,F Parnassian *(member of the Parnassian school of French poets)*

parodie [parɔdi] NF **1** *Littérature* parody **2** *(imitation grossière)* mockery; **une p. de procès** a mockery of a trial

parodier [9] [parɔdje] VT **1** *Beaux-Arts* to parody **2** *(singer)* to mimic, to parody; **je le parodie un peu, mais c'est ce qu'il a dit** I'm parodying him a little, but that's what he said

parodique [parɔdik] ADJ parodic

parodiste [parɔdist] NMF parodist

parodontal, -e, -aux, -ales [parɔdɔ̃tal, -o] ADJ *Méd* periodontal

parodonte [parɔdɔ̃t] NM *Anat* periodontium

parodontiste [parɔdɔ̃tist] NMF *Méd* periodontist

parodontite [parɔdɔ̃tit] NF *Méd* periodontitis

parodontologie [parɔdɔ̃tɔlɔʒi] NF *Méd* periodontology

parodontolyse [parɔdɔ̃tɔliz] NF *Méd* periodontosis

parodontopathie [parɔdɔ̃tɔpati] NF *Méd* periodontoclasia

parodontose [parɔdɔ̃toz] NF *Méd* periodontosis

paroi [parwa] NF **1** *(entre des pièces)* partition (wall); *(d'une pièce, d'un ascenseur)* wall; *(d'une citerne, d'un vase)* inside *or* inner surface **2** *Anat, Biol & Bot* wall; **p. des artères** artery wall; **p. cellulaire** cell wall **3** *Géol & (en alpinisme)* face, wall; **p. rocheuse** rock face

paroir [parwar] NM **1** *(en tannerie, en reliure)* parer, paring knife **2** *Métal* flatter, set hammer

paroisse [parwas] NF parish

paroissial, -e, -aux, -ales [parwasjal, -o] ADJ *(fête, église)* parish *(avant n)*; *(décision, don)* parish *(avant n)*, parochial

paroissien, -enne [parwasjɛ̃, -ɛn] NM,F **1** *Rel* parishioner **2** *Fam (type)* **c'est un drôle de p.** he's a weird one

NM *(livre → gén)* prayer book; *(→ catholique)* missal

parole [parɔl] NF **1** *(faculté de s'exprimer)* **la p.** speech; **il ne lui manque que la p., à ton chien** your dog does everything but talk; **être doué de p.** to be endowed with speech; **perdre/retrouver l'usage de la p.** to lose/to recover the power of speech; **avoir la p. facile** to be a fine talker, to have a way with words; *Prov* **la p. est d'argent, le silence est d'or** speech is silver, silence is golden

2 *(fait de parler)* **demander la p.** to ask for the right to speak; *Jur* to request leave to speak; **les délégués demandent la p.** the delegates want to speak; **prendre la p.** *(gén)* to speak; *(au parlement, au tribunal)* to take the floor; **vous avez la p.** *(à un avocat, un député)* you have the floor; *(dans un débat)* (it's) your turn to speak *or* over to you; **la p. est à la défense** the defence may now speak; **adresser la p. à qn** to talk *or* to speak to sb; **nous ne nous adressons plus la p.** we're not on speaking terms *or* we don't talk to each other any more; **couper la p. à qn** to interrupt sb; **passer la p. à qn** to hand over to sb; **je laisse maintenant la p. à mon collègue** I now hand over to my colleague; **droit de p.** right to speak; **temps de p.** speaking time; **votre temps de p. est révolu** your time is up

3 *Ling* speech, parole; **acte de p.** speech act

4 *(souvent pl) (propos)* word, remark; **des paroles blessantes** hurtful words *or* remarks; **jamais une p. gentille!** never a kind word!; **voilà une bonne p.!** well said!; **prononcer des paroles historiques** to utter historic words; **ce sont ses propres paroles** those are his very own words; **elle n'a jamais une p. plus haute que l'autre** she never raises her voice; **ce ne sont que des paroles en l'air** all that's just idle talk; **il s'y connaît en belles paroles** he's full of fine words; **en paroles, ça a l'air simple, mais...** it's easy enough to say it, but...; **en paroles et en actes** in word and deed; **répandre** *ou* **porter la bonne p.** to spread *or* to carry the good word; **la p. de Dieu** the Word of God; **c'est p. d'Évangile** it's the gospel truth; *Prov* **les paroles s'envolent, les écrits restent** verba volant, scripta manent

5 *(engagement)* word; **ma p. vaut bien la sienne** my word is as good as his/hers; **c'est votre p. contre la sienne** it's your word against his/hers; **il n'a qu'une p., il est de p.** his word is his bond, he's a man of his word; **tu n'as aucune p.** you never keep your word; **donner sa p. (d'honneur) à qn** to give sb one's word (of honour); **tenir p.** to keep one's word; **reprendre** *ou* **retirer sa p.** to go back on one's word; **c'est un homme de p.** he's a man of his word; **p. d'honneur!** I give you my word (of honour)!; **ma p.!** my word!; **p.!** cross my heart!, I swear to God!

6 *Cartes* **avoir la p.** to be the first to bid; **passer p.** to pass; **p.!** *(je passe)* pass!, your bid!

❑ **paroles** NFPL **1** *(d'une chanson)* words, lyrics; **paroles de Robbie Blondeau** lyrics by Robbie Blondeau

2 *(d'une illustration)* words; **histoire sans paroles** wordless cartoon; **sans paroles** no caption

❑ **sur parole** ADV *(prisonnier)* on parole

parolier, -ère [parɔlje, -ɛr] NM,F *(d'une chanson)* lyric writer, lyricist; *(d'un opéra)* librettist

paronomase [parɔnɔmaz] NF paronomasia

paronyme [parɔnim] ADJ paronymous

NM paronym

paronymie [parɔnimi] NF paronymy

paronymique [parɔnimik] ADJ paronymous

paros [parɔs] NM Parian marble

parotide [parɔtid] *Anat* ADJ F parotid

NF parotid gland

parotidien, -enne [parɔtidjɛ̃, -ɛn] ADJ *Anat* parotid, parotidian

parotidite [parɔtidit] NF *Méd* parotitis; **p. infectieuse** mumps

parousie [paruzi] NF *Rel* Parousia

paroxysmal, -e, -aux, -ales [parɔksismal, -o] = **paroxysmique**

paroxysme [parɔksism] NM **1** *(d'un état affectif)* paroxysm, height; **le mécontentement a atteint son p.** discontent is at its height; **au p. de la douleur** in paroxysms of pain; **être au p. de la joie** to be ecstatically happy; **les fans étaient au p. du délire** the fans' enthusiasm had reached fever pitch

2 *(d'un phénomène)* height; **l'incendie était à son p.** the fire was at its height

3 *Méd* paroxysm, crisis

4 *Géol* **p. volcanique** paroxysmal eruption

paroxysmique [parɔksismik], **paroxystique** [parɔksistik] ADJ paroxysmal, climactic

paroxyton [parɔksitɔ̃] *Gram* ADJ M paroxytone

NM paroxytone

parpaillot, -e [parpajo, -ɔt] **NM,F** *Hum ou Vieilli Péj* (French) Protestant

parpaing [parpɛ̃] **NM 1** *(pierre de taille)* perpend **2** *(aggloméré) Br* breezeblock, *Am* cinderblock

Parque [park] **NF** *Myth* **la P.** Fate; **les Parques** the Parcae, the Fates

parquer [3] [parke] **VT 1** *(mettre dans un parc → bétail)* to pen in *or* up; *(→ moutons)* to pen in *or* up, to fold; **p. les huîtres** to lay down an oyster-bed

2 *(enfermer → prisonniers)* to shut in *or* up, to confine; *(→ foule, multitude)* to pack *or* to cram in; **on parquait les réfugiés dans les camps** the refugees were herded into the camps

3 *(voiture)* to park

4 *Ordinat* to park

►**se parquer VPR** *(en voiture)* to park

parquet [parkɛ] **NM 1** *(revêtement de bois)* (wooden) floor *or* flooring; *(à chevrons)* parquet; **refaire le p.** to re-lay *or* to replace the floorboards; **p. à l'anglaise** strip flooring

2 *Jur* public prosecutor's department, *Br* ≃ Crown Prosecution Service, *Am* ≃ District Attorney's office; **déposer une plainte auprès du p.** to lodge a complaint with the public prosecutor; **p. général** ≃ Principal State Counsel's Office

3 *Bourse* **le p.** *(lieu)* the (trading) floor; *(personnes)* the Stock Exchange

4 *Beaux-Arts* wooden backing

parquetage [parkətaʒ] **NM 1** *Constr (installation)* laying of parquet flooring; *(sol)* (parquet) flooring **2** *Beaux-Arts* backing (with wood)

parqueter [27] [parkəte] **VT** to lay a parquet floor in, to put a parquet floor down in

parqueterie [parkɛtri] **NF** *(installation)* laying of parquet flooring; *(fabrication)* making of parquet flooring

parqueteur [parkətœr] **NM** *(fabricant)* parquet maker; *(poseur)* parquet layer

parquetier [parkətje] **NM** *Jur* prosecutor

parqueur, -euse [parkœr, -øz], **parquier, -ère** [parkje, -ɛr] **NM,F** oyster culturist

parrain [parɛ̃] **NM 1** *Rel* godfather; **être le p. d'un enfant** to be a child's godfather

2 *Com* sponsor

3 *(d'un projet)* promoter; *(d'un enfant du tiers-monde)* sponsor; *(d'une œuvre charitable)* patron; *Pol* proposer, *Am* sponsor

4 *(d'un navire)* namer, christener; *(d'une cloche)* christener

5 *(de la mafia)* godfather

'Le Parrain' *Puzo, Coppola* 'The Godfather'

parrainage [parɛnaʒ] **NM 1** *Rel* (act of) being a godparent

2 *Com* sponsorship, sponsoring; **p. d'entreprises** corporate sponsorship; **p. télévision** television sponsoring

3 *(d'un projet)* proposing, promoting; *(d'un enfant du tiers-monde)* sponsorship, sponsoring; *(d'une œuvre charitable)* patronage; *Pol* proposing, *Am* sponsoring

4 *(d'un navire)* naming, christening; *(d'une cloche)* christening

parrainer [4] [parɛne] **VT 1** *(candidat, postulant)* to propose, *Am* to sponsor; *(projet)* to propose, to support; *(enfant du tiers-monde)* to sponsor; *(œuvre charitable)* to patronize **2** *Com* to sponsor; **se faire p.** to be sponsored **3** *(navire)* to name, to christen; *(cloche)* to christen

parraineur [parɛnœr] **NM** sponsor

parricide [parisid] **ADJ** parricidal

NMF *(assassin)* parricide

NM *(crime)* parricide; **commettre un p.** to commit parricide

parsec [parsɛk] **NM** *Astron* parsec

parsemer [19] [parsəme] **VT 1** *(semer, saupoudrer)* **p. qch de qch** to scatter sth with sth

2 *(sujet: fleurs, étoiles)* **le ciel était parsemé d'étoiles** the sky was studded *or* scattered with stars; **un champ parsemé de pâquerettes** a field dotted with daisies; *Littéraire* **des feuilles parsemaient le chemin** the path was scattered *or* strewn with leaves, leaves were scattered *or* strewn all over the path; *Fig* **un texte parsemé de coquilles** a text littered with misprints; **un visage parsemé de taches de rousseur** a freckled face

pars *etc voir* **partir**

parsi, -e [parsi] **ADJ** Parsi, Parsee

NM *(langue)* Parsee

❑ **Parsi, -e NM,F** Parsi, Parsee

parsisme [parsism] **NM** *Rel* Parseeism

PART [par] **NF 1** *(dans un partage → de nourriture)* piece, portion; *(→ d'un butin, de profits, de travail etc)* share; **une p. de gâteau** a slice of cake; **donnez-moi deux parts de choucroute** I'd like two portions *or* servings *or* helpings of sauerkraut; **à chacun sa p.** share and share alike; **couper qch en parts égales** to cut sth into equal parts *or* portions; **elle a eu sa p. de soucis** she's had her share of worries; **repose-toi, tu as fait ta p.** have a rest, you've done your bit; **la p. du pauvre** a bit left aside *(for the poor should they come knocking at the door)*; **avoir p. à** to have a share in, to share (in); **avoir p. aux bénéfices** to share in the profits; **avoir la p. belle** to get a good deal; **faire la p. belle à qn** to give sb a good deal; *Fam aussi Fig* **vouloir sa p. de** *ou* **du gâteau** to want one's share of the cake; **se réserver** *ou* **se tailler la p. du lion** to keep *or* to take the lion's share; *Fam* **p. à deux!** let's go halves!

2 *Jur (pour les impôts)* = basic unit used for calculating personal income tax; **un couple avec un enfant a deux parts et demie** a couple with a child *Br* has a tax allowance worth two and a half *or Am* has two and a half tax exemptions; **p. virile** *(dans un héritage)* lawful share

3 *Écon & Fin* share; **p. d'association** partnership share; **p. bénéficiaire** founder's share; **p. de fondateur** founder's share; **p. d'intérêts** partner's share; **p. de marché** market share; **p. de marché relative** relative market share; **p. patronale** employer's contribution; **p. salariale** employee's contribution; **p. sociale** unquoted share; *Mktg* **p. de voix** share of voice

4 *(fraction)* part, portion; **ce n'est qu'une petite p. de la vérité** it's only a fraction *or* small part of the truth; **en grande p.** for the most part, largely, to a large extent; **les sociétés, pour la plus grande p., sont privatisées** firms, for the most part, are privatized; **elle ne participe que pour une petite p. aux frais d'exploitation** she only pays a fraction *or* small part of the running costs; **il y a toujours une p. d'affabulation dans ce qu'il dit** there's always a touch of fantasy in what he says; **il y a une grande p. de peur dans son échec** his/her failure is due largely to fear, fear goes a long way towards explaining his/her failure; *Rad & TV* **p. d'audience** audience share

5 *(participation)* **prendre p. à** *(discussion, compétition, manifestation)* to take part in; *(cérémonie, projet)* to join in, to play a part in; *(attentat)* to take part in, to play a part in; **deux cyclistes ne prendront pas p. à la course** two riders will not be (taking part) in the race; **prendre p. à la joie/peine de qn** to share (in) sb's joy/sorrow; **un acte où la volonté n'a eu aucune p.** an act in which willpower had no share *or* part; **la chance n'a aucune p. dans sa réussite** luck has nothing to do with his/her success; **il faut faire la p. du hasard/de la malchance** you have to recognize the part played by chance/ill-luck, you have to make allowances for chance/ill-luck; **faire la p. des choses** to take things into consideration; **faire la p. du feu** to cut one's losses

6 *Théât (aparté)* (artist's) cut

7 *(locutions)* **je viens de la p. de Paula** Paula sent me; **donne-le lui de ma p.** give it to him/her from me; **dis-lui au revoir/merci de ma p.** say goodbye/thank you for me; **je vous appelle de la p. de Jacques** I'm calling on behalf of Jacques; **de ta p., cela me surprend beaucoup** I'm surprised at you; **je ne m'attendais pas à une telle audace/mesquinerie de leur p.** I didn't expect such boldness/meanness from them; **c'est très généreux de ta p.** that's very generous of you; **cela demande un certain effort de votre p.** it requires a certain amount of effort on your part; **c'est de la p. de qui?** *(au téléphone, à un visiteur)* who (shall I say) is calling?; **pour ma/sa p.** (as) for me/him/her; **pour ma p., je n'ai rien contre** as for me *or Sout* for my part, I have nothing against it; **d'une p...., d'autre p....** on the one hand..., on the other hand...; **nous avons entamé des négociations avec les Américains d'une p. et les Japonais d'autre p.** we have started talks with the Americans and with the Japanese; **faire p. de qch à qn** to announce sth to sb, to inform sb of sth; **elle m'a fait p. à plusieurs reprises de ses difficultés financières** she told me about her financial problems on several occasions; **prendre qch en bonne p.** to take sth in good part; **prendre qch en mauvaise p.** to take offence at sth, to take sth amiss; **ne le prenez pas en mauvaise p., mais...** don't be offended *or* don't take this the wrong way, but...

❑ **à part ADJ 1** *(séparé → comptes, logement)* separate **2** *(original, marginal)* odd; **ce sont des gens à p.** these people are rather special **ADV 1** *(à l'écart)* **elle est restée à p. toute la soirée** she kept herself to herself all evening; **les stagiaires ont l'impression qu'on les met à p.** the trainees feel they're being left on the sidelines; **mets les dossiers bleus à p.** put the blue files to one side; **mis à p. deux ou trois détails, tout est prêt** except for *or* apart from two or three details, everything is ready **2** *(en aparté)* **prendre qn à p.** to take sb aside *or* to one side **3** *(séparément)* separately; **faites cuire la viande à p.** cook the meat separately *or* on its own **PRÉP 1** *(excepté)* except for, apart *or* aside from; **à p. toi, personne ne le sait** nobody knows apart from you; **à p. cela** apart from that, that aside **2 à p. soi** to oneself; **elle se disait à p. soi que...** she said to herself that...

❑ **à part entière ADJ un membre à p. entière de** a full *or* fully paid up member of; **citoyen à p. entière** person with full citizenship (status); **elle est devenue une actrice à p. entière** she's now a proper *or* a fully-fledged actress

❑ **à part que CONJ** *Fam* except that[■], if it weren't *or* except for the fact that[■]; **c'est une jolie maison, à p. qu'elle est un peu humide** it's a nice house, except that it's a bit damp

❑ **de part en part ADV** from end to end, throughout, right through; **la poutre est fendue de p. en p.** the beam is split from end to end

❑ **de part et d'autre ADV 1** *(des deux côtés)* on both sides, on either side

2 *(partout)* on all sides; **on entendait dire, de p. et d'autre, que...** people on all sides were saying that...

❑ **de part et d'autre de PRÉP** on both sides of

❑ **de toute part, de toutes parts ADV** (from) everywhere, from all sides *or* quarters; **ils accouraient de toutes parts vers le village** they were rushing towards the village from all directions; **l'eau fuyait de toutes parts** water was leaking out everywhere

❑ **pour une large part ADV** to a great extent

part. *(abrév écrite* **particulier***)* **p. vend moto état neuf** private sale: brand-new motorbike

partage [partaʒ] **NM 1** *(division → d'un domaine)* division, dividing *or* splitting up; *(→ d'un pays)* partition; *(→ d'un rôti)* carving; *(→ d'un gâteau)* slicing, cutting (up); **faire le p. de qch** to divide sth up; **à la mort des parents, il y aura p.** when the parents die, the estate will be split *or* divided up

2 *(répartition → d'une fortune, des devoirs, des tâches)* sharing out; *(→ des torts, des fautes)* sharing, apportioning; **p. des bénéfices** profit-sharing; *Aviat* **p. de code** code-sharing; **p. du pouvoir** power sharing, the sharing of power; **p. du travail** jobsharing

3 *Littéraire (lot)* lot; **la souffrance est le p. du genre humain** suffering is the lot of mankind

4 *Jur (acte juridique)* partition; **p. d'ascendant** partition in will

5 *Géom* division

6 *Ordinat* **p. des données** data sharing; **p. de fichiers** file sharing; **p. d'imprimantes** printer sharing; **p. de temps** time-sharing

❑ **en partage ADV donner qch en p. à qn** to leave sb sth (in one's will); **il donna en p. à ses fils dix hectares de terre** he left ten hectares of land to be shared out between his sons; *Fig Littéraire* **ce que la nature lui a donné en p.** the gifts bestowed upon him/her by nature; **je n'ai reçu en p. que la vieille horloge de mon père** all I got for my share was my father's old clock

▫ **sans partage** ADJ *(joie)* unmitigated; *(affection)* undivided; *(engagement, enthousiasme)* thoroughgoing

partagé, -e [partaʒe] ADJ **1** *(opposé)* split, divided; **les avis sont partagés** opinions are divided; **j'ai lu des critiques partagées** I've read mixed reviews

2 *(indécis)* torn; **je suis très p. sur ce point** I have very mixed feelings on the subject; **il était p. entre la joie et la crainte** he was torn between joy and fear

3 *(mutuel → haine)* mutual, reciprocal; *(→ amour)* mutual

4 *(commun → sentiments, douleur)* shared

5 *Vieilli* **être bien/mal p.** *(être bien/mal loti)* to have received one's share/less than one's share

6 *Ordinat* **en temps p.** on a time-sharing basis

partageable [partaʒabl] ADJ **1** *(bien, propriété)* which can be shared out *or* divided; *(nombre)* divisible **2** *(point de vue)* that can be shared; **votre opinion est difficilement p.** your opinion is not one that can easily be shared **3** *Jur* partible

partager [17] [partaʒe] VT **1** *(diviser → propriété)* to divide up, to share out; **p. qch en deux/par moitié** to divide sth in two/into two halves; **partage la tarte en huit** cut the pie into eight pieces; **la France était alors partagée en deux zones** at the time, France was split *or* divided into two zones; **p. son temps entre deux occupations** to divide *or* split one's time between two occupations

2 *(moralement → pays, société)* to divide; **la question du désarmement partage le pays** the country is divided *or* split over the question of disarmament; **être partagé entre** to be split *or* divided between; **je suis partagée entre l'envie de finir mes études et celle de travailler** I'm torn between finishing my studies and getting a job

3 *(répartir → bénéfices, provisions)* to share out; **ils ont partagé la nourriture entre les deux/trois familles** they shared out the food between both/all three families; **partagez le chocolat équitablement** share out the chocolate fairly; **je lui ai proposé de p. mon croissant** I offered him/her a share of my croissant

4 *(avoir en commun)* to share; **p. un lit/une chambre avec qn** to share a bed/room with sb; **on partage un appartement** we share a *Br* flat *or Am* apartment; **p. la joie/peine/surprise de qn** to share (in) sb's joy/sorrow/surprise; **je ne partage vraiment rien avec ces gens-là** I really have nothing in common with those people; **le pouvoir est partagé entre les deux assemblées** power is shared *or* split between the two Houses; **p. l'avis de qn** to share sb's opinion; **voici une opinion partagée par beaucoup de gens** this is an opinion shared *or* held by many (people); **j'ai été heureuse de pouvoir vous faire p. ma joie** I was pleased to be able to share my joy with you

5 *Fin* **p. proportionnellement** to divide pro rata

USAGE ABSOLU **elle n'aime pas p.** she doesn't like to share

▸**se partager** VPR **1** *(biens, travail, vivres, butin)* to share (out); *Sport* **Lyon et Marseille se partagent la première place** Lyons and Marseilles share first place *or Br* are equal first; **se p. les faveurs du public** to be joint favourites with the public

2 *(diviser son temps)* **elles se partagent entre leur carrière et leurs enfants** their time is divided between their professional lives and their families

3 *(se diviser)* to fork, to divide; **se p. en** to be split *or* divided into; **l'association se partage en deux tendances** the association is split into two groups

4 *(être communiqué)* **ces expériences ne se partagent pas facilement** it's not easy to share such experiences

partageur, -euse [partaʒœr, -øz] ADJ willing to share; **cet enfant n'est pas très p.** this child is not good at sharing

partageux, -euse [partaʒø, -øz] *Vieilli* ADJ *(idéologie, politique)* advocating the equal distribution of wealth

NM,F advocate of the equal distribution of wealth

partagiciel [partaʒisjɛl] NM *Offic Ordinat* shareware

partance [partɑ̃s] **en partance** ADJ *(train, voyageur)* due to leave; *(avion)* about to take off; *(navire)* about to sail; **le dernier train en p.** the last train; **en p. pour** bound for

partant¹ [partɑ̃] CONJ *Littéraire* therefore, consequently, thus; **et, p., elle n'avait aucun droit sur la succession** and thus she had no claim on the estate

partant², -e [partɑ̃, -ɑ̃t] ADJ **être p. pour faire qch** to be willing *or* ready to do sth; **êtes-vous toujours p.?** are you still game?, can I/we/*etc* still count you in?

NM,F *Sport (cheval)* runner; *(cycliste, coureur)* starter

part-antenne [parɑ̃tɛn] (*pl* **parts-antenne**) NF *TV* = advance purchase of broadcasting rights

partenaire [partənɛr] NMF **1** *(gén)* partner; **je suis son p. au tennis** I partner him/her at tennis, I'm his/her tennis partner **2** *Écon* (business) partner; **partenaires commerciaux** trading partners; **p. financier** financial partner; **les partenaires sociaux** unions and management **3** *Cin & Théât* **il était mon p. dans la pièce** I acted opposite him in the play

partenarial, -e, -aux, -ales [partənarjal, -o] ADJ joint

partenariat [partənarja] NM partnership; *Mktg* **p. télévision** television tie-in; **p. public-privé** Public-Private Partnership, private finance initiative

parterre [partɛr] NM **1** *Hort (en bordure)* border; *(plus large)* bed, flowerbed; **un p. de fleurs** a flowerbed **2** *Fam (sol)* floor■ **3** *Théât (emplacement) Br* stalls, *Am* orchestra; *(spectateurs)* (audience in the) *Br* stalls *or Am* orchestra; **il y avait hier un p. distingué** there was a distinguished *or* select audience yesterday

parthe [part] ADJ Parthian

NM *(langue)* Parthian

▫ **Parthe** NMF Parthian

parthénogenèse [partenoʒənɛz] NF *Biol* parthenogenesis

parthénogénétique [partenoʒenetik] ADJ *Biol* parthenogenic, parthenogenetic, parthenogenous

Parthénon [partenɔ̃] NM **le P.** the Parthenon

parti¹ [parti] NM **1** *Pol* **p. (politique)** (political) party; **le p. (communiste)** the (Communist) Party; **le p. conservateur/démocrate/républicain/socialiste** the Conservative/Democratic/Republican/Socialist Party; **les partis de droite/gauche** the parties of the right/left, the right-wing/left-wing parties; **le système du p. unique** the one-party system

2 *(choix, décision)* decision, course of action; **hésiter entre deux partis** to wonder which course of action to take; **prendre le p. de la modération** to opt for moderation; **prendre le p. de faire qch** to make up one's mind to do sth, to decide to do sth; **j'ai fini par prendre le p. de vendre** I eventually decided to sell; **prendre p.** *(prendre position)* to take sides *or* a stand; **l'heure est venue de prendre p.** the time has come to take a stand, it's time to come (down) off the fence; **prendre p. pour/contre qch** to come out for/against sth; **il a résolument pris p. pour la musique concrète** he came down firmly on the side of concrete music; **prendre p. pour qn** to side *or* to take sides with sb; **prendre p. contre qn** to take sides against sb; **son p. est pris** his/her mind is made up, he's/she's made up his/her mind; **vous avez suffisamment tergiversé, il faut prendre un p.** you've hummed and hawed long enough, it's time you made up your mind; **elle ne sera jamais musicienne, il faut que j'en prenne mon/qu'elle en prenne son p.** she'll never be a musician, I'll/she'll just have to accept it

3 *(avantage)* **tirer p. de** *(situation)* to take advantage of; *(équipement)* to put to good use; **tirer p. du matériel** to put the equipment to good use; **elle ne sait pas tirer p. de ses qualifications** she doesn't know how to get the most out of her qualifications; **elle tire p. de tout** she can turn anything to her advantage; **il tire le meilleur p. possible de ses relations** he uses his connections to the best possible advantage

4 *Vieilli ou Hum (personne à marier)* **c'est un beau** *ou* **bon p.** he's/she's a good catch

5 *(locution)* **faire un mauvais p. à qn** to ill-treat sb

▫ **parti pris** NM **1** *(prise de position)* commitment; **avoir un p. pris de modernisme/clarté** to be committed to modernism/clear-thinking

2 *(préjugé)* bias; **je n'ai aucun p. pris contre le tennis professionnel, mais...** I'm not biased against professional tennis, but...; **être de p. pris** to be biased; **faire qch de p. pris** to do sth deliberately *or* on purpose; **être sans p. pris** to be unbiased *or* objective; **pour une fois, sois sans p. pris!** try to be objective for once!; **je dirais, sans p. pris, qu'elle est la meilleure** without any bias on my part, I'd say that she's the best

parti², -e¹ [parti] ADJ *Fam (ivre)* wasted, plastered; **tu étais bien p. hier soir!** you were pretty far gone *or Br* well away last night!

partiaire [parsjɛr] ADJ *Jur* **colon p.** = farmer who shares the produce of his farm with the landlord

partial, -e, -aux, -ales [parsjal, -o] ADJ biased, partial

partialement [parsjalmɑ̃] ADV in a biased *or* partial way

partialité [parsjalite] NF *(favorable)* partiality; *(défavorable)* bias; **p. en faveur de qn** partiality for sb, bias in favour of sb; **p. contre qn** bias against sb; **il juge toujours avec p.** he's always biased *or* biassed in his judgments

partibus [partibys] *voir* **in partibus**

participant, -e [partisipɑ̃, -ɑ̃t] ADJ participant, participating; **les personnes participantes** the participants, the people taking part

NM,F *(gén)* participant; *Sport* competitor; **les participants au congrès** the participants in *or* those taking part in the congress

participatif, -ive [partisipatif, -iv] ADJ **prêt p.** participating capital loan

participation [partisipasjɔ̃] NF **1** *(engagement, contribution → gén)* participation, involvement (**à** in); *(→ en classe)* level of participation; **doit faire des efforts de p.** *(élève)* must try to take part more; **il nie sa p. à** *ou* **dans l'enlèvement du prince** he denies having participated *or* been involved in the prince's kidnapping; **malgré sa p. à de nombreux jeux télévisés** *(candidat)* in spite of his/her having been a contestant in many TV game shows; **sa p. aux jeux Olympiques semble compromise** there's a serious question mark hanging over his/her participation in the Olympic Games; **apporter sa p. à qch** to contribute to sth; **cela s'est fait avec leur p.** they were involved in it; **la décision a été prise sans sa p.** the decision was made without him/her being involved *or* having any part in it; **notre foire du livre a dû se faire sans la p. des éditeurs** our book fair had to be held in the absence of any *or* without any publishers

2 *(dans un spectacle)* appearance; **avec la p. des frères Jarry** featuring the Jarry Brothers; **avec la p. spéciale de Robert Vann** guest appearance by Robert Vann

3 *(contribution financière)* contribution (to costs); **il y a 20 euros de p. aux frais** you have to pay 20 euros towards costs; **nous demandons à chacun une petite p.** we're asking every one of you to contribute a small amount *or* to make a small contribution

4 *Pol* **p. (électorale)** (voter) turnout; **un faible taux de** *ou* **une faible p. aux élections** a poor *or* low turnout at the polls

5 *Écon & Pol (détention de capital)* interest, share; **avoir une p. majoritaire dans une société** to have a majority holding *or* interest in a company; **il détient une p. de 6 pour cent dans l'entreprise** he holds a 6 percent share in the company; *Hist* **la P.** = desire for increased worker participation prevalent in the late 1960s; **p. aux frais** cost sharing; **prendre des participations dans une entreprise** to buy into a company; **p. aux bénéfices** profit-sharing; **p. croisée** cross-holding; **p. ouvrière** worker participation; **p. des salariés aux bénéfices** profit-sharing scheme

6 *Jur* **p. aux acquêts** = sharing of spouse's purchases after marriage subsequent to divorce, *Br* ≃ property adjustment; **p. criminelle** complicity

▫ **en participation** ADJ profit-sharing *(avant n)*

participative [partisipativ] *voir* **participatif**

participe [partisip] NM *Gram* participle (form); **p. passé/présent** past/present participle; **proposition p., p. absolu** participial construction

participer [3] [partisipe] **participer à** VT IND **1** *(prendre part à → concours, négociation, cérémonie)* to take part in; *(→ discussion)* to contribute to; *(→ projet)* to be involved in; *(→ aventure)* to be involved in, to be part of; *(→ épreuve sportive)* to take part *or* to be in; *(→ attentat, vol)* to be involved in, to take part in; *(→ jeu)* to join in; *(→ émission)* to take part in; **tous ceux qui ont participé au jeu** all contestants *or* competitors; **c'est le premier rallye/marathon auquel je participe** it's the first rally/marathon I've been in; **elle participe activement au projet** she takes an active part in the project; **elle nie avoir participé au complot** she denies having been involved in the plot; **j'aimerais te voir p. plus souvent aux tâches ménagères!** I'd like to see you taking on a greater share of the household chores!

2 *(partager)* to share (in); **p. à la douleur/joie de qn** to share in sb's pain/joy

3 *(financièrement → achat, dépenses)* to share in, to contribute to; **tous ses collègues ont participé au cadeau** all his/her colleagues contributed something towards the present

4 *Écon & Fin (profits, pertes)* to share (in); **p. aux bénéfices** to share in the profits

USAGE ABSOLU *(dans un jeu)* to take part, to join in; *(à l'école)* to contribute (during class); **tu ne participes pas assez (en classe)** you don't contribute enough in class; **l'idée principale du metteur en scène est de faire p. le public** the director's basic idea is to get *or* encourage the public to participate in the show

❑ **participer de** VT IND to pertain to; **tout ce qui participe de la philosophie** everything pertaining *or* relating to philosophy

participial, -e, -aux, -ales [partisipjal, -o] *Gram* ADJ participial

❑ **participiale** NF participial clause

particularisation [partikylarizasjɔ̃] NF particularization

particulariser [3] [partikylarize] VT **1** *(restreindre à un cas particulier)* to particularize; **p. une proposition générale** to particularize (from) a general statement **2** *(distinguer, singulariser)* to distinguish, to characterize; **cette façon de parler particularise le provençal** this manner of speaking is peculiar *or* specific to Provençal **3** *Jur* **p. une affaire** to specify (the identity of) one of the accused (in a case)

▸**se particulariser** VPR **se p. par** to be distinguished *or* characterized by

particularisme [partikylarism] NM particularism

particulariste [partikylarist] ADJ particularist

NMF particularist

particularité [partikylarite] NF **1** *(trait distinctif → d'une personne, d'une culture, d'une langue etc)* particularity, (specific) feature *or* characteristic *or* trait; *(→ d'une région)* distinctive feature; *(→ d'une machine)* special feature; **la p. de cet aspirateur, c'est qu'il n'a pas de sac** what distinguishes this vacuum cleaner (from all the rest) *or* what is special about this vacuum cleaner is that it doesn't have a bag; **les tortues de mer ont la p. de pondre dans le sable** a distinctive feature of turtles is that they lay their eggs in the sand

2 *(élément)* detail, particular; **pourquoi insister sur cette p.?** why stress that particular *or* specific aspect?

particule [partikyl] NF **1** *Géol, Gram & Phys* particle; **p. alpha/bêta** alpha/beta particle; **p. élémentaire** elementary *or* fundamental particle **2** *(dans un nom)* particule *(the preposition "de" in a surname, indicating aristocratic origin)*

'Les Particules élémentaires' *Houellebecq* 'Atomised'

particulier, -ère [partikylje, -ɛr] ADJ **1** *(précis → circonstance, exemple, point)* particular, specific; **j'ai traité un aspect p. de son œuvre** I've dealt with a particular *or* specific aspect of his/her work

2 *(caractéristique → odeur, humour, parler, style)* distinctive, characteristic; **p. à** peculiar to, characteristic of; **une odeur particulière au pois de senteur** a fragrance peculiar to sweetpeas; **il a un humour qui lui est p.** he has his own special brand of humour; **un trait bien p.** a highly distinctive feature; *Littéraire* **une façon de marcher à lui particulière** his own particular way of walking

3 *(exceptionnel)* particular, special, unusual; **porter une attention toute particulière à qch** to pay particular *or* special attention to sth; **elle avait pour cette amie une tendresse toute particulière** she was particularly fond of that friend; **leurs photos n'offrent pas d'intérêt p.** their photographs are of *or* hold no particular interest; **il ne s'est rien passé de p.** nothing special *or* particular happened

4 *(bizarre → comportement, goûts, mœurs)* peculiar, odd; **elle a toujours été un peu particulière** she's always been a bit unusual; **ses tableaux sont très particuliers** his/her pictures are very peculiar

5 *(privé → avion, intérêts)* private; **j'ai une voiture particulière** I've got my own car *or* a car of my own; **cours p., leçon particulière** private lesson; **je donne des cours particuliers de latin** I give private lessons *or Br* tuition in Latin

6 *Can (minutieux)* meticulous, particular

NM **1** *(personne privée)* private individual; **simple p.** ordinary person, private citizen; **il loge chez des particuliers** *Br* he's in private lodgings, *Am* he rooms with a family; **vente de p. à p.** private sale

2 *Fam Péj (individu)* character; **un drôle de p.** an odd character

3 *(élément individuel)* **le p.** the particular; **passer du p. au général** to go from the particular to the general

❑ **en particulier** ADV **1** *(essentiellement)* in particular, particularly, especially; **vous avez été très désagréables, toi en p., Jacques** you've been most unpleasant, especially you *or* you in particular, Jacques; **les Français en général et les Parisiens en p.** French people in general and Parisians in particular

2 *(seul à seul)* in private; **puis-je vous parler en p.?** may I have a private word with you?; **recevoir qn en p.** to see sb privately *or* in private

particulièrement [partikyljɛrmɑ̃] ADV **1** *(surtout)* particularly, specifically, in particular; **nous nous attacherons plus p. à cet aspect de l'œuvre** we shall deal in particular *or* more specifically with this aspect of the work; **j'avais tout p. envie de cette robe-là** I particularly wanted that dress; **leurs enfants sont très beaux, p. leur fille** their children are very good-looking, especially their daughter

2 *(spécialement)* particularly, specially, especially; **il n'est pas p. laid/doué** he's not particularly ugly/gifted; **je n'aime pas p. cela** I'm not particularly keen on it; **je ne la connais pas p.** I don't know her very *or* particularly well; **tu aimes le whisky? – pas p.** do you like whisky? – not particularly

PARTIE² [parti]

> part **1, 2, 6, 8, 10** ■ game **3** ■ field **5** ■ party **7**

ADJ F *voir* **parti²**

NF **1** *(élément, composant)* part; **les parties du corps** the parts of the body; **les parties constituantes** the component parts; **faire p. de** *(comité)* to be a member of, to be on, to sit on; *(club, communauté)* to be a member of, to belong to; *(équipe)* to belong to, to be one of, to be in; *(licenciés)* to be among, to be one of; *(métier, inconvénients, risques)* to be part of; **tous ceux qui font p. de notre association** all the members of our association; **ils ne font pas p. de la Communauté européenne** they don't belong to *or* aren't a member of the European Community; **il ne fait plus p. de notre personnel** he's no longer on our staff, he's not a member of our staff any more; **il fait presque p. de la famille** he's almost one of the family; **faire p. intégrante de** to be an integral part of; **cela fait p. intégrante de la vie quotidienne** it's part and parcel of everyday life; **parties génitales** *ou* **sexuelles** genitals, private parts; **parties viriles** male (sexual) organs; *Fam* **ses parties** his privates

2 *(fraction, morceau)* part; **couper qch en deux parties** to cut sth into two (parts); **coupez le melon en trois parties** cut the melon into three parts; **la p. visible de la Lune** the visible side of the Moon; **la p. boisée de la colline** the wooded part *or* side of the hill; *Hum* **dans la p. charnue de mon anatomie** in the fleshy part of my anatomy; **une p. du blé est contaminée** some *or* part of the wheat is contaminated; **ce n'est qu'une p. de la vérité** it's only part of the truth; **une p. de l'héritage** (a) part of the inheritance; **une grande/petite p. de l'électorat** a large/small part of the electorate, a large/small section of the electorate; **il est absent une grande** *ou* **la plus grande p. du temps** he's away much of *or* most of the time; **pendant la plus grande p. du chemin** (for) most of the way; **la plus grande p. de ses concerts** most of his/her concerts; **j'ai lu une p. de ses livres** I've read some of his/her books; **je n'ai coupé qu'une p. des dahlias** I've only cut some of the dahlias

3 *Sport & (jeu)* game; **faire une p. de cartes** to have a game of cards; **on fait une p.?** shall we play *or* have a game?; **il va tous les soirs faire sa p. chez le docteur Ranton** he goes to Doctor Ranton's every night to play cards; *aussi Fig* **la p. n'est pas égale** it's an uneven match, it's not a fair match; *Fig* **la p. sera difficile à jouer** it's not going to be easy, we've got a tough time ahead of us; **p. d'échecs/de billard/de tennis/de cartes** game of chess/billiards/tennis/cards; **p. de golf** round of golf; *Fig* **abandonner** *ou* **quitter la p.** to give up the fight, to throw in the towel; *Fig* **avoir la p. belle** to be in a favourable position, to be well placed; *Fig* **avoir p. gagnée** to be bound to succeed; *Fig* **la p. est jouée/n'est pas jouée** the outcome is a foregone conclusion/is still wide open; *Golf* **p. par coups** stroke play; *Golf* **p. par points** stableford; *Golf* **p. par trous** match play

4 *(divertissement à plusieurs)* **p. de chasse/pêche** shooting/fishing party; **p. de campagne** day *or* outing in the country; *Fam* **p. carrée** foursome; *Fam* **p. fine** orgy▪; *Fam* **une p. de jambes en l'air** a bit of nooky; **p. de plaisir** pleasure trip; *Fam* **cette course était une véritable p. de plaisir** that race was a piece of cake; *Fam* **ça n'est pas une p. de plaisir!** it's no picnic *or* fun!; *Can* **p. de sucre** sugaring-off party *(celebration held during the maple sugar harvesting season)*; **on va lui faire une farce, qui veut être de la p.?** we're going to play a trick on him/her, who wants to join in?; **elle m'a déjà fait assez de reproches, ne te mets pas (aussi) de la p.** I've had enough criticism from her, don't you join in as well; **s'il se met aussi de la p., nous aurons les capitaux nécessaires** if he comes in on it too, we shall have the necessary capital; **je ne peux pas partir avec toi cette fois, mais ce n'est que p. remise** I can't go with you this time, but there'll be other opportunities; **ce n'est que p. remise, je me vengerai!** I'll get even some day!

5 *(domaine, spécialité)* field, line; **ce n'est pas ma p.** it's not my field *or* line; **elle est de la p.** it's her line; **moi qui suis de la p., je peux te dire que ce ne sera pas facile** being in that line of business myself, I can tell you it won't be easy

6 *Mus* part; **la p. de la clarinette/du soprano** the clarinet/soprano part

7 *(participant → gén) & Jur* party; **être p. dans** to be a party to *or* in; **être p. dans une négociation** to be a party to a negotiation; **les parties en présence** the parties; **les deux parties demandent le renvoi de l'affaire** both sides have requested an adjournment; **les parties belligérantes** the belligerent *or* warring parties; **p. adverse/intervenante** opposing/intervening party; **p. appelante** appellant; **p. civile** private party *(acting jointly with the public prosecutor in criminal cases)*, plaintiff *(for damages)*; **se constituer** *ou* **se porter p. civile** to act jointly with the public prosecutor; **parties communes** communal spaces; **p. comparante** appearer;

parties contractantes/intéressées contracting/interested parties; hautes parties contractantes sovereign contracting parties p. défaillante party failing to appear (in court), defaulting party; p. jointe co-plaintiff/co-defendant; p. lésée aggrieved party; les parties plaidantes the litigants; p. poursuivie defendant; p. prenante payee, receiver; Fig être p. prenante dans qch to be directly involved or concerned in sth; p. principale (gén) principal party; (ministère public) Br ≃ the Crown (in Crown proceedings), Am ≃ the District Attorney; parties privatives private spaces; la p. publique ou poursuivante public prosecutor, Br ≃ the Crown, Am ≃ the District Attorney; p. requérante claimant, petitioner; les parties signataires signatories;

8 Gram p. du discours part of speech

9 Math p. d'un ensemble subset

10 Chim p. par million part per million

11 (locution) avoir p. liée avec qn to be hand in glove with sb; ils avaient p. liée depuis le début they were working hand in glove together from the start

12 Compta en p. double double-entry; en p. simple single-entry

13 parties annexes (d'un ouvrage) end matter

❏ à partie ADV s'attaquer à qn à p. (s'attaquer à lui) to set on sb; (l'interpeller) to take sb to task

❏ en partie ADV in part, partly, partially; en p. dû au mauvais temps partly due to the bad weather; je ne l'ai cru qu'en p. I only half believed him; c'est en p. vrai it's partly true; c'est en p. de la fiction et en p. de la réalité it's part fiction and part truth; c'est en p. de l'or et en p. de l'argent it's partly gold and partly silver; en grande ou majeure p. for the most part, largely, mainly; c'est en grande p. à cause de lui it's largely because of him

❏ pour partie ADV partly, in part

'Partie de campagne' Renoir 'An Outing to the Country'

partiel, -elle [parsjɛl] ADJ partial; contrôle ou examen p. mid-term exam; (emploi à) temps p. part-time job; elle ne le fait qu'à temps p. she only does it part-time

NM **1** Univ mid-term exam **2** Phys partial

❏ partielle NF Pol by-election

partiellement [parsjɛlmɑ̃] ADV partially, partly; ce n'est que p. vrai it's only partly true

PARTIR [43] [partir]

VI to go 1–4, 9, 10 ■ to leave 1, 3, 6 ■ to pass away 1 ■ to set off 2 ■ to set out 2 ■ to start off 2, 7 ■ to go off 6 ■ to disappear 9 ■ to come out 9, 10 ■ to come off 10

VI **1** (s'en aller) to go, to leave; Euph (mourir) to pass on or away; quand je partirai when I depart this life or this world, when I pass on; pars, tu vas rater ton train (off you) go, or you'll miss your train; il faut que je parte I must be off, I must go or leave; je peux p. maintenant? can I go or leave now?; Paul est déjà parti Paul has gone or left already; empêche-la de p. stop her (going), don't let her go; je ne vous fais pas p., j'espère I hope I'm not chasing you away; p. en courant/boitant to run/to limp off; p. discrètement to leave discreetly, to slip off; laisser p. (prisonnier, otage) to set free, to let go, to release; (écolier) to let out; (employé) to let go; laisse-moi p. let me go; si ça ne vous plaît pas, vous pouvez toujours p. if you don't like it, you can always go or leave; sa femme est partie pour toujours/avec son meilleur ami his wife has gone for good/gone off with his best friend; il est parti avec la caisse he ran away or off with the till; faites-les p. ask them to leave; le climat les a fait p. the climate drove them away; tout son argent part en jeux vidéo all his/her money goes on computer games; p. de to leave; je ne peux pas p. du bureau avant 17h30 I can't leave the office before 5.30; je suis parti de chez moi à 10 heures I left home at 10; p. du

gouvernement to leave office or the government; une prime pour ceux qui partiront volontairement de l'entreprise a bonus for those who leave the company voluntarily

2 (se mettre en route) to set off or out, to start off; il faut p. de bonne heure pour éviter les bouchons we must set off early or make an early start if we want to beat the traffic jams; pars devant, je te rattrape go ahead, I'll catch up with you; Fam regarde cette circulation, on n'est pas encore partis! by the look of that traffic, we're not off yet!; le courrier n'est pas encore parti the post hasn't gone yet; p. en avion (personne) to fly (off); (courrier) to go air mail or by air; p. en bateau to go (off) by boat, to sail; p. à bicyclette to go (off) by bike, to cycle off; p. en voiture to go (off) by car, to drive off

3 (se rendre) to go, to leave; je pars à ou pour Toulon demain I'm leaving for or I'm off to Toulon tomorrow; nous partons en Espagne à Pâques we're going or we're off to Spain at Easter; dans quelle direction est-elle partie? which way did she go?; il est parti à la cuisine he's gone (off) to the kitchen; p. à la campagne/montagne/mer to go (off) to the countryside/mountains/seaside; p. vers le sud to go south; toutes les eaux usées partent dans les égouts all liquid waste goes (down) into the sewers

4 (aller → pour se livrer à une activité) to go; elle est partie au tennis/à la danse she's gone to play tennis/to her dance class; p. à la chasse/pêche to go shooting/fishing; p. à la recherche de to set off in search of, to go looking for; p. à la guerre to go (off) to war; p. en week-end to go off or away for the weekend; nous partons en excursion/voyage demain we're setting off on an excursion/a journey tomorrow; tu ne pars pas (en vacances) cet été? aren't you going on Br holiday or Am vacation this summer?; p. en congé maternité to go on maternity leave; p. skier/se promener to go skiing/for a walk; sa tête est partie heurter le buffet his/her head hit the sideboard

5 (s'engager) p. dans un discours to launch into a speech; p. dans une explication to embark on an explanation; p. sur un sujet to start off on a topic; Fam quand elles sont parties sur leur boulot, c'est difficile de les arrêter once they start on about their job, there's no stopping them; Fam les voilà partis à refaire toute la maison there they go doing up the entire house

6 (démarrer → machine, moteur, voiture) to start (up); (→ avion) to take off, to leave; (→ train) to leave, to depart; (→ fusée) to go up; (→ pétard) to go off; (→ plante) to take; ton avion n'est pas encore parti your plane hasn't left yet; le coup (de feu) est parti tout seul the gun went off on its own; il m'a insulté et la gifle est partie he insulted me and I just slapped him; excuse-moi, le mot est parti (tout seul) I'm sorry, the word just slipped out; faire p. (moteur) to start (up); (pétard) to set or to let off; (fusil) to let off; (plante) to get started; Fam je ferai p. ma daube à 11 heures I'll get my stew on at 11 o'clock

7 (se mettre en mouvement, débuter → coureur, match, concert) to start (off); la contrebasse est partie avant la mesure the double bass started off or came in before the beat; Sport il est parti trop vite he set or went off too fast; on est partis pour avoir des ennuis! we're headed for trouble!; elle est partie pour nous faire la tête toute la soirée she's all set to sulk the whole evening; le match est bien/mal parti pour notre équipe the match has started well/badly for our team; le projet est bien parti the project is off to a good start; je le vois mal parti pour récupérer son titre the way he's going, I just can't see him winning back his title; elle a l'air bien partie pour remporter l'élection she seems well set to win the election

8 (se vendre) to sell; le nouveau modèle part bien the new model is selling well

9 (disparaître, s'effacer → inscription) to disappear, to be rubbed off or out, to be worn off; (→ tache) to disappear, to go, to come out; (→ douleur) to go, to disappear; (→ bouton) to come off;

(→ pellicules, odeur) to go; ça partira au lavage it'll wash off, it'll come out in the wash; faire p. (salissure) to get rid of, to remove; (odeur) to get rid of, to clear; (douleur) to ease; je n'arrive pas à faire p. les traces de doigts sur la table I can't remove the finger marks from the table; ça ne fera pas p. ton mal de gorge it won't get rid of your sore throat; rien de tel que la toile émeri pour faire p. la rouille there's nothing like emery paper for removing rust

10 (se défaire, se détacher → attache, bouton) to come off, to go; (→ maille) to run; (→ étiquette) to come off

❏ à partir de PRÉP **1** (dans le temps) (as) from; à p. d'aujourd'hui from today onwards, (as) from today; à p. de mardi starting from Tuesday, from Tuesday onwards; à p. de 5 heures from 5 o'clock on or onwards; à p. de (ce moment-)là, il ne m'a plus adressé la parole from that moment on or from then on, he never spoke to me again **2** (dans l'espace) (starting) from; le deuxième à p. de la droite the second (one) from the right; comptez cinq espaces à p. de la marge count five spaces in from the margin; à p. du carrefour, c'est tout droit after the crossroads, it's straight on or ahead **3** (numériquement) imposé à p. de 2000 euros taxable from 2,000 euros upwards; compte à p. de dix count from ten **4** (avec, à base de) from; c'est fait à p. d'huiles végétales it's made from or with vegetable oils; on ne peut pas tirer de conclusions à p. de si peu de preuves you can't reach any conclusion on the basis of so little evidence; j'ai fait un résumé à p. de ses notes I've made a summary based on his/her notes

❏ partir de VT IND **1** (dans l'espace) pour teindre le cheveu, on part de la racine to dye hair, you start with the roots; de petites pousses partent du pied little sprouts are shooting up from the root; le ferry/marathon part de Brest the ferry sails from/the marathon starts in Brest; la rue part de la mairie the street starts at the town hall; la cicatrice part du poignet et va jusqu'au coude the scar goes or stretches from the wrist to the elbow; c'est le quatrième en partant de la droite/du haut it's the fourth (one) from the right/top **2** (dans le temps) nous allons faire p. le contrat du 15 janvier we'll make the contract effective (as) from 15 January; votre congé part de la fin mai your holidays begin at the end of May **3** (dans un raisonnement) p. du principe que… to start from the principle that…, to start by assuming that…; si l'on part de ce principe, il faudrait ne jamais contester on that basis, one should never protest; tu ne devrais pas p. du présupposé que… you shouldn't start (off) by presupposing that or start from the presupposition that… **4** (provenir de) tous les problèmes sont partis de là all the problems stemmed from that; ça partait d'un bon sentiment his/her intentions were good; sa remarque est partie du cœur his/her comment came or was (straight) from the heart, it was a heartfelt remark

partisan, -e [partizɑ̃, -an] ADJ (querelles, esprit) partisan; (choix) biased; être p. de qch/de faire qch to be in favour of sth/doing sth; elle n'est pas partisane de cette thèse she doesn't favour this theory

NM

1 (adepte, défenseur) supporter; c'est un p. de la censure he's for or in favour of censorship **2** (dans une guerre) partisan; guerre de partisans guerilla or guerrilla warfare

partisante [partizɑ̃t] ADJ F Fam être p. de qch ou faire qch to be in favour of sth/doing sth■; elle

n'est pas p. de cette thèse she doesn't favour this theory

partita [partita] **NF** partita

partiteur [partitœr] **NM** *Agr* irrigation sluice

partitif, -ive [partitif, -iv] *Gram* **ADJ** partitive
NM partitive (form)

partition [partisjɔ̃] **NF 1** *Mus (symboles)* score; *(livret)* score, music; **elle joue sans p.** she plays without music; **p. d'orchestre** full score **2** *Hist & Pol* partition, partitioning, splitting; **lors de la p. de l'Inde** when India was partitioned **3** *Ordinat & Math* partition

partitionner [partisjɔne] **VT** *Ordinat (disque)* to partition

partitive [partitiv] *voir* **partitif**

partousard, -e [partuzar, -ard] **NM,F** *Fam* = person who takes part in an orgy

partouse [partuz] **NF** *Fam* orgy▪

partouser [3] [partuze] **VI** *Fam* = to take part in an orgy

partout [partu] **ADV 1** *(dans l'espace)* everywhere; **chercher qch p.** to look everywhere for sth; **je ne peux pas être p. à la fois!** I can't be everywhere *or* in two places at the same time!; **les cloches sonnaient p. à la fois** the bells were ringing everywhere at once; **il laisse toujours traîner ses affaires p.** he always leaves his things all over the place; **il a voyagé un peu p.** he's been all over the place; **ils ont habité un peu p. en Italie** they've lived all over Italy; **j'ai mal p.** I ache all over; **le toit prend l'eau de p.** the roof leaks everywhere; **les gens accouraient de p.** people came rushing from all sides; **p. où** everywhere (that), wherever

2 *Sport* **3 buts p.** 3 (goals) all; **15 p.** *(au tennis)* 15 all; **40 p.** deuce

partouzard, -e [partuzar, -ard] = **partousard**

partouze [partuz] = **partouse**

partouzer [3] [partuze] = **partouser**

part-time, part time [partajm] **NM** *Belg & Can (emploi)* part-time job; *(travailleur)* part-time worker

parturiente [partyrjɑ̃t] **NF** parturient

parturition [partyrisjɔ̃] **NF** parturition

paru, -e [pary] **PP** *voir* **paraître[2]**

parulie [paryli] **NF** *Méd* gumboil, *Spéc* parulis

parure [paryr] **NF 1** *(ensemble)* set; **p. de berceau** *Br* cot *or Am* crib set; **p. de lit** set of bed linen

2 *(bijoux)* parure, set of jewels; *(colifichets)* matching set of costume jewellery

3 *Littéraire (ornements)* finery; **dans sa plus belle p.** in all her (best) finery; *Fig* **les arbres revêtus de leur p. de gel** the trees dressed in their coat of frost; *Fig* **la beauté sans p.** beauty unadorned

❑ **parures NFPL** *Culin* scraps, trimmings

parurerie [paryrri] **NF** costume jewellery and accessories trade

parurier, -ère [paryrje, -ɛr] **NM,F 1** *(fabricant)* manufacturer of costume jewellery and accessories **2** *(commerçant)* dealer in costume jewellery and accessories

parut *etc voir* **paraître[2]**

parution [parysjɔ̃] **NF** *(gén)* publication; *(d'une revue)* issue; **juste avant/après la p. du livre** just before/after the book came out; **date de p.** *(d'un livre, article)* date of publication, publication date; *(d'une revue)* date of issue

parvenir [40] [parvənir]

USAGE ABSOLU *Vieilli (s'élever socialement)* to succeed *or* get on (in life)

❑ **parvenir à VT IND** *(aux être)* **1** *(atteindre → sujet: voyageur, véhicule, lettre, son)* **p. à** *ou* **jusqu'à** to get to, to reach; **nous voici parvenus au sommet de la butte** we've now reached the top of the hill; **l'ambulance ne put p. jusqu'à lui** the ambulance couldn't get (through) to him; **faire p. un colis à qn** to send sb a parcel; **si cette carte vous parvient** if you get *or* receive this card; **votre demande doit nous p. avant le 4** your application must be in *or* reach us by the 4th; **l'histoire est parvenue aux oreilles de sa femme** the story reached his wife's ears; **des écrits anciens qui sont parvenus jusqu'à nous** ancient writings which have come down to us

2 *(obtenir → célébrité, réussite)* to achieve; **étant parvenu au faîte de la gloire** having reached *or* achieved the pinnacle of fame; **p. à une parfaite entente** to reach complete agreement

3 *(en venir à)* to reach; **elle était parvenue à un âge avancé** she had reached an advanced age; **une fois le projet parvenu à maturité** once the project had matured *or* had reached maturity

4 *(réussir à)* **p. à faire qch** to succeed in doing *or* to manage to do sth; **il ne parviendra jamais à la convaincre** he'll never succeed in convincing *or* manage to convince her

parvenu, -e [parvəny] *Péj* **ADJ** parvenu, upstart, nouveau riche
NM,F parvenu, upstart, nouveau riche

parvient, parvint *etc voir* **parvenir**

parvis [parvi] **NM** parvis, square *(in front of church or public building)*; **parking interdit sur le p. de la cathédrale** *(sur panneau)* no parking in front of the cathedral

PAS [peaɛs] **NM** *Pharm (abrév* **acide para-amino-salicylique***)* PAS

pas[1] [pɑ] **NM 1** *(déplacement)* step; **mes p. me conduisirent à une clairière** my steps took me to a clearing; **je vais faire quelques p. dans le parc** I'm going for a short *or* little walk in the park; **le convalescent fit quelques p. dehors** the convalescent took a few steps outside; **revenir** *ou* **retourner sur ses p.** to retrace one's steps *or* path, to turn back; **arriver sur les p. de qn** to follow close on sb's heels, to arrive just after sb; **avancer à** *ou* **faire de petits p.** to take short steps; **marcher à grands p.** to stride along; **faire un p. sur le côté** to take a step to the *or* to one side; **faire un p. en avant** to step forward, to take a step *or* pace forward; **faire un petit p. en avant** to take a small step *or* to inch forward; **faire un p. en arrière** to step back; **faire ses premiers p.** to learn to walk; *Fig* **il a fait ses premiers p. de comédien dans un film de Hitchcock** he made his debut as an actor in a Hitchcock film; **marcher à p. de velours** to pad around; *Fig* **marcher sur les p. de qn** to follow in sb's footsteps; *Belg* **faire** *ou* **donner un p. de conduite à qn** to go with sb part of the way

2 *Fig (progrès)* **avancer à petits p.** to make slow progress; **la stratégie des petits p.** the softly-softly approach; **avancer à grands p.** *(enquête)* to make great progress; *(technique, science)* to take big steps forward; *(échéance, événement)* to be looming; **avancer à p. comptés** *ou* **mesurés** *(lentement)* to make slow progress; *(prudemment)* to tread carefully; *Fig* to proceed slowly but surely; **faire un p. en avant** *(discussion, négociateur)* to take a step forward; **faire un grand p. en avant** to take a great step *or* leap forward; **faire un p. en arrière** to take a step back *or* backwards; **faire un p. en avant et deux (p.) en arrière** to take one step forward and two steps back *or* backwards; **faire le premier p.** to make the first move; **il n'y a que le premier p. qui coûte** the first step is the hardest; **c'est au moins un p. sur la bonne voie** at least it's a step in the right direction

3 *Fig (étape)* step; **c'est un p. difficile pour lui que de te parler directement** talking to you directly is a difficult step for him to take; **c'est un grand p. à faire** *ou* **franchir** it's a big step to take; **franchir** *ou* **sauter le p.** to take the plunge; **le p. est vite fait** *ou* **franchi** one thing very easily leads to the other

4 *(empreinte)* footprint; **des p. sur le sable** footprints in the sand

5 *(allure)* pace; **allonger** *ou* **doubler le p.** to quicken one's step *or* pace; **hâter** *ou* **presser le p.** to hurry on; **ralentir le p.** to slow one's pace, to slow down; **aller du** *ou* **marcher au même p.** to walk at the same pace; **aller** *ou* **marcher d'un bon p.** to walk at a good *or* brisk pace; **avancer** *ou* **marcher d'un p. lent** to walk slowly; **changer de p.** to change pace

6 *(démarche)* gait, tread; **marcher d'un p. alerte/léger/élastique** to walk with a sprightly/light/bouncy tread; **avancer d'un p. lourd** *ou* **pesant** to tread heavily, to walk with a heavy tread; **elle entendait son p. irrégulier/feutré sur la terrasse** she could hear his irregular/soft footfall on the terrace

7 *Mil* step; **p. accéléré** = marching step between quick march and double-quick; **p. cadencé** quick march; *Mil* **au p. de charge** at the charge; *Fig* charging along; **au p. redoublé** on the double, at double quick march; **p. de route** march at ease

8 *(danse)* pas, step; **apprendre le p. du tango** to learn the tango *or* how to (dance the) tango; **esquisser un p.** to dance a few steps, to do a little dance; **p. battu/tombé** pas battu/tombé; **p. de deux/trois** pas de deux/trois

9 *Sport* **au p. de course** at a run; *Fig* at a run, on the double; **au p. de gymnastique** at a jog trot; *Ski* **faire des p. tournants** to skate a turn; *Équitation* **p. allongé/rassemblé** extended/collected walk; *Ski* **p. alternatif** basic stride, hick-off and glide; *Ski* **p. de canard/de l'escalier** herringbone/side stepping climb; *Boxe* **p. de côté** side step; *Ski* **p. de patinage** *ou* **patineur** skating

10 *(mesure)* pace; *(espace approximatif)* pace, step; **comptez trente p.** count thirty steps *or* paces; **à quelques p. de là** a few steps *or* paces away; **l'église est à deux p.** the church is very close at hand *or* is only a stone's throw from here; **le restaurant n'est qu'à deux p. (de la gare)** the restaurant is (only) just round the corner (from the station); **il se tenait à quelques p. de moi** he was standing just a few yards from me; *Fig* **entre la consommation de drogue et la vente, il n'y a qu'un p.** there's only a small *or* short step from taking drugs to selling them; **ne pas quitter qn d'un p.** to follow sb's every footstep

11 *(marche d'escalier)* step; **attention au p. en descendant dans la cuisine** watch the step on the way (down) to the kitchen; **p. de porte** doorstep; **sur tous les p. de porte** on every doorstep; **ne reste pas sur le p. de la porte** don't stand at the door *or* on the doorstep *or* in the doorway

12 *Géog (en montagne)* pass; *(en mer)* strait; **le p. de Calais** the Strait of Dover

13 *Tech (d'une vis)* thread; *(d'une denture, d'un engrenage)* pitch; **p. à droite/gauche** right-hand/left-hand thread

14 *Aviat* pitch

15 *Mil* **p. de tir** *(pour missile)* launching site

16 *Math* pitch

17 *Élec* **p. de bobinage** winding pitch

18 *(locutions)* **prendre le p. sur qn/qch** to take precedence over sb/sth; **céder le p.** to give way; **les considérations financières ont fini par céder/prendre le p.** financial considerations eventually gave way/prevailed; **se tirer d'un mauvais p.** to get oneself out of a fix

❑ **à chaque pas ADV 1** *(partout)* everywhere, at every step; **je la rencontre à chaque p.** I meet her everywhere (I go)

2 *(constamment)* at every turn *or* step; **à chaque p. je dois corriger les mêmes erreurs** I keep having to correct the same mistakes

❑ **au pas ADV 1** *(en marchant)* at a walking pace; **ne courez pas, allez au p.** don't run, walk

2 *Aut* **aller** *ou* **rouler au p.** *(dans un embouteillage)* to crawl along; *(consigne de sécurité)* to go slow, *Br* to go dead slow

3 *Équitation* walking, at a walk; **mettre son cheval au p.** to walk one's horse; **mettre qn/qch au p.** to bring sb/sth to heel; **le président a mis le ministre au p.** the president forced the minister to toe the line *or* brought the minister back into line

❑ **de ce pas ADV** straightaway, at once; **je vais de ce p. lui dire ma façon de penser** I'm going to waste no time in telling him what I think

❑ **pas à pas ADV 1** *(de très près)* step by step; **il la suivait p. à p.** he followed her step by step

2 *(prudemment)* step by step, one step at a time; **il faut refaire l'expérience p. à p.** the experiment must be repeated step by step

3 *Ordinat* step by step

pas[2] [pɑ] **ADV 1** *(avec "ne", pour exprimer la négation)* **elle ne viendra p.** she won't come; **ils ne sont p. trop inquiets** they're not too worried; **je n'aime p. les légumes** I don't like vegetables; **ils n'ont p. de problèmes/d'avenir** they have no problems/no future, they haven't got any problems/a future; **il a décidé de ne p. accepter** he decided not to accept; **ce n'est p. que je ne veuille p., mais...** it's not that I don't want to, but...

2 *Fam (avec omission du "ne")* **elle sait p.** she

doesn't know■; **t'en fais p.!** don't (you) worry!■; **c'est p. sûr** it's not sure *or* definite■; **il est p. bête, lui!** that's good thinking!■; **c'est vraiment p. drôle!** *(pas amusant)* it's not in the least *or* slightest bit funny!■; *(ennuyeux)* it's no fun at all!■; **non, j'aime p.** no, I don't like it■

3 *(avec "non", pour renforcer la négation)* **non p.** not; **il était non p. sévère mais ferme** he wasn't strict, (he was) just firm; **elle est non p. belle mais jolie** she's not so much beautiful as pretty

4 *(employé seul)* **sincère ou p.** sincere or not; **fatigué ou p.** tired or not; **les garçons voulaient danser, les filles p.** the boys wanted to dance, the girls didn't; **tu comprends ou p.?** do you understand or not *or* or don't you?; **pourquoi p.?** why not?; **viendras-tu? – pourquoi p.?** will you come? – why not?; *Fam* **p. la peine** (it's) not worth it; **p. assez** not enough; **j'ai insisté, mais p. assez** I insisted but not sufficiently *or* enough; **des fraises p. mûres** unripe strawberries

5 *(dans des réponses négatives)* **p. de dessert pour moi, merci** no dessert for me, thank you; **qui l'a pris? – p. moi, en tout cas!** who took it? – not me, that's for sure!; **p. du tout** not at all; **c'est toi qui as fini les chocolats? – p. du tout!** was it you who finished the chocolates? – certainly not!; **je n'en suis p. du tout sûr** I'm not at all sure (about it); **p. le moins du monde** not in the least *or* slightest, not at all; **je vous dérange? – p. le moins du monde, entrez** am I disturbing you? – not in the least *or* not at all, come in; **absolument p.** not at all; **vous êtes bien d'accord? – absolument p.** do you agree? – absolutely not *or* not at all

6 *Fam (n'est-ce pas)* **on a fait ce qu'on a pu, p.?** we did what we could, didn't we *or* right?

❑ **pas mal** *Fam* **ADJ INV** not bad; **l'album n'est p. mal** the album isn't bad; **c'est p. mal comme idée** that's not a bad idea; **regarde mon dessin – ah, p. mal!** look at my drawing – ah, not bad! **ADV 1** *(bien)* **je ne m'en suis p. mal tiré** I handled it quite well; **on ferait p. mal de recommencer** we'd be better off starting again **2** *(très)* **il est p. mal soûl** he's pretty drunk; **la voiture est p. mal amochée** the car's pretty battered

❑ **pas mal de ADV** *Fam (suivi d'un nom dénombrable)* quite a few, quite a lot of; *(suivi d'un nom indénombrable)* quite a lot of; **p. mal de mensonges/journalistes** quite a few lies/journalists; **p. mal d'argent** quite a lot of money; **quand? – il y a p. mal de temps** when? – quite a while ago

❑ **pas plus mal ADV il a maigri – c'est p. plus mal** he's lost weight – good thing too *or* that's not such a bad thing *or* just as well; **il ne s'en est p. trouvé plus mal** he ended up none the worse for it

❑ **pas un, pas une ADJ** not a (single), not one; **p. une maison n'est restée debout** not a single *or* not one house was left standing; **p. un mot!** not a word!; **p. un bruit!** not a sound!; **p. un geste!** not one move! **PRON** not (a single) one; **p. une n'est arrivée à l'heure** not one *or* not a single one (of them) got there on time; **il n'y en a p. un d'acceptable** none of them are acceptable; **parmi elles, p. une qui ne veuille y aller** every one of them wants to go there; **p. un n'a bronché** there wasn't a peep out of any of them; **il s'y entend comme p. un pour déranger les gens à 2 heures du matin** he's a specialist at disturbing you at 2 in the morning; **il sait faire les crêpes comme p. un** he makes pancakes like nobody else (on earth)

pas-à-pas [pazapa] **ADJ INV** *Ordinat* step-by-step, single-step

NM INV 1 *Tech* step-by-step (mechanism) **2** *Ordinat* single-step operation

PASCAL [paskal] **NM INV** *Ordinat* PASCAL

pascal[1], -e, -als *ou* **-aux, -ales** [paskal, -o] **ADJ** *Rel (de la fête chrétienne)* Easter *(avant n)*, *Spéc* paschal; *(de la fête juive → gén)* paschal, Passover *(avant n)*; *(→ agneau)* paschal

pascal[2], -als [paskal] **NM 1** *Phys* pascal **2** *Anciennement Fam (billet)* **un p.** a 500-franc note■

pascalien, -enne [paskaljɛ̃, -ɛn] **ADJ** Pascalian, Pascal's; **le pari p.** Pascal's wager

> *Allusion*
> **Un pari pascalien**
> Blaise Pascal was both a mathematical genius and a Christian philosopher. One of the originators of probability theory, he suggested in his *Pensées* that if a man bets on the existence of God, he has everything to gain, and nothing to lose. In modern French, if one says **c'est un pari pascalien** it means that one has nothing to lose.

pascal-seconde [paskalsəgɔ̃d] *(pl* **pascals-seconde)** **NM** *Phys* pascal-second

pas-d'âne [pɑdɑn] **NM INV** *Bot* coltsfoot

Pas-de-Calais [pɑdəkalɛ] **NM le P.** Pas-de-Calais

pas-de-porte [pɑdpɔrt] **NM INV 1** *Com* ≃ commercial lease **2** *Jur* key money

pas-grand-chose [pagrɑ̃ʃoz] **NMF INV** *Péj* good-for-nothing

pashmina [paʃmina] **NM** *(laine, châle)* pashmina

pasionaria [pasjɔnarja] **NF** *(femme)* militant; **la p. du mouvement démocratique** the champion of the democratic movement

Pasiphaé [pazifae] **NPR** *Myth* Pasiphaë

paso doble [pasodɔbl] **NM INV** paso doble

passable [pɑsabl] **ADJ 1** *(acceptable)* passable, tolerable; **leur vin est p.** their wine is drinkable; **il écrit des vers passables** he writes quite good poetry **2** *Scol (tout juste moyen)* average **3** *Can (praticable)* negotiable, passable; **un chemin p.** a passable road

passablement [pɑsabləmɑ̃] **ADV 1** *(de façon satisfaisante)* passably well, tolerably (well); **je chante p.** my voice isn't bad **2** *(notablement)* fairly, rather, somewhat; **les deux chansons sont p. ressemblantes** the two songs are somewhat *or* rather similar; **ils avaient p. bu** they had drunk quite a lot

passacaille [pasakaj] **NF** *(musique → française)* passacaille; *(→ italienne)* passacaglia

passade [pɑsad] **NF 1** *(amourette)* fling, *Sout* amourette; **entre eux, ce ne fut qu'une p.** they just had a (little) fling **2** *(caprice)* passing fancy, fad

passage [pɑsaʒ] **NM A.** *MOUVEMENT* **1** *(allées et venues)* **prochain p. du car dans deux heures** the coach will be back *or* will pass through again in two hours' time; **chaque p. du train faisait trembler les vitres** the windows shook every time a train went past; **laisser le p. à qn/une ambulance** to let sb/an ambulance through, to make way for sb/an ambulance; **ils attendaient le p. des coureurs** they were waiting for the runners to go by; **p. de troupeaux** *(panneau sur la route)* cattle crossing; **moquette grand p.** heavy-duty carpeting

2 *(circulation)* traffic; **il y a peu/beaucoup de p. dans notre ville/rue** there's not much/a lot of traffic in our town/street

3 *(arrivée, venue)* **elle attend le p. de l'autobus** she's waiting for the bus; **guette le p. du facteur** watch out for the *Br* postman *or Am* mailman

4 *(visite)* call, visit; **c'est le seul souvenir qui me reste de mon p. chez eux** that's the only thing I remember of my visit to them; **lors de mon prochain p. à Paris** next time I'm in Paris; **le relevé du compteur sera fait lors de notre prochain p.** *(message laissé par EDF)* we will read your meter the next time we call

5 *(franchissement → d'une frontière, d'un fleuve)* crossing; *(→ d'un col)* passing; *(→ de la douane)* passing (through); **après le p. du sucre dans l'urine** after the sugar has gone *or* passed into the urine; **p. interdit** *(sur panneau)* no entry; *Mil* **p. à l'ennemi** going over to the enemy; *Naut* **le p. de la ligne** the crossing of the line

6 *(changement, transition)* change, transition; **le p. de l'hiver au printemps** the change *or* passage from winter to spring; **le p. de l'autocratie à la démocratie** the changeover *or* transition from autocracy to democracy; **depuis le p. à l'euro** since the changeover to the euro, since euros replaced francs/*etc*

7 *(dans une hiérarchie)* move; **p. d'un employé à l'échelon supérieur** promotion of an employee to a higher grade; *Scol* **le p. dans la classe supérieure** going *or* moving up to the next *Br* class *or Am* grade

8 *(voyage sur mer, traversée)* crossing; **ils travaillaient durement pour payer leur p.** they worked hard to pay for their passage *or* crossing; **pour limiter le nombre des passages clandestins vers les États-Unis** to reduce the number of illegal border crossings into the United States

9 *Astron* transit; **le p. d'un astre au méridien** the passage *or* transit of a star across the meridian

10 *Ordinat* **p. machine** run; **p. automatique à la ligne (suivante)** autoflow, wordwrap

11 *Psy* **p. à l'acte** acting out; **une pulsion criminelle ne s'accompagne pas nécessairement d'un p. à l'acte** criminal thoughts don't necessarily lead to criminal actions

12 *Rad, Théât & TV* **lors de son dernier p. à la télévision** *(personne)* last time he/she was on TV; *(film)* last time it was shown on TV; **pour son premier p. au Théâtre du Rocher** for his/her first appearance at the Théâtre du Rocher

13 *Sport* **temps de p.** split time; **p. du témoin** *(au relais)* (baton) changeover

B. *VOIE* **1** *(chemin)* passage, way; **enlève ton sac du p.** move your bag out of the way; **tu es dans le p.!** you're in the way!; **il y a des passages dangereux dans la grotte** there are some dangerous passages in the cave; **donner** *ou* **livrer p. à qn/qch** to let sb/sth in; **boucher** *ou* **obstruer le p. à qn** to block the way for sb; **le p. de Drake** Drake Passage; **le p. du nord-ouest** the Northwest Passage; **p. secret** secret passage

2 *(ruelle)* alley, passage; *(galerie commerçante)* arcade; **p. couvert** passageway

3 *(tapis de couloir)* runner

4 *Aut* **p. de roue** wheel housing

5 *Rail* **p. à niveau** *Br* level crossing, *Am* grade crossing

6 *(voie)* **p. clouté** *ou* **(pour) piétons** *Br* pedestrian *or* zebra crossing, *Am* crosswalk; **p. protégé** priority over secondary roads; **p. souterrain** underpass, *Br* (pedestrian) subway

C. *D'UN FILM, D'UN ROMAN* passage, section; **elle m'a lu quelques passages de la lettre de Paul** she read me a few passages from Paul's letter; **tu te souviens du p. où ils se rencontrent?** do you remember the bit *or* sequence where they meet?

❑ **au passage ADV 1** *(sur un trajet)* on one's way; **les enfants doivent attraper la cocarde au p.** the children have to catch the ribbon as they go past; **nous visiterons les caves de Reims au p.** we'll visit the cellars at Rheims on our way

2 *(dans le cours de l'action)* in passing; **j'ai noté deux bonnes répliques au p.** I noted down a couple of good lines in passing

3 *(à propos)* incidentally, by the way; **tiens, au p., je te signale trois fautes page 32** by the way, there are three mistakes on page 32

❑ **au passage de PRÉP au p. du carrosse, la foule applaudissait** when the carriage went past *or* through, the crowd clapped

❑ **de passage ADJ** *(client)* casual; **être de p.** *(voyageur)* to be passing through; **je suis de p. à Paris** I'm in Paris for a few days

❑ **sur le passage de PRÉP la foule s'est massée sur le p. du marathon** the crowd gathered on the marathon route

❑ **passage à tabac NM** beating up

❑ **passage à vide NM** momentary flagging; **avoir un p. à vide** *(moralement)* to feel a bit low *or* down; *(intellectuellement)* to have a lapse in concentration; **j'ai eu un petit p. à vide juste avant midi** I flagged a bit just before lunch; **il a eu un p. à vide et a perdu cinq secondes** *(sportif)* he had a lapse in concentration and lost five seconds

passager, -ère [pɑsaʒe, -ɛr] **ADJ 1** *(momentané → bonheur)* fleeting, short-lived; *(→ mauvaise humeur)* passing, short-lived; *(→ crise)* temporary, short-lived; *(→ engouement)* passing; **état p.** passing phase; **ne vous inquiétez pas, ces douleurs seront passagères** don't worry, the pain won't last; **ils ont eu une petite brouille passagère** they fell out momentarily

2 *(très fréquenté)* busy; **des rues très passagères** very busy roads, roads with very heavy traffic

NM,F passenger; **ce sont les passagers à destination d'Athènes qui ont le plus attendu** the people going to Athens waited the longest; **p. clandestin** stowaway; **p. en transit** transit passenger

passagèrement [pasaʒɛrmɑ̃] ADV for a short while, temporarily, momentarily

passant¹, -e [pasɑ̃, -ɑ̃t] ADJ *(voie, route)* busy **NM,F** passer-by; **les passants s'arrêtaient pour regarder** passers-by would stop and stare

passant² [pasɑ̃] NM *(belt)* loop

passation [pasasjɔ̃] NF 1 *Jur (d'un acte, d'un contrat)* drawing up (and signing) 2 *Pol* **p. des pouvoirs** transfer of power 3 *Compta (d'une écriture)* entering; *(d'un dividende)* payment; **p. d'écriture** journal entry; **p. par pertes et profits** write-off

passavant [pasavɑ̃] NM 1 *Jur* transire 2 *Naut* (fore-and-aft) catwalk, flying bridge

passe [pas] NM 1 *(passe-partout)* master *or* pass key

2 *(laissez-passer)* pass

NF 1 *Sport (aux jeux de ballon)* pass; **faire une p.** to pass (the ball), to make a pass; **fais-moi une p.** pass (me) the ball; *Ftbl* **p. en avant/en retrait** forward/back pass; *Escrime* **p. d'armes** sparring; *Fig* **il y a eu une belle p. d'armes entre les deux leaders** there was some fine sparring between the two leaders

2 *(en tauromachie)* pass; **p. de muleta** pass with the muleta

3 *Fam (d'une prostituée)* trick; **faire une p.** to turn a trick

4 *(situation)* **être dans une bonne p.** *(commerce)* to be thriving; *(mentalement)* to be going through a good period *or* patch; **leur couple traverse une mauvaise p.** their relationship is going through a rough *or* bad patch

5 *Géog (col)* pass; *(chenal)* pass, channel; **la p. de Khaybar** the Khyber Pass

6 *(d'un prestidigitateur)* pass

7 *Tech (d'une machine)* cut

8 *Can* **p. migratoire** fish ladder

9 *Typ* overs, overplus; **exemplaires de p.** surplus copies, over copies

10 *Fin* **p. de caisse** allowance for cashier's errors

11 *Ordinat* pass

12 *(mise)* stake; *(à la roulette)* passe; **p. anglaise** craps

13 *(sur un cours d'eau)* passage

14 *(d'un chapeau)* rim

❑ **en passe de** PRÉP about to, on the point of; **ils sont en p. de prendre le contrôle des médias** they're poised *or* set to gain control of the media

passé¹ [pase] PRÉP after; **p. minuit** after midnight; **p. le pont, c'est à droite** it's on the right after the bridge; **p. la première impression** once *or* after the first impression has worn off

passé, -e¹ [pase] ADJ 1 *(précédent → année, mois)* last, past; **au cours des mois passés** over the past *or* last few months

2 *(révolu)* **il est 3 heures passées** it's past *or Br* gone 3 o'clock; **elle a 30 ans passés** she's over 30; **à 15 ans passés, il ne savait toujours pas lire** he was over 15 and he still couldn't read

3 *(qui n'est plus)* past, former; **elle songeait au temps p.** she was thinking of times *or* days gone by

4 *(teinte, fleur)* faded

NM 1 *(temps révolu)* **le p.** the past; **oublions le p.** let bygones be bygones, let's forget the past; **dans le p.** in the past; **c'est du p., tout ça** it's all in the past *or* it's all behind us now

2 *(d'une personne, d'une ville)* past; **un pays au p. glorieux/sanglant** a country with a glorious/bloody past; **avoir honte/être fier de son p.** to be ashamed/proud of one's past; **il a un lourd p.** he's a man with a past

3 *Gram* past tense; **verbe au p.** verb in the past tense; **les temps du p.** past tenses; **p. antérieur** past anterior; **p. composé** (present) perfect; **p. simple** *ou* **historique** simple past, past historic

4 *Couture* **p. empiétant** encroaching (satin) stitch; **p. plat** satin stitch

❑ **par le passé** ADV in the past; **il est beaucoup plus indulgent que par le p.** he's much more indulgent than before *or* than he used to be; **soyons amis, comme par le p.** let's be friends, like before

passe-bande [pasbɑ̃d] ADJ INV *Électron* band-pass

passe-bas [pasba] ADJ INV *Électron* **filtre p.** low-pass filter

---

passe-boules [pasbul] NM INV ≃ Aunt Sally

passe-crassane [paskrasan] NF INV passe-crassane *(variety of winter pear)*

passe-droit [pasdrwa] *(pl* **passe-droits***)* NM privilege, special favour

passée² [pase] ADJ F *voir* **passé²**
NF *Chasse (du gibier d'eau)* flighting; *(d'un lièvre, d'un renard)* track; **chasse à la p.** *(du gibier d'eau)* flighting, flight-shooting, passshooting

passe-haut [paso] ADJ INV *Électron* high-pass

passéisme [paseism] NM *Péj* attachment to the past, backward-looking attitude

passéiste [paseist] *Péj* ADJ backward-looking **NMF** backward-looking person

passe-lacet [paslasɛ] *(pl* **passe-lacets***)* NM bodkin; *Fam* **raide comme un p.** completely broke *or Br* skint

passement [pasmɑ̃] NM (piece of) braid *or* braiding *or* cord *(used as trimming)*

passementer [3] [pasmɑ̃te] VT to braid

passementerie [pasmɑ̃tri] NF *(articles)* trimmings, soft furnishings; *(commerce)* soft furnishing trade

passementier, -ère [pasmɑ̃tje, -ɛr] ADJ *(commerce, industrie)* soft furnishing *(avant n)* **NM,F** soft furnishing manufacturer

passe-montagne [pasmɔ̃taɲ] *(pl* **passe-montagnes***)* NM balaclava

passe-partout [paspartu] ADJ INV 1 *(robe, instrument)* versatile, all-purpose *(avant n)*; **un discours p.** a speech for all occasions; **une réponse p.** a stock *or* all-purpose reply 2 *Rail* UIC standard *(avant n)*
NM INV 1 *(clé)* master *or* skeleton key 2 *Beaux-Arts & Typ* passe-partout 3 *(scie)* two-handed saw

passe-passe [paspas] NM INV **tour de p.** *(tour de magie)* (magic) trick; *(tromperie)* trick

passe-pied [paspje] *(pl* **passe-pieds***)* NM *(en danse)* passepied

passe-plat [paspla] *(pl* **passe-plats***)* NM serving hatch

passepoil [paspwal] NM piping *(UNCOUNT)*

passepoiler [3] [paspwale] VT *(vêtement)* to trim with piping, to pipe; **poche passepoilée** welted pocket

passeport [paspɔr] NM 1 *Admin* passport; **p. européen** EU *or* European passport; **p. biométrique** biometric passport 2 *Fig* passport; **ce diplôme est un p. pour la vie professionnelle** this diploma is a passport to a job

---

PASSER [3] [pase]

VI to pass A1, 6, 10, 12, B2, 4, 6, 9, D1, 2 ▪ to pass by A1 ▪ to go past A1, 7, 12 ▪ to flow A3 ▪ to go A5, 11, B3, 5 ▪ to call A7, 8 ▪ to run A3, 5 ▪ to get through A9 ▪ to be elected B6 ▪ to be on B7 ▪ to become C2 ▪ to go by D1 ▪ to disappear D2 ▪ to fade D2 ▪ to wear off D2 ▪ to die down D2 ▪ to go bad D3 **VT** to cross A1, 2 ▪ to pass A3, 9, B6 ▪ to go past A3 ▪ to take across A4 ▪ to put A6 ▪ to run A7 ▪ to clear A8 ▪ to take B1 ▪ to have B1 ▪ to get through B2 ▪ to leave out B3 ▪ to give B6 ▪ to put through B6 ▪ to lend B8 ▪ to apply B9 ▪ to put on B9, 11, 13 ▪ to show B5 ▪ to reach B14 ▪ to agree on B14 ▪ to draw up B16 ▪ to spend C1 ▪ to get through C2
USAGE ABSOLU to pass

VI *(aux être)* **A.** *EXPRIME UN DÉPLACEMENT* **1** *(se déplacer → personne, véhicule)* to pass (by), to go *or* to come past; **regarder p. les coureurs** to watch the runners go past; **p. à droite/gauche** to go right/left; **l'avion est passé au-dessus de la maison** the plane flew over the house; **un avion passait dans le ciel** a plane was flying in the sky; **pour empêcher les poids lourds de p. dans le village** to stop lorries from driving *or* going through the village; **p. devant qch** to go past sth; **puisque tu passes devant la boulangerie, rapporte du pain** seeing as you're going past the baker's, pick up some bread; **passe devant si tu ne vois pas** *(devant moi)* go in front of me if you can't see; *(devant tout le monde)* go to the front if you can't see; **p. sous une échelle** to go under a ladder; **p. sous une voiture** *(se faire*

écraser) to get run over (by a car); **p. sur un pont** to go over *or* to cross a bridge; **des péniches passaient sur le canal** barges were going past *or* were sailing on the canal

2 *(fugitivement)* **j'ai vu un éclair de rage p. dans son regard** I saw a flash of anger in his/her eyes; **un sourire passa sur ses lèvres** a smile played about his/her lips; **elle dit tout ce qui lui passe par la tête** she says the first thing that comes into her head; **qu'est-ce qui a bien pu lui p. par la tête** whatever was he/she thinking of?; **le pouvoir n'a fait que p. entre leurs mains** they knew power only briefly; *Fam Hum* **il y a que le train qui lui soit pas passé dessus** she's the town bike

3 *(s'écouler → fluide)* to flow, to run; **l'eau passe dans cette canalisation** the water flows *or* runs along this channel; **il y a de l'air qui passe sous la porte** there's a permanent draught coming under the door

4 *(emprunter un certain itinéraire)* **si vous passez à Paris, venez me voir** come and see me if you're in Paris; **le voleur est passé par la fenêtre** the burglar got in through the window; **passe par l'escalier de service** use the service stairs

5 *(fleuve, route)* to go, to run; **la nouvelle route ne passera pas dans le village** the new road won't go *or* run through the village; **le Rhône passe à Lyon** the Rhone goes *or* flows through Lyons; **le tunnel passera sous la montagne** the tunnel will go under the mountain; **le pont passe au-dessus de l'avenue** the bridge crosses the avenue

6 *Math* to pass; **soit une droite passant par deux points A et B** given a straight line between two points A and B

7 *(sur un parcours régulier → démarcheur, représentant)* to call; *(→ bateau, bus, train)* to come *or* to go past; **p. chez un client** to call on a client; **le facteur n'est pas encore passé** the *Br* postman *or Am* mailman hasn't been yet; **le facteur passe deux fois par jour** the *Br* postman *or Am* mailman delivers *or* comes twice a day; **le bus passe toutes les sept minutes** there's a bus every seven minutes; **le bateau/train est déjà passé** the boat/train has already gone *or* left; **le prochain bateau passera dans deux jours** the next boat will call *or* is due in two days

8 *(faire une visite)* to call; **p. chez qn** to call at sb's place; **j'ai demandé au médecin de p.** I asked the doctor to call (in) *or* to come *or* to visit; **j'essaierai de p. dans la soirée** I'll try and call in during the evening; **veuillez p. au commissariat demain** please report to the police station tomorrow; **je ne fais que p.** I'm not stopping; **p. voir qn** to call on sb; **je passerai te chercher** I'll come and fetch you; **passe la prévenir** go and tell her

9 *(franchir une limite)* to get through; **tu ne passeras pas, il y a trop de monde** you won't get through, there are too many people; **le piano ne passera jamais par la porte** the piano will never go *or* get through the door; **ne laisse p. personne** don't let anybody through; **il est passé au rouge** he went through a red light; **ça passe ou ça casse** it's make or break

10 *(s'infiltrer)* to pass; **p. dans le sang** to pass into *or* to enter the bloodstream; **la lumière passe à travers les rideaux** the light shines through the curtains; **le vent et la neige passaient entre les planches disjointes** the wind and snow got in through the gaps in the floorboards; **le café doit p. lentement** *(dans le filtre)* the coffee must filter through slowly

11 *(aller, se rendre)* to go; **où est-il passé?** where's he gone (to)?; **où sont passées mes lunettes?** where have my glasses disappeared to?; **passons à table** let's eat; **si l'on passait au wagon-restaurant?** shall we go to the dining-car?; **passons dans mon bureau** let's go into my office; **les invités passèrent de la salle à manger au salon** the guests went *or* moved from the dining room into the living room; **p. de Suisse en France** to cross over *or* to go from Switzerland to France; **p. à l'ennemi** to go over to the enemy; **elle est passée à l'opposition** she's gone over to *or* she's joined the opposition;

il est passé du côté du vainqueur he's switched to the winning side

12 *Chasse* to pass, to go *or* to come past; **ici, les bécasses passent en septembre** woodcock fly over here in September; **là où le gibier passe** where game animals pass

13 *Naut* **p. au vent** to sail to windward; **p. sur l'avant** to cut across the bow

14 *Théât* to cross the stage

B. *EXPRIME UNE ACTION* **1 p. à** *(se soumettre à)* to go for; **p. au scanner** to go for a scan; **p. à la visite médicale** to go for a medical examination; **ce matin, je suis passé au tableau** I was asked to explain something at the blackboard this morning; *Fam* **je ne veux pas me faire opérer – il faudra bien que tu y passes, pourtant!** I don't want to have an operation – you're going to have to!; *Fam* **avec lui, toutes les femmes du service y sont passées** he's had all the women in his department; *Fam* **y p.** *(mourir)* to croak, *Br* to snuff it; **tout le monde a cru que tu allais y p.** everybody thought you were a goner

2 *(être accepté)* to pass; **elle est passée à l'écrit mais pas à l'oral** she got through *or* she passed the written exam but not the oral; **j'ai un bout de pomme qui est passé de travers** a bit of my apple has gone down the wrong way; **j'ai mangé quelque chose qui ne passe pas** I've eaten something that won't go down; **sa dernière remarque n'est pas passée** his/her last remark stuck in my throat; **ce genre d'explication ne passera pas avec lui** he won't swallow an explanation like that; **ton petit discours est bien passé** your little speech went down well *or* was well received; **la deuxième scène ne passe pas du tout** the second scene doesn't work at all; **le film passe mal sur le petit écran/en noir et blanc** the film just isn't the same on TV/in black and white; **le fascisme ne passera pas!** no to fascism!; **l'injurier, passe encore, mais le frapper!** it's one thing to insult him, but quite another to hit him!; **une heure de retard, passe, mais trois!** an hour's delay would be forgivable, but (certainly not) three!

3 *(être transmis)* to go; **sa collection de tableaux passera à sa fille** his/her collection of paintings will go to his/her daughter; **la ferme est passée de père en fils depuis cinq générations** the farm has been handed down from father to son for five generations; **la carafe passa de main en main** the jug was passed around; **la locution est passée du latin à l'anglais** the phrase came *or* passed into English from Latin; **le pouvoir est passé de la gauche à la droite** the right has taken over from the left

4 *(entrer)* to pass; **c'est passé dans le langage courant** it's passed into *or* it's now part of everyday speech; **c'est passé dans les mœurs** it's become standard *or* normal practice

5 *(être utilisé, absorbé)* to go; **tout son salaire passe dans la maison** all his/her salary goes on the house; **400 à 500 euros passent chaque mois dans la nourriture** food accounts for 400 to 500 euros a month; **tout le fromage y est passé** every last bit of cheese went (in the end); **les deux bouteilles y sont passées** both bottles were drunk; **toutes ses économies y passent** all his/her savings go towards *or* into it

6 *Pol (être adopté → projet de loi, amendement)* to pass, to be passed; *(être élu → député)* to be elected, to get in; **la loi est passée** the law was passed; **si les socialistes passent** if the socialists get in *or* are elected

7 *Cin & Théât* to be on, to be showing; **son documentaire n'est jamais passé** his/her documentary was never shown; **sa dernière pièce passe au Galatée** his/her latest play is on at the Galatée; *Rad & TV* **les informations passent à 20 heures** the news is on at 8 p.m.; **p. à la radio** *(émission, personne)* to be on the radio *or* the air; **p. à la télévision** *(personne)* to be *or* to appear on television; *(film)* to be on television

8 *Jur (comparaître)* **p. devant le tribunal** to come up *or* to go before the court; **p. en correctionnelle** ≃ to go before the magistrate's court; **l'affaire passera en justice le mois prochain** the case will be heard next month

9 *(dans un jeu)* to pass; **je passe** pass

C. *EXPRIME UN CHANGEMENT D'ÉTAT* **1** *(accéder → à un niveau)* **p. dans la classe supérieure** to move up to the next *Br* form *or Am* grade; *Scol* **p. en seconde** ≃ to move up *Br* to the fifth form *orAm* to tenth grade; **p. à** to move to; **il est passé au grade supérieur** he's been promoted to the next highest rank; **p. du deuxième au troisième échelon** to move up from the second to the third grade

2 *(devenir)* to become; **p. entraîneur** to become a coach; **il est passé ailier** he plays on the wing now; **p. professionnel** to turn professional; **p. chef de service** to become *or* to be promoted head of department

3 *Aut* **p. en troisième** to change into third (gear); **la seconde passe mal** second gear is stiff

4 *(dans des locutions verbales)* **passons à l'ordre du jour** let us turn to the business on the agenda; **traduisons le texte, puis nous passerons au commentaire** let's translate the text first, then we'll analyse it; **p. à l'action** to take action; **p. de l'état liquide à l'état gazeux** to pass *or* to change from the liquid to the gaseous state; **la lumière passait du rose au mauve** the light changed from pink to mauve; **p. sans transition de la gaieté à la tristesse** to switch from joy to sadness; **quand on passe de l'adolescence à l'âge adulte** when you pass from adolescence to adulthood; **la production est passée de 20 à 30/de 30 à 20 tonnes** output has gone (up) from 20 to 30/(down) from 30 to 20 tonnes; **p. du français au russe** to switch from French to Russian; **comment êtes-vous passé du cinéma au théâtre?** how did you move *or* make the transition from the cinema to the stage?; **il passe d'une idée à l'autre** he jumps *or* flits from one idea to another; **le dernier vers de la fable est passé en proverbe** the last verse of the fable has become a proverb

D. *EXPRIME UNE ÉVOLUTION DANS LE TEMPS* **1** *(s'écouler → temps)* to pass, to go by; **la journée est passée agréablement** the day went off *or* passed pleasantly; **une heure est vite passée** an hour passes quickly; **à mesure que les jours passaient** as the days went by; **comme le temps passe!** how time flies!

2 *(s'estomper → douleur)* to fade (away), to wear off; *(→ malaise)* to disappear; *(→ mode, engouement)* to die out; *(→ enthousiasme)* to wear off, to fade; *(→ beauté)* to fade, to wane; *(→ chance, jeunesse)* to pass; *(→ mauvaise humeur)* to pass, to vanish; *(→ rage, tempête)* to die down; *(→ averse)* to die down, to stop; **mon envie est passée** I don't feel like it any more; **j'aimais regarder la télévision mais cela m'a passé** I used to like watching television but not any more; **cette habitude lui passera avec l'âge** he'll/she'll get over the habit as he/she gets older; **ce médicament fait p. la douleur très rapidement** this medicine relieves pain very quickly; **je vais te faire p. le goût de mentir, moi!** I'll make you think twice before you tell lies again!

3 *(s'altérer → fruit, denrées)* to spoil, to go bad, *Br* to go off; *(se faner → fleur)* to wilt; **le vin est ouvert depuis trop longtemps, il a passé** the wine's been open too long, it's gone off; **les roses sont passées** the roses have wilted

4 *(pâlir → teinte)* **le papier peint a passé au soleil** the sun has faded the wallpaper

5 *(aux avoir) Vieilli Euph (mourir)* **il a passé cette nuit** he passed on *or* away last night

VT *(aux avoir)* **A.** *EXPRIME UN DÉPLACEMENT* **1** *(traverser → pont, col de montagne)* to go over, to cross; *(→ écluse)* to go through, to cross; **p. une rivière à la nage** to swim across a river; **p. un ruisseau à gué** to ford a stream

2 *(franchir → frontière, ligne d'arrivée)* to cross, to go through; **une fois passé le pas de la porte, il fait frais** once you're over the threshold it gets cooler; **si je passe cette porte, je ne reviendrai plus jamais** if I go through that door I'll never come back; **nous passerons la frontière à Vintimille** we'll cross the border at Ventimiglia

3 *(dépasser → point de repère)* to pass, to go past; **vous passez l'escalier et c'est à droite** go past the stairs and it's on your right, it's on your right after you pass the stairs; **p. l'arrêt de l'autobus** *(le manquer)* to miss one's bus stop; **p. le cap Horn** to (go) round Cape Horn; **quand on passe les 1000 mètres d'altitude** when you go over 1,000 metres high; **l'or a passé les 400 dollars l'once** gold has broken through the $400 an ounce mark

4 *(transporter)* to ferry *or* to take across

5 *(introduire)* **p. de la drogue/des cigarettes en fraude** to smuggle drugs/cigarettes

6 *(engager → partie du corps)* to put; **p. son bras autour de la taille de qn** to put *or* to slip one's arm round sb's waist; **il passa son doigt à travers le grillage** he put *or* he stuck a finger through the wire netting; **je n'arrive pas à p. ma tête dans l'encolure de cette robe** my head won't go through the neck of the dress; **il a passé la tête par l'entrebâillement de la porte** he poked his head round the door

7 *(faire aller → instrument)* to run; **p. un peigne dans ses cheveux** to run a comb through one's hair; **p. une éponge sur la table** to wipe the table; **p. un chiffon sur les meubles** to dust the furniture; **p. l'aspirateur** to vacuum, *Br* to hoover; **p. le balai** to sweep up; **passe le balai dans l'escalier** give the stairs a sweep, sweep the stairs

8 *Équitation (haie)* to jump, to clear; **le cheval a passé le fossé** the horse cleared the ditch

9 *Sport (franchir → obstacle, haie)* to jump (over); *(transmettre → ballon)* to pass; *(dépasser → coureurs)* to overtake, to pass; **p. la barre à deux mètres** to clear the bar at two metres; **p. les autres concurrents** to overtake the other competitors; *Fig* **p. tous les obstacles** to overcome *or* to surmount all the obstacles

B. *EXPRIME UNE ACTION* **1** *(se soumettre à → permis de conduire)* to take; *(→ examen)* to take, *Br* to sit; *(→ scanner, visite médicale)* to have, to go for; **il passe sa thèse demain** he has his oral *or Br* viva for his thesis tomorrow; **la voiture doit p. un contrôle** the car must go (in) for a test *or* must be tested

2 *Vieilli (réussir → examen)* to pass; *(→ épreuve éliminatoire)* to get through; **elle a passé sa ceinture noire de karaté** she's got her black belt in karate now; **il a passé l'écrit, mais attendons l'oral** he's passed the written exam, but let's see what happens in the oral

3 *(omettre)* to miss *or* to leave out, to omit; **je passe toutes les descriptions dans ses romans** I miss out *or* I skip all the descriptions in his/her novels; **tu as tout de même passé plusieurs détails importants** you did miss out *or* omit several important details

4 *(tolérer)* **elle lui passe tout** she lets him/her get away with anything; **elle est gentille, alors on lui passe le reste** she's so nice that people make allowances (for the rest); **passez-moi l'expression/le mot** if you'll pardon the expression/excuse the term

5 *(soumettre à l'action de)* **p. une plaie à l'alcool** to put alcohol on a cut; **p. les parquets à l'encaustique** to polish the floors; **p. des légumes au mixeur** to put vegetables through the blender, to blend vegetables; **p. qch sous l'eau** to rinse sth *or* to give sth a rinse under the tap; **p. qch au four** to put sth in the oven; *Fam* **p. quelque chose à qn** *Br* to tick sb off, *Am* to chew sb out; *Fam* **se faire p. quelque chose** *Br* to get a good ticking off, *Am* to get a good chewing-out; *Can Fam* **p. un Québec** *ou* **un sapin à qn** to take sb in, to take sb for a ride

6 *(donner, transmettre → gén)* to pass, to hand, to give; *(→ rhume)* to pass on, to give; *(→ au téléphone)* to put through; **passe(-moi) le couteau** give me the knife, hand over the knife; **passe-moi le sel** pass me the salt; **fais p. à ton voisin** pass it to your neighbour; **p. la consigne à qn** to pass on orders to sb; **p. ses pouvoirs à son successeur** to hand over one's powers to one's successor; **il a passé sa grippe à tout le bureau** he gave his flu to everybody in the office; **je te passe Fred** here's Fred, I'll hand you over to Fred; **passe-moi Annie** let me talk to Annie, put Annie on

pas–pas

7 *(rendre public → annonce)* **faire p. une petite annonce** to place a small ad

8 *Fam (prêter)* to lend■; **peux-tu me p. 50 euros jusqu'à demain?** could you lend me 50 euros till tomorrow?; **tu me passes ton livre sur les abeilles?** could you lend me your book *or* let me have your book about bees?; **je lui passe ma chambre et je dors au salon** he/she can have my room and I'll sleep in the living room

9 *(appliquer → substance)* to apply, to put on; **p. de la cire sur qch** to wax sth; **p. une couche de peinture sur un mur** to apply a coat of paint to a wall; **il faudra p. une deuxième couche** it needs a second coat; **je vais te p. de la crème dans le dos** I'm going to put *or* to rub some cream on your back

10 *(filtrer, tamiser → thé, potage)* to strain; *(→ farine)* to sieve

11 *(enfiler → vêtement)* to slip *or* to put on; **je passe une robe moins chaude et j'arrive** I'll just put on a cooler dress and I'll be with you; **elle passa l'anneau à son doigt** she slipped the ring on her finger

12 *Aut* **p. une vitesse** to put the car in gear; **p. la marche arrière** to go into reverse; **p. la troisième** to change *or* to shift into third gear

13 *Cin & TV (film)* to show, to screen; *(diapositive)* to show; *Rad (émission)* to broadcast; *(cassette, disque)* to play, to put on; **on passe un western au Rex** there's a western on at the Rex

14 *Com (conclure → entente)* to conclude, to come to, to reach; *(→ marché)* to agree on, to strike, to reach; *(→ commande)* to place (**de qch** for sth; **à qn** with sb); **passez commande avant le 12** order before the 12th

15 *Compta* to enter, to post; **p. un article en compte** to enter a sale into a ledger; **p. écriture d'un article** to post an entry; **p. une somme au débit/au crédit** to debit/credit an account with a sum; **p. une somme en perte** to charge an amount to an account; **p. une somme en profit** to credit an amount to an account; **p. par pertes et profits** to transfer to profit and loss, to write off

16 *Jur (faire établir → acte juridique)* to draw up; **nous passons le contrat demain** we're drawing up the contract tomorrow; **un acte passé par-devant notaire** a deed drawn up in the presence of a lawyer

C. *EXPRIME UNE NOTION TEMPORELLE* 1 *(employer → durée)* to spend; **j'ai passé un an en Angleterre** I spent a year in England; **passez un bon week-end/une bonne soirée!** have a nice weekend/evening!; **j'ai passé deux heures sur la traduction** I spent two hours on the translation, it took me two hours to do the translation; **p. ses vacances à lire** to spend one's *Br* holidays *or Am* vacation reading; **il va venir p. quelques jours chez nous** he's coming to stay with us for a few days; **as-tu passé une bonne nuit?** did you sleep well last night?, did you have a good night?; **pour p. le temps** to pass the time; *Fam* **on ne va pas p. le réveillon là-dessus!** let's not spend all night on it!

2 *(aller au-delà de → durée)* to get through, to survive; **s'il arrive à p. la première semaine, il sera tiré d'affaire** if he gets through *or* survives the first week, he'll be out of danger; **elle ne passera pas la nuit** she won't see the night out, she won't last the night

3 *(assouvir → envie)* to satisfy; **p. sa colère sur qn** to work off *or* to vent one's anger on sb; **je passais ma colère en jouant de la batterie** I let off steam by playing the drums; **ne passe pas ta fureur sur moi!** don't take it out on me!

USAGE ABSOLU *(transmettre → ballon)* to pass; **il a passé à l'avant-centre** he passed to the centre forward

❑ **en passant ADV 1** *(dans la conversation)* in passing; **faire une remarque en passant** to remark in passing, to make a casual remark; **soit dit en passant** it must be said; **il n'est guère aimable soit dit en passant** he's not very likable it must *or* has to be said

2 *(sur son chemin)* **il s'arrête de temps à autre en passant** he calls on his way by *or* past from time to time; **l'avion, en passant, a laissé une traînée blanche** the plane left a white trail as it passed

❑ **en passant par PRÉP 1** *(dans l'espace)* via; **l'avion va à Athènes en passant par Londres** the plane goes to Athens via London *or* stops in London on its way to Athens

2 *(dans une énumération)* (and) including; **toutes les romancières de Sand à Sarraute en passant par Colette** every woman novelist from Sand to Sarraute including Colette

❑ **passer après VT IND le directeur commercial passe après lui** the sales manager comes after him; **il faut le faire libérer, le reste passe après** we must get him released, everything else is secondary

❑ **passer avant VT IND** to go *or* to come before; **ses intérêts passent avant tout** his/her own interests come before anything else; **le travail passe avant le plaisir** work (comes) before pleasure

❑ **passer par VT IND 1** *(dans une formation)* to go through; **il est passé par une grande école** he studied at a "grande école"; **elle est passée par tous les échelons** she rose through all the grades

2 *(dans une évolution)* to go through, to undergo; **le pays est passé par toutes les formes de gouvernement** the country has experienced every form of government; **la maladie passe par différentes phases** the illness goes through different stages; **elle est passée par des moments difficiles** she's been through some difficult times

3 *(recourir à)* to go through; **je passe par une agence pour avoir des billets** I get tickets through an agency; **p. par l'opératrice** to go through the operator; **il va falloir en p. par ses exigences** we'll just have to do what he/she says; **je suis passé par là** it's happened to me too, I've been through that too; **pour comprendre, il faut être passé par là** you have to have experienced it to understand

❑ **passer pour VT IND 1** *(avec nom)* to be thought of as; **dire qu'il passe pour un génie!** to think that he's considered a genius!; **je vais p. pour un idiot** I'll be taken for *or* people will take me for an idiot; **en te maquillant, tu pourrais facilement p. pour elle** with some make-up on, you could easily pass for her *or* you could easily be taken for her; **se faire p. pour qn** to pass oneself off as sb; **il se fait p. pour un professionnel** he claims to be a professional

2 *(avec adj)* **son livre passe pour sérieux** his/her book is considered to be serious; **il s'est fait p. pour fou** he pretended to be mad

3 *(avec verbe)* **elle passe pour descendre d'une famille noble** she is said to be descended from an aristocratic family

❑ **passer sur VT IND** *(ne pas mentionner)* to pass over, to skip; *(excuser)* to overlook; **passons sur les détails** let's pass over *or* skip the less important facts; **je passerai sur les lacunes de son exposé** I shall overlook the gaps in his/her essay; **je passerai sur votre attitude pour cette fois** I'll overlook your attitude this once; **il l'aime et passe sur tout** he loves him/her and forgives everything; **passons!** let's say no more about it!, let's drop it!; **tu me l'avais promis, mais passons!** you promised me, but never mind!

▶**se passer VPR 1** *(s'écouler → heures, semaines)* to go by, to pass; **la soirée s'est passée tranquillement** the evening went by *or* passed quietly; **la journée s'est passée dans l'angoisse pour les parents** it was a day of anguish for the parents; **si la journée de demain se passe sans incident** if everything goes off smoothly tomorrow

2 *(survenir → événement)* to take place, to happen; **l'histoire se passe en Corse/en 1789** the story takes place in Corsica/in 1789; **qu'est-ce qui se passe?** what's happening?, what's going on?; **que s'est-il passé?** what happened?; **qu'est-ce qui va se p. maintenant?** what's going to happen now?; **il se passe que ton frère vient d'être arrêté(, voilà ce qui se passe)!** your brother's just been arrested(, that's what's the matter!); **il ne se passe rien d'intéressant** nothing interesting's happening; **il ne se passe pas une semaine sans qu'il perde de l'argent aux courses** not a week goes by without him losing money on the horses

3 *(se dérouler → dans certaines conditions)* to go (off); **comment s'est passée ton audition?** how did your audition go?; **l'opération s'est bien/mal passée** the operation went (off) smoothly/badly; **si tout se passe bien, nous y serons demain** if all goes well, we'll be there tomorrow; **tout se passe très bien entre les membres de l'équipe** the team (members) get along very well together; **tout se passe comme prévu** everything's going according to plan *or* going as planned; **les choses ne se seraient pas passées ainsi avec moi!** I wouldn't have let that happen!, I wouldn't have stood for that!; **ça ne se passera pas comme ça!** it won't be as easy as that!

4 *(s'achever → douleur)* to go, to subside; *(→ malaise)* to vanish; **bois de l'eau, ton hoquet se passera** drink some water, it'll get rid of your hiccups *or* and your hiccups'll stop

5 *(s'appliquer, se mettre → produit)* to apply, to put on; **se p. de la crème sur les mains** to put some cream on one's hands; **il se passa un peigne/la main dans les cheveux** he ran a comb/his fingers through his hair; **elle se passait un mouchoir sur le front** she was wiping her forehead with a handkerchief

6 **se p. de** *(vivre sans)* to do *or* to go without; **il faudra te p. de jardinier/secrétaire** you'll have to do *or* to go *or* to manage without a gardener/secretary; **si tu crois pouvoir te p. de tout le monde!** if you think you can manage all by yourself!; **il ne peut pas se p. de télévision** he can't live without TV; **les plantes ne peuvent se p. d'eau** plants can't survive without water; **se p. de faire** to manage without doing; **il ne peut se p. de boire** he can't do without drink

7 **se p. de** *(s'abstenir)* to do without; **je me serais bien passée de garder ses enfants** I could have done without having to look after his/her children; **je me passerais (volontiers) de ses réflexions!** I can do very well without his/her remarks!; **sa déclaration se passe de tout commentaire** his/her statement needs no comment

---

passerage [pɑsraʒ] **NF** *Bot* pepperwort; **p. cultivée** garden cress

passereau, -x [pɑsro] **NM 1** *(oiseau)* passerine **2** *Vieilli (moineau)* sparrow

passerelle [pɑsrɛl] **NF 1** *(pour piétons)* footbridge **2** *Naut (plan incliné)* gangway, gangplank; *(escalier)* boarding steps; **la p. de commandement** the bridge; **p. de navigation** navigation bridge **3** *Aviat (amovible)* steps; *(fixe)* passenger bridge **4** *Théât* catwalk **5** *Univ (entre deux cycles)* link; **établir une p. entre deux cursus** to link two courses **6** *Ordinat* gateway

passériforme [pɑserifɔrm] **NM** *Orn* passerine, member of the Passeriformes

passerine [pɑsrin] **NF** *Orn* (North American) bunting

passerose [pɑsroz] **NF** *Bot* hollyhock

passet [pɑsɛ] **NM** *Belg* (small) stepladder

passe-temps [pɑstɑ̃] **NM INV** pastime, hobby

passe-thé [pɑste] **NM INV** tea strainer

passe-tout-grain [pɑstugrɛ̃] **NM INV** Passe-Tout-Grain (wine)

passeur, -euse [pɑsœr, -øz] **NM,F 1** *(sur un bac, un bateau etc)* ferryman, ferrywoman **2** *(de contrebande)* smuggler **3** *(d'immigrants clandestins)* smuggler; **il trouva un p. qui l'aida à gagner les États-Unis** he found someone to get him over the border into the United States **4** *Sport* passer

passe-velours [pɑsvəlur] **NM INV** *Bot* cockscomb

passe-vite [pɑsvit] **NM INV** *Belg & Suisse* vegetable mill

passible [pasibl] **ADJ p. de** liable to; **crime p. de la prison** crime punishable by imprisonment; **p. d'une contravention** liable to be fined; **p. de poursuites** actionable; **p. des tribunaux** liable to prosecution

passif[1] [pasif] **NM 1** *(dettes)* liabilities; **p. exigible** *ou* **circulant** current liabilities; **l'actif et le p.** assets and liabilities; **p. reporté** deferred liabilities **2** *(locution)* **cette décision est à mettre à son p.** this decision is a black mark against him

passif², -ive [pasif, -iv] **ADJ** *(gén) & Chim & Gram* passive
NM *Gram* passive (voice); **au p.** in the passive (voice)

passif-agressif, passive-agressive [pasifagrɛsif, pasivagresiv] *(mpl* **passifs-agressifs,** *fpl* **passives-agressives) ADJ** *Psy* passive-aggressive; **comportement p.** passive aggression, passive aggressivity

passifloracée [pasiflɔrase] *Bot* **NF** member of the passionflower family *or Spéc* the Passifloraceae
▫ **passifloracées NFPL** passionflowers, *Spéc* Passifloraceae

passiflore [pasiflɔr] **NF** *Bot* passionflower, *Spéc* passiflora

passim [pasim] **ADV** passim

passing-shot [pasiŋʃɔt] *(pl* **passing-shots) NM** passing shot; **faire un p.** to play a passing shot

passion [pasjɔ̃] **NF 1** *(amour fou)* passion, love; **ils ont vécu une grande p.** they had a passionate love affair, they were passionately in love; **aimer qn à la** *ou* **avec p.** to love sb passionately
2 *(du jeu, des voyages etc)* passion; **avoir la p. de qch, avoir une p. pour qch** to have a passion for sth, to be passionately interested in sth; **sa p. pour la musique** his/her passion for music; **la moto est sa p., la moto est une p. chez lui** he's mad about motorbikes
3 *(exaltation)* passion, feeling; **débattre de qch avec p.** to argue passionately about sth; **sans p.** dispassionately
4 *Rel* **la P. (du Christ)** the Passion; **la semaine de la P.** Passion Week; **le temps de la P.** Passiontide; *Rel* **la P. selon saint Jean** the Passion according to Saint John; *Mus* the (Saint) John Passion
▫ **passions NFPL** *(sentiments)* passions, emotions, feelings; **savoir dominer ses passions** to be able to control one's emotions

'La Passion de Jeanne d'Arc' *Dreyer* 'The Passion of Joan of Arc'

passioniste = **passionniste**

passionnant, -e [pasjɔnɑ̃, -ɑ̃t] **ADJ** *(voyage, débat)* fascinating, exciting; *(personne)* fascinating; *(récit)* fascinating, enthralling, gripping; **nous avons eu une discussion passionnante** we had a fascinating discussion; **ce boulot n'est pas très p.** this job's not very exciting

passionné, -e [pasjɔne] **ADJ 1** *(aimant → amant, lettre)* passionate
2 *(très vif → caractère, tempérament)* passionate, emotional; *(→ discours)* passionate, impassioned; *(→ débat)* heated, impassioned; *(→ intérêt, sentiment)* passionate, keen
3 *(intéressé → lecteur, joueur d'échecs etc)* avid, keen; **être p. de qch** to be mad about sth
NM,F 1 *(en amour)* passionate person
2 *(fervent)* enthusiast, devotee; **c'est une passionnée de moto** she's mad about motorbikes, she's a motorbike fanatic; **pour les passionnés de flamenco** for flamenco lovers

passionnel, -elle [pasjɔnɛl] **ADJ** passionate; **"drame p. à Bordeaux"** *(dans un titre)* "love tragedy in Bordeaux"

passionnellement [pasjɔnɛlmɑ̃] **ADV** passionately

passionnément [pasjɔnemɑ̃] **ADV 1** *(avec passion)* passionately, with passion **2** *(en intensif)* keenly, fervently, ardently; **je désire p. que tu réussisses** I very much hope that you will succeed

passionner [3] [pasjɔne] **VT 1** *(intéresser → sujet: récit)* to fascinate, to enthral, to grip; *(→ sujet: discussion, idée)* to fascinate, to grip; **la politique la passionne** politics is her passion, she has a passion for politics
2 *(animer → débat)* **elle ne sait pas parler politique sans p. le débat** every time she talks about politics it becomes very heated
►**se passionner VPR se p. pour qch** *(idée)* to feel passionately about sth; *(activité)* to have a passion for sth; **je me passionne pour le reggae** I have a passion for reggae

passionnette [pasjɔnɛt] **NF** *Vieilli* passing fancy

passionniste [pasjɔnist] **NM** *Rel* Passionist

passivation [pasivɑsjɔ̃] **NF 1** *Chim & Métal* passivization **2** *Gram* putting into the passive

passive [pasiv] *voir* **passif²**

passivement [pasivmɑ̃] **ADV** passively

passiver [3] [pasive] **VT** *Chim* to passivate

passivité [pasivite] **NF 1** *(attitude)* passivity, passiveness **2** *Métal* passivity

passoire [pɑswar] **NF 1** *(à petits trous)* sieve; *(à gros trous)* colander; **p. à thé** tea strainer; *Fam* **avoir la tête** *ou* **la mémoire comme une p.** to have a memory like a sieve; *Fam* **transformer qn en p.** to pump sb full of lead, to riddle sb with bullets
2 *Fam (personne, institution négligente)* **leur service de contre-espionnage est une p.** their counter-espionage service is leaking like a sieve; **cette frontière est une vraie p.** this border doesn't keep anyone in or out; **ce gardien est une vraie p.** *(au football)* this goalkeeper is really useless *or* lets everything in

pastaga [pastaga] **NM** *Fam (pastis)* pastis▪

pastel [pastɛl] **NM 1** *(crayon)* pastel; *(dessin)* pastel (drawing); **dessiner au p.** to draw in pastels **2** *(teinte douce)* pastel (shade) **3** *Bot* pastel woad **4** *(couleur bleue)* pastel blue
ADJ INV pastel; **tons p.** pastel shades

pastelliste [pastelist] **NMF** pastellist

pastenague [pastənag] **NF** *Ich* stingray

pastèque [pastɛk] **NF** *(plante)* watermelon plant; *(fruit)* watermelon

pasteur [pastœr] **NM 1** *Rel (protestant)* minister, pastor; *Vieilli (prêtre)* pastor; **le Bon P.** the Good Shepherd **2** *Littéraire (berger)* shepherd **3** *Fig Littéraire (guide, gardien)* shepherd **4** *(qui vit de l'élevage)* pastoralist, shepherd; **les Peuls sont un peuple de pasteurs** the Fulani are a pastoral people

pasteurella [pastœrɛla] **NF** *Méd* pasteurella

pasteurellose [pastœrɛloz] **NF** *Méd* pasteurellosis

pasteurien, -enne [pastœrjɛ̃, -ɛn] **ADJ** of Louis Pasteur; **les découvertes pasteuriennes** Pasteur's discoveries

pasteurisation [pastœrizɑsjɔ̃] **NF** pasteurization, pasteurizing

pasteuriser [3] [pastœrize] **VT** to pasteurize

pastiche [pastiʃ] **NM** pastiche

pasticher [3] [pastiʃe] **VT** to do a pastiche of

pasticheur, -euse [pastiʃœr, -øz] **NM,F 1** *(auteur de pastiches)* writer of pastiches **2** *(plagiaire)* plagiarist

pastillage [pastijaʒ] **NM 1** *Tech* pelletizing **2** *Culin* (non-edible) decorative sugarwork **3** *Cér* china ornamentation

pastille [pastij] **NF 1** *Pharm* pastille, lozenge; **p. pour la gorge** throat lozenge; **p. contre la toux** cough drop *or Br* sweet **2** *Culin* **p. de chocolat** chocolate drop; **p. de menthe** mint **3** *(pois)* polka dot; **un chemisier rouge à pastilles blanches** a red blouse with white polka dots **4** *(disque de papier, de tissu)* disc; **p. verte** = green label on a low-emission vehicle indicating that it may be driven on days when restrictions are placed on traffic due to high levels of atmospheric pollution **5** *Tech* pellet

pastilleuse [pastijøz] **NF** *Tech* pelletizer

pastis [pastis] **NM 1** *(boisson)* pastis **2** *Fam (situation embrouillée)* muddle, mess, fix

pastoral, -e, -aux, -ales [pastɔral, -o] **ADJ** *Littérature, Mus & Rel* pastoral
▫ **pastorale NF 1** *Littérature* pastoral; *Mus* pastorale **2** *Rel* pastoral

'La Symphonie pastorale' *Beethoven, Gide* 'The Pastoral Symphony'

pastoralisme [pastɔralism] **NM** *Agr* (cattle) grazing

pastorat [pastɔra] **NM** pastorate

pastorien, -enne [pastɔrjɛ̃, -ɛn] = **pasteurien**

pastoureau, -elle, -aux, -elles [pasturo, -ɛl] **NM,F** *Littéraire* shepherd boy, *f* girl
▫ **pastourelle NF 1** *Littérature* pastourelle **2** *(danse)* fourth figure of the quadrille

pat [pat] *Échecs* **ADJ INV le roi est p.** it's a stalemate
NM stalemate; **éviter le p.** to avoid stalemate

patache [pataʃ] **NF 1** *(diligence)* (rickety) four-wheeler **2** *Naut (des douaniers)* revenue vessel

patachon [pataʃɔ̃] **NM** *Fam* **mener une vie de p.** to lead a riotous existence

patagium [pataʒjɔm] **NM** *Orn & Zool* patagium

patagon, -e *ou* **-onne** [patagɔ̃, -ɔn] **ADJ** Patagonian
▫ **Patagon, -e** *ou* **-onne NM,F** Patagonian

Patagonie [patagɔni] **NF la P.** Patagonia

pataouète [patawɛt] **NM** *Fam* = French dialect spoken by working-class French settlers in Algeria

pataphysique [patafizik] **ADJ** pataphysic
NF pataphysics *(singulier)*

patapouf [patapuf] *Fam* **NM** fatty, podge; **un gros p.** a fatso, a fatty
EXCLAM crash!

pataquès [patakɛs] **NM 1** *(faute de liaison)* bad *or* incorrect liaison **2** *(faute de langage)* serious mistake *(in pronunciation etc)* **3** *Fam (situation confuse)* mess, shambles *(singulier)*; **faire un p.** to cause a stink, to set tongues wagging

patarafe [pataraf] **NF** *Can* insult

pataras [patara] **NM** *Naut* preventer shroud

patard [patar] **NM** *Anciennement* small coin; **je n'en donnerais pas un p.** I wouldn't give a (brass) farthing for it; **cela ne vaut pas un p.** it isn't worth a doit

patarin [patarɛ̃] **NM** *Hist* **1** *(au XIXème siècle)* Patarin **2** *(cathare d'Italie)* Italian Cathar

patas [patas] **NM** *Zool* patas monkey, red monkey, dancing monkey

patata [patata] *voir* **patati**

patate [patat] **NF 1** *Bot & Culin* **p. (douce)** sweet potato
2 *Fam (pomme de terre)* spud; *Can* **patates frites** *Br* chips, *Am* (French) fries
3 *Fam (coup)* thump, clout
4 *Fam (personne stupide)* dork, *Br* divvy, *Am* putz
5 *Anciennement Fam (dix mille francs)* ten thousand francs▪
6 *Math* = set diagram
7 *Can Fam (cœur)* heart▪, *Br* ticker; **monter les escaliers, c'est dur pour la p.** going up the stairs is hard on the old heart *or Br* ticker
8 *Fam (locutions)* **avoir la p.** to be on top form, to be full of beans; **en avoir gros sur la p.** to be down in the mouth; *Can* **être dans les patates** to be out to lunch; *Can* **ne pas lâcher la p.** to persevere▪, to hang in there

patati [patati] **et patati, et patata ADV** *Fam* blah blah blah, and so on and so forth

patatoïde [patatɔid] **ADJ** potato-shaped, oblong-shaped
NM oblong-shaped object

patatras [patatra] **EXCLAM** crash!

pataud, -e [pato, -od] **ADJ** *(maladroit)* clumsy; *(sans finesse)* gauche
NM,F 1 *(chiot)* (big-pawed) puppy **2** *Vieilli (personne → maladroite)* clumsy oaf; *(→ à l'esprit lent)* oaf

Pataugas® [patogas] **NMPL** = thick-soled hiking boots with canvas uppers

pataugeage [patoʒaʒ] **NM 1** *(dans l'eau)* paddling about; *(dans la boue)* squelching about **2** *Fig (embarras)* floundering

pataugeoire [patoʒwar] **NF** paddling pool

patauger [17] [patoʒe] **VI 1** *(dans l'eau)* to paddle about; *(dans la boue)* to squelch about **2** *(s'empêtrer)* to flounder; **il patauge dans ses réponses** he's getting more and more bogged down trying to answer; *Fam* **p. (dans la semoule)** to be totally lost▪ **3** *(ne pas progresser → enquête)* to get bogged down

patauger, -euse [patoʒœr, -øz] **NM,F** paddler
▫ **pataugeuse NF** *Can* paddling pool

patch [patʃ] **NM** *Méd* patch

patchouli [patʃuli] **NM** patchouli; **huile de p.** patchouli oil

patchwork [patʃwœrk] **NM 1** *Couture (technique)* patchwork; *(ouvrage)* (piece of) patchwork **2** *(ensemble hétérogène)* patchwork; **le pays est un p. de nationalités** the country is a patchwork of different nationalities
▫ **en patchwork ADJ** patchwork *(avant n)*

pâte [pɑt] **NF 1** *(à base de farine → à pain)* dough; *(→ à tarte) Br* pastry, *Am* dough; *(→ à gâteau) Br* mixture, *Am* batter; *(→ à frire)* batter; **p. à beignets** batter; **p. brisée** *Br* short *or* shortcrust pastry, *Am* pie dough; **p. à crêpes** pancake batter; **p. à choux** choux pastry; **p. feuilletée** flaky pastry, *Br* puff pastry; **p. à foncer** pastry (dough); **p. à frire** batter; **p. sablée** *Br* rich shortcrust pastry, *Am* sweet *or* sugar dough

2 *(pour fourrer, tartiner)* paste; **p. d'amandes** marzipan, almond paste; **p. d'anchois** anchovy paste *or* spread; **p. de coing** quince jelly; **une p. de fruits** fruit jelly *(made from thick fruit pulp)*; **une p. de fruits** a fruit jelly

3 *(en fromagerie)* **(fromage à) p. cuite** cheese made from scalded curds; **(fromage à) p. fermentée/molle** fermented/soft cheese

4 *(tempérament)* **il est d'une p. à vivre cent ans** he's the sort who'll live to be a hundred; **c'est une bonne p., il est bonne p.** he's a good sort; **une p. molle** *(personne sans caractère)* a wimp; *Can (personne paresseuse)* a shirker

5 *Beaux-Arts* paint, colours

6 *Cér* paste

7 *(en cosmétologie)* paste; **p. dentifrice,** *Can* **p. à dents** toothpaste

8 *Tech* **p. à bois** wood pulp; **p. à papier** paper pulp; *Ind* **p. de verre** molten glass; *(en joaillerie)* paste

9 p. à modeler Plasticine®, modelling clay

□ **pâtes** NFPL **1** *Culin* **pâtes (alimentaires)** pasta *(UNCOUNT)*; **les pâtes sont trop cuites** the pasta's overcooked; **pâtes fraîches** fresh pasta **2** *Pharm* **pâtes pectorales** cough lozenges *or* pastilles

pâté [pate] NM **1** *Culin* pâté; **p. de campagne** pâté de campagne *(coarse pâté made with pork)*; **p. de canard** duck pâté; *Can* **p. chinois** shepherd's pie; **p. en croûte** pâté en croûte, *Br* raised (crust) pie; **p. de foie** liver pâté; **p. impérial** spring roll; **p. à la viande** meat pie

2 *Belg (gâteau)* cake

3 *Fam (tache d'encre)* (ink) blot; **faire des pâtés** *(stylo)* to smudge; *(élève)* to make ink-blots

4 *(tas)* **p. de sable** sand pie; **faire des pâtés de sable** to make sand pies

□ **pâté de maisons** NM block

pâtée [pate] NF **1** *(pour animaux)* food, feed; **p. pour chat/chien** cat/dog food; **as-tu donné la p. aux porcs?** have you fed the pigs? **2** *(nourriture grossière)* pap **3** *Fam* trashing, hammering; **foutre la p. à qn** *(correction, défaite écrasante)* to give sb a thrashing *ou* a hammering

patelin¹ [patlɛ̃] NM *Fam (village)* village▪; *(petite ville)* small town▪; *Péj* **tout droit débarqué de son p.** fresh up from the country▪

patelin², -e [patlɛ̃, -in] ADJ *Littéraire* fawning, unctuous

pateliner [3] [patline] VI *Vieilli* to be fawning *or* unctuous

patelle [patɛl] NF **1** *Zool (mollusque)* limpet **2** *Archéol* patella

patène [patɛn] NF paten

patenôtre [patnotr] NF *Vieilli ou Littéraire* **1** *(prière)* prayer **2** *(paroles incompréhensibles)* gibberish

patent, -e¹ [patɑ̃, -ɑ̃t] ADJ **1** *(flagrant, incontestable)* obvious, patent; **c'est un fait p.** it's patently obvious; **il est p. que...** it is patently obvious that... **2** *Hist* patent

patentable [patɑ̃tabl] ADJ *Admin* subject to a licence, requiring a licence

patentage [patɑ̃taʒ] NM patenting *(UNCOUNT)*

patente² [patɑ̃t] NF **1** *Anciennement (taxe)* trading tax; **payer p.** to be duly licensed **2** *Hist (royal)* patent **3** *Naut* **p. de santé** bill of health **4** *Can Fam (chose)* thingy; *(invention)* gadget▪

patenté, -e [patɑ̃te] ADJ **1** *Fam (attesté)* established▪; **un raciste p.** an out-and-out racist **2** *(qui paie patente)* trading under licence, licensed

patenter [3] [patɑ̃te] VT to license

patenteux, -euse [patɑ̃tø, -øz] *Can Fam* ADJ *(adroit)* handy, good with one's hands▪; *(intelligent)* clever▪, *Am* smart▪

NM,F handyman, *f* handywoman

Pater [patɛr] NM INV Paternoster, Our Father

pater [patɛr] NM **1** *Fam (père)* old man, *Br* pater **2** *Rel* paternoster (bead)

patère [patɛr] NF **1** *(à vêtements)* coat peg **2** *(à rideaux)* curtain hook **3** *Antiq & Archit* patera

paterfamilias [patɛrfamiljas] NM **1** *Antiq* paterfamilias **2** *Hum* domineering father

paternalisme [patɛrnalism] NM paternalism

paternaliste [patɛrnalist] ADJ paternalist, paternalistic

paterne [patɛrn] ADJ *Littéraire* benevolent

paternel, -elle [patɛrnɛl] ADJ **1** *(du père)* paternal; **cousins du côté p.** cousins on the father's *or* paternal side; **ma grand-mère paternelle** my grandmother on my father's side, my father's mother **2** *(indulgent)* fatherly

NM *Fam Hum (père)* old man, *Br* pater

paternellement [patɛrnɛlmɑ̃] ADV paternally, in a fatherly way

paternité [patɛrnite] NF **1** *(d'un enfant)* fatherhood, *Sout* paternity; **il vit mal sa p.** he's finding fatherhood difficult, he's finding it difficult being a father; *Jur* **p. légitime/naturelle** legitimate/natural paternity **2** *(d'une œuvre)* authorship, *Sout* paternity; *(d'une théorie)* paternity; **revendiquer/désavouer la p. d'un livre** to claim/to repudiate authorship of a book

pâteux, -euse [patø, -øz] ADJ **1** *(gâteau)* doughy; **ces abricots sont p.** these apricots are like cotton wool; **avoir la bouche** *ou* **langue pâteuse** to have a furred tongue; **parler d'une voix pâteuse** to sound groggy **2** *(style)* heavy, clumsy, lumbering

pathétique [patetik] ADJ **1** *(émouvant)* pathetic, moving, poignant; **des descriptions pathétiques** descriptions full of pathos **2** *Anat* **nerf p.** pathetic nerve

NM **1** *(émotion)* pathos **2** *Anat* pathetic nerve

pathétiquement [patetikmɑ̃] ADV pathetically, movingly, poignantly

pathétisme [patetism] NM *Littéraire* pathos

pathogène [patɔʒɛn] *Méd* ADJ pathogenic, pathogenetic

NM pathogen

pathogenèse [patɔʒənɛz], **pathogénie** [patɔʒeni] NF *Méd* pathogenesis, pathogeny

pathogénique [patɔʒenik] ADJ *Méd* pathogenic, pathogenetic

pathognomonique [patɔgnɔmɔnik] ADJ pathognomonic, pathognomonic

pathologie [patɔlɔʒi] NF pathology

pathologique [patɔlɔʒik] ADJ **1** *Méd* pathologic, pathological **2** *Fam (excessif, anormal)* pathological

pathologiquement [patɔlɔʒikmɑ̃] ADV pathologically

pathologiste [patɔlɔʒist] ADJ pathologistic

NMF pathologist

pathomimie [patɔmimi] NF pathomimicry

pathos [patos] NM pathos

patibulaire [patibylɛr] ADJ sinister; **il avait une mine p.** he looked sinister

patiemment [pasjamɑ̃] ADV patiently

patience [pasjɑ̃s] NF **1** *(calme)* patience, *Sout* forbearance; **avec p.** patiently; **je n'ai aucune p. avec les enfants** I've no patience with children; **aie un peu de p.** be patient for a minute; **prends p.** be patient; **ma p. a des limites** there are limits to my patience; **prendre son mal en p.** to put up with it; **elle a une p. d'ange** she has the patience of a saint *or* of Job

2 *(persévérance)* patience, painstaking care; **sa p. a été récompensée** his/her patience was rewarded

3 *Cartes Br* patience, *Am* solitaire; **faire des patiences** to play *Br* patience *or* *Am* solitaire; **jeu de p.** puzzle; *Fig (travail minitieux)* test of patience

4 *Bot* dock

EXCLAM hold on!; **p., j'ai presque fini!** hold on *or* just a minute, I've almost finished!; **p., il va voir de quoi je suis capable!** just you wait (and see), I'll show him what I'm made of!

Patience et longueur de temps font plus que force ni que rage

This is the moral of a La Fontaine fable, *Le Lion et le rat*. A lion spares the life of a passing rat, and when the lion is later caught in the mesh of a hunting net, the rat patiently gnaws through it to release him. The lion's strength is much less effective than the rat's patience in this situation. The expression means "patience and the passage of time do more than strength and rage". Where a French parent says to a child **Patience et longueur de temps**, it is the equivalent of using the English expression "All in good time!" to curb the child's impatience.

---

patient, -e [pasjɑ̃, -ɑ̃t] ADJ patient

NM,F *(malade)* patient

NM *Gram (par opposition à agent)* patient

patienter [3] [pasjɑ̃te] VI *(attendre)* to wait; **faites-la p. un instant** ask her to wait for a minute; **p. en lisant le journal** to read the newspaper to while away *or* pass the time; *Tél* **c'est occupé, vous voulez p.?** it's *Br* engaged *or* *Am* busy, will you hold?

patin [patɛ̃] NM **1** *Sport* skate; *(de luge, de traîneau)* runner; **patins à glace/roulettes** ice/roller skates; **faire du p. à glace/roulettes** to go ice-skating/roller-skating; **sais-tu faire du p. à glace/à roulettes?** can you ice-skate/roller-skate?; *Can Fam* **être vite sur ses patins** to be quick on one's feet▪; *Can Fam* **accrocher ses patins** to hang up one's hat, to retire▪; *(sportif)* to hang up one's boots, to retire▪

2 *(pour marcher sur un parquet)* felt pad *(used to move around on a polished floor)*

3 *très Fam (baiser)* French kiss, *Br* snog; **rouler un p. à qn** to French kiss *or* *Br* snog sb

4 *Aviat* landing pad

5 *Aut* **p. de frein** brake shoe; *Fam* **donner** *ou* **filer un coup de p.** *(un coup de frein)* to slam on the brakes

6 *Constr (d'échafaudage)* sole plate *or* piece

7 *Tech* shoe, pad

8 *Rail* (rail) base

9 *(d'un blindé)* (track) link

patinage [patinaʒ] NM **1** *Sport* skating, ice-skating; **p. artistique** figure skating; **p. à roulettes** roller-skating; **p. de vitesse** speed skating **2** *(d'une roue)* spinning; *(de l'embrayage)* slipping **3** *(patine artificielle)* patination

patine [patin] NF **1** *(d'un meuble)* sheen; **la p. du temps** the patina of age *or* time **2** *Beaux-Arts & Géol* patina

patiné, -e [patine] ADJ patinated; **p. par le temps** patinated with age

patiner [3] [patine] VI **1** *Sport* to skate **2** *Aut (roue)* to spin; *(embrayage)* to slip; **ça patine!** it's very slippery!, it's like an ice rink *or* a skating rink! **3** *Fig (stagner)* to get nowhere **4** *Can Fig (locution)* **savoir p.** to avoid the issue

VT *(un meuble)* to patine, to patinize

▶ **se patiner** VPR to patinate, to become patinated

patinette [patinɛt] NF *(child's)* scooter

patineur, -euse [patinœr, -øz] NM,F *(sur glace)* skater, ice-skater; *(à roulettes)* roller-skater; *(en rollers)* rollerblader

NM *Can Entom (araignée)* water spider

patinoire [patinwar] NF **1** *Sport* ice *or* skating rink **2** *(surface trop glissante)* **ce trottoir est une véritable p.** this pavement is like an ice rink *or* a skating rink

patio [patjo, pasjo] NM patio

pâtir [32] [patir] **pâtir de** VT IND to suffer from, to suffer as a result of

pâtis [pati] NM grazing (ground), pasture

pâtisser [3] [patise] VT to work up

VI to make cakes; **elle pâtisse bien** she's a good pastry cook, she makes good cakes

pâtisserie [patisri] NF **1** *(gâteau)* cake, pastry; **elle mange trop de pâtisseries** she eats too many cakes **2** *(activité)* cake-making, pastry-making; **faire de la p.** to make *or* to bake cakes; **elle fait de la bonne p.** she makes good cakes **3** *(boutique)* pâtisserie, cake *Br* shop *or* *Am* store; **p.-confiserie** confectioner's **4** *Archit* plaster moulding *or* mouldings

pâtissier, -ère [patisje, -ɛr] NM,F pastry cook, confectioner; **son mari est très bon p.** her husband makes very good cakes

pâtisson [patisɔ̃] NM *Bot* squash

patoche [patɔʃ] NF *Fam Vieilli* (big) paw *or* mitt

patois [patwa] NM patois, dialect; **il parle encore le p.** he still speaks patois *or* the dialect

patoisant, -e [patwazɑ̃, -ɑ̃t] ADJ patois-speaking, dialect-speaking

NM,F patois *or* dialect speaker

patoiser [3] [patwaze] VI to speak patois *or* the dialect

pâton [patɔ̃] NM **1** *(pâte à pain)* ball of dough **2** *(pour la volaille)* ball of feed *(for cramming poultry)*

patouiller [3] [patuje] *Fam* VI *(patauger)* to slosh *or* to wallow about

VT *(tripoter)* to paw, to mess about with

patraque [patrak] ADJ *Fam* **1** *(souffrant)* out of sorts, under the weather **2** *Vieilli (cassé → pendule)* on the blink

Patras [patras] NM Patras

pâtre [pɑtr] NM *Littéraire* shepherd

patres [patrɛs] *voir* **ad patres**

patriarcal, -e, -aux, -ales [patrijarkal, -o] ADJ patriarchal

patriarcat [patrijarka] NM **1** *Rel (dignité, territoire)* patriarchate **2** *(en anthropologie)* patriarchy

patriarche [patrijarʃ] NM *(gén) & Rel* patriarch

patrice [patris] NM *Antiq* patrician

patricial, -e, -aux, -ales [patrisjal, -o] ADJ *Antiq* patrician; **dignité patriciale** patrician rank

patriciat [patrisja] NM **1** *Antiq (dignité)* patriciate, dignity of patrician; *(ordre)* patriciate, the order of the patricians **2** *Littéraire (élite)* élite

patricien, -enne [patrisjɛ̃, -ɛn] ADJ **1** *Antiq* patrician **2** *Littéraire (noble)* **l'orgueil p.** aristocratic pride; **une demeure patricienne** a stately home; **une famille patricienne** an aristocratic family
NM,F *Antiq* patrician

patriclan [patriklɑ̃] NM patriclan

patrie [patri] NF **1** *(pays natal)* homeland, native country; *(région natale)* native region; *(ville natale)* home town; **Paris, seconde p. de la comédienne** Paris, the actress's adoptive home *or* the city which has become the actress's second home; **morts pour la p.** *(sur monument aux morts)* they gave their lives for their country
2 *(communauté)* home; **trouver une nouvelle p.** to find a new home
3 *Fig* **la p. de** the home *or* birthplace of; **la Nouvelle-Orléans, la p. du jazz** New Orleans, the home *or* birthplace of jazz

patrilignage [patriliɲaʒ] NM patrilineage

patrilinéaire [patrilineɛr] ADJ patrilineal

patrilocal, -e, -aux, -ales [patrilɔkal, -o] ADJ patrilocal

patrimoine [patrimwan] NM **1** *(possessions héritées)* inheritance, *Sout* patrimony **2** *Fin (d'un individu)* property, wealth, personal assets; *(actif net)* net assets; **p. immobilier** *Br* property assets, *Am* real-estate assets; **p. social** social assets **3** *(artistique, culturel)* heritage **4** *Biol* **p. génétique** gene pool; **p. héréditaire** genotype

patrimonial, -e, -aux, -ales [patrimɔnjal, -o] ADJ patrimonial

patriotard, -e [patrijɔtar, -ard] *Péj* ADJ jingoistic
NM,F jingoist, chauvinist

patriote [patrijɔt] ADJ patriotic
NMF patriot

patriotique [patrijɔtik] ADJ patriotic

patriotiquement [patrijɔtikmɑ̃] ADV patriotically

patriotisme [patrijɔtism] NM patriotism

patristique [patristik] *Rel* ADJ patristic
NF patristics *(singulier)*, patrology

patrologie [patrɔlɔʒi] NF *Rel (collection d'écrits)* patrology; *(patristique)* patrology, patristics *(singulier)*

patron[1] [patrɔ̃] NM **1** *Couture* pattern; **p. de jupe** skirt pattern; **(taille) p.** medium size; **demi-p.** small size; **grand p.** large size **2** *Beaux-Arts* template **3** *Typ (plaque)* stencil (plate); **coloriage au p.** stencil-painting

patron[2], **-onne** [patrɔ̃, -ɔn] NM,F **1** *(d'une entreprise → propriétaire)* owner; *(→ gérant)* manager; *(→ directeur)* employer; *(→ de café, d'auberge)* owner, landlord, *f* landlady; **eh, la patronne, une bière!** a beer please, landlady!; **p. de presse** newspaper proprietor; **les grands patrons de presse** the press barons
2 *(maître de maison)* master, *f* mistress
3 *Univ* **p. de thèse** (doctoral) supervisor
4 *(d'un service hospitalier)* senior consultant
5 *Fam (conjoint)* old man; *(conjointe)* old lady
6 *Rel* patron saint; **la patronne des musiciens** the patron saint of musicians
NM **1** *(d'une entreprise → chef)* boss; **être son propre p.** to be one's own boss; *Fam* **c'est moi le p.!** I'm the boss!, I'm in charge!
2 *Antiq & Hist* patron
3 *Naut* skipper

patronage [patrɔnaʒ] NM **1** *(soutien officiel)* patronage; **sous le haut p. du président de la République** under the patronage of the President of the Republic **2** *(soutien financier)* sponsorship, sponsoring; **sous le p. de** sponsored by **3** *(pour les jeunes)* youth club **4** *(tutelle d'un saint)* protection; **placé sous le p. de saint André** under the protection of Saint Andrew
❑ **de patronage** ADJ moralistic; **une mentalité de p.** a Sunday school mentality

patronal, -e, -aux, -ales [patrɔnal, -o] ADJ **1** *Com & Ind* employer's, employers' **2** *Rel* patronal

patronat [patrɔna] NM **le p.** the employers; **le p. français** French employers

patronne [patrɔn] *voir* **patron**[2]

patronner [3] [patrɔne] VT **1** *(parrainer → gén)* to support; *(→ financièrement)* to sponsor; **p. une entreprise auprès des banques** to secure a company with the banks **2** *Couture* to make the pattern for

patronnesse [patrɔnɛs] ADJ F *voir* **dame**

patronyme [patrɔnim] NM patronymic

patronymique [patrɔnimik] ADJ patronymic

patrouille [patruj] NF patrol; *Aviat* **p. de chasse** fighter patrol; *Naut* **p. maritime** navy patrol; **faire une/être en p.** to go/to be on patrol

patrouiller [3] [patruje] VI to patrol

patrouilleur [patrujœr] NM **1** *Mil* man on patrol; **les patrouilleurs** the patrol **2** *Aviat (de chasse)* (patrolling) fighter; *(de détection)* spotter plane **3** *Naut* patrol ship

patte [pat] NF **1** *(jambe)* leg; *(pied → d'un félin, d'un chien)* paw; *(→ d'un oiseau)* foot; **donne la p., Rex!** Rex, give a paw!; **être bas** *ou* **court sur pattes** *(animal, personne)* to be short-legged; **être haut sur pattes** to be long-legged; **pattes de devant** *(membres)* forelegs; *(pieds)* forepaws, forefeet; **pattes de derrière** *(membres)* hind legs; *(pieds)* hind paws *or* feet; **p. de lapin** rabbit foot; *(favori)* sideburn, sidewhisker; **pattes de mouche** (spidery) scrawl; *Fam* **pantalon (à) pattes d'éléphant** *ou* **d'éph** bell-bottoms, *Br* flares; **bas les pattes!** *(à un chien)* down!; **faire p. de velours** *(chat)* to sheathe *or* to draw in its claws; *(personne)* to use the velvet glove (approach)
2 *Fam (jambe)* leg■, *Br* pin, *Am* gam; **se casser une p.** to break one's leg; **il a une p. folle** he's got a *Br* gammy leg *or Am* gimpy leg; **retomber sur ses pattes** to land on one's feet; **tirer dans les pattes à qn** to cause trouble for sb; **ils n'arrêtent pas de se tirer dans les pattes** they're always giving each other a hard time; **se faire faire aux pattes** to get collared
3 *Fam (main)* hand■, paw; **avoir les pattes sales** to have grubby paws; **un coup de p.** a swipe, a cutting remark; **eh, toi, bas les pattes!** *(à une personne)* hey, you, paws off!, keep your paws to yourself!; **tomber dans** *ou* **entre les pattes de qn** to fall into sb's clutches; **graisser la p. à qn** to grease sb's palm
4 *(savoir-faire → d'un peintre)* (fine) touch; *(→ d'un écrivain)* talent; **avoir de la p., avoir le coup de p.** *(d'un peintre)* to have a fine touch
5 *Constr (pour fixer)* (metal) tie, (heavy) fastener; *(de couverture)* saddle; **p. de scellement** *Br* expansion bolt, *Am* expansion anchor
6 *(d'un portefeuille, d'une chaussure)* tongue; *(sur l'épaule)* strap; **p. de boutonnage** fly (front)
7 *Naut (d'une ancre)* fluke, palm
8 *Tech (d'un grappin)* claw; **p. d'attache** gusset plate
9 *Suisse & (dans l'est de la France) (torchon)* cloth
❑ **pattes** NFPL *(favoris)* sideburns, sidewhiskers
❑ **à pattes** ADV *Fam* **allez, on y va à pattes!** come on, let's hoof it!

Allusion

Montrer patte blanche

In La Fontaine's fable *Le Loup, la chèvre et le chevreau* ("The Wolf, the Nanny Goat and the Kid"), a wolf overhears a password which should admit him to the nanny goat's house during her absence. When he comes to the door, and imitates the voice of a goat, the kid he is hoping to devour requires further proof of identity, telling him to **montrer patte blanche** ("show a white foot"). The wolf is foiled, his prey unscathed. **Montrer patte blanche** is used today to mean "to show that one has impeccable credentials" or "to prove that one is bona fide", often in some sort of screening process.

patté, -e [pate] ADJ *Hér* paty

patte-de-loup [patdəlu] *(pl* **pattes-de-loup***)* NF gipsywort

patte-d'oie [patdwa] *(pl* **pattes-d'oie***)* NF **1** *(ride)* crow's-foot **2** *(carrefour)* crossroads, junction **3** *Anat* pes anserinus **4** *Bot (Potentilla anserina)* silverweed; *(famille des Chénopodiacées)* goosefoot **5** *Constr* (crossbraced) truss **6** *(d'un pont)* starling; *(balise)* (marker) dolphin

patte-mâchoire [patmaʃwar] *(pl* **pattes-mâchoires***)* NF maxilliped

pattemouille [patmuj] NF damp cloth *(used when ironing)*

patte-nageoire [patnaʒwar] *(pl* **pattes-nageoires***)* NF uropod

pattern [patɛrn] NM *(en sciences humaines)* pattern

pattier [patje] NM *Suisse Fam* **jurer comme un p.** to swear like a trooper

pattinsonage [patinsɔnaʒ] NM *Métal* pattinsonization, Pattinson's process

pattu, -e [paty] ADJ **1** *Orn* feather-legged **2** *(chien)* big-pawed; *(personne)* big-legged

patudo [patydo] NM *Ich* bigeye tuna

pâturable [pɑtyrabl] ADJ pasturable

pâturage [pɑtyraʒ] NM **1** *(prairie)* pasture, pastureland **2** *(activité)* grazing

pâture [pɑtyr] NF **1** *(nourriture)* food, feed; **jeter** *ou* **donner qn en p. à qn** to serve sb up to sb **2** *(lieu)* pasture **3** *(pour l'esprit)* food, diet; **la poésie est sa p. favorite** poetry is his/her favourite reading matter

pâturer [3] [pɑtyre] VT to graze
VI to graze

pâturin [pɑtyrɛ̃] NM *Br* meadow grass, *Am* spear grass

paturon [patyrɔ̃] NM **1** *(du cheval)* pastern **2** *Fam* foot■, *Br* plate, *Am* dog

pauchouse [poʃuz] = **pochouse**

paulette [polɛt] NF *Hist* = tax paid every year by magistrates to guarantee the hereditary status of their office

paulinien, -enne [polinjɛ̃, -ɛn] ADJ Pauline

paulinisme [polinism] NM *Rel* Paulinism

pauliste[1] [polist] *Rel* ADJ Paulist
NMF Paulist

pauliste[2] [polist] ADJ *(de São Paulo)* of/from São Paulo
❑ **Pauliste** NMF = inhabitant of or person from São Paulo

paulownia [polɔnja] NM *Bot* paulownia

paume [pom] NF **1** *Anat* palm **2** *Menuis* halving (lap joint) **3** *Sport* real tennis; **jeu de p.** *(terrain)* real-tennis court **4** *(mesure)* hand

paumé, -e[1] [pome] *Fam* ADJ **1** *(désemparé, indécis)* confused■, mixed-up; *(marginal)* out of it **2** *(isolé)* remote, godforsaken; **un patelin complètement p.** a village in the middle of nowhere *or* in the back of beyond **3** *(perdu)* lost■
NM,F *(marginal)* dropout

paumée[2] [pome] NF *Hist* buffet

paumelle [pomɛl] NF **1** *Constr (gond)* (lift-off) hinge; *(partie du gond)* (hinge) plate **2** *(gant)* sailmaker's palm **3** *(pour assouplir le cuir)* pommel **4** *Bot* two-rowed barley

paumer [3] [pome] *Fam* VT **1** *(égarer)* to lose■ **2** *(recevoir)* to get■, to cop; **il a paumé un gnon dans la figure** he got himself a whack in the face **3** *(attraper → délinquant, fautif)* **se faire p.** to get busted *or Br* nicked
VI *(perdre)* to lose■; **celui qui paume paie à boire** the loser pays for the drinks
►**se paumer** VPR *Fam* to get lost■

paumier, -ère [pomje, -ɛr] *Chasse* ADJ F **bête paumière** deer with palmate antlers
NM deer with palmate antlers

paumoyer [13] [pomwaje] VT **1** *(cuir)* to make supple using a pommel **2** *Naut* to underrun

paumure [pomyr] NF palm *(of deer's antlers)*

paupérisation [poperizasjɔ̃] NF pauperization

paupériser [3] [poperize] VT to pauperize
►**se paupériser** VPR to become pauperized

paupérisme [poperism] NM pauperism

paupière [popjɛr] NF eyelid

paupiette [popjɛt] NF **p. (de veau)** paupiette of veal, veal olive

pause [poz] NF **1** *(moment de repos)* break; **faire une p.** to have *or* to take a break; **la p. de midi** the lunch break; **p.-cigarette** cigarette break; **p.-repas** meal break

2 *(temps d'arrêt → dans une conversation)* pause; **marquer une p.** to pause; **après une p., elle reprit son discours** after a pause *or* a short break, she went on

3 *(arrêt → d'un processus)* halt; **il a annoncé une p. dans les réformes** he declared a temporary halt to the reforms

4 *Mus* rest

5 *Sport* half-time

pause-café [pozkafe] (*pl* **pauses-café**) **NF** coffee break

pause-carrière [pozkarjɛr] (*pl* **pauses-carrière**) **NF** *Belg* career break *(on reduced pay)*

pauser [3] [poze] **VI** **1** *Mus (faire une pause)* to pause **2** *Fam* **faire p. qn** to keep sb hanging around

pauvre [povr] **ADJ** **1** *(sans richesse → personne, pays, quartier)* poor; **il recrute ses partisans dans les milieux pauvres** his supporters come from the poorer sections of the population

2 *(avant le nom) (pitoyable → demeure, décor)* humble, wretched; *(→ sourire)* weak, thin; *(→ personne)* poor; *Fam* **ce n'est qu'un p. gosse** he's only a poor kid; **p. femme/homme!** poor woman/man!; **laisse donc ce p. chien tranquille!** do leave that poor dog alone!; **mon p. frère le répétait souvent** as my poor brother used to say; **ah, ma p. dame, si vous saviez!** but my dear lady, if only you knew!; *Fam* **c'est la vie, mon p. vieux!** that's life, my friend!; *Fam* **p. crétin!** you idiot!; *Fam* **c'est un p. type** he's a sad case; **p. de moi!** woe is me! **p. de nous!** (the) Lord protect us!; **p. France!** what's the country coming to?

3 *(insuffisant)* poor; **gaz/minerai p.** lean gas/ore; **un sous-sol p.** a poor subsoil; **une végétation p.** sparse vegetation; **une plaine p.** an infertile *or* unproductive plain; **souffrir d'une alimentation p.** to suffer from a poor diet; **elle a un vocabulaire très p.** her vocabulary is very poor; **malgré une argumentation très p.** in spite of very poor *or* weak arguments; **être p. en qch** to lack sth, to be lacking in sth; **la ville est p. en espaces verts** the town is short of *or* lacks parks; **alimentation p. en sels minéraux** food lacking (in) minerals; **régime p. en calories** low-calorie diet

NMF **1** *(par compassion)* poor thing; **les pauvres, comme ils ont dû souffrir!** poor things, they must have suffered so much!; **mon p.!** you poor thing!

2 *(en appellatif)* **mais mon p./ma p., il ne m'obéit jamais!** *(pour susciter la pitié)* but my dear fellow/my dear, he never does as I say!; **tu es vraiment trop bête, ma p./mon p.!** *(avec mépris)* you're really too stupid for words, my dear girl/boy!

NM poor man, *Littéraire* pauper; **les pauvres** the poor; **elle allait voir ses pauvres** she visited the poor; **c'est le champagne du p.** it's poor man's champagne

pauvrement [povrəmɑ̃] **ADV** **1** *(misérablement → décoré, habillé)* poorly, shabbily; **vivre p.** to live in poverty **2** *(médiocrement)* poorly; **il traduit p.** he's a poor translator

pauvresse [povrɛs] **NF** *Vieilli* poor woman, pauperess; **une p. en haillons** a poor ragged woman

pauvret, -ette [povrɛ, ɛt] **ADJ** poor, poor-looking

NM,F **le p., la pauvrette** the poor (little) dear, the poor (little) thing

pauvreté [povrəte] **NF** **1** *(manque d'argent)* poverty; **il a fini ses jours dans la p.** he ended his days in poverty; *Prov* **p. n'est pas vice** poverty is not a vice; **p. infantile** child poverty

2 *(médiocrité)* poverty; **son article montre la p. de ses idées** his/her article demonstrates the poverty of his/her ideas; **avoir une imagination d'une extrême p.** to be extremely unimaginative

3 *(déficience)* poverty; **la p. du sol ne permet qu'un faible rendement** the poorness of the soil means that the yield is very low

pauvrette [povrɛt] *voir* **pauvret**

pavage [pavaʒ] **NM** **1** *(action → gén)* paving; *(→ aux pavés ronds)* cobbling; **le p. des rues piétonnières est en cours** the pedestrian precinct is being paved **2** *(surface → dallee)* paving; *(→ empierrée)* cobbles, cobblestones **3** *Géol* pavement; **p. de déflation** desert pavement *or* mosaic

pavane [pavan] **NF** pavane

pavaner [3] [pavane] **se pavaner VPR** to strut about

pavé [pave] **NM** **1** *(surface → dallée)* pavement, paving; *(→ empierrée)* cobbles, cobblestones; **tenir le haut du p.** to be on top; **être sur le p.** *(sans domicile)* to be on the street; *(au chômage)* to be jobless; **jeter** *ou* **mettre qn sur le p.** *(l'expulser de son domicile)* to throw sb out on the streets; *(le licencier)* to throw sb out of his/her job

2 *(pierre → gén)* paving stone; *(→ ronde)* cobblestone; *Fig* **avoir un p. sur l'estomac** to have a weight on one's stomach; **lui, quand il veut aider, c'est le p. de l'ours** with friends like him, who needs enemies?; **un** *ou* **le p. dans la mare** a bombshell; **son article a été le p. dans la mare** his/her article caused a bit of a furore; **jeter un p. dans la mare** to set the cat among the pigeons

3 *Culin (viande)* thick slab *or* chunk; **p. de romsteck** thick rump steak; *(gâteau)* **un p. au chocolat** a (thick) chocolate cake

4 *Presse & Typ (encart)* block (of text); *(publicité)* (large) display advertisement

5 *Ordinat* pad, keypad; **p. numérique** numeric keypad

6 *Fam (livre)* massive tome, doorstop; *(article)* huge article; *(dissertation)* huge essay

7 *Fam (dent)* tooth▪

> *Allusion*
>
> **Sous les pavés, la plage**
>
> This slogan became famous during the student riots in Paris in May 1968. It means "Beneath the cobbles, the beach". The cobbles were the cobbles from the streets that were pulled up and thrown at the police, and "the beach" was the layer of sand in which they were set. Figuratively speaking, the cobbles represented the dreary society the students wanted to overthrow, centred round work and stuffy conformity, while sand, "the beach", represented a life of liberty and peaceful co-existence to which they aspired. The slogan is used today to describe the possibility of a better world, or simply to allude to the idealism of this time.

pavement [pavmɑ̃] **NM** **1** *Constr* flooring *or* paving *(made of flags, tiles or mosaic)* **2** *Géog* sea floor

paver [3] [pave] **VT** *(avec des dalles)* to pave; *(avec des pavés ronds)* to cobble; **cour pavée** *(dallée)* paved (court)yard; *(aux pavés ronds)* cobbled (court)yard; *Can Fig* **être pavé de monde** to be full of *or* packed with people

paveton [pavtɔ̃] **NM** *Fam (pavé → gén)* paving stone▪; *(→ rond)* cobblestone▪

paveur [pavœr] **NM** *Constr* paver

pavie [pavi] **NF** = type of peach

pavillon [pavijɔ̃] **NM** **1** *(maison particulière)* detached house; **p. de banlieue** detached house *(in the suburbs)* **2** *(belvédère, gloriette)* lodge; **le p. du gardien** the keeper's lodge; **p. de chasse** hunting lodge; **p. de jardin** summerhouse, pavilion **3** *(dans un hôpital)* wing, wards; *(dans une cité universitaire)* house; *(dans une exposition)* pavilion; **il travaille au p. de pédiatrie** he works on the pediatric ward *or* in the pediatric wing; **le p. français à l'exposition** the French pavilion at the exhibition **4** *Aut* roof **5** *(ornement)* pavilion **6** *Anat (des trompes utérines)* pavilion; **p. (auriculaire)** auricle, pinna **7** *Mus (d'un instrument)* bell; *(d'un phonographe, d'un haut-parleur, d'une sirène)* horn **8** *Naut* flag; **p. en berne** flag at half-mast; **p. d'armateur** *ou* **de reconnaissance** house flag; **pavillons de signaux** *ou* **de signalisation** signal flags; **p. amiral** admiral's flag; **p. de complaisance** flag of convenience; **p. de détresse** flag of distress; **p. national** ensign; **p. de quarantaine** quarantine flag, yellow jack; **baisser p.** to lower *or* to strike one's flag; *Fig* to back down; **il a baissé p. devant elle!** he let her ride roughshod over him!

▫ **en pavillon ADJ** *Archit (toit)* pavilion *(avant n)*

'Le Pavillon des cancéreux' *Soljenitsyne* 'Cancer Ward'

pavillonnaire [pavijɔnɛr] **ADJ** **un quartier p.** an area of low-rise housing; **un hôpital p.** a hospital (constructed) in wings, a multiwing hospital

pavillonnerie [pavijɔnri] **NF** *Naut (atelier)* flag loft; *(entrepôt)* flag store

pavimenteux, -euse [pavimɑ̃tø, -øz] **ADJ** *Méd* pavement *(avant n)*

Pavlov [pavlɔf] **NPR** Pavlov; **les chiens de P.** Pavlov's dogs

pavlovien, -enne [pavlɔvjɛ̃, -ɛn] **ADJ** Pavlovian

pavois [pavwa] **NM** **1** *Hist* shield; **élever** *ou* **hisser** *ou* **porter qn sur le p.** to raise *or* to carry sb on high **2** *Naut (partie de la coque)* bulwark; *(pavillons)* flags and bunting; **hisser le grand p.** to dress ship *or* full; **hisser le petit p.** to dress (the ship) with masthead flags

pavoisement [pavwazmɑ̃] **NM** **1** *(d'un édifice, d'une rue)* decking out with flags *or* bunting **2** *Naut* dressing (with flags)

pavoiser [3] [pavwaze] **VT** **1** *(édifice, rue)* to deck with flags *or* bunting **2** *Naut* to dress (with flags)

VI **1** *(déployer des drapeaux)* to put out flags **2** *Naut* to dress ship **3** *Fam (faire le fier)* **il n'y a pas de quoi p.** that's nothing to be proud of▪

pavot [pavo] **NM** *Bot* poppy; **graines de p.** poppy seeds; **p. cornu** red-horned poppy; **p. somnifère** opium poppy

pavute [pavyt] **NF** *très Fam* whore, hooker

pâwâ [pɑwɑ] **NM** *Can (assemblée amérindienne)* pow-wow; *Fig (grand rassemblement)* jamboree

payable [pɛjabl] **ADJ** payable; **chèque p. à l'ordre de** cheque payable to; **facture p. le 5 du mois** invoice payable *or* due on the 5th of the month; **p. en douze mensualités** payable in twelve monthly instalments; **p. à l'arrivée** payable on arrival; **p. à la banque** payable at the bank; **p. à la commande** cash with order, payable with order; **p. comptant** payable in cash; **p. sur demande** payable on demand; **p. à l'échéance** payable at maturity; **p. à la livraison** payable on delivery; **p. au porteur** payable to bearer; **p. à vue** payable on sight

payant, -e [pɛjɑ̃, -ɑ̃t] **ADJ** **1** *(non gratuit)* **les consommations sont payantes** you have to pay for your drinks; **l'entrée est payante** there is an admission charge *or* a charge for admission; *Can* **téléphone p.** payphone

2 *(qui paie)* paying

3 *Fam (qui produit → de l'argent)* profitable▪; *(→ un résultat)* efficient▪; **une spéculation payante** a profitable speculation; **ses efforts du premier trimestre ont été payants** his/her efforts during the first term have paid off

NM *Fam* **le cochon de p.** the mug who has to pay

paye [pɛj] = **paie**

payé, -e [peje] **ADJ** **bien/mal p.** well-/low-paid

payement [pɛmɑ̃] = **paiement**

payer [11] [peje] **VT** **1** *(solder, régler)* to pay; **p. ses impôts au percepteur** to pay one's taxes to the collector; **j'ai une amende à p.** I've got a fine to pay; **p. sa dette à la société** to pay one's debt to society; **c'est le prix à p. si tu veux réussir** that's the price you have to pay for success; *Hum* **p. son tribut à la nature** to go to meet one's maker

2 *(rémunérer)* to pay; **combien paies-tu ta femme de ménage?** how much do you pay your cleaning lady?; **j'espère que tu t'es fait p. pour ces informations** I hope they paid you *or* you were paid for what you told them; **être payé pour savoir qch** to have learnt sth to one's cost; **tu es pourtant payé pour le savoir!** you of all people should know that!

3 *(acheter)* **p. qch à qn** to buy sth for sb; **p. à boire à qn** to buy sb a drink; **je lui ai payé un diamant** I bought him/her a diamond; **j'ai payé ma voiture 10 000 euros** I paid 10,000 euros for my car; **combien as-tu payé ta maison?** how much did your house cost you?, how much did you pay for your house?; **je te paie le théâtre** I'll take you out to the theatre; **combien il t'a fait p.?** how much did he charge?; **il me l'a fait p. trop cher** he overcharged me; **c'est payé?** is it paid for?

4 *Fig (obtenir au prix d'un sacrifice)* **p. qch de** to pay for sth with; **p. sa réussite de sa santé** to succeed at the expense *or* the cost of one's health; **elle me le paiera!** she'll pay for this!; **je te ferai p. ça, mon vieux!** I'll make you pay for this, mate!; **p. cher qch** to pay a high price for sth; **c'est p. cher la réussite** that's too high a price to pay for success

5 *(subir les conséquences de)* to pay for; **il paie maintenant son laisser-aller** now he's paying for his easy-going attitude; *Fig* **p. les pots cassés** to foot the bill; *Vieilli* **p. les violons** to be out of pocket for nothing
6 *(dédommager)* to compensate, to repay; **ses félicitations me paient de mes efforts** his/her congratulations repay me my efforts; **p. qn de belles paroles** to fob sb off with smooth talk; **p. qn d'ingratitude** to repay sb with ingratitude; **p. qn de retour** to repay sb in kind
7 *(acheter → criminel)* to hire; *(→ témoin)* to buy (off); **p. un tueur** to hire a gunman
8 *(compenser)* to pay; **son loyer ne paie même pas mes impôts locaux** his/her rent doesn't even pay *or* cover my local taxes
9 *(être soumis à → taxe)* **certaines marchandises paient un droit de douane** you have to pay duty on some goods, some goods are liable to duty
USAGE ABSOLU **p. comptant** *ou* **en liquide** *ou* **en espèces** to pay (in) cash; **p. à crédit** to pay by credit; **je paye par chèque/avec ma** *ou* **par carte de crédit** I'll pay by cheque/with my *or* by credit card; **p. d'avance** to pay in advance; **p. intégralement, p. en totalité** to pay in full; **p. à la livraison** to pay on delivery; **p. à l'ordre de...** *(sur chèque)* pay to the order of...; **payez au porteur** pay to bearer; **p. à présentation** to pay on presentation; **p. à vue** to pay at sight; **les chômeurs ne paient pas** the unemployed don't have to pay; **c'est moi qui paie** *(l'addition)* I'll pay, it's my treat; **p. de ses deniers** *ou* **de sa poche** to pay out of one's own pocket; **p. rubis sur l'ongle** to pay (cash) on the nail; **leur patron paie bien** their boss pays well; *Fig* **vous êtes coupable, vous devez p.** you're guilty, you're going to pay; **p. pour les autres** to be punished for others
VI **1** *(être profitable)* to pay; **l'ostréiculture ne paie plus** there's no money (to be made) in oyster farming nowadays; **c'est un travail qui paie mal** it's badly paid work, it's work that doesn't pay well; **l'honnêteté ne paie plus** it doesn't pay to be honest any more
2 *Fam (prêter à rire)* to be *or* to look a sight; **tu payes avec ces lunettes!** you're an amazing sight with those glasses on!
3 *(locutions) Littéraire* **p. d'audace** to risk one's all; *Fam* **la maison ne paie pas de mine, mais elle est confortable** the house isn't much to look at but it's very comfortable; **p. de sa personne** *(s'exposer au danger)* to put oneself on the line; *(se donner du mal)* to put in a lot of effort
▶**se payer 1** *(emploi réfléchi)* to compensate oneself; **tenez, payez-vous** here, take what I owe you; **se p. de mots** to talk a lot of fine words
2 *(emploi passif)* to have to be paid for; **la qualité se paie** you have to pay for quality; **tout se paie** everything has its price
3 *Fam (s'offrir)* to treat oneself to; **j'ai envie de me p. une robe** I feel like treating myself to a dress; **se p. la tête** *ou très Fam* **la tronche de qn** *(se moquer de)* to make a fool of sb, *Br* to take the mick *or* the mickey out of sb; *(duper)* to take sb for a ride; **se p. du bon temps,** *très Fam* **s'en p. (une tranche)** to have a fantastic time, to have a ball *or Am* a blast
4 *Fam (être chargé de)* to be landed *or* saddled with; **je me paie tout le boulot** I end up doing all the work▪
5 *Fam (recevoir)* to get▪, *Br* to land; **je me suis payé un 2 à l'oral** I got a 2 in the oral
6 *Fam (supporter)* to put up with▪; **on s'est payé leurs gosses pendant tout le week-end** we had to put up with their kids for the whole weekend; **il s'est payé une crève carabinée** he came down with a stinking cold
7 *Fam (percuter)* to run *or* to bump into▪; **il a brûlé un feu rouge et s'est payé un piéton** he went through a red light and hit a pedestrian▪; **il s'est payé un arbre en moto** he crashed *or* smashed his motorbike into a tree▪
8 *Fam (agresser)* to go for; **s'il continue à m'énerver, celui-là, je vais me le p.!** if he carries on annoying me, I'm going to thump him one!
9 *très Fam (avoir une relation sexuelle avec)* to screw, *Br* to shag

payer-prendre [pejeprɑ̃dr] NM INV cash-and-carry

payeur, -euse [pɛjœr, -øz] ADJ *(agent, fonctionnaire)* payments *(avant n)*
NM,F payer
NM **1** *Admin (distribuant → les salaires)* wages clerk; *(→ les remboursements de frais)* firm's accountant **2** *Mil* paymaster **3** *(débiteur)* **mauvais p.** bad debtor, defaulter

pay-per-view [pɛpœrvju] ADJ *TV* pay-per-view

pays[1] [pei] NM **1** *(nation)* country; **les nouveaux p. industrialisés** the newly industrialized countries; **les p. membres du pacte de Varsovie** the Warsaw Pact countries; **le p. d'accueil** the host country; *UE* **p. candidat** applicant country; **p. débiteur** debtor nation; **p. émergent** emerging country; **p. étranger** foreign country; **p. exportateur** exporting country; **p. importateur** importing country; **p. industrialisé** industrialized country; *UE* **p. membre** member state; **p. d'origine** country of origin; **p. pétrolier** oil-producing country; *UE* **p. en phase d'adhésion** accession country; **p. de provenance** country of origin; **les p. les moins avancés** the least developed countries; **les p. riches** affluent countries; **p. signataires** *(d'un accord)* signatory countries; **p. en (voie de) développement** developing country; **p. du tiers-monde** Third World country; *Can* **les vieux p.** *(pays d'Europe)* the old countries, the Old World; **ils se conduisent comme en p. conquis** they're acting *or* behaving as if they own the place; **voir du p.** to travel a lot; *Fam* **faire voir du p. à qn** to give sb a hard time
2 *(zone, contrée)* region, area; **p. chaud/sec** hot/dry region; **p. de montagnes/lacs** mountain/lake country; **quel p.! il pleut sans arrêt!** what a place! it never stops raining!; **le P. de la Loire** the Loire (region); **en p. de Loire** in the Loire area *or* valley; **au p. des rêves** *ou* **des songes** in the land of dreams; **être en p. de connaissance** *(avec des gens connus)* to be among familiar faces; *(sur un sujet)* to be on familiar *or* home ground
3 *(agglomération)* village, small town; **un petit p. de 2000 âmes** a small town of 2,000 souls; **ça s'est vite su dans tout le p.** the whole village *or* every man, woman and child in the village soon knew about it
4 *(peuple)* people, country; **s'adresser au p.** to talk to the nation; **tout le p. se demande encore qui est l'assassin** the whole country's still wondering who the murderer might be
5 *(région d'origine)* **le p.** *(nation)* one's country; *(région)* one's home (region); *(ville)* one's home (town); **les jeunes quittent le p.** there's an exodus of young people from the region; **c'est un enfant du p.** he's from these parts; **on voit bien que tu n'es pas du p.!** it's obvious you're not from around here!; **le mal du p.** homesickness; **avoir le mal du p.** to be homesick
6 *Admin* = group of neighbouring "communes" which have joined together to promote distinctive aspects of the locality
7 *Fig (berceau, foyer)* **le p. des tulipes** the country of the tulip; **le p. du bel canto** the cradle of bel canto; **l'Espagne, p. de la corrida** Spain, land of the bullfight
▫ **de** *ou* **du pays** ADJ *(produits)* local; **ils vendent des produits du p.** they sell local produce; **saucisson de p.** traditional *or* country-style sausage

pays[2], **-e** [pei, -iz] NM,F *Fam Vieilli* **il a rencontré un p. au régiment** he met somebody in the army from back home▪

paysage [peizaʒ] NM **1** *(étendue géographique)* landscape; **p. montagneux/vallonné** hilly/rolling landscape
2 *(panorama)* view, scenery, landscape; **du sommet, le p. est magnifique** the view from the top is beautiful; **cette région offre de merveilleux paysages** this area has marvellous scenery; *Fam Fig* **faire bien dans le p.** to look good
3 *(aspect d'ensemble)* landscape, scene; **p. politique/social** political/social landscape *or* scene; **le p. audiovisuel français** French broadcasting; **p. urbain** townscape, urban landscape
4 *Beaux-Arts* landscape (painting); **un p. de Millet** a Millet landscape, a landscape by Millet
5 *Ordinat* **(mode** *ou* **format) p.** landscape (mode); **imprimer qch en p.** to print sth in landscape

paysager, -ère [peizaʒe, -ɛr] ADJ landscape *(avant n)*; **parc p.** landscaped gardens

paysagiste [peizaʒist] ADJ landscape *(avant n)*
NMF **1** *Beaux-Arts* landscape painter, landscapist **2** *Hort* landscape gardener

paysan, -anne [peizɑ̃, -an] ADJ **1** *(population)* rural; *Hist & Péj* peasant *(avant n)*; **le malaise p.** discontent amongst small farmers; **le monde p.** the farming world
2 *(rustique → décor)* rustic; *(→ style, vêtements)* rustic, country *(avant n)*; *Péj* peasant
NM,F **1** *(cultivateur)* (small) farmer; *Hist & Péj* peasant; **les paysans veulent des réformes** the farming community wants *or* the farmers want reforms
2 *Péj (rustre)* peasant; **des manières de p.** rough manners; **un p. du Danube** a plain-speaking man
▫ **à la paysanne** ADJ *Culin* with small onions and diced bacon

'Le Paysan de Paris' *Aragon* 'The Night Walker'

paysannat [peizana] NM **1** *(ensemble des agriculteurs)* farming community, farmers; *Hist (classe)* peasantry **2** *(condition des paysans)* farming life; *Hist* peasant life

paysannerie [peizanri] NF farming community, farmers; *Hist* peasantry

Pays-Bas [peiba] NMPL **les P.** the Netherlands; **vivre aux P.** to live in the Netherlands; **aller aux P.** to go to the Netherlands

PC [pese] NM **1** *(abrév* **parti communiste***)* CP, Communist Party **2** *(abrév* **personal computer***)* PC **3** *(abrév* **prêt conventionné***)* = approved mortgage loan **4** *(abrév* **permis de construire***)* building permit *or* licence, *Br* planning permission **5** *Mil (abrév* **poste de commandement***)* HQ **6** *(abrév* **Petite Ceinture***) (bus)* = bus following the inner ring road in Paris
NF *Fin (abrév* **pièce de caisse***)* cash voucher

pc *(abrév écrite* **pièce***)* room; **à louer: 2 pc** one-bedroomed *Br* flat *or Am* apartment to let

PCB [pesebe] NM *Chim (abrév* **polychlorobiphényle***)* PCB

pcc *(abrév écrite* **pour copie conforme***)* certified accurate

Pce *(abrév écrite* **prince***)* prince

pce *(abrév écrite* **pièce***)* room; **à louer: 2 pce** one-bedroomed *Br* flat *or Am* apartment to let

Pcesse *(abrév écrite* **princesse***)* princess

PCF [peseɛf] NM *(abrév* **Parti communiste français***)* French Communist Party

PCG [peseʒe] NM *Compta (abrév* **plan comptable général***)* chart of accounts

PCI [pesei] NM **1** *(abrév* **Parti communiste italien***)* Communist Party of Italy **2** *(abrév* **Parti communiste international***)* International Communist Party

PCP [pesepe] NF *Chim (abrév* **phencyclidine***)* PCP

PCR [peseɛr] NF *Biol (abrév* **polymerase chain reaction***)* PCR

PCS [peseɛs] NFPL *(abrév* **professions et catégories sociales***)* socio-economic categories

PCV [peseve] NM *Tél (abrév* **à percevoir***) Br* reverse-charge call, *Am* collect call; **appeler Paris en P.** *Br* to make a reverse-charge call to Paris, *Am* to call Paris collect; **je les ai appelés en P.** *Br* I reversed the charges when I called them, *Am* I called them collect

PDA [pedea] NM *Ordinat (abrév* **personal digital assistant***)* PDA
NF *TV (abrév* **part d'audience***)* audience share

PDF [pedeɛf] NM *Ordinat (abrév* **portable document format***)* PDF

P-DG [pedeʒe] NMF INV *(abrév* **président-directeur général***) Br* ≃ MD, *Am* ≃ CEO

PDM [pedeɛm] NF *Com (abrév* **part de marché***)* market share

PDV [pedeve] NM *Com (abrév* **point de vente***)* POS

PEA [peəa] NM *Fin (abrév* **plan d'épargne en actions***)* ≃ investment trust, *Br* ≃ ISA

péage [peaʒ] NM **1** *(taxe)* toll **2** *(lieu → d'autoroute, de pont)* toll (gate); *Hist* tollhouse; **p. à 5 kilomètres** *(panneau sur la route)* toll 5 kilometres **3** *TV* **chaîne à p.** pay channel

péagiste [peaʒist] NMF toll collector

peak time [piktajm] **NM** *TV* peak time, prime time

péan [peɑ̃] **NM** *Antiq* paean

peau, -x [po] **NF 1** *Anat* skin; *(autour des ongles)* hangnail; **elle a la p. douce** she has soft skin; **avoir une p. de pêche** to have (soft and) velvety skin; **avoir la p. sèche/grasse** to have dry/greasy skin; **p. mixte** combination skin; **peaux mortes** dead skin; **n'avoir que la p. et les os, n'avoir que la p. sur les os** to be all skin and bone; **attraper qn par la p. du cou** to grab sb by the scruff of the neck; **prendre qn par la p. du cou** *ou* **du dos** *ou Fam* **des fesses** *ou très Fam* **du cul** to grab sb by the scruff of the neck; **être** *ou* **se sentir bien dans sa p.** to feel good about oneself, to be together; **être mal dans sa p.** to be ill at ease with oneself, to feel bad about oneself; **on sent qu'il est mal dans sa p.** you can tell he's not a very happy person; **entrer** *ou* **se mettre dans la p. de qn** to put oneself in sb's shoes *or* place; **je ne voudrais pas être dans sa p.** I wouldn't like to be in his shoes; **entrer dans la p. du personnage** to get right into the part; *Fam* **avoir qn dans la p.** to be crazy about sb▪, to have sb under one's skin; *Fam* **avoir qch dans la p.** to have sth in one's blood; *Fam* **il sait pas quoi faire de sa p.** he doesn't know what to do with himself; **changer de p.** to change one's look; *Fig* **faire p. neuve** to get a facelift; **l'université fait p. neuve** the university system is being completely overhauled; **c'est dur de faire p. neuve à 50 ans** it's hard to start a new life at 50; **avoir la p. dure** to be thick-skinned; *Fam* **si tu tiens à ta p.** if you value your life *or* hide; *Fam* **y laisser sa p.** to pay with one's life▪, to be killed▪; *Fam* **un jour, j'aurai ta p.!** I'll get you one of these days!; *Fam* **faire** *ou* **crever la p. à qn** to do sb in, to bump sb off; **ils lui ont fait la p.** they did him/her in; *Fam* **trouer la p. à qn** to fill *or* to pump sb full of lead; *Fam* **se faire trouer la p.** to get filled *or* pumped full of lead; **coûter la p.** *Fam* **des fesses** *ou très Fam* **du cul** to cost an arm and a leg

2 *Zool (gén)* skin; *(fourrure)* pelt; *(cuir → non tanné)* hide; *(→ tanné)* leather, (tanned) hide; **une valise en p.** a leather suitcase; **le commerce des peaux** the fur and leather trade; **p. d'ours** bearskin; **sac en p. de serpent** snakeskin bag; **cuir pleine p.** full leather; *Fam* **une p. d'âne** *(diplôme)* a diploma▪; **p. de chamois** *(chiffon)* chamois leather; **p. de tambour** (drum) skin; *Fam Péj* **vieille p.** old bag; *Fam Péj* **des révolutionnaires en p. de lapin** Mickey Mouse *or* tinpot revolutionaries

3 *(d'un fruit, d'un légume, du lait bouilli, d'un saucisson)* skin; **enlever la p. d'un fruit** to peel a fruit; **p. de pêche** *(tissu)* silky soft fabric; *aussi Fig* **p. de banane** banana skin

4 *Élec* **effet de p.** skin effect

5 *(locutions) Fam* **p. de balle (et balai de crin),** *Vulg* **p. de zébi** *(refus, mépris)* no chance, no way; **en fin de compte, tout ce qu'on a obtenu c'est p. de balle** in the end we got *Br* sod all *or Am* zilch; **tu me prêtes ta voiture? – p. de balle!** will you lend me your car? – no chance!

❑ **peau bleue NM** *Ich* blue shark

❑ **peau d'orange NF** orange peel; *Méd* orange-peel skin *(caused by cellulite)*

❑ **peau de vache NF** *Fam (femme)* bitch, *Br* cow; *(homme) Br* swine, *Am* stinker

'La Peau de chagrin' *Balzac* 'The Wild Ass's Skin'

'Peau d'âne' *Perrault, Demy* 'Donkey Skin'

Allusion

Vendre la peau de l'ours (avant de l'avoir tué)

In La Fontaine's fable *The Bear and the Two Friends*, two impoverished friends try to negotiate the price of a bearskin without having even caught and killed the bear. The English equivalent of the moral here is "Don't count your chickens before they're hatched". La Fontaine's exact wording was, in fact, **Il ne faut jamais vendre la peau de l'ours qu'on ne l'ait mis à terre** ("You should never sell the bearskin before bringing down the bear").

peaucier [posje] **ADJ M** dermal

NM p. (du cou) platysma

peaufiner [3] [pofine] **VT 1** *(à la peau de chamois)* to shammy-leather **2** *Fig* to put the finishing touches to

peau-rouge [poruʒ] *(pl* **peaux-rouges***)* **ADJ** Red Indian *(avant n)*, redskin *(avant n)*

❑ **Peau-Rouge NMF** Red Indian, Redskin

peausserie [posri] **NF 1** *(peaux)* leatherwear **2** *(industrie)* leather *or* skin trade

peaussier [posje] **NM 1** *(personne qui prépare les peaux)* skinner **2** *(commerçant)* leather dealer

PEbd [peəbede] **NM INV** *(abrév* **polyéthylène basse densité***)* LDPE

pébrine [pebrin] **NF** *(des vers à soie)* pebrine

pébroc, pébroque [pebrɔk] **NM** *Fam* umbrella▪, *Br* brolly

pécaïre [pekair] **EXCLAM** *Vieilli (dans le Midi)* good God!

pécan [pekɑ̃] **NM (noix de) p.** pecan

pécari [pekari] **NM 1** *Zool* peccary **2** *(cuir)* peccary (skin)

peccable [pɛkabl] **ADJ** peccable

peccadille [pekadij] **NF 1** *(péché)* peccadillo; **des peccadilles de jeunesse** youthful indiscretions **2** *(vétille)* **se disputer pour des peccadilles** to argue over trifles

peccant, -e [pekɑ̃, -ɑ̃t] **ADJ** *Méd Vieilli* peccant; **humeurs peccantes** peccant humours

pechblende [pɛʃblɛ̃d] **NF** *Minér* pitchblende

péché [peʃe] **NM 1** *(faute)* sin; **p. de (la) chair** sin of the flesh; **p. mortel/véniel** mortal/venial sin; **le p. originel** original sin; **p. de jeunesse** youthful indiscretion; **p. mignon** weakness; **mon p. mignon, c'est le chocolat** I just can't resist chocolate, chocolate is my little weakness; **le p. d'orgueil** the sin of pride; **les sept péchés capitaux** the seven deadly sins; *Prov* **à tout p. miséricorde** = every sin can be forgiven; *Bible* **que celui qui est sans p. lui jette la première pierre** let he who is without sin cast the first stone

2 *(état)* sin; **vivre dans le p.** *(gén)* to lead a life of sin *or* a sinful life; *(sans mariage religieux)* to live in sin; **retomber dans le p.** to relapse (into sin)

pêche[1] [pɛʃ] **NF 1** *(fruit)* peach; **p. abricot** *ou* **jaune/blanche** yellow/white peach; **p. de vigne** red-fleshed peach *(grown amongst vines)*; **elle a un teint de p.** she has a peaches and cream complexion; **p. Melba** peach Melba

2 *Fam (énergie)* get-up-and-go; **avoir la p.** to be on (top) form, to be full of go *or* beans; **ça va te donner la p.** it'll make you feel on top of the world

3 *Fam (coup)* thump, wallop; **prendre une p.** to get thumped *ou* walloped

4 *très Fam* **poser une p.** to *Br* have *or Am* take a dump

ADJ INV peach *(avant n)*, peach-coloured

pêche[2] [pɛʃ] **NF 1** *(activité → en mer)* fishing; *(→ en eau douce)* fishing, angling; **aller à la p.** *(en mer)* to go fishing; *(en eau douce)* to go fishing *or* angling; **p. réglementée** *(sur panneau)* fishing by permit only; **p. à la baleine** whaling, whale-hunting; *Can* **p. blanche** ice fishing; **p. à la cuiller** spinning; **p. à la dandinette** jigging; **p. éloignée, grande p., p. hauturière** distant-water fishery; **p. au gros** deep-sea fishing; **p. au lamparo** fishing by lamplight; **p. au lancer** cast fishing; **p. à la ligne** angling; *Fig* **aller à la p. à la ligne** *(au lieu de voter)* to abstain from voting; **p. maritime** sea fishing; **p. à la morue** cod fishing; **p. à la mouche** fly fishing; **p. sous la glace** ice fishing; **p. sous-marine** underwater fishing; **aller à la p. aux informations** to go in search of information

2 *(produit de la pêche)* catch; **la p. a été bonne** there was a good catch; *Fig* **alors, la p. a été bonne?** any luck?; *Bible* **p. miraculeuse** miraculous draught of fishes

3 *(lieu)* fishery, fishing ground; **pêches maritimes** sea fisheries; **p. côtière** coastal fishery; **p. gardée** restricted fishing area

pécher [18] [peʃe] **VI 1** *Rel* to sin; **p. par omission** to sin by omission; **p. par orgueil** to commit the sin of pride **2** *(commettre une erreur)* **cette enquête pèche sur un point** the inquiry falls down on one point; **p. par excès de minutie** to be overmeticulous; **elle a péché par imprudence** she was too careless, she was overcareless; **il est tombé par là où il avait péché** his sins were his undoing; **p. contre** to go against the rules of; **p. contre le bon goût** to go against the rules of good taste

pêcher[1] [peʃe] **NM 1** *Bot* peach tree **2** *Menuis* peach wood

pêcher[2] [4] [peʃe] **VT 1** *Pêche (essayer de prendre)* to fish for; *(prendre)* to catch; **j'ai pêché trois truites** I caught *or* landed three trout; **p. la crevette** to shrimp, to go shrimping; **p. des moules** to collect mussels; **p. la baleine** to hunt whales, to go whaling; **p. le corail/des perles** to dive for coral/pearls; **p. des grenouilles** to hunt frogs; **p. le hareng au chalut** to trawl for herring

2 *(tirer de l'eau)* to fish out; **p. une chaussure** to fish out a shoe

3 *Fam (dénicher)* to seek out▪, to hunt *or* to track down, to unearth; **il est allé p. des chansons inédites chez un auteur oublié** he dug up *or* unearthed some unpublished songs by a forgotten songwriter; **où a-t-il été p. que j'avais démissionné?** where did he get the idea that I'd resigned?▪

VI 1 *(aller à la pêche)* to fish; **il pêche tous les dimanches** he goes fishing every Sunday; **p. à la ligne/traîne** to angle/troll; **p. en mer** to go sea fishing; **p. en eau trouble** to fish in troubled waters

2 *Can (puiser)* to draw; **p. de l'eau dans un puits** to draw water from a well

pechère [pəʃɛr] = **peuchère**

pécheresse [peʃrɛs] *voir* **pécheur**

pêcherie [pɛʃri] **NF** fishery

pêchette [pɛʃɛt] **NF** dip net

pécheur, -eresse [peʃœr, peʃrɛs] **NM,F** sinner; **p. endurci** unrepentant sinner; *Fig* **ne pas vouloir la mort du p.** not to demand too harsh a punishment

pêcheur, -euse [pɛʃœr, -øz] **NM,F** *(en mer)* fisherman, *f* fisherwoman; *(en eau douce)* angler; **p. de baleines** whaler; **p. à la ligne** angler; *Fig* abstentionist; **p. au chalut** trawlerman; **p. de crevettes** shrimper; **p. de perles** pearl diver

'Pêcheur d'Islande' *Loti* 'An Iceland Fisherman'

Péchiney [peʃinɛ] **NM** = large metal-producing group

pêchu, -e [pɛʃy] **ADJ** *Fam* on (top) form, full of go

pécloter [3] [peklɔte] **VI** *Suisse Fam* **1** *(être en mauvaise santé) & Fig* to be in a bad way **2** *(mal fonctionner)* to play up

pecnot [pɛkno] = **péquenaud**

PECO [peko] **NM** *(abrév* **pays d'Europe centrale et orientale***)* CEEC

pécoptéris [pekɔpteris] **NM** *Bot* pecopteris

pécore [pekɔr] *Fam Péj* **NMF** *(paysan)* yokel, bumpkin, *Am* hick

NF quelle p., celle-là! she's so stuck-up!

pécos [pekos] **NM** *Fam* bomber, cone *(cannabis cigarette)*

pecten [pɛktɛn] **NM** *Zool* pecten, scallop

pectine [pɛktin] **NF** pectin

pectiné, -e [pɛktine] **ADJ 1** *Bot & Zool* pectinate, pectinated **2** *Anat* pectineal; **muscle p.** pectineus

NM *Anat* pectineus

pectique [pɛktik] **ADJ** pectic

pectoral, -e, -aux, -ales [pɛktɔral, -o] **ADJ 1** *Anat* pectoral **2** *Pharm (pâtes)* cough *(avant n)*; **sirop p.** expectorant

NM 1 *Anat* pectoral muscle; **travailler ses pectoraux** to work on one's pecs; **grand/petit p.** pectoralis major/minor **2** *Antiq & Rel* pectoral

pectose [pɛktoz] **NF** *Chim* pectose

pécu [peky] **NM** *Fam Br* bog roll, *Am* TP

péculat [pekyla] **NM** *Admin* peculation, embezzlement

pécule [pekyl] **NM 1** *(petit capital)* savings, nest egg; **se constituer un (petit) p.** to put some money aside **2** *Mil* (service) gratuity **3** *Jur* **p. de libération** prison earnings *(paid on discharge)* **4** *Hist* peculium **5** *Belg* **p. de vacances** holiday bonus payment

pécune [pekyn] **NF** *Vieilli ou Hum* money, lucre

pécuniaire [pekynjɛr] **ADJ** financial, *Sout* pecuniary; **des difficultés pécuniaires** financial *or* money problems

pécuniairement [pekynjɛrmã] **ADV** financially, *Sout* pecuniarily

PED [peəde] **NM** (*abrév* **pays en développement**) developing country

pédagogie [pedagɔʒi] **NF 1** (*méthodologie*) educational methods **2** (*pratique*) teaching skills; **il manque de p.** he lacks teaching skills **3** *Belg* (*foyer*) hostel for female students

pédagogique [pedagɔʒik] **ADJ** (*science, manière*) educational, teaching (*avant n*), *Sout* pedagogical; (*voyage, sortie*) educational; **elle n'a aucune formation p.** she's not been trained to teach *or* as a teacher; **aides** *ou* **supports pédagogiques** teaching materials

pédagogiquement [pedagɔʒikmã] **ADV** (*d'un point de vue pédagogique*) from an educational *or* a pedagogical point of view

pédagogue [pedagɔg] **ADJ il n'est pas très p.** he's not very good at teaching; **elle est très p.** she's a very good teacher

    NMF 1 (*enseignant*) teacher **2** (*éducateur*) educationalist **3** *Antiq* pedagogue

pédalage [pedalaʒ] **NM** pedalling

pédale [pedal] **NF 1** (*d'un vélo, d'un pédalo*) pedal; **appuyer sur les pédales** to pedal hard **2** (*d'une poubelle*) pedal; (*d'une machine à coudre, d'un tour*) treadle **3** *Aut* pedal; **p. d'embrayage** clutch; **appuyer sur la p. du frein** to step on *or* to use the brake pedal **4** *Mus* pedal; **p. douce** soft pedal; **p. forte** loud *or* sustaining pedal; *aussi Fig* **mettre la p. douce** to soft-pedal **5** *Fam* (*homosexuel*) queer, *Am* fag, = offensive term used to refer to a male homosexual; **il est de la p.** he's a queer *or Am* fag **6** *Fam* **perdre les pédales** to lose one's marbles, *Br* to lose the plot; **s'emmêler les pédales** to get all mixed up, to get hopelessly lost

    ❑ **à pédales ADJ** pedal (*avant n*); **auto à pédales** (*jouet*) pedal car

pédaler [3] [pedale] **VI 1** (*sur un vélo*) to pedal; **p. en danseuse** to pedal off the saddle **2** *Fam* (*locutions*) **p. dans la choucroute** *ou* **la semoule** *ou* **le yaourt** to get nowhere

pédaleur, -euse [pedalœr, -øz] **NM,F** *Fam* cyclist■

pédalier [pedalje] **NM 1** (*d'une bicyclette*) drive (mechanism) **2** *Mus* (*d'un orgue*) pedals, pedal board

Pédalo® [pedalo] **NM** pedalo, pedal-boat

pédant, -e [pedã, -ãt] **ADJ** (*exposé, ton*) pedantic

    NM,F

pédanterie [pedãtri] **NF** pedantry

pédantesque [pedãtɛsk] **ADJ** *Littéraire* pedantic

pédantisme [pedãtism] **NM** = **pédanterie**

pédé [pede] *très Fam* **ADJ** queer, *Br* bent, = offensive term used to refer to a male homosexual; **p. comme un phoque** *Br* as bent as a nine-bob note *or* as a three-pound note, *Am* as queer as a three-dollar bill

    NM queer, *Am* fag, = offensive term used to refer to a male homosexual

pédégé [pedeʒe] **NM** *Fam Hum Br* MD■, *Am* CEO■

pédéraste [pederast] **NM 1** (*avec des jeunes garçons*) pederast **2** (*entre hommes*) homosexual

pédérastie [pederasti] **NF 1** (*avec des jeunes garçons*) pederasty **2** (*entre hommes*) homosexuality

pédérastique [pederastik] **ADJ 1** (*avec des jeunes garçons*) pederastic **2** (*entre hommes*) homosexual

pédestre [pedɛstr] **ADJ 1** *voir* **randonnée 2** *voir* **statue**

pédestrement [pedɛstrəmã] **ADV** *Littéraire* on foot, afoot

pédiatre [pedjatr] **NMF** paediatrician

pédiatrie [pedjatri] **NF** paediatrics (*singulier*)

pédiatrique [pedjatrik] **ADJ** paediatric

pedibus [pedibys] **ADV** *Fam Hum* **p. (cum jambis)** on foot■, on Shanks's *Br* pony *or Am* mare

pédicellaire [pediselɛr] **NM** *Zool* pedicellaria

pédicelle [pedisɛl] **NM** pedicel

pédicellé, -e [pedisele] **ADJ** pedicellate

pédiculaire [pedikylɛr] **ADJ** *Bot & Entom* pedicular

    NF *Bot* **p. des forêts** lousewort; **p. feuillée** leafy lousewort; **p. des marais** marsh lousewort

pédicule [pedikyl] **NM 1** *Anat* peduncle **2** *Archit* stand, base **3** *Bot* (*pédicelle*) pedicle; (*pédoncule*) peduncle **4** *Zool* (*de crabe*) peduncle, pedicel, eyestalk

pédiculé, -e [pedikyle] **ADJ 1** *Anat* pedicled, pediculated **2** *Bot* pedunculed

pédiculose [pedikyloz] **NF** *Méd* pediculosis

pédicure [pedikyr] **NMF** chiropodist

pédicurie [pedikyri] **NF 1** (*profession*) chiropody **2** (*soins*) pedicure

pédieux, -euse [pedjø, -øz] **ADJ** *Anat* pedal

pedigree [pedigre] **NM** pedigree; **un chien avec p.** a pedigree dog

pédiluve [pedilyv] **NM** (*bassin*) foot bath

pédimane [pediman] **ADJ** *Zool* pedimanous

pédiment [pedimã] **NM** *Géol* pediment

pédipalpe [pedipalp] *Entom* **NM 1** (*appendice*) pedipalp **2** (*scorpion*) whip scorpion, *Spéc* pedipalp

pédiplaine [pediplɛn] **NF** pediplain, pediplane

pédodontie [pedodõsi] **NF** paedodontia, paedodontics (*singulier*)

pédogenèse [pedoʒənɛz] **NF 1** *Géol* pedogenesis, soil formation **2** *Biol* paedogenesis

pédologie [pedolɔʒi] **NF 1** *Géol* pedology **2** *Méd* paedology

pédologue [pedolɔg] **NMF** *Géol* pedologist

pédomètre [pedomɛtr] **NM** pedometer

pédonculaire [pedõkylɛr] **ADJ** peduncular

pédoncule [pedõkyl] **NM 1** *Anat & Bot* peduncle; **p. cérébral** restiform body; **p. ramifié** pedicel **2** *Zool* (*du crabe*) eyestalk, pedicel

pédonculé, -e [pedõkyle] **ADJ** pedunculate, pedunculated; **chêne p.** pedunculate oak

pédophile [pedofil] **ADJ** paedophiliac

    NMF paedophile

pédophilie [pedofili] **NF** paedophilia

pédopsychiatre [pedopsikjatr] **NMF** child psychiatrist

pédopsychiatrie [pedopsikjatri] **NF** child psychiatry

pedzouille [pedzuj] **NM** *Fam Péj* yokel, peasant, *Am* hick

PEE [peəə] **NM** (*abrév* **plan d'épargne d'entreprise**) company savings scheme

peeling [piliŋ] **NM** (*soin de beauté*) exfoliation (treatment); *Méd* dermabrasion; **p. chimique** chemical peel; **se faire faire un p.** to have exfoliation treatment; *Méd* to have dermabrasion; **se faire un p.** to use a facial scrub

peep-show [pipʃo] (*pl* **peep-shows**) **NM** peep-show

peer-to-peer [pirtupir] **ADJ** *Ordinat* peer-to-peer

Pégase [pegaz] **NPR** *Myth* Pegasus

    NF *Astron* Pegasus

pégase [pegaz] **NM** *Ich* pegasus

PEGC [peəʒese] **NMF** *Scol* (*abrév* **professeur d'enseignement général de collège**) = teacher qualified to teach one or two subjects to eleven-to-fifteen-year-olds in French secondary schools

pegmatite [pɛgmatit] **NF** pegmatite

pégosité [pegozite] **NF** adhesiveness

pègre [pɛgr] **NF** (*criminel*) underworld

pégueux, -euse [pegø, -øz] **ADJ 1** (*dans le Midi*) (*poisseux*) sticky **2** (*adhésif*) quick-drying

PEhd [peəa∫de] **NM INV** (*abrév* **polyéthylène haute densité**) HDPE

pehlvi [pɛlvi] = **pahlavi**

peï, pei [pɛj] **NM** *Belg Fam* guy, *Br* bloke

peignage [pɛɲaʒ] **NM** *Tex* (*du lin, de la laine*) combing; (*du chanvre*) hackling

peignait *etc* **1** *voir* **peindre 2** *voir* **peigner**

peigne [pɛɲ] **NM 1** (*pour les cheveux*) comb; **se donner un coup de p.** to run a comb through one's hair, to give one's hair a comb; **je viens pour un coup de p.** (*chez le coiffeur*) I just want a quick comb through; **un p. retenait ses cheveux en arrière** her hair was held back with a comb; **p. fin** fine-tooth comb; *Fig* **passer une région/un document au p. fin** to go over an area/a document with a fine-tooth comb **2** *Tex* (*d'un métier à tisser*) reed **5** *Zool* (*mollusque*) scallop, pecten; (*chez l'oiseau*) pecten; (*chez les scorpions*) comb

    ADJ *Can Fam Péj* (*avare*) stingy

peigné, -e[1] [peɲe] **ADJ** (*fil*) combed

    NM 1 (*ruban*) combed sliver **2** (*tissu*) combed yarn

peigne-cul [pɛɲkyl] (*pl inv ou* **peigne-culs**) **NM** *très Fam Péj* (*individu méprisable*) jerk, *Br* tosser; (*individu grossier*) pig, boor

peignée[2] [peɲe] **NF** *Fam* (*volée de coups*) thrashing, hiding, hammering; **flanquer une p. à qn** to give sb a thrashing *or* hiding *or* hammering; **recevoir une p.** to get a thrashing *or* hiding *or* hammering **2** *Tex* cardful

peigner [4] [peɲe] **VT 1** (*cheveux*) to comb; **viens ici que je te peigne** come here so that I can comb your hair; **je suis vraiment mal peignée aujourd'hui** my hair is all over the place today; *Fam* **faire ça ou p. la girafe** it's either that or some other pointless task **2** *Tex* (*lin, laine*) to comb; (*chanvre*) to hackle; **coton peigné** brushed cotton

    ▸**se peigner VPR** (*se coiffer*) to comb one's hair; **se p. la barbe** to comb one's beard

peigneur, -euse [peɲœr, -øz] **ADJ** combing

    NM,F (*personne*) comber

    NM (*cylindre*) doffer

    ❑ **peigneuse NF** (*machine*) comb, combing machine

peignier, -ère [peɲje, -ɛr] **NM,F** comb maker

peignoir [pɛɲwar] **NM 1** (*sortie de bain*) **p. (de bain)** bathrobe **2** (*robe de chambre*) dressing gown, *Am* bathrobe **3** (*chez le coiffeur*) *Br* cape, *Am* robe

peignure [peɲyr] **NF** *Can Fam* hairdo

    ❑ **peignures NFPL** combings

Pei-king [pejkin] = **Pékin**

peille [pɛj] **NF** *Tex* rag (*used in paper-making*)

peinard, -e [pɛnar, -ard] *Fam* **ADJ** (*vie, boulot*) cushy; **rester** *ou* **se tenir p.** to keep one's nose clean; **là-bas, on sera peinards** we'll have it easy there; **il sont peinards dans leur nouvelle baraque** they're nice and comfortable in their new place; **il a trouvé un coin p. pour pioncer** he found a quiet corner to crash out

    ADV (*tranquillement*) in peace■, peacefully■

peinardement [pɛnardəmã] **ADV** *Fam* coolly■

peindre [81] [pɛdr] **VT 1** (*mur, tableau*) to paint; **j'ai peint la porte en bleu** I painted the door blue; **p. à la bombe/au pistolet** to spray-paint; **p. au pinceau/rouleau** to paint with a brush/roller; **p. à l'huile/à l'eau** to paint in oils/in watercolours; *Suisse Fig* **p. le diable sur la muraille** to be pessimistic **2** (*décrire*) to portray, to depict

    VI to paint, to be a painter *or* an artist; **p. sur soie/verre** to paint on silk/glass

    ▸**se peindre VPR 1** (*emploi passif*) to be painted on; **c'est un revêtement qui se peint facilement** it's a covering which can easily be painted **2** (*se représenter* → *en peinture*) to paint one's (own) portrait; (→ *dans un écrit*) to portray oneself **3** (*se grimer*) **se p. le visage** to paint one's face **4** to show; **la stupéfaction se peignit sur son visage** amazement was written all over his/her face; *Littéraire* **déjà la mort se peint sur son visage** already his/her face is taking on the hue of death

---

PEINE [pɛn]

sentence **A1** ■ suffering **A2** ■ trouble **B1, C** ■ sadness **B2** ■ effort **C1** ■ worth **C1** ■ difficulty **C2**

NF A. 1 (*châtiment*) sentence; **infliger une lourde p. à qn** to pass a harsh sentence on sb; **p. accessoire** accessory penalty, ancillary penalty; **p. afflictive** afflictive penalty (*entailing imprisonment and loss of civic rights*); **p. complémentaire** additional penalty; **p. contractuelle** penalty for non-performance (of contract); **p. correctionnelle** = imprisonment for between two months and five years, or a fine; **p. criminelle** = imprisonment for more than five years; **p. de durée indéterminée** indeterminate sentence; **p. d'emprisonnement** prison sentence; **p. incompressible** sentence without remission; **p. infamante** = penalty involving loss of civil rights; **p. justifiée** = theory by which the "Cour de cassation" rejects an appeal based on an error of law, on the grounds that the penalty

imposed was the same as would have been imposed under the law that applied to the violation; **p. mitigée** reduced sentence; **la p. de mort** ou **la p. capitale** capital punishment, the death penalty; **p. obligatoire** mandatory sentence; **p. patrimoniale** property penalty, penalty affecting property *(fine and confiscation)*; **p. pécuniaire** pecuniary penalty; **p. de police** penalty for minor offences; **p. principale** principal penalty, primary penalty; **p. de prison** prison sentence; **p. de prison avec sursis** suspended (prison) sentence; **p. privative de droits** penalty entailing loss of rights; **p. privative de liberté** custodial sentence; **p. requise** recommended sentence; **p. restrictive de liberté** penalty restricting liberty; **p. de substitution** non-custodial sentence; *Littéraire* **porter la p. de la célébrité** to pay the price of fame

2 *Rel (damnation)* damnation, suffering; **les peines éternelles** eternal damnation *or* suffering, the fires of hell

B. 1 *(tourment, inquiétude)* trouble; **mes amis viennent souvent me raconter leurs peines** my friends often come to tell me their troubles; **faire p. à voir** to be a sorry sight; **tu faisais p. à voir avec tes deux bras dans le plâtre** you did look a sorry sight with both your arms in plaster; **peines de cœur** heartache(s); **se mettre en p. pour qn** to be extremely worried about sb

2 *(tristesse)* sadness, sorrow, grief; **il partageait sa p.** he shared his/her grief; **avoir de la p.** to be sad *or* upset; **faire de la p. à qn** to upset sb; **je ne voudrais pas lui faire de la p. en lui disant** I wouldn't like to upset him/her by telling him/her; **il me fait vraiment de la p.** I feel really sorry for him

C. 1 *(effort)* effort, trouble; **ce n'est pas la p.** it's not worth it, it's pointless; **ce n'est pas la p. de tout récrire/que tu y ailles** there's no point writing it all out again/your going; *Ironique* **c'était bien la p. que je mette une cravate!** it was a real waste of time putting a *or* my tie on!; **se donner de la p.** to go to a lot of trouble; **il s'est donné beaucoup de p. pour réussir** he went to a lot of trouble to succeed; **prendre** *ou* **se donner la p. de** to go to *or* to take the trouble to; **donnez-vous la p. d'entrer** please do come in, *Sout* (please) be so kind as to come in; **si vous voulez bien vous donner la p. d'attendre un instant** if you wouldn't mind waiting a moment; **il ne s'est même pas donné la p. de répondre** he didn't even bother replying; **ne vous donnez pas la p. de me reconduire, je connais le chemin** don't bother to show me out, I know the way; **s'il veut s'en donner la p., il peut très bien réussir** if he can be bothered to make the effort, he's perfectly capable of succeeding; **tu aurais pu prendre la p. de téléphoner** you could at least have phoned; **valoir la p.** to be worth it; **l'exposition vaut la p. d'être vue** the exhibition is worth seeing; **en être pour sa p.** to have nothing to show for one's trouble; **ne pas épargner** *ou* **ménager sa p.** to spare no effort; **n'essaie pas de le convaincre, c'est p. perdue** don't try to persuade him, it's a waste of time *or* you'd be wasting your breath

2 *(difficulté)* **avoir de la p. à marcher** to have trouble *or* difficulty walking; **j'ai p. à vous croire** I find it difficult *or* hard to believe you; **elle a eu toutes les peines du monde à venir à la réunion** she had a terrible time *or* the devil's own job getting to the meeting; **je serais bien en p. de vous l'expliquer** I'd have a hard job explaining it to you, I wouldn't really know how to explain it to you; **je ne suis pas en p. pour y aller** it's no trouble for me to get there, I'll have no problem getting there

❏ **à peine** ADV **1** *(presque pas)* hardly, barely, scarcely; **j'arrive à p. à soulever mon sac** I can hardly *or* barely lift my bag; **elle sait à p. lire** she can hardly read; **j'y vois à p.** *(ma vue est mauvaise)* I've very poor sight, I can hardly see; *(il fait sombre)* I can hardly see anything; **c'est à p. si je l'ai entrevu** I only just caught a glimpse of him; *Fam Hum* **je t'assure, je n'ai pas touché au gâteau – à p.!** I swear I didn't touch the cake – a likely story!

2 *(tout au plus)* barely; **il était à p. dix heures** it was only just ten o'clock; **il y a à p. une semaine/deux heures** not quite a week/two hours ago, barely a week/two hours ago

3 *(à l'instant)* just; **je termine à p.** I've only just finished

4 *(aussitôt)* **à p. guérie, elle a repris le travail** no sooner had she recovered than she went back to work; **à p. était-elle couchée que le téléphone se mit à sonner** no sooner had she gone to bed than *or* she'd only just gone to bed when the phone rang

❏ **avec peine** ADV **1** *(difficilement)* with difficulty; **je l'ai fait avec p.** I had trouble *or* a struggle doing it

2 *Sout (à regret)* **je vous quitte avec p.** it is with deep regret that I leave you

❏ **sans peine** ADV **1** *(aisément)* without difficulty, easily; **l'italien sans p.** Italian the easy way

2 *(sans regret)* with no regrets, with a light heart

❏ **sous peine de** PRÉP **défense de fumer sous p. d'amende** *(écriteau dans un lieu public)* smokers will be prosecuted; **sous p. de mort** on pain of death

---

❦

'Peines d'amour perdues' *Shakespeare* 'Love's Labour's Lost'

---

peiner [4] [pene] VT *(attrister)* to upset, to distress; **sa mort m'a profondément peiné** his/her death greatly grieved *or* distressed me; **je suis peiné par ton attitude** I'm unhappy with your attitude; **d'un ton peiné** in a sad tone

VI **1** *(personne)* to have trouble *or* difficulty; **j'ai peiné pour terminer dans les délais** I had to struggle to finish *or* I had a lot of trouble finishing on time; **il peinait sur son travail** he was toiling at *or* over his work; **p. à marcher** to have trouble *or* difficulty walking; **je peine à comprendre son point de vue** I find it hard to understand his/her point of view

2 *(machine)* to strain, to labour; **on entendait un moteur p. dans la montée** you could hear a car engine toiling up the hill

peint, -e [pɛ̃, pɛ̃t] PP *voir* **peindre**

peintre [pɛ̃tr] NM

Note that it is no longer considered a mistake to feminize this word and to say **une peintre** but some French speakers nonetheless regard this form as unacceptable, especially in France. See also the entry **féminisation**.

1 *(artiste)* painter; *Cin & TV* **p. de cache** matt artist **2** *(artisan, ouvrier)* painter; **p. en bâtiment** house painter; **p. de décors** specialist decorator; **p. en lettres** signwriter **3** *Fig (écrivain)* portrayer; **c'est un excellent p. de la vie à la campagne** his depictions of country life are superb

peintre-décorateur [pɛ̃trədekɔratœr] *(pl* **peintres-décorateurs)** NM painter and decorator

peintre-graveur [pɛ̃trəgravœr] *(pl* **peintres-graveurs)** NM painter-engraver, painter-etcher

peinture [pɛ̃tyr] NF **1** *(substance)* paint; **p. laquée/satinée/mate** gloss/satin-finish/matt paint; *Constr* **p. à l'eau** water *or* water-based paint; *Beaux-Arts* **p. à l'huile** oil paint

2 *(action)* painting; **faire de la p. au pistolet** to spray-paint; **faire de la p. au rouleau** to paint with a roller; **p. en bâtiment** (house) painting

3 *(couche de matière colorante)* paintwork; **donner un petit coup de p. à qch** to freshen sth up; **la porte a besoin d'un petit coup de p.** the door could do with a lick of paint; **la p. de la grille est écaillée** the paintwork on the gate is flaking off; **p. fraîche** *(sur un écriteau)* wet paint; **refaire la p. d'une porte** to repaint a door;

refaire la p. d'une pièce to redecorate a room; **il faudra refaire les peintures** the paintwork will have to be done; **p. de guerre** warpaint

4 *Beaux-Arts (art, technique)* painting; **elle est passée à la p. abstraite** she turned to abstract painting; **faire de la p.** to paint; **p. au couteau** palette-knife painting; **p. au doigt** finger-painting; **p. sur soie** silk painting

5 *(œuvre)* painting, picture, canvas; **une p. murale** a mural; **peintures rupestres** cave paintings; *Fam* **je ne peux pas la voir en p.** I can't stand *or Br* stick the sight of her

6 *(ensemble d'œuvres peintes)* painting; **la p. figurative** figurative painting; **la p. flamande** Flemish painting; **la p. de Picasso** Picasso's paintings

7 *(description)* portrayal, picture; **une p. de la société médiévale** a picture of medieval society

peinture-émulsion [pɛ̃tyremylsjɔ̃] *(pl* **peintures-émulsions)** NF emulsion (paint)

peinturer [3] [pɛ̃tyre] VT **1** *(barbouiller)* to daub with paint **2** *Can & (en Afrique francophone) (peindre)* to paint; **p. la salle de bains** to paint the bathroom

▶**se peinturer** VPR *Can* **se p. dans le coin** to dig oneself into a hole, to paint oneself into a corner

peinturlurer [3] [pɛ̃tyrlyre] *Fam* VT to daub with paint

▶**se peinturlurer** VPR **elle s'était peinturluré le visage** she'd plastered make-up on her face

péjoratif, -ive [peʒɔratif, -iv] ADJ pejorative, derogatory

NM pejorative (term)

péjoration [peʒɔrasjɔ̃] NF pejoration

péjorative [peʒɔrativ] *voir* **péjoratif**

péjorativement [peʒɔrativmɑ̃] ADV pejoratively, derogatorily

pékan [pekɑ̃] NM pekan, fisher

péket [pɛkɛ] = **péquet**

Pékin [pekɛ̃] NM Peking

pékin [pekɛ̃] NM **1** *Tex* Pekin (fabric) **2** *Fam Mil (civil)* civilian▪ **3** *Fam (individu)* guy, *Br* bloke

pékiné, -e [pekine] ADJ pekin *(avant n)*

NM pekin

pékinois, -e [pekinwa, -az] ADJ Pekinese, Pekingese

NM **1** *(langue)* Pekinese, Mandarin (Chinese) **2** *Zool* Pekinese, Pekingese

❏ **Pékinois, -e** NM,F Pekinese, Pekingese (person); **les P.** the people of Peking

pekoe [peko] NM pekoe (tea)

PEL [peɛl] NM *Banque (abrév* **plan (d')épargne logement)** *Br* ≃ building society account, *Am* ≃ savings and loan association account

pelade [pəlad] NF *Méd* alopecia areata, pelada

pelage [pəlaʒ] NM coat, fur

pélagianisme [pelaʒjanism] NM *Rel* Pelagianism

pélagien¹, -enne¹ [pelaʒjɛ̃, -ɛn] *Rel* ADJ Pelagian

NM,F Pelagian

pélagien², -enne² [pelaʒjɛ̃, -ɛn] ADJ *Vieilli Biol & Géol* pelagic

pélagique [pelaʒik] ADJ *Biol* pelagic

pelagos [pelagɔs] NM *Biol* pelagic life forms

pélamide [pelamid] NF **1** *(poisson)* Atlantic bonito **2** *(serpent)* sea snake

pelant, -e [pəlɑ̃, -ɑ̃t] ADJ *Belg Fam (agaçant)* annoying▪; *(assommant)* boring▪, deadly dull; **c'est p.!** *(agaçant)* it's a real pain in the neck!; *(assommant)* it's a real drag!

pelard [pəlar] *Tech* ADJ M **bois p.** barked wood

NM barked wood

pélargonium [pelargɔnjɔm] NM *Bot* pelargonium

pelé, -e [pəle] ADJ **1** *(chat, renard, fourrure)* mangy; *(vêtement)* threadbare **2** *(sans végétation)* bare, treeless **3** *(fruit)* peeled

NM *Fam (chauve)* bald *or* bald-headed man▪

2 *(locution)* **il y avait trois pelés et un tondu** there was hardly a (living) soul there, *Br* there was one man and his dog

pélécaniforme [pelekanifɔrm] *Orn* NM member of the Pelecaniformes

❏ **pélécaniformes** NMPL Pelecaniformes

Pelée [pəle] NF **la montagne P.** Mount Pelée

péléen, -enne [peleɛ̃, -ɛn] ADJ *Géol* Pelean

pêle-mêle [pɛlmɛl] ADV in a jumble, every which way; **les draps et les couvertures étaient p. sur le lit** sheets and covers were all jumbled up *or* in a heap on the bed; **les spectateurs se sont**

engouffrés p. dans la salle the spectators piled pell-mell into the room

NM INV *(cadre pour photos)* multiple (photo) frame

peler [25] [pǝle] **VT 1** *(fruit, légume)* to peel **2** *très Fam (locution)* **p. le jonc à qn** to get on sb's nerves *or Br* wick

VI 1 *(peau)* to peel; **j'ai le dos qui pèle** my back's peeling **2** *Fam (locution)* to be freezing (cold)▪; **ça pèle** it's freezing (cold) *or Br* brass monkeys

▸**se peler VPR qu'est-ce qu'on** *Fam* **se pèle** *ou très Fam* **se les pèle ici!** it's freezing in here!▪

pèlerin [pɛlrɛ̃] **NM 1** *Rel* pilgrim **2** *Ich (requin)* basking shark **3** *Orn* peregrine (falcon) **4** *Fam (individu)* guy, *Br* bloke

pèlerinage [pɛlrinaʒ] **NM 1** *(voyage)* pilgrimage; **faire un** *ou* **aller en p. à Lourdes** to go on a pilgrimage to Lourdes; **un p. littéraire sur les traces de Stendhal** a literary pilgrimage in Stendhal's footsteps **2** *(endroit)* place of pilgrimage

pèlerine [pɛlrin] **NF** cape

péliade [peljad] **NF** *Zool* adder, common viper

pélican [pelikɑ̃] **NM** *Orn* pelican

pelisse [pǝlis] **NF** pelisse

pellagre [pelagr] **NF** *Méd* pellagra

pellagreux, -euse [pelagrø, -øz] *Méd* **ADJ** pellagrous

NM,F pellagra sufferer

pelle [pɛl] **NF 1** *(pour ramasser)* shovel; *(pour creuser)* spade; **p. à charbon** coal shovel; **p. à ordures** dustpan

2 *Culin* **p. à poisson/tarte** fish/cake slice

3 *Constr* **p. mécanique** *(sur roues)* mechanical shovel; *(sur chenilles)* excavator

4 *(extrémité d'un aviron)* (oar) blade

5 *très Fam (baiser)* French kiss; **rouler une p. à qn** to French kiss sb, *Br* to snog sb

6 *Fam (locutions)* **(se) prendre** *ou* **(se) ramasser une p.** *(tomber, échouer) Br* to come a cropper, *Am* to take a spill

▫ **à la pelle ADV 1** *(avec une pelle)* **ramasser la neige à la p.** to shovel up the snow

2 *Fam (en grande quantité)* in spades, by the bucketful; **gagner** *ou* **ramasser de l'argent à la p.** to be raking it in; **il y en a à la p.** there's masses *or* loads (of it/them)

Allusion

Les feuilles mortes se ramassent à la pelle

This line continues **les souvenirs et les regrets aussi**, and it means "Dead leaves are everywhere, memories and regrets too". The lines come from a song with words by Jacques Prévert, sung by Yves Montand, Juliette Gréco and others. The expression evokes autumnal melancholy and nostalgia. Since **se ramasser à la pelle** means literally "to be picked up by the shovelful" the expression is often changed and used in jokes. If a schoolchild says **Les mauvaises notes se ramassent à la pelle**, this means "Bad marks are coming thick and fast"; if a driver says **Les contraventions se ramassent à la pelle**, it means "I'm getting one ticket after another".

---

pelle-bêche [pɛlbɛʃ] *(pl* **pelles-bêches)** **NF** digging shovel

pelle-pioche [pɛlpjɔʃ] *(pl* **pelles-pioches)** **NF** = combined pick and hoe

peller [4] [pɛle] **VT** *Suisse* to shovel

pellet [pɛlɛ] **NM** *Pharm & Métal* pellet

pelletage [pɛltaʒ] **NM** shovelling

pelletée [pɛlte] **NF 1** *(de terre → ramassée)* shovelful; *(→ creusée)* spadeful **2** *Fam (grande quantité)* heap, pile; **une p. d'injures** a stream of insults

pelleter [27] [pɛlte] **VT** to shovel (up); *Can* **p. des nuages** to dream up idle schemes

pelleterie [pɛltri] **NF 1** *(art)* fur dressing **2** *(peaux)* peltry, pelts **3** *(commerce)* fur trade

pelleteur, -euse [pɛltœr, -øz] **NM,F** *(personne)* shoveller

▫ **pelleteuse NF** mechanical shovel *or* digger; **pelleteuse chargeuse** loading shovel, wheel loader

pelletier, -ère [pɛltje, -ɛr] **NM,F** furrier

pelletiérine [pɛltjerin] **NF** pelletierine

pelliculage [pelikylaʒ] **NM** *Phot* stripping

pelliculaire [pelikylɛr] **ADJ** *(qui forme une pellicule)* filmy

pellicule [pelikyl] **NF 1** *(peau → gén)* skin, film; *(→ du raisin)* skin; **une p. s'était formée sur le lait** a skin had formed on the milk

2 *(mince croûte)* film, thin layer; **une p. de glace sur la mare** a thin layer of ice over the pond **3** *(pour emballer)* **p. cellulosique** regenerated cellulose film *or* foil

4 *Phot* film; **une p.** *(bobine)* a reel (of film); *(chargeur)* a (roll of) film; **p. en bobine** roll film; **p. (en) couleur** colour film; **p. rapide** fast film; **p. sensible** fast film; **p. vierge** film stock

▫ **pellicules NFPL** *(dans les cheveux)* dandruff (UNCOUNT); **avoir des pellicules** to have dandruff; **shampooing contre les pellicules** anti-dandruff shampoo

pelliculé, -e [pelikyle] **ADJ** *(livre)* plastic-covered; *(disque)* sealed, factory-sealed

pelliculer [3] [pelikyle] **VT** *Typ* to strip

pelliculeux, -euse [pelikylø, -øz] **ADJ** *(cuir chevelu)* scurfy

pelloche [pelɔʃ] **NF** *Fam* film▪ *(for camera)*

pellucide [pelysid] **ADJ** *Biol* pellucid

pélo [pelo] **NM** *Fam (individu)* guy, *Br* bloke

pélobate [pelɔbat] **NM** *Zool* pelobatid (toad), spadefoot toad; **p. brun** European spadefoot

pélodyte [pelɔdit] **NM** *Zool* parsley frog, *Spéc* pelodytid

Péloponnèse [pelɔpɔnɛz] **NM le P.** the Peloponnese

péloponnésien, -enne [pelɔpɔnezjɛ̃, -ɛn] **ADJ** Peloponnesian

▫ **Péloponnésien, -enne NM,F** Peloponnesian

pelotage [pǝlɔtaʒ] **NM** *Fam* (heavy) petting, necking

pelotant, -e [pǝlɔtɑ̃, -ɑ̃t] **ADJ** *Can (neige)* sticky, soft

pelotari [pǝlɔtari] **NM** pelota player, pelotari

pelote [pǝlɔt] **NF 1** *(de ficelle, de coton)* ball; **une p. de laine** a ball of wool; *Fam* **faire sa p.** to make one's nest egg *or* one's pile; **mettre de la laine en p.** to ball wool; **p. à épingles** pincushion

2 *Can (boule)* **p. de neige** snowball

3 *Couture (coussinet)* pincushion

4 *Zool (sticky)* pad

5 *Zool* **p. de régurgitation** regurgitation pellet

6 *Pêche* pellet

7 *Sport* pelota; **jouer à la p. (basque)** to play pelota

8 [plɔt] *Can Vulg (sexe de la femme)* pussy, *Br* fanny; *(femme)* a bit of *Br* skirt *or Am* tail

peloter [3] [plɔte] *Fam* **VT** to grope, to feel up; **elle s'est fait p. dans le métro** somebody groped her in the metro

▸**se peloter VPR** to grope each other

peloteur, -euse [plɔtœr, -øz] *Fam* **ADJ il est du genre p.** he can't keep his hands to himself, he's got wandering hands

NM,F quel p.! he can't keep his hands to himself!

peloton [plɔtɔ̃] **NM 1** *Mil (division)* platoon; *(unité)* squad; **p. de discipline** *ou* **de punition** punishment squad; **p. d'exécution** firing squad; **suivre** *ou* **faire le p. (d'instruction)** to attend the training unit

2 *Sport* pack; **être dans le p. de tête** to be up with the leaders; *Fig* to be among the front runners

3 *(de coton, de laine)* small ball

4 *(d'abeilles, de chenilles)* cluster

pelotonnement [plɔtɔnmɑ̃] **NM 1** *(d'un animal, d'un enfant)* curling up **2** *(d'un fil)* winding into a ball

pelotonner [3] [plɔtɔne] **VT** *(laine)* to wind up into a ball

▸**se pelotonner VPR** to curl up; *(pour avoir chaud)* to snuggle up

pelouse [pǝluz] **NF 1** *(terrain)* lawn; *(herbe)* grass; **arroser/tondre la p.** to water/to mow the lawn; **la p. a bien poussé** the grass has grown well; **p. interdite** *(sur panneau)* keep off the grass

2 *Sport* field, ground; *(d'un champ de courses)* paddock; **sur la p. du Parc des Princes** in the Parc des Princes stadium

3 *Géog (prairie)* short-grass prairie

4 *Fam (marijuana)* grass, weed

pelta [pɛlta] **NM** *OU* **NF** *Antiq* pelta

peltaste [pɛltast] **NM** *Antiq* peltast

pelté, -e [pɛlte] **ADJ** *Bot* peltate

peluche [pǝlyʃ] **NF 1** *(jouet)* cuddly toy; **elle garde toutes ses peluches sur son lit** she keeps all her soft *or* cuddly toys on her bed **2** *Tex* plush **3** *(poussière)* (piece of) fluff (UNCOUNT)

▫ **en peluche ADJ chien/canard en p.** (cuddly) toy dog/duck

peluché, -e [pǝlyʃe] **ADJ 1** *(à poils longs)* fluffy **2** *(tissu)* pilled

pelucher [3] [pǝlyʃe] **VI** to pill

pelucheux, -euse [pǝlyʃø, -øz] **ADJ 1** *(tissu)* fluffy **2** *(fruit)* downy

pelure [pǝlyr] **NF 1** *(peau)* peel (UNCOUNT); **p. d'oignon** onion skin; *(vin)* pale rosé wine **2** *Fam (vêtement)* coat▪

pelvien, -enne [pɛlvjɛ̃, -ɛn] **ADJ** *Anat (cavité, organe)* pelvic

pelvigraphie [pɛlvigrafi] **NF** X-ray pelvimetry

pelvimétrie [pɛlvimetri] **NF** pelvimetry

pelvis [pɛlvis] **NM** *Anat* pelvis

pemmican [pɛmikɑ̃] **NM** pemmican

pemphigus [pɑ̃figys] **NM** *Méd* pemphigus

pénal, -e, -aux, -ales [penal, -o] **ADJ** *(droit)* criminal; *(code, réforme)* penal

pénalement [penalmɑ̃] **ADV** penally; **être p. responsable** to be liable in criminal law

pénalisant, -e [penaliza, -ɑ̃t] **ADJ** disadvantageous, detrimental; **une mesure pénalisante pour certaines catégories d'usagers** a measure which will penalize certain categories of users

pénalisation [penalizasjɔ̃] **NF 1** *Sport* penalty (for infringement); *Équitation* **points de p.** faults, penalty points **2** *(désavantage)* penalization

pénaliser [3] [penalize] **VT 1** *Sport* to penalize **2** *(désavantager)* to penalize, to put *or* to place at a disadvantage; **ces enfants sont pénalisés dès leur entrée à l'école** these children are disadvantaged from the moment they start school

pénaliste [penalist] **NMF** specialist in criminal law

pénalité [penalite] **NF 1** *Fin* penalty; **p. libératoire** full and final penalty payment; *Jur* **p. par référence** = sentencing according to a general statutory tariff; **p. de retard** penalty for late *or* overdue payment; *(pour livraison tardive)* late delivery penalty **2** *Sport* penalty; **coup de pied de p.** penalty kick; **donner le coup de pied de p.** to take the penalty kick; **jouer les pénalités** to go into injury time

penalty [penalti] *(pl* **penaltys** *ou* **penalties)** **NM** penalty (kick); **siffler/tirer un p.** to award/to take a penalty

pénard [penar] = **peinard**

pénates [penat] **NMPL 1** *Myth* Penates **2** *Fam* **regagner ses p.** to go home▪

penaud, -e [pǝno, -od] **ADJ** sheepish, contrite; **prendre un air p.** to look sheepish; **d'un air tout p.** sheepishly, with a hangdog look

pence [pɛns] *pl voir* **penny**

penchant [pɑ̃ʃɑ̃] **NM 1** *(goût → pour quelque chose)* liking, penchant **(pour** for); *(→ pour quelqu'un)* fondness, liking **(pour** for); **un petit p. pour le chocolat** a weakness for chocolate; **éprouver un p. pour qn** to be fond of sb **2** *(tendance)* tendency, inclination; **de mauvais penchants** evil tendencies **3** *Vieilli ou Littéraire (pente)* slope

penché, -e [pɑ̃ʃe] **ADJ 1** *(tableau)* crooked, askew; *(mur, écriture)* sloping, slanting; *(objet)* tilting **2** *(personne)* leaning; **il était p. en avant** he was leaning forward; **je l'ai aperçu, p. à la fenêtre** I saw him, leaning out of the window; **il est toujours p. sur ses livres** he's always got his head in a book

pencher [3] [pɑ̃ʃe] **VI 1** *(aux être) (être déséquilibré → pile)* to lean (over), to tilt; *(→ bateau)* to list; **la tour/le mur penche vers la droite** the tower/the wall leans to the right; **le miroir penche encore un peu, redresse-le** the mirror is still crooked, straighten it; **ne faites pas p. le bateau** don't rock the boat; *Fig* **faire p. la balance en faveur de/contre qn** to tip the scales in favour of/against sb

2 *(aux être) (être en pente)* to slope (away); **le sol penche** the floor slopes *or* is on an incline

3 *(aux avoir)* **p. pour** *(préférer)* to be inclined to, to favour; **je penche pour cette solution** I

pel–pen

favour this solution; **je pencherais plutôt pour l'hypothèse du suicide** I'm inclined to favour the suicide theory; **son passé le fait p. pour une politique de droite** he has right-wing leanings because of his past; **je penche pour tout lui avouer** I'm in favour of telling him/her everything; **la décision a l'air de p. en ma faveur** the decision seems to weigh in my favour

VT to tilt, to tip up; **il pencha la bouteille pour lui servir du vin** he tilted the bottle to pour him/her some wine; **il pencha la tête en arrière pour l'embrasser** he leaned backwards to kiss him/her; **elle pencha la tête au-dessus du parapet** she leaned over the parapet; **p. la tête à droite** to lean one's head to the right

▸**se pencher VPR 1** *(s'incliner)* to lean, to bend; **se p. en avant/en arrière** to lean *or* bend forward/backwards; **j'ai dû me p. pour l'entendre** I had to lean forward *or* over to hear him/her; **se p. à** *ou* **par la fenêtre** to lean out (of) the window; **elle se pencha sur le berceau** she leaned over the cradle; **il se pencha sous la table pour ramasser son crayon** he reached under the table to pick up his pencil; **ne pas se p. au-dehors** *(sur écriteau)* do not lean out of the window

2 se p. sur to look into; **se p. sur un problème/un dossier** to look into a problem/a file

pendable [pɑ̃dabl] **ADJ 1** *Vieilli (passible de la pendaison)* **ce n'est pas un cas p.** it's not a hanging offence **2 jouer un tour p. à qn** to play a rotten trick on sb

pendage [pɑ̃daʒ] **NM** (angle of) dip

pendaison [pɑ̃dɛzɔ̃] **NF** hanging; **mort par p.** death by hanging

❑ **pendaison de crémaillère NF** housewarming (party)

pendant[1] [pɑ̃dɑ̃] **PRÉP** *(au cours de)* during; *(insistant sur la durée)* for; **il est arrivé p. la cérémonie** he came in during the ceremony; **p. les vacances, nous sommes passés par Bordeaux** during our holidays we stopped off at Bordeaux; **p. l'hiver** during the winter; **quelqu'un a appelé p. l'heure du déjeuner** somebody called while you were at lunch *or* during your lunch break; **il te l'a dit après la réunion? – non, p.** did he tell you after the meeting? – no, during it; **p. ce temps(-là)** in the meantime, meanwhile; **elle travaille, et lui, p. ce temps-là, il s'amuse!** she works while he just enjoys himself!; **je suis là p. tout l'été** I'm here during the *or* for the whole (of the) summer; **p. une heure** for an hour; **je m'absenterai p. un mois** I'll be away for a month; **je ne l'ai pas vu p. plusieurs années** I didn't see him for several years; **j'y ai habité p. un an** I lived there for a year; **nous avons roulé p. 20 kilomètres** we drove for 20 kilometres

❑ **pendant que CONJ 1** *(tandis que)* while; **surveille les valises p. que je vais chercher les billets** look after the suitcases while I go and get the tickets; **on a appelé p. que vous étiez absent** someone called while you were out

2 *(tant que)* while; **partons p. qu'il est encore temps** let's go while it's still possible; **p. que tu y es, pourras-tu passer à la banque?** while you're there *or* at it, could you stop off at the bank?; **traite-moi de menteur p. que tu y es!** call me a liar while you're at it!; **p. que j'y pense, voici l'argent que je te dois** while I think of it, here's the money I owe you

3 *(puisque)* since, while; **allons-y p. que nous y sommes** let's go, since we're here

pendant[2], **-e** [pɑ̃dɑ̃, -ɑ̃t] **ADJ 1** *(tombant → jambes)* dangling; *(→ seins, joues)* sagging; **il restait là, les bras pendants** he stood there with his arms hanging at his sides; **la langue pendante** *(de fatigue, de convoitise)* with one's tongue hanging out; **un chien aux oreilles pendantes** a dog with floppy ears

2 *Jur (en cours → d'instruction)* pending; *(→ de résolution)* pending, being dealt with

3 *Archit* **clef pendante** hanging keystone

NM 1 *(bijou)* pendant; **p. (d'oreilles)** (pendant) earring

2 *(symétrique → d'une chose)* matching piece (**de** to); **faire p. à qch** to match sth; **se faire p.** to match, to be a matching pair

3 *(alter ego → d'une personne)* counterpart, opposite number; **c'est le digne p. de son frère!** he's every bit as bad as his brother!

pendard, -e [pɑ̃dar, -ard] **NM,F** *Fam Vieilli* rogue, rapscallion

pendeloque [pɑ̃dlɔk] **NF 1** *(de boucle d'oreille)* pendant, eardrop **2** *(d'un lustre)* pendant, drop **3** *(d'une chèvre)* dewlap

pendentif [pɑ̃dɑ̃tif] **NM 1** *(bijou)* pendant **2** *Archit* pendentive

penderie [pɑ̃dri] **NF** *(meuble)* wardrobe; *(pièce)* walk-in wardrobe *or* closet

pendiller [3] [pɑ̃dije] **VI** to hang (down), to dangle; **des fanions pendillaient à la fenêtre** pennants hung from the window

pendillon [pɑ̃dijɔ̃] **NM 1** *Théât* proscenium paintings **2** *(d'une horloge)* pendulum rod *or* spindle

Pendjab [pɛndʒab] **NM le P.** the Punjab

pendjabi [pɛndʒabi] **NM** *(langue)* Punjabi

pendoir [pɑ̃dwar] **NM** butcher's *or* meat hook

pendouiller [3] [pɑ̃duje] **VI** *Fam* to hang down▪, to dangle▪; **ton ourlet pendouille** your hem is down▪

pendre [73] [pɑ̃dr] **VT 1** *(accrocher)* to hang (up); **p. un tableau à un clou** to hang a picture from a nail; **p. ses vêtements sur des cintres** to put one's clothes on hangers *or* coathangers; **p. son linge sur un fil** to hang up one's washing on a line; **p. la crémaillère** to have a housewarming (party)

2 *(exécuter)* to hang; **condamné à être pendu** sentenced to be hanged; **il sera pendu à l'aube** he'll hang *or* be hanged at dawn; **p. qn haut et court** to hang sb (by the neck); **se faire p.** to be hanged; *Fam* **qu'il aille se faire p. ailleurs** he can go to blazes *or* go hang; **je veux bien être pendu si j'y comprends quoi que ce soit** I'll be hanged if I understand any of it

3 *Fig* **être pendu au cou de qn** to cling to sb; **être (toujours) pendu après qn** *ou* **aux basques de qn** to dog sb's every footstep, to hang around sb; *Fam* **être pendu au téléphone** to be never off the phone, to spend one's life on the phone; *Fam* **elle est toujours pendue à ma sonnette** she's always on my doorstep

VI 1 *(être accroché)* to hang; **du linge pendait aux fenêtres** washing was hanging out of the windows; *Fam* **ça te pend au nez** you've got it coming to you

2 *(retomber)* to hang; *(bras, jambes)* to dangle; *(langue d'un animal)* to hang out; **sa natte pendait dans son dos** his/her plait was hanging down his/her back; **elle laisse toujours p. ses cheveux dans son dos** she always wears her hair loose; **ta jupe pend par derrière** your skirt's hanging down *or* dipping at the back; **avoir les joues/seins qui pendent** to have sagging cheeks/breasts; **des rideaux qui pendent jusqu'à terre** full-length curtains

▸**se pendre VPR 1** *(se suicider)* to hang oneself

2 *(s'accrocher)* to hang (**à** from); **les chauves-souris se pendent aux branches** the bats hang from the branches; **se p. au cou de qn** to fling one's arms around sb's neck

pendu, -e [pɑ̃dy] **NM,F** hanged man, *f* woman; **le (jeu du) p.** (the game of) hangman

pendulaire [pɑ̃dylɛr] **ADJ** oscillating, pendulous; **migration p.** commuting; **train p.** tilting train

NMF *Suisse* commuter

pendule [pɑ̃dyl] **NM** *(instrument, balancier)* pendulum

NF *(horloge)* clock; *Fig* **remettre les pendules à l'heure** to set the record straight; *Fam* **en faire une p.**, *Vulg* **en chier une p.** to make a big fuss

penduler [3] [pɑ̃dyle] **VI** *(en alpinisme)* to do a pendulum traverse

pendulette [pɑ̃dylɛt] **NF** small clock; **p. de voyage** travel (alarm) clock

pendulier, -ère [pɑ̃dylje, -ɛr] **NM,F** clockmaker

penduline [pɑ̃dylin] **NF** *Orn* penduline tit

pêne [pɛn] **NM** bolt (of lock); **p. demi-tour** latch

Pénélope [penelɔp] **NPR** *Myth* Penelope; **c'est un travail de P.** it's a never-ending task, *Br* it's like painting the Forth Bridge

pénéplaine [peneplɛn] **NF** peneplain, peneplane

pénétrabilité [penetrabilite] **NF** penetrability

pénétrable [penetrabl] **ADJ 1** *(où l'on peut entrer)* **une jungle difficilement p.** an impenetrable jungle **2** *Fig (compréhensible)* fathomable; **des poèmes/musiques peu pénétrables** rather abstruse poems/music

pénétrance [penetrɑ̃s] **NF** *Biol* penetrance

pénétrant, -e [penetrɑ̃, -ɑ̃t] **ADJ 1** *(humidité)* pervasive; *(pluie)* drenching; *(odeur)* penetrating, pervasive; **une petite bruine pénétrante** the kind of drizzle that soaks one through; **le froid était p.** it was bitterly cold **2** *(clairvoyant → esprit)* penetrating, sharp; *(→ regard)* piercing, penetrating; **lancer à qn un regard p.** to give sb a piercing look

❑ **pénétrante NF** = road leading into the city

pénétrateur [penetratœr] **NM** *(en astronautique)* penetrator

pénétration [penetrasjɔ̃] **NF 1** *(par un solide)* penetration; *(par un liquide)* seepage, seeping; *(par un corps gras)* absorption; **à cause de la p. de l'eau de pluie dans le sol** because of rainwater seeping into the ground; **masser doucement jusqu'à p. totale de la crème** gently massage *or* rub in the cream until it has been completely absorbed into the skin

2 *(acte sexuel)* penetration

3 *(invasion)* penetration, invasion; **une tentative de p.** an attempted raid

4 *Fig (perspicacité)* perception; **un esprit plein de p.** a very perceptive *or* sharp mind; **avec p.** perspicaciously

5 *Com (d'un produit)* (market) penetration; *(d'un marché)* penetration

pénétré, -e [penetre] **ADJ 1** *(rempli)* **être p. de joie/honte** to be filled with joy/shame; **il se sentit p. de la vérité de ces paroles** he felt convinced of the truth of these words; **un orateur p. de son sujet** a speaker who is completely immersed in his subject; *Péj* **p. de sa propre importance** full of one's own importance

2 *(convaincu)* earnest, serious; **d'un air p.** with an earnest air, earnestly; **prendre un ton p.** to adopt an earnest tone (of voice)

pénétrer [18] [penetre] **VI 1** *(entrer)* to go, to enter; **p. dans les bois** to go into the woods; **ils ont réussi à p. en Suisse** they managed to cross into *or* to enter Switzerland; **l'armée a pénétré en territoire ennemi** the army penetrated enemy territory; **p. dans la maison de qn** *(avec sa permission)* to enter sb's house; *(par effraction)* to break into sb's house; **l'informatique pénètre même dans les salles de concert** computers are even making their presence felt in concert halls; **comment faire pour p. dans le monde de la publicité?** how can one get into advertising?; **p. sur un marché** to break into a market, to make inroads into *or* on a market

2 *(passer → balle)* to penetrate; *(s'infiltrer → liquide)* to seep, to penetrate; **la balle a pénétré dans le poumon** the bullet entered *or* penetrated the lung; **l'eau a très vite pénétré dans la cale** water quickly flooded into the hold; **le vent pénètre par la cheminée** the wind comes in by the chimney; **la poussière pénètre partout** dust gets in everywhere; **faire p. la crème en massant doucement** gently rub *or* massage the cream in

3 p. dans *(approfondir)* to go (deeper) into; **p. dans les détails d'une théorie** to go into the details of a theory; **je m'efforce de p. dans la vie de mon client** I try to put myself into my client's situation

VT 1 *(traverser)* to penetrate, to go in *or* into, to get in *or* into; **la balle a pénétré l'os** the bullet penetrated *or* pierced the bone; **l'humidité a fini par p. ma veste** the damp finally soaked through my jacket; **la pluie m'a pénétré jusqu'aux os** I got soaked to the skin (in the rain); **un froid glacial me pénétra** I was chilled to the bone *or* to the marrow

2 *(imprégner)* to spread into *or* through; **ces idées ont pénétré toutes les couches de la société** these ideas have spread through all levels of society

3 *Com (un marché)* to penetrate, to enter

4 *(sexuellement)* to penetrate

5 *(deviner)* to penetrate, to perceive; **p. un mystère** to get to the heart of a mystery; **p. le sens d'un texte** to grasp the meaning of a text; **p. les intentions de qn** to guess *or* fathom sb's intentions

▸**se pénétrer VPR 1** *(emploi réciproque)* **les croyances hindoue et bouddhiste se sont mutuellement pénétrées** the Hindu and Buddhist faiths became intertwined

2 *(emploi réfléchi)* **se p. d'une vérité** to become

convinced of a truth; **se p. d'un principe** to internalize a principle; **il faut vous p. de l'importance du facteur religieux** you must be aware of *or* you must understand the importance of the religious element

pénétromètre [penetrɔmɛtr] **NM** *Tech* penetrometer

pénibilité [penibilite] **NF** onerousness

pénible [penibl] **ADJ 1** (*épuisant → voyage, ascension*) hard, tough; (→ *travail, tâche*) laborious, hard; (→ *vie*) hard, difficult; (→ *respiration*) laboured, heavy; **elle trouve de plus en plus p. de monter les escaliers** she finds it more and more difficult *or* harder and harder to climb the stairs
2 (*attristant*) distressing, painful; **annoncer une p. nouvelle** to break bad news; **il m'est p. de devoir vous annoncer que…** it is my painful duty to inform you that…; **en parler m'est très p.** I find it difficult to talk about (it); **ma présence lui est p.** my being here bothers him/her
3 (*difficile à supporter*) tiresome; **caractère p.** disagreeableness; **je trouve ça vraiment p.** I find it a real nuisance; **tu es p., tu sais!** you're a real pain in the neck *or* nuisance!

péniblement [peniblǝmã] **ADV 1** (*avec difficulté*) laboriously, with difficulty; **avancer p. dans la neige** to struggle through the snow; **il respire de plus en plus p.** he's finding it more and more difficult to breathe
2 (*tout juste*) just about; **j'arrive p. à boucler les fins de mois** I barely manage to make ends meet at the end of the month; **il atteint p. la moyenne en allemand** he just about scrapes through in German

péniche [penif] **NF** (*large*) barge; (*étroite*) narrow boat; *Mil* **p. de débarquement** landing craft
☐ **péniches** **NFPL** *Fam* (*grandes chaussures*) clodhoppers

pénicillé, -e [penisile] **ADJ** *Biol* penicillate
pénicillinase [penisilinaz] **NF** *Biol* penicillinase
pénicilline [penisilin] **NF** *Biol & Pharm* penicillin
pénicillinorésistant, -e [penisilinɔrezistã, -ãt] **ADJ** *Biol* (*microbe, staphylocoque*) penicillin-resistant
pénicillium [penisiljɔm] **NM** *Biol* penicillium
pénien, -enne [penjɛ̃, -ɛn] **ADJ** (*artère, étui*) penile
pénil [penil] **NM** mons veneris
péninsulaire [penɛ̃sylɛr] **ADJ** peninsular
NMF inhabitant of a peninsula
péninsule [penɛ̃syl] **NF** peninsula; **la p. antarctique** the Antarctic Peninsula; **la p. d'Arabie** the Arabian Peninsula; **la p. du Cap York** the Cape York Peninsula; **la p. Ibérique** the Iberian Peninsula
pénis [penis] **NM** penis
pénitence [penitãs] **NF 1** *Rel* (*repentir*) penitence; (*punition*) penance; (*sacrement*) penance, sacrament of reconciliation; **faire p.** to repent; **accomplir sa p. pour l'expiation de ses péchés** to do penance for one's sins; **le carême est une période de p.** Lent is a time for doing penance
2 (*punition*) punishment; **mettre qn en p.** to punish sb; **ce n'est pas la peine d'apprendre le piano si tu le fais comme une p.** there's no point learning the piano if you treat it as a punishment; **pour votre p.** as a punishment
3 (*dans un jeu*) forfeit
Pénitencerie [penitãsri] **NF** *Rel* (**Sacrée**) **P.** apostolique penitentiary (*in Rome*)
pénitencier [penitãsje] **NM 1** (*prison*) prison, jail, *Am* penitentiary **2** *Rel* penitentiary; **grand p.** grand penitentiary
pénitent, -e [penitã, -ãt] **ADJ** penitent
NM,F penitent
pénitentiaire [penitãsjɛr] **ADJ** prison (*avant n*)
pénitentiaux [penitãsjo] **ADJ MPL** *voir* psaume
pénitentiel, -elle [penitãsjɛl] **ADJ** penitential, penitence (*avant n*)
NM penitential (*book*)
pennage [pɛnaʒ] **NM** *Orn* plumage (*of bird of prey*)
penne¹ [pɛn] **NF 1** *Orn* quill, *Spéc* penna **2** (*d'une flèche*) flight, feather **3** (*d'une antenne*) tip
penne² [pene] **NMPL** (*pâtes*) penne
penné, -e [pɛne] **ADJ** pennaceous
penniforme [penifɔrm] **ADJ** pinnate, pinnated
pennon [penɔ̃] **NM 1** *Hist* pennon **2** *Naut* pennon
Pennsylvanie [pɛnsilvani] **NF la P.** Pennsylvania; **en P.** in Pennsylvania

pennsylvanien, -enne [pɛnsilvanjɛ̃, -ɛn] **ADJ** Pennsylvanian
☐ **Pennsylvanien, -enne** **NM,F** Pennsylvanian
penny [peni] (*pl sens* **1** pence [pɛns], *pl sens* **2** pennies [peniz]) **NM 1** (*somme*) penny; **ça coûte 90 pence** it costs 90 pence **2** (*pièce*) penny; **je n'ai que des pennies dans ma poche** I have only pennies in my pocket
péno [peno] **NM** *Fam* (*abrév* **penalty**) penalty■, *Br* pen (*in football*)
pénologie [penɔlɔʒi] **NF** penology
pénombre [penɔ̃br] **NF 1** (*obscurité*) half-light, dim light; **la p. nous empêchait de distinguer les visages** the light was too faint *or* dim to see any faces; **dans la p.** in the half-light; *Fig* in the background, out of the limelight **2** *Astron* penumbra
penon [pǝnɔ̃] **NM** *Naut* pennon
pensable [pãsabl] **ADJ à cette époque-là, de telles vitesses n'étaient pas pensables** in those days, such speeds were unthinkable; **cette histoire n'est pas p.!** this story is incredible!
pensant, -e [pãsã, -ãt] **ADJ** (*être*) thinking; **mal p.** unorthodox
pense-bête [pãsbɛt] (*pl* pense-bêtes) **NM** reminder; **fais-toi un p. pour ne pas oublier de téléphoner** make a note of it somewhere so that you don't forget to phone
pensée [pãse] **NF 1** (*idée*) thought, idea; **la seule p. d'une seringue me donne des sueurs froides** the very thought of a needle brings me out in a cold sweat; **à la seule p. des vacances, …** at the very thought of *or* just thinking of the holidays, …; **la p. que tu seras là me donne du courage** the thought that you will be there gives me courage; **cette p. me hante** I'm haunted by that thought; **tout à la p. de son rendez-vous, il n'a pas vu arriver la voiture** deeply absorbed in *or* by the thought of his meeting, he didn't see the car (coming); **être tout à** *ou* **perdu dans ses pensées** to be lost in thought; **avoir une p. pour qn** to think of sb; **avoir une p. émue pour qn** to spare a (kind) thought for sb; **avoir de mauvaises pensées** (*méchantes*) to have evil thoughts; (*sexuelles*) to have immoral *or* bad thoughts; **avoir de sombres pensées** to have gloomy thoughts
2 (*façon de raisonner*) thought; **elle a une p. rigoureuse** she's a rigorous thinker; **avoir une p. claire** to be clear-thinking
3 (*opinion*) thought, (way of) thinking; **j'avais deviné ta p.** I'd guessed what you were thinking; **veux-tu connaître ma p. sur ce livre?** do you want to know what I think of *or* about this book?; **dire sa p.** to speak one's mind, to say what one thinks; **dire le fond de sa p.** to say what one really thinks; **pour aller jusqu'au bout** *ou* **fond de ma p. je dirais que…** to be absolutely frank, I'd say that…; **allez donc jusqu'au bout de votre p.** come on, say what you really think *or* what's really on your mind; **il partage ma p.** he shares my opinion, he thinks the same way I do
4 (*esprit*) mind; **nous sommes avec vous par la** *ou* **en p.** our thoughts are with you; **je les vois en p.** I can see them in my mind *or* in my mind's eye; **transportez-vous par la p. dans une contrée exotique** let your thoughts take you to an exotic land
5 *Phil* thought; **la p. est distincte de la perception** thought is distinct from perception; **p. conceptuelle/logique/mathématique** conceptual/logical/mathematical thought
6 (*idéologie*) thinking, thought; **la p. marxiste** Marxist thinking, Marxist thought; **l'influence de la p. de Confucius sur la Chine** the influence of Confucius' thinking on China; **la p. unique** = new orthodoxy in politics driven by the principles of the free market
7 (*dans les formules*) **je vous envoie une tendre p. (à vous et à votre famille)** I send my love (to you and your family); **avec nos affectueuses** *ou* **meilleures pensées** with (all) our love *or* fondest regards
8 *Bot* pansy; **p. sauvage** wild pansy
☐ **pensées** **NFPL** *Littérature & Phil* thoughts; **les pensées de Marc Aurèle** the thoughts of Marcus Aurelius

'**La Pensée sauvage**' *Lévi-Strauss* 'The Savage Mind'

'**Pensées**' *Pascal* 'Pensées'

PENSER [3] [pãse]

| **VT** to think 1–6 ■ to assume 1 ■ to realize 4 ■ to remember 5 ■ to think out 7 |
| **VI** to think 1 |

VT 1 (*croire*) to think, to assume; **qu'en penses-tu?** what do you think of it?; **je ne sais qu'en p.** I don't know what to think *or* I can't make up my mind about it; **je pense que oui** (yes,) I think so; **je pense que non** (no,) I don't think so *or* I think not; **je pense que tu devrais lui dire** I think you should tell him/her; **pas aussi beau qu'on le penserait** not as beautiful as one might suppose; **je n'en pense que du bien/mal** I have the highest/lowest opinion of it; **on pensait du mal de lui dans le village** in the village, they thought ill of him *or* they had a low opinion of him; "**plutôt idiot!**", **pensa-t-elle** "rather foolish," she thought *or* reflected; **je pense qu'elle viendra demain** I think *or* assume that she'll come tomorrow; **qu'est-ce qui te fait p. qu'il ment?** what makes you think he's lying?; **j'ai pensé qu'un rôti, ce ne serait pas suffisant** it occurred to me *or* I thought that one joint wouldn't be enough; **quoi qu'on pense** whatever people (may) think; **quoi que tu puisses p.** whatever you (may) think; **je le pensais diplomate** I thought him tactful, I thought he was tactful; **je pensais la chose faisable, mais on me dit que non** I thought it was possible (to do), but I'm told it's not
2 (*escompter*) **je pense partir demain** I'm thinking of *or* planning on *or* reckoning on leaving tomorrow; **je pense avoir réussi** (*examen*) I think I passed
3 (*avoir à l'esprit*) to think; **je ne sais jamais ce que tu penses** I can never tell what you're thinking *or* what's on your mind; **au volant, pensez sécurité** when you're at the wheel, think safety (first); **dire tout haut ce que certains** *ou* **d'autres pensent tout bas** to say out loud what others are thinking in private; *Fam Euph* **ce que je pense** you-know-what; **il a marché dans ce que je pense** he trod in some you-know-what; *Fam Euph* **(là) où je pense** in the *Br* backside *or Am* butt; *Fam* **il peut se le mettre où je pense** he knows where he can stick it; *Fam* **elle lui a fichu un coup de pied où je pense** she gave him/her a kick up the you-know-where
4 (*comprendre*) to think, to realize; **pense qu'elle a près de cent ans** you must realize that she's nearly a hundred; **il faut p. que ces tribus n'avaient pas de tradition écrite** we must not lose sight of the fact that these tribes had no written tradition
5 (*se rappeler*) to remember, to think; **je n'ai plus pensé que c'était lundi** I forgot *or* I never thought it was Monday
6 (*pour exprimer la surprise, l'approbation, l'ironie*) **je n'aurais/on n'aurait jamais pensé que…** I'd never/nobody'd ever have thought that…; **il n'aurait jamais pensé qu'elle le relancerait jusque chez lui** he'd never have thought *or* dreamt *or* imagined that she'd track him down and harass him at home; **qui aurait pu p. que…** who'd have thought *or* guessed that…; **quand je pense que…** to think that…; **quand je pense que j'aurais pu être sa femme!** to think that I could've been his wife!; **quand on pense qu'il n'y avait pas le téléphone à l'époque!** when you think that there was no such thing as the phone in those days!; *Fam* **tu penses!** you bet!; *Ironique* you must be joking!; *Fam* **lui, me dire merci? tu penses** *ou* **penses-tu** *ou* **pense donc!** him? thank me? I should be so lucky *or* you must be joking!; *Fam* **tu penses bien que je lui ai tout raconté!** I told him/her everything, as you can well imagine; *Fam* **tu viendras à la fête? – je pense bien!** will

you come to the party? – just (you) try and stop me!; *Fam* **il est content? – je pense** *ou* **tu penses bien!** is he pleased? – you bet!; **tu penses bien que le voleur ne t'a pas attendu!** you can bet your life the thief didn't leave his name and address!

7 *(concevoir)* to think out *or* through; **le projet n'a pas été pensé dans toutes ses implications** the implications of the project weren't thought through (properly); **une architecture bien pensée** a well-planned *or* well-thought out architectural design

8 *Littéraire (être sur le point de)* **je pensai m'évanouir** I all but fainted; **elle pensa devenir folle** she was very nearly driven to distraction

VI 1 *(réfléchir)* to think, to ponder; **apprendre à p.** to learn to think; **p. tout haut** to think aloud *or* out loud; **donner** *ou* **laisser à p.** to make one think, to start one thinking; **voilà des statistiques qui donnent à p.!** these figures provide food for thought!; *Péj* **p. bien** to have conventional beliefs; **une ville dont les habitants pensent bien** a conservative town

2 *(avoir une opinion)* **je n'ai jamais pensé comme toi** I never did agree with you *or* share your views; **je ne dis rien mais je n'en pense pas moins** I say nothing but that doesn't stop me thinking

❑ **penser à** *VT IND* **1** *(envisager)* to think about *or* of; **p. à l'avenir** to think about *or* to ponder the future; **pense un peu à ce que tu dis!** just think for a moment (about) what you're saying!; **oui, c'est faisable, j'y penserai** yes, it can be done, I'll think about *or* I'll consider it; **vous éviteriez des ennuis, pensez-y** you'd save yourself a lot of trouble, think it over!; **c'est simple mais il fallait y p.** it's a simple enough idea but somebody had to think of it (in the first place); **sans y p.** *(par automatisme)* without thinking; **quand tu sauras conduire, tu changeras de vitesse sans y p.** when you know how to drive, you'll change gear without (even) thinking; **sans p. à mal** without *or* not meaning any harm (by it); **tu n'y penses pas** you can't be serious; **me rétracter, tu n'y penses pas!** me, go back on what I said, come off it *or* never!

2 *(rêver à)* to think about *or* of; **à quoi penses-tu?** what are you thinking about?; **je pense à toi** *(dans une lettre)* I'm thinking of you

3 *(se préoccuper de)* to think of, to care about; **elle ne pense qu'à elle** she only cares about herself; **essaye de p. un peu aux autres** try to think of others; **les économies d'énergie, pensez-y!** think about saving energy!; *Fam Euph* **il ne pense qu'à ça!** he's got a one-track mind

4 *(se remémorer)* to think *or* to remember to; **as-tu pensé au** *ou* **à apporter le tire-bouchon?** did you think *or* remember to bring the corkscrew?; **et mon livre? – j'y pense, je te le rapporte demain** what about my book? – I haven't forgotten (it), I'll bring it back tomorrow; **dis donc, j'y pense, qu'est devenu le vieux Georges?** by the way, whatever happened to old Georges?; **tu ne penses à rien!** you've a head *or* memory like a sieve!; **n'y pense plus!** forget (all about) it!; **cela me fait p. à mon frère** it reminds me of my brother; **fais-moi p. à l'appeler** remind me to call him/her; **ça me fait p. à des fleurs** it makes me think of flowers; **le poème me fait p. à ma jeunesse** the poem takes me back to my youth

penseur, -euse [pɑ̃sœr, -øz] *NM,F* thinker

'Le Penseur' *Rodin* 'The Thinker'

pensez-y-bien [pɑ̃sezibjɛ̃] *NM Can* **sa dernière mauvaise expérience au jeu lui a donné un p.** his/her last bad gambling experience gave him/her cause for reflection *or* gave him/her something to think about

pensif, -ive [pɑ̃sif, -iv] *ADJ* thoughtful, pensive, reflective; **elle était toute pensive** she was lost in thought; **d'un air p.** thoughtfully

pension [pɑ̃sjɔ̃] *NF* **1** *(somme allouée)* pension; **toucher une p.** to draw a pension; **p. alimentaire** *Br* maintenance, *Am* alimony; **p. de guerre** war

pension; **p. d'invalidité** disability pension; **p. de retraite** (retirement *or* old-age) pension; **p. de réversion** survivor's pension; **p. de veuve** widow's pension; **p. viagère** life annuity

2 *(logement et nourriture)* board and lodging; **la p. est de 100 euros par jour** it's 100 euros a day for room and board *or* board and lodging; **prendre p. chez qn** *(client)* to take board and lodgings with sb; *(ami)* to be staying with sb; **être en p. chez qn** to lodge with sb; **prendre qn en p.** to take sb in as a lodger; **l'oncle paye la p. de son neveu** the uncle is paying for board and lodging for his nephew; **être en p. complète** to be on full board

3 *(hôtel)* **p. (de famille)** ≃ boarding house, guesthouse

4 *(pensionnat)* boarding school; *(élèves)* boarders; **être en p.** to be a boarder *or* at boarding school; **envoyer qn en p.** to send sb to boarding school; **si tu ne travailles pas mieux, je vais t'envoyer en p.!** if your work doesn't improve, I'll send you away to boarding school!

5 *Banque* **p. d'effets** pawning of stock

6 *Belg (cessation d'activité)* retirement; **l'âge de la p.** retirement age; **prendre sa p.** to retire

pensionnaire [pɑ̃sjɔnɛr] *NMF* **1** *(d'un hôtel)* guest, resident; *(d'un particulier)* (paying) guest, lodger; *(d'une maison de retraites)* resident; *Fam (d'une prison)* inmate▪ **2** *Scol* boarder **3** *(à la Comédie-Française)* = actor or actress on a fixed salary with no share in the profits (as opposed to a "sociétaire"); *(à la villa Médicis)* = scholarship student

pensionnat [pɑ̃sjɔna] *NM* **1** *(école)* boarding school **2** *(pensionnaires)* boarders

pensionné, -e [pɑ̃sjɔne] *ADJ* **1** *(qui perçoit une pension)* **elle est pensionnée à 75 pour cent** her pension represents 75 percent of her income **2** *Belg (qui est à la retraite → gén)* retired; *(→ officier)* on the retired list

NM,F **1** *(personne qui perçoit une pension)* pensioner **2** *Belg (personne ne travaillant plus)* retired person

pensionner [3] [pɑ̃sjɔne] *VT* **p. qn** to (grant sb a) pension

VI *Can (être en pension)* to be a boarder

pensive [pɑ̃siv] *voir* **pensif**

pensivement [pɑ̃sivmɑ̃] *ADV* pensively, thoughtfully, reflectively

pensum [pɛ̃sɔm] *NM* **1** *Vieilli Scol* imposition, punishment; *(lignes)* lines **2** *(corvée)* chore; *Fam* **quel p.!** what a drag *or* nuisance!

pentacle [pɛ̃takl] *NM* pentacle

pentacorde [pɛ̃takɔrd] *NM Antiq (lyre, système)* pentachord

pentacrine [pɛ̃takrin] *NM Zool* pentacrinus, pentacrinite

pentadactyle [pɛ̃tadaktil] *ADJ Zool* pentadactyl

pentadécagone [pɛ̃tadekagon] *NM Géom* pentadecagon

pentaèdre [pɛ̃taɛdr] *Géom ADJ* pentahedral

NM pentahedron

pentagonal, -e, -aux, -ales [pɛ̃tagonal, -o] *ADJ Géom* pentagonal

Pentagone [pɛ̃tagon] *NM* **le P.** the Pentagon

pentagone [pɛ̃tagon] *NM Géom* pentagon

pentamère [pɛ̃tamɛr] *ADJ Biol* pentamerous

pentamètre [pɛ̃tamɛtr] *NM Littérature* pentameter

pentane [pɛ̃tan] *NM Chim* pentane

pentapole [pɛ̃tapɔl] *NF Antiq* pentapolis

pentaradié, -e [pɛ̃taradje] *ADJ Bot & Zool* pentamerous

pentarchie [pɛ̃tarʃi] *NF* pentarchy

Pentateuque [pɛ̃tatøk] *NM* **le P.** the Pentateuch

pentathlon [pɛ̃tatlɔ̃] *NM* pentathlon

pentathlonien, -enne [pɛ̃tatlɔnjɛ̃, -ɛn] *NM,F* pentathlete

pentatome [pɛ̃tatɔm] *NF Entom* forest bug, *Spéc* Pentatoma

pentatonique [pɛ̃tatɔnik] *ADJ Mus* pentatonic

pentavalent, -e [pɛ̃tavalɑ̃, -ɑ̃t] *ADJ Chim* pentavalent

pente [pɑ̃t] *NF* **1** *(inclinaison)* slope, incline; **une forte p.** a steep incline *or* slope

2 *(descente, montée)* slope; **gravir une p.** to climb a slope

3 *Constr* slope; *(d'un toit)* pitch; **une p. de 10 pour cent** a 1 in 10 gradient; **p. d'eau** lift

4 *Math (d'une courbe)* slope

5 *Littéraire (penchant)* inclination, leaning; **sa p. naturelle le conduit à être plutôt indulgent** he's of a lenient disposition, he's naturally inclined to be lenient

6 *Élec* mutual conductance

7 *Géog* **p. limite** angle of repose; **p. continentale** continental slope

8 *(locutions)* **être sur une mauvaise p.** to be heading for trouble; **il a bien remonté la p.** *(en meilleure santé)* he's back on his feet again; *(financièrement)* he's solvent again; **être sur une p. glissante** *ou* **savonneuse** to be on a slippery slope

❑ **en pente** *ADJ (route)* sloping; *(plage, côte)* shelving; **la route est en p.** the road is on a slope *or* an incline; **en p. douce** sloping gently; **en p. raide** on a steep incline *ADV* **descendre/ monter en p. douce** to slope gently down/up; **descendre/monter en p. raide** to slope sharply down/up

Pentecôte [pɑ̃tkot] *NF* **1** *(fête chrétienne)* Whitsun, Pentecost; **la semaine de la P.** Whit Week, Whitsuntide; **dimanche de P.** Whit Sunday; **lundi de P.** Whit Monday **2** *(fête juive)* Shabuoth

pentecôtisme [pɑ̃tkotism] *NM* Pentecostalism

pentecôtiste [pɑ̃tkotist] *NMF* Pentecostalist

pentédécagone [pɛ̃tedekagon] *NM Géom* pentadecagon

Penthésilée [pɛ̃tezile] *NPR Myth* Penthesileia

penthiobarbital, -als [pɛ̃tjɔbarbital] *NM Br* pentabarbitone, *Am* pentabarbital

penthode [pɛ̃tɔd] *NF Électron* pentode, five-electrode tube

pentode [pɛ̃tɔd] = **penthode**

pentose [pɛ̃toz] *NM Biol & Chim* pentose

Pentothal® [pɛ̃total] *NM INV Pharm* Pentothal®

pentoxyde [pɛ̃tɔksid] *NM Chim* pentoxide

pentrite [pɛ̃trit] *NF* pentryl

pentu, -e [pɑ̃ty] *ADJ (chemin)* steep, sloping; *(toit)* sloping, slanting, pointed; *(comble)* sloping

penture [pɑ̃tyr] *NF Tech (de porte, de volet)* strap hinge; **p. et gond** hook and hinge; *Naut* **pentures du gouvernail** rudder braces

pénultième [penyltjɛm] *ADJ* penultimate

NF penultimate (syllable)

pénurie [penyri] *NF* **1** *(pauvreté)* destitution, penury; **vivre dans la p.** to live in poverty **2** *(manque)* **p. de** lack *or* shortage of; **p. d'argent** shortage of money, money shortage; **il y a (une) p. de viande** there is a meat shortage, meat is in short supply; *Écon* **p. de main-d'œuvre** labour shortage

péon [peɔ̃] *NM* peon

people [pipɔl] *Fam ADJ INV* **la presse p.** the celebrity press▪

NMPL celebrities▪, celebs; **c'est très à la mode chez les p.** all the celebs are into it

PEP [pɛp] *NM Banque (abrév* **plan d'épargne populaire***)* = personal pension plan

pep [pɛp] *NM Fam* pep; **avoir du p.** to be full of pep

pépé [pepe] *NM Fam* **1** *(grand-père)* grandpa, *Br* granddad, *Am* gramps **2** *Péj (vieillard)* old codger *or* boy, *Am* old-timer

pépée [pepe] *NF Fam Vieilli* chick

pépère [pepɛr] *Fam ADJ (facile → travail)* cushy; *(tranquille → endroit)* quiet▪; **un petit boulot p.** a cushy little number *or* job; **une petite vie p.** a cosy little life; **on est arrivés pépères, le lendemain matin** we got there the following morning, no sweat

ADV leisurely▪; **on a fait ça p.** we took it easy, we did it at our own pace; **rouler p.** to potter along

NM **1** *(grand-père)* grandpa, *Br* granddad, *Am* gramps

2 *Péj (vieillard) Br* old boy *or* codger, *Am* old-timer

3 *Fam (location)* **gros p.** *(avec affection)* tubby; *(avec mépris)* fat slob

péperin [pepprɛ̃] *NM Géol* peperino

pépette, pépète [pepɛt] *Fam NF Belg* fear▪; **avoir la p.** to be scared stiff *or* witless

❑ **pépettes, pépètes** *NFPL* **1** *Vieilli (argent)* cash, dough; **t'as des pépettes?** have you got any cash? **2** *Belg (peur)* fear▪; **avoir les pépettes** to be scared stiff *or* witless

pépie [pepi] *NF* **1** *Orn* pip **2** *Fam (soif)* **avoir la p.** to be parched

pépiement [pepimã] NM chirping, tweeting, twittering

pépier [9] [pepje] VI to chirp, to tweet, to twitter

Pépin [pepɛ̃] NPR **P. le Bref** Pepin the Short

pépin [pepɛ̃] NM **1** *(de fruit)* pip; **pépins de pomme/poire** apple/pear pips; **des mandarines sans pépins** seedless tangerines **2** *Fam (problème)* hitch, snag; **il y a un petit p.** there's a slight hitch; **avoir un p.** to have a problem■; **il m'arrive un gros p.** I'm in big trouble; **en cas de p.** if there's a snag or hitch **3** *Fam (parapluie)* umbrella■, *Br* brolly

pépinière [pepinjɛr] NF **1** *Bot* (tree) nursery; *Fig* **une p. de futurs prix Nobel** a breeding-ground for future Nobel prizewinners **2 p. d'entreprise** business incubator

pépiniériste [pepinjerist] ADJ nursery *(avant n)* NMF nurseryman, *f* nurserywoman

pépite [pepit] NF nugget; **p. d'or** gold nugget; **pépites de chocolat** chocolate chips

péplum [peplɔm] NM **1** *Antiq (vêtement de femme)* peplum **2** *(film)* (historical) epic

pépon [pepɔ̃] NM *Bot* pepo

péponide [peponid] NM OU NF = **pépon**

peppermint [pepɛrmint] NM *(liqueur)* peppermint liqueur

PEPS [peapɛs] NM *Com & Compta (abrév premier entré, premier sorti)* FIFO

peps [peps] NM *Fam* energy■, get-up-and-go; **avoir du p.** to have plenty of get-up-and-go, to be full of life

pepsine [pepsin] NF *Biol & Chim* pepsin

peptide [peptid] NM *Biol & Chim* peptide

peptidique [peptidik] ADJ *Chim* peptide *(avant n)*, peptidic; **liaison p.** peptide bond, peptide linkage

peptique [peptik] ADJ *Biol & Chim* peptic

peptone [peptɔn] NF *Biol & Chim* peptone

péquenaud, -e [pekno, -od], **péquenot, -otte** [pekno, -ɔt] NM,F *Fam Péj (rustre)* yokel

péquet [pekɛ] NM *Belg* juniper brandy

péquin [pekɛ̃] = **pékin 2, 3**

péquiste [pekist] *Can* ADJ = of the Parti québécois ► NMF *(membre)* member of the Parti québécois; *(partisan)* supporter of the Parti québécois

PER [peɛr] NM **1** *Banque (abrév plan d'épargne retraite)* retirement savings plan or scheme **2** *(abrév price/earnings ratio)* p/e ratio

péramèle [peramɛl] *Zool* NM bandicoot ❑ **péramèles** NMPL Perameles

perborate [pɛrbɔrat] NM *Chim* perborate

perçage [pɛrsaʒ] NM **1** *(d'un trou)* drilling, boring **2** *Tex* punching

percale [pɛrkal] NF percale

percaline [pɛrkalin] NF percaline

perçant, -e [pɛrsã, -ãt] ADJ **1** *(voix)* piercing, shrill; *(regard)* piercing, sharp; **cris perçants** *(d'une personne)* earsplitting screams; *(d'un oiseau)* shrill cries; **pousser des cris perçants** to scream loudly; **avoir une vue perçante** to have a sharp eye; **elle a des yeux perçants** she has a piercing gaze **2** *(froid)* **le froid était p.** it was bitterly cold **3** *(outil)* piercing ► NM *Sport* **avoir du p.** to be penetrating

perce [pɛrs] NF **1** *(outil)* punch, drill, bore **2** *Mus* bore ❑ **en perce** ADV **mettre un tonneau en p.** to broach a barrel

percée [pɛrse] NF **1** *(ouverture → gén)* opening; *(→ dans un mur)* gap, breach; **ouvrir une p. dans un bois** to clear a path through a wood **2** *Sport* break; *Mil* breakthrough; **une p. à travers les lignes ennemies** a breakthrough into enemy lines; **faire une p.** to make a breakthrough, to break through; **tenter une p.** to try to break through **3** *Écon & Tech* breakthrough; **on note une p. de la bande dessinée japonaise sur le marché international** Japanese comics have begun to take a share of the international market; **faire une p. dans un marché** to break into a market; *Mktg* **p. commerciale** market thrust; **p. technologique** technological breakthrough **4** *Aviat* instrument letdown

percement [pɛrsəmã] NM *(d'une route)* building, opening; *(d'un tunnel)* driving; *(d'un canal)* cutting; *(d'une porte, d'une fenêtre)* opening

perce-muraille [pɛrsmyraj] *(pl* **perce-murailles)** NF *Bot* pellitory-of-the-wall

perce-neige [pɛrsənɛʒ] NF INV OU NM INV *Bot* snowdrop

perce-oreille [pɛrsɔrɛj] *(pl* **perce-oreilles)** NM *Entom* earwig

perce-pierre [pɛrspjɛr] *(pl* **perce-pierres)** NF *Bot (saxifrage)* saxifrage; *(criste-marine)* (rock) samphire

percepteur, -trice [pɛrsɛptœr, -tris] NM,F **1** *(receveur des impôts)* tax inspector, *m* taxman **2** *Belg (receveur des postes)* postmaster, *f* postmistress

perceptibilité [pɛrsɛptibilite] NF perceptibility

perceptible [pɛrsɛptibl] ADJ **1** *(sensible)* perceptible; **à peine p.** almost imperceptible; **p. à l'oreille** audible **2** *Jur & Fin* liable for collection or to be levied

perceptiblement [pɛrsɛptibləmã] ADV perceptibly

perceptif, -ive [pɛrsɛptif, -iv] ADJ perceptive

perception [pɛrsɛpsjɔ̃] NF **1** *(par les sens)* perception; *Mktg* **p. de marque** brand perception; *Mktg* **p. sélective** selective perception **2** *(notion)* perception, notion; **avoir une p. claire des problèmes** to be clearly aware of the problems **3** *Psy* perception **4** *Fin & Jur (encaissement → gén)* collection, levying; *(→ d'un impôt)* collection; *(lieu)* Br tax office, *Am* internal revenue office; **p. de dividende** receipt of a dividend; **p. douanière** collection of customs duties; **p. à la source** tax deduction at source

perceptive [pɛrsɛptiv] *voir* **perceptif**

perceptrice [pɛrsɛptris] *voir* **percepteur**

percer [16] [pɛrse] VT **1** *(trouer → gén)* to pierce (through); *(→ planche)* to drill (a hole) through; *(→ mur)* to make a hole in; **p. une membrane** to pierce or to puncture or to perforate a membrane; **la pointe a percé le ballon** the nail burst or pierced the balloon; **la malle d'osier était percée au fond** there was a hole in the bottom of the wickerwork trunk; **mes chaussures sont percées** I've got holes in my shoes; **se faire p. les oreilles** to have one's ears pierced; **il a eu le tympan percé dans l'accident** he suffered a burst or perforated eardrum in the accident; **un bruit à vous p. les oreilles** ou **tympans** an ear-splitting noise; **p. le cœur/bras à qn d'un coup de couteau** to stab sb through the heart/in the arm; **des montants percés de trous pour poser des étagères** uprights with holes for shelf brackets **2** *(pratiquer → trou)* to drill; *Constr (route)* to open, to build **(dans** through); *(tunnel)* to drive **(dans** through); *(canal)* to cut **(dans** through); **p. une porte dans un mur** to put a door in or into a wall **3** *(pénétrer avec difficulté)* to push through; **le soleil perça enfin le brouillard** at last the sun pierced through the fog; **ses yeux avaient du mal à p. l'obscurité** he/she had trouble making things out in the dark; **p. un mystère** to solve a mystery **4** *(déchirer)* to pierce, to tear, *Littéraire* to rend; **un cri perça le silence/la nuit** a scream rent the silence/night; **p. qn/qch à jour** to see right through sb/sth **5** *Méd* **p. la poche des eaux** to break the waters; **il faut p. l'abcès** the abscess will have to be lanced **6** *(sujet: bébé)* **p. ses dents** to be teething; **p. une dent** to cut a tooth or have a tooth coming through ► VI **1** *(poindre)* to come through; **des crocus percent sous la neige** crocuses are coming or pushing up through the snow; **le soleil perce enfin** the sun's finally broken through; **ses dents ont commencé à p.** his/her teeth have begun to come through **2** *(abcès)* to burst **3** *(filtrer)* to filter through, to emerge; **rien n'a percé de leur entrevue** nothing came out or emerged from their meeting; **elle ne laisse rien p. de ce qu'elle ressent** she doesn't let her feelings show, she keeps her feelings well hidden; **il laissa p. son impatience/sa jalousie** he let his impatience/jealousy show **4** *(réussir)* to become famous; **commencer à p.** to be on the way up; **un jeune chanteur en train de p.** an up-and-coming young singer; **p. sur le**

marché des lecteurs MP3 to break into the MP3 market

percerette [pɛrsəret] NF twist gimlet

perceur, -euse [pɛrsœr, -øz] NM,F *(personne)* driller; **p. de coffre-fort** safebreaker, safecracker ❑ **perceuse** NF *(machine-outil)* drill; **perceuse électrique (portative)** power or electric drill; **perceuse radiale/à percussion** radial/hammer drill

percevable [pɛrsəvabl] ADJ *Fin & Jur* liable to be levied or for collection

━━━━━━━━━━━━

'Perceval ou le conte du Graal' *Chrétien de Troyes* 'Perceval, the Story of the Grail'

percevoir [52] [pɛrsəvwar] VT **1** *(vibration, sensation, chaleur)* to feel; **j'ai cru p. une nuance de mépris dans sa voix** I thought I detected a note of contempt in his/her voice; **je ne perçois pas la différence** I can't make out or see the difference; **je commençais à p. la vérité** the truth was beginning to dawn on me; **être bien/mal perçu** *(personne)* to be well/badly thought of; *(produit)* to be well/badly perceived **2** *Fin (rente, intérêt)* to receive, to be paid; *(allocation, commission)* to receive; *(impôt)* to collect; **cotisations à p.** contributions still due

perchage[1] [pɛrʃaʒ] NM *Orn* perching

perchage[2] [pɛrʃaʒ] NM *Métal* poling

perchaude [pɛrʃod] NF *Can* Ich (yellow) perch

perche [pɛrʃ] NF **1** *(pièce de bois)* pole; *(tuteur)* beanpole, stake; *Rail* coupling pole; *Sport* pole; *(de téléski)* T-bar; **p. à houblon** hop pole; *Fig* **jeter** ou **tendre la p. à qn** to throw sb a line, to give sb a helping hand; *Fig* **prendre** ou **saisir la p.** to take or to rise to the bait **2** *Cin & TV* boom **3** *Fam (personne)* **grande p.** beanpole **4** *Ich* perch; **p. goujonnière** pope, ruff(e); **p. du Nil** Nile perch; **p. de mer** sea perch, comber; **p. truitée** black bass **5** *Zool (d'un cerf)* beam

perchée [pɛrʃe] NF roost

percher [3] [pɛrʃe] VI **1** *(oiseau)* to perch; *(poule)* to roost **2** *Fam (habiter)* to live■ ► VT *(placer)* to put; **pourquoi as-tu perché le bol sur l'étagère du haut?** why did you put the bowl on the top shelf?; *Fig* **une petite église perchée en haut de la colline** a little church perched on top of the hill ► **se percher** VPR **1** *(oiseau)* to perch; *(poule)* to roost **2** *(monter)* to perch; **ils se sont perchés sur le balcon pour mieux voir** they perched on the balcony to get a better view

percheron [pɛrʃərɔ̃] NM *Zool* percheron

perche-soleil [pɛrʃsɔlɛj] *(pl* **perches-soleils)** NM *Ich* pumpkinseed (sunfish)

percheur, -euse [pɛrʃœr, -øz] ADJ *(oiseau)* perching

perchis [pɛrʃi] NM pole plantation

perchiste [pɛrʃist] NMF **1** *Sport* pole-vaulter **2** *Cin & TV* boom operator), boom man

perchlorate [pɛrklɔrat] NM *Chim* perchlorate

perchlorique [pɛrklɔrik] ADJ *Chim* perchloric

perchman [pɛrʃman] NM boom (operator), boom man

perchoir [pɛrʃwar] NM **1** *(pour les oiseaux)* perch; *(pour la volaille)* roost **2** *Pol* = raised platform for the seat of the President of the French National Assembly; **obtenir le p.** to become President of the (French) National Assembly

perciforme [pɛrsiform] ADJ perciform ► NM perciform, member of the Perciformes

percipient [pɛrsipjã] NM percipient

perclus, -e [pɛrkly, -yz] ADJ crippled, paralysed; **être p. de rhumatismes** to be crippled with rheumatism; **être p. de douleur/terreur/timidité** to be paralysed with pain/fear/shyness

percnoptère [pɛrknɔptɛr] NM *Orn* **p. (d'Égypte)** Egyptian vulture

perçoir [pɛrswar] NM *(perceuse)* drill, borer; *(alêne)* awl; *(vrille)* gimlet; *(poinçon)* punch, punching machine

perçoit, perçoivent *etc voir* **percevoir**

percolateur [pɛrkɔlatœr] NM coffee (percolating) machine

percolation [pɛrkɔlasjɔ̃] NF percolation

perçu, -e [pɛrsy] PP *voir* **percevoir**

percussion [pɛrkysjɔ̃] NF *Méd, Mus & Tech* percussion; **fusil à p.** percussion gun

❑ **percussions** NFPL percussion ensemble; **aux percussions, Jack** on percussion, Jack

percussionniste [pɛrkysjɔnist] NMF percussionist

percutané, -e [pɛrkytane] ADJ *Méd* percutaneous

percutant, -e [pɛrkytɑ̃, -ɑ̃t] ADJ **1** *(qui percute)* percussion *(avant n)*; *Tech* percussive **2** *(argument, formule)* powerful, striking; *(style)* incisive; *(titre de journal)* hard-hitting; **leur slogan est p.** their slogan hits you right between the eyes

percuter [3] [pɛrkyte] VT **1** *(heurter)* to crash *or* to run into; **la moto a percuté le mur** the motorbike crashed into the wall **2** *Mil & Tech* to strike **3** *Méd* to percuss

VI **1** *Mil* to explode **2** *Fam (comprendre)* to catch on

❑ **percuter contre** VT IND **aller/venir p. contre** to crash into

perçut *etc voir* **percevoir**

percuteur [pɛrkytœr] NM **1** *Mil* firing pin, hammer **2** *Archéol* percussion tool **3** *Méd* plessor, plexor

perdable [pɛrdabl] ADJ loseable; **le match n'est plus p.** the match can't be lost now

perdant, -e [pɛrdɑ̃, -ɑ̃t] ADJ losing; **jouer un cheval p.** to bet on a losing horse; **être p.** *(gén)* to lose out; *(perdre de l'argent)* to be out of pocket; **il est p. dans cette affaire** he loses out *or* he comes out the loser in this deal; **partir p.** to start out with low expectations

NM,F loser; **être bon/mauvais p.** to be a good/bad loser

NM ebb (tide)

perditance [pɛrditɑ̃s] NF *Élec* leakage conductance, leakance

perdition [pɛrdisjɔ̃] NF *Rel* perdition

❑ **en perdition** ADJ **1** *Naut* in distress **2** *(en danger)* in trouble; **des adolescents en p.** adolescents heading for trouble *or* on the wrong path; **une entreprise en p.** a company in difficulties *or* in trouble

PERDRE [77] [pɛrdr]

> VT to lose **1–8** ▪ to waste **9** ▪ to ruin **10**
> VI to lose
> VPR to get lost **2, 3** ▪ to disappear **2, 4** ▪ to die out **5** ▪ to go to waste **6**

VT **1** *(égarer → clefs, lunettes)* to lose, to mislay

2 *(laisser tomber)* **p. de l'eau/de l'huile** to leak water/oil; **des sacs de sable qui perdaient leur contenu** sandbags spilling their contents; **la brosse perd ses poils** the brush is losing *or* shedding its bristles; **il perd son pantalon** his trousers are falling down; **tu perds des papiers/un gant!** you've dropped some papers/a glove!

3 *(laisser échapper)* to lose; **p. sa page** to lose one's page *or* place; *aussi Fig* **p. la trace de qn** to lose track of sb; *aussi Fig* **p. qn/qch de vue** to lose sight of sb/sth, to lose track of sb/sth; **ne perdons pas de vue le fait que l'inflation est de 5 pour cent** let's not lose sight of the fact that inflation is running at 5 percent; **je n'ai pas perdu un mot/une miette de leur entretien** I didn't miss a (single) word/scrap of their conversation; **ça ne sera pas perdu pour tout le monde, va!** somebody somewhere will be happy (about it)!; *Fam* **p. les pédales** *(ne plus comprendre)* to be completely lost▪ ; *(céder à la panique)* to lose one's head; *aussi Fig* **p. pied** to get out of one's depth

4 *(être privé de → bien, faculté)* to lose; **p. sa place** *(dans une réunion)* to lose one's seat; **p. sa fortune au jeu** to lose one's fortune gambling, to gamble one's fortune away; **p. son emploi** *ou* **sa situation** *ou* **sa place** to lose one's job; **n'avoir rien à p.** to have nothing to lose; **p. des/ses forces** to lose strength/one's strength; **p. la mémoire/l'appétit** to lose one's memory/appetite; **p. la parole** *(la voix)* to lose one's voice; *(dans une réunion)* to lose the floor; **p. un œil/ses dents** to lose an eye/one's teeth; **p. du sang/poids** to lose blood/weight; *Méd* **elle a perdu les eaux** her waters broke; **p. le contrôle de** to lose control of; **p. connaissance** to pass out, to faint; **p. le goût/sens de** to lose one's taste for/sense of; **p. espoir** to lose hope; **p. l'habitude de (faire)** to get out of the habit of (doing); **p. patience** to run out of *or* to lose patience; **p. (tous) ses moyens** to panic; **p. la raison** *ou* **la tête** to go mad; *Fam* **p. le nord** *ou* **la boule** to crack up, to go round the bend, *Br* to lose the plot; *Fam* **celui-là, il perd pas le nord!** he's certainly got his head screwed on!; **il en a perdu le boire et le manger** it worried him so much he lost his appetite; **j'y perds mon latin** I'm totally confused *or* baffled

5 *(avoir moins)* to lose; **la tapisserie n'a rien perdu de ses couleurs** the wallpaper has lost none of its colour; **les actions ont perdu de leur valeur** the shares have partially depreciated; **elle a beaucoup perdu de son anglais** she's forgotten a lot of her English

6 *(être délaissé par)* to lose; **tu vas p. tous tes amis si tu ne changes pas d'attitude** you'll lose all your friends if you don't change your attitude; **il a perdu toute sa clientèle** he has lost all his customers; *Fam* **un de perdu, dix de retrouvés** there's plenty more fish in the sea

7 *(par décès)* to lose; **il a perdu ses parents dans un accident** he lost his parents in an accident

8 *(contre quelqu'un)* to lose; *Sport (set)* to drop, to lose; **p. l'avantage** to lose the *or* one's advantage; **il a perdu la partie** *(dans un jeu)* he lost the game; **p. du terrain** to lose ground

9 *(gâcher → temps, argent)* to waste; **j'ai perdu ma journée** I've wasted the day; **comme ça je n'aurai pas perdu ma journée!** that way my day won't have been wasted after all!

10 *(causer la ruine de)* to ruin (the reputation of); **c'est le jeu qui le perdra** gambling will be the ruin of him *or* his downfall; *Hum* **toi, c'est le fromage qui te perdra!** you eat far too much cheese for your own good!; *Hum* **toi, c'est la curiosité qui te perdra!** you're far too inquisitive for your own good!

11 *(locution)* **tu ne perds rien pour attendre!** just (you) wait and see!

VI **1** *(dans un jeu, une compétition, une lutte etc)* to lose; **c'est le 35 qui est sorti, tu as perdu!** number 35 came up, you've lost!; **p. à la loterie/aux élections** to lose at the lottery/polls; **p. sur la marchandise** to lose on the goods; **je vous le vends 100 euros mais j'y perds** I'm selling it to you for 100 euros but I'm losing (money) on it; **p. au change** to lose out (on a deal); *Fig* to lose out; *aussi Fig* **je n'ai pas perdu au change** I've come out of it quite well; **jouer à qui perd gagne** to play (a game of) loser takes all

2 *(en qualité, psychologiquement)* to lose (out); *Fam* **on perd beaucoup en n'ayant pas la couleur** you lose a lot *or* miss out by not having colour TV; **ces vins blancs perdent à être conservés trop longtemps** these white wines don't improve with age; **on perd toujours à agir sans réfléchir** you're bound to be worse off if you act without thinking; **le récit perd en précision ce qu'il gagne en puissance d'évocation** what the story loses in accuracy, it gains in narrative power

▸**se perdre** VPR **1** *(emploi réciproque)* **se p. de vue** to lose sight of each other; **il ne faudra plus nous p. de vue** we must stay in touch from now on

2 *(emploi passif) (crayon, foulard, clef)* to get lost, to disappear; **si on ne les range pas, ces lunettes vont se p.!** these glasses will get lost if they're not put away!; *Fam* **il y a des paires de claques qui se perdent** somebody needs a good slap; *très Fam* **il y a des coups de pied au cul qui se perdent** somebody needs a good kick up the *Br* arse *or Am* ass

3 *(s'égarer → personne)* to get lost, to lose one's way; *(→ avion, bateau)* to get lost; **je me suis perdu** I got lost *or* couldn't find my way; **se p. dans le dédale des rues** to get lost in the maze of streets; **son regard se perdait dans le lointain** he/she had a faraway look in his/her eyes; **se p. dans les détails** to get bogged down in too much detail; **se p. dans ses calculs** to get one's calculations muddled up; **se p. en conjectures** to be lost in conjecture

4 *(disparaître)* to disappear, to become lost, to fade; **les sommets se perdaient dans la brume** the mountain tops were lost *or* shrouded in the mist; **ses appels se perdirent dans la foule** his/her calls were swallowed up by the crowd; **se p. dans la nuit des temps** to be lost in the mists of time

5 *(devenir désuet)* to become lost, to die out; **la coutume s'est perdue** the custom is (now) lost; **ce sont des métiers qui se perdent** these trades are dying out

6 *(nourriture, récolte → par pourrissement)* to rot; *(→ par surabondance)* to go to waste

perdreau, -x [pɛrdro] NM **1** *Orn* young partridge **2** *Fam Arg crime (policier)* cop

perdrix [pɛrdri] NF *Orn* partridge; **p. grise** grey partridge; **p. des neiges** ptarmigan; **p. rouge** red-legged partridge

perdu, -e [pɛrdy] PP *voir* **perdre**

ADJ **1** *(balle, coup)* stray; *(heure, moment)* spare; **à temps p.** in a spare moment; **fais-le à temps p.** do it if you've got a spare moment

2 *(inutilisable → emballage)* disposable, one-way; *(→ verre)* non-returnable; **comble p.** waste roof space

3 *(condamné)* lost; **sans votre intervention, j'étais un homme p.** if you hadn't intervened, I'd have been finished *or* lost

4 *Littéraire (ruiné)* **c'est un homme p. de dettes** he's heavily in debt

5 *(désespéré)* lost; **il est complètement p. depuis la mort de sa mère** he's been completely lost since his mother died

6 *(gâché → vêtement, chapeau)* ruined, spoiled; *(→ nourriture)* spoiled; **pleurant sa réputation perdue** crying for his/her lost *or* tainted reputation

7 *(de mauvaise vie)* **femme perdue** loose woman

8 *(isolé → coin, village)* lost, remote, godforsaken; **le continent p.** the lost continent

NM,F *Fam* **comme un p.** *(courir)* hell for leather; *(crier)* like a mad thing

perdurer [3] [pɛrdyre] VI to continue (on), to endure, to last

père [pɛr] NM **1** *(géniteur)* father; **le p. d'Anne** Anne's father; **tu es un p. pour moi** you're like a father to me; **devenir p.** to become a father; **p. inconnu** *(sur fiche d'état civil)* father unknown; **je suis né de p. inconnu** it's not known who my father was; **John Smith p.** John Smith senior; **Alexandre Dumas p.** Alexandre Dumas père; **maintenant que je suis p. de famille** now that I've got a family; **un p. de famille meurt noyé en laissant trois orphelins** *(titre de journal)* father of three drowns; **être bon p. de famille** to be a (good) father *or* family man; **en bon p. de famille** carefully; **c'est un investissement de p. de famille** it's a rock-solid *or* copper-bottomed investment; **p. naturel** natural father; *Théât* **jouer les pères nobles** to play elderly noblemen; **p. nourricier** foster father; *Prov* **tel p., tel fils** like father, like son; *Prov* **à p. avare, fils prodigue** = a miser's son will be a spendthrift

2 *(innovateur)* father; **le p. de la psychanalyse** the father of psychoanalysis; **p. fondateur** founding father

3 *(homme, enfant) Fam* **tu as vu ce gros p., il peut à peine se remuer** look at that tub of lard *or* fat lump, he can barely move; *Fam* **allez, mon gros p., au lit!** come on now, little fellow, off to bed!; *Fam* **mon petit p.** (my) little one *or* fellow; *Fam* **il pleure, pauvre petit p.!** he's crying, poor little thing!; **c'est un p. tranquille** he's a quiet sort; *Fam* **moi, je conduis en p. peinard** I like to drive nice and slowly; **le p. Fouettard** the Bogeyman; **le p. Durand/Dupont** old Durand/Dupont; **le p. Noël** Santa Claus, Father Christmas; **le petit p. des peuples** the little father of the people

4 *Rel* father; **le p. Lamotte** Father Lamotte; **merci, mon p.** thank you, Father; **il a fait ses études chez les pères** he was educated at a religious institution; **les Pères Blancs** the White Friars, the Carmelites; **le P. éternel** the

Heavenly Father; **le P., le Fils et le Saint-Esprit** the Father, the Son and the Holy Ghost *or* Spirit; **notre P. qui êtes aux cieux** our Father who art in Heaven

5 *Zool* sire

❏ **pères** **NMPL** *Littéraire (aïeux)* forefathers, fathers; **du temps de nos pères** in the days of our forefathers

❏ **de père en fils** **ADV ils sont menuisiers de p. en fils** they've been carpenters for generations; **cette tradition s'est transmise de p. en fils** this tradition has been handed down from father to son

pérégrin [peregrɛ̃] **NM** *Antiq* peregrine

pérégrination [peregrinasjɔ̃] **NF** peregrination; **au cours de ses pérégrinations** on *or* during his travels

Père-Lachaise [pɛrlaʃɛz] **NM le (cimetière du) P.** = the chief cemetery of Paris, where many famous people are buried

péremption [perɑ̃psjɔ̃] **NF** *Jur* lapsing; **au bout de trois ans il y a p. et vous ne pouvez plus réclamer la dette** there is a strict time limit of three years on claims after which payment may not be demanded; **p. de l'instance** = extinction of an action *(the statutory time limit having passed)*; **p. du jugement** = lapse of a judgment by default for failure to serve it within six months

péremptoire [perɑ̃ptwar] **ADJ 1** *(impérieux → ton)* peremptory; **de façon p.** peremptorily **2** *(tranchant → argument)* unanswerable

péremptoirement [perɑ̃ptwarmɑ̃] **ADV** peremptorily

pérennant, -e [perenɑ̃, -ɑ̃t] **ADJ** *Bot* perennating

pérenne [perɛn] **ADJ 1** *(durable)* perennial **2** *(source, rivière)* perennial **3** *Bot* perennating

pérennisation [perenizasjɔ̃] **NF** perpetuation

pérenniser [3] [perenize] **VT** to perpetuate

pérennité [perenite] **NF** perenniality, lasting quality

péréquation [perekwasjɔ̃] **NF** *Admin, Écon (d'impôts, de salaires)* equalization; *Rail (de tarifs)* standardizing; *Can Admin* **fonds de p.** equalization fund

perestroïka [perɛstrɔika] **NF** perestroika

perfectibilité [pɛrfɛktibilite] **NF** *Littéraire* perfectibility

perfectible [pɛrfɛktibl] **ADJ** perfectible; **l'appareil n'est plus guère p. maintenant** the machine can hardly be improved any further

perfectif, -ive [pɛrfɛktif, -iv] *Gram* **ADJ** perfective
     NM perfective aspect

perfection [pɛrfɛksjɔ̃] **NF 1** *(qualité)* perfection; **atteindre la p.** to achieve perfection **2** *(trésor)* gem, treasure; **cet ordinateur est une p.** this computer is an absolute gem

❏ **à la perfection** **ADV** to perfection, perfectly; **tout marche à la p.** things couldn't be better, everything's perfect

perfectionné, -e [pɛrfɛksjɔne] **ADJ** sophisticated

perfectionnement [pɛrfɛksjɔnmɑ̃] **NM 1** *(d'un art, d'une technique)* perfecting; **notre but est le p. de nos techniques** our aim is to perfect our techniques **2** *(d'un objet matériel)* improvement; **la vieille pompe avait besoin de quelques perfectionnements** the old pump needed to be improved somewhat **3** *(formation)* **stage/cours de p.** advanced course/classes

perfectionner [3] [pɛrfɛksjɔne] **VT 1** *(amener au plus haut niveau)* to (make) perfect; **des techniques très perfectionnées** very sophisticated techniques **2** *(améliorer)* to improve (upon); **il faudra que tu perfectionnes la présentation** you'll have to polish up *or* to improve the presentation

▸ **se perfectionner** **VPR** to improve oneself; **il s'est beaucoup perfectionné en français** his French has improved considerably; **prendre des cours de natation pour se p.** to take advanced swimming classes

perfectionnisme [pɛrfɛksjɔnism] **NM** perfectionism

perfectionniste [pɛrfɛksjɔnist] **ADJ être p.** to be a perfectionist
     NMF perfectionist

perfective [pɛrfɛktiv] *voir* **perfectif**

Perfecto® [pɛrfɛkto] **NM** biker's jacket

perfide [pɛrfid] *Littéraire* **ADJ** *(personne, conseil)*

perfidious, treacherous, faithless; **la p. Albion** perfidious Albion
     NMF traitor; **la p. a volé mon cœur** the perfidious creature has stolen my heart

perfidement [pɛrfidmɑ̃] **ADV** *Littéraire* perfidiously, treacherously

perfidie [pɛrfidi] **NF** *Littéraire* **1** *(caractère)* perfidy, treacherousness **2** *(acte)* piece of treachery, perfidy; *(parole)* perfidious *or* treacherous remark

perfluorocarbone [pɛrflyɔrɔkarbɔn] **NM** *Chim* perfluorocarbon

perfolié, -e [pɛrfɔlje] **ADJ** perfoliate

perforage [pɛrfɔraʒ] **NM 1** *Métal* piercing **2** *(du cuir)* punching **3** *Ordinat* punching **4** *Méd* perforating **5** *Mines* drilling

perforant, -e [pɛrfɔrɑ̃, -ɑ̃t] **ADJ 1** *(pointe, dispositif)* perforating **2** *(balle, obus)* armour-piercing **3** *(artère)* perforating; *(nerf)* perforans

perforateur, -trice [pɛrfɔratœr, -tris] **ADJ** perforating
     NM,F *Ordinat* punch-card operator
     NM *Méd* perforator **2** *(pour documents)* (hole) punch

❏ **perforatrice** **NF 1** *Mines* rock drill **2** *Ordinat* card punch

perforation [pɛrfɔrasjɔ̃] **NF 1** *(action)* piercing, perforating; *Ordinat* punching **2** *(trou → dans du papier, du cuir)* perforation; *(→ dans une pellicule)* sprocket hole; *Ordinat* punch (hole) **3** *Méd* perforation; **p. intestinale** perforation of the intestine

perforatrice [pɛrfɔratris] *voir* **perforateur**

perforer [3] [pɛrfɔre] **VT 1** *(percer)* to perforate **2** *(titre de transport)* & *Ordinat* to punch **3** *Méd* to perforate

perforeuse [pɛrfɔrøz] **NF** *Ordinat* card punch, (key) punch

performance [pɛrfɔrmɑ̃s] **NF 1** *(résultat)* result, performance; *Sport* **il a amélioré sa p. d'une seconde** he improved his performance by one second; **moteur haute p.** high-performance engine; **il faut améliorer les performances de notre entreprise** we must improve our company's performance; **les performances de l'année dernière sur le marché japonais** last year's results on the Japanese market

2 *(réussite)* achievement; **quelle p.!** what a feat!; **elle donne une p. éblouissante dans le rôle d'Antigone** she gives a dazzling performance in the role of Antigone

3 *Ling & Psy* performance

❏ **performances** **NFPL** *(d'ordinateur, de voiture etc)* (overall) performance

performant, -e [pɛrfɔrmɑ̃, -ɑ̃t] **ADJ** *(machine, système)* efficient; *(produit, entreprise)* competitive; *(employé)* effective; *(technicien)* first-class; *(résultats)* outstanding, impressive; *(investissement)* profitable, high-yield; **une voiture très performante** a high-performance car

performatif, -ive [pɛrfɔrmatif, -iv] **ADJ** performative
     NM performative (verb)

perfuser [3] [pɛrfyze] **VT** *Méd* to put on a drip *or Am* an IV, to perfuse

perfusion [pɛrfyzjɔ̃] **NF** *Méd* drip, perfusion, *Am* IV; **être sous p.** to be on a drip *or Am* an IV; **nourrir** *ou* **alimenter qn par p.** to drip-feed sb; **p. saline** saline drip *or Am* IV

Pergame [pɛrgam] **NM** Pergamum

pergélisol [pɛrʒelisɔl] **NM** permafrost (soil), *Spéc* pergelisol

pergola [pɛrgɔla] **NF** pergola

péri¹ [peri] **NF** *(fée, sorcière)* peri

péri², -e [peri] **ADJ** *Hér* couped

périanthaire [perjɑ̃tɛr] **ADJ** *Bot* perianthial

périanthe [perjɑ̃t] **NM** *Bot* perianth

périarthrite [periartrit] **NF** *Méd* periarthritis

périarticulaire [periartikylɛr] **ADJ** periarticular

périastre [periastr] **NM** periastron

péribole [peribɔl] **NM** *Antiq (enceinte, espace)* peribolus

péricarde [perikard] **NM** *Anat* pericardium

péricardique [perikardik] **ADJ** *Anat* pericardial

péricardite [perikardit] **NF** *Méd* pericarditis

péricarpe [perikarp] **NM** *Bot* pericarp

périchondre [perikɔ̃dr] **NM** *Anat* perichondrium

périclase [periklaz] **NM** *Chim* periclase

Périclès [periklɛs] **NPR** Pericles

péricliter [3] [periklite] **VI** to be on a downward slope, to be going downhill; **ses affaires périclitent dangereusement** his/her business is going downhill fast; **une industrie qui périclite** an industry with no future

péricrâne [perikrɑn] **NM** pericranium

péricycle [perisikl] **NM** pericycle

péridinien [peridinjɛ̃] **NM** *Zool* peridinian

péridot [perido] **NM** *Minér* peridot, chrysolite

péridotite [peridɔtit] **NF** *Minér* peridotite

péridural, -e, -aux, -ales [peridyral, -o] *Méd* **ADJ** epidural

❏ **péridurale** **NF** epidural (anaesthesia); **accoucher sous péridurale** to give birth under an epidural

périe [peri] *voir* **péri**

périf [perif] = **périph**

périgée [periʒe] **NM** perigee

périglaciaire [periglasjɛr] **ADJ** periglacial

Périgord [perigɔr] **NM le P.** Perigord

périgordien, -enne [perigɔrdjɛ̃, -ɛn] **ADJ** Perigordian
     NM Perigordian

périgourdin, -e [perigurdɛ̃, -in] **ADJ 1** *(de Périgueux)* of/from Périgueux **2** *(du Périgord)* of/from Périgord

❏ **Périgourdin, -e** **NM,F 1** *(de Périgueux)* = inhabitant of or person from Périgueux **2** *(du Périgord)* = inhabitant of or person from Périgord

périhélie [perieli] **NM** perihelion

périhépatite [periepatit] **NF** *Méd* perihepatitis

péri-informatique [periɛ̃fɔrmatik] *(pl* **péri-informatiques***)* **ADJ matériel p.** computer equipment
     NF computer environment

péril [peril] **NM 1** *(danger)* danger; **au p. de ma/leur**/*etc* **vie** at great risk to my/their/*etc* (own) life; *Littéraire* **il y a p. à juger trop hâtivement** it is dangerous to judge too hastily; *Littéraire* **se jeter dans le p.** to rush into peril; *Jur* **p. en la demeure** = state of urgency justifying a provisional execution of judgment; *Fig* **il n'y a pas p. en la demeure** it's not a matter of life and death

2 *(menace)* peril; *Péj* **le p. jaune** the yellow peril

3 *Naut* **les périls de la mer** the perils of the sea

❏ **en péril** **ADJ** *(monuments, animaux)* endangered; **être en p.** to be in danger *or* at risk; **ses jours sont en p.** his/her life is in danger **ADV mettre en p.** to endanger, to put at risk

périlleuse [perijøz] *voir* **périlleux**

périlleusement [perijøzmɑ̃] **ADV** perilously, dangerously

périlleux, -euse [perijø, -øz] **ADJ** perilous, hazardous, dangerous

périlune [perilyn] **NM** *Astron* perilune

périmé, -e [perime] **ADJ 1** *(expiré)* out-of-date; **mon passeport est p.** my passport is no longer valid *or* has expired **2** *(aliment)* past its sell-by date **3** *(démodé)* outdated, outmoded; **vous défendez des principes périmés** you're defending outdated principles

périmer [3] [perime] **se périmer** **VPR 1** *(expirer)* to expire; **laisser (se) p. un billet** to let a ticket go out of date; **laisser p. de la nourriture** to let food go off *or* bad **2** *Jur* to lapse **3** *(se démoder)* to become outdated *or* outmoded

périmètre [perimɛtr] **NM 1** *(contour)* & *Géom* perimeter; *(surface)* area; **des recherches ont été entreprises dans un vaste p.** searches were conducted over a vast area; **dans un p. de 50 kilomètres** within a 50-kilometre radius; **dans le p. de la centrale** on the premises of the power station; **p. de sécurité** safety zone **2** *Jur* **p. sensible** ≃ green belt

périnatal, -e, -als *ou* **-aux, -ales** [perinatal, -o] **ADJ** *Méd* perinatal

périnatalité [perinatalite] **NF** *Méd* perinatal period

périnatalogie [perinatalɔʒi] **NF** *Méd* perinatal paediatrics

périnéal, -e, -aux, -ales [perineal, -o] **ADJ** *Anat* perineal

périnée [perine] **NM** *Anat* perineum

périnéorraphie [perineɔrafi] **NF** *Méd* perineorrhaphy

périnéphrite [perinefrit] **NF** *Méd* perinephritis

période [perjɔd] **NF 1** *(époque)* period, time; **traverser une p. difficile** to go through a difficult period *or* time; **une longue p. de beau temps** a

long spell of fine weather; **la p. bleue de Picasso** Picasso's blue period; **c'était ma p. macramé** it was the time when I was keen on macramé; **elle a eu sa p. jazz** she went through a jazz period or phase; **nous avons eu une longue p. de froid** we had a long spell of cold weather; **pendant la p. électorale** during election time; **pendant la p. des fêtes** at Christmas time; **dans la p. allant de début juin à fin septembre** between the beginning of June and the end of September; Fin **p. d'amortissement** depreciation period; Fin **p. comptable** financial period, accounting period, Am fiscal period; Bourse **p. de cotation obligatoire** mandatory quote period; UE **p. de double circulation** (de la monnaie nationale et de l'euro) double circulation period; **p. d'essai** trial period; **p. d'essai gratuit** free trial period; **p. d'essor** boom; **p. de grâce** tax holiday; Jur **p. d'observation** period of observation; **p. de réflexion** cooling-off period; Jur **p. de sûreté** tariff (of imprisonment); Jur **p. suspecte** = period between functional insolvency and declaration of bankruptcy

2 Mil **p. (d'exercice)** training

3 Phys, Chim & Mus period; Math (d'une fonction) period; (d'une fraction) repetend; **p. de révolution** period of revolution; **p. (radioactive)** half-life

4 Transp **p. bleue/blanche/rouge** = period during which tickets are cheapest/medium-priced/most expensive

5 Gram period, complete sentence

NM Littéraire **le plus haut p. (de la gloire/de l'éloquence)** the height or acme (of glory/of eloquence); **le plus haut p. de son influence** the zenith of his influence

❏ **périodes** NFPL Vieilli (règles) period(s); **avoir ses périodes** to be having one's period

❏ **par périodes** ADV from time to time, every now and then, every so often; **c'est par périodes** it comes and goes; **ça le prend par périodes** it comes over him from time to time

périodicité [perjɔdisite] NF frequency

périodique [perjɔdik] ADJ **1** Chim, Phys, Psy & Mus periodic; Math (fonction) periodic; (fraction) recurring **2** (publication) periodical **3** Méd recurring

NM periodical

périodiquement [perjɔdikmɑ̃] ADV **1** Chim, Math & Phys periodically **2** (régulièrement) periodically, every so often; **les douleurs reviennent p.** the pain recurs periodically

péricœsophagien, -enne [periøzɔfaʒjɛ̃, -ɛn] ADJ peri(o)esophageal

périoste [perjɔst] NM Anat periosteum

périostite [perjɔstit] NF Méd periostitis

péripate [peripat] NM Zool peripatus

péripatéticien, -enne [peripatetisjɛ̃, -ɛn] ADJ Antiq Peripatetic

NM,F Antiq Peripatetic, member of the Peripatetic school

❏ **péripatéticienne** NF Littéraire ou Hum streetwalker

péripatétisme [peripatetism] NM peripateticism

péripétie [peripesi] NF **1** (événement) event, episode; (aventure) adventure; **une vie pleine/un voyage plein de péripéties** an eventful life/trip, a life/trip rich in incident; **après bien des péripéties, ils sont arrivés à destination** after many adventures, they finally managed to get there **2** Littérature peripeteia

périph [perif] NM Fam (abrév **boulevard périphérique**) **le p.** the Paris Br ring road or Am beltway▪

périphérie [periferi] NF **1** (bord) periphery; **sur la p. de la plaie** on the edges of the wound; **jaune au milieu et orangé à la p.** yellow in the middle and orange round the edge **2** (faubourg) outskirts; **à la p. des grandes villes** on the outskirts of cities

périphérique [periferik] ADJ **1** (quartier) outlying **2** Physiol & Ordinat peripheral

NM **1** (boulevard) Br ring road, Am beltway; **le p.** (à Paris) the Paris Br ring road or Am beltway **2** Ordinat peripheral (device); **p. d'entrée/de sortie** input/output device; **p. externe** external device

périphlébite [periflebit] NF periphlebitis

périphrase [perifraz] NF circumlocution, Spéc periphrasis

périphrastique [perifrastik] ADJ circumlocutory, Spéc periphrastic

périple [peripl] NM **1** (voyage d'exploration) voyage, expedition; **son dernier p. dans l'Antarctique** his/her latest expedition to the Antarctic **2** (voyage touristique) tour, trip; **faire un (long) p.** to go on a (long) tour **3** Littéraire (durée de la vie) life, lifetime

périptère [periptɛr] Archit ADJ peripteral

NM peripteros, periptery

périr [32] [perir] VI Littéraire **1** (personne) to perish; **péri en mer** lost at sea; **p. noyé** to drown, to be drowned; Fig **p. d'ennui** to die of boredom; **s'ennuyer à p.** to be bored to death **2** (souvenir) to perish; (idéal, gloire, liberté) to be destroyed, to perish; **son nom ne périra pas** his/her name will live (on)

périscolaire [periskɔlɛr] ADJ extracurricular

périscope [periskɔp] NM periscope

périscopique [periskɔpik] ADJ periscopic

périsélène [periselɛn] NM Astron perilune

périsperme [perispɛrm] NM perisperm

périssabilité [perisabilite] NF perishability

périssable [perisabl] ADJ perishable

périssodactyle [perisɔdaktil] Zool ADJ perissodactyl(ous), perissodactylate

NM perissodactyl

❏ **périssodactyles** NMPL Perissodactyla

périssoire [periswar] NF canoe

périssologie [perisɔlɔʒi] NF Ling pleonasm

péristaltique [peristaltik] ADJ Physiol peristaltic

péristaltisme [peristaltism] NM Physiol peristalsis

péristome [peristom] NM Bot & Zool peristome

péristyle [peristil] NM peristyle

Péritel® [peritɛl] ADJ INV prise P. scart plug; (qui reçoit) scart socket

péritéléphonie [peritelefɔni] NF Tech peripheral telephone equipment

péritélévision [peritelevizjɔ̃] NF TV video and computer technology

péritendinite [peritɑ̃dinit] NF Méd peritendinitis

périthèce [peritɛs] NM Bot perithecium

péritoine [peritwan] NM Anat peritoneum

péritonéal, -e, -aux, -ales [peritɔneal, -o] ADJ Anat peritoneal

péritonite [peritɔnit] NF Méd peritonitis

périityphlite [peritiflit] NF Méd perityphlitis

périurbain, -e [periyrbɛ̃, -ɛn] ADJ out-of-town

périvasculaire [perivaskylɛr] ADJ Anat perivascular

perlant, -e [pɛrlɑ̃, -ɑ̃t] ADJ slightly sparkling

NM slightly sparkling wine

perle [pɛrl] NF **1** (bijou) pearl; **p. fine/de culture** natural/cultured pearl; **p. noire** black pearl; **c'est la p. de ma collection** it's the prize piece of my collection; Fig **jeter des perles aux pourceaux** to cast pearls before swine

2 (bille) bead; **perles de verre** glass beads

3 (goutte) drop; **des perles de sueur** beads of sweat; **des perles de rosée** dewdrops; **une p. de sang** a drop of blood

4 (personne) gem, treasure; **sa femme est une p.!** his wife is a real gem!; **c'est la p. des maris!** he's the perfect husband!

5 Fam (bêtise) howler

6 Entom Perla (stonefly)

7 très Fam (pet) fart; **lâcher une p.** to fart

8 Can (prunelle) pupil (of the eye); **il tient à cette montre comme à la p. de ses yeux** he treasures that watch

ADJ INV pearl, pearl-grey

perlé, -e [pɛrle] ADJ **1** (nacré) pearly, pearl (avant n); **des dents perlées** pearl or pearly teeth **2** (orné de perles) beaded; **coton p.** (mercerisé) pearl or perlé cotton **3** (orge) pearl (avant n); (riz) polished **4** (rire, son) rippling **5** Zool pearl

perlèche [pɛrlɛʃ] NF perleche

perler [3] [pɛrle] VI to bead; **la sueur perlait sur son visage** beads of sweat stood out on his face

VT Vieilli (travail) to execute perfectly

perlier, -ère [pɛrlje, -ɛr] ADJ (barque) pearling; (industrie) pearl (avant n)

perlimpinpin [pɛrlɛ̃pɛ̃pɛ̃] NM voir poudre

perlingual, -e, -aux, -ales [pɛrlɛ̃gwal, -o] ADJ perlingual; **à prendre par voie perlinguale** (dans mode d'emploi) to be dissolved under the tongue

perlite [pɛrlit] NF Métal pearlite

perlon [pɛrlɔ̃] NM Ich seven gills

perlot¹ [pɛrlo] NM Zool = variety of small oyster found on the Channel coast

perlot² [pɛrlo] NM Fam Vieilli (tabac) baccy

perlouse, perlouze [pɛrluz] NF **1** Fam (perle) pearl▪ **2** Vulg (pet) fart; **lâcher une p.** to fart, Br to let off, Am to lay one

perm [pɛrm] NF Fam **1** Mil (abrév **permission**) leave▪; **être en p.** to be on leave **2** Scol (abrév **permanence**) (tranche horaire) study period▪; (salle) study Br room or Am hall▪; **aller en p.** to go to the study Br room or Am hall

permafrost [pɛrmafrɔst], **permagel** [pɛrmaʒɛl] NM permafrost, pergelisol

permanence [pɛrmanɑ̃s] NF **1** (persistance → gén) permanence, lasting quality; (→ d'une tradition) continuity

2 (service de garde) duty (period); **être de p.** to be on duty or call; **une p. est assurée à la mairie le mardi matin** council offices are open on Tuesday mornings; **le professeur d'anglais assure une p. tous les mercredis entre 15 heures et 16 heures** the English teacher is available to see students every Wednesday between 3 p.m. and 4 p.m.; **p. téléphonique** answering service

3 (local, bureau) office

4 Scol study Br room or Am hall; **aller en p.** to go to the study Br room or Am hall; **avoir deux heures de p.** to have a two-hour study period

❏ **en permanence** ADV permanently; **il est soûl en p.** he's permanently drunk; **elle me harcèle en p.** she's forever harassing me

permanencier, -ère [pɛrmanɑ̃sje, -ɛr] NM,F person on duty

permanent, -e [pɛrmanɑ̃, -ɑ̃t] ADJ **1** (constant) permanent; **subir une tension permanente** to suffer permanent tension; **avec elle, ce sont des reproches permanents** she's forever nagging

2 (fixe) permanent; **avoir un emploi p.** to have a permanent job; **armée permanente** standing army

3 Cin continuous, non-stop; **c'est le spectacle p. avec lui!** there's never a dull moment with him!; **cinéma p.** continuous showing; **(cinéma) p. de 14 heures à 22 heures** continuous showing from 2 p.m. to 10 p.m.

4 Ordinat permanent

NM,F (d'un parti) official; (d'une entreprise) salaried worker, worker on the payroll

❏ **permanente** NF perm; **se faire faire une permanente** to have a perm, to have one's hair permed

permanenté, -e [pɛrmanɑ̃te] ADJ (cheveux) permed

permanenter [3] [pɛrmanɑ̃te] VT to perm; **se faire p.** to have a perm, to have one's hair permed

permanganate [pɛrmɑ̃ganat] NM Chim permanganate

permanganique [pɛrmɑ̃ganik] ADJ Chim permanganic

perme [pɛrm] NF Fam Mil (abrév **permission**) leave▪; **être en p.** to be on leave

perméabilité [pɛrmeabilite] NF **1** Géol & Phys permeability **2** (d'une personne) susceptibility (à to)

perméable [pɛrmeabl] ADJ **1** Géol & Phys permeable (à to) **2** (personne) susceptible (à to)

PERMETTRE [84] [pɛrmɛtr] VT **1** (sujet: personne) to allow; (sujet: chose) to allow, to permit, to enable; **je ne permettrai aucun écart de conduite** I won't stand for or allow any misconduct; **p. à qn de faire qch, p. que qn fasse qch** to allow sb to do sth, to let sb do sth; **je ne vous permets pas de me parler sur ce ton** I won't have you speak to me in that tone of voice; **je ne te permets plus ce genre de commentaire** I won't take that sort of remark from you again; **il ne permettra pas qu'on insulte son frère** he won't allow his brother to be insulted; **le règlement permet de sortir à 5 heures** the regulations allow you to leave at 5; **mon régime ne me permet aucune viande** I'm on a meat-free diet; **le train à grande vitesse permettra d'y aller en moins de deux heures** the high-speed train will make it possible to get there in under two hours; **sa lettre permet toutes les craintes** his/her letter gives cause for concern; **ce document**

permet d'entrer dans le secteur turc this document enables *or* entitles you to enter the Turkish sector; **votre mission ne permet pas d'erreur** your mission leaves no room for error; **si le temps/sa santé le permet** weather/(his/her) health permitting

2 *(tournure impersonnelle)* **c'est permis?** is it allowed *or* permitted?; **il n'est pas/il est permis de boire de l'alcool** drinking is not/is allowed *or* permitted; **il est permis de ne pas aimer ce genre de poésie** one may *or* might well not like this type of poetry; **autant qu'il est permis d'en juger** as far as it is possible to judge; **est-il permis d'être aussi mal élevé?** how can anyone be so rude?; *Fam* **elle est belle/insolente comme c'est pas permis** she's outrageously beautiful/cheeky; **un tel mauvais goût, ça devrait pas être** *ou Fam* **c'est pas permis** there should be a law against such bad taste

3 *(dans des formules de politesse)* **il reste un sandwich, vous permettez?** may I have the last sandwich?; **si vous me permettez l'expression** if I may be allowed to say so, if you don't mind my saying; **permettez-moi de ne pas partager votre avis** I beg to differ; **tu n'es pas sincère non plus, permets-moi de te le dire** and you're not being honest either, let me tell you; *Fam* **non, mais tu permets que j'en place une?** I'd like to get a word in, if you don't mind; **ah permettez, j'étais là avant vous!** do you mind, I was there before you!; *Littéraire* **permettez-moi de vous présenter mon frère** let me introduce *or* allow me to introduce my brother

▶**se permettre VPR 1** *(s'accorder)* to allow *or* to permit oneself; **je me suis permis un petit verre de vin** I allowed myself a small glass of wine

2 *(oser)* to dare; **il se permet de petites entorses au règlement** he's not averse to bending the rules now and then; **elle se permettait n'importe quoi** she thought she could get away with anything; *Ironique* **des critiques, oh mais je ne me permettrais pas!** criticize? I wouldn't dare!; **si je peux me p., je ne pense pas que ce soit une bonne idée** if you don't mind my saying so, I don't think it's a very good idea

3 *(pouvoir payer)* to (be able to) afford; **pouvez-vous vous p. 1000 euros de plus?** can you afford 1,000 euros more?; **je ne peux pas me p. une bague à ce prix-là** I can't afford a ring at that price

4 se p. de faire qch to take the liberty of doing sth; **je me suis permis de vous apporter des fleurs** I took the liberty of bringing you some flowers; **puis-je me p. de vous rappeler mon nom/nos accords signés?** may I remind you of my name/our binding agreements?; **je me permets de vous écrire au sujet de mon fils** I'm writing to you about my son

---

permien, -enne [pɛrmjɛ̃, -ɛn] *Géol* **ADJ** Permian
NM Permian

permis[1] [pɛrmi] **NM** permit, licence; **vous avez un p. pour ce fusil?** do you have a licence for that gun?; **p. (de conduire)** *Br* driving licence, *Am* driver's license; **rater/réussir le p. (de conduire)** to fail/to pass one's (driving) test; **p. de conduire international** international driving licence; **p. à points** = driving licence with a penalty points system, introduced in France in 1992; **p. de construire** building permit *or* licence, *Br* planning permission; **p. de chasse** *(à courre)* hunting permit; *(au fusil)* shooting licence; **p. de débarquement** landing permit; **p. de douane** customs permit; **p. d'embarquement** shipping note; **p. d'exportation** export permit *or* licence; **p. d'inhumer** burial certificate; **p. de port d'armes** firearms licence; **p. de séjour/travail** residence/work permit

permis[2], **-e** [pɛrmi, -iz] **PP** *voir* **permettre**

permissif, -ive [pɛrmisif, -iv] **ADJ** permissive

permission [pɛrmisjɔ̃] **NF 1** *(autorisation)* permission, leave; **demander/accorder la p. de faire qch** to ask/to grant permission to do sth; **si tu veux inviter tes amis, tu as ma p.** you have my permission to invite your friends; **les enfants n'ont la p. de sortir qu'accompagnés** the children don't have permission *or* aren't allowed to go out unaccompanied; **avec votre p., je vais aller me coucher** if you don't mind, I'll go to bed; **sans demander la p.** without asking permission, without so much as a by-your-leave; **j'ai la p. de minuit** I'm allowed to stay out until midnight

2 *Mil (congé)* leave, furlough; *(certificat)* pass; **être en p.** to be on leave *or* furlough; **avoir une p. de six jours** to have six days' leave; **p. à terre** shore leave; **avoir la p. de minuit** to have a late pass; *Jur* **p. de sortir** *(de prison)* permission to leave

permissionnaire [pɛrmisjɔnɛr] **NM** man on leave *or* furlough

permissive [pɛrmisiv] *voir* **permissif**

permissivité [pɛrmisivite] **NF** permissiveness

permit *etc voir* **permettre**

permittivité [pɛrmitivite] **NF** permittivity

permsélectif, -ive [pɛrmselɛktif, -iv] **ADJ** *Chim* permselective

permutabilité [pɛrmytabilite] **NF** permutability, interchangeability

permutable [pɛrmytabl] **ADJ 1** *(interchangeable)* interchangeable **2** *Math* permutable

permutant, -e [pɛrmytɑ̃, -ɑ̃t] **NM,F** exchanger, = one who exchanges (posts etc) with someone; **fonctionnaire cherchant un p.** civil servant seeking an exchange

permutation [pɛrmytasjɔ̃] **NF 1** *(transposition → gén)* permutation; *(→ de postes)* exchange of posts; *Aut* **p. des roues** wheel interchange **2** *Math* permutation

permuter [3] [pɛrmyte] **VT 1** *(intervertir → gén)* to switch round, to permutate; *(→ lettres, chiffres)* to switch round **2** *Math* to permute
VI *(changer de place, de poste)* **les deux équipes permutent** the two teams swap shifts; **p. avec** to swap with; **je vois mal, alors j'ai permuté avec une fille du premier rang** my eyesight's poor, so I swapped places with a girl in the front row

pernicieuse [pɛrnisjøz] *voir* **pernicieux**

pernicieusement [pɛrnisjøzmɑ̃] **ADV** perniciously

pernicieux, -euse [pɛrnisjø, -øz] **ADJ 1** *(néfaste)* noxious, injurious, *Sout* pernicious; **l'abus d'alcool est p. pour la santé** excessive drinking is injurious *or* harmful to one's health; **des insinuations pernicieuses** insidious suggestions **2** *Méd* pernicious

péroné [perɔne] **NM** fibula

péronier, -ère [perɔnje, -ɛr] **ADJ** peroneal
NM peroneal muscle

péronisme [perɔnism] **NM** Peronism

péroniste [perɔnist] **ADJ** Peronist
NMF Peronist

péronnelle [perɔnɛl] **NF** scatterbrain

péronosporale [perɔnɔspɔral] *Bot* **NF** member of the Peronospora
▫ **péronosporales NFPL** Peronospora

péroraison [perɔrɛzɔ̃] **NF** *(conclusion)* peroration; **après toute une p. sur notre retard, elle en est venue au fait** *(discours)* after a long tirade about our being late, she came to the point

pérorer [3] [perɔre] **VI** *Péj (discourir)* to hold forth; **il peut p. devant un public pendant des heures** he can go on and on for hours in front of an audience

péroreur, -euse [perɔrœr, -øz] **NM,F** *Péj* speechifier

per os [pɛrɔs] **ADV** *Méd* orally

Pérou [peru] **NM le P.** Peru; **vivre au P.** to live in Peru; **aller au P.** to go to Peru; *Fam* **c'est pas le P.** it won't break the bank

Pérouse [peruz] **NM** Perugia

peroxydase [pɛrɔksidaz] **NF** *Biol & Chim* peroxidase

peroxydation [pɛrɔksidasjɔ̃] **NF** *Chim* peroxidation

peroxyde [pɛrɔksid] **NM** *Chim* peroxide

peroxyder [3] [pɛrɔkside] **VT** *Chim* to peroxidize

perpendiculaire [pɛrpɑ̃dikylɛr] **ADJ 1** *(gén) & Math* perpendicular (**à** to) **2** *Archit* perpendicular
NF perpendicular; **tirer une p.** to drop *or* draw a perpendicular

perpendiculairement [pɛrpɑ̃dikylɛrmɑ̃] **ADV** perpendicularly; **p. à la rue** at right angles *or* perpendicular to the street

perpendicularité [pɛrpɑ̃dikylarite] **NF** perpendicularity

perpète [pɛrpɛt] **NF** *Fam Arg crime* **il a pris p.** he got life
▫ **à perpète ADV** *Fam* **1** *(loin → habiter)* miles away, in the back of beyond; **il m'a envoyée à p.** he sent me miles away **2** *(très longtemps)* **jusqu'à p.** till Doomsday, forever **3** *(à vie)* **être condamné à p.** to get life

perpétration [pɛrpetrasjɔ̃] **NF** perpetration

perpétrer [18] [pɛrpetre] **VT** to commit, *Sout* to perpetrate

perpette [pɛrpɛt] = **perpète**

perpétuation [pɛrpetɥasjɔ̃] **NF** perpetuation

perpétuel, -elle [pɛrpetɥɛl] **ADJ 1** *(éternel)* perpetual, everlasting; **le chevalier jurait à sa belle un p. amour** the knight pledged everlasting love to his beloved; **être condamné à la prison perpétuelle** to be sentenced to life imprisonment; **un monde en p. devenir** a perpetually *or* an ever-changing world

2 *(constant)* perpetual, constant, never-ending; **de perpétuels reproches** perpetual *or* constant reproaches; **le malade a une perpétuelle envie de vomir** the patient is permanently nauseous

3 *(à vie → secrétaire, membre)* permanent

perpétuellement [pɛrpetɥɛlmɑ̃] **ADV** forever, constantly, perpetually; **il a p. soif** he's forever *or* permanently thirsty; **j'avais p. l'impression que...** I was constantly under the impression that...

perpétuer [7] [pɛrpetɥe] **VT 1** *(tradition, préjugé)* to carry on **2** *(souvenir)* to perpetuate, to pass on

▶**se perpétuer VPR 1** *(personne)* to perpetuate one's name; **se p. dans sa musique** to live on through *or* in one's music **2** *(tradition)* to live on; **certains rites se sont perpétués de père en fils** some rites have been handed down from father to son

perpétuité [pɛrpetɥite] **NF** *Littéraire* perpetuity; **la p. de l'espèce** the continuation of the species; **la p. des souvenirs que l'on laisse** the enduring memories one leaves behind
▫ **à perpétuité ADJ 1** *(condamnation)* life *(avant n)* **2** *(concession)* in perpetuity **ADV être condamné à p.** to be sentenced to life imprisonment

perplexe [pɛrplɛks] **ADJ** perplexed, puzzled; **avoir l'air p.** to look puzzled; **laisser p.** to perplex, to puzzle; **sa remarque m'a laissé p.** his/her remark perplexed *or* puzzled me; **rendre p.** to bewilder; **je restai p., ne sachant que faire** I was in a quandary about what to do

perplexité [pɛrplɛksite] **NF** confusion, perplexity, puzzlement; **la p. se lisait sur son visage** you could see that he/she was confused; **être dans une profonde p.** to be in a state of great confusion; **être plongé dans la p.** to be perplexed *or* puzzled; **l'incohérence de son récit nous a plongés dans la p.** the incoherence of his/her story perplexed *or* puzzled us

perquisition [pɛrkizisjɔ̃] **NF** search; **procéder à** *ou* **faire une p. chez qn** to carry out *or* to make a search of sb's home; **p. domiciliaire** house search

perquisitionner [3] [pɛrkizisjɔne] **VI** *Jur* to carry out a search, to conduct a search; **p. chez** *ou* **au domicile de qn** to search sb's home, to carry out *or* to conduct a search of sb's home
VT *Jur* to search

perré [pere] **NM** *Constr (d'une route, d'une digue)* stone pitching *or* facing

perrière [pɛrjɛr] **NF** *Hist* mangonel, perrier

perron [perɔ̃] **NM** steps *(outside a building)*; **sur le p. de l'Élysée** on the (front) steps of the Élysée palace

perroquet [perɔkɛ] **NM 1** *Orn* parrot; **apprendre/répéter qch comme un p.** to learn/to repeat sth parrot-fashion; **répéter comme un p. ce que dit qn** to parrot what sb says; *Ich* **p. de mer** parrot fish **2** *Naut* topgallant (sail) **3** *(boisson)* pastis and mint cocktail

perruche [peryʃ] **NF 1** *Orn* parakeet; **p. (ondulée)** budgerigar **2** *Fam (personne)* chatterbox **3** *Naut* mizzen topgallant sail

perruque [peryk] **NF 1** *(postiche)* wig; *Hist* periwig, peruke; *Fig Péj* **la justice à p.** fuddy-duddy

per-per

old judges **2** *Pêche* tangled line **3** *Fam (travail clandestin)* **faire de la p.** to work on the side■ *(during office hours)*

perruquier [perykje] **NM** wigmaker

pers, -e[1] [pɛr, pɛrs] **ADJ** *Littéraire* sea-green, perse

persan, -e [pɛrsɑ̃, -an] **ADJ** Persian

NM 1 *(langue)* Persian **2** *Zool* Persian cat

❑ **Persan, -e NM,F** Persian

Allusion

Comment peut-on être persan?

This expression means literally "How can one be Persian?" Montesquieu's *Lettres persanes* of 1721 poked fun at the French society of his day by presenting it through the eyes of a Persian visitor writing home with his impressions. At the time, nothing could have seemed more exotic than a Persian complete with turban and baggy trousers. At one point, the hero is quizzed by a Parisian: "Aha! So you are Persian, Sir! Amazing! And how exactly is one Persian?" This emphasizes the ignorance of the supposedly more civilized party. Today the expression is often varied, for example substituting **anglais** or **communiste**, but always with the intent of showing the limitations and bigotry of the speaker.

Perse [pɛrs] **NF la P.** Persia

perse[2] [pɛrs] **ADJ** Persian; **l'Empire p.** the Persian Empire

NM *(langue)* Persian; **moyen/vieux p.** Middle/Old Persian

NF *(tissu)* chintz

❑ **Perse NMF** Persian

persécuté, -e [pɛrsekyte] **ADJ** persecuted

NM,F 1 *(opprimé)* persecuted person; **les persécutés** the downtrodden, the persecuted **2** *Psy* persecution maniac

persécuter [3] [pɛrsekyte] **VT 1** *(opprimer)* to persecute **2** *(harceler)* to torment; **tu vas arrêter de p. ta petite sœur?** will you stop bullying *or* tormenting your little sister?; **se sentir persécuté** to feel persecuted

persécuteur, -trice [pɛrsekytœr, -tris] **ADJ** tormenting, *Sout* persecutory

NM,F persecutor; **ses persécuteurs** his/her tormentors

persécution [pɛrsekysjɔ̃] **NF 1** *(oppression)* persecution; **être victime d'une p. religieuse** to suffer religious persecution **2** *(harcèlement)* harassment, harassing, tormenting **3** *Psy* **délire de p.** persecution complex; **manie de p.** persecution mania

persécutrice [pɛrsekytris] *voir* **persécuteur**

Persée [pɛrse] **NPR** *Myth* Perseus

perséides [pɛrseid] **NFPL** *Astron* Perseids

persel [pɛrsɛl] **NM** *Chim* persalt, peroxy salt

Perséphone [pɛrsefɔn] **NPR** *Myth* Persephone

Persépolis [pɛrsepɔlis] **NM** Persepolis

persévérance [pɛrseverɑ̃s] **NF** perseverance, persistence, tenacity; **avec p.** doggedly; **travailler avec p.** to persevere in one's work, to work steadily

persévérant, -e [pɛrseverɑ̃, -ɑ̃t] **ADJ** persevering, persistent, tenacious; **être p. (dans qch)** to be persevering *or* to persevere (in sth)

persévération [pɛrseverasjɔ̃] **NF** perseveration

persévérer [18] [pɛrsevere] **VI** to persevere, to persist; **p. dans qch** to continue *or* to carry on doing sth; **si vous persévérez dans cette attitude de refus** if you continue with *or* keep up this negative attitude; **p. dans l'effort** to sustain one's effort; **persévère!** don't give up!, persevere!; *Littéraire* **p. à faire qch** to persevere in doing sth

Pershing [pɛrʃiŋ] **NPR** Pershing

persicaire [pɛrsikɛr] **NF** *Bot* persicaria, lady's thumb

persicot [pɛrsiko] **NM** *(liqueur)* persico, persicot, = liqueur flavoured with peach kernels

persienne [pɛrsjɛn] **NF** shutter, Persian blind

persiflage [pɛrsiflaʒ] **NM 1** *(attitude)* scoffing, jeering, mocking **2** *(propos)* taunts, scoffs, jeers

persifler [3] [pɛrsifle] **VT** *Littéraire* to scoff at, to jeer at, to deride

persifleur, -euse [pɛrsiflœr, -øz] **ADJ** *(moqueur)* scoffing, jeering, mocking

NM,F scoffer, mocker, derider

persil [pɛrsi] **NM** parsley; **faux p.** fool's parsley

persillade [pɛrsijad] **NF** = sauce made from chopped parsley and garlic; **p. de bœuf** cold beef sautéd with "persillade"

persillé, -e [pɛrsije] **ADJ 1** *(plat)* sprinkled with parsley **2** *(viande)* marbled **3 fromage p., fromage à pâte persillée** blue-veined cheese

persillère [pɛrsijɛr] **NF** parsley pot

Persique [pɛrsik] **ADJ le golfe P.** the Persian Gulf

persique [pɛrsik] **ADJ** *(de l'ancienne Perse)* (Ancient) Persian

persistance [pɛrsistɑ̃s] **NF 1** *(d'un phénomène)* persistence; **p. du mauvais temps sur tout le territoire demain** bad weather will continue in all areas tomorrow; **p. rétinienne** persistence of vision

2 *(de quelqu'un → dans le travail)* persistence, perseverance, tenacity; *(→ dans le refus)* obstinacy, stubbornness, *Sout* obdurateness; **sa p. dans le mensonge** his/her persistent lying; **je ne comprends pas sa p. à vouloir partir ce soir** I don't understand why he/she persists in wanting to leave tonight

❑ **avec persistance ADV** *(courageusement)* persistently, tenaciously, indefatigably; *(obstinément)* obstinately, stubbornly, *Sout* obdurately

persistant, -e [pɛrsistɑ̃, -ɑ̃t] **ADJ 1** *(tenace)* persistent, lasting, enduring; **une odeur persistante** a persistent *or* lingering smell **2** *Bot* evergreen; **arbre à feuilles persistantes** evergreen (tree)

persister [3] [pɛrsiste] **VI 1** *(durer)* to last, to continue, to persist; **la chaleur persistera demain** it will continue hot for another day; **il persiste un doute/une interrogation** there remains a doubt/question; **les doutes qui pouvaient encore p.** any lingering doubts

2 *(s'obstiner)* to persist; **il faut p.** you must persevere, you must keep at it; **p. à faire qch** to persist in doing sth; **pourquoi persistes-tu à lui faire faire du grec?** why do you persist in making him/her learn Greek?; **je persiste à croire que tu avais tort** I still think you were wrong; **malgré tout ce qui s'est passé, il persiste dans l'erreur** despite everything that's happened, he keeps on making the same mistake; **p. dans sa décision/son choix** to stick to one's decision/choice

3 *Jur* **persiste et signe** I certify the truth of the above; *Hum* **je persiste et signe!** I'm sticking to my guns!

perso [pɛrso] *Fam* **ADJ** *(abrév* **personnel***)* personal■, private■

ADV *(abrév* **personnellement***)* **il joue trop p.** he hogs the ball too much

persona grata [pɛrsɔnagrata] **ADJ INV** persona grata; **je ne suis plus p.** I'm now persona non grata

personale [pɛrsɔnal] **NF** personate flower

persona non grata [pɛrsɔnanɔngrata] **ADJ INV** persona non grata; **il est p.** he's persona non grata, *Fam* his name is mud

personé, -e [pɛrsɔne] **ADJ** *Bot* personate

personnage [pɛrsɔnaʒ] **NM 1** *(de fiction)* character; *(dans un tableau)* figure; **un p. de roman/de théâtre** a character in a novel/in a play; **un p. de bande dessinée** a cartoon character; *Théât & Fig* **les personnages du drame** the dramatis personae; **jouer un p.** *Cin & Théât* to play *or* to act a part; *Fig* to act a part, to put on an act; **elle a refusé de signer? c'est bien dans son p.!** so she wouldn't sign? that's typical of her!; **p. principal** main *or* leading character; **personnages secondaires** *Littérature* minor *or* secondary characters; *Cin, Théât & Fig* supporting roles

2 *(individu)* character, individual; **sinistre p.** evil customer; **grossier p.!** swine!; **curieux p. que ce juge au cœur tendre** this soft-hearted judge cuts an odd figure

3 *(personnalité importante)* person of note, important figure, big name; **p. connu** *ou* **célèbre** celebrity; **grands personnages de l'État** state dignitaries; **les grands personnages de l'histoire** the great names of history; **c'est qu'elle se prend pour un p.!** my, she doesn't half fancy herself (as a big shot)!; **c'est devenu un p.** he's become an important person *or Fam* a big shot

4 *(personne remarquable)* character; **ce Frédéric, c'est un p.!** that Frédéric's quite a character!

5 *(image publique)* (public) image, persona; **il s'est construit un p.** he's created an image for himself

personnalisation [pɛrsɔnalizasjɔ̃] **NF** personalization; **la p. d'une tenue** giving an outfit a personal touch; **p. d'un crédit** tailoring of a credit arrangement

personnaliser [3] [pɛrsɔnalize] **VT** *(papier à lettres)* to personalize; *(voiture, crédit)* to customize; **p. qch** *(retraite, contrat)* to tailor sth to personal requirements; **nous devons p. l'accueil** we must welcome our guests/clients/*etc* in a more personal manner; **comment p. votre cuisine** how to give your kitchen a personal touch

personnalisme [pɛrsɔnalism] **NM** *Phil* personalism

personnaliste [pɛrsɔnalist] *Phil* **ADJ** personalist

NMF personalist

personnalité [pɛrsɔnalite] **NF 1** *(caractère → d'une personne)* personality, character; *(→ d'une maison, d'une pièce etc)* character; **un homme sans aucune p.** a man with no personality (whatsoever); **c'est une forte p.** he/she has a strong personality; *Psy* **p. simultanée** dissociated personality

2 *(personne importante)* personality; **les personnalités du monde du spectacle** personalities *or* celebrities in the entertainment business; **les personnalités politiques** the key political figures

3 *Jur* **p. civile** *ou* **juridique** *ou* **morale** legal personality; **p. des lois** personality of laws; **p. des peines** personality of punishment

personne[1] [pɛrsɔn] **NF 1** *(individu)* person; **plusieurs personnes** several people *or Admin* persons; **quelques personnes** a few people; **toute p. intéressée peut** *ou* **les personnes intéressées peuvent s'adresser à Nora** all those interested *or* all interested parties should contact Nora; **une p. de ta/sa connaissance** somebody you know/he/she knows; **20 euros par p.** 20 euros each *or* per person *or* a head; **une p. âgée** an elderly person; **les personnes âgées** the elderly; **grande p.** grown-up; **les grandes personnes** grown-ups

2 *(être humain)* **s'en prendre aux biens et aux personnes** to attack property and people; **ce qui compte, c'est l'œuvre/le rang et non la p.** it's the work/the rank that matters and not the individual; **la p. humaine** the individual

3 *(femme)* lady; **une jeune p.** a young lady; **une petite p.** a little woman

4 *(corps)* **ma p.** myself; **ta p.** yourself; **sa p.** himself/herself; *Fam* **il s'occupe un peu trop de sa petite p.** he's a little too fond of number one; **ils s'en sont pris à la p. (même) du diplomate** they physically attacked the diplomat; **un attentat sur la p. du Président** an attempt on the President's life; **en la p. de** in the person of; **il trouva en la p. d'Élise une épouse et une inspiratrice** in Élise, he found both a wife and a muse; **en p.** in person; **venir en p.** to come in person; **j'y veillerai en p.** I'll see to it personally; **il dînait avec Napoléon en p.** he was dining with Napoleon himself *or* none other than Napoleon; **c'était lui? – en p.!** was it him? – none other!; **c'est la vindicte en p.** he's/she's vindictiveness itself *or* personified; **elle est la beauté en p.** she's the very embodiment of beauty, she's beauty personified; **être bien (fait) de sa p.** to have a good figure

5 *Gram* person; **première/deuxième/troisième p.** first/second/third person; **à la première p. du singulier** in the first person singular

6 *Jur* **p. à charge** dependent; **p. juridique** juristic person; **p. morale** legal entity; **p. physique** natural person; **p. à charge** dependant

❑ **par personne interposée ADV** through *or* via a third party; **dis-le-lui par p. interposée** have a go-between tell him/her

personne[2] [pɛrsɔn] **PRON INDÉFINI 1** *(avec un sens négatif)* no one, nobody; **qui me demande? – p.** who wants to see me? – nobody *or* no one; **p. n'a compris** nobody *or* no one understood; **p. ne peut rien y faire** nobody *or* no one can do anything about it; **p. ne vient jamais me voir**

nobody *or* no one ever comes to see me; **que p. ne sorte!** nobody *or* no one leave (the room)!; **p. d'autre que toi** nobody *or* no one (else) but you; *Fam* **p. le sait** nobody knows; *Fam* **p. en veut** nobody wants any

2 *(en fonction de complément)* anyone, anybody; **il n'y a p.** there's no one *or* nobody there, there isn't anyone *or* anybody there; **il n'y a jamais p. dans ce restaurant** there is never anyone *or* anybody in this restaurant; **je ne vois p. que je connaisse** I can't see anyone *or* anybody I know; **je ne connais p. d'aussi gentil qu'elle** I don't know anyone *or* anybody as nice as her; **elle ne parle à p. d'autre** she doesn't speak to anyone *or* anybody else; **cet appartement n'appartient à p.** this flat doesn't belong to anyone *or* anybody; **je n'y suis** *ou* **je ne suis là pour p.** if anyone *or* anybody calls, I'm not in; *Fam* **quand il s'agit de faire la vaisselle/de payer, il n'y a plus p.** when it's time to do the dishes/to pay, you can't see anyone *or* anybody for dust; *Fam* **il est charmant, mais quand on a besoin de lui, il n'y a plus p.!** he's very nice, but whenever you need him, he's nowhere to be found!

3 *(avec un sens positif)* anyone, anybody; **je me demande si p. arrivera un jour à le convaincre** I wonder if anyone *or* anybody will ever manage to convince him; **je doute que p. s'en soit aperçu** I doubt whether anyone *or* anybody noticed; **si tu le montres jamais à p....** if you never show it to anyone *or* anybody...; **il est parti sans que p. le remarque** he left without anyone *or* anybody noticing him; **sortez avant que p. vous voie** leave before anyone *or* anybody sees you; **avant de soupçonner p., renseigne-toi** before you start suspecting anyone *or* anybody, get some more information; **il est meilleur conseiller que p.** he's better at giving advice than anyone *or* anybody (else); **y a-t-il p. de plus rassurant que lui?** is there anyone *or* anybody more reassuring than him?; **c'est trop difficile pour laisser p. d'autre que lui s'en charger** it is too difficult to let anyone *or* anybody but him do it; **p. de blessé?** nobody *or* anybody injured?; **tu le sais mieux que p.** you know it better than anyone *or* anybody (else); **elle réussit les crêpes comme p.** there's no one *or* nobody who makes pancakes quite like her

personnel[1] [pɛrsɔnɛl] **NM** *(d'une entreprise)* staff, workforce; *(d'un service)* staff, personnel; *Mil* personnel; **le p. est en grève** the staff is *or* are on strike; **faire partie du p.** to be on the staff; **un membre du p.** a member of staff; **avoir trop/manquer de p.** to be overstaffed/understaffed *or* short-staffed; **le p. est autorisé à...** (members of) staff are authorized to...; **tout le p. touchera une prime** everybody on the payroll will receive a bonus; **p. (de maison)** servants, (domestic) staff; **p. administratif** administrative staff; **p. auxiliaire** ancillary staff; **p. de bureau** office staff, clerical staff; **p. de cabine** *(d'un avion)* flight personnel, cabin crew *or* staff; **p. dirigeant** managerial staff; **p. d'encadrement** supervisory personnel, management; **p. d'entretien** maintenance staff; **p. intérimaire** temporary staff; **p. navigant** flight personnel *or* staff *or* crew; **p. réduit** reduced *or* skeleton staff; **p. saisonnier** seasonal staff; **p. au sol** ground personnel *or* staff *or* crew; *Mktg* **p. de soutien commercial** sales support staff; **p. à temps partiel** part-time staff; **p. de vente** sales personnel; **p. volant** flight staff

personnel[2], **-elle** [pɛrsɔnɛl] **ADJ 1** *(privé → gén)* personal, individual; *(→ titre de transport, laissez-passer)* non-transferable; **pas d'allusions personnelles, s'il vous plaît** no personal comments *or* don't be personal, please; **c'est un appel p.** *(n'intéressant pas le travail)* it's a personal call; *(confidentiel)* it's a rather private call; **avoir son hélicoptère p.** to have one's own *or* a private helicopter; **il mène une campagne personnelle contre la pollution** he's conducting a one-man campaign against pollution; *Pol* **le pouvoir p.** (absolute) personal power

2 *(original)* **très p.** highly personal *or Sout* idiosyncratic

3 *(joueur)* selfish

4 *Phil* individual

5 *Rel* personal

6 *Gram (pronom)* personal; **les formes personnelles du verbe** finite verb forms

personnellement [pɛrsɔnɛlmɑ̃] **ADV** personally; **l'imprésario m'a contacté p.** the impresario contacted me personally; **je ne le connais pas p.** I don't know him personally; **p., je suis contre la peine de mort** I'm against the death penalty personally *or* myself

personne-ressource [pɛrsɔnrəsurs] *(pl* **personnes-ressources) NF** *Can* contact person

personnification [pɛrsɔnifikɑsjɔ̃] **NF** personification, embodiment; **Cupidon est la p. de l'amour** Cupid is the personification of *or* personifies love; **ma mère est la p. de la patience** my mother is patience itself *or* is patience personified

personnifié, -e [pɛrsɔnifje] **ADJ** personified; **Quasimodo est la laideur personnifiée** Quasimodo is the epitome of ugliness *or* is ugliness personified; **c'est la patience/bonté personnifiée** he/she is patience/kindness personified *or* patience/kindness itself

personnifier [9] [pɛrsɔnifje] **VT** to personify, to be the embodiment of; **l'Oncle Sam personnifie les États-Unis** Uncle Sam personifies the United States; **il personnifie la prudence paysanne** he typifies the cautious nature of the peasant

perspectif, -ive[1] [pɛrspɛktif, -iv] **ADJ** *(plan, vue)* perspective

perspective[2] [pɛrspɛktiv] **NF 1** *Beaux-Arts* perspective; **p. aérienne** aerial perspective; **p. albertienne** Albertian perspective; **p. atmosphérique** atmospheric perspective; **p. axonométrique** axonometric perspective; **p. baroque** baroque perspective; **p. bifocale** bifocal perspective; **p. brunelleschienne** Brunelleschian perspective; **p. cavalière** isometric projection; **p. centrale** central perspective; **p. classique** classical perspective; **p. intuitive** intuitive perspective; **p. linéaire** linear perspective; **p. parallèle** parallel perspective; **p. primitive** primitive perspective; **p. rationnelle** rational perspective; **manquer de p.** to be out of perspective

2 *(point de vue)* angle, viewpoint, standpoint; **dans une p. sociologique** from a sociological standpoint; **analysons maintenant ce texte sous une p. différente** let us now analyse this text from a different viewpoint

3 *(éventualité)* prospect, thought; **la p. de revoir mes parents** the prospect of seeing my parents again; **elle était très excitée à la p. de faire ce voyage** she was very excited at the prospect of going on the journey; **p. d'avenir** outlook, prospects

4 *(avenir)* (future) prospect, outlook; **perspectives d'activité** business outlook; **perspectives de carrière** job prospects; **perspectives commerciales** market prospects; **perspectives de croissance** prospects for growth; **perspectives économiques** economic forecast *or* outlook; **perspectives d'emploi** job prospects; **perspectives de profit** profit outlook; **ouvrir de nouvelles** *ou* **des perspectives (pour)** to open up new horizons (for)

5 *(vue)* view

▫ **en perspective ADV 1** *Beaux-Arts* in perspective; **en p. accélérée** in trompe-l'œil perspective **2** *(en vue)* on the horizon, in sight; **pas de reprise du travail en p.** no return to work in sight

perspicace [pɛrspikas] **ADJ** perceptive, *Sout* perspicacious; **être très p.** to have a sharp *or* clever mind

perspicacité [pɛrspikasite] **NF** (clearness of) insight, perceptiveness, perspicacity; **avec p.** astutely, perceptively; **d'une grande p.** of acute perspicacity

perspiration [pɛrspirasjɔ̃] **NF** perspiration

persuader [3] [pɛrsɥade] **VT 1** *(convaincre)* to persuade, to convince; **il ne se laissera pas p.** he won't be persuaded; **p. qn de qch** to persuade *or* convince sb of sth; **je l'ai persuadé de la nécessité d'un déménagement** I managed to persuade him that it was necessary to move; **p. qn de faire qch** to persuade sb to do sth, to talk sb into doing sth; **rien n'aurait pu la p. de repartir** nothing would have induced her to leave again; **être persuadé** *(être convaincu)* to be convinced; **les jurés sont persuadés de sa sincérité** the jurors are convinced of his/her sincerity; **j'en suis persuadé** I'm convinced *or* sure of it; **je n'en suis pas persuadé** I'm not convinced (of it)

2 *Vieilli ou Littéraire (faire admettre)* **p. qch à qn** to persuade sb of sth, to make sb believe sth; **toutes les sottises qu'un parleur insinuant pourrait p. au peuple** all the stupidities that an insinuating speaker could persuade people to believe

▸**se persuader VPR se p. de** to convince oneself of, to become convinced of; **elle s'est persuadée qu'elle est trop grosse** she's convinced herself that she's too fat

persuasif, -ive [pɛrsɥazif, -iv] **ADJ** *(personne)* persuasive; *(argument)* convincing, persuasive

persuasion [pɛrsɥazjɔ̃] **NF** persuasion; **avoir un grand pouvoir de p.** to have great powers of persuasion; **agir par la p.** to use persuasion

persuasive [pɛrsɥaziv] *voir* **persuasif**

persulfate [pɛrsylfat] **NM** persulphate

persulfure [pɛrsylfyr] **NM** persulphuric acid

perte [pɛrt] **NF 1** *(décès)* loss; **c'est pour vous une p. bien cruelle** you're suffering a very cruel *or* sad loss

2 *(privation → d'une faculté)* **p. de connaissance** fainting, blackout; **p. d'appétit** loss of appetite; **p. de mémoire** (memory) blank; **p. de la vue** loss of eyesight

3 *(disparition, destruction)* loss; **déclarer une p.** to declare the loss (of a thing); **la p. de l'avion (et de tous ses passagers)** the loss of the plane (and of all those on board); **ce n'est pas une grande** *ou* **grosse p.** it's no great loss; **avec pertes et fracas** unceremoniously

4 *(gaspillage)* waste; **quelle p. de temps!** what a waste of time!

5 *(réduction)* loss; **p. de chaleur** heat loss; **p. de charge** *(dans un tuyau)* pressure loss; **p. de poids** weight loss; **p. de compression/de vitesse** loss of compression/of engine speed; **en p. de vitesse** *(avion)* losing speed; *Fig* losing momentum; *Élec* **p. à la terre** earth *or Am* ground leakage

6 *Littéraire (ruine)* ruin, ruination; **courir** *ou* **aller (droit) à sa p.** to be on the road to ruin; **jurer la p. de qn** to vow to ruin sb

7 *Fin* loss, deficit; **travailler** *ou* **fonctionner à p.** to operate at a loss; **vendre qch à p.** to sell sth at a loss; **passer une p. par profits et pertes** to write off a loss; **subir de lourdes pertes** to suffer heavy losses; **l'entreprise a enregistré une p. de 2 millions** the company has chalked up losses of 2 million; **p. de bénéfice** loss of profit; **p. brute** gross loss; **p. en capitaux** capital loss; **p. de change** (foreign) exchange loss; **p. d'intérêts** loss of interest; **p. latente** unrealized loss; **p. nette** net loss; *Compta* **pertes et profits exceptionnels** extraordinary items; **p. sèche** dead loss; *Compta* **p. supportée** loss attributable; **p. totale** total loss; *Compta* **p. transférée** loss transferred

8 *(défaite)* loss; **très affecté par la p. de son procès** very upset at having lost his case; **la p. d'un set** *(au tennis)* the dropping of a set

9 *Géog* **p. de rivière** drying-up of a river

10 *Ordinat* **p. de données irréparable** irretrievable data loss

11 *Jur* **p. de validité** expiry

▫ **pertes NFPL 1** *Fin* losses, loss; **pertes et profits** profit and loss; **compte des pertes et profits** profit and loss account; *aussi Fig* **passer qch aux** *ou* **par pertes et profits** to write sth off (as a total loss); **pertes d'exploitation** operating loss

2 *Mil* losses; **les pertes ont été énormes** there were heavy losses, there was a heavy loss of life; **de lourdes pertes en hommes et en matériel** heavy losses of men and equipment

3 *Méd* **pertes (blanches)** whites, (vaginal) discharge; **pertes de sang** metrorrhagia

▫ **à perte ADV** at a loss; **vendre qch à p.** to sell sth at a loss

▫ **à perte de vue ADV 1** *(loin)* as far as the eye can see

2 *(longtemps)* endlessly, interminably, on and on

▫ **en pure perte ADV** for nothing, to no avail; **il a couru en pure p., il a quand même manqué son train** it was a waste of time *or* absolutely no use running, he missed the train all the same

Perth [pɛrs] NM Perth

pertinacité [pɛrtinasite] NF *Littéraire* pertinacity, pertinaciousness

pertinemment [pɛrtinamɑ̃] ADV 1 *(à propos)* appropriately, pertinently, fittingly; **elle ajouta p. que...** she added, rather pertinently, that... 2 *(parfaitement)* **je sais p. que ce n'est pas vrai** I know perfectly well *or* for a fact that it's not true

pertinence [pɛrtinɑ̃s] NF 1 *(bien-fondé)* pertinence, relevance, *Sout* appositeness 2 *Ling* distinctiveness

pertinent, -e [pɛrtinɑ̃, -ɑ̃t] ADJ *(propos)* pertinent, relevant, apt; **vos critiques ne sont pas pertinentes** your criticisms are irrelevant

pertuis [pɛrtɥi] NM 1 *Géog (détroit)* straits, channel; *(d'un fleuve)* narrows 2 *Naut* sluice

pertuisane [pɛrtɥizan] NF *Hist* partisan, halberd

perturbant, -e [pɛrtyrbɑ̃, -ɑ̃t] ADJ disturbing

perturbateur, -trice [pɛrtyrbatœr, -tris] ADJ *(élève)* disruptive; *(agent, militant)* subversive ▪ NM,F *(en classe)* troublemaker, rowdy element; *(agitateur)* troublemaker, subversive element

perturbation [pɛrtyrbasjɔ̃] NF 1 *(désordre)* disturbance, disruption; **jeter** *ou* **semer la p. dans qch** to disrupt sth; **les perturbations continuent à la poste** the postal service is still being disrupted 2 *Astron* perturbation 3 *Météo* disturbance; **p. atmosphérique** (atmospheric) disturbance 4 *Tél & Rad* interference

perturbatrice [pɛrtyrbatris] *voir* **perturbateur**

perturbé, -e [pɛrtyrbe] ADJ 1 *(affecté)* upset, perturbed; *(déconcerté)* disconcerted; **des enfants perturbés** children with behavioural problems 2 *(trafic, service)* disrupted; **j'ai un sommeil p.** I have difficulty sleeping

perturber [3] [pɛrtyrbe] VT 1 *(interrompre)* to disrupt; **p. le déroulement d'un match** to disrupt a match 2 *(déconcerter)* to disconcert; **il ne faut pas p. l'enfant par des changements trop fréquents** don't disorient the child by changing his/her routine too often; **ça n'a pas l'air de te p. outre mesure** you don't seem particularly bothered by it 3 *(affecter)* to upset, to perturb; **la mort de son frère l'a profondément perturbé** he was deeply upset by his/her brother's death

Pérugin [peryʒɛ̃] NPR **le P.** Il Perugino; **un tableau du P.** a painting by Il Perugino

pérugin, -e [peryʒɛ̃, -in] ADJ Perugian
□ **Pérugin, -e** NM,F Perugian

péruvien, -enne [peryvjɛ̃, -ɛn] ADJ Peruvian
□ **Péruvien, -enne** NM,F Peruvian

pervenche [pɛrvɑ̃ʃ] NF 1 *Bot* periwinkle 2 *Fam (contractuelle)* Br (female) traffic warden▪, *Am* meter maid▪
▪ ADJ INV **(bleu) p.** periwinkle blue; **des yeux p.** periwinkle blue eyes

pervers, -e [pɛrvɛr, -ɛrs] ADJ 1 *(dépravé)* perverted; **avoir l'esprit p., être p.** to have a perverted *or* twisted mind 2 *Littéraire (malfaisant)* wicked 3 *(effet)* perverse; **les effets p. de la dévaluation** the perverse effects of devaluation
▪ NM,F pervert; **p. (sexuel)** (sexual) pervert

perversion [pɛrvɛrsjɔ̃] NF 1 *Littéraire (corruption)* perversion, corruption 2 *Psy* perversion; **p. sexuelle** sexual perversion

perversité [pɛrvɛrsite] NF 1 *(caractère)* perversity 2 *(acte)* perverse act

perverti, -e [pɛrvɛrti] ADJ *(personne)* perverted, depraved
▪ NM,F pervert

pervertir [32] [pɛrvɛrtir] VT 1 *(corrompre → personne)* to pervert, to corrupt 2 *(déformer)* to pervert, to impair, to distort; **la consommation répétée de piment peut p. le goût** eating chilli too often can impair one's sense of taste
▪**se pervertir** VPR to become perverted

pervertissement [pɛrvɛrtismɑ̃] NM *Littéraire* perversion, corruption, corrupting

pervibrage [pɛrvibraʒ] NM = **pervibration**

pervibrateur [pɛrvibratœr] NM internal *or* immersion vibrator

pervibration [pɛrvibrasjɔ̃] NF vibration of concrete

pervibrer [3] [pɛrvibre] VT to vibrate *(concrete)*

pesade [pəzad] NF pesade

pesage [pəzaʒ] NM 1 *(action de peser)* weighing 2 *Sport (vérification)* weigh-in; *(lieu → pour les concurrents)* weighing room; *(→ pour les spectateurs)* enclosure *(inside race courses)*

pesamment [pəzamɑ̃] ADV heavily; **marcher p.** to walk with a heavy step, to tread heavily; **descendre p. l'escalier** to thump down the stairs; **il s'éloigna p.** he lumbered off

pesant, -e [pəzɑ̃, -ɑ̃t] ADJ 1 *(lourd → gén)* heavy, weighty; **marcher à pas pesants** *ou* **d'une démarche pesante** to tread heavily; **il descendit la colline d'un pas p.** he lumbered down the hill; **le vol p. des vautours** the unwieldy flight of the vultures; **je me sens la tête pesante/les jambes pesantes** my head feels/my legs feel heavy
2 *(astreignant)* hard, heavy, demanding; **dix heures par jour, c'est trop p. pour elle** ten hours a day is too heavy *or* too much for her
3 *(grave)* heavy, weighty, *Littéraire* burdensome
4 *(trop orné → architecture)* heavy, cumbersome
5 *(peu vivace → esprit)* slow, sluggish
6 *(insupportable)* heavy; **l'ambiance chez eux est toujours pesante** it always feels very oppressive in their house; **ses critiques sont pesantes à la longue** his/her criticisms are hard to bear in the long run
7 *Can (maussade → temps)* oppressive, close
▪ NM **valoir son p. d'or** to be worth one's weight in gold; *Fam Hum* **valoir son p. de nougat** *ou* **de moutarde** *ou* **de cacahuètes** to be pretty good; **son histoire valait son p. de nougat!** that was some story he/she told!

pesanteur [pəzɑ̃tœr] NF 1 *Phys* gravity 2 *(lourdeur → d'un objet)* heaviness, weightiness; *(→ d'une démarche)* heaviness; *(→ d'un style)* ponderousness; *(→ de l'esprit)* slowness, sluggishness; **j'ai une p. d'estomac** there's something lying heavy on my stomach; **les pesanteurs administratives** cumbersome administrative procedures

PESC [peɑɛssə] NF *UE (abrév politique étrangère et de sécurité commune)* CFSP

pesco-végétarien, -enne [pɛskoveʒetarjɛ̃, -ɛn] *(mpl* **pesco-végétariens**, *fpl* **pesco-végétariennes)** NM,F pescatarian

pèse [pɛz] = **pèze**

pèse-acide [pɛzasid] *(pl inv ou* **pèse-acides)** NM acidimeter

pèse-alcool [pɛzalkɔl] NM INV alcoholometer

pèse-bébé [pɛzbebe] *(pl inv ou* **pèse-bébés)** NM (set of) baby scales

pesée [pəze] NF 1 *(avec une balance)* weighing; **faire la p. d'un paquet** to weigh a parcel 2 *(pression)* **exercer une p. sur qch** to put one's whole weight on sth 3 *Méd* weighing 4 *Sport* weigh-in; **passer à la p.** to (go to the) weigh-in

pèse-esprit [pɛzɛspri] *(pl inv ou* **pèse-esprits)** NM *Vieilli* alcoholometer

pèse-lait [pɛzlɛ] NM INV galactometer, lactometer

pèse-lettre [pɛzlɛtr] *(pl inv ou* **pèse-lettres)** NM (set of) letter scales

pèse-liqueur [pɛzlikœr] *(pl inv ou* **pèse-liqueurs)** NM (liqueur) alcoholometer

pèse-moût [pɛzmu] *(pl inv ou* **pèse-moûts)** NM saccharimeter

pèse-personne [pɛzpɛrsɔn] *(pl inv ou* **pèse-personnes)** NM (set of) bathroom scales

peser [19] [pəze] VT 1 *(avec une balance)* to weigh; **p. qch dans sa main** to feel the weight of sth; **p. une livre de sucre par kilo de fruits** weigh out one pound of sugar per kilo of fruit; **faites p. vos fruits et légumes avant de passer à la caisse** get your fruit and vegetables weighed before going to the till
2 *Fam (valoir)* **un mec qui pèse 10 millions de dollars** a guy worth 10 million bucks
3 *(évaluer, choisir)* to weigh; **p. ses mots** to weigh *or* to choose one's words; **et je pèse mes mots!** and I'm not saying this lightly!; **p. le pour et le contre** to weigh (up) the pros and cons; **p. les risques** to weigh up the risk, to evaluate the risks; **tout bien pesé** all things considered, all in all
4 *Fig (entreprise)* to be worth; **cette entreprise pèse 20 millions de dollars** this company is worth 20 million dollars
VI 1 *(corps, objet → avoir comme poids)* to weigh; *(→ être lourd)* to be heavy; **combien pèses-tu/pèse le paquet?** how much do you/does the parcel weigh?; **la valise pesait 30 kilos** the suitcase weighed 30 kilos; *Fam* **ce truc-là pèse une tonne!** that thing weighs a ton!; *Sport* **il pèse 75 kilos** he weighs in at 165 pounds

2 *Fig (personne, opinion)* to weigh; **p. lourd** to weigh a lot; **il ne pèse pas lourd face à lui** he's no match for him; **mon avis ne pèse pas lourd** my opinion doesn't carry much weight *or* count for much; **la question d'argent a pesé très lourd dans mon choix** the question of money was a determining *or* major factor in my choice; **mes raisons ne pèsent pas lourd dans la balance** my arguments don't carry much weight *or* don't matter very much
3 **p. sur** *(faire pression sur → sujet: masse, poids)* to press (heavily) on; **p. sur un levier** to lean on a lever; *Can Joual* **p. sur les gaz** to step on it, *Am* to hit the gas
4 **p. sur** *(accabler)* to weigh down, to be a strain on; **les responsabilités qui pèsent sur moi** the responsibilities I have to bear; **un lourd silence pesait sur l'assemblée** a heavy silence hung over the meeting; **une menace qui pèse sur nous** a threat that is hanging over us; **des présomptions pèsent sur elle** she's under suspicion; **ça me pèse sur l'estomac/la conscience** it's lying on my stomach/weighing on my conscience
5 **p. sur** *(influer sur)* to influence, to affect; **ces actes peuvent p. sur la décision du jury** these acts may influence the jury's decision
6 *Suisse* **p. sur** *(appuyer)* to press
7 **p. à** *(être pénible pour)* to weigh down *or* heavy on; **ton absence me pèse** I find your absence difficult to bear; **la vie à deux commence à me p.** living with somebody else is beginning to weigh me down; **cette ambiance me pèse un peu** I'm finding this atmosphere a bit oppressive; **la solitude ne me pèse pas** being alone doesn't bother me
▪**se peser** VPR 1 *(emploi réfléchi)* to weigh oneself
2 *(emploi passif)* to be weighed; **les mangues ne se pèsent pas** *(au magasin)* mangoes are not sold by weight

pèse-sel [pɛzsɛl] *(pl inv ou* **pèse-sels)** NM salinometer

pèse-sirop [pɛzsiro] *(pl inv ou* **pèse-sirops)** NM syrup hydrometer

peseta [pezeta, peseta] NF *Anciennement* peseta

pesette [pəzɛt] NF (pair of) assay scales

peseur, -euse [pəzœr, øz] NM,F *(personne)* weigher
□ **peseuse** NF *(machine)* (automatic) weigher

pèse-urine [pɛzyrin] NM INV urinometer

peseuse-ensacheuse [pəzøzɑ̃saʃøz] *(pl peseuses-ensacheuses)* NF weighing and bagging device

pèse-vin [pɛzvɛ̃] NM INV oenometer

peso [pezo, peso] NM peso

peson [pəzɔ̃] NM balance

pessaire [pesɛr] NM *Méd* pessary

pesse [pɛs] NF *Bot* horsetail, *Spéc* equisetum; **p. d'eau** mare's-tail

pessière [pesjɛr] NF spruce plantation

pessimisme [pesimism] NM pessimism

pessimiste [pesimist] ADJ pessimistic; **pourquoi es-tu toujours aussi p.?** why are you always so pessimistic?, why do you always look on the dark side?
▪ NM,F pessimist

peste [pɛst] NF 1 *Méd* plague; **avoir la p., être atteint de la p.** to have the plague, to be stricken with the plague; **p. bubonique** bubonic plague; *Hist* **la Grande P., la P. noire** the Black Death; *Vét* **p. bovine** rinderpest, cattle plague; *Vét* **p. porcine** swine fever; **fuir qn comme la p.** to avoid sb like the plague; **je me méfie de lui comme de la p.** I don't trust him one little bit, I wouldn't trust him as far as I could throw him
2 *Fam (personne)* (regular) pest, pain in the neck; **petite p.** little devil, little pest
3 *Vieilli ou Littéraire* **(la) p. soit de toi!, (que) la p. t'étouffe!** a plague on you!
▪ EXCLAM *Vieilli* good gracious!, heavens!

═══◁▭▷═══

'**La Peste**' *Camus* 'The Plague'

pester [3] [pɛste] VI **p. contre qn/qch** to complain *or* to moan about sb/sth; **je l'entends qui peste dans sa barbe** I can hear him cursing under his breath

pesteux, -euse [pɛstø, -øz] ADJ pestiferous

pesticide [pɛstisid] **ADJ** pesticidal
NM pesticide

pestiféré, -e [pɛstifere] **ADJ** plague-stricken, plague-ridden
NM,F plague victim; *Fig* **traiter qn comme un p.** to treat sb like a pariah *or* a leper

pestilence [pɛstilɑ̃s] **NF** stench, foul smell

pestilentiel, -elle [pɛstilɑ̃sjɛl] **ADJ** foul, stinking, *Sout* pestilential

pet[1] [pɛ] **NM** *Fam* **1** *(vent)* fart; **lâcher un p.** to fart, to break wind; **p. de maçon** wet fart; **ça ne vaut pas un p. de lapin** it's not worth a monkey's fart; **elle a toujours un p. de travers** there's always something wrong with her■; **il n'y a pas un p. de vent** there's not a breath of wind■; **il n'a pas un p. d'amour-propre** he doesn't have an ounce of self-respect
2 *(bagarre)* **il va y avoir du p.** there's going to be hell to pay
3 faire le p. *(faire le guet)* to keep watch *or* a lookout■

pet[2] [pɛt] **NM** *Fam (coup brutal)* wallop, thump; *(trace de choc)* dent; **ma voiture a pris un p. sur le pare-chocs** my car took a thump on the bumper; **il y a des pets partout sur l'arrière de la voiture** the back of the car is all dented

pétage [petaʒ] **NM** *très Fam* **p. de plombs** *(fait de se mettre en colère)* going ballistic, hitting the *Br* roof *or Am* ceiling; *(fait de craquer nerveusement)* cracking up; **le patron nous a fait un p. de plombs quand il l'a su** the boss went totally ballistic *or* totally hit the *Br* roof *or Am* ceiling when he found out; **être au bord du p. de plombs** to be on the verge of cracking up

pétainisme [petenism] **NM** Pétain's doctrine, Pétainism

pétainiste [petenist] **ADJ** Pétainist; **régime/propagande p.** Pétain's regime/propaganda; **ils étaient pétainistes** they were Pétain supporters
NMF Pétain supporter, Pétainist

pétale [petal] **NM** petal; **pétales de maïs** cornflakes

pétalisme [petalism] **NM** *Antiq* petalism

pétaloïde [petalɔid] **ADJ** petal-like

pétanque [petɑ̃k] **NF** (game of) pétanque

> *Culture*
> **PÉTANQUE**
> Originally invented in the south of France, where it has become a local institution, this bowling game is equally popular with tourists. The game, which requires two teams and is played up to a score of thirteen points, is played outdoors on a flat sandy or earth surface. Each team consists of two to three players, each of whom has three steel "boules". Each player tosses or rolls their "boule" so that it ends up as near as possible to the "cochonnet" (a small wooden ball thrown from a distance of 6 to 10 metres), at the same time trying to hit the other team's "boules" so as to scatter them. Players take turns, and whoever ends up closest to the "cochonnet" when all balls are played, wins.

pétant, -e [petɑ̃, -ɑ̃t] **ADJ** *Fam* **à 3 heures pétantes** at 3 (o'clock) sharp *or* on the dot

Pétaouchnock [petauʃnɔk] **NM** *Fam* = imaginary distant place; **ils l'ont envoyé à P.** they sent him to some place in the back of beyond *or* to Timbuktu

pétaradant, -e [petaradɑ̃, -ɑ̃t] **ADJ** *Fam* put-putting

pétarade [petarad] **NF** **1** *(d'un cheval)* (succession of) farts **2** *(d'un moteur)* backfiring, put-putting; *(d'un feu d'artifice)* crackle, banging

pétarader [3] [petarade] **VI** **1** *(cheval)* to let off a succession of farts **2** *(feu d'artifice)* to crackle, to bang; *(moteur)* to backfire, to put-put; **ils descendirent la rue en pétaradant** they went backfiring *or* put-putting down the street

pétard [petar] **NM** **1** *(explosif → dans les fêtes)* firecracker, *Br* banger; **lancer** *ou* **tirer des pétards** to let off firecrackers; *Fig* **p. mouillé** damp squib; *Fig* **lancer un p.** to cause a sensation *or* a stir
2 *Fam* **faire du p.** *(bruit)* to make a racket *or* a din; *(scandale)* to kick up a fuss, to cause a stink
3 *Fam (pistolet)* shooter, *Am* piece
4 *Fam (cigarette de cannabis)* joint
5 *Fam (postérieur)* butt, *Br* bum, *Am* fanny
6 *Can très Fam (belle fille)* stunner, *Br* cracker
7 *Rail Br* detonator, *Am* torpedo
□ **en pétard** **ADJ** *Fam* **être en p.** *(en colère)* to be fuming *or* livid; **se mettre en p.** to go ballistic, to hit the *Br* roof *or Am* ceiling

pétase [petaz] **NM** *Antiq* petasus

pétasse [petas] **NF** *très Fam* **1** *(femme vulgaire)* slut, *Br* slapper, scrubber **2** *(prostituée)* whore, hooker **3** *(peur)* **avoir la p.** to be scared stiff

pétaudière [petodjɛr] **NF** *Fam (lieu)* shambles *(singulier)*; *Fig* disaster area; *(groupe)* motley crew

pétaure [petɔr] **NM** *Zool* flying phalanger, glider

pétauriste [petɔrist] **NM** *Zool* giant flying squirrel

pet-de-nonne [pɛdnɔn] *(pl* **pets-de-nonne***)*, *Can* **pet-de-sœur** [pɛdsœr] *(pl* **pets-de-sœur***)* **NM** doughnut

pète[1] [pɛt] **NF** *Belg Fam* **1** *(échec)* failure■ **2 p. de feu** *(étincelle)* spark■

pète[2] [pɛt] **NM** *Belg & Can (en langage enfantin → derrière)* bottom

pété, -e [pete] **ADJ** *très Fam* **1** *(ivre)* shit-faced, *Br* rat-arsed, pissed; *(drogué)* stoned, high (as a kite) **2** *(cassé)* broken■, bust **3 être p. de t(h)unes** to be loaded

pétéchie [peteʃi] **NF** *Méd* petechia

péter [18] [pete] *Fam* **VI** **1** *(faire un pet)* to fart; *très Fam* **il pète plus haut que son cul** *ou Can* **le trou** he thinks he's the bee's knees, he thinks he's it; *très Fam* **p. dans la soie** to live in the lap of luxury; *très Fam* **envoyer qn p.** to tell sb where to go *or* where to get off
2 *(exploser)* to blow up; **la grenade lui a pété en pleine figure** the grenade blew up right in his/her face; **faire p. qch** *(bâtiment, voiture)* to blow sth up; *(pétards)* to set *or* let off sth; **si ça continue comme ça entre eux, ça va finir par p.** if things carry on the way they are between them, all hell will break loose; **il faut que ça pète (ou que ça dise pourquoi)** let's have it all out in the open
3 *(faire du bruit → bois qui brûle)* to crack, to crackle; *(→ bouchon)* to pop
4 *(casser → corde, élastique)* to snap; **ma braguette a pété** my zip's bust; *Fig* **p. dans les mains de qn** *(projet, affaire)* to fall through
5 *très Fam* **tu vas la fermer? j'en ai rien à p. de tes histoires!** will you shut up? I don't give a *Br* monkey's *or Am* rat's ass about your nonsense
VT **1** *(casser)* to break■, to bust; **je crois que j'ai pété le magnétoscope** I think I've bust the *Br* video *or Am* VCR; *très Fam* **p. la gueule à qn** to smash sb's face in; **p. les plombs** *(se mettre en colère)* to go ballistic, to hit the *Br* roof *or Am* ceiling; *(craquer)* to crack up; **p. un câble** to crack up; *Can* **p. la cerise** to pop one's cherry
2 *(être plein de)* **p. la santé** to be bursting with health; **p. le feu** *ou* **des flammes** to be bursting with energy, to be full of beans; *Can très Fam* **p. de la broue** to show off■
3 la p. *(avoir très faim)* to be starving *or* ravenous
4 *Belg (recaler → candidat)* to fail■, *Am* to flunk; **il a été pété** he failed *or Am* flunked his exam
▸**se péter** **1 attention, ça va se p.!** watch out, it's going to break!■
2 *(se casser)* **se p. le poignet/la cheville** to break one's wrist/ankle■; **la poutre s'est pétée en deux** the beam broke in two■
3 *(locutions)* **se p. la gueule** *très Fam (tomber)* to fall flat on one's face; *(en voiture)* to get smashed up; *Vulg (s'enivrer)* to get shit-faced *or* pissed; *Can* **se p. les bretelles** to brag■, to be full of oneself■; **se la p.** to show off■; **il se la pète à la Rambo avec son bandeau** he thinks he's Rambo in that bandana■

Peter Pan [pitœrpɑ̃] **NPR** Peter Pan

pète-sec [pɛtsɛk] *Fam* **ADJ INV** abrupt■, curt■, snippy
NMF INV abrupt■ *or* curt■ *or* snippy person

péteur, -euse[1] [petœr, -øz] **NM,F** **1** *Fam* farter, person who constantly breaks wind■ **2** *Can très Fam Fig* **p. de broue** *(prétentieux)* boaster■, braggart■

péteux, -euse[2] [petø, -øz] *Fam* **ADJ** **1** *(lâche)* chicken, yellow-bellied **2** *(prétentieux)* stuck-up, snooty
NM,F **1** *(lâche)* chicken; **tu n'es qu'un petit p.!** you're just chicken! **2** *(prétentieux)* upstart; **quel petit p.!** he's so full of himself!

péthidine [petidin] **NF** *Pharm* pethidine

pétillant, -e [petijɑ̃, -ɑ̃t] **ADJ** **1** *(effervescent → eau, vin)* sparkling, fizzy **2** *(brillant)* **avoir le regard p.** to have a twinkle in one's eyes; **une réponse pétillante d'humour** an answer sparkling with wit; **une brune pétillante** a bubbly brunette
NM sparkling wine

pétillement [petijmɑ̃] **NM** **1** *(crépitement)* crackling, crackle **2** *(effervescence)* bubbling, sparkling **3** *(vivacité)* sparkle; **le p. de son regard** the sparkle in his/her eyes

pétiller [3] [petije] **VI** **1** *(crépiter)* to crackle **2** *(faire des bulles)* to bubble, to fizz **3** *(briller)* to sparkle; **p. d'esprit** to sparkle with wit; **son interprétation de Figaro pétille d'intelligence** his/her interpretation of Figaro shines *or* sparkles with intelligence; **un regard qui pétille de joie/d'intelligence** a look that sparkles with joy/with intelligence

pétiole [pesjɔl] **NM** *Bot* leafstalk, *Spéc* petiole

pétiolé, -e [pesjɔle] **ADJ** *Bot* petiolate, petiolated

Petiot [pɔtjo] **NPR le docteur P.** = mass murderer who lured people to his home by promising them safe passage to South America during the Occupation and who was found guilty of 27 killings and executed in 1946

petiot, -e [pɔtjo, -ɔt] *Fam* **ADJ** tiny, teenyweeny
NM,F (little) kiddy, tiny tot; **ma petiote** my little girl■

PETIT, -E [p(ə)ti, -it]

> **ADJ** little **1, 3, 8** ■ small **1–3, 5, 6** ■ short **1** ■ young **3** ■ baby **3** ■ slight **6, 7** ■ petty **9**
> **NM,F** boy **1–3** ■ girl **1–3** ■ son **1** ■ daughter **1** ■ child **2** ■ short person **4** ■ dear **5**

ADJ **1** *(en hauteur, en largeur)* small, little; *(en longueur)* little, small, short; **une personne de petite taille** a small *or* short person; **je suis trop petite pour être mannequin** I'm too small *or* short to be a model; **un p. gros** a tubby little man; **une petite femme sèche** a skinny little woman; **un homme p. et malingre** a short puny man; **il y a un p. mur entre les deux jardins** there's a low *or* small wall between the two gardens; *Fam* **une toute petite bonne femme** *(femme)* a tiny little woman; *(fillette)* a tiny little girl; **de petites jambes grassouillettes** *(de bébé)* little fat legs; *(d'adulte)* short fat legs; **petite distance** short distance; **à petite distance on voyait une chaumière** a cottage could be seen a short way *or* distance away; **la corde est un peu trop petite** the rope is a bit too short; **elle a de petits pieds** she's got small *or* little feet; **un p. "a"** a small "a"; **je voudrais ce tissu en petite largeur** I'd like that material in a narrow width; **un p. nuage** a small *or* little cloud; **un p. bout de papier** a scrap of paper; **une petite ossature** a small *or* frail bone structure; **une chambre assez petite** a smallish room; **une toute petite maison** a tiny little house; **acheter une petite tour Eiffel** to buy a miniature *or* model Eiffel Tower; **se faire tout p.** *(passer inaperçu)* to make oneself inconspicuous, to keep a low profile; **se faire tout p. devant qn** *(par respect ou timidité)* to humble oneself before sb; *(par poltronnerie)* to cower *or* to shrink before sb; **ça vaut un p. 12 sur 20** it's only worth 12 out of 20; **on y sera dans une petite heure** we'll be there in a bit less than *or* in just under an hour; **dans une petite huitaine** in a little less than a week; **je voudrais un p. kilo de rôti de bœuf** ≃ I'd like just under two pounds of beef for roasting; **il y a un p. kilomètre d'ici à la ferme** ≃ it's no more than *or* just under three quarters of a mile from here to the farm; *Can* **p. suisse** chipmunk
2 *(faible)* small; **petite averse** small *or* light shower; **expédition/émission à p. budget** low-budget expedition/programme; **p. loyer** low *or* moderate rent; **petite retraite/rente** small pension/annuity; **avec un p. effectif** with small numbers (of people)
3 *(jeune → personne)* small, little; *(→ plante)* young, baby *(avant n)*; *(plus jeune)* little, younger; **quand j'étais p.** when I was little; **je**

pes–pet

ne suis plus une petite fille! I'm not a little girl any more!; les petits Chiliens the children of Chile; les petits Français French children; une petite Chinoise a young or little Chinese girl; il est encore trop p. he's still too small or young; un p. chien a puppy; un p. chat a kitten; un p. lion/léopard a lion/leopard cub; un p. mouton a lamb; un p. éléphant a baby elephant, an elephant calf

4 (bref, court) short, brief; p. entracte short or brief interval; petite phrase (énoncé) sound-bite; les petites phrases des hommes politiques political soundbites; un p. séjour a short or brief stay; si on lui faisait une petite visite? shall we pop in to see him/her?; elle est partie faire un p. tour en ville she's gone off for a little walk round the town; donnez-moi un p. délai give me a little more time; un p. répit a short breathing space

5 (dans une hiérarchie) petite entreprise small company; les petites et moyennes entreprises small and medium-sized businesses; les petites et moyennes entreprises industrielles small industrial firms, SMIs; petite association small association; p. commerçant small trader, shopkeeper; les petits commerçants (owners of) small businesses; le p. commerce the small retail trade; la petite délinquance petty crime; la petite industrie small industry; les petits agriculteurs/propriétaires small farmers/landowners; p. fonctionnaire minor or Péj petty official; p. peintre/poète minor painter/poet; les petits salaires (sommes) low salaries, small wages; (employés) low-paid workers; Com p. porteur small investor or shareholder; il s'est trouvé un p. emploi au service exportation he found a minor post in the export department

6 (minime) small, slight, minor; (insignifiant) small, slight; p. changement small or slight or minor change; une petite touche de peinture a slight touch of paint; ce n'est qu'un p. détail it's just a minor detail; dans les plus petits détails down to the last detail; il y a de petits avantages there are a few small advantages; une petite intervention chirurgicale minor surgery, a small or minor operation; il a fallu lui faire de petites réparations it had to undergo minor repairs; un p. malentendu a small or slight misunderstanding; il y a un p. défaut there's a slight or small or minor defect; j'ai un p. ennui I've got a bit of a problem; j'ai eu un p. rhume I had a bit of a cold or a slight cold; de petites erreurs small or slight mistakes; j'ai eu une petite peur I was somewhat frightened, I had a bit of a fright

7 (léger) slight; un p. sourire a hint of a smile; un p. soupir a little sigh; elle a un p. accent she's got a slight accent; dit-elle d'une petite voix she said in a faint voice; petite montée gentle slope; petite brise gentle breeze; ça a un p. goût it tastes a bit strange; ça a un p. goût d'orange it tastes slightly of orange

8 (avec une valeur affective) little; mon p. mignon (my) little darling; Fam alors, la petite mère, ça va? all right, Br missus or Am little lady?; elle a ses petits préférés she's got her little favourites; j'ai trouvé une petite couturière/un p. garagiste I've found a very good little seamstress/garage; il ne faut pas changer ses petites habitudes! you shouldn't try to change his/her little ways!; je me suis octroyé un p. congé I allowed myself a little bit of time off; fais-moi une petite place make a little space for me, give me a (little) or tiny bit of room; j'élabore ma petite méthode au fur et à mesure I work out my own (little) method as I go along; il aimait faire son p. poker le soir he was fond of a game of poker in the evening; elle portait toujours sa petite robe noire en scène she always wore her little black dress on stage; tu mets ton p. ensemble? will you be wearing that nice little suit?; un p. roman distrayant an entertaining little novel; un p. vin sans prétention an unpretentious little wine; il y a un p. vent frais pas désagréable there's a nice little breeze; ma petite maman Br Mummy, Am Mommy, my Br Mum

or Am Mom; alors, mon p. Paul, comment ça va? (dit par une femme) how's life, Paul, dear?; (dit par un homme plus âgé) how's life, young Paul?; tu mangeras bien une petite glace! come on, have an ice cream!; un p. pourboire aiderait à le convaincre a small tip might persuade him; je n'ai pas le temps de faire un match – juste un p.! I've no time to play a match – come on, just a quick one!; c'est une petite futée she's a clever one; p. débrouillard! you're smart!, you don't miss a thing!; Euph c'est une petite surprise it's quite a surprise; c'est tout de même une petite victoire still, it's quite a victory; c'est un p. événement it's quite an event; c'est un p. exploit! it's quite an achievement!; p. imbécile! you idiot!; très Fam p. con! you Br arsehole or Am asshole!; mon p. monsieur, je vous prie de changer de ton look here, my (good) man, I'll thank you not to use that tone with me; j'en ai assez de ses petits mystères/petites manigances! I'm fed up with his/her little mysteries/intrigues!

9 Littéraire (mesquin) mean, mean-spirited, petty; il est p. he's small-minded or petty; il est avare, c'est le côté p. du personnage he's a skinflint, that's the petty side of his personality; comme c'est p., ce que vous avez fait là! that was really mean!

10 Bot petite bardane lesser burdock; petite camomille wild camomile

NM,F 1 (fils) little son or boy; (fille) little daughter or girl; c'est le p. de Monique it's Monique's son; Fam c'est la petite d'en face it's the girl from across the street, it's the daughter of the people across the street, Br it's across the road's daughter; elle va à la même école que le p. (des) Verneuil she goes to the same school as the Verneuil boy

2 (enfant) little or small child, little or small boy, f girl; quant aux petits, nous les emmènerons au zoo as for the younger children, we'll take them to the zoo; la cour des petits (garçons ou filles) the junior playground; la cour des petites the younger girls' or Br junior playground; c'est un livre qui fera les délices des petits comme des grands this book will delight young and old (alike); tu veux de la pâte à modeler? – c'est pour les petits! do you want some Plasticine®? – that's for children!

3 Fam (adolescent) (young) boy, f girl; le p./la petite de la boulangerie (employé) the boy/the girl who works at the baker's

4 (adulte de petite taille) short person; Fam Hum alors, le p., tu viens? coming, shorty?

5 (avec une valeur affective → à un jeune) dear; (→ à un bébé) little one; attention petite, ça brûle! careful, dear or darling, it's boiling hot!; mon p. dear, darling; mon p., je suis fier de toi (à un garçon) young man, I'm proud of you; (à une fille) young lady, I'm proud of you; viens, mon tout p. come here (my) little one; ça, ma petite, vous ne l'emporterez pas au paradis! you'll never get away with it, my dear!; pauvre p., il a perdu sa mère the poor little thing's lost his mother; la pauvre petite, comment va-t-elle faire? poor thing, however will she manage?

NM 1 (animal) baby; ses petits (gén) her young; (chatte) her kittens; (chienne) her puppies; (tigresse, louve) her cubs; l'éléphante protège son p. the elephant cow protects her calf or baby; quand les petits sortent de l'œuf when the fledglings or baby birds hatch out; le singe avec son p. sur le dos the monkey with its baby on its back; faire des petits (chienne) to have pups; (chatte) to have kittens; Fam mes économies ont fait des petits my savings have grown; Can Fam Fig faire ses petits to pack (up)■

2 (dans une hiérarchie) c'est toujours les petits qui doivent payer it's always the little man who's got to pay; dans la course aux marchés, les petits sont piétinés in the race to gain markets, small firms or businesses get trampled underfoot

3 (carte au tarot) lowest trump card

ADV 1 Com c'est un 38 mais ce modèle chausse/taille p. it says 38 but this style Br is a small fitting or Am runs small

2 (juste) voir/prévoir p. to see/to plan things on a small scale; un seul gâteau, tu as vu p.! only one cake, you're cutting it fine or that's stretching it a bit!

❏ en petit ADV (en petits caractères) in small characters or letters; (en miniature) in miniature; un univers en tout p. a miniature universe; je voudrais cette jupe (mais) en plus p. I'd like this skirt (but) in a smaller size

❏ en petite ADV Can Aut in low gear

❏ petit à petit ADV little by little, gradually

═══

'Le Petit soldat' Godard 'The Little Soldier'

petit-beurre [p(ə)tibœr] (pl petits-beurre) NM petit beurre, butter Br biscuit or Am cookie, Br ≃ rich tea biscuit

petit-bois [p(ə)tibwa] (pl petits-bois) NM glazing or window bar

petit-bourgeois, petite-bourgeoise [p(ə)tiburʒwa, p(ə)titburʒwaz] (mpl petits-bourgeois, fpl petites-bourgeoises) ADJ lower-middle class, petit bourgeois
NM,F member of the lower-middle class; les petits-bourgeois the lower-middle class, the petty bourgeoisie

Petit-Clamart [p(ə)tiklamar] NM le P. = town in the Paris suburbs where an unsuccessful attempt to assassinate Charles de Gaulle took place in 1962

petit-cousin, petite-cousine [p(ə)tikuzɛ̃, p(ə)titkuzin] (mpl petits-cousins, fpl petites-cousines) NM,F (au second degré) second cousin; (éloigné) distant cousin

petit-déj' [p(ə)tidɛʒ] (pl petits-déj') NM Fam breakfast■, Br brekkie

petit déjeuner [p(ə)tideʒœne] (pl petits déjeuners) NM breakfast

petit-déjeuner [5] [p(ə)tideʒœne] VI to have breakfast■

petite-fille [p(ə)titfij] (pl petites-filles) NF granddaughter

petitement [pətitmɑ̃] ADV 1 (modestement) humbly; vivre p. to live in lowly or humble circumstances; être p. logé to live in cramped accommodation 2 (mesquinement) pettily, meanly; agir p. to behave pettily

petite-nièce [p(ə)titnjɛs] (pl petites-nièces) NF great-niece

petitesse [pətitɛs] NF 1 (taille → d'un objet) smallness, small size; (→ d'une somme, d'un revenu) paltriness 2 (caractère mesquin) pettiness, meanness; p. d'esprit narrow-mindedness 3 (acte mesquin) piece of pettiness, petty act, mean-spirited action

petit-fils [p(ə)tifis] (pl petits-fils) NM grandson

petit-four [p(ə)tifur] (pl petits-fours) NM petit four

petit-gris [p(ə)tigri] (pl petits-gris) NM 1 (escargot) garden snail; Culin petit-gris 2 (écureuil) Siberian grey squirrel; (fourrure) squirrel fur

pétition [petisjɔ̃] NF 1 (texte) petition; adresser une p. à qn to petition sb; faire une p. to organize a petition 2 Phil p. de principe petitio principii; vous partez d'une p. de principe you're assuming that what we're trying to prove is true, you're begging the question 3 Jur p. d'hérédité = action in recognition of successoral rights

pétitionnaire [petisjɔnɛr] NMF petitioner

pétitionner [3] [petisjɔne] VI to petition

petit-lait [p(ə)tilɛ] (pl petits-laits) NM whey; ça se boit comme du p. it goes down like water; Fig boire du p. to be lapping it up

petit-maître, petite-maîtresse [p(ə)timɛtr, p(ə)titmɛtrəs] (mpl petits-maîtres, fpl petites-maîtresses) NM,F Vieilli dandy, fop, f young woman of fashion

petit-nègre [p(ə)tinɛgr] NM pidgin; Péj ce n'est pas du français, c'est du p. that isn't French, it's gibberish

petit-neveu [p(ə)tinəvø] (pl petits-neveux) NM great-nephew

pétitoire [petitwar] ADJ voir action

petits-enfants [pətizɑ̃fɑ̃] NMPL grandchildren

petit-suisse [p(ə)tisɥis] (pl petits-suisses) NM petit suisse = thick fromage frais sold in small individual portions

pétochard, -e [petɔʃar, -ard] *Fam* **ADJ** *(peureux)* chicken
NM,F *(personne peureuse)* chicken

pétoche [petɔʃ] **NF** *Fam* fear■; **avoir la p.** to be scared stiff *or* witless; **filer** *ou* **flanquer la p. à qn** to scare the living daylights out of sb

pétocher [3] [petɔʃe] **VI** *Fam* to be scared stiff *or* witless

pétoire [petwar] **NF 1** *(sarbacane)* peashooter **2** *Fam Hum (arme à feu)* old rifle■

pétole [petɔl] **NF** *Suisse (crotte)* goat shit

Pétomane [petɔman] **NM le P.** = late 19th and early 20th century French music-hall performer who delighted audiences with his farting skills

peton [pətɔ̃] **NM** *Fam* foot■, *Br* plate, *Am* dog

pétoncle [petɔ̃kl] **NM** (pilgrim) scallop

pétouiller [3] [petuje] **VI** *Suisse* to loaf about

pétouner [3] [petune] **VI** *Can (en acadien)* to moan, to grumble

Pétra [petra] **NM** Petra

Pétrarque [petrark] **NPR** Petrarch

pétrarquisme [petrarkism] **NM** Petrarchism

pétrel [petrɛl] **NM** *Orn* petrel; **p. des Bermudes, p. cahow** cahow

pétrel-tempête [petrɛltɑ̃pɛt] *(pl* **pétrels-tempête***)* **NM** *Orn* storm petrel

pétreux, -euse [petrø, -øz] **ADJ** *(os)* petrous; *(nerf)* petrosal

pétrifiant, -e [petrifjɑ̃, -ɑ̃t] **ADJ 1** *Littéraire (ahurissant)* stunning, stupefying **2** *Géol* petrifactive

pétrification [petrifikasjɔ̃] **NF** petrification, petrifaction; *Fig (du cœur)* hardening; *(de l'esprit)* sclerosis

pétrifier [9] [petrifje] **VT 1** *(abasourdir)* to petrify, to transfix; **être pétrifié de terreur** to be rooted to the spot *or* rigid with terror **2** *Géol* to petrify **3** *(couvrir de calcaire)* to encrust with lime
▸**se pétrifier VPR 1** *(se figer)* **son visage se pétrifia** his/her face froze **2** *Géol* to petrify, to become petrified **3** *Fig* **son esprit se pétrifiait** he/she was developing sclerosis of the mind

pétrin [petrɛ̃] **NM 1** *(à pain)* kneading trough; **p. mécanique** dough mixer, kneading machine **2** *Fam (embarras)* jam, fix; **être dans le p.** to be in a fix *or* a mess; **se fourrer dans un beau** *ou* **sacré p.** to get into a real mess; **on s'est fourrés dans un beau p.!** we're right up the creek (without a paddle)!; **mettre qn dans un beau** *ou* **sacré p.** *Br* to land sb (right) in it, *Am* to land sb in a tough spot

pétrir [32] [petrir] **VT 1** *(malaxer)* to knead; **il lui pétrissait le bras** he was kneading his/her arm **2** *(façonner → esprit, personne)* to mould, to shape **3** *(emplir)* **être pétri d'orgueil** to be filled with pride; **être pétri de préjugés** to be steeped in prejudice; **être pétri de contradictions** to be riddled with contradictions

pétrissage [petrisaʒ] **NM** kneading

pétrisseur, -euse [petrisœr, -øz] **NM,F (ouvrier) p.** dough mixer
▫ **pétrisseuse NF** *(machine)* kneading machine

pétrochimie [petrɔʃimi] **NF** petrochemistry

pétrochimique [petrɔʃimik] **ADJ** petrochemical

pétrochimiste [petrɔʃimist] **NMF** petrochemist

pétrodollar [petrɔdɔlar] **NM** petrodollar

pétrogale [petrɔgal] **NM** *Zool* rock wallaby

pétrogenèse [petrɔʒənɛz] **NF** petrogenesis

pétroglyphe [petrɔglif] **NM** petroglyph

pétrographe [petrɔgraf] **NMF** petrographer

pétrographie [petrɔgrafi] **NF** petrography

pétrographique [petrɔgrafik] **ADJ** petrographic, petrographical

pétrole [petrɔl] **NM** oil, petroleum; **p. brut** crude (oil); **p. lampant** *Br* paraffin oil, *Am* kerosene; **p. vert** food (processing) industry
ADJ INV *(couleur)* **bleu p.** petrol blue
▫ **à pétrole ADJ** *(lampe, réchaud) Br* oil *(avant n)*, *Am* kerosene *(avant n)*

pétrolette [petrɔlɛt] **NF** *Fam Hum (cyclomoteur)* moped■

pétroleuse [petrɔløz] **NF 1** *Hist* female arsonist *(active during the Paris Commune)* **2** *Fam (militante)* militant female political activist■

pétrolier, -ère [petrɔlje, -ɛr] **ADJ** *(industrie, compagnie, choc)* oil *(avant n)*; *(pays)* oil-producing
NM 1 *(navire)* (oil) tanker **2** *(industriel)* oil tycoon **3** *(technicien)* petroleum *or* oil engineer

pétrolier-minéralier [petrɔljemineralje] *(pl* **pétroliers-minéraliers***)* **NM** oil and ore tanker

pétrolifère [petrɔlifɛr] **ADJ** oil-bearing

pétrologie [petrɔlɔʒi] **NF** petrology

pétrologue [petrɔlɔg] **NMF** petrologist

pétromonarchie [petrɔmɔnarʃi] **NF** oil kingdom

pétromonnaie [petrɔmɔnɛ] **NF** petrocurrency

Pétrone [petrɔn] **NPR** Petronius

Pétrouchka [petruʃka] **NPR** Petruschka

pette[1] [pɛt] = **pète**[1]

pette[2] [pɛt] = **pète**[2]

pétulance [petylɑ̃s] **NF** exuberance, ebullience, high spirits

pétulant, -e [petylɑ̃, -ɑ̃t] **ADJ** exuberant, ebullient

pétun [petœ̃] **NM** *Vieilli* tobacco

pétuner [3] [petyne] **VI** *Vieilli (priser)* to take snuff; *(fumer)* to smoke

pétunia [petynja] **NM** petunia

PEU [pø]

little **A1, B1** ■ not much **A1** ■ not very **A2** ■ not long **B2** ■ few **B3** ■ a bit, a little **C**

ADV A. *EMPLOYÉ SEUL* **1** *(modifiant un verbe)* little, not much; **il travaille p.** he doesn't work much; **il mange/parle p.** he doesn't eat/talk much; **je le connais p.** I don't know him well; **c'est p. le connaître** it just shows how little you know him; **on a p. dormi** we didn't sleep much; **il vient très p.** he comes very rarely, he very seldom comes; **on s'est très p. vus** we saw very little of each other; **j'ai trop p. confiance en elle** I don't trust her enough

2 *(modifiant un adjectif, un adverbe etc)* not very; **un livre p. intéressant** a rather dull book; **une avenue p. fréquentée** a quiet street; **l'affaire est p. rentable** the business isn't very profitable; **il vient p. souvent** he doesn't come very often; **elle s'est défendue p. habilement** she defended herself rather clumsily; **il est assez p. soigneux** he doesn't take much care; **l'alibi est fort p. crédible** the alibi is highly implausible; **p. avant** shortly *or* not long before; **p. après** soon after, shortly *or* not long after; **pas p.** not a little, more than a little; **je ne suis pas p. fier du résultat** I'm more than a little proud of the result

B. *EMPLOI NOMINAL* **1** *(indiquant la faible quantité)* **le p. que tu manges** the little you eat; **le p. que tu gagnes** the little you earn; **il vit de p.** he lives off very little; **il est mon aîné de p.** he's only slightly older than me; *Fam* **il a raté son examen de p.** he just failed his exam■, he failed his exam by a hair's breadth; **c'est p.** it's not much; *Littéraire* **hommes/gens de p.** worthless men/people; **c'est p. (que) de le dire, encore faut-il le faire!** that's easier said than done!; **c'est p. dire** that's an understatement, that's putting it mildly; **ce n'est pas p. dire!** and that's saying something!; *Fam* **très p. pour moi!** not on your life!

2 *(dans le temps)* **ils sont partis il y a p.** they left a short while ago, they haven't long left; **d'ici p.** very soon, before long; **vous aurez de mes nouvelles avant p.** you'll hear from me before long; **je travaille ici depuis p.** I've only been working here for a while, I haven't been working here long

3 *(quelques personnes)* a few (people); **tout le monde en parle, p. le connaissent** everybody's talking about him but few know him; **p. avaient compris** few (people) had understood; **nous étions p. à le croire** only a few of us believed it

C. *PRÉCÉDÉ DE "UN"* **1** *(modifiant un verbe)* **un p.** a little, a bit; **je le connais un p.** I know him a little *or* a bit; **reste un p. avec moi** stay with me for a while; **il ressemble un p. à Cary Grant** he looks a bit *or* a little like Cary Grant; **veux-tu manger un p.?** do you want something to eat?; **pousse-toi un (tout) petit p.** move up a (little) bit; **viens un p. par là** come here a minute; **pose-lui un p. la question, et tu verras!** just ask him/her, and you'll see!; **fais voir un p....** let me have a look...; *Fam* **tu l'as vu? – un p.!** did you see it? – you bet I did *or* and how!; *Fam* **un p. que je vais lui dire ce que je pense!** I'll give him/her a piece of my mind, don't you worry (about that)!

2 *(modifiant un adjectif, un adverbe etc)* **un p.** a little, a bit; **il est un p. fatigué** he is a little *or* a bit tired; **je suis un p. pressée** I'm in a bit of a hurry; **votre devoir était un p. confus** your work was a little *or* a bit confused; **il est un p. poète** he's a bit of a poet; **un p. partout** just about *or* pretty much everywhere; **tu parles un p. fort** you're talking a little *or* a bit too loudly; **on roulait un p. vite** we were driving a little *or* a bit too fast; **un p. plus** a little *or* bit more; **pouvez-vous vous exprimer un p. plus clairement?** could you express yourself a little more clearly?; **un p. plus de** *(suivi d'un nom comptable)* a few more; *(suivi d'un nom non comptable)* a little (bit) more; **nous recevons un p. plus d'appels maintenant** we're getting a few more calls now; **un p. plus de lait?** a little more milk?; **un p. moins** a little *or* bit less; **roule un p. moins vite** drive a little more slowly; **un p. moins de** *(suivi d'un nom comptable)* slightly fewer, not so many; *(suivi d'un nom non comptable)* a little (bit) less; **nous avons un p. moins de difficultés** we're not having quite so many difficulties; **il y a un p. moins de vent** it's a little less windy; **un p. trop** a little *or* bit too (much); **il en fait vraiment un p. trop!** he's really making too much of it!; *Fam* **un p. beaucoup** a bit much; *Fam* **il est un p. bête, ce mec – un p. beaucoup!** the guy's a bit stupid – more than a bit!; *Fam* **tu as bu un p. beaucoup hier soir** you certainly had a few last night; *Fam* **un p.(, mon neveu)!** you bet!, sure thing!, *Br* too right!; *Fam* **elle est jolie – un p., oui!** she's pretty – just a bit!; *Fam* **il te reproche de lui avoir menti, c'est un (petit) p. ça, non?** he's blaming you for lying to him, isn't that it?■; *Fam* **un p. plus et l'évier débordait!** another minute and the sink would have overflowed!■; *Fam* **un p. plus et on se serait crus au bord de la mer** you could almost imagine that you were at the seaside■; *Fam* **un p. plus, et je partais** I was just about to leave■; *Fam* **un p. plus et je me faisais écraser!** I was within an inch of being run over!; *Fam* **pas qu'un p.** more than a little

▫ **peu à peu ADV** little by little, bit by bit, gradually; **on s'habitue, p. à p.** you get used to things, bit by bit *or* gradually; **la neige fondait p. à p.** the snow was gradually melting

▫ **peu de DÉT 1** *(suivi d'un nom non comptable)* not much, little; *(suivi d'un nom comptable)* not many, few; **il a p. de travail** he doesn't have much work; **cela a p. d'importance** that is of little importance, that doesn't matter much; **cela a p. d'intérêt** it's of little interest; **je ne reste que p. de temps** I'm only staying for a short while, I'm not staying long; **il n'a que p. de temps à me consacrer** he can only give me a small amount of time; **p. de temps avant/après** not long before/after; **il y avait p. de neige** there wasn't much snow; **il reste p. de jours** there are only a few days left; **j'ai p. d'amis** I have few friends, I don't have many friends; **en p. de mots** in a few words; **p. d'écrivains ont abordé cette question** few writers have dealt with this question; **on est p. de chose** what an insignificant thing man is; **c'est p. de chose** it's nothing; **ne me remerciez pas, c'est vraiment p. de chose** don't thank me, it's really nothing

2 *(avec un déterminant)* **le p. de** *(suivi d'un nom comptable)* the *or* what few; *(suivi d'un nom non comptable)* the *or* what little; **le p. de connaissances que j'ai** the *or* what few acquaintances I have; **le p. de fois où je l'ai vu** on the few *or* rare occasions when I've seen him; **le p. de leçons que j'ai prises** what few *or* the few lessons I've had; **le p. d'expérience que j'avais** what little experience I had; **son p. d'enthousiasme** his/her lack of enthusiasm; **avec mon p. de moyens** with my limited means; **avec ce p. de matériel/d'idées** with such limited material/ideas

▫ **peu ou prou ADV** *Littéraire* more or less

▫ **pour peu que CONJ pour p. qu'il le veuille, il réussira** if he wants to, he'll succeed; **pour p. qu'elle ait compris...** if she's got the message...

▫ **pour un peu ADV pour un p. il m'accuserait!** he's all but accusing me!; **pour un p., j'oubliais mes clés** I nearly forgot my keys

pet–peu

❑ **quelque peu** ADV **1** *(modifiant un verbe)* just a little; **vous ne trouvez pas que vous exagérez quelque p.?** don't you think you're exaggerating just a little?

2 *(modifiant un adjectif)* somewhat, rather; **il était quelque p. éméché** he was somewhat *or* rather tipsy

❑ **quelque peu de** DÉT not a little; **le chantier a été achevé avec quelque p. de hâte** the site was completed in not a little haste

❑ **si peu que** CONJ **si p. que j'y aille, j'apprécie toujours beaucoup l'opéra** although I don't go very often, I always like the opera very much

❑ **si peu... que** CONJ **si p. informé qu'il soit** however badly informed he may be; **si p. réaliste qu'il soit** however unrealistic he may be

❑ **sous peu** ADV before long, in a short while; **vous recevrez sous p. les résultats de vos analyses** you will receive the results of your tests in a short while

❑ **un peu de** DÉT a little (bit) of; **prends un p. de gâteau** have a little *or* some cake; **c'est meilleur avec un p. de crème dessus** it tastes better with a bit of cream on top; **pourrais-je avoir un (tout) petit p. de lait?** could I have (just) a little milk?; **un p. de tout** a bit of everything; **avec un p. de chance...** with a little luck...; **allons, un p. de patience!** come on, let's be patient!; **avec un (tout) petit p. de bonne volonté...** with (just) a little willingness...; **tu l'as quitté par dépit? – il y a un petit p. de ça** so you left him in a fit of pique? – that was partly it *or* that was part of the reason

peucédan [pøsedɑ̃] NM *Bot* peucedanum

peuchère [pøʃɛr] EXCLAM *(dans le Midi)* heck!, *Br* strewth!

peuh [pø] EXCLAM **1** *(avec indifférence)* bah! **2** *(avec dédain)* humph!

peul, -e [pøl] ADJ Fulani

NM *(langue)* Fulani

❑ **Peul, -e** NM,F Fulani, Fula, Fulah; **les Peuls** the Fulanis *or* Fulani, the Fulas *or* Fula, the Fulahs *or* Fulah

peulven [pølvɛn] NM *(menhir)* peulven, menhir

peuplade [pœplad] NF (small) tribe, people

peuple [pœpl] NM **1** *(communauté)* people; **un roi aimé de son p.** a king loved by his people *or* subjects; **les peuples d'Asie** the peoples of Asia; **le p. français a fait son choix** the French people have chosen; **le p. de Dieu** *(dans l'Ancien Testament)* the Hebrews; *(dans le Nouveau Testament)* the Christians; *Rel* **le p. élu** the chosen people *or* ones

2 le p. *(prolétariat)* the people; **le pouvoir revient au p.** power belongs to the people; **parti du p.** people's party; **homme du p.** ordinary man; *Vieilli* **le bas** *ou* **petit p.** the lower classes *or Br* orders

3 *Fam (foule)* crowd; **il va y avoir du p.** there's going to be tons of people there; **t'aurais vu le p.!** you should have seen how many people there were!■

4 *(locutions) Fam* **il se fiche** *ou* **se moque du p.** he's got some nerve; **encore une hausse de la TVA, faudrait pas se moquer du p.!** not another VAT increase, what kind of idiots do they take us for?; **que demande le p.?** what more could you ask for?

ADJ INV working-class; **se donner un genre p.** to try to look working-class; *Péj* **une expression qui fait p.** a vulgar *or* common turn of phrase

peuplé, -e [pœple] ADJ populated; **région peu/très peuplée** sparsely/densely populated region

peuplement [pœpləmɑ̃] NM **1** *(humain → action)* populating; *(→ état)* population; **au moment du p. des États-Unis** while the United States was being populated; **des régions à faible p.** sparsely populated areas **2** *École (d'une forêt)* planting (with trees); *(d'une rivière)* stocking (with fish); *(ensemble → des végétaux)* plant population, *Spéc* stand; *(→ des arbres)* tree population

peupler [5] [pœple] VT **1** *(région, ville)* to populate, to people; *(forêt)* to plant (with trees); *(rivière)* to stock (with fish)

2 *(vivre dans)* to live in, to inhabit; **les Indiens qui peuplent ces régions** the Indians who live in these areas; **peuplé de** inhabited by

3 *Fig Littéraire* to fill; **les monstres qui peuplent ses rêves** the monsters that fill his/her dreams; **un lieu peuplé de souvenirs** a place full of memories

▶**se peupler** VPR *(région, ville)* to become populated, to acquire a population; **la ville nouvelle se peuple petit à petit** people are gradually moving into the new town; **la rue s'est peuplée peu à peu** the street gradually filled (up) with people

peupleraie [pøplərɛ] NF poplar grove

peuplier [pøplije] NM poplar (tree); **p. blanc** white poplar; **p. d'Italie** Lombardy poplar; **p. tremble** aspen

peupons [pøpɔ̃] NFPL *(verlan de* **pompes***)* shoes■

peur [pœr] NF **1** *(sentiment)* fear, apprehension, alarm; **la p. lui donnait des ailes** fear gave him/her wings; **avoir p.** to be afraid *or* frightened *or* scared; **on a eu très p.** we were badly frightened; **je n'ai qu'une p., c'est de les décevoir** my one fear is that I might disappoint them; *Fam* **on a sonné tard, j'ai eu une de ces peurs!** someone rang the doorbell late at night and it gave me a terrible fright!; **avoir p. pour qn** to fear for sb; **avoir p. d'un rien** to scare easily, to be easily frightened; **avoir horriblement p. de qch** to have a dread of sth; **avoir grand-p.** to be very much afraid *or* frightened *or* scared; **n'aie pas p.** *(ne t'effraie pas)* don't be afraid; *(ne t'inquiète pas)* don't worry; **ça va, tu n'as pas besoin d'avoir p.!** don't you worry about that!, there's nothing to be afraid of!; **il double dans le virage, il n'a pas p., lui au moins!** *Br* overtaking *or Am* passing on the bend, he's certainly got some nerve!; **j'ai bien p. qu'elle ne vienne pas** I'm really worried (that) she won't come; **j'en ai (bien) p.** I'm (very much) afraid so; **il ne s'en remettra pas – j'en ai bien p.** he won't pull through – I'm very much afraid you might be right; **des monstres qui font p.** scary monsters; **faire p. à qn** to frighten *or* to scare sb; **le travail ne lui fait pas p.** he's/she's not workshy *or* afraid of hard work; **ils cherchent à te faire p.** they're trying to frighten you; **j'adore les films qui font p.** I love scary movies *or Br* films; **il nous fait p. avec ses histoires d'hôpital** he tells us scare *or* horror stories about the hospital; **à faire p.** frightening; **une tête à faire p.** a frightening face; **boiter/loucher à faire p.** to have a dreadful limp/squint; **prendre p.** to get frightened, to take fright; **être pris de p.** to be gripped by fear, to be overcome with fear, to take fright; **avoir une p. bleue de** to be scared stiff of; **faire une p. bleue à qn** to give sb a terrible fright; **tu m'as fait une p. bleue** you gave me such a fright; **la p. du gendarme** the fear of authority; **avec eux, il n'y a que la p. du gendarme qui marche** they only understand the language of repression; **avoir la p. au ventre** to be gripped by fear; **être mort** *ou* **vert de p.** to be frightened out of one's wits; **elle était morte de p. à cette idée** that idea scared her out of her wits; **on a eu plus de p. que de mal** we weren't hurt, just scared; **il y a eu plus de p. que de mal** nobody was hurt, but it was frightening; *Fam Ironique* **tu as l'air content, ça fait p.!** you don't exactly look beside yourself with joy!; *Fam Ironique* **ces bananes sont mûres, ça fait p.!** I've seen riper bananas!

2 *(phobie)* fear; **avoir p. de l'eau/du noir** to be afraid of water/of the dark; **il a p. en avion** he's afraid of flying

❑ **dans la peur de** PRÉP **vivre dans la p. de qch** to live in fear *or* in dread of sth

❑ **de peur de** PRÉP **de p. de faire** for fear of doing; **je ne disais rien de p. de lui faire du mal** I said nothing for fear that I might *or* in case I hurt him/her

❑ **de peur que** CONJ for fear that; **je préfère éteindre de p. qu'on nous voie** I'd rather switch the light off in case someone sees us; **il partit de p. qu'on ne l'accusât d'ingérence** he left for fear of being *or Sout* lest he should be accused of interfering

❑ **par peur de** PRÉP out of fear of; **il cèdera au chantage par p. du scandale** the fear of a scandal will make him give in to blackmail

❑ **sans peur** ADV fearlessly, undaunted; **affronter l'avenir sans p.** to face up to the future bravely

'Qui a peur de Virginia Woolf?' *Albee, Nichols*
'Who's Afraid of Virginia Woolf?'

peureuse [pœrøz] *voir* **peureux**

peureusement [pœrøzmɑ̃] ADV fearfully, timorously, apprehensively

peureux, -euse [pœrø, -øz] ADJ *(craintif)* timorous, fearful; **un enfant p.** a fearful child

NM,F *(poltron)* fearful person; **quel p.!** what a coward!

peut *etc voir* **pouvoir**[2]

peut-être [pøtɛtr] ADV maybe, perhaps; **ils sont p. sortis, p. sont-ils sortis** maybe they've gone out, they may *or* might have gone out; **il y a p. encore trois places de libres** there are maybe another three seats left; **elle est p. efficace, mais guère rapide** she might be efficient, but she is not very quick; **je n'ai p. pas d'expérience, mais j'ai de l'ambition** I may lack experience *or* maybe I lack experience, but I'm ambitious; **tu viendras? – p.** will you come? – maybe *or* perhaps; **p. pas** maybe *or* perhaps not; **il est p. bien déjà parti** he may well have already left; **p. bien, mais...** perhaps *or* maybe so but...; **j'y suis pour quelque chose, p.?** so you think it's my fault, do you!; **je suis ta bonne, p.?** what do you take me for? a maid?

❑ **peut-être que** CONJ perhaps, maybe; **p. qu'il est malade** perhaps *or* maybe he is ill; **je n'ai pas vu ce film, p. que c'est bien** I've never seen this film, maybe it's good; **p. qu'il viendrait si tu l'invitais** maybe he would come if you invited him; **p. (bien) qu'il viendra** he may well come; **p. (bien) que oui, p. (bien) que non** maybe, maybe not (who knows?); **tu viendras? – p. bien que oui, p. bien que non** will you come? – perhaps I will, perhaps I won't *or* maybe I will, maybe I won't

peuvent, peux *etc voir* **pouvoir**[2]

p. ex. *(abrév* **par exemple***)* eg

pey [pɛj] = peï

peyotl [pejɔtl] NM peyote

pèze [pɛz] NM *Fam* cash, dough; **ils sont pleins de p.** they're loaded *or* stinking rich

pezizale [pəzizal] NF fungus of the order Pezizales

❑ **pezizales** NFPL Pezizales

pezize [pəziz] NF *Bot* peziza

pfennig [pfenig] NM *Anciennement (monnaie)* pfennig

pff [pf], **pfft** [pft], **pfut** [pfyt] EXCLAM pooh!

PGCD [peʒesede] NM *Math (abrév* **plus grand commun diviseur***)* HCF

pH [peaʃ] NM *Chim (abrév* **potentiel hydrogène***)* pH; **savon/shampooing/***etc* **(à) p. neutre** pH balanced soap/shampoo/*etc*

phacochère [fakɔʃɛr] NM *Zool* warthog

Phaéton [faetɔ̃] NPR *Myth* Phaëthon

phaéton [faetɔ̃] NM **1** *(véhicule)* phaeton **2** *Orn* tropical bird

phage [faʒ] NM *Biol (abrév* **bactériophage***)* phage

phagédénisme [faʒedenism] NM *Méd* phaged(a)ena

phagocytaire [fagɔsitɛr] ADJ *Biol* phagocytic

phagocyte [fagɔsit] NM *Biol* phagocyte

phagocyter [3] [fagɔsite] VT **1** *Biol* to phagocytose **2** *Fig (absorber)* to engulf, to absorb; **après avoir phagocyté tous ses concurrents** after having swallowed up all its competitors

phagocytose [fagɔsitoz] NF *Biol* phagocytosis

phalan [falɑ̃] NM *Belg (partie du bœuf)* rump steak; *(morceau coupé)* slice of rump steak

phalange [falɑ̃ʒ] NF **1** *Anat* phalanx **2** *(groupe)* **la P. (espagnole)** the Falange; **les Phalanges libanaises** the (Lebanese) Phalangist Party **3** *Antiq (corps d'armée)* phalanx **4** *Littéraire (armée)* host, army

phalanger [falɑ̃ʒe] NM *Zool* phalanger; **p. volant** flying phalanger

phalangère [falɑ̃ʒɛr] NF *Bot* spider plant

phalangette [falɑ̃ʒɛt] NF *Anat* top joint *(of finger or toe)*, *Spéc* distal phalanx

phalangien, -enne [falɑ̃ʒjɛ̃, -ɛn] ADJ *Anat* phalangeal

phalangine [falɑ̃ʒin] NF *Anat* middle joint *(of finger or toe)*, *Spéc* phalanx media

phalangiste [falɑ̃ʒist] ADJ *(en Espagne)* Falangist; *(au Liban)* Phalangist

NMF *(en Espagne)* Falangist; *(au Liban)* Phalangist

phalanstère [falɑ̃stɛr] **NM 1** *(de Fourier)* phalanstery **2** *Littéraire (communauté)* community, group

phalanstérien, -enne [falɑ̃sterjɛ̃, -ɛn] **ADJ** Phalansterian

NM,F member of a phalanstery, Phalansterian

phalarope [falarɔp] **NM** *Orn* phalarope

phalène [falɛn] **NF** *Entom* geometer moth; **p. du bouleau** peppered moth

phalline [falin] **NF** phalloidin

phallique [falik] **ADJ** phallic

phallocentrique [falɔsɑ̃trik] **ADJ** phallocentric

phallocentrisme [falɔsɑ̃trism] **NM** phallocentrism

phallocrate [falɔkrat] **ADJ** male-chauvinist

NM male chauvinist

phallocratie [falɔkrasi] **NF** male chauvinism

phallocratique [falɔkratik] **ADJ** male-chauvinist

phalloïde [falɔid] **ADJ** phalloid

phallotoxine [falɔtɔksin] **NF** *Biol* phallotoxin

phallus [falys] **NM 1** *Anat* phallus **2** *Bot* **p. impudique** (common) stinkhorn

phanère [fanɛr] **NM** *Zool* superficial body growth

phanérogame [fanerɔgam] **NM OU NF** *Bot* phanerogam

phanie [fani] **NF** *Opt* luminosity

phanotron [fanɔtrɔ̃] **NM** mercury-vapour rectifier tube, *Am* phanotron tube

phantasme [fɑ̃tasm] = **fantasme**

phantasmer [fɑ̃tasme] = **fantasmer**

pharamineux, -euse [faraminø, -øz] = **faramineux**

pharaon [faraɔ̃] **NM 1** *Hist* pharaoh **2** *(jeu)* faro

pharaonien, -enne [faraɔnjɛ̃, -ɛn], **pharaonique** [faraɔnik] **ADJ 1** *Hist* pharaonic **2** *Fig (gigantesque)* huge, enormous

PHARE [far] **NM** *UE (abrév* **Pologne Hongrie Aide à la Reconstruction Économique)** PHARE

phare [far] **NM 1** *Naut* lighthouse; **p. à éclipses** *ou* **occultations** occulting light; **p. à feu fixe/tournant** fixed/revolving light; **p. flottant** lightship **2** *Aut* headlight, *Br* headlamp; **allumer** *ou* **mettre ses phares** to switch one's headlights on; **mettre les phares en code** *Br* to dip *or Am* to dim one's headlights; **p. antibrouillard** fog *Br* lamp *or Am* light; **p. à iode** quartz-iodine lamp; **p. de recul** *Br* reversing *or Am* back-up light **3** *Aviat* light, beacon; **phares d'atterrissage** landing lights **4** *Littéraire (guide)* beacon, leading light **5** *(comme adj; avec ou sans trait d'union) (exemplaire)* flagship *(avant n)*; **industrie p.** flagship *or* pioneering industry; **film-p.** seminal movie *or Br* film; **produit-p.** flagship (product)

pharillon [farijɔ̃] **NM** *Pêche* flare; **pêche au p.** flare fishing

pharisaïque [farizaik] **ADJ 1** *Hist & Rel* Pharisaic, Pharisaical **2** *Littéraire (hypocrite)* pharisaical

pharisaïsme [farizaism] **NM** *Hist & Rel* Pharisaism, Phariseeism

pharisien, -enne [farizjɛ̃, -ɛn] **ADJ 1** *Hist & Rel* Pharisaic, Pharisaical **2** *(moralisateur)* self-righteous **3** *Vieilli (hypocrite)* sanctimonious

NM,F 1 *Hist & Rel* Pharisee; **les Pharisiens** the Pharisees **2** *(moralisateur)* self-righteous person **3** *Vieilli (hypocrite)* sanctimonious person, *Littéraire* pharisee

pharmaceutique [farmasøtik] **ADJ** pharmaceutic, pharmaceutical

pharmacie [farmasi] **NF 1** *(magasin) Br* chemist's (shop), *Am* pharmacy, drugstore; *(dans un hôpital)* dispensary, pharmacy; **p. de garde** duty *Br* chemist *or Am* pharmacy *or* drugstore; **quelle est la p. de garde ce soir?** which *Br* chemist *or Am* pharmacy *or* drugstore is open all night tonight?; **aller à la p.** *Br* to go to the chemist *or* chemist's, *Am* to go to the pharmacy *or* drugstore **2** *(meuble)* medicine chest *or* cabinet *or Br* cupboard; *(boîte)* first-aid box; **p. de voyage** travelling first-aid kit **3** *Univ* pharmacy, pharmaceutics *(singulier)*

pharmacien, -enne [farmasjɛ̃, -ɛn] **NM,F 1** *(diplômé)* pharmacist, *Br* chemist **2** *(vendeur) Br* (dispensing) chemist, *Am* druggist

pharmacocinétique [farmakɔsinetik] **NF** pharmacokinetics *(singulier)*

pharmacodépendance [farmakɔdepɑ̃dɑ̃s] **NF** (pharmaceutical) drug dependency

pharmacodynamie [farmakɔdinami] **NF** pharmacodynamics *(singulier)*

pharmacodynamique [farmakɔdinamik] **ADJ** pharmacodynamic

pharmacogénétique [farmakɔʒenetik] **NF** pharmacogenetics *(singulier)*

pharmacologie [farmakɔlɔʒi] **NF** pharmacology

pharmacologique [farmakɔlɔʒik] **ADJ** pharmacological

pharmacologue [farmakɔlɔg], **pharmacologiste** [farmakɔlɔʒist] **NM,F** pharmacologist

pharmacomanie [farmakɔmani] **NF** (pharmaceutical) drug-addiction, *Spéc* pharmacomania

pharmacopée [farmakɔpe] **NF** pharmacopeia, pharmacopoeia; **la P. internationale** the International Pharmacopoeia

pharmacorésistance [farmakɔrezistɑ̃s] **NF** resistance to drugs

pharmacovigilance [farmakɔviʒilɑ̃s] **NF** (pharmaceutical) drug testing and control, pharmaceutical monitoring

pharyngal, -e, -aux, -ales [farɛ̃gal, -o] **ADJ** *Anat & Ling* pharyngal, pharyngeal

□ **pharyngale NF** *Ling* pharyngal *or* pharyngeal (consonant)

pharyngé, -e [farɛ̃ʒe], **pharyngien, -enne** [farɛ̃ʒjɛ̃, -ɛn] **ADJ** *Méd* pharyngal, pharyngeal

pharyngite [farɛ̃ʒit] **NF** *Méd* pharyngitis

pharyngo-laryngé, -e [farɛ̃gɔlarɛ̃ʒe] **ADJ** *Méd* pharyngolaryngeal

pharynx [farɛ̃ks] **NM** *Anat* pharynx

phase [faz] **NF 1** *(moment)* phase, stage; **être en p. de croissance/déclin** to be going through a period of growth/decline; **p. critique** critical stage; *Méd* critical phase; **p. de développement** development stage; **p. terminale** terminal phase; **cancer en p. terminale** terminal cancer; **le projet en arrive à sa p. d'exploitation** the project has moved into its first production run; **p. de fabrication** manufacturing stage; *Mktg* **p. de faisabilité** feasibility stage; *Mktg* **p. d'introduction** introduction stage **2** *Élec & Tech* phase; **différence de p.** difference in phase **3** *Astron* phase; **phases de la Lune** phases of the Moon, lunar phases; **entrer dans une nouvelle p.** *(Lune)* to change **4** *Phys* phase; **diagramme des phases** phase *or* constitution diagram; **règle des phases** phase rule **5** *Chim* phase **6** *Aviat* phase; **p. d'approche** approach phase; **p. d'atterrissage** landing phase; **p. de décollage** take-off phase

□ **en phase ADJ** *Élec, Phys & Tech* in phase; **les mouvements ne sont plus en p.** the movements are now out of phase; *Fig* **être en p.** to see eye to eye; **ils ne sont pas en p.** they don't see things the same way

phasemètre [fazmɛtr] **NM** *Élec* phasemeter; **p. enregistreur** phase recorder

phasianidé [fazjanide] *Orn* **NM** bird of the Phasianidae family

□ **phasianidés NMPL** Phasianidae

phasme [fasm] **NM** *Entom* stick insect, *Spéc* phasmid

phasmide [fasmid] **NM** *Entom* phasmid

phasmidé [fasmide] *Entom* **NM** phasmid

□ **phasmidés NMPL** Phasmidae

phasmoptère [fasmɔptɛr] = **phasmide**

Phébus [febys] **NPR** *Myth* Phoebus

Phèdre [fɛdr] **NPR** *Myth* Phaedra

phelloderme [felɔdɛrm] **NM** *Bot* phelloderm

phellogène [felɔʒɛn] **ADJ** *Bot* phellogenic, phellogenetic

phénacétine [fenasetin] **NF** *Pharm* phenacetin

phénakisticope [fenakistikɔp], **phénakistiscope** [fenakistiskɔp] **NM** phenakistoscope, thaumatrope, zoetrope

phénanthrène [fenɑ̃trɛn] **NM** *Chim* phenanthrene

phénate [fenat] = **phénolate**

phencyclidine [fɛ̃siklidin] **NF** *Chim* phencyclidine, PCP

phénétique [fenetik] *Biol* **ADJ** phenetic

NF phenetics *(singulier)*

Phénicie [fenisi] **NF** **la P.** Phoenicia

phénicien, -enne [fenisjɛ̃, -ɛn] **ADJ** Phoenician

NM *(langue)* Phoenician

□ **Phénicien, -enne NM,F** Phoenician

phénique [fenik] **ADJ** *voir* **acide**

phéniqué, -e [fenike] **ADJ** *Chim* phenolic, carbolic

phénix [feniks] **NM 1** *Myth* phoenix; **tel p.** like the proverbial phoenix **2** *Littéraire (prodige)* paragon **3** *Bot* palm tree

phénobarbital, -als [fenobarbital] **NM** *Pharm Br* phenobarbitone, *Am* phenobarbital

phénocristal, -aux [fenokristal, -o] **NM** phenocryst

phénol [fenɔl] **NM** *Chim* phenol, carbolic acid

phénolate [fenɔlat] **NM** *Chim* phenolate, phenoxide

phénolique [fenɔlik] **ADJ** *Chim* phenolic

phénologie [fenɔlɔʒi] **NF** phenology

phénolphtaléine [fenɔlftalein] **NF** *Chim* phenolphthalein

phénoménal, -e, -aux, -ales [fenɔmenal, -o] **ADJ 1** *(prodigieux)* phenomenal, tremendous, amazing; **son sens des affaires est p.** he/she has phenomenal *or* amazing business acumen; **un embouteillage p.** a most phenomenal *or* unbelievable traffic jam; **il a un toupet p.** he's got an outrageous nerve, *Br* he's outrageously cheeky **2** *Phil* phenomenal

phénoménalement [fenɔmenalmɑ̃] **ADV** phenomenally

phénomène [fenɔmɛn] **NM 1** phenomenon; **la grêle et autres phénomènes naturels** hail and other natural phenomena **2** *(manifestation)* phenomenon; **la communication de masse est un p. du XXème siècle** mass communication is a 20th-century phenomenon **3** *(prodige)* prodigy, wonder; **une truite de 10 kilos est un p.** a 10-kilo trout is a rare phenomenon **4** *Fam (excentrique)* character; **un drôle de p.** an odd customer; **cette gamine, quel p.!** that kid is a real character! **5** *(monstre)* **p. (de foire)** freak **6** *Phil* phenomenon

phénoménisme [fenɔmenism] **NM** phenomenalism

phénoméniste [fenɔmenist] **ADJ** phenomenalist

NMF phenomenalist

phénoménologie [fenɔmenɔlɔʒi] **NF** phenomenology

'**La Phénoménologie de l'esprit**' *Hegel* 'The Phenomenology of Mind'

phénoménologique [fenɔmenɔlɔʒik] **ADJ** phenomenological

phénoménologue [fenɔmenɔlɔg] **NMF** phenomenologist

phénoplaste [fenɔplast] **NM** *Chim* phenolic resin

phénothiazine [fenɔtjazin] **NF** *Chim* phenothiazine

phénotype [fenɔtip] **NM** *Biol* phenotype

phénotypique [fenɔtipik] **ADJ** *Biol* phenotypic, phenotypical

phénylalanine [fenilalanin] **NF** *Chim* phenylalanine

phénylbutazone [fenilbytazon] **NF** *Chim* phenylbutazone

phénylcétonurie [fenilsetɔnyri] **NF** *Méd* phenylketonuria

phényle [fenil] **NM** *Chim* phenyl radical

phénylique [fenilik] **ADJ** phenylic

phéochromocytome [feɔkrɔmɔsitom] **NM** pheochromocytoma

phéophycée [feɔfise] **NF** member of the Laminaria

□ **phéophycées NFPL** Laminaria

phéromone [ferɔmɔn], **phérormone** [ferɔrmɔn] **NF** pheromone

phi [fi] **NM INV** phi

Phidias [fidjas] **NPR** Phidias

Philadelphie [filadɛlfi] **NM** Philadelphia

Philaminte [filamɛ̃t] **NPR** = the principal bluestocking in Molière's 'Les Femmes savantes'

philanthe [filɑ̃t] **NM** *Entom* bee-killer wasp

philanthrope [filɑ̃trɔp] **ADJ** philanthropic

NMF philanthropist, philanthrope

philanthropie [filɑ̃trɔpi] **NF** philanthropy

philanthropique [filɑ̃trɔpik] **ADJ** philanthropic

philatélie [filateli] **NF** stamp-collecting, *Spéc* philately

philatélique [filatelik] **ADJ** philatelic

philatéliste [filatelist] **NMF** stamp-collector, *Spéc* philatelist

Philémon [filemɔ̃] **NPR** *Myth* Philemon; **P. et Baucis** Philemon and Baucis

philharmonie [filarmɔni] **NF** philharmonic *or* musical society

philharmonique [filarmɔnik] **ADJ** philharmonic **NM le p. de Boston/Berlin** the Boston/Berlin Philharmonic (Orchestra)

Philippe [filip] **NPR P. II (de Macédoine)** Philip II (of Macedon); **P. Auguste** Philip Augustus; **P. le Bel** Philip the Fair

philippin, -e[1] [filipɛ̃, -in] **ADJ** Filipino ◻ **Philippin, -e NM,F** Filipino

philippine[2] [filipin] **NF** *(jeu)* = game in which two people, having found and shared a double-kernelled almond, bet on who will remember to say "bonjour Philippine" first the next day

Philippines [filipin] **NFPL les P.** the Philippines, the Philippine Islands; **vivre aux P.** to live in the Philippines; **aller aux P.** to go to the Philippines

philippique [filipik] **NF** *Littéraire* philippic

philistin, -e [filistɛ̃, -in] *Littéraire* **ADJ** philistine, uncultured; **dédaignant les récriminations philistines** scorning the recriminations of the philistines **NM,F** philistine

philistinisme [filistinism] **NM** *Littéraire* philistinism

Philistins [filistɛ̃] **NMPL les P.** the Philistines

philo [filo] **NF** *Fam* *(abrév* **philosophie***)* philosophy■

philodendron [filodɛ̃drɔ̃] **NM** philodendron

philologie [filɔlɔʒi] **NF** philology

philologique [filɔlɔʒik] **ADJ** philological

philologue [filɔlɔg] **NMF** philologist

philosophale [filozɔfal] **ADJ F** *voir* **pierre**

philosophe [filozɔf] **ADJ** philosophical; **elle est très p.** she's very philosophical **NMF 1** *(penseur)* philosopher **2** *(sage)* **il a pris la chose en p.** he took it philosophically *or* calmly

philosopher [3] [filozɔfe] **VI** to philosophize (**sur** about)

philosophie [filozɔfi] **NF 1** *(étude)* philosophy; **faire des études de p.** to study *or* Br to read philosophy; **la p. de l'histoire/des sciences** the philosophy of history/science **2** *(conception, doctrine)* philosophy; **quelle est votre p. de la vie?** what's your philosophy of life? **3** *(sagesse)* **il est plein de p.** he is very wise ◻ **avec philosophie ADV** philosophically

philosophique [filozɔfik] **ADJ** philosophical

philosophiquement [filozɔfikmɑ̃] **ADV** philosophically

philtre [filtr] **NM p. (d'amour)** love-potion, philtre

phimosis [fimozis] **NM** *Méd* phimosis

phishing [fiʃiŋ] **NM** *Ordinat* phishing

phlébite [flebit] **NF** *Méd* phlebitis

phlébographie [flebografi] **NF** *Méd* phlebography

phlébologie [flebɔlɔʒi] **NF** *Méd* phlebology

phlébologue [flebɔlɔg] **NMF** vein specialist, *Spéc* phlebologist

phléborragie [fleboraʒi] **NF** *Méd* phleborrhagia

phlébothrombose [flebotrɔ̃boz] **NF** *Méd* phlebothrombosis

phlébotome [flebɔtɔm] **NM** *Entom* sand fly

phlébotomie [flebɔtɔmi] **NF** *Méd* phlebotomy

phlegmon [flɛgmɔ̃] **NM** *Méd* phlegmon

phlegmoneux, -euse [flɛgmɔnø, -øz] **ADJ** *Méd* phlegmonous

phléole [fleɔl] **NF** *Bot* phleum, cat's tail grass; **p. des prés** timothy grass, meadow cat's tail grass

phloème [flɔɛm] **NM** *Bot* phloem

phlogistique [flɔʒistik] **NM** *Chim* phlogiston

phlox [flɔks] **NM** *Bot* phlox

phlyctène [fliktɛn] **NF** *Méd* phlyctena

pH-mètre [peaʃmɛtr] *(pl* **pH-mètres***)* **NM** pH meter

Phnom Penh [pnɔmpɛn] **NM** Phnom Penh

phobie [fɔbi] **NF** phobia; **avoir la p. de qch** to have a phobia about sth

phobique [fɔbik] **ADJ** phobic

Phocée [fose] **NF** Phocaea

phocéen, -enne [fɔseɛ̃, -ɛn] **ADJ 1** *Antiq* Phocaean **2** *(de Marseille)* of/from Marseilles; **la cité phocéenne** = the city of Marseilles

◻ **Phocéen, -enne NM,F 1** *Antiq* Phocaean **2** *Vieilli* = inhabitant of or person from Marseilles

phocomèle [fɔkɔmɛl] *Méd* **ADJ** phocomelic, phocomelous **NM** phocomelus

phocomélie [fɔkɔmeli] **NF** *Méd* phocomelia

phœnix [feniks] **NM** = **phénix 3**

pholade [fɔlad] **NF** *Zool* piddock

pholcodine [fɔlkɔdin] **NF** *Pharm* pholcodine

pholidote [fɔlidɔt] *Zool* **ADJ** scaly **NM** pangolin ◻ **pholidotes NMPL** Pholidota, pangolins

pholiote [fɔljɔt] **NF** *Bot* pholiota

phonateur, -trice [fɔnatœr, -tris] **ADJ** phonatory; **l'appareil p.** the phonatory apparatus

phonation [fɔnasjɔ̃] **NF** phonation

phonatoire [fɔnatwar] **ADJ** phonatory; **acte p.** phonatory act

phonatrice [fɔnatris] *voir* **phonateur**

phone [fɔn] **NM** phon

-PHONE [fɔn] **SUFF**

The most interesting use of this suffix from a translation point of view is the creation, based on a root ending in -o, of adjectives and nouns referring to SPEAKERS of a particular language.

Although the equivalent form ending in *-phone* also exists in English in some cases, it is of a more formal register than the French, eg:

francophone French-speaking, Francophone; **un francophone** a French speaker, a Francophone; **anglophone** English-speaking, Anglophone; **un anglophone** an English speaker, an Anglophone; **germanophone** German-speaking; **un germanophone** a German speaker; **hispanophone** Spanish-speaking; **un hispanophone** a Spanish speaker

phonématique [fɔnematik] **ADJ** phonemic, phonematic **NF** phonemics *(singulier)*

phonème [fɔnɛm] **NM** phoneme

phonémique [fɔnemik] **ADJ** phonemic **NF** phonemics *(singulier)*

phonéticien, -enne [fɔnetisjɛ̃, -ɛn] **NM,F** phonetician

phonétique [fɔnetik] **ADJ** phonetic **NF** phonetics *(singulier)*

phonétiquement [fɔnetikmɑ̃] **ADV** phonetically

phonétisme [fɔnetism] **NM** *Ling* phonetism

phoniatre [fɔnjatr] **NMF** speech therapist

phoniatrie [fɔnjatri] **NF** speech therapy

phonie [fɔni] **NF** *Tél* **1** *(abrév* **radiotéléphonie***)* radiotelephony **2** *(abrév* **téléphonie***)* telephony

phoning [fɔniŋ] **NM** *Mktg* telesales

phonique [fɔnik] **ADJ 1** *Ling* phonic **2** *(relatif aux sons)* sound *(avant n)*

phono [fɔno] **NM** *Fam Vieilli (abrév* **phonographe***)* phonograph■, gramophone■

phonocapteur, -trice [fɔnɔkaptœr, -tris] **ADJ** sound-reproducing *(avant n)*

phonocardiographie [fɔnɔkardjografi] **NF** phonocardiography

phonogénie [fɔnɔʒeni] **NF** *(pour la radio)* good broadcasting quality; *(pour l'enregistrement)* good recording quality

phonogénique [fɔnɔʒenik] **ADJ voix p.** *(pour la radio)* good broadcasting voice; *(pour l'enregistrement)* good recording voice

phonogramme [fɔnɔgram] **NM** phonogram

phonographe [fɔnɔgraf] **NM** phonograph, gramophone

phonographique [fɔnɔgrafik] **ADJ** phonographic

phonolite, phonolithe [fɔnɔlit] **NF** *Minér* phonolite

phonolitique, phonolithique [fɔnɔlitik] **ADJ** *Minér* phonolitic

phonologie [fɔnɔlɔʒi] **NF** *Ling* phonology

phonologique [fɔnɔlɔʒik] **ADJ** *Ling* phonological

phonologue [fɔnɔlɔg] **NMF** *Ling* phonologist

phonométrie [fɔnɔmetri] **NF** phonometry

phonon [fɔnɔ̃] **NM** phonon

phonothèque [fɔnɔtɛk] **NF** sound archives

phoque [fɔk] **NM 1** *Zool* seal; **p. barbu** bearded seal; **p. à capuchon** hooded seal, bladdernose; **p. gris** grey seal; **p. du Groenland** harp seal; **p. marbré** ringed seal; **p. moine** monk seal; **p. veau-marin** common *or* harbour seal **2** *(fourrure)* sealskin

phormium [fɔrmjɔm] **NM** *Bot* phormium, New Zealand flax

phosgène [fɔsʒɛn] **NM** *Chim* phosgene

phosphatage [fɔsfataʒ] **NM** *Chim* phosphatization

phosphatase [fɔsfataz] **NF** *Chim* phosphatase

phosphatation [fɔsfatasjɔ̃] **NF** *Chim* phosphate coating

phosphate [fɔsfat] **NM** *Chim* phosphate; **sans phosphates** phosphate-free

phosphaté, -e [fɔsfate] **ADJ** *Chim* phosphated; **des engrais phosphatés** phosphate-enriched fertilizers

phosphater [3] [fɔsfate] **VT 1** *Agr* to phosphatize, to treat with phosphates **2** *Métal* to phosphate, to phosphatize

phosphatide [fɔsfatid] **NF** *Biol & Chim* phosphatide, phospolipid

phosphatique [fɔsfatik] **ADJ** *Chim* phosphatic

phosphène [fɔsfɛn] **NM** *Chim* phosphene

phosphine [fɔsfin] **NF** *Chim* phosphine; **phosphines primaires/secondaires/tertiaires** primary/secondary/tertiary phosphines

phosphite [fɔsfit] **NM** *Chim* phosphite

phosphocalcique [fɔsfɔkalsik] **ADJ** *Physiol* phosphocalcic

phosphoglycérique [fɔsfɔgliserik] **ADJ** *Chim* **acide p.** phosphoglyceric acid

phospholipase [fɔsfɔlipaz] **NF** *Biol & Chim* phospholipase

phospholipide [fɔsfɔlipid] **NM** *Biol & Chim* phospholipid

phosphoprotéine [fɔsfɔprɔtein] **NF** *Biol & Chim* phosphoprotein

phosphore [fɔsfɔr] **NM** *Chim* phosphorus

phosphoré, -e [fɔsfɔre] **ADJ** *Chim (naturellement)* phosphorated; *(artificiellement)* phosphoretted

phosphorer [3] [fɔsfɔre] **VI** *Fam (réfléchir)* to think hard■, *Hum* to cogitate; **qu'est-ce que ça phosphore ici!** I can see those brains are working overtime here!

phosphorescence [fɔsfɔresɑ̃s] **NF** *Phys* phosphorescence

phosphorescent, -e [fɔsfɔresɑ̃, -ɑ̃t] **ADJ 1** *Phys* phosphorescent **2** *(luisant)* luminous, glowing

phosphoreux, -euse [fɔsfɔrø, -øz] **ADJ** *Chim* phosphorous; **acide p.** phosphorous acid; **bronze p.** phosphor bronze

phosphorique [fɔsfɔrik] **ADJ** *Chim* phosphoric

phosphorisme [fɔsfɔrism] **NM** *Méd* phosphorism

phosphorite [fɔsfɔrit] **NF** *Minér* phosphorite, phosphate rock

phosphorylation [fɔsfɔrilasjɔ̃] **NF** *Biol & Chim* phosphorylation

phosphoryle [fɔsfɔril] **NM** *Biol & Chim* phosphoryl

phosphure [fɔsfyr] **NM** *Chim* phosphide

phot [fɔt] **NM** *Phys* phot

photo [foto] **NF 1** *(cliché)* photo, shot; **avez-vous fait des photos?** did you take any photos or pictures?; **sur la p.** in the photo; *Cin* **les photos du tournage** the shooting stills; **p. de famille** family portrait; *Fig* **poser pour la traditionnelle p. de famille** *(politiciens, sportifs)* to have the traditional group photograph taken; **p. d'identité** passport photo; **p. souvenir** souvenir photo; *Fam* **tu veux ma p.?** what are you staring at?; *Fam Fig* **y'a pas p.** there's no contest **2** *(activité)* photography; **faire de la p. en amateur/professionnel** to be an amateur/professional photographer; **p. de mode** fashion photography ◻ **en photo ADV** on a photograph; **des fleurs en p.** a photo of some flowers **ADV prendre qn en p.** to take sb's photo *or* picture; **prendre qch en p.** to take a photo *or* picture of sth; **il est bien en p.** he photographs well

photo- [foto] **PRÉF** photo-

photobiologie [fɔtɔbjɔlɔʒi] **NF** *Biol* photobiology

photocathode [fɔtɔkatɔd] **NF** *Chim* photocathode

photochimie [fɔtɔʃimi] **NF** *Chim* photochemistry

photochimique [fɔtɔʃimik] **ADJ** *Chim* photochemical

photocinèse [fɔtɔsinɛz] **NF** *Biol* photokinesis

photocomposer [3] [fɔtɔkɔ̃poze] **VT** *Typ* to photoset, to photocompose, *Br* to filmset

photocomposeuse [fɔtɔkɔ̃pozøz] **NF** *Typ* photocompositor, *Br* filmsetter

photocompositeur [fɔtɔkɔ̃pozitœr] **NM** *Typ* photocomposer, phototypesetter, *Br* filmsetter

photocomposition [fɔtɔkɔ̃pozisjɔ̃] **NF** *Typ* photocomposition, photosetting, *Br* filmsetting

photoconducteur, -trice [fɔtɔkɔ̃dyktœr, -tris] *Électron* **ADJ** photoconductive; **cellule photoconductrice** photoconductor cell **NM** photoconductor

photoconduction [fɔtɔkɔ̃dyksjɔ̃] **NF** *Électron* photoconductivity

photoconductrice [fɔtɔkɔ̃dyktris] *voir* **photoconducteur**

photocopie [fɔtɔkɔpi] **NF** photocopy; *(action)* photocopying

photocopier [9] [fɔtɔkɔpje] **VT** to photocopy; **photocopiez-moi ce document en trois exemplaires, s'il vous plaît** please make three photocopies or copies of this document for me

photocopieur [fɔtɔkɔpjœr] **NM** photocopier

photocopieuse [fɔtɔkɔpjøz] **NF** photocopier

photocopillage [fɔtɔkɔpijaʒ] **NM** = infringement of copyright through excessive use of photocopiers

photodésintégration [fɔtɔdezɛ̃tegrasjɔ̃] **NF** *Phys* photodisintegration

photodiode [fɔtɔdjɔd] **NF** *Électron* photodiode

photodissociation [fɔtɔdisɔsjasjɔ̃] **NF** *Chim* photodissociation

photodynamique [fɔtɔdinamik] *Biol* **ADJ** photodynamic **NF** photodynamics *(singulier)*

photoélasticimétrie [fɔtɔelastisimetri] **NF** *Phys* measurement of photoelasticity

photoélasticité [fɔtɔelastisite] **NF** *Phys* photoelasticity

photoélectricité [fɔtɔelɛktrisite] **NF** *Phys* photoelectricity

photoélectrique [fɔtɔelɛktrik] **ADJ** *Phys* photoelectric

photoélectron [fɔtɔelɛktrɔ̃] **NM** *Phys* photoelectron

photoémetteur, -trice [fɔtɔemetœr, -tris] **ADJ** photoemissive

photoémission [fɔtɔemisjɔ̃] **NF** photoemission

photo-finish [fɔtɔfiniʃ] *(pl* **photos-finish)** **NF** *(photographie)* photo finish; *(appareil)* photofinish camera; **l'arrivée a dû être vérifiée à la p.** it was a photo finish

photogène [fɔtɔʒɛn] **ADJ 1** *Phys* photogenic **2** *Biol* photogenic; **organe p.** photophore

photogenèse [fɔtɔʒənɛz] **NF** photogenesis

photogénique [fɔtɔʒenik] **ADJ** photogenic

photogéologie [fɔtɔʒeɔlɔʒi] **NF** *Géol* photogeology

photogramme [fɔtɔgram] **NM** photogram

photogrammétrie [fɔtɔgrametri] **NF** photogrammetry

photographe [fɔtɔgraf] **NMF 1** *(artiste)* photographer; **ils ont posé sur le perron pour les photographes** they had a photo call on the steps; **p. en chef** chief photographer; **p. de mode** fashion photographer; *Cin* **p. de plateau** unit photographer; **p. de presse** press photographer **2** *(commerçant)* dealer in photographic equipment; **je vais apporter cette pellicule chez le p.** I'm taking this film to the developer's or photo shop

photographie [fɔtɔgrafi] **NF 1** *(activité)* photography; **faire de la p.** *(professionnel)* to be a photographer; *(amateur)* to be an amateur photographer; **p. aérienne/en couleurs** aerial/colour photography; **p. au flash** flash photography; **p. fabriquée** fabricated photography; **p. manipulée** manipulated photography; **p. de mode** fashion photography; **p. plastique** artistic photography

2 *(cliché)* photograph, picture; **prendre une p. de qn** to take a photograph or a picture of sb; **nos photographies de Grèce** our photographs from Greece; **toutes les photographies du mariage** all the wedding pictures or photographs; **p. d'identité** passport photograph; **p. de plateau** still; **p. publicitaire** publicity still; **p. satellite** satellite photograph; **p. de tournage** still

3 *(reproduction)* **ce sondage est une p. de l'opinion** this survey is an accurate reflection of public opinion

photographier [9] [fɔtɔgrafje] **VT 1** *(prendre une photographie de)* to photograph, to take photographs or pictures of; **se faire p.** to have one's photograph or picture taken **2** *Fig (mémoriser)* to memorize (photographically)

photographique [fɔtɔgrafik] **ADJ 1** *Phot* photographic **2** *Fig (fidèle à la réalité)* **il nous a fait une description presque p. des lieux** he described the place in the minutest detail

photographiquement [fɔtɔgrafikmɑ̃] **ADV** photographically

photograveur [fɔtɔgravœr] **NM** photoengraver

photogravure [fɔtɔgravyr] **NF** photoengraving

photo-interprétation [fɔtɔɛ̃tɛrpretasjɔ̃] *(pl* **photos-interprétations)** **NF** photo-interpretation

photojournalisme [fɔtɔʒurnalism] **NM** photojournalism

photojournaliste [fɔtɔʒurnalist] **NMF** photojournalist

photolecture [fɔtɔlɛktyr] **NF** optical character recognition, OCR

photolithographie [fɔtɔlitɔgrafi] **NF 1** *(technique)* photolithography **2** *(image)* photolithograph

photoluminescence [fɔtɔlyminesɑ̃s] **NF** photoluminescence

photoluminescent, -e [fɔtɔlyminesɑ̃, -ɑ̃t] **ADJ** photoluminescent

photolyse [fɔtɔliz] **NF** *Chim* photolysis

photomacrographie [fɔtɔmakrɔgrafi] **NF** macrophotography

Photomaton® [fɔtɔmatɔ̃] **NM** photobooth

photomécanique [fɔtɔmekanik] **ADJ** *Typ* photomechanical

photomètre [fɔtɔmɛtr] **NM** photometer

photométrie [fɔtɔmetri] **NF** photometry

photométrique [fɔtɔmetrik] **ADJ** photometric

photomicrographie [fɔtɔmikrɔgrafi] **NF 1** *(technique)* photomicrography **2** *(image)* photomicrograph

photomontage [fɔtɔmɔ̃taʒ] **NM** photomontage

photomultiplicateur, -trice [fɔtɔmyltiplikatœr, -tris] **ADJ** photomultiplier *(avant n)* **NM** photomultiplier

photon [fɔtɔ̃] **NM** *Phys* photon

photonique [fɔtɔnik] **ADJ** *Phys* photon *(avant n)*, photonic

photopériode [fɔtɔperjɔd] **NF** *Biol* photoperiod

photopériodique [fɔtɔperjɔdik] **ADJ** *Biol* photoperiodic

photopériodisme [fɔtɔperjɔdism] **NM** *Biol* photoperiodism

photophilie [fɔtɔfili] **NF** *Biol & Bot* photophily

photophobie [fɔtɔfɔbi] **NF** *Méd* photophobia

photophobique [fɔtɔfɔbik] **ADJ** *Méd* photophobic

photophore [fɔtɔfɔr] **NM 1** *(lampe)* reflective lamp *(used by miner)* **2** *(pour bougie)* candle holder with glass shade **3** *Zool* photophore

photopile [fɔtɔpil] **NF** photovoltaic cell

photopolymère [fɔtɔpɔlimɛr] **ADJ** **plastique p.** photopolymer

photoréalisme [fɔtɔrealism] **NM** photorealism

photorécepteur [fɔtɔreseptœr] **NM** photoreceptor

photoreportage [fɔtɔrəpɔrtaʒ] **NM 1** *(discipline)* photojournalism **2** *(article)* report *(consisting mainly of photographs)*

photorésistance [fɔtɔrezistɑ̃s] **NF** *Électron* photoelectric resistor

photorésistant, -e [fɔtɔrezistɑ̃, -ɑ̃t] **ADJ** photoresistant

photo-robot [fɔtɔrɔbo] *(pl* **photos-robots)** **NF** Photofit® or Identikit® (picture)

photo-roman [fɔtɔrɔmɑ̃] *(pl* **photos-romans)** **NM** photonovel

photosensibilisation [fɔtɔsɑ̃sibilizasjɔ̃] **NF** photosensitization

photosensibilité [fɔtɔsɑ̃sibilite] **NF** photosensitivity

photosensible [fɔtɔsɑ̃sibl] **ADJ** photosensitive; **rendre qch p.** to photosensitize sth

photosphère [fɔtɔsfɛr] **NF** *Astron* photosphere

photostat [fɔtɔsta] **NM** *Tech* photostat

photostoppeur, -euse [fɔtɔstɔpœr, -øz] **NM,F** street photographer

photostyle [fɔtɔstil] **NM** *Ordinat* light pen

photosynthèse [fɔtɔsɛ̃tɛz] **NF** *Biol & Bot* photosynthesis; **fabriquer qch par la p.** to photosynthetize sth

photosynthétique [fɔtɔsɛ̃tetik] **ADJ** *Biol & Bot* photosynthetic

phototactisme [fɔtɔtaktism] **NM** *Biol* phototaxis, phototaxy

phototaxie [fɔtɔtaksi] **NF** *Biol* phototaxis, phototaxy

photothèque [fɔtɔtɛk] **NF** picture or photographic library

photothérapie [fɔtɔterapi] **NF** *Méd* phototherapy

phototransistor [fɔtɔtrɑ̃zistɔr] **NM** phototransistor

phototropisme [fɔtɔtrɔpism] **NM** *Biol* phototropism

phototype [fɔtɔtip] **NM** phototype

phototypie [fɔtɔtipi] **NF** *Typ* phototype (process)

photovoltaïque [fɔtɔvɔltaik] **ADJ** photovoltaic

phragmite [fragmit] **NM 1** *Bot* reed **2** *Orn* **p. aquatique** aquatic warbler; **p. des joncs** sedge warbler

phrase [fraz] **NF 1** *Ling* sentence; *(en grammaire transformationnelle)* phrase

2 *(énoncé)* **sa dernière p.** the last thing he/she said; **laisse-moi finir ma p.** let me finish (what I have to say); **p. célèbre** famous saying or remark; **p. toute faite** set phrase; *Pol* **petite p.** soundbite; **faire de grandes phrases** ou **des phrases** to talk in flowery language

3 *Mus* phrase

❑ **sans phrases** **ADV** straightforwardly

phrasé [fraze] **NM** *Mus* phrasing

phraséologie [frazeɔlɔʒi] **NF 1** *(style)* phraseology **2** *Littéraire (verbiage)* flowery or high-flown language

phraséologique [frazeɔlɔʒik] **ADJ 1** *(style)* phraseological **2** *Littéraire (verbiage)* flowery, high-flown

phraser [3] [fraze] **VT** *Mus* to phrase

phraseur, -euse [frazœr, -øz] **NM,F** *Péj* speechifier, person of fine words

phrastique [frastik] **ADJ** *Ling* sentence

phratrie [fratri] **NF** *(en anthropologie) & Antiq* phratry

phréatique [freatik] **ADJ** phreatic

phrénique [frenik] **ADJ** phrenic

phrénologie [frenɔlɔʒi] **NF** phrenology

phrygane [frigan] **NF** *Entom* caddis fly; **larve de p.** caddis worm

Phrygie [friʒi] **NF** **la P.** Phrygia

phrygien, -enne [friʒjɛ̃, -ɛn] **ADJ 1** *Antiq* Phrygian **2** *Mus* **mode p.** Phrygian mode **3** **bonnet p.** cap of liberty, Phrygian cap

❑ **Phrygien, -enne** **NM,F** Phrygian

Culture

BONNET PHRYGIEN

This red conical cloth cap was an emblem of the French Revolution, symbolising the freedom of the people. **Marianne** (the personification of the French Republic; see box at this entry) is always depicted wearing one.

---

phtaléine [ftalein] **NF** *Chim* phthalein

phtalique [ftalik] **ADJ M** *Chim* phthalic

phtiriase [ftirjaz] **NF** *Méd* phthiriasis

phtirius [ftirjys] **NM** pubic louse, *Spéc* Phthirus pubis

phtisie [ftizi] **NF** *Vieilli Méd* consumption, *Spéc* phthisis; **p. galopante** galloping consumption

phtisiologie [ftizjɔlɔʒi] **NF** *Vieilli Méd* phthisiology

phtisiologue [ftizjɔlɔg] **NMF** *Vieilli Méd* phthisiologist

phtisique [ftizik] *Vieilli Méd* **ADJ** consumptive, *Spéc* phthisic **NMF** person suffering from consumption or *Spéc* phthisis

Phuket [pukɛt] **NM** Phuket

phycocyanine [fikɔsjanin] **NF** phycocyanin

phycoérythrine [fikɔeritrin] **NF** phycoerythrin

phycomycète [fikɔmisɛt] *Biol* **NM** phycomycete

❑ **phycomycètes** **NMPL** Phycomyceteae, phycomycetes

phylactère [filaktɛr] **NM 1** *Rel* phylactery, teffilah **2** *Beaux-Arts* phylactery, scroll **3** *(dans une bande dessinée)* bubble, balloon

phylarque [filark] **NM** *Antiq* phylarch

phylétique [filetik] **ADJ** *Biol* phyletic, phylogenetic

phyllade [filad] **NM** *Géol* phyllite

phyllie [fili] **NF** *Entom* leaf insect

phylloquinone [filɔkinɔn] **NF** *Biol & Chim* phylloquinone

phyllotaxie [filɔtaksi] NF *Bot* phyllotaxis

phylloxéra, phylloxera [filɔksera] NM *Entom & Bot* phylloxera

phylloxéré, -e [filɔksere] ADJ phylloxerated

phylloxérien, -enne [filɔkserjɛ̃, -ɛn], **phylloxérique** [filɔkserik] ADJ *Entom & Bot* phylloxerna

phylogenèse [filɔʒənɛz] NF *Biol* phylogenesis, phylogeny

phylogénétique [filɔʒenetik] ADJ *Biol* phylogenetic, phylogenic

phylogénie [filɔʒeni] = **phylogenèse**

phylogénique [filɔʒenik] = **phylogénétique**

phylum [filɔm] NM *Biol* phylum

physalie [fizali] NF *Zool* Portuguese man-of-war, *Spéc* Physalia

physalis [fizalis] NM *Bot* winter *or* ground cherry, cape gooseberry, physalis

physe [fiz] NF *Zool* physa

physicalisme [fizikalism] NM *Phil* physicalism

physicien, -enne [fizisjɛ̃, -ɛn] NM,F physicist; **p. nucléaire** nuclear physicist

physico-chimie [fizikoʃimi] NF physical chemistry, physicochemistry

physico-chimique [fizikoʃimik] (*pl* **physico-chimiques**) ADJ physicochemical

physico-mathématique [fizikomatematik] (*pl* **physico-mathématiques**) ADJ physicomathematical

physiocrate [fizjɔkrat] *Hist* ADJ physiocratic
NMF physiocrat

physiocratie [fizjɔkrasi] NF *Hist* physiocracy

physiocratique [fizjɔkratik] ADJ *Hist* physiocratic

physiognomonie [fizjɔgnɔmɔni] NF physiognomy (*science*)

physiologie [fizjɔlɔʒi] NF physiology

physiologique [fizjɔlɔʒik] ADJ physiological

physiologiquement [fizjɔlɔʒikmɑ̃] ADV physiologically

physiologiste [fizjɔlɔʒist] NMF physiologist

physionomie [fizjɔnɔmi] NF 1 (*visage*) features, facial appearance; *Spéc* physiognomy; **il y a quelque chose dans sa p. qui attire la sympathie** there's something about his/her face that draws you to him/her; **il ne faut pas juger les gens sur leur p.** you shouldn't judge by appearances
2 (*aspect → d'une chose*) face, appearance; **la p. des choses** the face of things; **la p. du quartier a changé en dix ans** the appearance of the district has changed in ten years; **ceci a modifié la p. du marché** this has altered the appearance of the market

physionomique [fizjɔnɔmik] ADJ physionomical

physionomiste [fizjɔnɔmist] ADJ good at remembering faces, observant (of people's faces); **je ne suis pas très p.** I'm not very good at remembering faces
NMF *Vieilli* physiognomist

physiopathologie [fizjɔpatɔlɔʒi] NF physiopathology

physiopathologique [fizjɔpatɔlɔʒik] ADJ physiopathologic, physiopathological

physiothérapeute [fizjɔterapøt] NMF *Can & Suisse Méd* physiotherapist

physiothérapie [fizjɔterapi] NF natural medicine

physique¹ [fizik] NF physics (*singulier*); **p. expérimentale** experimental physics; *Vieilli* **p. du globe** geophysics; **p. nucléaire** nuclear physics; **p. des particules** particle physics; **p. du sol** soil mechanics

physique² [fizik] ADJ 1 *Phys & Chim* (*propriété*) physical
2 (*naturel → monde, univers*) physical, natural
3 (*corporel → exercice, force, effort*) physical, bodily; (*→ symptôme*) physical, *Spéc* somatic; (*→ souffrance*) physical, bodily; *Fam* **je ne le supporte pas, c'est p.** I can't stand him, it's a gut feeling
4 (*sexuel → plaisir, jouissance*) physical, carnal
NM 1 (*apparence*) **soigner son p.** to take care of *or* look after oneself; **avoir un p. ingrat** to be physically unattractive; **avoir un p. avantageux** to have a fine physique; *Théât & Fig* **avoir le p. de l'emploi** to look the part
2 (*constitution*) physical condition; **au p. comme au moral** physically as well as morally speaking

physiquement [fizikmɑ̃] ADV physically; **il n'est pas mal p.** he's quite good-looking

physisorption [fizisɔrpsjɔ̃] NF physisorption

physostigma [fizɔstigma] NM *Bot* physostigma

physostigmine [fizɔstigmin] NF *Chim* physostigmine

physostome [fizɔstɔm] NM *Ich* physostomous fish

phytéléphas [fitelefas] NM *Bot* phytelephas

phytobiologie [fitɔbjɔlɔʒi] NF phytobiology

phytocide [fitɔsid] ADJ phytocidal
NM phytocide

phytoflagellé [fitɔflaʒele] NM phytoflagellate

phytogéographie [fitɔʒeɔgrafi] NF phytogeography

phytohormone [fitɔɔrmɔn] NF phytohormone

phytonutriment [fitɔnytrimɑ̃] NM phytonutrient

phytopathologie [fitɔpatɔlɔʒi] NF phytopathology

phytophage [fitɔfaʒ] ADJ phytophagous

phytopharmacie [fitɔfarmasi] NF plant pharmacology

phytophthora [fitɔftɔra] NM *Bot* phytophthora

phytoplancton [fitɔplɑ̃ktɔ̃] NM phytoplankton

phytosanitaire [fitɔsanitɛr] ADJ plant-care (*avant n*), *Spéc* phytosanitary; **produit p.** (*engrais*) plant-care product; (*pesticide*) pesticide

phytosociologie [fitɔsɔsjɔlɔʒi] NF phytosociology

phytothérapeute [fitɔterapøt] NMF expert in herbal *or* plant medicine

phytothérapie [fitɔterapi] NF herbal medicine

phytotoxique [fitɔtɔksik] ADJ phytotoxic

phytotron [fitɔtrɔ̃] NM plant laboratory

phytozoaire [fitɔzɔɛr] NM phytozoon, zoophyte

pi [pi] NM INV 1 (*lettre*) pi 2 *Math* pi 3 *Phys* pion, pi meson

piaculaire [pjakylɛr] ADJ *Littéraire* expiatory

piaf [pjaf] NM *Fam* (*oiseau*) bird■; (*moineau*) sparrow■; *Fig* **cervelle** *ou* **crâne** *ou* **tête de p.!** birdbrain!

piaffant, -e [pjafɑ̃, -ɑ̃t] ADJ **être p. d'impatience** to be champing at the bit

piaffement [pjafmɑ̃] NM pawing (the ground)

piaffer [3] [pjafe] VI 1 (*cheval*) to paw the ground 2 (*personne*) to stamp one's feet; **p. d'impatience** to be champing at the bit, to be seething with impatience

piaffeur, -euse [pjafœr, -øz] ADJ (*cheval*) pawing

piaillard, -e [pjajar, -ard] = **piailleur**

piaillement [pjajmɑ̃] NM 1 (*d'oiseaux*) **un p.** a chirp, a cheep; **le p. des moineaux** the chirping *or* cheeping of the sparrows; **des piaillements** chirping, cheeping 2 *Fam* (*d'enfants*) squealing■ (UNCOUNT)

piailler [3] [pjaje] VI 1 (*oiseau*) to chirp, to cheep 2 *Fam* (*enfant*) to squeal■

piailleries [pjajri] NF 1 (*d'oiseau*) chirping, cheeping 2 *Fam* (*d'enfants*) squealing■

piailleur, -euse [pjajœr, -øz] *Fam* ADJ (*enfant*) squealing■
NM,F (*enfant*) squealer■

pian [pjɑ̃] NM *Méd* yaws (*singulier*), framboesia

piane-piane [pjanpjan] ADV *Fam* slowly■; **vas-y p.!** take your time!, there's no rush!

pianissimo [pjanisimo] ADV 1 *Mus* pianissimo 2 *Fam* (*doucement*) nice and slowly

pianiste [pjanist] NMF pianist, piano player; **p. de jazz** jazz pianist

'**La Pianiste**' *Haneke* 'The Piano Teacher'

pianistique [pjanistik] ADJ (*aptitude, technique*) piano (*avant n*), piano playing (*avant n*); **l'œuvre p. de Mozart** Mozart's works for piano

piano [pjano] NM (*instrument*) piano; **jouer** *ou* **faire du p.** to play the piano; **se mettre au p.** (*s'asseoir*) to sit at the piano; (*jouer*) to go to the piano (and start playing); (*apprendre*) to take up the piano; **au p., Clara Bell** (*classique*) the pianist is Clara Bell; (*jazz*) on piano, Clara Bell; **p. droit/à queue** upright/grand piano; *Fam* **p. à bretelles** *ou* **du pauvre** squeezebox; **p. de concert** concert grand; **p. crapaud** boudoir grand; **p. demi-queue** baby grand; **p. mécanique** Pianola®, player piano; **p. préparé** prepared piano; **p. quart de queue** miniature grand
ADV 1 *Mus* piano 2 *Fam* (*doucement*) slowly■; **vas-y p.(-p.)!** take your time!, there's no rush!

piano-bar [pjanobar] (*pl* **pianos-bars**) NM piano bar

pianoforte [pjanɔfɔrte] NM forte-piano

pianotage [pjanɔtaʒ] NM 1 (*sur un piano*) tinkling (on a piano) 2 (*sur une table*) drumming 3 *Fam* (*sur un clavier*) tapping away (at a keyboard)

pianoter [3] [pjanɔte] VI 1 (*jouer du piano*) to tinkle away on the piano 2 (*tambouriner*) to drum one's fingers 3 *Fam* (*taper sur un clavier*) to tap away; **p. sur un ordinateur** to tap away at a computer
VT (*sur un piano*) to tinkle out on the piano

piapiater [3] [pjapjate] VI *Fam* to chat, *Br* to natter

piassava [pjasava] NM piassaba, piassava; **balai en p.** piassaba brush, broom

piasse [pjas] NF *Can Fam* (*dollar*) dollar■, buck; (*argent*) money■, cash, *Br* dosh

piastre [pjastr] NF 1 (*au Proche-Orient*) piastre 2 *Can Fam* (*dollar*) dollar■, buck; (*argent*) money■, cash, *Br* dosh 3 *Hist* piastre, piece of eight

piaule [pjol] NF *Fam* 1 (*chambre*) room■ 2 (*logement*) place

piaulement [pjolmɑ̃] NM 1 (*d'un oiseau*) cheep; **les piaulements de l'oiseau** the cheeping of the bird 2 *Fam* (*d'un enfant*) whimpering■ (UNCOUNT)

piauler [3] [pjole] VI 1 (*oiseau*) to cheep 2 *Fam* (*enfant*) to whimper■

piazza [pjadza] NF *Br* piazza, *Am* gallery

PIB [peibe] NM (*abrév* **produit intérieur brut**) GDP; **P. nominal** nominal income; **P. potentiel** potential GDP; **P. réel** real GDP

pibale [pibal] NF (*terme de l'ouest de la France*) elver

pible [pibl] **à pible** ADJ *Naut* **mât à p.** pole-mast

pic [pik] NM 1 (*montagne*) peak
2 (*outil*) pick, pickaxe; **p. à glace** ice-pick
3 *Orn* woodpecker; **p. cendré** grey-headed woodpecker; **p. épeiche** great spotted woodpecker; **p. épeichette** lesser spotted woodpecker; **p. mar** middle-spotted woodpecker; **p. noir** black woodpecker; **p. vert** green woodpecker
4 (*d'une courbe*) peak
□ **à pic** ADJ (*paroi, falaise*) sheer ADV 1 (*verticalement*) straight down; **les rochers tombent à p. dans la mer** the sheer rocks go straight down to the sea; **couler à p.** to go straight down *or* straight to the bottom
2 *Fam* (*au bon moment*) just at the right time■, *Br* spot on; **tu tombes** *ou* **tu arrives à p., j'allais t'appeler** you've come just at the right time *or* right on cue, I was about to call you; **cet argent arrive on ne peut plus à p.** that money couldn't have come at a better moment

pica [pika] NM *Méd* pica

picador [pikadɔr] NM picador

picage [pikaʒ] NM *Orn & Vét* feather eating

picaillons [pikajɔ̃] NMPL *Fam* (*argent*) dough, bread; **avoir des p.** to be loaded

picard, -e [pikar, -ard] ADJ of/from Picardy
NM (*dialecte*) Picard *or* Picardy dialect
□ **Picard, -e** NM,F = inhabitant of or person from Picardy

Picardie [pikardi] NF **la P.** Picardy

picarel [pikarɛl] NM *Ich* picarel

picaresque [pikarɛsk] ADJ picaresque

pic-bois [pikbwa] (*pl* **pics-bois**) NM *Can Orn* woodpecker

piccolo [pikolo] NM piccolo

pichenette [piʃnɛt] NF flick; **d'une p., elle envoya la miette par terre** she flicked the crumb onto the ground

pichet [piʃɛ] NM jug, pitcher

picholine [pikɔlin] NF *Culin* pickled olive

pichtegorne [piʃtəgɔrn] NM *Fam* wine■, vino, *Br* plonk

pickles [pikɛlz] NMPL pickles

pickpocket [pikpɔkɛt] NM pickpocket

pick-up [pikœp] NM INV 1 (*lecteur*) pick-up (arm); *Vieilli* (*tourne-disque*) record player 2 (*camion*) pick-up (truck)

pico- [piko] PRÉF pico-

picole [pikɔl] NF *Fam* boozing

picoler [3] [pikɔle] VI *Fam* (*boire*) to booze, to knock it back; **qu'est-ce qu'on a picolé ce soir-là!** *Br* we didn't half knock it back *or Am* we sure knocked it back that night!; **il picole pas mal** he's a real boozer

picoleur, -euse [pikɔlœr, -øz] NM,F *Fam* (*buveur*) boozer, alky

picorer [3] [pikɔre] **VT 1** *(oiseau)* to peck (at) **2** *(personne)* to nibble (away) at, to pick at
USAGE ABSOLU *(oiseau)* to pick *or* scratch about; **cette enfant ne fait que p.** that child only picks at her food

picornavirus [pikɔrnavirys] **NM** *Biol* picornavirus

picoseconde [pikɔsəgɔ̃] **NF** picosecond

picot [piko] **NM 1** *Tech* barb, point; **p. d'entraînement** feed pin **2** *Constr* pick hammer **3** *(au crochet, en dentelle)* picot **4** *Pêche* flatfish net **5** *(sur du bois)* splinter **6** *Belg (piquant)* bristle; *(épine)* thorn; *(pointe)* spike **7** *Can (tache de rousseur)* freckle
❑ **à picots ADJ** *(dispositif, entraînement)* sprocket *(avant n)*

picotage [pikɔtaʒ] **NM** pecking

picote [pikɔt] **NF** *Can & Vieilli Méd* smallpox

picoté, -e [pikɔte] **ADJ** perforated

picotement [pikɔtmɑ̃] **NM** *(dans les yeux)* smarting *or* stinging (sensation); *(dans la gorge, le nez)* tickle; *(sur la peau)* tingle, prickle; **j'ai des picotements dans les doigts** my fingers are tingling; **j'ai des picotements dans les yeux** my eyes are smarting; **ça me donne des picotements partout** it makes my flesh crawl *or* creep

picoter [3] [pikɔte] **VT 1** *(piquer → yeux)* to sting, to smart; *(→ gorge)* to irritate, to tickle; *(→ peau, doigt)* to sting; **la fumée lui picotait les yeux** the smoke was stinging his/her eyes; **j'ai les orteils qui me picotent** my toes are tingling **2** *(sujet: oiseau)* to peck at **3** *(faire de petits trous dans)* to prick tiny holes in, to perforate

picotin [pikɔtɛ̃] **NM 1** *(mesure)* peck **2** *(ration)* **p. (d'avoine)** ration of oats

picouille [pikuj] **NM** *Can* old horse, old nag

picoulet [pikulɛ] **NM** *Suisse* = traditional folk dance of French-speaking Switzerland

picpoul [pikpul] **NM** = variety of white grape grown in the south of France

picrate [pikrat] **NM 1** *Chim* picrate **2** *Fam Péj (vin)* wine■, vino, *Br* plonk

picride [pikrid] **NF** = **picris**

picrique [pikrik] **ADJ M** *Chim* picric

picris [pikris] **NM** *Bot* picris

picrocholine [pikrɔkɔlin] **ADJ F guerre p.** *Littérature* = the war between Picrochole and Gargantua in Rabelais' 'Gargantua'; *Fig (au motif insignifiant)* petty wrangling

picrotoxine [pikrɔtɔksin] **NF** *Chim* picrotoxin

picte [pikt] **ADJ** Pictish
❑ **Picte NMF** Pict

pictogramme [piktɔgram] **NM** pictogram, pictograph

pictographie [piktɔgrafi] **NF** pictography

pictographique [piktɔgrafik] **ADJ** pictographic

pictorialisme [piktɔrjalism] **NM** pictorialism

pictural, -e, -aux, -ales [piktyral, -o] **ADJ** pictorial

pic-vert [pivɛr] *(pl* **pics-verts***)* = **pivert**

pidgin [pidʒin] **NM** pidgin

Pie [pi] **NPR** *(pape)* Pius

pie [pi] **ADJ INV** *(couleur)* pied; **cheval p.** piebald (horse); **vache p. noire** black and white cow; **voiture p.** patrol car, *Br* panda car
ADJ F *Littéraire (pieux)* **œuvre p.** pious work
NF 1 *Orn* magpie; **p. bleue à calotte noire** azure-winged magpie; **p. de mer** oystercatcher; **trouver la p. au nid** to make a lucky find **2** *Fam (bavard)* chatterbox

'La Pie voleuse' *Rossini* 'The Thieving Magpie'

PIÈCE [pjɛs]

> **NF** piece **1, 2, 6** ■ bit **1** ■ part **2** ■ patch **3** ■ room **4** ■ paper, document **5** ■ play **6** ■ coin **7** ■ gun **11**
> **ADV** each

NF 1 *(morceau)* piece, bit; **une p. de viande** *(flanc)* a side of meat; *(morceau découpé)* a piece *or* cut of meat; **une p. de tissu** *(coupée)* a piece *or* length of cloth; *(sur rouleau)* a roll of cloth; *Fam* **une belle p.** *(femme)* a babe, *Br* a nice bit of stuff, a bit of all right; *Belg Fam* **une belle p. d'homme** a great strapping fellow; **mettre qch en pièces** *(briser)* to smash sth to pieces; *(déchirer)* to tear *or* to pull sth to pieces; *(critiquer)* to tear sth to pieces; **je l'ai retrouvé en pièces** I found it in pieces; **p. à p.** piecemeal, gradually; **le domaine constitué p. à p. par mon père** the estate gradually built up by my father; **d'une seule p., tout d'une p.** all of a piece; *Fig* **il est tout d'une p.** he's very blunt *or* straightforward; **il n'a jamais travaillé pour nous, il a monté cela de toutes pièces** he never worked for us, he made up *or* invented the whole thing; **c'est un mensonge monté de toutes pièces** it's an out-and-out lie *or* a lie from start to finish; **fait de pièces et de morceaux** made up of bits and pieces, *Péj* cobbled together

2 *(d'une collection)* piece, item; *(d'un mécanisme)* part, component; *(d'un jeu)* piece; **ménagère de 36 pièces** 36-piece cutlery set; **p. détachée** (spare) part; **en pièces détachées** in separate pieces *or* parts; **le bureau est livré en pièces détachées** the desk comes in kit form; **pièces et main-d'œuvre** parts and labour; **p. maîtresse** centrepiece; **la p. maîtresse de ma collection** the centrepiece of *or* choicest piece in my collection; **la p. maîtresse d'une argumentation** the main part *or* the linchpin of an argument; *aussi Fig* **p. de musée** museum piece; **p. de rechange** spare *or* replacement part; *aussi Fig* **les pièces d'un puzzle** the pieces of a puzzle

3 *Couture* patch; **je vais y mettre une p.** I'll patch it *or* put a patch on it; **p. rapportée** patch; *Fig (personne)* odd person out

4 *(salle)* room; **un deux-pièces** a one-bedroom *Br* flat *or Am* apartment; **un trois-pièces cuisine** a two-bedroom *Br* flat *or Am* apartment

5 *(document)* paper, document; **p. annexe** attachment; **p. à l'appui** supporting document; *Compta* **p. de caisse** cash voucher; **p. comptable** (accounting) voucher; *Jur* **p. à conviction** exhibit; **p. d'identité** proof of identity, ID; **avez-vous une p. d'identité?** do you have any proof of identity *or* any ID?; **pièces jointes** enclosures; **pièces justificatives** supporting documents; **je vous le démontrerai pièces à l'appui** I'll show you (actual) proof of it

6 *Littérature & Mus* piece; **p. pour violoncelle** piece for cello; **p. de circonstance** situation piece; **p. (de théâtre)** play; **petite p.** playlet; **p. écrite pour la télévision** *Br* television play, *Am* play written for TV; **monter une p.** to put on *or* to stage a play

7 *(argent)* **p. (de monnaie)** coin; **une p. de 2 euros** a 2-euro coin *or* piece; **p. d'or** gold coin; **je n'ai que quelques pièces dans ma poche** I've only got some loose change in my pocket; *Vieilli* **donner la p. à qn** to tip sb, to give sb a tip

8 *(champ)* **une p. d'avoine** a field sown in oats; **mettre une p. en betteraves** to grow beetroot on a piece of land

9 *Culin* **p. montée** *(gâteau)* ≃ tiered cake; *(pyramide)* = pyramid of caramel-covered profiteroles often served at weddings and other special occasions; **p. de résistance** main dish; *Fig* pièce de résistance

10 p. de vin cask of wine

11 *Mil* **p. (d'artillerie)** gun

12 *Métal* **p. battue** draw-back

13 *Élec* **p. polaire** polar piece

14 *Zool* **pièces buccales** mouthparts

15 *Hér* ordinary, charge; **p. honorable** honourable ordinary

16 *(locutions)* **faire p. à qn** to set up in opposition to sb; *Belg* **avoir toujours une p. pour mettre sur le trou** *(tout savoir)* to have an answer for everything; *(avoir de la repartie)* to be always ready with an answer; *Belg* **ne plus tenir p. ensemble** to be falling to pieces

ADV *(chacun)* each, apiece; **les roses sont à 3 euros p.** the roses are 3 euros each *or* apiece
❑ **à la pièce ADV** *(à l'unité)* singly, separately; **ceux-ci sont vendus à la p.** these are sold separately *or* individually
❑ **à la pièce, aux pièces ADV travailler à la p.** to be on *or* to do piecework; **être payé à la p.** to be paid a *or* on piece rate; **le travail est payé à la p.** you get a piecework rate; *Fam* **on n'est pas aux pièces!** we're not on piecework!, there's no great hurry!
❑ **sur pièces ADV** on evidence; **juger sur pièces** to judge for oneself
❑ **pièce d'eau NF 1** *(lac)* (ornamental) lake **2** *(bassin)* (ornamental) pond

> *Culture*
> **PIÈCE**
> Flats in France are referred to in terms of the total number of rooms they have (excluding the kitchen and bathroom). "Un deux-pièces" is a flat with a living room and one bedroom; "un cinq-pièces" is a flat with five rooms.

piécette [pjesɛt] **NF** *(monnaie)* small coin

PIED [pje] **NM 1** *(d'une personne, d'un animal)* foot; **pieds nus** barefoot; **marcher/être pieds nus** to walk/to be barefoot; **ne va pas pieds nus dans le jardin** don't go into the garden barefoot *or* with nothing on your feet; **avoir** *ou* **marcher les pieds en dedans** to be pigeon-toed, to walk with one's feet turned in; **avoir** *ou* **marcher les pieds en dehors** to walk with one's feet turned out, to be splay-footed *or Am* duck-toed; **sauter à pieds joints** to make a standing jump; **le p. m'a manqué** my foot slipped, I lost my footing; **Achille aux pieds légers** swift-footed Achilles; **mettre le p. (en plein) dans qch** to step right in sth; *Euph* **je vais lui mettre mon p. quelque part** I'll kick him/her *or* give him/her a kick up the backside; **mettre p. à terre** *(à cheval, à moto)* to dismount; **lorsqu'ils mirent le p. sur le sol de France** when they set foot on French soil; *Fam* **je n'ai pas mis les pieds dehors/à l'église depuis longtemps** I haven't set foot outside/in church for a long time■; **je ne mettrai** *ou* **remettrai plus jamais les pieds là-bas** I'll never set foot there again; **ils ne remettront plus les pieds dans notre hôtel** they'll never set foot in our hotel again; *Méd* **avoir les pieds plats** to have flat feet, to be flat-footed; *Fam* **il ne remuait** *ou* **bougeait ni p. ni patte** he stood stock-still *or* didn't move a muscle; **aller** *ou* **avancer** *ou* **marcher d'un bon p.** to go apace; **aller** *ou* **marcher d'un p. léger** to have a spring in one's step; **avoir bon p. bon œil** to be fit as a fiddle *or* hale and hearty; **partir du bon/mauvais p.** to start off (in) the right/wrong way; **l'opération est partie du bon p.** the operation got off to a good start; **leur couple part du mauvais p.** their relationship is off to a bad start *or* off on the wrong foot; **avoir le p. marin** to be a good sailor; **je n'ai pas le p. marin** I'm prone to seasickness; **faire un p. de nez à qn** to thumb one's nose at sb; *Fam* **cette pièce est un p. de nez aux intellos** this play is a real slap in the face for intellectual types; **avoir les (deux) pieds sur terre** to have one's feet (firmly) on the ground *or* one's head screwed on (the right way); **elle a les pieds sur terre** she's got her feet *or* both her feet on the ground; **avoir p.** to touch bottom; **au secours, je n'ai plus p.!** help, I'm out of my depth *or* I've lost my footing!; **j'ai déjà un p. dans la place/l'entreprise** I've got a foot in the door/a foothold in the company already; **avoir un p. dans la tombe** to have one foot in the grave; *Can Fam* **avoir les deux pieds dans la même bottine** *(être maladroit)* to have two left feet, to be clumsy■; *(ne pas être débrouillard)* to be lacking in initiative *or* resourcefulness■; **avoir les deux pieds dans le même sabot** to be lacking in initiative *or* resourcefulness; **elle n'a pas les deux pieds dans le même sabot** there are no flies on her; *Fam* **bien fait pour tes/leurs/***etc* **pieds!, ça te/leur/***etc* **fera les pieds!** serves you/them/*etc* right!; **être pieds et poings liés** to have no room to manoeuvre; **je suis pieds et poings liés** my hands are tied; **faire des pieds et des mains pour** to bend over backwards *or* to pull out all the stops in order to; **faire du p. à qn** *(flirter)* to play footsie with sb; *(avertir)* to kick sb (under the table); **faire le p. de grue** to cool *or Br* to kick one's heels; **les pieds devant** feet first, in one's coffin; **elle en est partie les pieds devant** she left there feet first *or* in a box; *Fam* **avoir le p. au plancher** *(accélérer)* to have one's foot down; *Fam* **lever le p.** *(ralentir)* to ease off (on the accelerator), to slow down■; *(partir subrepticement)* to slip off; **il n'a pas levé le p. de tout le trajet** he never took his foot off the accelerator once during the

pic–pie

whole trip; *Belg Fam* **jouer avec les pieds de qn** *(se moquer de)* to make fun of sb■, *Br* to take the mick *or* the mickey out of sb; *(duper)* to take sb for a ride; *Can Fam* **mettre qn à p.** *(employé)* to give sb the push; **mettre le p. à l'étrier** to get into the saddle; *Fig* **il a fallu lui mettre le p. à l'étrier** he/she had to be given a leg up; *Fam* **mettre les pieds dans le plat** *(intervenir sans ménagements)* to steam in; *(commettre une maladresse) Br* to put one's foot in it, *Am* to put one's foot in one's mouth; **mettre qch sur p.** to set sth up; **il ne peut plus mettre un p. devant l'autre** *(ivre)* he can't walk in a straight line any more; *(fatigué)* his legs won't carry him any further; **reprendre p.** to get *or* to find one's footing again; *aussi Fig* **retomber sur ses pieds** to fall *or* to land on one's feet; **ne pas savoir sur quel p. danser** to be at a loss to know what to do; **se jeter** *ou* **se traîner aux pieds de qn** to throw oneself at sb's feet, to get down on one's knees to sb; **se lever du p. gauche** to get out of the wrong side of the bed; **elle s'est levée du p. gauche aujourd'hui** she got out of the wrong side of the bed today; *Fam* **je cuisine comme un p.** *(très mal)* I'm a useless cook, I can't even boil an egg; **il a fait ça comme un p.** he made a dog's breakfast *or Br* a pig's ear of it; **il chante/conduit comme un p.** he can't sing/drive to save his life; **on s'est débrouillés comme des pieds** we went about it the wrong way *or Br* in a cack-handed way; *Fam* **prendre son p.** *(s'amuser)* to get one's kicks; *(sexuellement)* to come; **il prend son p. en faisant du jazz!** he gets a real kick out of playing jazz!; *Fam* **c'est le p.** it's great *or* fantastic *or Br* fab *or Am* awesome; *Fam* **on a passé dix jours à Hawaï, quel p.!** we spent ten days in Hawaii, what a blast!; *Fam* **les cours d'anglais, ce n'est pas le p.!** the English class isn't exactly a barrel of laughs!; *Fam* **être bête comme ses pieds** *Br* to be thick (as two short planks), *Am* to have rocks in one's head; *Can Fam* **avoir les pieds ronds** to be three sheets to the wind, to be dead drunk

2 *(d'un mur, d'un lit)* foot; *(d'une table, d'une chaise)* leg; *(d'une lampe, d'une colonne)* base; *(d'un verre)* stem; *(d'un micro, d'un appareil photo)* stand, tripod; **donner du p. à une échelle** to give slope to a ladder

3 *Typ (d'une lettre)* bottom, foot; *Typ* **p. de mouche** paragraph mark; **p. de page** footer

4 *Bot* plant; *(de champignon)* foot; **p. de laitue** head of lettuce; **p. mère** stool; **p. de vigne** vine (plant), vinestock

5 *(mesure)* foot; **le mur fait 6 pieds de haut** the wall is 6-feet high; **un mur de 6 pieds de haut** a 6-foot high wall

6 *Tech Aut* **p. de bielle** end of connecting rod; **p. à coulisse** calliper rule; **p. milieu** centre pillar; *Can* **p. de roi** folding rule

7 *Littérature* foot; **vers de 12 pieds** 12-foot verse *or* line

8 *Culin* **p. de cochon** pig's *Br* trotter *or Am* foot; **p. de mouton** sheep's foot; **pieds paquets** stuffed mutton tripe dish *(from Marseilles)*; **p. de veau** calf's foot

9 *(d'un bas, d'une chaussette)* foot **10** *Mus* foot **11** *Cin & TV* **p. de sol** high-hat

❑ **à pied** ADV **1** *(en marchant)* on foot; **on ira au stade à p.** we'll walk to the stadium

2 *(au chômage)* **mettre qn à p.** *(mesure disciplinaire)* to suspend sb; *(mesure économique)* to lay sb off, *Br* to make sb redundant

❑ **à pied d'œuvre** ADJ **être à p. d'œuvre** to be ready to get down to the job; **trouver qn à p. d'œuvre** to find sb already at work

❑ **à pied sec** ADV without getting one's feet wet; **on peut traverser la rivière à p. sec** the river can be forded

❑ **au petit pied** ADJ *Vieilli* small-time

❑ **au pied de** PRÉP at the foot *or* bottom of; **au p. de la tour Eiffel** at *or* by the foot of the Eiffel Tower; **au p. des Alpes** in the foothills of the Alps; **être au p. du mur** to be faced with no alternative; **mettre qn au p. du mur** to get sb with his/her back to the wall, to leave sb with no alternative

❑ **au pied de la lettre** ADV literally; **prendre qch au p. de la lettre** to take *or* to interpret sth literally; **suivre des instructions au p. de la lettre** to follow instructions to the letter

❑ **au pied levé** ADV at a moment's notice; **il faut que tu sois prêt à le faire au p. levé** you must be ready to drop everything and do it

❑ **de pied en cap** ADV **en vert de p. en cap** dressed in green from top *or* head to toe; **habillé de p. en cap par un couturier japonais** wearing a complete outfit by a Japanese designer

❑ **de pied ferme** ADV resolutely; **je t'attends de p. ferme** I'll definitely be waiting for you; **les cambrioleurs, je les attends de p. ferme!** I've got a nasty surprise in store for potential burglars!

❑ **des pieds à la tête** ADV from top to toe *or* head to foot; **couvert de peinture des pieds à la tête** covered in paint from head to foot

❑ **en pied** ADJ *(photo, portrait)* full-length; *(statue)* full-size standing

❑ **pied à pied** ADV inch by inch; **lutter** *ou* **se battre p. à p.** to fight every inch of the way

❑ **sur le pied de guerre** ADV *Mil* on a war footing; *Hum* ready (for action); **dans la cuisine, tout le monde était sur le p. de guerre** it was action stations in the kitchen

❑ **sur pied** ADJ *(récolte)* uncut, standing; *(bétail)* on the hoof

ADV **être sur p.** *(en bonne santé)* to be up and about; **mettre qn sur p.** to set sb on his/her feet; **remettre qn sur p.** to put sb on his/her feet again, to make sb better

❑ **sur un pied d'égalité** ADV on an equal footing; **être sur un p. d'égalité avec** to stand on equal terms with

---

pied-à-terre [pjetatɛr] NM INV pied-à-terre

pied-bot [pjebo] *(pl* **pieds-bots***)* NMF club-footed person

pied-d'alouette [pjedalwɛt] *(pl* **pieds-d'alouette***)* NM *Bot* larkspur

pied-de-biche [pjedbiʃ] *(pl* **pieds-de-biche***)* NM **1** *(pince)* nail puller *or* extractor **2** *(levier)* crowbar **3** *(pied de meuble)* cabriole leg **4** *(d'une machine à coudre)* foot

pied-de-cheval [pjedʃəval] *(pl* **pieds-de-cheval***)* NM *Zool* large oyster

pied-de-coq [pjedkɔk] *(pl* **pieds-de-coq***)* NM hound's-tooth (check), dogtooth (check)

pied-de-lion [pjedljɔ̃] *(pl* **pieds-de-lion***)* NM *Bot* lion's foot

pied-de-loup [pjedlu] *(pl* **pieds-de-loup***)* NM *Bot* wolf's-foot, wolf's-claw, clubmoss

pied-de-mouton [pjedmutɔ̃] *(pl* **pieds-de-mouton***)* NM wood hedgehog (fungus)

pied-de-poule [pjedpul] *(pl* **pieds-de-poule***)* NM hound's-tooth (check), dogtooth (check)

ADJ INV **un tailleur p.** a hound's-tooth suit

pied-de-roi [pjedərwa] *(pl* **pieds-de-roi***)* NM *Can* folding rule

pied-de-veau [pjedvo] *(pl* **pieds-de-veau***)* NM *Bot* lords and ladies

pied-d'oiseau [pjedwazo] *(pl* **pieds-d'oiseau***)* NM *Bot* bird's foot

pied-droit [pjedrwa] *(pl* **pieds-droits***)* = **piédroit**

piédestal, -aux [pjedɛstal, -o] NM pedestal; **mettre qn sur un p.** to put *or* to set *or* to place sb on a pedestal; **tomber de son p.** to fall off one's pedestal

piedmont [pjemɔ̃] = **piémont**

pied-noir [pjenwar] *(pl* **pieds-noirs***)* ADJ pied-noir

NMF pied-noir *(French settler in North Africa, especially Algeria)*

> *Culture*
>
> **PIED-NOIR**
>
> This is the name given to the French settlers who settled in North Africa (most notably in Algeria) during the period of French colonial expansion. Most of them resettled in France (mainly on the south coast) after the colonies regained their independence. The largest wave of these settlers to arrive in France was in 1962, following the Algerian war.

piédouche [pjeduʃ] NM small pedestal

pied-du-roi [pjedyrwa] *(pl* **pieds-du-roi***)* NM *Can* folding ruler

pied-plat [pjepla] *(pl* **pieds-plats***)* NM *Vieilli (personne grossière)* lout; *(personne servile)* toady

piédroit [pjedrwa] NM *Archit (d'une voûte)* pier; *(d'une fenêtre)* jamb; *(jambage)* piedroit

pied-sabot [pjesabo] *(pl* **pieds-sabots***)* NM *Phot* hot shoe

Pieds Nickelés [pjenikle] NMPL **les P.** = well-known cartoon characters from a comic strip of the same name, first published in 1908

piège [pjɛʒ] NM **1** *(dispositif)* trap, snare; **prendre un animal au p.** to trap an animal; **poser** *ou* **tendre un p.** to set a trap; **tendre un p. à qn** to set a trap for sb; **attirer qn dans un p.** to lure sb into a trap; **être pris à son propre p.** to fall into one's own trap, *Sout* to be hoist by one's own petard; **se laisser prendre au p. de l'amour** to be taken in by love; **donner dans le p.** to fall into the trap; *Fam* **p. à cons** con, scam; *Fam* **élections, p. à cons!** election, deception!; **p. à mâchoires** jaw trap; **pris comme dans un p. à rats** caught like a rat in a trap; **p. à souris** mousetrap

2 *(difficulté)* trap, snare; **les pièges des contrats d'assurance** the traps hidden in the small print of insurance contracts; **la dictée était bourrée de pièges** the dictation was full of traps

3 *Électron* **p. à ions** ion trap

4 *Géol* trap

piégé, -e [pjeʒe] ADJ **engin** *ou* **objet p.** booby trap; **colis p.** parcel bomb; **lettre/voiture piégée** letter/car bomb

piégeage [pjeʒaʒ] NM **1** *Chasse* trapping **2** *Géol* trap formation

piégée [pjeʒe] *voir* **piégé**

piéger [22] [pjeʒe] VT **1** *(animal)* to trap, to ensnare; **la police les a piégés** the police trapped them; **se laisser p.** to fall into a trap, to get trapped; *Fig* **je me suis fait p. comme un débutant** I was taken in *or* caught out like a complete beginner **2** *(voiture, paquet)* to booby-trap

piégeur, -euse [pjeʒœr, -øz] NM,F trapper

pie-grièche [pigrijɛʃ] *(pl* **pies-grièches***)* NF **1** *Orn* shrike; **p. écorcheuse** red-backed shrike; **p. grise** great grey shrike, *Am* northern shrike; **p. migratrice** loggerhead shrike; **p. rousse** woodchat shrike **2** *Vieilli (mégère)* shrew

pie-mère [pimɛr] *(pl* **pies-mères***)* NF *Anat* pia mater

Piémont [pjemɔ̃] NM **le P.** Piedmont

piémont [pjemɔ̃] NM piedmont

piémontais, -e [pjemɔ̃tɛ, -ɛz] ADJ Piedmontese

NM *(dialecte)* Piedmontese dialect

❑ **Piémontais, -e** NM,F Piedmontese; **les P.** the Piedmontese

piercé, -e [pirse] ADJ *Fam* pierced■ *(part of body)*

piercing [pirsiŋ] NM **1** *(pratique)* (body) piercing **2** *(bijou)* piercing

piéride [pjerid] NF *Entom* pierid; **p. du chou** cabbage white (butterfly)

pierrade® [pjɛrad] NF *Culin* **1** *(appareil, méthode)* = hot stone on which thin pieces of meat are cooked at the table **2** *(mets)* = meal consisting of pieces of meat cooked at the table on a hot stone

pierraille [pjɛraj] NF loose stones, scree *(UNCOUNT)*

Pierre [pjɛr] NPR **P. l'Ermite** Peter the Hermit; **P. le Grand** Peter the Great

'Pierre et le loup' *Prokofiev* 'Peter and the Wolf'

pierre [pjɛr] NF **1** *(matière)* stone; *(caillou)* stone, *Am* rock; *(rocher)* rock, boulder; **d'un coup** *ou* **jet de p.** by throwing *or* hurling a stone; **tuer qn à coups de pierres** to stone sb to death; *Beaux-Arts* **la p.** stone; **sculpter la p.** to carve in stone; **la p.** *(immobilier)* the property *or Am* real estate business; **investir dans la p.** to invest in property *or* in bricks and mortar; **les vieilles pierres** old buildings; **p. d'achoppement** stumbling block; **p. levée** standing stone; **p. polie** neolith; **p. taillée** palaeolith, paleolith; **faire d'une p. deux coups** to kill two birds (with one stone); **jeter une p. à qn** to throw a stone at sb; **jeter la p. à qn** to cast a stone at sb; **qui va (lui) jeter la première p.?** who will cast the first stone?; **c'est une p. dans ton jardin** that remark was (meant) for you; **se mettre une p. autour du cou** to make things difficult for oneself; **la date est à marquer d'une p. blanche** it's a red-letter day; *Prov* **p. qui roule n'amasse pas mousse** a rolling stone gathers no moss

2 *Constr* stone; **p. de taille** *ou* **d'appareil** freestone; *aussi Fig* **p. angulaire** keystone, cornerstone; **p. à bâtir** building stone; **mur de** *ou* **en p.** stone wall; **mur de** *ou* **en pierres sèches**

pie–pie

drystone wall; **poser la première p. (de)** to lay down the first stone (of); *Fig* to lay the foundations (of)

3 *Minér & (en joaillerie)* stone; **p. brute** rough *or* uncut stone; **p. taillée** cut stone; **p. fine** *ou* **semi-précieuse** semi-precious stone; **p. d'aigle** eaglestone; **p. de lune** moonstone; **p. précieuse** gem, precious stone; *aussi Fig* **p. de touche** touchstone

4 *Géol* **p. calcaire** *ou* **à chaux** limestone; **p. meulière** = type of stone common in the Paris area once used for making millstones and as a building material; **p. ollaire** soapstone, *Spéc* steatite; **p. ponce** pumice stone

5 *(instrument)* **p. à affûter** *ou* **aiguiser** whetstone; **p. à briquet** (lighter) flint; **p. à feu** *ou* **fusil** gun flint

6 *(stèle)* **p. funéraire** *ou* **tombale** tombstone, gravestone

7 *Rel* **p. d'autel** altar stone; **p. noire** black stone

8 *Hist & Fig* **p. philosophale** philosopher's stone; *Fig* **chercher la p. philosophale** to search for the impossible

9 *(dans un fruit)* (piece of) grit

10 *Vieilli Méd* (kidney) stone, *Spéc* calculus

❑ **de pierre** ADJ stony, of stone; **être/rester de p.** to be/to remain icy-cool; **son cœur/visage restait de p.** he/she remained stony-hearted/stony-faced

❑ **pierre à pierre, pierre par pierre** ADV stone by stone; *Fig* painstakingly; **il a construit sa fortune p. par p.** he built up his fortune from nothing

❑ **pierre sur pierre** ADV *Littéraire* **après le tremblement de terre, il ne restait pas p. sur p.** not a stone was left standing after the earthquake; **ils n'ont pas laissé p. sur p. de la théorie d'origine** they shot the original theory to pieces

pierré [pjere] NM drystone drain

pierrée [pjere] NF drystone drain

pierreries [pjɛrri] NFPL precious stones, gems

pierreux, -euse [pjɛrø, -øz] ADJ **1** *(terrain)* stony, rocky; *(chemin)* stony; *(lit de rivière)* gravelly **2** *(fruit)* gritty **3** *Vieilli Méd* calculous

pierrier [pjɛrje] NM scree *(UNCOUNT)*

Pierrot [pjɛro] NPR Pierrot

pierrot [pjɛro] NM **1** *Théât* Pierrot; *(clown)* pierrot, clown **2** *Fam (moineau)* sparrow▪

pietà [pjeta] NF pietà

piétaille [pjetɑj] NF **1** *Hum (fantassins)* rank and file **2** *Péj (subalternes)* rank and file; **la direction nous considère comme de la p.** the management just thinks of us as *Br* skivvies *or Am* flunkies **3** *Hum (piétons)* pedestrians

piété [pjete] NF **1** *Rel* piety; **articles de p.** devotional objects **2** *(amour)* devotion, reverence; **p. filiale** filial devotion

piétement [pjɛtmɑ̃] NM *(d'un meuble)* legs, base

piéter [18] [pjete] VI *(oiseau)* to run *(instead of flying)*

piétin [pjetɛ̃] NM **1** *Agr* root rot **2** *Vét* foot rot

piétinant, -e [pjetinɑ̃, -ɑ̃t] ADJ **1** *(foule, démarche)* shuffling **2 nous voulons relancer cette enquête piétinante** we want to follow up this enquiry which has been going nowhere; **il va relancer sa carrière piétinante** he's going to make a fresh start on his career which has been stagnating

piétinement [pjetinmɑ̃] NM **1** *(marche sur place)* shuffling about **2** *(bruit)* **le p. des chevaux** the sound of the horses' hooves; **le p. de la foule** the sound of the crowd shuffling about **3** *Fig (stagnation)* **le p. de l'affaire arrange certaines personnes** the lack of progress in the case suits certain people

piétiner [3] [pjetine] VI **1** *(marcher sur place)* to shuffle about; *(avancer péniblement)* to shuffle along

2 *(trépigner)* **p. de rage** to stamp one's feet in rage; **p. d'impatience** to stamp one's feet impatiently; *Fig* to be champing at the bit

3 *Fig (stagner)* to fail to make (any) progress *or* headway; **l'enquête piétine** the enquiry is getting nowhere *or* is making no headway; **on piétine, il faut se décider!** we're not getting anywhere *or* we're just marking time, let's make up our minds!

VT **1** *(écraser)* to trample *or* to tread on; **ils sont morts piétinés par la foule** they were trampled to death by the crowd

2 *Fig (libertés, traditions)* to trample underfoot, to ride roughshod over

piétisme [pjetism] NM pietism

piétiste [pjetist] ADJ pietistic, pietistical

NMF pietist

piéton, -onne [pjetɔ̃, -ɔn] ADJ **rue piétonne** pedestrianized street; **zone piétonne** pedestrian precinct

NM,F pedestrian

piétonnier, -ère [pjetɔnje, -ɛr] ADJ pedestrian *(avant n)*; **circulation piétonnière** pedestrian traffic; **rue piétonnière** pedestrianized street; **zone piétonnière** pedestrian precinct

NM *Belg (zone piétonne)* pedestrian precinct

piétrain [pjetrɛ̃] ADJ M Pietrain

NM Pietrain

piètre [pjɛtr] ADJ *(avant n) (gén)* very poor, mediocre; *(excuse)* lame, paltry; **faire p. figure** to be a sorry sight; **de p. qualité** very mediocre; **c'est une p. consolation** that's small *or* not much comfort

piètrement [pjɛtrəmɑ̃] ADV very mediocrely; **je suis bien p. récompensée** this is (a) meagre recompense indeed for my effort

pieu, -x[1] [pjø] NM **1** *(poteau → pour délimiter)* post; *(→ pour attacher)* stake **2** *Fam (lit)* bed▪, pit; **aller** *ou* **se mettre au p.** to turn in, to hit the *Br* sack *or Am* hay **3** *Constr* pile; **p. de fondation** foundation pile

pieuse [pjøz] *voir* **pieux**[2]

pieusement [pjøzmɑ̃] ADV **1** *(dévotement)* piously, devoutly **2** *Littéraire (scrupuleusement)* religiously, scrupulously

pieuter [3] [pjøte] *Fam* VI **1** *(passer la nuit)* to crash (out) **2 p. avec qn** to bunk down with sb

▶**se pieuter** VPR to turn in, to hit the *Br* sack *or Am* hay

pieuvre [pjœvr] NF **1** *Zool* octopus **2** *Fig (personne)* leech

pieux[2], **-euse** [pjø, -øz] ADJ **1** *(dévot)* pious, devout **2** *(charitable)* **p. mensonge** white lie **3** *(respectueux → silence)* reverent

pièze [pjɛz] NF *Phys* pieze

piézo-électricité [pjezoelɛktrisite] *(pl* **piézo-électricités***)* NF *Phys* piezoelectricity

piézo-électrique [pjezoelɛtrik] *(pl* **piézo-électriques***)* ADJ *Phys* piezoelectric

piézographe [pjezɔgraf] NM *Phys* piezograph

piézomètre [pjezɔmɛtr] NM *Phys* piezometer

piézométrique [pjezɔmetrik] ADJ *Phys* piezometric

pif [pif] ONOMAT bang, smack; **p., paf!** bang! bang!

NM *Fam (nez) Br* conk, hooter, *Am* shnozzle; **je l'ai dans le p.** I can't stand the sight of him/her, *Br* he/she gets right up my nose

❑ **au pif** ADV *Fam* **faire qch au p.** to do sth by guesswork▪; **au p., je dirais trois** I'd say three, at a rough guess, off the top of my head I'd say three; **j'ai répondu au p.** I just guessed▪; **j'y suis allé au p. et il restait des places** I just went on the off chance and there were still some seats left; **j'ai pris celui-là au p.** I just took the first one that came to hand

pifer, piffer [3] [pife] VT *Fam (supporter)* **je ne peux pas le p.!** I can't stomach him!, I just can't stand him!▪

pifomètre [pifɔmɛtr] **au pifomètre** ADV *Fam* **j'ai dit ça au p.** I was just guessing▪; **faire qch au p.** to do sth by guesswork▪

Pigalle [pigal] NF = area of Paris famous for its nightclubs (including the Moulin Rouge) and as a red-light district

pigamon [pigamɔ̃] NM *Bot* meadow-rue; **petit p.** lesser meadow-rue; **p. des Alpes** Alpine meadow-rue

pige [piʒ] NF **1** *(tige graduée)* measuring stick

2 *Tech* gauge rod

3 *Fam Journ* **travailler à la p., faire des piges** to work freelance▪; **être payé à la p.** to be paid piece rate▪ *or* by the line▪

4 *(d'un typographe)* take *(amount of copy to be set up in a given time)*

5 *Fam (an)* year▪; **elle a déjà 70 piges** she's 70 already▪; **pour 40 piges, il est bien conservé** he still looks pretty good for a 40-year-old

6 *Mktg (de la publicité concurrente)* monitoring

7 *Fam (locution)* **faire la p. à qn** to go one better than sb

pigeon [piʒɔ̃] NM **1** *Orn* pigeon; **p. biset** rock dove; **p. colombin** stock dove; **p. cravaté** turbit; **p. culbutant** roller; **p. ramier** wood pigeon, ringdove; **p. rouleur** roller; **p. voyageur** carrier *or* homing pigeon

2 *(jeu)* **p. vole** = children's game consisting of a yes or no answer to the question: does X fly?

3 *Constr (plâtre)* handful of plaster; *(chaux)* lump (in lime)

4 *Sport* **p. d'argile** clay pigeon

5 *Fam (dupe) Br* mug, *Am* sucker; **et c'est encore moi le p.!** and yours truly *or Br* muggins here ends up holding the baby as usual!

pigeonnant, -e [piʒɔnɑ̃, -ɑ̃t] ADJ **soutien-gorge p.** uplift bra; **poitrine pigeonnante** full bosom

pigeonne [piʒɔn] NF hen pigeon

pigeonneau, -x [piʒɔno] NM **1** *Orn* young pigeon, *Spéc* squab **2** *Méd* chrome *or* tanner's ulcer

pigeonner [3] [piʒɔne] VT **1** *Constr* to plaster **2** *Fam (duper)* **p. qn** to take sb in *or* for a ride, to hoodwink sb; **se faire p.** *(tromper)* to be led up the garden path, to be taken for a ride; *(pour de l'argent)* to get ripped off

pigeonnier [piʒɔnje] NM **1** *(pour pigeons)* dovecote **2** *Fam (mansarde)* garret, attic

piger [17] [piʒe] VT **1** *Fam (comprendre)* to get it, to catch on, *Br* to twig; **j'ai mis une heure avant de p. ce qu'il disait** it took me an hour to catch on to what he was saying; **pigé?** got it?, got the picture?, *Br* have you twigged?; **elle pige rien** *ou* **que dalle à l'art** she hasn't got a clue about art; **impossible de lui faire p. quoi que ce soit!** you just can't get through to him/her at all! **2** *(mesurer)* to rule (out)

USAGE ABSOLU to get it; **tu piges?** get it?; **il a fini par p.** he finally got it *or* got the picture, *Br* the penny finally dropped

VI *Fam (travailler à la pige)* to work freelance▪

pigiste [piʒist] NMF **1** *Typ* piece-rate typographer **2** *Journ* freelance journalist, freelancer

pigment [pigmɑ̃] NM pigment

pigmentaire [pigmɑ̃tɛr] ADJ pigmentary

pigmentation [pigmɑ̃tasjɔ̃] NF pigmentation

pigmenter [3] [pigmɑ̃te] VT to pigment

pignada [piɲada], **pignade** [piɲad] NF *(dans le sud-ouest de la France)* plantation of maritime pines

pigne [piɲ] NF **1** *(cône)* pine cone **2** *(graine)* pine kernel

pignocher [3] [piɲɔʃe] VI **1** *Vieilli (manger)* to nibble *or* to pick at food **2** *(peindre)* = to paint with minutely fine strokes

pignoler [3] [piɲɔle] **se pignoler** VPR *très Fam* to jerk off, to beat off

pignon [piɲɔ̃] NM **1** *Archit (de mur)* gable; *(de bâtiments)* side wall; **p. chantourné** shaped gable; **p. à redents** *ou* **à pas d'oiseau** crow-step(ped) *or* corbie-step(ped) gable; **avoir p. sur rue** *(personne)* to be well-off (and respectable); *(entreprise)* to be well established

2 *Tech (roue dentée)* cogwheel, gear wheel; *(petite roue)* pinion; *(d'une bicyclette)* rear-wheel, sprocket; **p. baladeur** sliding-mesh gear; **p. de renvoi** transmission (gear) wheel

3 *Bot* pine kernel *or* nut

pignoratif, -ive [piɲɔratif, -iv] ADJ *Jur* with a repurchase option

pignouf [piɲuf] NM *Fam (rustre)* slob, boor

pika [pika] NM *Zool* pika, whistling hare

pilaf [pilaf] NM pilaf, pilau

pilage [pilaʒ] NM pounding, grinding

pilaire [pilɛr] ADJ pilar, pilary

pilastre [pilastr] NM *Archit* pilaster; *(d'escalier)* newel (post); *(d'un balcon)* pillar

Pilate [pilat] NPR **Ponce P.** Pontius Pilate; *Littéraire* **être renvoyé de Caïphe à P.** to be driven from pillar to post

Pilates [pilat] NM **(la méthode) P.** Pilates; **pratiquer la méthode P.** to do Pilates

pilaw [pilav] = **pilaf**

pilchard [pilʃar] NM pilchard

pile [pil] NF **1** *(tas → désordonné)* pile, heap; *(→ ordonné)* pile, stack; **mettre en p.** to stack (up), to pile (up)

2 *Ordinat* stack

3 *Constr (pilier)* pier

4 *(appui)* pier; *(pieu)* pile; **p. culée** abutment pier

5 *Élec* battery; **une radio à piles** a radio run on

batteries, a battery radio; **marcher avec des** *ou* **sur piles** to work on *or* off batteries; **p. atomique** pile reactor; **p. bouton** button battery; **p. à combustible** fuel cell; **p. sèche** dry battery; **p. solaire** solar cell

6 *Hér* pile

7 *(côté d'une pièce)* **le côté p.** the reverse side; **p. ou face?** heads or tails?; **p., je gagne** tails, I win; **jouer** *ou* **tirer à p. ou face** to toss a coin; **tirons à p. ou face** let's toss for it

8 *Tech (bac)* **p. défileuse/blanchisseuse** breaker (beater), poacher, bleacher

9 *Fam (coups)* belting, thrashing; **flanquer la p. à qn** to give sb a good beating *or* drubbing

10 *Fam (défaite)* beating; **recevoir** *ou* **prendre une (bonne) p.** to get a beating *or Br* hammering *or Am* shellacking; **flanquer une p. à une équipe** to hammer a team, to walk all over a team

ADV *Fam* **1** *(net)* dead; **s'arrêter p.** to stop dead

2 *(juste)* right; **p. au milieu** right in the middle; **ça commence à 8 heures p.** it begins at 8 o'clock sharp *or* on the dot; **nous étions p. à l'heure** we were (there) right on time *or* on the dot; **il y en a p. 250** there are 250 exactly; **tu es tombé p. sur le bon chapitre** you just hit (on) the right chapter; **vous tombez p., j'allais vous appeler** you're right on cue, I was about to call you

pilé, -e [pile] **ADJ** *Can Vieilli* mashed; **patates pilées** mashed potatoes

pile-poil [pilpwal] **ADV** *Fam* **ça rentre p.** it fits exactly■ ; **c'est tombé p.** *(au bon moment)* it came just at the right time■ ; **je suis arrivée p. à l'heure** I got there on the dot *or* bang on time

Allusion

Pile-poil

This expression comes from a satirical television programme *Les Guignols de l'Info* on Canal+, a French TV channel. This show is a take-off of a serious discussion programme, where media celebrities and politicians deal with serious issues. In the spoof, the people are replaced by puppets, **les guignols de l'Info** ("news puppets"), and the Jacques Chirac puppet is constantly saying **pile-poil**, which is supposed to mean "precisely" or "exactly". The word has now come to enter the French language with this meaning.

piler [3] [pile] **VT 1** *(broyer → gén)* to crush, to grind; *(→ noix, amandes)* to grind **2** *Fam (vaincre)* to make mincemeat of, to wipe the floor with; **il a pilé ses adversaires** he thrashed his opponents; **on s'est fait p. en beauté au foot!** they wiped the floor with us at football! **3** *Can Joual (empiler)* to pile up■ , to stack up■ **4** *Can Vieilli (marcher sur)* to step on, to tread on

VI 1 *Fam (freiner)* to slam on the brakes **2** *Can Vieilli* **p. sur les pieds de qn** to step on sb's toes

pilet [pilɛ] **NM** *Orn* pintail

pileur, -euse[1] [pilœr, -øz] **NM,F** crusher, grinder

pileux, -euse[2] [pilø, -øz] **ADJ** *(bulbe, follicule)* hair *(avant n)*

pilier [pilje] **NM 1** *Anat, Constr & Mines* pillar

2 *Fig (défenseur)* pillar; *(bastion)* bastion, bulwark; **c'était un p. du socialisme** he/she was a pillar of socialism; **la constitution, p. de la démocratie** the constitution, one of the pillars of democracy; *Fam Péj* **c'est un p. de bar** *ou* **bistrot** *(habitué) Br* he/she can always be found propping up the bar, *Am* he's/she's a regular barfly

3 *(au rugby)* prop (forward); **p. droit** tight-head prop; **p. gauche** loose-head prop

4 *(de montagne)* buttress

pilifère [pilifɛr] **ADJ** *Bot* piliferous

pili-pili [pilipili] **NM INV** bird pepper

pilipino [pilipino] **NM** *(langue)* Pilipino

pillage [pijaʒ] **NM 1** *(vol)* pillage, looting, plundering; **le p. de la ville par les soldats** the pillaging of the town by the soldiers; **mettre au p.** to pillage **2** *(plagiat)* plagiarism, pirating **3** *(d'une ruche)* robbing

pillard, -e [pijar, -ard] **ADJ** pillaging, looting, plundering

NM,F *(d'une ville, d'un village)* pillager, looter, plunderer; *(lors d'une émeute)* looter

pillaver [3] [pijave] **VI** *Fam* to knock it back, to booze

piller [3] [pije] **VT 1** *(dépouiller → village, ville)* to pillage, to loot, to plunder; *(→ magasin)* to loot **2** *(détourner)* to siphon off, *Br* to cream off; **p. les caisses de l'État** to siphon off *or Br* to cream off taxpayers' money **3** *(plagier)* to plagiarize

pilleur, -euse [pijœr, -øz] **NM,F** *(d'une ville, d'un village)* pillager, looter, plunderer; *(lors d'une émeute)* looter; **p. d'épaves** wrecker

pillow-lava [pilolava] *(pl* **pillow-lavas***)* **NF** *Géol* pillow lava

pilocarpe [pilɔkarp] **NM** *Bot* pilocarpus

pilocarpine [pilɔkarpin] **NF** *Chim* pilocarpine

pilon [pilɔ̃] **NM 1** *(de mortier)* pestle; *Tech* pounder **2** *Typ* **mettre un livre au p.** to pulp a book; **tous ces livres iront au p.** all these books will be pulped; **on a eu plus de 2000 pilons** we had to pulp more than 2,000 copies **3** *(jambe de bois)* (straight) wooden leg **4** *(de volaille)* drumstick

pilonnage [pilɔnaʒ] **NM 1** *(broyage)* pounding **2** *Typ* pulping **3** *(bombardement)* (heavy) bombardment, shelling; *Fig* **p. publicitaire** barrage of publicity

pilonner [3] [pilɔne] **VT 1** *(broyer)* to pound **2** *Typ* to pulp **3** *(bombarder)* to bombard, to shell

pilori [pilɔri] **NM 1** *Hist* pillory **2** *Fig* **clouer** *ou* **mettre qn au p.** to pillory sb

pilo-sébacé, -e [pilɔsebase] *(mpl* **pilo-sébacés,** *fpl* **pilo-sébacées***)* **ADJ** pilosebaceous

piloselle [pilɔzɛl] **NF** *Bot* mouse-ear (hawkweed)

pilosisme [pilozism] **NM** pilosis

pilosité [pilozite] **NF** pilosity; **p. excessive/normale** excessive/normal hair growth; **p. faciale** facial hair

pilot [pilo] **NM 1** *Constr* pile; **p. de pont** bridge pile **2** *Tech (chiffons)* = cloth used in paper-making

pilotable [pilɔtabl] **ADJ** *(avion)* flyable; *(bateau)* sailable; *(voiture)* driveable; *(moto)* rideable

pilotage [pilɔtaʒ] **NM 1** *Naut* piloting; **droits de p.** pilotage dues **2** *Aviat* pilotage, piloting; **école de p.** flying school; **p. automatique** automatic piloting; **sur p. automatique** on automatic pilot *or* autopilot; **p. sans visibilité** blind flying **3** *(d'une voiture)* driving; *(d'une moto)* riding **4** *Fig (direction)* **le p. d'une entreprise** running a business

pilote [pilɔt] **NM**

Note that it is no longer considered a mistake to feminize this word and to say **une pilote** in senses 1, 2 and 3 but some French speakers nonetheless regard this form as unacceptable, especially in France. See also the entry **féminisation**.

1 *Aviat & Naut* pilot; **p. de chasse** fighter pilot; **p. d'essai** test pilot; **p. de ligne** airline pilot

2 *(guide)* guide

3 *(de voiture de course)* driver; *(de moto de course)* rider; **p. automobile** *ou* **de course** racing driver

4 *Tech* **p. automatique** autopilot, automatic pilot; *Fig* **je ne me rappelle de rien, j'ai dû rentrer chez moi en** *ou* **sur p. automatique** I don't remember anything, I must have got home on autopilot

5 *Élec* pilot

6 *(poisson)* pilot fish

7 *Ordinat (d'affichage, d'imprimante)* driver; **p. de mise en file d'attente** spooler

8 *Rail* pilot, pilotman

9 *TV* pilot

10 *Presse* **P.** = French cartoon magazine

ADJ 1 *(expérimental)* experimental; *(promotionnel)* promotional; **école p.** experimental school; **usine/installation p.** pilot factory/plant; **produit p.** promotional item, special offer

2 *Mktg (échantillon, étude, prix)* pilot

piloter [3] [pilɔte] **VT 1** *(conduire → avion)* to pilot, to fly; *(→ bateau)* to pilot; *(→ voiture)* to drive; *(→ moto)* to ride **2** *(guider → personne)* to guide, to show around; *(→ outil)* to guide **3** *Ordinat* to drive; **piloté par menu** menu-driven; **piloté par ordinateur** computer-driven **4** *Constr* to drive piles into **5** *(étude, campagne)* to pilot

pilotin [pilɔtɛ̃] **NM** = apprentice in the French merchant navy

pilotis [pilɔti] **NM** piling; **maison sur p.** house built on piles *or* stilts

pilou [pilu] **NM** flannelette

pils [pils] **NF** *Belg* lager

pilulaire[1] [pilylɛr] **ADJ** pilular

NM *Vét* balling gun

pilulaire[2] [pilylɛr] **NF** *Bot* pillwort

pilule [pilyl] **NF 1** *(médicament)* pill; *Fam* **dorer la p. à qn** to *Br* sugar *or Am* sweeten the pill for sb; *Fam* **se dorer la p.** to catch some rays; *Fam Fig* **faire passer la p.** to get sb to swallow the pill *or* to take their medicine; **il a dit ça pour faire passer la p.** he said it to *Br* sugar *or Am* sweeten the pill; *Fam Fig* **trouver la p. amère** to find it a bitter pill to swallow; *Fin* **p. empoisonnée** *(contre-OPA)* poison pill

2 *(contraceptif)* **p. contraceptive** *ou* **anticonceptionnelle** contraceptive pill; **la p.** the pill; **prendre la p.** to be on the pill; **p. abortive** abortion pill; **p. du lendemain** morning-after pill

pilulier [pilylje] **NM 1** *(boîte)* pill box **2** *(instrument)* pill machine

pilum [pilɔm] **NM** *Antiq* pilum, javelin

pimbêche [pɛ̃bɛʃ] **ADJ** stuck up; **ce qu'elle peut être p.!** she thinks she's the queen bee *or Br* Lady Muck!

NF c'est une p. she's really stuck-up

pimbina [pɛ̃bina] **NM** *Can Bot (fruit)* highbush cranberry; *(plante)* highbush cranberry bush

piment [pimɑ̃] **NM 1** *Bot & Culin* chili, chilli; **p. doux** (sweet) pepper; **p. rouge** red chili; **p. fort** hot pepper, pimento **2** *(saveur, charme)* **ça met un peu de p. dans la vie!** it adds some spice to life!; **une histoire/vie qui ne manque pas de p.** a story/life that is anything but dull; **cette fille a du p.** she's certainly got character

pimenté, -e [pimɑ̃te] **ADJ** *(sauce)* hot, spicy

pimenter [3] [pimɑ̃te] **VT 1** *Culin* to season with chili, to spice up **2** *(corser)* **p. une histoire** to lace a story with spicy details; **p. la vie** to add spice to life

pimpant, -e [pɛ̃pɑ̃, -ɑ̃t] **ADJ** *(net)* spruce, neat, smart; *(frais)* fresh, bright; **elle est arrivée toute pimpante** she turned up all bright-eyed and bushy tailed

pimprenelle [pɛ̃prənɛl] **NF** *Bot* salad burnet

❑ **Pimprenelle NPR** *TV* **P. et Nicolas** = popular children's programme of the 1960s

PIN [peiɛn] **NM** *Écon (abrév* **produit intérieur net***)* NDP

pin [pɛ̃] **NM 1** *Bot* pine; **p. d'Alep** Aleppo pine; **p. australien** Australian pine, river oak; **p. cembro** Swiss stone pine, arolla pine; **p. maritime** maritime pine; **p. noir** Austrian pine; **p. d'Oregon** Douglas fir; **p. parasol** *ou* **pignon** stone pine; **p. sylvestre** Scots *or* Scotch pine **2** *Menuis* pine, pinewood

pinacée [pinase] *Bot* **NF** member of the Pinaceae

❑ **pinacées NFPL** Pinaceae

pinacle [pinakl] **NM 1** *Archit* pinnacle **2** *Fig* zenith, acme; **être au p.** to be at the top; **mettre** *ou* **porter qn au p.** to praise sb to the skies, to put sb on a pedestal

pinacothèque [pinakɔtɛk] **NF** art gallery

pinaillage [pinajaʒ] **NM** *Fam* nitpicking, hair-splitting

pinailler [3] [pinaje] **VI** *Fam* to split hairs, to nitpick; **p. sur qch** to quibble over sth

pinaillerie [pinajri] **NF** nagging

pinailleur, -euse [pinajœr, -øz] *Fam* **ADJ** fussy, nitpicking, quibbling

NM,F nitpicker

pinard [pinar] **NM** *Fam* wine■ , vino

pinardier [pinardje] **NM 1** *(navire)* wine tanker **2** *Fam (marchand)* wine merchant■

pinasse [pinas] **NF** (flat-bottomed) pinnace

pinastre [pinastr] **NM** maritime pine, pinaster

pinçage [pɛ̃saʒ] **NM** nipping off, pinching out

pinçard, -e [pɛ̃sard, -ard] **ADJ** that lands toe-first

NM,F = horse that lands toe-first

pince [pɛ̃s] **NF 1** *(outil)* (pair of) pliers *or* pincers; *(pour l'âtre, de forgeron)* tongs; *(pour tenir en place)* clip; *Élec* **p. ampèremétrique** grip current tester; **p. à cheveux** hair clip; **p. coupante** wire cutters; **p. crocodile** crocodile clip; **p. à dénuder** wire-strippers; **p. à dessin** bulldog clip; **p. à épiler** (pair of) tweezers; **p. à glaçons** ice tongs; **p. à linge** clothes peg *or Am* pin; **p. multiprise**

multiple pliers; **p. à ongles** (nail) clippers; **p. à palettes** pallet pusher; **p. plate** flat (nose) pliers; **p. à sucre** sugar tongs; **p. universelle** universal *or* all-purpose pliers; **p. à vélo** bicycle clip
2 *Biol & Méd* **p. (à disséquer)** (dissecting) forceps; **pinces hémostatiques** artery clip, *Spéc* haemostat
3 *Zool* (*d'un crabe, d'un homard*) claw, pincer; (*d'un sabot de cheval*) toe; (*incisive*) incisor
4 *Couture* dart, tuck; **ouvrir** *ou* **retirer des pinces** to take out tucks; **p. de poitrine** dart
5 *Cin & TV* **p. pour projecteur** gaffer grip
6 *Fam* (*main*) paw, mitt; **serrer la p. à qn** to shake hands with sb▪
□ **à pinces** ADJ *Couture* pleated; **pantalon à pinces** front-pleated trousers ADV *Fam* (*à pied*) on foot▪, on shanks's *Br* pony *or Am* mare; **j'irai à pinces** I'll hoof it

pincé, -e¹ [pɛ̃se] ADJ 1 (*dédaigneux → sourire*) tight-lipped; **il avait un air p.** he had a stiff *or* starchy manner; ..., **répondit-elle d'un ton p.** ..., she answered stiffly *or* starchily 2 (*serré*) tight; **aux lèvres pincées** tight-lipped

pinceau, -x [pɛ̃so] NM 1 (*brosse → de peintre*) paintbrush, brush; (*→ de maquillage*) brush; **coup de p.** brush stroke; **il a un bon coup de p.** he paints well 2 (*style*) brushwork; **on reconnaît bien là le p. d'Utrillo** this is obviously Utrillo's brushwork 3 (*de lumière*) beam, pencil; *Opt* **p. lumineux** light pencil
□ **pinceaux** NMPL *Fam* (*jambes*) legs▪, *Br* pins, *Am* gams; (*pieds*) feet▪, *Br* plates, *Am* dogs; **s'emmêler les pinceaux** (*trébucher*) to trip up▪, to stumble▪; (*s'embrouiller*) to tie oneself in knots

pincée² [pɛ̃se] ADJF *voir* **pincé**
NF pinch

pincelier [pɛ̃səlje] NM dipper, dip cup

pincement [pɛ̃smɑ̃] NM 1 (*émotion*) twinge, pang; **j'ai eu un p. au cœur** it tugged at my heartstrings 2 (*fait de serrer*) pinching, nipping 3 *Mus* plucking 4 *Hort* nipping off, *Br* deadheading 5 *Aut* toe-in

pince-monseigneur [pɛ̃smɔ̃sɛɲœr] (*pl* **pinces-monseigneur**) NF jemmy

pince-nez [pɛ̃sne] NM INV pince-nez

pince-oreille [pɛ̃sɔrɛj] (*pl* **pince-oreilles**) NM *Entom* earwig

pincer [16] [pɛ̃se] VT 1 (*serrer*) to pinch, to nip; **se faire p. par un crabe** to get nipped by a crab; **arrête de p. ton frère** stop pinching your brother; **son grand-père lui pinça la joue** his/her grandfather pinched his/her cheek; **pince-moi, je rêve!** pinch me, I must be dreaming!; **se faire p. les fesses** to have one's bottom pinched, to be goosed; **p. les lèvres** to go tight-lipped; **une veste/robe qui pince la taille** a fitted jacket/dress
2 (*sujet: vent, froid*) to nip at; **le vent pinçait mes joues** the wind nipped at my cheeks
3 *Mus* to pluck
4 *Hort* to pinch out, to nip off, *Br* to deadhead
5 *Fam* (*arrêter*) to collar, to nab; **un jour, tu vas te faire p. par les flics** one day, you'll get nabbed *or Am* collared; **elle s'est fait p. en sortant du magasin** she got collared as she was about to leave the *Br* shop *or Am* store
6 *Fam* (*locution*) **en p. pour qn** to be crazy about sb, to have the hots for sb, *Br* to fancy sb like mad
USAGE ABSOLU *Fam* (*faire froid*) **ça pince** it's nippy, there's a nip in the air; **ça pince (dur) aujourd'hui!** it's bitterly *or* freezing cold today!▪
▶ **se pincer** VPR 1 (*soi-même*) to pinch oneself; **se p. le nez** to hold *or* to pinch one's nose
2 (*par accident → doigt*) to catch; **je me suis pincé le doigt dans le tiroir** I caught my finger in the drawer, my finger got caught in the drawer

pince-sans-rire [pɛ̃sɑ̃rir] ADJ INV **elle est très p.** she's got a very dry sense of humour; **répondre d'un air p.** to answer drily *or* deadpan
NMF INV person with a deadpan *or* dry sense of humour

pincette [pɛ̃sɛt] NF 1 (*d'horloger*) (pair of) tweezers 2 *Suisse* (*pince à linge*) clothes peg *or Am* pin
□ **pincettes** NFPL (*pour attiser*) (fireplace) tongs; *Fam* **il n'est pas à prendre avec des**

pincettes (*très énervé*) he's like a bear with a sore head

pinchard, -e [pɛ̃ʃar, -ard] ADJ iron grey, dark grey
NM,F iron *or* dark grey horse

pinçon [pɛ̃sɔ̃] NM pinch mark

pinçure [pɛ̃syr] NF pinch-ache

Pindare [pɛ̃dar] NPR Pindar

pindarique [pɛ̃darik] ADJ Pindaric

pine [pin] NF *Vulg* (*pénis*) dick, prick, cock; **rentrer la p. sous le bras** to go home without getting laid *or Br* without getting one's oats

pinéal, -e, -aux, -ales [pineal, -o] ADJ pineal

Pineau [pino] NM 1 (*vin*) **P. (des Charentes)** Pineau (des Charentes) (*aperitif made from unfermented grape juice and brandy*) 2 (*cépage*) Pineau grape

pinède [pinɛd] NF pinewood, pine grove

pinène [pinɛn] NM *Chim* pinene

piner [3] [pine] VI *Can Vulg* to fuck, *Br* to shag

pineraie [pinrɛ] = **pinède**

pinglot [pɛ̃glo] NM *Fam* (*pied*) foot▪, *Br* plate, *Am* dog

pingouin [pɛ̃gwɛ̃] NM (*alcidé*) auk; (*manchot*) penguin; **grand p.** great auk; **petit p., p. torda** razorbill

ping-pong [piŋpɔ̃g] NM (*pl* **ping-pongs**) table tennis, ping-pong

pingre [pɛ̃gr] ADJ (*avare*) stingy, mean, tight-fisted
NMF skinflint, penny-pincher

pingrerie [pɛ̃grəri] NF (*avarice*) stinginess, meanness

pinière [pinjɛr] NF = **pinède**

pinne [pin] NF *Zool* pinna (mollusc)

pinnipède [pinipɛd] NM pinniped, pinnipedian

pinnothère [pinɔtɛr] NM pinnothere, pea-crab

pinnule [pinyl] NF 1 *Bot* pinnule 2 *Métal* sight vane, sight (*of alidade, sextant etc*); **p. à fils** cross-hair sight; **p. à œilleton** aperture sight

Pinocchio [pinɔkjo] NPR Pinocchio

pinocytose [pinɔsitoz] NF *Biol* pinocytosis

pinot [pino] NM pinot

pin-pon [pɛ̃pɔ̃] EXCLAM (*langage enfantin*) = noise made by a fire engine's two-tone siren

pin's [pins] NM INV *Br* badge, *Am* button

pinscher [pinʃer] NM (*doberman*) pinscher

pinson [pɛ̃sɔ̃] NM *Orn* chaffinch; **p. du Nord** brambling

pinta [pɛ̃ta] NM *Méd* pinta

pintade [pɛ̃tad] NF *Orn* guinea fowl; **p. vulturine** vulturine guinea fowl

pintadeau, -x [pɛ̃tado] NM *Orn* young guinea fowl

pintadine [pɛ̃tadin] NF *Zool* pearl oyster

pinte [pɛ̃t] NF 1 (*mesure → française*) ≃ quart (*0.93 litre*); (*→ anglo-saxonne*) pint; (*→ canadienne*) quart 2 (*verre*) pint 3 *Suisse* café-bar 4 *Fam* (*locutions*) **s'offrir** *ou* **se faire** *ou* **se payer une p. de bon sang** to have a good laugh; *Can* **se faire une p. de mauvais sang** to worry oneself sick

pinté, -e [pɛ̃te] ADJ *Fam* (*saoul*) smashed, sozzled

pinter [3] [pɛ̃te] *Fam* VI (*se saouler*) to booze
VT (*boire*) to swill, to knock back
▶ **se pinter** VPR *très Fam* **se p. (la gueule)** to get smashed *or* sozzled

pinteur, -euse [pɛ̃tœr, -øz] NM,F *Belg & Suisse Fam* boozer, alky

pintocher [3] [pɛ̃tɔʃe] VI *Suisse Fam* to booze

pin-up [pinœp] NF INV (*photo*) pinup; (*jolie fille*) sexy-looking girl

pinyin [pinjin] NM *Ling* Pinyin

piochage [pjɔʃaʒ] NM digging (up)

pioche [pjɔʃ] NF 1 (*outil*) pick, pickaxe, mattock; **ils ont démoli le mur à coups de p.** they demolished the wall with a pick 2 (*aux dominos*) stock; (*aux cartes*) talon, stock

piocher [3] [pjɔʃe] VT 1 (*creuser*) to dig (up)
2 (*tirer*) to draw; **p. une carte/un domino** to draw a card/a domino (from the stock); **p. des prunes dans un compotier** to dig into a bowl for plums
3 *Fam* (*étudier*) to cram, *Br* to swot at, *Am* to grind away at
VI 1 (*puiser*) to dig (**dans** into); **les cerises sont délicieuses, vas-y, pioche (dans le tas)** the cherries are delicious, go ahead, dig in
2 (*aux dominos, aux cartes*) to draw from the stock; **pioche!** (*aux cartes*) take a card!

piocheur, -euse [pjɔʃœr, -øz] ADJ *Fam* hardworking▪
NM,F 1 (*ouvrier*) digger 2 *Fam* (*étudiant*) *Br* swot, *Am* grind

piolet [pjɔlɛ] NM ice-axe

pion¹ [pjɔ̃] NM 1 (*de jeux de société*) piece; (*de dames*) draughtsman, *Am* checker; (*d'échecs*) pawn 2 *Fig* (*personne*) **n'être qu'un p. sur l'échiquier** to be just a cog in the machine *or* a pawn in the game 3 *Phys* pion

pion², pionne [pjɔ̃, pjɔn] NM,F *Fam Arg scol* (*surveillant*) supervisor▪

Culture

PION

In French lycées, the "pions" (officially called "surveillants") are responsible for supervising pupils outside class hours; they are often university students who do the job to make a little extra money.

pioncer [16] [pjɔ̃se] VI *Fam* to sleep▪

pionicat, pionnicat [pjɔnika] NM *Fam Arg scol* (*activité du surveillant*) = working as a "pion"

pionnier, -ère [pjɔnje, -ɛr] ADJ pioneering; **une entreprise pionnière dans le domaine du multimédia** a pioneering company in the world of multimedia
NM,F 1 (*inventeur*) pioneer; **une pionnière de la physique nucléaire** a pioneer of nuclear physics 2 (*colon*) pioneer; **les pionniers de l'Ouest américain** the pioneers of the Wild West
NM 1 *Mil* sapper 2 (*société, produit*) pioneer; **entrer en p. sur le marché** to be the first on the market

piorne [pjɔrn] NF *Suisse Fam* sniveller

piorner [3] [pjɔrne] VI *Suisse Fam* to snivel

pioupiou [pjupju] NM *Fam Vieilli* soldier▪, *Br* squaddie, *Am* GI (Joe)

pipa [pipa] NM *Zool* Surinam toad

pipe [pip] NF 1 (*à fumer → contenant*) pipe; (*→ contenu*) pipe, pipeful; **une p. en écume/terre** a meerschaum/clay pipe; **une p. de bruyère** a briar pipe
2 *Tech* pipe
3 (*tonneau*) wine cask
4 *Vulg* (*fellation*) blow-job; **faire** *ou* **tailler une p. à qn** to give sb a blow-job
5 *Fam* (*cigarette*) *Br* fag, *Am* butt
6 (*futaille*) (large) cask, barrel
7 (*tuyau*) pipe(line) (*for liquid, gas*)
8 *Fam* **casser sa p.** (*mourir*) to croak, to kick the bucket
9 *Can Vieilli* (*distance*) distance; **ça fait une sacrée p.!** that's quite a long way!, that's quite a distance!

pipeau, -x [pipo] NM 1 *Mus* (*reed*) pipe; *Fam Fig* **c'est du p.** it's a load of garbage *or Br* rubbish 2 *Chasse* bird call
□ **pipeaux** NMPL (*pour les oiseaux*) birdlimed *or* limed twigs

pipeauter [3] [pipote] VI *Fam* to talk garbage *or Br* rubbish

pipée [pipe] NF bird snaring, bird catching (*with bird calls and limed twigs*)

pipelet, -ette [piplɛ, ɛt] NM,F *Fam* 1 *Vieilli* (*concierge*) concierge▪, *Am* doorman▪ 2 (*bavard*) chatterbox, gasbag

pipe-line, pipeline [pajplajn, piplin] (*pl* **pipe-lines**) NM pipeline

piper [3] [pipe] VT 1 (*truquer → dés*) to load; (*→ cartes*) to mark; *aussi Fig* **les dés sont pipés** the dice are loaded 2 *Chasse* to hunt with a bird call 3 (*locution*) **ne pas p. (mot)** to keep mum; **je te conseille de ne pas p. mot** mum's the word, you'd better keep your mouth shut

pipéracée [piperase] *Bot* NF member of the Piperaceae *or* pepper family
□ **pipéracées** NFPL Piperaceae

piperade [piperad] NF piperade (*rich stew of tomatoes and sweet peppers, mixed with beaten eggs and slightly scrambled*)

piperie [pipri] NF *Littéraire* ruse, trick

pipérin [piperɛ̃] NM *Chim* piperin(e)

pipérine [piperin] NF *Chim* piperin(e)

pipéronal, -als [piperɔnal] NM *Chim* piperonal

pipette [pipɛt] NF pipette; *Suisse* **ça ne vaut pas p.** it's not worth a bean *or Am* a red cent

pipeur, -euse [pipœr, -øz] NM,F *Vieilli* deceiver

pipi [pipi] NM *Fam (urine)* pee; **faire p.** to have a pee, to pee; **le chien a fait p. sur le tapis** the dog's made a puddle *or* peed on the carpet; **aller faire p.** to go for a pee, to go to the loo *or Am* john; **faire p. au lit** to wet the bed; **c'est du p. de chat** *(sans goût)* it's like gnat's pee, it's like dishwater; *(sans intérêt)* it's a load of bilge *or Br* tripe

pipier, -ère [pipje, -ɛr] ADJ pipe-making *(avant n)*

NM,F pipe-maker

pipi-room [pipirum] *(pl* **pipi-rooms***)* NM *Fam Br* loo, *Am* john

pipistrelle [pipistrɛl] NF *Zool* pipistrelle

pipit [pipit] NM *Orn* pipit; **p. des arbres** tree pipit; **p. à gorge rousse** red-throated pipit; **p. maritime** *ou* **obscur** rock pipit; **p. des prés** meadow pipit; **p. rousseline** tawny pipit; **p. spioncelle** water pipit

pipo [pipo] NMF *Fam Arg scol* = student at the "École Polytechnique"

pipole [pipɔl] NMF celebrity, *Fam* celeb; **c'est un bar fréquenté par les pipoles** the bar is a popular celeb hang-out

piquage [pikaʒ] NM **1** Couture stitching **2** *Tex* punching

piquant, -e [pikɑ̃, -ɑ̃t] ADJ **1** *(plante)* thorny; *(ortie)* stinging; **sa barbe est piquante** his beard's all prickly

2 *(vif → air, vent)* biting

3 *Culin (moutarde, radis)* hot; *(plat, sauce)* hot, spicy

4 *(caustique → remarque, ton)* cutting, biting

5 *(excitant → récit, détail)* spicy, juicy; *(charmant → beauté, brunette)* striking

6 *Fam (eau)* fizzy

NM **1** *(de plante)* thorn, prickle; *(d'oursin, de hérisson)* spine; *(de barbelé)* barb, spike; **couvert de piquants** prickly

2 *(intérêt)* **le p. de l'histoire, c'est qu'elle n'est même pas venue!** the best part of it is that *or* to crown it all she didn't even show up!; **des détails qui ne manquent pas de p.** juicy details; **le changement donne du p. à la vie** variety is the spice of life; **cette fille a du p.** that girl is rather striking *or* is strikingly attractive

pique [pik] NF **1** *(arme)* pike; *(de picador)* pic, lance **2** *(propos)* barb, cutting remark; **envoyer** *ou* **lancer des piques à qn** to make cutting remarks to sb

NM *Cartes* **du p.** spades; **le roi de p.** the king of spades; **jouer à** *ou* **du p.** to play spades

piqué, -e [pike] ADJ **1** *(abîmé → vin)* sour; *(→ miroir)* mildewed; *(→ bois)* wormeaten; *(→ papier)* foxed

2 *Fam (fou)* crazy, loopy

3 *Mus* staccato; **note piquée** dotted note

4 *Culin (de lard)* larded, piqué; *(d'ail)* studded with garlic, piqué

5 *(dessus de lit, vêtement)* quilted

6 *(locutions) Fam* **une histoire pas piquée des hannetons** *ou* **des vers** a heck of a good story; **un alibi pas p. des hannetons** *ou* **des vers** the perfect alibi■ ; **il est pas p. des hannetons** *ou* **des vers, ton frangin!** your brother is really something else!; **un rhume pas p. des vers** *ou* **des hannetons** a stinking cold

NM **1** *Tex* piqué

2 *Aviat* nosedive; **attaquer en p.** to dive-bomb; **descendre en p.** to (go into a) nosedive

3 *(en danse)* piqué

pique-assiette [pikasjɛt] *(pl* **inv** *ou* **pique-assiettes***)* NMF *Fam* sponger, scrounger, freeloader; **jouer les p.** to gatecrash

pique-bœuf [pikbœf] *(pl* **inv** *ou* **pique-bœufs** [pikbø]*)* NM *Orn* oxpecker

pique-bois [pikbwa] NM INV *Can Orn* woodpecker

pique-feu [pikfø] *(pl* **inv** *ou* **pique-feux***)* NM poker

pique-fleur, pique-fleurs [pikflœr] *(pl* **pique-fleurs***)* NM flower holder

pique-nique [piknik] *(pl* **pique-niques***)* NM picnic; **faire un p.** to go on *or* for a picnic

pique-niquer [3] [piknike] VI to picnic, to go on *or* for a picnic; **un bon endroit pour p.** a nice place to have *or* for a picnic

pique-niqueur, -euse [piknikœr, -øz] *(mpl* **pique-niqueurs**, *fpl* **pique-niqueuses***)* NM,F picnicker

pique-note, pique-notes [piknɔt] *(pl* **pique-notes***)* NM spike file, bill file

piquer [3] [pike] VT **1** *Méd (avec une seringue)* **p. qn** to give sb an injection

2 *Vét (tuer)* **p. un animal** to put an animal down, to put an animal to sleep; **faire p. un chien** to have a dog put down

3 *(avec une pointe)* to prick; **p. un morceau de viande avec une fourchette/la pointe d'un couteau** to stick a fork/the tip of a knife into a piece of meat; **p. un bœuf avec un aiguillon** to goad an ox; **p. qn avec une épingle** to prick sb with a pin

4 *(sujet: animal, plante)* to sting, to bite; **être piqué** *ou* **se faire p. par une abeille** to get stung by a bee; **se faire p. par un moustique** to get bitten by a mosquito; **être piqué par des orties/méduses** to get stung by nettles/jellyfish

5 *(enfoncer)* to stick; **p. une aiguille dans une pelote** to stick a needle into a ball; **p. une fleur dans ses cheveux** to put a flower in *or* to stick a flower in one's hair; **p. une fourchette dans un steak** to stick a fork into a steak; **p. une photo sur le mur** to pin a picture on *or* onto the wall; **p. une broche sur un chemisier** to pin a brooch on *or* onto a blouse

6 *(brûler)* to tickle, to tingle, to prickle; **ça pique la gorge** it gives you a tickle in your *or* the throat; **le poivre pique la langue** pepper burns the tongue; **la fumée me pique les yeux** the smoke is making my eyes sting; **le vent me pique les joues** the wind is biting *or* stinging my cheeks; **un tissu rêche qui pique la peau** a rough material which chafes the skin

7 *(stimuler → curiosité, jalousie)* to arouse, to awaken; *(→ amour-propre)* to pique; *(→ intérêt)* to stir (up)

8 *Fam (faire de manière soudaine)* **p. un cent mètres** *ou* **un sprint** to sprint off; *Fig* to take off in a flash; **p. une colère** to go ballistic, to hit the roof; **p. une crise (de nerfs)** to get hysterical; **p. un galop** to gallop off; **p. un somme** *ou* **un roupillon** to take a nap, to grab some shut-eye; **p. un fard** to turn red *or* crimson; **p. une tête** *(plonger)* to dive in; *(se baigner)* to have a dip

9 *Fam (dérober)* to pinch, *Br* to nick; **p. une voiture** to pinch *or Br* nick a car; **p. un porte-monnaie** to snatch a wallet; **il a piqué la femme de son copain** he ran off with his friend's wife; **p. une phrase dans un livre/à un auteur** to lift a sentence from a book/an author; **je me suis fait p. ma voiture ce matin** my car was pinched *or Br* nicked this morning

10 *Fam (arrêter)* to nab, to collar, *Br* to nick; **la police l'a piqué la main dans le sac** he was caught red-handed; **se faire p.** *(arrêter)* to get nabbed *or Am* nailed; *(surprendre)* to get caught

11 *Mus* **p. une note** to dot a note, to play a note staccato

12 *Couture* to sew; *(cuir)* to stitch

13 *Culin* **p. un rôti d'ail** to stick pieces of garlic into a roast; **p. une viande de lardons** to lard a piece of meat

14 *(en danse)* **p. la pointe** to prick the pointe

15 *Tech (rouille)* to hammer off

16 *Pêche* to gaff, to strike (with a gaff)

17 *Naut* **p. l'heure** to strike the hour

VI **1** *(brûler → barbe)* to prickle; *(→ désinfectant, alcool)* to sting; *(→ yeux)* to burn, to smart; **aïe! ça pique!** ouch! that stings!; **tu piques!** *(tu es mal rasé)* you're all prickly!; **radis/moutarde qui pique** hot radish/mustard; *Fam* **eau qui pique** fizzy water■ ; **vin qui pique** sour wine; **odeur qui pique** pungent smell; **gorge qui pique** sore throat

2 *(descendre → avion)* to (go into a) dive; *(→ oiseau)* to swoop down; *(→ personne)* to head straight towards; **p. (droit) vers** to head (straight) for

3 *(locutions)* **p. du nez** *(avion)* to (go into a) nosedive; *(bateau)* to tilt forward; *(fleur)* to droop; *(personne)* to (begin to) drop off; **tu es fatigué, tu commences à p. du nez** you're tired, you keep nodding off; *Équitation* **p. des deux** to spur; *Fig* to run away full tilt

►**se piquer** VPR **1** *(avec une seringue → malade)* to inject oneself; *(→ drogué)* to shoot up; **il se pique à l'héroïne** he shoots *or* does heroin

2 *(par accident)* to prick oneself

3 *(s'abîmer → papier, linge)* to turn mildewy, to go mouldy; *(→ métal)* to pit, to get pitted; *(→ vin)* to turn sour

4 *Fam* **se p. le nez** *ou* **la ruche** to get plastered

5 *Littéraire* **se p. de** to pride oneself on; **il se pique de connaissances médicales** he prides himself on his knowledge of medicine

6 *(locution)* **elle s'est piquée au jeu** it grew on her

piquet [pikɛ] NM **1** *(pieu)* post, stake, picket; *(plus petit)* peg; **planter un p. dans le sol** to drive a stake into the ground; **p. de tente** tent peg; **être planté comme un p.** to stand there like a lemon *or* dummy

2 *(groupe → de soldats, de grévistes)* picket; **p. d'incendie** fire fighting squad; **p. de grève** picket; **piquets de grève volants** flying pickets

3 *(coin)* **mettre un enfant au p.** to send a child to stand in the corner; *aussi Hum* **au p.!** go to the back of the class!

4 *(jeu)* piquet; **faire une partie de p.** to play a hand of piquet

piquetage [piktaʒ] NM **1** *(d'une route, d'un chemin)* staking (out), pegging (out) **2** *Can* picketing

piqueter [27] [pikte] VT **1** *(route, chemin)* to stake *or* to peg (out) **2** *Littéraire (parsemer)* to stud, to dot; **un ciel piqueté d'étoiles** a sky studded with stars, a star-studded sky

VI *Can* to picket

piqueteur, -euse [piktœr, -øz] NM,F *Can* picketer

piquette [pikɛt] NF *Fam* **1** *(vin)* cheap wine■ , *Br* plonk **2** *(défaite)* thrashing, pasting; **foutre la p. à qn** to thrash *or* paste sb **3** *(locution)* **c'est de la p.** it's a mere trifle

piqueur, -euse [pikœr, -øz] ADJ *Entom* stinging *(avant n)*

NM,F **1** *Couture* stitcher; *(dans l'industrie de la chaussure)* upper stitcher **2** *Fam (voleur)* thief■ ; **un p. d'idées** a stealer of ideas■ **3** *Chasse* whipper-in **4** *(surveillant d'écurie)* groom

NM **1** *Constr* overseer **2** *Mines* hewer, getter

piqueux [pikø] NM *Chasse* (chief) whipper-in

piquier [pikje] NM *Mil & Hist* pike-bearer, pike-man

piquoir [pikwar] NM *Tech* (draughtsman's) needle, pricker

piquouse [pikuz] NF *Fam* shot, *Br* jab; **se faire une p.** to have a jab

piqûre [pikyr] NF **1** *(d'aiguille)* prick; **p. d'épingle** pinprick **2** *(de guêpe, d'abeille)* sting; *(de moustique, de puce)* bite **3** *(de plante)* sting; **piqûres d'orties** nettle stings **4** *Méd* injection, shot; **p. antitétanique** antitetanus *or* tetanus injection *or* shot; **faire une p. à qn** to give sb an injection; **p. de rappel** booster (injection *or* shot) **5** *Couture (point)* stitch; *(rangs, couture)* stitching *(UNCOUNT)* **6** *(altération → du bois)* wormhole; *(→ du métal)* pit; **piqûres** *(sur une page)* foxing **7** *(tache → de rouille, de moisi)* spot, speck; **piqûres de mouches** fly specks

piranha [piraɲa] NM *Ich* piranha

pirarucu [piraruku] NM *Ich* pirarucu, arapaima

piratage [pirataʒ] NM pirating *(UNCOUNT)*, piracy; **p. informatique** (computer) hacking; **p. de logiciels** software piracy; **p. musical** music piracy; **p. téléphonique** phreaking

pirate [pirat] NM **1** *(sur les mers)* pirate; **p. de l'air** hijacker **2** *(escroc)* swindler, thief; **c'est tous des pirates, dans la grand-rue** the traders in the high street are a bunch of thieves **3** *(de logiciels, de DVD)* pirate; **p. informatique** cracker, hacker; **p. du téléphone** phreaker **4** *(comme adj; avec ou sans trait d'union)* pirate *(avant n)*; **enregistrement p.** pirate *or* bootleg recording

pirater [3] [pirate] VT **1** *Fam (voler)* to rip off, to rob; **p. des idées** to pinch ideas **2** *(copier illégalement)* to pirate; *Ordinat* to hack; **p. un film/un DVD** to make a pirate copy of a movie *or Br* film/a DVD

VI to pirate

piraterie [piratri] NF **1** *(sur les mers → activité)* piracy; *(→ acte)* act of piracy; **p. aérienne** air piracy, hijacking **2** *(escroquerie)* swindle, sharp practice **3** *(plagiat)* piracy, pirating; **p. audiovisuelle** unauthorized copying *or* reproduction; **p. commerciale** industrial piracy; **p. informatique** hacking

piraya [piraja] = **piranha**

pire [pir] ADJ **1** *(comparatif)* worse; **si je dors, c'est p. encore** if I sleep, it's even worse; **les conditions sont pires que jamais** the conditions are worse than ever; **ça ne pourrait pas**

être p. it couldn't be worse; **c'est de p. en p.** it's getting worse and worse; *Prov* **il n'est p. eau que l'eau qui dort** still waters run deep; *Prov* **il n'est p. sourd que celui qui ne veut pas entendre** there's none so deaf as he who will not hear; *Can Fam* **il est pas p., ton gâteau!** your cake's not bad!; *Can Fam* **p. que p.** dire, as bad as it can get■
2 *(superlatif)* worst; **mon p. ennemi** my worst enemy; **se livrer aux pires horreurs** to commit the worst *or* foulest abominations; **c'est la p. chose qui pouvait lui arriver** it's the worst thing that could happen to him/her
NM il y a p. you could find worse, there is *or* are worse; **le p.** the worst; **s'attendre au p.** to expect the worst; **craindre le p.** to fear the worst; **le p. est qu'elle en aime un autre** the worst (part) of it is that she's in love with someone else; **dans le p. des cas, (en mettant les choses) au p.** at worst

Pirée [pire] **NM Le P.** Piraeus; *Littéraire* **prendre Le P. pour un homme** to make a crude mistake

piriforme [piriform] **ADJ** pear-shaped, *Spéc* pyriform

pirogue [pirɔg] **NF** pirogue, dugout; **p. à balancier** outrigger

piroguier [pirɔgje] **NM** pirogue boatman

pirole [pirɔl] **NF** *Bot* wintergreen, pyrola

piroplasmose [pirɔplasmoz] **NF** *Vét* piroplasmosis

pirouette [pirwɛt] **NF 1** *(tour sur soi-même)* pirouette, body spin; **faire une p.** to pirouette, to spin (on one's heels) **2** *Équitation & (en danse)* pirouette **3** *(changement d'opinion)* about-face, about-turn **4** *(dérobade)* **répondre** *ou* **s'en tirer par une p.** to answer flippantly

pirouettement [pirwɛtmɑ̃] **NM** *Littéraire* (succession of) pirouettes, pirouetting *(UNCOUNT)*

pirouetter [4] [pirwete] **VI 1** *(pivoter)* to pivot; **p. sur ses talons** to turn on one's heels **2** *(faire une pirouette → danseur)* to pirouette

pis[1] [pi] **NM** *(de vache)* udder

pis[2] [pi] *Littéraire* **ADJ** worse; **c'est p. que jamais** it's worse than ever
NM le p. *(le pire)* the worst; **il y a p.** you could find worse, there is *or* are worse; **dire p. que pendre de qn** to vilify sb; **on m'a dit p. que pendre de cet homme-là** I've been told the most dreadful things about that man; **le nouveau musée? on en dit p. que pendre** the new museum? nobody has a good word to say about it
ADV worse; **il a fait p. encore** he's done worse things still
❑ **au pis ADV** if the worst comes to the worst
❑ **au pis aller ADV** at the very worst
❑ **qui pis est ADV** what's *or* what is worse

pis-aller [pizale] **NM INV** *(expédient)* last resort; **on va l'engager mais c'est un p.** we'll take him/her on but it's far from ideal, we'll take him/her on, it's the best we can do under the circumstances; **disons lundi, mais ce serait un p.** let's say Monday, but that's if the worst comes to the worst

pisan, -e [pizɑ̃, -an] **ADJ** of/from Pisa
❑ **Pisan, -e NM,F** Pisan

piscicole [pisikɔl] **ADJ** fish-farming *(avant n)*, *Spéc* piscicultural

pisciculteur, -trice [pisikyltœr, -tris] **NM,F** fish-farmer, *Spéc* pisciculturist

pisciculture [pisikyltyr] **NF** fish-farming, *Spéc* pisciculture

pisciforme [pisifɔrm] **ADJ** fish-shaped, *Spéc* pisciform

piscine [pisin] **NF 1** *(de natation)* (swimming) pool; **p. couverte/découverte** *ou* **en plein air** indoor/outdoor (swimming) pool; **p. d'eau de mer** sea-water pool; **p. municipale** public (swimming) pool; **p. olympique** Olympic-size(d) (swimming) pool; **p. à vagues** wave pool **2** *Rel* piscina **3** *Fam Arg crime* **la p.** = the French secret service

piscivore [pisivɔr] **ADJ** fish-eating, *Spéc* piscivorous
NMF fish-eating *or Spéc* piscivorous animal

Pise [piz] **NM** Pisa; **la tour de P.** the Leaning Tower of Pisa

pisé [pize] **NM** pisé, rammed clay

pisiforme [pizifɔrm] *Anat* **ADJ M** pisiform
NM pisiform

pisolite, pisolithe [pizɔlit] **NF** *Géol* pisolite, peastone

pisolitique, pisolithique [pizɔlitik] **ADJ** *Géol* pisolitic; **calcaire p.** pisolite

pissaladière [pisaladjɛr] **NF** = onion, olive and anchovy tart *(from Nice)*

pissat [pisa] **NM** urine *(of certain animals)*

pisse [pis] **NF** *très Fam* piss; **c'est de la p. d'âne, ta bière!** your beer's like (gnat's) piss!

pisse-copie [piskɔpi] **NMF INV** *Fam* hack

pisse-froid [pisfrwa] **NM INV** *Fam* cold fish

pissement [pismɑ̃] **NM** *très Fam* pissing

pissenlit [pisɑ̃li] **NM 1** *Bot* dandelion; *Fam* **manger les pissenlits par la racine** *(être mort)* to be pushing up the daisies **2** *Can Fam (enfant)* bedwetter■, child who wets his/her bed■

pisser [3] [pise] *très Fam* **VI 1** *(uriner)* to piss, to (have a) pee; **je dois aller p.** I've got to have a piss *or* a leak; **le chien a pissé sur le tapis** the dog peed on the carpet; **il a pissé dans sa culotte** he's pissed in *or* peed in *or* wet his pants; **p. au lit** to wet the bed; *Vulg Fig* **je lui pisse dessus** screw him/her, *Br* he/she can get stuffed; *Vulg* **je te pisse à la raie!** up yours!; **c'est comme si on pissait dans un violon** it's like pissing into the wind, *Br* it's a bloody waste of time; **laisse p. (le mérinos)** bugger it, forget it; **ça ne pisse pas** *ou* **ne va pas p. loin** it's no big deal *or* great shakes; **envoyer p. qn** to tell sb to piss off; **ne plus se sentir p.** to think one's shit doesn't stink; **c'était à p. de rire** it was an absolute scream; **elle me fait p. de rire** she has me in stitches; **ils en pissaient dans leur culotte** *ou* **froc** they were pissing themselves (laughing); **ça lui a pris comme une envie de p.** the urge just came over him/her
2 *(fuir)* to leak■; **le tonneau/réservoir pisse** the barrel/tank is leaking
VT 1 *(uriner)* to piss; **p. du sang** to piss blood; **p. des lames de rasoir** *(souffrir au cour de la miction)* to piss razor blades
2 *(laisser s'écouler)* **ça pissait le sang** there was blood gushing *or* spurting everywhere; **mon nez pissait le sang** I had blood pouring from my nose; **elle pissait le sang** blood was pouring out of her; **le moteur commençait à p. de l'huile** oil started to gush from the engine
3 *(locution)* **p. de la copie** to churn it out, to write reams

pissette [pisɛt] **NF 1** *Chim* wash(ing) bottle **2** *Can Vulg (pénis)* dick, prick

pisseur, -euse[1] [pisœr, -øz] *très Fam* **NM,F** *(gén)* person with a weak bladder■; *(enfant qui fait au lit)* bedwetter■; **p. de copie** hack *(who writes a lot)*
❑ **pisseuse NF** little madam, little brat

pisseux, -euse[2] [pisø, øz] **ADJ** *Fam* **1** *(imprégné d'urine)* urine-soaked■; **des draps p.** sheets soaked with pee; **les couloirs sont p.** *(sentent mauvais)* the corridors reek of pee **2** *(délavé)* washed-out■; **les papiers peints ont fini par devenir p.** the wallpaper has faded over the years■; **un vert p.** a washed-out shade of green■ **3** *(jauni)* yellowing■

pisse-vinaigre [pisvinɛgr] **NM INV** *Fam* **1** *(avare)* skinflint, miser **2** *(rabat-joie)* wet blanket

pissodrome [pisɔdrɔm] **NM** *Belg très Fam* public urinal■

pissoir [piswar] **NM** *Fam* public urinal■

pissotière [pisɔtjɛr] **NF** *Fam* public urinal■

pissou, -x [pisu] **NM** *Can Fam* chicken, coward■

pistache [pistaʃ] **NF** pistachio (nut); **glace à la p.** pistachio ice-cream
ADJ INV (vert) p. pistachio (green)

pistachier [pistaʃje] **NM** pistachio (tree)

pistage [pistaʒ] **NM** *(de personne)* tailing; *(d'animal)* tracking, trailing

pistard [pistar] **NM** track cyclist

piste [pist] **NF 1** *(trace)* track, trail; **être sur la p. de qn** to be on sb's trail; **les policiers sont sur sa p.** the police are on his/her trail; **ils sont sur la bonne/une fausse p.** they're on the right/wrong track; **jeu de p.** treasure hunt
2 *(indice)* lead; **la police cherche une p.** the police are looking for leads
3 *Sport (de course à pied)* running track; *(pour les courses de chevaux)* (race)course, (race)-track; *(de patinage)* rink; *(de course cycliste)* cycling track; *(de course automobile)* racing track; *(d'athlétisme)* lane; *(d'escrime)* piste; **p. cendrée** cinder track; **p. de cirque** circus ring; **p. de danse** dance floor; **p. de patinage** skating rink; **p. de ski** ski slope, run, piste; **p. de ski artificielle** dry ski slope
4 *(chemin, sentier)* trail, track; **p. cavalière** bridle path; **p. cyclable** *(sur la route)* cycle lane; *(à côté)* cycle track
5 *Aviat* runway; **en bout de p.** at the end of the runway; **p. d'envol/d'atterrissage** take-off/ landing runway
6 *Cin & Ordinat* track; **magnéto 4 pistes** 4-track tape recorder; **p. de localisation** buzz track; **p. magnétique** *(sur carte)* magnetic strip; **p. métronome** click track; **p. non synchrone** wild track; **p. sonore** soundtrack; **p. de travail** working track
7 *Ordinat* **p. d'amorçage** boot track
8 *Chasse* trail
9 *(de dés)* dice run *or* baize
❑ **en piste EXCLAM** off you go! **ADV entrer en p.** to come into play, to join in

pister [3] [piste] **VT** *(suivre → personne)* to tail; *(→ animal)* to track, to trail

pisteur [pistœr] **NM** *Ski (pour entretien)* ski slope maintenance man; *(pour surveillance)* ski patrolman

pistil [pistil] **NM** pistil

pistoche [pistɔʃ] **NF** *Fam* (swimming) pool■

pistole [pistɔl] **NF** *Hist* pistole

pistolet [pistɔlɛ] **NM 1** *(arme à feu)* pistol, gun; **p. à air comprimé** air pistol; **p. d'alarme** alarm pistol; **p. d'arçon** horse pistol; **p. automatique** pistol; *Sport* **p. de starter** starting pistol
2 *(instrument)* **p. agrafeur** staple gun; **p. à peinture** spray gun; **p. de scellement** cartridge-operated hammer; *Can Fam* **être en p.** to be hopping mad *or* fuming
3 *(de dessinateur)* French curve
4 *(jouet)* **p. à bouchon** popgun; **p. à eau** water pistol
5 *Fam (urinal)* bottle■
6 *Fam (type bizarre)* **un drôle de p.** a shady *or Br* dodgy character
7 *Belg (petit pain)* bread roll

pistolet-mitrailleur [pistɔlɛmitrajœr] *(pl* **pistolets-mitrailleurs) NM** sub-machine-gun

pistoleur [pistɔlœr] **NM** spray gun painter

piston [pistɔ̃] **NM 1** *Tech* piston; **p. de frein** brake piston; **p. plongeur** ram, plunger piston
2 *Mus (d'un instrument à vent)* valve, piston; *(cornet)* cornet
3 *Fam (recommandation, protection)* string-pulling; **il est rentré par p.** he got in by knowing the right people; **elle a du p.** she has friends in the right places; **elle a fait marcher le p. pour se faire embaucher** she got somebody to pull a few strings for her to get the job
4 *Fam Arg scol (élève)* = student of the "École centrale des arts et manufactures"; **P.** *(l'ECAM)* = nickname of the "École centrale des arts et manufactures"

pistonné, -e [pistɔne] **NM,F** *Fam* **c'est un p.** he got where he is thanks to a bit of string-pulling

pistonner [3] [pistɔne] **VT** *Fam* to pull strings for; **elle s'est fait p. pour entrer au ministère** she used her connections to get into the Ministry■

pistou [pistu] **NM** *(sauce)* pesto; *(soupe)* = vegetable soup with pesto

pita [pita] **NF** pitta bread

pitahaya [pitaaja] **NF** *Bot* dragon fruit, pitahaya

pitance [pitɑ̃s] **NF** *Littéraire* sustenance, daily bread; **une maigre p.** scanty *or* meagre fare; **gagner sa p.** to earn a living

pitaya [pitaja] = **pitahaya**

pitbull [pitbul] **NM** pitbull (terrier)

pitch [pitʃ] **NM** *(au golf)* pitch (shot)

pitcher [3] [pitʃe] **VT** *Cin* to pitch

pitchoun, -e [pitʃun], **pitchounet, -ette** [pitʃunɛ, -ɛt] **NM,F** *(dans le Midi)* little one; **où il est, le p.?** where's the little one?

pitchpin [pitʃpɛ̃] **NM** pitch pine

pite [pit] **NF 1** *(plante)* American aloe **2** *(matière)* silk grass

piteuse [pitøz] *voir* **piteux**

piteusement [pitøzmɑ̃] **ADV** miserably, pathetically

piteux, -euse [pitø, -øz] **ADJ 1** *(pitoyable)* pitiful, piteous; **être en p. état** to be in a pitiful

condition; **un manteau en p. état** a shabby coat
2 *(mauvais, médiocre)* poor, mediocre; **des résultats p.** poor results
3 *(triste)* **faire piteuse mine** to look crestfallen
4 *(honteux)* sheepish; **il a un air plutôt p.** he doesn't look too pleased with himself; **elle s'est excusée de façon piteuse** she apologized shamefacedly

pithécanthrope [pitekɑ̃trɔp] NM pithecanthropus

pithiatique [pitjatik] ADJ *Méd* pithiatic

pithiatisme [pitjatism] NM *Méd* pithiatism

pithiviers [pitivje] NF puff-pastry cake *(filled with almond cream)*

pitié [pitje] NF 1 *(compassion)* pity; **elle l'a fait par p. pour lui** she did it out of pity for him; **avoir p. de qn** *(s'apitoyer)* to feel pity for *or* to pity sb; **elle me fait p.** I feel sorry for her; **vous me faites p.!** you look awful!; *(avec mépris)* you're pitiful!; **cela faisait p. à voir** it was pitiful to see; **la pièce? c'était à faire p.** the play? it was wretched *or* pitiful; **prendre qn en p.** to take pity on sb
2 *(désolation)* pity; **quelle p.!, c'est une p.!** what a pity!; *Littéraire* **elle est si pauvre que c'en est p.** she's so poor it is a pity to behold
3 *(clémence)* mercy, pity; **il a eu p. de ses ennemis** he had mercy on *or* took pity on his enemies; **elle avait l'air si fatiguée que j'ai eu p. d'elle et j'ai fait la vaisselle à sa place** she looked so tired that I took pity on her and did the dishes for her
EXCLAM **(par) p.!** (have) mercy!; *(avec agacement)* for pity's sake!; **par p., taisez-vous!** for pity's sake, be quiet!; *Hum* **p. pour ma pauvre carcasse!** have mercy on my poor old bones!
❑ **sans pitié** ADJ ruthless, merciless; **ils ont été sans p.** *(jurés)* they showed no mercy; *(terroristes)* they were ruthless

piton [pitɔ̃] NM 1 *(clou → gén)* eye *or* eye-headed nail; *(→ d'alpiniste)* piton 2 *Géog (dans la mer)* submarine mountain; *(pic)* piton, needle; **p. rocheux** rocky outcrop 3 *Can Fam (d'une sonnette)* button■; *(d'un clavier)* key■

pitonnage [pitɔnaʒ] NM *Sport* hammering (in) pitons

pitonner [3] [pitɔne] VI 1 *Sport* to hammer (in) pitons 2 *Can Fam (zapper)* to zap, to channel-hop; *(sur un clavier, une calculatrice)* to tap■

pitonneux, -euse [pitɔnø, -øz] NM,F *Can Fam* 1 *(personne qui zappe sans arrêt)* channel-hopper, channel-surfer 2 *(adepte de l'informatique)* computer nut, techie

pitoune [pitun] NF *Can* 1 *(bille de bois)* pulpwood bolt 2 *Fam (femme bien en chair)* plump woman■; **grosse p.** fat lump (of a woman) 3 *Fam Péj (femme de mœurs légères)* tramp, tart 4 *Fam (terme d'affection)* darling, sweetheart

pitoyable [pitwajabl] ADJ 1 *(triste → destin)* pitiful; **c'est p. à voir** it's a pitiful *or* pathetic sight 2 *(mauvais → effort, résultat)* pitiful, deplorable, dismal; *(→ excuse, argument)* pathetic, pitiful

pitoyablement [pitwajabləmɑ̃] ADV 1 *(tristement)* pitifully 2 *(médiocrement)* pitifully, deplorably; **échouer p.** to fail miserably

pitpit [pitpit] = **pipit**

pitre [pitr] NM 1 *(plaisantin)* clown; **faire le p.** to clown *or* to fool around 2 *(bouffon)* clown

pitrerie [pitrəri] NF tomfoolery *(UNCOUNT)*; **faire des pitreries** to clown *or* fool around; **arrête tes pitreries!** stop clowning *or* fooling around!

pittoresque [pitɔrɛsk] ADJ picturesque, colourful
NM picturesqueness

pittosporum [pitɔspɔrɔm] NM *Bot* pittosporum, pittospore

Pittsburgh [pitsbœrg] NM Pittsburgh

pituitaire [pitɥitɛr] ADJ *Anat* pituitary; **fosse p.** pituitary fossa

pituite [pitɥit] NF *Méd* gastrorrhoea

pityriasis [pitirjazis] NM *Méd* pityriasis; **p. capitis/rosé** pityriasis capitis/rosea

pive [piv] NF *Suisse* pine cone

pivelé, -e [pivle] ADJ *Can (moucheté → gén)* spotted; *(→ de taches de rousseur)* freckled

pivert [pivɛr] NM *Orn* (green) woodpecker

pivoine [pivwan] NF *Bot* peony

pivot [pivo] NM 1 *(axe → gén)* pivot; *(→ de levier)* fulcrum; *(→ de compas, de boussole)* centre pin; **à p., monté sur p.** pivoted, swivelling; *Aut* **p. de fusée** kingpin, kingbolt 2 *(centre)* pivot, hub; **le p. de toute son argumentation** the crux of his/her argument 3 *Sport* centre 4 *(en dentisterie)* post 5 *Bot* taproot 6 *UE* **cours p.** central rate; **taux p.** designated rate

pivotant, -e [pivɔtɑ̃, -ɑ̃t] ADJ *(qui tourne)* revolving, swivelling; **fauteuil p.** swivel chair

pivotement [pivɔtmɑ̃] NM revolving, swivelling

pivoter [3] [pivɔte] VI 1 *(autour d'un axe → porte)* to revolve (**sur/autour de** on/around); *(→ fauteuil)* to swivel; *(→ aiguille)* to swivel around, to pivot; *(→ pan de mur)* to pivot; **faire p. qch** to swing sth (round) 2 *(personne)* to turn; **p. sur ses talons** to spin round, to pivot on one's heels 3 *Mil* to wheel round

pixel [piksɛl] NM pixel

pixélisé, -e [pikselise] ADJ *Ordinat* pixellated, bitmapped, bitmap *(avant n)*

pixillation [piksilasjɔ̃] NF *Cin & TV* pixillation

pizza [pidza] NF pizza

pizzaiolo [pidzajolo] *(pl* **pizzaiolos** *ou* **pizzaioli** [-li]) NM *Belg* pizza chef

pizzeria [pidzerja] NF pizzeria

pizzicato [pidzikato] *(pl* **pizzicati** [-ti]) NM *Mus* pizzicato

PJ[1] [peʒi] NF *Fam (abrév* **police judiciaire**) *Br* ≃ CID, *Am* ≃ FBI

PJ[2] *(abrév écrite* **pièces jointes**) encl.

pK [peka] NM *Chim* pK

PL *Transp (abrév écrite* **poids lourd**) HGV

Pl., pl.[1] *(abrév écrite* **place**) Sq.

pl.[2] *(abrév écrite* **planche**) pl

PL/1 [peɛlɛ̃] NM *Ordinat (abrév* **Programming Language One**) PL/1

placage [plakaʒ] NM 1 *(revêtement → de bois)* veneering; *(→ de pierre, de marbre)* facing, cladding; *(→ de métal)* plating; **bois de p.** veneer 2 *Sport* tackle 3 *Littérature & Mus Fam* patchwork (composition)

placard [plakar] NM 1 *(armoire)* cupboard, *Am* closet; **p. à balais** broom cupboard; **p. de cuisine** kitchen cupboard; **p. mural** wall cupboard; **p. à provisions** store cupboard; **p. de salle de bains** bathroom cabinet; **p. à vêtements** *Br* wardrobe, *Am* closet; **avoir un cadavre dans le p.** to have a skeleton in the *Br* cupboard *or Am* closet; *Fam* **mettre qn au p.** *(l'écarter)* to sideline sb■; *Fam* **mettre qch au p.** *(le retirer de la circulation)* to put sth in cold storage *or* in mothballs; *Fam* **mettre qn dans un p. doré** to kick sb upstairs
2 *(affiche)* poster; **p. publicitaire** display advertisement; *(grand)* large display advertisement; *(de pleine page)* full-page advertisement
3 *Typ* galley (proof)
4 *Naut* patch
5 *Fam (prison)* slammer, clink; **faire 20 ans de p.** to do 20 years inside *or* in the clink; **mettre qn au p.** to put sb behind bars *or* inside *or* away
6 *Fam (couche de maquillage)* dollop
7 *Vieilli (avis écrit)* proclamation

placarder [3] [plakarde] VT 1 *(afficher → photo, affiche)* to stick up, to put up; **j'ai placardé des photos sur les murs** I plastered the walls with photos 2 *(couvrir → mur)* **p. qch de qch** to cover sth with sth 3 *Typ* **p. un ouvrage** to set a book in galleys

placardisation [plakardizasjɔ̃] NF *Fam* sidelining■

placardiser [3] [plakardize] VT *Fam* to sideline■

PLACE [plas]

> space **1, 4** ■ room **1** ■ place **2, 7** ■ seat **3** ■ ticket **3** ■ square **5** ■ job, position **6** ■ rank **7**

NF 1 *(espace disponible)* space *(UNCOUNT)*, room *(UNCOUNT)*; **je n'ai pas la p. pour un piano** I haven't got enough room *or* space for a piano; **faire de la p.** to make room *or* space; **fais une p. sur le bureau pour l'ordinateur** make some room *or* clear a space on the desk for the computer; **faites-lui une petite p.** give him/her a bit of room; **il reste de la p. pour quatre personnes** there's enough space *or* room left for four people; **il y a encore de la p. au dernier rang** there's still some room in the back row; **prendre de la p.** to take up a lot of space *or* room; **ne prends pas toute la p.** *(à table, au lit)* don't take up so much room; *(sur la page)* don't use up all the space; **laisser la** *ou* **faire p. à** to make room *or* way for; **la machine à écrire a fait p. au traitement de texte** word processors have taken over from *or* superseded typewriters; **ce travail ne laisse aucune p. à la créativité** there's no place *or* room for creativity in this kind of work; **les anciens font p. aux jeunes** older people are giving way to the young generation; **p. aux jeunes!** make room for the younger generation!; **et maintenant, p. aux artistes** and now, on with the show; **la musique tient une grande p. dans ma vie** music is a very important part of my life; **sa famille ne tient qu'une petite p. dans son emploi du temps** he/she devotes very little time to his/her family; **p. au sol** *(d'un ordinateur, d'une voiture)* footprint; **faire p. nette** to tidy up; *Fig* to clear up, to make a clean sweep; **j'ai fait p. nette dans la cuisine** I cleared up the kitchen; **j'ai fait p. nette dans mes tiroirs** I cleared out my drawers
2 *(endroit précis)* place, spot; **changer les meubles de p.** to move the furniture around; **changer la cuisinière de p.** to move the *Br* cooker *or Am* stove (to a new place); **mets/remets les clefs à leur p.** put the keys/put the keys back where they belong; **la statue est toujours à la même p.** the statue is still in the same place *or* spot; **ce plateau n'est pas à sa p.** this tray isn't in its proper place *or* doesn't belong here; **est-ce que tout est à sa p.?** is everything in order *or* in its proper place?; **savoir rester à sa p.** to know one's place; **je ne me sens pas à ma p. parmi eux** I feel out of place among them; **ta p. n'est pas ici** you're out of place here; **trouver sa p. dans l'existence** to find one's niche in life; **il a rapidement trouvé sa p. dans notre équipe** he quickly fitted into our team; *Fig* **avoir une** *ou* **sa p. quelque part** to have one's place somewhere; **tu auras toujours une p. dans mon cœur** there'll always be a place in my heart for you; **reprendre sa p.** *(sa position)* to go back to one's place; *(son rôle)* to go back to where one belongs; **notre collègue ne pourra pas reprendre sa p. parmi nous** our colleague is unable to resume his/her post with us; **pour rien au monde je ne donnerais ma p.** I wouldn't swop places for anything in the world; **remettre qn à sa p.** to put sb in his/her place; **te voilà remis à ta p.!** that's put you in your place!; **se faire une p. au soleil** to make a success of things, to find one's place in the sun; **une p. pour chaque chose et chaque chose à sa p.** a place for everything and everything in its place
3 *(siège)* seat; *(fauteuil au spectacle)* seat; *(billet)* ticket; **retourne à ta p.** go back to your seat; **céder** *ou* **laisser sa p. à qn** to give up *or* to offer one's seat to sb; **avoir la p. d'honneur** *(sur l'estrade)* to sit at the centre of the stage; *(à table)* to sit at the top *or* head of the table; **à la p. du conducteur** in the driver's seat; **une voiture à deux places** a two-seater car; **une caravane à quatre places** a caravan that sleeps four; **une salle de 500 places** a room that can seat 500 people; **un autobus de 46 places** a 46-seater bus; **réserver une p. d'avion/de train** to make a plane/train reservation; **payer p. entière** to pay full price; **il a pris le train sans payer sa p.** he got on the train without buying a ticket; **j'ai trois places de concert** I have three tickets for the concert; **toutes les places sont à 30 euros** all tickets *or* seats are 30 euros; **ça vous ennuierait de changer de p.?** would you mind swopping places?; **est-ce que cette p. est prise?** is anybody sitting here?; **prendre p.** *(s'asseoir)* to sit down; **p. assise** seat; **25 places debout** *(sign)* 25 standing; **il ne reste plus que des places debout** it's now standing room only; **à la p. du mort** in the (front) passenger seat; **dans le monde du spectacle, les places sont chères** it's difficult to gain a foothold in show business; *aussi Fig* **la p. est toute chaude** the seat's still warm
4 *(dans un parking)* (parking) space; **un parking de 1000 places** a car park with space for 1,000 cars; *Suisse* **p. de parc** *(individuel)* parking

space; *(collectif) Br* car park, *Am* parking lot

5 *(espace urbain)* square; **la p. du marché** the market place, the market square; **la p. du village** the village square; **médecin connu sur la p. de Paris** doctor well-known in Paris; **le plus cher sur la p. de Paris** the most expensive in Paris; **sur la p. publique** in public; **porter le débat sur la p. publique** to make the debate public; *Suisse* **p. de jeu(x)** playground; *Suisse* **p. de sport** sportsground; **la p. Beauvau** = the Ministry of the Interior (situated on the square of the same name in Paris); **la p. de la Concorde** = one of the biggest and busiest squares in Paris, laid out in the reign of Louis XV; **la p. du Colonel-Fabien** = the Communist party headquarters (situated on the square of the same name in Paris); **la p. de Grève** = former name of the "Place de l'Hôtel de Ville" in Paris; **la p. Rouge** Red Square; **la p. Saint-Marc** Saint Mark's Square; **la p. Tian'anmen** Tiananmen Square; **la p. Vendôme** = opulent square in Paris where the Ritz hotel and famous jewellery shops are situated; **la p. des Vosges** = elegant and fashionable square in the Marais district of Paris, built under Henri IV

6 *(poste, emploi)* position, post; **quitter/perdre sa p.** to leave/to lose one's job; **une bonne p.** a good job; **il y a peu de places libres** there are few situations vacant; **je cherche une p. de secrétaire** I'm looking for a job as a secretary; *Suisse* **p. de travail** job

7 *(rang → dans une compétition)* place, rank; **avoir la première p.** to come first *or* top; **avoir la dernière p.** to come last *or Br* bottom; **elle est en bonne p. au dernier tour** she's well placed on the last lap; **être** *ou* **partir en bonne p. pour gagner** to be (all) set to win; **les filles occupent les meilleures places en biologie** girls get the best grades in biology

8 *Bourse* **p. boursière** stock market; **p. financière** financial centre; **p. financière internationale** money market; **le dollar est à la hausse sur la p. financière de New York** the dollar has risen on the New York exchange; **les places mondiales** the global markets

9 *Mil* **p. d'armes** parade ground, *Am* parade; *Suisse* = army camp with barracks and rifle range; **p. (forte)** fortress, stronghold; **nous voici dans la p.** *(ville assiégée)* here we are, inside the walls (of the city); *(endroit quelconque)* here we are; *Fig* we've now gained a foothold

10 *Belg (pièce d'habitation)* room

❑ **à la place** ADV instead; **on ira en Espagne à la p.** we'll go to Spain instead; **j'ai rapporté la jupe et j'ai pris un pantalon à la p.** I returned the skirt and exchanged it for a pair of trousers; **je préfère travailler le dimanche et avoir des heures libres en semaine à la p.** I prefer to work Sundays and have time off during the week instead

❑ **à la place de** PRÉP **1** *(au lieu de)* instead of; **à la p. du documentaire, on a eu un vieux feuilleton** instead of the documentary, we were shown an old series; **j'irai à sa p.** I'll go instead of him/her

2 *(dans la situation de)* **à ma p.** in my situation; **à sa p.** in his/her situation; **à ta p., j'irais** if I were you I'd go; **mettez-vous à ma p.** put yourself in my place *or* shoes; **je ne voudrais pas être à sa p.** rather him/her than me

❑ **de place en place** ADV here and there

❑ **en place** ADJ **1** *(important)* established; **un homme politique en p.** a well-established politician; **les gens en p. disent que...** the powers that be say that... **2** *Mines* in situ ADV **1** *(là)* in position; **les forces de police sont déjà en p.** the police have already taken up their position; **est-ce que tout est en p.?** is everything in order *or* in its proper place? **2** *(locutions)* **mettre en p.** *(équipement)* to set up; *(plan)* to set up, to put into action; *(réseau)* to set up; **la méthode sera mise en p. progressivement** the method will be phased in (gradually); **ça va lui mettre/remettre les idées en p.** it'll give him/her a more realistic view of things/set him/her thinking straight again; **il ne tient pas en p.** *(il est turbulent)* he can't keep still; *(il est anxieux)* he's nervous; *(il voyage beaucoup)* he's always on the move

❑ **par places** ADV here and there

❑ **sur place** ADV there, on the spot; **je serai déjà sur p.** I'll already be there; **tué sur p.** killed on the spot; **s'approvisionner sur p.** to use local suppliers; **engager du personnel sur p.** to hire staff locally

---

placé, -e [plase] ADJ **1** *(aux courses)* **cheval p.** placed horse; **arriver p.** to be placed

2 *(situé)* **bien p.** *(magasin, appartement)* well-situated; *(fermeture, bouton, couture)* well-positioned; **mal p.** *(magasin, appartement)* badly-located; *(fermeture, bouton, couture)* poorly-positioned; *(coup)* below the belt; *(abcès)* in an awkward spot; *Euph* in an embarrassing place; *(orgueil)* misplaced; **on était très bien/mal placés** *(au spectacle)* we had really good/bad seats; *Fig* **être bien/mal p. pour faire qch** to be in a good position/no position to do sth; **il est mal p. pour en parler** he's in no position to talk (about it)

3 *(socialement)* **haut p.** well up *or* high up in the hierarchy; **des gens haut placés** people in high places

placebo [plasebo] NM placebo

placement [plasmɑ̃] NM **1** *(investissement)* investment; **un bon/mauvais p.** a sound/bad investment; **faire un p.** to make an investment, to invest; **nous avons acheté la maison pour faire un p.** we bought the house as an investment; **un p. de père de famille** a gilt-edged investment, a blue chip; **p. en actions** equity investment; **p. à court terme/à long terme** short-term/long-term investment; **p. éthique** ethical investment; **p. financier** Stock Market investment; **p. obligataire** bond investment; **p. à revenus fixes** fixed-income *or* fixed-yield investment; **p. à revenus variables** variable-income *or* variable-yield investment

2 *(de chômeurs)* placing

3 *Jur (d'un mineur dans une famille d'accueil ou dans un organisme)* placement; **je m'occupe du p. des jeunes dans les familles** my job is finding homes for young people

4 *(attribution d'un siège)* seating; **le p. des invités autour de la table** the seating of the guests around the table

5 *(internement)* **p. d'office** hospitalization order; **p. volontaire** ≃ voluntary admission *(including detention for observation)*

6 *Mktg* placement; *Cin & TV* **p. de produit** product placement

7 *Belg (installation)* installation

8 *Jur* **p. sous surveillance électronique** electronic tagging; **p. sous surveillance judiciaire** placing under judicial supervision

placenta [plasɛ̃ta] NM placenta

placentaire [plasɛ̃tɛr] *Zool* ADJ placental
NM placental mammal

❑ **placentaires** NMPL Eutheria

placentation [plasɛ̃tasjɔ̃] NF placentation

placer[1] [plasɛr] NM placer (deposit)

PLACER[2] **[16]** [plase]

> **VT** to place **1, 3–5** ▪ to seat **2** ▪ to put **3, 5, 8** ▪ to set **6** ▪ to locate **7** ▪ to sell **10** ▪ to invest **11** ▪ to find a job for **12**
> **VPR** to stand, to sit **1** ▪ to consider **3** ▪ to finish **4** ▪ to find a job **5** ▪ to sell **7**

VT **1** *(mettre dans une position précise)* to place; **p. un patron sur du tissu** to lay a pattern on *or* over a piece of fabric; **p. ses doigts sur le clavier** to place one's fingers on the keyboard; *Sport* **p. la balle** to place the ball; *Mus* **p. sa voix** to pitch one's voice

2 *(faire asseoir)* to seat; **l'ouvreuse va vous p.** the usherette will show you to your seats; **p. des convives à table** to seat guests around a table; **pourvu qu'ils ne me placent pas à côté d'Anne!** I hope they don't put me next to Anne!

3 *(établir → dans une position, un état)* to put, to place; **p. qn devant ses responsabilités** to force sb to face up to his/her responsibilities

4 *(établir → dans une institution)* to place; **p. un enfant à l'Assistance publique** to place *or* to put a child in care; **p. qn à l'hospice** to put sb in an old people's home

5 *(classer)* to put, to place; **p. la loi au-dessus de tout** to set the law above everything else; **moi, je le placerais parmi les grands écrivains** I would rate *or* rank him among the great writers

6 *(situer dans le temps)* **il a placé l'action du film en l'an 2000** he set the film in the year 2000

7 *(situer dans l'espace)* to locate; **je n'arrive pas à p. Nice sur la carte** I can't tell you where Nice is on the map

8 *(mettre)* to put; **orchestre placé sous la direction de...** orchestra conducted by...; **p. sa confiance en qn** to put one's trust in sb; **elle a placé tous ses espoirs dans ce projet** she's pinned all her hopes on this project

9 *(dans la conversation)* **il essaie toujours de p. quelques boutades** he always tries to slip in a few jokes; **je n'ai pas pu p. un mot** I couldn't get a word in edgeways; *Fam* **je peux en p. une?** can I get a word in?

10 *(vendre)* to sell; **facile/difficile à p.** easy/difficult to sell; **nous aurons du mal à p. notre stock invendu** it will be hard to get rid of our excess stock; **les enfants sont chargés de p. les billets de loterie** the children are to sell the lottery tickets; *Hum* **j'essaie désespérément de p. mon vieux canapé!** I'm desperately trying to find a home for my old sofa!

11 *Fin* to invest; **p. ses économies en Bourse** to invest one's savings on the stock market; **le banquier s'est chargé de p. mon argent** the banker helped me invest my money; **p. de l'argent sur un compte** to put *or* deposit money in an account

12 *(procurer un emploi à)* to find a job for; **p. les jeunes chômeurs** to find jobs for unemployed young people; **p. qn comme apprenti chez qn** to apprentice sb to sb; **elle a été placée à la direction commerciale** she was appointed head of the sales department

13 *Belg (installer → gaz, téléphone)* to install

▸**se placer** VPR **1** *(dans l'espace)* **place-toi près de la fenêtre** *(debout)* stand near the window; *(assis)* sit near the window; **placez-vous en cercle** get into a circle; **venez vous p. autour de la table** come and sit at the table; **plaçons-nous plus près de l'écran** let's move closer to the screen

2 *(dans le temps)* **plaçons-nous un instant au début du siècle** let's go back for a moment to the turn of the century

3 *(dans un jugement, une analyse)* to look at *or* to consider things; **si l'on se place de son point de vue** if you look at things from his/her point of view

4 *(occuper un rang)* to rank, to finish; **se p. premier/troisième** to finish first/third

5 *(trouver un emploi)* **elle s'est placée comme infirmière** she found *or* got a job as a nurse

6 *Fam (se présenter avantageusement)* **se p. auprès du patron** to butter up *or* to sweet-talk the boss

7 *(se vendre)* to sell; **ces marchandises se placent facilement** these goods sell easily

---

placet [plasɛ] NM **1** *Arch (demande écrite)* petition, address **2** *Jur (réquisition d'audience)* (plaintiff's) claim **3** *Suisse (de siège)* seat

placette [plasɛt] NF (small) square

placeur, -euse [plasœr, -øz] NM,F **1** *(dans une salle de spectacle)* usher, *f* usherette **2** *(dans une agence pour l'emploi)* employment agent

placide [plasid] ADJ placid, calm

placidement [plasidmɑ̃] ADV placidly, calmly

placidité [plasidite] NF placidness, calmness

placier [plasje] NM **1** *(forain)* market superintendent, market pitch agent **2** *(représentant de commerce)* sales representative; *(qui fait du porte-à-porte)* door-to-door salesman, *f* saleswoman

placoderme [plakɔdɛrm] NM placoderm

❑ **placodermes** NMPL Placodermi

Placoplâtre® [plakoplɑtr] NM plasterboard

placotage [plakɔtaʒ] NM *Can Fam* chatter, gossip▪

placoter [3] [plakɔte] VI *Can Fam* to gossip▪

placoteur, -euse [plakɔtœr, -øz], **placoteux, -euse** [plakɔtø, -øz] **NM,F** *Can Fam* gossip■, gossipy person■

plaçure [plasyr] **NF** *Typ* collation

plafond [plafɔ̃] **NM 1** *(d'un bâtiment)* ceiling; *(d'une voiture, d'une galerie)* roof; **faux p.** false ceiling; **p. à caissons** coffered ceiling; **p. flottant** *ou* **suspendu** drop *or* suspended ceiling; **la pièce est basse de p.** the room has got a low ceiling; *Fig* **il est un peu bas de p.** he's a bit slow on the uptake
2 *Beaux-Arts* ceiling painting
3 *Aviat* ceiling
4 *Météo* **p. (nuageux)** (cloud) ceiling
5 *(limite supérieure)* ceiling; **le p. des salaires** the wage ceiling, the ceiling on wages; **fixer un p. à un budget** to put a ceiling on a budget, to cap a budget; **p. des charges budgétaires** spending limit, budgetary limit; **p. de crédit** credit ceiling *or* limit; *Banque* **p. de découvert** overdraft limit; **p. de l'impôt** tax ceiling; *Banque* **p. d'autorisation de retrait, p. de retrait** withdrawal limit
6 *(comme adj: avec ou sans trait d'union)* ceiling *(avant n)*; **vitesse p.** maximum speed; **des prix plafonds** ceiling *or* top prices
7 *(au bridge)* ceiling

plafonnage [plafɔnaʒ] **NM 1** *(d'une pièce)* ceiling installation **2** *Belg Constr (plâtrage → action)* plastering; *(→ ouvrage)* plasterwork

plafonné, -e [plafɔne] **ADJ salaire p.** = upper limit of a salary on which contributions are payable

plafonnement [plafɔnmɑ̃] **NM p. des salaires/cotisations** *(fait de limiter)* setting a ceiling on wages/contributions; *(fait d'atteindre un plafond)* levelling off of wages/contributions

plafonner [3] [plafɔne] **VT 1** *(pièce, maison)* to put a ceiling in *or* into
2 *(impôts, salaires etc)* to set a ceiling on; **les cotisations sont plafonnées à 12 pour cent** contributions have a ceiling *or* upper limit of 12 percent
3 *Belg Constr (couvrir)* to plaster (over); *(colmater)* to plaster over *or* up
VI 1 *(avion)* to fly at the ceiling; *(voiture)* to go at maximum *or* top speed
2 *(ventes, salaires)* to level off; *(taux d'intérêt, prix)* to peak; **la production plafonne** output has reached its ceiling; **je plafonne à 1500 euros depuis un an** my monthly income hasn't exceeded 1,500 euros for over a year

plafonneur [plafɔnœr] **NM 1** *(plâtrier)* ceiling plasterer **2** *Belg Constr (maçon)* plasterer

plafonnier [plafɔnje] **NM 1** *(d'appartement)* ceiling light **2** *Aut* (overhead) courtesy *or* guide light

plagal, -e, -aux, -ales [plagal, -o] **ADJ** *Mus* plagal

plage [plaʒ] **NF 1** *(grève)* beach; **p. de galets/de sable** pebble/sandy beach; **aller en vacances à la p.** to go on holiday to the seaside
2 *(espace de temps)* **p. horaire** (allotted) slot; **p. musicale** musical intermission; **p. publicitaire** commercial break
3 *(écart)* range; **p. des longueurs d'onde** wavelength range; **p. de prix** price range; **p. de taux** rate band
4 *Littéraire (surface)* zone, area; **une p. d'ombre** an area of shadow; **une p. de lumière** a sunny area; *Opt* **p. lumineuse** light area, highlight
5 *Naut (d'un cuirassé)* freeboard deck; **p. avant** foredeck; **p. arrière** quarterdeck, afterdeck
6 *Aut* **p. arrière** parcel shelf, back shelf
7 *(d'un disque)* track
❑ **de plage ADJ** beach *(avant n)*; **serviette de p.** beach towel; **vêtements de p.** beachwear

---

'Pauline à la plage' *Rohmer* 'Pauline at the Beach'

---

plagiaire [plaʒjɛr] **NMF** plagiarizer, plagiarist

plagiat [plaʒja] **NM** plagiary, plagiarism

plagier [9] [plaʒje] **VT** *(œuvre, auteur)* to plagiarize

plagioclase [plaʒjɔklaz] **NM** *Minér* plagioclase, triclinic feldspar

plagiste [plaʒist] **NMF** beach attendant

plaid[1] [plɛ] **NM** *Hist (assemblée)* court; *(jugement)* finding, judgement

plaid[2] [plɛd] **NM** *(pièce de tissu)* plaid; *(couverture)* car rug

plaidable [plɛdabl] **ADJ** pleadable

plaidant, -e [plɛdɑ̃, -ɑ̃t] **ADJ** *voir* **avocat**[2], **parti**[1]

plaider [4] [plede] **VI 1** *Jur* to plead; **ce matin, je plaide** I'm pleading this morning; **p. pour qn** to defend sb, to plead for *or* on behalf of sb; **p. contre qn** to plead (the case) against sb
2 *(présenter des arguments) aussi Fig* **p. en faveur de qn/qch** to speak in sb's/sth's favour; *aussi Fig* **p. contre qn/qch** to speak against sb/sth; **ton attitude ne plaide guère en ta faveur** your attitude hardly speaks for you *or* is hardly a strong point in your favour; **nous plaidons ici pour le respect des droits de l'homme** we are here to defend human rights
VT to plead; *Jur* **p. une cause** to plead a case; **l'affaire sera plaidée en juin** the case will be heard in June; **p. coupable/non coupable** to plead guilty/not guilty, to make a plea of guilty/not guilty; **plaidez-vous coupable ou non coupable?** how do you plead (guilty or not guilty)?; **p. la légitime défense** to plead self-defence; *Fig* **p. la cause de qn** to speak in favour of *or* defend sb, to plead sb's cause; **p. sa propre cause** to speak in one's own defence; **p. le faux pour savoir le vrai** to get at the truth by telling a lie
►**se plaider VPR la cause s'est plaidée hier** the case was heard yesterday

plaider coupable, plaider-coupable [plɛdekupabl] **NM** *Jur* plea-bargaining

plaideur, -euse [plɛdœr, -øz] **NM,F** litigant

plaidoirie [plɛdwari] **NF 1** *(exposé) Jur* speech for the defence; *Fig* defence **2** *(action de plaider)* pleading

plaidoyer [plɛdwaje] **NM 1** *Jur* speech for the defence **2** *(supplication)* plea

plaie [plɛ] **NF 1** *(blessure)* wound; **p. pénétrante** perforating wound; **p. profonde** deep wound; **p. superficielle** surface wound; **une p. vive** an open wound; **le départ de sa femme est resté pour lui une p. vive** his wife's departure scarred him for life
2 *Littéraire (tourment)* wound; *Prov* **p. d'argent n'est pas mortelle** = money isn't everything
3 *Bible* **les dix plaies d'Égypte** the ten plagues of Egypt
4 *Fam (personne ennuyeuse)* pest, pain, nuisance■; *(chose ennuyeuse)* pain, nuisance■; **quelle p., cette femme!** what a pest *or* pain *or* nuisance that woman is!

plaignait *etc voir* **plaindre**

plaignant, -e [plɛɲɑ̃, -ɑ̃t] *Jur* **ADJ la partie plaignante** the plaintiff
NM,F plaintiff

plain [plɛ̃] **ADJ 1** *Fam Vieilli (terrain, surface)* flat■, level■, even■ **2** *Hér* plain
NM le p. high tide

plain-chant [plɛ̃ʃɑ̃] *(pl* **plains-chants)** **NM** plainsong, plainchant

plaindre [80] [plɛ̃dr] **VT 1** *(avoir pitié de)* to feel sorry for, to pity; **je plains celle qui l'épousera!** I feel sorry for *or* I pity whoever's going to marry him!; **je vous plains de voyager dans ces conditions** I feel sorry for you *or* I pity you having to travel in those conditions; **comme je vous plains** I do feel sorry for you; **il adore se faire p.** he's always looking for sympathy; **il est plus à p. qu'à blâmer** he is more to be pitied than blamed; **elle est bien à p. avec des enfants pareils!** with children like that, you can't help but feel sorry for her!; **avec tout l'argent qu'ils gagnent, ils ne sont vraiment pas à p.** with all the money they're making, they've got nothing to worry about
2 *Vieilli (donner parcimonieusement)* to give grudgingly, to spare; **ne pas p. sa peine** to be unstinting in one's efforts; **je n'ai jamais plaint mon temps passé auprès des enfants** I never begrudged the time I spent with the children
►**se plaindre VPR 1** *(protester)* to complain; **arrête de te p. tout le temps** stop complaining all the time; *Ironique* **plains-toi (donc)!** my heart bleeds for you!; **se p. de** *(symptôme)* to complain of; *(personne, situation)* to complain about; **le patient se plaint de manquer** *ou* **de son manque d'appétit** the patient is complaining of loss of appetite; **il est venu se p. à moi de sa femme** he came and complained to me about his wife; **elle se plaint de ce qu'on la traite comme une servante** she complains that they treat her like a servant; **ce n'est pas moi qui m'en plaindrai!** I'm not complaining!
2 *(geindre)* to moan, to groan

plaine [plɛn] **NF 1** *(étendue plate)* plain; **p. abyssale/bathyale** abyssal/bathial zone; **la p. de Sibérie occidentale** the West Siberian Plain **2** *Hist* **la P.** the Plain, = central area of the French National Convention, where the moderates were seated **3** *Belg* **p. de jeux** playground; **p. de(s) manœuvres** exercise ground; **p. de(s) sports** sports field *or* ground

plain-pied [plɛ̃pje] **de plain-pied ADV 1** *(au même niveau)* on the same level (**avec** as), on a level (**avec** with); **la chambre et le salon sont de p.** the bedroom and the living room are on the same level *or* on a level; **une maison construite de p.** *(avec le sol extérieur) Br* a bungalow, *Am* a ranch house
2 *(d'emblée)* **entrons de p. dans le sujet** let's get straight to the point
3 *(sur un pied d'égalité)* **être de p. avec qn** to be on an equal footing with sb

plaint, -e [plɛ̃, -ɛ̃t] **PP** *voir* **plaindre**
❑ **plainte NF 1** *(gémissement → d'un malade)* moan, groan; *Littéraire* **les plaintes du vent** the howling of the wind
2 *(protestation)* complaining *(UNCOUNT)*, moaning *(UNCOUNT)*; **c'est un sujet de plainte assez répandu** it's a common complaint; **je n'ai aucun sujet de plainte** I have no complaints, I have nothing to complain about
3 *Jur* complaint; **déposer une plainte** to lodge *or* to file a complaint; **retirer une plainte** to withdraw a complaint; **porter plainte contre qn** to bring an action against sb; **désirez-vous porter plainte?** do you wish to begin proceedings?; **plainte en diffamation** action for libel; **plainte contre X** action against person or persons unknown

plaintif, -ive [plɛ̃tif, -iv] **ADJ 1** *(de douleur)* plaintive, mournful; **d'un ton p.** plaintively; **un cri p.** a plaintive cry **2** *Littéraire (désignant des choses)* plaintive

plaintivement [plɛ̃tivmɑ̃] **ADV** plaintively, mournfully

plaire [110] [plɛr] **plaire à VT IND 1** *(être apprécié par)* **cela me plaît** I like it; **l'album m'a plu** I liked the album; **le potage ne vous a pas plu?** didn't you like the soup?; **ça vous plaît, le commerce?** how do you like business life?; **elle vous plaît, la maison?** how do you like the house?; **si le karaté me plaît, je continuerai** if I like karate, I'll keep it up; **le nouveau professeur ne me plaît pas du tout** I really don't like *or* care for the new teacher; **rien ne lui plaît** there's no pleasing him/her; **cette idée ne me plaît pas du tout** I'm not at all keen on this idea; *Fam* **il commence à me p., celui-là!** he's starting to bug me *or Br* get on my wick!; **offre du parfum, ça plaît toujours** give perfume, it's always appreciated
2 *(convenir à)* **si ça me plaît** if I feel like it; **quand ça me plaît** whenever I feel like it; **elle ne lit que ce qui lui plaît** she only reads what she feels like (reading)
3 *(séduire)* to be appealing *or* attractive to; **il cherche à p. aux femmes** he tries hard to make himself attractive to women; **c'est le genre de fille qui plaît aux hommes** she's the kind of girl that men find attractive
USAGE ABSOLU il a vraiment tout pour p.! he's got everything going for him!; *Ironique* he's so marvellous!; **aimer p.** to take pleasure in being attractive; **une robe doit p. avant tout** a dress must above all be appealing
V IMPERSONNEL 1 *(convenir)* **il lui plaît de croire que...** he/she likes to think that...; **te plairait-il de nous accompagner?** would you like to come with us?; **comme** *ou* **tant qu'il te plaira** *(exprime l'indifférence)* see if I care; **tu le prends sur ce ton? comme il te plaira** if you choose to take it like that, see if I care; **plaise à Dieu** *ou* **au ciel que...** *(souhait)* please God that...; **plût à Dieu** *ou* **au ciel que...** *(regret)* if only...; *Jur* **plaise au tribunal de déclarer mon client innocent** I ask the court to find my client innocent
2 *(locutions)* **s'il te plaît, s'il vous plaît** please; **s'il vous plaît!** *(dit par un client)* excuse me!; *Belg (dit par un serveur)* here you are!; **prête-moi un stylo, s'il te plaît** lend me a pen, please; **sors**

d'ici, et plus vite que ça, s'il te plaît! get out of here and please be quick about it!; *Fam* du caviar, s'il vous plaît, on ne se refuse rien! caviar! my, my, we're splashing out a bit, aren't we?; *Can Fam* il fait froid en s'il vous plaît aujourd'hui! it's really cold■ or *Br* it isn't half cold today!; *Vieilli ou Hum* plaît-il? I beg your pardon?

▸se plaire VPR 1 *(emploi réciproque)* ces deux jeunes gens se plaisent, c'est évident it's obvious that those two like each other

2 *(dans un endroit)* je me plais (bien) dans ma nouvelle maison I enjoy living in my new house, I like it in my new house; alors, vous vous plaisez à Paris? so, how do you like living in *or* like it in Paris?; mes plantes se plaisent ici my plants are happy here

3 se p. à to enjoy, to delight *or* take pleasure in; il se plaît à la contredire he loves *or* enjoys contradicting her; *Ironique* je me plais à penser que tu as fait tes devoirs avant de sortir I suppose you've done your homework before going out

plaisamment [plɛzamɑ̃] ADV 1 *(agréablement)* pleasantly, agreeably 2 *(de façon amusante)* amusingly 3 *(risiblement)* ridiculously, laughably

Plaisance [plɛzɑ̃s] NM Piacenza

plaisance [plɛzɑ̃s] NF (pleasure) boating
▫ de plaisance ADJ *(navigation, bateau)* pleasure *(avant n)*

plaisancier, -ère [plɛzɑ̃sje, -ɛr] NM,F amateur yachtsman, *f* yachtswoman

plaisant, -e [plɛzɑ̃, -ɑ̃t] ADJ 1 *(agréable)* pleasant, nice; p. à l'œil pleasing to the eye, nice to look at

2 *(drôle)* funny, amusing

3 *(ridicule)* ridiculous, laughable

NM 1 *(aspect)* le p. de l'histoire the funny part of it; le p. de cette aventure the funny thing about this adventure

2 *Vieilli (farceur)* wag, joker

3 mauvais p. joker; un mauvais p. avait débranché la télé some joker had unplugged the TV

plaisanter [3] [plɛzɑ̃te] VI 1 *(faire de l'esprit)* to joke; *(faire une plaisanterie)* to (crack a) joke; elle aime bien p. she enjoys a joke; elle n'était pas d'humeur à p. she wasn't in a joking mood; assez plaisanté, au travail! enough horsing around, back to work!; il faut bien p., n'est-ce pas? we all have to have a laugh from time to time, don't we?; p. sur to make fun of; p. sur le nom de qn to make fun of sb's name; en plaisantant jokingly; je l'ai dit pour p. I meant it as a joke

2 *(parler à la légère)* to joke; c'est vrai, je ne plaisante pas it's true, I'm not joking; je ne plaisante pas, obéis! I'm not joking, do as I say!; tu plaisantes! you can't be serious!, you've got to be joking!

3 *(prendre à la légère)* on ne plaisante pas avec ces choses-là you mustn't joke about such things; le patron ne plaisante pas avec la discipline the boss takes discipline very seriously *or* is a stickler for discipline; on ne plaisante pas avec la loi you shouldn't fool around with the law; on ne plaisante pas avec la santé you shouldn't take any chances with your health

VT to make fun of, to tease; ils n'arrêtent pas de le p. sur son accent they're always teasing him about his accent

plaisanterie [plɛzɑ̃tri] NF 1 *(parole amusante)* joke; faire des plaisanteries to tell *or* crack jokes; lancer une p. to make a joke; c'est une p., j'espère? I trust *or* hope you're joking; c'est une p.! *(ça ne peut être sérieux)* it must be a joke!; la p. a assez duré this has gone far enough; une p. de mauvais goût a joke in bad *or* poor taste; les plaisanteries les plus courtes sont les meilleures brevity is the soul of wit

2 *(humour)* joking; comprendre *ou* entendre la p. to be able to take a joke; elle ne comprend *ou* n'entend pas la p. she can't take a joke; je l'ai dit par p. I meant it as a joke; pousser trop loin la p. to take the joke too far, to go too far; p. à part joking apart; tourner qch en p. to make a joke of sth

3 *(raillerie)* joke, jibe; faire des plaisanteries sur le nom/l'allure de qn to make fun of sb's name/appearance; elle est en butte aux plaisanteries de ses collègues she's the laughing stock of her colleagues; mauvaise p. cruel joke

4 *(chose facile)* child's play *(UNCOUNT)*; c'est une p., cet exercice! there's nothing to this exercise!, this exercise is child's play!

plaisantin [plɛzɑ̃tɛ̃] NM 1 *(farceur)* joker, clown; quel est le petit p. qui m'a donné un faux numéro? which joker gave me a wrong number? 2 *(fumiste)* ce n'est qu'un p. he's nothing but a fly-by-night

plaisir [plezir] NM 1 *(joie)* pleasure; j'éprouve toujours du p. à écouter du jazz I always get pleasure out of listening to jazz; avoir (du) p. *ou* prendre (du) p. à faire qch to take pleasure in doing sth; j'ai eu grand p. à voyager avec vous it was a real pleasure travelling with you; faire p. à qn to please sb; ça va lui faire p. he'll/she'll be pleased *or* delighted (with this); on prend son p. où on le trouve! you only live once!; le bon p. de qn sb's wish *or* desire; on ne déciderait jamais rien s'il fallait attendre son bon p.! we'd never make any decisions if we always had to wait until he/she felt like it!

2 *(dans des formules de politesse)* vous me feriez p. en restant dîner I'd be delighted if you stayed for dinner; cela fait p. de vous voir en bonne santé it's a pleasure to see you in good health; faites-moi le p. d'accepter won't you grant me the pleasure of accepting?; tu me feras le p. de ne plus revoir ce garçon I don't want you to see that boy again; fais-moi le p. d'éteindre cette télévision do me a favour, will you, and turn off the television; elle se fera un p. de vous raccompagner she'll be (only too) glad to take you home; je me ferai un p. de vous renseigner I'll be delighted *or* happy to give you all the information; cette chipie se fera un p. de répandre la nouvelle that little minx will take great pleasure in spreading the news; aurai-je le p. de vous avoir parmi nous? will I have the pleasure of your company?; j'ai le p. de vous informer que... I am pleased to inform you that...; tout le p. est pour moi the pleasure is all mine, (it's) my pleasure; au p. (de vous revoir) see you again *or* soon

3 *(agrément)* pleasure; le caviar est un p. coûteux caviar is an expensive pleasure; les plaisirs de la vie life's pleasures; elle aime les plaisirs de la table she loves good food

4 *(sexualité)* pleasures; les plaisirs de la chair pleasures of the flesh; les plaisirs défendus forbidden pleasures; *Euph* p. solitaire self-abuse

▫ à plaisir ADV 1 *(sans motif sérieux)* il se tourmente à p. he's a born worrier

2 *(sans retenue)* unrestrainedly; elle ment à p. she lies through her teeth

▫ avec plaisir ADV with pleasure; pourrez-vous m'aider? – avec p.! will you be able to help me? – I'd be delighted (to) *or* with pleasure!

▫ par plaisir, pour le plaisir ADV for its own sake, just for the fun of it; il joue aux cartes par p., non pas pour l'argent he doesn't play cards for money, just for the fun of it

plaisons *etc voir* **plaire**

PLAN[1] [plɑ̃]

> plan B, C ■ project B1, 3, 5 ■ map C1 ■ blueprint C2, 3 ■ plane A1, 3, 5 ■ surface A2 ■ shot A4

NM A. 1 *(surface plane)* plane

2 *Constr (surface)* surface; p. de cuisson hob; p. snack fold-down table; p. de travail *(d'une cuisine)* worktop, working surface

3 *Beaux-Arts & Phot* plane; p. focal focal plane

4 *Cin & TV* shot; gros p. close-up; très gros p. big close-up, extreme close-up, detail shot; p. américain American shot, two-shot; p. de coupe reaction shot, cutaway shot; p. de demi-ensemble medium-long shot; p. de détail detail shot; p. éloigné long shot; p. d'ensemble wide shot; p. d'extérieur exterior (shot); p. général long shot; p. genoux knee-length shot; p. de grand ensemble full shot; p. de groupe group shot; p. de mise en place establishing shot; p. moyen medium shot; p. à niveau level shot; p. en plongée high-angle shot, overhead shot, bird's-eye shot; p. rapproché close shot; p. de secours *ou* p. de sécurité cover shot; p. serré close-up, tight shot; p. de situation establishing shot; p. subjectif point-of-view shot; p. de transition bridging shot, neutral shot; p. travelling travelling shot; p. très éloigné extreme long shot, extra-long shot; p. très rapproché extreme close-up; p. de visage face shot

5 *Géom* plane; p. horizontal/incliné/médian/tangent level/inclined/median/tangent plane; en p. incliné sloping

6 *Aviat* p. de sustentation aerofoil

B. 1 *(projet)* plan, project; *Fam* ne vous inquiétez pas, j'ai un p. don't worry, I've got a plan■; *Fam* j'ai un bon p. pour les vacances I've got a great idea for the holidays; *Fam* lui et ses plans foireux! him and his lousy plans!; *Fam* on se fait un p. ciné/resto? shall we go to the *Br* cinema *or Am* movies/go out for a meal?■; un p. d'action a plan of action; un p. de bataille a battle plan; un p. de carrière a career plan *or* strategy; *Can Vieilli* p. de nègre harebrained scheme

2 *(structure)* plan, framework, outline; le p. d'un roman the plan *or* the narrative framework of a novel; je veux un p. détaillé de votre thèse I want a detailed outline *or* a synopsis of your thesis

3 *Admin* plan, project; p. d'aménagement rural rural development plan *or* scheme; p. de modernisation modernization project *or* scheme; p. d'occupation des sols, *Belg* p. de secteur = document laying out local land development plans; p. de santé health scheme; p. de sauvegarde zoning plan; p. d'urbanisme town planning scheme

4 *Écon* plan; *Compta* p. d'amortissement depreciation schedule; p. d'assainissement stabilization plan; *Écon* p. d'austérité austerity programme; *Pol* p. de campagne campaign plan; *Compta* p. comptable ≃ Statement of Standard Accounting Practices; *Compta* p. comptable général, p. de comptes chart of accounts; p. d'échantillonnage *(en statistique)* sample survey; p. d'échéances instalment plan; p. économique economic plan; *Banque* p. d'épargne savings scheme *or* plan; *Banque* p. d'épargne en actions investment trust, *Br* ≃ ISA; p. d'épargne entreprise employee *Br* share *or Am* stock ownership plan; *Banque* p. d'épargne logement *ou* p. épargne-logement *Br* ≃ building society account, *Am* ≃ savings and loan association account; *Banque* p. d'épargne populaire special savings account; *Banque* p. d'épargne retraite = retirement savings plan *or* scheme; *Compta* p. de financement funding *or* financial plan; p. financier financial plan; p. d'investissement investment plan; p. de licenciement planned redundancy scheme; *Bourse* p. d'options sur titres stock option plan; p. prévisionnel forecast plan; p. quinquennal five-year plan; p. de redressement recovery plan; p. de restructuration restructuring plan; p. de retraite pension plan *or* scheme; p. social *(du gouvernement)* = corporate restructuring plan, usually involving job losses; p. stratégique d'entreprise strategic business plan; p. de trésorerie cash flow forecast

5 *Mktg (projet)* plan, project; p. d'action action plan; p. de campagne campaign plan; p. de développement des produits product planning; p. marketing marketing plan; p. média media plan; p. prévisionnel forecast plan; p. prix price plan

6 *Cin & TV* p. de production production schedule; p. de tournage shooting schedule; p. de travail production schedule

7 *Typ (en publication assistée par ordinateur)* p. de maquette layout card; p. de mise en page(s) page plan

C. 1 *(carte)* map, plan; un p. de Paris a map *or* plan of Paris; p. de métro *Br* underground *or Am* subway map; p. de vol flight plan

2 *Archit (dessin)* plan, *Am* blueprint; acheter un appartement sur plans to buy *Br* a flat off-plan *or Am* an apartment as shown on the blueprint; lever un p. to make a survey; p. d'ensemble outline; p. de masse overall plan; *Fig* tirer des

plans sur la comète to build castles in the air; *Belg* **tirer son p.** to manage
3 *Tech* plan, blueprint; **p. d'une machine/voiture** blueprint of a machine/car

◻ **de second plan** ADJ *(question)* of secondary importance; *(artiste, personnalité)* second-rate

◻ **en plan** ADV *Fam* in the lurch; **laisser qn en p.** to leave sb in the lurch; **laisser qch en p.** to drop sth; **il m'a laissée en p.** he left me in the lurch; **j'ai tout laissé en p. et j'ai filé à l'hôpital** I dropped everything and rushed to the hospital; **je suis resté en p.** *(seul)* I was left stranded *or* high and dry; **tous mes projets sont restés en p.** none of my plans came to anything■

◻ **sur le plan de** PRÉP as regards, as far as... is concerned; **sur le p. du salaire, ça me convient** as far as the salary is concerned, it suits me fine; **sur le p. de la conduite** as far as behaviour goes; **sur le p. intellectuel** intellectually speaking; **sur le p. personnel** on a personal level; **c'est le meilleur sur tous les plans** he's the best whichever way you look at it

◻ **plan d'eau** NM *(naturel)* stretch of water; *(artificiel)* reservoir; *(ornemental)* ornamental lake

◻ **premier plan** NM **1** *Cin* foreground; **au premier p.** in the foreground
2 *Fig* **au premier p. de l'actualité** in the forefront of today's news; **de (tout) premier p.** *(personnage)* leading, prominent; **jouer un rôle de tout premier p. dans qch** to play a leading *or* major part in sth

plan², -e¹ [plɑ̃, plan] ADJ **1** *(miroir)* plane; *(terrain, surface)* flat
2 *Math* plane, planar; **surface plane** plane

planage [planaʒ] NM *(d'une surface)* planing; *(d'un métal)* planishing; *(pour rendre la forme)* straightening, flattening (out)

planaire [planɛr] NF *Zool* planarian

planant, -e [planɑ̃, -ɑ̃t] ADJ *Fam (drogue)* relaxing■; *(musique)* mellow

planarisation [planarizasjɔ̃] NF *Électron* planar process

planche [plɑ̃ʃ] NF **1** *(de bois)* plank, board; **p. à billets** printing press *(for printing banknotes)*; *Fam* **recourir à** *ou* **faire marcher la p. à billets** to pump (more) money into the economy■; **p. à découper** chopping board; **p. à dessin** drawing board; **p. à laver** washboard; **p. à pain** breadboard; *Fam* **c'est une p. à pain** she's (as) flat as a board *or* a pancake; *Fam* **avoir du pain sur la p.** to have a lot on one's plate; **p. à pâtisserie** pastry board; **p. à repasser** ironing board; **p. de salut** last hope; *Fam* **c'est une p. pourrie** he/she can't be relied on■; *Can Fam* **conduire à la p.** to drive at top speed■ *or* like a maniac; *Can Fam* **ça marche à la p.** everything's going like clockwork
2 *Naut* gangplank; **jour de p.** lay day
3 *Fam (ski)* ski■
4 *Typ* plate; **planches en couleurs** colour plates
5 *Hort (de légumes)* patch; *(de plantes, de fleurs)* bed
6 *Aviat* **p. de bord** instrument panel
7 *Sport* **faire la p.** to float on one's back; **p. d'appel** take-off board; **p. à neige** snowboard; **p. de surf** surfboard

ADJ *Can (surface, terre)* flat, even

◻ **planches** NFPL **1** *Théât* **les planches** the boards, the stage; **son amour des planches** his/her love of the stage; **monter sur les planches** to go on the stage, to tread the boards; **remonter sur les planches** to go back on the stage
2 *(chemin)* *Br* promenade, *Am* boardwalk; **les planches de Deauville** the *Br* promenade *or Am* boardwalk at Deauville

◻ **planche à roulettes** NF skateboard; **faire de la p. à roulettes** to go skateboarding, to skateboard

◻ **planche à voile** NF sailboard, windsurfer; **faire de la p. à voile** to go windsurfing, to windsurf

planche-contact [plɑ̃ʃkɔ̃takt] *(pl* **planches-contacts)** NF *Phot* contact sheet

planchéiage [plɑ̃ʃejaʒ] NM **1** *(parquetage)* flooring **2** *(lambrissage)* planking, boarding

planchéier [4] [plɑ̃ʃeje] VT **1** *(parqueter)* to floor **2** *(lambrisser)* to board

plancher¹ [plɑ̃ʃe] NM **1** *Archit & Constr* floor; **refaire le p. d'une pièce** to refloor a room *(with floorboards)*; **p. creux/plein** hollow/solid floor; *Fam* **le p. des vaches** dry land■, terra firma■; *Fam* **débarrasse-moi le p.!** clear off!, get lost!; *Fam* **avoir un feu de p.** to be wearing ankle-swingers *or* trousers that are too short■
2 *Aut* floor
3 *Can Joual (étage)* floor, storey; *Fig* **prendre le p.** to take the floor, to speak
4 *Anat* floor; **le p. buccal** *ou* **de la bouche** the floor of the mouth; **p. pelvien** pelvic floor
5 *(limite inférieure)* floor; **une augmentation de 3 pour cent avec un p. de 100 euros** a 3 percent rise with a lower limit *or* a floor of 100 euros; **p. des salaires** wage floor
6 *(comme adj; avec ou sans trait d'union)* minimum; **prix p.** minimum *or* bottom price

plancher² [3] [plɑ̃ʃe] VI *Fam Arg scol* to have a test■; **demain on planche en maths** we've got a *Br* maths *or Am* math test tomorrow

◻ **plancher sur** VT IND *Fam (travailler sur)* to work on■

planchette [plɑ̃ʃɛt] NF **1** *(petite planche)* small board; *(étagère)* (small) shelf **2** *(topographique)* plane-table

planchiste [plɑ̃ʃist] NMF windsurfer

plançon [plɑ̃sɔ̃] NM *(jeune arbre)* sapling; *(plante)* set, slip

plan-concave [plɑ̃kɔ̃kav] *(pl* **plan-concaves)** ADJ plano-concave

plan-convexe [plɑ̃kɔ̃vɛks] *(pl* **plan-convexes)** ADJ plano-convex

plancton [plɑ̃ktɔ̃] NM plankton; **p. aérien** aerial plankton; **p. végétal** vegetable plankton

planctonique [plɑ̃ktɔnik] ADJ planktonic

planctonivore [plɑ̃ktɔnivɔr], **planctophage** [plɑ̃ktɔfaʒ] ADJ plankton-eating

plane² [plan] NF *(outil)* drawknife

plané, -e [plane] ADJ *Aviat* **vol p.** gliding; **descendre en vol p.** to glide down; *Fam* **faire un vol p.** *(tomber)* to go flying

planéité [planeite] NF planeness, flatness, evenness

planelle [planɛl] NF *Suisse* ceramic tile

planer [3] [plane] VI **1** *(oiseau)* to soar; *(avion)* to glide; *(fumée, ballon)* to float; **laisser son regard** *ou* **ses regards p. sur** to gaze out over
2 *(danger, doute, mystère)* to hover; **p. sur** to hover over, to hang over; **le danger planait sur l'Europe** danger hung *or* hovered over Europe; **le doute plane encore sur cette affaire** this affair is still shrouded in mystery
3 *(être en dehors des réalités)* to be (way) above things; **il plane au-dessus de ces petits détails** he's way above such insignificant details
4 *Fam (être sous l'influence d'une drogue)* to be high, to be spaced out; *(ne pas avoir le sens des réalités)* to have one's head in the clouds; *(penser à autre chose)* to be miles away, to have one's head in the clouds; **cette musique me fait p.!** this music really blows me away!; **ça plane pour moi!** everything's hunky-dory!

VT *(surface)* to make smooth; *(bois)* to plane; *(métal)* to planish

planétaire [planetɛr] ADJ **1** *Astron* planetary **2** *(mondial)* worldwide, global; **à l'échelle p.** on a global scale **3** *Phys (électrons)* orbital, orbiting

NM **1** *Astron* orrery **2** *Tech* sun gear

planétairement [planetɛrmɑ̃] ADV worldwide

planétarisation [planetarizasjɔ̃] NF globalization; **la p. économique** the growth of a world economy

planétarium [planetarjɔm] NM planetarium

planète [planɛt] NF planet; **planètes inférieures/supérieures** inferior/superior planets; **sur la p. tout entière** *(la Terre)* all over the Earth *or* world

📖 🎬
'La Planète des singes' Boulle, Schaffner, Burton 'Planet of the Apes'

🎬
'La Planète Sauvage' Laloux 'The Fantastic Planet'

planétoïde [planetɔid] NM planetoid

planétologie [planetɔlɔʒi] NF planetology

planeur, -euse [planœr, -øz] NM,F *(de métal)* planisher; *(d'orfèvrerie)* chaser

NM *Aviat* glider; **faire du p.** to go gliding

◻ **planeuse** NF *(machine → pour bois)* planing machine; *(→ pour métal)* planishing machine

planèze [planɛz] NF *Géol* planeze

planifiable [planifjabl] ADJ which can be planned

planificateur, -trice [planifikatœr, -tris] ADJ planning *(avant n)*, relating to (economic) planning

NM,F planner

planification [planifikasjɔ̃] NF planning; **p. budgétaire** budget planning; **p. à court terme** short-term planning; **p. économique** economic planning; **p. de l'entreprise** company *or* corporate planning; **p. à long terme** long-term planning; **p. des naissances** population control; **p. des opérations** operational planning; *Mktg* **p. du produit** product planning; *Mktg* **p. stratégique** strategic planning; *Ordinat* **p. des systèmes** systems engineering; **p. des ventes** sales planning

planificatrice [planifikatris] *voir* **planificateur**

planifié, -e [planifje] ADJ *(économie)* planned

planifier [9] [planifje] VT *(gén)* & *Écon* to plan

planigramme [planigram] NM flow chart

planimétrage [planimetraʒ] NM planimetric measurement

planimètre [planimɛtr] NM planimeter; **p. polaire** polar planimeter

planimétrie [planimetri] NF planimetry

planimétrique [planimetrik] ADJ planimetric

planipenne [planipɛn] *Entom* NM planipennine, member of the Planipennia

◻ **planipennes** NMPL Planipennia

planisme [planism] NM support for *or Péj* over-reliance on economic planning

planisphère [planisfɛr] NM planisphere

planiste [planist] NMF supporter *or Péj* uncritical advocate of economic planning

plan-masse [plɑ̃mas] *(pl* **plans-masses)** NM overall plan

planning [planiŋ] NM *(programme)* plan, schedule; **le p. de la semaine** the week's schedule; **faire un p.** to work out a schedule; **nous avons un p. très chargé cette semaine** we have a very busy schedule this week; *Compta* **p. des charges** expenditure planning; *Mktg* **p. de distribution** distribution schedule; **p. de livraison** delivery schedule

◻ **planning familial** NM *(méthode)* family planning; *(organisme)* family planning clinic

planoir [planwar] NM = small flat-ended chisel

planorbe [planɔrb] NF *Zool* planorbid

plan-plan [plɑ̃plɑ̃] ADJ INV *Fam* routine■, humdrum■

planque [plɑ̃k] NF *Fam* **1** *(cachette → d'une personne)* hideout■, hideaway■; *(→ d'une chose)* hiding place■ **2** *(travail → gén)* cushy job; *(→ en temps de guerre)* safe job■ **3** *(guet)* stakeout; **faire une p.** to stake a place out; **la police est en p. devant la maison** the police are staking out the house

planqué, -e [plɑ̃ke] *Fam* NM,F = person with a cushy job; **quelle planquée!** what a cushy job she's got!

NM *Mil* draft dodger

planquer [3] [plɑ̃ke] *Fam* VT *(cacher)* to hide■, to stash; **planque ton bouquin, voilà le prof** hide your book, the teacher's coming; **on a planqué son frère chez nous pendant une semaine** we hid his/her brother at our place for a week

VI *(surveiller)* to keep watch■

▸ **se planquer** VPR *(se cacher)* to hide■; *(se mettre à l'abri)* to take cover■

plan-relief [plɑ̃rəljɛf] *(pl* **plans-reliefs)** NM street model

plan-séquence [plɑ̃sekɑ̃s] *(pl* **plans-séquences)** NM *Cin* sequence shot

plansichter [plɑ̃siʃter] NM plansifter

plant [plɑ̃] NM **1** *(jeune plante → gén)* young plant; *(→ issue d'une graine)* seedling; *(jeune arbre)* sapling; **p. de vigne** young vine; **p. de tomate** young tomato plant **2** *(ensemble → de légumes)* patch; *(→ de plantes, de fleurs)* bed; *(→ d'arbres, d'arbustes)* nursery) plantation

plantage [plɑ̃taʒ] NM **1** *Fam (erreur)* mistake■, *Br* boob, *Am* goof **2** *Fam (échec)* flop **3** *Fam Ordinat (d'un réseau, d'un logiciel)* crash **4** *Suisse (potager)* vegetable *or* kitchen garden

Plantagenêt [plɑ̃taʒnɛ] NPR Plantagenet

plantain [plɑ̃tɛ̃] NM *(herbe, bananier)* plantain

plantaire [plɑ̃tɛr] ADJ *Anat* plantar

plantard [plɑ̃tar] = **plançon**

plantation [plɑ̃tasjɔ̃] NF **1** *(opération)* planting **2** *(culture)* plant, crop; **p. d'oranges** orange grove **3** *(exploitation agricole)* plantation

plante[1] [plɑ̃t] NF *Bot* plant; **p. verte/à fleurs** green/flowering plant; **p. fourragère** fodder plant; **p. grasse** succulent plant; **p. d'appartement** house *or* pot plant; **p. grimpante** creeper, climbing plant; **p. d'intérieur** pot plant, indoor plant; **p. médicinale** medicinal herb; **p. potagère** vegetable; **p. de serre** hothouse plant; *Fig (personne)* delicate flower, fragile person; **p. textile** fibre plant; **p. vivace** perennial plant; **médecine par les plantes** herbal medicine, herbalism; **se soigner par les plantes** to use herbal remedies; *Fam* **c'est une belle p.** she's a fine figure of a woman

plante[2] [plɑ̃t] NF *Anat* **la p. du pied** the sole of the foot; **la p. des pieds** the soles of the feet

planté, -e [plɑ̃te] ADJ **1 bien p.** *(enfant)* lusty, robust; *(dent)* well-positioned, well-placed; **avoir les dents mal plantées** to have crooked *or* uneven teeth; **avoir les cheveux plantés bas/haut** to have a low/receding hairline **2** *Fam Ordinat* **être p.** *(réseau, ordinateur)* to be down

planter [3] [plɑ̃te] VT **1** *Agr & Hort* to plant; **p. des choux** to plant cabbages; *Fam Fig* **aller p. ses choux** to go and live in the country■; **une allée plantée d'acacias** an avenue lined with acacia trees; **une colline plantée d'arbres** a hill planted with trees

2 *(enfoncer)* to stick *or* to drive in; *(avec un marteau)* to hammer in; **p. un pieu dans le sol** to drive a stake into the ground; **il ne sait même pas p. un clou** he can't even hammer a nail in properly; **p. un couteau dans le dos de qn** to stab sb in the back, to stick a knife in sb's back; **le lion lui a planté ses griffes dans la cuisse** the lion dug its claws into his/her thigh; *Can Fig* **p. des clous** to doze off (in one's chair)

3 *(tente)* to pitch, to put up; *Fig* **il a fini par p. sa tente en Provence** he finally settled in Provence

4 *(poser résolument)* **p. un baiser sur les lèvres de qn** to kiss sb full on the lips; **il planta ses yeux dans les miens** he stared into my eyes

5 *(dépeindre → personnage)* to sketch (in); **les personnages sont plantés dès la page 20** the characters have all been sketched in by page 20; **p. le décor** *Théât* to set up the scenery; *Littérature* to set the scene

6 *Fam (abandonner → personne, voiture)* to dump, to ditch; *(→ travail, projet)* to pack in, to drop; **je l'ai planté là** I just dumped him there; **ne la laissez pas plantée là** don't leave her standing there■; **je crois que je vais tout p. là** I think I'll pack it all in *or* ditch the whole thing

7 *Fam (tuer à l'arme blanche)* to knife to death■; *(blesser à l'arme blanche)* to knife■, *Am* to shank, to shiv

8 *Can Fam (critiquer violemment)* to slate, to pan; **pour son dernier livre, il s'est fait p. par la critique** he was slated *or* panned by the critics for his last book

9 *Can Fam (battre → équipe, candidat aux élections)* to thrash; **ils se sont fait p. par une petite équipe** they got thrashed by a small team

VI *Fam Ordinat (réseau, logiciel)* to go down, to crash

▸**se planter** VPR **1** *(s'enfoncer)* to become stuck *or* embedded, to embed itself; **l'écharde s'est plantée dans la chair** the splinter embedded itself in the flesh

2 *Fam (se tenir immobile)* to stand■; **j'irai me p. sous leur nez** I'll go and stand right in front of them; **ne reste pas planté là comme une souche** don't just stand there like a fool *or Br* a lemon

3 *Fam (se tromper)* to get it wrong; **j'ai dû me p.** I must have got it wrong *or Br* boobed; **on s'est complètement plantés, c'est infaisable** we've got it completely wrong, it can't be done

4 *Fam (dans un accident)* to have a crash■; **je me suis planté en vélo** I had a crash on my bike; **se p. contre un arbre** to smash into a tree■

5 *Fam (échouer)* to fail■; **il s'est planté à son examen** he failed■ *or Am* flunked his exam

6 *Fam (ordinateur)* to go down, to crash

planteur, -euse [plɑ̃tœr, -øz] NM,F *Agr* planter; **des planteurs de pommes de terre** potato planters

NM **1** *(dans les pays tropicaux)* planter **2** *(cocktail)* **(punch) p.** planter's punch

▫ **planteuse** NF *(machine)* planter, planting machine

plantigrade [plɑ̃tigrad] ADJ plantigrade

NM plantigrade

plantoir [plɑ̃twar] NM dibble

planton [plɑ̃tɔ̃] NM **1** *Mil* orderly; **être de p.** to be on orderly duty; *Fam* **faire le p.** to stand about *or* around (waiting)■ **2** *Suisse (jeune plante)* seedling, young plant **3** *(en Afrique francophone) (garçon de bureau)* office boy

plantule [plɑ̃tyl] NF (plant) germ

plantureuse [plɑ̃tyrøz] *voir* **plantureux**

plantureusement [plɑ̃tyrøzmɑ̃] ADV *Littéraire* copiously, lavishly

plantureux, -euse [plɑ̃tyrø, -øz] ADJ **1** *(aux formes pleines → femme, beauté)* buxom; *(→ poitrine)* full, generous **2** *(copieux → repas)* copious, lavish **3** *Littéraire (fertile)* fertile; **la plantureuse province** the lush province

plaquage [plakaʒ] NM **1** *(revêtement)* cladding, coating **2** *Sport* tackling *(UNCOUNT)*, tackle **3** *Fam (abandon → d'une personne)* ditching, dumping; *(→ d'une activité)* dropping

plaque [plak] NF **1** *(surface → de métal)* plate; *(→ de marbre)* slab; *(→ de verre)* plate, pane; *(→ de chocolat)* bar; *(→ de beurre)* pack; *(revêtement)* plate; *(pour commémorer)* plaque; **p. de blindage** armour plate; **p. de cheminée** fire back; **p. d'égout** manhole cover; **p. minéralogique** *ou* **d'immatriculation** *Br* number plate, *Am* license plate; **p. de plâtre** plasterboard; **p. de propreté** fingerplate; **p. de rue** street name plate, street sign; **p. de verglas** icy patch; *Fam* **être à côté de la p.** to be wide of the mark, to be off-target, to be barking up the wrong tree

2 *(inscription professionnelle)* nameplate, plaque; *(insigne)* badge

3 *(au casino)* chip; *Anciennement Fam* **une p.** *(dix mille francs)* ten thousand francs■

4 *Élec* plate; *Électron* plate, anode; **p. d'accumulateur** accumulator plate; **p. de déviation** deflector plate

5 *Phot* plate

6 *Culin (de four)* baking tray; **p. (de cuisson** *ou* **chauffante)** hot plate; *Suisse* **p. (à gâteau)** cake tin; **p. à induction** induction hob; **p. vitrocéramique** ceramic hob

7 *Anat & Méd (sur la peau)* patch; **des plaques rouges dues au froid** red blotches due to the cold; **p. dentaire** (dental) plaque; **p. muqueuse** mucous plaque; **plaques d'eczéma** eczema patches

8 *Géog* **p. à vent** wind slab

9 *Géol* **p. (lithosphérique)** plate; **p. mince** thin section

10 *Typ* **p. gravée** gravure; **p. offset** offset plate

▫ **en plaques, par plaques** ADV **sa peau part en** *ou* **par plaques** his/her skin is flaking

▫ **plaque tournante** NF **1** *Rail* turntable

2 *Fig* nerve centre; **la p. tournante du trafic de drogue** the nerve centre of the drug-running industry; **cette ville deviendra la p. tournante de l'Europe** this city will become the hub of Europe

plaqué, -e [plake] ADJ plated; **p. d'or** *ou* **or** gold-plated; **p. d'argent** *ou* **argent** silver-plated

NM **1** *(en joaillerie)* **montre en p. or** gold-plated watch; **c'est du p.** *(or)* it's gold-plated; *(argent)* it's silver-plated **2** *Menuis* veneer

plaquemine [plakmin] NF (Japanese) persimmon, kaki

plaqueminier [plakminje] NM (Japanese) persimmon (tree)

plaque-modèle [plakmɔdɛl] *(pl* **plaques-modèles)** NF *Métal* die

plaquer [3] [plake] VT **1** *Menuis* to veneer

2 *(en joaillerie)* to plate

3 *Métal* to clad

4 *(mettre à plat)* to lay flat; **le vent plaquait son écharpe/ses cheveux sur sa figure** the wind blew his/her scarf/hair flat against his/her face; **la sueur plaquait sa chemise contre son corps** his/her shirt was stuck to his/her chest with sweat; **les cheveux plaqués sur le front** hair plastered down on the forehead; **je l'ai plaqué contre le mur/au sol** I pinned him to the wall/ground; **le dos plaqué contre la porte** standing flat against the door; **il avait les épaules plaquées au mur** he had his shoulders pinned *or* pressed to the wall; **p. sa cavalière contre soi** to clasp one's partner to one; **p. un baiser sur la joue de qn** to give sb a smacking kiss on the cheek; **p. sa main sur la bouche de qn** to put one's hand over sb's mouth

5 *(ajouter)* **la conclusion semble plaquée** the conclusion reads like an afterthought *or* feels as though it's just been tacked on

6 *Fam (abandonner → personne, travail, situation)* to dump, to ditch; *(→ famille)* to walk out on; **j'ai envie de tout p.** I feel like *Br* packing *or* chucking it all in *or Am* chucking everything; **il s'est fait p. par sa femme** his wife walked out on him

7 *Sport* to tackle; *Fig (personne en fuite)* to rugby-tackle

8 *Mus (accord)* to strike, to play; **je ne sais que p. quelques accords** I only know a few chords

9 *Belg (coller)* to stick

▸**se plaquer** VPR **se p. au sol** to throw oneself flat on the ground; **se p. contre un mur** to flatten oneself against a wall

plaquettaire [plaketɛr] ADJ *Biol* platelet *(avant n)*

plaquette [plakɛt] NF **1** *(livre)* booklet; **p. publicitaire** (advertising) brochure **2** *Physiol* (blood) platelet, thrombocyte **3** *(petite plaque)* (small) plate; **p. commémorative** commemorative plaque **4** *Com (de beurre)* pack; *(de chocolat)* bar; *(de pilules)* blister-pack; **p. insecticide** insecticide diffuser **5** *Aut* **p. de frein** brake pad **6** *Ordinat* circuit board

plaqueur [plakœr] NM **1** *Menuis* veneerer **2** *Métal* plater

plasma [plasma] NM **1** *Biol* plasma; **p. sanguin** blood plasma **2** *Phys* plasma; **jet de p.** plasma jet

plasmaphérèse [plasmaferɛz] NF *Méd* plasmapheresis

plasmatique [plasmatik] ADJ *Biol* plasmatic

plasmide [plasmid] NM *Biol* plasmid

plasmifier [9] [plasmifje] VT *Phys* to transform into plasma

plasmine [plasmin] NF *Biol & Chim* plasmin

plasminogène [plasminɔʒɛn] NM *Biol & Chim* plasminogen

plasmique [plasmik] ADJ *Phys* plasmic

plasmocytaire [plasmɔsitɛr] ADJ *Biol* plasmocyte *(avant n)*

plasmocyte [plasmɔsit] NM *Biol* plasmocyte

plasmode [plasmɔd] NM *Biol* plasmodium

plasmodium [plasmɔdjɔm] NM *Biol & Méd (parasite)* plasmodium

plasmolyse [plasmɔliz] NF *Physiol* plasmolysis

plasmopara [plasmɔpara] NM *Bot* plasmopara

plaste [plast] NM *Bot* plastid

plastic [plastik] NM plastic explosive

plasticage [plastikaʒ] = **plastiquage**

plasticien, -enne [plastisjɛ̃, -ɛn] NM,F **1** *Beaux-Arts* (plastic) artist **2** *Méd* plastic surgeon **3** *Tech* plastics technician

plasticité [plastisite] NF **1** *(d'un matériau)* plasticity **2** *(du caractère)* pliability, malleability **3** *Beaux-Arts* plastic quality, plasticity

plasticulture [plastikyltyr] NF *Hort* plasticulture

plastie [plasti] NF plastic surgery

plastifiant [plastifjɑ̃] NM **1** *Chim* plasticizer **2** *Constr* (mortar) plasticizer

plastification [plastifikasjɔ̃] NF **1** *(revêtement)* plastic-coating **2** *(ajout d'un plastifiant)* plastication **3** *(d'un document)* lamination

plastifier [9] [plastifje] VT **1** *(recouvrir de plastique)* to cover in *or* with plastic; **une couverture plastifiée** a plastic-coated cover **2** *(ajouter un plastifiant à)* to plasticize **3** *(document)* to laminate

plastigel [plastiʒɛl] NM *Chim* plastigel

plastination [plastinasjɔ̃] NF plastination

plastiner [3] [plastine] VT to plastinate

plastiquage [plastikaʒ] NM bombing *(UNCOUNT)*, bomb attack *(with plastic explosives)*; **après le p. de l'ambassade** after the embassy was blown up, after the bombing of *or* bomb attack on the embassy

plastique [plastik] ADJ **1** *(malléable)* plastic **2** *Beaux-Arts* plastic
NM **1** *(matière)* plastic **2** *(explosif)* plastic explosive
NF **1** *Beaux-Arts* (art of) modelling *or* moulding; **la p. grecque** Greek sculpture **2** *(forme du corps)* figure
❑ **en plastique** ADJ plastic *(avant n)*

plastiquement [plastikmɑ̃] ADV plastically, in plastic terms

plastiquer [3] [plastike] VT to blow up, to bomb *(with plastic explosives)*; **ils ont plastiqué l'ambassade cette nuit** they bombed the embassy last night

plastiqueur, -euse [plastikœr, -øz] NM,F bomber *(using plastic explosives)*

plastisol [plastisɔl] NM *Chim* plastisol

plastoc, plastoque [plastɔk] NM *Fam* plastic■

plastron [plastrɔ̃] NM **1** *(de chemise → non amovible)* shirtfront; *(→ amovible)* plastron, dickey; **chemise à p.** dinner shirt **2** *(de cuirasse)* plastron, breastplate **3** *Escrime* plastron **4** *Zool (de tortue)* plastron

plastronner [3] [plastrɔne] VI **1** *(se rengorger)* to throw out one's chest **2** *(parader)* to swagger *or* to strut around

plasturgie [plastyrʒi] NF **1** *(techniques)* plastics processing **2** *(industrie)* plastics industry

plasturgiste [plastyrʒist] NMF person working in the plastics industry

plat[1] [pla] NM **1** *(contenant)* dish; **p. ovale/à poisson** oval/fish dish; **p. à gratin** baking dish; **p. de service** serving dish; **p. à tarte** flan dish; **p. à barbe** shaving dish
2 *(préparation culinaire)* dish; **c'est mon p. préféré** it's my favourite dish; **un p. froid/chaud** a cold/hot dish; **p. cuisiné** precooked *or* ready-cooked dish; **p. garni** main dish served with vegetables; **un p. en sauce** a dish cooked *or* made with a sauce; **un petit p.** a delicacy; **elle aime les bons petits plats** she enjoys good food; **je t'ai préparé un bon petit p.** I've cooked something special for you; *Fig* **vendre qch contre un p. de lentilles** to sell something for a song; *Fam* **quel p. de nouilles!** what a *Br* twit *or Am* meathead!
3 *(partie du menu)* course; **deux plats au choix** a choice of two main courses; **le p. du jour** today's special, the dish of the day; **le p. principal** *ou* **de résistance** the main course *or* dish
4 *(locutions)* **mettre les petits plats dans les grands** to put on a big spread; *Fam* **faire (tout) un p. de qch** to make a big song and dance *or* a big fuss about sth; **il n'y a pas de quoi en faire tout un p.** it's not worth getting all worked up about; **il en fait un p.** *(il fait très chaud)* it's a scorcher, *Br* it's roasting; *Fam* **faire du p. à qn** *(à une femme) Br* to chat sb up, *Am* to give sb a line; *(à son patron)* to sweet-talk sb, *Br* to butter sb up

plat[2], **-e** [pla, plat] ADJ **1** *(plan, horizontal → terrain)* flat, level; *(→ mer)* still; **en terrain p.** on level ground; **un p. pays** *(plaine)* a plain; **la mer était plate** the sea was still
2 *(non profond)* flat, shallow; **bateau p.** shallow *or* shallow-bottomed boat
3 *(non saillant)* flat; **avoir un ventre p.** to have a flat stomach; **avoir la poitrine plate** to be flat-chested; *Fam* **elle est plate comme une planche à pain** *ou* **comme une limande** she's (as) flat as a board *or* pancake
4 *(non épais → montre, calculatrice)* slimline; *(→ écran)* flat
5 *(sans hauteur → casquette)* flat; **ma coiffure est trop plate** my hair lacks body; **chaussures plates** *ou* **à talons plats** flat shoes
6 *(médiocre → style)* flat, dull, unexciting; *(sans saveur → vin)* insipid; **une plate imitation** a pale imitation; **sa vie a été bien plate** he/she led rather a dull existence
7 *(obséquieux)* cringing, fawning; **être p. devant ses supérieurs** to cringe before *or* to kowtow to one's superiors; **je vous fais mes plus plates excuses** please accept my most humble apologies; **elle a dû faire de plates excuses** she was forced to make abject apologies; **p. comme une punaise** spineless
8 *(non gazeux)* still, non-sparkling
9 *Littérature voir* **rime**
10 *Géom (angle)* straight
NM **1** *(partie plate → gén)* flat (part); *(→ d'un aviron)* blade; **le p. de la main/d'une épée** the flat of the hand/a sword
2 *(lieu plan)* **sur le p.** on the flat *or* level
3 *(en sport)* **le p.** the flat; **spécialiste du p.** flat-racing specialist; *Équitation* **(course de) p.** flat race
4 *Fam (plongeon)* belly-flop; **faire un p.** to do a belly-flop
5 *(de bœuf)* **p. de côtes** *Br* best *or Am* short rib
6 *Typ* **plats** boards
7 *Métal* (small) flat (bar)
8 *(édition)* **p. couverture** case cover
❑ **plate** NF **1** *(bateau)* monkey-boat
2 *Belg (flasque)* flask
❑ **à plat** ADJ **1** *Fam (fatigué)* (all) washed out; **je suis complètement à p.** I've had it, I feel totally washed out **2** *Fam (déprimé)* down; **il est très à p.** he's feeling very low *or* down **3** *(pneu, batterie, pile)* flat ADV **1** *(horizontalement)* flat; **couché à p.** lying flat on his back; **dormir à p.** to sleep without a pillow; **les mains à p. sur la table** hands flat on the table; **mettre à p.** *(robe)* to unpick (and lay out the pieces); *(projet, problème)* to examine from all angles; **tomber à p.** *(plaisanterie)* to fall flat **2** *(rouler)* with a flat (tyre)
❑ **à plat ventre** ADV face down *or* downwards; **couché à p. ventre** lying face downwards; **se mettre à p. ventre** *(après avoir été allongé)* to flop over onto one's stomach; *(après avoir été debout)* to lie face downwards; **tomber à p. ventre** to fall flat on one's face; *Fig* **ils sont tous à p. ventre devant elle** they all bow down to her

platane [platan] NM plane tree; **faux p.** sycamore; *Fam* **rentrer dans un p.** to crash into a tree■

plataniste [platanist] NM *Zool* Indus river dolphin, Ganges river dolphin

plat-bord [plabɔr] *(pl* **plats-bords)** NM *Naut* gunwale, gunnel

plateau, -x [plato] NM **1** *(présentoir)* tray; **j'ai fait monter un p. dans ma chambre pour le dîner** I had a dinner tray brought up to my room; **p. de viandes froides** selection of *Br* cold meats *or Am* cold cuts; **p. à fromages** cheeseboard; **p. de fruits de mer** seafood platter; **p. d'argent** silver salver; *Fig* **il attend que tout lui soit apporté sur un p. (d'argent)** he expects everything to be handed to him on a (silver) plate
2 *Théât* stage; *Cin* set; *TV* panel; **sur le p.** *Théât* on stage; *Cin* on set; *TV* **nous avons un beau p. ce soir** we have a wonderful line-up for you in the studio tonight; *Cin* **p. fermé** closed set; *Cin* **p. de tournage** film set
3 *Tech (d'un électrophone, d'un micro-ondes)* turntable; *(d'une balance)* plate, pan; *(d'un véhicule)* platform; **p. de chargement** platform trolley; **p. d'embrayage** pressure plate; **p. de frein** brake backing plate; **p. de pédalier** front chain wheel; *Fig* **mettre qch sur les plateaux de la balance** to weigh sth up
4 *(d'une courbe)* plateau; **faire un** *ou* **atteindre son p.** to reach a plateau, to level off
5 *Géog* plateau, tableland; **hauts plateaux** high plateau; **p. continental** continental shelf; **le p. Ozark** the Ozark Plateau; **le p. de Sibérie centrale** the Central Siberian Plateau
6 *(en anthropologie)* plate, labret
7 *(d'une table)* top
8 *Sport* clay pigeon
9 **p. technique** *(d'un hôpital)* technical equipment

plateau-repas [platorəpa] *(pl* **plateaux-repas)** NM *(à la maison)* dinner; *(dans un avion)* in-flight meal

plate-bande [platbɑ̃d] *(pl* **plates-bandes)** NF **1** *Hort (pour fleurs)* flowerbed, bed; *(pour arbustes, herbes)* bed **2** *Archit (linteau)* platband; *(moulure)* frieze **3** *Fam (locutions)* **marcher sur** *ou* **piétiner les plates-bandes de qn** to tread on sb's toes; **ne marche pas sur mes plates-bandes** keep off my patch

platée [plate] NF **1** *(pleine assiette)* plate, plateful; *(plein plat)* dish, dishful; *Fam (portion)* big helping■ **2** *Constr* continuous foundation

plate-forme [platfɔrm] *(pl* **plates-formes)** NF **1** *Transp (d'un train, d'un bus)* platform
2 *Géog* shelf; **p. continentale** *ou* **insulaire** continental shelf; **p. de glace** ice shelf
3 *Pétr* rig; **p. de forage** drilling rig; **p. de forage en mer** offshore oil rig; **p. off-shore** offshore platform; **p. pétrolière** oil rig; **p. de production** production platform
4 *Pol* platform; **p. électorale** election platform
5 *Astron & Géol* platform
6 *(pour armement)* (gun) platform
7 *(d'une voie)* road level (width)
8 *Ind* **p. auto-élévatrice** jack-up accommodation platform; **p. élévatrice** elevator platform
9 *Constr (terrassement)* subgrade; **toit en p.** flat roof
10 *Ordinat & TV* platform; **p. numérique** digital platform; **p. satellite** satellite platform

platelage [platlaʒ] NM **1** *Naut* plating *(upon which armour is bolted)* **2** *(en travaux publics)* floor(-ing), planking

platelonge, plate-longe [platlɔ̃ʒ] *(pl* **platelonges** *ou* **plates-longes)** NF *(longe)* leading rein

platement [platmɑ̃] ADV **1** *(banalement)* dully, stolidly, bluntly **2** *(servilement)* cringingly, fawningly; **s'excuser p.** to give a cringing apology

plateresque [platərɛsk] ADJ *Archit* plateresque

plateure [platyr, platœr] NF *Mines* flat seam

plathelminthe [platɛlmɛ̃t] *Zool* NM flatworm, *Spéc* platyhelminth
❑ **plathelminthes** NMPL flatworms, *Spéc* Platyhelminthes

platinage [platinaʒ] NM platinization

platine [platin] ADJ INV *voir* **blond**
NM **1** *(métal)* platinum; **p. iridié** platiniridium
2 *Belg (pain moulé)* large tin loaf
NF **1** *Tech (d'une serrure, d'une horloge)* plate; *(d'une machine à coudre)* sinker; *(d'un microscope)* stage
2 *Mus* **p. cassette** cassette deck; **p. CD** CD player; **p. disque** *ou* **tourne-disque** record deck; **p. double cassette** twin cassette deck; **p. laser** CD player; **p. de magnétophone** tape deck
3 *Opt* stage
4 *Typ* platen
5 *(d'une arme)* (gun) lock
6 *(dans une tuyauterie)* (insert) washer
7 *Belg (moule) Br* baking tin, *Am* baking pan

platiné, -e [platine] ADJ *(blond → cheveux)* platinum blond; **une blonde platinée** a platinum blonde

platiner [3] [platine] VT *(recouvrir de platine)* to platinize

platineux, -euse [platinø, -øz] ADJ *Chim* platinous

platinifère [platinifɛr] ADJ platiniferous

platiniste [platinist] NMF *Fam* DJ■

platinite [platinit] NF platinite

platinoïde [platinɔid] *Chim* ADJ platinoid
NM platinoid

platitude [platityd] NF **1** *(absence d'originalité)* dullness, flatness, triteness; **ce film est d'une p.!** this movie *or Br* film is so dull! **2** *(lieu commun)* platitude, commonplace, trite remark; **débiter des platitudes** to talk in platitudes **3** *Littéraire (obséquiosité)* obsequiousness, grovelling; **elle ne reculera devant aucune p. pour avoir ce poste** she'll stoop to anything to get the job

platode [platɔd] NM *Zool* flatworm

Platon [platɔ̃] NPR Plato

platonicien, -enne [platɔnisjɛ̃, -ɛn] ADJ Platonic
NM,F Platonist

platonique [platɔnik] ADJ **1** *Phil* Platonic **2** *(amour)* platonic **3** *Littéraire (de pure forme)* token; **la France a formulé une protestation p.** France has made a token protest

platoniquement [platɔnikmɑ̃] ADV **1** *(aimer, admirer)* platonically **2** *Littéraire (sans produire d'effet)* futilely, to no effect

platonisme [platɔnism] NM Platonism

plâtrage [plɑtraʒ] NM *Constr (action)* plastering; *(ouvrage)* plasterwork

plâtras [plɑtra] NM **1** *(débris)* (plaster) rubble *(UNCOUNT)* **2** *Constr* rubblework *(UNCOUNT)*

plâtre [plɑtr] NM **1** *Constr* plaster; **plafond en p.** plastered ceiling; *Fam* **ton camembert, c'est du vrai p.** your camembert tastes like chalk (it's so unripe)■
2 *Méd (matériau)* plaster; *(appareil)* plaster cast; **ils lui ont mis un bras dans le p.** they put his arm in plaster; **être dans le p.** to be in plaster; **il devra garder son p.** he'll have to keep his cast on; **p. de marche** walking cast

3 *Beaux-Arts (matériau)* plaster; *(objet)* plaster cast *or* model; **p. de Paris** *ou* **à modeler** plaster of Paris; **p. à mouler** moulding plaster
❑ **plâtres NMPL les plâtres** *(revêtements)* the plasterwork

plâtrée [plɑtre] **NF** *Fam* huge helping; **une p. de nouilles** a huge helping of noodles

plâtrer [3] [plɑtre] **VT 1** *Méd (accidenté)* to plaster (up); *(membre)* to put in a cast *or* in plaster; **être plâtré de la taille jusqu'aux pieds** to be in a cast from the waist down; **aura-t-il besoin d'être plâtré?** will he have to have a cast?; **je suis allé à l'hôpital pour me faire p. le bras** I went to hospital to have my arm put in plaster **2** *Constr (couvrir)* to plaster (over); *(colmater)* to plaster over *or* up **3** *Agr (sol)* to dress with sulphate

plâtrerie [plɑtrəri] **NF 1** *(usine)* plasterworks **2** *(travaux)* plasterwork, plastering

plâtreux, -euse [plɑtrø, -øz] **ADJ 1** *(fromage)* chalky **2** *(mur)* plastered, covered with plaster **3** *(couleur, teint)* pasty

plâtrier [plɑtrije] **NM 1** *(maçon)* plasterer **2** *(commerçant)* builder's merchant **3** *(industriel)* plaster manufacturer

plâtrière [plɑtrijɛr] **NF 1** *(carrière)* gypsum *or* lime quarry **2** *(usine)* plasterworks **3** *(four)* plaster kiln, gypsum kiln
ADJ F brique p. moulded brick

plattekees, plattekeis [plat(ə)kes] **NM** *Belg* fromage frais

platy [plati] **NM** *Ich* platy

platyrhinien [platirinjɛ̃] **NM** *Zool* platyrrhine

plausibilité [plozibilite] **NF** plausibility

plausible [plozibl] **ADJ** plausible, credible, believable; **pas très** *ou* **peu p.** implausible

Plaute [plot] **NPR** Plautus

play-back [plɛbak] **NM INV** miming; **il chante en p.** he's miming (to a tape); **c'est du p.** he's/she's/*etc* miming

play-boy [plɛbɔj] *(pl* **play-boys)** **NM** playboy

playlist [plɛlist] **NM** *Rad* playlist

playon [plɛjɔ̃] = **pleyon**

plèbe [plɛb] **NF 1** *Littéraire Péj* **la p.** the hoi polloi, the plebs **2** *Antiq* **la p.** the plebs

plébéien, -enne [plebejɛ̃, -ɛn] **ADJ 1** *Littéraire Péj (du bas peuple)* plebeian; **des manières plébéiennes** plebeian manners **2** *Antiq* plebeian
NM,F 1 *Littéraire Péj (personne vulgaire)* plebeian **2** *Antiq* plebeian

plébiscitaire [plebisitɛr] **ADJ** plebiscitary

plébiscite [plebisit] **NM** plebiscite

plébisciter [3] [plebisite] **VT 1** *(élire → par plébiscite)* to elect by (a) plebiscite; *(→ à une large majorité)* to elect by a large majority **2** *(approuver)* to approve (by a large majority); **les spectateurs plébiscitent notre émission** viewers overwhelmingly support our programme

plécoptère [plekɔptɛr] *Entom* **NM** stonefly, *Spéc* plecopteran
❑ **plécoptères NMPL** stoneflies, *Spéc* Plecoptera

plectre [plɛktr] **NM** plectrum

pléiade [plejad] **NF 1** *Littéraire (grand nombre de)* group, pleiad; **une p. de vedettes** a glittering array of stars **2** *Littérature* **la P.** *(poètes)* = group of seven French poets in the 16th century, including du Bellay and Ronsard; *(édition)* = prestigious edition of literary classics

> *Culture*
> **LA PLÉIADE**
> Founded in 1931 by Jacques Schiffrin and bought by Gallimard in 1933, this series of literary classics is unique in its genre: in France, having one's works published as part of this collection is considered to be the ultimate accolade for a writer. The series was designed to provide the public with handsomely-produced literary classics, and the books are characterized by the extremely delicate bible paper on which they are printed (allowing a large amount of text to be fitted into one volume) and by their luxurious gilt leather binding. The Pléiade series became a byword for erudition in 1961, when it began including critical introductions and prefaces written, often over a period of years, by distinguished specialists.

Pléiades [plejad] **NFPL** *Astron & Myth* Pleiades

PLEIN, -E [plɛ̃, plɛn]

> **ADJ** full **1, 3–7, 9–11** ■ solid **2** ■ busy **4**
> **NM** full tank **1**
> **PRÉP** all over

ADJ 1 *(rempli)* full; **avoir l'estomac** *ou* **le ventre p.** to have a full stomach; **avoir les mains pleines** to have one's hands full; **avoir le nez p.** to have a blocked nose; **verre à demi p.** half-full glass; **p. à ras bord** full to the brim; **p. à ras bord de** brimming with; **p. de** full of; **la casserole est pleine d'eau** the pan is full of water; **une pièce pleine de livres** a room full of books; **un roman p. d'intérêt** a very interesting novel; **être p. d'enthousiasme/de bonne volonté** to show great enthusiasm/willingness; *Fam* **p. aux as** loaded, stinking rich; **p. à craquer** *(valise)* bulging, bursting, crammed full; *(salle)* packed; *Fam* **un gros p. de soupe** a tub of lard, a fat slob; *Fam* **être p. comme un œuf** *(valise, salle)* to be chock-a-block; *(personne repue)* to be stuffed; *Fam* **être p. (comme) une barrique** *ou* **une outre** to be plastered, to have had a skinful

2 *(massif)* solid; **une porte pleine** a solid door; **des briques pleines** solid bricks; **en bois p.** solid-wood; **mur p.** blind wall

3 *(complet)* full; **année pleine** full (calendar) year; **mois p.** full (calendar) month; **p. temps, temps p.** full-time; **être** *ou* **travailler à temps p.** to work full-time; **pleine page** *(gén)* full page; *(en publicité, sur une page)* full-page ad; *(en publicité, sur deux pages)* (double-page) spread; **pleins pouvoirs** (full) power of attorney; **avoir les pleins pouvoirs** to have full powers; **être en p. travail** *(usine)* to be in full production

4 *(chargé)* busy, full; **j'ai eu une journée pleine** I've had a busy day; **ma vie a été pleine** I've led a full life; **la pleine saison** the height of the season, the high season

5 *(en intensif)* **une pleine carafe de** a jugful of; **une pleine valise de** a suitcase full of; **de son p. gré** of his/her own volition *or* free will; **obtenir un p. succès** to achieve complete success; **une industrie en p. essor** a booming *or* fast-growing industry; **j'ai pleine conscience de ce qui m'attend** I know exactly what to expect; **être en pleine forme** to be on top form; **couler à pleins bords** to be overflowing; **embrasser qn à pleine bouche** to kiss sb full on the mouth; **manger des mûres à pleine bouche** to eat mouthfuls of blackberries; **ramasser qch à pleins bras** to pick up armfuls of sth; **rire à pleine gorge** to laugh one's head off; **chanter/crier à p. gosier** to sing/to shout at the top of one's voice; **ramasser qch à pleines mains** to pick up handfuls of sth; **sentir qch à p. nez** to reek of sth; **respirer à pleins poumons** to take deep breaths; *Fam* **mettre la radio à p. tube** *ou* **pleins tubes** to put the radio on full blast; *Fam* **foncer/rouler à p. tube** to go/to drive flat out; *très Fam* **déconner à p. tube** *ou* **pleins tubes** to talk a lot of crap *or* *Br* bollocks; *Archit* **arc p. cintre** round arch; **pleine charge moteur** full throttle; **pleins feux sur** spotlight on; **pleins gaz**, *Fam* **pleins pots** full throttle; **allez, vas-y pleins gaz!** go on, put your foot down *or* step on it!; **pleins phares** *Br* full beam, *Am* high beams; **rouler (en) pleins phares** to drive on full headlights *or* *Br* on full beam *or* *Am* on high beams

6 *(milieu, cœur)* **en p. air** *(concert, marché)* open-air, outdoor; **des activités de p. air** outdoor activities; **en pleine campagne** right out in the country, in the middle of the countryside; **en p. cœur de la ville** right in the heart of the city; *Fam* **en pleine figure** *ou* **poire** right in the face■; **en p. jour** in broad daylight; **en pleine mer** (out) in the open sea; **en p. midi** at twelve (noon) on the dot; **en pleine nuit** in the middle of the night; **en pleine rue** (right) in the middle of the street; **en p. soleil** in full sunlight; **en pleine terre** in the open ground; **en p. vent** in the wind; **en p. vol** in mid-flight

7 *(arrondi)* full; **avoir des formes pleines** to have a well-rounded *or* full figure; **avoir des joues pleines** to be chubby-cheeked; **avoir le visage p.** to be moon-faced

8 *Zool (vache)* in calf; *(jument)* in foal; *(truie)* in pig; *(brebis)* in lamb; *(chatte)* pregnant

9 *Littéraire (préoccupé)* **ses lettres sont pleines de vous** she talks about nothing but you in her letters; **être p. de soi-même/son sujet** to be full of oneself/one's subject

10 *(au billard→ couleur)* full

11 *Astron & Météo* full; **la lune est pleine** the moon is full; **la pleine mer** high tide

NM 1 *(de carburant)* full tank; **on fait le p. une fois par mois au supermarché** *(de courses)* we stock up once a month at the supermarket; **avec un p., tu iras jusqu'à Versailles** you'll get as far as Versailles on a full tank; **faire le p.** to fill up; **le p., s'il vous plaît** fill her *or* it up, please; *Fig* **faire le p. de vitamines/soleil** to stock up on vitamins/sunshine; **il a fait le p. de ses voix** he got as many votes as he's ever likely to get

2 *(maximum)* **donner son p.** *(personne)* to give one's best, to give one's all; **le p. de la lune** the moon at its full; **le p. de la mer** the tide at its highest

3 *(en calligraphie)* downstroke; **les pleins et les déliés** the downstrokes and the upstrokes

4 *Constr* solid *or* massive parts; **le p. d'un mur** the solid section of a wall

ADV 1 *Fam* **tout p.** *(très)* really■; **il est mignon tout p., ce bébé** what a totally cute little baby

2 *(non creux)* **sonner p.** to sound solid

PRÉP *(partout dans)* all over; **j'ai des plantes p. ma maison** my house is full of plants, I have plants all over the house; **il a de la boue p. son pantalon** his trousers are covered in mud, he's got mud all over his trousers; *Fig* **avoir de l'argent p. les poches** to have loads of money; *Fam* **il en a p. la bouche, de sa nouvelle voiture** he keeps on about *or* he's full of his new car; *Fam* **en avoir p. les bottes de qch** to be fed up with sth; *Fam* **j'en ai p. les bottes** *ou* **pattes** my feet are killing me; **j'en ai p. le** *Fam* **dos** *ou* *Vulg* **cul** I've had it up to here; *Fam* **s'en mettre p. la lampe** to stuff one's face; *Fam* **en mettre p. la vue à qn** to put on a show for sb; **en prendre p.** *Fam* **les dents** *ou* **les gencives** *ou très Fam* **la gueule** *(se faire reprendre)* to get bawled out, *Br* to get a right rollocking; *(être éperdu d'admiration)* to be bowled over

❑ **à plein ADV les moteurs/usines tournent à p.** the engines/factories are working to full capacity; **utiliser des ressources à p.** to make full use of resources

❑ **de plein droit ADV exiger** *ou* **réclamer qch de p. droit** to demand sth as of right *or* as one's right

❑ **de plein fouet ADJ** head-on **ADV** head-on, full on; **les deux véhicules se sont heurtés de p. fouet** the vehicles hit each other full on

❑ **en plein ADV 1** *(en entier)* in full, entirely; **le soleil éclaire la pièce en p.** the sun lights up the entire room

2 *(complètement, exactement)* **en p. dans/sur** right in the middle of/on top of; **j'ai mis le pied en p. dans une flaque** I stepped right in the middle of a puddle; **donner en p. dans un piège** to fall right into a trap

❑ **plein de DÉT** *Fam* lots of■; **il y avait p. de gens dans la rue** there were crowds *or* masses of people in the street; **tu veux des bonbons/de l'argent? j'en ai p.** do you want some sweets/money? I've got lots; **j'ai (p., p.,) p. d'argent** I've got lots (and lots) *or* loads (and loads) of money

pleinement [plɛnmɑ̃] **ADV** wholly, fully, entirely; **vivre p. sa passion** to live one's passion to the full; **je suis p. convaincu** I'm fully convinced; **profiter p. de qch** to make the most of sth

plein(-)emploi [plɛnɑ̃plwa] **NM** *Écon* full employment

plein-temps [plɛ̃tɑ̃] *(pl* **pleins-temps)** **ADJ INV** full-time
NM full-time job; **faire un p.** to work full-time, to have a full-time job
❑ **à plein-temps ADV travailler à p.** to work full-time

plein-vent [plɛ̃vɑ̃] *(pl* **pleins-vents)** **NM** isolated *or* exposed tree

pléistocène [pleistɔsɛn] **NM** *Géol* Pleistocene (period)

plénier, -ère [plenje, -ɛr] **ADJ** plenary

pla–ple

plénipotentiaire [plenipɔtɑ̃sjɛr] **ADJ** plenipotentiary
 NMF plenipotentiary

plénitude [plenityd] **NF** 1 *Littéraire (des formes, d'un son)* fullness; **être dans la p. de son talent** to be at the peak of one's talent 2 *(satisfaction totale)* fulfilment; **un sentiment de p.** a feeling of fulfilment 3 *Jur* **p. de juridiction** full jurisdiction, unlimited jurisdiction

plénum [plenɔm] **NM** *Pol* plenum

pléonasme [pleɔnasm] **NM** pleonasm

pléonastique [pleɔnastik] **ADJ** pleonastic

plésiomorphe [plezjɔmɔrf] **ADJ** *Biol* plesiomorphous

plésiomorphie [plezjɔmɔrfi] **NF** *Biol* plesiomorphous character

plésiosaure [plezjɔzɔr] **NM** plesiosaur

pléthore [pletɔr] **NF** *(excès)* excess, plethora; **p. de** an excess of, a plethora of; **il y a p. de candidats à ce poste** far too many candidates have applied for the post

pléthorique [pletɔrik] **ADJ** *(excessif)* excessive, overabundant

pleur [plœr] **NM** *Vieilli ou Littéraire* tear; **répandre ou verser des pleurs (sur)** to shed tears (for), to weep (for); **en pleurs** in tears; **il y aura des pleurs et des grincements de dents** there will be a great wailing and gnashing of teeth; *Ironique* **verser un p. pour** to shed a tear for, to weep for

pleurage [plœraʒ] **NM** 1 *(basse fréquence)* wow; *(haute fréquence)* flutter 2 *Can (pleurnicherie)* whining *(UNCOUNT)*, *Br* whingeing *(UNCOUNT)*

pleural, -e, -aux, -ales [plœral, -o] **ADJ** *Anat* pleural

pleurant [plœrɑ̃] **NM** *Beaux-Arts* weeping figure, weeper

pleurard, -e [plœrar, -ard] **ADJ** 1 *Fam (sanglotant)* whimpering 2 *(plaintif)* whining, *Br* whingeing
 NM,F 1 *Fam (qui sanglote)* whimperer 2 *(qui se plaint)* whiner, *Br* whinger

pleurer [5] [plœre] **VI** 1 *(verser des larmes)* to cry; **le bébé pleure** the baby's crying; **s'endormir en pleurant** to cry oneself to sleep; **p. de joie/rage** to weep for joy/with rage; **j'en pleurais de rire!** I laughed so much that I cried!; **j'en aurais pleuré** I could have wept or cried; **à p.** enough to make you weep or cry; **l'histoire est bête/triste à p.** the story is so stupid/sad you could weep; **faire p. qn** to make sb cry; *Ironique* **arrête, tu vas me faire p.!** my heart bleeds for you!; **p. à chaudes larmes** to cry one's eyes out; *Fam* **p. comme une Madeleine ou comme un veau ou comme une fontaine** to bawl one's eyes out; **ne laisser à qn que les yeux pour p.** to leave sb nothing but the clothes they stand up in; **il ne lui reste ou il n'a plus que les yeux pour p.** he has nothing left to his name; *Fam* **dans le gilet de qn** to go crying to sb■; **elle pleurait d'un œil et riait de l'autre** she didn't know whether to laugh or cry; **elle n'avait pas assez de ses yeux pour p.** she was grief-stricken
 2 *Physiol* to cry; **avoir un œil qui pleure** to have a weepy or watery eye
 3 *Fam (réclamer)* to beg■; **il est allé p. auprès du directeur pour avoir une promotion** he went cap in hand to the boss or went and begged the boss for a promotion; **p. après** to beg for; **p. après des subventions** to go begging for subsidies
 4 *(se lamenter)* **p. sur** to lament, to bemoan, to bewail; **p. sur soi-même ou son sort** to bemoan one's fate
 5 *Littéraire (vent)* to wail, to howl; *(animal)* to wail
 VT 1 *(répandre)* to cry, to shed, to weep; **p. des larmes de joie** to cry or to shed tears of joy; **p. toutes les larmes de son corps** to cry one's eyes out
 2 *(être en deuil de)* to mourn; **nous pleurons notre cher père** we're mourning (for) our dear father; **p. la mort de qn** to mourn sb's death
 3 *(regretter)* to lament, to bemoan; **p. une occasion perdue** to lament a lost opportunity
 4 *Fam (donner à regret)* to begrudge■; **il ne pleure pas sa peine** he doesn't mind putting himself out; **tu ne vas pas p. les quelques euros que tu lui donnes par mois?** surely you

don't begrudge him/her the few euros you give him/her a month?
 5 *(se plaindre)* **elle est allée p. qu'on l'avait trompée** she went complaining that she'd been deceived
 6 *(locution)* **p. misère** to cry over or to bemoan one's lot; **il est allé p. misère chez ses parents** he went to his parents asking for money

pleurésie [plœrezi] **NF** *Méd* pleurisy

pleurétique [plœretik] *Méd* **ADJ** pleuritic
 NMF pleurisy sufferer, pleuritic

pleureur, -euse [plœrœr, -øz] **ADJ** 1 *(personne)* who cries a lot; **c'est un enfant très p.** he cries a lot 2 *(arbre)* weeping *(avant n)*
 NM,F **c'est un p.** he cries a lot; **quelle pleureuse, celle-là!** doesn't she cry a lot!
 ❑ **pleureuse NF** *(aux enterrements)* (professional) mourner

pleurite [plœrit] **NF** *Méd* dry pleurisy

pleurnichard, -e [plœrniʃar, -ard] = **pleurnicheur**

pleurnichement [plœrniʃmɑ̃] **NM** = **pleurnicherie**

pleurnicher [3] [plœrniʃe] **VI** *(sangloter)* to whimper; *(se plaindre)* to whine, *Br* to whinge; **et après, ne viens pas p.!** and don't come crying to me!; **p. auprès de qn** to go crying to sb

pleurnicherie [plœrniʃri] **NF** whining *(UNCOUNT)*, *Br* whingeing *(UNCOUNT)*; **lui, on l'aura toujours avec quelques pleurnicheries** you can always get round him if you whine a bit

pleurnicheur, -euse [plœrniʃœr, -øz] **ADJ** *(sanglotant)* whimpering; *(plaintif)* whining, *Br* whingeing
 NM,F *(qui sanglote)* whimperer; *(qui se plaint)* whiner, *Br* whinger

pleurodynie [plœrɔdini] **NF** *Méd* pleurodynia

pleuronecte [plœrɔnɛkt] *Ich* **NM** pleuronect
 ❑ **pleuronectes NMPL** Pleuronectidae

pleuronectidé [plœrɔnɛktide] *Ich* **NM** pleuronectid
 ❑ **pleuronectidés NMPL** Pleuronectidae

pleuronectiforme [plœrɔnɛktifɔrm] *Ich* **NM** flatfish, *Spéc* pleuronectiform
 ❑ **pleuronectiformes NMPL** flatfishes, *Spéc* Pleuronectiforms

pleuropneumonie [plœrɔpnømɔni] **NF** *Méd* pleuropneumonia

pleurote [plœrɔt] **NM** oyster mushroom

pleurotomie [plœrɔtɔmi] **NF** *Méd* pleurotomy

pleut *voir* **pleuvoir**

pleutre [pløtr] *Littéraire* **ADJ** cowardly, faint-hearted, lily-livered; **il est trop p. pour se battre** he's too lily-livered to put up a fight
 NM coward

pleutrerie [pløtrəri] **NF** *Littéraire* 1 *(caractère lâche)* cowardice, pusillanimity 2 *(acte)* act of cowardice or pusillanimity

pleuvasser [3] [pløvase] **V** **IMPERSONNEL** *Fam* to drizzle■

pleuviner [3] [pløvine] **V** **IMPERSONNEL** to drizzle■

pleuvioter [3] [pløvjɔte] **V** **IMPERSONNEL** *Fam* to drizzle■

pleuvoir [68] [pløvwar] **V** **IMPERSONNEL** to rain; **il pleut** it's raining; **il a plu toute la journée** it's been raining all day; **il pleut à grosses gouttes** it's raining heavily; **il pleut quelques gouttes** there's a spatter of rain; **on dirait qu'il va p.** it looks like rain; **il pleut à seaux** ou **à verse** ou *Fam* **des cordes** ou *Fam* **des hallebardes** it's raining cats and dogs, *Br* it's bucketing down; *Fam* **il pleut comme vache qui pisse,** *Can* **il pleut à boire debout** it's raining cats and dogs, *Br* it's bucketing down; **qu'il pleuve ou qu'il vente** come rain come shine; **des récompenses comme s'il en pleuvait** rewards galore; **elle dépense de l'argent comme s'il en pleuvait** she's spending money like there was no tomorrow; **il pleut, il mouille(, c'est la fête à la grenouille)** ≃ it's raining, it's pouring(, the old man is snoring)
 VI *(coups)* to rain down, to fall like rain; *(insultes)* to shower down; **les punitions pleuvaient sur les élèves** punishments were showering down upon or on the pupils; **les coups pleuvaient sur sa tête** blows were raining down upon or on his/her head; **faire p. des coups sur qn** to rain blows (down) on sb, to shower sb with blows; **faire p. les malédictions sur qn** to rain curses upon or on sb's head

pleuvoter [3] [pløvɔte] **V** **IMPERSONNEL** *Fam* to drizzle■

plèvre [plɛvr] **NF** *Anat* pleura; *Méd* **cancer de la p.** pleural cancer

Plexiglas® [plɛksiglas] **NM** *Br* Perspex®, *Am* Plexiglas®

plexus [plɛksys] **NM** *Anat* plexus; **p. solaire** solar plexus

Pleyel [plejɛl] **NF** **la salle P.** = large auditorium in Paris used for classical music concerts

pleyon [plejɔ̃] **NM** *Agr* withe, osier tie

pli [pli] **NM** 1 *(repli → d'un éventail, d'un rideau, du papier)* fold; *(→ d'un pantalon)* crease; **le drap fait des plis** the sheet is creased or rumpled; **un tissu qui ne fait pas de plis** a material that doesn't crease; **faux p.** crease; *Fam* **ça ne fait pas un p.** there's no doubt about it■; **je me doutais qu'il se blesserait, et ça n'a pas fait un p.** I was just waiting for him to hurt himself, and sure enough he did
 2 *Couture* pleat; **p. d'aisance** inverted pleat; **p. couché** knife pleat; **p. creux** box pleat; **p. plat** flat pleat
 3 *(habitude)* habit; **c'est un p. à prendre** you've (just) got to get into the habit; **il a pris le p. de marcher tous les jours** he got into the habit of going for a walk every day; **p. était pris** I/he/etc had got used to it; **ses enfants ont pris un mauvais p. dès le début** his/her children got into a bad habit right from the start
 4 *(ride)* wrinkle, line, crease; *(bourrelet)* fold; **des petits plis apparaissent autour de ses yeux** little lines are showing around his/her eyes; **les plis de son ventre** *(petits)* the creases in his/her belly; *(gros)* the rolls of fat on his/her belly; **p. du bras** bend of the arm; **p. de l'aine** crease or fold of the groin
 5 *(enveloppe)* envelope; *(lettre)* letter; **veuillez trouver sous ce p. le document demandé** please find enclosed the required document; **sous p. cacheté** in a sealed envelope; **la copie vous sera envoyée sous p. séparé** the copy will be sent to you under separate cover; **sous p. recommandé** by registered letter
 6 *Cartes* trick; **faire un p.** to win or to take a trick
 7 *Géog* **p. (de terrain)** fold; **p. couché** recumbent fold
 8 *Menuis* ply
 ❑ **à plis ADJ** pleated

pliable [plijabl] **ADJ** foldable; **difficilement p.** hard to fold

pliage [plijaʒ] **NM** *(action)* folding; *(objet)* folded-paper model; **à p. accordéon** fan-fold, *Am* Z-fold

pliant, -e [plijɑ̃, -ɑ̃t] **ADJ** folding, collapsible
 NM folding stool

plic-ploc, plic ploc [plikplɔk] **ADV** *Belg* 1 *(dans l'espace)* here and there 2 *(dans le temps)* (every) now and then, from time to time

plie [pli] **NF** *Ich* plaice

plié [plije] **NM** plié

pliement [plimɑ̃] **NM** *(fait de plier)* folding

plier [10] [plije] **VT** 1 *(journal, carte, drap, vêtement)* to fold; **p. bagage** to pack up and go
 2 *(tordre → fil de fer, doigt, genou)* to bend; **p. les jambes/bras** to bend one's legs/arms; **la douleur le plia en deux** he was doubled up in pain; **être plié en deux** ou **en quatre (de rire)** doubled up (with laughter)■
 3 *(rabattre → parapluie, chaise)* to fold up or away
 4 *(soumettre)* **je n'ai jamais pu la p. à mes désirs/pu p. sa volonté** I never managed to get her to submit to my desires/to bend her will; **p. qn à une habitude** to get sb into a habit
 5 *Fam (détruire)* to smash up■, to wreck■
 6 *Fam* **c'est plié** *(c'est fait)* it's done and dusted; *(les dés sont jetés)* the die is cast
 VI 1 *(se courber)* to bend (over), to bow; **les branches pliaient sous le poids des fruits/de la neige** the branches were weighed down with fruit/snow; **p. sous le poids des responsabilités** to be weighed down by responsibility
 2 *(se soumettre)* to yield, to give in, to give way; **tu plieras!** you'll just have to knuckle under!; **p. devant qn** to submit or to yield to sb; **faire p. qn** to subdue sb, to make sb give in; **tu ne me feras pas p.** I won't give in (to you)
 ▸**se plier VPR** 1 *(chaise, parapluie)* to fold up or

away; *(personne, corps)* to bend, to stoop; **se p. en deux** to bend double

  2 se p. à *(se soumettre à)* to submit to; *(s'adapter à)* to adapt to; **il faut se p. aux usages locaux** you have to respect local customs; **se p. à des méthodes nouvelles** to adapt to *or* to accept new methods; **c'est une discipline à laquelle il faut se p.** you have to accept the discipline; **se p. aux caprices/volontés de qn** to give in to sb's whims/wishes

plieur, -euse [plijœr, -øz] NM,F **1** *(en bonneterie)* folder **2** *(de papier)* folder
  ▫ **plieuse** NF *Typ (machine)* folder, folding machine *or* unit

Pline [plin] NPR **P. l'Ancien/le Jeune** Pliny the Elder/Younger

plinthe [plɛ̃t] NF **1** *Constr (en bois) Br* skirting (board), *Am* baseboard, mopboard; *(en pierre)* skirting; **p. chauffante** skirting fan convector **2** *Archit* plinth

pliocène [plijɔsɛn] *Géol* ADJ Pliocene *(avant n)* ◊ NM Pliocene *(period)*

plioir [plijwar] NM **1** *(coupe-papier)* paper knife **2** *(pour ligne de pêche)* winder

plissage [plisaʒ] NM pleating

plissé, -e [plise] ADJ **1** *(jupe)* pleated **2** *(ridé → front, visage)* wrinkled, creased; **une petite figure toute plissée** a wrinkled little face **3** *Géol (terrain)* folded
  ◊ NM *(plis)* pleats; **p. soleil** sunray *or Am* sunburst pleats

plissement [plismɑ̃] NM **1** *Géog (phénomène)* folding; **p. (de terrain)** *(résultat)* fold; **montagnes formées par plissements** fold mountains; **le p. hercynien** the Armorican *or* Hercynian fold **2** *(du front, du visage)* wrinkling *(UNCOUNT)*; *(des yeux)* screwing up

plisser [3] [plise] VT **1** *(faire des plis à → volontairement)* to fold; *(→ involontairement)* to crease
  2 *(froncer → yeux)* to screw up; *(→ nez, front)* to wrinkle; **la contrariété plissait son front** his/her brow was furrowed with worry; **p. la bouche** *ou* **les lèvres** to pucker one's lips
  3 *Géog* to fold
  4 *Couture* to pleat
  ◊ VI *(se froisser → pantalon, robe, nappe)* to crease, to become creased; *(→ collant)* to wrinkle
  ▶ **se plisser** VPR **1** *(se froisser)* to crease; **la soie se plisse facilement** silk creases easily
  2 *(se rider)* to crease, to wrinkle; **son front se plissa** he/she frowned; **ses yeux se plissent quand elle sourit** her eyes go all crinkly when she smiles

plisseur, -euse [plisœr, -øz] *Tex* NM,F *(personne)* pleater
  ◊ **plisseuse** NF *(machine)* pleating machine

pliure [plijyr] NF **1** *(marque)* fold **2** *(pliage)* folding; *Typ* **p. en accordéon** accordion fold, concertina fold; **p. à la française** French fold; **p. parallèle** parallel fold **3** *(du genou, du bras)* bend

ploc [plɔk] ONOMAT plop; **on entendait le p. des gouttes d'eau dans l'évier** we could hear the sound of water dripping into the sink

plocéidé [plɔseide] *Orn* NM ploceid
  ◊ **plocéidés** NMPL Ploceidae

plogue [plɔg] NF *Can Joual* **1** *(prise de courant)* plug■ **2** *(publicité)* plug; **ils ont fait une** *ou* **de la p. pour la nouvelle émission** they plugged the new programme

ploguer [3] [plɔge] VT *Can Joual* **1** *(brancher)* to plug in■ **2** *(faire de la publicité pour)* to plug; **il a plogué son disque pendant l'émission** he plugged his album during the show

ploïdie [plɔidi] NF *Biol* ploidy

ploie *etc voir* **ployer**

ploiement [plwamɑ̃] NM *Littéraire* bending

plomb [plɔ̃] NM **1** *Métal* lead; **j'ai du p. dans l'estomac** I feel as though I have a lead weight in my stomach; *Fam* **il n'a pas de p. dans la tête** *ou* **cervelle** he's featherbrained, he's got nothing between the ears; **ça te mettra un peu de p. dans la tête** *ou* **cervelle** that'll knock some sense into you
  2 *(d'arme à feu)* leadshot, shot; **un p.** a piece of shot; **du gros p.** buckshot; **le petit p.** small shot; **avoir du p. dans l'aile** *(entreprise)* to be in a sorry state *or* a bad way; *(personne)* to be in bad shape *or* on one's last legs

3 *Élec* fuse; **un p. a sauté** a fuse has blown; **faire sauter les plombs** to blow the fuses; *Fam* **péter les plombs** *(se mettre en colère)* to go ballistic, to hit the *Br* roof *or Am* ceiling; *(craquer)* to crack up
  4 *Pêche* sinker
  5 *Couture* lead (weight)
  6 *(de vitrail)* lead, came
  7 *(sceau)* lead seal
  8 *Constr* plumb, bob, plummet
  9 *Typ* type; **lire sur le p.** to read from the metal
  10 *Naut* **p. (de sonde)** lead
  ◊ **à plomb** *(le mur n'est pas/est à p.* the wall is off plumb/is plumb ADV **mettre qch à p.** to plumb sth
  ◊ **de plomb** ADJ *(gouttière, tuyau etc)* lead *(avant n)*; **un ciel de p.** a leaden sky

plombage [plɔ̃baʒ] NM **1** *(d'une dent)* filling; **faire un p. à qn** to fill sb's tooth; **se faire faire un p.** to have a tooth filled *or* a filling (put in) **2** *(d'un colis)* sealing (with lead) **3** *Pêche* leading **4** *Agr & Hort* tamping down **5** *(de la céramique)* lead glazing

plombaginacée [plɔ̃baʒinase] *Bot* NF plumbago, leadwort
  ◊ **plombaginacées** NFPL Plumbaginaceae

plombagine [plɔ̃baʒin] NF graphite, plumbago

plombe [plɔ̃b] NF *Fam* hour■; **ça fait des plombes que je t'attends** I've been waiting for you for ages■; **elle met toujours trois plombes à se préparer** she always takes ages to get ready■

plombé, -e [plɔ̃be] ADJ **1** *(teint)* leaden, pallid; *(ciel)* leaden, heavy **2** *(scellé → colis, wagon)* sealed (with lead) **3** *Pêche* weighted (with lead) *or* with a sinker **4** *(dent)* filled **5** *très Fam (atteint par une MST)* **être p.** to have a dose

plombée [plɔ̃be] NF **1** *Pêche* sinker, shot **2** *Hist (arme)* lead mace

plomber [3] [plɔ̃be] VT **1** *(dent)* to fill, to put a filling in
  2 *(colis)* to seal with lead
  3 *Pêche* to weight (with lead), to lead
  4 *Agr & Hort* to tamp down
  5 *(mur)* to plumb
  6 *(toit)* to lead
  7 *(céramique)* to glaze
  8 *Littéraire (rendre gris → teint, ciel)* **p. qch** to turn sth the colour of lead
  9 *Fam (tuer à l'aide d'une arme à feu)* **p. qn** to fill sb with lead, to pump sb full of lead
  10 *très Fam (transmettre une maladie vénérienne à)* **p. qn** to give sb a dose
  11 *Fig (handicaper, compromettre)* to jeopardize, to undermine; **un parti plombé par les scandales** a party plagued by scandal
  ◊ VI *(au jeu de boules)* = to throw the bowl in such a way that it lands on the ground without rolling
  ▶ **se plomber** VPR *(ciel)* to turn leaden *or* the colour of lead

plomberie [plɔ̃bri] NF **1** *(installation)* plumbing; **toute la p. est à refaire** all the plumbing in the house must be redone **2** *(profession)* plumbing **3** *(atelier)* plumber's shop

plombeur [plɔ̃bœr] NM *Agr* (heavily weighted) roller

plombeux, -euse [plɔ̃bø, -øz] ADJ leaden

plombier [plɔ̃bje] NM **1** *(artisan)* plumber **2** *Fam (espion)* spy■ *(who plants bugs)*

---

plombières [plɔ̃bjɛr] NF tutti-frutti (ice cream)

plombifère [plɔ̃bifɛr] ADJ *Chim* plumbiferous

plombique [plɔ̃bik] ADJ *Chim* plumbic

plombure [plɔ̃byr] NF *(de vitrail)* leads, cames

plonge [plɔ̃ʒ] NF *Fam* washing-up■, washing the dishes■; **faire la p.** to wash dishes■ *(in a restaurant)*

plongeant, -e [plɔ̃ʒɑ̃, -ɑ̃t] ADJ plunging; **il y a une vue plongeante jusqu'à la mer** the view plunges down to the sea

plongée [plɔ̃ʒe] NF **1** *Sport* (underwater) diving; **faire de la p.** to go diving; **il fait de la p. depuis deux ans** he has been diving for two years; **p. sous-marine** skin *or* scuba diving **2** *(de sous-marin)* dive, diving *(UNCOUNT)*, submersion *(UNCOUNT)*; **effectuer sa p.** to dive, to submerge; **être en p.** to be submerged **3** *Cin* high-angle shot **4** *(descente rapide)* swoop, plunge, dive

plongement [plɔ̃ʒmɑ̃] NM *(dans un liquide)* plunging

plongeoir [plɔ̃ʒwar] NM diving board

plongeon [plɔ̃ʒɔ̃] NM **1** *(dans l'eau)* dive; **faire un p.** to dive; **faire un p. (en) arrière** to do a back dive *or* a back flip; **p. de haut vol** high dive; *Fam aussi Fig* **faire le p.** to take a tumble, *Br* to come a cropper; **son entrepôt a brûlé, il a fait le grand p.** his warehouse burned down and he lost everything■
  2 *Ftbl* dive; **faire un p.** to dive
  3 *Orn Br* diver, *Am* loon; **p. arctique** black-throated *Br* diver *or Am* loon; **p. catmarin** *ou* **à gorge rousse** red-throated *Br* diver *or Am* loon; **p. imbrin** *Br* great northern diver, *Am* common loon

plonger [17] [plɔ̃ʒe] VI **1** *(dans l'eau)* to dive; *(en profondeur)* to dive, to go skin *or* scuba diving; **il plongea du haut du rocher** he dived off the rock **2** *Ftbl* to dive
  3 *(descendre → avion)* to dive; *(→ sous-marin)* to dive; *(→ oiseau)* to dive, to swoop; *(→ racine)* to go down; *Fig* **le roman plonge dans la suspense dès la première page** the novel plunges (the reader) into suspense from the very first page; **depuis le balcon, la vue plonge dans le jardin des voisins** there's a bird's-eye view of next door's garden from the balcony
  4 p. dans *(s'absorber dans)* to plunge into, to absorb oneself in; **elle plongea dans la dépression** she plunged into depression
  5 p. dans *(avoir ses sources dans)* to go back to; **cette tradition plonge dans la nuit des temps** this tradition goes back to the dawn of time
  6 *Fam (échouer)* to decline■, to fall off■; *(faire faillite)* to go bankrupt■, to fold; **beaucoup d'élèves plongent au deuxième trimestre** a lot of pupils' work deteriorates in the second term; **de nombreux petits commerçants ont plongé** a lot of small businesses folded; **c'est ça qui a fait p. la boîte** that's what sent the company to the wall; **c'est ce qui l'a fait p.** that's what caused his demise
  7 *Fam Arg crime (être envoyé en prison)* to be put inside *or* away, *Br* to be sent down
  8 *Fam (prendre une décision importante)* to take the plunge, to go for it
  ◊ VT **1** *(enfoncer)* to plunge, to thrust; **p. la main dans l'eau** to plunge one's hand into the water; **il plongea la main dans sa poche** he thrust his hand deep into his pocket; **elle lui plongea un couteau entre les épaules** she thrust a knife between his/her shoulder blades; **plongez les crustacés dans l'eau bouillante** plunge the shellfish into a pan of boiling water
  2 *(mettre)* to plunge; **la panne a plongé la pièce dans l'obscurité** the power failure plunged the room into darkness; **la pièce fut plongée dans l'obscurité** the room was plunged into darkness; **p. son regard** *ou* **ses regards dans** to look deep *or* deeply into; **p. qn dans l'embarras** to put sb in a difficult spot; **la remarque nous plongea tous dans la consternation** the remark appalled us all; **être plongé dans** to be deep in; **j'étais plongé dans mes pensées/comptes** I was deep in thought/in my accounts; **être plongé dans le désespoir** to be deep in despair; **je suis plongé dans Proust pour l'instant** at the moment I'm completely immersed in Proust; **il est plongé dans ses dossiers** he's engrossed in his files; **plongé dans un sommeil profond, il ne nous a pas entendus** as he was sound asleep, he didn't hear us
  ▶ **se plonger** VPR **se p. dans** *(bain)* to sink into;

(études, travail) to throw oneself into; *(livre)* to bury oneself in

plongeur, -euse [plɔ̃ʒœr, -øz] NM,F **1** *Sport* diver; **p. sous-marin** skin *or* scuba diver **2** *(dans un café) Br* washer-up, *Am* dishwasher

　NM *(oiseau) Br* diver, *Am* loon

plot [plo] NM **1** *Élec* contact; *(dans un commutateur)* contact block **2** *(bille de bois)* block; *Suisse* **p. de boucherie** butcher's block **3** *Sport* block **4** *Suisse (billot)* (woodchopping) block **5** *Suisse (bille)* length of tree trunk; *(sciée)* plank **6** *Suisse (parpaing) Br* breeze block, *Am* cinder block **7** *Suisse (cube de jeu d'enfant)* (building) block

plouc [pluk] NM **1** *Fam Péj* yokel, peasant, *Am* hick; **qu'est-ce qu'il fait p.!** he's so uncouth!▪; **son chapeau fait p.** he/she looks like a complete yokel in that hat **2** *Fam Arg mil Br* squaddie, *Am* grunt

plouf [pluf] ONOMAT splash!; **elle a fait p. dans l'eau** she went splash into the water

ploutocrate [plutɔkrat] NMF plutocrat

ploutocratie [plutɔkrasi] NF plutocracy

ploutocratique [plutɔkratik] ADJ plutocratic

ployable [plwajabl] ADJ *Littéraire* pliable, flexible

ployer [13] [plwaje] VT **1** *Littéraire (courber)* to bend, to bow; **le vent ploie la cime des arbres** the wind bends the tops of the trees

　2 *(fléchir)* to bend, to flex; **p. les genoux** to bend one's knees; *Fig* to toe the line, to submit

　VI *Littéraire* **1** *(arbre)* to bend; *(étagère, poutre)* to sag; **les étagères ploient sous le poids des livres** the shelves are sagging under the weight of the books; **ses jambes ployèrent sous lui** his legs gave way beneath him

　2 *Fig* **p. sous le poids des ans** to be weighed down by age; **p. sous le joug** to bend beneath the yoke, to be subjugated

PLS [peɛlɛs] NF *Méd (abrév* **position latérale de sécurité)** recovery position

PLU [ply] NM *(abrév* **plan local d'urbanisme)** = local town planning scheme

plu [ply] PP **1** *voir* **plaire 2** *voir* **pleuvoir**

pluché, -e [plyʃe] = **peluché**

plucher [3] [plyʃe] = **pelucher**

pluches [plyʃ] NFPL *Fam* **1** *(épluchage)* peeling▪; **faire les p.** to peel the veggies *or Br* veg; **je suis de p.** *(gén)* I'm peeling the veggies *or Br* veg; *(soldat)* I'm on spud-bashing (duty) **2** *(épluchures)* (vegetable) peelings▪

plucheux, -euse [plyʃø, -øz] = **pelucheux**

plug [plœg] = **plogue**

plug-and-play [plœgɛ̃dplɛ] *Ordinat* ADJ INV plug-and-play

　NM plug-and-play

plugiciel [plyʒisjɛl] NM *Can Ordinat* plug-in

pluie [plɥi] NF **1** *Météo* rain; **le temps est à la p.** it looks like rain; **sous la p.** in the rain; **sous une p. diluvienne** in the pouring rain; **p. battante** driving rain; **p. torrentielle** torrential rain; **(petite) p. fine** drizzle; *Écol* **pluies acides** acid rain; **ennuyeux comme la p.** deadly boring; **triste comme la p.** terribly sad; *Fig* **faire la p. et le beau temps** to rule the roost; **parler de la p. et du beau temps** to talk about this and that; *Prov* **après la p., le beau temps** it'll all be alright in the end; *Prov* **petite p. abat grand vent** a soft answer turneth away wrath

　2 *(retombée)* shower; **une p. de cendres s'échappa du volcan** the volcano sent out a shower of ashes; **une p. d'étoiles filantes** a meteor shower

　3 *(série → de coups, de balles, de pierres)* hail, shower; *(→ d'injures, de compliments)* stream

　4 *très Fam (pratique sexuelle)* **p. d'or** golden showers

　▫ **en pluie** ADV **les cendres tombaient en p. sur la ville** ashes rained *or* showered down on the town; **verser la farine en p. dans le lait** sprinkle the flour into the milk

plumage [plymaʒ] NM plumage, feathers

plumaison [plymɛzɔ̃] NF plucking

plumard [plymar] NM *Fam* bed▪, sack; **aller au p.** to hit the hay *or* sack

plumasserie [plymasri] NF feather trade

plumassier, -ère [plymasje, -ɛr] NM,F *(artisan)* feather dresser, plumassier; *(commerçant)* feather dealer, plumassier

plum-cake [plumkɛk, plœmkɛk] *(pl* **plum-cakes)** NM fruit cake

plume¹ [plym] NF **1** *(d'oiseau)* feather; **un édredon de p.** *ou* **plumes** a feather quilt; **une couette en p.** *ou* **plumes d'oie** a goose-feather quilt *or Br* duvet; *Fam* **j'y ai laissé des plumes** I didn't come out of it unscathed; *Fig Hum* **perdre ses plumes** to go thin on top, to go bald; *Fam* **voler dans les plumes à qn** to go for sb, to let fly at sb; *Littéraire* **passer une** *ou* **la p. par le bec à qn** to frustrate sb's hopes, to thwart sb

　2 *(pour écrire)* quill; *(de stylo)* nib; **dessiner à la p.** to draw in pen and ink; **je prends la p. pour te dire que...** I take up my pen to tell you that...; **je passe la p. à ton frère pour qu'il te donne tous les détails** I'll hand over to your brother who'll give you all the details; *Ironique* **j'ai pris ma plus belle p. pour écrire aux Réclamations/ à la Direction du personnel** I wrote the complaints/the personnel department a very nice letter; **c'est un critique à la p. acérée** he's a scathing critic; **les idées se pressent sous sa p.** he/she can't write his ideas down quickly enough, his/her ideas are coming thick and fast; **p. d'oie** goose quill; **laisser aller** *ou* **courir sa p.** to write as the ideas come; **avoir la p. facile** to have a gift for writing; **vivre de sa p.** to make one's living by writing, to live by one's pen

　3 *(écrivain)* pen

　4 *Méd* **p. à vaccin** vaccine point

　5 *(d'un mollusque)* pen; **p. de mer** sea pen

　6 *Vulg (fellation)* blow-job; **tailler une p. à qn** to give sb a blow-job, to go down on sb

　▫ **à plumes** ADJ **1** *Orn* feathered, *Spéc* pennaceous

　　2 *(vêtement)* (decorated) with feathers

　▫ **en plumes** ADJ feather *(avant n)*, feathered

plume² [plym] = **plumard**

plumeau, -x [plymo] NM feather duster

plume-fontaine [plymfɔ̃tɛn] *(pl* **plumes-fontaines)** NM *Can Joual* fountain pen

plumer [3] [plyme] VT **1** *(oiseau)* to pluck **2** *Fam (escroquer)* to fleece

plumet [plymɛ] NM plume

plumeté, -e [plymte] ADJ **1** *Vieilli (ornement)* feather-like **2** *Hér* plumetty

plumetis [plymti] NM **1** *(broderie)* **(broderie au) p.** raised satin stitch; **collant (à) p.** dotted tights **2** *Tex* Swiss muslin

plumeur, -euse¹ [plymœr, -øz] NM,F *(personne)* (poultry) plucker

plumeux, -euse² [plymø, -øz] ADJ *Littéraire* feathery

　▫ **plumeuse** NF *(machine)* plucking machine

plumier [plymje] NM pencil box *or* case

plumitif [plymitif] NM **1** *Péj (employé)* pen pusher **2** *Péj (journaliste)* hack; *(écrivain)* bad writer▪ **3** *Jur (registre)* (written) court record, court minute-book

plum-pudding [plumpudiŋ] *(pl* **plum-puddings)** NM Christmas pudding, plum pudding

plumule [plymyl] NF *Orn & Bot* plumule

plupart [plypar] **la plupart** NF most; **quelques-uns sont partis mais la p. ont attendu** some left but most (of them) waited

　▫ **la plupart de** PRÉP most (of); **la p. des enfants** *(du monde)* the majority of *or* most children; *(d'un groupe)* the majority *or* most of the children; **la p. des chanteurs étaient Anglais** most of the singers were English, the singers were mostly English; **la p. d'entre eux** most of them, the majority of them; **la p. du temps** *(d'habitude)* most of the time; *(en général)* in most cases; **dans la p. des cas** in the majority of *or* in most cases

　▫ **pour la plupart** ADV mostly, for the most part; **les clients sont pour la p. satisfaits** the customers are mostly satisfied *or* for the most part satisfied; **ils te croient? – oui, pour la p.** do they believe you? – most of them do *or* for the most part, yes

plural, -e, -aux, -ales [plyral, -o] ADJ plural; **vote p.** plural voting

pluralisme [plyralism] NM pluralism

pluraliste [plyralist] ADJ pluralist, pluralistic

　NMF pluralist

pluralité [plyralite] NF plurality

pluriannuel, -elle [plyrianɥɛl] ADJ **1** *Jur* running over several years **2** *Bot (plante)* perennial

pluricausal, -e, -als *ou* **-aux, -ales** [plyrikozal, -o] ADJ pluricausal

pluricellulaire [plyriselylɛr] ADJ *Biol* multicellular

pluridimensionnel, -elle [plyridimɑ̃sjɔnɛl] ADJ multidimensional

pluridisciplinaire [plyridisiplinɛr] ADJ multidisciplinary, joint *(avant n)*; **cursus p.** joint *or* interdisciplinary course

pluridisciplinarité [plyridisiplinarite] NF **la p. de notre formation** the interdisciplinary nature of our training programme; **nous encourageons la p. dans les études universitaires** we encourage students to take up a range of subjects

pluriel, -elle [plyrjɛl] ADJ **1** *Gram* plural **2** *(diversifié)* diverse, multifarious; **une société plurielle** a pluralist society

　NM plural; **la troisième personne du p.** the third person plural; **au p.** in the plural; **mettre au p.** to put in *or* into the plural; **le p. de majesté** the royal "we"

pluriethnique [plyriɛtnik] ADJ multiethnic

plurihebdomadaire [plyriɛbdɔmadɛr] ADJ published several times weekly

　NM = publication appearing several times weekly

plurilatéral, -e, -aux, -ales [plyrilateral, -o] ADJ multilateral

plurilingue [plyrilɛ̃g] ADJ multilingual, polyglot

plurilinguisme [plyrilɛ̃gwism] NM multilingualism

plurinational, -e, -aux, -ales [plyrinasjɔnal, -o] ADJ multinational

plurinominal, -e, -aux, -ales [plyrinɔminal, -o] *voir* **scrutin**

pluripartisme [plyripartism] NM *Pol* pluralist (party) *or* multiparty system

pluripartite [plyripartit] ADJ *Pol* pluralist, multiparty

pluriséculaire [plyrisekylɛr] ADJ lasting several centuries

plurivalent, -e [plyrivalɑ̃, -ɑ̃t] ADJ multivalent, polyvalent

plurivoque [plyrivɔk] ADJ equivocal, ambiguous

PLUS

ADV	more **A** ▪ most **B** ▪ not any more **C1**
	▪ no more **C2**
CONJ	plus
NM	plus sign **1** ▪ plus **2**

ADV [ply] **A.** *COMPARATIF DE SUPÉRIORITÉ* **1** *(suivi d'un adverbe, d'un adjectif)* more; **viens p. souvent** *(do)* come more often; **p. tôt** earlier; **p. tard** later; **c'est p. loin** it's further *or* farther; **maniez-le p. doucement** handle it more gently *or* with more care; **c'est p. court/petit** it's shorter/smaller; **sois p. modeste** be more modest; **elle est p. intéressante/sophistiquée** she's more interesting/sophisticated; **tu es p. patient que moi** you're more patient than I am *or* than me; **c'est p. fatigant qu'on ne le croit** it's more tiring than it seems; **c'est p. rouge qu'orange** it's red rather than *or* it's more red than orange; **elle est p. réservée que timide** she's reserved rather than shy; **c'est p. que gênant** it's embarrassing, to say the least; **on a obtenu des résultats p. qu'encourageants** our results were more than encouraging; **elle a eu le prix mais elle n'en est pas p. fière pour ça** she got the award, but it didn't make her any prouder for all that; **je veux la même, en p. large** I want the same, only bigger; **c'est sa mère mais en p. mince** she looks exactly like her mother, only slimmer; **bien p. beau** much more handsome; **bien p. gros** much fatter; **encore p. beau** more handsome still, even more handsome; **ça ira infiniment p. vite** it'll be infinitely faster; **il est autrement p. calme que son père** he's certainly much calmer than his father; **cinq fois p. cher** five times dearer *or* as dear *or* more expensive; **deux fois p. cher** twice as expensive; **il l'a fait deux fois p. vite (qu'elle)** he did it twice as quickly (as she did)

　2 *(avec un verbe)* more; **j'apprécie p. son frère** I like his/her brother more *or* better; **je m'intéresse à la question p. que tu ne penses** I'm more interested in the question than you think; **je ne peux vous en dire p.** I can't tell you any

more; **la verte coûtait p.** the green one was more expensive

3 *(avec un nom)* **cela représente p. qu'une simple victoire** it means more than just a victory; **c'est p. qu'un problème, c'est une catastrophe!** it's more than just a problem, it's a disaster!

B. *SUPERLATIF DE SUPÉRIORITÉ* **1** *(suivi d'un adverbe, d'un adjectif)* most; **le p. loin** the furthest *or* farthest; **la montagne la p. haute** the highest mountain; **sur la branche la p. haute** on the topmost *or* highest branch; **l'homme le p. riche du monde** the richest man in the world, the world's richest man; **j'ai répondu le p. gentiment que j'ai pu** I answered as kindly as I could; **j'y vais le p. rarement possible** I go there as seldom as possible; **le p. souvent** most of the time; **le p. rouge/laid** the reddest/ugliest; **la p. amusante** the most amusing one; **tu es le p. gentil de tous** you're the kindest of all; **le festival le p. populaire de France** the most popular festival in France; **un de ses tableaux les p. connus** one of his/her best-known paintings; **le p. gros des deux** the bigger of the two; **le p. gros des trois** the biggest of the three; **c'est ce qu'il y a de p. original dans sa collection d'été** it's the most original feature of his/her summer collection; **c'est en hiver que les fleurs sont le p. chères** in winter, flowers are at their dearest *or* most expensive; **choisis les fruits les p. mûrs possible** select the ripest possible fruit; **faites au p. vite** do it the quickest possible way *or* as quickly as possible; **aller au p. pressé** *ou* **urgent** to deal with the most urgent priority first

2 *(précédé d'un verbe)* most; **c'est moi qui travaille le p.** I'm the one who works most *or* the hardest; **dans le groupe, c'est lui qui y croyait le p.** of all the group, he was the one who believed in it most; **ce qui me tourmente le p.** what worries me (the) most; **faites-en le p. possible** do as much as you can

C. *ADVERBE DE NÉGATION* **1** *(avec "ne")* **je n'y retournerai p.** I won't go back there any more; **je ne m'en souviens p.** I don't remember (any more); **je ne les vois p.** I don't see them any more, *Sout* I no longer see them

2 *(tour elliptique)* **p. de** no more; **p. de glace pour moi, merci** no more ice cream for me, thanks; **p. de tergiversations!** let's not shilly-shally any longer!; **p. un mot!** not another word!

ADJ [plys] *Scol* **B p.** B plus; *Chim* **H p.** H plus

CONJ [plys] **1** *Math* plus; **3 p. 3 égale 6** 3 plus 3 is *or* makes 6; **p. 4 moins p. 3 égale p. 1** plus 4 minus plus 3 is *or* makes plus 1; **il fait p. 5°** it's 5° above freezing, it's plus 5°

2 *(en sus de)* plus; **le transport, p. le logement, p. la nourriture, ça revient cher** travel, plus *or* and accommodation, plus *or* then food, (all) work out quite expensive; **ça fait 1000 euros, p. la TVA** it's 1,000 euros plus VAT; **p. le fait que...** plus *or* together with the fact that...

NM [plys] **1** *Math* plus (sign); **mets un p. avant le chiffre 4** put a plus sign in front of the figure 4

2 *(avantage, atout)* plus, bonus, asset; **la connaissance de l'anglais est toujours un p.** knowledge of English is always a plus; **la proximité de la gare est un p.** the closeness of the station is an advantage *or* a plus (factor)

❑ **au plus ADV** *(au maximum)* at the most *or* outside; **il a au p. 20 ans** he's 20 at the most, he can't be more than 20; **ça coûtera au p. 50 euros** it'll cost a maximum of 50 euros *or* 50 euros at most; **il y a 15 km au p.** it's 15 km at the outside

❑ **de plus ADV 1** *(en supplément)* extra, another, more; **mets deux couverts de p.** lay two extra *or* more places; **raison de p. pour y aller** all the more reason for going; **je ne veux rien de p.** I don't want anything more; **tu n'auras rien de p.** you'll have nothing more; **il est content, que te faut-il de p.?** he's happy, what more do you want?; **un mot/une minute de p. et je m'en allais** another word/minute and I would have left; **10 euros de p. ou de moins, quelle différence?** 10 euros either way, what difference does it make?

2 *(en trop)* too many; **en recomptant, je trouve 30 points de p.** when I add it up again, I get 30 points too many

3 *(en outre)* furthermore, what's more, moreover; **elle fait mal son travail et de p. elle prend trop cher** she doesn't do her work properly, and what's more her fees are too high; **de p., il m'a menti** what's more, he lied to me

❑ **de plus en plus ADV 1** *(suivi d'un adjectif)* more and more, increasingly; *(suivi d'un adverbe)* more and more; **de p. en p. souvent** more and more often; **de p. en p. dangereux** more and more *or* increasingly dangerous; **ça devient de p. en p. facile/compliqué** it's getting easier and easier/more and more complicated; **le ciel devenait de p. en p. sombre** the sky was growing darker and darker

2 *(précédé d'un verbe)* **les prix augmentent de p. en p.** prices are increasing all the time

❑ **de plus en plus de DÉT** *(suivi d'un nom dénombrable)* more and more, a growing number of; *(suivi d'un nom non dénombrable)* more and more; **de p. en p. de gens** more and more people, an increasing number of people; **il y a de p. en p. de demande pour ce produit** demand for this product is increasing, there is more and more demand for this product; **elle a de p. en p. de fièvre** her temperature is rising

❑ **des plus ADV** most; **son attitude est des p. compréhensibles** his/her attitude is most *or* quite understandable; **un juge des p. impartiaux** a most unbiased judge

❑ **en plus ADV 1** *(en supplément)* extra *(avant n)*; **c'est le même appartement avec un balcon en p.** it's the same *Br* flat *or Am* apartment with a balcony as well; **les boissons sont en p.** drinks are extra, you pay extra for the drinks; **ça fait 45 minutes de transport en p.** it adds 45 minutes to the journey; **10 euros en p. ou en moins, quelle différence?** 10 euros either way, what difference does it make?

2 *(en trop)* spare; **tu n'as pas des tickets en p.?** do you have any spare tickets?; **j'ai une carte en p.** *(à la fin du jeu)* I've got one card left over; *(en distribuant)* I've got one card too many

3 *(en cadeau)* as well, on top of that; **et vous emportez une bouteille de champagne en p.!** and you get a bottle of champagne as well *or* on top of that *or* into the bargain!

4 *(en outre)* further, furthermore, what's more; **elle a une excellente technique et en p., elle a de la force** her technique's first-class and she's got strength; *Fam* **mais c'est qu'elle est méchante en p.!** and she's nasty to cap it all *or* to boot!; **et elle m'avait menti, en p.!** not only that but she'd lied to me (as well)!; **c'est lui qui s'est trompé, et en p., il se plaint!** he makes the mistake and, to crown it all, complains about it!

5 *(d'ailleurs)* besides, what's more, moreover; **je ne tiens pas à le faire et, en p., je n'ai pas le temps** I'm not too keen on doing it, and besides *or* what's more, I've no time

❑ **en plus de PRÉP** *(en supplément de)* besides, on top of, in addition to; **en p. du squash, elle fait du tennis** besides (playing) squash, she plays tennis

❑ **et plus ADV** over; **deux ans et p.** over two years; **45 kilos et p.** over 45 kilos, 45 odd kilos; **les gens de 30 ans et p.** people aged 30 and over; **des chemisiers à 35 euros et p.** blouses at 35 euros and over *or* more

❑ **ni plus ni moins ADV** no more no less, that's all; **je te donne une livre, ni p. ni moins** I'll give you one pound, no more no less; **tu t'es trompé, ni p. ni moins** you were mistaken, that's all

❑ **non plus ADV moi non p. je n'irai pas** I won't go either; **je n'en ai pas moi non p.** I haven't got any either; **je ne sais pas – moi non p.!** I don't know – neither do I *or* nor do I *or* me neither!

❑ **on ne peut plus ADV je suis on ne peut p. désolé de vous voir partir** I'm ever so sorry you're leaving; **c'est on ne peut p. compliqué** it couldn't be more complicated; **il était on ne peut p. heureux de te voir** he couldn't have been more delighted to see you; **des gens on ne peut p. charmants** the most charming people you could ever wish to meet

❑ **plus de DÉT 1** *(comparatif, suivi d'un nom)* more; **nous voulons p. d'autonomie!** we want more autonomy!; **tu as fait p. de fautes que moi** you made more mistakes than I did *or* than me; **je n'ai pas p. de courage qu'elle** I'm no braver than she is *or* her; **c'est p. de l'insouciance que de l'incompétence** it's more (a matter of) carelessness than incompetence; **elle a p. de facilité que son frère pour apprendre** she's better at learning than her brother

2 *(comparatif, suivi d'un nombre)* more than, over; **il y a p. de 15 ans de cela** it's more than 15 years ago now; **elle a bien p. de 40 ans** she's well over 40; **elle roulait à p. de 150 km/h** she was driving at more than 150 km/h *or* doing over 150 km/h; *Fam* **vous avez un peu p. du kilo** you've got *or* that's a bit over one kilo; **il y en a p. d'un qui s'est plaint** more than one person complained; **il est p. de 5 heures** it's past 5 o'clock *or* after 5

3 *(superlatif, suivi d'un nom)* **le p. de** (the) most; **c'est ce qui m'a fait le p. de peine** that's what hurt me (the) most; **c'est notre équipe qui a le p. de points** our team has (the) most points; **celui qui a le p. de chances de réussir** the one (who's the) most likely to succeed; **le p. possible de cerises** as many cherries as possible; **le p. d'argent possible** as much money as possible; **les p. de 20 ans** people over 20, the over-20s; **les p. de 10 tonnes** vehicles over 10 tons

❑ **plus... moins** the more... the less; **p. il vieillit, moins il a envie de sortir** the older he gets, the less he feels like going out; **p. ça va, moins je la comprends** I understand her less and less (as time goes on)

❑ **plus ou moins ADV** more or less; **c'est p. ou moins cher, selon les endroits** prices vary according to where you are; **j'ai p. ou moins compris ce qu'elle disait** I understood more or less what she was talking about; **je ne l'ai que p. ou moins cru** I only half believed him; **tous ces partis, c'est p. ou moins la même chose** all these parties amount to more or less the same thing; **c'était p. ou moins prévu** it was more or less expected

❑ **plus... plus** the more... the more; **p. je réfléchis, p. je me dis que...** the more I think (about it), the more I'm convinced that...; **p. j'attendais, p. j'étais en colère** the longer I waited, the angrier I got; **p. j'avançais, p. la forêt s'épaississait** the further *or* the deeper I went into the forest, the thicker it got; **p. ça va, p. il est agressif** he's getting more and more aggressive (all the time); **p. ça va, p. je me demande si...** the longer it goes on, the more I wonder if...

❑ **qui plus est ADV** what's *or* what is more

❑ **sans plus ADV** nothing more; **c'était bien, sans p.** it was nice, but nothing more; **une fille assez sympathique, sans p.** quite a nice girl, but nothing more *or* no more than that

❑ **tout au plus ADV** at the most; **c'est une mauvaise grippe, tout au p.** it's a bad case of flu, at the most

---

plusieurs [plyzjœr] **ADJ INDÉFINI** several; **il y a eu p. témoins** there were several witnesses; **en p. endroits** in several places; **p. fois, à p. reprises** several times

PRON INDÉFINI 1 *(désignant des personnes)* several people; **se mettre à p. pour faire qch** to do sth as a group; **ils s'y sont mis à p.** several people got together; **vous venez à p.?** will there be several of you coming?; **nous serons p. à la réunion** there will be several of us at the meeting; **p. (d'entre eux) ont refusé** several of them refused; **p. parmi les enfants avaient envie de rentrer** several of the children wanted to go back

2 *(reprenant le substantif)* several; **il n'y a pas une seule solution mais p.** there is no single solution, but several; **n'utilisez pas une seule couleur, mais p.** don't use just one colour, but several; **il ne sera pas le seul intervenant, il y en aura p.** he won't be the only contributor, there will be several of them

plus-produit [plysprɔdɥi] *(pl* **plus-produits***)* **NM** *Mktg* competitive advantage

plus-que-parfait [plyskəparfɛ] *(pl* **plus-que-parfaits***)* **NM** pluperfect, past perfect; **p. de**

l'indicatif/du subjonctif pluperfect indicative/ subjunctive

plus-value [plyvaly] (*pl* **plus-values**) **NF 1** *(augmentation de la valeur)* increase (in value), appreciation **2** *(excédent d'impôts)* (tax) budget surplus **3** *(surcoût)* surplus value **4** *(somme ajoutée au salaire)* bonus **5** *(bénéfice)* capital gain, profit; **réaliser une p. sur la vente d'un produit** to make a profit on the sale of a product; **p. sur titres** paper profit

Plutarque [plytark] **NPR** Plutarch

plut *etc* **1** *voir* **plaire 2** *voir* **pleuvoir**

Pluton [plytɔ̃] **NPR** *Myth* Pluto
  NF *Astron* Pluto

pluton [plytɔ̃] **NM** *Géol* pluton

plutonien, -enne [plytɔnjɛ̃, -ɛn] **ADJ 1** *Myth* Plutonian, Plutonic **2** *Vieilli Géol* plutonic

plutonique [plytɔnik] **ADJ** *Géol* plutonic

plutonisme [plytɔnism] **NM** *Géol (théorie, formation de roches)* plutonism

plutonium [plytɔnjɔm] **NM** *Chim* plutonium

plutôt [plyto] **ADV 1** *(de préférence)* rather; *(à la place)* instead; **p. mourir!** I'd rather die!; **mets p. mon manteau, tu auras plus chaud** put my coat on instead, you'll be warmer; **n'y va pas en voiture, prends p. le train** don't go by car, take the train instead; **demande p. à un spécialiste** you'd better ask a specialist; **ne te plains pas, travaille p.!** don't complain, just work!; **p. que** rather than, instead of; **p. que de travailler, je vais aller faire des courses** I'm going to do some shopping instead of working; **p. que de faire les choses en cachette** rather than do things in secret; **p. la mort que l'esclavage!** death before slavery!, rather *or* sooner death than slavery!; **p. mourir que de céder!** I'd rather die than give in!

2 *(plus précisément)* rather; **la situation n'est pas désespérée, disons p. qu'elle est délicate** the situation is not hopeless, let's say rather that it is delicate; **ce n'était pas une maison de campagne, mais p. un manoir** it wasn't a country house, it was more of a country manor; **elle n'est pas bête, p. étourdie** she's not so much stupid as absent-minded, she's not stupid, just absent-minded; **elle a l'air sévère ou p. austère** she looks severe, or rather austere; **elle le méprise p. qu'elle ne le hait** she doesn't so much hate as despise him

3 *(assez, passablement)* rather, quite; **il s'est montré p. aimable** he was rather nice, he behaved rather nicely; **elle est p. jolie** she's rather pretty; **sa vie est p. monotone** his/her life is rather dull; **comment va-t-il? – p. bien** how is he? – quite well; **c'est p. mieux que la dernière fois** it's rather better than last time; **c'est p. une bonne idée, tu ne trouves pas?** it's rather a good idea, isn't it?

4 *(en intensif) Fam* **il est p. collant, ce type!** that guy's a bit of a leech!; **il est idiot, ce film! – p., oui!** it's stupid, this film! – you can say that again *or* you're telling me!

pluvial, -e, -aux, -ales [plyvjal, -o] **ADJ** pluvial; **eau pluviale** rainwater

pluvian [plyvjɑ̃] **NM** *Orn* crocodile bird, Egyptian plover

pluvier [plyvje] **NM** *Orn* plover; **p. argenté** grey plover; **grand p. à collier** ringed plover; **p. doré** golden plover; **p. doré américain** American golden plover; **p. guignard** dotterel

pluvieux, -euse [plyvjø, -øz] **ADJ** *(temps, journée)* rainy, wet; *(climat)* wet, damp

pluviner [3] [plyvine] = **pleuvasser**

pluviomètre [plyvjɔmɛtr] **NM** rain gauge, *Spéc* pluviometer

pluviométrie [plyvjɔmetri] **NF** pluviometry

pluviométrique [plyvjɔmetrik] **ADJ** pluviometric

pluviôse [plyvjoz] **NM** = 5th month of the French Revolutionary calendar (from 20/21/22 January to 18/19/20 February)

pluviosité [plyvjozite] **NF** (average) rainfall

PLV [peɛlve] **NF** *Mktg (abrév* **publicité sur le lieu de vente**) point-of-sale promotion

Plymouth [plimus] **NM** Plymouth

PM [peɛm] **NF** *Mil* **1** *(abrév* **préparation militaire**) pre-call-up training **2** *(abrév* **police militaire**) MP
  NM *(abrév* **pistolet-mitrailleur**) sub-machine-gun

PMA [peɛma] **NF** *(abrév* **procréation médicalement assistée**) assisted conception
  NMPL *(abrév* **pays les moins avancés**) LDCs

PmaC *Écon (abrév écrite* **propension marginale à consommer**) APC

PmaE *Écon (abrév écrite* **propension marginale à épargner**) APS

PME [peɛmə] **NF INV** *(abrév* **petite et moyenne entreprise**) small business; **les P.** small and medium-sized enterprises
  NM *(abrév* **porte-monnaie électronique**) electronic wallet, electronic purse

PMI [peɛmi] **NF INV** *(abrév* **petite et moyenne industrie**) small industry; **les P.** small and medium-sized industries
  NF *(abrév* **protection maternelle et infantile**) mother and child care *(including antenatal and postnatal clinics and family planning)*

PMO [peɛmo] **NFPL** *(abrév* **pièces et main-d'œuvre**) parts and labour

PmoC *Écon (abrév écrite* **propension moyenne à consommer**) APC

PmoE *Écon (abrév écrite* **propension moyenne à épargner**) APS

PMU [peɛmy] **NM** *(abrév* **Pari mutuel urbain**) = French betting authority, *Br* ≃ tote, *Am* ≃ parimutuel

PN *(abrév écrite* **Parc National**) National Park

PNB [peɛnbe] **NM** *(abrév* **produit national brut**) GNP

pneu [pnø] **NM 1** *Aut* tyre; **avoir un p. à plat/crevé** to have a flat (tyre)/a puncture; **p. à carcasse biaise** *ou* **croisée** crossply tyre; **p. à carcasse radiale, p. radial** radial (ply) tyre; **p. à chambre à air** tubetype; **p. sans chambre à air** tubeless *or* solid tyre; **p. clouté** spiked tyre; *Can* **p. d'hiver** winter tyre; **p. neige** snow tyre; **p. pluie** wet-weather tyre; *Can* **p. quatre-saisons** all-season *or* all-weather tyre; **p. taille basse** low-profile tyre; **p. tout-temps** all-weather tyre; **p. tout-terrain** all-terrain tyre

2 *Fam (lettre)* message■ *(sent through a compressed air tube system)*, pneumatic (dispatch)■

pneumallergène [pnømalɛrʒɛn] **NM** respiratory allergen

pneumatique [pnømatik] **ADJ 1** *(gonflable)* inflatable, blow-up *(avant n)* **2** *Phys & Rel* pneumatic
  NM 1 *Aut* tyre **2** *(lettre)* message *(sent through a compressed air tube system)*, pneumatic (dispatch)

pneumatophore [pnømatɔfɔr] *Bot & Zool* **ADJ** pneumatophorous
  NM pneumatophore

pneumo [pnømo] **NM** *Méd (traitement)* artificial pneumothorax

pneumococcie [pnømɔkɔksi] **NF** *Méd* pneumococcia

pneumoconiose [pnømɔkɔnjoz] **NF** *Méd* pneumoconiosis

pneumocoque [pnømɔkɔk] **NM** *Biol & Méd* pneumococcus

pneumocystose [pnømɔsistoz] **NF** *Méd* pneumonitis, pneumocystis pneumonia

pneumogastrique [pnømɔgastrik] *Anat* **ADJ M** pneumogastric, vagal
  NM vagus nerve

pneumologie [pnømɔlɔʒi] **NF** *Méd* pneumology

pneumologue [pnømɔlɔg] **NMF** *Méd* lung specialist

pneumonectomie [pnømɔnɛktɔmi] **NF** *Méd* pneumectomy, pneumonectomy

pneumonie [pnømɔni] **NF** *Méd* pneumonia; **p. atypique** atypical pneumonia

pneumonique [pnømɔnik] **ADJ** *Méd* pneumonic

pneumopathie [pnømɔpati] **NF** *Méd* lung disease

pneumopéritoine [pnømɔperitwan] **NM** *Anat* pneumoperitoneum

pneumo-phtisiologue [pnømɔftizjɔlɔg] *(pl* **pneumo-phtisiologues**) **NMF** *Méd* lung specialist

pneumopleurésie [pnømɔplœrezi] **NF** *Méd* pleuropneumonia

pneumothorax [pnømɔtɔraks] **NM** *Méd* pneumothorax

PNN [peɛnɛn] **NM** *Écon (abrév* **produit national net**) NNP

PNUD, Pnud [pnyd] **NM** *(abrév* **Programme des Nations unies pour le développement**) UNDP

PNUE, Pnue [pny] **NM** *(abrév* **Programme des Nations unies pour l'environnement**) UNEP

PO 1 *Rad (abrév écrite* **petites ondes**) MW **2** *Com (abrév* **par ordre**) by order

Pô [po] **NM le Pô** the (River) Po

pochade [pɔʃad] **NF 1** *(peinture)* (quick) sketch, thumbnail sketch **2** *(écrit)* sketch

pochard, -e [pɔʃar, -ard] **NM,F** *Fam* alky, boozer

pocharder [3] [pɔʃarde] **se pocharder VPR** *Fam Br* to get legless, *Am* to tie one on

poche [pɔʃ] **NF 1** *(d'un vêtement)* pocket; *(d'un sac)* pocket, pouch; **je n'ai même pas cinq euros en p.** I don't even have five euros on me; **p. intérieure** inside (breast) pocket; **p. plaquée** patch pocket; **p. (de) poitrine** breast pocket; **p. à rabat** flapped pocket; **p. revolver** hip pocket; **avoir les poches percées** to be a spendthrift; **j'ai les poches percées** money just burns a hole in my pocket; *Fam* **se remplir les poches, s'en mettre plein les poches,** *très Fam* **s'en foutre plein les poches** to rake it in; *Fam* **faire les poches à qn** to go through *or* to rifle (through) sb's pockets; *Fam* **j'en ai été de ma p.** I was out of pocket; *Fam* **c'est dans la p.!** it's in the bag!; *Fam* **il a mis tout le monde dans sa p.** he twisted everyone round his little finger, he took everyone in; *Fam* **mets ça dans ta p. (et ton mouchoir par-dessus)!** put that in your pipe and smoke it!; *Fam* **ne pas avoir les yeux dans sa p.** to have eyes in the back of one's head

2 *(boursouflure)* bag; **avoir des poches sous les yeux** to have bags under one's eyes; **faire des poches aux genoux/coudes** to go baggy at the knees/elbows

3 *(amas)* pocket; **p. d'air** air pocket; **p. d'eau/de gaz** pocket of water/gas; *Mines* **p. de grisou** pocket of firedamp

4 *Méd* sac; **p. des eaux** (sac of) waters, amniotic sac; **la p. des eaux s'est rompue** her waters broke; **p. de pus** pus sac

5 *Zool (d'un kangourou)* pouch; *(d'un poulpe)* sac; *(d'un oiseau)* crop; **p. marsupiale** marsupium

6 *(contenant)* **p. plastique** plastic bag; *Culin* **p. à douille** piping bag

7 *Métal* **p. de coulée** foundry ladle

8 *(secteur)* pocket; **p. de résistance/pauvreté** pocket of resistance/deprivation

9 *Suisse (louche)* ladle
  NM *(livre)* paperback (book)
  ADJ *Can Fam (nul)* lousy, *Br* rubbish; **c'est assez p. comme émission** it's a pretty lousy *or Br* rubbish programme

❑ **de poche ADJ** *(collection, édition)* pocket *(avant n)*; *(cuirassé, théâtre)* pocket *(avant n)*, miniature *(avant n)*

❑ **en poche ADV 1** *(avec soi → argent)* on me/you/*etc*; *(→ diplôme)* under one's belt; **elle est repartie, contrat en p.** she left with the contract signed and sealed
  2 *(livre)* in paperback; **il est sorti en p.** it's come out in paperback

poché, -e [pɔʃe] **ADJ** *(œuf)* poached **2** *(meurtri)* **avoir un œil p.** to have a black eye

pocher [3] [pɔʃe] **VT 1** *Culin (œuf, poisson)* to poach **2** *(meurtrir)* **p. un œil à qn** to give sb a black eye **3** *Beaux-Arts (peinture)* to dash off
  VI *(vêtement)* to go baggy

pochetée [pɔʃte] **NF** *Fam Vieilli* nitwit, dumbo

pochetron [pɔʃtrɔ̃] **NM** *Fam* alky, boozer

pochette [pɔʃɛt] **NF 1** *(d'un vêtement)* (breast) pocket handkerchief **2** *(sac → de femme)* clutch bag, (small) handbag; *(→ d'homme)* clutch bag **3** *(sachet → pour documents)* (plastic) wallet, (plastic) document holder; *(→ d'allumettes)* book **4** *(d'un disque)* sleeve, cover **5** *Mus (violon)* kit (violin)

pochette-surprise [pɔʃɛtsyrpriz] *(pl* **pochettes-surprises**) **NF** *Br* lucky bag, *Am* surprise pack; *Fam Hum* **tu l'as trouvé dans une p., ton permis de conduire?, tu l'as eu dans une p., ton permis?** did you get your *Br* driving licence *or Am* driver's license in a cornflakes packet *or* in a Christmas cracker?

pocheuse [pɔʃøz] **NF** egg poacher

pochoir [pɔʃwar] **NM 1** *(plaque évidée)* stencil; **décor au p.** stencils, stencilled motifs *or* patterns; **faire une frise au p.** to make a wall frieze

with stencils, to stencil a wall frieze **2** *Tex* printing block

pochon [pɔʃɔ̃] NM **1** *(poche)* belt pouch; *(sachet)* (small) bag **2** *(dans l'est de la France et le canton de Genève) (louche)* ladle

pochothèque [pɔʃɔtɛk] NF *(librairie)* paperback *Br* bookshop *or Am* bookstore; *(rayon)* paperback section

pochouse [pɔʃuz] NF *Culin* fish stew *(with white wine and onions)*

podagre [pɔdagr] *Arch Méd* ADJ gouty
NMF gout sufferer
NF *(goutte)* gout

podcast [pɔdkast] NM podcast

podcasting [pɔdkastiŋ] NM podcasting

podestat [pɔdɛsta] NM *Hist* Podesta

podiatre [pɔdjatr] NMF *Can Br* chiropodist, *esp Am* podiatrist

podie [pɔdi] NM *Zool* podium

podium [pɔdjɔm] NM **1** *(plate-forme)* podium; *Sport* **monter sur le p.** to mount the podium; *(à la télévision, dans un jeu)* to step onto the platform **2** *Archit* podium **3** *Zool* podium

podologie [pɔdɔlɔʒi] NF *Br* chiropody, *esp Am* podiatry

podologue [pɔdɔlɔg] NMF *Br* chiropodist, *esp Am* podiatrist

podomètre [pɔdɔmɛtr] NM pedometer

podure [pɔdyr] NF *Entom* springtail

podzol [pɔdzɔl] NM *Géol* podzol

podzolique [pɔdzɔlik] ADJ *Géol* podzolic

podzolisation [pɔdzɔlizasjɔ̃] NF *Géol* podzolization

pœcile [pesil] NM *Antiq* painted portico, poecile

pœcilogale [pesilɔgal] NM *Zool* African striped weasel

pœcilotherme [pesilɔtɛrm], **pœcilothermie** [pesilɔtɛrmi] = **poïkilotherme, poïkilothermie**

poêle [pwal] NM **1** *(chauffage)* stove; *(en céramique)* furnace; **p. à accumulation** storage heater; **p. à bois** wood *or* wood-burning stove; **p. à mazout** oil *or* oil-fired stove **2** *(drap)* pall; **tenir les cordons du p.** to be a pallbearer
NF *(ustensile)* **p. (à frire)** *Br* frying pan, *Am* fry pan; **p. à marrons** pan for toasting chestnuts *(with holes in the bottom)*; **passer qch à la p.** to fry sth

poêlé, -e [pwale] ADJ pan-fried
❏ **poêlée** NF **1** *(contenu d'une poêle)* **une p. de pommes de terre** a *Br* frying pan *or Am* fry pan full of potatoes **2** *Culin* **p. de champignons** pan-fried mushrooms

poêler [pwale] VT **1** *(frire)* to fry **2** *(braiser)* to braise *(in a shallow pan)*

poêlon [pwalɔ̃] NM casserole

poème [pɔɛm] NM **1** *Littérature* poem; **un p. en prose** a prose poem; **un p. en vers** a poem **2** *Mus* **p. symphonique** symphonic *or* tone poem **3** *Fam (locutions)* **ç'a été (tout) un p., pour venir de l'aéroport jusqu'ici!** what a to-do or business getting here from the airport!; **ta fille, c'est (tout) un p.!** your daughter's really something else!

poésie [pɔezi] NF **1** *(genre)* poetry; **écrire de la p.** to write poems *or* poetry **2** *(poème)* poem; **des poésies pour enfants** poems *or* verse for children **3** *Littéraire (charme)* poetry; **la p. du vieux Montmartre** the poetic charm of old Montmartre **4** *(sensibilité)* **tu manques de p.** you don't have any soul

poète [pɔɛt] NM

> Note that it is no longer considered a mistake to feminize this word and to say **une poète** but some French speakers nonetheless regard this form as unacceptable, especially in France. See also the entry **féminisation**.

(auteur) poet; **il est p. à ses heures** he writes the occasional poem; **femme p.** (woman) poet; **comme l'a dit le p.** in the words of the poet
ADJ *(allure, air)* poetic, of a poet

poétereau, -x [pɔetro] NM poetaster

poétesse [pɔetɛs] NF poetess

poétique [pɔetik] ADJ poetic
NF poetics *(singulier)*

poétiquement [pɔetikmã] ADV poetically

poétisation [pɔetizasjɔ̃] NF *Littéraire* poetization, poeticization

---

poétiser [pɔetize] VT *Littéraire* to poetize, to poeticize

pogne [pɔɲ] NF *Fam* hand∎, mitt; *Vulg* **se faire une p.** to jerk off, *Br* to have a wank

pogner [pɔɲe] VT *Can* **1** *(empoigner)* to grab; *Fig* **son histoire m'a pogné au cœur** his/her story went straight to my heart
2 *Fam (caresser)* to grope, to feel up
VI *Can Vulg (se caresser)* to grope each other, to feel each other up; *(avoir des relations sexuelles)* to screw, *Br* to have it off
▶**se pogner** VPR *Vulg* to jerk off, *Br* to have a wank; *Can* **se p. le cul** *(se caresser mutuellement)* to grope each other, to feel each other up; *(avoir des relations sexuelles)* to screw, *Br* to have it off

pognon [pɔɲɔ̃] NM *Fam* cash, *Br* dosh, *Am* bucks; **ils ont plein de p.** they're rolling *Br* in it *or Am* in dough

pogo [pogo] NM *Fam* pogo *(dance)*

pogoter [pɔgɔte] VI *Fam* to pogo

pogrom, pogrome [pɔgrɔm] NM pogrom

poids [pwa] NM **1** *(gén)* & *Phys* weight; **son p. est de 52 kilos** he/she weighs 52 kilos; **faire attention à** *ou* **surveiller son p.** to watch one's weight; **prendre/perdre du p.** to gain/to lose weight; **reprendre du p.** to put weight back on *or* on again; **je suis tombé de tout mon p. sur le bras** I fell on my arm with all my weight; **p. brut/net** gross/net weight; *Rail* **p. adhérent** adhesive weight; **p. atomique** atomic weight; **p. en charge** (fully) loaded weight; **p. mort** dead weight; **p. net à l'emballage** net weight when packed; **p. net embarqué** loaded net weight; *Com* **p. rendu** delivered weight; **p. spécifique** unit weight; *Com* **p. de taxation** chargeable weight; **p. utile** *Aviat* useful load; *Astron* payload; **p. à vide** unladen weight, tare; *Com* **faire bon p.** to give good weight; **il y a un kilo de cerises bon p.** there's a little more than *or* just over a kilo of cherries; **faire le p.** *Com* to make up the weight; *Fig* to hold one's own; **il ne fait pas le p. face aux spécialistes** he's no match for *or* not in the same league as the experts; **j'ai peur de ne pas faire le p.** I'm afraid of being out of my depth
2 *(objet → gén, d'une horloge)* weight; **avoir un p. sur l'estomac** to feel bloated; *Fam* **les p. et mesures** weights and measures
3 *(charge pénible)* burden; **le p. des impôts** the burden of taxation; **le p. de ses soucis** the burden of his/her worries; **ça m'a enlevé un p.** it's taken a weight off my mind
4 *Sport (lancer)* shotputting, shot; *(instrument)* shot; *(aux courses)* weight; **p. et haltères** weightlifting; *Boxe* **p. coq** bantamweight; *Boxe* **p. léger** lightweight; *Boxe* **p. lourd** heavyweight; *Fig* **un p. lourd de la politique** a political heavyweight; *Boxe* **p. mi-lourd** light heavyweight; *Boxe* **p. mi-moyen** light middleweight; *Boxe* **p. mouche** flyweight; *Boxe* **p. moyen** middleweight; *Boxe* **p. plume** featherweight; *Fig* **c'est un p. plume, cette petite!** that little one weighs next to nothing!
5 *(importance)* influence, weight; **son avis a du p. auprès du reste du groupe** his/her opinion carries weight with the rest of the group; **donner du p. à un argument** to lend weight to an argument
❏ **au poids** ADV *(vendre)* by weight
❏ **au poids de** PRÉP by the weight of; **au p. de l'or** by the weight of gold
❏ **de poids** ADJ *(alibi, argument)* weighty; **un homme de p.** an influential man
❏ **sous le poids de** PRÉP **1** *(sous la masse de)* under the weight of; **elle avançait, courbée sous le p. d'un gros sac** she walked along, bowed down by *or* bent under the weight of a heavy bag
2 *Fig* under the burden of; **écrasé sous le p. des responsabilités** weighed down by responsibilities
❏ **poids lourd** NM **1** *Transp* heavy (goods) vehicle *or Br* lorry *or Am* truck
2 *voir* **poids** NM **4**
❏ **poids mort** NM *Tech* & *Fig* dead weight; *Mktg (produit)* dog, dodo

poignait *voir* **poindre**

poignant, -e [pwaɲã, -ãt] ADJ heartrending, poignant; **de façon poignante** poignantly; **le**

---

souvenir p. de leur dernière rencontre the poignant memory of the last time they met

poignard [pwaɲar] NM dagger; **coup de p.** stab; **donner un coup de p. à qn** to stab sb; **recevoir un coup de p.** to get stabbed; *Fig* **un coup de p. dans le dos** a stab in the back

poignarder [pwaɲarde] VT to stab, to knife; *aussi Fig* **p. qn dans le dos** to stab sb in the back; **se faire p.** to be knifed *or* stabbed; **c'est comme si on me poignardait** *(douleur, angoisse)* it feels as if I were being stabbed

poigne [pwaɲ] NF grip; **avoir de la p.** to have a strong grip; *Fig* to rule with a firm hand
❏ **à poigne** ADJ firm, authoritarian, iron-handed

poignée [pwaɲe] NF **1** *(contenu → gén)* handful; *(→ de billets de banque)* fistful; **une p. de riz** a handful of rice
2 *(petit nombre)* handful; **une p. de manifestants** a handful of demonstrators
3 *(pour saisir → gén)* handle; *(→ d'un sabre, d'une épée)* hilt; *(→ d'un pistolet)* grip; **la p. d'un tiroir/d'une valise** a drawer/suitcase handle; *Cin* & *TV* **p. de panoramique** panning handle; **p. de porte** door handle; **c'est la p. qui a lâché** the handle broke
❏ **à poignées** ADV **1** *(en quantité)* **prendre des bonbons à poignées** to take handfuls of sweets
2 *(avec prodigalité)* hand over fist; **dépenser l'argent à poignées** to spend money hand over fist
❏ **par poignées** ADV in handfuls; **je perds mes cheveux par poignées** my hair's coming out in handfuls
❏ **poignée de main** NF handshake; **distribuer des poignées de main à la foule** to shake hands with people in the crowd; **donner une p. de main à qn** to shake hands with sb, to shake sb's hand
❏ **poignées d'amour** NFPL *Fam* love handles

'**Pour une poignée de dollars**' *Leone* 'A Fistful of Dollars'

poigner [pwaɲe] VT *Can (empoigner)* to grab, to grasp; *Fig* **son histoire m'a poigné au cœur** his/her story went straight to my heart
❏ **poigner dans** VT IND *Belg* to grab, to grasp

poignet [pwaɲɛ] NM **1** *Anat* wrist **2** *(extrémité d'une manche)* cuff; *(bande de tissu)* wristband

poïkilotherme [pɔikilɔtɛrm] *Physiol* ADJ poikilothermic
NM poikilotherm

poïkilothermie [pɔikilɔtɛrmi] NF *Physiol* poikilothermia, poikilothermy

poil [pwal] NM **1** *(d'une personne, d'un animal)* hair; **le lavabo était plein de poils** the washbasin was full of hairs; **avoir le p. dur** *ou* **dru** *(barbe)* to have a rough beard; *Fam* **je n'ai plus un p. de sec** *(mouillé)* I'm soaked through; *(en sueur)* I'm sweating like a pig; *(mort de peur)* I'm in a cold sweat; *Fam* **il n'a plus un p. sur le caillou** he's bald as an egg *or Br* a coot; **p. pubien** pubic hair; *Fam* **avoir un p. dans la main** to be bone-idle; **avoir du p. au menton** to have grown up; **même pas encore de p. au menton et monsieur se permet d'avoir un avis!** hardly a hair on his lip and he thinks he can have an opinion!; *Fam* **avoir du p. aux pattes** to have hairy legs; *Fam* **être de bon/mauvais p.** to be in a good/bad mood∎; *Fam* **reprendre du p. de la bête** *(guérir)* to perk up again; *(reprendre des forces)* to regain some strength for a fresh

onslaught■ ; *Fam* **tomber sur le p. à qn** to jump on sb, to go for sb; **d'un seul coup, elle m'est tombée sur le p.** she came down on me like a ton of bricks; **p. follet** down

2 *Fam (infime quantité)* **pas un p. de** not an ounce of; **il n'a pas un p. d'intégrité** he doesn't have one ounce *or* a shred of integrity; **il n'y a pas un p. de vrai dans ce qu'il dit** there's not an ounce of truth in what he says; **à un p. près, il était tué** he missed being killed by a hair's breadth, he came within an inch of his life; **à un p. près il ratait son examen** he very nearly failed his exam■ ; **nous avons payé la même chose à un p. près** we paid more or less the same■ ; *Fam* **un p. plus haut/moins vite** a fraction *or* a touch higher/slower

3 *(pelage → long)* hair, coat; *(→ court)* coat; **il a le p. luisant** his coat is shiny; **chien à p. ras/long** smooth-haired/long-haired dog; **manteau en p. de chameau** camel-hair coat; **en poils de sanglier** made of bristle; *Can Vieilli* **manteau/chapeau de poils** fur coat/hat

4 *(d'une brosse)* bristle; *(d'un pinceau)* hair, bristle; *(d'un tapis)* pile; *(d'un pull angora)* down

5 *Bot* hair; **poils absorbants** root hairs; **p. à gratter** itching powder

6 *Fam* **torse p.** *(homme)* barechested■ ; *(femme)* topless■

□ **à poil** *Fam* **ADJ** stark naked, *Br* starkers **ADV** stark naked, *Br* starkers; **se mettre à p.** to strip (off); **aller se baigner à p.** to go skinny-dipping; **à p., à p.!** *(huées)* get 'em off!

□ **au poil** *Fam* **ADJ** terrific, great; **être au (petit) p.** to be just the ticket; **il est au p., ton copain!** your friend's terrific! **ADV** terrifically; **ils avaient tout préparé au p.** they'd done everything to a T; **tu peux venir samedi, au p.!** you can come on Saturday, great!; **tomber au p.** to arrive just at the right moment■

□ **au petit poil, au quart de poil** **ADV** *Fam* terrifically; **ça a marché au petit p.** it's all gone exactly according to plan; **rentrer dans qch au quart de p.** to fit into sth perfectly■ ; **démarrer au quart de p.** to start right away or first time■

□ **de tout poil, de tous poils** **ADJ** *Fam Hum* of all kinds■ ; **voleurs et escrocs de tout p.** all manner of thieves and crooks

poilant, -e [pwalɑ̃, -ɑ̃t] **ADJ** *Fam* hysterical, side-splitting

poil de carotte [pwaldəkarɔt] **ADJ INV** *(cheveux)* red; *(enfant)* red-haired; **il est p.** he's red-haired, he has carroty-red hair

□ **Poil de carotte** **NPR** = the red-headed boy in Jules Renard's novel of the same name, which recounts an unhappy childhood

poiler [3] [pwale] **se poiler** **VPR** *Fam (rire)* to kill oneself (laughing); *(s'amuser)* to have a ball

poilu, -e [pwaly] **ADJ** hairy; **p. comme un singe** hairy as an ape

NM *Hist* poilu; **les poilus de 14 *ou* de 1914** (French) soldiers in the 1914–18 war

poinçon [pwɛ̃sɔ̃] **NM** **1** *(marque)* hallmark; **marquer une bague au p.** to hallmark a ring **2** *(de brodeuse, de couturière)* bodkin; *(de cordonnier)* awl, bradawl; *(de graveur)* stylus; *(de sculpteur)* chisel **3** *Typ* (matrice) punch **4** *Métal* die, stamp **5** *Menuis* point, awl **6** *(pièce de charpente)* *Br* king post, *Am* joggle post

poinçonnage [pwɛ̃sɔnaʒ], **poinçonnement** [pwɛ̃sɔnmɑ̃] **NM** **1** *(d'un ticket)* punching **2** *(en joaillerie)* hallmarking **3** *Métal* stamping, die-stamping **4** *Typ* drive, strike

poinçonner [3] [pwɛ̃sɔne] **VT** **1** *(ticket)* to punch **2** *(en joaillerie)* to hallmark **3** *Métal* to stamp

poinçonneur, -euse [pwɛ̃sɔnœr, -øz] **NM,F** **1** *(employé)* ticket puncher **2** *Métal* punching machine operator

□ **poinçonneuse** **NF** *(machine)* punching machine

poindre [82] [pwɛ̃dr] *Littéraire* **VI** **1** *(lumière, jour)* to break; *(plante)* to appear, to come out; **dès que le jour poindra** as soon as dawn breaks, at daybreak

2 *(mouvement, idée)* **alors je vis p. un sourire sur son visage** then I saw the beginnings of a smile on his/her face; **une idée commençait à p. dans son esprit** an idea was growing in his/her mind

VT **1** *(tourmenter)* to stab; **ce souvenir le poignait parfois** the memory would stab him painfully from time to time

2 *(stimuler)* to prick, to spur on; **le désir de vérité et de justice ne cessait de la p.** she was forever spurred on by the desire for truth and justice

poing [pwɛ̃] **NM** fist; **le p. levé** with one's fist raised; **lever le p.** to raise one's fist; **montrer le p. à qn** to shake one's fist at sb; **les poings sur les hanches** with arms akimbo; **se battre à poings nus** to fight with one's bare fists; **donner *ou* taper du p. sur la table** to bang one's fist on *or* to thump the table; *Fam* **mettre son p. dans la figure à qn** to punch■ *or* to smack sb in the face; *très Fam* **tu veux (prendre) mon p. dans la gueule?** fancy a knuckle sandwich *or Br* a bunch of fives, do you?; **ils sont entrés, revolvers/armes au p.** they came in, guns/arms at the ready; **gros comme le p.** (as) big as your fist; *Suisse* **faire le p. dans sa poche** to swallow one's anger

poinsettia [pwɛ̃setja] **NM** *Bot* poinsettia

point[1] [pwɛ̃] *voir* **poindre**

POINT[2] [pwɛ̃]

> point **1, 3, 6, 7, 9–12, 18** ■ dot **1, 3, 16, 17** ■ spot **1, 2, 7** ■ blob **2** ■ full stop, period **3** ■ position **4** ■ place **7** ■ twinge **8** ■ stitch **8, 14, 15**

NM **1** *(marque)* point, dot, spot; *(sur un dé, un domino)* pip, spot; **un corsage à petits points bleus** a blouse with blue polka dots; **elle a des petits points blancs dans la gorge** she's got small white spots in her throat; **je t'ai fait un p. sur la carte pour indiquer où c'est** I put a dot on the map to show you where it is; **la voiture n'était plus qu'un p. à l'horizon** the car was now no more than a speck on the horizon; **p. lumineux** spot *or* point of light; *Cin & TV* **points de repère au sol** location marks

2 *(petite quantité)* spot, dab, blob; **un p. de soudure** a spot *or* blob of solder; **mets-y un p. de colle** put a dab of glue on it; **p. de rouille** speck *or* spot of rust

3 *(symbole graphique → en fin de phrase)* *Br* full stop, *Am* period; *(→ sur un i ou un j)* dot; *(→ en morse, en musique)* dot; *Math* point; **deux points, trois traits** two dots, three dashes; **a p. b** a point b; *Fam Fig* **p. barre** end of story; **tu rentres à minuit ou bien tu n'y vas pas, p. barre** you'll be home by midnight or you're not going at all and that's it, end of story; **p. d'exclamation** *Br* exclamation mark, *Am* exclamation point; **p. d'insertion** insertion point; *aussi Fig* **p. d'interrogation** *Br* question mark, *Am* query mark; **p. typographique** point; **points de conduite** (dot) leaders; **points de suspension** ellipsis, suspension points; **p. final** full stop, *Am* period *(at the end of a piece of text)*; *Fig* **j'ai dit non, p. final *ou* un p. c'est tout!** I said no and that's that *or* that's final *or* there's an end to it!; **mettre un p. final à une discussion** to terminate a discussion, to bring a discussion to an end; **p., à la ligne!** new paragraph!; *Fig* **il a fait une bêtise, p. à la ligne!** he did something stupid, let's leave it at that!

4 *Aviat & Naut (position)* position; **donner/recevoir le p.** to give/to be given one's position; **porter le p. sur la carte** to mark one's position on the map; **p. estimé/observé** estimated/observed position; **p. fixe** run-up; *Naut* **faire le p.** to take a bearing, to plot one's position

5 *(bilan)* **faire le p.** to take stock (of the situation); **à 40 ans, on s'arrête et on fait le p.** when you reach 40, you stand back and take stock of your life; **on fera le p. vendredi** we'll get together on Friday and see how things are progressing; **et maintenant, le p. sur la circulation** and now, the latest traffic news; **nous ferons le p. sur les matches à Wimbledon à 11 heures** we'll bring you a round-up of play at Wimbledon at 11 o'clock

6 *Géom* point; **le p. B** point B; **par deux points distincts ne passe qu'une seule droite** only one line passes through two distinct points; **p. commun à deux lignes** crossing point of two lines; **p. d'intersection/de tangence** intersection/tangential point; **p. double** double point

7 *(endroit)* point, spot, place; **en plusieurs points de la planète** in different places *or* spots on the planet; *Com* **p. d'achat** point of purchase; *Anat* **p. aveugle** blind spot; **p. de contrôle** checkpoint; **p. de convergence** focus point; **quel est le p. culminant des Alpes?** what is the highest point of the Alps?; *Com* **p. de distribution** distribution outlet; *Anat* **points lacrymaux** puncta lacrimalia; **p. névralgique** *Méd* nerve centre; *Fig* sensitive spot; **p. de rencontre** meeting point; *Banque* **p. retrait** *Br* cashpoint, *Am* ATM; *Com* **p. de vente** point of sale; *Com* **p. de vente au détail** retail outlet; *Com* **p. de vente électronique** electronic point of sale; *Mktg* **p. de vente multimarque** multibrand store; **disponible dans votre p. de vente habituel** available at your local stockist

8 *(douleur)* twinge, sharp pain; *Méd* pressure point; **j'ai un p. au poumon** I can feel a twinge (of pain) in my chest; **p. de côté** stitch

9 *(moment, stade)* point, stage; **à ce p. de la discussion** at this point in the discussion; **à ce p. de nos recherches** at this point *or* stage in our research; **nous nous retrouvons au même p. qu'avant** we're back to where we started; **les pourparlers en sont toujours au même p.** the negotiations haven't got any further; **p. de bascule** tipping point; *Fin* **p. critique** break-even point; *Mktg* **p. mort** break-even point; *Mktg* **p. prix** price point

10 *(degré)* point; **porter qch à son plus haut p.** to carry sth to extremes; **si tu savais à quel p. je te méprise!** if you only knew how much I despise you!; *Fam* **il est radin, mais à un p.!** you wouldn't believe how tight-fisted he is!; *Chim* **p. d'éclair** flashpoint; *Chim* **p. de fusion/liquéfaction** melting/liquefaction point; *aussi Fig* **p. de saturation** saturation point

11 *(élément → d'un texte, d'une théorie)* point; *(→ d'un raisonnement)* point, item; *(→ d'une description)* feature, trait; **il reste quelques points obscurs dans votre thèse** a few points in your thesis still need clarifying; **le second p. à l'ordre du jour** the second item on the agenda; **un programme social en trois points** a three-point social programme; **voici un p. d'histoire que je souhaiterais éclaircir** I'd like to make clear what happened at that particular point in history; **c'est au moins un p. d'acquis** we all agree on at least one point; **p. d'entente/de désaccord** point of agreement/of disagreement; **p. commun** common feature; **nous n'avons aucun p. commun** we have nothing in common; *Jur* **un p. de droit** a point of law

12 *(unité de valeur → dans un sondage, à la Bourse)* point; *(→ de retraite)* unit; *(→ du salaire de base)* (grading) point; *(→ sur une carte de fidélité)* point; *Scol* point, *Br* mark; *Sport & (dans un jeu)* point; **sa cote de popularité a gagné/perdu trois points** his/her popularity rating has gone up/down by three points; **il me manquait 12 points pour avoir l'examen** I was 12 marks short of passing the exam; **une faute d'orthographe, c'est quatre points de moins** four marks are taken off for each spelling mistake; **la dame rapporte six points** the queen's worth six points; **avoir plus de points que qn** to outpoint sb, to have more points than sb; *Boxe* **battu aux points** beaten on points; **elle est à deux points du set** she's two points from winning the set; **faire le p.** *(le gagner)* to win the point; *Scol* **bon p.** *(image)* = card or cardboard picture given to schoolchildren as a reward, ≃ gold star; *(appréciation)* mark *(for good behaviour)*; *Fig Hum* **un bon p. pour toi!** you get a brownie point!, good for *or Br* on you!; *Scol* **mauvais p.** black mark *(against someone's name)*; *Fig Hum* **un mauvais p. pour toi!** go to the back of the class!; **points d'annonce** points in hand; **points cadeau** points *(awarded when making a purchase and collected by the customer to receive a discount off subsequent purchases)*; *aussi Fig* **marquer un p.** to score a point; **rendre des points à qn** to be way above sb; **points de retraite** = units used

by the French social security system to calculate an individual's pension

13 *Astron* **p. gamma** *ou* **vernal** First Point of Aries, vernal equinox

14 *Couture* stitch; **faire un p. à** to put a stitch *or* a few stitches in; **bâtir à grands points** to tack; **coudre à grands points** to sew using a long stitch; **p. de couture/crochet/tricot** sewing/crochet/knitting stitch; **p. arrière** backstitch; **p. de devant** front stitch; **p. de jersey** stocking stitch; **p. mousse** moss stitch; **p. de riz** moss stitch; **tapisserie au petit p.** petit point tapestry; *Fig* **c'est un travail au petit p.** it's a highly demanding piece of work

15 *Méd* **p. de suture** stitch; **il a fallu lui faire dix points de suture au visage** he/she had to have ten stitches in his/her face

16 *Ordinat (unité graphique)* dot; *(emplacement)* **p. d'accès/de retour** entry/reentry point; **p. de branchement** branch point; **p. de sonde** probing point

17 *Tél* dot

18 *Beaux-Arts & (en joaillerie)* point

19 *Presse* **le P.** = French weekly news magazine

20 *Cin & TV* **p. diffus** soft focus; **p. d'entrée** *(sur bande, film)* in-point

▫ **à ce point, à un tel point** ADV *(tellement)* so, that; **ton travail est dur à ce p.?** is your job so (very) *or* that hard?; **comment peux-tu être maladroit/paresseux à un tel p.?** how can you be so clumsy/lazy?; **j'en ai tellement assez que je vais démissionner – à ce p.?** I'm so fed up that I'm going to resign – that bad, is it?

▫ **à ce point que, à (un) tel point que** CONJ so much so that, to such a point that; **il faisait très chaud, à tel p. que plusieurs personnes se sont évanouies** it was very hot, so much so that several people fainted; **les choses en étaient arrivées à un tel p. que...** things had reached such a pitch that...; **elle est déprimée, à ce p. qu'elle ne veut plus voir personne** she's so depressed that she won't see anyone any more

▫ **à point** ADJ *(steak)* medium; *(rôti)* done to a turn; *(fromage)* ripe, just right; *(poire)* just *or* nicely ripe; *Fam Fig* **ton bonhomme est à p., tu n'as plus qu'à enregistrer ses aveux** your man's nice and ready now, all you've got to do is get the confession down on tape ADV **1** *Culin* **le gâteau est cuit à p.** the cake is just cooked through

2 *(au bon moment)* **tomber à p.** *(personne)* to come (just) at the right time; *(arrivée, décision)* to be very timely

▫ **à point nommé** ADV **faire qch à p. nommé** to do sth (just) at the right time *or* on time; **arriver à p. nommé** to arrive (just) at the right moment *or* when needed, to arrive in the nick of time

▫ **au plus haut point** ADV *(énervé, généreux, irrespectueux)* extremely, most; *(méfiant)* highly, extremely; **je le respecte/déteste au plus haut p.** I couldn't respect/hate him more; **elle m'inquiète au plus haut p.** I'm really worried about her

▫ **au point** ADJ *Phot* in focus; *(moteur)* tuned; *(machine)* in perfect running order; *(technique)* perfected; *(discours, plaidoyer)* finalized; *(spectacle, artiste)* ready; **ton revers n'est pas encore au p.** your backhand isn't good enough *or* up to scratch yet; **le son/l'image n'est pas au p.** the sound/the image isn't right; **quand ma technique sera au p.** when my technique has been refined *or* polished; **mes élèves sont maintenant au p. pour l'examen** my students are now ready for the exam ADV **mettre au p.** *(texte à imprimer)* to edit; *(discours, projet, rapport)* to finalize, to put the finishing touches to; *(spectacle)* to perfect; *(moteur)* to tune; *(appareil photo)* to (bring into) focus; *(affaire)* to settle, to finalize; **mettre les choses au p.** to put the record straight; **mettons les choses au p.: je refuse de travailler le dimanche** let's get things straight: I refuse to work Sundays; **après cette discussion, j'ai tenu à mettre les choses au p.** following that discussion, I insisted on putting the record straight; **tu devrais mettre les choses au p. avec lui** you should sort things out between you

▫ **au point de** PRÉP **méticuleux au p. d'en être agaçant** meticulous to the point of being exasperating; **il n'est pas stupide au p. de le leur répéter** he's not so stupid as to tell them

▫ **au point du jour** ADV *Littéraire* at dawn *or* daybreak

▫ **au point où** CONJ **nous sommes arrivés au p. où...** we've reached the point *or* stage where...; **au p. où j'en suis, autant que je continue** having got this far, I might as well carry on; **au p. où en sont les choses** as things stand, the way things are now

▫ **au point que** CONJ so much that, so... that; **il était très effrayé, au p. qu'il a essayé de se sauver** he was so frightened that he tried to run away; **ils maltraitaient leur enfant, au p. qu'on a dû le leur retirer** they mistreated their child so much that he had to be taken away from them

▫ **de point en point** ADV point by point, punctiliously, to the letter; **le programme a été exécuté de p. en p.** the programme was followed point by point

▫ **point d'ancrage** NM **1** *Aut* seat-belt anchorage **2** *Fig* cornerstone

▫ **point d'appui** NM **1** *(d'un levier)* fulcrum **2** *Mil* strongpoint **3** *Fig (soutien)* support

▫ **point chaud** NM **1** *Géog aussi Fig* hot spot **2** *Ordinat* hotspot

▫ **point de chute** NM **1** *(d'un objet)* point of impact **2** *Fig* **j'ai un p. de chute à Milan** I have somewhere to stay in Milan

▫ **point culminant** NM *Astron* zenith; *Géog* peak, summit, highest point; *Fig* acme, apex; **les investissements sont à leur p. culminant** investment has reached a peak

▫ **point de départ** NM starting point; *aussi Fig* **nous voilà revenus au p. de départ** now we're back where we started

▫ **point faible** NM weak spot; **son p. faible, c'est sa susceptibilité** his/her touchiness is his/her weak spot *or* point

▫ **point fort** NM *(d'une personne, d'une entreprise)* strong point; *(d'un joueur de tennis)* best shot; **les coups francs/les pénalités ne sont pas son p. fort** he's/she's not very good at free kicks/penalties; **les maths n'ont jamais été mon p. fort** I was never any good at maths, maths was never my strong point

▫ **point mort** NM *Aut* neutral; **au p. mort** *Aut* in neutral; *Fig* at a standstill

▫ **point noir** NM **1** *Méd* blackhead **2** *(difficulté)* difficulty, headache; **un p. noir de la circulation** *(encombré)* a heavily congested area; *(dangereux)* an accident blackspot

▫ **point par point** ADV point by point

▫ **point sensible** NM **1** *(endroit douloureux)* tender *or* sore spot **2** *Mil* key *or* strategic target **3** *Fig* **toucher un p. sensible** *(chez quelqu'un)* to touch a sore point *or* on a sore spot; *(dans un problème)* to touch on a sensitive area

▫ **sur le point de** PRÉP **être sur le p. de faire qch** to be about to do *or* on the point of doing *or* on the verge of doing sth; **j'étais sur le p. de partir** I was about to *or* going to leave; **sur le p. de pleurer** on the verge of tears *or* of crying

---

point[3] [pwɛ̃] ADV *Arch ou Littéraire* **1** *(en corrélation avec "ne")* **je ne l'ai p. encore vu** I haven't seen him yet; **p. n'est besoin de** there's no need to; **p. n'était besoin de partir de si bonne heure** there was no need *or* it was unnecessary to leave so early

2 *(employé seul)* **du vin il y en avait, mais de champagne p.** there was wine, but no champagne *or* not a drop of champagne; **il eut beau chercher, p. de John** he searched in vain, John was nowhere to be found; **p. de démocratie sans liberté de critiquer** (there can be) no democracy without the freedom to criticize

3 *(en réponse négative)* **p. du tout!** not at all!, not in the least!; **cela vous dérange? – p. du tout!** do you mind? – not in the least!

pointage [pwɛ̃taʒ] NM **1** *(d'une liste)* ticking off *(UNCOUNT)*, checking (off) *(UNCOUNT)*; *(de votes)* counting **2** *(d'un fusil)* aiming; *(d'un télescope)* pointing, training **3** *(des ouvriers → système)* timekeeping; *(→ à l'arrivée)* clocking in *or* on; *(→ à la sortie)* clocking out *or* off **4** *Tech* tack welding

pointal, -aux [pwɛ̃tal, -o] NM *Tech* stay, strut, prop

point de vue [pwɛ̃dvy] *(pl* **points de vue***)* NM **1** *(panorama)* vista, view; **là-haut, le p. est magnifique** the view from up there is magnificent

2 *(opinion)* point of view, standpoint; **quel est ton p.?** what is your opinion?, where do you stand on this?; **du p. des prix, du p. prix** pricewise, as far as prices are concerned; **de ce p., il n'a pas tort** from that point of view *or* viewed in this light, he's right; **adopter un p. différent** to view things from a different angle

pointe [pwɛ̃t] NF **1** *(extrémité → gén)* point, pointed end, tip; *(→ d'un cheveu)* tip; *(→ d'une flèche)* tip, head; *(→ d'une chaussure)* toe; **la p. du sein** the nipple; **à la p. de l'épée** at the point of a sword; **mets-toi sur la p. des pieds** stand on tiptoe *or* on the tips of your toes; **elle traversa la pièce/monta l'escalier sur la p. des pieds** she tiptoed across the room/up the stairs; **allons jusqu'à la p. de l'île** let's go to the farthest point of the island; **p. d'asperge** asparagus tip; **p. feutre** fibre tip

2 *Géog* **p. (de terre)** headland, foreland

3 *Sport* spike

4 *(foulard)* headscarf *(folded so as to form a triangle)*; *(lange) Br* nappy, *Am* diaper

5 *Mil (avancée)* advanced party; *Fig* **faire** *ou* **pousser une p. jusqu'au village suivant** to push *or* to press on as far as the next village

6 *(accès)* peak, burst; **p. (de vitesse)** burst of speed; **faire une p. à plus de 200 km/h** to put on a burst of speed of over 200 km/h; **avec des pointes à 160 km/h** with a top speed of 160 km/h

7 *(moquerie)* barb, taunt; *(mot d'esprit)* witticism; **lancer des pointes à qn** to taunt sb

8 *(petite quantité → d'ail)* hint; *(→ d'ironie, de jalousie)* trace, hint, note; **il a une p. d'accent** he's got a slight accent; **il n'a pas une p. d'accent** he hasn't got the slightest trace of an accent

9 p. de lecture *(d'un tourne-disque)* stylus

10 *Beaux-Arts* **p. sèche** *(outil)* dry point; *(procédé)* dry-point (engraving); **compas à pointes sèches** (pair of) dividers

11 *(outil de maçon)* point

12 *Élec* surge; **pouvoir des pointes** point effect

13 *Ind (d'un tour)* (lathe) centre; *(d'une machine-outil)* cone

14 *(clou)* nail, sprig, brad

15 *Pêche* point

16 *Méd* **pointes de feu** ignipuncture

▫ **pointes** NFPL *(en danse)* points; **faire des pointes** to dance on points

▫ **à la pointe de** PRÉP to the forefront of; *aussi Fig* **à la p. du combat** in the front line of battle; **à la p. de l'actualité** right up to date; **à la p. du progrès** in the vanguard (of progress)

▫ **à la pointe du jour** ADV *Littéraire* at daybreak *or* dawn, at the break of day

▫ **de pointe** ADJ **1** *(puissance, période)* peak *(avant n)*; **heure de p.** rush hour; **vitesse de p.** maximum *or* top speed

2 *(secteur, industrie)* high-tech; *(technologie)* cutting-edge

▫ **en pointe** ADJ **1** *(menton)* pointed; *(décolleté)* plunging ADV **1** *(en forme de pointe)* to a point; **s'avancer en p.** to taper (to a point); **tailler en p.** *(barbe)* to shape to a point; *(diamant)* to cut to a point **2** *(à grande vitesse)* at top speed; *Fam* **je fais plus de 200 en p.** I can do over 200, *Br* I can do 200 plus top whack

pointé, -e [pwɛ̃te] ADJ *Mus* dotted

pointeau, -x [pwɛ̃to] NM **1** *Tech* centre punch; *(d'un carburateur)* needle **2** *(pour trouer)* punch **3** *(pour régler une ouverture)* nozzle valve **4** *(surveillant)* timekeeper

pointer[1] [pwɛ̃tœr] NM *(chien)* pointer

pointer[2] [3] [pwɛ̃te] VT **1** *(dresser)* **l'animal pointa les oreilles** the animal pricked up its ears; *Fig* **p. son nez** *ou* **sa tête quelque part** to show one's face somewhere

2 *(diriger → arme)* to aim (**sur** *ou* **vers** at); *(→ télescope)* to point (**sur** *ou* **vers** at), to train (**sur** *ou* **vers** on); *(→ spot, projecteur)* to train (**sur** *ou* **vers** on); *(→ doigt)* to point (**vers** at); *Ordinat (→ curseur)* to position (**sur** on); **p. un mot** to point to a word; **le mot pointé** the word where the cursor is

3 *(à la pétanque)* **p. une boule** to make a draw shot

4 (*marquer → liste*) to check (off), to tick off; (*votes*) to count; **p. la liste des participants** to check or to tick off the list of participants

5 (*contrôler → à l'arrivée*) to check in; (*→ à la sortie*) to check out

6 *Naut* (*carte marine*) to prick

VI 1 (*monter en pointe → jeune pousse*) to come up or through; **p. vers le ciel** (*arbre, oiseau*) to rise (up) towards the sky

2 (*faire saillie*) to stick or to jut out, to protrude; **ses seins pointaient sous son corsage** her nipples showed beneath her blouse

3 (*apparaître → aube, jour*) to be dawning; (*→ jalousie, remords*) to be breaking or seeping through; **j'ai vu une lueur d'effroi p. dans son regard** I saw fear flashing in his/her eyes

4 (*à la pétanque*) to draw (the jack)

5 (*ouvrier → en arrivant*) to clock in or on; (*→ en sortant*) to clock out or off; **p. à l'ANPE** ou **au chômage** to register as unemployed, *Br* to sign on

6 *Ordinat* **p. et cliquer** to point-and-click (**sur** on)

▸**se pointer VPR** *Fam* to show (up), to turn up; **il s'est pas pointé** he never showed; **alors, tu te pointes?** are you coming or aren't you?■

pointeur, -euse [pwɛ̃tœr, -øz] NM,F **1** (*surveillant*) timekeeper **2** *Sport* scorer, marker **3** (*à la pétanque*) drawer (of the jack)
   NM *Ordinat & Mil* pointer; **p. laser** laser pointer
   □ **pointeuse NF 1** (*machine-outil*) jig borer **2** (*horloge*) time clock

pointil [pwɛ̃til] = **pontil**

pointillage [pwɛ̃tijaʒ] NM **1** (*d'une surface*) stippling **2** (*d'une ligne*) marking out with dots, dotting

pointillé [pwɛ̃tije] NM **1** (*trait*) dotted line; **découper suivant le p.** cut along the dotted line
   2 (*technique de dessin*) stippling; **dessin au p.** stippled design
   □ **en pointillé ADJ les frontières sont en p. sur la carte** the frontiers are drawn as dotted lines on the map **ADV** *Fig* **une solution lui apparaissait en p.** he/she was beginning to see the outline of a solution; **on pouvait lire en p. des allusions à son passé glorieux** reading between the lines we saw certain allusions to his/her glorious past

pointiller [3] [pwɛ̃tije] VT **1** (*surface*) to stipple **2** (*ligne*) to dot, to mark with dots
   VI to draw in stipple

pointilleuse [pwɛ̃tijøz] *voir* **pointilleux**

pointilleusement [pwɛ̃tijøzmɑ̃] ADV fussily, fastidiously

pointilleux, -euse [pwɛ̃tijø, -øz] ADJ (*personne*) fussy, fastidious; (*commentaire*) nitpicking; **il est très p. sur l'horaire** he's very particular about or he's a stickler for time-keeping

pointillisme [pwɛ̃tijism] NM *Beaux-Arts* pointillism

pointilliste [pwɛ̃tijist] *Beaux-Arts* ADJ pointillist
   NMF pointillist

pointu, -e [pwɛ̃ty] ADJ **1** (*effilé*) sharp, pointed
   2 (*perspicace → esprit*) sharp, astute; (*→ étude*) in-depth, astute; **une lecture pointue de l'œuvre** an astute or perceptive interpretation of the work; **elle avait un esprit très p.** her mind was razor-sharp
   3 (*revêche → air, caractère*) querulous, petulant; **prendre un air p.** to bridle
   4 (*aigu → voix, ton*) shrill, sharp; **il avait une voix pointue** he had a shrill voice; **un accent p.** (*parisien*) a clipped Parisian accent
   5 (*spécialisé → formation, marché*) (very) narrowly specialized, narrowly targeted
   6 (*aux courses*) **arrivée pointue** bunched finish
   ADV **parler p.** (*en France*) = to talk in a clipped (Parisian) way; (*au Canada*) = to talk in a posh pseudo-French way

pointure [pwɛ̃tyr] NF **1** (*de chaussures*) size; **quelle est ta p.?** what size do you take? **2** *Fam Fig* (*personne remarquable en son genre*) **une (grosse) p.** a big name; **une (grosse) p. de la boxe** a big name in boxing

point-virgule [pwɛ̃virgyl] (*pl* **points-virgules**) NM semicolon

poire [pwar] NF **1** (*fruit*) pear; **nous en avons parlé entre la p. et le fromage** we talked idly about it

at the end of the meal; **en forme de p.** pear-shaped; *Belg* **p. de coing** quince; **p. conférence** conference pear; **p. Williams** Williams pear
   2 (*alcool*) pear brandy
   3 (*objet en forme de poire*) **p. en caoutchouc** rubber syringe; **p. électrique** (pear-shaped) switch; **p. à injections** douche; **p. à lavement** enema; **p. à poudre** powder horn or flask
   4 *Fam* (*visage*) face■ , mug; **prendre qch en pleine p.** to get smacked in the face with sth; **il s'est pris le ballon en pleine p.** the ball hit him right in the face■ or between the eyes; **il s'est pris la remarque en pleine p.** the remark hit him where it hurt
   5 *Fam* (*imbécile*) sucker, *Br* mug; **une bonne p.** a real sucker or *Br* mug; **tu es vraiment trop bonne p.** you're a real sucker or *Br* mug; **et moi, bonne p., j'ai accepté** and sucker or *Br* mug that I am, I accepted
   6 (*en joaillerie*) pear, pear-shaped jewel
   7 (*morceau de viande*) = pear-shaped end of the round of beef
   ADJ *Fam* **ce que tu peux être p.!** you're such a sucker or *Br* mug!
   □ **en poire ADJ** (*sein, perle*) pear-shaped
   □ **poire d'angoisse NF 1** *Hist* (iron) gag
   2 *Fig Littéraire* awful obligation to say nothing

poiré [pware] NM perry

poireau, -x [pwaro] NM **1** (*légume*) leek; *Fam* **faire le p.** to hang about or around **2** *Vulg* (*pénis*) dick, cock; **souffler dans le p. à qn** to give sb a blowjob

poireauter [3] [pwarote] VI *Fam* to hang about or around; **faire p. qn** to keep sb hanging about or around

poirée [pware] NF *Bot* white beet

poirier [pwarje] NM **1** *Bot* pear tree **2** *Menuis* pear, pearwood **3** *Sport* **faire le p.** to do a headstand

pois [pwa] NM **1** *Bot & Culin* pea; **petits p.** (green) peas, garden peas; (*extrafins*) petit pois; **p. cassé** split pea; **p. chiche** chickpea; **p. de senteur** sweet pea **2** (*motif*) (polka) dot, spot; **un corsage à p. blancs** a blouse with white polka dots or white spots

poiscaille [pwaskaj] NF *Fam* fish■

poise [pwaz] NM ou NF *Phys* poise

poison [pwazɔ̃] NM **1** (*substance*) poison; **ils avaient mis du p. dans son café** they had poisoned his/her coffee **2** *Fam* (*corvée*) drag, hassle **3** *Littéraire* (*vice*) poison; **le p. de l'oisiveté** the poison of idleness
   NMF (*enfant, personne insupportable*) pest

poissard, -e [pwasar, -ard] *Vieilli Péj* ADJ (*faubourien*) coarse, common, vulgar
   □ **poissarde NF** fishwife

poisse [pwas] NF *Fam* bad or rotten luck■ ; **quelle p.!** what rotten luck!; **avoir la p.** to be unlucky■ ; **porter la p. (à qn)** to bring (sb) bad luck

poisser [3] [pwase] VT **1** (*rendre poisseux*) **p. qch** to make sth sticky **2** *Fam* (*attraper*) to nail, to nab; **se faire p.** to get nabbed **3** (*enduire de poix*) to (cover with) pitch

poisseux, -euse [pwasø, -øz] ADJ sticky

poisson [pwasɔ̃] NM **1** (*animal*) fish; **attraper du p.** to catch fish; **p. d'eau douce/de mer** freshwater/saltwater fish; **p. cartilagineux** cartilaginous fish; **p. cavernicole** cave fish; **p. combattant** fighting fish; **poissons osseux** bony fish; **p. papillon** butterfly fish; **les poissons plats** flatfish; *Can* **petit p. des chenaux** tomcod; **p. porc-épic** porcupine fish; **p. rouge** goldfish; **p. volant** flying fish; **être comme un p. dans l'eau** to be in one's element; **être heureux comme un p. dans l'eau** to be as happy as a lark or *Br* as a sandboy or *Am* as a clam; *Fam* **engueuler qn comme du p. pourri** to call sb every name under the sun; *Prov* **petit p. deviendra grand** tall oaks from little acorns grow
   2 *Culin* fish; **en entrée, nous avons du p.** we have fish or a fish dish as a starter
   3 *Entom* **p. d'argent** silverfish
   □ **poisson d'avril NM 1** (*farce*) April fool; **p. d'avril!** April fool!
   2 (*papier découpé*) = cut-out paper fish placed on someone's back as a prank on 1 April
   □ **Poissons NMPL 1** *Astron* Pisces
   2 *Astrol* Pisces; **être Poissons** to be Pisces or a Piscean

Culture
POISSON D'AVRIL
In France and other French-speaking countries, on the first of April, children cut fish shapes out of paper and stick them on their unsuspecting classmates' backs and people play practical jokes on one another before crying out "Poisson d'avril!" ("April fool!").This custom is referred to in Quebec as "courir le poisson d'avril".

poisson-chat [pwasɔ̃ʃa] (*pl* **poissons-chats**) NM *Ich* catfish

poisson-coffre [pwasɔ̃kɔfr] (*pl* **poissons-coffres**) NM *Ich* boxfish, trunkfish, coffer fish

poisson-crapaud [pwasɔ̃krapo] (*pl* **poissons-crapauds**) NM *Ich* toadfish

poisson-épée [pwasɔ̃epe] (*pl* **poissons-épées**) NM *Ich* swordfish

poisson-globe [pwasɔ̃glɔb] (*pl* **poissons-globes**) NM *Ich* globefish, puffer (fish)

poisson-lanterne [pwasɔ̃lɑ̃tɛrn] (*pl* **poissons-lanternes**) NM *Ich* lantern fish

poisson-lune [pwasɔ̃lyn] (*pl* **poissons-lunes**) NM *Ich* sunfish

poissonnerie [pwasɔnri] NF **1** (*magasin*) fish shop, *Br* fishmonger's; (*au marché*) fish stall; (*marché*) fish market **2** (*industrie*) fish industry

poissonneux, -euse [pwasɔnø, -øz] ADJ full of fish; **des eaux poissonneuses** waters rich in fish

poissonnier, -ère [pwasɔnje, -ɛr] NM,F (*personne*) *Br* fishmonger, *Am* fish merchant
   □ **poissonnière NF** (*ustensile*) fish-kettle

poisson-paradis [pwasɔ̃paradi] (*pl* **poissons-paradis**) NM *Ich* paradise fish

poisson-perroquet [pwasɔ̃perɔke] (*pl* **poissons-perroquets**) NM *Ich* parrot fish

poisson-pierre [pwasɔ̃pjɛr] (*pl* **poissons-pierres**) NM *Ich* stonefish

poisson-pilote [pwasɔ̃pilɔt] (*pl* **poissons-pilotes**) NM *Ich* pilot fish

poisson-sabre [pwasɔ̃sabr] (*pl* **poissons-sabres**) NM *Ich* scabbard fish

poisson-scie [pwasɔ̃si] (*pl* **poissons-scies**) NM *Ich* sawfish

poisson-soldat [pwasɔ̃sɔlda] (*pl* **poissons-soldats**) NM *Ich* soldier fish

poitevin, -e [pwatvɛ̃, -in] ADJ **1** (*du Poitou*) of/from Poitou **2** (*de Poitiers*) of/from Poitiers
   NM (*dialecte du Poitou*) Poitou dialect
   □ **Poitevin, -e NM,F 1** (*du Poitou*) = inhabitant of or person from Poitou **2** (*de Poitiers*) = inhabitant of or person from Poitiers

Poitiers [pwatje] NM Poitiers

Poitou [pwatu] NM **le P.** Poitou

Poitou-Charentes [pwatuʃarɑ̃t] NM **le P.** Poitou-Charentes

poitrail [pwatraj] NM **1** *Zool* breast **2** (*partie de harnais*) breastplate **3** *Hum* (*poitrine*) chest

poitrinaire [pwatrinɛr] *Vieilli* ADJ phtisic, consumptive
   NMF phtisic, consumptive

poitrine [pwatrin] NF **1** (*thorax*) chest; (*seins*) bust, chest; **serrer qn contre** ou **sur sa p.** to hold or press or clasp sb to one's breast; **elle a une p. opulente** she's got a big bust or bosom; **elle a commencé à avoir de la p. vers 12 ans** she started developing breasts at about 12 years old; **elle n'a pas encore de p.** she's still flat-chested, she hasn't got any bust yet; **elle n'a pas beaucoup de p.** she's flat-chested
   2 (*poumons*) chest, lungs; **être fragile de la p.** to have weak lungs or a weak chest; *Arch* **s'en aller de la p.** to be dying of consumption
   3 *Culin* **p. de bœuf** beef brisket, brisket of beef; **p. fumée** ≃ smoked bacon; **p. de porc** belly pork; **p. salée** *Br* ≃ salt belly pork, *Am* ≃ salt pork; **p. de veau** breast of veal

poivrade [pwavrad] NF (*sauce*) pepper sauce
   □ **à la poivrade ADJ** *Culin* with a pepper sauce

poivre [pwavr] NM pepper; **p. blanc** white pepper; **p. de Cayenne** Cayenne (pepper); **p. noir** ou **gris** (black) pepper; **p. vert** green pepper; **p. en grains** peppercorns, whole pepper; **p. moulu** ground pepper
   □ **poivre et sel ADJ INV** pepper-and-salt; **cheveux/barbe p. et sel** pepper-and-salt hair/beard

poivré, -e [pwavre] **ADJ 1** *Culin* peppery **2** *(parfum)* peppery, spicy **3** *(chanson, histoire)* spicy, racy **4** *Fam (ivre)* wasted, *Br* sloshed

poivrer [3] [pwavre] **VT** *Culin* to pepper; **tu devrais p. un peu plus ta sauce** you should put a little more pepper in your sauce
▸**se poivrer VPR** *Fam* to get wasted *or Br* sloshed

poivrier [pwavrije] **NM 1** *Bot* pepper plant **2** *(contenant)* pepper pot; *(moulin)* pepper mill

poivrière [pwavrijer] **NF 1** *Archit* pepper box *(fortification)* **2** *(ustensile)* pepper pot **3** *(plantation)* pepper plantation

poivron [pwavrɔ̃] **NM** (sweet) pepper, capsicum; **p. vert/jaune/rouge** green/yellow/red pepper

poivrot, -e [pwavro, -ɔt] **NM,F** *Fam* alky, boozer

poix [pwa] **NF** pitch

poker [pɔkɛr] **NM** *Cartes* poker; **jouer au p.** to play poker; **faire un p.** *ou* **une partie de p.** to have a game of poker; **p. d'as** *(dés)* poker dice; *(cartes)* four aces; **p. menteur** liar poker

Polac, Polack [pɔlak] **NMF** *Fam* Polack, = offensive term used to refer to a Polish person

polacre [pɔlakr] **NF** *(voilier)* polacca

Polaire [pɔlɛr] **NF la P.** Polaris, the Pole Star, the North Star

polaire [pɔlɛr] **ADJ** *Math, Phys & Tech* polar
NF 1 *Phys* polar curve **2** *Math* polar axis

polaque [pɔlak] **NM** *Hist* Polack, Polish cavalryman *(in the French army during the 17th and 18th centuries)*

polar [pɔlar] **NM** *Fam (livre, film)* thriller■, whodunnit

polard, -e [pɔlar, -ard] *Fam* **ADJ être complètement p.** to be a total *Br* swot *or Am* grind
NM,F *Br* swot, *Am* grind

polarimètre [pɔlarimetr] **NM** *Opt* polarimeter

polarimétrie [pɔlarimetri] **NF** *Opt* polarimetry

polarisable [pɔlarizabl] **ADJ** *Phys* polarizable

polarisant, -e [pɔlarizã, -ãt] **ADJ** *Phys* polarizing

polarisation [pɔlarizasjɔ̃] **NF 1** *Phys* polarization **2** *(de l'intérêt, des activités)* focusing, concentrating

polariser [3] [pɔlarize] **VT 1** *Phys* to polarize
2 *(concentrer → son attention, son énergie, ses ressources)* to focus; **il a polarisé l'attention de l'auditoire** he made the audience sit up and listen
3 *(faire se concentrer)* **p. qn sur qch** to make sb concentrate (exclusively) on sth; **le programme polarise trop les élèves sur les mathématiques** the syllabus forces the students to concentrate too much on mathematics
▸**se polariser VPR 1** *Phys* to polarize
2 se p. sur qch *(se concentrer → personne, attention)* to focus on sth; **il s'est trop polarisé sur sa carrière** he was too wrapped up in his career; **être polarisé sur ses ennuis personnels/ses études** to be obsessed by one's personal problems/one's studies; **être polarisé sur un seul aspect de qch** to focus on a single aspect of sth

polariseur [pɔlarizœr] **NM** *Opt* polarizer

polarité [pɔlarite] **NF** polarity

polarographie [pɔlarɔgrafi] **NF** polarography

Polaroid® [pɔlarɔid] **NM 1** *(appareil)* Polaroid® (camera) **2** *(photo)* Polaroid® (picture)

polatouche [pɔlatuʃ] **NM** *Zool* flying squirrel

polder [pɔldɛr] **NM** *Géog* polder

poldérisation [pɔlderizasjɔ̃] **NF** *Géog* reclamation (of land from the sea)

pôle [pol] **NM 1** *Phys, Géog & Math* pole; **le p. Nord/Sud** the North/South Pole; **pôles magnétiques** magnetic poles
2 *(extrême)* pole; **le gouvernement a réussi à concilier les deux pôles de l'opinion sur cette question** the government managed to reconcile the two poles of opinion on this subject
3 *Écon* **p. de compétitivité** competitiveness cluster *(area in which a large number of businesses and R&D companies have been set up and encouraged to work together, with the aim of boosting innovation and making French industry more competitive)*; **p. de conversion** special economic zone; **pôles de croissance** main centres of economic growth; **les pôles de croissance** the main centres of economic growth; **p. économique** economic hub; **Toulouse est**

devenue le p. (d'attraction) économique de la **région** Toulouse has become the focus *or* hub of economic development in the region; **p. de reconversion** development *or* reconversion zone
4 *Élec* pole; **p. saillant** salient pole
5 *Anat* pole *(of an organ)*
6 *Pol* **P. Républicain** = French political party created in 2002 by Jean-Pierre Chevènement with a republican and anti-EU agenda

polémarque [pɔlemark] **NM** *Antiq* polemarch

polémique [pɔlemik] **ADJ 1** *(article)* polemic, polemical, provocative; *(attitude)* polemic, polemical, embattled **2** *(journaliste, écrivain)* provocative
NF controversy; **une vive p. s'ensuivit** a heated argument ensued

polémiquer [3] [pɔlemike] **VI** to be polemical; **sans vouloir p., je pense que...** I don't want to be controversial, but I think ...

polémiste [pɔlemist] **NMF** polemist, polemicist

polémologie [pɔlemɔlɔʒi] **NF** war studies, *Spéc* polemology

polémologue [pɔlemɔlɔg] **NMF** war studies expert, *Spéc* polemologist

polémoniacée [pɔlemɔnjase] *Bot* **NF** member of the Polemoniaceae
❑ **polémoniacées NFPL** Polemoniaceae

polenta [pɔlɛnta] **NF** polenta

pole position [polpozisjɔ̃] *(pl* **pole positions)** **NF** pole position; **être en p.** to be in pole position

poli, -e [pɔli] **ADJ 1** *(bien élevé)* polite, courteous; **être très p. avec qn** to be very polite *or* very courteous to sb; **ce n'est pas p. de répondre!** it's rude to answer back!; **vous pourriez être p.!** keep a civil tongue in your head!; **il est trop p. pour être honnête** he's too sweet to be wholesome
2 *(pierre)* smooth; *(métal)* polished; *(marbre)* glassed
NM *(éclat)* shine, sheen; **la table a un beau p.** the table has a nice shiny finish *or* a high polish *or* a rich sheen

police [pɔlis] **NF 1** *(institution)* police; **la p. est alertée** *ou* **prévenue** the police have been called; **entrer dans la p.** to join the police, to go into the police force; **toutes les polices de France sont à ses trousses** the entire French police force is chasing him/her, police throughout France are chasing him/her; *Fam* **je vais à la p.** I'm going to the police■; *Fig Hum* **tu es de la p. ou quoi?** what is this, the Spanish Inquisition?, what is this, Twenty Questions?; **p.! les mains en l'air!** police! hands up!; **p. administrative** law enforcement; **p. de l'air et des frontières** airport and border police; **p. judiciaire** *Br* ≃ Criminal Investigation Department, *Am* ≃ Federal Bureau of Investigation; **p. militaire** military police; **p. mondaine** *ou* **des mœurs** vice squad; **p. montée** mounted police; **p. municipale** ≃ local police; **la P. nationale** the police force *(excluding "gendarmes")*; **p. parallèle** paramilitary police; **p. du roulage** *Br* traffic police, *Am* state highway patrol; **p. secours** (police) emergency services; **p. secrète** secret police; **la guerre des polices** = rivalry between different police departments; *Fam* **la p. des polices** ≃ the police complaints committee
2 *(maintien de l'ordre)* (enforcement of) law and order; *(par les policiers)* policing; **faire la p. dans les centres commerciaux** to maintain security in shopping *Br* centres *or Am* malls; **il n'a jamais voulu faire la p. chez lui** he never tried to keep his family in order
3 *Typ & Ordinat* **p. (de caractères)** font; **p. bitmap** *ou* **pixélisée** bitmap font; **p. par défaut** default font
4 *Assur* **p. d'assurance** insurance policy; **p. d'assurance (sur la) vie** life (insurance) policy; **prendre** *ou* **contracter une p. d'assurance** to take out a policy; **p. conjointe** joint policy; **p. individuelle crédit acheteur** individual buyer credit policy; **p. individuelle crédit fournisseur** individual supplier credit policy; **p. ouverte** open policy; **p. tous risques** fully comprehensive policy; **p. universelle** worldwide policy
5 *Com* **p. de chargement** bill of lading
❑ **de police ADJ** police *(avant n)*

POLICE NATIONALE
The "Police nationale" operates under the authority of the Ministry of the Interior, unlike the "Gendarmerie", which is an army corps.

policé, -e [pɔlise] **ADJ** *Littéraire* highly civilized, urbane

policeman [pɔlisman] *(pl* **policemans** *ou* **policemen** [-mɛn]) **NM** (British) policeman

policer [16] [pɔlise] **VT** *Littéraire* to civilize

Polichinelle [pɔliʃinɛl] **NPR** *(aux marionnettes)* Punchinello; *(à la commedia dell'arte)* Pulcinella; **aller voir P.** to go to a Punch-and-Judy show

polichinelle [pɔliʃinɛl] **NM 1** *(pantin)* (Punch) puppet; *Fam* **avoir un p. dans le tiroir** to have a bun in the oven **2** *Fam Péj (personne)* clown, buffoon; **arrête de faire le p.** stop clowning around

policier, -ère [pɔlisje, -ɛr] **ADJ 1** *(de la police)* police *(avant n)* **2** *(roman, film)* detective *(avant n)*
NM

Note that it is no longer considered a mistake to feminize this word in sense 1 and to say **une policière** but some French speakers nonetheless regard this form as unacceptable, especially in France. See also the entry **féminisation**.

1 *(agent)* policeman, police officer; **une femme p.** a policewoman, a woman *or* female police officer; **p. en civil** detective; **une femme p. en civil** a woman *or* female detective; **plusieurs policiers sont entrés dans l'immeuble** several police officers went into the building **2** *(livre)* detective novel; *(film)* detective film

policlinique [pɔliklinik] **NF** outpatient clinic

policologie [pɔlikɔlɔʒi] **NF** police procedure

poliment [pɔlimã] **ADV** politely; **il s'effaça p. pour la laisser passer** he politely stepped aside to let her pass

polio [pɔljo] **Méd NMF** polio victim
NF polio; **avoir la p.** to have polio

poliomyélite [pɔljomjelit] **NF** *Méd* poliomyelitis

poliomyélitique [pɔljomjelitik] **ADJ** *(gén)* polio *(avant n)*; *(personne)* suffering from polio; **il est p.** he has polio
NMF polio victim

polonium [pɔlɔnjɔm] **NM** *Chim* polonium

poliorcétique [pɔljɔrsetik] *Mil* **ADJ** poliorcetic
NF poliorcetics *(singulier)*

polir [32] [pɔlir] **VT 1** *(métal)* to polish (up), to burnish; *(pierre, meuble)* to polish; *(chaussures)* to polish, to clean, to shine; *(ongles)* to buff; **poli par l'érosion/le temps** made smooth by erosion/the passage of time **2** *(parfaire)* to polish, to refine; **p. ses phrases** to polish one's sentences
▸**se polir VPR se p. les ongles** to polish *or* buff one's nails

polissable [pɔlisabl] **ADJ** *(métal)* polishable, burnishable

polissage [pɔlisaʒ] **NM 1** *(d'un meuble)* polishing; *(des ongles)* buffing **2** *Métal* polishing, burnishing; **p. électrolytique** electrolytic polishing, electropolishing

polisseur, -euse [pɔlisœr, -øz] **NM,F** *(personne)* polisher
NM *(machine → de riz)* rice-polishing machine
❑ **polisseuse NF 1** *(machine → pour la pierre)* glassing *or* polishing machine **2** *Métal* polishing head *or* stick

polissoir [pɔliswar] **NM** *(machine)* polishing machine; *(outil)* polishing head *or* lathe, polisher; **p. à ongles** (nail) buffer

polisson, -onne [pɔlisɔ̃, -ɔn] **ADJ 1** *(taquin)* mischievous, cheeky **2** *(égrillard)* saucy, naughty; **une chanson polissonne** a racy *or* saucy song
NM,F *(espiègle)* little devil *or* rogue *or* scamp

polissonner [3] [pɔlisɔne] **VI** *Vieilli* **1** *(badiner)* to fool around **2** *(faire des sottises)* to get up to mischief

polissonnerie [pɔlisɔnri] **NF 1** *(facétie)* piece of mischief **2** *(parole grivoise)* risqué *or* saucy remark; **dire des polissonneries** to make risqué

or saucy remarks 3 *(acte grivois)* **des polissonneries** naughty goings-on

poliste [pɔlist] NM *Entom* paper wasp

Politburo [pɔlitbyro] NM Politburo

politesse [pɔlitɛs] NF 1 *(bonne éducation)* politeness, courteousness; **il est toujours d'une grande p.** he is always very polite *or* courteous; **faire/dire qch par p.** to do/to say sth out of politeness; **brûler la p. à qn** to leave sb abruptly

2 *(propos)* polite remark; **échanger des politesses** to exchange polite small-talk; *Ironique* to trade insults

3 *(acte)* polite gesture; **rendre la p. à qn** to pay sb back for a favour; *Ironique* to give sb a taste of his/her own medicine

❑ **de politesse** ADJ *(lettre, visite)* courtesy *(avant n)*

politicaillerie [pɔlitikajri] NF *Fam Péj* backroom politics■

politicard, -e [pɔlitikar, -ard] *Fam Péj* ADJ careerist■

NM,F careerist politician■

politicien, -enne [pɔlitisjɛ̃, -ɛn] ADJ 1 *(d'habile politique)* political; **une manœuvre politicienne** a successful political move 2 *Péj* scheming

NM,F politician

politico-économique [pɔlitikoekɔnɔmik] *(pl* **politico-économiques)** ADJ politico-economic

politicologie [pɔlitikɔlɔʒi] = **politologie**

politicologue [pɔlitikɔlɔg] = **politologue**

politique [pɔlitik] ADJ 1 *(du pouvoir de l'État → institution, carte)* political

2 *(de la vie publique)* political; **quelles sont ses opinions politiques?** what are his/her politics?; **une carrière p.** a career in politics; **dans les milieux politiques** in political circles; **homme p., femme p.** politician; **les partis politiques** the political parties

3 *Littéraire (diplomate)* diplomatic, politic; **ce n'était pas très p. de le licencier** it wasn't a very wise move to fire him

NF 1 *(activité)* politics; **faire de la p.** to be involved in politics; **je ne fais pas de p.!** *(je refuse de prendre parti)* I don't want to bring politics into this!, no politics please!; **elle se destine à la p.** she wants to go into politics; **parler p.** to talk politics; **p. de juste milieu** middle-of-the-road politics; **p. locale** local politics; **p. minoritaire** minority politics; **p. de parti** party politics; **p. partisane** partisan politics; *Péj* **la p. politicienne** party politics

2 *(stratégie)* policy; **suivre** *ou* **adopter une nouvelle p.** to follow *or* adopt a new policy; **une p. de gauche** a left-wing policy; **c'est de bonne p.** *Pol* it's good political practice; *Fig* it's good practice; **p. d'accommodement** give-and-take policy; *UE* **la p. agricole commune** the Common Agricultural Policy; **p. antichômage** policy that aims to reduce unemployment; **p. antiprotectionniste** free-trade policy; **p. d'apaisement** policy of appeasement; *Mktg* **p. d'assortiment diversifié** mixed merchandising; **p. d'austérité** austerity policy; **p. budgétaire** budgetary *or* fiscal policy; **p. commerciale** trade policy; **p. de commercialisation** marketing policy; *UE* **p. communautaire** EU policy; **p. commune de la pêche** Common Fisheries Policy; *Mktg* **p. de communication** promotional policy; **p. conjoncturelle** economic policy *(responding to changes in the business cycle)*; **la p. consensuelle** consensus politics; **p. conventionnelle** = policy relating to union-management agreements; **p. de la corde raide** political brinkmanship; **p. à court terme** short-termism; **p. de crédit** credit policy; **p. déflationniste** *ou* **p. de déflation** deflationary policy; **p. de distribution** distribution policy; *Pol* **p. économique** economic policy; **p. d'élargissement européenne** policy of enlarging the European Union; **p. électoraliste** vote-catching policies; **p. d'endiguement** policy of containment; **p. étrangère** foreign policy; *UE* **p. étrangère et de sécurité commune** Common Foreign and Security Policy; **p. extérieure** foreign policy; **p. fiscale** fiscal policy; **p. de gestion** business policy; **p. industrielle** industrial policy; **p. inflationniste** inflationary policy; **p. intérieure** domestic policy; **p. d'investissement** investment policy; **p. du laissez-faire** laissez-faire policy; **p. de libre-échange** free-trade policy; **p. à long terme** long-term policy; **p. de la main tendue** policy of the outstretched hand; **pratiquer la p. de la main tendue** to make friendly overtures, to be conciliatory; *Mktg* **p. de marque** brand policy; *Com* **p. en matière de change** exchange policy; **p. monétaire** monetary policy; **p. d'open-market** open-market policy; **p. d'ouverture** consensus politics; **p. de la porte ouverte** open-door policy; **p. des prix** pricing *or* prices policy; **p. des prix et des salaires** prices and incomes policy; *Mktg* **p. de produit** product policy; *Mktg* **p. de promotion** promotional policy; **p. de relance** reflationary policy; **p. des revenus** incomes policy; **p. de rigueur** policy of austerity; **p. des salaires** wages policy; **p. sécuritaire** repressive law-and-order policy; **p. de stabilité** stabilizing policy; **p. de la terre brûlée** scorched-earth policy; *Mktg* **p. de vente** sales policy; **pratiquer la p. de l'autruche** to bury one's head in the sand; **pratiquer la p. de la chaise vide** to make a political point by not attending meetings; **la p. du pire** = deliberately worsening the situation to further one's ends

NMF 1 *(politicien)* politician

2 *(prisonnier)* political prisoner

NM politics; **faire passer le p. avant le social** to accord more importance to politics than to welfare

politique-fiction [pɔlitikfiksjɔ̃] NF futuristic political fiction; **un roman de p.** a futuristic political novel

politiquement [pɔlitikmɑ̃] ADV 1 *Pol* politically; **p. correct** politically correct 2 *Littéraire (adroitement)* diplomatically

politisation [pɔlitizasjɔ̃] NF politicization; **la p. du sport** the politicization of sport, bringing politics into sport

politiser [3] [pɔlitize] VT to politicize, to bring politics into; **ils sont moins/plus politisés** they are less/more interested in politics; **p. une grève** to give a political dimension to a strike

▶**se politiser** VPR to become political

politologie [pɔlitɔlɔʒi] NF political science

politologue [pɔlitɔlɔg] NMF political scientist

poljé [pɔlje] NM *Géog* polje

polka [pɔlka] NF polka

pollakiurie [pɔlakiyri] NF *Méd* pollakiuria

pollen [pɔlɛn] NM pollen

pollicitant, -e [pɔlisitɑ̃, -ɑ̃t] NM,F *Jur* offeror

pollicitation [pɔlisitasjɔ̃] NF *Jur* pollicitation, tentative offer

pollinie [pɔlini] NF *Bot* pollinium

pollinique [pɔlinik] ADJ *Bot* pollinic

pollinisation [pɔlinizasjɔ̃] NF pollination; **féconder par p.** to cross-pollinate

polliniser [3] [pɔlinize] VT to pollinate

pollinose [pɔlinoz] NF *Méd* pollinosis

polluant, -e [pɔlɥɑ̃, -ɑ̃t] ADJ polluting; **un produit p.** a pollutant

NM polluting agent, pollutant; **p. organique persistant** persistent organic pollutant

pollué, -e [pɔlɥe] ADJ polluted; **une région fortement polluée** a highly polluted region, a region with a high level of pollution

polluer [7] [pɔlɥe] VT 1 *Écol* to pollute 2 *Fig (souiller)* to pollute, to sully; **la presse à scandale pollue toute la profession** the gutter press is a disgrace to the whole profession

pollueur, -euse [pɔlɥœr, -øz] ADJ *(industrie)* polluting

NM,F polluter; **les pollueurs devront payer les dégâts** the polluters will have to pay for the damage; **principe du pollueur-payeur** polluter pays principle

pollution [pɔlysjɔ̃] NF 1 *Écol* pollution; **p. atmosphérique** atmospheric *or* air pollution 2 *Fig* pollution

❑ **pollutions** NFPL *Méd* **pollutions nocturnes** wet dreams, *Spéc* nocturnal emissions

polo [pɔlo] NM 1 *Sport* polo 2 *(chemise)* polo shirt

polochon [pɔlɔʃɔ̃] NM *Fam* bolster■

Pologne [pɔlɔɲ] NF **la P.** Poland; **vivre en P.** to live in Poland; **aller en P.** to go to Poland

polonais, -e [pɔlɔnɛ, -ɛz] ADJ Polish; *Ordinat* **notation polonaise** Polish notation

NM *(langue)* Polish

❑ **Polonais, -e** NM,F Pole

❑ **polonaise** NF 1 *Mus (danse)* polonaise 2 *Culin* polonaise *(brioche layered with candied fruit and covered with meringue)* 3 *(vêtement)* polonaise

❑ **à la polonaise** ADJ *Culin* à la polonaise, = covered with chopped hard-boiled egg yolk, herbs and fried breadcrumbs

polonium [pɔlɔnjɔm] NM *Chim* polonium

poltron, -onne [pɔltrɔ̃, -ɔn] ADJ cowardly, faint-hearted, lily-livered

NM,F coward, *Littéraire* poltroon

poltronnerie [pɔltrɔnri] NF cowardice, faint-heartedness

poly- [pɔli] PRÉF poly-

polyacide [pɔliasid] NM *Chim* polyacid

polyacrylate [pɔliakrilat] NM *Chim* polyacrylate

polyacrylique [pɔliakrilik] *Chim* ADJ polyacrylic

NM polyacrylic

polyaddition [pɔliadisjɔ̃] NF *Chim* polyaddition

polyalcool [pɔlialkɔl] NM *Chim* polyalcohol

polyamide [pɔliamid] NM *Chim* polyamide

polyamine [pɔliamin] NF *Chim* polyamine

polyamour [pɔliamur] NM polyamory

polyandre [pɔljɑ̃dr] ADJ polyandrous

polyandrie [pɔliɑ̃dri] NF polyandry

polyarchie [pɔliarʃi] NF *Pol* polyarchy

polyarthrite [pɔliartrit] NF *Méd* polyarthritis; **p. rhumatoïde** rheumatoid arthritis; **p. rhumatoïde de l'enfant** juvenile rheumatoid arthritis, Still's disease

polyatomique [pɔliatɔmik] ADJ *Chim* polyatomic

polybasique [pɔlibasik] ADJ *Chim* polybasic

polybutadiène [pɔlibytadjɛn] NM *Chim* polybutadiene

polycarbonate [pɔlikarbɔnat] NM *Chim* polycarbonate

polycarpique [pɔlikarpik] ADJ *Bot* polycarpous, polycarpic

polycentrique [pɔlisɑ̃trik] ADJ *Biol* polycentric

polycentrisme [pɔlisɑ̃trism] NM *Pol* polycentrism

polycentriste [pɔlisɑ̃trist] ADJ *Pol* polycentrist

polychète [pɔlikɛt] *Zool* NM polychaete

❑ **polychètes** NMPL Polychaeta

polychlorobiphényle [pɔliklɔrɔbifenil] NM *Chim* polychlorinated biphenyl

polychlorure [pɔliklɔryr] NM **p. de vinyle** polyvinyl chloride

polychroïsme [pɔlikrɔism] NM pleochroism

polychrome [pɔlikrom] ADJ polychromatic, polychrome

polychromie [pɔlikrɔmi] NF polychromy

polyclinique [pɔliklinik] NF polyclinic

polycondensat [pɔlikɔ̃dɑ̃sa] NM *Chim* polycondensate, condensation polymer

polycondensation [pɔlikɔ̃dɑ̃sasjɔ̃] NF *Chim* polycondensation, condensation polymerization

polycopie [pɔlikɔpi] NF 1 *(procédé)* duplication; **envoyer un texte à la p.** to send a text to be duplicated 2 *(document)* duplicate

polycopié [pɔlikɔpje] NM *(gén)* (duplicated) notes; *Univ* handout

polycopier [9] [pɔlikɔpje] VT to duplicate

polycourant [pɔlikurɑ̃] ADJ INV *Rail* multi-current *(avant n)*

polycrystallin, -e [pɔlikristalɛ̃, -in] ADJ *Minér* polycristalline

polyculture [pɔlikyltyr] NF polyculture, mixed farming

polycyclique [pɔlisiklik] ADJ *Biol & Chim* polycyclic

polydactyle [pɔlidaktil] ADJ polydactyl, polydactylous

NMF polydactyl

polydactylie [pɔlidaktili] NF polydactyly, polydactylism

polydipsie [pɔlidipsi] NF *Méd* polydipsia

Polydore [pɔlidɔr] NPR *Myth* Polydorus

polyèdre [pɔliɛdr] *Géom* ADJ polyhedral

NM polyhedron

polyédrique [pɔliedrik] ADJ *Géom* polyhedral

polyélectrolyte [pɔlielɛktrɔlit] *Chim* ADJ polyelectrolytic

NM polyelectrolyte

polyembryonie [pɔliɑ̃brijɔni] NF *Biol* polyembryony

polyester [pɔliɛstɛr] NM *Chim* polyester

polyéther [pɔlietɛr] NM *Chim* polyether

polyéthylène [pɔlietilɛn] NM *Chim* polythene, *esp Am* polyethylene; **p. haute densité** high density polythene

pol-pol

polygale [pɔligal] NM *Bot* polygala

polygame [pɔligam] ADJ polygamous
NM polygamist

polygamie [pɔligami] NF polygamy

polygène [pɔliʒɛn] NM *Biol* polygen

polygénie [pɔliʒeni] NF *Biol* polygenesis

polygénique [pɔliʒenik] ADJ **1** *Biol* polygenic **2** *Géol* polygenetic

polygénisme [pɔliʒenism] NM polygenesis

polyglobulie [pɔliglɔbyli] NF *Méd* polycythaemia

polyglotte [pɔliglɔt] ADJ polyglot
NMF polyglot

polygonacée [pɔligɔnase] NF *Bot* polygonaceous plant
□ **polygonacées** NFPL Polygonaceae

polygonal, -e, -aux, -ales [pɔligɔnal, -o] ADJ *Géom* polygonal; *Géol* **sol p. arctique** patterned ground

polygonation [pɔligɔnasjɔ̃] NF polygonation

polygone [pɔligɔn] NM **1** *Géom* polygon **2** *Mil* **p. de tir** shooting range **3** *(dans des statistiques)* **p. des fréquences** frequency polygon

polygraphe [pɔligraf] NM *(écrivain)* versatile writer; *Péj* = writer who writes on too many subjects

polygynie [pɔliʒini] NF polygyny

polyholoside [pɔliɔlɔsid] NM *Chim* polysaccharide

polyinsaturé, -e [pɔliɛ̃satyre] ADJ polyunsaturated

polykystose [pɔlikistoz] NF *Méd* **p. rénale** polycystic kidney disease, PKD

polylobé, -e [pɔlilɔbe] ADJ *Archit* multifoiled

polymérase [pɔlimeraz] NF *Chim* polymerase

polymère [pɔlimɛr] *Chim* ADJ polymeric
NM polymer

polymérie [pɔlimeri] NF *Chim* polymerism

polymérisable [pɔlimerizabl] ADJ *Chim* polymerizable

polymérisation [pɔlimerizasjɔ̃] NF *Chim* polymerization

polymériser [3] [pɔlimerize] VT *Chim* to polymerize

polymétallique [pɔlimetalik] ADJ polymetallic; **nodule p.** polymetallic nodule

polymorphe [pɔlimɔrf] ADJ **1** *(gén)* & *Biol* polymorphous, polymorphic; **espèce p.** polymorph **2** *Chim* polymorphic

polymorphie [pɔlimɔrfi] NF *Chim* polymorphism

polymorphisme [pɔlimɔrfism] NM polymorphism

polymyxine [pɔlimiksin] NF *Pharm* polymyxin

Polynésie [pɔlinezi] NF **la P.** Polynesia; **vivre en P.** to live in Polynesia; **aller en P.** to go to Polynesia; **la P. française** French Polynesia

polynésien, -enne [pɔlinezjɛ̃, -ɛn] ADJ Polynesian
NM *(langue)* Polynesian
□ **Polynésien, -enne** NM,F Polynesian

polynévrite [pɔlinevrit] NF *Méd* polyneuritis

polynôme [pɔlinom] NM *Math* polynomial

polynomial, -e, -aux, -ales [pɔlinɔmjal, -o] ADJ *Math* polynomial

polynucléaire [pɔlinykleɛr] *Biol* ADJ polynuclear, polynucleate
NM polymorphonuclear leucocyte

polynucléotide [pɔlinykleotid] NM *Biol* & *Chim* polynucleotide

polyol [pɔljɔl] NM *Chim* polyalcohol

polyoléfine [pɔliolefin] NF *Chim* polyolefine

polyoside [pɔliozid] NM *Chim* polysaccharide

polype [pɔlip] NM **1** *Méd* polyp, polypus **2** *Zool* polyp

polypeptide [pɔlipɛptid] NM *Biol* & *Chim* polypeptide

polypeptidique [pɔlipɛptidik] ADJ *Biol* & *Chim* polypeptide *(avant n)*

polypeux, -euse [pɔlipø, -øz] ADJ *Méd* & *Zool* polypous

polyphagie [pɔlifaʒi] NF *Méd* polyphagia

polyphasé, -e [pɔlifaze] ADJ *Élec* polyphase *(avant n)*

Polyphème [pɔlifɛm] NPR *Myth* Polyphemus

polyphénol [pɔlifenɔl] NM *Chim* polyphenol

polyphonie [pɔlifɔni] NF *Mus* polyphony

polyphonique [pɔlifɔnik] ADJ *Mus* polyphonic

polyphoniste [pɔlifɔnist] NMF *Mus* polyphonist

polypier [pɔlipje] NM *Zool* polypary

polyplacophore [pɔliplakɔfɔr] *Zool* NM polyplacophoran
□ **polyplacophores** NMPL Polyplacophora

polyploïde [pɔliplɔid] *Biol* ADJ polyploid
NMF polyploid

polyploïdie [pɔliplɔidi] NF *Biol* polyploidy

polypnée [pɔlipne] NF *Méd* polypnoea

polypode [pɔlipɔd] NM *Bot* polypody

polypore [pɔlipɔr] NM *Bot* polypore; **p. écailleux** dryad's saddle

polypropène [pɔliprɔpɛn], **polypropylène** [pɔliprɔpilɛn] NM polypropylene

polyptère [pɔliptɛr] NM *Ich* polypterid

polyptyque [pɔliptik] NM *Beaux-Arts* polyptych

polyradiculonévrite [pɔliradikylɔnevrit] NF *Méd* polyradiculoneuritis

polyribosome [pɔliribozɔm] NM *Biol* & *Chim* polyribosome

polysaccharide [pɔlisakarid] NM *Chim* polysaccharide

polysémie [pɔlisemi] NF *Ling* polysemy

polysémique [pɔlisemik] ADJ *Ling* polysemous

polysoc [pɔlisɔk] ADJ *Agr* multiple

polysome [pɔlisɔm] NM *Biol* & *Chim* polysome

polysorbate [pɔlisɔrbat] NM *Chim* polysorbate

polystyrène [pɔlistirɛn] NM polystyrene; **p. expansé** expanded polystyrene

polysulfure [pɔlisylfyr] NM *Chim* polysulphide

polysyllabe [pɔlisilab], **polysyllabique** [pɔlisilabik] ADJ polysyllabic
NM polysyllable

polysynodie [pɔlisinɔdi] NF *Hist* & *Pol* = system of government by aristocratic council rather than ministers during the regency of Louis XV, from 1715 to 1719

polysynthétique [pɔlisɛ̃tetik] ADJ *Ling* polysynthetic

polytechnicien, -enne [pɔlitɛkniʒɛ̃, -ɛn] NM,F *(étudiant)* student at the "École Polytechnique"; *(diplômé)* graduate of the "École Polytechnique"

polytechnique [pɔlitɛknik] ADJ **1** *(polyvalent)* polytechnic **2** *Univ* polytechnic; **(l'École) P.** = "grande école" for engineers

Culture

ÉCOLE POLYTECHNIQUE

Founded in 1794, this prestigious engineering college has close connections with the Ministry of Defence. Formerly situated in the heart of Paris's 5th arrondissement, the college moved to Palaiseau, near Paris, in the 1970s. It is popularly known as "l'X". Students are effectively enlisted in the army and must repay their education through government service.

Culture

LA TUERIE DE L'ÉCOLE POLYTECHNIQUE

This tragedy (also known as "le massacre de l'École Polytechnique") took place in December 1989 when a man walked into the engineering school of the "École polytechnique" (technical college) in Montreal, Quebec, and shot dead 14 women before taking his own life. The fact that only women were shot was no coincidence. Before starting his shooting spree the man shouted about how much he hated women and blamed feminism for much of what had gone wrong in his life, most notably for his failure to be admitted to study engineering at the college (even though women accounted for only 20% of students). The incident profoundly shocked Canada, putting issues of violence against women at the forefront of the political agenda and leading to tighter gun-control laws.

polytétrafluoroéthylène [pɔlitetraflyɔrɔetilɛn] NM *Chim* polytetrafluoroethylene

polythéisme [pɔliteism] NM polytheism

polythéiste [pɔliteist] ADJ polytheistic
NMF polytheist

Polythène® [pɔlitɛn] NM *Chim* polythene

polytonal, -e, -aux, -ales [pɔlitɔnal, -o] ADJ *Mus* polytonal

polytonalité [pɔlitɔnalite] NF *Mus* polytonality, polytonalism

polytoxicomanie [pɔlitɔksikɔmani] NF multiple (drug) addiction

polytransfusé, -e [pɔlitrɑ̃sfyze] ADJ = who has received multiple blood transfusions
NM,F = person who has received multiple blood transfusions

polytraumatisé, -e [pɔlitromatize] *Méd* ADJ suffering from multiple trauma
NM,F multiple trauma sufferer

polytraumatisme [pɔlitromatism] NM *Méd* multiple trauma

polytric [pɔlitrik] NM *Bot* polytrichum

polyuréthane, polyuréthanne [pɔliyretan] NM *Chim* polyurethan, polyurethane

polyurie [pɔliyri] NF *Méd* polyuria, polyuresis

polyurique [pɔliyrik] ADJ *Méd* polyuric

polyvalence [pɔlivalɑ̃s] NF *(gén)* versatility, adaptability; *Chim* polyvalence, polyvalency

polyvalent, -e [pɔlivalɑ̃, -ɑ̃t] ADJ *(gén)* versatile, adaptable; *(salle)* multi-purpose; *Chim* polyvalent
NM,F **1** *Fin* & *Jur* tax inspector **2** *(dans les services sociaux)* social worker
□ **polyvalente** NF *Can (école)* = secondary school offering both general and vocational courses

polyvinyle [pɔlivinil] NM polyvinyl

polyvinylique [pɔlivinilik] ADJ polyvinyl *(avant n)*

polyvitamine [pɔlivitamin] NF *Pharm* multivitamin

pomelo, pomélo [pomelo] NM pomelo

Poméranie [pɔmerani] NF **la P.** Pomerania

poméranien, -enne [pɔmeranjɛ̃, -ɛn] ADJ Pomeranian
□ **Poméranien, -enne** NM,F Pomeranian

pomerium [pɔmerjɔm] = **pomœrium**

pomerol [pɔmerɔl] NM Pomerol *(wine)*

pomiculteur, -trice [pɔmikyltœr, -tris] NM,F orchardist, fruit grower

pommade [pɔmad] NF **1** *Méd (pour brûlures)* ointment; *(pour foulures)* liniment; *Vieilli (cosmétique)* cream; **p. pour les lèvres** lip balm *or* salve; *Fam* **passer de la p. à qn** to butter sb up **2** *Culin* cream, paste *(made from pounding various ingredients together)*

pommader [3] [pɔmade] VT *(cheveux)* to put cream on, to pomade

pommard [pɔmar] NM Pommard *(wine)*

pomme [pɔm] NF **1** *(fruit)* apple; **p. d'api** = variety of small, sweet apple; **p. (de) cajou** cashew apple *or* pear; **p. cannelle** custard apple; **p. à cidre** cider apple; **p. à couteau** dessert *or* eating apple; **p. à cuire** cooking apple, *Br* cooker; **p. de reinette** pippin; *Fig* **la p. de discorde** the bone of contention; *Myth* **les pommes d'or du jardin des Hespérides** the golden apples of Hesperides; *Fam Fig* **tomber dans les pommes** to pass out■, to keel over

2 *(légume)* potato; **pommes allumettes** (very thin) fries; **pommes chips** (potato) *Br* crisps *or Am* chips; **pommes dauphine/duchesse** dauphine/duchesse potatoes; **pommes frites** *Br* chips, *Am* (French) fries; **pommes noisettes** pommes noisettes, = deep-fried potato balls; **pommes vapeur** steamed potatoes

3 *(cœur → du chou, de la salade)* heart

4 *(objet rond → d'une canne)* knob; **p. d'arrosoir** rose *(of a watering can)*; **p. de douche** shower head

5 *Fam (figure)* face■, mug; **t'en fais une drôle de p.!** you're looking funny *or* weird!

6 **p. (à l'eau** *ou* **à l'huile)** *(naïf)* sucker, *Br* mug; **être bonne p.** to be a sucker *or Br* a mug; **t'es trop bonne p.!** you're such a soft touch *or* a pushover!

7 *Fam (locutions)* **ma p.** *(moi)* yours truly; **ta/sa p.** *(toi/lui ou elle)* you■/him■/her■; **et l'addition, c'est encore pour ma p.!** and yours truly *or Br* muggins has to fork out again!; **et les papiers à remplir, ce sera pour sa p.!** and he/she can damn well cope with the paperwork himself/herself!
□ **aux pommes** ADJ **1** *Culin* apple *(avant n)*
2 *Fam (extraordinaire)* terrific, great
□ **pomme d'Adam** NF Adam's apple
□ **pomme d'amour** NF **1** *(tomate)* tomato
2 *(friandise)* toffee apple
□ **pomme de pin** NF pine *or* fir cone
□ **pomme de terre** NF potato; **pommes de terre à l'eau** boiled potatoes; **pommes de terre frites** *Br* chips, *Am* (French) fries; **p. en robe de chambre** *ou* **en robe des champs** baked potato, jacket potato

pommé, -e [pɔme] ADJ **1** *(salade, chou)* hearty, firm **2** *Fam Vieilli (idiot, gaffe)* complete■, downright■

pommeau, -x [pɔmo] **NM** *(d'une canne)* knob, pommel; *(d'une selle, d'une épée)* pommel; *(d'un fût de pistolet)* pommel, cascabel; **p. de douche** shower head

pommelé, -e [pɔmle] **ADJ 1** *(cheval)* dappled; **gris p.** dapple-grey **2** *(ciel)* mackerel *(avant n)*, dappled

pommeler [24] [pɔmle] **se pommeler VPR le ciel se pommelait** the sky was becoming dappled with clouds

pommelle [pɔmɛl] **NF** drain grating *or* cover

pommer [3] [pɔme] **VI** *(chou, laitue)* to heart

pommeraie [pɔmrɛ] **NF** apple orchard

pommeté, -e [pɔmte] **ADJ** *Hér* bourdonné

pommette [pɔmɛt] **NF 1** *(de la joue)* cheekbone **2** *Can (pomme sauvage)* wild apple, crab apple

pommeté, -e [pɔmte] = **pommeté**

pommier [pɔmje] **NM 1** *(arbre)* apple tree **2** *(bois)* apple wood

pomœrium [pɔmerjɔm] **NM** *Antiq* pomœrium

pomologie [pɔmɔlɔʒi] **NF** *Hort* pomology

pomologiste [pɔmɔlɔʒist], **pomologue** [pɔmɔlɔg] **NMF** *Hort* pomologist

pompage [pɔ̃paʒ] **NM** pumping

pompe [pɔ̃p] **NF 1** *(machine)* pump; **va prendre de l'eau à la p.** go and get some water from the pump; **p. à air/chaleur** air/heat pump; **p. à balancier** pumping jack; **p. centrifuge/volumétrique** centrifuge/displacement pump; **p. à vide/d'injection** vacuum/injection pump; **p. aspirante** suction pump; **p. à bicyclette** *ou* **à vélo** bicycle pump; **p. à essence** *(distributeur)* **Br** petrol pump, *Am* gas pump; *(station)* **Br** petrol *or Am* gas station; **s'arrêter à une p. (à essence)** to stop at a *Br* petrol *or Am* gas station; **les prix à la p.** pump prices; **p. foulante** force pump; *Aut* **p. à huile** oil pump; **p. à incendie** water pump *(on a fire engine)*; *Fam* **avoir un coup de p.** to suddenly feel *Br* knackered *or Am* bushed

2 *Fam (chaussure)* shoe■; **un coup de p.** a kick■; **être** *ou* **marcher à côté de ses pompes** to be screwed up; **il est à côté de ses pompes aujourd'hui** he's not quite with it today

3 *Physiol* **p. membranaire** *(membrane)* pump

4 *(apparat)* pomp; **la p. des mariages princiers** the pomp (and circumstance) of royal weddings; **en grande p.** with great pomp and ceremony; **renoncer aux pompes du siècle** to renounce the pomps and vanities of this wicked world

5 *Fam Arg mil* **(soldat de) deuxième p.** *Br* squaddie, *Am* grunt

6 *Fam (aide-mémoire) Br* crib, *Am* trot

7 *Fam Arg drogue (seringue)* hype, hypo

☐ **pompes NFPL** *Sport Br* press-ups, *Am* push-ups

☐ **à toute(s) pompe(s) ADV** *Fam* like lightning, *Am* like sixty; **il est parti à toutes pompes** he was off like a shot

☐ **pompes funèbres NFPL** *(entreprise de)* **pompes funèbres** funeral parlour; **les pompes funèbres sont venues à 9 heures** the undertakers came at 9 o'clock

pompé, -e [pɔ̃pe] **ADJ** *Fam (épuisé) Br* knackered, *Am* bushed; **je suis p.!** I've had it!, I'm just about ready to drop!

Pompée [pɔ̃pe] **NPR** Pompey

Pompéi [pɔ̃pei] **NM** Pompeii

pompéien, -enne [pɔ̃pejɛ̃, -ɛn] **ADJ** Pompeiian, Pompeian

☐ **Pompéien, -enne NM,F** Pompeiian, Pompeian

pomper [3] [pɔ̃pe] **VT 1** *(aspirer → pour évacuer)* to pump (out); *(→ pour faire monter)* to pump up; *(→ pour boire)* to suck up; **il va falloir p. l'eau du bateau** we'll have to pump the water out of the boat; **p. de l'eau du puits** to pump (up) water from the well; **des parasites qui pompent le sang** parasites that suck blood; *Fam* **p. qn, p. l'air à qn** *(l'importuner)* to get on sb's nerves, to bug sb

2 *(absorber → sujet: éponge)* to soak up; *(→ sujet: sol)* to soak *or* to drink up

3 *Fam Fig (utiliser → économies, réserves)* to take up■, to eat up; **notre voyage aux Seychelles a pompé toutes nos économies** our trip to the Seychelles just ate up all our savings; **il se fait p. tout son argent par son ex-femme** his ex-wife is bleeding him dry

4 *Fam (fatiguer)* to wear out, to do in; **ce**

déménagement **m'a pompé** that move's done me in

5 *très Fam (boire)* to knock back

6 *Fam Arg scol (copier)* to crib **(sur** from); **il a tout pompé sur sa voisine** he cribbed the lot from his neighbour

7 *Vulg* **p. qn, p. le dard à qn** *(lui faire une fellation)* to give sb a blow-job, to suck sb off

VI 1 *(faire marcher une pompe, appuyer)* to pump; **p. sur la pédale du frein** to pump the brake pedal

2 *Fam Arg scol (copier)* to crib; **j'ai pompé sur Anne** I cribbed from Anne

3 *Pêche* to pump

pompette [pɔ̃pɛt] **ADJ** *Fam* tipsy, merry; **elle était complètement/un peu p.** she was far gone/a bit tipsy

pompeuse [pɔ̃pøz] *voir* **pompeux**

pompeusement [pɔ̃pøzmɑ̃] **ADV** pompously, bombastically

pompeux, -euse [pɔ̃pø, -øz] **ADJ** pompous, bombastic

pompidolien, -enne [pɔ̃pidɔljɛ̃, -ɛn] **ADJ** = relating to the Pompidou era *(1969–74, when Georges Pompidou was French President)*; **l'ère pompidolienne** the Pompidou era; **la France pompidolienne** France under Georges Pompidou

pompier, -ère [pɔ̃pje, -ɛr] **ADJ** *Beaux-Arts* pompier; *Péj (style, décor)* pretentious, pompous; **art p.** = official paintings of the second half of the 19th century, today often considered grandiloquent and over-conventional (eg certain paintings by Gérôme and Meissonier)

NM 1 *(sapeur)* fireman; **les pompiers** the fire *Br* brigade *or Am* department

2 *Beaux-Arts (style)* pompier (style); *(artiste)* pompier

3 *Vulg (locution)* **faire un p. à qn** to give sb a blowjob, to suck sb off

pompiérisme [pɔ̃pjerism] **NM** *Beaux-Arts* pompier style *or* genre

pompile [pɔ̃pil] **NM** *Entom* pompilid, hunting wasp

pompiste [pɔ̃pist] **NMF** *Br* petrol *or* pump attendant, *Am* gas station attendant

pom-pom girl [pɔmpɔmgœrl] **NF** cheerleader

pompon [pɔ̃pɔ̃] **NM 1** *Tex* pompom; **bonnet à p.** bobble hat **2** *Fam (locutions)* **dans le genre désagréable, il tient le p.!** when it comes to unpleasantness, he certainly takes the *Br* biscuit *or Am* cake!; **ça, c'est le p.!** that's the limit!

pomponner [3] [pɔ̃pɔne] **VT p. qn** to do sb up, to doll sb up; **se faire p.** to get dolled up

▶**se pomponner VPR** to do oneself up, to doll oneself up

ponant [pɔnɑ̃] **NM** *Littéraire* West

ponantais, -e [pɔnɑ̃tɛ, -ɛz] *Vieilli* **ADJ** Western
NM,F 1 *(de l'ouest)* Westerner **2** *(marin)* sailor *(from the French Atlantic coast)*

ponçage [pɔ̃saʒ] **NM 1** *(au papier de verre → d'un mur)* sanding (down), sandpapering; *(→ de peinture)* rubbing down; *(avec une ponceuse)* sanding; *(à la pierre ponce)* pumicing **2** *Beaux-Arts* pouncing

ponce [pɔ̃s] **ADJ pierre p.** pumice (stone)
NF 1 *Beaux-Arts* pounce bag, pouncer **2** *Can Vieilli (boisson)* grog, hot toddy

ponceau, -x [pɔ̃so] **NM** small bridge

Ponce Pilate [pɔ̃spilat] *voir* **Pilate**

poncer [16] [pɔ̃se] **VT 1** *(polir au papier de verre → mur)* to sandpaper, to sand (down); *(→ peinture)* to rub down; *(polir avec une ponceuse)* to sand (down); *(polir à la pierre ponce)* to pumice (off) **2** *Beaux-Arts* to pounce

ponceur, -euse[1] [pɔ̃sœr, -øz] **NM,F 1** *(de murs)* sander **2** *Beaux-Arts* pouncer

☐ **ponceuse NF** *(machine)* sander, sanding machine

ponceux, -euse[2] [pɔ̃sø, -øz] **ADJ** pumiceous

poncho [pɔ̃tʃo] **NM 1** *(cape)* poncho **2** *(chausson)* Afghan-style sock

poncif [pɔ̃sif] **NM 1** *Péj (cliché)* cliché, commonplace **2** *Beaux-Arts* pouncing pattern **3** *Métal* parting compound

ponction [pɔ̃ksjɔ̃] **NF 1** *Méd* puncture; *(de poumon)* tapping; **p. lombaire/du ventricule** lumbar/ventricular puncture

2 *(retrait)* withdrawal; **faire une grosse p. sur**

un compte to withdraw a large sum from an account; **c'est une p. importante sur mes revenus** it makes quite a big hole *or* dent in my income; *Admin* **p. fiscale** taxation; **p. sociale** = contributions to the social security scheme, *Br* ≃ National Insurance contributions

ponctionner [3] [pɔ̃ksjɔne] **VT 1** *Méd (poumon)* to tap; *(région lombaire)* to puncture **2** *(compte en banque)* to withdraw money from; *(économies)* to make a hole *or* dent in; **on nous ponctionne un tiers de notre salaire en impôts** a third of our salary goes in tax

ponctualité [pɔ̃ktɥalite] **NF** *(exactitude)* punctuality, promptness; **avec p.** promptly, on time

ponctuation [pɔ̃ktɥasjɔ̃] **NF** punctuation

ponctuel, -elle [pɔ̃ktɥɛl] **ADJ 1** *(exact)* punctual; **être p.** to be on time

2 *(action) Br* one-off, *Am* one-shot; *(problèmes, difficultés)* occasional; *(expérience)* isolated; **ses interventions ponctuelles étaient vitales pour le projet** the contributions he/she made at various stages of the project were invaluable; **l'État accorde une aide ponctuelle aux entreprises en difficulté** the state gives backing to companies to see them through periods of financial difficulty; **les terroristes ne se livraient qu'à des actions ponctuelles** the terrorists made only sporadic attacks

3 *Ling & Math* punctual; *Phys* **source ponctuelle de chaleur** pinpoint flame; **source lumineuse ponctuelle** point source

ponctuellement [pɔ̃ktɥɛlmɑ̃] **ADV 1** *(avec exactitude)* punctually **2** *(de façon limitée)* on an ad hoc basis; **agir p.** to take action on an ad hoc basis *or* as the need arises

ponctuer [7] [pɔ̃ktɥe] **VT 1** *Gram* to punctuate **2** *Fig* to punctuate; **ses conférences étaient toujours ponctuées de plaisanteries** his/her lectures were always punctuated *or* peppered with jokes; **elle ponctuait les mots importants d'un hochement de tête** she emphasized *or* stressed the important words with a nod **3** *Mus* to phrase

USAGE ABSOLU *Gram* **savoir p.** to know how to use punctuation

pondaison [pɔ̃dɛzɔ̃] **NF** laying season

pondérable [pɔ̃derabl] **ADJ** weighable, ponderable

pondéral, -e, -aux, -ales [pɔ̃deral, -o] **ADJ** weight *(avant n)*

pondérateur, -trice [pɔ̃deratœr, -tris] **ADJ** stabilizing

pondération [pɔ̃derasjɔ̃] **NF 1** *(sang-froid)* levelheadedness; **agir/parler avec p.** to act/speak levelheadedly **2** *Bourse & Écon* weighting **3** *Pol (de pouvoirs)* balance, equilibrium **4** *Beaux-Arts & Littérature* proper balance (of parts); **conserver quelque p.** to retain a sense of measure

pondératrice [pɔ̃deratris] *voir* **pondérateur**

pondéré, -e [pɔ̃dere] **ADJ 1** *(personne)* levelheaded, steady; *(esprit)* well balanced **2** *Bourse & Écon* weighted

pondérer [18] [pɔ̃dere] **VT 1** *(pouvoirs)* to balance (out), to counterbalance **2** *Bourse & Écon* to weight

pondéreux, -euse [pɔ̃derø, -øz] *Ind* **ADJ** heavy **NM** heavy material; **les p.** heavy goods

pondeur, -euse [pɔ̃dœr, -øz] **ADJ** *(poule)* laying
☐ **pondeuse NF 1** *(poule)* laying hen, layer; **c'est une bonne pondeuse** she's a good layer **2** *Fam Péj ou Hum (femme)* **c'est une vraie pondeuse** she breeds like a rabbit

Pondichéry [pɔ̃diʃeri] **NM** Pondicherry

pondoir [pɔ̃dwar] **NM** laying place

pondre [75] [pɔ̃dr] **VT 1** *(sujet: oiseau)* to lay; **un œuf frais pondu** a new(ly)-laid egg, a freshly-laid egg

2 *Fam Péj (sujet: femme → enfant)* to produce■, to drop

3 *Fam (créer → gén)* to come up with; *(→ en série)* to churn out; **il pond un article tous les jours** he churns out an article every day; **je n'ai pondu que trois pages sur le sujet** I could only produce *or* come up with three pages on the subject

VI *(poule)* to lay (an egg/eggs); *(moustique, saumon etc)* to lay its eggs

ponette [pɔnɛt] **NF** female pony

poney [pɔnɛ] **NM** pony

pongé [pɔ̃ʒe] NM *Tex* pongee

pongidé [pɔ̃ʒide] *Zool* NM pongid
❑ **pongidés** NMPL Pongidae

pongiste [pɔ̃ʒist] NMF table tennis player

Pont [ləpɔ̃] NM *Antiq* **le P.** the (Kingdom of) Pontus

pont [pɔ̃] NM **1** *Constr* bridge; **dormir** *ou* **vivre sous les ponts** to be homeless, *Br* to sleep under the arches; **p. autoroutier** *Br* motorway *or Am* freeway flyover; **p. à bascule** bascule *or* balance bridge; **p. ferroviaire** railway bridge; **p. à haubans** cable-stayed bridge; **p. levant** lift bridge; **p. mobile** swing bridge, movable bridge; **p. à péage** toll-bridge; **p. routier** road bridge; **p. suspendu** suspension bridge; **p. tournant** *(routier)* swing bridge; *(ferroviaire)* turntable; **faire/promettre un p. d'or à qn** to offer/to promise sb a golden hello; *Fig* **jeter un p.** to build bridges; **se porter** *ou* **être solide comme le P.-Neuf** to be as fit as a fiddle; **de quoi vous plaignez-vous, vous êtes solide comme le P.-Neuf!** what are you complaining about, you'll bury us all!; **le p. du Gard** = the enormous Roman aqueduct at Nîmes; **les Ponts** = nickname of the ''École des Ponts et Chaussées''

2 *Naut* deck; **elle prend le soleil sur le p.** she's sunbathing on the sun deck; **bateau à deux/trois ponts** two-/three-decker; **p. arrière** aft *or* after deck; **p. avant** foredeck; **p. d'envol** flight deck; **p. inférieur/principal** lower/main deck; **p. supérieur** upper *or* top deck; **tout le monde sur le p.!** all hands on deck!

3 *(week-end)* long weekend; *(jour)* = day off between a national holiday and a weekend; **faire le p.** *(employé)* = to take the intervening working day or days off; **le 14 juillet tombe un jeudi, je vais faire le p.** the 14th of July falls on a Thursday, I'll take the Friday off (and have a long weekend)

4 *(structure de manutention)* **p. de chargement** loading platform; **p. élévateur** *ou* **de graissage** garage ramp, car lift, elevator platform; **p. roulant** gantry *or* travelling crane

5 *Aut* axle; **p. arrière** rear axle (and drive)

6 *Aviat* **p. aérien** airlift

7 *Anat* **p. de Varole** pons (Varolii)

8 *Élec* **p. de Wheatstone** Wheatstone bridge

9 **p. aux ânes** *Géom* pons asinorum; *Fig* old chestnut

10 *Mil* **p. d'assaut** assault bridge; **p. Bailey** Bailey bridge; **p. de bateaux** pontoon bridge

11 *Mus* bridge; *Cin & TV* **p. sonore** bridge

12 *Sport* bridge; **faire le p.** to do the crab

13 *Théât* **p. de service** catwalk bridge

❑ **Ponts et Chaussées** NMPL **les Ponts et Chaussées** *Admin* Department of Civil Engineering; *Univ* College of Civil Engineering

'**Le Pont de la rivière Kwaï**' *Lean, Boulle* 'The Bridge on the River Kwai'

Ponta Delgada [pɔ̃tadɛlgada] NM Ponta Delgada

pontage [pɔ̃taʒ] NM **1** *Méd* bypass (operation); **p. coronarien** heart bypass (operation); **on lui a fait un p.** he's/she's had a bypass, he's/she's had bypass surgery **2** *Constr* (gantry) bridging **3** *Naut* decking **4** *Chim* bridging

Pont-Aven [pɔ̃tavɑ̃n] NM *Beaux-Arts* **l'école de P.** the Pont-Aven School

pont-bascule [pɔ̃baskyl] *(pl* ponts-bascules*)* NM weighbridge

pont-canal [pɔ̃kanal] *(pl* ponts-canaux [-kano]*)* NM canal(-carrying) bridge

ponte[1] [pɔ̃t] NM **1** *Fam (autorité)* **un (grand) p.** a big shot, a bigwig; **ce sont tous de grands pontes de l'université/de la médecine** they're all top-flight academics/high up in the medical profession **2** *(dans les jeux de hasard)* punter

ponte[2] [pɔ̃t] NF **1** *Zool (action)* laying (of eggs); *(œufs → d'un oiseau)* clutch, eggs; *(→ d'un insecte, un poisson)* eggs **2** *Physiol* **p. ovulaire** ovulation

ponté, -e [pɔ̃te] *Naut* ADJ *(à un pont)* single-deck *(avant n)*; *(à plusieurs ponts)* multi-deck *(avant n)*
❑ **pontée** NF deck load

ponter [3] [pɔ̃te] VI *(aux jeux de hasard)* to punt
VT **1** *(miser)* to bet **2** *Naut* to deck

pontet [pɔ̃tɛ] NM trigger guard

Pont-Euxin [pɔ̃tøksɛ̃] NM **le P.** the Euxine Sea

pontier [pɔ̃tje] NM **1** *(qui manœuvre un pont mobile)* swing-bridge keeper **2** *(qui conduit un pont roulant)* travelling-crane operator

pontife [pɔ̃tif] NM **1** *Fam (autorité)* pundit, bigwig, big shot **2** *Antiq* pontifex, pontiff **3** *Rel* pontiff

pontifiant, -e [pɔ̃tifjɑ̃, -ɑ̃t] ADJ pontificating

pontifical, -e, -aux, -ales [pɔ̃tifikal, -o] ADJ **1** *Rel (insignes, cérémonie)* pontifical; *(État, trône)* papal **2** *Antiq* pontifical
NM pontifical

pontificat [pɔ̃tifika] NM pontificate; **sous le p. de Jean-Paul II** during the pontificate of John-Paul II

pontifier [9] [pɔ̃tifje] VI to pontificate; **arrête de p.** stop pontificating

pontil [pɔ̃til] NM *Tech (verre)* button of hot glass *(used to fix the glass object to the punty)*; *(barre)* punty, pontil (rod)

pont-l'évêque [pɔ̃levɛk] NM INV Pont l'Évêque (cheese)

pont-levis [pɔ̃ləvi] *(pl* ponts-levis*)* NM drawbridge

ponton [pɔ̃tɔ̃] NM **1** *(d'un port de commerce)* pontoon, floating dock; *(d'un port de plaisance)* landing stage, jetty; *(pour nageurs)* (floating) platform **2** *(chaland)* hulk, lighter; *(vieux vaisseau)* hulk

ponton-grue [pɔ̃tɔ̃gry] *(pl* pontons-grues*)* NM floating crane

pontonnier [pɔ̃tɔnje] NM *Mil* pontonier

pont-promenade [pɔ̃prɔmnad] *(pl* ponts-promenade *ou* ponts-promenades*)* NM promenade deck

pont-rail [pɔ̃raj] *(pl* ponts-rails*)* NM *Br* railway *or Am* railroad bridge

pont-route [pɔ̃rut] *(pl* ponts-routes*)* NM road bridge

pontuseau, -x [pɔ̃tyzo] NM *Tech* **1** *(tige)* chain wire **2** *(trace)* chain line **3** *(rouleau)* register roll, table roll

pool [pul] NM **1** *Écon* pool; **p. d'assurances** insurance pool; **p. bancaire** banking pool; **p. de l'or** gold pool **2** *(équipe)* pool; **p. de dactylos** typing pool; **p. de secrétaires** secretarial pool

Poona [puna] NM Poona

POP [peɔpe] NM *Chim (abrév* **polluant organique persistant)** POP

pop [pɔp] ADJ INV *(art, chanteur, mouvement)* pop; **musique p.** pop (music); **p. électronique** electropop
NM OU NF pop (music)

pop art [pɔpart] *(pl* pop arts*)* NM pop art

Popaul [pɔpol] NM *Vulg (pénis)* dick, prick, cock; **étrangler P.** to beat one's meat, to bang *or Br* bash the bishop

pop-corn [pɔpkɔrn] NM INV popcorn

pope [pɔp] NM *(Eastern Orthodox Church)* priest

popeline [pɔplin] NF *Tex* poplin; **en** *ou* **de p.** poplin *(avant n)*

poplité, -e [pɔplite] ADJ *Anat* popliteal; **creux p.** popliteal space

pop music [pɔpmyzik, pɔpmjuzik] *(pl* pop musics*)* NF pop (music)

popote [pɔpɔt] *Fam* NF **1** *(cuisine)* cooking▪; **faire la p.** to do the cooking **2** *(matériel)* mess kit▪ **3** *Mil (mess)* officers' mess▪
ADJ INV overly houseproud▪ **elle est très p.** she's very much the stay-at-home type

popotin [pɔpɔtɛ̃] NM *Fam* butt, *Br* bum

popov [pɔpɔf] *Fam* ADJ Russian▪
NMF Russki

poppers [pɔpœrz] NMPL *Fam Arg drogue* poppers

popu [pɔpy] ADJ *Fam* working-class▪

populace [pɔpylas] NF *Fam Péj* rabble, hoi polloi, plebs

populacier, -ère [pɔpylasje, -ɛr] ADJ vulgar, common

populage [pɔpylaʒ] NM *Bot* marsh marigold

populaire [pɔpylɛr] ADJ **1** *(ouvrier)* working-class; **les quartiers populaires** the working-class areas; **les classes populaires** the working classes

2 *(tradition, croyance)* popular; **bon sens p.** popular wisdom

3 *Pol (gouvernement)* popular; *(démocratie, tribunal)* people's *(avant n)*; *(soulèvement)* mass *(avant n)*; **la volonté p.** the will of the people

4 *(destiné au peuple)* popular; **art p.** popular art; **romans populaires** popular fiction

5 *(qui a du succès → chanteur, mesures)* popular; **elle s'est rendue très p. auprès des étudiants** she made herself very popular with the students; **la voile devient très p.** sailing is growing in popularity *or* becoming more and more popular

6 *Ling (étymologie)* popular; *(niveau de langue)* colloquial

populairement [pɔpylɛrmɑ̃] ADV *Ling* colloquially; **comme on dit p.** as the popular phrase goes

popularisation [pɔpylarizasjɔ̃] NF popularization

populariser [3] [pɔpylarize] VT to popularize

popularité [pɔpylarite] NF popularity; **elle jouit d'une grande p. parmi les étudiants** she's very popular with the students; **le président a perdu de sa p.** there's been a decline in the president's popularity

population [pɔpylasjɔ̃] NF **1** *(nombre d'individus)* population; **p. active/civile** working/civilian population; **p. canine** dog *or* canine population; **p. excédentaire** surplus population; **p. inactive** non-working population; **p. mondiale** world population

2 *(peuple)* people; **la p. locale** the local people, the locals

3 *Mktg* **p. cible** target population; **p. mère** basic population; **p. prévue** projected population

4 *Astron & Phys* population

populationniste [pɔpylasjɔnist] ADJ encouraging population growth; **politique p.** policy of population growth; **gouvernement p.** government in favour of population growth
NMF = supporter of measures encouraging population growth

populeux, -euse [pɔpylø, -øz] ADJ *(quartier)* heavily *or* densely populated, populous; *(place, rue)* crowded, very busy

populiculteur [pɔpylikyltœr] NM poplar grower

populiculture [pɔpylikyltyr] NF poplar cultivation *or* growing

populisme [pɔpylism] NM **1** *Hist* populism **2** *Littérature* populism *(literary movement in the 1920s and 1930s that set out to describe the lives of working-class people)*

populiste [pɔpylist] ADJ **1** *Hist* populist **2** *Littérature* populist
NMF **1** *Hist* populist **2** *Littérature* populist *(writer)* *(member of the literary movement in the 1920s and 1930s that set out to describe the lives of working-class people)*

populo [pɔpylo] NM *Fam* **1** *(foule)* crowd▪; **il y avait un de ces populos en ville** the town was jam-packed *or Br* chock-a-block *or* heaving **2** *(peuple)* **le p.** the plebs, the riff-raff, the rabble

poque [pɔk] NF *Can Joual (contusion)* bruise▪; *(bosse)* bump▪; *(égratignure)* scratch▪

poqué, -e [pɔke] ADJ *Can Joual (fatigué)* worn out, done in

poquer [3] [pɔke] VT *Can Joual (contusionner)* to bruise▪; *(emboutir)* to dent▪, to bump▪; *(érafler)* to scratch▪; *(frapper)* to hit▪; *Fam* **se faire p. la gueule** to get one's face smashed up
VI = in boules, to throw the boule in such a way that it does not roll on landing

poquet [pɔkɛ] NM *Agr* seed hole

poquettes [pɔkɛt] NFPL *Belg Méd* chickenpox

porc [pɔr] NM **1** *Zool Br* pig, *Am* hog; **manger comme un p.** to eat like a pig; **p. sauvage** wild boar **2** *Culin* pork **3** *(peau)* pigskin **4** *Fam (personne)* pig, swine
❑ **de porc** ADJ **1** *Culin* pork *(avant n)* **2** *(en peau)* pigskin *(avant n)*

porcelaine [pɔrsəlɛn] NF **1** *(produit)* china, porcelain; **p. dure/tendre** hard-paste/softpaste porcelain; **p. phosphatique** *ou* **tendre naturelle** bone china

2 *(pièce)* piece of china *or* porcelain

3 *(ensemble)* **la p.** china, chinaware, porcelain; **p. de Chine** china; **p. de Limoges** Limoges porcelain; **p. de Saxe** Dresden china; **p. de Sèvres** Sèvres china

4 *Zool (mollusque)* cowrie
❑ **de porcelaine** ADJ **1** *(tasse, objet)* china *(avant n)*, porcelain *(avant n)*

2 *(teint)* porcelain *(avant n)*, peaches-and-cream *(avant n)*

porcelainier, -ère [pɔrsəlenje, -ɛr] **ADJ** china *(avant n)*, porcelain *(avant n)*
NM,F porcelain *or* china manufacturer

porcelet [pɔrsəlɛ] **NM** piglet

porc-épic [pɔrkepik] *(pl* **porcs-épics)** **NM 1** *Zool* porcupine; **p. d'Amérique** North American porcupine, Canada porcupine **2** *(personne revêche)* prickly person **3** *Fam (homme mal rasé)* **c'est un vrai p.** he's really bristly

porchaison [pɔrʃɛzɔ̃] **NF** *Chasse* boar(-hunting) season

porche [pɔrʃ] **NM** porch

porcher, -ère [pɔrʃe, -ɛr] **NM,F** swineherd

porcherie [pɔrʃəri] **NF** *aussi Fig* pigsty, *Am* pigpen

porcin, -e [pɔrsɛ̃, -in] **ADJ 1** *(industrie, production)* pig *(avant n)* **2** *(yeux, figure)* pig-like, piggy
NM pig; **les porcins** the pig family, *Spéc* the suidians

pore [pɔr] **NM** pore; **avoir les pores dilatés** to have open pores; *Fig* **elle sue la suffisance par tous les pores** she exudes *or* oozes self-importance

poreux, -euse [pɔrø, -øz] **ADJ** porous

porion [pɔrjɔ̃] **NM** *(dans le nord de la France)* overman, foreman *(in coalmine)*

porno [pɔrno] *Fam* **ADJ** *(abrév* **pornographique)** *(film, magazine, scène)* porn *(avant n)*, porno *(avant n)*; **des photos pornos** dirty pictures
NM *(abrév* **pornographie) 1 le p.** *(genre)* porn; *(industrie)* the porn industry **2** *(film)* blue movie, *Br* porno film

pornographe [pɔrnɔgraf] **NMF** pornographer

pornographie [pɔrnɔgrafi] **NF** pornography

pornographique [pɔrnɔgrafik] **ADJ** pornographic

porophore [pɔrɔfɔr] **NM** expanding agent

porosité [pɔrozite] **NF** porosity

porphyra [pɔrfira] **NF** *Bot* Porphyra

porphyre [pɔrfir] **NM** *Minér* porphyry

porphyrie [pɔrfiri] **NF** *Méd* porphyria, royal purple disease

porphyrine [pɔfirin] **NF** *Biol & Chim* porphyrin

porphyrique [pɔrfirik] **ADJ** *Minér* porphyritic

porphyrogénète [pɔrfirɔʒenɛt] *Hist* **ADJ** porphyrogenitus, born in the purple
NM porphyrogenitus

porphyroïde [pɔrfirɔid] **ADJ** *Minér* porphyroid

porque [pɔrk] **NF** *Naut* web frame *(to strengthen ship)*

porreau, -x [pɔro] **NM** *Suisse* leek

porridge [pɔridʒ] **NM** porridge

port¹ [pɔr] **NM 1** *(pour bateaux)* harbour; *(plus important, ville)* port; **dans le p. de Dunkerque** in Dunkirk harbour; **sur le p.** on the quayside; **entrer au p.** to come into port *or* harbour; **quitter le p.** to leave port *or* harbour; **p. artificiel** artificial port; **p. d'attache** port of registry, home port; *Fig* home base; **p. de commerce** commercial port; **p. d'embarquement** *(de marchandises)* port of shipment; *(de personnes)* port of embarkation; **p. d'entrée** port of entry; **p. d'escale** port of call; **p. fluvial** river port; **p. franc** free port; **p. de guerre** *ou* **militaire** naval base; **p. maritime** *ou* **de mer** sea port; **P. Moresby** Port Moresby; **p. naturel** natural harbour; **p. de pêche** fishing port; **p. de plaisance** marina; **p. de relâche** port of call; **P. of Spain** Port of Spain; **p. de transit** port of transit; *Fig* **nous touchons** *ou* **arrivons au p.** we're on the home straight; **faire naufrage (en arrivant) au p., échouer en vue du p.** to fall at the last fence
2 *Littéraire (havre, refuge)* haven
3 *Ordinat* port; *(pour Internet)* socket; **p. de communication** comms port, communications port; **p. d'imprimante** printer port; **p. modem** modem port; **p. parallèle** parallel port; **p. série** serial port; **p. série universel** USB, universal serial bus; **p. souris** mouse port
❏ **à bon port ADV** safely, safe and sound; **nous sommes arrivés à bon p.** we got there safe and sound; **les verres sont arrivés à bon p.** the glasses got there in one piece *or* without mishap; **le chauffeur les a conduits à bon p.** the driver brought them safely to the right place

'Port au soleil couchant' *Lorrain* 'Seaport at Sunset'

port² [pɔr] **NM 1** *(d'une lettre, d'un colis)* postage; **frais de p.** (cost of) postage; **(en) p. dû/payé** postage due/paid; **p. et emballage** postage and packing; **p. franc, p. payé** postage paid; **p. compris** postage included
2 *Transp (de marchandises)* carriage; **p. franc, franco de p.** carriage paid *or* included; **p. avancé** carriage forward, freight collect; **p. dû** carriage forward; **p. franc, p. payé** carriage paid; **p. payé, assurance comprise** carriage insurance paid
3 *(possession → d'une arme)* carrying; *(→ d'un uniforme, d'un casque)* wearing; **p. d'armes prohibé** illegal carrying of weapons; *Mil* **se mettre au p. d'armes** to shoulder arms; **le p. du casque est obligatoire** *(sur panneau)* safety helmets must be worn
4 *(maintien)* bearing, deportment; **elle a un p. de tête très gracieux** she holds her head very gracefully; **avoir un p. de reine** to have a regal *or* queenly bearing
5 *(d'une plante)* habit
6 *Mus* **p. de voix** port de voix, appogiatura
7 *Naut* **p. en lourd** dead weight

port³ [pɔr] **NM** *(mot occitan) (col)* pass *(in the Pyrenees)*

portabilité [pɔrtabilite] **NF** *Ordinat* portability; *Tél* **p. du numéro** number portability

portable [pɔrtabl] **ADJ 1** *(téléviseur, machine à écrire, ordinateur)* portable; *(téléphone) Br* mobile *(avant n)*, *Am* cellular *(avant n)* **2** *(vêtement)* wearable **3** *Fin* to be paid in person
NM *(ordinateur)* laptop; *(téléphone) Br* mobile, mobile phone, *Am* cell, cellphone

portage [pɔrtaʒ] **NM 1** *(d'équipement)* porterage **2** *Naut* portage **3** *Banque & Écon* piggybacking **4** *(distribution d'un journal à domicile)* home delivery

portail [pɔrtaj] **NM 1** *(d'une église)* portal; *(d'un jardin, d'une école)* gate **2** *Ordinat* portal

portal, -e, -aux, -ales [pɔrtal, -o] **ADJ** *Anat* portal

portance [pɔrtɑ̃s] **NF 1** *Aviat* lift **2** *(d'un terrain)* bearing capacity

portant, -e [pɔrtɑ̃, -ɑ̃t] **ADJ 1** *Naut* **vent p.** fair wind **2** *(mur)* load-bearing **3** *(locution)* **bien/mal p.** in good/poor health; **il est bien p.** he's very well
NM 1 *Naut* outrigger **2** *Théât* upright, support *(for flats)* **3** *(pour vêtements)* rail **4** *(poignée)* handle

portatif, -ive [pɔrtatif, -iv] **ADJ** *(gén)* portable; *(ordinateur)* laptop
NM *(ordinateur)* laptop

Port-au-Prince [pɔroprɛ̃s] **NM** Port-au-Prince

porte [pɔrt] **NF 1** *(d'une maison, d'un véhicule, d'un meuble)* door; *(d'un passe-plat)* hatch; **on vient de sonner, tu vas ouvrir la p.?** someone's just rung the bell, could you answer *or* open the door?; **le piano est resté coincé dans la p.** the piano got stuck in the door *or* doorway; **fermer** *ou* **interdire** *ou* **refuser sa p. à qn** to bar sb from one's house; **fermer ses portes** *(magasin)* to close down; **ouvrir sa p. à qn** to welcome sb; **ouvrir la p. toute grande à qn** to welcome sb with open arms; **ouvrir ses portes** *(magasin, musée)* to open; **un père ministre, ça ouvre pas mal de portes** a father who happens to be a minister can open quite a few doors; *Aut* **p. arrière** rear passenger door; *Aut* **p. avant** *(côté conducteur)* driver door; *(côté passager)* front passenger door; **p. coupe-feu** firedoor; **p. dérobée** hidden door; **p. de derrière/devant** back/front door; **p. d'entrée** front door; *Belg* **p. de rue** front door; **p. de secours** emergency exit; **p. de service** trademen's entrance; **p. de sortie** way out, exit; *Fig* way out, let-out; **trouver une p. de sortie** to find a way out; **ménager à qn une p. de sortie** to leave sb a way out; *aussi Fig* **à ma/sa p.** at my/his/her door, on my/his/her doorstep; **l'hiver est à nos portes** winter is at the door; **Lyon, ce n'est pas la p. à côté** it's a fair way to Lyons; **il n'habite pas la p. à côté** he doesn't exactly live round the corner; **elle est entrée dans l'entreprise par la grande p.** she went straight in at the top of the company; **entrer dans une profession par la petite p.** to get into a profession by the back door; **l'équipe quitte le tournoi par la grande p.** the team is leaving the tournament in style; **après le scandale, il est sorti par la petite p.** after the scandal, he made a discreet exit; *Fig* **ouvrir la p. à qch** to pave the way for sth; **ouvrir la p. à l'espoir** to allow a measure of hope; **cette décision ouvre toute grande la p. à l'injustice** this decision throws the door wide open to injustice; **prendre la p.** to leave; **il lui a dit de prendre la p.** he showed him/her the door; **j'y suis allé mais j'ai trouvé p. close** *ou Belg* **p. de bois** I went round but nobody was in *or* at home; **il a essayé tous les éditeurs, mais partout il a trouvé p. close** *ou Belg* **p. de bois** he tried all the publishers, but without success; **c'est la p. ouverte à tous les abus** it leaves the door wide open for all kinds of abuses; *Prov* **il faut qu'une p. soit ouverte ou fermée** = it has to be either one way or the other
2 *(passage dans une enceinte)* gate; **les portes de Paris** = the old city gates around Paris; **p. d'écluse** lock gate; **p. d'embarquement** (departure) gate; **p. triomphale** triumphal arch; **les portes de l'enfer** the gates of hell; **les portes du paradis** heaven's gates, the pearly gates; **la P. d'Orléans/de Clichy** Porte d'Orléans/de Clichy; **la P., la Sublime-P.** the (Sublime) Porte; **la p. de Versailles** = site of a large exhibition complex in Paris where major trade fairs take place
3 *(panneau)* door (panel); **p. basculante/battante** up-and-over/swing door; **p. coulissante** *ou* **roulante** sliding door; **p. à deux battants** double door; **p. coupée** half-door, stable door; **p. escamotable** folding door; **p. palière** *(qui donne sur un palier)* landing door; **portes palières** *(dans le métro)* platform screen doors, platform-edge doors; **p. tournante** revolving door; **p. vitrée** glass door
4 *Sport* gate
5 *Ordinat* gate
ADJ F *Anat (veine)* portal
❏ **à la porte ADV 1 à la p.!** out of here!; **ne reste pas à la p.** don't stay on the doorstep; **je suis à la p. de chez moi** *(sans clefs)* I'm locked out; *(chassé)* I've been thrown out (of my home); **mettre qn à la p.** *(importun)* to throw sb out; *(élève)* to expel sb; *(employé)* to fire *or* to dismiss sb
2 *Belg (dehors)* outside; **quelle température fait-il à la p.?** what's the temperature outside?
❏ **de porte à porte, porte à porte ADV** from door to door; **je mets 40 minutes p. à p.** it takes me 40 minutes door to door
❏ **de porte en porte ADV** from door to door

'La Porte étroite' *Gide* 'Strait is the Gate'

porté [pɔrte] **NM** *(en danse)* porté

porte-aéronefs [pɔrtaerɔnɛf] **NM INV** aircraft carrier

porte-à-faux [pɔrtafo] **NM INV** overhang; *Constr* cantilever
❏ **en porte-à-faux ADV être en p.** *(mur)* to be out of plumb, to be out of true; *(roche)* to be in a precarious position; *Fig* to be in an awkward position; **mettre qn en p.** to put sb in an awkward position; **il est en p. par rapport à la politique officielle du parti** he's at odds with the official party line

porte-affiches [pɔrtafiʃ] **NM INV** noticeboard

porte-aiguille [pɔrtegɥij] *(pl* **inv** *ou* **porte-aiguilles)** **NM 1** *Méd* needle holder **2** *Couture (d'une machine)* needle holder; *(étui)* needle case

porte-amarre [pɔrtamar] **NM INV** line-throwing machine; **fusil p.** line-throwing gun

porte-à-porte [pɔrtapɔrt] **NM INV** *(pour vendre)* door-to-door selling; *(démarchage électoral)* door-to-door canvassing, doorstepping; **faire du p.** *(pour vendre)* to sell from door to door, to be a door-to-door salesman, *f* saleswoman; *(pour un candidat, un parti)* to go canvassing from door-to-door, to go doorstepping

porte-autos [pɔrtoto] **ADJ INV** car-carrying, transporter *(avant n)*

porte-avions [pɔrtavjɔ̃] **NM INV** aircraft carrier

porte-bagages [pɔrtbagaʒ] **NM INV** *(d'un vélo)* rack; *(d'un train)* (luggage) rack; *(d'une voiture)* roof rack

porte-balai [pɔrtbalɛ] *(pl* **inv** *ou* **porte-balais)** **NM** *Élec* brush holder

porte-bannière [pɔrtbanjɛr] *(pl* **inv** *ou* **porte-bannières)** **NMF** banner bearer

porte-barge [pɔrtəbarʒ] *(pl* **inv** *ou* **porte-barges)** **NM** container barge

porte-bébé [pɔrtbebe] *(pl* **inv** *ou* **porte-bébés)** **NM 1** *(nacelle)* carry-cot **2** *(harnais)* baby sling

porte-billet, porte-billets [pɔrtbijɛ] (*pl* **porte-billets**) NM *Br* wallet, *Am* billfold

porte-bois [pɔrtbwa] NM INV *Entom* caddisworm

porte-bombes [pɔrtbɔ̃b] NM INV *Mil & Aviat* bomb rack

porte-bonheur [pɔrtbɔnœr] NM INV lucky charm; **une patte de lapin p.** a lucky rabbit's foot

porte-bouquet [pɔrtbukɛ] (*pl* **porte-bouquets**) NM flower holder, flower vase

porte-bouteille, porte-bouteilles [pɔrtbutɛj] (*pl* **porte-bouteilles**) NM 1 (*châssis*) wine rack 2 (*panier*) bottle-carrier 3 (*d'un réfrigérateur*) bottle rack

porte-brancard [pɔrtbrɑ̃kar] (*pl* **inv** *ou* **porte-brancards**) NM tug

porte-carte, porte-cartes [pɔrtəkart] (*pl* **porte-cartes**) NM 1 (*portefeuille*) card-holder, *Br* wallet, *Am* billfold (*with spaces for cards, photos etc*) 2 (*de cartes géographiques*) map holder

porte-chapeaux [pɔrtʃapo] NM INV hatstand

porte-chars [pɔrtʃar] NM INV *Mil* tank transporter

porte-chéquier [pɔrtʃekje] (*pl* **porte-chéquiers**) NM chequebook holder

porte-cigare, porte-cigares [pɔrtsigar] (*pl* **porte-cigares**) NM cigar case

porte-cigarette, porte-cigarettes [pɔrtsigarɛt] (*pl* **porte-cigarettes**) NM cigarette case

porte-clefs, porte-clés [pɔrtəkle] NM INV 1 (*anneau*) key ring 2 (*étui*) key case 3 *Vieilli* (*gardien*) turnkey

porte-conteneurs [pɔrtkɔ̃tnœr] NM INV container ship

porte-copie [pɔrtkɔpi] (*pl* **inv** *ou* **porte-copies**) NM *Typ* copy holder

porte-couteau [pɔrtkuto] (*pl* **inv** *ou* **porte-couteaux**) NM knife rest

porte-cravate [pɔrtkravat] (*pl* **inv** *ou* **porte-cravates**) NM tie rack

porte-crayon [pɔrtkrɛjɔ̃] (*pl* **inv** *ou* **porte-crayons**) NM pencil holder

porte-croix [pɔrtəkrwa] NM INV cross bearer

porte-document, porte-documents [pɔrtdɔkymɑ̃] (*pl* **porte-documents**) NM briefcase, document case

porte-drapeau [pɔrtdrapo] (*pl* **inv** *ou* **porte-drapeaux**) NM *aussi Fig* standard bearer

portée [pɔrte] NF 1 *Mil & Opt* range; (*de la voix*) range, compass; **(à) courte p.** short-range; **(à) grande p.** long-range; **(à) longue p.** long-range; **(à) moyenne p.** medium-range

2 (*champ d'action → d'une mesure, d'une loi*) scope; (*impact → d'une décision*) impact, significance; (*→ d'un événement*) consequences, repercussions; (*→ d'une déclaration, des mots*) (full) significance *or* import; (*→ d'une publicité, d'une campagne*) reach; **l'incident a eu une p. considérable** the incident had far-reaching consequences; **une découverte d'une grande p.** a far-reaching discovery; **ces idées furent sans grande p. jusqu'en 1940** these ideas had very little impact until 1940

3 *Zool* (*gén*) litter; (*d'une truie*) farrow

4 *Mus* staff, stave

5 *Constr* (*dimension*) span; (*charge*) load

6 *Élec* span

7 *Tech* area of bearing

8 (*d'un navire*) burden, tonnage; **p. en lourd** deadweight (capacity); **p. utile** load-carrying capacity

□ **à la portée de** PRÉP 1 (*près de*) close *or* near to; **ne pas laisser à la p. des enfants** (*sur emballage*) keep out of the reach of children

2 (*pouvant être compris par*) **son livre est à la p. de tous** his/her book is easily accessible to the ordinary reader; **l'article n'est pas à ma p.** the article is beyond me; **un jeu à la p. des 10–12 ans** a game suitable for 10–12 year olds

3 (*locution*) **à la p. de toutes les bourses** easily affordable, to suit all pockets; **ce n'est pas à la p. de toutes les bourses** not everyone can afford it

□ **à portée de** PRÉP within reach of; **à p. de fusil** within (firing) range, within gunshot; **à p. de canon** within gun range; **à p. de (la) main** within (easy) reach; **avoir** *ou* **garder qch à p. de (la) main** to keep sth handy *or* close at hand *or* within (easy) reach; **gardez la trousse de secours à p. de la main** keep the first-aid kit in a handy place; **à p. de voix** within earshot

porte-épée [pɔrtepe] (*pl* **inv** *ou* **porte-épées**) NM 1 (*pièce de cuir*) sword knot, frog 2 *Ich* swordtail

porte-étendard [pɔrtetɑ̃dar] (*pl* **inv** *ou* **porte-étendards**) NM 1 (*officier*) standard bearer 2 (*étui*) standard pocket

porte-étrivière [pɔrtetrivjɛr] (*pl* **inv** *ou* **porte-étrivières**) NM stirrup leather holder

portefaix [pɔrtəfɛ] NM INV (*porteur*) porter

porte-fanion [pɔrtəfanjɔ̃] (*pl* **inv** *ou* **porte-fanions**) NM pennant bearer

porte-fenêtre [pɔrtfənɛtr] (*pl* **portes-fenêtres**) NF French window

portefeuille [pɔrtəfœj] NM 1 (*étui*) *Br* wallet, *Am* billfold; *Fam* **avoir le p. rembourré** *ou* **bien garni** to be comfortably off

2 *Fin* (*ensemble*) portfolio; **p. d'actions** share portfolio; **p. d'activités** business portfolio, portfolio mix; **p. d'assurances** insurance portfolio; *Com* **p. effets** bills in hand, holdings; **p. indexé** indexed portfolio; **p. d'investissements** investment portfolio; **p. avec mandat** discretionary portfolio; *Mktg* **p. de marques** brand portfolio; *Mktg* **p. de produits** product portfolio; **p. de titres** portfolio of securities

3 *Pol* portfolio; **on lui a confié le p. des Affaires étrangères** he/she has been given *or* he/she holds the foreign affairs portfolio

porte-fort [pɔrtfɔr] NM INV *Jur* 1 (*engagement*) guarantee 2 (*personne*) guarantor

porte-glaive [pɔrtglɛv] (*pl* **inv** *ou* **porte-glaives**) NM 1 *Hist* (**chevalier**) p. sword bearer 2 *Ich* swordtail

porte-greffe [pɔrtəgrɛf] (*pl* **inv** *ou* **porte-greffes**) NM *Hort* stock

porte-hauban [pɔrtəoba̅] (*pl* **inv** *ou* **porte-haubans**) NM *Naut* chainwale, channel

porte-hélicoptères [pɔrtelikɔptɛr] NM INV helicopter carrier *or* ship

porte-jarretelles [pɔrtʒartɛl] NM INV *Br* suspender belt, *Am* garter belt

porte-journaux [pɔrtʒurno] NM INV newspaper rack

porte-lame [pɔrtəlam] (*pl* **inv** *ou* **porte-lames**) NM blade holder

portelone [pɔrtəlɔn] NM *Naut* cargo door, cargo port

porte-malheur [pɔrtmalœr] NM INV 1 (*personne*) jinx, *Littéraire* Jonah 2 (*objet*) jinx; **les plumes de paon sont considérées comme un p.** peacock feathers are thought to bring bad luck

portemanteau, -x [pɔrtmɑ̃to] NM 1 (*sur pied*) coat stand, hatstand; (*mural*) coat rack 2 (*cintre*) coathanger 3 *Arch* (*malle*) portmanteau

portement [pɔrtəmɑ̃] NM **p. de croix** (Christ's) bearing of the Cross

porte-menu [pɔrtmənu] (*pl* **inv** *ou* **porte-menus**) NM menu holder

porte-missile [pɔrtmisil] (*pl* **inv** *ou* **porte-missiles**) NM missile carrier

porte-monnaie [pɔrtmɔnɛ] NM INV *Br* purse, *Am* change purse; **p. électronique** electronic purse *or* wallet; *Fam* **avoir le p. rembourré** *ou* **bien garni** to be comfortably off

porte-montre [pɔrtmɔ̃tr] (*pl* **inv** *ou* **porte-montres**) NM 1 (*support*) watch stand 2 (*vitrine*) show case (for watches)

porte-musc [pɔrtmysk] (*pl* **inv** *ou* **porte-muscs**) NM *Zool* musk deer

porte-musique [pɔrtmyzik] NM INV music case

porte-objet [pɔrtɔbʒɛ] (*pl* **inv** *ou* **porte-objets**) NM 1 (*de microscope*) slide 2 (*platine*) stage

porte-outil [pɔrtuti] (*pl* **inv** *ou* **porte-outils**) NM (*gén*) tool holder; (*d'une perceuse*) chuck; (*d'une raboteuse*) stock; (*d'un tour*) slide rest

porte-papier [pɔrtpapje] NM INV toilet paper holder; (*pour rouleau*) toilet roll holder

porte-paquet [pɔrtpakɛ] (*pl* **porte-paquets**) NM *Belg* (*d'un vélo*) rack

porte-parapluie [pɔrtparaplɥi] (*pl* **inv** *ou* **porte-parapluies**) NM umbrella stand

porte-parole [pɔrtparɔl] NM INV

Note that it is no longer considered a mistake to feminize this word in sense 1 and to say **une porte-parole** but some French speakers nonetheless regard this form as unacceptable, especially in France. See also the entry **féminisation**.

1 (*personne*) spokesperson, spokesman, *f* spokeswoman; **se faire le p. de qn** to speak on sb's behalf 2 (*périodique*) mouthpiece, organ

porte-plume [pɔrtplym] (*pl* **inv** *ou* **porte-plumes**) NM pen holder

porte-poisse [pɔrtpwas] NM INV *Fam* jinx ∎

porte-poussière, porte-poussières (*pl* **porte-poussières**) [pɔrtpusjɛr] NM *Can* dustpan

porte-queue [pɔrtəkø] (*pl* **inv** *ou* **porte-queues**) NM *Orn* swallowtail

porter¹ [pɔrte] = **porté**

porter² [pɔrter] NM (*bière*) porter

PORTER³ [3] [pɔrte]

VT ∎ to carry A1, C1, 4–6 ∎ to bear A1, C1, 2, 4, 7 ∎ to take A2 ∎ to give strength to A2 ∎ to write down B3 ∎ to direct B4 ∎ to feel B6 ∎ to wear C1 ∎ to show C2 ∎ to have C1, 3

VI ∎ to carry 1 ∎ to hit home 3

VT **A.** *TENIR, SUPPORTER* 1 (*soutenir → colis, fardeau, meuble*) to carry; (*→ bannière, pancarte, cercueil*) to carry, to bear; **aide-moi à p. le sac jusqu'à la cuisine** help me to carry the bag to the kitchen; **j'ai porté sa malle jusqu'au grenier** I carried his/her trunk up to the attic; **tu peux p. combien?** how much can you carry?; **son cheval portera 56 kilos** his/her horse will carry 56 kilos; **deux piliers portent le toit** two pillars take the weight of *or* support the roof; **la glace n'est pas assez épaisse pour nous p.** the ice is too thin to bear our weight; *Sport* **celui qui porte le ballon** the player with *or* in possession of the ball; *Mil* **portez armes!** shoulder arms!; **p. qn sur son dos/dans ses bras** to carry sb on one's back/in one's arms; **le kangourou porte son petit dans une poche** the kangaroo carries its young in a pouch; **ses jambes ne la portaient plus** her legs couldn't carry her any more; **se laisser p. par le courant** to let oneself be carried (away) by the current; *Équitation* **p. son cheval** to carry one's horse, to keep one's horse together; *Fig* **elle porte bien son âge** she looks young for her age; *Littéraire* **p. beau** to be sprightly; **p. la responsabilité de qch** to bear (the) responsibility for sth; **il a trouvé cette responsabilité bien lourde à p.** this responsibility weighed heavily upon him

2 (*soutenir moralement → sujet: foi, religion*) to give strength to, to support; **c'est l'espoir de le retrouver qui la porte** the hope of finding him again keeps her going

B. *METTRE, AMENER* 1 (*amener*) to take; **p. qch à qn** to take sth to sb; **p. un message à qn** to take *or* to convey a message to sb; **porte-lui ce colis** take him/her this parcel, deliver this parcel to him/her; **p. des fleurs sur la tombe de qn** to take flowers to sb's grave; **portez-le sur le canapé** take *or* carry him to the settee; **se faire p. un repas** to have a meal brought (to one); **p. une œuvre à l'écran/à la scène** to adapt a work for the screen/the stage; **p. le débat sur la place publique** to make the debate public; **p. une affaire devant les tribunaux** to take *or* to bring a matter before the courts; **elle a porté sa requête jusqu'au Président de la République** she took her petition as far as the President; **p. qn au pouvoir** to bring sb to power; **p. une émotion/crise à son paroxysme** to bring an emotion to a peak/a crisis to a head; **p. son art à la perfection** to perfect one's art; **cela porte le total à 210 euros** that brings the total (up) to 210 euros; **les frais d'inscription ont été portés à 35 euros** the registration fees have been increased *or* raised to 35 euros; **il vient de p. le score de 110 à 123** he's just raised the score from 110 to 123; *Culin* **p. qch à ébullition** to bring sth to the boil; *Métal* **p. qch au rouge** to heat sth to red-heat

2 (*diriger*) **p. sa** *ou* **la main à sa tête** to raise one's hand to one's head; **p. sa** *ou* **la main à son chapeau** to raise one's hand to one's hat; **il porta la main à sa poche** he put his hand to his pocket; **il porta la main à son revolver** he reached for his gun; **p. une tasse à ses lèvres** to lift *or* to raise a cup to one's lips; **p. le buste en**

avant to lean forward; **p. son regard vers** *ou* **sur** to look towards *or* in the direction of; **p. ses pas vers** to make one's way towards, to head for; *Littéraire* **les pavés sur lesquels il avait tant de fois porté ses pas** the pavement on which he had so often walked; *Mil* **p. des troupes en avant** to move troops forward

3 *(enregistrer → donnée)* to write down, to put down; **p. sa signature sur un registre** to sign a register; **porte ce point sur le graphique** plot that point onto the graph; **p. qn absent** to report sb absent; **se faire p. absent/malade** to go absent/sick; **p. qn disparu** to report sb missing; **p. qn déserteur** to report *or* to declare sb a deserter; **portez le vin à mon compte** put the wine on my account; *Compta* **p. un achat sur un compte** to enter a purchase on an account; *Fin* **p. une somme au compte clients** to post a sum to accounts receivable; **p. 200 euros au crédit de qn** to credit sb's account with 200 euros, to credit 200 euros to sb's account; **p. 200 euros au débit de qn** to debit 200 euros from sb's account

4 *(appliquer → effort, énergie)* to direct, to bring, to bear; **p. son attention sur** to focus one's attention on, to turn one's attention to; **p. son choix sur** to choose; **p. une accusation contre qn** to bring a charge against sb; **il a fait p. tout son effort** *ou* **ses efforts sur la réussite du projet** he did his utmost to make the project successful; **p. une attaque contre qn** to direct an attack at *or* to attack sb; **p. ses vues sur qn** *(pour accomplir une tâche)* to have sb in mind *(for a job)*; *(pour l'épouser)* to have one's eye on sb

5 *(inciter)* **mon intervention l'a portée à plus de clémence** my intervention made her inclined *or* prompted her to be more lenient; **le paysage portait à la mélancolie** the scenery elicited feelings of melancholy; **l'alcool peut p. les gens à des excès/à la violence** alcohol can drive people to excesses/induce people to be violent; **qu'est-ce qui vous a porté à faire du théâtre?** what made you take up acting?; **tout porte à croire que...** everything leads one to believe that...; **tous les indices portent à penser que c'est lui le coupable** all the evidence suggests he is the guilty one; **être porté à faire** to be inclined to do; *Fam* **il est porté sur la boisson** *ou* **bouteille** he's fond of the bottle; *Fam Euph* **être porté sur la chose** to have a one-track mind

6 *(éprouver)* **p. de l'intérêt à qn/qch** to be interested in sb/sth; **p. de l'admiration à qn** to admire sb; **je lui porte beaucoup d'amitié** I hold him/her very dear; **l'amour qu'il lui portait** the love he felt for him/her; **la haine qu'il lui portait** the hatred he felt towards him/her *or* bore him/her

C. *AVOIR SUR SOI, EN SOI* **1** *(bijou, chaussures, lunettes, vêtement)* to wear, to have on; *(badge, décoration)* to wear; *(barbe, couettes, moustache, perruque)* to have; *(cicatrice)* to bear, to have, to carry; *(pistolet, stylo)* to carry; **je porte toujours sur moi de quoi écrire** I always carry something to write with; **il porte le dossard numéro 12** he's wearing number 12; **son cheval porte le numéro 5** his/her horse is number 5; **elle porte toujours du noir** she always dresses in *or* wears black; **p. les cheveux longs/courts/relevés** to wear one's hair long/short/up; **je porte bien/mal les pantalons** trousers look good/don't look good on me

2 *(laisser voir → trace)* to show, to bear; *(→ date, inscription)* to bear; **l'étui portait ses initiales gravées** the case was engraved with his/her initials; **la lettre porte la date du 13 mars** the letter is dated 13 March *or Sout* bears the date 13 March; **le couteau ne porte aucune empreinte** there are no fingerprints on the knife; **la signature que porte le tableau** the signature (which appears *or* is) on the painting; **le rapport portait le nom de plusieurs hauts fonctionnaires** the report bore *or* carried the names of several senior officials; **elle portait la résignation sur son visage** resignation was written on *or* all over her face; *Ling* **la syllabe portant l'accent tonique** the stressed syllable

3 *(nom, prénom, patronyme)* to have; **nous portons le même nom** we have *or* bear the same name; **il porte le nom de Legrand** he's called Legrand; **elle porte le nom de son mari** she has taken her husband's name; **c'est un nom difficile à p.** it's not an easy name to be called by; **le roman et la pièce portent le même titre** the novel and the play have the same title

4 *(en soi)* to carry, to bear; **p. qch en soi** to carry *or* to bear sth within oneself; **l'espoir/la rancune que je portais en moi** the hope/resentment I bore within me

5 *Méd (virus)* to carry; **tous ceux qui portent le virus** all carriers of the virus

6 *(sujet: femme, femelle → enfant, petit, portée)* to carry

7 *Agr & Hort (fruits)* to bear; **la tige porte trois feuilles** there are three leaves on the stem; **lorsque l'arbre porte ses fleurs** when the tree's in bloom; *Fig* **p. ses fruits** to bear fruit

USAGE ABSOLU *(soutenir)* **l'eau de mer porte plus que l'eau douce** sea water is more buoyant than fresh water

VI 1 *(son, voix)* to carry; **sa voix ne porte pas assez** his/her voice doesn't carry well; **aussi loin que porte la vue** as far as the eye can see

2 *(canon, fusil)* **p. à** to have a range of; **le coup de feu a porté à plus de 2 km** the shot carried more than 2 km

3 *(faire mouche → critique, mot, plaisanterie)* to hit *or* to strike home; *(→ observation)* to be heard *or* heeded; *(→ coup)* to hit home, to tell

4 *(cogner)* **c'est le crâne qui a porté** the skull took the impact *or* the full force; **p. sur** *ou* **contre** to hit; **sa tête a porté sur** *ou* **contre le pilier** his/her head hit the pillar

5 *Naut* **laisser p.** to bear away, to let (her) go; **p. à la terre** to stand in for the shore; **p. (bon) plein** to sail clean full; **p. au vent** to stand to windward

6 *(dans l'habillement masculin)* **p. à droite/gauche** to dress on the right/left

❑ **porter de VT IND** *Hér* to bear

❑ **porter sur VT IND 1** *(concerner → sujet: discussion, discours, chapitre, recherches)* to be about, to be concerned with; *(→ sujet: critiques)* to be aimed at; *(→ sujet: loi, mesures)* to concern; *(→ sujet: dossier, reportage)* to be about *or* on; **le détournement porte sur plusieurs millions d'euros** the embezzlement concerns several million euros

2 *(reposer sur → sujet: charpente)* to rest on; *Ling* **l'accent porte sur la deuxième syllabe** the accent falls on the second syllable, the second syllable is stressed

▶**se porter VPR 1** *(bijou, chaussures, vêtement)* to be worn; **je veux une veste qui se porte avec tout** I want a jacket which can be worn *or* which goes with anything; **c'est une robe qui se porte avec une ceinture** this dress is worn with a belt; **les manteaux se porteront longs cet hiver** coats will be (worn) long this winter

2 *(personne)* **comment vous portez-vous?** how do you feel?, how are you (feeling)?; **il se porte très bien maintenant** he's (feeling) fine now; **à bientôt, portez-vous bien!** see you soon, look after yourself!; **il va bientôt s'en aller, je ne m'en porterai que mieux** he's going to leave soon and I'll feel all the better for it; **nos parents ne prenaient pas de congés et ne s'en portaient pas plus mal** our parents never took time off and they were none the worse for it

3 *(se proposer comme)* **se p. acquéreur de qch** to offer to buy sth; **se p. candidat** to put oneself up *or Br* to stand *or Am* to run as a candidate; **se p. caution** to stand security; **se p. volontaire pour faire** to volunteer to do; **se p. fort pour qn** to act as a guarantor for sb; **se p. fort de qch** to guarantee sth, to vouch for sth

4 *(aller)* to go; **se p. au-devant de qn** to go to meet sb; **se p. en tête d'une procession/course** to take the lead in a procession/race; *Mil* **se p. en avant** to move forward, to advance; **il s'est porté à l'avant du peloton** he went to the head of the pack; **tout son sang s'est porté à sa tête** the blood rushed to his/her head

5 se p. à *(se livrer à)* to give oneself over to, to indulge in; **se p. à des actes de violence** to indulge in violent acts; **comment a-t-il pu se p. à de telles extrémités?** how could he go to such extremes?

6 se p. sur *(sujet: choix, soupçon)* to fall on; *(sujet: conversation)* to turn to; **tous les regards se portèrent sur elle** all eyes turned towards her

---

porte-revues [pɔrtrəvy] **NM INV** magazine rack

porterie [pɔrtəri] **NF** gatehouse

porte-savon [pɔrtsavɔ̃] *(pl inv ou* **porte-savons***)* **NM** soap dish

porte-serviette[1], porte-serviettes [pɔrtsɛrvjɛt] *(pl* **porte-serviettes***)* **NM** *(support)* towel rail

porte-serviette[2] [pɔrtsɛrvjɛt] **NM INV** *(pochette)* napkin holder

porte-skis [pɔrtski] **NM INV** *Aut* ski rack, ski carrier

porte-toasts [pɔrtətost] **NM INV** toast rack

porteur, -euse [pɔrtœr, -øz] **ADJ 1** *(plein d'avenir)* flourishing; **un marché p.** a buoyant market; **l'informatique est un secteur p.** IT is a flourishing *or* booming industry; **une idée porteuse** an idea with great potential

2 *(chargé)* **un vaccin p. d'espoir** a vaccine which brings new hope; **un livre p. de doutes** a book expressing doubt

3 *Tech (essieu)* load-bearing; *(roue)* carrying

4 *Phys* **onde/fréquence porteuse** carrier wave/frequency

5 *Astron (fusée)* booster *(avant n)*

6 *Constr (mur)* load-bearing

7 *Méd* **les individus porteurs du virus** individuals who carry the virus, (individuals who are) carriers of the virus

NM,F 1 *Méd* carrier; **p. sain** (unaffected) carrier

2 *(de bagages)* porter; *(d'un cercueil, d'un brancard, d'un étendard)* bearer; *(d'eau)* carrier; *(de nouvelles, d'une lettre)* bearer; **p. d'eau** water-carrier; **le p. du message attend votre réponse** the messenger *or Sout* the bearer of the message is waiting for your answer; **j'arrivais, p. d'heureuses nouvelles** I arrived bringing *or* bearing good news; **il était p. de faux papiers** he was carrying false papers; **par p.** by messenger

3 *Sport* **le p. du ballon** the player in possession of *or* with the ball

NM 1 *Banque & Bourse* bearer; *(actionnaire)* shareholder, *Am* stockholder; **chèque/obligations au p.** bearer cheque/bonds; **les petits/gros porteurs** small/big investors; **p. d'actions** shareholder; *Am* stockholder; **p. d'actions nominatives** registered shareholder *or Am* stockholder; **p. d'obligations** debenture holder, bondholder; **p. de parts** shareholder, *Am* stockholder; **p. de titres** holder of stock, stockholder; **payable au p.** payable to bearer

2 *Can (aux funérailles)* pallbearer

❑ **porteuse NF 1** *Tél* carrier

2 *Can (marraine)* godmother

porte-vélos [pɔrtəvelo] **NM INV** bicycle rack

porte-vent [pɔrtəvɑ̃] *(pl inv ou* **porte-vents***)* **NM** air duct

porte-voix [pɔrtəvwa] **NM INV** *(simple)* megaphone; *(électrique) Br* loudhailer, *Am* bullhorn; **parler dans un p.** *(simple)* to talk through a megaphone; *(électrique)* to talk through a *Br* loudhailer *or Am* bullhorn; **mettre ses mains en p.** to cup one's hands round one's mouth

portfolio [pɔrtfoljo] **NM** portfolio

portier, -ère [pɔrtje, -ɛr] **ADJ** *Rel* **frère p.** porter; **sœur portière** portress

NM,F 1 *(gardien → d'un établissement public)* doorman, *f* doorwoman; *(→ d'un hôtel)* commissionaire; **p. de nuit** night porter; **p. électronique** electronic door-entry system

2 *Littéraire (d'un domaine, d'un monastère)* gatekeeper; **Saint Pierre, p. du paradis** St Peter, who guards the gates of Paradise

NM *Rel* porter

❑ **portière NF 1** *(d'un véhicule)* door

2 *(tenture)* portière, door curtain

'Portier de nuit' *Cavani* 'The Night Porter'

---

portillon [pɔrtijɔ̃] **NM** *(d'une porte cochère)* wicket; *(d'un passage à niveaux)* side gate; *(d'une gare)* gate, barrier; **p. automatique** *(dans le métro)* ticket barrier; *Fam* **ça se bouscule au**

p. *(il y a affluence)* there's a huge crowd trying to get in; *(il/elle/etc bafouille)* he/she/*etc* can't get his/her/*etc* words out; *Fam Hum* **ça ne se bouscule pas au p.** people are staying away in droves

portion [pɔrsjɔ̃] **NF 1** *(part → de gâteau, de quiche)* portion; *(→ de viande, de légumes etc)* portion, helping; *(→ d'argent)* share, cut; **p. congrue** (income providing) a meagre living; **être réduit à la p. congrue** to have just enough to live on, to make a meagre living **2** *(d'un groupe, d'une population)* portion, section **3** *(segment → de ligne, d'autoroute)* stretch

❑ **en portions ADJ** in individual helpings

portique [pɔrtik] **NM 1** *Archit* portico **2** *Sport* crossbeam **3** *(dispositif de sécurité)* security gate **4** *Ind* gantry crane **5** *Rail* **p. à signaux** signal gantry

portland [pɔrtlɑ̃d] **NM (ciment) p.** Portland cement

Port-Louis [pɔrlwi] **NM** Port Louis

Porto [pɔrto] **NM** Oporto

porto [pɔrto] **NM** port (wine)

Porto Novo [pɔrtonɔvo] **NM** Porto Novo

portor [pɔrtɔr] **NM** yellow-veined black marble

portoricain, -e [pɔrtɔrikɛ̃, -ɛn] **ADJ** Puerto Rican

❑ **Portoricain, -e NM,F** Puerto Rican

Porto Rico [pɔrtoriko] **NM** Puerto Rico; **à P.** in Puerto Rico

portos [pɔrtos] **NMF INV** *Fam* dago *(from Portugal)*, = offensive term used to refer to a Portuguese

portraire [112] [pɔrtrɛr] **VT** *Arch ou Littéraire* **1** *(sujet: artiste)* to draw/to paint the portrait of **2** *(sujet: auteur)* to portray

portrait [pɔrtrɛ] **NM 1** *(dessin, peinture, photo)* portrait; **le p. n'est pas très ressemblant** it is not a very good likeness; **faire le p. de qn** *(dessinateur)* to draw sb's portrait; *(peintre)* to paint sb's portrait; *Fam* **se faire tirer le p.** to have one's photo taken▪; **votre p. en 5 minutes** *(sur panneau)* your photo in 5 minutes; **p. de famille** family portrait; **être tout le p.** *ou* **le p. vivant de qn** to be the spitting image of sb

2 *Beaux-Arts* **l'art du p., le p.** portraiture

3 *Fam (figure)* **abîmer le p. à qn** to waste sb's face, to rearrange sb's features; **elle s'est fait arranger le p.** she got her face rearranged

4 *(description)* portrayal, description, portrait; **faire** *ou* **tracer le p. de qn** to portray sb

5 *(jeux de société)* ≃ Botticelli; **p. chinois** ≃ animal, vegetable or mineral

6 *Ordinat* **(mode** *ou* **format) p.** portrait (mode); **imprimer qch en p.** to print sth in portrait

'Portrait de l'artiste au chevalet' *Rembrandt* 'Portrait of the Artist at his Easel'

'Portrait des époux Arnolfini' *Van Eyck* 'Portrait of Giovanni Arnolfini and his Wife'

'Portrait de femme' *James, Campion* 'The Portrait of a Lady'

portrait-charge [pɔrtrɛʃarʒ] *(pl* **portraits-charges) NM** *Littéraire* unkind character sketch

portrait-interview [pɔrtrɛɛ̃tɛrvju] *(pl* **portraits-interviews) NM** close-up *(interview)*

portraitiste [pɔrtretist] **NMF** portraitist

portrait-robot [pɔrtrɛrɔbo] *(pl* **portraits-robots) NM 1** *(d'un criminel)* Photofit® *or* Identikit® picture **2** *(caractéristiques)* typical profile

portraiture [pɔrtretyr] **NF** *Arch ou Littéraire* **1** *(dessin)* portrait **2** *(description)* portrayal, portraiture

portraiturer [3] [pɔrtretyre] **VT** *Littéraire* to portray, to depict

Port-Saïd [pɔrsaid] **NM** Port Said

Port-Salut® [pɔrsaly] **NM INV** Port-Salut (cheese)

portuaire [pɔrtɥɛr] **ADJ** port *(avant n)*, harbour *(avant n)*

portugais, -e [pɔrtygɛ, -ɛz] **ADJ** Portuguese

NM *(langue)* Portuguese

❑ **Portugais, -e NM,F** Portuguese; **les P.** the Portuguese

❑ **portugaise NF** *(huître)* Portuguese oyster

❑ **portugaises NFPL** *Fam* ears▪, *Br* lugholes; **avoir les portugaises ensablées** to be as deaf as a post

Portugal [pɔrtygal] **NM le P.** Portugal; **vivre au P.** to live in Portugal; **aller au P.** to go to Portugal

portulan [pɔrtylɑ̃] **NM** portolano

POS, Pos [pɔs] **NM** *(abrév* **plan d'occupation des sols)** = document detailing local land development plans

pose [poz] **NF 1** *(mise en place → d'appareils)* putting in, installing; *(→ de rideaux)* putting up, hanging; *(→ de carrelage, de câbles)* laying; *(→ de moquette)* fitting, laying; *(→ d'une bombe)* planting; **la p. de la fenêtre vous coûtera 300 euros** it will cost you 300 euros to have the window put in; **la p. de la moquette a pris une demi-journée** it took half a day to fit *or* lay the carpet(s); **train de p.** track-laying train

2 *(attitude)* position, posture; *(pour un artiste)* pose; **dans une p. peu élégante** in a rather inelegant position *or* posture; **prendre une p. avantageuse** to strike a flattering pose; **prendre la p.** to start posing, to take up a pose; **garder** *ou* **tenir la p.** to hold the pose

3 *Phot (cliché, durée)* exposure; **une pellicule de 24/36 poses** a 24-/36-exposure film

4 *(affectation)* affectation

5 *Typ* **p. de marges** margin setting; **p. de tabulations** tabbing, setting of tabs

posé, -e [poze] **ADJ 1** *(mesuré → personne)* self-possessed, collected, composed; *(→ manières, ton)* calm, cool, tranquil **2** *Mus* **voix bien/mal posée** steady/unsteady voice

Poséidon [pɔzeidɔ̃] **NPR** *Myth* Poseidon

posément [pozemɑ̃] **ADV** calmly, coolly

posemètre [pozmɛtr] **NM** *Phot* exposure meter

poser[1] [poze] **NM** *Mil* landing *(of a helicopter)*

POSER[2] [3] [poze]

> **VT** to put **1** ▪ to lay **1, 3** ▪ to place **1, 9** ▪ to put away **2** ▪ to put up **3** ▪ to put in **3** ▪ to install **3** ▪ to ask **4** ▪ to state **5** ▪ to land **10**
> **VI** to pose **1, 2** ▪ to put on airs **2, 3**
> **VPR** to land **3** ▪ to arise **5**

VT 1 *(mettre)* to put, to lay, to place; **p. ses coudes sur la table** to rest *or* to put one's elbows on the table; **je ne sais plus où j'ai posé la clef** I can't remember where I've put *or* left the key; **p. un sac par terre** to put a bag (down) on the floor; **elle avait posé sa bicyclette contre la palissade** she'd leant *or* put her bike against the fence; **ne pose pas ton chapeau sur le lit** don't put your hat (down) on the bed; **elle a posé le pied sur la première marche** she put *or* placed her foot on *or* onto the first step; **j'ai tellement mal que je ne peux plus p. le pied par terre** my foot hurts so much, I can't put my weight on it any longer; **dès que je pose la tête sur l'oreiller, je m'endors** I fall asleep as soon as my head touches the pillow; **il posa un baiser sur ses paupières** he kissed her on the eyelids; *Fam Hum* **je ne sais pas où p. mes fesses** I don't know where to park my *Br* bum *or Am* butt

2 *(cesser d'utiliser)* to put away *or* down; **pose ton ballon et viens dîner** put away your ball and come and have dinner; **posez vos stylos et écoutez-moi** put your pens down and listen to me

3 *(installer → papier peint, cadre, tentures, affiche)* to put up; *(→ antenne)* to put up, to install; *(→ radiateur, alarme)* to put in, to install; *(→ verrou)* to fit; *(→ cadenas)* to put on; *(→ moquette)* to fit, to lay; *(→ carrelage, câble, mine, rail, tuyau)* to lay; *(→ vitre)* to put in; *(→ placard)* to put in, to install; *(→ prothèse)* to fit, to put in; *(→ enduit)* to put on; *(→ bombe)* to plant; **faire p. un double vitrage** to have double-glazing put in *or* fitted; **se faire p. une couronne** to have a crown fitted

4 *(énoncer → question)* to ask; *(→ devinette)* to ask, to set; **p. une question à qn** to ask sb a question, to put a question to sb; **je peux p. la question autrement** I can put *or* ask the question another way; **p. un problème** *(causer des difficultés)* to raise *or* to pose a problem; *(l'énoncer)* to set a problem; **de la façon dont il m'avait posé le problème...** the way he'd put *or* outlined the problem to me...; **elle me pose de gros problèmes** she's a great problem *or* source of anxiety to me; **si ça ne pose pas de problème, je viendrai avec mon chien** if it's not a problem (for you) I'll bring my dog

5 *(établir → condition)* to state, to lay down; *(→ principe, règle)* to lay *or* to set down, to state; **une fois posées les bases du projet** once the foundations of the project have been laid down; **p. qch comme condition/principe** to lay sth down as a condition/principle; **si l'on pose que...** if we assume *or* suppose that...; **si l'on pose comme hypothèse que...** if we take as a hypothesis that...; **cela posé, nous pouvons dire que...** taking this as read, we can say that...; **posons cela comme acquis** let's take that as read

6 *Fam (mettre en valeur)* to establish the reputation of▪, to give standing to▪; **il n'y a rien qui pose un chercheur comme le Nobel** there's nothing quite like the Nobel prize to get a scientist noticed▪ *or* to boost a scientist's reputation▪; **une voiture comme ça, ça vous pose** that kind of car gives you a certain status▪

7 *Math* to put down; **je pose 2 et je retiens 1** put down 2, carry 1; **p. une opération** to set out a sum

8 *Mus* **p. sa voix** to pitch one's voice

9 *Sport* to place; **il a bien posé sa volée** he placed his volley perfectly

10 *Aviat (avion, hélicoptère)* to land, to set down

11 *Can (photographier)* to photograph, to take a photograph *or* picture of; **il s'est fait p. avec sa copine** he had his picture taken with his girlfriend

USAGE ABSOLU à toi de p.! *(aux dominos)* your turn!

VI 1 *(pour un peintre, un photographe)* to pose, to sit; **j'ai souvent posé pour elle** I used to pose *or* to sit for her regularly; **p. pour une photo/un magazine** to pose for a photo/magazine; **et maintenant, tout le monde va p. pour la photo souvenir** let's have everyone together now for the souvenir photograph; *Fam* **faire p. qn** *(le faire attendre)* to keep sb hanging around

2 *(fanfaronner)* to put on airs, to show off, to pose; **regardez-le p. devant ces dames!** just look at him showing off in front of those ladies!; **il adore p.** he can't resist showing off

3 *(faire semblant)* to put on airs, to strike a pose *or* an attitude; **elle n'est pas vraiment malheureuse, elle pose** she's not really unhappy, it's just a façade *or* it's all show; *Fam* **p. au justicier** *(se faire passer pour)* to act the avenger

►**se poser VPR 1** *(emploi passif)* **se p. facilement** *(chaudière)* to be easy to install; *(moquette)* to be easy to lay

2 *(faire surgir)* **se p. la question** *ou* **le problème de savoir si...** to ask oneself *or* to wonder whether...; **il va finir par se p. des questions** he's going to start having doubts

3 *(descendre → avion, hélicoptère)* to land, to touch down; *(→ papillon)* to land, to alight; *(→ oiseau)* to land, to perch; **se p. en catastrophe** to make an emergency landing; **se p. en douceur** to make a smooth landing; **les hirondelles se posent sur les fils électriques** the swallows land *or* perch on the electric wires; **une plume est venue se p. sur sa tête** a feather floated down onto his/her head; **tous les regards se posèrent sur elle** all eyes turned to her; **il sentit leurs yeux se p. sur lui** he could feel their eyes on him; **sa main se posa sur la mienne** he/she put her hand on mine

4 *Fam (s'asseoir)* **pose-toi là** sit yourself down here

5 *(surgir → question, problème)* to arise, to come up; **la question s'est déjà posée plusieurs fois** the question has come up several times already; **la question ne se pose plus maintenant** the question is irrelevant now; **la question qui se pose maintenant est la suivante** the question which must now be asked is the following; **le problème qui se pose à moi** the problem I've got to face *or* to solve; **le problème se pose de savoir si l'on doit négocier** there's the problem of whether or not we should negotiate; **le problème ne se pose pas exactement en ces termes** that's not exactly where the problem lies

6 se p. en *ou* **comme** *(se faire passer pour)* to pass oneself off as; **il veut se p. comme arbitre du goût** he wants to pass himself off as *or* to pose as an arbiter of taste; **je ne me suis jamais posé en expert** I never set myself up to be *or* I never pretended I was an expert

7 *Fam (locutions)* **pour l'intelligence, son frère se pose là!** *(il est brillant)* his/her brother's got quite a brain!; **elle se pose là, leur bagnole!** *(avec admiration)* their car's an impressive bit of machinery!; **comme plombier, tu te poses là!** call yourself a plumber, do you?; **comme enquiquineuse, elle se pose un peu là!** she's such a pain in the neck!; **comme gaffe, ça se pose là!** that's what you might call a blunder!

poseur, -euse [pozœr, -øz] **ADJ** *(prétentieux)* affected, pretentious, mannered; **elle est très poseuse** she's terribly pretentious

NM,F 1 *(m'as-tu-vu)* show-off, *Br* poseur

2 *(installateur)* **p. de parquet/carrelage/câbles** floor/tile/cable layer; **p. d'affiches** billsticker, billposter; **p. de mines** mine layer; **p. de rails** tracklayer, platelayer; **les poseurs de bombes se sont enfuis** those responsible for planting the bombs *or* the bombers ran away

posidonie [pozidɔni] **NF** *Bot* neptune-grass

positif, -ive [pozitif, -iv] **ADJ 1** *(constructif → mesures, suggestion, attitude)* positive, constructive; *(→ réaction, échos, critique)* favourable

2 *(réaliste)* pragmatic, practical-minded

3 *(affirmatif → réponse)* positive; **si sa réponse est positive** if he/she says yes

4 *(certain → fait)* positive, actual

5 *Math, Méd, Phot & Phys* positive

NM 1 *(quelque chose de constructif)* **il nous faut du p.** we need something positive

2 *Ling, Math & Phot* positive; *Typ* **p. en couleur** colour positive

3 *Mus (orgue)* positive organ; *(clavier secondaire)* choir *or* positive organ

POSITION [pozisjɔ̃] **NF 1** *Mil (lieu d'où l'on mène une action)* position; **une p. dominante** a commanding position; **p. avancée/défensive** advanced/defensive position; **p. clef** key position; **être en p. de combat** to be ready to attack; **des positions fortifiées** a fortified position; *aussi Fig* **p. de repli** fall-back position; **p. retranchée** entrenched *or* dug-in position

2 *(lieu où l'on se trouve)* position; **donnez-nous votre p.** what is your position?; **déterminer sa p.** to find one's bearings; **déterminer la p. de qch** to locate sth

3 *(dans un sondage, une course)* position, place; **nous sommes en dernière/première p. dans le championnat** we're bottom of the league/in the lead in the championship; **arriver en première/dernière p.** *(coureur)* to come first/last; *(candidat)* to come top/be last; **elle est en sixième p.** she's in sixth position *or* place, she's lying sixth; **ils ont rétrogradé en quatrième p. au hit-parade** they went down to number four in the charts

4 *(d'une entreprise, d'un produit)* position; **p. clé** key position; **p. concurrentielle** competitive position; **p. stratégique** strategic position

5 *(posture)* posture, position; **changer de p.** to change (one's) position, to shift; **tu as une mauvaise p.** you've got bad posture; **tu as une mauvaise p. à cheval/lorsque tu fais le stem** your posture on horseback/when doing the stem turn is incorrect; **la p. debout est inconfortable** standing up is uncomfortable; **dans la** *ou* **en p. verticale** when standing up; **dans la** *ou* **en p. allongée** when lying down; **dans la** *ou* **en p. assise** when sitting, in a sitting position; **p. latérale de sécurité** *(en secourisme)* recovery position; **la p. du missionnaire** the missionary position; **p. de sécurité** *(en avion)* brace position

6 *(angle, orientation)* position, setting; **quelle est la p. de l'aiguille?** where is the needle pointing?, what's the position of the needle?; **mettez le siège en p. inclinée** tilt the seat back; **éclairage à plusieurs positions** lamp with several settings

7 *(opinion)* position, stance, standpoint; **prendre p. (sur qch)** to take a stand *or* to take up a position (on sth); **prendre p. pour** *ou* **en faveur de qch** to come down in favour of sth; **prendre p. contre qch** to come out against sth; **rester sur ses positions** to stand one's ground, to stick to one's guns; **quelle est la p. de la France dans ce conflit?** what's France's position on this conflict?; *Pol* **p. commune** common stance; **p. de principe** policy position

8 *(situation)* position, situation; **vous me mettez dans une p. délicate** you're putting me in a difficult situation *or* position; **en p. de force** in a strong position *or* a position of strength; **p. sociale** social standing; *Belg* **être en p., être dans une p. intéressante** to be expecting; **être en p. de faire qch** to be in a position to do sth

9 *(dans une entreprise)* position, post; **dans sa p., elle devrait se sentir responsable** a woman in her position should feel responsible; **j'ai une p. à tenir** I have my position to think of

10 *Banque* balance (of account); *Bourse* position; **j'aimerais avoir ma p., s'il vous plaît** could you tell me my balance, please?; *Banque* **feuille de p.** interim statement; *Bourse* **liquider une p.** to close (out) a position; *Bourse* **prendre une p. inverse sur le marché** to offset; *Bourse* **p. acheteur** long position, bull position; *Banque* **p. de compte** balance; *Banque* **p. créditrice** credit balance; *Banque* **p. débitrice** debit balance; *Bourse* **p. de place** market position; *Banque* **p. de trésorerie** cash(flow) situation; *Bourse* **p. vendeur** short position, bear position

11 *Ling (d'un terme, d'une syllabe, d'une voyelle)* position; **phonème en p. forte/faible** stressed/unstressed phoneme

12 *(en danse)* position

13 *Mus (accord, doigté)* position

14 *Géom & Psy* position

15 *Jur* status

❑ **de position ADJ** *(balise)* position *(avant n)*

positionnement [pozisjɔnmɑ̃] **NM 1** *Com & Mktg* positioning; **p. concurrentiel** competitive positioning; **p. de la marque** brand positioning; **p. de prix** price positioning; **p. du produit** product positioning; **p. par la qualité** quality positioning; **p. stratégique** strategic positioning **2** *Tech* positioning **3** *Fin (d'un compte)* calculation of the balance

positionner [3] [pozisjɔne] **VT 1** *Com & Mktg (produit)* to position **2** *Tech* to position **3** *(localiser)* to locate, to determine the position of **4** *Fin (compte)* to calculate the balance of

▶ **se positionner VPR** to position oneself, to get into position; **se p. par rapport à la concurrence** to position oneself in relation to the competition; **se p. à la hausse sur le marché** to move upmarket

positionneur [pozisjɔnœr] **NM** positioner

positive [pozitiv] *voir* **positif**

positivement [pozitivmɑ̃] **ADV 1** *Élec* positively; **chargé p.** positively charged **2** *(réagir)* positively **3** *(tout à fait)* absolutely, positively; **c'est p. honteux** it's absolutely shameful; **il est p. idiot** he's an absolute *or* perfect idiot **4** *(avec certitude)* **je ne le sais pas p.** I don't know it for certain, I can't be positive about it

positiver [3] [pozitive] **VI** to think positively

positivisme [pozitivism] **NM** *Phil* positivism; **p. logique** logical positivism

positiviste [pozitivist] *Phil* **ADJ** positivist

NMF positivist

positivité [pozitivite] **NF** positivity

positon [pozitɔ̃] **NM** *Phys* positron

positonium [pozitonjɔm] **NM** *Phys* positronium

positron [pozitrɔ̃] **NM** positron

positronium [pozitrɔnjɔm] = **positonium**

posologie [pozɔlɔʒi] **NF** *Méd* **1** *(instructions)* dosage; **respectez la p.** use as directed **2** *(science)* posology

posse [posi] **NF** *Fam (bande)* posse

possédant, -e [posedɑ̃, -ɑ̃t] **ADJ** propertied, property-owning

❑ **possédants NMPL** property owners

possédé, -e [posede] **ADJ** *(par le démon)* possessed

NM,F person possessed; **comme un p.** like a man possessed

posséder [18] [posede] **VT 1** *(détenir → demeure, collection, fortune, terres)* to own, to possess, to have; *(→ colonies)* to have; *(→ preuve, document, titre, ticket)* to hold, to have; *(→ arme, armée)* to possess; **les gens qui ne possèdent rien** those who have nothing; **le pays ne possédait pas d'armée puissante** the country did not possess a powerful army; **tu ne possèdes pas la vérité, tu sais** you don't know everything, you know

2 *(être doté de → talent, mémoire)* to possess, to have; **cette région possède de grandes réserves d'eau** this region has large water reserves

3 *Littéraire (maîtriser → art, langue)* to have mastered; **(bien) p. son sujet** to be master of *or* on top of one's subject; **un conférencier qui possède parfaitement son sujet** a lecturer who knows exactly what he's talking about

4 *(habiter → sujet: démon)* to possess; **la jalousie le possède** he's consumed with *or* eaten up with jealousy; **il était possédé par la haine** he was consumed with *or* full of hatred; **le démon qui le possède** the devil within him; **être possédé du diable** *ou* **du démon** to be possessed by the devil

5 *Fam (tromper → sujet: escroc)* to con, to have; **je me suis fait p.** I've been conned *or* had

6 *Littéraire (sexuellement)* to possess, to have carnal knowledge of; **quand il la posséda enfin** when finally she was his

▶ **se posséder VPR** *(se dominer)* **je ne me possédais plus** I was not myself any more, I was no longer master of myself; **elle ne se possédait plus de joie/rage** she was beside herself with joy/rage

possesseur [posesœr] **NM 1** *(propriétaire → d'une maison, d'une collection, d'une fortune)* owner, possessor; *(→ d'un hôtel, d'une ferme)* owner, proprietor; *(→ d'une charge, d'un ticket, de valeurs)* holder; *(→ d'un titre)* incumbent, holder; *(→ de documents)* possessor, holder; **être le p. d'une propriété** to own *or* to possess a property

2 *(détenteur → d'une preuve)* possessor

possessif, -ive [posesif, -iv] **ADJ** *Gram & Psy* possessive

NM *Gram* possessive (form)

possession [posesjɔ̃] **NF 1** *(détention → d'une maison, d'un hôtel, d'une collection, d'une fortune)* ownership, possession; *(→ d'informations)* possession; *(→ d'actions, d'un diplôme)* holding; *(→ d'une charge, d'un titre)* possession, holding; *(→ d'un poste)* tenure; **avoir qch en sa p.** to have sth in one's possession; **être en p. de qch** to be in possession of sth; **prendre p. de** *(maison)* to take possession of; *(fonctions)* to take up; **entrer en p. de** to come into possession of, to come by; **comment êtes-vous entré en p. de ces documents?** how did you come to have *or* come by these documents?; **tomber en la p. de qn** to come into sb's possession

2 *Jur* possession; **p. d'état** = de facto enjoyment of a certain status; **p. de fait** actual possession; **p. utile** quiet possession

3 *Fin (d'une société)* assets

4 *(territoire)* possession, dominion

5 *(contrôle)* control; **une force étrange a pris p. de lui** a strange force has gained possession of him; **reprendre p. de soi-même** to regain *or* recover one's self-control *or* composure; **être en p. de toutes ses facultés** to be in (full) possession of one's faculties; **être en pleine p. de ses moyens** to be at the peak of one's powers *or* abilities

6 *Psy & Rel* possession

possessionnel, -elle [posesjɔnɛl] **ADJ** *Jur* possessional

possessive [posesiv] *voir* **possessif**

possessivité [posesivite] **NF** possessiveness

possessoire [poseswar] *Jur* **ADJ** possessory

NM 1 *(droit)* (right of) possession **2** *(action)* possessory action

possibilité [posibilite] **NF 1** *(chose envisageable ou faisable)* possibility; **p. (de) cuisine séparée** *(dans une petite annonce)* separate kitchen possible

2 *(moyen)* possibility; *(occasion)* opportunity; **il n'a pas vraiment la p. de refuser** he can't really refuse; **mon travail me donne la p. de voyager** my job gives me the opportunity of travelling; **on ne m'en a jamais donné la p.** I was never given the opportunity *or* chance

3 *(éventualité)* possibility; **c'est une p. que je n'avais pas envisagée** it's a possibility that I

hadn't envisaged; **le syndicat n'a pas nié la p. d'une reprise des négociations** the *Br* trade union *or Am* labor union has not ruled out the possible re-opening of negotiations

❏ **possibilités** NFPL **1** *(financières)* means; **50 euros, c'est dans mes possibilités** 50 euros, that's within my means; **chacun doit payer selon ses possibilités** from each according to his means; **la maison était au-dessus de nos possibilités** we couldn't afford the house **2** *(intellectuelles, physiques)* possibilities, potential; **c'est un pianiste qui a de grandes possibilités** this pianist has got great possibilities *or* potential; **écrire une thèse serait au-dessus de mes possibilités** I couldn't cope with writing a thesis; **connaître ses possibilités** to be aware of one's (own) capabilities **3** *(techniques)* facilities; **machine qui offre de multiples possibilités d'utilisation** machine with many features; *Ordinat* **possibilités d'extension** upgradeability

━━━━━━━━━

'**La Possibilité d'une île**' *Houellebecq* 'The Possibility of an Island'

possible [pɔsibl] ADJ **1** *(réalisable → gén)* possible; *(→ construction)* feasible; **est-il p. de vivre sur Mars?** is life possible on Mars?; **rendre qch p.** to make sth possible; **il est p. de dire/de faire** it is possible to say/to do; **il est toujours p. d'annuler la réunion** the meeting can always be cancelled; **il ne m'est financièrement pas p. de partir pour l'étranger** I can't afford to go abroad; **j'ai fait tout ce qu'il m'était techniquement p. de faire** I did everything that was technically possible; **ce n'est pas p. d'être aussi maladroit!** how can anyone be so clumsy!; **il faut qu'on divorce, ce n'est pas autrement** we've got to get a divorce, it's the only solution; **on a dû le pousser, ce n'est pas p. autrement!** somebody MUST have pushed him!; *Fam* **il est pas p., ce mec!** this guy's just too much!

2 *(probable)* possible; **il est p. que je vous rejoigne plus tard** I may *or* might join you later; **serait-il p. qu'il m'ait menti?** could he (possibly) have lied to me?; **il t'aime – c'est bien p., mais moi pas!** he loves you – quite possibly *or* that's as may be, but I don't love him!; **tu devrais lui écrire – c'est p., mais je n'en ai pas envie** you should write to him/her – maybe (I should), but I don't feel like it

3 *(pour exprimer l'étonnement)* *Fam* **elle est morte hier – c'est pas p.!** she died yesterday – I can't believe it!*; *Fam* **pas p.! c'est ta fille?** is this your daughter? impossible *or* surely not!; *Ironique* **Noël c'est le 25 – pas p.!** Christmas is on the 25th – never *or* you don't say!

4 *(envisageable → interprétation, explication, option)* possible; **le 24 février serait une date p.** 24 February would be a possible date *or* a possibility; **voici la sélection p. pour le match de demain** here is the possible selection for tomorrow's match

5 *(potentiel)* possible; **je l'ai cherché dans tous les endroits possibles** I looked for it everywhere imaginable *or* in every possible place; **as-tu considéré tous les cas possibles?** have you considered every possible *or* conceivable explanation?; **il a eu tous les problèmes possibles et imaginables pour récupérer son argent** he had all kinds of problems getting his money back; **bougez le moins p.** move as little as possible; **roulez le plus lentement p.** drive as slowly as possible; **je veux un rapport aussi détaillé que p.** I want as detailed a report as possible; **j'ai acheté les moins chers p.** I bought the cheapest I could find; **il mange le plus/le moins de gâteaux p. *ou* possibles** he eats as many/as few cakes as possible

❏ NM **le p.** the possible; **c'est dans le domaine du p.** it's within the bounds of possibility, it's quite possible; **faire (tout) son p.** to do one's best *or* all one (possibly) can *or* one's utmost

❏ **au possible** ADV in the extreme; **ennuyeux au p.** extremely boring; **elle a été désagréable/serviable au p.** she couldn't have been more unpleasant/helpful

possiblement [pɔsibləmɑ̃] ADV *Can* possibly

post-achat [pɔstaʃa] *(pl* **post-achats***)* ADJ post-purchase

post-acheminement [pɔstaʃminmɑ̃] *(pl* **post-acheminements***)* NM transfer from main airport

postage [pɔstaʒ] NM mailing, *Br* posting

postal, -e, -aux, -ales [pɔstal, -o] ADJ *(colis)* (sent) by mail *or Br* post; *(frais, service, tarif)* postal; *(train, camion, wagon)* mail *(avant n)*

postchèque [pɔstʃɛk] NM Post Office traveller's cheque

postclassique [pɔstklasik] ADJ postclassical

postcombustion [pɔstkɔ̃bystjɔ̃] NF **1** *(combustion)* reheat, after-burning **2** *(dispositif)* afterburner

postcommunion [pɔstkɔmynjɔ̃] NF *Rel* postcommunion

postcommunisme [pɔstkɔmynism] NM postcommunism

postcommuniste [pɔstkɔmynist] ADJ postcommunist

postcure [pɔstkyr] NF *Méd* rehabilitation, aftercare; **foyer de p.** rehabilitation centre; **elle est en p.** she's in aftercare

postdate [pɔstdat] NF post-date

postdater [3] [pɔstdate] VT to postdate

post-doctoral, -e, -aux, -ales [pɔstdɔktɔral, -o] ADJ *Univ* post-doctoral, post-doctorate

post-doctorat [pɔstdɔktɔra] NM *Univ* postdoctorate

poste[1] [pɔst] NM **1** *Rad & TV* **p. (de) radio/télévision** radio/television set; *Fam* **ouvrir/fermer le p.** to switch the radio/television on/off■; **p. émetteur/récepteur** transmitting/receiving set; **p. émetteur pirate** pirate station; **p. d'émission** transmitter; **p. à galène** crystal set

2 *Tél (appareil)* telephone; *(d'un standard)* extension; **passez-moi le p. 1421** give me extension 1421; **le p. est occupé** the extension is *Br* engaged *or Am* busy; **je vous passe le p.** I'm putting you through; **p. cellulaire** cellphone

3 *(métier)* post, job, position; **un p. à pourvoir** a post to be filled, a (job) vacancy; **présenter sa candidature à un p. de technicien** to apply for a job as a technician; **elle a un p. très élevé au ministère** she has a very senior position *or* post in the ministry; **il a obtenu le p. de directeur financier** he was given the post of *or* he was appointed financial director; **p. d'encadrement** managerial position; **p. évolutif** job with prospects (for promotion)

4 *(local, installation)* **p. d'aiguillage** signal box; **p. de douane** customs post; **p. d'équipage** crew's quarters; **p. d'essence** *Br* petrol *or Am* gas station; **p. d'incendie** fire point; **p. de pilotage** *Aviat* flight deck; *Naut* cockpit; **p. de police** police station; **passer la nuit au p.** to spend the night at the station; **p. de ravitaillement** service station; **p. de secours** first-aid post

5 *Mil* post; *aussi Fig* **être/rester à son p.** to be/to stay at one's post; **à vos postes!** to your posts!, stand by!; **p. avancé** advanced *or* outlying post; **p. de combat** action *or* battle station; **p. de commandement** command post; **p. de contrôle** checkpoint; **p. de garde** guardroom; *aussi Fig* **p. d'observation/d'écoute/de surveillance** observation/listening/look-out post

6 *Fin (d'un compte)* item, entry; *(d'un budget)* item; **p. de bilan** balance sheet item; **p. créditeur/débiteur** credit/debit item; **p. extraordinaire** extraordinary item; **p. de mémoire** reminder entry

7 *Ind (division du temps)* shift; **p. de 10 heures** 10-hour shift; **p. de nuit** nightshift; **p. de travail** *(emplacement)* workplace

8 *Ordinat* **p. autonome** stand-alone; **p. terminal** terminal; **p. de travail** workstation

9 *Chasse* hide

poste[2] [pɔst] NF **1** *(établissement)* post office; **grande p.** main post office; **p. restante** poste restante

2 *(moyen d'acheminement)* mail, *Br* post; **envoyer qch par la p.** to mail sth, to send sth by mail *or Br* post; **mettre une lettre à la p.** to mail *or Br* to post a letter; **je venais de la mettre à la p. quand je m'aperçus que j'avais oublié le timbre** I'd just dropped it in the mail *or Br* letter box when I realized I hadn't put a stamp on it; **p. aérienne** airmail

3 *Admin* **la p.** ≃ the Post Office; **travailler à la p.** ≃ to work for the Post Office; **les Postes et Télécommunications** = the French postal and telecommunications service; **grève des postes** postal *or* mail strike

4 *Hist (relais)* post

❏ **postes** NFPL *Archit* wave moulding

posté, -e [pɔste] ADJ **travail p.** shift work; **ouvrier p.** shift worker

poste-à-poste [pɔstapɔst] ADJ INV *Ordinat* point-to-point

Postéclair [pɔsteklɛr] NM = fax service offered by France Télécom

poste-frontière [pɔstəfrɔ̃tjɛr] *(pl* **postes-frontières***)* NM customs post

poster[1] [pɔstɛr] NM poster

poster[2] [3] [pɔste] VT **1** *(envoyer → colis, courrier)* to mail, *Br* to post; **la lettre a été postée le 2 mai** the letter was sent *or* was mailed *or Br* was posted on 2 May

2 *(placer → garde, complice, troupes)* to post, to station; **l'inspecteur fit p. un homme à chaque issue** the inspector gave orders for a man to be stationed at each exit

▸**se poster** VPR *(sentinelle)* to station *or* to post *or* to position oneself; **se p. sur le parcours d'une course/d'un cortège** to go and stand on the route of a race/procession

postérieur, -e [pɔsterjœr] ADJ **1** *(ultérieur → date, époque)* later; *(→ fait, invention)* subsequent, later; **le tableau est p. à 1930** the picture was painted after 1930; **la rechute est très postérieure à son opération** the relapse came a long time after his/her operation **2** *(de derrière → pattes)* hind, rear, back; *(→ partie)* back, *Sout* posterior **3** *Ling (voyelle, articulation)* back

NM *Fam Hum* behind, posterior

postérieurement [pɔsterjœrmɑ̃] ADV later, subsequently, at a later date; **p. à** later than, after

posteriori [pɔsterjɔri] *voir* **a posteriori**

postériorité [pɔsterjɔrite] NF posteriority

postérité [pɔsterite] NF **1** *Littéraire (lignée)* posterity, descendants; **mourir sans p.** to die without issue; *Fig* **la p. du nouveau roman** the legacy of the nouveau roman

2 *(générations futures)* posterity; **nous travaillons pour la p.** we are working for posterity; **passer à la p.** *(artiste)* to become famous, to go down in history; *(mot, œuvre)* to be handed down to posterity *or* to future generations

postface [pɔstfas] NF postscript, afterword

postglaciaire [pɔstglasjɛr] ADJ *Géol* postglacial

posthite [pɔstit] NF *Méd* posthitis

posthume [pɔstym] ADJ *(enfant, ouvrage)* posthumous; **médaille décernée à titre p.** posthumously awarded medal

posthypophyse [pɔstipofiz] NF *Anat* posthypophysis

postiche [pɔstiʃ] ADJ **1** *(cheveux, barbe, chignon)* false **2** *(fictif)* sham, spurious

NM hairpiece

postier, -ère [pɔstje, -ɛr] NM,F postal worker

postillon [pɔstijɔ̃] NM **1** *(de salive)* **postillons** spluttering; **envoyer des postillons** to splutter **2** *(cocher)* postilion

postillonner [3] [pɔstijɔne] VI to splutter; "**jamais!**", **dit-il en postillonnant** "never!" he spluttered; **il nous postillonnait dessus** he spluttered all over us

postimpressionnisme [pɔstɛ̃presjɔnism] NM *Beaux-Arts* Postimpressionism

postimpressionniste [pɔstɛ̃presjɔnist] *Beaux-Arts* ADJ Postimpressionist

NMF Postimpressionist

postindustriel, -elle [pɔstɛ̃dystrijɛl] ADJ postindustrial

Post-it® [pɔstit] NM INV Post-it®

post-marché [pɔstmarʃe] *(pl* **post-marchés***)* NM back office

postminimalisme [pɔstminimalism] NM postminimalism

post-minimaliste [pɔstminimalist] **1** ADJ postminimalist

NMF post-minimaliste

postmoderne [pɔstmɔdɛrn] ADJ postmodern

postmodernisme [pɔstmɔdɛrnism] NM postmodernism

postmoderniste [pɔstmɔdɛrnist] ADJ postmodernist

NMF postmodernist

postmodernité [pɔstmɔdɛrnite] **NF** postmodernism

postnatal, -e, -als *ou* **-aux, -ales** [pɔstnatal, -o] **ADJ** postnatal

postopératoire [pɔstɔperatwar] **ADJ** postoperative

post-partum [pɔstpartɔm] **NM INV** postpartum period

postposer [3] [pɔstpoze] **VT 1** *Gram* to place after; **un adjectif postposé** a postpositive adjective, an adjective that comes after the noun **2** *Belg (remettre à plus tard)* to postpone

postposition [pɔstpozisjɔ̃] **NF** *Gram* **1** *(particule)* postposition **2** *(fait de postposer)* **la p. de l'adjectif** placing the adjective after the noun

postprandial, -e, -aux, -ales [pɔstprɑ̃djal, -o] **ADJ** postprandial

postprod [pɔstprɔd] **NF** *Fam Cin & TV (abrév* **postproduction)** postproduction■

postproduction [pɔstprɔdyksjɔ̃] **NF** *Cin & TV* postproduction

postromantique [pɔstrɔmɑ̃tik] **ADJ** post-Romantic

postscolaire [pɔstskɔlɛr] **ADJ** further education *(avant n)*; **enseignement p.** further education

PostScript® [pɔstskript] **NM** *Ordinat* PostScript®

post-scriptum [pɔstskriptɔm] **NM INV** postscript

postsériel, -elle [pɔstserjɛl] **ADJ** post-serial; **musique postsérielle** post-serial music

postsonorisation [pɔstsɔnɔrizasjɔ̃] **NF** *Cin* post-synchronization, dubbing

postsonoriser [pɔstsɔnɔrize] **VT** *Cin* to postsynchronize, to dub

postsynchro [pɔstsɛ̃kro] **NF** *Cin* post-synching

postsynchronisation [pɔstsɛ̃krɔnizasjɔ̃] **NF** post-synchronization

postsynchroniser [3] [pɔstsɛ̃krɔnize] **VT** to post-synchronize

post-test [pɔsttɛst] *(pl* **post-tests)** **NM** *Mktg* post-test

post-tester [3] [pɔsttɛste] **VT** *Mktg* to post-test

postulant, -e [pɔstylɑ̃, -ɑ̃t] **NM,F 1** *(à un emploi)* applicant, candidate **2** *Rel* postulant

postulat [pɔstyla] **NM 1** *Math* postulate; **nous partons du p. que...** we take it as axiomatic that... **2** *(principe de base)* postulate **3** *Rel* postulancy

postulation [pɔstylasjɔ̃] **NF** *Jur* representation, proxy

postuler [3] [pɔstyle] **VT 1** *(poste)* to apply for **2** *Math* to postulate, to assume
VI *Jur* **p. pour un client** to act on behalf of *or* to represent a client
❏ **postuler à VT IND** *(emploi)* to apply for

post-universitaire [pɔstyniversitɛr] *(pl* **post-universitaires)** **ADJ** postgraduate

postural, -e, -aux, -ales [pɔstyral, -o] **ADJ** postural

posture [pɔstyr] **NF 1** *(position du corps)* posture, position; **prendre une p. comique** to strike a comic pose; **dans une p. inconfortable** in an uncomfortable position
2 *(situation)* position; **être en bonne/en mauvaise p.** to be in a good/in an awkward position; **être en fâcheuse p.** to be in an awkward position; **être en p. de faire qch** to be in a position to do sth
3 *Belg (statuette)* statuette

pot [po] **NM 1** *(contenant)* pot; **p. en étain/verre/terre** tin/glass/earthenware pot; **mettre en p.** *(plantes)* to pot; *(fruits, confitures)* to put into jars; **p. à eau/lait** water/milk jug; **p. à *ou* de yaourt** yoghurt pot; **p. de chambre** (chamber) pot; **p. à confiture** *ou* **à confitures** jam jar; **p. de fleurs** *(vide)* flowerpot, plant pot; *(planté)* flowers in a pot, potted flowers; **p. à moutarde** mustard pot; **p. à tabac** tobacco jar; *Fig* tubby little person; **tourner autour du p.** to beat about the bush; *Prov* **c'est dans les vieux pots qu'on fait les bonnes** *ou* **les meilleures soupes** = experience always wins the day; *Fam* **être sourd comme un p.** to be as deaf as a post
2 *(contenu)* pot, potful; **p. de confiture/miel** jar of jam/honey; *Ordinat* **p. de miel** *(pour piéger les pirates informatiques)* honeypot; **p. de peinture** pot *or* can of paint; *Péj* **être un vrai p. de peinture** *(très maquillée)* to wear make-up an inch thick, to put one's make-up on with a trowel; **petit p. (pour bébé)** (jar of) baby food; **elle ne**

lui donne que des petits pots she only feeds him/her prepared baby foods
3 *(pour enfant)* pot, potty; **mets-le sur son p.** put him on his potty; **aller sur le p.** to use the potty
4 *Vieilli (marmite)* (cooking) pot
5 *Fam (boisson)* drink■, *Br* jar, *Am* snort; **prendre un p.** to have a drink; **viens, je t'offre un p.** come on, I'll buy you a drink; **ils font un p. pour son départ à la retraite** they're having a little get-together for his retirement; **je suis invité à un p. ce soir** I've been invited out for drinks tonight
6 *Fam (chance)* luck■; **avoir du p.** *(souvent)* to be lucky■; *(à un certain moment)* to be in luck; **il n'a pas de p.** *(jamais)* he's unlucky■; *(en ce moment)* he's out of luck; **pas de p.!** hard *or* tough luck!; **manque de p., la banque était fermée** as (bad) luck would have it, the bank was closed; **coup de p.** stroke of luck
7 *Fam (derrière)* butt, *Br* bum
8 *Cartes (talon)* stock; *(enjeux)* pot
9 *Aut* **p. d'échappement** *(silencieux)* silencer, *Am* muffler; *(tuyau)* *Br* exhaust (pipe), *Am* tail pipe; **p. catalytique** catalytic converter
10 *Fam* **plein p.** *(à toute vitesse)* *Br* like the clappers, *Am* like sixty
11 *Naut* **p. au noir** doldrums
❏ **en pot** **ADJ** *(plante)* pot *(avant n)*, potted; *(confiture, miel)* in a jar
❏ **pot de colle** **NM** *Fam Fig* nuisance■; **quel p. de colle!** he/she sticks to you like glue!, you can't shake him/her off *or* get rid of him/her!; **elle est p. de colle** she sticks to you like glue, you just can't get rid of her

C'est le pot de terre contre le pot de fer
In the La Fontaine fable *Le pot de terre et le pot de fer*, an earthenware pot suggests to a cast-iron one that they go travelling together. On the bumpy road, the two are thrown together, and the earthenware pot smashed to pieces; the weaker vessel, so to speak, is destroyed. The moral of the story is that one should associate with one's equals and not confront someone more powerful. The expression when used today refers to an unequal contest.

potable [pɔtabl] **ADJ 1** *(buvable)* **eau p.** drinking water; **eau non p.** water unsuitable for drinking **2** *Fam (acceptable → travail)* reasonable■, just about OK; *(→ vêtement)* wearable

potache [pɔtaʃ] **NM** *Fam* schoolkid; **blague de p.** schoolboy joke

potage [pɔtaʒ] **NM 1** *Culin* soup; **p. aux légumes** vegetable soup; *Fam* **être dans le p.** *(être évanoui)* to be out cold; *(être dans une situation pénible)* to be in the soup **2** *Vieilli ou Littéraire* **n'ayant pour tout p. que son diplôme de masseur** with only his masseur's diploma to his name

potager, -ère [pɔtaʒe, -ɛr] **ADJ** *(culture)* vegetable *(avant n)*; *(plante)* grown for food, food *(avant n)*; **jardin p.** kitchen garden, vegetable plot
NM 1 *(jardin)* kitchen garden, vegetable plot **2** *Suisse (fourneau)* stove, range; *(cuisinière)* cooker

potamochère [pɔtamɔʃɛr] **NM** *Zool* bushpig, red river hog, *Spéc* potamochoerus

potamologie [pɔtamɔlɔʒi] **NF** *Géog* potamology

potamot [pɔtamo] **NM** *Bot* pondweed, water spike

potard [pɔtar] **NM** *Fam Vieilli (pharmacien)* *Br* chemist■, *Am* druggist■; *(étudiant)* pharmacy student■

potasse [pɔtas] **NF** *Chim* **1** *(hydroxyde)* potassium hydroxide, (caustic) potash **2** *(carbonate)* (impure) potassium carbonate, potash

potasser [3] [pɔtase] *Fam* **VT** *(discipline, leçon)* *Br* to swot up on, *Am* to bone up on; *(examen)* to cram for
VI *Br* to swot, *Am* to bone up

potassique [pɔtasik] **ADJ** *Chim (gén)* potassium *(avant n)*; *(sel)* potassic

potassium [pɔtasjɔm] **NM** *Chim* potassium

pot-au-feu [pɔtofø] **NM INV** *Culin* pot-au-feu, boiled beef with vegetables
ADJ INV *Fam (pantouflard)* **être p.** to be a homebody

pot-de-vin [podvɛ̃] *(pl* **pots-de-vin)** **NM** bribe; **verser des pots-de-vin à qn** to grease sb's palm, to bribe sb

pote [pɔt] *Fam* **ADJ** **être p. avec qn** to be pally with sb; **ils sont très potes** they're very pally
NM *pal*, *Br* mate, *Am* buddy; **salut mon p.!** hi pal *or Br* mate *or Am* buddy!

Touche pas à mon pote
In the early 1980s, the "Front national", an extreme right-wing political party, had a high profile in France. To combat its ideology, Harlem Désir founded a group called "SOS-Racisme", and this is its slogan ("Lay off my pal"). The expression caught on, and is used to express group solidarity when defending something from a threat, with the relevant word being substituted for "mon pote", for example **Touche pas à ma retraite!** ("Leave my pension alone!").

poteau, -x [pɔto] **NM 1** *(mât)* post, pole; *Belg* **p. d'éclairage** street lamp, streetlight; **p. électrique** electricity pylon; **p. indicateur** signpost; **p. télégraphique** telegraph pole *or* post; **p. (d'exécution)** (execution) stake; **envoyer qn au p.** to sentence sb to execution by firing squad; *Fam* **le proviseur, au p.!** down with the headmaster!; *Fam* **avoir des jambes comme des poteaux** to have legs like tree-trunks; **elle a de ces poteaux!** her legs are like tree-trunks!
2 *(support de but)* post, goalpost; **entre les poteaux** between the goalposts; **le premier/second p.** the near/back post
3 *(dans une course)* **p. d'arrivée** winning post; **p. de départ** starting post; **rester au p.** *(cheval)* to be left at the starting post; **se faire coiffer au** *ou* **battre sur le p. (d'arrivée)** to be beaten at the (finishing) post; *Fig* to be pipped at the post, *Am* to be beaten by a nose
4 *Fam Vieilli (ami)* *Br* mate, *Am* buddy

potée [pɔte] **NF 1** *Culin* pork hotpot *(with cabbage and root vegetables)* **2** *Métal (pour mouler)* moulding clay **3** *Tech (d'étain)* putty powder; *(de fer)* crocus, jeweller's rouge

potelé, -e [pɔtle] **ADJ** plump, chubby; **une petite bonne femme potelée** a dumpy little woman

potence [pɔtɑ̃s] **NF 1** *(supplice, instrument)* gallows **2** *Constr (d'une charpente)* post and braces; *(d'une lanterne, d'une enseigne)* support; *(d'une perfusion)* stand; **en p.** bracket-shaped, L-shaped **3** *(d'une grue)* crane jib **4** *(pour panneaux de signalisation)* overhead signpost

potencé, -e [pɔtɑ̃se] **ADJ** *Hér* potent; **croix potencée** potent cross

potentat [pɔtɑ̃ta] **NM 1** *(monarque)* potentate **2** *(despote)* despot; **il se comporte en vrai p. avec ses employés** he's a real despot as far as his employees are concerned

potentialisation [pɔtɑ̃sjalizasjɔ̃] **NF** *Physiol* potentiation

potentialiser [3] [pɔtɑ̃sjalize] **VT** *Physiol* to potentiate

potentialité [pɔtɑ̃sjalite] **NF 1** *Gram* potentiality **2** *(possibilité)* **ce projet offre de multiples potentialités de développement** this project has a lot of potential for development

potentiel, -elle [pɔtɑ̃sjɛl] **ADJ** potential; **un client p.** a prospective client
NM 1 *Élec, Math, Phys & Physiol* potential; **p. de repos** resting potential
2 *(possibilités)* potential, potentiality; **avoir un certain p.** *(personne)* to have promising qualities, to have potential; **p. de croissance** growth potential; *Pol* **p. électoral** chances of electoral success; **p. du marché** market potential *(of market)*; **p. sur le marché** market potential *(of product)*; **p. militaire** military potential; **p. de production** production potential *or* capacity; **p. publicitaire** advertising potential; **p. de vente** sales potential
3 *Ling* potential (mood)

potentiellement [pɔtɑ̃sjɛlmɑ̃] **ADV** potentially

potentille [pɔtɑ̃tij] **NF** *Bot* potentilla; **p. rampante** cinquefoil

potentiomètre [pɔtɑ̃sjɔmɛtr] **NM** potentiometer; **p. général** group fader

poterie [pɔtri] **NF 1** *(art)* pottery; **faire de la p.** to

do *or* make pottery **2** *(article)* piece of pottery; **des poteries grecques** Greek pottery **3** *(atelier)* potter's workshop *or* studio; *(usine)* pottery (works) **4** *Métal* **p. d'étain/de cuivre** pewter(-ware)/copper(ware)

poterne [pɔtɛrn] NF *(porte)* postern

potestatif, -ive [pɔtɛstatif, -iv] ADJ *Jur* **condition potestative** potestative condition

potiche [pɔtiʃ] NF **1** *(vase)* rounded vase **2** *Fam (personne sans pouvoir)* figurehead■; **jouer les potiches** *(femme)* to look decorative

potier, -ère [pɔtje, -ɛr] NM,F potter

potimarron [pɔtimarɔ̃] NM *Bot* Chinese okra

potin [pɔtɛ̃] NM *Fam (bruit)* racket, din; **faire du p.** *(machine, personne)* to make a racket; *(scandale, affaire)* to cause a furore

❏ **potins** NMPL *Fam (commérages)* gossip, idle rumours■; **(rubrique des) potins mondains** society gossip (column)

potiner [pɔtine] VI *Fam* to gossip, to spread rumours■

potinier, -ère [pɔtinje, -ɛr] ADJ *Fam* gossipy, scandal-mongering

potion [pɔsjɔ̃] NF potion, draught; **p. magique** magic potion

potiquet [pɔtikɛ] NM *Belg* pot

potiron [pɔtirɔ̃] NM pumpkin

potlatch [pɔtlatʃ] NM potlatch

potomanie [pɔtɔmani] NF *Méd* potomania, dipso-mania

potomètre [pɔtɔmɛtr] NM potometer

poto-poto [pɔtɔpɔtɔ] NM INV **1** *(boue)* mud; *(matériau)* dried mud *(used as a building material)* **2** *Belg Fam (cafouillage, imbroglio)* shambles, muddle

potoroo, potorou [pɔtɔru] NM *Zool* potoroo, rat kangaroo

pot-pourri [popuri] *(pl* **pots-pourris**) NM **1** *Mus* potpourri, medley **2** *Littérature* potpourri **3** *(fleurs)* potpourri

potron-jaquet [pɔtrɔ̃ʒakɛ], **potron-minet** [pɔtrɔ̃-minɛ] NM INV *Vieilli ou Hum* **dès p.** at the crack of dawn

Potsdam [pɔtsdam] NM Potsdam

Pott [pɔt] NPR *Méd* **mal de P.** Pott's disease

potto [pɔtɔ] NM *Zool* potto; **p. (de Calabar)** ag-wantibo

pottock [pɔtjɔk] NM pony *(from the Basque country)*

pou, -x [pu] NM **1** *(parasite de l'homme)* louse; **des poux** lice; **p. de tête/du corps** head/body louse; **poux du pubis** crab *or* pubic lice, crabs; *Fam Fig* **chercher des poux dans la tête à qn** to pick a quarrel with sb

2 *Entom* **p. collant** *ou* **des serres** cochineal (insect); **p. des livres** (common) book louse **3** *(locutions)* **être laid** *ou* **moche comme un p.** to be as ugly as sin; **être fier** *ou* **orgueilleux comme un p.** to be as proud as a peacock

pouacre [pwakr] *Fam Vieilli* ADJ **1** *(sale)* dirty■, filthy■, unwashed■ **2** *(avare)* mean■, stingy

NM,F **1** *(personne sale)* dirty *or* filthy *or* un-washed person■ **2** *(personne avare)* mean■ *or* stingy person

pouah [pwa] EXCLAM ugh!, yuck!

poubelle [pubɛl] NF **1** *(récipient à déchets) Br* dustbin, *Am* trash *or* garbage can; **mettre** *ou* **jeter qch à la p.** to put *or* to throw sth in the *Br* dustbin *or Am* trash can; **je vais mettre ces vieilles chaussures à la p.** I'm going to throw these old shoes out; **descendre la p.** to put the *Br* rubbish *or Am* garbage out; **bon pour la p.** fit for the *Br* bin *or Am* trash can; **faire les poubelles** to go scavenging (from the *Br* dustbins *or Am* trash cans); *Fig* **les poubelles de l'histoire** the scrapheap of history; **p. à pédale** pedal bin

2 *(dépotoir)* dumping-ground, *Br* rubbish *or Am* garbage dump; **ne prenez pas la mer pour une p.** don't use the sea as a dumping-ground **3** *Fam (voiture)* heap, banger, rustbucket **4** *(utilisé en apposition)* **pétrolier p.** = old, poorly-maintained oil tanker which poses a threat to the environment; **usines poubelles** dirty factories, factories which damage the environment; **la télé p.** trash TV

5 *Ordinat* wastebasket, *Am* trash

pouce [pus] NM **1** *Anat (doigt)* thumb; *(orteil)* big toe; *Fam* **se tourner les pouces** to twiddle one's thumbs; *Suisse* **tenir les pouces à qn** to keep one's fingers crossed for sb; *Belg* **sucer de son**

p. to guess; *Fam* **et le p.!** and a bit more besides! **2** *(mesure)* inch; *Fig* **on n'avançait pas d'un p. sur la route** the traffic was solid; *Fig* **je ne changerai pas d'un p. les dispositions de mon testament** I won't change one jot *or* iota of my will; *Fig* **ne pas céder un p. de terrain** not to yield *or* budge an inch

3 *Can Fam (locutions)* **avoir les mains pleines de pouces** to be all thumbs; **donner un p.** to give a lift to a hitchhiker■; **faire du p., voyager sur le p.** to thumb a *Br* lift *or Am* ride

EXCLAM *(dans un jeu) Br* pax!, *Am* time out!

pouce-pied [puspje] *(pl* **pouces-pieds**) NM *Zool* goose barnacle

poucer [3] [puse] VI *Can Fam (faire de l'auto-stop)* to thumb a *Br* lift *or Am* ride

Poucet [pusɛ] NPR **le Petit P.** Hop-o'-my-thumb, Tom Thumb *(from Perrault's tale)*

poucettes [pusɛt] NFPL = metal rings formerly attached to the thumbs of prisoners

Pouchkine [puʃkin] NPR Pushkin

poucier [pusje] NM *(doigtier)* thumbstall

pou-de-soie [pudswa] *(pl* **poux-de-soie**) NM *Tex (tissu)* poult-de-soie; *(vêtement)* garment made of poult-de-soie

pouding [pudiŋ], **poudingue** [pudɛ̃g] = **pudding**

poudrage [pudraʒ] NM **1** *(gén)* (light) powdering *or* sprinkling **2** *Tech* powdering **3** *Agr* dusting, crop-dusting

poudre [pudr] NF **1** *(aliment, médicament)* pow-der; *(de craie, d'os, de diamant, d'or)* dust, powder; **mettre** *ou* **réduire qch en p.** to reduce sth to powder, to pulverize *or* to powder sth; **p. à éternuer** sneezing powder; **p. à laver,** *Belg* **p. à lessiver** soap *or Br* washing powder; *Suisse* **p. à lever** baking powder; **p. à récurer** scouring powder

2 *Mil* powder, gunpowder; **p. à canon** gunpow-der; **faire parler la p.** to settle the argument with guns; **ça sent la p.** there's talk of war

3 *(cosmétique → pour le visage)* (face) powder; *(→ pour une perruque)* powder; **p. de riz** face powder; **p. compacte/libre** pressed/loose pow-der; **se mettre de la p.** to powder one's face *or* nose

4 *Fam Arg drogue (héroïne)* smack, skag, H; *(cocaïne)* coke, charlie, *Am* nose candy

5 *Vieilli (poussière)* dust

6 *(locutions)* **prendre la p. d'escampette** to decamp; **jeter de la p. aux yeux à qn** to try to dazzle *or* to impress sb; **tout ça c'est de la p. aux yeux** all that's just for show; **p. de perlimpinpin** *(faux remède)* quack remedy; **leur politique, c'est de la p. de perlimpinpin** their policy is just a magic cure-all

❏ **en poudre** ADJ *(amandes, lait)* powdered; **chocolat en p.** drinking chocolate; **noix de muscade en p.** ground nutmeg

poudrer [3] [pudre] VT **1** *(maquiller)* to powder; **une femme poudrée** a woman with a powdered face **2** *Littérature (saupoudrer)* **la neige poudrait les arbres** the trees had a light powdering *or* sprinkling of snow

▸**se poudrer** VPR to powder one's nose *or* face

poudrerie [pudrəri] NF **1** *(fabrique)* gun-powder factory **2** *Can (neige)* flurry of snow

poudrette [pudrɛt] NF *(engrais)* = dried and pow-dered night-soil used as manure

poudreux, -euse [pudrø, -øz] ADJ **1** *(terre)* dusty; *(substance, neige)* powdery **2** *Vieilli (couvert de poussière)* dusty

❏ **poudreuse** NF **1** *(neige)* powdery snow, pow-der **2** *Agr* sprinkler, powder-sprinkler

poudrier [pudrije] NM *(powder)* compact

poudrière [pudrijɛr] NF **1** *Mil* (gun)powder store; **la maison était une vraie p.** the house was packed with explosives **2** *Fig (région)* powder keg

poudrin [pudrɛ̃] NM spindrift

poudroie *etc voir* **poudroyer**

poudroiement [pudrwamɑ̃] NM *Littéraire (de la neige)* sparkle; *(de la poussière)* fine cloud

poudroyer [13] [pudrwaje] VI *Littéraire (sable, neige)* to rise in clouds; *(soleil, lumière)* to shine hazily; **au loin, la route poudroyait** in the dis-tance, fine clouds of dust could be seen rising up from the road

pouf¹ [puf] NM *(siège)* pouf, pouffe

❏ **à pouf** ADV *Belg* **1** *(à crédit)* on tick **2 taper à p.** *(au hasard)* to make a wild guess

pouf² [puf] ONOMAT *(dans une chute)* thump, bump; **faire p.** to go thump; **et p., par terre!** whoops-a-daisy!

pouffe [puf] = **poufiasse**

pouffer [3] [pufe] VI **p. (de rire)** to titter

pouffiasse, poufiasse [pufjas] NF *très Fam Péj* **1** *(prostituée)* whore, hooker **2** *(femme aux mœurs légères)* slut, tart **3** *(femme désagréable)* bitch, *Br* cow

pouic [pwik] **que pouic** PRON *Fam* zilch, *Br* bug-ger all, sod all; **j'y comprends que p.** I don't understand a damn *or Br* bloody thing

pouillard [pujar] NM *Orn (jeune perdreau)* poult, young partridge; *(jeune faisan)* young pheasant

Pouille [puj] NF **la P., les Pouilles** Apulia

pouillé [puje] NM *Hist* terrier *(of diocese, abbey etc)*

pouillerie [pujri] NF *Vieilli* **1** *(pauvreté sordide)* squalor **2** *(lieu)* filthy place, lousy hole

pouilles [puj] NFPL *Vieilli* jeers; *Littéraire* **dire** *ou* **chanter p. à qn** to jeer at sb, to revile sb

pouilleux, -euse [pujø, -øz] ADJ **1** *(couvert de poux)* covered in lice, lousy, verminous **2** *(pauvre et sale → individu)* grubby, filthy; *(→ restaurant, quartier)* shabby, seedy **3** *Géog (sté-rile)* **la Champagne pouilleuse** = the barren part of the Champagne region

NM,F *Péj* grubby person; **sur ce, arrive une espèce de p.** in comes a scruffy wretch

pouillot [pujo] NM *Orn* **p. fitis** willow warbler; **p. siffleur** wood warbler; **p. véloce** chiffchaff

pouilly [puji] NM Pouilly (wine)

poujadisme [puʒadism] NM *Pol & Fig Péj* Pouja-dism

poujadiste [puʒadist] NM,F *Pol & Fig Péj* Poujadist

Poulaga [pulaga] NF *Fam Arg crime* **la maison P.** the cops, *Br* the pigs, the fuzz

poulaille [pulaj] NF *Fam* **la p.** the cops, *Br* the pigs, the fuzz

poulailler [pulaje] NM **1** *(hangar)* hen house; *(cour)* hen run **2** *Fam Théât* **le p.** *Br* the gods, *Am* the peanut gallery; **nous avons des places au p.** we've got seats up in *Br* the gods *or Am* the peanut gallery

poulain [pulɛ̃] NM **1** *Zool* colt; *(très jeune)* foal **2** *(protégé)* (young) protégé; **il avait plusieurs poulains** he had several young people under his patronage **3** *Tech* **p. (de chargement)** skid

poulaine [pulɛn] NF **1** *(chaussure)* **(soulier à la) p.** poulaine **2** *Naut* head

poulamon [pulamɔ̃] NM *Can* (Atlantic) tomcod

poularde [pulard] NF fattened hen, poulard, pou-larde

poulbot [pulbo] NM *(Montmartre)* urchin

poule [pul] NF **1** *Orn* hen; **p. de bruyère** grey hen; **p. d'eau** moorhen; **p. faisane** hen pheasant; **p. pondeuse** laying hen; **p. des prairies** prairie chicken; **la p. aux œufs d'or** the goose that laid the golden eggs; **se coucher avec les poules** to go to bed very early; **p. mouillée** drip; **ton argent, tu le reverras quand les poules auront des dents** you can kiss your money goodbye; **tu crois qu'on va avoir une augmentation? – c'est ça, quand les poules auront des dents!** do you think we're going to get a pay rise? – yeah, and pigs might fly!; **une p. n'y retrouverait pas ses poussins** it's an awful mess; **être comme une p. qui a trouvé un couteau** to be all flustered; *Prov* **la p. ne doit pas chanter devant le coq** = it's the man who should wear the trousers

2 *Culin (boiling)* fowl; **p. au riz** boiled chicken with rice; **p. au pot** = casseroled chicken with vegetables

3 *Fam (maîtresse)* mistress■; *Vieilli (prostituée)* whore; **p. de luxe** *(prostituée)* high-class whore *or* prostitute

4 *Fam (terme d'affection)* **ma p.** sweetheart, honey, babe

5 (comme adj) **c'est une mère p.** she's a real mother hen; **c'est un papa p.** he's a real mother hen

6 Sport group, pool; **en p. A, Metz bat Béziers** in group or pool A, Metz beat Béziers; Équitation **p. d'essai** 1,600 m maiden race

7 (cagnotte) pool, kitty

Allusion

La poule aux œufs d'or

This is the title of a fable by La Fontaine, about a hen that lays a golden egg each day. The greedy owner kills her, hoping to find even more gold, but finds an ordinary chicken carcass instead. He has thus put paid to the source of all his wealth. In English we speak of the goose, rather than the hen, that lays the golden eggs; otherwise the expression works the same in both languages.

---

poulet [pulɛ] NM **1** Culin & Orn chicken; **p. fermier** free-range chicken; **p. de grain** corn-fed chicken **2** Fam (policier) cop, Br pig **3** Fam (terme d'affection) **mon p.** my pet, (my) love **4** Fam Vieilli (lettre galante) love letter■

'**Poulet au vinaigre**' Chabrol 'Coq au vin'

poulette [pulɛt] NF **1** Orn pullet **2** Fam (terme d'affection) **ma p.** sweetheart, honey, babe **3** Fam (femme) Br bird, Am chick **4** Culin **sauce (à la) p.** = sauce made from butter, egg yolks and vinegar

pouliche [pulif] NF filly

Poulidor [pulidɔr] NPR = popular Tour de France cyclist, best-known for coming second

poulie [puli] NF (roue) pulley; (avec enveloppe) block; **p. folle** idler; **p. simple/double/fixe** single/double/fixed block; **p. trapézoïdale** V-belt pulley

pouliner [3] [puline] VI to foal

poulinière [pulinjɛr] NF brood mare

ADJ F voir **jument**

pouliot¹ [puljo] NM Bot pennyroyal

pouliot² [puljo] NM (sur charrette) windlass

poulot, -otte [pulo, -ɔt] NM,F Vieilli **mon p.** (my) pet, (my) darling

poulpe [pulp] NM octopus

pouls [pu] NM Méd pulse; **prendre le p. à qn** to take sb's pulse; **tâter le p. à qn** to feel sb's pulse; **prendre** ou **tâter le p. de** (électorat) to feel the pulse of, to sound out; (entreprise, secteur) to feel the pulse of; **p. veineux** venous pulse

poult-de-soie [putswa] (pl **poults-de-soie**) = **pou-de-soie**

poumon [pumɔ̃] NM **1** Anat lung; **p. artificiel** ou **d'acier** artificial ou iron lung; Méd **cancer du p.** lung cancer; **avoir de bons poumons** ou **des poumons** (chanteur) to have a powerful voice; (baby) to have a good pair of lungs; Fig **Central Park, le p. vert de New York** Central Park, New York's green lung ou main green park **2** Fam Hum **poumons** (seins) knockers, jugs, Am hooters **3** Zool **p. de mer** rhizostoma octopus

poupard [pupar] NM Vieilli (bébé) chubby-cheeked baby

poupe [pup] NF Naut stern

poupée [pupe] NF **1** (figurine) doll; **jouer à la p.** to play with dolls; **p. de chiffon/cire/porcelaine** rag/wax/china doll; **p. qui parle/marche** talking/walking doll; **p. Barbie®** ou **mannequin** Barbie® doll; **p. de son** stuffed doll; **p. gonflable** inflatable or blow-up doll; **des poupées gigognes** ou **russes** a set of Russian dolls **2** Fam (fille, femme) babe, doll **3** Fam (bandage) (large) finger bandage■; **faire une p. à qn** to bandage sb's finger **4** Tech (gén) headstock; (d'un tour) poppet □ **de poupée** ADJ **une chambre de p.** a doll's bedroom; **un visage de p.** a doll-like face

'**Les Poupées russes**' Klapisch 'The Russian Dolls'

poupin, -e [pupɛ̃, -in] ADJ (visage, personne) chubby

poupon [pupɔ̃] NM **1** (bébé) little baby **2** (jouet) baby doll

pouponner [3] [pupɔne] VI Fam to play the doting mother/father

pouponnière [pupɔnjɛr] NF nursery (for babies and toddlers who can neither stay with their parents nor be fostered)

poupoule [pupul] NF Fam **ma p.** sweetheart, honey, babe

poupoune [pupun] NF Can Fam sweetie, honey

POUR [pur]

for **1–4, 7, 10–12, 14, 16** ■ to **5** ■ per **9** ■ on behalf of **12** ■ in order to **15** ■ in favour of **16**

PRÉP 1 (indiquant le lieu où l'on va) for; **partir p. l'Italie** to leave for Italy; **un billet p. Paris** a ticket for or to Paris; **p. Granville, prendre à gauche** turn left for Granville; **le train p. Séville** the train for Seville, the Seville train; **je m'envole p. Rome** I'm flying to Rome; **partir p. la campagne** to go to the country

2 (dans le temps → indiquant le moment) for; **pourriez-vous avoir fini p. lundi/demain?** could you have it finished for Monday/tomorrow?; **p. dans une semaine** for a week's time; **p. le 10 mai** for 10 May; **vous partez en Italie p. Pâques?** are you going to Italy for Easter?; **p. la première fois** for the first time; **p. le moment** for the moment; **tu organises quelque chose p. ton anniversaire?** are you doing anything for your birthday?; **j'ai repeint la chambre p. quand tu viendras** I've redecorated the room for when you visit

3 (dans le temps → indiquant la durée) for; **partir p. 10 jours** to go away for 10 days; **elle est absente p. une semaine** she's away for a week; **il n'en a plus p. longtemps** he won't be long now; (à vivre) he hasn't got long to live; **j'en ai bien p. cinq heures** it'll take me at least five hours

4 (exprimant la cause) for; **je l'ai remercié p. son amabilité** I thanked him for his kindness; **il a été grassement récompensé p. son aide** he was handsomely rewarded for his help; **fermé p. travaux** (sur vitrine d'un magasin) closed for repairs; **un restaurant apprécié p. ses fruits de mer** a restaurant famous for its seafood; **ils se querellent p. des broutilles** they quarrel over the slightest thing; **désolé p. dimanche** sorry about Sunday; **il est tombé malade p. avoir mangé trop d'huîtres** he fell ill after eating or because he ate too many oysters; **condamné p. vol** found guilty of theft; **elle a obtenu un prix p. son premier film** she won an award for her first movie or Br film; **sa bonne constitution y est p. quelque chose** his/her strong constitution had something to do with or played a part in it; **elle est p. beaucoup dans le succès de la pièce** the success of the play is to a large extent due to her, she has had a great deal to do with the success of the play; **ne me remerciez pas, je n'y suis p. rien** don't thank me, I didn't have anything to do with it

5 (exprimant la conséquence) to; **p. son malheur** to his/her misfortune; **p. la plus grande joie des enfants** to the children's great delight; **il a erré trois heures en forêt p. se retrouver à son point de départ** he wandered for three hours in the forest, only to find he was back where he'd started from; **ses paroles n'étaient pas p. me rassurer** his/her words were far from reassuring to me; **ce n'est pas p. me déplaire** I can't say I'm displeased with it

6 (capable de) **je me suis trompé et il ne s'est trouvé personne p. me le dire** I made a mistake and nobody was capable of telling me; **il y a toujours des gens p. rire du malheur des autres** there will always be people who'll laugh at other people's misfortune

7 (par rapport à) for; **il est en avance p. son âge** he's advanced for his age; **pas mal p. un début** not bad for a start; **il fait froid p. un mois de mai** it's cold for May; **c'est cher p. ce que c'est** it's expensive for what it is

8 (avec une valeur emphatique) **mot p. mot** word for word; **p. un champion, c'est un champion!** that's what I call a (real) champion!; **p. une surprise, c'est une surprise!** well, talk about (a) surprise!; **perdre p. perdre, autant que ce**

soit en beauté if we are going to lose, we might as well do it in style; **p. être en colère, je l'étais!** I was SO angry!

9 (indiquant une proportion, un pourcentage) per; **cinq p. cent** five percent; **p. mille** per thousand; **il faut 200 g de farine p. une demi-livre de beurre** take 200 g of flour to or for half a pound of butter

10 (moyennant) for; **p. 50 euros** for 50 euros; **p. la somme de** for the sum of; **p. rien** for nothing; **il y en a bien p. 300 euros de réparation** the repairs will cost at least 300 euros

11 (à la place de) for; **prendre un mot p. un autre** to mistake a word for another; **on l'a prise p. sa fille** they mistook her for her daughter

12 (au nom de) for, on behalf of; **parler p. qn** to speak on sb's behalf or for sb; **remercie-le p. moi** thank him from me or for me or on my behalf; **son tuteur prend toutes les décisions p. lui** his guardian makes all the decisions for him or on his behalf; **p. le directeur** (dans la correspondance) pp Director

13 (en guise de, en qualité de) **prendre qn p. époux/épouse** to take sb to be one's husband/wife; **avoir qn p. ami/professeur** to have sb as a friend/teacher; **j'ai son fils p. élève** his/her son is one of my pupils; **p. tout remerciement voilà ce que j'ai eu** that's all the thanks I got; **avoir p. conséquence** to have as a consequence; **j'ai p. principe que...** I believe on principle that...; **il se fait passer p. un antiquaire** he claims to be an antique dealer; **le livre a p. titre...** the book's title is..., the book is entitled...

14 (indiquant l'attribution, la destination, le but) for; **acheter un cadeau p. qn** to buy a present for sb; **il y a quelqu'un p. vous au téléphone** there's someone on the phone for you; **j'ai beaucoup d'admiration p. lui** I've got a lot of admiration for him; **son amour p. moi** his/her love for me; **mes sentiments p. elle** my feelings towards or for her; **tant pis p. lui!** that's too bad (for him)!; **c'est p. quoi faire, ce truc?** what's that thing for?; **sirop p. la toux** cough mixture; **un journal p. enfants** a newspaper for children; **des vêtements chauds p. l'hiver** warm clothes for winter; **tout est bon p. son ambition** everything feeds his/her ambition; **il est mort p. la patrie** he died for his country; **voyager p. son plaisir** to travel for pleasure; **l'art p. l'art** art for art's sake; **la discipline p. la discipline c'est idiot** discipline (just) for the sake of discipline is stupid; **p. quatre personnes** (recette) serves four; (couchage) sleeps four; **c'est fait p.** that's what it's (there) for

15 (suivi de l'infinitif) (afin de) (in order) to; **je suis venu p. vous voir** I'm here or I've come to see you; **nous sommes là p. vous informer** we're here to inform you; **p. mieux comprendre** in order to understand more clearly; **p. en finir avec toutes ces rumeurs...** in order to put a stop to these rumours...; **si tu veux réussir, il faut tout faire p.** if you want to succeed you have to do everything possible

16 (en faveur de) for, in favour of; **voter p. qn** to vote for or in favour of sb; **manifester p. les droits de l'homme** to demonstrate for or in favour of human rights; **il a p. lui de nombreuses qualités** he has a number of qualities in his favour; **être p.** to be in favour; **qui est p.?** who's in favour?; **on est p.** ou **contre** you're either for or against (it); **ceux qui sont p. cette solution** the supporters of this solution, those who are in favour of this solution; **je suis p. qu'on s'y mette tout de suite** I'm in favour of getting down to it immediately

17 (du point de vue de) **ça compte peu p. toi, mais p. moi c'est tellement important** it matters little to you but to or for me it's so important; **p. moi, il a dû se réconcilier avec elle** if you ask me, he must have made it up with her; **p. moi, c'est comme s'il était toujours là** to or for me, it's as though he's still here or around

18 (en ce qui concerne) **et p. le salaire?** and what about the salary?; **ne t'en fais pas p. moi** don't worry about me; **p. certains de nos collègues, la situation est inchangée** as far as some

of our colleagues are concerned, the situation has not changed; **p. ce qui est de l'avancement, voyez avec le responsable du personnel** as far as promotion is concerned, see the personnel officer

19 *(exprimant la concession)* **p. être gentil il n'en est pas moins bête** he may be kind but he's still stupid, for all his kindness he's no less stupid; **p. être jeune, elle n'en est pas moins compétente** young though she is she's very able; **p. grands que soient les rois, ils sont ce que nous sommes** great though kings are, they are but as we are; **p. patient qu'il soit, il ne supportera pas cette situation** for all his patience, he won't put up with this situation

20 *Littéraire (sur le point de)* about to, on the point of; **il était p. partir** he was about to leave *or* on the point of leaving

NM INV **il y a du p. et du contre** there are things to be said on both sides (of the argument); **peser le p. et le contre** to weigh up the pros and cons; **les p. l'emportent** the argument in favour is overwhelming; *Pol ou Hum* the ayes have it

❑ **pour que** CONJ **1** *(exprimant le but)* so that, *Sout* in order that; **venez tôt p. que nous ayons le temps de faire connaissance** come early so that we have time to get to know each other; **j'ai pris des places non-fumeurs p. que vous ne soyez pas incommodés par la fumée** I've got non-smoking seats so that you won't be bothered by the smoke

2 *(exprimant la conséquence)* **il est assez malin p. qu'on ne l'arrête pas** he is cunning enough to avoid being caught; **mon appartement est trop petit p. qu'on puisse tous y dormir** my flat is too small for us all to be able to sleep there

pourave [purav] ADJ *Fam (très mauvais)* crap, garbage, *Br* rubbish

pourboire [purbwar] NM tip; **donner un p. à qn** to give a tip to sb, to tip sb; **j'ai laissé deux euros de p.** I left a two-euro tip; **être payé au p.** to depend on tips for one's pay

pourceau, -x [purso] NM *Littéraire* **1** *(porc)* pig, *Am* hog **2** *(homme → sale)* pig; *(→ vicieux)* animal

pour-cent [pursɑ̃] NM INV *Fin* percentage

pourcent [pursɑ̃] NM *Fam* **quelques pourcents d'électeurs se sont abstenus** quite a few voters abstained

pourcentage [pursɑ̃taʒ] NM **1** *Fin & Math* percentage; **ça fait combien, en p.?** what's the percentage figure? **2** *Com* percentage, commission; **travailler au p.** to work on a commission *or* percentage basis; **être payé au p.** to be paid on commission *or* on a commission basis

pourchasser [3] [purʃase] VT **1** *(criminel)* to chase, to pursue; **pourchassé par ses créanciers** pursued *or* hounded by his creditors **2** *(erreur, abus)* to track down; **nous pourchasserons les injustices** we'll root out injustice wherever we find it

pourfendeur, -euse [purfɑ̃dœr, -øz] NM,F *Littéraire* **p. d'idées reçues/de l'hypocrisie** declared *or* sworn enemy of received ideas/of hypocrisy

pourfendre [73] [purfɑ̃dr] VT *Littéraire* **1** *(avec une épée → ennemi)* to kill (by the sword) **2** *(hypocrisie, préjugés)* to combat

pourim [purim] NM *Rel* Purim

pourlèche [purlɛʃ] = **perlèche**

pourlécher [18] [purleʃe] **se pourlécher** VPR to lick one's lips; **se p. les babines** to lick one's lips; *Hum* **je m'en pourlèche les babines à l'avance** my mouth is watering already

pourliche [purliʃ] NM *Fam* tip■ *(in bar, restaurant)*

pourparlers [purparle] NMPL negotiations, talks; **être/entrer en p. avec qn** to have/to enter into talks *or* negotiations with sb; **les p. vont reprendre** negotiations will be resumed; *UE* **p. d'adhésion** entry talks; **p. bilatéraux** bilateral talks; **p. de paix** peace talks

pourpier [purpje] NM *Bot* purslane

pourpoint [purpwɛ̃] NM doublet, pourpoint; **des personnages en p.** characters wearing doublet and hose

pourpre [purpr] ADJ crimson; **son visage devint p.** he/she went *or* turned crimson

NM **1** *(couleur)* crimson; **le p. de la honte lui monta au visage** he/she turned crimson with shame

2 *(mollusque)* murex, purple fish

3 *Biol* **p. rétinien** visual purple

NF **1** *(teinte)* purple (dye)

2 *Rel* **la p.** *(robe)* the purple; **revêtir la p. cardinalice** to don the red hat; **né dans la p.** born in *or* to the purple

pourpré, -e [purpre] ADJ **1** *Littéraire* crimson **2** *Vieilli Méd* **fièvre pourprée** hives

pourprin, -e [purprɛ̃, -in] ADJ *Vieilli* crimson

pourquoi [purkwa] ADV why; **p. pars-tu?, p. est-ce que tu pars?** why are you going?; **p. m'avoir menti?** why did you lie to me?; **p. cet air triste?** why are you looking so sad?; **p. chercher des difficultés?** why make things more complicated?; **p. lutter?** what's the use of fighting?; **p. tant d'efforts?** why so much effort?; **p. tant de simagrées?** what's the point of all this play-acting?; **mais p.?** but why?; **p. pas?** why not?; **elle a bien réussi l'examen, p. pas moi?** she passed the exam, why shouldn't I?; **p. ça?** why?; **et p. donc?** but why?; **et p., s'il vous plaît?** and why, may I ask?; **p. je n'ai rien dit? parce que ça ne me regarde pas!** why didn't I say anything? because it's none of my business!; **je ne sais pas p. tu dis ça** I don't know why you're saying that; **voilà p. je démissionne** that's (the reason) why I am resigning, that's the reason for my resignation; **c'est p. je n'y suis pas allée** that's why I didn't go; **personne ne m'a dit p.** nobody has told me why; **il boude, va savoir** *ou* **comprendre p.!** he's sulking, don't ask me why!; **je l'ai fait sans savoir p.** I did it without knowing why; **c'est une opération délicate, et voici p....** it is a tricky operation and this is why...

NM INV **nous ne saurons jamais le p. de cette affaire** we'll never get to the bottom of this affair; **il s'interroge toujours sur le p. et le comment des choses** he's always bothered about the whys and wherefores of everything; **dans sa lettre, il explique le p. de son suicide** in his letter, he explains the reason *or* reasons for his suicide

pourra *etc voir* **pouvoir**[2]

pourri, -e [puri] ADJ **1** *(nourriture → gén)* rotten, bad; *(→ œufs)* bad; *(→ planche, arbre, plante)* rotten; *(→ dent)* rotten, decayed; *(→ chairs)* decomposed, putrefied; **complètement p.** rotten to the core

2 *Fam (mauvais → climat, saison)* rotten; **il a fait un temps p.** the weather was rotten

3 *(en mauvais état)* falling apart, *Br* knackered; **elle est complètement pourrie ta voiture!** your car is a wreck *or* a heap of junk!

4 *(de mauvaise qualité)* crappy, *Br* rubbish, *Am* rinky-dink

5 *Fam (corrompu → individu, système)* rotten to the core, *Br* bent; **votre société est pourrie!** your society is rotten!

6 *(trop gâté → enfant)* spoilt

7 *Fam (plein)* **il est p. de fric** he's stinking rich, he's loaded; **il est p. de talent** he's amazingly talented, he's bursting with talent; **il est p. de vices** he's rotten to the core; **être p. d'orgueil/d'ambition** to be eaten up with pride/ambition

NM,F *Fam* **1** *(homme méprisable)* scumbag, *Br* swine, *Am* stinker; *(femme méprisable)* bitch, *Br* cow; **tas de pourris!** you rotten swines!

2 *Belg (paresseux)* lazy so-and-so

NM *(partie pourrie)* rotten *or* bad part; **enlève le p.** cut off the bad bit/bits; **sentir le p.** to stink

pourridié [puridje] NM *Hort* root rot

pourriel [purjɛl] NM *Ordinat* spam e-mail; **pourriels** spam

pourrir [32] [purir] VI **1** *(se gâter → fruit, légume, viande, œuf)* to go rotten, to go bad *or Br* off; *(→ planche, arbre)* to rot; *(→ végétation, dent)* to decay, to rot; *(→ chairs)* to decay, to putrefy; **p. sur pied** to rot on the stalk; **la pluie a fait p. toute la récolte** the rain rotted the entire harvest; *Fig* **laisser p. la situation** to let the situation deteriorate

2 *Fam (croupir → personne)* to rot; **p. en prison** to rot in prison

VT **1** *(putréfier → nourriture)* to rot, to putrefy; *(→ végétation, dent)* to decay

2 *(gâter → enfant)* to spoil

3 *(pervertir → individu)* to corrupt, to spoil; *(→ société)* to corrupt

4 *(gâcher)* **elle me pourrit l'existence** she's ruining my life

5 *Fam (dire du mal de)* to badmouth, *Br* to slag off

pourrissage [purisaʒ] NM *Cér* ageing *(of clay, in humid caves)*

pourrissant, -e [purisɑ̃, -ɑ̃t] ADJ *(chairs)* putrescent, putrefying, decaying; **des fruits pourrissants** rotting fruit

pourrissement [purismɑ̃] NM **1** *(de fruits, du bois, de la viande)* rotting; *(de chairs)* putrefaction; *(d'une dent, de la végétation)* decay, rotting, decaying **2** *(d'une situation)* deterioration

pourriture [purityr] NF **1** *(partie pourrie)* rotten part *or* bit **2** *(processus)* rotting, rot, decay; *(état)* rottenness **3** *(corruption)* rottenness, corruption **4** *Fam (personne)* rotten swine **5 p. noble** *(en œnologie)* noble rot, pourriture noble

pour-soi [purswa] NM INV *Phil* pour-soi

poursuit *etc voir* **poursuivre**

poursuite [pursɥit] NF **1** *(pour rattraper un animal, un fugitif)* chase; **p. en voiture** car chase; **les voilà partis dans une p. effrénée** off they go in hot pursuit; **ils sont à la p. des voleurs** *(ils courent)* they're chasing the thieves; *(ils enquêtent)* they're on the trail of the thieves; **se mettre** *ou* **se lancer à la p. de qn** to set off in pursuit of sb, to give chase to sb

2 *(prolongation → de pourparlers, d'études, de recherches)* continuation; **la panne d'électricité a empêché la p. de l'opération** the power cut prevented the operation from going on *or* being carried out; **ils ont décidé la p. de la grève** they've decided to carry on *or* to continue with the strike

3 *(recherche → du bonheur, d'un rêve)* pursuit

4 *Astron* tracking

5 *Sport* pursuit

6 *Théât (projecteur)* follow spot

7 *Jur* **p. disciplinaire** disciplinary action

❑ **poursuites** NFPL *Jur* **poursuites (judiciaires)** *(en droit civil)* (legal) proceedings; *(en droit pénal)* prosecution; **entamer** *ou* **engager des poursuites contre qn** *(en droit civil)* to institute (legal) proceedings *or* to take legal action against sb; *(en droit pénal)* to prosecute sb; **vous pouvez faire l'objet de poursuites** you're liable to prosecution

'La Poursuite infernale' *Ford* 'My Darling Clementine'

poursuiteur, -euse [pursɥitœr, -øz] NM,F *Sport* pursuit rider

poursuivant, -e [pursɥivɑ̃, -ɑ̃t] ADJ *Jur* **la partie poursuivante** the plaintiff

NM,F **1** *(dans une course)* pursuer **2** *Jur* plaintiff

poursuivre [89] [pursɥivr] VT **1** *(courir après → animal, voleur, voiture)* to chase (after), *Sout* to pursue; **je me suis fait p. par une bande de voyous/une voiture de police** I was chased by a gang of hoodlums/a police car; **il sentait leurs regards qui le poursuivaient** he could feel their eyes pursuing *or* following him

2 *(s'acharner contre → sujet: créancier, rival)* to hound, to harry, to pursue; *(→ sujet: image, passé, remords)* to haunt, to hound, to pursue; **p. qn de ses assiduités** to pester sb with one's attentions; **p. qn de sa haine** to hound sb through hatred; **il est poursuivi par la malchance** he is dogged *or* pursued by misfortune

3 *(continuer → interrogatoire, récit, recherche, voyage)* to go *or* to carry on with, to continue; *(→ lutte)* to continue, to pursue; **p. son chemin** to press on; **elle poursuivit sa lecture** she carried on reading, she read on; **ils poursuivirent la discussion jusqu'à une heure tardive** they went on talking till late at night; **poursuivez votre travail** get on with your work; **"quelques années plus tard", poursuivit-il** "a few years later," he went on

4 *(aspirer à → objectif)* to pursue, to strive towards; *(→ rêve)* to pursue; *(→ plaisirs)* to pursue, to seek

5 *Jur* **p. qn (en justice)** *(en droit civil)* to institute (legal) proceedings against *or* to sue sb; *(en droit pénal)* to prosecute sb; **être poursuivi pour détournement de fonds** to be

prosecuted for embezzlement; **être poursuivi en diffamation** to be sued for libel

USAGE ABSOLU *(continuer)* **veuillez p., Monsieur** please proceed, sir; **bien, poursuivons** right, let's go on *or* continue

►**se poursuivre VPR 1** *(se courir après)* to chase one another *or* each other

2 *(se prolonger → pourparlers, recherches)* to go on, to continue; *(→ opération)* to go on

pourtant [purtɑ̃] **ADV 1** *(malgré tout)* yet, even so, all the same; **elle est p. bien gentille** and yet she's very nice; **il faut p. bien que quelqu'un le fasse** somebody has to do it all the same; **cette histoire est p. vraie** and yet this story is true; **et p.** and yet; **c'est une avenue résidentielle, et p. bruyante** it's a residential street and yet it's still noisy; **et p., toutes les conditions étaient réunies!** and yet, all the conditions were right!

2 *(emploi expressif)* **c'est p. simple!** but it's quite simple!; **ce n'est p. pas compliqué!** it's not exactly complicated!; **il n'est pas bête, p.!** he's not exactly stupid!; **je t'avais p. prévenu!** I did warn you!; **les instructions étaient p. claires** the instructions were quite clear; **ma montre ne s'est p. pas envolée!** my watch didn't just vanish into thin air!; **c'est p. vrai qu'il est déjà midi!** 12 o'clock already!

pourtour [purtur] **NM 1** *(délimitation → d'un terrain)* perimeter; *(→ d'un globe)* circumference; **les pays du p. méditerranéen** the countries around the Mediterranean **2** *(bordure → d'un plat)* edge, rim; *(→ d'une feuille)* edge; *(→ d'une baignoire)* surround

pourvoi [purvwa] **NM** *Jur* appeal; **il a présenté un p. en cassation** he has taken his case to the final court of appeal; **p. en cassation** appeal to the final court of appeal; **p. en grâce** appeal for clemency; **p. incident** incidental petition; **p. provoqué** = cross-appeal by a party against whom the original appeal was not directed; **p. en révision** review

pourvoir [64] [purvwar] **VT 1** *(équiper)* **p. qn de** *ou* **en** *(outils)* to equip *or* to provide sb with; *(vivres, documents)* to provide sb with; **p. qch de** to equip *or* to fit sth with; **p. une maison du chauffage central** to fit out *or* equip a house with central heating; **la salle est pourvue d'un excellent système acoustique** the auditorium has been fitted with an excellent sound system

2 *(doter)* **p. de** to endow with; **la nature l'a pourvue d'une remarquable intelligence** nature has endowed *or* graced her with extraordinary intelligence; **ses parents l'ont pourvu d'une solide éducation** his parents provided him with a sound education; **la cigogne est pourvue d'un long bec** storks have *or* possess long beaks

3 *(remplir → emploi)* to fill; **le poste est toujours à p.** the post is still vacant *or* is still to be filled

❑ **pourvoir à VT IND** *(besoin)* to provide *or* to cater for; *(dépense)* to pay for; **nous pourvoirons au transport des médicaments** we will provide for *or* deal with the transport of medicine

►**se pourvoir VPR 1** *Jur* to appeal; **se p. en cassation** to take one's case to the final court of appeal

2 se p. de *(outils)* to equip oneself with; *(vivres)* to provide oneself with

pourvoirie [purvwari] **NF** *Can* outdoor equipment shop

pourvoyeur, -euse [purvwajœr, -øz] **NM,F 1** *(d'armes, de marchandises)* supplier; *(de drogue)* dealer **2** *Littéraire* **p. de fausses nouvelles** rumour monger

NM *Mil* ammunition server

pourvoyons *etc voir* **pourvoir**

pourvu, -e [purvy] **PP** *voir* **pourvoir**

ADJ bien p. well-off, well-provided for

pourvu que [purvykə] **CONJ 1** *(exprimant un souhait)* **pourvu qu'il vienne!** I hope *or* let's hope he's coming!; **p. ça dure!** let's hope it lasts!; **pourvu qu'il ne pleuve pas!** let's hope it doesn't rain! **2** *(exprimant une condition)* provided (that), so *or* as long as; **tout ira bien p. vous soyez à l'heure** everything will be fine so long as you're on time

pourvut *etc voir* **pourvoir**

poussage [pusaʒ] **NM** pushing

poussah [pusa] **NM 1** *(figurine)* tumbler (toy) **2** *(homme)* portly (little) man

pousse [pus] **NF 1** *Anat* growth

2 *Bot (bourgeon)* (young) shoot, sprout; *(début de croissance)* sprouting; *(développement)* growth; **une plante à p. lente/rapide** a slow-growing/fast-growing plant; **ma plante fait des pousses** my plant is sprouting new leaves; **pousses de bambou** bamboo shoots; **pousses de soja** beansprouts

3 *Com & Ordinat* **jeune p. (d'entreprise)** start-up

4 *(de la pâte à pain)* proving

5 *(en œnologie)* shooting, *Spéc* malolactic fermentation

6 *Vét* broken wind

NM INV = pousse-pousse 1

poussé, -e[1] [puse] **ADJ 1** *(fouillé → interrogatoire)* thorough, probing, searching; *(→ recherche, technique)* advanced; *(→ connaissances)* extensive; *(→ description)* thorough, extensive, exhaustive; **d'une efficacité très poussée** highly efficient; **elle fera des études poussées** she'll go on to advanced studies; **je n'ai pas fait d'études poussées** I didn't stay in education very long

2 *(exagéré)* excessive; **60 euros pour une coupe, c'est un peu p.!** 60 euros for a haircut is a bit steep!; **la plaisanterie est un peu poussée** that's taking the joke too far

3 *Aut (moteur)* customized

pousse-au-crime [pusokrim] *Fam* **ADJ INV** that encourages crime■

NM INV 1 *(eau-de-vie)* firewater, rotgut **2 c'est du p.** it encourages crime■

pousse-café [puskafe] **NM INV** *Fam* liqueur■, pousse-café■; **voulez-vous un p.?** would you like a liqueur with your coffee?

poussée[2] [puse] **NF 1** *Constr, Géol, Phys & Aviat* thrust; **p. d'Archimède** upthrust buoyancy; **centre de p.** *Phys* aerodynamic centre, centre of pressure; *(de liquide)* centre of buoyancy

2 *(pression)* push, shove, thrust; **la barrière a cédé sous la p. des manifestants** the barrier gave way under the pressure of the demonstrators; **écarter qch d'une p.** to push *or* shove sth aside

3 *Méd* eruption, outbreak; **le bébé fait une petite p. de boutons rouges** the baby has a rash; **faire une p. de fièvre** to have a sudden rise in temperature; **une p. d'adrénaline** a surge of adrenalin; **faire une p. de croissance** to shoot up

4 *Bot* **p. radiculaire** root pressure

5 *(progression)* upsurge, rise; **une p. de racisme** an upsurge of racism; **une p. de l'inflation, une p. inflationniste** a rise in inflation

6 *(attaque)* thrust; **la p. des troupes hitlériennes contre la Pologne** the thrust *or* offensive of Hitler's troops against Poland

7 *Aviat & Astron* thrust

pousse-pied [puspje] **NM INV** = small light flat-bottomed boat

pousse-pousse [puspus] **NM INV 1** *(en Extrême-Orient)* rickshaw **2** *Suisse (poussette) Br* push-chair, buggy, *Am* stroller

POUSSER [3] [puse]

> **VT** to push **1–4, 7, 8** ▪ to press **2** ▪ to spur on **5** ▪ to carry on, to continue **6**
> **VI** to grow **1** ▪ to push on **2** ▪ to push **4–6**
> **VPR** to move **3**

VT 1 *(faire avancer → caddie, fauteuil roulant, landau)* to push, to wheel (along); *(→ moto en panne)* to push, to walk; *(→ caisse)* to push (along), to push forward; *(→ pion)* to move forward; **j'ai dû p. mon vélo jusqu'à la maison** I had to push *or* to wheel my bike home; **on va p. la voiture** *(sur une distance)* we'll push the car (along); *(pour la faire démarrer)* we'll push-start the car, we'll give the car a push (to start it); **il poussait son troupeau devant lui** he was driving his flock before him; **ils essayaient de p. les manifestants vers la place** they were trying to drive *or* to push the demonstrators towards the square; **le vent pousse le radeau loin de la côte** the wind is pushing the raft away from the coast; **le courant poussait le canot** the stream was carrying *or* pushing the canoe along; **des rafales de vent poussaient les nuages** gusts of wind sent the clouds scudding across the sky; **je me sentais irrésistiblement poussé vers elle** I was irresistibly attracted to her; *Fam* **faut pas p. (mémé** *ou* **mémère dans les orties)** that's pushing it a bit

2 *(enclencher, appuyer sur → bouton, interrupteur)* to push (in), to press; **p. un levier vers le haut/bas** to push a lever up/down; **le ressort pousse le percuteur** the spring pushes the hammer in *or* home; **p. un verrou** *(pour ouvrir)* to slide a bolt out; *(pour fermer)* to slide a bolt in *or* home; **pousse le volet** *(pour l'ouvrir)* push the shutter open *or* out; *(pour le fermer)* push the shutter to; **p. une porte** *(doucement, pour l'ouvrir)* to push a door open; *(doucement, pour la fermer)* to push a door to *or* shut; **la porte à peine poussée, il me racontait ce qu'il avait fait dans la journée** no sooner was he inside the door, than he began telling me all about his day

3 *(bousculer)* to push, to shove; **p. qn du coude** *(pour l'alerter, accidentellement)* to nudge sb with one's elbow; **j'ai été obligé de p. plusieurs personnes pour pouvoir sortir** I had to push past several people to get out; **elle l'a poussé par-dessus bord** she pushed him overboard

4 *(enlever)* to push (away), to push *or* to shove aside; **pousse le vase/ton pied, je ne vois pas la télévision** move the vase/your foot out of the way, I can't see the television; *Fam* **pousse ton derrière de là!** shove over!, *Br* shift up!; **pousse le journal, je vais mettre la table** move *or* shift the paper, I'm going to lay the table

5 *(inciter, entraîner → personne)* to spur on, to drive; **c'est l'orgueil qui le pousse** he is spurred on *or* driven by pride; **on n'a pas eu à le p. beaucoup pour qu'il accepte** he didn't need much pressing *or* persuasion to accept; **p. qn à la consommation** to encourage sb to buy *or* to consume; **p. qn à la dépense** to encourage sb to spend more; **p. qn au désespoir/suicide** to drive sb to despair/suicide; **ici, tout pousse à la paresse** this place encourages idleness; **sa curiosité l'a poussé à l'indiscrétion** his curiosity made him indiscreet; **p. qn à faire qch** *(sujet: curiosité, jalousie)* to drive sb to do sth; *(sujet: pitié soudaine)* to prompt sb to do sth; *(sujet: personne)* to incite sb to do *or* to push sb into doing *or* to prompt sb to do sth; **p. qn à se droguer** to push sb into taking drugs; **p. qn à boire** to drive sb to drink; **sa tyrannie les avait poussés à se révolter** his/her tyranny had driven them to revolt; **un désir inexplicable me poussa à y retourner** I was mysteriously compelled to go back there; **mes parents ne m'ont jamais poussé à faire des études** my parents never encouraged me to study; **elle le pousse à divorcer** *(elle l'en persuade)* she's talking him into getting a divorce; **mais qu'est-ce qui a bien pu te p. à lui dire la vérité?** what on earth possessed you to tell him/her the truth?

6 *(poursuivre → recherches)* to press on *or* to carry on with; *(→ discussion, études, analyse)* to continue, to carry on (with); *(→ argumentation)* to carry on (with), to push further; *(→ comparaison, interrogatoire)* to take further; *(→ avantage)* to press home; **en poussant plus loin l'examen de leur comptabilité** by probing deeper into their accounts; **vous auriez dû p. un peu plus votre réflexion sur ce point** you should have developed that point further; **p. la plaisanterie un peu loin** to take *or* to carry the joke a bit too far; **tu pousses un peu loin le cynisme** you're being a bit too cynical; **p. la promenade jusqu'à** to push on to, to walk as far as; **p. la sévérité jusqu'à la cruauté** to carry severity to the point of cruelty; **elle a poussé l'audace jusqu'à...** she was bold enough to...; **il a poussé le vice jusqu'à ne pas la saluer** his spite was such that he refused even to greet her

7 *(forcer → moteur)* to push; *(→ voiture)* to drive hard *or* fast; *(→ chauffage, son)* to turn up; *(exiger un effort de → étudiant, employé)* to push; *(→ cheval)* to urge *or* to spur on; **je suis à 130, je**

pou–pou

préfère ne pas p. le moteur I'm doing 130, I'd rather not push the engine any further; *Fam* **p. la sono à fond** to turn the sound up full (blast); **on ne m'a pas assez poussé quand j'étais à l'école** I wasn't pushed hard enough when I was at school

8 *(encourager → candidat, jeune artiste)* to push; **elle a poussé son fils pour qu'il entre dans l'enseignement** she pushed her son towards a teaching career; **si tu la pousses un peu sur le sujet, tu verras qu'elle ne sait pas grand-chose** if you push her a bit on the subject, you'll see that she doesn't know much about it

9 *(émettre)* **p. un cri** *(personne)* to cry, to utter *or* to let out a cry; *(oiseau)* to call; **p. une exclamation** to cry out; **p. un gémissement** to groan; **p. une plainte** to moan; **p. un soupir** to sigh, to heave a sigh; **p. des cris/hurlements de douleur** to scream/to yell with pain; *Fam* **p. la chansonnette, en p. une** to sing a song■; **allez, grand-père, tu nous en pousses une?** come on, grandpa, give us a song

10 *Agr & Bot (plante, animal)* to force; **les fermiers poussent les veaux** farmers force calves

11 *Phot* to push-process

12 *Mil (troupes)* to push forward, to drive on; **p. une charge** to charge; **p. une reconnaissance** to go on a (wide-ranging) reconnaissance; *aussi Fig* **p. une attaque** to drive an attack home

13 *Écon* **p. à la hausse/la baisse** to have an inflationary/a deflationary effect; **poussé par les profits** profit-driven; **p. la vente de qch** to push the sale of sth; **p. qch aux enchères** to up the bidding for sth

VI 1 *(grandir → arbre, poil, ongle)* to grow; *(→ dent)* to come through; **le banian ne pousse qu'en Inde** banyans only grow *or* are only found in India; **pour empêcher les mauvaises herbes de p.** to stop weeds from growing; **des mauvaises herbes poussées entre les pierres** weeds which have sprung up between the stones; **les plants de tomates poussent bien** the tomato plants are doing well; **ses dents commencent à p.** he's/she's cutting his/her teeth, he's/she's teething; *Fig* **il a poussé trop vite** he's grown too fast; *Fam* **et les enfants, ça pousse?** how're the kids (then), growing *or* shooting up?; **des tours poussent partout dans mon quartier** there are high-rise blocks springing up all over the place where I live; **faire p.** *(légumes, plantes)* to grow; **faire p. du blé** to grow *or* to cultivate wheat; *Littéraire* **dès que les blés seront poussés** as soon as the corn has sprung up; **on fait p. de la vigne dans la région** they grow grapes in this region; **mets de l'engrais, ça fera p. tes laitues plus vite** use fertilizer, it'll make your lettuces grow faster; **laisser p.** to grow; **et si tu laissais p. ta barbe?** what about growing *or* why don't you grow a beard?; **elle a laissé p. ses cheveux** she's let her hair grow

2 *(avancer)* to push on; **ils ont poussé jusqu'au manoir** they went on *or* pushed on *or* carried on as far as the manor house; **poussons un peu plus loin** let's go on *or* push on a bit further

3 *Fam (exagérer)* **deux heures de retard, tu pousses!** you're two hours late, that's a bit much!; **60 euros par personne, ils poussent un peu!** 60 euros per person, that's a bit much *or* steep!; **je veux 25 pour cent d'augmentation – tu ne trouves pas que tu pousses un peu?** I want a 25 percent pay rise – don't you think that's pushing it a bit?; **faut pas p.!** enough's enough!

4 *(bousculer)* to push, to shove; **ne poussez pas, il y en aura pour tout le monde!** stop shoving *or* pushing, there's plenty for everyone!; *Fam* **ça poussait dans la file d'attente** there was a lot of shoving *or* jostling in the queue

5 *(appuyer)* to push; **on a tous poussé en même temps pour désembourber la voiture** we all pushed together to get the car out of the mud; **p. sur un bouton** to push a button; **p. sur ses pieds/jambes** to push with one's feet/legs; **poussez sur vos bâtons dans la descente** use your poles as you go downhill; **p. dans le sens de qn** to push sb's cause

6 *Physiol (à la selle)* to strain; *(dans l'enfantement)* to push; **poussez!** *(femme en travail)* push!

7 *(en œnologie)* to undergo secondary fermentation *(in the spring)*

▶**se pousser VPR 1** *(emploi passif)* to be pushed; **la manette se pousse d'un seul doigt** the lever can be pushed with a single finger

2 *(emploi réciproque)* **les gens se poussaient pour voir arriver le Président** people were pushing and shoving to get a look at the President

3 *(se déplacer)* to move; **tu peux te p. un peu?** *(dans une rangée de chaises)* could you move along a bit *or* a few places?; *(sur un canapé, dans un lit)* could you move over slightly?; **la foule s'est poussée pour laisser passer l'ambulance** the crowd moved out of the way of the ambulance; *Fam* **pousse-toi de là, tu vois bien que tu gênes!** move over *or* shove over, can't you see you're in the way?; *Fam* **pousse-toi de devant la télé!** stop blocking the TV!

4 *Fam (hiérarchiquement)* **se p. dans une entreprise** to make one's way up (the ladder) in a company■; **il faut une fortune pour se p. dans la finance** you need a private fortune to get ahead in the world of finance■

5 *Can Fam (s'enfuir)* to run away■, *Br* to scarper; **il faut se p.!** we've got to go, we have to make a move

---

poussette [pusɛt] **NF 1** *(pour enfant) Br* pushchair, *Am* stroller; *Suisse (landau) Br* pram, *Am* baby carriage **2** *(à provisions)* shopping *Br* trolley *or Am* cart **3** *Fam* **faire la p. à un coureur cycliste** to give a rider a little push *or* shove

poussette-canne [pusɛtkan] *(pl* **poussettes-cannes) NF** folding *Br* pushchair *or Am* stroller

pousseur [pusœr] **NM 1** *Naut* push tug **2** *Astron* booster **3** *Littéraire (de soupirs)* heaver; *(de belles phrases)* utterer

poussier [pusje] **NM** coal dust

poussière [pusjɛr] **NF 1** *(terre sèche, salissures)* dust *(UNCOUNT)*; *(grain)* speck of dust; **la voiture souleva un nuage de p.** the car raised a cloud of dust; **tu en fais de la p. en balayant!** you're making *or* raising a lot of dust with your broom!; **prendre la p.** *ou Belg* **les poussières** to collect dust; **les tapisseries prennent facilement la p.** the wall-hangings are dust traps; **recouvert de p.** dusty, covered with dust; **faire la p.** *ou Belg* **les poussières** to dust, to do the dusting; **essuie la p. sur les meubles/dans ta chambre** dust the furniture/your room; **mettre** *ou* **réduire qch en p.** to smash sth to smithereens; **tomber en p.** to crumble into dust; **les parchemins/os tombent en p.** the pieces of parchment/the bones are crumbling into dust

2 *(dans l'œil)* piece of grit

3 *(particules → de roche, de charbon, d'or)* dust *(UNCOUNT)*; **p. cosmique/interstellaire** cosmic/interstellar dust; **poussières industrielles** industrial dust; **p. lunaire** lunar *or* moon dust; **p. radioactive** radioactive particles *or* dust

▫ **poussières NFPL** *Fam* **dix euros et des poussières** just over ten euros■; **ça fait trois kilos et des poussières** it's a little over three kilos■

poussiéreux, -euse [pusjerø, -øz] **ADJ 1** *(couvert de poussière)* dusty, dust-covered; **vitres poussiéreuses** grimy windows; **de vieux grimoires tout p.** old volumes all covered with dust **2** *(dépassé → législation, théorie)* outmoded, outdated

poussif, -ive [pusif, -iv] **ADJ 1** *(essoufflé → cheval)* broken-winded; *(→ vieillard)* short-winded, wheezy; *(→ locomotive)* puffing, wheezing **2** *(laborieux → prose)* dull, flat, laboured; *(→ campagne électorale, émission)* sluggish, dull

poussin [pusɛ̃] **NM 1** *Orn* chick; *Culin* spring chicken, *Br* poussin **2** *Fam (terme d'affection)* **mon p.** my pet *or* darling; **pauvre petit p.!** poor little thing! **3** *Sport* junior *(9 years old)* **4** *Fam Arg mil* = first-year student in the French Air Force training school

poussine [pusin] **NF** *Suisse* pullet

poussinière [pusinjɛr] **NF** chick house

poussive [pusiv] *voir* **poussif**

poussivement [pusivmɑ̃] **ADV monter p.** to puff *or* to wheeze (one's way) up; **le train avançait p.** the train was wheezing *or* puffing along

poussoir [puswar] **NM 1** *(d'une montre)* button; *(d'une sonnerie électrique)* (push) button **2** *Tech* tappet

poutargue [putarg] **NF** = salted and pressed mullet roe

pout-de-soie [putswa] *(pl* **pouts-de-soie)** = **pou-de-soie**

Poutine [putin] **NPR** Putin

poutine [putin] **NF** *Can* **1** *(plat cuisiné)* = French fries served with sauce (usually chicken gravy) and curd cheese, a Quebec speciality; **p. râpée** *(plat acadien)* = balls of grated potato stuffed with pork **2** *(dessert)* = traditional pudding served with maple syrup **3** *Fam Fig (grosse femme)* fat lump (of a woman)

poutou [putu] **NM** *Fam (bise)* kiss■

poutrage [putraʒ] **NM** *Constr (de bois)* (framework of) beams; *(de fer, d'acier)* (framework of) girders

poutraison [putrɛzɔ̃] **NF** *Constr (de bois)* (framework of) beams; *(de fer, d'acier)* (framework of) girders

poutre [putr] **NF 1** *Constr (en bois)* beam; *(en fer)* girder; **p. armée/en treillis** lattice/trussed girder; **p. apparente** exposed beam; **p. de faîte** ridge beam **2** *Sport* beam; **exercices à la p.** beam exercises

poutrelle [putrɛl] **NF** *Constr (en bois)* small beam; *(en acier)* girder

poutser [3] [putse] **VT** *Suisse Fam* to clean■

pouture [putyr] **NF** *Agr* stall fattening

pouvoir[1] [puvwar] **NM 1** *(aptitude, possibilité)* power; **avoir un grand p. de concentration/de persuasion** to have great powers of concentration/persuasion; **avoir un grand p. d'adaptation** to be very adaptable; **je n'ai pas le p. de lire l'avenir!** I can't predict the future!; **il n'est plus en notre p. de décider de la question** we're no longer in a position to decide on this matter; **je ferai tout ce qui est en mon p. pour t'aider** I'll do everything *or* all in my power to help you; *Écon* **p. d'achat** purchasing power, buying power; **p. d'achat réel** real purchasing *or* buying power; *Fin* **p. libératoire** legal tender

2 *Admin & Jur (d'un président, d'un tuteur)* power; **le p. décisionnaire des actionnaires** the decision-making powers of shareholders; **le roi avait un p. absolu** the king had absolute power; **avoir p. de décision** to have the authority to decide; **je n'ai pas p. de vous libérer** I have no authority *or* it is not in my power to release you; **je lui ai donné p. de décider à ma place par-devant notaire** I gave him/her power of attorney; **p. absolu** absolute power; **p. disciplinaire** disciplinary powers

3 *Pol* **le p.** *(exercice)* power; *(gouvernants)* government; **elle est trop proche du p. pour comprendre** she's too close to those in power to understand; **arriver au p.** to come to power; **être au p.** *(parti élu)* to be in power *or* office; *(junte)* to be in power; **les gens au p. ne connaissent pas nos problèmes** those in power *or* the powers that be don't understand our difficulties; **prendre le p.** *(élus)* to take office; *(dictateur)* to seize power; **exercer le p.** to exercise power, to govern, to rule; **le p. central** central government; **p. constituant** constituent power; **le p. exécutif** executive power, the executive; **le p. judiciaire** judicial power, the judiciary; **le p. législatif** legislative power, the legislature; **le p. local** local government, the local authorities

4 *(influence)* power, influence; **avoir du p. sur qn** to have power *or* influence over sb; **il a beaucoup de p. au sein du comité** he's very influential *or* he has a lot of influence within the committee; **avoir qn en son p.** to have sb in one's power; **la ville est tombée en leur p.** the town has fallen into their hands; **le p. de la télévision/des sens** the power of television/the senses

5 *Phys & Tech* power, quality; **p. absorbant** absorbency; **p. calorifique (inférieur/supérieur)** (net/gross) calorific value; **p. couvrant (d'une peinture)** opacity (of a paint); **p. isolant** insulating capacity

▫ **pouvoirs NMPL 1** *(fonctions)* powers, authority; **outrepasser ses pouvoirs** to overstep *or* to exceed one's authority; **avoir tous pouvoirs pour faire qch** *(administrateur)* to have full

powers to do sth; *(architecte, animateur)* to have carte blanche to do sth; *Pol* **pouvoirs exceptionnels** special powers *(available to the President of the French Republic in an emergency)*; **pouvoirs partagés** shared powers

2 *(gouvernants)* **les pouvoirs constitués** the legally constituted government; **les pouvoirs publics** the authorities

3 *(surnaturels)* powers

POUVOIR² [58] [puvwar] **V AUX 1** *(avoir la possibilité, la capacité de)* **je peux revenir en France** I'm able to *or* I can return to France; **comme vous pouvez le voir sur ces images** as you can see on these pictures; **je peux vous aider?** *(gén, dans un magasin)* can I help you?; **on peut toujours s'arranger** some sort of an arrangement can always be worked out; **si seulement je pouvais me souvenir de son nom** if only I could remember his/her name; **pourriez-vous m'indiquer la gare?** could you tell me the way to the station?; **comment as-tu pu lui mentir!** how could you lie to him/her!; **je te l'apporte dès que je peux** I'll bring it to you as soon as I can *or* as soon as possible; **quand il pourra de nouveau marcher** when he's able to walk again; **c'est plus que je ne peux payer** it's more than I can afford (to pay); **je ne peux (pas) m'empêcher de penser que...** I can't help thinking that...; **ce modèle peut se ranger dans une valise** this model packs *or* can be packed into a suitcase; **l'argument peut aisément être retourné** the argument cuts both ways *or* can easily be turned around; **je ne peux pas dormir** I'm unable to *or* I can't sleep; **jamais plus elle ne pourra chanter** she'll never be able to sing again; **tout le monde ne peut pas le faire/en dire autant!** not everybody can do it/say that!; **le projet ne pourra pas se faire sans sa collaboration** the project can't be carried out without his/her collaboration; **il ne peut pas suivre d'études universitaires** *(il n'est pas assez brillant)* he's not up to going to university; **fais ce que tu veux, je ne peux pas mieux te dire!** do as you please, that's all I can say!; **tu ne peux pas ne pas l'aider** you MUST help him/her, you can't refuse to help him/her; *Fam* **il ne peut pas la voir (en peinture)** he can't stand (the sight of) her; *Fam* **je n'ai jamais pu le voir (en peinture)** I never could stand him

2 *(parvenir à)* to manage *or* to be able to; **avez-vous pu entrer en contact avec lui?** did you manage to contact him?; **c'est construit de telle manière que l'on ne puisse pas s'échapper** it's built in such a way that it's impossible to escape *or* as to make escape impossible

3 *(avoir la permission de)* **vous pouvez disposer** you may *or* can go now; **si je peux** *ou* **si je puis m'exprimer ainsi** if I may use the phrase; **vous pouvez dire ce que vous voulez, on ne vous croira pas** say what you will *or* you can say whatever you like, nobody'll believe you; **si on ne peut plus plaisanter, maintenant!** it's a pretty sad day if you can't have a laugh any more!

4 *(avoir des raisons de)* **on ne peut que s'en féliciter** one can't but feel happy about it; *Fam* **je suis désolé – ça, tu peux (l'être)!** I'm so sorry – so you should be *or* and with good reason *or* and I should think so too!

5 *(exprime une éventualité, un doute, un risque)* **la maladie peut revenir** the disease can *or* may recur; **attention, tu pourrais glisser** careful, you might *or* could slip; **ça peut exploser à tout moment** it could *or* may *or* might explode at any time; **un accident peut toujours se produire** accidents do happen; **il a pu les oublier dans le bus** he could *or* may have left them on the bus; **ce ne peut être déjà les invités!** (surely) it can't be the guests already!; **j'aurais pu l'attendre longtemps, elle n'arrive que demain!** I could have waited a long time, she's not coming until tomorrow!; **la gauche pourrait bien ne pas être élue** the left could well not get *or* be elected; **après tout, il pourrait bien ne pas avoir menti** he may well have been telling the truth after all; **d'aucuns pourront mettre sa sincérité en doute** some people might question his/her sincerity; **c'est plus facile qu'on ne pourrait le croire** it's easier than you might think; **elle a très bien pu arriver entre-temps** she may well have arrived in the meantime; **je peux toujours m'être trompé** it's possible I might have got it wrong; **ça aurait pu être pire** it could have been worse; **on a pu dire de lui qu'il était le précurseur du romantisme** some consider him to be the precursor of the Romantic movement; **il pourrait** *(tournure impersonnelle)* it could *or* may (possibly); **il pourrait s'agir d'un suicide** it could *or* may *or* might be suicide; **il peut arriver que...** it may (so) *or* can happen that...; **il ne peut pas y avoir d'erreur** there can't (possibly) be a mistake

6 *(exprime une approximation)* **elle pouvait avoir entre 50 et 60 ans** she could have been between 50 and 60 (years of age); **il pouvait être deux heures quand nous sommes sortis** it could *or* might have been two o'clock when we came out

7 *(exprime une suggestion, une hypothèse)* **tu peux toujours essayer de lui téléphoner** you could always try phoning him/her; **tu pourrais te lever pour donner ta place à la dame, quand même!** you might get up and let the lady have your seat!; **tu pourrais au moins t'excuser!** you could at least apologize!, the least you could do is apologize!; **il aurait pu me prévenir!** he could've *or* might've warned me!; **on peut s'attendre à tout avec elle** anything's possible with her

8 *(en intensif)* **où ai-je bien pu laisser mes lunettes?** what on earth can I have done with my glasses?; **qu'a-t-elle (bien) pu leur dire pour les mettre dans cet état?** what can she possibly have said for them to be in such a state!

9 *Littéraire (exprime le souhait)* **puisse ce fléau nous épargner!** let us hope *or* pray we may be spared this plague!; **puisse-t-il vous entendre!** let us hope he can hear you!; **puissé-je ne jamais revivre des moments pareils!** may I never have to live through that again!

VT *(être capable de faire)* **qu'y puis-je?** what can I do about it?; **vous seul y pouvez quelque chose** only you can do anything about it; **tu y peux quelque chose, toi?** can YOU do anything about it?; **on n'y peut rien,** *Belg* **on n'en peux rien** it can't be helped, nothing can be done about it; **que puis-je pour vous?** what can I do for you?; **elle peut beaucoup pour notre cause** she can do a lot for our cause; **j'ai fait tout ce que j'ai pu** I did my level best *or* all I could; *Fam Hum* **je fais ce que je peux et je peux peu** I do what I can, which isn't very much; **je n'en peux plus** *(physiquement)* I'm exhausted; *(moralement)* I can't take any more *or* stand it any longer; *(je suis rassasié)* I'm full (up); *Fam* **ma voiture n'en peut plus** my car's had it; **je n'en peux plus de l'entendre se plaindre sans cesse** I just can't take his/her continual moaning any more; *Fam* **regarde-le danser avec elle, il n'en peut plus!** just look at him dancing with her, he's in seventh heaven!

▶**se pouvoir V IMPERSONNEL ça se peut** it may *or* could be; **ça se peut, mais...** that's as may be, but...; **il va pleuvoir – ça se pourrait bien!** it's going to rain – that's quite possible!; **est-ce qu'ils vont se marier? – cela se pourrait** are they going to get married? – they might *or* it's possible; **sois calme, et s'il se peut, diplomate** keep calm and, if (at all) possible, be tactful; **il** *ou* **ça se peut qu'il soit malade** he might be ill, maybe he's ill; **il se peut que je vienne** I might come, maybe I'll come; **il se pourrait bien qu'il n'y ait plus de places** it might *or* could well be fully booked; *Littéraire* **il s'est pu faire que...** it may have happened that...

---

pouzzolane [puzɔlan] **NF** pozzuolana, pozzolana

poya [pɔja] **NF** *Suisse (dans le canton de Fribourg)* = moving of cattle up to higher mountain pastures at the beginning of summer, or a painting of this

Poznan [pɔznan] **NM** Poznan

PP [pepe] **ADJ** *(abrév* **préventive de la pellagre)** **vitamine PP** niacin

pp 1 *(abrév écrite* **pages)** pp **2** *(abrév écrite* **par procuration)** pp

PPCM [pepeseɛm] **NM** *Math (abrév* **plus petit commun multiple)** LCM

PPE [pepeə] **NF** *(abrév* **prime pour l'emploi)** = tax credit awarded to low wage-earners, as an incentive to continue working and not claim benefit instead

ppm [pepeɛm] **NFPL 1** *Chim (abrév* **parties par million)** ppm **2** *Ordinat (abrév écrite* **pages per minute)** ppm

PPP [pepepe] **NM** *(abrév* **partenariat public-privé)** PPP

ppp *(abrév écrite* **points par pouce)** dpi

PQ¹ [peky] **NM** *très Fam (abrév* **papier-cul)** *Br* bog roll, *Am* TP

PQ² 1 *(abrév écrite* **province de Québec)** PQ **2** *(abrév écrite* **premier quartier (de lune))** = first quarter

PQR [pekyɛr] **NF** *(abrév* **presse quotidienne régionale)** local daily press

PR¹ [peɛr] **NM** *(abrév* **parti républicain)** = right-wing French political party

PR² *(abrév écrite* **poste restante)** PR

Pr *(abrév écrite* **professeur)** Prof

practice [praktis] **NM** *Golf* driving range

Prado [prado] **NM le (musée national du) P.** the Prado

praesidium [prezidjɔm] **NM** praesidium, presidium

pragmatique [pragmatik] **ADJ** *(politique)* pragmatic; *(personne, attitude)* pragmatic, practical

NF pragmatics *(singulier)*

pragmatisme [pragmatism] **NM** pragmatism

pragmatiste [pragmatist] **ADJ** pragmatist

NMF pragmatist

pragois, -e [pragwa, -az] = **praguois**

Prague [prag] **NM** Prague

praguois, -e [pragwa, -az] **ADJ** of/from Prague

▫ **Praguois, -e NM,F** = inhabitant of or person from Prague

praire [prɛr] **NF** clam

prairial, -als [prɛrjal] **NM** *Hist* = 9th month of the French Republican Calendar (from 20 May to 18 June)

prairie [preri] **NF 1** *(terrain)* meadow **2** *(formation végétale)* grassland; **p. artificielle** cultivated grassland **3 la P.** *(aux États-Unis)* the Prairie; **les Prairies** *(au Canada)* the Prairies

prakrit [prɑkri] **NM** *Ling* Prakrit

pralin [pralɛ̃] **NM 1** *Culin* praline *(toasted nuts in caramelized sugar)* **2** *Hort* dressing *(for roots and seeds before planting)*

pralinage [pralinaʒ] **NM 1** *Culin* browning in sugar **2** *Hort* dressing *(of roots and seeds before planting)*

praline [pralin] **NF 1** *Culin (amande)* praline; *Belg (chocolat)* (filled) chocolate **2** *Fam (balle d'arme à feu)* slug **3** *Fam (coup)* belt, wallop **4** *Vulg (clitoris)* clit

praliné, -e [praline] **ADJ** *(glace, entremets)* praline-flavoured; *(amande)* browned in sugar; *(chocolat)* with a praline centre

NM chocolate with a praline centre

praliner [3] [praline] **VT 1** *Culin* to brown in sugar **2** *Hort* to dress *(before planting)*

prame [pram] **NF** *Naut* praam, pram

prandial, -e, -aux, -ales [prɑ̃djal, -o] **ADJ** *Méd* prandial

prao [prao] **NM** *Naut* **1** *(bateau malais)* proa, prau **2** *(voilier)* proa

praséodyme [prazeɔdim] **NM** *Chim* praseodymium

prasin, -e [prazɛ̃, -in] **ADJ** *Littéraire* prasine, prasinous

praticable [pratikabl] **ADJ 1** *(sentier)* passable, practicable **2** *(réalisable → suggestion, solution)* practicable, feasible **3** *(porte, fenêtre)* practicable

NM 1 *Cin & TV* dolly **2** *Théât* platform **3** *Ind* cradle **4** *Sport* (floor) mat

praticien, -enne [pratisjɛ̃, -ɛn] **NM,F 1** *(médecin, dentiste etc)* practitioner **2** *(technicien)* practitioner **3** *Beaux-Arts* sculptor's assistant

praticité [pratisite] **NF** *(commodité)* convenience; *(utilité)* usefulness

pratiquant, -e [pratikɑ̃, -ɑ̃t] **ADJ** practising; **catholique p.** practising Catholic; **je ne suis pas p.** *(gén)* I'm not religious *or* a believer, I don't practise (my religion); *(chrétien)* I don't attend church regularly, I'm not a (regular) churchgoer; **non p.** nonpractising

NM,F 1 *Rel (catholique)* practising Catholic; *(protestant)* practising Protestant; *(juif)* practising Jew; *(musulman)* practising Muslim **2** *(adepte)* adherent

pratique¹ [pratik] **ADJ 1** *(utile → gadget, outil, voiture, dictionnaire)* practical, handy; *(→ vêtement)* practical; **peu p.** not very practical; **quand on a des invités, c'est bien p. un lave-vaisselle!** when you've got guests, a dishwasher comes in handy!; **c'est très p. d'avoir l'école si près de la maison** it's very practical *or* handy to have the school so close to the house

2 *(facile → horaires)* convenient; **il faut changer de bus trois fois, ce n'est pas p.!** you have to change buses three times, it's very inconvenient!; **ce n'est pas p. de courir avec une jupe étroite** it's not easy to run in a tight skirt; **cette crème n'est pas p. à appliquer** this cream isn't easy to apply

3 *(concret → application, connaissance, conseil, formation)* practical; **régler les détails pratiques d'une excursion** to sort out the practical details of an excursion

4 *(pragmatique)* practical; **avoir le sens ou l'esprit p.** to have a practical turn of mind, to be practical

pratique² [pratik] **NF 1** *(application → d'une philosophie, d'une politique)* practice; *(→ de l'autocritique, d'une vertu)* exercise; *(→ d'une technique, de la censure)* application; **mettre en p.** *(conseils, préceptes)* to put into practice; *(vertu)* to exercise; **en ou dans la p.** in (actual) practice

2 *(d'une activité)* practice; **la p. régulière du tennis/vélo** playing tennis/cycling on a regular basis; **la p. d'un sport est encouragée** sporting activity *or* practising a sport is encouraged; **p. illégale de la médecine** illegal practice of medicine; **la p. religieuse** religious observance

3 *Can (entraînement)* training session; **une p. de hockey** a hockey training session

4 *(expérience)* practical experience; **on voit que tu as de la p.** you've obviously done this before; **j'ai plusieurs années de p.** I have several years' practical experience

5 *(usage)* practice; **des pratiques religieuses** religious practices; **pratiques déloyales** unfair (business) dealings; **pratiques d'excellence** best practice; **pratiques restrictives** restrictive practices; **une p. courante** common practice; **le marchandage est une p. courante là-bas** over there, it's common practice to barter

6 *Vieilli (clientèle)* customers

7 *Jur* **terme de p.** legal term

8 *Naut* **avoir libre p.** to be out of quarantine

pratiquement [pratikmã] **ADV 1** *(presque)* practically, virtually; **il n'y avait p. personne** there was hardly anybody *or* practically nobody **2** *(concrètement)* in practice; *(en fait)* in practice *or* (actual) fact

pratiquer [3] [pratike] **VT 1** *(faire → entaille, incision, ouverture)* to make; *(→ passage)* to open up; *(→ intervention chirurgicale, tests)* to carry out, to perform; **des marches avaient été pratiquées dans la roche** steps had been carved out in the rock; **p. un trou** *(à la vrille)* to bore *or* to drill a hole; *(aux ciseaux)* to cut (out) a hole

2 *(appliquer → préceptes, politique)* to practise; *(→ autocritique, vertu)* to practise, to exercise; *(→ technique)* to use, to apply; *(→ censure)* to apply; *(→ sélection)* to make; **je ne pratiquerai jamais ce genre de chantage** I will never resort to *or* use this kind of blackmail; **la vivisection est encore pratiquée dans certains laboratoires** vivisection is still carried out *or* practised in some laboratories

3 *(s'adonner à → jeu de ballon)* to play; *(→ art martial, athlétisme)* to do; *(→ art, médecine, religion, charité)* to practise; *(→ langue)* to speak; *(→ humour, ironie)* to use; **p. un sport** to take part in a sporting activity; **est-ce que vous pratiquez un sport?** do you do anything in the way of sport?; **p. la natation** to swim; **p. la boxe** to box

4 *(fréquenter)* **p. un auteur** to read an author's works regularly; *Hum* **ça fait des années que je pratique l'animal** I've known this guy for years

5 *Com (rabais)* to make, to give; **ce sont les prix pratiqués dans tous nos supermarchés** these are the current prices in all our supermarkets

USAGE ABSOLU **il a appris le piano mais ne pratique plus beaucoup** he learnt the piano but doesn't play it much any more

VI 1 *Rel* to practise (one's religion); **il est catholique, mais il ne pratique pas** he is not a practising Catholic

2 *(travailler → médecin, avocat)* to practise

▸**se pratiquer VPR** **cette coutume se pratique encore dans certains pays** this custom still exists in certain countries; **le commerce de l'ivoire se pratique encore** ivory trading still goes on *or* is still practised; **les prix qui se pratiquent à Paris** current Paris prices; **cela se pratique couramment dans leur pays** it is common practice in their country

Pravda [pravda] **NF la P.** Pravda

praxie [praksi] **NF** *Psy* praxis

praxis [praksis] **NF** *Phil* praxis

Praxitèle [praksitɛl] **NPR** Praxiteles

pré [pre] **NM 1** *Agr* meadow **2** *(locutions)* **p. carré** domain, preserve; *Littéraire* **aller sur le p.** to fight a duel

préaccord [preakɔr] **NM** draft agreement

préachat [preaʃa] **NM** *Rad & TV* advance purchase of broadcasting rights

pré-acheminement [preaʃminmã] *(pl* **pré-acheminements)** **NM** *Transp* transfer to main airport

préadaptation [preadaptasjɔ̃] **NF** *Biol* preadaptation

préadhésion [preadezjɔ̃] **NF** *UE* pre-accession

préadolescence [preadɔlesãs] **NF** preadolescence, preteen years

préadolescent, -e [preadɔlesã, -ãt] **NM,F** preadolescent, preteen

préalable [prealabl] **ADJ** *(discussion, entrevue, sélection)* preliminary (**à** to); *(travail, formation)* preparatory (**à** to); *(accord, avertissement)* prior (**à** to); **faites un essai p. sur un bout de tissu** test first *or* beforehand on a piece of cloth; **…mais il y a quelques formalités préalables** …but there are a few formalities to be gone through first; **sans avertissement p.** without prior notice

NM prerequisite, precondition

□ **au préalable ADV** first, beforehand

préalablement [prealablmã] **ADV** first, beforehand; **appliquer sur la plaie p. nettoyée** apply after cleansing the wound

□ **préalablement à PRÉP** prior to, before

préallumage [prealymaʒ] **NM** *Aut* pre-ignition

Préalpes [prealp] **NFPL les P.** the Pre-Alps, the Lower Alps

préalpin, -e [prealpɛ̃, -in] **ADJ** of the Pre-Alps

préambule [preãbyl] **NM 1** *(d'une constitution, d'une conférence)* preamble; **épargnez-nous les préambules!** spare us the preliminaries!, get straight to the point! **2** *(prémices)* prelude (**de** to); **cet incident a été le p. d'une crise grave** this incident was the prelude to a serious crisis

□ **sans préambule ADV** without preliminaries, straight off

préampli [preãpli] **NM** *Fam (abrév* **préamplificateur)** preamp

préamplificateur [preãplifikatœr] **NM** preamplifier

PréAO [preao] **NF** *Ordinat (abrév* **présentation assistée par ordinateur)** computer-assisted presentation

préapprentissage [preaprãtisaʒ] **NM** pre-apprenticeship training

préau, -x [preo] **NM** *(d'une école)* covered part of the playground; *(d'un pénitencier)* yard; *(d'un cloître)* inner courtyard

préavis [preavi] **NM** (advance) notice; **mon propriétaire m'a donné un mois de p.** my landlord gave me a month's notice (to move out); **p. de grève** strike notice, notice of strike action; **déposer un p. de grève** to give notice of strike action; **p. (de licenciement)** notice (of dismissal); *Banque* **dépôt à sept jours de p.** deposit at seven days' notice

□ **sans préavis ADV** *Admin* without prior notice *or* notification

préaviser [3] [preavize] **VT** *Jur* to give (advance) notice to

prébende [prebãd] **NF 1** *Rel* prebend **2** *Littéraire (emploi)* sinecure; *(argent)* handsome payment *or Littéraire* emolument

prébendé [prebãde] *Rel* **ADJ m** prebendal

NM prebendary, prebend

prébendier [prebãdje] **NM** *Rel* prebendary, prebend

prébiotique [prebjɔtik] **ADJ** prebiotic

précâblé, -e [prekable] **ADJ** prewired

précaire [prekɛr] **ADJ** *(équilibre)* fragile, precarious; *(vie, situation)* precarious; *(santé)* delicate, frail; *(abri)* precarious, rickety; **il a un emploi p.** he's got no job security

□ **précaires NMPL les précaires** people living on the poverty line

précairement [prekɛrmã] **ADV** precariously

précambrien, -enne [prekãbrijɛ̃, -ɛn] *Géol* **ADJ** Precambrian

NM Precambrian (era)

précampagne [prekãpaɲ] **NF** pre-campaign period

précancéreux, -euse [prekãserø, -øz] **ADJ** precancerous

précarisation [prekarizasjɔ̃] **NF** **on assiste à une p. croissante de l'emploi** we are seeing job security increasingly threatened

précariser [3] [prekarize] **VT** **p. l'emploi** to threaten job security; **la crise a précarisé leur situation** the recession has made them more vulnerable

précarité [prekarite] **NF** precariousness; **la p. de l'emploi** the lack of job security

précatif, -ive [prekatif, -iv] **ADJ** *Jur* precative, precatory

précaution [prekosjɔ̃] **NF 1** *(disposition préventive)* precaution; **prendre la p. de faire qch** to take the precaution of doing *or* to be especially careful to do sth; *aussi Euph* **prendre des ou ses précautions** to take precautions; **prenez des précautions avant de vous engager dans cette affaire** take all necessary precautions before getting involved; **avec beaucoup de précautions oratoires** in carefully chosen phrases; **précautions d'emploi** caution (before use)

2 *(prudence)* caution, care

□ **avec précaution ADV** cautiously, warily

□ **par (mesure de) précaution ADV** as a precaution *or* precautionary measure

□ **pour plus de précaution ADV** to be on the safe side, to make absolutely certain

□ **sans précaution ADV** carelessly, rashly; **elle manipule les produits toxiques sans la moindre p.** she handles toxic substances without taking the slightest precaution

précautionner [3] [prekosjɔne] **se précautionner VPR** *Littéraire* **se p. contre qch** to guard against sth

précautionneuse [prekosjɔnøz] *voir* **précautionneux**

précautionneusement [prekosjɔnøzmã] **ADV 1** *(avec circonspection)* cautiously, warily **2** *(avec soin)* carefully, with care

précautionneux, -euse [prekosjɔnø, -øz] **ADJ 1** *(circonspect)* cautious, wary **2** *(soigneux)* careful

précédemment [presedamã] **ADV** before (that), previously; **comme je l'ai dit p.** as I have said *or* mentioned before

précédent, -e [presedã, -ãt] **ADJ** previous; **la semaine précédente** the week before, the previous week; **lors de rencontres précédentes** during previous *or* earlier meetings

NM precedent; **créer un p.** to create *or* set a precedent

□ **sans précédent ADJ** without precedent, unprecedented

précéder [18] [presede] **VT 1** *(être devant)* to precede; **je vais vous p. dans le tunnel** I'll go into the tunnel first; **le groupe, précédé par le guide** the group, led *or* preceded by the guide; **l'antichambre qui précède le salon** the antechamber leading to the drawing room

2 *(être placé avant)* to precede, to be in front of; **l'adresse doit p. le numéro de téléphone** the address should come before the telephone number; **faire p. son nom de ses initiales** to write one's initials in front of one's name

3 *(avoir lieu avant)* to precede; **le film sera précédé par un ou d'un documentaire** the film will be preceded by *or* will follow a documentary; **le jour qui précéda son arrestation** the day before *or* prior to his/her arrest; **celui qui vous a précédé à ce poste** the person who held the post before you, your predecessor

4 *(arriver en avance sur)* to precede, to arrive ahead of *or* before; **elle m'a précédé sur le court de quelques minutes** she got to the court a few minutes before me; **il précède le favori de trois secondes** he has a three-second lead over the favourite; **il avait été précédé de sa mauvaise réputation** his bad reputation had preceded him

VI to precede; **as-tu lu ce qui précède?** have you read what comes before?; **les semaines qui précédèrent** the preceding weeks; **faites p. votre signature de la mention "lu et approuvé"** before your signature add the words "lu et approuvé"

préceinte [presɛ̃t] **NF** *Naut* bend, wale

précellence [presɛlɑ̃s] **NF** *Littéraire* pre-eminence

précepte [presɛpt] **NM** precept

précepteur [presɛptœr] **NM** private *or* home tutor

préceptorat [presɛptɔra] **NM** private *or* home tutorship

préceptrice [presɛptris] **NF** governess

précéramique [preseramik] **ADJ** preceramic

précession [presesjɔ̃] **NF** precession; **p. des équinoxes** precession of the equinoxes

préchambre [preʃɑ̃br] **NF** precombustion chamber

préchantre [preʃɑ̃tr] **NM** *Rel* precentor

précharge [preʃarʒ] **NF** *Aut* pre-load

préchargé, -e [preʃarʒe] **ADJ** *Ordinat (logiciel)* pre-loaded

préchauffage [preʃofaʒ] **NM** *(d'un four)* preheating; *(d'un moteur)* warm-up

préchauffer [3] [preʃofe] **VT** *(four)* to preheat; *(moteur)* to warm up

prêche [prɛʃ] **NM** sermon

prêcher [4] [preʃe] **VT** 1 *Rel (Évangile, religion)* to preach; *(carême, retraite)* to preach for; *(personne)* to preach to; **vous prêchez un converti** you're preaching to the *Br* converted *or Am* choir; *Hum* **p. la bonne parole** to spread the good word

2 *(recommander → doctrine, bonté, vengeance)* to preach; **p. le faux pour savoir le vrai** to make false statements in order to discover the truth

VI *(prêtre, moralisateur)* to preach; **p. d'exemple** *ou* **par l'exemple** to practise what one preaches; **p. dans le désert** to preach in the wilderness; **p. pour son saint** *ou* **son clocher** *ou* **sa paroisse** to look after one's own interests

prêcheur, -euse [prɛʃœr, -øz] **ADJ** 1 *Fam Péj (sermonneur)* moralizing■, preachy 2 *Rel* **frères prêcheurs** preaching friars

NM,F 1 *Fam Péj (sermonneur)* moralizer■ 2 *Rel* preacher

prêchi-prêcha [preʃipreʃa] **NM INV** *Fam Péj* sermonizing■, lecturing■

précieuse [presjøz] *voir* **précieux**

précieusement [presjøzmɑ̃] **ADV** 1 *(soigneusement)* preciously; **conserver qch p.** to look after sth very carefully, to take great care of sth 2 *(avec affectation)* **c'est écrit un peu p.** the style is a little bit precious

précieux, -euse [presjø, -øz] **ADJ** 1 *(de valeur → temps, santé)* precious; *(→ pierre, métal)* precious; *(→ ami, amitié)* precious, valued; *(→ objet, trésor, bijou)* precious, priceless

2 *(très utile)* invaluable; **c'était un p. conseiller** he was an invaluable *or* irreplaceable adviser; **elle fut d'une aide précieuse** her help was invaluable; **elle m'a été d'un p. secours** her help was invaluable to me

3 *(maniéré)* mannered, affected, precious

4 *Beaux-Arts & Littérature* precious

NM *Beaux-Arts & Littérature* preciosity

▫ **précieuse NF** *Hist* précieuse *(member of an aristocratic movement of ladies in 17th-century France who espoused refinement in language and social behaviour and held literary salons)*

▫ **précieuses NFPL** *très Fam Hum (testicules)* balls, nuts

préciosité [presjozite] **NF** 1 *(maniérisme)* affectedness, mannered style 2 *Beaux-Arts & Littérature* preciosity

précipice [presipis] **NM** 1 *(gouffre)* precipice 2 *(catastrophe)* **être au bord du p.** to be on the brink of disaster

précipitamment [presipitamɑ̃] **ADV** *(annuler, changer)* hastily, hurriedly; **monter/traverser p.** to dash up/across; **agir trop p.** to be too hasty *or* overhasty, to act too hastily

précipitant [presipitɑ̃] **NM** *Chim* precipitant

précipitation [presipitasjɔ̃] **NF** 1 *(hâte)* haste; **les ouvriers ont quitté l'usine avec p.** the workers rushed *or* hurried out of the factory; **dans ma p., j'ai oublié l'adresse** in the rush, I forgot the address; **tout s'est fait dans la plus grande p.** everything was done in a great hurry

2 *(irréflexion)* rashness; **agir avec p.** to act rashly

3 *Chim* precipitation

▫ **précipitations NFPL** *Météo* precipitation; **fortes précipitations sur l'ouest du pays demain** tomorrow, it will rain heavily in the west

précipité, -e [presipite] **ADJ** 1 *(pressé → pas)* hurried; *(→ fuite)* headlong 2 *(rapide → respiration)* rapid; **tout cela a été si p.** it all happened so fast 3 *(hâtif → retour)* hurried, hasty; *(→ décision)* hasty, rash

NM *Chim* precipitate

précipiter [3] [presipite] **VT** 1 *(faire tomber)* to throw *or* to hurl (down); **ils ont précipité leur voiture dans la mer** they pushed their car into the sea; **le choc précipita les passagers vers l'avant** the shock sent the passengers flying *or* hurtling to the front

2 *Fig (plonger)* to plunge; **p. qn dans le désespoir/le malheur** to plunge sb into despair/misfortune; **p. un pays dans la guerre/crise** to plunge a country into war/a crisis

3 *(faire à la hâte)* **il ne faut rien p.** we mustn't rush (into) things *or* be hasty; **nous avons dû p. notre départ/mariage** we had to leave/get married sooner than planned

4 *(accélérer → pas, cadence)* to quicken, to speed up; *(→ mouvement, mort)* to hasten

5 *Chim* to precipitate (out)

VI *Chim* to precipitate (out)

▸**se précipiter VPR** 1 *(d'en haut)* to hurl oneself; **il s'est précipité du septième étage** he threw *or* hurled himself from the seventh floor; **se p. dans le vide** to hurl oneself into space

2 *(se ruer)* to rush (**sur** at); **on s'est tous précipités dehors** we all rushed out; **il s'est précipité dans l'escalier pour la rattraper** *(vers le bas)* he rushed downstairs after her; *(vers le haut)* he rushed upstairs after her; **il s'est précipité dans l'ascenseur** he rushed into the *Br* lift *or Am* elevator; **se p. vers** *ou* **au-devant de qn** to rush to meet sb; **dès qu'il rentre à la maison, il se précipite devant la télévision** as soon as he gets home he throws himself down in front of the television

3 *(s'accélérer → pouls, cadence)* to speed up, to quicken; **depuis peu, les événements se précipitent** things have been moving really fast recently

4 *(se dépêcher)* to rush, to hurry; **on a tout notre temps, pourquoi se p.?** we've got plenty of time, what's the rush?; **ne te précipite pas pour répondre** take your time before answering

préciput [presipyt] **NM** *Jur* = portion of an estate or inheritance that devolves upon one of the co-heirs over and above his/her equal share with the others

préciputaire [presipytɛr] **ADJ** *Jur* = relating to a "préciput"

précis, -e [presi, -iz] **ADJ** 1 *(exact → horloge, tir, instrument)* precise, exact; *(→ description)* precise, accurate; **les dimensions précises de la maison** the exact measurements of the house; **la balance n'est pas très précise** the scales aren't very accurate; **le signalement p. du meurtrier** a precise *or* an accurate description of the murderer; **pour être plus p.** to be more precise; **à 20 heures précises** at precisely 8 p.m., at 8 p.m. sharp; **à cet instant p.** at that precise *or* very moment; **il arriva à l'instant p. où je partais** he arrived just as I was leaving

2 *(clair, net)* precise, specific; **instructions précises** precise orders; **je voudrais une réponse précise** I'd like a clear answer; **je n'ai aucun souvenir p. de cette année-là** I don't remember that year clearly at all; **il est très p. dans son travail** he's very meticulous *or* precise *or* exact in his work; **le geste p. du chirurgien** the surgeon's sure hand

3 *(particulier)* particular, specific; **sans raison précise** for no particular reason; **sans but p.** with no specific aim in mind; **rien de p.** nothing in particular; **tu penses à quelqu'un de p.?** do you have a specific person in mind?

NM 1 *(manuel)* handbook; **un p. d'histoire de France** a short history of France

2 *(résumé)* précis, summary

précisément [presizemɑ̃] **ADV** 1 *(exactement)* precisely; **il nous reste très p. 4,55 euros** we've got precisely *or* exactly 4.55 euros left; **ce n'est pas p. ce à quoi je pensais** that's not exactly what I had in mind; *Euph* **pas p.** not exactly; **ce n'est pas p. une réussite** it's not exactly a success, it's not (exactly) what you'd call a success; **ou plus p....** or more precisely..., or to be more precise...

2 *(justement, par coïncidence)* precisely, exactly; **c'est p. le problème** that's exactly *or* precisely what the problem is; **M. Lebrun? c'est p. de lui que nous parlions** Mr. Lebrun? that's precisely who we were talking about

3 *(oui)* that's right

préciser [3] [presize] **VT** 1 *(clarifier → intentions, pensée)* to make clear; **cette fois-ci, je me suis bien fait p. les conditions d'admission** this time I made sure they explained the conditions of entry clearly to me

2 *(spécifier)* **l'invitation ne précise pas si l'on peut venir accompagné** the invitation doesn't specify *or* say whether you can bring somebody with you; **p. qch à qn** to make sth clear to sb; **j'ai oublié de leur p. le lieu du rendez-vous** I forgot to tell them where the meeting is taking place; **la Maison-Blanche précise que la rencontre n'est pas officielle** the White House has made it clear that this is not an official meeting; **"cela s'est fait sans mon accord", précisa-t-il** "this was done without my agreement," he pointed out

USAGE ABSOLU vous dites avoir vu quelqu'un, pourriez-vous p.? you said you saw somebody, could you be more specific?

▸**se préciser VPR** *(idée, projet)* to take shape; *(situation, menace)* to become clearer; **les vacances se précisent** the holiday plans are taking shape

précision [presizjɔ̃] **NF** 1 *(exactitude → d'une information, d'une description)* accuracy; *(→ de mouvements)* preciseness, precision; **avec p.** accurately, precisely; **avec une p. mathématique** with mathematical precision

2 *(netteté)* precision, distinctness; **les visages sont peints avec une extraordinaire p.** the faces are painted with extraordinary precision *or* attention to detail

3 *(explication)* **apporter une p. à qch** to clarify sth; **demander des précisions sur qch** to ask for more *or* further information *or* details about sth; **nous y reviendrons dès que nous aurons plus de précisions** we'll come back to that as soon as we have further information *or* details; **je vous remercie de vos précisions** thank you for your informative comments; **raconter qch avec maintes précisions** to recount sth in great detail

▫ **de précision ADJ** precision *(avant n)*; **instrument de p.** precision instrument; **horlogerie de haute p.** high-precision watchmaking

précisionnisme [presizjɔnism] **NM** *Beaux-Arts* precisionism

précisionniste [presizjɔnist] *Beaux-Arts* **ADJ** precisionist

NMF precisionist

précité, -e [presite] **ADJ** *(oralement)* aforesaid, aforementioned; *(par écrit)* above-mentioned, aforesaid; **les auteurs précités** the authors quoted above

préclassique [preklasik] **ADJ** preclassical

précoce [prekɔs] **ADJ** 1 *(prématuré → surdité, mariage)* premature 2 *(en avance → intellectuellement)* precocious, mature (beyond one's years); *(→ sexuellement)* precocious; **les enfants précoces** precocious children; **j'étais un garçon p. pour mon âge** I was advanced for a boy of my age 3 *Bot & Météo* early; **les gelées précoces** early frost; **poire p.** early *or* early-fruiting pear

précocement [prekɔsmɑ̃] **ADV** prematurely, precociously; **marié/vieilli p.** prematurely married/aged

précocité [prekɔsite] **NF 1** *(d'un enfant)* precociousness, precocity; *(d'une faculté, d'un talent)* early manifestation, precociousness; **p. sexuelle** sexual precociousness **2** *Bot & Météo* early arrival, earliness

précolombien, -enne [prekɔlɔ̃bjɛ̃, -ɛn] **ADJ** pre-Columbian

précombustion [prekɔ̃bystjɔ̃] **NF** precombustion

pré-commercialisation [prekɔmɛrsjalizasjɔ̃] **NF** *Mktg* pre-marketing

précompte [prekɔ̃t] **NM 1** *(retenue) Br* tax deduction (from one's salary), *Am* withholding tax; **p. mobilier** (withholding) tax on company income **2** *(estimation)* (deduction) schedule

précompter [3] [prekɔ̃te] **VT 1** *(déduire)* to deduct; *(cotisations, impôts)* to deduct at source; **vos cotisations sont précomptées sur votre salaire** your contribution is deducted automatically from your salary **2** *(estimer)* to schedule, to estimate

préconception [prekɔ̃sɛpsjɔ̃] **NF** preconception, prejudice

préconçu, -e [prekɔ̃sy] **ADJ** set, preconceived; **idée préconçue** preconceived idea; **agir sans plan p.** to act without a preconceived *or* set plan

préconditionné, -e [prekɔ̃disjɔne] **ADJ** pre-packed, pre-packaged

préconditionner [3] [prekɔ̃disjɔne] **VT** to pre-pack, to pre-package

préconfiguré, -e [prekɔ̃figyre] **ADJ** *Ordinat* preconfigured

préconisateur [prekɔnizatœr] **NM** *Mktg* influencer, opinion leader

préconisation [prekɔnizasjɔ̃] **NF 1** *(d'un remède)* recommendation; *(d'une méthode)* advocacy **2** *Rel* preconization

préconiser [3] [prekɔnize] **VT 1** *(recommander →* solution, méthode*)* to advocate; *(→ remède)* to recommend; **il préconise d'augmenter les tarifs douaniers** he advocates *or* is an advocate of higher trade tariffs **2** *Rel* to preconize

préconscient, -e [prekɔ̃sjɑ̃, -ɑ̃t] *Psy* **ADJ** preconscious

     NM preconscious

précontraint, -e [prekɔ̃trɛ̃, -ɛ̃t] *Tech* **ADJ** prestressed

     NM prestressed concrete

     ❏ **précontrainte NF** prestress

précordial, -e, -aux, -ales [prekɔrdjal, -o] **ADJ** *Anat* precordial

précordialgie [prekɔrdjalʒi] **NF** *Méd* precordialgia

précuire [98] [prekɥir] **VT** to precook

précuisson [prekɥisɔ̃] **NF** precooking

précuit, -e [prekɥi, -it] **ADJ** precooked, ready-cooked

précurseur [prekyrsœr] **ADJ M** warning *(avant n)*; **signe p.** forewarning, portent

     NM forerunner, precursor; **faire figure** *ou* **œuvre de p.** to break new ground

prédaté, -e [predate] **ADJ** predated

prédateur, -trice [predatœr, -tris] *Bot & Zool* **ADJ** predatory

     NM predator

prédation [predasjɔ̃] **NF** predation

prédatrice [predatris] *voir* **prédateur**

prédécesseur [predesesœr] **NM** predecessor

     ❏ **prédécesseurs NMPL** *(ancêtres)* forebears

prédécoupé, -e [predekupe] **ADJ** precut, ready-cut

prédéfini, -e [predefini] **ADJ** predefined

prédéfinition [predefinisjɔ̃] **NF** *Ordinat* **p. des secteurs** hard sectoring

prédélinquant, -e [predelɛ̃kɑ̃, -ɑ̃t] **NM,F** predelinquent

prédelle [predɛl] **NF** *Beaux-Arts* predella

prédestination [predɛstinasjɔ̃] **NF** predestination

prédestiné, -e [predɛstine] **ADJ** *(voué à tel sort)* predestined, fated; **être p. à faire qch** to be predestined *or* fated to do sth; **un nom p.** an appropriate name

     NM,F *Rel* chosen *or* predestined one

prédestiner [3] [predɛstine] **VT 1** *(vouer)* to prepare, to predestine; **rien ne me prédestinait à devenir acteur** nothing marked me out to become an actor *or* for an acting career **2** *Rel* to predestine, to predestinate

prédétermination [predetɛrminasjɔ̃] **NF** predetermination

prédéterminer [3] [predetɛrmine] **VT** to predetermine

prédicable [predikabl] **ADJ** predicable

prédicant [predikɑ̃] **NM** *Rel* preacher

prédicat [predika] **NM 1** *Ling (verbe)* predicator; *(adjectif)* predicate **2** *(en logique)* predicate

prédicateur, -trice [predikatœr, -tris] **NM,F** preacher

prédicatif, -ive [predikatif, -iv] **ADJ 1** *Ling & (en logique)* predicative **2** *Rel* predicatory, predicant

prédication [predikasjɔ̃] **NF 1** *Ling & (en logique)* predication **2** *Rel* **la p.** *(action)* preaching; *(prêche)* sermon

prédicative [predikativ] *voir* **prédicatif**

prédicatrice [predikatris] *voir* **prédicateur**

prédictibilité [prediktibilite] **NF** predictability

prédictible [prediktibl] **ADJ** predictable

prédictif, -ive [prediktif, -iv] **ADJ** predictive; *Tél* **écriture prédictive** predictive texting, predictive text input; *Méd* **médecine prédictive** predictive medicine

prédiction [prediksjɔ̃] **NF** *(prophétie)* prediction; **tes prédictions se sont accomplies** *ou* **réalisées** what you predicted came true

prédictive [prediktiv] *voir* **prédictif**

prédigéré, -e [prediʒere] **ADJ** predigested

prédilection [predilɛksjɔ̃] **NF** predilection, partiality; **avoir une p. pour qch** to be partial to sth, to have a predilection for sth

     ❏ **de prédilection ADJ** favourite

prédiquer [3] [predike] **VT** to predicate

prédire [103] [predir] **VT** to predict, to foretell; **ils avaient prédit la guerre** they'd predicted the war *or* that there would be a war; **p. l'avenir** *(par hasard ou estimation)* to predict the future; *(voyant)* to tell fortunes; **elle m'a prédit un grand avenir/que je voyagerais** she predicted a great future ahead of me/that I would travel; **je lui prédis des jours difficiles** I can see difficult times ahead for him/her

prédisposer [3] [predispoze] **VT 1** *(préparer)* to predispose; **sa taille la prédisposait à devenir mannequin** her height made modelling an obvious choice for her **2** *(incliner)* **être prédisposé en faveur de qn** to be favourably disposed to sb **USAGE ABSOLU cette époque-là ne prédisposait pas à la frivolité** that period was not conducive to frivolity

prédisposition [predispozisjɔ̃] **NF 1** *(tendance)* predisposition (à to); *Mktg* **p. à l'achat** buyer-readiness **2** *(talent)* gift, talent

prédit, -e [predi, -it] **PP** *voir* **prédire**

prednisone [prednizɔn] **NM** *Pharm* prednisone

prédominance [predɔminɑ̃s] **NF** predominance

prédominant, -e [predɔminɑ̃, -ɑ̃t] **ADJ** *(principal →* couleur, trait*)* predominant, main; *(→ opinion, tendance)* prevailing; *(→ souci)* chief, major

prédominer [3] [predɔmine] **VI** *(couleur, trait)* to predominate; *(sentiment, tendance)* to prevail; **le soleil va p. sur presque tout le pays** the weather will be sunny in most parts of the country; **c'est ce qui prédomine dans tous ses romans** that's the predominant feature of all his/her novels; **ce qui prédomine chez lui, c'est la générosité** generosity is his chief *or* predominant quality

prééclampsie [preeklɑ̃psi] **NF** *Méd* pre-eclampsia

préélectoral, -e, -aux, -ales [preelɛktɔral, -o] **ADJ** pre-electoral

préélémentaire [preelemɑ̃tɛr] **ADJ** *Scol Br* pre-primary, *Am* pre-elementary

préemballé, -e [preãbale] **ADJ** pre-packed, pre-packaged

préemballer [3] [preãbale] **VT** to pre-pack, to pre-package

pré-embarquement [preãbarkəmã] **NM** *(à un aéroport)* pre-boarding

pré-embarquer [preãbarke] **VI** *(à un aéroport)* to pre-board

préembryon [preãbrijɔ̃] **NM** *Biol & Méd* pre-embryo

prééminence [preeminɑ̃s] **NF** pre-eminence, dominance; **donner la p. à qch** to put sth first

prééminent, -e [preeminɑ̃, -ɑ̃t] **ADJ** pre-eminent; **occuper un rang p.** to hold a prominent position

préempter [3] [preãpte] **VT** *Jur* to pre-empt

préemption [preãpsjɔ̃] **NF** *Jur* pre-emption

préencollé, -e [preãkɔle] **ADJ** prepasted

préenregistré, -e [preãrəʒistre] **ADJ** prerecorded

préenregistrement [preãrəʒistrəmã] **NM** prerecording

préenregistrer [3] [preãrəʒistre] **VT** to prerecord

préétabli, -e [preetabli] **ADJ** pre-established

préétablir [32] [preetablir] **VT** to pre-establish, to establish in advance

préétude [preetyd] **NF** *Mktg* pilot study

préexcellence [preeksɛlɑ̃s] **NF** *Littéraire* preeminence, incomparable superiority

préexistant, -e [preɛgzistɑ̃, -ɑ̃t] **ADJ** existing; **les immeubles préexistants seront détruits** existing buildings will be torn down

préexistence [preɛgzistɑ̃s] **NF** preexistence

préexister [3] [preɛgziste] **préexister à VT IND** *(gén)* to exist before; *(loi)* to predate

préfabrication [prefabrikasjɔ̃] **NF** prefabrication

préfabriqué, -e [prefabrike] **ADJ** prefabricated; *Fig* **un sourire p.** an artificial smile

     NM 1 *(construction)* prefab **2** *(matériau)* prefabricated material; **en p.** prefabricated

préfabriquer [3] [prefabrike] **VT** to prefabricate

préface [prefas] **NF 1** *(avant-propos)* preface (**de** to) **2** *Rel* preface

préfacer [16] [prefase] **VT** to write a preface to, to preface

préfacier [prefasje] **NM** prefacer, preface writer

préfacturation [prefaktyrasjɔ̃] **NF** *Compta* prebilling

préfectoral, -e, -aux, -ales [prefɛktɔral, -o] **ADJ 1** *(du préfet)* prefectorial, prefectural; **par arrêté p., par mesure préfectorale** by order **2** *Belg Scol* of a *Br* head teacher *or* *Am* principal *(of a secondary school)*

préfecture [prefɛktyr] **NF 1** *Admin (chef-lieu)* prefecture; *(édifice)* prefecture building; *(services)* prefectural office; *(emploi)* post of prefect; **briguer la p.** to aspire to the prefecture; **p. maritime** port prefecture; **p. de police** (Paris) police headquarters **2** *Antiq* prefecture

PRÉFECTURE

This refers to the main administrative office of each "département". The word has also come to refer to the town where the office is located. One goes to the "préfecture" to obtain a driving licence or a "carte de séjour", for example.

préfecturier [prefɛktyrje] **NM** *Journ* = journalist who reports on events relating to the "préfecture"

préférable [preferabl] **ADJ** preferable; **cette solution est nettement p.** that solution is preferable *or* to be preferred; **ne va pas trop loin, c'est p.** it'd be better if you didn't go too far away; **il serait p. de le revoir** *ou* **qu'on le revoie** it would be preferable *or* better to see him again; **p. à** preferable to, better than; **tout est p. à cette vie de reclus** anything is better than this hermit's life

préférablement [preferabləmã] **ADV** *Littéraire* **p. à** *(de préférence à)* in preference to

préféré, -e [prefere] **ADJ** favourite; **quel est ton passe-temps p.?** what is your favourite hobby?

     NM,F favourite; **la petite dernière est la préférée de mon mari** our youngest child is my husband's favourite

préférence [preferɑ̃s] **NF 1** *(prédilection)* preference; **par ordre de p.** in order of preference; **donner** *ou* **accorder la p. à** to give preference to; **avoir une p. pour** to have a preference for; **montrer une p. pour** to show a preference for, to favour; **ma p. va aux tissus unis** I prefer *or* have a preference for plain fabrics; **ça m'est égal, je n'ai pas de p.** it doesn't matter to me *or* I don't mind, I've no particular preference; **avoir la p. sur qn** to have preference over sb; **sur 200 candidates, c'est elle qui a eu la p.** she was chosen out of 200 candidates; *Mktg* **p. du consommateur** consumer preference

     2 *Jur* **droit de p.** right to preferential treatment **3** *Écon* **p. douanière** preferential duties; **p. pour la liquidité** liquidity preference **4** *Pol* **la p. nationale** = policy of discrimination in favour of a country's own nationals as opposed to immigrants

     ❏ **de préférence ADV** preferably; **donne-moi un**

verre de vin, et du bon de p. give me a glass of wine, preferably a good one; **à consommer de p. avant fin 2008** (*sur emballage*) best before end 2008

◽ **de préférence à** PRÉP in preference to, rather than

préférentiel, -elle [preferãsjɛl] ADJ (*traitement, tarif, vote*) preferential

préférentiellement [preferãsjɛlmã] ADV preferentially

préférer [18] [prefere] VT to prefer; **la bruyère préfère une terre tourbeuse** heather does better in *or* prefers peaty soil; **ils préfèrent les échecs aux cartes** they prefer chess to playing cards; **je préférerais du thé** I'd prefer tea, I'd rather have tea; **je me préfère avec un chignon** I think I look better with my hair up; **il préférait mourir plutôt que (de) partir** he would rather die than leave; **il y a des moments où l'on préfère rester seul** there are times when one would rather be alone; **je préfère que tu n'en dises rien à personne** I'd prefer it if *or* I'd rather you didn't tell anybody

USAGE ABSOLU **si tu préfères, nous allons rentrer** if you'd prefer, we'll go home

préfet [prefɛ] NM **1** *Admin* prefect; **elle était p. du Lot** she used to be prefect of the Lot department; **le p. de Paris** the prefect of Paris; **p. de police** (*en France*) prefect *or* chief of police; (*en Grande-Bretagne*) ≃ chief constable, ≃ head of the constabulary; **p. de région** regional prefect **2** *Rel* prefect; **p. apostolique** prefect apostolic; **p. des études** master of studies (*in a religious school*) **3** *Naut* **p. maritime** = port admiral overseeing the defence of certain maritime departments **4** *Belg Scol Br* head teacher, *Am* principal (*of a secondary school*) **5** *Antiq* prefect

---

Culture
PRÉFET

In France a "préfet" is a high-ranking official, one of a body of civil servants created by Napoleon in 1800. The "préfet" is the general administrator of the "département", the chief executive officer and the executive chief of police.

---

préfète [prefɛt] NF **1** (*épouse*) prefect's wife **2** (*titulaire*) (woman) prefect **3** *Belg Scol Br* headmistress, *Am* principal (*of a secondary school*)

préfiguration [prefigyrasjõ] NF prefiguration, foreshadowing; **ce rêve était-il la p. de mon avenir?** was this dream a premonition?

préfigurer [3] [prefigyre] VT (*annoncer*) to prefigure

préfinancement [prefinãsmã] NM advance funding, prefinancing

préfinancer [16] [prefinãse] VT to fund in advance, to pre-finance

préfix, -e¹ [prefiks] ADJ *Jur* prescribed, set

préfixal, -e, -aux, -ales [prefiksal, -o] ADJ préfixal, prefix (*avant n*)

préfixation [prefiksasjõ] NF *Ling* prefixing, prefixation; **la p. d'un morphème** the use of a morpheme as a prefix

préfixe² [prefiks] NM *Ling* prefix

préfixé, -e [prefikse] ADJ **1** *Ling* prefixed **2** *Jur* (*date, délai*) prescribed, set

préfixer [3] [prefikse] VT *Ling* to prefix

préfloraison [preflɔrɛzõ] NF *Bot* aestivation, prefloration

préfoliaison [prefɔljɛzõ], **préfoliation** [prefɔljasjõ] NF *Bot* vernation, prefoliation

pré-fondu [prefõdy] NM *Cin & TV* prefade

préformage [preformaʒ] NM preforming

préformaté, -e [preformate] ADJ *Ordinat* preformatted

préformater [3] [preformate] VT *Ordinat* to preformat

préformation [preformasjõ] NF preformation

préforme [preform] NF preform

préformer [3] [preforme] VT to preform

préfourrière [prefurjɛr] NF = place where cars that have been parked illegally are taken before being impounded

pré-gardiennat, prégardiennat [pregardjɛna] (*pl* **pré-gardiennats** *ou* **prégardiennats**) NM *Belg* (*jardin d'enfants*) *Br* nursery school, *Am* kindergarten

---

prégénital, -e, -aux, -ales [preʒenital, -o] ADJ *Psy* pregenital

préglaciaire [preglasjɛr] ADJ *Géol* preglacial

prégnance [preɲɑ̃s] NF **1** *Littéraire* (*importance*) significance, meaningfulness **2** *Psy* pregnance, Prägnanz

prégnant, -e [preɲɑ̃, -ɑ̃t] ADJ *Littéraire* significant, pregnant (with meaning)

préhellénique [preelenik] ADJ pre-Hellenic

préhenseur [preɑ̃sœr] ADJ M prehensile

préhensile [preɑ̃sil] ADJ prehensile

préhension [preɑ̃sjõ] NF prehension; **doué de p.** able to grip

préhispanique [preispanik] ADJ prehispanic

préhistoire [preistwar] NF prehistory

préhistorien, -enne [preistɔrjɛ̃, -ɛn] NM,F prehistorian

préhistorique [preistɔrik] ADJ **1** (*ère, temps*) prehistoric, prehistorical **2** *Fam* (*dépassé*) ancient, prehistoric; **elle est p., sa bagnole!** his/her car's virtually an antique!

préhominien [preɔminjɛ̃] NM prehominid

préimplantatoire [preɛ̃plɑ̃tatwar] ADJ *Biol & Med* (*diagnostic, embryon*) preimplantation (*avant n*)

pré-impression [preɛ̃presjõ] NF *Typ* pre-press

pré-imprimé [preɛ̃prime] (*pl* **pré-imprimés**) NM pre-printed form

pré-imprimée NF = **pré-imprimé**

pré-imputation [preɛ̃pytasjõ] NF *Compta* pre-input preparation

préindustriel, -elle [preɛ̃dystrijɛl] ADJ preindustrial

préinscription [preɛ̃skripsjõ] NF preregistration

préinstallé, -e [preɛ̃stale] ADJ *Ordinat* preinstalled

préinstaller [3] [preɛ̃stale] VT *Ordinat* to preinstall

préislamique [preislamik] ADJ pre-Islamic

préjudice [preʒydis] NM harm (*UNCOUNT*), wrong (*UNCOUNT*); **causer un** *ou* **porter p. à qn** to harm sb, to do sb harm; **les magnétoscopes ont-ils porté p. au cinéma?** have *Br* video recorders *or Am* VCRs been detrimental to the cinema?; **p. d'agrément** loss of amenity, loss of enjoyment of life; **p. corporel** bodily harm; **p. esthétique** aesthetic damage, disfiguration; **p. financier** financial loss; **p. grave** substantial wrong; **p. matériel** material injury; **subir un p. matériel/financier** to sustain damage/financial loss; **p. moral** non-pecuniary damages; **subir un p. moral** to suffer mental distress; **p. personnel** personal injury; **p. psychologique** mental injury

◽ **au préjudice de** PRÉP (*chose*) to the detriment *or* at the expense of; (*personne*) to the detriment *or Sout* prejudice of; **on développe le tourisme au p. des traditions locales** tourism is being developed at the expense of local traditions

◽ **sans préjudice de** PRÉP without prejudice to; **vous devez payer un million d'euros sans p. de vos dettes antérieures** you must pay a million euros, without prejudice to the money previously owed

préjudiciable [preʒydisjabl] ADJ prejudicial, detrimental (**à** to); **de telles déclarations seraient préjudiciables à votre candidature** such statements would be harmful *or* injurious to your candidature

préjudiciel, -elle [preʒydisjɛl] ADJ (*question*) interlocutory; (*action*) prejudicial

préjugé [preʒyʒe] NM prejudice; **préjugés raciaux** racial prejudice; **avoir un p. contre qn** to be prejudiced against sb; **avoir un p. favorable pour** *ou* **à l'égard de qn** to be prejudiced in sb's favour, to be biased towards sb; **n'avoir aucun p.** to be totally unprejudiced *or* unbiased

préjuger [17] [preʒyʒe] *Littéraire* VT to prejudge; **autant qu'on puisse le p.** as far as one can judge beforehand

◽ **préjuger de** VT IND **p. de qch** to judge sth in advance, to prejudge sth; **autant qu'on puisse en p.** as far as one can judge beforehand; **son attitude ne laisse rien p. de sa décision** his/her attitude gives us no indication of what he/she is going to decide; **on ne peut p. de l'avenir** you can't tell what the future has in store; **je crains d'avoir préjugé de mes forces** I'm afraid I've overestimated my strength

prélart [prelar] NM **1** (*bâche*) tarpaulin **2** *Can* (*linoléum*) linoleum

---

prélasser [3] [prelase] **se prélasser** VPR to be stretched out, to lounge (around), to laze around; **se p. au soleil** to laze *or* bask in the sun

prélat [prela] NM prelate

prélatin, -e [prelatɛ̃, -in] ADJ pre-Latin

prélature [prelatyr] NF prelacy

prélavage [prelavaʒ] NM prewash

prélaver [3] [prelave] VT to prewash

prêle, prèle [prɛl] NF *Bot* horsetail, scouring rush

prélegs [prelɛg] NM *Jur* preference legacy

prélèvement [prelɛvmɑ̃] NM **1** *Méd & Ind* (*action*) sampling; (*échantillon → gén*) sample; (*→ sur les tissus*) swab; **il faut faire un p. dans la partie infectée** we have to take a swab of the infected area; **faire des prélèvements à qn** to do tests on sb

2 *Banque* (*retrait*) withdrawal; **p. automatique** *ou* **bancaire** direct debit; **p. en espèces** cash withdrawal; **faire un p. sur un compte** to debit an account

3 *Fin* (*retenue → sur le salaire*) deduction; (*→ sur les biens*) levy; **p. sur le capital** capital levy; **les cotisations sont payées par p. à la source** contributions are deducted at source; *UE* **prélèvements agricoles** agricultural levies; *UE* **p. compensatoire** compensatory levy; **p. à l'exportation** export levy; **prélèvements fiscaux** taxes; **p. à l'importation** import levy; **p. de l'impôt à la source** taxation at source; **prélèvements obligatoires** tax and social security contributions; **p. salarial** deduction from wages; **prélèvements sociaux** social security contributions

prélever [19] [prelave] VT **1** *Méd & Ind* (*échantillon*) to take; (*organe*) to remove; (*en prévision de transplantations futures*) to harvest; **p. du sang** to take a blood sample

2 *Banque* (*somme → en espèces*) to withdraw; **la somme sera prélevée sur votre compte tous les mois** the sum will be deducted *or* debited from your account every month; **aller à la banque p. de l'argent** to go to the bank and withdraw some money

3 *Fin* (*sur un salaire*) to deduct, to withdraw; **p. qch à la source** to deduct sth at source; **p. une commission de 2 pour cent sur une opération** to charge a 2 percent commission on a transaction; **dividende prélevé sur le capital** dividend paid out of capital

préliminaire [prelimin ɛr] ADJ preliminary; **remarque p.** preliminary *or* prefatory remark

◽ **préliminaires** NMPL (*préparatifs*) preliminaries; (*discussions*) preliminary talks

prélogique [prelɔʒik] ADJ prelogical

prélude [prelyd] NM **1** *Mus* prelude **2** (*préliminaire*) prelude (**de** *ou* **à** to); **cette première rencontre fut le p. de bien d'autres** this was the first of many meetings

'**Prélude à l'après-midi d'un faune**' Mallarmé, Debussy 'L'après-midi d'un faune' (poem), 'Prelude to the Afternoon of a Faun' (music)

préluder [3] [prelyde] VI *Mus* to warm up, to prelude; **p. par des vocalises** to warm up by doing vocal exercises

◽ **préluder à** VT IND to be a prelude to

prémaquette [premakɛt] NF *Typ* rough layout

pré-marketing [premarketiŋ] NM *Mktg* pre-marketing

prématuré, -e [prematyre] ADJ **1** (*naissance, bébé*) premature; **être p. de six semaines** to be six weeks premature *or* early **2** (*décision*) premature; (*décès*) untimely; **il est p. de dresser un bilan de la situation** it is too early to assess the situation

NM,F premature baby *or* infant

prématurément [prematyremã] ADV prematurely; **il nous a quittés p.** his was an untimely death

prématurité [prematyrite] NF prematurity

prémédication [premedikasjõ] NF *Méd* premedication

prémédiquer [premedike] VT *Méd* to premedicate

préméditation [premeditasjõ] NF premeditation; **avec p.** with malice aforethought; **meurtre avec p.** premeditated murder; **meurtre sans p.** unpremeditated murder, murder without

premeditation; **si on ne peut pas prouver la p.** if proof of intent cannot be shown

prémédité, -e [premedite] ADJ **1** *Jur (crime)* premeditated, wilful **2** *(insulte, réponse)* deliberate

préméditer [3] [premedite] VT *(crime, vol)* to premeditate; **p. de faire qch** to plan to do sth; **ils avaient bien prémédité leur coup** they'd thought the whole thing out really well

prémenstruel, -elle [premɑ̃stryɛl] ADJ premenstrual

prémices [premis] NFPL **1** *Littéraire (début)* beginnings; **les p. de l'été** the first *or* early signs of summer; **les p. d'un grand talent** the first *or* early stirrings of a great talent **2** *Antiq (récolte)* premices, primices, first fruits; *(animaux)* premices, primices

PREMIER, -ÈRE [prəmje, -ɛr] ADJ **1** *(souvent avant le nom) (initial)* early; **les premiers hommes** early man; **ses premières œuvres** his/her early works; **les premiers temps** at the beginning, early on; **il n'est plus de la première jeunesse** he's not as young as he used to be; **un Matisse de la première période** an early Matisse

2 *(proche)* nearest; **je réussis à attraper les premières branches** I managed to grasp the nearest branches; **au p. rang** *Cin & Théât* in the first *or* front row; *Scol* in the first row

3 *(à venir)* next, first; **le p. venu** the first person who comes along; **ce n'est pas le p. venu** he's not just anybody; **le p. imbécile venu pourrait le faire** any idiot could do it; **on s'est arrêtés dans le p. hôtel venu** we stopped at the first hotel we came to *or* happened to come to

4 *(dans une série)* first; **chapitre p.** Chapter One; **à la première heure** first thing, at first light; **à première vue** at first (sight); **au p. abord** at first; **au p. abord, on le prendrait pour un prêtre** on first meeting him you'd think he was a priest; *Littéraire* **au p. chant du coq** when the cock crows, at cock crow; **dans un p. temps** (at) first, to start with, to begin with; **de la première à la dernière ligne** from beginning to end; **de la première à la dernière page** from cover to cover; **le p. nom d'une liste** the top name on a list; *Can* **p. nom** first *or* Christian name, *Am* given name; *Fam* **du p. coup** first off, at the first attempt; **faire ses premières armes** to make one's debut; **il a fait ses premières armes à la 'Gazette du Nord'** he cut his teeth at the 'Gazette du Nord'; **j'ai fait mes premières armes dans le métier comme apprenti cuisinier** I started in the trade as a cook's apprentice; **p. amour** first love; **le p. arrivé** the first person to arrive; **p. jet** (first) *or* rough *or* initial draft; *Jur* **p. occupant** first occupant; *Cin* **première prise** first take *or* shot; **premiers secours** *(personnes et matériel)* emergency services; *(soins)* first aid; **c'est la première fois que...** it's the first time that...; **il y a toujours une première fois** there's always a first time; *Journ* **première page** front page; **mets-le en première page** put it on the front page; **faire la première page des journaux** to be headline news; **première partie** *(gén)* first part; *(au spectacle)* opening act; **qui va (lui) jeter** *ou* **lancer la première pierre?** who will cast the first stone?; *Can Joual* **p. plancher** *Br* ground floor▪, *Am* first floor▪

5 *(principal)* main; **de (toute) première nécessité/urgence** (absolutely) essential/urgent; **c'est vous le p. intéressé** you're the main person concerned *or* the one who's got most at stake; **le p. pays producteur de vin au monde** the world's leading wine-producing country; **la première collection de fossiles au monde** the world's greatest *or* foremost collection of fossils; *Bourse* **p. marché** main market

6 *(haut placé → clerc, commis)* chief; *(→ danseur)* leading; **le p. personnage de l'État** the country's Head of State; **sortir p. d'une grande école** to be first on the pass list *(in the final exam of a "grande école")*; *Hum* **il se prend pour le p. moutardier du pape** he thinks he's God's gift to humanity; **p. avocat général** Principal Advocate-General; **première chambre** upper chamber *or* court; **p. maître** chief petty officer; **P. Ministre** Prime Minister; **p. secrétaire (du parti)** first secretary (of the party); *Jur* **p. substitut** ≃ Senior Assistant State Counsel

7 *(après le nom) (originel)* first, original, initial; **il n'a jamais retrouvé son inspiration première** he never recovered his initial inspiration; **l'idée première était de...** the original idea was to...

8 *(spontané)* first; **son p. mouvement** his/her first *or* spontaneous impulse; **quelles sont vos premières réactions?** what are your first *or* initial reactions?

9 *(après le nom) (fondamental)* first; *Math (nombre)* prime; *(polynôme)* irreducible; **cause première** first cause; **principe p.** first *or* basic principle

10 *(moindre)* **et ta récitation, tu n'en connais pas le p. mot!** you haven't a clue about your recitation, have you?; **la robe coûte 300 euros et je n'en ai pas le p. sou** the dress costs 300 euros and I haven't a *Br* penny *or Am* cent to my name

11 *Gram* **première personne (du) singulier/pluriel** first person singular/plural

12 *Culin* **côte/côtelette première** prime rib/cutlet

NM,F **1** *(personne)* **le p.** the first; **entre la première** go in first; **elle a fini dans les cinq premières** she finished amongst the top five; **elle est la première de sa classe/au hit-parade** she's top of her class/the charts; **si c'est moi qui pars le p.** if I go first; *Fam* **mon p. m'a fait une rougeole** my eldest has had measles▪; *Cin & Théât* **jeune p.** juvenile lead; **jeune première** young female lead; *Pol* **le P. (britannique)** the (British) Prime Minister *or* Premier; *Bible* **les premiers seront les derniers** the first shall be last

2 *(chose)* **le p.** the first (one); **de toutes les maisons où j'ai vécu, c'est la première que je regrette le plus** of all the houses in which I have lived, I miss the first (one) most of all

3 le p. *(celui-là)* the former; **plantez des roses ou des tulipes, mais les premières durent plus longtemps** plant roses or tulips, but the former last longer

NM **1** *(dans une charade)* **mon p. sent mauvais** my first has a nasty smell

2 *(étage) Br* first floor, *Am* second floor; **la dame du p.** the lady on the *Br* first floor *or Am* second floor

3 *(dans des dates)* **le p. du mois** the first of the month; **tous les premiers du mois** every first (day) of the month; **Aix, le p. juin** Aix, *Br* 1 June *or Am* June 1; **le p. avril** April Fool's *or* All Fools Day; **le P. Mai** May Day; **le p. janvier** *ou* **de l'an** New Year's Day

❑ **première** NF **1** *Cin & Théât* first night, opening night; **première mondiale** world première

2 *(exploit)* **c'est une (grande) première chirurgicale** it's a first for surgery; **la première des Grandes Jorasses** the first ascent of the Grandes Jorasses

3 *Scol Br* lower sixth (form), *Am* eleventh grade; **première supérieure** = class leading to the entrance exam for the "École normale supérieure"

4 *Aut* first (gear); **être/passer en première** to be in/to go into first

5 *Transp* first class; **voyager en première** to travel first class; **billet/wagon de première** first-class ticket/carriage

6 *Couture* head seamstress

7 *(en danse)* first (position)

8 *Typ (épreuve)* first proof; *(édition → d'un livre)* first edition; *(→ d'un journal)* early edition

9 *(d'une chaussure)* insole

❑ **de première** ADJ *Fam* first-rate; **un imbécile de première** a prize idiot

❑ **en premier** ADV first, in the first place, first of all; **je dois m'occuper en p. de mon visa** the first thing I must do is to see about my visa

❑ **premier de cordée** NM leader *(of a roped climbing team)*

❑ **premier degré** NM **1** *Scol Br* primary *or Am* elementary education

2 *(phase initiale)* first step; **brûlure au p. degré** first-degree burn

3 *Fig* **des gags à ne pas prendre au p. degré** jokes which mustn't be taken at face value

❑ **premier prix** NM **1** *Com* lowest *or* cheapest price; **dans les premiers prix** at the cheaper *or* lower end of the scale

2 *(récompense)* first prize; **elle a eu le p. prix d'interprétation** she's won the award for best actress

premièrement [prəmjɛrmɑ̃] ADV **1** *(dans une énumération)* in the first place, first; **p. il faut de l'argent, deuxièmement il faut du temps** first you need the money, then you need the time **2** *(pour objecter)* firstly, in the first place, to start with; **p., ça ne te regarde pas!** to begin *or* to start with, it's none of your business!

premier-lieutenant [prəmjeljøtnɑ̃] *(pl* **premiers-lieutenants)** NM *Suisse* lieutenant

premier-ministrable [prəmjeministrabl] *(pl* **premier-ministrables)** ADJ *(politicien)* suitable for Prime Minister

NMF potential Prime Minister

premier-né, première-née [prəmjene, prəmjɛrne] *(mpl* **premiers-nés**, *fpl* **premières-nées)** ADJ first-born

NM,F first-born

prémilitaire [premilitɛr] ADJ premilitary

prémisse [premis] NF premise

prémix [premiks] NM *(boisson)* ready-mixed alcoholic drink

prémolaire [premɔlɛr] NF premolar

prémonition [premɔnisjɔ̃] NF premonition

prémonitoire [premɔnitwar] ADJ premonitory; **j'ai fait un rêve p.** I had a premonition in my dream

prémontré, -e [premɔ̃tre] *Rel* ADJ Premonstrant, Premonstratensian

NM,F Premonstrant, Premonstratensian

prems [prəms] = **preums**

prémunir [32] [premynir] VT **p. qn contre qch** *(protéger)* to protect sb against sth; *(mettre en garde)* to put sb on his/her guard against sth

►**se prémunir** VPR **se p. contre qch** to protect oneself *or* to guard against sth

prenable [prənabl] ADJ pregnable

prenait *etc voir* **prendre**

prenant, -e [prənɑ̃, -ɑ̃t] ADJ **1** *(captivant)* engrossing, gripping **2** *(qui prend du temps)* time-consuming **3** *(préhensile)* prehensile

prénatal, -e, -als *ou* **-aux, -ales** [prenatal, -o] ADJ *Br* antenatal, *Am* prenatal

PRENDRE [79] [prɑ̃dr]

to take **A1–4, B2–5, 7, 8, C1–3, 6, D2, 3, 5, E1–3, F, G1–4** ▪ to pick up **A1** ▪ to hold **A2** ▪ to get **A5–7, D6** ▪ to buy **A7** ▪ to use **B1** ▪ to borrow **B2** ▪ to eat **B3** ▪ to drink **B3** ▪ to travel by **B5** ▪ to catch **B6, C5** ▪ to capture **C1** ▪ to take up **C3** ▪ to come over **C4** ▪ to consider **E3** ▪ to write down **F1** ▪ to have **G1, 3** ▪ to assume **G5**

VI to take **1** ▪ to catch on **1** ▪ to set **2** ▪ to thicken **2** ▪ to start **4**

VT **A.** *SAISIR, ACQUÉRIR* **1** *(ramasser)* to pick up; **la chatte prend ses chatons par la peau du cou** the cat picks up her kittens by the scruff of the neck; **elle prit sa guitare sur le sol** she picked her guitar up off the floor; **quand il prend son saxophone, tout le monde se tait** when he picks *or* takes up his saxophone, everybody quietens down; **prends la casserole par le manche** pick the pan up by the handle; **il prit son manteau à la patère** he took his coat off the hook; **p. qch des mains de qn** to take sth off sb; **va p. du persil/des fleurs dans le jardin** go and pick some parsley/flowers in the garden; **p. un peigne dans sa poche/dans un tiroir** to take a comb out of one's pocket/a drawer; **prends le bébé** pick the baby up

2 *(saisir et garder)* to take (hold of), to hold; **tu peux p. mon sac un instant?** could you hold on to *or* take my bag for a minute?; **p. sa tête entre ses mains** to hold one's head in one's hands; **il m'a pris par les épaules et m'a secoué** he took (hold of) me by the shoulders and shook me; **prenez cette médaille qui vous est offerte par tous vos collègues** accept this medal as a gift from all your colleagues; **p. un siège** to take a seat, to sit down

3 *(emporter → lunettes, document, en-cas)* to take; **tu as pris tes papiers (avec toi)?** have you got your papers (with you)?; **inutile de p. un parapluie** there's no need to take *or* no need for an umbrella; **p. des vivres pour un mois** to

take one month's supply of food; **quand prendrez-vous le colis?** when will you collect the parcel?

4 *(emmener)* to take (along); **l'inspecteur prit trois hommes avec lui** the inspector took three men with him; **je suis passé la p. chez elle à midi** I picked her up at *or* collected her from her home at 12 noon; **p. qn en voiture** to give sb a lift; **p. un auto-stoppeur** to give a hitchhiker a lift, to pick up a hitchhiker; **je fais p. les enfants à la sortie de l'école par la baby-sitter** I get the babysitter to pick the children up from school

5 *(trouver)* to get; **où as-tu pris ce couteau?** where did you get that knife (from)?; **où as-tu pris cette idée/cette citation/ces manières?** where did you get that idea/this quotation/those manners?; **où as-tu pris qu'on est plus heureux à la campagne?** where did you get the idea that people are happier in the country?

6 *(se procurer)* **p. des renseignements** to get some information

7 *(acheter → nourriture, billet de loterie)* to get, to buy; *(→ abonnement, assurance)* to take out; *(réserver → chambre d'hôtel, place de spectacle)* to book; **j'ai pris des artichauts pour ce soir** I've got *or* bought some artichokes for tonight; **je vais vous p. un petit poulet aujourd'hui** I'll have *or* take a small chicken today; **je ne prends plus de fruits au supermarché** I don't buy fruit at the supermarket any more

8 *(demander → argent)* to charge; **je prends une commission de 3 pour cent** I take a 3 percent commission; *Fam* **mon coiffeur ne prend pas cher** my hairdresser isn't too expensive *or* doesn't charge too much; **je prends 20 euros de l'heure** I charge 20 euros per hour; **elle l'a réparé sans rien nous p.** she fixed it free of charge *or* without charging us (anything) for it

9 *(retirer)* **les impôts sont pris à la source** tax is deducted at source; **p. de l'argent sur son compte** to withdraw money from one's account

B. *AVOIR RECOURS À, SE SERVIR DE* **1** *(utiliser → outil)* to use; **prends un marteau, ce sera plus facile** use a hammer, you'll find it's easier; **je ne prends jamais de dé pour coudre** I never use a thimble when I'm sewing; **ne prends pas ça, ça raye l'émail** don't use that, it scratches the enamel

2 *(emprunter)* to take, to borrow; **je peux p. ta voiture?** can I take *or* borrow your car?; **tu peux p. ma jupe** you can take *or* borrow my skirt

3 *(consommer → nourriture)* to eat; *(→ boisson)* to drink, to have; *(→ médicament)* to take; *(→ sucre)* to take; **je ne prends jamais de somnifères** I never take sleeping pills; **nous en discuterons en prenant le café** we'll discuss it over a cup of coffee; **tu prends du lait?** do you take milk?; **qu'est-ce que tu prends?** what would you like to drink?, what will it be?; **je prendrais bien une bière** I could do with a beer; **si on allait p. un verre** how about (going for) a drink?; **elle prend de la cocaïne** she takes cocaine; **à p. matin, midi et soir** to be taken three times a day; **elle n'a rien pris depuis trois jours** she hasn't eaten anything for three days; **tu leur as fait p. leurs médicaments?** did you make sure they took their medicine?

4 *(comme ingrédient)* to take; **p. 50 g de beurre et 200 g de farine** take 50 g of butter and 200 g of flour

5 *(se déplacer en)* to take, to go *or* to travel by; **p. l'avion** to take the plane, to fly; **p. le bateau** to take the boat, to sail; **p. le bus/le train** to take the bus/train, to go by bus/train; **p. un taxi** to take *or* to use a taxi; **je ne prends jamais la voiture** I never use the car; **elle prend sa bicyclette pour aller au travail** she goes to work on a bike, she cycles to work

6 *(monter dans → bus, train)* to catch, to get on; **elle a pris le vol suivant/le mauvais avion** she caught the next plane/got on the wrong plane

7 *(louer)* to take; **on a pris une chambre dans un petit hôtel** we took a room in a small hotel; **j'ai pris un petit studio** I rented a little studio *Br* flat *or Am* apartment

8 *(suivre → voie)* to take; **prends la première à droite** take the first (on the) right; **prenez la**

direction de Lille follow the signs for Lille; **j'ai pris un sens interdit** I drove down a one-way street

C. *PRENDRE POSSESSION DE, CONTRÔLER* **1** *(retenir par la force → fugitif)* to capture; *(→ prisonnier)* to take; *(→ animal)* to capture, to catch; *Mil (→ ville, position)* to take; **p. qn en otage** to take sb hostage; **les pêcheurs n'ont rien pris** the fishermen didn't catch anything

2 *(voler)* to take; **il a tout pris dans la maison** he took everything in the house; **p. une citation dans un livre** *(sans permission)* to lift *or* to poach a quotation from a book; **combien vous a-t-on pris?** how much was taken *or* stolen from you?; **elle m'a pris mon tour** she took my turn; **elle m'a pris mon idée/petit ami** she stole my idea/boyfriend; *Littéraire* **la mort lui a pris son fils** death has robbed him/her *or* deprived him/her of his/her son

3 *(occuper → temps)* to take (up), *Sout* to require; *(→ place)* to take (up); **il prenait le banc à lui tout seul** he was taking up all the space on the bench; **ça prend combien de temps pour y aller?** how long does it take to get there?; **ça (m')a pris deux heures** it took (me) two hours; **ça va te p. des heures de le coudre à la main!** it'll take you ages to sew it by hand!; **chercher un appartement prend du temps** *Br* flat-hunting *or Am* apartment-hunting is time-consuming

4 *(envahir → sujet: malaise, rage)* to come over; *(→ sujet: peur)* to seize, to take hold of; **quand ses quintes de toux le prennent** when he has a bout of coughing; **la fièvre du jeu la prit** she was gripped by gambling fever; **une douleur le prit dans le dos** he suddenly felt a twinge of pain in his back; **quand le doute me prend** when doubt gets a hold of me, when I am seized by doubt; **l'envie le** *ou* **lui prit d'aller nager** he felt like going for a swim; **je me suis laissé p. par le charme du lieu** I fell under the spell of the place; **qu'est-ce qui te prend?** what's wrong with *or* what's the matter with *or* what's come over you?; **qu'est-ce qui le** *ou* **lui prend de ne pas répondre?** why on earth isn't he answering?; *Fam* **ça te prend souvent?** do you make a habit of this?; *Fam* **quand ça le** *ou* **lui prend, il casse tout** when he gets into this state, he just smashes everything in sight; **il me prend parfois le désir de tout abandonner** I sometimes feel like giving it all up; **il est rentré chez lui et bien/mal lui en a pris** he went home and it was just as well he did/but he'd have done better to stay where he was; *très Fam* **ça me prend la tête** it's a real pain; **il me prend la tête** he's really getting on my nerves; **arrête de me p. la tête** stop being such a pain

5 *(surprendre → voleur, tricheur)* to catch; **si tu veux le voir, il faut le p. au saut du lit** if you want to see him, you must catch him as he gets up; **l'orage/la pluie nous a pris en rase campagne** the storm/rain crept up on us *or* caught us unawares in the open countryside; **ils se sont fait p. à la frontière** they were caught at the border; **p. qn à faire qch** to catch sb doing sth; **que je ne te prenne plus à écouter aux portes!** don't let me catch you listening at keyholes again!; **on ne me prendra plus à l'aider!** you'll never catch me helping him/her again!; **je t'y prends, petit galopin!** caught *or* got you, you little rascal!; **il se jura qu'on ne l'y prendrait plus** he swore to himself he'd never get caught again

6 *(pion, dame)* to take; **le roi prend la dame** the King is higher than *or* takes the Queen

7 *Sport* **p. le service de qn** to break sb's service; **il est venu p. la deuxième place** *(pendant la course)* he moved into second place; *(à l'arrivée)* he came in second

8 *Fam (affronter → adversaire)* to take on; **demain, je te prends aux échecs** tomorrow I'll take you on at *or* play you at chess

D. *ADMETTRE, RECEVOIR* **1** *(recevoir)* **le docteur ne pourra pas vous p. avant demain** the doctor won't be able to see you before tomorrow; **après 22 heures, nous ne prenons plus de clients** after 10 p.m., we don't let any more customers in

2 *(cours)* to take

3 *(accueillir → pensionnaire, locataire)* to take in; *(→ passager)* to take; *(admettre par règlement)* to take, to allow; *(engager → employé, candidat)* to take on; **le lycée prend des pensionnaires** the school takes boarders; **le ferry/train ne prend que les passagers qui ont réservé** the ferry/train only takes passengers with reservations; **nous ne pouvons pas p. votre chien à bord** we can't allow your dog on board; **nous ne prenons pas les cartes de crédit/les bagages en cabine** we don't take credit cards/cabin baggage; **après son opération, je le prendrai dans mon service** after his operation, I'll have him transferred to my department; **p. un comptable** to take on *or* to hire an accountant; **ils ne prennent que des gens qui ont de l'expérience** they only take *or* employ *or* use experienced people; **p. qn à titre d'essai** *ou* **à l'essai** to take sb (on) *or* to employ sb on a trial basis; **p. qn comme stagiaire** to take sb on as a trainee; **on l'a prise comme assistante de direction** she's been taken on as (an) executive assistant

4 *(acquérir, gagner)* **p. de l'avance/du retard** to be earlier/later than scheduled; **j'ai pris trois centimètres de tour de taille** I've put on three centimetres round the waist; **quand le gâteau commence à p. une jolie couleur dorée** when the cake starts to take on a nice golden colour; **le projet commence à p. forme** *ou* **tournure** the project's starting to take shape

5 *(terminaison)* to take; **"gaz" ne prend pas d's au pluriel** "gaz" doesn't take an s in the plural; **ça prend un e au féminin** it takes an e in the feminine (form); **le a prend un accent circonflexe** there's a circumflex on the a

6 *(subir)* to get; **p. un coup de soleil** to get sunburnt; *Vieilli* **p. froid** *ou* **du mal** to catch *or* to get a cold; *Fam* **tu vas p. une fessée/claque!** you'll get a smack/a clout!; **p. des coups de pied** to get kicked; *Sport & Fig* **il prend bien les coups** he can take a lot of punishment; **j'ai pris la tuile en plein sur la tête** the tile hit me right on the head; *Fam* **c'est elle qui a tout pris** *(coups, reproches)* she got the worst *or* took the brunt of it; *(éclaboussures)* she got most *or* the worst of it; *Fam* **qu'est-ce qu'on a pris!, on a pris quelque chose!** *(averse)* we got soaked *or* drenched!; *(réprimande)* we got a real dressing down!; *(critique)* we got panned!; *(défaite)* we got thrashed!; *Fam* **qu'est-ce que le gouvernement a pris dans les journaux du matin!** the government got a roasting in the morning papers!; *Fam* **il en a pris pour 15 ans** he got 15 years, he got put away for 15 years

E. *CONSIDÉRER DE TELLE MANIÈRE* **1** *(accepter)* to take; **il faut p. les choses comme elles viennent/sont** you've got to take things as they come/are; **il a essayé de le p. avec le sourire** *ou* **en souriant** he tried to pass it off with a smile; **elle a pris sa défaite avec le sourire** she accepted her defeat with a smile; **bien/mal p. qch** to take sth well/badly; **elle prend très mal la critique** she doesn't take kindly to being criticized

2 *(interpréter)* to take; **ne prends pas ça pour toi** *(ne te sens pas visé)* don't take it personally; **p. qch en bien/en mal** to take sth as a compliment/badly; **elle a pris mon silence pour de la désapprobation** she took my silence as a criticism; **c'est ce qu'il a dit, prends-le pour ce que ça vaut** that's what he said, (take it) for what it's worth

3 *(considérer)* to take, to consider; **prenons un exemple** let's take *or* consider an example; **prends Pierre, il n'est pas brillant, et pourtant il a réussi** take Pierre, he's not very bright but he's got on in life; **p. qn en amitié** to grow fond of sb; **p. qn en pitié** to take pity on sb; **j'ai pris cette maison en horreur** I grew to loathe that house; **p. qn/qch pour** *(par méprise)* to mistake sb/sth for; *(volontairement)* to take sb/sth for, to consider sb/sth to be; **on me prend souvent pour ma sœur** I'm often mistaken for my sister; **je vous avais pris pour Robert** I thought you were Robert; **de dos, on pourrait le p. pour mon mari** seen from behind, you could mistake him for my husband; **pour qui me prenez-vous?** what do you take me for?, who do you

think I am?; **tu me prends pour ta bonne?** do you think I'm your maid?; **elle va me p. pour un idiot** she'll think I'm a fool; **p. qn/qch comme** to take sb/sth as; **p. qch comme excuse** to use *or* to take sth as an excuse; **p. un monument comme point de repère** to use a monument as a landmark; **à tout p.** all in all, by and large, all things considered; **à tout p., je préférerais le faire moi-même** all things considered I'd rather do it myself

4 *(traiter → personne)* to handle, to deal with; **p. qn par la douceur** to use gentle persuasion on sb; **elle sait très bien p. les enfants** she knows how to handle children; *Mil & Fig* **p. l'ennemi de front/à revers** to tackle the enemy head on/from the rear

F. *ENREGISTRER* **1** *(consigner → notes)* to take *or* to write down; *(→ empreintes, mesures, température, tension)* to take; **je n'ai pas eu le temps de p. son numéro** I didn't have time to take (down) his/her number; **je peux p. jusqu'à 90 mots par minute** I can take down up to 90 words per minute; **p. les dimensions d'une pièce** to measure a room; **p. les mensurations d'un client** to take a customer's measurements

2 *Phot* **p. qn/qch (en photo)** to take a picture *or* photo *or* photograph of sb/sth; **ne prends pas la tour, elle est affreuse** don't take (a picture of) the tower, it's hideous

G. *DÉCIDER DE, ADOPTER* **1** *(s'octroyer → vacances)* to take, to have; *(→ bain, douche)* to have, to take; **p. un jour de congé** to take *or* to have the day off; **p. un congé maternité** to take maternity leave; **p. du repos** to rest, to have a rest; **p. du bon temps** to have fun *or* a good time; **p. le temps de faire qch** to take the time to do sth; **p. son temps** to take one's time; **p. un amant** to take a lover; **tu n'as pas le droit! – je le prends!** you've no right! – that's what you think!

2 *(s'engager dans → mesure, risque)* to take; **p. une décision** *(gén)* to make a decision; *(après avoir hésité)* to make up one's mind, to come to a decision; **p. la décision de faire qch** to make up one's mind to do sth, to decide to do sth; **p. l'initiative** to take the initiative; **p. l'initiative de qch** to initiate sth; **p. l'initiative de faire qch** to take the initiative in doing sth, to take it upon oneself to do sth; **p. une (bonne) résolution** to make a (good) resolution; **p. de bonnes résolutions pour l'avenir** to resolve to do better in the future; **p. la résolution de faire qch** to resolve to do sth

3 *(choisir → sujet d'examen, cadeau)* to take, to choose, to have; **j'ai pris le docteur Valiet comme médecin** I chose Dr Valiet to be *or* as my GP; **je prends la cravate rouge** I'll take *or* have the red tie; **je ne sais pas quel poster p. pour elle** I don't know which poster to choose *or* to buy for her; **qu'est-ce qu'on lui prend comme glace?** which ice cream shall we get him/her?; **ils n'ont pris que les 20 premiers** they only took *or* selected the top 20; **c'est à p. ou à laisser** (you can) take it or leave it; **il y a à p. et à laisser dans son livre** his book is good in parts *or Br* is a bit of a curate's egg

4 *(se charger de → poste)* to take, to accept; **p. ses fonctions** to start work; *Fam* **j'ai fini par p. des ménages** in the end I took on some cleaning jobs; **j'ai un appel pour toi, tu le prends?** I've got a call for you, will you take it?

5 *(adopter → air)* to put on, to assume; *(→ ton)* to assume; **elle a pris de grands airs pour me le dire** she told me very condescendingly; **il avait pris une voix doucereuse** he'd assumed a suave tone

USAGE ABSOLU 1 *Cartes* **je prends** I'll try it; **j'ai pris à cœur** I went hearts

2 *Fam (subir)* **quand les deux frères font une bêtise, c'est toujours l'aîné qui prend** when the two brothers have been up to some mischief, the eldest always gets the blame▪ *or* gets it in the neck; **c'est toujours les mêmes qui prennent!** they always pick on the same ones!, it's always the same ones who get it in the neck!

VI 1 *(se fixer durablement → végétal)* to take (root); *(→ bouture, greffe, vaccin)* to take; *(→ mode, slogan)* to catch on; **la peinture ne prend pas sur le plastique** the plastic won't take the paint; **ça ne prendra pas avec elle** *(mensonge)* it won't work with her, she won't be taken in; *Fam* **ça prend pas!** give me a break!, yeah right!, *Br* pull the other one!

2 *(durcir → crème, ciment, colle)* to set; *(→ lac, étang)* to freeze (over); *(→ mayonnaise)* to thicken

3 *(passer)* **prends à gauche** *(tourne à gauche)* turn left; **tu peux p. par Le Mans** you can go via Le Mans; **p. à travers bois/champs** to cut through the woods/fields

4 *(commencer)* to start, to get going; **le feu a pris dans la grange** the fire started in the barn; **je n'arrive pas à faire p. le feu/les brindilles** I can't get the fire going/the twigs to catch; **le sapin prend bien** pine is easy to get going *or* to light

5 *Mus & Théât* **prenons avant la sixième mesure/à la scène 2** let's take it from just before bar six/from scene 2

▫ **prendre sur VT IND 1** *(entamer)* to use (some of); **désolé d'avoir pris sur votre temps d'antenne** sorry to have encroached on *or* cut into your air time; **p. sur son capital pour payer qch** to use some of *or* to dig into one's capital to pay for sth; **je ne prendrai pas sur mon week-end pour finir le travail!** I'm not going to give up *or* to sacrifice part of my weekend to finish the job!; **après quelques jours sans nourriture, l'organisme prend sur ses réserves** after a few days without food, the body starts using up its reserves

2 *(locutions)* **p. sur soi** to grin and bear it; **p. sur soi de faire qch** to take (it) upon oneself to do sth

▸**se prendre VPR 1** *(emploi passif)* **ces cachets se prennent avant les repas** these tablets should be taken before meals

2 *(emploi réciproque)* **ils se sont pris pour époux** they were united in matrimony

3 *(se coincer → emploi passif)* to get caught *or* trapped; **le foulard s'est pris dans la portière** the scarf got caught *or* shut in the door

4 *(se coincer → personne)* **attention, tu vas te p. les doigts dans la charnière!** careful, you'll trap your fingers *or* get your fingers caught in the hinge!; **se p. les pieds dans qch** to trip over sth

5 *Fam (choisir)* **se p. qch** to get sth for oneself; **prends-toi un gâteau** get yourself a cake; **elle s'est pris un nouvel amant** she's taken a new lover

6 *(se laisser aller)* **se p. à qch** to get (drawn) into sth; **on se prend au charme de sa musique** you gradually succumb to the charm of his/her music; **se p. à faire qch** to find oneself starting to do sth; **se p. à rêver** to find oneself dreaming; **je me pris à l'aimer/le haïr** I found myself falling in love with him/starting to hate him

7 se p. d'amitié pour qn to feel a growing affection for sb

8 *(se considérer)* **elle se prend pour une artiste/un génie** she likes to think she's an artist/a genius; **il ne se prend pas pour rien** *ou* **pour n'importe qui** he thinks he's God's gift to humanity; **tu te prends pour qui pour me parler sur ce ton?** who do you think you are, talking to me like that?

9 s'en p. à qn/qch *(l'attaquer)* to attack sb/sth; *(le rendre responsable)* to put the blame on sb/sth; **pourquoi faut-il toujours que tu t'en prennes à moi?** why do you always take it out on me?; **l'équipe perd un match et l'on s'en prend tout de suite à l'entraîneur** the team loses a match and the coach automatically gets the blame; **ne t'en prends qu'à toi-même** you've only (got) yourself to blame; **s'en p. à une institution/un système** *(l'accuser)* to put the blame on an institution/a system; *(le critiquer)* to attack an institution/a system

10 *(locutions)* **comment pourrions-nous nous y p.?** how could we go about it?; **tu t'y prends un peu tard pour t'inscrire!** you've left it a bit late to enrol!; **il faut s'y p. deux mois à l'avance pour avoir des places** you have to book two months in advance to be sure of getting seats; **elle s'y est prise à trois fois pour faire démarrer la tondeuse** she made three attempts before the lawnmower would start; **s'y p. bien/mal avec qn** to handle sb the right/wrong way; **elle s'y prend bien** *ou* **sait s'y p. avec les enfants** she's good with children; **si tu t'y prends bien avec lui** if you get on the right side of him; **je n'arrive pas à repasser le col – c'est parce que tu t'y prends mal** I can't iron the collar properly – that's because you're going about it the wrong way *or* doing it wrong

---

preneur, -euse [prənœr, -øz] **NM,F 1** *(acheteur)* buyer; *(d'un chèque, d'une lettre de change)* payee; **trouver p. pour qch** to find someone (willing) to buy sth, to find a buyer for sth; **si vous me le laissez à 20 euros, je suis p.** I'll buy it if you'll take 20 euros for it

2 *(locataire)* lessee, leaseholder

3 *(ravisseur)* **p. d'otages** hostage-taker

▫ **preneur de son, preneuse de son NM,F** sound engineer, sound technician

prenne *etc voir* **prendre**

prénom [prenɔ̃] **NM** first *or Am* given name

prénommé, -e [prenɔme] **ADJ un garçon p. Julien** a boy called *or esp Am* named Julien; *aussi Hum* **la prénommée Maria** the said Maria

NM,F *Jur* above-named (person); **le p.** the above-named

prénommer [3] [prenɔme] **VT** to call, *esp Am* to name; **si c'est une fille, nous la prénommerons Léa** if it's a girl, we'll call *or* name her Léa

▸**se prénommer VPR comment se prénomme-t-il?** what's his first name?; **il se prénomme Robin** his first name is Robin

prénotion [prenosjɔ̃] **NF** *(en sociologie) & Phil* prenotion

prénuptial, -e, -aux, -ales [prenypsjal, -o] **ADJ** premarital, antenuptial; **examen p.** premarital medical check

préoccupant, -e [preɔkypɑ̃, -ɑ̃t] **ADJ** worrying; **la situation est préoccupante** the situation gives cause for concern *or* is worrying

préoccupation [preɔkypasjɔ̃] **NF 1** *(souci)* concern, worry; **le chômage reste notre p. première** unemployment remains our major cause for concern; **ceux pour qui l'argent n'est pas une p.** those who don't have to worry about money *or* who don't have money worries; **j'ai d'autres préoccupations** I have other things to worry about; **j'ai été un sujet de p. pour mes parents** I was a worry to my parents; **préoccupations d'ordre moral/esthétique** moral/aesthetic considerations

2 *(priorité)* concern, preoccupation; **ma seule p. est de divertir le public** my only concern *or* sole preoccupation is to keep the audience entertained; **depuis qu'elle est partie, il n'a plus qu'une p., la retrouver** since she left his one thought is to find her again

préoccupé, -e [preɔkype] **ADJ** *(inquiet)* worried, preoccupied, concerned; **elle avait l'air p.** she looked worried, there was a look of concern on her face; **d'un ton p.** in a worried tone

préoccuper [3] [preɔkype] **VT 1** *(tracasser → sujet: avenir, question)* to worry; **sa santé me préoccupe** I'm worried *or* anxious *or* concerned about his/her health; **son avenir professionnel n'a pas l'air de la p.** she doesn't seem to be concerned about her career, her career doesn't seem to worry her

2 *(obséder)* to preoccupy, to concern, to be of concern to; **l'environnement est un sujet qui nous préoccupe beaucoup** we are deeply concerned with environmental issues; **le foot est tout ce qui le préoccupe** football is all he thinks about; **il est trop préoccupé de sa petite personne** he's too wrapped up in himself

▸**se préoccuper VPR se p. de** to be concerned with, to care about; **se p. de l'avenir** to care about the future; **se p. de ses enfants** to worry about one's children; **il ne s'est pas beaucoup préoccupé de savoir si j'allais bien** he didn't bother himself much to find out if I was all right; **ne te préoccupe donc pas de ça!** don't you worry *or* bother about that!

préœdipien, -enne [preødipjɛ̃, -ɛn] **ADJ** *Psy* pre-Oedipal

préolympique [preɔlɛ̃pik] **ADJ** pre-Olympic

préopératoire [preɔperatwar] **ADJ** preoperative, presurgical, *Fam* preop

préoral, -e, -aux, -ales [preɔral, -o] **ADJ** *Zool* preoral

prépa [prepa] **NF** *Fam Univ* = class preparing for the competitive entrance exam to a "grande école"; **faire une p., être en p.** = to be studying for the entrance exam to a "grande école"

prépaiement [prepɛmɑ̃] **NM** prepayment

préparamétré, -e [preparametre] **ADJ** *Ordinat* pre-configured

préparateur, -trice [preparatœr, -tris] **NM,F 1** *Univ* = assistant to a professor of science **2** *Pharm* **p. en pharmacie** assistant to a dispensing *Br* chemist *or Am* pharmacist

préparatifs [preparatif] **NMPL** preparations; **p. de départ/guerre** preparations for leaving/war; **commencer les p. du voyage** to start preparing for the trip; **j'étais en pleins p. de départ quand...** I was in the middle of preparing *or* getting ready to leave when...

préparation [preparasjɔ̃] **NF 1** (*réalisation → d'un plat, d'un médicament*) preparation; (*apprêt → d'une peau, de la laine*) dressing; **les moules ne demandent pas une longue p.** mussels don't take long to prepare

2 (*organisation → d'un voyage, d'une fête, d'un attentat*) preparation; **la randonnée avait fait l'objet d'une soigneuse p.** the ramble had been carefully thought out *or* prepared

3 (*entraînement → pour un examen*) preparation; (*→ pour une épreuve sportive*) training, preparation; **la p. d'un examen** preparing *or* working for an exam; **manquer de p.** to be insufficiently prepared; *Mil* **p. d'artillerie** initial artillery bombardment; **p. militaire** pre-call-up training

4 (*chose préparée*) preparation; **p. culinaire** dish; **p. pour gâteau/sauce** cake/sauce mix; **p. (pharmaceutique)** (pharmaceutical) preparation

5 *Scol* **faire une p. à une grande école** = to be studying for the entrance exam to a "grande école"

6 *Vieilli* (*exercice*) exercise; (*fait à la maison*) homework; **as-tu fait ta p. latine?** did you do your Latin homework?

7 *Mines* **p. mécanique** mechanical processing **8** *Beaux-Arts* primer

❑ **en préparation ADV** being prepared, in hand; **avoir un livre/disque en p.** to have a book/record in the pipeline

❑ **sans préparation ADV** (*courir*) without preparation, cold; (*parler*) extempore, ad lib; **tu ne peux pas le lui dire sans p.** you can't tell him/her just like that

préparatoire [preparatwar] **ADJ** **travail p.** groundwork; **p. à** preparatory to, in preparation for

préparer [3] [prepare] **VT 1** (*réaliser → plat, sandwich*) to prepare, to make; (*→ médicament, cataplasme*) to prepare; **qu'est-ce que tu nous as préparé de bon?** what delicious dish have you cooked for us?; **plats tout préparés** pre-cooked *or* ready-cooked meals

2 (*rendre prêt → valise*) to pack; (*→ repas, chambre, champ*) to prepare, to get ready; (*→ poisson, poulet*) to prepare, to dress; (*→ peaux, laine*) to dress; (*→ document*) to prepare, to draw up; (*→ ordonnance*) to make up; **préparez la monnaie, s'il vous plaît** please have change ready; **poulet tout préparé** oven-ready *or* dressed chicken; *Fam* **on dirait qu'il nous prépare une rougeole** (it) looks like he's getting the measles; **p. le terrain (pour)** to prepare the ground *or* to lay the ground (for); *Fig* to pave the way (for)

3 (*organiser → attentat, conférence*) to prepare, to organize; (*→ vacances*) to plan, to arrange; (*→ complot*) to prepare, to hatch; **p. un coup** to be hatching something, to be cooking something up; **je suis sûr qu'il nous prépare quelque chose** I'm sure he's up to something; **elle avait bien préparé son histoire** she'd got her story off to a T; **elle avait préparé sa réponse** she'd got her *or* an answer ready; **p. une surprise à qn** to have a surprise in store for sb

4 (*travailler à → œuvre*) to be preparing, to be working on; (*→ examen*) to be preparing for;

(*→ épreuve sportive*) to be in training for; (*→ discours*) to prepare; *Fam* **tu as préparé quelque chose en géographie?** did you prepare *or* revise any geography?" ; **il prépare une grande école** he's studying for the entrance exam to a "grande école"

5 (*former → élève*) to prepare; (*→ athlète*) to train; **p. qn à qch** (*examen*) to prepare sb for sth; (*épreuve sportive*) to train sb for sth; **on les prépare intensivement à l'examen** they're being coached for the exam; **rien ne m'avait préparé à ce type de problème** nothing had prepared me for this kind of problem

6 (*habituer*) to accustom; **nous avons préparé les enfants à l'idée qu'ils vont changer d'école** we've got the children used to the idea of changing schools

▸ **se préparer VPR 1** (*s'apprêter*) to get ready; **le temps qu'elle se prépare, on aura raté la séance** by the time she's ready, we'll have missed the show; **se p. à qch/à faire qch** to prepare *or* to get ready for sth/to do sth; **se p. au combat** to prepare for action *or* combat; **nous nous préparions à répondre à ses critiques** we got ready to reply to his/her criticism

2 (*s'entraîner*) to train; **se p. pour Roland-Garros** to train *or* to prepare for the French Open tennis tournament

3 (*être sur le point d'arriver*) **un orage se prépare** there's a storm brewing; **je sens qu'il se prépare quelque chose** I can feel there's something afoot *or* in the air

4 (*pour soi-même*) **se p. un café** to make oneself a coffee; **tu te prépares bien des ennuis/des désillusions** you're in for trouble/a disappointment

5 se p. à qch (*être disposé à*) to be ready *or* prepared for sth; **préparez-vous à vous faire tremper!** be ready *or* prepared to get soaked!; **je ne m'étais pas préparé à un tel accueil** I wasn't prepared for *or* I wasn't expecting such a welcome

6 se p. à faire qch (*être sur le point de*) to be about to do sth; **on se préparait à passer à table** we were about to sit down to eat

prépayé, -e [prepeje] **ADJ** prepaid

prépayer [11] [prepeje] **VT** to pay in advance, to prepay

prépension [prepɑ̃sjɔ̃] **NF** *Belg* early retirement

prépensionné, -e [prepɑ̃sjɔne] **NM,F** *Belg* = person who has taken or been given early retirement

préplanification [preplanifikasjɔ̃] **NF** preplanning

prépondérance [prepɔ̃derɑ̃s] **NF** predominance, primacy (**sur** over)

prépondérant, -e [prepɔ̃derɑ̃, -ɑ̃t] **ADJ** predominant; **jouer un rôle p.** to play a prominent part *or* role; **sa voix sera prépondérante** he/she will have the casting vote

préposé, -e [prepoze] **NM,F 1** (*employé*) **p. des douanes** customs official *or* officer; **p. à la caisse** cashier; **p. au vestiaire** cloakroom attendant **2** *Admin* **p. (des postes)** *Br* postman, *Am* mailman **3** *Jur* agent

préposer [3] [prepoze] **VT** (*affecter*) **p. qn à** to place *or* to put sb in charge of; **il a été préposé à l'accueil** he was put in charge of reception

prépositif, -ive [prepozitif, -iv] = **prépositionnel**

préposition [prepozisjɔ̃] **NF** preposition

prépositionnel, -elle [prepozisjɔnɛl] **ADJ** *Gram* prepositional

prépositive [prepozitiv] *voir* **prépositif**

prépositivement [prepozitivmɑ̃] **ADV** *Gram* prepositionally; **adverbe employé p.** adverb used as a preposition

prépresse [prepres] **NM** *Typ* pre-press

préproduction [preprɔdyksjɔ̃] **NF** *Cin & TV* pre-production

préprogrammé, -e [preprɔgrame] **ADJ** *Ordinat* preprogrammed

préprogrammer [3] [preprɔgrame] **VT** *Ordinat* to preprogram

prépsychose [prepsikoz] **NF** prepsychosis

prépsychotique [prepsikɔtik] **ADJ** prepsychotic **NMF** prepsychotic

prépubère [prepybɛr] **ADJ** prepubescent

prépublication [prepyblikasjɔ̃] **NF** prepublication

prépuce [prepys] **NM** foreskin, *Spéc* prepuce

préraphaélisme [prerafaelism] **NM** *Beaux-Arts* Pre-Raphaelism

préraphaélite [prerafaelit] *Beaux-Arts* **ADJ** Pre-Raphaelite **NMF** Pre-Raphaelite

préréglage [preregla ʒ] **NM** *Tech* preselection, presetting

prérégler [18] [preregle] **VT** *Tech* to preselect, to preset

prérentrée [prerɑ̃tre] **NF** *Scol* = start of the new school year for teachers (a few days before the pupils)

prérequis, -e [preʀəki, -iz] *Belg* **ADJ** (*préalable → travail, formation*) preparatory; (*requis → connaissance*) required **NM** (*condition préalable*) prerequisite, precondition; (*connaissance requise*) required knowledge

préretraite [preʀətʀɛt] **NF 1** (*allocation*) early retirement allowance **2** (*période*) early retirement; **partir en p.** to take early retirement; **être mis en p.** to be retired early; **elle est en p.** she's taken early retirement

préretraité, -e [preʀətʀɛte] **NM,F** = person who has taken *or* who has been given early retirement

prérévolutionnaire [preʀevolysjɔnɛr] **ADJ** prerevolutionary

prérogative [prerɔgativ] **NF** prerogative, privilege

préroman, -e [prerɔmɑ̃, -an] **ADJ** pre-Romanesque

préromantique [prerɔmɑ̃tik] **ADJ** pre-Romantic **NMF** pre-Romantic (*poet or artist*)

préromantisme [prerɔmɑ̃tism] **NM** pre-Romanticism

PRÈS [pʀɛ] **ADV 1** (*dans l'espace*) near, close; **cent mètres plus p.** one hundred metres nearer *or* closer; **aussi p. que** as near *or* close as; **le bureau est tout p.** the office is very near *or* just around the corner

2 (*dans le temps*) near, close, soon; **Noël, c'est tout p. maintenant** it'll be Christmas very soon now, Christmas will be here very soon now; **jeudi c'est trop p., disons plutôt samedi** Thursday is too soon, let's say Saturday

PRÉP ambassadeur p. le Saint-Siège ambassador to the Holy See; **expert p. la chambre de commerce** expert (appointed) to the Chamber of Commerce

❑ **à... près ADV c'est parfait, à un détail p.** it's perfect but for *or* except for one thing; **j'ai raté mon train à quelques secondes p.** I missed my train by a few seconds; **vous n'en êtes plus à un procès p.** what's one more trial to you?; **on n'est pas à cinq euros p.** we can spare five euros; **tu n'es plus à cinq minutes p.** another five minutes won't make much difference

❑ **à cela près que CONJ** except that; **tout s'est bien passé, à cela p. que j'ai perdu mon portefeuille** everything went well except that I lost my wallet

❑ **à peu de choses près ADV** more or less; **à peu de choses p., il y en a 50** there are 50 of them, more or less *or* give or take a few

❑ **à peu près ADV 1** (*environ*) about, around; **il habite à peu p. à dix kilomètres** he lives about *or* around ten kilometres away; **il est à peu p. cinq heures** it's about *or* around five o'clock; **on était à peu p. 50** there were about *or* around 50 of us

2 (*plus ou moins*) more or less; **il sait à peu p. comment y aller** he knows more or less *or* roughly how to get there

❑ **de près ADV** at close range *or* quarters; **elle y voit mal de p.** she can't see very well close up *or* at close range; **il est rasé de p.** he's clean-shaven; **surveiller qn de p.** to keep a close watch *or* eye on sb; **frôler qch de p.** to come within an inch of sth; **les explosions se sont suivies de très p.** the explosions took place within seconds of each other; **ses enfants se suivent de p.** his/her children are close together in age; **regarder qch de (très) p.** to look at sth very closely; *Fig* to look (very) closely at sth, to look carefully into sth; **avant de donner de l'argent pour la recherche, il faut y regarder de p.** before giving money away for research, you must look into it carefully; **étudions la question de plus p.** let's take a closer look at the problem; **de p. ou de loin** however *or* whichever way you look at it;

cela ressemble, de p. ou de loin, à une habile escroquerie however *or* whichever way you look at it, it's a skilful piece of fraud; **tout ce qui touche, de p. ou de loin à...** everything (which is) even remotely connected with...

❑ **près de** PRÉP **1** *(dans l'espace)* near; **il habite p. de Paris** he lives near Paris; **ils habitent p. d'ici** they live near here; **il vit p. de chez moi** he lives near me; **assieds-toi p. de lui** sit near him *or* next to him; *Naut* **naviguer p. du vent** to sail close to the wind; **vêtements p. du corps** close-fitting *or* tight-fitting clothes

2 *(affectivement, qualitativement)* close to; **il a toujours été p. de ses parents** he's always been close to his parents; **les premiers candidats sont très p. les uns des autres** there's very little difference between the first few candidates; **ce comportement est plus p. de la bêtise que de la méchanceté** this behaviour is more like *or* closer to stupidity than malice; **être p. de ses sous** *ou* **de son argent** to be tightfisted

3 *(dans le temps)* **Noël est trop p. du jour de l'an** Christmas is too close to New Year's Day; **on est p. des vacances** it's nearly the holidays; **il doit être p. de la retraite** he must be about to retire; **nous étions p. de partir** we were about to leave; **vous êtes p. d'avoir deviné** you've nearly guessed; **je ne suis pas p. d'oublier ça** I'm not about to *or* it'll be a long time before I forget that; **je ne suis pas p. de me remarier** I'm not about *or* in no hurry to get married again; **ils ne sont pas p. de me revoir dans leur restaurant!** I shan't visit their restaurant again in a hurry!

4 *(environ, presque)* nearly, almost; **cela fait p. d'un mois qu'il est absent** he's been gone for almost a month; **il est p. de midi** it's nearly midday; **on était p. de 50** there were almost *or* nearly 50 of us; **ça nous a coûté p. de 100 euros** it cost us nearly 100 euros

présage [prezaʒ] NM **1** *(signe)* omen, *Littéraire* portent; **heureux/mauvais p.** good/bad omen; **j'y ai vu le p. d'un avenir meilleur** I viewed it as a sign of better days to come **2** *(prédiction)* prediction; **tirer un p. de qch** to make a prediction on the basis of sth

présager [17] [prezaʒe] VT **1** *(être le signe de)* to be a sign of, *Littéraire* to portend; **cela ne présage rien de bon** that doesn't bode well **2** *(prévoir)* to predict; **je n'aurais pu p. qu'il en arriverait à cette extrémité** I would never have guessed that he would go so far; **laisser p. qch** to be a sign of sth

présalaire [presalɛr] NM = allowance paid to students

pré-salé [presale] *(pl* **prés-salés***)* NM *(mouton)* salt-meadow sheep; *(viande)* salt-meadow *or* pré-salé lamb; **un gigot de p.** a salt-meadow leg of lamb

presbyophrénie [prɛsbjɔfreni] NF *Méd* presbyophrenia

presbyopie [prɛsbjɔpi] NF *Opt Br* longsightedness, *Am* farsightedness, *Spéc* presbyopia

presbyte [prɛsbit] *Opt* ADJ *Br* longsighted, *Am* farsighted, *Spéc* presbyopic

NMF *Br* longsighted *or Am* farsighted person, *Spéc* presbyope

presbytéral, -e, -aux, -ales [prɛsbiteral, -o] ADJ presbyteral, presbyterial, priestly

presbytère [prɛsbitɛr] NM presbytery

presbytérianisme [prɛsbiterjanism] NM Presbyterianism

presbytérien, -enne [prɛsbiterjɛ̃, -ɛn] ADJ Presbyterian

NM,F Presbyterian

presbyterium [prɛsbitɛrjɔm] NM presbytery

presbytie [prɛsbisi] NF *Opt Br* longsightedness, *Am* farsightedness, *Spéc* presbyopia

prescience [presjɑ̃s] NF **1** *(pressentiment)* foreknowledge, foresight, *Littéraire* prescience; **avoir la p. de qch** to have a premonition of sth **2** *Rel* prescience

prescient, -e [presjɑ̃, -ɑ̃t] ADJ *Littéraire* prescient

préscientifique [presjɑ̃tifik] ADJ prescientific

préscolaire [preskɔlɛr] ADJ preschool *(avant n)*

préscolarisation [preskɔlarisasjɔ̃] NF preschool education

prescripteur, -trice [prɛskriptœr, -tris] NM,F prescriber; *Mktg* opinion leader

prescriptible [prɛskriptibl] ADJ *Jur* prescriptible

prescription [prɛskripsjɔ̃] NF **1** *Jur* prescription; **p. de la peine** lapse *or* lapsing of the sentence; **y a-t-il p. pour les crimes de guerre?** is there a statutory limitation relating to war crimes?; *Fig* **il y a p.** it's all in the past now; **p. de l'action publique** = time limit after which a prosecution may not be brought; **p. acquisitive** positive *or* acquisitive prescription; **p. civile** prescription; **p. extinctive** negative prescription; **p. légale** statute of limitations

2 *(instruction)* **se conformer aux prescriptions** to conform to instructions *or* regulations; **les prescriptions de la morale** moral dictates

3 *Méd (ordonnance)* prescription; **il ne doit pas y avoir p. d'antibiotiques dans ce cas** antibiotics should not be prescribed in this case; **prescriptions** *(recommandations)* orders, instructions

prescriptrice [prɛskriptris] *voir* **prescripteur**

prescrire [99] [prɛskrir] VT **1** *(recommander)* to prescribe; **p. qch à qn** to prescribe sth for sb; **on lui a prescrit du repos** he/she was ordered to rest; **p. à qn de faire qch** to order sb to do sth

2 *(stipuler)* to prescribe, to stipulate; **accomplir les formalités que prescrit le règlement** to go through the procedures stipulated in the regulations; **ce que l'honneur prescrit** the demands *or* dictates of honour

3 *Jur (propriété)* to obtain by prescription; *(sanction, peine)* to lapse; **il faut 20 ans pour p. la peine** the sentence only lapses after 20 years

USAGE ABSOLU *Jur* **on ne prescrit pas contre les mineurs** one cannot obtain property from minors by prescription

▸**se prescrire** VPR *Jur (s'acquérir)* to be obtained by prescription; *(se périmer)* to lapse; **la peine se prescrit par cinq ans** the penalty lapses after five years

prescrit, -e [prɛskri, -it] ADJ **1** *(conseillé → dose)* prescribed, recommended; **agir dans les limites prescrites** to act within prescribed limits **2** *(fixé)* **au jour p.** on the set day; **à la date prescrite** on the date laid down, on the prescribed date; **à l'heure prescrite** at the agreed hour; **dans le délai p.** within the agreed time

NM *Belg Jur & Fig* prescription

prescrivait *etc voir* **prescrire**

préséance [preseɑ̃s] NF **1** *(priorité)* precedence, priority (**sur** over); **avoir la p. sur qn** to have precedence over sb **2** *(étiquette)* **la p. veut qu'on le serve avant vous** according to (the rules of) etiquette, he should be served before you

présélecteur [preselɛktœr] NM *Tech* preselector

présélection [preselɛksjɔ̃] NF **1** *(premier choix)* short-listing **2** *Aut* **boîte de vitesses à p.** preselector gearbox **3** *Rad* **poste avec/sans p.** radio with/without preset

présélectionné, -e [preselɛksjɔne] NM,F short-listed candidate

présélectionner [3] [preselɛksjɔne] VT **1** *(faire un premier choix parmi)* to short-list **2** *(fixer à l'avance → heure, programme)* to preset, to preselect

présence [prezɑ̃s] NF **1** *(fait d'être là)* presence; **si ma p. vous gêne, je peux partir** if my presence disturbs you, I can leave; **j'ignorais ta p.** I didn't know you were here; **je sentais une p. derrière moi** I could feel a presence behind me; **merci de nous avoir honorés de votre p.** thank you for honouring us with your presence; **cela s'est passé hors de ma p.** I wasn't present when it happened; **faire acte de p., faire de la p.** to put in an appearance; **réunion à neuf heures, p. obligatoire** meeting at nine o'clock, attendance compulsory; **p. assidue aux cours** regular attendance in class; **p. policière** police presence

2 *(existence)* presence; **la p. de sang dans les urines** the presence of blood in the urine; **expliquez-moi la p. de cette arme ici** explain to me how this weapon comes to be here

3 *Théât (personnalité)* presence; **avoir de la p.** to have great presence; **il n'a aucune p. sur scène** he has no stage presence whatsoever

4 *(influence)* presence; **la p. française en Afrique** the French presence in Africa

5 *Rel* **p. réelle** real presence

❑ **en présence** ADJ **1** *(en opposition)* **les armées/équipes en p.** the opposing armies/teams **2** *Jur* **les parties en p.** the opposing parties, *Spéc* the litigants ADV **mettre deux personnes en p.** to bring two people together *or* face-to-face

❑ **en présence de** PRÉP **la lecture du testament s'est faite en p. de toute la famille** the will was read out in the presence of the entire family; **je ne parlerai qu'en p. de mon avocat** I refuse to talk unless my lawyer is present; **en ma p.** in my presence; **nous nous trouvons en p. d'un problème insoluble** we are faced with an insoluble problem

❑ **présence d'esprit** NF presence of mind; **mon voisin a eu la p. d'esprit de me prévenir** my neighbour had the presence of mind to warn me; **conserver sa p. d'esprit** to keep one's presence of mind, to keep one's wits about one

présénescence [presenesɑ̃s] NF presenility

présénile [presenil] ADJ presenile

présent, -e [prezɑ̃, -ɑ̃t] ADJ **1** *(dans le lieu dont on parle)* present; **les personnes ici présentes** the people here present; **qui était p. quand la bagarre a éclaté?** who was present when the fight broke out?; **le racisme est p. à tous les niveaux** racism can be found at all levels; **croyez bien que je suis p. en pensée** *ou* **par le cœur** I can assure you I am with you in spirit *or* that my thoughts are with you; **être p. à une conférence** to be present at *or* to attend a conference; **étaient présents à la cérémonie les amis et proches du défunt** present at *or* attending the ceremony were the friends and relatives of the deceased; *Mil* **être p. à l'appel** to be present at roll call; **Duval? – p.!** Duval? – here *or* present!; **avoir qch p. à l'esprit** to bear *or* to keep sth in mind; **je n'ai pas p. à l'esprit le terme exact qu'il a employé** I can't bring *or* call to mind the precise word he used; **des images que nous garderons longtemps présentes à l'esprit** images which will linger in our minds; **répondre p.** *Scol* to answer to one's name, to be present at roll call; *Fig* to rise to the challenge; **des centaines de jeunes ont répondu p. à l'appel du pape** hundreds of young people answered the Pope's call

2 *(actif)* **il a été très p. après la mort de mon mari** he was very supportive after my husband died; **les Français ne sont pas du tout présents dans le jeu** the French team is making no impact on the game at all; **on a rarement vu un chanteur aussi p. sur scène** seldom has one seen a singer with such stage presence

3 *(en cours)* **dans le cas p.** in the present case; **la présente convention** this agreement

NM,F **il y avait 20 présents à la réunion** 20 people were present at *or* attended the meeting

NM **1** *(moment)* present; **vivre dans le p.** to live in the present; **pour le p.** for the time being, for the moment

2 *Gram* present (tense); **au p.** in the present; **le p. historique** *ou* **de narration** the historical present; **p. de l'indicatif/du subjonctif** present indicative/subjunctive; **p. historique** historic present; **p. progressif** present progressive; **p. simple** simple present

3 *Littéraire (cadeau)* gift, present; **faire p. de qch à qn** to present sb with sth

❑ **présente** NF *Admin (lettre)* **la présente** the present (letter), this letter; **le porteur de la présente** the bearer of this letter; **je vous informe par la présente que...** I hereby inform you that...; **je joins à la présente un chèque à votre nom** I herewith enclose a cheque payable to you

❑ **à présent** ADV now; **tu peux t'en aller à p.** you may go now; **je travaille à p. dans une laiterie** I'm working in a dairy at present

❑ **à présent que** CONJ now that

❑ **d'à présent** ADJ modern-day, present-day; **les hommes politiques d'à p.** today's *or* present-day politicians, the politicians of today

présentable [prezɑ̃tabl] ADJ presentable; **ta tenue n'est pas p.** you're not fit to be seen in that outfit; **griffonnés comme ça, les documents ne sont pas présentables** these hastily scribbled documents are not fit to be seen

présentateur, -trice [prezɑ̃tatœr, -tris] NM,F *Rad & TV (des programmes)* announcer, presenter; *(du journal)* newscaster, *Am* anchorman, *f* anchorwoman; *(de variétés)* host, *Br* compere; **p.**

de talk-show *Br* chat show *or Am* talk show host; **p. de télévision** television presenter; **p. de (vidéo)clips** video jockey, VJ

présentatif [prezɑ̃tatif] **NM** *Gram* presentative construction

présentation [prezɑ̃tasjɔ̃] **NF 1** *(dans un groupe)* introduction; **faire la p. de qn à la Cour** to present sb at Court; **faire les présentations** to do the introductions; **Robert, faites donc les présentations** *(entre plusieurs personnes)* Robert, could you introduce everybody?; **venez par ici, vous deux, je vais faire les présentations** come over here, you two, I want to introduce you; **maintenant que les présentations sont faites** now that everybody's been introduced

2 *Rad & TV (des informations)* presentation, reading; *(des variétés, d'un jeu)* hosting, *Br* compering; **assurer la p. d'une séquence** to present a news story

3 *Couture* fashion show; **aller à une p. de collection** *ou* **couture** *ou* **mode** to attend a fashion show

4 *(exposition)* presenting, showing; *Com (à un client potentiel)* presentation; **la p. des modèles a d'abord provoqué une vive controverse** there was fierce controversy when the models were first presented *or* unveiled; **la p. du projet gagnant aura lieu devant la presse** the winning project will be presented to *or* unveiled before the press

5 *(aspect formel → d'un texte)* presentation; *(→ d'une lettre)* layout; **bon devoir mais soignez davantage la p.** a good piece of work, but take more care with the presentation; **l'idée de départ est bonne mais la p. des arguments n'est pas convaincante** the original idea is good but the arguments are not presented in a convincing manner

6 *Com (emballage)* presentation, packaging

7 *Mktg (étalage)* display; **la p. des objets dans une vitrine** the presentation *or* display of items in a shop window; **p. sur le lieu de vente** point-of-sale display; **p. en masse** mass display; **p. du produit** product display; **p. au sol** floor display; **p. à la sortie** check-out display; **p. en vrac** dump display

8 *(allure)* **il a une mauvaise/bonne p.** he doesn't look/he looks very presentable; **recherche hôtesses, excellente p.** *(dans une annonce)* receptionists required, must be of smart appearance

9 *(d'un document, d'un laissez-passer)* showing; *(d'un compte, d'une facture)* presentation; **la p. de la facture a lieu un mois après** the bill is presented a month later; *Banque* **p. à l'encaissement** paying in, *Br* encashment; **p. au paiement** presentation for payment

10 *Obst* **p. par le sommet/siège** head/breech presentation; **p. céphalique/transversale** cephalic/transverse presentation

11 *Rel* **la P. du Seigneur/de la Vierge** the Presentation of Christ (in the Temple)/of the Virgin Mary

☐ **sur présentation de** PRÉP on presentation of; **vous n'entrerez que sur p. d'une invitation/de ce coupon** you'll only be admitted on presentation of an invitation/this coupon

présentatrice [prezɑ̃tatris] *voir* **présentateur**

présentement [prezɑ̃tmɑ̃] **ADV** at present, *Am* presently

PRÉSENTER [3] [prezɑ̃te]

VT to introduce **1, 7** ■ to describe **2** ■ to present **3–9, 11** ■ **13** ■ to show **3, 11** ■ to submit **7** ■ to enter **8** ■ to explain **9** ■ to offer **10,** ■ **12** ■ to have **11**
VPR to introduce oneself **1** ■ to appear **3** ■ to look **4** ■ to arise **6** ■ to present **7**

VT 1 *(faire connaître)* to introduce; **je te présente ma sœur Blanche** this is *or* let me introduce my sister Blanche; **nous n'avons pas été présentés** we haven't been introduced; **on ne vous présente plus** *(personne célèbre)* you need no introduction from me; **p. qn à la Cour/au Roi** to present sb at Court/to the King

2 *(décrire)* to describe, to portray; **on me l'a présenté comme un homme de parole** he

was described to me as a man of his word; **on vous présente souvent comme une mélomane** you're often spoken of *or* portrayed as a music lover; **je présente mon héros sous les traits d'un jeune banquier** I have portrayed my hero as a young banker

3 *(remettre → ticket, papiers)* to present, to show; *(→ facture, devis)* to present; **p. une traite à l'acceptation** to present a bill for acceptance; **p. un chèque à l'encaissement** to present a cheque for payment

4 *(montrer publiquement)* to present; **le nouveau musée sera présenté à la presse demain** the new museum will be presented *or* opened to the press tomorrow; **les Ballets de la Lune (vous) présentent...** the Moon Ballet Company presents...

5 *Com (conditionner)* to present, to package; **c'est aussi présenté en granulés** it also comes in granules; **bouteille/vitrine joliment présentée** attractively packaged bottle/dressed window

6 *Rad & TV (informations)* to present, to read; *(variétés, jeu)* to host, *Br* to compere; **les informations vous sont présentées par Claude Mart** the news is presented *or* read by Claude Mart; **l'émission de ce soir est présentée par Margot Collet** your host for tonight's programme is Margot Collet

7 *(soumettre → démission)* to present, to submit, to hand in; *(→ pétition)* to put in, to submit; *(→ projet de loi)* to present, to introduce; **p. sa candidature à un poste** to apply for a position

8 *(dans un festival)* to present; *(dans un concours)* to enter; **pourquoi présentez-vous votre film hors festival?** why aren't you showing your film as part of the festival?; *Scol & Univ* **p. l'anglais à l'oral** to take English at the oral exam; **il a présenté un de ses élèves au Conservatoire** he has entered one of his pupils for the Conservatoire entrance exam; **p. un candidat** *(à un concours)* to enter a candidate; *Pol* to put up a candidate

9 *(expliquer → dossier)* to present, to explain; *(→ rapport)* to present, to bring in; **vous avez présenté votre cas de manière fort convaincante** you have set out *or* stated your case most convincingly; **présentez-leur la chose gentiment** put it to them nicely; **tout dépend de la façon dont on présentera la décision à la réunion** it all depends on the way the decision is put *or* explained to the meeting; **présentez vos objections** state your objections

10 *(dans des formules de politesse)* to offer; **p. ses condoléances à qn** to offer one's condolences to sb, to offer sb one's condolences; **je vous présente mes condoléances** please accept *or* I'd like to offer my condolences; **p. ses hommages à qn** to pay one's respects to sb; **p. ses excuses** to offer (one's) apologies; **p. ses félicitations à qn** to congratulate sb

11 *(comporter → anomalie, particularité)* to have, to present; *(→ symptômes, traces, signes)* to show; *(→ difficulté, risque)* to involve; **la colonne vertébrale présente une déviation** the spine shows *or* presents curvature; **p. l'avantage de** to have the advantage of; **la cuisine est petite, mais elle présente l'avantage d'être équipée** the kitchen may be small, but it has the advantage of being fully equipped; **cette œuvre présente un intérêt particulier** this work is of particular interest; **les deux systèmes présentent peu de différences** the two systems present or display very few differences; **votre compte présente un découvert de 500 euros** your account shows a 500 euro overdraft *or* is overdrawn by 500 euros

12 *(offrir)* **p. son bras à une dame** to offer one's arm to a lady; **p. sa main à qn** to hold out one's hand to sb; **p. des petits fours** to offer *or* to pass round petit fours

13 *Mil (armes)* to present; **présentez armes!** present arms!

VI *Fam* **il présente bien, ton ami** your friend looks good; **le type présentait plutôt mal** the guy didn't look too presentable

▶**se présenter** VPR **1** *(décliner son identité)* to introduce oneself

2 *(emploi passif)* **ça se présente sous forme de poudre ou de liquide** it comes as a powder or a liquid

3 *(se manifester)* to appear; **se p. au QG** to report to HQ; **aucun témoin ne s'est encore présenté** no witness has come forward as yet; **vous devez vous p. au tribunal à 14 heures** you are required to be in court at 2 p.m.; **elle s'est présentée à son entretien avec une heure de retard** she arrived one hour late for the interview; **se p. chez qn** to call on sb, to go to sb's house; **après cette soirée, il n'a pas osé se p. chez elle** after the party, he didn't dare show his face at her place; **il ne s'est présenté aucun acheteur/volontaire** no buyer/volunteer has come forward; **ne pas écrire, se p.** *(dans une petite annonce)* applicants should apply in person, no letters please

4 *(avoir telle tournure)* **les choses se présentent plutôt mal** things aren't looking too good; **ça se présente mal pour qu'on ait fini mardi** it doesn't look as if we'll have finished by Tuesday; **tout cela se présente fort bien** it all looks very promising; **l'affaire se présente sous un jour nouveau** the matter can be seen *or* appears in a new light

5 *(être candidat)* **se p. aux présidentielles** to run for president; **se p. à un examen** to take an exam; **se p. à un concours de beauté** to go in for *or* to enter a beauty contest; **se p. pour un poste** to apply for a job; **pour le moment, deux personnes se sont présentées** *(pour une offre d'emploi)* two people have applied so far

6 *(survenir)* to arise; **une image terrible se présenta à mon esprit** a ghastly vision came into *or* sprang into my mind; **la scène qui se présentait à nos yeux** the scene that met our eyes; **si l'occasion se présente** if an opportunity arises; **si une difficulté se présente** if any difficulty should arise; **elle a épousé le premier qui s'est présenté** she married the first man that came along; **j'attends que quelque chose d'intéressant se présente** I'm waiting for something interesting to turn up *or* to come my way

7 *Obst* to present; **le bébé se présente par le siège** the baby is in a breech position, it's a breech baby; **le bébé se présente par la tête** the baby's presentation is normal, the baby's in a head position

présentoir [prezɑ̃twar] **NM** *Mktg (étagère)* (display) shelf; *(support)* (display) stand, display unit; *(panier)* dump bin; **p. de caisse** check-out display; **p. au sol** floor display, floor stand

présérie [preseri] **NF** *Ind* test series, pilot series

préservateur, -trice [prezɛrvatœr, -tris] **ADJ** *Vieilli* preservative; *(mesures)* preventive
NM *(dans la nourriture)* preservative

préservatif, -ive [prezɛrvatif, -iv] **ADJ** *Littéraire* preventive, protective
NM condom, sheath; **p. féminin** female condom; *(diaphragme)* diaphragm

préservation [prezɛrvasjɔ̃] **NF** preservation, protection; **la p. de l'espèce/de la faune** the preservation of the species/of wildlife; **la p. de l'emploi** safeguarding jobs

préservative [prezɛrvativ] *voir* **préservatif**

préservatrice [prezɛrvatris] *voir* **préservateur**

préserver [3] [prezɛrve] **VT 1** *(maintenir)* to preserve, to keep; **notre peuple tient à p. son identité culturelle** our people want to preserve their cultural identity; **pour p. l'intégrité de notre territoire** in order to retain our territorial integrity

2 *(protéger)* **p. de** to protect *or* to preserve from; **à p. de l'humidité/la chaleur** *(sur emballage)* to be kept in a dry/cool place; **Dieu** *ou* **le ciel me préserve de tomber jamais aussi bas!** God *or* Heaven forbid that I should ever fall so low!; **le ciel m'en préserve!** heaven forbid!

▶**se préserver** VPR **se p. de** to guard against; **pour se p. du froid** to guard against *or* to protect oneself from the cold; **tu apprendras à te p. des dangers** you'll learn to guard against *or* to keep yourself safe from danger

préside [prezid] **NM** *Hist* fortified post, presidio

présidence [prezidɑ̃s] **NF 1** *(fonction)* & *Pol* presidency; *Univ* principalship, *Br* vice-chancellorship, *Am* presidency; *(d'un homme) Com* chairmanship, directorship; *Admin* chairmanship; *Univ* **la p. du jury** the chief examinership; **une femme a été nommée à la p.** *Pol* a woman was made President; *Admin* a woman was appointed to the chair *or* made chairperson; **sous la p. de M. Fabre** under the chairmanship of Mr Fabre; *UE* **p. tournante** rotating presidency

2 *(durée → prévue)* term of office; *(→ effectuée)* period in office; **sa p. aura duré un an** he'll/she'll have been in office for a year

3 *(lieu)* presidential residence *or* palace

4 *(services)* presidential office; **vous avez la p. en ligne** you're through to the President's *or* the Presidential office; **à la p., on ne dit rien** presidential aides are keeping silent

président [prezidɑ̃] **NM 1** *Pol* president; **p. de l'Assemblée nationale** President of the National Assembly; **p. de la Commission européenne** President of the European Commission; **p. de la Confédération helvétique** President of the Swiss Confederation; **le p. du Conseil** ≃ the Prime Minister *(during the Fourth Republic)*; **p. élu** president elect; **p. fantoche** puppet president; **le p. du Parlement européen** the President of the European Parliament; **le p. de la République française** the French President; **p. du Sénat** President of the Senate; **p. à vie** life president

2 *Admin* chairperson, chairman, *f* chairwoman; **p. d'honneur** honorary chairman *or* president

3 *Com* chairman, *f* chairwoman; **p.-directeur général** *Br* chairman and managing director, *Am* (president and) chief executive officer; **p. du conseil d'administration** Chairman of the Board

4 *Jur* **p. adjoint** = deputy president of the Judicial Division of the "Conseil d'État"; **p. d'audience** presiding magistrate *or* judge; **p. de chambre** = president of a division of the Court of Cassation; **p. de section** head of division; **p. du tribunal** presiding judge

5 *Univ* principal, *Br* vice-chancellor, *Am* president; **p. du jury (d'examen)** chief examiner

6 *Sport* **p. d'un club de football** president of a football club; **le p. du comité olympique** the chairman of the Olympic Committee; **p. du jury** chairman of the panel of judges

7 *Suisse (dans les cantons de Neuchâtel et Valais)* mayor

présidente [prezidɑ̃t] **NF 1** *Pol (titulaire)* (woman) president; *Vieilli (épouse du président)* president's wife

2 *Admin* chairwoman; **p. d'honneur** honorary chairwoman *or* president

3 *Com (titulaire)* chairwoman; *Vieilli (épouse du président)* chairman's wife; **p.-directrice générale** *Br* chairwoman and managing director, *Am* (president and) chief executive officer; **p. du conseil d'administration** Chairwoman of the Board

4 *Jur* **p. adjointe** = deputy president of the Judicial Division of the "Conseil d'État"; **p. d'audience** presiding magistrate; **p. de chambre** = president of a division of the Court of Cassation; **p. de section** head of division; **p. du tribunal** presiding judge

5 *Univ* principal, *Br* vice-chancellor, *Am* president; **p. du jury (d'examen)** chief examiner

6 *Sport* **p. d'un club de football** president of a football club; **la p. du comité olympique** the chairwoman of the Olympic Committee; **p. du jury** chairwoman of the panel of judges

7 *Suisse (dans les cantons de Neuchâtel et Valais)* mayor, *f* mayoress

présidentiable [prezidɑ̃sjabl] **NMF** would-be presidential candidate

présidentialisme [prezidɑ̃sjalism] **NM** presidential (government) system

présidentiel, -elle [prezidɑ̃sjɛl] **ADJ 1** *(du président → gén)* presidential, president's *(avant n)*; *(→ élection)* presidential; **dans l'entourage p.** among the president's close associates **2** *(centralisé → régime)* presidential

▫ **présidentielles NFPL** presidential election *or* elections

Culture

LES PRÉSIDENTIELLES

In France, since 1873, the president has been traditionally elected for a renewable seven-year term ("le septennat"). However, as a result of a referendum held in September 2000 the seven-year term of office was replaced in 2002 by a five-year term ("le quinquennat"). Candidates are usually nominated by the main political parties, but anyone who collects the requisite number of sponsors can run. If no candidate wins an outright majority in the first round of voting, a runoff between the two frontrunners is held two weeks later.

présider [3] [prezide] **VT** *(diriger → séance)* to preside at *or* over; *(→ réunion)* to chair; *(→ œuvre de bienfaisance, commission)* to preside over, to be the president of; *(table)* to be at the head of

▫ **présider à VT IND p. aux destinées d'un pays** to rule over a country; **un réel esprit de coopération a présidé à nos entretiens** a genuine spirit of cooperation prevailed during our talks; **les règles qui président à cette cérémonie** the rules governing this ceremony

présidial, -e, -aux, -ales [prezidjal, -o] *Hist* **ADJ** presidial

NM presidial

présidialité [prezidjalite] **NF** *Hist* jurisdiction of a presidial

présidium [prezidjɔm] = **praesidium**

présocratique [presɔkratik] **ADJ** Presocratic

NMF Presocratic

présomptif, -ive [prezɔ̃ptif, -iv] **ADJ** presumptive

présomption [prezɔ̃psjɔ̃] **NF 1** *(prétention)* presumption, presumptuousness

2 *(supposition)* presumption, assumption; **il s'agit là d'une simple p. de votre part** you're only assuming this (to be the case)

3 *Jur* presumption; **de fortes présomptions pèsent sur lui** he is under great suspicion; **p. absolue** *ou* **irréfragable** irrefutable presumption; **p. d'imputabilité** presumption of imputability; **p. d'innocence** presumption of innocence; **p. légale** presumption of law; **p. de paternité** presumption of legitimacy; **p. simple** rebuttable presumption

présomptive [prezɔ̃ptiv] *voir* **présomptif**

présomptueux, -euse [prezɔ̃ptɥø, -øz] **ADJ** presumptuous

NM un jeune p. a presumptuous young man

présono [presɔno] **NF** *Fam TV & Rad* playback

présonorisation [presɔnɔrizasjɔ̃] **NF** *TV & Rad* playback

présonoriser [3] [presɔnɔrize] **VT** *TV & Rad* to play back

presque [prɛsk] **ADV 1** *(dans des phrases affirmatives)* almost, nearly; **les cerises sont p. mûres** the cherries are almost *or* nearly ripe; **il a p. tout perdu au jeu** he gambled away almost *or* nearly all his money; **l'espèce a p. entièrement disparu** the species is virtually *or* all but extinct; **l'ambulance est arrivée p. aussitôt** the ambulance arrived almost immediately *or* at once; **il est p. minuit** it's almost *or* nearly midnight; **de l'avis de p. tous les collègues,...** in the opinion of almost all of our colleagues,...; **il termine p.** he's just finishing; **nous y sommes p.** we're almost there; **il a p. terminé** he has nearly *or* almost finished; **ça n'est pas sûr mais p.** it's not certain, but just about *or* but as good as; **c'est p. de l'inconscience!** it's little short of madness!

2 *(dans des phrases négatives)* hardly, scarcely; **ils ne se sont p. pas parlé** they hardly spoke to each other; **je n'avais p. pas mangé de la journée** I'd eaten next to *or* almost *or* virtually nothing all day; **tu fumes beaucoup en ce moment? – non, p. pas** do you smoke much at the moment? – no, hardly at all; **est-ce qu'il reste des gâteaux? – non, p. pas** are there any cakes left? – hardly any; **je ne dors p. plus** I hardly *or* scarcely get any sleep any more; **il n'y a p. plus de café** there's hardly any coffee left; **p. jamais** scarcely *or* hardly ever, almost never; **je n'ai p. rien fait de la journée** I've done virtually *or* almost nothing all day; *Fam* **c'est p. rien** it's hardly anything

3 *(quasi)* **avoir la p. certitude de qch** to be almost *or* practically certain of sth; **la p. totalité des électeurs** almost *or* nearly all the voters

▫ **ou presque ADV des écrivains ignorés ou p.** writers who are unknown or almost unknown; **c'est sûr, ou p.** it's almost *or* practically certain; **j'ai vu tout le monde ou p.** I saw everybody or almost *or* virtually everybody

presqu'île [prɛskil] **NF** peninsula

pressage [prɛsaʒ] **NM 1** *(d'un vêtement, d'un tissu)* pressing; **p. à la vapeur** steam-pressing **2** *(d'un disque)* pressing **3** *Tech* press moulding **4** *(du fromage)* draining *or* pressing of curds

pressant, -e [prɛsɑ̃, -ɑ̃t] **ADJ 1** *(urgent)* urgent; **un travail p.** an urgent piece of work **2** *(insistant → question, invitation)* pressing, insistent; **elle se faisait de plus en plus pressante** she was becoming more and more insistent

press-book [prɛsbuk] *(pl* **press-books)** **NM** portfolio

presse [prɛs] **NF 1** *(journaux, magazines etc)* **la p. (écrite)** the press, the papers; **que dit la p.?** what do the papers say?; **la grande p.** large-circulation newspapers and magazines; **p. de bas étage** popular press, gutter press, ≃ tabloids; **p. de charme** soft-porn magazines; **la p. du cœur** romantic fiction (magazines); **la p. féminine** women's magazines; **la p. financière** the financial press; **la p. généraliste** the general (-interest) press; **p. gratuite** free press; **la p. magazine** news magazines; **p. masculine** men's magazines; **p. musicale** music press; **la p. nationale** the national press; **la p. d'opinion** the quality newspapers; **p. people** celebrity press; **p. périodique** periodical press; **la p. poubelle** the gutter press; **la p. professionnelle** the trade press; **p. de qualité** quality newspapers; **p. quotidienne** daily press; **la p. quotidienne régionale** the local daily press; **p. régionale** regional press; **la p. à sensation** *ou* **à scandale** the popular press, ≃ the tabloids, *Péj* the gutter press; **la p. du soir** the evening newspapers; **la p. spécialisée** the specialist press; **la p. sportive** the sports press; **avoir bonne/mauvaise p.** to have a good/bad press; *Fig* to be well/badly thought of; **le nucléaire n'a pas très bonne p.** nuclear power has a bad image *or* press

2 *Typ* press; **sous p.** in the press; **être mis sous p.** to go to press; **au moment où nous mettons sous presse** at the time of going to press; **sortir de p.** to come out; *Typ* **p. d'imprimerie** printing press; **p. à retiration** perfecting machine; **p. à rogner** plough; **p. rotative** rotary press; **p. typographique** printing press *or* machine

3 *Agr, Tech & Tex* press; *Menuis* bench vice; **p. à balancier** (mechanical) fly press; **p. à forger** forging machine; **p. hydraulique/mécanique** hydraulic/power press; **p. à main** *ou* **à serrer** hand *or* screw press; **p. monétaire** coining press

4 *(pour le vin)* winepress

5 *Littéraire (foule, bousculade)* press, throng; **au moment de Noël, il y a toujours p.** it's always busy at Christmas

6 *Can (urgence)* urgency; **il n'y a pas de p.!** there's no urgency!, there's no need to panic!

7 *Presse* **La P.** = major French-language daily newspaper in Canada

▫ **de presse ADJ 1** *(campagne, coupure, attaché)* press *(avant n)*

2 *(moment, période)* peak *(avant n)*; **nous avons des moments de p.** we get very busy at times

pressé, -e [prese] **ADJ 1** *(personne)* **être p.** to be pressed for time, to be in a hurry *or* rush; **je suis horriblement p.** I'm in an awful hurry *or* rush; **ils ne sont jamais pressés** they're never in a hurry; **tu n'as pas l'air p. de la revoir** you seem in no hurry *or* you don't seem eager to see her again; **je suis p. d'en finir** I'm anxious to get the whole thing over with; **je ne suis pas pressée de me remarier!** I'm in no rush to get married again!

2 *(précipité → démarche, geste)* hurried; **aller d'un pas p.** to walk hurriedly

3 *(urgent → réparation, achat)* urgent; **cette réparation, c'est p.?** is this repair urgent?; **si vous n'avez rien de plus p. à faire** if you've got nothing more urgent to do; **il n'a rien trouvé de plus p. que d'aller tout raconter à sa femme** he wasted no time in telling his wife the whole story; **le plus p., c'est de prévenir son mari** the first thing to do is to tell her husband

4 *(exprimé → agrume)* freshly squeezed; **p. à froid** cold-pressed

5 *Tech* pressed

presse-agrumes [prɛsagrym] **NM INV** juicer, juice extractor

presse-ail [prɛsaj] **NM INV** garlic press

presse-bouton [prɛsbutɔ̃] **ADJ INV** *voir* **guerre**

presse-citron [prɛssitrɔ̃] *(pl* **inv** *ou* **presse-citrons)** **NM** lemon squeezer

pressée [prese] **NF** *(de raisins)* (grape) pressings

presse-étoupe [prɛsetup] *(pl* **inv** *ou* **presse-étoupes)** **NM** *Tech* stuffing box, packing box (and gland); **garniture de p.** packing

pressens *etc voir* **pressentir**

pressentiment [presɑ̃timɑ̃] **NM** premonition; **avoir le p. de.../que...** to have a feeling of.../that...; **avoir le p. de malheurs à venir** to have a premonition of disaster; **avoir le p. que la mort est proche** to have a feeling of impending death, to have a foreboding *or* premonition of death; **j'ai eu le curieux p. que je reviendrais ici un jour** I had the odd feeling *or* a hunch that I'd be back again some day

pressentir [37] [presɑ̃tir] **VT 1** *(prévoir → gén)* to sense (in advance), to have a premonition of; *(→ malheur)* to have a premonition *or* foreboding of; **p. un danger/des difficultés** to sense danger/trouble; **p. que...** to have a feeling *or* premonition that...; **son attitude me fait p. que...** I get the feeling *or* I can sense from his attitude that...; **rien ne laissait p. qu'elle allait démissionner** nothing indicated *or* suggested that she would resign

2 *(contacter)* to approach, to contact; **il a été pressenti pour jouer le Christ à l'écran** he's been approached about portraying Christ on the screen; **toutes les personnes pressenties** all the people who were contacted

presse-papiers [prɛspapje] **NM INV 1** *(objet lourd)* paperweight **2** *Ordinat* clipboard

presse-purée [prɛspyre] **NM INV** potato masher

presser [4] [prese] **VT 1** *(extraire le jus de)* to squeeze; **p. le raisin** to press grapes; *Fam* **p. le citron à qn, p. qn comme un citron** to exploit sb to the full■, to squeeze sb dry; *Fig* **on presse l'orange et on jette l'écorce** you use people and then cast them aside

2 *(faire se hâter)* to rush; **j'ai horreur qu'on me presse** I hate being rushed; **qu'est-ce qui te presse?** what's the hurry?, what's (all) the rush for?; **rien ne nous presse** we're not in any hurry *or* rush; **p. le pas** to speed up; *Littéraire* **nous presserons notre départ** we shall hasten our departure

3 *(serrer)* to squeeze; **elle pressait sa poupée dans ses bras** she was hugging her doll; **il pressait sur son cœur la photo de sa fille** he was clasping a picture of his daughter to his heart; **p. la main à qn** to squeeze sb's hand, to give sb's hand a squeeze; **nous étions pressés contre les barrières** we were pressed *or* crushed against the gates; **pressés les uns contre les autres** packed *or* squashed together

4 *(appuyer sur → commutateur, bouton)* to press, to push

5 **p. qn de faire qch** *(l'inciter à faire)* to urge sb to do sth; **je le pressai de quitter le pays** I urged him to leave the country; **il m'a pressé de lui donner la combinaison du coffre** he pressured *or* pressurized me into giving him the combination of the safe

6 *(accabler, harceler)* **pressé par ses créanciers** pressed by his creditors; **p. qn de questions** to ply *or* to bombard sb with questions; **être pressé par le temps/l'argent** to be pressed for time/money

7 *Tech (disque, pli)* to press

VI le temps presse time is short; **l'affaire presse** it's an urgent matter; **rien ne presse, ça ne presse pas** there's no (need to) rush *or* hurry; **pressons!** come on, let's hurry up!

►**se presser VPR 1** *(se dépêcher)* to hurry; **il n'est que deux heures, il n'y a pas de raison de se p.** it's only two o'clock, there's no point in rushing *or* no need to hurry; **allons les enfants, pressons-nous un peu** come on children, get a move on; **faire qch sans se p.** to take one's time over doing sth; **répondre sans se p.** to answer deliberately *or* leisurely, to give an unhurried answer; **se p. de faire qch** to be in a hurry to do sth; **je ne me pressai pas de répondre** I was in no hurry to reply; **pressons-nous de rentrer** let's hurry back; **heureusement que tu les as fait se p. un peu ou on y serait encore!** thank goodness you hurried them up a bit, otherwise we'd still be there!

2 *(se serrer)* **il se pressait contre moi tant il avait peur** he was pressing up against me in fear; **les gens se pressaient au guichet** there was a crush at the box office; **on se pressait pour entrer** people were pushing to get in; **les badauds se pressaient autour de la victime** the onlookers crowded *or* clustered around the victim; **le temps où les photographes se pressaient à ma porte** the days when photographers would crowd *or* press round my door; **les mots se pressaient dans sa bouche** he/she couldn't get his/her words out (fast enough)

3 *Fam* **se p. le citron** to rack one's brains

presse-raquette [prɛsrakɛt] *(pl* **inv** *ou* **presse-raquettes)** **NM** racket press

presseur, -euse [prɛsœr, -øz] *Tech* **ADJ** pressing **NM,F** presser

presse-viande [prɛsvjɑ̃d] **NM INV** juice extractor *(for meat)*

pressier [prɛsje] **NM** *Typ* pressman

pressing [presiŋ] **NM 1** *(repassage)* pressing; **p. à la vapeur** steam-pressing **2** *(boutique)* dry cleaner's **3** *Fam* **faire le p.** to put *or* to pile on the pressure

pression [prɛsjɔ̃] **NF 1** *(action)* pressure; **une simple p. de la main suffit** you just have to press lightly; **exercer une p. sur qch, faire p. sur qch** to exert pressure on sth

2 *Phys* pressure; **la p. de l'eau** water pressure; **p. de vapeur saturante** saturated vapour pressure; *Aut* **p. des pneus** tyre pressure; **p. acoustique** sound pressure; *Méd* **p. artérielle** blood pressure; *Météo* **p. atmosphérique** atmospheric pressure; **zone de hautes/basses pressions** area of high/low pressure; **à haute/basse p.** high-/low-pressure; **mettre sous p.** to pressurize; **récipient/cabine sous p.** pressurized container/cabin; *Fig* **être sous p.** to be stressed *or* under pressure; **entre midi et deux heures, on est sous p.** we're always under pressure between twelve and two; **faire monter la p.** to pile on *or* increase the pressure; *Fam* **mettre la p. à qn** to pressurize sb■, to put pressure on sb■

3 *(contrainte morale)* pressure; **céder à la p. populaire/familiale** to give in to popular/family pressure; **faire p. sur qn** to put pressure on sb; **on a fait p. sur lui pour qu'il démissionne** they put pressure on him to resign, they pressured *or* pressurized him into resigning; **il faut exercer une p. sur la classe politique** we must put pressure on *or* bring pressure to bear on the political community; **il y a une forte p. sur le dollar/l'équipe belge** the dollar/the Belgian team is under heavy pressure; **sous la p. des événements, il dut démissionner** the pressure of events was such that he had to resign

4 *(bouton-pression) Br* press stud, *Am* snap (fastener)

5 *(bière)* draught (beer); **garçon, trois pressions!** waiter, *Br* three half pints of lager *or Am* three beers!

6 *Écon* **p. fiscale** tax burden; **p. inflationniste** inflationary pressure

❑ **à la pression ADJ** *(bière)* draught

pressoir [prɛswar] **NM 1** *(appareil)* **p. (à vin)** winepress; **p. à cidre/huile** cider/oil press **2** *(lieu)* presshouse

pressostat [prɛsɔsta] **NM** manostat, pressure controller

presspahn [prɛspan] **NM** press board

pressurage [presyraʒ] **NM** *(du raisin)* pressing

pressurer [3] [presyre] **VT 1** *(raisin)* to press; *(citron)* to squeeze **2** *Fig (exploiter)* to squeeze, to exploit

►**se pressurer VPR** *Fam* **se p. le cerveau** to rack one's brains

pressureur, -euse [presyrœr, -øz] **NM,F 1** *(ouvrier)* press-house hand **2** *Fig (exploiteur)* exploiter

pressurisation [presyrizasjɔ̃] **NF** pressurization

pressuriser [3] [presyrize] **VT** to pressurize

prestance [prɛstɑ̃s] **NF un jeune homme de belle/noble p.** a handsome/noble-looking young man; **il a de la p.** he is a fine figure of a man; **son costume anglais lui donne une certaine p.** his English suit gives him a certain air of elegance

prestant [prɛstɑ̃] **NM** *Mus (d'un orgue)* diapason (stop)

prestataire [prɛstatɛr] **NMF 1** *(bénéficiaire)* recipient *(of an allowance)*; **depuis la majorité de mes enfants, je ne suis plus p. des allocations familiales** since my children came of age, I have not been able to claim child benefit **2** *(fournisseur)* **p. de service** service provider

prestation [prɛstasjɔ̃] **NF 1** *(allocation)* allowance, benefit; **les diverses prestations auxquelles vous avez droit** the various benefits to which you are entitled; **verser les prestations** to pay out benefits; **recevoir des prestations** to receive benefits; **p. compensatoire** *(en cas de divorce)* compensation; *Mil* **p. en deniers** allowance in money; **prestations familiales** family benefits *(such as child benefit, rent allowance etc)*; **p. indemnitaire** allowance, benefit; **p. d'invalidité** (industrial) disablement benefit; **prestations maladie** sickness benefit; *Mil* **p. en nature** benefit in kind; **prestations sociales** social security benefits; **p. de vieillesse** old-age pension

2 *Com* **p. de service** provision *or* delivery of a service; **p. de capitaux** provision of capital

3 *(d'un artiste, d'un sportif etc)* performance; **faire une bonne/mauvaise p.** to perform well/badly; **faire une bonne p. scénique/télévisuelle** to put on a good stage/television performance

4 *Jur & Hist* **p. de serment** taking the oath; **sa p. de serment aura lieu mardi** he/she will be sworn in on Tuesday; **p. de foi** oath of fealty

5 *Jur & Admin* **prestations locatives** service charge *(paid by the tenant to the landlord)*

preste [prɛst] **ADJ** swift, nimble; **avoir la main p.** *(être adroit)* to have a light touch

prestement [prɛstəmɑ̃] **ADV** *(se faufiler)* swiftly, nimbly; *(travailler)* swiftly, quickly

prester [3] [preste] *Belg* **VT** *(service)* to provide

VI *Sport* **bien p.** to perform well

prestesse [prɛstɛs] **NF** *Littéraire* swiftness, nimbleness

prestidigitateur, -trice [prɛstidiʒitatœr, -tris] **NM,F** conjuror, magician

prestidigitation [prɛstidiʒitasjɔ̃] **NF** conjuring, *Sout* prestidigitation; **faire de la p.** *(en amateur)* to do conjuring (tricks); *(en professionnel)* to be a conjuror; *Fig* **c'est de la p.!** it's magic!

prestidigitatrice [prɛstidiʒitatris] *voir* **prestidigitateur**

prestige [prɛstiʒ] **NM** prestige; **jouir d'un grand p.** to enjoy great prestige; **redonner du p. à une institution** to restore prestige to an institution; **le p. de l'uniforme** the glamour of the uniform

❑ **de prestige ADJ** *(politique, publicité, magazine)* prestige *(avant n)*; *(résidence)* luxury *(avant n)*

❑ **pour le prestige ADV** for the sake of prestige; **collectionner les œuvres d'art pour le p.** to collect works of art for their prestige value

prestigieux, -euse [prɛstiʒjø, -øz] **ADJ 1** *(magnifique)* prestigious; **notre prestigieuse collection "Histoire"** our magnificent History collection **2** *(renommé → produit)* renowned, famous, world-famous; **la Californie exporte ses p. produits dans le monde entier** California exports its renowned products worldwide

prestissimo [prɛstisimo] **ADV** *Mus* prestissimo

presto [prɛsto] **ADV 1** *Mus* presto **2** *Fam (vite)* at *or* on the double, double-quick; **il faudra que tu me rembourses p.** you'll have to repay me double-quick

présumable [prezymabl] **ADJ** presumable; **il est p. que...** it is to be presumed that...

présumé, -e [prezyme] **ADJ 1** *(considéré comme)* presumed; **tout accusé, en l'absence de preuves, est p. innocent** in the absence of proof, all defendants are presumed innocent **2** *(supposé)* presumed, putative; **Max Dalbon est l'auteur p. du pamphlet** Max Dalbon is presumed to be the author of this pamphlet

présumer [3] [prezyme] **VT** *(supposer)* to presume, to assume; **je présume que vous êtes sa sœur** I take it *or* presume you're his/her sister;

p. qn innocent to presume sb (to be) innocent; **tu viens aussi, je présume?** you're coming too, presumably?, you're coming too, I presume *or* assume?

▫ **présumer de** VT IND *(surestimer)* **j'ai un peu présumé de mes forces** I overdid things somewhat; **sans p. de son intelligence** without overrating his/her intelligence; **p. de qn** to rely on sb too much

présupposé [presypoze] NM presupposition

présupposer [3] [presypoze] VT to presuppose; **la question présuppose une grande culture historique** the question calls for *or* presupposes a thorough grasp of history

présupposition [presypozisjɔ̃] NF presupposition

présure [prezyr] NF *Biol & Chim* **1** *(enzyme)* rennin **2** *(pour le fromage etc)* rennet

présurer [3] [prezyre] VT to curdle with rennet

prêt[1] [prɛ] NM **1** *(action)* lending, loaning; **c'est seulement un p.** it's only a loan; **le p. de livres est réservé aux étudiants** the lending of books is restricted to students; **conditions de p.** lending conditions

2 *(bancaire)* loan; **solliciter un p.** to apply for a loan; **obtenir un p. d'une banque** to secure a bank loan; **accorder un p. à qn** to lend money to sb; **p. à court/moyen/long terme** short-/ medium-/long-term loan; **p. d'accession à la propriété** home loan; **prêts d'aide à l'investissement** *ou* **au développement des entreprises** loan guaranteed scheme; **p. avantageux** soft loan; **p. bancaire** bank loan; **p. de banque à banque** interbank loan; **p. bonifié** loan at reduced rate of interest, soft loan; **p. conditionnel, p. à condition** tied loan; **p. à des conditions avantageuses** soft loan; **p. aux conditions du marché** hard loan; **p. à la consommation** consumer loan; **p. à la construction** building loan; **p. conventionné** = approved mortgage loan; **p. à découvert** overdraft loan; **p. de démarrage** start-up loan; **p. en devises étrangères** foreign currency loan; **p. douteux** doutful loan; **p. d'épargne-logement** home loan; **p. escompté** discounted loan; **p. à fonds perdus** loan without security, unsecured loan; **p. sur gage** loan against security; **p. gagé** *ou* **garanti** guaranteed *or* secured loan, collateral loan; **p. garanti par l'État** sovereign loan; **p. d'honneur** loan on trust; **p. hypothécaire** mortgage loan; **p. sur hypothèque** mortgage loan; **p. immobilier** home loan, ≃ mortgage; **p. à intérêt** loan at *or* with interest, interest-bearing loan; **p. sans intérêt** interest-free loan; **p. au jour le jour** loan at call; **p. sur nantissement** loan on collateral; **p. non-garanti** unsecured loan; **p. participatif** equity loan; **p. en participation** syndicated loan; **prêts aux particuliers** personal loans; **p. personnalisé** *ou* **personnel** personal loan; **p. à la petite semaine** = short-term loan at high rate of interest; **p. relais** bridging loan; **p. remboursable sur demande** loan at call, loan repayable on demand; **p. de remboursement** refunding loan; **p. en souffrance** non-performing loan; **p. à taux zéro** interest-free loan; **p. à tempérament** instalment loan; **p. à terme (fixe)** term loan; **p. sur titres** loan against securities; **p. à vue** loan at call, loan repayable on demand

3 *Jur & Naut* **p. à la grosse** bottomry loan

4 *Mil* pay; **p. franc** (subsistence) allowance *(paid in money)*

5 *(dans une bibliothèque → document)* loan, issue, book issued; *Fam* **allez aux prêts** go to the issuing desk▪

prêt[2], **-e** [prɛ, prɛt] ADJ **1** *(préparé)* ready; **le dîner/votre costume est p.** dinner/your suit is ready; **je suis p., on peut partir** I'm ready, we can go now; **mes valises sont prêtes** my bags are packed; **p. à l'emploi** ready for use; **p. à emporter** *Br* take-away *(avant n)*, *Am* take-out *(avant n)*; **poulet p. à cuire** *ou* **rôtir** oven-ready *or* dressed chicken; **être (fin) p. au départ** to be all set to go; **l'armée se tient prête à intervenir** the army is ready to step in *or* to intervene; **vous n'êtes pas encore p. pour la compétition** you're not ready for competition yet; **tout est (fin) p. pour la cérémonie** everything is ready for the ceremony; *Fam* **j'ai toujours une cassette de prête** I always have a tape ready

2 *(disposé)* **toujours p.** *(devise des scouts)* be prepared; **p. à faire qch** ready *or* willing to do sth; **ils ne sont pas prêts à vendre** they aren't ready *or* willing to sell; **être p. à tout** to be game for anything; **il est p. à tout (faire) pour réussir** he'd do anything *or* stop at nothing to succeed; **Paul est tout p. à te remplacer** Paul is ready and willing to stand in for you

3 *Littéraire (sur le point de)* **p. à faire qch** on the point of doing sth; **p. à mourir** at the point of death

prêt-à-boire [prɛtabwar] *(pl* **prêts-à-boire***)* NM ready-mixed alcoholic drink

prêt-à-coudre [prɛtakudr] *(pl* **prêts-à-coudre***)* NM ready-to-sew garment, garment in kit form

prêt-à-manger [prɛtamɑ̃ʒe] *(pl* **prêts-à-manger***)* NM **1** *(nourriture)* fast food **2** *(restaurant)* fast-food restaurant

prêt-à-monter [prɛtamɔ̃te] *(pl* **prêts-à-monter***)* NM kit

prétantaine [pretɑ̃tɛn] NF *Vieilli* **courir la p.** to chase (after) women

prêt-à-porter [prɛtapɔrte] *(pl* **prêts-à-porter***)* NM ready-to-wear fashion; **le salon du p.** the ready-to-wear fashion fair; **une collection de p. féminin** a women's ready-to-wear collection; **elle n'achète que du p.** she only buys ready-to-wear *or Br* off-the-peg clothes

prêt-bail [prɛbaj] NM *Écon* lend-lease; **loi de p.** lend-lease act

prêté [prete] NM *(locution)* **c'est un p. pour un rendu** it's tit for tat

prétendant, -e [pretɑ̃dɑ̃, -ɑ̃t] NM,F *(à un bien, à un titre)* claimant (**à** to); **p. au trône** pretender to the throne

NM **1** *Hum (soupirant)* suitor, wooer **2** *Mktg* challenger

prétendre [73] [pretɑ̃dr] VT **1** *(se vanter de)* to claim; **il prétend qu'il peut rester 10 minutes sans respirer** he claims he can go 10 minutes without breathing; **je n'ai jamais prétendu détenir la clé de la sagesse** I never claimed to hold the key to wisdom

2 *(affirmer)* to claim, to say, to maintain; **il prétendait être un descendant de Napoléon** he claimed to be descended from Napoleon; **elle prétend avoir quelque chose d'important à te dire** she claims to have *or* she says she has something important to tell you; **je ne prétends pas que ce soit** *ou* **que c'est de ta faute** I'm not saying *or* I don't say it's your fault; **on prétend que …** people say that …, it is said that …; **on la prétend folle** she's said *or* alleged to be mad; **à ce qu'elle prétend, son mari est ambassadeur** according to her, her husband is an ambassador; **ce n'est pas le chef-d'œuvre qu'on prétend** it's not the masterpiece it's made out to be

3 *(avoir l'intention de)* to intend, to mean; **qui prétendez-vous choisir comme successeur?** whom do you intend to choose as your successor?; **mon père prétend être respecté de tous** my father means to be respected by all; *Belg* **il ne prétend pas le faire** he doesn't intend to do it

▫ **prétendre à** VT IND **1** *(revendiquer)* to claim; **vous pouvez p. à une indemnisation** you can claim compensation

2 *Littéraire (aspirer à)* to aspire to; **p. aux honneurs** to aspire to honours; **il prétend au titre de champion** he is aiming for the championship; **p. à la main de qn** to aspire to marry sb

▸**se prétendre** VPR *(se dire)* to claim to be; **il se prétend avocat** he claims to be a lawyer; **elle se prétend infirme** she claims to be disabled; *Fam* **et ça se prétend original en plus!** and what's more it claims to be original!

prétendu, -e [pretɑ̃dy] ADJ *(par soi-même)* so-called, self-styled; *(par autrui)* so-called, alleged; **le p. professeur était en fait un espion** the so-called professor was in fact a spy

NM,F *Vieilli (fiancé, fiancée)* betrothed, intended

prétendument [pretɑ̃dymɑ̃] ADV *(par soi-même)* supposedly; *(par autrui)* supposedly, allegedly; **cet individu p. architecte nous avait construit une horreur** this so-called architect built us a monstrosity

prête-nom [prɛtnɔ̃] *(pl* **prête-noms***)* NM **1** *(homme de paille)* figurehead, man of straw; **servir de p. à qch** to act as a figurehead for sth **2** *Fin (société)* nominee company

prétensionneur [pretɑ̃sjɔnœr] NM *Aut* pre-tensioner

prétentaine [pretɑ̃tɛn] NF *Vieilli* **courir la p.** to chase (after) women

prétentieuse [pretɑ̃sjøz] *voir* **prétentieux**

prétentieusement [pretɑ̃sjøzmɑ̃] ADV pretentiously, self-importantly

prétentieux, -euse [pretɑ̃sjø, -øz] ADJ *(personne, style, remarque)* pretentious; **mauvaise langue, et en plus prétentieuse!** she's a scandalmonger and pretentious into the bargain!

NM,F conceited *or* self-important person, poseur; **un jeune p.** a conceited young man; **regarde-la, quelle prétentieuse!** look at her, she's so full of herself *or* she really fancies herself!

prétention [pretɑ̃sjɔ̃] NF **1** *(orgueil)* pretentiousness, conceit, self-conceit; **il est plein de p.** he's so conceited

2 *(ambition)* pretension, claim; **tu n'as tout de même pas la p. de te représenter?** do you really have the nerve to *Br* run *or Am* stand again?; **je n'ai pas la p. d'avoir été complet sur ce sujet** I don't claim to have fully covered the subject; **avoir une p. à la sagesse** to pretend to wisdom; **l'article a des prétentions littéraires** the article has literary pretensions

▫ **prétentions** NFPL **1** *(exigences)* claims; **avoir des prétentions sur un héritage/une propriété** to lay claim to an inheritance/a property; **renoncer à ses prétentions** to renounce one's claims

2 *(financières)* **prétentions (de salaire)** expected salary, target earnings; **vos prétentions sont trop élevées** you're asking for too high a salary; **envoyez une lettre spécifiant vos prétentions** send a letter specifying your salary expectations

▫ **sans prétention** ADJ unpretentious; **un écrivain sans p.** an unassuming writer; **c'est un scénario sans p.** it's an unpretentious script; **un repas sans p.** a simple meal

prêter [4] [prete] VT **1** *(argent, bien)* to lend, to loan; **peux-tu me p. ta voiture?** can you lend me *or* can I borrow your car?; **je lui avais prêté 50 euros/mes livres d'art** I had lent him/her 50 euros/my art books

2 *(attribuer)* to attribute, to accord; **p. de l'importance à qch** to attach importance to sth; **on lui a parfois prêté des pouvoirs magiques** he/she was sometimes alleged *or* claimed to have magical powers; **on me prête des talents que je n'ai malheureusement pas** I am credited with skills that I unfortunately do not possess; **l'opposition vous prête l'intention d'organiser un coup d'État** the opposition claims *or* alleges that you intend to stage a coup; **ce sont les propos prêtés au sénateur** these are the words attributed to the senator

3 *(offrir)* to give; **p. asile à qn** to give *or* to offer sb shelter; **p. assistance** *ou* **secours à qn** to give *or* to lend assistance to sb; **p. attention à** to pay attention to; **ne pas p. attention à** to ignore; **p. l'oreille** to listen; **p. une oreille attentive à qn** to listen attentively to sb; **p. une oreille distraite à qn** to listen to sb with only half an ear; **p. sa voix à** *(chanter)* to sing the part of; *(parler)* to speak the part of; *(soutenir)* to speak on behalf *or* in support of; **p. serment** to take the oath; *Pol* to be sworn in; **faire p. serment à qn** to put sb under oath; **p. son nom à une cause** to lend one's name to a cause; **p. le flanc à la critique** to lay oneself open to *or* to invite criticism; **p. le flanc à l'adversaire** to give the adversary an opening

USAGE ABSOLU **la banque prête à 9 pour cent** the bank lends at 9 percent; **p. sur gages** to lend (money) against security; *Prov* **on ne prête qu'aux riches** = people don't lend money to those who really need it; *Fig* = people are judged according to their reputation

VI *(tissu, cuir)* to give, to stretch

▫ **prêter à** VT IND *(donner lieu à)* to give rise to, to invite; **le texte prête à confusion** the text is open to misinterpretation; **la déclaration prête à équivoque** the statement is ambiguous; **il est d'une naïveté qui prête à rire** he is ridiculously naive

▸**se prêter** VPR **1 se p. à** *(consentir à)* to lend oneself to; **se p. à un arrangement** to lend oneself to *or* to consent to an arrangement; **se**

p. à une fraude to countenance a fraud; **se p. au jeu** to enter into the spirit of the game

2 se p. à (être adapté à) to be suitable for; **si le temps s'y prête** weather permitting; **les circonstances ne se prêtaient guère aux confidences** it was no time for confidences; **ma petite maison ne se prête pas à une grande réception** my little house is hardly the (ideal) place for a big party

prétérit [preterit] NM Gram preterite; **au p.** in the preterite

prétériter [3] [preterite] VT Suisse (personne) to wrong

prétérition [preterisjɔ̃] NF preterition

pré-test [pretɛst] (pl **pré-tests**) NM Mktg pre-test; **p. publicitaire** copy test

pré-tester [3] [pretɛste] VT Mktg to pre-test

préteur [pretœr] NM Antiq praetor

prêteur, -euse [prɛtœr, -øz] ADJ **elle n'est pas prêteuse** she doesn't like lending, she's very possessive about her belongings

NM,F lender, moneylender; **p. sur gages** pawnbroker; **p. sur hypothèque** mortgagee; **p. en dernier ressort** lender of last resort; **p. sur titre** money broker

prétexte¹ [pretɛkst] ADJ F Antiq (toge) praetexta
NF Antiq toga praetexta

prétexte² [pretɛkst] NM **1** (excuse) pretext, excuse; **trouver un bon p.** to come up with a good excuse; **un mauvais p.** a lame or feeble excuse; **servir de p. à qn** to provide sb with a pretext; **prendre p. de qch** to use sth as an excuse; **pour toi, tous les prétextes sont bons pour ne pas travailler** any excuse is good for avoiding work as far as you're concerned

2 (occasion) **pour toi, tout est p. à rire/au sarcasme** you find cause for laughter/sarcasm in everything

❏ **sous aucun prétexte** ADV on no account; **vous ne quitterez cette pièce sous aucun p.** on no account or under no circumstances will you leave this room, you will not leave this room on any account

❏ **sous prétexte de** PRÉP **il est sorti sous p. d'aller acheter du pain** he went out on the pretext of buying some bread

❏ **sous prétexte que** CONJ **sous p. qu'elle a été malade, on lui passe tout** just because she's been ill, she can get away with anything

prétexter [4] [pretɛkste] VT to give as a pretext, to use as an excuse; **j'ai prétexté un rendez-vous chez le dentiste** I used a dental appointment as an excuse; **tu n'aurais pas pu p. autre chose?** couldn't you have found another excuse?; **p. que** to give as a pretext or excuse that; **elle va sûrement p. qu'elle n'a pas trouvé de taxi** she'll certainly pretend or come up with the excuse that she couldn't find a taxi; **p. la fatigue** to plead fatigue

pretium doloris [presjɔmdɔlɔris] NM INV Jur (financial) compensation

prétoire [pretwar] NM **1** Jur court **2** Antiq (tente, palais) praetorium

Pretoria [pretɔrja] NM Pretoria

prétorial, -e, -aux, -ales [pretɔrjal, -o] ADJ Antiq praetorial

prétorien, -enne [pretɔrjɛ̃, -ɛn] ADJ Antiq (d'un magistrat) pretorian, praetorian; (d'un garde) praetorian; aussi Fig **garde prétorienne** praetorian guard
NM Praetorian Guard

prétraille [pretraj] NF Péj Vieilli **la p.** the priests, the clergy

prétraité, -e [pretrete] ADJ Tech pretreated

prétraitement [pretrɛtmɑ̃] NM **1** Ordinat preprocessing **2** Tech pretreatment

prêtre [prɛtr] NM **1** Rel priest; **les prêtres** the clergy; aussi Fig **grand p.** high priest **2** Ich sand smelt

prêt-relais [prɛrəlɛ] (pl **prêts-relais**) NM Br bridging loan, Am bridge loan

prêtre-ouvrier [prɛtruvrije] (pl **prêtres-ouvriers**) NM worker-priest

prêtresse [prɛtrɛs] NF Rel priestess; aussi Fig **grande p.** high priestess

prêtrise [pretriz] NF priesthood; **recevoir la p.** to be ordained a priest

préture [pretyr] NF Antiq praetorship

preums [prɔms] Fam ADJ **first▪**; **je suis p.!** I'm first!
NMF first▪

preuve [prœv] NF **1** (indice) proof, piece of evidence, evidence (UNCOUNT); **avoir la p. que...** to have proof that...; **avez-vous des preuves de ce que vous avancez?** can you produce evidence of or can you prove what you're saying?; **avoir la p. que.../de...** to have proof that.../ of...; **c'est à nous de fournir la p.** it's up to us to show proof, the onus of proof is on us; **p. d'amour** token of love; **p. par commune renommée** hearsay evidence; **p. indiciaire** circumstantial evidence; **p. par écrit** written evidence; **p. intrinsèque** intrinsic evidence; **p. littérale** documentary evidence; **p. par ouï-dire** hearsay evidence; **p. recevable** admissible evidence; **p. tangible** hard evidence; **p. testimoniale** testimony

2 (démonstration) proof; **faire la p. de qch** to prove sth; **mon avocat fera la p. de mon innocence** my lawyer will prove that I'm innocent, my lawyer will prove my innocence; **ce n'est pas une p.** that proves nothing or doesn't prove anything; **la p. de son inexpérience, c'est qu'il n'a pas demandé de reçu** his not asking for a receipt goes to show or proves that he lacks experience; Fam **il n'est pas fiable, la p., il est déjà en retard** you can never rely on him, look, he's already late; **j'en veux pour p....** the proof of it is...; **faire p. d'un grand sang-froid** to show or to display great presence of mind; **c'est un produit qui a fait ses preuves** it's a tried and tested product; **la mission exige des gens ayant fait leurs preuves** the mission calls for experienced people; **il avait fait ses preuves dans le maquis** he'd won his spurs or proved himself in the Maquis

3 Tech = test measuring the alcohol content of a liquid

4 Math **p. par neuf** casting out nines; **faire la p. par neuf** to cast out nines

❏ **à preuve** ADV Fam **tout le monde peut devenir célèbre, à p. moi-même** anybody can become famous, take me for instance or just look at me; **le directeur est un incapable, à p. le déficit de la maison** the manager is incompetent, witness the firm's deficit

❏ **à preuve que** CONJ Fam which goes to show that; **il m'a trahi, à p. qu'on ne peut se fier à personne** he betrayed me, which (just) goes to show that you can't trust anybody

❏ **preuves en main** ADV with cast-iron proof available; **affirmer qch preuves en main** to back sth up with cast-iron evidence or proof

preux [prø] Arch ou Littéraire ADJ M valiant, gallant; **p. chevalier** gallant knight
NM valiant or gallant knight

prévalence [prevalɑ̃s] NF prevalence

prévaloir [61] [prevalwar] VI (prédominer) to prevail (sur/contre over ou against/against); **l'optimisme prévaut encore dans les milieux financiers** optimism still prevails in financial circles; **nous lutterons pour faire p. nos droits légitimes** we will fight for our legitimate rights; **faire p. son opinion** to win acceptance for one's opinion; **en l'occurrence, mon avis a prévalu sur le sien** in the event, my opinion prevailed over or against his/hers; **ce principe prévaut sur tous les autres** this principle takes precedence or prevails over all others; **rien ne prévalut contre son obstination** nothing could prevail against or overcome his/her obstinacy

▸**se prévaloir** VPR **1 se p. de** (profiter de) to take advantage of; (faire valoir → droit) to exercise; **elle se prévalait de son ancienneté pour imposer ses goûts** she took advantage of her seniority to impose her preferences

2 se p. de (se vanter de) to boast of or about; **il se prévalait de ses origines aristocratiques** he boasted of or about his aristocratic background

prévaricateur, -trice [prevarikatœr, -tris] Jur ADJ corrupt
NM,F corrupt official

prévarication [prevarikasjɔ̃] NF Jur (corruption) breach of trust, corrupt practice

prévaricatrice [prevarikatris] voir **prévaricateur**

prévariquer [3] [prevarike] VI Jur to depart from justice

prévaudrai, prévaux etc voir **prévaloir**

prévenance [prevnɑ̃s] NF consideration, thoughtfulness; **être plein de p. à l'égard de qn** to show consideration for or to be considerate

towards sb; **entourer qn de prévenances** to do or to show sb many kindnesses

prévenant, -e [prevnɑ̃, -ɑ̃t] ADJ **1** (personne) considerate, thoughtful (**envers** towards); (geste) thoughtful; **des manières prévenantes** attentive manners **2** Vieilli (engageant) **un homme à p.** a man of engaging appearance

prévenir [40] [prevnir] VT **1** (informer) **p. qn (de qch)** to inform sb (about or of sth), to let sb know (about or of sth); **si tu m'avais prévenu, j'aurais préparé à dîner** if you'd let me know, I'd have prepared something for dinner; **je vais le p. que vous êtes ici** I'll tell him or let him know that you're here; **préviens-moi s'il y a du nouveau** let me know if anything new comes up; **en cas d'accident, qui dois-je p.?** who should I inform or notify in case of an accident?; **p. la police** to call or to notify the police

2 (mettre en garde) to warn, to tell; **on m'avait prévenu de n'ouvrir à personne** I had been warned or told not to open to anybody; **je te préviens, si tu recommences, c'est la fessée!** I'm warning you, if you do that again I'll spank you!; **tu es** ou **te voilà prévenu!** you've been warned!

3 (empêcher → maladie) to prevent; (→ catastrophe) to avert; (→ danger) to ward or stave off; **p. une rechute** to prevent a relapse; **comment p. d'autres tragédies de ce genre?** how can we prevent other such disasters from happening?; Prov **mieux vaut p. que guérir** prevention is better than cure

4 (anticiper → désir, besoin) to anticipate; (→ accusation, critique) to forestall; **j'ai écrit cette préface pour p. toute accusation de parti pris politique** I've written this preface in order to forestall any charges of political prejudice

5 (influencer) **p. qn en faveur de** to predispose sb towards; **p. qn contre** to prejudice sb against

USAGE ABSOLU **partir sans p.** to leave without warning or notice

préventif, -ive [prevɑ̃tif, -iv] ADJ preventive, preventative; **prendre des mesures préventives** to take preventive or precautionary measures; **prenez ce médicament à titre p.** take this medicine as a precaution

❏ **préventive** NF custody (pending trial); **faire de la préventive** to be remanded in custody; **ils ont fait trois mois de préventive** they were imprisoned without trial for three months

prévention [prevɑ̃sjɔ̃] NF **1** (ensemble de mesures) prevention; **nous nous attachons à la p. des accidents** we endeavour to prevent accidents; **la p. joue un grand rôle dans la lutte contre le SIDA** prevention plays an important role in the fight against Aids; **la p. routière** the road safety administration, Br ≃ the Royal Society for the Prevention of Accidents

2 (parti pris → positif) predisposition, bias (**en faveur de** in favour of); (→ négatif) prejudice, bias (**contre** against); **avoir des préventions à l'égard de** ou **contre qn** to be prejudiced or biased against sb; **toute innovation dans ce domaine se heurte aux préventions du public** any innovation in this domain meets with public resistance

3 Jur custody; **il a fait un an de p. avant d'être jugé** he was remanded in custody for one year before being tried

préventive [prevɑ̃tiv] voir **préventif**

préventivement [prevɑ̃tivmɑ̃] ADV (comme précaution) preventatively, as a precaution or preventive

préventologie [prevɑ̃tɔlɔʒi] NF preventative or preventive medicine

préventorium [prevɑ̃tɔrjɔm] NM tuberculosis sanatorium, preventorium

prévenu, -e [prevny] PP voir **prévenir**
ADJ **1** (partial) biased (**en faveur de** or **pour/contre** in favour of/against) **2** Jur (poursuivi judiciairement) charged; **il est p. de meurtre avec préméditation** he is charged with premeditated murder
NM,F (à un procès) defendant; (en prison) prisoner; **le p. nie toute participation aux faits** the defendant denies being involved

préverbe [prevɛrb] NM preverb

prévient, prévint etc voir **prévenir**

prévisibilité [previzibilite] NF foreseeability

prévisible [previzibl] ADJ foreseeable, predictable; **ses réactions ne sont pas toujours prévisibles** his/her reactions are sometimes unexpected or unpredictable; **son échec était p.** it was to be expected that he'd/she'd fail; **c'était difficilement p.** it was hard to foresee

prévision [previzjɔ̃] NF 1 (gén pl) (calcul) expectation; **le coût de la maison a dépassé nos prévisions** the house cost more than we expected; **selon nos prévisions** according to our forecast; **réussir au-delà de toute p.** to succeed beyond all expectation

2 Écon (activité) forecasting; (résultat) forecast; **p. de la base** grass-roots forecasting; **p. boursière** Stock Market forecast; **prévisions budgétaires** budget forecasts or estimates; **prévisions conjoncturelles** economic forecasts; **p. de la demande** forecast of demand; **prévisions économiques** economic forecasts; **p. événementielle** hazard forecasting; **p. du marché** market forecasting; **prévisions qualitatives** qualitative forecasting; **prévisions quantitatives** quantitative forecasting; **p. de ventes** sales forecast; **p. des ventes et profits** sales and profit forecast

3 Météo (technique) (weather) forecasting; **prévisions météorologiques** (bulletin) weather forecast

▫ **en prévision de** PRÉP in anticipation of; **isoler une maison en p. du froid** to insulate a house in anticipation of cold weather

prévisionnel, -elle [previzjɔnɛl] ADJ (analyse, étude) forward-looking; (coût, budget) estimated

prévisionner [previzjɔne] VT Cin & TV to preview

prévisionniste [previzjɔnist] NMF Écon forecaster

prévisualisation [previzɥalizasjɔ̃] NF Ordinat print preview

prévoir [63] [prevwar] VT 1 (prédire → gén) to foresee, to anticipate; (→ augmentation, baisse, ventes) to forecast; Météo to forecast; **p. une augmentation du trafic** to anticipate or to expect an increase in traffic; **j'avais prévu que ça arriverait** I anticipated it would happen; **on ne peut pas toujours tout p.** you can't always think of everything in advance; Fam **alors ça, ça n'était pas prévu au programme** we weren't expecting that to happen▪; Fam **heureusement qu'on avait prévu le coup!** luckily we had anticipated this!▪; **et maintenant, le temps prévu pour demain** and now, tomorrow's weather; **rien ne laissait p. pareil accident** nothing indicated that such an accident could happen; **rien ne laissait p. qu'il nous quitterait si rapidement** we never expected him to pass away so soon; **tout laisse p. que...** everything points or all signs point to...

2 (projeter) to plan; **tout s'est passé comme prévu** everything went according to plan or smoothly; **on a dîné plus tôt que prévu** we had dinner earlier than planned; **tout est prévu pour les invités** everything has been laid on or arranged for the guests; **le repas est prévu pour 100 personnes** a meal for 100 people has been planned; **l'ouverture du centre commercial est prévue pour le mois prochain** the opening of the shopping Br centre or Am mall is scheduled for next month; **l'argent que nous avions prévu pour le voyage n'a pas suffi** the money we allowed for or budgeted for or set aside for the trip wasn't enough; **nous avions prévu une heure pour la correspondance** we'd allowed an hour for the connection; **dépenses prévues au budget** expenses provided for or included in the budget; **p. de faire qch** to plan to do sth; **j'ai prévu d'apporter des boissons chaudes pour tout le monde** I'm planning to bring hot drinks for everyone

3 (emporter → repas, imperméable) to bring; **prévoyez des vêtements chauds** make sure you bring some warm clothes

4 Jur to provide for; **dans tous les cas prévus par la loi** in all cases provided for by law; **la loi n'a pas prévu un cas semblable** the law makes no provision for a case of this kind

prévôt [prevo] NM 1 Hist provost 2 Mil provost marshal

prévôtal, -e, -aux, -ales [prevotal, -o] ADJ 1 Hist provostal, relating to provost duty; **cour prévôtale** provostal court (temporary criminal court

without appeal), summary court 2 Mil **service p.** provost duty

prévôté [prevote] NF 1 Hist provostship 2 Mil military police

prévoyait etc voir **prévoir**

prévoyance [prevwajɑ̃s] NF foresight, foresightedness, forethought; **faire preuve de p.** to be provident; **elle a manqué de p. en achetant cette voiture** it was rather short-sighted or unwise of her to buy that car; **p. sociale** social security provisions

prévoyant, -e [prevwajɑ̃, -ɑ̃t] ADJ provident, prudent; **ses parents ont été prévoyants** his/her parents made provision for the future

prévu, -e [prevy] PP voir **prévoir**

PRG [peɛrʒe] NM Pol (abrév **Parti radical de gauche**) = left-of-centre French political party

Priam [prijam] NPR Myth Priam

priant [prijɑ̃] NM kneeling statue

Priape [prijap] NPR Priapus

priapée [prijape] NF 1 Antiq (chant) song in honour of Priapus; (fête) Priapic fertility rite 2 Vieilli (poésie) lewd verse

priapisme [prijapism] NM Méd priapism

prie-Dieu [pridjø] NM INV prie-dieu, prayer stool

prier [10] [prije] VT 1 (ciel, Dieu) to pray to; **p. la Vierge Marie** to pray to the Virgin Mary; **je prie Dieu (et tous ses saints) que...** I pray (to) God (and all his saints) that...

2 (supplier) to beg, to beseech; **je vous en prie, emmenez-moi** I beg you to take me with you; **je te prie de me pardonner** please forgive me; **les enfants, je vous en prie, ça suffit!** children, please, that's enough!; **il adore se faire p.** he loves to be coaxed; **elle ne s'est pas fait p. pour venir** she didn't need any persuasion to come along; **après s'être fait un peu p.** after a bit of persuasion or persuading or coaxing; **j'ai accepté sans me faire p.** I said yes without any hesitation

3 (enjoindre) to request; **vous êtes priés d'arriver à l'heure** you're requested to arrive on time; **je te prie de ne pas t'occuper de ça!** I'd be obliged if you minded your own business!, kindly or please mind your own business!; **je vous prie de croire qu'il m'a écouté cette fois!** believe (you) me, he listened to me this time!

4 (dans des formules de politesse) **merci – je vous en prie** thank you – (please) don't mention it; **je vous remercie d'être venu – je vous en prie** thank you for coming – you're welcome or (please) don't mention it; **puis-je entrer? – je vous en prie** may I come in? – please do; **pourriez-vous m'indiquer où est le commissariat, je vous prie?** could you please tell me or would you be kind enough to tell me where the police station is?; **M. et Mme Lemet vous prient de bien vouloir assister au mariage de leur fille** (sur une invitation) Mr and Mrs Lemet request the pleasure of your company at their daughter's wedding; **je vous prie de croire à mes sentiments distingués** ou **les meilleurs** (à quelqu'un dont on connaît le nom) Br yours sincerely, Am sincerely (yours); (à quelqu'un dont on ne connaît pas le nom) Br yours faithfully, Am sincerely (yours)

5 Littéraire (inviter) **p. qn à qch** to ask or to invite sb for sth, Littéraire to request sb's presence at sth; **il nous a priés à déjeuner** he asked or invited us to lunch

VI to pray; **elle a prié longtemps** she prayed for a long time; **p. de toute son âme** to pray with all one's soul; **p. pour qn** to pray for sb; **prions pour la paix** let us pray for peace

prière [prijɛr] NF 1 Rel prayer; **dire** ou **faire** ou **réciter ses prières** to pray, to say one's prayers; **être en p.** to be praying; **je l'ai trouvé en p.** I found him at prayer; **pensez à moi dans vos prières** remember me in your prayers; **tu peux faire tes prières** (menace) say your prayers

2 (requête) request, plea, entreaty; **elle a fini par céder aux prières de ses enfants** she finally gave in to her children's pleas; **p. de ne pas ouvrir la fenêtre** (sur panneau) please keep the window closed; **p. de ne pas fumer** (sur panneau) no smoking (please)

3 (utilisé dans la correspondance) **p. de nous couvrir par chèque** kindly remit by cheque; **p. de faire suivre** please forward

▫ **prière d'insérer** NM OU NF insert (publisher's blurb for press release)

prieur, -e [prijœr] ADJ **père p.** prior; **mère prieure** prioress
NM prior
▫ **prieure** NF prioress

prieuré [prijœre] NM (communauté) priory; (église) priory (church)

prima donna [primadɔna] (pl **prime donne** [primedɔne]) NF prima donna

primage [primaʒ] NM Tech priming

primaire [primɛr] ADJ 1 (premier → d'une série) primary; **élection p.** primary election; **école/enseignement p.** Br primary or Am elementary school/education; Géol **ère p.** Palaeozoic (age)

2 (couleur) primary

3 (de base) **connaissances primaires** basic knowledge

4 (borné → personne) narrow (in outlook), unsophisticated; (→ attitude) simplistic, unsophisticated; **faire de l'anticommunisme p.** to be a dyed-in-the-wool or an out-and-out anticommunist; **il est plutôt p. dans ses raisonnements** his arguments are rather simplistic

NMF (personne bornée) person of narrow outlook; **ces gens sont des primaires, ils voteront pour n'importe quel démagogue** these people aren't very sophisticated, they'll vote for any rabble-rouser

NM 1 Scol **le p.** Br primary or Am elementary education; **être en p.** to be at Br primary or Am elementary school; **dans le p.** in Br primary or Am elementary schools; **les classes du p.** Br primary or Am elementary school classes

2 Géol **le p.** the Palaeozoic age

3 Écon **le p.** the primary sector

NF Pol primary (election); **les primaires** the primaries

primal, -e, -aux, -ales [primal, -o] ADJ primal; **cri p.** primal scream

primarité [primarite] NF simplemindedness

primat [prima] NM 1 Rel primate; **le p. des Gaules** the Archbishop of Lyons 2 Littéraire (supériorité) sway, primacy; **le p. des émotions sur l'esprit** the primacy of emotions over the mind

primate [primat] NM 1 Zool primate; **les primates** the Primates 2 Fam (homme grossier) ape, brute

primatial, -e, -aux, -ales [primasjal, -o] Rel ADJ primatial
▫ **primatiale** NF primatial church

primatie [primasi] NF Rel (dignité) primateship, primacy; (siège) primacy

primatologie [primatɔlɔʒi] NF primatology

primatologue [primatɔlɔg] NMF primatologist

primauté [primote] NF 1 (supériorité) primacy; **avoir la p.** to have priority, to come first; **avoir la p. sur** to have priority over; **donner la p. à la théorie sur la pratique** to accord more importance to theory than to practice; Littéraire **gagner qn de p.** to forestall sb 2 Rel primacy; **la p. du pape** the primacy of the Pope

prime [prim] ADJ 1 Math prime; **m p.** m prime

2 Littéraire (premier) **dès sa p. enfance** ou **jeunesse** from his/her earliest childhood; **elle n'est plus vraiment dans sa p. jeunesse** she's not that young any more; **de p. saut** (à la première impulsion) on the first impulse; (dès la première fois) at the first attempt, at once

NF 1 (gratification) bonus; **p. d'ancienneté** bonus for long service; **p. de départ** severance pay, golden handshake; **p. d'encouragement** incentive; **p. d'intéressement** incentive bonus; **p. d'objectif** incentive bonus; **p. de rendement** productivity bonus; (pour mission réussie) success fee

2 (indemnisation → par un organisme) allowance; (→ par l'État) subsidy; UE **p. à l'arrachage (des pommiers/de la vigne)** subsidy for uprooting (apple trees/vines); **p. pour l'emploi** = tax credit awarded to low wage-earners, as an incentive to continue working and not claim benefit instead; **p. de transport/déménagement** travel/relocation allowance; **p. de licenciement** redundancy payment; **p. de risque** danger money; **p. de vie chère** cost-of-living allowance

3 (incitation) subsidy; Fig **cette mesure est une p. à la délation** this measure will only encourage people to denounce others; **p. de**

développement industriel industrial development subsidy; **p. de développement régional** regional development subsidy; **p. à l'exportation** export subsidy; **p. à l'investissement** investment subsidy; **p. au retour** repatriation allowance

4 Fin (cotisation) premium; (indemnité) indemnity; **p. d'assurance** insurance premium; **ils ne toucheront pas la p.** (bonus) they will not qualify for the no-claims bonus; **p. de renouvellement** renewal premium; **p. unique** single premium

5 Bourse (taux) option rate; (somme) option money; **faire p.** to stand at a premium; **lever la p.** to exercise or take up an option; **réponse des primes** declaration of options; **p. acheteur** buyer's option; **p. du change** agio; **p. de conversion** conversion premium; **p. d'émission** premium on option to buy shares; **p. de remboursement** premium on redemption, redemption fee; **p. de risque de marché** risk premium; **p. vendeur** seller's option

6 Mktg (cadeau) free gift, giveaway; **p. auto-payante** self-liquidating premium; **p. contenant** container premium; **p. différée** on-pack offer; **p. directe** with-pack premium; **p. à l'échantillon** free sample; **p. produit en plus** bonus pack

7 Rel prime; **chanter p.** to sing the prime
□ **de prime abord** ADV at first sight or glance
□ **en prime** ADV as a bonus; **en p. vous recevrez trois tasses à café** as a bonus, you will get a free gift of three coffee cups; **recette donnée en p. avec ce produit** free recipe when you buy this product; **non seulement il ne fait rien mais en p. il se plaint!** not only does he do nothing, but he complains as well!

primé, -e [prime] ADJ (film, vin, fromage) award-winning; (animal) prizewinning

prime donne [primedɔne] voir **prima donna**

primer [3] [prime] VT **1** (récompenser → animal, invention) to award a prize to; **les races traditionnelles ne sont plus souvent primées** awards are seldom given or seldom go to the traditional breeds nowadays; **elle a été primée au concours du plus beau bébé** she won or was awarded a prize in the beautiful baby contest; **un film primé à Cannes l'année dernière** a film which won an award at Cannes last year
2 (prédominer sur) to take precedence over
VI (avoir l'avantage) to take precedence; **pour lui, c'est l'intelligence qui prime** intelligence is what counts most for him; **ce qui prime chez lui, c'est l'honnêteté** honesty is his most outstanding quality; **p. sur** to take precedence over; **le salaire a primé sur tous les autres avantages** the salary took precedence over all the other advantages; **son dernier argument a primé sur tous les autres** his/her final argument won out over all the others

primerose [primroz] NF Bot hollyhock, rose mallow

primesaut [primso] NM Littéraire first impulse
primesautier, -ère [primsotje, -ɛr] ADJ **1** (spontané) impulsive, spontaneous **2** (vif → humeur) jaunty

prime time [prajmtajm] NM TV prime time

primeur [primœr] NF (exclusivité) **notre chaîne a eu la p. de l'information** our channel was first with the news; **je vous réserve la p. de mon reportage** you'll be the first one to have or you'll have first refusal of my article; **merci de me donner la p.** thank you for letting me know first
□ **primeurs** NFPL early fruit and vegetables

primeuriste [primœrist] NMF early fruit and vegetable grower

primevère [primvɛr] NF Bot (sauvage) primrose; (cultivée) primula; **p. élevée** oxlip; **p. officinale** cowslip

prim'holstein [primɔlʃtajn] ADJ INV = relating to the Prim'holstein breed of cattle
NMF INV Prim'holstein, Holstein-Friesian (breed of dairy cow)

primidi [primidi] NM Hist = first day of a ten-day period in the Republican calendar
primipare [primipar] ADJ primiparous
NF primipara

primipile [primipil] NM Antiq = highest rank of a centurion in the Roman army

primitif, -ive [primitif, -iv] ADJ **1** (initial) primitive, original; **voici notre projet dans sa forme primitive** here is our project in its original form; **mes gants ont perdu leur teinte primitive** my gloves have lost their original colour; **le sens p. du mot a disparu** the original meaning of the word has disappeared; **l'Église primitive** the early or primitive Church; **l'homme p.** primitive or early man; **langage p.** primitive language; Suisse **la Suisse primitive, les cantons primitifs** = the original four cantons that unified in 1291 to form a confederation, the beginning of modern-day Switzerland; Ling **temps p.** basic tense; Géol **terrain p.** primeval or primitive formations
2 (non industrialisé → société) primitive; **leur technologie est plus que primitive** their technology is definitely primitive or archaic; **la vie dans ces montagnes est restée très primitive** life in these mountains is still very primitive; Fig **ton installation électrique est plutôt primitive!** the wiring in your place is a bit primitive!
3 (fruste → personne) primitive, unsophisticated; **il est gentil mais un peu p.** he's nice but a bit unsophisticated
4 Beaux-Arts primitive; **la peinture primitive flamande/italienne** primitive Flemish/Italian painting
5 Opt **couleurs primitives** major colours
6 Math **fonction primitive** primitive (function)
NM,F **1** (en anthropologie) member of a primitive society, primitive
2 Beaux-Arts primitive (painter)
□ **primitive** NF Ordinat & Math primitive

primitivement [primitivmã] ADV originally, in the first place; **p., mon intention était de rester une semaine** I originally intended to stay for one week

primitivisme [primitivism] NM Beaux-Arts primitivism

primo [primo] ADV Fam first of all■, for starters; **p., je n'en ai pas envie, (et) secundo je n'ai pas le temps** first of all, I don't feel like it, (and) second, I haven't got the time

primo-accédant [primoaksedã] (pl primo-accédants) NM first-time buyer

primo-arrivant, primo-arrivante [primoarivã, -ãt] (mpl primo-arrivants, fpl primo-arrivantes) ADJ recently immigrated
NM,F recent immigrant

primogéniture [primoʒenityr] NF primogeniture
primo-infection [primoɛ̃fɛksjɔ̃] (pl primo-infections) NF primary infection

primordial, -e, -aux, -ales [primɔrdjal, -o] ADJ **1** (essentiel) fundamental, essential; **d'une importance primordiale** of prime importance; **elle a eu un rôle p. dans les négociations** she played a crucial role in the negotiations; **il est p. que tu sois présent** it's essential for you to be there; **il est p. de leur faire parvenir de la nourriture** it's essential or vital to get food to them
2 (originel → élément, molécule) primordial, primeval; **les instincts primordiaux de l'homme** man's primal instincts

primulacée [primylase] Bot NF member of the Primulaceae
□ **primulacées** NFPL Primulaceae

prince [prɛ̃s] NM **1** (souverain, fils de roi) prince; **le p. consort** the prince consort; **le p. héritier** the crown prince; **le p. de Galles** the Prince of Wales; **le P. Noir** the Black Prince; **le p. régent** the Prince Regent; **les princes du sang** princes of royal blood; **les princes qui nous gouvernent** the powers that be; **le P. Charmant** Prince Charming; **être ou se montrer bon p.** to behave generously; **je suis bon p., je vous pardonne** I'll be magnanimous or generous and forgive you; **tu as été bon p.** that was generous of you; **il a agi en p.** he behaved royally; **cet enfant est traité/vêtu comme un p.** that child is treated/dressed like a prince
2 (personnage important) prince; **les princes de l'Église** princes of the Church (cardinals and bishops); **le p. des enfers ou des ténèbres** Satan, the prince of darkness; **le p. des Apôtres** (saint Pierre) the prince of the Apostles
3 (sommité) prince; **le p. des poètes** the prince of poets
4 Fam (homme généreux) real gem or Br gent; **merci, mon p.!** thanks, Br squire or Am buddy!

'Le Petit Prince' Saint-Exupéry 'The Little Prince'

prince-de-galles [prɛ̃sdəgal] ADJ INV Prince-of-Wales check (avant n)
NM INV Prince-of-Wales check material
princeps [prɛ̃sɛps] ADJ INV **édition p.** first edition
princesse [prɛ̃sɛs] NF **1** (souveraine, fille de roi) princess; **habillée comme une p.** dressed like a princess; **arrête de faire la p., tu veux!** stop giving yourself airs! **2** (robe) princess dress **3** Belg (haricot) (very thin) string bean

'La Princesse de Clèves' Madame de La Fayette 'The Princess of Clèves'

princier, -ère [prɛ̃sje, -ɛr] ADJ **1** (du prince) prince's (avant n), royal; **dans la loge princière** in the royal box **2** (luxueux → don) princely; **ils ont donné un cadeau p./une somme princière** they gave a princely gift/sum

princièrement [prɛ̃sjɛrmã] ADV (dîner, recevoir, être traité) in grand style, royally; **nous avons été accueillis p.** we were given a (right) royal welcome

principal, -e, -aux, -ales [prɛ̃sipal, -o] ADJ **1** (essentiel) main; **les principaux intéressés** the main parties involved; **la porte/l'entrée principale** the main gate/entrance; **c'est lui l'acteur p.** he's the leading man
2 Gram (verbe, proposition) main
3 (supérieur) principal, chief; **clerc p.** chief clerk
NM **1** (essentiel) **le p.** the most important thing; **le p., c'est que tu ne sois pas blessé** what is most important is that you're not hurt; **c'est fini, c'est le p.** it's over, that's the main thing
2 Fin (capital) principal; (de l'impôt) = original amount of tax payable before surcharges; **p. et intérêts** principal and interest
3 Mus principal
NM,F Scol (school) principal
□ **principale** NF Ling main clause

principalement [prɛ̃sipalmã] ADV chiefly, mostly, principally; **nous avons besoin p. d'un nouveau directeur** what we need most is a new manager

principat [prɛ̃sipa] NM Hist **1** (dignité) principate **2** (règne) principate

principauté [prɛ̃sipote] NF principality; Rel **les principautés** the principalities

principe [prɛ̃sip] NM **1** (règle morale) principle, rule of conduct; **j'ai des principes** I've got principles; **cela ne fait pas partie de mes principes** it's against my principles; **j'ai toujours eu pour p. d'agir honnêtement** I have always made it a principle to act with honesty; **c'est une question de p.** it's a matter of principle; **vivre selon ses principes** to live in accordance with one's principles; **manquer à tous ses principes** to fail to live up to one's principles; **elle est sans principes** she has no principles
2 (axiome) principle, law, axiom; **les principes de la philosophie** the principles of philosophy; **je pars du p. que...** I start from the principle or I assume that...; **posons comme p. que nous avons les crédits nécessaires** let us assume that we get the necessary credits; **un p. de base** a basic principle; **le p. d'Archimède** Archimedes' principle; Compta **p. de la partie double/simple** double-entry/single-entry method; **c'est le p. des vases communicants** it's the principle of communicating vessels; Fig there's been a knock-on effect
3 (notion → d'une science) principle; **enseigner les principes de la biologie** to teach the basic principles of biology
4 (fonctionnement) principle; **ces deux appareils sont construits selon le même p.** these two appliances are built according to the same principle; **le p. de la vente par correspondance, c'est...** the (basic) principle of mail-order selling is...
5 (fondement) principle, constituent; **votre déclaration contredit le p. même de notre Constitution** your statement goes against the very principle or basis of our Constitution; **le fromage est riche en principes nutritifs** cheese

pri-pri

has a high nutritional value; **p. de précaution** precautionary principle; **p. de précaution sanitaire** precautionary principle

6 *(origine)* origin; **le p. de la vie** the origin of life; **remonter au p. des choses** to go back to first principles

7 *Chim (extrait)* principle; **p. actif** active principle *or* constituent

❑ **de principe** ADJ *(accord, approbation)* provisional

❑ **en principe** ADV **1** *(en théorie)* in principle, in theory, theoretically; **en p., je devrais pouvoir venir** all being well, I should be able to come

2 *(d'habitude)* usually; **en p., nous descendons à l'hôtel** we usually stop at a hotel

❑ **par principe** ADV on principle; **il refuse de l'écouter par p.** he refuses to listen to him/her on principle

❑ **pour le principe** ADV on principle; **je viendrai juste pour le p.** I'll come just on principle; **tu refuses de signer pour le p. ou pour des raisons personnelles?** are you refusing to sign on principle or for personal reasons?

printanier, -ère [prɛ̃tanje, -ɛr] ADJ **1** *(du printemps)* spring *(avant n)*; **il fait un temps p.** it feels like spring, spring is in the air; **une température printanière** springlike weather

2 *(gai et jeune → tenue, couleur)* springlike; **vêtue de couleurs printanières** dressed in springlike colours; **comme tu es printanière avec cette robe!** how (fresh and) springlike you look in that dress!

3 *Culin (potage, salade)* printanier *(garnished with early mixed vegetables, diced)*

printanisation [prɛ̃tanizasjɔ̃] NF *Agr* vernalization

printemps [prɛ̃tɑ̃] NM **1** *(saison)* spring; **au p.** in (the) spring, in (the) springtime; **p. précoce/tardif** early/late spring; **le P. de Bourges** = annual music festival in Bourges **2** *Littéraire (année)* summer; **une jeune fille de vingt p.** a young girl of twenty summers **3** *Littéraire (commencement)* spring; **au p. de la vie** in the springtime of life

'Le Printemps' *Botticelli* 'Spring'

priodonte [prijɔdɔ̃t] NM *Zool* giant armadillo

prion [prijɔ̃] NM *Biol* prion

priorat [prijɔra] NM *Rel* priorate

priori [prijɔri] *voir* **a priori**

priorisation [prijɔrizasjɔ̃] NF prioritizing, prioritization

prioritaire [prijɔritɛr] ADJ **1** *Transp* priority *(avant n)*, having priority; **ce véhicule est p. lorsqu'il quitte son arrêt** this vehicle has (the) right of way *or* has priority when leaving a stop

2 *(usager, industrie)* priority *(avant n)*; **notre projet est p. sur tous les autres** our project has priority over all the others; **mon souci p., c'est de trouver un logement** my main *or* first problem is to find somewhere to live

NMF person with priority; **cette place est réservée aux prioritaires titulaires d'une carte** this seat is reserved for priority cardholders

prioritairement [prijɔritɛrmɑ̃] ADV as a priority, as a matter of urgency

priorité [prijɔrite] NF **1** *(sur route)* right of way; **avoir la p.** to have the right of way; **tu as la p.** it's your right of way; **laisser la p. à une voiture** *Br* to give way *or Am* to yield to a car; **il y a p. à droite** *ou Belg* **de droite** you must *Br* give way to *or Am* yield to traffic coming from the right

2 *(en vertu d'un règlement)* priority; **les handicapés ont la p. pour monter à bord** disabled people are entitled to board first

3 *(antériorité)* priority, precedence

4 *(primauté)* priority; **donner** *ou* **accorder la p. à qch** to prioritize sth, to give priority to sth; **la p. sera donnée à la lutte contre le cancer** priority will be given to the fight against cancer; **ce dossier a la p. absolue** this file is top priority; **avoir la p. sur** to have *or* take priority *or* precedence over

5 *Bourse* **action de p.** *Br* preference share, *Am* preferred stock

6 *Phot* **p. à la vitesse** shutter priority

❑ **en priorité, par priorité** ADV as a priority, as a matter of urgency; **nous discuterons en p. des droits de l'homme** we'll discuss human rights as a priority; **leur dossier sera traité en p.** their file will get priority treatment

pris, -e [pri, -iz] PP *voir* **prendre**

ADJ **1** *(occupé → personne)* busy; *(siège, place)* taken; **une femme très prise** a very busy woman; **je suis déjà p. ce jour-là** I've already got something on that day, that day's booked already; **aide-moi, tu vois bien que j'ai les mains prises** help me, can't you see my hands are full?

2 *Méd* **avoir le nez p.** to have a blocked nose; **avoir la gorge prise** to have a sore throat

3 *(crème, colle, ciment)* set; *(eau, rivière)* frozen

4 *(envahi)* **p. de pitié/peur** stricken by pity/fear; **p. de panique** panic-stricken; **p. de remords** smitten with remorse; **p. d'une violente douleur** seized with a terrible pain; **p. de boisson** under the influence of alcohol

5 *Can* **être bien p.** to be strongly built

❑ **prise** NF **1** *(point de saisie)* grip, hold; *(en escalade)* hold; *(pour le pied)* foothold; **trouve une prise et dis-moi quand tu es prêt** get a grip and tell me when you're ready; **avoir prise sur qn** to have a hold over sb; **je n'ai aucune prise sur mes filles** I can't control my daughters at all; **les menaces n'ont aucune prise sur lui** threats have no effect *or* make no impression on him; **donner prise à la critique** *(personne)* to lay oneself open to attack; *(idée, réalisation)* to be open to attack; *aussi Fig* **lâcher prise** to let go

2 *(de judo, de lutte)* hold; **faire une prise de judo à qn** to use a judo throw on sb

3 *(absorption → d'un médicament)* taking; **la prise du médicament doit se faire à heures régulières** the medication must be taken regularly; **la prise d'insuline doit se faire aux heures prescrites** insulin must be injected at the prescribed times

4 *(dose → de tabac)* pinch; *(→ de cocaïne)* snort

5 *(capture → de contrebande, de drogue)* seizure, catch; *(dans un jeu)* capture; *Pêche* catch; *Mil* **la prise de la Bastille** the storming of the Bastille; **prises de guerre** spoils of war

6 *Élec* **prise (de courant), prise électrique** *(mâle)* plug; *(femelle)* socket; **prise murale** wall socket; **prise multiple** adaptor; **prise Péritel®** Scart plug; *(qui reçoit)* Scart socket; **prise de terre** *Br* earth, *Am* ground; **l'appareil n'a pas de prise de terre** the appliance is not *Br* earthed *or Am* grounded

7 *Tech* **prise d'air** *(ouverture)* air inlet; *(introduction d'air)* ventilation; **prise d'eau** water point; *Aut* **prise directe** direct drive; **prise de vapeur** steam outlet

8 *(durcissement → du ciment, de la colle)* setting; *(→ d'un fromage)* hardening; **à prise rapide** *(ciment, colle)* quick-setting

9 *Cin & TV* **prise longue** long take; **prise des marques** blocking; **prise panoramique** panning shot; **prise unique** single take

10 *(dans des expressions) Fin* **prise de bénéfices** profit-taking; **prise de commandement** taking command (of a regiment); **prise de conscience** realization; **ma première prise de conscience de la souffrance humaine** the first time I became aware of human suffering; **prise en considération** taking into account; **nous insistons sur la prise en considération des circonstances individuelles** we stress that personal circumstances must be taken into account; **prise de contact** meeting; **ce ne sont que les premières prises de contact entre nous** we're just meeting to get to know each other better; *Écon* **prise de contrôle** takeover; *Vieilli* **prise de corps** arrest (by warrant); **prise de décision(s)** decision-making; *Com* **prise à domicile** receipt at domicile; *Rel* **prise d'habit** *(action)* taking the habit; *(cérémonie)* profession; **prise de mousse** secondary champagne fermentation; **prise de notes** note-taking; **prise d'otages** hostage-taking; **encore trois prises de parole avant la fin de la session** three more speeches to go before the end of the session; *Écon* **prise de participation** *(dans une entreprise)* acquisition of an interest in a company; **prise de position** opinion, stand; *Bourse* position taking; **à l'origine, vos prises de position étaient moins libérales** originally, your position was less liberal *or* you took a less liberal stand; **prise de possession** *(d'un héritage)* acquisition; *(d'un territoire)* taking possession; **prise de pouvoir** *(légale)* (political) takeover; *(illégale)* seizure of power; *Fam* **prise de tête** hassle; *Rel* **prise de voile** taking the veil; **à sa prise de voile** when she took the veil

❑ **aux prises avec** PRÉP grappling *or* battling with; **être aux prises avec qch** to be grappling *or* battling with sth; **je l'ai laissé aux prises avec un problème de géométrie** I left him grappling *or* wrestling with a geometry problem

❑ **en prise** ADV *Aut* in gear; **mets-toi en prise** put the car in *or* into gear ADJ *Fig* **être en prise (directe) avec la réalité** to have a good hold on *or* to have a firm grip on reality

❑ **prise d'armes** NF (military) parade

❑ **prise de bec** NF row, squabble; **des petites prises de bec** petty squables

❑ **prise à partie** NF *Jur* = civil action against a judge or magistrate

❑ **prise de sang** NF blood test

❑ **prise de son** NF sound (recording); **la prise de son est de Raoul Fleck** sound (engineer), Raoul Fleck

❑ **prise de vues** NF *Cin & TV (technique)* shooting; *(cliché)* (camera) shot; *(de tournage)* take; **prise de vues: Jaroslaw Mitchell** camera: Jaroslaw Mitchell; **prise de vues images par images** stop-motion photography; **prise de vue aérienne** aerial shot; **prise de vue sur grue** crane shot; **prise de vue en mouvement** running shot; **prise de vue par transparence** process shot; **prise de vue en travelling** travelling shot

❑ **prise en charge** NF **1** *(par la Sécurité sociale)* refunding *(of medical expenses through the social security system)*

2 *(par un taxi)* minimum (pick-up) charge

3 *Fin (de frais)* payment, covering

prisable [prizabl] ADJ *Littéraire* worthy of esteem

prisé, -e[1] [prize] ADJ valued; **des qualités très prisées** highly valued qualities

prisée[2] [prize] NF *Jur* valuation

priser [3] [prize] VT **1** *Littéraire (estimer)* to prize, to value highly; **je ne prise guère sa compagnie** I don't particularly relish his/her company **2** *(tabac)* to take; *(cocaïne)* to snort

VI to take snuff

priseur, -euse [prizœr, -øz] NM,F *(de tabac)* snuff-taker

prismatique [prismatik] ADJ prismatic

prisme [prism] NM **1** *Phys* prism; **jumelles à p.** prismatic binoculars **2** *Fig* **tu vois toujours la réalité à travers un p.** you always distort reality **3** *Géol* **prismes basaltiques** (basalt) columnar structure

prison [prizɔ̃] NF **1** *(lieu)* prison, jail; **être/aller en p.** to be in/to go to prison *or* jail; **mettre qn en p.** to put sb in prison *or* jail; **sortir de p.** to get out (of prison *or* jail); **l'otage a raconté sa vie dans sa p.** the hostage told of (his/her) life in captivity; **pour lui, la pension a été une véritable p.** boarding school was like a prison for him; **p. ouverte** open prison

2 *(peine)* imprisonment; **faire de la p.** to be in prison *or* jail, to serve time; **elle a fait de la p. dans sa jeunesse** she was jailed in her youth; **elle a fait deux ans de p.** she spent two years in prison *or* jail; **il a été condamné à cinq ans de p.** he was sentenced to five years in prison *or* jail; **il risque la p.** he risks going to prison *or* jail; **p. à vie** *ou* **à perpétuité** life sentence; **p. ferme** imprisonment

3 *Fig* prison; **son amour était une p.** I felt caged in by his/her love

prisonnier, -ère [prizɔnje, -ɛr] ADJ **1** *(séquestré)* captive; **plusieurs mineurs sont encore prisonniers au fond de la mine** several miners are still trapped at the bottom of the shaft; **je ne sortais pas et restais p. dans mon petit studio** I shut myself away in my little bedsit and never went out; **il gardait ma main prisonnière** he wouldn't let go of my hand

2 *Fig* **être p. de ses promesses** to be the prisoner of *or* to be trapped by one's promises; **être p. de ses principes** to be a slave to one's principles; **être p. de ses habitudes** to be a creature of habit; **on est p. de son éducation** we're prisoners of our upbringing

NM,F prisoner; **il a été fait p.** he was taken prisoner; **se constituer p.** to give oneself up, to

turn oneself in; **les prisonniers sont montés sur le toit pour protester** the inmates staged a rooftop protest; **p. de droit commun** = prisoner convicted under ordinary criminal law; **les prisonniers de droit commun et les prisonniers politiques** common criminals and political prisoners; **p. de guerre** prisoner of war, POW; **p. en instance de libération** prisoner waiting for *or* pending release; **p. d'opinion** prisoner of conscience; **p. politique** political prisoner

NM 1 *(tige filetée)* stud (bolt)

2 *(pièce sertie)* insert

'La Prisonnière du désert' *Ford* 'The Searchers'

prit *etc voir* **prendre**

privat-docent *(pl* **privat-docents)** **NM 1** [privadɔsɛ̃t] *(professeur libre)* privat-dozent, privat-docent **2** [privadɔsɑ̃] *Suisse (professeur bénévole)* = unpaid university lecturer who gives classes on subjects of his/her choice

privatif, -ive [privatif, -iv] **ADJ 1** *(privé)* private; **avec jardin p.** with a private garden **2** *(réservé à une personne)* exclusive **3** *Jur* **peine privative de liberté** detention **4** *Ling (élément, préfixe)* privative

NM *Ling* privative prefix

privation [privasjɔ̃] **NF** *(perte)* loss, deprivation; **pour moi, arrêter de boire n'a pas été une p.** giving up drinking was no deprivation for me; **p. des droits civiques** loss *or* deprivation of civil rights

❑ **privations NFPL** *(sacrifices)* hardship, hardships; **une vie de privations** a life of hardship; **les privations de la guerre** the hardships of war; **à force de privations** through constant sacrifice, by constantly doing without; **affaibli par les privations** weakened by deprivation

privatique [privatik] **NF** stand-alone technology

privatisable [privatizabl] **ADJ** which can be privatized, privatizable

privatisation [privatizasjɔ̃] **NF** privatization, privatizing

privatisée [privatize] **NF** *(société)* privatized company; *(industrie)* privatized industry

privatiser [3] [privatize] **VT** to privatize

►**se privatiser VPR** to go private

privatiste [privatist] **NMF** private law specialist

privative [privativ] *voir* **privatif**

privauté [privote] **NF** *(familiarité)* **p. de langage** crude *or* coarse language; **une telle p. de langage n'est pas de mise** there's no call for that sort of language

❑ **privautés NFPL** *(libertés déplacées)* liberties; **avoir** *ou* **se permettre des privautés avec qn** to take liberties with sb

privé, -e [prive] **ADJ 1** *(personnel)* private; **ma correspondance privée** my private correspondence; **ma vie privée** my private life

2 *(non public)* private; **une audience privée** a private audience; **nous avons eu droit à une visite privée du château** we were given a private tour of the castle

3 *(officieux)* unofficial; **nous avons appris sa démission de source privée** we've learned unofficially that he/she has resigned

4 *(non géré par l'État)* private

NM 1 *Ind* private sector; **travailler dans le p.** to work for the private sector *or* a private company; *Fam* **elle est médecin à l'hôpital mais elle fait aussi du p.** she works as a doctor in a hospital but she also has *or* takes private patients

2 *(enseignement privé)* private education; **elle a mis ses filles dans le p.** she sent her daughters to a private school

3 *(intimité)* private life; **dans le p., c'est un homme très agréable** in private life, he's very pleasant

4 *Fam (détective privé)* private eye, *Am* dick, shamus

❑ **en privé ADV** in private; **pourrais-je vous parler en p.?** could I talk to you privately *or* in private?; **intimidante en public, elle est pourtant charmante en p.** she may be intimidating in public, but in private life she's charming

priver [3] [prive] **VT 1** *(démunir)* to deprive; **prenez mon écharpe, ça ne me prive guère** have my scarf, I won't miss *or* don't need it; **je ne vous en prive pas?** can you spare it?, I'm not depriving you, am I?; **ça la prive beaucoup de ne plus fumer** she misses smoking a lot; **être privé de** to be deprived of, to have no; **nous avons été privés de trains pendant quatre semaines à cause de la grève** we had no trains for four weeks because of the strike; **nous sommes privés de voiture depuis une semaine** we've been without a car for a week; **privé d'eau/d'air/de sommeil** deprived of water/air/sleep; *Littéraire* **privé de connaissance** bereft of consciousness; **ce genre de situation me prive de tous mes moyens** I completely lose my head *or* I go completely to pieces in that kind of situation; **le cancer/la guerre m'a privé de mon meilleur ami** I lost my best friend to cancer/in the war, cancer/the war took my best friend (away) from me

2 *(comme sanction)* to deprive; **p. qn de qch** to make sb go *or* do without sth; **tu seras privé de dessert/télévision** no dessert/television for you; **il a été privé de sortie** he was grounded, he wasn't allowed to go out; **il a été privé de ses droits de citoyen** he was deprived *or* stripped of his civil rights

►**se priver VPR 1** *(faire des sacrifices)* **elle s'est privée pour leur payer des études** she made great sacrifices to pay for their education; **il n'aime pas se p.** he hates denying himself anything; **ne pas se p.** to deny oneself nothing; **un jour de congé supplémentaire, il ne se prive pas!** another day off, he certainly looks after himself!

2 se p. de *(renoncer à)* to deprive oneself of, to do without; **il se prive d'alcool** he cuts out alcohol, he goes without alcohol

3 *(se gêner)* **il ne s'est pas privé de se moquer de toi** he didn't hesitate to make fun of you; **je ne vais pas me p. de le lui dire!** I'll make no bones about telling him/her!; **tu peux te reposer cinq minutes, elle ne s'en est pas privée!** you can have a rest for five minutes, SHE did!

privilège [privilɛʒ] **NM 1** *(avantage)* privilege; **l'éducation est un droit et non un p.** education is a right, not a privilege; **le p. de l'âge** the prerogative of old age; **j'ai eu le p. de la voir sur scène** I was privileged (enough) to see her perform; **j'ai le triste p. de vous annoncer...** it is my sad duty to inform you...; **j'ai eu le triste p. de connaître cet individu** it was once my misfortune to be acquainted with this individual

2 *(exclusivité)* **l'homme a le p. de la parole** man is unique in being endowed with the power of speech

3 *(faveur)* privilege, favour; **accorder des privilèges à qn** to grant sb favours

4 *Hist (dans l'Ancien Régime)* **les privilèges** privileges

5 *Fin & Jur* **p. de créancier** creditor's preferential claim; **p. fiscal** tax privilege; **p. général/spécial** general/particular lien; **p. du premier saisissant** = priority of payment for the fist creditor to make a claim

6 *Banque* **p. d'émission** right to issue (banknotes)

privilégié, -e [privileʒje] **ADJ 1** *(avantagé)* privileged; **l'île jouit d'un climat p.** the island enjoys an excellent climate; **appartenir aux classes privilégiées** to belong to the privileged classes; **la minorité privilégiée** the privileged few

2 *(choisi → client, partenaire)* favoured; **avoir des relations privilégiées avec un pays** to have a special relationship with a country

3 *(préféré)* favourite, preferred; **le moyen d'expression p. de cet artiste** the artist's favourite *or* preferred means of expression, the means of expression favoured by the artist

4 *Fin (action) Br* preference *(avant n)*, *Am* preferred *(avant n)*; *Jur* **créancier p.** preferential creditor

NM,F privileged person; **quelques privilégiés ont assisté à la représentation** a privileged few attended the performance; **nous faisons partie des privilégiés** we are among the privileged

privilégier [9] [privileʒje] **VT 1** *(préférer)* to privilege; **nous avons privilégié cette méthode pour l'enseignement de la langue** we've singled out this method for language teaching; **je ne veux pas p. telle lecture de 'Tartuffe' plutôt que telle autre** I don't wish to favour this particular interpretation of 'Tartuffe' over any other

2 *(avantager)* to favour; **les basketteurs adverses sont privilégiés par leur haute taille** the basketball players in the opposing team are helped by the fact that they're taller; **cette augmentation privilégie les hauts salaires** this increase is of particular benefit to high earners

3 *(banque)* to grant a charter to

prix [pri] **NM 1** *(tarif fixe)* price, cost; **p. écrasés** *ou* **sacrifiés!** *(sur panneau)* prices slashed!; **à moitié p.** half price; **p. et conditions de transport d'un produit** freight rates and conditions for a product; **le p. de l'essence à la pompe** the cost of *Br* petrol *or Am* gas to the motorist; **six yaourts pour le p. de quatre** six yoghurts for the price of four; **ça coûte un p. fou** it costs a fortune *or* the earth; **mes bottes, dis un p. pour voir!** how much do you think my boots cost?; **le p. du voyage comprend le repas de midi** the cost of the trip includes lunch; **laissez-moi au moins régler le p. des places** let me at least pay for the tickets; **à bas** *ou* **vil p.** very cheaply; **acheter qch à bas p.** to buy sth at a low price *or* very cheaply; **j'ai acheté le lot à vil p.** I bought the lot for next to nothing; **à ce p.-là** at that price; **à ce p.-là, ce serait bête de se le refuser** at that price, it would be silly not to buy it; **dans mes p.** within my (price) range; **c'est tout à fait dans mes p.** it's well within what I can afford *or* within my price range; **ce n'est déjà plus tout à fait dans ses p.** that's already a little more than he/she wanted to spend; **le p. fort** *(maximal)* top *or* maximum price; *(excessif)* high price; **j'ai payé le p. fort pour ma promotion** I was promoted but I paid a high price for it *or* it cost me dear; **je l'ai acheté un bon p.** I bought it for a very reasonable price; **je l'ai vendu un bon p.** I got a good price for it; **on achète aujourd'hui ses esquisses à p. d'or** his sketches are now worth their weight in gold *or* now cost the earth; **je l'ai acheté à p. d'or** I paid a small fortune for it; *Fam* **au p. où sont les choses** *ou* **où est le beurre** seeing how expensive everything is▪; **j'ai fini par trouver le cuir que je voulais mais j'ai dû y mettre le p.** I finally found the type of leather I was looking for, but I had to pay top price for it; *Fig* **elle a été reçue à son examen, mais il a fallu qu'elle y mette le p.** she passed her exam, but she really had to work hard for it; **mettre un p. à qch** to price sth, to put a price on sth; **p. d'acceptabilité** psychological price; **p. d'achat** purchase price; *Bourse* bid price; *Bourse* **p. acheteur** bid price; **p. affiché** sticker price, displayed price; **p. d'appel** loss leader price; **p. cassés** knockdown prices; **p. catalogue** catalogue price, list price; **p. (au) comptant** cash price; *Bourse* spot price; **p. conseillé** recommended retail price; **p. conseillé par le fabricant** manufacturer's recommended price; **p. à la consommation** retail price; **p. courant** going *or* market price; **p. coûtant** cost price; **à p. coûtant** at cost price; **acheter/vendre qch à p. coûtant** to buy/sell sth at cost (price); **p. demandé** asking price; **p. de demi-gros** trade price; **p. départ usine** price ex-works, factory price; **p. de déséquilibre** disequilibrium price; **p. de détail** retail price; **p. directeur** price leader; **p. d'écrémage** skimming price; **p. d'équilibre** target price; **p. d'équilibre concurrentiel** competitive equilibrium price; *Bourse* **p. du disponible** spot price; *Bourse* **p. d'émission** *(d'actions)* issue price; **p. exceptionnel** bargain price; **p. à l'exportation, p. (à l')export** export price; **p. de fabrique** manufacturer's price; **p. facturé, p. de facture** invoiced price; **p. de faveur** preferential price; **p. fixe** fixed price; **p. forfaitaire, p. à forfait** fixed price, all-inclusive price; **p. de gros** wholesale price; **p. homologué** authorized price; **p. hors taxe(s)** price net of tax, price before tax; **p. à l'importation, p. (à l')import** import price; **p. imposé** fixed price; **p. indicatif** approximate price; **p. initial** basic price, prime cost, starting price; *UE* **p. d'intervention** intervention price; **p. au kilo** price per kilo; **p. de lancement** introductory price; **p. libre** deregulated price; **p. marchand** trade price; *Bourse* **p. du marché** market price; **p. marqué** marked price; **p. minimum rentable** break-even price; **p. de négociation** trade

price; **p. net** net price; *(sur un menu)* price inclusive of service; **p. offert** offer price, selling price; **p. officiel** standard price; *Bourse* **p. de l'option** option price; **p. optimum** optimal price; *Mktg* **p. de pénétration** penetration price; **p. plafond** ceiling price; **p. plancher** floor price; **p. pratiqué** current price; **p. préférentiel** preferential price; **p. de prestige** premium price, prestige price; **p. promotionnel** promotional price; **p. psychologique** psychological price; **p. psychologique optimum** optimal psychological price; **p. public** (normal) retail price; **p. de rabais** reduced price, discount price; **p. de rachat** redemption price; **p. recommandé** recommended retail price; **p. réduit** reduced price, discount price; *Bourse* **p. du report** contango rate; **p. de revient** cost price; **p. seuil** floor price; **p. de solde** bargain price; **p. de soutien** support price; **p. standard** standard price; **p. taxé** standard price; **p. taxe comprise** price inclusive of tax; *Bourse* **p. à terme** forward price; **p. tout compris** *ou* **tous frais compris** *ou* **toutes taxes comprises** all-inclusive price; **p. de transport** freight price; **p. unique** flat price; **p. unitaire, p. à l'unité** unit price; **p. d'usine** factory price; **p. vendeur** offer price, selling price; **p. à la vente** sticker price, displayed price; **p. de vente** selling price; **p. de vente imposé** resale price maintenance; **p. de vente publique** public selling price

2 *(étiquette)* price (tag), price label; **il n'y avait pas de p. dessus** it wasn't priced, there was no price (tag) on it

3 *(barème convenu)* price; **votre p. sera le mien** name your price; **faire un p. (d'ami) à qn** to do a special deal for sb; **c'était la fin du marché, elle m'a fait un p. pour les deux cageots** the market was nearly over, so she let me have both boxes cheap; **mettre qch à p.** *(aux enchères)* to set *Br* a reserve *or Am* an upset price on sth; **les deux chandeliers mis à p.** the two chandeliers with *Br* a reserve *or Am* an upset price; *Fig* **sa tête a été mise à p.** there's a price on his/her head *or* a reward for his/her capture

4 *(valeur)* price, value; **le p. de la vie/liberté** the price of life/freedom; **j'ai pris conscience du p. de mon indépendance** I realized how valuable my independence was to me; **donner du p. à qch** to make sth worthwhile; **il donne** *ou* **attache plus de p. à sa famille depuis sa maladie** his family is more important to him since his illness; **on attache plus de p. à la vie quand on a failli la perdre** life is more precious to you when you have nearly lost it; **ça n'a pas de p.** you can't put a price on it; **le sourire d'un enfant, ça n'a pas de p.** a child's smile is the most precious thing in the world

5 *(contrepartie)* **à ce p.** at that *or* such a price; **il fallait céder tous ses droits d'auteur, et à ce p. j'ai refusé** giving up the copyright was too high a price to pay, so I refused (to do it); **oui, mais à quel p.!** yes, but at what cost!

6 *(dans un concours commercial, un jeu)* prize; **premier/deuxième p.** first/second prize

7 *(dans un concours artistique, un festival)* prize, award; **p. littéraire** literary prize; **elle a eu le p. de la meilleure interprétation** she got the award for best actress; *Sport* **le Grand P. (automobile)** the Grand Prix; **le film qui a gagné le Grand P. d'Avoriaz** the film which won the Grand Prix at the Avoriaz festival; **le P. de l'arc de triomphe** = annual horserace at Longchamp; **le P. d'Amérique** = annual trotting race at Vincennes; **le P. de Diane** = annual horserace at Chantilly; **le p. Femina** = annual literary prize whose winner is chosen by a jury of women; **le p. Goncourt** = the most prestigious French annual literary prize; **le p. Louis-Delluc** the Louis Delluc *Br* film *or Am* movie award *(annual prize for a French film)*; **le p. Nobel** the Nobel prize; **le P. de Novembre** = annual literary prize; **le p. Pulitzer** the Pulitzer prize; **le P. Renaudot** = annual literary prize; **le p. Veuve-Clicquot** = businesswoman of the year award

8 *(œuvre primée → livre)* award-winning book or title; *(→ disque)* award-winning record; *(→ film)* award-winning movie *or Br* film

9 *(lauréat)* prizewinner; **il a été P. de Rome** he won the Prix de Rome; **Cannes rend hommage à ses P. d'interprétation féminine** Cannes salutes its award-winning actresses; **nous recevons aujourd'hui le P. Nobel de la Paix** we welcome today the winner of the Nobel Peace prize; **p. de vertu** paragon of virtue; **je n'ai jamais été un p. de vertu** I was never a paragon of virtue

10 *Scol (distinction)* **jour de la distribution des p.** prize *or* prizegiving day; **p. de consolation** consolation prize; **p. d'excellence** first prize; **p. d'honneur** second prize

❑ **à aucun prix ADV** not at any price, not for all the world, on no account; **je ne quitterais le pays à aucun p.!** nothing would induce me to leave the country!; **il ne se séparera de son chien à aucun p.** nothing would ever make him part with his dog

❑ **à n'importe quel prix ADV** at any price, no matter what (the cost); **il veut se faire un nom à n'importe quel p.** he'll stop at nothing to make a name for himself

❑ **à tout prix ADV 1** *(obligatoirement)* at all costs; **tu dois à tout p. être rentré à minuit** you must be back by midnight at all costs

2 *(coûte que coûte)* at any cost, no matter what (the cost); **nous voulons un enfant à tout p.** we want a child no matter what (the cost)

❑ **au prix de PRÉP** at the cost of; **ma mère m'a élevé au p. de grands sacrifices** my mother made great sacrifices to bring me up; **je ne veux pas du succès au p. de ma santé/notre amitié** I don't want success at the cost *or* expense of my health/our friendship; **collaborer avec eux au p. d'une trahison, jamais!** if collaborating with them means becoming a traitor, never!; **qu'est-ce qu'un peu de temps perdu, au p. de ta santé?** what's a little wasted time when your health is at stake?

❑ **de prix ADJ** *(bijou, objet)* valuable

❑ **pour prix de PRÉP** in return for; **pour p. de sa patience** as a reward for *or* in return for his/her patience

❑ **sans prix ADJ** invaluable, priceless; **sa flûte du dix-huitième siècle est sans p.** his/her eighteenth-century flute is priceless; **l'estime de mes amis est sans p.** I value the esteem of my friends above all else

prix-courant [prikurɑ̃] *(pl* **prix-courants***)* **NM** *Com* price list, catalogue

prix-étalon [prietalɔ̃] *(pl* **prix-étalons***)* **NM** *Com* standard cost *or* price

pro [pro] *Fam (abrév* **professionnel***)* **ADJ 1** *(émission, film)* professional■ **2** *Sport* professional■; **il est joueur p. maintenant** he's turned pro

NMF pro; **c'est une vraie p.** she's a real pro; **passer p.** to turn pro; **ils ont fait un vrai travail de p.** they did a really professional job■; **elle a fait ça en p.** she did it like a pro

proactif, -ive [prɔaktif, -iv] **ADJ** proactive

probabilisme [prɔbabilism] **NM** *Phil* probabilism

probabiliste [prɔbabilist] *Phil* **ADJ** probabilist, probabilistic

NMF probabilist

probabilité [prɔbabilite] **NF 1** *(vraisemblance)* probability, likelihood; **selon toute p.** in all probability *or* likelihood **2** *(supposition)* probability; **je ne dis pas qu'il l'a volé, c'est une p.** I'm not saying he stole it, but it's probable; **la p. qu'il gagne est plutôt faible** there's little chance of him winning **3** *Math & Phys* probability

probable [prɔbabl] **ADJ 1** *(vraisemblable)* likely, probable; **il est peu p. qu'elle soit sa sœur** it's not very likely that she's his/her sister; **il est peu p. qu'il réussisse** there is little chance of his succeeding

2 *(possible)* probable; **il est p. qu'elle viendra** she'll probably come; **est-il à Paris? – c'est p.** is he in Paris? – quite probably (he is); *Fam* **je parie qu'elle va refuser – p.!** I bet she'll say no – more than likely!

probablement [prɔbabləmɑ̃] **ADV** probably; **tu as p. raison** you're probably right; **tu viendras demain? – très p.** will you come tomorrow? – very probably *or* quite likely; *Fam* **p. qu'il acceptera** he's likely to accept, he'll probably say yes

probant, -e [prɔbɑ̃, -ɑ̃t] **ADJ 1** *(convaincant → argument, fait, expérience)* convincing; **peu p.** unconvincing **2** *Jur (pièce)* probative

probation [prɔbasjɔ̃] **NF** *Jur & Rel* probation; **être en p.** to be on probation

probationnaire [prɔbasjɔnɛr] **NMF** *Jur* probationer

probatoire [prɔbatwar] **ADJ** probationary; **examen p.** probationary examination; **période p.** trial period; *Jur* **délai p.** probation

probe [prɔb] **ADJ** *Littéraire* upright, endowed with integrity; **homme p.** man of integrity

probité [prɔbite] **NF** probity, integrity, uprightness

problématique [prɔblematik] **ADJ** problematic, problematical

NF *(problèmes)* set of problems *or* issues; *Phil* problematics

problématiquement [prɔblematikmɑ̃] **ADV** problematically

problème [prɔblɛm] **NM 1** *Math* problem; **p. de géométrie** geometry problem; **résoudre un p. d'algèbre** to solve an algebra *or* algebraic problem; **problèmes de robinet** = mathematical problems for schoolchildren, typically about the volume of water in a container

2 *(difficulté)* problem, difficulty; **avoir des problèmes** to have problems; **ne t'inquiète pas, tu n'auras aucun p.** don't worry, you'll be all right; **tu n'auras aucun p. à la convaincre** you won't have any problem convincing her; **pas de p., viens quand tu veux** no problem, you can come whenever you want; *Fam* **tu pourras passer me prendre? – oui, sans p.** could you come and pick me up? – sure, no problem; **nous avons un gros p.** we have a major problem, we're in big trouble here; **un p. personnel** a personal matter; **il a toujours eu des problèmes d'argent** he always had money troubles *or* problems; *Fam* **dis donc, c'est ton p., pas le mien** listen, it's your problem, not mine; **avoir des problèmes psychologiques** to be psychologically disturbed

3 *(question)* problem, issue, question; **soulever un p.** to raise a question *or* an issue; **la clé du p.** the key to the problem; *Fig* **faux p.** red herring; **nous discutons d'un faux p.** we're not discussing the real problem here

❑ **à problèmes ADJ** *(peau, cheveux)* problem *(avant n)*; *Fam* **ma cousine, c'est une femme à problèmes** my cousin's always got problems■

proboscide [prɔbɔsid] **NF** *Arch ou Littéraire (d'éléphant)* trunk

proboscidien, -enne [prɔbɔsidjɛ̃, -ɛn] *Zool* **NM** proboscidian

❑ **proboscidiens NMPL** Proboscidea

procaïne [prɔkain] **NF** *Pharm* Novocaine

procaryote [prɔkarjɔt] *Biol* **ADJ** prokaryotic, procaryotic

NM prokaryote, procaryote

procédé [prɔsede] **NM 1** *(comportement)* conduct, behaviour; **vos procédés sont indignes** your behaviour is shameful; **je n'ai pas du tout apprécié son p.** I wasn't very impressed with what he/she did

2 *(technique)* process; **mettre un p. au point** to perfect a process; **p. de fabrication** manufacturing process; *Chim* **p. Haber-Bosch** Haber process

3 *Péj (artifice)* **toute la pièce sent le p.** the whole play seems contrived

4 *(au billard)* tip

procéder [18] [prɔsede] **VI 1** *(progresser)* to proceed; **p. méthodiquement/par tâtonnements** to proceed methodically/by trial and error; **p. par ordre** to take things in order; **procédons par ordre** let's do one thing at a time

2 *(se conduire)* to behave; **j'apprécie sa manière de p. avec nous** I like the way he deals with us

❑ **procéder à VT IND 1** *(effectuer)* to conduct; **p. à une étude** to conduct a study; **p. à un examen approfondi de la situation** to examine the situation thoroughly; **p. à l'élection du bureau national du parti** to elect the national executive of the party; **p. à l'éviction d'un locataire** to evict a tenant **2** *Jur* **p. à l'arrestation d'un criminel** to arrest a criminal; **p. à l'ouverture d'un testament** to open a will

❑ **procéder de VT IND 1** *Littéraire (provenir de)* to proceed from, to originate in; **tous ses problèmes procèdent d'une mauvaise administration**

all his/her problems spring *or* derive from poor management **2** *Rel* to proceed from

procédural, -e, -aux, -ales [prɔsedyral] **ADJ** procedural

procédure [prɔsedyr] **NF 1** *(démarche)* procedure, way to proceed; **nous suivrons la p. habituelle** we'll follow the usual procedure; **voici la p. à suivre** this is the way to proceed; **procédures de sécurité** safety procedures

2 *Jur (ensemble des règles)* procedure, practice; *(action)* proceedings; **Code de p. civile/pénale** civil law/criminal law procedure; **engager** *ou* **entamer une p. contre qn** to start proceedings against sb; **p. accusatoire** accusatory procedure; **p. civile** civil procedure; **p. contradictoire** adversarial procedure; **p. par défaut** default procedure; **p. de divorce** divorce proceedings; **p. de faillite** bankruptcy proceedings; **p. générale** general procedure; **p. inquisitoire** inquisitorial procedure; **p. à jour fixe** fixed-date procedure; **p. en matière contentieuse** procedure in contentious matters; **p. en matière gracieuse** procedure in non-contentious matters; **p. ordinaire** ordinary procedure; **p. pénale** criminal procedure; **p. sommaire** summary procedure

3 *Ordinat* procedure; **p. de chargement** loading procedure

4 p. scientifique scientific procedure

procédurier, -ère [prɔsedyrje, -ɛr] **ADJ 1** *Péj (personne)* pettifogging, quibbling; **être p.** to be a pettifogger *or* a quibbler **2** *(action, démarche)* litigious; **formalités procédurières** procedural formalities, red tape

NM,F *Péj* pettifogger, quibbler

procellariiforme [prɔselariifɔrm] *Orn* **NM** procellariiform

❑ **procellariiformes NMPL** Procellariiformes

procès [prɔsɛ] **NM 1** *Jur (pénal)* trial; *(civil)* lawsuit, legal proceedings; **p. civil** lawsuit; **p. criminel** (criminal) trial; **p. en diffamation** libel case, libel suit; **p. équitable** fair trial; **faire** *ou* **intenter un p. à qn** to institute legal proceedings against sb; **intenter un p. en divorce à qn** to institute divorce proceedings against sb; **entreprendre** *ou* **engager un p. contre qn** to take sb to court; **instruire un p.** to prepare a lawsuit; **être en p. avec qn** to be involved in a lawsuit with sb; **il a gagné/perdu son p. contre nous** he won/lost his case against us; **un p. pour meurtre** a murder trial; *Fig* **sans autre forme de p.** without further ado; **renvoyé sans autre forme de p.** unceremoniously dismissed

2 *(critique)* **faire le p. de qn/qch** to put sb/sth on trial; **vous me faites un p. d'intention** you're assuming too much about my intentions; **pas de p. d'intention, s'il vous plaît!** don't put words in my mouth, please!; **faire un mauvais p. à qn** to make groundless accusations against sb; **tu lui fais un mauvais p.** you're being unfair to him/her

3 *Anat* process; **p. ciliaire** ciliary process

4 *Ling* process

'Le Procès' *Kafka, Welles* 'The Trial'

processeur [prɔsesœr] **NM** *Ordinat* **1** *(organe)* (hardware) processor; *(unité centrale)* central processing unit

2 *(ensemble de programmes)* (language) processor; **p. entrée/sortie** input/output processor, I/O processor; **p. de données** data processor; **p. frontal/graphique/maître/matriciel** front-end/display/master/array processor; **p. d'image tramée** raster image processor; **p. RISC** RISC processor

processif, -ive [prɔsesif, -iv] **ADJ** *Littéraire (procédurier)* pettifogging, quibbling

procession [prɔsesjɔ̃] **NF 1** *Rel* procession; **p. rituelle** religious procession **2** *(cortège)* procession; **une p. de voitures** a motorcade; **les manifestants s'avançaient en p. vers la place** the demonstrators were marching towards the square in procession

processionnaire [prɔsesjɔnɛr] *Entom* **ADJ** processionary

NF *(papillon)* processionary moth; *(chenille)* processionary caterpillar; **p. du pin** (pine) processionary moth

processionnel, -elle [prɔsesjɔnɛl] **ADJ** processional

processive [prɔsesiv] *voir* **processif**

processualiste [prɔsɛsɥalist] **NMF** *Jur* litigation expert

processus [prɔsesys] **NM 1** *(méthode, démarche, évolution)* process; **le p. d'acquisition de la lecture** learning how to read; **le p. de démocratisation est en marche** the democratization process is under way; *Mktg* **p. d'achat** purchasing process; *UE* **p. de convergence** convergence process; **p. décisionnel** *ou* **de décision** decision-making process; **p. de diffusion** *ou* **de distribution** distribution process; **p. de fabrication** manufacturing process; **p. industriel** industrial processing; **p. de paix** peace process

2 *Psy* **p. primaire/secondaire** primary/secondary process

3 *Méd* process; **p. pathologique** pathology

procès-verbal [prɔsɛvɛrbal] *(pl* **procès-verbaux** [-o]) **NM 1** *Jur (acte → d'un magistrat)* (official) report, record; *(→ d'un agent de police)* (police) report **2** *(pour une contravention)* parking ticket; **dresser un p. à qn** to give sb a parking ticket **3** *(résumé → d'une réunion, d'une assemblée)* minutes; *(→ d'un colloque)* proceedings; *(→ d'un témoignage)* record; **tenir le p. des réunions** to keep the minutes of the meetings

prochain, -e [prɔʃɛ̃, -ɛn] **ADJ 1** *(dans le temps)* next; **je te verrai la semaine prochaine** I'll see you next week; **à samedi p.!** see you next Saturday!; **le mois p.** next month, this coming month; **ça sera pour une prochaine fois** we'll do it some other time; **la prochaine fois, fais attention** next time, be careful

2 *(dans l'espace)* next; **je descends au p. arrêt** I'm getting off at the next stop; **tourne à gauche au p. carrefour** turn left at the next crossroads

3 *(imminent)* imminent, near; **nous nous reverrons dans un avenir p.** we will see each other again in the near future; **un jour p.** one day soon; **leur p. départ** their imminent departure; **il savait sa fin prochaine** he knew his death was imminent, he knew he was not long for this world

4 *(immédiat → cause, pouvoir)* immediate

NM son p. one's fellow man; **aime ton p. comme toi-même** love your neighbour as yourself

❑ **prochaine NF** *Fam* **1** *(arrêt)* next stop; **je descends à la prochaine** I'm getting off at the next stop

2 *(locution)* **à la prochaine!** see you (soon)!, be seeing you!, *Am* so long!

prochainement [prɔʃɛnmɑ̃] **ADV** shortly, soon; **il revient p.** he'll be back soon; **p. sur vos écrans** *(film)* coming soon

PROCHE [prɔʃ]

> **ADJ** nearby **1** ▪ near **1, 2** ▪ imminent **2** ▪ close **3, 4** ▪ similar **5**
> **NM** close relative

ADJ 1 *(avoisinant)* nearby; **elle entra dans une église p.** she went into a nearby church; **le bureau est tout p.** the office is close at hand *or* very near; **le village le plus p. est Pigny** Pigny's the nearest village

2 *(dans l'avenir)* near, imminent; *(dans le passé)* in the recent past; **dans un avenir p.** in the near future; **le dénouement est p.** the end is in sight; **Noël est p.** we're getting close to Christmas; **lampions et drapeaux dans les rues, la fête est p.** there are lanterns and bunting in the streets, the celebrations are about to begin; **la fin du monde est p.** the end of the world is nigh; **la dernière guerre est encore p. de nous** the last war belongs to the not too distant past

3 *(cousin, parent)* close; **adresse de votre plus p. parent** address of your next of kin

4 *(intime)* close; **nous sommes plus proches depuis ce deuil** we've grown closer since we were bereaved; **l'un des proches conseillers du président** one of the president's trusted *or* close advisors

5 *(semblable)* similar; **nos goûts sont très proches** we have very similar tastes

NM close relative *or* relation; **la mort d'un p.** the death of a loved-one; **perdre un p.** to lose a close relative; **ses proches** his/her friends and relatives

❑ **de proche en proche ADV** *(petit à petit)* gradually, step by step; **l'infection gagne de p. en p.** the infection is spreading gradually; **de p. en p., j'ai fini par reconstituer les événements** step by step, I finally reconstructed the events

❑ **proche de PRÉP 1** *(dans l'espace)* near (to), close to, not far from; **la villa est p. de la mer** the villa is close to *or* near the sea; **plus p. de chez lui** closer to his home

2 *(dans le temps)* close; **la guerre est encore p. de nous** the war is still close to us

3 *(en contact avec)* close to; **il est resté p. de son père** he remained close to his father; **elle est très p. de ses élèves/malades** she's close to her pupils/patients; **être p. de la nature** to be close to *or* in touch with nature; **d'après des sources proches de la Maison-Blanche** according to sources close to the White House

4 *(semblable à → langage, espèce animale)* closely related to; *(→ style, solution)* similar to; **la haine est p. de l'amour** hatred is akin to love; **portrait p. de la réalité** accurate *or* lifelike portrait; **une obsession p. de la névrose** an obsession verging on the neurotic; **ils sont proches de nous par la religion et la culture** religiously and culturally they have a lot in common with us

5 *(sans différence de rang, d'âge avec)* close to; **les candidats sont proches les uns des autres** there's little to choose between the candidates; **mes frères et moi sommes proches les uns des autres** my brothers and I are close together (in age)

Proche-Orient [prɔʃɔrjɑ̃] **NM le P.** the Middle East, the Near East

proche-oriental, -e [prɔʃɔrjɑ̃tal] *(mpl* **proche-orientaux** [-o], *fpl* **proche-orientales)** **ADJ** Middle-Eastern, Near-Eastern

prochinois, -e [prɔʃinwa, -waz] *Pol* **ADJ** pro-Chinese; *(maoïste)* Maoist

NM,F pro-Chinese; *(Maoïste)* Maoist

prochordé [prɔkɔrde] = **procordé**

procidence [prɔsidɑ̃s] **NF** *Obst* prolapse of the umbilical cord

proclamation [prɔklamasjɔ̃] **NF 1** *(annonce)* (official) announcement *or* statement; **p. du résultat des élections à 20 heures** the results of the election will be announced at 8 p.m. **2** *(texte)* proclamation; **la p. sera affichée dans toutes les mairies** the proclamation will be displayed in every town hall

proclamer [3] [prɔklame] **VT 1** *(déclarer → innocence, vérité)* to proclaim, to declare; **p. que...** to declare that…; **nous proclamons que la paix sera bientôt instaurée** we declare that we will soon be at peace; **elle est allée p. partout qu'il la battait** she went around telling everybody that he beat her

2 *(annoncer publiquement)* to publicly announce *or* state, to proclaim; **p. la république** to proclaim the republic; **p. le résultat des élections** to announce the results of the election; **p. qn empereur** to proclaim sb emperor

proclitique [prɔklitik] *Ling* **ADJ** proclitic

NM proclitic

proclive [prɔkliv] **ADJ** *Anat* proclivous

proconsul [prɔkɔ̃syl] **NM 1** *Antiq* proconsul **2** *(primate fossile)* Proconsul

proconsulaire [prɔkɔ̃sylɛr] **ADJ** *Antiq* proconsular

proconsulat [prɔkɔ̃syla] **NM** *Antiq* proconsulate

procordé [prɔkɔrde] *Zool* **NM** protochordate

❑ **procordés NMPL** Protochordata

procréateur, -trice [prɔkreatœr, -tris] *Littéraire*

ADJ procreant, procreative

NM,F procreator

procréation [prɔkreasjɔ̃] **NF** procreation; **p. artificielle** artificial reproduction; **p. médicalement assistée** assisted conception

procréatique [prɔkreatik] **NF** *Biol* = field of study relating to the techniques of artificial reproduction

procréatrice [prɔkreatris] *voir* **procréateur**

procréer [15] [prɔkree] *Littéraire* **VT** to procreate

VI to procreate

proctalgie [prɔktalʒi] **NF** *Méd* proctalgia

proctite [prɔktit] **NF** *Méd* proctitis

pro–pro

proctologie [prɔktɔlɔʒi] NF Méd proctology

proctologue [prɔktɔlɔg] NMF Méd proctologist

procurateur [prɔkyratœr] NM Hist procurator

procuratie [prɔkyrasi] NF Hist 1 (palais) procurators' palace 2 (dignité) procuratorship

procuration [prɔkyrasjɔ̃] NF 1 Jur (pouvoir → gén) power or letter of attorney; (→ pour une élection) proxy (form); **donner p. à qn** to authorize or to empower sb; **p. générale** full power of attorney 2 Banque mandate; **il a une p. sur mon compte** he has a mandate to operate my account □ **par procuration** ADJ (vote) proxy (avant n) ADV 1 (voter) by proxy 2 Fig vicariously; **vivre/ voyager par p.** to live/to travel vicariously

procure [prɔkyr] NF Rel procuracy

procurer [3] [prɔkyre] VT 1 (fournir) to provide; **p. de l'argent à qn** to provide sb with money, to obtain money for sb; **p. un renseignement à qn** to get hold of information for sb; **je lui ai procuré un emploi** I found him/her a job; **son travail lui procure d'importants revenus** his/ her job provides him/her with or brings in a substantial income; **les places qu'il m'a procurées étaient excellentes** the seats he found or obtained for me were superb

2 (apporter) to bring; **la lecture me procure beaucoup de plaisir** reading brings me great pleasure, I get a lot of pleasure out of reading; **les joies procurées par les sens** pleasures afforded by the senses

►**se procurer** VPR to get, to obtain; **essaye de te p. son dernier livre** try to get his/her latest book; **il faut que je me procure un visa** I must get a visa

procureur [prɔkyrœr] NM

> Note that it is no longer considered a mistake to feminize this word in sense 1 and to say **une procureure** (with a final **e**) but some French speakers nonetheless regard this form as unacceptable, especially in France. See also the entry **féminisation**.

1 Jur prosecutor; **p. adjoint** ≃ Deputy State Counsel; **p. général** = public prosecutor at the "Parquet", Br ≃ Director of Public Prosecutions, Am ≃ district attorney; **p. de la République** = public prosecutor at a "tribunal de grande instance", ≃ Attorney General 2 Hist (syndic) procurer 3 Rel procurator

procyonidé [prɔsjɔnide] Zool NM procyonid □ **procyonidés** NMPL Procyonidae

prodigalité [prɔdigalite] NF 1 (générosité) extravagance, Sout prodigality, profligacy; **donner avec p.** to be extremely generous 2 (dépenses) extravagance, Sout prodigality; **connu pour ses prodigalités** well-known for his/her extravagance or for his/her extravagant spending habits 3 Littéraire (surabondance) (lavish) abundance, Sout prodigality

prodige [prɔdiʒ] NM 1 (miracle) marvel, wonder; **faire des prodiges** to work wonders, to achieve miracles; **ton médicament a fait des prodiges** your medicine worked wonders; **tenir du p.** to be nothing short of miraculous or a miracle; **cela tient du p. que personne ne soit mort** it's nothing short of a miracle that nobody was killed; **un p. de...** a wonder of...; **cet appareil est un p. de la technique moderne** this machine is a wonder of modern technology; **il nous a fallu déployer des prodiges d'ingéniosité pour tout ranger** we had to use boundless ingenuity to find space for everything

2 (personne) prodigy; **à dix ans, on la considérait comme un p. en mathématiques** at ten years of age she was considered a mathematical genius

ADJ **musicien p.** musical prodigy

prodigieuse [prɔdiʒjøz] voir **prodigieux**

prodigieusement [prɔdiʒjøzmɑ̃] ADV 1 (beaucoup) enormously, tremendously; **je me suis p. amusé** I enjoyed myself tremendously; **il m'agace p.** he really gets on my nerves 2 (magnifiquement) fantastically, magnificently; **elle dessine p. bien** she draws fantastically well

prodigieux, -euse [prɔdiʒjø, -øz] ADJ 1 (extrême) huge, tremendous; **sa chanson a eu un succès p.** his/her song was hugely successful; **être d'une bêtise prodigieuse** to be prodigiously

---

stupid; **être d'une force prodigieuse** to be tremendously strong; **une quantité prodigieuse** a huge amount

2 (peu commun) prodigious, astounding, amazing; **une connaissance prodigieuse d'histoire** an astounding knowledge of history

3 Littéraire (miraculeux) prodigious, miraculous; **guérison prodigieuse** miracle cure

prodigue [prɔdig] ADJ 1 (dépensier) extravagant, Sout profligate 2 Fig **p. de** generous or over-generous with; **elle n'est guère p. de détails** she doesn't go in much for detail; **p. de compliments** lavish with compliments; **tu es toujours p. de bons conseils** you're always full of good advice

NMF spender, spendthrift

prodiguer [3] [prɔdige] VT 1 (faire don de) to be lavish with; **la nature nous prodigue ses bienfaits** nature is profuse or lavish in its bounty; **elle a prodigué des soins incessants à son fils** she lavished endless care on her son; **il lui prodiguait ses conseils** he was generous with his advice, he lavished advice on him/her; aussi Péj **prodiguant des sourires à tous** smiling bountifully at everybody 2 (gaspiller) to waste, to squander

►**se prodiguer** VPR Littéraire **il se prodigue sans compter** he gives generously of himself

pro domo [prodomo] ADJ INV **faire un plaidoyer p.** to defend oneself or one's own cause

prodrome [prɔdrom] NM 1 Méd warning symptom, Spéc prodrome 2 Littéraire (signe) forerunner, early sign

prodromique [prɔdrɔmik] ADJ Méd prodromal

producteur, -trice [prɔdyktœr, -tris] ADJ producing; **les pays producteurs de pétrole** oil-producing countries; **zone productrice de betteraves** beetroot-producing or beetroot-growing area; Fin **p. d'intérêt** interest-bearing; Cin **société productrice** production company

NM,F Cin, Rad, Théât & TV (personne) producer; **p. associé** associate producer, production associate; **p. de cinéma** movie or Br film producer; **p. délégué** executive producer; **p. de disques** record producer; **p. d'émissions de radio** radio producer; **p. exécutif** executive producer

NM Agr & Écon producer; (société) production company; **directement du p. au consommateur** directly from the producer to the consumer; Agr **les producteurs sont mécontents** the farmers are up in arms; **les producteurs de melons** melon growers or producers; **ce pays est le premier p. de composants électroniques du monde** this country is the world's largest producer of electronic components

productibilité [prɔdyktibilite] NF maximum energy yield (from a hydroelectric power station)

productible [prɔdyktibl] ADJ (marchandise) producible

productif, -ive [prɔdyktif, -iv] ADJ 1 (travailleur) productive; (auteur) prolific; **de manière productive** productively; **c'est l'un de nos auteurs les plus productifs** he is one of our most prolific or productive authors 2 Fin **capital p.** interest-bearing or interest-yielding capital; **p. d'intérêts** interest-bearing 3 Agr & Mines productive; **le sol est peu p.** the yield from the soil is poor

production [prɔdyksjɔ̃] NF 1 (activité économique) **la p.** production; **la p. ne suit plus la consommation** supply is failing to keep up with demand; **à ce stade de la p., nous perdons de l'argent** at this stage of production, we're losing money

2 (rendement) & Ind output; Agr yield; **la p. a augmenté/diminué** Ind output has risen/ dropped; Agr the yield is higher/lower; **l'usine a une p. de 10 000 voitures par an** the factory turns out or produces 10,000 cars a year; **p. globale** aggregate production or output

3 (produits) & Agr produce (UNCOUNT), production (UNCOUNT); Ind products, production; **les productions maraîchères de la région** the Br market-garden or Am truck-garden produce of the area; **le pays veut écouler sa p. de maïs** the country wants to sell off its maize crop or the maize it has produced; **p. excédentaire** surplus production; Compta **p. stockée** (poste de bilan) stored production, production left in stock; **p. vendue** sales

---

4 (fabrication → gén) production, manufacturing; (→ d'électricité) production, generation; **p. à la chaîne** production line system, mass production; **p. sur** ou **à la commande** production to order; **p. discontinue** production in batches; **p. juste à temps** just-in-time production; **p. manufacturée** secondary production; **p. de matières premières** primary production; **p. textile** textile manufacturing

5 (d'une œuvre d'art → action de créer) production, creation; Cin, Théât & TV production

6 (d'une œuvre d'art → résultat créé) Cin production, Br film, Am movie; Rad production, programme; Théât production, play; **la p. contemporaine** contemporary works; **la p. dramatique/romanesque du XVIIIème siècle** 18th-century plays/novels; **une importante p. littéraire** a large literary output; **les productions de l'esprit** intellectual work

7 (d'une œuvre d'art → financement) production; **assurer la p. de** to produce; **assistant/ directeur de p.** production assistant/manager; **société de p.** production company

8 (présentation) presentation; **sur p. d'un acte de naissance** on presentation of a birth certificate

9 (fait d'occasionner) production, producing, making; **la p. d'un son** making a sound

10 Tech **p. combinée** heat and power (generation)

11 Fin **p. immobilisée** = fixed assets produced for use by the company

productique [prɔdyktik] NF industrial automation

productive [prɔdyktiv] voir **productif**

productivisme [prɔdyktivism] NM Péj obsession with productivity

productiviste [prɔdyktivist] ADJ Péj that emphasizes productivity to an obsessive degree

productivité [prɔdyktivite] NF 1 (fertilité → d'un sol, d'une région) productivity, productiveness 2 (rendement) productivity; **accroissement de la p.** increase in productivity; Fin **p. de l'impôt** (net) tax revenue; Écon **p. marginale** marginal productivity 3 Écol productivity, production

productrice [prɔdyktris] voir **producteur**

produire [98] [prɔdɥir] VT 1 (fabriquer → bien de consommation) to produce, to manufacture; (→ énergie, électricité) to produce, to generate; Agr (faire pousser) to produce, to grow; **p. qch en masse** to mass-produce sth; **p. qch en série** ou **à la chaîne** to produce sth on an assembly line

2 (fournir → sujet: usine) to produce; (→ sujet: sol) to produce, to yield; Fin (bénéfice) to yield, to return

3 (causer → bruit, vapeur) to produce, to make; (→ douleur, démangeaison) to produce, to cause; (→ sensation) to create, to generate; (→ changement) to effect, to bring about; (→ résultat) to produce; **la lumière produit une illusion spectaculaire** the light creates a spectacular illusion; **l'effet produit par son discours a été catastrophique** the effect of his/her speech was disastrous; **p. une impression favorable sur qn** to produce or make a favourable impression on sb

4 (créer → sujet: artiste) to produce; **il a produit quelques bons romans** he has written or produced a few good novels

5 Cin, Rad, Théât & TV to produce

6 (engendrer) to produce; **combien le XIXème siècle/Mexique a-t-il produit de romancières?** how many female novelists did the 19th century produce/has Mexico produced?

7 (présenter → passeport) to produce, to show; (→ preuve) to produce, Sout to adduce; (→ témoin) to produce

USAGE ABSOLU Écon to produce, to be productive; **tes arbres ne produiront jamais** your trees will never bear fruit; **il produit beaucoup** (écrivain) he writes a lot; (musicien) he writes or composes a lot; (cinéaste) he makes a lot of movies or Br films

►**se produire** VPR 1 (événement) to happen, to occur; **ça peut encore se p.** it may happen again; **il s'est produit un très grave accident près d'ici** there was a very serious accident near here; **une transformation majeure s'est produite** a major change has taken place

2 (personne) to appear, to give a performance;

se p. sur scène to appear on stage; **se p. en public** to give a public performance

produit [prɔdɥi] NM **1** *Ind* product, article; *Agr* product, produce *(UNCOUNT)*; **les produits de la terre** the produce of the land; **produits d'achat courant** convenience goods; **produits agricoles** agricultural produce, farm products; **produits alimentaires, produits d'alimentation** food products, foodstuffs; *Mktg* **p. d'appel** loss leader, traffic builder; **p. augmenté** augmented product; **p. bactéricide** bactericide; **p. de beauté** beauty product; **les produits de beauté** cosmetics, beauty products; **produits blancs** white goods; **produits bruns** brown goods; **p. brut** raw product; **produits chimiques** chemicals; **garanti sans produits chimiques** guaranteed no (chemical) additives; *Mktg* **p. ciblé** niche product; **p. colorant** colouring agent; **produits de consommation** consumables, consumable goods; **produits de consommation courante** consumer goods; **p. dérivé** by-product; *Mktg* **p. drapeau** own-brand product; **p. écologique** green product; *Mktg* **p. d'élite** premium product; **p. d'entretien** (household) cleaning product; **produits étrangers** foreign produce, foreign goods; **produits exotiques** exotic goods; **p. final** end product; **p. fini** finished product, end product; **p. générique** own-brand product; **produits de grande consommation** consumer products; **produits gris** = IT and office equipment, such as computers, telephones and photocopiers; **p. de haut niveau** high standard product; **p. d'imitation** imitative product; **produits de luxe** luxury goods *or* articles; **p. manufacturé** manufactured product; **produits manufacturés** manufactured goods *or* products; **produits maraîchers** *Br* market-garden *or Am* truck-farm produce; **produits de marque** branded *or* brand-name goods *or* products; **p. sans marque** unbranded product; *Mktg* **p. à marque du distributeur** own-brand product; **produits naturels** natural produce; *Mktg* **p. sans nom** no-name product; **p. novateur** innovative product; **produits d'origine nationale** domestic products; **p. ouvré** finished product, end product; **produits du pays** home produce; **produits périssables** perishable goods, non-durable goods; **produits pharmaceutiques** drugs, pharmaceuticals, pharmaceutical products; *Mktg* **p. de prestige** premium product; **produits "prêts-à-consommer"** convenience goods; **produits de second choix** seconds, rejects; **produits spécialisés** speciality goods; **p. de substitution** substitute; **p. substitut** substitute product; **p. de synthèse** synthetic product; *Mktg* **p. tactique** me-too product, follow-me product; **p. à vaisselle** washing-up liquid; *Mktg* **p. vedette** first-off; **p. vert** green product

2 *(résultat)* product, outcome; **le p. d'une matinée de travail** the result *or* product of a morning's work; **c'est un pur p. de ton imagination** it's a complete figment of your imagination

3 *(bénéfice)* profit; **le p. de la vente** the profit made on the sale; *Com* **le p. de la journée** the day's takings *or* proceeds; **il vit du p. de ses terres** he lives off his land; **vivre du p. de son travail** to work for a living; **produits accessoires** sundry income; **p. brut** gross proceeds, gross income; **produits d'exploitation** operating income, income from operations; **p. financier** *(recette)* interest received; **p. de l'impôt** tax revenue; **produits à recevoir** accrued income, accruals

4 *Fin* **p. financier** *(dispositif d'investissement)* financial product; **p. structuré** structured fund; **p. de taux** interest-bearing financial product

5 *Écon* **le p. industriel** industrial earnings; **p. intérieur brut** gross (domestic) product; **p. intérieur net** net domestic product; **p. national brut/net** gross/net national product

6 *Chim & Math* product; **p. cartésien** Cartesian product; **p. vectoriel** vector product

7 *Zool* offspring

8 *Pétr* **produits blancs/noirs** white/black products

proembryon [proɑ̃brijɔ̃] NM *Biol* proembryo

proéminence [proeminɑ̃s] NF **1** *Littéraire (caractère)* prominence, conspicuousness **2** *(saillie)* protuberance; **la montagne présente une p. à gauche du pic** the mountain juts out *or* protrudes left of the peak

proéminent, -e [proeminɑ̃, -ɑ̃t] ADJ prominent

prof [prɔf] NMF *Fam (abrév* **professeur***)* **1** *Scol* teacher▪; **ma p. de maths** my maths teacher **2** *Univ (sans chaire) Br* ≃ lecturer▪, *Am* ≃ instructor▪; *(titulaire de chaire)* prof; **elle est p. de fac** ≃ she's *Br* a lecturer *or Am* an instructor **3** *(hors d'un établissement scolaire)* teacher▪, tutor▪; **ma p. de piano** my piano teacher

profanateur, -trice [prɔfanatœr, -tris] *Littéraire* ADJ blasphemous, sacrilegious

NM,F profaner

profanation [prɔfanasjɔ̃] NF **1** *(sacrilège)* blasphemy, sacrilege, profanation; *(d'une sépulture)* desecration **2** *(avilissement)* defilement, debasement; **une p. de la justice** a travesty of justice

profanatrice [prɔfanatris] *voir* **profanateur**

profane [prɔfan] ADJ **1** *(ignorant)* uninitiated; **je suis p. en la matière** I know nothing about the subject **2** *(non religieux)* secular, non-religious

NMF **1** *(ignorant)* lay person, layman, *f* laywoman; **je n'ai jamais fait de ski, je suis un p.** I've never skied, I'm a complete beginner; **pour le p.** to the layman *or* uninitiated **2** *(non religieux)* lay person, non-initiate

NM **le p.** *(le non-religieux)* the secular, the profane; **le p. et le sacré** the sacred and the profane

profaner [3] [prɔfane] VT **1** *Rel (tombe, église, hostie)* to desecrate, to violate the sanctity of, to profane **2** *(dégrader → justice, talent)* to debase, to defile, *Sout* to profane; *(→ innocence)* to defile

profeciat, proféciat [prɔfesjat] EXCLAM *Belg* congratulations!; **souhaiter p. à qn** to congratulate sb

profectif, -ive [prɔfektif, -iv] ADJ *Littéraire* profectitious

proférer [18] [prɔfere] VT *(insultes, menaces)* to utter; **p. des injures contre qn** to heap insults on sb; **sans p. une seule parole** without so much as a word

profès, -esse [prɔfɛ, -ɛs] *Rel* ADJ professed

NM,F professed monk, *f* professed nun

professer [4] [prɔfese] VT **1** *Littéraire (opinion)* to profess; **p. des opinions révolutionnaires** to profess revolutionary opinions; **il a toujours professé qu'il haïssait la religion** he has always professed hatred for *or* claimed that he hated religion **2** *Vieilli (enseigner)* to teach; **p. l'anglais/l'histoire à l'université** to teach English/history at university

professeur [prɔfɛsœr] NM

> Note that it is no longer considered a mistake to feminize this word and to say **une professeure** (with a final **e**) but some French speakers nonetheless regard this form as unacceptable, especially in France. See also the entry **féminisation**.

1 *(du primaire, du secondaire)* teacher, schoolteacher; **mon p. d'anglais** my English teacher; **p. agrégé** qualified teacher *(who has passed the "agrégation")*; **p. certifié** qualified teacher *(who has passed the "CAPES")*; **p. des écoles** *Br* primary *or Am* elementary school teacher; **p. principal** *Br* ≃ form tutor, *Am* ≃ homeroom teacher

2 *(de l'enseignement supérieur → assistant) Br* ≃ lecturer, *Am* ≃ instructor; *(→ au grade supérieur)* professor; **elle est p. à l'université de Lyon** she teaches at Lyons University; *Méd* **p. agrégé** = professor qualified to teach medicine

3 *Can Univ* **p. adjoint** assistant professor; *Univ* **p. agrégé** associate professor; **p. titulaire** *Scol* staff teacher, member of (teaching) staff; *Univ Br* tenured lecturer, lecturer with full tenure, *Am* full professor

4 *Belg & Suisse Univ* **p. ordinaire** *Br* tenured lecturer, *Am* full professor; **p. extraordinaire** = lecturer with a reduced teaching schedule (because of other professional commitments)

5 *(hors d'un établissement scolaire)* teacher, tutor; **elle est p. de piano** she's a piano teacher, she teaches (the) piano

profession [prɔfɛsjɔ̃] NF **1** *(métier)* occupation, job, profession; *(d'un commerçant, d'un artisan)* trade; *(d'un artiste, d'un industriel)* profession; **quelle est votre p.?** what is your occupation?, what do you do (for a living)?; **de p.** professional; **je suis mécanicien de p.** I'm a mechanic by trade; *Hum* **rebelle de p.** professional rebel; **p. libérale** (liberal) profession; **les professions libérales** *(métiers)* the professions; *(gens)* professional people

2 *(corporation → de commerçants, d'artisans)* trade; *(→ d'artistes, d'industriels)* profession

3 *(déclaration)* **faire p. de** to profess, to declare; **faire p. de libéralisme/socialisme** to declare oneself a liberal/socialist

4 *Rel* **p. religieuse** profession; **p. de foi** profession of faith

❑ **sans profession** *Admin* ADJ unemployed NMF unemployed; **les sans p. recevront une indemnité** the unemployed will receive benefit

professionnalisation [prɔfɛsjɔnalizasjɔ̃] NF *(d'une activité)* professionalization; *(d'un sportif)* turning professional

professionnaliser [3] [prɔfɛsjɔnalize] VT *(joueur, sportif)* **p. qn** to make sb into a professional

►**se professionnaliser** VPR *(sportif)* to turn professional; *(sport)* to become professional *or* a professional sport

professionnalisme [prɔfɛsjɔnalism] NM professionalism

professionnel, -elle [prɔfɛsjɔnɛl] ADJ **1** *(lié à une profession → maladie, risque)* occupational; *(→ enseignement)* vocational; **avoir des soucis professionnels** to have work problems; **aucun changement au niveau p.** nothing new on the job front; **je suis satisfait sur le plan p.** I'm satisfied with my job; **une vie professionnelle satisfaisante** a rewarding job; **améliorer sa vie professionnelle** to improve one's job situation; **école professionnelle** ≃ technical college

2 *(non amateur → musicien, sportif)* professional

3 *(compétent)* professional, accomplished; **elle a réagi d'une manière très professionnelle** she reacted in a very professional way; **le jeu des jeunes acteurs était très p.** the young actors performed like real professionals

NM,F **1** *Sport* professional; **les professionnels de la boxe** professional boxers; **passer p.** to turn professional

2 *(personne expérimentée)* professional; **c'est l'œuvre d'un p.** this is the work of a professional; **ce n'est pas digne d'un p.** it's unworthy of a professional; **p. de (la) santé** healthcare professional, *Am* healthcare provider

❑ **professionnelle** NF *Fam (prostituée)* pro, streetwalker

professionnellement [prɔfɛsjɔnɛlmɑ̃] ADV professionally; **p., il a plutôt réussi** he did rather well in his professional life; **je n'ai affaire à elle que p.** I only have a professional relationship with her, my relations with her are strictly business

professoral, -e, -aux, -ales [prɔfɛsɔral, -o] ADJ **1** *(de professeur)* professorial **2** *(pédant)* patronizing, lecturing

professorat [prɔfɛsɔra] NM teaching; **il a choisi le p.** he chose teaching as a *or* his profession

proficiat [profisjat] = **profeciat**

profil [prɔfil] NM **1** *(côté du visage)* profile; **mon meilleur p.** my best profile; **avoir un p. de médaille** to have very regular features

2 *(silhouette)* profile, outline; **on devinait le p. du volcan dans la brume** the volcano was silhouetted in the mist; *Fig* **adopter/garder un p. bas** to adopt/to keep a low profile

3 *(aptitude)* profile; **elle a le p. de l'emploi** she seems right for the job; **il a le p. idéal pour être président** he's ideal presidential material; **son p. de carrière** his/her career profile

4 *(description)* profile; *Mktg* **p. de la clientèle** customer profile; *Mktg* **p. du** *ou* **des consommateurs** consumer profile; **p. démographique** demographic profile; **p. d'entreprise** company profile; **p. géodémographique** geodemographic profile; **p. du marché** market profile; **p. médical** medical history; *Banque* **p. patrimonial** personal assets profile; **p. de poste** job description; *Mktg* **p. de produit** product profile; *Psy & Mktg* **p. psychologique** psychological profile; **p. socio-démographique** sociodemographic profile

5 *Géog* profile; **p. d'équilibre** profile of equilibrium; **p. fluvial en long** long profile of a river; **p. fluvial en travers** river section

6 *Com* **le p. des ventes montre une augmentation** the sales outline *or* profile shows a definite increase

7 *Archit* (perpendicular) section

❑ **de profil ADV** in profile; **être de p.** to be in profile *or* side-on; **se mettre de p.** to turn to one side *(so that one's face is in profile)*; **mettez-vous de p. par rapport à la caméra** show your profile *or* stand side-on to the camera

profilage [prɔfilaʒ] **NM 1** *Menuis* profiling, moulding; *Métal* shaping, forming; *Aut (d'une carrosserie)* streamlining **2** *(en criminologie)* criminal profiling **3** *Mktg* customer profiling

profilé, -e [prɔfile] **ADJ** *Menuis* profiled, moulded; *Métal* shaped, formed; *Aut (carrosserie)* streamlined

NM *Métal* section

profiler [3] [prɔfile] **VT 1** *Menuis* to profile, to mould; *Métal* to shape, to form; *Aut (carrosserie)* to streamline

2 *(représenter de profil)* to draw in section

3 *Littéraire (laisser voir)* **les montagnes au loin profilaient leur silhouette** the mountains were silhouetted in the distance

4 *(en criminologie)* to profile

▸**se profiler VPR 1** *(se découper)* to stand out, to be silhouetted (**sur** *ou* **contre** against); **l'église se profile en haut de la colline** the church stands out on top of the hill

2 *(apparaître)* to emerge; **une solution se profile enfin** a solution is finally emerging; **des nuages noirs se profilent à l'horizon** black clouds are coming up on the horizon; **des périodes difficiles/des ennuis se profilent à l'horizon** a difficult time/trouble is looming on the horizon

profileur [prɔfilœr] **NM** (psychological) profiler

profilographe [prɔfilɔgraf] **NM** *(en travaux publics)* profilograph

profit [prɔfi] **NM 1** *(avantage)* profit, advantage; **elle ne cherche que son p.** she's only interested in personal gain; **tirer p. de ses lectures** to benefit from one's reading; **tirer p. de l'expérience des autres** to profit from other people's experience; **tirer p. d'une situation** to take advantage of *or* make the most of a situation; **j'ai lu ton livre avec p.** reading your book taught me a lot; **il a étudié avec p.** he gained a lot from his studies; **vous étudierez avec p. la préface** you will find it enlightening to study the preface; **mettre qch à p.** to take advantage of *or* to make the most of sth; **essayez de mettre à p. les connaissances acquises** try to make the most of what you already know; **faire son p. de qch** to profit by *or* from sth; *Fam* **ta veste t'aura fait du p.** you certainly got your money's worth out of that jacket; **il y a trouvé son p., sinon il ne l'aurait pas fait** he got something out of it otherwise he wouldn't have done it

2 *Com & Fin (bénéfice)* profit; **faire** *ou* **réaliser des profits** to make a profit; **vendre à p.** to sell at a profit; **le p. réalisé sur la vente de la propriété** the return on *or* the revenue from the sale of the property; **l'exploitation de la mine ne rapporte que de faibles profits** working the mine brings in only small profits; **p. brut** gross profit; **p. espéré** anticipated profit; **profits exceptionnels** windfall profits; **profits de l'exercice** year's profits; **p. d'exploitation** operating profit; **profits fictifs** paper profits; **profits non matérialisés** paper profits; **p. minimal** minimum trading profit; **profits mis en réserve** capital reserves; **p. net** net profit; **profits et pertes** profit and loss; **p. pur** pure profit; **p. réel** real profit; **p. tout clair** clear profit; **il n'y a pas de petits profits** every little helps

3 *Jur* **p. du défaut** = (legal) advantage accruing to the appearing party when the other party is in default

❑ **au profit de PRÉP** *(organisation caritative, handicapés etc)* in aid of; **à son/mon seul p.** for his/her/my sole benefit; **il a été écarté de la direction au p. de son fils** he was replaced as manager by his son; **les socialistes perdront des voix au p. des communistes** votes will swing from the Socialists to the Communists, the Communists will pick up votes from the Socialists

profitabilité [prɔfitabilite] **NF** profitability

profitable [prɔfitabl] **ADJ** profitable; **la lecture de cet ouvrage vous serait tout à fait p.** it would be of great benefit to you to read this work; **ce séjour en Italie lui a été p.** the time he/she spent in Italy did him/her a lot of good

profitablement [prɔfitabləmɑ̃] **ADV** profitably

profitant, -e [prɔfitɑ̃, -ɑ̃t] **ADJ** *Fam Vieilli* profitable▪

profiter [3] [prɔfite] **VI** *Fam* to thrive▪, to do well▪; **cet enfant profite (bien)** this child is thriving

❑ **profiter à VT IND** to benefit, to be beneficial to; **cet argent ne profite à personne** this money's not benefitting anyone; **les études ne t'ont guère profité** studying didn't do you much good; **il mange comme quatre mais ça ne lui profite guère!** he eats like a horse but it doesn't do him any good!; **ces chaussures m'ont bien profité** these shoes have lasted me a long time, I've got a lot of wear out of these shoes

❑ **profiter de VT IND 1** *(financièrement)* to profit from; **tous n'ont pas profité de l'expansion** not everybody gained by the expansion

2 *(jouir de)* to enjoy; **p. de sa retraite/de la vie** to enjoy *or* make the most of one's retirement/of life; *Fam* **vivement Noël que je puisse p. de mes petits-enfants!** I can't wait for Christmas so I can be with my grandchildren!

3 *(tirer parti de)* to take advantage of; **p. du soleil** to make the most of the sun; **p. du beau temps pour aller se promener** to take advantage of the good weather to go for a walk; **il profite de ce qu'elle est absente** he's taking advantage of the fact that she's away; **p. de l'occasion** to make the most of *or* seize the opportunity; **p. de la situation** to take advantage of the situation; **je profite d'un moment de calme pour vous dire que…** I'm using these few moments of peace and quiet to tell you that…; **profites-en, ça ne va pas durer!** make the most of it, it won't last!; **comme j'avais un deuxième billet, j'en ai fait p. ma copine** since I had a second ticket, I took my girlfriend along

4 *(exploiter)* to exploit, to take advantage of, to use; **elle a profité de nous tant qu'elle a pu** she exploited us as long as she could; **tu profites de moi, c'est tout!** you're taking advantage of me *or* using me, that's all!

profiteroles [prɔfitrɔl] **NFPL** profiteroles; **p. au chocolat** chocolate profiteroles

profiteur, -euse [prɔfitœr, -øz] **NM,F** profiteer; **les profiteurs de guerre** war profiteers

profond, -e [prɔfɔ̃, -ɔ̃d] **ADJ 1** *(enfoncé → lac, racine, blessure)* deep; **peu p.** shallow; **un puits p. de 10 mètres** a well 10 metres deep; **dans les couches profondes du sol** deep in *or* in the deepest layers of the earth; **des préjugés dont l'origine est profonde** deep-rooted *or* deep-seated prejudices; **la haine de l'ennemi est profonde** hatred of the enemy runs deep; **la France profonde** *(rurale)* provincial France; **la France profonde semble être réfractaire à ces changements** the man in the street *or* the average person in France seems to be opposed to these changes; **l'Amérique/l'Angleterre profonde** *(d'un point de vue sociologique)* middle America/England; *(rurale)* provincial America/England

2 *(plongeant → révérence, salut)* deep, low; *(→ regard)* penetrating; *(→ décolleté)* plunging

3 *(intense → respiration)* deep; *(→ soupir, sommeil)* deep, heavy; *(→ silence)* profound, utter; *(→ changement)* profound; *(→ mépris, respect, amour, tristesse)* deep, profound; **dans une solitude profonde** in extreme isolation; **absorbé dans de profondes pensées** deep in thought; **ma surprise fut profonde** I was extremely surprised; **de profonds bouleversements** profound changes; **cette expérience a laissé en elle des marques profondes** the experience marked her for life

4 *(grave → voix)* deep

5 *(obscur)* deep, dark; **dans la nuit profonde** at dead of night

6 *(foncé → couleur)* deep; **bleu p.** deep blue

7 *(sagace)* deep, profound; **avoir un esprit p.** to have profound insight; **elle leur reproche de ne pas être assez profonds** she reproaches them for their shallowness *or* with being shallow

8 *(véritable → cause)* deep, underlying, primary; **la raison profonde de son acte** his/her basic *or* primary *or* underlying motivation; **je ne connais pas ses intentions profondes** I don't know what his/her intentions are deep down

9 *Ling* deep

ADV *(aller, creuser)* deep

NM au plus p. de in the depths of; **au plus p. de la terre** in the depths *or* bowels of the earth; **au plus p. de la nuit** at dead of night; **au plus p. de mon cœur** deep in my heart

profondément [prɔfɔ̃demɑ̃] **ADV 1** *(creuser, enfouir)* deep; **il salua p. la foule** he greeted the crowd with a deep bow

2 *(respirer)* deeply; *(soupirer)* heavily, deeply; **dormir p.** to be sound asleep; **d'habitude, je dors très p.** I usually sleep very heavily, I'm usually a sound sleeper; **p. endormi** sound *or* fast asleep

3 *(en intensif)* profoundly, deeply; **je suis p. choqué** I'm deeply shocked; **elle est p. convaincue de son bon droit** she's utterly convinced she's right; **ce que je ressens pour lui est p. différent** what I feel for him is completely different; **je regrette p.!** I'm deeply sorry!

profondeur [prɔfɔ̃dœr] **NF 1** *(dimension)* depth; **quelle est la p. du puits?** how deep is the well?; **un trou de trois mètres de p.** a hole three metres deep; **on s'est arrêtés à huit mètres de p.** we stopped eight metres down; **une armoire de 60 centimètres de p.** a wardrobe 60 centimetres deep; **de grande p.** very deep; **de faible p.** shallow; **la faible p. de l'étang** the shallowness of the lake

2 *(intensité → d'un sentiment)* depth, *Sout* profundity

3 *(perspicacité)* profoundness, profundity; **un film sans p.** a film with no depth, a shallow *or* superficial film; **sa p. d'esprit** his/her insight

4 *Opt & Phot* **p. de champ** depth of field; **p. de foyer** depth of focus

5 *Aviat (d'une aile)* chord (length)

❑ **profondeurs NFPL** *Littéraire* depths

❑ **en profondeur ADJ** *(étude)* in-depth, thorough; **il nous faut des changements en p.** we need fundamental changes **ADV** *(creuser)* deep; **notre crème antirides agit en p.** our anti-wrinkle cream works deep into the skin; **il faut agir en p.** we need to make fundamental changes

pro forma [prɔfɔrma] **ADJ facture p.** pro forma invoice

profus, -e [prɔfy, -yz] **ADJ** profuse

profusément [prɔfyzemɑ̃] **ADV** profusely

profusion [prɔfyzjɔ̃] **NF 1** *(abondance)* profusion, abundance; **avec une p. d'exemples** with abundant examples **2** *(excès)* excess; **avec une p. de détails** with too much detail

❑ **à profusion ADV** galore, plenty; **il y avait à boire et à manger à p.** there was food and drink galore, there was plenty to eat and drink

progéniture [prɔʒenityr] **NF** offspring, *Sout* progeny; *Hum* **que fais-tu de ta nombreuse p. le dimanche?** what do you do with your brood *or* all your offspring on Sundays?

progénote [prɔʒenɔt] **NM** *Biol* progenote

progéria [prɔʒerja] **NF** *Méd* progéria

progestatif, -ive [prɔʒɛstatif, -iv] *Physiol* **ADJ** *(hormones)* progestative; **corps p.** corpus luteum

NM progestin, progestogen

progestérone [prɔʒɛsterɔn] **NF** *Physiol* progesterone

progiciel [prɔʒisjɛl] **NM** *Ordinat* package; **p. de communication** comms package; **p. intégré** integrated package

proglottis [prɔglɔtis] **NM** *Zool* proglottis, proglottid

prognathe [prɔgnat] **ADJ** prognathous, prognathic

NMF prognathous subject

prognathisme [prɔgnatism] **NM** prognathism

programmable [prɔgramabl] **ADJ** programmable

programmateur, -trice [prɔgramatœr, -tris] **NM,F** *Rad & TV* programme planner; *Ordinat* programmer

NM *(d'une cuisinière)* programmer, autotimer; *(d'une machine à laver)* programme selector

programmation [prɔgramasjɔ̃] **NF 1** *Rad & TV* programme planning; **un changement de p.** a change to the advertised *or* scheduled programme **2** *Ordinat* programming; **p. absolue/dynamique/linéaire** absolute/dynamic/linear

programming; **p. orientée objet, p. par objets** object-oriented programming **3** *Écon* programming **4** *Belg* **p. sociale** = end-of-year bonus allocated to public sector workers

programmatique [prɔgramatik] ADJ programmatic

programmatrice [prɔgramatris] *voir* **programmateur**

programme [prɔgram] NM **1** *(contenu → d'une cérémonie, d'un spectacle)* programme; **qu'est-ce qu'il y a au p. ce soir à l'Opéra?** what's on tonight at the Opéra?; **il y a un bon p. ce soir à la télé** it's a good night on TV tonight; *TV* **programmes d'été** summer schedule *or* programmes; *Rad & TV* **p. minimum** minimum programme schedule *(provided during strike action by journalists and technicians)*

2 *(brochure → d'un concert, d'une soirée)* programme; *(→ de cinéma, de télévision)* listings, guide; **demandez le p.!** programmes on sale here!; **le p. de télévision est en page 4** the TV guide is on page 4

3 *(emploi du temps)* schedule, programme; **arrêter un p.** to draw up *or* arrange a programme; **notre p. est très chargé cette semaine** we have a busy schedule this week; **qu'avons-nous au p. aujourd'hui?** what's our schedule (for) today?, what's on the agenda for today?; **remplir son p.** to fulfil (the requirements of) one's schedule; **inscrire qch au p.** to schedule sth; *Mktg* **p. des annonces** advertising schedule; **p. de production** production programme *or* schedule; *Com* **p. des ventes** sales programme *or* schedule

4 *Scol (d'une année)* curriculum; *(dans une matière)* syllabus; **une question hors p.** a question not covered by the syllabus; **Shakespeare est** *ou* **figure au p. cette année** Shakespeare is on this year's syllabus; **les auteurs au p.** the set authors; **le p. de première année à l'université** the first-year programme *or* syllabus at college

5 *Pol (plate-forme) Br* manifesto, *Am* platform; **p. commun** common *or* joint manifesto; **p. électoral** (election) platform; **p. de gouvernement** government manifesto; **le P. commun** *(en France)* = joint platform adopted by the Communist and Socialist Parties in the 1970s

6 *(projet)* programme; **lancer un p. de réformes** to launch a package *or* programme of reforms; **le p. nucléaire/spatial français** the French nuclear/space programme; **quel est ton p. pour les vacances?** what have you got planned *or* arranged for the holidays?; **on n'a pas de p., on verra au jour le jour** we haven't any definite plans *or* anything definite planned, we'll play it by ear; *Fam* **ton voyage, c'est tout un p.!** this trip sounds like it's quite something!; *Hum* **je voudrais l'intéresser à l'actualité – tout un p.!** I'd like to get him/her interested in current affairs – that's a tall order!; **p. alimentaire mondial** world food programme; *Mktg* **p. d'amélioration de la qualité** quality improvement programme; **p. économique** economic programme *or* plan; **p. de fabrication** production programme *or* schedule; *Mktg* **p. de fidélisation** loyalty programme; **p. de formation** training programme; **p. d'investissement** investment programme; **p. d'investissements à long terme** long-term investment programme; **p. de licenciement** planned redundancy scheme; **p. des Nations unies pour le développement** United Nations Development Programme; *Mktg* **p. de stimulation** incentive scheme

7 *Ordinat* program; **p. objet/source** object/source program; **p. d'affiliation par mots-clés** keyword sponsorship; **p. amorce** initial program loader, bootstrap; **p. antivirus** antivirus program; **p. d'assemblage** assembler; **p. de chargement** loader; **p. de commande d'impression** printer driver; **p. de commande de la souris** mouse driver; **p. de conversion** conversion program; **p. en cours d'éxécution** active program; **p. de création de pages Web** web authoring program; **p. de dessin** drawing program, paint program; **p. de diagnostic** malfunction routine; **p. de gestion** driver; **p. d'installation** setup program, installer; **p. sentinelle** watchdog program; **p. de service** utility program; **p. de test** check program; **p. utilitaire** utility program; **p. virus** virus program

8 *Can Rad & TV (émission)* programme

programmé, -e [prɔgrame] ADJ computerized

programmer [3] [prɔgrame] VT **1** *Cin, Rad, Théât & TV* to bill, to programme; **le débat n'a jamais été programmé** the debate was never shown *or* screened; **les deux chaînes programment la même émission** both channels are running the same programme

2 *(planifier)* to plan; **j'ai programmé tout le week-end** I planned the entire weekend

3 *Électron* to set, to programme; **comment p. votre magnétoscope** how to set (up) your *Br* video recorder *or Am* VCR

4 *Ordinat* to program; **p. qch en assembleur** to program sth in assembly language

VI *Ordinat* to program

programmeur, -euse [prɔgramœr, -øz] NM,F *Ordinat* programmer

progrès [prɔgrɛ] NM **1** *(amélioration)* progress *(UNCOUNT)*; *(avancée)* breakthrough, advance; **faire des p.** *(élève, malade, enquêteurs)* to make progress; **être en p.** to be making progress, to be improving; **il y a du p., continuez** that's better, keep it up; **le XXème siècle a connu de grands p. scientifiques** the 20th century witnessed some great scientific breakthroughs; **la science a fait de grands p.** science has made great progress *or* great strides (forward); **le p.** progress; **croire au p.** to believe in progress; *Pol* **le parti du p.** the party of progress; *aussi Ironique* **tu vois, c'est ça le p.!** that's progress for you!; *Presse* **Le P.** = daily newspaper published in Lyons

2 *(progression)* **les p. de** *(armée)* the progress *or* advance of; *(incendie)* the progress of; *(criminalité)* the upsurge *or* increase in; *(maladie)* the progress *or* progression of

3 *Mil* advance

progresser [4] [prɔgrese] VI **1** *(s'améliorer → élève)* to improve, to (make) progress; *(→ projet)* to progress, to make progress; *(→ enquête, enquêteur)* to make progress *or* headway; **vous avez bien progressé depuis le début de l'année** you've improved a lot *or* made great strides since the beginning of the year; **elle a progressé en français mais pas en musique** she has made some progress in French but not in music

2 *(gagner du terrain → ennemi)* to advance, to gain ground; *(→ marcheur)* to make progress; *(→ maladie)* to progress; *(→ inflation)* to creep up, to rise; **p. lentement/rapidement** to make slow/rapid progress; **nos bénéfices ont progressé de 2 pour cent l'année dernière** our profits rose by 2 percent last year; **la recherche scientifique progresse de jour en jour/à grands pas** scientific research is making progress every day/is advancing by leaps and bounds

progressif, -ive [prɔgresif, -iv] ADJ **1** *(graduel → gén)* gradual, progressive; *(→ taux)* graduated, increasing; **exercices progressifs** graded exercises **2** *Ling* continuous, progressive; **la forme progressive en anglais** the progressive *or* continuous form in English **3** *Méd (maladie)* progressive

progression [prɔgresjɔ̃] NF **1** *(avancée)* progress, advance; **l'ennemi a poursuivi sa p. vers l'intérieur des terres** the enemy advanced *or* progressed inland

2 *(développement → d'une maladie, d'un parti politique)* progression, progress; *(→ du racisme)* spread, development; *(→ de la délinquance, du chômage)* rise (**de** in); *(→ d'un secteur économique)* expansion; *Bourse (→ des cours)* rise, improvement (**de** in); *(→ dans une carrière)* progress, advancement; **la p. du mal est inévitable** the progression of the disease is unavoidable; **notre chiffre d'affaires est en constante p.** our turnover is constantly increasing *or* improving; **un chiffre d'affaires en p. de 22 pour cent** turnover up by 22 percent

3 *Math* progression; **p. arithmétique** arithmetical progression

4 *Mus* progression; **p. harmonique** harmonic progression

progressisme [prɔgresism] NM belief in the possibility of (social) progress, progressivism

progressiste [prɔgresist] ADJ *(politique, parti)* progressive

NMF progressive

progressive [prɔgresiv] *voir* **progressif**

progressivement [prɔgresivmɑ̃] ADV progressively, gradually

progressivité [prɔgresivite] NF progressiveness; *Fin* **p. de l'impôt** progressive increase in taxation

prohibé, -e [prɔibe] ADJ **1** *(interdit)* prohibited, banned, illegal; **le port d'armes est p.** it is illegal to carry weapons, people are forbidden to carry weapons **2** *Jur* **temps p.** proscribed *or* prohibited period

prohiber [3] [prɔibe] VT to prohibit, to ban

prohibitif, -ive [prɔibitif, -iv] ADJ **1** *(prix, tarif)* prohibitive **2** *(loi)* prohibitory

prohibition [prɔibisjɔ̃] NF **1** *(interdiction)* prohibition; **la p. du port d'armes** the ban on carrying weapons; **p. d'entrée** *ou* **à l'importation** import ban; **p. de sortie** export ban **2** *Hist* **la P.** Prohibition

prohibitionnisme [prɔibisjɔnism] NM prohibitionism

prohibitionniste [prɔibisjɔnist] ADJ prohibitionist

NMF prohibitionist

prohibitive [prɔibitiv] *voir* **prohibitif**

proie [prwa] NF **1** *(animal)* prey

2 *(victime)* prey; **vu son grand âge, il est une p. facile pour les cambrioleurs** being so old makes him easy prey for burglars; **être la p. de qn** to be the prey *or* victim of sb; **les enfants sont la p. de la publicité** children are the victims of advertising; **la ville devint rapidement la p. des flammes** the city rapidly became engulfed in flames

❑ **en proie à** PRÉP in the grip of; **en p. au doute** racked with *or* beset by doubt; **être en p. à des hallucinations** to suffer from hallucinations

projecteur [prɔʒɛktœr] NM **1** *(pour illuminer un spectacle)* spotlight; *(pour illuminer un édifice)* floodlight; *(pour surveiller)* searchlight; **éclairé par des projecteurs** floodlit; *Fig* **sous les projecteurs de l'actualité** in the spotlight; **p. de décrochement** kicker (light); **p. ponctuel** spotlight **2** *(d'images)* projector; **p. de cinéma** cine-projector; **p. (de diapositives)** slide projector **3** *Aut* headlight; **p. halogène** halogen headlight

projectif, -ive [prɔʒɛktif, -iv] ADJ *Géom & Psy* projective

projectile [prɔʒɛktil] NM **1** *Mil* projectile **2** *(objet lancé)* projectile, missile

projection [prɔʒɛksjɔ̃] NF **1** *Cin & Phot (action)* projection; *(séance)* screening, showing; **ils durent interrompre la p.** they had to stop the film; **une p. de diapos** a slide show; **une conférence avec p.** a lecture (illustrated) with slides; **appareil de p.** projector; *Cin & TV* **p. frontale** front projection; **p. privée** private showing; *Cin & TV* **p. en transparence** rear projection

2 *(jet → d'un liquide)* splashing; *(→ de boue)* splashing, splattering; *(→ de graisse)* spattering; **sali par des projections de boue** splattered *or* splashed with mud; **quand vous cuisinez, attention aux projections d'huile** when cooking, be careful of the hot oil spattering; *Géol* **p. de cendres** ash fall; **projections volcaniques** ejecta, volcanic debris

3 *Psy* projection (**sur** onto); *Fam* **tu fais une p.** you're projecting

4 *Math* projection; **p. orthogonale** orthogonal projection

5 *Géom* **p. (cartographique)** (map) projection; **p. de Mercator** Mercator *or* Mercator's projection

6 *(prévision)* projection; **p. des ventes** sales projection

7 *(dans un récit, un film)* **p. en avant** flashforward

projectionniste [prɔʒɛksjɔnist] NMF projectionist

projective [prɔʒɛktiv] *voir* **projectif**

projet [prɔʒɛ] NM **1** *(intention)* plan; **faire** *ou* **former le p. de faire qch** to plan to do sth; **j'ai fait le p. de me rendre en Italie** I'm planning on going to Italy; **j'ai formé le p. de m'arrêter de travailler dès que possible** I'm planning on stopping work as soon as possible; **faire des projets** to make plans; **faire des projets d'avenir** to plan *or* make plans for the future; **il a**

plusieurs projets de spectacle he has plans for several new shows; **je n'ai pas de projets pour ce soir** I have no plans for tonight; **le P. génome humain** the Human Genome Project

2 *(esquisse)* plan, outline; **tous les projets doivent nous parvenir le 4 décembre au plus tard** all outlines to be in by 4 December at the latest; **ma pièce n'est encore qu'à l'état de p.** my play is still only a draft *or* at the planning stage; *Jur* **p. d'accord/de contrat** draft agreement/contract; **p. de budget** budget estimates; *Jur* **p. de loi** bill; **avoir des projets dans ses cartons** to have some outline plans in one's folder; *Fig* to have plans for the future

3 *(d'un bâtiment)* plan; *(d'une machine)* blueprint; **p. de construction** building project

❑ **en projet** ADV **qu'avez-vous en p. pour le printemps?** what are your plans for the spring?; **nous avons un nouveau modèle d'avion en p.** we're working on (the plans for) a new design of aircraft

Culture

LES GRANDS PROJETS

The concept of a "grand projet" is central to the way France has been developing its infrastructure, most notably in the fields of transport, urban planning, energy and telecommunications. "Grands projets" – such as the development of the TGV network – typically involve a great deal of preparation and planning and often colossal investment. Even though the "grands projets" are always the initiative of government planners, whether at national or regional level, the financing of the projects usually comes from a mixture of public and private money.

projeté [prɔʃte] NM *Math* projection

projeter [27] [prɔʃte] VT **1** *(prévoir)* to plan, to arrange; **j'ai projeté un voyage pour cet été** I've planned a trip for this summer; **je n'ai pas projeté de sortir ce soir** I haven't planned *or* arranged to go out tonight; **nous avons projeté de monter une affaire ensemble** we're planning on setting up a business together; **nous avons dû abandonner la promenade projetée** we had to abandon our plans for a walk

2 *(lancer → gén)* to throw; *(→ violemment)* to hurl; *(→ liquide)* to splash; *(→ boue)* to splatter, to splash; *(→ graisse)* to spatter; **être projeté au sol** to be hurled to the ground; **elle a été projetée hors de la voiture** she was thrown out of the car; **le volcan projette des cendres** the volcano throws up ashes; **le train projette des gravillons en passant** the train throws up loose stones as it passes

3 *(faire apparaître → ombre, lumière)* to project, to cast, to throw; **son chapeau projette une ombre légère sur son visage** his/her hat is casting a slight shadow on his/her face

4 *Cin & Phot* to show, to project; **si tu nous projetais tes diapos d'Italie!** why don't you show us your slides of Italy!

5 *Psy* to project; **p. ses fantasmes sur qn** to project one's fantasies onto sb

6 *Math* to project; **p. un cercle/une droite sur un plan** to project a circle/a straight line onto a plane

7 *(voix)* to project

▸**se projeter** VPR **1** *(ombre)* to fall, to be cast; **son ombre se projetait sur l'écran** he was silhouetted against the screen

2 *Psy* **se p. sur qn** to project oneself onto sb

projeteur [prɔʃtœr] NM **1** *(technicien)* design engineer **2** *(dessinateur)* industrial (design) draughtsman

projette *etc voir* **projeter**

projo [prɔʒo] NM *Fam* projector■

Prokofiev [prɔkɔfjɛf] NPR Prokofiev

prolabé, -e [prɔlabe] ADJ *Méd* prolapsed

prolactine [prɔlaktin] NF *Physiol* prolactin

prolamine [prɔlamin] NF *Biol & Chim* prolamin, prolamine

prolapsus [prɔlapsys] NM *Méd* prolapse; **p. de l'utérus** prolapse of the womb

prolégomènes [prɔlegɔmɛn] NMPL prolegomena

prolepse [prɔlɛps] NF *Littérature* prolepsis, anticipation

prolétaire [prɔletɛr] ADJ **1** *Vieilli (masse, parti)* proletarian **2** *(quartier)* working-class

NMF proletarian, member of the proletariat

prolétariat [prɔletarja] NM proletariat

prolétarien, -enne [prɔletarjɛ̃, -ɛn] ADJ proletarian; **solidarité prolétarienne** solidarity of the working class

prolétarisation [prɔletarizasjɔ̃] NF proletarianization

prolétariser [3] [prɔletarize] VT to proletarianize, to make working-class

▸**se prolétariser** VPR to become proletarianized *or* working-class

prolifératif, -ive [prɔliferatif, -iv] ADJ proliferative

prolifération [prɔliferasjɔ̃] NF **1** *(gén)* proliferation, multiplication; **p. des armes** arms proliferation; **la p. des industries** the mushrooming of industry **2** *Biol & Nucl* proliferation

prolifère [prɔlifɛr] ADJ *Bot* proliferous

proliférer [18] [prɔlifere] VI to proliferate; **les insectes prolifèrent dans le marécage** insects proliferate in the swamp; **les affichages illégaux prolifèrent** flyposting is on the increase; **les clichés prolifèrent dans ses derniers poèmes** his/her later poems abound in clichés

prolifique [prɔlifik] ADJ **1** *(fécond)* prolific **2** *Fig (auteur, peintre)* prolific, productive

proligère [prɔligɛr] ADJ *Biol* proligerous

proline [prɔlin] NF *Biol & Chim* proline

prolixe [prɔliks] ADJ **1** *(description, style)* wordy, verbose, *Sout* prolix **2** *(écrivain)* verbose, *Sout* prolix; **il n'est pas p.** *(bavard)* he's a man of few words

prolixement [prɔliksəmɑ̃] ADV *(parler, écrire)* at great length

prolixité [prɔliksite] NF **1** *(d'un discours)* wordiness, verbosity **2** *(d'un auteur)* verbosity, prolixity

prolo [prɔlo] *Fam* ADJ plebby

NMF pleb, prole; **les prolos** the working class■

PROLOG, prolog [prɔlɔg] NM *Ordinat* PROLOG, prolog

prologue [prɔlɔg] NM **1** *Littérature, Mus & Théât* prologue (**de** to) **2** *(début)* prologue, prelude, preamble; **en p. à la réunion** as a prologue *or* prelude *or* preamble to the meeting

prolongateur [prɔlɔ̃gatœr] NM *Élec* extension

prolongation [prɔlɔ̃gasjɔ̃] NF **1** *(allongement)* extension; **obtenir une p. de congé** to get an extension of leave **2** *Sport Br* extra time, *Am* overtime; **jouer les prolongations** to play *or* to go into *Br* extra time *or Am* overtime

prolonge [prɔlɔ̃ʒ] NF *Mil* ammunition wagon; **p. d'artillerie** gun carriage

prolongé, -e [prɔlɔ̃ʒe] ADJ **1** *(long → applaudissements, séjour, absence)* lengthy, prolonged

2 *(trop long)* protracted, prolonged; **le séjour p. au soleil abîme la peau** prolonged exposure to the sun is harmful to the skin; **en cas d'arrêt p. entre deux stations** in the event of unduly long halts between stations; **attention à la station debout/assise prolongée** be careful not to spend too much time standing/sitting

3 *(attardé)* **un adolescent p.** an overgrown schoolboy; *Vieilli* **une jeune fille prolongée** a spinster

prolongement [prɔlɔ̃ʒmɑ̃] NM **1** *(extension → d'une route)* continuation; *(→ d'un mur, d'une voie ferrée, d'une période)* extension

2 *(suite)* outcome, consequence; **cette loi est le p. logique d'un long processus de réforme** this law is the logical outcome *or* consequence of a long process of reform

❑ **prolongements** NMPL *(conséquences)* effects, consequences, repercussions; **cette affaire aura des prolongements** this matter will have significant repercussions; **les prolongements du scandale se font encore sentir** the effects of *or* ripples from the scandal can still be felt

❑ **dans le prolongement de** PRÉP **les deux rues sont dans le p. l'une de l'autre** the two streets are a continuation of each other; **je veux installer le frigidaire dans le p. de l'évier** I want the fridge in line with the sink; **la maison que vous cherchez se trouve dans le p. du parc** the house you're looking for is just past the park on the same side of the road; **c'est tout à fait dans le p. de mes préoccupations actuelles** that's along exactly the same lines as what I'm concerned with at the moment

prolonger [17] [prɔlɔ̃ʒe] VT **1** *(dans le temps)* to extend, to prolong; **p. son séjour** to extend one's stay, to stay longer than planned; **p. un délai** to extend a deadline; **comment p. la vie** how to prolong life

2 *(dans l'espace)* to extend, to continue; **la route sera prolongée de deux kilomètres** the road will be made 2 km longer *or* will be extended by 2 km; **la ligne de métro n° 7 a été prolongée jusqu'en banlieue** the no. 7 *Br* underground *or Am* subway line was extended to the suburbs; **il a fallu p. le fil de la télévision** we had to extend the lead for the television set; **rue Crinas prolongée** = continuation of rue Crinas

3 *Mus (note)* to hold

▸**se prolonger** VPR **1** *(dans le temps → situation)* to persist, to go on; *(→ effet)* to last; *(→ réunion)* to be prolonged, to go on; **la guerre semble se p. indéfiniment** the war seems to be going on forever; **notre discussion s'est prolongée tard** our conversation went on until late

2 *(dans l'espace)* to go on, to continue; **le sentier se prolonge dans la forêt** the path continues through the forest

promenade [prɔmnad] NF **1** *(à pied → gén)* walk; *(→ courte)* stroll; *(à bicyclette, à cheval)* ride; *(en voiture)* ride, drive; **faire une p.** *(à pied)* to go for a walk *or* stroll; *(à bicyclette, à cheval)* to go for a ride; **faire une p. en voiture** to go for a drive; **et si on faisait une p. en mer?** shall we go for a sail?; **je lui ai fait faire une p.** I took him/her out for a walk; **l'heure de la p.** *(d'un détenu)* exercise time; **aller en Angleterre de nos jours, c'est presque devenu une p.** going to England nowadays is almost like going next door; *Fam* **ç'a été une vraie p.** *(victoire facile)* it was a real walkover

2 *(allée → gén)* walk(way); *(en bord de mer)* promenade; **la P. des Anglais** the Promenade des Anglais *(fashionable street running along the seafront in Nice)*

3 *(en danse)* promenade

❑ **en promenade** ADV *(à pied)* out walking, out for a walk; *(à bicyclette, à cheval)* out riding, out for a ride; *(en voiture)* out riding *or* driving, out for a ride *or* drive

promener [19] [prɔmne] VT **1** *(sortir → à pied)* to take (out) for a walk *or* stroll; *(→ en voiture)* to take (out) for a drive; **j'ai passé le week-end à p. un ami étranger dans Paris** I spent the weekend showing a foreign friend around Paris; **p. le chien** to walk the dog, to take the dog for a walk; **cela vous promènera un peu** it'll get you out (of the house) a bit; *Fam* **envoyer p. qn** *(l'éconduire)* to send sb packing, to tell sb where to go; *Fam* **tout envoyer p.** *Br* to chuck *or* to pack it all in, *Am* to chuck everything

2 *Fig (emmener → personne)* **il m'a promené de bureau en bureau** he dragged me from office to office; **j'en ai assez d'être promené de poste en poste** I've had enough of being sent *or* shunted around from one job to another; *Littéraire* **p. partout le carnage** to carry death and destruction everywhere

3 *(mentir à)* **il m'a promené pendant trois semaines** he kept me hanging on for three weeks

4 *(déplacer)* **elle promène son regard sur la foule** her eyes scan the crowd; **p. ses doigts sur le piano** *(en jouant)* to run one's fingers over the keys; *(pour le toucher)* to finger the piano; **il promenait le faisceau électrique sur le mur** he ran *or* played the torch beam over the wall

5 *(traîner)* **p. son ennui/désespoir** to go around looking bored/disconsolate

6 *(transporter)* to take around; **le roman nous promène dans la France du XIXème siècle** the novel takes us for a stroll round 19th-century France; **ses récits de voyage nous ont promenés dans le monde entier** his/her travel stories have taken us all around the world

▸**se promener** VPR **1** *(à pied)* to go for a walk *or* stroll; *(en voiture)* to go for a drive; *(à bicyclette, à cheval)* to go for a ride; *(en bateau)* to go for a sail; **viens te p. avec moi** come for *or* on a walk with me; **emmener p. qn** to take sb (out) for a walk; *Fam* **va te p.!** (go) get lost!

2 *(mains, regard)* **ses doigts se promenaient sur le clavier** his/her fingers wandered over the keyboard

3 *Fam (traîner)* **j'en ai assez que tes affaires se promènent dans toute la maison!** I've had enough of your things lying about all over the house!; **où sont-elles encore allées se p., ces lunettes?** where have those glasses got to this time? **4** *Fam (éprouver de la facilité)* **il se promène en anglais** he finds English a pushover

promeneur, -euse [prɔmnœr, -øz] NM,F *(dans un parc, en ville)* stroller, walker; *(randonneur)* walker, rambler

promenoir [prɔmnwar] NM **1** *Théât* promenade **2** *(dans un parc)* covered walk **3** *Constr* gallery, arcade, walkway

promériter [3] [prɔmerite] VT *Belg* to be (officially) entitled to

promesse [prɔmɛs] NF **1** *(engagement)* promise, assurance; **faire une p.** to (make a) promise; **faire des promesses** to make promises; **manquer à/tenir sa p.** to break/to keep one's promise; **je ne vous fais pas de p.** I won't promise anything; **rappelle-toi, j'ai ta p.** remember, you promised (me) *or* gave your word; **il m'a fait la p. de revenir** he promised me he would come back; **elle m'avait fait de grandes promesses** she promised me great things; **encore une p. en l'air** *ou* **d'ivrogne** *ou* **de Gascon!** promises, promises!; *Pol* **p. électorale** electoral promise; **p. de mariage** promise of marriage **2** *Com & Fin* commitment; **p. d'action** (debenture) scrip; **p. écrite** written promise, written undertaking; **p. d'achat/de vente** promise to buy/to sell; **p. unique de vente** unique selling point *or* proposition; **3** *Mktg* claim; **p. mensongère** false claim; **p. produit** claim *(made about a product)* **4** *Littéraire (espoir)* promise; **la p. d'une journée magnifique/d'un avenir meilleur** the promise of a beautiful day/of a better future **5** *Jur* **p. de porte-fort** porte-fort; **p. post mortem** = clause pursuant to which the obligations in the agreement will be performed only on the death of one of the parties
▫ **promesses** NFPL *(avenir)* promise; **un jeune joueur plein de promesses** a young player showing great promise, a very promising young player

promet *etc voir* **promettre**

prométhazine [prɔmetazin] NF promethazine

Prométhée [prɔmete] NPR *Myth* Prometheus

prométhéen, -enne [prɔmeteɛ̃, -ɛn] ADJ Promethean

prométhéum [prɔmeteɔm] NM *Chim* promethium

promettant, -e [prɔmetɑ̃, -ɑ̃t] NM,F *Jur* promisor

prometteur, -euse [prɔmetœr, -øz] ADJ **1** *(début, situation)* promising, encouraging; *(sourire)* full of promise; *aussi Ironique* **voilà qui est p.!** that's a good sign! **2** *(musicien, acteur)* promising, of promise

promettre [84] [prɔmɛtr] VT **1** *(jurer)* to promise; **je te l'ai promis** I promised (you); **je ne peux rien vous p.** I can't promise anything; **je te promets de ne pas lui en parler** I promise I won't say a word to him/her about it; **je te promets que je ne dirai rien** I promise (you) I won't say anything; **on nous a promis de l'aide** we were promised help; **p. une récompense** to offer a reward; **je te rembourserai, c'est promis** I'll pay you back, I promise; **p. la lune, p. monts et merveilles** to promise the earth, to promise the moon and the stars; *Prov* **p. et tenir sont deux** = it's easier to make a promise than to keep one **2** *(annoncer)* to promise; **la météo nous promet du beau temps pour toute la semaine** the weather forecast promises nice weather for the whole week; **tout cela ne promet rien de bon** it doesn't look *or* sound too good; **voilà une émission qui promet d'être intéressante** this programme should be interesting, it sounds like an interesting programme **3** *(destiner)* to destine; **ses récents succès le promettent à une brillante carrière** considering his recent successes, he has a brilliant career ahead of him; **il est promis à un grand avenir** he is destined for a great future, he has a great future ahead of him **4** *Fam (affirmer)* to assure; **je te promets qu'il s'en souviendra, de ce dîner!** I can assure you

or you can take my word for it that he'll remember that dinner!
VI **1** *(faire naître des espérances)* to promise; **un jeune auteur qui promet** a promising young author; **des débuts qui promettent** a promising start **2** *Fam (laisser présager des difficultés)* **ce gamin promet!** that kid's got a great future ahead of him!; *Ironique* **eh bien, ça promet!** that's a good start!; **eh bien, ça promet pour la fin de la semaine!** well then, it looks as if we're in for a great weekend!
▶ **se promettre** VPR **1** *(emploi réciproque)* **ils se sont promis de se revoir** they promised (each other) that they would meet again **2** *(espérer)* **je m'étais promis beaucoup de joie de cette rencontre** I'd been looking forward to the meeting; **se p. du bon temps** to look forward to enjoying oneself **3** *(se jurer à soi-même)* to swear, to promise (to) oneself; **je me suis bien promis de ne jamais recommencer** I swore never to do it again, I promised myself I would never do it again; **je me suis promis d'aller lui rendre visite un de ces jours** I mean to visit him/her one of these days **4** *Vieilli* **se p. à qn** to plight one's troth to sb; **elle s'était promise à un médecin de province** she was promised *or* betrothed to a provincial doctor

promeut, promeuvent *etc voir* **promouvoir**

promis, -e [prɔmi, -iz] ADJ promised; **voici le document p.** here is the promised document
NM,F *Vieilli* betrothed

promiscuité [prɔmiskɥite] NF **1** *(voisinage)* overcrowding; **vivre dans la p.** to live in overcrowded conditions; **la p. des plages en été/de l'hôpital** the overcrowding of beaches in summer/lack of privacy in hospital; **je ne supporte pas la p.** *(dans un hôpital etc)* I can't stand the lack of privacy; *(dans le métro)* I can't stand the overcrowding **2** **p. sexuelle** (sexual) promiscuity

promit *etc voir* **promettre**

promo [prɔmo] NF *Fam* **1** *Mil, Scol & Univ Br* year, *Am* class; **la p. 64** the class of '64 **2** *Com* promotion■, promo; **en p.** on special offer **3** *TV* promotional video

promontoire [prɔmɔ̃twar] NM **1** *Géog* headland, promontory **2** *Anat* promontory

promoteur, -trice [prɔmɔtœr, -tris] ADJ **société promotrice privée** development company
NM,F **1** *Littéraire (créateur)* promoter, instigator; **le p. de la réforme** the instigator of the reform **2** *Com* promoter; **p. des ventes** sales promoter **3** *Constr* **p. (immobilier)** property developer
NM *Chim* promoter

promotion [prɔmɔsjɔ̃] NF **1** *(avancement)* promotion; **j'ai eu une p.** I've been promoted; **fêter la p. de qn** to celebrate sb's promotion; **p. au mérite/à l'ancienneté** promotion on merit/by seniority; **p. des cadres** executive promotion; **p. interne** internal promotion, **p. sociale** upward mobility **2** *Com & Mktg (publicité)* promotion; *(offre spéciale)* special offer, promotion; **faire une p. sur un produit** to promote a product; **faire la p. de qch** to promote sth; **la p. du jour** *(sur la vitrine d'un magasin, dans un marché)* today's special offer; **p. de la semaine** this week's special offer *or Am* special; **p. collective** tie-in promotion; **p. d'entreprises** corporate identity; **p. sur le lieu de vente** point-of-sale promotion, in-store promotion; **p. on-pack** on-pack promotion; **p. sur point d'achat** point-of-purchase promotion; **p. de prestige** prestige promotion; **p. spéciale** special promotion; **p. des ventes** sales promotion **3** *Mil, Scol & Univ Br* year, *Am* class; **ils étaient camarades de p.** they were in the same class *or* year; **le premier de sa p.** the first in his year **4** *Constr* **p. immobilière** property development **5** *Échecs* queening
▫ **promotions** NFPL *Suisse (remise de diplômes)* = school prize-giving ceremony marking the move up to the next class
▫ **en promotion** ADJ *Com* on special offer, on promotion, *Am* on special

promotionnel, -elle [prɔmɔsjɔnɛl] ADJ *(brochure)*

promotional; *(tarif)* special; *(budget)* promotional, publicity; **tarifs promotionnels sur ce voyage en Israël!** special offer on this trip to Israel!

promotionner [3] [prɔmɔsjɔne] VT to promote

promotrice [prɔmɔtris] *voir* **promoteur**

promouvoir [56] [prɔmuvwar] VT **1** *(faire monter en grade)* to promote; **il a été promu capitaine** he was promoted (to the rank of) captain **2** *(encourager → réforme)* to advocate, to push for; *(→ recherche, création d'entreprise)* to promote, to further **3** *Com (article)* to promote, to publicize

prompt, -e [prɔ̃, prɔ̃t] ADJ prompt, quick, swift; **p. à répondre** quick with an answer; **vous avez été trop p. à agir** you acted rashly; **p. à la colère** easily moved to anger; **p. à la riposte** quick with a riposte; **avoir l'esprit p.** to be quick-witted; **l'esprit est p. et la chair infirme** the spirit is willing but the flesh is weak; **avoir la repartie prompte** to have a ready wit, to always be ready with an answer

promptement [prɔ̃tmɑ̃] ADV quickly, swiftly; **répondre p.** to give a prompt reply; **exécuter p. des ordres** to waste no time in carrying out orders

prompteur [prɔ̃ptœr] NM teleprompter, *Br* Autocue®; **p. déroulant** roller prompter

promptitude [prɔ̃tityd] NF quickness, swiftness

promu, -e [prɔmy] PP *voir* **promouvoir**
NM,F promoted person; **voici la liste des promus dans l'ordre de la Légion d'honneur** here is the list of those decorated with the Legion of Honour; *Univ* **les nouveaux promus** = this year's graduates of a "grande école"

promulgation [prɔmylgasjɔ̃] NF promulgation

promulguer [3] [prɔmylge] VT to promulgate

promyélocyte [prɔmjelɔsit] NM promyelocyte

pronaos [prɔnaɔs] NM *Antiq* pronaos

pronateur, -trice [prɔnatœr] *Physiol* ADJ **muscle p.** pronator
NM pronator

pronation [prɔnasjɔ̃] NF *Physiol* prone position, pronation

pronatrice [prɔnatris] *voir* **pronateur**

prône [pron] NM *Rel* (Sunday) sermon

prôner [3] [prone] VT *(patience, indulgence, tolérance)* to strongly recommend, to advocate, to urge; *(méthode)* to strongly recommend, to advocate

prôneur, -euse [pronœr, -øz] NM,F *Littéraire* advocate

pronom [prɔnɔ̃] NM pronoun; **p. indéfini/interrogatif/personnel/relatif** indefinite/interrogative/personal/relative pronoun

pronominal, -e, -aux, -ales [prɔnɔminal, -o] *Gram* ADJ *(adjectif, adverbe)* pronominal; *(verbe)* reflexive
NM reflexive verb

pronominalement [prɔnɔminalmɑ̃] ADV *Gram* pronominally; **adjectif fonctionnant p.** adjective functioning as a pronoun *or* pronominally; **verbe employé p.** verb employed pronominally *or* reflexively

prononçable [prɔnɔ̃sabl] ADJ pronounceable; **un nom qui n'est pas p.** an unpronounceable name

prononcé, -e [prɔnɔ̃se] ADJ *(traits)* strong; *(forme)* strong, definite; *(tendance)* marked; *(accent)* broad, pronounced, strong; **avoir un goût p. pour qch** to have a strong *or* distinct taste for sth; **un accent peu p.** a faint *or* slight accent
NM *Jur* (announcement of) decision

prononcer [16] [prɔnɔ̃se] VT **1** *(dire → parole)* to say, to utter; *(→ discours)* to make, to deliver; **sans p. un mot** without a word; **il a prononcé quelques mots sur la situation en Chine** he said a few words about the situation in China; **ne prononce plus jamais son nom** never mention his/her name again; **il a prononcé son nom entre ses dents** *ou* **dans sa barbe** he mumbled his/her name **2** *(proclamer → jugement)* to pronounce; **p. un divorce** to issue a divorce decree, to pronounce a couple divorced; **p. la sentence** to pronounce *or* to pass sentence; **p. le huis clos de l'audience** to order that the case be heard in camera; **il a prononcé lui-même sa condamnation** he's condemned himself **3** *Rel* **p. ses vœux** to take one's vows

4 *(articuler → mot, langue)* to pronounce; *(→ phonème)* to articulate; **je ne sais pas le p.** I don't know how to pronounce or say it; **c'est un mot que je prononce toujours de travers** I always mispronounce that word; **mal p. qch** to mispronounce sth

USAGE ABSOLU **apprendre à p.** to learn to pronounce one's words properly, to learn proper pronunciation; **il prononce mal** his pronunciation is poor; **c'est la mode chez certains acteurs de ne pas p. clairement** it is the fashion among certain actors to slur their speech

VI **1** *Jur* to deliver or to give a verdict (**sur** on); **le tribunal a prononcé** the court delivered its verdict

2 *Vieilli ou Littéraire (choisir)* to pronounce; **p. en faveur de/contre** to pronounce in favour of/against

▶**se prononcer** VPR **1** *(mot)* to be pronounced; **le "a" se prononce en ouvrant la bouche** "a" is pronounced by opening the mouth; **le deuxième "i" ne se prononce pas** the second "i" isn't sounded or is silent; **comment ça se prononce?** how do you say it?; **ça s'écrit comme ça se prononce** it's spelled as it sounds

2 *(s'exprimer → gén)* to give one's opinion; *(→ juge)* to give a verdict; *(→ médecin)* to give one's prognosis; **ils se sont prononcés pour/contre la peine de mort** they pronounced or declared themselves in favour of/against the death penalty; **ne se prononcent pas** *(dans un sondage)* don't know

prononciation [prɔnɔ̃sjasjɔ̃] NF **1** *(d'un mot)* pronunciation; **un mot avec deux prononciations différentes** a word with two different pronunciations; **la p. du "th" anglais est difficile pour un Français** pronouncing the English "th" is difficult for a French person; **la p. du "t" final est facultative** the final "t" doesn't have to be sounded

2 *(d'une personne)* pronunciation; **elle a une bonne/mauvaise p. en allemand** her German pronunciation is good/bad; **étant petit, j'ai pris des leçons particulières pour corriger ma mauvaise p.** when I was young, I had private tuition to improve my speech

3 *(d'un jugement)* pronouncing; **j'attends la p. du divorce** I'm waiting for the divorce to be made final or to come through

pronostic [prɔnɔstik] NM **1** *Sport* forecast; *(pour les courses)* forecast, (racing) tip; **vos pronostics sur le match Bordeaux-Marseille?** what's your forecast or prediction for the Bordeaux-Marseilles match? **2** *(conjecture)* forecast; **les pronostics économiques** economic forecasts; **p. du marché** market forecast **3** *Méd* prognosis

pronostique [prɔnɔstik] ADJ *(gén) & Méd* prognostic

pronostiquer [3] [prɔnɔstike] VT **1** *(prévoir)* to forecast, *Sout* to prognosticate **2** *(être signe de)* to be a sign or forerunner of; **le vent d'ouest pronostique la pluie** westerly winds are a sign or harbinger of rain

pronostiqueur, -euse [prɔnɔstikœr, -øz] NM,F **1** *Écon* forecaster **2** *Sport* tipster

pronto [prɔ̃to] ADV *Fam* pronto

pronucléus [prɔnykleys] NM *Biol* pronucleus

pronunciamiento [prɔnunsjamjɛnto] NM *(gén)* military coup; *(en pays de langue espagnole)* pronunciamento

pro-occidental, -e, -aux, -ales [prɔɔksidɑtal, -o] ADJ pro-Western
     NM,F pro-Westerner

propadiène [prɔpadjɛn] NM *Chim* propadiene

propagande [prɔpagɑ̃d] NF **1** *(politique)* propaganda; **p. électorale** electioneering **2** *(publicité)* publicity, plugging; **faire de la p. pour qn/qch** to advertise sb/sth; **tu me fais de la p.!** you're a good advert for my cause!
     ❑ **de propagande** ADJ *(film, journal)* propaganda *(avant n)*

propagandisme [prɔpagɑ̃dism] NM propagandism

propagandiste [prɔpagɑ̃dist] ADJ propagandist
     NMF propagandist

propagateur, -trice [prɔpagatœr, -tris] NM,F *(de nouvelles)* propagator, spreader; *(d'idées)* disseminator

propagation [prɔpagasjɔ̃] NF **1** *Littéraire (reproduction)* propagation, spreading; **la p. de**

l'espèce humaine the propagation of the human race

2 *(diffusion → d'un incendie, d'une doctrine, d'une rumeur)* spreading; **la p. des idées révolutionnaires** the spreading of revolutionary ideas; **ils n'ont pu empêcher la p. de l'incendie** they couldn't stop the fire (from) spreading

3 *Élec & Phys* propagation; **p. en espace libre** propagation in free space, free-space propagation; **p. guidée** guided (wave) propagation; **vitesse de p. d'une onde** velocity of propagation of a wave

propagatrice [prɔpagatris] *voir* **propagateur**

propager [17] [prɔpaʒe] VT **1** *(répandre → foi, idées)* to propagate, to disseminate, to spread; *(→ épidémie, feu, rumeur, mode)* to spread; **la télévision a propagé la nouvelle très rapidement** television spread the news very quickly; **sa spécialité c'est de p. des rumeurs** he's/she's a specialist in spreading gossip; **le vent a propagé l'incendie jusqu'à la pinède voisine** the wind spread the fire to the nearby pine wood; **p. une maladie** to transmit or to spread a disease

2 *Bot & Zool* to propagate; **p. des fleurs par semis** to propagate flowers by sowing seed

▶**se propager** VPR **1** *(s'étendre → nouvelle, épidémie etc)* to spread; **la nouvelle de l'accident s'est propagée à toute allure** the news of the accident spread like wildfire; **l'épidémie se propage dans les bidonvilles** the epidemic is spreading in the slums

2 *Phys (onde, son)* to be propagated

3 *(plante)* to propagate, to reproduce

propagule [prɔpagyl] NF *Bot* propagulum, propagule

propane [prɔpan] NM *Chim* propane

propanier [prɔpanje] NM propane tanker or carrier

propanol [prɔpanɔl] NM *Chim* propanol

proparoxyton [prɔparɔksitɔ̃] *Ling* ADJ M proparoxytone
     NM proparoxytone

propédeutique [prɔpedøtik] NF **1** *(enseignement préparatoire)* propaedeutics **2** *Anciennement Univ* = first year of university course

propène [prɔpɛn] = **propylène**

propension [prɔpɑ̃sjɔ̃] NF **1** *(tendance)* propensity (à to); **avoir une forte p. à qch/à faire qch** to have a strong tendency to do sth **2** *Écon* propensity; **p. à consommer/épargner** propensity to consume/to save; **p. à importer** propensity to import; **p. marginale à consommer** marginal propensity to consume; **p. marginale à épargner** marginal propensity to save; **p. moyenne à consommer** average propensity to consume; **p. moyenne à épargner** average propensity to save

propergol [prɔpɛrgɔl] NM propellant; **p. liquide/solide** liquid/solid propellant

propharmacien, -enne [prɔfarmasjɛ̃, -ɛn] NM,F dispensing doctor

prophase [prɔfaz] NF *Biol* prophase

prophète [prɔfɛt] NM prophet; **grands/petits prophètes** major/minor prophets; **le P.** the Prophet; **p. de malheur** prophet of doom; **faux p.** false prophet

prophétesse [prɔfetɛs] NF prophetess

prophétie [prɔfesi] NF prophecy; **faire une p.** to prophesy; **ses prophéties sur l'imminence d'une guerre** his/her prophecies about a war being imminent

prophétique [prɔfetik] ADJ **1** *Rel* prophetic **2** *Fig (prémonitoire)* prophetic, premonitory; **il a eu une vue p. de la catastrophe** he had a premonition of the catastrophe

prophétiquement [prɔfetikmɑ̃] ADV prophetically

prophétiser [3] [prɔfetize] VT **1** *Rel* to prophesy **2** *Fig (prédire)* to foretell, to predict, to prophesy
     VI *(prédire)* to make pompous predictions

prophétisme [prɔfetism] NM *Rel* **p. (biblique)** prophetism

prophylactique [prɔfilaktik] ADJ *(mesure)* prophylactic

prophylaxie [prɔfilaksi] NF prophylaxis

propice [prɔpis] ADJ **1** *(favorable → temps, période, vent)* favourable; **les cieux n'ont pas l'air bien propices** the sky looks rather menacing; **l'automne est p. à la méditation** autumn is conducive

to or is an appropriate time for meditation; **les festivals sont propices aux rencontres** festivals are good places to meet people; **que les dieux vous soient propices!** may the gods smile upon you!; **si la fortune nous est p.** if Fortune smiles on us

2 *(opportun)* suitable; **peu p.** inauspicious; **au moment p.** at the right moment; **un endroit plus p.** a more suitable place

propithèque [prɔpitek] NM *Zool* sifaka; **p. à diadème** diademed sifaka; **p. de Verreaux** Verreaux's sifaka

propitiation [prɔpisjasjɔ̃] NF *Rel* propitiation

propitiatoire [prɔpisjatwar] ADJ *Rel* propitiatory; **offrande/sacrifice p.** propitiatory gift/sacrifice
     NM *Bible* **le p.** the mercy seat

propolis [prɔpolis] NF propolis, bee glue

proportion [prɔpɔrsjɔ̃] NF **1** *(rapport)* proportion, ratio; **une égale p. de oui et de non dans les deux échantillons** the same ratio or proportion of yeses to noes in both samples; **la p. d'alcool dans un vin** the percentage of alcohol in a wine, the alcohol content of a wine; **la p. des maisons individuelles est stationnaire** the proportion or comparative number of detached houses remains stable; **tu n'as pas respecté les proportions dans le dessin** your drawing isn't in proportion; **dans la** ou **une p. de 15 pour cent** in the ratio of 15 percent; **dans la** ou **une p. de cent contre un** in the ratio of a hundred to one; **dans la même p.** in equal proportions; **dans une juste p.** in the correct proportion; **hors de p. avec** out of proportion to; **sans p. avec** out of (all) proportion with

2 *Chim* **loi des proportions définies** law of constant or definite proportions; **loi des proportions multiples** law of multiple proportions
     ❑ **proportions** NFPL **1** *(importance)* (great) importance; **prendre des proportions énormes** to grow out of all proportion; **pourquoi un incident aussi minime a-t-il pris de telles proportions?** why was such a trivial incident blown out of all proportion?; **si les commandes diminuent dans de sérieuses proportions** if orders should decrease to any great extent

2 *(dimensions)* dimensions, size; **tout dépendra des proportions de l'armoire** it will all depend on the size of the wardrobe; **c'est la même chose, toutes proportions gardées** it's the same thing but on a different scale
     ❑ **à proportion** ADV proportionately, at the same rate; **tout augmente, et les salaires à p.** everything is going up, and salaries are keeping pace
     ❑ **à proportion de** PRÉP in proportion to
     ❑ **en proportion** ADJ in proportion; **il a de gros frais, mais son salaire est en p.** he has a lot of expenses, but he has a correspondingly high salary ADV proportionately, at the same rate; **vous serez récompensé en p.** you'll be rewarded accordingly
     ❑ **en proportion de** PRÉP in proportion to; **son succès est en p. de son talent** his/her success is proportional or in proportion to his/her talent; **il est payé en p. des risques qu'il court** he is payed in proportion to the risks he takes

proportionnalité [prɔpɔrsjɔnalite] NF **1** *Math* proportionality **2** *(rapport)* balance, (good) proportions **3** *(répartition)* equal distribution **4** *Écon* **p. de l'impôt** fixed rate system of taxation

proportionné, -e [prɔpɔrsjɔne] ADJ **1** *(harmonieux)* **bien p.** well-proportioned; **mal p.** out of proportion **2** *(adapté)* **p. à** commensurate with, in proportion to, proportional to; **la cotisation est proportionnée à vos revenus** payment is commensurate with or proportional to your income

proportionnel, -elle [prɔpɔrsjɔnɛl] ADJ **1 p. à** *(en rapport avec)* proportional to, in proportion with, commensurate with; **ils gagnent un salaire p. à leur travail** they earn a salary in proportion to the work they do; **directement/inversement p. (à)** directly/inversely proportional (to)

2 *Com & Écon (droits, impôt)* ad valorem

3 *Math & Pol* proportional
     ❑ **proportionnelle** NF *Pol* **la proportionnelle** *(processus)* proportional system; *(résultat)* proportional representation; **être élu à la proportionnelle** to be elected by proportional

representation; **proportionnelle intégrale** list system

proportionnellement [prɔpɔrsjɔnɛlmɑ̃] ADV *(gén)* proportionately (**à** to); *Math & Écon* proportionally, in direct ratio (**à** to)

proportionner [3] [prɔpɔrsjɔne] VT to match; **il est juste de p. le délit et la sanction** the punishment must fit the crime; **il faudrait p. la note à l'effort fourni par l'élève** the mark should reflect *or* match the amount of effort put in by the pupil

propos [prɔpo] NM **1** *(sujet)* subject, topic; **à ce p.** in this respect *or* connection; **à ce p., que penses-tu de ma suggestion?** which reminds me, what do you think of my suggestion?; **c'est à quel p.?** what's it about?; **elle veut te voir – à quel p.?** she wants to see you – what about *or* what for?; **à quel p. a-t-elle téléphoné?** what was the reason for her telephone call?

2 *Littéraire (but)* intention, aim; **mon p. n'est pas de vous convaincre** my aim is not to convince you; **là n'est pas le/mon p.** that is not the/my point; **avoir le ferme p. de faire qch** to firmly intend to do sth, to have the firm intention of doing sth

NMPL *(paroles)* words, talk; **menus p.** small talk; **tenir des p. injurieux** to make offensive remarks; **elle tient des p. sibyllins** she talks in riddles; **les p. qu'ils échangèrent sont restés confidentiels** their talk *or* conversation has remained confidential; **il était si fatigué que ses p. étaient à peine audibles** he was so tired that his words could hardly be heard

❑ **à propos** ADJ appropriate; **il serait à p. de changer de cap** it would be appropriate *or* timely to change course; **elle n'a pas jugé à p. de nous le dire** she didn't think it appropriate to tell us ADV **1** *(opportunément)* at the right moment; **arriver** *ou* **tomber à p.** to occur at the right time; **répondre à p.** *(pertinemment)* to answer appropriately; *(au bon moment)* to answer at the right moment; **mal à p.** at the wrong moment; **tu ne pouvais pas tomber plus mal à p.** you couldn't have come at a worse time; **très mal à p.** at the worst possible moment

2 *(au fait)* by the way, incidentally; **à p., as-tu reçu ma carte?** by the way *or* incidentally, did you get my postcard?

❑ **à propos de** PRÉP about, concerning, regarding; **j'ai quelques remarques à faire à p. de votre devoir** I have a few things to say to you about your homework; **dis donc, à p. d'argent** hey, (talking) about money *or* on the subject of money; **elle se met en colère à p. de tout et de rien** *ou* **à p. d'un rien** she gets angry for no reason at all

❑ **à tout propos** ADV constantly, at the slightest provocation

❑ **de propos délibéré** ADV deliberately, on purpose

proposable [prɔpozabl] ADJ proposable

proposer [3] [prɔpoze] VT **1** *(suggérer)* to suggest; **qu'est-ce que tu proposes?** what would *or* do you suggest?; **je propose qu'on aille au cinéma** I suggest going to the cinema; **je vous propose de rester dîner** I suggest (that) you stay for dinner; **écoutez, voilà ce que je vous propose** listen, this is what I suggest; **l'agence nous a proposé un projet original** the agency submitted an original project to us; **proposez vos idées** put forward your ideas; **le chef vous propose sa quiche au saumon** the chef's suggestion *or* recommendation is the salmon quiche; **le cinéma le César vous propose cette semaine…** this week at le César:…; **"asseyons-nous", proposa-t-elle** "let's sit down," she said

2 *(offrir)* to offer; **il a proposé sa place à la vieille dame** he offered the old lady his seat; **puis-je vous p. mon parapluie?** would you like *or* can I offer you my umbrella?; **on m'a proposé une vieille horloge** I have been offered an old clock; **on m'en propose un bon prix** I've been offered a good price for it; **p. ses services à qn** to offer *or* to volunteer one's services to sb; **elle m'a proposé de m'aider** she offered to help me; **ils (vous) proposent deux semaines aux Seychelles pour 600 euros** they're offering two weeks in the Seychelles for 600 euros

3 *(personne)* to recommend, to put forward; **p. la candidature de qn** to nominate sb; **p. qn pour un oscar** to nominate sb for an Oscar

4 *Scol (sujet) Br* to set, *Am* to assign; **proposez-leur des exercices gradués** *Br* set *or Am* assign them increasingly difficult exercises

5 *Admin & Pol* **p. une loi** to introduce a bill; **p. un ordre du jour** to move an agenda; **p. la suspension de la séance** to move that the session be suspended

►**se proposer** VPR **1** *(être volontaire)* to offer one's services; **se p. comme secrétaire** to offer to act as secretary, to offer one's services as secretary; **je me propose pour coller les enveloppes** I'm volunteering to stick the envelopes; **se p. pour un poste** to apply for a post

2 se p. de *(avoir l'intention de)* to intend to; **ils se proposaient de passer ensemble une semaine tranquille** they intended to spend a quiet week together

proposition [prɔpozisjɔ̃] NF **1** *(suggestion)* suggestion, proposal; **faire une p.** to make a suggestion *or* proposal; **quelqu'un a-t-il une autre p. à faire?** has anyone any other suggestions *or* anything else to suggest?; **vos propositions ne sont pas recevables** what you're suggesting *or* proposing is unacceptable; **faire une p. à qn** to make sb a proposition; **je vais te faire une p., partons dimanche!** I tell you what, why don't we leave on Sunday!

2 *(offre)* offer; **faire une p. à qn** to make sb an offer; **faire** *ou* **formuler une p.** to make a proposal; **refuser une p.** to turn down an offer; **j'ai déjà eu quelques propositions de tournage** I've already had one or two film offers; *Euph* **faire des propositions à qn** to proposition sb; **p. d'affaires** business proposition; **p. de paiement** payment proposal; **p. de prix** price proposal; **p. de rachat** offer to buy

3 *Phil & (en logique)* proposition; **calcul des propositions** propositional calculus

4 *(recommandation)* recommendation; **sur (la) p. du comité** on the committee's recommendation

5 *Pol* **propositions et contre-propositions** proposals and counterproposals; **mettre une p. aux voix** to put a motion to the vote; **la p. est votée** the motion is passed; **p. européenne** proposed European legislation; **p. de loi** *Br* private member's bill, *Am* private bill; **p. de réforme** reform proposal; **propositions de paix** peace proposals

6 *Gram* clause; **p. principale/subordonnée/relative** main/subordinate/relative clause; **p. circonstancielle de temps/lieu/but** adverbial clause of time/place/purpose

7 *Mktg* **p. unique de vente** unique selling proposition *or* point, USP

propositionnel, -elle [prɔpozisjɔnɛl] ADJ propositional; **calcul p.** propositional calculus

PROPRE [prɔpr]

> **ADJ** clean **A1** ▪ neat **A1, 4** ▪ toilet-trained **A2** ▪ honest **A3** ▪ non-polluting **A5** ▪ own **B1** ▪ proper **B2, 4–6** ▪ specific **B3**
> **NM** cleanliness **1** ▪ tidiness **1** ▪ distinctive feature **2**

ADJ **A. 1** *(nettoyé, lavé)* clean; *(rangé)* neat, tidy; **chez eux c'est bien p.** their house is neat and tidy; **gardez votre ville p.** *Br* don't drop litter!, *Am* don't litter!; *Péj* **p. sur lui** neat and proper; *Ironique* **nous voilà propres!** now we're in a fine mess!; **p. comme un sou neuf** spick and span, clean as a new pin

2 *Euph (éduqué → bébé)* toilet-trained, potty-trained; *(→ chiot) Br* house-trained, *Am* house-broken

3 *(honnête)* honest; **de l'argent p.** honest money; **il n'a jamais rien fait de p.** he's never done anything honest; **une affaire pas très p.** a shady business

4 *(bien exécuté → travail)* neat, well done

5 *Écol* clean, non-polluting, non-pollutant; *Nucl* clean

B. 1 *(avant le nom) (en intensif)* own; *(privé)* own, private; **ma p. maison/fille** my own house/daughter; **de mes propres yeux** with my own eyes; **de sa p. main** personally; **de son p. chef** on his/her own initiative *or* authority; **les propres paroles du Prophète** the Prophet's very *or* own words; **son p. hélicoptère** his/her own helicopter, a helicopter of his/her own, his/her private helicopter

2 *(légitime)* proper, legitimate; **l'objet p. de la diplomatie** the proper *or* legitimate purpose of diplomacy

3 *(caractéristique)* **p. à** specific *or* peculiar to; **pour des raisons qui lui sont propres** for reasons of his/her own; **sa méthode de travail lui est p.** he/she has his/her own particular way of working; **une habitude p. à notre génération** a habit peculiar to *or* specific to our generation

4 *(adapté)* proper; **le mot p.** the proper *or* correct term; **p. à** suited to, fit for, appropriate to; **p. à la consommation humaine** fit for human consumption; **mesures propres à stimuler la production** appropriate measures for boosting production

5 *Ling (nom)* proper; *(sens)* literal

6 *Astron* **mouvement p.** proper motion

7 *Phys* **oscillation p.** natural oscillation

8 *Ordinat* **erreur p.** inherent error

9 *Math (nombre, valeur)* characteristic; *(partie)* proper

10 *Fin* **capitaux** *ou* **fonds propres** capital stock

NM **1** *(propreté)* cleanliness, tidiness; **sentir le p.** to smell clean; *Belg* **faire du p.** to spring-clean; *Fam Ironique* **c'est du p.!** *(gâchis)* what a mess!; *(action scandaleuse)* shame on you!

2 *(caractéristique)* peculiarity, distinctive feature; **la raison est le p. de l'homme** reason is unique to man

3 *Rel* proper

❑ **propres** NMPL *Jur* separate property (of each spouse)

❑ **au propre** ADV **1** *(en version définitive)* **mettre qch au p.** to copy sth out neatly, to make a fair copy of sth

2 *Ling* literally; **le mot peut s'employer au p. et au figuré** the word can be used both literally and figuratively

❑ **en propre** ADV by rights; **avoir en p.** to possess (by rights); **la fortune qu'il a en p.** his own fortune, the fortune that's his by rights

❑ **propre en ordre** ADJ *Suisse* neat and tidy

propre-à-rien [prɔprarjɛ̃] *(pl* **propres-à-rien***)* NMF good-for-nothing; **ce sera toujours un p.** he'll never amount to anything

proprement [prɔprəmɑ̃] ADV **1** *(sans salir → gén)* cleanly, tidily; *(→ écrire)* neatly; **l'hôtel est très p. tenu** the hotel is spotlessly clean; **habillé p.** neatly *or* tidily dressed; **manger p.** to eat without making a mess; **coupe ta viande p.!** cut your meat without making a mess!; **elle rangea p. ses affaires** she set her things out neatly

2 *(absolument)* truly, totally, absolutely; **elle est p. insupportable!** she's absolutely unbearable!; **c'est p. scandaleux!** it's an absolute disgrace!

3 *(comme il faut)* well and truly; **il s'est fait p. éjecter** he was thrown out unceremoniously *or* well and truly thrown out; **il l'a p. ridiculisée** he made an absolute fool of her

4 *(spécifiquement)* specifically, strictly; **l'aspect p. éducatif du projet leur a échappé** they missed the specifically educational significance of the project

5 *Littéraire (convenablement)* decently, properly, honourably; **elle ne s'est pas conduite très p.** she didn't behave very properly

❑ **à proprement parler** ADV strictly speaking

❑ **proprement dit, proprement dite** ADJ actual; **la maison p. dite** the house proper, the actual house, the house itself

propret, -ette [prɔprɛ, -ɛt] ADJ neat and tidy; **elle est toujours bien proprette** she's always neat and tidy; **un petit jardin bien p.** a neat little garden

propreté [prɔprəte] NF **1** *(hygiène, soin)* cleanliness; *(des vêtements, de la vaisselle)* cleanness; *(d'une pièce, d'un travail)* neatness, tidiness; *(absence de saleté)* cleanness, cleanliness; *Euph* **l'apprentissage de la p.** *(chez l'enfant)* toilet-training, potty-training; **ils ne connaissent pas les règles élémentaires de p.** they don't know the basic rules of hygiene **2** *Écol* cleanness, absence of pollution

propréteur [prɔpretœr] **NM** *Antiq* propraetor
propréture [prɔpretyr] **NF** *Antiq* propraetorship
propriétaire [prɔprijetɛr] **NMF 1** *(celui qui possède)* owner; **ce sont eux les propriétaires du club/de l'hôtel** they are the owners *or* proprietors of the club/hotel; **c'est moi le p.** I am the owner; **ils ont voulu être propriétaires** they wanted to own their own place; **devenir p. de qch** to acquire sth; **tous les propriétaires seront soumis à la taxe** all householders *or* homeowners will be liable to tax; **qui est le p. de cette valise?** to whom does this case belong?; **vous êtes maintenant l'heureux p. d'une machine à laver** you are now the proud owner *or* possessor of a washing machine; **p. foncier** property owner; **p. indivis** joint owner; **p. légitime** rightful *or* legal owner; **p. occupant** owner-occupier; **p. terrien** landowner; **p. unique** sole owner
2 *(celui qui loue)* landlord, *f* landlady
propriétaire-éleveur [prɔprijetɛrelvœr] *(pl* **propriétaires-éleveurs)** **NM** *Agr & Sport* owner-breeder
propriétaire-récoltant [prɔprijetɛrrekɔltɑ̃] *(pl* **propriétaires-récoltants)** **NM** wine grower
propriété [prɔprijete] **NF 1** *(chose possédée)* property; *(terres)* property, estate; **une très belle/une grande/une petite p.** an excellent/a large/a small property; **p. foncière/immobilière** landed/real estate; **p. de l'État** government *or* state property; **p. grevée d'hypothèques** encumbered estate; **p. en indivision** jointly-owned property; *Jur* **p. mobilière** personal property, movables; **p. privée** private (property); **p. privée, défense d'entrer** *(sur panneau)* private property, keep out
2 *(fait de posséder)* ownership
3 *Jur* ownership; **posséder en toute p.** to hold in fee simple; **p. collective des moyens de production** collective ownership of the means of production; **p. commerciale** leasehold ownership *(covenant to extend lease)*; **p. commune** joint ownership; **p. exclusive de l'auteur** exclusive property of the author; **p. incorporelle** incorporeal hereditaments; **p. individuelle** personal *or* private property; **p. indivise** joint ownership; **p. industrielle** patent rights; **p. intellectuelle** intellectual property; **p. littéraire et artistique** copyright
4 *(propriétaires)* property owners; **la grande/petite p.** the big/small landowners
5 *(qualité)* property, characteristic, feature; **la codéine a des propriétés antitussives** codeine suppresses coughing; **ce plastique a la p. d'être souple** this plastic has the characteristic of being flexible
6 *(exactitude → d'un terme)* aptness, appropriateness; **sans p. dans les termes, pas de clarté** if the correct terms are not used, clarity is lost
proprio [prɔprijo] **NMF** *Fam* landlord, *f* landlady▪
propriocepteur [prɔprijosɛptœr] **NM** *Physiol* proprioceptor
proprioceptif, -ive [prɔprijosɛptif, -iv] **ADJ** *Physiol* proprioceptive
proprioception [prɔprijosɛpsjɔ̃] **NF** *Physiol* proprioception
proprioceptive [prɔprijosɛptiv] *voir* **proprioceptif**
propulser [3] [prɔpylse] **VT 1** *Aut* to drive; *Astron* to propel; *Tech* to propel, to drive; **propulsé par un moteur puissant** driven by a powerful engine
2 *(pousser)* to push, to fling; **il s'est trouvé propulsé sur le devant de la scène** he was pushed towards the front of the stage; **le vélo a été propulsé sous le camion** the bicycle was flung *or* thrown under the lorry; *Fig* **elle s'est trouvée propulsée à la tête de l'entreprise** she suddenly found herself in charge of the business
►**se propulser VPR** *Fam* to shoot; **il s'est propulsé dans le bureau du patron** he shot off to the boss's office
propulseur [prɔpylsœr] **NM 1** *Tech & Naut (hélice)* (screw) propeller; *(moteur)* power unit; *(carburant)* propellant; **p. d'étrave** bow propeller **2** *Astron* rocket engine; **p. auxiliaire** booster
propulsif, -ive [prɔpylsif, -iv] **ADJ** propellant, propelling, propulsive; **roue propulsive** driving wheel
propulsion [prɔpylsjɔ̃] **NF 1** *Aviat, Tech & Naut (phénomène)* propulsion, propelling force; *(résultat)* propulsion, propulsive motion, drive; **fusée à p. atomique/nucléaire** atomic-powered/nuclear-powered rocket **2** *Élec* **p. électrique** electric drive; **p. turbo-électrique** turbo-electric propulsion; **p. par photons** photonic drive
propulsive [prɔpylsiv] *voir* **propulsif**
propyle [prɔpil] **NM** *Chim* propyl
propylée [prɔpile] **NM** propylaeum; **les propylées de l'Acropole** the Propylaea
propylène [prɔpilɛn] **NM** *Chim* propylene, propene
prorata [prɔrata] **NM INV** proportion; **en respectant le p.** in due ratio
❑ **au prorata ADV** proportionally, pro rata
❑ **au prorata de PRÉP** in proportion to; **bénéfices au p. du nombre d'actions** profits shared out pro rata to (the number of) shares held
prorogatif, -ive [prɔrɔgatif, -iv] **ADJ** *Jur* prorogating
prorogation [prɔrɔgasjɔ̃] **NF 1** *Admin & Jur (d'un délai)* extension; *(d'un visa, d'un contrat)* renewal; **p. de compétence** *ou* **de juridiction** extension of jurisdiction **2** *Pol (suspension → d'une assemblée)* adjournment, *Spéc* prorogation
prorogative [prɔrɔgativ] *voir* **prorogatif**
proroger [17] [prɔrɔʒe] **VT 1** *Admin & Jur (délai, compétence)* to extend; *(traité, contrat, visa)* to renew; *(échéance)* to defer **2** *Pol (suspendre → assemblée)* to adjourn, *Spéc* to prorogue
prosaïque [prozaik] **ADJ** mundane, pedestrian, prosaic; *Hum* **pour en revenir à des préoccupations plus prosaïques, qu'est-ce qu'on mange ce soir?** to get back to more mundane matters, what are we having for dinner?
prosaïquement [prozaikmɑ̃] **ADV** mundanely, prosaically
prosaïsme [prozaism] **NM** ordinariness, prosaicness; **quel p.!** how romantic!
prosateur, -trice [prozatœr, -tris] **NM,F** prose writer
proscenium [prɔsenjɔm] **NM 1** *Théât* apron, proscenium **2** *Antiq* proscenium
proscripteur [prɔskriptœr] **NM** proscriber
proscription [prɔskripsjɔ̃] **NF 1** *Hist (exil)* exiling, banishment; *Antiq* proscription **2** *(interdiction)* prohibition, banning, proscription
proscrire [99] [prɔskrir] **VT 1** *(exiler)* to banish, to proscribe; **p. qn de la société** to ostracize sb **2** *(interdire → gén)* to forbid; *(→ par la loi)* to outlaw; *(déconseiller)* to advise against; **cet usage est à p.** this expression is to be avoided
proscrit, -e [prɔskri, -it] **ADJ 1** *(exilé)* proscribed **2** *(interdit)* forbidden; **c'est un usage p.** *(déconseillé)* the expression is to be avoided; *(tabou)* the expression is taboo
NM,F outlaw
proscrivait *etc voir* **proscrire**
prose [proz] **NF 1** *Littérature* prose **2** *Fam (style)* (writing) style; **sa p. se lit sans déplaisir** his/her work reads quite well **3** *Fam Hum (écrit)* work▪ ; *Ironique* masterpiece; **vous, au fond de la classe, apportez-moi votre p.!** you there, in the back row, bring me over your masterpiece!
❑ **en prose ADJ** prose *(avant n)*; **texte en p.** prose text **ADV écrire en p.** to write (in) prose

Allusion

Faire de la prose sans le savoir

In Molière's comedy *Le Bourgeois gentilhomme*, the social climber, monsieur Jourdain, tries to ape the aristocracy. He engages various teachers who are out to fleece him, and learns in one lesson that language can be divided into poetry or prose. The thought strikes him that he has been "talking prose without realizing it". In modern French, other words can be substituted for **prose** when people give signs of some natural aptitude not previously recognized, eg **Tu fais de la politique/de la philosophie sans le savoir, comme monsieur Jourdain faisait de la prose.** ("You were a politician/philosopher all along, you just didn't realize it.") There are echoes here of the English rhyme, "He's a poet and doesn't know it".

prosecteur [prɔsɛktœr] **NM** *Univ* prosector, demonstrator (in anatomy)
prosélyte [prozelit] **NMF 1** *(adepte)* proselyte; **l'idée a fait de nombreux prosélytes** there were many converts to the idea, many people espoused the idea **2** *Hist & Rel* convert, proselyte
prosélytisme [prozelitism] **NM 1** *Rel* proselytism **2** *(propagande)* proselytism, missionary zeal; **faire du p.** *Br* to proselytize, *Am* to proselyte
prosencéphale [prozɑ̃sefal] **NM** *Anat* forebrain, *Spéc* prosencephalon
Proserpine [prozɛrpin] **NPR** *Myth* Proserpina
prosimien [prosimjɛ̃] *Zool* **NM** prosimian
❑ **prosimiens NMPL** Prosimii, Lemuroidea, prosimians
prosobranche [prozɔbrɑ̃ʃ] *Zool* **NM** prosobranch
❑ **prosobranches NMPL** Prosobranchia, Prosobranchiata, Streptoneura
prosodie [prozɔdi] **NF 1** *Littérature* prosody **2** *Mus* rules of musical arrangement
prosodique [prozɔdik] **ADJ** prosodic
prosopagnosie [prozɔpagnɔzi] **NF** *Psy* prosopagnosia
prosopopée [prozɔpɔpe] **NF** prosopopoeia
prospect[1] [prɔspɛ] **NM** *Mktg* prospective customer, prospect; **prospects à forte potentialité** hot prospect pool
prospect[2] [prɔspɛkt] **NM** *Constr & Jur* minimum distance between buildings
prospecté, -e [prɔspɛkte] **NM,F** *Mktg* prospective customer, prospect
prospecter [4] [prɔspɛkte] **VT 1** *Mktg (région)* to comb; *(clientèle)* to canvass; *(marché)* to explore, to investigate **2** *Mines* to prospect; **p. une région pour trouver de l'or** to prospect an area for gold; **on prospecte la région pour trouver du pétrole** they're looking for oil in the area
USAGE ABSOLU *Mktg* to canvass customers; *Mines* to prospect
prospecteur, -trice [prɔspɛktœr, -tris] **ADJ** prospecting, investigating
NM,F 1 *Mktg* canvasser **2** *Mines* prospector
prospecteur-placier [prɔspɛktœrplasje] *(pl* **prospecteurs-placiers)** **NM** employment officer
prospectif, -ive [prɔspɛktif, -iv] **ADJ** prospective
❑ **prospective NF 1** *(dans l'administration, le management)* long-term planning; *Écon* (long-term) forecasting **2** *(science)* futurology
prospection [prɔspɛksjɔ̃] **NF 1** *Mines* prospecting; **p. minière/pétrolière** mining/oil exploration **2** *Mktg (de la clientèle)* canvassing, prospecting; *(des tendances, du marché)* exploring; **faire de la p.** to explore the market; **p. commerciale** business development; **p. du marché** market exploration; **p. téléphonique** *ou* **par téléphone** telephone canvassing; **p. sur le terrain** field research
prospective [prɔspɛktiv] *voir* **prospectif**
prospectiviste [prɔspɛktivist] **ADJ 1** *(ayant rapport à la futurologie)* futurological **2** *Écon (analyse, approche)* that forecasts future *or* long-term trends
NMF 1 *(futurologue)* futurologist **2** *(dans l'administration, le management)* long-term planner; *Écon* (economic) forecaster
prospectrice [prɔspɛktris] *voir* **prospecteur**
prospectus [prɔspɛktys] **NM 1** *Com (de publicité)* leaflet; *(de plusieurs pages)* brochure; **il n'y a rien que des p. dans la boîte aux lettres** there's nothing but advertising leaflets in the letter box; **nous avons envoyé des p. à tous nos clients** we have sent a mailshot to *or* we have circularized all our customers; **p. de publicité directe** fly sheet **2** *Bourse* prospectus
prospère [prɔspɛr] **ADJ 1** *(florissant → ville, région, commerce)* flourishing, thriving; *(→ santé)* glowing; **les affaires sont prospères** business is booming **2** *(riche)* prosperous
prospérer [18] [prɔspere] **VI** *(entreprise)* to flourish, to thrive; *(pays)* to prosper, to thrive, to do well; *(personne)* to fare well, to thrive; *(plante)* to thrive; **le tourisme a fait p. toute la région** tourism brought wealth to the whole area
prospérité [prɔsperite] **NF** prosperity, success; **une période de (grande) p.** a boom; **être en pleine p.** to be thriving; **(santé et) p. à tous!** here's to health and prosperity!
prostaglandine [prɔstaglɑ̃din] **NF** *Physiol* prostaglandin
prostate [prɔstat] **NF** *Anat* prostate (gland); **se**

pro–pro

faire opérer de la p. to have a prostate operation; *Méd* **cancer de la p.** prostate cancer

prostatectomie [prɔstatɛktɔmi] NF *Méd* prostatectomy

prostatique [prɔstatik] *Méd* ADJ prostatic; **calcul p.** prostatic calculus, prostatolith
   NM prostate sufferer

prostatite [prɔstatit] NF *Méd* prostatitis

prosternation [prɔstɛrnasjɔ̃] NF 1 *Rel* bowing-down, *Sout* prosternation 2 *Fig Littéraire (servilité)* toadying

prosternement [prɔstɛrnəmɑ̃] NM 1 *Rel* bowing-down, *Sout* prosternation 2 *Fig Littéraire (servilité)* toadying

prosterner [3] [prɔstɛrne] VT *Arch ou Littéraire* **le vent prosterne les arbres** the wind is laying the trees flat *or* is bending the trees to the ground
   ▸ **se prosterner** VPR *Rel* to bow down (**devant** before); *Fig* **se p. devant qn** to grovel to sb

prosthèse [prɔstɛz] NF *Ling* pro(s)thesis

prosthétique [prɔstetik] ADJ *Ling* pro(s)thetic

prostitué, -e [prɔstitɥe] NM,F *(homme)* male prostitute; *(femme)* prostitute

prostituer [7] [prɔstitɥe] VT 1 *(personne)* to make a prostitute of, to prostitute 2 *Fig* **p. son talent** to sell *or* to prostitute one's talent
   ▸ **se prostituer** VPR *aussi Fig* to prostitute oneself

prostitution [prɔstitysjɔ̃] NF *aussi Fig* prostitution

prostration [prɔstrasjɔ̃] NF 1 *Méd & Rel* prostration 2 *Écon* collapse, crash

prostré, -e [prɔstre] ADJ 1 *(accablé)* prostrate, despondent 2 *Méd* prostrate

prostyle [prɔstil] *Archit* ADJ **temple p.** prostyle temple
   NM prostyle

protactinium [prɔtaktinjɔm] NM *Chim* prot(o)actinium

protagoniste [prɔtagɔnist] NMF 1 *(principal participant)* protagonist; **les protagonistes du conflit vont entamer des pourparlers** the protagonists in the conflict are to start negotiations 2 *Cin & Littérature* (chief) protagonist, main character 3 *Antiq* protagonist

protal, -als [prɔtal] NM *Fam Br* headmaster▪, head, *Am* principal▪

protamine [prɔtamin] NF protamine

protandrie [prɔtɑ̃dri] = **protérandrie**

protase [prɔtaz] NF *Gram & (en rhétorique)* protasis

prote [prɔt] NM *Vieilli* foreman *(in printing works)*

protéagineux, -euse [prɔteaʒinø, -øz] ADJ proteinaceous
   NM proteinaceous plant

protéase [prɔteaz] NF protease

Protecteur [prɔtɛktœr] NM *Hist* Protector

protecteur, -trice [prɔtɛktœr, -tris] ADJ 1 *(qui protège)* protective; **il est très p. avec ses enfants** he is very protective towards his children; **crème protectrice** barrier cream 2 *(condescendant)* patronizing 3 *Écon* protectionist
   NM,F 1 *(gardien)* custodian, guardian, guarantor 2 *(mécène)* patron
   NM *(d'une prostituée)* procurer

protectif, -ive [prɔtɛktif, -iv] ADJ *Littéraire* protective; **erreur protective** protective illusion

protection [prɔtɛksjɔ̃] NF 1 *(défense)* protection; **assurer la p. de qn** to protect sb; **demander la p. des services de police** to ask for police protection; **prendre qn sous sa p.** to take sb under one's wing; **ne t'inquiète pas, tu es sous ma p.** don't worry, I'll protect *or* shield you; *Mil* **p. aérienne** aerial protection; **p. civile** *(en temps de guerre)* civil defence; *(en temps de paix)* disaster management; **p. du consommateur** consumer protection; *Nucl* **p. contre les rayonnements** radiological protection; **p. diplomatique** diplomatic protection; **p. de l'emploi** personal security, job protection; **p. de l'enfance** child welfare; **p. de l'environnement** environmental protection, protection of the environment; **p. des espèces menacées** protection of endangered species; **p. fiscale** tax shield; **p. judiciaire** (court) supervision (of a minor), wardship; **p. maternelle et infantile** mother and child care *(including antenatal and postnatal clinics and family planning)*; **p. de la nature** nature conservation *or* conservancy; **p. rapprochée** *(d'une personne)* police protection; **p. sociale** social welfare (system)

2 *(prévention)* protection, preservation, conservation; **c'est une bonne p. contre la rouille/les fraudes** it's a good protection against rust/fraud

3 *(soutien)* **solliciter la p. de qn** to ask for sb's support, to ask sb to use their influence on one's behalf; **par p.** through (personal) influence

4 *Beaux-Arts & Sport* patronage

5 *(serviette hygiénique)* **p. (féminine)** *Br* sanitary towel, *Am* sanitary napkin

6 *Ordinat* security; **p. contre la copie** copy protection; **p. contre l'écriture** *ou* **en écriture** write-protection; **p. de fichier** file protection, protected file access; **p. de l'information** data protection; **p. mémoire** protected location; **p. par mot de passe** password protection

7 *Métal* coating; **p. cathodique** cathodic protection
   □ **de protection** ADJ protective, safety *(avant n)*; **gaine de p.** protective cover; **couche/vernis de p.** protective coating/varnish

protectionnisme [prɔtɛksjɔnism] NM protectionism

protectionniste [prɔtɛksjɔnist] ADJ protectionist
   NMF protectionist

protectorat [prɔtɛktɔra] NM protectorate

protectrice [prɔtɛktris] *voir* **protecteur**

Protée [prɔte] NPR *Myth* Proteus

protée [prɔte] NM 1 *Littéraire (personne)* chameleon 2 *(amphibien)* olm 3 *Bot* protea

protégé, -e [prɔteʒe] ADJ 1 *Aviat* **espace aérien p.** protected airspace 2 *Écol (espèce, zone)* protected 3 *Électron* protected 4 *Ordinat* **p. contre la copie** copy-protected; **p. contre l'écriture** *ou* **en écriture** write-protected; **p. par mot de passe** password-protected 5 *(relations sexuelles)* protected; **rapports non protégés** unprotected sex
   NM,F protégé

protège-bas [prɔtɛʒba] NM INV socklet *(worn to protect stocking from rough shoes)*

protège-cahier [prɔtɛʒkaje] *(pl* **protège-cahiers***)* NM exercise-book cover

protège-couche [prɔtɛʒkuʃ] *(pl* **protège-couches***)* NM nappy liner

protège-dents [prɔtɛʒdɑ̃] NM INV gum-shield

protège-lange [prɔtɛʒlɑ̃ʒ] *(pl* **protège-langes***)* = **protège-couches**

protège-matelas [prɔtɛʒmatla] NM INV mattress cover

protéger [22] [prɔteʒe] VT 1 *(assurer → la sécurité de)* to protect, to defend; *(→ la santé, la survie de)* to protect, to look after; **les verres fumés protègent bien les yeux** tinted lenses offer good protection for the eyes; **p. qch contre le** *ou* **du froid** to protect *or* to insulate sth against the cold; **p. qch contre** *ou* **de la chaleur** to heatproof sth, to protect sth against heat; **p. qch contre les radiations** to shield sth from radiation; **les arbres protègent la maison du vent** the trees shelter the house from the wind; **il fit p. sa fille par des gardes du corps** he employed bodyguards to protect his daughter; **c'est pour p. son frère qu'elle a dit cela** she said it in order to protect *or* to shield her brother

2 *Com & Écon (position)* to hedge; *Jur* **p. qch par un brevet** to patent sth

3 *(aider → les arts)* to be a patron of; *(→ le sport)* to encourage, to be a patron of; **on la protège en haut lieu** she has friends in high places

4 *(sujet: racketteur)* to protect

5 *Euph (prostituée)* to act as a procurer, *f* procuress for

6 *Ordinat* **p. contre la copie** to copy-protect; **p. contre l'écriture** *ou* **en écriture** to write-protect; **p. par mot de passe** to password-protect
   ▸ **se protéger** VPR to protect oneself; **protégez-vous contre la grippe** protect yourself against the flu; **se p. contre le** *ou* **du soleil** to shield oneself from the sun; **les jeunes sont encouragés à se p. lors de leurs relations sexuelles** young people are encouraged to protect themselves (by using a condom); **elle a su se p. grâce à des relations haut placées** she was able to protect herself thanks to friends in high places

protège-slip [prɔtɛʒslip] *(pl* **protège-slips***)* NM panty liner

protège-tibia [prɔtɛʒtibja] *(pl* **protège-tibias***)* NM shin pad

protège-tympan [prɔtɛʒtɛ̃pɑ̃] NM INV earplug

protéide [prɔteid] NM protein

protéiforme [prɔteifɔrm] ADJ multiform, *Littéraire* protean

protéine [prɔtein] NF protein; **p. biogène** biogen; **p. plasmatique/spécifique** plasma/specific protein; **protéines animales/végétales** animal/vegetable proteins

protéiné, -e [prɔteine] ADJ *(enrichi en protéines)* protein-enriched; *(qui contient des protéines)* containing protein

protéinique [prɔteinik] ADJ containing protein

protéinurie [prɔteinyri] NF *Méd* proteinuria

protéique [prɔteik] ADJ proteinaceous, protein *(avant n)*

protèle [prɔtɛl] NM *Zool* aardwolf

protéolyse [prɔteoliz] NF *Biol & Chim* proteolysis

protéolytique [prɔteolitik] ADJ *Biol & Chim* proteolytic

protéomique [prɔteomik] *Biol & Chim* ADJ proteomic
   NF proteomics *(singulier)*

protérandrie [prɔterɑ̃dri] NF *Bot* protandry, proterandry

protérogynie [prɔterɔʒini] = **protogynie**

protérozoïque [prɔterɔzɔik] *Géol* ADJ Proterozoic
   NM Proterozoic

protestable [prɔtɛstabl] ADJ *Banque* protestable; *Jur* which may be protested

protestant, -e [prɔtɛstɑ̃, -ɑ̃t] ADJ Protestant
   NM,F Protestant

protestantisme [prɔtɛstɑ̃tism] NM *(doctrine)* Protestantism; *(ensemble des protestants)* Protestant churches, Protestant community

protestataire [prɔtɛstatɛr] ADJ *(délégué)* protesting; *(mesure)* protest *(avant n)*
   NMF protester, protestor

protestation [prɔtɛstasjɔ̃] NF 1 *(mécontentement)* protest, discontent; **grand mouvement/grande manifestation de p. demain à 14 heures** a big protest rally/demonstration will be held tomorrow at 2 p.m.

2 *(opposition)* protest; **paroles/geste de p.** words/gesture of protest; **en signe de p.** as a protest; **sans p.** without protest; **sans une p.** without a murmur

3 *Jur* protesting, protestation
   □ **protestations** NFPL *Littéraire (déclarations)* **protestations d'amitié** protestations *or* assurances of friendship; **faire à qn des protestations d'amour/de loyauté** to profess one's love/loyalty to sb

protester [3] [prɔtɛste] VI *(dire non)* to protest (**contre** against *ou* about); **je proteste!** I protest!, I object!; **elle a protesté auprès du directeur** she complained to the manager; **p. mollement** to make a feeble protest
   VT 1 *Jur* to protest

2 *Vieilli (affirmer)* to protest, to declare; **je proteste avec la dernière énergie que je n'ai pas reçu votre convocation** I strongly protest that *or* I solemnly declare that I didn't receive your notification
   □ **protester de** VT IND *Littéraire* **p. de son innocence** to protest one's innocence

protêt [prɔtɛ] NM *Jur* protest; **faire dresser un p.** to (make a) protest; **p. authentique** certified protest; **p. faute d'acceptation/faute de paiement** protest for non-acceptance/non-payment

prothalame [prɔtalam] NM *Littérature* prothalamion

prothalle [prɔtal] NM *Bot* prothallium, prothallus

prothèse [prɔtɛz] *Méd* NF 1 *(technique)* prosthetics (*UNCOUNT*); **p. dentaire** prosthodontics *(singulier)* 2 *(dispositif)* prosthesis; **p. auditive** hearing aid; **p. dentaire totale** (set of) dentures; **p. dentaire fixe** bridge, *Spéc* fixed dental prosthesis

prothésiste [prɔtezist] NMF *Méd* prosthetist; **p. dentaire** prosthodontist, dental prosthetist

prothétique [prɔtetik] *Méd* ADJ prosthetic
   NF prosthetics *(singulier)*

prothorax [prɔtɔraks] NM *Entom* prothorax

prothrombine [prɔtrɔ̃bin] NF *Physiol* prothrombin

protide [prɔtid] NM protein

protidique [prɔtidik] ADJ proteinaceous, protein *(avant n)*

protique [prɔkreatik] **ADJ** *Chim* **acide p.** protic acid

protiste [prɔtist] **NM** *Biol* protist

protium [prɔtjɔm] **NM** *Chim* protium

proto- [prɔto] **PRÉF** proto-

protococcus [prɔtɔkɔkys] **NM** *Bot* protococcus

protocolaire [prɔtɔkɔlɛr] **ADJ** *(respectueux des usages)* formal; *(conforme à l'étiquette)* mindful of *or* conforming to etiquette; **le prince dans une attitude peu p.** the Prince in a relaxed pose

protocole [prɔtɔkɔl] **NM 1** *Jur & Pol* protocol; **p. d'accord** draft agreement; **p. d'intention** statement of intent; **le P. de Kyoto** the Kyoto Protocol

2 *Ordinat (gén)* protocol; *(de réseau)* frame format; *(de traitement)* procedure; **p. HTTP sécurisé** secure HTTP; **p. multivoie** multi-channel protocol; **p. Internet** Internet protocol; **p. de téléchargement** download protocol; **p. de transfert anonyme** anonymous FTP; **p. de transfert de fichiers** file transfer protocol; **p. de transmission** transmission protocol; **p. univoie** single-channel protocol

3 *Typ* style sheet

4 *(cérémonial)* **le p.** protocole, etiquette; **le chef du p.** the chief of protocol; **le bain de foule n'était pas prévu par le p.** the walkabout was not part of the (prearranged) schedule

5 *Phys, Chim & Biol* **p. d'une expérience** experimental procedure

6 *Méd* **p. opératoire** protocol

7 *Com* **p. d'achat et de vente** buy-sell agreement

protocordé [prɔtɔkɔrde] *Zool* **NM** protochordate
□ **protocordés NMPL** Protochordata

protoétoile [prɔtɔetwal] **NF** *Astron* protostar

protogalaxie [prɔtɔgalaksi] **NF** *Astron* protogalaxy

protogine [prɔtɔʒin] **NM OU NF** *Géol* protogine

protogynie [prɔtɔʒini] **NF** *Bot* protogyny

protohistoire [prɔtɔistwar] **NF** protohistory

protohistorien, -enne [prɔtɔistɔrjɛ̃, -ɛn] **NM,F** protohistorian

protohistorique [prɔtɔistɔrik] **ADJ** protohistoric

proto-industralisation [prɔtɔɛ̃dystrijalizasjɔ̃] **NF** proto-industrialization

protomé [prɔtɔme] **NM** *Archéol* protome

proton [prɔtɔ̃] **NM** *Phys* proton

protonéma [prɔtɔnema] **NM** *Bot* protonema

protonique [prɔtɔnik] **ADJ** *Chim* protonic

protophyte [prɔtɔfit] **NM** protophyte
□ **protophytes NMPL** Protophyta

protoplanète [prɔtɔplanɛt] **NF** *Astron* protoplanet

protoplasma [prɔtɔplasma], **protoplasme** [prɔtɔplasm] **NM** *Biol* protoplasm

protoplasmique [prɔtɔplasmik] **ADJ** *Biol* protoplasmic

protoplaste [prɔtɔplast] **NM** *Biol* protoplast

protoptère [prɔtɔptɛr] **NM** *Ich* protopterus, African lung fish

protostomien [prɔtɔstɔmjɛ̃] **NM** *Entom* protostome

protothérien [prɔtɔterjɛ̃] *Zool* **NM** prototherian
□ **protothériens NMPL** Prototheria

prototypage [prɔtɔtipaʒ] **NM** *Ordinat* prototyping; **p. rapide** rapid prototyping

prototype [prɔtɔtip] **NM 1** *Ind* prototype **2** *(archétype)* standard; **c'est le p. du vieil imprimeur** he's the archetypal old printer **3** *(comme adj; avec ou sans trait d'union)* prototype *(avant n)*

prototypique [prɔtɔtipik] **ADJ** prototypic, prototypical

protoure [prɔtur] *Entom* **NM** proturan
□ **protoures NMPL** Protura

protoxyde [prɔtɔksid] **NM** *Chim* protoxide; **p. d'azote** nitrous oxide

protozoaire [prɔtɔzɔɛr] *Zool* **NM** protozoan, protozoon
ADJ protozoal, protozoic
□ **protozoaires NMPL** Protozoa

protractile [prɔtraktil] **ADJ** protractile

protrusion [prɔtryzjɔ̃] **NF** protrusion

protubérance [prɔtyberɑ̃s] **NF 1** *(bosse)* bump; *(enflure)* bulge, *Spéc* protuberance **2** *Anat* protuberance; **p. cérébrale** mesencephalon **3** *Astron* **p. solaire** solar prominence

protubérant, -e [prɔtyberɑ̃, -ɑ̃t] **ADJ** *(muscle)* bulging; *(menton, front)* prominent; *(œil, ventre)* protruding, bulging

protubérantiel, -elle [prɔtyberɑ̃sjɛl] **ADJ** *Astron* prominence *(avant n)*

protuteur, -trice [prɔtytœr, -tris] **NM,F** *Jur* acting guardian

prou [pru] *voir* **peu**

proudhonien, -enne [prudɔnjɛ̃, -ɛn] **ADJ** Proudhonian
NM,F follower of Proudhon

proue [pru] **NF** *Naut* bow, bows, prow
□ **en proue ADJ** projecting **ADV s'avancer en p.** to protrude

prouesse [pruɛs] **NF 1** *Littéraire (acte héroïque)* deed of valour
2 *(action remarquable)* exploit, feat; *Fig* **le convaincre a été une p.** convincing him was quite a feat; **faire des prouesses** *(briller)* to perform outstandingly; *(faire des efforts)* to do one's utmost; **j'ai fait des prouesses pour finir dans les délais** I did my utmost to finish on time; **j'ai dû faire des prouesses pour le convaincre** it took everything I had *or* I had to work very hard to convince him; *Hum* **il n'a pas/je n'ai pas fait de prouesses** he/I didn't exactly shine

proustien, -enne [prustjɛ̃, -ɛn] **ADJ** Proustian

prout [prut] **NM** *Fam* **1** *(pet)* fart; **faire un p.** to fart, *Br* to let off, *Am* to lay one **2 p., ma chère!** *(pour singer un homosexuel)* ooh, ducky!

prout-prout [prutprut] **ADJ** *Fam* snobby, up oneself; **qu'est-ce qu'elle peut être p., sa gonzesse!** his girlfriend can be so up herself!

prouvable [pruvabl] **ADJ** provable; **ce n'est pas p.** it can't be proved; **c'est facilement/difficilement p.** it's easy/difficult to prove

prouver [3] [pruve] **VT 1** *(faire la preuve de)* to prove; **cela n'est pas encore prouvé, cela reste à p.** it remains to be proved; **il n'est pas prouvé que...** there's no proof that...; **les faits ont prouvé qu'elle était bel et bien absente** the facts proved her to have indeed been absent; **p. qch à qn** to prove sth to sb, to give sb proof of sth; **prouve-moi le contraire!** give me proof of *or* to the contrary!; **il t'a menti – prouve-le-moi!** he lied to you – prove it!; *Jur* **p. le bien-fondé d'une accusation** to substantiate a charge; **il m'a prouvé par A + B que j'avais tort** he demonstrated that I was wrong in a very logical way

2 *(mettre en évidence)* to show; **cela prouve bien que j'avais raison** it shows that I was right; **tous les tests ont prouvé la supériorité du nouveau système** all the tests showed *or* demonstrated the superiority of the new system; **son désintéressement n'est plus à p.** his/her impartiality is no longer open to question

3 *(témoigner)* to demonstrate; **p. à qn son amitié/sa reconnaissance** to demonstrate one's friendship/gratitude to sb, to give sb proof of one's friendship/gratitude

▶**se prouver VPR se p. qch (à soi-même)** to prove sth (to oneself); **que cherche-t-il à se p.?** what's he trying to prove to himself?

provenance [prɔvnɑ̃s] **NF** *(d'un mot)* origin; *(d'une rumeur)* source; **des marchandises de p. étrangère** imported goods; **des produits de p. anglaise** goods of English origin; **pays de p.** country of origin; **quelle est la p. de ces légumes?** where do these vegetables come from?
□ **en provenance de PRÉP** (coming) from; **le train en p. de Genève** the train from Geneva, the Geneva train; **les voyageurs en p. de Montréal** passengers (recently arrived) from Montreal

provençal, -e, -aux, -ales [prɔvɑ̃sal, -o] **ADJ** Provençal
NM *Ling* Provençal
□ **Provençal, -e, -aux, -ales NM,F** = inhabitant of or person from Provence
□ **à la provençale ADJ** *Culin* à la provençale *(cooked with olive oil, garlic, tomatoes and chopped parsley)*

Provence [prɔvɑ̃s] **NF la P.** Provence

Provence-Alpes-Côte-d'Azur [prɔvɑ̃salpkotdazyr] **NF la région P.** Provence-Alpes-Côte-d'Azur

provende [prɔvɑ̃d] **NF** *Vieilli* provender

provenir [40] [prɔvnir] **provenir de VT IND 1** *(lieu)* to come from; **d'où provient cette statuette?** where does this statuette come from?; **des produits provenant du Japon** products from

Japan **2** *(résulter de)* to arise *or* to result from, to arise out of

proverbe [prɔvɛrb] **NM** proverb, adage; **comme dit le p.** as the proverb goes; **passer en p.** to become proverbial
□ **Proverbes NMPL** *Bible* Proverbs

proverbial, -e, -aux, -ales [prɔvɛrbjal, -o] **ADJ 1** *(de proverbe)* proverbial **2** *(connu)* well-known, proverbial; **au lycée, son talent d'imitateur est p.** he's become well-known throughout the school for his impersonations

proverbialement [prɔvɛrbjalmɑ̃] **ADV** proverbially

providence [prɔvidɑ̃s] **NF 1** *Rel* Providence; **les voies de la P.** the ways of Providence **2** *(aubaine)* salvation, piece of luck **3** *(personne)* **tu es ma p.!** you're my saviour!; **vous rentrez à Nice en voiture? vous êtes ma p.!** you're driving back to Nice? you've saved my life!

providentiel, -elle [prɔvidɑ̃sjɛl] **ADJ** providential, miraculous; **c'est l'homme p.!** he's the man we need!; **sans cette grève providentielle, nous n'aurions jamais fait connaissance** if that strike hadn't happened at just the right time, we'd never have met

providentiellement [prɔvidɑ̃sjɛlmɑ̃] **ADV** providentially, miraculously

provient *etc voir* **provenir**

provignage [prɔviɲaʒ], **provignement** [prɔviɲəmɑ̃] **NM** *Agr* provining

provigner [3] [prɔviɲe] **VT** *Agr* to provine
VI 1 *Agr (se multiplier)* to be propagated by layering **2** *Fig Vieilli (se répandre)* to be propagated

provin [prɔvɛ̃] **NM** layered runner, sucker

province [prɔvɛ̃s] **NF 1** *(régions en dehors de la capitale)* **la p.** *(en France)* provincial France; *(dans d'autres pays)* the provinces; **il doit bientôt partir en p.** he'll soon be leaving town; **un week-end en p.** a weekend out of town; **ils vivent en p.** they live in the provinces; **nous avons également des bureaux en p.** we also have provincial branches; **arriver** *ou* **débarquer tout droit de sa p.** to be fresh from the country *or* the provinces; **une petite ville de p.** a small country town; **Bordeaux est une grande ville de p.** Bordeaux is a major provincial town

2 *Belg & Can Admin* = administrative district similar to the French "département"

3 *Hist* province; **la Gaule cisalpine était une p. romaine** Cisalpine Gaul was a Roman province; **la p. de Bourgogne** the province of Burgundy; *Can* **la Belle P.** Quebec

ADJ INV notre quartier est encore très p. there's still a small-town feeling to our area; **sa famille est restée un peu p.** his/her family's kept up a rather provincial way of life

Provinces Maritimes [prɔvɛ̃smaritim] **NFPL** *(au Canada)* **les P.** the Maritime Provinces, the Maritimes

Provinces-Unies [prɔvɛ̃syni] **NFPL** *Hist (aux Pays-Bas)* **les P.** the United Provinces

provincial, -e, -aux, -ales [prɔvɛ̃sjal, -o] **ADJ 1** *(en dehors de Paris)* provincial; **sa tournée provinciale** his/her tour of the provinces; **la vie provinciale** provincial life, life in the provinces

2 *Belg & Can Admin* relating to a "province"; *Belg* **conseil p.** ≃ county council; *Belg* **conseiller p.** ≃ county councillor; *Belg* **palais p.** ≃ county council building

3 *Péj (personne, comportement)* provincial, parochial
NM,F provincial
NM 1 *Rel* provincial
2 *Can* **le P.** the Provincial Government

'La Provinciale' *Goretta* 'A Girl From Lorraine'

'Les Provinciales' *Pascal* 'Provincial Letters'

provincialat [prɔvɛ̃sjala] **NM** *Rel* provincialate

provincialisme [prɔvɛ̃sjalism] **NM 1** *Ling* provincialism **2** *Péj (étroitesse d'esprit)* small-town *or* parish-pump mentality, parochialism

provint *etc voir* **provenir**

provirus [prɔvirys] **NM** *Biol* provirus

proviseur [prɔvizœr] NM

> Note that it is no longer considered a mistake to feminize this word and to say **une proviseure** (with a final **e**) but some French speakers nonetheless regard this form as unacceptable, especially in France. See also the entry **féminisation**.

1 (*directeur*) Br head teacher, headmaster, f headmistress, Am principal **2** Belg (*adjoint*) deputy head (*with overall responsibility for discipline within the school*)

provision [prɔvizjɔ̃] NF **1** (*réserve* → *de bois, de nourriture*) stock, store, supply; (*d'eau*) supply; **une p. de pommes de terre** a stock of potatoes; **nos provisions d'eau/de bois** our water/wood supply; **avoir une bonne p. de chocolat/patience** to have a good supply of chocolate/plenty of patience; **ma grand-mère avait une p. de boutons de nacre** my grandmother had plenty of spare mother-of-pearl buttons; **faire p. de** (*nourriture, enveloppes*) to stock up with; (*bois de chauffage*) to build up a stock of; **les écureuils font p. de noix pour l'hiver** squirrels store up nuts for the winter; **faire des provisions** to stock up on food, to lay in stocks of food; **faire des provisions de qch** to stock up with sth
2 (*acompte*) advance or down payment; *Banque* (sufficient) funds; **je n'ai pas de p.** I don't have sufficient funds or enough money in my account; **manque de p.** (*sur chèque*) no funds; **verser de la p.** ou **des provisions** to deposit funds; **faire p. pour une lettre de change** to provide for or to protect a bill of exchange
3 (*d'un bilan comptable*) provision; (*couverture*) cover; **p. pour amortissement, p. pour dépréciation** provision for depreciation, depreciation allowance; **p. pour créances douteuses** provision for bad debts; **p. pour risques et charges** contingency and loss provision
4 (*honoraires*) retainer
5 *Jur* interim payment, interlocutory relief; **par p.** (*décision, acte*) provisional, interim; **p. ad litem** security or provision for costs (*during divorce proceedings*)
□ **provisions** NFPL (*courses*) provisions (de bouche) shopping (UNCOUNT), groceries; **qu'est-ce que tu as fait des provisions?** what have you done with the groceries?
□ **à provisions** ADJ (*filet, sac*) shopping (*avant n*); **armoire à provisions** store cupboard; **c'est mon étagère à provisions** it's the shelf where I keep my food

provisionnel, -elle [prɔvizjɔnɛl] ADJ provisional

provisionnement [prɔvizjɔnmɑ̃] NM *Banque* funding

provisionner [3] [prɔvizjɔne] VT *Banque* (*compte*) to deposit funds into; (*lettre de change*) to provide for, to protect; **son compte n'a pas été provisionné depuis plusieurs mois** there has been no money paid into his/her account for several months

provisoire [prɔvizwar] ADJ **1** (*momentané*) temporary, provisional; **c'est une solution p.** it's a temporary solution or a stopgap
2 (*précaire*) makeshift; **une réparation p.** a makeshift repair
3 (*intérimaire* → *gouvernement*) provisional; (→ *directeur*) acting
4 *Jur* (*jugement*) provisional, interlocutory; (*mise en liberté*) conditional
NM **ça n'est que du p.** it's only temporary, it's only for the time being; *Hum* **ces préfabriqués devaient être remplacés par des nouveaux bâtiments, c'est du p. qui dure** those prefabs were meant to be replaced by new buildings, unfortunately it's a case of a temporary solution becoming permanent; **il s'est installé dans le p.** he's got used to living on a day-to-day basis; **je ne veux plus vivre dans le p.** I'm tired of living in uncertainty

provisoirement [prɔvizwarmɑ̃] ADV temporarily, provisionally; **la piscine est p. fermée** the swimming-pool is temporarily closed; **je fais repeindre la chambre et, p., je couche dans le salon** I'm having the bedroom redecorated and I'm sleeping in the living room for the time

being; **p., je fais des ménages** for the time being, I do cleaning for people

provisorat [prɔvizɔra] NM *Br* headship, *Am* principalship

provitamine [prɔvitamin] NF provitamin

provo [prɔvo] NM **1** *Fam Arg scol* (*proviseur*) head (*of a school*) **2** (*aux Pays-Bas*) provo

provoc [prɔvɔk] NF *Fam* provocation▪; **tu fais de la p. ou quoi?** are you trying to *Br* wind me up or *Am* tick me off?

provocant, -e [prɔvɔkɑ̃, -ɑ̃t] ADJ **1** (*agressif*) aggressive, provocative; **une remarque provocante** an aggressive remark; **sur un ton p.** provocatively; **de façon provocante** provocatively **2** (*osé*) blatant; **un modernisme p.** blatant modernism **3** (*aguicheur*) provocative
NM,f *Pol* provocateur

provocation [prɔvɔkasjɔ̃] NF **1** (*stratégie*) provocation, incitement; (*acte*) provocation; **c'est de la p.!** it's an act of provocation!; **faire qch par p.** to do sth as an act of provocation; **se livrer à des provocations à l'égard de qn** to provoke sb; **les provocations policières** police provocation; **il a dit ça par pure p.** he only said it to try and shock people **2** *Littéraire* (*séduction*) teasing, provocativeness

provocatrice [prɔvɔkatris] *voir* **provocateur**

provolone [prɔvɔlɔn] NM (*fromage*) provolone

provoquer [3] [prɔvɔke] VT **1** (*défier*) to provoke, to push (to breaking point); **ne me provoque pas!** don't push me!; **c'est lui qui m'a provoqué!** he started it!; **il semblait vouloir p. le policier** he seemed to be trying to provoke the policeman; **p. le destin** to tempt fate; **p. qn en duel** to challenge sb to a duel
2 (*sexuellement*) to tease, arouse
3 (*occasionner* → *maladie, sommeil*) to cause, to induce; (→ *sentiment*) to arouse, to stir up; to give rise to; (→ *réaction, explosion, changement*) to cause; (→ *événement*) to cause, to be the cause of, to bring about; **les vapeurs d'essence peuvent p. des migraines** *Br* petrol or *Am* gas fumes can cause migraines; **ce médicament peut p. une légère somnolence** this medicine may cause drowsiness; **pouvant p. la mort** potentially fatal; **il ne se doutait pas qu'il allait p. sa jalousie** he didn't realize that he would make him/her jealous; **il disait cela pour p. les rires de ses camarades** he said that to make his schoolfriends laugh; **ses dénégations ne provoquèrent aucune réaction chez le juge** his/her denials brought no reaction from the judge; **l'explosion provoqua la panique générale** the explosion caused general panic; **le krach a provoqué de nombreuses faillites** the stock exchange crash caused a great number of bankruptcies; **elle fit cette déclaration pour p. une nouvelle enquête** she made that statement so that there would be a new enquiry
4 (*inciter*) **p. les jeunes à la violence/au crime** to incite young people to violence/to crime
5 *Méd* **p. l'accouchement** to induce labour

prox. (*abrév écrite* **proximité**) **p. commerces** near shops

proxémique [prɔksemik] NF *Ling* proxemics

proxène [prɔksɛn] NM *Antiq* = official appointed to look after foreign residents in a city

proxénète [prɔksenɛt] NMF procurer, f procuress

proxénétisme [prɔksenetism] NM procuring

proximal, -e, -aux, -ales [prɔksimal, -o] ADJ proximal

proximité [prɔksimite] NF **1** (*dans l'espace*) closeness, nearness, proximity; **la p. du casino est une grande tentation** having the casino so close (by) is very tempting
2 (*dans le temps*) closeness, imminence; **la p. de Noël** Christmas being near; **la p. du départ les rend fébriles** the approaching departure is making them excited
3 *Vieilli* (*parenté*) kinship; **p. du sang** blood kinship
□ **à proximité** ADV nearby, close at hand; **ses parents habitent à p.** his/her parents live near or close by
□ **à proximité de** PRÉP near, close to, not far

from; **la maison est à p. de la mer** the house is not far from the sea
□ **de proximité** ADJ **1** *Tech* proximity (*avant n*)
2 (*de quartier*) **commerces de p.** local shops; **commerçants de p.** local shopkeepers; **emplois de p.** = employment in the community (*as a way of reducing unemployment*); **des actions de p.** community work

proxo [prɔxo] NM *Fam* pimp, *Am* mack

proyer [prwaje] NM *Orn* bunting

Prozac® [prozak] NM *Pharm* Prozac®

proze [prɔz], **prozinard** [prɔzinar] NM *très Fam* butt, *Br* bum, *Am* fanny

pruche [pryʃ] NF *Can* Eastern hemlock

prude [pryd] ADJ prudish, prim and proper; **et pourtant, je ne suis pas p.** and yet I'm not afraid to call a spade a spade
NMF prude, puritan; **ne fais pas la p.!** don't be so prudish!, don't be such a prude!

prudemment [prydamɑ̃] ADV (*avec précaution*) carefully, cautiously, prudently; **regarde p. des deux côtés avant de traverser** be careful to look right and left before crossing **2** (*avec sagesse*) wisely, prudently; **il préféra p. battre en retraite** he was wise enough to retreat

prudence [prydɑ̃s] NF **1** (*précaution*) caution, carefully; **elle conduit avec la plus grande p.** she's a very careful driver; **la p. avant tout!** safety first!; *Prov* **p. est mère de sûreté** look before you leap
2 (*méfiance*) wariness, caginess; (*ruse*) cunning; **avoir la p. du serpent** to be a sly fox
3 *Vieilli* (*sagesse*) wisdom, good judgment, prudence
□ **prudences** NFPL *Littéraire* wariness (UNCOUNT), caginess (UNCOUNT); **ses prudences en matière de musique contemporaine** his/her wariness of modern music
□ **avec prudence** ADV (*avec attention*) cautiously, carefully
□ **par prudence, par mesure de prudence** ADV as a precaution; **par p., je n'ai pas voulu lui en parler tout de suite** I thought it wiser not to speak of it to him/her right away

prudent, -e [prydɑ̃, -ɑ̃t] ADJ **1** (*attentif*) careful, prudent; **sois p.!** be careful!; **tu peux lui confier tes enfants, elle est très prudente** you can safely leave your children with her, she's very sensible
2 (*mesuré*) discreet, circumspect, cautious; **une réponse prudente** a diplomatic or circumspect answer; **il faut se montrer p. en matière d'investissements** one should be cautious when investing money; **trop p.** overcautious
3 (*prévoyant* → *gén*) judicious, wise; (→ *décision*) wise, sensible; **un homme de loi p.** a wise lawyer; **tu sors sans écharpe, ce n'est pas p.** you're going out without a scarf, that's not very sensible; **vous avez raison, c'est plus p.** you're right, it's wiser or more sensible; **ses parents s'étaient montrés prudents et avaient mis de l'argent de côté pour lui** his parents had looked ahead or had been provident and had put aside some money for him; **on n'est jamais trop p.** you can't be too careful
4 (*préférable*) advisable, better; **il serait p. de partir avant la nuit** it would be better for us to leave before nightfall; **il est p. de réserver ses places** advance booking is advisable

pruderie [prydri] NF prudishness, prudery

prud'homal, -e, -aux, -ales [prydɔmal, -o] *Jur* ADJ **conseiller p.** = member of an industrial tribunal; **élections prud'homales** industrial tribunal election

prud'homie [prydɔmi] NF *Jur* jurisdiction of an industrial tribunal

prud'homme [prydɔm] *Jur* NM (*conseiller*) **p.** member of an industrial tribunal
□ **prud'hommes** NMPL (*tribunal*) **les prud'hommes, le conseil de prud'hommes** the industrial tribunal; **aller aux prud'hommes** to go before an industrial tribunal

pruine [prɥin] NF (*sur un fruit*) bloom

prune [pryn] NF **1** (*fruit*) plum; **p. de Damas** damson **2** (*alcool*) plum brandy **3** *Fam* (*balle*) bullet▪, slug; (*coup*) clout, thump **4** *Fam* (*contravention*) fine▪ **5** *Fam* (*locutions*) **des prunes!** no way!, nothing doing!; **pour des prunes** for nothing▪; **je suis allé en classe pour des**

prunes, le prof n'était pas là I went to school for nothing, the teacher wasn't there; *Vieilli* **elle aura 15 ans aux prunes** she'll be 15 next summer

ADJ INV plum-coloured

pruneau, -x [pryno] **NM 1** *(fruit sec)* prune **2** *Suisse (prune)* red plum **3** *Fam Vieilli (personne hâlée)* **c'est un vrai p.** he's/she's as brown as a berry **4** *Fam (balle)* bullet■ , slug; **il s'est pris un p. dans le buffet** someone filled his belly with lead

prunelaie [prynlɛ] **NF** *Hort* plum orchard

prunelée [prynle] **NF** plum jam

prunelle [prynɛl] **NF 1** *Bot* sloe **2** *(alcool)* sloe gin **3** *Anat* pupil; **je tiens à ce livre comme à la p. de mes yeux** I wouldn't give this book up *or* away for the world **4** *(regard)* eye; *Fam* **jouer de la p.** to flutter one's eyelashes

prunellier [prynelje] **NM** sloe, blackthorn

prunier [prynje] **NM** plumtree; **p. myrobolan** cherry plum, myrobalan; **p. du Japon** Japanese cherry

prunus [prynys] **NM** *Bot* prunus, Japanese flowering cherry

prurigineux, -euse [pryriʒinø, -øz] **ADJ** *Méd* pruritic

prurigo [pryrigo] **NM** *Méd* prurigo

prurit [pryrit] **NM** *Méd* pruritus

Prusse [prys] **NF la P.** Prussia

Prusse-Orientale [prysɔrjãtal] **NF** *Hist* **la P.** East Prussia

prussiate [prysjat] **NM** *Vieilli* cyanide; **p. jaune** potassium ferrocyanide

prussien, -enne [prysjɛ̃, -ɛn] **ADJ** Prussian
□ **Prussien, -enne NM,F** Prussian

prussik [prysik] **NM** *(en alpinisme)* **(nœud de) p.** prusik knot

prussique [prysik] **ADJ** prussic

prytane [pritan] **NM** *Antiq* prytanis

prytanée [pritane] **NM 1** *Antiq* prytaneum **2** *(école)* **le P. militaire de La Flèche** the La Flèche military academy *(free school for sons of members of the armed forces)*

PS¹ [peɛs] **NM** *(abrév* **parti socialiste***)* = French socialist party

P.S., PS² [peɛs] **NM** *(abrév* **post-scriptum***)* PS, ps

psallette [psalɛt] **NF** choir school

psalliote [psaljɔt] **NF p. des forêts** pine wood mushroom

psalmiste [psalmist] **NM** psalmist

psalmodie [psalmɔdi] **NF 1** *Rel* psalmody, intoning **2** *Fig Littéraire* drone

psalmodier [9] [psalmɔdje] **VI 1** *Rel* to chant **2** *Fig Littéraire* to drone (on)
VT 1 *Rel* to chant **2** *Fig* to intone, to drone (out)

psaltérion [psalterjɔ̃] **NM** *Mus* psaltery

psaume [psom] **NM** psalm; **le livre des Psaumes** Psalms; **psaumes pénitentiaux** Penitential Psalms; **P. 27** Psalm XXVII

psautier [psotje] **NM** psalter

PSC [peɛsse] **NM** *UE (abrév* **Pacte de stabilité et de croissance***)* SGP

pschent [pskɛnt] **NM** *Antiq* pschent

pseudarthrose [psødartroz] **NF** pseudoarthrosis, nearthrosis

pseudo [psødo] **NM** *Fam (abrév* **pseudonyme***)* pseudonym

pseudo- [psødo] **PRÉF** pseudo-, false; **méfie-toi de leur pseudo-contrat** beware of their so-called contract; **ses pseudo-excuses** his/her fake apologies; **des p.-intellectuels** pseudo-intellectuals; **le pseudo-démarcheur attaquait les vieilles dames** the bogus salesman preyed on old ladies; **c'est du pseudo-style anglais** it's in pseudo-English style

pseudocarpe [psødokarp] **NM** *Bot* pseudocarp

pseudohermaphrodisme [psødɛrmafrɔdism] **NM** *Méd* pseudohermaphroditism

pseudomembrane [psødomãbran] **NF** *Méd* pseudomembrane, false membrane

pseudomembraneux, -euse [psødomãbranø, -øz] **ADJ** *Méd* pseudomembranous

pseudomorphe [psødomɔrf] **NM** *Minér* pseudomorph

pseudonyme [psødɔnim] **NM** *(nom d'emprunt →* *gén)* assumed name; *(→ d'un écrivain)* pen name, pseudonym; *(→ d'acteur)* stage name; *(→ de criminel)* alias; **prendre un p.** to adopt a

pseudonym; **sous le p. de** under the pseudonym of

pseudopode [psødopɔd] **NM** *Biol* pseudopodium

pseudoscience [psødosjãs] **NF** pseudoscience

pseudotumeur [psødotymœr] **NF** *Méd* false tumour

PS-G, PSG [peɛsʒe] **NM** *Ftbl (abrév* **Paris St-Germain***)* = Paris football team

psi [psi] **NM 1** *(lettre grecque)* psi **2** *Nucl* psi *(particle)*, J

PSIG [peɛsiʒe] **NM** *(abrév* **Peloton de surveillance et d'intervention de la gendarmerie***)* = gendarmerie commando squad

psilocybe [psilɔsib] **NM** *Bot* psilocybe (mushroom)

psilocybine [psilɔsibin] **NF** *Bot* psilocybin

psilophyte [psilɔfit] **NM** Psilophyton

psilosis [psilɔzis] **NM** *Méd* psilosis, sprue

psilotum [psilɔtɔm] **NM** Psilotum

psitt [psit] **EXCLAM** psst!, hey!

psittacidé [psitaside] **NM** psittacine

psittacisme [psitasism] **NM** *Psy* parrot-like repetition, *Spéc* psittacism

psittacose [psitakoz] **NF** psittacosis

psoas [psoas] **NM** *Anat* **ADJ muscle p.** psoas muscle
NM psoas (muscle); **p. iliaque** psoas major, psoas magnus; **petit p.** psoas minor, psoas parvus

psoque [psɔk] **NM** *Entom* psocid

psoralène [psɔralen] **NM** psoralen

psoriasis [psɔrjazis] **NM** psoriasis

pst [pst] **= psitt**

PSU [peɛsy] **NM** *Anciennement (abrév* **parti socialiste unifié***)* = former French socialist party

psy [psi] *Fam* **NMF** *(psychanalyste)* shrink, *Am* bug doctor
NF *(psychanalyse)* psychoanalysis■ ; **il est très branché p.** he's really into psychoanalysis

psychanalyse [psikanaliz] **NF** *(discipline)* psychoanalyse; *(traitement)* analysis, psychoanalysis; **il fait une p.** he's in *or* undergoing (psycho)analysis

psychanalyser [3] [psikanalize] **VT** to psychoanalyse, to analyse; **elle se fait p.** she's undergoing psychoanalysis, she's in therapy; **je me suis fait p. pendant cinq ans** I went to see an analyst *or* therapist for five years

psychanalyste [psikanalist] **NMF** analyst, psychoanalyst

psychanalytique [psikanalitik] **ADJ** analytical, psychoanalytical

psychasthénie [psikasteni] **NF** psychasthenia, psychastheny

psychasthénique [psikastenik] **ADJ** psychasthenic
NMF psychasthenic

Psyché [psiʃe] **NPR** *Myth* Psyche

psyché [psiʃe] **NF 1** *Psy* psyche **2** *(miroir)* cheval glass

psychédélique [psikedelik] **ADJ** psychedelic

psychédélisme [psikedelism] **NM** psychedelic state

psychiatre [psikjatr] **NMF** psychiatrist

psychiatrie [psikjatri] **NF** psychiatry; **p. infantile** child psychiatry

psychiatrique [psikjatrik] **ADJ** psychiatric

psychiatrisation [psikjatrizasjɔ̃] **NF 1** *Péj (traitement)* psychiatrization, subjection to psychiatric therapy **2** *(interprétation)* interpretation in psychiatric terms

psychiatriser [3] [psikjatrize] **VT 1** *Péj (traiter)* to psychiatrize, to subject to psychiatric therapy **2** *(interpréter)* to interpret in psychiatric terms

psychique [psiʃik] **ADJ 1** *Méd (blocage)* mental; *(troubles)* mental, *Spéc* psychic; **les maux de tête peuvent être d'origine p.** headaches may be psychosomatic
2 *Fam (psychologique)* psychological; **je ne peux pas voir une souris sans défaillir, c'est p.** I feel faint whenever I see a mouse, I know it's all in the mind but I can't help it
NM *Fam* mind, psychological side; **chez lui, c'est le p. qui va mal** he's got a psychological problem

psychisme [psiʃism] **NM** psyche, mind; **son p. est perturbé** the balance of his/her mind is disturbed

psycho [psiko] **NF** *Fam (psychologie)* **il a fait (des**

études de) p. he studied psychology■ ; **il t'a plu, le cours de p.?** did you like the psychology lecture?■

psycho- [psiko] **PRÉF** psycho-

psychoactif, -ive [psikoaktif, -iv] **ADJ** psychoactive; **agent p.** psychoactive agent

psychoaffectif, -ive [psikoafɛktif, -iv] **ADJ** psycho-affective

psychoanaleptique [psikɔanalɛptik] **ADJ** psychoanaleptic
NM psychoanaleptic

psychobiologie [psikɔbjɔlɔʒi] **NF** psychobiology

psychochirurgie [psikɔʃiryrʒi] **NF** psychosurgery

psychocritique [psikɔkritik] **NMF** psychological critic
NF psychological criticism

psychodramatique [psikɔdramatik] **ADJ** psychodramatic

psychodrame [psikɔdram] **NM 1** *(thérapie)* role-play techniques, psychodrama **2** *(séance)* (psychotherapeutic) role-play session

psychodysleptique [psikɔdislɛptik] **ADJ** psychodysleptic
NM psychodysleptic

psychogène [psikɔgɛn] **ADJ** psychogenic

psychogenèse [psikɔgɛnɛz] **NF** psychogenesis

psychogénétique [psikɔʒenetik] **ADJ** psychogenetic
NF psychogenetics *(singulier)*

psychographie [psikɔgrafi] **NF** psychographics *(singulier)*

psychographique [psikɔgrafik] **ADJ** psychographic

psychokinésie [psikɔkinezi] **NF** psychokinesis

psycholeptique [psikɔlɛptik] **ADJ** psycholeptic
NM psycholeptic drug, tranquillizer

psycholinguiste [psikɔlɛ̃gɥist] **NMF** psycholinguist

psycholinguistique [psikɔlɛ̃gɥistik] **ADJ** psycholinguistic
NF psycholinguistics *(singulier)*

psychologie [psikɔlɔʒi] **NF 1** *(étude)* psychology; **faire de** *ou* **étudier la p.** to do *or* study psychology; **p. appliquée/comparative** applied/comparative psychology; **p. expérimentale/clinique/sociale** experimental/clinical/social psychology; **p. commerciale** psychology of marketing; **p. des consommateurs** consumer psychology; **p. des profondeurs** analytical psychology; **p. de la publicité** advertising psychology; **p. du travail** occupational psychology
2 *(intuition)* perception; **faire preuve de p.** to have good psychological insight, to be perceptive; **tu manques de p.** you're not very perceptive
3 *(mentalité)* psychology, mind; **la p. des citadins** the psychology *or* mind of the town-dweller; **il faut comprendre sa p.** you have to understand the way his/her mind works; **p. des foules** crowd psychology
4 *(dimension psychologique)* psychology; **étudiez la p. des personnages** study the psychological make-up of the characters; **la p. de son dernier film est tout à fait sommaire** the psychological content of his/her last movie *or* Br film leaves a lot to be desired

psychologique [psikɔlɔʒik] **ADJ 1** *(méthode, théorie)* psychological
2 *Méd (état, troubles)* psychological, mental; **il a des problèmes psychologiques** he has psychological problems; **son état p. n'était pas bon du tout** he/she wasn't in a good state of mind *or* frame of mind at all; **il suffit qu'elle parle à son médecin pour aller mieux, c'est p.** she only has to talk to her doctor to feel better, it's all in her mind
3 *(dimension)* psychological; **la vérité p. de ses personnages** his/her true-to-life characters
4 *(propice)* **le moment** *ou* **l'instant p.** the right *or* appropriate moment

psychologiquement [psikɔlɔʒikmã] **ADV** psychologically

psychologisme [psikɔlɔʒism] **NM** psychologism

psychologue [psikɔlɔg] **ADJ** insightful, perceptive
NMF psychologist; **p. scolaire** educational psychologist; **p. du travail** occupational psychologist

psychométricien, -enne [psikɔmetrisjɛ̃, -ɛn] **NM,F** psychometrist

psychométrie [psikɔmetri] **NF** psychometrics *(singulier)*

psychométrique [psikɔmetrik] **ADJ** psychometric

psychomoteur, -trice [psikɔmɔtœr, -tris] **ADJ** psychomotor

psychomotricien, -enne [psikɔmɔtrisjɛ̃, -ɛn] **NM,F** psychomotricity specialist

psychomotricité [psikɔmɔtrisite] **NF** psychomotricity

psychopathe [psikɔpat] **NMF** psychopath

psychopathie [psikɔpati] **NF** psychopathy, psychopathic personality

psychopathologie [psikɔpatɔlɔʒi] **NF** psychopathology

psychopathologique [psikɔpatɔlɔʒik] **ADJ** psychopathological

psychopédagogie [psikɔpedagɔʒi] **NF** educational psychology

psychopédagogique [psikɔpedagɔʒik] **ADJ centre p.** centre for educational psychology

psychopédagogue [psikɔpedagɔg] **NMF** educational psychologist

psychopharmacologie [psikɔfarmakɔlɔʒi] **NF** psychopharmacology

psychophysiologie [psikɔfizjɔlɔʒi] **NF** psychophysiology

psychophysiologique [psikɔfizjɔlɔʒik] **ADJ** psychophysiological

psychophysiologiste [psikɔfizjɔlɔʒist] **NMF** psychophysiologist

psychophysique [psikɔfizik] **NF** psychophysics *(singulier)*

psychoplasticité [psikɔplastisite] **NF** suggestibility

psychopompe [psikɔpɔ̃p] **NMF** *Rel* psychopomp

psychoprophylactique [psikɔprɔfilaktik] **ADJ méthode p.** psychoprophylaxis

psychorigide [psikɔriʒid] **ADJ** resisting change
NMF = person who resists change

psychorigidité [psikɔriʒidite] **NF** pathological conservatism, resistance to change or progress

psychose [psikoz] **NF 1** *Psy* psychosis; **p. maniaco-dépressive** manic depression **2** *(angoisse → individuelle)* (obsessive) fear **(de** of); *(→ collective)* fear; **il a la p. du cambriolage** he has an obsessive fear of being *Br* burgled *or Am* burglarized; **il règne ici une véritable p. de guerre** people here are in the grip of war hysteria

psychosensoriel, -elle [psikɔsɑ̃sɔrjɛl] **ADJ** psychosensory

psychosocial, -e, -aux, -ales [psikɔsɔsjal, -o] **ADJ** psychosocial

psychosociologie [psikɔsɔsjɔlɔʒi] **NF** psychosociology

psychosociologique [psikɔsɔsjɔlɔʒik] **ADJ** psychosociological

psychosociologue [psikɔsɔsjɔlɔg] **NMF** psychosociologist

psychosomatique [psikɔsɔmatik] **ADJ** *(médecine, trouble)* psychosomatic
NF psychosomatics *(singulier)*

psychostimulant, -e [psikɔstimylɑ̃, -ɑ̃t] *Pharm* **ADJ** psychostimulating, psychostimulant
NM psychostimulant

psychotechnicien, -enne [psikɔtɛknisjɛ̃, -ɛn] **NM,F** psychotechnician

psychotechnique [psikɔtɛknik] **ADJ** psychotechnical
NF psychotechnology

psychothérapeute [psikɔterapøt] **NMF** psychotherapist

psychothérapeutique [psikɔterapøtik] = **psychothérapique**

psychothérapie [psikɔterapi] **NF** psychotherapy; **faire une p.** to be in therapy; **faire une p. de groupe** to go to or to do group therapy; **p. analytique** analytical (psycho)therapy; **p. non directive** nondirective therapy

psychothérapique [psikɔterapik] **ADJ** psychotherapeutic

psychotique [psikɔtik] **ADJ** psychotic
NMF psychotic

psychotonique [psikɔtɔnik] **ADJ** mood-elevating, *Spéc* psychotonic
NM mood elevator, *Spéc* psychotonic (drug)

psychotrope [psikɔtrɔp] **ADJ** psychotropic, psychoactive
NM psychotropic (drug)

psychromètre [psikrɔmɛtr] **NM** *Météo* psychrometer

psychrométrie [psikrɔmetri] **NF** *Météo* psychrometry

psylle¹ [psil] **NM** *(charmeur de serpents)* snake charmer

psylle² [psil] **NM OU NF** *Entom* psylla, jumping plant louse

psyllium [psiljɔm] **NM** *Bot & Pharm* psyllium

PTA *Anciennement (abrév écrite* **peseta**) Pta, P

PTCA [petesea] **NM** *Transp (abrév* **poids total en charge autorisé**) = maximum authorized load

Pte 1 *(abrév écrite* **porte**) door **2** *(abrév écrite* **pointe**) pt

ptéranodon [pteranodɔ̃] **NM** *Zool* pteranodon

ptéridophyte [pteridɔfit] *Bot* **NM** pteridophyte
□ **ptéridophytes NMPL** Pteridophyta

ptéridospermée [pteridɔspɛrme] **NF** pteridosperm

ptérobranche [pterɔbrɑ̃ʃ] *Zool* **NM** pterobranch
□ **ptérobranches NMPL** Pterobranchia

ptérodactyle [pterɔdaktil] **NM** pterodactyl

ptéropode [pterɔpɔd] *Zool* **NM** pteropod
□ **ptéropodes NMPL** Pteropoda, pteropods

ptérosaurien [pterɔsɔrjɛ̃] **NM** pterosaur

ptérygoïde [pterigɔid] *Anat* **ADJ apophyse p.** pterygoid process
NF pterygoid

ptérygoïdien, -enne [pterigɔidjɛ̃, -ɛn] *Anat* **ADJ** pterygoid
NM pterygoid (muscle)

ptérygote [pterigɔt] *Entom* **NM** pterygote
□ **ptérygotes NMPL** Pterygota; **ptérygotes paléoptères** Palaeodictyoptera

PTFE [peteɛfø] **NM** *Chim (abrév* **polytétrafluoroéthylène**) PTFE

ptolémaïque [ptɔlemaik] **ADJ** Ptolemaic

Ptolémée [ptɔleme] **NPR** Ptolemy

ptomaïne [ptɔmain] **NF** *Biol* ptomaine

ptose, ptôse [ptoz] **NF** *Méd* ptosis, prolapse

ptosis, ptôsis [ptɔzis] **NM** *Méd* ptosis *(of eyelid)*

PTT [petete] **NFPL** *Anciennement (abrév* **Postes, Télécommunications et Télédiffusion**) = former French post office and telecommunications network

ptyaline [ptjalin] **NF** *Biol & Chim* ptyalin

ptyalisme [ptjalism] **NM** *Méd* ptyalism

pu [py] **PP** *voir* **pouvoir²**

PU [pey] **NM** *Com (abrév* **prix unitaire**) unit price

puant, -e [pɥɑ̃, -ɑ̃t] **ADJ 1** *(nauséabond)* stinking, foul-smelling **2** *Fam (très vaniteux)* cocky; **il est vraiment p.!** he really thinks he's something special!
NM *Fam (fromage)* smelly cheese■

puanteur [pɥɑ̃tœr] **NF** foul smell, stench

pub¹ [pyb] **NF** *Fam* **1** *(publicité)* advertising■; **il travaille dans la p.** he's or he works in advertising; **faire de la p. pour qch** to advertise sth■; **un coup de p.** a plug; **ils ont fait un gros coup de p. autour de ce livre** they really hyped the book **2** *(annonce → gén)* ad, advertisement■; *Rad & TV* commercial■

pub² [pœb] **NM** *(bar)* pub

pubalgie [pybalʒi] **NF** *Méd* pubalgia

pubère [pybɛr] **ADJ** pubescent; **il est p.** he's reached (the age of) puberty

pubertaire [pybɛrtɛr] **ADJ** pubertal

puberté [pybɛrte] **NF** puberty

pubescence [pybesɑ̃s] **NF** *Bot* pubescence

pubescent, -e [pybesɑ̃, -ɑ̃t] **ADJ** *Bot* pubescent, puberulent

pubien, -enne [pybjɛ̃, -ɛn] **ADJ** pubic

pubis [pybis] **NM** *(os)* pubis; *(bas-ventre)* pubis, *Spéc* pubes

publiable [pyblijabl] **ADJ** publishable; **ce n'est guère p.** it's hardly fit for publication or to be printed

public, -ique [pyblik] **ADJ 1** *(ouvert à tous)* public; **chemin p.** public footpath; **la séance est publique** it's an open session
2 *(connu)* public, well-known; **sa nomination a été rendue publique ce matin** his/her nomination was officially announced or was made public this morning; **l'homme p.** the man the public sees
3 *(de l'État)* public, state *(avant n)*

NM 1 *(population)* public; **le grand p.** the general public, the public at large
2 *(audience → d'un spectacle)* public, audience; *(→ d'un écrivain)* readership, readers; *(→ d'un match)* spectators; *(→ d'un produit, d'une publicité)* audience; **p. féminin/familial** female/family audience; **s'adresser à un vaste p./à un p. restreint** to address a vast/limited audience; **c'est un excellent livre, mais qui n'a pas encore trouvé son p.** although the book is excellent, it hasn't yet found the readership it deserves; **p. cible** target audience; **être bon p.** to be easy to please
3 *(secteur)* **le p.** the public sector
□ **en public ADV** publicly, in public; **les livres ont été brûlés en p.** the books were publicly burnt; **faire une déclaration en p.** to make a public statement; **cette émission a été enregistrée en p.** this programme was recorded before a live audience; **faire honte à qn en p.** to show sb up in public
□ **grand public ADV INV produits grand p.** consumer goods; **émission grand p.** programme designed to appeal to a wide audience; **film grand p.** blockbuster; **l'électronique grand p.** consumer electronics

publicain [pyblikɛ̃] **NM** *Antiq* tax gatherer; *Bible* publican

publication [pyblikasjɔ̃] **NF 1** *(d'un livre, d'un journal)* publication, publishing; **le journal a dû cesser sa p.** the paper had to cease publication or to fold; **j'attends la p. pour consulter mon avocat** I'm waiting for publication or for the book to be published before I consult my lawyer; **interdire la p. de qch** to stop sth coming out or being published; **date de p.** publication date, date of publication; **p. assistée par ordinateur** desktop publishing
2 *Jur (d'un arrêté, d'une loi)* promulgation, publication; **la p. des bans** announcement of or publishing the banns; **p. du commandement** publication of sentence; **p. des condamnations** publication of sentences; **p. de mariage** publication of the banns
3 *(document)* publication, magazine; *Fin* **p. des comptes** disclosure (of accounts); **p. scientifique** scientific publication or journal; **p. spécialisée** specialist review

publiciel [pyblisjɛl] **NM** *Can Ordinat* public domain software

publiciste [pyblisist] **NMF 1** *Jur* specialist in public law **2** = **publicitaire**

publicitaire [pyblisitɛr] **ADJ** *(gén)* advertising *(avant n)*, promotional; *(vente)* promotional; **budget p.** advertising budget; **documents publicitaires** advertising or promotional material
NMF *(personne)* advertising man, *f* woman; **c'est un p.** he's in or he works in advertising; **c'est une p.** she's in or she works in advertising

publicité [pyblisite] **NF 1** *(action commerciale, profession)* advertising; **être dans la p.** to be or to work in advertising; **faire de la p. pour qch** to advertise or to publicize sth; **en ce moment, ils font de la p. pour les banques** there are a lot of advertisements for banks at the moment; **passer une p. à la télévision** to advertise on TV; **p. aérienne** sky writing; **p. par affichage** poster advertising; **p. agressive** hard sell; **p. ambiante** ambient advertising; **p. d'amorçage** advance publicity; **p. audiovisuelle** audiovisual advertising; **p. de bouche à oreille** word-of-mouth advertising; **p. clandestine** underhand advertising; **p. collective** group advertising; **p. comparative** comparative advertising; **p. concurrentielle** competitive advertising; **p. continue** drip advertising; **p. directe** direct advertising, direct mail advertising; **p. d'entreprise** corporate advertising; **p. extérieure** outdoor advertising; **p. générique** generic advertising; **p. goutte-à-goutte** drip advertising; **p. informative** informative advertising; **p. institutionnelle** institutional advertising, corporate advertising; **p. intensive** saturation advertising; **p. isolée** solus advertisement; **p. sur le lieu de vente** *(activité)* point-of-sale advertising; *(promotion)* point-of-sale promotion; **p. de marque** brand advertising; **p. média** media advertising; **p. mensongère** misleading advertising; **p. par mots clés** keyword advertising; **p. sur panneau**

billboard advertising; **p. périphérique** perimeter advertising; **p. au point de vente** point-of-sale advertising; **p. de prestige** prestige advertising; **p. de produit** product advertising; **p. par publipostage** direct mail advertising; **p. rédactionnelle** advertorial; **p. à réponse directe** direct response advertising; **p. subliminale** subliminal advertising; **p. télévisée** television advertising; **p. par voie d'affiches** poster advertising

2 (*diffusion*) publicity; **ça ne peut que lui faire de la p.** it's bound to be publicity for him/her; **faire sa propre p.** to sell oneself; **il a fait de la p. pour toi, tu sais!** he gave you a good press, you know!; **faire de la p. pour qch** to publicize sth

3 (*annonce commerciale*) advertisement, advert; *Rad & TV* commercial; **passer une p. à la télévision** to advertise on TV; **p. mensongère** misleading advertisement; **p. télévisée** television advertisement *or* commercial

4 (*caractère public*) public nature; **la p. de cette déclaration ne lui laisse pas la possibilité de se rétracter** the fact that he/she made the statement publicly leaves him/her no room to retract; **la p. des débats parlementaires garantit-elle la démocratie?** is democracy safeguarded by the fact that debates in Parliament are (held in) public?; **p. des débats** public hearings

5 *Jur* (*en droit civil*) public announcement

publicité-médias [pyblisitemedja] NF *Mktg* media advertising, above-the-line advertising

publicité-produit [pyblisiteprɔdɥi] NF *Mktg* product advertising

publier [10] [pyblije] VT **1** (*éditer → auteur, texte*) to publish; **elle a été publiée aux États-Unis** she's been published in the States; **dans un article qui n'a jamais été publié** in an unpublished article

2 (*rendre public → communiqué*) to make public, to release; (→ *brochure*) to publish, to issue, to release; (→ *bans*) to publish, to announce; (→ *décret, loi*) to promulgate, to publish; **le journal publie les cours de l'or** the paper publishes gold prices

publi-information [pybliɛ̃fɔrmasjɔ̃] (*pl* **publi-informations**) NF special advertising section, *Am* advertorial

publiphobe [pyblifɔb] ADJ anti-advertising
  NMF = person who is against advertising

Publiphone® [pyblifɔn] NM cardphone

publipostage [pyblipɔstaʒ] NM mailshot, mailing; **faire un p.** to send a mailshot *or* mailing; **p. d'essai** test *or* cold mailing; **p. groupé** volume mailing; **p. massif** blanket mailing

publique [pyblik] *voir* **public**

publiquement [pyblikmɑ̃] ADV publicly, in public; **il s'est confessé p.** he admitted his fault in public; **sa mère lui a fait honte p.** his/her mother showed him/her up in front of everybody

publireportage [pyblirəpɔrtaʒ] NM special advertising section, *Am* advertorial

puccinia [pyksinja] NM *Bot* puccinia

puccinie [pyksini] NF *Bot* puccinia

puce [pys] NF **1** *Entom* flea; **p. de mer** sandflea, sandhopper; **p. d'eau** water flea; **ce nom m'a mis la p. à l'oreille** the name gave me a clue *or* set me thinking; *Fam* **il est excité comme une p.** he's so excited he can't sit still; **elle est rentrée de l'école excitée comme une p.** she came home jumping up and down with excitement

2 *Fam* (*par affection*) ma p. sweetie; **tu veux quelque chose, ma p.?** do you want something, sweetie?; **où elle est, la petite p.?** where's my little girl then?

3 *Électron* (*composant*) chip; **p. à ADN** DNA chip; *TV* **p. antiviolence** V-chip; **p. logique** logic chip; **p. mémoire** memory chip; **p. de reconnaissance vocale** voice recognition chip

4 *Ordinat & Typ* (*symbole*) bullet (point)
  ADJ INV (*couleur*) puce

□ **puces** NFPL **1** (*jeu*) jeu de puces tiddly-winks

2 (*marché*) flea market; **elle s'habille aux puces** she wears secondhand clothes

puceau, -elle [pyso, -ɛl] *Fam* ADJ **il est p.** he's a virgin▪
  NM,F virgin▪

pucelage [pyslaʒ] NM *Fam* virginity▪; **perdre son p.** to lose one's virginity

Pucelle [pysɛl] NF **la P. d'Orléans, Jeanne la P.** the Maid of Orléans, Joan of Arc

pucelle [pysɛl] *voir* **puceau**

puceron [pysrɔ̃] NM greenfly, aphid, plant louse

puche [pyʃ] NF (*terme normand*) shrimping net

pucheux [pyʃø] NM **1** (*grande cuiller*) ladle, scoop

2 *Tech* (*pour le raffinage du sucre*) syrup ladle

pucier [pysje] NM *très Fam* (*lit*) bed▪, *Br* pit

puck [pœk] NM *Suisse* puck

pudding [pudiŋ] NM **1** (*au pain rassis*) = bread pudding **2** (*anglais*) (plum) pudding, Christmas pudding

puddlage [pœdlaʒ] NM *Métal* puddling

puddler [3] [pœdle] VT *Métal* to puddle

puddleur [pœdlœr] NM *Métal* puddler; **p. mécanique** puddling machine

pudeur [pydœr] NF **1** (*décence*) modesty, decency, propriety; **avec p.** modestly; **par p., il n'a pas abordé le sujet** out of a sense of decency *or* propriety he did not mention the subject; **manquer de p.** to have no sense of decency; **fausse p.** false modesty **2** (*délicatesse*) tact, sense of propriety; **il aurait pu avoir la p. de se taire** he could have been tactful enough to keep quiet

pudibond, -e [pydibɔ̃, -ɔ̃d] ADJ prudish, prim
  NM,F prude

pudibonderie [pydibɔ̃dri] NF prudishness

pudicité [pydisite] NF *Littéraire* modesty

pudique [pydik] ADJ **1** (*chaste*) chaste, modest; **une jeune fille très p.** a very demure young lady **2** (*discret*) discreet; **quelques remarques pudiques sur ses difficultés financières** a few discreet remarks about his/her financial difficulties

pudiquement [pydikmɑ̃] ADV **1** (*avec pudeur*) modestly; **elle tira p. sa jupe sur ses genoux** she modestly drew her skirt over her knees **2** (*avec tact*) discreetly

pudu [pydy] NM *Zool* pudu

Pueblo [pweblo] NMF **les Pueblos** the Pueblo

pue-la-sueur [pylasɥœr] NM INV *Péj* workman▪

puer [7] [pɥe] VI to stink; **ça pue ici!** what a stink *or* stench!

  VT **1** (*répandre → odeur*) to stink of; **p. le vin/l'éther** to stink of wine/ether; **il pue l'ail à quinze pas!** he *or* his breath reeks of garlic!; *Fam* **tu pues des pieds** your feet stink; *très Fam* **il pue de la gueule** his breath stinks **2** (*laisser paraître → défaut*) **p. la méchanceté/l'hypocrisie** to be oozing spitefulness/hypocrisy; **il pue l'arriviste** you can smell the social climber (in him) a mile off

puériculteur, -trice [pɥerikyltœr, -tris] NF **1** (*dans une crèche*) nursery nurse **2** (*à l'hôpital*) pediatric nurse

puériculture [pɥerikyltyr] NF **1** (*gén*) child care *or* welfare **2** *Scol* nursery nursing **3** (*à l'hôpital*) pediatric nursing

puéril, -e [pɥeril] ADJ **1** (*enfantin*) childlike; **un enthousiasme p.** a childish excitement **2** (*immature, naïf*) childish, infantile, puerile

puérilement [pɥerilmɑ̃] ADV childishly

puérilisme [pɥerilism] NM puerilism

puérilité [pɥerilite] NF (*non-maturité*) childishness, puerility

□ **puérilités** NFPL childish *or* petty trifles

puerpéral, -e, -aux, -ales [pɥɛrperal, -o] ADJ *Méd* puerperal; **fièvre puerpérale** childbed *or* puerperal fever

puerpéralité [pɥɛrperalite] NF *Méd* puerperium

Puerto Rico [pwɛrtoriko] = **Porto Rico**

puffin [pyfɛ̃] NM *Orn* shearwater; **p. des Anglais** Manx shearwater

pugilat [pyʒila] NM **1** (*bagarre*) brawl, scuffle, *Br* (bout of) fisticuffs **2** *Antiq* boxing

pugiliste [pyʒilist] NM **1** *Littéraire* (*boxeur*) pugilist **2** *Antiq* boxer

pugilistique [pyʒilistik] ADJ *Littéraire* pugilistic

pugnace [pygnas] ADJ *Littéraire* **1** (*combatif*) belligerent **2** (*dans la discussion*) pugnacious

pugnacité [pygnasite] NF *Littéraire* **1** (*combativité*) belligerence **2** (*dans la discussion*) pugnacity

puîné, -e [pɥine] *Vieilli* ADJ (*de deux enfants*) younger; (*de plusieurs enfants*) youngest
  NM,F (*de deux enfants*) younger child; (*de plusieurs enfants*) youngest child; **les puînés n'avaient pas droit à l'héritage paternel** the younger children had no right to their father's inheritance

puis¹ [pɥi] *voir* **pouvoir²**

puis² [pɥi] ADV **1** (*indiquant la succession*) then; **il a regardé un moment, p. a semblé s'en désintéresser** he looked for a while, then seemed to lose interest; **il sortit p. se mit à courir** he went out and (then) started to run; **prenez à gauche p. à droite** turn left then right; **vous verrez une grande ferme à droite, p. un groupe de maisons** you'll see a big farm on the right, then a group of houses

2 (*dans une énumération*) then; **elle a mangé une cerise, p. une autre, p. une troisième** she ate a cherry, then another, then another

□ **et puis** ADV **1** (*indiquant la succession*) **il a dîné rapidement et p. il s'est couché** he ate quickly and then he went to bed; **en tête du cortège, le ministre et p. les conseillers** at the head of the procession the minister followed by the counsellors; **et p. qu'est-ce qui s'est passé?** then what happened?, what happened then *or* next?; **et p. après?** (*pour solliciter la suite*) what then?, what happened next?; (*pour couper court*) it's none of your business!; (*exprimant l'indifférence*) so what!; **oui, je vais vendre ma voiture, et p. après?** yes, I'll sell my car, if it's any of your business!; **et p. c'est tout!, et p. voilà!** and that's all!, and that's that!, and that's all there is to it!; **tu n'iras pas, et p. c'est tout!** you're not going, and that's that!

2 (*dans une énumération*) **il y avait mes parents, mes frères et p. aussi mes cousins** there were my parents, my brothers and also my cousins

3 (*d'ailleurs*) **je n'ai pas envie de sortir, et p. il fait trop froid** I don't feel like going out, and anyway *or* and what's more it's too cold

□ **puis... que** ADV *Arch* since, seeing that; **p. donc qu'il en est ainsi** since matters stand thus

puisage [pɥizaʒ] NM drawing (of water)

puisard [pɥizar] NM **1** (*pour l'évacuation*) sump; **p. de rue** catch pit **2** (*pour l'épuration*) cesspool, drainage well **3** *Naut* bilge well **4** *Mines* sump

puisatier [pɥizatje] NM **1** (*terrassier*) well sinker **2** *Mines* sumpman

puisement [pɥizmɑ̃] = **puisage**

puiser [3] [pɥize] VT **1** (*eau*) to draw; **p. l'eau d'un puits/d'une citerne** to draw water from a well/a tank

2 (*extraire*) to get, to take, to derive; **où a-t-il puisé le courage de parler ainsi?** where did he get the nerve to say such things?; **p. sa force dans** to draw one's strength from; **p. son inspiration dans** to take *or* to draw one's inspiration from

3 (*prélever*) to draw, to take; **tu peux p. de l'argent sur mon compte si tu en as besoin** you can draw some money from my account if you need any

  VI (*se servir*) to draw; **p. dans ses économies** to draw on *or* upon one's savings; **j'ai trop puisé dans mes économies** I've depleted my savings; **est-ce que je peux p. dans ta réserve de crayons?** can I dip into *or* help myself from your stock of pencils?; **p. dans son expérience** to draw on one's experience; **ils n'ont pas puisé dans la même documentation** they didn't use the same source material

puisette [pɥizɛt] NF (*en Afrique francophone*) *ou Vieilli* ladle, scoop (*for drawing water*)

puisque [pɥiskə] CONJ **1** (*parce que*) since, because; **tu ne peux pas acheter de voiture, p. tu n'as pas d'argent** you can't buy a car because *or* since you don't have any money; **la terrasse est très ensoleillée puisqu'exposée au sud** because *or* since the terrace faces south it gets a lot of sun

2 (*étant donné que*) since; **je viendrai dîner, p. vous insistez** I will come to dinner, since you insist; **je ne sortirai pas, p. ça t'inquiète** since it worries you, I won't go out; **p. vous voulez me parler, allons dans mon bureau** since you wish to speak to me, let's go into my office; **bon, p. tu le dis/y tiens** all right, if that's what you say/want; **p. c'est comme ça, je m'en vais!** if that's how it is, I'm leaving!; **puisqu'il en est ainsi** since that's the way things are; **ce chantage, puisqu'il faut l'appeler ainsi...** this blackmail, since there's no other word for it...; **cette erreur, puisqu'erreur il y a...** this mistake, since there is a mistake...

3 *(emploi exclamatif)* **mais p. je te dis que je ne veux pas!** but I'm telling you that I don't want to!; **mais puisqu'il m'attend!** but I'm telling you he's waiting for me!; **p. je te dis que je vais le faire!** I've told you I'm going to do it!; **tu vas vraiment y aller? – p. je te le dis!** so are you really going? – isn't that what I said?

puissamment [pɥisamɑ̃] **ADV** **1** *(avec efficacité)* greatly; **ils ont p. contribué à la victoire** their part in the victory was decisive; *Ironique* **p. raisonné!** brilliant thinking! **2** *(avec force)* powerfully, *Sout* mightily; **un corps p. musclé** a powerfully muscular body

puissance [pɥisɑ̃s] **NF** **1** *(force physique → d'une personne, d'une armée)* power, force, strength

2 *(pouvoir, autorité)* power; **un État au sommet de sa p.** a state at the height of its power

3 *(capacité)* power, capacity; **une grande p. de travail** a great capacity for work; **une grande p. de séduction** great powers of seduction

4 *(d'un appareil)* power, capacity, capability; *(d'une arme nucléaire)* yield; **augmenter/diminuer la p.** to turn the volume up/down; *Élec* **p. active/instantanée/réactive** active/instantaneous/reactive power; *Aut* **p. effective** power output; *Élec* **p. d'entrée/de sortie** input/output (power); *Mil* **p. de feu** fire power; *Aut* **p. administrative** *ou* **fiscale** engine rating; *Aut* **p. nominale/au frein** nominal/brake horsepower

5 *Com* power; **p. d'achat** buying *or* puchasing power; **p. commerciale** sales power; **p. publicitaire** *ou* **de vente** selling power

6 *Math* power; **six p. cinq** six to the power (of) five; **deux (à la) p. trois égale huit** two cubed *or* two to the power (of) three is eight; *Fig* **c'est comme une étincelle, mais à la p. mille** it's like a spark, but a thousand times bigger

7 *Jur* authority; **p. maritale** authority of husband over wife; **p. paternelle** paternal authority; **p. tutélaire** power of guardianship; **être en p. de mari** to be under a husband's authority *or* control

8 *Admin* **la p. publique** the authorities

9 *(pays puissant)* power; **p. économique** economic power; **p. mondiale** world power

10 *Opt* (optical) power

11 *Équitation* puissance

12 *Géol* thickness, depth

❑ **puissances** **NFPL** powers; **les puissances de l'argent** the moneyed classes; *Bible* **les puissances** the powers; **les puissances des ténèbres** the powers of darkness; *Pol* **les grandes puissances** the great powers

❑ **en puissance** **ADJ** *(virtuel)* potential, prospective; **un candidat en p.** a potential candidate; **un client en p.** a prospective customer; **c'est un fasciste en p.** he's got latent fascist tendencies

puissant, -e [pɥisɑ̃, -ɑ̃t] **ADJ** **1** *(efficace → remède)* powerful, potent, *Sout* efficacious; *(→ antidote, armée, moteur, ordinateur)* powerful; *(→ membre, mouvement)* strong, powerful, *Littéraire* mighty; **une théorie qui soit assez puissante pour expliquer l'évolution** a theory powerful enough to explain evolution

2 *(intense → odeur, voix)* strong, powerful

3 *(influent)* powerful, *Littéraire* mighty; **riche et p.** rich and powerful; **ils craignent leurs puissants voisins** they fear their powerful neighbours

4 *(profond)* powerful; **un p. instinct de conservation** a powerful instinct of self-preservation

5 *Fam (remarquable)* wicked, *Br* fab, *Am* awesome

6 *Géol* thick

❑ **puissants** **NMPL** **les puissants** the powerful

puisse *etc voir* **pouvoir**[2]

puits [pɥi] **NM** **1** *(pour l'eau)* well; **p. artésien** artesian well; **p. à ciel ouvert** open well; **p. perdu** cesspool

2 *Pétr* **p. de pétrole** oil well; **p. d'exploration** exploration *or* wild cat well; **p. d'intervention** relief *or* killer well; **p. sec** *ou* **improductif** duster

3 *Mines* shaft, pit; **p. d'aérage** ventilation *or* ventilating shaft; **p. d'extraction** extraction shaft

4 *Constr* **p. d'amarrage** *ou* **d'ancrage** anchor block (hole)

5 *Fig* **un p. de science** a walking encyclopedia, a fount of knowledge, a mine of information

6 *Géog* pothole

7 *Écol* **p. de carbone** carbon sink

❑ **puits d'amour** **NM** *Culin* cream puff

puja [pudʒa] **NF** *(dans l'hindouisme)* puja

pulicaire [pylikɛr] **NF** *Bot* pulicaria, fleabane

pull [pyl] **NM** sweater, *Br* jumper

pullman [pulman] **NM** **1** *Rail* Pullman® (car) **2** *(autocar)* luxury touring bus, *Br* luxury coach

pullorose [pylɔroz] **NF** *Vét* pullorum disease

pull-over [pylɔvɛr] *(pl* **pull-overs***)* **NM** sweater, *Br* jumper

pullulation [pylylasjɔ̃] **NF** pullulation

pullulement [pylylmɑ̃] **NM** **1** *(processus)* proliferation; **empêcher le p. des bactéries** to stop bacteria from proliferating **2** *(grand nombre)* **un p. d'insectes** swarms of insects; **un p. de touristes** hordes of tourists

pulluler [3] [pylyle] **VI** **1** *(abonder)* to congregate, to swarm; **au lever du jour, les mouettes pullulent sur la falaise** seagulls congregate *or* swarm on the cliffs at dawn; **les marchands de chaussures pullulent dans ce coin de la ville** there are lots of shoe shops in this part of town, this part of town is full of *or* swarming with shoe shops; **des égouts où les rats pullulent** sewers overrun by rats

2 *(se multiplier)* to multiply, to proliferate; **les mauvaises herbes pullulaient dans le jardin abandonné** weeds were taking over the abandoned garden

3 **p. de** *(fourmiller de)* to swarm *or* to be alive with; **la plage pullule de baigneurs** the seashore is swarming with bathers; **ce texte pullule de fautes de frappe** this text is riddled with typing errors

pulmonaire [pylmɔnɛr] **ADJ** **1** *Anat* pulmonary **2** *Méd* pulmonary, lung *(avant n)*

NF *Bot* lungwort

pulmoné, -e [pylmɔne] *Zool* **ADJ** pulmonate

NM pulmonate

❑ **pulmonés** **NMPL** Pulmonata

pulpaire [pylpɛr] **ADJ** pulpal

pulpe [pylp] **NF** **1** *(de fruit)* pulp; **p. d'agrumes** citrus pulp; **yaourt/boisson à la p. de fruit** yoghurt/drink with real fruit **2** *Anat* pulp; *(des doigts)* pad, *Spéc* digital pulp; **p. dentaire** tooth *or* dental pulp

pulpectomie [pylpɛktɔmi] **NF** *Méd* **1** *(dévitalisation)* pulpectomy **2** *(ablation du testicule)* = type of orchidectomy

pulpeux, -euse [pylpø, -øz] **ADJ** **1** *Anat & Bot* pulpy **2** *(charnu → lèvres, formes)* fleshy, voluptuous; **une blonde pulpeuse** a curvaceous blonde

pulpite [pylpit] **NF** *Méd* pulpitis

pulque [pulke] **NM** *(alcool)* pulque

pulsant, -e [pylsɑ̃, -ɑ̃t] **ADJ** *Astron* pulsating

pulsar [pylsar] **NM** *Astron* pulsar

pulsatif, -ive [pylsatif, -iv] **ADJ** pulsatory, pulsatile

pulsation [pylsasjɔ̃] **NF** **1** *Anat (du cœur)* beat; *(du pouls)* pulsation; **pulsations cardiaques** heartbeats **2** *Astron* pulsation **3** *Élec* pulsatance, angular frequency **4** *Phys* (mechanical) pulsation **5** *Mus* beat

pulsative [pylsativ] *voir* **pulsatif**

pulser [3] [pylse] **VT** *(air)* to extract, to pump out

VI **1** *Méd & Mus* to throb **2** *Astron* to pulsate

pulsion [pylsjɔ̃] **NF** **1** *(motivation)* impulse, unconscious motive; **mû par des pulsions inexplicables** spurred on *or* driven by mysterious impulses **2** *Psy* drive, urge; **pulsions sexuelles** sexual desire, sexual urge; **p. de mort** death wish

pulsionnel, -elle [pylsjɔnɛl] **ADJ** drive *(avant n)*

pulsoréacteur [pylsɔreaktœr] **NM** pulse-jet (engine)

pultacé, -e [pyltase] **ADJ** *Méd* pultaceous, pulpy

pultrusion [pyltryzjɔ̃] **NF** pultrusion

pulvérin [pylverɛ̃] **NM** **1** *Hist (pour armes à feu)* mealed gunpowder **2** *(pour mélanges pyrotechniques)* = powder used in firework manufacture

pulvérisable [pylverizabl] **ADJ** **1** *(qui peut être réduit en poudre)* that can be crushed **2** *(liquide)* that can be sprayed

pulvérisateur [pylverizatœr] **NM** **1** *(vaporisateur)* spray **2** *Agr* sprayer; **p. rotatif/va-et-vient** rotary/travelling sprayer

pulvérisation [pylverizasjɔ̃] **NF** **1** *(d'un liquide)* spraying **2** *(broyage)* pulverizing, crushing; **p. cathodique** cathode sputtering **3** *(de médicament)* **prendre un médicament en pulvérisations** to take a medicine in the form of a spray

pulvériser [3] [pylverize] **VT** **1** *(broyer)* to pulverize, to turn into powder, to crush **2** *Fig (détruire)* to demolish, to smash to pieces; **les bombes ont pulvérisé la ville** the bombs reduced the town to ashes *or* to a heap of rubble; **p. un record** to smash a record; *Fam* **je vais le p., ce type!** I'm going to flatten *or* make mincemeat out of the guy! **3** *(vaporiser)* to spray

pulvériseur [pylverizœr] **NM** disc harrow

pulvérulence [pylverylɑ̃s] **NF** powderiness, dustiness

pulvérulent, -e [pylverylɑ̃, -ɑ̃t] **ADJ** powdery, dusty

puma [pyma] **NM** puma, cougar, mountain lion

puna [pyna] **NF** **1** *Géog (haut plateau)* puna (of the Andes) **2** *(mal des montagnes)* mountain sickness

punaise [pynɛz] **NF** **1** *Entom* bug; **p. des lits** bed bug; **p. des bois** *(pentatome)* forest bug **2** *(clou)* tack, *Br* drawing pin, *Am* thumbtack; **p. d'architecte** three-pointed tack **3** *Fam (personne)* vixen **4** *Fam Péj* **p. de sacristie** sanctimonious person▪

EXCLAM *Fam Br* sugar!, *Am* shoot!

punaiser [4] [pyneze] **VT** to pin up, to put up with *Br* drawing pins *or Am* thumbtacks; **p. des affiches au mur** to pin posters to the wall

punch[1] [pɔ̃ʃ] **NM** *(boisson)* punch

punch[2] [pœnʃ] **NM INV** **1** *Fam (dynamisme)* pep, get-up-and-go; **avoir du p.** to be full of get-up-and-go; **une politique qui a du p.** a hard-hitting policy; **ça vous donnera du p. pour la suite!** it'll give you energy *or* set you up for what's to come! **2** *Sport (d'un boxeur)* **il a le p.** he's got a knock-out *or* devastating punch

puncheur [pœnʃœr] **NM** *Sport* powerful boxer

punching-ball [pœnʃiŋbol] *(pl* **punching-balls***)* **NM** punch *or* speed ball

punctation [pɔ̃ktasjɔ̃] **NF** *Jur* = partial agreement

punctum [pɔ̃ktɔm] **NM** *Physiol* punctiform

puncture [pɔ̃ktyr] **NF** *Méd* puncture

puni, -e [pyni] **NM,F** punished pupil; **les punis resteront dans la classe pendant la récréation** those who have been punished will stay in during break

punique [pynik] **ADJ** *(civilisation)* Carthaginian, Punic; *(guerre)* Punic

NM *(langue)* Punic

punir [32] [pynir] **VT** **1** *(élève, enfant)* to punish

2 *Jur* to punish, to penalize; **être puni par la loi** to be punished by law, to be prosecuted; **être puni de prison** to be sentenced to prison; **le kidnapping est puni de la prison à vie** kidnapping is punishable by life imprisonment; **tout abus sera puni** *(sur panneau)* penalty for improper use; *Bible* **tu seras puni par où tu as péché** as you sow, so you shall reap; **p. qn de qch** *(à cause de)* to punish sb for sth; **elle est bien punie de sa méchanceté** she's paying the price for her spitefulness; **me voilà puni de ma gourmandise!** it serves me right for being greedy!, that'll teach me to be greedy!; **se faire p.** to be punished; *Fam* **c'est le ciel** *ou* **le bon Dieu qui t'a puni** it serves you right

punissable [pynisabl] **ADJ** punishable, deserving (of) punishment; **p. de trois mois de prison** *(délit)* carrying a penalty of three months imprisonment; *(criminel)* liable to three months in jail

punitif, -ive [pynitif, -iv] **ADJ** *(expédition, mesures)* punitive; **en agissant ainsi, je n'ai pas d'intentions punitives** I do not intend this as punishment

punition [pynisjɔ̃] **NF** **1** *(sanction)* punishment; **donner une p. à un enfant** to punish a child; **en guise de p.** as (a) punishment; **il est en p.** he is being kept in detention; **p. corporelle** corporal punishment; **p. de Dieu** *ou* **du ciel** divine retribution

2 *Fam (défaite)* thrashing; **les Bordelais ont infligé une rude p. aux Parisiens** the Bordeaux team wiped the floor with *or* thrashed *or Br* hammered the Paris club

3 (conséquence) punishment, penalty; **la p. est lourde** it's a heavy price to pay

❏ **en punition de** PRÉP as a punishment for

Punjab [pœndʒab] = **Pendjab**

punk [pœnk] ADJ INV punk

NMF punk

punkette [pœnkɛt] NF Fam punkette

puntarelle [pɛtarɛl] NF coral chippings

pupe [pyp] NF Entom pupa, chrysalis

pupillaire [pypilɛr] ADJ 1 Jur pupillary 2 Anat pupillary

pupillarité [pypilarite] NF Jur wardship

pupille¹ [pypij] NMF 1 (en tutelle) ward (of court) 2 (orphelin) orphan; **p. de l'État** child in care; **pupilles de la Nation** war orphans

pupille² [pypij] NF Anat pupil

pupilloscopie [pypijɔskɔpi] NF Méd skiascopy, sciascopy

pupinisation [pypinizasjɔ̃] NF Tél loading (of line) with inductances, pupinization

pupipare [pypipar] Entom ADJ pupiparous

❏ **pupipares** NMPL Pupipara

pupitre [pypitr] NM 1 Aviat & Ordinat console; (clavier) keyboard; Ordinat **p. (de commande)** console (desk); **p. de mélange** ou **de mixage** mixing desk, mixing console, audio-mixer; **p. de poursuite** tracking console; Ordinat **p. de visualisation** visual display unit

2 Mus (support → sur pied) music stand; (→ sur un instrument) music rest; (groupe) section; **le p. des violons** the violin section, the violins; **p. d'orchestre** orchestra stand

3 (tablette de lecture) (table) lectern

4 Vieilli (bureau d'écolier) desk

pupitreur, -euse [pypitrœr, -øz] NM,F console operator; (claviste) keyboarder

pur, -e [pyr] ADJ 1 (non pollué → eau) pure, clear, uncontaminated; (→ air) clean, pure, unpolluted; (→ ciel) clear

2 (sans mélange → liquide) undiluted; (→ whisky, gin etc) straight, neat; (→ race) pure; (→ bonheur, joie) unalloyed, pure; (→ note, voyelle, couleur) pure; **du lait p.** unadulterated milk; **le cognac se boit p.** cognac should be taken straight or neat; **p. style dorique** pure Doric style; **pure laine (vierge)** pure (new) wool; **biscuits p. beurre** (100 percent) butter biscuits; **cheval p. sang** thoroughbred horse; **c'est un p. produit de la bourgeoisie** he's/she's a genuine middle-class product; **c'est un p. produit de mai 68** he's/she's a true child of May 68; Euph **ce n'est pas un p. esprit** he's/she's made of flesh and blood; **à l'état p.** pure, unalloyed, unadulterated; **p. et dur** (fidèle) strict; (intransigeant) hard-line; Hum **les amateurs de café purs et durs** serious or dedicated coffee drinkers; **c'est un socialiste p. jus** he's a socialist through and through

3 (sans défaut) faultless, perfect; **des lignes pures** neat or perfect lines; **l'ovale p. de son visage** the faultless or perfect oval of his/her face; **un style p.** an unaffected style; **elle parle un italien très p.** she speaks very refined or polished Italian

4 (innocent) pure, clean; **être p.** to be pure at heart; **ses pensées sont pures** his/her thoughts are clean or pure; **une conscience pure** a clear conscience; **le regard p. d'un enfant** a child's innocent gaze; **une jeune fille pure** a young innocent girl

5 (théorique) pure, theoretical; **sciences pures** pure science

6 (en intensif) sheer, utter, pure; **c'est de la folie pure!** it's sheer lunacy!; **par pure méchanceté** out of sheer malice; **c'est un p. hasard qu'il se soit trouvé là** it was pure or sheer chance that he was there; **p. et simple** pure and simple; **c'est de la lâcheté pure et simple** it's sheer cowardice, it's cowardice pure and simple

7 Fam (excellent) wicked, cool, Am awesome

8 Chim & Opt pure

9 Minér flawless

NM,F 1 Pol (fidèle) dedicated follower; (intransigeant) hardliner

2 Rel true believer

pureau, -x [pyro] NM Constr bare, gauge (of roofing slate, tile etc)

purée [pyre] NF 1 Culin (de légumes) purée; **p. de tomates/carottes** tomato/carrot purée; **p. (de pommes de terre)** mashed potatoes; **p. en flocons** instant mashed potato; **p. Mousseline** instant mashed potato; **réduire qch en p.** Culin to purée sth; Fig to smash sth to a pulp; **j'ai retrouvé mes coquillages en p. au fond du sac** my shells were all crushed at the bottom of the bag

2 Fam (misère) **être dans la p.** to be broke

3 **balancer la p.** Vulg (éjaculer) to shoot one's load; très Fam (tirer avec une arme à feu) to open fire■

EXCLAM Fam (colère, agacement) hell!, blast (it)!; (surprise) wow!

❏ **purée de pois** NF Fam (brouillard) pea souper

purement [pyrmã] ADV 1 (uniquement) purely, only, solely; **ses connaissances sont p. techniques** his/her knowledge is purely technical 2 (entièrement) purely, wholly; **une existence p. mystique** a purely mystical life; **p. et simplement** purely and simply; **le contrat est p. et simplement annulé** the contract is unconditionally cancelled; **non, c'est p. et simplement impossible!** no, it's quite simply out of the question!

pureté [pyrte] NF 1 (propreté) cleanness, purity; **la p. de l'eau** the cleanness of the water; **la p. du ciel** the clearness of the sky

2 Chim & Opt purity; Minér purity, flawlessness; **la p. de l'or** the purity of gold; **une émeraude d'une grande p.** a perfect or flawless emerald

3 (harmonie → d'un contour) neatness, purity; (→ d'une ligne, d'un style) purity, refinement; **la p. de ses traits** the perfection in his/her face or of his/her features

4 (innocence) purity, chastity; **je doute de la p. de ses intentions** I doubt whether his/her intentions are honourable

purgatif, -ive [pyrgatif, -iv] ADJ purgative

NM purgative

purgation [pyrgasjɔ̃] NF 1 Méd (remède) purgative; (processus) purging, cleansing 2 Rel purgation

purgative [pyrgativ] voir purgatif

purgatoire [pyrgatwar] NM Rel & Fig purgatory; **au p.** in purgatory

purge [pyrʒ] NF 1 Tech (processus → gén) draining, bleeding; (→ d'un radiateur, des freins) bleeding; (dispositif) bleed key; **robinet de p.** drain or bleed cock 2 Méd purge, purging 3 Fig (au sein d'un groupe) purge 4 Jur **p. d'hypothèque** redemption of mortgage 5 Tex cleaning

purgeoir [pyrʒwar] NM purifying tank, filtering tank

purger [17] [pyrʒe] VT 1 Tech (radiateur, freins) to bleed; (réservoir) to drain; (tuyau à gaz) to allow to blow off, to blow off

2 Chim (métal) to refine; (substance) to purify

3 Jur (peine) to serve, **il a purgé six mois de prison** he served six months in prison; **p. sa peine** to serve one's sentence

4 (dette) to pay off; (hypothèque) to redeem

5 Méd (personne) to purge, to give a laxative to

6 (débarrasser) **le parti a été purgé de ses contestataires** the party has been purged of disloyal elements; **p. un quartier** to clean up an area

7 (nettoyer, purifier) **ils ont purgé le texte de toute allusion politique** they removed all political references from the text

▶ **se purger** VPR to take a purgative

purgeur [pyrʒœr] NM (vidange) drain cock, bleed cock; (trop-plein) bleed tap; **p. d'air** air cock; **p. de vapeur** pet cock

purifiant, -e [pyrifjã, -ãt] ADJ 1 (crème, lotion) cleansing, purifying 2 (air) healthy

purificateur, -trice [pyrifikatœr, -tris] ADJ purifying

NM **p. (d'air** ou **d'atmosphère)** (air) purifier

purification [pyrifikasjɔ̃] NF 1 Chim purifying; Métal refining; **p. de l'air/l'eau** air/water purifying 2 Fig (de l'âme) cleansing; **p. ethnique** ethnic cleansing 3 Rel purification; **la P.** Candlemas, the Purification

purificatoire [pyrifikatwar] ADJ purificatory

NM Rel purificator (napkin)

purificatrice [pyrifikatris] voir purificateur

purifier [9] [pyrifje] VT 1 (nettoyer → air) to purify, to clear; (→ peau) to cleanse; **la pluie a purifié l'atmosphère** the rain has cleared the air

2 (âme) to cleanse

3 (corriger → langue, style) to purify

4 Chim (filtrer) to purify, to decontaminate; **eau purifiée** purified or decontaminated water

5 Métal to refine; **or purifié** refined gold

▶ **se purifier** VPR 1 (devenir propre) to become clean or pure; **plus on monte, plus l'air se purifie** the higher you go, the purer the air becomes

2 Rel to be cleansed or purified; **l'âme se purifie dans la prière** the soul is purified by prayer

purin [pyrɛ̃] NM liquid manure, slurry

purine [pyrin] NF Chim 1 (composé) purine 2 (base purique) purine (base)

purique [pyrik] ADJ Chim **base p.** purine base

purisme [pyrism] NM 1 (gén) & Ling purism 2 Beaux-Arts Purism

puriste [pyrist] ADJ 1 (gén) & Ling purist 2 Beaux-Arts Purist

NMF 1 (gén) & Ling purist 2 Beaux-Arts Purist

puritain, -e [pyritɛ̃, -ɛn] ADJ 1 (strict) puritan, puritanical 2 Hist Puritan

NM,F 1 (personne stricte) puritan 2 Hist **les puritains** the Puritans

puritanisme [pyritanism] NM 1 (austérité) puritanism, austerity 2 Hist Puritanism

purot [pyro] NM Agr liquid manure pit

purotin [pyrotɛ̃] NM Fam Vieilli hard-up person, person who is always broke

purpura [pyrpyra] NM Méd purpura

purpurin, -e [pyrpyrɛ̃, -in] ADJ Littéraire crimson, purpurine

❏ **purpurine** NF Chim purpurin

pur-sang [pyrsã] NM INV Zool thoroughbred

purulence [pyrylãs] NF purulence, purulency

purulent, -e [pyrylã, -ãt] ADJ Méd (plaie) suppurating; (sinusite) purulent

pus [py] NM Méd pus

puseyisme [pjuzeism] NM Rel Puseyism

push-pull [puʃpul] ADJ INV push-pull

NM INV push-pull

pusillanime [pyzilanim] ADJ Littéraire pusillanimous

pusillanimité [pyzilanimite] NF Littéraire pusillanimity

pustule [pystyl] NF 1 Méd pustule; **p. maligne** malignant pustule 2 Bot & Zool pustule

pustuleux, -euse [pystylø, -øz] ADJ Méd pustular, pustulous

put¹ etc voir pouvoir¹

put² [put] NM Bourse put (option)

putain [pytɛ̃] très Fam NF (prostituée) whore, hooker; (femme aux mœurs légères) tart, slut, Br slag; **faire la p.** (chercher à plaire) to prostitute oneself■; (renoncer à ses principes) to sell out

ADJ **il est très p.** he's a real bootlicker

EXCLAM fuck!, fucking hell!; **p., j'ai oublié mon parapluie!** shit, I've forgotten my umbrella!; **p. de bagnole/de temps!** (this) fucking car/weather!; **p. d'autobus, encore en retard!** that fucking bus is always late!; **p. de merde!** oh, fuck!

putassier, -ère [pytasje, -ɛr] ADJ Vulg 1 (vulgaire → manières) tarty 2 (servile, obséquieux) ingratiating■

putatif, -ive [pytatif, -iv] ADJ 1 Jur putative 2 (supposé) assumed, supposed

pute [pyt] NF Vulg 1 (prostituée) whore; **aller chez les** ou **aux putes** to go (out) whoring; **fils de p.!** you son of a bitch!; **faire la p.** (chercher à plaire) to prostitute oneself■ 2 (femme facile) tart, slut, Br slag 3 (femme méprisable) bitch

putier [pytje], **putiet** [pytjɛ] NM Bot wild cherry, bird cherry (tree)

putois [pytwa] NM 1 Zool polecat 2 (fourrure) fitch, polecat fur

putréfaction [pytrefaksjɔ̃] NF putrefaction, decomposition; **matière en (état de) p.** putrefying matter; **en état de p. avancée** in an advanced state of decomposition

putréfiable [pytrefjabl] ADJ putrefiable

putréfié, -e [pytrefje] ADJ putrefied, putrid, rotten

putréfier [9] [pytrefje] VT to putrefy, to rot

▶ **se putréfier** VPR to putrefy, to rot, to become putrid

putrescence [pytresãs] NF putrescence

putrescent, -e [pytresɑ̃, -ɑ̃t] ADJ putrescent, rotting

putrescibilité [pytresibilite] NF putrescibility

putrescible [pytresibl] ADJ putrescible, putrefiable

putride [pytrid] ADJ **1** *(pourri → viande, cadavre)* decomposed, putrid; *(→ eau)* putrid, contaminated **2** *(nauséabond)* foul, putrid; **odeur p.** putrid smell, foul stench **3** *Littéraire (immoral → lettre, pièce)* depraved

putridité [pytridite] NF *Littéraire* rottenness, putridness

putsch [putʃ] NM military coup, putsch

putschiste [putʃist] ADJ *(officiers)* involved in the putsch
⟶ NMF putschist, author of a military coup

putt [pœt] NM putt

putter [pœtœr] NM putter (club)

putting [pœtiŋ] = **putt**

putto [pyto] *(pl* **puttos** *ou* **putti**) NM *Beaux-Arts* putto

puvathérapie [pyvaterapi] NF puvatherapy

puy [pɥi] NM puy, mountain *(in the Auvergne)*

Puy-de-Dôme [pɥidədom] NM **le P.** Puy-de-Dôme

puzzle [pœzl] NM **1** *(jeu de société)* (jigsaw) puzzle **2** *(énigme)* puzzle, puzzling question, riddle; **je commence à rassembler les morceaux du p.** I'm beginning to fit the pieces of the puzzle together; **il ne lui restait plus qu'à placer la dernière pièce du p.** he/she just had the last piece of the jigsaw to put into place

PV [peve] NM *Fam (abrév* **procès-verbal**) (parking) ticket; **j'ai eu un PV ce matin** I got a ticket this morning; **mettre un PV à qn** to give sb a ticket

PVC [pevese] NM *(abrév* **polyvinyl chloride**) PVC; **un siège en P.** a PVC seat

PVD [pevede] NM *(abrév* **pays en voie de développement**) developing country

PVP [pevepe] NM *Com (abrév* **prix de vente publique**) public selling price

px *(abrév écrite* **prix**) **px à déb** offers

pycnique [piknik] ADJ pyknic
⟶ NMF pyknic type

pycnogonide [piknɔgɔnid] *Entom* NM sea spider, *Spéc* pycnogonid
❑ **pycnogonides** NMPL Pycnogonida

pycnomètre [piknɔmɛtr] NM *Tech* pycnometer, picnometer

pycnose [piknoz] NF *Biol* pycnosis

pyélite [pjelit] NF *Méd* pyelitis

pyélonéphrite [pjelonefrit] NF *Méd* pyelonephritis

pyémie [pjemi] NF *Méd* pyaemia

pygargue [pigarg] NM *Orn* **p. à tête blanche** bald eagle; **p. à queue blanche** white-tailed sea eagle

Pygmalion [pigmaljɔ̃] NPR *Myth* Pygmalion

pygmée [pigme] ADJ Pygmy
⟶ NMF *Péj* **1** *Arch (nain)* pygmy, dwarf **2** *(personne insignifiante)* nobody, pygmy
❑ **Pygmée** NMF Pygmy

pyhémie = **pyémie**

pyjama [piʒama] NM **un p.** (a pair of) pyjamas; **encore en p. à cette heure-ci?** you're still in your *or* wearing pyjamas at this time of day?; **j'y suis comme dans un p.** it's really comfortable

pylône [pilon] NM **1** *(d'électricité, de téléphone)* pylon; *(pour fils télégraphiques)* lattice mast; **p. électrique** electricity pylon **2** *Archit* monumental column, pylon **3** *Antiq* pylon **4** *Constr* tower

pylore [pilɔr] NM *Anat* pylorus

pylorique [pilɔrik] ADJ *Anat* pyloric

pyocyanique [pjɔsjanik] ADJ **bacille p.** bacillus pyocyaneus

pyodermite [pjɔdɛrmit] NF *Méd* pyodermatitis

pyogène [pjɔʒɛn] ADJ *Méd* pyogenic

pyohémie [pjɔemi] = **pyémie**

Pyongyang [pjɔ̃gjɑ̃g] NM Pyongyang

pyorrhée [pjɔre] NF *Méd* pyorrhoea

pyothorax [pjɔtɔraks] NM *Méd* pyothorax, empyema

pyrale [piral] NF *Entom* pyralis, meal moth, bee moth; **p. des pommes** codling moth

pyralène [piralɛn] NM pyralene

pyramidal, -e, -aux, -ales [piramidal, -o] ADJ **1** *Écon, Géom & Méd* pyramidal **2** *(objet)* pyramid-shaped; **forme pyramidale** pyramid shape **3** *Anat* **muscle p. de l'abdomen** pyramidalis; **voie pyramidale** pyramidal tract

pyramide [piramid] NF **1** *Archit & Géom* pyramid; **la p. de Khéops** the (Great) Pyramid of Cheops; **la P. du Louvre** = glass pyramid in the courtyard of the Louvre which acts as its main entrance
2 *(empilement)* **une p. de fruits** a pyramid of fruit; **entasser des oranges en p.** to pile up oranges in a pyramid; **p. humaine** human pyramid
3 *(en sociologie)* **p. des âges** population pyramid
4 *Écol* **p. alimentaire** food pyramid
5 *Anat* pyramid; **p. de Malpighi** pyramid of Malpighi
6 *Fin* **p. des salaires** wage pyramid

pyramidé, -e [piramide] ADJ pyramidal

pyramidion [piramidjɔ̃] NM *Archit* pyramidion

pyranne [piran] NM pyran

pyrène [pirɛn] NM *Chim* pyrene

pyrénéen, -enne [pireneɛ̃, -ɛn] ADJ Pyrenean
❑ **Pyrénéen, -enne** NM,F Pyrenean

Pyrénées [pirene] NFPL **les P.** the Pyrenees

Pyrénées-Atlantiques [pireneatlɑ̃tik] NFPL **les P.** Pyrénées-Atlantiques

Pyrénées-Orientales [pirenezɔrjɑ̃tal] NFPL **les P.** Pyrénées-Orientales

pyrénéite [pireneit] NF *Minér* Pyrenean black garnet

pyrénomycète [pirenɔmisɛt] *Bot* NM pyrenomycete
❑ **pyrénomycètes** NMPL pyrenomycetes

pyrétique [piretik] ADJ *Méd* piretic

pyrèthre [pirɛtr] NM *Bot* feverfew, pyrethrum; **poudre de p.** insect powder

pyréthrine [piretrin] NF *Pharm* pyrethrin

Pyrex® [pirɛks] NM Pyrex®; **en P.** Pyrex®; **plat en P.** Pyrex® dish

pyrexie [pirɛksi] NF *Méd* pyrexia

pyridine [piridin] NF *Chim* pyridin(e)

pyridoxine [piridɔksin] NF *Biol & Chim* pyridoxin

pyrimidine [pirimidin] NF *Chim* pyrimidin(e)

pyrimidique [pirimidik] ADJ *Chim* **base p.** pyrimidic base

pyrite [pirit] NF *Minér* pyrite; **p. cuivreuse** copper pyrite *or* pyrites; **p. blanche** marcasite

pyroclastique [pirɔklastik] ADJ *Géol* pyroclastic

pyrocorise [pirɔkɔriz] = **pyrrhocoris**

pyroélectricité [pirɔelɛktrisite] NF pyroelectricity

pyrogallique [pirɔgalik] ADJ *Chim* pyrogallic

pyrogallol [pirɔgalɔl] NM *Chim* pyrogallol

pyrogénation [pirɔʒenasjɔ̃] NF pyrogenation

pyrogène [pirɔʒɛn] ADJ *Méd* pyrogenic

pyrographe [pirɔgraf] NM pyrographic apparatus

pyrograver [3] [pirɔgrave] VT **p. qch** to work sth with a heated stylus, *Spéc* to pyrograph sth

pyrogravure [pirɔgravyr] NF *(procédé)* poker-work, *Spéc* pyrography; *(résultat)* pyrograph

pyroligneux, -euse [pirɔliɲø, -øz] *Chim* ADJ pyroligneous
⟶ NM pyroligneous acid

pyrolusite [pirɔlyzit] NF *Minér* pyrolusite, polianite

pyrolyse [pirɔliz] NF pyrolysis

pyromane [pirɔman] NMF *Psy* pyromaniac; *Jur (incendiaire)* arsonist

pyromanie [pirɔmani] NF pyromania

pyromécanisme [pirɔmekanism] NM pyromechanism

pyromètre [pirɔmɛtr] NM pyrometer

pyrométrie [pirɔmetri] NF pyrometry

pyrométrique [pirɔmetrik] ADJ pyrometric(al)

pyrophore [pirɔfɔr] NM *Chim* pyrophorus

pyrophosphorique [pirɔfɔsfɔrik] ADJ *Chim* pyrophosphoric

pyrophyte [pirɔfit] *Bot* ADJ pyrophytic
⟶ NF pyrophyte

pyrosis [pirɔzis] NM heartburn, *Spéc* pyrosis

pyrosulfurique [pirɔsylfyrik] ADJ *Chim* pyrosulphuric

pyrotechnicien, -enne [pirɔtɛknisjɛ̃, -ɛn] NM,F pyrotechnician

pyrotechnie [pirɔtɛkni] NF pyrotechnics *(singulier)*, pyrotechny, fireworks

pyrotechnique [pirɔtɛknik] ADJ pyrotechnic, pyrotechnical; **un spectacle p.** a firework display

pyroxène [pirɔksɛn] NM pyroxene

pyroxyle [pirɔksil] NM *Vieilli* pyroxilin, guncotton

pyrrhique [pirik] NF *Antiq (danse)* Pyrrhic

pyrrhocoris [pirɔkɔris] NM *Entom* linden bug, *Spéc* pyrrhocorid

pyrrhonien, -enne [pirɔnjɛ̃, -ɛn] *Phil* ADJ Pyrrhonic, Pyrrhonian
⟶ NM,F Pyrrhonist

pyrrhonisme [pirɔnism] NM *Phil* Pyrrhonism

pyrrhotite [pirɔtit] NF *Minér* pyrrhotite

Pyrrhus [pirys] NPR Pyrrhus

pyrrol, pirrole [pirɔl] NM *Chim* pyrrol(e)

pyrrolique [pirɔlik] ADJ *Chim* pyrrolic

Pythagore [pitagɔr] NPR Pythagoras

pythagoricien, -enne [pitagɔrisjɛ̃, -ɛn] ADJ Pythagorean; **la gamme pythagoricienne** the Pythagorean scale
⟶ NM,F Pythagorean

pythagorique [pitagɔrik] ADJ **nombres pythagoriques** Pythagorean numbers

pythagorisme [pitagɔrism] NM *Phil* Pythagoreanism

pythie [piti] NF **1** *Antiq* **la p. (de Delphes)** Pythia (of Delphi) **2** *Littéraire (prophétesse)* pythoness

pythien, -enne [pitjɛ̃, -ɛn] ADJ *Antiq* Pythian; **Apollon p.** Pythian Apollo

pythiques [pitik] *Antiq* ADJ MPL **Jeux p.** Pythian Games
❑ **Pythiques** NFPL **les P.** the Pythians, the Pythian Odes (of Pindar)

python [pitɔ̃] NM *Zool* python; **p. molure** Indian python; **p. réticulé** reticulated python

pythonisse [pitɔnis] NF **1** *Antiq* pythoness **2** *Littéraire (prophétesse)* prophetess, (female) soothsayer

pyurie [pjyri] NF *Méd* pyuria

pyxide [piksid] NF **1** *(boîte à couvercle)* pyxis **2** *Rel* pyx **3** *Bot* pyxidium, pyxis

Q, q¹ [ky] NM INV *(lettre)* Q, q; **Q comme quintal** ≃ Q for Quentin

q² *(abrév écrite* **quintal***)* q

qanun [kanun] NM *Mus* qanun *(traditional trapezoidal-shaped zither used in Arab music)*

qaraïte [karait] = **karaïte**

qasida [kasida] NF *Littérature* qasida

qat [kat] NM khat

Qatar [katar] NM **le Q.** Qatar, Katar; **vivre au Q.** to live in Qatar; **aller au Q.** to go to Qatar

QCM [kyseɛm] NM *(abrév* **questionnaire à choix multiple***)* multiple-choice questionnaire

QG [kyʒe] NM *(abrév* **quartier général***)* HQ

QHS [kyaʃɛs] NM *(abrév* **quartier de haute sécurité***)* high-security *or* top-security wing

QI [kyi] NM *Psy (abrév* **quotient intellectuel***)* IQ

qibla [kibla] NF INV kiblah, qibla

Qom [kɔm] NF Qom, Qum

qsp *(abrév écrite* **quantité suffisante pour***)* qs

QSR [kyesɛr] NM *(abrév* **quartier de sécurité renforcée***)* high-security *or* top-security wing

quad [kwad] NM **1** *(moto)* quad bike; *(sport)* quad biking; **faire du q.** to go quad biking **2** *(patin à roulettes)* quad (roller) skate

quadra [kwadra, kadra] *Fam (abrév* **quadragénaire***)* ADJ quadragenarian■; **être q.** to be in one's forties■

  NMF *(personne)* person in his/her forties■; **c'est un q.** he's in his forties

quadragénaire [kwadraʒenɛr, kadraʒenɛr] ADJ quadragenarian; **être q.** to be in one's forties

  NMF person in his/her forties, quadragenarian; **un sémillant q.** a dashing forty-year-old

quadragésimal, -e, -aux, -ales [kwadraʒezimal, -o, kadraʒezimal, -o] ADJ quadragesimal, Lenten

quadragésime [kwadraʒezim, kadraʒezim] NF Quadragesima (Sunday)

quadrangle [kwadrãgl, kadrãgl] NM *Géom* quadrangle

quadrangulaire [kwadrãgylɛr, kadrãgylɛr] ADJ *(figure)* quadrangular, four-angled; *(tour, bâtiment)* four-sided

quadrant [kwadrã, kadrã] NM *Géom* quadrant

quadratique [kwadratik, kadratik] ADJ **1** *Math* quadratic **2** *Minér* tetragonal; **système q.** tetragonal system

quadrature [kwadratyr, kadratyr] NF **1** *Géom* quadrature, squaring; **q. du cercle** squaring the circle; **c'est la q. du cercle** it's like trying to square a circle *or* to get a quart into a pint pot **2** *Astron* quadrature **3** *Math* integration

quadrette [kwadrɛt, kadrɛt] NF team of four bowls players

quadri [kwadri, kadri] NF **1** *(quadriphonie)* quadraphony, quadraphonics *(singulier)* **2** *(quadrichromie)* four-colour processing *or* printing

quadricentenaire [kwadrisãtənɛr, kadrisãtənɛr] NM quadricentennial

quadriceps [kwadrisɛps] NM *Anat* quadriceps

quadrichromie [kwadrikrɔmi, kadrikrɔmi] NF four-colour processing *or* printing

quadridimensionnel, -elle [kwadridimãsjɔnɛl, kadridimãsjɔnɛl] ADJ four-dimensional

quadriennal, -e, -aux, -ales [kwadrijenal, -o, kadrijenal, -o] ADJ quadrennial, four-year *(avant n)*; **les jeux Olympiques sont quadriennaux** the Olympic Games take place every four years

quadrifide [kwadrifid] ADJ *Bot* quadrifid

quadrige [kwadriʒ, kadriʒ] NM *Antiq* quadriga

quadrijumeaux [kwadriʒymo, kadriʒymo] ADJ MPL *Anat* **tubercules q.** quadrigeminal bodies, corpora quadrigemina

  NMPL *Biol* quadruplets

quadrilatéral, -e, -aux, -ales [kwadrilateral, -o, kadrilateral, -o] ADJ *Géom* quadrilateral, four-sided

quadrilatère [kwadrilatɛr, kadrilatɛr] ADJ *Géom* quadrilateral

  NM *Géom & Mil* quadrilateral

quadrillage [kadrijaʒ] NM **1** *(réseau)* grid; **q. international** standard grid; **q. des rues** grid arrangement *or* layout of streets

  2 *(tracé)* grid *or* criss-cross pattern; **pour dessiner, tu peux utiliser le q. de ton cahier** you can use the squares on your exercise-book to do your drawing

  3 *(division)* division; **q. administratif** division into administrative areas; **q. hospitalier** hospital area division

  4 *(contrôle)* surveillance; **les gangsters se sont enfuis malgré le q. mis en place par la police** the gangsters got away despite the tight police controls

  5 *(sur une carte)* grid, graticule

quadrille [kadrij] NM quadrille; **le q. des lanciers** the lancers

quadrillé, -e [kadrije] ADJ squared, cross-ruled

quadriller [3] [kadrije] VT **1** *(papier)* to criss-cross, to mark into squares

  2 *(surveiller)* to put under tight surveillance; **la police quadrille le quartier** police presence is heavy in the district; **tout le quartier est quadrillé** the whole district is under tight surveillance

  3 *(être réparti sur)* to be scattered about *or* dotted over; **les pylônes quadrillent la région** pylons criss-cross *or* are dotted all over the area

quadrilobe [kwadrilɔb, kadrilɔb] NM *Archit* quatrefoil

quadrimestriel, -elle [kadrimɛstrijɛl] ADJ four-monthly

  NM = publication appearing every four months

quadrimoteur [kwadrimɔtœr, kadrimɔtœr] ADJ M four-engined

  NM four-engined plane

quadriparti, -e [kwadriparti, kadriparti] = **quadripartite**

quadripartite [kwadripartit, kadripartit] ADJ **1** *Bot* quadripartite **2** *(conférence, commission)* quadripartite; **réunion q.** *(de groupements)* quadripartite meeting; *(de pays)* meeting between four countries; *(de partis)* four-party meeting

quadriphonie [kwadrifɔni, kadrifɔni] NF quadraphony, quadraphonics *(singulier)*

quadriplégie [kwadripleʒi] NF *Méd* quadriplegia, tetraplegia

quadripolaire [kwadripɔlɛr, kadripɔlɛr] ADJ *Élec* quadripolar

quadripôle [kwadripol, kadripol] NM *Élec* quadripole

quadrique [kwadrik, kadrik] *Math* ADJ quadric

  NF quadric (curve)

quadriréacteur [kwadrireaktœr, kadrireaktœr] ADJ M four-engined

  NM four-engined plane *or* jet

quadrirème [kwadrirɛm, kadrirɛm] NF *Antiq* quadrireme

quadrisyllabe [kwadrisilab] NM quadrisyllable, tetrasyllable

quadrisyllabique [kwadrisilabik] ADJ quadrisyllabic, tetrasyllabic

quadrivalent, -e [kwadrivalã, -ãt, kadrivalã, -ãt] ADJ *Chim* quadrivalent, tetravalent

quadrumane [kwadryman, kadryman] *Zool* ADJ quadrumanous, four-handed

  NM quadrumane; **les quadrumanes** the quadrumana

quadrupède [kwadrypɛd, kadrypɛd] ADJ quadruped, quadrupedal, four-footed

  NM quadruped

quadruple [kwadrypl, kadrypl] ADJ **1** *(à quatre éléments)* quadruple; **un q. meurtre** a quadruple murder; **un q. rang de perles** four rows *or* a quadruple row of pearls; **en q. exemplaire** in quadruplicate

  2 *Mus* **q. croche** *Br* hemidemisemiquaver, *Am* sixty-fourth note

  NM quadruple; **le q. (de)** *(quantité, prix)* four times as much (as); *(nombre)* four times as many (as); **douze est le q. de trois** twelve is four times three; **j'ai gagné 100 euros et le vendeur le q.** I earned 100 euros and the seller four times that; **elle gagne le q. de ce que je gagne** she earns four times as much as I do

quadrupler [3] [kwadryple, kadryple] VI to increase fourfold, to quadruple; **ses revenus ont quadruplé depuis l'année dernière** his/her income has increased fourfold *or* quadrupled since last year, he/she earns four times more than he/she did last year; **la peur du conflit a fait q. les ventes de boîtes de conserve** fears of war pushed sales of tinned food up by 400 percent

  VT to increase fourfold, to quadruple

quadruplés, -ées [kwadryple, kadryple] NM,F PL quadruplets, quads

quadruplet [kwadryplɛ, kadryplɛ] NM *Math* quadruplet, quadruple, tetrad

quadruplex [kwadryplɛks, kadryplɛks] ADJ INV quadruplex

  NM INV **1** *Tél* quadruplex system **2** *Can (habitation)* = residence divided into four apartments, *Am* quadruplex

quai [kɛ] NM **1** *(d'une gare)* platform; **le train est à q.** the train is in; **arrivée du train q. numéro 5** train arriving on platform 5; **accès aux quais** *(sur panneau)* to the trains

  2 *Naut* quay, wharf; **arriver** *ou* **venir à q.** to berth; **le navire est à q.** the ship has berthed; *Com* **livrable à q.** *(marchandises)* ex-quay, ex-wharf; **droit de q.** wharfage; **q. de chargement** loading platform; **q. de déchargement** offloading platform; **q. d'embarquement** loading platform

  3 *(berge)* bank, embankment; **sur les quais de la Seine** on the banks of the Seine

  4 *(rue bordant un fleuve)* street; **prendre les quais** to drive along the river *(in a town)*; **le Q.** *(le Quai d'Orsay)* the (French) Foreign Ministry; *(le Quai des Orfèvres)* Police Headquarters *(in Paris)*

  5 *Tech* platform

'**Quai des brumes**' *Carné* 'Port of Shadows'

quaker, -eresse [kwɛkœr, kwɛkrɛs] NM,F Quaker, *f* Quakeress; **les quakers** the Quakers, the Society of Friends

quakerisme [kwɛkœrism] NM Quakerism

qualifiable [kalifjabl] **ADJ 1** *Sport (athlète, concurrent)* liable to qualify **2** *(descriptible)* **sa conduite n'est pas q.** his/her behaviour is indescribable; **les atrocités qu'ils ont commises ne sont pas qualifiables** there are no words to describe the atrocities they committed

qualifiant, -e [kalifjɑ̃, -ɑ̃t] **ADJ** leading to a qualification

qualificatif, -ive [kalifikatif, -iv] **ADJ** qualifying
NM 1 *(mot)* term, word; **il n'y a pas de q. assez fort pour la décrire** there's no word strong enough to describe her; **ce q. suave ne lui convient guère!** he/she hardly deserves to be described in such a pleasant way! **2** *Gram* qualifier, modifier

qualification [kalifikasjɔ̃] **NF 1** *(formation)* qualification, skill; **elle n'a aucune q. pour s'occuper d'enfants** she's not qualified to look after children; **sans q.** unskilled; **il n'a pas les qualifications requises pour ce poste** he's not qualified *or* he hasn't got the right qualifications for this job; **q. professionnelle** professional qualification
2 *Sport* preliminary, qualifying; **obtenir sa q.** to qualify; **leur q. est assurée** they are sure to qualify; **épreuves/match de q.** qualifying heats/match
3 *(appellation)* name; **la q. de faussaire paraît exagérée** the term forger seems a bit extreme
4 *Jur* legal definition
5 *Bourse* qualification *(by acquisition of shares)*

qualificative [kalifikativ] *voir* **qualificatif**

qualifié, -e [kalifje] **ADJ 1** *(compétent)* skilled, qualified; **elle est qualifiée pour remplir cette tâche** she's qualified to do this task; **je suis certainement q. pour en parler** I am certainly qualified to speak about it; **un professeur q.** a qualified teacher; **non q. pour** ineligible for **2** *Sport (choisi)* qualifying; **les joueurs qualifiés** the qualifying players **3** *Jur* aggravated

qualifier [9] [kalifje] **VT 1** *(appeler)* **q. qn/qch de...** to describe sb/sth as...; **il qualifie tout le monde de snob** he calls *or* dubs everybody a snob; **un incident que l'ambassade qualifie de grave** an incident described as serious by the embassy; **je ne sais comment q. son attitude** I don't know how to describe his/her attitude
2 *(professionnellement)* to qualify; **son expérience la qualifie parfaitement pour ce poste** her experience qualifies her perfectly for this job
3 *Sport* to qualify
4 *Ling* to qualify, to modify
►**se qualifier VPR 1 se q. de...** *(se dire)* to call oneself...; **elle se qualifie volontiers d'artiste** she likes to call herself an artist
2 *(être choisi)* to qualify; **se q. pour la finale** to qualify for *or* to get through to the final

qualitatif, -ive [kalitatif, -iv] **ADJ** qualitative; **d'un point de vue q.** from a qualitative point of view

qualitativement [kalitativmɑ̃] **ADV** qualitatively

qualitativiste [kalitativist] **NMF** *Mktg* market researcher

qualité [kalite] **NF 1** *(côté positif → d'une personne)* quality, virtue; *(→ d'une chose)* good point, positive feature; **elle a beaucoup de qualités** she has many (good) qualities; **elle n'a pas que des qualités** she isn't all good; **les qualités et les défauts** good and bad qualities; **qualités morales/intellectuelles** moral/intellectual qualities; **qualités de cœur** human qualities; **avoir des qualités de cœur** to have a good heart; **q. marchande** merchantable quality; **qualités relationnelles** interpersonal skills
2 *(propriété)* quality, property; **cette plante a des qualités laxatives** this plant has laxative properties; **q. substantielle** *(d'un objet)* fundamental characteristic
3 *(niveau)* quality, grade; **q. ordinaire** standard *or* regular grade; **q. médiocre** poor quality; **q. inférieure** low grade; **de q. inférieure, de mauvaise q.** low-quality, poor-quality; **de q. supérieure** good-quality, high-quality; **de bonne q.** quality, good-quality; **de première q.** *(gén)* top-quality, first-rate; *(viande)* prime; **la q. de l'impression est insuffisante/bonne** the quality of the printing is inadequate/good; **10 points pour la q. artistique** 10 points for artistic merit; **un pneumologue de sa q. devrait le savoir** a lung specialist of his/her calibre should know; **q. de vie** quality of life; *Mktg* **q. perçue** perceived quality; *Com* **q. totale** total quality management
4 *(statut)* position; *Jur* quality, capacity; **nom, prénom, âge et q.** surname, first name, age and occupation; **avoir q. pour faire qch** *(être habilité)* to be entitled to do sth; *(être capable)* to be qualified to do sth; **qui a q. pour décider, ici?** who's entitled *or* empowered to decide around here?
5 *(valeur supérieure)* quality; **la q. et la quantité** quality and quantity; **la q. se paie** you get what you pay for
6 *Ordinat* **q. brouillon** draft quality; **q. courrier** (near) letter quality; **q. d'impression** print quality
7 *Phil* quality
8 *Élec & Tél* **facteur de q.** quality factor
❑ **qualités NFPL** *(mérites)* skills, qualities; **pensez-vous avoir les qualités requises?** do you think you've got the required skills?; **nous l'avons choisi pour ses qualités de gestionnaire** we chose him for his managerial skills
❑ **de qualité ADJ 1** *(de luxe)* quality *(avant n)*, high-standard; **vêtements de q.** quality clothes; **un immeuble de q. dans un cadre agréable** a luxury residence in pleasant surroundings
2 *Vieilli (noble)* **gens de q.** gentlefolk, people of quality
❑ **en qualité de PRÉP en q. de tuteur, je peux intervenir** (in my capacity) as guardian, I can intervene; **en ma q. de chef de l'opposition, je...** as leader of the opposition, I...
❑ **ès qualités ADV** *Admin & Jur* in one's official capacity; **le ministre n'est pas intervenu ès qualités, mais à titre personnel** the minister intervened in a personal rather than an official capacity

qualiticien, -enne [kalitisjɛ̃, -ɛn] **NM,F** *(dans une entreprise)* quality maintenance manager *or* officer

QUAND [kɑ̃] **CONJ 1** *(lorsque)* when; **réveille-moi q. tu partiras** wake me when you leave; **q. tu le verras, demande-lui de me téléphoner** when you see him, ask him to ring me; **elle venait de partir q. il arriva** she had just left when he arrived; **je te donnerai une réponse q. j'aurai reçu sa lettre** I'll give you a reply when I get his/her letter; **je le préfère q. il est de bonne humeur** I prefer him when he's in a good mood; **q. j'ai le temps, j'aime bien aller au cinéma** when I have the time, I like to go to the *Br* cinema *or Am* movies; **q. je te disais qu'il serait en retard!** I TOLD you he'd be late!; **q. je pense à l'argent que j'ai dépensé!** when I think *or* to think of the money I spent!; *Fam* **q. il n'y en a plus il y en a encore** there's plenty more where that came from; *Prov* **q. le vin est tiré, il faut le boire** you've made your bed, now you must lie in it
2 *(alors que)* when; **elle se promène q. elle doit garder la chambre** she's up and about when she should be in bed; **pourquoi rester enfermé q. il fait si beau dehors?** why stay cooped up when it's so lovely outside?; **pourquoi rester ici q. on pourrait partir en week-end?** why stay here when we could go away for the weekend?
3 *(introduisant une hypothèse)* even if; **q. il serait le plus riche des hommes, elle n'en voudrait pas** even if he were the richest man in the world, she wouldn't want to have anything to do with him; **et q. ce serait, j'ai bien le droit de rêver** even if that is the case, I'm allowed to dream, aren't I?
ADV when; **q. travaille-t-il?** when does he work?; **q. viendras-tu nous voir?** when will you come and visit us?; **je ne sais pas encore q. je pars** I don't know when I'm leaving yet; **depuis q. es-tu là?** how long have you been here?; **à q. le mariage?** when's the wedding?; **c'est pour q., ce mariage?** when is this wedding going to happen?; **jusqu'à q. restez-vous?** until when *or* how long are you staying?; *Fam* **q. est-ce que tu y vas?** when are you going there?
❑ **quand bien même CONJ** even if; **j'irai, q. bien même je devrais y aller à pied!** I'll go, even if I have to go on foot!
❑ **quand même CONJ** even though, even if; **q. même tu lui dirais vingt fois, elle oublierait toujours** even if you told her twenty times, she would still forget **ADV 1** *(malgré tout)* all the same, even so; **c'était q. même bien** it was still good, it was good all the same; **je pense qu'il ne viendra pas, mais je l'inviterai q. même** I don't think he'll come but I'll invite him all the same **2** *(en intensif)* **tu pourrais faire attention q. même!** you really should be more careful!

---

quant [kɑ̃] **quant à PRÉP** as for *or* to; **q. aux photos, je ne les ai même jamais vues** as for the photographs, I never even saw them; **q. à la publication de l'ouvrage, elle devrait avoir lieu en juin** as for *or* regarding the publication of the work, it should take place in June; **je partage votre opinion q. à ses capacités** I share your opinion about his/her ability; **q. à moi** as for me, for my part, as far as I am concerned; **q. à vous, tenez-vous tranquilles** as for you, just keep quiet; **q. à ce que vous nous proposez...** as for your proposal...; **q. à le faire vraiment, c'est une autre histoire** as for actually doing it *or* as far as actually doing it is concerned, that's quite another matter

quanta [kwɑ̃ta] *pl de* **quantum**

quant-à-soi [kɑ̃taswa] **NM INV rester** *ou* **se tenir sur son q.** to remain distant *or* aloof; **chacun reste sur son q.** everyone remains aloof

quantième [kɑ̃tjɛm] **NM** day (and date) of the month; **la lettre ne spécifie pas le q. du mois pour la livraison** the letter doesn't specify what day of the month delivery is to be made; *Jur* **dû le jour ayant le même q.** due on the same day and date

quantifiable [kɑ̃tifjabl] **ADJ** quantifiable

quantificateur [kɑ̃tifikatœr] **NM** *Math* quantifier

quantification [kɑ̃tifikasjɔ̃] **NF 1** *(gén) & Phil* quantification **2** *Phys* quantization

quantifié, -e [kɑ̃tifje] **ADJ** *Phys* quantized; **grandeur quantifiée** quantized magnitude

quantifier [9] [kɑ̃tifje] **VT 1** *(gén) & Phil* to quantify **2** *Phys* to quantize

quantique [kwɑ̃tik, kɑ̃tik] **ADJ** *(mécanique, nombre, théorie)* quantum
NF quantum mechanics *(singulier)*

quantitatif, -ive [kɑ̃titatif, -iv] **ADJ 1** *(concernant la quantité)* quantitative; **évaluation quantitative des résultats des tests** quantitative analysis of test results **2** *(reposant sur des statistiques)* quantitative; **l'histoire quantitative** quantitative history **3** *Ling* quantitative; **terme q.** quantifier

quantitativement [kɑ̃titativmɑ̃] **ADV** quantitatively

quantité [kɑ̃tite] **NF 1** *(mesure)* amount, quantity; **quelle q. de lessive faut-il mettre?** how much detergent do you have to put in?; **petites quantités de peinture/vitamines** small amounts of paint/doses of vitamins; **une q. de, des quantités de** lots of, a lot of, a great many; **il y a une q.** *ou* **des quantités de boîtes en carton dans le couloir** there are a lot of cardboard boxes in the corridor; **il n'en reste pas des quantités** there aren't a lot left; **en grande/petite q.** in large/small quantities; **acheter qch en grande q.** to buy sth in bulk; *Fam* **une q. industrielle de** masses and masses of, heaps and heaps of; **en quantités industrielles** in industrial quantities; *Com* **q. économique de commande** economic order quantity; *Écon* **q. d'équilibre** equilibrium quantity
2 *Phys (grandeur)* quantity; **q. constante/variable** constant/variable quantity; **q. d'électricité** quantity *or* charge of electricity; **q. de lumière** quantity of light; **q. de mouvement** linear momentum
3 *Phil & Ling* quantity
4 *(locutions)* **tenir qn/qch pour q. négligeable** to disregard sb/sth; **traiter qn/qch comme une q. négligeable** to treat sb/sth as unworthy of consideration; **il considère mon avis comme q. négligeable** he doesn't care a jot for my opinion
❑ **en quantité ADV du vin/des prix en q.** lots of wine/prizes; **il y avait du saumon en q. dans le torrent** there was plenty of salmon in the stream
❑ **quantité de DÉT** a great many, lots of; **q. de femmes vous diront que...** a large number of women will tell you that...; **elle trouve q. de**

raisons pour ne pas le faire she finds any number *or* lots of reasons not to do it

quanton [kwãtɔ̃, kãtɔ̃] NM *Phys* quanton

quantum [kwãtɔm] (*pl* **quanta** [-ta]) NM **1** *Math & Phys* quantum; **théorie des quanta** quantum theory **2** (*montant*) amount; **q. des dommages et intérêts** sum of damages **3** (*proportion*) proportion, ratio

quaquaversal, -e, -aux, -ales [kwakwavɛrsal, -o] ADJ *Géol* quaquaversal

quarantaine [karãtɛn] NF **1** (*quantité*) une q. around *or* about forty, forty or so; **une q. de voitures** around *or* about forty cars; **elle a une q. d'années** she's around *or* about forty (years old)

2 (*âge*) **avoir la q.** to be around *or* about forty; **les problèmes typiques de la q.** the typical problems of the fortysomething generation; **quand on arrive à** *ou* **atteint la q.** when you hit forty

3 *Méd & Vét* (*isolement*) quarantine

4 *Bot* annual *or* hairy stock

□ **en quarantaine** ADJ **1** *Méd & Vét* in quarantine **2** *Fig* excluded, ostracized ▪ **mettre en q.** to quarantine; *Fig* to ostracize, to exclude

quarante [karãt] ADJ **1** (*gén*) forty; **elle a q. de fièvre** she has a temperature of forty (degrees); **en q.** (*en 1940*) in 1940

2 (*dans des séries*) fortieth; **page/numéro q.** page/number forty; *Can* **vieux comme l'an q.** ancient, as old as the hills

PRON forty

NM INV **1** (*gén*) forty; **les Q.** = the members of the Académie française

2 (*numéro d'ordre*) number forty

3 (*chiffre écrit*) forty

4 (*au tennis*) forty; **q. partout** deuce; *voir aussi* **cinquante**

quarante-huitard, -e [karãtɥitar, -ard] (*mpl* **quarante-huitards**, *fpl* **quarante-huitardes**) *Hist* ADJ of the revolution of 1848

NM revolutionary of 1848

quarantenaire [karãtnɛr] ADJ **1** (*qui dure quarante ans*) forty-year (*avant n*)

2 *Méd* quarantine (*avant n*); (*maladie*) *Br* notifiable, *Am* quarantinable

NMF (*personne*) quarantined person

NM (*lieu*) quarantine

NF (*maladie*) *Br* notifiable *or* *Am* quarantinable disease

quarantième [karãtjɛm] ADJ fortieth

NMF **1** (*personne*) fortieth **2** (*objet*) fortieth (one)

NM **1** (*partie*) fortieth **2** (*étage*) *Br* fortieth floor, *Am* forty-first floor **3** *Naut* **les quarantièmes rugissants** the roaring forties; *voir aussi* **cinquième**

quarantièmement [karãtjɛmmã] ADV in fortieth place

quark [kwark] NM *Phys* quark

quart¹ [kar] NM **1** (*quatrième partie*) quarter; **5 est le q. de 20** 5 is a quarter of 20; **un q. de beurre** a quarter (of a pound) of butter; **un q. de la tarte** one quarter of the tart; **un q. de cidre** a quarter (of a litre) of cider; **un kilo un q.** a kilo and a quarter, one and a quarter kilos; **un q. de cercle** (*gén*) a quarter (of a) circle; *Géom* a quadrant; **q. de finale** quarter final; **un q. de tour** a quarter turn; **démarrer** *ou* **partir au q. de tour** to start first go; *Fam* **le débat a démarré au q. de tour** the debate took off right away; *Fam* **il a réagi au q. de tour** he reacted straight away; *Fam* **elle a compris au q. de tour** she understood straight off *or* right away; *Fam* **au q. de poil** perfectly▪; **le frigo rentre au q. de poil** the fridge just fits▪

2 *Mus* **q. de soupir** *Br* semiquaver rest, *Am* sixteenth rest; **q. de ton** quarter tone

3 (*quinze minutes*) *Br* quarter of an hour, *Am* quarter hour; **l'horloge sonne tous les quarts** the clock chimes on the quarter of every hour; **c'est le q. qui sonne** that's the bell for quarter past; **une heure et q.**, **une heure un q.**, *Belg* **une heure q.** a quarter past one; **une heure moins le q.**, *Belg* **une heure moins q.** a quarter to one; *Fam* **viens au q.** get here at a quarter past; *Fam* **j'étais là à moins le q.** I was there at a quarter to

4 (*petite quantité*) fraction; **il dit cela mais il**

n'en pense pas le q. that's what he says but he doesn't really mean it

5 *Naut* (*garde*) watch; (*aire de vent*) rhumb; **prendre le q.** to take the watch; **être de q.** to be on watch *or* duty; **officier de q.** officer of the watch; **homme de q.** watch keeper; **petit q.** dogwatch; **grand q.** six-hour (evening) watch

6 (*bouteille ou pichet*) quarter litre

7 (*gobelet*) (quarter litre) mug *or* beaker

8 *Fam* **q. de brie** (*nez*) beak, *Br* conk, hooter

quart², -e¹ [kar, kart] ADJ *Vieilli* fourth

quartager [17] [kartaʒe] VT *Agr* to plough a fourth time

quartanier, quartannier [kartanje] NM = four-year-old wild boar

quart-arrière [kararjɛr] (*pl* **quart-arrières**) NMF *Can* quarterback

quartaut [karto] NM quarter cask

quart-bouillon [karbujɔ̃] NM *Hist* **pays de q.** = region in France which enjoyed the right to free salt production, subject to paying the equivalent of a quarter of its production as duty to the crown

quart-de-finaliste [kardəfinalist] (*pl* **quart-de-finalistes**) NMF quarterfinalist

quart-de-pouce [kardəpus] (*pl* **quarts-de-pouce**) NM *Tex* thread counter, weaver's glass

quart-de-rond [kardərɔ̃] (*pl* **quarts-de-rond**) NM quarter-round, ovolo

quart d'heure [kardœr] (*pl* **quarts d'heure**) NM **1** (*quinze minutes*) *Br* quarter of an hour, *Am* quarter hour; **je suis resté un q. devant la porte** I stood at the door for *Br* a quarter of an hour *or Am* a quarter hour; **cela va te prendre au moins trois quarts d'heure** it'll take you at least three quarters of an hour

2 (*locutions*) *Belg* **le q. académique** = the quarter of an hour between the official and actual starting times of a lecture etc; **le q. américain** = the time when the girls can invite the boys to dance (at a party); *Fam* **passer un mauvais q.** to have a bad time of it; *Fam* **faire passer un mauvais q. à qn** to give sb hell; *Hum* **le q. de Rabelais** the hour of reckoning, the dreaded moment; **le dernier q.** the very last minutes; **tous les quarts d'heure** (*souvent*) every five minutes

quarte² [kart] NF voir **quart²**

NF **1** *Élec* quad **2** *Mus* fourth **3** *Escrime* quarte **4** *Cartes* quart

quarté [karte] NM *Courses de chevaux* = bet in which the punter predicts the first four horses to finish a race

quarteron, -onne [kartərɔ̃, -ɔn] NM,F (*métis*) quadroon

NM *Péj* (*petit nombre*) bunch, gang; **un q. de politiciens véreux** a bunch of shady politicians

quartet [kwartɛ] NM *Ordinat* fourbit byte

quartette [kwartɛt] NM *Mus* quartet, quartette

quartidi [kwartidi] NM *Hist* = fourth day of a tenday period in the Republican calendar

quartier [kartje] NM **1** (*partie d'une ville*) district, area; *Admin* district; **le q. des affaires** the business district; **le q. juif** the Jewish quarter *or* area; **le q. chinois** Chinatown; **le q.** (*le voisinage*) the neighbourhood; **tout le q. en parle** the whole neighbourhood is talking about it; **je ne suis pas du q.** I'm not from around here; **demandez aux gens du q.** ask the locals *or* the local people; **q. commerçant** shopping area; **les beaux quartiers** the fashionable districts; **les bas quartiers** the less salubrious parts of town; **les quartiers nord de la ville** the north side of (the) town; **les vieux quartiers** the old town *or* quarter (of town); **le Q. latin** the Latin Quarter (*area on the Left Bank of the Seine traditionally associated with students and artists*)

2 *Mil* quarters; **le q. est à l'autre bout de la ville** the barracks are on the other side of the town; *aussi Fig* **q. général** headquarters; **la bande a établi son q. général près de la gare** the gang set up its headquarters near the station; **grand q. général** General Headquarters; **quartiers d'hiver** winter quarters; *Fig* **prendre ses quartiers d'hiver** to winter at *or* in; **avoir q. libre** *Mil* to be off duty; *Fig* to be free

3 (*partie d'une prison*) wing; **q. de haute sécurité** *ou* **de sécurité renforcée** high- *or* top-security wing; **q. de semi-liberté** semi-custodial

centre, semi-custodial wing (*from which prisoner may be released to engage in certain activities*)

4 (*quart*) quarter; (*morceau*) portion, section; **un q. de pomme** a quarter of an apple; **un q. d'orange** an orange segment; **un q. de bœuf** a quarter of beef; **cinquième q.** offal

5 *Astron* quarter; **la Lune est dans son premier/dernier q.** the Moon is in its first/last quarter

6 *Hér* quarter

7 (*degré de descendance noble*) **un prince à seize quartiers** = a prince of noble descent through all of his great-great-grandparents; **quartiers de noblesse** degree of noble descent; *Fig* **avoir ses quartiers de noblesse** to be well established

8 (*pitié*) mercy, quarter; *Vieilli* **demander q.** to ask for quarter; **l'armée victorieuse n'a pas fait de q.** the victorious army gave no quarter; **pas de q.!** no quarter!

9 (*d'une chaussure*) quarter; (*d'une selle*) (half) panel

10 *Zool* (*partie du sabot*) quarter

11 *Mines* (overseers) district

12 *Belg* (*appartement*) furnished one-bedroom *Br* flat *or* *Am* apartment

□ **de quartier** ADJ (*médecin, cinéma*) local

quartier-maître [kartjemɛtr] (*pl* **quartiers-maîtres**) NM **1** *Hist & Mil* quartermaster **2** *Naut* leading seaman

quartile [kwartil] NM *Math* quartile

quart-monde, quart monde [karmɔ̃d] (*pl* **quarts-mondes, quarts mondes**) NM **le q.** (*ensemble de pays*) the least developed countries, the Fourth World; (*dans un pays*) the poor

quarto [kwarto] ADV fourthly

quartz [kwarts] NM quartz

□ **à quartz** ADJ quartz (*avant n*)

quartzeux, -euse [kwartsø, -øz] ADJ quartz (*avant n*)

quartzifère [kwartsifɛr] ADJ *Minér* quartziferous

quartzite [kwartsit] NM *Minér* quartzite

quasar [kazar] NM *Astron* quasar

quasi [kazi] ADV = **quasiment**

NM chump end

quasi- [kazi] PRÉF quasi-, near, almost; **j'en ai la quasi-certitude** I'm virtually certain; **la quasitotalité du budget** almost the whole *or* entire budget; **la quasi-totalité des femmes** almost all (the) women

quasi-collision [kazikɔlizjɔ̃] (*pl* **quasi-collisions**) NF *Av* (*aérienne*) air miss

quasi-contrat [kazikɔ̃tra] (*pl* **quasi-contrats**) NM *Jur* quasi-contract, implied contract

quasi-cristal [kazikristal] (*pl* **quasi-cristaux** [-kristo]) NM *Phys* quasi-crystal

quasi-délit [kazideli] (*pl* **quasi-délits**) NM criminal negligence

quasi-espèces [kaziɛspɛs] NFPL cash equivalents

quasiment [kazimã] ADV *Fam* almost▪, practically▪; **attends-moi, j'ai q. fini** wait for me, I've nearly finished▪; **c'est q. la même chose** it's more or less the same▪; **je n'ai q. rien senti** I hardly *or* barely *or* scarcely felt a thing▪

Quasimodo [kazimɔdo] NF *Rel* Quasimodo, Low Sunday

NPR Quasimodo, the hunchback of Notre-Dame

quasi-monnaie [kazimɔnɛ] (*pl* **quasi-monnaies**) NF *Fin* near money, quasi-money

quasistellaire [kazistɛlɛr] ADJ *Astron* quasi-stellar

quasi-trésorerie [kazitrezɔrri] NF *Compta* cash equivalents

quasi-usufruit [kaziyzyfrɥi] NM *Jur* quasi-usufruct

quassia [kwasja, kasja], **quassier** [kwasje, kasje] NM *Bot* quassia (tree)

quater [kwater] ADV (*quatrièmement*) fourthly, in the fourth place

quaternaire [kwatɛrnɛr] ADJ **1** *Géol* Quaternary; **ère q.** Quaternary era **2** *Chim & Math* quaternary

NM *Géol* Quaternary (period)

quaterne [kwatɛrn] NM = group of four winning numbers on the same line (of a "Loto" ticket)

quaternion [kwatɛrnjɔ̃] NM *Math* quaternion

quatorze [katɔrz] ADJ **1** (*gén*) fourteen

2 (*dans des séries*) fourteenth; **page/numéro q.** page/number fourteen; **le 14 juillet** Bastille Day; **en q.** during World War I; **la guerre de q.**

World War I, the First World War; *Fam Hum*
c'est (re)parti comme en q.! once more into
the breach!
  PRON fourteen
  NM INV 1 *(gén)* fourteen
  2 *(numéro d'ordre)* number fourteen
  3 *(chiffre écrit)* fourteen; *voir aussi* **cinq**

quatorzième [katɔrzjɛm] **ADJ** fourteenth
  NMF 1 *(personne)* fourteenth **2** *(objet)* fourteenth (one)
  NM 1 *(partie)* fourteenth **2** *(étage) Br* fourteenth floor, *Am* fifteenth floor **3** *(arrondisse-*
  ment de Paris) fourteenth (arrondissement)
  NF *Mus* fourteenth; *voir aussi* **cinquième**

quatorzièmement [katɔrzjɛmmɑ̃] **ADV** in fourteenth place

quatrain [katrɛ̃] **NM** *Littérature* quatrain

quatre [katr] **ADJ 1** *(gén)* four; **les q. vertus**
cardinales the cardinal virtues
  2 *(dans des séries)* fourth; **page/numéro q.**
  page/number four
  3 *Aut* **4L** Renault 4; **4 × 4** = quatre-quatre
  4 *(locutions)* **il lui fallait se tenir à q. pour ne**
  pas rire/parler he/she had to bite his/her lip not
  to laugh/to bite his/her tongue not to speak; **il a**
  fait les q. cents coups dans sa jeunesse he
  sowed his wild oats when he was young; **cet**
  enfant fait les q. cents coups that child's a bit
  of a handful; **il n'y est pas allé par q. chemins**
  he came straight to the point *or* didn't beat
  about the bush; **aux q. coins de la chambre** in
  the four corners of the room; **ils viennent des q.**
  coins du monde they come from the four corners of the world; **jouer aux q. coins** = to run
  from one corner of a room to another trying to
  reach a corner before the player standing in the
  middle; **être tiré à q. épingles** to be immaculately dressed *or* dressed to the nines; *Fam* **les**
  q. fers en l'air flat on one's back; **il s'est re-**
  trouvé les q. fers en l'air he fell flat on his back;
  Fam **ton q. heures** your afternoon snack; **un de**
  ces q. matins, *Fam* **un de ces q.** one of these
  days; **être enfermé entre q. murs** to be shut
  away indoors; *Fam* **être entre q. planches** to be
  six feet under; **il a eu vite dépensé ses q. sous**
  he soon spent the little money he had; **ça ne**
  vaut pas q. sous it's not worth *Br* tuppence *or*
  Am a red cent; **une bague de q. sous** a cheap
  ring; **un hôtel de q. sous** a cut-price *or* low-rate
  hotel; *Littéraire* **les q. vents** *(les quatre points*
  cardinaux) the four points of the compass; **être**
  logé aux q. vents to live in a draughty old place;
  dire ses q. vérités à qn to tell sb a few home
  truths; **faire les q. volontés de qn** to pander to
  sb's every whim; **se mettre en q. pour qn** to go
  to no end of trouble *or* to bend over backwards
  for sb; **se mettre en q. pour faire qch** to go out of
  one's way to do sth
  PRON four
  NM INV 1 *(gén)* four
  2 *(numéro d'ordre)* number four
  3 *(chiffre écrit)* four
  4 *Cartes* four
  5 *(en aviron)* four; **q. de couple** quadruple; **q.**
  de pointe avec barreur coxed four; **q. de pointe**
  sans barreur coxless *or* straight four; *voir aussi*
  cinq
  ❑ **à quatre mains** *Mus* **morceau à q. mains**
  piece for four hands **ADV jouer à q. mains** to
  play a duet
  ❑ **à quatre pattes ADV** on all fours; **marcher à q.**
  pattes to walk on all fours; **se mettre à q. pattes**
  to go down on all fours
  ❑ **comme quatre ADV boire/manger/parler**
  comme q. to eat/to drink/to talk a lot; **avoir de**
  l'esprit comme q. to be a bit of a wit

'**Quatre Apôtres**' *Dürer* 'The Four Apostles'

'**Les 400 coups**' *Truffaut* 'The 400 Blows'

Quatre-Cantons [katrkɑ̃tɔ̃] **NMPL le lac des Q.**
Lake Lucerne

quatre-cent-vingt-et-un [katrəsɑ̃vɛ̃teœ̃] **NM INV** =
simple dice game usually played in cafés; the
loser pays for a round of drinks

quatre-de-chiffre [katrədəʃifr] **NM INV** *Chasse*
figure-four trap

quatre-épices [katrepis] **NM INV** allspice
quatre-feuilles [katrəfœj] **NM INV** *Archit* quatrefoil
quatre-mâts [katrəma] **NM INV** four-master
quatre-quarts [katkar] **NM INV** ≃ pound cake
  (without fruit)
quatre-quatre [katkatr] **ADJ INV** four-wheel drive
  NM INV OU NF INV four-wheel drive (vehicle), *Am*
  SUV
quatre-roues [katrəru] **NM INV** *Can (voiture à*
  cheval) buggy, gig; *(véhicule tout-terrain)* quad
  (bike)
quatre-saisons [katrəsɛzɔ̃] **NF INV** *(légume)*
  second-crop *or* second-cropping vegetable;
  (fruit) second-crop *or* second-cropping fruit;
  une fraise q. a second-crop *or* second-cropping strawberry, a perpetual-fruiting strawberry
quatre-temps [katrətɑ̃] **NMPL** *Rel* Ember days
quatre-vingt-dix [katrəvɛ̃dis] **ADJ 1** *(gén)* ninety
  2 *(dans des séries)* ninetieth; **page/numéro q.**
  page/number ninety
  PRON ninety
  NM INV 1 *(gén)* ninety
  2 *(numéro d'ordre)* number ninety
  3 *(chiffre écrit)* ninety
  4 *Fam (sur une voiture)* = sticker showing the
  maximum speed at which a new licence holder
  can drive a car; **pas étonnant, c'est un q.!** no
  wonder, he's only just passed his test!; *voir aussi*
  cinquante
quatre-vingt-dixième [katrəvɛ̃dizjɛm] *(pl* **qua-**
  tre-vingt-dixièmes) **ADJ** ninetieth
  NMF 1 *(personne)* ninetieth **2** *(objet)* ninetieth
  (one)
  NM 1 *(partie)* ninetieth **2** *(étage) Br* ninetieth
  floor, *Am* ninety-first floor; *voir aussi* **cinquième**
quatre-vingt-dixième ment [katrəvɛ̃dizjɛmmɑ̃]
  ADV in ninetieth place
quatre-vingtième [katrəvɛ̃tjɛm] *(pl* **quatre-ving-**
  tièmes) **ADJ** eightieth
  NMF 1 *(personne)* eightieth **2** *(objet)* eightieth
  (one)
  NM 1 *(partie)* eightieth **2** *(étage) Br* eightieth
  floor, *Am* eighty-first floor; *voir aussi* **cinquième**
quatre-vingtièmement [katrəvɛ̃tjɛmmɑ̃] **ADV** in
  eightieth place
quatre-vingts [katrəvɛ̃] **ADJ 1** *(gén)* eighty; **q.**
  personnes eighty people; **quatre-vingt-deux**
  eighty-two **2** *(dans des séries)* eightieth; **page/**
  numéro quatre-vingt page/number eighty
  PRON eighty
  NM INV 1 *(gén)* eighty **2** *(numéro d'ordre)* number eighty **3** *(chiffre écrit)* eighty; *voir aussi*
  cinquante
quatrième [katrijɛm] **ADJ** fourth; **le q. âge** *(pé-*
  riode) advanced old age; *(groupe social)* very
  old people
  NMF 1 *(personne)* fourth
  2 *(objet)* fourth (one)
  NM 1 *(partie)* fourth
  2 *(étage) Br* fourth floor, *Am* fifth floor
  3 *(arrondissement de Paris)* fourth (arrondissement)
  NF 1 *Scol Br* ≃ third year, *Am* ≃ eighth grade
  2 *Aut* fourth gear
  3 *(en danse)* fourth position; *voir aussi* **cin-**
  quième
  ❑ **en quatrième vitesse ADV** *Fam* in a hurry,
  at breakneck speed; **rapporte ce livre à la bi-**
  bliothèque, et en q. vitesse! take this book
  back to the library and be quick about it!; **j'ai**
  bu mon café en q. vitesse I drank my coffee in a
  rush

'**En quatrième vitesse**' *Aldrich* 'Kiss Me Deadly'

quatrièmement [katrijɛmmɑ̃] **ADV** fourthly, in
  fourth place

quatrillion [katriljɔ̃] **NM** *Br* quadrillion, *Am* septil-
  lion

quattrocentiste [kwatrɔtʃɛntist] **NMF** *Beaux-Arts*
  & Littérature quattrocentist

quattrocento [kwatrɔtʃɛnto] **NM** *Beaux-Arts & Lit-*
  térature quattrocento

quatuor [kwatɥɔr] **NM 1** *Mus* quartet; **q. à cordes/**
  vent string/wind quartet **2** *Can Fam (groupe)*
  foursome

quat'zarts [katzar] **NMPL bal des q.** = ball formerly organized at the end of the academic year by

the students of the four sections of the "École
Nationale des Beaux-Arts"

quat'zyeux [katzjø] **entre quat'zyeux ADV** *Fam* in
  private ∎

QUE [kə]

qu' is used instead of **que** before a word
beginning with a vowel or mute h.

En anglais, le pronom relatif objet peut être
omis. La conjonction **that** peut être omise
après les verbes d'opinion, ainsi que **say, know**
etc, p. ex. **je sais que c'est possible** I know
(that) it's possible.

ADV 1 *(combien, comme)* **q. tu es naïf!** you're so
  naive!, aren't you naive!; **q. de bruit ici!** it's so
  noisy here!, what a lot of noise there is in here!;
  q. d'assurance chez une femme si jeune! so
  much self-confidence in such a young woman!;
  q. de choses à faire dans une maison! there
  are so many things to do in a house!; **qu'il a un**
  grand nez! he's got such a big nose!; *Fam*
  qu'est-ce q. tu es bête! you're (ever) so stupid!;
  qu'est-ce q. c'est bon! it's delicious!, it's so
  good!; *Fam* **qu'est-ce qu'il m'a déçu!** he really
  disappointed me!; *Littéraire* **qu'avec plaisir je**
  vous revois! with what pleasure I behold you
  again!
  2 *(exprimant l'indignation)* **q. m'importent ses**
  états d'âme! what do I care about what he/she
  feels!
  3 *(pourquoi)* why; **q. ne l'as-tu (pas) dit plus**
  tôt! why didn't you say so earlier?, I wish you
  had said so *or* that earlier!; **q. viens-tu parler**
  de rendement? why on earth are you talking
  about productivity?
  PRON RELATIF 1 *(représente une personne)* who,
  that, *Sout* whom; **la fille qu'il a épousée** the girl
  (whom) he married; **sa sœur, q. je n'avais pas**
  vue depuis dix ans, était là aussi his/her sister, whom *or* who I hadn't seen for ten years,
  was there too; **le responsable q. j'ai vu** the official (whom) *or* that I saw; **la femme qu'elle était**
  devenue the woman (that) she'd become
  2 *(représente un animal)* which, that; **les che-**
  nilles q. les enfants ont rapportées the caterpillars (which) *or* that the children brought back
  3 *(représente une chose, une idée)* which, that; **le**
  contrat q. j'ai signé the contract (which) *or* that
  I signed; **la dernière lettre qu'il a écrite** the last
  letter (which) *or* that he wrote; **la chose la plus**
  drôle q. j'aie jamais entendue the funniest
  thing I've ever heard; **je ne suis pas la seule,**
  q. je sache I'm not the only one as far as I know
  4 *(pour souligner une caractéristique)* **malheu-**
  reux q. vous êtes! you unfortunate man!; **fati-**
  guée qu'elle était, elle continuait à l'aider
  tired though *or* as she was, she carried on helping him/her; **de timide qu'il était, il est devenu**
  expansif once a shy man, he's now an extrovert;
  Fam **toute jaune qu'elle était, l'eau!** the water
  was all yellow, really it was!; **en bon père/électri-**
  cien qu'il était being the good father/electri-
  cian he was; **bel exploit q. le sien!** what he's/
  she's done is quite a feat!; **drôles de gens q.**
  ces gens-là! strange people, those!; **une**
  chance, q. cette panne! very lucky, this breakdown!
  5 *(dans des expressions de temps, de durée)* **voi-**
  ci trois mois q. je ne joue plus it's three months
  since I stopped playing, I haven't played for three
  months; **ça fait deux heures q. j'attends** I've
  been waiting for two hours; **un jour q.…** one
  day when…; **un soir qu'il faisait très chaud**
  one very hot evening, one evening when the
  weather was very hot; **le temps q. tu te pré-**
  pares, il sera trop tard by the time you're ready
  it'll be too late; **il n'y a pas longtemps qu'elle**
  l'a vendu it wasn't long ago that she sold it; **il y**
  a bien longtemps q. je le sais I've known for a
  long time; **chaque fois q. je m'absente, il télé-**
  phone every time I'm out he phones; *Littéraire*
  du temps q. les bêtes parlaient at the time
  when animals could speak
  PRON INTERROGATIF 1 *(dans le discours direct)*
  what; **q. se passe-t-il?** what's happening?;

qu'y a-t-il? what's the matter?; **q. dis-tu?** what are you saying?; **q. devient-elle?** what's become of her?; **qu'est-ce q. ça veut dire?** what does it mean?; **qu'est-ce q. tu lis/fais?** what are you reading/doing?; **qu'est-ce q. je vois/j'entends?** *(ton menaçant ou humoristique)* what's this I see/hear?; **qu'est-ce qui t'arrive?** what's the matter with you?; **qu'est-ce q. la liberté?** what is freedom?; **qu'est-ce q. c'est q. cette horreur?** what's this monstrosity?

2 *(dans le discours indirect)* what; **je ne sais plus q. penser** I don't know what to think any more; **je ne sais q. devenir** I don't know what to do with myself

CONJ 1 *(après des verbes déclaratifs ou des verbes d'évaluation)* that; **je sais q. je peux le faire** I know (that) I can do it; **crois-tu qu'il se serait excusé?** do you think he'd have apologized?; **ne crains-tu pas qu'il oublie** *ou* **qu'il n'oublie?** aren't you afraid (that) he might forget?; **il est possible q. je revienne** I may come back; **il est surprenant qu'elle n'ait pas téléphoné** it's strange (that) she hasn't phoned; **il est fort dommage q. vous n'ayez pas été là** it's a real shame (that) you weren't there; **exigez qu'on vous indemnise** demand compensation *or* to be compensated; **je préférerais qu'on me laisse à l'écart de tout cela** I'd rather be left out of all this; **il dit qu'il était déçu** he said (that) he was disappointed; **elle murmura qu'elle devait s'en aller** she whispered that she had to go; **où il est dit q. la nature se suffit à elle-même** in which the reader learns that nature is sufficient unto itself

2 *(en début de proposition)* **q. leur fils ait fugué, cela ne devrait pas nous surprendre** the fact that their son ran away shouldn't come as a surprise to us; **q. vous ayez raison, c'est bien évident** it's quite obvious (that) you're right; **q. tu pleures ne changera rien** your *or* you crying won't change anything

3 *(et déjà)* than; **il n'a pas fini de lire un roman qu'il en commence un autre** no sooner has he finished one novel than he starts reading another

4 *(afin que)* so that; **approche-toi, q. je te voie mieux** come closer so that I can see you better; **parle plus fort, q. l'on t'entende** speak up so that we can hear you

5 *Fam (tellement que)* **elle tousse q. ça réveille tout le monde** she coughs so much (that) she wakes everybody up; **il est têtu q. ça en devient un vrai problème** he's so stubborn (that) it's a real problem; *Littéraire* **êtes-vous fou q. vous risquiez votre vie pour un inconnu?** are you so crazy that you're willing to risk your life for a stranger?

6 *Fam (parce que)* cos, coz; **ne viens pas, q. si je te vois je te tue!** don't come, coz if I see you I'll kill you!

7 *(suivi du subjonctif) (pour formuler un ordre, un souhait, une éventualité)* **qu'elle parle!** *(faites-la parler)* make her talk!; *(laissez-la parler)* let her speak!; **q. l'on apporte à boire!** bring some drinks!; **q. le bal commence!** let the dancing begin!; **eh bien, qu'il s'en aille s'il n'est pas content!** he can leave if he doesn't like it!; **q. Dieu nous pardonne** may God forgive us; **qu'il m'attaque et je dis tout** just let him (try and) attack me, and I'll reveal everything

8 *(dans une double hypothèse)* **il me l'interdirait q. je le ferais quand même** I would do it even if he forbade me to; **aurais-je le moyen d'y aller q. je n'en aurais pas envie** even had I the means of going, I still would not have the will

9 *(répète la conjonction précédente)* **quand je serai grande et q. j'aurai un métier** when I'm grown up and (I) have a job; **comme il l'aime/s'il l'aime et qu'elle l'aime...** as/if he loves her and she loves him...; **comme/puisque j'ai horreur de cuisiner et q. Pierre aussi...** as/since I hate cooking and Pierre (does) too...

10 *(formule de présentation et d'insistance)* **je croyais l'affaire faite et voilà qu'elle n'est pas d'accord** I thought the deal was clinched and now I find she disagrees; **si je n'ai rien dit, c'est q. je craignais de te vexer** if I said nothing, it

was because I was afraid of upsetting you; **q. oui!** oh yes indeed!; **q. non!** certainly not!; **tu n'iras pas – q. si!** you won't go – oh yes I will *or* I will too!; **tu ne le savais pas? – q. si!** didn't you know? – oh yes, I did!; *Fam* **q. tu crois/dis!** that's what YOU think/say!

11 *(dans une formule interrogative)* **est-ce q. tu viendras?** will you come?; *Fam* **comment qu'il a fait?** how did he manage?"; *Fam* **où qu'elle est partie?** where did she go (to)?"

12 *(suivi de "faire")* **je n'ai q. faire de vos souhaits** I don't want your good wishes; *Littéraire* **vous n'aviez q. faire de parler** you had no business to speak

□ **que... ne CONJ** without; **aucune décision n'est prise q. je ne sois préalablement consulté** no decision is made without my being consulted first

□ **que... ou non CONJ** whether... or not; **q. tu me croies ou non** whether you believe me or not

□ **que... (ou) que CONJ** whether... or; **q. je parte ou q. je reste** whether I go or (whether I) stay; **qu'il fasse beau, qu'il pleuve, je sors me promener** come rain or come shine, I go out for a walk

□ **que si CONJ** *Littéraire* if; **q. si vous savez la vérité, il est de votre devoir de la révéler** if you know the truth, it is your duty to reveal it

Québec [kebɛk] **NM 1** *(province)* **le Q.** Quebec; **au Q.** in Quebec; **la province de** *ou* **du Q.** Quebec State **2** *(ville)* Quebec; **à Q.** in (the city of) Quebec

québécisme [kebesism] **NM** Quebec French word/phrase

québécité [kebesite] **NF** Quebec identity

québécois, -e [kebekwa, -az] **ADJ** from Quebec **NM** *Ling* Quebec French

□ **Québécois, -e NM,F** Québecois, Quebecker

quebracho [kebratʃo] **NM** *Bot* quebracho

quebri [kəbri] **NF** *Anciennement Fam (verlan de brique)* ten thousand francs"

quechua [ketʃwa] **NM** *(langue)* Quechua

□ **Quechua NMF INV** Quechua; **les Q.** the Quechua

Queensland [kwinslãd] **NM le Q.** Queensland

quel, -elle [kɛl] **ADJ INTERROGATIF** *(personne)* which; *(animal, chose)* which, what; **quelle actrice serait capable de jouer ce rôle?** which actress could play this part?; **de q. côté es-tu?** which *or* whose side are you on?; **de q. magasin parlez-vous?** which shop are you talking about?; **je ne sais quels sont ses projets** I don't know what his/her plans are; **quelle heure est-il?** what's the time?, what time is it?; **quelle sorte d'homme est-ce?** what kind of man is he?

ADJ EXCLAMATIF what; **q. dommage!** what a pity!; **q. idiot!** what a fool!; **q. sale temps!** what terrible weather!; **q. talent chez ce peintre!** what talent this painter has!, what a talented painter!; **quelle bêtise d'avoir oublié le tire-bouchon!** how stupid to have forgotten the corkscrew!; **il s'est exprimé en japonais, et avec quelle aisance!** he spoke in Japanese, and so fluently too!; **si tu savais q. point il tient à cette montre** if you knew how fond he is of this watch; **quelle ne fut pas ma surprise (quand je le vis entrer)!** imagine my surprise (when I saw him come in)!; *Littéraire* **quelle audace que la vôtre!** what audacity on your part!

ADJ RELATIF *(en corrélation avec "que"* → *personne)* whoever; *(→ animal)* whichever; *(→ chose)* whichever, whatever; **il a refusé de recevoir les nouveaux arrivants, quels qu'ils fussent** he refused to see the new arrivals, whoever they were; **les mammifères quels qu'ils soient** all mammals; **quelle que soit**

l'assurance que vous choisissiez... whichever insurance policy you choose...; **quelle que soit mon affection pour elle** however great my affection for her, much as I love her; **il se baigne q. que soit le temps** he goes swimming whatever the weather

PRON INTERROGATIF which (one); **q. est le plus jeune des deux?** which one is the younger of the two?; **de tous vos matchs, q. fut le plus difficile?** of all the matches you've played, which (one) was the most difficult *or* which was the most difficult one?

quelconque [kɛlkɔ̃k] **ADJ INDÉFINI 1** *(quel qu'il soit)* any, some or other; **si, pour une raison q., tu ne pouvais pas venir** if, for some reason or other *or* if, for any reason, you can't come; **s'il y a un problème q.** if there is any problem (whatever); **je trouverai bien une excuse q.** I'll find some excuse or other; **une q. de ses connaissances** some acquaintance of his/hers; **as-tu une q. idée du prix?** have you got any idea of the price?; **a-t-il une chance q. de gagner?** has he got any chance *or* does he stand the slightest chance of winning?

2 *Math* any; **un quadrilatère q.** any quadrilateral figure; **un cercle passant par trois points quelconques** a circle passing through any three points

ADJ *(insignifiant, banal →* nourriture, visage*)* ordinary, plain; *(→* personne*)* average, ordinary; *(→* comédien, film, spectacle*)* run-of-the-mill, second-rate, (pretty) average; *(→* exécution, réalisation*)* mediocre, lacklustre; **on ne peut pas lui donner un emploi q.** we can't give him/her an ordinary job *or Fam* any old job; **moi, je le trouve très q.** I don't think there's anything special about him

quéléa [kelea] **NM** *Orn* quelea

quelle [kɛl] *voir* **quel**

quelles [kɛl] *voir* **quel**

QUELQUE [kɛlkə] **ADJ INDÉFINI 1** *(un peu de)* some; **j'ai eu q. peine à le reconnaître** I had some difficulty (in) recognizing him; **elle est bizarre depuis q. temps** she's been acting strangely for a time now *or* for some time now

2 *(n'importe quel)* some; **je trouverai bien q. prétexte** no doubt I'll think of some excuse (or other); **q. passant aura ramassé l'argent** some passer-by will have picked up the money; **il trouvera bien une q. autre excuse** he's bound to find some new excuse or other

3 *(en corrélation avec "que")* **dans q. pays que tu sois** whichever *or* whatever country you may be in; **à q. heure que ce soit** whatever the time, at whatever time

ADV 1 *(approximativement)* around, about; **il y a q. 40 ans de cela** that was about 40 years ago, that was 40 or so years ago

2 *(en corrélation avec "que")* **nous y arriverons, q. difficile que ce soit** we will manage, however difficult it may be

□ **quelques ADJ INDÉFINI 1** *(sans déterminant)* a few, some; **quelques jours plus tard** a few days later; **amène quelques amis** bring some *or* a few friends along; **quelques dizaines de journalistes** a few dozen journalists; *Fam* **ça pèse deux kilos et quelques** it's a little *or* a bit over two kilos; *Fam* **il était 5 heures et quelques** it was just after 5 o'clock; *Fam* **50 euros et quelques** just over 50 euros

2 *(avec déterminant)* few; **les quelques millions de téléspectateurs qui nous regardent** the few million viewers watching us; **elle n'a laissé que ces quelques vêtements** she only left these few clothes

□ **en quelque sorte ADV 1** *(en un sens)* as it were, so to speak, in a manner of speaking; **c'est en q. sorte un cheval avec un buste d'homme** it is, as it were *or* so to speak, a horse with the head and shoulders of a man

2 *(en résumé)* in a nutshell, in fact; **tu veux, en q. sorte, refaire le monde** in a nutshell *or* in fact, you want to set the world to rights

□ **quelque chose PRON INDÉFINI 1** *(dans une affirmation)* something; **elle a q. chose aux poumons** she's got something wrong with her lungs; **q. chose me dit que...** something tells me that..., I've got the feeling that...; **ça m'a fait q. chose de le revoir 20 ans plus tard** it was

really weird to see him 20 years later; **quand il est parti, ça m'a vraiment fait q. chose** when he left it really affected me; **q. chose de blanc/rouge** something white/red; **q. chose de beau** something beautiful; **elle a fait q. chose de bien** she did a very good thing, she did something very good; **il trouvera encore q. chose de pire à faire** he'll find (still) worse to do *or* something even worse to do

2 *(dans une question, une négation, une hypothèse)* anything, something; **tu veux q. chose à manger?** do you want something *or* anything to eat?; **s'il m'arrivait q. chose, contactez mon notaire** if anything *or* something should happen to me, contact my solicitor; **q. chose ne va pas?** is there anything wrong?, is there something wrong?, is anything the matter?; **ça te ferait vraiment q. chose si je partais?** would it really matter to you *or* would you feel anything if I left?; **tu n'as pas q. chose d'autre?** haven't you got something *or* anything else?

3 *Fam (dans une approximation)* **elle a q. chose comme 80 ans** she's about 80 *or* 80 or so; **c'était une Renault 5 ou q. chose comme ça** it was a Renault 5 or something (of the kind *or* like that); **elle est q. chose au parti socialiste** she's something in the Socialist Party; **Anne q. chose a téléphoné** Anne something *or* somebody phoned

4 *Fam (emploi expressif)* **il s'est viandé, q. chose de bien** he got smashed up something awful; **il lui a passé un savon, q. chose de bien** he gave him/her an almighty telling-off; **il tenait q. chose comme cuite!** he was totally plastered!; **il y a q. chose comme vent dehors** there's a terrible wind outside; **c'est q. chose!** *(ton exaspéré)* that's a bit much!; *(ton admiratif)* that's quite something!; **je t'ai dit trois fois de ranger ta chambre, c'est q. chose!** I've told you three times to tidy up your room, for God's sake!; **partie de rien, elle dirige l'entreprise, c'est q. chose, non?** she started from nothing and now runs the firm, quite something, eh?

❑ **quelque part** ADV **1** *(dans un lieu)* somewhere; **tu vas q. part à Noël?** are you going anywhere (special) for Christmas?

2 *Fam Euph (aux toilettes)* **elle est allée q. part** she went to powder her nose

3 *Fam Euph (au derrière)* **il a mal q. part** he's got a pain in his you-know-what; **c'est mon pied q. part que tu veux?** do you want a kick up the backside?; **elle lui a foutu un coup de genou q. part** *(dans les testicules)* she kneed him in the you-know-where *or* where it hurts most

❑ **quelque part que** CONJ *Littéraire* **q. part qu'elle regardât** wherever she looked

---

quelquefois [kɛlkəfwa] ADV sometimes, from time to time; **je vais q. au concert** sometimes *or* from time to time I go to concerts; **q., je me demande si j'ai raison d'insister** sometimes I wonder if I'm right to insist

quelques-uns, quelques-unes [kɛlkəzœ̃, -yn] PRON INDÉFINI **1** *(certains)* some; **q. parmi eux avaient beaucoup lu** some of them had read a lot; **q. de ses collaborateurs étaient au courant** some of his/her colleagues knew about it; **il y en a toujours q. pour se plaindre** certain *or* some people always complain

2 *(un petit nombre)* a few; **tu connais ses pièces? – seulement quelques-unes** do you know his/her plays? – only a few of them

quelqu'un, -e [kɛlkœ̃, -yn] PRON INDÉFINI *Littéraire (l'un, l'une)* **q. de** one of; **quelqu'une de ces demoiselles va vous conduire** one of these young ladies will show you the way

❑ **quelqu'un** PRON INDÉFINI **1** *(dans une affirmation)* someone, somebody; **q. devra le faire!** someone *or* somebody will have to do it!; **q. te demande au téléphone** there's someone *or* somebody on the phone for you; **demande à q. du village** ask one of the villagers, ask someone *or* somebody from the village; **q. de très grand est venu** someone *or* somebody very tall called; **q. de frisé/barbu** someone *or* somebody with curly hair/a beard; **c'est q. de bien** he's a nice person; **tu peux lui parler, c'est q. de sûr** you can talk to him/her, he's/she's a reliable person; **il faut q. de plus** one more (person) is needed; **c'est q.!** *(ton admiratif)* he's/she's quite somebody!; *Péj* **ce garçon, c'est q.!** that boy's a little horror!; **elle veut devenir q. (dans le monde de l'art)** she wants to become someone famous (in the world of art); *Péj* **il se prend pour** *ou* **se croit q.** he thinks he's really something, he thinks he's it

2 *(dans une question, une négation, une hypothèse)* anyone, anybody; **il y a q.?** is (there) anyone *or* anybody in?; **si q. me demande** if someone *or* somebody *or* anyone *or* anybody asks for me; **y a-t-il eu q. de blessé?** was anyone *or* anybody *or* someone *or* somebody hurt?; **q. parmi vous le connaît-il?** do any of you know him?

quels [kɛl] *voir* **quel**

quémander [3] [kemɑ̃de] VT *(aide, argent, nourriture)* to beg for; *(compliment)* to fish *or* to angle for; **ton chien est toujours à q. des caresses** your dog is always wanting to be stroked; **q. qch auprès de qn** to beg for sth from sb

quémandeur, -euse [kemɑ̃dœr, -øz] NM,F *Littéraire (mendiant)* beggar

qu'en-dira-t-on [kɑ̃diratɔ̃] NM INV gossip; **elle a peur du q.** she's afraid of what people will say; **je me moque du q.** I don't care what people say

quenelle [kənɛl] NF *Culin* quenelle

quenotte [kənɔt] NF *Fam (dent d'un enfant)* tooth▪

quenouille [kənuj] NF **1** *Tex* distaff; *Hist* **tomber en q.** to fall to the distaff; *(échouer)* to go to rack and ruin **2** *(d'un lit)* bedpost **3** *Métal* stopper **4** *Bot (tige)* bulrush

❑ **quenouilles** NFPL *Can Fam Péj* long skinny legs▪, matchstick legs

quéquette [kekɛt] NF *Fam Br* willy, *Am* peter

quérable [kerabl] ADJ = that must be applied for or called for in person; *Assur* **primes quérables** premiums collected by the company's representatives

quercétine [kɛrsetin] NF *Chim* quercetin, quercitin

quercinois, -e [kɛrsinwa, -az] ADJ of/from Quercy

❑ **Quercinois, -e** NM,F = inhabitant of or person from Quercy

quercitrin [kɛrsitrɛ̃] NM *Chim* quercitrin

quercitrine [kɛrsitrin] NF *Chim* quercitrin

quercitron [kɛrsitrɔ̃] NM *Bot* quercitron (oak), dyer's oak

Quercy [kɛrsi] NM **le Q.** Quercy

quercynois, -e [kɛrsinwa, -az] = **quercinois**

querelle [kərɛl] NF quarrel; *(verbale)* quarrel, argument; **avoir une q. avec qn** to have a quarrel *or* a row with sb; **une vieille q.** a long-standing quarrel; **ce n'est qu'une q. d'amoureux** it's only a lovers' tiff; **q. de famille** *(brouille)* family squabble; *(sérieuse)* family feud; **q. d'ivrognes** drunken brawl; **la q. déclenchée au sein du gouvernement** the row sparked off within the cabinet; **vaines querelles** pointless squabbles; **q. d'Allemand, mauvaise q.** quarrel for quarrelling's sake; **q. de personnes** ad personam quarrel

quereller [4] [kərele] VT *Vieilli* to reprimand

▸**se quereller** VPR to quarrel (with one another); **elles se querellent pour des riens** they quarrel *or* squabble over nothing; **se q. avec qn** to have an argument *or* to quarrel with sb

querelleur, -euse [kərɛlœr, -øz] ADJ quarrelsome, belligerent; **il est très q.** he's always picking fights *or* looking for arguments

NM,F quarrelsome person

quérir [kerir] VT *Littéraire (à l'infinitif seulement)* **envoyer** *ou* **faire q. qn** to summon sb; **le roi le fit q.** the king bade him come; **venir/aller q. qn** to come/to go and fetch sb

quérulence [kerylɑ̃s] NF querulousness, whining

quérulent, -e [kerylɑ̃, -ɑ̃t] ADJ querulous, whining

quèsaco [kezako] ADV *Fam* what's that (thing)?▪

Que Sais-je? [kəsɛʒ] NM *(collection)* = series of informative paperbacks on a wide range of subjects

quesot [kəzo] NM *Élec* exhaust tube

qu'est-ce que [kɛskə], **qu'est-ce qui** [kɛski] *voir* **que** PRON INTERROGATIF

questeur [kɛstœr] NM **1** *Antiq* quaestor **2** *Pol* parliamentary administrator

question [kɛstjɔ̃] NF **1** *(interrogation)* question; **je ferme la porte à clé? – bien sûr, quelle** *ou* **cette q.!** shall I lock the door? – of course, what a question!; **y a-t-il des questions?** are there any questions?; **peut-on lui faire confiance, toute la q. est là** *ou* **voilà la q.!** can he/she be trusted, that's the question!; **poser une q. à qn** to ask sb a question; **c'est moi qui pose les questions!** I'm (the one) asking the questions!, I do the asking!; *Pol* **poser une q.** to table a question; **c'est une q. que je me pose depuis longtemps** that's something *or* a question I've been asking myself for a long time; **je commence à me poser des questions sur sa compétence** I'm beginning to have (my) doubts about *or* to wonder how competent he/she is; **se poser la q. de savoir si...** to ask oneself whether...; **q. à choix multiple** multiple-choice question; *Mktg* **q. de contrôle** check question, control question; *Mktg* **q. dichotomique** dichotomous question; *Pol* **q. écrite/orale** written/oral question; **q. fermée** closed-ended *or* yes/no question; *Mktg* **q. filtre** check question; **q. ouverte** open-ended question; *Pol* **poser la q. de confiance** to ask for a vote of confidence; **q. piège** *(dans un jeu)* trick question; *(dans un interrogatoire)* loaded *or* leading question; **q. subsidiaire** *(dans un jeu)* tie-breaker

2 *(sujet)* question, topic; **j'en connais un bout sur la q.!** I know quite a bit about this (topic)!; **de quoi est-il q. dans ce paragraphe?** what is this paragraph about?; **il a beaucoup été q. d'échanges culturels à la réunion** during the meeting they talked a lot about cultural exchanges *or* the overriding topic was cultural exchanges; **dans notre prochaine émission, il sera q. de l'architecture romane** in our next programme, we will examine Roman architecture; **il n'est jamais q. de la répression dans son livre** repression is never mentioned in his/her book; *Fam* **prête-moi 100 euros – pas q.!** lend me 100 euros – no way *or Br* nothing doing!; **il ne saurait être q. que vous régliez l'addition** there's no question of your settling the bill; **il n'en est pas q.!, c'est hors de q.!** it's out of the question!; **avec mon salaire, une voiture c'est hors de q.** with my salary, a car is out of the question; **je veux sortir ce soir – c'est hors de q.!** I want to go out tonight – you can forget it *or* it's out of the question!; **il n'est pas q.** *ou* **il est hors de q. que je le voie!** there's no way I'll see him!, there's no question of my seeing him!; *Fam* **q. salaire, je ne me plains pas** as far as the salary is concerned *or* salary-wise, I'm not complaining; *Fam* **q. soleil, on n'a pas été gâtés** we didn't see much in the way of sunshine

3 *(affaire, difficulté)* question, matter, point (at issue); **la q. du nucléaire** the nuclear energy question *or* issue; **là n'est pas la q.** that's not the point *or* the issue; **(une) q. de** a question of; **ce n'est plus qu'une q. de temps** it's only a question *or* matter of time; **c'est une q. d'habitude/de politesse** it's a question of habit/of politeness; **c'est une q. de vie ou de mort** it's a matter of life and death; **ils se sont disputés pour des questions d'argent** they had an argument over *or* about money; **je ne lis pas les critiques, q. de principe!** I don't read reviews on principle!; **ça c'est une autre q.!** that's another problem *or* story!; *Jur* **q. préalable** preliminary point of law; **q. préjudicielle** preliminary ruling; **q. principale** subject matter

4 son talent ne fait pas (de) q. his/her talent is beyond (all) question *or* (any) doubt; **c'est son passé qui fait q.** what's doubtful is his/her past

5 *Hist* question; **mettre** *ou* **soumettre qn à la q.** to put sb to the question

❑ **en question** ADJ in question, concerned; **la personne en q. veut garder l'anonymat** the person in question wishes to remain anonymous ADV **mettre qch en q.** *(mettre en doute)* to call sth into question, to challenge *or* question sth; **mettez-vous mon honnêteté en q.?** are you questioning my honesty?; **remettre en q.** *(mettre en doute)* to (call into) question, to challenge; *(compromettre)* to call into question; **la moindre querelle et leur couple est remis en q.** the slightest argument and their relationship is put in jeopardy; **se remettre en q.** to do some soul-searching

questionnaire [kɛstjɔnɛr] NM questionnaire; **q. à choix multiple** multiple-choice questionnaire; **q. pilote** pilot questionnaire

questionnement [kɛstjɔnəmɑ̃] NM questioning

questionner [3] [kɛstjɔne] VT (interroger) **q. qn** to question sb, to ask sb questions; **elle m'a questionné sur mon emploi du temps** she asked me questions about or questioned me on my timetable; **se faire q.** to be questioned
▸ **se questionner** VPR to question each other

questionneur, -euse [kɛstjɔnœr, -øz] ADJ (enfant, air) inquisitive
   NM,F Littéraire questioner; **les enfants sont souvent des questionneurs** children often ask a lot of questions

questure [kɛstyr] NF 1 Antiq quaestorship 2 Pol = treasury and administrative department of the French Parliament

quétaine [kɛtɛn] Can Fam NMF tacky person; **quel q.!** he's so tacky!
   ADJ tacky

quétainerie [ketɛnri] NF Can Fam kitsch; **ce film est une vraie q.** this film is so cheesy

quête [kɛt] NF 1 (d'argent) collection; **faire une q.** to collect money, to make a collection; **faire la q.** (à l'église) to take (the) collection; (dans la rue) to go round with the hat, to pass the hat round; **ils font la q. pour la fête de l'école** they're collecting money or making a collection for the school fête
   2 Littéraire (recherche) quest (de for); **la q. du Graal** the Quest for the Holy Grail; **q. initiatique** journey of self-discovery
   3 Chasse search
   4 Naut rake
   □ **en quête de** PRÉP Littéraire in search or pursuit of, searching for; **le poète en q. de la beauté** the poet in search or pursuit of beauty; **se mettre en q. de** to go in search of; **elle est en q. d'un travail** she's job-hunting

quêter [4] [kete] VI (à l'église) to take (the) collection; (parmi un groupe) to collect money, to make a collection; (dans la rue) to pass the hat round, to go round with the hat; **q. pour les pauvres/handicapés** to collect money for the poor/disabled
   VT 1 Littéraire (approbation, louanges) to seek; (compliments) to fish for, to angle for 2 Chasse (gibier) to search

quêteur, -euse [ketœr, -øz] NM,F 1 (personne qui fait la quête) collector 2 Can (mendiant) beggar

quetsche [kwɛtʃ] NF 1 Bot quetsch (plum) 2 (eau-de-vie) quetsch brandy

quetzal¹, -als [kɛtzal] NM Orn quetzal

quetzal², -es [kɛtzal, -ɛs] NM (monnaie) quetzal

queue [kø] NF 1 Zool tail; **q. de renard** fox's brush; Aut **faire une q. de poisson à qn** to cut in in front of sb; **leur relation a fini en q. de poisson** their relationship fizzled out; Fam **il est parti la q. basse** ou **entre les jambes** he left with his tail between his legs
   2 Bot (d'une cerise, d'une feuille) stalk; (d'une fleur) stalk, stem; Suisse Fam **ne pas se prendre pour la q. de la poire** to think one is the bee's knees
   3 (extrémité → d'une poêle, d'une casserole) handle; (→ d'un avion, d'une comète, d'un cerf-volant) tail; (→ d'une étoile filante) trail; (→ d'un cortège) back, tail (end); (→ d'un orage, d'un tourbillon) tail (end); (→ d'une procession, d'un train) rear; **les voitures de q.** the rear carriages; **être à la q.** ou **en q.** (d'un cortège) to be at the rear; **je monte toujours en q.** I always get on at the rear (of the train); Sport **il est en q. de peloton** he is at the back or rear of the bunch; Fam **on pourrait prendre un taxi – je n'en ai pas encore vu la q. d'un** we could get a taxi – I haven't seen hide nor hair of one yet; Fam **il y en avait pas la q. d'un/d'une** there wasn't a single one ■, there wasn't one to be seen ■; Fam **ne pas en avoir la q. d'un** (argent) to be broke or Br skint; Fam **ce que tu dis n'a ni q. ni tête** you're making no sense at all, you're talking nonsense; Fam **la pièce n'avait ni q. ni tête** you couldn't make head or nor tail of the play; Fam **une histoire sans q. ni tête** a shaggy-dog story
   4 (dans un classement) bottom; **être à la q. de la classe/du championnat** to be at the bottom of the class/league
   5 (file d'attente) Br queue, Am line; **faire la q.** Br to queue (up), Am to stand in line; **vous faites la q.?** Br are you queuing up?, Am are you in line?;

allez à la q.! go to the back of the Br queue or Am line!
   6 Vulg (pénis) cock, prick; **se faire** ou **se taper une q.** to jerk off, Br to have a wank
   7 (au billard) **q. (de billard)** (billiard) cue; **(faire une) fausse q.** (to) miscue
   8 Constr (d'une marche) tail; (d'une pierre) (inner) tail; **q. d'aronde** dovetail
   9 Pétr tails, bottoms
   10 Typ (d'une lettre) stem, tail, Spéc descender; (d'une note de musique) stem; (d'une page) tail, foot; **tranche de q.** tail edge
   11 Entom **grande q. fourchue** puss moth
   □ **queues** NFPL Vulg **des queues!** no way!, no chance!
   □ **à la queue leu leu** ADV in single or Indian file

queue-d'aronde [kødarɔ̃d] (pl **queues-d'aronde**) NF Menuis dovetail; **assemblage à q.** dove-tail(ed) joint

queue-de-cheval [kødʃəval] (pl **queues-de-cheval**) NF 1 (cheveux) ponytail; **avoir une q.** to have a ponytail, to wear one's hair in a ponytail 2 Anat cauda equina

queue-de-cochon [kødkɔʃɔ̃] (pl **queues-de-cochon**) NF 1 (vrille) auger 2 (ornement) wrought-iron twist

queue-de-morue [kødmɔry] (pl **queues-de-morue**) NF 1 (habit) tailcoat, Fam tails 2 (brosse) flat (paint) brush

queue-de-pie [kødpi] (pl **queues-de-pie**) NF tail-coat

queue-de-rat [kødra] (pl **queues-de-rat**) NF Menuis rat-tail file

queue-de-renard [kødrənar] (pl **queues-de-renard**) NF Bot (amarante) love-lies-bleeding; (mélampyre) cow-wheat; (vulpin) foxtail fescue

queutard [køtar] NM Vulg horny bastard

queuter [3] [køte] VI 1 (au billard) to hit through the ball 2 très Fam (rater) to screw up
   VT Vulg (forniquer avec) to screw, to shaft

queux [kø] voir **maître**

QUI [ki]

En anglais, le pronom relatif objet peut être omis lorsque la préposition qui l'introduit est rejetée en fin de phrase, p. ex. **l'amie avec qui j'ai passé mes vacances** the friend (who) I spent my holiday with.

PRON RELATIF 1 (représente une personne) who, that; **il y a des gens qui aiment ça** there are people who like that; **toi q. connais le problème, tu pourras m'aider** you who or as you are acquainted with the problem, you can help me out; **c'est Pierre q. me l'a dit** Pierre told me, it was Pierre who told me
   2 (après une préposition) whom, who; **la personne à q. je l'ai prêté** the person I lent it to or Sout to whom I lent it; **il ne peut résister à q. lui fait des compliments** he can't resist anyone who pays him compliments; **c'est à q. aura le dernier mot** each tries or they all try to have the last word; **c'était à q. crierait le plus fort** it was down to who could shout the loudest; **le collègue avec q. j'ai déjeuné** the colleague I had lunch with or Sout whom I had lunch with or with whom I had lunch; **les personnes au nom de q. ils ont agi** the people in whose name they acted; **l'homme en q. j'avais confiance** the man (whom) I trusted; **l'amie par q. j'ai eu cette adresse** the friend I got this address from or Sout from whom I got this address; **le couturier pour q. elle travaille** the designer she works for or Sout whom she works for or for whom she works; **c'est rebutant pour q. n'est pas habitué** it's disconcerting for somebody who isn't or for whoever isn't used to it; **la personne sans q. nous n'aurions jamais pu écrire ce livre** the person without whom this book would never have been written; **le peintre sur q. a été faite cette monographie** the painter about whom this monography was written; **je ne sais plus sur q. compter** I don't know who or Sout whom to rely on any more; **à q. de droit…** to whom it may concern…
   3 (sans antécédent) whoever, anyone (who); **vienne q. voudra** anyone who wants to can come; **emmenez q. vous voulez** take whoever you

like with you; **j'ai peur de négliger q. j'aime** I worry about neglecting those (whom) I love; **faites-vous aider par q. vous voulez** get help from anyone or whoever you like; **q. tu sais, q. vous savez** you know who; **q. tu sais doit venir ce soir** you know who is coming tonight; **nous avons contacté q. vous savez** we contacted you know who or Sout whom; **il est allé chez q. tu sais hier soir** he went to you know who's last night; **c'est la responsabilité de q. vous savez** it's you know who's responsibility
   4 (représente un animal) which, that; **les animaux q. parcourent la jungle** the animals which or that roam the jungle
   5 (représente une chose, une idée) which, that; **le festival, q. débutera en mai** the festival, which will start in May; **donne-moi le magazine q. est sur la table** give me the magazine (that) or which is on the table; **elle veut une poupée q. marche** she wants a walking doll, she wants a doll that can walk; **l'année q. suivit son divorce** the year following or after his/her divorce; **la seule q. me plaise** the only one (that) I like
   6 (après des verbes de perception) **je l'ai entendu q. se plaignait** I heard him moaning; **tu ne la vois pas q. descend?** can't you see her coming down?
   7 (formule de présentation) **le voilà q. pleure maintenant!** now he's crying!; **voilà q. ne m'aide pas beaucoup** that doesn't help me much; **voilà q. est bien** that is a good thing
   8 (en corrélation avec "que") **q. que tu sois, q. que vous soyez** whoever you are or Sout you may be; **q. que ce soit** (sujet) whoever; (objet) anybody, anyone; **q. que ce soit q. téléphone, répondez que je suis absent** whoever phones, tell them I'm not here; **je défie q. que ce soit de faire mieux que je n'ai fait** I challenge anybody to improve on what I did
   9 (locutions) **q. aime bien châtie bien** spare the rod and spoil the child; **q. a bu boira** a leopard never changes its spots; **q. ne dit mot consent** silence is consent; **q. sème le vent récolte la tempête** he who sows the wind shall reap the whirlwind; **q. vole un œuf vole un bœuf** he that will steal a penny will steal a pound

   PRON INTERROGATIF 1 (sujet ou attribut dans le discours direct) who; **q. m'appelle?** who's calling (me)?; **q. sait?** who knows?; Mil **q. vive?, q. va là?** who goes there?; **q. suis-je?** who am I?; **q. est votre médecin?** who's your doctor?; **on me l'a donné – q. donc?** I was given it – by who? or who by? or Sout by whom?; **q. donc t'a frappé?** who hit you?; **q. est-ce q.** who; **q. est-ce q. en veut?** who wants some?; Fam **c'est q. q., q. c'est q.** who; Fam **c'est q. q. ou q. c'est q. te l'a dit?** who told you?
   2 (objet dans le discours direct) who, Sout whom; **q. cherchez-vous?** who are you looking for?; **c'est à q.?** whose is it?; **à q. le tour?** whose turn (is it)?; **à q. mens-tu?** who are you lying to?; **de q. parles-tu?** who or Sout whom are you talking about?; **chez q. dors-tu ce soir?** whose place are you staying at tonight?, who or Sout whom are you staying with tonight?; **vers q. me tourner?** to whom can I turn?, who or whom can I turn to?; **q. est-ce que** who; **q. est-ce que tu connais ici?** who do you know around here?; **à q. est-ce que je dois de l'argent?** who do I owe money to?
   3 (sujet dans le discours indirect) who; **je ne vois pas q. pourrait t'aider** I can't see who could or I can't think of anyone who could help you
   4 (objet dans le discours indirect) who, Sout whom; **sais-tu q. j'ai rencontré ce matin?** do you know who I met this morning?; **je ne me souviens pas à q. je l'ai donné** I can't remember who I gave it to; **sais-tu q. ça appartient?** do you know who it belongs to or Sout to whom it belongs?; **tu ne m'as pas dit pour q. tu travailles** you haven't told me who you work for
   □ **qui… qui** PRON INDÉFINI **ils étaient déguisés, q. en Pierrot, q. en bergère** they were in fancy dress, some as Pierrots, others as shepherdesses

quia [kɥija] **à quia** ADV Littéraire **être à q.** to be at a loss for an answer; **mettre** ou **réduire qn à q.** to confound sb

Quiberon [kibrɔ̃] NPR Quiberon; **la presqu'île de Q.** the Quiberon peninsula

quicageon [kikaʒɔ̃] NM *Suisse* summer house

quiche [kiʃ] NF quiche; **q. lorraine** quiche lorraine

quichenotte [kiʃnɔt] NF = coiffe worn by women in Vendée as part of traditional costume

quick [kwik] NM = porous cement tennis court

quiconque [kikɔ̃k] PRON RELATIF INDÉFINI whoever, anyone *or* anybody who; **q. désobéira sera puni** whoever disobeys *or* anyone who *or* anybody who disobeys will be punished; *Bible* **q. frappera par l'épée périra par l'épée** he who lives by the sword shall die by the sword

  PRON INDÉFINI anyone *or* anybody (else); **il connaît les volcans mieux que q.** he knows volcanoes better than anyone *or* anybody else

Quid® [kwid] NM = annually updated one-volume encyclopedia of facts and figures

quid [kwid] PRON INTERROGATIF *Hum* **q. de...?** what about...?

quidam [kidam] NM *Hum* fellow, individual

quiddité [kɥidite] NF *Phil* quiddity

quiescence [kɥiɛsɑ̃s] NF *Biol* quiescence

quiescent, -e [kɥiɛsɑ̃, -ɑ̃t] ADJ *Biol* quiescent

qui est-ce que [kiɛskə], **qui est-ce qui** [kiɛski] *voir* **qui** PRON INTERROGATIF

quiet, -ète [kjɛ, kjɛt] ADJ *Littéraire* calm, tranquil

quiétisme [kjetism] NM quietism

quiétiste [kjetist] ADJ quietist

  NMF quietist

quiétude [kjetyd] NF *Littéraire* **1** *(d'une demeure)* quiet, tranquillity, *Littéraire* quietude **2** *(d'esprit)* peace of mind; **elle attendait les résultats en toute q.** she was calmly waiting for the results

quignon [kiɲɔ̃] NM **q. (de pain)** *(morceau)* (crusty) chunk of bread; *(extrémité)* end crust (of the loaf)

quillard [kijar] NM *Fam Arg mil* = soldier about to be discharged *or* nearing the end of his national service

quille [kij] NF **1** *(jeu)* skittle, pin; **jouer aux quilles** to play ninepins *or* skittles **2** *Fam (jambe)* leg■, *esp Br* pin; **il ne tient pas sur ses quilles** he's shaky on his pins; *Fig* **jouer des quilles** to beat it, to leg it **3** *Fam (petite fille)* little girl■ **4** *Fam Arg mil (fin du service)* discharge■, *Br* demob; *Fig* **vivement la q.!** I can't wait to get out of here! **5** *Naut* keel; **la q. en l'air** bottom up; **q. de roulis** bilge keel

quilleur, -euse [kijœr, -øz] NM,F *Can* bowler *(person)*

quillon [kijɔ̃] NM **1** *(d'épée, de baïonnette)* cross bar, cross guard **2** *(de fusil)* piling pin

quimboiseur [kɛ̃bwazœr] NM *(sorcier antillais)* sorcerer

quinaire [kinɛr] ADJ *Math* quinary

quinaud, -e [kino, -od] ADJ *Vieilli ou Littéraire* ashamed, abashed

quincaillerie [kɛ̃kajri] NF **1** *(articles, commerce)* hardware **2** *(boutique) Br* ironmonger's, *Am* hardware store **3** *Fam Péj (bijoux)* cheap costume jewellery■; *(armes)* weapons■, hardware; **elle a mis toute sa q.** she's wearing every bit of jewellery she's got; **il ne sort jamais sans toute sa q.** he's always armed to the teeth when he goes out

quincaillier, -ère [kɛ̃kaje, -ɛr] NM,F hardware dealer, *Br* ironmonger

quinconce [kɛ̃kɔ̃s] NM quincunx; **en q.** arranged in a quincunx

quindécemvir [kɥɛ̃desɛmvir] NM *Antiq* quindecemvir

quine [kin] NM OU NF *(au Loto)* series of five winning numbers, quinto; *Vieilli* **c'est un q. à la loterie** it's one chance in ten thousand

quiné, -e [kine] ADJ *Bot* quinate

quinidine [kinidin] NF *Chim* quinidine

quinine [kinin] NF *Pharm* quinine

quinoa [kinɔa] NM *Bot & Culin* quinoa

quinoléine [kinɔlein] NF *Chim* quinoline

quinolone [kinɔlɔn] NF *Pharm* quinolone

quinone [kinɔn] NF *Chim* quinone

quinqua [kɛ̃ka] *Fam (abrév* **quinquagénaire)** ADJ fiftysomething■; **être q.** to be fiftysomething *or* in one's fifties

  NMF person in his/her fifties, fiftysomething■; **c'est un q.** he's fiftysomething *or* in his fifties

quinquagénaire [kɛ̃kaʒenɛr] ADJ quinquagenarian; **être q.** to be in one's fifties

  NMF **1** *(personne)* fifteenth **2** *(objet)* fifteenth (one)

  NM **1** *(partie)* fifteenth **2** *(étage) Br* fifteenth floor, *Am* sixteenth floor **3** *(arrondissement de Paris)* fifteenth (arrondissement)

  NMF *Mus* fifteenth; *voir aussi* **cinquième**

quinzièmement [kɛ̃zjɛmmɑ̃] ADV in fifteenth place

quinziste [kɛ̃zist] NM rugby union player

quinzomadaire [kɛ̃zɔmadɛr] *Fam Journ* ADJ bimonthly■, *Br* fortnightly■

  NM *(gén)* bimonthly *or Br* fortnightly publication■

quiproquo [kipɔrko] NM *(sur l'identité d'une personne)* mistake; *(sur le sujet d'une conversation)* misunderstanding; **l'intrigue est fondée sur un q.** the plot revolves round a case of mistaken identity; **il croyait que j'étais ton frère, j'ai entretenu le q.** he mistook me for your brother and I didn't let on; **il y a q., nous ne parlons pas du même étudiant** there is a misunderstanding, we're not talking about the same student

quiquajon [kikaʒɔ̃] = **quicageon**

quiquette [kikɛt] = **quéquette**

quirat [kira] NM *Jur* joint ownership *(in a ship)*

quirataire [kiratɛr] NM *Jur* joint owner *(of a ship)*

Quirinal [kirinal] *voir* **mont**

quirite [kɥirit] NM *Antiq* Roman citizen

quiscale [kɥiskal] NM *Orn* grackle, crow blackbird; **q. bronzé** common grackle; **q. rouilleux** rusty blackbird

Quito [kito] NM Quito

quittance [kitɑ̃s] NF **q. comptable** accountable receipt; **q. de gaz/d'électricité** gas/electricity bill; **q. de loyer** rent receipt; **q. finale, q. libératoire** receipt in full; **q. pour solde** receipt in full; *Banque* **q. pour solde de tout compte** closing account balance

quittancer [16] [kitɑ̃se] VT to give a receipt for

quinquennal, -e, -aux, -ales [kɛ̃kenal, -o] ADJ *(plan)* five-year *(avant n)*; *(élection, foire)* five-yearly, quinquennial

quinquennat [kɛ̃kena] NM five-year period, quinquennium, lustrum

quinquérème [kɛ̃kerɛm] NF *Antiq* quinquereme

quinquet [kɛ̃kɛ] NM *(Argand)* oil lamp

  □ **quinquets** NMPL *Fam (yeux)* peepers, eyes■; **ouvrez/fermez les quinquets!** open/close your eyes!

quinquina [kɛ̃kina] NM **1** *Bot & Pharm* cinchona **2** *(boisson)* quinine tonic wine

quint, -e¹ [kɛ̃, kɛ̃t] *voir* **fièvre**

quintaine [kɛ̃tɛn] NF *Hist* quintain

quintal², -aux [kɛ̃tal, -o] NM *(metric)* quintal

quinte² [kɛ̃t] NF **1** *Méd* **q. (de toux)** coughing fit, fit of coughing **2** *Mus* fifth; **q. juste** perfect fifth **3** *Cartes (gén)* quint; *(au poker)* straight; **q. flush** straight flush; **q. flush royale** royal flush **4** *Escrime* quinte

quinté [kɛ̃te] NM = bet in which the punter predicts the first five horses to finish a race

quintefeuille [kɛ̃tfœj] NF *Hér & Bot* cinquefoil

  NM *Archit* cinquefoil

quintessence [kɛ̃tesɑ̃s] NF *Littéraire* quintessence; **la q. du romantisme** the epitome *or* quintessence *or* very essence of Romanticism

quintet [kɛ̃tɛt] NM *(jazz)* quintet

quintette [kɛ̃tɛt] NM quintet, quintette; **q. à cordes/vent** string/wind quintet

quinteux, -euse [kɛ̃tø, -øz] ADJ **1** *Méd (toux)* fitful **2** *Littéraire (acariâtre)* crotchety, testy **3** *(cheval)* restive

quintidi [kɛ̃tidi] NM *Hist* = fifth day of a ten-day period in the Republican calendar

Quintillien [kɛ̃tiljɛ̃] NPR Quintilian

quintillion [kɛ̃tiljɔ̃] NM *Br* quintillion, *Am* nonillion

quinto [kɥɛ̃to, kɛ̃to] ADV in (the) fifth place, fifthly

quintolet [kɛ̃tɔlɛ] NM *Mus* quintole(t), quintuplet

quintuple [kɛ̃typl] ADJ *(à cinq éléments)* quintuple, five-fold; **un q. meurtre** a quintuple murder

  NM quintuple; **le q. (de)** *(quantité, prix)* five times as much (as); *(nombre)* five times as many (as); **vingt-cinq est le q. de cinq** twenty-five is five times five; **le q. de sa valeur** five times its value

quintupler [3] [kɛ̃typle] VI to increase fivefold, to quintuple; **la paix a fait q. le nombre des naissances** peace has multiplied the number of births by five

  VT to increase fivefold, to quintuple

quintuplés, -ées [kɛ̃typle] NM,F PL quintuplets, *Br* quins, *Am* quints

quinzaine [kɛ̃zɛn] NF **1** *(durée)* **une q. (de jours)** two weeks, *Br* a fortnight; **venez me voir dans une q.** come and see me in a couple of weeks *or* in two weeks *or Br* in a fortnight's time

  2 *(quantité)* **une q. de** about fifteen; **une q. de crayons** about fifteen pencils, fifteen pencils or so

  3 *Com* **q. commerciale** two-week sale; **la grande q. des prix littéraires** the literary prize season *(two-week period in November and December when all the major French literary prizes are awarded)*; *Cin* **Q. des réalisateurs** = competition forming part of the Cannes film festival which frequently gives awards to less mainstream films and less well-known directors

  4 *(salaire)* two weeks' pay, *Br* a fortnight's pay

quinze [kɛ̃z] ADJ **1** *(gén)* fifteen; **q. jours** two weeks, *Br* a fortnight **2** *(dans des séries)* fifteenth; **page/numéro q.** page/number fifteen

  PRON fifteen

  NM INV **1** *(gén)* fifteen; **lundi en q.** two weeks from *or Br* a fortnight on Monday **2** *(numéro d'ordre)* number fifteen **3** *(chiffre écrit)* fifteen **4** *Sport* **le q. de France** the French Fifteen **5** *Anciennement Pol & UE* **les Q.** = the fifteen member states of the European Union *(before ten new countries joined in 2004)*; *voir aussi* **cinq**

quitte [kit] ADJ **1** *(libéré → d'une dette, d'une obligation)* **être q. envers qn** to be even *or* quits *or* (all) square with sb; **être q. d'une dette** to be rid *or* clear of a debt; **donne-moi seulement 50 euros, tu es q. du reste** just give me 50 euros, let's not worry about the rest *or* I'll let you off the rest; **considérer** *ou* **estimer qn q. de** to consider sb to be rid *or* clear of; **vous êtes tenu q. de ce que vous me devez** consider your debt to me (to be) paid; **être q. envers la société** *(après une peine de prison)* to have paid one's debt to society; **je ne te tiens pas q. de ta promesse!** I don't consider that you have fulfilled your promise!

  2 *(au même niveau)* **être quittes** to be quits *or* all square

  3 **en être q. pour qch** *(s'en tirer avec quelque chose)* to get away with sth; **il en a été q. pour quelques égratignures/la peur** he got away with a few scratches/a bit of a fright

  4 **en être q. pour faire** *(devoir faire)* to have to do sth; **j'ai oublié mes papiers à la banque, j'en suis q. pour y retourner** I've left my papers at the bank, so I have to go back there now

  5 **q. ou double** *(dans un jeu de hasard)* nothing *or Br* double or quits; *Fig* **c'est jouer à q. ou double** it's a big gamble *or* risk

  6 *Belg* **être q. de qch** to be deprived of sth

  □ **quitte à** PRÉP **1** *(au risque de)* even if it means; **je lui dirai, q. à me faire renvoyer** I'll tell him/her, even if it means being fired

  2 *(puisqu'il faut)* since it is necessary to; **q. à les inviter, autant le faire dans les règles** since we have to invite them, we may as well do things properly

QUITTER [3] [kite] VT **1** *(lieu)* to leave; *(ami, époux)* to leave, to split up with; *(emploi)* to leave, to quit, to give up; *(fonction, chambre d'hôtel)* to vacate; *(habitude)* to drop, to get rid of; **je quitte (le bureau) à 5 heures** I leave the office *or* I finish at 5 o'clock; *Naut* **q. le port** to leave port; *Rail* **q. les rails** to be derailed, to derail, to leave the track; **la voiture a quitté la route** the car came off *or* ran off *or* left the road; **il ne peut pas encore q. son lit** he can't leave his bed yet, he's still confined to bed; **elle ne quitte pratiquement pas son atelier** she hardly ever sets foot outside *or* leaves her workshop; **il faut que je te quitte** I must be going, I must go; **je ne te**

quitterai jamais I'll never leave you; **il ne la quitta pas des yeux** *ou* **du regard** he never took his eyes off her, he watched her every move; **il suffit que je la quitte des yeux une seconde pour qu'elle fasse des bêtises** if I let her out of my sight *or* if I take my eyes off her for a second, she gets up to some mischief; **il a quitté les affaires/le théâtre** he retired from business/gave up the stage; **quel plaisir de tout q.!** how nice to get away from it all!; *Euph* **il nous a quittés hier** he passed away yesterday; *Euph* **elle a quitté ce monde** she has departed this world *or* this life

2 *(abandonner → sujet: courage, force)* to leave, to desert, *Sout* to forsake; **son optimisme ne l'a jamais quitté** he remained optimistic throughout; **son bon sens semblait l'avoir quitté** he seemed to have taken leave of his senses; **c'est une idée qui ne me quitte pas** I can't get the idea out of my head; *Littéraire* **la vie le quittait lentement** his life was slowly ebbing away

3 *(retirer → habit)* to take off; **il ne quitte jamais son chapeau** he never takes his hat off, he always has his hat on; **tu vas adorer ce pull, tu ne le quitteras plus** you'll love this sweater, you won't want to take it off; **q. le deuil** to come out of mourning

4 *(au téléphone)* **ne quittez pas** hold on, hold the line

5 *Ordinat (base de données, programme)* to quit; **q. le système** to quit

▶**se quitter** VPR *(amis)* to part; *(époux)* to part, to break *or* to split up; **il est tard, nous devons nous q.** it's late, we have to say goodbye now; **quittons-nous bons amis** let's part on good terms; **depuis qu'ils se sont rencontrés, ils ne se quittent plus** ever since they met they have been inseparable

quitus [kitys] NM *Jur* (full) discharge, quietus; **donner q. à qn** to discharge sb

qui-vive [kiviv] NM INV **être sur le q.** *(soldat)* to be on the alert *or* the qui vive; *(animal)* to be on the alert; **je la sentais sur le q.** I felt she was on edge, I felt she was waiting for something to happen

quiz [kwiz] NM quiz

Qum [kɔm] = **Qom**

quôc-ngu [kɔkngu] NM INV *Ling* = system for writing modern Vietnamese, based on the Roman alphabet

QUOI [kwa] PRON RELATIF what, which; **c'est ce à q. je voulais en venir** that's what I was getting at; **c'est ce à q. je me suis intéressé** that's what I was interested in; **il a refusé, ce en q. il a eu raison** he refused, which was quite right of him; **on est allés au jardin, après q. il a fallu rentrer** we went to the garden, and then we had to come back in; **prends de q. boire/écrire/payer** get something to drink/to write/to pay with; **il y a de q. nourrir au moins dix per-**

sonnes there's enough to feed at least ten people; **il n'y a pas de q. se faire du souci** there's nothing to worry about; **il y a de q. être satisfait** there are good grounds for satisfaction; *Fam* **je suis en colère – il y a de q.!** I'm angry – it's no wonder *or* with good reason!; **...sur q. il se lève et   sort** whereupon he got up and left; **merci! – il n'y a pas de q.** thank you! – not at all *or* you're welcome *or* don't mention it

ADV INTERROGATIF **1** *(quelle chose)* what; **c'est q.?** what's that?; *Fam* **c'est q. ton nom?** what's your name?■; *Fam* **tu fais q. ce soir?** what are you doing this evening?■; **à q. penses-tu?** what are you thinking about?; *Fam* **elle est à q. ta glace?** what flavour is your ice cream?■; **je me demande à q. ça sert/il pense** I wonder what it's for/what he's thinking about; **en q. puis-je vous être utile?** how can I help you?; **par q. se sent-il concerné?** what does he feel concerned about?; **je voudrais parler au directeur – c'est pour q.?** I'd like to talk to the manager – what (is it) about?; **sur q. va-t-elle travailler?** what is she going to work on?; **elle ne sait plus q. lui dire** she doesn't know what to say to him/her any more; *Fam* **salut, alors q. de neuf?** hi, what have you been up to *or* what's new?; **q. de plus naturel?** what could be more natural?; **à q. bon?** what's the use?; **à q. bon l'attendre?** what's the use of waiting for him?; **q. encore?** what else?; *(ton irrité)* what is it now?

2 *Fam (pour faire répéter)* **q.?** what?; **q., qu'est-ce que tu dis?** what did you say?

3 *(emplois expressifs)* **eh bien q., qu'est-ce que tu as?** well, what's the matter with you?; **enfin q.,** *ou* **eh bien q., tu pourrais regarder où tu vas!** come on now, watch where you're going!; **de q.? tu n'es pas d'accord?** what's that, you don't agree?; **tu viens (oui) ou q.?** are you coming or not?; **décide-toi, q.!** well, make up your mind!; **mais puisque je l'ai vue, q.!** but I saw her, I'm telling you!; **si je comprends bien, tu es fauché, q.!** if I've understood you, you're broke, aren't you?; **je vais lui acheter ce livre, pour lui faire un petit cadeau, q.** I'm going to buy him/her this book... you know, just as a little present

❑ **quoi que** CONJ **q. qu'il arrive** whatever happens; **q. qu'il en soit** be that as it may, however that may be; **q. qu'il dise** whatever he may say; **q. que vous en pensiez** whatever you may think of it; **je te défends de lui dire q. que ce soit!** I forbid you to tell him/her anything (whatsoever)!; **trouve un moyen, q. que ce soit qui nous tire d'affaire** find a way, any way that will get us out of this mess; **si je peux t'aider en q. que ce soit** if I can help you in any way; **q. qu'il en ait** whatever he feels about it

quoique [kwakə] CONJ **1** *(bien que)* though, although; **quoiqu'il fût déjà minuit** though *or* although it was already midnight; **q. riche, il**

n'était guère généreux although rich, he was hardly generous; **q. née en France, elle a passé sa vie en Angleterre** though *or* although born in France, she spent her life in England

2 *(introduisant une restriction)* **bien sûr 500 euros c'est cher, q. tu sais, ce n'est pas exagéré** of course 500 euros is a lot of money, although you know *or* but mind you it's not excessive; **je vous installerais bien dans cette chambre... q. vous seriez mieux dans celle qui donne sur la cour** I'd like to put you in this room... although you'd be better off in the one which overlooks the courtyard; **il a l'air compétent... q....** he seems competent... mind you...

quokka [kwɔka] NM *Zool* quokka

quolibet [kɔlibɛ] NM gibe, jeer, taunt; **les enfants le poursuivaient de leurs quolibets** the children jeered at him *or* taunted him relentlessly

quorum [kwɔrɔm, kɔrɔm] NM quorum; **nous avons atteint le q.** we're quorate, we have a quorum

quota [kɔta] NM quota; *Mktg* **q. d'échantillonnage** sampling quota; **q. à l'exportation** *ou* **d'exportation** export quota; **q. à l'importation** *ou* **d'importation** import quota; **q. laitier** milk quota; **q. de ventes** sales quota; **quotas volontaires à l'export** voluntary export restraint; *Can Fig* **avoir son q.** to be fed up

quote-part [kɔtpar] (*pl* **quotes-parts**) NF share; **q. des bénéfices** share in the profits

quotidien, -enne [kɔtidjɛ̃, -ɛn] ADJ **1** *(de chaque jour → entraînement, promenade, repas)* daily; *(→ préoccupations)* everyday; **leurs disputes étaient devenues presque quotidiennes** they'd got to the stage where they were arguing almost every day

2 *(routinier → tâche)* run-of-the-mill, humdrum NM daily (paper); **un grand q.** a (major) national daily; *Presse* **Le Q. de Paris** = daily Paris newspaper; **q. du septième jour** Sunday paper *or* newspaper

❑ **au quotidien** ADV *Fam* on a day-to-day basis; **le cancer/le sida au q.** living with cancer/Aids (from day to day)

quotidiennement [kɔtidjɛnmã] ADV daily, every day

quotidienneté [kɔtidjɛnte] NF everyday nature; **la q. de leur existence** the routine of their everyday life

quotient [kɔsjã] NM **1** *Math* quotient **2** *Psy* **q. intellectuel** intelligence quotient **3** *Jur* **q. électoral** electoral quota; **q. familial** dependants' allowance **4** *Physiol* **q. respiratoire** respiratory quotient

quotité [kɔtite] NF **1** *Fin* quota; **la q. du dégrèvement fiscal** the portion of income not subject to taxation; *Com* **q. imposable** taxable portion of income **2** *Jur* **q. disponible** disposable portion (of estate)

QWERTY [kwɛrti] ADJ INV **clavier Q.** Qwerty keyboard

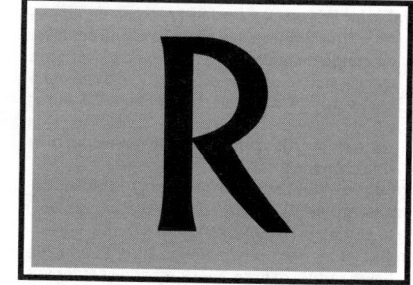

R

R¹, r [ɛr] **NM INV** (lettre) R, r; **R comme Raoul** ≃ R for Robert

R² [ɛr] (abrév **Renault**) **une R19/21/25** a Renault 19/21/25

R³ 1 Vieilli Phys (abrév écrite roentgen) R **2** (abrév écrite rand) R

R., r. (abrév écrite **rue**) St

R-, RE-, RÉ- [r, rə, re] **PRÉF**

• This prefix is often used to express REPETITION and as such it is very frequent.

When used with verbs it is mostly translated using **again**, or more rarely using the prefix **re-**: **redire** to say again; **revoir** to see again; **redemander** to ask again; **remanger** to eat again; **repasser** to call again; **redonner** to give again (as in **redonne-moi ton numéro de téléphone**), **réélire** to re-elect; **relire** to reread; **réécrire** to rewrite

It can also be used with nouns, eg:
réélection re-election; **redéploiement** redeployment; **rediffusion** repeat

In informal usage it is widely used, for example in **rebonjour** (sometimes abbreviated to just **re**), meaning "hello again"

It is also used in telegraphic style to indicate the repetition of an event:
le lendemain, re-pluie the next day it rained again; **au retour, re-embouteillage** on the way back we were stuck in a traffic jam again; **pour le dîner, re-haricots** for dinner we had beans again

Re- can even be used more than once as a prefix: **on a crevé une fois à l'aller, on a recrevé au retour, et re-recrevé en allant au garage** we had a puncture on the way there, another one on the way back and yet another one when driving to the garage

• As in English, the prefix re- may signal a RETURN TO A PREVIOUS STATE that had been interrupted:
réarmer to rearm; **rétablir** to re-establish; **reconstruire** to rebuild; **réchauffer** to reheat

In other cases, English will use the adverb **back** instead of a prefix:
redescendre to come back down; **revenir** to come back; **rallumer** to switch back on; **redonner** to give back (as in **redonne-moi le stylo que je t'ai prêté**).

• Note that in many instances the prefix **re-** has lost its original meaning. Some words starting with **re-** have superseded the words they were derived from:
raffiner to refine; **refroidir** to cool; **remplir** to fill up

Some words have different meanings depending on the meaning of the prefix **re-**. The verb **rechercher** is one of them:
la police recherche le prisonnier qui s'est évadé the police are looking for the escaped prisoner; **il n'y a plus de lait, il faut que j'aille en rechercher** there's no milk left, I'll have to go and get some more

---

ra [ra] **NM INV** short drumroll, ruffle

Râ [ra] = **Rê**

raag [rag] = **raga**

rab [rab] Fam **NM** (excédent) leftovers■, extra■; **il y a du r. de poulet** there's some chicken left over; **qui veut du r.?** who wants seconds?; **faire du r.** (au travail) to put in a bit of overtime or a few extra hours; (à l'armée) to serve extra time; **j'ai eu deux heures de r. au lit** I had an extra two hours in bed

□ **en rab ADJ il y a des patates en r.** there are some spuds left (over); **t'aurais pas une clope en r.?** can I bum a smoke or Br fag?, have you got a spare smoke or Br fag?; **vous auriez pas un oreiller en r.?** do you have a spare pillow?■

rabab [rabab] = **rebab**

rabâchage [rabaʃaʒ] **NM** Fam **son cours, c'est vraiment du r.** he's/she's always going over the same old things in class

rabâcher [3] [rabaʃe] Fam **VT 1** (conseils) to keep (on) repeating■; (malheurs) to keep harping on about; **tu n'arrêtes pas de r. la même chose** you're like a broken record, you do go on; **elle nous a rabâché qu'il fallait faire attention au verglas** she kept on at us about being careful of the ice; **des arguments rabâchés** the same old arguments; **le prof rabâche le même cours depuis dix ans** the teacher's been regurgitating or churning out the same old course for ten years

2 (leçon) to go over and over

VI to keep repeating oneself■, to keep harping on

rabâcheur, -euse [rabaʃœr, -øz] Fam **ADJ il est très r.** he's always repeating himself■ or harping on about the same thing; **elle devient un peu rabâcheuse** she's starting to repeat herself■

NM,F drone, bore

rabais [rabɛ] **NM** reduction, discount; **avec un r. de 15 pour cent, avec 15 pour cent de r.** with a 15 percent discount or reduction; **faire un r. de 10 pour cent sur le prix** to knock 10 percent off the price; **faire** ou **accorder un r. sur qch** to give a discount on sth; **il m'a fait un r. de 20 pour cent** he gave me 20 percent off or a 20 percent discount; **r. différé** deferred rebate

□ **au rabais ADJ** (vente) cut-price; Péj (formation) second-rate; (travail) underpaid **ADV** acheter/vendre qch au r. to buy/to sell sth at a reduced price or at a discount; Péj **elle travaille au r.** she works for a pittance

rabaissant, -e [rabɛsɑ̃, -ɑ̃t] **ADJ** degrading, debasing

rabaissement [rabɛsmɑ̃] **NM** (de l'être humain) debasement

rabaisser [4] [rabɛse] **VT 1** (diminuer → prétentions) to moderate, to reduce; (→ niveau) to lower; (→ orgueil) to humble; (→ prix) to reduce, to lower

2 (dévaloriser → mérites) to devalue, to belittle; (→ personne) to belittle, to run or to put down; **il prend un malin plaisir à la r. devant ses collègues** he takes a perverse pleasure in putting her down in front of his/her colleagues; **de tels actes rabaissent l'homme au niveau de l'animal** such actions reduce man to the level of an animal

3 (voilette, jupe) to pull (back) down

▶**se rabaisser VPR 1** (se dévaloriser) to belittle oneself, to run or to put oneself down, to sell oneself short; **il est toujours en train de se r. devant ses collègues** he's always putting or running himself down in front of his colleagues

2 (s'avilir) to degrade oneself

raban [rabɑ̃] **NM** Naut (short) rope or line

rabane [raban] **NF** (matière) raffia fabric; (tapis) raffia mat

Rabat [raba] **NM** Rabat

rabat [raba] voir **rabattre**

NM 1 (d'un sac, d'une poche) flap; (de toge) bands **2** Jur **r. d'arrêt** = quashing of a decision due to procedural error **3** Chasse beating, driving; **chasse au r.** beating, driving

rabat-joie [rabaʒwa] **ADJ INV ce qu'ils sont r.!** what a bunch of killjoys they are!

NMF INV killjoy, spoilsport

rabattable [rabatabl] **ADJ** (siège) folding

rabattage [rabataʒ] **NM** Chasse beating

rabattant, -e [rabatɑ̃, -ɑ̃t] **ADJ** Minér **exploitation rabattante** retreating system

rabattement [rabatmɑ̃] **NM** Géom rabatment

rabatteur, -euse [rabatœr, -øz] **NM,F 1** Chasse beater **2** Com tout **3** Pol canvasser

NM Agr reel

rabattre [83] [rabatr] **VT 1** (toit ouvrant, strapontin → pour baisser) to pull down; (→ pour lever) to pull up; (couvercle, siège des toilettes) to close, to shut; (chapeau) to pull down; (col, visière) to turn down; **rabats le drap sur la couverture** fold the sheet back over the blanket; **rabattez le tissu avant de coudre** fold the material over before sewing; **les cheveux rabattus sur le front** hair brushed forward or down over the forehead; **rabats le capot de la voiture** close the bonnet of the car; **une bourrasque rabattit le volet contre le mur** a gust of wind blew the shutter back against the wall; **de la fumée rabattue par le vent** smoke blown back by the wind; **le vent rabattait la pluie contre son visage** the wind was driving the rain against his/her face; **r. la balle** (au tennis) to smash the ball; **l'oiseau se posa et rabattit ses ailes** the bird landed and folded back its wings

2 (ramener → gibier) to drive; **la police rabattait les manifestants vers** ou **sur la place** the police were driving the demonstrators (back) towards the square; Fam **r. des clients** (racoler) to tout for customers

3 (déduire) to take off, to deduct; **il a rabattu 5 pour cent sur le prix affiché** he took or knocked 5 percent off the marked price

4 (diminuer) **r. l'orgueil de qn** to humble sb; **en r.** (modérer ses exigences) to climb down, to lower one's sights

5 Couture to stitch down; **r. une couture** to fell a seam; **r. deux mailles** (en tricot) to decrease two stitches; **r. toutes les mailles** to cast off

6 Géom to rabat

7 Hort to cut (down), to prune away

8 Tex to tone down

VI (quitter la direction suivie) **nous rabattîmes sur le château** we turned off towards the castle

▶**se rabattre VPR 1** (véhicule → graduellement) to move back into position; (→ brusquement) to cut in; (coureur) to cut in or across; **le car s'est rabattu juste devant moi** the bus cut in just in front of me

2 (se fermer → volet) to slam shut; (→ siège de voiture) to fold down; (→ table) to fold away

3 (oiseau) to land

4 se r. sur (se contenter de) to fall back on, to make do with; **il a dû se r. sur un emploi de veilleur de nuit** he had to make do with a night watchman's job

rabbi [rabi] **NM** Hist rabbi

rabbin [rabɛ̃] **NM** rabbi; **grand r.** chief rabbi

rabbinat [rabina] **NM** rabbinate

rabbinique [rabinik] **ADJ** rabbinical, rabbinic

rabbinisme [rabinism] **NM** rabbinism

rabbiniste [rabinist] **NMF** rabbinist

rabe [rab] = **rab**

rabelaisien, -enne [rablɛzjɛ̃, -ɛn] **ADJ** Rabelaisian

rabibocher [3] [rabiboʃe] Fam **VT 1** (réconcilier) to patch things up between **2** Vieilli (réparer) to fix or to patch up

▶**se rabibocher VPR** to make up; **se r. avec qn** to patch things up with sb

rabiot [rabjo] = **rab**

rabioter [3] [rabjɔte] *Fam* **VT 1** *(obtenir en supplément)* to wangle; **elle a réussi à r. une semaine de congé de maladie** she managed to wangle a week's sick leave **2** *(s'octroyer)* **il m'a rabioté 5 euros sur la monnaie** he pocketed 5 euros when he gave me my change

VI to skimp; **ils rabiotent sur la nourriture** they skimp on the food

rabique [rabik] **ADJ** rabies *(avant n)*, rabic

rabistoquer [3] [rabistɔke] **VT** *Belg Fam (réparer)* to patch up; *(remonter le moral à)* to buck up

râble [rɑbl] **NM 1** *Zool* back, saddle; *Culin* **r. de lièvre** saddle of hare; *Fam* **tomber** *ou* **sauter sur le r. à qn** *(attaquer)* to lay into sb, to go for sb; *(critiquer)* to go for sb; *Fam* **je ne pouvais pas me douter de ce qui allait me tomber sur le r.** I didn't suspect what was waiting for me round the corner **2** *Métal* rabble, rake; *Tech* rake

râblé, -e [rɑble] **ADJ 1** *(animal)* broad-backed **2** *(personne)* stocky

râbler [3] [rɑble] **VT** *Métal* to rabble; *Tech* to rake (out)

râblure [rɑblyr] **NF** *Naut* rabbet, groove

rabonnir [32] [rabɔnir] **VI** *Vieilli* to improve

rabot [rabo] **NM** *Menuis* plane; **dent r.** straight tooth *(in raker set)*; **passer qch au r., donner un coup de r. à qch** to plane sth

rabotage [rabɔtaʒ], **rabotement** [rabɔtmɑ̃] **NM** planing (down)

raboter [3] [rabɔte] **VT** to plane (down)

►**se raboter VPR je me suis raboté le genou contre le mur** I scraped my knee on the wall

raboteur [rabɔtœr] **NM** *(ouvrier)* planer

raboteux, -euse [rabɔtø, -øz] **ADJ 1** *(sentier)* bumpy, rugged; *(plancher)* uneven, rough; *(bois)* knotty **2** *Littéraire (style)* rugged, unpolished, rough

❑ **raboteuse NF** *(outil)* planing machine, planer

raboudiner [3] [rabudine] **VT** *Can Fam* **1** *(mal rapiécer)* to patch up; *(mal réparer)* to repair shoddily[■] **2** *(bafouiller)* to mumble[■], to mutter[■]

raboudineur, -euse [rabudinœr, -øz] **NM,F** *Can Fam* **1** *(mauvais ouvrier)* slapdash *or* shoddy worker **2** *(bafouilleur)* mumbler[■]

rabougri, -e [rabugri] **ADJ 1** *(plante)* shrivelled **2** *(personne)* shrivelled, wizened

rabougrir [32] [rabugrir] **VT** *(dessécher)* to shrivel (up); *(entraver la croissance de)* to stunt (the growth of)

►**se rabougrir VPR 1** *(plante)* to shrivel (up) **2** *(personne)* to become wizened, to become shrivelled (with age)

rabouillère [rabujɛr] **NF** *Zool* nest burrow

raboutage [rabutaʒ] **NM** *(de tuyaux)* joining, putting end to end; *(de cordes)* tying together, putting end to end

rabouter [3] [rabute] **VT** *(tuyaux)* to join, to put end to end; *(cordes)* to tie together, to put end to end; *Fig* **ce n'est pas une anthologie, seulement quelques textes raboutés** it's not an anthology, only a few bits of prose thrown *or* stuck together

rabrouer [6] [rabrue] **VT** to send packing; **se faire r. par qn** to feel the sharp end of sb's tongue

rac [rak] **NF** *Belg Fam* **1** *Naut (bassin)* (natural) harbour[■] **2** *Fig (locution)* **être en r.** to have broken down[■]

racage [rakaʒ] **NM** *Naut* parrel, parral

racagnac [rakaɲak] **NM** *Belg* **1** *(crécelle)* rattle **2** *(tournevis)* (ratchet) screwdriver **3** *Fam* **vieux r.** old fossil

racahout [rakaut] **NM** *Culin* racahout, raccahout

racaille [rakaj] **NF 1** *Vieilli (populace)* rabble, riff-raff **2** *Péj (voyous)* trash, *Br* yobs; **la r. de banlieue** *Br* ≃ council estate yobs, *Am* ≃ hoods from the projects **3** *Péj (voyou)* lout, *Br* yob

raccard [rakar] **NM** *Suisse* = grain store typical of the Valais canton

raccommodable [rakɔmɔdabl] **ADJ** mendable, repairable

raccommodage [rakɔmɔdaʒ] **NM** *(de linge, d'un filet)* mending, repairing; *(d'une chaussette)* darning, mending; **j'ai du r. à faire** I've got some mending to do; **un r. bien fait** a neat bit of mending

raccommodement [rakɔmɔdmɑ̃] **NM** *Fam* patching things up

raccommoder [3] [rakɔmɔde] **VT 1** *(réparer → linge, filet)* to repair, to mend; *(→ chaussette)* to darn, to mend; **peux-tu r. mon pantalon/mes chaussettes?** can you mend my trousers/darn my socks? **2** *Fam (réconcilier)* to patch things up between; **je suis raccommodé avec elle** I've patched things up *or* made it up with her

►**se raccommoder VPR** *Fam (se réconcilier)* to make it up, to patch things up (**avec** with)

raccommodeur, -euse [rakɔmɔdœr, -øz] **NM,F** mender

raccompagnateur, -trice [rakɔ̃paɲatœr, -tris] **NM,F** *Can* = volunteer who drives people home in their own cars after a night out

raccompagner [3] [rakɔ̃paɲe] **VT 1** *(reconduire à la porte)* **r. qn** to show *or* to see sb out

2 *(accompagner)* **je vais te r. chez toi** *(à pied)* I'll walk *or* take you back home; *(en voiture)* I'll give you a *Br* lift *or Am* ride home, I'll drive *or* run you home; **tu me raccompagnes jusqu'au bout de la rue?** will you walk me *or* see me to the end of the street?; **r. qn à la gare/à l'aéroport** to see sb off at the station/airport; **fais-toi r.** get a *Br* lift *or Am* ride home; **je me suis fait r. en voiture après la soirée** I asked someone to give me a *Br* lift *or Am* ride home after the party

raccord [rakɔr] **NM 1** *(en décoration)* join; **papier avec r.** wallpaper with pattern match; **tissu sans r.** random match material; **compte 33 centimètres pour le r.** allow 33 centimetres for pattern match

2 *Cin (liaison de scènes)* continuity; *(plan)* link shot; **scène de r.** link scene; *Littérature* link; *Cin* **r. sur le regard** eyeline match

3 *(retouche)* touch-up; **la peinture de la cuisine a besoin de quelques raccords** the kitchen paintwork needs some touching up; *Fam* **elle s'est fait un petit r. devant la glace** she touched up her make-up in front of the mirror

4 *Tech (pour tuyaux différents)* adaptor; *(joint)* connector; **r. en T** T-union

raccordement [rakɔrdəmɑ̃] **NM 1** *(opération de connexion) & Rail* linking, joining; *(travaux publics)* connecting, linking, joining; *Élec* joining, connecting; *Tél* **faire le r. (au réseau)** to connect the phone **2** *(voie ferrée)* junction **3** *Ordinat* link

raccorder [3] [rakɔrde] **VT 1** *(route, chemin de fer)* to link up, to join up; **la ville nouvelle est raccordée à l'autoroute** the new town is linked up to the motorway *or* has a motorway link-up

2 *(morceaux cassés, papier peint)* to align, to join (up); *(bandes magnétiques)* to splice; **les motifs ne sont pas raccordés** the pattern doesn't line up

3 *Élec (au secteur)* to couple; *(à un circuit)* to join; **nous ne sommes toujours pas raccordés au réseau électrique** we still don't have mains electricity

4 *Tél* **r. qn au réseau** to connect (up) sb's phone

5 *Fig (indices, faits)* to link up, to connect

6 *Cin (scènes)* to link up

►**se raccorder VPR 1 se r. à** *(route, voie ferrée)* to join up with

2 se r. à *(être lié à)* to tie in with; **le dernier paragraphe ne se raccorde pas au reste** the last paragraph doesn't tie in with the rest

3 *Ordinat* **se r. à** to link up to

raccourci [rakursi] **NM 1** *(trajet)* shortcut; **prendre un r.** to take a shortcut **2** *(énoncé)* **un r. saisissant** a pithy turn of phrase **3** *Beaux-Arts* foreshortening *(UNCOUNT)* **4** *Ordinat* **r. clavier** keyboard shortcut

❑ **en raccourci ADV** *(en résumé)* in brief, in a nutshell; *(en miniature)* on a small scale, in miniature

raccourcir [32] [rakursir] **VT 1** *(vêtement, rideau)* to shorten, to take up; *(cheveux, barbe)* to trim; *(discours, texte, trajet, film)* to shorten; *(séjour)* to cut short; **j'ai raccourci la robe de 3 centimètres** I've shortened the dress by 3 centimetres, I've taken the dress up by 3 centimetres; **tu as trop raccourci les manches** you've made the sleeves too short; **le sentier raccourcit le trajet de deux kilomètres** the path shortens the trip by two kilometres; **elle a dû r. ses vacances d'une semaine** she had to come back from her holidays a week early

2 *Fam (décapiter)* **r. qn** to chop sb's head off

VI 1 *(en durée)* **les jours raccourcissent** the days are growing shorter *or* drawing in

2 *(en longueur)* **son tee-shirt a raccourci au lavage** his/her T-shirt has shrunk in the wash; **les manteaux vont r. à l'automne prochain** coats will be shorter next autumn

3 *(distance)* **ça raccourcit** it's shorter

►**se raccourcir VPR** *(diminuer)* **les délais de livraison se sont considérablement raccourcis** delivery times have been considerably shortened *or* reduced

raccourcissement [rakursismɑ̃] **NM** *(des jours)* shortening, drawing in; *(d'un vêtement au lavage)* shrinking; *(des délais)* shortening, reducing; **on remarque un r. des jupes dans la collection automne–hiver** hemlines are higher in this year's autumn–winter collection

raccroc [rakro] **par raccroc ADV** by a stroke of good luck

raccrochage [rakrɔʃaʒ] **NM 1** *(du téléphone)* hanging up **2** *(de wagons)* coupling **3** *Fam (racolage)* soliciting[■], *Am* hustling

raccrocher [3] [rakrɔʃe] **VT 1** *(remettre en place → habit, rideau)* to hang back up; *(→ tableau)* to put back on the hook, to hang *or* to put back up; *(→ téléphone)* to put down, to hang up; *Fam* **r. les gants** *(boxeur)* to hang up one's gloves; *Fam* **r. le client** *(prostituée)* to solicit[■], *Am* to hustle, to hook

2 *(relier → wagons)* to couple, to hitch together; **la remorque a été mal raccrochée à la voiture** the trailer wasn't properly hitched up to the car; *Fig* **c'est la seule chose qui la raccroche à la vie** it's the only thing which keeps her going, it's her only lifeline

3 *(rattraper → affaire)* to save at the last minute; **ils ont raccroché les négociations** they managed to rescue the negotiations at the last minute

4 *Fam (obtenir par chance → commande)* to pull off, to bring off

VI 1 *(au téléphone)* to hang up, to put the receiver down; **elle m'a raccroché au nez** she hung up on me; **je n'ai pas envie de me faire r. au nez** I don't want to have the phone put down on me

2 *Fam (cesser une activité → gén)* to pack it in, *Am* to hang it up; *(→ boxeur)* to hang up one's gloves

►**se raccrocher VPR 1 se r. à** *(se rattraper à)* to grab *or* to catch hold of; *Fig* **il n'a personne à qui se r.** he has nobody to turn to; *Fig* **il se raccrochait à cet espoir** he hung on to that hope

2 se r. à *(être relié à)* to be linked *or* related to

raccrocheur, -euse [rakrɔʃœr, -øz] **ADJ** *(publicité)* eye-catching

raccuser [3] [rakyze] **VT** *Belg Fam* to snitch on

raccusette [rakyzɛt] **NF** *Belg Fam* snitch

race [ras] **NF 1** *(d'un humain)* race; **la r. blanche/noire** the white/black race; **de r. blanche** white; **de r. noire** black; **il est de r. asiatique** he's of Asian origin

2 *(catégorie)* **la r. des honnêtes gens est en voie de disparition** decent people are a dying breed; **il est de la r. des gens qui se plaignent tout le temps** he's one of those people who are always moaning; **elle est de la r. des gagnants** she's a born winner; *très Fam* **(quelle) sale r.!** (what) scum!

3 *(d'un animal)* breed; **la r. canine/féline/bovine/porcine** dogs/cats/cattle/pigs

4 *Littéraire (lignée)* line; **être de r. noble** to be of noble stock *or* blood

5 *(distinction)* **avoir de la r.** to have breeding

6 *très Fam* **ta r.!** *Br* piss off!, *Am* take a hike!; *Vulg* **enculé de ta r.!** you fucking prick!; *très Fam* **défoncer** *ou* **faire** *ou* **éclater sa r. à qn** to waste sb's face, *Br* to punch sb's lights out, *Am* to punch sb out; *Vulg* **niquer sa r. à qn** to beat the shit out of sb

❑ **de race ADJ** *(chien, chat)* purebred, pedigree *(avant n)*; *(cheval)* thoroughbred; **avoir de la r.** *(chien, chat)* to be purebred; *(cheval)* to be a thoroughbred

racé, -e [rase] **ADJ 1** *(chien, chat)* purebred, pedigree *(avant n)*; *(cheval)* thoroughbred **2** *(personne)* distinguished(-looking), tall and aristocratic-looking **3** *(voilier, voiture)* handsome

racémique [rasemik] ADJ *Chim* racemic

racer [rɛsœr] NM racer *(car, boat)*

rachat [raʃa] NM **1** *(de ce qu'on avait vendu)* repurchase, buying back; *Jur* **avec faculté de r.** with option of repurchase

2 *Com (achat)* **nous vous proposons le r. de votre ancienne voiture!** we offer to take your old car as a trade-in *or Br* in part-exchange!

3 *Fin (d'actions, d'obligations)* buying up *or* in; *(d'une affaire)* takeover; *(d'une franchise, d'une rente)* redemption; *Bourse (d'actions)* buy-back, repurchase; *(de police d'assurance)* surrender; **r. d'entreprise financé par l'endettement** leveraged buy-out; **r. de l'entreprise par la direction** management buy-out; **r. d'entreprise par les salariés** staff *or* employee buy-out; *Compta* **r. forfaitaire des créances** lump-sum purchase of accounts receivable; *Bourse* **r. gagnant** repurchase at a profit

4 *(de captifs)* **ils ont convenu du r. des captifs** they came to an agreement over the prisoners' ransom; **l'opposition a condamné le r. des otages** the opposition condemned the ransom being paid to free the hostages

5 *(des péchés)* redemption

Rachel [raʃɛl] NPR *Bible* Rachel

rachetable [raʃtabl] ADJ **1** *Fam (remplaçable)* **un vase, c'est r.** a vase is replaceable **2** *Littéraire (dette, rente, péché)* redeemable

racheter [28] [raʃte] VT **1** *(en plus)* to buy some more (of); **rachète du pain** buy some more bread; **r. des actions** *(en supplément)* to buy some more shares; *(pour remplacer celles qu'on a vendues)* to buy back *or* to repurchase shares; **je vais r. un service à café** I'm going to buy another *or* a new coffee set

2 *(acheter → gén)* to buy; *(→ entreprise)* to take over; *Bourse (actions)* to repurchase, to buy back; **r. qch à qn** *(à un particulier)* to buy sth from sb; *Com* **on vous rachète vos anciens meubles** your old furniture taken *Br* in part-exchange *or Am* as a trade-in; *Fin* **j'ai racheté sa part/son affaire** I've bought him/her out (of the business)/bought him/her out; *Bourse* **se couvrir en rachetant** to cover a short position by buying back

3 *(rente, cotisations, obligation)* to redeem

4 *(erreur, défaut)* to make up for, to compensate for; *(péché)* to atone for, *Sout* to expiate; *(vie dissolue)* to make amends for, to make up for; *(pécheur)* to redeem; **Jésus-Christ est mort pour r. les hommes** Christ died to redeem mankind; **il n'y en a pas un pour r. l'autre** one's as bad as the other; **l'humour ne rachète pas la lourdeur du style** the humour doesn't compensate for *or* make up for the clumsiness of the style

5 *Constr* to modify, to compensate

6 *Hist (soldat)* to buy out; *(prisonnier, esclave)* to ransom, to buy the freedom of

7 *Scol & Univ* **r. un candidat** to pass a candidate *(in spite of insufficient marks)*; **r. une (mauvaise) note** to make up for a (poor) *Br* mark *or Am* grade

▸**se racheter** VPR *(gén)* to make amends, to redeem oneself; *(pécheur)* to redeem oneself; **que puis-je faire pour me r.?** what can I do to make up for it?, how can I redeem myself?; **ce n'est pas en m'offrant des fleurs que tu vas te r.!** it'll take more than flowers to bring me round!

racheteur [raʃtœr] NM purchaser

rachialgie [raʃjalʒi] NF *Méd* rachialgia

rachianalgésie [raʃianalʒezi], **rachianesthésie** [raʃianɛstezi] NF *Méd* rachianaesthesia

rachidien, -enne [raʃidjɛ̃, -ɛn] ADJ rachidian, rachidial

rachis [raʃis] NM *Anat, Bot & Orn* rachis; **r. cervical** cervical vertebrae; **r. lombaire** lumbar vertebrae

rachitique [raʃitik] ADJ **1** *Méd* suffering from rickets, *Spéc* rachitic **2** *(chétif → plante)* stunted; *(→ chien, personne)* puny, scrawny

NMF person suffering from rickets

rachitisme [raʃitism] NM *Méd* rickets *(singulier)*, *Spéc* rachitis

Rachmaninov [rakmaninɔf] NPR Rachmaninov, Rachmaninoff

racho [raʃo] *Fam* ADJ *(personne, arbre)* weedy, scrawny; *(portion)* mean, stingy

NMF scrawny person

racial, -e, -aux, -ales [rasjal, -o] ADJ racial, race *(avant n)*; **attiser la haine raciale** to stir up racial hatred; **émeute raciale** race riot

racinage [rasinaʒ] NM *(en reliure)* tree-marbling

racinal, -aux [rasinal, -o] NM **1** *(pièce de charpente)* purlin **2** *Constr* member

racine [rasin] NF **1** *Bot* root; **r. aérienne** aerial root; **r. pivotante** taproot; **racines alimentaires** root crops; **racines (comestibles)** root vegetables; **r. de gingembre** root ginger; **prendre r.** to take root; *Fam* **il prend r.** *(il s'installe)* he's getting a bit too comfortably settled■; *Fam* **tu vas prendre r.!** *(l'attente est longue)* you'll take root!; *Littéraire* **ces vices jettent dans l'âme de profondes racines** these vices become deeply rooted in the soul

2 *Anat (d'un cheveu, d'un poil, d'une dent)* root; *(du nez)* base; *Fam* **se faire faire les racines** *(chez le coiffeur)* to have one's roots done

3 *Ling & Math* root; **r. carrée/cubique/énième** square/cube/nth root

4 *Ordinat* root directory

▫ **racines** NFPL *(origines)* roots; **elle a ses racines en Écosse** her roots are in Scotland; **je suis sans racines** I don't have any roots, I don't belong anywhere; **retrouver ses racines** to go back to one's roots; **cette croyance a ses racines dans le folklore breton** this belief is rooted in Breton folklore

raciner [3] [rasine] VT *(en reliure)* to tree-marble

racinien, -enne [rasinjɛ̃, -ɛn] ADJ Racinian

racisme [rasism] NM racism, racial prejudice; **c'est du r. anti-vieux** that's ageism; **c'est du r. anti-jeunes** that's prejudice against young people

raciste [rasist] ADJ racist

NMF racist

rack [rak] NM *(meuble)* (stereo) rack

racket [rakɛt] NM *(activité)* racketeering; *(contre protection)* (protection) racket; **la lutte contre le r. à l'école** the fight to stop schoolchildren being bullied into handing over their money or possessions

racketter [4] [rakete] VT to extort money from; **se faire r.** *(gén)* to be a victim of extortion; *(contre protection)* to pay protection money; **il est inadmissible que les enfants se fassent r. dans les écoles** it is unacceptable for schoolchildren to be bullied into handing over their money or possessions

racketteur, -euse [rakɛtœr, -øz] NM,F racketeer

raclage [raklaʒ] NM scraping

racle [rakl] NF *(instrument)* squeegee

raclée [rakle] NF *Fam* **1** *(coups)* thrashing, hiding; **flanquer une r. à qn** to give sb a good thrashing *or* hiding; **prendre** *ou* **recevoir une r.** to get a good thrashing *or* hiding **2** *(défaite)* thrashing, hammering; **mettre une r. à qn** to thrash sb; **il a pris une** *ou* **sa r. en finale** he got thrashed *or* hammered in the final

raclement [rakləmɑ̃] NM scraping (noise); **on entendit quelques raclements de gorge** some people could be heard clearing their throats

racler [3] [rakle] VT **1** *(frotter → gén)* to scrape; *(→ pour enlever)* to scrape off; **r. la semelle de ses souliers** to scrape the soles of one's shoes; **r. la peinture de la table** to scrape the paint off the table; **un petit vin blanc qui racle le gosier** a white wine that is rough on *or* that burns your throat; *Fig* **r. les fonds de tiroir** to scrape some money together

2 *Péj (instrument)* **r. du violon** to scrape away at the fiddle

▸**se racler** VPR **se r. la gorge** to clear one's throat

râcler [3] [rakle] VT *Can Vieilli* to rake

raclette [raklɛt] NF **1** *Culin (plat)* raclette, = Swiss speciality consisting of melted cheese prepared at the table using a special heater or grill, served with potatoes and cold meats; *(fromage)* raclette *(cheese)* **2** *(grattoir)* scraper **3** *(pour vitres)* squeegee

racleur, -euse [raklœr, -øz] NM,F **ce n'est qu'un r. de violon** he's a third-rate fiddler

racli [rakli] NF *Fam* chick, *Br* bird

raclo [raklo] NM *Fam* guy, *Br* bloke

racloir [raklwar] NM **1** *Mines* scraper **2** *Menuis* scraper plane **3** *Métal* strickle **4** *Archéol* racloir, side scraper

raclure [raklyr] NF **1** *(résidu)* scraping **2** *très Fam (homme méprisable)* bastard, *Am* son-of-a-bitch; *(femme méprisable)* bitch

racolage [rakɔlaʒ] NM **1** *(par une prostituée)* soliciting; *(par un vendeur)* touting (for customers); *(par un militant)* canvassing; **faire du r.** *(prostituée)* to solicit; *(commerçant)* to tout (for customers); *(militant)* to canvass (support) **2** *Hist (de soldats)* press-ganging

racoler [3] [rakɔle] VT **1** *(clients → sujet: prostituée)* to accost; *(→ sujet: vendeur)* to tout for; *(électeurs)* to canvass **2** *Hist (soldat)* to press-gang

VI *(prostituée)* to solicit

racoleur, -euse [rakɔlœr, -øz] ADJ *(sourire)* enticing; *(affiche)* eye-catching; *(titre, journal)* sensationalist; *(campagne électorale)* vote-catching

NM,F *(politicien)* canvasser; *(commerçant)* tout

NM *Hist* crimp

▫ **racoleuse** NF *(prostituée)* prostitute *(soliciting on the street)*

racontable [rakɔ̃tabl] ADJ **ce n'est pas r. devant des enfants** I can't say it in front of children; **alors que s'est-il passé? – ce n'est pas r.!** so what happened? – it defies description!

racontar [rakɔ̃tar] NM *Fam* piece of gossip; **n'écoute pas les racontars** don't listen to gossip; **tout ça, c'est des racontars** that's just gossip *or* talk

raconter [3] [rakɔ̃te] VT **1** *(conte, histoire)* to tell; **la tapisserie de Bayeux raconte la conquête de l'Angleterre** the Bayeux tapestry tells (the story) of the conquest of England; **il a raconté l'histoire à son voisin** he told his neighbour the story, he told the story to his neighbour

2 *(événement, voyage)* to tell, to relate; **il a raconté l'accident à sa mère** he told his mother about the accident; **r. ses malheurs à qn** to tell sb all one's troubles, to pour one's heart out to sb; *Fam* **r. sa vie** to tell one's (whole) life story; *Fam* **nous raconte pas ta vie!** we don't want to hear your life story!

3 *(dire)* to tell; **ne crois pas tout ce qu'on raconte** don't believe everything people tell you; **on raconte beaucoup de choses sur lui** you hear all sorts of stories about him; **on m'avait raconté que vous étiez malade** I heard that you were ill; **on raconte qu'il a été marié plusieurs fois** people say he's been married several times; **à ce qu'on raconte, elle était la maîtresse du docteur** she was the doctor's mistress, at least that's what people say; **elle est allée tout lui r.** she went and told him/her everything; **mais enfin qu'est-ce que tu racontes?** what (on earth) are you on about?; **ne raconte pas de bêtises** don't be silly; **qu'est-ce que tu racontes (de beau)?** so, what's new?; *Fam* **je te raconte pas!** you can't imagine!; **on s'est pris une de ces cuites, je te raconte pas...** you can't imagine how plastered we got

USAGE ABSOLU **vite, raconte!** go on, *or* quick, tell me!; **r. bien/mal** to be a good/bad storyteller

▸**se raconter** VPR **1** *(événement)* **des choses pareilles ne se racontent pas** such things are best left unsaid; **il faut l'avoir vécu, ça ne se raconte pas** I couldn't describe what it was like, you had to be there

2 *(parler de soi)* to talk about oneself

3 *Fam (à soi-même)* **se r. des histoires** to fool *or* to delude oneself■; **se la r.** to show off

raconteur, -euse [rakɔ̃tœr, -øz] NM,F storyteller; **c'est un bon r.** he tells a good story

racorni, -e [rakɔrni] ADJ **1** *(vieillard)* wizened, shrivelled; *(mains)* gnarled; *(plante)* shrivelled; *(parchemin)* dried-up **2** *(esprit)* hardened

racornir [32] [rakɔrnir] VT **1** *(peau)* to toughen; *(cuir, parchemin)* to stiffen; *(cœur)* to harden **2** *(plante)* to shrivel up

▸**se racornir** VPR **1** *(peau, viande)* to become tough; *(cuir, parchemin)* to stiffen, to become stiff **2** *(plante)* to shrivel up, to become shrivelled up **3** *(personne)* to become hardened *or* hardhearted

racornissement [rakɔrnismɑ̃] NM **1** *(de la peau)* toughening; *(du cuir, du parchemin)* stiffening; *(du cœur)* hardening **2** *(d'une plante)* shrivelling up

racquet-ball [rakɛtbol] **NM** raquetball

racrapoter [3] [rakrapɔte] **se racrapoter VPR** *Belg (confortablement)* to curl up; *(dans l'inconfort)* to huddle up; *Fig* to retreat into *or* to turn in on oneself

rad [rad] **NM** rad

radar [radar] **NM** radar; **r. d'autoguidage** homing radar; **r. de navigation** navigation radar; **r. de veille** military surveillance radar; **écran/système r.** radar screen/system; **contrôle-r.** *(sur la route)* radar speed trap; *Fam* **marcher au r.** *(ne pas être bien réveillé)* to be on automatic pilot

radarastronomie [radarastrɔnɔmi] **NF** radar astronomy

radariste [radarist] **NMF** radar specialist *or* engineer

radasse [radas] **NF** *Vulg* **1** *(prostituée)* tart, hooker **2** *(femme)* tart, *Br* slapper

rade [rad] **NF 1** *Naut (bassin)* (natural) harbour, *Spéc* roads, roadstead; **en r. de San Francisco** in San Francisco harbour; **mouiller en r. de Brest** to lie at anchor off Brest (harbour); **le navire a coulé en r. de Toulon** the ship sank off Toulon (harbour)
  2 *Fam (locutions)* **laisser qn en r.** *(abandonner)* to leave sb stranded *or* in the lurch; **on est restés en r.** we were left stranded; **être en r.** *(en panne)* to have broken down■ *or* conked out; **tomber en r.** *(en panne)* to break down■, to conk out
  NM *Fam (bar)* joint

radeau, -x [rado] **NM** raft; **r. de sauvetage** life raft; **r. pneumatique** inflatable raft

═══════════════════════

'Le Radeau de la Méduse' *Géricault* 'The Raft of the Medusa'

rader [3] [rade] **VT** *(bloc de pierre)* to split

radeuse [radøz] **NF** *Fam Arg* crime *Vieilli* streetwalker

radiaire [radjɛr] **ADJ** radiate, radiated

radial, -e, -aux, -ales [radjal, -o] **ADJ** *Math & Anat* radial
  □ **radiale NF** *(autoroute urbaine)* urban expressway *(leading out from the city centre)*

radian [radjɑ̃] **NM** radian

radiance [radjɑ̃s] **NF** *Vieilli* radiance

radiant, -e [radjɑ̃, -ɑ̃t] **ADJ** radiant
  NM radiant

radiateur [radjatœr] **NM** *(à eau, d'un véhicule)* radiator; **r. à bain d'huile** oil-filled radiator; **r. à gaz** gas heater; **r. électrique** electric radiator *or* heater; **r. soufflant** fan heater

radiatif, -ive [radjatif, -iv] **ADJ** radiative

radiation [radjasjɔ̃] **NF 1** *Biol & Phys* radiation **2** *(élimination → d'un candidat, d'un médecin)* striking off; *(→ d'un avocat)* disbarment; *(→ d'une dette)* cancellation; **ils ont demandé sa r. de l'ordre des médecins/du barreau** they asked that he/she should be struck off the medical register/that he/she should be disbarred from practising law; *Bourse* **r. de la cote** delisting

radiative [radjativ] *voir* **radiatif**

radical, -e, -aux, -ales [radikal, -o] **ADJ 1** *(complet)* radical, drastic; **un changement r.** a drastic *or* radical change; **une réorganisation radicale** a thoroughgoing *or* root and branch reorganization
  2 *(efficace)* **l'eucalyptus c'est r. contre le rhume** eucalyptus is just the thing for colds; *Fam* **il s'endort quand je mets la radio, c'est r.** he goes to sleep as soon as I put the radio on, it works like a dream
  3 *Pol* radical
  4 *Bot* radical, root *(avant n)*
  5 *Ling* root *(avant n)*
  NM,F *Pol* radical; **r. de gauche** member of the ''Parti radical de gauche''
  NM 1 *Ling* radical, stem
  2 *Chim* radical; **r. divalent** dyad; **r. libre** free radical
  3 *Math* radical (sign)

radicalaire [radikalɛr] **ADJ** *Chim* free radical *(avant n)*

radicalement [radikalmɑ̃] **ADV** radically, completely; **r. faux** completely untrue; **il a r. changé**

he's completely different, he's a different person

radicalisation [radikalizasjɔ̃] **NF** radicalization; **il est pour la r. des revendications** he wants the demands to be made more radical; **la r. du conflit** the heightening of the conflict

radicaliser [3] [radikalize] **VT** to radicalize, to make more radical
  ▶**se radicaliser VPR le mouvement étudiant s'est radicalisé** the student movement has become more radical

radicalisme [radikalism] **NM** radicalism

radicalité [radikalite] **NF** radicality

radical-socialisme [radikalsɔsjalism] *(pl* **radical-socialismes***)* **NM** radical-socialism

radical-socialiste, radicale-socialiste [radikalsɔsjalist] *(mpl* **radicaux-socialistes** [radikosɔsjalist]*, fpl* **radicales-socialistes***)* **ADJ** radical-socialist
  NM,F radical-socialist

radicant, -e [radikɑ̃, -ɑ̃t] **ADJ** radicant

radicelle [radisɛl] **NF** rootlet, *Spéc* radicel

radicivore [radisivɔr] **ADJ** *Zool* root-eating

radicotomie [radikɔtɔmi] **NF** *Méd* radicotomy

radiculaire [radikylɛr] **ADJ** radicular

radiculalgie [radikylalʒi] **NF** *Méd* radiculalgia

radicule [radikyl] **NF** radicle

radiculite [radikylit] **NF** *Méd* radiculitis

radié, -e [radje] **ADJ 1** *(cadran)* marked in rays, *Spéc* radiate **2** *Bot* radiate, rayed
  □ **radiée NF** *Bot* radiate plant

radier[1] [radje] **NM 1** *Constr (dalle)* concrete slab; *(revêtement)* apron **2** *Mines* sill

radier[2] [9] [radje] **VT** *(éliminer → candidat, médecin)* to strike off; *(→ avocat)* to disbar; *(→ dette)* to cancel; **elle a été radiée de l'ordre des médecins/du barreau** she was struck off the medical register/disbarred from practising law; *Bourse* **r. qch de la cote** *(société, actions)* to delist sth

radiesthésie [radjɛstezi] **NF** divination, divining

radiesthésiste [radjɛstezist] **NMF** diviner

radieux, -euse [radjø, -øz] **ADJ** *(matinée, temps)* glorious; *(soleil, beauté)* brilliant, radiant; *(visage, personne)* radiant, glowing (with happiness); **un sourire r.** a beaming smile; **elle était radieuse à son retour de vacances** she was positively glowing when she got back from her holidays

radin, -e [radɛ̃, -in] *Fam* **ADJ** tightfisted, stingy
  NM,F skinflint, tightwad

radiner [3] [radine] **VI** *Fam (arriver)* to turn *or* to show *or* to roll up; **alors, tu radines?** are you coming then?
  ▶**se radiner VPR** *Fam* to turn *or* to show *or* to roll up; **allez, vite, radine-toi!** come on, get a move on!

radinerie [radinri] **NF** *Fam* tightfistedness, stinginess

radio [radjo] **NF 1** *(récepteur)* radio
  2 *(diffusion)* **la r.** radio (broadcasting); **faire de la r.** to be *or* to work as a radio presenter; **à la r.** on the radio; **passer à la r.** *(personne)* to be on the radio; *(chanson)* to be played on the radio; *(jeu, concert)* to be broadcast (on the radio), *Am* to be radiocast
  3 *(station)* radio station; **sur toutes les radios** on all stations; **écoutez r. TSW!** tune in to TSW!; **R. France** = state-owned radio broadcasting company; **R. France Internationale** = French overseas broadcasting service; **r. commerciale** commercial radio station; **r. communautaire** community radio station; **r. locale** local radio station; **r. locale privée** ou **libre** independent local radio station; **r. musicale** music station; **r. périphérique** = radio station broadcasting from outside national territory; **r. pirate** pirate radio station; **r. privée** independent *or* commercial radio station
  4 *(radiotéléphonie)* radiotelephony
  5 *Méd* X-ray (photograph); **passer une r.** *ou* *Fam* **à la r.** to have an X-ray (done), to be X-rayed; **faire une r. de qch** to X-ray sth
  NM 1 *Vieilli (télégramme)* radio(gram)
  2 *(opérateur)* radio operator
  ADJ INV radio *(avant n)*; **message r.** radio message

radioactif, -ive [radjoaktif, -iv] **ADJ** radioactive

radioactivation [radjoaktivasjɔ̃] **NF** radioactivation

radioactive [radjoaktiv] *voir* **radioactif**

radioactivité [radjoaktivite] **NF** radioactivity

radioalignement [radjoalinmɑ̃] **NM** *(méthode)* radio navigation; *(dispositif)* radio direction finder

radioaltimètre [radjoaltimɛtr] **NM** radio altimeter

radioamateur [radjoamatœr] **NM** radio ham

radioastronome [radjoastrɔnɔm] **NMF** radio astronomer

radioastronomie [radjoastrɔnɔmi] **NF** radio astronomy

radiobalisage [radjobalizaʒ] **NM** radio beacon signalling

radiobalise [radjobaliz] **NF** radio beacon

radiobaliser [3] [radjobalize] **VT** to equip with a radio beacon signalling system

radiobiologie [radjobjɔlɔʒi] **NF** radiobiology

radiocarbone [radjokarbɔn] **NM** radiocarbon

radiocassette [radjokasɛt] **NM** radio cassette player

radiochimie [radjoʃimi] **NF** radiochemistry

radiochronologie [radjokrɔnɔlɔʒi] **NF** radiochronology

radiocobalt [radjokɔbalt] **NM** radiocobalt

radiocommande [radjokɔmɑ̃d] **NF** radio control

radiocommunication [radjokɔmynikasjɔ̃] **NF** radiocommunication

radiocompas [radjokɔ̃pa] **NM** radio compass

radioconcentrique [radjokɔ̃sɑ̃trik] **ADJ** radio-concentric

radioconducteur [radjokɔ̃dyktœr] **NM** *Phys* radioconductor

radiocristallographie [radjokristalɔgrafi] **NF** *Phys* radio crystallography

radiodermite [radjodɛrmit] **NF** *Méd* radiodermatitis

radiodétection [radjodetɛksjɔ̃] **NF** radiodetection

radiodiagnostic [radjodjagnɔstik] **NM** *Méd* X-ray diagnosis

radiodiffraction [radjodifraksjɔ̃] **NF** X-ray diffraction

radiodiffusé, -e [radjodifyze] **ADJ** radio *(avant n)*

radiodiffuser [3] [radjodifyze] **VT** to broadcast (on radio), *Am* to radiocast

radiodiffusion [radjodifyzjɔ̃] **NF** (radio) broadcasting

radioélectricien, -enne [radjoelɛktrisjɛ̃, -ɛn] **NM,F** radio engineer

radioélectricité [radjoelɛktrisite] **NF** radio engineering

radioélectrique [radjoelɛktrik] **ADJ** *Élec* radio *(avant n)*

radioélément [radjoelemɑ̃] **NM** radioelement

radiofréquence [radjofrekɑ̃s] **NF** radio frequency

radiogalaxie [radjogalaksi] **NF** radio galaxy

radiogénique [radjoʒenik] **ADJ** **voix r.** good broadcasting voice; **elle est très r.** she's good radio material

radiogoniomètre [radjogɔnjɔmɛtr] **NM** (radio) direction finder, radiogoniometer

radiogoniométrie [radjogɔnjɔmetri] **NF** (radio) direction finding, radiogoniometry

radiogramme [radjogram] **NM** radiogram

radiographie [radjografi] **NF** *(technique)* radiography, X-ray photography; *(image)* X-ray

radiographier [9] [radjografje] **VT** to X-ray

radiographique [radjografik] **ADJ** *(technique)* radiographic; *(examen)* X-ray *(avant n)*

radioguidage [radjogidaʒ] **NM 1** *Aviat* radio direction finding, radio guidance; *(de missile)* homing **2** *Aut* traffic news

radioguidé, -e [radjogide] **ADJ** *(avion)* radio-controlled; *(projectile, missile)* guided

radioguider [3] [radjogide] **VT** to radio-control

radio-immunologie [radjoimynɔlɔʒi] **NF** radioimmunology

radio-immunologique [radjoimynɔlɔʒik] *(pl* **radio-immunologiques***)* **ADJ** **dosage r.** radioimmunoassay

radio-isotope [radjoizɔtɔp] *(pl* **radio-isotopes***)* **NM** radioisotope

radiolaire [radjolɛr] *Zool* **NM** radiolarian
  □ **radiolaires NMPL** Radiolaria

radiolarite [radjolarit] **NF** *Minér* radiolarite, radiolarian ooze

radiolésion [radjolezjɔ̃] **NF** radiation injury, radiolesion

radiolocalisation [radjɔlɔkalizasjɔ̃] NF radioloca-tion

radiologie [radjɔlɔʒi] NF radiology

radiologique [radjɔlɔʒik] ADJ radiological; **exa-men r.** X-ray examination

radiologiste [radjɔlɔʒist], **radiologue** [radjɔlɔg] NMF radiologist

radioluminescence [radjɔlyminɛsɑ̃s] NF radio-luminescence

radiolyse [radjɔliz] NF radiolysis

radiomessagerie [radjɔmesaʒri] NF radio-paging

radiométallographie [radjɔmetalɔgrafi] NF radio metallography

radiomètre [radjɔmɛtr] NM radiometer; **r. à ba-layage** scanning radiometer

radionavigant [radjɔnavigɑ̃] NM radio officer *or* operator

radionavigation [radjɔnavigasjɔ̃] NF radio navi-gation; **aide à la r.** radio navigational aid; **techniques de r.** radio navigational techniques

radionécrose [radjɔnekroz] NF *Méd* radionecro-sis, X-ray necrosis

radiophare [radjɔfar] NM radio beacon

radiophonie [radjɔfɔni] NF broadcasting, radio-telephony

radiophonique [radjɔfɔnik] ADJ *(émission, feuille-ton)* radio *(avant n)*; *(studio)* broadcasting *(avant n)*

radiophotographie [radjɔfɔtɔgrafi] NF *(image)* X-ray photograph; *(procédé)* radiophotography

radioprotection [radjɔprɔtɛksjɔ̃] NF defence against radiation

radiorécepteur [radjɔresɛptœr] NM radio receiver

radiorepérage [radjɔrɔperaʒ] NM radiolocation

radioreportage [radjɔrɔpɔrtaʒ] NM *(émission)* (radio) report; *(commentaire)* (radio) com-mentary

radioreporter [radjɔrɔpɔrtɛr] NM (radio) reporter *or* correspondent

radiorésistance [radjɔrezistɑ̃s] NF radioresist-ance

radioréveil [radjɔrevɛj] NM radio alarm (clock)

radioscopie [radjɔskɔpi] NF 1 *Méd* radioscopy 2 *(étude)* in-depth analysis

radioscopique [radjɔskɔpik] ADJ X-ray *(avant n)*

radiosensibilité [radjɔsɑ̃sibilite] NF radiosensi-tivity

radiosensible [radjɔsɑ̃sibl] ADJ radiosensitive, radiation-sensitive

radiosondage [radjɔsɔ̃daʒ] NM radiosondage, radiosonde sounding; **station de r.** radiosonde station

radiosonde [radjɔsɔ̃d] NF *Météo* radiosonde, ra-diometeorograph

Radio-Sorbonne [radjɔsɔrbɔn] NF = radio service broadcasting distance learning programmes

radiosource [radjɔsurs] NF *Astron* radio-source, radio star, star source

radio-taxi [radjɔtaksi] *(pl* **radio-taxis)** NM radio cab, radio-taxi

radiotechnique [radjɔtɛknik] ADJ radiotechnical NF radiotechnics *(singulier)*, radio technology

radiotélégramme [radjɔtelegram] NM radiotele-gram

radiotélégraphie [radjɔtelegrafi] NF radiotelegra-phy, wireless telegraphy

radiotélégraphiste [radjɔtelegrafist] NMF radio operator, radiotelegrapher

radiotéléphone [radjɔtelefɔn] NM radiotele-phone

radiotéléphonie [radjɔtelefɔni] NF radioteleph-ony, radiocommunication; **r. cellulaire** cellular radio

radiotéléphoniste [radjɔtelefɔnist] NMF radio-telephonist

radiotélescope [radjɔteleskɔp] NM radio tele-scope

radiotélévisé, -e [radjɔtelevize] ADJ broadcast simultaneously on radio and TV, simulcast

radiotélévision [radjɔtelevizjɔ̃] NF radio and tele-vision

radiothérapeute [radjɔterapøt] NMF radiothera-pist

radiothérapie [radjɔterapi] NF radiotherapy

radiotrottoir [radjɔtrɔtwar] NM OU NF *Fam (en Afrique francophone)* = news spread by public rumour

radis [radi] NM 1 *Bot* radish; **r. noir** black radish 2 *Fam (sou)* **j'ai plus un r.** I haven't a bean *or Am* a red cent; **sans un r.** broke, *Br* skint

radium [radjɔm] NM *Chim* radium

radius [radjys] NM radius

radjah [radʒa] = **raja**

radôme [radom] NM radome

radon [radɔ̃] NM *Chim* radon

radotage [radɔtaʒ] NM drivel

radoter [3] [radɔte] *Fam* **vi** *(se répéter)* to witter on; *(divaguer)* to ramble on; **excuse-moi si je radote, mais...** sorry to go on and on about it, but...; **là, il radote!** he's going soft in the head! **vt 1** *(raconter)* **qu'est-ce que tu radotes?** what are you drivelling *or Br* wittering on about? **2** *(répéter)* **il radote cent fois les mêmes histoires** he's always going on about the same old things

radoteur, -euse [radɔtœr, -øz] NM,F drivelling fool

radoub [radu] NM **1** *(réparation)* repair, refitting; **le voilier est au r.** the yacht is being refitted **2** *(cale)* dry dock

radouber [3] [radube] **vt 1** *(bateau)* to repair, to refit **2** *(filet)* to mend **3** *Vieilli (vêtement)* to patch up

radoucir [32] [radusir] **vt 1** *(caractère)* to soften; *(personne)* to calm down, to mollify
2 *Météo* to make milder; **les chutes de neige ont radouci le temps** there's been a slight rise in temperature due to the snowfall
▸**se radoucir VPR 1** *(voix)* to soften, to become gentler; *(personne)* to yield, to soften; **elle a fini par se r. devant leurs prières** her attitude softened *or* she relented in the face of their pleas
2 *(température)* to get milder; **le temps s'est radouci** the weather's milder

radoucissement [radusismɑ̃] NM **1** *Météo* (slight) rise in temperature; **net r. des températures ce matin** a marked rise in temperature this morn-ing **2** *(d'une personne)* softening

radsoc [radsɔk] *Fam Vieilli* ADJ radical-socialist■ NMF radical-socialist■

radula [radyla] NF *Zool* radula

rafale [rafal] NF **1** *Météo (de vent, de pluie → gén)* gust; *(→ en mer)* squall; *(de neige)* flurry; **le vent souffle en ou par rafales** it's blustery **2** *Mil* burst; **une r. de mitraillette** a burst of machine-gun fire **3** *Fig* burst; **par ou en rafales** intermittently

raffermir [32] [rafɛrmir] **vt 1** *(muscle, peau)* to tone *or* to firm up; *(chair)* to firm up, to make firm(er)
2 *(consolider)* to strengthen, to reinforce; **r. sa position** to consolidate one's position; **r. le courage de qn** to bolster up sb's courage; **l'équipe gouvernementale est sortie raffermie du conflit** the government team came out of the conflict stronger
▸**se raffermir VPR 1** *(muscle, peau)* to tone *or* to firm up; *(chair)* to firm up, to become firmer
2 *(se consolider)* to get stronger; **son autorité se raffermit** he/she is recovering *or* regaining his/her authority; **se r. dans ses intentions** to stiffen one's resolve
3 *Fin (monnaie, prix)* to strengthen

raffermissement [rafɛrmismɑ̃] NM *(de muscle, de la peau)* toning *or* firming up; *(de chair)* firming up; *(de la voix)* steadying; *(de l'autorité, du pouvoir)* strengthening, consolidation; **r. des tendances à la Bourse** strengthening of trends on the Stock Exchange

raffinage [rafinaʒ] NM refining

raffinat [rafina] NM refined product

raffiné, -e [rafine] ADJ **1** *Ind* refined; **pétrole r.** refined oil **2** *(élégant → personne, style)* refined, sophisticated **3** *(subtil → raisonnement)* subtle; *(→ politesse)* extreme, exquisite; *(→ goût)* re-fined, discriminating
NM,F person of taste

raffinement [rafinmɑ̃] NM **1** *(élégance → d'une personne, d'un style)* refinement, sophistication **2** *(subtilité → d'un raisonnement)* subtlety; *(→ des goûts)* refinement **3** *(détail élégant)* sub-tlety, refinement **4** *(surenchère)* **avec un r. de cruauté** with exquisite *or* refined cruelty

raffiner [3] [rafine] **vt 1** *Ind* to refine **2** *(rendre plus délicat)* to polish, to refine
vi to be overparticular *(sur* about); **pas le temps de r., il faut agir!** there's no time for fussing over details, we need to act!; **elle raffine beaucoup sur la toilette** she's overparticular about her appearance; **je n'ai pas eu le temps de r. sur les détails** I didn't have time to pay that much attention to the details

raffinerie [rafinri] NF refinery; **r. de pétrole/sucre** oil/sugar refinery

raffineur, -euse [rafinœr, -øz] NM,F *Pétr* refiner NM (paper) refiner

raffle = **rafle 3**

rafflesia [raflezja] NM *Bot* rafflesia

rafflésie [raflezi] NF *Bot* rafflesia

raffoler [3] [rafɔle] **raffoler de vt IND** to be crazy *or* mad about; **il raffole de ses petits-enfants** he's mad about his grandchildren; **super, de la glace, j'en raffole!** ooh, ice cream, I LOVE ice cream!

raffut [rafy] NM *Fam* **1** *(bruit)* racket, din; **qu'est-ce que c'est que tout ce r.?** *(voix)* what's all this shouting about? **2** *(scandale)* **faire du r.** to cause a stink, to set tongues wagging

raffûter [3] [rafyte] **vt** *Sport* to hand off

rafiot [rafjo] NM *Fam (bateau)* **vieux r.** old tub

rafistolage [rafistɔlaʒ] NM *Fam* patching up; **c'est le roi du r.** he's always making do; *Fig* **ces changements ne sont que du r.** these changes will do nothing more than patch things up, these are nothing more than cosmetic changes

rafistoler [3] [rafistɔle] **vt** *Fam* to patch up

rafle [rafl] NF **1** *(arrestation)* raid; **une r. de police** a police raid; **la police a fait une r. dans le club** the police raided the club; *Hist* **la r. du Vel' d'Hiv** = the rounding up of Jews in the Paris Vélodrome d'Hiver in 1942
2 *Fig* **il y a eu une r. sur le sucre en prévision de l'embargo** all the sugar available in the shops was snatched up in anticipation of the embargo; **les cambrioleurs ont fait une r. dans les bijouteries du quartier** the burglars made a clean sweep of *or* cleaned out all the *Br* jewel-lers' shops *or Am* jewelry stores in the area
3 *Bot* stalk; *(du maïs)* cob

rafler [3] [rafle] **vt** *Fam* **1** *(voler)* to swipe, *Br* to nick **2** *(saisir)* to grab; *Com* to buy up; **les clients ont tout raflé en moins de deux heures** the customers cleared the shelves in less than two hours; **les enfants ont tout raflé dans la cuisine** the children have made off with everything in the kitchen **3** *(remporter → prix)* to walk off with; **le film a raflé toutes les récompenses** the film made a clean sweep of the awards

rafraîchir [32] [rafrɛʃir] **vt 1** *(refroidir)* to cool (down); **ces averses ont rafraîchi le temps** the weather's a bit cooler because of the showers; **un verre d'eau te rafraîchira** a glass of water will cool you down
2 *(remettre en état → vêtement)* to smarten *or* to brighten up; *(→ barbe)* to trim; *(→ peintures, maquillage)* to freshen up; **la cuisine a besoin d'être rafraîchie** the kitchen needs a lick of paint; **à r.** *(logement)* needs some redecoration
3 *Fam Fig (raviver)* **r. la mémoire à qn** to refresh *or* to jog sb's memory; **je vais te r. les idées ou la mémoire, moi!** I'll refresh your memory for you!
USAGE ABSOLU **je coupe ou je rafraîchis simple-ment?** *(chez le coiffeur)* do you want me to cut it or just tidy it up *or* give it a trim?
vi 1 *Météo* to get cooler or colder; **le temps rafraîchit** it's getting colder
2 *Culin* to chill; **mettre qch à r.** to chill sth
3 *Ordinat* to refresh
▸**se rafraîchir VPR 1** *(se refroidir)* to get colder
2 *(faire sa toilette)* to freshen up
3 *(boire)* to have a cool drink

rafraîchissant, -e [rafrɛʃisɑ̃, -ɑ̃t] ADJ **1** *(froid)* cool, refreshing; *(tonique)* refreshing, invig-orating; **une boisson rafraîchissante** a refresh-ing drink **2** *(charmant)* refreshing; **d'une simplicité/spontanéité rafraîchissante** refresh-ingly simple/spontaneous

rafraîchissement [rafrɛʃismɑ̃] NM **1** *(refroidisse-ment)* cooling; **net r. des températures sur tout le pays** temperatures are noticeably cooler throughout the country **2** *(boisson)* cool *or* cold drink **3** *Ordinat* refresh; **cycle/vitesse de r.** re-fresh cycle/rate

raft [raft], **rafting** [raftiŋ] NM white-water rafting

raga [raga] NM INV *Mus* raga

ragaillardir [32] [ragajardir] **vt** to buck *or* to perk

up; **ragaillardi par une nuit de sommeil** refreshed *or* reinvigorated after a good night's sleep

rage [raʒ] **NF 1** *Méd & Vét* **la r.** rabies; **r. de dents** (severe) toothache

2 *(colère → d'adulte)* rage, fury; *(→ d'enfant)* tantrum; **être fou de r.** to be absolutely furious; **mettre qn en r.** to infuriate sb; **elle est repartie la r. au cœur** she went off boiling *or* seething with rage; **j'ai accepté, mais la r. au cœur** I accepted, but actually I was furious about it; **r. de l'air** air rage; **r. au volant** road rage

3 *(passion)* passion, mania (**de** for); **ils ont la r. du jeu** they're mad on gambling; **avoir la r. de vivre** to have an insatiable lust for life; **avoir la r. d'apprendre** to have a passionate desire to learn

4 *(locution)* **faire r.** *(incendie, ouragan)* to rage; *(mode)* to be all the rage

Allusion

Ô rage! Ô désespoir!

In Corneille's play *Le Cid* of 1636, Rodrigo ("Rodrigue" in French and better known as Le Cid) is a young nobleman intent on avenging an insult to his father (Don Diego, "Don Diègue" in French) by the father of the woman he loves. These words are uttered by Don Diego in a monologue where he bewails his own inability to right the wrong inflicted on him as he is an old man. Today, this is a mock-melodramatic cry: one might say, for example, **Ô rage! Ô désespoir! Jamais je n'aurai fini mon travail dans les délais**, the English equivalent being "Curses! I'll never get this work done on time."

rageant, -e [raʒɑ̃, -ɑ̃t] **ADJ** *Fam* infuriating■

rager [17] [raʒe] **VI** to fume, to be furious; **r. contre qn** to be furious with sb; **je rage de la voir se pavaner** it makes me mad *or* it infuriates me to see her strutting about; **ça (vous) fait r.!** it's absolutely infuriating!; **ça me fait r. de voir tout cet argent dépensé pour rien** it makes my blood boil to see all that money just wasted

rageur, -euse [raʒœr, -øz] **ADJ 1** *(irrité → ton)* angry, enraged; *(→ geste, réponse)* bad-tempered, angry; **...dit-elle d'un ton r.** ...she said furiously; **"va au diable!" dit-il, r.** "go to hell!" he said furiously **2** *(coléreux)* hot-tempered

rageusement [raʒøzmɑ̃] **ADV** furiously, angrily; **il claqua r. la porte** he slammed the door angrily

raggamuffin [ragamœfin] **NM** *Mus* ragga, raggamuffin

raglan [raglɑ̃] **ADJ INV** raglan; **des manches r.** raglan sleeves

NM raglan coat

ragnagnas [raɲaɲa] **NMPL** *très Fam* **avoir ses r.** to be on the rag

ragondin [ragɔ̃dɛ̃] **NM 1** *Zool* coypu **2** *(fourrure)* nutria

ragot[1] [rago] **NM** piece of gossip; **des ragots** gossip; **les ragots ne m'intéressent pas** I'm not interested in gossip

ragot[2], **-e**[1] [rago, -ɔt] *Chasse & Zool* **ADJ F laie ragote** sow in its third year

NM boar in its third year

ragot[3], **-e**[2] [rago, -ɔt] **ADJ** *Vieilli* dumpy, squat

ragougnasse [raguɲas] **NF** *Fam (mauvais ragoût, mauvaise nourriture)* pigswill

ragoût [ragu] **NM** stew, ragout

❑ **en ragoût ADJ** stewed; **faire qch en r.** to stew sth

ragoûtant, -e [ragutɑ̃, -ɑ̃t] **ADJ peu r.** *(mets)* unappetizing; *(personne)* unsavoury; *(lieu)* insalubrious

ragréer [15] [ragree] **VT** *Constr* to finish off

ragtime [ragtajm] **NM** *Mus* ragtime

raguenasser [3] [ragənase] **VI** *Can (en acadien) (se répéter)* to repeat oneself, to witter on; *(divaguer)* to ramble

raguer [3] [rage] **VI** *Naut* to chafe, to rub

rahat-loukoum [raatlukum] *(pl* **rahat-loukoums***),* **rahat-lokoum** [raatlɔkum] *(pl* **rahat-lokoums***)* **NM** piece of Turkish delight; **des rahat-loukoums** Turkish delight

rai [rɛ] **NM 1** *Littéraire (rayon)* **un r. de lumière** a shaft of light **2** *(d'une roue)* spoke

raï [raj] **NM** *Mus* rai *(mixture of North African and Western music)*

raïa [raja] = **raya**

raid [rɛd] **NM 1** *Mil* raid, surprise attack; **r. aérien** air raid **2** *Sport (avec des véhicules)* long-distance rally; *(à pied)* trek **3** *Bourse* raid; **lancer un r. contre** *ou* **sur** to mount a raid on

raide [rɛd] **ADJ 1** *(rigide → baguette, étoffe)* stiff, rigid; *(tendu → fil, ficelle)* taut, tight; *(droit)* straight; **avoir une jambe r.** to have a stiff leg; **assis tout r. sur un tabouret/dans son lit** sitting stiffly on a stool/bolt upright in his bed; **avoir les cheveux raides (comme des baguettes de tambour)** to have (poker-)straight hair; **se tenir r. comme un piquet** to stand as stiff as a pole *or* a poker

2 *(guindé → personne, démarche)* stiff; *(→ style, jeu de scène)* wooden; *(inébranlable → personne, comportement)* rigid, inflexible; *Littéraire* **être r. comme la justice** to be totally unbending *or* inflexible

3 *(abrupt)* steep; **la côte est (en pente) r.** the hill climbs steeply; **la descente est en pente r.** *(piste de ski)* the slope is very steep; *(route)* the way down is very steep

4 *Fam (fort → café)* strong■; *(→ alcool)* rough; **vraiment r., cette vodka!** that vodka's really rough!

5 *Fam (osé → détail, récit, scène)* risqué■; **le vieux canapé a dû en voir de raides** the old sofa has seen a thing or two

6 *Fam (surprenant)* **elle est r., celle-là!** that's a bit far-fetched *or* hard to swallow!; **je vais t'en raconter une r.** I'll tell you an amazing story; **elle m'en a dit de raides sur toi** *(méchancetés)* she told me some pretty nasty things about you

7 *Fam (désargenté)* broke, *Br* skint; **être r. comme un passe-lacet** to be flat broke *or* cleaned out

8 *Fam (drogué)* stoned, wasted; *(ivre)* plastered, *Br* legless

ADV 1 *(à pic)* steeply; **ça descend/monte r. derrière chez eux** the ground slopes steeply downwards/upwards behind their house

2 *Fam (en intensif)* **tomber r.** to fall to the ground; **r. mort** dead as a doornail, *Br* stone dead

raider [rɛdœr] **NM** raider

raideur [rɛdœr] **NF 1** *(d'une étoffe, d'une attitude)* stiffness; *(d'une baguette)* stiffness, rigidity; *(d'une corde)* tautness; *(des cheveux)* straightness; *(d'un sentier)* steepness; *(d'un style, d'un jeu de scène)* woodenness; *(du caractère)* inflexibility, rigidity; **elle répondit avec r.** she answered stiffly **2** *(d'un muscle)* stiffness; **avoir une r. dans l'épaule** to have a stiff shoulder **3** *(d'une pente)* steepness

raidillon [rɛdijɔ̃] **NM** steep path *or* climb; **juste avant le r.** just before the road starts climbing

raidir [32] [rɛdir] **VT 1** *(tendre → corde, câble)* to tighten, to pull tight *or* taut; **r. les bras/jambes** to brace one's arms/legs

2 *(faire perdre sa souplesse à)* to stiffen; **l'eau calcaire raidit le tissu** hard water stiffens fabric

▸**se raidir VPR 1** *(perdre sa souplesse)* to stiffen, to go stiff, to become stiffer

2 *(se tendre → muscle, corps)* to tense (up), to stiffen; *(→ cordage)* to tighten, to grow taut

3 *(rassembler sa volonté)* to steel *or* to brace oneself; **se r. contre l'adversité** to stand firm in the face of adversity

raidissement [rɛdismɑ̃] **NM 1** *(physique)* tensing, stiffening **2** *(moral)* **face au r. des patrons** faced with the tougher line taken by the employers

raidisseur [rɛdisœr] **NM 1** *(tendeur)* stretcher **2** *Aviat* stiffener, stringer **3** *Constr & Naut* stringer

raie [rɛ] *voir* **rayer**

NF 1 *(trait)* line; *(rayure)* stripe; *(griffure)* scratch, mark; **raies creusées dans le bois** marks cut into the wood; **une r. de lumière** a ray of light

2 *(dans les cheveux) Br* parting, *Am* part; **une r. sur le côté** a side *Br* parting *or Am* part; **se coiffer avec la r. à gauche/droite** to part one's hair on the left/right; **je ne porte pas de r.** I don't have a *Br* parting *or Am* part

3 *Anat* slit; **r. des fesses** cleft of the buttocks; *Vulg* **taper dans la r. à qn** *(sodomiser)* to fuck sb up the *Br* arse *or Am* ass

4 *Agr* furrow

5 *Opt & Phys* line; **raies spectrales** spectrum lines; **r. d'absorption/d'émission** absorption/emission spectrum

6 *Ich* ray, skate; *Culin* skate; **r. bouclée** thornback; **r. cornue, r. manta** devilfish, manta ray; **r. électrique/venimeuse** electric/sting ray; *Culin* **r. au beurre noir** skate in brown butter sauce

raifort [rɛfɔr] **NM** *Bot* horseradish; **sauce au r.** horseradish sauce

rail [raj] **NM 1** *(barre d'acier)* rail; **les rails** *(la voie)* the tracks, the rails; **les rails s'arrêtent en rase campagne** the track comes to an end in the middle of the countryside; **poser des rails** to lay track; **r. conducteur** live rail; **r. fixe** main rail; **r. mobile** switch (rail); **sortir des rails** to leave the rails, to go *or* to come off the rails; *Fig* **remettre qn/qch sur les rails** to put sb/sth back on the rails; **elle a remis l'entreprise sur ses** *ou* **les rails** she put *or* set the firm (back) on the rails again

2 *(moyen de transport)* **le r.** rail; **une grève du r.** a rail strike; **les usagers du r.** rail users; **transport par r.** rail transport

3 *(glissière)* track; **r. d'éclairage** lighting track; **r. de sécurité** *(sur la route)* crash barrier; **r. de travelling** dolly (tracks)

4 *Naut* shipping lane

5 *Fam Arg drogue (de cocaïne)* line; **se faire un r.** to do a line

railler [3] [raje] *Littéraire* **VT** to mock, to laugh *or* to scoff at; **il en a eu assez de se faire r. par tout le monde** he was fed up with everyone laughing at him

VI to jest; *Hum* **vous raillez?** you jest, surely!

▸**se railler VPR se r. de qn/qch** to scoff at sb/sth

raillerie [rajri] **NF 1** *(attitude)* mocking, *Littéraire* raillery; *Vieilli* **il n'entend pas r. sur les choses religieuses** he will not have jokes made about religion **2** *(remarque)* jibe; **il décida d'ignorer leurs railleries** he decided to ignore their scoffing

railleur, -euse [rajœr, -øz] **ADJ** mocking, scoffing

NM,F mocker, scoffer; **faire taire les railleurs** to silence the scoffers

rail-route [rajrut] **ADJ INV** road-rail *(avant n)*

rainer [4] [rene] **VT** to groove

rainette[1] [renɛt] **NF** *Zool (grenouille)* tree frog

rainette[2] [renɛt] **NF 1** *(en maréchalerie)* paring knife **2** *Menuis* tracing iron **3** *(en tannerie)* race knife

rainurage [rɛnyraʒ] **NM** *(sur route)* grooved surface

rainure [rɛnyr] **NF 1** *(sillon)* groove; *(guide)* channel, slot; **les rainures du parquet** the gaps between the floorboards; **à rainures** grooved **2** *Anat* groove

rainurer [3] [rɛnyre] **VT** to (cut a) groove (in)

raiponce [rɛpɔ̃s] **NF** *Bot* rampion

raire [112] [rɛr] **VI** to bell, to troat

raïs [rais] **NM** head of state *(in Arab countries)*

rais-de-cœur [rɛdəkœr] **NMPL** *Beaux-Arts* heart leaves

raisin [rɛzɛ̃] **NM 1** *(en grappes)* grapes; **acheter du r.** to buy grapes; **r. blanc/noir** white/black grapes; **r. de cuve/table** wine/eating grapes **2** *Culin* **raisins de Corinthe** currants; **raisins secs** raisins; **raisins de Smyrne** *Br* sultanas, *Am* golden raisins **3** *Bot* **r. de renard** herb Paris; **r. d'ours** bearberry

'Les Raisins de la colère' *Steinbeck, Ford* 'The Grapes of Wrath'

raisiné [rezine] **NM 1** *(confiture)* = fruit preserved in grape jelly **2** *Fam Arg crime (sang)* blood ■, *Br* claret

raisinet [rezinɛ] **NM** *Suisse* redcurrant

raison [rɛzɔ̃] **NF 1** *(motif)* reason; **j'aurais cent raisons de vous mettre à la porte** I can think of a hundred reasons why I should dismiss you; **il n'y a aucune r. pour que vous partiez** there's no reason for you to leave; **y a-t-il une r. de s'inquiéter?** is there any reason to worry?; **quelle est la r. de...?** what's the reason for...?; **quelle est la r. de son départ?** why is he/she leaving?; **la r. pour laquelle je vous écris** the reason (why *or* that) I'm writing to you; **la r. en est que...** the reason is (that)..., it's because...; **pour quelle r.?** why?; **pour des raisons familiales/personnelles** for family/personal reasons; **pour raisons de santé** for reasons of ill-health, for health reasons; **avoir de bonnes raisons** *ou*

des raisons (de faire qch) to have good reasons (for doing sth); **avoir ses raisons** to have one's reasons; **je n'ai pas de raisons à te donner!** I don't have to tell you why!; **avec r.** with good reason; **sans r.** for no reason (at all); **pour une r. ou pour une autre** for one reason or another; **pour la (bonne et) simple r. que** for the simple reason that; **elle n'est pas venue, pour la (bonne et) simple r. qu'elle était malade** the reason she didn't come was simply that she was ill; **ce n'est pas une r.!** that's no excuse!; **ce n'est pas une r. pour vous fâcher** that's no reason for you to get angry; **r. de vivre** reason to live; **cet enfant c'est sa r. de vivre** he/she lives for that child; **à plus forte r.** all the more so; **mais je suis malade! – r. de plus!** but I'm not feeling well! – all the more reason!; **r. de plus pour le faire** that's one more reason for doing so; *Fam* **qu'elle se débrouille toute seule, y a pas de r.!** there's no reason why she shouldn't sort it out for herself!; **se rendre aux raisons de qn** to yield to sb's arguments

2 *(lucidité)* **il n'a pas/plus toute sa r.** he's not/he's no longer in his right mind; **il n'a plus toute sa r. depuis la catastrophe** the disaster affected his mind; **perdre la r.** to lose one's mind; **recouvrer la r.** to recover one's faculties; **troubler la r. de qn** to affect sb's mind

3 *(bon sens)* reason; **agir contre toute r.** to behave quite unreasonably; **faire entendre r. à qn, ramener qn à la r.** to make sb see reason; **rappeler qn à la r.** to bring sb to his/her senses; **revenir à la r.** to come to one's senses; **plus que de r.** to excess, more than is reasonable; **elle boit plus que de r.** she drinks to excess or more than is good for her; **il faut r. garder** one must keep one's head

4 *(faculté de penser)* reason; **l'homme est un être doué de r.** man is a thinking being

5 *Math* proportion; **en r. inverse/directe (de)** in inverse/direct proportion (to)

6 *(locutions)* **avoir r.** to be right; **avoir (bien) r. de faire qch** to be (quite) right to do or justified in doing sth; **donner r. à qn** *(personne)* to agree that sb is right; *(événement)* to prove sb right; **se faire une r.** to resign oneself; **fais-toi une r., c'est trop tard** you'll just have to put up with or to accept the fact that it's too late; **avoir r. de qn/qch** to get the better of sb/sth, to overcome sb/sth; **le traitement a finalement eu r. de son eczéma** the treatment finally cured his/her eczema; **demander r. à qn (de)** to demand satisfaction from sb (for); **rendre r. de qch à qn** to justify sth to sb; *Prov* **la r. du plus fort est toujours la meilleure** might is right

□ **à raison de** PRÉP at the rate of

□ **comme de raison** ADV and rightly so

□ **en raison de** PRÉP **1** *(à cause de)* on account of, because of; **le vol est annulé en r. du mauvais temps** the flight has been cancelled because of bad weather

2 *(en proportion de)* according to

□ **raison commerciale** NF trademark

□ **raison d'État** NF reasons of State, raison d'état; **le gouvernement a invoqué la r. d'État pour justifier cette mesure** the government justified the measure on the grounds of reasons of State

□ **raison d'être** NF raison d'être; **sa présence n'a plus aucune r. d'être** there's no longer any reason for him/her to be here

□ **raison sociale** NF corporate or company name

raisonnable [rɛzɔnabl] ADJ **1** *(sensé → personne,*

solution, décision) sensible; **sois r.!** be reasonable!; **tu n'es (vraiment) pas r. de boire autant** it's not sensible to drink so much; **ce n'est pas r. d'imposer une semaine de soixante heures à ses employés** it's unreasonable to expect one's employees to work a sixty-hour week; **à cet âge ils sont raisonnables** when they get to that age they know how to behave sensibly; **soyez raisonnables, les enfants, je reviens dans une minute** behave yourselves children, I'll be back in a minute; **je sais, je devrais être plus r.** I know, I should be more careful or sensible; **il devrait/tu devrais être plus r.** he/you should know better; *Hum* **est-ce bien r.?** is that wise?

2 *(normal, naturel)* reasonable; **il est r. de penser que...** it's reasonable to think that...

3 *(acceptable → prix, heure, conditions)* reasonable; *(→ salaire)* decent; **un appartement de taille r.** a reasonably or fairly large *Br* flat or *Am* apartment; **leurs exigences restent très raisonnables** they're very moderate in their demands

4 *(doué de raison)* rational

raisonnablement [rɛzɔnabləmɑ̃] ADV **1** *(de manière sensée)* sensibly, properly; **quand donc te conduiras-tu r.?** when are you going to behave sensibly or properly? **2** *(normalement)* reasonably; **elle peut r. espérer une augmentation** she can reasonably expect a pay rise **3** *(modérément)* in moderation; **vous pouvez boire, mais r.** you may drink, but in moderation

raisonné, -e [rɛzɔne] ADJ **1** *(analyse, projet, décision)* reasoned; **voilà qui est bien r.!** well worked out! **2** *(grammaire, méthode)* structured

raisonnement [rɛzɔnmɑ̃] NM **1** *(faculté, réflexion)* **le r.** reasoning; **r. par l'absurde** reductio ad absurdum; **r. par analogie** analogical reasoning; *Jur* **r. a contrario** = inversion of the premises of a law or judgment to deduce the opposite result; **r. déductif/inductif** deductive/inductive reasoning

2 *(argumentation)* reasoning; **mon r. est le suivant** my reasoning is as follows; **la conclusion de mon r. est la suivante** after careful thought, I have come to the following conclusion; **je ne suis pas bien votre r.** I don't follow your line of argument or thought; **son r. est assez convaincant** his/her arguments are quite convincing; **il ne faudra pas tenir ce r. avec lui** we mustn't use that argument with him; **ce n'est pas un r.!** you're wrong to think like that!

□ **raisonnements** NMPL *Littéraire* (endless) arguing *(UNCOUNT)*

raisonner [3] [rɛzɔne] VI **1** *(penser)* to think; **r. avant d'agir** to think before doing something; **r. comme un tambour** ou **une pantoufle** to talk nonsense, to talk through one's hat

2 *(enchaîner des arguments)* **non, là vous raisonnez mal!** no, your reasoning isn't sound there!; **r. par analogie** to use analogy as the basis of one's argument; **r. par induction/déduction** to use inductive/deductive reasoning

3 *(discuter)* **r. sur** to argue about; **r. avec qn** to reason with sb; **r. avec lui, c'est perdre son temps** it's a waste of time trying to reason with him

VT **1** *(faire appel à la raison de)* to reason with; **j'ai essayé de le r., rien à faire** I tried to reason with him or to make him see reason, but it was no use; **il faut absolument la r.** she must be made to see reason or sense

2 *(examiner)* to think out or through; **r. ses choix** to make reasoned choices

▶**se raisonner** VPR **1** *(emploi réfléchi)* **raisonne-toi, essaie de manger moins** be reasonable and try not to eat so much

2 *(emploi passif)* **la passion ne se raisonne pas** there's no reasoning with passion, passion knows no reason

raisonneur, -euse [rɛzɔnœr, -øz] ADJ **1** *(discutailleur)* argumentative **2** *(qui pense)* reasoning, rational

NM,F **1** *(discutailleur)* arguer, quibbler **2** *(penseur)* reasoner

raja(h) [raʒa] NM rajah

rajeunir [32] [raʒœnir] VI **1** *(redevenir jeune)* to grow young again; **elle voudrait r.** she'd like to be younger; **je ne rajeunis pas** I'm not getting any younger

2 *(paraître plus jeune)* to look or to seem younger; **je le trouve rajeuni** he looks younger to me; **il a rajeuni de plusieurs années depuis son mariage** he looks years younger since he got married; **elle rajeunit de jour en jour, on dirait!** she seems to get younger every day!

3 *(retrouver de l'éclat → façade)* to look like new

VT **1** *(rendre jeune)* **r. qn** to rejuvenate sb, to make sb younger; *Fig* to make sb look younger; **cette coiffure/robe la rajeunit** that hairstyle/dress makes her look younger; **il a perdu des kilos, ça le rajeunit** he's lost weight, it takes years off him; **r. le personnel d'une société** to bring new blood into a company

2 *(attribuer un âge moins avancé à)* **très aimable à vous, mais vous me rajeunissez!** that's very kind of you but you're making me younger than I am!; **vous me rajeunissez de cinq ans** I'm five years older than you said

3 *(faire se sentir plus jeune)* **cette soirée m'a rajeuni de dix ans!** this party's made me feel ten years younger!; **ça me rajeunit!** it makes me feel younger!; **ça ne nous rajeunit pas!** it makes you realize how old we are!, it makes you feel your age!

4 *(moderniser → mobilier, équipement)* to modernize; *(→ robe, veste)* to update

▶**se rajeunir** VPR **1** *(se faire paraître plus jeune)* to make oneself look younger

2 *(se dire plus jeune)* to lie about one's age, to make oneself out to be younger than one is; **elle se rajeunit de cinq ans** she claims to be five years younger than she really is

rajeunissant, -e [raʒœnisɑ̃, -ɑ̃t] ADJ rejuvenating

rajeunissement [raʒœnismɑ̃] NM **1** *Biol & Physiol* rejuvenation; **elle a fait une cure de r.** she went to a health farm **2** *(modernisation → d'un équipement, d'une entreprise)* modernization **3** *(abaissement de l'âge)* **le r. de la population** the decreasing average age of the population; **il y a aujourd'hui un net r. des amateurs de musique classique** there has been a marked drop in the average age of classical music lovers

rajout [raʒu] NM **1** addition; **faire des rajouts à qch** to make additions to sth, to add things to sth **2** *(pour les cheveux)* **rajouts** extensions

rajouter [3] [raʒute] VT **1** *(ajouter)* to add *(à* to) **2** *(dire en plus)* to add *(à* to); **je n'ai rien à r.** I have nothing to add, I have nothing more to say; **r. que...** to add that... **3** *Fam (locution)* **en r.** to lay it on a bit thick; **je t'en prie, n'en rajoute pas!** oh, for God's sake, give it a rest!

rajustement [raʒystəmɑ̃] NM adjustment; **r. des prix** price adjustment; **un r. des salaires** a wage adjustment

rajuster [3] [raʒyste] VT **1** *(prix, salaires, vêtements)* to adjust; *(chignon)* to fix, to tidy **2** *(rectifier)* **r. le tir** to adjust or to correct one's aim

▶**se rajuster** VPR to tidy oneself up; **il avait oublié de se r.** he'd forgotten to do up his fly or to adjust his dress

raki [raki] NM raki

râlant, -e [rɑlɑ̃, -ɑ̃t] ADJ *Fam* infuriating■, exasperating■

râle [rɑl] NM **1** *(respiration)* rattle; **r. (d'agonie)** death rattle **2** *Méd* rale **3** *Orn* rail; **r. d'eau** water rail; **r. des genêts** corncrake; **r. de Virginie** Virginia rail

ralécher [raleʃe] = **relécher**

râlement [rɑlmɑ̃] NM *Littéraire* moaning, groaning

ralenti, -e [ralɑ̃ti] ADJ **mener une vie ralentie** to live quietly; **depuis son infarctus, il mène une vie ralentie** since his coronary, he's been taking things easy

NM **1** *Cin* slow motion

2 *Aut & Tech* idling speed; **régler le r.** to adjust the idling speed

□ **au ralenti** ADV **1** *Cin* **passer une scène au r.** to show a scene in slow motion

2 *(à vitesse réduite)* **avancer au r.** to move slowly forward; **tourner au r.** *(moteur)* to idle; **l'usine tourne au r.** the factory is running under capacity; **depuis qu'il est à la retraite, il vit au r.** now that he's retired, he doesn't do as much as he used to; **ils travaillent au r.** *(pour protester)* they're on *Br* a go-slow or *Am* a slowdown; *(par nécessité)* they're working at a slower pace

ralentir [32] [ralɑ̃tir] VI to slow down; **l'autobus**

n'a même pas ralenti the bus didn't even slow down; **attention, r.** *(panneau sur route)* reduce speed now; **r., travaux** *(sur panneau)* slow, roadworks ahead

VT 1 *(mouvement, effort)* to slow down; **r. sa course** *ou* **l'allure** to reduce speed, to slow down; **r. le pas** to slow down **2** *(processus)* to slow down

▸**se ralentir** VPR to slow down

ralentissement [ralɑ̃tismɑ̃] NM **1** *(décélération)* decrease in speed, slowing-down; **un r. de 10 kilomètres sur la N10** slow-moving traffic for 10 kilometres on the N10

2 *(diminution)* reduction; **un r. des ventes** a fall-off in sales; **un r. des fonctions cérébrales** a reduction in brain activity; **un r. de l'économie** economic downturn; **le commerce entre les deux pays a connu un net r.** trade between the two countries has fallen off considerably

ralentisseur [ralɑ̃tisœr] NM **1** *(sur une route)* speed bump, *Br* sleeping policeman **2** *Aut & Tech* idler, speed reducer **3** *Phys* moderator; **r. de particules/neutrons** particle/neutron moderator

râler [3] [rɑle] VI **1** *(blessé)* to moan, to groan; *(agonisant)* to give a death rattle **2** *Fam (se plaindre)* to grumble, to moan; **mais qu'est-ce qu'elle a encore à r.?** what is she moaning about now?; **r. contre qch** to moan about sth; **ça me fait r.!** it makes me so mad!; **juste pour la faire r.** just to make her mad **3** *(tigre)* to growl

râleur, -euse [rɑlœr, -øz] *Fam* ADJ bad-tempered ∎, grumpy

NM,F grouch, moaner; **quel r.!** he never stops moaning!

ralingue [ralɛ̃g] NF *Naut* bolt rope; **voile en r.** shivering sail

ralinguer [3] [ralɛ̃ge] *Naut* VT to rope

VI to shiver

ralléger [22] [raleʒe] VI *Fam (venir)* to come ∎; *(revenir)* to come back ∎

rallidé [rallide] *Orn* NM Rallus

❏ **rallidés** NMPL Rallidae

rallié, -e [ralje] NM,F new supporter

ralliement [ralimɑ̃] NM **1** *(adhésion)* **lors de son r. à notre parti/notre cause** when he/she came over to our party/cause **2** *(rassemblement)* rally, gathering; **signe/cri de r.** rallying sign/cry; **point de r.** rallying point; **ce bar est un bon point de r.** the bar is a good meeting place

rallier [9] [ralje] VT **1** *(rejoindre → groupe, poste)* to go back to; **des permissionnaires qui rallient leur régiment** soldiers on their way back to their units

2 *(adhérer à)* to join; **c'est pour cela que j'ai fini par r. ce parti** that's why I ended up joining this party

3 *(rassembler → autour de soi, d'un projet)* to win over; *(→ des troupes)* to gather together, to rally; **r. les indécis** to win over *or* to persuade the undecided; **il a su r. la majorité des actionnaires à son projet** he managed to convince the majority of the shareholders that his project was a good idea; **r. tous les suffrages** to meet with general approval; **r. qn à sa cause** to win sb over

4 *Chasse (chiens)* to call in

5 *Naut* **r. la terre** to haul in for the coast; **r. le bord** to rejoin ship

▸**se rallier** VPR **1** *(se joindre)* **il a fini par se r.** he ended up joining; **se r. à qn** to join forces with sb; **se r. à un parti** to join a party

2 **se r. à un avis/un point de vue** *(se montrer favorable à)* to come round to an opinion/a point of view; **se r. à l'avis général** to come round to *or* to rally to the opinion of the majority

---

Allusion

Ralliez-vous à mon panache blanc!

This was the rallying cry of Henry IV of France at the Battle of Ivry, near Évreux, on 14 March 1590, during the war of the Holy Catholic League. The meaning is "Rally round my white plume" (ie on the king's helmet). The phrase is used today allusively to rally one's friends and supporters around one (in somewhat grandiloquent language), meaning simply "Follow me!"

---

rallonge [ralɔ̃ʒ] NF **1** *(électrique)* extension (cable)

2 *(d'une table)* extension; *Can (d'un bâtiment) Br* extension, *Am* addition

3 *(tuyau)* extension tube *(of a vacuum cleaner)*

4 *Fam (délai)* extra time *(UNCOUNT)*; **une r. de quelques jours** a few extra days

5 *Fam (supplément)* extra money *(UNCOUNT)*; **il nous a donné une r. de 20 euros** he gave us an extra 20 euros; **r. budgétaire** addition to the budget

❏ **à rallonge(s)** ADJ **1 table à r.** *ou* **rallonges** extending table

2 *(week-end)* long *(avant n)*; *(histoire)* never-ending; *(nom)* double-barrelled

rallongement [ralɔ̃ʒmɑ̃] NM *(gén)* lengthening, extension; *(d'un vêtement)* letting down

rallonger [17] [ralɔ̃ʒe] VT **1** *(gén)* to extend; *(durée, liste)* to lengthen, to make longer, to extend; **r. un article de quelques lignes** to extend an article by a few lines; **l'autoroute a été rallongée de 20 kilomètres** the motorway has been extended by 20 kilometres

2 *(vêtement → en défaisant l'ourlet)* to let down; *(→ en ajoutant du tissu)* to make longer; **r. qch de dix centimètres** to make sth ten centimetres longer; **j'ai fait r. cette jupe de dix centimètres** I had this skirt let down ten centimetres

3 *Fam (sujet: trajet, itinéraire)* **ça nous rallonge** it's taking us out of our way; **en passant par Lille, ça te rallonge d'une heure** if you go via Lille, it'll add an hour to your journey time

USAGE ABSOLU **ça rallonge de passer par Lille** it takes longer if you go via Lille

VI **les jours rallongent** the days are getting longer; **la mode rallonge** hemlines are coming down again

rallumer [3] [ralyme] VT **1** *(feu)* to rekindle, to light again; *(lampe, télévision)* to put back on, to switch on again; *(électricité)* to turn on again; **r. une cigarette** *(éteinte)* to relight a cigarette; *(une autre)* to light up another cigarette

2 *(faire renaître → haine, passion)* to rekindle; **cet événement a rallumé la guerre** this event sparked the war off again

USAGE ABSOLU *(lampe)* **rallume!** put the light back on!

▸**se rallumer** VPR **1** *(feu, incendie)* to flare up again; *(lampe, appareil)* to come back on

2 *(espoir)* to be revived; *(conflit)* to break out again; *(passion)* to flare up

3 elle se ralluma une énième cigarette she lit yet another cigarette

rallye [rali] NM **1** *(course)* **r. (automobile)** (car) rally **2** *(soirée)* = exclusive upper-class ball for young people **3** *Bourse* **r. boursier** stock-market rally

RAM, Ram [ram] NF *Ordinat (abrév* **random access memory)** RAM; **R. sur carte** on-board RAM

ramadan [ramadɑ̃] NM *Rel* Ramadan, Ramadhan; **faire** *ou* **observer le r.** to observe Ramadan

ramage [ramaʒ] NM *Littéraire (d'un oiseau)* song

❏ **ramages** NMPL floral pattern; **un tissu à grands ramages** material with a bold floral pattern

ramager [17] [ramaʒe] VT *(étoffe)* to print a floral pattern on

VI *(oiseau)* to sing, to warble

ramancher [17] [ramɑ̃ʃe] VT *Can Vieilli* **1** *(fracture)* to set **2** *(réparer)* to repair, to mend

ramancheur, -euse [ramɑ̃ʃœr, -øz] NM,F *Can Vieilli* bonesetter; *Hum Péj* chiropractor

ramas [rama] NM *Vieilli ou Littéraire* raggle-taggle assortment, hotchpotch

ramassage [ramasaʒ] NM **1** *(cueillette → du bois, des fruits)* gathering; *(→ des pommes de terre)* picking, digging up; *(→ des champignons)* picking, gathering; **r. manuel** hand picking

2 *(collecte)* collection; **r. du lait** milk collection; **r. des ordures** *Br* rubbish *or Am* garbage collection

3 *(transport)* picking up; **ils se chargent du r. des ouvriers** they pick up the workers; **point/ zone de r.** pick-up point/area; **r. scolaire** school bus service

4 *Bourse (d'actions)* buying up

ramassé, -e [ramase] ADJ **1** *(trapu → homme, corps)* stocky, squat; *(→ bâtisse, forme)* squat **2** *(recroquevillé)* huddled; **un village r. autour de son église** a village huddled *or* clustering round its church **3** *(style)* terse

ramasse-miettes [ramasmjɛt] NM INV crumb sweeper

ramasse-poussière, ramasse-poussières *(pl* ramasse-poussières) [ramaspusjɛr] NM *Belg* dustpan

---

RAMASSER [3] [ramase]

VT to pick up **1, 7** ∎ to pick **2** ∎ to gather **2, 3** ∎ to collect **3, 4** ∎ to condense **5** ∎ to buy up **6** ∎ to get **8** ∎ to catch **9**
VPR to be picked (up) **1** ∎ to pick oneself up **2** ∎ to crouch **4** ∎ to come a cropper **5**

VT 1 *(objet à terre)* to pick up; *Fam* **ils ramassent des fraises à la pelle dans leur jardin** they get loads of strawberries from their garden; *Fam* **des mauvaises notes, il en a ramassé à la pelle cette année** he's been getting bad *Br* marks *or Am* grades by the dozen this year; *Fig* **r. qn dans le ruisseau** to pick sb up out of the gutter; *Fam* **il était à r. à la petite cuillère** *(épuisé)* he was all washed out; *(blessé)* you could have scraped him off the ground; **encore un pas et je serai bon à r. à la petite cuillère!** one more step and I'll fall to bits!

2 *(cueillir → champignons)* to pick, to gather; *(→ pommes de terre)* to dig; *(→ marrons)* to gather

3 *(rassembler → copies)* to collect, to take in; *(→ cartes à jouer)* to gather up; *(→ feuilles mortes)* to sweep up; **r. du bois** to gather wood; *Fig* **r. les débris d'une armée** to rally the remnants of an army; *Fam* **il a ramassé pas mal d'argent** he's picked up *or* made quite a bit of money; **r. ses forces** to gather one's strength; **r. la monnaie** to pick up the change; *Fam* **r. le paquet** to hit the jackpot

4 *(élèves, ouvriers)* to collect; **r. les ordures** to collect the *Br* rubbish *or Am* garbage

5 *(résumer)* to condense; **ramassez vos idées en quelques lignes** condense your ideas into just a few lines

6 *Bourse (actions)* to buy up

7 *Fam (trouver)* to pick up, to dig up; **où as-tu ramassé cet affreux roquet?** where did you pick up *or* dig up that ugly mutt?

8 *Fam (recevoir)* to get ∎; **r. une gifle/un coup/ un PV** to get a slap/a clout/a parking ticket

9 *Fam (attraper → maladie)* to catch ∎

10 *Fam (arrêter)* to nab; **se faire r.** *(se faire emmener par la police)* to get picked up *or* nabbed *or Br* lifted; *(échouer)* to fail ∎, *Br* to come a cropper

▸**se ramasser** VPR **1** *(emploi passif)* to be picked (up); **les cèpes se ramassent en automne** ceps are picked in the autumn; *Fam* **les truffes se ramassent à la pelle dans cette région** there are loads of truffles around here

2 *Fam (se relever)* to pick oneself up ∎

3 *Fam (recevoir)* **se r. une gifle/un coup/un PV** to get a slap/a clout/a parking ticket

4 *(avant de bondir)* to crouch

5 *Fam (tomber)* to fall flat on one's face, to go flying; *(échouer)* to fail ∎, *Br* to come a cropper

ramassette [ramasɛt] NF *Belg* dustpan

ramasseur, -euse [ramasœr, -øz] NM,F gatherer; **r./ramasseuse de balles** *(au tennis)* ball boy/girl; **r. de lait** milk collector

NM *Agr (machine)* pick-up

ramasseuse-presse [ramasøzprɛs] *(pl* ramasseuses-presses) NF *Agr* pick-up baler

ramassis [ramasi] NM *Péj (d'objets)* jumble; *(de personnes)* bunch; *(d'idées)* collection, hotchpotch; **un r. de petits voyous** a bunch of young louts; **un r. de mensonges** a tissue of lies

ramassoire [ramaswar] NF *Suisse* dustpan

rambarde [rɑ̃bard] NF rail, guardrail

rambo [rɑ̃bo] NM *Fam* = security officer patrolling the Parisian railway network and underground

Rambouillet [rɑ̃buje] NM **le château de R.** = one of the residences used by the President of France, mainly for international conferences

ramboutan [rɑ̃butɑ̃] NM *Bot* **1** *(fruit)* rambutan **2** *(arbre)* rambutan tree

ramdam [ramdam] NM *Fam (vacarme)* racket, din; **faire du r.** to make a racket *or* a din

rame [ram] NF **1** *(aviron)* oar; **nous avons rejoint le port à la r.** we rowed into port **2** *(de papier)*

ream **3** *(train)* train; **r. de métro** *Br* underground *or Am* subway train **4** *(branche)* prop, stake; **haricots à rames** stick beans, *Br* runner beans, *Am* pole beans **5 ne pas** *Fam* **en ficher** *ou très Fam* **en foutre une r.** to do zilch *or Br* bugger *or* sod all

rameau, -x [ramo] **NM 1** *(branche)* (small) branch; **r. d'olivier** olive branch **2** *Fig (division)* branch, subdivision **3** *Anat* ramification
❑ **Rameaux NMPL** *Rel* **les Rameaux, le dimanche des Rameaux** Palm Sunday

ramée [rame] **NF 1** *Littéraire (feuillage)* foliage; **sous la r.** under the leafy boughs **2** *Vieilli (branches coupées)* cut branches **3** *(locution) Fam* **il n'en a pas fichu une r.** he hasn't done a stroke (of work)

ramender [3] [ramɑ̃de] **VT 1** *Agr* to add more manure to **2** *(réparer → filet)* to mend **3** *(redorer)* to gild, to regild

ramendeur, -euse [ramɑ̃dœr, -øz] **NM,F** = repairer of fishing nets

ramener [19] [ramne] **VT 1** *(personne, véhicule → au point de départ)* to take back; *(→ à soi)* to bring back; **je vous ramène?** *(chez vous)* shall I give you a *Br* lift *or Am* ride home?; *(à votre point de départ)* shall I give you a *Br* lift *or Am* ride back?; **son chauffeur le ramène tous les soirs** his chauffeur drives him back every evening; **je te ramènerai la voiture lundi** I'll bring the car back on Monday; **r. à** *(un endroit)* to take back to; **r. les enfants à l'école** to take the children back to school; **il a fallu le r. à l'hôpital** he had to be taken back into hospital

2 *(rapporter)* **ramène-moi un journal** bring me back a newspaper; **je te ramènerai un souvenir d'Italie** I'll bring you back a souvenir from Italy; **elle a vécu dix ans en Inde et en a ramené mari et enfants** she lived in India for ten years, returning with a husband and children; **il faut que je ramène les clefs à l'agence** I've got to take the keys back to the estate agent

3 *(rétablir)* to bring back, to restore; **r. la paix** to restore peace; **r. l'espérance** to bring back *or* to revive hope

4 *(placer)* **elle ramena le châle sur ses épaules** she pulled the shawl around her shoulders; **r. ses cheveux en arrière** to draw one's hair back; **r. ses genoux sous son menton** to pull one's knees up under one's chin

5 *(faire revenir)* **l'été a ramené les visiteurs** the summer has brought back the tourists; **l'orage le ramena chez lui** the storm obliged him to return home; **le film m'a ramené dix ans en arrière** the film took me back ten years; **r. le débat au sujet principal** to lead *or* to steer the discussion back to the main subject; **ce qui nous ramène au problème de...** which brings us back to the problem of...; **r. la conversation à** *ou* **sur qch** to bring the conversation back (round) to sth; **r. qn à la vie** to bring sb back to life, to revive sb; **r. un malade à lui** to bring a patient round; **r. qn dans le rang** to pull sb back into line

6 *(réduire)* **cela ramène le problème à sa dimension financière** it reduces the problem to its purely financial aspects; **ne ramenons pas son attitude à de la jalousie** let's not reduce his/her attitude to simple jealousy; **r. tout à soi** to bring everything back to *or* to relate everything to oneself

7 *(locution) Fam* **la r., r. sa fraise** *(vouloir s'imposer)* to stick one's oar in, to butt in; *(faire l'important)* to show off

▸**se ramener VPR 1** *Fam (arriver)* to turn up, to show up; **ramène-toi en vitesse!** come on, hurry up!

2 se r. à *(se réduire à)* to boil down to; **toute l'affaire se ramenait finalement à une querelle de famille** in the end the whole business boiled down to *or* was nothing more than a family quarrel

ramequin [ramkɛ̃] **NM 1** *(récipient)* ramekin (mould) **2** *(tartelette)* (small) cheese tart

ramer [3] [rame] **VI 1** *(pagayer)* to row; **r. en couple** to scull

2 *Fam (avoir des difficultés)* to have a hard time of it; **r. pour faire qch** to sweat blood *or* to bust a gut to do sth; **j'ai assez ramé, maintenant j'ai envie d'un boulot stable** I've struggled to make ends meet for long enough, now I want a secure job; **qu'est-ce qu'on a ramé pour trouver cet appartement!** it was such a hassle finding this *Br* flat *or Am* apartment!

VT 1 *Hort* to stick, to stake

2 *Fam* **ne pas en r. une** to do zilch *or Br* bugger all *or* sod all

ramescence [ramesɑ̃s] **NF** *Bot* ramification, branching

ramette [ramɛt] **NF** ream *(of 125 sheets)*, five quires

rameur, -euse[1] [ramœr, -øz] **NM,F** rower, oarsman, *f* oarswoman; **r. de couple** sculler

rameuter [5] [ramøte] **VT 1** *(regrouper → foule)* to draw; **son manège avait rameuté les gens autour de lui** his antics had attracted *or* drawn a crowd of people around him **2** *(mobiliser → militants, partisans)* to rouse; **r. les populations** to stir people into action **3** *Chasse (chiens)* to round up

rameux, -euse[2] [ramø, -øz] **ADJ** branching, *Spéc* ramose

rami [rami] **NM** *Cartes* rummy; **faire r.** to go rummy

ramie [rami] **NM** *Tex* ramie
NF *Bot* ramie

ramier [ramje] **ADJ M 1 pigeon r.** ringdove, wood pigeon **2** *Fam (fainéant)* lazy■
NM 1 *(pigeon)* ringdove, wood pigeon; **petit r.** stock dove **2** *Fam (fainéant)* lazybones, lazy so-and-so

ramification [ramifikasjɔ̃] **NF 1** *Bot* offshoot, *Spéc* ramification **2** *Anat* ramification; **ramifications nerveuses** nerve plexus **3** *(d'un fleuve)* ramification, distributary; *(d'une voie ferrée)* branch line; *(d'un réseau, d'une organisation)* branch; *(d'un complot)* ramification

ramifier [9] [ramifje] **se ramifier VPR 1** *Anat & Bot* to ramify, to divide **2** *(se subdiviser → réseau)* to split; **la famille s'est ramifiée en trois branches** the family split into three branches

ramille [ramij] **NF** twig, branchlet

ramingue [ramɛ̃g] **ADJ** *Équitation* stubborn, disobedient to the spur

ramolli, -e [ramɔli] **ADJ 1** *(mou)* soft; **beurre r.** soft butter; **le beurre est tout r.** the butter's (gone) all soft **2** *Fam (gâteux)* soft; **il est un peu r. du cerveau, il a le cerveau un peu r.** he's gone a bit soft (in the head) *or* soft-headed **3** *Fam (sans énergie)* **se sentir tout r.** to feel washed out
NM,F *Fam* **un vieux r.** an old dodderer

ramollir [32] [ramɔlir] **VT 1** *(rendre mou)* to soften
2 *(affaiblir)* to weaken; **ces vacances m'ont ramolli** this holiday has left me without any energy
3 *Fam (rendre gâteux)* **l'âge l'a ramolli** he's gone soft in the head with age
VI to go soft; **faire r. du beurre** to soften butter
▸**se ramollir VPR 1** *(devenir mou)* to go soft
2 *Fam (perdre son tonus)* **depuis que j'ai arrêté le sport, je me suis ramolli** I've been out of condition since I stopped doing sport■
3 *Fam (devenir gâteux)* **j'ai l'impression que je me ramollis** I feel like I'm going soft in the head; **son cerveau se ramollit** he's/she's going soft in the head

ramollissant, -e [ramɔlisɑ̃, -ɑ̃t] **ADJ 1** *Pharm* emollient **2** *(climat)* debilitating

ramollissement [ramɔlismɑ̃] **NM** *(du beurre, de la cire)* softening; **r. cérébral** softening of the brain

ramollo [ramɔlo] *Fam* **ADJ 1** *(mou)* washed out, wiped (out); **se sentir tout r.** to feel like a wet rag **2** *(gâteux)* doddery
NMF wet rag *(person)*

ramon [ramɔ̃] **NM** *Belg* broom

ramonace [ramɔnas], **ramonache** [ramɔnaʃ] **NF** *Belg* horseradish

ramonage [ramɔnaʒ] **NM 1** *(d'une cheminée)* chimney-sweeping; *(d'une machine)* cleaning; *(d'une pipe)* cleaning (out) **2** *Sport (en alpinisme)* chimneying

ramonasse [ramɔnas] = **ramonace**

ramoner [3] [ramɔne] **VT 1** *(cheminée)* to sweep; *(machine)* to clean; *(pipe)* to clean (out) **2** *(en alpinisme)* to chimney **3** *Vulg (posséder sexuellement)* to screw, *Br* to shag
VI *(en alpinisme)* to (climb a) chimney

ramoneur [ramɔnœr] **NM** chimney sweep

rampant, -e [rɑ̃pɑ̃, -ɑ̃t] **ADJ 1** *Biol (animal)* creeping, crawling, *Spéc* reptant; **insecte r.** flightless insect
2 *Bot* creeping; **fraisiers rampants** creeping strawberries; **plante rampante** creeper
3 *(évoluant lentement)* **inflation rampante** creeping inflation
4 *Péj (personne, caractère)* crawling, grovelling
5 *Hér* rampant; **lion/dragon r.** lion/dragon rampant
6 *Archit (arc)* rampant; *(pièce)* raked
7 *Fam* **personnel r.** *(de compagnie aérienne)* ground staff
NM 1 *Fam (de compagnie aérienne)* member of the ground staff; **les rampants** the ground staff
2 *Archit* pitch

rampe [rɑ̃p] **NF 1** *(main courante)* handrail, banister; **r. (d'escalier)** banister; *Fam* **tiens bon la r.!** hang in there!, don't give in!; *Fam Euph* **lâcher la r.** *(mourir)* to croak, to kick the bucket
2 *(plan incliné)* ramp; **r. d'un échangeur** sloping approach to an interchange; **r. d'accès** approach ramp; **r. de chargement** loading ramp; **r. de graissage** lubricating rack; *Astron* **r. de lancement** launch pad, launching pad; *Fig* launch pad
3 *(côte)* slope, incline
4 *Théât* footlights; **passer la r.** to get across to the audience; **il passe mal la r.** he doesn't come across well
5 *Aviat* **r. (de balisage)** marker *or* runway lights

rampeau, -x [rɑ̃po] **NM** *(aux dés)* deciding throw; **faire r.** to be all square

rampement [rɑ̃pmɑ̃] **NM** creeping, crawling

ramper [3] [rɑ̃pe] **VI 1** *(lierre)* to creep; *(personne)* to crawl; *(serpent)* to slither, to crawl; **entrer/sortir en rampant** to crawl in/out **2** *(doute, inquiétude)* to lurk **3** *Fig (s'abaisser)* to grovel; **r. devant qn** to grovel before sb

rampon [rɑ̃pɔ̃] **NM** *Suisse* lamb's lettuce

ramponneau, -x [rɑ̃pɔno] **NM** *Fam (coup)* clout; **(se) prendre un r.** to get a clout

Ramsès [ramsɛs] **NPR** Ramsès, Rameses

ramule [ramyl] **NM** twig, branchlet

ramure [ramyr] **NF 1** *Bot* **la r.** the branches, the tree tops **2** *(d'un cerf)* antlers

ranatre [ranatr] **NF** *Entom* ranatra

rancard [rɑ̃kar] **NM 1** *Fam (rendez-vous → gén)* appointment■; *(→ amoureux)* date■; **j'ai r. avec lui à 15 heures** I'm meeting him at 3; **filer (un) r. à qn** to arrange to meet sb■; **on s'est filé (un) r. pour la semaine prochaine** we arranged to meet next week, we made a date for next week **2** *Fam Arg crime (renseignement)* info■ *(UNCOUNT)*, *Br* gen *(UNCOUNT)*; *(tuyau)* tip, tip-off

rancarder [3] [rɑ̃karde] **VT 1** *Fam Arg crime (renseigner)* to tip sb off; **qui t'a rancardé?** who tipped you off?; **r. qn sur qch** to give sb the lowdown on sth **2** *Fam (donner un rendez-vous à)* **r. qn** to arrange to meet sb■
▸**se rancarder VPR** *Fam Arg crime* to get information■

rancart [rɑ̃kar] **NM 1** = **rancard 2 mettre** *ou* **jeter qn au r.** to throw sb on the scrap heap; **mettre** *ou* **jeter qch au r.** *(objet)* to chuck sth out, *(projet)* to scrap sth

rance [rɑ̃s] **ADJ** *(beurre, huile)* rancid; *(noix)* stale
NM odeur/goût de r. rancid smell/taste; **avoir un goût de r.** to taste rancid; **sentir le r.** to smell rancid

ranch [rɑ̃tʃ] *(pl* **ranchs** *ou* **ranches)** **NM** ranch

ranche [rɑ̃ʃ] **NF** peg, rung

rancher [rɑ̃ʃe] **NM** peg ladder

ranci [rɑ̃si] **NM enlève le r.** take off the rancid bit; **sentir le r.** to have a rancid smell

rancio [rɑ̃sjo] **NM 1** *(goût)* rancio **2** *(vin)* rancio wine *(sweet wine which has acquired a smooth, lingering taste with ageing)*

rancir [32] [rɑ̃sir] **VI 1** *(beurre, huile)* to go rancid; *(noix)* to go stale **2** *Fig Littéraire* to become stale

rancissement [rɑ̃sismɑ̃] **NM pour éviter le r. du beurre/des noix** to avoid the butter going rancid/the walnuts going stale

rancœur [rɑ̃kœr] **NF** resentment, rancour; **avoir de la r. envers qn** to feel resentful towards sb; **plein de r.** *(personne, ton)* resentful, bitter

rançon [rɑ̃sɔ̃] **NF 1** *(somme d'argent)* ransom; *Arch ou Littéraire* **mettre qn à r.** to hold sb to ransom **2** *(contrepartie)* **c'est la r. de la gloire/du succès** that's the price you have to pay for being famous/successful

rançonnement [rɑ̃sɔnmɑ̃] **NM** **1** *Littéraire (demande de rançon)* holding to ransom **2** *(vol)* holding up (and robbing) **3** *Fam (exploitation)* fleecing, swindling

rançonner [3] [rɑ̃sɔne] **VT** **1** *Littéraire (exiger une rançon de)* to hold to ransom; **ils ont rançonné la ville** they held the town to ransom **2** *(voler → voyageur)* to hold up (and rob) **3** *Fam (exploiter)* to fleece, to swindle

rançonneur, -euse [rɑ̃sɔnœr, -øz] **NM,F** **1** *(qui exige une rançon)* ransomer **2** *(voleur)* highwayman, *f* highwaywoman **3** *Fam (exploiteur)* swindler

rancune [rɑ̃kyn] **NF** grudge; **plein de r.** spiteful; **garder r. à qn, avoir de la r. contre qn** to bear *or* to harbour a grudge against sb; **elle garde r. à son frère de son refus** she has a grudge against her brother because of his refusal; **sans r.?** no hard feelings?; **sans r.!** no hard feelings!, let's shake hands and forget it!

rancunier, -ère [rɑ̃kynje, -ɛr] **ADJ** spiteful; **être r.** to bear grudges

NM,F spiteful person

Rand [rɑ̃d] **NM** *Géog* **le R.** the Rand

rand [rɑ̃d] **NM** *(monnaie)* rand

rando [rɑ̃do] **NF** *Fam* hiking■; **ski de r.** cross-country skiing■

randomisation [rɑ̃dɔmizasjɔ̃] **NF** randomization

randomiser [3] [rɑ̃dɔmize] **VT** to randomize

randonnée [rɑ̃dɔne] **NF** **1** *(promenade → à pied sur le plat)* ramble, hike; *(→ à pied en montagne)* trek; *(→ à bicyclette)* ride; *(→ à skis)* cross-country hike; *(→ à cheval)* trek; **r. équestre** pony trek; **r. à pied** *ou* **pédestre** *(sur le plat)* ramble, hike; *(en montagne)* trek; **faire une r. (à pied** *ou* **pédestre)** *(sur le plat)* to go rambling *or* hiking; *(en montagne)* to go trekking; **faire une r. à bicyclette** to go for a bike ride; **faire une r. à skis** to go cross-country skiing; **faire une r. à cheval** to go pony-trekking

2 *(sport → à pied sur le plat)* rambling, hiking; *(→ à pied en montagne)* hill-walking, trekking; *(→ à skis)* cross-country skiing; **la r. pédestre** *(sur le plat)* rambling, hiking; *(en montagne)* trekking; **grande r.** long-distance hiking; **faire de la r.** *(à pied sur le plat)* to go rambling *or* hiking; *(à pied en montagne)* to go hill-walking *or* trekking; *(à bicyclette)* to go cycling; *(à skis)* to go cross-country skiing; *(à cheval)* to go pony-trekking

randonner [3] [rɑ̃dɔne] **VI** *(à pied sur le plat)* to go rambling *or* hiking; *(à pied en montagne)* to go hill-walking *or* trekking; *(à bicyclette)* to go cycling; *(à skis)* to go cross-country skiing; *(à cheval)* to go pony-trekking

randonneur, -euse [rɑ̃dɔnœr, -øz] **NM,F** *(à pied sur le plat)* rambler, hiker; *(à pied en montagne)* hill-walker; *(à bicyclette)* cyclist; *(à skis)* cross-country skier; *(à cheval)* pony-trekker

rang [rɑ̃] **NM** **1** *(rangée → de personnes)* row, line; *(→ de fauteuils)* row; *(→ de crochet, de tricot)* row (of stitches); **sur un r.** in one row; **un collier à double r. de perles** a double string of pearls; **le premier/dernier r.** the front/back row; **on était au premier r.** we were in the front row

2 *(dans une hiérarchie)* rank; **cette entreprise occupe le premier r. mondial du marché des composants électroniques** this company is number one in the world in the electronic component market; **l'entreprise a été reléguée au cinquième r. pour la production d'appareils électroménagers** the company has slipped to fifth place in the white goods market; **ce problème devrait être au premier r. de nos préoccupations** this problem should be at the top of our list of priorities; **venir au deuxième/troisième r.** to rank second/third; **par r. d'âge** according to age; **par r. d'ancienneté** in order of seniority; **il a pris r. parmi les meilleurs** he ranks among the best; **avoir r. d'ambassadeur** to hold the office of ambassador; **de r. inférieur/supérieur** low-/high-ranking; **de premier r.** high-ranking, first-class, top-class; **de second r.** second-rate; **r. des hypothèques** priority of mortgage; **r. de préséance** order of precedence

3 *(condition sociale)* (social) standing; **le respect qui est dû à son r.** the respect which his/her position commands; **un homme du meilleur r.** a man of the highest standing; **elle a épousé quelqu'un d'un r. plus élevé** she married above her station; **tenir son r.** to maintain one's position in society; **être digne de son r.** to be worthy of one's standing; **de haut r.** of high standing

4 *Mil* **le r.** the ranks; **les militaires du r.** the rank and file; **sortir du r.** to come up through the ranks; *Fig* to stand out; **un officier sorti du r.** an officer who came up through *or* was promoted from the ranks; **rentrer dans le r.** to return to the ranks; *Fig* to give in, to submit

5 *Can* = group of farms in long strips of land, at right angles to a road or a river; *Fig* **les rangs** the countryside; **ils sont des rangs** they're from good country stock; *Péj* they're from the back of beyond

❑ **rangs NMPL** ranks; *Mil* **à vos rangs fixe!** fall in!; *Mil* **en rangs serrés** in close order; **être** *ou* **se mettre sur les rangs** to line up; **trois candidats sont sur les rangs** three candidates are lined up for *or* are in the running for the job; **servir dans les rangs d'une armée** to serve in the ranks of an army; **servir dans les rangs d'un parti/syndicat** to be a member *or* to serve in the ranks of a party/union; **rentrer dans les rangs** to fall in

❑ **au rang de PRÉP** **1** *(dans la catégorie de)* **une habitude élevée** *ou* **passée au r. de rite sacré** a habit which has been raised to the status of a sacred rite

2 *(au nombre de)* **mettre qn au r. de ses amis** to count sb among one's friends

3 *(à la fonction de)* **élever qn au r. de ministre** to raise *or* to promote sb to the rank of minister

❑ **de rang ADV** **trois heures de r.** three hours in a row

❑ **en rang ADV** in a line *or* row; **entrez/sortez en r.** go in/out in single file; **se mettre en r.** to line up, to form a line; **en r. d'oignons** in a line *or* row

rangé, -e[1] [rɑ̃ʒe] **ADJ** **1** *(en ordre → chambre, vêtements)* tidy **2** *(raisonnable → personne)* steady, level-headed; *(→ vie)* settled; **une jeune personne rangée** a very sober *or* well-behaved young person; **il mène une petite vie bien rangée** he leads a very settled existence **3** *Fam (assagi)* settled■; **être r. des voitures** to have settled down■; *(criminel)* to have gone straight

rangée[2] [rɑ̃ʒe] **NF** row

rangement [rɑ̃ʒmɑ̃] **NM** **1** *(mise en ordre → d'une pièce)* tidying (up); **faire du r.** to tidy up; **avoir la manie du r.** to have a mania for tidiness, to be fanatically tidy

2 *(d'objets, de vêtements)* putting away

3 *(agencement)* arrangement, classification

4 *(meuble)* storage unit; *(cagibi)* storage room; *(espace)* storage space; **quelques solutions de r.** a few storage ideas; **cette cuisine manque de rangements** this kitchen lacks storage space

ranger[1] [rɑ̃dʒœr] **NM** *Mil* ranger

❑ **rangers NMPL** combat boots

ranger[2] [17] [rɑ̃ʒe] **VT** **1** *(mettre en ordre → pièce)* to tidy (up)

2 *(mettre à sa place → vêtement, objets)* to put away; *(→ document)* to file away; **peux-tu r. les verres?** can you put the glasses away?; **où range-t-on les photocopies?** where do you keep *or* file the photocopies?; **j'ai rangé la voiture au garage** I've put the car in the garage; **je ne sais pas, je l'ai rangé là** I don't know, I put it there; **tout est si bien rangé!** everything is arranged so neatly *or* tidily!; *Ordinat* **r. en mémoire** to store

3 *(classer)* to sort (out); **je vais r. mes cartes postales** I'm going to sort (out) my postcards; **r. des dossiers par année** to file documents according to year; *Fig* **r. qn parmi** to rank sb amongst; **peut-on le r. parmi les grands?** can he be ranked *or* does he rank amongst the greats?

4 *Littéraire (faire adhérer)* **r. un auditoire à son avis** to win over an audience

5 *(mettre en rang → troupes)* to draw up; *(→ élèves)* to line up

►**se ranger VPR** **1** *(emploi passif)* **où se rangent les serviettes?** where do the towels go?, where are the towels kept?

2 *(s'écarter → piéton)* to stand aside; *(→ véhicule)* to pull over; **rangez-vous!** stand aside!

3 *(se mettre en rang → élèves, coureurs)* to line up; **rangez-vous deux par deux** get into rows of two, line up in twos; **les concurrents se rangent sur la ligne de départ** the competitors are lining up at the start

4 *(se placer)* **se r. du côté de qn** to side with sb; **se r. contre** to pull up next to; **la voiture se rangea le long du trottoir** the car pulled up beside the kerb

5 *Fam (s'assagir)* to settle down■; **se r. des voitures** to settle down; *(criminel)* to go straight

6 *Naut* **se r. à quai** to berth

7 se r. à *(adhérer à → avis)* to go along with; *(→ décision)* to abide by, to go along with; **se r. au choix de qn** to go along with sb's decision; **ils se sont finalement rangés à mon avis** they ended up coming round to my point of view

Rangoon [rɑ̃gun] **NM** Rangoon

rani [rani] **NF INV** rani, ranee

ranidé [ranide] *Zool* **NM** member of the frog family *or Spéc* the Ranidae

❑ **ranidés NMPL** frogs, *Spéc* Ranidae

ranimation [ranimasjɔ̃] **NF** resuscitation

ranimer [3] [ranime] **VT** **1** *(feu)* to rekindle, to relight

2 *(conversation)* to bring back to life; *(haine, passion, souvenir)* to rekindle, to revive; *(douleur)* to bring back; *(ville, industrie)* to revive, to put new life into; **r. le moral des troupes** to restore the morale of the troops; **r. le courage de qn** to put new heart into sb; **on ne peut r. le passé** you can't bring back the past; **r. le débat** to revive the controversy

3 *(malade)* to revive, to bring round; *(après un arrêt cardiaque)* to resuscitate

►**se ranimer VPR** *(conversation)* to pick up again; *(personne)* to come round; *(visage)* to light up; *(haine, passion)* to flare up again, to be rekindled; **leurs espoirs se ranimèrent** their hopes were revived

rantanplan [rɑ̃tɑ̃plɑ̃] **ONOMAT** = noise of a drum-roll

ranz [rɑ̃, rɑ̃z] **NM** *Suisse* **r. (des vaches)** pastoral melody *(played on the alphorn)*

raousse [raus] **EXCLAM** *Fam* (get) out!, *Br* on your bike!, *Am* take a hike!

raout [raut] **NM** *Arch ou Hum* (social) gathering

rap [rap] **NM** *Mus* rap

rapace [rapas] **ADJ** **1** *Orn* predatory **2** *Fig (avare)* grasping, avaricious

NM **1** *Orn* bird of prey **2** *Fig (avare)* vulture

rapacité [rapasite] **NF** *Littéraire* **1** *(avarice)* rapaciousness, rapacity; **avec r.** rapaciously **2** *(d'un animal)* rapacity

râpage [rɑpaʒ] **NM** *(du métal, du bois)* filing down

rapatriable [rapatrijabl] **ADJ** **est-il r. dans l'état où il est?** can he be repatriated in his present state?

rapatrié, -e [rapatrije] **NM,F** repatriate; **les rapatriés d'Algérie** = French settlers in Algeria who were repatriated as a result of Algerian independence in 1962

rapatriement [rapatrimɑ̃] **NM** repatriation; **le r. des bénéfices** repatriation of profits; **r. sanitaire** repatriation for health reasons

rapatrier [10] [rapatrije] **VT** *(personnes, capitaux)* to repatriate; *(objets)* to send *or* to bring home; **son corps a été rapatrié le mois dernier** his/her body was sent home last month; **se faire r.** to be sent back to one's home country

râpe [rɑp] **NF** **1** *(de cuisine)* grater; **r. à fromage/muscade** cheese/nutmeg grater **2** *Tech (en distillerie)* rotary peeler; *(en outillage)* rasp *or* rough file **3** *Bot* rape **4** *Suisse Fam (avare)* skinflint; **quelle r.!** he's/she's such a skinflint! **5** *Fam (guitare)* guitar■, axe

râpé, -e [rɑpe] **ADJ** **1** *(carotte, fromage etc)* grated **2** *(vêtement)* worn out, threadbare **3** *Fam (raté)* **c'est r.!** we've/you've/*etc* had it!; **c'est r. pour nos vacances en Australie!** bang goes our holiday in Australia!, that's our holiday in Australia out the window!

NM **1** *(fromage)* grated cheese **2** *(tabac)* scraped tobacco **3** *(vin)* rape wine

râper [3] [rɑpe] **VT** **1** *(carotte, fromage etc)* to grate **2** *Tech* to file down **3** *Fig* **un vin qui râpe la gorge** a rough wine

rapercher [3] [rapɛrʃe] **VT** *Suisse Fam* **1** *(dénicher)* to find■, to get■; **va r. ton père à la pinte** go and

haul your dad out of the bar **2** *(rassembler)* to get together■, to collect■

râperie [ʀɑpʀi] NF crushing mill

rapetassage [ʀaptasaʒ] NM *Fam* patching up, mending■

rapetasser [3] [ʀaptase] VT *Fam* to patch up, to mend■

rapetissement [ʀaptismɑ̃] NM **1** *(réduction)* **il observa le r. de l'image sur l'écran** he watched the picture get smaller and smaller on the screen **2** *Fig (fait de dévaloriser)* belittling

rapetisser [3] [ʀaptise] VT **1** *(rendre plus petit)* to make smaller

2 *(faire paraître plus petit)* **r. qn/qch** to make sb/ sth seem smaller; **la distance rapetisse les objets** distance makes things look smaller

3 *(dévaloriser)* to belittle

VI *(gén)* to get smaller; *(au lavage)* to shrink; **la piste rapetissait à vue d'œil** the runway grew rapidly smaller and smaller

►**se rapetisser** VPR *(se dévaloriser)* **se r. aux yeux de qn** to belittle oneself in front of sb

râpeux, -euse [ʀɑpø, -øz] ADJ *(vin)* rough; *(voix)* rasping

Raphaël [ʀafaɛl] NPR Raphael

raphaélesque [ʀafaelɛsk], **raphaélique** [ʀafaelik] ADJ Raphaelesque

raphé [ʀafe] NM *Anat & Bot* raphe

raphia [ʀafja] NM **1** *Bot* raffia *or* raphia palm **2** *Tex* raffia, raphia

raphide [ʀafid] NF *Bot* raphide

rapiat, -e [ʀapja, -at] *Fam* ADJ *(avare)* tight-fisted, stingy; **qu'est-ce qu'elle est rapiate!** she's so stingy!

NM,F skinflint, tightwad

rapide [ʀapid] ADJ **1** *(véhicule, sportif, cheval)* fast; *(courant)* fast-flowing; *Aviat* **approche r.** fast approach; *Aviat* **décélération/descente r.** rapid deceleration/descent; **être r. à la course** to be a fast *or* quick runner; to run fast; *Sport* **une piste r.** a quick *or* fast track; **piste r. aujourd'hui sur l'hippodrome d'Auteuil** the going is good today at Auteuil; **r. comme l'éclair** quick as lightning; **r. comme une flèche** swift as an arrow

2 *(esprit, intelligence, travail)* quick; *(progrès, réaction, changement)* rapid; **c'est l'homme des décisions rapides** he's good at making quick decisions; **une réponse r.** a quick *or* speedy reply; **il n'a pas l'esprit très r.** he's a bit slow on the uptake; **être r. à la détente** to be quick off the mark

3 *(rythme)* quick, fast; **marcher d'un pas r.** to walk at a brisk *or* quick pace; *Méd* **battements de cœur rapides** rapid heartbeat

4 *Tech* **acier r.** high-speed steel; **colle à prise r.** quick-setting adhesive; **déblocage r.** quick release; *Ordinat* **imprimante/lecteur r.** high-speed printer/drive; *Phot* **pellicule r.** fast film

5 *(court, sommaire)* quick; **le chemin le plus r.** the shortest *or* quickest way; **c'est plus r. si tu passes par là** it's faster *or* quicker if you go that way; **un examen r. des dossiers** a quick *or* cursory glance through the documents; **jeter un coup d'œil r. sur qch** to have a quick glance at sth

6 *(hâtif → jugement, décision)* hurried, hasty; **une visite r.** a hurried visit

7 *(facile → recette)* quick

NMF *Fam (personne)* **c'est un r.** *(il comprend vite)* he's really quick on the uptake; *(il travaille vite)* he's a fast worker; **ce n'est pas un r.** *(il ne comprend pas vite)* he's a bit slow on the uptake; *(il ne travaille pas vite)* he's not a fast worker

NM **1** *(cours d'eau)* rapid

2 *(train)* express (train), fast train

rapidement [ʀapidmɑ̃] ADV **1** *(vite)* quickly, rapidly; **aussi r. que possible** as quickly as possible; **la situation se détériore r.** the situation is deteriorating rapidly; **il faut que je réponde r.** I must reply quickly **2** *(superficiellement)* briefly; **j'ai lu r. les journaux de ce matin** I had a quick look at *or* I briefly glanced at the morning papers

rapidité [ʀapidite] NF **1** *(vitesse → d'une course, d'une attaque)* speed; *(→ d'une réponse)* quickness; **avec r.** quickly, speedily, rapidly; **célèbre pour sa r. à la course** famous for being a fast runner; **le chat a une r. de détente remarquable**

the speed with which the cat is able to pounce is remarkable; **grâce à sa r. d'esprit** because of his/her quick mind, because of the speed with which he/she grasps things; **la r. de son geste m'étonna** I was surprised at how quickly his/her hand moved; **la r. avec laquelle elle faisait des progrès** the speed *or* rapidity with which she progressed; **avec la r. de l'éclair** in a flash, with lightning speed

2 *(d'une piste)* **la r. de cette piste favorisait les coureurs** the fast surface of the track helped the runners

3 *(du pouls)* rapidity

4 *Ordinat* **r. d'impression** print speed; **r. de traitement** processing speed

rapido [ʀapido], **rapidos** [ʀapidos] ADV *Fam* quickly■; **boire un coup rapidos** to have a quick drink■ *or* a quick one

rapiècement [ʀapjɛsmɑ̃], **rapiéçage** [ʀapjesaʒ] NM **1** *(raccommodage)* patching (up) **2** *(pièce de tissu, de cuir)* patch

rapiécer [20] [ʀapjese] VT to patch up

rapière [ʀapjɛʀ] NF rapier

rapin [ʀapɛ̃] NM **1** *Vieilli (apprenti chez un artiste)* artist's apprentice **2** *Péj (peintre sans talent)* dauber

rapine [ʀapin] NF *Littéraire* **1** *(pillage)* pillage, plunder **2** *(butin)* plunder

rapiner [3] [ʀapine] *Littéraire* VT to pillage

VI to pillage

rapinerie [ʀapinʀi] NF *Littéraire* plundering, pillaging

raplapla [ʀaplapla] ADJ INV *Fam* **1** *(fatigué)* washed out, wiped (out); **je me sens tout r. aujourd'hui** I don't have any go in me at all today **2** *(plat)* flat; **il est r., ton ballon!** your ball's as flat as a pancake!

raplatir [32] [ʀaplatir] VT to make flatter, to flatten

rappareiller [4] [ʀapaʀeje] VT to match up again

rappariement [ʀapaʀimɑ̃] NM matching up, pairing up

rapparier [9] [ʀapaʀje] VT to match *or* to pair up; **r. des gants** to pair gloves

rappel [ʀapɛl] NM **1** *(remise en mémoire)* reminder; *(en publicité)* follow-up; **le r. de ces événements tragiques la bouleversait** she was deeply upset to be reminded of those tragic events; **commençons par un r. historique** let's start by recalling the historical background; **voici un r. des titres de l'actualité** here's a summary of today's news; **r.! défense de stationner** *(sur panneau)* no parking; **r.! défense de doubler** *(sur panneau)* *Br* no overtaking, *Am* no passing; **(lettre de) r.** *(lettre)* reminder; *Fin* **r. de compte** reminder; **r. d'échéance** reminder of due date, prompt note; **r. à l'ordre** *(gén)* call to order; *Br Pol* ≃ naming; **il a fallu trois rappels à l'ordre pour qu'il se taise** he had to be called to order three times before he stopped talking

2 *(d'un ambassadeur, de produits défectueux)* recall; *Com (d'une somme avancée)* calling in; **r. sous les drapeaux** *(de réservistes)* (reservists') call-up *or* recall

3 *Théât* curtain call; *(à un concert)* encore; **il y a eu plusieurs rappels** *(au théâtre)* he/she/etc took several curtain calls *or* was called back several times; *(à un concert)* there were several encores

4 *(répétition → dans un tableau, une toilette)* **r. de couleur** colour repeat

5 *Méd* booster; **dose/vaccination de r.** booster dose/injection; **piqûre de r.** booster (shot); **ne pas oublier le r. l'an prochain** don't forget to renew the vaccination next year

6 *(arriéré)* **r. de salaire** back pay; **r. de cotisation** payment of contribution arrears

7 *Tél* **r. automatique** recall

8 *Tech (retour)* return; **ressort/vis de r.** return spring/screw

9 *Sport (en alpinisme → activité)* abseiling, rappelling; *(→ descente)* abseil, rappel; **descendre en r.** to rope *or* to abseil down; **faire un r.** to abseil; **faire du r.** *(en voile)* to sit *or* to lean out

10 *Math* **ligne de r.** line of projection

11 *Ordinat* calling up

rappelable [ʀaplabl] ADJ *Mil* recallable

rappelé, -e [ʀaple] ADJ recalled

NM,F *Mil* reservist *(who has been recalled)*

VT to remind **1** ■ to recall **2** ■ to call back **2**, **3** ■ to phone back **3** ■ to call up **5**

VPR to remember **3**

VT **1** *(remettre en mémoire)* **r. qch à qn** to remind sb of sth; **est-il nécessaire de r. le talent qu'il a?** do I need to remind you how talented he is?; **rappelez-moi votre nom** what was your name again, please?; **rappelle-moi de lui écrire** remind me to write to him/her; **rappelle-moi que c'est son anniversaire** remind me it's his/her birthday; **il faut r. que...** it should be borne in mind *or* remembered that...; **les portes ferment à 8 heures, je vous le rappelle** let me remind you that the doors are closed at 8; **le premier mouvement n'est pas sans r. Brahms** the first movement is somewhat reminiscent of Brahms; **ça m'a rappelé mes vacances en Grèce** it reminded me of my holiday in Greece; **ça me rappelle quelque chose** that rings a bell; **numéro à r. dans toute correspondance** *(dans une lettre)* please quote this number in all correspondence

2 *(faire revenir → personne)* to recall, to call back; *(→ marchandises défectueuses)* to recall; **rappelez donc votre chien!** call your dog off!; **r. un ambassadeur** to recall an ambassador; *Mil* **r. des réservistes** to recall reservists; *Euph* **le Seigneur a rappelé à lui son serviteur** he has been called to a better *or* higher place; **l'acteur a été rappelé plusieurs fois** the actor had several curtain calls; **la mort de sa mère l'a rappelé à Aix** the death of his mother took him back to Aix

3 *(au téléphone)* to call back, to phone *or Br* to ring back; **rappelez-moi plus tard** call me back later

4 *(faire écho à)* **son collier de turquoise rappelle la couleur de ses yeux** her turquoise necklace echoes the colour of her eyes; **les rideaux rappellent la couleur de la moquette** the curtains pick out the colour of the carpet

5 *Ordinat* to call up; **r. un sous-programme/ une procédure** to call up a subroutine/a procedure

6 *(locution)* **r. qn à la vie** to bring sb back to life

►**se rappeler** VPR **1** *(emploi réciproque)* **on se rappelle demain?** shall we talk again tomorrow?

2 *(emploi réfléchi)* **se r. au bon souvenir de qn** to send sb one's best regards

3 *(se souvenir de)* to remember; **tu te rappelles mon frère?** do you remember my brother?; **rappelle-toi que je t'attends!** remember *or* don't forget (that) I'm waiting for you!; **elle se rappelle avoir reçu une lettre** she remembers receiving a letter; **je me rappelle bien que tu étais là** I'm sure *or* I well remember that you were here

rapper [3] [ʀape] VI to rap

rappeur, -euse [ʀapœʀ, -øz] NM,F rapper

rappliquer [3] [ʀaplike] VI *Fam (arriver)* to turn up, to show up, to roll up; *(revenir)* to get back

rappointir [32] [ʀapwɛ̃tir] VT to sharpen the tip of

rappointis [ʀapwɛ̃ti] NM *Constr* key

rappondre [75] [ʀapɔ̃dr] *Suisse* VT to join (together); *(cordes, fils)* to tie together

►**se rappondre** VPR to be added

rapponse [ʀapɔ̃s] NF *Suisse (nœud)* knot; *(couture)* seam

NM report **1** ■ profit **2** ■ ratio **3** ■ connection **4** ■ link **4**

NMPL relationship

NM **1** *(compte rendu → gén)* report; *Mil* briefing; **faire** *ou* **rédiger un r. (sur)** to make *or* to draw up a report (on); **soumettre un r. à qn** to submit a report to sb; **faire un r. sur les conditions de travail** to report on working conditions; **r. d'activité** progress report; **r. annuel** annual report; **r. commercial** market report; **r. du commissaire aux comptes** auditor's report; **r. détaillé** item-by-item report, full rundown; **r. d'étude de**

marché market study report; **r. d'expert** audit report; *Compta* **r. d'exploitation** operating statement; **r. de faisabilité** feasibility report; **r. financier** annual (financial) report *or* statement; **r. de gestion** management report; **r. intérimaire** interim report; **r. périodique** progress report; **r. de police** police report; *Mil* **r. quotidien** (daily) briefing; **r. du président** chairman's report; **r. récapitulatif** summary report; **r. de recherche** research paper; **r. réservé** qualified report; **r. de situation journalière** daily trading report; **r. de vente** sales report; **au r.!** read!; *Fig Hum* let's hear it then!

2 *(profit)* profit; **en r.** *(capital)* interest-bearing, productive; **il vit du r. de son capital** he lives on the income from his investments; **d'un bon r.** profitable; **d'un mauvais r.** unprofitable; **cette terre est d'un bon r.** this land gives a good yield; **r. annuel** annual return

3 *(proportion)* ratio; **dans le r. de 1 à 5** in a ratio of 1 to 5; *Aut* **r. du changement de vitesse** gear ratio; **r. cours-bénéfice** price-earnings ratio; **r. coût-efficacité** cost-effectiveness ratio; **r. coût-profit** cost-benefit ratio; *Cin* **r. hauteur/largeur** aspect ratio; **r. de parité** parity ratio; **r. profit-ventes** profit-volume *or* profit-to-volume ratio; **r. qualité-prix** *(gén)* value for money; *Com* quality-price ratio; **c'est d'un bon r. qualité-prix** it's good value for money; **r. signal-bruit** signal-to-noise ratio

4 *(relation)* connection, link; **avoir r. à** to be connected with, to relate to; **n'avoir aucun r. avec qch** to have no connection with *or* to bear no relation to sth; **son dernier album n'a aucun r. avec les précédents** his/her latest album is nothing like his/her earlier ones; **c'est sans r. avec le sujet** that's beside the point, that's irrelevant; **je ne vois pas le r.** I don't see the connection; **où est le r.?** what's that got to do with it?; **mais ça n'a aucun r.!** but that's got nothing to do with it!; **cette décision n'est pas sans r. avec les récents événements** this decision isn't totally unconnected to recent events; **établir un r. entre deux événements** to establish a link *or* connection between two events; **le r. de forces entre les deux pays** the balance of power between the two countries; **il y a un r. de forces entre eux** they are always trying to see who can get the upper hand; **r. de causalité** causal relation; **rapports patrons-syndicats** relations between the employers and the unions

5 *Jur* **r. contractuel** privity of contract; **r. des dettes** = operation whereby an heir deducts from his/her share of the estate his/her debts to the decedent or to a co-heir; **r. des dons et des legs à fin de réduction** abatement of a legacy; **r. des dons et des legs à fin d'égalité** abatement of a legacy; **r. à succession** hotchpot

❑ **rapports** NMPL *(relations)* relationship, relations; **des rapports sociaux/culturels** social/cultural relations; **rapports entre l'Est et l'Ouest** East-West relations; **cesser tous rapports avec qn** to break off all relations with sb; **nous n'avons plus de rapports avec cette société** we no longer deal with that company; **entretenir de bons rapports avec qn** to be on good terms with sb; **rapports sexuels** (sexual) intercourse; **avoir des rapports (avec qn)** to have sex (with sb)

❑ **de rapport** *voir* **immeuble**

❑ **en rapport avec** PRÉP **1** *(qui correspond à)* in keeping with

2 *(en relation avec)* **mettre qn en r. avec qn** to put sb in touch with sb; **il les a mis en r. (l'un avec l'autre)** he put them in contact (with each other); **mettre qch en r. avec** to link sth to; **se mettre en r. avec qn** to get in touch *or* contact with sb; **être en r. avec qn** to be in touch with sb

❑ **par rapport à** PRÉP **1** *(en ce qui concerne)* regarding

2 *(comparativement à)* compared with, in comparison to; **on constate un retrait de l'euro par r. au dollar** the euro has dropped sharply against the dollar

❑ **par rapport que** PRÉP *Can Fam* because■

❑ **rapport à** PRÉP *Fam* **1** *(en ce qui concerne)* about■; **r. à notre affaire, tu as du nouveau?** any news about our little business?

2 *(à cause de)* because of■

❑ **sous le rapport de** PRÉP as regards; **sous le r. des prix** as far as prices are concerned, as regards prices; **sous ce r.** in this respect

❑ **sous tous (les) rapports** ADV in every respect; **jeune homme bien sous tous rapports** *(petite annonce)* respectable young man

---

rapporté, -e [rapɔrte] ADJ added on; **sans élément r.** plain; **poche rapportée** patch *or* sewn-on pocket; **poignée rapportée** detachable handle; **terre rapportée** made ground

rapporter [3] [rapɔrte] VT **1** *(remettre à sa place)* to bring back; **tu rapporteras la clé** bring back the key

2 *(apporter avec soi)* to bring; *Chasse* to retrieve; **j'ai rapporté des fleurs du jardin** I brought some flowers in from the garden; **as-tu rapporté le journal?** did you get *or* buy the paper?; **le chien rapporte la balle** the dog brings back the ball; **je rapporte une impression favorable de cet entretien** I came away with a favourable impression of that meeting

3 *(apporter de nouveau ou en plus)* **rapportez-nous un peu plus de vin** bring us a little more wine

4 *(rendre)* to take back, to return; **pouvez-vous r. ces livres à la bibliothèque?** could you take these books back *or* return these books to the library?; **quelqu'un a rapporté le sac que tu avais oublié** somebody has brought back *or* returned the bag you left behind

5 *(ajouter)* to add; *Couture* to sew on; *Math* **r. un angle** to plot an angle

6 *(produire)* to produce, to yield; **r. des bénéfices** to yield a profit; **r. des intérêts** to yield interest; **le compte d'épargne vous rapporte 3,5 pour cent** the savings account has a yield of 3.5 percent *or* carries 3.5 percent interest; **sa boutique lui rapporte beaucoup d'argent** his/her shop brings in a lot of money; **et qu'est-ce que ça t'a rapporté en fin de compte?** what did you get out of it in the end?; **ça peut r. gros!** it could make you a lot of money!

7 *(répéter → propos)* to tell, to say; **on m'a rapporté que les travaux n'étaient pas terminés** I was told that the work was not finished; **ce n'est pas ce qui a été rapporté** that's not quite what was said

8 *(faire le compte rendu de)* to report (on); *Pol* **r. les décisions d'une commission** to report on the decisions of a committee

9 *Admin & Jur (annuler)* to cancel, to revoke; **r. un projet de loi** to throw out a bill

10 r. qch à *(rattacher)* to relate sth to; **elle rapporte tout à elle** she always brings everything back to herself

11 *Compta (écriture)* to post

VI **1** *(être rentable)* to yield a profit; **c'est un métier qui rapporte** it's a profitable career; *Fam* **ça rapporte** it pays

2 *Chasse* to retrieve; **rapporte, mon chien!** fetch, boy!

3 *Fam (enfant)* to tell tales, to sneak; **je n'aime pas les enfants qui rapportent!** I don't like children who tell tales!

▶**se rapporter** VPR **1 se r. à** *(avoir un lien avec)* to refer *or* to relate to; **l'affiche ne se rapporte pas au sujet de la pièce** the poster bears no relation to the play itself

2 *Gram* **se r. à** to relate to

3 s'en r. à *(s'en remettre à)* to rely on; **je m'en rapporterai à votre expérience** I'll rely on *or* trust your experience

rapporteur, -euse [rapɔrtœr, -øz] ADJ telltale, *Br* sneaky

NM,F **1** *(personne indiscrète)* telltale, *Br* sneak, *Am* tattletale **2** *Admin & Pol (porte-parole)* reporter, recorder; **r. officiel** official recorder; **r. de la commission** = committee member who acts as spokesperson

NM *Géom* protractor

rapprendre [raprɑ̃dr] = **réapprendre**

rapprochage [raprɔʃaʒ] NM *Agr* thinning

rapproché, -e [raprɔʃe] ADJ *(dans l'espace, dans le temps)* close; *(yeux)* close-set; **des maisons très rapprochées** houses very close together; **j'ai trois réunions très rapprochées dans la journée** I've got three meetings one right after the other

rapprochement [raprɔʃmɑ̃] NM **1** *(réconciliation → entre groupes, personnes)* rapprochement, reconciliation; **des tentatives de r.** attempts at reconciliation; **un r. israélo-palestinien** an Israeli-Palestinian rapprochement

2 *(comparaison)* link, connection; **elle fait un r. saisissant entre Mao et Jung** she draws a striking parallel between Mao and Jung; **tu n'avais pas fait le r.?** hadn't you made the connection?; **quand j'ai eu fait le r.** once I made the connection *or* put two and two together; **le r. de ces deux textes établit le plagiat** comparing the two texts provides proof of plagiarism

3 *(convergence)* coming together; **on assiste à un r. des thèses des deux parties** the arguments of the two parties are coming closer together

4 *Compta* **r. bancaire** bank reconciliation

5 *Jur* **r. des législations** approximation of laws

rapprocher [3] [raprɔʃe] VT **1** *(approcher)* to bring closer *or* nearer; **il a rapproché son tabouret du piano** he brought *or* moved his stool closer to the piano; **rapprochez les deux toiles** bring the two canvases closer together; *Couture* **r. les morceaux bord à bord** to put the two pieces edge to edge; *Typ* **à r.** close up

2 *(dans le temps)* **chaque minute le rapprochait du moment fatidique** every minute brought the fateful moment closer; **l'émission/la fête a été rapprochée à cause des événements** the programme/party has been brought forward because of what's happened; **je vais r. mes rendez-vous** I'm going to group my appointments together

3 *(faire paraître proche)* to bring closer; **le dessin japonais rapproche les différents plans** Japanese drawing techniques foreshorten perspective

4 r. qn *(de sa destination)* to take *or* to bring sb closer; **je te dépose à Concorde, ça te rapprochera** I'll drop you off at Concorde, that'll get you a bit closer to where you're going

5 *(affectivement)* to bring (closer) together; **cette naissance n'a pas suffi à les r.** that baby wasn't enough to bring them together; **ça m'a rapproché de mon père** it's brought me closer to my father, it's brought my father and me closer together; **qu'est-ce qui vous rapproche?** what do you have in common?

6 *(comparer)* to compare

7 *Compta* to reconcile

USAGE ABSOLU **mon nouveau zoom rapproche 15 fois** my new zoom lens magnifies 15 times

▶**se rapprocher** VPR **1** *(emploi réciproque)* **les deux pays cherchent à se r.** the two countries are seeking a rapprochement

2 *(venir près)* to come close *or* closer; **la date du mariage/le vacarme des moteurs se rapproche** the wedding day/the roar of the engines is getting closer; **rapprochez-vous de moi** come closer (to me); **rapprochez-vous de l'estrade** move closer to the stage

3 se r. de *(se réconcilier avec)* to get *or* to become closer to; **j'ai essayé sans succès de me r. d'elle avant sa mort** I tried in vain to get closer to her before she died; **il se rapproche actuellement des catholiques** he's now moving closer to Catholicism

4 se r. de *(être comparable à)* to be similar to; **le style se rapproche du reggae** the style is similar to *or* resembles reggae

rapsode [rapsɔd] = **rhapsode**

rapsodie [rapsɔdi] = **rhapsodie**

rapt [rapt] NM *(kidnapping)* abduction, kidnapping; **r. d'enfant** abduction of a child; **r. de séduction** = non-violent abduction of a minor; **r. de violence** unlawful imprisonment, hostage-taking

raptus [raptys] NM *Psy* raptus

râpure [rɑpyr] NF filings

raqué, -e [rake] ADJ *Can Fam (en panne, en ruine)* wrecked; *Fig (épuisé) Br* knackered, *Am* bushed

raquer [3] [rake] *Fam* VT to cough up, to fork out

VI to pay up, to cough up

raquette [rakɛt] NF **1** *(de tennis)* racket; *(de ping-pong)* bat; *Fam* **c'est une bonne r.** *(joueur)* he's/she's a good tennis player■ **2** *(pour la neige)*

snowshoe; **ils sont montés en raquettes** they snowshoed up **3** *Bot* prickly pear

raquetteur, -euse [rakɛtœr, -øz] **NM,F** *Can* snowshoer

rare [rar] **ADJ 1** *(difficile à trouver)* rare, uncommon; **ce qui est r. est cher** anything that is in short supply is expensive; **l'amour vrai est un sentiment si r.** true love is such a rare feeling; **un musicien d'un r. talent** an exceptionally talented musician; **plantes/timbres rares** rare plants/stamps; **être d'une beauté r.** to be uncommonly beautiful

2 *(peu fréquent)* rare; **à de rares intervalles** at rare *or* infrequent intervals; **on le voyait chez nous à de rares intervalles** once in a (very long) while, he'd turn up at our house; **lors d'une de ses rares visites** on one of his/her rare *or* few visits; **tes visites sont trop rares** you don't visit us nearly often enough; **il est r. qu'elle veuille bien venir avec moi** she rarely *or* seldom agrees to come with me; **ça n'a rien de r.** there's nothing unusual about that; **il n'est pas r. de le voir ici** it's not uncommon *or* unusual to see him here; *Fam* **tu te fais r. ces derniers temps** you've become quite a stranger lately, where have you been hiding lately?; **c'est un mot r.** that's a rare word

3 *(peu nombreux)* few; **les rares électeurs qui ont voté pour lui** the few who voted for him; **les rares amis qu'elle s'est faits** the few friends she made; **rares sont ceux qui l'apprécient** not many people like him/her; **à de rares exceptions près** with only *or* apart from a few exceptions; **elle est une des rares personnes que je connaisse à aimer le jazz** she's one of the very few people I know who enjoys jazz; **je suis un des rares à aimer la pluie** I'm one of the few people who like rain; **ces animaux deviennent rares** these animals are becoming rare; **les visiteurs se font rares** there are fewer and fewer visitors; **les bons pâtissiers se font rares** good pastry chefs are hard to find nowadays

4 *(peu abondant)* scarce; **la nourriture était r. pendant la guerre** food was scarce during the war; **la main-d'œuvre/l'argent était r.** there was a shortage of labour/money, labour/money was scarce; **les denrées de base se font rares** basic food items are becoming scarce

5 *(clairsemé)* thin, sparse; **une herbe r.** sparse clumps of grass; **elle a toujours eu le cheveu r.** she always had very thin hair; **il a le cheveu r.** his hair is thinning

6 *Phys (raréfié)* rare

raréfaction [rarefaksjɔ̃] **NF 1** *Phys (de l'air)* rarefaction **2** *(des denrées, de l'argent)* increasing scarcity

raréfiable [rarefjabl] **ADJ** rarefiable

raréfier [9] [rarefje] **VT 1** *Phys (air, oxygène)* to rarefy, to rarify **2** *(argent, denrées)* to make scarce

►**se raréfier VPR 1** *Phys (air)* to rarefy, to rarify **2** *(argent, denrées)* to become scarce; *(visites)* to become less frequent

rarement [rarmɑ̃] **ADV** rarely, seldom; **elle téléphone r., pour ne pas dire jamais** she seldom, if ever, calls

rarescent, -e [raresɑ̃, -ɑ̃t] **ADJ** *Littéraire* becoming rarer

rareté [rarte] **NF 1** *(d'un fait, d'un phénomène)* rarity; *(d'un mot, d'une maladie)* rareness; *(de visites)* infrequency; *(d'une denrée)* scarcity; **une poterie d'une très grande r.** an extremely rare piece of pottery **2** *(objet → rare)* rarity, rare object; *(→ bizarre)* curio

rarissime [rarisim] **ADJ** extremely rare, most unusual

RAS [ɛraɛs] **ADV** *Fam (abrév* **rien à signaler**) nothing to report

ras[1] [ra] **NM** *(radeau)* raft

ras[2] [ras] **NM** *(titre éthiopien)* ras

ras[3], **-e** [ra, raz] **ADJ 1** *(cheveux)* close-cropped, very short; *(tête)* close-cropped; *(barbe)* very short

2 *(végétation)* short; *(pelouse)* closely-mown

3 *(plein)* **mesure rase** full measure; **deux cuillerées rases de sucre** two level spoonfuls of sugar

4 *Tex* short-piled

5 *(locution)* **en rase campagne** in the open countryside; **la voiture est tombée en panne en rase campagne** the car broke down in the middle of nowhere

ADV 1 *(très court)* short; **avoir les ongles coupés r.** to keep one's nails cut short; **une haie taillée r.** a closely-clipped hedge

2 *Fam* **en avoir r. le bol** *ou* **la casquette** *ou Vulg* **le cul (de qch)** to have had it up to here (with sth), to be fed up (to the back teeth) (with sth); *Fam* **r. le bol!** enough is enough!; **ah non, r. le bol, on l'a assez vu!** not HIM again!

❑ **à ras ADV coupé à r.** cut short

❑ **à ras bord, à ras bords ADV** to the brim *or* top

❑ **à ras de PRÉP** level with; **à r. de terre** level with the ground

❑ **au ras de PRÉP au r. de l'eau** just above water level, level with the water; *Fam* **elle portait une minijupe qui lui arrivait au r. des fesses** she was wearing a mini-skirt which was more like a belt; *Fam* **ses remarques étaient au r. des pâquerettes** he/she came out with some very uninspired comments; *Fam* **le débat est au r. des pâquerettes** the discussion isn't exactly highbrow, the tone of the discussion is rather low

rasade [razad] **NF** *(dans un verre)* glassful; *(au goulot)* swig

rasage [razaʒ] **NM 1** *(de la barbe)* shaving **2** *Tex* shearing **3** *Métal* (machine) shaving

rasance [razɑ̃s] **NF** *Mil* grazing

rasant, -e [razɑ̃, -ɑ̃t] **ADJ 1** *(bas)* **vue rasante** panoramic view; **un soleil r.** a low sun; **lumière rasante** oblique *or* low-angled light **2** *Mil* **tir r.** grazing fire **3** *Fam (assommant)* deadly dull; **c'était r.** it was a real drag

rascasse [raskas] **NF** *Ich* scorpion fish

ras-du-cou [radyku] **ADJ INV** round-neck *(avant n)*; **un pull r.** a round-neck sweater

NM INV round-neck sweater

rase-bitume [razbitym] **NMF INV** *Fam* runt, squirt

rase-mottes [razmɔt] **NM INV 1** *Aviat* hedgehopping; **voler en** *ou* **faire du r.** to hedgehop **2** *Péj* runt, shortie

raser [3] [raze] **VT 1** *(cheveux, poils)* to shave off; *(crâne, personne)* to shave; **mal rasé** ill-shaven; **être rasé de près** to be close-shaven; **se faire r.** *(la barbe)* to be given a shave

2 *(détruire)* to raze; **la vieille église a été rasée** the old church was razed to the ground

3 *(frôler → sol, eau)* to skim; **la balle lui rasa l'épaule** the bullet grazed his/her shoulder; **r. les murs** to hug the walls

4 *Fam (lasser)* to bore■ ; **tu nous rases!** you're boring us to tears!

5 *Tex* to shear

❑ **à raser ADJ** shaving *(avant n)*; **mousse à r.** shaving foam

►**se raser VPR 1** *(couper ses poils)* to shave; **se r. de près** to shave closely; **se r. les jambes** to shave one's legs; **se r. la barbe** to shave off one's beard

2 *Fam (s'ennuyer)* to be bored stiff *or* to tears; **qu'est-ce qu'on se rase ici!** it's deadly dull here!

3 *Chasse (lièvre)* to squat, to crouch

rasette [razɛt] **NF** *Agr* skim coulter

raseur, -euse [razœr, -øz] **NM,F** *Fam* bore, drag; **quel r.!** what a bore *or* drag!

rash [raʃ] *(pl* **rashs** *ou* **rashes**) **NM** *Méd* rash

rasibus [razibys] **ADV** *Fam* **1** *(court)* short■ , very close■ ; **il s'est fait couper les cheveux r.** he's been scalped **2** *(très près)* very close■ ; **la balle est passée r.** the bullet whizzed past

raskol [raskɔl] **NM** *Hist* = schism in the Russian Orthodox Church in the 17th century

ras-le-bol [ralbɔl] **NM INV** *Fam* **il y a un r. général dans la population** people in general are sick and tired of *or* fed up with the way things are going

rasoir [razwar] **NM** razor; **r. électrique** (electric) shaver; **r. mécanique** *ou* **de sûreté** safety razor; **demander une coupe au r.** to ask for a razor cut; **coupé au r.** cut with a razor

ADJ *Fam* deadly dull; **ce qu'il peut être r.!** he's such a bore!

raspatoire [raspatwar] **ADJ** *Méd* raspatory

Raspoutine [rasputin] **NPR** Rasputin

raspoutitsa [rasputitsa] **NF** *(en Russie)* = period of thaw which turns the surface soil into mud

rasquette [raskɛt] **NF** *Fam Mil* combat ration

rassasiement [rasazimɑ̃] **NM** satisfaction

rassasier [9] [rasazje] **VT 1** *(faim)* to satisfy; **r. qn** to satisfy sb's hunger; **je suis rassasié** I'm full

2 *Fig* **alors, vous êtes rassasiés de plein air?** so, have you had your fill of fresh air?; **il n'est jamais rassasié de la voir** he never tires of seeing her

USAGE ABSOLU les fruits ne rassasient pas fruit isn't very filling *or* doesn't satisfy your hunger

►**se rassasier VPR 1** *(apaiser sa faim)* to eat one's fill; **se r. d'un plat** to eat one's fill of a dish

2 *(assouvir son désir)* **se r. de qch** to get one's fill of sth; **je ne me rassasie pas de cette vue/sa présence** I never tire of this view/his/her presence

rassemblement [rasɑ̃bləmɑ̃] **NM 1** *(réunion sur la voie publique → gén)* gathering, group; *(→ en politique)* rally; **disperser un r.** to break up *or* to disperse a gathering; **r. électoral** campaign rally; **r. pour la paix** peace rally

2 *(dans un nom de parti)* party, union, alliance; **votez pour le R. écologiste** vote for the Green party; *Anciennement* **R. pour la République** = right-wing French political party

3 *(fait de se rassembler)* gathering; **tous les rassemblements sont strictement interdits** all rallies *or* gatherings are strictly forbidden; **vous devez empêcher le r. des élèves dans le hall** you must prevent the pupils from gathering in the hall

4 *(union)* union; **œuvrer au r. de la gauche** to work towards the union of the left

5 *Mil* **sonner le r.** to sound the assembly; **r.!** fall in!

6 *(d'objets, d'idées, de preuves)* collecting, gathering; *(de documents, d'outils)* collecting, assembling, gathering

7 *Ordinat (de données)* gathering

rassembler [3] [rasɑ̃ble] **VT 1** *(objets, idées, preuves)* to collect, to gather; *(documents, outils)* to collect, to assemble, to gather; *Ordinat (données)* to gather; **elle rassembla tous les journaux de la semaine passée** she gathered together all the previous week's newspapers; **r. des preuves pour une inculpation** to gather *or* to collect evidence for a charge; **il a rassemblé des documents pour écrire une biographie** he has collected *or* assembled documents to write a biography; **faites r. toutes mes affaires et envoyez-les-moi** have all my belongings collected together and send them to me; **j'eus à peine le temps de r. quelques affaires** I hardly had enough time to gather *or* to put a few things together; **r. ses forces** to gather *or* to muster one's strength; **r. ses esprits** to gather *or* to collect one's wits; **r. ses idées** to gather one's thoughts; **r. son courage** to summon up one's courage

2 *(personnes)* to gather together; *(troupes)* to assemble, to muster; *(animaux)* to round up; **puisque nous voici ici rassemblés** since we are (gathered) here together; **leur manifestation a rassemblé des milliers de personnes** their demonstration drew *or* attracted thousands of people; **ce qui nous rassemble ici ce soir, c'est la passion du théâtre** it is a passion for the theatre which has brought us here this evening

3 *Équitation* to collect

►**se rassembler VPR** *(gén)* to gather together, to assemble; *(foule)* to collect, to gather; *(troupes)* to fall in, to muster, to assemble; **ils se sont rassemblés devant chez moi** they gathered together *or* assembled outside my home; **nous nous rassemblons tous les jeudis dans ce bar** we meet *or* get together in this bar every Thursday; **rassemblez-vous!** assemble!

rassembleur, -euse [rasɑ̃blœr, -øz] **NM,F ce fut un grand r.** he was a great leader who could appeal to all sides

rasseoir [65] [raswar] **VT 1** *(asseoir de nouveau)* **r. qn** *(qui était debout)* to sit sb down (again); **veuillez r. le malade** *(dans son lit)* please sit the patient up again; **je vous en prie, faites r. tout le monde** please, have everybody sit down again

2 *(replacer)* to put back; **r. une statue sur son socle** to put a statue back on its plinth

►**se rasseoir VPR 1** *(personne)* to sit down again; **il a fait se r. tous les invités** he made all

the guests sit down again; **allez vous r.** go back to your seat, go and sit down again

2 *(liquide)* to settle

rasséréner [18] [raserene] *Littéraire* **VT r. qn** to put sb's mind at rest; **ses déclarations m'ont complètement rasséréné** what he/she said put my mind completely at rest

▸**se rasséréner VPR** to become calm *or* serene again

rasseyait, rassied *etc voir* **rasseoir**

rassir [32] [rasir] **VI** *(gâteau, pain)* to go stale; **laisser r. un morceau de bœuf** to let a piece of beef hang; **faire r. du pain** to let bread go stale

▸**se rassir VPR** to go stale

rassis[1], **-e** [1] [rasi, -iz] **PP** *voir* **rasseoir**

rassis[2], **-e** [2] [rasi, -iz] **ADJ 1** *(gâteau, pain)* stale; *(viande)* properly hung **2** *Littéraire (calme)* calm, composed; *(pondéré)* balanced

rassissement [rasismã] **NM** *(d'un gâteau, du pain)* going stale

rassoit *etc voir* **rasseoir**

rassortiment [rasɔrtimã] = **réassortiment**

rassortir [rasɔrtir] = **réassortir**

rassoyait *etc voir* **rasseoir**

rassurant, -e [rasyrã, -ãt] **ADJ 1** *(personne)* reassuring; **le président n'a pas été très r. dans ses dernières déclarations** the president's most recent statements were not very reassuring; **elle a été rassurante pour tout le monde** she comforted everybody

2 *(nouvelle, déclaration, ton, voix)* reassuring, comforting; *aussi Ironique* **voilà qui est r.!** well, that's reassuring!

rassurer [3] [rasyre] **VT** to reassure; **j'aimerais pouvoir te r.** I wish I could reassure you *or* put your mind at ease; **va vite r. ta mère** go and tell your mother she has nothing to worry about, go and set your mother's mind at ease; **je te rassure tout de suite, je ne vais pas te demander de le faire à ma place!** I can assure you, I won't ask you to do it for me!; **je n'étais pas très rassuré** I felt rather worried; **je ne suis pas très rassuré de la savoir seule** I have my worries about her being alone; **il n'a pas l'air très rassuré** he's not looking too happy; **ah, me voilà rassuré!** that's a relief!

▸**se rassurer VPR 1** *(se raisonner)* to reassure oneself; **j'essaie de me r. en me disant que tout n'est pas fini** I try to reassure myself by saying it's not all over

2 *(cesser de s'inquiéter)* **elle a mis longtemps à se r.** it took her a while to calm down; **rassure-toi** don't worry

rasta [rasta] *Fam* **ADJ INV** Rasta

NMF Rasta

NM *Vieilli* = racist term used with reference to wealthy foreigners

rastafari [rastafari] **ADJ** Rastafarian

NMF Rastafarian

rastaquouère [rastakwɛr] **NM** *Fam Vieilli* = racist term used with reference to wealthy foreigners

rastel [rastɛl] **NM** *(dans le Midi)* = gathering of people invited for a drink

rastériser [3] [rasterize] **VT** *TV* to rasterize

Rastignac [rastiɲak] **NPR** = character from Balzac's 'la Comédie humaine', the typical young man from the provinces trying to make good in the capital

rat [ra] **NM 1** *(animal)* rat; **faire la chasse aux rats** to go ratting; **r. d'Amérique** muskrat, musquash; **r. des bois** wood rat, *Am* pack rat; **r. des champs** field mouse; **r. d'eau** water vole *or* rat; **r. d'égout** common *or* brown *or* Norway *or* sewer rat; **r. géant** giant rat; **r. gris** common *or* brown *or* Norway *or* sewer rat; **r. musqué** muskrat, musquash; **r. noir** black rat; **r. palmiste** ground squirrel; **r. surmulot** common *or* brown *or* Norway *or* sewer rat; **les rats quittent le navire** the rats are leaving the sinking ship; *très Fam* **être fait comme un r.** to have no escape, to be cornered; **vous êtes faits comme des rats!** you're caught like rats in a trap!; *Fam* **être comme un r. dans un fromage** to be in clover, to be like a pig in mud; *très Fam* **s'emmerder** *ou* **se faire chier comme un r. mort** to be bored shitless

2 *Fig (personne)* **r. de bibliothèque** bookworm, *Am* library rat; **r. d'hôtel** hotel thief

3 **petit r. de l'Opéra** ballet student *(at the Opéra de Paris)*

4 *Fam Péj (avare)* skinflint, tightwad

5 *(par affection)* **mon (petit) r.** my darling

6 *Can Fam Péj (personne sournoise)* sly customer; *(non gréviste)* scab, strikebreaker■

ADJ M *Fam Péj* **1** *(avare)* stingy, tight-fisted; **il est tellement r.!** he's so stingy!, he's such a miser *or* skinflint!

2 *Can (sournois)* wily■, sly■

Allusion

Le rat des villes et le rat des champs

This is the title of a La Fontaine fable (*The Town Mouse and the Country Mouse*). In this fable, a town mouse invites a country mouse to a lavish dinner but they are interrupted by some noise and have to run away. When they return, the country mouse suggests that instead the town mouse comes to dine in the countryside the next day, when they could enjoy more humble fare but in peace. The expression is used today to emphasize the difference between people who live in the city and those who live in the countryside, and more generally between rich but stressful city life and frugal but peaceful country life.

rata [rata] **NM** *Fam* food■, grub; **ne pas s'endormir sur le r.** not to fall asleep on the job

ratafia [ratafja] **NM** ratafia (liqueur)

ratage [rataʒ] **NM** failure; **un r. complet** a complete failure; **après un ou deux ratages, il a réussi son soufflé à la perfection** after one or two disastrous attempts, he got the soufflé just right

rataplan [rataplã] **ONOMAT** rat-a-tat

ratatiné, -e [ratatine] **ADJ 1** *(fruit)* shrivelled (up) **2** *(visage)* wrinkled, wizened **3** *Fam (voiture, vélo)* smashed up; *(soufflé)* flat

ratatiner [3] [ratatine] **VT 1** *Fam (démolir)* **le bâtiment a été ratatiné en quelques secondes** the building was reduced to a pile of rubble within seconds; **la voiture a été complètement ratatinée** the car was completely smashed up

2 *(flétrir)* **l'âge l'a complètement ratatiné** he has become wizened with age

3 *Fam (battre)* to thrash; **je me suis fait r. au tennis/aux échecs** I got thrashed at tennis/chess

4 *Fam (assassiner)* to do in; **il s'est fait r.** he got done in

▸**se ratatiner VPR 1** *(se dessécher)* to shrivel; **son visage s'est ratatiné** his/her face has become all wizened

2 *(rapetisser)* to shrink; **elle se ratatine en vieillissant** she's shrinking with age

3 *Fam (s'écraser)* to crash■; **la voiture s'est ratatinée contre un mur** the car crashed *or* smashed into a wall

ratatouille [ratatuj] **NF 1** *Culin* **r. (niçoise)** ratatouille **2** *Fam Péj (ragoût grossier)* **ils ont servi une affreuse r.** they served up some ghastly mess **3** *Fam (raclée)* walloping, hammering

rat-de-cave [radkav] *(pl* **rats-de-cave**) **NM** wax taper

rate [rat] **NF 1** *Zool* she-rat, female rat **2** *Anat* spleen; *Fam* **se dilater la r.** to be in stitches, to kill oneself (laughing), to split one's sides

raté, -e [rate] **ADJ 1** *(photo, sauce)* spoilt; *(coupe de cheveux)* disastrous; **il est complètement r., ce gâteau** this cake is a complete disaster

2 *(attentat)* failed; *(vie)* wasted; *(occasion)* missed; *(tentative)* failed, abortive, unsuccessful; **un musicien r.** a failed musician

NM,F failure, loser

NM 1 *(bruit)* misfiring *(UNCOUNT)*; **le moteur a des ratés** the engine is misfiring

2 *(difficulté)* hitch

3 *Mil* misfire

râteau, -x [rɑto] **NM 1** *(de jardin)* rake; **ramasser les feuilles mortes avec un r.** to rake up the dead leaves; **donner un coup de r. à l'allée** to give the path a rake; **r. faneur** tedder; **r. mécanique** raker

2 *(de croupier)* rake

3 *(de métier à tisser)* comb

4 *Fam (peigne)* comb■

5 *Fam (locutions)* **mettre un r. à qn** to turn sb down■, *Br* to knock sb back; **se prendre un r.** to get turned down■, *Br* to get a knockback

6 *Suisse Fam (avare)* miser, skinflint

ratel [ratɛl] **NM** *Zool* ratel, honey badger

râtelage [rɑtlaʒ] **NM** raking up

râtelée [rɑtle] **NF** rakeful

râteler [24] [rɑtle] **VT** to rake up

râteleur, -euse [rɑtlœr, -øz] **NM,F** raker *(of hay)*

râtelier [rɑtəlje] **NM 1** *(support)* rack; **r. à fusils/outils/pipes** gun/tool/pipe rack **2** *(mangeoire)* rack; *Fam* **manger à tous les râteliers** to have a finger in every pie **3** *Fam (dentier)* dentures■

rater [3] [rate] **VI 1** *Fam (échouer)* to fail; **je t'avais dit qu'elle serait en retard, et ça n'a pas raté!** I told you she'd be late, and sure enough she was!; **ça ne rate jamais** it never fails; **tais-toi, tu vas tout faire r.!** shut up or you'll ruin everything!

2 *Mil* **le coup a raté** the gun failed to go off

VT 1 *(but)* to miss; **vous avez de la chance, la balle a bien failli ne pas vous r.** you're lucky, that bullet missed you by a fraction of an inch *or* a hair's breadth; **elle a raté la marche** she missed the step; **j'ai raté ma chance** I missed my opportunity *or* chance; *Fam* **j'ai raté mon coup** I made a mess of it; *Fam* **s'il recommence, je te jure que je ne le raterai pas!** if he does it again, I swear I'll get him!; *Fam* **le coiffeur ne t'a pas raté, dis donc!** the hairdresser really did a job on you!

2 *(avion, rendez-vous, visiteur, occasion)* to miss; **je n'ai pas vu le concert – tu n'as rien raté/tu as raté quelque chose!** I didn't see the concert – you didn't miss anything!/you really missed something!; **c'est une émission à ne pas r.** this programme is a must *or* is unmissable; **tu vas nous faire r. la séance!** you're going to make us miss the film!; *Fam* **tu n'en rates pas une!** you're always putting your foot in it!

3 *(ne pas réussir)* **il a complètement raté son oral** he made a complete mess of his oral; **j'ai encore raté mon permis de conduire** I've failed my driving test again; **il a raté son effet** he didn't achieve the desired effect; **il a raté sa sortie** his exit didn't quite come off; **il rate toujours les mayonnaises** his mayonnaise always goes wrong; **j'ai raté mon gâteau** I made a mess of the cake; **r. sa vie** to make a mess of one's life; **c'est raté, il ne reste plus de places** we've had it, there are no tickets left; **si tu voulais lui parler, c'est raté, il vient de partir** if you wanted to talk to him, you're too late, he's just gone

▸**se rater VPR** *Fam* **1** *(personnes)* to miss each other■; **on avait rendez-vous à l'Arc de Triomphe mais on s'est ratés** we were supposed to meet at the Arc de Triomphe but we missed each other

2 *(soi-même)* **il s'est coupé les cheveux lui-même, il s'est complètement raté!** he cut his hair himself and made a complete mess of it!; **elle est tombée de vélo, elle ne s'est pas ratée!** she really *or Br* didn't half hurt herself when she fell off her bike!; **elle s'est ratée pour la troisième fois** that's her third (unsuccessful) suicide attempt

ratiboiser [3] [ratibwaze] **VT** *Fam* **1** *(voler)* **r. qch à qn** to pinch *or Br* to nick sth from sb

2 *(ruiner)* to clean out; **je suis ratiboisé!** I'm cleaned out!; **on s'est fait r. au casino** we were cleaned out at the casino

3 *(tuer)* to bump off, to do in; *Fig* **les critiques l'ont ratiboisé** the critics tore him to shreds, *esp Br* he was slated by the critics

4 *(cheveux)* **je suis ressorti ratiboisé de chez le coiffeur** I got scalped at the hairdresser's; **se faire r. (la colline)** to get scalped

ratiche [ratiʃ] **NF** *Fam* tooth■

raticide [ratisid] **NM** rat poison

ratier [ratje] **ADJ M** ratter

NM ratter

ratière [ratjɛr] **NF 1** *(piège)* rat trap **2** *Tex* dobby

ratification [ratifikasjɔ̃] **NF** *Jur* ratification

ratifier [9] [ratifje] **VT 1** *Jur* to ratify; **ils ont fait r. le traité par le gouvernement** they put the treaty before Parliament for ratification **2** *Littéraire (confirmer)* to confirm

ratinage [ratinaʒ] **NM** *Tex* friezing

ratine [ratin] **NF** *Tex* ratine
ratiner [3] [ratine] **VT** *Tex* to frieze, to friz(z)
ratineuse [ratinøz] **NF** *Tex* friezing machine
rating [ratiŋ] **NM** *Écon & Naut* rating; **r. de la dette** debt rating
ratio [rasjo] **NM 1** *Écon & Fin* ratio; **r. de capitalisation** p/e ratio, price/earnings ratio; **r. capital-travail** capital-labour ratio; *Compta* **r. capitaux empruntés-fonds propres** debt-to-equity ratio; **r. cours-bénéfices** price-earnings ratio; **r. de couverture de l'intérêt** interest coverage; **r. d'endettement** debt ratio; *Compta* **r. d'exploitation** performance ratio, operating ratio; *Compta* **r. de gestion** financial ratio; **r. d'intensité de capital** capital-output ratio; **r. de levier** leverage; *Compta* **r. de liquidité (générale)** liquidity ratio; *Compta* **r. de liquidité immédiate** quick ratio, acid test ratio; *Compta* **r. de rentabilité (nette)** (net) profit ratio; *Compta* **r. de solvabilité** solvency ratio; *Compta* **r. de trésorerie** cash ratio; **r. des ventes** sales ratio; **r. de volume de bénéfices** profit/volume ratio, P/V
2 *Jur* **ratio decidendi** ratio decidendi, = the legal principle on which a court's decision is founded; **r. legis** ratio legis, = legislative motivation; **ratio scripta** ratio scripta, = written reason
ratiocination [rasjɔsinasjɔ̃] **NF** quibble; **ce sont des ratiocinations!** you're just splitting hairs!
ratiociner [3] [rasjɔsine] **VI** to quibble, to split hairs
ration [rasjɔ̃] **NF 1** *(portion)* ration; **rations de guerre** war rations; *Fig* **il a eu sa r. de problèmes** he's had his share of problems; *Hum* **non merci, j'ai eu ma r.!** no thanks, I've had my fill (of it)!
2 *(quantité nécessaire)* daily intake; **r. alimentaire** food intake; **r. d'entretien** maintenance ration
3 *Mil* rations; **r. de combat** combat rations; **avoir une r. réduite** to be on short rations; **rations de survie** survival rations
rational, -aux [rasjɔnal, -o] **NM** *Antiq* breastplate, pectoral
rationalisation [rasjɔnalizasjɔ̃] **NF** rationalization; *Compta* **r. des choix budgétaires** planning-programming-budgeting system
rationalisé, -e [rasjɔnalize] **ADJ** rationalized
rationaliser [3] [rasjɔnalize] **VT** to rationalize
rationalisme [rasjɔnalism] **NM** rationalism
rationaliste [rasjɔnalist] **ADJ** rationalist
NMF rationalist
rationalité [rasjɔnalite] **NF** rationality
rationaux [rasjɔno] *voir* **rational**
rationnaire [rasjɔnɛr] **NMF** ration-book holder
rationnel, -elle [rasjɔnɛl] **ADJ 1** *Math & Phil* rational **2** *(sensé)* rational; **il n'a pas une attitude très rationnelle** his attitude is not very rational **3** *Écon* **l'organisation rationnelle de l'industrie** the rationalization *or* streamlining of industry
rationnellement [rasjɔnɛlmɑ̃] **ADV 1** *Math & Phil* rationally **2** *(avec bon sens)* rationally, sensibly, logically
rationnement [rasjɔnmɑ̃] **NM** rationing
rationner [3] [rasjɔne] **VT 1** *(quelque chose)* to ration; **on nous rationne même l'électricité!** they're even rationing electricity!
2 *(quelqu'un)* to put on rations, to ration; **je vais vous r. à deux tasses de café par jour** I'm going to ration you to two cups of coffee a day; *Hum* **il va bientôt falloir le r.!** we'll have to put him on (short) rations soon!
▶**se rationner VPR** to ration oneself
Ratisbonne [ratisbɔn] **NM** Regensburg
ratissage [ratisaʒ] **NM 1** *(nettoyage)* raking **2** *(fouille)* combing, thorough search
ratisser [3] [ratise] **VT 1** *(gravier, allée)* to rake; *(feuilles, herbe coupée)* to rake up **2** *Fam (voler)* to pinch, *Br* to nick; **je me suis fait r. mon sac** I got my bag pinched *or Br* nicked **3** *(ruiner)* to clean out; **il s'est fait r. au poker** he got cleaned out playing poker **4** *(fouiller)* to comb **5** *Sport* to heel
VI *Fam Fig* **r. large** to cast one's net wide
ratite [ratit] *Orn* **NM** ratite
❑ **ratites NMPL** Ratitae
rat-kangourou [rakɑ̃guru] **NM** *Zool* kangaroo rat, rat kangaroo
raton [ratɔ̃] **NM 1** *(animal)* young rat; **r. laveur** raccoon **2** *(par affection)* **mon r.!** my darling! **3** *Vulg* = offensive term used to refer to North African Arabs
ratonnade [ratɔnad] **NF** = violent racist attack on North African Arab immigrants
ratoureux, -euse [raturø, -øz] *Can* **ADJ** wily, devious; **parfois le bonheur est un peu r.** sometimes happiness is not all it seems
NM,F shady customer
RATP [ɛratepe] **NF** *(abrév* **Régie autonome des transports parisiens**) = Paris transport authority
rattachement [rataʃmɑ̃] **NM 1** *Admin & Pol* **le r. de la Savoie à la France** the incorporation of Savoy into France; **opérer le r. de territoires à la métropole** to bring territories under the jurisdiction of the home country; **demander son r. à un service** to ask to be attached to a department **2** *Compta* matching
rattacher [3] [rataʃe] **VT 1** *(paquet)* to tie up again, to do up again; *(ceinture, lacet)* to do up again; *(cheveux → en chignon)* to put up (again); *(→ en queue-de-cheval)* to tie back; *(chien)* to tie up again; *(plante grimpante)* to tie back
2 *Admin & Pol* **r. plusieurs services à une même direction** to bring several departments under the same management; **nous sommes rattachés à l'Hôpital Broussais** we're attached to the Broussais Hospital; **r. un territoire à un pays** to bring a territory under the jurisdiction of a country; **les abonnés ont été rattachés à un nouveau central** the subscribers were connected to a new exchange
3 *(lier → idée)* **r. qch à** to connect *or* to link sth with, to relate sth to; **les liens qui nous rattachent à notre famille** the ties that bind us to our family; **c'était la seule chose qui nous rattachait l'un à l'autre** it was the only thing that bound us together
▶**se rattacher VPR 1 se r. à** *(découler de)* to derive from; **des dialectes qui se rattachent à une langue** dialects which derive from the same language
2 se r. à *(avoir un lien avec)* to be connected *or* linked with, to be related to; **laissez de côté tout ce qui ne se rattache pas au problème central** put everything that isn't (directly) related to the key issue to one side; **voici le rapport et toutes les pièces qui s'y rattachent** here is the report and its related documents
rattachiste [rataʃist] *Belg* **ADJ** *(personne, politique)* = advocating the integration of French-speaking regions of Belgium into France
NMF = advocate of the integration of French-speaking regions of Belgium into France
rat-taupe [ratop] *(pl* **rats-taupes**) **NM** *Zool* mole rat
ratte [rat] **NF** = variety of small yellow-skinned potato
rattrapable [ratrapabl] **ADJ une telle erreur ne serait pas r.** a mistake like that couldn't be put right
rattrapage [ratrapaʒ] **NM 1** *(au bac)* **être admis au r.** = to be allowed to sit further oral examinations to gain a pass mark in the "baccalauréat"; **l'oral de r.** = further oral examination to gain a pass mark in the "baccalauréat"
2 *(remise à niveau)* **r. scolaire** ≃ remedial teaching; **cours de r.** = extra class for pupils who need to catch up
3 *(d'une maille)* picking up
4 *Écon* **r. des salaires** wage adjustment
rattraper [3] [ratrape] **VT 1** *(animal, prisonnier)* to recapture, to catch again
2 *(objet qui tombe)* to catch (hold of); **je l'ai rattrapé de justesse** I caught (hold of) it just in time; **r. la balle au vol/bond** to catch the ball in the air/on the bounce
3 *(quelqu'un parti plus tôt)* to catch up with; **passe devant, je te rattraperai** go on ahead, I'll catch up with you *or* catch you up
4 *(compenser)* **r. le temps perdu** *ou* **son retard** to make up for lost time; **il a rattrapé les cours manqués** he has caught up on the lessons he missed; **r. du sommeil** to catch up on one's sleep; **pour r. nos pertes** to make good our losses
5 *(erreur, maladresse)* to put right; *(situation, mayonnaise)* to salvage; **dis-moi comment r. le mal que je t'ai fait** tell me how I can make up for the hurt I've caused you
6 *(étudiant)* to let through
7 *(maille)* to pick up
8 *Écon* to adjust
▶**se rattraper VPR 1** *(emploi passif) Prov* **le temps perdu ne se rattrape jamais** = you can never make up for lost time
2 *(éviter la chute)* to catch oneself (in time); **heureusement il s'est rattrapé** luckily he managed to avoid falling; **se r. à qn/qch** to grab *or* to catch hold of sb/sth to stop oneself falling
3 *(avant de faire une erreur)* to stop oneself; **...mais je me suis rattrapé de justesse** ...but I caught *or* stopped myself just in time
4 *(compenser)* **j'ai l'intention de me r.!** I'm going to make up for it!; **la limonade est en promotion, mais ils se rattrapent sur le café** lemonade is on special offer, but they've put up the price of coffee to make up for it; *Hum* **enfant, c'était un ange, mais elle s'est bien rattrapée depuis!** she used to be an angel when she was a child, but she's certainly made up for it since!
5 *(élève)* to catch up
raturage [ratyraʒ] **NM** crossing out, scoring out *(UNCOUNT)*
rature [ratyr] **NF** crossing out, deletion; **tu as fait trop de ratures** you've crossed too many things out; **sans ratures ni surcharges** *(dans un formulaire)* without deletions or alterations
raturer [3] [ratyre] **VT** to cross out, to delete; **les devoirs raturés ne seront pas corrigés** homework with too many crossings-out in it will not be marked
RAU [ɛray] **NF** *(abrév* **République Arabe Unie**) UAR, United Arab Republic
raucité [rosite] **NF** *Littéraire* **1** *(enrouement)* hoarseness; *(caractère voilé)* huskiness **2** *(d'un cri)* raucousness
rauque [rok] **ADJ 1** *(voix → enrouée)* hoarse; *(→ voilée)* husky **2** *(cri)* raucous **3** *Belg (personne → enrouée)* hoarse
rauquer [3] [roke] **VI** to growl
rauwolfia [rowɔlfja] **NM** *Bot* rauwolfia
ravagé, -e [ravaʒe] **ADJ 1** *(pays)* ravaged, devastated; *(personne → par la fatigue)* haggard; *(→ par le désespoir, le chagrin)* devastated, torn apart; *(→ par la maladie, la douleur)* ravaged; **les traits ravagés par l'alcool** his/her features ravaged by alcohol **2** *Fam (fou)* crazy, nuts
ravager [17] [ravaʒe] **VT** *(région, ville)* to ravage, to lay waste, to devastate; *(récoltes)* to ravage, to devastate, to play havoc with; *(visage)* to ravage; **la guerre a ravagé leur vie** the war wreaked havoc upon their lives
ravages [ravaʒ] **NMPL** *(destruction)* devastation; **les r. du feu/de la tempête** the devastation *or* destruction caused by the fire/the storm; **les r. de la maladie/du temps** the ravages of disease/of time; **faire des r.** to wreak havoc; *Fig* **l'alcoolisme faisait des r.** alcoholism was rife; **notre cousin fait des r. (dans les cœurs)!** our cousin is a heartbreaker!; **elle va faire des r. dans cette tenue!** she's dressed to kill!
ravageur, -euse [ravaʒœr, -øz] **ADJ 1** *(destructeur)* destructive, devastating; **des insectes ravageurs** insect pests; **les effets ravageurs du chômage** the devastating effects of unemployment **2** *(sourire)* devastating; *(humour)* scathing
NM,F ravager
raval, -als [raval] **NM** *Minér* (shaft) deepening
ravalement [ravalmɑ̃] **NM 1** *(d'une façade → nettoyage)* cleaning; *(→ recrépissage)* re-roughcasting **2** *Fam Fig* **se faire faire un r. (de façade)** *(opération)* to have a facelift▪; *(maquillage)* to put on one's warpaint **3** *(d'un arbre)* pruning, cutting back
ravaler [3] [ravale] **VT 1** *Constr* to redo; *Fam* **se faire r. la façade** *ou* **le portrait** to have a facelift▪
2 *(salive)* to swallow; *(larmes)* to hold *or* to choke back; *(colère)* to stifle, to choke back; *(fierté)* to swallow; *Fam* **faire r. ses paroles à qn** to make sb eat his/her words; *Fam* **je lui ferai r. ses insultes!** I'll make him/her choke on his/her insults!
3 *(abaisser)* to lower; **de tels sentiments nous**

ravalent au niveau de la bête such feelings lower *or* reduce us to the level of animals
4 *(arbre)* to prune, to cut back
5 *Mines* to deepen
VI *Chasse & Zool (cerf)* to age
▸**se ravaler VPR 1** *(s'abaisser)* to debase *or* to lower oneself; **se r. aux pires bassesses** to stoop to the meanest acts; **se r. au rang de la brute** to be reduced to the level of animals
2 *Fam* **se r. la façade** *(se maquiller)* to slap some make-up on, to put on one's warpaint
ravaleur [ravalœr] **NM** cleaner, stone-cleaner
ravaudage [ravodaʒ] **NM** *Vieilli* **1** *(action → de chaussettes)* darning; *(→ de vêtements)* mending **2** *(résultat → de chaussettes)* darn; *(→ d'un vêtement)* mend
ravauder [3] [ravode] **VT** *Vieilli (chaussettes)* to darn; *(vêtements)* to mend
VI *Can* **1** *(errer)* to wander about; *(faire l'idiot)* to fool *or* to clown around **2** *Can (faire du bruit)* to make a racket
ravaudeur, -euse [ravodœr, -øz] **NM,F** *Vieilli (de chaussettes)* darner; *(de vêtements)* mender
rave¹ [rav] **NF** *(radis)* radish; *(navet)* turnip
rave² [rɛv] **NF** *(soirée)* rave
ravelin [ravlɛ̃] **NM** *Archit* ravelin
ravenala [ravənala] **NM** *Bot* ravenala
ravenelle [ravnɛl] **NF** *Bot* **1** *(radis sauvage)* wild radish **2** *(giroflée)* wallflower, gillyflower
Ravenne [ravɛn] **NM** Ravenna
ravi, -e [ravi] **ADJ** delighted (**de qch** with sth); **il n'a pas eu l'air r.** he didn't look too pleased; **d'un air r.** delightedly; **je suis r. de vous voir** I'm delighted to see you; **r. (de faire votre connaissance)** (I'm) delighted *or* very pleased to meet you; **eh bien, vous m'en voyez r.!** I'm positively delighted!
NM,F *(simple d'esprit)* simpleton, halfwit
ravier [ravje] **NM** hors-d'œuvres dish
ravière [ravjɛr] **NF** turnip field
ravigotant, -e [ravigɔtɑ̃, -ɑ̃t] **ADJ** *Fam (vent)* invigorating▪, bracing▪; *(soupe, vin)* warming▪
ravigote [ravigɔt] *Culin* **NF** ravigote sauce *(vinaigrette with herbs and hard-boiled eggs)*
❑ **à la ravigote ADJ** with a ravigote sauce
ravigoter [3] [ravigɔte] **VT** *Fam* to buck up; **cette promenade/ce petit whisky m'a ravigotée** that walk/that little whisky bucked me up; **la voilà toute ravigotée** she's full of life again; **ravigoté par une nuit de repos** refreshed *or* restored by a good night's sleep
ravilir [32] [ravilir] **VT** to degrade, to debase
ravin [ravɛ̃] **NM** gully, ravine
ravine [ravin] **NF** gully
ravinement [ravinmɑ̃] **NM 1** *(action)* gullying **2** *(résultat)* **ravinements** gullies
raviner [3] [ravine] **VT 1** *Géog* to gully **2** *Fig* to furrow; **un visage raviné** a deeply lined face
raviole [ravjɔl] **NF** *Culin* = small cheese-filled piece of ravioli
ravioli [ravjɔli] *(pl* **inv** *ou* **raviolis) NM** piece of ravioli; **des raviolis** ravioli
ravir [82] [ravir] **VT 1** *(enchanter)* to delight; **son dernier film ravira les amateurs d'humour noir** his/her latest film will delight lovers of black humour; **cette naissance les a ravis** they were thrilled with the new baby
2 *Littéraire (enlever → femme)* to ravish; *(→ enfant)* to abduct; **r. qch à qn** to rob sb of sth; **il s'est fait r. la première place par un jeune inconnu** he was beaten to first place by a youngster nobody had heard of; **prématurément ravi à l'affection des siens** taken too early from (the bosom of) family and friends
❑ **à ravir ADV** *(merveilleusement)* **la robe lui va à r.** the dress looks lovely on her; **il dessine à r.** he draws beautifully; **elle est belle à r.** she's ravishing
raviser [3] [ravize] **se raviser VPR** to change one's mind; **il s'est ravisé** he changed his mind, he thought better of it, he had second thoughts
ravissant, -e [ravisɑ̃, -ɑ̃t] **ADJ** *(vêtement)* gorgeous, beautiful; *(endroit, maison)* delightful, beautiful; *(femme)* strikingly *or* ravishingly beautiful
ravissement [ravismɑ̃] **NM 1** *(enchantement)* **c'est un véritable r. (pour les yeux)** it is an enchanting sight; **avec r.** *(écouter, contempler)* in delight, delightedly; **c'est ce que nous avons découvert avec r.** that's what we found out to our delight; **mettre** *ou* **plonger qn dans le r.** to send sb into raptures; **dans le plus grand r. (de tous les sens)** totally enraptured
2 *Littéraire (enlèvement → d'une femme)* ravishment; *(→ d'un enfant)* abduction
3 *Rel* rapture
ravisseur, -euse [ravisœr, -øz] **ADJ** *Entom* **patte ravisseuse** grasping tibia
NM,F kidnapper, *Sout* abductor
ravitaillement [ravitajmɑ̃] **NM 1** *Mil & Naut* supplying; **assurer le r. de qn en munitions/carburant/vivres** to supply sb with ammunition/fuel/food; **le r. des grandes villes est l'un des problèmes majeurs en temps de guerre** maintaining supplies in large cities is one of the major problems in wartime; **bateau/véhicule de r.** supply ship/vehicle
2 *Aviat* refuelling; **r. en vol** in-flight *or* mid-air refuelling
3 *(denrées)* food supplies; *Fam Hum* **je vais au r.** I'm off to buy some food▪, I'm going for fresh supplies
ravitailler [3] [ravitaje] **VT 1** *Mil* to supply; **r. un régiment en vivres** to supply a regiment with food, to supply food to a regiment **2** *Aviat & Naut* to refuel; **r. un avion en vol** to refuel a plane in flight **3** *(famille, campement)* **r. qn en** to supply sb with, to give sb fresh supplies of
▸**se ravitailler VPR 1** *(en nourriture)* to get (fresh) supplies **2** *(en carburant)* to refuel
ravitailleur, -euse [ravitajœr, -øz] **ADJ avion r.** supply plane, (air) tanker; **véhicule/navire r.** supply vehicle/ship
NM,F *Mil* quartermaster; *Naut* supply officer
NM 1 *Aviat (avion)* tanker aircraft; **r. d'avions** *(camion-citerne)* (airport) supply tanker **2** *Mil* supply vehicle **3** *Naut (d'escadre, de sous-marin)* supply ship; *(pour travaux en mer)* refurbishment ship
ravivage [ravivaʒ] **NM 1** *Métal (gén)* cleaning; *(à l'abrasif)* scouring; *(à l'acide)* pickling; *(au chalumeau)* burning off **2** *Tex (d'une couleur)* brightening up, reviving
raviver [3] [ravive] **VT 1** *(feu)* to rekindle, to revive; *(couleur)* to brighten up
2 *(sensation, sentiment)* to rekindle, to revive; **r. le chagrin/la douleur de qn** to revive sb's feelings of grief/sorrow; **le procès va r. l'horreur/les souffrances de la guerre** the trial will bring back the horrors/sufferings of the war
3 *Métal (gén)* to clean; *(à l'abrasif)* to scour; *(à l'acide)* to pickle; *(au chalumeau)* to burn off
▸**se raviver VPR** *(sentiment)* to return; **sa haine se ravivait dès qu'il le voyait** every time he saw him, his hatred flared up again
ravoir [ravwar] *(à l'infinitif seulement)* **VT 1** *(récupérer)* to get back **2** *(nettoyer)* **r. une chemise/casserole** to get a shirt/pan clean **3** *(maladie)* **je ne veux pas r. la grippe** I don't want to get flu again
▸**se ravoir VPR** *Belg (reprendre haleine)* to get one's breath back; *(retrouver ses esprits)* to come to one's senses
rawette [rawɛt] **NF** *Belg Fam (rabiot)* extra helping▪; *(fonds)* residue▪
ray [rɛ] **NM** *(en Asie du Sud-Est)* slash-and-burn farming
raya [raja] **NM** *Hist* rayah
rayage [rɛjaʒ] **NM 1** *(éraflement)* scratching **2** *(rature)* scoring **3** *(d'arme à feu)* rifling
rayé, -e [rɛje] **ADJ 1** *(à raies → papier)* lined, ruled; *(→ vêtement)* striped; **tissu r. bleu et rouge** blue and red striped fabric, fabric with blue and red stripes **2** *(éraflé → verre, disque, carrosserie)* scratched **3** *(arme à feu)* rifled
rayer [11] [rɛje] **VT 1** *(abîmer)* to scratch; **les branches avaient rayé la peinture** the branches had scratched the paintwork
2 *(éliminer → faute, coquille)* to cross *or* to score out; *(→ clause, codicille)* to cancel; *(→ médecin)* to strike off; *(→ avocat)* to debar; **on vous a rayé** *ou* **on a rayé votre nom de la liste** your name has been struck off *or* crossed off the list; **r. la mention inutile** *(dans un formulaire)* delete where inapplicable; **j'ai rayé son souvenir de ma mémoire** I've erased his/her memory from my mind; **rayé, balayé, je n'existe plus!** out of sight, out of mind, it's as if I'd never existed!; **rayé de la carte** wiped off the face of the earth
3 *(fusil)* to rifle
4 *Mil* **r. qn des contrôles** to strike sb off the strength
rayère [rɛjɛr] **NF** *Archit* dreamhole
ray-grass [rɛgras] **NM INV** *Bot* rye grass
raymond [rɛmɔ̃] *Fam* **ADJ** square, straight
NM square, straight
rayon¹ [rɛjɔ̃] **NM 1** *Opt & Phys* ray; **r. cathodique** cathode ray; **r. laser** laser beam; **r. lumineux** (light) ray; **r. vert** green flash
2 *(de lumière)* beam, shaft; *(du soleil)* ray; *Fig (d'espoir)* ray; **un r. de lune** a moonbeam; **un r. de soleil** a ray of sunshine, a sunbeam; *Météo* a brief sunny spell; *Fig* a ray of sunshine; **cet enfant est un peu notre r. de soleil** this child has brought a ray of sunshine into our life
3 *Math (vecteur)* radius vector; *(d'un cercle)* radius
4 *(de roue)* spoke
5 *(distance)* radius; **dans un r. de 20 kilomètres autour de** within (a radius of) 20 kilometres of
6 *Aut* **r. de braquage** turning circle
7 **r. d'action** range; **à grand r. d'action** long-range; *Fig* **étendre son r. d'action** to increase *or* to widen the scope of one's activities
8 *Beaux-Arts* **r. visuel principal** line of vision
❑ **rayons NMPL 1** *Méd* radiation treatment *(UNCOUNT) (for cancer)*; *Fam* **on lui fait des rayons** he's/she's having radiotherapy *or* radiation treatment; **mal** *ou* **maladie des rayons** radiation sickness
2 *Phys* **rayons bêta** beta rays; **rayons cathodiques** cathode rays; **rayons cosmiques** cosmic rays; **rayons gamma** gamma rays; **rayons infrarouges** infrared light; **rayons X** X-rays; **passer qch aux rayons X** to X-ray sth; **rayons ultraviolets** ultraviolet light
rayon² [rɛjɔ̃] **NM 1** *(étagère → gén)* shelf; *(→ à livres)* shelf, bookshelf
2 *Com (dans un magasin)* department; **le r. des jouets/des surgelés** the toy/the frozen food department; **nous n'en avons plus en r.** we're out of stock; **r. des soldes** bargain counter
3 *Fam (domaine)* **demande à ton père, c'est son r.** ask your father, that's his department; **il en connaît un r. en électricité** he really knows a thing or two about electricity; **c'est/c'est pas mon r.** that's/that's not my department
4 *Entom* comb; *(d'abeilles)* honeycomb
5 *Hort* small furrow, drill
rayonnage [rɛjɔnaʒ] **NM 1** *(étagères)* shelving *(UNCOUNT)*, shelves; **sur les rayonnages** on the shelves **2** *Hort* drilling
rayonnant, -e [rɛjɔnɑ̃, -ɑ̃t] **ADJ 1** *(radieux)* radiant; **r. de joie** radiant with joy; **r. de santé** glowing *or* blooming with health **2** *Archit & Beaux-Arts* radiating; **chapelles rayonnantes** radiating chapels; **motif r.** radiating pattern; **gothique r.** High Gothic **3** *Phys* **chaleur/énergie rayonnante** radiant heat/energy **4** *Méd* **douleur rayonnante** radiating pain
rayonne [rɛjɔn] **NF** *Tex* rayon
rayonné, -e [rɛjɔne] **ADJ** radiating
rayonnement [rɛjɔnmɑ̃] **NM 1** *(influence)* influence; **le r. de la France au siècle des Lumières** the influence of France during the Enlightenment
2 *Littéraire (éclat)* radiance; **un r. émanait de tout son être** his/her entire being was radiant with joy
3 *(lumière → d'une étoile, du feu)* radiance
4 *Phys* radiation; **r. électromagnétique/optique/visible** electromagnetic/optical/visible radiation; **r. cosmologique/solaire** cosmic/solar radiation; **r. fossile** fossil radiation; **chauffage par r.** radiant heating; **énergie de r.** radiant energy
rayonner [3] [rɛjɔne] **VI 1** *(personne, physionomie)* to be radiant; **r. de joie** to be radiant with joy; **r. de bonheur** to radiate happiness; **r. de santé** to be blooming with health; **son visage rayonnait/ses yeux rayonnaient d'allégresse** he/she was beaming/his/her eyes were shining with joy
2 *Littéraire (soleil)* to shine
3 *(circuler → influence)* to spread; *(→ touriste)* to tour around; *(→ chaleur)* to radiate; **nos cars**

rav–ray

rayonnent dans toute la région our coaches cover every corner of the region; **nous avons rayonné autour d'Avignon** we toured the region around Avignon
  4 *(être disposé en rayons)* to radiate; **sept avenues rayonnent à partir de la place** seven avenues radiate (out) from the square
  5 *Opt & Phys* to radiate
  6 *Méd* **douleur qui rayonne** radiating pain
  VT 1 *Hort* to furrow
  2 *(mettre des étagères dans)* to fit with shelves, to put shelves up in

rayonneur [rɛjɔnœr] **NM** drill (tool)
rayonnisme [rɛjɔnism] **NM** *Beaux-Arts* rayonism
rayonniste [rɛjɔnist] *Beaux-Arts* **ADJ** Rayonist
  NMF Rayonist
rayure [rɛjyr] **NF 1** *(ligne)* line, stripe; *(du pelage)* stripe; **papier à rayures** lined *or* ruled paper; **tissu à rayures** striped fabric; **une chemise à rayures bleues** a blue-striped shirt; **un drapeau à rayures bleues** a flag with blue stripes **2** *(éraflure)* score, scratch **3** *(d'une arme à feu)* groove, rifling
raz [ra] **NM 1** *(détroit)* strait *(run by fast tidal races, in Brittany)* **2** *(courant)* race
raz-de-marée, raz de marée [radmare] **NM INV 1** *Géog* tidal wave, tsunami **2** *Fig (bouleversement)* tidal wave; **r. électoral** landslide victory
razzia [razja, radzja] **NF 1** *Mil* foray, raid **2** *Fam Fig* raid; **faire une r. sur qch** to raid sth

'L'Ultime razzia' Kubrick 'The Killing'

razzier [9] [razje, radzje] **VT 1** *Mil* to raid **2** *Fam Fig (en prenant)* to raid; *(en achetant)* to buy up
RBE [ɛrbeə] **NM** *(abrév* **revenu brut d'exploitation)** gross profit
RBL *(abrév écrite* **rouble)** R, Rub
R-C *(abrév écrite* **rez-de-chaussée)** *Br* ground floor, *Am* first floor
RCS [ɛrseɛs] **NM** *(abrév* **Registre du commerce et des sociétés)** register of companies
R-D [ɛrde] **NM** *(abrév* **recherche et développement)** R & D, R and D
r.d. *(abrév écrite* **rive droite)** right bank
RDA [ɛrdea] **NF** *Anciennement (abrév* **République démocratique allemande)** GDR; **vivre en R.** to live in the GDR; **aller en R.** to go to the GDR
RDB [ɛrdebe] **NM** *(abrév* **revenu disponible brut)** gross disposable income
RDC [ɛrdese] **NF** *(abrév* **République démocratique du Congo)** **la R.** the DRC
RdC *(abrév écrite* **rez-de-chaussée)** *Br* ground floor, *Am* first floor
RDS [ɛrdeɛs] **NM 1** *Fin (abrév* **remboursement de la dette sociale)** = contribution paid by every taxpayer towards the social security deficit **2** *Tech (abrév* **radio data system)** RDS
Rê [rɛ] **NPR** *Myth* Rā
ré [re] **NM INV** D; *(chanté)* re, ray
réa¹ [rea] **NM** pulley (wheel)
réa² [rea] **NF** *Fam (abrév* **réanimation)** **être en salle de r.** to be in intensive care■ *or Am* the ICU
réabonnement [reabɔnmɑ̃] **NM** *(au cinéma, au théâtre etc)* renewal of one's season ticket (**à** for); *(à une revue)* renewal of one's subscription (**à** to); *(à un club)* renewal of one's membership (**à** of)
réabonner [3] [reabɔne] **VT r. qn au théâtre** to renew sb's season ticket for the theatre; **r. qn à une revue** to renew sb's subscription to a magazine
  ▶**se réabonner VPR** *(au cinéma, au théâtre etc)* to renew one's season ticket (**à** for); *(à une revue)* to renew one's subscription (**à** to); *(à un club)* to renew one's membership (**à** of)
réabsorber [3] [reapsɔrbe] **VT** to reabsorb; **elle commence à r. un peu de nourriture** she has started to take a little food again
réabsorption [reapsɔrpsjɔ̃] **NF** reabsorption
réac [reak] *Fam Péj* **ADJ** reactionary■
  NMF reactionary■
réaccoutumer [3] [reakutyme] **VT** to reaccustom; **r. qn à qch** to reaccustom sb to sth, to get sb used to sth again
  ▶**se réaccoutumer VPR se r. à qch** to reaccustom oneself to sth, to get used to sth again; **j'aurais du mal à me r.** I'd have trouble getting used to it again

réachat [reaʃa] **NM** *Com* rebuy, repurchase; **r. modifié** modified rebuy
réacheminement [reaʃəminmɑ̃] **NM** *(de marchandises)* rerouting; *(de message)* redirecting
réacheminer [3] [reaʃəmine] **VT** *(marchandises)* to reroute; *(message)* to redirect
réacheter [28] [reaʃte] **VT** *Com* to rebuy, to repurchase
réactance [reaktɑ̃s] **NF** reactance; **bobine de r.** reaction coil
réactant [reaktɑ̃] **NM** *Chim* reactant
réacteur [reaktœr] **NM 1** *Aviat* jet (engine) **2** *Chim, Nucl & Phys* reactor; **r. à eau sous pression** pressurized water reactor; **r. à neutrons rapides** fast (neutron) reactor; **r. nucléaire** nuclear reactor
réactif, -ive [reaktif, -iv] **ADJ 1** *Chim & Phys* reactive; **papier r.** reagent paper; **peinture primaire réactive** primer; **substance réactive** reactant **2** *(entreprise, économie)* reactive, responsive
  NM 1 *Chim* reagent **2** *Psy* reactive
réaction [reaksjɔ̃] **NF 1** *(réponse)* reaction, response; *(des consommateurs)* feedback; **la nouvelle l'a laissée sans r.** she showed no reaction to the news; **elle eut une r. de peur/de colère** her reaction was one of fear/anger; **il a eu une r. très violente** he reacted very violently; **il n'a eu aucune r.** he didn't react at all; **avoir des réactions lentes** to be slow to react; **la voiture a de très bonnes réactions** the car responds well *or* handles well; **r. à un stimulus** stimulus response, response to a stimulus; **temps de r.** *Méd* reaction time; *Psy* latent period *or* time; **r. affective** emotional response; **r. auditive** response to auditory stimulus; *Méd* **r. de Bordet-Wassermann** Wassermann's reaction; *Psy* **r. conditionnée** conditioned response; **r. cutanée** skin *or Spéc* cutaneous reaction; **r. émotionnelle** emotional response; *Méd* **r. immunitaire** immune response, immunoreaction; **r. motrice** motor response; **r. tactile** tactile response; *Mktg* **r. des ventes** sales response
  2 *(riposte)* reaction; **en** *ou* **par r. contre** as a reaction against; **la décision a été prise en r. à...** the decision was taken in response to...
  3 *Pol (mouvement)* reaction; *(personnes)* reactionaries; **gouvernement/vote de r.** reactionary government/vote
  4 *Aviat, Astron, Chim & Phys* reaction; **propulsion par r. atomique** atomic-powered propulsion; **r. en chaîne** chain reaction; *Fig* chain reaction, domino effect
  5 *Électron* **r. négative** negative feedback
réactionnaire [reaksjɔnɛr] **ADJ** reactionary
  NMF reactionary
réactionnel, -elle [reaksjɔnɛl] **ADJ 1** *Chim & Physiol* reactional; **formation réactionnelle** reaction formation **2** *Psy* reactive
réactique [reaktik] **NF** *Com* business intelligence system
réactivation [reaktivasjɔ̃] **NF** reactivation
réactive [reaktiv] *voir* **réactif**
réactiver [3] [reaktive] **VT 1** *(feu)* to rekindle; *(circulation sanguine)* to restore; *(système)* to reactivate; *(négociations)* to revive **2** *Chim* to reactivate
réactivité [reaktivite] **NF 1** *Chim* reactivity **2** *Biol* reactivity, excitability **3** *(capacité à réagir)* reactivity, responsiveness
réactogène [reaktɔʒɛn] **ADJ** reactogenic
  NM reactogen, (general) allergen
réactualisation [reaktɥalizasjɔ̃] **NF 1** *(ajustement)* adapting, readjustment **2** *(modernisation)* updating, bringing up to date
réactualiser [3] [reaktɥalize] **VT 1** *(ajuster)* to adapt, to readjust **2** *(moderniser)* to update, to bring up to date
réadaptation [readaptasjɔ̃] **NF 1** *(rééducation →* *d'un invalide, d'un prisonnier)* rehabilitation; *(→ d'un muscle)* re-education **2** *(réaccoutumance)* readjustment, readaptation (**à** to); **son équilibre dépendra aussi de sa r. à la vie familiale et sociale** his/her mental stability will also depend on how he/she readjusts *or* readapts to his/her home and social life
réadapter [3] [readapte] **VT** *(invalide, prisonnier)* to rehabilitate; *(muscle)* to re-educate
  ▶**se réadapter VPR** *(invalide, handicapé, exilé)* to readjust (**à** to); **après 20 ans d'exil, ils ont du**

mal à se r. after 20 years in exile they're finding it hard to adjust *or* to readjust *or* to adapt
réadjudication [readʒydikasjɔ̃] **NF** = resale by auction
réadmettre [84] [readmɛtr] **VT** to readmit
réadmission [readmisjɔ̃] **NF** readmission, readmittance
ready-made [rɛdimɛd] *(pl inv ou* **ready-mades)** **NM** *Beaux-Arts* ready-made
réaffectation [reafɛktasjɔ̃] **NF 1** *(de ressources, de subventions)* reassignment, reallocation **2** *(d'un employé)* reassignment; **il a demandé sa r. à son poste initial** he asked to be reassigned to his original job **3** *Ordinat* reallocation
réaffecter [4] [reafɛkte] **VT 1** *(ressources, subventions)* to reassign, to reallocate **2** *(employé → à une fonction)* to reassign; *(→ à une région, à un pays)* to post back **3** *Ordinat* to reallocate
réafficher [3] [reafiʃe] **VT** *Ordinat* to redisplay
réaffirmer [3] [reafirme] **VT** to reaffirm, to reassert
réagir [32] [reaʒir] **VI 1** *Chim, Phot & Phys* to react
  2 *(répondre)* to react; **il a bien/mal réagi à son départ** he reacted well/badly to his/her leaving; **il faut absolument r.** we really have to do something; **tu réagis trop violemment** you're overreacting; **et tu restes là sans r.!** how can you just sit there (and do nothing)?; **au moins ça l'a fait r.** at least it got a reaction from him/her
  3 *Méd* to respond; **elle réagit bien au traitement** she's responding well to the treatment; **il a très fortement réagi au vaccin** he had a very strong reaction to the vaccine
  4 *(avoir des répercussions)* **r. sur** to have an effect on, to affect; **les phénomènes mondiaux réagissent sur les économies nationales** world events have an effect *or* repercussions on countries' economies
réajustement [reaʒystəmɑ̃] = **rajustement**
réajuster [reaʒyste] = **rajuster**
réal¹, -aux [real, -o] **NM** *(monnaie)* real
réal², -e, -aux, -ales [real, -o] **ADJ** *Hist* **galère réale** royal galley
réalésage [realeza3] **NM** *(action)* reboring; *(résultat)* rebore
réaléser [18] [realeze] **VT** to rebore
réalgar [realgar] **NM** *Minér* realgar, red arsenic
réalignement [realiɲmɑ̃] **NM** realignment; **r. monétaire** realignment of currencies
réaligner [3] [realiɲe] **VT** to realign
réalisable [realizabl] **ADJ 1** *(projet)* feasible, workable; *(rêve)* attainable; **tu sais bien que ce n'est pas r.!** you know it can't *or* it won't work! **2** *Fin* realizable
réalisateur, -trice [realizatœr, -tris] **NM,F 1** *Cin* director, film-maker; *Rad & TV* producer **2** *(maître d'œuvre)* **il a été le r. du projet** he was the one who brought the project to fruition
réalisation [realizasjɔ̃] **NF 1** *(d'un projet)* carrying out, execution; *(d'une œuvre d'art)* creation; *(d'un rêve)* fulfilment; *(d'un exploit)* achievement; **être en cours de r.** to be under way; **pour moi, c'est la r. d'un vieux rêve** for me it's an old dream come true
  2 *(chose réalisée)* achievement; **le nouveau centre commercial est une r. remarquable** the new shopping centre is a major achievement; **l'une des dernières réalisations du grand architecte** one of the great architect's last works
  3 *Jur (d'un contrat)* fulfilment; *Com (d'une vente)* clinching, closing; *Fin (liquidation)* realization; **r. du stock** clearance sale
  4 *Cin (mise en scène)* directing; *(film)* production; **r. (de) George Cukor** *(dans un film)* directed by George Cukor; **beaucoup de comédiens se lancent dans la r. (de films)** many actors are taking up film directing; **la r. de ce film coûterait trop cher** to make this movie *or Br* film would cost too much
  5 *Rad & TV (processus)* production; *(enregistrement)* recording; **à la r., Fred X** sound engineer, Fred X
  6 *Mus* realization
  7 *Fin (d'actions)* selling out; *(d'un bénéfice)* making
réalisatrice [realizatris] *voir* **réalisateur**
réaliser [3] [realize] **VT 1** *(rendre réel → projet)* to carry out; *(→ rêve, ambition)* to fulfil, to realize; *(→ espoir)* to realize

2 *(accomplir → œuvre)* to complete, to carry out; *(→ œuvre d'art)* to create; *(→ exploit)* to achieve, to perform; **les efforts réalisés** the efforts that have been made

3 *Com (vente)* to make; *Fin (capital, valeurs)* to realize; *(bénéfice)* to make; *(actions)* to sell out; **r. des économies** to make savings; **r. un chiffre d'affaires de 10 millions d'euros** to have a turnover of 10 million euros, to have a 10 million-euro turnover

4 *Cin* to direct, to make; *Rad & TV* to produce

5 *Mus* to realize

6 *(comprendre)* to realize; **as-tu réalisé que la situation est grave?** do you realize how serious the situation is?

USAGE ABSOLU **je ne réalise pas encore** it hasn't sunk in yet; **laisse-lui le temps de r.** give him/her time for it to sink in; **elle est encore sous le choc, mais quand elle va r.!** she's still in a state of shock, but wait till it hits her!

►**se réaliser** VPR 1 *(s'accomplir → projet)* to be carried out; *(→ rêve, vœu)* to come true, to be fulfilled; *(→ prédiction)* to come true

2 *(personne)* to fulfil oneself

réalisme [realism] NM 1 *(gén)* realism; **faire preuve de r.** to be realistic; **r. politique** political realism *or* pragmatism 2 *Beaux-Arts & Littérature* realism; **r. moderne** modern realism; **r. social** social realism; **r. socialiste** Socialist Realism

réaliste [realist] ADJ 1 *(gén)* realistic 2 *Beaux-Arts & Littérature* realist

NMF realist

réalité [realite] NF 1 *(existence)* reality; **douter de la r. d'un fait** to doubt the reality of a fact

2 *(univers réel)* **la r.** reality; **regarder la r. en face** to face up to reality; **la dure r. quotidienne** the harsh reality of everyday existence; **dans la r.** in real life; **quand la r. dépasse la fiction** when truth is stranger than fiction; *Ordinat* **r. virtuelle** virtual reality

3 *(fait)* fact; **n'en doutez pas, c'est une r.!** you'd better believe it, it's the truth!; **prendre conscience des réalités (de la vie)** to face facts; **les réalités de ce monde** the realities of this world; **elle n'a pas le sens des réalités** she has no sense of reality, she doesn't live in the real world

❑ **en réalité** ADV 1 *(en fait)* in (actual) fact; **on m'en avait dit beaucoup de mal, mais en r. il est charmant** I'd heard a lot of bad things about him, but in (actual) fact he is charming

2 *(vraiment)* in real life; **à la scène, elle paraît plus jeune qu'elle n'est en r.** on stage, she looks younger than she is in real life

reality show [realitiʃo] NM *TV* reality show

realpolitik [realpɔlitik] NF realpolitik

réaménagement [reamenaʒmɑ̃] NM 1 *(d'un bâtiment, d'une salle)* refitting *(UNCOUNT)*; *(d'un projet)* reorganization, replanning *(UNCOUNT)*; **r. urbain** urban redevelopment 2 *(d'un horaire)* replanning *(UNCOUNT)*, readjustment *(UNCOUNT)* 3 *Fin (d'une dette)* rescheduling *(UNCOUNT)*

réaménager [17] [reamenaʒe] VT 1 *(bâtiment, salle)* to refit, to refurbish; *(projet)* to reorganize, to replan 2 *(horaire)* to replan, to readjust; *(politique)* to reshape 3 *Fin (dette)* to reschedule

réamorcer [16] [reamɔrse] VT 1 *(pompe)* to prime again; *Fig* **r. la pompe** to get things rolling again 2 *(discussion)* to begin *or* to start again, to reinitiate 3 *Ordinat* to reboot

►**se réamorcer** VPR *Ordinat* to reboot

réanimateur, -trice [reanimatœr, -tris] NM,F resuscitator

réanimation [reanimasjɔ̃] NF *(action)* resuscitation; **service de r. (intensive)** intensive care unit; **admis en r.** *(service)* put in intensive care

réanimatrice [reanimatris] *voir* **réanimateur**

réanimer [3] [reanime] VT 1 *(malade)* to resuscitate 2 *(conversation, intérêt)* to revive

réapparaître [91] [reaparɛtr] VI *(aux être ou avoir)* *(gén)* to come back, to reappear again; *(douleur)* to come back, to recur, to return; *(thème, métaphore, motif)* to recur, to be repeated; **tous ces facteurs ont contribué à faire r. les conflits entre les ethnies** all of these factors have contributed to the resurgence of ethnic conflicts

réapparition [reaparisjɔ̃] NF 1 *(du soleil, d'une personne)* reappearance; *(d'une douleur)* recurrence; *(du nationalisme, d'une maladie)* resurgence 2 *(d'une vedette)* comeback

réapparu, -e [reapary] PP *voir* **réapparaître**

réapprendre [79] [reaprɑ̃dr] VT to learn again; **elle a dû r. à marcher après son accident** she had to learn to walk again after her accident; **r. le bonheur** to learn how to be happy again

réapprovisionnement [reaprɔvizjɔnmɑ̃] NM *Com (d'un magasin)* restocking; *(d'un commerçant)* resupplying; **assurer le r. d'un magasin** to restock a *Br* shop *or Am* store

réapprovisionner [3] [reaprɔvizjɔne] VT *Com (magasin)* to restock (**en** with); *(commerçant)* to resupply (**en** with)

►**se réapprovisionner** VPR *(magasin, commerçant)* to stock up again, to restock (**en** with); *(famille)* to replenish one's supplies (**en** of), to stock up (**en** on)

réargenter [3] [rearʒɑ̃te] VT to resilver

réarmement [rearməmɑ̃] NM 1 *Mil* rearmament, rearming; *Pol* rearmament; **r. moral** moral rearmament 2 *Naut* refitting 3 *(d'arme à feu)* cocking 4 *(d'un appareil photo)* winding on, resetting

réarmer [3] [rearme] VT 1 *Mil & Pol* to rearm 2 *Naut* to refit 3 *(arme à feu)* to cock 4 *(appareil photo)* to wind on, to reset

VI *(pays)* to rearm

réarrangement [rearɑ̃ʒmɑ̃] NM 1 *(processus)* rearranging, rearrangement; *(résultat)* rearrangement 2 *Chim* rearrangement

réarranger [17] [rearɑ̃ʒe] VT to rearrange, to redo

réassignation [reasiɲasjɔ̃] NF 1 *Jur* resummons *(singulier)* 2 *Méd* **r. sexuelle** gender reassignment

réassigner [3] [reasiɲe] VT *Jur* to resummon

réassort [reasɔr] NM new stock

réassortiment [reasɔrtimɑ̃] NM 1 *Com (d'un magasin)* restocking; *(d'un stock)* renewing; *(de marchandises)* new stock, fresh supplies 2 *(de pièces d'un service)* matching (up); *(d'une soucoupe)* replacing

réassortir [32] [reasɔrtir] VT 1 *Com (magasin)* to restock; *(stock)* to renew 2 *(tissu, parure de lit, etc)* to match

►**se réassortir** VPR to replenish one's stock (**en** of)

réassurance [reasyrɑ̃s] NF reinsurance

réassurer [3] [reasyre] VT to reinsure

►**se réassurer** VPR to reinsure

réassureur [reasyrœr] NM reinsurer

rebab [rəbab] NM *Mus* rebab

rebaisser [4] [rəbese] VI to go down again, to drop *or* to fall again

VT *(prix)* to bring down again, to lower again; *(chauffage, feu, son)* to turn down again, to turn down low again

rebaptiser [3] [rəbatize] VT to rename

rébarbatif, -ive [rebarbatif, -iv] ADJ 1 *(personne)* cantankerous, surly 2 *(sujet, tâche, idée)* daunting; *(style)* off-putting

rebat *etc voir* **rebattre**

rebâtir [32] [rəbɑtir] VT to rebuild

rebattre [83] [rəbatr] VT 1 *(cartes)* to reshuffle 2 *(locution)* **elle m'a rebattu les oreilles de son divorce** she went on and on *or* she kept harping on about her divorce

rebattu, -e [rəbaty] ADJ *(éculé → histoire, thème)* hackneyed, trite

rebec [rəbɛk] NM *Mus* rebec(k)

Rébecca [rebeka] NPR *Bible* Rebecca

rebelle [rəbɛl] ADJ 1 *Pol* rebel *(avant n)* 2 *(indomptable → cheval)* rebellious; *(→ cœur, esprit)* rebellious, intractable; *(→ enfant)* rebellious, wilful; *(→ mèche)* unruly, wild 3 **r. à** *(réfractaire à)* impervious to; **r. à tout conseil** unwilling to heed advice, impervious to advice; **r. à toute discipline** unamenable to discipline 4 *(acné, fièvre)* stubborn, *Spéc* refractory

NMF rebel

rebeller [4] [rəbɛle] **se rebeller** VPR to rebel; **se r. contre** to rebel against; **la jeune génération de cinéastes qui se rebellent contre les conventions** the younger generation of film-makers who flout established conventions

rébellion [rebɛljɔ̃] NF 1 *(révolte)* rebellion; **entrer en r. (contre)** to rebel (against) 2 *(rebelles)* **la r.** the rebels

rebelote [rəbəlɔt] NF *Cartes* rebelote *(said when playing the second card of a pair of king and queen of trumps while playing belote)*

EXCLAM *Fam* here we go again!

rébétiko [rebetiko] NM *Mus* rebetiko

rebeu [rəbø] NM *Fam (verlan de* **beur**) = person born and living in France of North African immigrant parents

rebibes [rəbib] NFPL *Suisse (de fromage)* = thin slices of cheese; *(de viande)* = small pieces of cured meat

rebiffer [3] [rəbife] **se rebiffer** VPR *Fam* **quand je lui fais une remarque, il se rebiffe** when I say anything to him he reacts really badly *or* he immediately takes offence; **se r. contre qch** to kick out against sth

rebiquer [3] [rəbike] VI *Fam* to stick up

rebirth [ribœrs], **rebirthing** [ribœrsiŋ] NM *Psy* rebirthing

reblanchir [32] [rəblɑ̃ʃir] VT *(gén)* to rewhiten; *(à la chaux)* to rewhitewash

reblochon [rəblɔʃɔ̃] NM Reblochon (cheese)

reboire [108] [rəbwar] VT to drink again; **jamais je ne reboirai de ce vin** I'll never drink *or* touch that wine again

VI to drink again

reboisement [rəbwazmɑ̃] NM reafforestation

reboiser [3] [rəbwaze] VT to reafforest

rebond [rəbɔ̃] NM 1 *(d'une balle)* bounce, rebound; **je l'ai attrapé au r.** I caught it on the rebound 2 *Fin (d'actions, de marché, de monnaie)* recovery

rebondi, -e [rəbɔ̃di] ADJ *(joue, face)* chubby, plump; *(formes)* well-rounded; **ventre r.** paunch; **une jeune fille aux formes rebondies** a curvaceous young woman; **à la poitrine rebondie** buxom

rebondir [32] [rəbɔ̃dir] VI 1 *(balle, ballon)* to bounce; **le ballon rebondit mal** the ball doesn't bounce well; **il fait toujours r. la balle trois fois avant de servir** he always bounces the ball three times before serving

2 *(conversation, intrigue)* to get going *or* moving again; *(intérêt)* to revive, to be renewed; **faire r. qch** *(procès, scandale)* to give new impetus to sth

3 *(se remettre → économie)* to recover, to pick up again; **il n'a jamais vraiment rebondi après cet échec** he never really recovered from that setback

4 *Can Fam (chèque)* to bounce

rebondissement [rəbɔ̃dismɑ̃] NM 1 *(d'une balle)* bouncing 2 *(d'une affaire)* (new) development

rebord [rəbɔr] NM *(d'un fossé, d'une étagère, d'un puits)* edge; *(d'une assiette, d'un verre)* rim; *(d'une cheminée)* mantelpiece; *(d'une fenêtre)* (window) ledge *or* sill; **le savon est sur le r. de la baignoire** the soap is on the side *or* edge of the bath

reborder [3] [rəbɔrde] VT 1 *(chapeau, vêtement)* to renew the edging on 2 *(enfant, drap)* to tuck in again

rebot [rəbo] NM *Sport* pelota

rébou [rebu] ADJ INV *Fam (verlan de* **bourré**) *(ivre)* *Br* pissed, *Am* bombed

rebouchage [rəbuʃaʒ] NM 1 *(d'un trou)* filling (in) 2 *Constr (d'une surface)* stopping, making good 3 *(d'un puits)* stopping (up)

reboucher [3] [rəbuʃe] VT 1 *(bouteille de vin)* to recork; *(flacon, carafe)* to restopper; *(tube de colle, de dentifrice)* to put the top back on; **r. après usage** *(sur emballage)* replace lid after use 2 *(évier)* to block again 3 *Constr (trou)* to fill, to plug; *(fissure)* to fill, to stop

►**se reboucher** VPR *(évier)* to get blocked again

rebours [rəbur] **à rebours** ADV 1 *(à l'envers → compter, lire)* backwards; *(dans le mauvais sens)* the wrong way; **tu as compris à r.** you've got the wrong idea, *Br* you've got the wrong end of the stick; **il ne faut pas le prendre à r.!** you mustn't rub him up the wrong way!; **tu prends tout à r.!** you're always getting the wrong idea!, *Br* you're always getting the wrong end of the stick!

2 *Tex* against the nap *or* the pile

❑ **à rebours de** PRÉP **aller à r. de tout le monde** to go *or* to run counter to the general trend; **elle fait tout à r. de ce qu'on lui dit** she does the exact opposite of what people tell her

'À Rebours' *Huysmans* 'Against Nature'

reboutement [rəbutmɑ̃] **NM** *Méd* bonesetting
rebouteur, -euse [rəbutœr, -øz], **rebouteux, -euse** [rəbutø, -øz] **NM,F** *Méd* bonesetter
reboutonner [3] [rəbutɔne] **VT** to button up again, to rebutton
▸**se reboutonner VPR** to do oneself up again
rebras [rəbra] **NM** *(de manche)* cuff; *(de gant)* gauntlet
rebroder [3] [rəbrɔde] **VT** *Couture* to re-embroider; **un tissu rebrodé d'or** a fabric re-embroidered with gold
rebrousse-poil [rəbruspwal] **à rebrousse-poil ADV 1** *(brosser)* against the nap *or* the pile; **caresser un chat à r.** to stroke a cat the wrong way *or* against its fur **2** *(maladroitement)* the wrong way; **mieux vaut ne pas prendre le patron à r.** better not rub the boss up the wrong way
rebrousser [3] [rəbruse] **VT 1** *(cheveux)* to ruffle **2** *(poil)* to brush the wrong way; *Fam* **r. le poil à qn** to rub sb up the wrong way **3** *Tex (drap)* to brush against the nap **4** *(locution)* **r. chemin** to turn back, to retrace one's steps
VI *Chasse (gibier)* to break back through the line of beaters
rebrûler [3] [rəbryle] **VT** *(objet en verre)* to fire-polish
rebuffade [rəbyfad] **NF** rebuff; **essuyer une r.** to suffer a rebuff
rébus [rebys] **NM** rebus; *Fig* **ce texte est un r. pour moi** this text is a real puzzle for me
rebuse [rəbyz] **NF** *Suisse* cold snap *(in spring)*
rebut [rəby] **NM 1** *(article défectueux)* second, reject; **cette boutique leur sert à écouler les rebuts de fabrication** they use that shop to sell off all their seconds *or* rejects
2 *(poubelle, casse)* **mettre** *ou* **jeter au r.** to throw away, to discard; **bon à mettre au r.** *(vêtement)* only fit to be thrown out; *(véhicule)* ready for the scrapheap
3 *Fig Littéraire* **le r. de la société** the dregs of society
4 *(envoi postal)* dead letter
▫ **de rebut ADJ 1** *(sans valeur)* **meubles de r.** unwanted furniture; **vêtements de r.** cast-offs
2 *(défectueux)* **marchandises de r.** seconds, rejects
rebutant, -e [rəbytɑ̃, -ɑ̃t] **ADJ 1** *(repoussant)* repulsive; **un visage r.** a repulsive face **2** *(décourageant → style, vocabulaire)* unappealing, *esp Br* off-putting; *(→ méthode, programme)* discouraging, *esp Br* off-putting; *(→ tâche)* unpleasant
rebuter [3] [rəbyte] **VT 1** *(décourager)* to discourage, to put off; **ses façons ont de quoi vous r.** his/her manners are enough to put you off **2** *(dégoûter)* to put off; **cette nourriture rebuterait un homme affamé** even a starving man would be put off by that food **3** *(choquer)* **ses manières me rebutent** I find his/her behaviour quite shocking
▸**se rebuter VPR** *(se lasser)* **il était plein d'ardeur mais il s'est vite rebuté** he used to be very keen but he soon lost heart *or* his enthusiasm
recacheter [27] [rəkaʃte] **VT** to reseal
recadrage [rəkadraʒ] **NM** *Phot* cropping; *Cin* framing; *Fig* refocusing, reorientation
recadrer [3] [rəkadre] **VT** *Phot* to crop; *Cin* to frame; *Fig* to refocus, to reorientate
recalage [rəkalaʒ] **NM** *Fam (à un examen)* failing■, *Am* flunking
recalcification [rəkalsifikasjɔ̃] **NF** recalcification
recalcifier [9] [rəkalsifje] **VT** to recalcify
récalcitrant, -e [rekalsitrɑ̃, -ɑ̃t] **ADJ** *(animal)* stubborn; *(personne)* recalcitrant, rebellious
NM,F recalcitrant
recalculer [3] [rəkalkyle] **VT** to work out again, to recalculate
recalé, -e [rəkale] *Fam* **ADJ recalée en juin, j'ai réussi en septembre** I failed■ *or Am* flunked in June but passed in September
NM,F failed candidate■; **il y a eu cinq recalés dans la classe** five people in the class have failed■ *or Am* flunked
recaler [3] [rəkale] **VT** *Fam (candidat)* to fail■, *Am* to flunk; **il s'est fait r. à l'examen pour la deuxième fois** he failed■ *or Am* flunked the exam for the second time
recapitalisation [rəkapitalizasjɔ̃] **NF** *Fin* recapitalization
recapitaliser [3] [rəkapitalize] **VT** *Fin* to recapitalize
récapitulatif, -ive [rekapitylatif, -iv] **ADJ 1** *(note)* summarizing; *(tableau)* summary *(avant n)* **2** *Banque* **tableau r. (d'un compte)** (summary) statement
NM summary, recapitulation, résumé
récapitulation [rekapitylasjɔ̃] **NF 1** *(résumé)* summary, recapitulation, résumé; *(liste)* recapitulation, summary; **faire la r. de qch** to recap *or* to sum up sth **2** *Banque* (summary) statement
récapitulative [rekapitylativ] *voir* **récapitulatif**
récapituler [3] [rekapityle] **VT 1** *(résumer)* to summarize, to recapitulate **2** *(énumérer)* to go *or* to run over; **récapitulons vos arguments** let's run over *or* go over your arguments
USAGE ABSOLU to recap, to sum up; **alors, je récapitule...** so, I'll recap...
recapturer [3] [rəkaptyre] **VT** to recapture
recarburation [rəkarbyrasjɔ̃] **NF** recarburization
recarburé, -e [rəkarbyre] **ADJ** recarburized
recarreler [24] [rəkarle] **VT** to retile
recaser [3] [rəkaze] *Fam* **VT** *(dans un emploi)* to find a new job for■
▸**se recaser VPR** *(retrouver un emploi)* to get fixed up with a new job; *(se remarier)* to get hitched again, to settle down again■
recauser [3] [rəcoze] **VI r. de qn/qch** to talk about sb/sth again; **je dois en r. avec lui** I must speak *or* talk about it to him again
recéder [18] [rəsede] **VT 1** *(à l'ancien propriétaire)* to sell back **2** *(vendre)* to resell; **les circonstances l'ont obligé à r. sa maison** circumstances forced him to resell his house
▫ **recéder à VT IND r. à qch** to give oneself up to sth again
recel [rəsɛl] **NM** *Jur* **1** *(d'objets → action)* receiving stolen goods; *(→ résultat)* possession of stolen goods; **faire du r.** to deal in stolen goods; **condamné pour r. de bijoux volés** convicted for possession of stolen jewels **2** *(de personnes)* **r. de cadavre/naissance** concealment of a death/birth; **r. de déserteur/malfaiteur** harbouring a deserter/a (known) criminal
receler [25] [rəsəle] **VT 1** *Jur (bijoux, trésor)* to receive; *(personne)* to harbour **2** *(mystère, ressources)* to hold; **la maison recèle un secret** the house holds a secret; **le sous-sol recèle beaucoup de pétrole** the subsoil holds a great deal of oil
VI *Chasse (cerf)* to lie in covert
▸**se receler VPR** *Chasse (cerf)* to lie in covert
receleur, -euse [rəsəlœr, -øz] **NM,F** *Jur* receiver (of stolen goods)
récemment [resamɑ̃] **ADV 1** *(dernièrement)* recently, not (very) long ago; **un journaliste r. rentré d'Afrique** a journalist just back from Africa; **ils ont emménagé r.** they moved in recently *or* not (very) long ago; **tout r. encore** just recently; **l'as-tu rencontrée r.?** have you met her lately? **2** *(nouvellement)* recently, newly; **membres r. inscrits** newly registered members
récence [resɑ̃s] **NF** *Littéraire* recency, recentness
recensement [rəsɑ̃smɑ̃] **NM 1** *(inventaire → gén)* count, inventory; *(→ de population)* census; **faire un r.** to make a count *or* an inventory; **faire le r. de la population** to take a census of the population; **employé au r.** census taker **2** *Pol* **r. des votes** registering *or* counting of the votes **3** *Mil (des futurs conscrits)* registering (for military service); *(des équipements)* inventorying
recenser [3] [rəsɑ̃se] **VT 1** *(population)* to take *or* to make a census of; *(votes)* to count, to register **2** *(objets)* to count, to make an inventory of; *(marchandises)* to inventory, to take stock of; **r. les marchandises en magasin** to do the stocktaking **3** *Mil (futurs conscrits)* to register; *(équipements)* to inventory; **se faire r.** to register for military service
recenseur, -euse [rəsɑ̃sœr, -øz] **NM,F** census taker
recension [rəsɑ̃sjɔ̃] **NF** recension
récent, -e [resɑ̃, -ɑ̃t] **ADJ 1** *(événement)* recent; **leur mariage est tout r.** they've just *or* recently got married; **ils sont de noblesse récente** they're of recent nobility; **jusqu'à une date récente** until recently; **c'est une mode récente** it's a recent fashion **2** *(bourgeois, immigré)* new
recentrage [rəsɑ̃traʒ] **NM 1** *Aut* recentring; *Tech* realigning **2** *Écon* streamlining, rationalization **3** *Pol* refocusing, redefinition
recentrer [3] [rəsɑ̃tre] **VT 1** *Aut* to recentre; *Tech* to realign **2** *Écon* to streamline, to rationalize **3** *Pol* to refocus, to redefine **4** *Sport* to cross again
▸**se recentrer VPR** to become refocused
recepage [rəsəpaʒ], **recépage** [rəsepaʒ] **NM** *Agr* (severe) pruning, cutting *or* lopping (back)
receper [19] [rəsəpe], **recéper** [18] [rəsepe] **VT** *Agr* to prune (severely), to cut *or* to lop back
récépissé [resepise] **NM** (acknowledgment of) receipt; **r. de dépôt** deposit receipt; **r. de douane** customs receipt; **r. d'entrepôt** warehouse receipt
réceptacle [resɛptakl] **NM 1** *(réservoir)* container, vessel, receptacle; **la mer est le r. des déchets de la ville** the sea is the receptacle *or* dumping ground for the city's waste **2** *Fig Littéraire (lieu de rendez-vous)* meeting place **3** *Bot* receptacle
récepteur, -trice [resɛptœr, -tris] **ADJ** *Rad, Tél & TV* receiving, receiver *(avant n)*
NM 1 *Électron* receiver; **r. électroacoustique** electroacoustic transducer *or* receiver
2 *Rad & TV* (receiving) set, receiver; *TV* **r. de contrôle** monitor; **r. de radio** radio receiver; **r. de télévision** television receiver
3 *(téléphonique)* receiver; **décrocher le r.** to lift the receiver
4 *Méd* receptor; *(en neurologie)* receptor (molecule); **r. olfactif/auditif/tactile** olfactory/auditory/tactile receptor
5 *Ling* receiver
réceptice [resɛptis] **ADJ** *Jur (acte)* = valid only when the party concerned is notified
réceptif, -ive [resɛptif, -iv] **ADJ 1** *(ouvert)* receptive; **r. à** open *or* receptive to **2** *Méd* susceptible (to infection)
NM *Mktg* **r. précoce** early adopter
réception [resɛpsjɔ̃] **NF 1** *(du courrier, d'une commande)* receipt; **dès r. de la présente** on receipt of this letter; **à payer à la r.** *Br* cash *or Am* collect on delivery; **acquitter** *ou* **payer à la r.** to pay on receipt *or* delivery; *Com* **r. définitive** final acceptance
2 *Rad & TV* reception; **ma télévision a une bonne/mauvaise r.** I get good/bad reception on my TV; **r. multiple** multiple reception
3 *(accueil)* welcome, reception; **une r. chaleureuse** a warm welcome; **une r. glaciale** an icy reception; **faire une bonne r. à qn** to give sb a good reception *or* warm welcome, to receive *or* welcome sb warmly
4 *(fête, dîner)* party, reception; **r. mondaine** society event; **pour toutes vos réceptions** for whenever you have guests
5 *(d'un hôtel, d'une société → lieu)* reception area *or* desk; *(→ personnel)* reception staff; **demandez à la r.** ask at reception
6 *(cérémonie d'admission)* admission; **discours de r.** induction speech
7 *Constr* **r. des travaux** acceptance (of work done)
8 *Sport (d'un sauteur)* landing; *(du ballon → avec la main)* catch; **bonne r. de Pareta qui passe à Loval** *(avec le pied)* good control by Pareta who passes to Loval; **mauvaise r. de Petit** Petit miscontrols the pass; **il s'est blessé à la r.** *(sauteur)* he hurt himself on landing
réceptionnaire [resɛpsjɔnɛr] **NMF 1** *(dans un hôtel)* head of reception **2** *Com (de marchandises)* consignee **3** *Naut* receiving agent, receiver, consignee
réceptionner [3] [resɛpsjɔne] **VT 1** *(marchandises)* to check and sign for, to take delivery of **2** *Sport (balle → avec la main)* to catch; *(→ avec le pied)* to control, to trap **3** *(recevoir)* to receive
▸**se réceptionner VPR** to land; **il s'est bien/mal réceptionné** he made a good/poor landing
réceptionniste [resɛpsjɔnist] **NMF** receptionist
réceptive [resɛptiv] *voir* **réceptif**
réceptivité [resɛptivite] **NF 1** *(sensibilité)* receptiveness, responsiveness **2** *Méd* susceptibility (to infection); **la r. à certaines maladies augmente avec l'âge** susceptibility to certain ill-

reb–rec

nesses increases with age **3** *Psy* receptiveness **4** *Mktg* **r. des consommateurs** consumer acceptance

réceptrice [resɛptris] *voir* **récepteur**

recercler [3] [rəsɛrkle] **VT** *(tonneau)* to rehoop

recès [rəsɛ] = **recez**

récessif, -ive [resesif, -iv] **ADJ 1** *Biol (gène)* recessive **2** *Écon* recessionary

récession [resesjɔ̃] **NF 1** *(crise économique)* recession; **r. économique** economic recession **2** *Astron & Géog* receding *(UNCOUNT)*

récessive [resesiv] *voir* **récessif**

récessivité [resesivite] **NF** *Biol* recessiveness

recette [rəsɛt] **NF 1** *Com Br* takings, *Am* take; **on a fait une bonne/mauvaise r.** the *Br* takings were *or Am* take was good/poor; **la r. était meilleure la semaine dernière** *Br* takings were *or Am* the take was up last week; **faire r.** *Com* to be profitable; *(film, pièce)* to be a (box-office) success, to be a hit at the box office; *(idée)* to catch on; *(mode)* to be all the rage; *(personne)* to be a great success, to be a hit; **r. annuelle** annual earnings; **r. brute** gross income *or* earnings; **recettes de caisse** cash receipts; *Cin* **r. guichet** box-office receipts; **r. journalière** daily *Br* takings *or Am* take; **r. nette** net income *or* receipts; *Cin* **r. en salles** box-office receipts

2 *Jur & Fin (recouvrement)* collection; *(bureau)* tax (collector's) office; **faire la r. des contributions** to collect the contributions; **r. fiscale** *(administration)* revenue service, *Br* Inland Revenue, *Am* IRS; *(revenus)* tax revenue; **r. municipale** local tax office; **recettes non gagées** unassigned *or* unpledged revenue; **r. principale** *(de la poste)* main post office; *(des impôts)* main tax office

3 *Culin* **r. (de cuisine)** recipe; **elle m'a donné la r. des crêpes** she gave me the pancake recipe; **livre de recettes** cookbook, *Br* cookery book

4 *Pharm* formula

5 *Fig (méthode)* **elle a une r. pour enlever les taches** she's got a foolproof method of getting rid of stains; **la r. du bonheur** the secret of *or* recipe for happiness

6 *Mines* landing; **r. de fond/jour** bottom/top landing

▫ **recettes NFPL** *(sommes touchées)* income *(UNCOUNT)*, receipts, incomings; **recettes et dépenses** *(gén)* income and expenses, incomings and outgoings; *(en comptabilité)* credit and debit; **recettes en devises** foreign currency earnings; **recettes de l'État** public revenue, state revenue; **recettes publiques** public revenue, statute income

recevabilité [rəsəvabilite] **NF** *Jur* admissibility

recevable [rəsəvabl] **ADJ 1** *(offre, excuse)* acceptable **2** *Jur (témoignage)* admissible; *(demande)* allowable; *(personne)* entitled; **témoignage non r.** inadmissible evidence; **être déclaré r. dans une demande** to be declared entitled to proceed with a claim **3** *(marchandises)* fit for acceptance

recevant, -e [rəsəvɑ̃, -ɑ̃t] **ADJ** *Can (personne)* hospitable, who likes to entertain

receveur, -euse [rəsəvœr, -øz] **NM,F 1** *Transp* **r. (d'autobus)** (bus) conductor

2 *Admin* **r. (des postes)** postmaster, *f* postmistress; **r. (des impôts)** tax collector *or* officer; **r. des contributions** income tax collector; **r. des douanes** collector of customs; **r. des finances** district tax collector; **r. municipal** = collector of municipal taxes

3 *Méd* recipient; **r. universel** universal recipient

RECEVOIR [52] [rəsəvwar]

> **VT** to receive **1–3, 8, 10–12** ▪ to get **1–3, 10** ▪ to greet **4** ▪ to entertain **4** ▪ to put up **4** ▪ to see **5** ▪ to admit **6** ▪ to pass **9**
> **VI** to entertain **1** ▪ to see clients/patients **2**
> **VPR** to visit each other **1** ▪ to land **2**

VT 1 *(courrier, commandes, coup de téléphone, compliments)* to receive, to get; *(salaire, somme)* to receive, to get, to be paid; *(cadeau)* to get, to receive, to be given; *(prix, titre)* to receive, to get, to be awarded; *(déposition, réclamation, ordre)* to receive; **nous n'avons toujours rien reçu** we still haven't received anything; **voilà longtemps que je n'ai pas reçu de ses nouvelles** it's a long time since I last heard from him/her; **nous avons bien reçu votre courrier du 12 mai** we acknowledge receipt *or* confirm receipt of your letter dated *Br* 12 May *or Am* May 12; **je reçois une livraison chaque semaine** I get weekly deliveries; **c'est le nom que j'ai reçu de mes parents** it's the name I was given by my parents; **la rose a reçu le nom de la cantatrice** the rose took its name from *or* was named after the singer; **cette hypothèse n'a pas encore reçu de confirmation** that hypothesis has yet to receive confirmation *or* to be confirmed; **je n'ai de conseils à r. de personne!** I don't have to take advice from anybody!; **je n'ai pas l'habitude de r. des ordres** I'm not in the habit of taking orders; **veuillez r., Madame, l'expression de mes sentiments les meilleurs** *ou* **mes salutations distinguées** *(à quelqu'un dont on connaît le nom) Br* yours sincerely, *Am* sincerely (yours); *(à quelqu'un dont on ne connaît pas le nom) Br* yours faithfully, *Am* sincerely (yours); **ma requête n'a pas été reçue** my request was turned down

2 *(attention)* to receive, to get; *(affection, soins)* to receive; *(éducation)* to get

3 *(subir → coups)* to get, to receive; **il a reçu un choc terrible** he got *or* had *or* received a terrible shock; **r. un coup sur la tête** to receive a blow to *or* to get hit on the head; **elle a reçu plusieurs coups de couteau** she was stabbed several times; **la bouteille est tombée et c'est lui qui a tout reçu** the bottle fell over and it went all over him

4 *(chez soi → accueillir)* to greet, to welcome; *(→ inviter)* to entertain; *(→ héberger)* to take in, to put up; **je reçois quelques amis lundi, serez-vous des nôtres?** I'm having a few friends round on Monday, will you join us?; **r. qn à dîner** *(avec simplicité)* to have sb round for dinner, to invite sb to dinner; *(solennellement)* to entertain sb to dinner; **ils m'ont reçu à bras ouverts** they welcomed me with open arms; **j'ai été très bien reçu** I was made (to feel) most welcome; **j'ai été mal reçu** I was made to feel unwelcome; **elle est reçue partout** she's welcomed in all circles; **ils ont reçu la visite de cambrioleurs** they were visited by burglars; **ils ont reçu la visite de la police** they received a visit from the police; **je reçois mes parents pour une semaine** I'm having my parents to stay for a week; **nous ne pouvons guère r. plus de deux personnes** we can hardly have more than two people; *Fam* **se faire r.** to get told off

5 *(à son lieu de travail → client, représentant)* to see; **crois-tu qu'elle va nous r.?** do you think she'll see us?; **ils furent reçus par le Pape** they had an audience with *or* were received by the Pope

6 *(dans un club, une société → nouveau membre)* to admit; **Livot a été reçu à l'Académie française** Livot has been admitted to the Académie Française

7 *(abriter)* **l'école peut r. 800 élèves** the school can take up to 800 pupils; **l'hôtel peut r. 100 personnes** the hotel can accommodate 100 people; **le chalet peut r. six personnes** the chalet sleeps six (people); **ce port peut r. les gros pétroliers** the port can handle large oil tankers; **le stade peut r. jusqu'à 75 000 personnes** the stadium can hold up to 75,000 people *or* has a capacity of 75,000

8 *(eaux de pluie)* to collect; *(lumière)* to receive

9 *(surtout au passif) (candidat)* to pass; **elle a été reçue à l'épreuve de français** she passed her French exam; **je ne suis pas reçu** I didn't pass; **cette année on a reçu 60 pour cent des candidats** this year we passed 60 percent of the candidates

10 *Rad & TV* to receive, to get; **vous recevez la huitième chaîne?** do you get the eighth channel?

11 *Rel (sacrement, vœux)* to receive; *(confession)* to hear

12 *Fin* **à r.** *(effets, intérêts)* receivable

VI 1 *(donner une réception)* to entertain; **elle sait merveilleusement r.** she's marvellous at entertaining, she's a marvellous hostess; **la comtesse recevait le mardi** *(tenait salon)* the countess used to be at home (to visitors) on Tuesdays

2 *(avocat, conseiller)* to be available (to see clients); *(médecin)* to see patients; **le médecin reçoit/ne reçoit pas aujourd'hui** the doctor is/isn't seeing patients today

►**se recevoir VPR 1** *(s'inviter)* to visit each other **2** *Sport* to land; **elle s'est mal reçue** she landed badly *or* awkwardly

recez [rəsɛ] **NM 1** *Hist* recess, ordinance *(of the Holy Roman Empire)* **2** *(en diplomatie)* minutes (of convention)

réchampi [reʃɑ̃pi], **rechampi** [rəʃɑ̃pi] **NM** *Beaux-Arts & Constr* = ornamental feature of contrasting colour

réchampir [reʃɑ̃pir], **rechampir** [32] [rəʃɑ̃pir] **VT** *Beaux-Arts & Constr* to set off

réchampissage [reʃɑ̃pisaʒ], **rechampissage** [rəʃɑ̃pisaʒ] **NM** *Beaux-Arts & Constr* setting off

rechange [rəʃɑ̃ʒ] **NM 1** *Banque (d'un effet)* redraft **2** *(vêtements)* change of clothes, spare set of clothes

▫ **de rechange ADJ 1** *(de secours → pièce, vêtement)* spare; **elle n'avait même pas de linge de r.** she didn't even have a change of clothes; **apporte un maillot de r.** bring an extra *or* a spare swimming costume **2** *(de remplacement → solution, politique)* alternative

rechanger [17] [rəʃɑ̃ʒe] **VT** to change (again), to exchange (again)

rechanter [3] [rəʃɑ̃te] **VT** to sing again

rechapage [rəʃapaʒ] **NM** *Aut* retreading

rechaper [3] [rəʃape] **VT** *Aut* to retread; **pneus rechapés** retreads

réchapper [3] [reʃape] **réchapper à, réchapper de VT IND** *(maladie)* to pull through; *(accident)* to survive, to come through; **il ne réchappera pas à ce scandale** his reputation won't survive the scandal; **en r.** *(rester en vie)* to come through, to escape alive; **si j'en réchappe** if I come through this, if I survive

recharge [rəʃarʒ] **NF 1** *(d'arme)* reload; *(de stylo, de briquet, de parfum)* refill; *(de téléphone portable)* top-up card **2** *(action) & Mil* reloading; *Élec* recharging; **mettre l'accumulateur en r.** to put the battery on charge

rechargeable [rəʃarʒabl] **ADJ** *(briquet, stylo, vaporisateur)* refillable; *(pile, batterie)* rechargeable

rechargement [rəʃarʒəmɑ̃] **NM 1** *(d'une arme, d'un appareil photo)* reloading; *(d'une pile, d'une batterie)* recharging; *(d'un briquet, d'un stylo, d'un vaporisateur)* refilling; *(d'un poêle à bois, à charbon, à mazout)* refuelling **2** *(voiture, camion)* reloading **3** *(d'une route)* remetalling; *(d'une voie ferrée)* reballasting, relaying

recharger [17] [rəʃarʒe] **VT 1** *(réapprovisionner → arme, appareil photo)* to reload; *(→ pile, batterie)* to recharge; *(→ briquet, stylo, vaporisateur)* to refill; *(→ poêle à bois, à charbon, à mazout)* to refuel; *Fam Fig* **r. ses accus** to recharge one's batteries; **r. un téléphone portable** *(recharger la batterie)* to charge (up) *or* recharge a *Br* mobile phone *or Am* cellphone; *(ajouter des unités)* to credit *or Br* top up a mobile phone, *Am* to refill a cellphone

2 *(voiture, camion)* to load again; **il a fallu r. les bagages dans la voiture** we had to load the bags back into the car

3 *(route)* to remetal; *(voie ferrée)* to reballast, to relay

4 *Ind* to strengthen, to consolidate

5 *Ordinat* to reload

réchaud [reʃo] **NM 1** *(de cuisson)* (portable) stove; **r. à alcool** spirit stove; **r. de camping** *(à gaz)* camping stove; *(à pétrole)* Primus® (stove); **r. à gaz** (portable) gas stove **2** *(chauffe-plats)* plate warmer, chafing dish

réchauffage [reʃofaʒ] **NM** reheating

réchauffé, -e [reʃofe] **ADJ 1** *(nourriture)* reheated, warmed-up, heated-up **2** *Fig (plaisanterie)* stale

NM ça a un goût de r. it tastes like it's been reheated; *Fig Péj* **c'est du r.** that's old hat; **rien de nouveau dans le journal sur l'affaire, il n'y a que du r.** there's nothing new in the paper about the business, just a rehash of what's been said already

rec–rec

réchauffement [reʃofmɑ̃] **NM** warming up *(UNCOUNT)*; **r. de l'atmosphère, r. de la planète** *ou* **planétaire** global warming; **on annonce un léger r. pour le week-end** temperatures will rise slightly this weekend

réchauffer [3] [reʃofe] **VT 1** *(nourriture)* to heat *or* to warm up (again); **je vais faire r. la soupe** I'll heat up the soup

2 *(personne, salle)* to warm up; **il frappait ses mains l'une contre l'autre pour les r.** he was clapping his hands together to warm them up; **le soleil commençait à nous r.** we were beginning to feel warmer in the sun; **tu as l'air** *ou* **tu es bien réchauffé!** don't you feel the cold?; *Littéraire* **r. un serpent dans son sein** to nourish a viper in one's bosom

3 *Fig (ambiance)* to warm up; *(ardeur)* to rekindle; **ça vous réchauffe le cœur de les voir** it warms (the cockles of) your heart to see them; **ses bonnes paroles m'avaient réchauffé le cœur** his/her kind words had warmed my heart

USAGE ABSOLU ça réchauffe, hein? it really warms you up *or* gives you a nice warm glow inside, doesn't it?

▸**se réchauffer VPR 1** *(emploi passif)* **un soufflé ne se réchauffe pas** you can't reheat a soufflé

2 *(personne)* to warm up; **je n'arrive pas à me r. aujourd'hui** I just can't get warm today; **alors, tu te réchauffes?** well now, are you warming up a bit?; **se r. les pieds/mains** to warm one's feet/hands (up)

3 *(pièce, sol, temps)* to warm up, to get warmer; **ça ne se réchauffe guère!** the weather isn't exactly getting warmer!

réchauffeur [reʃofœr] **NM** heater; **r. d'air/d'eau/d'huile** air/water/oil heater; **r. à mélange** (liquid) mixture preheater; **r. à surface** surface preheater

rechaussement [rəʃosmɑ̃] **NM 1** *Agr & Hort* earthing *or* banking up **2** *Constr* consolidating

rechausser [3] [rəʃose] **VT 1** *(personne)* **r. qn** to put sb's shoes back on for him/her **2** *(skis)* to put on again **3** *Agr & Hort* to earth *or* to bank up **4** *Constr* to consolidate (the base of)

▸**se rechausser VPR** to put one's shoes back on

rêche [rɛʃ] **ADJ 1** *(matière, vin)* rough; *(fruit)* bitter **2** *Fig (voix, ton)* harsh, rough

recherche [rəʃɛrʃ] **NF 1** *(d'un objet, d'une personne, d'un emploi, de la vérité)* search (**de** for); *(du bonheur, de la gloire, du plaisir)* pursuit (**de** of); *(d'informations)* research (**de** into); **la r. du virus devrait être plus systématique** tests to detect the virus should be more systematic; **la r. d'un bon avocat m'a déjà pris deux mois** I've already spent two months looking for *or* searching for a good lawyer

2 *Ordinat* search, searching *(UNCOUNT)*; *(de données, d'un fichier)* retrieval; **faire une r.** to do a search; **r. arrière** backward search; **r. avant, r. vers le bas** forward search; **r. booléenne** Boolean search; **r. documentaire** information retrieval; **r. de données** data retrieval; **r. globale** global search; **r. et remplacement** search and replace; **r. et remplacement globale** global search and replace; **r. vers le haut** backward search

3 *Jur* search; **action en r. de paternité** paternity proceedings *or Am* suit; **r. de maternité naturelle** search for the natural mother; **r. de paternité naturelle** search for the natural father

4 *(prospection)* **r. minière** mining; **r. pétrolière** oil prospecting

5 *(en sciences, en art, en lettres)* **la r.** research; **le budget de la r.** the research budget; **la r. sur le cancer** cancer research; **bourse/travaux de r.** research grant/work; **faire de la r.** to do research; **elle fait de la r. en chimie** *(spécialiste)* she's a research chemist; *(étudiante)* she's a chemistry research student; **r. biomédicale** biomedical research; **r. documentaire** documentary research; **r. fondamentale** fundamental research; **r. opérationnelle** *Br* operational *or Am* operations research; **r. scientifique** scientific research

6 *Mktg* research; **r. ad hoc** ad hoc research; **recherches sur les besoins des consommateurs** consumer research; **r. commerciale** marketing research; **r. et développement** research and development; **r. documentaire** desk research; **r. longitudinale** longitudinal *or* continuous research; **r. marketing** market research; **r. de motivation** motivation *or* motivational research; **r. opérationnelle** operational research; **recherches par panel** panel research; **r. sur les prix** pricing research; **r. de produits** product research; **r. par sondage** survey research; **recherches sur le terrain** field research

7 *(raffinement)* sophistication, refinement; *(affectation)* affectation, ostentatiousness; **vêtu avec r.** elegantly dressed; **s'habiller avec r.** to be a fastidious dresser; **s'exprimer avec r.** to be highly articulate; **sans r.** *(style)* simple, plain; **trop de r. nuit à la clarté du style** an overelaborate style works against *or* undermines clarity

▫ **recherches NFPL 1** *(enquête)* search; **les recherches de la police pour rattraper le fuyard sont restées vaines** despite a police search, the runaway has not been found; **dans l'affaire Mennesson, la police continue les** *ou* **ses recherches** the police are continuing their enquiry into the Mennesson affair; **faire des recherches (sur qch)** *(gén)* to inquire (into sth); *(sujet: chercheur)* to do research (into sth); **faire faire des recherches pour retrouver un parent disparu** to have a search carried out for a missing relative

2 *(travaux → gén)* work, research; *(→ de médecine)* research; **une équipe d'archéologues mène déjà des recherches sur le site** a team of archeologists is already working on *or* researching the site

▫ **à la recherche de PRÉP** in search of, looking *or* searching for; **être/partir/se mettre à la r. de** to be/to set off/to go in search of; **ils ont fait tout Paris à la r. d'un vase identique** they searched the whole of Paris for an identical vase; **nous sommes toujours à la r. d'un remède** we're still looking for a cure; **je suis toujours à la r. d'un prétexte pour ne pas y aller** I'm always looking for an excuse not to go; **depuis combien de temps êtes-vous à la r. d'un emploi?** how long have you been looking for a job?; **une vie passée à la r. des plaisirs/de la fortune** a life spent in pursuit of pleasure/riches

---

'À la recherche du temps perdu' *Proust* 'In Search of Lost Time' *or* 'Remembrance of Things Past'

---

recherché, -e [rəʃɛrʃe] **ADJ 1** *(prisé → mets)* choice *(avant n)*; *(→ comédien)* in demand, much sought-after; *(→ objet rare)* much sought-after; **ce style de fauteuil est très r.** there's a lot of demand for this type of chair **2** *(raffiné → langage)* studied, recherché; *(→ tenue)* elegant; *(→ style)* ornate, elaborate; *Péj (affecté)* affected; **dans sa toilette la plus recherchée** in her best finery

recherche-action [rəʃɛrʃaksjɔ̃] *(pl* **recherches-actions)** **NF** *Psy* action research

recherche-développement [rəʃɛrʃdevəlɔpmɑ̃] *(pl* **recherches-développements)** **NF** *Écon* research and development

rechercher [3] [rəʃɛrʃe] **VT 1** *(document, objet)* to look *or* to search for; *(disparu)* to search for; *(assassin)* to look for; **r. un passage dans un livre** to try and find a passage in a book; *Tél* **nous recherchons votre correspondant** we're trying to connect you; **il est recherché par la police** the police are looking for him; **on recherche pour meurtre homme brun, 32 ans** wanted for murder brown-haired, 32-year-old man; **la police recherche les témoins de l'accident** the police are appealing for anyone who witnessed the accident to come forward

2 *(dans une annonce)* **(on) recherche jeunes gens pour travail bien rémunéré** young people wanted for well-paid job

3 *(cause)* to look into, to investigate; **on recherche toujours la cause du sinistre** the cause of the fire is still being investigated

4 *(compliments, pouvoir, gloire)* to seek (out); *(sécurité, solitude)* to look for; *(fortune, plaisirs)* to be in search of; *(beauté, pureté)* to strive for, to aim at; **r. l'affection/la compagnie de qn** to seek out sb's affection/company

5 *(récupérer → personne)* to collect, to fetch back (again); **je viendrai te r.** I'll come and fetch you; **j'ai laissé ma bicyclette chez Paul, il va falloir que j'aille la r.** I left my bike at Paul's place, I'll have to go and get it back

6 *(chercher à nouveau)* to search *or* to look for again

7 *(prendre à nouveau)* **va me r. du pain chez le boulanger/à la cuisine** go and get me some more bread from the baker's/kitchen

8 *Ordinat* to search; **r. et remplacer qch** to search and replace sth; **r. vers le bas/haut** to search forwards/backwards

recherchiste [rəʃɛrʃist] **NMF** *Can* researcher, research assistant; *Rad & TV* (programme) researcher

rechigner [3] [rəʃiɲe] **VI 1** *(montrer sa mauvaise humeur)* to grimace, to frown

2 *(protester)* to grumble; **fais-le sans r.** do it without making a fuss

▫ **rechigner à VT IND elle rechigne à faire cette vérification** she's reluctant to carry out this check; **r. à la tâche** *ou* **à l'ouvrage** to be unwilling to do it; **la vieille Marie, en voilà une qui ne rechignait pas à l'ouvrage!** old Marie didn't mind a bit of hard work!

rechristianiser [3] [rəkristjanize] **VT** to reconvert to Christianity

rechute [rəʃyt] **NF 1** *Méd* relapse; **avoir** *ou* **faire une r.** to (have a) relapse **2** *(d'une mauvaise habitude)* relapse **3** *Écon* **on craint une r. de l'activité économique** there are fears of a further slump

rechuter [3] [rəʃyte] **VI 1** *Méd* to (have a) relapse **2** *(dans une mauvaise habitude)* to relapse

récidivant, -e [residivɑ̃, -ɑ̃t] **ADJ** recurring

récidive [residiv] **NF 1** *Jur (après première condamnation)* second offence; *(après deuxième condamnation)* subsequent offence; **il y a r.** this is a second offence; **en cas de r.** in the event of a second *or* subsequent offence; **elle n'en est pas à sa première r.** this is the latest in a long line of offences, she has reoffended on more than one occasion; *Fig* **à la première r., je confisque ton vélo!** if you do that once more, I'll confiscate your bike! **2** *Méd* recurrence

récidiver [3] [residive] **VI 1** *Jur (après première condamnation)* to commit a second offence; *(après deuxième condamnation)* to commit a subsequent offence **2** *(recommencer)* **il récidive dans ses plaintes** he keeps making the same complaints (over and over again) **3** *Méd* to recur, to be recurrent

récidivisme [residivism] **NM** persistent *or* habitual offending, *Spéc* recidivism

récidiviste [residivist] **ADJ** reoffending, recidivist

NMF *(pour la première fois)* second offender, *Spéc* recidivist; *(de longue date)* persistent *or* habitual offender, *Spéc* recidivist

récif [resif] **NM** reef; **r. corallien** *ou* **de corail** coral reef; **r. frangeant** fringing reef

récifal, -e, -aux, -ales [resifal, -o] **ADJ** *(poisson, écosystème, habitat)* reef *(avant n)*; **un aquarium r.** a reef aquarium

récif-barrière [resifbarjɛr] *(pl* **récifs-barrières)** **NM** barrier reef

Recife [resif] **NM** Recife

récipiendaire [resipjɑ̃dɛr] **NMF 1** *(nouveau venu)* member elect **2** *(d'une médaille, d'un diplôme)* recipient

récipient [resipjɑ̃] **NM** container

réciprocité [resiprɔsite] **NF** reciprocity; **mais à titre de r., laissez-moi vous inviter à déjeuner** but allow me to repay you by inviting you to lunch

réciproque [resiprɔk] **ADJ 1** *(mutuel)* mutual; **des sentiments réciproques** mutual feelings; **je vous hais! – c'est r.!** I hate you! – I hate you too *or* the feeling's mutual!; **l'affection qu'elle portait au jeune homme n'était pas r.** her affection for the young man was not reciprocated *or* returned

2 *(bilatéral → accord, convention)* reciprocal

3 *(en logique)* converse; **proposition r.** converse (proposition)

4 *Gram & Math* reciprocal

NF 1 la r. *(l'inverse)* the reverse, the opposite; **pourtant la r. n'est pas vraie** though the reverse isn't true, but not vice versa; **je ne l'aime pas, et la r. est vraie** I don't like him/her and he/she doesn't like me either *or* and the feeling's mutual

2 **la r.** *(la même chose)* the same; **ils vous ont invités, à vous de leur rendre la r.** they invited you, now it's up to you to do the same *or* to invite them in return; **elle m'a roulé, mais j'ai bien l'intention de lui rendre la r.** she conned me, but I fully intend to get even with her *or* to get my own back

3 *Math* reciprocal function

réciproquement [resiprɔkmɑ̃] ADV 1 *(mutuellement)* **ils ont le devoir de se protéger r.** it is their duty to protect each other *or* one another, they must provide each other with mutual protection 2 *(inversement)* vice versa; **ce qui est blanc ici est noir là-bas et r.** what is white here is black over there and vice versa

réciproquer [3] [resiprɔke] *Belg* VI **je vous souhaite une bonne année! – je réciproque!** happy New Year! – same to you!

VT *(voeux)* to return

récit [resi] NM 1 *(histoire racontée)* story, tale, *Sout* narration; **il nous fit le r. de ses aventures** he gave us an account of his adventures; **faites le r. de vos dernières vacances** write an account of your last *Br* holidays *or Am* vacation; **nous avons tous frémi au r. de cette histoire** we all shivered when we heard the tale

2 *(exposé)* account; **le r. chronologique des faits** a chronological account of the facts; **un r. circonstancié** a blow-by-blow account

3 *Littérature & Théât* narrative; **r. de voyage** *(livre)* travel book

4 *Mus (dans un opéra)* recitative; *(solo)* solo; *(clavier d'orgue)* third manual, choir (organ)

récital, -als [resital] NM recital; **r. de piano** piano recital

récitant, -e [resitɑ̃, -ɑ̃t] ADJ *Mus* solo

NM,F *Cin & Théât* narrator; *Mus* soloist

récitatif [resitatif] NM recitative

récitation [resitasjɔ̃] NF 1 *(d'un texte)* recitation 2 *Scol (poème)* recitation piece; **on leur a fait apprendre une belle r.** they were given a beautiful poem to learn (by heart)

réciter [3] [resite] VT 1 *(dire par cœur* → *leçon)* to repeat, to recite; *(*→ *discours)* to give; *(*→ *poème, prière)* to say, to recite; *(*→ *formule)* to recite 2 *(dire sans sincérité)* **elle avait l'air de r. un texte** she sounded as if she was reading from a book; **le témoin a récité sa déposition** the witness reeled off his/her statement

reck [rɛk] NM *Suisse* 1 *Sport* horizontal bar 2 *(pente)* steep slope

réclamant, -e [reklamɑ̃, -ɑ̃t] NM,F *Jur* claimant

réclamation [reklamasjɔ̃] NF 1 *Admin (plainte)* complaint; **pour toute r., s'adresser au guichet 16** all complaints should be addressed *or* referred to desk 16; **faire une r.** to lodge a complaint; **service/bureau des réclamations** complaints department/office

2 *Jur (demande)* claim, demand; **faire une r.** to lodge a claim; **faire droit à une r.** to allow *or* to satisfy a claim; **r. en dommages-intérêts** claim for damages; **r. d'état** claim of status; **r. d'indemnité** claim for compensation; **r. litigieuse** contentious claim

3 *(récrimination)* complaining *(UNCOUNT)*; **les réclamations continuelles des enfants** the children's incessant complaining

4 *(dans le domaine fiscal)* tax adjustment claim

réclame [reklam] NF *Vieilli* 1 **la r.** *(la publicité)* advertising *(UNCOUNT)*; **faire de la r. pour qch** to advertise sth; *Fig* **faire de la r. à qn** *(chanter ses louanges)* to sing sb's praises; *Fig* **ça ne va pas lui faire de r.** it's not a very good advertisement for him/her

2 *(annonce, panneau)* advertisement; **j'ai vu la r. de cette voiture à la télé** I saw the commercial *or Br* advert for this car on TV; **r. lumineuse** illuminated sign

▫ **en réclame** ADJ on (special) offer; **article en r.** special offer; **le café est en r. cette semaine** there's a special offer on coffee *or* coffee's on special offer this week ADV at a discount

réclamer [3] [reklame] VT 1 *(argent, augmentation* → *gén)* to ask for; *(*→ *avec insistance)* to demand; *(attention, silence)* to call for, to demand; *(personne)* to ask *or* to clamour for; **l'enfant ne cesse de r. sa mère** the child is continually asking for his/her mother; **les enfants réclament leur dessert** the children are clamouring for *or* demanding their dessert; **je réclame le silence!** silence, please!; **Monsieur le Président, je réclame la parole** Mr President, may I say something?; **elle me doit encore de l'argent mais je n'ose pas le lui r.** she still owes me money but I daren't ask for it back; **r. le secours de qn** to ask sb for assistance; **ils réclament la semaine de 35 heures** they demand a 35-hour week

2 *(revendiquer* → *droit)* to claim; *(*→ *somme due)* to put in for, to claim; **r. des dommages et intérêts** to claim compensation *or* damages; **r. sa part d'héritage** to claim one's share of the inheritance; **je ne fais que r. mon dû** I am merely claiming what is mine

3 *(nécessiter* → *précautions)* to call for; *(*→ *soins)* to require; *(*→ *explication)* to require, to demand; **la situation réclame des mesures d'exception** the situation calls for special measures

USAGE ABSOLU *Fam* **le chien est toujours à r.** the dog's always begging; *Fam* **le bébé est toujours à r.** the baby's always wanting to be fed

VI 1 *(se plaindre)* to complain; **r. auprès de qn** to complain to sb

2 *(protester)* **r. contre qch** to cry out against sth

▸**se réclamer** VPR **se r. de qn** *(utiliser son nom)* to use sb's name; *(se prévaloir de lui)* to invoke sb's name; **elle ne se réclame d'aucun mouvement politique** she doesn't identify with any political movement; **les organisations se réclamant du marxisme** organizations calling *or* labelling themselves Marxist

reclaper, reclapper [3] [rəklape] VT *Belg* to slam

reclaquer [3] [rəklake] VT *Belg* to slam

reclassement [rəklasmɑ̃] NM 1 *(de données* → *alphabétiques)* reordering; *(*→ *numériques)* reordering, resequencing 2 *(d'un dossier* → *remise en place)* refiling; *(*→ *nouveau classement)* reclassifying 3 *Admin (d'un fonctionnaire)* regrading; **r. de la fonction publique** restructuring of the state sector 4 *(d'un chômeur)* placement; *(d'un handicapé, d'un ex-détenu)* rehabilitation

reclasser [3] [rəklase] VT 1 *(par ordre alphabétique)* to reorder; *(par ordre numérique)* to reorder, to resequence

2 *(ranger)* to put back, to refile; *(réorganiser)* to reclassify, to reorganize; **r. les dossiers par ordre chronologique** to reclassify the files in chronological order

3 *Admin (salaires)* to restructure; *(fonctionnaire)* to regrade

4 *(chômeur)* to place; *(handicapé, ex-détenu)* to rehabilitate

reclouer [6] [rəklue] VT to nail back together

reclus, -e [rəkly, -yz] ADJ solitary, secluded; **mener une vie recluse** to lead a secluded existence

NM,F recluse; **vivre en r.** to live like a hermit *or* recluse

réclusion [reklyzjɔ̃] NF 1 *Littéraire (solitude)* reclusion, seclusion 2 *Jur* imprisonment; **r. criminelle** imprisonment with labour; **condamné à la r. criminelle à perpétuité** sentenced to life (imprisonment), given a life sentence

réclusionnaire [reklyzjɔnɛr] NMF prisoner

récognitif, -ive [rekɔgnitif, -iv] ADJ *Jur* recognitive, recognitory; **acte r.** deed of recognition

récognition [rekɔgnisjɔ̃] NF recognition

récognitive [rekɔgnitiv] *voir* **récognitif**

recoiffer [3] [rəkwafe] VT **r. ses cheveux** to do *or* to redo one's hair; **r. qn** *(le peigner)* to redo sb's hair, to do sb's hair (again); *(lui remettre un chapeau)* to put sb's hat back on

▸**se recoiffer** VPR 1 *(se peigner)* to do *or* to redo one's hair 2 *(remettre son chapeau)* to put one's hat back on

recoin [rəkwɛ̃] NM 1 *(coin)* corner, nook; **elle a dû le cacher dans quelque r.** she must have hidden it in some corner or other; **une maison pleine de recoins** a rambling house, a house full of nooks and crannies; **chercher dans le moindre r.** *ou* **dans tous les (coins et) recoins** to search every nook and cranny

2 *Fig (partie secrète)* recess; **les recoins de l'inconscient** the (hidden) recesses of the unconscious

reçoit, reçoivent *etc voir* **recevoir**

récolement [rekɔlmɑ̃] NM *Jur (des meubles saisis, d'une coupe de bois)* verification, checking; **le r. des témoins** reading over their depositions to witnesses

récoler [3] [rekɔle] VT *Jur (meubles saisis, coupe de bois)* to verify, to check; **r. les témoins** to read over their depositions to witnesses

recollage [rəkɔlaʒ] NM resticking

récollection [rekɔlɛksjɔ̃] NF *Rel (recueillement)* meditation, recollection; *(retraite spirituelle)* retreat

recollement [rəkɔlmɑ̃] = **recollage**

recoller [3] [rəkɔle] VT 1 *(objet brisé)* to stick *or* to glue back together; *(timbre)* to stick back on; *(enveloppe)* to stick back down, to restick; *(semelle)* to stick *or* to glue back on; **r. les morceaux** *(avec de la colle)* to stick *or* to glue the pieces back together (again); *(avec de l'adhésif)* to tape the pieces back together (again); *Fig* to patch things up

2 *(appuyer)* **il recolla son front à la vitre glacée** he pressed his forehead back against the frosted window pane

3 *Fam (redonner)* **on m'a recollé une amende** I've been landed with another fine; **on nous a recollé un prof nul** we've been landed with another useless teacher

4 *Fam (remettre)* to stick *or* to shove back; **ils l'ont recollé à l'hôpital** they stuck him back in hospital

▫ **recoller à** VT IND *Sport* **r. au peloton** to catch up with the bunch

▸**se recoller** VPR 1 *(emploi passif)* **ça se recolle très facilement** it can easily be stuck back together

2 *(se ressouder* → *os)* to knit (together), to mend; *(*→ *objet)* to stick (together)

3 *Fam Fig* **se r. avec qn** *(se réinstaller avec)* to move back in with sb▪

récollet [rekɔlɛ] NM *Rel* Recollect (friar)

récoltable [rekɔltabl] ADJ ready for harvesting

récoltant, -e [rekɔltɑ̃, -ɑ̃t] ADJ **propriétaire** *ou* **viticulteur r.** = winegrower who harvests his own grapes

NM,F grower

récolte [rekɔlt] NF 1 *(des céréales)* harvest *(UNCOUNT)*; *(des légumes, des fruits)* picking *(UNCOUNT)*; *(des pommes de terre)* lifting *(UNCOUNT)*; *(du miel)* gathering, collecting *(UNCOUNT)*; **ils ont déjà commencé à faire la r.** they've already started harvesting

2 *(quantité récoltée)* harvest; *(denrées récoltées)* crop; **la r. a été bonne cette année** the harvest *or* crop was good this year

3 *(de documents, d'informations)* gathering, collecting

récolter [3] [rekɔlte] VT 1 *(céréales)* to harvest, to gather; *(légumes, fruits)* to pick; *(pommes de terre)* to lift, to pick; *(miel)* to collect, to gather; *Fig* **il récolte ce qu'il a semé** it's his own fault, he's reaping what he sowed

2 *(informations, argent)* to collect, to gather; **la police a pu r. quelques indices** the police were able to gather a few clues; **r. une somme importante** to collect a large sum; **r. des voix** to get votes

3 *Fam (ennuis, maladie, etc)* to get; **tout ce que j'ai récolté, c'est un bon rhume** all I got (out of it) was a bad cold; **elle a récolté toute une série de mauvaises notes** she got a whole crop *or* series of bad *Br* marks *or Am* grades; **depuis qu'il a acheté cette maison, il n'a récolté que des ennuis** he's had nothing but trouble since he bought that house

recombinaison [rəkɔ̃binɛzɔ̃] NF *Biol & Chim* recombination

recombinant, -e [rəkɔ̃binɑ̃, -ɑ̃t] ADJ *Biol & Chim* recombinant

recombiner [3] [rəkɔ̃bine] VT *Biol & Chim* to recombine

recommandable [rəkɔmɑ̃dabl] ADJ commendable; **r. à tous égards** *(personne)* highly respectable; **un individu/hôtel peu r.** a rather disreputable character/hotel; **le procédé est peu r.** that isn't a very commendable thing to do

recommandataire [rəkɔmɑ̃datɛr] NMF *Com* case of need, referral drawee

recommandation [rəkɔmɑ̃dasjɔ̃] NF 1 *(conseil)* advice, recommendation; **tout ira bien si tu suis mes recommandations** everything will be all right if you follow my advice; **faire qch sur la**

r. de qn to do sth on sb's recommendation; **je lui ai fait mes dernières recommandations** I gave him/her some last-minute advice; **elle nous a fait mille recommandations** she gave us all kinds of advice, she told us a thousand things to do and not to do; **r. importante, ne pas dépasser la dose prescrite** (sur emballage) caution: do not exceed the stated dose

2 (appui) recommendation, reference; **je me suis procuré des recommandations** I've got some people to give me a reference; **je vous mets un mot de r. pour le spécialiste** I'll write you a referral for the specialist

3 (d'un courrier → sans avis de réception) Br registering, Am certifying; (→ avec avis de réception) recording

4 Pol **r. de l'ONU** UN recommendation

recommandé, -e [rǝkɔmɑ̃de] ADJ **1** (conseillé) advisable; **dans votre cas le sport n'est pas r.** in your case sport isn't advisable or recommended; **il est r. de...** it is advisable to...; **il est r. aux visiteurs de se munir de leurs passeports** visitors are advised to take their passports; Euph **ce n'est pas (très) r. d'être constamment en retard** it's not really advisable to be late all the time; **la réservation est fortement recommandée** you are strongly advised to book in advance

2 (courrier → avec avis de réception) Br recorded, Am certified; (→ à valeur assurée) registered

NM (courrier → avec avis de réception) Br recorded or Am certified delivery item; (→ à valeur assurée) registered item; **par courrier r.** by Br recorded delivery or Am certified mail; **en r.** (avec avis de réception) by Br recorded delivery or Am certified mail; (à valeur assurée) by registered Br post or Am mail

recommander [3] [rǝkɔmɑ̃de] VT **1** (conseiller → produit, personne) to recommend; **cet hôtel est recommandé par tous les guides** this hotel is recommended in all the guidebooks; **je te recommande vivement mon médecin** I (can) heartily recommend my doctor to you; **un homme aux ses états de service recommandent** a man with a very commendable service record or whose service record commends him

2 (exhorter à) to recommend, to advise; **je vous recommande la prudence** I recommend or I advise you to be cautious, I advise caution; **r. à qn de faire qch** to advise sb to do sth; **je ne saurais trop vous r. d'être vigilant** I cannot advise you too strongly to be watchful

3 (confier) **r. qn à qn** to place sb in sb's care; Rel **r. son âme à Dieu** to commend one's soul or oneself to God

4 (courrier → pour attester sa réception) Br to record, Am to certify; (→ pour l'assurer) to register

5 (boisson) **r. un café/whisky** to order another coffee/whisky

▸ **se recommander** VPR **1 se r. à** (s'en remettre à) to commend oneself to; **recommandons-nous à Dieu** let us commend our souls to God

2 se r. de qn (postulant) to give sb's name as a reference; **tu peux te r. de moi** (chez un marchand) you can say I sent you; (à un postulant) you can give my name as a referee

3 Littéraire (montrer sa valeur) **elle se recommande par son efficacité** her efficiency commends her or is a strong point in her favour

4 Suisse (insister) **se r. auprès de qn que...** to point out to sb that...; **je me recommande pour que vous fermiez bien la porte à clé** I'd just like to remind you to make sure you lock the door

recommencement [rǝkɔmɑ̃smɑ̃] NM resumption; **la vie est un éternel r.** every day is a new beginning; **l'histoire est un éternel r.** history is always repeating itself

recommencer [16] [rǝkɔmɑ̃se] VT **1** (refaire → dessin, lettre, travail etc) to start or to begin again; (→ attaque) to renew, to start again; (→ expérience) to repeat; (→ erreur) to repeat, to make again; **recommence ta phrase depuis le début** start your sentence again from the beginning; **ne recommence pas tes bêtises** don't start that nonsense again; **recommençons la scène 4** let's do scene 4 again; **si seulement on pouvait r. sa vie!** if only one could start one's life afresh or begin one's life all over again!;

c'est la quatrième fois que je recommence cette rangée de tricot that's the fourth time I've had to start this row of knitting; **tout est à r., il faut tout r.** we have to start or to begin all over again

2 (reprendre → histoire, conversation) to resume, to carry on with; (→ lecture, travail) to resume, to go back to; (→ campagne, lutte) to resume, to take up again; **la vie est une lutte toujours recommencée** life is an ongoing or continuous struggle

USAGE ABSOLU **ça fait trois fois que je recommence** I've started this three times; **ne recommence pas!** don't do that again!; **le voilà qui recommence!** he's at it again!

VI **1** (depuis le début) to start or to begin again; (après interruption) to resume; **les cours ne recommencent qu'en octobre** term doesn't begin or start again until October; **pour moi, la vie va r.** my life is about to begin anew, a new life is beginning for me; **tenez-vous tranquilles, ça ne va pas r. comme hier, non?** calm down, you're not going to start behaving like you did yesterday, are you?; **ça y est, ça recommence!** here we go again!

2 (se remettre) **r. à faire qch** to start doing or to do sth again; **elle a recommencé à danser deux mois après son accident** she started dancing again or she went back to dancing two months after her accident; **depuis quand a-t-il recommencé à boire?** when did he start drinking again?; **mon genou recommence à me faire mal** my knee's started aching again

3 (tournure impersonnelle) **il a recommencé à neiger dans la nuit** it started snowing again during the night; **il recommence à faire froid** it's beginning or starting to get cold again; **il recommence à y avoir des moustiques** the mosquitoes are back (again)

recommercialiser [3] [rǝkɔmɛrsjalize] VT to remarket

recomparaître [91] [rǝkɔ̃parɛtr] VI Jur to appear again

récompense [rekɔ̃pɑ̃s] NF **1** (d'un acte) reward, Sout recompense; **en r. de** as a reward or in return for; **en r. ou pour ta r., accepte ce cadeau** please accept this gift as a reward; Fam Ironique **il a trimé toute sa vie, et voilà sa r.!** he's slaved away all his life and that's all the thanks or the reward he gets!; **qu'il soit heureux, ce serait là ma plus belle r.** as long as he is happy, that will be ample recompense or reward for me; **la juste r. de ses crimes** just retribution for his/her crimes; **forte r.** (petite annonce) generous reward

2 (prix) award, prize; **la remise des récompenses** the presentation of awards

3 Jur financial provision

4 Mil award

récompenser [3] [rekɔ̃pɑ̃se] VT **1** (pour un acte) to reward, Sout to recompense (**de** for); **tu mérites d'être récompensé** you deserve a reward or to be rewarded; Ironique **voilà comment je suis récompensé de ma peine!** that's all the reward I get for my troubles! **2** (primer) to give an award or a prize to, to reward; **le scénario a été récompensé à Cannes** the script won an award at Cannes

recomposable [rǝkɔ̃pozabl] ADJ reconstructable

recomposé, -e [rǝkɔ̃poze] ADJ **famille recomposée** = family that includes stepchildren from partners' previous marriages, Am blended family

recomposer [3] [rǝkɔ̃poze] VT **1** (reconstituer) to piece or to put together (again), to reconstruct; **son esprit recomposait peu à peu la scène** he/she gradually reconstructed the scene in his/her mind **2** Typ (page) to reset; (texte) to rekey **3** (réarranger → chanson) to rewrite; (→ photo) to compose again **4** Chim & Ling to recompose **5** Tél to redial, to dial again

recomposition [rǝkɔ̃pozisjɔ̃] NF **1** (reconstitution) reconstruction **2** Typ (d'une page) resetting; (d'un texte) rekeying **3** (d'une chanson) rewriting; (d'une photo) recomposition **4** Chim & Ling recomposition

recompter [3] [rǝkɔ̃te] VT to count again

réconciliation [rekɔ̃siljasjɔ̃] NF **1** (entente) reconciliation; **leur r. a été de courte durée** their

reconciliation didn't last long **2** Jur & Rel reconciliation

réconcilier [9] [rekɔ̃silje] VT **1** (deux personnes) to reconcile; **nous devons les r.** we have to reconcile them with each other

2 Fig (réunir, allier) **r. qn avec** (doctrine, religion) to reconcile sb with; (idée) to reconcile sb to; **ça m'a réconcilié avec la vie** it renewed my appetite for life, it made life seem worth living again; **r. qch avec qch** to reconcile sth with sth; **il voulait r. classicisme et romantisme** he wanted to bridge the gap between classicism and romanticism

3 Rel to reconcile

▸ **se réconcilier** VPR (personnes) to make up; (pays) to make peace; Hum **se r. sur l'oreiller** to make up in bed; **se r. avec soi-même** to come to terms with oneself

recondamner [3] [rǝkɔ̃dane] VT to sentence again

reconditionner [3] [rǝkɔ̃disjone] VT (marchandises) to repackage

reconductible [rǝkɔ̃dyktibl] ADJ Jur renewable

reconduction [rǝkɔ̃dyksjɔ̃] NF (d'un contrat, d'un budget, d'un mandat) renewal; (de mesures, d'une politique, d'une grève) continuation; (d'un bail) renewal, extension; **voter la r. de la grève** to vote for the continuation of the strike or for continued strike action; **r. tacite** tacit renewal

reconduire [98] [rǝkɔ̃dɥir] VT **1** (accompagner) **r. qn** (chez lui) to see sb home; (vers la sortie) to show sb to the door; **laisse-moi te r.** let me see you home; **r. qn à pied/en voiture** to walk/to drive sb home; **inutile de me r., je connais le chemin** please don't trouble yourself, I know the way

2 (expulser) to escort; **les terroristes ont été reconduits à la frontière sous bonne escorte** the terrorists were taken (back) to the border under police escort

3 (renouveler → contrat, budget, mandat) to renew; (→ mesures, politique, grève) to continue; (→ bail) to renew, to extend

reconduite [rǝkɔ̃dɥit] NF Jur **la r. des réfugiés à la frontière** the escorting of the refugees (back) to the border

reconfiguration [rǝkɔ̃figyrasjɔ̃] NF **1** (d'une société) re-engineering **2** Ordinat reconfiguration

reconfigurer [3] [rǝkɔ̃figyre] VT **1** (société) to re-engineer **2** Ordinat to reconfigure

réconfort [rekɔ̃fɔr] NM comfort; **tu m'es d'un grand r.** you're a great comfort to me; **avoir besoin de r.** to need cheering up

réconfortant, -e [rekɔ̃fɔrtɑ̃, -ɑ̃t] ADJ **1** (rassurant) comforting, reassuring **2** (revigorant) fortifying, invigorating, stimulating

réconforter [3] [rekɔ̃fɔrte] VT **1** (consoler) to comfort, to reassure; **tes bonnes paroles m'ont réconfortée** your kind words comforted or consoled me or gave me hope; **cela me réconforte de voir que je ne suis pas la seule** it cheers me up or I'm glad to see I'm not the only one

2 (revigorer) **bois ça, ça va te r.** drink this, it'll make you feel better

▸ **se réconforter** VPR **1** (physiquement) to make oneself feel better

2 (moralement) to cheer oneself up, to console oneself

reconnais etc voir **reconnaître**

reconnaissable [rǝkɔnɛsabl] ADJ recognizable; **après trois mois de prison il était à peine r.** after three months in prison he was hardly recognizable or you could hardly recognize him; **r. entre tous** unmistakeable; **r. à** identifiable by

reconnaissait etc voir **reconnaître**

reconnaissance [rǝkɔnɛsɑ̃s] NF **1** (gratitude) gratitude; **avoir/éprouver de la r. envers qn** to be/to feel grateful to or towards sb; **je lui en ai une vive r.** I am most grateful to him/her; **témoigner de la r. à qn** to show gratitude to sb; **vous avez toute ma r.** I'm most grateful to you; **avec r.** gratefully, with gratitude; **en r. de votre dévouement** as a token of my/our/etc gratitude for or in recognition of your devotion; Fam **il n'a même pas la r. du ventre!** he'd bite the hand that fed him!; **le chat vient vers toi mais c'est la r. du ventre** the cat comes to you but it's only cupboard love

2 *(exploration)* reconnaissance; **envoyer des hommes en r.** to send men out on reconnaissance; **partir en r.** to go on reconnaissance; *Fig* **elle est partie en r.** *ou* **est allée faire une r. des lieux** she went to check the place out; **patrouille de r.** reconnaissance patrol; **vol de r.** reconnaissance flight

3 *(identification)* recognition; **je porterai un canotier, ce sera notre signe de r.** I'll be wearing a boater, that's how you'll recognize me; *Mktg* **r. des besoins** need recognition; **r. des empreintes digitales** fingerprint recognition; **r. de l'iris** iris recognition; **r. de la main** hand recognition

4 *(aveu)* admission; **la r. de ses torts lui a valu l'indulgence du jury** his/her admission of his/her wrongs won him/her the leniency of the jury; *Jur* **r. de culpabilité** guilty plea

5 *Pol (d'un gouvernement, d'un État, de l'indépendance)* recognition; **la r. de la Palestine** the recognition of Palestine

6 *Jur (d'un droit)* recognition, acknowledgment; **r. de dette** acknowledgment of a debt, IOU; **r. d'enfant** legal recognition of a child; *Admin* **r. d'utilité publique** official approval

7 *(reçu)* **acte de r. (du mont-de-piété)** pawn ticket

8 *Ordinat* recognition; **r. de formes/de caractères** pattern/character recognition; **r. optique des caractères** optical character recognition; **r. de la parole, r. vocale** speech recognition

9 *Psy* recognition

reconnaissant, -e [rəkɔnɛsɑ̃, -ɑ̃t] **ADJ** grateful; **se montrer r.** to show one's gratitude; **je te suis r. de ta patience** I'm most grateful to you for your patience; **je vous en suis très r.** I'm very grateful, I'm in your debt; **je vous serais r. de me fournir ces renseignements dans les meilleurs délais** I would be (most) obliged *or* grateful if you would provide me with this information as soon as possible

reconnaître [91] [rəkɔnɛtr] **VT 1** *(air, personne, pas)* to recognize; **je t'ai reconnu à ta démarche** I recognized you *or* I could tell it was you by your walk; **je ne l'aurais pas reconnue, elle a vieilli de dix ans!** I wouldn't have known (it was) her, she looks ten years older!; **on ne le reconnaît plus** you wouldn't recognize *or* know him now; **je te reconnais bien (là)!** that's just like you!, that's you all over!; **tu veux fonder une famille? je ne te reconnais plus!** you want to start a family? that's not like you at all *or* you've changed your tune!; **il a été reconnu par plusieurs témoins** he was identified by several witnesses; **on reconnaît bien là la marque du génie** you can't fail to recognize the stamp of genius; **je reconnais bien là ta mauvaise foi!** that's just typical of your insincerity!

2 *(admettre → torts)* to recognize, to acknowledge, to admit; *(→ aptitude, talent, vérité)* to acknowledge, to recognize; **il faut au moins lui r. cette qualité** you have to say this for him/her; **l'accusé reconnaît-il les faits?** does the accused acknowledge the facts?; **il est difficile de lui faire r. ses erreurs** it's hard to get him/her to acknowledge he's/she's wrong; **sa prestation fut décevante, il faut bien le r.** it has to be admitted that his/her performance was disappointing; **elle est douée, il faut le r.!** she's clever, you've got to admit it *or* give her that!; **je reconnais que j'ai eu tort** I admit I was wrong; **elle refuse de r. qu'elle est malade** she won't admit *or* acknowledge that she's ill; **il n'a jamais reconnu avoir falsifié les documents** he never admitted to having falsified the documents

3 *Jur & Pol (État, chef de file)* to recognize; *(enfant)* to recognize legally; *(dette, document, signature)* to authenticate; **tous le reconnaissent comme leur maître** they all acknowledge him as their master; **la presse a reconnu en lui le futur chef du parti** the press acknowledged him as the future leader of the party; *Jur* **r. la compétence d'un tribunal** to acknowledge the competence of a court; **être reconnu coupable** to be found guilty; **organisme reconnu d'utilité publique** officially approved organization; **r. un droit à qn** to recognize *or* to acknowledge sb's right; **je ne reconnais à personne le droit de me juger** nobody has the right to judge me

4 *(explorer)* to reconnoitre; **il envoya dix hommes r. le terrain** he ordered ten men to go and reconnoitre the ground; **l'équipe de tournage est allée r. les lieux** the film crew went to have a look round (the place)

▸**se reconnaître VPR 1** *(emploi réfléchi) (physiquement, moralement)* to see oneself; **je me reconnais dans la réaction de ma sœur** I can see myself reacting in the same way as my sister; **je ne me reconnais pas dans votre description** I don't recognize myself in your description

2 *(emploi réciproque)* to recognize each other

3 *(emploi passif)* to be recognizable; **un poisson frais se reconnaît à l'odeur** you can tell a fresh fish by the smell

4 *(se retrouver)* **je ne me reconnais plus dans ma propre ville** I can't even find my way about *or* around my own home town any more; **mets des étiquettes sur tes dossiers, sinon comment veux-tu qu'on s'y reconnaisse?** label your files, otherwise we'll get completely confused; **la situation est trop embrouillée, je ne m'y reconnais plus** the situation is too complicated, I'm totally confused

5 *(s'avouer)* **se r. coupable** to admit one's guilt

reconnecter [3] [rəkɔnɛkte] **VT** to reconnect

▸**se reconnecter VPR** *Ordinat* to reconnect, to get back on line

reconnu, -e [rəkɔny] **PP** *voir* **reconnaître**

ADJ 1 *(admis)* recognized, accepted; **c'est un fait r.** it's a recognized *or* an accepted fact; **ce diplôme n'est pas r. dans tous les pays** this diploma is not recognized in all countries **2** *(célébré)* famous, well-known

reconquérir [39] [rəkɔ̃kerir] **VT 1** *(territoire, peuple)* to reconquer, to recapture **2** *(liberté, honneur, avantage)* to win back, to recover **3** *(personne, estime, amitié)* to win back

reconquête [rəkɔ̃kɛt] **NF 1** *(d'un territoire, d'un peuple)* reconquest, recapture **2** *(de la liberté, de l'honneur, d'un avantage)* winning back *(UNCOUNT)*, recovery

reconquiert *etc voir* **reconquérir**

reconquis, -e [rəkɔ̃ki, -iz] **PP** *voir* **reconquérir**

reconsidérer [18] [rəkɔ̃sidere] **VT** to reconsider

reconstituant, -e [rəkɔ̃stitɥɑ̃, -ɑ̃t] **ADJ** *(aliment, boisson)* fortifying; *(traitement)* restorative

NM restorative

reconstituer [7] [rəkɔ̃stitɥe] **VT 1** *(reformer → groupe)* to bring together again, to reconstitute; *(→ armée, gouvernement)* to reconstitute; *(→ société, parti)* to revive; *(→ capital)* to rebuild, to build up again; *(→ fichier)* to recreate; **r. des stocks** to replenish stocks, to restock; **bois reconstitué** chipboard; **lait reconstitué** reconstituted milk

2 *(recréer → objet archéologique)* to piece *or* to put back together; *(→ histoire, meurtre)* to reconstruct; **ils ont reconstitué un décor d'époque** they created a period setting

reconstitution [rəkɔ̃stitysjɔ̃] **NF 1** *(d'un groupe)* reconstituting *(UNCOUNT)*, bringing together again *(UNCOUNT)*; *(d'une armée, d'un gouvernement)* reconstitution; *(d'une société, d'un parti)* revival; *(d'un capital)* rebuilding *(UNCOUNT)*, building up again; *(d'un fichier)* recreating *(UNCOUNT)* **2** *(d'un objet archéologique)* piecing back together; *(d'une histoire, d'un meurtre)* reconstruction; **r. historique** *(spectacle)* historical reconstruction

reconstructeur, -trice [rəkɔ̃stryktœr, -tris] **ADJ** reconstructive; **chirurgie reconstructrice** reconstructive surgery

reconstruction [rəkɔ̃stryksjɔ̃] **NF 1** *(gén)* reconstruction, rebuilding; **en r.** being rebuilt **2** *Ling* reconstruction

reconstructrice [rəkɔ̃stryktris] *voir* **reconstructeur**

reconstruire [98] [rəkɔ̃strɥir] **VT 1** *(bâtiment)* to reconstruct, to rebuild; *(fortune, réputation)* to rebuild, to build up again; **r. sa vie** to put one's life back together, to rebuild one's life **2** *Ling* to reconstruct

reconvention [rəkɔ̃vɑ̃sjɔ̃] **NF** *Jur* counterclaim

reconventionnel, -elle [rəkɔ̃vɑ̃sjɔnɛl] **ADJ** *Jur* **demande reconventionnelle** counterclaim

reconventionnellement [rəkɔ̃vɑ̃sjɔnɛlmɑ̃] **ADV** by counterclaim

reconversion [rəkɔ̃vɛrsjɔ̃] **NF** *(d'une usine)* conversion (**en** into); *(d'un individu)* retraining; **r. économique** economic restructuring; **r. industrielle** industrial redeployment

reconvertir [32] [rəkɔ̃vɛrtir] **VT 1** *(usine)* to convert (**en** into) **2** *(armes)* to convert

▸**se reconvertir VPR** *(employé)* to retrain; **il s'est reconverti dans l'informatique** he retrained and went into IT; **l'entreprise s'est reconvertie dans le bâtiment** the company moved into construction

reconvocation [rəkɔ̃vɔkasjɔ̃] **NF** *Pol (du Parlement, d'un ministre)* recall

reconvoquer [3] [rəkɔ̃vɔke] **VT** *Pol (Parlement, ministre)* to recall

recopier [9] [rəkɔpje] **VT 1** *(mettre au propre)* to write up, to make *or* to take a fair copy of **2** *(copier à nouveau)* to copy again, to make another copy of

record [rəkɔr] **NM 1** *Sport & Fig* record; **battre un r. de vitesse** to break a speed record; **r. de hauteur/longueur** high/*Br* long *or Am* broad jump record; **le r. du monde** the world record; **la marque affiche partout des records de vente** the brand is achieving record sales everywhere; *Fam* **tu bats tous les records d'idiotie!** they don't come any more stupid than you!; *Fam* **ça bat tous les records** that beats everything *or* the lot

2 *(comme adj, avec ou sans trait d'union)* record *(avant n)*; **l'inflation a atteint le chiffre-r. de 200 pour cent** inflation has risen to a record *or* record-breaking 200 percent; **en un temps-r.** in record time

recordage [rəkɔrdaʒ] **NM** *(d'une raquette)* restringing

recorder [3] [rəkɔrde] **VT** *(raquette)* to restring

recordman [rəkɔrdman] *(pl* **recordmans** *ou* **recordmen** [-mɛn]) **NM** (men's) record holder; **le r. du 5000 mètres** the record holder for the (men's) 5,000 metres

recordwoman [rəkɔrdwuman] *(pl* **recordwomans** *ou* **recordwomen** [-mɛn]) **NF** (women's) record holder; **la r. du saut en hauteur** the record holder for the women's high jump

recorriger [17] [rəkɔriʒe] **VT** *(erreur)* to recorrect, to correct again; *(dissertation)* to *Br* mark *or Am* grade again

recoucher [3] [rəkuʃe] **VT** *(personne)* to put back to bed; *(objet)* to lay down again

VI *Fam* **r. avec qn** to sleep with sb again

▸**se recoucher VPR** to go back to bed

recoudre [86] [rəkudr] **VT 1** *(bouton, badge etc)* to sew on again; *(accroc, ourlet etc)* to sew up again **2** *Méd* to sew *or* to stitch up (again)

recoupage [rəkupaʒ] **NM** *Couture* recutting

recoupe [rəkup] **NF 1** *(boisson)* diluted spirits **2** *Agr (de fourrage)* aftermath; *(en meunerie)* middlings

recoupement [rəkupmɑ̃] **NM 1** *(vérification)* crosschecking; **faire un r.** to crosscheck, to do a crosscheck; **procéder par recoupements** to carry out a crosscheck **2** *Constr (action)* stepping; *(résultat)* retreat **3** *Géom* resection

recouper [3] [rəkupe] **VT 1** *(couper à nouveau)* **r. de la viande** to cut *or* to carve some more meat; **je vous recoupe une tranche de gâteau?** shall I cut you another slice *or* piece of cake?

2 *Couture* to cut again, to recut

3 *(concorder avec)* to tally with, to match up with

VI *Cartes* to cut again

▸**se recouper VPR 1** *(se blesser → personne)* to cut oneself again

2 *(ensembles, routes)* to intersect

3 *(statistiques, témoignages)* to tally, to confirm one another; **les deux versions ne se recoupent pas** the two stories don't tally

recouponnement [rəkupɔnmɑ̃] **NM** *Bourse* renewal of coupons

recouponner [3] [rəkupɔne] **VT** *Bourse* to renew the coupons of

recourbé, -e [rəkurbe] **ADJ** *(gén)* bent, curved; *(cils)* curved; *(nez)* hooked

recourbement [rəkurbəmɑ̃] **NM** *(état)* curve; *(action)* curving

recourber [3] [rəkurbe] **VT** to bend, to curve

▸**se recourber VPR** to bend, to curve

recourbure [rəkurbyr] **NF** bend, curve

rec–rec

recourir [45] [rəkurir] **VT** to run again; **r. une course** to (run a) race again

VI 1 *Sport* to run *or* to race again; **il n'a pas pu r. après sa chute** he wasn't able to run again after his fall **2** *Jur* to appeal (**contre** against)

❑ **recourir à VT IND 1** *(personne)* **r. à qn** to appeal *or* to turn to sb; **en cas de désaccord, il faudra r. à un expert** in the event of a disagreement you will have to turn to *or* to seek the help of an expert **2** *(objet, méthode etc)* **r. à qch** to resort to sth

recours [rəkur] **NM 1** *(ressource)* recourse, resort; **c'est notre dernier r.** this is our last resort *or* the last course left open to us; **c'est sans r.** there's nothing we can do about it; **avoir r. à** *(moyen)* to resort to; *(personne)* to turn to; **nous n'aurons r. à l'expulsion qu'en dernière limite** we shall only resort to *or* have recourse to eviction if absolutely necessary; **je me vois contraint d'avoir r. à vous** I am forced to turn to you

2 *Jur* appeal; **r. en annulation** = application for a judicial review of administrative action; **r. en appréciation de légalité** = application for review of legality; **r. en cassation** appeal (to the appellate court); *Can* **r. collectif** class action; **r. pour excès de pouvoir** (demand for) remedy of ultra vires; **r. en grâce** *(pour une remise de peine)* petition for pardon; *(pour une commutation de peine)* petition for clemency *or* remission; **r. gracieux** application for an ex gratia settlement; **r. en indemnité** action for damages *(in the administrative courts)*; **r. en interprétation** petition for interpretation; **r. de pleine juridiction** = claim against the state made in the administrative courts; **r. en référé** = emergency appeal to a judge; **r. en révision** application to reopen proceedings; **r. contre des tiers** recourse against third parties; *Assur* **s'assurer contre le r. des tiers** to insure against a third-party claim

❑ **en dernier recours ADV** as a last resort

recouru, -e [rəkury] **PP** *voir* **recourir**

recousait *etc voir* **recoudre**

recouvert, -e [rəkuvɛr, -ɛrt] **PP** *voir* **recouvrir**

recouvrable [rəkuvrabl] **ADJ** *(dette, facture)* collectable, recoverable; *(impôt)* collectable

recouvrage [rəkuvraʒ] **NM** recovering, re-upholstering

recouvrement [rəkuvrəmɑ̃] **NM 1** *(récupération → d'une somme)* collecting, collection; *(→ de la santé)* recovering, recovery

2 *Fin (perception)* collection; *(d'une créance)* recovery; **l'impôt est mis en r. après le 31 octobre** payment of tax is due from *Br* 31 October *or Am* October 31; **date de mise en r.** date due, due date; **modalités de r.** methods of payment; **r. amiable des créances** amicable recovery of debt; **r. des pensions alimentaires** recovery of alimony

3 *(d'une surface)* covering (over)

4 *Constr & Menuis* lap

5 *Ordinat & Math* overlap

6 *Géol* overlap, overthrust

❑ **recouvrements NMPL** *(dettes)* outstanding debts

recouvrer [3] [rəkuvre] **VT 1** *(récupérer → santé, biens)* to recover; *(→ liberté)* to regain; **elle n'a pas recouvré tous ses moyens** she hasn't recovered *or* regained the full use of her faculties; **il a recouvré l'usage de sa jambe** he got back *or* recovered the use of his leg; **laissez-lui le temps de r. ses esprits** give him/her time to recover his/her wits **2** *Fin (percevoir)* to collect, to recover; **créances à r.** outstanding debts

recouvrir [34] [rəkuvrir] **VT 1** *(couvrir)* to cover (**de** in *or* with); **r. un gâteau de chocolat** to coat a cake with chocolate; **un fauteuil recouvert de velours** an armchair covered in velvet; **ajouter suffisamment d'eau pour r. les légumes** add enough water to cover the vegetables

2 *(couvrir à nouveau → personne)* to cover (up) again; *(→ siège)* to re-cover, to reupholster; *(→ livre)* to re-cover

3 *(englober)* to cover; **le mot ne recouvre pas les mêmes notions dans les deux langues** the word doesn't cover the same concepts in the two languages

▶**se recouvrir VPR 1** *(remettre des vêtements)* **recouvre-toi, le soleil s'est caché** cover yourself up again, the sun's gone in

2 *Météo* to get cloudy again

3 *(surface)* **se r. de moisissure** to become covered with *or* in mould; **la glace s'est recouverte de buée** the mirror steamed up

recracher [3] [rəkraʃe] **VT 1** *(cracher)* to spit out (again); **r. un noyau** to spit out a stone; *Fam* **le distributeur de billets a recraché ma carte** the *Br* cashpoint *or Am* ATM spat out my card **2** *Fam (cours, leçon)* to regurgitate

VI to spit again

récré [rekre] **NF** *Fam (dans le primaire) Br* playtime, *Am* recess; *(dans le secondaire) Br* break, *Am* recess

récréance [rekreɑ̃s] **NF 1** *Anciennement Jur* = provisional usufruct of ecclesiastical estate under dispute at law **2** *(en diplomatie)* **lettres de r.** (ambassador's) letters of recall

récréatif, -ive [rekreatif, -iv] **ADJ** recreational; **une journée récréative** a day of recreation *or* relaxation; **lecture récréative** light reading

recréation [rəkreasjɔ̃] **NF** *Ordinat* **la r. de tous les fichiers me prendra des heures** it will take me hours to recreate all the files

récréation [rekreasjɔ̃] **NF 1** *Scol (dans le primaire) Br* playtime, *Am* recess; *(dans le secondaire) Br* break, *Am* recess **2** *(délassement)* recreation, leisure activity; **le tricot/la télé, c'est ma r.** knitting/watching TV is how I relax, I relax by knitting/watching TV

récréative [rekreativ] *voir* **récréatif**

recréer [15] [rəkree] **VT 1** *(suivant un modèle)* to recreate **2** *(créer)* to create; **il recrée un décor à son goût** he is creating a decor more to his liking

récréer [15] [rekree] *Arch ou Littéraire* **VT** to entertain, to amuse, to divert

▶**se récréer VPR** to entertain *or* to amuse *or* to divert oneself

récrément [rekremɑ̃] **NM** *Arch* recrement

recrépir [32] [rəkrepir] **VT** *Constr* to roughcast

recrépissage [rəkrepisaʒ] **NM** resurfacing *or* redoing with roughcast

recreuser [5] [rəkrøze] **VT** *(creuser → davantage)* to dig deeper; *(→ un nouveau trou)* to dig again; *Fig (question)* to dig deeper *or* to go deeper into

récrier [10] [rekrije] **se récrier VPR 1** *(protester)* to cry out, to protest (**contre** against) **2** *Littéraire (s'exclamer)* to cry out, to exclaim; **se r. de surprise/joie** to cry out *or* to exclaim in surprise/joy

récriminateur, -trice [rekriminatœr, -tris] **ADJ** recriminative, recriminatory

NM,F recriminator

récrimination [rekriminasjɔ̃] **NF** recrimination, protest

récriminatrice [rekriminatris] *voir* **récriminateur**

récriminer [3] [rekrimine] **VI** *(critiquer)* to recriminate (**contre** against)

récrire [rekrir] = **réécrire**

recristallisation [rəkristalizasjɔ̃] **NF** recrystallization

recristalliser [3] [rəkristalize] **VT** to recrystallize

VI to recrystallize

recroître [93] [rəkrwatr] **VI** to grow again

recroquevillé, -e [rəkrɔkvije] **ADJ 1** *(confortablement)* curled up; *(dans l'inconfort)* hunched *or* huddled up **2** *(feuille, pétale)* curled *or* shrivelled up

recroqueviller [3] [rəkrɔkvije] **se recroqueviller VPR 1** *(confortablement)* to curl up; *(dans l'inconfort)* to hunch *or* to huddle up **2** *(feuille, pétale)* to shrivel *or* to curl (up)

recru, -e[1] [rəkry] **ADJ** *Littéraire* **être r. de fatigue** to be exhausted

recrû [rəkry] **NM** new growth

recrudescence [rəkrydɛsɑ̃s] **NF** *(aggravation → d'une maladie)* aggravation, worsening; *(→ de la fièvre)* new bout; *(→ d'une épidémie, d'un incendie)* fresh *or* new outbreak; *(→ du froid)* new spell; *(→ de la délinquance)* upsurge (**de** in *or* of); **la r. du terrorisme** the new wave *or* outbreak of terrorism; **la r. de la violence/des bombardements** the renewed violence/bombing; **nous nous attendons à une r. des pluies** we are expecting more frequent spells of rain

recrudescent, -e [rəkrydɛsɑ̃, -ɑ̃t] **ADJ** *Littéraire* increasing, mounting, *Sout* recrudescent

recrue[2] [rəkry] **NF 1** *Mil* recruit **2** *Fig* recruit, new member; **faire de nouvelles recrues** to gain new recruits

recrutement [rəkrytmɑ̃] **NM** recruiting, recruitment *(UNCOUNT)*; **le r. du personnel s'effectue par concours** staff are recruited by competitive examination

recruter [3] [rəkryte] **VT 1** *(engager)* to recruit; **l'entreprise recrute des ingénieurs en informatique** the firm is recruiting computer engineers; *Hum* **nous recrutons des bonnes volontés pour déménager** do we have any volunteers to help with the move?

2 *Mil & Pol* to recruit, to enlist; **les membres du parti sont recrutés dans les milieux ouvriers** party members are recruited from the working classes

USAGE ABSOLU to recruit; **en ce moment, les sociétés d'informatique recrutent** computing companies are recruiting (new staff) at the moment

▶**se recruter VPR 1** *(être engagé)* to be recruited (**parmi** from among); **les ingénieurs se recrutent sur diplôme** engineers are recruited on the basis of their qualifications

2 se r. dans *(provenir de)* to come from; **les futurs ministres se recrutent généralement dans les grandes écoles** future ministers generally come from the "grandes écoles"

recruteur, -euse [rəkrytœr, -øz] **ADJ** recruiting; **sergent r.** recruiting sergeant

NM,F recruiter

recta [rɛkta] **ADV** *Fam* **payer r.** to pay on the nail

rectal, -e, -aux, -ales [rɛktal, -o] **ADJ** *Anat* rectal

rectangle [rɛktɑ̃gl] **NM 1** *(forme)* rectangle, oblong; *Ordinat* **r. de sélection** selection box **2** *Géom* rectangle

ADJ triangle r. right-angled triangle

rectangulaire [rɛktɑ̃gylɛr] **ADJ 1** *(forme)* rectangular, oblong **2** *Géom* rectangular

recteur, -trice [rɛktœr, -tris] **ADJ 1** *Orn* **penne rectrice** tail feather

2 père r. *(chez les jésuites)* rector

NM,F 1 *Scol & Univ (d'académie)* = chief administrative officer of an education authority, *Br* ≃ (Chief) Education Officer, *Am* ≃ Commissioner of the State Board of Education; *(d'une université catholique)* ≃ rector

2 *Belg Univ* principal, *Br* vice-chancellor, *Am* president

NM *Rel (d'un sanctuaire)* ≃ rector; *(en Bretagne)* priest, rector

❑ **rectrice NF** *Orn* rectrix

> *Culture*
>
> **RECTEUR**
>
> The head of an "académie", this representative of the Minister of Education administers scholastic and university regulations (overseeing curriculum, staffing etc).

rectifiable [rɛktifjabl] **ADJ 1** *(réparable)* rectifiable; **les erreurs ne sont pas rectifiables après coup** mistakes cannot be rectified afterwards **2** *Chim* rectifiable

rectificateur [rɛktifikatœr] **NM** *Chim* rectifier

rectificatif, -ive [rɛktifikatif, -iv] **ADJ** correcting; **mention rectificative** correction

NM correction, rectification

rectification [rɛktifikasjɔ̃] **NF 1** *(d'un document, d'un texte)* amendment, correction; *(d'un calcul)* correction, adjustment; *(d'une erreur)* rectification, correction; *(d'un compte, d'un instrument)* adjustment; *(d'une courbe, d'une frontière)* adjustment, rectification; *(d'un alignement)* straightening; **je voudrais faire** *ou* **apporter une r.** I'd like to make a correction; **apporter une r. à une déclaration** to correct a statement; *Journ* **droit de r.** ≃ right of reply

2 *Chim & Math* rectification

3 *Tech* precision grinding

rectificative [rɛktifikativ] *voir* **rectificatif**

rectifier [9] [rɛktifje] **VT 1** *(corriger → document, texte)* to amend, to correct; *(→ calcul)* to correct, to adjust; *(→ erreur)* to rectify, to correct; *(ajuster → compte, instrument)* to adjust; *(→ courbe, frontière)* to adjust, to rectify; *(→ alignement)* to straighten; **r. le tir** *Mil* to adjust the range; *Fig* to take a slightly different tack; **"il est banquier", rectifia-t-elle** "he's a banker," she corrected him/me/*etc*

2 *Chim & Math* to rectify

3 *Tech* to precision grind

4 *Fam (casser)* to break▪

5 *Fam (dépouiller)* to rob■, to mug, *Br* to do over

6 *Fam (tuer)* to bump off; **se faire r.** to get bumped off

▶**se rectifier** VPR *Fam (s'enivrer)* to have a skinful, to get wasted

rectifieur, -euse [rɛktifjœr, -øz] *Tech* NM,F grinding-machine operator

◻ **rectifieuse** NF *(machine)* grinding machine

rectiligne [rɛktiliɲ] ADJ *(droit)* straight; *Math* rectilinear

NM *Math* rectilinear angle

rectilinéaire [rɛktilineɛr] ADJ rectilinear

rection [rɛksjɔ̃] NF *Ling* rection

rectite [rɛktit] NF *Méd* proctitis

rectitude [rɛktityd] NF **1** *(droiture)* (moral) rectitude, uprightness; **agir avec r.** to behave correctly *or* with integrity **2** *Littéraire (exactitude → d'un raisonnement)* correctness, soundness **3** *Littéraire (d'une ligne)* straightness

recto [rɛkto] NM front of a page, *Spéc* recto; **n'écrivez qu'au r.** write on this side only; **voir au r.** see over

◻ **recto verso** ADV on both sides

recto-colite [rɛktɔkɔlit] *(pl* **recto-colites)** NF *Méd* proctocolitis

rectoral, -e, -aux, -ales [rɛktɔral, -o] ADJ *Br* ≃ of the (Chief) Education Officer, *Am* ≃ of the State Board of Education; **décision rectorale** ≃ decision by *or* emanating from *Br* the Education Office *or Am* the State Board of Education

rectorat [rɛktɔra] NM **1** *Univ (d'une académie → administration) Br* ≃ Education Office, *Am* ≃ State Board of Education; *(→ bâtiment) Br* ≃ Education offices, *Am* ≃ Board of Education offices **2** *(chez les jésuites)* rectorship

rectoraux [rɛktɔro] *voir* **rectoral**

rectoscope [rɛktɔskɔp] NM *Méd* proctoscope

rectoscopie [rɛktɔskɔpi] NF proctoscopy

rectrice [rɛktris] *voir* **recteur**

rectum [rɛktɔm] NM *Anat* rectum

reçu, -e [rəsy] PP *voir* **recevoir**

ADJ *(usages)* accepted, recognized; *(opinion)* received

NM,F *(candidat)* successful candidate; **il n'y a que dix reçus** only ten people passed

NM *(quittance)* receipt; *Can* **r. de caisse** (till) receipt; **r. certifié** accountable receipt; **r. en duplicata** receipt in duplicate; **r. d'espèces** cash receipt; **r. libératoire** receipt in full discharge

recueil [rəkœj] NM *(de chansons, de recettes)* collection; *(de poèmes)* collection, selection, anthology; *(de lois)* compendium, body; **r. de morceaux choisis** selection, anthology; *Ordinat* **r. de données** data collection

recueillement [rəkœjmɑ̃] NM contemplation, meditation; **écouter qch avec r.** to listen reverently to sth

recueillera *etc voir* **recueillir**

recueilli, -e [rəkœji] ADJ contemplative, meditative; **un public très r.** a very attentive audience; **un visage r.** a composed expression

recueillir [41] [rəkœjir] VT **1** *(récolter → miel, pollen)* to gather, to collect; *(→ eaux de pluie)* to collect; *(→ votes, suffrages)* to win; *Fig* **il a recueilli les félicitations du jury** he was congratulated by the board of examiners; *Fig* **r. le fruit de son travail** to reap the fruit of one's labour

2 *(renseignements)* to collect, to obtain; *(déposition)* to take; *(argent, fonds)* to collect; **r. les traditions locales** to collect *or* to record local traditions; *Littéraire* **j'ai recueilli ses dernières paroles** I received his/her last words; **propos recueillis par Daniel Renault** *(dans un article de journal)* (story by) Daniel Renault

3 *(héberger → personne)* to take in; **r. un oiseau tombé du nid** to take care of a bird which has fallen from its nest

▶**se recueillir** VPR *(penser)* to spend some moments in silence; *(prier)* to pray; **recueillons-nous un instant avant de nous séparer** before we go our separate ways let us pray for a moment; **le chef de l'État s'est recueilli devant le cénotaphe** the head of state reflected a while in front of the cenotaph; **aller se r. sur la tombe de qn** to spend some moments in silence at sb's graveside

recuire [98] [rəkɥir] VT **1** *Culin (à l'eau)* to cook longer; *(au four)* to cook longer in the oven **2** *(métal, verre)* to anneal; *(lingot)* to soak

VI **faire r. un rôti** to recook a joint; **faire r. un gâteau** to rebake a cake

recuit [rəkɥi] NM *(du métal, du verre)* annealing; **r. de normalisation/recristallisation** full normalizing/annealing

recul [rəkyl] NM **1** *(mouvement → gén)* backward movement; *(→ d'un glacier, d'une armée)* retreat; *(→ d'un cheval)* backing; *(→ d'un fusil)* recoil, kick; *(→ d'un canon)* recoil; **il eut un mouvement de r.** he stepped back; *(brusquement)* he recoiled

2 *(distance)* **as-tu assez de r. pour juger du tableau/prendre la photo?** are you far enough away to judge the painting/to take the photograph?; **on n'a pas assez de r. pour admirer le bâtiment** *(dans une rue étroite)* you can't get back far enough to admire the building

3 *(réflexion)* **avec le r.** retrospectively, with (the benefit of) hindsight; **prendre du r. par rapport à un événement** to stand back (in order) to assess an event; **je manque de r. pour juger** I'm too closely involved *or* too close to be able to judge; **nous n'avons pas assez de r. pour juger des effets à long terme** it's too early *or* not enough time has passed to assess what long-term effects there might be

4 *(baisse)* fall, drop, decline; **le r. de la mortalité** the downturn *or* decline in the death rate; **le r. de l'industrie textile** the decline of the textile industry; **le r. du yen par rapport au dollar** the fall of the yen against the dollar; **les ventes ont subi un r.** sales have dropped; **un r. des valeurs morales** a falling off of moral values

reculade [rəkylad] NF *(d'une armée)* retreat; *(politique)* climbdown, back-tracking *(UNCOUNT)*

reculé, -e [rəkyle] ADJ **1** *(dans l'espace)* remote, far-off; **ils habitent dans un coin r.** they live in an out-of-the-way place **2** *(dans le temps)* remote, far-off, distant; **les temps les plus reculés** the distant past

◻ **reculée** NF *Géog* blind valley

reculement [rəkylmɑ̃] NM *(pièce de harnais)* breeching

reculer [3] [rəkyle] VT **1** *(dans l'espace)* to push *or* to move back; **r. une clôture d'un mètre** to move a fence back by one metre; *Fig* **r. les limites du possible** to push back the frontiers of what is considered possible

2 *(dans le temps → rendez-vous)* to delay, to postpone, to defer; *(→ date)* to postpone, to put back; *(→ décision)* to defer, to postpone, to put off; **r. la date de son départ** to postpone one's departure

VI **1** *(aller en arrière → à pied)* to step *or* to go *or* to move back; *(→ en voiture)* to reverse, to move back; **recule d'un pas!** take one step backwards!; **elle recula de dégoût** she recoiled *or* drew back in disgust; **reculez ou je tire!** back off *or* get back or I'll shoot!; **mets le frein à main, la voiture recule!** put the handbrake on, the car is rolling backwards!; **il a heurté le mur en reculant** he backed *or* reversed into the wall; **faire r. un cheval** to back a horse; **la police a fait r. la foule** the police moved the crowd back

2 *(céder du terrain → falaise, forêt, eaux)* to recede; *Mil* to fall back, to retreat; *Fig* **faire r. les frontières de la science** to push *or* to roll back the frontiers of science

3 *(renoncer)* to retreat, to shrink (back), to draw back; **il est trop tard pour r.** it's too late to draw back *or* to pull out; **il n'est pas homme à r. devant les difficultés** he is not the kind of man to shrink back in the face of difficulties; **il ne recule devant rien** nothing daunts him; **r. devant l'ennemi** to retreat in the face of the enemy; **r. devant le danger** to retreat in the face of danger; **cela en a fait r. plus d'un** that's put off *or* daunted more than one person; **le prix m'a fait r.** I backed down when I saw the price; **c'est r. pour mieux sauter** that's just putting off the inevitable

4 *(faiblir → cours, valeur)* to fall, to weaken; *(→ épidémie, criminalité, mortalité)* to recede; **le yen recule par rapport au dollar** the yen is losing ground *or* falling against the dollar; **faire r. la pauvreté** to reduce (the level of) poverty; **l'isolement des malades a fait r. l'épidémie** they managed to get the epidemic under control by putting people in quarantine

5 *(avoir un mouvement de recul)* to recoil

▶**se reculer** VPR *Fam* to step *or* to move back; **recule-toi!** get back!

reculons [rəkylɔ̃] **à reculons** ADV **1** *(en marche arrière)* backwards; **marcher** *ou* **aller à r.** to walk backwards; **descendre un escalier à r.** to go downstairs backwards; **sortir à r.** to back out; *Hum* **avancer à r.** to be getting nowhere **2** *(avec réticence)* under protest; **faire qch à r.** to do sth unwillingly *or* under protest

reculotter [3] [rəkylɔte] VT **r. un enfant** to put a child's *Br* trousers *or Am* pants back on

▶**se reculotter** VPR to put one's *Br* trousers *or Am* pants back on

récup [rekyp] NF *Fam* **1 de la r.** *(des matériaux de récupération)* scrap **2** *Pol (récupération idéologique)* hijacking■, takeover■

récupérabilité [rekyperabilite] NF *(d'un objet)* salvage value

récupérable [rekyperabl] ADJ **1** *(objet)* salvageable, worth rescuing; **vêtements récupérables** (still) serviceable clothes

2 *(personne)* redeemable; **les récidivistes sont-ils récupérables?** can persistent offenders be re-educated?

3 *(temps)* recoverable; **ces heures supplémentaires sont récupérables** time off will be given in lieu of overtime worked

4 *Fin (TVA)* reclaimable

récupérateur, -trice [rekyperatœr, -tris] ADJ **1** *(qui recycle)* **industrie récupératrice** = industry based on reclaimed or recycled materials **2** *(qui repose)* **sommeil r.** refreshing *or* restorative sleep

NM,F = industrialist or builder working with reclaimed materials

NM *Tech* recuperator; **r. de chaleur** heat economizer

récupération [rekyperasjɔ̃] NF **1** *(après séparation, perte)* recovery; **la r. de sa voiture à la fourrière lui a coûté cher** it cost him/her a lot to get his/her car out of the pound

2 *École* recycling, reclaiming; **matériau de r.** scrap *(UNCOUNT)*

3 *(de sportif)* recovery

4 *Pétr* **r. assistée** enhanced recovery; **taux de r.** (rate of) recovery

5 *Ind* **r. de chaleur** heat recovery; **chaudière à r.** recuperative *or* regenerative heater

6 *Pol* hijacking, takeover; **il y a eu r. du mouvement par les extrémistes** the movement has been hijacked *or* taken over by extremists

7 *(au travail)* making up; **quand je fais des heures supplémentaires, j'ai des jours de r.** when I work overtime, I get time off in exchange *or* in lieu

8 *Astron* recovery

9 *Ordinat (d'un fichier, de données)* retrieval, recovery

10 *Fin (d'une dette)* recovery; *(de TVA)* reclaiming; *(des débours)* recoupment

récupératrice [rekyperatris] *voir* **récupérateur**

récupérer [18] [rekypere] VT **1** *(retrouver → gén)* to get back; *(→ bagages)* to retrieve, to reclaim; **il doit r. son chien au chenil** he's got to pick up *or* to collect his dog from the kennels; **elle est passée r. ses affaires** she dropped by to pick up her things; **je passe te r. en voiture** I'll come and pick you up; **je n'ai jamais pu r. mon livre** I never managed to get my book back; **veux-tu r. ton anorak?** do you want your anorak back?; **j'ai récupéré l'usage de ma main gauche** I recovered the use of my left hand; **il a récupéré toutes ses forces** *(il s'est reposé)* he has recuperated, he's back to normal; **tout a brûlé, ils n'ont rien pu r.** everything was destroyed by the fire, they didn't manage to salvage anything

2 *(pour utiliser → chiffons, papier, verre, ferraille)* to salvage; *(→ chaleur, énergie)* to save; **j'ai récupéré des chaises dont personne ne voulait** I've rescued some chairs no one wanted; **je ne jette rien, je récupère tout** I don't throw anything away, I save everything; **regarde si tu peux r. quelques pommes** see if you can save a few apples

3 *(jour de congé)* to make up for, to compensate for; **on récupère ce jour férié vendredi prochain** we are making up for this public

holiday by working next Friday; **les jours fériés travaillés seront récupérés** employees will be allowed time off in lieu of public holidays worked

4 *Pol* to hijack, to take over; **le mouvement a été récupéré par le gouvernement** the movement has been hijacked by the government for its own ends

5 *Ordinat (fichier, données)* to retrieve, to recover

6 *Fin (TVA)* to reclaim; *(dette)* to recover; **r. ses débours** to recoup one's expenditure; **r. sa mise** to recoup one's outlay

VI *(se remettre)* to recover, to recuperate; **il en a pour plusieurs jours à r., avec le décalage horaire** with the time difference it will take him a few days to get back to normal *or* to recover *or* to recuperate; **j'ai besoin de r.** *(de prendre des vacances)* I need to get my breath back, I need to relax

récurage [rekyraʒ] **NM** *(nettoyage)* scouring; *(avec une brosse)* scrubbing

récurant, -e [rekyrɑ̃, -ɑ̃t] **ADJ** scouring

NM scouring cream *or* agent

récurer [3] [rekyre] **VT** *(nettoyer)* to scour; *(avec une brosse)* to scrub

récurrence [rekyrɑ̃s] **NF 1** *(gén) & Méd* recurrence **2** *Math (d'une décimale)* recurrence; *(induction)* induction

récurrent, -e [rekyrɑ̃, -ɑ̃t] **ADJ 1** *(thème, son, mot)* recurrent, recurring; *Littérature* **héros r.** recurring character **2** *Méd (fièvre)* recurrent, relapsing **3** *Anat* **nerf r.** nervus laryngeus recurrens **4** *Ordinat & Math* **suite** *ou* **série récurrente** recursion series **5** *Écon* **chômage r.** periodic *or* recurrent unemployment; **coûts récurrents** recurrent *or* running costs

récursif, -ive [rekyrsif, -iv] **ADJ** recursive

récursivité [rekyrsivite] **NF** recursiveness

récursoire [rekyrswar] **ADJ action r.** cross claim

récusable [rekyzabl] **ADJ** *Jur (témoignage)* challengeable, *Sout* impugnable; *(juré, témoin)* challengeable; **c'est une affirmation r.** that statement is open to challenge

récusation [rekyzasjɔ̃] **NF** *(d'une thèse, d'un témoin)* challenging; **r. de juré/d'arbitre** challenge of *or* exception to *or* objection to a member of the jury/an arbitrator; **droit de r.** right to challenge

récuser [3] [rekyze] **VT** *(thèse)* to challenge; *Jur (juge, juré, expert)* to challenge, to take exception to, to object to; *(décision, témoignage)* to challenge, *Sout* to impugn; **r. la compétence de la cour** to challenge the competence of the court

▶**se récuser VPR 1** *(lors d'un procès)* to declare oneself incompetent

2 *(lors d'une entrevue, d'un débat)* to refuse to give an opinion, to decline to (make any) comment

reçut *etc voir* **recevoir**

recyclabilité [rəsiklabilite] **NF** recyclability

recyclable [rəsiklabl] **ADJ** recyclable

recyclage [rəsiklaʒ] **NM 1** *Ind* recycling; *Aut* **r. des gaz d'échappement** exhaust gas recirculation **2** *(perfectionnement)* refresher course; *(reconversion)* retraining **3** *(stage → pour employés, chômeurs)* retraining course

recycler [3] [rəsikle] **VT 1** *Ind* to recycle; **papier recyclé** recycled paper; **la municipalité fait r. le verre, le papier et le plastique** the town council organizes the recycling of glass, paper and plastic

2 *(perfectionner)* to send on a refresher course; *(reconvertir)* to retrain

▶**se recycler VPR** *(pour se perfectionner)* to go on a refresher course; *(pour se reconvertir)* to retrain; **se r. dans la comptabilité** to retrain as an accountant; *Hum* **le vocabulaire des jeunes change, j'ai dû me r.** young people speak differently nowadays, I've had to bring myself up to date

recycleur [rəsiklœr] **NM 1** *(industriel du recyclage)* recycling company **2** *(appareil pour recycler l'eau)* water recycler

rédacteur, -trice [redaktœr, -tris] **NM,F 1** *(auteur → d'un livre)* writer; *(→ d'un guide, d'un dictionnaire)* compiler; **les rédacteurs de l'encyclopédie** the contributors to the encyclopedia; **le r. du contrat n'a pas prévu cela** the person who drew up the contract didn't foresee this

2 *Journ* writer, contributor; **r. artistique** art editor; **r. associé** associate editor; **r. en chef** *(d'une revue)* (chief) editor; *(du journal télévisé)* television news editor; **r. en chef des actualités** news editor; **r. en chef technique** production editor; **r. politique** political editor; **r. publicitaire** copywriter; **r. sportif** sports editor

rédaction [redaksjɔ̃] **NF 1** *(écriture)* writing; *(d'un guide, d'un dictionnaire)* compiling; **il vient d'achever la r. de son roman** he's just finished writing his novel; **la r. de la thèse a pris moins de temps que la recherche** writing up the thesis took less time than researching it; **équipe chargée de la r. d'un guide/dictionnaire** team responsible for compiling a guide/dictionary; **la r. d'un projet de loi/d'un contrat d'assurance** the drafting of a bill/of an insurance contract

2 *Journ (lieu)* editorial office; *TV* newsdesk, newsroom; *(équipe)* editorial staff; **la r. est en grève** the editorial staff is *or* are on strike

3 *Scol (composition)* ≃ essay

4 *(dans l'édition)* **r. électronique** on-line publishing; **r. publicitaire** copywriting

rédactionnel, -elle [redaksjɔnɛl] **ADJ** editorial

rédactrice [redaktris] *voir* **rédacteur**

redan [rədɑ̃] **NM 1** *(ouvrage de fortification)* redan

2 *Archit (découpure)* cusp; *(ressaut)* step

reddition [redisjɔ̃] **NF 1** *Mil* surrender **2** *Fin & Jur* rendering; **r. de compte** presentation of account

redécoupage [rədekupaʒ] **NM** *Pol* **r. électoral** redrawing of electoral *or* constituency boundaries; **procéder à** *ou* **effectuer un r. électoral** to redraw the electoral boundaries

redécouverte [rədekuvɛrt] **NF** rediscovery

redécouvrir [34] [rədekuvrir] **VT** to rediscover

redéfaire [109] [rədefɛr] **VT** *(nœud)* to undo again; *(tricot, couture)* to unstitch again; *(lit, coiffure)* to mess up again

redéfinir [32] [rədefinir] **VT** to redefine; **r. la politique du logement** to lay down new housing policy guidelines

redéfinition [rədefinisjɔ̃] **NF** redefinition

redéfit, redéfont *etc voir* **redéfaire**

redemander [3] [rədəmɑ̃de] **VT 1** *(demander à nouveau)* to ask again; **je lui ai redemandé son nom** I asked him/her his/her name again; **r. de l'aide à qn** to ask sb again for help; **je lui ai redemandé de fermer la porte** I asked him/her again to close the door; **j'ai redemandé qu'il nous écrive un article** I asked again if he would write an article for us

2 *(demander davantage)* to ask for more; **il a redemandé de la soupe** he asked for some more soup; *Fig* **tout le monde en redemande** everybody is clamouring *or* keeps asking for more, they can't get enough of it; **sa correction ne lui a pas suffi, il en redemande** one punishment obviously wasn't enough because he's asking for another one

3 *(après un prêt)* to ask for; **redemande ton vélo dès que tu en as besoin** ask for your bike back as soon as you need it

redémarrage [rədemaraʒ] **NM 1** *(d'une machine)* starting up again *(UNCOUNT)*; *Ordinat* reboot, restart; **r. à chaud** warm boot, warm start **2** *(économique)* recovery, upturn

redémarrer [3] [rədemare] **VI 1** *(moteur)* to start up again **2** *(processus)* to get going *or* to take off again; **l'économie redémarre** the economy is looking up again; **les cours redémarrent fin octobre** classes start again at the end of October **3** *Ordinat* to reboot

rédempteur, -trice [redɑ̃ptœr, -tris] **ADJ** redeeming, *Sout* redemptive; **œuvre rédemptrice** redemptive act, act of redemption

NM,F redeemer; **le R.** the Redeemer

rédemption [redɑ̃psjɔ̃] **NF** *Rel* **la R.** Redemption

rédemptoriste [redɑ̃ptɔrist] **NM** *Rel* Redemptorist (father)

rédemptrice [redɑ̃ptris] *voir* **rédempteur**

redent [rədɑ̃] = **redan**

redenté, -e [rədɑ̃te] **ADJ** *Beaux-Arts* cuspate

redéploiement [rədeplwamɑ̃] **NM 1** *Mil* redeployment **2** *Écon* reorganization, restructuring

redéployer [13] [rədeplwaje] **VT 1** *Mil* to redeploy **2** *Écon* to reorganize, to restructure

▶**se redéployer VPR 1** *Mil* to redeploy **2** *Écon (entreprise)* to reorganize its operations

redescendre [73] [rədesɑ̃dr] **VT 1** *(colline, montagne etc → en voiture)* to drive (back) down; *(→ à pied)* to walk (back) down; *(sujet: alpiniste)* to climb back down

2 *(apporter) (du point de vue de quelqu'un qui est en haut)* to take down again, to take back down; *(du point de vue de quelqu'un qui est en bas)* to bring down again, to bring back down; **je redescendrai les cartons plus tard** *(je suis en haut)* I'll take the cardboard boxes back down later; *(je suis en bas)* I'll bring the cardboard boxes back down later

VI *(aux être)* **1** *(descendre → du point de vue de quelqu'un qui est en haut)* to go down again, to go back down; *(du point de vue de quelqu'un qui est en bas)* to come down again, to come back down; *(alpiniste)* to climb back down; *Fam (après une prise de drogue)* to come down; **quand tu redescendras, veux-tu...?** *(nous sommes en haut)* when you go down again *or* go back down, will you...?; *(je suis à l'étage inférieur)* when you come down again *or* come back down, will you...?; **la température/le niveau de l'eau redescend** the temperature/the water level is falling (again); **je suis redescendu en chasse-neige** I snowploughed (back) down; **et maintenant, comment r.?** and now, how do we get back down?

2 *(descendre à nouveau → du point de vue de quelqu'un qui est en haut)* to go down again; *(du point de vue de quelqu'un qui est en bas)* to come down again; **r. de voiture** to get out of the car again

redevable [rədəvabl] **ADJ 1** *Fin* **être r. d'une somme d'argent à qn** to owe sb a sum of money; **vous êtes r. d'un acompte provisionnel** you are liable for an interim payment; **être r. de l'impôt** to be liable to tax

2 *Fig (moralement)* **être r. de qch à qn** to be indebted to sb for sth; **je lui suis r. de ma promotion** I owe him/her my promotion, I owe it to him/her that I was promoted

redevait *etc voir* **redevoir**

redevance [rədəvɑ̃s] **NF 1** *TV* licence fee; *Tél* rental charge **2** *Com & Fin (pour un service)* dues, fees; *(royalties)* royalties; **r. pétrolière** oil royalty **3** *Hist* tax

redevenir [40] [rədəvnir] **VI** *(aux être)* to become again; **le ciel redevient nuageux** the sky is clouding over again; **r. amis** to become friends again; **r. silencieux** to fall silent again; **j'ai l'impression d'être redevenu moi-même** I feel like my old self again

redevoir [53] [rədəvwar] **VT** *(aux temps simples seulement)* **il redoit cinquante mille euros** he still owes fifty thousand euros

rédhibition [redibisjɔ̃] **NF** *Jur* = cancellation of sale due to a latent defect

rédhibitoire [redibitwar] **ADJ 1** *Jur* **action r.** remedy for latent defect; **vice r.** latent defect

2 *Fig (insurmontable)* **le prix est élevé mais pas r.** the price is high but not prohibitive; **une mauvaise note à l'écrit, c'est r.** a bad *Br* mark *or Am* grade in the written exam is enough to fail the candidate; **dans ce métier, être petit est r.** being small is a bar to entering this profession

rédie [redi] **NF** *Zool* redia

rediffuser [3] [rədifyze] **VT** to repeat, to rebroadcast; **nous rediffuserons ces images** we'll be showing these scenes again, we'll be rebroadcasting these scenes

rediffusion [rədifyzjɔ̃] **NF** repeating, rebroadcasting; *(programme rediffusé)* repeat

rédiger [17] [rediʒe] **VT** *(manifeste, contrat)* to write, to draw up; *(thèse, rapport)* to write up; *(ordonnance)* to write out; *(lettre)* to write, to compose; *(article)* to write; *(guide, dictionnaire)* to compile; **il a rédigé sa lettre en termes énergiques** he wrote a strongly worded letter

USAGE ABSOLU il rédige bien he writes well

rédimé, -e [redime] **ADJ** *Hist* **province/ville rédimée** = province/town in France which, in 1553, had bought back the duty levied by the monarchy on sales of salt; *Belg Hist* **cantons rédimés** = territory transferred from Germany to Belgium by the Treaty of Versailles in 1919

redimensionnement [rədimɑ̃sjɔnmɑ̃] NM **1** *Ordinat (d'une fenêtre)* resizing **2** *Suisse (d'une industrie, d'une entreprise)* downsizing

redimensionner [3] [rədimɑ̃sjɔne] VT **1** *Ordinat (fenêtre)* to resize **2** *Suisse (industrie, entreprise)* to downsize

rédimer [3] [redime] *Rel* VT to redeem, to buy off
  ▸ **se rédimer** VPR to redeem oneself

redingote [rədɛ̃gɔt] NF **1** *(de femme)* tailored *or* fitted coat **2** *(d'homme)* frock coat

rédintégration [redɛ̃tegrasjɔ̃] NF **1** *Psy* redintegration **2** *r. des cristaux* redintegration of crystals

redire [102] [rədir] VT **1** *(répéter)* to say *or* to tell again, to repeat; *(rabâcher)* to keep saying, to repeat; **je tiens à vous r. combien j'ai été heureux de vous voir** I'd like to say again how happy I was to see you; **redites lentement les mots après moi** repeat slowly after me; **et que je n'aie pas à te le r.!** and I don't want to have to tell you again!; **on le lui a dit et redit** he's/she's been told again and again; **elle a redit la même chose tout au long de son discours** throughout her speech she repeated the same thing
  2 *(rapporter)* to (go and) tell, to repeat; **surtout, n'allez pas le lui r.** whatever you do, don't go and tell him/her
  3 *(locutions)* **quelque chose/rien à r.** something/nothing to object to; **elle ne voit rien à r. aux nouvelles mesures** she can't see anything wrong with *or* she has no objections to the new measures; **il n'y avait rien à r. à cela** there was nothing wrong with *or* nothing to object to in that; **trouver à r. (à)** to find fault (with); **l'organisation était parfaite, je n'y ai pas trouvé à r.** the organization was perfect, there was nothing I could find fault with *or* I had no complaint to make

rediscuter [3] [rədiskyte] VT to discuss again, to have further discussion(s) about
  ▫ **rediscuter de** VT IND to talk about *or* to discuss again

redisons *etc voir* **redire**

redistribuer [7] [rədistribɥe] VT *(cartes)* to deal again; *(fortune)* to redistribute; *(emplois)* to reallocate; **r. les rôles** to recast the show; *Fig* to reallocate the tasks

redistribution [rədistribysjɔ̃] NF *(des revenus, des terres, des richesses)* redistribution

redit, -e [rədi, -it] PP *voir* **redire**
  ▫ **redite** NF superfluous *or* needless repetition; **son texte est plein de redites** his/her text is very repetitive

redites [rədit] *voir* **redire**

redoit, redoivent *etc voir* **redevoir**

redondance [rədɔ̃dɑ̃s] NF **1** *(répétition)* redundancy; **de nombreuses redondances** a lot of redundancy **2** *Ordinat, Ling & Tél* redundancy; **vérification par r.** redundancy check

redondant, -e [rədɔ̃dɑ̃, -ɑ̃t] ADJ **1** *(mot)* redundant, superfluous; *(style)* redundant, verbose, wordy **2** *Ordinat, Ling & Tél* redundant

redonner [3] [rədɔne] VT **1** *(donner de nouveau)* to give again; **j'ai redonné les chaussures au cordonnier** I took the shoes back *or* returned the shoes to the cobbler's; **elle lui a redonné un coup de pied** she kicked him/her again; **cette promenade m'a redonné faim** that walk has made me hungry again
  2 *(donner davantage de)* to give more of; **redonnez-lui du sirop** give him/her some more cough mixture; **r. à manger/de l'argent/du travail à qn** to give sb some more food/money/work
  3 *(rendre)* to give back; **ce médicament va vous r. des forces** the medicine will give you back your strength; **r. de l'appétit à qn** to restore sb's appetite, to give sb back his/her appetite; **ça m'a redonné confiance/courage** it restored my confidence/my courage; **ça m'a redonné envie de voyager** it made me want to travel again; **ces vacances lui ont redonné bonne mine** the holiday put the colour back in his/her cheeks; **la lessive qui redonne l'éclat du neuf à tout votre linge** the powder that puts the brightness back into your washing
  4 *Théât* to stage again; **r. 'Hamlet' au théâtre** to stage 'Hamlet' again
  ▫ **redonner dans** VT IND to lapse *or* to fall back into

redorer [3] [rədɔre] VT **1** *Tech* to regild **2** *(société, image)* to repackage

redormir [36] [rədɔrmir] VI *(plus longtemps)* to sleep some more; *(à nouveau)* to sleep again; **je n'ai pas pu r.** I couldn't get back to sleep

redoublant, -e [rədublɑ̃, -ɑ̃t] NM,F *Br* pupil repeating a year, *Am* student repeating a grade; **combien y a-t-il de redoublants?** *Br* how many pupils are repeating their year?, *Am* how many students are repeating their grade?

redoublé, -e [rəduble] ADJ **1** *(lettre)* double **2** *(intensifié)* **faire des efforts redoublés** to redouble one's efforts; **frapper à coups redoublés** *(à la porte)* to knock even harder

redoublement [rədubləmɑ̃] NM *Scol* repeating a *Br* year *or Am* grade; **son r. l'a fait progresser** he's/she's doing much better at school since he/she repeated a *Br* year *or Am* grade
  2 *Ling* reduplication
  3 *(accroissement)* increase, intensification; **seul un r. d'efforts lui permettra de réussir** he/she will only succeed if he/she works much harder; **avec un r. de zèle** with renewed *or* redoubled zeal

redoubler [3] [rəduble] VT **1** *(rendre double)* **r. une consonne** to double a consonant
  2 *Scol* **r. une classe** to repeat a *Br* year *or Am* grade
  3 *(augmenter → sentiment, chagrin)* to add to; **r. ses efforts** to redouble one's efforts
  USAGE ABSOLU **ils l'ont fait r.** they made him/her repeat the *Br* year *or Am* grade
  VI *(froid, tempête)* to increase, to intensify
  ▫ **redoubler de** VT IND to increase in; **les coups redoublèrent de violence** the blows rained down more heavily; **r. d'efforts** to redouble one's efforts; **r. de patience** to be doubly *or* extra patient; **r. de ruse** to be doubly *or* extra cunning

redoul [rədul] NM *Bot* myrtle-leaved (tanner's) sumach

redoutable [rədutabl] ADJ **1** *(dangereux → personne, adversaire)* formidable; *(→ ennemi)* fearsome, formidable; *(→ maladie)* dreadful; **la compagnie d'assurances a des enquêteurs redoutables** the insurance company has very able investigators; **elle a un revers r.** she has a lethal backhand **2** *(effrayant → aspect, réputation)* awesome, fearsome, awe-inspiring

redoutablement [rədutabləmɑ̃] ADV *(très)* extremely, terribly

Redoute [rədut] NF **la R.** = French mail-order company

redoute [rədut] NF *(fortification)* redoubt

redouter [3] [rədute] VT to dread; **un professeur redouté de tous les élèves** a much-dreaded teacher; **il redoute de te rencontrer** he dreads meeting you; **elle redoute que tu (ne) lui en parles** she's terrified that you'll mention it to him/her

redouteux, -euse [rədutø, -øz] *Can Vieilli* ADJ distrustful, suspicious
  NM,F distrustful *or* suspicious person

redoux [rədu] NM milder spell of weather *(during winter)*

redowa [rədɔva] NF redowa

redox [rədɔks] ADJ *Chim* **couple r.** redox couple

redressage [rədrɛsaʒ] NM straightening (up)

redresse [rədrɛs] NF *Fam* **à la redresse** ADJ **un type à la r.** a tough guy

redressement [rədrɛsmɑ̃] NM **1** *(du corps, d'une barre)* straightening up; *(de la tête)* lifting up, raising
  2 *(d'un véhicule)* **son pneu a explosé juste après un r. dans un virage** his/her tyre burst just after he/she straightened up coming out of a bend
  3 *Com & Écon* recovery; **plan de r.** recovery programme; **r. économique** economic recovery
  4 *Compta* adjustment; **r. financier** gearing adjustment; *Admin* **r. fiscal, r. d'impôt** tax adjustment
  5 *Jur* **r. judiciaire** receivership; **être mis en r. judiciaire** to go into receivership
  6 *Électron* rectification

redresser [4] [rədrɛse] VT **1** *(arbre, poteau)* to straighten (up), to set upright; *(véhicule, volant)* to straighten (up); *(bateau)* to right;

(avion) to right, to straighten up, to lift the nose of; **r. la tête** *(la lever)* to lift up one's head; *(avec fierté)* to hold one's head up high; **r. les épaules** to straighten one's shoulders
  2 *(corriger → courbure)* to put right, to straighten out; *(→ anomalie)* to rectify, to put right; *(→ situation)* to sort out, to put right, to put back on an even keel; *(→ compte)* to adjust
  3 *(entreprise)* to put back on its feet; **pour r. l'économie** in order to bring about an economic recovery
  4 *Électron* to rectify
  USAGE ABSOLU *Aut* to straighten up, to recover; **il n'a pas redressé assez vite à la sortie du virage** he didn't straighten up quickly enough after he came out of the bend
  ▸ **se redresser** VPR **1** *(personne assise)* to sit up straight; *(personne allongée)* to sit up; *(personne voûtée ou penchée)* to straighten up; *(avec fierté)* to draw oneself up, to hold one's head up; **redresse-toi!** *(personne assise)* sit up straight!; *(personne debout)* stand up straight!
  2 *Fig (remonter)* to recover; **les résultats se redressent depuis mai** output figures have been looking up *or* have been recovering since May; **la situation se redresse un peu** the situation is on the mend; **le dollar se redressait nettement jeudi matin** the dollar made a marked recovery on Thursday morning

redresseur, -euse [rədrɛsœr, -øz] ADJ **1** *Élec* rectifying **2** *Opt* erecting
  NM **1** *Élec* rectifier **2** *(personne)* **r. de torts** righter of wrongs; *Hist ou Hum (chevalier)* knight errant; **r. d'entreprise** company doctor

redû, -ue [rədy] PP *voir* **redevoir**
  NM *Fin* balance due, amount owed

réduc [redyk] NF *Fam (réduction)* discount ∎

réductase [redyktaz] NF *Biol & Chim* reductase

réducteur, -trice [redyktœr, -tris] ADJ **1** *(limitatif)* simplistic **2** *Tech* reduction *(avant n)* **3** *Chim* reducing
  NM **1** *Tech* reduction gear **2** *Chim* reducer, reductant, reducing agent **3** **r. de têtes** head-shrinker

réductibilité [redyktibilite] NF reducibility

réductible [redyktibl] ADJ **1** *(dépenses, dimensions)* which can be reduced; *(théorie)* which can be reduced *or* simplified **2** *Chim, Math & Méd* reducible

réduction [redyksjɔ̃] NF **1** *(remise)* discount, rebate; **accorder** *ou* **faire une r. de 5 euros sur le prix total** to give a 5-euro discount on the overall cost; **faire une r. à qn** to give sb a reduction; **carte de r.** discount card
  2 *(baisse)* reduction, cut *(de* in); *Fin (du capital)* writing down; **ils nous ont imposé une r. des dépenses/salaires** they've cut our expenditure/wages; **r. de capacité** *ou* **d'effectifs** staff cuts, downsizing; **r. des prix** price reduction; **la r. du temps de travail** = reduction of the working week in France from 39 to 35 hours, introduced by the government of Lionel Jospin in 1998 and phased in from 2000 onwards; **ils ont promis une r. des impôts** they promised to reduce *or* to lower taxes
  3 *(copie plus petite → d'une œuvre)* (scale) model
  4 *Biol, Chim & Métal* reduction
  5 *Méd* setting, reducing; **la r. d'une fracture** setting a broken bone
  6 *Math, Mus & Phil* reduction
  7 **r. à l'absurde** *(en logique)* reductio ad absurdum
  8 *Jur* **r. de peine** mitigation (of sentence); **il a eu une r. de peine** he got his sentence cut *or* reduced
  ▫ **en réduction** ADJ scaled-down

réductionnisme [redyksjɔnism] NM reductionism

réductionniste [redyksjɔnist] ADJ reductionist
  NMF reductionist

réductrice [redyktris] *voir* **réducteur**

réduire [98] [redɥir] VT **1** *(restreindre → consommation)* to reduce, to cut down on; *(→ inflation, chômage)* to reduce, to bring down, to curb; *(→ dépenses, effectifs)* to reduce, to cut back on; *(→ distance)* to reduce, to decrease; *(→ chauffage)* to lower, to turn down; *Fin (→ capital)* to write down; **réduis la flamme** turn down the

gas; **on a nettement réduit les dépenses d'armement** arms spending has been cut right back *or* sharply reduced; **il a réduit le prix de 10 pour cent** he cut *or* reduced the price by 10 percent; **j'ai réduit mon budget vêtements à 50 euros par mois/mon texte à trois pages** I've cut down my spending on clothes to 50 euros a month/my text to three pages; **ils ont réduit le temps d'attente de deux jours** they've cut *or* they've shortened the waiting time by two days; **r. qch de moitié** to cut sth by half, to halve sth

2 *(rapetisser → photo)* to reduce; *(→ schéma)* to scale down; *(→ texte)* to shorten, to cut (**de** by); *Ordinat (→ fenêtre)* to minimize

3 *(changer)* **r. qch à l'essentiel** to boil sth down; **il a réussi à r. à néant le travail de dix années** he managed to reduce ten years' work to nothing; **r. qch en miettes** to smash sth to bits *or* pieces; **r. qch en cendres** to reduce sth to ashes; **r. qch à sa plus simple expression** to reduce sth to its simplest expression

4 *(forcer)* **r. qn à** to reduce sb to; **r. la presse/l'opposition au silence** to silence the press/the opposition; **r. à la clandestinité** to drive underground; **r. qn au désespoir** to drive sb to despair; **en être réduit à des expédients/au suicide** to be driven to using expedients/to suicide; **ils en sont réduits aux dernières extrémités** they are in dire straits; **voilà où nous en sommes réduits!** look what we're *or* we've been reduced to!; **r. qn à faire qch** to force *or* to compel *or* to drive sb to do sth; **j'en suis réduit à mendier** I'm reduced to begging

5 *(vaincre)* to quell, to subdue, to crush; **r. les poches de résistance** to crush the last pockets of resistance; **une armée que rien n'a pu r.** an army which no one *or* nothing has been able to beat

6 *Chim & Culin* to reduce

7 *Méd* to set, to reduce

8 *Math & Mus* to reduce

9 *Suisse (ranger)* to put away

VI *Culin* to reduce; **faire r.** to reduce

▸**se réduire** VPR 1 *(économiser)* to cut down; **il va falloir se r. sur les sorties au restaurant** we're going to have to cut down on eating out

2 **se r. à** *(consister en)* to amount to; **la rencontre s'est réduite à un échange poli** the meeting amounted to nothing more than a polite exchange of views; **son influence se réduit à peu de chose** his/her influence amounts to very little

réduit, -e [redɥi, -it] ADJ 1 *(échelle, format etc)* scaled-down, small-scale

2 *(taille)* small; *(tarif)* reduced, cut; **à vitesse réduite** at reduced *or* low speed; **billet à prix r.** cheap *or* cut-price ticket; **voyager à prix r.** to travel at reduced rates; **la fréquentation est réduite l'hiver** attendance is lower in the winter

3 *(peu nombreux → débouchés)* limited, restricted

NM 1 *Péj (logement)* cubbyhole; **il vit dans un r. mal chauffé** he lives in an unheated little cubbyhole

2 *(recoin)* recess; *(placard)* cupboard

3 *(fortification)* reduit

réduplication [redyplikasjɔ̃] NF *Ling* reduplication

réduve [redyv] NM *Entom* reduvius, assassin bug

rééchelonnement [reeʃlɔnmɑ̃] NM *(d'une dette)* rescheduling

rééchelonner [3] [reeʃəlɔne] VT *(dette)* to reschedule

réécouter [3] [reekute] VT **r. qch** to listen to sth again; **fais-moi r. ce passage** let me listen to that bit again

réécrire [99] [reekrir] VT to rewrite; **r. l'histoire** to rewrite history

VI **r. à qn** to write to sb again, to send sb another letter

réécriture [reekrityr] NF rewriting

réécrivait *etc voir* **réécrire**

réédification [reedifikasjɔ̃] NF reconstruction, re-erection

réédifier [9] [reedifje] VT to reconstruct, to re-erect

rééditer [3] [reedite] VT 1 *Typ* to republish; **son livre a été réédité chez Leroux** his/her book has been republished by Leroux *or* brought out again by Leroux 2 *Fam (refaire)* to repeat; **r. la même erreur** to make *or* to repeat the same mistake

réédition [reedisjɔ̃] NF 1 *Typ (nouvelle édition)* new edition; *(action de rééditer)* republishing, republication 2 *Fam (répétition)* repeat, repetition

rééducation [reedykasjɔ̃] NF 1 *Méd (d'un membre)* re-education; *(d'un malade)* rehabilitation, re-education; **faire de la r.** to undergo *Br* physiotherapy *or Am* physical therapy; **r. motrice** motor re-education; **r. de la parole** speech therapy 2 *(morale)* re-education; *Jur (d'un délinquant)* rehabilitation

rééduquer [3] [reedyke] VT 1 *Méd (membre)* to re-educate; *(malade)* to give *Br* physiotherapy *or Am* physical therapy to 2 *Jur (délinquant)* to rehabilitate

réel, -elle [reɛl] ADJ 1 *(concret → gén)* real; *(→ date)* effective; *(→ résultats, fait)* actual; **besoins réels** genuine needs; **dans la vie réelle, c'est différent** it's different in real life; **en termes réels** in real terms

2 *(avant le nom) (appréciable)* genuine, real; **une réelle amélioration** real *or* genuine progress; **elle a fait preuve d'un r. talent** she's shown true *or* genuine talent; **prendre un r. plaisir à faire qch** to take real *or* great pleasure in doing sth

NM **le r.** reality, the real

réélection [reelɛksjɔ̃] NF re-election

rééligible [reeliʒibl] ADJ re-eligible; **ils sont/ne sont pas rééligibles** they are/aren't entitled to stand for election again

réélire [106] [reelir] VT to re-elect; **elle compte bien se faire r.** she's pretty sure she'll be re-elected

réellement [reɛlmɑ̃] ADV really; **ces faits ont r. eu lieu** these events really did take place

réélu, -e [reely] PP *voir* **réélire**

réembaucher [3] [reɑ̃boʃe] VT to take back on, to take on again, to re-employ; **sa société l'a réembauché** his company took him on again; **le P-DG l'a fait r. dans l'une de ses usines** the managing director made sure he/she was given another job in one of his factories; **il a réussi à se faire r.** he managed to get another job (in the same company)

VI to hire again; **l'entreprise réembauche** the company is taking people on again

réémetteur [reemetœr] NM relay transmitter

réemploi [reɑ̃plwa] = **remploi**

réemployer [reɑ̃plwaje] = **remployer**

réemprunter [reɑ̃prœ̃te] = **remprunter**

réengagement [reɑ̃gaʒmɑ̃] = **rengagement**

réengager [reɑ̃gaʒe] = **rengager**

réenregistrable [reɑ̃rəʒistrabl] ADJ rerecordable

réenregistrement [reɑ̃rəʒistrəmɑ̃] NM rerecording

réenregistrer [3] [reɑ̃rəʒistre] VT to rerecord

réensemencement [reɑ̃smɑ̃smɑ̃] NM resowing

réensemencer [16] [reɑ̃smɑ̃se] VT to sow again, to resow

réenvisager [17] [reɑ̃vizaʒe] VT *(de nouveau)* to consider again, to think about again; *(différemment)* to rethink, to review

rééquilibrage [reekilibraʒ] NM *(de roues)* balancing; *(du budget)* rebalancing; **le r. des forces européennes** the restabilizing of power in Europe; **r. du budget** rebalancing the budget, balancing the budget again

rééquilibre [reekilibr] NM restoration of balance

rééquilibrer [3] [reekilibre] VT 1 *(roues)* to balance; *(budget)* to rebalance, to balance again; *(situation)* to restabilize 2 *(personne)* **son séjour à l'étranger l'a rééquilibré** his stay abroad has helped him (to) find his feet again

réer [15] [ree] VI to bell, to troat

réescompte [reɛskɔ̃t] NM rediscount

réescompter [3] [reɛskɔ̃te] VT to rediscount

réessayage [reesɛjaʒ] NM *(séance)* second fitting

réessayer [11] [reeseje] VT *(voiture, produit, méthode)* to try again; *(vêtement)* to try on again

réétudier [9] [reetydje] VT 1 *(discipline)* to study again; **se mettre à r. le grec** to go back to studying Greek 2 *(projet, idée)* to study *or* to examine again; **on va r. la question** we're going to give the question some more thought

réévaluation [reevalɥasjɔ̃] NF *(d'une devise, d'une monnaie)* revaluation; *(d'un budget, d'un salaire → gén)* reappraisal, reassessment; *(→ à la hausse)* upgrade, upgrading; *(→ à la baisse)* downgrade, downgrading

réévaluer [7] [reevalɥe] VT 1 *Fin (devise, monnaie)* to revalue; *(budget, salaire)* to reappraise; *(à la hausse)* to upgrade; *(à la baisse)* to downgrade 2 *(qualité, travail)* to reassess, to reevaluate

réexamen [reɛgzamɛ̃] NM *(d'une politique, d'une situation)* re-examination, reassessment; *(d'une décision)* reconsideration; *(d'un dossier, d'une question)* re-examination

réexaminer [3] [reɛgzamine] VT *(politique, situation)* to re-examine, to reassess; *(décision)* to reconsider; *(dossier, question)* to re-examine, to examine again

réexpédier [9] [reɛkspedje] VT 1 *(courrier → à l'expéditeur)* to return (to sender), to send back; *(→ au destinataire)* to forward 2 *Fam (personne)* to throw out; **je l'ai réexpédié vite fait** I got rid of him in no time

réexpédition [reɛkspedisjɔ̃] NF *(à l'expéditeur)* sending back, returning (to sender); *(au destinataire)* forwarding, redirecting; **service de r. du courrier** mail-forwarding *or* mail-redirecting service

réexportation [reɛkspɔrtasjɔ̃] NF *(activité)* re-exportation; *(produit)* re-export

réexporter [3] [reɛkspɔrte] VT to re-export

réf. *(abrév écrite* **référence***)* ref

refaçonner [3] [rəfasɔne] VT to reshape, to remodel

réfaction [refaksjɔ̃] NF 1 *Com* reimbursement, allowance 2 *Fin* adjustment

refaire [109] [rəfɛr] VT 1 *(à nouveau → travail, traduction etc)* to redo, to do again; *(→ voyage)* to make again; **tout est à r.** everything will have to be done (all over) again; **r. une addition** to do a sum again; **r. une opération pour la vérifier** to do a calculation again to check it; **r. un pansement** to redo a bandage; **r. une piqûre à qn** to give sb another injection; **r. le numéro** *(de téléphone)* to redial; **r. ses lacets** to tie one's laces again; **quand pourras-tu r. du sport?** when will you be able to start doing sport again?; **je vais r. quelques longueurs de bassin** I'm going to swim a few more lengths; **j'ai dû r. du riz** I had to make (some) more rice; **il a refait le dessin en tenant compte de nos remarques** he redid the drawing taking our comments into account; **nous avons refait à pied les 10 kilomètres qui nous séparaient du village** we walked the 10 kilometres back to the village; **tu ne vas pas me r. une scène!** you're not going to start again!; *Fig* **vous ne la referez pas** you won't change her; **r. le monde** to put *or* to set the world to rights; **r. sa vie** to start a new life, to make a fresh start (in life); **r. sa vie avec qn** to make *or* to start a new life with sb; **si c'était à r., je ne l'épouserais pas** if I could start all over again, I wouldn't marry him/her; **si c'était à r.? – je suis prêt à recommencer** and if you had to do it all again? – I would do the same thing; *Chasse* **r. sa tête** *(cerf)* to grow new antlers

2 *(réparer)* to redo; **r. la toiture** to redo the roof; **r. la peinture** to redo the paintwork; **ils refont la route** they are resurfacing the road; **le moteur a été complètement refait à neuf** the engine has had a complete overhaul; *Méd* **se faire r. le nez** to have a nose job

3 *Fam (berner)* to do, to have, to con; **j'ai été refait!** I've been done *or* had *or* conned!; **il m'a refait de 10 euros** he did me out of 10 euros

V IMPERSONNEL **il refait soleil/froid** it's sunny/cold again

▸**se refaire** VPR 1 *(se changer)* **on ne se refait pas** you can't change the way you are

2 *Fam (financièrement)* to recoup one's losses; **j'ai besoin de me r.** I need to get hold of some more cash

3 **se r. une tasse de thé** to make oneself another cup of tea; **se r. une beauté** to powder one's nose; **se r. une santé** to recuperate

4 **se r. à qch** to get used to sth again; **il a du mal à se r. à la vie urbaine** he's finding it hard getting used to city life again *or* getting reaccustomed to city life

refait [rəfɛ] NM *Chasse & Zool (du cerf)* new antlers; **temps du r.** antler-growing season

réfection [refɛksjɔ̃] NF *(gén)* redoing; *(d'une pièce)* redecorating; *(d'une maison)* redoing, doing up; *(d'une route)* repairs; **pendant les travaux de r.** *(d'une maison)* while the house is being done up; *(d'une route)* during repairs to the road, while there are roadworks

réfectoire [refɛktwar] NM *(dans une communauté)* refectory; *Scol* dining hall, canteen; *Univ* (dining) hall

refend [rəfɑ̃] NM *Archit & Constr* **bois de r.** (wood in) planks; **pierre de r.** corner stone; **mur de r.** partition (wall)

refendre [78] [rəfɑ̃dr] VT **1** *(ardoise)* to split **2** *voir* **scie**

refera *etc voir* **refaire**

référé [refere] NM *Jur (procédure)* summary proceedings; *(arrêt)* summary judgement; *(ordonnance)* temporary injunction; **assigner qn en r.** to bring *or* to institute summary proceedings against sb, to apply for a summary judgement to be granted against sb

référé-liberté [refereliberte] *(pl* **référés-libertés***)* NM *Jur* = provision in French law whereby a person placed on remand can make an emergency appeal to be released from custody

référence [referɑ̃s] NF **1** *(renvoi)* reference

2 *Admin & Com* reference number; **r. à rappeler dans toute correspondance** *(correspondance administrative)* reference number to be quoted in all correspondence

3 *(base d'évaluation)* reference; **un prix littéraire, c'est une r.** a literary prize is a good recommendation for a book; **le film a été primé à Cannes mais ce n'est pas une r.** the film won a prize at Cannes but that's no recommendation; **ton ami n'est pas une r.** your friend is nothing to go by; **faire r. à** to refer to, to make (a) reference to; **la biographie fait plusieurs fois r. à son éthylisme** the biography makes several references to his/her alcoholism; **dans ce passage il fait r. à Platon** in this passage he is referring to Plato; **servir de r. (pour)** to be a benchmark (for)

4 *Ling* reference

5 *Mktg (produit)* listed product

6 *Compta* **r. au meilleur** benchmarking

❑ **références** NFPL *(pour un emploi → témoignages)* references, credentials; *(→ document)* reference letter, testimonial; **sérieuses références exigées** *(petite annonce)* good references required; **quelles sont les références de votre société?** what are your company's credentials?

❑ **de référence** ADJ reference *(avant n)*; **ouvrage/livre de r.** reference work/book; *Fin* **année de r.** base year; *Psy* **groupe de r.** reference group; **prix de r.** reference price

référencé, -e [referɑ̃se] ADJ **être r.** to have a reference number; **votre lettre référencée 450/198** your letter reference number 450/198

référencement [referɑ̃smɑ̃] NM **1** *Com (d'un produit)* listing **2** *Ordinat* referencing

référencer [16] [referɑ̃se] VT **1** *Com (produit)* to list **2** *Ordinat* to reference

référendaire [referɑ̃dɛr] ADJ referendum *(avant n)*; **conseiller r.** ≃ public auditor

référendum [referɛ̃dɔm] NM referendum; **les Norvégiens ont décidé par r. de ne pas entrer dans l'Union européenne** the Norwegians have voted in a referendum *or* by referendum not to join the European Union; **r. révocatoire** = referendum in which voters decide whether or not to dismiss an elected representative (who may be a member of Parliament, civil servant, head of state etc)

référent [referɑ̃] NM referent

référentiel, -elle [referɑ̃sjɛl] ADJ referential

NM frame of reference

référer [18] [refere] **référer à** VT IND *Ling* to refer to

❑ **en référer à** VT IND to refer back to; **il ne peut rien décider sans en r. à son supérieur** he can't decide anything without referring back to his boss

▸**se référer** VPR **1 se r. à** *(se rapporter à)* to refer to; **l'article se réfère à l'affaire Dreyfus** the article refers to the Dreyfus affair; **nous nous référons à la définition ci-dessus** the reader is referred to the above definition; **tout ce qui ne se réfère pas directement à notre affaire** anything that is not directly connected with *or* related to our business

2 se r. à *ou* **s'en r. à qn, se r. à** *ou* **s'en r. à l'avis de qn** *(s'en remettre à)* to leave it up to sb to decide

refermer [3] [rəfɛrme] VT to close, to shut; **r. ses mâchoires sur qch** to clamp one's jaws on sth

▸**se refermer** VPR *(porte)* to close, to shut; *(blessure)* to close *or* to heal up; *(piège)* to snap shut; **la porte s'est refermée sur mes doigts** the door closed on my fingers; *Fig* **le piège se referme sur l'espion** the net is closing in around the spy

refiler [3] [rəfile] VT *Fam* **1** *(donner)* to give▪ ; **il m'a refilé sa grippe/son vieux blouson** he gave me the flu/his old jacket; **ils vont nous r. les enfants pour le week-end** they're palming the kids off on us *or* dumping the kids on us for the weekend; **on s'est fait r. de la camelote** we got given some real *Br* rubbish *or Am* garbage

2 *(locution)* **r. le bébé à qn** to unload a problem onto sb, to pass the buck onto sb

refinancement [rəfinɑ̃smɑ̃] NM refinancing; **r. de dette** debt refinancing

refinancer [16] [rəfinɑ̃se] VT to refinance

refit *etc voir* **refaire**

réfléchi, -e [refleʃi] ADJ **1** *(caractère, personne)* reflective, thoughtful; *(action, opinion)* deliberate, considered; **une analyse réfléchie** a thoughtful *or* well thought-out analysis; **un enfant très r. pour son âge** a child who thinks very seriously for his age **2** *Ling* reflexive

réfléchir [32] [refleʃir] VT **1** *Phot & Phys* to reflect

2 *(s'aviser)* **il réfléchit que son argent ne suffirait pas** it occurred to him that he wouldn't have enough money

VI to think, to reflect; **as-tu bien réfléchi?** have you thought about it carefully?; **je n'ai pas eu le temps de r.** I haven't had a chance to reflect; **laisse-moi le temps de r.** give me time to think; **parler sans r.** to speak without thinking; **il fallait r. avant de parler!** you should have thought before you spoke!; **j'ai longuement réfléchi** I gave it a lot of thought; **r. vite** to think quickly; **quand on voit comment ça se passe, ça fait r.** when you see what's happening, it makes you think; **tes mésaventures m'ont donné à r.** your mishaps have given me food for thought; **r. à qch** to think about sth, to reflect on sth, to consider sth; **réfléchissez à ma proposition** do think about my offer; **as-tu réfléchi aux conséquences de ton départ?** have you thought about *or* considered the consequences of your going?; **j'ai beaucoup réfléchi au problème** I've given the problem a great deal of thought; **tout bien réfléchi** all things considered, after careful consideration; **c'est tout réfléchi** it's all settled, my mind's made up; **c'est tout réfléchi, je refuse!** my mind's made up, the answer is no!

▸**se réfléchir** VPR *(lumière, son)* to be reflected

réfléchissant, -e [refleʃisɑ̃, -ɑ̃t] ADJ *Phys* reflecting

réflecteur, -trice [reflɛktœr, -tris] ADJ reflecting

NM **1** *Astron* reflector, reflecting telescope **2** *Phys & Aut* reflector

réflectif, -ive [reflɛktif, -iv] ADJ *Physiol* reflexive

réflectorisé, -e [reflɛktɔrize] ADJ reflective

réflectrice [reflɛktris] *voir* **réflecteur**

reflet [rəflɛ] NM **1** *(lumière)* reflection, glint, light; **les reflets du soleil sur l'eau** the reflection of the sun on the water

2 *(couleur → gén)* tinge, glint, highlight; *(→ de la soie)* sheen, shimmer; **des cheveux châtains avec des reflets dorés** brown hair with tints of gold; **se faire faire des reflets** to have highlights put in; **avoir des reflets changeants** to shimmer

3 *(image)* reflection; **je vois ton r. dans la vitre** I can see your reflection in the window; **on voit le r. du flash dans la fenêtre** you can see the reflection of the flash on the windowpane; **ses lettres sont le r. de son caractère** his/her letters reflect *or* mirror his/her character

refléter [18] [rəflete] VT **1** *(renvoyer → lumière)* to reflect; *(→ image)* to reflect, to mirror

2 *(représenter)* to reflect, to mirror; **son air perplexe reflétait son trouble intérieur** his/her puzzled look indicated *or* betrayed his/her inner turmoil; **ce qu'il dit ne reflète pas ce qu'il pense/mon opinion** his words are not a fair reflection of what he thinks/of my opinion

▸**se refléter** VPR **1** *(lumière, rayon)* to be reflected

2 *(se manifester)* to be reflected; **son éducation religieuse se reflète dans sa manière de vivre** his/her religious education is reflected in the way he/she lives; **le bonheur se reflète sur son visage** you can see the happiness in his/her face

refleurir [32] [rəflœrir] VI **1** *(plante)* to flower again, to blossom again **2** *Fig Littéraire* to blossom *or* to flourish again

reflex [reflɛks] ADJ INV reflex *(avant n)*

NM INV reflex (camera); **r. mono-objectif** single-lens reflex

réflexe [reflɛks] NM **1** *Biol & Physiol* reflex (action); **avoir de bons réflexes** to have good reflexes; **r. conditionné** conditioned reflex; **r. inné** instinctive reflex; **r. rotulien** knee reflex *or* jerk

2 *(réaction)* reaction; **il a eu/n'a pas eu le r. de tirer le signal d'alarme** he instinctively pulled/he didn't think to pull the alarm; **son premier r. a été d'appeler à l'aide** his/her immediate reaction was to call for help; **ses réflexes de conducteur sont émoussés** his reflexes when he's behind the wheel aren't what they used to be; **c'est devenu un r.** it's become automatic

ADJ reflex *(avant n)*

réflexible [reflɛksibl] ADJ reflexible

réflexif, -ive [reflɛksif, -iv] ADJ *Math & Phil* reflexive

réflexion [reflɛksjɔ̃] NF **1** *(méditation)* thought; **après mûre r.** after careful consideration, after much thought; **leur proposition demande r.** their offer will need thinking over; **donner matière à r.** to provide food for thought; **s'absorber dans ses réflexions** to be deep *or* lost in thought; **r. faite, à la r.** *(finalement)* on reflection; *(quand on change d'avis)* on further consideration, on second thoughts

2 *(discernement)* **agir sans r.** to act without thinking, to act thoughtlessly; **son rapport manque de r.** his/her report hasn't been properly thought out *or* through

3 *(remarque)* remark, comment; **faire des réflexions à qn** to make remarks to sb; **elle ne supporte pas qu'on lui fasse la moindre r.** she can't stand the slightest criticism; **elle a fait d'amères réflexions sur son passé** she commented bitterly on his/her past life; **sa r. ne m'a pas plu** I didn't like his/her remark *or* what he/she said; *Euph* **elle a eu des réflexions de la direction** the management have had a word with her

4 *Tech (de la lumière)* reflection; **angle de r.** angle of reflection

réflexive [reflɛksiv] *voir* **réflexif**

réflexivité [reflɛksivite] NF reflexivity

réflexogène [reflɛksɔʒɛn] ADJ *Physiol* reflexogenic, reflexogenous; **zone r.** trigger area

réflexogramme [reflɛksɔgram] NM *Vieilli* reflexogram

réflexologie [reflɛksɔlɔʒi] NF reflexology; **r. plantaire** foot reflexology

refluer [7] [rəflye] VI **1** *(liquide)* to flow back; *(marée)* to ebb; *(foule, public)* to surge back; **faire r. les manifestants** to push back the demonstrators; *Fin* **faire r. le dollar/yen** to keep down the value of the dollar/yen **2** *Fig Littéraire (pensée, souvenir)* to come flooding *or* rushing back

reflux [rəfly] NM **1** *(de la marée)* ebb **2** *(d'une foule)* backward surge **3** *Méd* reflux; **r. gastro-œsophagien** gastro-oesophageal reflux (disease)

refondateur, -trice [rəfɔ̃datœr, -tris] ADJ reformative

NM,F reformer, reinventor

refondation [rəfɔ̃dasjɔ̃] NF *(d'un parti politique)* radical reform

refondatrice [rəfɔ̃datris] *voir* **refondateur**

refonder [3] [rəfɔ̃de] VT *(parti politique)* to radically reform

refondre [75] [rəfɔ̃dr] VT **1** *(métal)* to remelt, to melt down again; *(cloche)* to recast; *(monnaie)* to recoin, to remint

2 *Fig (remanier)* to recast, to reshape, to refashion; **r. un projet de loi** to redraft *or* to recast a bill; **la troisième édition a été entièrement**

ref–ref

refondue the third edition has been entirely revised

VI *(neige, glace)* to melt again

refont [rəfɔ̃] *voir* **refaire**

refonte [rəfɔ̃t] NF **1** *Métal (nouvelle fonte)* remelting; *(nouvelle coulée)* recasting; *(de la monnaie)* recoinage **2** *Fig (remaniement)* recasting, reshaping, refashioning; **il y a eu r. de l'ouvrage** the work has been completely *or* entirely revised

reforestation [rəfɔrɛstasjɔ̃] NF reforestation

réformable [refɔrmabl] ADJ **1** *Mil* = liable for exemption from military service **2** *(modifiable)* reformable, capable of being modified

reformage [rəfɔrmaʒ] NM reforming; **r. catalytique/à la vapeur** catalytic/steam reforming

reformatage [rəfɔrmataʒ] NM *Ordinat* reformatting

reformater [3] [rəfɔrmate] VT *Ordinat* to reformat

réformateur, -trice [refɔrmatœr, -tris] ADJ reforming; **idées réformatrices** ideas of reform

NM,F reformer

réformation [refɔrmasjɔ̃] NF **1** *Littéraire (action)* reform, reformation **2** *Vieilli Rel* **la R.** the Reformation **3** *Jur* reversal

réformatrice [refɔrmatris] *voir* **réformateur**

réforme [refɔrm] NF **1** *(modification)* reform; **nombreux sont ceux qui demandent la r. de l'orthographe** there are many people calling for spelling reform; *Pol* **r. constitutionnelle** constitutional reform; **r. électorale** electoral reform; **r. monétaire** monetary reform; **réformes sociales** social reforms; **nous choisirons la voie des réformes** we shall opt for reformism *or* a policy of reform *or* reforms; **la r. de l'orthographe** = attempt by the Académie française to simplify spelling rules

2 *Mil (de matériel)* scrapping; *(d'un soldat)* discharge; *(d'un appelé)* declaration of unfitness for service; **r. temporaire** deferment; **commission de r.** ≃ Army Medical Board

3 *Rel* **la R.** the Reformation

réformé, -e [refɔrme] ADJ *(religion, Église)* Reformed, Protestant

NM,F *(calviniste)* Protestant; *(moine)* member of a Reformed Order

NM *Mil (recrue)* = conscript declared unfit for service; *(soldat)* discharged soldier

reformer [3] [rəfɔrme] VT **1** *(à nouveau)* to re-form, to form again; **r. un groupe** to bring a group back together; **reformez les groupes!** get back into your groups!; **r. les rangs** to fall into line again

2 *Pétr* to reform

▸**se reformer** VPR to re-form, to form again; **la fissure se reforme tous les hivers** the crack reappears every winter; **l'association va se r. autour d'une nouvelle équipe** the association will be set up again *or* re-formed around a new team

réformer [3] [refɔrme] VT **1** *(modifier)* to reform

2 *Littéraire (supprimer)* to put an end to; **r. les abus** to put an end to injustice

3 *(mettre au rebut)* to scrap, to discard

4 *Mil (recrue)* to declare unfit for service; *(soldat)* to discharge; *(tank, arme)* to scrap; **se faire r.** to be exempted from military service; **être réformé P4** to be discharged for reasons of mental health

5 *Rail* to overhaul

6 *Jur (décision)* to reverse

réformette [refɔrmɛt] NF *Fam Péj* petty reform

reformeur [rəfɔrmœr] NM *Pétr* reformer

réformisme [refɔrmism] NM reformism

réformiste [refɔrmist] ADJ reformist

NMF reformist

reformulation [rəfɔrmylasjɔ̃] NF rewording

reformuler [3] [rəfɔrmyle] VT to rephrase, to reword; **je ne comprends pas votre question, pouvez-vous la r.?** I don't understand your question, could you rephrase it?

refouiller [3] [rəfuje] VT to carve out

refoulant, -e [rəfulɑ̃, -ɑ̃t] ADJ pumping *(avant n)*; **pompe refoulante** force pump

refoulé, -e [rəfule] ADJ *(instinct, sentiment)* repressed; *(ambition)* frustrated; *(personne)* inhibited

NM,F inhibited person

NM *Psy* **le r.** repressed content; **retour du r.** return of the repressed

refoulement [rəfulmɑ̃] NM **1** *(d'assaillants)* driving *or* pushing back; *(d'immigrants)* turning back *or* away **2** *Psy* repression **3** *Rail* backing

refouler [3] [rəfule] VT **1** *(assaillants)* to drive *or* to push back, to repulse; *(immigrants)* to turn back *or* away; **les forces de police ont refoulé les manifestants hors de la place** the police drove the demonstrators out of the square; **on nous a refoulés à l'entrée** we got turned away at the door; **ils se sont fait r. à la frontière** they were turned back at the border

2 *(liquide)* to force to flow back; *(courant)* to stem; *(air)* to pump out

3 *(retenir)* **r. ses larmes** to hold *or* to choke back one's tears; **r. sa colère** to keep one's anger in check

4 *Psy* to repress

5 *Rail* to back

VI **1** *(pieu, cheville)* to balk

2 *(mal fonctionner)* **l'égout refoule** a stench is coming up from the sewer; **la cheminée refoule** the fire is blowing back

3 *Vulg (sentir mauvais)* to stink▪, *Br* to pong, to niff

refouloir [rəfulwar] NM *(en artillerie)* rammer

réfractaire [refraktɛr] ADJ **1** *(matériau)* refractory, heat-resistant

2 *(personne)* **r. à** resistant *or* unamenable to; **être r. à l'autorité** to reject authority; **je suis r. aux mathématiques** I'm incapable of understanding mathematics, mathematics is a closed book to me; **r. aux charmes de la nature** impervious to nature's charms

3 *Méd & Tech* refractory

4 *Physiol* **période r.** refractory period *or* phase

NM **1** *Tech* refractory (material)

2 *Mil* defaulter

3 *Hist* = French citizen refusing to work in Germany during World War II

réfracter [3] [refrakte] VT to refract

▸**se réfracter** VPR to be refracted

réfracteur, -trice [refraktœr, -tris] ADJ refracting

NM refracting telescope, refractor

réfraction [refraksjɔ̃] NF refraction; **indice de r.** refractive index

réfractomètre [refraktɔmɛtr] NM **1** *Opt* refractometer **2** *Méd* optometer

réfractrice [refraktris] *voir* **réfracteur**

réfragable [refragabl] ADJ *Jur* refragable

refrain [rəfrɛ̃] NM **1** *(d'une chanson, d'un poème)* chorus, refrain; *(chanson)* tune, song; **reprendre le r. en chœur** to sing the chorus; **chanter de vieux refrains** to sing old songs *or* tunes; **r. publicitaire** (advertising) jingle **2** *Péj (sujet)* **change de r.** can't you talk about something else?; **avec toi c'est toujours le même r.** it's always the same old story with you

réfrangibilité [refrɑ̃ʒibilite] NF refrangibility, refrangibleness

réfrangible [refrɑ̃ʒibl] ADJ refrangible

refrènement [rəfrɛnmɑ̃], **réfrènement** [refrɛnmɑ̃] NM *Littéraire* repressing, curbing

refréner [rəfrene], **réfréner** [18] [refrene] VT to hold back, to hold in check, to curb; **r. sa colère** to stifle one's anger

réfrigérant, -e [refriʒerɑ̃, -ɑ̃t] ADJ **1** *(liquide)* cooling *(avant n)*, *Spéc* refrigerant; **mélange r.** refrigerant **2** *Fig (comportement, individu)* frosty, icy

NM *Ind (appareil)* cooler

réfrigérateur [refriʒeratœr] NM refrigerator, *Br* fridge, *Am* icebox; **conserver au r.** keep refrigerated; *Fig* **mettre qn au r.** to sideline sb; *Fig* **mettre un projet au r.** to shelve a plan, to put a plan on ice *or* in cold storage

réfrigérateur-congélateur [refriʒeratœrkɔ̃ʒelatœr] *(pl* **réfrigérateurs-congélateurs***)* NM fridge-freezer

réfrigération [refriʒerasjɔ̃] NF refrigeration; **appareils de r.** refrigeration appliances; **r. industrielle** industrial refrigeration

réfrigéré, -e [refriʒere] ADJ **1** *(personne)* frozen **2** *(véhicule)* refrigerated

réfrigérer [18] [refriʒere] VT **1** *(denrée)* to cool, to refrigerate; *Fam* **je suis réfrigérée!** I'm freezing!

2 *Fig* **son abord glacial m'a réfrigéré** his/her icy manner cut me dead

réfringence [refrɛ̃ʒɑ̃s] NF refringence, refringency

réfringent, -e [refrɛ̃ʒɑ̃, -ɑ̃t] ADJ refringent

refroidir [32] [rəfrwadir] VT **1** *Tech (moteur, fluide)* to cool; *(métal)* to quench

2 *Fig (personne)* to cool (down); *(sentiment, enthousiasme)* to dampen, to put a damper on; **cet échec l'a refroidi** this failure has dampened his enthusiasm

3 *Fam (assassiner)* to bump off

VI **1** *(devenir froid)* to get cold; *(devenir moins chaud)* to cool down; **faites r. pendant deux heures au réfrigérateur** cool *or* leave to cool in the refrigerator for two hours; **viens manger, le potage va r.!** come and eat, the soup's getting cold!; **ne laisse pas r. ton thé** don't let your tea get cold; **le temps a refroidi** *(légèrement)* it *or* the weather has got cooler; *(sensiblement)* it *or* the weather has got colder

2 *Fam Fig* **laisser r. qch** to leave *or* to keep *or* to put sth on ice

3 *(à cache-cache)* **tu refroidis!** you're getting colder!

▸**se refroidir** VPR **1** *(devenir froid)* to get cold; *(devenir moins chaud)* to cool down; **le temps va se r.** *(légèrement)* it's going to get cooler; *(sensiblement)* it's going to get cold *or* colder; **attendez que le métal se soit refroidi** wait till the metal has cooled (down); **ne laissez pas vos muscles se r.** don't let your muscles get cold

2 *(diminuer)* to cool off; **sa passion s'est refroidie** his/her passion has cooled

3 *(prendre froid)* to catch a chill

refroidissement [rəfrwadismɑ̃] NM **1** *Tech (de l'eau, d'un moteur)* cooling; *(du métal)* quenching; **à r. par circulation d'eau** water-cooled; **à r. par ventilation** air-cooled; **plaque/tour de r.** cooling plate/tower

2 *(du temps)* drop in temperature

3 *(rhume)* chill; **elle a pris un r.** she caught a chill

4 *Fig (dans une relation)* cooling (off); **il y a eu un net r. dans leurs relations** there's been a definite cooling off in their relationship

refroidisseur [rəfrwadisœr] NM *Tech* cooler

refuge [rəfyʒ] NM **1** *(abri)* refuge; **servir de r. à qn** to offer refuge to sb, to provide a roof for sb; **chercher/trouver r. dans une grange** to seek/to find shelter in a barn; **donner r. à** to give shelter to, to shelter

2 *(en montagne)* (mountain) refuge; **l'hébergement est en r.** accommodation is provided at the mountain refuge

3 *(réconfort)* haven; **chercher r. dans les livres** to seek refuge in books; **ce quartier est le r. des artistes** this area is a haven for artists

4 *(dans une rue)* refuge, (traffic) island

5 *Biol* refugium

6 *(comme adj) voir* **valeur**

réfugié, -e [refyʒje] NM,F refugee; **r. non-statutaire** unrecognized refugee; **r. statutaire** recognized refugee

réfugier [9] [refyʒje] **se réfugier** VPR **1** *(s'abriter)* to take refuge *or* shelter; **ils se sont réfugiés dans une grotte** they took refuge in a cave; **ils se sont réfugiés sous un arbre** they sheltered under a tree **2** *Fig* **elle se réfugie dans ses livres** she takes refuge in her books

refuite [rəfɥit] NF *Chasse (passage)* run, pass, path

refumer [3] [rəfyme] VI to start smoking again

refus [rəfy] NM **1** *(réponse négative)* refusal, rebuff; *(rejet → d'une proposition, d'un candidat, d'un manuscrit)* rejection; **s'exposer à un r.** to run the risk of a refusal *or* of being turned down; **opposer un r. à qn** to turn sb down; **opposer un r. catégorique à qn** to give an outright refusal to sb; **r. de vente/de priorité/d'obéissance** refusal to sell/to give way/to comply; **r. d'acceptation** non-acceptance; **r. de coopérer** non-cooperation; *Admin* **r. du dépôt** = refusal to register a mortgage because the applicant has not completed the required administrative formalities; *Journ* **r. d'insertion** refusal to publish; **r. d'obéissance** refusal to comply; **r. d'obtempérer** obstruction; **r. de paiement** non-payment; **r. de vente** refusal to sell; *Fam* **ce n'est pas de r.!** I wouldn't say no!, I don't mind if I do!

2 *Équitation* refusal

refusable [rəfyzabl] ADJ *(gén)* refusable; *(offre)* which can be rejected

refusé, -e [rəfyze] **NM,F** *Univ* failed candidate

refuser [3] [rəfyze] **VT 1** *(don)* to refuse to accept; *(livraison)* to reject; *(offre, proposition)* to turn down, to refuse; *(invitation)* to turn down, to decline; *(candidat)* to turn down; *(chèque)* to bounce; **r. une marchandise pour non-conformité** to refuse to accept an unfit *or* a faulty product; **il a refusé tous les cadeaux** he's refused to accept any present, he's turned down every present; **je suis obligé de r. du travail** I have to turn jobs down *or* to refuse work; **le restaurant refuse du monde tous les soirs** the restaurant turns people away every evening; **être refusé** *(à un examen)* to fail

2 *(autorisation)* to refuse, to turn down; *(service)* to refuse, to deny; **je lui ai refusé l'accès au jardin** I denied him/her access to the garden; **je lui ai refusé la visite du jardin** I wouldn't allow him/her to visit the garden; **r. sa porte à qn** to refuse to see sb; **r. de faire qch** to refuse to do sth; **il refuse de sortir de sa chambre** he refuses to leave his room; **r. de payer une somme** to withhold a sum of money; **il ne peut rien lui r.** he can refuse him/her nothing; **comment peux-tu lui r. ça?** how can you deny him/her that?; **on leur a refusé l'entrée du château** they weren't allowed in the castle; **il s'est vu r. l'autorisation** he was refused *or* denied permission

3 *(objet)* **le tiroir refuse de s'ouvrir** the drawer refuses to *or* won't open

4 *Équitation* to refuse

5 *(maladie, responsabilité)* to refuse, to reject; **je refusais tout à fait cette idée** I wouldn't accept that idea at all; **r. le combat** to refuse battle *or* to fight; **r. de lutter contre la maladie/d'utiliser la force** to refuse to combat illness/to use force; **r. les responsabilités** to shun responsibilities, to refuse to take on responsibilities; **on ne peut lui r. une réelle maîtrise du sujet** there's no denying he/she really knows the subject

VI 1 *Constr* to resist, to balk

2 *Naut* to haul, to turn

▸**se refuser VPR 1** *(emploi passif)* **une telle offre ne se refuse pas** such an offer is not to be refused *or* can't be turned down; **un séjour au bord de la mer, ça ne se refuse pas** a stay at the seaside, you can't say no to that

2 *(à soi-même)* to deny oneself; *Fam* **des vacances au Brésil, on ne se refuse rien!** a holiday in Brazil, you're certainly spoiling yourself!

3 se r. à faire qch to refuse to do sth; **je me refuse à croire de pareilles sornettes!** I refuse to believe such twaddle!; **l'avocat se refuse à tout commentaire** the lawyer is refusing to make any comment *or* is declining to comment; **je me refuse à de telles manœuvres!** I refuse to engage in such scheming!; **se r. à l'évidence** to shut one's eyes to the facts

réfutabilité [refytabilite] **NF** refutability

réfutable [refytabl] **ADJ** refutable; **des arguments qui ne sont pas réfutables** arguments which cannot be refuted

réfutation [refytasjɔ̃] **NF** refutation

réfuter [3] [refyte] **VT 1** *(en prouvant)* to refute, to disprove **2** *(contredire)* to contradict

refuznik [rəfyznik] **NMF** refusnik, refusenik

reg [rɛg] **NM** *Géog* reg

regagner [3] [rəgaɲe] **VT 1** *(gagner → à nouveau)* to win back, to regain; *(→ après une perte)* to win back; **le dollar regagne quelques centimes sur le marché des changes** the dollar has regained a few cents on the foreign exchange market; **r. la confiance de ses électeurs** to win back the voters' trust; **r. le temps perdu** to make up for lost time; **r. du terrain** to recover lost ground

2 *(retourner à)* to go back *or* to return to; **r. la ville/la France** to return to (the) town/to France; **il a regagné la côte à la nage** he swam (back) to the shore; **r. sa place** to get back to one's seat *or* place

regain [rəgɛ̃] **NM 1** *(retour, accroissement)* renewal, revival; **un r. de vie** a new lease of life; **avec un r. de bonne humeur** with renewed cheerfulness; **un r. d'énergie** fresh energy; **un r. d'espoir** renewed hope; **on constate un r. d'activité sur les marchés boursiers** we can see renewed activity *or* a renewal of activity on the Stock Market **2** *Agr* aftermath

régal, -als [regal] **NM 1** *(délice)* delight, treat; **ce repas est un vrai r.** this meal is a real treat **2** *(plaisir)* delight; **la mousse au chocolat est son r.** chocolate mousse is his/her favourite; **c'est un vrai r. de l'écouter** it's a treat *or* a pleasure to listen to him/her; **c'est un r. pour les yeux** it's a sight for sore eyes

régalade [regalad] **NF boire à la r.** = to drink without letting the bottle touch one's lips

régalage [regalaʒ] **NM** *(d'un terrain)* levelling

régale [regal] **ADJ F** *Chim* **eau r.** aqua regia

régalec [regalɛk] **NM** *Ich* oarfish

régalement [regalmɑ̃] **NM** (tax) apportioning

régaler [3] [regale] **VT 1** *(offrir à manger, à boire à)* to treat; **r. ses amis d'un excellent vin** to treat one's friends to an excellent wine

2 *Fig* to regale; **elle régalait ses collègues d'anecdotes croustillantes** she regaled her colleagues with *or* treated her colleagues to spicy anecdotes

3 *(terrain)* to level

4 *Fin* to apportion (a tax)

USAGE ABSOLU *Fam* **aujourd'hui, c'est moi qui régale** today it's on me *or* I'm treating you *or* it's my treat

▸**se régaler VPR 1** *(en mangeant)* **je me suis régalé** it was a real treat, I really enjoyed it

2 *Fig* **je me régale à l'écouter** it's a real treat for me to listen to him/her; **elle se régale avec ses petits-enfants** she's having the time of her life with her grandchildren

régalien, -enne [regaljɛ̃, -ɛn] **ADJ** kingly, royal; **droit r.** royal prerogative

regard [rəgar] **NM 1** *(expression)* look, expression; **son r. était haineux** he/she had a look of hatred in his/her eye *or* eyes, his/her eyes were full of hatred; **il a un r. doux/torve** he has a gentle/menacing look in his eyes; **un r. vitreux** a glassy stare; **un r. concupiscent** a leer; **un r. méfiant** a suspicious look

2 *(coup d'œil)* look, glance, gaze; **mon r. s'arrêta sur une fleur** my eyes fell on a flower; **attirer les regards** to be the centre of attention; **nos regards se croisèrent** our eyes met; **je sentis son r. se poser sur moi** I felt him/her looking at me, I felt his/her gaze on me; **il a détourné le r.** he averted his gaze, he looked away; **ils échangèrent un r. de connivence** they exchanged knowing *or* conspiring looks; **un r. qui en disait long** an eloquent look; **chercher du r.** to look (around) for; **interroger qn du r.** to give sb a questioning look; **il est parti sans même un r.** he left without even a backward glance; **jeter** *ou* **lancer un r. à qn** to glance *or* to cast a glance at sb; **il lançait aux visiteurs des regards mauvais** he glared at the visitors *or* gave the visitors nasty looks; **caché aux regards du public** out of the public eye; **loin des regards curieux** far from prying eyes; **sous les regards de la foule** while the crowd looked on; **elle attire tous les regards** everyone turns to look at her; *Fig* **porter un r. nouveau sur qn/qch** to look at sb/sth in a new light; **couver qn/qch du r.** to stare at sb/sth with greedy eyes; *Hum* **suivez mon r.** mentioning no names

3 *(d'égout)* manhole; *(de four)* peephole

4 *(contrôle)* **droit de r.** right of inspection; **je demande un droit de r. sur tous les textes qui sortent de ce bureau** I demand the right to check all texts leaving this office

□ **au regard de PRÉP 1** *(aux termes de)* in the eyes of; **mes papiers sont en règle au r. de la loi** my papers are in order from a legal point of view

2 *(en comparaison avec)* in comparison with, compared to; **ce n'est pas grand-chose au r. de ce que je dois au percepteur** that's not much compared to what I owe the *Br* taxman *or Am* IRS

□ **en regard ADV un texte latin avec la traduction en r.** a Latin text with a translation on the opposite page

□ **en regard de PRÉP 1** *(face à)* **en r. de la colonne des chiffres** facing *or* opposite the column of figures

2 *(en comparaison avec)* compared with

regardant, -e [rəgardɑ̃, -ɑ̃t] **ADJ 1** *(avare)* sparing, grudging, *Euph* careful with money **2** *(pointilleux)* demanding; **elle n'est pas très regardante sur la propreté** she's not very particular when it comes to cleanliness

REGARDER [3] [rəgarde]

> **VT** to look at **1, 2, 5** ▪ to see **1** ▪ to watch **1** ▪ to examine **2** ▪ to look up **3** ▪ to concern **4** ▪ to regard **5**
> **VI** to look **1** ▪ to face **2**

VT 1 *(voir)* to look at, to see; *(observer)* to watch, to see; **r. qch rapidement** to glance at sth; **r. qch fixement** to stare at sth; **r. qch longuement** to gaze at sth; **regarde s'il arrive** see if he's coming; **si tu veux t'instruire, regarde-le faire** if you want to learn, watch how he does it; **il n'aime pas qu'on le regarde manger** he doesn't like people watching him eat; **as-tu regardé le match?** did you watch *or* see the match?; *Fam* **regarde voir dans la chambre** go and look *or* have a look in the bedroom; *Fam* **regarde voir si ton petit frère dort** look *or* check and see if your little brother is sleeping, will you?; *Fam* **regarde-moi ça!** just look at that!; *Fam* **regarde-moi ce travail!** just look at this mess!; *Fam* **tu ne m'as pas regardé!** what do you take me for?, who do you think I am?; *Fam* **tu veux que j'y aille à ta place? non mais, tu m'as bien regardé?** you want me to go instead of you? what sort of a sucker do you take me for?

2 *(examiner → moteur, blessure)* to look at, to check; *(→ notes, travail)* to look over *or* through; **as-tu eu le temps de r. le dossier?** did you have time to look at the file?

3 *(vérifier)* to look up; **regarde son prénom dans le dictionnaire** look up his/her first name in the dictionary; **tu regardes constamment la pendule!** you're always looking at *or* watching the clock!; *Fam* **non mais, tu as regardé l'heure?** *(il est tard)* have you seen the time?, do you realize what time it is?; **je vais r. quelle heure il est** *ou* **l'heure** I'm going to see *or* to check what time it is

4 *(concerner)* to concern; **bien sûr que ça me regarde!** of course it concerns me!; **ceci ne regarde que toi et moi** this is (just) between you and me; **ça ne te regarde pas!** that's *or* it's none of your business!; **cette affaire ne me regarde plus** this affair is no longer any concern *or* business of mine; **cela ne les regarde en rien** it's absolutely no business of theirs; **en quoi est-ce que ça me regarde?** what's that got to do with me?

5 *(considérer → sujet, situation)* to look at, to view; **elle ne regarde pas les choses de la même façon que moi** she looks at *or* sees things differently from me; **si l'on regarde la situation de son point de vue** if you look at *or* view the situation from his/her standpoint; **un projet que l'on regardait alors avec suspicion** a project which was regarded *or* viewed with suspicion at the time; **nous regardons l'avenir avec confiance** we look to the future with confidence; **il regarde avec envie la réussite de son frère** he casts an envious eye upon his brother's success, he looks upon his brother's success with envy; **ne r. que** *(ne penser qu'à)* to be concerned only with, to think only about; **il ne regarde que ses intérêts** he thinks only about his own interests; **r. qn comme** to consider sb as, to regard sb as, to look upon sb as; **je l'ai toujours regardé comme un frère** I've always looked upon him as a brother; **on le regarde comme un futur champion** he is seen *or* regarded as a future champion; **r. qch comme** to regard sth as, to look upon sth as, to think of sth as

USAGE ABSOLU regarde à la lettre D look through the D's, look at *or* under the letter D

VI 1 *(personne)* to look; **nous avons regardé partout** we looked *or* searched everywhere; **il passe des heures à r. dans son télescope** he spends hours peering into his telescope; **tu ne sais pas r.** you should learn to use your eyes; **ne reste pas là à r., fais quelque chose!** don't just stand there (staring), do something!

2 *(bâtiment, pièce)* **r. à l'ouest** to face West; **le balcon regarde vers la mer** the balcony looks out over *or* faces the sea

□ **regarder à VT IND 1** *(morale, principes)* to think of *or* about, to take into account; *(apparence, détail)* to pay attention to; **je regarde avant tout à**

ref–reg

la qualité I'm particularly or primarily concerned with quality; **nous regardons d'abord au bien-être de nos patients** we are primarily concerned with the welfare of our patients; **regarde à ne pas faire d'erreur** watch you don't make a mistake; **r. à la dépense** to be careful with one's money; **ne regardons pas à la dépense!** let's not think about the money!; **acheter sans r. à la dépense** to buy things regardless of the expense; **tu ne vas pas r. à 3 euros, non!** you're not going to worry about 3 euros, are you?; **y r. à deux** ou **à plusieurs fois avant de faire qch** to think twice before doing sth; **à y bien r., à y r. de plus près** when you think it over, on thinking it over; **il ne faut pas y r. de trop près** don't look too closely; Fig don't be too fussy

2 Belg (veiller sur) to look after
□ **regarder après** = **regarder à 2**
□ **regarder de** vt ind Belg **r. de faire qch** to make sure or to take care to do sth

▸**se regarder** vpr **1** (emploi réfléchi) aussi Fig to look at oneself; **se r. dans un miroir** to look at oneself in a mirror; **elle se regardait sans complaisance** she examined herself critically; Fam **tu ne t'es pas regardé!** you should take a (good) look at yourself!

2 (emploi réciproque) (personnes) to look at each other or at one another; (bâtiments) to be opposite one another, to face each other; **elles se regardaient dans les yeux** they were looking or staring into each other's eyes

3 (emploi passif) (spectacle) **cette émission se regarde en famille** this is a family show, this show is family viewing; **ça se regarde volontiers** it's quite enjoyable to watch

regardeur, -euse [rəgardœr, -øz] nm,f Littéraire watcher
regarnir [32] [rəgarnir] vt (rayons, garde-manger) to restock, to refill, to stock up again; (maison) to refurnish
régate [regat] nfNaut regatta; **faire une r.** to sail in a regatta
régater [3] [regate] vi **1** Naut to race or to sail in a regatta; **r. avec qn** to race sb in a regatta **2** Suisse (être à la hauteur) to measure up, to match up
régatier [regatje] nm Naut entrant or competitor in a regatta
regel [rəʒɛl] nm renewed frost
regeler [25] [rəʒəle] vt to freeze again
    vi to freeze again
    v impersonnel **il regèle** it's freezing again
régence [reʒɑ̃s] nf regency
    □ **Régence** nf **la R.** the Regency of Philippe II (in France) adj inv (style) (French) Regency; **un fauteuil R.** a Regency armchair; Fig **elle est très R.** she's very genteel
Regency [reʒɑ̃si] adj inv (style britannique) Regency
régendat [reʒɑ̃da] nm Belg = teacher training course for "régents"
régénérateur, -trice [reʒeneratœr, -tris] adj regenerative; Rel **eau régénératrice** baptismal water
    nm,f Littéraire regenerator
    nm regenerator
régénération [reʒenerasjɔ̃] nf regeneration; Ordinat **r. de l'écran** screen refresh
régénératrice [reʒeneratris] voir **régénérateur**
régénéré, -e [reʒenere] adj regenerated; **caoutchouc r.** regenerated rubber (fibres)
régénérer [18] [reʒenere] vt **1** Biol & Chim to regenerate **2** (rénover) to regenerate, to restore; **je me sens régénéré après cette douche** I feel refreshed or revived after that shower
    ▸**se régénérer** vpr Biol & Chim to regenerate (itself)
régent, -e [reʒɑ̃, -ɑ̃t] adj **reine régente** Queen Regent; **prince r.** Prince Regent
    nm,f **1** Pol regent **2** Belg = qualified secondary school teacher
    nm Anciennement (de la Banque de France) director
régenter [3] [reʒɑ̃te] vt to rule over, to run; **il veut tout r.** he wants to run everything or the show; **il veut r. tout le monde** he wants everybody to be at his beck and call

reggae [rege] nm Mus reggae
régicide [reʒisid] adj regicidal
    nmf (personne) regicide
    nm (acte) regicide
régie [reʒi] nf **1** (d'une entreprise publique → par l'État) state control; (→ par le département) local government control; (→ par la commune) local authority control; **(société en) r.** (par l'État) state-controlled corporation; (par le département) local government controlled company; (par la commune) ≃ local authority controlled company; **il travaille à la r. municipale des eaux** he works for the local water board; Hist **la R.** = collection of taxes by state functionaries, Br ≃ Customs and Excise; Can **R. des Loyers** rental board

2 (pièce → dans un studio de télévision ou de radio) control room; (→ dans un théâtre) lighting box; (équipe) production team; **r. centrale** master control room; **r. mobile** mobile control room

3 Écon **travaux en r.** (net) timework
4 Mktg **r. publicitaire** advertising sales agency
5 Fin excise
6 r. de quartier = neighbourhood group made up of members of the local authority and local residents, who work together to develop public services, improve communication and tackle social issues in their community
regimber [3] [rəʒɛ̃be] vi **1** (cheval) to rear up, to jib **2** (personne) to grumble, to complain; **faire qch sans r.** to do sth without grumbling or complaining; **inutile de r.** it's no use grumbling or complaining
regimbeur, -euse [rəʒɛ̃bœr, -øz] nm,f Littéraire complainer, grumbler
régime [reʒim] nm **1** Pol (système) regime, (system of) government; (gouvernement) regime; **r. militaire/parlementaire/totalitaire** military/parliamentary/totalitarian regime; **la chute du r.** the fall of the regime or the government; **sous le r. de Pompidou/Clinton** during the Pompidou/Clinton administration

2 Admin & Jur (système) system, scheme; (règlement) rules, regulations; **le r. des visites à l'hôpital** hospital visiting hours and conditions; **r. de Sécurité sociale** = subdivision of the French social security system applying to certain professional groups; **être marié sous le r. de la communauté/de la séparation de biens** to have opted for a marriage based on joint ownership of property/on separate ownership of property; **r. d'assurance vieillesse** old-age pension fund or scheme; **r. complémentaire** additional retirement cover; **r. contractuel** contractual regime; **r. douanier** customs regulations; **r. fiscal** tax regime or system; Fin **r. du forfait** standard assessment system, fixed-rate tax assessment system; **le r. général de la Sécurité sociale** the social security system; **r. légal** statutory regime; **r. matrimonial** marriage settlement; **r. matrimonial primaire** basic matrimonial property regime; **régimes matrimoniaux** matrimonial property regimes; **r. pénitentiaire** prison system; Fin **r. du réel** full assessment system; **r. de retraite** retirement scheme; **r. de retraite des artisans, commerçants et professions libérales** self-employed pension; **r. de retraite par capitalisation** funded pension scheme; **r. simplifié** simplified system; **r. de transit** transit system; **le r. du travail** the organization of labour

3 Écon **r. préférentiel** special arrangements
4 (alimentaire) diet; **faire un r.,** Belg **faire r.** to go on a diet; **être au r.** to be on a diet, to be dieting; **se mettre au r.** to go on a diet; **r. alimentaire** diet; **r. amaigrissant** Br slimming or Am reducing diet; **r. grossissant** fattening diet; **r. lacté** milk diet; Fam Hum **je suis au r.** I'm on an alcohol-free diet■; **r. sans sel** salt-free diet; **se mettre au r. jockey** to go on a starvation diet

5 Ind & Tech engine speed; **fonctionner à plein r.** (usine) to work to full capacity; **travailler à plein r.** (personne) to work flat out; **à ce r. vous ne tiendrez pas longtemps** at this rate you won't last long; **r. de croisière** economic or cruising speed; **r. de production** production rate

6 Géog (d'un cours d'eau) rate of flow, regimen;

r. glaciaire/nivo-glaciaire/nivo-pluvial glacial/snow and ice/snow and rain regime; **r. des pluies** rainfall pattern; **le r. des vents** the prevailing winds or wind system
7 Ling **r. direct/indirect** direct/indirect object; **cas r.** objective case
8 Phys regimen, flow rate; **r. laminaire** laminary flow
9 Bot (de bananes) hand, stem, bunch; (de dattes) bunch, cluster

régiment [reʒimɑ̃] nm **1** Mil (unité) regiment; **r. d'infanterie** infantry regiment
2 Vieilli (service militaire) **faire son r. dans l'infanterie** Br ≃ to do one's military service in the infantry, Am ≃ to be drafted into the infantry; **un de mes camarades de r.** a friend from my military service days
3 Fam (grand nombre) **il a tout un r. de cousins** he's got a whole army of cousins; **il y en a pour un r.** there's enough for a whole army
régimentaire [reʒimɑ̃tɛr] adj Mil regimental
région [reʒjɔ̃] nf **1** Géog region, area; **r. industrielle/agricole** industrial/agricultural region or area; **les régions tempérées/polaires** the temperate/polar regions; **la Sologne est une r. marécageuse** the Sologne is a marshy area or region; **dans la r. de Nantes** in the Nantes area, in the region of Nantes; **les habitants de Paris et sa r.** the inhabitants of Paris and the surrounding region or area; **le nouveau médecin n'est pas de la r.** the new doctor isn't from the area or from around here; **si jamais tu passes dans la r....** if you're ever in the area...; **la r. parisienne** the Paris area, the area around Paris; Pol **r. tampon** buffer zone; Mktg **r. test** test area

2 Anat **r. cervicale/lombaire** cervical/lumbar region; **une douleur dans la r. du foie** a pain somewhere around or near the liver
    □ **Région** nf Admin region (French administrative area made up of several departments); **je suis financé par la R.** I get funding from the region
régional, -e, -aux, -ales [reʒjɔnal, -o] adj **1** (de la région) regional; (de la localité) local **2** (sur le plan international) local, regional; **un conflit r.** a regional conflict
    nm Tél area telephone system
    □ **régionale** nf Belg (fédération) = regionally-based organization; (amicale d'étudiants) = regionally-based students' association
régionalisation [reʒjɔnalizasjɔ̃] nf regionalization
régionaliser [3] [reʒjɔnalize] vt to regionalize
régionalisme [reʒjɔnalism] nm regionalism
régionaliste [reʒjɔnalist] adj regionalist
    nmf (gén) & Pol regionalist; (écrivain) regional writer
régir [32] [reʒir] vt **1** (déterminer) to govern **2** Vieilli (domaine) to manage
régisseur, -euse [reʒisœr, -øz] nm,f **1** (d'un domaine) steward **2** Cin & TV assistant director; Théât stage manager; **r. d'extérieurs** location manager; **r. de plateau** floor manager; **r. de plateau adjoint** assistant floor manager **3** Écon comptroller
registraire [reʒistrɛr] nmf Can Admin registrar
registration [reʒistrasjɔ̃] nf Mus registration
registre [rəʒistr] nm **1** Admin & Jur register; (de comptes) account book; **noter qch dans un r.** to write sth down in or to enter sth into a register; **signer le r.** (d'un hôtel) to sign the register; Jur **r. d'audience** record; **s'inscrire au r. du commerce** to register one's company; **r. de l'état civil** ≃ register of births, marriages and deaths;

Bourse **r. des actionnaires** register of *Br* shareholders *or Am* stockholders, *Br* shareholders' *or Am* stockholders' register; *Bourse* **r. des actions** share register; **R. du commerce et des sociétés** the Registrar of companies; *Compta* **r. de comptabilité** account book, ledger; **r. des dépôts** mortgage register; **r. foncier** land register; **r. national des brevets** national patent register; **r. national des dessins et modèles** national register of designs and models; **r. national des marques** national trademark register; **r. des procès-verbaux** minutes book; **r. des salaires** payroll; *Fin* **r. des transferts** transfer register

2 *Typ* register

3 *Mus (d'un orgue)* stop; *(d'une voix)* range, register; **avoir un r. étendu** to have a wide range; **un r. aigu/grave** a high/low pitch

4 *Ling* register, level of language

5 *(style)* tone, style; **le livre est écrit dans un r. plaisant** the book is written in a humorous style

6 *Tech (dans un conduit)* damper

7 *Ordinat* register; *(de Windows®)* registry; **r. d'accès mémoire** memory access register

registrer [3] [rəʒistre] **VT** *Mus* to registrate

réglable [reglabl] **ADJ 1** *(adaptable)* adjustable; **position/hauteur r.** adjustable position/height; **le dossier est r. en hauteur** the height of the seat is adjustable; **température/intensité r.** adjustable temperature/intensity **2** *(payable)* payable; **r. par mensualités** payable in monthly instalments

réglage [reglaʒ] **NM 1** *(mise au point)* adjustment, regulation; **procéder au r. des phares** to adjust the headlights; **r. d'un thermostat** thermostat setting; **levier de r.** adjusting lever

2 *Aut, Rad & TV* tuning; **r. du contraste/de la luminosité de l'écran** contrast/brightness control; *Phot* **le r. de l'appareil est automatique** the camera is fully automatic

3 *Mil* **r. du tir** range finding *or* adjustment

4 *(du papier)* ruling

règle [rɛgl] **NF 1** *(instrument)* ruler, rule; **r. à calcul** slide rule

2 *(principe, code)* rule; **c'est la r.** that's the rule; **se plier à une r.** to abide by a rule; **les règles de l'honneur** the rules *or* code of honour; **les règles de la politesse exigent que...** courtesy demands that...; **enfreindre la r.** to break the rule *or* rules; **j'ai pour r. de me coucher de bonne heure** I make it a rule to go to bed early; **il est de r. de porter une cravate ici** it's customary to wear a tie here; **les règles de base en grammaire** the basic rules of grammar; **les règles des échecs** the rules of chess; **règles d'exploitation** operating regulations; *Jur* **r. de droit** Rule of Law; **la r. du jeu** the rules of the game; **respecter la r. du jeu** to play by the rules; **r. d'or** golden rule; **règles de sécurité** safety regulations; **r. de trois** rule of three; **dans les règles (de l'art)** according to the (rule) book, by the book

▫ **règles NFPL** *Physiol (en général)* periods; *(d'un cycle)* period; **avoir ses règles** to be menstruating, to have one's period; **je n'ai plus de** *ou* **mes règles depuis trois mois** I haven't had a period for three months; **avoir des règles douloureuses** to have painful periods, *Br* to suffer from period pain *or* pains, *Am* to suffer from menstrual cramps

▫ **en règle ADJ être en r.** *(document)* to be in order; *(personne)* to have one's papers in order, to be in possession of valid papers; **se mettre en r.** to sort out one's situation; **une bataille en r.** a battle according to the rules; **recevoir un avertissement en r.** to be given an official warning; **tenir sa comptabilité en r.** to keep one's accounts in order

▫ **en règle générale ADV** generally, as a (general) rule

'La Règle du jeu' *Renoir* 'The Rules of the Game'

réglé, -e [regle] **ADJ 1** *(organisé)* regular, well-ordered; **une vie bien réglée** a well-ordered existence

2 *(rayé ou quadrillé)* **papier r.** ruled *or* lined paper; **c'est r. comme du papier à musique** it's as regular as clockwork

▫ **réglée ADJ F** *(jeune fille)* **depuis combien de temps êtes-vous réglée?** how long have you been having your periods?; **est-elle réglée?** has she started her periods (yet)?

règlement [rɛgləmɑ̃] **NM 1** *Admin* regulation, rules; **observer le r.** to abide by the rules; **d'après le r., il est interdit de...** it's against the regulations to...; **le r. a été affiché dans chaque classe** the rules have been pinned up in each classroom; **r. administratif** ≃ statutory policy; **r. d'administration publique** ≃ statutory decree *or* declaration; **r. d'application** implementing regulation; **r. autonome** autonomous regulation; **r. intérieur** *(d'une école)* school rules; *(d'un bureau)* company *or* staff regulations; **r. de police municipale** *ou* **municipal** ≃ by-law; **r. sanitaire** health regulations

2 *(d'un compte)* settlement; *(d'une facture)* payment, settlement; **en r. de votre compte** in settlement of your account; **faire un r. par chèque** to pay by cheque; **r. à la commande** cash with order; **pour r. de tout compte** in full settlement; **r. par carte de crédit/au comptant** payment by credit card/in cash; **r. en espèces** cash payment *or* settlement; **r. en nature** settlement in kind

3 *(résolution)* settlement, settling; **r. de compte** *ou* **comptes** settling of scores; **il y a eu des règlements de comptes** some old scores were settled; *Jur* **r. à l'amiable** amicable settlement; *(sans procès)* out-of-court settlement; **r. de gré à gré** amicable settlement, settlement by negotiation; *Jur* **r. judiciaire** compulsory liquidation, *Br* winding-up; **se mettre en r. judiciaire** to go into liquidation *or* receivership; *Jur* **r. de juges** settlement of a conflict of jurisdictions by a superior court

4 *Bourse* settlement; **(marché du) r. mensuel** forward market

'Règlement de comptes à O.K. Corral' *Sturges* 'Gunfight at the O.K. Corral'

réglementaire [rɛgləmɑ̃tɛr] **ADJ 1** *(conforme)* regulation *(avant n)*; **longueur/uniforme r.** regulation length/uniform; **modèle de chaudière r.** approved *or* standard type of boiler; **il a passé l'âge r.** he's above the statutory age limit; **le score était de 0–0 à l'issue du temps r.** *(au foot)* the score was 0–0 after ninety minutes; **ce que vous avez fait là n'est pas r.** it's against the rules to do that, that's against the rules; *Fam* **sa tenue n'était pas des plus réglementaires** his/her outfit was somewhat unorthodox

2 *Jur* **pouvoir r.** statutory *or* regulative power

3 *Admin (décision)* statutory; **dispositions réglementaires** regulations

réglementairement [rɛgləmɑ̃tɛrmɑ̃] **ADV** according to regulations, statutorily

réglementarisme [rɛgləmɑ̃tarism] **NM** tendency to over-regulation

réglementation [rɛgləmɑ̃tasjɔ̃] **NF 1** *(mesures)* regulations; **r. fiscale** tax regulations; **la r. du travail** labour regulations *or* legislation **2** *(limitation)* control, regulation; **la r. des prix** price regulation; **r. des changes** exchange control

réglementer [3] [rɛgləmɑ̃te] **VT** to regulate, to control; **la vente des boissons alcoolisées est très réglementée** the sale of alcoholic drinks is under strict control *or* is strictly controlled

régler [18] [regle] **VT 1** *(résoudre → litige)* to settle, to resolve; *(→ problème)* to solve, to iron out, to sort out; **alors c'est réglé, nous irons au bord de la mer** it's settled then, we'll go to the seaside; **c'est une affaire réglée** it is (all) settled now

2 *(payer → achat)* to pay (for); *(→ facture, mensualité)* to pay, to settle; *(→ compte)* to settle; *(→ épicier, femme de ménage, loyer)* to pay; *(→ créancier)* to settle up with; **mon salaire ne m'a pas été réglé** my salary hasn't been paid (in); **r. l'addition** to pay *or* to settle the bill; **r. qch en espèces** to pay cash for sth; **r. qch par chèque/par carte de crédit** to pay for sth by cheque/by credit card; **je peux vous r. par chèque?** will you take a cheque?, can I pay by cheque?; **désirez-vous r. par chèque ou par carte de crédit?** would you like to pay by cheque or credit card?; *Assur* **r. un sinistre** to settle a claim; **r. ses comptes (avec qn)** to settle up (with sb); *Fig* to settle (one's) scores (with sb); **r. quelques comptes** to settle a few scores; **j'ai un compte à r. avec toi** I've got a bone to pick with you; *Fam* **r. son compte à qn** *(se venger de lui)* to get even with sb; *(le tuer)* to take care of sb

3 *(volume, allumage, phare etc)* to adjust; *(vitesse, thermostat)* to set; *(température)* to regulate; *(circulation)* to control; *(moteur)* to tune; **j'ai réglé mon réveil sur sept heures/le four à 200°** I've set my alarm for seven o'clock/the oven at 200°; **comment r. la radio sur France-Musique?** how do you tune in to France-Musique?; *Sport* **r. l'allure** to set the pace; **r. qch sur** *(accorder par rapport à)* to set sth by; **r. sa montre sur l'horloge parlante** to set one's watch by the speaking clock; **r. son rythme sur celui du soleil** to model one's rhythm of life on the movement of the sun; **r. son allure sur celle de qn** to adjust one's pace to that of sb

4 *(déterminer)* to decide (on), to settle; **quelques détails à r.** a few details to be settled; **r. les pas d'un ballet** to set (down) the steps for a ballet

5 *(papier)* to rule

6 *Jur (résoudre)* to settle; **r. qch à l'amiable** to settle sth amicably; *(sans procès)* to settle sth out of court

▸**se régler VPR 1** *(mécanisme)* to be set *or* regulated; *(luminosité, phare)* to be adjusted; *(récepteur)* to be tuned

2 *(se résoudre)* to be settled; **ça s'est réglé à l'amiable** it was settled amicably

3 se r. sur *(imiter)* to model oneself on, to follow (the example of); **elle a tendance à se r. sur (l'exemple de) sa mère** she has a tendency to model herself on her mother

réglet [reglɛ] **NM 1** *Archit* reglet **2** *(pour mesurer)* carpenter's rule

réglette [reglɛt] **NF 1** *(petite règle)* short ruler, straightedge **2** *Typ* lead, reglet **3** *(au Scrabble®)* rack **4** *Ordinat (pour un clavier)* template

régleur, -euse [reglœr, -øz] **ADJ** adjusting

NM,F setter

NM 1 *(dans l'industrie du froid)* regulator *(of freezing mixture)* **2** *Assur* **(inspecteur) r.** loss adjuster

▫ **régleuse NF** *Ind* ruling machine

réglisse [reglis] **NF** liquorice; **bâton de r.** stick of liquorice; **bonbon à la r.** liquorice-flavoured *Br* sweet *or Am* candy

réglo [reglo] *Fam* **ADJ INV** *(personne)* straight, on the level; *(opération, transaction)* legit, kosher; **un type r.** an OK *or Am* a regular guy; **elle a été très r.** she played by the rules; **il n'a pas été très r. avec moi** he didn't treat me right; **il trempe toujours dans des affaires pas très r.** he's always mixed up in some kind of shady business

ADV by the book, fair and square; **il a intérêt à jouer r.** he'd better play fair; **on fait ça r., hein?** we'll do it by the book, OK?

réglure [reglyr] **NF** ruling

régnant, -e [reɲɑ̃, -ɑ̃t] **ADJ 1** *(qui règne)* reigning **2** *(qui prédomine)* prevailing, reigning, dominant; **la mode régnante** prevailing fashion

règne [rɛɲ] **NM 1** *(gouvernement)* reign; **sous le r. de Catherine II** in the reign of Catherine II **2** *(domination → de la bêtise, de la justice)* rule, reign; **c'est le r. de l'argent/de la technologie** money/technology reigns supreme **3** *Biol* **r. animal/végétal** animal/plant kingdom

régner [8] [reɲe] **VI 1** *(gouverner)* to reign, to rule; **r. sur un pays** to reign over *or* to rule (over) a country

2 *(dominer → idée)* to predominate, to prevail; *(→ ordre, silence)* to reign, to prevail; **le chaos règne** chaos reigns *or* prevails; **la courtoisie qui règne dans nos rapports** the courtesy which prevails in our dealings with each other; **la suspicion qui règne au bureau** the climate of suspicion in the office *or* which pervades the office; **r. sur** to rule over; **en maître (sur)** to rule supreme (over); *Littéraire* **elle règne dans mon cœur** she reigns in my heart; **faire r. la paix** to keep the peace; **faire r. le silence** to keep everybody quiet; **faire r. l'ordre** to keep things under control; **un dictateur qui a fait r. la terreur** a dictator who established a reign of terror; *Ironique* **la confiance règne!** there's trust *or* confidence for you!

3 *(tournure impersonnelle)* **il règne enfin une paix profonde** a great peace reigns at last; **il règne dans la famille une atmosphère de haine** an atmosphere of hatred reigns in the family

régolite [regɔlit] **NM** *Géol* regolith

regonflage [rəgɔ̃flaʒ], **regonflement** [rəgɔ̃fləmɑ̃] **NM** *(de ballon, de bouée)* blowing up again, reinflating; *(de matelas pneumatique)* pumping up again, reinflating

regonfler [3] [rəgɔ̃fle] **VT 1** *(gonfler de nouveau → ballon, bouée)* to blow up (again), to reinflate; *(→ matelas pneumatique)* to pump up (again), to reinflate; *Fam* **son séjour à la mer l'a regonflée à bloc** her stay at the seaside has bucked her up (no end); *Fam* **je suis regonflé à bloc!** I'm back on form!

2 *(gonfler davantage → pneus)* to put more air in *or* into; **faites le plein et regonflez les pneus avant** fill her up and put some air in the front tyres

VI *(gén) & Méd* to swell (up) again

►**se regonfler VPR** *Fam* **je me suis regonflé en allant passer un week-end à la mer** I spent a weekend at the seaside and it really did me good

regorgement [rəgɔrʒəmɑ̃] **NM** *Littéraire* overflow, overflowing

regorger [17] [rəgɔrʒe] **VI** *Littéraire (liquide)* to overflow

▫ **regorger de VT IND** to overflow with, to abound in; **la terre regorge d'eau** the ground is waterlogged; **les vitrines regorgent de marchandises** the shop windows are packed with goods; **les cafés regorgent de clients** the cafés are packed with customers; **la ville regorge de musées** the town has an abundance of museums

regratter [3] [rəgrate] **VT** to scrape again

regrattier, -ère [rəgratje, -ɛr] **NM,F** *Hist* regrater

regréer [15] [rəgree] **VT** to rig again

regreffer [4] [rəgrefe] **VT** to regraft

régresser [4] [regrese] **VI 1** *(baisser → chiffre, population)* to drop; *(→ douleur)* to improve; **le chiffre d'affaires a régressé** there has been a drop in turnover **2** *(décliner → civilisation)* to regress; *(→ industrie)* to be in decline; **j'ai régressé en maths** my maths has deteriorated **3** *(s'atténuer)* **la maladie a régressé** the patient's condition has improved **4** *Biol & Psy* to regress

régressif, -ive [regresif, -iv] **ADJ** *(gén)* regressive; *(impôt)* degressive; *Biol* **forme régressive** throwback

régression [regresjɔ̃] **NF 1** *(recul)* decline, decrease, regression; **être en r.** *(épidémie)* to be on the decline, to be losing ground; *(chômage, production)* to be on the decline, to be declining; **r. sociale** downward mobility **2** *Psy & Biol* regression; **r. atavique** throwback **3** *Géog* **r. (marine)** (marine) regression

régressive [regresiv] *voir* **régressif**

regret [rəgrɛ] **NM 1** *(remords)* regret; **elle m'a fait part de ses regrets** she expressed her regret to me; **je n'ai aucun r.** I have no regrets; **je n'ai qu'un r., c'est d'avoir dû lui mentir** my only regret is that I had to lie to him/her; **tu l'achètes, pas de regrets?** so you're buying it, no regrets?; **sans un r.** without a single regret; **tous mes regrets** I'm terribly *or* awfully sorry; **regrets éternels** *(faire-part de décès)* deeply regretted, greatly lamented

2 *(tristesse)* regret; **je vous quitte avec beaucoup de r.** I leave you with great regret, I'm very sorry I have to leave you; **nous nous en sommes séparés avec r.** we were sorry to part with it; **nous sommes au** *ou* **nous avons le r. de vous annoncer que...** we are sorry *or* we regret to have to inform you that...; **j'ai le r. de te le dire** I'm sorry *or* I regret to have to tell you this; **à mon grand r.** (much) to my regret

▫ **à regret ADV** *(partir, sévir)* regretfully, with regret; **il s'éloigna comme à r.** he walked away with apparent reluctance

regrettable [rəgrɛtabl] **ADJ** regrettable, unfortunate; **il est r. que...** it's unfortunate that...; **il est r. que tu n'aies pas été informée à temps** it is unfortunate *or* a pity (that) you were not informed in time

regretter [4] [rəgrete] **VT 1** *(éprouver de la nostalgie pour → personne, pays)* to miss; *(→ jeunesse, passé)* to be nostalgic for; **il sera regretté de tous** he'll be greatly *or* sorely missed; **son regretté mari** her late lamented husband

2 *(se repentir de)* to be sorry about, to regret; **tu n'as rien à r.** you've got nothing to feel sorry about *or* to regret; **je ne regrette pas le temps passé là-dessus/l'argent que ça m'a coûté** I'm not sorry I spent time/money on it; **il me ferait presque r. ma gentillesse** I'm almost sorry I was so kind to him; **je ne regrette rien** I've no regrets; **je saurai te faire r. ta plaisanterie** I'll make you sorry for that joke; **tu ne le regretteras pas!** you won't regret it!, you won't be sorry!; **vous le regretterez!** you'll regret it!, you'll be sorry!, you'll rue the day!; **vous regretterez vos paroles!** you'll be sorry you said that!, you'll regret those words!; **je regrette qu'elle soit partie si tôt** I'm sorry that she left so early, I wish she hadn't left so early

USAGE ABSOLU pouvez-vous venir? – non, je regrette will you be able to come? – no, I'm afraid not *or* – sorry, no; **ah non! je regrette! j'étais là avant toi!** I'm sorry but I was here first!

▫ **regretter de VT IND 1** *(se reprocher de)* **tu ne regretteras pas de m'avoir écouté** you won't be sorry you listened to me, you won't regret having listened to me

2 *(dans des expressions de politesse)* **nous regrettons de ne pouvoir donner suite à votre appel** *(au téléphone)* we regret *or* we are sorry we are unable to connect you; **je regrette de devoir vous annoncer que...** I regret to inform you that...

regrèvement [rəgrɛvmɑ̃] **NM** *Fin* tax increase

regrimper [3] [rəgrɛ̃pe] **VT** to climb (up) again

VI 1 *(sur une montagne, sur un arbre)* to climb (up) again **2** *(augmenter → température, taux)* to go up *or* to rise again

regros [rəgro] **NM** tanner's bark, tanbark

regrossir [32] [rəgrosir] **VI** to put on weight again

regroupement [rəgrupmɑ̃] **NM 1** *(d'animaux, d'enfants)* rounding up, round-up; *(de troupes)* gathering together, rallying; *(d'une équipe, d'un parti)* regrouping; **le r. des différentes tendances politiques** the rallying (together) of various shades of political opinion; **r. familial** = policy of authorizing the families of immigrant workers in possession of long-term work permits to join their relatives in France

2 *(de sociétés, de services)* merger, amalgamation

3 *(de comptes)* consolidation

regrouper [3] [rəgrupe] **VT 1** *(rassembler → animaux, enfants)* to round up, to gather together; *(→ troupes)* to gather together, to rally; *(→ équipe, parti)* to regroup

2 *(unir → sociétés, services)* to merge, to amalgamate; **regroupons le parti autour d'une idée-force** let us unite the party around a key idea

3 *(contenir)* to contain; **le centre culturel regroupe sous un même toit un cinéma et un théâtre** the arts centre accommodates *or* has a cinema and a theatre (under the same roof)

4 *(comptes)* to consolidate

►**se regrouper VPR** *(institutions)* to group together; *(foule)* to gather; *(équipe, parti, troupes)* to regroup; **les sociétés se sont regroupées pour mieux faire face à la concurrence** the companies have joined forces to deal more effectively with the competition; **les manifestants se regroupent devant la mairie** demonstrators are gathering *or* assembling in front of the town hall

régulage [regylaʒ] **NM** *Métal* babbitting

régularisation [regylarizasjɔ̃] **NF 1** *(d'une situation)* straightening out, regularization **2** *Fin (d'un compte, des stocks, des charges)* adjustment; *(de dividende)* equalization; **paiement de dix mensualités avec r. annuelle** ten monthly payments with end-of-year adjustments **3** *Géog* grading

régulariser [3] [regylarize] **VT 1** *(rendre légal)* to regularize; **il a fait r. son permis de séjour** he got his residence permit sorted out *or* put in order; **r. sa situation** to have one's papers sorted out *or* put in order; *Hum (se marier)* to tie the knot

2 *(rendre régulier)* to regulate; **des pilules qui régularisent le rythme cardiaque** pills which regulate the heartbeat

3 *Fin (compte, stocks, charge)* to adjust; *(dividende)* to equalize

4 *Géog* to grade

régularité [regylarite] **NF 1** *(dans le temps)* regularity, steadiness; **la r. des battements de son cœur** the regularity of his/her heartbeat; **un emploi du temps d'une parfaite r.** a schedule that is (as) regular as clockwork; **faire preuve de r.** *(dans son travail)* to be reliable; **les factures tombent avec r.** there's a steady flow of bills to pay; **les lettres me parvenaient sans aucune r.** letters would reach me fairly erratically

2 *(dans l'espace → de la dentition)* evenness; *(→ d'une surface)* smoothness; *(→ de plantations)* straightness

3 *(en valeur, en intensité)* consistency; **élève d'une grande r.** very consistent pupil; **travailler avec r.** to work steadily

4 *(légalité)* lawfulness, legality; *Fin* **r. et sincérité des charges** true and fair nature of expenses

régulateur, -trice [regylatœr, -tris] **ADJ** regulating, control *(avant n)*

NM 1 *(dispositif, horloge)* regulator; **r. de tension** voltage smoother; **r. de vitesse** cruise control **2** *Biol (gène)* regulator *or* regulatory gene **3** *Électron* controller **4** *Rail (personne)* controller, *Am* dispatcher

régulation [regylasjɔ̃] **NF 1** *(contrôle)* control, regulation; *(réglage)* regulation, correction; **r. de la circulation** traffic control; **r. de la consommation électrique** regulation *or* control of electricity consumption; *Fin* **la r. du marché des changes** foreign exchange control; **r. des naissances** birth control

2 *Biol* regulation; **r. thermique** (body) temperature control

3 *Électron* regulation

4 *Rail* control

régulatrice [regylatris] *voir* **régulateur**

régule [regyl] **NM** *Tech* antifriction metal, babbitt metal

réguler [3] [regyle] **VT** to control

régulier, -ère [regylje, -ɛr] **ADJ 1** *(fixe, permanent)* regular; **des revenus réguliers** a regular *or* steady income; **manger à heures régulières** to eat regularly *or* at regular times; **de façon régulière** on a regular basis; **liaisons régulières** *(en avion)* regular flights; **les vols réguliers** scheduled flights; **armée régulière** regular *or* standing army; **troupes régulières** regular troops, regulars

2 *(dans l'espace → gén)* regular, even; *(→ plantations)* evenly distributed; **des espacements réguliers** regular intervals; **une écriture régulière** regular *or* neat handwriting; **il peignit un trait bien r.** he painted an even line

3 *(uniforme → montée, déclin)* steady; *(→ distribution)* even; **être r. dans son travail** to be a steady worker; **c'est un élève r.** he's a consistent pupil

4 *(harmonieux → traits)* regular

5 *(conforme à la règle → transaction)* legitimate; *(→ procédure)* correct, fair; *(conforme à la loi)* legal; *Sport* permissible; **l'expulsion n'était pas régulière** the eviction wasn't legal; **c'est un procédé pas très r.** that's not quite above board; **le coup n'était pas r.** it was a bit of a dirty trick, it was a low blow; **être en situation régulière** to be in line with the law

6 *Fam (honnête)* on the level, straight; **ils sont réguliers en affaires** they're straight *or* honest in business; **il n'a pas été très r. avec moi** he didn't play fair with me, he wasn't straight *or* on the level with me

7 *Bot, Géom, Ling & Zool* regular

8 *Rel (clergé, abbé)* regular

NM *Mil & Rel* regular

▫ **régulière NF** *Fam Hum (épouse)* old lady, *Br* missus; *(maîtresse)* mistress■, *Br* bit on the side

▫ **à la régulière ADV** *Fam* fair and square, above board; **ça a été fait à la régulière** it was all (done) above board, there was nothing shady about it

régulièrement [regyljɛrmɑ̃] **ADV 1** *(dans l'espace → disposer)* evenly, regularly, uniformly; **les arbres sont plantés r.** the trees are evenly *or* regularly spaced

2 *(dans le temps → progresser)* steadily;

(→ *mettre à jour, rendre visite*) regularly; **donne de tes nouvelles r.** write often *or* regularly *or* on a regular basis; **elle avait r. de bonnes notes** she got consistently good *Br* marks *or Am* grades; **je la vois assez r.** I see her quite regularly *or* quite frequently

3 *(selon la règle)* lawfully; **assemblée élue r.** lawfully *or* properly elected assembly

4 *Fam (normalement)* in principle, normally; **r., c'est lui qui devrait gagner** ordinarily *or* in principle, he should win

régur [regyr] **NM** *Géol* regur (soil), black cotton soil

régurgitation [regyrʒitasjɔ̃] **NF** regurgitation

régurgiter [3] [regyrʒite] **VT** to regurgitate

réhabilitable [reabilitabl] **ADJ** *(condamné)* who can be rehabilitated

réhabilitation [reabilitasjɔ̃] **NF 1** *Jur* rehabilitation; **r. d'un failli** discharge of a bankrupt; **obtenir la r. de qn** to clear sb's name; **r. judiciaire** judicial discharge; **r. légale** legal discharge **2** *(d'une personne)* rehabilitation, clearing the name of **3** *(d'un quartier)* rehabilitation

réhabilité, -e [reabilite] **ADJ** rehabilitated; *Fin* discharged

NM,F *Jur* rehabilitated person; *Fin* discharged bankrupt

réhabiliter [3] [reabilite] **VT 1** *Jur (condamné)* to rehabilitate; *(failli)* to discharge; **r. la mémoire de qn** to clear sb's name; **r. qn dans ses fonctions** to reinstate sb **2** *(revaloriser* → *profession)* to rehabilitate, to restore to favour; (→ *quartier)* to rehabilitate

▶**se réhabiliter VPR** to rehabilitate oneself, to restore one's reputation

réhabituer [7] [reabitɥe] **VT r. qn à qch/à faire qch** to get sb used to sth again/to doing sth again; **il va falloir r. les enfants à un peu plus de discipline** the children are going to have to get used to a little more discipline again

▶**se réhabituer VPR se r. à** to get used to again; **j'ai eu du mal à me r. à la vie à Paris** I had a hard time getting used to life in Paris again *or* getting reaccustomed to life in Paris; **se r. à faire qch** to get back into the habit of doing sth, to get used to doing sth again

rehaussage [rəosaʒ] **NM** *Beaux-Arts* enhancing

rehaussement [rəosmɑ̃] **NM 1** *Constr (d'un plafond)* raising; *(d'un mur)* raising, building up *or* higher **2** *Fin* upward adjustment, increment

rehausser [3] [rəose] **VT 1** *Constr (surélever* → *plafond)* to raise; (→ *mur)* to make higher; **nous avons rehaussé la clôture** we made the fence higher

2 *(faire ressortir* → *goût)* to bring out; (→ *beauté, couleur)* to emphasize, to enhance; **du velours noir rehaussé de broderies** black velvet set off by embroidery

3 *(revaloriser)* to enhance, to increase; **une nouvelle victoire pour r. le prestige de l'équipe** a further victory which will increase *or* enhance the team's prestige

rehausseur [rəosœr] *Aut* **ADJ M** *(siège)* booster *(avant n)*

NM booster seat

rehaut [rəo] **NM** *Beaux-Arts* highlight

réhoboam [reobɔam] **NM** *(bouteille de champagne)* rehoboam

réhydratation [reidratasjɔ̃] **NF** moisturizing, *Spéc* rehydration; **pour une meilleure r. de votre peau** to ensure that your skin retains its moisture

réhydrater [3] [reidrate] **VT** *(peau)* to moisturize, *Spéc* to rehydrate

reichien, -enne [rɛʃjɛ̃, -ɛn] *Psy* **ADJ** Reichian

NM,F Reichian

reichsmark [rajʃmark] **NM** *Hist* reichsmark

réification [reifikasjɔ̃] **NF** reification

réifier [9] [reifje] **VT** to reify

reiki [reki] **NM** reiki

réimperméabiliser [3] [reɛ̃pɛrmeabilize] **VT** to re-proof

réimplantation [reɛ̃plɑ̃tasjɔ̃] **NF 1** *Méd* reimplantation **2** *(d'une industrie, d'une usine)* re-establishment; *(d'une tribu)* resettling

réimplanter [3] [reɛ̃plɑ̃te] **VT 1** *Méd* to reimplant **2** *(industrie, usine)* to set up again, to re-establish; *(tribu)* to resettle

réimportation [reɛ̃pɔrtasjɔ̃] **NF** *(activité)* reimportation, reimporting; *(produit)* reimport

réimporter [3] [reɛ̃pɔrte] **VT** to reimport

réimposer [3] [reɛ̃poze] **VT 1** *(taxer à nouveau)* to tax again **2** *Typ* to reimpose

réimposition [reɛ̃pozisjɔ̃] **NF 1** *(taxe)* further taxation **2** *Typ* reimposition

réimpression [reɛ̃prɛsjɔ̃] **NF** *(processus)* reprinting; *(résultat)* reprint; **en cours de r.** *(sur catalogue)* being reprinted, new edition pending; **ce livre est en cours de r.** this book is being reprinted

réimprimer [3] [reɛ̃prime] **VT** to reprint

Reims [rɛ̃s] **NM** Reims, Rheims

rein [rɛ̃] **NM 1** *Anat* kidney; **r. artificiel** artificial kidney, kidney machine; **coup de r.** heave

2 *Constr* springer

▫ **reins NMPL** *(dos)* back; *Littéraire (taille)* waist; **avoir mal aux reins** to have (a) backache; **avoir mal dans le bas des** *ou* **au creux des reins** to have a pain in the small of one's back; **les cheveux lui tombaient jusqu'aux reins** his/her hair came down to the small of his/her back; **donner un coup de reins** to heave; *Fig* to pull oneself together; **j'ai dû donner un coup de reins pour soulever l'armoire** I had to heave the wardrobe up; *Fam* **avoir les reins solides** to have good financial backing▪; *Fam* **je lui briserai** *ou* **casserai les reins** I'll break him/her

réincarcération [reɛ̃karserasjɔ̃] **NF** reimprisonment; **après sa r.** after he/she was sent back to jail

réincarcérer [18] [reɛ̃karsere] **VT r. qn** to send sb back to jail, to reimprison sb

réincarnation [reɛ̃karnasjɔ̃] **NF** reincarnation

réincarner [3] [reɛ̃karne] **se réincarner VPR** to be reincarnated (**en** as)

réincorporer [3] [reɛ̃kɔrpɔre] **VT** *(militaire, soldat)* to re-enlist

reine [rɛn] **NF 1** *(femme du roi)* queen (consort); *(souveraine)* queen; **la r. Anne** Queen Anne; **la r. mère** the Queen Mother; **la r. de Saba** the Queen of Sheba; **la r. de Suède/des Pays-Bas** the Queen of Sweden/of the Netherlands; **s'habiller comme une r.** to be dressed up to the nines *or* like a princess; **elle est heureuse comme une r.** she is as happy as a lark

2 *Cartes & Échecs* queen; *Cartes* **la r. de cœur/pique** the queen of hearts/spades

3 *Fig* queen; **la r. de la soirée** the belle of the ball, the star of the party; **tu es vraiment la r. des imbéciles** you're the most stupid woman I've ever come across; **r. de beauté** beauty queen; *Vieilli* **la petite r.** the bicycle

4 *Entom* queen; **la r. des abeilles/termites** the queen bee/termite

5 *Hort* **r. des reinettes** rennet *(apple)*

6 *Suisse (vache)* **r. (à cornes)** = champion Hérens cow of a herd that has won a cowfighting competition; **r. (à lait)** best milker

reine-claude [rɛnklod] *(pl* **reines-claudes)** **NF** (Reine Claude) greengage

reine-des-prés [rɛndepre] *(pl* **reines-des-prés)** **NF** *Bot* meadowsweet *(UNCOUNT)*

reine-marguerite [rɛnmargərit] *(pl* **reines-marguerites)** **NF** *Bot* (China *or* annual) aster

reinette [rɛnɛt] **NF** ≃ pippin; **r. grise** russet *(apple)*

réinfecter [4] [reɛ̃fɛkte] **VT** to reinfect

▶**se réinfecter VPR** to become reinfected

réinfection [reɛ̃fɛksjɔ̃] **NF** reinfection

réinitialisation [reinisjalizasjɔ̃] **NF** *Ordinat* reset; *(de la mémoire)* reinitialization

réinitialiser [3] [reinisjalize] **VT** *Ordinat* to reset; *(mémoire)* to reinitialize

ré-injection [reɛ̃ʒɛksjɔ̃] **NF** *TV* foldback

réinscriptible [reɛ̃skriptibl] **ADJ** *Ordinat (support)* rewritable

réinscription [reɛ̃skripsjɔ̃] **NF** reregistration

réinscrire [99] [reɛ̃skrir] **VT** *(étudiant)* to reregister, to re-enrol; *(électeur)* to reregister; *(sur un agenda)* to put down again

▶**se réinscrire VPR** to reregister, to re-enrol; **je me suis réinscrit au cours de poterie** I put my name down for *or* I joined the pottery class again; **se r. au chômage** to reregister as unemployed

réinsérer [18] [reɛ̃sere] **VT 1** *(paragraphe, bloc)* to reinsert **2** *(détenu, drogué)* to rehabilitate, to reintegrate (**dans** into *or* in)

▶**se réinsérer VPR** to rehabilitate oneself, to become rehabilitated *or* reintegrated

réinsertion [reɛ̃sɛrsjɔ̃] **NF 1** *(d'un paragraphe, d'un bloc)* reinsertion **2** *(d'un détenu, d'un drogué)* rehabilitation; **r. professionnelle** = getting back into the job market; **la r. sociale** social rehabilitation, reintegration into society; **pour eux, la r. sociale est très difficile** they find it very difficult to get back into the community (again)

réinstallation [reɛ̃stalasjɔ̃] **NF notre r. en Europe a été facile** settling in Europe again *or* moving back to Europe was easy

réinstaller [3] [reɛ̃stale] **VT 1** *(chauffage, électricité, téléphone)* to reinstall, to put back

2 *(déplacer)* to move; *(remettre au même endroit)* to move back; **j'ai réinstallé mon bureau au premier étage** I've moved my office back to the *Br* first floor *or Am* second floor

▶**se réinstaller VPR 1** *(déménager)* to move; *(revenir au même endroit)* to go back, to settle again; **il s'est réinstallé dans son ancien bureau** he's gone *or* moved back to his old office

2 *(se rasseoir)* to settle (back) down in one's seat

réintégrable [reɛ̃tegrabl] **ADJ il est difficilement r.** he cannot be easily reinstated

réintégrande [reɛ̃tegrɑ̃d] **NF** *Jur* action of recovery

réintégration [reɛ̃tegrasjɔ̃] **NF 1** *(d'un fonctionnaire)* reinstatement; *(dans un parti)* readmission **2** *(d'un évadé)* reimprisonment **3** *(recouvrement d'un droit)* reintegration **4** *Jur* **r. du domicile conjugal** return to the marital home

réintégrer [18] [reɛ̃tegre] **VT 1** *(fonctionnaire)* to reinstate; *(membre d'un parti)* to readmit; **il a été réintégré dans l'Administration** he was reinstated in the Civil Service **2** *(regagner)* to go back *or* to return to; *Jur* **r. le domicile conjugal** to return to the marital home

réintroduction [reɛ̃trɔdyksjɔ̃] **NF** reintroduction

réintroduire [98] [reɛ̃trɔdɥir] **VT r. qch** *(dans un texte)* to reintroduce sth, to put sth back in; *(projet de loi)* to put up again, to reintroduce

réinventer [3] [reɛ̃vɑ̃te] **VT** to reinvent; **il a su r. la mise en scène** he has a totally new approach to theatre direction

réinvestir [32] [reɛ̃vɛstir] **VT** to reinvest

réinviter [3] [reɛ̃vite] **VT** to invite again; **il faudra les r.** we'll have to ask *or* invite them (round) again

reis [reis] **NM** *Hist* = title conferred upon certain dignitaries of the Ottoman Empire

réitératif, -ive [reiteratif, -iv] **ADJ** reiterative

réitération [reiterasjɔ̃] **NF** reiteration

réitérative [reiterativ] *voir* **réitératif**

réitérer [18] [reitere] **VT** *(interdiction, demande)* to reiterate, to repeat

reître [rɛtr] **NM 1** *Hist* reiter **2** *Littéraire (soudard)* ruffianly soldier

rejaillir [32] [rəʒajir] **VI 1** *(gicler* → *gén)* to splash (back); (→ *violemment)* to spurt (up); **le champagne lui a rejailli à la figure** champagne spurted up into his/her face; **avec le vent, l'eau de la fontaine rejaillit sur la place** because of the wind, the water from the fountain is splashing onto the square

2 *(se répercuter)* **r. sur** to reflect on *or* upon; **sa notoriété a rejailli sur nous tous** his/her fame reflected on *or* was shared by all of us; **la honte rejaillit sur lui** he was covered in shame

rejaillissement [rəʒajismɑ̃] **NM** *Littéraire* **1** *(d'une fontaine)* splashing up **2** *Fig (retombées)* repercussion, reflection

rejet [rəʒɛ] **NM 1** *(physique)* throwing back *or* up, driving back; **interdire le r. de substances polluantes** to prohibit the discharge of pollutants; **rejets toxiques** toxic waste

2 *(refus)* rejection; *Jur (d'une réclamation, d'un appel)* dismissal; **elle a été très déçue par le r. de son manuscrit/de son offre** she was very disappointed when her manuscript/her offer was turned down; **il y a eu r. de toutes les accusations par le juge** the judge dismissed all charges; **on constate un r. des idées modernes** a rejection of modern ideas is apparent; **ne lui**

parle pas de sport, il fait un r. don't talk to him about sport, he can't stand it; **les enfants handicapés sont parfois victimes d'un phénomène de r. à l'école** disabled children are sometimes rejected by other children at school

3 *Littérature (enjambement)* run-on; *Gram* **il y a r. du verbe à la fin de la proposition subordonnée** the verb is put *or* goes at the end of the subordinate clause

4 *Méd (d'une greffe)* rejection

5 *Géol* throw; **r. horizontal** heave

6 *Bot* shoot

7 *Ordinat* ignore (character)

8 *Entom* cast (swarm)

rejetable [rəʒtabl] **ADJ** *(gén &) Jur* which can be rejected *or* dismissed

rejeter [27] [rəʒte] **VT 1** *(relancer)* to throw back; *(violemment)* to hurl back; **les cahots les ont rejetés à l'arrière de la camionnette** they were thrown to the back of the van by the jolting; **il rejeta son chapeau en arrière** he tilted his hat back; **elle rejeta ses cheveux en arrière** she tossed her hair back; **r. la tête en arrière** to throw one's head back; **r. les épaules en arrière** to put one's shoulders back; **r. un verbe en fin de phrase** to put a verb at the end of a sentence

2 *(repousser → ennemi)* to drive *or* to push back; *(bannir)* to reject, to cast out, to expel; **r. une armée au-delà des frontières** to drive an army back over the border; **elle a été rejetée par sa famille** her family rejected *or* disowned her; **la société les rejette** society rejects them *or* casts them out; **se faire r.** to be rejected

3 *(rendre → nourriture)* to spew out, to throw up, to reject; *(→ déchets)* to throw out, to expel; **son estomac rejette tout ce qu'elle absorbe** she can't keep anything down; **r. de la bile/du sang** to throw up *or* to bring up bile/blood; **la mer a rejeté plusieurs épaves** several wrecks were washed up *or* cast up by the sea

4 *(refuser → gén)* to reject, to turn down; *(→ projet de loi)* to throw out; *Jur (→ réclamation, appel)* to dismiss; **r. une offre/une demande** to reject an offer/a request; **ne rejette pas d'emblée cette idée/hypothèse** don't dismiss this idea/hypothesis out of hand

5 *(déplacer)* **r. la faute/la responsabilité sur qn** to shift the blame/responsibility on to sb

6 *Méd (greffe)* to reject

VI *Bot* to shoot

►**se rejeter VPR 1 se r. en arrière** to jump backwards

2 *(se renvoyer)* **ils se rejettent mutuellement la responsabilité de l'accident** they blame each other for the accident

rejeton [rəʒtɔ̃] **NM 1** *Péj ou Hum (enfant)* kid; **que fais-tu de tes rejetons cet été?** what will you do with your offspring *or* kids this summer? **2** *Bot* offshoot, shoot

rejette *etc voir* **rejeter**

rejoindre [82] [rəʒwɛ̃dr] **VT 1** *(retrouver)* to meet (up with), to join; *(avec effort)* to catch up with; **tu me rejoins au café en bas?** can you meet (up with) me in the café downstairs?; **je viendrai vous r. dans le Midi dès que je pourrai** I'll come and meet up with you *or* join you in the Midi as soon as I can; **il est parti r. sa femme** he went to meet up with *or* join *or* rejoin his wife; **il a rejoint le gros du peloton** he's caught up with the pack

2 *(retourner à)* to get back *or* to return to; **elle a rejoint Paris** she got back *or* she returned to Paris; **l'ambassadeur a rejoint son poste à Moscou** the ambassador has returned to his post in Moscow; **le nageur eut du mal à r. le rivage** the swimmer had difficulty reaching the shore; **il a reçu l'ordre de r. son régiment** he was ordered to rejoin his regiment

3 *(aboutir à)* to join *or* to meet (up with); **le chemin rejoint la route à la hauteur de la borne** the path meets *or* joins (up with) the road at the milestone

4 *(être d'accord avec) (ressembler à)* to be along the same lines as; **ses propos rejoignent les miens** he/she echoes what I say; **cela rejoint ce que je disais tout à l'heure** that fits in with what I was saying just now

5 *Pol (adhérer à)* to join; **elle a fini par r. l'opposition** she ended up joining the opposition

►**se rejoindre VPR 1** *(se réunir)* to meet again *or* up; **nous nous rejoindrons à Marseille** we'll meet up in Marseilles

2 *(rivières, routes, lignes)* to join (up), to meet (up)

3 *(concorder)* **nos opinions se rejoignent entièrement** our views concur perfectly, we are in total agreement; **nous avons voulu faire se r. différents témoignages** we aimed to bring together different accounts

rejointoiement [rəʒwɛ̃twamɑ̃] **NM** repointing

rejointoyer [13] [rəʒwɛ̃twaje] **VT** to repoint

rejointoyeur [rəʒwɛ̃twajœr] **NM** *Belg* cleaner, stone-cleaner

rejouer [6] [rəʒwe] **VT 1** *(refaire → jeu)* to play again; *(→ match)* to replay, to play again; **r. le même cheval** to bet on the same horse again; **elle a rejoué toute sa fortune sur le 7** she gambled her whole fortune on the 7 again; *Cartes* **tu devrais r. atout** you should lead trumps again

2 *(pièce de théâtre)* to perform again; *(morceau)* to play again; **il leur a fait r. la scène au moins 50 fois** he made them go through the scene at least 50 times

VI *(en sport, aux cartes etc)* to play again; *(au casino)* to start gambling again

réjoui, -e [reʒwi] **ADJ** joyful, happy, pleased; **avoir** *ou* **prendre un air r.** to look cheerful; **je voyais à sa mine réjouie que les nouvelles étaient bonnes** I could see from the joyful expression on his/her face *or* from his/her joyful expression that it was good news

réjouir [32] [reʒwir] **VT** to delight; **la nouvelle a réjoui tout le monde** everyone was delighted at the news; **ça ne me réjouit guère d'y aller** I'm not particularly keen on *or* thrilled at going; **ça lui a réjoui le cœur** it gladdened his/her heart

►**se réjouir VPR** to be delighted (**de qch** at sth); **je me réjouis de vous accueillir chez moi** I'm delighted to welcome you to my home; **se r. du malheur des autres** to gloat over other people's misfortunes; **je me réjouis de votre succès** I'm glad to hear of your success; **je me réjouis à la pensée de les retrouver** I'm thrilled *or* delighted at the idea of meeting them again; **je m'en réjouis d'avance** I'm really looking forward to it; *Suisse* **se r. de qch/de faire qch** to look forward to sth/to doing sth

réjouissance [reʒwisɑ̃s] **NF** *(gaieté)* rejoicing; **les occasions de r. manquent** opportunities for rejoicing are scarce

❑ **réjouissances NFPL** *(fête)* festivities; **réjouissances publiques** public festivities; *Hum* **quel est le programme des réjouissances?** what exciting things lie in store for us today?

réjouissant, -e [reʒwisɑ̃, -ɑ̃t] **ADJ** *(spectacle)* delightful; *(nouvelles)* joyful; **peu r.** rather grim; *Ironique* **c'est r.!** that's just great!; **je ne vois pas ce que tu trouves de si r. à cette histoire** I don't see what you find so funny *or* amusing about this story

rejuger [17] [rəʒyʒe] **VT** *Jur* to retry

relâche [rəlaʃ] **NF 1** *(pause)* respite, rest; **accordons-nous un peu de r.** let's rest a while *or* take a short break

2 *Cin & Théât (fermeture)* **le dimanche est notre jour de r.** there is no performance on Sundays; **nous ferons r. en août** no performances in August; **r. le mardi** *(salle de spectacle)* no performance on Tuesdays

3 *Naut* **le navire a fait r. à Nice** the boat called in at Nice; **(port de) r.** port of call

❑ **sans relâche ADV** without respite, continuously; **travailler sans r.** to work continuously *or* without respite; **il écrit sans r. jusqu'à l'aube** he writes without letting up *or* without a break until dawn

relâché, -e [rəlaʃe] **ADJ 1** *(négligé → discipline, effort)* lax, loose; *(→ style)* flowing, *Péj* loose; **la surveillance était plutôt relâchée** surveillance was a bit lax **2** *(détendu → muscle, corde)* lax, relaxed; *Méd* **intestin r.** lax bowels

relâchement [rəlaʃmɑ̃] **NM 1** *(laisser-aller)* laxity, loosening; *(de la discipline)* relaxation; *(des efforts)* let-up; *(de l'attention)* wavering; **il y a du r. dans votre travail** you're letting your work slide; **le r. des mœurs** the laxity of *or* decline in moral standards **2** *Méd (de l'intestin)* loosening; *(d'un muscle)* relaxation **3** *(d'une corde, d'un lien)* loosening, slackening **4** *Jur* **r. du lien conjugal** = release from conjugal obligations without divorce

relâcher [3] [rəlaʃe] **VT 1** *(libérer → animal)* to free; *(→ prisonnier)* to release, to set free; **les otages ont été relâchés** the hostages have been released *or* set free; **il a relâché l'oiseau** he let the bird go, he freed the bird; **le ministre l'a fait r. immédiatement** the minister arranged for his immediate release

2 *(diminuer)* to relax, to slacken; **r. son attention** to let one's attention wander; **ne relâchons pas nos efforts** we must not relax *or* slacken our efforts

3 *(détendre → câble, corde)* to loosen, to slacken; *(→ muscle)* to relax; **elle a relâché son étreinte** she relaxed *or* loosened her grip

4 *Littéraire (abandonner)* to give up; **il n'a rien relâché de ses exigences** he didn't let up in *or* didn't give up any of his demands

5 *Méd (intestin)* to loosen

VI *Naut* to put into port; **nous avons relâché à Cannes** we put in at Cannes

►**se relâcher VPR 1** *(muscle)* to relax, to loosen; *(câble, corde)* to loosen, to slacken; *(étreinte)* to relax, to loosen

2 *(devenir moins rigoureux → personne, mœurs, discipline)* to become lax *or* laxer; **se r. dans son travail** to become lax about one's work; **elle se relâche en tout** she's letting things slide; **son attention se relâche** his/her attention is flagging

relaie *etc voir* **relayer**

relais [rəlɛ] **NM 1** *(succession)* shift; **travail par r.** shift work; **ouvriers de r.** shift workers; **passer le r. à qn** to hand over to sb; **il est temps que je passe le r.** it's time I handed over (control); **prendre le r. (de qn)** to take over (from sb); **j'ai commencé le travail, tu n'as plus qu'à prendre le r.** I started the work, just carry on *or* take over; **il m'a déjà réprimandé, ne prends pas le r.!** he's already told me off, don't you start as well!

2 *(intermédiaire)* **je leur sers de r. quand ils ont quelque chose à se dire** they communicate with each other through me; **le graphiste sert de r. entre le client et l'imprimeur** the graphic artist is the link between the customer and the printer

3 *Sport* relay; **courir le r. 4 x 400 mètres** to run the 4 x 400 metres relay

4 *Hist (lieu)* coaching inn; *(chevaux)* relay

5 *Chasse (chiens)* relay

6 *(auberge)* inn; **r. autoroutier** *Br* motorway café, *Am* truck stop; **ce restaurant est donné comme r. gastronomique dans le guide** this restaurant is recommended in the guide as an excellent place to eat

7 *(en alpinisme)* belay (station)

8 *(comme adj; avec ou sans trait d'union) Élec (appareil, station)* relay *(avant n)*; *(processus)* relaying

9 *Phys* **r. statique/de mesure/de tout ou rien** static/measuring/all-or-nothing relay

10 *Tél* **r. hertzien** radio relay; **r. de télévision** television relay station; **r. temporaire** hook-up

11 *Banque* **(crédit) r.** bridging loan

relaisser [4] [rəlɛse] **se relaisser VPR** *Chasse* to come to a halt *or* a standstill

relance [rəlɑ̃s] **NF 1** *(nouvelle impulsion)* revival, boost

2 *Écon* **il y a une r. de la production sidérurgique** steel production is being boosted *or* increased; **politique de r.** reflationary policy; **r. économique** reflation, economic revival;

3 *Admin & Com (d'un client)* follow-up; **des relances téléphoniques** follow-up calls; **lettre de r.** follow-up letter

4 *Mktg (d'un produit, d'une marque, d'une entreprise)* relaunch

5 *Cartes* raise; **faire une r.** to raise (the stakes); **limiter la r.** to limit the raise

relancement [rəlɑ̃smɑ̃] **NM** *Mktg (d'un produit)* relaunch

relancer [16] [rəlɑ̃se] **VT 1** *(donner un nouvel essor à → gén)* to relaunch, to revive; *(→ ventes)* to boost; *(→ produit)* to relaunch; **r. l'économie d'un pays** to give a boost to *or* to boost *or* to reflate a country's economy

2 *(solliciter à nouveau → client)* to follow up; *Fig* to chase after, *Br* to chase up; **il faudra le r. pour**

obtenir un rendez-vous you'll have to chase after him *or Br* to chase him up if you want an appointment; **c'est à lui de r. ses clients** it's his job to follow up on *or Br* to chase up his clients; **je l'ai relancée plusieurs fois pour qu'elle vienne dîner à la maison** I pestered her several times to come to dinner; **arrête de me r.!** stop badgering me!; **elle s'est déjà fait r. trois fois par la banque** she's already had three reminders from her bank

3 *(jeter → à nouveau)* to throw again; *(→ pour rendre)* to throw back

4 *Chasse* to start again

5 *(faire redémarrer → moteur)* to restart; *Ordinat (→ programme)* to rerun; *(→ logiciel)* to restart

VI *Cartes* to raise (the bid) (**de** by)

►**se relancer** VPR **se r. dans le tissage** to take up weaving again; **se r. dans de longues explications** to re-embark on a long explanation

relaps, -e [rəlaps] ADJ relapsed

NM,F *Rel* relapsed person, backslider

rélargir [32] [relarʒir] VT to widen

relater [3] [rəlate] VT 1 *(raconter)* to relate, to recount; **les faits ont été relatés dans la presse** the facts were reported *or* detailed in the papers

2 *Jur (consigner)* to record

relatif, -ive [rəlatif, -iv] ADJ 1 *(gén) & Gram & Math* relative; **donner une valeur relative** to give a relative value; **comparer les mérites relatifs de...** to compare the relative merits of...; **tout est r.** it's all relative

2 **r. à** *(concernant)* relating to, concerning

3 *(approximatif)* **les élèves sont rentrés dans un ordre r.** the pupils went back inside in a more or less orderly fashion; **jouir d'un respect r.** to enjoy a limited amount of respect; **un confort très r.** very limited comfort; **nous avons goûté un repos tout r.** we enjoyed a rest of sorts; **un isolement r.** relative *or* comparative isolation

4 *Mus* relative

NM 1 *Gram* relative pronoun

2 *(proportions)* **avoir le sens du r.** to have a sense of proportion

▫ **relative** NF *Gram* relative clause

relation [rəlasjɔ̃] NF 1 *(corrélation)* relationship, connection; **r. de cause à effet** relation *or* relationship of cause and effect; **mettre deux questions en r. l'une avec l'autre, faire la r. entre deux questions** to make the connection between *or* to connect two questions; **c'est sans r. avec..., il n'y a aucune r. avec...** there's no connection with..., it's nothing to do with...

2 *(rapport)* relationship; **nouer des relations professionnelles** to form professional contacts; **nos relations sont purement professionnelles** our relationship is purely professional; **les relations sino-japonaises** relations between China and Japan, Sino-Japanese relations; **les deux pays ont cessé toute r.** the two countries have broken off all relations; **nos relations sont assez tendues** relations between us are rather strained; **avoir** *ou* **entretenir des relations avec qn** to be in touch with sb; **entretenir des relations de bon voisinage avec qn** to be on good terms with sb; **avoir de bonnes/mauvaises relations avec qn** to be on good/bad terms with sb; **être en r. avec qn** to be in touch *or* in communication with sb; **nous sommes en r. d'affaires depuis des années** we've had business dealings *or* a business relationship for years; **en excellentes/mauvaises relations avec ses collègues** on excellent/bad terms with one's colleagues; **entrer en r. avec qn** *(le contacter)* to get in touch *or* to make contact with sb; **mettre qn en r. avec un ami/une organisation** to put sb in touch with a friend/an organization; **r. (amoureuse)** love affair; **avoir une r. (amoureuse) avec qn** to have a relationship with sb; *Mktg* **relations clientèle** customer relations; **relations diplomatiques** diplomatic relations *or* links; **relations extérieures** foreign affairs; **relations humaines** *(gén)* dealings between people; *(en sociologie)* human relations; **relations industrielles** industrial relations; **relations internationales** international relations; **relations presse** press relations; **relations publiques** public relations; **relations sexuelles** sexual relations *or* intercourse; **relations sexuelles avant le mariage** sex before marriage; *Ind* **relations sociales** labour relations

3 *(connaissance)* acquaintance; **une r. d'affaires** a business acquaintance *or* connection; **c'est une r. de travail** he's a colleague; **avoir de nombreuses relations** to know a lot of people; **utilise tes relations** use your connections; **heureusement que j'ai des relations!** it's a good thing I'm well connected *or* I know the right people!; **j'ai trouvé à me loger par relations** I found a place to live through knowing the right people *or* through the grapevine

4 *Math* relation; **r. de Chasles** Chasles relation; **relations spatiales** spatial relations

5 *(compte rendu)* relation, narration; **sa r. des faits** his/her account of the story; **faire la r. de qch** to give an account of sth

6 *Jur* account

relationnel, -elle [rəlasjɔnɛl] ADJ 1 *Psy* relationship *(avant n)*; **avoir des difficultés relationnelles** to have trouble relating to people 2 *Ling* relational, relation *(avant n)*

relationniste [rəlasjɔnist] NMF *Can* public relations officer

relative [rəlativ] *voir* **relatif**

relativement [rəlativmɑ̃] ADV 1 *(passablement)* relatively, comparatively, reasonably 2 *(de façon relative)* relatively, *Sout* contingently

▫ **relativement à** PRÉP 1 *(par rapport à)* compared to, in relation to 2 *(concernant)* concerning; **entendre un témoin r. à une affaire** to hear a witness in relation to a case

relativisation [rəlativizasjɔ̃] NF relativization

relativiser [3] [rəlativize] VT **r. qch** to consider sth in context, *Spéc* to relativize sth

USAGE ABSOLU **il faut r., ça pourrait être pire** you've got to keep things in perspective, it could be worse

relativisme [rəlativism] NM *Phil* relativism

relativiste [rəlativist] ADJ 1 *Phys* relativistic 2 *Phil* relativist, relativistic

NMF *Phil* relativist

relativité [rəlativite] NF 1 *(gén)* relativity; **la r. des connaissances humaines** the relative nature *or* relativeness of human knowledge 2 *Phys* relativity; **(théorie de) la r. générale/restreinte** general/special (theory of) relativity 3 *Jur* **r. aquilienne** = principle whereby only those protected by the law breached may claim damages; **r. des conventions** privity of contract

relaver [3] [rəlave] VT 1 *(laver de nouveau)* to wash again, to rewash 2 *Belg & Suisse (vaisselle)* to wash

relax [rəlaks] ADJ INV 1 *Fam (personne, ambiance)* easy-going, laid-back; *(activité, vacances)* relaxing; **c'est une fille plutôt r.** she's an easy-going sort of girl; **r. Max!** *(locution)* chill out! 2 **fauteuil r.** reclining chair

ADV *Fam* **on va réviser, mais r., OK?** we'll do some revision, but we'll take it easy, OK?

NM *(fauteuil)* reclining chair

relaxant, -e [rəlaksɑ̃, -ɑ̃t] ADJ relaxing, soothing

relaxation [rəlaksasjɔ̃] NF 1 *(détente)* relaxation, relaxing; **faire de la r.** to do relaxation exercises 2 *Phys & Psy* relaxation

relaxe [rəlaks] ADJ = **relax** ADJ 2

NF *Jur* discharge, release

relaxer [3] [rəlakse] VT 1 *(relâcher → muscle)* to relax 2 *(détendre)* to relax; **ce bain m'a bien relaxé** I feel really relaxed after my bath 3 *Jur (prisonnier)* to discharge, to release

►**se relaxer** VPR to relax

relaxine [rəlaksin] NF *Physiol* relaxin

relayer [11] [rəlɛje] VT 1 *(suppléer)* to relieve, to take over from; **il l'a relayée au chevet du malade** he took over from her at the patient's bedside

2 *(transmettre → information)* to relay, to transmit

3 *Rad & TV* to relay

4 *Sport* to take over, to take the baton

VI *Arch* to relay, to change horses

►**se relayer** VPR to take turns (**pour faire qch** doing sth); *Sport* to take over from each other; **se r. auprès d'un malade** to take turns at a sick person's bedside; **se r. au volant** to take turns at the wheel

relayeur, -euse [rəlɛjœr, -øz] NM,F *Sport* relay runner

releasing factor [rəliziŋfaktɔr] *(pl* **releasing factors***)* NM *Physiol* releasing factor

relécher [18] [rəleʃe] VT *Belg (lécher)* to lick

relecture [rəlɛktyr] NF **une r. de sa lettre m'a donné l'impression que quelque chose n'allait pas** a closer (second) reading of his/her letter gave me the impression something was wrong; **la r. du manuscrit a pris une heure** it took an hour to reread the manuscript; **à la r., j'ai trouvé que...** on reading it again *or* when I reread it, I found that...; **le metteur en scène nous propose une véritable r. de la pièce** the director gives us a totally new interpretation to the play; *Typ* **r. d'épreuves** proofreading

relégation [rəlegasjɔ̃] NF 1 *Sport* relegation 2 *Jur* relegation 3 *Hist* banishment

relégué, -e [rəlege] ADJ 1 *Sport* relegated 2 *Jur* relegated 3 *Hist* banished

NM,F 1 *Sport* relegated team 2 *Jur* relegated person 3 *Hist* banished person

reléguer [18] [rəlege] VT 1 *(cantonner)* to relegate; **r. qn au second plan** to put sb in the background; **r. un tableau au grenier** to relegate *or* consign a picture to the attic; *Sport* **leur équipe a été reléguée en deuxième division cette année** their team was relegated to the second division this year 2 *Jur* to relegate 3 *Hist* to banish

relent [rəlɑ̃] NM 1 *(gén pl) (mauvaise odeur)* stink *(UNCOUNT)*, stench *(UNCOUNT)*; **des relents de tabac froid** a stench of stale tobacco; *Fig* **un r. de scandale entoure ce politicien** there is a whiff of scandal about this politician 2 *(trace)* residue, hint, trace

relessiver [3] [rəlɛsive] VT *Belg (lessiver)* to wash

relevable [rəlvabl] ADJ *(siège, appuie-tête)* (vertically) adjustable; *(accoudoir)* folding; **siège à dossier r.** reclinable seat

relevage [rəlvaʒ] NM *Tech* lifting; **système de r.** lift system

relevailles [rəlvaj] NFPL *Rel* churching

relevance [rələvɑ̃s] NF *Belg Jur (pertinence)* relevance

relevant, -e [rələvɑ̃, -ɑ̃t] ADJ *Belg Jur (pertinent)* relevant

relevé, -e [rəlve] ADJ 1 *(redressé → col, nez)* turned-up; **ses manches étaient relevées jusqu'au coude** his/her sleeves were rolled up to the elbows; **elle portait un chapeau à bords relevés** she wore a hat with a turned-up brim

2 *Culin (assaisonné)* seasoned, well-seasoned; *(pimenté)* spicy, hot; **je n'aime pas trop les plats relevés** I don't like spicy food much

3 *(distingué)* elevated, refined

4 *(virage)* banked

NM 1 *(de recettes, de dépenses)* summary, statement; *(de gaz, d'électricité)* reading; *(de noms)* list; **faire le r. du gaz** to read the gas meter; *Mktg* **r. d'achat** purchase report; *Mktg* **r. d'achat journalier** purchase diary; **r. de caisse** cash statement; *Banque* **r. de compte** bank statement; **r. de compte d'auteur** *(dans l'édition)* rights statement; *Fin* **r. des dépenses** statement of expenditure; *Fin* **r. des dettes actives et passives** statement of assets and liabilities; *Fin* **r. de factures** statement of invoices; *Fin* **r. de fin de mois** monthly *or* end-of-month statement; *Jur* **r. de forclusion** = leave to proceed out of time; *Banque* **r. d'identité bancaire** = document giving details of one's bank account; *Banque* **r. d'identité postal** = document giving details of one's post office account; *Banque* **r. mensuel** monthly statement; **demander son r. (de compte)** to ask for one's bank statement; *Scol* **r. de notes** examination results; *Fin* **r. remis** account tendered; **r. de température** temperature recording; **r. de vente** sales report

2 *(en topographie)* survey; **faire le r. d'un terrain** to plot a piece of land

3 *Archit* layout

4 *(en danse)* relevé

Culture

RELEVÉ D'IDENTITÉ BANCAIRE

An "RIB" is a small slip of paper showing all of a person's bank details. Employers, utility companies and other financial institutions may ask for one to effect standing orders.

relève [rəlɛv] NF 1 *(manœuvre)* relieving, changing; **prendre la r. (de qn)** to take over (from sb); **la r. de la garde** the changing of the guard 2 *(groupe)* replacement, stand-in; **la r.** *(au*

rel–rel

travail) the relief team; *Mil* the relief troops; *(garde)* the relief guard

relèvement [rəlɛvmɑ̃] **NM 1** *(rétablissement)* recovery, restoring; **contribuer au r. d'un pays/ d'une économie** to help a country/an economy recover; **mesures prises pour favoriser le r. d'une société** measures adopted to help put a company back on its feet *or* to help a company recover

2 *(fait d'augmenter)* raising; *(résultat)* increase, rise; **le r. des impôts/des salaires** tax/salary increase

3 *(reconstruction)* re-erecting, rebuilding

4 *(rehaussement)* raising, increase; **le r. du niveau des eaux** the rise in the water level

5 *Jur* release

6 *Naut* bearing *(UNCOUNT)*; **faire un r. (de sa position)** to plot *or* to chart one's position

7 *Rad* (radio) direction finding

8 *Constr* **station de r.** pumping station

RELEVER [19] [rəlve]

> to stand up again **1** ■ to pick up **1, 4, 12, 14** ■ to raise **2, 3, 13** ■ to put up **2, 3** ■ to increase **3** ■ to re-erect **5** ■ to enhance **6** ■ to season **7** ■ to notice **8** ■ to record, to note down **9** ■ to relieve **10** ■ to release **11**

VT 1 *(redresser → lampe, statue)* to stand up again; *(→ chaise)* to pick up; *(→ tête)* to lift up again; **ils m'ont relevé** *(debout)* they helped me (back) to my feet; *(assis)* they sat me up *or* helped me to sit up

2 *(remonter → store)* to raise; *(→ cheveux)* to put up; *(→ col, visière)* to turn up; *(→ pantalon, manches)* to roll up; *(→ rideaux)* to tie back; *(→ strapontin)* to tie up; **le virage est trop relevé** the banking on the bend has been made too steep

3 *(augmenter → prix, salaires)* to increase, to raise, to put up; *(→ notes)* to put up, to raise; **ils ont relevé les notes d'un point** they put up *or* raised the *Br* marks *or Am* grades by one point

4 *(ramasser, recueillir)* to pick up; *Scol* **r. les copies** to collect the papers

5 *(remettre en état → mur)* to rebuild, to re-erect; *(→ pylône)* to re-erect, to put up again; **r. des ruines** *(ville)* to reconstruct *or* to rebuild a ruined city; *(maison)* to rebuild a ruined house; *Fig* **c'est lui qui a relevé la nation** he's the one who put the country back on its feet (again) *or* got the country going again; **r. l'économie** to rebuild the economy; **r. le moral des troupes** to boost the troops' morale

6 *(mettre en valeur)* to enhance

7 *Culin* to season, to spice up; **relevez l'assaisonnement** make the seasoning more spicy

8 *(remarquer)* to notice; **r. des fautes** to notice *or* to pick out mistakes; **elle n'a pas relevé l'allusion** *(elle n'a pas réagi)* she didn't pick up the hint; *(elle l'a sciemment ignorée)* she pretended not to notice the hint

9 *(enregistrer → empreinte digitale)* to record; *(→ cote, mesure)* to take down, to plot; *(→ informations)* to take *or* to note down; *(→ plan)* to sketch; **on a relevé des traces de boue sur ses chaussures** traces of mud were found *or* discovered on his/her shoes; *Fam* **r. l'eau** *ou* **le compteur d'eau** to read the water meter; *Fam* **r. le gaz** *ou* **le compteur du gaz** to read the gas meter; **ayant relevé les détails dans son carnet...** having noted down *or* recorded the details in his/her notebook...; **les faits relevés ne plaident pas en ta faveur** the facts as they have been recorded do not help your case; *Météo* **températures relevées à 16 heures** temperatures recorded at 4 p.m.; *Compta* **r. un compte** to make out a statement of account; *Naut* **r. sa position** to plot *or* to chart one's position; **r. un point** to take a bearing

10 *(relayer → garde)* to relieve; *(→ coéquipier)* to take over from; **r. qn de ses vœux** to release sb from his/her vows; **r. qn de ses fonctions** to relieve sb of his/her duties

11 *Jur (prisonnier)* to release

12 *(en tricot)* to pick up

13 *Constr (parquet)* to lift, to raise

14 *Cartes* to pick up (one's cards)

15 *Naut* **r. un navire** to refloat a ship

USAGE ABSOLU *(remarquer)* **ce ne sont que des ragots, il vaut mieux ne pas r.** it's just gossip, (best) ignore it; **je ne relèverai pas!** I'll ignore that!

VI *(remonter → vêtement)* to ride up; **ta jupe relève derrière** your skirt rides up at the back

▫ **relever de VT IND 1** *(être de la compétence de → juridiction)* to fall *or* to come under; *(→ spécialiste)* to be a matter for; *(→ magistrat)* to come under the jurisdiction of; **cela relève des tribunaux/de la psychiatrie** it's a matter for the courts/the psychiatrists

2 *(tenir de)* **cela relève du miracle** it's truly miraculous

3 *(se rétablir de)* **r. de couches** to come out of confinement; **elle relève d'une grippe** she is recovering from flu

▸**se relever VPR 1** *(être inclinable)* to lift up

2 *(se remettre → debout)* to get *or* to stand up again; *(→ assis)* to sit up again; **il l'aida à se r.** he helped him/her to his/her feet again; **se r. la nuit** to get up in the night; **je ne veux pas avoir à me r.!** I don't want to have to get up (again)!

3 *(remonter)* **les commissures de ses lèvres se relevèrent** the corners of his/her mouth curled up

4 *Fig* **se r. de** to recover from, to get over; **le parti se relève de ses cendres** *ou* **ruines** the party is rising from the ashes; **je ne m'en relèverai/ils ne s'en relèveront pas** I'll/they'll never get over it

releveur, -euse [rəlvœr, -øz] **ADJ** *Anat* **muscle r.** levator muscle

NM,F *(employé)* meter reader

NM 1 *Anat* levator **2** *(sur une moissonneuse)* elevator

reliage [rəljaʒ] **NM** *(de tonneaux)* hooping

relief [rəljɛf] **NM 1** *Beaux-Arts, Géog & Opt* relief; **la région a un r. accidenté** the area is hilly; **pays sans (aucun) r.** flat country; **un r. calcaire** limestone relief

2 *(contraste)* relief, highlight; **donner du r. à qch** to highlight sth; **sans r.** *(paysage, style)* flat; **son discours manquait de r.** his speech was a rather lacklustre affair; **le personnage est brossé avec beaucoup de r.** the character is brought out *or* stands out very well

3 *(en acoustique)* **r. acoustique** spatial effect (of a sound)

4 *Ordinat* highlight; **mettre en r.** to highlight

▫ **reliefs NMPL** *Littéraire* **les reliefs** *(d'un repas)* the remnants *or* leftovers

▫ **en relief ADJ** *Beaux-Arts & Typ* relief *(avant n)*, raised; **cinéma/photographie en r.** stereoscopic cinema/photography; **impression en r.** relief printing; **lettres en r.** embossed letters; **motif en r.** raised design, design in relief **ADV** *(en valeur)* **mettre qch en r.** to bring sth out; *Ordinat* to highlight sth; **le jus de citron met en r. le goût des fraises** lemon juice brings out *or* accentuates the taste of strawberries; **mets ce paragraphe en r. en faisant des marges plus larges** make this paragraph stand out by making the margins wider

relier [9] [rəlje] **VT 1** *(faire communiquer)* to link up, to link (together), to connect; **les deux pièces sont reliées par un long couloir** the two rooms are linked (together) *or* connected by a long corridor; **un vol quotidien relie Paris à Lourdes** a daily flight links Paris to Lourdes; **la route qui relie Bruxelles à Ostende** the road running from *or* linking Brussels to Ostend; **le cordon ombilical relie la mère à l'enfant** the umbilical cord attaches *or* connects the mother to the baby

2 *(mettre en rapport)* to connect, to link (together), to relate; **les deux paragraphes ne sont pas reliés** there is no link *or* connection between the two paragraphs; **vos idées sont bien/mal reliées entre elles** your ideas are well/ badly linked together

3 *(livre)* to bind; **relié en cuir** leather-bound; **relié toile** cloth-bound

4 *(tonneau)* to hoop

relieur, -euse [rəljœr, -øz] **NM,F** bookbinder

religieuse [rəliʒjøz] *voir* **religieux**

religieusement [rəliʒjøzmɑ̃] **ADV 1** *(pieusement)* religiously; **se marier r.** to get married in church **2** *(soigneusement)* religiously, rigorously, scrupulously; *(avec vénération)* reverently, devoutly; **il lit 'L'Humanité' r. tous les jours** he reads 'L'Humanité' religiously every day

religieux, -euse [rəliʒjø, -øz] **ADJ 1** *(cérémonie, éducation, ordre, art)* religious; *(mariage, école)* church *(avant n)*; **l'état r.** the religious state

2 *(personne)* religious; **il n'a jamais été très r.** he was never very religious

3 *(empreint de gravité)* religious; **un silence r. se fit dans la salle** a reverent silence fell on the room; **elle nettoyait les cuivres avec un soin r.** she cleaned the brasses with almost religious care, she took an almost religious care over the brasses

NM member of a religious order

▫ **religieuse NF 1** *Rel* nun

2 *Culin* cream puff; **religieuse au chocolat/au café** chocolate/coffee cream puff

3 *Suisse Culin (de raclette)* = crusty burnt edges of a raclette cheese casing; *(de fondue)* = burnt cheese at the bottom of a fondue dish

religion [rəliʒjɔ̃] **NF 1** *(croyance)* religion; **l'histoire de la r.** the history of religion; **r. organisée** organized religion; **la r. juive** the Jewish religion *or* faith; **être sans** *ou* **n'avoir pas de r.** to have no religion, to be of no religious faith; **se convertir à la r. catholique/musulmane** to be converted to Catholicism/Islam; **le football est une r. pour certains** football is a religion with some people, some people make a religion out of football; **entrer en r.** to join a religious order; **la r. est l'opium du peuple** religion is the opium of the people; **les religions du Livre** the religions of the Book

2 *(piété)* religious faith; *Littéraire* **avoir de la r.** to be religious *or* devout; **connu pour sa r.** well-known for the strength of his religious faith; *Arch* **se faire une r. de qch** to be obsessed with sth

religionnaire [rəliʒjɔnɛr] **NMF** *Vieilli* Calvinist

religiosité [rəliʒjozite] **NF** religiosity, religiousness

reliquaire [rəlikɛr] **NM** reliquary

reliquat [rəlika] **NM** *(d'une somme)* remainder, balance; *(d'un compte)* balance; **un r. de vacances** outstanding leave; **r. d'impôts** outstanding taxes; **après apurement des comptes, il n'y a plus aucun r.** after balancing the accounts, there is nothing left over *or* there is no surplus

relique [rəlik] **NF 1** *Rel & Fig* relic; **conserver qch comme une r.** to treasure sth **2** *Biol* relict

relire [106] [rəlir] **VT** *(lire à nouveau)* to read again, to reread; *(pour corriger → épreuves)* to read; *(→ texte, lettre)* to read over

▸**se relire VPR** to read (over) what one has written; **j'ai du mal à me r.** I have difficulty reading my own writing

reliure [rəljyr] **NF 1** *(technique)* binding, bookbinding; **atelier de r.** bindery **2** *(couverture)* binding; **r. d'amateur** amateur *or* threequarter binding; **r. demi-toile** half-cloth binding; **r. à nerfs** band *or* banded binding; **r. pleine** full binding; **r. pleine toile** cloth binding; **r. sans couture** perfect binding; **r. à spirale** spiral binding

relocalisation [rəlɔkalizasjɔ̃] **NF** relocation

relocaliser [3] [rəlɔkalize] **VT** to relocate

relogement [rəlɔʒmɑ̃] **NM** rehousing

reloger [17] [rəlɔʒe] **VT** to rehouse

relookage [rəlukaʒ] **NM** *Fam (d'une personne)* makeover; *(d'un produit, d'un modèle)* revamping; *(d'un magasin)* revamping, makeover

relooker [3] [rəluke] *Fam* **VT** *(personne)* to give a makeover to; *(produit, modèle)* to revamp; *(magasin)* to revamp, to give a makeover to

▸**se relooker VPR** to change one's image■, to give oneself a makeover

relooking [rəlukiŋ] = **relookage**

reloquer [3] [rəlɔke] **se reloquer VPR** *Fam* to put one's clothes back on■, *Br* to get one's kit back on

reloqueter [27] [rəlɔkte] **VT** *Belg Hum* to wipe with a floorcloth

relou [rəlu] **ADJ INV** *Fam* (verlan de **lourd**) *(qui manque de subtilité)* unsubtle■, in your face, *Br* OTT

relouer [6] [rəlwe] **VT** *(sujet: propriétaire)* to rent out again, to relet; *(sujet: locataire)* to rent again; **nous relouons chaque année le même appartement** we rent *or* take the same *Br* flat *or Am* apartment every year

relu, -e [rəly] **PP** *voir* **relire**

réluctance [relyktɑ̃s] **NF** *Phys* reluctance

reluire [97] [rəlɥir] **VI 1** *(casque, casserole, parquet)* to gleam, to shine; *(pavé mouillé)* to glisten; **faire r. ses cuivres** to do *or* to polish the brasses **2** *Fam (atteindre l'orgasme)* to come

reluisant, -e [rəlɥizɑ̃, -ɑ̃t] **ADJ 1** *Fam (gén nég)* **peu** *ou* **pas r.** *(médiocre)* shabby; **un individu peu r.** an unsavoury character; **notre avenir n'apparaît guère r.** our future hardly looks bright **2** *(brillant)* shining, shiny, gleaming

reluisent *etc voir* **reluire**

reluquer [3] [rəlyke] **VT** *Fam (personne)* to eye up, to check out, *Am* to scope (out); *(objet, fortune)* to have one's eye on, to covet▪; **se faire r.** to be *or* get stared at

relut *etc voir* **relire**

relutif, -ive [rəlytif, -iv] **ADJ** *Fin* **avoir un effet r.** to strengthen the equity capital of a company

relution [rəlysjɔ̃] **NF** *Fin* strengthening of equity capital

relutive [rəlytiv] *voir* **relutif**

rem [rɛm] **NM** *Nucl (abrév* **roentgen equivalent man)** rem

remâcher [3] [rəmaʃe] **VT 1** *(mâcher de nouveau)* to chew again; *(sujet: ruminant)* to ruminate **2** *(ressasser)* to brood over

remaillage [rəmajaʒ] **NM** *(d'un filet)* mending; *(d'un bas, d'une chaussette)* darning

remailler [3] [rəmaje] **VT** *(filet)* to mend; *(bas, chaussette)* to darn

remake [rimɛk] **NM** *Cin* remake; **à quand le r.?** when are you doing the remake?

rémanence [remanɑ̃s] **NF 1** *Phys* remanence, retentivity **2** *Physiol (durabilité)* persistence **3** *Opt* after-image; *TV* **r. à l'extinction** after-image

rémanent, -e [remanɑ̃, -ɑ̃t] **ADJ 1** *Phys (aimantation)* remanent, retentive; *(magnétisme)* residual **2** *(gén)* & *Chim* persistent; **image rémanente** after-image

remanger [17] [rəmɑ̃ʒe] **VT** *(manger à nouveau)* to have *or* to eat again; *(manger davantage de)* to have *or* to eat some more; **je n'ai plus jamais remangé d'huîtres depuis** I've never eaten oysters since; **j'en ai remangé** I had some more *or* a second helping

VI to eat again

remaniable [rəmanjabl] **ADJ** *(discours, projet, texte)* revisable, amendable; **son plan sera difficilement r.** his/her plan is going to be hard to revise *or* to rework

remaniement [rəmanimɑ̃] **NM 1** *(d'un projet de loi)* redrafting, amending, altering; *(d'un discours)* revision, altering; *(d'un programme)* modification; **procéder au r. d'un projet de loi** to redraft *or* amend *or* alter a bill **2** *(d'un gouvernement, d'un ministère)* reshuffle; **r. ministériel** cabinet reshuffle

remanier [9] [rəmanje] **VT 1** *(texte, discours)* to revise; *(projet de loi)* to amend, to redraft, to alter; *(programme)* to modify **2** *(gouvernement, ministère)* to reshuffle; **l'équipe a été complètement remaniée** the team was completely reshuffled

remaquiller [3] [rəmakije] **VT** to make up again

▸**se remaquiller VPR** *(entièrement)* to reapply one's make-up; *(partiellement)* to touch up one's make-up

remarcher [3] [rəmarʃe] **VI 1** *(accidenté, handicapé)* to walk again **2** *(mécanisme, méthode)* to work again; **ça a l'air de bien r. entre eux** they seem to be getting on again

remariage [rəmarjaʒ] **NM** remarriage; **son r. avec...** his/her remarriage to...

remarier [9] [rəmarje] **VT** to remarry; **finalement, il a réussi à r. son fils** he eventually managed to marry off his son again

▸**se remarier VPR** to get married *or* to marry again, to remarry; **se r. avec qn** to remarry sb

remarquable [rəmarkabl] **ADJ 1** *(marquant)* striking, notable, noteworthy; **un événement r.** a noteworthy event; **de façon r.** remarkably; **il est r. qu'il n'ait rien entendu** it's remarkable *or* strange that he heard nothing

2 *(émérite → personne)* remarkable, outstanding, exceptional; **un travail r.** a remarkable *or* an outstanding piece of work; **d'un courage r.** remarkably brave

3 *(particulier)* conspicuous, prominent; **la girafe est r. par la longueur de son cou** the giraffe is notable for its long neck

remarquablement [rəmarkabləmɑ̃] **ADV** remarkably, strikingly, outstandingly; **elle joue r. du violon** she plays the violin outstandingly well

remarque [rəmark] **NF 1** *(opinion exprimée)* remark, comment; *(critique)* (critical) remark; **je l'ai trouvée insolente et je lui en ai fait la r.** I thought she was insolent and (I) told her so; **tu sais, je m'en étais fait la r.** it had crossed my mind, you know; **j'en ai assez de tes remarques** I've had enough of your remarks *or* criticism; **cette r. t'était destinée** that remark was aimed at you, that was a dig at you; **faire une r. à qn sur qch** to pass a remark to sb about sth; **si le service n'est pas assez rapide, fais-en la r. au garçon** if service isn't fast enough, have a word with *or* complain to the waiter about it

2 *(commentaire écrit)* note; **j'ai ajouté quelques remarques grammaticales en fin de chapitre** I have added a few grammatical notes at the end of the chapter

3 *Vieilli ou Littéraire* **digne de r.** noteworthy, (worthy) of note

remarqué, -e [rəmarke] **ADJ** conspicuous, noticeable, striking; **il a fait une intervention très remarquée** the speech he made attracted a great deal of attention; **une entrée remarquée** a conspicuous entrance

remarquer [3] [rəmarke] **VT 1** *(constater)* to notice; **je n'ai même pas remarqué que tu étais parti** I didn't even notice you had left; **je remarque que personne n'en a parlé** I notice *or* note that no one has spoken about it; **faire r. qch à qn** to point sth out to sb, to call sb's attention to sth; **on m'a fait r. que...** it's been pointed out to me *or* it's been drawn to my attention that...; **puis-je vous faire r. que nous sommes en retard?** may I point out to you that we're late?; **je te ferai r. qu'il est déjà minuit** look, it's already midnight; **remarque, je m'en moque éperdument** mind you, I really couldn't care less; **remarque qu'elle** *ou* **remarque, elle a sûrement raison** mind you, she's most probably right

2 *(distinguer)* to catch sight of, to notice; **il l'avait déjà remarquée la semaine précédente** he'd already noticed *or* spotted her the week before; **il est entré sans que je le remarque** he came in without me noticing (him); **elle a été remarquée par un metteur en scène** she attracted the attention of a producer; **se faire r.** to draw attention to oneself; **elle partit sans se faire r.** she left unnoticed *or* without drawing attention to herself

3 *(dire)* to remark; **"il ne viendra pas", remarqua-t-il** "he won't come," he remarked

4 *(marquer de nouveau → date, adresse)* to write *or* to note down again; *(→ linge)* to tag *or* to mark again

▸**se remarquer VPR** *(être visible)* to be noticed, to show; **le défaut du tissu se remarque à peine** the flaw in the material is scarcely noticeable *or* hardly shows; **ça ne se remarquera pas** it won't show, it won't be noticed; **si elle continue à bouder, ça va se r.** if she keeps (on) sulking, people are going to notice

remastériser [3] [rəmasterize] **VT** to remaster

remasticage [rəmastikaʒ] **NM** reapplication of putty

remastiquer [3] [rəmastike] **VT** *(vitre)* to reapply putty to

remballage [rɑ̃balaʒ] **NM** *(d'affaires personnelles)* packing up again; *(d'un paquet)* rewrapping

remballer [3] [rɑ̃bale] **VT 1** *(marchandise)* to pack up again; *(paquet)* to wrap (up) again, to rewrap; *Fam Hum* **r. ses outils** to put one's *Br* trousers▪ *or* keks *or Am* pants▪ back on **2** *Fam Fig* **tu peux r. tes compliments** you can keep your compliments to yourself

rembarquement [rɑ̃barkəmɑ̃] **NM** *(de produits)* reloading; *(de passagers)* re-embarkation

rembarquer [3] [rɑ̃barke] **VT** *(produits)* to reload; *(passagers)* to re-embark

VI *(passagers)* to re-embark

▸**se rembarquer VPR 1** *(passagers)* to re-embark **2** *Fig* **se r. dans qch** to get involved in sth again; **tu ne vas pas te r. dans une histoire pareille** you're not going to get mixed up in a mess like that again

rembarrer [3] [rɑ̃bare] **VT** *Fam* **r. qn** to tell sb where to go *or* where to get off; **je me suis fait (drôlement) r.!** I was told (in no uncertain terms) where to get off!

rembaucher [3] [rɑ̃boʃe] = **réembaucher**

remblai [rɑ̃blɛ] **NM 1** *(action → de talus)* embanking, banking (up); *(→ de fossé)* backfilling **2** *Rail & Constr (talus)* embankment; **route en r.** (em)banked road **3** *(terre rapportée)* **(terre de) r.** *(pour chemin de fer, route)* ballast; *(pour excavation)* backfill **4** *Mines* packing, backfill

remblaie *etc voir* **remblayer**

remblaiement [rɑ̃blɛmɑ̃] **NM** *Géol* depositing

remblaver [3] [rɑ̃blave] **VT** *Agr* to sow again

remblayage [rɑ̃blɛjaʒ] **NM 1** *(de talus)* embanking, banking (up); *(de fossé)* backfilling **2** *Mines* backfilling, stowing

remblayer [11] [rɑ̃bleje] **VT 1** *Constr* to bank up; **r. un fossé** to fill up a ditch **2** *Mines* to backfill, to pack

remblayeuse [rɑ̃blɛjøz] **NF** *(machine)* backfiller

rembobiner [3] [rɑ̃bɔbine] **VT** *(film, bande magnétique)* to rewind, to spool back

▸**se rembobiner VPR** to rewind

remboîtage [rɑ̃bwataʒ], **remboîtement** [rɑ̃bwatmɑ̃] **NM 1** *Méd (d'une articulation, d'un os)* repositioning, resetting **2** *Typ (d'un livre)* recasing

remboîter [3] [rɑ̃bwate] **VT 1** *Méd (articulation, os)* to reposition, to reset **2** *(pièces, tuyaux)* to fit together again **3** *Typ (livre)* to recase

rembourrage [rɑ̃buraʒ] **NM** *(d'un vêtement, d'un coussin)* padding; *(d'un siège)* stuffing

rembourrer [3] [rɑ̃bure] **VT** *(vêtement, coussin)* to pad; *(siège)* to stuff; *Fam* **il est plutôt bien rembourré** he's a bit podgy *or* a bit on the plump side; *Hum* **rembourré avec des noyaux de pêches** as hard as bricks

rembourrure [rɑ̃buryr] **NF** = **rembourrage**

remboursable [rɑ̃bursabl] **ADJ** *(billet, frais)* refundable; *(prêt)* repayable; *Fin (rente, obligation)* redeemable; **r. en 20 mensualités** repayable in 20 monthly instalments; **non r.** non-redeemable

remboursement [rɑ̃bursəmɑ̃] **NM** *(d'un billet, d'un achat)* refund; *(d'un prêt)* repayment, settlement; *(d'une dépense)* reimbursement; *Fin (d'une rente, d'une obligation)* redemption; **le r. de ses dettes lui a pris deux ans** it took him/her two years to pay off his/her debts; **j'ai obtenu le r. de mes frais de déplacement** I got my travelling expenses reimbursed *or* refunded *or* paid; **envoi** *ou* **expédition contre r.** cash on delivery; **r. anticipé** early repayment; **r. de la dette sociale** = contribution paid by every taxpayer towards the social security deficit; **r. des droits de douane** customs drawback; **r. in fine** bullet repayment

rembourser [3] [rɑ̃burse] **VT** *(argent)* to pay back *or* off, to repay; *(dépense, achat)* to reimburse, to refund; *(personne)* to pay back, to reimburse; *(prêt)* to repay; *Fin (rente, obligation)* to redeem; **les billets non utilisés seront remboursés** unused tickets will be reimbursed *or* refunded; **frais de port remboursés** postage refunded; **r. qn de qch** to reimburse *or* refund sb for sth; **tous les délégués seront remboursés de leurs frais** we will refund *or* reimburse all delegates' expenses; **est-ce que tu peux me r.?** can you pay me back?; **se faire r.** to get a refund; **tu t'es fait r. pour ton trajet en taxi?** did they reimburse you for your taxi journey?; **remboursez, remboursez!** we want a refund!, give us our money back!; **ce médicament n'est remboursé qu'à 40 pour cent (par la Sécurité sociale)** only 40 percent of the price of this drug is refunded (by the Health Service)

▸**se rembourser VPR** to get one's money back; **elle s'est remboursée dans la caisse** she paid herself back out of the till

Rembrandt [rɑ̃brɑ̃] **NPR** Rembrandt

rembranesque [rɑ̃branɛsk] **ADJ** *Beaux-Arts* Rembrandtesque

rembrunir [32] [rɑ̃brynir] **se rembrunir VPR 1**

Littéraire (s'assombrir) to darken, to cloud (over); **le ciel s'est rembruni** the sky has clouded over **2** *(se renfrogner)* to darken; **son visage s'est rembruni à l'annonce de la nouvelle** his/her face darkened when he/she heard the news

rembuchement [rãbyʃmã] **NM** *Chasse* return to cover

rembucher [3] [rãbyʃe] *Chasse* **VT** to drive to cover

▸**se rembucher VPR** to take cover, to enter cover

remède [rəmɛd] **NM 1** *(solution)* remedy, cure; **trouver un r. au désespoir/à l'inflation** to find a cure for despair/for inflation; *Fig* **le chômage est-il sans r.?** is there no cure for *or* no answer to unemployment?; **porter r. à qch** to cure *or* to find a cure for sth

2 *(thérapeutique)* cure, remedy; **un r. contre le cancer/le Sida** a cure for cancer/for Aids; *Fig* **le r. est pire que le mal** the cure is worse than the disease; *Fam* **c'est un (vrai) r. contre l'amour** he's/she's a real turn-off

3 *Vieilli (médicament)* remedy; **un r. de bonne femme** a traditional *or* an old-fashioned remedy; **un r. de cheval** a drastic remedy; *Prov* **aux grands maux les grands remèdes** desperate times call for desperate measures

remédiable [rəmedjabl] **ADJ** curable, *Littéraire* remediable

remédier [9] [rəmedje] **remédier à VT IND 1** *(maladie)* to cure; *(douleur)* to alleviate, to relieve **2** *(problème)* to remedy, to find a remedy *or* solution for; *(manque)* to remedy; *(défaut)* to make up for, to compensate for; *(erreur)* to put right; **nous ne savons pas comment r. à la situation** we don't know how to remedy the situation

remembrement [rəmãbrəmã] **NM** land consolidation *or* reallotment

remembrer [3] [rəmãbre] **VT** to redistribute *or* to reallot

remémoration [rəmemɔrasjɔ̃] **NF** *Littéraire* recalling

remémorer [3] [rəmemɔre] *Littéraire* **VT r. qch à qn** to remind sb of sth, to bring sth to sb's mind

▸**se remémorer VPR** to recollect, to recall, to remember

remerciement [rəmɛrsimã] **NM 1** *(action)* thanks, thanking; **une lettre de r.** a letter of thanks, a thank-you letter; **un geste/un mot de r.** a gesture/a word of thanks

2 *(parole)* thanks; **remerciements** *(dans un livre)* acknowledgements; **je crois que j'ai droit à un r.** *ou* **des remerciements** I think I deserve a thank you; **(je vous adresse) tous mes remerciements pour ce que vous avez fait** (I) thank you for what you did; **il a balbutié quelques remerciements et s'est enfui** he mumbled a few words of thanks and ran off; **avec mes remerciements** with (many) thanks

remercier [9] [rəmɛrsje] **VT 1** *(témoigner sa gratitude à)* to thank **(de** *ou* **pour** for); **je te remercie** thank you; **comment vous r. pour ce que vous avez fait?** I don't know how to thank you for what you did; **tu peux r. le Ciel!** you can count yourself lucky!; **elle nous a remerciés par un superbe bouquet de fleurs** she thanked us with a beautiful bunch of flowers; **il me remercia d'un sourire** he smiled his thanks, he thanked me with a smile; **je te remercie de m'avoir aidé** thank you for helping me *or* for your help; **et c'est comme ça que tu me remercies!** and that's all the thanks I get!

2 *(pour décliner une offre)* **encore un peu de thé? – je vous remercie** would you like some more tea? – no, thank you; **je te remercie mais je n'ai que faire de ton aide** I can do without your help, thanks all the same; *Ironique* **je te remercie du conseil** thanks for the advice

3 *Euph (licencier)* to let go; **ils ont décidé de la r.** they decided to dispense with her services

réméré [remere] **NM** *Jur* repurchase (clause); **vente à r.** sale with option of repurchase

remettant [rəmɛtã] **NM** *Fin* remitter

remetteur, -euse [rəmɛtœr, -øz] **ADJ** *(banque)* remitting
NM,F remitter

REMETTRE [84] [rəmɛtr]

VT to put back **1** ▪ to put **1** ▪ to add **4** ▪ to put on again **5** ▪ to hand over **7** ▪ to give **7** ▪ to hand in **7** ▪ to place **8** ▪ to give back **9** ▪ to put off **10** ▪ to remember **12** ▪ to remit **13**
VPR to recover **4** ▪ to start doing again **5** ▪ to rely on **6**

VT 1 *(replacer → gén)* to put back; *(→ horizontalement)* to lay, to put; **remets le livre où tu l'as trouvé** put the book back where you found it; **remets les cartes face dessous** lay *or* place the cards face down again; **il remit son fusil par terre** he laid *or* put his gun down on the floor again; **r. qch à plat** to lay sth flat again *or* back (down) flat; **l'oiseau remit sa tête sous son aile** the bird put *or* tucked its head back under its wing; **r. qn debout** to stand sb up again *or* sb back up; **je l'ai remis en pension** I sent him back to boarding school; *Fig* **r. qn sur la voie** to put sb back on the right track; *Fig* **r. qn sur le droit chemin** to set sb on the straight and narrow again; **r. qch à cuire** to put sth back on to cook; **r. qch à sécher/tremper** to put sth back up to dry/back in to soak

2 *(remplacer)* **il faut simplement lui r. des piles** you just have to put new batteries in (it); **faire r. un verre à ses lunettes** to have a lens replaced *or* to have a new lens put in one's glasses

3 *(rétablir dans un état)* **r. qch en marche** to get sth going again; **r. qch en état** to repair sth; **r. qch à neuf** to restore sth; **r. une pendule à l'heure** to set a clock right (again); **ces mots me remirent en confiance** those words restored my faith; *Fam* **elle a remis la pagaille dans toute la maison** she plunged the whole household into chaos again

4 *(rajouter)* to add; **remets un peu de sel** put in a bit more salt, add some (more) salt; *Fam* **en r.** *(exagérer)* to overstate one's case ▪; *Fam* **il est assez puni comme ça, n'en remets pas** he's been punished enough already, no need to rub it in

5 *(vêtements, chaussures)* to put on again, to put back on; **remets tes skis/ta casquette** put your skis/cap back on

6 *(recommencer)* **la balle est à r.** *(au tennis)* play a let; *Fam* **voilà qu'elle remet ça!** there she goes again!, she's at it again!; *Fam* **tu ne vas pas r. ça avec ma mère!** don't you start going on again about my mother!; *Fam* **les voilà qui remettent ça avec leur grève!** here they go striking again!; *Fam* **je n'ai pas envie de r. ça!** I don't want to go through that again!; *Fam* **allez, on remet ça!** *(au café)* come on, let's have another round *or* another one!; *Fam* **remettez-nous ça!** same again, please!; *Belg Fam* **r. le couvert** to start again ▪

7 *(donner → colis, lettre, message)* to deliver, to hand over; *(→ objet, dossier à régler, rançon)* to hand over, to give; *(→ dossier d'inscription, dissertation)* to hand *or* to give in; *(→ pétition, rapport)* to present, to hand in; *(→ démission)* to hand in, to tender; *(→ médaille, récompense)* to present, to give; **on nous a remis 10 euros à chacun** we were each given 10 euros; **r. qn aux autorités** to hand *or* to turn sb over to the authorities; **on lui a remis le prix Nobel** he/she was presented with *or* awarded the Nobel prize; *Banque* **r. un chèque à l'encaissement** to cash a cheque

8 *(confier)* to place; **r. son sort/sa vie entre les mains de qn** to place one's fate/life in sb's hands; **r. son âme à Dieu** to commit one's soul to God, to place one's soul in God's keeping

9 *(rendre → copies)* to hand *or* to give back; *(→ clés)* to hand back, to return; **l'enfant a été remis à sa famille** the child was returned to his family

10 *(ajourner → entrevue)* to put off, to postpone, *Br* to put back; *(→ décision)* to put off, to defer; **r. qch à huitaine** to postpone sth *or* to put sth off for a week; **la réunion a été remise à lundi** the meeting has been put off *or* postponed until Monday; **r. qch à plus tard** to put sth off until later

11 *Méd (replacer → articulation, os)* to put back in place; **sa cheville n'est pas vraiment encore remise** his/her ankle isn't reset yet

12 *Fam (reconnaître → personne)* to remember ▪; **je ne la remets pas** I don't remember her, I can't place her

13 *(faire grâce de → peine de prison)* to remit; *(pardonner → péché)* to forgive, *Sout* to remit; *(→ offense)* to forgive, to pardon; **r. une dette à qn** to let sb off a debt

14 *Chasse (gibier)* to drive to cover

15 *Belg (vomir)* to vomit (up)

16 *Belg (rendre → monnaie)* **il m'a remis 3 euros** he gave me 3 euros change

17 *Belg & Suisse (céder)* to sell; **ils ont remis leur boutique** they gave up *or* sold their shop

VI *Naut* **r. à la route** to get back on course; **r. à la voile** to hoist sail again

❑ **remettre à VT IND** *Belg (identifier avec)* to identify with; *(associer à)* to associate with

▸**se remettre VPR 1** *(se livrer)* **se r. à la police** to give oneself up to the police; **se r. entre les mains de qn** to put *or* to place oneself in sb's hands

2 *Vieilli* **se r. qn** *(reconnaître)* to remember *or* to place sb

3 *(se replacer → dans une position, dans un état)* **se r. au lit** to go back to bed; **se r. debout** to stand up again, to get back up; **se r. en route** to get started *or* going again; **tu ne vas pas te r. en colère!** don't go getting angry again!; **se r. avec qn** *(se réconcilier)* to make it up with sb; *(se réinstaller)* to go *or* to be back with sb again

4 *(guérir)* to recover, to get better; **je vais me r., c'est simplement que je suis encore sous le choc** I'll be all right, it's just that I'm still in shock; **elle se remettra, ne t'inquiète pas** *(d'un choc)* she'll get over it, don't worry; *(d'une dépression)* she'll pull out of it, don't worry; **se r. de qch** to get over sth; **se r. d'un accident** to recover from *or* to get over an accident; **il ne s'est pas encore complètement remis de son opération** he's not fully recovered from his operation yet; **allons, remets-toi!** come on, pull yourself together *or* get a grip on yourself!; **je ne m'en remets pas** I can't get over it; **elle va s'en r.** she'll get over it

5 **se r. à qch/à faire qch** *(reprendre, recommencer à)* to start *or* to take up sth/doing sth again; **il s'est remis à fumer** he started smoking again; **je me suis remis à l'espagnol** I've taken up Spanish again; **la pluie se remet à tomber, il se remet à pleuvoir** the rain's starting again, it's started raining again; **le temps se remet au beau** it's brightening up; **le temps se remet à la neige** it looks like snow again

6 **s'en r. à** *(se fier à)* to rely on, to leave it (up) to; **tu peux t'en r. à moi** you can rely on me *or* leave it (up) to me; **je m'en remets à lui pour tout ce qui concerne le financement du projet** I'm leaving the financial arrangements of the plan to him *or* in his hands; **s'en r. à la décision de qn** to leave it (up) to sb to decide; **s'en r. au bon sens de qn** to rely on sb's common sense

remeubler [5] [rəmœble] **VT** *(de nouveau)* to refurnish; *(avec de nouveaux meubles)* to put new furniture into

▸**se remeubler VPR** to refurnish one's house/*Br* flat *or Am* apartment

rémige [remiʒ] **NF** *Orn* remex; **les rémiges** remiges

remilitarisation [rəmilitarizasjɔ̃] **NF** remilitarization

remilitariser [3] [rəmilitarize] **VT** to remilitarize

▸**se remilitariser VPR** to become remilitarized

reminéralisation [rəmineralizasjɔ̃] **NF** remineralization

reminéraliser [3] [rəmineralize] **VT** to remineralize

réminiscence [reminisɑ̃s] **NF 1** *(souvenir)* reminiscence, recollection; **quelques réminiscences de ce qu'elle avait appris à l'école** a few vague memories of what she'd learned at school; **des réminiscences de mon enfance** reminiscences *or* recollections of my childhood

2 *(influence)* overtone; **il y a des réminiscences de Mahler dans ce morceau** there are some echoes of Mahler in this piece, this piece is reminiscent of Mahler

3 *Phil & Psy* reminiscence

remis, -e [rəmi, -iz] **PP** *voir* **remettre**

ADJ être r. to be well again; **une semaine de repos et me voilà r.** a week's rest and I'm back on my feet (again); **être r. de** to have recovered from, to have got over; **il n'est pas encore r. de sa frayeur/son cauchemar** he hasn't yet got over his fright/nightmare

❑ **remise NF 1** *(dans un état antérieur)* **la remise en place des meubles/en ordre des documents nous a pris du temps** putting all the furniture back into place/sorting out the papers again took us some time; **remise en cause** *ou* **question** calling into question; **ses remises en question continuelles** his/her constant doubts *or* questioning; **remise en état** *(d'une maison)* restoration; **remise en jeu** *ou* **en touche** *(au hockey)* push-in; *(au rugby)* line-out; *(au foot)* throw-in; **la remise en marche du moteur** restarting the engine; **remise à neuf** restoration; **il a besoin d'une remise à niveau** he needs a refresher course; *Ordinat* **remise à zéro** *(effacement)* core flush; *(réinitialisation)* resetting; *Aut* **la remise à zéro du compteur kilométrique a été faite récemment** the mileometer has recently been put back to zero

2 *(livraison)* delivery; **remise d'une lettre/d'un paquet en mains propres** personal delivery of a letter/package; **la remise des clés sera faite par l'agence** the agency will be responsible for handing over the keys; **la remise de la rançon aura lieu derrière le garage** the ransom will be handed over *or* paid behind the garage; *Scol* **remise des prix** prize-giving

3 *Com (réduction)* discount, reduction, *Spéc* remittance; **une remise de 15 pour cent** a 15 percent discount, 15 percent off; **faire une remise sur qch** to allow a discount on sth; **faire une remise à qn** to give sb a discount; **remise de caisse** cash discount; **remise de fidélité** customer loyalty discount; **remise de marchandisage** merchandising allowance; **remise sur marchandises** trade discount; **remise promotionnelle** promotional discount; **remise quantitative** *ou* **pour quantité** *ou* **sur la quantité** bulk *or* quantity discount; **remise saisonnière** seasonal discount; **remise d'usage** trade discount

4 *(d'effet, de chèque)* remittance; **faire une remise de fonds à qn** to send sb a remittance, to remit funds to sb; **faire une remise de chèque** to pay in a cheque; **remise documentaire** documentary remittance; **remise d'effets** remittance of bills; **remise de fonds** remittance of funds; **remise à vue** demand deposit

5 *Fin (d'un impôt)* allowance

6 *Jur* remission; **faire remise d'une dette** to discharge a debt; **faire remise d'une amende** to remit *or* to reduce a fine; **remise de peine** reduction of (the) sentence; **bénéficier d'une r. de peine** to be granted a reduction in one's sentence, to have one's sentence reduced

7 *(ajournement)* putting off, postponement; **la remise à huitaine de l'ouverture du procès** the postponement *or Sout* deferment of the opening of the trial for a week; **r. de cause** postponement of hearing

8 *(resserre)* shed

9 *Aut* **voiture de grande remise** chauffeur-driven hire limousine

10 *Chasse* covert

11 *Belg (cession)* sale, selling

remisage [rəmizaʒ] **NM** *(gén)* putting away, storing (away)

remise [rəmiz] *voir* **remis**

remiser [3] [rəmize] **VT 1** *(ranger)* to store away, to put away **2** *Fam Vieilli (rabrouer)* **r. qn** to send sb packing

VI *(parier à nouveau)* to place another bet

▸**se remiser VPR** *(gibier)* to take cover

remisier [rəmizje] **NM** *Bourse* intermediate broker

rémissible [remisibl] **ADJ** *Littéraire (crime, faute, péché)* remissible, subject to remission

rémission [remisjɔ̃] **NF 1** *Rel* remission, forgiveness; **la r. des péchés** the remission of sins

2 *Jur* remission; **la r. d'une peine** the remission of a sentence

3 *Méd (d'une maladie)* remission; *(de la douleur, de la fièvre)* abatement; **la r. fut de courte durée** the remission didn't last; **être en r.** to be in remission

❑ **sans rémission ADJ** *(implacable)* merciless, pitiless; **ses jugements sont sans r.** his/her judgements are merciless **ADV 1** *(sans pardon possible)* mercilessly, without mercy; **tu seras puni sans r.** you will be mercilessly punished **2** *(sans relâche)* unremittingly, relentlessly; **travailler sans r.** to work unremittingly *or* relentlessly

remit *etc voir* **remettre**

rémittence [remitɑ̃s] **NF** *Méd (d'une fièvre, d'un mal)* remittence, remittency

rémittent, -e [remitɑ̃, -ɑ̃t] **ADJ** *Méd (fièvre, mal)* remittent

remix [rəmiks] **NM** *Mus* remix

remixer [3] [rəmikse] **VT** *Mus* to remix

rémiz [remiz] **NM** *Orn* penduline (tit)

remmaillage [rɑ̃majaʒ] = **remaillage**

remmailler [rɑ̃maje] = **remailler**

remmailleuse [rɑ̃majøz] **NF** *Tex* **1** *(ouvrière)* looper **2** *(machine)* looping machine

remmailloter [3] [rɑ̃majɔte] **VT** *(bébé)* to wrap in swaddling clothes again

remmancher [3] [rɑ̃mɑ̃ʃe] **VT** to put a handle back on

remmener [19] [rɑ̃mne] **VT** *(au point de départ)* to take back; *(à soi)* to bring back; **je te remmènerai chez toi en voiture** I'll drive you back home; **nous l'avons remmené au zoo** we took him to the zoo again *or* back to the zoo

remmoulage [rɑ̃mulaʒ] **NM** *Métal* mould assembly

remmouler [3] [rɑ̃mule] **VT** *Métal (moule)* to assemble

remnographie [remnɔgrafi] **NF** *Tech* nuclear magnetic resonance imaging

remodelage [rəmɔdlaʒ] **NM 1** *(d'une silhouette, des traits)* remodelling **2** *(d'un quartier)* replanning **3** *(d'une institution)* reorganization; *(d'un projet)* redesigning, revising

remodeler [25] [rəmɔdle] **VT 1** *(silhouette, traits)* to remodel **2** *(quartier)* to replan **3** *(institution)* to reorganize; *(projet)* to redesign, to revise

rémois, -e [remwa, -az] **ADJ** of/from Rheims *or* Reims

❑ **Rémois, -e NM,F** = inhabitant of or person from Rheims

remontage [rəmɔ̃taʒ] **NM 1** *(d'une pendule)* winding up, rewinding **2** *(d'une étagère, d'un mécanisme)* reassembly, reassembling

remontant, -e [rəmɔ̃tɑ̃, -ɑ̃t] **ADJ 1** *Bot (fraisier)* double-cropping, *Spéc* remontant; *(rosier)* remontant **2** *(fortifiant)* invigorating

NM tonic

remonte [rəmɔ̃t] **NF 1** *Mil* remount **2** *Naut* sailing upstream *or* upriver **3** *(d'un poisson qui fraie)* run

remonté, -e [rəmɔ̃te] **ADJ** *Fam* **1** *(plein d'énergie)* full of beans

2 *Fam (irrité)* **r. contre qn/qch** up in arms about sb/sth

❑ **remontée NF 1** *(d'une côte)* ascent, climb; **la remontée du fleuve** the trip upriver *or* upstream; **la remontée des mineurs a lieu à 4 heures** the miners are brought back up at 4 o'clock

2 *(rattrapage)* catching up; *(augmentation → d'une monnaie, d'un cours, des valeurs, des prix)* recovery; **faire une belle r.** to make a good recovery; **le coureur colombien a fait une belle remontée face à ses adversaires** the Colombian competitor has managed to catch up with his opponents; **on constate une brusque remontée de la cote du président** the popularity of the President has shot up

3 *Géog* upwelling

❑ **remontée mécanique NF** ski lift

remonte-pente [rəmɔ̃tpɑ̃t] *(pl* **remonte-pentes**) **NM** ski tow, T-bar

remonter [3] [rəmɔ̃te] **VT 1** *(côte, étage)* to go *or* to climb back up; **r. l'escalier** to go *or* to climb back up the stairs

2 *(porter à nouveau)* to take back up; **r. une valise au grenier** to take a suitcase back up to the attic

3 *(parcourir → en voiture, en bateau etc)* to go up; **r. le Nil** to sail up the Nile; **les saumons remontent le fleuve** the salmon are swimming upstream; **nous avons remonté la Seine en voiture jusqu'à Rouen** we drove along the Seine (upriver) to Rouen; **r. le défilé** *(aller en tête)* to work one's way to the front of the procession; **r. la rue** to go *or* to walk back up the street; **en remontant le cours des siècles** *ou* **du temps** going back several centuries

4 *(relever → chaussette)* to pull up; *(→ manche)* to roll up; *(→ col, visière)* to raise, to turn up; *(→ robe)* to raise, to lift; *(→ store)* to pull up, to raise; **r. qch** to put sth higher up, to raise sth; **remonte ton pantalon** pull your *Br* trousers *or Am* pants up; **elle a remonté la vitre** she wound the window up

5 *(augmenter → salaire, notation)* to increase, to raise, to put up; **tous les résultats des examens ont été remontés de deux points** all exam results have been put up *or* raised by two *Br* marks *or Am* grades

6 *(assembler à nouveau → moteur, kit)* to reassemble, to put back together (again); *(→ étagère)* to put back up; *Cin (→ film)* to re-edit

7 *Com (rouvrir)* to set up again; **à sa sortie de prison, il a remonté une petite affaire de plomberie** when he came out of prison he started up another small plumbing business

8 *(faire prospérer à nouveau)* **il a su r. l'entreprise** he managed to set *or* to put the business back on its feet; **elle a remonté la scierie après la mort de son père** she got the sawmill going again after her father died

9 *(renouveler)* to restock, to stock up again; **r. sa cave** to stock up one's cellar again, to restock one's cellar; **r. son stock (de DVD)** to stock up again (on DVDs); **il faut que je remonte ma garde-robe pour l'hiver** I must buy myself some new clothes *or* a new wardrobe for the winter

10 *(mécanisme, montre)* to wind (up); **pas besoin de la r., elle est à piles** there's no need to wind it (up), it's battery-operated; **continue à la r.** keep on winding it (up)

11 *(ragaillardir → physiquement)* to pick up; *(→ moralement)* to cheer up; *Fam* **prends un whisky, ça te remontera** have a whisky, it'll perk you up; **r. le moral à qn** to cheer sb up

12 *Sport (concurrent)* to catch up (with)

13 *Théât* to stage again, to put on (the stage) again; **une pièce oubliée que personne n'avait jamais remontée** a forgotten play which had never been revived

VI *(surtout aux être)* **1** *(monter de nouveau)* to go back up, to go up again; **l'enfant remonta dans la brouette/sur l'escabeau** the child got back into the wheelbarrow/up onto the stool; **remonte dans ta chambre** go back up to your room; **r. au troisième étage** to go back up to the third floor; **r. à Paris** to go back to Paris

2 *Transp* **r. dans** *(bateau, bus, train)* to get back onto; *(voiture)* to get back into; **r. à cheval** *(se remettre en selle)* to remount; *(refaire de l'équitation)* to take up riding again

3 *(s'élever → route)* to go back up, to go up again; **le sentier remonte jusqu'à la villa** the path goes up to the villa; **la rivière a remonté cette nuit** *(a un niveau supérieur)* the level of the river rose again last night; **la mer remonte** the tide's coming in (again); **le baromètre remonte** the barometer is rising; **le prix du sucre a remonté** *(après une baisse)* the price of sugar has gone back up again; **sa fièvre remonte de plus belle** his/her temperature is going up even higher; **tu remontes dans mon estime** you've gone up in my esteem; *Fig* **sa cote remonte** he's/she's becoming more popular; *Fig* **ses actions remontent** things are looking up *or* picking up for him/her

4 *(jupe)* to ride up, to go up

5 *(faire surface → mauvaise odeur)* to come back up; **r. à la surface** *(noyé)* to float back (up) to the surface; *(plongeur)* to resurface; *(scandale)* to re-emerge, to resurface; **un sentiment de culpabilité remontait à sa conscience de temps en temps** a guilty feeling would well up in him/her from time to time

6 *(retourner vers l'origine)* **r. dans le temps** to go back in time; **il avait beau r. dans ses souvenirs, il ne la reconnaissait pas** however far back he tried to remember, he couldn't place

her; **il est remonté très loin dans l'histoire de sa famille** he delved back a long way into his family history; **si l'on remonte encore plus loin dans le passé** looking *or* going back even further into the past; **r. à** *(se reporter à)* to go back to, to return to; **r. à la cause première/à l'origine de qch** to go back to the primary cause/the origins of sth; **le renseignement qui nous a permis de r. jusqu'à vous** the piece of information which enabled us to trace you; **r. de l'effet à la cause** to trace the effect back to the cause; **r. à** *(dater de)* to go *or* to date back to; **ça remonte à loin maintenant** it happened a long time *or* years *or* ages ago; **leur brouille remonte à loin** their quarrel is of long standing, they quarrelled a long time ago; **cela remonte à plusieurs mois** this goes *or* dates back several months; **cela remonte à 1958** this goes *or* dates back to 1958; **les recherches font r. sa famille à 1518** research shows that his/her family goes back to 1518; **on fait généralement r. la crise à 1910** the crisis is generally believed to have started in 1910

7 *Hort (framboisier)* to crop twice; *(dahlia)* to reflower

8 *Théât* to go upstage

9 *Naut (navire)* to sail north; *(vent)* to come round the north; **r. au vent** to tack into the wind

►**se remonter** VPR **1** *(emploi passif)* **ces montres ne se remontent pas** these watches don't have to be wound up; **ça se remonte avec une clé** you wind it up with a key

2 *(emploi réfléchi) (physiquement)* to recover one's strength; *(moralement)* to cheer oneself up; **elle dit qu'elle boit pour se r.** she says she drinks to cheer herself up *or* to make herself feel better; **il s'est bien remonté depuis hier** he's cheered up a lot since yesterday; **se r. le moral** to cheer oneself up

3 *Fam* **se r. en** *(se réapprovisionner en)* to replenish one's stock of▪; **il s'est remonté en cravates/en chaussettes** he's replenished his stock of ties/socks

remonteur, -euse [rəmɔ̃tœr, -øz] NM,F *(gén)* fitter, assembler; *(d'horloges, de montres)* winder

remontoir [rəmɔ̃twar] NM *(d'une montre)* winder

remontrance [rəmɔ̃trɑ̃s] NF **1** *(gén pl) (reproche)* remonstrance, reproof; **faire des remontrances à qn** to reprimand *or* to admonish sb **2** *Hist* remonstrance

remontrer [3] [rəmɔ̃tre] VT **1** *(montrer de nouveau)* to show again; **tu peux me r. ton livre?** can you show me your book again?; **j'aimerais que tu me remontres comment tu as fait** I'd like you to show me again *or* once more how you did it

2 *Littéraire (faute, tort)* to point out

3 *(locutions)* **crois-tu vraiment pouvoir m'en r.?** do you really think you have anything to teach me?; **il veut toujours en r. à tout le monde** he's always trying to show off to people; **il en remontrerait à ses professeurs** he could teach *or* show his teachers a thing or two

►**se remontrer** VPR to show up again; **et ne t'avise pas de te r. ici!** and don't ever show your face (around) here again!

rémora [remɔra] NM *Ich* remora, sharksucker

remordre [76] [rəmɔrdr] VT to bite again

▫ **remordre à** VT IND *(se remettre à)* **elle ne veut plus r. à l'informatique** she doesn't want to have anything more to do with computers

remords [rəmɔr] NM **1** *(repentir)* remorse; **avoir des r.** to be full of remorse; **j'ai des r. de l'avoir laissé partir à pied** I feel bad about leaving him to walk; **je n'ai aucun r.!** I'm not the slightest bit sorry!; **des r. de conscience** twinges of conscience; **être bourrelé de** *ou* **torturé par le r.** to be stricken with remorse; **elle est rongée par le r.** she is consumed with remorse; **il a été pris de r.** his conscience got the better of him; **sans aucun r.** without a qualm, without any compunction, without (the slightest) remorse

2 *(regret)* **tu ne veux vraiment pas l'acheter, c'est sans r.?** you're sure you won't regret not buying it?

remorquage [rəmɔrkaʒ] NM towing

remorque [rəmɔrk] NF **1** *(traction → d'une voiture)* towing; *(→ d'un navire)* tugging, towing; **câble de r.** towline, towrope; **prendre une voiture en r.** to tow a car; **être en r.** to be *Br* on tow *or Am* in tow; **véhicule accidenté en r.** *Br* on tow, *Am* in tow

2 *(véhicule)* trailer

3 *(câble)* towline, towrope

4 *Fig* **être à la r. de qn** to tag (along) behind sb; **toujours à la r. de ton frère!** always tagging (along) behind your brother!; **il est toujours à la r.** he always lags behind

remorquer [3] [rəmɔrke] VT **1** *(voiture)* to tow; *(navire)* to tug, to tow; *(masse)* to haul; **se faire r. jusqu'au garage** to get a tow to the garage **2** *Fam (traîner → enfant, famille)* to drag along

remorqueur, -euse [rəmɔrkœr, -øz] ADJ *(avion, bateau, train)* towing

NM **1** *Naut* towboat, tug; **r. de haute mer** ocean-going tug **2** *Astron* space tug

remoudre [85] [rəmudr] VT to regrind, to grind again

remouiller [3] [rəmuje] VT **1** *(éponge, linge)* to wet again **2** *Naut* **nous avons remouillé l'ancre à Nice** we anchored in Nice again

rémoulade [remulad] NF *Culin* rémoulade (sauce)

remoulage [rəmulaʒ] NM **1** *(du café)* regrinding **2** *(en meunerie → action)* remilling; *(→ résultat)* middlings

remouler [3] [rəmule] VT to remould

rémouleur [remulœr] NM (itinerant) knife grinder

remous [rəmu] NM **1** *(tourbillon)* swirl, eddy; *(derrière un bateau)* wash, backwash; **r. d'air** eddy

2 *(mouvement)* ripple, stir; **un r. parcourut la foule** a ripple *or* stir went through the crowd

3 *(réaction)* stir, flurry; **l'article va sûrement provoquer quelques r. dans la classe politique** the article will doubtless cause a stir *or* raise a few eyebrows in the political world; **sa nomination n'a pas provoqué de r.** his/her appointment didn't cause a stir

rempaillage [rɑ̃pajaʒ] NM *(d'une chaise)* reseating (with rushes), rushing

rempailler [3] [rɑ̃paje] VT *(chaise)* to reseat (with rushes)

rempailleur, -euse [rɑ̃pajœr, -øz] NM,F chair-rusher

rempaqueter [27] [rɑ̃pakte] VT to wrap (up) again, to rewrap

rempart [rɑ̃par] NM **1** *(enceinte)* rampart, bulwark; **les remparts** *(d'une ville)* ramparts, city walls **2** *Fig Littéraire* bulwark, bastion; **elle lui fit un r. de son corps** she shielded him/her with her body; **le r. de nos libertés** the bulwark *or* bastion of our liberties

rempiètement [rɑ̃pjɛtmɑ̃] NM *Constr* underpinning

rempiéter [18] [rɑ̃pjete] VT *Constr* to underpin

rempiler [3] [rɑ̃pile] VT to pile (up) again

VI *Fam Arg mil* to re-enlist▪, to sign up again▪, *Am* to re-up; **il a rempilé pour cinq ans** he signed up for five more years

rempirer [3] [rɑ̃pire] VI *Can Vieilli* to worsen, to get worse

remplaçable [rɑ̃plasabl] ADJ replaceable; **difficilement r.** hard to replace

remplaçant, -e [rɑ̃plasɑ̃, -ɑ̃t] NM,F **1** *(gén)* replacement, stand-in; *Univ Br* supply *or Am* substitute teacher; *(d'un médecin, d'un dentiste)* replacement, *Br* locum **2** *Sport* reserve; *(au cours du match)* substitute **3** *Mus, Théât & TV* understudy

remplacement [rɑ̃plasmɑ̃] NM **1** *(substitution)* replacement; **le juge a procédé au r. de deux jurés** the judge has replaced two members of the jury; **il y a eu quelques remplacements dans le personnel** some members of staff have been replaced; **le r. des pneus va me coûter cher** it's going to cost me a lot to replace the tyres; **en r. de** in place of, as a replacement *or* substitute for

2 *(suppléance)* **je ne trouve que des remplacements** I can only find work standing in *or* covering for other people; **faire un r.** to stand in, to fill in; **faire des remplacements** *(gén)* to do temporary replacement work; *(comme secrétaire)* to do temporary secretarial work; *(comme enseignant)* to work as a *Br* supply *or Am* substitute teacher

▫ **de remplacement** ADJ **un avion arrive avec du matériel de r.** a plane is arriving with replacement equipment *or* with spares; **produit de r.** substitute product; **solution de r.** alternative *or* fallback (solution)

remplacer [16] [rɑ̃plase] VT **1** *(renouveler → pièce usagée)* to replace, to change; **r. une tuile cassée/un fusible** to replace a broken tile/a fuse; **il va falloir r. les poignées de porte** we'll have to replace the door handles

2 *(mettre à la place de)* to replace (**par** with); **nous avons remplacé les vieux bâtiments par un grand jardin** we have made a big garden where the old buildings used to be; **remplacez les adjectifs par d'autres expressions** replace the adjectives with other phrases

3 *(prendre la place de)* to replace, to take the place of; **dans de nombreuses tâches, la machine remplace maintenant l'homme** for a lot of tasks, machines are now taking over from men; **le pétrole a remplacé le charbon** oil has taken the place of coal

4 *(suppléer)* to stand in *or* to substitute for; **tu dois absolument trouver quelqu'un pour le r.** you must find someone to replace him; **rien ne peut r. une mère** there is no substitute for a mother; **personne ne peut la r.** she's irreplaceable; **si vous ne pouvez pas venir, faites-vous r.** if you can't come, get someone to stand in for you; **il l'a remplacé deux fois comme capitaine de l'équipe nationale** he's stood in for him twice as captain of his country's team; **on l'a remplacé pendant la seconde mi-temps** he was taken off *or* substituted during the second half; **tu as l'air épuisé, je vais te r.** you look exhausted, I'll take over from you; **je me suis fait r. par un collègue pendant mon absence** I got a colleague to replace me while I was away

►**se remplacer** VPR to be replaced; **cette pièce se remplace facilement** the part is easy to replace *or* easily replaced; **une sœur, ça ne se remplace pas** there's no substitute for a sister; **une secrétaire comme ça, ça ne se remplace pas** you won't find another secretary like her

remplage [rɑ̃plaʒ] NM *Archit (d'une fenêtre gothique)* tracery

rempli, -e [rɑ̃pli] ADJ **j'ai eu une journée bien remplie** I've had a very full *or* busy day; **un emploi du temps très** *ou* **bien r.** a very busy schedule; *Fam* **j'ai le ventre bien r., ça va mieux!** I feel a lot better for that meal!

NM *Couture* tuck

remplier [9] [rɑ̃plije] VT **1** *(en cordonnerie)* to fold **2** *(en reliure)* to turn over and glue

remplir [32] [rɑ̃plir] VT **1** *(emplir)* to fill; **il a rempli mon verre d'un excellent vin** he filled my glass with an excellent wine; **remplissez votre casserole d'eau** fill your saucepan with water; **le vase est rempli à ras bord** the vase is full to the brim; **la foule a rapidement rempli la rue** the crowd quickly filled the street; **cela a rempli ma journée** it took up my whole day; **on ne remplit plus les salles avec des comédies** comedies don't pull audiences *or* aren't box-office hits any more; **la cave est remplie de bons vins** the cellar is filled *or* stocked with good wines; **elle a déjà rempli dix pages** she has already written *or* filled ten pages; **l'accident a rempli les premières pages des journaux** the accident was front-page news; **le corsage est joli mais tu ne le remplis pas** it's a pretty blouse but you're a bit too thin for it

2 *(compléter → questionnaire, dossier)* to fill in *or* out; *(→ chèque)* to fill *or* to make out; **je n'ai pas rempli le formulaire** I didn't fill in the form; **elle a rempli des pages et des pages** she wrote pages and pages

3 *(combler → trou)* to fill in

4 *(accomplir → engagement, rôle)* to fulfil; *(→ fonction, mission)* to carry out; **dès que j'aurai rempli mes obligations, je vous rejoindrai** as soon as I've fulfilled my obligations I'll join you

5 *(satisfaire → condition)* to fulfil, to satisfy, to meet; *(→ besoin)* to meet, to satisfy; **elle ne remplit pas les conditions nécessaires** she doesn't fulfil *or* meet the necessary conditions

6 *(d'émotion)* **r. qn de joie/d'espoir** to fill sb with joy/with hope; **être rempli de colère/de désespoir** to be filled with anger/with despair; **être rempli de soi-même/de son importance** to be full of oneself/of one's own importance

►**se remplir** VPR **1** to fill (up); **le ciel s'est rapidement rempli de nuages noirs** the sky quickly filled with dark clouds; **ses yeux se remplirent de larmes** his/her eyes filled with tears; **le fossé s'est rempli d'eau en quelques minutes** the ditch filled (up) with water within a few minutes

2 *Fam* **se r. l'estomac** *ou* **la panse** to stuff oneself *or* one's face; **se r. les poches** to line one's pockets

remplissage [rɑ̃plisaʒ] NM **1** *(d'une fosse, d'un récipient)* filling (up) **2** *Fig (d'un texte)* padding; **faire du r.** to pad **3** *Constr* studwork; **r. en briques** nogging **4** *Mus* filling-in

remploi [rɑ̃plwa] NM **1** *(d'un travailleur)* re-employment **2** *(d'une machine, de matériaux)* reuse **3** *Fin* reinvestment

remployer [13] [rɑ̃plwaje] VT **1** *(travailleur)* to take on again, to re-employ **2** *(machine, matériaux)* to reuse, to use again **3** *Fin* to reinvest

remplumer [3] [rɑ̃plyme] **se remplumer** VPR **1** *(d'un oiseau)* to get new feathers *or* new plumage

2 *Fam (physiquement)* to put a bit of weight back on▪; **elle s'est remplumée depuis l'année dernière** she's put a bit of weight back on since last year

3 *Fam (financièrement)* to improve one's cash flow▪, to get back on one's feet; **il a réussi à se r. en vendant ses tableaux** he managed to improve his cash flow situation by selling his paintings

rempocher [3] [rɑ̃pɔʃe] VT to pocket again, to put back in one's pocket

rempoissonnement [rɑ̃pwasɔnmɑ̃] NM restocking (with fish)

rempoissonner [3] [rɑ̃pwasɔne] VT to restock (with fish)

remporter [3] [rɑ̃pɔrte] VT **1** *(reprendre)* to take back; **n'oublie pas de r. ton livre** don't forget to take your book with you **2** *(obtenir)* to win, to get; **r. un prix** to carry off *or* to win a prize; **r. un succès** to be successful **3** *Sport* to win

rempotage [rɑ̃pɔtaʒ] NM *(d'une plante)* repotting

rempoter [3] [rɑ̃pɔte] VT *(plante)* to repot

remprunter [3] [rɑ̃prœ̃te] VT **1** *(emprunter → de nouveau)* to borrow again; *(→ en supplément)* to borrow more **2** *(route)* **r. le même chemin** to take the same road again

remuage [rəmɥaʒ] NM **1** *Agr (du blé)* turning (over) **2** *(de bouteilles de champagne)* turning *(of champagne bottles)*, remuage

remuant, -e [rəmɥɑ̃, -ɑ̃t] ADJ **1** *(agité)* restless, fidgety; **que cet enfant est r.!** that child never sits still! **2** *(entreprenant)* energetic, active, lively; *Euph* **son parti trouve qu'il est un peu trop r.** his party finds him somewhat over-enthusiastic

remue [rəmy] NF *(dans les Alpes)* **1** *(migration)* transhumance **2** *(pâturage)* seasonal pasture

remue-ménage [rəmymenaʒ] NM INV **1** *(d'objets)* jumble, disorder; **il a fallu tout déménager, tu aurais vu le r. dans le bureau hier** we had to move out all the furniture, you should've seen the mess *or* shambles in the office yesterday

2 *(agitation bruyante)* commotion, hurly-burly, rumpus; **les gens du dessus font leur r. habituel** the people upstairs are making their usual rumpus; *Fig* **la nouvelle de sa démission a fait un de ces r.!** the news of his/her resignation caused quite a commotion *or* stir

remue-méninges [rəmymenɛ̃ʒ] NM INV *Offic* brainstorming; **un r.** a brainstorming session

remuement [rəmymɑ̃] NM *Littéraire* movement, moving, stirring

remuer [7] [rəmɥe] VT **1** *(agiter → tête, jambes)* to move; *(→ oreilles)* to waggle; **r. les lèvres** to move one's lips; **r. les bras** to wave one's arms (about); **la brise remue les branches/les herbes** the breeze is stirring the branches/the grass; **le chien remuait la queue** the dog was wagging its tail

2 *(déplacer → objet)* to move, to shift; **je l'entends r. ses livres/son tabouret** I can hear him/her shifting his/her books/stool (about); **il faudrait pouvoir r. ces meubles** it would be better if we could move the furniture

3 *(retourner → cendres)* to poke; *(→ terre, compost)* to turn over; *(→ salade)* to toss; *(→ boisson, préparation)* to stir; **remuez délicatement le chocolat et les blancs d'œufs** gently fold the chocolate into the egg whites; **r. des fortunes** *ou* **de grosses sommes** to handle huge amounts of money; *Fam* **r. l'or à la pelle** to be rolling in money; **r. ciel et terre** to move heaven and earth, to leave no stone unturned

4 *(ressasser)* to stir up, to brood over; **à quoi bon r. le passé?** what's the good of stirring up *or* raking over the past?; **r. des souvenirs** to turn *or* to go over memories

5 *(troubler)* to move; **être (tout)/profondément remué** to be (very)/deeply moved; **ton histoire m'a remué** your story moved me

VI **1** *(s'agiter → nez, oreille)* to twitch; **la queue du chien/du chat/du cheval remuait** the dog was wagging/the cat was wagging/the horse was flicking its tail

2 *(branler → dent, manche)* to be loose

3 *(personne, animal → bouger)* to move; *(→ gigoter)* to fidget; *Fam* **les gosses, ça remue tout le temps** kids can't stop fidgeting *or* never keep still; **qu'est-ce qui remue dans le panier?** what's that moving about in the basket?

4 *Fig* to get restless; **les mineurs commencent à r.** the miners are getting restless

►**se remuer** VPR **1** *(bouger)* to move; **j'ai besoin de me r. un peu** I need to get some exercise

2 *(se démener)* to put oneself out; **il a fallu que je me remue pour t'inscrire** I had to go to a lot of trouble to get you on the course; *Fam* **remue-toi un peu!** *(agis)* get a move on!, shift yourself!, *Br* get up off your backside!

remueur, -euse [rəmɥœr, -øz] NM,F *Littéraire* **un r. d'idées** an ideas man

remugle [rəmygl] NM *Littéraire* mustiness, fustiness

rémunérateur, -trice [remyneratœr, -tris] ADJ *(investissement)* remunerative; *(emploi)* lucrative, well-paid

rémunération [remynerasjɔ̃] NF remuneration, payment (**de** for); *(salaire)* pay; **r. du capital** interest on capital; **r. de départ** starting salary

rémunératoire [remyneratwar] ADJ *Jur* remunerative; **legs r.** legacy in consideration of service rendered

rémunératrice [remyneratris] *voir* **rémunérateur**

rémunérer [18] [remynere] VT *(personne)* to remunerate, to pay; *(travail, services)* to pay for; **travail bien/mal rémunéré** well-paid/badly-paid work; **avoir un emploi rémunéré** to be gainfully employed, to be in gainful employment; **vous êtes-vous fait r. pour ce travail?** did you get paid for this job?

Rémus [remys] NPR *Myth* Remus

renâcler [3] [rənakle] VI **1** *(cheval)* to snort **2** *(personne)* to grumble, to moan; *Fig* **il a un peu renâclé** he dragged his feet a bit; **il a accepté en renâclant** he reluctantly accepted; **r. à faire qch** to be (very) loath *or* reluctant to do sth; **r. à la besogne** to be workshy

renais, renaissait *etc voir* **renaître**

Renaissance [rənɛsɑ̃s] NF **la R.** the Renaissance (period)

ADJ INV *Archit & Beaux-Arts* Renaissance *(avant n)*

renaissance [rənɛsɑ̃s] NF **1** *(réincarnation)* rebirth **2** *(renouveau)* revival, rebirth

renaissant, -e [rənɛsɑ̃, -ɑ̃t] ADJ **1** *(intérêt, enthousiasme)* renewed; *(passion)* reawakening; *(douleur)* recurring; *(économie)* reviving; **leur amour r.** their rekindled love; **sans cesse r.** *(espoir)* ever renewed; *(problème)* ever recurring **2** *Archit & Beaux-Arts* Renaissance *(avant n)*; **l'art r.** Renaissance art, the art of the Renaissance

renaître [92] [rənɛtr] VI *(inusité aux temps composés)* **1** *(naître de nouveau → gén)* to come back to life, to come to life again; *(→ végétation)* to spring up again; **se sentir r.** to feel like a new person; *Rel* **r. par le baptême/la pénitence** to be born again through baptism/repentance; *Littéraire* **r. à la vie** to come alive again; *Littéraire* **r. à l'espoir/l'amour** to find new hope/a new love; *Fig* **r. de ses cendres** to rise from the ashes

2 *(revenir → jour)* to dawn; *(→ courage, économie)* to revive, to recover; *(→ lettres, arts)* to revive; *(→ bonheur, espoir)* to return; **faire r. le passé/un antagonisme** to revive the past/an antagonism; **faire r. les espérances de qn** to revive sb's hopes, to get sb's hopes up again; **faire r. la confiance** to restore confidence; **l'espoir renaît dans l'équipe/le village** the team/the village has found fresh hope; **l'espoir** *ou* **l'espérance renaît toujours** hope springs eternal

Rénal [renal] NPR **Madame de R.** = a bourgeois woman who is Julien Sorel's first love in Stendhal's 'Le Rouge et le Noir' (1830)

rénal, -e, -aux, -ales [renal, -o] ADJ *Anat* kidney *(avant n)*, *Spéc* renal

renaquit *etc voir* **renaître**

renard [rənar] NM **1** *Zool* fox; **r. argenté/bleu** silver/blue fox; **r. corsac** corsac fox; **r. polaire** Arctic fox; **r. roux** common *or* red fox **2** *(fourrure)* fox fur; **un manteau en r. argenté** a silver fox fur coat **3** *Fig* **vieux r.** (sly) old fox, cunning old devil; **c'est un fin r.** he's as sly as a fox **4** *Tech (brèche)* breach, leakage **5** *Ich* **r. de mer** thresher (shark)

renarde [rənard] NF *Zool* vixen

renardeau, -x [rənardo] NM fox cub

renardière [rənardjɛr] NF **1** *(tanière)* fox's earth *or* den **2** *Can (élevage)* fox farm

renauder [3] [rənode] VI *Fam Vieilli* to whinge, to moan and groan

Renaudot [rənodo] NM **le prix R.** = annual literary prize for a work of fiction

rencaissage [rɑ̃kɛsaʒ] NM *(d'une plante)* reboxing

rencaissement [rɑ̃kɛsmɑ̃] NM *Fin* cashing (in) again

rencaisser [4] [rɑ̃kɛse] VT **1** *(plante)* to rebox **2** *Fin (toucher)* to cash again; *(remettre en caisse)* to put back in the till

rencard [rɑ̃kar] = **rancard**

rencarder [rɑ̃karde] = **rancarder**

renchérir [32] [rɑ̃ʃerir] VI **1** *(devenir plus cher)* to become more expensive, to go up

2 *(faire une surenchère)* to make a higher bid, to bid higher

VT *(rendre plus cher)* **la crise a renchéri les produits courants** the crisis has pushed up the price of everyday goods

USAGE ABSOLU **"un homme fort aimable", renchérit-elle** "a most likable man," she added

▫ **renchérir sur** VT IND **1** *(personne)* to outbid; *(enchère)* to bid higher than

2 *(en actes ou en paroles)* to go further than, to outdo; **il renchérit toujours sur ce que dit sa femme** he always goes further *or* one better than his wife

renchérissement [rɑ̃ʃerismɑ̃] NM increase, rise; **un r. des produits laitiers** an increase *or* a rise in the price of dairy products

renchérisseur, -euse [rɑ̃ʃerisœr, -øz] NM,F *(aux enchères)* outbidder

rencogner [3] [rɑ̃kɔɲe] VT *Fam* to corner

►**se rencogner** VPR to huddle up

rencontre [rɑ̃kɔ̃tr] NF **1** *(entrevue)* meeting, encounter; **une r. de hasard** a chance meeting *or* encounter; **c'était une r. tout à fait inattendue** it was a completely unexpected encounter; **faire la r. de qn** to meet sb; **faire beaucoup de rencontres** to meet a lot of people; **faire une r.** to meet someone; **faire une mauvaise r.** to have an unpleasant encounter; **faire de mauvaises rencontres** to meet the wrong kind of people; **aller** *ou* **marcher à la r. de qn** to go to meet sb; **je pars à sa r.** I'm going to go and meet him/her; **rencontres en ligne** on-line dating

2 *(conférence)* meeting, conference; **une r. internationale sur l'énergie nucléaire** an international meeting *or* conference on nuclear energy; **r. au sommet** summit meeting

3 *Sport* match, game, *Br* fixture; *(en boxe)* fight; **une r. de tennis** a tennis match *or Br* fixture; **une r. d'athlétisme** an athletics meeting

4 *(combat)* engagement, encounter; *(duel)* duel

5 *(jonction → de deux fleuves)* confluence; *(→ de deux routes)* junction; *(collision → de deux voitures)* collision

6 *Arch ou Littéraire (conjoncture)* occasion, conjuncture; **par r.** by chance

▫ **de rencontre** ADJ *(liaison)* passing, casual; *(amitié)* chance *(avant n)*

rem–ren

'Rencontres du troisième type' *Spielberg* 'Close Encounters of theThird Kind'

Allusion

Rencontre du troisième type
Steven Spielberg's 1977 film *Close Encounters of the Third Kind* gave rise to this expression. The phrase is used in French today, with allusive reference to the film, to refer to unexpected get-togethers between different sorts of people, or odd juxtapositions of disparate objects.

rencontrer [3] [rɑ̃kɔ̃tre] VT **1** *(croiser)* to meet, *Sout* to encounter; *(faire la connaissance de)* to meet; **je l'ai rencontré (par hasard) au marché** I met him (by chance) *or* bumped into him at the market; **je lui ai fait r. quelqu'un qui peut l'aider professionnellement** I've put him/her in touch with somebody who can offer him/her professional help; **c'est moi qui lui ai fait r. son mari** I was the one who introduced her to her future husband

2 *(avoir une réunion avec)* to meet, to have a meeting with; **il ne peut pas vous r. avant lundi** he can't meet you before Monday

3 *(affronter)* to meet; *Sport* to play (against), to meet; **attention, vous allez r. les meilleurs** watch out, you're going to be up against the best; **Nantes rencontre Bordeaux samedi** Nantes *Br* are *or Am* is playing Bordeaux on Saturday

4 *(heurter)* to strike, to hit; *(entrer en contact avec)* to meet; **la fourche rencontra une grosse pierre** the fork struck *or* hit a big stone; **r. les yeux de qn** to meet sb's eyes; **sa main rencontra quelque chose de froid** his/her hand came up against *or* met something cold

5 *(trouver → thème, plante, arbre)* to come across, to encounter; *(→ opposition, difficulté, obstacle)* to encounter, to meet with, to come *or* run up against; **r. l'assentiment de tous** to meet with everyone's approval; **sans r. la moindre résistance** without meeting with *or* experiencing the least resistance; **l'une des plus belles villes qu'il m'ait été donné de r.** one of the most beautiful cities I've had the opportunity to visit; **c'est un écrivain comme on n'en rencontre plus guère** he's the sort of writer you hardly ever come across nowadays; **r. l'amour/Dieu** to find love/God

6 *Belg (argument, objection)* to counter; *(besoin, exigence)* to meet, to satisfy

▶**se rencontrer** VPR **1** *(se trouver en présence)* to meet; **c'est elle qui les a fait se r.** she arranged for them to meet; **où vous êtes-vous rencontrés?** where did you meet?; **comme on se rencontre!** it's a small world!

2 *Sport* to play (against), to meet

3 *(se rejoindre → fleuves)* to meet, to join; *(→ routes)* to meet, to merge; *(se heurter)* to collide, to run into each other; **leurs yeux** *ou* **regards se sont rencontrés** their eyes met

4 *(être d'accord → personnes)* to agree

5 *(emploi passif)* **un homme intègre, ça ne se rencontre pas souvent** it's not often you come across *or* meet an honest man

6 *(tournure impersonnelle)* **il se rencontrera toujours des gens pour nier la vérité** you will always find people who deny the truth

7 *Fig Littéraire* **se r. avec qn** to see eye to eye with sb

rendement [rɑ̃dmɑ̃] NM **1** *(production)* output; **le r. d'un puits de pétrole** the output of an oil well; **travailler à plein r.** *(usine)* to work at full capacity; **r. d'ensemble** *ou* **global** *ou* **total** aggregate output; **r. à l'heure, r. horaire** output per hour; **r. optimal** *ou* **maximum** maximum *or* peak output

2 *(rentabilité → gén)* productivity; *(→ d'un ordinateur)* throughput; **le r. de cette machine est supérieur** this machine is more productive

3 *(efficacité)* efficiency; **mon r. s'en est trouvé affecté** it's affected my efficiency; **r. économique** commercial efficiency; **r. effectif** performance rating; **r. thermodynamique** thermodynamic efficiency

4 *Agr* yield; **le r. de ces champs est faible** those fields give a low yield; **une terre sans aucun r.** a land that yields no return

5 *Fin* yield, return; **à haut/bas r.** high-/low-yield; **r. actuariel** actuarial return; **r. actuariel brut** gross redemption yield, gross actuarial return; **r. annuel** annual return; **r. brut** gross yield *or* return; **r. constant** fixed yield; **r. coupon** coupon yield; **rendements croissants** increasing returns; **rendements décroissants** diminishing returns; **r. à l'échéance** yield to maturity, redemption yield; **r. sur fonds propres** return on equity; **r. marginal du capital** marginal return on capital; **r. moyen** average yield; **r. net** net return; **r. réel** inflation-adjusted yield

6 *Chim* yield

7 *Élec & Phys* efficiency

rendez-vous [rɑ̃devu] NM INV **1** *(rencontre → gén)* appointment; *(→ d'amoureux)* date; **prendre r. avec qn/un r. chez le coiffeur** to make an appointment with sb/at the hairdresser's; **j'ai r. chez le médecin** I have an appointment with the doctor; **donner r. à qn** to arrange to meet sb; **se donner r.** to arrange to meet; **avez-vous r.?** do you have an appointment?; **le réceptionniste m'a pris r. pour 11 heures** the receptionist made an appointment for me for 11 o'clock; **être en r.** to be in a meeting; **lieu de r.: devant l'église** meet in front of the church; **r. chez mes parents à 10 heures** let's meet at 10 o'clock at my parents' (house); **un r. manqué** a missed meeting; **c'était un r. manqué** we/they didn't meet up; *Fig* **le soleil était au r.** the sun was shining; **r. d'affaires** business meeting *or* appointment; **r. citoyen** = name sometimes given to the "journée d'appel de préparation à la défense"; *Astron* **r. spatial** docking in space

2 *(endroit)* meeting place; **j'étais le premier au r.** I was the first one to turn up *or* to arrive; **ici, c'est le r. des étudiants** this is a student haunt; **r. de chasse** *(lieu de rassemblement)* meet; *(bâtiment)* hunting lodge

3 *(personne)* **votre r. est arrivé** your client/patient/*etc* is here

rendormir [36] [rɑ̃dɔrmir] VT to put *or* to send back to sleep

▶**se rendormir** VPR to go back to sleep, to fall asleep again; **je n'arrive pas à me r.** I can't get back to sleep

rendosser [3] [rɑ̃dose] VT to put on again; *Fig* **r. l'uniforme** to return to military life

RENDRE [73] [rɑ̃dr]

> **VT** to give back **1** ▪ to return **1, 2, 10** ▪ to make **3** ▪ to portray **5** ▪ to render **5** ▪ to sound **6** ▪ to look **6** ▪ to give out **7** ▪ to vomit **8** ▪ to pronounce **10** ▪ to yield **11**
> **VI** to be productive **1** ▪ to be effective **2** ▪ to vomit **3**
> **VPR** to surrender **1** ▪ to make oneself **2** ▪ to go **3** ▪ to give in **1, 4**

VT **1** *(restituer → objet prêté, volé ou donné)* to give back, to return; *(→ objet défectueux)* to take back, to return; *(→ somme)* to pay back; *(→ réponse)* to give; **il est venu r. la chaise** he brought the chair back; **donne-moi 10 euros, je te les rendrai demain** give me 10 euros, I'll pay you back *or* I'll give it back to you tomorrow; **r. un devoir** *(sujet: élève)* to hand *or* to give in a piece of work; *(sujet: professeur)* to hand *or* to give back a piece of work; **l'enfant a été rendu à sa famille** the child was handed back *or* returned to his family; **r. un otage** to return *or* to hand over a hostage

2 *(donner en retour)* to return; **r. un baiser à qn** to kiss sb back; **r. le bien pour le mal/coup pour coup** to return good for evil/blow for blow; **rends-moi 3 euros** give me 3 euros back *or* 3 euros change; **elle m'a rendu 2 euros de trop** she gave me back 2 euros too much; **r. la monnaie (sur)** to give change (out of *or* from); **elle me méprise, mais je le lui rends bien** she despises me, but the feeling's mutual

3 *(suivi d'un adj) (faire devenir)* to make; **r. qch public** to make sth public; **la nouvelle n'a pas encore été rendue publique** the news hasn't been made public *or* been released yet; **r. qn aveugle** to make sb (go) blind, to blind sb; *Fig* to blind sb; **r. qn célèbre** to make sb famous; **r. qn fou** to drive *or* to make sb mad; **r. qn heureux/idiot/malade** to make sb happy/stupid/ill; **rien que de penser aux examens, ça me rend malade** just thinking about the exams makes me (feel) ill; **r. qn responsable** to make *or* to hold sb responsible; **r. qn sourd** to make sb (go) deaf; **l'absence de ponctuation rend le texte incompréhensible** the lack of punctuation makes the text incomprehensible; **ils veulent r. la Loire navigable** they want to make the river Loire navigable

4 *(faire recouvrer)* **r. l'ouïe/la santé/la vue à qn** to restore sb's hearing/health/sight, to give sb back his/her hearing/health/sight; **l'opération ne lui a pas rendu l'usage de la parole/de son bras** the operation did not give him/her back the power of speech/the use of his/her arm; **tu m'as rendu l'espoir** you've given me new hope; **r. son honneur à qn** to restore sb's honour; **r. sa forme à un chapeau** to pull a hat back into shape; **Brillax rend à vos sols l'éclat du neuf!** Brillax puts the shine back into your floors!

5 *(exprimer → personnalité)* to portray, to capture; *(→ nuances, pensée)* to convey, *Sout* to render; **la traduction rend bien sa pensée** the translation successfully conveys *or Sout* renders his/her thought; **voyons comment il a rendu cette scène à l'écran** *(metteur en scène)* let's see how he transferred this scene to the screen; **l'enregistrement ne rend pas la qualité de sa voix** the recording doesn't do justice to the quality of his/her voice

6 *(produire)* **r. un son métallique/cristallin** to sound metallic/like glass; **ici le mur rend un son creux** the wall sounds hollow here; **ça ne rend rien** *ou* **pas grand-chose** *(décor, couleurs)* it doesn't look much; **les photos n'ont pas rendu grand-chose** the pictures didn't come out very well; **mes recherches n'ont encore rien rendu** my research hasn't come up with anything yet *or* hasn't produced any results yet

7 *Culin* to give out; **quand les champignons ont rendu toute leur eau** when the mushrooms have released all their juices

8 *(vomir → repas)* to vomit, to bring up; **il a tout rendu** he's brought everything back up

9 *Sport* **r. du poids** to have a weight handicap; **r. 150 mètres** to have a 150 metres handicap; **r. 5 kilos** to give *or* to carry 5 kilos

10 *(prononcer → jugement, arrêt)* to pronounce; *(→ verdict)* to deliver, to return; **r. une sentence** to pass *or* to pronounce sentence; **r. un oracle** to prophesy

11 *Agr & Hort (produire)* to yield, to have a yield of; **cette terre rend peu de blé à l'hectare** ≃ this land doesn't yield much wheat per acre; **ce blé rend beaucoup de farine** this wheat has a high flour yield

VI **1** *Agr & Hort* to be productive; **les vignes ont bien rendu** the vineyards have given a good yield *or* have produced well; **cette terre ne rend pas** this land is unproductive *or* yields no return; **le verger rend peu** the orchard is not very productive

2 *(ressortir)* to be effective; **ce tapis rend très bien/ne rend pas très bien avec les rideaux** this carpet looks really good/doesn't look much with the curtains; **le tableau rendrait mieux sous un autre éclairage** the picture would be more effective *or* would look better with different lighting

3 *(vomir)* to vomit, to be sick; **j'ai envie de r.** I want to be *or* I feel sick; **il a rendu la nuit dernière** he was sick last night

▶**se rendre** VPR **1** *(criminel)* to give oneself up, to surrender; *(ville)* to surrender; **se r. à la police** to give oneself up to the police; **rendez-vous!** give yourself up!, surrender!; *Fig* **il a fini par se r.** he finally gave in

2 *(suivi d'un adj) (devenir)* to make oneself; **elle sait se r. indispensable** she knows how to make herself indispensable; **rends-toi utile!** make yourself useful!; **tu vas te r. malade** you'll make yourself ill; **ne te rends pas malade pour ça!** it's not worth making yourself ill about *or* over it!

3 *(aller)* to go; **je me rends à l'école à pied/à**

vélo/en voiture I walk/ride (my bike)/drive to school, I go to school on foot/by bike/by car; **il s'y rend en train** he goes or gets or travels there by train; **je me rendais chez elle quand je l'ai vue** I was going to or I was on my way to her place when I saw her; **les pompiers se sont rendus sur les lieux** the fire brigade went to or arrived on the scene

4 se r. à (accepter) to yield to; **se r. à l'avis de ses supérieurs** to bow to the opinion of one's superiors; **se r. à la raison** to give in to reason; **il ne s'est pas rendu à leurs raisons** he didn't give in to their arguments; **se r. à l'évidence** (être lucide) to face facts; (reconnaître les faits) to acknowledge or to recognize the facts; **se r. aux prières de qn** to give way or to yield to sb's entreaties

rendu, -e [rɑ̃dy] ADJ **1** (arrivé) **nous/vous voilà rendus** here we/you are; **tu seras plus vite r. par le train** you'll get there quicker by train; Can **r. à la porte, il a changé d'idée** having got as far as the door, he changed his mind

2 (harassé) exhausted, worn or tired out; **les chevaux étaient rendus** the horses were worn out

3 Com **droits acquittés/non acquittés** delivery duty paid/unpaid; **r. à domicile** delivered to your door; **r. franco à bord** (delivered) free on board, f.o.b.; **r. frontière** delivered at frontier

4 Can (devenu) **et la voilà rendue maîtresse d'école!** and now she's become a schoolteacher!

NM **1** Com returned article, return; **faire un r.** to return or exchange an article

2 Beaux-Arts & Ordinat rendering

rendzine [rɑ̃dzin] NF Géol rendsina, rendzina

rêne [rɛn] NF (courroie) rein; Fig **lâcher les rênes** to let go; Fig **prendre les rênes** to take over the reins; Fig **c'est lui qui tient les rênes** he's the one who's really in charge

renégat, -e [rənega, -at] NM,F renegade

renégociation [rənegɔsjasjɔ̃] NF (d'un contrat) renegotiation; (d'une dette) rescheduling

renégocier [9] [rənegɔsje] VT (contrat) to renegotiate; (dette) to reschedule

reneiger [23] [rəneʒe] V IMPERSONNEL to snow again; **il reneige** it's snowing again

rénette [rənɛt] NF **1** (en maréchalerie) paring knife **2** Menuis tracing iron **3** (en tannerie) race knife

renettoyer [13] [rənetwaje] VT Belg (nettoyer) to clean

renfaîter [4] [rɑ̃fɛte] VT (toit) to new-ridge

renfermé, -e [rɑ̃fɛrme] ADJ uncommunicative, withdrawn, silent; **elle est du genre r.** she's the uncommunicative type

NM **une odeur de r.** a stale or musty smell; **ça sent le r. ici** it smells musty in here

renfermer [3] [rɑ̃fɛrme] VT **1** (contenir) to hold, to contain; **son histoire renferme une part de vérité** there's some truth in what he/she says **2** (enfermer de nouveau) to shut up again **3** Vieilli (ranger) to put away

▸**se renfermer** VPR to withdraw (into oneself)

renfiler [3] [rɑ̃file] VT (aiguille) to rethread, to thread again; (perles) to restring; (vêtement) to slip back into

renflé, -e [rɑ̃fle] ADJ (colonne, forme) bulging, bulbous

renflement [rɑ̃fləmɑ̃] NM (d'une colonne, d'un vase) bulge; **la poche forme un r. à hauteur de la hanche** the pocket bulges (out) at the hip

renfler [3] [rɑ̃fle] VT **le pigeon renfla ses plumes** the pigeon fluffed up its feathers

▸**se renfler** VPR to bulge out

renflouage [rɑ̃flua ʒ], **renflouement** [rɑ̃flumɑ̃] NM **1** Naut (d'un bateau échoué) refloating, floating off; (d'un bateau coulé) raising **2** Écon (d'une entreprise, d'un projet) bailing out, re-floating

renflouer [6] [rɑ̃flue] VT **1** Naut (bateau échoué) to refloat, to float off; (bateau coulé) to raise **2** Écon (entreprise, projet) to bail out; **r. les caisses de l'État** to swell the government's coffers; **ça va r. nos finances** that will bail us out

renfoncement [rɑ̃fɔ̃smɑ̃] NM **1** (dans un mur) recess, hollow; **r. d'une porte** doorway **2** Typ indentation

renfoncer [16] [rɑ̃fɔ̃se] VT **1** (bouchon) to push

further in; (clou) to knock further in; (chapeau) to pull down; Fig **je voulais lui r. ses paroles dans la gorge** I wanted to shove the words down his/her throat **2** Typ to indent

renforçateur [rɑ̃fɔrsatœr] NM **1** Phot intensifier **2** (de mise en pli) setting lotion **3** Psy reinforcer

renforcement [rɑ̃fɔrsəmɑ̃] NM **1** (consolidation → d'une poutre, d'un mur) reinforcement; (→ des pouvoirs, d'une équipe) strengthening **2** Phot intensification **3** Psy reinforcement

renforcer [16] [rɑ̃fɔrse] VT **1** Constr & Couture to reinforce

2 (augmenter → effectif, service d'ordre) to reinforce, to strengthen; **le candidat choisi viendra r. notre équipe de chercheurs** the ideal candidate will join our team of researchers; **le dispositif de sécurité a été renforcé** security has been increased or tightened up

3 (affermir → conviction) to reinforce, to strengthen, to intensify; (→ craintes) to heighten; (→ impression) to strengthen, to heighten; **sa méchanceté a renforcé ma détermination** his/her nastiness made me all the more or even more determined; **il m'a renforcé dans mon opinion** he confirmed me in my belief

4 (mettre en relief) to set off, to enhance; **utilisez un adverbe pour r. l'adjectif** use an adverb to reinforce or underline the adjective

5 Psy to reinforce

6 Scol **suivre des cours d'anglais renforcé** to do extra English

▸**se renforcer** VPR (devenir plus fort → pouvoir) to be consolidated, to increase; (→ conviction, sentiment) to grow stronger; (→ tendance) to increase; **sa popularité s'est beaucoup renforcée** his/her popularity has greatly increased or has grown considerably; **notre équipe se renforce maintenant de plusieurs jeunes ingénieurs** our team has now been strengthened by the arrival of several young engineers

renformir [32] [rɑ̃fɔrmir] VT Constr to repair and roughcast

renformis [rɑ̃fɔrmi] NM Constr repairing and roughcasting

renfort [rɑ̃fɔr] NM **1** (aide) reinforcement; **demander du r.** (gén) to ask for help; (sujet: policiers, pompiers) to ask for backup; **nous avons reçu le r. de bénévoles** we were aided by volunteers, we had backup from a team of volunteers; Hum **j'ai besoin de r. pour faire la cuisine** I need some extra pairs of hands to help me do the cooking; **il amène toujours sa sœur en r.** he always brings his sister along to back him up; **des troupes furent envoyées en r.** troops were sent in as reinforcements

2 (pièce de tissu) lining; **collant avec renforts aux talons/à l'entrejambe** tights with reinforced heels/gusset

3 Tech reinforcement

❑ **renforts** NMPL Mil (soldats) reinforcements; (matériel) (fresh) supplies

❑ **à grand renfort de** PRÉP with a lot of, with much/many; **ils ont fait sortir tout le monde à grand r. de hurlements** they got everyone out with much yelling (and shouting); **il s'expliquait à grand r. de gestes** he expressed himself with the help of a great many gestures; **son nouveau film, dont la sortie a été annoncée à grand r. de publicité** his/her much publicized new movie (or Br film)

❑ **de renfort** ADJ reinforcement (avant n)

renfrogné, -e [rɑ̃frɔɲe] ADJ (air, visage) sullen, dour; (personne) sulky, dour; **il est toujours r.** he's always sulking

renfrogner [3] [rɑ̃frɔɲe] **se renfrogner** VPR to scowl, to frown; **elle se renfrognait quand on parlait de lui** she became sullen whenever his name was mentioned

rengagé [rɑ̃ga ʒe] NM Mil re-enlisted man

rengagement [rɑ̃gaʒmɑ̃] NM (d'un soldat) re-enlistment; (d'un combat) re-engagement; (d'argent) reinvestment; **la banque a annoncé son r.** (employé) the bank announced it was taking him/her on again

rengager [17] [rɑ̃ga ʒe] VT (combat) to re-engage; (conversation) to start again, to take up again; (employé) to re-engage, to take on again; (argent) to reinvest, to plough back

VI Mil to re-enlist

▸**se rengager** VPR Mil to re-enlist, to join up again

rengaine [rɑ̃gɛn] NF **1** (refrain) (old) tune, (old) song **2** Fig **avec eux, c'est toujours la même r.** they never change their tune, with them it's always the same (old) story; **tais-toi, je la connais, ta r.!** save your breath, I know what you're going to say!

rengainer [4] [rɑ̃gene] VT **1** (arme) **r. un revolver** to put a revolver back in its holster; **r. une épée** to put a sword back in its sheath **2** Fig to hold back, to contain; **tu peux r. tes compliments** you can keep your compliments to yourself

rengorger [17] [rɑ̃gɔrʒe] **se rengorger** VPR **1** (volatile) to puff out its throat **2** (personne) to puff oneself up; **il se rengorge quand on lui parle de sa pièce** he puffs up with pride when you talk to him about his play

rengraisser [4] [rɑ̃grese] VI to put weight back on, to put on weight again

rengrégement [rɑ̃greʒmɑ̃] NM Arch (de difficultés, problèmes etc) increase, aggravation

rengréger [22] [rɑ̃greʒe] Arch VT (difficultés, problèmes etc) to increase, to aggravate

VI (difficultés, problèmes etc) to increase

rengrènement [rɑ̃grɛnmɑ̃] NM Tech re-engaging

rengréner [18] [rɑ̃grene], **rengrener** [19] [rɑ̃grəne] VT Tech (pignon) to re-engage

reniement [rənimɑ̃] NM (d'une promesse) breaking; (de sa famille) disowning, Sout repudiation; (de sa religion, d'un principe, de ses convictions) renouncing, abandonment; Rel (du Christ) denial

renier [9] [rənje] VT (promesse) to break; (famille, patrie) to disown, Sout to repudiate; (religion, principe, convictions) to renounce, to abandon; **il a renié ses engagements** he's reneged on or broken his promises; **Pierre a renié Jésus par trois fois** Peter denied Christ three times

▸**se renier** VPR to retract

reniflard [rəniflar] NM Aut breather; (dans une canalisation) breather, vent

reniflement [rɑ̃nifləmɑ̃] NM (action → en pleurant) sniffing, sniffling; (→ à cause d'un rhume) snuffling; (bruit) sniff, sniffle, snuffle; **reniflements snivelling**

renifler [3] [rənifle] VT **1** (humer) to sniff at; **r. le bouquet d'un vin** to smell a wine's bouquet; **il renifla la bonne odeur qui s'échappait de la cuisine** his nose picked up the lovely smell coming from the kitchen

2 (aspirer par le nez → tabac, cocaïne) to sniff

3 Fam Fig to sniff out; **r. une histoire louche** to smell a rat; **il sait r. une bonne affaire** he's got a (good) nose for a bargain, he's good at sniffing out bargains

VI **1** (en pleurant) to sniffle; (à cause d'un rhume) to snuffle, to sniff; **arrête de r.** stop sniffling or snuffling

2 Fam (sentir mauvais) to stink, Br to pong, to niff

renifleur, -euse [rəniflœr, -øz] ADJ **1** Fam (enfant) sniffing, sniffling, snuffling **2** Aviat **avion r.** sniffer plane

NM,F Fam sniffer, sniffler, snuffler

réniforme [reniform] ADJ kidney-shaped, Spéc reniform

rénine [renin] NF Physiol renin

renipper [3] [rənipe] Can VT (rénover → maison, pièce) to do up, to renovate

▸**se renipper** VPR to smarten oneself up, to smarten up one's appearance

rénitence [renitɑ̃s] NF Méd resistance to pressure, renitency

rénitent, -e [renitɑ̃, -ɑ̃t] ADJ Méd resisting pressure, renitent

rennais, -e [rɛnɛ, -ɛz] ADJ of/from Rennes

❑ **Rennais, -e** NM,F = inhabitant of or person from Rennes

renne [rɛn] NM Zool reindeer

Rennes [rɛn] NM Rennes

renoi [rənwa] NM Fam (verlan de noir) Black ∎

renom [rənɔ̃] NM **1** (notoriété) fame, renown; **il doit son r. à son invention** he became famous thanks to his invention

2 Littéraire (réputation) reputation; **votre attitude est préjudiciable à votre r.** your attitude is detrimental to your reputation

❑ **de renom, en renom** ADJ famous, renowned;

un musicien de (grand) r. a musician of high renown *or* repute; **une école en r.** a famous *or* renowned school

renommé, -e [rənɔme] **ADJ** *(célèbre)* famous, renowned, celebrated; **chez un fourreur r.** at a celebrated *or* famous furrier's; **elle est renommée pour ses omelettes** she's famous for her omelettes

❑ **renommée NF 1** *(notoriété)* fame, repute; **un musicien de renommée internationale** a world-famous musician, a musician of international repute; **ce vin est digne de sa renommée** this wine is worthy of its reputation; **de bonne/fâcheuse renommée** of good/ill repute; *Prov* **bonne renommée vaut mieux que ceinture dorée** = a good name is worth more than wealth

2 *Littéraire (rumeur publique)* public opinion

renommer [3] [rənɔme] **VT 1** *(à un poste)* to reappoint, to renominate **2** *Ordinat* to rename

renon [rənɔ̃] **NM** *Belg* lease cancellation; **il a donné son r.** he has terminated his lease

renonçant [rənɔ̃sɑ̃] **NM** *Rel (dans l'hindouisme)* renouncer

renonce [rənɔ̃s] **NF** *Cartes* renounce, inability to follow suit; **je fais une r.** I can't follow suit; **avoir une r. à cœur** to be short of hearts; **faire une fausse r.** to revoke

renoncement [rənɔ̃smɑ̃] **NM** renunciation; **vivre dans le r.** to live a life of renunciation *or* abnegation

renoncer [16] [rənɔ̃se] **VI** *Cartes* to renounce, to fail to follow suit; *(faire une fausse renonce)* to revoke

VT 1 *Belg (bail)* to cancel

2 *Arch (renier → personne)* to disown

USAGE ABSOLU je renonce! I give up!; **je ne renoncerai jamais** I'll never give up

❑ **renoncer à VT IND** *(gén)* to renounce, to give up; *(projet, métier)* to give up, to abandon; *(habitude)* to give up; *(pouvoir, couronne)* to relinquish; *(droit)* to waive, to relinquish; *(vacances)* to sacrifice, to forgo; **il a renoncé au trône** he renounced *or* gave up the throne; **elle ne veut à aucun prix r. à son indépendance** nothing would make her give up her independence; **r. au tabac** to give up smoking; *Rel* **r. au monde** to renounce the world; **r. à faire qch** *(en cours de route)* to give up doing sth; *(avant d'avoir commencé)* to give up the idea of doing sth; **je renonce à la convaincre** I've given up trying to convince her

renonciataire [rənɔ̃sjatɛr] **NMF** = person in favour of whom a right has been renounced

renonciateur, -trice [rənɔ̃sjatœr, -tris] **NM,F** *Jur* renouncer

renonciation [rənɔ̃sjasjɔ̃] **NF 1** *(à la couronne, à sa carrière, à la violence)* renunciation (**à** of); *(à un projet)* abandonment (**à** of); *(à un droit)* waiver, waiving (**à** of) **2** *Jur* release

renonciatrice [rənɔ̃sjatris] *voir* **renonciateur**

renonculacée [rənɔ̃kylase] *Bot* **NF** member of the Ranunculaceae

❑ **renonculacées NFPL** Ranunculaceae

renoncule [rənɔ̃kyl] **NF** *Bot* buttercup, *Spéc* ranunculus; **r. des marais** marsh marigold, kingcup; **fausse r.** lesser celandine

renoter [3] [rənɔte] **VT** *Can* to ramble

renouée [rənwe] **NF** *Bot* knotgrass; **r. des oiseaux** hogweed; **r. poivre-d'eau** water pepper

renouer [6] [rənwe] **VT 1** *(rattacher → ruban, lacet)* to retie, to tie (up) again; *(cravate)* to reknot, to tie again

2 *(reprendre → discussion, relations)* to resume, to renew; **r. une liaison** to rekindle *or* to revive an old affair

VI to get back together again; **j'ai renoué avec mes vieux amis** I've taken up with my old friends again; **r. avec la tradition/l'usage** to revive traditions/customs; **r. avec le succès** to enjoy renewed success

renouveau, -x [rənuvo] **NM 1** *(renaissance)* revival; **connaître un r.** to undergo a revival **2** *(recrudescence)* **un r. de succès** renewed success **3** *Littéraire (retour du printemps)* springtime, springtide

renouvelable [rənuvlabl] **ADJ 1** *(offre)* repeatable; *(permis, bail, abonnement)* renewable; **l'expérience est facilement r.** the experience is easy to repeat; **l'offre ne sera pas r.** it's an unrepeatable offer; **l'abonnement n'est pas r. par téléphone** the subscription cannot be renewed by phone; *École* **énergie r.** renewable energy; **non r.** non-renewable

2 *Admin & Pol* **le comité est r. tous les ans** the committee must *Br* stand *or Am* run for office each year; **mon mandat est r.** I am eligible to *Br* stand *or Am* run (for office) again

3 *École & Jur* renewable

renouvelant, -e [rənuvlɑ̃, -ɑ̃t] **NM,F** *Rel* confirmand

renouveler [24] [rənuvle] **VT 1** *(prolonger → abonnement, passeport, contrat)* to renew; **le crédit a été renouvelé pour six mois** the credit arrangement was extended for a further six months; *Méd* **ordonnance à r.** repeat prescription, prescription to be renewed

2 *(répéter)* to renew, to repeat; **r. un exploit/une tentative** to repeat a feat/an attempt; **r. une question** to repeat a question, to ask a question again; **r. une promesse/une plainte** to repeat a promise/a complaint; *Rel* **r. ses vœux** to renew one's vows; **il nous a renouvelé ses vœux pour la nouvelle année** he wished us all a happy New Year again; **je vous renouvelle mes félicitations** I congratulate you once more *or* again; **il faudra r. votre candidature** you'll have to apply again *or* to reapply; **avec une ardeur renouvelée** with renewed vigour; **j'ai préféré ne pas r. l'expérience** I chose not to repeat the experience

3 *(changer)* to renew, to change; *(→ commande, achat)* to repeat; **r. l'eau d'un aquarium** to change the water in an aquarium; **r. l'air d'une pièce** to let some fresh air into a room; **elle a renouvelé son stock de confitures** she renewed *or* replenished her stock of jams; **r. sa garde-robe** to get *or* to buy some new clothes; **on a renouvelé mon plâtre** they gave me a new plaster; **r. la composition d'un groupe** to change the line-up of a band; **il nous revient avec un répertoire entièrement renouvelé** he's back with an entirely new repertoire; **elle a renouvelé le genre policier** she gave the detective story a new lease of life; **une découverte qui renouvelle totalement notre conception du temps** a discovery which radically alters our conception of time

4 *(réélire → groupe, assemblée)* to re-elect

►**se renouveler VPR 1** *(se reformer → épiderme)* to be renewed

2 *(se reproduire)* to recur, to occur again and again; **les appels anonymes se sont renouvelés pendant un mois** the anonymous phone calls persisted for a month; **je te promets que cela ne se renouvellera pas** I promise you it won't happen again

3 *(changer de style)* to change one's style; **c'est un bon acteur mais il ne se renouvelle pas assez** he's a good actor but he doesn't vary his roles enough

4 *(groupe, assemblée)* to be re-elected *or* replaced

renouvellement [rənuvɛlmɑ̃] **NM 1** *(reconduction → d'un abonnement, d'un passeport, d'un contrat)* renewal; **solliciter le r. d'un mandat** *Br* to stand *or Am* to run for re-election

2 *(répétition)* repetition, recurrence

3 *(changement)* **procéder au r. d'une équipe** to change the line-up of a team; **procéder au r. de sa garde-robe** to buy some new clothes; **la marée assure le r. de l'eau dans les viviers** the water in the tanks is changed by the action of the tide; **ce produit active le r. cellulaire** this product encourages the cells to renew themselves; **dans la mode actuelle, il n'y a aucun r.** there are no new ideas in (the world of) fashion today

4 *Rel* confirmation; **faire son r.** to be confirmed

5 *Com (de marchandises)* restocking, reordering; *(de matériel)* replacement; **r. du personnel** staff turnover; **r. de stock** restocking

6 *Fin (d'un crédit)* extension

renouvellerai *etc voir* **renouveler**

rénovateur, -trice [renɔvatœr, -tris] **ADJ** reformist, reforming

NM,F reformer; **les grands rénovateurs de la science** the people who revolutionized *or* radically transformed science

NM *(pour nettoyer)* restorer

rénovation [renɔvasjɔ̃] **NF 1** *(d'un meuble, d'un immeuble)* renovation; *(d'un quartier)* redevelopment, renovation; **la maison est en r.** the house is being done up *or* is having a complete facelift; **r. urbaine** urban renewal **2** *Fig (rajeunissement → d'une méthode)* updating; *(→ d'une institution)* updating, reform

rénovatrice [renɔvatris] *voir* **rénovateur**

rénové, -e [renɔve] **ADJ 1** *(remis à neuf)* renovated

2 *Belg* **enseignement r.** = restructured secondary education system set up in the 1960s

rénover [3] [renɔve] **VT 1** *(remettre à neuf → meuble)* to restore, to renovate; *(→ immeuble)* to renovate, to do up; *(→ quartier)* to redevelop, to renovate; *(→ salle de bains)* to modernize; **toute la façade ouest a été rénovée** the whole of the west front has been done up *or* has been given a facelift **2** *(rajeunir → méthode)* to update; **r. les institutions politiques** to reform political institutions

renseignement [rɑ̃sɛɲəmɑ̃] **NM 1** *(information)* piece of information, information *(UNCOUNT)*; **un précieux r.** an invaluable piece of information, some invaluable information; **de précieux renseignements** (some) invaluable information; **pour tout r., veuillez appeler ce numéro** for information *or* if you have any queries, please call this number; **demander un r.** *ou* **des renseignements à qn** to ask sb for information; **prendre des renseignements sur qn/qch** to make enquiries about sb/sth; **ayant pris des renseignements sur le prix, il a fait sa réservation** having found out about the price, he made his reservation; **renseignements pris, elle était la seule héritière** after making some enquiries it turned out (that) she was the sole heir; **tu n'obtiendras aucun r.** you won't get any information; *aussi Ironique* **merci pour le r.** thanks for letting me know; **aller aux renseignements** to go and (see what one can) find out

2 *Fam (surveillance)* **être/travailler dans le r.** to be/to work in intelligence▪

❑ **renseignements NMPL 1** *Admin (service)* enquiries (department); *(réception)* information *or* enquiries (desk); *Tél* **appeler les renseignements** to phone *Br* directory enquiries *or Am* information

2 *(espionnage)* intelligence; **agent/services de renseignements** intelligence agent/services; **elle travaille pour les services de renseignements** she works in intelligence; **les Renseignements généraux** = the secret intelligence branch of the French police force, *Br* ≃ the Special Branch, *Am* ≃ the FBI; **renseignements humains** human intelligence, *Fam* humint

3 *Fin* **renseignements de crédit** status *or* credit enquiry

Culture

LES RENSEIGNEMENTS GÉNÉRAUX

Created under Vichy, this agency is the intelligence arm of the Ministry of the Interior. It keeps tabs on political parties, trade unions, lobby groups and various individuals.

renseigner [4] [rɑ̃seɲe] **VT 1** *(mettre au courant → étranger, journaliste)* to give information to, to inform; *(→ automobiliste)* to give directions to; **elle vous renseignera sur les prix** she'll tell you the prices, she'll give you more information about the prices; **pardon, Monsieur, pouvez-vous me r.?** excuse me, sir, could you help me, please?; **r. qn sur qn/qch** to tell sb about sb/sth; **bien renseigné** well-informed; **mal renseigné** misinformed; **on vous a mal renseigné** you have been misinformed; **je suis mal renseigné sur l'horaire des marées** I don't have much information about the times of the tides; **l'office du tourisme nous a très bien/très mal renseignés** the tourist board gave us excellent information/totally the wrong information

2 *(donner des indices à)* **ça ne me renseigne pas sur ses motivations** that doesn't tell me anything about his/her motives; **seule sa biographie peut nous r. sur son passé militaire** only his biography can tell us something of *or* about his military career; *Ironique* **nous voilà bien renseignés!** that doesn't get us very far!, that doesn't give us much to go on!

3 *Belg* *(indiquer)* **pouvez-vous me r. le chemin?** could you show me the way?; **pouvez-vous me r. un livre?** *(conseiller)* could you recommend a book?

▸ **se renseigner** VPR to make enquiries; **se r. sur qn/qch** to find out about sb/sth; **il aurait fallu se r. sur son compte** you should have made (some) enquiries about him/her; **essaie de te r. pour savoir combien coûterait un billet** try to find out how much a ticket would cost; **renseignez-vous auprès de votre agence de voyages** ask your travel agent for further information

rentabilisable [rãtabilizabl] ADJ profitable

rentabilisation [rãtabilizasjõ] NF **la r. de l'affaire prendra peu de temps** it will not be long before the business becomes profitable *or* starts to make a profit

rentabiliser [3] [rãtabilize] VT *(affaire)* to make profitable; *(investissement)* to obtain a return on

rentabilité [rãtabilite] NF profitability, cost-effectiveness (**de** of); *(d'une affaire)* profitability; *(d'un investissement)* rate of return; *(des ventes)* return (**de** on); **taux de r.** rate of profit; **r. directe du produit** direct product profitability; **r. nette d'exploitation** net operating profit

rentable [rãtabl] ADJ profitable, cost-effective; **l'opération s'est avérée r.** the operation turned out to be profitable *or* has paid off; **si je les vends moins cher, ce n'est plus r.** if I sell them any cheaper, I no longer make a profit *or* any money; **c'est plus r. d'acheter que de louer en ce moment** you're better off buying than renting at the moment

rentamer [3] [rãtame] VT *(recommencer)* to start *or* to begin again

rente [rãt] NF **1** *(revenu)* private income; **avoir des rentes** to have a private income, to have independent means; **vivre de ses rentes** to live on *or* off one's private income; **r. de situation** secure income
2 *(pension)* pension, annuity, *Spéc* rente; **servir une r. à qn** to pay sb an allowance; **r. foncière** ground rent; **r. viagère** life annuity
3 *Écon* rent
4 *Bourse* (government) bond; **rentes amortissables** redeemable securities *or* bonds; **r. annuelle** annuity; *Banque* **rentes consolidées** consols; **rentes sur l'État** government stock *or* funds; **r. à paiement différé** deferred annuity; **rentes perpétuelles** undated *or* irredeemable securities; **r. de situation** guaranteed income; **r. à terme** terminable annuity; **r. viagère** life annuity, life interest

renter [3] [rãte] VT *Vieilli (personne)* to pay an allowance to

rentier, -ère [rãtje, -ɛr] NM,F person of private means; **mener une vie de r.** to live a life of ease; **petit r.** person with a small private income; **r. viager** life annuitant

rentoilage [rãtwalaʒ] NM *(d'un tableau)* relining

rentoiler [3] [rãtwale] VT *(tableau)* to reline

rentoileur, -euse [rãtwalœr, -øz] NM,F *(de tableaux)* reliner

rentrage [rãtraʒ] NM **1** *(du bois, du foin)* taking *or* bringing in **2** *Tex* looming, healding

rentraire [112] [rãtrɛr] VT *Couture (raccommoder)* to mend

rentraiture [rãtrɛtyr] NF *Couture* mending

rentrant, -e [rãtrã, -ãt] ADJ **1** *Math voir* **angle** 2 *Aviat* **train d'atterrissage r.** retractable undercarriage **3** *Ordinat* re-entrant

rentrayer [11] [rãtrɛje] VT *Couture* to mend

rentré, -e[1] [rãtre] ADJ **1** *(refoulé)* suppressed; **colère/jalousie rentrée** suppressed anger/jealousy **2** *(creux → joues)* hollow, sunken; *(→ yeux)* sunken, deep-set
NM *Couture* turn in

rentre-dedans [rãtrədədã] NM INV *Fam* **faire du r. à qn** to come on to sb, *Br* to chat sb up, *Am* to hit on sb

rentrée[2] [rãtre] NF **1** *Scol* **r. (scolaire** *ou* **des classes)** start of the (new) academic year; **la r. des élèves/des professeurs** the day the pupils/teachers go back; **depuis la r. de Noël/Pâques** since the spring/summer term began, since the Christmas/Easter break; **la r. est fixée au 6 septembre** school starts again *or* schools reopen on 6 September; **j'irai le mardi de la r.** I'll go on the first Tuesday of the (new) term; **c'est quand, la r., chez vous?** when do you go back? *(to school, college etc)*; **on se revoit à la r.!** see you next term!, see you after the holidays!; **les vitrines de la r.** back-to-school window displays
2 *(au Parlement)* reopening (of Parliament), new (parliamentary) session; **les députés vont devoir avancer leur r.** Parliament will have to start the new session earlier than usual; **à la prochaine r. parlementaire** at the beginning of the new parliamentary session; **faire sa r. politique** *(après les vacances)* to start the new political season *(after the summer)*; *(après une absence)* to make one's (political) comeback
3 *(saison artistique)* **la r. musicale/théâtrale** the new musical/theatrical season *(after the summer break)*; **la r. littéraire** the autumn's new books; **le disque sortira à la r.** the record will be released in the *Br* autumn *or Am* fall; **pour votre r. parisienne** *(après les vacances)* for the start of your *Br* autumn *or Am* fall season in Paris; *(après une absence)* for your Paris comeback
4 *(retour → des vacances d'été)* (beginning of the) *Br* autumn *or Am* fall; *(→ de congé ou de week-end)* return to work; *Transp* city-bound traffic; **la r. a été dure** it was hard to get back to work after the summer *Br* holidays *or Am* vacation; **grosses rentrées prévues ce soir** inbound traffic will be heavy tonight; **r. sociale** = return to work after the summer holidays
5 *(d'argent)* receipt; **j'attends une r. d'argent** I'm expecting some money
6 *Astron* **r. (atmosphérique)** re-entry (into the atmosphere)
7 *Cartes* pick-up
8 *Agr (des foins)* bringing *or* taking in
◻ **rentrées** NFPL *Fin* income, money coming in; **avoir des rentrées (d'argent) régulières** to have a regular income *or* money coming in regularly; **rentrées de caisse** cash receipts; **rentrées fiscales** tax receipts *or* revenue; **rentrées journalières** daily takings; *Compta* **rentrées et sorties de caisse** cash receipts and payments

RENTRER [3] [rãtre]

VI	to go in **1** ▪ to come in **1, 6** ▪ to fit in **1** ▪ to be part of **2** ▪ to return **4** ▪ to come/go home **4** ▪ to go back **5** ▪ to start again **5** ▪ to sink in **6**
VT	to bring in **1** ▪ to put in **2** ▪ to hold back **3** ▪ to input **4**

VI *(aux être)* **1** *(personne → vue de l'intérieur)* to come in; *(→ vue de l'extérieur)* to go in; *(chose)* to go in; *(s'emboîter)* to go in, to fit in; **une souris essayait de r. dans le placard** a mouse was trying to get into the cupboard; **tu es rentré dans Lyon par quelle route?** which way did you come to Lyons?, which road did you take into Lyons?; **fais r. le chien** bring the dog back inside; **impossible de faire r. ce clou dans le mur** I can't get this nail to go into the wall; **la clé ne rentre pas dans la serrure** the key won't go into the keyhole; **tu n'arriveras pas à tout faire r. dans cette valise** you'll never fit everything in this case; **c'est par là que l'eau rentre** that's where the water is coming *or* getting in; **les rallonges rentrent sous la table** the leaves fit in under the table; **r. dans** *(poteau)* to crash into; *(véhicule)* to collide with; **les deux voitures sont rentrées l'une dans l'autre** the two cars crashed into each other; **je lui suis rentré dedans** *(en voiture)* I drove straight *or* right into him/her; *Fam (verbalement)* I laid into him/her; *Fam* **rentre-lui dedans!** *(frappe-le)* smack him/her one!; *Fam* **il n'a pas arrêté de me r. dedans** *(verbalement)* he was constantly knocking me *or Br* having a go at me
2 *(faire partie de)* to be part of, to be included in; **la mesure en question ne rentre pas dans le cadre de la réforme** the measure under discussion is not part of the reform; **cela ne rentre pas dans mes attributions** that is not part of my duties
3 *(pour travailler)* **r. dans les affaires/la police** to go into business/join the police; **il est rentré dans la société grâce à son oncle** he got a job with the company thanks to his uncle
4 *(retourner → gén)* to return, to come *or* to get back; *(revenir chez soi)* to come *or* to get (back) home; *(aller chez soi)* to go (back) *or* to return home; **nous rentrerons dimanche** we'll come *or* be back home on Sunday; **je rentre tout de suite!** I'm on my way home!, I'm coming home straightaway!; **les enfants, rentrez!** children, get *or* come back in!; **il n'est pas encore rentré de (faire) ses commissions** he hasn't got back from shopping yet; **je ne rentrerai pas dîner** I won't be home for dinner; **je rentre chez moi pour déjeuner** *(tous les jours)* I go home for lunch; **je suis inquiète, elle n'est pas rentrée hier soir** I'm worried, she didn't come home last night; **les élèves sont rentrés au lycée enchantés de leur visite** the students got back to school thrilled by their visit; **il est rentré à cinq heures** he got in at five o'clock; **je vous laisse, il faut que je rentre** I've got to leave you now, I must get (back) home; **en rentrant de l'école** on the way home *or* back from school; **r. dans son pays** to go back *or* to return home (to one's country); **le bateau n'est pas rentré au port** the boat hasn't come (back) in
5 *(reprendre ses occupations → lycéen)* to go back to school, to start school again; *(→ étudiant)* to go back, to start the new term; *(→ école)* to start again, to go back; *(→ parlementaire)* to start the new session, to return to take one's seat; *(→ Parlement)* to reopen, to reassemble; *(→ cinéaste)* to start the season
6 *(être perçu → argent)* to come in; **l'argent rentre mal** there isn't much money coming in; **faire r. l'argent/les devises** to bring in money/ foreign currency; **faire r. l'impôt/les cotisations** to collect taxes/dues; **faire r. ses créances** to collect one's money *or* debts; *Com* **la commande n'est pas encore rentrée** the order isn't in *or* hasn't come in yet
7 *Fam (explication, idée, connaissances)* to sink in; **ça rentre, l'informatique?** are you getting the hang of computing?; **le russe, ça rentre tout seul avec Sophie!** *(elle apprend bien)* Sophie is having no trouble picking up Russian!; *(elle enseigne bien)* Sophie makes learning Russian easy!; **je le lui ai expliqué dix fois, mais ça n'est toujours pas rentré** I've told him/her ten times but it hasn't gone *or* sunk in yet; **faire r. qch dans la tête de qn** to get sth into sb's head, to drum sth into sb; **tu ne lui feras jamais r. dans la tête que c'est impossible!** you'll never get it into his/her head *or* convince him/ her that it's impossible!
8 *Sport* **r. dans la mêlée** to scrum down; *Ftbl* **faire r. le ballon dans les buts** to get the ball into the back of the net; **faire r. une bille** *(en billard)* to pot a ball

VT *(aux avoir)* **1** *(mettre à l'abri → linge, moisson)* to bring in, to get in; *(→ bétail)* to bring in, to take in; *(→ véhicule)* to put away; *(→ chaise)* to carry in, to take in; **il faut r. les plantes avant les grands froids** we must bring the plants in before it gets really cold; **rentre ta moto au garage** put your motorbike (away) in the garage; **r. les foins** to bring in the hay
2 *(mettre → gén)* to put in; *(faire disparaître → antenne)* to put down; *(→ train d'atterrissage)* to raise, to retract; *(→ griffes)* to draw in, to retract; **r. une clé dans une serrure** to put a key in a lock; **r. son chemisier dans sa jupe** to tuck one's blouse into one's skirt; **elle rentra ses mains sous sa cape/dans son manchon** she put her hands under her cloak/into her muff; **rentre ton ventre/tes fesses!** pull your stomach/bottom in!; **r. la tête dans les épaules** to

hunch (up) one's shoulders; **avec la tête rentrée dans les épaules** with hunched shoulders

3 *(réprimer → colère)* to hold back, to suppress; **r. ses larmes/son humiliation** to swallow one's tears/humiliation

4 *Ordinat* to input, to key in

5 *Typ* **r. une ligne** to indent a line

6 *Naut* **r. le pavillon** to lower the colours; **rentrez!** ship oars!

□ **rentrer dans** **VT IND** *(recouvrer)* to recover; **r. dans son argent/ses dépenses** to recover one's money/expenses, to get one's money/expenses back; **r. dans ses fonds** to recoup (one's) costs; **r. dans ses droits** to recover one's rights; **r. dans la légalité** *(sujet: criminel)* to reform; *(sujet: opération, manœuvre)* to become legal

□ **rentrer en** **VT IND** **r. en grâce auprès de qn** to get back into sb's good graces *or* good books; **r. en faveur auprès de qn** to regain favour with sb; **r. en possession de** to regain possession of

►**se rentrer** **VPR** **1** *(emploi passif)* **les foins ne se rentrent pas avant juillet** the hay isn't brought in until July; **les rallonges se rentrent sous la table** the extension leaves fit in under the table

2 *Fam* **se r. dedans** *(se heurter)* they smashed *or* banged into one another; *(se disputer)* they laid into one another

renuméroter [3] [rənymerɔte] **VT** *Tech* to renumber, to reserialize

renversant, -e [rɑ̃vɛrsɑ̃, -ɑ̃t] **ADJ** *(nouvelle)* astounding, amazing, staggering; *(personne)* amazing, incredible; **elle est d'une bêtise renversante** she is incredibly stupid

renverse [rɑ̃vɛrs] **NF** *Naut (du vent)* change; *(du courant)* turn (of tide)

□ **à la renverse** **ADV** **tomber** *ou* **partir à la r.** *(sur le dos)* to fall flat on one's back; **j'ai failli tomber à la r.** I almost fell over backwards; *Fig* **il y a de quoi tomber à la r.** it's amazing *or* staggering

renversé, -e [rɑ̃vɛrse] **ADJ** **1** *(image)* reverse *(avant n)*, reversed, inverted; *(objet)* upside down, overturned **2** *(penché → écriture)* backhanded, that slopes backwards; **le corps r. en arrière** with the body leaning *or* tilted back **3** *(stupéfait)* **être r.** to be staggered

NM *Suisse* milky coffee

renversement [rɑ̃vɛrsəmɑ̃] **NM** **1** *(inversion → d'une image)* inversion

2 *(changement)* **r. des alliances** reversal *or* switch of alliances; **il y eut un brusque r. du vent/du courant** the wind/the current changed direction suddenly; **ils ont attendu le r. de la marée** they waited for the tide to turn; **r. des rôles** role reversal; **r. de situation** reversal of the situation; **r. de tendance** shift *or* swing (in the opposite direction)

3 *(chute → d'un régime, d'un gouvernement)* overthrow

4 *(inclinaison → du buste, de la tête)* tipping *or* tilting back

5 *Mus* inversion

6 *Méd* retroversion

renverser [3] [rɑ̃vɛrse] **VT** **1** *(répandre → liquide)* to spill; *(faire tomber → bouteille, casserole)* to spill, to knock over, to upset; *(→ table, voiture)* to overturn; *(→ bateau)* to capsize, to overturn; *(retourner exprès)* to turn upside down; **r. qch d'un coup de pied** to kick sth over

2 *(faire tomber → personne)* to knock down; **être renversé par qn** to be knocked down *or* run over by sb; **il m'a renversé de mon tabouret** he tipped me off my stool; **se faire r. par une voiture** to get *or* be knocked down by a car

3 *(inverser)* to reverse; **r. l'ordre des mots** to reverse the word order; *Math* **r. une fraction** to invert a fraction; **le Suédois renversa la situation au cours du troisième set** the Swedish player managed to turn the situation round during the third set; **r. les rôles** to reverse the roles; **r. la vapeur** to reverse engines; *Fig* to change direction

4 *(détruire → obstacle)* to overcome; *(→ valeurs)* to overthrow; *(→ régime)* to overthrow, to topple; **le président a été renversé** the President was thrown out of *or* removed from office; **r. un gouvernement** *(par la force)* to overthrow *or* to topple a government; *(par un vote)* to bring down *or* to topple a government

5 *(incliner en arrière)* to tilt *or* to tip back

6 *(stupéfier)* to amaze, to astound; **la nouvelle de leur divorce m'a renversé** I was completely taken aback *or* amazed when I heard they'd got divorced

►**se renverser** **VPR** **1** *(bouteille)* to fall over; *(liquide)* to spill; *(véhicule)* to overturn; *(bateau)* to overturn, to capsize; *(marée)* to turn

2 *(personne)* to lean over backwards; **l'acrobate se renverse en arrière et touche le sol avec ses mains** the acrobat bends over backwards and touches the floor with his/her hands; **se r. sur sa chaise** to tilt back on one's chair; **se r. dans un fauteuil** to lie back in an armchair

renvidage [rɑ̃vidaʒ] **NM** *Tex* winding on

renvider [3] [rɑ̃vide] **VT** *Tex* to wind on

renvideur [rɑ̃vidœr] **NM** *Tex (métier)* mule (jenny)

renvoi [rɑ̃vwa] **NM** **1** *(d'un colis, de marchandises → gén)* return, sending back; *(→ par avion)* flying back; *(→ par bateau)* shipping back; **r. à l'expéditeur** *(sur enveloppe, sur colis)* return to sender

2 *Tél* **r. automatique d'appels** call forwarding

3 *Sport (d'une balle → gén)* sending back; *(→ à la main)* throwing back; *(→ au pied)* kicking back; *(→ au tennis)* return; **r. aux 22 mètres** 22 metre drop-out; **r. en touche** touch kick, kick for touch

4 *(congédiement → d'un employé)* dismissal, *Br* sacking; *(→ d'un élève)* expulsion; **demander le r. d'un élève/d'un employé** to ask for a pupil to be expelled/an employee to be dismissed; **au bout de trois avertissements, c'est le r. définitif** *(d'un employé)* after three warnings it's the sack; *(d'un élève)* after three warnings it's expulsion

5 *(ajournement)* postponement; **le tribunal décida le r. du procès à huitaine** the court decided to put off *or* to adjourn the trial for a week

6 *(transfert)* transfer; **ordonnance de r. aux assises** order of transfer to the High Court; **après le r. du texte en commission** after the text was sent to a committee

7 *(référence)* cross-reference; *(note au bas du texte)* footnote; **faire un r. à** to make a cross-reference to, to cross-refer to

8 *(éructation)* belch, burp; **avoir un r.** to belch, to burp; **ça me donne des renvois** it makes me belch *or* burp, it repeats on me

9 *Jur* amendment; **r. des fins de poursuite** discharge of case; **demande de r.** application for removal of action; **r. préjudiciel** preliminary ruling

10 *Mus* repeat mark

11 *Tech* **levier de r.** reversing lever; **poulie de r.** return pulley

renvoyé [rɑ̃vwaje] **NM** *Jur* **r. des fins de la poursuite** acquittal

renvoyer [30] [rɑ̃vwaje] **VT** **1** *(colis, formulaire, personne)* to send back; *(marchandises)* to return, to send back; *(cadeau)* to return, to give back; *(importun)* to send away; *(soldat, troupes)* to discharge; **r. qch à l'expéditeur** to return sth to sender; **on les a renvoyés chez eux** they were sent (back) home *or* discharged; **je le renvoie chez sa mère demain** I'm sending him back *or* off to his mother's tomorrow

2 *(lancer de nouveau → ballon)* to send back, to return; **j'étais renvoyé de vendeur en vendeur** I was being passed *or* shunted around from one salesman to the next; **r. la balle à qn** *Sport* to throw *or* to pass the ball back to sb; *Ftbl* to kick *or* to pass the ball back to sb; *(au tennis)* to return to sb; *Fig* to answer sb tit for tat; *Fig* **savoir r. la balle** to give as good as one gets; **r. l'ascenseur à qn** to send the *Br* lift *or Am* elevator back to sb; *Fig* to return sb's favour

3 *(congédier → employé)* to dismiss; *(→ élève)* to expel; **tu vas te faire r.** *(de ton travail)* you're going to lose your job; *(de ton lycée)* you're going to get yourself expelled

4 *(différer)* to postpone, to put off; *Jur* to adjourn; **r. une affaire à huitaine** to adjourn a case for a week; **la réunion est renvoyée à mardi prochain** the meeting has been put off until *or* put back to next Tuesday

5 *(transférer → affaire)* to refer; **l'affaire a été renvoyée en cour d'assises** the matter has been referred to the High Court; **r. qn en cour d'assises** to send sb before the High Court

6 *(faire se reporter)* to refer; **je vous renvoie à l'article publié dans 'La Tribune'** I refer you to the article published in 'La Tribune'; **les numéros renvoient aux notes de fin de chapitre** the numbers refer to notes at the end of each chapter; **cet article renvoie à un autre** *(dans un dictionnaire)* this entry is cross-referred to another

7 *(réverbérer → chaleur, lumière)* to reflect; *(→ son)* to throw back, to echo; **la glace lui renvoyait son image** he/she saw his/her reflection in the mirror; **la falaise nous renvoyait nos cris** the cliff echoed our cries

VI *Can* to vomit, to throw up

►**se renvoyer** **VPR** *(locution)* **on peut se r. la balle comme ça longtemps!** we could go on forever blaming each other like this!; **dans cette affaire d'évasion, les autorités françaises et suisses se renvoient la balle** in this escape business, the French and Swiss authorities are trying to make each other carry the can

réoccupation [reɔkypasjɔ̃] **NF** *(action militante)* reoccupation; *(réinstallation)* moving (back) in again; **nous envisageons la r. immédiate du bâtiment** *(pour y vivre)* we expect people to move straight back into the building

réoccuper [3] [reɔkype] **VT** *(usine, lieu public)* to reoccupy; *(habitation)* to move back into; *(emploi)* to take up again

réopérer [18] [reɔpere] **VT** *Méd* to operate again on; **il va falloir vous r.** you'll have to have another operation, you're going to require further surgery

réorchestration [reɔrkɛstrasjɔ̃] **NF** reorchestration

réorchestrer [3] [reɔrkɛstre] **VT** to reorchestrate

réorganisateur, -trice [reɔrganizatœr, -tris] **ADJ** reorganizing

NM,F reorganizer

réorganisation [reɔrganizasjɔ̃] **NF** reorganization; *Com* **r. des processus** *(dans une entreprise)* business process re-engineering

réorganisatrice [reɔrganizatris] *voir* **réorganisateur**

réorganiser [3] [reɔrganize] **VT** to reorganize

►**se réorganiser** **VPR** to reorganize oneself, to get reorganized

réorientation [reɔrjɑ̃tasjɔ̃] **NF** **1** *Pol* redirecting **2** *Univ* changing to a different course

réorienter [3] [reɔrjɑ̃te] **VT** **1** *Pol* to reorientate, to redirect **2** *Univ* to put onto a different course

réouverture [reuvɛrtyr] **NF** **1** *(d'un magasin, d'un guichet, d'un musée, d'une route, d'un col)* reopening; **r. du cabinet médical à 14 heures** surgery reopens at 2 p.m. **2** *(reprise → d'un débat)* resumption; *Bourse* **à la r. des marchés ce matin** when trading resumed this morning

repaginer [3] [rəpaʒine] **VT** *Ordinat* to repaginate

repaie *etc voir* **repayer**

repaire [rəpɛr] **NM** **1** *(d'animaux)* den, lair **2** *(d'individus)* den, haunt; **un r. d'espions/de malfaiteurs** a den of spies/of criminals

repairer [4] [rəpɛre] **VI** *(animal)* to hide in its den *or* lair

repaître [91] [rəpɛtr] **VT** *Littéraire (nourrir)* to feed; **r. son esprit de connaissances nouvelles** to feast one's mind on knowledge; **r. ses yeux de qch** to feast one's eyes on sth; **r. qn d'espérance** to feed sb's hopes

►**se repaître** **VPR** **1** *Littéraire* **se r. de** *(manger)* to feed on

2 *Fig (savourer)* **se r. de bandes dessinées** to feast on comic strips; **se r. de chimères** to indulge in vain imaginings; **se r. de sang** to wallow in blood

répandre [74] [repɑ̃dr] **VT** **1** *(renverser accidentellement → liquide, sel)* to spill; *(verser → sable, sciure)* to spread, to sprinkle, to scatter; **r. des larmes** to shed tears; **r. le sang** to spill *or* to shed blood

2 *(propager → rumeur, terreur, usage)* to spread

3 *(dégager → odeur)* to give off; *(→ lumière)* to shed, to give out; *(→ chaleur, fumée)* to give out *or* off; **le poêle répand une douce chaleur dans la maison** the stove spreads a gentle warmth throughout the house

ren–rep

4 *(dispenser → bienfaits)* to pour out, to spread (around); **cette nouvelle répandit la tristesse dans la ville** the news cast a gloom over *or* spread gloom throughout the town; **cette nouvelle répandit le bonheur dans toute la maison** the news brought a general air of happiness to the house

▸**se répandre VPR 1** *(eau, vin)* to spill; **les eaux se sont répandues dans toute la ville** the water spread throughout the town; *Fig* **les supporters se sont répandus sur le terrain** the fans spilled (out) *or* poured onto the field

2 *(se propager → nouvelle, mode, coutume)* to spread, to become widespread; **les boutons rouges se répandent ensuite sur tout l'abdomen** the red pimples then spread to the whole abdominal area; **l'usage de la carte de crédit s'est répandu parmi les jeunes** credit card use has become widespread among young people; **se r. comme une traînée de poudre** to spread like wildfire

3 *(se dégager → odeur)* to spread, to be given off; **la fumée se répandit dans la carlingue** smoke spread through the cabin; **il se répandit une odeur de brûlé** the smell of burning filled the air

4 *(prodiguer)* **se r. en compliments/en propos blessants** to be full of compliments/hurtful remarks; **se r. en excuses** to apologize profusely; **se r. en invectives contre qn** to heap abuse on sb; **se r. en louanges sur qn** to heap praise on sb; **inutile de se r. en commentaires là-dessus** no need to keep on (making comments) about it

répandu, -e [repɑ̃dy] **ADJ** widespread; **un préjugé (très) r.** a very widespread *or* widely held prejudice; **une vue (très) répandue** a commonly held *or* widely found view; **la technique n'est pas encore très répandue ici** the technique isn't widely used here yet

réparable [reparabl] **ADJ 1** *(appareil)* repairable; **j'espère que c'est r.** I hope it can be mended *or* repaired, I hope it's not beyond repair; **c'est facilement/difficilement r.** it's easy/difficult to repair; **la voiture n'est pas r.** *(après un accident)* the car is a write-off; *(à cause de sa vétusté)* the car isn't worth repairing

2 *(erreur, perte)* reparable; **une maladresse difficilement r.** a blunder which will be hard to correct *or* to put right

reparaître [91] [rəparɛtr] **VI 1** *(journal, revue)* to be out again, to be published again **2** = **réapparaître**

réparateur, -trice [reparatœr, -tris] **ADJ un sommeil r.** restorative *or* refreshing sleep

NM,F repairer, repairman, *f* repairwoman; **r. d'antiquités** antiques restorer; **r. de radios** radio repairman

réparation [reparasjɔ̃] **NF 1** *(processus)* repairing, fixing, mending; *(résultat)* repair; **pendant les réparations** during (the) repairs; **les réparations de l'appartement/de la toiture** the repairs to the *Br* flat *or Am* apartment/the roof; **toutes les réparations sont à la charge du locataire** the tenant is liable for all repair work *or* all repairs; **atelier/service de r.** repair shop/department; **r. d'entretien** maintenance

2 *(compensation)* redress, compensation; **en r. des dégâts occasionnés** in compensation for *or* to make up for the damage caused; **en r. d'un tort** to make up for *or Sout* in atonement for a wrong; *Littéraire* **demander/obtenir r.** to demand/to obtain redress; **demander/obtenir r. par les armes** to demand/to obtain satisfaction by a duel

3 *Jur* damages, compensation; **r. civile** compensation; **r. de dommages** damages; **r. par équivalent** compensatory damages; **r. légale** legal redress

4 *(correction → d'une négligence)* correction; *(→ d'une omission)* rectification

▫ **réparations NFPL** *Hist* **les réparations** (war) reparations

▫ **de réparation ADJ** *Sport* penalty *(avant n)*; **surface de r.** penalty area; **point de r.** penalty spot; **coup de pied de r.** penalty (kick)

▫ **en réparation ADJ** under repair, being repaired

réparatrice [reparatris] *voir* **réparateur**

réparer [3] [repare] **VT 1** *(appareil, chaussure)* to repair, to mend; *(maison)* to repair; *(défaut de construction)* to repair, to make good; *(meuble, porcelaine)* to restore; **faire r. qch** to get sth repaired *or* put right; **donner ses chaussures à r.** to take one's shoes to the mender's

2 *(compenser → gén)* to make up for, to compensate for; *(→ pertes)* to repair, to make good; **il est encore temps de r. le mal qui a été fait** there's still time to make up for *or* to undo the harm that's been done; **r. les dégâts** to repair the damage; *Fig* to pick up the pieces

3 *(corriger → omission)* to rectify, to repair; *(→ négligence, erreur)* to correct, to rectify; **c'était une négligence qu'il ne pouvait plus r.** it was too late for him to correct the mistake

4 *(santé, forces)* to restore

USAGE ABSOLU aujourd'hui, les gens ne réparent plus, ils jettent people today don't mend things, they just throw them away

▸**se réparer VPR** to mend; **ça ne se répare pas** it can't be mended

reparler [3] [rəparle] **VT** *(langue)* to speak again; **ce voyage m'a donné l'occasion de r. arabe** this trip gave me the opportunity to speak Arabic again

VI to speak again; **il a reparlé de son roman** he talked about his novel again; **retenez bien son nom, c'est un chanteur dont on reparlera** remember this singer's name, you'll be hearing more of him; **je laisse là les Incas, nous allons en r.** I won't say any more about the Incas now, we'll come back to them later; **il n'en a plus reparlé** he never mentioned it again; **r. à qn (de qch)** to speak to sb (about sth) again; **elle ne lui a pas reparlé depuis** she hasn't spoken (another word) to him/her since; **si je vous surprends à r. ensemble...** if I catch you two talking again...

▸**se reparler VPR** *(se réconcilier)* to be back on speaking terms; **nous ne nous sommes pas reparlé depuis** we haven't spoken to one another since

repars *etc voir* **repartir**[1,2]

repartager [17] [rəpartaʒe] **VT** to share out again

repartie [rəparti], **répartie** [reparti] **NF** *(réplique)* retort, repartee; **une r. adroite/spirituelle** a clever/witty retort; **avoir de la r., avoir l'esprit de r., avoir la r. prompte** to have a good sense of repartee

repartir[1] [43] [rəpartir] **VT** *aux avoir Littéraire (répliquer)* to retort, to reply, to rejoin; **on me repartit que le maître serait bientôt de retour** I received the reply that the master would soon be back

repartir[2] [43] [rəpartir] **VI** *(aux être)* **1** *(se remettre en chemin)* to start *or* to set off again; *(se remettre à fonctionner → machine)* to start (up) again; **quand repars-tu?** when are you off *or* leaving again?; **je repars pour Paris** I'm off to Paris again; **l'économie est bien repartie** the economy has picked up again; **votre carrière semble être bien repartie** your career seems to have taken off well again; **c'est reparti, encore une hausse de l'électricité!** here we go again, another rise in the price of electricity!; **r. à l'assaut** *ou* **à l'attaque** *Mil* to mount a fresh assault; *Fig* to try again; **r. à zéro** to start again from scratch, to go back to square one; **r. du bon pied** to make a fresh start; **il est reparti d'un éclat de rire** he burst out laughing again

2 *Hort* to start growing *or* to sprout again

répartir [32] [repartir] **VT 1** *(distribuer → encouragements, sanctions)* to give; *(→ héritage, travail)* to share out, to divide up (**entre** among); *(→ tâches, responsabilités)* to allocate, to apportion; *(→ frais, risques)* to share; *(→ soldats, policiers)* to deploy, to spread out; *(→ poids, chaleur, ventilation)* to distribute; **les bénéfices seront répartis entre les actionnaires** profits will be shared out *or* distributed among the shareholders; **le tout, c'est de bien r. les livres dans les cartons** the important thing is for the books to be evenly *or* properly distributed in the boxes; **répartissez les enfants en trois groupes** get *or* split up the children into three groups

2 *(étaler → confiture, cirage)* to spread

3 *(dans le temps)* **r. des remboursements** to pay back in instalments; **r. des paiements** to spread out the payments

4 *Ordinat* **être réparti** to be distributed *(over a network)*

▸**se répartir VPR 1** *(se diviser)* to split, to divide (up); **répartissez-vous en deux équipes** get yourselves *or* split into two teams; **les dépenses se répartissent en trois catégories** expenditure falls under three headings

2 *(partager)* **se r. le travail/les responsabilités** to share out the work/the responsibility

répartiteur, -trice [repartitœr, -tris] **NM,F 1** *Littéraire* distributor, apportioner **2** *Fin* tax assessor **3** *Assur* **r. d'avaries** average adjuster

répartition [repartisjɔ̃] **NF 1** *(partage → de l'impôt, des bénéfices)* distribution; *(→ d'un butin)* sharing out, dividing up; *(→ d'allocations, de prestations)* allotment, sharing out; *Bourse (de titres)* allotment, allocation; **comment se fera la r. des frais?** how will the expenses be shared out?; **comment se fera la r. des tâches?** how will the tasks be shared out *or* allocated?; **la r. des portefeuilles ministériels** the distribution of ministerial posts; **la r. des richesses est très inégale** the distribution of wealth is very unequal; *Bourse* **première et unique r.** first and final dividend; *Bourse* **dernière r.** final dividend; **r. des actifs** asset allocation; **r. optimale des ressources** optimal resource allocation; **r. des risques** risk spreading; *Pol* **r. des votes** voting pattern

2 *(agencement → dans un appartement)* layout; **la r. des pièces est la suivante** the layout of the rooms is as follows, the rooms are laid out as follows

3 *(étalement → dans l'espace)* distribution; *(→ dans le temps)* spreading; **la r. géographique des gisements** the geographical distribution of the deposits

4 *Écon* assessment

5 *Assur* **r. d'avarie** average adjustment

répartitrice [repartitris] *voir* **répartiteur**

reparu, -e [rəpary] **PP** *voir* **reparaître**

reparution [rəparysjɔ̃] **NF** *(d'un journal)* republishing, reappearance; **le jour de sa r., le quotidien s'est vendu à un million d'exemplaires** on the day the paper was back on the newsstands *or* resumed publication, it sold a million copies

repas [rəpa] **NM 1** *(gén)* meal; *(d'un nourrisson, d'un animal) Br* feed, *Am* feeding; **faire un bon r.** to have a square *or* good meal; **faire quatre r. par jour** to have four meals a day, to eat four times a day; **prendre ses r. à la cantine** *(de l'école)* to have school lunches *or Br* dinners; *(de l'usine)* to eat in the (works) canteen; **à l'heure** *ou* **aux heures des r.** at mealtimes; **r. d'affaires** business lunch; **r. à la carte** à la carte meal; **r. chaud** hot meal; **r. livrés à domicile** meals on wheels; **r. de midi** lunch, *Br* midday *or Am* noon meal; **r. de noces** wedding meal; **r. du soir** dinner, evening meal

2 *(comme adj; avec ou sans trait d'union)* **plateau-r.** lunch *or* dinner tray; *Br* **ticket-r.** luncheon voucher, *Am* meal ticket

repassage [rəpasaʒ] **NM 1** *(du linge)* ironing; **faire du r.** to do some ironing; **faire un premier r. avant de bâtir la couture** go over it with an iron before tacking the seam; **r. superflu** *(sur étiquette d'un vêtement)* wash and wear, non-iron **2** *(aiguisage → gén)* sharpening; *(→ avec une pierre)* whetting

repasser [3] [rəpase] **VI 1** *(passer à nouveau dans un lieu)* to go (back) again; **elle repassera** she'll drop by again; **je suis repassé la voir à l'hôpital** I went to see her in the hospital again; **je ne suis jamais plus repassé dans cette rue** I never again went down *or* visited that street; **si tu repasses à Berlin, fais-moi signe** if you're in *or* passing through Berlin again, let me know; **r. par le même chemin** to go back the way one came; **il passait et repassait sous l'horloge de la gare** he kept walking up and down under the station clock; **faire r. le fromage** to pass the cheese round again; **r. sur un dessin** to go over a drawing again, to go back over a drawing; **j'ai horreur qu'on repasse derrière moi** I hate to have people go over what I've done; **la livre est repassé au-dessous des 2 dollars** the pound has fallen *or* dropped below 2 dollars again; *Fam* **il peut toujours r.** he hasn't a hope, he's got another think coming;

rep–rep

Fam **tu repasseras!** no way!, no chance!, not on your life!

2 *Cin & TV* to be on *or* to be shown again

VT 1 *(défriper)* to iron; **r. les plis** to iron out the creases

2 *(aiguiser → gén)* to sharpen; *(→ avec une pierre)* to whet

3 *(réviser) Scol* **r. ses leçons/le programme de physique** to go over one's homework/the physics course; *Compta* **r. des comptes** to re-examine a set of accounts

4 *Fam (donner)* **elle m'a repassé sa tunique** she let me have her smock

5 *(traverser à nouveau)* **r. un fleuve** to go back across a river, to cross a river again

6 *(subir à nouveau)* **r. un examen** to take an exam again, *Br* to resit an exam; **je dois r. l'allemand/le permis demain** I have to retake German/my driving test tomorrow; **r. une échographie** to go for another ultrasound scan

7 *(à nouveau)* to pass again; **repasse-moi la confiture** pass me (over) the jam again; **voulez-vous r. la salade?** would you hand *or* pass the salad round again?; **repasse-moi mon mouchoir** hand me back my handkerchief

8 *(remettre)* **r. une couche de vernis** to put on another coat of varnish; **r. un manteau** *(le réessayer)* to try a coat on again; **r. un poisson sur le gril** to put a fish back on the grill, to give a fish a bit more time on the grill; **repasse ta sauce au mixer** put your sauce through the blender again; **repasse les chaussettes en machine** stick the socks in the washing machine again; **repasse-moi la diapo 3** show me slide 3 again; **repasse-moi la face A du disque** play me the A-side of the record again

9 *(au téléphone)* **je te repasse Paul** I'll put Paul on again, I'll hand you back to Paul; **repassez-moi le standard** put me through to the switchboard again

10 *Fam (escroquer)* to do, to rip off

►**se repasser VPR** to iron; **le voile ne se repasse pas** *(ne doit pas être repassé)* the veil mustn't be ironed; *(n'a pas besoin de repassage)* the veil doesn't need ironing

repasseur, -euse [rəpasœr, -øz] **NM,F 1** *(de linge)* ironer **2** *(rémouleur)* knife-grinder, knife-sharpener

❑ **repasseuse NF** *(machine)* ironing machine

repavage [rəpavaʒ] **NM** repaving

repaver [3] [rəpave] **VT** to repave

repayer [11] [rəpeje] **VT** *(payer à nouveau)* to pay again; *(payer en plus)* to pay more for; **je lui ai repayé un café** I bought him/her another coffee; **si l'on veut visiter la maison des reptiles, il faut r.** if you wish to visit the reptile house, you have to pay extra

repêchage [rəpeʃaʒ] **NM 1** *(d'un objet)* fishing out; *(d'un corps)* recovery **2** *Univ (d'un candidat)* letting through; **épreuve de r.** resit **3** *Sport* repechage

repêcher [4] [rəpeʃe] **VT 1** *(noyé)* to fish out, to recover; **r. un corps/une voiture dans le fleuve** to fish a body/a car out of the river **2** *Univ* to let through; **j'ai été repêché à deux points** I was let through although I was two points short of the pass mark; **j'ai été repêché à l'oral** I passed on my oral **3** *Sport* to let through on the repechage

repeindre [81] [rəpɛ̃dr] **VT** to repaint, to paint again

repeint [rəpɛ̃] **NM** *Beaux-Arts* touched-up area

rependre [73] [rəpɑ̃dr] **VT** to rehang, to hang again

repens *etc voir* **repentir²**

repenser [3] [rəpɑ̃se] **VT** to reconsider, to rethink; **l'entrepôt a été entièrement repensé** the layout of the warehouse has been completely redesigned; **il faudra r. notre stratégie** we'll have to rethink our strategy

❑ **repenser à VT IND** to think about again; **en y repensant** thinking back on it all; **je n'ai plus jamais repensé à elle** I never thought of her again *or* gave her another thought; **ah mais oui, j'y repense, elle t'a appelé ce matin** oh yes, now I come to think of it, she phoned you this morning; **tout à coup, ça m'a fait r. à ce qu'il avait dit** suddenly it made me think of what he had said

repentance [rəpɑ̃tɑ̃s] **NF** *Littéraire* repentance

repentant, -e [rəpɑ̃tɑ̃, -ɑ̃t] **ADJ** repentant, penitent; **pécheur r.** repentant sinner

repenti, -e [rəpɑ̃ti] **ADJ** repentant, penitent; **alcoolique/fumeur r.** reformed alcoholic/smoker; *Vieilli* **fille repentie** reformed prostitute

NM,F 1 *(ancien terroriste)* = former terrorist who now collaborates with the police **2** *Jur Br* = Crown witness, *Am* = State witness

repentir¹ [rəpɑ̃tir] **NM 1** *(remords)* remorse; **verser des larmes de r.** to shed tears of remorse *or* regret

2 *Rel* repentance; **mener une vie de r.** to live a life of repentance *or* penance

3 *(correction)* alteration

4 *Beaux-Arts* reworking, retouching

repentir² [37] [rəpɑ̃tir] **se repentir VPR 1** to repent

2 **se r. de qch** to regret, to be sorry for sth; **elle se repent d'avoir été trop sévère** she's sorry for having been too harsh; **il s'en repentira, croismoi** believe me, he'll regret that *or* he'll be sorry for that; **j'ai refusé son offre et je m'en suis amèrement repenti** I turned down his/her offer and I've lived to rue the day *or* I bitterly regret it; **se r. d'une faute/d'avoir péché** to repent of a fault/of having sinned; **elle s'en repentira** she'll be sorry, she'll rue the day

repérable [rəperabl] **ADJ** *(maison)* easily found; *(changement, signe)* easily spotted; **le bar est facilement r.** the bar is easy to find; **les oiseaux de cette espèce sont repérables à leur bec coloré** birds of this species are recognizable *or* identifiable by their coloured beaks

repérage [rəperaʒ] **NM 1** *(localisation)* spotting, pinpointing **2** *Mil* location **3** *Cin* **être en r.** to be looking for locations *or* choosing settings **4** *Typ* registry, laying

repercer [16] [rəpɛrse] **VT** *(en orfèvrerie)* to pierce

répercussion [repɛrkysjɔ̃] **NF 1** *(conséquence)* repercussion, consequence (**sur** on) **2** *(renvoi → d'un son)* repercussion, echo **3** *Fin* **le coût final est aggravé par la r. de l'impôt** the final cost is increased because taxes levied are passed on (to the buyer)

répercuter [3] [repɛrkyte] **VT 1** *(renvoyer → son)* to echo, to reflect; **un coup de feu répercuté par l'écho** the sound of an echoing shot

2 *Fin* to pass on; **r. l'impôt sur le prix de revient** to pass a tax on in the selling price; **r. l'augmentation des salaires sur les prix** to pass the wage increase on to prices

3 *(transmettre → ordre)* to pass on *or* along

►**se répercuter VPR 1** *(bruit)* to echo

2 **se r. sur** to have an effect on *or* upon, to affect; **les problèmes familiaux se répercutent sur le travail scolaire** family problems have repercussions on *or* affect children's performances at school

reperdre [77] [rəpɛrdr] **VT** to lose again; **j'ai reperdu 2 kilos** my weight's gone back down by 2 kilos

repère [rəpɛr] **NM 1** *(marque)* line, mark; *(indice → matériel)* landmark; *(→ qui permet de juger)* benchmark, reference mark; **verser le liquide jusqu'au r.** pour in the liquid until it reaches the mark; **point de r.** landmark; *Cin* **repères de changement** changeover marks; *Typ* **repères de coupe** corner marks

2 *Tech* (index) mark; **r. de montage** assembly *or* match mark

3 *(référence)* reference point, landmark; **la date de son mariage me sert de r.** I use the date of his/her wedding as a reference point *or* to help me remember; *Fig* **j'ai l'impression de n'avoir plus aucun (point de) r.** I've lost my bearings

4 *Math* **r. projectif** projective point

5 *(comme adj; avec ou sans trait d'union)* reference *(avant n)*; **date/point r.** reference date/point

repérer [18] [rəpere] **VT 1** *(indiquer par un repère)* to mark; *Tech* to mark out *or* off

2 *(localiser)* to locate, to pinpoint; **r. d'abord l'église sur la carte** first locate the church on the map

3 *(remarquer)* to spot, to pick out, to notice; **je l'avais repéré au premier rang** I'd noticed *or* spotted him in the first row; **tu vas nous faire r. avec tes éternuements** you'll get us caught *or* spotted with your sneezing; **les ravisseurs se sont fait r. près de l'hôpital** the kidnappers were spotted near the hospital

4 *(dénicher)* to discover; **j'ai repéré un très bon petit restaurant** I've discovered a really nice little restaurant

►**se repérer VPR 1** *(déterminer sa position)* to find *or* to get one's bearings; **on n'arrive jamais à se r. dans un aéroport** you can never find your way about *or* around in an airport

2 *Fig* **beaucoup de jeunes ont du mal à se r. dans la jungle universitaire** many young people find it difficult to get *or* to find their bearings in the jungle of the university; **je n'arrive plus à me r. dans ses mensonges** I don't know where I am any more with all those lies he/she tells

répertoire [repɛrtwar] **NM 1** *(liste)* index, list; **r. alphabétique/thématique** alphabetical/thematic index

2 *(livre)* notebook, book; **ils notent le vocabulaire dans un r.** they write down the vocabulary in a notebook; **r. d'adresses** address book; **r. à onglets** thumb-index notebook *or* book; **r. des rues** street index

3 *Mus & (en danse)* repertoire; *Théât* repertoire, repertory; *Fig (de plaisanteries, d'injures, etc)* repertoire; **jouer une pièce du r.** *(acteur)* to be in rep; *(théâtre)* to put on a play from the repertoire *or* a stock play; **elle a joué tout le r. classique** she's played every part in the classical repertory; **on a inscrit une pièce de Brecht à notre r.** we have put a play by Brecht on *or* in our repertoire; *Fig* **tu devrais ajouter ça à ton r.** that could be another string to your bow

4 *Jur* **r. civil** civil register; **r. général** record of cases

5 *Ordinat* directory; **r. central** *ou* **principal** main directory

répertorier [9] [repɛrtɔrje] **VT 1** *(inventorier)* to index, to list; **r. les erreurs** to list *or* to pick out the mistakes **2** *(inscrire dans une liste)* to list; **répertorié par adresses/professions** listed under addresses/professions

répéter [18] [repete] **VT 1** *(dire encore)* to repeat; **je n'arrête pas de vous le r.** that's what I've been trying to tell you; **je t'ai répété cent fois de ne pas le faire** I've told you a hundred times not to do it; **je vous répète que ce n'est pas possible!** it's not possible, I tell you!, I repeat, it's not possible!; **je ne veux pas avoir à le r.** I don't want to have to say it again *or* to repeat it; **elle ne se l'est pas fait r. (deux fois)** she didn't need telling twice

2 *(raconter → fait)* to repeat; *(→ histoire)* to retell, to relate; **répète-moi exactement ce qu'il a dit** tell me (again) exactly what he said; **ne lui répète pas** don't tell him/her, don't repeat this to him/her; **ne va pas le r. (à tout le monde)** don't go telling everybody

3 *(recommencer)* to repeat, to do again; **des tentatives répétées de chantage** repeated attempts to blackmail people

4 *(mémoriser → leçon)* to go over, to practise; *(→ morceau de musique)* to practise; *(→ pièce, film)* to rehearse; **répétons la séquence une dernière fois** let's run through the sequence one more time; **faire r. son rôle à qn** to help sb rehearse his/her lines, to go over sb's lines with him/her; **faire r. ses leçons à un enfant** to go over a child's lessons with him/her

5 *(reproduire → motif)* to repeat, to duplicate; *(→ refrain)* to repeat; **l'écho répétait nos rires à l'infini** our laughter echoed *or* reverberated endlessly

6 *Jur* to obtain recovery of

USAGE ABSOLU répétez après moi repeat after me; **répète un peu pour voir?** let's hear you repeat that (if you dare)!; **on ne répète pas demain** *(au cinéma, au théâtre)* there's no rehearsal tomorrow

►**se répéter VPR 1** *(redire la même chose)* to repeat oneself; **au risque de me r.** at the risk of repeating myself; **depuis son premier roman, elle se répète** since her first novel, she's just been rewriting the same thing

2 *(se reproduire → situation, événement)* to recur, to reoccur, to be repeated; *(→ motif)* to be repeated; **et que ça ne se répète plus!** don't let it happen again!; **la disposition des locaux se répète à tous les étages** the layout of the rooms is the same on every floor; **l'histoire se répète** history repeats itself

Allusion

Vous pouvez répéter la question?

This expression has its origin in a sketch by the French comedians Les Inconnus in which they parody general knowledgeTV quiz shows where contestants have to correctly answer questions which are definitions. The sketch features a very stupid contestant who says "Can you repeat the question?" to every question, and then always gives the same answer: Stéphanie de Monaco (the princess beloved of sections of the French popular press). When one does not hear or understand a question, one can use this phrase in a mock-imbecile fashion, in an allusion to the Les Inconnus sketch.

répéteur [repetœr] **NM** *Élec* repeater

répétiteur, -trice [repetitœr, -tris] **NM,F** *Vieilli* coach *(at home or in school)*; *Cin & TV* **r. de dialogues** dialogue coach

répétitif, -ive [repetitif, -iv] **ADJ** repetitive, repetitious

répétition [repetisjɔ̃] **NF 1** *(d'un mot, d'un geste)* repetition

2 *(d'un événement)* repetition

3 *(séance de travail)* rehearsal; **être en r.** to be rehearsing; **r. générale** dress rehearsal; **r. technique** technical run, technical walk-through

4 *Jur* **r. de l'indu** recovery of payment made in error

□ **à répétition ADJ 1** *(en armurerie, en horlogerie)* repeater *(avant n)*

2 *Fam (renouvelé)* **il fait des bêtises à r.** he keeps doing stupid things; **des laryngites à r.** repeated bouts of laryngitis

répétitive [repetitiv] *voir* **répétitif**

répétitivité [repetitivite] **NF** repetitiveness, repetitiousness

répétitrice [repetitris] *voir* **répétiteur**

repeuplement [rəpœpləmɑ̃] **NM** *(par des hommes)* repopulation; *(par des animaux)* restocking; *(par des plantes)* replantation, replanting *(UNCOUNT)*; *(d'une forêt)* replanting

repeupler [5] [rəpœple] **VT** *(pays, secteur)* to repopulate; *(étang)* to restock; *(forêt)* to replant

▸**se repeupler VPR cette région commence à se r.** people are starting to move back to the area; **la rivière se repeuple** life is coming back to the river

repic [rəpik] **NM** *Cartes* repique; **faire qn r. (et capot)** to outwit sb

repiquage [rəpikaʒ] **NM 1** *Agr & Hort* planting *or* bedding out **2** *(sur bande)* rerecording, taping; *(sur disque)* transfer **3** *Couture* restitching **4** *(de la chaussée)* repaving **5** *Phot* touching up

repique [rəpik] **NF** *Phot* spotting

repiquer [3] [rəpike] **VT 1** *Agr & Hort (planter → riz, salades)* to plant *or* to pick *or* to bed out

2 *Fam (attraper de nouveau)* to catch *or* to nab again; **et que je ne te repique pas à faire ça!** don't let me catch you doing that again!

3 *(enregistrer → sur cassette)* to rerecord, to tape; *(→ sur disque)* to transfer

4 *Couture* to restitch

5 *Fam Arg scol (classe)* to repeat▪

6 *(repaver)* to repave

7 *Phot* to touch up

VI 1 *Fam (recommencer)* to start again▪; **r. à un plat** to have a second helping▪; **r. au truc** to be at it again

2 *Fam Arg scol (redoubler une classe)* to repeat a *Br* year *or Am* grade▪

répit [repi] **NM** respite, rest; **un moment de r.** a breathing space; **mes enfants ne me laissent pas un instant de r.** my children never give me a minute's rest; **s'accorder quelques minutes de r.** to give oneself a few minutes' rest; **la douleur ne lui laisse aucun r.** he/she is in constant pain, he/she has no respite from the pain

□ **sans répit ADV** *(lutter)* tirelessly; *(poursuivre, interroger)* relentlessly, without respite

replacement [rəplasmɑ̃] **NM 1** *(remise en place)* replacing, putting back **2** *(de capitaux)* reinvestment **3** *(de personnes)* **des mesures pour permettre le r. des licenciés** steps to find new employment for workers made redundant

replacer [16] [rəplase] **VT 1** *(remettre)* to replace, to put back; **replace ça là où tu l'as trouvé** put that back where you found it; **r. les événements dans leur contexte** to put events into their context

2 *Fam (réutiliser)* to put in again▪; **elle est bonne, celle-là, je la replacerai!** that's a good one, I must remember it *or* use it myself sometime!▪

3 *(capitaux)* to reinvest

4 *(trouver un nouvel emploi pour)* to find a new position for

5 *Can (reconnaître)* to recognize; **je ne l'avais pas vue depuis si longtemps que je n'arrivais pas à la r.** it was so long since I'd seen her that I couldn't place her

▸**se replacer VPR 1** *(se remettre en place)* to take up one's position again; **les joueurs se replacent sur le terrain** the players are taking up their positions again on the field

2 *(domestique)* to find (oneself) a new job

3 *(dans une situation déterminée)* to imagine oneself, to visualize oneself; **il faut se r. dans les conditions de l'examen pour comprendre son échec** you have to imagine yourself in the exam situation to understand why he/she failed

replantation [rəplɑ̃tasjɔ̃] **NF** replanting *(UNCOUNT)*

replanter [3] [rəplɑ̃te] **VT** to replant; **r. une forêt en sapins** to replant a forest with firs; **après le phylloxéra, ils ont replanté en blé** after the phylloxera epidemic they planted the area with wheat

replat [rəpla] **NM** *Géog* sloping ledge, shoulder

replâtrage [rəplatraʒ] **NM 1** *Constr* replastering **2** *Fam Fig (réconciliation)* patching-up; *(réarrangement)* tinkering

replâtrer [3] [rəplatre] **VT 1** *Constr* to replaster **2** *Fam Fig* to patch up; **ces capitaux ne suffiront pas à r. les finances de l'entreprise** this capital won't be sufficient to paper over the cracks in the company's finances; **ils n'ont fait que r. le texte** they just doctored *or Br* rejigged the text a bit

replet, -ète [rəplɛ, -ɛt] **ADJ** *(personne)* plump, podgy, portly; *(visage)* plump, chubby; *(ventre)* full, rounded; **un petit garçon au visage r.** a chubby-faced little boy

réplétion [replesjɔ̃] **NF** *Physiol* repletion

repleuvoir [68] [rəpløvwar] **V IMPERSONNEL il repleut** it's (started) raining again; **il n'a pas replu depuis** it hasn't rained (again) since

repli [rəpli] **NM 1** *(pli → du terrain)* fold; *(→ de l'intestin)* coil; *(courbe → d'une rivière)* bend, meander

2 *Mil* withdrawal, falling back *(UNCOUNT)*; **solution** *ou* **stratégie de r.** fallback option; *Mil & Mktg* **r. stratégique** strategic withdrawal

3 *Fig Littéraire (recoin)* recess; **les sombres replis de l'âme** the dark recesses *or* reaches of the soul

4 *(baisse)* fall, drop; **on note un léger r. de la livre sterling** sterling has fallen slightly *or* has eased (back); **la livre est en r. de 0,15 pour cent** the pound is down 0.15 percent

5 *(introversion)* **un r. sur soi** a turning in on oneself

repliable [rəplijabl] **ADJ** folding

réplicase [replikaz] **NF** *Biol* replicase

réplication [replikasjɔ̃] **NF** *Biol* replication

repliement [rəplimɑ̃] **NM** *(introversion)* withdrawal; **r. sur soi-même** withdrawal (into oneself), turning in on oneself, self-absorption

replier [10] [rəplije] **VT 1** *(plier → journal)* to fold up again; *(→ bord, coin)* to turn *or* fold down; *(→ couteau)* to fold, to close; **replie le bas de ton pantalon** turn up the bottom of your *Br* trousers *or Am* pants

2 *(ramener → ailes)* to fold; *(→ jambes)* to tuck under; **l'oiseau a replié sa tête sous son aile** the bird tucked its head under its wing

3 *Mil (troupes)* to withdraw; **r. les populations civiles** to move the civilian population back

▸**se replier VPR 1** *(emploi passif)* to fold back; **la lame se replie dans le manche** the blade folds back into the handle

2 *Mil* to withdraw, to fall back; *Bourse (monnaie)* to fall back

3 *(emploi réfléchi)* **se r. sur soi-même** to withdraw into oneself, to turn in on oneself; **il est trop replié sur lui-même** he's too much of an introvert; **la secte s'est repliée sur elle-même** the sect has cut itself off from the outside world

réplique [replik] **NF 1** *(réponse)* reply, retort, *Sout* rejoinder; **la r. ne s'est pas fait attendre** his/her/*etc* reply wasn't long in coming; **ce gamin a la r. facile** that kid is always ready with *or* is never short of an answer; **je cite toujours la r. de de Gaulle le jour où...** I like to quote the reply made by de Gaulle when...; **avoir le sens de la r.** to be always ready with an answer; **argument sans r.** irrefutable *or* unanswerable argument; **c'est sans r.** what can you say to that!, there's no answer to that!; **quand elle a décidé quelque chose, c'est sans r.** when she's made up her mind about something, she's quite adamant!; **obéissez, et pas de r.!** do as you're told and no argument!; **un échange de répliques assez vives** a rather lively exchange

2 *(dans une pièce, dans un film)* line, cue; **manquer sa r.** to miss one's cue; **oublier sa r.** to forget one's lines; **donner la r. à un acteur** *(en répétition)* to give an actor his cues; *(dans une distribution)* to play opposite an actor

3 *(reproduction)* replica, studio copy; **il est la r. vivante de son père** he's the spitting image of *or* a dead ringer for his father; **réaliser la r. de qch** to design a replica of sth

4 *Géol* aftershock

répliquer [3] [replike] **VT** *(répondre)* to reply, to retort; **elle répliqua que ça ne le regardait pas** she replied *or* retorted that it was none of his business; **il n'y a rien à r. à un tel argument** there's no answer to an argument like that; **que r. à ça?** how can you reply to that?; **"il n'en est pas question", répliqua-t-il** "it's out of the question," he replied *or* retorted

USAGE ABSOLU monte te coucher et ne réplique pas! go upstairs to bed and no argument!; **le pays a été attaqué et a répliqué immédiatement** the country was attacked and immediately retaliated; **il répliqua par un coup de pied** he answered with a kick

□ **répliquer à VT IND 1** *(répondre à → remarque, insulte)* to reply to; **r. à une critique** to reply to *or* to answer criticism; **r. à qn** to answer sb back; **ne t'avise plus de me r.!** don't you ever dare answer me back again!

2 *(contre-attaquer)* to respond to; **la France a répliqué à cette déclaration en rappelant son ambassadeur** France has responded to this declaration by recalling her ambassador

▸**se répliquer VPR** *Biol* to replicate

replisser [3] [rəplise] **VT** *(tissu)* to pleat again

reploiement [rəplwamɑ̃] **NM** *Littéraire (introversion)* withdrawal

replonger [17] [rəplɔ̃ʒe] **VT 1** *(plonger à nouveau)* to dip back; **r. la louche dans la marmite** to dip the ladle back into the pot; **l'enfant replongea ses doigts dans la confiture** the child plunged *or* stuck his/her fingers back into the jam

2 *Fig (faire sombrer à nouveau)* to plunge back, to push back; **le choc la replongea dans la démence** the shock pushed *or* tipped her back into madness; **le film m'a replongé dans le Paris de mon enfance** the film takes me right back to the Paris of my childhood

VI 1 *(plonger à nouveau)* to dive again; **on replonge?** shall we dive in again *or* have another dive?

2 *Fam Fig (reprendre une habitude)* to be at it again; **r. dans l'alcoolisme/la délinquance** to relapse into drinking/delinquency; **r. dans la dépression** to sink back *or* to relapse into depression; **un rien peut faire r. un alcoolique** it doesn't take much to push an alcoholic back into his old ways

3 *Fam Arg crime (retourner en prison)* to go back inside

4 **se r. dans** to go back to; **se r. dans son travail** to immerse oneself in work again, to go back to one's work; **se r. dans ses recherches** to get involved in one's research again

replu [rəply] **PP** *voir* **repleuvoir**

repolir [32] [rəpɔlir] **VT** to polish up again

repolissage [rəpɔlisaʒ] **NM** repolishing, polishing up again

répondant, -e [repɔ̃dɑ̃, -ɑ̃t] **NM,F 1** *(garant)* guarantor, surety; **être le r. de qn** *(financièrement)* to stand surety for sb, to be sb's guarantor; *(moralement)* to answer *or* to vouch for sb

2 *(d'un questionnaire)* respondent

NM 1 *Vieilli Rel* server

2 *(statuette funéraire égyptienne)* shawabti

3 *(locution)* **avoir du r.** *(avoir des économies)* to have plenty of cash stashed away; *(avoir de la répartie)* to have quick repartee, to be quick at repartee

répondeur, -euse [repɔ̃dœr, -øz] **ADJ** *(insolent)* who answers back; **il est déjà r. à son âge** *Br* he's got a lot of cheek *or Am* he's very sassy for his age

NM r. (téléphonique) (telephone) answering machine; **r. enregistreur** answering machine; **r. interrogeable à distance** remote-control answering machine

RÉPONDRE [75] [repɔ̃dr]

> **VT** to answer **1, 3, 4** ▪ to reply **1, 3** ▪ to answer back **2** ▪ to write back **3** ▪ to respond **5**
> **VT** to answer **1, 2** ▪ to reply **1, 2** ▪ to write back **2**

VI 1 *(répliquer)* to answer, to reply; **réponds quand je t'appelle!** answer (me) when I call you!; **ma sœur a répondu pour moi** my sister answered for me *or* in my place; **bien répondu!** well said *or* spoken!; **répondez par oui ou par non** answer *or* say yes or no; **il n'a répondu que par des grognements** his only answer *or* reply was a series of grunts; **elle répondit en riant** she answered *or* replied with a laugh; **il lui a répondu par un crochet du gauche** he answered *or* replied with a left hook; **r. par un clin d'œil/hochement de tête** to wink/to nod in reply; **r. par l'affirmative/la négative** to answer in the affirmative/negative; **seul l'écho me/lui/** *etc* **répondit** the only reply was an echo; **r. à qn** to answer sb; **réponds à la dame** answer the lady; **r. à qch** to answer sth; **vous ne répondez pas à ma question** you haven't answered my question; **je ne répondrai pas à cet interrogatoire** I refuse to answer these questions *or* to undergo this interrogation

2 *(être insolent)* to answer back; **r. à ses parents/professeurs** to answer one's parents/teachers back; **et ne réponds pas!** and no answering back!, and no *Br* backchat *or Am* back talk!

3 *(à une lettre)* to answer, to reply, to write back; **r. par écrit** to answer *or* to reply in writing; **il faut leur r. par écrit** you must give them a written answer *or* reply; **je n'ai jamais répondu** I never wrote back *or* answered *or* replied; **il ne m'a pas encore répondu** he hasn't written back to me yet, I still haven't had a reply from him; **r. à une note** to answer *or* to reply to a note; **répondez au questionnaire suivant** answer the following questions, fill in the following questionnaire; **je réponds toujours aux vœux qu'on m'envoie** I always reply to any messages of goodwill that people send me; **r. à une invitation** *(dire qu'on l'a reçue)* to reply to *or* to answer an invitation; **je suis ravi que vous ayez pu r. à mon invitation** *(que vous soyez venu)* I'm delighted that you were able to accept my invitation; **vous devez r. à la convocation** *(dire que vous l'avez reçue)* you must acknowledge receipt of the notification; *Jur* **r. à une citation à comparaître** *(sujet: témoin)* to comply with a subpoena, to answer a court summons; *(sujet: inculpé)* to attend a summons

4 *(à la porte, au téléphone)* to answer; **ne réponds pas!** don't answer!; **je vais r.** *(à la porte)* I'll go; *(au téléphone)* I'll answer it, I'll get it; **ça ne répond pas** nobody's answering, there's no answer; **r. au téléphone** to answer the phone *or* telephone

5 *(réagir → véhicule, personne, cheval)* to respond (**à** to); **les gens répondent par milliers** people are responding in their thousands; **le public répond mal** there is a low level of public response; **les freins répondent bien** the brakes respond well; **une voiture qui répond bien** a car that responds well; **son organisme ne répond plus au traitement** his/her body isn't responding to treatment any more; **r. à l'amitié de qn** to respond to *or* to return sb's friendship; **r. au sourire/à l'amour de qn** to return sb's smile/love; **elle répondit à son accueil par un sourire glacial** she responded to *or* met his/her welcome with an icy smile; **r. à un coup** *ou* **à une attaque** to fight back, to retaliate; **r. à une accusation/critique** to counter an accusation/a criticism; **r. à la force par la force** to meet *or* to answer force with force; *Équitation* **r. aux aides** to respond (well) to aids

VT 1 *(gén)* to answer, to reply; *(après une attaque)* to retort; **r. (que) oui/non** to say yes/no in reply, to answer yes/no; **"à trois heures et demie", répondit-elle** "at half past three," she answered *or* replied; **qu'as-tu répondu?** what did you say?, what was your answer?; **que puis-je r. à cela?** what can I say to that?; **je n'ai rien trouvé à r.** I could find no answer *or* reply; **est-ce qu'elle a répondu quelque chose?** did she give any answer?, did she say anything in reply?; **si on me demande pourquoi, je répondrai ceci** if I'm asked the reason why, this is what I'll say *or* answer; **ils m'ont répondu des bêtises** they answered me with a lot of nonsense; **j'ai répondu à Joseph que je ne le ferais pas** I told Joseph I wouldn't do it; **je me suis vu r. que cela ne me regardait pas** I was told it was none of my business; **elle m'a répondu de le faire moi-même** she told me to do it myself; **que r. à cela?** there's no answer to that (, is there?); **il répondit ne pas s'en soucier** he answered *or* replied that he did not care about it

2 *(par lettre)* to answer, to reply (in writing *or* by letter); **r. que...** to write (back) that...

3 *Rel* **r. la messe** to give the responses (at Mass)

❑ **répondre à VT IND 1** *(satisfaire → besoin, demande)* to answer, to meet; *(→ attente, espoir)* to come *or* to live up to, to fulfil; *(correspondre à → norme)* to meet; *(→ condition)* to fulfil; *(→ description, signalement)* to answer, to fit; **nos produits répondent à ces exigences de qualité** our products meet these quality requirements; **les dédommagements ne répondent pas à l'attente des sinistrés** the amount offered in compensation falls short of the victims' expectations

2 *(s'harmoniser avec)* to match; **au bleu du ciel répond le bleu de la mer** the blue of the sky matches the blue of the sea; **la frise de la nef répond à celle du transept** the frieze in the nave matches with the one in the transept

3 r. au nom de *(s'appeler)* to answer to the name (of)

❑ **répondre de VT IND 1** *(cautionner → filleul, protégé)* to answer for; **r. de l'exactitude de qch/de l'intégrité de qn** to vouch for the accuracy of sth/sb's integrity; **je réponds de lui comme de moi-même** I can fully vouch for him; **je ne réponds plus de rien** I am no longer responsible for anything; **elle répond des dettes de son mari jusqu'au divorce** she's responsible *or* answerable for her husband's debts until the divorce

2 *(assurer)* **elle cédera, je vous en réponds!** she'll give in, you can take it from me *or* take my word for it!; **je vous en réponds que cela ne se renouvellera pas!** I guarantee (you) it won't happen again!

3 *(expliquer)* to answer *or* to account for, to be accountable for; **je n'ai pas à r. de mes décisions** I do not have to account for my decisions; **les ministres répondent de leurs actes devant le Parlement** ministers are accountable for their actions before Parliament; *Jur* **r. d'un crime** to answer for a crime; **il lui faudra r. de plusieurs tentatives de viol** he'll have to answer several charges of attempted rape

▸**se répondre VPR** *(instruments de musique)* to answer each other; *(sculptures, tableaux)* to match each other; *(couleurs, formes, sons)* to harmonize

répons [repɔ̃] **NM** *Rel* response

réponse [repɔ̃s] **NF 1** *(réplique)* answer, reply; **elle a toujours r. à tout** *(elle sait tout)* she has an answer for everything; *(elle a de la repartie)* she's never at a loss for *or* she's always ready with an answer; **elle fait toujours les questions et les réponses** she does all the talking; **pour toute r., elle me claqua la porte au nez** her only reply was to slam the door in my face; **une r. de Normand** an evasive answer; **c'est la r. du berger à la bergère** it's tit for tat; *Mktg* **r. stimulée** stimulus reponse

2 *(à un courrier)* reply, answer, response; *(à une demande)* reply, response; *(à une offre d'emploi)* reply; **en r. à votre courrier du 2 mai** in reply *or* response to your letter dated *Br* 2 May *or Am* May 2; **leur lettre est restée sans r.** their letter remained *or* was left unanswered; **leur demande est restée sans r.** there was no reply *or* response to their request; **j'ai sonné plusieurs fois, mais pas de r.** I've rung several times, but there's no answer; **r. par retour du courrier** reply by return of post; **je lui ai donné une r. positive** *(à son offre)* I accepted his/her offer; *(à sa candidature)* I told him/her his/her application had been successful; **je lui ai donné une r. négative** I turned him/her down; *Tél* **r. payée** reply paid; **télégramme avec r. payée** reply-paid telegram

3 *(réaction)* response; **la r. du gouvernement fut d'imposer le couvre-feu** the government's response was to impose a curfew

4 *(solution)* answer; **je n'ai pas la r. (à ton problème)** I don't have the answer (to your problem), I don't know what the answer (to your problem) is; **la r. à la question numéro 5 est fausse** the answer to number 5 is wrong

5 *Tech* response; **temps de r. d'un appareil** response time of a device

6 *Mus* answer

7 *Psy* response, reaction; **r. inconditionnelle** unconditioned response

8 *Jur* **r. au fond** defendant's plea

9 *(comme adj; avec ou sans trait d'union)* **bulletin-r.** reply slip; **coupon-r.** reply coupon

repopulation [rəpɔpylasjɔ̃] **NF** repopulation

report [rəpɔr] **NM 1** *(renvoi à plus tard)* postponement, deferment; *Jur* **r. du jugement sine die** deferment of the verdict to an unspecified date; *Fin* **r. d'échéance** extension of due date

2 *Compta* carrying forward *or* over; *(en haut du page)* (balance) brought forward; **faire le r. d'une somme** to carry forward *or* over an amount; **r. déficitaire sur les exercices précédents/ultérieurs** loss carried back/forward; **r. d'écritures** posting; **r. de l'exercice précédent** carried forward from the previous financial year; **r. à l'exercice suivant** carried forward to the next financial year; **r. à nouveau** balance (carried forward); *(en haut de colonne)* brought forward; *(en bas de colonne)* carried forward

3 *(au turf)* rebetting

4 *(transfert → de corrections)* transfer; **r. des voix** transfer of votes

5 *Bourse* contango, carry over; **prendre des actions en r.** to take in *or* carry over shares

6 *Phot* transfer

7 *Typ* **papier à r.** transfer paper

reportage [rəpɔrtaʒ] **NM 1** *(récit, émission)* report; **r. filmé/télévisé/photo** film/television/photo report; **r. en direct** live coverage; **r. en exclusivité** scoop, exclusive (report); **r. d'investigation** investigative report; **faire un r. sur qch** to do a report on sth; **j'ai fait mon premier grand r. pour 'Nice-Matin'** I covered my first big story for 'Nice-Matin'; **r. publicitaire** special advertising feature, *Am* advertorial

2 *(métier)* (news) reporting, reportage; **faire du r.** to be a news reporter; **être en r.** to be on an assignment; **faire du grand r.** to do international reporting, to cover stories from all over the world; **r. filmé** film reporting; **r. d'investigation** investigative reporting; **r. télévisé** television reporting

reporté, -e [rəpɔrte] **NM,F** *Bourse (d'actions)* giver

reporter[1] [rəpɔrtɛr] **NM** *Rad, TV & Journ* (news) reporter; **grand r.** international reporter; **r. en chef** chief reporter; **r. local** local reporter, stringer; **r. photographe** photojournalist; **r. de la presse écrite** newspaper reporter, press reporter; **r. sportif** sports reporter; **sac (de) r.** organizer bag

reporter[2] [3] [rəpɔrte] **VT 1** *(rapporter)* to take back; **r. un livre à la bibliothèque** to take a book back to the library

2 *(transcrire → note, insertion)* to transfer, to copy out; *Compta* to carry forward; **r. votre appréciation sous la photo du candidat** put your assessment under the candidate's photograph; *Compta* **solde à r.** balance (to be) carried forward; *Compta* **tu dois r. le total à la page suivante** you must carry the total forward to the

next page; *Compta* **r. à nouveau** to carry forward (to new account); *Compta* **r. le montant des exportations dans le livre des comptes** to post exports (to the ledger)

3 *(retarder → conférence, rendez-vous)* to postpone, to put off; *(→ annonce, verdict)* to put off, to defer; *(→ date)* to defer, *esp Br* to put back; **r. qch à une prochaine fois** to put sth off until another time

4 *(faire revenir en arrière)* to take back; **ces photos me reportent à l'été 43** these photographs take me back to the summer of '43

5 *(transférer)* to shift, to transfer; **elle a reporté ses notes dans son cahier bleu** she copied out her notes into her blue notebook; **les votes ont été reportés sur le candidat communiste** the votes were transferred to the communist candidate; **il a reporté toute son amertume sur sa fille** he's transferred *or* shifted all his bitterness onto his daughter

6 *(miser)* to put, to place, to transfer; **r. tous ses gains sur le 8** to put *or* to place all one's winnings on the 8

7 *Compta (écriture)* to enter up, to post

8 *Bourse* to continue, to contango; **faire r. des titres** to give on *or* to lend stock

▸**se reporter** VPR **1 se r. à** *(se référer à)* to turn *or* to refer to, to see; **reportez-vous à notre dernier numéro** see our last issue

2 se r. à *(revenir en arrière)* to look *or* think back to, to cast one's mind back to; **se r. au passé/à la période de l'après-guerre** to look back *or* think back to the past/to the post-war period

3 se r. sur *(se transférer sur)* to be transferred to; **tout son amour s'est reporté sur sa fille** all his/her love was switched to his/her daughter

reporter-cameraman [rəpɔrtɛrkameraman] *(pl* **reporters-cameramans** *ou* **reporters-cameramen** [-mɛn]) NM television news reporter

reporter-photographe [rəpɔrtɛrfɔtɔgraf] *(pl* **reporters-photographes**) NM news photographer, photojournalist

reporteur [rəpɔrtœr] NM **1** *Bourse (d'actions)* taker (of stock) **2** *Typ* transfer printer (person) **3** *Journ* **r. d'images** television news reporter

repos [rəpo] NM **1** *(détente)* rest; **prendre quelques jours de r.** to take *or* to have a few days' rest; **un moment de r.** a short rest; **trois jours de r. complet** three days of complete rest; **j'ai besoin d'un peu de r.** I need a bit of a rest, I need to rest a little; **mon médecin m'a conseillé le r.** my doctor has advised me to rest; **ces enfants ne lui laissent aucun r.** those children give him/her no rest

2 *(période d'inactivité)* rest (period), time off; **trois jours de r., un r. de trois jours** three days off; **après un mois de r.** after a month's rest; **le dimanche est mon seul jour de r.** Sunday is my only day off *or* day of rest; **r. compensateur** ≃ time off in lieu; **r. dominical** Sunday rest; **r. hebdomadaire** weekly time off

3 *Littéraire (tranquillité → de la nature)* peace and quiet; *(→ intérieure)* peace of mind; **trouver le r.** to relax; **troubler le r. de qn** to disturb sb; **la peur d'être expulsé lui ôtait tout r.** fear of expulsion took away his/her peace of mind; **je n'aurai pas de r. tant que...** I won't rest as long as...

4 *Littéraire (sommeil)* sleep, rest; **respecte le r. des autres** let other people sleep (in peace); **r. éternel** eternal rest; **le r. de la tombe** *ou* **de la mort** the sleep of the dead; **le champ de r.** the churchyard, God's acre

5 *Mus* cadence; *Littérature* break

6 *Mil* **r.!** at ease!

7 *Constr* (small) landing

8 *Géol* dormancy

9 *Phys* rest

10 *Sport* break

▫ **au repos** ADJ *(moteur, animal)* at rest; *(volcan)* dormant, inactive; *(muscle, corps)* relaxed ADV **1** *Agr* **laisser un champ au r.** to let a field lie fallow **2** *Mil* **mettre la troupe au r.** to order the troops to stand at ease

▫ **de tout repos** ADJ **le voyage n'était pas de tout r.** it wasn't exactly a restful journey; **des placements de tout r.** gilt-edged investments

▫ **en repos** ADJ **1** *(inactif)* **l'imagination de l'artiste ne reste jamais en r.** an artist's imagination never rests *or* is never at rest **2** *(serein)* **elle a la conscience en r.** she has an easy *or* a clear conscience

reposant, -e [rəpozɑ̃, -ɑ̃t] ADJ *(vacances)* relaxing; *(ambiance, lumière, musique)* soothing

repose [rəpoz] NF *(d'une serrure, d'une porte)* refitting *(UNCOUNT)*; *(d'un tissu, d'une moquette)* relaying *(UNCOUNT)*, putting (back) down again *(UNCOUNT)*

reposé, -e[1] [rəpoze] ADJ fresh, rested; **on repartira quand tu seras bien r.** we'll set off again once you've had a good rest; **tu as l'air r.** you look rested

reposée[2] [rəpoze] NF *Chasse* lair

repose-pieds [rəpozpje] NM INV footrest

repose-poignets [rəpozpwaɲe] NM INV wrist rest

REPOSER [3] [rəpoze]

> VT to rest **3** ▪ to ask again **1** ▪ to put down **2**
> VI to rest **1–3** ▪ to lie **1, 3**
> VPR to rest **1** ▪ to rely on **2**

VT **1** *(question)* to ask again, to repeat; *(problème)* to raise again, to bring up again

2 *(objet)* to put down (again) *or* back down; **on a dû faire r. de la moquette** we had to have the carpet relaid; **r. une serrure** to refit a lock

3 *(personne, corps, esprit)* to rest; **r. ses jambes** to rest one's legs; **la peinture me repose les nerfs** painting rests my nerves; **ça le repose de tous ses soucis** it gives him a rest from all his worries

4 *Mil* **reposez armes!** order arms!

VI **1** *(être placé)* to rest, to lie; **sa tête reposait sur l'oreiller** his/her head rested *or* lay on the pillow

2 *Littéraire (dormir)* to sleep; *(être allongé)* to rest, to be lying down; *(être enterré)* to rest, to be buried; **r. sur son lit de mort** to be lying on one's deathbed; **elle repose non loin de son village natal** she rests *or* she's buried not far from her native village; **ici reposent les victimes de la guerre** here lie the victims of the war

3 *(être posé)* to rest, to lie, to stand; **l'épave reposait par 100 mètres de fond** the wreck lay 100 metres down

4 *(liquide, mélange)* **laissez le vin r.** leave the wine to settle, let the wine stand; **laissez r. la pâte/colle** leave the dough to stand/glue to set

5 *Agr* **laisser la terre r.** to let the land lie fallow

▫ **reposer sur** VT IND **1** *(être posé sur)* to rest on, to lie on, to stand on; *Constr* to be built *or* to rest on; **la statue repose sur un socle de marbre** the statue stands *or* sits on a marble pedestal

2 *(être fondé sur → sujet: témoignage, conception)* to rest on; **sur quelles preuves repose votre affirmation?** what evidence do you have to support your assertion?, on what evidence do you base your assertion?; **l'ordre social repose sur la famille** social order hinges *or* is based on the family

▸**se reposer** VPR **1** *(se détendre)* to rest; **va te r. une heure** go and rest *or* go take a rest for an hour; **se r. des fatigues de la journée** to rest after a tiring day; *Fig* **se r. sur ses lauriers** to rest on one's laurels

2 se r. sur *(s'en remettre à)* to rely on; **le Président se repose trop sur ses conseillers** the President relies *or* depends too much on his advisers; **je me repose sur elle pour les histoires d'argent** I rely on her as far as money matters are concerned

repose-tête [rəpoztɛt] NM INV headrest

repositionnement [rəpozisjɔnmɑ̃] NM *Com (d'un produit)* repositioning; **r. réel** real repositioning

repositionner [3] [rəpozisjɔne] VT **1** *(remettre en position)* to reposition **2** *Com (produit)* to reposition

▸**se repositionner** VPR *Com* **se r. sur le marché** to reposition oneself in the market; **se r. à la baisse** to move downmarket; **se r. à la hausse** to move upmarket

reposoir [rəpozwar] NM *(dans une église)* altar of repose; *(dans une maison)* (temporary) altar

repourvoir [64] [rəpurvwar] VT *Suisse (poste)* to fill

repoussage [rəpusaʒ] NM **1** *Beaux-Arts* repoussé (work) *(UNCOUNT)*, chasing *(UNCOUNT)*, embossing *(UNCOUNT)*; *(travail du cuir)* embossing *(UNCOUNT)* **2** *Métal* repoussé

repoussant, -e [rəpusɑ̃, -ɑ̃t] ADJ repulsive, repellent; **être d'une laideur repoussante** to be repulsively *or* horribly ugly

repousse [rəpus] NF new growth; **des pilules qui facilitent la r. des cheveux** hair-restoring pills

repoussé [rəpuse] ADJ M repoussé *(avant n)*

NM *(technique → gén)* repoussé (work); *(→ au marteau)* chasing; *(relief)* repoussé

repousse-peaux [rəpuspo] NM INV cuticle remover

repousser [3] [rəpuse] VT **1** *(faire reculer → manifestants)* to push *or* to drive back; *(→ agresseur)* to drive off, to beat off, to repel; *(→ attaque)* to drive back, to repel; **r. les frontières de l'imaginaire/l'horreur** to push back the frontiers of imagination/horror

2 *(écarter)* to push aside *or* away; **elle repoussa violemment l'assiette** she pushed the plate away violently; **r. qn d'un geste brusque** to push *or* to shove sb out of the way roughly; **il repoussa du pied la bouteille vide** *(violemment)* he kicked the empty bottle away; *(doucement)* he nudged *or* edged the empty bottle out of the way with his foot; **repoussons les meubles** let's push back the furniture

3 *(refuser → offre, mesure, demande en mariage)* to turn down, to reject; *(→ solution, thèse)* to reject, to dismiss, to rule out; *(→ tentation, idées noires)* to resist, to reject, to drive away; **r. un projet de loi** to throw out *or* to reject a bill; **r. les avances de qn** to reject sb's advances

4 *(mendiant)* to turn away; *(prétendant)* to reject

5 *(dégoûter)* to repel, to put off; **il me repousse** he repels me

6 *(retarder → conférence, travail)* to postpone, to put off; *(→ date)* to defer, *Br* to put back; *(→ décision, jugement)* to defer; **repoussé au 26 juin** postponed until *Br* 26 June *or Am* June 26

7 *Tech (cuir)* to emboss; *(métal)* to chase, to work in repoussé

VI **1** *(barbe, plante)* to grow again *or* back; **elle se laisse r. les cheveux** she's letting her hair grow again

2 *Fam (sentir mauvais)* to stink, *Br* to pong, to niff; **il repousse du goulot** his breath stinks, he's got foul breath

▸**se repousser** VPR *(particules)* to repel each other

repoussoir [rəpuswar] NM **1** *(faire-valoir)* foil; **servir de r. à (la beauté de) qn** to act as a foil to sb's beauty **2** *(laideron)* ugly duckling; **sa sœur est un véritable r.** his/her sister's really ugly **3** *Beaux-Arts* repoussoir **4** *Constr (ciseau)* drift (chisel) **5** *(spatule de manucure)* orange stick

répréhensible [repreɑ̃sibl] ADJ reprehensible, blameworthy; **un acte r.** a reprehensible *or* an objectionable deed; **je ne vois pas ce que ma conduite a de r.** I don't see what's reproachable about my behaviour

REPRENDRE [79] [rəprɑ̃dr]

> VT to pick up again **1** ▪ to retake, to recapture **2** ▪ to take hold of again **3** ▪ to pick up **4** ▪ to get back **4** ▪ to take back **4, 5, 11** ▪ to collect **4** ▪ to have back **5** ▪ to go back to **6** ▪ to have more **7** ▪ to resume **8** ▪ to restart **8** ▪ to take up again **8** ▪ to repeat **9** ▪ to carry on **10** ▪ to take up **12** ▪ to rework **13** ▪ to alter **14** ▪ to repair **15** ▪ to reprimand **16** ▪ to catch **17** ▪ to return **18** ▪ to take over **19**
> VI to pick up **1** ▪ to recover **1** ▪ to improve **1** ▪ to resume **2** ▪ to start again **2, 3**
> VPR to pull oneself together **1** ▪ to settle down **1** ▪ to recover **2** ▪ to correct oneself **3** ▪ to start again **4**

VT **1** *(saisir à nouveau → objet)* to pick up again, to take again; **reprenez vos crayons et notez** pick up your pencils again and write; **r. les rênes** *Équitation* to take in the reins; *Fig* to resume control

2 *Mil (s'emparer à nouveau de → position, ville)* to retake, to recapture; *(→ prisonnier)* to recapture, to catch again

3 *(sujet: maladie, doutes)* to take hold of again;

quand la douleur me reprend when the pain comes back; **l'angoisse me reprit** anxiety took hold of me again; **ça y est, ça le reprend!** there he goes again!

4 *(aller rechercher → personne)* to pick up; *(→ objet)* to get back, to collect; *(remporter)* to take back; **va r. ton argent** go and collect your money *or* get your money back; **je (te) reprendrai mon écharpe demain** I'll get my scarf back (from you) tomorrow; **ils reprennent aux uns ce qu'ils donnent aux autres** they take away from some in order to give to others; **tu peux r. ton cadeau, je n'en ai que faire** you can keep your present, I don't want it; **tu peux r. ton parapluie, je n'en ai plus besoin** I don't need your umbrella any more, you can take it back; **je te reprendrai à la sortie de l'école** I'll pick you up *or* I'll collect you *or* I'll come and fetch you after school; **je suis venu r. Nathalie** I've come to pick Nathalie up, I've come to fetch Nathalie; **r. ses bagages à la consigne** to collect *or* to pick up one's luggage from the left-luggage office; **vous pouvez (passer) r. votre montre demain** you can come (by) and collect *or* pick up your watch tomorrow; **je laisserai la voiture à l'aéroport et je la reprendrai en revenant** I'll leave the car at the airport and I'll pick it up *or* collect it on the way back

5 *(réengager → employé)* to take back, to have back; *(réadmettre → élève)* to take back, to have back; **nous ne pouvons r. votre enfant en septembre** we can't take *or* have your child back in September

6 *(retrouver → un état antérieur)* to go back to; **elle a repris son nom de jeune fille** she went back to her maiden name; **il a repris sa bonhomie coutumière** he has recovered his usual good spirits; **je n'arrivais plus à r. ma respiration** I couldn't get my breath back; **r. son sang-froid** to calm down; **r. courage** to regain *or* to recover courage; **si tu le fais sécher à plat, il reprendra sa forme** if you dry it flat, it'll regain its shape *or* it'll get its shape back

7 *(se resservir)* **reprends un biscuit** have another biscuit; **reprenez-en (un peu)** have some more *or* a little more; **son ragoût était tellement bon que j'en ai repris deux fois** his/her stew was so good that I had three helpings; **reprends un comprimé dans deux heures** take another tablet in two hours' time; **j'ai changé d'avis, je vais en r. trois** *(chez un commerçant)* I've changed my mind, I'll have another three; **votre poulet était bon la dernière fois, je vais en r.** your chicken was good last time, I'll have some again *or* more

8 *(recommencer, se remettre à → recherche, combat)* to resume; *(→ projet)* to take up again; *(→ enquête)* to restart, to reopen; *(→ lecture)* to go back to, to resume; *(→ hostilités)* to resume, to reopen; *(→ discussion, voyage)* to resume, to carry on (with), to continue; *Ordinat (programme)* to restart; **r. ses études** to take up one's studies again, to resume one's studies; **je reprends l'école le 15 septembre** I start school again *or* I go back to school on 15 September; **r. le travail** *(après des vacances)* to go back to work, to start work again; *(après une pause)* to get back to work, to start work again; *(après une grève)* to go back to work; **r. contact avec qn** to get in touch with sb again; **r. la plume/la caméra/le pinceau** to take up one's pen/movie camera/brush once more; **les évadés ont repris leur course vers la mer** the fugitives have resumed their flight towards the coast; **r. la route** *ou* **son chemin** to set off again, to resume one's journey; **elle a repris le volant après quelques heures** she took the wheel again after a few hours; **je reprends des antibiotiques depuis une semaine** I've been taking antibiotics again for a week; **r. la mer** *(sujet: marin)* to go back to sea; *(sujet: navire)* to (set) sail again; *Journ* **Dupin reprendra sa chronique en janvier** Dupin will resume his regular column in January; *Jur* **r. une instance** to resume a hearing

9 *(répéter → texte)* to read again; *(→ argument, passage musical)* to repeat; *(→ refrain)* to take up; *(récapituler → faits)* to go over again; *TV* to

repeat; *Cin* to rerun; *Théât* to revive, to put on again, to put back on the stage; **il reprend toujours les mêmes thèmes** he always repeats the same themes, *Péj* he always harps on the same themes; **j'ai inlassablement repris mes arguments** I repeated *or* used the same arguments over and over again; **elle leur a fait r. en chœur les trois dernières mesures** she made them repeat the last three bars in chorus; **on reprend tout depuis le** *ou* **au début** *(on recommence)* let's start (all over) again from the beginning; **reprends la lecture depuis le début du paragraphe** start reading again from the beginning of the paragraph; **un sujet repris par tous vos hebdomadaires** an issue taken up by all your weeklies; **quand j'ai repris le rôle de Tosca** *(que j'avais déjà chanté)* when I took on the part of Tosca again; *(que je n'avais jamais chanté)* when I took on *or* over the part of Tosca; **il faut r. les événements bien plus loin** we have to take up the story much earlier

10 *(dire)* to go on, to carry on; **"et lui?" reprit-elle** "and what about him?" she went on

11 *Com (article refusé)* to take back; **les vêtements ne sont ni repris ni échangés** clothes cannot be returned or exchanged; **nous vous reprenons votre vieux salon pour tout achat de plus de 1000 euros** your old lounge suite accepted in part exchange for any purchase over 1,000 euros; **ils m'ont repris ma voiture pour 1000 euros** I traded my car in for 1,000 euros

12 *(adopter → idée, programme politique)* to take up; **j'ai repris leur devise** I've taken up their motto, I've made their motto mine; **r. à son compte les idées de qn** to take up sb's ideas

13 *(modifier → texte)* to rework, to go over again; *(→ peinture)* to touch up; **il a fallu tout r.** it all had to be gone over *or* done again; **c'était parfait, je n'ai rien eu à r.** it was perfect, I didn't have to make a single correction *or* alteration; **il faudra que tu reprennes le début du premier paragraphe** you'll have to rework the beginning of the first paragraph; **il faudra r. le projet de fond en comble** the plan has to be completely reviewed

14 *Couture (gén)* to alter; *(rétrécir)* to take in; **je vais r. le pantalon à la taille** I'll take in the trousers at the waist; **r. une maille** *(en tricot)* to pick up a stitch

15 *Constr* to repair; *Tech (pièce)* to rework, to machine; **r. un mur en sous-œuvre** to underpin a wall

16 *(réprimander)* to pull up, to pick up, *Sout* to reprimand; *(corriger)* to correct, to pull up; **j'ai été obligé de la r. en public** I had to put her straight in front of everybody; **sa femme est toujours en train de le r.** his wife is always pulling him up

17 *(surprendre)* **r. qn à voler/fumer** to catch sb stealing/smoking again; **que je ne t'y reprenne plus!** don't let me catch you at it again!; **on ne m'y reprendra plus!** that's the last time you'll catch me doing that!

18 *Sport* to return; **r. la balle en revers** to take *or* to return the ball on one's backhand; *Équitation* **r. un cheval** to rein a horse; *Chasse* **r. la voie** *(sujet: chien)* to pick up the scent again

19 *Fin (acheter → entreprise)* to take over, to buy out; *(prendre à son compte → cabinet, boutique)* to take over; **après l'accident de son père, elle a repris l'entreprise/le stock** she took over the firm/stock after her father's accident

VI 1 *(s'améliorer → affaires)* to improve, to recover, to pick up, to look up; *Bourse* to rally; *(repousser → plante)* to pick up, to recover; *Bourse* **les cours ont repris** the market rallied; **les affaires reprennent** business is picking *or* looking up; **avec le nouveau gérant, le restaurant a bien repris** with the new manager, the restaurant is picking up well

2 *(recommencer → lutte)* to start (up) again, to resume; *(→ pluie, vacarme)* to start (up) again; *(→ cours, école)* to start again, to resume; *(→ feu)* to rekindle; *(→ fièvre, douleur)* to return, to start again; **si la fièvre reprend, donnez-lui un comprimé** if his/her temperature goes up again or if the fever returns give him/her a tablet; **le**

feu ne veut pas r. the fire just won't get going again *or* rekindle; **je n'arrive pas à faire r. le feu** I can't get the fire going again; **l'incendie a repris au dernier étage** the fire has started again on the top floor; **la tempête reprit de plus belle** the storm started again with renewed ferocity; **le froid a repris** the cold weather has set in again *or* has returned

3 *(retourner au travail → employé)* to start again; **je reprends à 2 heures** I'm back (at work) at 2, I start again at 2

▶**se reprendre** VPR **1** *(recouvrer ses esprits)* to get a grip on oneself, to pull oneself together; *(retrouver son calme)* to settle down; **ils ne nous laissent pas le temps de nous r. entre deux questions** they don't give us time to take a breather between questions

2 *Sport (au cours d'un match)* to recover, to rally; **après un mauvais début de saison, il s'est très bien repris** he started the season badly but has come back strongly *or* has staged a good comeback

3 *(se ressaisir → après une erreur)* to correct oneself; **se r. à temps** *(avant une bévue)* to stop oneself in time

4 se r. à faire qch to start doing sth again; **elle se reprit à divaguer** she started rambling again; **je me repris à l'aimer** I started to fall in love with him/her again; **je m'y suis reprise à trois fois** I had to start again three times *or* to make three attempts

repreneur [rəprənœr] NM *Écon* buyer; **les repreneurs de la chaîne** the people who bought up *or* acquired the channel

reprennent, reprenons *etc voir* **reprendre**

représailles [rəprezaj] NFPL reprisals, retaliation (UNCOUNT); **user de r. contre un pays** to take retaliatory measures *or* to retaliate against a country; **exercer des r. contre** *ou* **envers qn** to take reprisals against sb; **en (guise de)** *ou* **par r. contre** in retaliation for, as a reprisal for; **nos r. seront militaires et économiques** we shall retaliate both militarily and economically

représentable [rəprezɑ̃tabl] ADJ representable

représentant, -e [rəprezɑ̃tɑ̃, -ɑ̃t] NM,F **1** *Pol* (elected) representative; **les représentants du peuple** the people's representatives

2 *(porte-parole)* representative; **un des derniers représentants de la Nouvelle Vague** one of the last representatives of New Wave cinema

3 *(délégué)* delegate, representative; **le r. de la France à l'ONU** France's *or* the French representative at the UN; **où sont les représentants des élèves?** where are the class *or* student delegates?; **r. légal** legal representative; **r. du personnel** staff delegate *or* representative; **r. syndical** union representative, *esp Br* shop steward

4 *Com* representative, agent; **je suis r. en électroménager** I'm a representative for an electrical appliances company; **notre r. au Japon** our agent in Japan; **r. (de commerce), r. commercial** (sales) representative; **r. dûment accrédité** duly authorized representative; **r. exclusif** sole agent; **r. multi-carte** freelance representative *(working for several companies)*; **r. du personnel** staff representative

représentatif, -ive [rəprezɑ̃tatif, -iv] ADJ representative; **vous ne pouvez prétendre être r.** you cannot claim to represent anybody; **voilà des photos, mais elles ne sont pas très représentatives** here are some photos but they don't really give you the right idea; **être r. de qn/qch** to be representative of sb/sth; **un échantillon r. de la population** a representative sample of the population; **c'est assez r. de la mentalité des jeunes** it's fairly typical of the way young people think

représentation [rəprezɑ̃tasjɔ̃] NF **1** *(image)* representation, illustration; **c'est une r. très fidèle des lieux** it's a very accurate description of the place

2 *Théât* performance; **r. en matinée** matinee (performance); **r. en soirée** evening performance; **il y aura 150 représentations** there will be 150 performances

3 *(évocation)* description, portrayal; **une r. féroce des milieux d'affaires** a vitriolic portrayal of the business world

rep-rep

4 *(matérialisation par un signe)* representing *(UNCOUNT)*; **l'écriture est un système de r. de la langue** writing is a way of representing language

5 *Admin & Pol* representation; **assurer la r. d'un pays** to represent a country, to act as a country's representative; **réduire sa r. diplomatique dans un pays** to cut down on *or* to reduce one's diplomatic representation in a country; **r. proportionnelle** proportional representation

6 *Jur* **r. en justice** legal representation

7 *Com* (sales) representation; *(agence)* agency; **avoir une r. à l'étranger** to have an office abroad; **faire de la r., être dans la r.** to be a (sales) representative; **je fais de la r. en chaussures** I'm a footwear salesman; **r. exclusive** sole agency; **avoir la r. exclusive de** to be sole agents for

8 *Psy* representation

9 *Beaux-Arts* representation; **une r. de la Vierge** a representation of the Virgin

10 *Géog* **r. plane** projection

□ **représentations** NFPL *Arch* **faire des représentations à qn** to make representations to sb

□ **en représentation** ADJ **1** *(personne)* **il est toujours en r.** he's always trying to project a certain image of himself

2 *(pièce de théâtre)* in performance

représentative [rəprezɑ̃tativ] *voir* **représentatif**

représentativité [rəprezɑ̃tativite] NF representativeness; **quelle est la r. de cet exemple?** how representative *or* typical is this example?

représenter [3] [rəprezɑ̃te] VT **1** *(montrer)* to depict, to show, to represent; **r. qch par un graphique** to show sth with a diagram; **le tableau représente une femme assise** the picture shows a seated woman; **la scène représente un intérieur bourgeois** the scene is *or* represents a middle-class interior; **je ne vois pas ce que cette sculpture est censée r.** I can't see what this sculpture is supposed to be *or* to represent

2 *(incarner)* to represent; *(symboliser)* to represent, to stand for; **elle représentait pour lui l'idéal féminin** she represented *or* symbolized *or* embodied the feminine ideal for him; **tu ne représentes plus rien pour moi** you don't mean anything to me any more; **chaque signe représente un son** each sign stands for *or* represents a sound

3 *(constituer)* to account for, to make up, to represent; **les produits de luxe représentent 60 pour cent de nos exportations** luxury items account for *or* make up *or* represent 60 percent of our exports; **le loyer représente un tiers de mon salaire** the rent amounts *or* comes to one third of my salary; **les immigrés représentent dix pour cent de l'échantillon** immigrants account for *or* make up *or* represent ten percent of the sample; **cela représente 200 heures de travail** 200 hours of work went into this, this represents 200 hours' work

4 *Théât (faire jouer)* to stage, to put on; *(jouer)* to play, to perform

5 *(être le représentant de)* to represent; **120 athlètes représentent la France aux jeux Olympiques** 120 athletes are representing France in the Olympic Games; **le maire s'est fait r. par son adjoint** the mayor was represented by his deputy, the mayor sent his deputy to represent him; **si vous n'êtes pas disponible, faites-vous r.** if you are not available, have someone stand in for you *or* delegate someone

6 *Com (agir au nom de)* to represent, to be a representative for

7 *Littéraire (faire remarquer)* to explain, to outline; *(mettre en garde quant à)* to point out; **elle me représenta les avantages fiscaux de son plan** she pointed out to me the tax benefits of her plan

8 *(traite)* to present for payment again

VI *Littéraire (présenter)* **il représente bien** he certainly has presence

▸**se représenter** VPR **1** *(à une élection)* to *Br* stand *or Am* to run (for election) again; *(à un examen)* to take *or Br* to sit an examination again

2 *(se manifester à nouveau → problème)* to crop *or* to come up again; **une occasion qui ne se représentera sans doute jamais** an opportunity which doubtless will never again present itself; **la même pensée se représenta à mon esprit** the same thought crossed my mind once more

3 *(imaginer)* to imagine, to picture; **j'essaie de me la r. avec 20 ans de moins** I try to imagine *or* picture her (as she was) 20 years ago; **le métier d'actrice n'est pas comme je me l'étais représenté** being an actress isn't what I imagined *or* thought it would be; **représentez-vous le scandale que c'était à l'époque!** just imagine *or* think how scandalous it was in those days!

répresseur [represœr] NM *Biol* repressor

répressif, -ive [represif, -iv] ADJ repressive; **par des moyens répressifs** through coercion

répression [represjɔ̃] NF **1** *(punition)* **ils exigent une r. plus sévère des actes terroristes** they are demanding a crackdown on terrorist activities; **mesures de r. de la fraude fiscale** measures to suppress tax evasion; **r. des fraudes** *(service gouvernemental)* consumer protection office

2 *(étouffement → d'une révolte)* suppression, repression; **la r. ne mène à rien** coercive methods are no use

3 *Psy* repression

répressive [represiv] *voir* **répressif**

réprimande [reprimɑ̃d] NF *(semonce → amicale)* scolding, rebuke; *(→ par un supérieur hiérarchique)* reprimand; **faire** *ou* **adresser une r. à qn** to rebuke *or* to reprimand sb; **face aux réprimandes de toute la famille** reprimanded by the whole family; **sur un ton de r.** in a reproving tone (of voice), in a tone of rebuke

réprimander [3] [reprimɑ̃de] VT *(gronder)* to reprimand, to rebuke; **il s'est fait r.** *(par son père)* he was told off; *(par son patron)* he was given a reprimand

réprimer [3] [reprime] VT **1** *(étouffer → rébellion)* to suppress, to quell, to put down **2** *(punir → délit, vandalisme)* to punish; **r. le banditisme/terrorisme** to crack down on crime/terrorism **3** *(sourire, colère)* to suppress; *(larmes)* to hold *or* to choke back; *(bâillement)* to stifle; *(juron)* to suppress, to smother; **des rires réprimés** repressed *or* stifled laughter

reprint [rəprint] NM *(livre)* reprint; *(réimpression)* reprinting

repris, -e [rəpri, -iz] PP *voir* **reprendre**

NM **r. de justice** ex-convict

□ **reprise** NF **1** *(d'une activité, d'un dialogue)* resumption; *Com (des affaires)* recovery, upturn; *Ordinat (d'un programme)* restart; **reprise des hostilités hier sur le front oriental** hostilities resumed on the eastern front yesterday; **la reprise du travail a été votée à la majorité** the majority voted in favour of going back *or* returning to work; *Bourse* **à la reprise des cotations** when trading resumed; *Com* **une reprise des affaires** an upturn *or* a recovery in business activity; **reprise (économique)** (economic) recovery; *Jur* **r. d'instance** resumption of a hearing; **reprise de travail** return to work; **les grévistes ont voté la reprise de travail** the strikers have voted to return to work

2 *Rad & TV* repeat, rerun; *Cin* rerun, reshowing; *Théât* revival, reprise; *Mus (d'un passage)* repeat, reprise; **une reprise d'une chanson des Beatles** a cover (version) of a Beatles song

3 *(rachat)* **deux hommes sont candidats à la reprise de la chaîne** two men have put in an offer to take over *or* to buy out the channel; **reprise de l'entreprise par ses salariés** employee *or* staff buy-out

4 *Com (de marchandises invendues, d'articles en solde)* taking back, return; **nous ne faisons pas de reprise** goods cannot be returned; **il m'offre une reprise de 500 euros pour ma vieille voiture** he'll give me 500 euros as a trade-in *or Br* in part exchange for my old car

5 *(entre locataires)* = payment made to an outgoing tenant (when renting property); **la reprise comprend l'équipement de la cuisine** the sum due to the former tenant includes the kitchen equipment; **ils demandent une reprise de 1500 euros** they're asking 1,500 euros for the furnishings *or Br* for furniture and fittings

6 *Aut* speeding up, acceleration; **une voiture qui a de bonnes reprises** a car with good acceleration; **je n'ai plus de reprise** I've got no acceleration

7 *Sport (à la boxe)* round; *Escrime* bout; *Équitation (leçon)* riding lesson; *(cavaliers)* riding team; **reprise de volée** *(au tennis)* return volley; *Ftbl* **à la reprise, la Corée menait 2 à 0** Korea was leading 2–0 when the game resumed after half-time *or* at the start of the second half

8 *Couture (dans la maille)* darn; *(dans le tissu)* mend; **faire une reprise à une chemise** to mend a shirt; **reprise perdue** invisible mend

9 *Compta* **reprises sur provisions** recovery of provisions, write-back of provisions

10 *Constr (des fondations)* consolidation

11 *Jur* **droit de reprise** right of repossession *or* re-entry; **reprise des propres** recovery of personal property

12 *Hort* regrowth

13 *Ind* overhauling, repairing; **reprise d'usinage** remachining

14 *Métal* misrun, scabbling

15 *Tex* **taux de reprise** regain *(of moisture)*

16 *Chasse* **reprise de gibier** capture of game

□ **reprises** NFPL **à diverses/multiples reprises** on several/numerous occasions; **à maintes reprises** on several *or* many occasions; **à trois ou quatre reprises** three or four times, on three or four occasions

reprisage [rəprizaʒ] NM *Couture (d'une chaussette, d'une moufle)* darning, mending; *(d'un vêtement)* mending

reprise [rəpriz] *voir* **repris**

repriser [3] [rəprize] VT *Couture (raccommoder → chaussette, moufle)* to darn, to mend; *(→ pantalon)* to mend

reprit *etc voir* **reprendre**

réprobateur, -trice [reprɔbatœr, -tris] ADJ reproving, reproachful; **jeter un regard r. à qn** to give sb a reproving look, to look at sb reprovingly *or* reproachfully; **..., dit-elle d'un ton r.** ..., she said reproachfully *or* in a reproving tone

réprobation [reprɔbasjɔ̃] NF **1** *(blâme)* disapproval, censure, *Sout* reprobation; **soulever la r. générale** to give rise to general reprobation, to be unanimously reproved; **encourir la r. générale** to meet with general disapproval **2** *Rel* reprobation

réprobatrice [reprɔbatris] *voir* **réprobateur**

reproche [rəprɔʃ] NM **1** *(blâme)* reproach; **accabler qn de reproches** to heap reproaches on sb; **faire un r. à qn** to reproach sb; **les reproches qu'on lui fait sont injustifiés** the reproaches levelled *or* directed at him/her are unjustified; **il y avait un léger r. dans sa voix/remarque** there was a hint of reproach in his/her voice/remark; **regarder qn d'un air plein de r.** to look at sb reproachfully; **d'un ton de r.** in a tone of reproach *or* reproachful tone; **faire r. à qn de qch** to upbraid sb for sth; **je ne vous fais pas r. de vous être trompé, mais d'avoir menti** what I hold against you is not the fact that you made a mistake, but the fact that you lied

2 *(critique)* **le seul r. que je ferais à la pièce, c'est sa longueur** the only thing I'd say against the play *or* my only criticism of the play is that it's too long

3 *Jur* **r. de témoin** barring of a witness

□ **sans reproche** ADJ *(parfait)* above *or* beyond reproach, irreproachable; *(qui n'a pas commis d'erreur)* blameless ADV **soit dit sans r., tu n'aurais pas dû y aller** I don't mean to blame *or* to reproach you, but you shouldn't have gone

reprocher [3] [rəprɔʃe] VT **1 r. qch à qn** *(erreur, faute)* to blame *or* to reproach sb for sth; **je lui reproche son manque de ponctualité** what I don't like about him/her is his/her lack of punctuality; **on ne peut pas r. au gouvernement son laxisme** you can't criticize the government for being too soft; **je ne vous reproche rien** I'm not blaming you for anything; **il n'y a absolument rien à lui r.** he's/she's totally blameless; **r. à qn de faire qch** to blame sb for doing sth; **il lui a toujours reproché de l'avoir quitté** he always blamed him/her for leaving him; **il s'est fait r. un certain laisser-aller dans le service** he was accused of a certain slackness in his department

2 r. qch à qch *(défaut)* to criticize sth for sth; **ce que je reproche à ce beaujolais, c'est sa verdeur** the criticism I would make of this Beaujolais is that it's too young; **je n'ai rien à r. à son interprétation** in my view his/her interpretation is faultless, I can't find fault with his/her

interpretation; *Fam* **tu lui reproches quelque chose à ma moto?** something wrong with my bike, is there?; **r. à qch d'être...** to criticize sth for being...; **on a reproché à ma thèse d'être trop courte** my thesis was criticized for being too short

3 *Jur (témoin)* to bar

►**se reprocher** VPR **n'avoir rien à se r.** to have nothing to feel guilty about, to have nothing with which to reproach oneself; **tu n'as pas à te r. son départ** you shouldn't blame yourself for his/her departure; **je me reproche de lui avoir fait confiance** I blame myself for trusting him/her

reproducteur, -trice [rəprɔdyktœr, -tris] ADJ *(organe, cellule)* reproductive; **cheval r.** studhorse, stallion; **poule reproductrice** breeder hen

NM,F *(poule)* breeder; *(cheval)* stud

NM *Tech* template

❑ **reproductrice** NF *(machine)* **reproductrice de cartes** *(card)* reproducer

reproductibilité [rəprɔdyktibilite] NF reproducibility, repeatability

reproductible [rəprɔdyktibl] ADJ reproducible, repeatable

reproductif, -ive [rəprɔdyktif, -iv] ADJ reproductive

reproduction [rəprɔdyksjɔ̃] NF **1** *Biol & Bot* reproduction; *Agr* breeding; **cycle/organes de la r.** reproductive cycle/organs; **l'époque de la r.** the breeding season; **r. asexuée** asexual reproduction; **r. par mitose** replication; **r. sexuée** sexual reproduction

2 *(restitution)* reproduction, reproducing; **cela se prête bien à la r.** it reproduces well; **techniques de r. des sons** sound reproduction techniques

3 *Typ (nouvelle publication)* reprinting, reissuing; *(technique)* reproduction, duplication; **droits de r.** reproduction rights; **tous droits de r. réservés pour tous pays** all rights of reproduction reserved for all countries; **r. interdite** *(sur vidéocassette, disque)* all rights reserved

4 *(réplique)* reproduction, copy; **la qualité des reproductions dans un ouvrage d'art** the quality of the reproduction or reproductions in an art book; **une r. du 'Baiser' de Rodin/de 'Guernica'** a copy of Rodin's 'Kiss'/of 'Guernica'; **une r. en couleur(s)** a colour print; **une r. en plâtre** a plaster cast; **une r. en résine** a resin replica

5 *(département)* reprographic department; **les documents sont partis à la r.** the documents have gone off to repro

reproductive [rəprɔdyktiv] *voir* **reproductif**

reproductrice [rəprɔdyktris] *voir* **reproducteur**

reproduire [98] [rəprɔdɥir] VT **1** *(faire un autre exemplaire de* → *gén)* to copy; *(*→ *clé)* to cut; **r. une médaille par moulage** to copy a medal by taking a mould of it; **ce tableau a été reproduit à des milliers d'exemplaires** thousands of reproductions have been made of this picture

2 *(renouveler)* to repeat; **cette expérience peut être reproduite** this experiment can be repeated; **tu as reproduit les mêmes erreurs** you've made the same mistakes as before

3 *(imiter)* to reproduce, to copy; **les enfants reproduisent les attitudes des adultes** children copy or mimic adult attitudes; **peintre qui reproduit le réel** painter who reproduces reality

4 *(représenter)* to show, to depict, to portray; **la tapisserie reproduit une scène de chasse** the tapestry depicts a hunting scene

5 *(restituer* → *son)* to reproduce

6 *Typ (republier* → *texte)* to reissue; *(*→ *livre)* to reprint; *(photocopier)* to photocopy; *(reprographier)* to duplicate, to reproduce; *(polycopier)* to duplicate

7 *Hort* to reproduce, to breed; **plantes reproduites en serre** plants propagated in a greenhouse

►**se reproduire** VPR **1** *Biol & Bot* to reproduce, to breed

2 *(se renouveler)* to recur; **ces tendances se reproduisent de génération en génération** these trends recur or are repeated with each successive generation; **et que cela ne se reproduise plus!** don't let it happen again!

reprogrammable [rəprɔgramabl] ADJ *Ordinat (touche)* reprogrammable

reprogrammer [3] [rəprɔgrame] VT **1** *Cin & TV* to reschedule **2** *Ordinat* to reprogram

reprographie [rəprɔgrafi] NF reprography, repro

reprographier [9] [rəprɔgrafje] VT *(polycopier)* to duplicate; *(photocopier)* to photocopy

reprographique [rəprɔgrafik] NF reprographic

réprouvé, -e [repruve] ADJ *Rel* reprobate

NM,F **1** *Rel* reprobate **2** *(personne rejetée)* **vivre en r.** to live as an outcast

réprouver [3] [repruve] VT **1** *(attitude, pratique)* to condemn, to disapprove of; **r. l'attitude de qn** to reprove or to condemn sb's attitude; **nous réprouvons l'usage qui a été fait de cet argent** we disapprove of or condemn the way this money has been used; **des pratiques/tendances que la morale réprouve** morally unacceptable practices/tendencies **2** *Rel* to reprobate, to damn

reps [rɛps] NM *Tex* rep, repp

reptation [rɛptasjɔ̃] NF crawling, *Spéc* reptation

reptile [rɛptil] ADJ reptile, reptant; *Littéraire* **âmes reptiles** grovelling souls

NM reptile

reptilien, -enne [rɛptiljɛ̃, -ɛn] ADJ reptilian

repu, -e [rəpy] PP *voir* **repaître**

ADJ *Sout (rassasié)* sated, satiated; **être r.** to be full (up), to have eaten one's fill; **je suis r. de films policiers** I've had my fill of detective films

républicain, -e [repyblikɛ̃, -ɛn] ADJ *(esprit, système)* republican

NM,F *(gén)* republican; *(aux États-Unis, en Irlande)* Republican; *Hist* **Républicains indépendants** Independent Republicans *(conservative Gaullist party founded in the early 1960s)*

NM **1** *Orn* sociable weaver **2** *Presse* **Le R. lorrain** = daily newspaper published in Metz

républicanisme [repyblikanism] NM republicanism

république [repyblik] NF **1** *(régime politique)* republic; **vivre en r.** to live in a republic; *Fam* **je fais ce que je veux, on est en r., non?** I'll do as I like, it's a free country, isn't it?; *Presse* **La R. du Centre** = daily newspaper published in Orléans; *Presse* **La Nouvelle R.** = daily newspaper published in Tours

2 *(État)* Republic; **la R. arabe unie** the United Arab Republic; *Péj* **r. bananière** banana republic; *Anciennement* **la R. démocratique allemande** the German Democratic Republic; **la R. démocratique du Congo** the Democratic Republic of the Congo; **la R. dominicaine** the Dominican Republic; *Anciennement* **la R. fédérale d'Allemagne** the Federal Republic of Germany; **la R. française** the French Republic; **la R. d'Irlande** the Irish Republic, the Republic of Ireland; **la R. islamique d'Iran** the Islamic Republic of Iran; **la R. populaire de Chine** the People's Republic of China; **la R. serbe de Bosnie** the Serb Republic of Bosnia-Herzegovina; **la R. tchèque** the Czech Republic; **la r. une et indivisible** = Jacobin concept of a unified state which is one of the basic principles of the French Republic; *Hist* **la R. de Weimar** the Weimar Republic

3 *(confrérie)* **dans la r. des lettres** in the literary world, in the world of letters

'**La République**' *Platon* 'The Republic'

répudiation [repydjasjɔ̃] NF **1** *(d'une épouse)* repudiation, disowning **2** *(d'une nationalité, d'un héritage)* renunciation, relinquishment; *(d'un principe, d'un devoir)* renunciation, renouncement

répudier [9] [repydje] VT **1** *(renvoyer* → *épouse)* to repudiate, to disown; **se faire r.** to be rejected **2** *(renoncer à* → *nationalité, héritage)* to renounce, to relinquish; *(*→ *principe, devoir)* to renounce; **r. ses anciennes convictions** to go back on or to renounce one's former beliefs

répugnance [repyɲɑ̃s] NF **1** *(dégoût)* repugnance (**pour** for), loathing (**pour** of or for), disgust; **avoir de la r. pour qn/qch** to loathe sb/sth

2 *(mauvaise volonté)* reluctance; **éprouver une certaine r. à faire qch** to be somewhat reluctant or loath to do sth; **je m'attelai à la tâche avec r.** I set about the task reluctantly or unwillingly; **la r. du syndicat à relancer le dialogue** the union's reluctance to resume talks

répugnant, -e [repyɲɑ̃, -ɑ̃t] ADJ **1** *(physiquement)* repugnant, loathsome, disgusting; **avoir un physique r.** to be repulsive; **odeur répugnante** disgusting smell; **tâche répugnante** revolting task; **une chambre d'une saleté répugnante** a revolting or disgustingly filthy room

2 *(moralement* → *individu, crime)* repugnant; *(*→ *livre, image)* disgusting, revolting; **il s'est conduit de façon répugnante avec ses employés** he behaved disgracefully or abominably towards his employees

répugner [3] [repyɲe] VT *Littéraire (personne)* to be repugnant to

❑ **répugner à** VT IND **1** *(être peu disposé à)* **r. à faire qch** to be reluctant or loath to do sth; **elle répugnait à le revoir** she was reluctant to see him again; **je répugne à accuser un ami** I am reluctant or loath to accuse a friend; **il ne répugnait pas à faire ce voyage** he didn't hesitate to make this trip

2 *(dégoûter)* **r. à qn** to repel sb, to be repugnant to sb; **tout ce qui est tâche domestique me répugne** I can't bear anything to do with housework; **ça ne te répugne pas, l'idée de manger du serpent?** doesn't the idea of eating snake disgust you or put you off?; **tout en cet homme me répugne** I loathe everything about that man, everything about that man is repulsive (to me)

3 *(tournure impersonnelle)* **il me répugne de travailler avec lui** I hate or loathe working with him

répulsif, -ive [repylsif, -iv] ADJ **1** *Phys* repulsive **2** *Littéraire (répugnant)* repulsive, repugnant, repellent

répulsion [repylsjɔ̃] NF **1** *(dégoût)* repulsion, repugnance; **éprouver de la r. pour qch** to feel repulsion for sth, to find sth repugnant; **leurs méthodes m'inspirent une grande r.** I find their methods repugnant **2** *Phys* repulsion

répulsive [repylsiv] *voir* **répulsif**

réputation [repytasjɔ̃] NF **1** *(renommée)* reputation, repute; **avoir (une) bonne/mauvaise r.** to have a good/bad reputation; **jouir d'une bonne r.** to have or to enjoy a good reputation; **se faire une r.** to make a reputation or name for oneself; **un hôtel de bonne/mauvaise r.** a hotel of good/ill repute; *Fam* **il n'a pas volé sa r. de frimeur** they don't call him a show-off for nothing; **elle a la r. de noter sévèrement** she has a reputation or she's well-known for being a tough *Br* marker or *Am* grader; **marque de r. mondiale** *ou* **internationale** world-famous brand, brand of international repute; **c'est ce qui a fait leur r.** that's what made their name, that's how they made their name; *Fam* **tu me fais une sale r.** you're giving me a bad name ▪; **leur r. n'est plus à faire** their reputation is well-established; **je vous présente un restaurateur dont la r. n'est plus à faire** here is someone who has built up a fine reputation as a restaurant owner; **connaître qn de r.** to know sb by repute or reputation

2 *(honorabilité)* reputation, good name; **je suis prêt à mettre ma r. en jeu** I'm willing to stake my reputation on it; **porter atteinte à la r. de qn** to damage or to blacken sb's good name

réputé, -e [repyte] ADJ **1** *(illustre* → *orchestre, restaurant)* famous, renowned; **l'un des musiciens les plus réputés de son temps** one of the most famous musicians of his day; **des vins très**

réputés wines of great repute; **un écrivain pas très r.** a little-known writer; **elle est réputée pour ses colères** she's famous *or* renowned for her fits of rage; **il est r. pour être un avocat efficace** he has the reputation of being *or* he's reputed to be a good lawyer

2 *(considéré comme)* reputed; **elle est réputée intelligente** she has a reputation for intelligence, she's reputed to be intelligent; **il est r. ne rien ignorer de cette science** he is reputed *or* said to know everything about the science

requalification [rəkalifikasjɔ̃] **NF** *Jur (d'une accusation)* amendment

requalifier [9] [rəkalifje] **VT 1** *Jur (accusation)* to amend **2** *(redéfinir)* **r. un contrat à durée déterminée en contrat à durée indéterminée** to redefine *or* recategorize a fixed-term contract as a permanent contract

requérant, -e [rəkerɑ̃, -ɑ̃t] *Jur* **ADJ** claiming; **la partie requérante** the claimant, the petitioner

NM,F claimant, petitioner

requérir [39] [rəkerir] **VT 1** *(solliciter → aide, présence)* to request; *(nécessiter)* to call for, to require; **ce travail requiert beaucoup d'attention** the work requires *or* demands great concentration; **r. la force publique** to ask the police to intervene; **r. les civils** to call upon civilian help

2 *Jur* to call for, to demand; **le juge a requis une peine de deux ans de prison** the judge recommended a two-year prison sentence

3 *(sommer)* **r. qn de faire qch** to request that sb do sth

USAGE ABSOLU pendant qu'il requérait during his summing-up

requeté [rekete] **NM** *Hist* **1** *(en Espagne au XIXème siècle)* Carlist volunteer **2** *(pendant la guerre civile espagnole)* = soldier recruited by the nationalist army

requête [rəkɛt] **NF 1** *(demande)* request, petition; **adresser une r. à qn** to make a request to sb, *Sout* to petition sb; **soumettre une r. à un service** to put in *or* to submit a request to a department; **à la** *ou* **sur la r. de qn** at sb's request *or* behest; **elle est venue à ma r.** she came at my request

2 *Jur* petition; **adresser une r. au tribunal** to petition the court, to apply for legal remedy **r. en cassation** application for appeal; **r. civile** extraordinary petition *(against a judgment)*; **r. conjointe** joint petition

3 *Ordinat* query

requiem [rekɥijɛm] **NM INV** *Rel & Mus* requiem

requiert *etc voir* **requérir**

requin [rəkɛ̃] **NM 1** *Ich* shark; **(grand) r. blanc** (great) white shark; **r. bleu** blue shark; **r. bouledogue** bull shark; **r. côtier** coastal shark; **r. dormeur taureau, r. de Port Jackson** Port Jackson shark **2** *(personne)* shark; *Fin* **r. (de la finance)** shark, raider; **les requins du show-business** the sharks of the show business world

requin-baleine [rəkɛ̃balɛn] *(pl* **requins-baleines)** **NM** *Ich* whale shark

requin-chabot [rəkɛ̃ʃabo] *(pl* **requins-chabots)** **NM** *Ich* bamboo shark; **r. épaulette** epaulette shark

requin-marteau [rəkɛ̃marto] *(pl* **requins-marteaux)** **NM** *Ich* hammerhead (shark)

requin-pèlerin [rəkɛ̃pɛlrɛ̃] *(pl* **requins-pèlerins)** **NM** *Ich* basking shark

requinquer [3] [rəkɛ̃ke] *Fam* **VT** *(redonner des forces à)* to pep up, to buck up; **le voilà requinqué** he's (back to) his old self again

▸**se requinquer VPR** to recover[■], to perk up; **il a eu du mal à se r.** it took him a while to recover *or* to get back to his old self again

requin-taupe [rəkɛ̃top] *(pl* **requins-taupes)** **NM** *Ich* mackerel shark, porbeagle

requin-taureau [rəkɛ̃toro] *(pl* **requins-taureaux)** **NM** *Ich* sand tiger shark

requin-tigre [rəkɛ̃tigr] *(pl* **requins-tigres)** **NM** *Ich* tiger shark

requis, -e [rəki, -iz] **PP** *voir* **requérir**

ADJ 1 *(prescrit)* required, requisite; **remplir les conditions requises** to meet the required *or* prescribed conditions; **les conditions requises sont simples** the requirements are simple; **avoir l'âge r.** to meet the age requirements; **avoir les qualifications requises** to have the requisite *or* necessary qualifications

2 *(réquisitionné)* commandeered, requisitioned; **fonctionnaire r.** commandeered civil servant; **gréviste r.** requisitioned striker

NM commandeered civilian; **les r. du travail (obligatoire)** labour conscripts

réquisit [rekizit] **NM** *Phil* necessary condition, requisite

réquisition [rekizisjɔ̃] **NF 1** *Mil & Fig* requisition, requisitioning, commandeering; **on a annoncé la r. des ouvriers grévistes** it has been announced that the striking workers are to be requisitioned; **il y a eu r. de tous les véhicules par l'armée** the army has requisitioned *or* commandeered all vehicles

2 *Jur* **r. d'audience** petition to the court

3 *Fin* **r. de paiement** demand for payment

▫ **réquisitions NFPL** *Jur (conclusions)* closing speech (for the prosecution); *(réquisitoire)* charge

réquisitionner [3] [rekizisjɔne] **VT 1** *(matériel, troupe, employé)* to requisition, to commandeer **2** *Hum (faire appel à)* **r. qn pour faire qch** to rope sb into doing sth; **elle nous a réquisitionnés pour faire la vaisselle** she requisitioned us to do the washing-up, she dragooned us into doing the washing-up

réquisitoire [rekizitwar] **NM 1** *Jur (dans un procès)* prosecutor's arraignment *or* speech *or* charge; **r. définitif** final application *(made by the public prosecutor to the investigating judge for following up an investigation)*; **r. à fin d'informer** = prosecutor's application for a judicial investigation; **r. introductif** = prosecutor's application for a judicial investigation; **r. supplétif** supplementary application *(made by the public prosecutor to the investigating judge for investigation of other matters)* **2** *Fig* indictment (**contre** of); **ces résultats constituent un véritable r. contre la politique du gouvernement** these results are an indictment of the government's policy

réquisitorial, -e, -aux, -ales [rekizitɔrjal, -o] **ADJ** accusatorial

requit *etc voir* **requérir**

requitter [3] [rəkite] **VT** to leave again

RER [ɛrəɛr] **NM** *Rail (abrév* **Réseau express régional**) = Paris metropolitan and regional rail system

RES [ɛrəɛs] **NM** *Fin (abrév* **rachat de l'entreprise par ses salariés**) employee buy-out

RESA [reza] **NF** *(abrév* **réservation**) = TGV seat reservation ticket

résa [reza] **NF** *(abrév* **réservation**) reservation, booking

resaler [3] [rəsale] **VT** to put more salt in, to add more salt to

resalir [32] [rəsalir] **VT** to make dirty again; **j'ai resali le tailleur que je viens de faire nettoyer** I've just got my suit back from the cleaners and I've got it dirty again; **évitez de r. des assiettes** try not to dirty any more plates

▸**se resalir VPR** to get oneself dirty again

rescapé, -e [rɛskape] **ADJ** surviving

NM,F 1 *(d'un accident)* survivor; **les rescapés de la catastrophe** the survivors of the catastrophe **2** *Fig* **les quelques rescapés du Tour de France** the few remaining participants in the Tour de France

rescindable [rəsɛ̃dabl] **ADJ** rescindable

rescindant, -e [rəsɛ̃dɑ̃, -ɑ̃t] **ADJ** rescissory

rescinder [3] [rəsɛ̃de] **VT** to rescind

rescision [resizjɔ̃] **NF** *Jur* rescission

rescisoire [resizwar] **ADJ** *Jur* rescissory; **action r.** rescissory action

rescousse [rɛskus] **à la rescousse ADV aller/venir à la r. de qn** to go/to come to sb's rescue; **arriver à la r.** to come to the rescue; **nous avons appelé quelques amis à la r.** we called on a few friends for help; **tout le monde à la r.!** rally round, everybody!

rescrit [rɛskri] **NM** *Rel, Antiq & Hist* rescript

réseau, -x [rezo] **NM 1** *(de fils, de veines)* network; *Mil* **r. de barbelés** barbed wire entanglement

2 *Transp* network; **r. aérien/ferroviaire/routier** air/rail/road network; **r. urbain** city bus network; **R. express régional** = Paris metropolitan and regional rail system

3 *Tél & TV* network; **r. câblé** cable network; *Rad* **r. hertzien** radio relay network; **r. satellitaire** satellite network; **r. satellite** satellite network; **r. de télécommunications** telecommunications network; **r. de télédistribution** television broadcasting network; **r. de téléphonie mobile** *Br* mobile phone *or Am* cellphone network; **r. téléphonique** telephone network; **r. de télévision** television network; **r. télévisuel** television network

4 *(organisation)* network; **développer un r. commercial** to develop *or* to expand a sales network; **r. d'affichage** outdoor network; **r. de distribution** distribution network; **r. d'espionnage** spy ring, network of spies; *Hist* **r. de résistance** resistance network *or* group; **r. de trafiquants de drogue** drug ring; **r. de vente** sales network

5 *Littéraire* network, web; **je suis pris dans un r. de contraintes** I'm caught in a network *or* web of constraints

6 *Archit* tracery

7 *Élec* grid; **r. bouclé** ring main

8 *Géog* **r. fluvial** river system

9 *Ordinat* network; **mettre en r.** to network; **r. analogique** analogue network; **r. en anneau** ring network; **r. de communication de données** datacomms network; **r. à commutation par paquets** packet-switching network; **r. de données** data network; **r. en étoile/maillé** star/mesh network; **r. informatique** computer network; **r. à large bande** broadband network; **r. local** local-area network, LAN; **r. longue distance** wide-area network, WAN; **r. national d'interconnexion** backbone; **r. numérique** digital network; **r. numérique à intégration de services** integrated services digital network; **r. de télématique** datacomms network; **r. d'utilisateurs** user network

10 *Opt* (diffraction) grating

réseautage [rezotaʒ] **NM** *Ordinat* networking

reseauter [rezɔte] **VT** *Ordinat* to network

résection [resɛksjɔ̃] **NF** *Méd* resection

réséda [rezeda] **ADJ INV** *(couleur)* reseda

NM 1 *Bot* reseda; **r. des teinturiers** weld, dyer's rocket **2** *Hort* mignonette; **r. jaune** wild mignonette; **r. raiponce** corn mignonette **3** *(couleur)* reseda

réséquer [18] [reseke] **VT** *Méd* to resect

réserpine [rezɛrpin] **NF** *Pharm* reserpine

réservataire [rezɛrvatɛr] **ADJ** *Jur* **elle est r. pour un tiers** a third of the legacy devolves to her by law; **héritier r.** heir who cannot be totally disinherited

NMF heir who cannot be totally disinherited

réservation [rezɛrvasjɔ̃] **NF 1** *(d'un billet, d'une chambre, d'une table)* reservation, booking; **faire une r.** *(à l'hôtel)* to make a reservation; *(au restaurant)* to reserve a table; **faut-il faire une r.?** is it necessary to reserve *or* to book?; **la r. est obligatoire** reservations are necessary; **souhaitez-vous un billet avec ou sans r.?** do you wish to reserve a seat with your ticket or not? **2** *Jur* reservation

réserve [rezɛrv] **NF 1** *(stock)* reserve, stock; **nous ne disposons pas d'une r. suffisante d'eau potable** we do not have sufficient reserves of drinking water; **une r. d'argent** some money put by; **faire des réserves de** to lay in supplies *or* provisions of; *Fam Hum* **il a des réserves!** he's got plenty of fat in reserve!; *Banque* **r. d'achat** credit limit; **r. latente** hidden reserve; *Écon* **r. légale** reserve assets; **r. liquide** liquid assets, cash reserve; **r. métallique** bullion reserve; **r. occulte** secret reserve; **r. de prévoyance** contingency reserve; **r. statutaire** statutory reserve

2 *(réticence)* reservation; **permettez-moi de formuler quelques réserves** I have some reservations which I should like to express; **avoir des réserves au sujet d'un projet** to have (some) reservations about a project; **faire** *ou* **émettre des réserves** to express reservations

3 *(modestie, retenue)* reserve; **une jeune femme pleine de r.** a very reserved young woman; **elle est** *ou* **demeure** *ou* **se tient sur la r.** she's being *or* remaining reserved (about it); **il a accueilli mon frère avec une grande r.** he welcomed my brother with great restraint

4 *(en anthropologie)* reservation; *École* reserve,

sanctuary; **r. de chasse/pêche** hunting/fishing preserve; *Can* **r. faunique** wildlife reserve; *Can* **r. indienne** Indian reservation; **r. naturelle** nature reserve; **r. ornithologique** *ou* **d'oiseaux** bird sanctuary

5 *(resserre → dans un magasin)* storeroom; *(collections réservées → dans un musée, dans une bibliothèque)* reserve collection

6 *Jur (clause)* reservation; *Jur* **sous toutes réserves** without prejudice; **r. (héréditaire)** = that part of a legacy legally apportioned to a rightful heir; **sous r. de la signature du contrat** subject to contract

7 *Mil* **la r.** the reserve

8 *Naut* **r. de flottabilité** reserves buoyancy

9 *Physiol* **r. alcaline (du sang)** concentration of alkaline substance (in the blood)

10 *Tech & Tex* resist

❑ **réserves** NFPL **1** *Fin* reserves; **réserves bancaires** bank reserves; **réserves de change** monetary reserves; **réserves en espèces** cash reserves; **réserves excédentaires** excess reserves; **réserves monétaires/de devises** monetary/currency reserves; **réserves monétaires internationales** international monetary reserves; **réserves non distribuées** capital reserves; **réserves obligatoires** statutory reserves

2 *(naturelles)* reserves; *Mines* **les réserves de charbon d'un pays** *(gisements)* a country's coal reserves; *(stocks)* a country's coal stocks; **réserves mondiales** *(de matières premières)* world reserves; *Pétr* **réserves prouvées** proven reserves

❑ **de réserve** ADJ **1** *(conservé pour plus tard)* reserve *(avant n)*; **nous avons un stock de r.** we have a reserve supply

2 *Fin* **monnaie de r.** reserve currency

3 *Mil* **officier de r.** officer of the reserve; **régiment de r.** reserve regiment

❑ **en réserve** ADV **1** *(de côté)* in reserve; **avoir de la nourriture en r.** to have food put by, to have food in reserve; **mettre de la nourriture en r.** to put food aside; **je tiens en r. quelques bouteilles pour notre anniversaire** I've put a few bottles aside *or* to one side for our anniversary

2 *Com* in stock; **avoir qch en r.** to have sth in stock; **nous avons du papier en r. pour un mois** we have one month's supply *or* stock of paper in reserve

❑ **sans réserve** ADJ *(admiration)* unreserved; *(dévotion)* unreserved, unstinting; *(approbation)* unreserved, unqualified ADV without reservation, unreservedly

❑ **sous réserve de** PRÉP subject to; **sous r. de vérification** subject to verification, pending checks; **le départ aura lieu à 8 heures sous r. d'annulation** departure, subject to cancellation, will be at 8 o'clock

❑ **sous toute réserve** ADV with all proper reserves; **attention, c'est sous toute r.!** there's no guarantee as to the accuracy of this!; **la nouvelle a été publiée sous toute r.** the news was published with no guarantee as to its accuracy

réservé, -e [rezɛrve] ADJ **1** *(non public)* **chasse réservée** *(sur panneau)* private hunting; **cuvée réservée** reserved vintage, vintage cuvée; *Euph* **quartier r.** red-light district

2 *(retenu)* reserved, *Br* booked; **désolé Monsieur, cette table est réservée** I'm sorry, sir, this table is reserved; **r.** *(table dans un restaurant)* reserved

3 *(distant)* reserved; **une jeune fille très réservée** a very reserved young girl; **il a toujours eu une attitude très réservée à mon égard** he was always very reserved towards me

4 *Jur* reserved

réserver [3] [rezɛrve] VT **1** *(retenir à l'avance)* to reserve, to book; **on vous a réservé une chambre** a room has been reserved for you; **je vous ai réservé une place sur le prochain vol** I've booked *or* reserved a seat for you *or* I've booked you on the next flight; **r. une place de concert** to book *or* to reserve a ticket for a concert; **nous réservons toujours cette table à nos meilleurs clients** we always reserve this table for our best customers

2 *(conserver → gén)* to reserve, to keep; *(→ pour un usage particulier)* to save, to keep, to set *or* to put aside; **il a réservé une partie de sa maison pour peindre** he keeps *or* he's set aside part of his house to paint in; **il a promis de nous r. une partie de sa récolte** he promised to put aside *or* to keep part of his crop for us; **j'avais réservé des fonds pour l'achat d'une maison** I had put *or* set some money aside to buy a house; **r. qn pour une mission spéciale** to keep sb for a special mission; **r. le meilleur pour la fin** to keep *or* to save the best till last; **r. sa réponse** to delay one's answer; **r. son opinion** to reserve one's opinion; **r. son jugement** to reserve judgement; **être réservé à qn** to be reserved for sb; **un privilège/sport réservé aux gens riches** a privilege/sport enjoyed solely by rich people; **toilettes réservées aux handicapés** toilets (reserved) for the disabled; **emplacements réservés aux médecins** parking (reserved) for doctors only; **les nouvelles installations seront réservées aux superpétroliers** the new installations will be reserved for the use of supertankers

3 *(destiner)* to reserve, to have in store; **r. une surprise à qn** to have a surprise (in store) for sb; **r. un accueil glacial/chaleureux à qn** to reserve an icy/a warm welcome for sb; **que nous réserve l'avenir?** what does the future have in store for us?; **nous ignorons le sort qui lui sera réservé** we do not know what fate has in store for him/her

USAGE ABSOLU **Mesdames, bonsoir, avez-vous réservé?** good evening, ladies, do you have a reservation *or Br* have you booked?; **j'ai réservé au nom de Roux** I have a reservation in the name of Roux; **pour r., appeler...** for reservations, call...

▶**se réserver** VPR **1** *(par prudence)* to hold back; **je me réserve pour le fromage** I'm keeping some room *or* saving myself for the cheese

2 *Sport & Fig* to save one's strength; **je me réserve pour le match de ce soir** I'm saving my strength for this evening's match

3 **se r. qch** to reserve *or* to keep sth (for oneself); **je me suis réservé le blanc du poulet/la chambre du haut** I've saved the chicken breast/ I've kept the top bedroom for myself; **se r. un droit de regard sur** to retain the right to inspect sth; **se r. le droit de faire qch** to reserve the right to do sth

réserviste [rezɛrvist] NM *Mil* reservist

réservoir [rezɛrvwar] NM **1** *(d'essence, de mazout)* tank; *Aut* (fuel *or Br* petrol) tank; *(d'eau)* (water) tank; *(des W-C)* cistern; **r. d'eau chaude** hot water tank; **r. d'encre** ink reservoir; *Aut* **r. de liquide de frein** brake fluid reservoir; *Com* **r. de main-d'œuvre** labour pool; *Fig* **un r. de jeunes talents** a breeding ground for young talent

2 *(étang, lac)* reservoir; *(pour poissons)* fish pond

résidanat [rezidana] NM *Br* housemanship, *Am* internship

résidant, -e [rezidɑ̃, -ɑ̃t] ADJ resident

NM,F resident

résidence [rezidɑ̃s] NF **1** *(domicile)* residence; **établir sa r. à Nice** to take up residence in Nice; **avoir sa r. à Lyon** to be resident *or* to live in Lyons; **r. effective** actual residence; **r. d'été** summer quarters; **r. officielle** official residence; **r. principale/secondaire** main/second home

2 *(bâtiment) Br* block of (luxury) flats, *Am* (luxury) apartment block; **r. hôtelière** apartment hotel; **r. médicalisée** nursing home; *Univ* **r. universitaire** *Br* hall of residence, *Am* dormitory

3 *(maison)* residential property; **il a acheté une jolie petite r. pas trop loin de Paris** he bought a nice little place not too far from Paris

4 *Jur* residence; **assigner qn à r.** to put sb under house arrest; **être en r. surveillée** to be under house arrest

résident, -e [rezidɑ̃, -ɑ̃t] NM,F **1** resident, (foreign) national; **tous les résidents français de Londres** all French nationals living in London

2 *Belg* **second r.** weekender, holiday resident

ADJ *Ordinat* resident

résidentiel, -elle [rezidɑ̃sjɛl] ADJ residential

résider [3] [rezide] VI **1** *(habiter)* **r. à** to live in, *Sout* to reside; **r. à l'étranger/à Genève** to live abroad/in Geneva **2** *Fig* **r. dans** to lie in; **sa force réside dans son influence sur l'armée** his/her strength lies in *or* is based on his/her influence over the army; **c'est là que réside tout l'intérêt du film** that is where the strength of the film lies

résidu [rezidy] NM *(portion restante)* residue

❑ **résidus** NMPL *(détritus)* residue, remnants; *Nucl* **résidus de fission** radioactive waste; **résidus de raffinage** waste oil

résiduaire [rezidɥɛr] ADJ residuary

résiduel, -elle [rezidɥɛl] ADJ **1** *(qui constitue un résidu → huile, matière)* residual **2** *(persistant → chômage)* residual; **fatigue résiduelle** constant tiredness **3** *Géog* **relief r.** residual relief

résignation [reziɲasjɔ̃] NF **1** *(acceptation)* resignation, resignedness; **accepter son destin avec r.** to accept one's fate resignedly *or* with resignation **2** *Jur* abandonment (of a right)

résigné, -e [reziɲe] ADJ resigned (**à** to); **prendre un air r.** to look resigned; **parler d'un ton r.** to speak in a resigned *or* philosophical tone of voice; **je suis r.** I've resigned myself

NM,F resigned person; **les résignés** people who have accepted their fate

résigner [3] [reziɲe] VT *(se démettre de)* to resign, to relinquish

▶**se résigner** VPR **1** *(se soumettre)* **il n'a jamais voulu se r.** he would never give up *or* in, he would never submit; **il faut se r.** you must resign yourself to it *or* accept it

2 **se r. à** *(accepter)* to resign oneself to; **il s'est résigné à vivre dans la pauvreté** he has resigned himself to living in poverty; **se r. à une perte** to resign oneself to a loss

résiliable [reziljabl] ADJ *Jur (bail, contrat, marché)* cancellable, terminable, voidable; **non r.** indefeasible

résiliation [reziljasjɔ̃] NF *Jur (d'un bail, d'un contrat, d'un marché → en cours)* cancellation, avoidance; *(→ arrivant à expiration)* termination

résilience [reziljɑ̃s] NF resilience; **r. d'impact** impact toughness *or* strength

résilient, -e [reziljɑ̃, -ɑ̃t] ADJ resilient

résilier [9] [rezilje] VT *(bail, contrat, marché → en cours)* to cancel; *(→ arrivant à expiration)* to terminate

résille [rezij] NF **1** *(à cheveux)* hairnet **2** *(d'un vitrail)* cames, leading, leads

résine [rezin] NF *Bot & Tech* resin; **r. époxyde** *ou* **epoxy** epoxy resin; **r. synthétique** synthetic resin; **r. thermodurcissable** thermosetting resin; **r. vinylique** vinyl resin

résiné, -e [rezine] ADJ resinated

NM resinated wine

résiner [3] [rezine] VT **1** *(enduire)* to resin **2** *(gemmer)* to tap

résineux, -euse [rezinø, -øz] ADJ **1** *(essence, odeur)* resinous **2** *(arbre, bois)* resiniferous, coniferous

NM conifer

résinier, -ère [rezinje, -ɛr] ADJ *(industrie)* resin *(avant n)*; *(produit)* resin-based

NM,F (resin) tapper

résinifère [rezinifɛr] ADJ *(arbre)* resiniferous; **canal r.** resin duct *or* canal

résipiscence [resipisɑ̃s] NF *Littéraire* resipiscence; **venir à r.** to see the error of one's ways

résistance [rezistɑ̃s] NF **1** *(combativité)* resistance (**à** to); **la r. de l'armée** resistance by the troops, the troops' resistance; **n'offrir aucune r.** to put up *or* offer no resistance; **elle a opposé une r. farouche à ses agresseurs** she put up a fierce resistance to her attackers; **il s'est laissé emmener sans r.** he let himself be taken away quietly *or* without resistance; **je sens une r. de sa part quand j'essaie de lui en parler** I can feel a reluctance on his/her part to talk about it; *Mktg* **r. des consommateurs** consumer resistance

2 *(rébellion)* resistance; **r. active/passive** active/passive resistance; **faire de la r. passive** to engage in passive resistance; *Hist* **la R.** the (French) Resistance; **il est entré dans la R. dès 1940** he joined the Resistance as early as 1940

3 *(obstacle)* resistance; **son projet n'a pas rencontré de r.** his/her project met no opposition *or* was unopposed; **venir à bout de toutes**

les résistances to overcome all obstacles or all resistance; **en fermant le tiroir j'ai senti une r.** when I shut the drawer I felt some resistance

4 (robustesse) resistance, stamina; **elle a sur-vécu grâce à sa r. exceptionnelle** she survived thanks to her great powers of resistance; **r. à la fatigue/au froid** resistance to tiredness/cold; **les limites de la r. humaine** the limits of human resistance or endurance

5 Tech (solidité) resistance, strength; (propriété physique) resistance; **r. aux chocs** resilience; **r. à la traction/à la flexion** tensile/bending strength; **la r. d'un pont/d'une poutre** the resistance of a bridge/beam; **r. des maté-riaux** strength of materials; **acier à haute r.** high-resistance or high-tensile steel; **r. de l'air** air resistance

6 Élec resistance; (dispositif chauffant) element; (conducteur) resistor; **quelle est l'unité de r. en électricité?** what's the unit of electrical resistance?

7 Psy resistance

LA RÉSISTANCE

This underground anti-German movement was created after the French–German armistice, in 1940, and gained in momentum after General de Gaulle's radio call from London on 18 June of the same year. The movement won the active support of the French Communist Party after German troops invaded the USSR. In his ambition to impose himself as the leader of a united resistance movement, General de Gaulle integrated all major clandestine groups into the "Conseil national de la Résistance". In May 1943, he created the French Committee of National Liberation in Algeria, which later became the provisional government for France in 1944.

Papy fait de la résistance

This is the title of a very popular French comedy film released in 1983 by director Jean-Marie Poiré. It is set during the Nazi occupation of France and tells the story of an apparently completely ordinary family who turn out to be secret Resistance fighters. The title, which means "Grandad is a Resistance fighter", can be adapted to suit most contexts where people are fighting back or resisting change. For instance, if the national football squad triumphs after losing several games, you may read **Les Bleus font de la résistance** ("The French team fight back") in the press. Or if workers are fighting the closure of their company, it is more than likely that some papers will use the headline **Les employés font de la résistance** ("The workers are fighting back").

résistant, -e [rezistã, -ãt] **ADJ 1** (personne) resistant, tough; (plante) hardy; (emballage) resistant, strong, solid; (couleur) fast; **c'est une enfant peu résistante** she's not a very strong child; **nos soldats sont résistants, bien entraînés** our soldiers are tough and well-trained

2 Élec & Phys resistant; **r. au froid/gel** cold/frost resistant; **r. aux chocs** shockproof; **r. à la chaleur** heatproof, heat-resistant

NM,F freedom fighter; Hist (en France) (French) Resistance fighter

résister [3] [reziste] **résister à VT IND 1** (agresseur, attaque) to resist, to hold out against; (autorité) to resist, to stand up to; (gendarme, huissier) to put up resistance to; (pression) to resist; **il a résisté aux officiers venus l'arrêter** he resisted arrest; **il n'a pas pu r. au courant** he couldn't fight against the current; **j'ai toujours résisté à ses caprices** I've always stood up to or opposed his/her whims; **je ne peux pas lui r., il est si gentil** I can't resist him, he's so nice

2 (fatigue, faim) to withstand, to put up with; (maladie, épidémie) to overcome; (solitude, douleur) to stand, to withstand; **r. à la tentation** to resist temptation; **r. à ses désirs/penchants** to fight against one's desires/inclinations

3 (à l'usure, à l'action des éléments) to withstand, to resist, to be proof against; **qui résiste**

au feu fireproof; **qui résiste à la chaleur** heatproof; **qui résiste aux chocs** shockproof; **r. au temps** to stand the test of time; **couleurs qui résistent au lavage** fast colours; **la porte a résisté à ma poussée** the door wouldn't open when I pushed it

4 (sujet: livre, projet) to stand up to; **r. à l'ana-lyse/l'examen** to stand up to analysis/investiga-tion; **son œuvre ne résistera pas à la critique** his/her work won't stand up to criticism

USAGE ABSOLU toute la famille a résisté (a fait partie de la Résistance) the whole family fought in the Resistance; **je n'ai pas pu r., je les ai achetés** I couldn't resist them so I bought them; **la serrure résiste** the lock is sticking; **la toiture/théière n'a pas résisté** the roof/teapot didn't stand up to the shock

résistible [rezistibl] **ADJ** Littéraire resistible

résistivité [rezistivite] **NF** Élec resistivity, specific resistance

résistor [rezistɔr] **NM** Élec resistor

resituer [7] [rǝsitɥe] **VT** to place (dans in); **il faut r. cet événement dans son contexte** the event needs to be placed or put into context

resocialisation [rǝsɔsjalizasjɔ̃] **NF** (d'un délin-quant, malade mental etc) reintegration into society

resocialiser [3] [rǝsɔsjalize] **VT** (délinquant, ma-lade mental etc) to reintegrate into society

résolu, -e [rezɔly] **PP** voir **résoudre**

ADJ 1 (personne) resolute, determined; **d'un air r.** determinedly, with an air of determin-ation, resolutely; **il m'a paru plutôt r.** he looked quite determined to me; **je suis r. à ne pas céder** I'm determined not to give in **2** (attitude) **une foi résolue en l'avenir** an unshakeable faith in the future

résoluble [rezɔlybl] **ADJ 1** (question, situation) soluble, solvable; **le problème est aisément r.** the problem is easy to solve or can be solved easily **2** Jur (bail, contrat) annullable, cancel-lable

résolument [rezɔlymã] **ADV 1** (fermement) reso-lutely, firmly, determinedly; **je m'oppose r. à cette décision** I'm strongly or firmly opposed to this decision **2** (vaillamment) resolutely, stead-fastly, unwaveringly

résolut etc voir **résoudre**

résolutif, -ive [rezɔlytif, -iv] **ADJ** (médicament, substance) resolvent

NM resolvent

résolution [rezɔlysjɔ̃] **NF 1** (décision) resolution; **prendre une r.** to make a resolution; **prendre la r. de faire qch** to make up one's mind or to resolve to do sth; **sa r. est prise** his/her mind is made up; **bonnes résolutions** (gén) good intentions; (du nouvel an) New Year resolu-tions

2 (détermination) determination, resolve, single-mindedness; **avec r.** resolutely, deter-minedly; **elle a fait preuve de beaucoup de r.** she showed great determination or resolution or resolve

3 (solution) solution, resolution; **la r. d'une énigme/d'un problème** the solution to an en-igma/a problem

4 Pol resolution; **prendre une r.** to pass a reso-lution; **la r. a été votée à l'unanimité par l'As-semblée** the resolution was unanimously adopted by the Assembly

5 Jur (d'un contrat) annulment, cancellation

6 Ordinat & TV (d'un écran) resolution; **mau-vaise/bonne r.** poor/high resolution; **écran à haute r.** high-resolution screen

7 Chim & Mus resolution

8 Méd resolution; **r. des membres** muscular relaxation

9 Opt **pouvoir de r.** resolving power

résolutive [rezɔlytiv] voir **résolutif**

résolutoire [rezɔlytwar] **ADJ** Jur resolutive

résolvait etc voir **résoudre**

résolvante [rezɔlvãt] **NF** Math resolvant equation

résonance [rezɔnãs] **NF 1** (gén) & Phys & Tél resonance; **entrer en r.** to start resonating; Fig **avoir une r. ou des résonances (dans)** to find an echo (in); **sa déclaration a eu quelque r. dans la classe politique** his/her statement found an echo or had a certain effect amongst politicians; **ces images éveillèrent en lui une**

étrange r. these pictures touched a chord deep within him/her; **r. magnétique** magnetic res-onance; **r. magnétique nucléaire** nuclear magnetic resonance

2 Littéraire (tonalité) connotation, colouring (UNCOUNT); **un poème de Donne aux résonan-ces très modernes** a poem by Donne with very modern overtones; **ce mot prend une r. toute particulière dans ce contexte** in this context, the word has particular connotations

résonant, -e [rezonã, -ãt] = **résonnant**

résonateur [rezonatœr] **NM** Phys resonator

résonnant, -e [rezonã, -ãt] **ADJ** (gén) & Phys resonant; **r. de cris** resounding or echoing with cries

resonner [3] [rǝsone] **VT** Belg (rappeler au télé-phone) to call or phone back; Br to ring back

résonner [3] [rezone] **VI 1** (sonner) to resonate, to resound; **sa voix résonnait dans les hauts-parleurs** his/her voice blared out or boomed out over the loudspeakers; **la cloche résonne faiblement** the bell rings feebly

2 (renvoyer le son) to resound, to be resonant; **la pièce résonne** sound reverberates or echoes in the room; **ça résonne!** there's an echo, it echoes!; **la halle résonnait des cris des ven-deurs** the hall resounded or echoed or rever-berated with the cries of the traders

résorbable [rezɔrbabl] **ADJ 1** Méd resorbable **2** (qui peut être éliminé) **un surplus difficilement r.** a surplus (which is) difficult to reduce or to absorb

résorber [3] [rezɔrbe] **VT 1** (éliminer → chômage, inflation, déficit) to reduce, to bring down, to curb; (→ dettes) to wipe out, to clear; (→ excé-dent) to absorb **2** Méd to resorb

▸**se résorber VPR 1** (chômage, inflation, déficit) to be reduced; (excédent) to be absorbed; **la crise ne va pas se r. toute seule** the crisis isn't going to just disappear **2** Méd to be resorbed

résorcine [rezɔrsin] **NF** Chim resorcin

résorcinol [rezɔrsinɔl] **NM** Chim resorcinol

résorption [rezɔrpsjɔ̃] **NF 1** (de l'inflation, du chômage, d'un déficit) curbing, reduction; (de dettes) clearing, wiping out; **la r. des excédents prendra plusieurs années** it will take several years for the surplus to be absorbed **2** Méd resorption

résoudre [88] [rezudr] **VT 1** (querelle, conflit) to settle, to resolve; (crise) to solve, to resolve; (énigme, mystère) to solve; (difficulté) to re-solve, to sort out; (problème) to solve, to re-solve; **le problème a été résolu en cinq minutes/après des années** the problem was solved in five minutes/was resolved over the years; **non résolu** unresolved

2 Math to resolve; **r. une équation** to solve an equation; **r. une parenthèse** to remove the brackets

3 (décider) to decide (on); **ils ont résolu sa perte** they decided on his/her ruin; **r. de faire qch** to decide to do sth; **je résolus finalement de rentrer chez moi** in the end I decided to go back home

4 (entraîner) **r. qn à faire qch** to induce or to move sb to do sth

5 Chim, Méd & Mus to resolve (**en** into)

6 Jur (bail, contrat) to annul, to avoid

▸**se résoudre VPR 1** Méd to resolve; **la tumeur s'est résolue lentement** the tumour slowly re-solved itself

2 se r. à faire qch (se résigner à) to resign or reconcile oneself to doing sth; **il faudra te r. à voir tout le monde** you'll just have to see everyone whether you like it or not; **je ne peux m'y r.** I can't bring myself to do it

3 se r. à (consister en) to amount to, to result in; **son aide se résout à peu de chose** his/her help amounts to little (in the end)

4 Chim **se r. à** to resolve itself (**en** into)

respect [rɛspɛ] **NM** (estime) respect (**pour** for); **avec r.** with respect, respectfully; **faire qch par r. pour qn** to do sth out of respect or regard for sb; **r. de soi** self-respect; **elle m'inspire beau-coup de r.** I have a great deal of respect for her; **élevé dans le r. des traditions** brought up to respect traditions; **avoir du r. pour qn** to re-spect sb, to have respect for sb; **avoir le r. des lois/des convenances** to respect or have

respect for *or* have regard for the law/the conventions; **r. du droit** observance of the law; **r. des droits de l'homme** respect for human rights; **manquer de r. à qn** to be disrespectful to sb; **marquer son r. à qn** to show respect to sb; **avec (tout)** *ou* **sauf le r. que je vous dois** with all due respect; **sauf votre r.** with respect; **tenir qn en r.** to keep sb at bay *or* at a (respectful) distance; **il nous tenait en r. avec un couteau** he kept us back *or* at bay with a knife

▫ **respects** NMPL respects, regards; **présenter ses respects à qn** to present one's respects to sb; **mes respects à madame votre mère** please give my respects to your mother

respectabiliser [3] [rɛspɛktabilize] VT to make respectable

respectabilité [rɛspɛktabilite] NF respectability

respectable [rɛspɛktabl] ADJ **1** *(estimable)* respectable, deserving of respect; *Hum* respectable; *Hum* **c'est une dame fort r.!** she's a real pillar of society! **2** *(important)* respectable; **un nombre r. de manifestants** a respectable *or* fair number of demonstrators; *Sport* **avec une avance r.** with an impressive lead; *Hum* **une calvitie r.** a fair-sized bald patch

respecter [4] [rɛspɛkte] VT **1** *(honorer → personne)* to respect, to have *or* to show respect for; **dans le pays, tout le monde le respecte** everyone respects him in our country; **il a un nom respecté dans notre ville** his name is held in respect in our city; **elle sait se faire r.** she commands respect; **il faut savoir se faire r. dans son travail** you have to earn people's respect at work; **il n'a pas su se faire r.** he was unable to gain respect

2 *(se conformer à)* to respect, to keep to; **si les formes sont respectées, vous obtiendrez ce que vous voulez** if the conventions are adhered to *or* respected, you'll get what you want; **r. les dernières volontés de qn** to abide by sb's last wishes; **r. les délais de livraison** to meet delivery schedules; **r. l'ordre alphabétique** to keep to alphabetical order; **r. la parole donnée** to keep one's word; **vous n'avez pas respecté la priorité** *(sur la route)* you didn't *Br* give way *or Am* yield; **r. les lois** to respect *or* to obey the law; **faire r. la loi** to enforce the law

3 *(ne pas porter atteinte à)* to show respect for; **les jeunes d'aujourd'hui ne respectent plus rien** today's young people do not show any respect for anything; **r. la tranquillité/le repos de qn** to respect sb's need for peace and quiet/rest; *Vieilli* **r. une femme** to respect a woman's honour

▸**se respecter** VPR **1** *(soi-même)* to respect oneself; **il s'est toujours respecté** he's always had self-respect *or* self-esteem; **elle ne se respecte plus** she's lost all her self-respect; **une chanteuse qui se respecte ne prend pas de micro** no self-respecting singer would use a microphone; **comme tout enseignant qui se respecte** like any self-respecting teacher

2 *(mutuellement)* to respect each other

respectif, -ive [rɛspɛktif, -iv] ADJ respective; **nous sommes rentrés dans nos foyers respectifs** we went back to our respective homes

respectivement [rɛspɛktivmɑ̃] ADV respectively; **Paul et Jean sont âgés r. de trois et cinq ans** Paul and Jean are three and five years old respectively

respectueuse [rɛspɛktɥøz] *voir* **respectueux**

respectueusement [rɛspɛktɥøzmɑ̃] ADV respectfully, with respect; **puis-je vous faire r. remarquer que vous vous êtes trompé?** may I respectfully point out that you have made a mistake?

respectueux, -euse [rɛspɛktɥø, -øz] ADJ **1** *(personne)* respectful; **se montrer r. envers qn** to be respectful to sb; **être r. de** to be respectful of; **r. des lois** law-abiding

2 *(lettre, salut)* respectful; **prendre un ton r. pour parler à qn** to adopt a respectful tone towards sb; *Fig* **se tenir à distance respectueuse** to keep a respectful distance

3 *(dans des formules de politesse)* **je vous prie d'agréer mes respectueuses salutations** *(à quelqu'un dont on connaît le nom) Br* yours sincerely, *Am* sincerely (yours); *(à quelqu'un dont on ne connaît pas le nom) Br* yours faithfully, *Am* sincerely (yours)

▫ **respectueuse** NF *Fam Euph* lady of the night

respirable [rɛspirabl] ADJ **1** *(qu'on peut respirer)* breathable; **l'air est difficilement r. ici** it's hard to breathe in here **2** *Fig (supportable)* **l'ambiance du bureau est à peine r.** the atmosphere at the office is almost unbearable

respirateur [rɛspiratœr] NM **1** *(masque)* gas mask, respirator **2** *Méd (poumon d'acier)* iron lung; *(à insufflation)* positive pressure respirator; **r. artificiel** respirator, ventilator

respiration [rɛspirasjɔ̃] NF **1** *Physiol (action)* breathing, *Spéc* respiration; *(résultat)* breath; **reprendre sa r.** to get one's breath back; **retenir sa r.** to hold one's breath; **avoir la r. difficile** *ou* **des difficultés de r.** to have trouble *or* difficulty breathing; *aussi Fig* **j'en ai eu la r. coupée** it took my breath away; *Méd* **r. artificielle** artificial respiration; **pratiquer la r. artificielle sur qn** to give sb artificial respiration; *Méd* **r. assistée** assisted respiration; *Psy* **r. consciente** rebirthing; *Méd* **r. contrôlée** controlled respiration

2 *(de plante)* respiration

3 *Mus* phrasing

respiratoire [rɛspiratwar] ADJ *(organe)* respiratory; *(appareil, exercice, problème)* breathing *(avant n)*; *Méd* **défaillance r.** respiratory failure; *Méd* **difficultés respiratoires** difficulty in breathing; *Bot* **quotient r.** respiratory quotient; *Méd* **troubles respiratoires** breathing *or* respiratory problems; *Anat* **voies respiratoires** respiratory tract

respirer [3] [rɛspire] VI **1** *Physiol* to breathe; **ça l'empêche de r.** it prevents him/her from breathing; **il a du mal à r., il respire avec difficulté** he has difficulty breathing, he's breathing with difficulty; **r. par la bouche/le nez** to breathe through one's mouth/nose; **respirez à fond, expirez!** breathe in, and (breathe) out!

2 *(plante, peau, vin)* to breathe

3 *(être rassuré)* to breathe again; **il est sauf, je respire** he's safe, I can breathe again; **ouf, je respire!** phew, thank goodness for that!

4 *(faire une pause)* **du calme, laissez-moi r.!** give me a break!; **on n'a jamais cinq minutes pour r.** you can't even take a breather for five minutes

VT **1** *Physiol* to breathe (in), *Spéc* to inhale; *(sentir → fleur, parfum)* to smell

2 *(exprimer)* to radiate, to exude; **elle respire la santé** she radiates good health; **il respire le bonheur** he's the very picture of happiness; **la maison respire la douceur de vivre** the whole house is bathed in *or* alive with the joy of living

resplendir [32] [rɛsplɑ̃dir] VI *Littéraire* **1** *(étinceler → casque, chaussure)* to gleam, to shine; **r. de propreté** to be spotlessly clean; **la mer resplendit au soleil** the sea is glinting in the sun **2** *(s'épanouir)* **son visage resplendit de bonheur** his/her face is shining *or* radiant with happiness; **les jeunes mariés resplendissent de joie** the newlyweds are radiant with joy

resplendissant, -e [rɛsplɑ̃disɑ̃, -ɑ̃t] ADJ **1** *(éclatant → meuble, parquet)* shining; *(→ casserole, émail)* gleaming; *(→ soleil, temps)* glorious **2** *(radieux)* resplendent, radiant; **tu as une mine resplendissante** you look radiant; **r. de santé** radiant *or* blooming with health; **r. de joie** radiant with joy; **une femme d'une beauté resplendissante** a radiantly beautiful woman

resplendissement [rɛsplɑ̃dismɑ̃] NM *Littéraire* resplendence, radiance

responsabilisation [rɛspɔ̃sabilizasjɔ̃] NF **développer la r. des jeunes** to make young people aware of their responsibilities

responsabiliser [3] [rɛspɔ̃sabilize] VT **1** *(donner des responsabilités à)* **tu ne le responsabilises pas assez** you don't give him enough responsibility **2** *(rendre conscient de ses responsabilités)* **r. qn** to make sb aware of their responsibilities

responsabilité [rɛspɔ̃sabilite] NF **1** *(obligation morale)* responsibility (**de** for); **nous déclinons toute r. en cas de vol** we take no responsibility in the event of theft; **c'est une grosse r.!** it's a big responsibility!; **prends tes responsabilités!** face up to your responsibilities!; **fuir les responsabilités** to evade *or* avoid responsibility; **faire porter la r. de qch à qn** to hold sb responsible for sth; **ils ont une r. morale vis-à-vis de nous** they have a moral obligation towards us; **assumer entièrement la r. de qch** to take on *or* to shoulder the entire responsibility for sth; **faire qch sous sa propre r.** to do sth on one's own responsibility

2 *(charge administrative)* function, position; **des responsabilités gouvernementales/ministérielles** a post in the government/cabinet; **il a accepté de nouvelles responsabilités au sein de notre compagnie** he took on new responsibilities within our company; **démis de ses responsabilités** relieved of his responsibilities *or* position; **avoir un poste à responsabilités** to have a responsible job; **elle a la r. du département publicité** she's in charge of the advertising department

3 *Jur* liability, responsibility (**de** for); *(acte moral)* responsibility; **r. des agents publics** personal liability of civil servants; **r. atténuée** diminished responsibility; **r. civile** *(d'un individu)* civil liability, strict liability; *(d'une société)* business liability; **être assuré r. civile** to have personal liability insurance; **r. collective** collective responsibility; **r. conjointe et solidaire** joint and several liability; **r. contractuelle/délictuelle** contractual/negligent liability; **r. de l'employeur** employer's liability; **r. (sociale) de l'entreprise** corporate responsibility; **r. du fabricant** manufacturer's liability; **r. du fait d'autrui** ≃ parental liability; **r. du fait des choses** = liability for objects in one's custody; **r. du fait du fonctionnement défectueux de la justice** liability for miscarriage of justice; **r. du fait des produits défectueux** liabilty for faulty products; **r. illimitée** unlimited liability; **r. limitée** limited liability; **r. pénale** legal responsibility; **r. pénale pour autrui** third-party legal liability; **r. pénale du chef d'entreprise** manager's legal liability; *Mktg* **r. du produit** product liability; **r. au tiers** third-party liability

4 *(rapport causal)* **la r. du tabac dans les affections respiratoires a été démontrée** it has been proved that smoking is the main contributing factor in respiratory diseases

responsable [rɛspɔ̃sabl] ADJ **1** *(garant)* responsible (**de** for); **j'en suis r.** I'm responsible for it; **les parents sont légalement responsables de leurs enfants** parents are legally responsible for their children; *Jur* **il n'est pas r. de ses actes** he cannot be held responsible for his (own) actions

2 *(chargé)* in charge (**de** of), responsible (**de** for); **il est r. du service après-vente** he's in charge of the after-sales department

3 *(à l'origine)* responsible (**de** for); **tenir qn/qch pour r. de qch** to hold sb/sth responsible for sth; **on l'a toujours considéré comme r. de nos problèmes** he has always been considered responsible for our problems; **l'abus des graisses animales est largement r. des affections cardiaques** the main contributing factor to heart disease is over-consumption of animal fats; **il est r. de l'accident** he is responsible for (causing) the accident

4 *Jur* liable; **r. civilement** liable in civil law

5 *Pol* **le ministre est r. devant le Parlement** the Minister is responsible *or* answerable *or* accountable to Parliament

6 *(réfléchi)* responsible; **ce n'est pas très r. de sa part** that isn't very responsible of him/her; **elle s'est toujours comportée en personne r.** she has always acted responsibly

NMF **1** *(coupable)* person responsible *or* to blame (**de** for); **qui est le r. de l'accident?** who's responsible for the accident?; **nous retrouverons les responsables** we will find the people *or* those responsible; **il n'y a jamais de responsables!** nobody is ever to blame!

2 *(dirigeant → politique)* leader; *(→ d'une société)* manager; *(→ d'un service)* head; **parler avec les responsables politiques** to speak with the political leaders; **réunion avec les responsables syndicaux** meeting with the union representatives *or* officials; **je veux parler au r.** I want to speak to the person in charge; **r. de** *ou*

du budget account executive; **r. commercial** business manager; **r. des comptes-clients** account handler; **r. d'événements** event manager; **r. (du) marketing** marketing manager; **r. politique** political leader; **r. produit** product manager; **r. des relations publiques** public relations officer; **r. syndical** union official

resquillage [rɛskijaʒ] NM *Fam (sans payer)* sneaking in; *(dans l'autobus, dans le métro etc)* fare-dodging; *(sans attendre son tour) Br* queue-jumping, *Am* line-jumping

resquille [rɛskij] NF = **resquillage**

resquiller [3] [rɛskije] *Fam* VI *(ne pas payer)* to sneak in; *(dans l'autobus, dans le métro etc)* to dodge the fare; *(ne pas attendre son tour)* to push in, *Br* to jump the queue, *Am* to cut in the line

VT to fiddle, to wangle; **r. une place pour le concert** to fiddle *or* to wangle oneself a seat for the concert

resquilleur, -euse [rɛskijœr, -øz] NM,F *Fam (qui ne paie pas)* = person who sneaks in without paying; *(dans l'autobus, dans le métro etc)* fare-dodger; *(qui n'attend pas son tour) Br* queue-jumper, *Am* line-jumper

ressac [rəsak] NM backwash *(of a wave)*

ressaigner [4] [rəseɲe] VI to bleed again

ressaisir [32] [rəsezir] VT **1** *(agripper de nouveau)* to catch *or* to grab again, to seize again; **le chien ressaisit sa proie** the dog got hold of *or* caught his prey again; *Fig* **la peur l'a ressaisi** fear gripped him again

2 *(occasion)* to seize again

3 *Ordinat* to rekey

▶**se ressaisir** VPR *(se calmer)* to pull oneself together; **ressaisis-toi!** pull yourself together!, get a hold of *or* a grip on yourself!; **il s'est ressaisi et a finalement gagné le deuxième set** he recovered *or* rallied and finally won the second set; **heureusement, elle s'est ressaisie au second trimestre** luckily, she improved *or* made more of an effort in the second term

ressaisissement [rəsezismɑ̃] NM *Littéraire* recovery of one's self-possession

ressasser [3] [rəsase] VT **1** *(répéter)* to go *or* harp on about; **r. les exploits de sa jeunesse** to go *or* to harp on about one's youthful exploits; **les mêmes histoires ressassées l'amusent toujours** he's/she's still amused by the same worn-out old stories **2** *(repenser à)* to turn over in one's mind

ressat [rəsa] NM *Suisse* **1** *(à la fin des vendanges)* = celebratory meal to mark the end of harvest **2** *(banquet)* wine-producer's banquet

ressaut [rəso] NM **1** *Géog* rise; *(en alpinisme)* step, projection **2** *Constr (en saillie)* step; *(en recul)* offset; **faire r.** to jut out **3** *(niveau des eaux)* jump

ressauter [3] [rəsote] VT *(barrière)* to jump again; **le cavalier revint sur ses pas et ressauta l'obstacle** the rider retraced his steps and jumped over the fence again

VI to jump again; **tous les enfants ont ressauté dans l'eau en même temps** all the children jumped into the water again at the same time

ressayage [resejaʒ] = **réessayage**

ressayer [reseje] = **réessayer**

ressemblance [rəsɑ̃blɑ̃s] NF **1** *(entre êtres humains)* likeness, resemblance; **la r. entre la mère et la fille est étonnante** mother and daughter look amazingly alike; **il y a une r. entre les deux cousins** the two cousins look alike; **il y a quelques ressemblances entre eux** they resemble each other in a few respects, there are a few points of similarity *or* likeness between them; **toute r. avec des personnes existantes ou ayant existé ne peut être que fortuite** *(dans un film)* any resemblance to persons living or dead is purely accidental

2 *(entre choses)* similarity; **il existe une certaine r. entre les deux livres** both books are somehow similar; **il n'y a aucune r. entre ta situation et la mienne** there's no similarity *or* comparison between your situation and mine

ressemblant, -e [rəsɑ̃blɑ̃, -ɑ̃t] ADJ *(photo, portrait)* true to life, lifelike; **ta photo n'est pas très ressemblante** your photo doesn't look like you; **elle est très ressemblante sur le dessin** the drawing really looks like her

ressembler [3] [rəsɑ̃ble] **ressembler à** VT IND **1** *(avoir la même apparence que)* to resemble, to look like; **il ressemble à sa mère** he looks like his mother, *Sout* he favours his mother; **elle me ressemble un peu** she looks a bit like me; **ça ne ressemble en rien à une maison** that doesn't look like a house at all; **la moustache le fait r. à son père** his moustache makes him look like his father; **à quoi ressemble-t-elle?** what's she like?, what does she look like?

2 *(avoir la même nature que)* to resemble, to be like; **il a toujours cherché à r. à son père** he always tried to be like his father; **je n'ai rien qui ressemble à une tenue de soirée** I have nothing that you could even vaguely call evening wear

3 *Fam (locutions)* **ça ne ressemble à rien** *(ça ne veut rien dire)* it makes no sense at all; *(c'est laid)* it looks like nothing on earth; **ça ne ressemble à rien de ne pas vouloir venir** there's no sense in not wanting to come; **à quoi ça ressemble de quitter la réunion sans même s'excuser?** what's the idea *or* meaning of leaving the meeting without even apologizing?; **cela ne me/te/leur ressemble pas** that's not like me/you/them; **ça lui ressemble bien d'oublier mon anniversaire** it's just like him/her to forget my birthday

▶**se ressembler** VPR **1** *(emploi réciproque)* to look alike, to resemble each other; **ils se ressemblent** they look alike *or* like each other; **tous les amoureux se ressemblent** all lovers are alike, lovers are all alike; **se r. comme deux gouttes d'eau** to be like two peas (in a pod); *Prov* **qui se ressemble s'assemble** birds of a feather flock together

2 *(emploi réfléchi)* **depuis sa maladie, il ne se ressemble plus** he's not been himself since his illness

ressemelage [rəsəmlaʒ] NM *(action)* soling, resoling; *(nouvelle semelle)* new sole

ressemeler [24] [rəsəmle] VT to sole, to resole

ressemer [19] [rəsəme] VT *(graine, champ)* to resow, to sow again

ressens *etc voir* **ressentir**

ressentiment [rəsɑ̃timɑ̃] NM resentment, ill will; **éprouver du r. à l'égard de qn** to feel resentment against sb, to feel resentful towards sb; **je n'ai aucun r. à ton égard** I don't bear you any resentment *or* ill will; **c'est un homme aigri, plein de r.** he's embittered and full of resentment

ressentir [37] [rəsɑ̃tir] VT **1** *(éprouver → bienfait, douleur, haine)* to feel; **j'ai ressenti la même impression que vous quand je l'ai vu** I felt the same way you did *or* I had the same feeling as you when I saw him; **je ne ressens aucune tendresse pour elle** I don't feel any affection for her

2 *(être affecté par)* to feel, to be affected by; **il a ressenti très vivement la perte de son père** he was deeply affected by his father's death; **j'ai ressenti ses propos comme une véritable insulte** I felt *or* was extremely insulted by his/her remarks

▶**se ressentir** VPR **1 se r. de** to feel the effect of; **je me ressens encore des suites de mon accident** I still feel *or* I'm still suffering from the effects of my accident; **la production a été accélérée et la qualité s'en ressent** they've speeded up production at the expense of quality; **elle est inquiète et son travail s'en ressent** she's worried and it shows in her work

2 *Fam* **s'en r. pour** to feel fit for, to feel up to

resserre [rəsɛr] NF *(à outils)* shed, outhouse; *(à produits)* storeroom; *(à provisions)* store cupboard, larder

resserré, -e [rəsere] ADJ *(étroit)* narrow

resserrement [rəsɛrmɑ̃] NM **1** *(d'une route → contraction)* narrowing; *(→ passage étroit)* narrow part; **il y a un r. de la route après le pont** the road narrows after the bridge

2 *(d'un nœud, d'un boulon)* tightening

3 *(limitation)* tightening; *Écon* **r. du crédit** credit squeeze; **r. monétaire** monetary squeeze

4 *(renforcement → d'un lien affectif, d'une amitié)* strengthening; *(→ de la discipline)* tightening (up)

5 *(des pores)* closing

resserrer [4] [rəsere] VT **1** *(nœud, boulon → serrer de nouveau)* to retighten, to tighten again; *(→ serrer davantage)* to tighten up; **resserre-le** tighten it (up)

2 *(renforcer → lien affectif, amitié)* to strengthen; *(→ discipline)* to tighten (up)

3 *(fermer)* to close (up); **pour r. les pores** to close *or* tighten the pores

4 *(diminuer → texte, exposé)* to condense, to compress

▶**se resserrer** VPR **1** *(devenir plus étroit)* to narrow; **la route se resserre après le village** the road narrows past the village

2 *(se refermer → nœud, boulon)* to tighten; *Fig* **les mailles du filet se resserrent** the net is closing in

3 *(devenir plus fort)* **nos relations se sont resserrées depuis l'année dernière** we have become closer (to each other) *or* our relationship has grown stronger since last year

resservir [38] [rəsɛrvir] VT **1** *(de nouveau)* to serve again; **elle nous a resservi les pâtes d'hier en gratin** she served up yesterday's pasta in a gratin

2 *(davantage)* to serve (out) some more *or* another helping; **donne-moi ton assiette, je vais te r.** give me your plate, I'll give you another helping

3 *Fam (répéter)* **il nous ressert la même excuse tous les ans** he comes out with *or* he trots out the same (old) excuse every year

VI **1** *(être utile)* **j'ai une vieille robe longue qui pourra bien r. pour l'occasion** I have an old full-length dress which would do for this occasion; **garde-le, ça pourra toujours r.** keep it, it might come in handy *or* useful again (one day)

2 *Mil & (au tennis)* to serve again

▶**se resservir** VPR **1** *(reprendre à manger)* to help oneself to some more *or* to a second helping; **ressers-toi** help yourself to (some) more; **puis-je me r.?** may I help myself to some more *or* take a second helping?; **resservez-vous du riz** help yourself to *or* have some more rice *or* another helping of rice

2 se r. de *(réutiliser)* to use again

ressors *etc voir* **ressortir**[1]

ressort [rəsɔr] NM **1** *(mécanisme)* spring; **faire r.** to act as a spring; **actionné** *ou* **mû par r.** spring-driven; **r. à boudin** coil spring; **r. hélicoïdal/spiral** helical/spiral spring; **r. à lames** leaf *or* coach spring; **r. de montre** watch spring, hairspring; **r. de sommier** bedspring

2 *(force morale)* spirit, drive; **manquer de r.** to lack drive

3 *(mobile)* motivation; **les ressorts de l'âme humaine** the deepest motivations of the human soul *or* spirit

4 *Phys (propriété)* springiness, *Spéc* elasticity

5 *(compétence)* **les problèmes qui sont de mon r.** problems I am qualified to deal with; **ce n'est pas de mon/ton r.** it is not my/your responsibility

6 *Jur* jurisdiction; **cette affaire est du r. de la cour** this case is *or* falls within the competence of the court; **juger une affaire en premier/dernier r.** to judge a case in the first instance/in a court of last resort

❑ **à ressort(s)** ADJ spring-loaded; **matelas à ressorts** spring mattress

❑ **en dernier ressort** ADV as a last resort

ressortir[1] [43] [rəsɔrtir] VT *(aux avoir)* **1** *(vêtement, ustensile)* to take out again

2 *(film)* to rerelease, to bring out again; *(pièce de théâtre)* to rerun

3 *Fam (répéter)* to trot out again; **tu ne vas pas r. cette vieille histoire?** you're not going to come out with that old story again, are you?

VI *(aux être)* **1** *(sortir à nouveau → vu de l'intérieur)* to go out again, to leave again; *(→ vu de l'extérieur)* to come out again; *(sortir → vu de l'intérieur)* to go out, to leave; *(→ vu de l'extérieur)* to come out; **je n'ai pas envie de r., il fait trop froid** I don't feel like going out again, it's too cold; **il n'est pas encore ressorti de chez le médecin** he hasn't left the doctor's yet

2 *(se détacher)* to stand out (**sur** against); **le rouge ressortira mieux** red will stand out better; **le foulard qu'elle porte fait r. ses yeux bleus** the scarf she's wearing brings out the blue of her eyes; **faire r. les avantages d'une solution** to stress *or* to highlight the advantages

res–res

of a solution; **ce rapport fait r. un certain nombre de problèmes importants** the report brings out a number of important points

3 *(réapparaître)* **la pointe est ressortie de l'autre côté du mur** the tip came through the other side of the wall; **la balle est ressortie par l'épaule** the bullet came out *or* exited through the shoulder

4 *(film)* to show again, to be rereleased; **ses films viennent de r. à Paris** his/her movies *or Br* films have just started showing again in Paris *or* have just been rereleased in Paris

5 *(chiffre, carte)* to come up again

❑ **ressortir de** VT IND to emerge *or* to flow from; **il ressort de votre analyse que les affaires vont bien** according to your analysis, business is good; **il ressort de tout cela qu'il a menti** the upshot of all this is that he's been lying

ressortir[2] [32] [rəsɔrtir] **ressortir à** VT IND **1** *Jur* to come under the jurisdiction of

2 *Littéraire (relever de)* to pertain to; **pareil sujet ressortit au roman plutôt qu'à l'essai** such a subject pertains to the novel rather than to the essay (genre)

ressortissant, -e [rəsɔrtisɑ̃, -ɑ̃t] NM,F *(d'un pays)* national; **r. d'un pays de l'Union européenne** EU national

ressouder [3] [rəsude] VT **1** *(tuyau)* to resolder, to reweld, to weld together again **2** *Fig (alliance, couple)* to bring *or* to get together again, to reunite

▸**se ressouder** VPR *(os, fracture)* to knit (again)

ressource [rəsurs] NF **1** *(secours)* recourse, resort; **tu es mon unique r.** you're the only person who can help me *or* my only hope; **elle n'a eu d'autre r. que la mendicité** there was no other course (of action) open *or* left to her but to become a beggar; **être à bout de ressources** to have exhausted all one's possibilities; **en dernière r.** as a last resort

2 *(présence d'esprit)* **un homme/une femme de r.** *ou* **ressources** a resourceful man/woman

3 *(endurance, courage)* **avoir de la r.** to have strength in reserve

4 *Aviat* flattening out, pull-out

❑ **ressources** NFPL **1** *(fonds)* funds, resources, income; **25 ans et sans ressources** 25 years old and no visible means of support; **ressources d'appoint** additional sources of income; **ressources du budget** budgetary resources; **ressources de l'État** government resources; **ressources financières** financial resources; **ressources fiscales** tax resources; **ressources personnelles** private means

2 *(réserves)* resources; **ressources humaines** human resources, personnel; **ressources naturelles/minières d'un pays** natural/mineral resources of a country; **des ressources en hommes** manpower resources

3 *(moyens)* resources, possibilities; **nous mobilisons toutes nos ressources pour retrouver les marins disparus** we're mobilizing all our resources *or* all the means at our disposal to find the missing sailors; **toutes les ressources de notre langue** all the possibilities *or* resources of our language

ressourcement [rəsursəmɑ̃] NM return to one's roots

ressourcer [16] [rəsurse] **se ressourcer** VPR **1** *(retourner aux sources)* to go back to one's roots **2** *(reprendre des forces)* to recharge one's batteries

ressouvenir [40] [rəsuvnir] **se ressouvenir** VPR *Littéraire* **se r. de** to remember, to recall; **à chaque retour dans son village natal, il se ressouvenait de son enfance** each time he returned to his home village, he would recall his childhood

ressuage [rəsɥaʒ] NM *Métal (du plomb, de l'argent)* sweating

ressuer [7] [rəsɥe] VI *Métal* **faire r.** *(plomb, argent)* to sweat

ressui [resɥi] NM *Chasse (refuge)* cover(t), refuge; **vent de r.** drying wind

ressurgir [32] [rəsyrʒir] VI **1** *(source)* to reappear **2** *(problème)* to arise again, to reoccur; **faire r. de vieux souvenirs** to bring back old memories; **cette idée ressurgit dans mon esprit** the idea suddenly came back to me

ressuscité, -e [resysite] NM,F **1** *Rel* resurrected person; **les ressuscités** those who have risen again, the risen **2** *Fig* **tu as l'air d'un r.** you look like death warmed up

ressusciter [3] [resysite] VT *(aux avoir)* **1** *Rel* to resurrect, to raise from the dead; **le Christ ressuscitera les morts** Christ will raise the dead to life

2 *(ranimer)* to resuscitate; *Méd* to bring back to life, to revive; **vos piqûres m'ont littéralement ressuscité** those injections you gave me literally brought me back to life; *Hum* **un whisky à r. les morts** whisky strong enough to bring the dead back to life; **tes larmes ne vont pas le r.** crying won't bring him back (to life); **r. une mode** to bring back a fashion

3 *Littéraire (faire ressurgir → tradition, mode)* to revive, to resurrect; **r. le passé** to summon up *or* to revive the past

VI **1** *(aux être) Rel* to rise again *or* from the dead; **le Christ est ressuscité (d'entre les morts)** Christ has risen (from the dead)

2 *(aux avoir) (revivre → sentiment, nature)* to come back to life, to revive

ressuyage [resɥijaʒ] NM *Hort* cleaning *(of vegetables for market)*

ressuyer [14] [resɥije] VT **1** *(faire sécher)* to dry; *Vieilli ou Littéraire* **le soleil a ressuyé la route, la route s'est ressuyée au soleil** the sun has dried the road **2** *Belg (essuyer)* to wipe, to dry

restant, -e [rɛstɑ̃, -ɑ̃t] ADJ remaining; **les 5 euros restants** the remaining 5 euros, the 5 euros remaining *or* left (over); **ils se sont partagé les chocolats restants** they shared the chocolates that were left; **c'est le seul héritier r.** he's the sole remaining heir

NM *(reste)* rest, remainder; *Chim* residuary **dépenser le r. de son argent** to spend the rest of one's money *or* one's remaining money; **un r. de tissu** a leftover piece of material; **pour le r. de mes/leurs/***etc* **jours** until my/their/*etc* dying day; *Com* **r. en caisse** cash surplus

❑ **restants** NMPL *Can (de nourriture)* leftovers

restau [rɛsto] NM *Fam* restaurant▪

restaurant [rɛstɔrɑ̃] NM restaurant; **manger au r.** to eat out; **ce soir, on dîne au r.** we're eating out tonight; **ils vont souvent au r.** they often eat out; **r. d'entreprise** (staff) canteen; **r. gastronomique** gourmet restaurant; **r. routier** *Br* transport café, *Am* truck stop; **r. universitaire** university canteen *or* cafeteria *or* refectory

restaurateur, -trice [rɛstɔratœr, -tris] NM,F **1** *(d'œuvres d'art)* restorer **2** *(qui tient un restaurant)* restaurant owner, *Sout* restaurateur **3** *Littéraire (d'un régime, d'une monarchie etc)* restorer

restauration [rɛstɔrasjɔ̃] NF **1** *(d'œuvres d'art)* restoration; **la r. des vitraux a pris plusieurs années** it took several years to restore the stained-glass windows

2 *(rétablissement)* restoration; *Hist* **la R.** = the restoration of the Bourbon monarchy in France, from 1815 to 1830

3 *(hôtellerie)* catering; **dans la r.** in the restaurant trade *or* the catering industry; **la r. collective** institutional catering; **la r. rapide** the fast-food industry

4 *Ordinat* restore

restauratrice [rɛstɔratris] *voir* **restaurateur**

restaurer [3] [rɛstɔre] VT **1** *(édifice, œuvre d'art)* to restore **2** *Littéraire (rétablir → discipline, autorité)* to restore, to re-establish; **r. la paix** to restore peace **3** *Littéraire (nourrir)* to feed

▸**se restaurer** VPR to have something to eat; **nous nous arrêterons vers midi pour nous r. un peu** we'll stop around noon to have a bite to eat

restau-U [rɛstoy] *(pl* **restaus-U***)* NM *Fam* university canteen *or* cafeteria *or* refectory▪

reste [rɛst] NM **1** *(suite, fin)* rest; **il en a mangé une partie et a jeté le r.** he ate part of it and threw the rest away; **puis-je vous payer le r. à la fin du mois?** can I pay you the rest at the end of the month?; **il a dormi le r. de la journée** he slept for the rest of the day; **le r. du temps** the rest of the time; **le r. de ta vie** the rest of your life; **si vous êtes sages, je vous raconterai le r. demain** if you're good, I'll tell you the rest of the story tomorrow; **pour le r., quant au r.** as for the rest; **et (tout) le r.!** and so on (and so forth)!; **tout le r. n'est que littérature/qu'illusion** everything else is just insignificant/an illusion; **sans attendre** *ou* **demander son r.** without (any) further ado; **elle s'est enfuie sans demander son r.** she left without further ado; **j'irai encaisser le chèque sans attendre mon r.** I'll go and cash in the cheque and have done with it; **être** *ou* **demeurer en r.** to be outdone, to be at a loss

2 *(résidu → de nourriture)* food left over, leftovers (of food); *(→ de boisson)* drink left over; *(→ de tissu, de papier)* remnant, scrap; *Cin* outtakes; **il y avait un r. de beurre/lait** there was a bit of butter/milk left (over); **accommoder un r. de viande** to use up the leftover meat; **un r. de jour** *ou* **de lumière** a glimmer of daylight; **un r. de courage/d'espoir** some remnants of courage/hope; **un r. de sa gloire passée** a vestige *or* remnant of his/her past glory

3 *Math* remainder; **le r. égale cinq** the remainder is five

❑ **restes** NMPL **1** *(d'un repas)* leftovers; **on mangera les restes ce soir** we'll have the leftovers tonight; *Fig* **je ne veux pas de ses restes!** I don't want his/her leftovers!

2 *(vestiges)* remains

3 *(ossements)* (last) remains

4 *Fam (locution)* **elle a de beaux restes** she's still beautiful despite her age▪

❑ **au reste** = **du reste**

❑ **de reste** ADJ surplus *(avant n)*, spare; **vous auriez du pain de r.?** do you have any bread left (over)?, do you have any bread to spare?; **passez me voir demain, j'aurai du temps de r.** come and see me tomorrow, I'll have some spare time; **il a de la patience de r.** he has patience to spare

❑ **du reste** ADV besides, furthermore, moreover; **inutile de discuter, du r., ça ne dépend pas de moi** there's no point in arguing and, besides, it's not up to me to decide; **du r., je ne suis pas d'accord avec toi** what's more, I don't agree with you

RESTER [3] [rɛste]

> to stay **1** ▪ to remain **1, 2** ▪ to be left **2** ▪ to live **4** ▪ to die **5** ▪ to endure **6**

VI **1** *(dans un lieu, une situation)* to stay, to remain; **le dard est resté dans son doigt** the sting is still *or* has stayed in his/her finger; **c'est mieux si la voiture reste au garage** it's better if the car stays in the garage; **malgré mes efforts, la tache est restée** despite my efforts, the stain wouldn't come out; **ceci doit r. entre nous** this is strictly between me and you, this is for our ears only; **restez donc à déjeuner/dîner** do stay for lunch/dinner; **je ne reste pas** I'm not staying *or* stopping; *Fig* **savoir r. à sa place** to know one's place; **r. debout/assis** to remain standing/seated; **elle est restée debout toute la nuit** she stayed up all night; **r. paralysé** to be left paralysed; **r. fidèle à qn** to be *or* to stay faithful to sb; **r. en fonction** to remain in office; **r. dans l'ignorance** to remain in ignorance; **r. célibataire** to remain single; **r. sans rien faire** to sit around doing nothing; **elle ne reste pas en place** she never keeps still; **tu veux bien r. tranquille!** will you keep still!; **r. en contact avec qn** to keep *or* to stay in touch with sb; **je reste sur une impression désagréable** I'm left with an unpleasant impression; **je n'aime pas r. sur un échec** I don't like to stop at failure; **r. dans les mémoires** *ou* **les annales** to go down in history; **nous en sommes restés à la page 160** we left off at *or* got as far as page 160; **nous en resterons à cet accord** we will limit ourselves to *or* go no further than this agreement; **restons-en là!** let's leave it at that!; *Fam* **r. en rade** *ou* **en carafe** to be left high and dry *or* stranded; **ça m'est resté sur le cœur** it still rankles with *or* galls me; **j'y suis, j'y reste!** here I am and here I stay!

2 *(subsister)* to be left; **r. sans résultat** to remain ineffective; **c'est tout ce qui me reste** that's all I have left; **cette mauvaise habitude lui est restée** he/she still has that bad habit;

res–res

restent les deux dernières questions à traiter the last two questions still have to be dealt with; **reste à savoir qui ira** there still remains the problem of deciding who is to go

3 *(tournure impersonnelle)* **il me reste une bague de ma grand-mère** I still have a ring my grandmother left me; **il nous reste un peu de pain et de fromage** we have a little bit of bread and cheese left; **il me reste la moitié à payer** I (still) have half of it to pay; **il nous reste de quoi vivre** we have enough left to live on; **lisez beaucoup, il en restera toujours quelque chose** do a lot of reading, there will always be something to show for it *or* there's always something to be got out of it; **cinq ôté de quinze, il reste dix** five (taken away) from fifteen leaves ten; **il reste un doute** a doubt still remains; **il reste encore à examiner les points a et c** points a and c still remain to be examined; **il ne reste plus rien à faire** there's nothing left to be done; **il reste à faire l'ourlet** the hem is all that remains *or* that's left to be done; **il reste encore 12 kilomètres à faire** there's still 12 kilometres to go; **il reste que le problème de succession n'est pas réglé** the fact remains that the problem of the inheritance hasn't been solved; **il n'en reste pas moins que vous avez tort** you are nevertheless wrong; **et s'il n'en reste qu'un, je serai celui-là** and if anyone will be there at the finish, it will be me

4 *Can & (en Afrique francophone) (habiter)* to live

5 *Euph (mourir)* to meet one's end; **il est resté sur le champ de bataille** he died on the battlefield; *Fam* **y r.** to kick the bucket

6 *(durer)* to live on, to endure; **son souvenir restera** his/her memory will live on

7 *Belg* **r. faire qch** to go on *or* continue doing sth

VT *Can Fam* **être resté** to be *Br* knackered *or Am* bushed

restituable [rɛstitɥabl] **ADJ** *(somme)* repayable

restituer [7] [rɛstitɥe] **VT 1** *(rendre → bien)* to return, to restore; *(→ argent)* to refund, to return; **r. qch à qn** to return sth to sb; **elle dut r. les fonds détournés** she had to pay back *or* to return the embezzled funds

2 *(reconstituer → œuvre endommagée)* to restore, to reconstruct; *(→ ambiance)* to reconstitute, to render; **r. fidèlement les sons/les couleurs** to reproduce sounds/colours faithfully

3 *(vomir)* to bring up; **r. son repas** to bring up one's meal

restitution [rɛstitysjɔ̃] **NF 1** *(d'un bien)* return, restitution; *(d'argent)* refund; **r. d'impôts** tax refund; *Jur* **r. d'indu** return of payment made in error **2** *(d'une œuvre endommagée)* restoration; *(d'une ambiance)* reconstitution; *(d'un son, d'une couleur)* reproduction

resto [rɛsto] **NM** *Fam* restaurant; **les restos du cœur** = charity food distribution centres

Culture

LES RESTOS DU CŒUR

Set up by the comedian Coluche in 1985, the "restos du cœur" (full name, "les Restaurants du Cœur") are run by volunteers who distribute free meals to the poor and homeless, especially in the winter months.

restoroute [rɛstorut] **NM** *(sur autoroute)* ≃ *Br* motorway *or Am* freeway restaurant; *(sur route)* roadside restaurant

resto-U [rɛstoy] *(pl* **restos-U)** = **restau-U**

restreindre [81] [rɛstrɛ̃dr] **VT** *(ambition, dépense)* to restrict, to limit, to curb; *(sorties, achats)* to cut back (on), to restrict, to limit; *(consommation)* to cut down; *(budget)* to restrict; *(autorité, pouvoir)* to limit, to restrict; **r. les libertés** to restrict liberties; **en raison de son âge, il a dû r. ses activités** he had to limit his activities because of his age; **elle a dû r. ses recherches à un domaine précis** she had to limit her research to a precise field

▸**se restreindre VPR 1** *(se rationner)* to cut down; **tu ne sais pas te r.** you don't know when to stop

2 *(diminuer)* **le champ d'activités de l'entreprise s'est restreint** the company's activities have become more limited; **son cercle d'amis s'est restreint** his/her circle of friends has got smaller

restreint, -e [rɛstrɛ̃, -ɛ̃t] **ADJ 1** *(réduit)* limited; **l'espace est r.** there's not much room; **édition à tirage r.** limited edition **2** *(limité)* restricted **(à** to); **une offre restreinte aux abonnés** an offer restricted to subscribers; **la distribution de ces produits est restreinte à Paris et à sa région** these products are sold exclusively in the Paris area

restrictif, -ive [rɛstriktif, -iv] **ADJ** restrictive

restriction [rɛstriksjɔ̃] **NF 1** *(réserve)* reservation; **émettre quelques restrictions à l'égard d'un projet** to express some reservations about a project; **r. mentale** mental reservation

2 *(limitation)* restriction, limitation; **r. de la concurrence** anti-competitive practices; **r. de crédit** restriction on credit, credit squeeze

3 *Ordinat* **r. d'accès** access restriction

□ **restrictions NFPL** restrictions; **les restrictions en temps de guerre** wartime restrictions *or* austerity; **restrictions budgétaires** budget restrictions; **restrictions salariales, restrictions des salaires** wage restraint

□ **sans restriction ADV** *(entièrement)* **je vous approuve sans r.** you have my unreserved approval

restrictive [rɛstriktiv] *voir* **restrictif**

restructuration [rəstryktyrasjɔ̃] **NF 1** *(d'un quartier, d'une ville)* redevelopment **2** *(d'une société, d'un service)* restructuring, reorganization **3** *(de dette)* rescheduling

restructurer [3] [rəstryktyre] **VT** *(société, service)* to restructure, to reorganize

▸**se restructurer VPR** to be restructured

resucée [rəsyse] **NF** *Fam* **1** *(quantité supplémentaire)* **une r.** some more; **t'en prendras bien une petite r.?** will you have some more? **2** *(répétition)* rehash; **ils ne montrent que des resucées à la télévision** all they ever show on TV is (old) repeats

résultant, -e [rezyltɑ̃, -ɑ̃t] **ADJ** resulting

□ **résultante NF 1** *(résultat)* result, outcome **2** *Math & Phys* resultant

résultat [rezylta] **NM 1** *(réalisation positive)* result; **on arrive à d'excellents résultats avec ce médicament** we're getting excellent results with this drug; **sans r.** *(action)* fruitless; **j'ai essayé de le lui faire comprendre, sans r.** I tried unsuccessfully to make him/her understand; **ne donner aucun r.** to have no effect; **il n'y a pas que le r. qui compte** the (end) result is not the only important thing

2 *(aboutissement)* result, outcome; **le r. final** the end result; **voici le r. de nombreuses années de recherche** this is the result of several years of research; **son attitude a eu pour r. de rapprocher le frère et la sœur** his/her attitude led to *or* resulted in closer ties between brother and sister; **ça a eu pour r. de le mettre en colère** it made him angry, he got angry as a result

3 *Fam (introduisant une conclusion)* **il a voulu trop en faire, r., il est malade** he tried to do too much and sure enough he fell ill; **r., je n'ai toujours pas compris** so I'm still none the wiser; **r. des courses...** the upshot was..., as a result...; **r. des courses, on s'est retrouvés au poste** the whole thing ended up with us in the police station

4 *Math* result; **peux-tu me donner le r. de la soustraction?** can you give me the result of *or* the answer to the subtraction?; **j'ai le même r. que toi** I get the same result as you

5 *Pol & Sport* result; **nous avons un dernier r. en tennis** here is the latest tennis score; **r. partiel** by-election result; **r. partiel pour la Corse et les Alpes-Maritimes** by-election result for Corsica and the Alpes-Maritimes; **le r. des courses** *Sport* the racing results; *Fig* the outcome (of the situation); **r.** *ou* **résultats des courses: il a été licencié** as a result he was dismissed, the upshot of it all was that he was dismissed

6 *Compta* profit; **dégager un r.** to make a profit; **r. brut** gross return; **r. courant** profit before tax and extraordinary items; **r. économique** economic profit; **r. exceptionnel** extraordinary profit or loss; **r. de l'exercice** profit or loss for the financial year, statement of income; **r. d'exploitation** operating profit or loss; **r. final** final statement; **r. financier** financial profit or loss; **r. net** net profit; **r. de la période** profit or loss for the financial period; **résultats prévisionnels** earnings forecast

□ **résultats NMPL** *Fin, Pol & Sport* results; *Com* performance; *Scol* results, *Br* marks, *Am* grades; *Mktg* **résultats antérieurs** past performance; **les résultats de l'exercice en cours sont mauvais** the results are poor for the current (financial) year; **les résultats du Loto** the winning lottery numbers

résulter [3] [rezylte] **résulter de VT IND** to result *or* to ensue from; **il est difficile de dire ce qui en résultera** at the moment it's difficult to say what the result *or* outcome will be; **je ne sais pas ce qui en résultera** I don't know what the end result will be *or* what's going to come out of this; **le travail/souci qui en résulte** the ensuing work/worry; **il résulte de l'enquête que...** the result of the investigation shows that..., it has emerged from the investigation that...; **il en a résulté que...** the result *or* the outcome was that...

résumé [rezyme] **NM 1** *(sommaire)* summary, résumé; **faites un r. du passage suivant** write a summary *or* a précis of the following passage; **r. des épisodes précédents** the story so far

2 *(bref exposé)* summary; **faites-nous le r. de la situation** sum up *or* summarize the situation for us

3 *(ouvrage)* summary, précis

□ **en résumé ADV** *(en conclusion)* to sum up; *(en bref)* in short, in brief, briefly; **en r., nous ne sommes d'accord sur aucun des points soulevés** in short, we do not agree on any of the points raised

résumer [3] [rezyme] **VT 1** *(récapituler)* to summarize, to sum up; **je vais vous r. notre conversation** let me summarize our conversation; **voici le problème résumé en quelques chiffres** here is the problem summed up in a few figures; **résume-lui l'histoire en quelques mots** sum up the story for him/her in a few words; **voilà toute l'affaire résumée en un mot** that's the whole thing in a nutshell; **pour r. les faits** to sum up

2 *(symboliser)* to typify, to symbolize; **ce cas résume tous les autres du même genre** this case sums up all others of the same type

▸**se résumer VPR 1** *(récapituler)* to sum up; **pour me r., je dirai que nous devons être vigilants** to sum up, I would say that we must be vigilant

2 **se r. à** to come down to; **cela se résume à peu de chose** it doesn't amount to much

resurchauffe [rəsyrʃof] **NF** reheating, *Spéc* resuperheating

resurchauffer [3] [rəsyrʃofe] **VT** to reheat, *Spéc* to resuperheat

resurchauffeur [rəsyrʃofœr] **NM** reheater, resuperheating machine

résurgence [rezyrʒɑ̃s] **NF 1** *Géog* resurgence **2** *(réapparition)* resurgence, revival

résurgent, -e [rezyrʒɑ̃, -ɑ̃t] **ADJ** resurgent

resurgir [rəsyrʒir] = **ressurgir**

résurrection [rezyrɛksjɔ̃] **NF 1** *Rel* resurrection; **la R. (du Christ)** the Resurrection (of Christ); **r. de la chair** resurrection of the body

2 *(renaissance)* revival; **nous attendons la r. du cinéma français** we're waiting for French cinema to take on a new lease of life

3 *(guérison)* **depuis qu'il sait que sa fille est saine et sauve, c'est une véritable r.!** now he knows his daughter is safe, he's made a miraculous recovery!

retable [rətabl] **NM** *(sur l'autel)* retable; *(derrière l'autel)* reredos

'Retable des Ermites' *Bosch* 'The Altarpiece of the Hermits'

rétablir [32] [retablir] **VT 1** *(établir de nouveau)* to restore; **le courant a été rétabli dans l'après-midi** the power was reconnected *or* restored in the afternoon; **r. le calme/l'ordre/une vieille coutume** to restore calm/order/an old custom;

r. l'équilibre to redress the balance; **nous prendrons les mesures nécessaires pour r. la situation** we'll take the measures required to restore the situation to normal; **r. un texte** to restore a text *(to its original form)*; **r. qn dans son emploi** to reinstate sb; **elle a été rétablie dans tous ses droits** all her rights were restored

2 *(guérir)* **r. qn** to restore sb to health; **c'est un traitement assez long mais il vous rétablira** it's a rather long treatment but it will restore you to health; **son séjour l'a complètement rétabli** his holiday brought about his complete recovery

3 *(rectifier)* to re-establish; **rétablissons les faits** let's re-establish the facts, let's get down to what really happened

►**se rétablir** VPR **1** *(guérir)* to recover; **il ne se rétablit pas très vite** he's not recovering very quickly; **elle est partie se r. à la campagne** she went to the country to recuperate *or* to recover

2 *(revenir → ordre, calme)* to be restored; *(→ silence)* to return

3 *Sport* to pull oneself up

rétablissement [retablismɑ̃] NM **1** *(de l'ordre, des communications)* restoration; **le r. du courant prendra deux heures** it will be two hours before the power comes back on; **nous souhaitons tous le r. de la paix** we all want peace to be restored

2 *(d'un fonctionnaire)* reinstatement

3 *(guérison)* recovery; **nous vous souhaitons un prompt r.** we wish you a speedy recovery

4 *Sport* **faire un r. à la barre fixe** to do a pull-up on the horizontal bar

retaille [rətaj] NF *(de diamant)* recutting

retailler [3] [rətaje] VT *(rosier, vigne)* to reprune; *(diamant, vêtement)* to recut; *(crayon)* to resharpen; *(haie)* to retrim; *(cartes à jouer)* to shuffle and cut again

rétamage [retamaʒ] NM retinning

rétamé, -e [retame] ADJ **1** *(étamé de nouveau)* retinned **2** *Fam (épuisé) Br* knackered, *Am* bushed; *(ivre)* wasted, trashed; *(hors d'usage)* wrecked, bust

rétamer [3] [retame] VT **1** *(étamer de nouveau)* to retin

2 *Fam (enivrer)* to knock out; **un verre de champagne suffit à me r.** one glass of champagne is enough to knock me out

3 *Fam (battre au jeu)* to clean out; **je me suis fait r. au casino** I got cleaned out at the casino

4 *Fam (épuiser)* to wear out, *Br* to knacker

5 *Fam (mettre hors d'usage)* to wreck, to bust; **il a complètement rétamé sa voiture** *Br* he wrote his car off, *Am* he totaled his car

6 *Fam (refuser → candidat)* to fail▪, *Am* to flunk; **ils ont rétamé la moitié des candidats** they failed *or Am* flunked half the candidates; **je me suis fait r. en anglais** I failed *or Am* flunked my English exam

►**se rétamer** VPR *Fam* **1** *(tomber)* to go flying, to take a tumble; **je me suis drôlement rétamé au ski** I took a real tumble when I went skiing

2 *(échouer)* to fail▪, *Am* to flunk; **je me suis rétamé à l'oral** I messed up *or Am* flunked my oral exam

rétameur [retamœr] NM tinker, tinsmith

retapage [rətapaʒ] NM *Fam (d'un lit)* straightening▪, making▪; *(d'une maison, d'une voiture)* doing up

retape [rətap] NF *Fam* **1** *(racolage)* **faire (de) la r.** *Br* to be on the game, *Am* to hustle **2** *(publicité)* loud advertising▪, hyping (up), plugging; **faire de la r. pour** to plug

retaper [3] [rətape] VT **1** *Fam (lit)* to straighten, to make▪

2 *Fam (maison, voiture)* to do up

3 *Fam (malade)* to buck up; **mon séjour à la montagne m'a retapé** my stay in the mountains set me back on my feet again

4 *(lettre, texte)* to retype, to type again

►**se retaper** VPR *Fam* **1** *(physiquement)* to get back on one's feet again; **elle a grand besoin de se r.** she badly needs to recharge her batteries

2 *(financièrement)* to sort out one's finances▪, to get straightened out (financially)

3 *(refaire)* **j'ai dû me r. la lecture du rapport** I had to read through the blasted report again; **on se retape une belote?** how about another game of belote?; **je me retaperais bien une petite bière** I wouldn't mind another beer, I wouldn't say no to another beer

retapisser [3] [rətapise] VT **1** *(pièce, mur → avec du papier peint)* to repaper; *(→ avec du tissu)* to hang with new material; *(fauteuil)* to recover **2** *Fam Arg crime (reconnaître)* to clock

retard [rətar] NM **1** *(manque de ponctualité)* lateness; *(temps écoulé)* delay; **il ne s'est même pas excusé pour son r.** he didn't even apologize for being late; **mon r. est dû à...** I'm late because of...; **avoir du r.** to be late; **j'avais plus d'une heure de r.** I was more than an hour late; **prendre du r.** *(sujet: personne)* to fall behind; *(sujet: train)* to be running late; **l'avion Londres–Paris est annoncé avec deux heures de r.** a two-hour delay is expected on the London to Paris flight; **son bébé est né avec cinq jours de r.** her baby was born five days late; **rapportez vos livres sans r.** return your books without delay; **r. de paiement** delay in payment, late payment; **tout r. dans le paiement des intérêts sera sanctionné** all late payments of interest *or* any delay in paying interest will incur a penalty

2 *(intervalle de temps, distance)* **il a un tour de r. sur son principal adversaire** he's a lap behind his main opponent; **le peloton est arrivé avec cinq minutes de r. sur le vainqueur** the pack arrived five minutes after *or* behind the winner

3 *(d'une horloge)* **ma montre a plusieurs minutes de r.** my watch is several minutes slow

4 *(d'un élève)* backwardness; **il a du r. en allemand** he's behind in German; **il doit combler son r. en physique** he's got to catch up in physics; **r. scolaire** learning difficulties

5 *(handicap)* **nous avons comblé notre r. industriel en quelques années** we caught up on *or* we closed the gap in our industrial development in a few years; **nous avons des années de r. (sur eux)** we're years behind (them); **r. mental** backwardness

6 *Tech* **r. à l'allumage** retarded ignition

ADJ INV *Pharm* delayed(-action) *(avant n)*; **insuline/pénicilline r.** slow-release insulin/penicillin

❑ **en retard** ADJ **je suis en r. pour la réunion** I'm late for the meeting; **j'ai des lettres/du tricot en r.** I'm behind with my mail/knitting; **un élève en r. sur les autres** a pupil lagging behind the others; **un élève en r. dans ses études** a pupil who is behind in his studies; **elle est très en r. pour son âge** *Psy* she's rather immature *or* slow for her age; *Scol* she's rather behind for her age; **paiement en r.** *(qui n'est pas fait)* arrears, overdue payment; *(qui est fait)* late payment; **il est en r. dans ses paiements** he's behind *or* in arrears with (his) payments; **un pays en r. sur les autres** a backward country, a country lagging behind the others; **être en r. sur son époque** *ou* **son temps** to be behind the times ADV late; **arriver en r.** to arrive late; **elle s'est mise en r.** she made herself late; **nous avons rendu nos épreuves en r.** we were late handing in our tests

retardataire [rətardatɛr] ADJ **1** *(qui n'est pas à l'heure)* late; *(qui a été retardé)* delayed **2** *(désuet)* obsolete, old-fashioned; **vous avez vraiment des méthodes retardataires** your methods are completely obsolete *or* outdated

NMF latecomer

retardateur, -trice [rətardatœr, -tris] ADJ retarding; *Mil* **action retardatrice** delaying tactics; *Phys & Tech* **frottement r.** (friction) drag

NM **1** *Chim* retarder, negative catalyst **2** *Constr* retarding agent, retarder **3** *Phot* (camera) self-timer

retardé, -e [rətarde] ADJ *Fam (arriéré)* retarded, backward, *Péj* slow

NM,F **r. (mental)** (mentally) retarded person

retardement [rətardəmɑ̃] **à retardement** ADJ *(mécanisme)* delayed-action *(avant n)*

ADV **comprendre à r.** to understand after the event

retarder [3] [rətarde] VT **1** *(ralentir → visiteur, passager)* to delay, to make late; *(entraver → enquête, progrès, travaux)* to delay, to hamper, to slow down; **la pluie/grève m'a retardé** the rain/strike made me late; **les problèmes financiers l'ont retardé dans ses études** financial problems slowed him down *or* hampered him in his studies

2 *(ajourner)* to postpone, to put back; **nous avons dû r. la date d'ouverture du congrès** we had to put back the date for *or* postpone the start of the congress; **l'intervention du Président a été retardée d'une heure** the President's address has been moved back one hour; **elle retarde par tous les moyens le moment de le rencontrer** she's using every opportunity to put off *or* to postpone *or* to delay meeting him

3 *(montre)* to put back; **j'ai retardé la pendule de quelques minutes** I put the clock back a few minutes

VI **1** *(montre)* to be slow; **la pendule retarde** the clock is slow; **mon réveil retarde de cinq minutes** my alarm (clock) is five minutes slow; *Fam* **je retarde de quelques minutes** I'm *or* my watch is a few minutes slow

2 *Fam (personne)* to be out of touch; **r. sur son temps** *ou* **son siècle** to be behind the times; **il retarde de 20 ans sur notre époque** *ou* **temps** he's 20 years behind the times; **r. (d'un métro)** to be out of touch

►**se retarder** VPR to make oneself late; **ne te retarde pas pour ça** don't let this hold you up *or* delay you

retassure [rətasyr] NF *Métal* shrinkage hole *or* pipe

retâter [3] [rətate] VT *(étoffe)* to feel again

❑ **retâter de** VT IND *Fam* **il n'a pas envie de r. de la prison** he doesn't want to sample the delights of prison life again

reteindre [81] [rətɛ̃dr] VT to dye again, to redye

retendoir [rətɑ̃dwar] NM piano tuning key

retendre [73] [rətɑ̃dr] VT **1** *(corde, câble)* to retighten, to tauten (again); *(ressort)* to reset; *(corde de raquette)* to tauten (again) **2** *(piège)* to reset

RETENIR [40] [rətənir]

> VT to hold **1** ▪ to hold back **2, 3** ▪ to book **4** ▪ to remember **5** ▪ to retain **6, 8** ▪ to deduct **7** ▪ to carry **9**
> VPR to restrain oneself **1** ▪ to hold on **2, 3**

VT **1** *(immobiliser)* to hold, to keep; **retiens le chien, il va sauter!** hold the dog back, it's going to jump!; **j'ai retenu la chaise juste à temps** I caught the chair just in time; **le mur est retenu par un échafaudage** the wall is held up by scaffolding; **r. le regard de qn** to arrest sb's gaze; **r. l'attention de qn** to hold sb's attention; **votre CV a retenu toute mon attention** I studied your *Br* CV *or Am* résumé with great interest; **r. qn prisonnier** to hold sb prisoner; **r. qn en otage** to hold sb hostage; **r. qn à dîner** to invite sb for dinner; **je ne vous retiens pas, je sais que vous êtes pressé** I won't keep you, I know you're in a hurry

2 *(empêcher d'agir)* to hold back; **quand il est en colère, personne ne peut le r.** when he's angry, there's no holding him *or* nobody can stop him; *Fam* **je ne sais pas ce qui me retient de l'envoyer promener** I don't know what's stopping *or* keeping me from telling him/her to go to hell; *Fam* **retiens-moi ou je fais un malheur** hold me back or I'll do something desperate

3 *(refouler → émotion)* to curb, to hold in check, to hold back; *(→ larmes, sourire)* to hold back; *(→ cri)* to stifle; **elle ne pouvait r. ses larmes/un sourire** she couldn't hold back her tears/a smile; **r. un geste d'impatience** to hold back *or* to check a gesture of impatience; **r. son souffle** *ou* **sa respiration** to hold one's breath

4 *(réserver)* to book, to reserve; **r. une chambre dans un hôtel** to book a room in a hotel; **retiens la date du 20 juin pour notre réunion** keep 20 June free for our meeting

5 *(se rappeler)* to remember; **r. qch** to remember *or* to recall sth; **et surtout, retiens bien ce qu'on t'a dit** and above all, remember *or* don't forget what you've been told; *Fam* **je te retiens, toi et tes soi-disant bonnes idées!** I'll remember you and your so-called good ideas!

6 *(candidature, suggestion)* to retain, to accept; **r. une accusation contre qn** to uphold a charge against sb

7 *(décompter)* to deduct, to keep back; **j'ai retenu 50 euros sur votre salaire** I've deducted 50 euros from your salary; **sommes retenues à la base** *ou* **source** sums deducted at source

8 *(conserver → chaleur)* to keep in, to retain, to conserve; *(→ eau)* to retain; *(→ lumière)* to reflect; **un filtre retient les impuretés** a filter retains the impurities

9 *Math* to carry; **je pose 5 et je retiens 4** I put down 5 and carry 4

10 *Can* **r. de qn** to look like sb; **elle retient de sa mère** she looks like her mother

►**se retenir** VPR **1** *(se contrôler)* to restrain oneself; **se r. de pleurer** to stop oneself crying

2 *Fam Euph* to hold on; **il n'a pas pu se r.** he couldn't wait (to go to the toilet)

3 *(s'agripper)* to hold on; **retiens-toi à la branche** hold on to the branch

retenter [3] [rətɑ̃te] VT to try again; **r. sa chance** to try one's luck again

rétenteur, -trice [retɑ̃tœr, -tris] ADJ *(force)* retaining; *Anat* **muscle r.** retentor (muscle)
NM *Jur* lien holder

rétention [retɑ̃sjɔ̃] NF **1** *Méd* retention; **faire de la r. d'urines/d'eau** to suffer from urine/water retention

2 *Géog* retention

3 *(refus de communiquer)* **faire de la r. d'information** to hold back *or* withhold information

4 *Jur* **droit de r.** lien; **r. administrative** = detention of illegal immigrants or of asylum seekers due to be deported; **r. douanière** detention by customs; **r. des mineurs** detention of minors

5 *Mktg (d'un message publicitaire)* retention; **r. sélective** selective retention

6 *Psy* retention

7 **r. du personnel** staff retention; **taux de r. du personnel** staff retention rate

retentir [32] [rətɑ̃tir] VI **1** *(résonner → gén)* to resound, to ring, to echo; *(→ Klaxon®)* to sound, to honk; *(→ tonnerre, canon)* to crash; *(→ alarme)* to ring, to sound; *(→ coup de feu, cri)* to ring out; **de bruyants applaudissements retentirent dans la salle** the auditorium resounded with deafening applause, loud applause rang out *or* burst forth in the auditorium; **la voix des enfants retentissait dans l'escalier** the children's voices rang out *or* echoed in the stairway; **l'explosion a retenti dans toute la ville** the explosion was heard right across the city; **la maison retentit du bruit des ouvriers** the house is filled with the noise of the workers; **faire r. qch** *(instrument musical)* to blow sth

2 *(avoir des répercussions)* **r. sur** to have an effect on; **l'accident de sa femme a retenti sur son moral** his wife's accident shook him a great deal

retentissant, -e [rətɑ̃tisɑ̃, -ɑ̃t] ADJ **1** *(éclatant → cri, bruit, gifle)* resounding, ringing; *(→ voix)* ringing; *(→ sonnerie)* loud **2** *(remarquable)* tremendous; **un succès r.** a resounding success; *Fam* **un bide r.** a resounding flop; **faire une découverte retentissante** to make a tremendous *or* sensational discovery

retentissement [rətɑ̃tismɑ̃] NM **1** *(contrecoup)* repercussion; **ça n'a aucun r. sur notre pouvoir d'achat** it doesn't affect our purchasing power in any way

2 *(impact)* effect, impact; **le r. dans l'opinion publique a été considérable/nul** there was considerable/no effect on public opinion; **cette déclaration devrait avoir un certain r.** this statement should create quite a stir

3 *Littéraire (bruit)* ringing, resounding

rétentrice [retɑ̃tris] *voir* **rétenteur**

retenu, -e [rətny] PP *voir* **retenir**

ADJ *(discret → personne)* subdued; **s'exprimer de façon retenue** to express oneself in restrained terms, to be restrained

▫ **retenue** NF **1** *(déduction)* deduction; **opérer une retenue de 9 pour cent sur les salaires** to deduct *or* to stop 9 percent from salaries; **faire une r. de 5% sur les salaires** to deduct *or* withhold 5% from salaries; **on a fait une retenue de 50 euros sur son salaire** 50 euros have been docked from his/her wages; **moins 5,6 pour cent en retenues diverses** less 5.6 percent in deductions *or Br* stoppages; **retenue fiscale** withholding tax; **retenue à la source** payment (of income tax) at source, *Br* ≃ PAYE, *Am* ≃ pay as you go

2 *(réserve)* reserve, self-control, restraint; **s'exprimer sans retenue** to express oneself without restraint, to speak freely; **se confier à qn sans retenue** to confide in sb unreservedly *or* freely; **rire sans retenue** to laugh uproariously *or* uncontrollably; **c'est une jeune femme pleine de retenue** she's a very reserved *or* reticent young woman; **un peu de retenue!** show some restraint!, keep a hold of yourself!

3 *Transp (ralentissement)* tailback

4 *Scol (punition)* detention; **mettre qn en retenue** to keep sb in after school, to put sb in detention; **j'ai quatre heures de retenue la semaine prochaine** I've got four hours' detention next week

5 *Math* **reporter la retenue** to carry over; **la retenue, c'est combien?** how much is there to carry over?

6 *Constr (d'une poutre)* pinning

7 *Naut (entre écluses)* reach

8 *(d'eau)* damming up *(UNCOUNT)*; **lac de retenue** impoundment, dam reservoir; **retenue d'eau** volume of water *(in dam)*

reterçage [rətɛrsaʒ] NM *Agr* reploughing

retercer [16] [rətɛrse] VT *Agr* to replough

rétiaire [retjɛr, resjɛr] NM *Antiq* retiarius, retiary

réticence [retisɑ̃s] NF **1** *(hésitation)* reluctance, reticence; **avec quelque r.** with some reticence *or* reservations; **avoir des réticences (sur qch)** to feel reticent *or* to have reservations (about sth); **j'ai remarqué un peu de r. dans son accord** I noticed he/she agreed somewhat reluctantly; **après bien des réticences, il a dit oui** after much hesitation he said yes; **parler avec r.** to speak reticently; **parlez sans r.** don't be reticent, feel free to speak quite openly

2 *(omission)* omission; *Jur* **r. dolosive** deceit by omission

réticent, -e [retisɑ̃, -ɑ̃t] ADJ **1** *(hésitant)* reticent, reluctant, reserved; **je suis un peu r. à l'égard de votre proposition** I feel slightly reluctant about your proposal; **se montrer r.** to seem rather doubtful; **se montrer r. à faire qch** to be hesitant about doing sth, to be reluctant *or* unwilling to do sth **2** *Littéraire (discret)* reticent

réticulaire [retikylɛr] ADJ reticular

réticulation [retikylasjɔ̃] NF *Chim* cross-linkage

réticule [retikyl] NM **1** *(sac)* reticule **2** *Opt* reticle

réticulé, -e [retikyle] ADJ **1** *Archit* reticulated, reticular **2** *Anat & Bot* reticulate

réticuler [3] [retikyle] VT *Chim* to cross-link

réticuline [retikylin] NF *Physiol* reticulin

réticulocyte [retikylɔsit] NM *Biol* reticulocyte

réticulo-endothélial, -e, -aux, -ales [retikylɔɑ̃dɔteljal, -o] ADJ *Anat* reticuloendothelial

réticulo-endothéliose [retikylɔɑ̃dɔteljoz] NF *Méd* reticuloendotheliosis

réticulose [retikyloz] NF *Méd* reticulosis

réticulum [retikylɔm] NM reticulum

retient *etc voir* **retenir**

rétif, -ive [retif, -iv] ADJ **1** *(cheval)* stubborn **2** *(enfant)* restive, fractious, *Sout* recalcitrant

rétine [retin] NF retina; *Méd* **r. décollée** detached retina

rétinien, -enne [retinjɛ̃, -ɛn] ADJ retinal

rétinite [retinit] NF **1** *Minér* retinite **2** *Méd* retinitis

rétinoïde [retinoid] NM retinoid

rétinol [retinɔl] NM retinol

rétinopathie [retinɔpati] NF *Méd* retinopathy; **r. diabétique** diabetic retinopathy

retint *etc voir* **retenir**

rétique [retik] = **rhétique**

retirable [rətirabl] NM withdrawable, that may be withdrawn *or* removed

retirage [rətiraʒ] NM *(processus)* reprinting; *(résultat)* reprint; **je voudrais faire un r. de ces photos** I'd like prints of these photos

retiration [rətirasjɔ̃] NF *Typ* perfecting; **imprimer une feuille en r.** to perfect a sheet; **presse** *ou* **machine à r.** perfecting machine

retiré, -e [rətire] ADJ **1** *(isolé)* remote, secluded, out-of-the-way; **ils cherchent une maison retirée** they're looking for a secluded house; **elle habite un quartier r.** she lives in an out-of-the-way neighbourhood **2** *(solitaire)* secluded; **mener une vie retirée à la campagne** to live a secluded life in the country; **vivre r. du monde** to live in seclusion **3** *(à la retraite)* retired

RETIRER [3] [rətire]

> **VT** to take off **1** ▪ to remove **1, 3** ▪ to take away **1, 4, 5** ▪ to take out **3, 6** ▪ to withdraw **4, 6** ▪ to collect **6** ▪ to get **7** ▪ to fire again **8** ▪ to reprint **9**
> **VI** to fire again **1** ▪ to shoot again **2**
> **VPR** to withdraw **1, 2** ▪ to retire **2** ▪ to recede **3** ▪ to vanish **4**

VT **1** *(ôter)* to take off *or* away, to remove; **retire tes gants** take off your gloves; **il aida l'enfant à r. son manteau** he helped the child off with his/her coat

2 *(ramener à soi)* **retire ta main** take your hand away; **retire tes jambes** move your legs back

3 *(faire sortir)* to take out, to remove; **on a retiré de nombreux corps du bâtiment** a large number of bodies were removed from *or* taken out of the building; **elle a été obligée de r. son fils de l'école** she had to remove her son from the school

4 *(annuler → droit)* to take away; *(→ plainte, offre)* to withdraw; *(→ accusation)* to take back; **r. sa candidature** to withdraw one's candidature, to stand down; **d'accord, je retire tout ce que j'ai dit sur lui** OK, I take back all I said about him; **r. un magazine de la circulation** to withdraw a magazine (from circulation); **la pièce a été retirée de l'affiche après une semaine** the play came off *or* closed after a week

5 *(confisquer)* **r. qch à qn** to take sth away from sb; **retire-lui le verre des mains** take the glass away from him/her; **on lui a retiré la garde des enfants** he/she lost custody of the children; **on lui a retiré son permis de conduire** he's/she's been banned from driving; **r. son emploi à qn** to take away sb's job; **r. sa confiance à qn** to no longer trust sb

6 *(récupérer → argent)* to withdraw, to take out, to draw; *(→ bagage, ticket)* to pick up, to collect; **j'ai retiré un peu d'argent de mon compte** I withdrew some money from my bank account; **retire 80 euros, ça suffira** take *or* get 80 euros out, that will be enough

7 *(obtenir)* to gain, to get; **r. un bénéfice important d'une affaire** to make a large profit out of a deal; **je n'ai retiré que des désagréments de cet emploi** I got nothing but trouble from that job

8 *(coup de feu)* to fire again

9 *Typ* to reprint; **r. une photo** to make a new *or* fresh print (from a photo)

VI **1** *(refaire feu)* to fire again

2 *Sport* to shoot again

►**se retirer** VPR **1** *(s'éloigner)* to withdraw; **il est tard, je vais me r.** it's late, I'm going to retire *or* to withdraw; **ils se sont retirés discrètement pour pouvoir parler entre eux** they withdrew discreetly so that they could talk together; **les manifestants se sont retirés** the demonstrators withdrew; **se r. de** to withdraw from; **se r. de la politique/compétition** to withdraw from politics/the competition; **se r. de la vie active** to retire; *Hum* **se r. dans ses appartements** to retire *or* to withdraw to one's room

2 *(s'établir)* to retire; *(se cloîtrer)* to retire, to withdraw; **il s'est retiré dans le Midi** he retired to the South of France; **se r. du monde** to cut oneself off from the world

3 *(mer)* to recede, to ebb; *(inondations)* to recede

4 *(disparaître)* to disappear, to vanish; **toute joie s'est retirée de leur maison à la mort de leur fille** joy vanished from their home when their daughter died

retirons [rətirɔ̃] NMPL *Tex* combings

retisser [3] [rətise] VT to weave again, to reweave

rétive [retiv] *voir* **rétif**

rétivité [retivite] NF *Littéraire* fractiousness, intractability

retombant, -e [rətɔ̃bɑ̃, -ɑ̃t] ADJ hanging, trailing, *Péj* drooping

retombé [rətɔ̃be] NM *(en danse)* landing

retombée [rətɔ̃be] NF **1** *Littéraire (déclin)* **la r. de**

l'enthousiasme populaire the decline in popular enthusiasm

2 *Archit & Constr* springing

❏ **retombées** NFPL **1 retombées radioactives** radioactive fallout

2 *Fig (répercussions)* repercussions, effects; **les retombées d'une campagne publicitaire** the results of an advertising campaign; **la grève aura des retombées sur les prix** the strike will have repercussions *or* a knock-on effect on prices; **les retombées du scandale/de l'affaire** the fallout from *or* the repercussions of the scandal/affair

retombement [rətɔ̃bmɑ̃] NM *Littéraire (fait de retomber)* falling down; *Fig* **j'étais trahi; mon r. fut atroce** I had been betrayed; I felt bitter disillusionment

retomber [3] [rətɔ̃be] VI *(aux être)* **1** *(bouteille, balai)* to fall over again; *(mur, livres empilés)* to fall down again *or* back down; *(ivrogne, bambin)* to fall over *or* down again; **se laisser r. par terre/sur une chaise** to fall *or* to drop back onto the ground/onto a chair; **se laisser r. sur son lit** to flop *or* to fall back onto one's bed; **se laisser r. sur son oreiller** to sink back into one's pillow; **r. de cheval** to fall off a horse again; **faire r. qch** to drop sth again; **le savon est retombé dans l'eau** the soap has fallen into the water again

2 *(atterrir → chat, sauteur, parachutiste, missile)* to land; *(→ balle)* to come (back) down; *(redescendre → couvercle, rideau de fer, clapet)* to close; *(→ soufflé, mousse)* to collapse; **laissez r. votre main droite** let your right hand come down *or* drop down; *Fig* **r. sur ses pattes** to land on one's feet

3 *(devenir moins fort → fièvre, prix)* to drop; *(→ agitation)* to fall, to tail off, to die away; *(→ enthousiasme)* to fall, to wane; **le dollar est retombé** the dollar has fallen *or* dropped again

4 *(dans un état, une habitude)* to fall back, *Sout* to lapse; **r. dans la pénurie/l'ennui** to fall back into poverty/boredom; **r. dans les mêmes erreurs** to make the same mistakes again; **r. en enfance** to go into one's second childhood

5 *Météo (vent)* to fall (again), to drop, to die down; *(brume)* to disappear, to be dispelled; *(tournure impersonnelle)* **il retombe de la pluie/neige/grêle** it's raining/snowing/hailing again

6 *(pendre → drapé, guirlande, ourlet)* to hang; **les fleurs retombent en lourdes grappes** the flowers are hanging in heavy clusters

7 *(redevenir)* **r. amoureux** to fall in love again; **r. d'accord** to come to *or* to reach an agreement again; **r. enceinte** to get pregnant again; **r. malade** to become *or* to fall ill again

8 *(dans l'expression des dates)* **mon anniversaire retombe un lundi cette année** my birthday falls on a Monday again this year

❏ **retomber sur** VT IND **1** *(rejaillir)* **la responsabilité retombe sur moi** the blame for it falls on me; **tous les torts sont retombés sur elle** she had to bear the brunt of all the blame; **la malédiction retombera sur votre tête** the curse shall be visited upon you; *Fam* **un de ces jours ça va te r. sur le nez!** one of these days you'll get your comeuppance *or* what's coming to you!

2 *Fam (rencontrer à nouveau)* **r. sur qn** to bump into *or* to come across sb again; **r. sur qch** to come across sth again; **je suis retombé sur le même prof/sujet à l'oral** I got the same examiner/question for the oral exam; **en tournant à droite, vous retombez sur l'avenue** if you turn right you're back on the avenue again

retoquer [3] [rətɔke] VT *Fam* to reject ■

retordage [rətɔrdaʒ], **retordement** [rətɔrdəmɑ̃] NM *Tex* twisting

retordeur, -euse [rətɔrdœr, -øz] *Tex* NM,F *(personne)* twister

❏ **retordeuse** NF *(machine)* twister, twisting machine

retordre [76] [rətɔrdr] VT *Tex* to twist

rétorquer [3] [retɔrke] VT **1** *(répliquer)* to retort; **il a rétorqué que ça ne me regardait pas** he retorted *or* rejoined that it was none of my business; **"certainement pas!" rétorqua-t-elle vivement** "certainly not!" she snapped back *or* replied indignantly **2** *Arch ou Littéraire (accusation)* to cast back, to hurl back; **r. un argument contre qn** to turn sb's argument against him/her

retors, -e [rətɔr, -ɔrs] ADJ **1** *(machiavélique)*

crafty, tricky; **méfie-toi, il est r.** be careful, he's a wily customer *or* he knows all the tricks of the trade **2** *Tex* **fil r.** twisted *or* warp yarn

rétorsion [retɔrsjɔ̃] NF **1** *(représailles)* retaliation; **mesures de r.** retaliatory measures; **par r.** in retaliation; **user de r. envers** to retaliate against **2** *Jur* retortion

retouche [rətuʃ] NF **1** *(correction)* alteration; **faire des retouches à un texte** to make alterations to a text; **je dois apporter quelques retouches à mon texte** I need to make a few alterations to my text; **sans retouches** unaltered

2 *Beaux-Arts (action)* retouching *(UNCOUNT)*; *(résultat)* retouch; **je veux faire des retouches à cette sculpture avant de l'exposer** I want to work a little more on this sculpture before exhibiting it

3 *Couture* alteration; **faire des retouches à un vêtement** to make alterations to a garment; **il faudra faire une r. dans le dos** it will have to be altered at the back

4 *Phot* touching up *(UNCOUNT)*; **l'agrandissement demande quelques retouches** the enlargement needs a little touching up

5 *Ordinat* **r. d'images** photo editing

retoucher [3] [rətuʃe] VT *(modifier → texte, vêtement)* to alter; *(→ œuvre)* to retouch; *(→ photo)* to retouch, to touch up; **j'ai seulement retouché les ombres** I just touched up the shadows

❏ **retoucher à** VT IND *(se remettre à)* to go back to; **et depuis, tu n'as plus jamais retouché à une cigarette** and since then you haven't touched a *or* another cigarette?; **il n'a plus jamais retouché à son piano** he never touched *or* played his piano again; **n'avez-vous pas envie de r. à la peinture, à présent?** don't you feel like doing a bit of painting again, now?

retoucheur, -euse [rətuʃœr, -øz] NM,F **1** *Couture* alterer **2** *Phot* retoucher

RETOUR [rətur] NM **1** *(chez soi, au point de départ)* return; **à ton r.** when you get back; **à son r. de l'hôpital nous l'inviterons au restaurant** when he/she gets out of hospital we'll take him/her out for a meal; **à son r. de l'usine il prenait le temps de lire le journal** when he got back from the factory he would take the time to read the newspaper; **nous comptons sur ton r. pour Noël** we expect you back (home) for Christmas; **après dix années d'exil, c'est le r. au pays** after a ten-year exile he's/she's coming home; **partir sans espoir de r.** to leave without any hope of returning; **r. à un stade antérieur** reverting *or* returning to an earlier stage; **sur le chemin ou la route du r.** on the way back; **voyage/vol de r.** return journey *or* trip/flight; **r. à la nature/au calme** return to nature/a state of calm; **r. à la normale** return to normal; **r. aux sources** return to one's roots; **c'est un r. aux sources qu'il fait en se rendant à Varsovie** he's going back to his roots on this trip to Warsaw; **r. à la terre** return to the land; **être sur le r.** to be about to return, to be on the point of returning; *Fig* to be past one's prime; **ils doivent être sur le r. à présent** they must be on their way back now; **un don Juan sur le r.** an ageing Don Juan; **une beauté sur le r.** a fading beauty

2 *(nouvelle apparition → d'une célébrité)* return, reappearance; *(récurrence → d'une mode, d'un thème)* return, recurrence; **ses retours répétés sur la scène londonienne** his/her regular reappearances on the London stage; **on note un r. des jupes longues** long skirts are back (in fashion); **le r. d'un thème** the recurrence of a theme

3 *(mouvement inverse)* **faire un r. sur soi-même** to review one's past life; **r. de bâton** kickback; **r. (de) chariot** carriage return; *Tech & Fig* **r. de flamme** backfire; **r. offensif** renewed outbreak; **r. rapide** *(d'une cassette)* rewind; *Élec* **r. par la terre** *Br* earthing, *Am* grounding; **r. à la case départ** *(dans un jeu)* back to the start; *Fig* back to square one *or* to the drawing board; **par un juste r. des choses il a été licencié** he was sacked, which seemed fair enough under the circumstances

4 *(réexpédition)* return; **r. à l'envoyeur** *ou* **à l'expéditeur** return to sender; **par r. du courrier** by return of post

5 *Transp (trajet)* return (journey), journey back;

combien coûte le r.? how much is the return fare?

6 *(sur un clavier)* return; **touche r.** return key; **appuyez sur la touche r.** press return; **r. arrière** backspace; **r. à la ligne automatique** word wrap; **r. à la ligne forcé** hard return

7 *Jur* reversion; **faire r. à** to revert to

8 *(au tennis)* return; **r. de service** return of serve, service return

9 *Ordinat* **r. (d'information)** (information) feedback

10 *Archit* return, (corner) angle; **en r. d'équerre** right-angle *(avant n)*

11 *Fin (amortissement)* return; *(effet)* dishonoured bill, bill returned dishonoured; **r. sur achat** purchase return; **r. sans frais** return free of charge; **r. sur investissements** return on investments; **r. sur ventes** return on sales

12 *Com (de marchandises)* return; **marchandises de r., retours** returns; **vendu avec possibilité de r.** sold on a sale or return basis

13 *(meuble)* **bureau avec r.** desk with a right-angled extension unit

14 *Chasse (ruse)* doubling back; **faire un r.** to double back

ADJ INV *Sport* **match r.** return match

❏ **retours** NMPL *(de vacances)* return traffic *(from weekends etc)*; **il y a beaucoup de retours ce soir** many people are driving back to the city tonight

❏ **de retour** ADV back; **je serai de r. demain** I'll be back tomorrow; **les hirondelles sont de r.** the swallows are back (again) *or* with us again; **de r. chez lui, il réfléchit** (once he was) back home, he thought it over

❏ **de retour de** PRÉP back from; **de r. de Rio, je tentai de la voir** on my return from Rio, I tried to see her

❏ **en retour** ADV in return

❏ **retour d'âge** NM change of life

❏ **retour de manivelle** NM **1** *Tech* kickback

2 *(choc en retour)* backlash; *(conséquence néfaste)* backlash, repercussion

❏ **retour en arrière** NM **1** *Cin & Littérature* flashback; **faire un r. en arrière** to flash back

2 *Fig (régression)* step backwards

❏ **sans retour** ADV *Littéraire (pour toujours)* forever, irrevocably

retournage [rəturnaʒ] NM turning inside out *(and repairing)*

retourne [rəturn] NF **1** *Cartes* **la r. est à cœur** hearts are trumps **2** *Fam* **les avoir à la r.** to be bone idle

retourné [rəturne] NM *(en football)* overhead flick

retournement [rəturnəmɑ̃] NM **1** *(revirement)* **un r. de situation** a turnaround *or* a reversal (of the situation) **2** *Écon (du marché)* collapse; **on craint un r. du marché de l'immobilier** there are fears that the housing market will collapse *or* that the housing bubble will burst **3** *Géom* turning (over)

RETOURNER [3] [rəturne]

VT to turn round **1, 3** ■ to send back **2** ■ to turn over **3** ■ to toss **4** ■ to turn upside down **5**	
VI to return, to go back	
VPR to turn round **1** ■ to turn over **2, 3** ■ to overturn **3** ■ to sort things out **4** ■ to change completely **5**	

VT *(aux avoir)* **1** *(orienter dans le sens contraire)* to turn round *or* around; *(renverser → situation)* to reverse, to turn inside out *or* back to front; **retourne le plan** turn the map round *or* around *or* the other way round; **r. une arme contre ou sur qn** to turn a weapon on sb; **puis il a retourné son arme contre lui-même** then he turned his weapon on himself, then he shot himself; **je lui ai retourné son** *ou* **le compliment** I returned the compliment

2 *(renvoyer → colis, lettre)* to send back

3 *(mettre à l'envers → literie)* to turn round *or* around; *(→ carte à jouer)* to turn up; *(→ champ, paille)* to turn over; *(→ verre)* to turn upside down; *(→ grillade)* to turn over; *(→ gant, poche)* to turn inside out; **il a retourné la photo contre le mur** he turned the photo against the wall; *Fig*

r. sa veste to sell out; **il te retournera comme une crêpe** *ou* **un gant** he'll twist you round his little finger

4 *(mélanger → salade)* to toss

5 *(fouiller → maison, pièce)* to turn upside down

6 *(examiner → pensée)* **tourner et r. une idée dans sa tête** to mull over an idea (in one's head)

7 *Fam (émouvoir)* **j'en suis encore tout retourné!** I'm still reeling from the shock!

VI *(aux être)* **1** *(aller à nouveau)* to return, to go again *or* back; **jamais je ne retournerai là-bas** I will never go there again *or* go back there; **je n'y étais pas retourné depuis des années** I had not been back there for years; **si tu étais à ma place, tu retournerais le voir?** if you were me, would you (ever) go and see him again?; **je retournai la voir une dernière fois** I paid her one *or* my last visit; **la pièce m'a tellement plu que je suis retourné la voir** I liked the play so much that I went (back) to see it again; **elle m'a fait r. à la maison** she sent me back home

2 *(revenir)* to go back, to return; **r. chez soi** to go (back) home; **r. à sa place** *(sur son siège)* to go back to one's seat

V IMPERSONNEL peut-on savoir de quoi il retourne? what is it all about?, what exactly is going on?

❑ **retourner à VT IND** *(reprendre, retrouver)* to return to, to go back to; **r. à l'ouvrage** to go back to work; **r. à un stade antérieur** to revert to an earlier stage; *Fig* **r. à ses premières amours** to go back to one's first loves

▶**se retourner VPR 1** *(tourner la tête)* to turn round; **partir sans se r.** to leave without looking back; **tout le monde se retournait sur eux** everybody turned round to look at them

2 *(se mettre sur l'autre face)* to turn over; **se r. sur le dos/ventre** to turn over on one's back/ stomach; **je me suis retourné dans mon lit toute la nuit** I tossed and turned all night; **elle doit se r. dans sa tombe** she must be turning in her grave

3 *(se renverser → auto, tracteur)* to overturn, to turn over

4 *(réagir)* to sort things out; **ils ne me laissent pas le temps de me r.** *(de décider)* they won't give me time to make a decision; *(de me reprendre)* they won't give me time to sort things out

5 *(situation)* to be reversed, to change completely; **le lendemain, la situation s'était retournée** the following day, the situation had changed beyond recognition

6 **s'en r.** *(partir)* to depart, to leave; *(rentrer)* to make one's way back

7 **se r. un ongle/doigt** to twist a nail/finger

8 **se r. contre qn** *(agir contre)* to turn against sb; **tout cela finira par se r. contre toi** all this will eventually backfire on you

9 *Jur* **se r. contre** to take (legal) action against

10 *Belg (locution)* **ne pas se r. après** *ou* **pour** *ou* **sur qch** not to pay attention to sth, not to care about sth

retracer [16] [rətrase] **VT 1** *(relater)* to relate *or* *Sout* to recount, to tell of; **retraçons les faits** let's go back over the facts **2** *(dessiner à nouveau → trait, cercle)* to draw again, to redraw; *(→ sentier)* to mark out again

rétractabilité [retraktabilite] **NF** propensity to shrink, shrinkability

rétractable [retraktabl] **ADJ 1** *Jur* retractable, revocable **2** *(emballage)* **film r.** shrink wrap **3** *(pointe)* retractable; **stylo à pointe r.** propelling pen

rétractation [retraktasjɔ̃] **NF** *(d'un aveu, d'un témoignage)* withdrawal, retraction, *Sout* retractation

rétracter [3] [retrakte] **VT 1** *Zool (griffes)* to retract, to draw back; *(cornes)* to retract, to draw in **2** *(aveu, témoignage)* to retract, to withdraw

▶**se rétracter VPR 1** *(griffes)* to draw back, *Spéc* to retract **2** *(témoin)* to retract, *Sout* to recant; **il lui a fallu se r.** he/she had to withdraw his/her statement

rétracteur [retraktœr] **ADJ M muscle r.** retractor (muscle)

rétractif, -ive [retraktif, -iv] **ADJ** retractive

rétractile [retraktil] **ADJ** retractile

rétractilité [retraktilite] **NF** retractility

rétraction [retraksjɔ̃] **NF 1** *Méd* retraction **2** *Tech* shrink-wrapping

rétractive [retraktiv] *voir* **rétractif**

retraduction [rətradyksjɔ̃] **NF 1** *(d'un texte traduit d'une autre langue)* retranslation **2** *(nouvelle traduction)* new translation

retraduire [98] [rətradɥir] **VT 1** *(texte traduit d'une autre langue)* to retranslate **2** *(à nouveau)* to make a new translation of

retrait [rətrɛ] **NM 1** *(annulation → d'une licence)* cancelling; *(→ d'un mot d'ordre)* calling off; **un r. de l'ordre de grève est hors de question** calling off the strike is out of the question; *Jur* **r. d'autorité parentale** withdrawal of parental authority; **r. de candidature** *(par un prestataire)* withdrawal of application; *(par un député)* standing down, withdrawal; **r. de permis (de conduire)** revocation of *Br* driving licence *or* *Am* driver's license; **r. du rôle** removal of a case from the *Br* cause list *or* *Am* docket

2 *Banque (d'un effet)* withdrawal; *(de monnaies)* withdrawal from circulation, calling in; **faire un r.** to withdraw money; **je veux faire un r. de 200 euros** I want to take out *or* to withdraw 200 euros; **r. automatique** automated withdrawal; **r. d'espèces** cash withdrawal

3 *(récupération)* **le r. des billets/bagages se fera dès onze heures** tickets/luggage may be collected from eleven o'clock onwards; **r. des bagages** *(dans un aéroport)* baggage reclaim

4 *(départ → d'un joueur, du contingent)* withdrawal

5 *(recul → des eaux d'inondation)* subsiding, receding; *(→ de la marée)* ebbing; *(→ des glaces)* retreat

6 *Jur (d'un acte administratif)* revocation; *(d'un acte de vente)* redemption; **r. successoral** redemption of an estate

7 *Tech* shrinkage

❑ **en retrait ADV** set back; **en r. par rapport au mur** *(clôture)* set back from the wall; *(étagère)* recessed; *Typ* **mettre en r.** to indent; **rester en r.** to stand back; *Fig* to remain in the background; **vivre en r.** to lead a quiet life

❑ **en retrait de PRÉP 1** *(en arrière de)* set back from; **la maison est en r. de la route** the house is set back from the road

2 *(en dessous de)* below, beneath; **son offre est en r. de ce qu'il avait laissé entendre** his offer doesn't come up to what he'd led us to expect

retraitant, -e [rətrɛtɑ̃, -ɑ̃t] **NM,F** *Rel* retreatant

retraite [rətrɛt] **NF 1** *Admin (pension)* pension; **toucher** *ou* **percevoir sa r.** to get *or* to draw one's pension; **r. par capitalisation** self-funded pension scheme; **r. complémentaire** supplementary pension; **r. des fonctionnaires/des non-salariés** public service/self-employed pension; **r. indexée sur le revenu** earnings-related pension; **r. minimum** guaranteed minimum pension; **r. par répartition** contributory pension scheme; **r. vieillesse** retirement pension

2 *(cessation d'activité)* retirement; **il est à la** *ou* **en r.** *(gén)* he has retired; *(officier)* he is on the retired list; **un médecin/policier à la r.** a retired doctor/police officer; **un militaire à la** *ou* **en r.** an army pensioner; **prendre sa r.** to retire; **mettre qn à la r.** to make sb take retirement, to retire sb; **être mis à la r.** to be made to take retirement, to be retired; **l'âge de la r.** retirement age; **r. anticipée** early retirement; **prendre sa r. anticipée** to take early retirement; **r. forcée** compulsory retirement; **r. d'office** compulsory retirement

3 *Chasse & Mil* retreat; **sonner la r.** to sound the retreat

4 *Rel* retreat; **suivre** *ou* **faire une r.** to go on a retreat

5 *Littéraire (cachette → gén)* hiding place, refuge, shelter; *(→ de voleurs)* hideout

6 *Constr* tapering, offsetting

retraité, -e [rətrete] **ADJ** *(qui est à la retraite → gén)* retired; *(→ officier)* on the retired list

NM,F *Admin* pensioner; *(personne ne travaillant plus)* retired person; **les retraités** retired people, senior citizens

retraitement [rətrɛtmɑ̃] **NM** *Ind & Nucl* reprocessing; **centre** *ou* **usine de r. (des déchets nucléaires)** (nuclear) reprocessing plant

retraiter [4] [rətrɛte] **VT** *Ind & Nucl* to reprocess

retranchement [rətrɑ̃ʃmɑ̃] **NM** *Mil* retrenchment, entrenchment; *Fig* **pousser** *ou* **forcer qn dans ses derniers retranchements** to force sb to the wall

retrancher [3] [rətrɑ̃ʃe] **VT 1** *Math* to subtract; **r. 10 de 20** to take 10 away from 20, to subtract 10 from 20

2 *(enlever)* to remove, to excise; **r. un passage d'un livre** to remove *or* to excise a passage from a book

3 *(déduire → pour des raisons administratives)* to deduct (**de** from); *(→ par sanction)* to deduct, to dock (**de** from)

▶**se retrancher VPR 1** *(se protéger)* **se r. derrière** *(se cacher)* to hide behind; *(se réfugier)* to take refuge behind; **se r. dans le silence** *ou* **le mutisme** to take refuge in silence; **ils se sont retranchés derrière la raison d'État/les statistiques** they hid behind the public interest/statistics; **se r. sur ses positions** to remain entrenched in one's position

2 *Mil* to entrench oneself

retranscription [rətrɑ̃skripsjɔ̃] **NF 1** *(processus)* retranscription **2** *(résultat)* new transcript

retranscrire [99] [rətrɑ̃skrir] **VT** to retranscribe

retransmettre [84] [rətrɑ̃smɛtr] **VT 1** *Rad* to broadcast; *TV* to broadcast, to screen, to show; **concert retransmis en direct** live concert; **r. une émission en direct/différé** to broadcast a programme live/a recorded programme **2** *(ordre, information)* to pass on, to relay

retransmission [rətrɑ̃smisjɔ̃] **NF** *Rad* broadcast; *TV* broadcast, screening, showing; **la r. du match est prévue pour 14h45** *(à la télévision)* the match will be shown *or* broadcast at 2.45 p.m.; *(à la radio)* the match will be broadcast at 2.45 p.m.; **r. en direct/différé** live/prerecorded broadcast; **r. par satellite** satellite broadcast; *(action)* satellite broadcasting

retransmit *etc voir* **retransmettre**

retravailler [3] [rətravaje] **VT** *(texte, mouvement de gym)* to work on again; *(argile, pâte)* to work again; **votre thèse a besoin d'être retravaillée** your thesis needs reworking

VI to (start) work again

retraverser [3] [rətravɛrse] **VT 1** *(à nouveau)* to cross again, to recross; **là où la voie ferrée retraverse la route** where the railway crosses the road again **2** *(en sens inverse)* to go *or* to cross back over; **l'ayant saluée, il retraversa la rue** once he'd said hello to her, he crossed back over the road; **elle a retraversé l'estuaire à la nage** she swam back across the estuary

retrayant, -e [rətrɛjɑ̃, -ɑ̃t] **NM,F** *Jur* redemptor

retrayé, -e [rətrɛje] **NM,F** *Jur* seller *(against whom right of redemption is exercised)*

rétrécir [32] [retresir] **VT 1** *(tissu, vêtement → au lavage)* to shrink; *Couture* **r. une jupe** to take in a skirt

2 *(route)* to narrow

VI *(tissu, vêtement)* to shrink; **r. au lavage** to shrink in the wash

▶**se rétrécir VPR** *(allée, goulot)* to narrow, to get narrower; *(cercle, diaphragme)* to contract, to get smaller; *(budget)* to shrink, to dwindle

rétrécissement [retresismɑ̃] **NM 1** *(d'un couloir, d'un diaphragme)* narrowing *(UNCOUNT)*; **en haut de la ruelle, il y a un r.** the lane narrows at the top; **r. de la chaussée** bottleneck **2** *Méd* stricture **3** *(d'un tissu, d'un vêtement)* shrinkage

retreindre [81] [rətrɛ̃dr] **VT** *Métal* to hammer (out)

retreint [rətrɛ̃] **NM** *Métal* hammering (out)

retreinte [rətrɛ̃t] **NF** *Métal* hammering (out)

retrempe [rətrɑ̃p] **NF** *Métal* requenching

retremper [3] [rətrɑ̃pe] **VT 1** *Métal* to requench **2** *(doigt)* to dip again; *(linge)* to soak again **3** *Fig* **cette épreuve lui a retrempé le caractère** this experience gave him/her new strength

▶**se retremper VPR 1** *(dans l'eau)* to have another dip **2 se r. dans** *(un milieu, un sujet)* to go back into; *Littéraire* **se r. aux sources** to go back to basics

rétribuer [7] [retribɥe] **VT** *(employé)* to pay, to remunerate; *(travail, service rendu)* to pay for; **travail rétribué** paid work

rétribution [retribysjɔ̃] **NF 1** *(salaire)* remuneration, salary **2** *(récompense)* recompense, reward

retriever [rətrivœr] NM (chien) retriever

rétro[1] [retro] ADJ INV retro; **mode r.** retro fashion
NM 1 (style) **le r.** retro style 2 (au billard) screw shot
ADV **s'habiller r.** to wear retro clothes; **leur appartement est meublé r.** their Br flat or Am apartment is furnished in retro style

rétro[2] [retro] NM Fam rearview mirror■

rétro- [retro] PRÉF retro-

rétroactes [retroakt] NMPL Belg antecedents; **j'ignore tout des r. de cette affaire** I know nothing of the events which gave rise to this situation

rétroactif, -ive [retroaktif, -iv] ADJ retroactive; **avec effet r. au 1er janvier** backdated to 1 January; **la loi a été votée, avec effet r. à dater de mars** the bill was passed, retroactive or retrospective to March

rétroaction [retroaksjɔ̃] NF 1 (action en retour) retrospective or retroactive effect, retroaction 2 Biol feedback 3 **r. acoustique** acoustic feedback

rétroactive [retroaktiv] voir **rétroactif**

rétroactivement [retroaktivmã] ADV retrospectively, retroactively, with retrospective or retroactive effect

rétroactivité [retroaktivite] NF retroactivity; Jur retrospectiveness

rétroagir [32] [retroaʒir] VI Littéraire to be retroactive, to retroact; **r. sur qch** to have a retroactive effect on sth

rétrocéder [18] [retrosede] VT 1 (rendre) to cede back, to retrocede 2 (revendre) to resell

rétrocession [retrosesjɔ̃] NF Jur retrocedence, retrocession

rétrocontrôle [retrokɔ̃trol] NM Physiol negative feedback control (of endocrine system)

rétroéclairage [retroeklera3] NM Ordinat (d'écran) backlight

rétroéclairé, -e [retroeklere] ADJ Ordinat backlit

rétroflexe [retrofleks] Ling ADJ retroflex
NF retroflex consonant

rétroflexion [retrofleksjɔ̃] NF Ling retroflexion

rétrofusée [retrofyze] NF Aviat & Astron retrorocket

rétrogradation [retrogradasjɔ̃] NF 1 Admin demotion, downgrading; Mil demotion 2 Aut Br changing down or Am shifting down (to a lower gear) 3 Astron retrogradation, retrograde motion 4 Littéraire (dans un développement) regression, retrogression

rétrograde [retrograd] ADJ 1 (passéiste → esprit) reactionary, backward; (→ mesure, politique) reactionary, backward-looking, Sout retrograde 2 (de recul → mouvement) backward, Sout retrograde 3 Astron, Géol, Méd & Mus retrograde 4 (en billard) **effet r.** screw

rétrograder [3] [retrograde] VT (fonctionnaire) to downgrade, to demote; (officier) to demote; **il a été rétrogradé** he was demoted
VI 1 Aut Br to change down, Am to shift down 2 (dans une hiérarchie) to move down; Sport **il a rétrogradé en cinquième position** he's fallen back to fifth place 3 Astron to retrograde

rétrogressif, -ive [retrogresif, -iv] ADJ retrogressive

rétrogression [retrogresjɔ̃] NF retrogression

rétrogressive [retrogresiv] voir **rétrogressif**

rétropédalage [retropedala3] NM Cyclisme backpedalling

rétroprojecteur [retroproʒektœr] NM overhead projector

rétroprojection [retroproʒeksjɔ̃] NF Cin & TV back projection

rétropropulsion [retropropylsjɔ̃] NF reverse thrust

rétrospectif, -ive [retrospɛktif, -iv] ADJ (étude) retrospective; **examen r.** retrospective study
❑ **rétrospective** NF 1 Beaux-Arts retrospective; Cin season, retrospective; **une rétrospective Richard Burton** a Richard Burton season; **une rétrospective de l'année 1944** a look back at the events of 1944 2 Fin review

rétrospectivement [retrospɛktivmã] ADV 1 (à la réflexion) looking back; **r., je me rends compte que j'ai eu tort** looking back, I realize I was wrong 2 (après coup) in retrospect; **tout est devenu clair r.** it all became clear in retrospect

rétrosynthétique [retrosɛ̃tetik] ADJ Chim **analyse r.** retrosynthetic analysis

retroussé, -e [rətruse] ADJ 1 (jupe) bunched or pulled up; (manches, pantalon) rolled or turned up 2 (nez) turned up 3 (babines) curled up; (moustache) curled or twisted up

retroussement [rətrusmã] NM (d'une jupe) bunching or pulling up; (d'un pantalon) rolling or turning up; (de manches) rolling up; **avec un r. des lèvres** with a curl of the lip

retrousser [3] [rətruse] VT 1 (jupe) to bunch or to pull up; (pantalon) to roll or to turn up; (manches) to roll up; aussi Fig **il va falloir r. nos manches** we'll have to roll our sleeves up
2 (babines) to curl up; (moustache) to curl or to twist up
▸**se retrousser** VPR 1 to pull or to hitch up one's skirt/trousers/etc; **j'ai dû me r. jusqu'aux genoux pour ne pas mouiller ma robe** I had to pull my dress up around my knees to stop it getting wet
2 (bords, feuille) to curl up

retroussis [rətrusi] NM (revers) lapel; (d'un uniforme) lappet; **chapeau à r.** cocked hat; **bottes à r.** topboots

retrouvailles [rətruvaj] NFPL 1 (après une querelle) getting back on friendly terms again; (après une absence) reunion, getting together again 2 (retour → dans un lieu) rediscovery, return; (→ à un travail) return; **mes r. avec le train-train quotidien** getting back into my daily routine

---

RETROUVER [3] [rətruve]

> VT to find 1, 2 ■ to meet up with 2 ■ to come across 2 ■ to remember 3 ■ to uncover 4 ■ to get back 5 ■ to recognize 6
> VPR to meet 1, 3 ■ to get together 2 ■ to find oneself back 4 ■ to end up 5 ■ to find one's way 6 ■ to go back to one's roots 7

VT 1 (clés, lunettes) to find (again); **je ne le retrouve plus** I can't find it; **il a retrouvé ma bague** he found my ring; **a-t-elle retrouvé sa clé?** (elle-même) did she find her key?; (grâce à autrui) did she get her key back?; **elle n'a toujours pas retrouvé de travail** she still hasn't found any work; **r. un poste** to find a (new) job; **r. son (ancien) poste** to get one's (old) job back; **r. son chemin** to find one's way (again); **là vous retrouvez la Nationale** that's where you join up with the main road; **r. la trace de qch** to find trace of sth; **on n'a rien retrouvé après l'explosion** there was nothing left after the blast; **r. tout propre/sens dessus dessous** to find everything clean/upside down; **r. qn affaibli/changé** to find sb weaker/a different person

2 (ami, parent) to be reunited with, to meet up with (again); (voleur) to catch up with (again), to find; (revoir par hasard) to come across (again), to run into again; (rejoindre) to meet up with again; **et que je ne vous retrouve pas ici!** don't let me catch you (around) here again!; **celle-là, je la retrouverai** I'll get even with her (one day); **retrouve-moi en bas** meet me downstairs

3 (se rappeler) to remember, Sout to recall; **ça y est, j'ai retrouvé le mot!** that's it, the word's come back to me now!

4 (redécouvrir → secret, parchemin, formule) to uncover

5 (jouir à nouveau de) **à partir de la semaine prochaine nous allons r. nos émissions littéraires** our book programmes will be back on as from next week; **nous avons retrouvé notre petite plage/maison** here we are back on our little beach/in our little house; **r. son calme** to regain one's composure; **r. l'appétit/ses forces/sa santé** to get one's appetite/strength/ health back; **r. la forme** to get fit again, to be back on form; **r. la foi** to find (one's) faith again; **r. la mémoire** to get one's memory back again; **r. le sommeil** to go back to sleep; **il a retrouvé le sourire** he's smiling again now, he's found his smile again; **j'avais retrouvé mes 20 ans** I felt 20 years old again; **le bonheur/l'amour retrouvé** new-found happiness/love; **elle m'a fait r. la joie de vivre** she made me feel or thanks to her I began to feel that life was worth living again

6 (reconnaître) to recognize, to trace; **on retrouve dans le premier mouvement des accents mozartiens** the influence of Mozart is

recognizable or noticeable in the first movement; **on retrouve les mêmes propriétés dans les polymères** the same properties are to be found in polymers; **je n'ai pas retrouvé la jeune fille gaie d'autrefois** she's not the happy young girl I used to know; **enfin, je te retrouve!** I'm glad to see you're back to your old self again!

▸**se retrouver** VPR 1 (avoir rendez-vous) to meet (one another); **on se retrouve demain** see you tomorrow; **retrouvons-nous sous l'horloge** let's meet under the clock

2 (se réunir) to get together; **ils aiment se r. entre eux** they like to get together; **on se retrouve entre gourmets/jeunes au Cheval Blanc** foodies/young people get together at the Cheval Blanc

3 (se rencontrer à nouveau) to meet again; Fam **on se retrouvera, mon bonhomme!** I'll get even with you, chum!; **comme on se retrouve!** fancy meeting you here!, well, well, well, look who's here!

4 (être de nouveau) to find oneself back (again); **se r. dans la même situation (qu'avant)** to find oneself back in the same situation (as before)

5 (par hasard) to end up; **je me suis retrouvé de l'autre côté de la frontière** I ended up on the other side of the border; **se r. dans la même situation (que quelqu'un d'autre)** to find oneself in or to end up in the same situation (as someone else); **à 40 ans, il s'est retrouvé veuf** he (suddenly) found himself a widower at 40; **tu vas te r. à l'hôpital** you'll end up in hospital

6 (se repérer) to find one's way; **je ne m'y retrouve plus dans tous ces formulaires à remplir** I can't make head or tail of all these forms to fill in; **s'y r.** (résoudre un problème) to sort things out; (faire un bénéfice) to make a profit; **il s'y retrouve (largement)!** he does more than break even!

7 (se ressourcer) to find oneself again, to go back to one's roots

---

rétroversé, -e [retroverse] ADJ Méd (utérus) retroverted

rétroversion [retroversjɔ̃] NF Méd retroversion

rétrovirus [retrovirys] NM Méd retrovirus; **r. spumeux** foamy virus, Spéc spumaretrovirus

rétroviseur [retrovizœr] NM Aut **r. (central)** (rearview) mirror; **r. extérieur** Br wing mirror, Am side-view mirror; **r. latéral** Br wing mirror, Am side-view mirror

rets [rɛ] NM 1 (gén pl) Littéraire (piège) snare; Fig **attraper** ou **prendre qn dans ses r.** to ensnare sb; Fig **tomber dans les r. de qn** to be caught in sb's trap 2 (filet → de chasse) net, snare; (→ de pêche) (fishing) net

retsina [retsina] NM retsina

retuber [3] [rətybe] VT Tech to retube

reuch [rœʃ] ADJ INV Fam (verlan de cher) expensive■, pricey

reuf [rœf] NM Fam (verlan de frère) brother■, bro

reum [rœm] NF Fam (verlan de mère) old lady, Br old dear

réunification [reynifikasjɔ̃] NF reunification

réunifier [9] [reynifje] VT to reunify, to reunite

Réunion [reynjɔ̃] NF (l'île de) **la R.** Réunion; **vivre à la R.** to live in Réunion; **aller à la R.** to go to Réunion

réunion [reynjɔ̃] NF 1 (rassemblement) gathering, get-together; **r. de famille** family reunion or gathering; **c'est l'occasion d'une r. familiale** it's an opportunity to bring the family together; **droit de r.** right of assembly

2 (fête) gathering, party; **j'organise une petite r. entre amis** I'm having a small party for my friends, I'm entertaining a few friends

3 (retrouvailles) reunion; **r. d'anciens élèves** school reunion

4 (congrès) meeting; (séance) session, sitting; **dites que je suis en r.** say that I'm in a meeting; **r. d'actionnaires** shareholders' meeting; **r. de comité** committee meeting; **r. du conseil d'administration** board meeting; **r. de la Cour** court session; **r. électorale** election meeting; **r. de groupe** (pour étude de marché) group meeting; **r. paritaire** round-table conference; **r. du Parlement** Parliamentary session; **r. du personnel** staff meeting; **r. préparatoire** briefing;

r. publique public *or* open meeting; **r. de remue-méninges** brainstorming session; **r. au sommet** summit (meeting *or* conference); **r. syndicale** union meeting

5 *(regroupement → de faits, de preuves)* bringing together, assembling, gathering; *(→ de sociétés, de services)* merging; *(→ d'États)* union; **la r. de ces territoires à la France a eu lieu en 1823** these territories were united with France in 1823

6 *Sport* meeting; **r. (sportive)** sports meeting, sporting event; **r. d'athlétisme** athletics meeting; **r. hippique** horse show

7 *Math* union

réunionnais, -e [reynjɔnɛ, -ɛz] **ADJ** of/from Réunion

▫ **Réunionnais, -e NM,F** = inhabitant of or person from Réunion

réunionnite [reynjɔnit] **NF** *Fam* meeting mania

réunion-téléphone® [reynjɔ̃telefɔn] *(pl* **réunions-téléphone) NF** *(appel)* conference call; *(système)* conference calling

réunir [32] [reynir] **VT 1** *(relier → pôles, tuyaux)* to join (together); *(→ brins, câbles)* to tie together

2 *(mettre ensemble → objets)* to collect together; *(→ bétail)* to round up; **le spectacle réunit ses meilleures chansons** the show is a collection of his/her best hits; **r. qch à qch** *(province)* to join sth to sth; **propriétés réunies au domaine royal en 1823** land acquired by the Crown in 1823

3 *(combiner → goûts, couleurs)* to combine; *(→ qualités)* to have; *(conditions requises)* to meet, to satisfy

4 *(recueillir → statistiques, propositions, informations)* to put *or* to collect together; *(→ preuves)* to put together; *(→ fonds)* to raise

5 *(personnes → rassembler)* to bring together; *(→ après une séparation)* to reunite; **nous sommes enfin réunis!** *(après rendez-vous manqué)* here we are together at last!, we found each other at last!; *(après querelle)* we're back together again!; **le séminaire réunira des chercheurs émérites** some highly talented researchers will be attending the conference; **réunissez les élèves par groupes de dix** gather *or* put the pupils into groups of ten

▸ **se réunir VPR 1** *(se retrouver ensemble → amis)* to meet, to get together; **l'assemblée se réunit une fois par semaine** the assembly meets once a week

2 *(fusionner)* to unite, to join (together)

réunis, -ies [reyni] **ADJ PL 1** *(rassemblés)* combined; **les influences lunaire et solaire réunies** the combined influence of the moon and the sun **2** *(dans un titre commercial)* **les Cavistes/Mareyeurs R.** United Vintners/Fisheries

réunissage [reynisaʒ] **NM** *Tex* doubling

reunoi [rənwa] = **renoi**

reup [rœp] **NM** *Fam (verlan de* **père***)* old man

reuss [rœs] **NF** *Fam (verlan de* **sœur***)* sister■, sis

réussi, -e [reysi] **ADJ** successful; **ton tricot/soufflé est très r.** your sweater/soufflé is a real success; **ce fut un retour r.** the homecoming was a success; *Ironique* **comme fête, c'était r.!** call that a party!; *Ironique* **ah c'est r.!, la voilà en larmes!** well done *or* very clever!, she's in tears now!

réussir [32] [reysir] **VT** *(manœuvre, œuvre, recette)* to make a success of, to carry off; *(exercice)* to succeed in doing; *(examen)* to pass; **il a réussi son saut périlleux/sa nature morte** his somersault/still life was a success; **elle réussit bien les omelettes** she makes very good omelettes; *Fam* **j'ai bien réussi mon coup** it worked out (well) for me, I managed to pull it off; *Ironique* **ah bravo, tu as bien réussi ton coup!** well done!, very clever!; **r. sa vie** to make a success of one's life; **r. son effet** to achieve the desired effect; **avec ce concert, il réussit un tour de force** his concert is a great achievement

VI 1 *(dans la vie, à l'école)* to do well, to be successful; **je veux r.** I want to succeed *or* to be a success *or* to be successful; **il a réussi dans la vie** he's done well in life, he's a successful man; **un jeune acteur qui va r.** an up-and-coming young actor; **une femme d'affaires qui a réussi** a successful businesswoman; **r. à un examen** to pass an exam; **nous sommes ravis d'apprendre que vous avez réussi** we're delighted to hear of your success

2 *(affaire, entreprise)* to succeed, to be a success; **l'opération n'a pas vraiment réussi** the operation wasn't really a success

3 *(parvenir)* **r. à faire qch** to manage to do sth, to succeed in doing sth; **j'ai réussi à le réparer/à me couper** I managed to mend it/to cut myself; **il réussit finalement à s'échapper** he finally managed to escape; **je n'ai pas réussi à la convaincre** I didn't manage *or* I failed to persuade her

4 *(convenir)* **r. à qn** *(climat, nourriture)* to agree with sb, to do sb good; **le café lui réussit/ne lui réussit pas** coffee agrees/doesn't agree with him/her; **on dirait que ça te réussit, le mariage!** being married *or* married life seems to suit you!; **il a essayé de les rouler, mais ça ne lui a pas réussi** he tried to swindle them but it didn't do him any good *or* it didn't get him very far; **tout lui réussit** he's/she's successful in everything he/she does, everything he/she does turns out well; **rien ne lui réussit** he/she can't do anything right

5 *Agr & Hort* to thrive, to do well

réussite [reysit] **NF 1** *(succès)* success; **c'est une r.!** it's a (real) success!; **son premier album est une r.** his/her first album is a success; **à quoi attribuez-vous votre r.?** what is the secret of your success?; **fêter sa r. à un examen** to celebrate passing an exam *or* getting through an exam; **r. (sociale)** (social) success; **tout ce qui lui importe, c'est la r.** the only thing that matters to him/her is success

2 *Cartes* patience; **faire une r.** to have a game of patience

réutilisable [reytilizabl] **ADJ** reusable; **non r.** disposable, throwaway

réutilisation [reytilizasjɔ̃] **NF** reuse

réutiliser [3] [reytilize] **VT** to reuse, to use again

revaccination [rəvaksinasjɔ̃] **NF** revaccination

revacciner [3] [rəvaksine] **VT** to revaccinate

revaloir [60] [rəvalwar] **VT je te revaudrai ça** *(en remerciant)* I'll repay you some day; *(en menaçant)* I'll get even with you for that, I'll pay you back for that

revalorisation [rəvalɔrizasjɔ̃] **NF 1** *(d'une monnaie)* revaluation **2** *(des salaires, des retraites)* raising, revaluation, increment **3** *(d'une théorie, d'une profession)* upgrading, reassertion; **on assiste à une r. du rôle des pères** the role of the father is becoming more important

revaloriser [3] [rəvalɔrize] **VT 1** *(monnaie)* to revaluate **2** *(salaires, retraites)* to raise, to revalue **3** *(théorie, profession)* to improve the status *or* prestige *or* standing of, to upgrade

revanchard, -e [rəvɑ̃ʃar, -ard] *Péj* **ADJ** *(attitude, politique)* of revenge, revengeful, *Sout* revanchard; *(personne)* revengeful, set on revenge, *Sout* revanchist

NM,F revanchist

revanche [rəvɑ̃ʃ] **NF 1** *(sur un ennemi)* revenge; **prendre sa r. (sur qn)** to take *or* to get one's revenge (on sb) **2** *Sport & (dans un jeu)* return game; **donner sa r. à qn** to give sb his/her revenge

▫ **en revanche ADV** on the other hand

revancher [3] [rəvɑ̃ʃe] **se revancher VPR** *Vieilli ou Littéraire (prendre sa revanche)* to revenge oneself; **se r. d'un bienfait** to return a favour

revanchisme [rəvɑ̃ʃism] **NM** revanchism, spirit of revenge

revascularisation [rəvaskylarizasjɔ̃] **NF** *Méd* revascularization

revasculariser [3] [rəvaskylarize] **VT** *Méd* to revascularize

rêvasser [3] [rɛvase] **VI** to daydream, to dream away, to muse; **arrête de r.** stop daydreaming!

rêvasserie [rɛvasri] **NF** daydream; **des rêvasseries sans fin** endless musing *or* daydreaming

rêvasseur, -euse [rɛvasœr, -øz] **ADJ** dreamlike, dreamy

NM,F daydreamer

revaudra *etc voir* **revaloir**

rêve [rɛv] **NM 1** *(d'un dormeur)* dream; **un mauvais r.** a nightmare, a bad dream; **faire un r.** to have a dream; **je l'ai vu en r.** I saw him in my *or* in a dream; **comme dans un r.** as if in a dream; **bonne nuit, fais de beaux rêves!** good night, sweet dreams!; *Psy* **le r.** dreams, dreaming

2 *(d'un utopiste)* dream, fantasy, pipe dream; **mon r., ce serait d'aller au Japon** my dream is to go to Japan, I dream of going to Japan; **tout ça, ce sont des rêves** that's all (just) fantasy *or* cloud-cuckoo-land; **rêves de gloire/célébrité** dreams of glory/fame; **un r. devenu réalité** a dream come true; **dans mes rêves les plus fous** in my wildest dreams *or* imaginings; **perdu dans son r.** *ou* **ses rêves** lost in his/her dream world; **un r. éveillé** a waking dream

3 *Fam* **le r.** *(l'idéal)* the ideal thing; **c'est/ce n'est pas le r.** it's/it isn't ideal; **c'est le r. pour un pique-nique, ici!** this place is just perfect for a picnic!; **ce n'est pas le r. mais il faudra faire avec** it's not exactly what I'd/we'd/*etc* dreamt of but it'll have to do

▫ **de mes/ses/***etc* **rêves ADJ** of my/his/*etc* dreams; **j'ai le métier de mes rêves** I've got the job I always dreamed of having; **la maison de leurs rêves** the house of their dreams, their dream house; **la femme de ses rêves** the woman of his dreams, his dream woman

▫ **de rêve ADJ** ideal, perfect; **une vie de r.** a sublime *or* an ideal existence; **un mariage de r.** a perfect marriage; **il fait un temps de r.** the weather is perfect

rêvé, -e [rɛve] **ADJ** perfect, ideal; **c'est l'endroit r. pour camper** this is the ideal place *or* just the place to camp

revêche [rəvɛʃ] **ADJ** *(personne)* surly, cantankerous, tetchy; *(voix, air)* surly, grumpy

revécu, -e [rəveky] **PP** *voir* **revivre**

réveil [revɛj] **NM 1** *(après le sommeil)* waking (up), *Littéraire* awakening; **je déteste l'heure du r.** I hate waking up *or* having to wake up (in the morning); **j'attendrai ton r. pour partir** I'll wait until you've woken up *or* until you're awake before I leave; **j'ai des réveils difficiles** *ou* **le r. difficile** I find it hard to wake up; **à mon r. il était là** when I woke up he was there

2 *(prise de conscience)* awakening

3 *Mil* reveille; **r. au clairon** (bugle) reveille; *Fig* **j'ai eu droit à un r. en fanfare, ce matin!** I was treated to a very noisy awakening this morning!

4 *(de la mémoire, de la nature)* reawakening; *(d'une douleur)* return, new onset; *(d'un volcan)* (new) stirring, fresh eruption

5 *(pendule)* alarm (clock); **j'ai mis le r. (à 7 heures)** I've set the alarm (for 7 o'clock); **r. téléphonique** wake-up service; **r. de voyage** travelling alarm clock

réveille-matin [revɛjmatɛ̃] **NM INV** *Vieilli* alarm (clock)

réveiller [4] [reveje] **VT 1** *(tirer → du sommeil, de l'évanouissement)* to wake (up); *(→ d'une réflexion, d'une rêverie)* to rouse, to stir; **il faut que l'on se fasse r. à 7 heures si on ne veut pas rater l'avion** we need to make sure somebody wakes us up at 7 am if we don't want to miss the plane; **un bruit/une explosion à r. les morts** a noise/an explosion loud enough to wake the dead; **le soleil réveillait peu à peu la nature** nature gradually began to stir under the sun's rays; **r. les consciences** to stir people's consciences

2 *(faire renaître → enthousiasme, rancœur, souvenirs)* to reawaken, to revive

▸ **se réveiller VPR 1** *(sortir → du sommeil, de l'évanouissement)* to wake (up), to awake *or* to awaken; *(→ d'une réflexion, de la torpeur)* to wake up, to stir *or* to rouse oneself; **se r. en retard** to oversleep; **se r. en sursaut** to wake up with a start; **il faut vous r.!** you'd better pull yourself together!; **le pays est en train de se r.** the country is beginning to stir itself *or* shake itself *or* waken up

2 *(se ranimer → passion, souvenir)* to revive, to be stirred up *or* aroused (again); *(→ volcan)* to stir *or* to erupt again; *(→ nature)* to revive; *(→ maladie, douleur)* to start up again, to return

réveillon [revɛjɔ̃] **NM** = family meal eaten on Christmas Eve or New Year's Eve; **r. (de Noël)** *(fête)* Christmas Eve party; *(repas)* Christmas Eve supper; **r. (de la Saint-Sylvestre** *ou* **du jour de l'an)** *(fête)* New Year's Eve party; *(repas)* New Year's Eve supper

réveillonner [3] [revɛjɔne] **VI** *(faire une fête → à Noël)* to have a Christmas Eve party; *(→ pour la Saint-Sylvestre)* to have a New Year's Eve party; *(faire un repas → à Noël)* to have a Christmas Eve supper; *(→ pour la Saint-Sylvestre)* to have a New Year's Eve supper; **nous avons trop bien réveillonné** we had too much to eat and drink *(on Christmas Eve or New Year's Eve)*

révélateur, -trice [revelatœr, -tris] **ADJ** *(détail)* revealing, indicative, significant; *(lapsus, sourire)* revealing, telltale; **une interview révélatrice** a revealing interview; **les chiffres sont révélateurs** the figures speak volumes; **ce sondage est très r. de la tendance actuelle** this poll tells us *or* reveals a lot about the current trend; **c'est tout à fait r. de notre époque** it says a lot about our times; **c'est r. de son manque de confiance en lui** it reveals *or* shows his lack of confidence; **un décolleté r.** a plunging neckline
NM,F revealer
NM 1 *(indice)* telltale sign
2 *Phot* developer

révélation [revelasjɔ̃] **NF 1** *(information)* revelation, disclosure; **faire des révélations à la presse/police** to give the press a scoop/the police important information; **Mylène Jauvert nous fait ses révélations!** Mylène Jauvert tells *or* reveals all (her secrets)!
2 *(personne)* **il pourrait bien être la r. musicale de l'année** he could well turn out to be this year's musical revelation *or* discovery
3 *(prise de conscience)* revelation; **ce voyage en Égypte a été une r.** that trip to Egypt was an eye-opener *or* a revelation; **avoir une r.** to have a brainwave
4 *(divulgation)* disclosure, revealing; **la r. d'un complot** the revealing *or* uncovering of a plot; *Jur* **r. de secret** breach of secrecy
5 *Rel* revelation

révélatrice [revelatris] *voir* **révélateur**

révélé, -e [revele] **ADJ** *(religion)* revealed

révéler [18] [revele] **VT 1** *(secret, information, intention)* to reveal, to disclose; *(état de fait)* to reveal, to bring to light; *(vérité)* to reveal, to tell; **j'ai des choses importantes à r. à la police** I have important information to give to the police; **qui sait ce que ces murs révéleraient s'ils pouvaient parler** who knows what these walls would tell if they could speak!; **elle a révélé mon secret** *(intentionnellement)* she revealed my secret; *(involontairement)* she gave away my secret; **le nom de la victime n'a toujours pas été révélé** the victim's name has still not been disclosed *or* released; **il refuse de r. son identité** he's refusing to disclose his identity *or* to say who he is; **Journ r. ses sources** to reveal one's sources; **le monde de corruption révélé par cette enquête** the world of corruption brought to light by this investigation
2 *(montrer → don, qualité, anomalie)* to reveal, to show; **ce comportement révèle une nature violente** this behaviour reveals a violent temperament; **la mauvaise gestion révélée par ces chiffres** the bad management brought to light *or* evidenced by these results; *Méd* **une grosseur que les radios n'avaient pas révélée** a growth which hadn't shown up on the X-rays; **l'actrice révèle dans cette scène un talent prometteur** the actress shows promising talent in this scene

3 *(faire connaître)* **r. qn** to make sb famous; **révélé par un important metteur en scène** discovered by an important director; **dans l'album qui l'a révélé (au public)** on the album which brought him fame
4 *Phot* to develop
►se révéler VPR 1 *(s'avérer)* **se r. coûteux/utile** to prove (to be) expensive/useful; **il s'est révélé d'un égoïsme effrayant** he proved to be dreadfully selfish; **l'expérience ne s'est pas révélée concluante** the experiment wasn't conclusive *or* turned out to be inconclusive; **elle se révéla piètre vendeuse** she turned out *or* proved to be a poor sales assistant; **il s'est révélé être un escroc** he turned out to be a crook
2 *(se faire connaître)* to be revealed *or* discovered, to come to light; **tu t'es révélé sous ton vrai jour** you've showed yourself in your true colours; **elle s'est révélée (au grand public) dans 'Carmen'** she had her first big success in 'Carmen'

revenant, -e [rəvnɑ̃, -ɑ̃t] **NM,F** *Fam Hum* **tiens, un r.!** hello, stranger!, long time no see!
NM *(fantôme)* ghost, spirit; **une histoire de revenants** a ghost story

revendable [rəvɑ̃dabl] **ADJ** resaleable

revendeur, -euse [rəvɑ̃dœr, -øz] **NM,F 1** *(détaillant)* retailer, dealer; **vous trouverez le dernier modèle chez votre r. habituel** you'll find the latest model at your local dealer **2** *(de billets, de tickets)* *Br* tout, *Am* scalper; *(d'articles d'occasion)* second-hand dealer; **r. de drogue** drug dealer; **r. de voitures** second-hand car dealer

revendicateur, -trice [rəvɑ̃dikatœr, -tris] **ADJ des discours revendicateurs** speeches setting out demands *or* claims
NM,F les revendicateurs demandaient une augmentation de salaire the claimants *or* protestors were pushing for a wage increase

revendicatif, -ive [rəvɑ̃dikatif, -iv] **ADJ** protest *(avant n)*; **un mouvement r.** a protest movement; **journée revendicative** day of action *or* protest

revendication [rəvɑ̃dikasjɔ̃] **NF 1** *(réclamation)* demand; **journée de r.** day of action *or* of protest; **revendications salariales** wage demands *or* claims; **revendications syndicales** union demands **2** *Jur* claim; **mener une action en r. contre qn** to set up *or* to lodge a claim against sb

revendicative [rəvɑ̃dikativ] *voir* **revendicatif**

revendicatrice [rəvɑ̃dikatris] *voir* **revendicateur**

revendiquer [3] [rəvɑ̃dike] **VT 1** *(réclamer → dû, droit, part d'héritage)* to claim; *(→ hausse de salaire)* to demand; **il revendique le droit de s'exprimer librement** he claims the right of free speech
2 *(assumer)* to lay claim to, to claim; **r. la responsabilité de qch** to claim responsibility for sth; **l'attentat n'a pas été revendiqué** nobody has claimed responsibility for the attack; **c'est un nom que je revendique** it's a name I am proud to bear; **il n'a jamais revendiqué cette paternité** he never claimed this child as his; **j'ai eu ma part de misère et je la revendique!** I've known what it is to be poor and I'm not ashamed of it!
3 *Jur* to lay claim to, to claim
USAGE ABSOLU le personnel revendique the staff are making demands *or* have put in a claim
❑ se revendiquer VPR il se revendique comme anarchiste he's a staunch anarchist

revendre [73] [rəvɑ̃dr] **VT 1** *(vendre → gén)* to sell; *(sujet: détaillant)* to retail; *Bourse (titres)* to sell out; **j'ai revendu ma maison plus cher que je ne l'avais achetée** I sold my house for more than I paid for it; **revends ta voiture, si tu as besoin d'argent** if you need money, sell your car
2 *Fam (locutions)* **des crayons, j'en ai à r.** I've got loads of pencils; **avoir du talent/de l'ambition à r.** she's got masses of talent/ambition; **avoir de l'énergie à r.** to be bubbling over with energy
►se revendre VPR ce genre d'appareil ne se revend pas facilement this sort of equipment isn't easy to resell; **dans cinq ans, cette maison se revendra beaucoup plus cher** in five years this house will be worth far more than it is now

revenez-y [rəvnezi] **NM INV 1** *Littéraire (retour vers* le passé) reversion, throwback **2** *Fam (locution)* **ce vin a un petit goût de r.!** this wine is rather moreish!

REVENIR [40] [rəvnir]

> to come back 1–3 ■ to return 1, 2 ■ to recur 2 ■ to reappear 2 ■ to crop up again 2

VI 1 *(venir à nouveau → gén)* to come back; *(→ chez soi)* to come back, to come (back) home, to return home; *(→ au point de départ)* to return, to come *or* to get back; **pouvez-vous r. plus tard?** could you come back later?; **elle est passée ce matin et a dit qu'elle reviendrait** she popped in this morning and said she would be *or* come back; **une fois revenue chez elle** once she'd got (back) home; **je suis revenue de Rome hier** I came *or* I got back from Rome yesterday; **passe me voir en revenant du bureau** call in to see me on your way back *or* home from the office; **je reviens (tout de suite)** I'll be (right) back; **les gens sont revenus à leur place** people are back in *or* have returned to their seats; **il n'est pas encore revenu de faire ses commissions** he hasn't come *or* got back from his errands yet; **je suis revenu déçu de la visite** I came back disappointed after the visit; **le boomerang revient vers celui qui l'a lancé** boomerangs return to the thrower; **la lettre m'est revenue** the letter was returned to me; **ça ne sert à rien de pleurer, ça ne va pas le faire r.!** it's no use crying, it's not going to bring him back!; **r. à qn** *(renouer le contact avec)* to come back to sb; **enfin tu me reviens!** at last, you've come back to me!; **d'où nous revenez-vous?** and where have you been?; **nous aimons r. ici** we like coming (back) here; **je ne reviendrai jamais chez ce coiffeur** I'll never come back to this hairdresser again; **je suis très satisfait de mes achats, je reviendrai** I'm very pleased with what I've bought, I'll be back; **r. en arrière** *(dans le temps)* to go back (in time); *(dans l'espace)* to retrace one's steps, to go back; **revenons en arrière, au début de l'année 1914** let's go back to the beginning of (the year) 1914; **r. au point de départ** to go back to the starting point; *Fig* to be back to square one
2 *(se manifester à nouveau → doute, inquiétude)* to return, to come back; *(→ calme, paix)* to return, to be restored; *(→ symptôme)* to recur, to return, to reappear; *(→ problème)* to crop up *or* to arise again; *(→ occasion)* to crop up again; *(→ thème, rime)* to recur, to reappear; *(→ célébration)* to come round again; *(→ saison)* to return, to come back; *(→ soleil)* to come out again, to reappear; **le temps des fêtes est revenu** the festive season is with us again *or* has come round again; **la question qui revient le plus fréquemment dans les entretiens** the most commonly asked question *or* the question that crops up most often in interviews; **la question revient toujours sur le tapis** that question always comes up for discussion; **c'est un thème qui revient toujours dans ses romans** it's a recurring theme in his/her novels; **c'est une erreur qui revient souvent dans vos devoirs** you often make this mistake in your homework; **ses crises reviennent de plus en plus souvent** his/her fits are becoming more and more frequent; **j'ai désherbé, mais les orties reviennent de plus belle** I've weeded, but the nettles are even worse than before
3 *Sport (dans une course)* to come back, to catch up; **le peloton est en train de r. sur les échappés** the pack is catching up with *or* gaining on the breakaway group; **et voici Bapow qui revient pour prendre la troisième place!** and it's Bapow who comes back to take third place!
4 *(coûter)* **r. cher** to be expensive; **r. à** to cost, to amount to, to come to; **elle a dû te r. cher, ta petite sortie!** your little night out must have cost you a lot!; **le voyage nous est revenu à 300 euros** the trip cost us 300 euros; **le tout ne reviendra pas à plus de 100 euros** it won't come to *or* cost any more than 100 euros for everything
5 *Culin* **faire r.** to brown; **une fois les oignons**

revenus once the onions have browned *or* are brown

6 *Fam (retrouver son état normal → tissu)* **les draps sont bien revenus au lavage** the sheets came up like new in the wash

▫ **revenir à** **VT IND** **1** *(équivaloir à)* to come down to, to amount to; **cela reviendrait à une rupture de contrat** that would amount to *or* mean a breach of contract; **cela revient toujours à une question de relations** it always boils down *or* comes down to having the right connections; **ce qui revient à dire que...** which amounts to saying that...; **ça revient au même!** it amounts to *or* comes to the same thing!; **pour moi, ça revient au même, il faudra que j'y aille** it's all the same to me, I'll have to go anyway

2 *(reprendre → mode, procédé, thème)* to go back to, to revert to, to return to; **le gouvernement veut r. à la liberté des prix** the government wants to return to price deregulation; **on revient aux** *ou* **à la mode des cheveux courts** short hair is coming back *or* on its way back; **r. à une plus juste vision des choses** to come round to a more balanced view of things; **r. à de meilleures dispositions** *ou* **à de meilleurs sentiments** to return to a better frame of mind; **on (en) revient à des formes d'énergie naturelles** natural sources of energy are coming back into use, we're reverting to natural sources of energy; **mais revenons** *ou* **revenons-en à cette affaire** but let's get *or* come back to this matter; **bon, pour (en) r. à notre histoire...** right, to get back to *or* to go on with our story...; **j'en** *ou* **je reviens à ma question, où étiez-vous hier?** I'm asking you again, where were you yesterday?; **et si nous (en) revenions à vous, M. Lebrun?** now what about you, Mr Lebrun?; **voilà 20 euros, et n'y reviens plus!** here's 20 euros, and don't ask me again!; **il n'y a pas** *ou* **plus à y r.!** and that's final *or* that's that!; **r. à soi** to come to, to come round

3 *(sujet: part, récompense)* to go *or* to fall to, to devolve on; *(sujet: droit, tâche)* to fall to; **à chacun ce qui lui revient** to each his due; **avec les honneurs qui lui reviennent** with the honours (which are) due to him/her; **ses terrains sont revenus à l'État** his/her lands passed *or* went to the State; **il devrait encore me r. 20 euros** I should still get 20 euros; **oui, il m'est quand même revenu un rang de perles** yes, I was left a string of pearls all the same; **ce titre lui revient de droit** this title is his/hers by right; **tout le mérite t'en revient** the credit is all yours, you get all the credit for it; **la décision nous revient, il nous revient de décider** it's for us *or* up to us to decide

4 *(sujet: faculté, souvenir)* to come back to; **l'appétit lui revient** he's/she's recovering his/her appetite *or* getting his/her appetite back; **l'usage de son bras gauche ne lui est jamais revenu** he/she never recovered the use of his/her left arm; **la mémoire lui revient** his/her memory is coming back; **son nom ne me revient pas (à la mémoire)** his/her name escapes me *or* has slipped my mind; **attends, ça me revient!** wait, I've got it now *or* it's coming back to me now!; **ça me revient seulement maintenant, ils ont divorcé** I've just remembered, they got divorced; **tu ne te souviens pas de cet article? – si, ça me revient maintenant!** don't you remember that article? – yes, I'm with you now *or* it's coming back to me now!

5 *(tournure impersonnelle)* **il me revient que tu étais riche à l'époque** as I recall, you were rich at the time; **r. à qn** *ou* **aux oreilles de qn** to get back to sb, to reach sb's ears; **il m'est revenu que...** word has got back to me *or* has reached me that...

6 *Fam (plaire à)* **ses manières ne me reviennent pas** his/her manners aren't to my liking; **elle a une tête qui ne me revient pas** I don't really like the look of her

▫ **revenir de** **VT IND** **1** *(émotion, étonnement, maladie)* to get over, to recover from; *(évanouissement)* to come round from, to come to after; **alors, tu es revenu de ta grande frayeur?** so, are you less frightened now *or* have you got over the fright now?; *Euph* **elle revient de loin!** *(elle a failli mourir)* it was touch and go (for her)!; *(elle a eu de graves ennuis)* she's had a close shave!; **en r.** *(guérir)* to come *or* to pull through it, to recover; *(échapper à un danger)* to come through (it); **je n'en reviens pas!** I can't get over it!; **je n'en reviens pas qu'il ait dit ça!** it's amazing he should say that!, I can't get over him saying that!; **quand je vais te le raconter, tu n'en reviendras pas** when I tell you the story you won't believe your ears

2 *(idée, préjugé)* to put *or* to cast aside, to throw over; *(illusion)* to shake off; *(principe)* to give up, to leave behind; **r. de ses erreurs** to realize *or* to recognize one's mistakes; *Fam* **moi, l'homéopathie, j'en suis revenu!** as far as I'm concerned, I've done *or* I'm through with homeopathy!; *Fam* **ce type-là, j'en suis bien revenue!** I'm totally over that guy now!; **il est revenu de tout** he's seen it all (before)

3 **s'en r.** to be on one's way back; **nous nous en revenions tranquillement lorsque...** we were slowly making our way home when...

▫ **revenir sur** **VT IND** **1** *(question)* to go back over, to hark back to; **elle ne peut s'empêcher de r. sur cette triste affaire** she can't help going *or* mulling over that sad business; **la question est réglée, ne revenons pas dessus** the matter's settled, let's not go back over it again

2 *(décision, déclaration, promesse)* to go back on; **ma décision est prise, je ne reviendrai pas dessus** my mind is made up and I'm not going to change it; **r. sur sa parole** *ou* **sur la parole donnée** to go back on one's word, to break one's promise

3 *Belg (locution)* **ne pas r. sur** not to remember

revente [rəvɑ̃t] **NF** resale; *Bourse (de titres)* selling out; **la r. d'un tableau** the resale of a painting

revenu[1] [rəvəny] **NM** **1** *(rétribution → d'une personne)* income *(UNCOUNT)*; **elle a de gros/petits revenus** she has a large/small income; **sans revenus** without any income; **revenus accessoires** incidental income; **revenus actuels** current earnings *or* income; **r. annuel** annual income; **r. brut** gross income; **r. brut global** total gross income; **r. cumulé** cumulative revenue; **r. disponible** disposable income; **r. disponible brut** gross disposable income; *Admin* **r. familial** family income; **r. fictif** notional income; **r. fixe** fixed income; **r. foncier** income from *Br* property *or Am* real estate; **r. par habitant** *ou* **par tête** per capita income; **r. imposable** taxable income; **r. des intérêts** earned interest, interest income; **r. locatif** rental income; **r. marginal** marginal revenue *or* income; **r. minimum d'insertion** = minimum welfare payment paid to people with no other source of income, *Br* income support, *Am* welfare; **r. net** net income; **r. net global** total net income; **r. nominal** nominal income; **r. par habitant** per capita income; **r. personnel disponible** disposable personal income; **r. réel** real income; **r. résiduel** residual income; **revenus salariaux, r. du travail** earned income; **r. de société** corporate income; **r. de transfert** transfer income

2 *(recettes → de l'État)* revenue; *Écon* **r. national** national income; *Écon* **r. national brut/net** gross/net national income; **revenus de l'exportation** export revenue, export earnings; **revenus publics** *ou* **de l'État** public revenue; **revenus du secteur public** public sector earnings

3 *(intérêt)* income, return; *(dividende → d'une action)* yield (**de** on); **un investissement produisant un r. de 7 pour cent** an investment with a 7 percent rate of return; *Bourse* **r.** *ou* **revenus obligataire(s), r.** *ou* **revenus des obligations** income from bonds

4 *(bénéfice)* **r. brut d'exploitation** gross profit

5 *Métal* tempering

revenu[2], **-e**[1] [rəvəny] **PP** *voir* **revenir**

revenue[2] [rəvəny] **NF** *(en sylviculture)* new growth, young wood

rêver [4] [rɛve] **VI** **1** *(en dormant)* to dream (**de** of); **r. tout haut** to talk in one's sleep; **j'ai l'impression d'avoir rêvé!** I feel as if I've been dreaming!; **elle rêve (tout) éveillée** she's a daydreamer, she's lost in a dream *or* daydream; **c'est ce qu'il m'a dit, je n'ai pas rêvé!** that's what he said, I didn't dream it up *or* imagine it!; **toi ici? (dites moi que) je rêve!** you here? I must be dreaming!; **r. de** to dream of; **j'ai rêvé d'un monstre** I dreamed of *or* dreamt of *or* had a dream about a monster; **on croit r.!** *(ton irrité)* is this a joke?; **elle en rêve la nuit** she dreams about it at night; *Fig* she's obsessed by it

2 *(divaguer)* to be imagining things, to be in cloud-cuckoo-land; **dis-moi aussi que je rêve!** go ahead, tell me I'm imagining things!; **toi, gagner ta vie tout seul, non mais tu rêves!** you, earn your own living? you must be joking!; **ça fait r.!** that's the stuff that dreams are made of!; **13 pour cent d'intérêt, ça fait r., hein?** 13 percent interest, isn't that just great?; **des plages/salaires à faire r.** dream beaches/wages; **(quand on voit) des paysages comme ça, ça fait r.** scenery like that is just out of this world; **des mots qui font r.** words that fire the imagination; **on peut toujours r.** there's no harm in dreaming!, there's no harm in a little fantasizing!; **faut pas r.!** let's not get carried away!; **la semaine de 25 heures? faut pas r.!** the 25-hour week? that'll be the day!

3 *(rêvasser)* to dream, to daydream; **aide-nous, au lieu de r.!** give us a hand instead of dreaming *or* daydreaming!; **r. à** to dream of, *Sout* to muse over; **j'étais en train de r. à ma jeunesse** I was lost in thoughts of my youth

VT **1** *(sujet: dormeur)* to dream; **vous l'avez rêvé!** you must have imagined *or* dreamt it!, you must have been dreaming!; **r. que...** to dream that...

2 *(souhaiter)* to dream of; **on ne saurait r. (une) occasion plus propice** you couldn't wish for a more appropriate occasion; **je n'ai jamais rêvé mariage/fortune!** I've never dreamed of marriage/being wealthy!; **il ne rêve que plaies et bosses** he's always spoiling for a fight

3 *(inventer de toutes pièces)* to dream up; **il a dû r. toute cette histoire** he must have dreamt up the whole story

▫ **rêver de** **VT IND** *(espérer)* to dream of; **j'avais tellement rêvé de ton retour** I so longed for your return; **l'homme dont toutes les femmes rêvent** the man every woman dreams about *or* desires; **je n'avais jamais osé r. d'un bonheur pareil!** I'd never have dared dream of such happiness!; **r. de faire qch** to be longing to do sth

réverbérant, -e [revɛrberɑ̃, -ɑ̃t] **ADJ** reverberating, reverberant

réverbération [revɛrberasjɔ̃] **NF** **1** *(du son)* reverberation; *(de la chaleur, de la lumière)* reflection; **à cause de la r. du soleil sur la neige** because of the glare of the sun on the snow **2** *(en acoustique)* **durée** *ou* **temps de r.** reverberation time

réverbère [revɛrbɛr] **NM** **1** *(lampe)* streetlamp, streetlight; *(poteau)* lamppost; *Presse* **Le R.** = newspaper produced and sold by the homeless, *Br* ≃ The Big Issue **2** *(réflecteur)* reflector

réverbérer [18] [revɛrbere] **VT** *(chaleur, lumière)* to reflect; *(son)* to reverberate, to send back

reverchon [rəvɛrʃɔ̃] **NM** = variety of sweet cherry

reverdir [32] [rəvɛrdir] **VI** to grow *or* to turn green again; *Fig Littéraire* to grow young again

VT to paint *or* make green again; **le printemps reverdit les champs** spring makes the fields green again

reverdoir [rəvɛrdwar] **NM** *(en brasserie)* underback

révérence [reverɑ̃s] **NF** **1** *Littéraire (déférence)* reverence; **traiter qn avec r.** to treat sb with reverence *or* reverently; *Vieilli* **r. parler** saving your reverence, begging your pardon

2 *(salut → d'homme)* bow; *(→ de femme)* curtsy; **faire la r. à qn** *(sujet: homme)* to bow to sb; *(sujet: femme)* to curtsy to sb; **tirer sa r. à qn** to walk out on sb; **je vous tire ma r.** I'm off; **tirer sa r. à qch** to bow out of sth

3 *Rel* **Votre R.** Your Reverence

révérencieux, -euse [reverɑ̃sjø, -øz] **ADJ** *Littéraire* reverent

révérend, -e [reverɑ̃, -ɑ̃d] **ADJ** reverend; **la révérende mère supérieure** the Reverend Mother (Superior); **le r. père Thomas** (the) Reverend Father Thomas

NM reverend; **oui, mon r.** yes, Reverend

révérendissime [reverɑ̃disim] ADJ *(archevêque)* Most Reverend

révérer [18] [revere] VT to revere, *Sout* to reverence; **il révère son frère** he's devoted to *or* he reveres his brother

rêverie [rɛvri] NF **1** *(réflexion)* daydreaming *(UNCOUNT)*, reverie; **plongé dans mes/ses/***etc* **rêveries** *ou* **ma/sa/***etc* **r.** deep in thought **2** *(chimère)* dream, daydream, delusion

revérifier [9] [rəverifje] VT to check again, to double-check

revernir [32] [rəvɛrnir] VT to revarnish

reverra *etc voir* **revoir**[2]

revers [rəvɛr] NM **1** *(d'une blouse, d'un veston)* lapel; *(d'un pantalon) Br* turn-up, *Am* cuff; *(d'une manche)* (turned-back) cuff; *(d'un uniforme)* facing; **peignoir à r. de soie** dressing gown with silk lapels; **col/bottes à r.** turned-down collar/boots

2 *(d'une feuille, d'un tissu, d'un tableau, de la main)* back; *(d'une médaille, d'une pièce)* reverse (side); **essuyant d'un r. de main la sueur qui coulait de son front** wiping the sweat from his/her forehead with the back of his/her hand; *Fig* **le r. de la médaille** the other side of the coin

3 *(échec, défaite)* setback; **essuyer un r.** to suffer a setback; **r. économiques** economic setbacks; **r. de fortune** reverse of fortune, setback (in one's fortunes)

4 *(au tennis)* backhand (shot); **faire un r.** to play a backhand shot; **jouer en r.** to play backhand

❑ **à revers** ADV *Mil* from *or* in the rear

réversal, -e, -aux, -ales [revɛrsal, -o] *Jur* ADJ **lettres réversales** letters of mutual concessions

❑ **réversales** NFPL letters of mutual concessions

reversement [rəvɛrsəmɑ̃] NM *Fin* transfer

reverser [3] [rəvɛrse] VT **1** *(verser → de nouveau)* to pour again, to pour (out) more (of); *(→ dans le récipient d'origine)* to pour back; **je vous reverse un verre?** shall I pour you another glass?

2 *Fin (reporter)* to transfer; **r. des intérêts sur un compte** to pay interest on an account; **la prime d'assurance vous sera intégralement reversée au bout d'un an** the total premium will be paid back to you after one year

reversi [rəvɛrsi] NM *(avec des cartes)* reversis; *(avec des pions)* reversi

réversibilité [revɛrsibilite] NF **1** *(d'un processus)* reversibility **2** *Jur (d'un bien, d'une pension)* revertibility

réversible [revɛrsibl] ADJ **1** *(vêtement)* reversible **2** *Jur (bien, pension)* revertible; **annuité r.** reversionary annuity **3** *Chim & Phys* reversible

réversion [revɛrsjɔ̃] NF *Biol, Jur & Métal* reversion

reversoir [rəvɛrswar] NM barrage, weir

revêtement [rəvɛtmɑ̃] NM **1** *(intérieur → peinture)* covering; *(→ enduit)* coating; *(extérieur → gén)* facing; *(→ crépi)* rendering; **r. de sol** flooring; **r. de sol stratifié** laminate flooring; **r. mural** wall covering

2 *Constr (d'une voie)* surface (material); **refaire le r. d'une route** to resurface a road

3 *Tech (d'un câble électrique)* housing, sheathing; *(d'un pneu)* casing; *(d'un conduit)* lining; **r. calorifuge** lagging; **r. galvanique** electroplating

4 *Aviat* skin

5 *Archit* revetment

6 *Mines* lining

revêtir [44] [rəvɛtir] VT **1** *Sout (endosser)* to don; **r. ses plus beaux atours** to array oneself in *or* to don one's finest attire; **la montagne a revêtu son habit de bruyère** the mountain is clad in its cloak of heather; **champs revêtus de verdure** verdure-clad fields

2 *Sout (habiller)* **r. qn de** to dress *or* to array sb in, to clothe sb in *or* with; **on l'avait revêtue d'une lourde cape** she had been arrayed *or* garbed in a heavy cloak; **un mur revêtu de lierre** an ivy-clad wall; *Fig* **r. qn d'une dignité/d'une autorité** to invest sb with a dignity/an authority

3 *(importance, signification)* to take on, to assume; *(forme)* to appear in, to take on, to assume; **ses propos revêtent un caractère dangereux** there's something dangerous in what he/she says; **Merlin revêtit l'aspect d'une souris** Merlin took on *or* assumed the appearance of a mouse

4 *Archit & Constr (rue → asphalter)* to surface; *(→ paver)* to pave; **r. une surface de** to cover a surface with; **des murs revêtus de boiseries** panelled walls

5 *Tech (chaudière)* to line, to lag; *(puits de mine)* to line

6 *Jur* **r. un contrat de signatures** to append signatures to a contract; **laissez-passer revêtu du tampon obligatoire** authorization bearing the regulation stamp

▶**se revêtir** VPR *Sout* **se r. de** *(endosser)* to don

reveulent *voir* **revouloir**

rêveur, -euse [rɛvœr, -øz] ADJ **1** *(distrait)* dreamy; **avoir un caractère r.** to be a daydreamer; **d'un air r.** dreamily; **d'un ton r.** dreamily

2 *(perplexe)* **laisser qn r.** to leave sb baffled *or* in a state of bafflement; **cette dernière phrase me laissa r.** these last words puzzled *or* baffled me; **ça laisse r.!** it makes you wonder!

NM,F dreamer, daydreamer

rêveusement [rɛvøzmɑ̃] ADV dreamily; **regarder r. par la fenêtre** to gaze absent-mindedly out of the window

reveut, reveux *voir* **revouloir**

reviens [rəvjɛ̃] NM *Fam* **je te prête mon dico mais il s'appelle r.** I'll lend you my dictionary but I'll need it back■

revient[1] *etc voir* **revenir**

revient[2] [rəvjɛ̃] NM *voir* **prix**

revif [rəvif] NM **1** *(de la marée)* rising of water (between low and high tide) **2** *Littéraire (regain)* renewal, revival; **un r. d'énergie** fresh energy; **un r. d'espoir** renewed hope

revigorant, -e [rəvigɔrɑ̃, -ɑ̃t] ADJ *(gén)* invigorating; *(vent, promenade)* bracing; *(bain)* invigorating, refreshing; *(boisson, aliment)* reviving, refreshing

revigorer [3] [rəvigɔre] VT **1** *(stimuler → sujet: vent, promenade)* to invigorate; *(→ sujet: bain)* to invigorate, to refresh; *(→ sujet: boisson, aliment)* to revive, to refresh; **une petite promenade pour vous r.?** how about a bracing little walk?

2 *(relancer → économie)* to boost, to give a boost to; **les subventions ont revigoré l'entreprise** the subsidies gave the company a new lease of life

revint *etc voir* **revenir**

revirement [rəvirmɑ̃] NM *(changement → d'avis)* about-face, change of mind; *(→ de situation)* turnaround, about-face, sudden turn; **un r. dans l'opinion publique** a complete swing *or* turnaround in public opinion; **un r. de la tendance sur le marché des valeurs** a sudden reversal of stock market trends

revirer [3] [rəvire] VI *Can Fam (changer)* **r. de capot** to switch allegiances■

révisable [revizabl] ADJ **1** *(gén)* revisable **2** *Jur* reviewable

réviser [3] [revize] VT **1** *Scol & Univ* to revise, to go over (again)

2 *(réévaluer → jugement, situation)* to review, to re-examine, to reappraise; *(→ contrat, salaire)* to review; **r. à la baisse/hausse** to downgrade/upgrade, to scale down/up; **il a fallu r. à la baisse les prévisions pour l'an prochain** the projected figures for next year have had to be scaled down

3 *Jur (jugement)* to review; **r. un procès** to reopen a trial; **r. le procès de qn** to retry sb

4 *(voiture)* to service; *(machine)* to overhaul; **faire r. une voiture** to have a car serviced; **la voiture a été révisée récemment** the car was serviced not long ago; **faire r. les freins** to have the brakes checked

5 *(clause)* to revise; *(liste électorale)* to update, to revise; *(manuscrit)* to check, to go over; *(épreuves)* to revise, *Spéc* to line edit

USAGE ABSOLU *Scol & Univ* **on a passé le week-end à r.** we spent the weekend revising *or* doing revision work; **je ne peux pas venir, je révise pour l'exam de linguistique** I can't come, I'm revising for the linguistics exam

réviseur, -euse [revizœr, -øz] NM,F **1** *Écon* **r. comptable** auditor; **r. externe/interne** external/internal auditor; *Belg* **r. d'entreprises** auditor **2** *(d'épreuves → gén)* reviser, checker; *(→ correcteur)* proofreader; **il est traducteur-r.** he translates and edits, he's a translator and editor

révision [revizjɔ̃] NF **1** *Scol & Univ* revision *(UNCOUNT)*, revising *(UNCOUNT)*; **faire des révisions** to revise; **où en es-tu de tes révisions?** how far have you got with your revision?

2 *(d'une clause)* revision; *(d'une liste électorale)* updating, revision; *(d'un manuscrit)* checking; *(d'épreuves)* checking, revising

3 *(d'une voiture)* service; *(d'une machine)* overhaul, overhauling; **la r. des 5000 km** the 5,000 km service

4 *(réévaluation → d'un jugement, d'une situation)* reappraisal, review; *(→ d'un contrat)* revision; *(→ d'un salaire)* review; **la r. à la baisse/hausse des prévisions** the downgrading/upgrading of the forecast figures; **les prix peuvent faire l'objet d'une r.** prices are subject to review

5 *Jur (d'un procès)* rehearing; *(d'un jugement)* reviewing

révisionnel, -elle [revizjɔnɛl] ADJ revisionary, review *(avant n)*

révisionnisme [revizjɔnism] NM revisionism

révisionniste [revizjɔnist] ADJ revisionist

NMF revisionist

revisiter [3] [rəvizite] VT **1** *(visiter à nouveau)* to revisit **2** *(voir sous un jour nouveau)* to reinterpret; **r. un auteur/une époque** to reinterpret a writer/an era; **Racine revisité par le célèbre metteur en scène** a new angle *or* a new take on Racine by the famous director

revisser [3] [rəvise] VT to screw back again

revit 1 *voir* **revivre 2** *voir* **revoir**[2]

revitalisant, -e [rəvitalizɑ̃, -ɑ̃t] ADJ revitalizing

revitalisation [rəvitalizasjɔ̃] NF revitalization

revitaliser [3] [rəvitalize] VT **1** *(ranimer → économie)* to revitalize; **ce nouveau plan économique est destiné à r. la région** this new economic programme is designed to revitalize *or* bring new life to the area **2** *(régénérer → peau)* to revitalize; **cette crème revitalisera votre épiderme** this cream will revitalize your skin

revival, -als [rivajvœl, rəvival] NM revival

revivifiant, -e [rəvivifjɑ̃, -ɑ̃t] ADJ bracing, revivifying

revivification [rəvivifikasjɔ̃] NF *Littéraire* **1** *(d'une personne)* revitalization **2** *(d'un souvenir)* reviving

revivifier [9] [rəvivifje] VT **1** *(personne)* to revitalize **2** *Littéraire (souvenir)* to bring back to life, to revive

reviviscence [rəvivisɑ̃s] NF **1** *Biol* anabiosis, reviviscence **2** *Littéraire* revival, reappearance

reviviscent, -e [rəvivisɑ̃, -ɑ̃t] ADJ *Biol* anabiotic, reviviscent

revivre [90] [rəvivr] VI **1** *(renaître)* to come alive (again); **les examens sont terminés, je revis!** the exams are over, I can breathe again *or* what a weight off my mind!; **quel calme, je me sens r.!** how quiet it is around here, I feel like a new person!

2 *(nature, campagne)* to come alive again

3 *(personne ou animal mort)* to come back to life; **r. dans** *ou* **par qn** to live again in *or* through sb

4 *(redevenir actuel)* **faire r. la tradition** to restore *or* to revive tradition; **faire r. les années de guerre** to bring back the war years

VT **1** *(se souvenir de)* to relive, to live *or* to go through (again); **toutes les nuits je revis l'accident** I relive the accident every night

2 *(vivre à nouveau)* to relive; **avec lui, elle revit un grand amour** with him, she's reliving a grand passion

révocabilité [revɔkabilite] NF **1** *Admin (d'un fonctionnaire)* dismissibility **2** *Jur (d'un acte juridique)* revocability **3** *Pol (d'un élu)* recallability

révocable [revɔkabl] ADJ **1** *Admin (fonctionnaire)* dismissible **2** *Jur (acte juridique)* revocable, subject to repeal **3** *Pol (élu)* recallable, subject to recall

révocation [revɔkasjɔ̃] NF **1** *Admin (d'un fonctionnaire)* dismissal; *(d'un dirigeant)* removal **2** *Jur (d'un acte juridique)* repeal, revocation; *(d'un testament)* revocation; *(d'un ordre)* rescinding; **la r. de l'édit de Nantes** the revocation of the Edict of Nantes; **r. ad nutum** unilateral revocation of a contract **3** *Pol (d'un élu)* removal, recall

révocatoire [revɔkatwar] ADJ revocatory

revoici [rəvwasi] PRÉP **me r.!** here I am again!, it's me again!; **nous r. à Paris** here we are in Paris

again *or* back in Paris; **la r. qui pleure** she's crying again

revoilà [rəvwala] PRÉP **r. le printemps!** it looks like spring's here again!; **enfin, te r.!** you're back at last!; **les r.!** there they are again!; **nous r. à Paris** here we are in Paris again *or* back in Paris; **la r. qui pleure** she's crying again; **nous y r., je m'y attendais!** here we go again! I just knew it

revoir[1] [rəvwar] NM **1** *Littéraire* **le charme du r.** the delights of meeting again
 2 *Chasse* trail
 ◻ **au revoir** EXCLAM goodbye! NM goodbye; **ce n'est qu'un au r.** we'll meet again

revoir[2] [62] [rəvwar] VT **1** *(rencontrer à nouveau)* to see *or* to meet again; **il y a longtemps que tu le revois?** is it a long time since you started seeing him again?; **tu ne croyais pas me r. de sitôt, hein?** you didn't expect to see me again so soon, did you?; **et que je ne te revoie plus ici, compris?** and don't let me see *or* catch you around here again, is that clear?
 2 *(retourner à)* to see again, to go back to; **c'est bon de r. son pays** it's good to be back in *or* to see one's country (again); **elle ne devait plus r. sa terre natale** she was never to see her native land again
 3 *(examiner à nouveau → images)* to see again, to have another look at; *(→ exposition, spectacle)* to see again; *(→ dossier)* to re-examine, to look at again; *(→ vidéocassette)* to watch again; **c'est un documentaire qu'il faut r.** the documentary is well worth seeing a second time; **je l'ai revu trois fois à la télévision** I've seen it three times on television
 4 *(assister de nouveau à → incident)* to see *or* to witness again; **nous ne voulons plus jamais r. ces scènes sur nos écrans** we never want to witness *or* to see such scenes on our screens again
 5 *(par l'imagination)* **je nous revois encore, autour du feu de camp** I can still see *or* picture us around the campfire; **je la revois petite** I can picture her when she was little; **quand je revois ces moments de bonheur** when I think back to those happy times
 6 *(vérifier → installation, mécanisme, moteur)* to check, to look at again
 7 *(réexaminer → texte)* to re-examine, to revise; *(→ épreuves)* to read; *(→ comptes)* to go over *or* look over again; *(→ opinion)* to modify, to revise; **je voudrais r. quelques points avec toi** I'd like to go over a few points with you; **la première partie de ta thèse est à r.** the first part of your thesis will have to be gone over again *or* revised; **édition revue et corrigée** *(dans un livre)* revised edition; **r. à la hausse/baisse** to revise upwards/downwards
 8 *Scol & Univ (cours)* to go over (again), *Br* to revise, *Am* to review; **revoyez les racines carrées pour demain** go over the section on square roots for tomorrow; **tu ferais bien de r. ta physique!** *(réviser)* you'd better revise your physics!; *(réapprendre)* you'd better study *or* learn your physics again!
 ▸**se revoir** VPR **1** *(emploi réciproque)* to meet again, to see each other again; **nous reverrons-nous?** will we see each other *or* meet again?
 2 *(emploi réfléchi)* to see *or* to picture oneself again; **je me revois enfant, chez ma grand-mère** I can still see myself as a child at my grandmother's

revoler [3] [rəvɔle] VI **1** *(voler à nouveau)* to fly again **2** *Can (être projeté dans toutes les directions → objets, personnes)* to fly in every direction; *(jaillir → liquide, sang)* to splatter; **les fenêtres ont revolé en miettes** the windows were smashed to smithereens

révoltant, -e [revɔltɑ̃, -ɑ̃t] ADJ *(violence, lâcheté, injustice)* appalling, shocking; *(grossièreté)* revolting, outrageous, scandalous; **il est d'un égoïsme r.** he's horribly self-centred

révolte [revɔlt] NF **1** *(sédition)* revolt, rebellion; *(dans une prison)* riot; **la r. fut durement réprimée** the revolt was harshly repressed
 2 *(insoumission)* rebellion, revolt; **être en r. contre qn** to be in revolt against sb; **elle est en r. contre ses parents** she's rebelling against her parents; **esprit de r.** spirit of revolt *or* rebellion
 3 *(réprobation)* outrage; **nous manifestons notre r. contre la vivisection** we're expressing our outrage against vivisection

révolté, -e [revɔlte] ADJ **1** *(rebelle)* rebellious, rebel *(avant n)*; **r. contre** in revolt against **2** *(indigné)* outraged **3** *Mil* mutinous
 NM,F **1** *(gén)* rebel **2** *Mil* rebel, mutineer

révolter [3] [revɔlte] VT *(scandaliser)* to appal, to revolt, to shock; **ça ne te révolte pas, toi?** don't you think that's disgusting *or* revolting *or* shocking?; **révolté par la misère/tant de violence** outraged by poverty/at so much violence
 ▸**se révolter** VPR **1** *(gén)* to revolt; **les mineurs se révoltent contre leurs syndicats** the miners are revolting *or* are in revolt against their unions; **adolescent, il s'est révolté contre ses parents** he rebelled against his parents when he was a teenager
 2 *(marin, soldat)* to mutiny

révolu, -e [revɔly] ADJ **1** *Littéraire (d'autrefois)* **aux jours révolus de ma jeunesse** in the bygone days of my youth; **en des temps révolus** in days gone by **2** *(fini)* past; **l'époque des hippies est révolue** the hippie era is over **3** *Admin* **âgé de 18 ans révolus** over 18 (years of age); **au bout de trois années révolues** after three full years

révolution [revɔlysjɔ̃] NF **1** *Pol & Hist* revolution; **faire la r.** to have a revolution; **la r. industrielle** the Industrial Revolution; **une r. de palais** a palace coup *or* revolution; **la première/seconde r. d'Angleterre** the English/Glorious Revolution; **la R. culturelle** *(en Chine)* the Cultural Revolution; **la R. (française)** the French Revolution; **la r. d'octobre** the October Revolution; *Can* **la R. tranquille** the Quiet Revolution *(period of social, political and economic change in Quebec in the 1960s)*; **r. verte** green revolution **2** *(changement)* revolution; **une r. dans** a revolution in; **faire** *ou* **causer une r. dans qch** to revolutionize sth **3** *(agitation)* turmoil; **tout le service est en r.** the whole department is in turmoil; **tous ces cambriolages ont mis la ville en r.** the town is up in arms *or* in uproar because of all these burglaries **4** *Astron & Math* revolution

> *Culture*
>
> **LA RÉVOLUTION FRANÇAISE**
>
> The French Revolution is the most important event in the history of modern France, from which the country emerged as a Republic with an egalitarian constitution. Precipitated by the social and financial abuses of the "Ancien Régime" monarchy, it was a turbulent period lasting from the Fall of the Bastille in 1789 until the end of the century, marked by the Declaration of Human Rights, the execution of Louis XVI and the Terror (1793), and war against the other European powers.

> *Culture*
>
> **LA RÉVOLUTION TRANQUILLE**
>
> "La Révolution tranquille" ("the quiet revolution") is the name given to the period in French Canadian history starting in the 1960s which saw a radical transformation of Quebec society. The role of the Catholic Church in the running of the province was considerably reduced, most notably with the transfer of educational affairs from the Church to the State. It was also a time when Quebec changed from a mainly agrarian province into a modern industrial one whose economy developed rapidly. The "Révolution tranquille" also saw the emergence of a new-found pride and self-confidence among French Canadians, reflected in a similarly vibrant cultural scene.

révolutionnaire [revɔlysjɔnɛr] ADJ *Pol, Hist & Fig* revolutionary; **une découverte r.** a revolutionary discovery
 NMF *Pol & Hist* revolutionary; *Fig* innovator

révolutionnairement [revɔlysjɔnɛrmɑ̃] ADV in a revolutionary manner

révolutionnarisation [revɔlysjɔnarizasjɔ̃] NF revolutionizing, revolutionization

révolutionnarisme [revɔlysjɔnarism] NM revolutionism

révolutionnariste [revɔlysjɔnarist] ADJ revolutionist
 NMF revolutionist

révolutionner [3] [revɔlysjɔne] VT **1** *(système, domaine)* to revolutionize; *(vie)* to change radically **2** *Fam (bouleverser → personne)* to upset (deeply)▪; *(→ village, service)* to cause a stir in; **cette nouvelle l'a révolutionnée** the news made a deep impression on her

revolver [revɔlvɛr] NM **1** revolver; **un coup de r.** a gunshot; **r. à six coups** six-shooter **2** *Opt* revolving nose piece **3** *Tech* capstan, turret

revolving [revɔlviŋ] ADJ INV revolving; *Banque* **crédit r.** revolving credit

révoquer [3] [revɔke] VT **1** *Admin (fonctionnaire)* to dismiss; *(dirigeant)* to remove (from office) **2** *Jur (acte juridique)* to revoke, to repeal; *(testament, contrat)* to revoke; *(ordre)* to revoke, to rescind **3** *Pol (élu)* to recall **4** *Littéraire* **r. qch en doute** to call sth into question

revoter [3] [rəvɔte] VI to vote again
 VT *(personne, parti)* to vote for again; *(loi)* to pass *or* adopt again

revouloir [57] [rəvulwar] VT *Fam (davantage de)* to want some more; *(de nouveau)* to want again; **j'en reveux!** I want some more!

revoyait *etc voir* **revoir**[2]

revoyure [rəvwajyr] NF *Fam* **à la r.!** see you (around)!

revu, -e[1] [rəvy] PP *voir* **revoir**[2]

revue[2] [rəvy] NF **1** *(publication → gén)* magazine; *(→ spécialisée)* review, journal; **r. économique** economic journal *or* review; **r. financière** financial review; **r. de linguistique** review of linguistics; **r. littéraire** literary journal; **r. de mode** fashion magazine; *Fam* **r. porno** porno *or* porn magazine; **r. scientifique** science journal; **r. spécialisée** trade paper, journal, review
 2 *(de music-hall)* variety show; *(de chansonniers)* revue; **r. à grand spectacle** spectacular
 3 *Mil (inspection)* inspection, review; *(défilé)* review, march-past; **la r. du 14 juillet** the 14 July (military) parade; **r. de détail/d'armement** kit/arms inspection; **passer en r.** *(troupes)* to hold a review of, to review; *(uniformes)* to inspect; *Fam* **être de la r.** to have to go without
 4 *(inventaire)* **faire la r. de qch, passer qch en r.** *(vêtements, documents)* to go *or* to look through sth; *(solutions)* to go over sth in one's mind, to review sth; **r. stratégique** strategic review
 ◻ **revue de presse** NF review of the press *or* of what the papers say

revuiste [rəvyist] NMF revue *or* sketch writer

révulsé, -e [revylse] ADJ *(traits, visage)* contorted; **r. de douleur** *(visage)* contorted with pain; **les yeux révulsés** with one's eyes rolled upwards

révulser [3] [revylse] VT **1** *(dégoûter)* to revolt, to fill with loathing, to disgust **2** *(crisper)* to contort **3** *Méd* to counter-irritate
 ▸**se révulser** VPR *(traits, visage)* to contort, to become contorted; *(yeux)* to roll upwards

révulsif, -ive [revylsif, -iv] *Méd* ADJ revulsant
 NM revulsant, revulsive

révulsion [revylsjɔ̃] NF **1** *Méd* revulsion, counter-irritation **2** *(dégoût)* revulsion, loathing; **éprouver de la r. pour** to be repelled by

révulsive [revylsiv] *voir* **révulsif**

rewriter[1] [rirajtœr] NM rewriter

rewriter[2] [3] [rirajte] VT to rewrite

rewriting [rirajtiŋ] NM rewriting

rexisme [rɛksism] NM *Belg Hist* Rexism

rexiste [rɛksist] *Belg Hist* ADJ Rexist
 NMF Rexist

Reykjavik [rɛkjavik] NM Reykjavik

rez-de-chaussée [redʃose] NM INV *Br* ground floor, *Am* first floor; **au r.** on the *Br* ground *or Am* first floor; **habiter un r.** to live in a *Br* ground floor flat *or Am* first floor apartment

rez-de-jardin [redʒardɛ̃] NM INV ground *or* garden level; **pièces en r.** ground-level rooms; **appartement en r.** garden *Br* flat *or Am* apartment

RF *(abrév écrite* **République française***)* French Republic

RFA [ɛrɛfa] NF *Anciennement (abrév* **République fédérale d'Allemagne***)* FRG, West Germany; **vivre en R.** to live in West Germany; **aller en R.** to go to West Germany

RFI [ɛrɛfi] NF *(abrév* **Radio France Internationale***)* = French World Service radio station

RFO [ɛrɛfo] NF *(abrév* **Radio-télévision française d'outre-mer***)* = French overseas broadcasting service

RG [ɛrʒe] NMPL (abrév **Renseignements généraux**) = secret intelligence branch of the French police, Br ≃ Special Branch, Am ≃ the FBI

r.g. (abrév écrite **rive gauche**) left bank

RH [ɛraʃ] NFPL (abrév **ressources humaines**) HR

Rh Physiol (abrév écrite **Rhésus**) Rh

rhabdomancie [rabdɔmãsi] NF rhabdomancy

rhabdomancien, -enne [rabdɔmãsjɛ̃, -ɛn] NM,F rhabdomancer

rhabillage [rabijaʒ] NM 1 (d'une meule) dressing; (d'une montre) overhaul 2 (d'une personne) **le r. des enfants après la gymnastique prend beaucoup de temps** the children take a long time getting dressed again after gym

rhabiller [3] [rabije] VT 1 (habiller à nouveau) to dress again; (acheter de nouveaux vêtements pour) to buy new clothes for; **rhabille-le, il va prendre froid** put his clothes back on, he'll catch cold

2 Archit to revamp, to refurbish; **on a rhabillé tout le foyer du théâtre** the entire foyer of the theatre has been refurbished

3 Fig (idée rebattue) to give a new look to

4 Tech (montre) to overhaul; (meule) to dress

▸**se rhabiller** VPR 1 (s'habiller à nouveau) to put one's clothes back on, to dress or to get dressed again

2 Fam (locution) **tu peux aller te/il peut aller se r.!** you can/he can forget it!

rhabilleur, -euse [rabijœr, -øz] NM,F (de montres) repairer

rhagades [ragad] NFPL Méd rhagades

rhamnacée [ramnase] Bot NF member of the Rhamnaceae

❏ **rhamnacées** NFPL Rhamnaceae

rhapsode [rapsɔd] NM Antiq rhapsode, rhapsodist

rhapsodie [rapsɔdi] NF Mus rhapsody

Rhénan [renã] NM **le R.** the Rhineland (Mountains)

rhénan, -e [renã, -an] ADJ 1 (du Rhin) of the Rhine, Rhenish; **le pays r.** the Rhineland 2 (de la Rhénanie) of the Rhineland

Rhénanie [renani] NF **la R.** the Rhineland

Rhénanie-du-Nord-Westphalie [renanidynɔrvɛsfali] NF **la R.** North Rhine-Westphalia

Rhénanie-Palatinat [renanipalatina] NF **la R.** Rhineland-Palatinate

rhénium [renjɔm] NM Chim rhenium

rhéobase [reɔbaz] NF Physiol rheobase

rhéologie [reɔlɔʒi] NF Phys rheology

rhéologique [reɔlɔʒik] ADJ Phys rheological

rhéologue [reɔlɔg] NMF Phys rheologist

rhéomètre [reɔmɛtr] NM Méd rheometer

rhéostat [reɔsta] NM Élec rheostat; **r. de glissement** slip regulator

Rhésus [rezys] NM Physiol (système sanguin) **facteur R.** rhesus or Rh factor; **R. positif/négatif** rhesus positive/negative

rhésus [rezys] NM Zool rhesus monkey

rhéteur [retœr] NM 1 Antiq rhetor 2 Littéraire rhetorician

rhétien, -enne [retjɛ̃, -ɛn] Géol ADJ Rhaetic
NM Rhaetic

rhétique [retik] ADJ Rhaetian
NM Rhaetian

rhétoricien, -enne [retɔrisjɛ̃, -ɛn] ADJ rhetorical
NM,F 1 (spécialiste) rhetorician 2 Belg Scol Br ≃ lower sixth-former, Am ≃ student in eleventh grade

rhétorique [retɔrik] ADJ rhetoric, rhetorical
NF 1 (art) rhetoric; **figure de r.** figure of speech 2 Péj (affectation) **ce n'est que de la r.** it's just rhetoric or posturing 3 Belg Scol Br ≃ lower sixth form, Am ≃ eleventh grade

rhétoriqueur [retɔrikœr] NM Littérature **les grands rhétoriqueurs** = school of poets of the 15th and 16th centuries noted for their formal and verbal virtuosity

rhéto-roman, -e [retɔrɔmã, -an] (mpl **rhéto-romans,** fpl **rhéto-romanes**) Ling ADJ Rhaeto-Romance (avant n)
NM Rhaeto-Romance

rhexistasie [reksistazi] NF Géol rhexistasy

Rhin [rɛ̃] NM **le R.** the Rhine

rhinanthe [rinãt] NM Bot yellow rattle, Spéc rhinanthus

rhinencéphale [rinãsefal] NM Anat rhinencephalon

rhingrave [rɛ̃grav] Hist NM (prince) Rhinegrave
NF (haut-de-chausses) petticoat-breeches, rhinegrave

rhinite [rinit] NF Méd rhinitis; **r. allergique** allergic rhinitis

rhinocéros [rinɔserɔs] NM 1 Zool rhinoceros, rhino; **r. blanc** white or square-lipped rhinoceros; **r. noir** black or hook-lipped rhinoceros 2 Entom rhinoceros beetle

rhinologie [rinɔlɔʒi] NF Méd rhinology

rhinolophe [rinɔlɔf] NM Zool horseshoe bat, Spéc rhinolophid

rhino-pharyngé, -e [rinɔfarɛ̃ʒe] (mpl **rhino-pharyngés,** fpl **rhino-pharyngées**) ADJ rhinopharyngal, rhinopharyngeal

rhino-pharyngien, -enne [rinɔfarɛ̃ʒjɛ̃, -ɛn] (mpl **rhino-pharyngiens,** fpl **rhino-pharyngiennes**) ADJ rhinopharyngal, rhinopharyngeal

rhino-pharyngite [rinɔfarɛ̃ʒit] (pl **rhino-pharyngites**) NF Méd inflammation of the nasal passages, Spéc rhinopharyngitis

rhino-pharynx [rinɔfarɛ̃ks] NM INV rhinopharynx

rhinoplastie [rinɔplasti] NF Méd rhinoplasty

rhinosclérome [rinɔsklerom] NM Méd scleroma

rhinoscopie [rinɔskɔpi] NF Méd rhinoscopy

rhinovirus [rinovirys] NM Biol rhinovirus

rhizobium [rizɔbjɔm] NM rhizobium

rhizocarpé, -e [rizɔkarpe] ADJ rhizocarpous, rhizocarpic

rhizoctone [rizɔktɔn] NM rhizoctonia

rhizoctonie [rizɔktɔni] NF rhizoctonia

rhizoflagellé [rizɔflaʒele] NM rhizoflagellate

rhizoïde [rizɔid] NM rhizoid

rhizomateux, -euse [rizɔmatø, -øz] ADJ rhizomatous

rhizome [rizom] NM rhizome

rhizophage [rizɔfaʒ] ADJ rhizophagous

rhizopode [rizɔpɔd] NM Zool rhizopod

❏ **rhizopodes** NMPL Rhizopoda

rhizopus [rizɔpy] NM rhizopus

rhizostome [rizɔstɔm] NM Zool rhizostome

rhizotome [rizɔtɔm] NM root slicer

rhô [ro] NM INV rho

rhodamine [rɔdamin] NF Chim rhodamin(e)

rhodanien, -enne [rɔdanjɛ̃, -ɛn] ADJ (du Rhône) from the Rhône; **le couloir r.** the Rhône corridor
NM (dialecte) = Rhône valley variety of Provençal

Rhode Island [rɔdajlãd] NM **le R.** Rhode Island; **à R.** in Rhode Island

Rhodes [rɔd] NM (ville) Rhodes
NFPL (en Suisse) **les R.-Extérieures** (Appenzell) Ausserrhoden; **les R.-Intérieures** (Appenzell) Innerrhoden

Rhodésie [rɔdezi] NF Anciennement **la R.** Rhodésia; **la R. du Nord** Northern Rhodesia; **la R. du Sud** Southern Rhodesia

rhodésien, -enne [rɔdezjɛ̃, -ɛn] ADJ Rhodesian
❏ **Rhodésien, -enne** NM,F Rhodesian

rhodiage [rɔdjaʒ] NM Métal rhodium plating

rhodié, -e [rɔdje] ADJ Chim rhodium (avant n)

rhodien, -enne [rɔdjɛ̃, -ɛn] ADJ Rhodian
❏ **Rhodien, -enne** NM,F Rhodian

rhodinol [rɔdinɔl] NM Chim rhodinol

rhodite [rɔdit] NF Chim rhodium gold

rhodium [rɔdjɔm] NM Chim rhodium

rhododendron [rɔdɔdɛ̃drɔ̃] NM rhododendron

Rhodoïd® [rɔdɔid] NM Rhodoïd®

rhodophycée [rɔdɔfise] Bot NF rhodophyte
❏ **rhodophycées** NFPL rhodophytes, Spéc Rhodophyceae

rhodopsine [rɔdɔpsin] NF Biol & Chim rhodopsin

rhombe [rɔ̃b] NM 1 (instrument de musique) bull-roarer 2 Vieilli (losange) rhombus

rhombencéphale [rɔ̃bãsefal] NM Anat rhombencephalon

rhombique [rɔ̃bik] ADJ rhombic

rhomboèdre [rɔ̃bɔɛdr] NM rhombohedron

rhomboédrique [rɔ̃bɔedrik] ADJ rhombohedral; **système r.** rhombohedral system

rhomboïdal, -e, -aux, -ales [rɔ̃bɔidal, -o] ADJ rhomboid, rhomboidal

rhomboïde [rɔ̃bɔid] NM 1 Géom rhomboid 2 Anat rhomboideus

rhônalpin, -e [ronalpɛ̃, -in] ADJ of/from the Rhône-Alpes region
NM,F = inhabitant of or person from the Rhône-Alpes region

rhoncus [rɔ̃kys] NM Méd rhoncus

Rhône [ron] NM 1 (fleuve) **le R.** the (River) Rhône 2 (département) **le R.** the Rhône

Rhône-Alpes [ronalp] NM Rhône-Alpes

Rhône-Poulenc [ronpulɛ̃k] NM = large chemicals manufacturing group

rhotacisme [rɔtasism] NM Ling rhotacism

Rhovyl® [rɔvil] NM = man-made fibre used in warm clothing

rhubarbe [rybarb] NF rhubarb; **confiture/tarte à la r.** rhubarb jam/tart

rhum [rɔm] NM rum; **au r.** (dessert) rum-flavoured; (boisson) rum-based; **r. blanc** white rum

rhumatisant, -e [rymatizã, -ãt] ADJ rheumatic
NM,F rheumatic

rhumatismal, -e, -aux, -ales [rymatismal, -o] ADJ rheumatic

rhumatisme [rymatism] NM rheumatism (UNCOUNT); **mes rhumatismes me font souffrir** my rheumatism is playing up; **avoir un r. ou des rhumatismes au genou** to have rheumatism in one's knee; **r. articulaire aigu** rheumatic fever; **r. déformant** polyarthritis

rhumatoïde [rymatɔid] ADJ rheumatoid

rhumatologie [rymatɔlɔʒi] NF rheumatology

rhumatologique [rymatɔlɔʒik] ADJ rheumatological

rhumatologue [rymatɔlɔg] NMF rheumatologist

rhumb [rɔ̃b] NM Naut rhumb

rhume [rym] NM cold; **avoir un r.** to have a cold; Fam **je tiens un bon r.!** I've got a nasty cold!; **un gros r.** a bad or heavy cold; **tu vas attraper un r.** you're going to catch (a) cold; **r. de cerveau** head cold; **r. des foins** hay fever

rhumer [3] [rɔme] VT to add rum to; **eau-de-vie rhumée** brandy and rum

rhumerie [rɔmri] NF rum distillery

rhynchite [rɛ̃kit] NM Entom rhynchites

rhynchocéphale [rɛ̃kosefal] NM Zool rhynchocephalian

rhynchonelle [rɛ̃kɔnɛl] NF Zool rhynchonellid, Spéc Rhynchonella

rhyolite, rhyolithe [rijɔlit] NF Géol rhyolite

rhythm and blues [ritmɛ̃dbluz] NM INV Mus rhythm and blues

rhytidectomie [ritidɛktɔmi] NF Méd facelift, Spéc rhytidectomy

rhytidome [ritidɔm] NM Bot rhytidome

rhytine [ritin] NF Zool **r. de Steller** Steller's sea cow, rhytina

rhyton [ritɔ̃] NM Archéol rhyton

RI [ɛri] NM Mil (abrév **régiment d'infanterie**) infantry regiment
NMPL (abrév **Républicains indépendants**) Independent Republicans (conservative Gaullist party founded in the early 1960s)

ri [ri] PP voir **rire**

ria [rija] NF Géol ria

Riad [rijad] = **Riyad**

rial, -als [rial] NM rial

Rialto [rialto] NM **le (pont du) R.** the Rialto Bridge

riant, -e [rijã, -ãt] ADJ 1 (visage, yeux) smiling 2 (nature, paysage) pleasant; **une riante vallée** a pleasant valley 3 Littéraire (heureux) happy

RIB [rib] NM (abrév **relevé d'identité bancaire**) = document giving details of one's bank account

ribambelle [ribãbɛl] NF 1 (d'enfants) flock, swarm; (de noms) string, torrent; Fam **suivi d'une r. de gamins** followed by a long string of or a swarm of kids; **une r. de jurons** a flood or torrent of oaths 2 (papier découpé) paper dolls
❏ **en ribambelle** ADV **les enfants sortent de l'école en r.** the children stream out of the school

ribat [ribat] NM INV = fortified convent in the Maghreb

ribaud, -e [ribo, -od] Arch ou Littéraire ADJ ribald
NM,F un r. a ribald fellow; **une ribaude** a brazen wench

ribaudequin [ribodkɛ̃] NM Hist ribaudequin

ribésiacée [ribezjase] Bot NF saxifrage, Spéc member of the Saxifragaceae
❏ **ribésiacées** NFPL Saxifragaceae

ribler [3] [rible] VT Tech (moulin) to true up, to dress

riblon [riblɔ̃] NM Métal scrap, swarf

riboflavine [riboflavin] NF Biol riboflavin, riboflavine

rg–rib

ribonucléase [ribonykleaz] **NF** *Biol & Chim* ribonuclease
ribonucléique [ribonykleik] **ADJ** *Biol & Chim* ribonucleic
ribonucléotide [ribonykleɔtid] **NM** *Biol & Chim* ribonucleotide
ribose [riboz] **NM** *Chim* ribose
ribosomal, -e, -aux, -ales [ribozɔmal, -o] **ADJ** *Chim* ribosomal
ribosome [ribozom] **NM** *Chim* ribosome
ribosomique [ribozɔmik] **ADJ** *Chim* ribosomal
ribote [ribɔt] **NF** *Vieilli ou Littéraire* high living; **en r.** *(ivre)* drunk; **faire r.** *(s'enivrer)* to go drinking
ribouis [ribwi] **NM** *Fam Vieilli* battered old shoe
riboulant, -e [ribulɑ̃, -ɑ̃t] **ADJ** *Fam Vieilli* staring; **yeux riboulants** staring eyes
ribouldingue [ribuldɛ̃g] **NF** *Fam Vieilli* **une sacrée r.** a real shindig; **faire la r.** to go on a spree *or* binge
ribouler [3] [ribule] **VI** *Fam Vieilli* **r. des yeux** to roll one's eyes (with amazement)
ribovirus [ribɔvirys] **NM** ribovirus
ribozyme [ribɔzim] **NM** *Chim* ribozyme
ricain, -e [rikɛ̃, -ɛn] *Fam* **ADJ** Yank, *Br* Yankee
❑ **Ricain, -e NM,F** Yank, *Br* Yankee, = pejorative or humorous term used with reference to Americans
ricanant, -e [rikanɑ̃, -ɑ̃t] **ADJ** sniggering
ricanement [rikanmɑ̃] **NM** *(rire → méchant)* snigger; *(→ nerveux, bête)* giggle; **ricanements** *(méchants)* sniggering; *(nerveux, bêtes)* giggling
ricaner [3] [rikane] **VI** *(rire → méchamment)* to snigger; *(→ nerveusement, bêtement)* to giggle
ricaneur, -euse [rikanœr, -øz] **ADJ** *(riant → méchamment)* sniggering; *(→ bêtement)* giggling
NM,F *(méchant)* sniggerer; *(bête)* giggler; **les ricaneurs en seront pour leurs frais** anybody who laughs *or* sniggers gets it
Ricard® [rikar] **NM** = brand of pastis
riccie [riksi] **NF** *Bot* riccia
RICE [ris] **NM** *Banque (abrév* **relevé d'identité de caisse d'épargne**) = savings account identification slip
ricercare [ritʃɛrkare] **NM** *Mus* ricercar(e)
Richard [riʃar] **NPR R. Cœur de Lion** Richard the Lion-Heart, Richard Cœur de Lion
richard, -e [riʃar, -ard] **NM,F** *Fam Péj* moneybags, *Br* nob; **un gros r.** a fat cat

RICHE [riʃ]

ADJ rich **1, 3–5** ▪ wealthy **1** ▪ lavish **2** ▪ lush **3** ▪ fertile **3** ▪ full **5**
NMF rich person

ADJ 1 *(fortuné → famille, personne)* rich, wealthy, well-off; *(→ nation)* rich, wealthy; **une r. héritière** a wealthy heiress; **ils ont l'air r.** they look wealthy; **elle a fait un r. mariage** she's married into a rich family *or* into money; **on n'est pas bien r. chez nous** we're not very well-off; **je te paie le restaurant, aujourd'hui, je suis r.** I'll treat you to a meal, I'm feeling rich today; **je suis plus r. de 500 euros maintenant** I'm 500 euros better off *or* richer now; **être r. comme Crésus** *ou* **à millions** to be as rich as Croesus *or* Midas; **elle est r. à millions** she's extremely wealthy

2 *(avant le nom) (demeure, décor)* lavish, sumptuous, luxurious; *(étoffe, enluminure)* magnificent, splendid; **un r. cadre doré** a heavy gilt frame; **elle le couvre de riches présents** she lavishes fabulous *or* expensive gifts on him

3 *(végétation)* lush, luxuriant, profuse; *(terre)* fertile, rich; *(aliment, vie)* rich; **un sol r.** a rich soil; **ce qu'il vous faut, c'est une alimentation r.** what you need is a nutritious diet; **le gâteau est un peu trop r.** the cake is a little too rich; *Fam* **c'est une r. nature** he is a hearty *or* an exuberant person; **la ville a une histoire très r.** the town has had a very varied history; **vous y trouverez une documentation très r. sur Proust** you'll find a wide range of documents on Proust there; *Fam ou Ironique* **c'est une r. idée que tu as eue là** that's a wonderful *or* great idea you've just had

4 *(complexe)* rich; **des tons riches** rich hues; **elle a un vocabulaire/une langue r.** she has a rich vocabulary/a tremendous command of the language; **une imagination r.** a fertile imagination

5 r. en *(vitamines, minerais)* rich in; *(événements)* full of; **r. en lipides** with a high lipid content; **régime r. en calcium** calcium-rich diet; **texte r. en superlatifs** text overflowing with superlatives; **la journée fut r. en émotions** the day was packed full of excitement; **la journée fut r. en rebondissements** spectacular things happened all day; **leur bibliothèque n'est pas r. en livres d'art** they don't have a very large collection *or* choice of art books; *Fam* **je ne suis pas r. en papier/farine!** I'm not very well-off for paper/flour!

6 *(qualités, possibilités)* **un livre r. d'enseignements** a very informative book; **un magazine féminin r. d'idées** a women's magazine packed full of ideas; **son premier roman est r. de promesses** his/her first novel is full of promise *or* shows great promise; *Littéraire* **jeune homme r. de mine** handsome-looking young man

NMF rich person; **les riches** the rich, the wealthy; **voiture de r.** rich man's car

ADV *Fam* **ça fait r.** it looks classy *or Br* posh

richelieu [riʃəljø] *(pl* **inv** *ou* **richelieus**) **NM** lace-up shoe
richement [riʃmɑ̃] **ADV 1** *(luxueusement)* richly, handsomely; **cette pièce est r. meublée** this room is richly *or* handsomely furnished **2** *(abondamment)* lavishly, sumptuously, richly; **r. illustré** lavishly illustrated **3** *(de manière à rendre riche)* **il a r. marié sa fille** *ou* **marié sa fille r.** he married his daughter into a wealthy family
richesse [riʃɛs] **NF 1** *(fortune → d'une personne)* wealth; *(→ d'une région, d'une nation)* wealth, affluence, prosperity; **vivre dans la r.** to be wealthy; **ses livres sont sa seule r.** his/her books are all he/she has; **le tourisme est la seule r. de la région** tourism is the region's only resource *or* only source of income; **ces traditions ancestrales font la r. de ce peuple** these ancestral traditions make up the rich cultural heritage of this people; *Mktg* **la r. vive** consumer purchasing power

2 *(d'un décor)* luxuriousness, lavishness, sumptuousness; *(d'un tissu)* beauty, splendour

3 *(luxuriance → de la végétation)* richness, lushness, profuseness, luxuriance; **la r. du sous-sol** the wealth of (underground) mineral deposits; **la r. en fer d'un légume** the high iron content of a vegetable; **notre r. en matières premières** our wealth of raw materials; **pour préserver notre r. en forêts** in order to protect our many forests

4 *(complexité → du vocabulaire, de la langue)* richness; *(→ de l'imagination)* creativeness, inventiveness; *(→ d'une description)* detailed nature; **la r. culturelle de notre capitale** the cultural wealth of our capital city

5 *(réconfort)* blessing; **avoir un ami fidèle est une grande r.** to have a faithful friend is to be rich indeed

❑ **richesses NFPL** *(biens, capital)* riches, wealth *(UNCOUNT)*; *(articles de valeur)* treasures, wealth; *(ressources)* resources; **richesses minières/naturelles** mining/natural resources; **les richesses que recèle ce site archéologique** the treasures contained in this archeological site

'La Richesse des nations' *Smith* 'The Wealth of Nations'

richissime [riʃisim] **ADJ** *Fam* fantastically wealthy, loaded
Richter [riʃtɛr] **NPR échelle de R.** Richter scale
ricin [risɛ̃] **NM** *Bot* castor-oil plant, *Spéc* ricinus
riciné, -e [risine] **ADJ** containing castor oil
rickettsie [rikɛtsi] **NF** *Biol & Méd* rickettsia
rickettsiose [rikɛtsjoz] **NF** *Méd* rickettsiosis
rickshaw [rikʃo] **NM** rickshaw
ricocher [3] [rikɔʃe] **VI 1** *(caillou)* to ricochet, to bounce, to glance (**sur** off); **les enfants font r. des pierres sur l'eau** the children are skimming pebbles across the water *or* are playing ducks and drakes **2** *(balle)* to ricochet (**sur** off)
ricochet [rikɔʃɛ] **NM 1** *(d'un caillou)* bounce, rebound; **faire des ricochets (sur l'eau)** to skim pebbles, to play ducks and drakes; **j'ai fait trois ricochets!** I made the pebble bounce three times!; *Fig* **par r.** indirectly; **les épargnants ont perdu de l'argent par r.** savers lost money as an indirect consequence; *Fig* **ces mesures feront r.** these measures will have a knock-on effect **2** *(d'une balle)* ricochet
ricotta [rikɔta] **NF** ricotta
ric-rac [rikrak] **ADV** *Fam* **1** *(très exactement)* **il nous a payés r.** he paid us right down to the last *Br* penny *or Am* cent **2** *(de justesse)* **avec mon petit salaire, à la fin du mois c'est r.** on my salary, money gets a bit tight at the end of the month; **il a réussi l'examen r.** he only just scraped through the exam; **c'était r.** it was touch and go, it was a close thing
rictus [riktys] **NM** grimace, *Sout* rictus; **un affreux r. déformait son visage** his/her face was twisted into a hideous grimace; **il eut un horrible r.** a hideous grimace passed across his face; **un r. de colère** an angry scowl *or* grimace
ridage [ridaʒ] **NM** *Naut* tightening, hauling taut
ride [rid] **NF 1** *(d'un visage)* line, wrinkle; *(sur un fruit)* wrinkle; **creusé de rides** furrowed with wrinkles; **prendre des rides** to age; *Fig* **le documentaire n'a pas pris une r.** the documentary hasn't dated in the slightest **2** *(sur l'eau, sur le sable)* ripple, ridge; **les dunes où le vent traçait ses rides** the dunes ridged by the wind **3** *Naut* **r. de hauban** shroud lanyard
ridé, -e [ride] **ADJ 1** *(visage)* wrinkled, lined; *(pomme)* wrinkled; **un front r.** a deeply lined forehead; **r. comme une vieille pomme** wrinkled like a prune **2** *(eau, sable)* ridged, rippled
rideau, -x [rido] **NM 1** *(en décoration intérieure)* curtain, *Am* drape; **fermé par un r.** curtained off; **mettre des rideaux aux fenêtres** to put curtains up; **tirer** *ou* **ouvrir les rideaux** to draw *or* to open the curtains; **tirer** *ou* **fermer les rideaux** to draw *or* to close the curtains; **r. de douche** shower curtain; **rideaux de lit** bed hangings; **doubles rideaux** thick curtains; **rideaux bonne femme** tieback curtains; *Fig* **tirer le r. sur qch** to draw a veil over sth; *Belg Fig Hum* **le r. de betteraves** = the linguistic frontier between Flemish and French speakers in Belgium

2 *Théât* curtain; **le r. se lève sur un jardin japonais** the curtain rises on a Japanese garden; **r. à la guillotine/à la grecque** drop/draw curtain; **r.!** curtain!; *Fam* **ça suffit, r.!** enough!, that'll do!

3 *(écran)* screen, curtain; **r. de bambou** bamboo curtain; **r. de cyprès** screen of cypress trees; *Mil* **r. de feu** covering fire; **r. de fumée** smokescreen; **r. de pluie** sheet of rain; *Mil* **r. de troupes** screen of troops

4 *(d'un bureau)* roll-top; **classeur à r.** tambour-door filing cabinet, roll-shutter cabinet

5 *TV* **r. de fond** sky cloth

6 *Rad* **r. d'antennes** aerial curtain

❑ **rideau de fer NM 1** *(d'un magasin)* (metal) shutter
2 *Théât* safety curtain
3 *Hist & Pol* Iron Curtain
4 *Constr (de cheminée)* damper, flue shutter
5 *Phot* shutter
6 *Géog* embankment

ridée [ride] **NF** lark net
ridelle [ridɛl] **NF** *(d'un camion)* side panel
ridement [ridmɑ̃] **NM** *(de la peau, du front)* wrinkling, lining, furrowing
rider [3] [ride] **VT 1** *(peau, front)* to wrinkle, to line, to furrow; *(fruit)* to wrinkle, to shrivel **2** *(eau, sable)* to ripple, to ruffle the surface of **3** *Naut* to tighten
▸**se rider VPR 1** *(fruit)* to shrivel, to go wrinkly; *(visage, peau)* to become wrinkled **2** *(eau)* to ripple, to become rippled
ridicule [ridikyl] **ADJ 1** *(risible → personne)* ridiculous, laughable; *(→ tenue)* ridiculous, ludicrous; **se sentir r.** to feel ridiculous; **se rendre r.** to make a fool of oneself, to make oneself look ridiculous; **tu es r. avec cette perruque** you look ridiculous with that wig on

2 *(absurde)* ridiculous, ludicrous, preposterous; **c'est r. d'avoir peur de l'avion** it's ridiculous to be afraid of flying

3 *(dérisoire)* ridiculous, laughable, derisory; **un salaire r.** *(trop bas)* a ridiculously low salary

NM 1 *(ce qui rend ridicule)* ridicule; **craindre le r.** to fear ridicule; **se couvrir de r.** to make

oneself a laughing stock, to make a complete fool of oneself; **couvrir qn de r.** to heap ridicule on sb; **tourner qn/qch en r.** to ridicule sb/sth, to hold sb/sth up to ridicule; **s'exposer au r.** to lay oneself open to ridicule; **tomber** *ou* **donner dans le r.** to become ridiculous; **le r. ne tue pas** ridicule never did anyone any real harm

2 *(absurdité → d'une situation)* ridiculousness; **c'est d'un r. (achevé** *ou* **fini)!** it's utterly ridiculous!, it's a farce!

❑ **ridicules** NMPL *Littéraire (traits absurdes)* ridiculous ways

ridiculement [ridikylmɑ̃] ADV **1** *(dérisoirement)* ridiculously, ludicrously; **r. petit/bas/grand** ridiculously small/low/big **2** *(risiblement)* ridiculously, laughably

ridiculiser [3] [ridikylize] VT to ridicule, to hold up to ridicule

▶**se ridiculiser** VPR to make oneself (look) ridiculous, to make a fool of oneself

ridoir [ridwar] NM *Naut* (rigging-)stretching device, turnbuckle

ridule [ridyl] NF small wrinkle

riel [rjɛl] NM riel

riemannien, -enne [remanjɛ̃, -ɛn] ADJ Riemann *(avant n)*; **géométrie riemannienne** Riemann geometry

RIEN [rjɛ̃]

nothing **1, 2** ■ anything **3** ■ love **5**

PRON INDÉFINI **1** *(nulle chose)* nothing; **créer qch à partir de r.** to create something out of nothing; **faire qch à partir de r.** to do sth from scratch; **passer son temps à r. faire** to spend one's time doing nothing; **réduire à r.** to reduce to nothing; **la tisane, r. de tel pour dormir!** there's nothing like herbal tea to help you sleep!; **r. de tel qu'un bon (roman) policier** there's nothing like a good detective story; **r. de cassé/grave, j'espère?** nothing broken/serious, I hope?; **r. d'autre** nothing else; **r. de nouveau** no new developments; **r. de plus** nothing else *or* more; **j'ai fait mon devoir, r. de plus** I've done my duty, nothing more; **r. de moins** nothing less; **il veut le poste de directeur, r. de moins** he wants the post of director, nothing less or no less; **qu'est-ce qui ne va pas? – r.!** what's wrong? – nothing!; **à quoi tu penses? – à r.!** what are you thinking about? – nothing!; **qu'est-ce que tu lui laisses? – r. de r.!** what are you leaving him/her? – not a thing!; **r. du tout** nothing at all; **je vous remercie – de r.!** thanks – you're welcome *or* not at all *or* don't mention it!; *Péj* **une fille de r.** a worthless girl; **une affaire de r. du tout** a trifling *or* trivial matter; **une égratignure de r. du tout** a little scratch; **c'est ça ou r.** take it or leave it; **c'est tout ou r.** it's all or nothing; **avec lui c'est toujours tout ou r.** with him it's always all or nothing; **r. à dire, c'est parfait!** what can I say, it's perfect!; **r. à faire, il n'entend pas** it's no good, he can't hear; **r. à faire, la voiture ne veut pas démarrer** it's no good, the car (just) won't start; *Douanes* **r. à déclarer** nothing to declare; **j'en ai r.** *Fam* **à faire** *ou très Fam* **à foutre** I don't give a damn *or* a toss; **faire semblant de r.** to pretend that nothing happened; *Fam* **c'est r. de le dire** you can say that again, you said it

2 *(en corrélation avec "ne")* **r. n'est plus beau que...** there's nothing more beautiful than...; **r. ne la fatigue** nothing tires her *or* makes her tired; **plus r. n'a d'importance** nothing matters any more; **r. de grave n'est arrivé** nothing serious happened; **r. n'y a fait, elle a refusé** (there was) nothing doing, she said no; **ce n'est r., ça va guérir** it's nothing, it'll get better; **ce n'est pas r.** it's no small thing *or* matter; **repeindre la cuisine, ce n'est pas r.** redecorating the kitchen is no small thing *or* no easy task; **ce n'est r. en comparaison de** *ou* **à côté de...** it's nothing compared to...; **je croyais avoir perdu, il n'en est r.** I thought I'd lost, but not at all *or* quite the contrary; **ils se disaient mariés, en fait il n'en est r.** they claimed they were married but they're nothing of the sort; **sans elle il n'est r.** without her he's nothing; **je ne suis r. sans mes livres** I'm lost without my books; **il n'est (plus) r. pour moi** he's *or* he means nothing to me (any more); **et moi alors, je ne suis r. (dans tout ça)?** and what about me (in all this), don't I count for anything *or* don't I matter?; **je ne comprends r.** I don't understand anything; **je n'ai r. compris** I haven't understood anything, I've understood nothing; **je ne me souviens de r.** I remember nothing, I don't remember anything; **on ne voit r. avec cette fumée** you can't see anything *or* a thing with all this smoke; **il ne croit à r.** he doesn't believe in anything; **ce soupçon ne repose sur r.** the suspicion is without foundation *or* based on nothing; **il n'y a r. entre nous** there is nothing between us; **cela** *ou* **ça ne fait r.** it doesn't matter; **ça ne (te) fait r. si je te dépose en dernier?** would you mind if I dropped you off last?, is it OK with you if I drop you off last?; **cela ne fait r. à l'affaire** that makes no difference (to the matter in hand); **dis-lui – je n'en ferai r.** tell him/her – I shall do nothing of the sort; **ça n'a r. à voir** it's got nothing to do with it; **ça n'a r. à voir avec toi** it's got nothing to do with you, it doesn't concern you; **Paul et Fred n'ont r. à voir l'un avec l'autre** there's no connection between Paul and Fred; **n'avoir r. contre qn/qch** to have nothing against sb/sth; **je n'ai r. contre lui** I have nothing against him, I don't have anything against him; **elle veut déménager, je n'ai r. contre** she wants to move, I've got nothing against it; **ne t'inquiète pas, tu n'y es pour r.** don't worry, it's not your fault; **ça n'a r. d'un chef-d'œuvre** it's far from being a masterpiece; **il n'a r. du séducteur** there's nothing of the ladykiller about him; **il n'y a r. de moins sûr** nothing could be less certain; **r. de moins que** nothing less than; **elle n'est r. de moins qu'une sotte** she's nothing less than an idiot; **ils ne veulent r. de moins que sa démission** they want nothing less than his/her resignation; **r. tant que** nothing so much as; **je ne méprise r. tant que le mensonge** I despise nothing so much as lying; **elle n'aime r. tant qu'à rester à lire sur le balcon** she likes nothing better than sitting reading on the balcony; **elle n'a r. fait que ce qu'on lui a demandé** she only did what she was asked to do; **il n'y a plus r. à faire** there's nothing more to be done; **pour ne r. vous cacher...** to be completely open with you...; **elle n'avait jamais r. vu de semblable** she had never seen such a thing *or* anything like it; **je ne sais r. de r.** I don't know a thing; **r. ne sert de courir (il faut partir à point)** slow and steady wins the race

3 *(quelque chose)* anything; **y a-t-il r. d'autre?** is there anything else?; **y a-t-il r. que je puisse faire?** is there nothing I can do?; **y a-t-il eu jamais r. de plus beau?** was there ever anything more beautiful?; **je me demande s'il y entend r.** I wonder whether he actually knows anything about it; **j'ai compris sans qu'il dise r.** I understood without him having to say anything; **j'ai compris avant qu'il dise r.** I understood before he said anything; **on ne peut pas vivre sans r. faire** you can't live without doing anything; **appelle-moi avant de r. faire** call me before you do *or* before doing anything; **il fait trop chaud pour r. manger** it's too hot to eat anything

4 r. ne va plus *(dans un jeu)* rien ne va plus

5 *(au tennis)* love; **r. partout** love all; **40 à r.** 40 love

6 *(locutions)* **elle est r. moins que décidée à le poursuivre en justice** *(bel et bien)* she's well and truly determined to take him to court; **elle est r. moins que sotte** *(nullement)* she is far from stupid

ADV *Fam (très)* very■, really; **elle est r. moche, sa copine** his girlfriend's a real dog *or Am* beast; **ils sont r. riches** *Br* they really are rolling in it, *Am* they sure as hell are rich

NM **1** *(néant)* **le r.** nothingness

2 *(chose sans importance)* **un r.** the merest trifle *or* slightest thing; **un r. la met en colère** the slightest thing *or* every little thing makes her angry; **un r. l'habille** he/she looks good in anything; **on se faisait gronder pour un r.** we used to get told off for the slightest thing; **il se fâche pour un r.** he loses his temper over the slightest little thing; **il a passé son examen comme un r.** he took the exam in his stride; **perdre son temps à des riens** to waste one's time over trivia *or* trifles; **les petits riens dont la vie est faite** the little things in life

3 un r. de *(très peu de)* a touch of; **un r. de cannelle** a touch *or* hint of cinnamon; **un r. de canard/vin** a taste of duck/wine; **un r. de frivolité** a touch *or* tinge *or* hint of frivolity; **en un r. de temps** in (next to) no time; **tout a été exécuté en un r. de temps** everything was done in next to no time

❑ **en rien** ADV **ça ne me dérange en r.** that doesn't bother me at all *or* in the least; **il ne ressemble en r. à son père** he looks nothing like his father; **ça n'a en r. affecté ma décision** it hasn't influenced my decision at all *or* in the least *or* in any way

❑ **pour rien** ADV **ne le dérange pas pour r.** don't disturb him for no reason; **il est venu pour r.** he came for nothing; **ça compte pour r.** that doesn't mean anything; **j'ai acheté ça pour r. chez un brocanteur** I bought it for next to nothing in a second-hand shop; **pour deux/trois fois r.** for next to nothing

❑ **rien du tout** NMF **un/une r. du tout** a nobody

❑ **rien que** ADV **r. que pour toi** just *or* only for you; **r. que cette fois** just this once; **r. qu'une fois** just *or* only once; **viens, r. qu'un jour** do come, (even) if only for a day; **r. que le billet coûte une fortune** the ticket alone costs a fortune; **r. que d'y penser, j'ai des frissons** the mere thought of it *or* just thinking about it makes me shiver; **la vérité, r. que la vérité** the truth and nothing but the truth; *Ironique* **r. que ça?** is that all?

❑ **un rien** ADV a touch, a shade, a tiny bit; **sa robe est un r. trop étroite** her dress is a touch *or* a touch *or* a tiny bit too tight; **c'est un r. trop sucré pour moi** it's a shade *or* tiny bit too sweet for me; *Fam Vieilli* **elle est un r. farce!** she's a bit of a clown!

riesling [rislinŋ] NM Riesling

rieur, -euse [rijœr, -øz] ADJ *(enfant)* cheery, cheerful; *(visage, regard)* laughing

NM,F laugher; **les rieurs** those who laugh; **avoir les rieurs de son côté** to have the last laugh

❑ **rieuse** NF *Orn* black-headed gull

Rif [rif] NM *Géog* **le R.** Er *or* El Rif, the Rif

rif [rif] NM *Fam Arg mil* combat■; **aller au r.** to go into battle■

rifain, -e [rifɛ̃, -ɛn] ADJ Riffian

❑ **Rifain, -e** NM,F Riff, Riffian

riff [rif] NM *Mus* riff

rififi [rififi] NM *Fam (bagarre)* trouble, *Br* aggro; **il va y avoir du r.** there's going to be trouble *or Br* aggro

riflard [riflar] NM **1** *Constr* paring chisel **2** *Menuis* jack (plane) **3** *Métal* coarse file **4** *Fam Vieilli (parapluie)* umbrella■, *Br* brolly

rifle [rifl] NM rifle; **carabine (de) 22 long r.** 22 calibre (rifle)

rifler [3] [rifle] VT **1** *Constr* to pare **2** *Menuis* to plane **3** *Métal* to file

riflette [riflɛt] NF *Fam Vieilli (guerre)* war■; *(zone des combats)* front■; **partir pour la r.** to go off to war *or* to the front■

rifloir [riflwar] NM riffler

rift [rift] NM *Géol* rift valley

Rift Valley [riftvalɛ] NM **le R.** the Rift Valley

Riga [riga] NM Riga

rigaudon [rigodɔ̃] NM *(danse, air)* rigadoon

rigide [riʒid] ADJ **1** *(solide → gén)* rigid; *(→ couverture de livre)* stiff **2** *(intransigeant)* rigid, inflexible, unbending **3** *(austère, strict)* rigid, strict; **une éducation r.** a strict upbringing

rigidement [riʒidmɑ̃] ADV rigidly, inflexibly, strictly

rigidifier [9] [riʒidifje] VT to rigidify, to stiffen

rigidité [riʒidite] NF **1** *(raideur)* rigidity, stiffness; **r. cadavérique** rigor mortis **2** *(caractère strict)* strictness, inflexibility

rigodon [rigodɔ̃] NM *(danse, air)* rigadoon

rigolade [rigolad] NF *Fam* **1** *(amusement)* fun■; **il n'y a pas que la r. dans la vie** there's more to life than just having fun *or* a good laugh; **prendre qch à la r.** *(avec humour)* to see the funny side of sth, to treat sth as a joke; *(avec*

légèreté) not to take sth too seriously■; **chez eux, l'ambiance n'est pas/est franchement à la r.** it isn't exactly/it's a laugh a minute round their place; **la vie n'est qu'une vaste r.** life is one big joke *or* farce; **élever quatre enfants, ce n'est pas une (partie de) r.** raising four children is no laughing matter; **soulever des poids est une r. pour elle** lifting weights is child's play for her; **c'est de la r.!** *(ce n'est pas sérieux)* it's a joke!; *(c'est sans importance)* it's nothing!; *(c'est très facile)* it's a piece of cake!; **c'est pas de la r.!** it's no picnic!

2 *(fou rire)* fit of laughter■; **ah, la r.!, quelle r.!** what a hoot *or* scream!

rigolage [rigɔlaʒ] NM *Hort* furrowing

rigolard, -e [rigɔlar, -ard] *Fam* ADJ *(personne)* fond of a joke *or* a laugh■; **il a toujours un air r.** he's always got a grin on his face, something always seems to be amusing him

NM,F **c'est un r.** he likes a good laugh

rigole [rigɔl] NF 1 *(filet d'eau)* rivulet, rill 2 *Constr (d'un mur)* ditch; *(d'une fenêtre)* drainage groove 3 *(conduit)* trench, channel; *(fossé)* ditch; *Hort (sillon)* furrow; **r. d'irrigation** irrigation channel; **r. d'écoulement** *ou* **d'évacuation** *(fossé)* drainage ditch; *(conduit)* flume

rigoler [3] [rigɔle] VI *Fam* 1 *(rire)* to laugh■; **moi, il ne me fait pas r. du tout** I don't find him funny *or* he doesn't make me laugh at all; *Ironique* **tu me fais r. avec tes remords!** you, sorry? don't make me laugh!

2 *(plaisanter)* to joke■; **il a dit ça pour r.** he said that in jest, he meant it as a joke; **histoire de r., pour r.** for a laugh, for fun; **tu rigoles!** you're joking *or* kidding!; **fais ce que je te dis, je ne rigole pas!** do as you're told, I'm not kidding *or* joking!; **il ne faut pas r. avec le fisc** you shouldn't mess about with the *Br* taxman *or Am* IRS; **ils rigolent pas avec la sécurité dans cet aéroport** they don't mess about *or* take any chances with security at this airport

3 *(s'amuser)* to have fun■; **on a bien rigolé cette année-là** we had some good laughs *or* great fun that year; **avec lui comme prof, tu ne vas pas r. tous les jours** it won't be much fun for you having him as a teacher

rigoleur, -euse [rigɔlœr, -øz] *Fam Vieilli* ADJ jovial■

NM,F jovial type■; **c'est un r.** he likes a (good) laugh

rigollot [rigɔlo] NM *Pharm* mustard leaf paper

rigolo, -ote [rigɔlo, -ɔt] *Fam* ADJ 1 *(amusant)* funny■; **il est r., ce gosse!** that kid is so funny!; **elle a des copains très rigolos** her friends are a scream; **ce serait r. que tu aies des jumeaux** wouldn't it be funny if you had twins; **c'est pas r. de bosser avec lui** working with him is no joke

2 *(étrange)* funny■, odd■; **c'est r., mais est-ce pratique?** it's certainly funny, but is it useful?

NM,F 1 *(rieur)* hoot, scream; **c'est une rigolote** she's a hoot

2 *(incompétent)* joker, clown, *Péj* comedian; **c'est un (petit) r.** he's a real comedian; **qui est le petit r. qui a débranché la prise?** what joker pulled the plug out?

NM *Fam Arg crime Vieilli (revolver)* revolver■

rigorisme [rigɔrism] NM rigorism

rigoriste [rigɔrist] ADJ rigid, rigoristic

NMF rigorist

rigotte [rigɔt] NF ≃ cottage cheese *(made from cow's and goat's milk)*

rigoureuse [rigurøz] *voir* **rigoureux**

rigoureusement [rigurøzmɑ̃] ADV 1 *(scrupuleusement)* rigorously; **son classement est r. fait** his/her filing system is very thorough; **suivre r. les consignes** to follow the instructions to the letter

2 *(complètement)* **r. interdit** strictly forbidden; **les deux portraits sont r. identiques** the two portraits are exactly the same *or* absolutely identical; **c'est r. vrai** it's perfectly true

3 *(sévèrement)* harshly, severely

rigoureux, -euse [rigurø, -øz] ADJ 1 *(scrupuleux → analyse, définition, entraînement)* rigorous; *(→ contrôle)* strict, stringent; *(→ raisonnement)* careful; *(→ description)* minute, precise; *(→ discipline)* strict; **observer une rigoureuse neutralité** to remain strictly neutral; **soyez plus r. dans votre travail** be more thorough in your work

2 *(sévère → personne)* severe, strict; *(→ sanction)* harsh, severe; *(→ discipline)* severe; *(→ principe)* strict

3 *(rude → climat)* harsh; *(→ hiver)* hard, harsh

rigueur [rigœr] NF 1 *(sévérité)* harshness, severity, rigour; **traiter qn avec r.** to be extremely strict with sb, to treat sb harshly; **tenir r. à qn de qch** to hold sth against sb; **elle me tient r. d'avoir oublié son anniversaire** I forgot her birthday, and now she holds it against me

2 *(austérité → d'une gestion)* austerity, stringency; *(→ d'une morale)* rigour, strictness, sternness; **politique de r.** austerity (measures); *Pol* **la R.** = economic squeeze applied by Mitterrand in 1982 after the relative failure of the reflation policy initially pursued by the socialist government

3 *(âpreté → d'un climat, d'une existence)* rigour, harshness, toughness; **l'hiver a été d'une r. exceptionnelle** the winter has been exceptionally harsh

4 *(précision → d'un calcul)* exactness, precision; *(→ d'une analyse, d'une logique, d'un esprit)* rigour; **il manque de r. dans son analyse** he's not rigorous enough in his analysis; **r. professionnelle** professionalism

❑ **rigueurs** NFPL *Littéraire* rigours; **les rigueurs de l'hiver/de la vie carcérale** the rigours of winter/of prison life

❑ **à la rigueur** ADV 1 *(peut-être)* **il a bu deux verres à la r., mais pas plus** he may possibly have had two drinks but no more

2 *(s'il le faut)* at a pinch, if need be; **à la r., on pourrait y aller à pied** at a pinch *or* if need be *or* if the worst comes to the worst we could walk there

❑ **de rigueur** ADJ **la ponctualité est de r.** punctuality is insisted upon, *Sout* it's de rigueur to be on time; **tenue de soirée de r.** *(sur carton d'invitation, dans un restaurant)* dress formal; **délai de r.** deadline

rikiki [rikiki] = **riquiqui**

rillettes [rijɛt] NFPL *Culin* rillettes *(potted meat)*

rillons [rijɔ̃] NMPL *Culin* greaves

Rilsan® [rilsɑ̃] NM *Tex* Rilsan®

rimailler [3] [rimaje] VI *Fam Vieilli Péj* to write poetry of a sort, to dabble in writing poetry

rimailleur, -euse [rimajœr, -øz] NM,F *Fam Vieilli Péj* rhymester, versifier, poetaster

rimaye [rimɑj] NF *Géog* bergschrund, rimaye

rimbaldien, -enne [rɛ̃baldjɛ̃, -ɛn] ADJ **la poésie rimbaldienne** Rimbaud's poetry, the poetry of Rimbaud; **avoir des accents rimbaldiens** *(écrit)* to be reminiscent of Rimbaud, to have Rimbaud-like overtones; **ce film a un côté r.** the film has a touch of Rimbaud about it

rime [rim] NF 1 *Littérature* rhyme; **créer un mot pour la r.** to coin a word for the sake of rhyme; **rimes croisées** *ou* **alternées** alternate rhymes; **rimes embrassées** abba rhyme scheme; **r. interne** internal rhyme; **r. masculine/féminine** masculine/feminine rhyme; **r. pour l'œil** eye rhyme; **r. pour l'oreille** rhyme for the ear; **r. pauvre** poor rhyme; **rimes plates** rhyming couplets; **r. riche** rich *or* perfect rhyme; **rimes tiercées** terza rima

2 *(locution)* **sans r. ni raison** *(partir, décider)* without rhyme or reason; **il me tenait des propos sans r. ni raison** what he was telling me had neither rhyme nor reason to it, there was neither rhyme nor reason in what he was telling me

rimer [3] [rime] VT to versify, to put into verse; **poésie rimée** rhyming verse

VI 1 *Littéraire (faire de la poésie)* to write poetry *or* verse

2 *(finir par le même son)* to rhyme (**avec** with); **les premier et dernier vers riment** the first and last lines rhyme

3 *(équivaloir à)* **pour beaucoup de gens bonheur rime avec argent** many people equate happiness with money; **amour ne rime pas toujours avec fidélité** love and fidelity don't aways go together *or* hand in hand

❑ **rimer à** VT IND **à quoi rime cette scène de jalousie?** what's the meaning of this jealous outburst?; **tout cela ne rime à rien** none of this makes any sense, there's no sense in any of this; **ça ne rime à rien de le gronder** there's absolutely no point in telling him off, it makes absolutely no sense to tell him off

rimeur, -euse [rimœr, -øz] NM,F *Péj* versifier, rhymester, poetaster

Rimmel® [rimɛl] NM mascara

Rimski-Korsakov [rimskikɔrsakɔf] NPR Rimsky-Korsakov

rinçage [rɛ̃saʒ] NM 1 *(au cours d'une lessive)* rinse, rinsing; **les draps ont besoin d'un r.** the sheets need rinsing (out) *or* a rinse; **produit de r.** *(pour lave-vaisselle)* rinsing agent *or* aid 2 *(pour les cheveux)* (colour) rinse

rinceaux [rɛ̃so] NMPL *Beaux-Arts* foliated pattern

rince-bouche [rɛ̃sbuʃ] NM INV *Arch* = goblet of warm flavoured water used to rinse the mouth after eating

rince-bouteilles [rɛ̃sbutɛj] NM INV 1 *(brosse)* bottlebrush 2 *(machine)* bottle-washing machine

rince-doigts [rɛ̃sdwa] NM INV finger bowl

rincée [rɛ̃se] NF *Fam* 1 *Vieilli (défaite)* licking, hammering, thrashing; *(coups)* thrashing; **prendre une r.** *(défaite)* to get hammered *or* licked *or* thrashed; *(coups)* to get thrashed 2 *(averse)* downpour■; **prendre une r.** to get caught in a downpour

rincer [16] [rɛ̃se] VT 1 *(passer à l'eau)* to rinse; **r. qch abondamment** to rinse sth thoroughly, to give sth a thorough rinse

2 *Fam (mouiller)* **se faire r.** to get caught in a downpour■

3 *Fam (ruiner)* **il s'est fait r. au jeu** he got cleaned out at the gambling table

VI *Fam (offrir à boire)* to buy the drinks■; **c'est moi qui rince!** I'm buying the drinks!, the drinks are on me!; **c'est le patron qui rince!** the drinks are on the house!

►**se rincer** VPR **se r. la bouche/les mains** to rinse one's mouth (out)/one's hands; *Fam* **se r. le bec** *ou* **la dalle** *ou* **le gosier** *(boire)* to wet one's whistle; *Fam* **se r. l'œil** *(regarder)* to get an eyeful; **alors, on se rince l'œil?** seen enough, have you?

rincette [rɛ̃sɛt] NF *Fam (eau-de-vie)* nip of brandy■, brandy chaser■ *(after coffee)*

rinceur, -euse [rɛ̃sœr, -øz] ADJ *(dispositif)* rinsing

❑ **rinceuse** NF *(machine)* bottle-washing machine

rinçure [rɛ̃syr] NF 1 *(eau de vaisselle)* dishwater 2 *Fam Vieilli (mauvaise boisson)* **leur vin, c'est de la r.** their wine tastes like dishwater

rinforzando [rinfɔrsɑ̃do] ADV *Mus* rinforzando

ring [riŋ] NM 1 *(estrade)* (boxing) ring; **monter sur le r.** *(au début d'un combat)* to get into the ring; **quand il est monté sur le r.** *(quand il a débuté)* when he took up boxing 2 *(boxe)* **le r.** the ring; **une légende du r.** a boxing legend, a legend of the ring 3 *Belg (rocade)* ring road

ringard[1] [rɛ̃gar] NM *Métal* rabble

ringard[2], **-e** [rɛ̃gar, -ard] *Fam Péj* ADJ *(démodé → gén)* corny, *Br* naff; *(→ chanson)* corny, cheesy; *(→ décor)* tacky, *Br* naff; **elle est ringarde** she's such a geek

NM,F 1 *(acteur)* second-rate actor■ 2 *(individu démodé)* geek, nerd, *Br* anorak

ringardage [rɛ̃gardaʒ] NM *Métal* rabbling

ringarder [3] [rɛ̃garde] VT *Métal* to rabble

ringardise [rɛ̃gardiz] NF *Fam* tackiness, *Br* naffness; **la déco était d'une r., je te dis pas!** the decor was unbelievably tacky *or Br* naff!

ringardiser [3] [rɛ̃gardize] VT *Fam* to make tacky

ringardissime [rɛ̃gardisim] ADJ *Fam* incredibly tacky *or Br* naff

ringuette [rɛ̃gɛt] NF ringette *(women's sport similar to ice hockey)*

rink-hockey [rinkɔkɛ] NM roller hockey

Rio de Janeiro [rijodədʒanɛro] NM 1 *(état)* Rio de Janeiro 2 *(ville)* Rio de Janeiro

Rio de la Plata [rijodlaplata] NM **le R.** the River Plate

Rio Grande [rijogrɑ̃de] NM **le R.** the Rio Grande

rioja [rjɔχa] NM Rioja

Rio Negro [rijonegro] NM **le R.** the Rio Negro

riotte [rjɔt] NF *Littéraire* row, quarrel

RIP [rip, ɛripe] NM *Banque (abrév* **relevé d'identité postale***)* = document giving details of one's post office account

ripage [ripaʒ] NM 1 *Constr* scraping 2 *Naut* cargo displacement

ripaille [ripaj] NF *Fam Vieilli* feast■ ; **faire r.** to have a feast

ripailler [3] [ripaje] VI *Fam Vieilli* to have a feast■

ripailleur, -euse [ripajœr, -øz] *Fam Vieilli* NM,F reveller■

ADJ revelling■ , feasting■

ripaton [ripatɔ̃] NM *Fam* foot■ ; **attention les ripatons!** mind your feet!

ripe [rip] NF *Constr* scraper

ripement [ripmɑ̃] NM = **ripage**

riper [3] [ripe] VT **1** *Constr* to scrape **2** *Naut* **r. un cordage** to let a rope out *or* slip **3** *(faire glisser → chargement)* to slide along; *Rail* **r. une voie** to shift a track

VI **1** *(glisser)* to slip **2** *Fam (s'en aller)* to beat it, to push off

ripieno [ripjeno] NM *Mus* ripieno

Ripolin® [ripɔlɛ̃] NM enamel paint, Ripolin®

ripoliner [3] [ripɔline] VT to paint *(with enamel paint)*; **murs ripolinés** walls painted with enamel paint *or* with Ripolin®

riposte [ripɔst] NF **1** *(réplique)* retort, riposte; **avoir la r. rapide** to be good at repartee; **elle a été prompte à la r.** she was quick to retort, she was ready with an answer

2 *(réaction)* reaction; **quand on l'attaque, la r. ne se fait pas attendre** when he's/she's attacked, he/she doesn't take long to react

3 *Mil (contre-attaque)* counterattack, reprisal; **r. graduée** flexible response

4 *Escrime* riposte

riposter [3] [ripɔste] VI **1** *(rétorquer)* to answer back

2 *(réagir)* to respond; **il a riposté à son insulte par une gifle** he countered his/her insult with a slap; **ils ont riposté par une rafale de mitraillette** they responded with a burst of machine-gun fire; **nous riposterons immédiatement** we will take immediate retaliatory action

3 *(contre-attaquer)* to counterattack; **r. à un assaut** to counterattack; **r. à une agression** to counter an aggression

4 *Escrime* to riposte

VT **elle riposta que ça ne le regardait pas** she retorted that it was none of his business; **"pas question", riposta-t-il** "no way," he snapped

ripou, -x *ou* **-s** [ripu] *Fam (verlan de* **pourri***)* ADJ *(mauvais)* rotten; *(personne)* corrupt■ ; **des flics ripoux** *Br* bent *or Am* bad cops; **ce monde r.** this rotten lousy world

NM *Br* bent *or Am* bad cop; **ce flic est un r.** he's a *Br* bent *or Am* bad cop

'Les Ripoux' *Zidi* 'Le Cop' (UK), 'My New Partner' (US)

ripper [ripɛr] NM *Tech* ripper

ripple-mark [ripœlmark] *(pl* **ripple-marks***)* NF *Géol* tide mark, ripple mark

ripuaire [ripɥɛr] *Hist* ADJ Ripuarian; **les Francs ripuaires** the Ripuarian Franks

▫ **Ripuaires** NMPL **les Ripuaires** the Ripuarians

riquettes [rikɛt] NFPL *Belg* scrap (iron); **jeter aux r.** to throw out

riquiqui [rikiki] ADJ INV *Fam* **1** *(minuscule)* teeny-weeny; **une portion r.** a minute *or* minuscule helping; **une natte r.** a dinky little plait **2** *(étriqué → mobilier)* shabby, grotty; *(→ vêtement)* skimpy; **ça fait r.** *(mesquin)* it looks a bit stingy *or* mean

rire [95] [rir] VI **1** *(de joie)* to laugh; **ta lettre nous a beaucoup fait r.** your letter made us all laugh a lot; **ça ne me fait pas r.** that's not funny; **fais-moi r.** make me laugh, say *or* do something funny; **"c'est vrai", dit-il en riant** "that's true," he said with a laugh; **sa gêne/tenue prêtait à r.** his/her embarrassment/outfit was really funny; **r. bêtement** to giggle, to titter; **r. de bon cœur** to laugh heartily; **r. bruyamment** to guffaw; **il n'y a pas de quoi r.** this is no joke *or* no laughing matter; **il vaut mieux en r.** it's best to laugh, you might as well laugh; **je ris de voir que toi aussi tu t'es trompé** it makes me laugh to see that *or* I find it funny that you made a mistake too; **je n'en pouvais plus de r.** I was helpless with laughter; *Fam* **j'étais morte de r.** I nearly died laughing, I was doubled up with laughter; *Fam* **c'est à mourir** *ou* **crever de r.** it's a hoot *or* a scream; **il vaut mieux en r. qu'en pleurer** you have to laugh or else you cry; **r. aux éclats** *ou* **à gorge déployée** to howl with laughter; **il m'a fait r. aux larmes avec ses histoires** his jokes made me laugh until I cried; **r. du bout des dents** *ou* **des lèvres** to force a laugh; **r. dans sa barbe** *ou* **sous cape** to laugh up one's sleeve, to laugh to oneself; **r. au nez** *ou* **à la barbe de qn** to laugh in sb's face; *Fam* **r. comme un bossu** *ou* **une baleine** to laugh oneself silly, *Br* to laugh like a drain; **se tenir les côtes** *ou* **se tordre de r.** to split one's sides (with laughter), to be in stitches; **r. jaune** to give a hollow laugh; *Ironique* **tu me fais r., laisse-moi r., ne me fais pas r.!** don't make me laugh!; **tu me fais r. toi, avec tes principes** you don't really think I take your so-called principles seriously, do you?; *Can Fam* **il fait froid pour pas en r. aujourd'hui!** it's freezing *or Br* baltic today!; *Can Fam* **il y avait du monde en pas pour r. à la manifestation** there were quite a few *or* quite a lot of people at the demonstration■ ; *Prov* **rira bien qui rira le dernier** he who laughs last laughs *Br* longest *or Am* best

2 *Fam (plaisanter)* to joke; **j'ai dit ça pour r.** *ou* **pour de r.** I (only) said it in jest, I was only joking; **c'était pour r.** it was only for fun; **je te le disais en riant** it was a joke, I was pulling your leg; **elle a pris ça en riant** it just made her laugh; **tu veux r.!** you must be joking!, you've got to be kidding!; **sans r., tu comptes y aller?** joking apart *or* aside, do you intend to go?

3 *(se distraire)* to have fun; **qu'est-ce qu'on a pu r. pendant ses cours!** we had such fun in his/her lessons!

4 *Littéraire (yeux)* to shine *or* to sparkle (with laughter); *(visage)* to beam (with happiness)

NM laugh, laughter *(UNCOUNT)*; **j'adore son r.** I love his/her laugh *or* the way he/she laughs; **le r. est une bonne thérapie** laughter is the best medicine; **j'entends des rires** I hear laughter *or* people laughing; **r. jovial** hearty laugh; **gros r.** guffaw; **il eut un gros r.** he roared with laughter; **r. gras** coarse laugh, cackle; **r. moqueur** sneer; **un petit r. sot** a silly giggle; **un petit r. méchant** a wicked little laugh, a snigger; **ce n'est pas avec des rires que vous me ferez taire** I won't be laughed down; *Rad & TV* **rires préenregistrés** *ou Fam* **en boîte** prerecorded *or* canned laughter

▫ **rire de** VT IND *(se moquer de)* to laugh at; **un jour nous rirons de tout cela** we'll have a good laugh over all this some day

►**se rire** VPR **1 se r. de** *(conseil, doute)* to laugh off, to make fun of; *(danger, maladie, difficultés)* to make light of

2 *Littéraire* **se r. de** *(se moquer de)* to laugh *or* to scoff at

ris [ri] NM **1** *Culin* sweetbread; **r. de veau** calf sweetbreads **2** *Naut* reef; **prendre/larguer un r.** to take in/to shake out a reef; **prendre les r.** to reef the sails **3** *Arch (rire)* laughter; **aimer les jeux et les r.** *(les amusements)* to enjoy the pleasures of life

risberme [risbɛrm] NF *(d'un barrage)* berm

RISC [risk] NM INV *(abrév* **reduced instruction set computer***)* *Ordinat* RISC

risée [rize] NF **1** *(moquerie)* mockery, ridicule; **être un objet de r.** to be a laughing stock; **devenir la r. du village/de la presse** to become the laughing stock of the village/the butt of the press's jokes; **tu t'exposerais à la r. de tout le monde** you'd lay yourself open to public ridicule **2** *(brise)* flurry (of wind)

riser [rajzœr, rizer] NM *Pétr* riser

risette[1] [rizɛt] NF *Fam* **1** *(sourire d'enfant)* **allez, fais r. à mamie** come on, give grandma a nice little smile **2** *(flagornerie)* **faire r.** *ou* **des risettes à qn** *Br* to smarm up *or Am* to play up to sb

risette[2] [rizɛt] NF *Suisse* **brosse à r.** stiff brush

risible [rizibl] ADJ **1** *(amusant)* funny, comical; **la situation n'avait rien de r.** the situation was not at all funny, there was nothing to laugh at in the situation **2** *(ridicule)* ridiculous, laughable

risorius [rizɔrjys] NM *Anat* risorius

risotto [rizɔto] NM *Culin* risotto

risque [risk] NM **1** *(danger)* risk, hazard, danger; **il y a un r. de contagion/d'explosion** there's a risk of contamination/of an explosion; **est-ce qu'il y a un r. que cela se reproduise?** is there any risk of that happening again?; **au r. de te décevoir/de le faire souffrir** at the risk of disappointing you/of hurting him; **r. professionnel** occupational hazard; **à r.** *(groupe, comportement, pratique)* high-risk; **l'alpinisme est une activité à r.** mountaineering is a high-risk activity; **zone/population à haut r.** high-risk area/population; **à mes/tes risques et périls** at my/your own risk; **aux risques et périls du propriétaire** at owner's risk; **ce sont les risques du métier** it's an occupational hazard; *Mktg* **r. perçu** perceived risk

2 *(initiative hasardeuse)* risk, chance; **il y a une part de r.** there's an element of risk; **cela n'est pas sans r.** it is not without its risks *or* dangers; **prendre un r.** to run a risk, to take a chance; **ne prenez pas de risques inutiles** don't take any unnecessary risks *or* chances; **courir le r. de se faire prendre** to run the risk of getting caught; **j'ai toujours gagné en ne prenant pas de risques** I've always won by playing safe; **avoir le goût du r., aimer le r.** to enjoy taking chances; **r. calculé** calculated risk

3 *(préjudice)* risk; **r. de cambriolage** risk of burglary; *Fin* **r. de change** foreign exchange risk; *Fin* **r. de contrepartie** credit risk; **r. d'incendie** fire hazard *or* risk; **r. locatif** tenant's third-party risk; **r. de marché** market risk; *Fin* **capitaux à risques** risk *or* venture capital; **la délégation aux Risques majeurs** the commission on natural disasters; *Assur* **souscrire un r.** to underwrite a risk

risqué, -e [riske] ADJ **1** *(dangereux)* risky, dangerous; **c'est une entreprise risquée** it's a risky business **2** *(osé)* risqué, racy

risque-pays [riskəpei] NM *Pol* country risk

risquer [3] [riske] VT **1** *(engager → fortune, crédibilité)* to risk; **r. sa vie** *ou Fam* **sa peau** to risk one's life *or* neck; *Fam* **r. le paquet** to chance one's arm, to stake one's all; **on risque le coup** *ou* **la partie?** shall we have a shot at it?, shall we chance it?; *Prov* **qui ne risque rien n'a rien** nothing ventured nothing gained

2 *(s'exposer à)* to risk; **elle risque la mort/la paralysie** she runs the risk of dying/of being left paralysed; **on ne risque rien à essayer** we can always try; **tu ne risques rien avec ce masque/avec moi à tes côtés** you'll be safe with this mask/with me beside you; **tu peux laisser ça dehors, ça ne risque rien** you can leave it outside, it'll be safe; **ne t'en fais pas, ces gants ne risquent rien** don't worry, I'm not bothered about those gloves; **après tout, qu'est-ce que tu risques?** what have you got to lose, after all?

3 *(oser)* to venture; **r. une comparaison** to risk drawing a comparison, to venture a comparison; **risquerai-je la question?** shall I be bold enough to put *or* shall I risk putting the question?; *Fam* **r. un regard** *ou* **un œil** to venture a look *or* a peep; *Fam* **r. le nez dehors** to poke one's nose outside

▫ **risquer de** VT IND to risk; **ton idée risque de ne pas marcher** there's a chance your idea mightn't work; **ça risque d'être long** this might take a long time; **il risque de se faire mal** he might hurt himself; **ils risquent d'être renvoyés** they run the risk of being sacked; **le plafond risquait de s'écrouler d'une minute à l'autre** the ceiling was likely to collapse at any minute; **ne m'attends pas, je risque d'être en retard** don't wait for me, I'm likely to be late *or* the chances are I'll be late; **il risque de gagner** he has *or* stands a good chance of winning, he might well win; *Hum* **je ne risque pas de me remarier!** (there's) no danger of my getting married again!; **ça ne risque pas de se faire!** there's no chance of that happening!; **ça ne risque pas!** no chance!

►**se risquer** VPR **se r. dehors** to venture outside; **se r. à faire qch** to venture *or* to dare to do sth; **je ne m'y risquerais pas si j'étais toi** I wouldn't take a chance on it if I were you; **se r. dans qch** *(entreprise, aventure)* to get involved in sth

risque-tout [riskətu] ADJ INV **il est très r.** he's a daredevil

NMF INV daredevil

riss [ris] NM *Géol* Riss

rissole [risɔl] NF **1** *Culin* rissole **2** *Pêche* = close-meshed fishing net for sardine and anchovy fishing

rissoler [3] [risɔle] *Culin* VT to brown; **pommes rissolées** sauté *or* sautéed potatoes
VI faire r. to brown

ristourne [risturn] NF **1** *(réduction)* discount, reduction; **faire une r. à qn** to give sb a discount; **j'ai eu une r. de 20 pour cent sur la moto** I got a 20 percent discount on the motorbike; **r. de fidélité** customer loyalty discount; **r. de prime** premium discount **2** *(remboursement)* refund, reimbursement **3** *Jur* cancellation *(of a maritime policy)* **4** *Com (versement)* bonus

ristourner [3] [risturne] VT **1** *(faire une ristourne de)* to give a discount of; **il nous a ristourné 20 pour cent du prix** he gave us a 20 percent discount *or* 20 percent off **2** *(rembourser)* to refund, to give a refund of **3** *Jur* to cancel *(a maritime policy)*
USAGE ABSOLU *Com* **r. à qn** to give a bonus to sb

ristrette [ristrɛt], **ristretto** [ristretɔ] NM *Suisse* very strong black coffee

rital, -e, -als, -ales [rital] *Fam* ADJ = racist term used to refer to an Italian
NM,F *Br* wop, Eyetie, *Am* Macaroni, = racist term used to refer to an Italian

Ritaline® [ritalin] NF *Pharm* Ritalin®

ritardando [ritardãdo] ADV *Mus* ritardando

rite [rit] NM **1** *Rel* rite; **rites d'initiation** initiation rites; **r. de passage** rite of passage **2** *(coutume)* ritual

ritournelle [riturnɛl] NF **1** *Fam (histoire)* **avec lui c'est toujours la même r.** he's always giving us the same old story **2** *Mus* ritornello

ritualisation [rityalizasjɔ̃] NF ritualization

ritualiser [3] [rityalize] VT to ritualize

ritualisme [rityalism] NM ritualism

ritualiste [rityalist] ADJ ritualistic
NMF ritualist

rituel, -elle [rityɛl] ADJ **1** *(réglé par un rite)* ritual **2** *(habituel)* ritual, usual, customary
NM **1** *(rite)* ritual; **r. d'initiation** initiation rite(s) *or* ritual **2** *Rel (livre)* ceremonial

rituellement [rityɛlmã] ADV **1** *(selon un rite)* ritually **2** *(invariablement)* without fail, religiously; **ils y vont r. chaque année** they go without fail *or* religiously every year

riv. *(abrév écrite rivière)* river

rivage [rivaʒ] NM **1** *(littoral)* shore; *Littéraire* **de lointains rivages** distant shores **2** *(plage)* **r. de sable/de galets** sand/pebble beach

rival, -e, -aux, -ales [rival, -o] ADJ *(antagonique)* rival *(avant n)*
NM,F **1** *(adversaire)* rival, opponent; **r. politique** political rival *or* opponent **2** *(concurrent)* rival; **elle n'a pas eu de rivale en son temps** she was unrivalled in her day
□ **sans rival** ADJ unrivalled

rivaliser [3] [rivalize] VI to compete *(avec* with); **ils rivalisent avec nous pour la conquête du marché** they're competing with us to dominate the market; **nos vins peuvent r. avec les meilleurs crus français** our wines can compare with *or* hold their own against *or* rival French vintages; **elles rivalisent d'élégance** they are trying to outdo each other in elegance; **ne rivalise pas de vitesse avec lui** don't try to match his pace

rivalité [rivalite] NF *(gén)* rivalry; *(en affaires)* competition; **des rivalités d'intérêts** conflicting interests

rive [riv] NF **1** *(bord → d'un lac, d'une mer)* shore; *(→ d'une rivière)* bank; **r. droite/gauche** *(gén)* right/left bank; **mode/intellectuels r. gauche** *(à Paris)* Left Bank fashion/intellectuals *(in Paris)* **2** *Constr* **poutre de r.** continuous girder *or* beam **3** *Métal* face; **r. d'un four** lip of an oven **4** *Littéraire* seashore

---

Culture
RIVE DROITE, RIVE GAUCHE
The Right (north) Bank of the Seine is traditionally associated with business and trade, and has a reputation for being more conservative than the Left Bank. The Left (south) Bank includes districts traditionally favoured by artists, students and intellectuals, and has a reputation for being Bohemian and unconventional.

---

rivelaine [rivlɛn] NF (miner's) pick

river [3] [rive] VT **1** *(joindre → plaques)* to rivet; *(→ clou)* to clinch; *Fam* **r. son clou à qn** to shut sb up
2 *Fig (fixer)* to rivet; **il avait les yeux rivés sur elle/les diamants** he couldn't take his eyes off her/the diamonds; **être rivé à la télévision/à son travail** to be glued to the television/chained to one's work; **rester rivé sur place** to be riveted *or* rooted to the spot; **ils étaient rivés au sol par une force invisible** an invisible force held *or* pinned them to the ground

riverain, -e [rivrɛ̃, -ɛn] ADJ *(d'un lac)* lakeside, waterside; *(d'une rivière)* riverside, waterside, *Sout* riparian; **les restaurants riverains de la Seine** the restaurants along the banks of the Seine; **les maisons riveraines de la grande route** the houses stretching along *or* bordering the main road
NM,F *(qui vit au bord → d'un lac)* lakeside resident; *(→ d'une rivière)* riverside resident; **les riverains du parc s'opposent au concert** residents living near the park are against the concert; **interdit sauf aux riverains** *(sur panneau)* residents only, no entry except for access

riveraineté [rivrɛnte] NF *Jur* riparian rights

rivesaltes [rivzalt] NM Rivesaltes (wine)

rivet [rivɛ] NM rivet; **r. bifurqué/fendu** slotted/split rivet

rivetage [rivtaʒ] NM riveting

riveter [27] [rivte] VT to rivet

riveteuse [rivtøz] NF riveting machine

riveur, -euse [rivœr, -øz] NM,F riveter

Riviera [rivjera] NF **la R.** the (Italian) Riviera

rivière [rivjɛr] NF **1** *Géog* river; **remonter/descendre une r.** to go up/down a river; **pêche en r.** river fishing; *Fig* **une r. de feu coule du Vésuve** a river of fire is flowing from Vesuvius **2** *(collier)* **r. de diamants** (diamond) rivière **3** *Équitation* water jump

rivoir [rivwar] NM *(marteau)* riveting hammer; *(machine)* riveting machine

rivulaire [rivylɛr] NF rivularia

rivure [rivyr] NF **1** *(tête de rivet)* rivet head **2** *(opération)* riveting; **r. simple/double** single/double riveting

rixe [riks] NF brawl, scuffle

Riyad [rijad] NM Riyadh

riyal, -als [rijal] NM riyal

riz [ri] NM rice; **r. blanc** white rice; **r. complet** brown rice; **r. court/long** short-grain/long-grain rice; **r. au lait** rice pudding; **r. pilaf/cantonnais/créole** pilaff/Cantonese/Creole rice; **r. rond** pudding rice; **r. sauvage** wild rice

rizerie [rizri] NF rice-processing plant

rizette [rizɛt] = **risette²**

rizicole [rizikɔl] ADJ *(région)* rice-producing, rice-growing; *(production)* rice *(avant n)*

riziculteur, -trice [rizikyltœr, -tris] NM,F rice grower

riziculture [rizikyltyr] NF *(processus)* rice-growing; *(secteur)* rice production

rizière [rizjɛr] NF rice field, paddyfield

riz-pain-sel [ripɛsɛl] NM INV *Fam Arg mil Br* quartermaster, *Am* commissary

RMC [ɛrɛmse] NF *(abrév* **Radio Monte-Carlo***)* = independent radio station

RMI [ɛrɛmi] NM *(abrév* **revenu minimum d'insertion***)* = minimum welfare payment paid to people with no other source of income, *Br* ≃ income support, *Am* ≃ welfare

RMIste [ɛrɛmist] NMF = person receiving the "RMI"

RMN [ɛrɛmɛn] NF *(abrév* **résonance magnétique nucléaire***)* NMR

RN [ɛrɛn] NF *(abrév* **route nationale***)* *Br* ≃ A-road, *Am* ≃ state highway

RNIS [ɛrɛnies] NM *Ordinat (abrév* **réseau numérique à intégration de services***)* ISDN; **envoyer qch par R.** to ISDN sth, to send sth by ISDN

ro *(abrév écrite* **recto***)* first side *or* front of a page, *Spéc* recto

road-movie, road movie [rodmuvi] *(pl* **road(-)movies***)* NM road movie

roadster [rodstɛr] NM *Aut* roadster

roaming [romiŋ] NM *Ordinat & Tél* roaming

roast-beef [rostbif] *(pl* **roast-beefs***)* NM *Vieilli Culin* roast beef

rob [rɔb] NM **1** *Pharm* syrup **2** *Cartes (au whist, au bridge)* rubber

robage [robaʒ] NM *(de cigares)* wrapping

robe [rɔb] NF **1** dress; **je me mets en r. ou en jupe?** shall I wear a dress or a skirt?; **r. de bal** ball-gown; **r. de baptême** christening robe; **r. de chambre** *Br* dressing gown, *Am* bathrobe; **pomme de terre en r. de chambre** baked *or* jacket potato; **r.-chasuble** *Br* pinafore dress, *Am* jumper; **r.-chemisier** *Br* shirtwaister, *Am* shirtwaist; **r. de grossesse** maternity dress; **r. d'intérieur** housecoat; **r. de mariée** wedding dress, bridal gown; **une r. à paniers** a dress with panniers; **r. de plage** sundress; **r.-sac** sack-dress; **r. du soir** evening dress; **r.-tablier** *Br* pinafore dress, *Am* jumper
2 *(tenue → d'un professeur)* gown; *(→ d'un cardinal, d'un magistrat)* robe; **les gens de r., la r.** the legal profession; *Can Rel* **prendre la r.** to take the habit, to take holy orders
3 *(pelage)* coat
4 *(enveloppe → d'un fruit)* skin; *(→ d'une plante)* husk
5 *(feuille de tabac)* wrapper leaf
6 *(en œnologie)* colour *(general aspect of wine in terms of colour and clarity)*

rober [3] [robe] VT *(cigare)* to wrap

roberts [robɛr] NMPL *Fam* tits, boobs

robin [robɛ̃] NM *Péj Littéraire* lawyer, gownsman

Robin des Bois [robɛ̃debwa] NPR Robin Hood

robinet [robinɛ] NM **1** *(à eau, à gaz)* *Br* tap, *Am* faucet; *(de tonneau)* spigot; **ouvrir/fermer le r.** to turn the *Br* tap *or* *Am* faucet on/off; **r. d'eau chaude/froide** hot/cold (water) *Br* tap *or* *Am* faucet; **r. d'arrivée d'eau** stopcock; **r. mélangeur/mitigeur** *Br* mixer tap, *Am* mixing faucet; **r. à tournant** plug cock **2** *Fam (sexe masculin) Br* willy, *Am* peter

robinetier [robintje] NM **1** *(fabricant)* *Br* tap *or Am* faucet manufacturer **2** *(commerçant)* = supplier of taps and plumbing accessories

robinetterie [robinɛtri] NF **1** *(dispositif)* plumbing **2** *(usine)* *Br* tap *or Am* faucet factory; *(commerce)* *Br* tap *or Am* faucet trade

robineux [robinø] NM *Can Fam* tramp, *Am* hobo

robinier [robinje] NM *Bot* acacia; **r. faux acacia** false acacia, robinia, locust tree

Robinson Crusoé [robɛ̃sɔ̃kryzoe] NPR Robinson Crusoe

roboratif, -ive [roboratif, -iv] ADJ *Littéraire (activité)* invigorating; *(mets)* hearty; *(climat)* bracing

robot [robo] NM robot; **comme un r.** robot-like, like an automaton; **r. ménager** *ou* **de cuisine, R. Marie** food processor

roboticien, -enne [robotisjɛ̃, -ɛn] NM,F robotics expert, robotician

robotique [robotik] ADJ robotic
NF robotics *(singulier)*

robotisation [robotizasjɔ̃] NF robotizing; *(d'un atelier, d'une usine)* automation

robotiser [3] [robotize] VT **1** *(atelier, usine, travail)* to automate, to robotize **2** *(personne)* to robotize

robre [rɔbr] NM *Cartes (au whist, au bridge)* rubber

roburite [robyrit] NF roburite

robusta [robysta] NM robusta (coffee)

robuste [robyst] ADJ **1** *(personne)* robust, sturdy, strong; **des jambes robustes** sturdy legs **2** *(santé)* sound; *(appétit)* robust, healthy; **doté d'une r. constitution** blessed with a robust *or* sound constitution **3** *(arbre, plante)* hardy **4** *(meuble, voiture, moteur)* sturdy, robust **5** *(conviction)* firm, strong

robustesse [robystɛs] NF **1** *(d'une personne)* robustness **2** *(d'un arbre, d'une plante)* hardiness **3** *(d'un meuble, d'une voiture, d'un moteur)* sturdiness, robustness

ROC [ɛrose] NF *Ordinat (abrév* **reconnaissance optique des caractères***)* OCR

roc [rɔk] NM **1** *(pierre)* rock; **dur** *ou* **ferme comme un r.** solid *or* firm as a rock; *Fig* **Jules, c'est un r.** Jules is as solid as a rock **2** *Échecs (pièce)* rook, castle; *(action)* castling

rocade [rɔkad] NF **1** *Constr* bypass **2** *Mil* communications line

rocaillage [rɔkajaʒ] NM *Archit* rocaille ornamentation

rocaille [rɔkaj] NF **1** *(pierraille)* loose stones; *(terrain)* stony ground **2** *(jardin)* rock garden, rockery **3** *Archit* rocaille; **style r.** rocaille style; **grotte/fontaine en r.** rocaille grotto/fountain

rocailleur [rɔkajœr] NM *Constr* = specialist in rocaille work

rocailleux, -euse [rɔkajø, -øz] ADJ **1** *(terrain)* rocky, stony **2** *(voix)* gravelly **3** *(style)* rough, rugged

rocamadour [rɔkamadur] NM Rocamadour cheese *(creamy French cheese made from goat's milk)*

rocambole [rɔkãbɔl] NF *Bot* rocambole, sand leek, giant *or* elephant garlic
  ▫ **Rocambole** NPR = hero of a series of fantastic adventure stories (1859–84) by Ponson du Terrail, from which the adjective "rocambolesque" is derived

rocambolesque [rɔkãbɔlɛsk] ADJ *(aventures)* fantastic; *(histoire)* incredible; **le scénario est r.** the script is all thrills and spills

rocelle [rɔsɛl] NF *Bot* orchil, dyer's moss

rochage [rɔʃaʒ] NM *Métal* spitting

rochassier, -ère [rɔʃasje, -ɛr] NM,F *Sport* rock climber

roche [rɔʃ] NF **1** *Géol* rock; **r. ignée/métamorphique/sédimentaire** igneous/metamorphic/sedimentary rock; **r. mère** parent rock
  2 *(pierre)* rock, boulder; **sculpté à même la r. ou dans la r.** *(bas-relief)* carved in the rock; *(statue)* carved out of the rock; **le sentier serpentait à travers les éboulis de roches** the path wound its way across a scree of boulders; *Antiq* **la r. Tarpéienne** the Tarpeian Rock

roche-magasin [rɔʃmagazɛ̃] *(pl* **roches-magasins***)* NF *Géol* reservoir rock

roche-mère [rɔʃmɛr] *(pl* **roches-mères***)* NF *Géol* mother *or* parent rock, gangue, matrix; **roche mère de pétrole** (oil) source rock

rocher¹ [rɔʃe] NM rock; **grimper/pousser à flanc de r.** to climb up/to grow on the rock face; **côte hérissée de rochers** rocky coast; **r. branlant** rocking *or* logan stone; **le R.** = the town of Monaco; **le r. de Gibraltar** the Rock of Gibraltar; *Littéraire* **quel r. de Sisyphe!** what a Sisyphean *or* never-ending task!
  2 *Sport* **faire du r.** to go rock-climbing
  3 *Anat* petrous bone
  4 *(en chocolat)* rocher *(rock-shaped chocolate)*

rocher² [rɔʃe] VI **1** *Métal* to spit
  2 *(bière)* to froth

roche-réservoir [rɔʃrezɛrvwar] *(pl* **roches-réservoirs***)* = **roche-magasin**

rochet [rɔʃɛ] NM **1** *Tex* spool **2** *Tech* **roue à r.** ratchet wheel

rocheuse [rɔʃøz] *voir* **rocheux**

Rocheuses [rɔʃøz] NFPL **les (montagnes) R.** the (Great) Rocky Mountains, the Rockies

rocheux, -euse [rɔʃø, -øz] ADJ *(paysage, région)* rocky

Roch Ha-Shana [rɔʃaʃana] NM INV *Rel* Rosh Hashanah

rochier [rɔʃje] NM *Ich* **1** *(poisson de roche)* wrasse
  2 *(requin)* dogfish

rock [rɔk] ADJ INV *Mus* rock
  NM **1** *Mus (musique)* rock (music); *(danse)* rock (and roll), jive; **danser le r.** to jive (and roll); **un groupe/chanteur de r.** a rock group/singer; **r. alternatif** alternative rock; **r. FM, r. mélodique** AOR **2** *Littérature & Myth (oiseau)* roc

rock and roll [rɔkɛnrɔl] NM INV *(musique)* rock and roll, rock'n'roll; *(danse)* rock (and roll), jive; **danser le r.** to jive, to rock (and roll)

rocker [rɔkœr] NM **1** *(artiste)* rock singer *or* musician **2** *Fam (fan)* rocker

rocket [rɔkɛt] = **roquette 1**

rockeur, -euse [rɔkœr, -øz] NM,F **1** *(artiste)* rock singer *or* musician; **les plus grands rockeurs** the greatest rock stars **2** *Fam (fan)* rocker

rocking-chair [rɔkiɲtʃɛr] *(pl* **rocking-chairs***)* NM rocking chair

rockumentaire [rɔkymãtɛr] NM *Cin* rockumentary

rococo [rɔkoko] ADJ INV **1** *Beaux-Arts* rococo **2** *Péj (tarabiscoté)* over-ornate, rococo; *(démodé)* antiquated, rococo
  NM *Beaux-Arts* rococo

rocou [rɔku] NM annatto, roucou

rocouer [6] [rɔkwe] VT to dye with annatto *or* roucou

rocouyer [rɔkuje] NM *Bot* annatto tree, roucou (tree)

rodage [rɔdaʒ] NM **1** *(d'un moteur, d'une voiture)* *Br* running in, *Am* breaking in; **tant que la voiture est en r.** while the car is being *Br* run in *or Am* broken in
  2 *Fig (mise au point)* **la démocratie est récente et demande un certain r.** democracy is in its infancy and needs time to get over its teething troubles; **le r. de ce service va prendre plusieurs mois** it'll take several months to get this new service running smoothly
  3 *Tech* grinding; **r. de soupape** valve grinding

rôdailler [3] [rodaje] VI *Fam (traînasser)* to roam *or* to wander about

rodéo [rodeo] NM **1** *(à cheval)* rodeo; **faire du r.** *(métier)* to be a rodeo rider; **r. mécanique** (mechanical) bucking bronco **2** *Fam (en voiture)* **les policiers et les gangsters ont fait un r. dans le quartier** the police and the gangsters had a high-speed car chase through the streets■; **ils font du r. en voitures volées** they go joyriding

roder [3] [rode] VT **1** *(moteur, voiture)* *Br* to run in, *Am* to break in **2** *Fig (mettre au point)* **r. un service/une équipe** to get a department/a team up and running; **r. un spectacle** to get a show into its stride; **il est rodé maintenant** he knows the ropes now; **tout est bien rodé** everything is running smoothly **3** *Tech (surface)* to grind

rôder [3] [rode] VI *(traîner → sans but)* to hang around, to roam *or* to loiter about; *(→ avec une mauvaise intention)* to lurk *or* to skulk around; **r. dans les rues** to prowl about *or* hang about the streets; **il rôdait autour de la banque** he was lurking *or* loitering around the bank; **l'animal rôde toujours** the animal is still on the prowl *or* prowling about; **arrêtez de r. autour de ma fille** stop hanging round my daughter

rôdeur, -euse [rodœr, -øz] NM,F prowler

rodoir [rodwar] NM *Tech* grinding tool, grinder

rodomont [rodomɔ̃] NM *Littéraire ou Vieilli* braggart

rodomontade [rodomɔ̃tad] NF *Littéraire* bragging *(UNCOUNT)*, swaggering *(UNCOUNT)*; **il est connu pour ses rodomontades** he's notorious for being a braggart; **faire des rodomontades** to brag, to bluster

Rodrigue [rodrig] NPR = character from Corneille's play 'le Cid', a dashing hero torn between passion for Chimène and duty towards his family and country

roentgen [rœntgɛn] NM *Phys* roentgen, röntgen

rœsti [røʃti] NMPL *Suisse Culin* roesti, potato pancake

rogations [rɔgasjɔ̃] NFPL *Cathol* rogations

rogatoire [rɔgatwar] ADJ *Jur* rogatory

rogaton [rɔgatɔ̃] NM *Fam* **1** *Vieilli (objet de rebut)* piece of rubbish
  ▫ **rogatons** NMPL *(restes de nourriture)* scraps (of food), leftovers

rognage [rɔɲaʒ] NM *(action → du cuir, du métal)* paring; *(→ du papier)* trimming; *Ordinat (d'image)* cropping

rogne [rɔɲ] NF *Fam* anger■, rage■; **être/se mettre en r. (contre qn)** to be/go mad *or* crazy (with/at sb); **mettre qn en r.** to make sb hopping mad

rogner [3] [rɔɲe] VT **1** *(couper → métal)* to pare, to clip; *(→ cuir)* to pare, to trim; *(→ papier)* to trim; *(→ livre)* to guillotine, to trim; *Ordinat (image)* to crop; **r. les griffes à un oiseau** to clip *or* to pare a bird's claws
  2 *(réduire → budget, salaire)* to cut (back)
  VI *Fam Vieilli (être en colère)* to be hopping mad
  ▫ **rogner sur** VT IND to cut back *or* down on; **r. sur la nourriture** to cut back *or* to skimp on food

rogneur, -euse [rɔɲœr, -øz] NM,F *(de papier)* trimmer
  ▫ **rogneuse** NF *(machine)* trimming machine

rognoir [rɔɲwar] NM trimmer

rognon [rɔɲɔ̃] NM **1** *Culin* kidney **2** *Géol* nodule
  ▫ **rognons** NMPL *Vulg (testicules)* balls, nuts, *Br* bollocks

rognonnade [rɔɲɔnad] NF *Culin* **r. de veau** = loin of veal cooked with kidneys

rognonner [3] [rɔɲɔne] VI *Fam Vieilli* to grumble, to grouse

rognures [rɔɲyr] NFPL *(de métal, de carton, d'étoffe)* clippings, trimmings; *(d'ongles)* clippings, parings; *(de viande)* scraps, offcuts

rogomme [rɔgɔm] NM *Fam* **voix de r.** hoarse *or* gruff voice■

rogue [rɔg] ADJ *(arrogant)* arrogant, haughty
  NF *Ich & Pêche* roe

rogué, -e [rɔge] ADJ *Pêche* roed

rohart [rɔar] NM *(de morse)* walrus ivory; *(d'hippopotame)* hippopotamus ivory

roi [rwa] NM **1** *(monarque)* king; **le r. Louis XIII** (King) Louis XIII; **r. constitutionnel** constitutional monarch; **r. de droit divin** king by divine right; **le r. de Rome** the King of Rome; **le R. des rois** the King of Kings; *Hist* **le R. Très Chrétien** the King of France; *Hist* **les rois fainéants** = the last Merovingian kings, in the 7th century; *Bible* **les Rois mages** the Magi, the Three Wise Men; *Rel* **les Rois** *(Épiphanie)* Twelfth Night; **tirer les Rois** to eat "galette des Rois"; **digne d'un r.** fit for a king; **être heureux comme un r.** to be as happy as a king *or Br* a sandboy; **vivre comme un r.** to live like a king *or* a lord; **je r. n'est pas son cousin** he's terribly stuck-up; **le r. dit "nous voulons"** "I want" doesn't get; *Hum* **je vais où le r. va à pied** I'm going to the toilet *or* to sit on the throne; **le r. est mort, vive le r.!** the King is dead, long live the King!; **le r. est nu** the emperor has no clothes
  2 *Fig* **le r. de notre petite fête** the prince of our little gathering; **le r. des animaux** the king of beasts; **les rois du pétrole** the oil tycoons *or* magnates; **le r. du surgelé** the leading name in frozen food, the frozen food king; *Hum* **c'est le r. de la resquille** he's a champion *Br* queue-jumper *or Am* line-jumper; **tu es vraiment le r. de la gaffe!** you're an expert at putting your foot in it!; **c'est vraiment le r. des imbéciles** he's a prize idiot; *très Fam* **c'est le r. des cons** he's a complete prick
  3 *Cartes* king; **r. de carreau/pique** king of diamonds/spades
  4 *Ich* **r. des harengs** oarfish

TIRER LES ROIS
The French traditionally celebrate Epiphany with a round, almond-flavoured pastry ("la galette des Rois") containing a small porcelain figurine ("la fève" – originally a dried bean). The pastry is shared out and the person who finds the "fève" is appointed "king" or "queen" and given a cardboard crown to wear. This tradition is called "tirer les Rois".

roide [rwad], **roideur** [rwadœr], **roidir** [rwadir] *Arch* = **raide, raideur, raidir**

roille [rɔj] NF *Suisse Fam* downpour■; **pleuvoir à la r.** to pee down, *Br* to chuck it down

roiller [3] [rɔje] V IMPERSONNEL *Suisse Fam* to pee down, *Br* to chuck it down

Roi-Soleil [rwasɔlɛj] NM *Hist* **le R.** the Sun King (Louis XIV)

Roissy [rwasi] NM *(aéroport)* = commonly-used name for Charles-de-Gaulle airport

roitelet [rwatlɛ] NM **1** *Péj (roi)* kinglet **2** *Orn* wren, *Am* winter wren; **r. huppé** goldcrest

rôlage [rolaʒ] NM twisting of tobacco

Roland-Garros [rolãgaros] NM **(le stade) R.** = stadium in Paris where international tennis championships are held

rôle [rol] NM **1** *Cin, Théât & TV* role, part; **apprendre son r.** to learn one's part *or* lines; **il joue le r. d'un espion** he plays (the part of) a spy; **distribuer les rôles** to do the casting, to cast; **il a toujours des rôles de névropathe** he's always cast as a neurotic, he always gets to play neurotics; **avec Jean Dumay dans le r. du Grand Inquisiteur** starring Jean Dumay as the Inquisitor General; **r. de composition** character part *or* role; **r. muet** non-speaking part; **r. parlant** speaking part, speaking role; **r. principal** leading role, starring role, lead; **r. secondaire** supporting role; **r. sérieux** straight part; **petit r.** walk-on part; **premier r.** *(acteur)* leading actor,f actress; *(personnage)* lead; **avoir le premier r. ou le r. principal** to have the starring role, to play the leading role; *Fig* to be the star of the show; **second r.** secondary *or* supporting role;

jouer les seconds rôles (auprès de qn) to play second fiddle (to sb); **meilleur second r. masculin/féminin** best supporting actor/actress; **jeu de r.** role play; **avoir le beau r.** to have it *or* things easy

2 *(fonction)* role; **jouer un r. important dans qch** to play an important part in sth; **cet élément ne joue qu'un r. secondaire dans le processus** this factor plays a secondary role in the process; **le r. du cœur dans la circulation du sang** the role *or* the part played by the heart in blood circulation; **le r. de l'exécutif** the role *or* function of the executive; **il prend très à cœur son r. de père** he takes his role as father *or* his paternal duties very seriously; **les femmes n'ont pas toujours un r. facile** a woman's role is not always easy, women do not always have it easy; **ce n'est pas mon r. de m'occuper de ça** it's not my job *or* it's not up to me to do it

3 *(liste)* roll; *Naut* **r. d'équipage** muster roll, crew list; **r. des malades** sick list

4 *Jur* **mettre une affaire au** *ou* **sur le r.** to put a case on the cause list; *Fin* **r. d'impôt** tax roll; *Fin* **r. nominatif** income tax (units) list

5 *(en sociologie)* role

6 *(de tabac)* twist of tobacco

rôle-titre [roltitr] *(pl* **rôles-titres***)* NM *Cin & Théât* title role

roller [rɔlœr] NM rollerblading; **faire du r.** to go rollerblading; **r. in-line** in-line skating; **faire du r. in-line** to go in-line skating
▫ **rollers** NMPL rollerblades; **rollers in-line** in-line skates

---

LE ROLLER

The past ten years or so have seen the emergence of a roller-skating "culture" in France, particularly in Paris. Nowadays it is common to see Parisians zooming through the streets of the capital on their rollerblades. Moreover, the Friday night rollerblading rally is now a well-established Parisian tradition: what started out as impromptu gatherings of a few roller-skating enthusiasts in the early 90s has developed into a weekly event involving hundreds of skaters rollerblading through the streets of Paris every Friday night. So popular is this means of transport that the French national police has created its own rollerblade brigade, the first of its kind in the world.

---

rolleur, -euse [rɔlœr, -øz] NM,F rollerblader
NM rollerblading; **faire du r.** to go rollerblading
▫ **rolleurs** NMPL rollerblades

rollier [rɔlje] NM *Orn* roller

rollmops [rɔlmɔps] NM *Culin* rollmop (herring)

roll on-roll off [rɔlɔnrɔlɔf] ADJ INV *(navire)* roll-on-roll-off, ro-ro
NM INV **1** *(roulage)* roll-on-roll-off **2** *(navire)* roll-on-roll-off ship, ro-ro ship

rollot [rɔlo] NM Rollot (cheese) *(traditional heart-shaped cheese produced in Picardy)*

ROM [rɔm] NF *Ordinat (abrév* **read only memory***)* ROM, Rom

rom [rɔm] ADJ INV Romany *(avant n)*

Romagne [rɔmaɲ] NF **la R.** the Romagna

romain, -e [rɔmɛ̃, -ɛn] ADJ **1** Roman; **l'Église romaine** the Church of Rome

2 *Belg Pol* Christian Socialist
▫ **Romain, -e** NM,F Roman NM *Typ* roman
▫ **romaine** NF **1** *(salade)* Br cos lettuce, *Am* romaine (lettuce)

2 *(balance)* steelyard

3 *Fam (locution)* **être bon comme la romaine** *(bienveillant)* to be too kind-hearted for one's own good; **on est bons comme la romaine** *(on a perdu)* we've had it; *(on va supporter les conséquences)* we're in for it

romaïque [rɔmaik] *Ling* ADJ Romaic
NM modern Greek

roman¹ [rɔmɑ̃] NM **1** *Littérature* novel; **il n'écrit que des romans** he only writes novels *or* fiction; **on dirait un mauvais r.** it sounds like something out of a cheap novel; **sa vie est un vrai r.** you could write a book about his/her life; **tout ça c'est du r.** it's all fantasy *or* make-believe; **r. d'anticipation** science-fiction novel;

r. d'apprentissage Bildungsroman; **r. d'aventures/d'amour** adventure/love story; **r. de cape et d'épée** swashbuckling tale; **r. de chevalerie** tale of chivalry; **r. à clef** roman à clef; **r. d'épouvante** horror novel; **r. d'espionnage** spy novel; *Péj* **r. de gare** airport *or* Am dime novel; **r. historique** historical novel; **r. de mœurs** social novel; **r. noir** thriller; **r. policier** detective story *or* novel; **r. psychologique** psychological novel; **r. de science-fiction** science-fiction *or* sci-fi novel; **r. à thèse** roman à thèse, novel of ideas

2 *(genre médiéval)* romance

3 *Psy* **r. familial** family romance

'Roman de la Rose' de Loris, de Meung 'Romance of the Rose'

---

roman², -e [rɔmɑ̃, -an] ADJ **1** *Ling* Romance *(avant n)* **2** *Archit* Romanesque; *(en Angleterre → architecture, style)* Norman; *(→ portail)* Romanesque
NM **1** *(langue)* Romance **2** *Archit* **le r.** Romanesque architecture; *(en Angleterre)* Norman architecture, the Norman style

romance [rɔmɑ̃s] NF *(poème, musique)* romance; *(chanson sentimentale)* sentimental love song *or* ballad

romancer [16] [rɔmɑ̃se] VT *(histoire)* to novelize; **r. une biographie** to write a biography in the form of a novel
VI *Fig* **avoir tendance à r.** to have a tendency to embroider the facts

romancero [rɔmɑ̃sero] NM *Littérature* **le r. du Cid** the romances of El Cid

romanche [rɔmɑ̃ʃ] ADJ Romansh
NM Romansh

romancier, -ère [rɔmɑ̃sje, -ɛr] *Littérature* NM,F novelist, novel *or* fiction writer
NM *(écrivain de genre médiéval)* writer of romances, romance writer

romand, -e [rɔmɑ̃, -ɑ̃d] ADJ of French-speaking Switzerland
▫ **Romand, -e** NM,F French-speaking Swiss; **les Romands** the French-speaking Swiss

romanée [rɔmane] NM (Vosne-)Romanée *(fine red wine produced in Burgundy)*

romanesque [rɔmanɛsk] ADJ **1** *Littérature (héros, personnage)* fictional, in a novel; *(technique, style)* novelistic; **l'œuvre r. de Sartre** Sartre's fiction *or* novels

2 *Fig (aventure)* fantastic(al), fabulous; *(imagination, amour)* romantic; **c'est un personnage r.** he's/she's like something out of a novel
NM *Littérature* **les règles du r.** the rules of fiction writing

roman-feuilleton [rɔmɑ̃fœjtɔ̃] *(pl* **romans-feuilletons***)* NM *Littérature* serialized novel, serial; **sa vie est un vrai r.** his/her life is a real adventure story

roman-fleuve [rɔmɑ̃flœv] *(pl* **romans-fleuves***)* NM *Littérature* roman-fleuve, saga; **il m'a écrit un r.** the letter he sent me was one long *or* endless saga

romani [rɔmani] NM *(langue)* Romany

romanichel, -elle [rɔmaniʃɛl] NM,F *Péj* **1** *(Tsigane)* Romany, gypsy **2** *(nomade)* gypsy

romanisation [rɔmanizasjɔ̃] NF romanization

romaniser [3] [rɔmanize] VT to romanize

romanisme [rɔmanism] NM *Rel* Romanism

romaniste [rɔmanist] NMF **1** *Rel* Romanist **2** *Ling* specialist in Romance languages **3** *Beaux-Arts & Jur* romanist

romanité [rɔmanite] NF **1** *(civilisation)* the (Ancient) Roman civilization *or* way of life **2** *(pays)* Roman Empire

romano [rɔmano] NMF *Fam* gippo, = offensive term used to refer to a gypsy

roman-photo [rɔmɑ̃foto] *(pl* **romans-photos***)* NM photo novel, photo romance; **une héroïne de r.** a soap-opera heroine

romantique [rɔmɑ̃tik] ADJ **1** *Beaux-Arts, Littérature & Mus* Romantic **2** *(sentimental)* romantic
NMF **1** *Beaux-Arts, Littérature & Mus* Romantic; **les romantiques** the Romantics **2** *(sentimental)* romantic

romantisme [rɔmɑ̃tism] NM **1** *Beaux-Arts, Littérature & Mus* Romanticism **2** *(sentimentalisme)*

romanticism; **ça ne manque pas de r.** it's quite romantic

romarin [rɔmarɛ̃] NM rosemary

rombière [rɔbjɛr] NF *Fam* **une vieille r.** a stuck-up old cow

rombosse [rɔbɔs] NF *Belg Culin* = type of apple turnover where the whole apple is baked in pastry

Rome [rɔm] NF Rome; **la R. antique** Ancient Rome; **le concours de R.** = former annual competition for artists, winners of which were entitled to spend three years at the French Academy in Rome

---

'Rome, ville ouverte' Rossellini 'Open City'

Roméo [rɔmeo] NPR Romeo

'Roméo et Juliette' Shakespeare, Zeffirelli, Luhrmann 'Romeo and Juliet'

---

rompre [78] [rɔpr] VT **1** *(mettre fin à → jeûne, silence, contrat)* to break; *(→ fiançailles, relations)* to break off; *(→ marché)* to call off; *(→ équilibre)* to upset; **r. le charme** to break the spell; **prenez des vacances pour r. la monotonie quotidienne!** take a holiday to break the monotony of everyday life!; **ne rompez pas le rythme** keep up the rhythm; *Hum* **désolé de r. ce doux entretien** sorry to break in on your tête-à-tête; **r. les chiens** to call off the hounds; *Fig* to change the subject

2 *(briser)* to break; **le fleuve a rompu ses digues** the river has burst its banks; *Littéraire* **r. ses chaînes** *ou* **fers** to break one's chains; *Naut* **r. les amarres** to break (free from) the moorings; **r. le pain** to break bread; *Littéraire* **r. le pain avec qn** to break bread with sb; *Fig* **r. des lances contre qn** to cross swords with sb; *Littéraire* **r. en visière avec qn** to quarrel openly with sb

3 *(accoutumer)* to break in; **r. qn à qch** to break sb in to sth; **r. qn à une discipline** to initiate sb into *or* to train sb in a discipline; **sa vie à la ferme l'a rompu aux travaux pénibles** life on the farm has inured him to hard labour

4 *Mil* to break; **r. les rangs** to break ranks; **rompez (les rangs)!** dismiss!, fall out!

VI **1** *(se séparer)* to break up; **r. avec** to break with; **r. avec ses amis/son milieu** to break with one's friends/one's milieu; **r. avec l'étiquette/la tradition** to break with etiquette/tradition; **r. avec une habitude** to break (oneself of) a habit

2 *(se briser → corde, branche)* to break, to snap; *(→ digue)* to break, to burst

3 *Sport (reculer)* to break

► **se rompre** VPR **1** *(se briser → branche)* to break *or* to snap (off); *(→ corde)* to break *or* to snap; *(→ digue)* to burst, to break; *(→ vaisseau sanguin)* to rupture

2 se r. les os *ou* **le cou** to break one's neck

rompu, -e [rɔpy] ADJ **1** *(épuisé)* **r. (de fatigue)** tired out, worn out, exhausted; **r. de travail** worn out *or* tired out by work; **j'ai les jambes rompues** my legs are giving way under me

2 *(habitué)* **r. aux affaires/à la diplomatie** experienced in business/in diplomacy; **il est r. à ce genre d'exercice** he's accustomed *or* used to this kind of exercise; **je suis peu r. au droit anglais** I'm not well-grounded in *or* I have little experience of English law; **r. aux rigueurs de** accustomed *or* inured to the rigours of

3 *Beaux-Arts* **couleur rompue** colour with a shot effect
NM *Bourse* fraction

romsteck [rɔmstɛk] NM *(partie du bœuf)* rumpsteak; *(morceau coupé)* slice of rumpsteak

Romulus [rɔmylys] NPR *Myth* **R. et Rémus** Romulus and Remus

ronce [rɔs] NF **1** *Bot* blackberry bush; **les ronces** *(buissons)* the brambles; **r. artificielle** barbed wire **2** *(nœud dans le bois)* burr, *Spéc* swirl; **r. de noyer** burr walnut

ronceraie [rɔsrɛ] NF bramble patch, brambles

ronceux, -euse [rɔsø, -øz] ADJ **1** *(bois)* knotty **2** *Littéraire (chemin)* brambly, thorny

Roncevaux [rɔsvo] NM Roncesvalles

ronchon, -onne [rɔ̃ʃɔ̃, -ɔn] *Fam* **ADJ** crotchety, grumpy, grouchy
   NM,F grumbler, grouse, *Am* grouch

ronchonnement [rɔ̃ʃɔnmɑ̃] **NM** *Fam* grousing (UNCOUNT), grouching (UNCOUNT), griping (UNCOUNT)

ronchonner [3] [rɔ̃ʃɔne] **VI** *Fam* to grouse, to gripe, to grouch (**après** at)

ronchonneur, -euse [rɔ̃ʃɔnœr, -øz] = **ronchon**

ronchopathie [rɔ̃kopati] **NF** = type of snoring associated with sleep apnoea

roncier [rɔ̃sje] **NM** *Bot* bramble (bush)

roncière [rɔ̃sjɛr] **NF** *Bot* bramble (bush)

rond, -e[1] [rɔ̃, rɔ̃d] **ADJ** 1 *(circulaire)* round, circular; **faire** *ou* **ouvrir des yeux ronds** to stare in disbelief

   2 *(bien en chair)* round, full, plump; **un petit bébé tout r.** a chubby little baby; **un petit nez r.** a button nose; **de jolies épaules bien rondes** well-rounded *or* well-turned shoulders; **des seins ronds** full breasts; **un ventre r.** a rounded belly; **un visage tout r.** a round face, *Péj* a moon face; **un petit homme r.** a *Br* podgy *or* *Am* pudgy little man

   3 *Fam (ivre)* wasted, loaded; **il était complètement r.** he was totally wasted; **r. comme une queue de pelle** *ou* **comme un boudin** *Br* as pissed as a newt, *Am* stewed to the gills

   4 *(franc)* straightforward, straight; **il est r. en affaires** he's very direct *or* straightforward *or* up front when it comes to business; **elle me l'a dit de façon très ronde** she told me straight (out)

   5 *(chiffre, somme)* round

   NM 1 *(cercle)* circle, ring; **faire des ronds de fumée** to blow *or* to make smoke rings; **faire des ronds dans l'eau** to make rings in the water; *Fig* to fritter away one's time

   2 *(anneau)* ring; **r. de serviette** napkin ring; *Ftbl* **r. central** centre circle

   3 *Fam (sou)* **je n'ai plus un r.** I'm flat broke, *Br* I'm skint; **je n'ai pas un r. sur moi** I don't have a *Br* penny *or* *Am* cent on me; **ils ont des ronds** they're rolling in it, they're loaded

   4 *Bot* **r. de sorcière** fairy ring *(on ground)*

   5 *(en danse)* **r. de jambe** rond de jambe; *Fig* **faire des ronds de jambe** to bow and scrape

   ADV *Fam (locutions)* **tourner r.** to go well■, to run smoothly■; **qu'est-ce qui ne tourne pas r.?** what's the matter?■, what's the problem?■; **ça ne tourne pas r.** things aren't going (very) well■; **ne pas tourner r.** *(machine)* to be on the blink; *(personne)* to be not all there, to have a screw *or* *Br* a slate loose; **tout r.** *(en entier → avaler)* whole■; *(exactement)* exactly■; **tu me dois 20 euros tout r.** you owe me exactly 20 euros

   □ **en rond** **ADV** *(se placer, s'asseoir)* in a circle; *(danser)* in a ring; *aussi Fig* **tourner en r.** *(ne pas parvenir à une solution)* to go round (and round) in circles; *(ne pas savoir quoi faire)* to hang around aimlessly

rondache [rɔ̃daʃ] **NF** *Hist* rondache, roundel

rondade [rɔ̃dad] **NF** *Sport* run-up

rond-de-cuir [rɔ̃dkɥir] *(pl* **ronds-de-cuir***)* **NM** *Péj* penpusher

ronde[2] [rɔ̃d] **NF** 1 *(inspection → d'un vigile)* round, rounds, patrol; *(→ d'un soldat)* patrol; *(→ d'un policier)* beat, round, rounds; **faire sa r.** *(sujet: veilleur)* to make one's round *or* rounds; *(sujet: policier)* to be on patrol *or* on the beat; **croiser une r. de police** to come across a police patrol

   2 *(mouvement circulaire)* circling, turning; **nous regardions la r. incessante des voitures** we were watching the cars go round and round

   3 *Mus Br* semibreve, *Am* whole note

   4 *(danse)* round (dance), ronde; **faire la r.** to dance round in a circle *or* ring; **allez les enfants, on fait la r.!** come on children, let's join hands in a ring!

   5 *(écriture)* round hand

□ **à la ronde** **ADV** **il n'y a pas une seule maison à 20 kilomètres à la r.** there's no house within 20 kilometres, there's no house within *or* in a 20-kilometre radius; **visible à 10 kilomètres à la r.** visible for 10 kilometres around; **(faire) passer le vin à la r.** to pass the wine round, to hand round the wine; **répétez-le à la r.** go round and tell everybody

□ **rondes** **NFPL** *Suisse Culin* jacket potatoes

![Night Watch icon]

'La Ronde de nuit' *Rembrandt* 'The Night Watch'

rondeau, -x [rɔ̃do] **NM** 1 *Littérature* rondeau 2 *Mus* rondo

ronde-bosse [rɔ̃dbɔs] *(pl* **rondes-bosses***)* **NF** sculpture in the round; **en r.** in the round

rondel [rɔ̃dɛl] **NM** *Vieilli* 1 *Littérature* rondel 2 *Mus* rondo

rondelet, -ette [rɔ̃dlɛ, -ɛt] **ADJ** *Fam* 1 *(potelé)* chubby, plump, plumpish 2 *(important)* **une somme rondelette** a tidy *or* nice little sum

rondelle [rɔ̃dɛl] **NF** 1 *(de salami, de citron)* slice; **couper qch en rondelles** to slice sth, to cut sth into slices 2 *Tech* disc; *(d'un écrou)* washer; *(d'une canette)* ring 3 *(au hockey)* puck

rondement [rɔ̃dmɑ̃] **ADV** 1 *(promptement)* briskly, promptly, quickly and efficiently; **des négociations r. menées** competently conducted negotiations 2 *(franchement)* frankly, outspokenly; **il me l'a dit r.** he told me straight out

rondeur [rɔ̃dœr] **NF** 1 *(forme → d'un visage, d'un bras)* roundness, plumpness, chubbiness; *(→ d'un sein)* fullness; *(→ d'une épaule)* roundness 2 *(franchise)* frankness; **avec r.** frankly

   □ **rondeurs** **NFPL** *Euph* curves; **rondeurs disgracieuses** unsightly bulges; **une jeune femme tout en rondeurs** a curvaceous young woman

rondier [rɔ̃dje] **NM** *Bot* palmyra

rondin [rɔ̃dɛ̃] **NM** *(bois)* round billet, log; **cabane en rondins** log cabin

rondo [rɔ̃do] **NM** *Mus* rondo

rondouillard, -e [rɔ̃dujar, -ard] **ADJ** *Fam* tubby, *Br* podgy, *Am* pudgy

rond-point [rɔ̃pwɛ̃] *(pl* **ronds-points***)* **NM** *Br* roundabout, *Am* traffic circle

Ronéo® [rɔneo] **NF** Roneo®

ronéoter [3] [rɔneɔte], **ronéotyper** [3] [rɔneɔtipe] **VT** to Roneo®, to duplicate

rôneraie [rɔnərɛ] **NF** palmyra grove

ronflant, -e [rɔ̃flɑ̃, -ɑ̃t] **ADJ** 1 *(moteur)* purring, throbbing; *(feu)* roaring 2 *Péj (discours)* bombastic, high-flown; *(titre)* grand-sounding; *(promesses)* grand

ronflement [rɔ̃fləmɑ̃] **NM** 1 *(d'un dormeur)* snore, snoring (UNCOUNT) 2 *(bruit → sourd)* humming (UNCOUNT), droning (UNCOUNT); *(→ fort)* roar, roaring (UNCOUNT), throbbing (UNCOUNT)

ronfler [3] [rɔ̃fle] **VI** 1 *(en dormant)* to snore; **r. comme un soufflet de forge** to snore like anything 2 *Fam (dormir)* to snooze, to snore away 3 *(vrombir → doucement)* to drone, to hum; *(→ fort)* to roar, to throb; **faire r. le moteur** to rev up the engine

ronflette [rɔ̃flɛt] **NF** *Fam* snooze; **piquer une r.** to have a nap *or* a snooze

ronfleur, -euse [rɔ̃flœr, -øz] **NM,F** snorer
   NM *Élec & Tél* buzzer

ronge [rɔ̃ʒ] **NM** *Zool* **faire son r.** to chew the cud, *Spéc* to ruminate

rongement [rɔ̃ʒmɑ̃] **NM** *Littéraire* gnawing

ronger [17] [rɔ̃ʒe] **VT** 1 *(mordiller)* to gnaw (away) at, to eat into; **r. un os** to gnaw at a bone; **rongé par les vers/mites** worm-/moth-eaten; *Fig* **r. son frein** to champ at the bit

   2 *(corroder → sujet: mer)* to wear away; *(→ sujet: acide, rouille)* to eat into; **rongé par la rouille** eaten away with rust, rusted away; **être rongé par la maladie** to be wasted by disease; **le mal qui ronge la société** the evil that eats away at society; **être rongé par les soucis** to be careworn; *Littéraire* **le chagrin qui me ronge le cœur** the sorrow that eats away *or* gnaws at my heart

   ► **se ronger** **VPR** **se r. les ongles** to bite one's nails

rongeur, -euse [rɔ̃ʒœr, -øz] **ADJ** rodent-like
   NM *Zool* rodent

rônier [rɔnje] **NM** *Bot* palmyra

ronron [rɔ̃rɔ̃] **NM** 1 *(d'un chat)* purr, purring (UNCOUNT); **faire r.** to purr 2 *(d'une machine)* whirr, hum 3 *(routine)* routine; **le r. de la vie quotidienne** the daily routine

ronronnement [rɔ̃rɔnmɑ̃] **NM** 1 *(d'un chat)* purr, purring (UNCOUNT) 2 *(d'une machine)* whirr, hum, whirring (UNCOUNT), humming (UNCOUNT); *(d'un bon moteur)* purr, purring (UNCOUNT); *(d'un avion)* drone, droning (UNCOUNT)

ronronner [3] [rɔ̃rɔne] **VI** 1 *(chat)* to purr; **r. de plaisir** to purr with pleasure 2 *(machine)* to whirr, to hum; *(bon moteur)* to purr; *(avion)* to drone 3 *Fig* to tick over, to chug along

röntgen [rœntgɛn] **NM** *Phys* roentgen, röntgen

roof [ruf] = **rouf**

roofing [rufiŋ] **NM** *Belg* roofing felt

roploplos [roploplo] **NMPL** *très Fam (seins)* tits, knockers, jugs

roque [rɔk] **NM** *Échecs* castling; **petit/grand r.** king's/queen's side castling

roquefort [rɔkfɔr] **NM** Roquefort (cheese)

roquentin [rɔkɑ̃tɛ̃] **NM** *Arch ou Littéraire* old fop, old beau

roquer [3] [rɔke] **VI** 1 *Échecs* to castle 2 *(au croquet)* to croquet the ball

roquerie [rɔkri] **NF** rookery *(of penguins or sea lions)*

roquet [rɔkɛ] **NM** 1 *(chien)* yappy *or* noisy dog; **sale r.!** damn *or* *Br* bloody animal! 2 *Fam Péj (personne)* pest; **espèce de petit r.!** you little pest!

roquetin [rɔktɛ̃] **NM** *Tex* 1 *(bobine)* silk spool 2 *(gros fil)* braiding yarn

roquette [rɔkɛt] **NF** 1 *(projectile)* rocket; **r. antichar** anti-tank rocket 2 *Bot & Culin Br* rocket, *Am* arugula; **r. blanche/de mer** wall/sea rocket; **r. maritime** sea rocket

rorqual, -als [rɔrkwal] **NM** *Zool* rorqual; **grand r.** blue whale; **petit r.** minke (whale); **r. commun** fin whale

Rorschach [rɔrʃa] **NPR** *Psy* **test de R.** Rorschach test

rosace [rozas] **NF** *Archit (moulure)* (ceiling) rose; *(vitrail)* rose window, rosace; *(figure)* rosette

rosacé, -e[1] [rozase] **ADJ** 1 *Bot* rose-like, *Spéc* rosaceous 2 *Méd* **acné rosacée** acne rosacea

rosacée[2] [rozase] **NF** 1 *Bot* rosaceous plant, rosacean 2 *Méd* rosacea
   □ **rosacées** **NFPL** Rosaceae

rosaire [rozɛr] **NM** 1 *(chapelet)* rosary; **égrener un r.** to count *or* *Am* to tell one's beads 2 *(prières)* **dire** *ou* **réciter son r.** to say the rosary, *Am* to tell one's beads

rosalbin [rozalbɛ̃] **NM** *Orn* (Australian) rose-breasted cockatoo

rosaniline [rozanilin] **NF** *Chim* rosaniline

rosat [roza] **ADJ INV** *Pharm* prepared with roses

Rosati [rosati] **NMPL** **les R.** = literary society founded in Arras in 1778

rosâtre [rozatr] **ADJ** pinkish, *Littéraire* roseate

Rosbif [rɔsbif] **NMF** *Fam (Britannique)* Brit, = pejorative or humorous term used with reference to British people

rosbif [rɔzbif] **NM** *(cru)* roasting beef (UNCOUNT), joint *or* piece of beef *(for roasting)*; *(cuit)* roast beef (UNCOUNT), joint of roast beef

rose [roz] **ADJ** 1 *(gén)* pink; *(teint, joue)* rosy; **r. bonbon/saumon** candy/salmon pink; **r. fluo** fluorescent *or* dayglo pink; **r. thé** tea rose; **vieux r.** old rose

   2 *(agréable)* **la vie d'un athlète n'est pas toujours r.** an athlete's life isn't all roses; **ce n'est pas (tout) r.** it isn't exactly a bed of roses

   3 *(érotique)* erotic, soft-porn *(avant n)*

   4 *Pol* left-wing *(relating to the French Socialist Party)*

   NF 1 *Bot* rose; **r. blanche/rouge** white/red rose; **r. de Damas** damask rose; **r. de Jéricho** rose of Jericho, resurrection plant; **r. de Noël** Christmas rose; **r. pompon** fairy rose; **r. sauvage** wild rose; **r. trémière** rose mallow, *Br* hollyhock; **teint de r.** rosy complexion; *Fam Euph* **ça ne sent pas la r. ici** it stinks a bit, *Br* it's a bit whiffy; *Fam* **envoyer qn sur les roses** to send sb packing, to tell sb where to go *or* where to get off; *Prov* **il n'y a pas de r. sans épines** there's no rose without a thorn

   2 *Archit* rose window, rosace

3 *(en joaillerie)* **(diamant en) r.** rose (diamond) **NM 1** *(couleur)* pink; **r. nacré** oyster pink; *Littéraire* **l'aurore aux doigts de r.** rosy-fingered Dawn

2 *(locution)* **voir la vie** *ou* **tout en r.** to see things through rose-tinted *Br* spectacles *or Am* glasses

▫ **rose des sables, rose du désert NF** gypsum flower

▫ **rose des vents NF** wind rose

rosé, -e¹ [roze] **ADJ 1** *(teinte)* pinkish, rosy **2** *(vin)* rosé
    NM rosé (wine)

Roseau [rozo] **NM** *Géog* Roseau

roseau, -x [rozo] **NM** *Bot* reed; **le r. plie mais ne rompt pas** the reed bends but does not break

roseau-massue [rozomasy] *(pl* **roseaux-massues)** **NM** *Bot* bulrush, reed mace

rose-croix [rozkrwa] **NM INV** Rosicrucian; **les r.** the Rosicrucians
    NF la r. Rosicrucianism

rosé-des-prés [rozedepre] *(pl* **rosés-des-prés)** **NM** *(champêtre)* field mushroom; *(des jachères)* horse mushroom

rosée² [roze] **NF** dew; *Phys* **point de r.** dew point

roselet [rozlɛ] **NM** *(fourrure)* ermine

roselier, -ère [rozəlje, -ɛr] **ADJ marais r.** reed marsh
    ▫ **roselière NF** reed bed

roselin [rozlɛ̃] **NM** *Orn* **r. rouge** rosefinch

roséole [rozeol] **NF** *Méd* roseola

roser [3] [roze] **VT** *Littéraire* **r. qch** to make *or* turn sth pink

roseraie [rozrɛ] **NF** rose garden, rosery, rosarium

Rosette [rozɛt] **NPR** Rosetta; **la pierre de R.** the Rosetta stone

rosette [rozɛt] **NF 1** *(nœud)* bow; **faire une r.** to tie a bow **2** *(cocarde)* rosette; **avoir/recevoir la r.** *(de la Légion d'honneur)* to have been awarded/be awarded the Legion of Honour **3** *Culin* **r. (de Lyon)** = broad type of salami **4** *Bot* rosette; **en r.** rosulate **5** *très Fam (anus)* ring, *Br* arsehole, *Am* asshole

roseur [rozœr] **NF** *Littéraire* pinkness, rosiness

roseval, -als [rozval] **NF** = variety of pink potato

Rosh Ha-Shana [roʃaʃana] **NM INV** *Rel* Rosh Ha-shanah

rosicrucien, -enne [rozikrysjɛ̃, -ɛn] **ADJ** Rosicrucian
    NM,F Rosicrucian

rosier [rozje] **NM** *Bot* rosebush, rose tree; **r. grimpant/nain** climbing/dwarf rose; **r. sauvage** wild dog *or* rose

rosière [rozjɛr] **NF** = young girl traditionally awarded a crown of roses and a prize for virgin

purity; *Fam Vieilli* **quelle r., celle-là!** she's as pure as the driven snow!

rosiériste [rozjerist] **NMF** rose grower, rosarian

rosir [32] [rozir] **VT** to give a pink hue to; **l'air de la montagne avait rosi ses joues** the mountain air had tinged *or* suffused his/her cheeks with pink
    VI *(ciel)* to turn pink; *(personne)* to go pink; **son visage rosit à la première gorgée de champagne** his/her face went pink as he/she took his/her first mouthful of champagne

rossard, -e [rosar, -ard] **NM,F** *Fam Péj* cad, *Br* rotter, blighter

rosse [rɔs] **ADJ** *(chanson, portrait)* nasty*,* vicious*; (conduite)* rotten, lousy, horrid*; (personne)* nasty*,* horrid*,* catty; **être r. envers** *ou* **avec qn** to be horrid *or* nasty to sb; **un professeur r.** a hard* *or* tough* teacher; *Vieilli Littéraire* **comédie r.** = drama in which virtue goes unrewarded and vice unpunished
    NF 1 *(personne)* rotten beast, *Br* rotter **2** *Vieilli (cheval)* nag, jade

rossée [rose] **NF** *Fam* hiding, thrashing; **flanquer une r. à qn** to give sb a good hiding *or* thrashing

rosser [3] [rose] **VT** *Fam* **1** *(frapper)* to thrash; **se faire r.** to get thrashed **2** *(vaincre)* to thrash, to hammer; **se faire r.** to get thrashed, to get hammered

rosserie [rosri] **NF** *Fam* **1** *(remarque)* nasty remark*; (acte)* dirty trick; **dire des rosseries sur qn** to say nasty* *or* rotten things about sb **2** *(caractère)* nastiness*,* rottenness; **il/elle est d'une r.!** he's/she's rotten *or Br* a rotter!

rossignol [rosiɲɔl] **NM 1** *Orn* nightingale; **r. des murailles** redstart **2** *(clef)* picklock, skeleton key **3** *Fam (objet démodé)* piece of junk; **on t'a refilé un r.** they've sold you a dud *or* a piece of junk

rossinante [rosinɑ̃t] **NF** *Littéraire (cheval)* scrag, nag

rossolis [rosoli] **NM** *Bot* sundew

rösti [røʃti] **=** **rœsti**

Rostov-sur-le-Don [rostofsyrlədɔ̃] **NM** Rostov

rostral, -e, -aux, -ales [rostral, -o] **ADJ** *Antiq* **colonne rostrale** rostral column

rostre [rostr] **NM** *Antiq & Zool* rostrum
    ▫ **rostres NMPL** *(tribune)* rostrum

rot¹ [rɔt] **NM** *Bot* rot

rot² [ro] **NM** *(renvoi)* belch, burp; **faire** *ou* **lâcher un r.** to (let out a) belch *or* burp; **il a fait son r.?** *(bébé)* has he burped?; **faire faire son r. à un bébé** to burp a baby

rôt [ro] **NM** *Arch (rôti)* roast

rotacé, -e [rotase] **ADJ** wheel-shaped

rotang [rotɑ̃g] **NM** *Bot* rattan

rotary [rotari] **NM 1** *Pétr* rotary drill **2** *Tél* uniselector system **3 le R.-Club** the Rotary Club

rotateur [rotatœr] **Anat ADJ M muscle r.** rotator
    NM rotator

rotatif, -ive [rotatif, -iv] **ADJ** *(mouvement)* rotary, rotating; *(moteur, pompe)* rotary
    ▫ **rotative NF** *Typ (rotary)* press; *Fig* **faire tourner** *ou* **marcher les rotatives** to give the newspapers something to write about

rotation [rotasjɔ̃] **NF 1** *(mouvement)* & *Géom* rotation; *(sur un axe)* spinning; *Sport* turn, turning *(UNCOUNT)*; **angle/sens/vitesse de r.** angle/direction/speed of rotation; **mouvement de r.** rotational *or Spéc* rotary motion; **masse en r.** rotating mass; **effectuer une r.** to rotate, to spin round

    2 *(renouvellement)* turnover; **r. des stocks/du personnel** inventory/staff turnover; **le délai de r. des stocks est de quatre mois** stocks are turned round every four months; **r. des postes** job rotation

    3 *Fin* turnover; **r. des capitaux** turnover of capital; **r. des clients** debtors' turnover; **r. des fournisseurs** creditors' turnover; *Bourse* **r. de portefeuille** churning; *Bourse* **r. de portefeuille-action** equity switching; *Bourse* **r. de portefeuille-obligation** gilt switching

    4 *Transp Br* turnround, *Am* turnaround

    5 *Agr* **la r. des cultures** crop rotation

rotative [rotativ] *voir* **rotatif**

rotativiste [rotativist] **NMF** *Typ* rotary printer

rotatoire [rotatwar] **ADJ 1** *(mouvement)* rotatory, rotary **2** *Chim* **pouvoir r.** rotatory power

rote¹ [rɔt] **NF** *Cathol (tribunal)* Rota

rote² [rɔt] **NF** *Belg Fam* anger*,* rage*; **être/se**

mettre en r. (contre qn) to be/go mad *or* crazy (at sb); **mettre qn en r.** to make sb hopping mad

rotengle [rotɑ̃gl] **NM** *Ich* red eye, rudd

roténone [rotenon] **NF** *Chim* rotenone

roter [3] [rote] **VI** to belch, to burp

roteuse [rotøz] **NF** *Fam (bouteille de champagne)* bottle of bubbly *or Br* champers

rôti [roti] **NM 1** *(viande → crue)* joint *(of meat for roasting)*; *(→ cuite)* joint, roast; **r. de porc** *(cru)* joint *or* piece of pork for roasting; *(cuit)* piece of roast pork **2** *(poisson)* **r. de lotte** baked monkfish *(UNCOUNT)*

rôtie [roti] **NF** *(pain grillé)* slice of toast; *(pain frit)* slice of fried bread

rotifère [rotifɛr] *Zool* **NM** rotifer
    ▫ **rotifères NMPL** Rotifera

rotin [rotɛ̃] **NM 1** *Bot (tige)* rattan; **chaise en r.** rattan chair **2** *Fam (sou)* **il n'a plus un r.** he's totally broke *or Br* skint

rôtir [32] [rotir] **VT 1** *(cuire)* to roast; **faire r. une viande** to roast a piece of meat; **dinde rôtie** roast turkey; **quand la viande est bien rôtie** when the meat is done to a turn; **ça ne va pas te tomber tout r. dans le bec** it's not going to just fall into your lap

    2 *Fam (dessécher → terre)* to parch; *(→ plantes)* to dry up, to parch; **le soleil me rôtissait le dos** my back was getting roasted by the sun

    VI *(cuire)* to roast; **mettre une oie à r.** to roast a goose; *Fam* **baisse le thermostat, on va r.** turn the thermostat down or we'll roast

    ►**se rôtir VPR** *Fam* **se r. au soleil** to bask *or* to fry in the sun; **se r. les jambes devant le feu** to roast one's legs in front of the fire

rôtissage [rotisaʒ] **NM** *Culin* roasting

rôtisserie [rotisri] **NF 1** *(restaurant)* grillroom, steakhouse, rotisserie **2** *(magasin)* rotisserie *(shop selling roast meat)*

rôtisseur, -euse [rotisœr, -øz] **NM,F 1** *(restaurateur)* grillroom *or* steakhouse owner; *(commis de cuisine)* roaster *(chef)* **2** *(vendeur)* seller of roast meat

rôtissoire [rotiswar] **NF 1** *(appareil)* roaster; *(broche)* (roasting) spit, rotisserie

roto [roto] **NF** *Fam Typ* rotary press

rotogravure [rotogravyr] **NF** rotogravure

rotonde [rotɔ̃d] **NF 1** *Archit* rotunda; **disposition en r.** circular layout **2** *(dans les autobus)* semi-circular bench seat *(at rear)* **3** *Rail* (circular) engine shed, roundhouse

rotondité [rotɔ̃dite] **NF 1** *(forme sphérique)* rotundity, roundness **2** *(corpulence)* plumpness, rotundity; *Hum* **rotondités** *(de femme)* curves

rotoplots [rotoplo] **NMPL** *très Fam (seins)* tits, knockers, jugs

rotor [rotɔr] **NM** rotor; *(d'un hélicoptère)* rotor arm

Rotring® [rotrin] **NM** Rotring® pen

Rotterdam [rotɛrdam] **NM** Rotterdam

rottweiler, rottweiller [rotvajlœr] **NM** *(chien)* Rottweiler

rotule [rotyl] **NF 1** *Anat* kneecap, *Spéc* patella; *Fam* **être sur les rotules** to be wiped *or Br* knackered; *Fam* **mettre qn sur les rotules** to wipe sb out, *Br* to knacker sb **2** *Tech* ball-and-socket joint; **à r.** ball-and-socket *(avant n)*

rotulien, -enne [rotyljɛ̃, -ɛn] **ADJ** *Anat* patellar

roture [rotyr] **NF** *Littéraire* commonalty; **né dans la r.** born a commoner; **elle a épousé quelqu'un de la r.** she married a commoner

roturier, -ère [rotyrje, -ɛr] **ADJ 1** *Hist (non noble)* common; **être d'origine roturière** to be of common birth *or* stock **2** *(vulgaire)* low, common, vulgar; **des façons roturières** plebeian manners
    NM,F *Hist* commoner, plebeian

rouable [rwabl] **NM 1** *(perche de boulanger)* fire rake **2** *(râteau de saline)* salt rake

rouage [rwaʒ] **NM 1** *Tech* moving part, movement; *(engrenage)* cogwheel; **les rouages d'une horloge** the works *or* movement of a clock

    2 *Fig* cog; **il n'était qu'un r. dans la vaste machine politique** he was only a cog in the huge political machine; **les rouages de la justice** the wheels of justice; **une organisation aux rouages bien huilés** a smooth-running organization, an organization that runs like clockwork

rouan, -anne¹ [rwɑ̃, -an] **ADJ** roan
    NM roan (horse)

rouanne[2] [rwan] NF 1 *(outil de marquage)* marking tool, rasing knife 2 *Menuis* paring-knife

roubignoles [rubiɲɔl] NF *Vulg (testicules)* balls, *Br* bollocks

roublard, -e [rublar, -ard] *Fam* ADJ *(rusé)* sly■, wily■, crafty■

NM,F dodger; **c'est un fin r.** he's a sly (old) fox *or* devil, he's an artful dodger

roublardise [rublardiz] NF *Fam* 1 *(habileté)* slyness■, craftiness■, wiliness■ 2 *(manœuvre)* clever *or* crafty trick, dodge

rouble [rubl] NM rouble

roucaou [rukau] NM *Ich* wrasse

rouchi [ruʃi] NM = dialect of Valenciennes and its surroundings

roucoulade [rukulad] NF 1 *(d'un pigeon)* (billing and) cooing *(UNCOUNT)* 2 *(des amoureux)* billing and cooing *(UNCOUNT)*

roucoulant, -e [rukulɑ̃, -ɑ̃t] ADJ cooing

roucoulement [rukulmɑ̃] NM 1 *(cri du pigeon)* (billing and) cooing *(UNCOUNT)* 2 *(propos tendres)* billing and cooing 3 *Péj (d'un chanteur)* crooning *(UNCOUNT)*

roucouler [3] [rukule] VI 1 *(pigeon)* to (bill and) coo 2 *(amoureux)* to bill and coo, to whisper sweet nothings 3 *Péj (chanteur)* to croon

VT 1 *(sujet: amoureux)* to coo 2 *Péj (sujet: chanteur)* to croon

roucoulis [rukuli] NM 1 *(d'un pigeon)* (billing and) cooing *(UNCOUNT)* 2 *(des amoureux)* billing and cooing

roudoudou [rududu] NM *Fam Br* hard sweet, *Am* candy *(licked out of a small round box or shell)*

roue [ru] NF 1 *Transp* wheel; **véhicule à deux/trois roues** two-wheeled/three-wheeled vehicle; **j'étais dans sa r.** I was right behind him/her; **r. directrice** guiding *or* leading wheel; **r. motrice** drive *or* driving wheel; **r. de secours** spare (wheel); **pousser à la r.** to give a helping hand; **je voudrais les empêcher de s'engager dans l'armée mais leur père pousse à la r.** I'd like to stop them joining up but their father is egging them on

2 *Tech* (cog *or* gear) wheel; **r. d'angle** bevel gear wheel; **r. crantée** toothed wheel; **r. dentée** cog (wheel), toothed wheel; **r. folle** idle wheel; **r. de friction** friction gear wheel; **r. à godets** bucket wheel; **r. hydraulique** waterwheel; **r. libre** freewheel; **j'ai descendu la côte en r. libre** I freewheeled down the hill; **r. à réaction** reaction wheel

3 *(objet circulaire)* wheel; **une r. de gruyère** a large round Gruyère cheese; **la grande r.** the Ferris wheel, *Br* the big wheel; **la r. de la Fortune** the wheel of Fortune; **la r. tourne** the wheel of Fortune is turning; **faire la r.** *(paon)* to spread *or* to fan its tail; *(gymnaste)* to do a cartwheel; *(séducteur)* to strut about

4 *Hist* **(le supplice de) la r.** the wheel

5 *Typ* **r. à caractères** *ou* **d'impression** print *or* type wheel

6 *Naut* **r. à aubes** *ou* **à palettes** paddle wheel; **r. du gouvernail** helm

7 *(locution)* **être la cinquième r. du carrosse** to feel utterly superfluous, to feel like a fifth wheel

roué, -e [rwe] ADJ sly, tricky, wily

NM,F 1 *(fripon)* sly fox 2 *Hist (homme)* roué, rake; *(femme)* hussy, trollop, jezebel

rouelle [rwɛl] NF 1 *Culin* **r. (de veau)** thick round of veal 2 *(rondelle)* (round) slice

Rouen [rwɑ̃] NM Rouen

rouennais, -e [rwanɛ, -ɛz] ADJ of/from Rouen

❑ **Rouennais, -e** NM,F = inhabitant of or person from Rouen

roue-pelle [rupɛl] *(pl* **roues-pelles**) NF bucket dredge *or* dredger

rouer [6] [rwe] VT 1 *Hist* **r. qn** to break sb on the wheel 2 *(locution)* **r. qn de coups** to pummel sb

rouergat, -e [rwɛrga, -at] ADJ of/from Rouergue

NM,F = inhabitant of or person from the Rouergue region

rouerie [ruri] NF *Littéraire* 1 *(caractère)* cunning, foxiness, wiliness 2 *(manœuvre)* sly *or* cunning trick

rouet [ruɛ] NM 1 *(pour filer)* spinning wheel 2 *Tech (de poulie)* sheave; *(de serrure)* ward

rouf [ruf] NM *Naut* deckhouse

rouflaquette [ruflakɛt] *Fam* NF *(accroche-cœur) Br* kiss *or Am* spit curl

❑ **rouflaquettes** NFPL *(favoris)* sideburns■

rouf-rouf, rouf rouf [rufruf] **à la rouf-rouf** ADV *Belg* in a rush *or* hurry

rougail [rugaj] NM *Culin* = spicy chutney used in La Réunion

rouge [ruʒ] ADJ 1 *(gén)* red; **être r.** *(après un effort)* to be flushed, to be red in the face; **être r. de plaisir/de colère** to be flushed with pleasure/anger; **être r. de honte** to be red in the face (with shame), to be red-faced; **r. brique** brick-red; **r. sang** blood-red; **r. vermillon** vermilion; **être r. comme un coq** *ou* **un coquelicot** *ou* **une écrevisse** *ou* **une pivoine** *ou* **une tomate** to be as red as a lobster *or Br* a beetroot; **quand il est arrivé il était tout r. tellement il avait couru** when he arrived he was all red in the face *or* his face was all flushed from having run so much; **la mer R.** the Red Sea; **la place R.** Red Square

2 *(pelage, cheveux)* red, ginger, *Péj* carroty

3 *Métal* red-hot

4 *Péj (communiste)* red

NMF *Péj (communiste)* Red

NM 1 *(couleur)* red; **le r. lui monta au visage** he/she went red in the face, his/her face went red; **r. cerise** cherry red; **r. sang** blood-red

2 *Transp* **le feu est passé au r.** the lights turned to *or* went red; **la voiture est passée au r.** the car went through a red light

3 *Rad & TV* **le r. est mis!** you're on (the) air!

4 *Fam (vin)* red wine■; **une bouteille de r.** a bottle of red; **un coup de r.** a glass of red wine■; **du gros r.** cheap red wine■; **du gros r. qui tache** (red) plonk

5 *(cosmétique)* **r. (à joues)** blusher, rouge

6 *Métal* **porté au r.** red-hot; **portez le métal au r.** heat the metal until it's red-hot

7 *(dans un jeu)* red; **tout miser sur le r.** to stake all on the red; *Fam* **le r. est mis** the die is cast

8 *Banque* red; **je suis dans le r.** I'm in the red *or* overdrawn; **sortir du r.** *(cesser d'être en déficit)* to get out of the red, to get rid of one's overdraft

NF *(au billard)* red (ball)

ADV 1 *Péj Pol* **voter r.** to vote communist

2 *(locution)* **voir r.** to see red

❑ **rouge à lèvres** NM lipstick

'Le Rouge et le noir' *Stendhal* 'Scarlet and Black'

rougeâtre [ruʒatr] ADJ reddish, reddy

rougeaud, -e [ruʒo, -od] ADJ ruddy, ruddy-cheeked

NM,F ruddy *or* ruddy-cheeked person

rouge-gorge [ruʒgɔrʒ] *(pl* **rouges-gorges**) NM *Orn* robin

rougeoie *etc voir* **rougeoyer**

rougeoiement [ruʒwamɑ̃] NM reddish glow

rougeole [ruʒɔl] NF measles *(singulier)*; **avoir la r.** to have (the) measles

rougeoleux, -euse [ruʒɔlø, -øz] ADJ *(enfant)* suffering from measles

NM,F person with measles

rougeoyant, -e [ruʒwajɑ̃, -ɑ̃t] ADJ glowing (red); **lueur rougeoyante** flush of red, red glow

rougeoyer [13] [ruʒwaje] VI 1 *(briller)* to glow (red) 2 *(devenir rouge)* to turn red, to redden, to take on a reddish hue

rouge-queue [ruʒkø] *(pl* **rouges-queues**) NM *Orn* redstart; **r. noir** black redstart

rouget [ruʒɛ] NM 1 *Ich* **r. barbet** *ou* **de vase** red mullet; **r. grondin** red gurnard; **r. de roche** surmullet 2 *Vét* swine erysipelas

rougeur [ruʒœr] NF 1 *(couleur → du ciel)* redness, glow; *(→ des joues)* redness, ruddiness 2 *(rougissement)* flush, blush; **sa r. l'a trahie** her blush gave her away 3 *Méd* red patch *or* blotch; **être sujet aux rougeurs** to be prone to developing red patches *(on one's skin)*

rough [rœf] NM 1 *Sport* **le r.** the rough 2 *(avant-projet)* mock-up

rougir [32] [ruʒir] VT 1 *(colorer en rouge)* **un dernier rayon de soleil rougissait le firmament** one last ray of sun spread a red glow across the skies; **r. son eau** to put a drop of (red) wine in one's water; **des yeux rougis par les larmes/la poussière** eyes red with weeping/with the dust

2 *Métal* to heat to red heat *or* until red-hot

3 *Fig Littéraire* **mes mains sont rougies de (son) sang** my hands are stained with (his/her) blood

VI 1 *(chose, personne → gén)* to go *or* to turn red; *(personne → de gêne)* to blush; *(→ d'excitation)* to flush; **les pommes/mes joues rougissent** the apples/my cheeks are turning red; *Littéraire* **au moment où rougit l'horizon** when the horizon reddens *or* becomes suffused with red; **menteur, tu rougis!** you liar, you're blushing!; **r. de plaisir/colère** to flush with pleasure/anger; **r. de honte** to blush with shame; **il se rassit en rougissant de honte** red-faced with shame, he sat down again; **"je vous aime", dit-il en rougissant** "I love you," he said, blushing *or* with a blush; **je me sentais r.** I could feel myself going red (in the face); **faire r. qn** to make sb blush; *Hum* **arrête, tu vas me faire r.** spare my blushes, please; **r. jusqu'au blanc des yeux** *ou* **jusqu'aux oreilles** to blush to the roots of one's hair

2 *Fig* **r. de qn/qch** *(avoir honte de)* to be ashamed of sb/sth; **j'en ai rougi pour elle** I felt ashamed for her; **tu n'as pas/il n'y a pas à en r.** there's nothing for you/nothing to be ashamed of; **je n'ai pas à r. de ma conduite** I'm not ashamed of what I did; **ne r. de rien** to be shameless

3 *Métal* to become red-hot

rougissant, -e [ruʒisɑ̃, -ɑ̃t] ADJ reddening; *(de gêne)* blushing; *(d'excitation)* flushing

rougissement [ruʒismɑ̃] NM reddening; *(de gêne)* blushing; *(d'excitation)* flushing

rouille [ruj] NF 1 *(corrosion d'un métal)* rust; **couche de r.** layer of rust; **tache de r.** spot of rust; **traiter une surface contre la r.** to rustproof a surface 2 *Bot & Agr* **r. blanche** white rust; **r. du blé** wheat rust; **r. des feuilles** leaf mould; **r. noire des céréales** stem rust 3 *Culin* = spicy sauce made with hot red peppers and garlic, served with fish soup and bouillabaisse

ADJ INV rust, rust-coloured

rouillé, -e [ruje] ADJ 1 *(grille, clef)* rusty, rusted; **la serrure est complètement rouillée** the lock is rusted up 2 *Fig (muscles)* stiff; **être r.** *(physiquement → gén)* to feel stiff; *(→ athlète)* to be out of practice; *(intellectuellement)* to feel a bit rusty; **mes réflexes au volant sont un peu rouillés** my driving reflexes are a bit rusty 3 *Bot (blé)* affected by rust, rusted; *(feuille)* mouldy

rouiller [3] [ruje] VT 1 *(métal)* to rust 2 *(intellect, mémoire)* to make rusty

VI to rust, to go rusty

►**se rouiller** VPR 1 *(métal, outil, machine)* to rust up, to get rusty 2 *(esprit, mémoire)* to become *or* to get rusty; **je me rouille** my brain's going 3 *(muscle)* to grow *or* to get stiff; *(athlète)* to get out of practice

rouillure [rujyr] NF 1 *Chim* rustiness 2 *Bot* rust, rusting *(UNCOUNT)* 3 *Mines* kerf

rouir [32] [rwir] VT to ret

rouissage [rwisaʒ] NM **r. à l'eau/à terre** water/ground retting

rouissoir [rwiswar] NM retting pit, rettery

roulade [rulad] NF 1 *Mus* roulade, run 2 *(d'un oiseau)* trill 3 *Culin* rolled meat, roulade; **r. de bœuf** rolled (piece of) beef, beef roulade 4 *(culbute)* roll; **r. avant/arrière** forward/backward roll; **faire des roulades** to do rolls

roulage [rulaʒ] NM 1 *Agr & Métal* rolling 2 *(transport)* haulage; *Mines* haulage, hauling; **entreprise de r.** carrier, haulier, *Am* hauler 3 *Naut* **manutention par r.** roll-on-roll-off 4 *Belg (circulation)* traffic; **accident de r.** traffic accident

roulant, -e [rulɑ̃, -ɑ̃t] ADJ 1 *(surface)* moving; *(meuble)* on wheels 2 *Rail* **matériel r.** rolling stock; **personnel r.** train crews 3 *Fin (capital, fonds)* working 4 *Fam Vieilli (drôle)* comical■

NM *Fam* crewman■

❑ **roulante** NF field *or* mobile kitchen

roule [rul] NM 1 *(tronc)* tree trunk 2 *(de carrier, de tailleur)* roller

roulé, -e [rule] ADJ 1 *Couture* rolled; **foulard r. main** hand-rolled scarf 2 *Ling* **r r.** rolled *or* trilled r 3 *Culin (gâteau, viande)* rolled 4 *Fam (locution)* **elle est bien roulée** she's curvy

NM 1 *Culin (gâteau)* Swiss roll; *(viande)* = meat in a roll of puff pastry; **r. au chocolat** chocolate Swiss roll 2 *Constr* rolled pebbles

rouleau, -x [rulo] NM 1 *(de papier, de tissu, de*

pellicule) roll; *(de fil)* coil; **r. de papier hygiénique** roll of toilet paper, *Br* toilet roll; **r. de parchemin** roll *or* scroll of parchment; **r. de pièces** roll of coins; **r. de réglisse** liquorice roll
2 *(outil → de peintre, de jardinier, de relieur)* roller; *(cylindre → de machine à écrire)* barrel, platen; **r. imprimeur** *ou* **encreur** (press) cylinder; **r. à pâtisserie,** *Can & Suisse* **r. à pâte** rolling pin
3 *(bigoudi)* roller, curler
4 *Culin* **r. de printemps** spring roll
5 *Sport (en saut en hauteur)* roll; **sauter en r.** to do a roll; **r. costal** western roll; **r. dorsal** Fosbury flop; **r. ventral** straddle
6 *(vague)* roller
7 *Beaux-Arts (vase)* rouleau
8 *Archit* arch moulding
9 *Constr* roller; **r. compresseur** *(à gazole)* roadroller; *(à vapeur)* steamroller; *Fig* steamroller; **le r. compresseur de la mondialisation** the steamroller of globalization

rouleauté, -e [rulote] *Couture* **ADJ** *(ourlet)* rolled
NM rolled hem

roulé-boulé [rulebule] *(pl* **roulés-boulés)** **NM** *(culbute)* roll; **faire des roulés-boulés** to roll

roulement [rulmɑ̃] **NM** **1** *(mouvement)* **un r. d'yeux** a roll of the eyes; **un r. de hanches** a swing of the hips
2 *(grondement)* rumble, rumbling *(UNCOUNT)*; **le r. du tonnerre** the rumble *or* roll *or* peal of thunder; **un r. de tonnerre** a roll *or* rumble of thunder, a thunderclap; **le r. des canons** the rumble *or* roar of the cannons; **r. de tambour** drum roll
3 *(tour de rôle)* rotation; **établir un r.** to set up *Br* a rota *or Am* a rotation system; **par r.** in rotation
4 *Tech (déplacement)* rolling; *(organe)* bearing; **r. à billes/à rouleaux/à aiguilles** ball/roller/needle bearings; **frottement de r.** rolling friction
5 *Fin* **r. des capitaux** circulation of capital
6 *Transp* rolling motion
7 *Mil (d'un char)* bogie and tread, tracking
8 *Méd* **r. diastolique** diastolic murmur

ROULER [3] [rule]

VT to roll **1–3, 6–8** ▪ to roll up **2** ▪ to diddle, to swindle **4** ▪ to sway **5** ▪ to roll out **6**
VI to go **1** ▪ to drive **1** ▪ to roll **2–4** ▪ to take turns **5**

VT **1** *(faire tourner)* to roll; **r. les yeux** to roll one's eyes; **les graviers que roulait le fleuve** the gravel that was being rolled along by the river; **r. de sombres pensées** to turn dark thoughts over in one's mind; *très Fam* **r. une pelle** *ou* **une galoche** *ou* **un pallot** *ou* **un patin à qn** to French-kiss sb, *Br* to snog sb; *Fig* **r. qn dans la farine** to pull the wool over sb's eyes
2 *(poster, tapis, bas de pantalon)* to roll up; *(corde, câble)* to roll up, to wind up; *(cigarette)* to roll; **aide-moi à r. la laine en pelote** help me to wind the wool up into a ball; **r. du fil sur une bobine** to spool *or* to wind thread around a reel; **r. un blessé dans une couverture** to wrap an injured person in a blanket
3 *(déplacer → Caddie®)* to push (along); *(→ balle, tronc, fût)* to roll (along); **il a roulé le rocher jusqu'en bas de la colline** he rolled the rock right down the hill; *Vieilli* **r. carrosse** to have an expensive lifestyle; *Fam* **j'ai roulé ma bosse** I've been around, I've seen it all
4 *Fam (escroquer → lors d'un paiement)* to diddle; *(→ dans une affaire)* to swindle▪; **elle m'a roulé de 5 euros** she diddled *or* did me out of 5 euros; **se faire r.** to be conned *or* had; **ce n'est pas du cuir, je me suis fait r.** it's not genuine leather, I've been done *or* had
5 *(balancer)* **r. des** *ou* **les épaules** to sway one's shoulders; **r. des** *ou* **les hanches** to swing one's hips; *Fam* **r. des mécaniques** to walk with a swagger; *Fig* to come *or* to play the tough guy
6 *(aplatir → gazon, court de tennis)* to roll; *Culin (pâte)* to roll out
7 *Ling* **r. les r** to roll one's r's
8 *Métal* to roll

VI **1** *(véhicule)* to go, to run; *(conducteur)* to drive; **une voiture qui a peu/beaucoup roulé** a car with a low/high mileage; **et ta Renault, elle roule toujours?** is your Renault still going *or* running?; **la moto roulait au milieu de la route** the motorbike was going *or* driving down the middle of the road; **à quelle vitesse rouliez-vous?** what speed were you travelling at?, what speed were you doing?, how fast were you going?; **il est interdit de r. sur la bande d'arrêt d'urgence** do not drive on the *Br* hard shoulder *or Am* shoulder; **j'ai beaucoup roulé quand j'étais jeune** I did a lot of driving when I was young; **seulement deux heures? tu as bien roulé!** only two hours? you've made good time!; **r. au pas** to go at a walking pace, to crawl along; **roulez au pas** *(sur panneau)* dead slow; **roule moins vite** slow down, drive more slowly; **elle roule en Jaguar** she drives (around in) a Jaguar; **r. à moto/à bicyclette** to ride a motorbike/a bicycle; **ça roule mal/bien dans Anvers** there's a lot of traffic/there's no traffic through Antwerp
2 *(balle, dé, rocher)* to roll; **ses billes allèrent r. dans le caniveau** his/her marbles rolled down into the gutter; **des larmes roulaient sur sa joue** tears were rolling down his/her cheeks; **faire r.** *(balle)* to roll; *(chariot)* to wheel (along); *(roue)* to roll along; **il a roulé jusqu'en bas du champ** he rolled *or* tumbled down to the bottom of the field; *Fam* **r. sous la table** to end up (dead drunk) under the table
3 *Naut* to roll
4 *(gronder → tonnerre)* to roll, to rumble; *(→ tambour)* to roll
5 *(se succéder)* to take turns; **nous ferons r. les équipes dès janvier** as from January, we'll start the teams off on *Br* a rota system *or Am* rotation
6 *(argent)* to circulate; **il sait faire r. l'argent** he knows how to make money work
7 r. sur *(conversation)* to be centred upon; **la conversation a d'abord roulé sur la politique** we started off talking about politics
8 *Fam (locutions) (aller bien)* **ça roule** things are fine, everything's OK; **salut! ça roule?** hi, how are things?; **r. sur l'or** to be rolling in money *or* in it; **mon salaire est correct, mais je ne roule pas sur l'or** I've got a decent salary, but I'm not exactly well-off *or* rolling in it

▸**se rouler** **VPR** **1** *(se vautrer)* **se r. par terre** *(de colère)* to have a fit; *(de douleur)* to be doubled up with pain; *(de rire)* to be doubled up with laughter; **c'était à se r. par terre** *(de rire)* it was hysterically funny; *(de douleur)* it was sheer agony
2 *très Fam* **se r. une pelle** *Br* to snog, *Am* to make out; *Fam* **s'en r. une** to roll a smoke *or Br* a fag; *Fam* **se les r.** to twiddle one's thumbs

Allusion

Rouler pour quelqu'un

French lorry-drivers decided to upgrade their image by displaying the slogan **Je roule pour vous** ("I'm driving for you") on their vehicles. The aim was to dispel the hostility of other road-users, by suggesting that the transport of goods was ultimately in their interest. **Rouler pour quelqu'un** came to mean "to serve someone's interests, to be backing someone". One could say of a French politician who seems to champion the "have-nots", **Il roule en fait pour les nantis** ("He is actually serving the interests of the haves", or "He is on the side of the haves").

roulette [rulɛt] **NF** **1** *(roue → libre)* wheel; *(→ sur pivot)* caster, castor; **à roulettes** *(libres)* with wheels; *(sur pivot)* on casters *or* castors; *Fam* **marcher** *ou* **aller comme sur des roulettes** *(opération)* to go off without a hitch; *(organisation, projet)* to go like clockwork; *Fam* **et ton entrevue? – ça a marché comme sur des roulettes** what about your interview? – it all went off very smoothly *or* without a hitch
2 *(ustensile → de relieur)* fillet (wheel); *(→ de graveur)* roulette; *Couture* tracing wheel; **r. de dentiste** dentist's drill; **r. à pâte** pastry cutting wheel
3 *(jeu)* roulette; *(roue)* roulette wheel; **r. russe** Russian roulette; *aussi Fig* **jouer à la r. russe** to play Russian roulette; **c'est un peu la r. russe, ta proposition** your proposal is a bit dicy *or* is pretty much of a gamble

rouleur [rulœr] **NM** **1** *Cyclisme* flat racer; **c'est un bon r.** he's good on the flat **2** *Fam* **r. de mécaniques** *(fanfaron)* poser **3** *Orn* roller

roulier [rulje] **NM** **1** *Hist* cart driver **2** *Naut* roll-on-roll-off ship

rouli-roulant [rulirulɑ̃] *(pl* **roulis-roulants)** **NM** *Can* skateboard

roulis [ruli] **NM** *Aviat & Naut* roll, rolling; **il y a du r.** the ship is rolling; **coup de r.** strong roll; **il y eut un grand coup de r.** the ship started to roll violently

roulotte [rulɔt] **NF** **1** *(tirée par des chevaux)* horse-drawn caravan **2** *(caravane)* caravan, mobile home

roulotté, -e [rulɔte] *Couture* **ADJ** *(ourlet)* rolled
NM rolled hem

roulottier [rulɔtje] **NM** *Fam (voleur)* = thief who robs parked cars

roulure [rulyr] **NF** *très Fam Péj* **1** *(prostituée)* hooker, whore **2** *(homme méprisable)* bastard, *Am* son-of-a-bitch; *(femme méprisable)* bitch

roumain, -e [rumɛ̃, -ɛn] **ADJ** Rumanian, Ro(u)manian
NM *(langue)* Romanian
❑ **Roumain, -e** **NM,F** Rumanian, Ro(u)manian

Roumanie [rumani] **NF** **la R.** Rumania, Ro(u)mania; **vivre en R.** to live in Romania; **aller en R.** to go to Romania

roumi [rumi] **NM** Christian *(for Muslims)*

round [rawnd, rund] **NM** *(à la boxe, dans un débat)* round

roupettes [rupɛt] **NFPL** *très Fam (testicules)* nuts, balls

roupie [rupi] **NF** **1** *(monnaie)* rupee **2** *(locutions)* **c'est de la r. de sansonnet** that's (worthless) rubbish; **ce n'est pas de la r. de sansonnet** it's not to be sniffed at; *Arch* **avoir la r.** to have a drippy nose

roupiller [3] [rupije] **VI** *Fam (dormir)* to sleep▪, *Br* to kip; *(faire un somme)* to get some shut-eye, *Br* to have a kip; **c'est pas le moment de r.!** this is no time for lying down on the job!

roupillon [rupijɔ̃] **NM** *Fam* snooze, nap, *Br* kip; **faire** *ou* **piquer un r.** to have a snooze *or* a nap *or Br* a kip

rouquette [rukɛt] = **roquette 2**

rouquier [rukje] **NM** *Ich* wrasse

rouquin, -e [rukɛ̃, -in] *Fam* **ADJ** *(personne)* red-haired▪, ginger-haired▪, ginger; *(chevelure)* red▪, ginger▪, *Péj* carroty; **elle est rouquine** she has red *or* ginger *or Péj* carroty hair
NM,F redhead
NM *(vin)* red wine▪

rouscailler [3] [ruskaje] **VI** *très Fam* to whinge, to moan (and groan); **arrête de r.!** stop whinging *or* moaning!

rouspétance [ruspetɑ̃s] **NF** *Fam* moaning (and groaning), grumbling; **pas de r.!** I don't want to hear any moaning (and groaning) *or* grumbling!

rouspéter [18] [ruspete] **VI** *Fam* to moan (and groan), to grumble (**contre** about)

rouspéteur, -euse [ruspetœr, -øz] *Fam* **ADJ** grumpy, grouchy
NM,F moaner, grumbler; **il n'y a que les rouspéteurs qui obtiennent satisfaction** you only get what you want if you complain▪, *Am Hum* it's the squeaky wheel that gets the grease *or* oil

roussâtre [rusatr] **ADJ** *(eau)* reddish; *(feuilles)* reddish-brown, russet

rousse [rus] *voir* **roux**

rousseau, -x [ruso] **NM** *Ich* red sea bream

roussélé, -e [rusle] **ADJ** *Can (visage, peau)* freckled, freckly

rousselet [ruslɛ] **NM** russet pear

rousserolle [rusrɔl] **NF** *Orn* **r. effarvatte** reed warbler; **r. isabelle** paddyfield warbler; **r. turdoïde** great reed warbler; **r. verderolle** marsh warbler

roussette [rusɛt] **NF** **1** *Ich* spotted dogfish; *Culin* rock salmon **2** *Zool (chauve-souris)* flying fox **3** *Zool (grenouille)* common frog

rousseur [rusœr] **NF** *(teinte)* redness, gingery colour
❑ **rousseurs** **NFPL** *(sur le papier)* foxing

roussi [rusi] **NM** **ça sent le r.** something's burning; *Fam Fig* there's trouble ahead *or* brewing; **il**

a démissionné quand ça a commencé à sentir **le r.** he resigned when things started going wrong

Roussillon [rusijɔ̃] NM **le R.** Roussillon

roussillonnais, -e [rusijɔnɛ, -ɛz] ADJ of/from Roussillon

NM,F = inhabitant of or person from Roussillon

roussin[1] [rusɛ̃] NM *Hist (cheval)* charger; **r. d'Arcadie** ass, Jerusalem pony

roussin[2] [rusɛ̃] NM *Fam Vieilli (policier)* policeman▪; *(espion)* police spy▪

roussir [32] [rusir] VT 1 *(rendre roux)* **r. qch** to turn sth brown 2 *(brûler)* to scorch, to singe; **la gelée a roussi l'herbe** the grass has turned brown with the frost

VI 1 *(feuillage, arbre)* to turn brown or russet 2 *Culin* **faire r. qch** to brown sth

roussissement [rusismɑ̃] NM turning brown

roussissure [rusisyr] NF turning brown

rouste [rust] NF *Fam* thrashing, hammering; **flanquer une r. à qn** to give sb a thrashing or a hammering

roustons [rustɔ̃] NMPL *très Fam (testicules)* balls, nuts

routage [rutaʒ] NM 1 *(de courrier)* sorting and mailing 2 *Naut* routing; **assurer le r. d'un navire** to plot the course of a ship

routard, -e [rutar, -ard] NM,F *Fam (auto-stoppeur)* hitchhiker▪; *(marcheur)* trekker▪; *(touriste avec sac à dos)* backpacker▪

ROUTE [rut]

road 1, 2, 5 ▪ route 3 ▪ way 3–5 ▪ journey 4 ▪ path 5	

NF 1 *(voie de circulation)* road; **les petites routes (de campagne)** small country roads; **c'est la r. de Genève** it's the road to Geneva; **sur r., la voiture consomme moins** when cruising or on the open road, the car's fuel consumption is lower; **il va y avoir du monde sur la r.** ou **les routes** there'll be a lot of cars on the roads or a lot of traffic; **je n'aime pas le savoir sur la r.** I don't like the idea of him driving; **tenir la r.** *(sujet: voiture)* to hold the road; *Fig* **cette politique ne tient pas la r.** there's no mileage in that policy; **r. départementale** secondary road; **r. nationale** major road, *Br* trunk road; **r. de montagne** mountain road

2 *(moyen de transport)* **par la r.** by road; **les transports sur r.** road transport; **les accidents de la r.** road accidents; **les victimes de la r.** road casualties

3 *(itinéraire)* way; **chercher sa r.** to try and find one's way; **c'est sur ma r.** it's on my way; **faire r. vers** *(sujet: bateau)* to be headed for, to be en route for, to steer a course for; *(sujet: voiture, avion)* to head for or towards; *(sujet: personne)* to be on one's way to, to head for; **en r. pour** ou **vers** bound for; **faisant r. vers** *(sujet: bateau, avion)* bound for, heading for, on its way to; *(sujet: personne)* on one's way to, heading for; **prendre la r. des vacances/du soleil** to set off on holiday/to the south; **r. aérienne** air route; **r. commerciale** commercial route, trade route; **la r. des épices** the spice trail or route; **la r. des Indes** the road to India; **r. maritime** shipping or sea route; **la r. de la soie** the silk road; **la R. des Vins** = tourist trail passing through wine country; **faire fausse r.** *(sujet: conducteur)* to go the wrong way, to take the wrong road; *Fig (dans un raisonnement)* to be on the wrong track

4 *(trajet)* journey; **j'ai fait la r. à pied** I did the journey on foot; **il y a six heures de r.** *(en voiture)* it's a six-hour drive or ride or journey; *(à bicyclette)* it's a six-hour ride or journey; **il y a une bonne heure de r.** it takes at least an hour to get there; **(faites) bonne r.!** have a good or safe journey!; **faire r. avec qn** to travel with sb; **faire de la r.** to do a lot of driving or mileage; **en r.** on the way; **j'ai dû perdre ma montre en r.** I must have lost my watch on the way; **prendre la** ou **se mettre en r.** to set off, to get going; **reprendre la r., se remettre en r.** to set off again, to resume one's journey; **allez, en r.!** come on, let's go!; *Fam Hum* **en r., mauvaise troupe!** c'mon you lot, we're off!

5 *Fig (voie)* road, way, path; **la r. du succès** the

road to success; **la r. est toute tracée pour lui** the path is all laid out for him

6 **mettre en r.** *(appareil, véhicule)* to start (up); *(projet)* to set in motion, to get started or under way; **se mettre en r.** *(machine)* to start (up); *Fam* **j'ai du mal à me mettre en r. le matin** I find it hard to get started or going in the morning

router [3] [rute] VT 1 *(courrier)* to sort and mail 2 *Naut (navire)* to plot a course for, to route

routeur, -euse [rutœr, -øz] NM,F 1 *Typ* sorting-and-mailing clerk 2 *Naut* route planner
NM *Ordinat* router

routier, -ère [rutje, -ɛr] ADJ road *(avant n)*
NM

> Note that it is no longer considered a mistake to feminize this word in sense 1 and to say **une routière**. Some French speakers nonetheless regard this form as unacceptable, especially in France. See also the entry **féminisation**.

1 *(chauffeur)* (long-distance) *Br* lorry or *Am* truck driver; *Fig* **c'est un vieux r. du journalisme** he's a veteran journalist

2 *Fam (restaurant) Br* transport café, *Am* truck-stop

3 *Sport (cycliste)* road racer or rider

4 *Naut (plotting)* chart

□ **routière** NF *Aut* touring car; **c'est une excellente routière** it's an ideal car for long-distance trips, it's an excellent touring car

routine [rutin] NF 1 *(habitude)* routine; **la r. quotidienne** the daily routine or *Péj* grind; **se laisser enfermer dans la r.** to get into a rut; **sortir de la r.** to get out of a rut 2 *Ordinat* routine

□ **de routine** ADJ *(contrôle, visite)* routine *(avant n)*; **c'est une procédure de r.** it's routine procedure; **une vérification de r.** a routine check

routinier, -ère [rutinje, -ɛr] ADJ *(tâche, corvée)* routine *(avant n)*, *Péj* humdrum; *(vérification, méthode)* routine *(avant n)*; **être r.** *(personne)* to be a creature of habit, to like one's routine; **de façon routinière** routinely
NM,F **c'est un r.** he's a creature of habit, he's tied to or he likes his routine

rouverain, rouverin [ruvrɛ̃] ADJ M **fer r.** red-short or brittle iron

rouvert, -e [ruvɛr, -ɛrt] PP *voir* **rouvrir**

rouvraie [ruvrɛ] NF robur plantation

rouvre [ruvr] NM *Bot* robur

rouvrir [34] [ruvrir] VT 1 *(livre, hôtel, débat, dossier)* to reopen 2 *Fig (raviver)* **r. une blessure** ou **plaie** to open an old wound
VI *(magasin)* to reopen, to open again
►**se rouvrir** VPR *(porte, fenêtre)* to reopen; *(blessure)* to reopen, to open up again

roux, rousse [ru, rus] ADJ *(feuillage, fourrure)* reddish-brown, russet; *(chevelure, moustache)* red, ginger; *(vache)* brown; **une petite fille rousse** a little girl with red hair, a little redhead
NM,F redhead
□ **rousse** NF *Fam Arg crime Vieilli* **la rousse** *(la police)* the fuzz, *Br* the Old Bill
NM 1 *(teinte → d'un feuillage)* reddish-brown *(colour)*, russet; *(→ d'une chevelure, d'une moustache)* reddish or gingery colour
2 *Culin* roux

royal, -e, -aux, -ales [rwajal, -o] ADJ 1 *Hist & Pol (puissance)* royal, regal; *(bijoux, insignes, appartements, palais, académie)* royal; **la famille royale** *(en Grande-Bretagne)* the Royal Family; *(ailleurs)* the royal family; **prince r.** crown prince, heir apparent

2 *(somptueux → cadeau)* magnificent, princely; *(→ pourboire)* lavish; *(→ salaire)* princely; *(→ accueil)* royal; **un train de vie r.** a sumptuous lifestyle

3 *(extrême → mépris)* total; *Fam* **il m'a fichu une paix royale** he left me in total peace

4 *Cartes* **quinte royale** royal flush

□ **royale** NF 1 *(barbe)* royale, imperial

2 *Fam (marine)* **la Royale** = the French Navy

□ **à la royale** ADJ *Culin* **lièvre à la royale** hare royale

royalement [rwajalmɑ̃] ADV 1 *(avec magnificence)* royally, regally; **ils nous ont reçus r.** they treated us like royalty; **il l'a r. payé** he paid

him a princely sum 2 *Fam (complètement)* totally▪; **je m'en fiche** ou **moque r.!** I really couldn't care less!, I don't give a damn!

royalisme [rwajalism] NM royalism

royaliste [rwajalist] ADJ royalist; **il ne faut pas être plus r. que le roi** one mustn't try to out-Herod Herod or to be more Catholic than the Pope
NMF royalist

royalties [rwajalti] NFPL royalties *(for landowner or owner of patent)*

royaume [rwajom] NM 1 *Hist & Pol* kingdom

2 *Rel* **le r. céleste** ou **des cieux** the kingdom of Heaven; *Littéraire* **le r. des morts** the kingdom of the dead

3 *Fig (domaine)* realm; **le r. de l'imagination** the realm of the imagination; **le cinéaste nous fait entrer dans le r. de la fantaisie** the film-maker takes us into the realm of fantasy; **mon atelier, c'est mon r.** my workshop is my private world or domain; **le r. éternel** the hereafter; **le r. des ombres** the netherworld

4 *(locutions)* **je ne le ferais pas/je n'en voudrais pas pour un r.** I wouldn't do it/have it for all the tea in China; *Prov* **au r. des aveugles, les borgnes sont rois** in the kingdom of the blind the one-eyed man is king

royaumer [3] [rwajome] **se royaumer** VPR *Suisse Fam* to lounge about

Royaume-Uni [rwajomyni] NM **le R. (de Grande-Bretagne et d'Irlande du Nord)** the United Kingdom (of Great Britain and Northern Ireland), the UK; **aller au R.** to go to the UK; **vivre au R.** to live in the UK

royauté [rwajote] NF 1 *(monarchie)* monarchy 2 *(rang)* royalty, kingship; **il aspirait à la r.** he had designs on the throne

RP[1] [ɛrpe] NFPL *(abrév* **relations publiques***)* PR
NF *(abrév* **recette principale***) (de la poste)* main post office; *(des impôts)* main tax office

RP[2] *(abrév écrite* **région parisienne***)* Paris area or region

R.P. *Rel (abrév écrite* **Révérend Père***)* Rev

RPR [ɛrpeɛr] NM *Anciennement Pol (abrév* **Rassemblement pour la République***)* = right-wing French political party

RSFSR [ɛrɛsɛfɛsɛr] NF *(abrév* **République socialiste fédérative soviétique de Russie***)* **la R.** RSFSR

RSVP *(abrév écrite* **répondez s'il vous plaît***)* RSVP

RTB [ɛrtebe] NF *(abrév* **Radio-télévision belge***)* = Belgian broadcasting company

RTC [ɛrtese] NM *Tél (abrév* **Réseau Téléphonique Commuté***)* PSTN

rte *(abrév écrite* **route***)* rd

RTGS [ɛrteʒeɛs] NM *Banque & UE (abrév* **Real-Time Gross Settlement***)* RTGS; **système R.** RTGS system

RTL [ɛrteɛl] NF 1 *(abrév* **Radio-télévision Luxembourg***)* = private broadcasting network based in Luxembourg 2 *Élec (abrév* **résistance transistor logique***)* RTL

RTT [ɛrtete] NF *(abrév* **réduction du temps de travail***)* = reduction of the working week in France from 39 to 35 hours, introduced by the government of Lionel Jospin in 1998 and phased in from 2000 onwards; **être en R.** to have time off *(because one has accumulated annual leave through the "RTT" system)*

RTVE [ɛrteveə] NF *(abrév* **Radio-télévision española***)* = Spanish broadcasting company

RU [ry] NM *Fam (abrév* **restaurant universitaire***)* university cafeteria or *Br* canteen or refectory▪

ru [ry] NM *Littéraire* brook, rill

ruade [ryad] NF kick; **lancer** ou **décocher une r. à** to kick or to lash out at

Ruanda [rwɑ̃da] = Rwanda

ruandais, -e [rwɑ̃dɛ, -ɛz] = rwandais

ruban [rybɑ̃] NM 1 *(ornement)* ribbon; *(liseré)* ribbon, tape; *(bolduc)* tape; *(sur chapeau)* band; **le r. bleu** the blue ribbon; **le r. rouge** the ribbon of the "Légion d'honneur"; *Fam* **le r. violet** = decoration for services to education in France

2 *Littéraire* **la rivière déroule son long r.** the river winds before us like a long ribbon

3 *(de cassette)* tape; *(de machine à écrire)* ribbon; **r. adhésif** adhesive tape; **r. adhésif en toile** gaffer tape; **r. correcteur** correction tape;

r. d'enregistrement recording tape; **r. isolant** insulating tape; **r. magnétique** magnetic *or* recording tape; *Ordinat* **r. perforé** perforated tape **4** *(en gymnastique rythmique)* ribbon

rubané, -e [rybane] ADJ **1** *Géol* ribbon *(avant n)*, banded **2** *Archéol* ribbon *(avant n)*

rubaner [3] [rybane] VT *Vieilli* to decorate *or* adorn with ribbons

rubanerie [rybanri] NF *(fabrication)* ribbon manufacture; *(commerce)* ribbon trade

rubanier, -ère [rybanje, -ɛr] ADJ ribbon *(avant n)* NM,F **1** *(fabricant)* ribbon maker **2** *(marchand)* ribbon seller

NM *Bot* branched bur-reed

rubato [rubato] *Mus* ADV rubato NM rubato

rubéfaction [rybefaksjɔ̃] NF *Méd* rubefaction

rubéfiant, -e [rybefjɑ̃, -ɑ̃t] *Méd* ADJ rubefacient NM rubefacient

rubéfier [9] [rybefje] VT to rubefy

rubellite [rybelit] NF *Minér* rubellite

rubénien, -enne [rybenjɛ̃, -ɛn] ADJ *Beaux-Arts* Rubenesque

rubéole [rybeɔl] NF German measles (UNCOUNT), *Spéc* rubella

rubéoleux, -euse [rybeɔlø, -øz] ADJ rubella *(avant n)*; *(patient)* suffering from German measles; *(symptômes)* of German measles NM,F German measles sufferer

rubescent, -e [rybesɑ̃, -ɑ̃t] ADJ *Littéraire* rubescent

rubiacée [rybjase] *Bot* NF rubiacea
  ❑ **rubiacées** NFPL Rubiaceae

rubican [rybikɑ̃] ADJ M roan NM roan

rubicelle [rybisɛl] NF *Minér* rubicelle

Rubicon [rybikɔ̃] NM *Géog & Hist* Rubicon; *Fig* **franchir** *ou* **passer le R.** to cross the Rubicon; *Hist* **le passage du R.** the crossing of the Rubicon

rubicond, -e [rybikɔ̃, -ɔ̃d] ADJ *Littéraire* rubicund, ruddy, rosy-cheeked

rubidium [rybidjɔm] NM *Chim* rubidium

rubigineux, -euse [rybiʒinø, -øz] ADJ *Littéraire* **1** *(couvert de rouille)* rust-covered **2** *(couleur de rouille)* rust-coloured

rubis [rybi] NM **1** *(pierre précieuse)* ruby **2** *(couleur)* ruby (colour) **3** *(d'une montre)* jewel, ruby **4** *Orn* red colibri; **petit r. de la Caroline** ruby-throated hummingbird

rubricard, -e [rybrikar, -ard] NM,F *Journ* columnist

rubrique [rybrik] NF **1** *(dans la presse → article)* column; *(→ page)* page; *(→ cahier)* section; **la r. des affaires** the business section; **la r. littéraire** the book column/page/section; **r. mondaine** society column; **la r. nécrologique** the obituaries; **r. pratique** advice column; **la r. scientifique** the science column/page/section; **elle tient la r. cinéma** *(critiques)* she writes the movie *or Br* film reviews
  2 *(catégorie)* heading; **la somme se trouve dans** *ou* **sous la r. frais généraux** the sum comes under the heading of overheads *or* is entered as an overhead
  3 *(d'un livre liturgique)* rubric; *(d'un dictionnaire)* field label

rubriquer [3] [rybrike] VT *(article, texte)* to provide with headings

ruche [ryʃ] NF **1** *(abri → en bois)* beehive; *(→ en paille)* beehive, *Spéc* skep; *(colonie d'abeilles)* hive; *Fam* **se piquer la r.** *(s'enivrer)* to get wasted *or Br* pissed **2** *Fig* hive of activity **3** *Couture* ruche, rouche

ruché [ryʃe] NM *Couture* ruche, rouche; **des ruchés** ruching

ruchée [ryʃe] NF hive

rucher [ryʃe] NM apiary

ruclon [ryklɔ̃] NM *Suisse* garden rubbish heap

rudbeckia [rydbekja] NM *Bot* rudbeckia, cone flower

rude [ryd] ADJ **1** *(rugueux → surface, vin, peau)* rough; *(→ toile)* rough, coarse; *(→ brosse)* stiff, hard; *(→ voix)* gruff; *(→ son)* rough, harsh
  2 *(→ manières, paysan)* rough, uncouth, unrefined; *(→ traits)* rugged
  3 *(difficile → climat, hiver)* harsh, severe; *(→ conditions, concurrent)* tough; *(→ concurrence)* severe, tough; *(→ vie, tâche)* hard, tough; *(→ métier)* demanding; *(→ côte)* hard, stiff; **être**

mis à r. épreuve *(personne)* to be severely tested, to be put through the mill; *(vêtement, matériel)* to get a lot of wear and tear; **ma patience a été mise à r. épreuve** it was a severe strain on my patience
  4 *(sévère → ton, voix)* rough, harsh, hard; *(→ personne)* harsh, hard, severe
  5 *Fam (important, remarquable)* **avoir un r. appétit** to have a hearty appetite"; **un r. gaillard** a hearty fellow"; **ça a été un r. coup pour lui** it was a hard blow for him"

rudement [rydmɑ̃] ADV **1** *Fam (diablement)* **c'est r. bon** it's really good"; **c'est r. beau** it's really lovely"; **c'est r. cher** it's incredibly *or* awfully expensive"; **il est r. plus intelligent que son frère** he's a damn sight more intelligent than his brother; **elle est r. culottée!** she's got some gall *or Br* cheek!; **ça m'a fait r. mal!** it hurt like hell!; **ils étaient r. nombreux** there were a heck of a lot of them
  2 *(sans ménagement)* roughly, harshly; **tu lui parles trop r.** you talk to him/her too roughly
  3 *(brutalement)* hard; **il a frappé à la porte r.** he banged hard on the door

rudenté, -e [rydɑ̃te] ADJ *Archit* cabled

rudenture [rydɑ̃tyr] NF *Archit* cabling

rudéral, -e, -aux, -ales [ryderal, -o] ADJ *Bot* ruderal

rudération [ryderasjɔ̃] NF cobble paving

rudesse [rydɛs] NF **1** *(rugosité → d'une surface, d'un vin, de la peau)* roughness; *(→ d'une toile)* roughness, coarseness; *(→ d'une voix)* gruffness; *(→ d'un son)* roughness, harshness
  2 *(rusticité → des manières, d'un paysan)* roughness, uncouthness; *(→ des traits)* ruggedness
  3 *(sévérité → d'un ton, d'une voix)* roughness, harshness, hardness; *(→ d'un maître)* severity, harshness; **traiter qn avec r.** to treat sb harshly
  4 *(dureté → d'un climat, d'un hiver)* hardness, harshness, severity; *(→ d'une concurrence, d'une tâche)* toughness

rudiment [rydimɑ̃] NM **1** *Littéraire (début, ébauche)* rudiment; **il en est encore au r.** he's still learning the basics; **je n'ai encore acquis qu'un r. de technique** my technique is still rudimentary
  2 *Biol* rudiment; **un r. de queue** a rudimentary tail
  ❑ **rudiments** NMPL *(d'un art, d'une science)* basics, rudiments; **tu apprendras vite les rudiments** you'll soon learn the basics; **apprendre les rudiments de la grammaire** to learn some basic grammar, to get a basic (working) knowledge of grammar; **je n'ai que des rudiments d'informatique** I have only a rudimentary knowledge of computing; **avoir des rudiments de chinois** to speak basic Chinese

rudimentaire [rydimɑ̃tɛr] ADJ **1** *(élémentaire)* rudimentary, basic; **des notions rudimentaires d'informatique** basic notions of computing **2** *(commençant)* rudimentary, undeveloped; **cette technique est encore r.** the technique is still in its infancy **3** *(succinct)* basic; **des informations trop rudimentaires** inadequate information **4** *Biol* rudimentary

rudiste [rydist] NM *Zool* rudist, Rudista

rudoie *etc voir* **rudoyer**

rudoiement [rydwamɑ̃] NM *Littéraire* harsh treatment

rudoyer [13] [rydwaje] VT to treat harshly; **il les a un peu rudoyés** he was a bit harsh with them

rue [ry] NF **1** *(voie, habitants)* street; **de la r., des rues** street *(avant n)*; *Fig* **c'est la r. qui dicte sa loi aujourd'hui** it's mob rule these days; **toute la r. en parle** the whole street *or* neighbourhood is talking about it; **r. pavée** paved street *(with small, flat paving stones)*; **r. piétonnière** *ou* **piétonne** pedestrian street; **r. principale** main street; **r. à sens unique** one-way street; **la grande r.** the main *or Br* high street; **les petites rues** the side streets; **être/se retrouver à la r.** to be/find oneself on the streets; **tu sais que tu n'es pas à la r., tu peux compter sur nous** you know we'll always put you up; **mettre** *ou* **jeter qn à la r.** to turn *or* to put sb out into the street; *Belg* **à r.** *(fenêtre)* looking out over the street; *(façade)* facing the street
  2 *Bot* rue

RUE

ruée [rɥe] NF rush; **à l'heure de la r. hors des bureaux** during the evening rush hour; **il y a eu une r. vers le buffet** everybody made a mad dash for the buffet; **il y a eu une r. sur les tickets de loterie** there's been a big run on lottery tickets; **dès que les portes se sont ouvertes, ç'a été la r.** the minute the doors opened, there was a mad rush; *Hist* **la r. vers l'or** the gold rush

'**La Ruée vers l'or**' *Chaplin* 'The Gold Rush'

ruelle [rɥɛl] NF **1** *(voie)* lane, narrow street, alley **2** *(de lit)* space between bed and wall **3** *Hist (pour réception)* ruelle *(part of bedchamber used by aristocratic ladies to hold morning receptions in the 16th and 17th centuries)*

ruer [7] [rɥe] VI **1** *(animal)* to kick (out)
  2 *Fam (locution)* **r. dans les brancards** *(verbalement)* to kick up a fuss; *(par ses actions)* to kick *or* to lash out
  ▶**se ruer** VPR **se r. sur qn** *(gén)* to rush at sb; *(agressivement)* to hurl *or* to throw oneself at sb; **se r. vers la sortie** to dash *or* to rush towards the exit; **ils se sont tous rués sur le buffet** they made a mad dash for the buffet; **dès qu'une chambre se libère, tout le monde se rue dessus** as soon as a room becomes vacant, everybody pounces on it; **on se rue pour aller voir son dernier film** people are flocking to see his/her latest movie *or Br* film; **se r. à l'attaque** to charge into the attack

ruffian [ryfjɑ̃] NM **1** *Arch (souteneur)* whoremonger **2** *(aventurier)* adventurer

rufflette® [ryflɛt] NF Rufflette® tape

rufian [ryfjɑ̃] = **ruffian**

rugby [rygbi] NM rugby (football); **r. à quinze** Rugby Union; **r. à treize** Rugby League

rugbyman [rygbiman] *(pl* **rugbymen** [-mɛn]) NM rugby player

rugine [ryʒin] NF *Méd* xyster

rugir [32] [ryʒir] VI **1** *(fauve)* to roar **2** *(personne)* to bellow, to howl *(de* with) **3** *(moteur)* to roar; *(vent)* to howl
  VT *(insultes, menaces)* to bellow out, to roar out

rugissant, -e [ryʒisɑ̃, -ɑ̃t] ADJ **1** *(fauve, moteur)* roaring **2** *Littéraire (flots)* roaring; *(vent, tempête)* roaring, howling

rugissement [ryʒismɑ̃] NM **1** *(d'un lion, d'un moteur)* roar, roaring **2** *Littéraire (des flots)* roar, roaring; *(du vent, de la tempête)* roar, roaring, howling **3** *(d'une personne)* roar; **r. de fureur** roar of fury, howl of rage; **r. de douleur** howl of pain; **pousser des rugissements de colère** to roar *or* howl with anger

rugosité [rygozite] NF *(d'une écorce, d'un plancher, de la peau)* roughness; *(d'une toile)* roughness, coarseness
  ❑ **rugosités** NFPL bumps, rough patches; **de petites rugosités sur la main** little rough patches (of skin) on the hand

rugueux, -euse [rygø, -øz] ADJ *(écorce, plancher, peau)* rough; *(toile)* rough, coarse

Ruhr [rur] NF **la R.** the Ruhr

ruiler [3] [rɥile] VT *Constr* to fillet

ruine [rɥin] NF **1** *(faillite financière)* ruin; **le jeu a causé sa r.** gambling ruined him/her *or* caused his/her ruin; **aller** *ou* **courir à la r.** to head for ruin; **être au bord de la r.** to be on the verge of ruin *or* bankruptcy
  2 *Fam (dépense exorbitante)* ruinous expense; **20 euros, ce n'est pas la r.!** 20 euros won't break *or* ruin you!; **l'entretien du bateau est une r.** maintaining the boat is ruinously expensive

3 (*bâtiment délabré*) ruin; **leur château est une vieille r.** their castle is an old ruin

4 (*personne usée*) wreck; **c'est une vraie r.** he's a real wreck

5 (*destruction → d'une institution*) downfall, ruin; *Fig* ruin; **il veut ma r.** he wants to ruin *or* finish me; **ce fut la r. de notre mariage** it wrecked *or* ruined our marriage; **le scandale fut la r. de sa carrière politique** the scandal ruined his/her political career; **c'est la r. de tous nos espoirs/projets** all our hopes/plans are in ruins, it's the downfall of all our hopes/plans

□ **ruines** NFPL ruins; **les ruines d'un vieux château** the ruins *or* remains of an old castle

□ **en ruine** ADJ ruined; **la ferme est en r.** the farmhouse is in ruins; **il y a beaucoup de moulins en r. dans la région** there are a lot of ruined windmills in the area ADV in ruins; **tomber en r.** to go to ruin

ruine-babines [ʀɥinbabin] NF INV *Can Fam* harmonica■, mouth organ■

ruine-de-Rome [ʀɥindəʀɔm] (*pl* **ruines-de-Rome**) NF *Bot* ivy-leaved toadflax

ruiner [3] [ʀɥine] VT **1** (*financièrement*) to ruin, to cause the ruin of, *Sout* to bring ruin upon; **les études de mes enfants me ruinent** my children's education is ruining me; **ça ne va pas te r.!** it won't break *or* ruin you!; **tu vas me r.!** you'll be the ruin *or* the ruination of me!

2 *Littéraire* (*endommager → architecture, cultures*) to ruin, to destroy; (→ *espérances*) to ruin, to dash; (→ *carrière, santé*) to ruin, to wreck; **cet échec ruine tous ses espoirs** this failure wrecks all his/her hopes

► **se ruiner** VPR **1** (*perdre sa fortune*) to ruin *or* to bankrupt oneself; (*dépenser beaucoup*) to spend a fortune; **il s'est ruiné aux courses** he ruined *or* bankrupted himself at the races; **je me ruine à te payer des études** I'm bleeding myself dry *or* ruining myself paying for your studies; **je ne me suis pas ruiné** I didn't spend much; **se r. en** to spend a fortune on; **elle se ruine en vêtements/livres** she spends a fortune on clothes/books

2 se r. la santé/la vue to ruin one's health/eyesight

ruineux, -euse [ʀɥinø, -øz] ADJ extravagantly expensive, ruinous; **20 euros, ce n'est pas r.** 20 euros is hardly extravagant

ruiniforme [ʀɥiniform] ADJ ruiniform

ruiniste [ʀɥinist] NMF *Beaux-Arts* painter of ruins

ruinure [ʀɥinyr] NF *Menuis* = notch in a joist *or* post designed to provide grip for the masonry

ruisseau, -x [ʀɥiso] NM **1** (*ru*) brook, stream

2 (*lit du cours d'eau*) bed of a stream; **un r. à sec** a dried-up stream

3 *Littéraire* (*torrent*) stream; **ruisseaux de sang/sueur** streams of blood/sweat; **ruisseaux de larmes** floods of tears; **il coulait des ruisseaux de lave/de boue** the lava/mud was flowing in streams; *Prov* **les petits ruisseaux font les grandes rivières** tall oaks from little acorns grow

4 (*rigole*) gutter

5 *Péj* (*caniveau*) gutter; **rouler dans le r.** to end up in the gutter; **tirer qn du r.** to pull *or* to drag sb out of the gutter

ruisselant, -e [ʀɥislɑ̃, -ɑ̃t] ADJ **1** (*inondé*) **r. (d'eau)** (*imperméable, personne*) dripping (wet); (*paroi*) streaming *or* running with water; **le visage r. de sueur** his/her face streaming *or* dripping with sweat; **les joues ruisselantes de larmes** his/her cheeks streaming with tears; **une pièce ruisselante de lumière** a room bathed in *or* flooded with light

2 (*qui ne cesse de couler*) **eaux ruisselantes** running waters

ruisseler [24] [ʀɥisle] VI (*couler → eau, sang, sueur*) to stream, to drip; **la sueur ruisselait sur son front** his/her brow was streaming *or* dripping with sweat; *Fig* **la lumière ruisselait par la fenêtre** light flooded in through the window; *Littéraire* **r. sur** (*sujet: chevelure*) to flow over; (*sujet: air, lumière*) to stream over

□ **ruisseler de** VT IND (*être inondé de*) to stream with; **r. de sang/sueur** to stream with blood/sweat; **les murs ruisselaient d'humidité** the walls were streaming *or* oozing with damp; **ses**

joues ruisselaient de larmes tears were streaming down his/her cheeks, his/her cheeks were streaming with tears; *Fig* **le palais ruisselait de lumière** the palace was bathed in *or* flooded with *or* awash with light

ruisselet [ʀɥislε] NM *Littéraire* little stream, brook

ruisselle *etc voir* **ruisseler**

ruissellement [ʀɥisεlmɑ̃] NM **1** (*écoulement*) **le r. de la pluie sur les vitres** the rain streaming *or* running down the window panes; *Littéraire* **r. de lumière** stream of light **2** *Géol* **r. pluvial, eaux de r.** (*immédiate*) runoff

rumb [ʀɔ̃b] NM *Naut* rhumb

rumba [ʀumba] NF rumba

rumen [ʀymεn] NM *Zool* rumen

rumeur [ʀymœʀ] NF **1** (*information*) rumour; **il y a des rumeurs de guerre** there's talk of war; **selon certaines rumeurs, le réacteur fuirait toujours** rumour has it *or* it's rumoured that the reactor is still leaking; **j'ai entendu des rumeurs selon lesquelles…** I've heard rumours *or* whispers *or* a whisper that…

2 (*bruit → d'un stade, d'une classe*) hubbub, hum; (→ *de l'océan*) murmur; (→ *de la circulation*) rumbling, hum; **la r. lointaine de la ville/de l'usine** the distant sound of the city/the factory

3 (*manifestation*) **r. de mécontentement** rumblings of discontent

4 (*opinion*) **la r. publique le tient pour coupable** rumour has it that he is guilty; **victime de la r. publique, elle dut quitter la ville** a victim of local gossip, she had to leave town

rumex [ʀymεks] NM *Bot* rumex

ruminant [ʀyminɑ̃] NM *Zool* ruminant

rumination [ʀyminasjɔ̃] NF *Zool* rumination

ruminer [3] [ʀymine] VI *Zool* to chew the cud, *Spéc* to ruminate

VT **1** (*ressasser → idée*) to ponder, to chew over; (→ *malheurs*) to brood over; (→ *vengeance*) to ponder **2** *Zool* to ruminate

rumsteck [ʀɔmstεk] = **romsteck**

runabout [ʀœnəbawt] NM *Naut* runabout

rune [ʀyn] NF rune

Rungis [ʀɔ̃ʒis] NM = large wholesale food market in the Paris suburbs

runique [ʀynik] ADJ runic

ruolz [ʀɥɔlts] NM = gold or silver plating

ruper [3] [ʀype] VT *Suisse très Fam* to stuff oneself with

rupestre [ʀypεstʀ] ADJ **1** *Archéol & Beaux-Arts* (*dessin*) rock (*avant n*); (*peinture*) cave (*avant n*) **2** *Bot* rock (*avant n*), *Spéc* rupestrine

RUPI (*abrév écrite* **roupie indienne**) Re

rupiah [ʀypja] NF *Méd* rupiah

rupicole [ʀypikɔl] NM *Orn* rock cock

rupin, -e [ʀypε̃, -in] *Fam* ADJ (*quartier*) plush, *Br* posh; (*intérieur*) ritzy, *Br* posh; (*personne*) loaded, *Br* rolling in it

NM,F moneybags; **c'est des rupins** they're rolling in money *or Br* rolling in it; **les rupins** the rich■

RUPP (*abrév écrite* **roupie du Pakistan**) Re, Pre

rupteur [ʀyptœʀ] NM **1** *Élec* (*d'une bobine*) circuit breaker **2** *Aut* **r. (d'allumage)** (*contact*) breaker

rupture [ʀyptyʀ] NF **1** (*d'une corde, d'une poutre etc*) breaking; (*d'un barrage*) bursting

2 *Méd* (*dans une membrane*) breaking, tearing, splitting; (*dans un vaisseau*) bursting; **il y a eu r. du ligament** the ligament tore; **r. d'anévrysme** aneurysmal rupture

3 *Tech* **r. de circuit** circuit break

4 (*cessation → de négociations, de fiançailles*) breaking off; (→ *de relations diplomatiques*) severance, breaking off; **la r. des pourparlers était inévitable** the talks were bound to break down; **une r. avec le passé** a break with the past; **la r. est complète avec ma famille** I've broken off *or* severed all ties with my family

5 (*dans un couple*) break-up; **scène de r.** break-up scene; **leur couple semble toujours au bord de la r.** they always seem on the verge of splitting *or* breaking up

6 (*changement*) break; **r. de cadence** sudden break in rhythm; **r. de ton** sudden change in *or* of tone

7 *Com* **être en r. de stock** to be out of stock

8 *Jur* **r. de ban** illegal return (from banishment); *Fig* **être en r. de ban avec son milieu/sa**

famille to be at odds with one's environment/one's family; **r. de contrat/garantie** breach of contract/guarantee; **r. prolongée de la vie commune** estrangement; **r. abusive (de contrat)** ≃ illegal dismissal

9 *Ind* **r. de charge** break of load, transshipment
10 *Mil* breakthrough

□ **en rupture avec** PRÉP **être en r. avec le parti** to be at odds with the party; **ils se sont mariés à la mairie, en r. avec la tradition** in a break with tradition, they got married at the town hall

rural, -e, -aux, -ales [ʀyʀal, -o] ADJ (*droit, population*) rural; (*vie, paysage*) country (*avant n*), rural; (*chemin*) country (*avant n*); **en milieu r.** in rural areas

NM,F country person; **les ruraux** country people, countryfolk

NM *Suisse* farm building

ruralisme [ʀyʀalism] NM idealization of the countryside

ruralité [ʀyʀalite] NF rurality

rurbain, -e [ʀyʀbε̃, -εn] ADJ of the newly suburbanized countryside

NM,F = person who lives in the newly suburbanized countryside

rurbanisation [ʀyʀbanizasjɔ̃] NF incorporation of villages into suburbia

ruse [ʀyz] NF **1** (*trait de caractère*) cunning, craftiness, slyness; **s'approprier qch par (la) r.** to obtain sth through *or* by trickery; **elle a dû recourir à la r. pour s'échapper** she had to resort to cunning to escape **2** (*procédé*) trick, ruse, wile; **r. de guerre** tactics, stratagem; *Fig* good trick; *Fam* **ruses de Sioux** crafty tactics, fox's cunning

□ **ruses** NFPL *Belg* trouble (UNCOUNT)

rusé, -e [ʀyze] ADJ (*personne*) crafty, sly, wily; (*air, regard*) sly; **il est r. comme un renard** he's as sly *or* cunning *or* wily as a fox

NM,F **tu es une petite rusée!** you're a crafty one *or* a sly one, my girl!

ruser [3] [ʀyze] VI to use cunning *or* trickery *or* guile; **il va falloir r.!** we'll have to be clever!; **r. avec qn** to outsmart sb; **r. avec qch** to get round sth by using cunning

rush [ʀœʃ] (*pl* **rushs** *ou* **rushes**) NM **1** (*ruée*) rush, stampede **2** *Sport* (*effort soudain*) spurt

rushes [ʀœʃ] NMPL *Cin* rushes

Ruskoff [ʀyskɔf] NMF *Péj* = **russkof**

russe [ʀys] ADJ Russian

NM (*langue*) Russian

□ **Russe** NMF Russian; **R. blanc** White Russian

□ **à la russe** ADV Russian-style; **boire à la r.** to drink Russian-style

Russie [ʀysi] NF **la R.** Russia; **vivre en R.** to live in Russia; **aller en R.** to go to Russia; **la R. soviétique** Soviet Russia

russification [ʀysifikasjɔ̃] NF Russification, Russianization

russifier [9] [ʀysifje] VT to Russianize, to Russify

russkof [ʀyskɔf] NMF *Fam* ≃ Russky, = offensive term used with reference to Russian people

russophile [ʀysɔfil] ADJ Russophile
NMF Russophile

russophobe [ʀysɔfɔb] ADJ Russophobe
NMF Russophobe

russophone [ʀysɔfɔn] ADJ Russian-speaking
NMF Russian speaker

russule [ʀysyl] NF *Bot* russula; **r. émétique** sickener

rustaud, -e [ʀysto, -od] *Péj* ADJ yokelish

NM,F yokel, (country) bumpkin; *Fam* **les rustauds du coin** the locals■

rusticage [ʀystikaʒ] NM *Constr* (*mortier*) light mortar; (*opération*) rusticating

rusticité [ʀystisite] NF **1** (*d'un comportement, d'une personne*) uncouthness, boorishness **2** (*d'un mobilier*) rusticity **3** *Agr* hardiness

Rustine® [ʀystin] NF = (bicycle tyre) rubber repair patch

rustique [ʀystik] ADJ **1** (*de la campagne → vie*) rustic, rural **2** (*meubles, poterie*) rusticated **3** *Littéraire* (*fruste → manières, personne*) country (*avant n*), rustic **4** *Agr* hardy **5** *Archit* rusticated

NM **le r.** (*style*) rustic style; (*mobilier*) rustic furniture

rustiquer [3] [ʀystike] VT *Constr* (*mur*) to rusticate

rustre [ʀystʀ] ADJ boorish, uncouth

NMF boor, lout

rut [ryt] NM *Zool (de mâle)* rut; *(de femelle)* heat; **au moment du r.** during the rutting season; **être en r.** *(mâle)* to (be in) rut; *(femelle)* to be *Br* on or *Am* in heat

rutabaga [rytabaga] NM swede, *Am* rutabaga, *Scot* turnip

rutacée [rytase] NF rutaceous plant
□ **rutacées** NFPL **les rutacées** the Rutaceae

ruthène [rytɛn] ADJ Ruthenian
□ **Ruthène** NMF Ruthenian

Ruthénie [ryteni] NF **la R.** Ruthenia

ruthénium [rytenjɔm] NM *Chim* ruthenium

ruthénois, -e [rytenwa, -az] ADJ of/from Rodez
NM,F = inhabitant of or person from Rodez (in south-west France)

rutherford [ryvœfɔr] NM *Phys* rutherford

rutherfordium [ryvœfɔrdjɔm] NM *Chim* rutherfordium

rutilance [rytilɑ̃s] NF gleam, shine; *(rouge)* red glow

rutilant, -e [rytilɑ̃, -ɑ̃t] ADJ **1** *(propre → carrosserie, armure)* gleaming, shining **2** *Littéraire (rouge → cuivre)* rutilant; *(→ visage)* ruddy

rutile [rytil] NM *Minér* rutile

rutilement [rytilmɑ̃] NM gleam, shine; *(rouge)* red glow

rutiler [3] [rytile] VI **1** *(étinceler)* to gleam, to shine **2** *Littéraire (d'un éclat rouge)* to glow red

rutine [rytin] NF *Chim* rutin

rutoside [rytɔzid] NM *Chim* rutin

ruz [ry] NM *Géol (dans le Jura)* cataclinal ravine

R-V *(abrév écrite* **rendez-vous***)* meeting, appointment

RVB [ɛrvebe] NM *(abrév* **rouge, vert et bleu***)* RGB

RVE [ɛrvɛ] NF *Écon (abrév* **restriction volontaire des exportations***)* VER

Rwanda [rwɑ̃da] NM **le R.** Rwanda; **aller au R.** to go to Rwanda; **vivre au R.** to live in Rwanda

rwandais, -e [rwɑ̃dɛ, -ɛz] ADJ Rwandan
□ **Rwandais, -e** NM,F Rwandan

rye [raj] NM rye (whisky)

rythme [ritm] NM **1** *Mus* rhythm; **ils dansaient sur/à un r. endiablé** they were dancing to/at a furious rhythm; **avoir du r.** *(sujet: musique)* to have a good (strong) beat *or* rhythm; **avoir le sens du r.** *(sujet: personne)* to have rhythm; **avoir le r. dans la peau** to have a natural sense of rhythm, to have rhythm; **marquer le r.** to mark time; **suivre le r.** to follow the beat
2 *Cin, Théât & Littérature* rhythm; **le spectacle/film manque de r.** the show is a bit slow-moving or lacks pace
3 *(allure → d'une production)* rate; *(→ des battements du cœur)* rate, speed; *(→ de vie)* tempo, pace; **il te faudra changer de r. quand tu auras des enfants** once you have children, you'll have to change pace *or* slow down a bit; **travailler à un r. soutenu** to work at a sustained pace; **au r. auquel il écrit ses romans** at the rate at which he writes novels; **à ce r.-là** at that rate;

suivre le r. to keep up the pace; **ils avaient du mal à suivre le r.** they had trouble keeping up the pace; **les rythmes scolaires** = the way in which the school year is organized; **r. de travail** work rate
4 *(succession → de marées, de saisons)* rhythm
5 *Anat & Biol* **r. biologique** biorhythm; **r. cardiaque** heartbeat, *Spéc* cardiac rhythm; **r. respiratoire** breathing rate
□ **au rythme de** PRÉP **1** *(au son de)* to the rhythm of; **ils défilaient au r. d'une marche militaire** they paraded to the rhythm of a military march
2 *(à la cadence de)* at the rate of; **au r. d'un milliard d'habitants en plus par décennie** at the rate of an extra one billion inhabitants per decade

rythmé, -e [ritme] ADJ *(musique)* rhythmic, rhythmical; *(prose)* rhythmical; **musique très rythmée** music with a good rhythm *or* beat

rythmer [3] [ritme] VT **1** *(mouvements de danse, texte)* to put rhythm into, to give rhythm to; **r. une chanson** to mark time to a song; **je n'ai pas pu m'empêcher de r. la chanson du pied** I couldn't help tapping my foot to the song **2** *(ponctuer)* **ces événements ont rythmé sa vie** these events gave a certain rhythm to *or* punctuated his/her life

rythmique [ritmik] ADJ rhythmic, rhythmical
NF **1** *Littérature* rhythmics *(UNCOUNT)* **2** *(gymnastique)* rhythmic gymnastics *(UNCOUNT)*

S

S¹, s¹ [ɛs] NM INV **1** *(lettre)* S, s **2** *(forme)* S-shape; **faire des S** *(voiture)* to zigzag; *(sentier)* to twist and turn; **à cet endroit, la route fait un S** at this point, there's a double bend *or* an S bend in the road
▫ **en S** ADJ *(crochet)* S-shaped; *(route, sentier)* winding, zigzagging; *(rivière)* meandering

S² *(abrév écrite Sud)* S

s² *(abrév écrite seconde)* s

s/ *(abrév écrite sur)* on

s' [s] *voir* **se, si²**

SA [ɛsɑ] NF *(abrév* **société anonyme)** *Br* ≃ plc, *Am* ≃ Corp.; **une SA** a limited company

S.A. *(abrév écrite* **Son Altesse)** HH

sa [sa] *voir* **son³**

saanen [sɑnən] NF *(chèvre)* Saanen

Saba [saba] NPR Sheba

sabayon [sabajɔ̃] NM *(entremets)* zabaglione; *(sauce)* sabayon sauce

sabbat [saba] NM **1** *Rel* Sabbath; **que faites-vous le jour du s.?** what do you do on the Sabbath? **2** *(de sorcières)* witches' sabbath **3** *Fam Vieilli (raffut)* din, racket

sabbatique [sabatik] ADJ **1** *Rel* sabbatical **2** *Univ* **demander une année s.** to ask for a sabbatical (year); **être en congé s.** to be on sabbatical **3** *Littéraire (digne d'un sabbat, très agité)* chaotic, tumultuous

sabéen, -enne [sabeɛ̃, -ɛn] ADJ *Hist* Sabean, Sabaean
   NM,F *Hist* Sabean, Sabaean
   NM *Rel* Sabian

sabéisme [sabeism] NM *Rel* Sabianism

sabelle [sabɛl] NF *Zool* sabella

sabellianisme [sabeljanism] NM *Rel* Sabellianism

Sabin, -e [sabɛ̃, -in] NM,F Sabine

sabine [sabin] NF savin (bush)

sabir [sabir] NM **1** *Ling* lingua franca **2** *Fam (jargon)* gobbledegook, mumbo-jumbo; **ils parlent un s. incompréhensible** they speak some incomprehensible gobbledegook; **dans leur s.** in their lingo

sablage [sabla3] NM **1** *(en travaux publics)* gritting **2** *Constr* sandblasting

sable [sabl] NM **1** *Géol* sand; **s. fin** fine sand; **s. de construction** coarse sand; *Fam Fig* **être sur le s.** *(sans argent)* to be broke *or* strapped *or Br* skint; *(sans emploi)* to be out of a job; **ils m'ont mis sur le s.** *(ruiné)* they've ruined *or* bankrupted me
   2 *Métal (moulding)* sand; **s. de fer** fine iron filings; *Constr* **s. liant** *ou* **mordant** sharp sand
   3 *Hér* sable
   ADJ INV sand-coloured, sandy
   ▫ **sables** NMPL **les sables (du désert)** the desert sands; **sables mouvants** quicksand *(UNCOUNT)*
   ▫ **de sable** ADJ *(château)* sand *(avant n)*; *(dune)* sand *(avant n)*, sandy; *(fond)* sandy

sablé, -e [sable] ADJ *(allée)* sandy
   NM shortbread *(Br* biscuit *or Am* cookie), piece of shortbread

sabler [sable] VT **1** *(route)* to grit **2** *(mur)* to sandblast **3** *(locution)* **s. le champagne** to crack open a bottle of champagne

sablerie [sabləri] NF sand plant

sableur [sablœr] NM **1** *(en travaux publics)* sander *(person)* **2** *Constr* sandblaster operator **3** *Métal (sand)* moulder

sableux, -euse [sablø, -øz] ADJ **1** *(mêlé de sable →eau, terrain)* sandy; *(→ champignons, moules)* gritty; **alluvions sableuses** sandy alluvium **2** *(rugueux → pâte)* grainy

---

▫ **sableuse** NF **1** *(en travaux publics)* sander, sandspreader **2** *Constr* sandblaster

sablier, -ère [sablije, -ɛr] ADJ *(industrie, commerce)* sand *(avant n)*
   NM **1** *(gén)* hourglass, sand glass; *(de cuisine)* egg timer **2** *(pour sécher l'encre)* sandbox **3** *Bot* sandbox tree
   ▫ **sablière** NF **1** *(lieu)* sand quarry, sandpit **2** *Constr (de toiture)* inferior purlin; *(dans un mur)* wall plate; **sablière haute** head rail **3** *(de locomotive)* sandbox

sabline [sablin] NF *Bot* sandwort

sablon [sablɔ̃] NM fine sand

sablonner [sablɔne] VT *Tech (surface)* to cover with sand

sablonneux, -euse [sablɔnø, -øz] ADJ sandy

sablonnière [sablɔnjɛr] NF sand quarry, sandpit

sabord [sabɔr] NM scuttle, porthole; **s. de charge** cargo door

sabordage [sabɔrda3], **sabordement** [sabɔrdəmɑ̃] NM *Naut & Fig* scuttling

saborder [sabɔrde] VT **1** *Naut* to scuttle, to sink **2** *(stopper → entreprise, journal)* to scuttle, to sink, to wind up **3** *(faire échouer → plans, recherche)* to scuttle, to put paid to, *Br* to scupper
   ▸ **se saborder** VPR **1** *(équipage)* to scuttle one's ship **2** *(entreprise)* to fold, to close down; *(parti)* to wind (oneself) up

sabot [sabo] NM **1** *(soulier)* clog, sabot; *Fam* **je te vois venir avec tes gros sabots** I know what you're after, I can see you coming a mile off; *Fam* **elle danse comme un s.** she's got two left feet; *Fam* **je chante comme un s.** I can't sing to save my life
   2 *Zool* hoof; **animaux à sabots** hoofed animals
   3 *Fam Péj (instrument, machine)* pile of junk
   4 *Cartes* shoe
   5 *Tech* **s. d'arrêt** chock; **s. de Denver** *Br* wheel clamp, *Am* Denver boot; **mettre le s. de Denver à une voiture** to *Br* clamp *or Am* to (Denver) boot a car; *Rail* **s. d'enrayage** skidpan; **s. de frein** brake shoe *or* block
   6 *(d'un meuble)* metal shoe; *(d'un tube)* ferrule
   7 *(jouet)* whipping top
   8 *(en travaux publics)* shoe

sabotage [sabɔta3] NM **1** *(destruction → de matériel)* sabotage; *Fig* **c'est du s.!** this is sheer sabotage!; **le s. d'un plan de paix** the sabotage *or* sabotaging of a peace plan **2** *(acte)* **un s.** an act *or* a piece of sabotage **3** *(travail bâclé)* botched work **4** *Rail* chairing **5** *(en travaux publics)* shoeing

sabot-de-Vénus [sabodvenys] *(pl* **sabots-de-Vénus)** NM *Bot* lady's slipper

saboter [sabɔte] VT **1** *(détruire, empêcher volontairement)* to sabotage; **s. une voie ferrée** to sabotage a train line; **des manifestants sont venus s. l'émission** demonstrators came to sabotage *or* to disrupt the programme **2** *(bâcler)* to bungle **3** *Rail* to chair **4** *(en travaux publics)* to shoe
   USAGE ABSOLU **tu sabotes!** you're making a mess of the whole thing!

saboterie [sabɔtri] NF sabot factory

saboteur, -euse [sabɔtœr, -øz] NM,F **1** *(destructeur)* saboteur **2** *(mauvais travailleur)* bungler

sabotier, -ère [sabɔtje, -ɛr] NM,F **1** *(fabricant)* clogmaker **2** *(commerçant)* clog seller

sabouler [sabule] VT *Vieilli (malmener)* to bully, to push around; *(réprimander)* to upbraid

sabra [sabra] NMF Sabra

---

sabre [sabr] NM **1** *(épée)* sabre; **tirer son s.** to draw one's sword; **s. d'abattis** machete; **s. d'abordage** cutlass; **s. de cavalerie** cavalry sabre; **s. au clair** with drawn sword; **le s. et le goupillon** the Army and the Church **2** *Ich* scabbard fish

sabre-baïonnette [sabrəbajɔnɛt] *(pl* **sabres-baïonnettes)** NM sword bayonet

sabrer [sabre] VT **1** *(texte)* to make drastic cuts in; *(paragraphe, phrases)* to cut; **s. tout un passage dans un chapitre** to cut a whole section out of a chapter
   2 *Fam (critiquer → auteur, pièce, film)* to savage, to rubbish
   3 *Fam (étudiant → noter sévèrement)* to give a lousy mark to; *(→ recaler)* to fail■, *Am* to flunk; *(employé → renvoyer)* to fire, *Br* to sack, *Am* to can; **se faire s.** to get the chop *or* the boot *or Br* the sack
   4 *(marquer vigoureusement)* to slash; *Fig* **la toile avait été sabrée à coups de crayon** great pencil slashes marked the canvas
   5 *(bâcler)* to botch, to bungle
   6 *(ouvrir)* **s. le champagne** to crack open a bottle of champagne *(originally, using a sabre)*
   7 *Vulg (posséder sexuellement)* to poke, *Br* to shaft
   USAGE ABSOLU **je vais devoir s.** I'll have to do some drastic editing

sabretache [sabrətaʃ] NF *Hist* sabretache

sabreur [sabrœr] NM **1** *Escrime* fencer *(specializing in the sabre)* **2** *Mil* sabreur

saburral, -e, -aux, -ales [sabyral, -o] ADJ *Vieilli Méd (langue)* furred, coated

saburre [sabyr] NF *Vieilli Méd* saburra

sac [sak] NM **1** *(contenant → petit, léger)* bag; *(→ grand, solide)* sack; **s. à bandoulière** shoulder bag; **s. de billes** bag of marbles; *Vieilli* **s. de classe** *ou* **d'école** satchel, school bag; **s. de couchage** sleeping bag; **s. à dos** rucksack, knapsack; *Aut* **s. gonflable** airbag; **s. à main** *(à poignée)* *Br* handbag, *Am* purse; *(à bandoulière)* shoulder bag; **s. de marin** kitbag; *Mil* **s. à munitions** cartridge pouch; **s. à ouvrage** workbag, sewing bag; **s. à pain** bread bag *(made of cloth)*; **s. en papier** paper bag; **s. de plage** beach bag; **s. (en) plastique** plastic bag; *(solide et grand)* *Br* plastic carrier (bag), *Am* large plastic bag; **s. à pommes de terre** potato sack; **s. à poussière** *(d'un aspirateur)* dust bag; **s. à provisions** shopping bag; **s. de sable** *Mil* sandbag; *Sport* punchbag; **s. seau** bucket bag; *Fam* **s. à viande** inner sheet■ *(of a sleeping bag)*; **s. de voyage** overnight *or* travelling bag; **je ne prendrai pas de valise, juste un s.** I won't pack a suitcase, just an overnight bag
   2 *(contenu → petit, moyen)* bag, bagful; *(→ grand)* sack, sackful
   3 *Anciennement Fam (dix francs)* ten francs■; **dix sacs** a hundred francs■
   4 *Anat & Bot* sac; **s. lacrymal** lacrymal sac; **s. membraneux** cyst
   5 *Rel* **le s. et la cendre** sackcloth and ashes
   6 *(pillage)* sack, pillage; **mettre qch à s.** *(ville, région)* to ransack *or* to plunder sth; *(maison)* to ransack sth
   7 *(locutions)* *Fam* **méfie-toi, c'est un s. de nœuds, leur affaire** that business of theirs is a real hornets' nest; *Fam* **voyons un peu ce s. d'embrouilles!** let's try and sort out this muddle!; **s. à malices** bag of tricks; *Fam* **c'est un s. d'os** he's/she's all skin and bone *or* a bag of bones; *Fam* **s. à puces** *(chien)* fleabag; *Fam* **s. à vin** drunk, lush; *Littéraire* **homme de s.**

et de corde rogue, jailbird; **être fagoté** *ou* **ficelé comme un s.** to look like a feather bed tied in the middle; *Fam* **ça y est, l'affaire est** *ou* **c'est dans le s.!** it's as good as done!, it's in the bag!; **ils sont tous à mettre dans le même s.** they're all as bad as each other; **attention, ne mettons pas racisme et sexisme dans le même s.!** let's not lump racism and sexism together!; *Fam Vieilli* **avoir le (gros) s.** to be loaded, to be rolling in it; *Fam Vieilli* **épouser le (gros) s.** to marry (into) money

saccade [sakad] NF jerk, jolt, (sudden) start; **après quelques saccades, le moteur s'arrêta** the engine jolted to a halt
☐ **par saccades** ADV jerkingly, joltingly, in fits and starts; **la voiture avançait par saccades** the car was lurching *or* jerking forward; **elle parlait par saccades** she spoke haltingly *or* in a disjointed manner

saccadé, -e [sakade] ADJ *(pas)* jerky; *(mouvement)* disjointed; *(voix)* halting; *(débit)* jerky, staccato; *(respiration)* irregular

saccader [3] [sakade] VT *Équitation (rênes)* to jerk

saccage [sakaʒ] NM *(wanton)* destruction; **quel s.!** what a mess!

saccager [17] [sakaʒe] VT 1 *(dévaster → maison, parc)* to wreck, to wreak havoc in, to devastate; *(→ matériel, livres)* to wreck, to ruin; *(→ cultures)* to lay waste, to devastate; **le village a été saccagé par l'inondation/par le tourbillon** the village was devastated by the flood/by the hurricane; **les cambrioleurs ont (tout) saccagé (dans) le salon** the burglars wrecked (everything in) the living room
2 *(piller → ville, région)* to lay waste, to sack

saccageur, -euse [sakaʒœr, -øz] NM,F vandal

saccharase [sakaraz] NF *Chim* saccharase

saccharate [sakarat] NM *Chim* saccharate

saccharide [sakarid] NM *Chim* saccharide

saccharifère [sakarifɛr] ADJ *Chim* sacchariferous

saccharification [sakarifikasjɔ̃] NF *Chim* saccharification, saccharization

saccharifier [9] [sakarifje] VT *Chim* to saccharify, to saccharize

saccharimètre [sakarimɛtr] NM *Chim* saccharimeter

saccharimétrie [sakarimetri] NF *Chim* saccharimetry

saccharimétrique [sakarimetrik] ADJ *Chim* saccharimetric

saccharin, -e [sakarɛ̃, -in] ADJ sugar *(avant n)*, saccharine
☐ **saccharine** NF saccharin

saccchariné, -e [sakarine] ADJ saccharined

saccharoïde [sakarɔid] ADJ *Minér* saccharoidal

saccharomyces [sakarɔmisɛs] NM saccharomyces

saccharose [sakaroz] NM *Chim* saccharose

sacciforme [saksifɔrm] ADJ sacciform, saccular

sacco [sako] NM *(siège)* beanbag

saccule [sakyl] NM *Anat* saccule

sacculine [sakylin] NF *Zool (crustacé)* parasitic barnacle

SACD [ɛsasede] NF *(abrév* **Société des auteurs et compositeurs dramatiques**) = association of writers and performers founded by Beaumarchais in 1777 which protects copyright and ensures royalties are paid

SACEM, Sacem [sasɛm] NF *Mus (abrév* **Société des auteurs, compositeurs et éditeurs de musique)** = body responsible for collecting and distributing royalties, *Br* ≃ Performing Rights Society, *Am* ≃ Copyright Royalty Tribunal

sacerdoce [sasɛrdɔs] NM 1 *Rel* priesthood 2 *(vocation)* vocation, calling; **l'enseignement est un s.** teaching is a real vocation *or* calling; **la vie d'un militant est un s.** being a militant calls for great dedication

sacerdotal, -e, -aux, -ales [sasɛrdɔtal, -o] ADJ priestly, sacerdotal

sachant *voir* **savoir**

sachée [saʃe] NF bagful

sachem [saʃɛm] NM sachem

sacherie [saʃri] NF bag and sack trade

sachet [saʃɛ] NM 1 *(petit sac)* (small) bag; **s. de lavande** lavender bag *or* sachet; **s. pour garniture périodique** sanitary disposal bag
2 *(dose → de soupe, d'entremets)* packet, sachet; *(→ d'herbes aromatiques)* sachet; **un s.**

d'aspirine a dose of aspirin; **un s. de thé** a teabag; **du thé en sachets** teabags; **soupe en sachets** packet soup
3 *Belg (sac)* bag; **s. poubelle** *Br* dustbin *or Am* garbage can liner, binbag

sachet-cuisson [saʃɛkɥisɔ̃] *(pl* **sachets-cuissons)** NM *(de riz)* bag *(in which rice is boiled)*; **en s.** boil-in-the-bag

sacoche [sakɔʃ] NF 1 *(besace → du facteur)* bag, mailbag, *Br (→ du vélo)* saddlebag, *Br* pannier 3 *(d'encaisseur)* money bag 4 *Belg & Can (sac à main) Br* handbag, *Am* purse

sac-poubelle [sakpubɛl] *(pl* **sacs-poubelle)** NM *Br* dustbin *or Am* garbage can liner, binbag

sacquer [3] [sake] *Fam* VT 1 *(employé)* **s. qn** to give sb the *Br* sack *or Am* ax, *Br* to sack *or Am* to can sb; **se faire s.** to get the *Br* sack *or Am* ax
2 *(étudiant)* to *Br* mark *or Am* grade strictly[*]; **me suis encore fait s. par le prof!** I got another rotten *Br* mark *or Am* grade from the teacher!; **elle va se faire s. à l'examen** she'll get slaughtered in the exam
3 *(locution)* **il ne peut pas la s.** he can't stand (the sight of) her
USAGE ABSOLU **le prof de maths saque vachement** the *Br* maths *or Am* math teacher is a really tough *Br* marker *or Am* grader

sacral, -e, -aux, -ales [sakral, -o] ADJ sacred

sacralisation [sakralizasjɔ̃] NF 1 *(d'une chose profane)* **notre époque voit la s. de la liberté individuelle** today, individual freedom is considered to be sacred *or* a sacred right; **la s. des ancêtres permet à cette société de faire face à la mort** the sacred respect they have for their ancestors is this society's way of coping with death 2 *Méd* sacralization

sacraliser [3] [sakralize] VT to regard as sacred

sacramentaire [sakramɑ̃tɛr] *Rel* NM *(livre de prières)* sacramentary
NMF sacramentarian, sacramentary

sacramental, -aux [sakramɑ̃tal, -o] NM sacramental

sacramentel, -elle [sakramɑ̃tɛl] ADJ 1 *Rel* sacramental 2 *Fig Littér (moment, paroles)* ritual, sacramental

sacrant, -e [sakrɑ̃, -ɑ̃t] ADJ *Can Fam* 1 *(fâcheux)* annoying[*], bothersome; **cet accident est bien s.!** this accident is a real pain! 2 **au plus s.** as quickly as possible[*]

sacre [sakr] NM 1 *(d'un empereur)* coronation and anointment; *(d'un évêque)* consecration; **recevoir le prix Goncourt, c'est le s. pour un écrivain** being awarded the prix Goncourt is the crowning achievement of a writer's career 2 *Orn* saker 3 *Can (juron)* swear word, expletive *(usually the name of a religious object)*

'Le Sacre' *David* 'Anointing of Napoleon'

'Le Sacre du printemps' *Stravinski* 'The Rite of Spring'

sacré, -e [sakre] ADJ 1 *Rel (édifice)* sacred, holy; *(art, textes, musique)* sacred, religious; *(animal)* sacred; **dans l'enceinte sacrée** within the place of worship; **le S. Collège** the Sacred College (of Cardinals)
2 *(devoir, promesse)* sacred, sacrosanct; *(droit)* sacred, hallowed; **les lois sacrées de l'hospitalité** the sacred laws of hospitality; **sa voiture, c'est s.!** his/her car is sacred!; **rien de plus s. que sa promenade après le repas** his/her after-dinner walk is sacrosanct
3 *(avant le nom) Fam (en intensif)* **j'ai un s. mal de dents!** I've got raging toothache!; **j'ai un s. boulot en ce moment!** I've got a hell of a lot of work on at the moment!; **il a un s. culot!** he's got a lot of nerve!; **elle a eu une sacrée vie** she's had quite a life; **c'est un s. cuisinier, ton mari!** your husband is a damn good cook *or* a terrific cook!; *aussi Ironique* **s. Marcel, toujours le mot pour rire!** good old Marcel, never a dull moment with him!; **s. farceur!** you old devil!; **c'est un s. veinard** he's a lucky *or Br* jammy devil!; **t'as eu une sacrée veine!** you were damn lucky!; *très Fam* **un s. con** a total *Br* arsehole *or Am*

asshole; *très Fam* **un s. fouteur de merde** a hell of a shit-stirrer; **c'est un s. numéro** he's quite a character *or* case!; **cette sacrée bagnole est encore en panne** the damn *or Br* bloody car's broken down again
4 *(avant le nom) Fam (satané)* damned, blasted; **s. nom de nom!** damn and blast it!; **s. nom de Dieu!** bloody hell!; **s. nom d'un chien!** *Br* damn it!, *Am* goddamn!
5 *Anat* sacral; **plexus s.** sacral plexus
NM **le s.** the sacred

sacrebleu [sakrəblø] EXCLAM *Arch* zounds!; *Hum* hell's bells!

Sacré-Cœur [sakrekœr] NM 1 *(édifice)* **le S., la basilique du S.** Sacré-Cœur *(one of the landmarks of Paris, the church situated on the Butte Montmartre)* 2 *(fête)* **le S., la fête du S.** the (Feast of the) Sacred Heart

Culture

LE SACRÉ-CŒUR

Perched at the top of "la butte Montmartre" (Montmartre Hill, in the north of Paris), the Sacré-Cœur basilica, with its neo-Byzantine architecture, is one of the most distinctive landmarks of the Paris skyline. It was built over a period of nearly 40 years, from 1875 to 1914. The decision to build it was taken in 1873 in the aftermath of the revolutionary insurrection of the Paris Commune (see note at entry "Commune"). Indeed, the pro-monarchy ultra-Conservative and ultra-religious cabinet of President MacMahon and Prime Minister duc de Broglie (which took office in 1873) were determined to restore what they called "l'ordre moral" ("moral order") after the decadence and irreligiosity that in their eyes had characterized the Paris Commune. The Sacré-Cœur basilica was therefore built in a spirit of atonement for the events of the insurrection and was meant as a symbol of the return to a strict social, moral and religious order, visible from all over Paris.

sacredieu [sakrədjø] EXCLAM *Arch* zounds!; *Hum* hell's bells!

sacrement [sakrəmɑ̃] NM sacrament; **les derniers sacrements** the last rites

sacrément [sakremɑ̃] ADV *très Fam* damn, *Br* bloody; **il s'est s. foutu de notre gueule** he made a total damn *or Br* bloody fool of us; **il est s. radin, celui-là!** he's so damn *or Br* bloody tight!; **il fait s. froid** it's damn *or Br* bloody cold

sacrer [3] [sakre] VT 1 *(empereur)* to crown and anoint, *Arch* to sacre; *(évêque)* to consecrate; **s. qn roi/empereur** to crown sb king/emperor
2 *(nommer, instituer)* to consecrate; **on l'a sacré meilleur acteur du siècle** he was acclaimed *or* hailed as the greatest actor of the century; **il a été sacré champion de France en 2003** he won the French championship in 2003, he was crowned French champion in 2003
3 *Can Fam (donner)* to give[*]; **s. une claque à qn** to slap sb, to give sb a slap
4 *Can Fam (mettre)* to chuck; **s. qn dehors** to chuck sb out
5 *Can Fam* **s. le** *ou* **son camp** *(s'en aller)* to beat it, *Br* to bugger off
VI *Can & Vieilli* to swear, to curse

sacret [sakre] NM *Orn* sakeret

sacreur, -euse [sakrœr, -øz] NM,F *Can* swearer, person who swears a lot

sacrifiable [sakrifjabl] ADJ expendable

sacrificateur, -trice [sakrifikatœr, -tris] NM,F *Antiq* sacrificer; **le grand s.** the (Jewish) High Priest

sacrifice [sakrifis] NM 1 *Rel* sacrifice, offering; **offrir qch en s. à Dieu** to offer sth as a sacrifice to God, to sacrifice sth to God; **offrir qn en s. aux divinités** to sacrifice sb to the gods; **le s. de la Croix** the Sacrifice of the Cross
2 *(effort, compromis)* sacrifice; **je n'ai pas le goût du s.** I have no desire to sacrifice myself; **faire des sacrifices/un s.** to make sacrifices/a sacrifice; **sacrifices financiers** financial sacrifices; **elle a fait de grands sacrifices pour monter la pièce/pour ses enfants** she's sacrificed a lot to put on the play/for her children;

faire le s. de sa vie pour qn to lay down or to sacrifice one's life for sb

❑ au sacrifice de PRÉP at the cost of; au s. de sa vie at the cost of his/her own life; au s. de mon bien-être personnel to the detriment of or at the cost of my personal well-being

sacrificiel, -elle [sakrifisjɛl] ADJ 1 Rel sacrificial 2 Métal sacrificial

sacrifié, -e [sakrifje] ADJ sacrificed, lost; (prix) rock-bottom; (article) at a rock-bottom price; prix sacrifiés! (sur panneau) rock-bottom prices!; la génération sacrifiée the lost generation

NM,F (sacrificial) victim

sacrifier [9] [sakrifje] VT 1 Rel to sacrifice; Fig c'est toute une génération qui a été sacrifiée a whole generation was sacrificed

2 (renoncer à → carrière, santé) to sacrifice (à for or to); (→ loisirs) to give up (à for or to); s. sa vie to make the ultimate sacrifice; s. sa vie à une cause to devote one's (entire) life to a cause; il a sacrifié sa vie pour sa patrie he sacrificed or laid down his life for his country; s. ses amis à sa carrière to sacrifice one's friends to one's career; s. l'emploi au nom de la rentabilité to sacrifice jobs for profits

3 Com (articles) to sell at rock-bottom prices; je les sacrifie, Mesdames! ladies, I'm giving them away!

❑ sacrifier à VT IND 1 Rel to sacrifice to; s. aux idoles to sacrifice to idols

2 (se conformer à) to conform to; s. à la mode to conform to or to go along with (the dictates of) fashion; à Noël, sacrifiez à la tradition keep tradition alive at Christmas

►se sacrifier VPR to sacrifice oneself; se s. pour son pays/pour ses enfants to sacrifice oneself for one's country/for one's children; se s. pour la bonne cause to sacrifice oneself in a good cause; Fam Hum il reste des frites – allez, je me sacrifie! there are some chips left over – oh well, I'll force them down!

sacrilège [sakrilɛʒ] ADJ sacrilegious

NMF profaner

NM 1 Rel sacrilege, profanation 2 Fig (crime) sacrilege, crime; ce serait un s. de retoucher la photo it would be criminal or a sacrilege to touch up the photograph; Hum je mets toujours un peu d'eau dans mon vin – s.! I always put a drop of water in my wine – that's sacrilege!

sacripant [sakripã] NM Vieilli scoundrel, rogue, scallywag

sacristain [sakristɛ̃] NM 1 Rel (catholique) sacristan; (protestant) sexton 2 Culin = small puff pastry cake in the shape of a paper twist

sacristi [sakristi] EXCLAM Vieilli (exprimant l'étonnement) heavens!; (exprimant la colère) Great Scott!

sacristie [sakristi] NF (d'une église catholique) sacristy; (d'une église protestante) vestry

sacristine [sakristin] NF sacristan

sacro-iliaque [sakroiljak] (pl sacro-iliaques) ADJ sacroiliac; articulation s. sacroiliac joint

sacro-saint, -e [sakrosɛ̃, -ɛ̃t] (mpl sacro-saints, fpl sacro-saintes) ADJ 1 Vieilli sacrosanct 2 Fam (intouchable) sacred, sacrosanct

sacrum [sakrɔm] NM sacrum

SADC [ɛsadese] NF Écon (abrév Southern African Development Community) SADC

sadducéen, -enne [sadyseɛ̃, -ɛn] Rel ADJ Sadducean

NM,F Sadducee

sadique [sadik] ADJ sadistic

NMF sadist

sadique-anal, -e [sadikanal] (mpl sadiques-anaux [-o], fpl sadiques-anales) ADJ anal, anal-sadistic

sadiquement [sadikmã] ADV sadistically

sadisme [sadism] NM sadism

sado [sado] Fam (abrév sadique) ADJ sadistic▪; il est un peu s. he's a bit of a sadist

NMF sadist▪

sado-maso [sadomazo] (pl sado-masos) Fam (abrév sadomasochiste) ADJ SM, S & M; il a des tendances sado-masos he's into S & M, he has S & M tendencies

NMF sadomasochist▪; c'est un s. he's into S & M

sadomasochisme [sadomazɔʃism] NM sadomasochism

sadomasochiste [sadomazɔʃist] ADJ sadomasochistic

NMF sadomasochist

saducéen, -enne = sadducéen

SAE [ɛsaə] (abrév Society of Automotive Engineers) ADJ INV SAE

NF SAE

safari [safari] NM safari; faire un s. to go on (a) safari

safari-photo [safarifoto] (pl safaris-photos) NM photographic or camera safari

SAFER, Safer [safɛr] NF Agr (abrév Société d'aménagement foncier et d'établissement rural) = agency entitled to buy land and earmark it for agricultural use

safran [safrã] NM 1 Bot & Culin saffron 2 Naut rudder blade

ADJ INV saffron (avant n), saffron-yellow

safrané, -e [safrane] ADJ 1 (teinte) saffron (avant n), saffron-yellow 2 Culin saffron-flavoured

safraner [3] [safrane] VT Culin to flavour with saffron, to saffron

safre [safr] NM sapphire glass

saga [saga] NF Littérature saga

sagace [sagas] ADJ sharp, acute, Sout sagacious

sagacité [sagasite] NF judiciousness, wisdom, Sout sagacity; avec s. shrewdly, judiciously; pour une fois, il a fait preuve de s. for once, he behaved shrewdly

sagaie [sagɛ] NF assagai, assegai

sagard [sagar] NM (dans les Vosges) sawmill worker

sage [saʒ] ADJ 1 (tranquille, obéissant) good, well-behaved; sois s., Paul! (recommandation) be a good boy, Paul!; (remontrance) behave yourself, Paul!; les enfants ont été sages the children behaved themselves; l'école l'a rendu plus s. school has quietened him down; être s. comme une image to be as good as gold

2 (sensé, raisonnable → personne) wise, sensible; (→ avis, conduite, décision) wise, sensible, reasonable; une politique peu s. an unwise policy, not a very sensible policy; le plus s. serait de... the most sensible thing (to do) would be...; il serait plus s. que tu prennes une assurance it would be wiser for you to take out insurance

3 (sobre → tenue) modest, sober; (→ robe) demure; (→ vie sentimentale) quiet; (→ film, livre) restrained, understated; (→ goûts) tame, Péj unadventurous; elle était habillée de façon très s. she was very soberly dressed; cette année, la mode est très s. the demure look is in this year

4 Euph Vieilli (chaste) elle est s. she's a good girl

NM 1 (personne) wise person; un vieux s. a wise old man

2 Pol une commission de sages an advisory committee

3 Antiq sage

sage-femme [saʒfam] (pl sages-femmes) NF midwife; un homme s. a male midwife

sagement [saʒmã] ADV 1 (tranquillement) quietly, nicely; attends-moi s. ici, Marie wait for me here like a good girl, Marie; il est en train de dessiner bien s. he's drawing nice and quietly 2 (raisonnablement) wisely, sensibly; il a s. refusé he quite wisely or sensibly refused 3 (pudiquement) elle baissa s. les yeux she modestly lowered her eyes

sagesse [saʒɛs] NF 1 (discernement → d'une personne) good sense, insight, wisdom; (→ d'une décision, d'une suggestion) good sense, wisdom; la s. voudrait que tu refuses you'd be better advised or it'd be wiser to refuse; elle a eu la s. de ne pas en parler she was wise or sensible enough not to mention it; elle n'a pas eu la s. d'attendre she wasn't sensible enough or didn't have the good sense to wait; agir avec s. to act wisely or sensibly; plein de s. (remarque) very sensible; (décision) very sensible or wise; la s. des nations popular wisdom

2 (obéissance) good behaviour; elle n'a pas été d'une grande s. aujourd'hui! she wasn't particularly well behaved today!

3 (sobriété → d'une toilette, d'un livre) soberness, tameness; (→ d'une vie sentimentale)

quietness; la trop grande s. de leur projet leur fera du tort the lack of ambition of their project will work against them

4 Euph (chasteté) proper behaviour

sagette [saʒɛt] NF 1 Vieilli (flèche) arrow 2 Bot arrowhead

sagine [saʒin] NF Bot pearlwort, pearlgrass

Sagittaire [saʒitɛr] NM 1 Astron Sagittarius 2 Astrol Sagittarius; être S. to be Sagittarius or a Sagittarian

sagittaire [saʒitɛr] NF arrowhead

sagittal, -e, -aux, -ales [saʒital, -o] ADJ Anat & Math sagittal

sagitté, -e [saʒite] ADJ Bot sagittate

sagou [sagu] NM sago

sagouin, -e [sagwɛ̃, -in] NM,F Fam (personne → malpropre) filthy pig; (→ incompétente) slob; travailler comme un s. to be a sloppy worker; manger comme un s. to eat like a pig

NM Zool marmoset, sagouin

❑ sagouine NF Can (en acadien) 1 (femme de ménage) cleaning woman, charwoman 2 (femme aux mœurs douteuses) loose woman

sagoutier [sagutje] NM Bot sago palm

Sahara [saara] NM le (désert du) S. the Sahara (desert); au S. in the Sahara; le S. occidental the Western Sahara

saharien, -enne [saarjɛ̃, -ɛn] ADJ (gén) Saharan; (troupes) desert (avant n); Fig (température) scorching, sizzling

NM Ling Saharan

❑ Saharien, -enne NM,F Saharan

❑ saharienne NF (veste) safari jacket

Sahel [saɛl] NM le S. the Sahel

sahélien, -enne [saeljɛ̃, -ɛn] ADJ Sahelian

❑ Sahélien, -enne NM,F Sahelian

sahib [saib] NM sahib

sahraoui, -e [sarawi] ADJ Sahrawi, from Western Sahara, of Western Sahara

❑ Sahraoui, -e NM,F Sahrawi, Western Saharan

saï [sai] NM Zool capuchin monkey

Saïda [saida] NM Saida

saie[1] [sɛ] NF Tex sagum

saie[2] [sɛ] NF Tech goldsmith's bench brush

saïga [sajga] NM Zool saiga

saignant, -e [sɛɲã, -ãt] ADJ 1 Culin (steak) rare 2 (blessure) bleeding

saignée [sɛɲe] NF 1 Méd bleeding (UNCOUNT), bloodletting (UNCOUNT); faire une s. à qn to bleed sb, to let sb's blood

2 (pertes humaines) la terrible s. de la Première Guerre mondiale the terrible slaughter of the First World War

3 Anat à la s. du bras at the crook of the arm

4 (dépenses) drain; des saignées dans le budget drains on the budget

5 (entaille) notch; Constr (dans un mur, pour un tuyau, pour un câble) hole; faire une s. sur un pin to tap a pine tree

6 (rigole) drainage channel

7 Tech (de tournage) sideways kerf

8 Mines kerf, undercut

saignement [sɛɲmã] NM bleeding; s. de nez nosebleed, Spéc epistaxis

saigner [4] [sɛɲe] VI 1 (plaie, blessé) to bleed; je saigne du nez my nose is bleeding, I've got a nosebleed; elle a tendance à s. du nez she tends to get nosebleeds; il saigne de la bouche (coupure superficielle) his mouth is bleeding; (hémorragie interne) he's bleeding from the mouth; Fig c'est une plaie qui saigne encore it's an open wound, it still rankles; s. comme un bœuf to bleed profusely

2 Fig Littéraire son cœur saigne à cette pensée his/her heart bleeds at the thought

VT 1 (malade, animal) to bleed; (cochon) to stick

2 (faire payer → contribuable) to bleed, to fleece; (épuiser → pays) to drain the resources of, to drain or to suck the lifeblood from; s. qn à blanc to bleed sb dry, to clean sb out

3 Fam (tuer à l'arme blanche) to stab to death▪

4 (arbre) to tap

5 (fossé) to cut

VI Fam ça va s. there's going to be trouble; c'est France–All Blacks aujourd'hui, ça va s.! France are playing the All Blacks today, the fur's going to fly!

▸**se saigner** VPR **se s. pour qn** to work one's fingers to the bone for sb; **se s. aux quatre veines pour qn** to bleed oneself dry for sb

saigneur [sɛɲœr] NM slaughterer, slaughterman

saigneux, -euse [sɛɲø, -øz] ADJ bleeding

saillant, -e [sajɑ̃, -ɑ̃t] ADJ 1 (en relief → veines) prominent; (→ os, tendon, menton) protruding; (→ muscle, yeux) bulging, protruding; (→ rocher) protruding; (→ corniche) projecting; **avoir les pommettes saillantes** to have prominent or high cheekbones
2 (remarquable → trait, fait) salient, outstanding; **l'ouvrage est plein de traits saillants** the work is full of striking features; **les faits saillants de l'année** the highlights of the year
NM 1 (de fortification) salient
2 (angle) salient angle

saillie [saji] NF 1 (d'un mur, d'une montagne) ledge; (d'un os) protuberance; **faire s., être en s.** (balcon, roche) to jut out; **une des briques faisait s.** one of the bricks was jutting or sticking out 2 Constr projection 3 Littéraire (trait d'esprit) sally, witticism, flash of wit 4 Zool covering, serving

saillir[1] [32] [sajir] VT Zool to cover, to serve

saillir[2] [50] [sajir] VI (rocher, poutre) to project, to jut out; (menton) to protrude; (os) to protrude, to stick out; (yeux) to bulge, to protrude; (muscle, veine) to stand out, to bulge; **l'effort faisait s. les veines de son cou** the veins on his/her neck were swelling or bulging with the strain

saïmiri [saimiri] NM Zool squirrel monkey

sain, -e [sɛ̃, sɛn] ADJ 1 (robuste → enfant) healthy, robust; (→ cheveux, peau) healthy; (→ dent) sound, healthy; **des dents très saines** teeth in perfect condition, healthy teeth; **être s. d'esprit** to be sane; **s. de corps et d'esprit** sound in mind and body; **un esprit s. dans un corps s.** a healthy mind in a healthy body
2 (en bon état → charpente, fondations, structure) sound; (→ situation financière, entreprise, gestion) sound, healthy; (→ viande) good; **ne gardez que les parties saines de l'ananas** keep only the unblemished parts of the pineapple; **la gestion de l'entreprise n'était pas saine** the company was mismanaged
3 (salutaire → alimentation, mode de vie) wholesome, healthy; (→ air, climat) healthy, invigorating; **tu ne devrais pas rester enfermé toute la journée, ce n'est pas s.** you shouldn't stay in all day long, it's not good for you or it's unhealthy
4 (irréprochable → opinion) sane, sound; (→ lectures) wholesome; **son rapport avec sa fille n'a jamais été très s.** his/her relationship with his/her daughter was never very healthy
5 Naut safe
❑ **sain et sauf, saine et sauve** ADJ safe and sound, unhurt, unharmed; **j'en suis sorti s. et sauf** I escaped unharmed or without a scratch

sainbois [sɛ̃bwa] NM Bot spurge flax

saindoux [sɛ̃du] NM lard

sainement [sɛnmɑ̃] ADV 1 (hygiéniquement) healthily; **se nourrir s.** to eat wholesome or healthy food; **vivre s.** to lead a healthy life 2 (sagement) soundly; **juger s. (de)** to make a sound judgment (on)

sainfoin [sɛ̃fwɛ̃] NM Bot sainfoin

saint, -e [sɛ̃, sɛ̃t] ADJ 1 (après le nom) (sacré → lieu, livre, image, guerre) holy; **la semaine sainte** Holy Week; **le s. carême** chrism; **les Saintes Écritures** the Scriptures; **la Sainte Église** the Holy Church; **la Sainte Famille** the Holy Family; **les saints Innocents** the Innocents; **leur s. patron** their patron saint; **le s. sacrement** the sacrament of Holy Communion, the Eucharist; Fam **elle le promène comme le s. sacrement** she shows it off as if it was the crown jewels; **le s. sacrifice de la messe** the Holy Sacrifice of the Mass; **le s. suaire (de Turin)** the Turin Shroud; **la Sainte Vierge** the Blessed Virgin; **une petite sainte vierge en ivoire** an ivory miniature of the Blessed Virgin
2 (canonisé) Saint; **s. Ambroise** Saint Ambrose; **s. André** Saint Andrew; **sainte Anne** Saint Anne; **s. Antoine** Saint Anthony; **s. Augustin** Saint Augustine; **s. Benoît** Saint Benedict; **sainte Catherine** Saint Catherine; Fig

coiffer sainte Catherine = to be 25 and still unmarried on Saint Catherine's Day (25th November); **sainte Cécile** Saint Cecilia; **s. Christophe** Saint Christopher; **s. Clément** Saint Clement; **s. Dominique** Saint Dominic; **sainte Élisabeth** Saint Elizabeth; **s. Étienne** Saint Stephen; **s. Eustache** Saint Eustace; **s. François (d'Assise)** Saint Francis (of Assisi); **sainte Geneviève** Saint Genevieve; **s. Georges** Saint George; **s. Jean** Saint John; **s. Jean-Baptiste** Saint John the Baptist; **s. Jérôme** Saint Jerome; **s. Joseph** Saint Joseph; **s. Julien** Saint Julian; **s. Louis** Saint Louis; **s. Luc** Saint Luke; **s. Marc** Saint Mark; **s. Matthieu** Saint Matthew; **s. Michel** Saint Michael; **s. Nicolas** Saint Nicholas; **s. Patrick** Saint Patrick; **s. Paul** Saint Paul; **s. Pierre** Saint Peter; **s. Sylvestre** Saint Sylvester; **sainte Thérèse d'Avila** Saint Teresa of Avila; **s. Thomas** Saint Thomas; **s. Thomas d'Aquin** Thomas Aquinas
3 (avant le nom) (exemplaire) holy; **le curé est un s. homme** the priest is a holy man; **sa mère était une sainte femme** his/her mother was a real saint; **être saisi** ou **pris d'une sainte colère/indignation** to be seething with righteous anger/indignation
4 (en intensif) **toute la sainte journée** the whole blessed day; **j'ai une sainte horreur des araignées** I have a real horror of spiders
NM,F 1 Rel saint; **le s. du jour** the Saint of the day; **les saints de glace** = the three Saints (Mamert, Gervase and Pancras) on whose name days (11, 12 and 13 May) late frosts often occur, according to tradition; **les saints du dernier jour** the Latter-Day Saints, the Mormons; **il lasserait la patience d'un s.** he'd try the patience of a saint; **je ne sais (plus) à quel s. me vouer** I don't know which way to turn (any more); Prov **comme on connaît ses saints on les honore** = treat each person according to their merits
2 Beaux-Arts (statue or effigy of a) saint
3 Fig saint; **vous êtes une sainte** you're a saint; **les promoteurs ne sont pas des petits saints** property developers are no angels; Fam **arrête de faire ton petit s.** stop being such a prig!
NM Rel **le s. des saints** the Holy of Holies; Fig the inner sanctum
❑ **saint, -e** ADJ (avec trait d'union) (dans des noms de lieux, de fêtes) **c'est la S.-Marc aujourd'hui** it's Saint Mark's day today, it's the feast of Saint Mark today; **ils vont à la messe à S.-Augustin** they attend Mass at Saint Augustine's (church)

saint-amour [sɛ̃tamur] NM INV Saint-Amour (wine)

Saint-Barthélémy [sɛ̃bartelemi] NF 1 (le massacre de) **la S.** the Saint Bartholomew's Day Massacre 2 Géog Saint Bart's

---

Culture

LA SAINT-BARTHÉLÉMY

La Saint-Barthélémy (Saint Bartholomew's Day Massacre) has become synonymous with the massacre of French Protestants, or Huguenots, that began in Paris on 23 August 1572. It was probably the single most horrific event in the course of the wars of religion that affected France in the Renaissance. It followed an unsuccessful attempt on the life of the Huguenot leader Gaspard de Coligny, ordered by Catherine de Medici, mother of King Charles IX, who was worried by the influence that Coligny held over her son and his support to the Protestant Netherlands against Catholic Spain. The massacre was made possible by the presence in Paris of a large number of Huguenots for the wedding of Henry of Navarre (later to become King Henry IV of France) and Margaret of Valois. About 3,000 people were murdered in Paris. The massacre then spread to the provinces where many more lost their lives.

---

saint-bernard [sɛ̃bernar] NM INV 1 Zool Saint Bernard (dog) 2 Hum (personne généreuse) **c'est un vrai s.** he's a good Samaritan

saint-crépin [sɛ̃krepɛ̃] NM Fam Vieilli shoemaker's tools▪, grindery▪; Fig **tout le s.** the whole (kit and) caboodle

Saint-Cyr [sɛ̃sir] NM Saint-Cyr military academy

saint-cyrien, -enne [sɛ̃sirjɛ̃, -ɛn] (mpl **saint-cyriens**, fpl **saint-cyriennes**) NM,F (élève) = cadet training at the Saint-Cyr military academy

Saint-Cyr-l'École [sɛ̃sirlekɔl] NF = military training school near Versailles

Saint-Domingue [sɛ̃dɔmɛ̃g] NM Santo Domingo

sainte-barbe [sɛ̃tbarb] (pl **saintes-barbes**) NF Mil (sur navire de guerre) = storeroom for weapons and gunpowder

Sainte-Chapelle [sɛ̃tʃapɛl] NF **la S.** = thirteenth-century church within the Palais de Justice on the Île de la Cité

Sainte-Hélène [sɛ̃telɛn] NF St Helena; **à S.** on St Helena

Sainte-Elme [sɛ̃tɛlm] NM **feu S.** corposant, Saint-Elmo's fire

Sainte-Lucie [sɛ̃tlysi] NF St Lucia; **à S.** in St Lucia

sainte-maure [sɛ̃tmɔr] NM INV Sainte-Maure (cheese)

saintement [sɛ̃tmɑ̃] ADV **vivre s.** to lead a saintly life; **mourir s.** to die a saintly death

Sainte-Mère-Église [sɛ̃tmɛregliz] NF = site of the first Normandy landings when American parachute troops landed there on the night of 5–6 June 1944

saint-émilion [sɛ̃temiljɔ̃] NM INV (vin) Saint Emilion

Saint Empire romain germanique [sɛ̃tɑ̃pirrɔmɛ̃ʒɛrmanik] NM Holy Roman Empire

sainte-nitouche [sɛ̃tnituʃ] (pl **saintes-nitouches**) NF Péj goody-two-shoes; **avec ses airs de s.** looking as though butter wouldn't melt in his/her mouth

Saintes [sɛ̃t] NFPL **les (îles des) S.** the Îles des Saintes

Saint-Esprit [sɛ̃tɛspri] NM **le S.** the Holy Spirit or Ghost; Orn **faire le S.** (oiseau de proie) to hover

sainteté [sɛ̃te] NF 1 (d'une personne) saintliness, godliness; (d'une action, d'une vie) saintliness; (d'un édifice, des Écritures, de la Vierge) holiness, sanctity; (du mariage) sanctity 2 (titre) **Votre S.** Your Holiness; **Sa S. (le pape)** His Holiness (the Pope)

Saint-Étienne [sɛ̃tetjɛn] NM Saint-Étienne

Sainte-Trinité [sɛ̃ttrinite] NF Rel **la S.** the Holy Trinity

saint-florentin [sɛ̃florɑ̃tɛ̃] NM INV Saint-Florentin (cheese)

saint-frusquin [sɛ̃fryskɛ̃] NM INV Fam **tout le s.** the whole caboodle, Br the full monty, Am the whole megilla

Saint-Gall [sɛ̃gal] NM Saint Gall; **le canton de S.** Saint-Gall

Saint-Germain-des-Prés [sɛ̃ʒɛrmɛ̃depre] NM Saint-Germain-des-Prés (area of Paris)

Culture

SAINT-GERMAIN-DES-PRÉS

This is the literary centre of Paris on the left bank of the Seine, famous for its bookshops, publishing houses, literary cafés and nightclubs. Its heyday was in the years following the Second World War, when Sartre and other existentialist intellectuals met regularly in its cafés, and singers and artists such as Juliette Gréco and Boris Vian performed there.

Saint-Glinglin [sɛ̃glɛ̃glɛ̃] NF Fam **attendre jusqu'à la S.** to wait forever or until doomsday; **c'est maintenant qu'il faut le faire, pas à la S.** it has to be done now, not whenever

Saint-Gobain [sɛ̃gɔbɛ̃] NF = large glassmaking company

Saint-Gothard [sɛ̃gɔtar] voir **col**

Saint-Graal [sɛ̃gral] NM **le S.** the (Holy) Grail

Saint-Guy [sɛ̃gi] NF **la danse de S.** Saint Vitus' dance

saint-honoré [sɛ̃tɔnɔre] NM INV = gateau consisting of a layer of caramel-covered profiteroles on top of a layer of pastry

saint-hubert [sɛ̃tybɛr] NM INV Zool bloodhound

Saint-Jacques [sɛ̃ʒak] NF **coquille S.** scallop

Saint-Jacques-de-Compostelle [sɛ̃ʒakdəkɔ̃pɔstɛl] NM Santiago de Compostela

Saint-Jean [sɛ̃ʒɑ̃] NF **la S.** Midsummer's Day; Can **la S.-Baptiste** = the Quebec national day

LA SAINT-JEAN-BAPTISTE

The "Société Saint-Jean-Baptiste" was founded in 1834 by Ludger Duvernay, to protect the Catholic faith and the French language in Canada. In 1927, it obtained from the Taschereau government a proclamation making 24 June, John the Baptist's day, the Quebec national day. From then on, a large parade was held annually on that day in Montreal. The traditional values and heroes of French Canada were displayed on large floats in a celebration of Quebec's past. In 1968, trouble erupted during the parade as a result of the presence of the newly elected Canadian Prime Minister, Pierre Trudeau, and it was subsequently abolished. The celebration was reinstated under the René Lévesque government, in 1977.

Saint-Laurent [sɛloʀɑ̃] **NM le S.** *(fleuve)* the St Lawrence (River); **le golfe du S.** the St Lawrence Seaway

Saint-Malo [sɛmalo] **NM** Saint-Malo

Saint-Marc [sɛmaʀ] **NF la place S.** Saint Mark's Square

saint-marcellin [sɛmaʀsəlɛ̃] **NM INV** = small round cheese produced in the Lyons area

Saint-Marin [sɛmaʀɛ̃] **NM** San Marino; **vivre à S.** to live in San Marino; **aller à S.** to go to San Marino

saint-marinais, -e [sɛmaʀinɛ, -ɛz] **ADJ** San Marinese □ **Saint-Marinais, -e NM,F** San Marinese; **les S.** the San Marinese

Saint-Martin [sɛmaʀtɛ̃] **NM** *Suisse* = holiday held in the canton of Jura around 11 November

Saint-Médard [sɛmedaʀ] **NF** *Prov* **s'il** *ou* **quand il pleut à la S., il pleut quarante jours plus tard** ≃ St Swithin's day if thou dost rain, for forty days it will remain. St Swithin's day if thou be fair, for forty days 'twill rain nae mair

Saint-Michel [sɛmiʃɛl] **NF la S.** Michaelmas

saint-nectaire [sɛnɛktɛʀ] **NM INV** Saint Nectaire *(cheese)*

Saint-Nicolas [sɛnikola] **NF la S.** Saint Nicholas' Day *(6 December, celebrated especially in Belgium and the north of France)*

Saint-Nom-la-Bretèche [sɛ̃nɔ̃labʀətɛʃ] **NM** = village and golf course near Paris where the French Open is held

Saint-Office [sɛtɔfis] **NM** *Hist* **le S.** the Holy Office

saintpaulia [sɛpolja] **NM** *Bot* African violet, saintpaulia

saint-paulin [sɛpolɛ̃] **NM INV** Saint Paulin *(cheese)*

Saint-Père [sɛpɛʀ] *(pl* **Saints-Pères) NM** Holy Father

Saint-Pétersbourg [sɛpetɛʀsbuʀ] **NM** St Petersburg

Saint-Pierre [sɛpjɛʀ] **NM la basilique S.** Saint Peter's Basilica

saint-pierre [sɛpjɛʀ] **NM INV** *Ich* John Dory, Saint Peter's fish

Saint-Pierre-et-Miquelon [sɛpjɛʀemiklɔ̃] **NM** St Pierre and Miquelon

Saint-Sébastien [sɛsebastjɛ̃] **NM** San Sebastian

Saint-Sépulcre [sɛsepylkʀ] **NM le S.** the Holy Sepulchre

Saint-Siège [sɛsjɛʒ] **NM le S.** the Holy See

saint-simonien, -enne [sɛsimɔnjɛ̃, -ɛn] *(mpl* **saint-simoniens,** *fpl* **saint-simoniennes) ADJ** Saint-Simonian □ **NM,F** Saint-Simonian

saint-simonisme [sɛsimɔnism] **NM** Saint-Simonism

Saint-Sylvestre [sɛsilvɛstʀ] **NF la S.** = New Year's Eve; **le réveillon de la S.** = New Year's Eve dinner and party

saint-synode [sɛsinɔd] *(pl* **saints-synodes) NM** *Hist & Rel* Holy Synod

Saint-Valentin [sɛvalɑ̃tɛ̃] **NF la S.** Saint Valentine's Day

Saint-Vincent-de-Paul [sɛvɛsɑ̃dpɔl] **NF la société S.** = Catholic charity founded in 1833

saisi, -e [sezi] **NM,F** *Jur* distrainee □ **saisie NF 1** *Ordinat* keyboarding, keying; **saisie de données** data capture, keyboarding; **saisie automatique/manuelle** automatic/manual input **2** *Typ (clavetage)* keyboarding

3 *Jur (d'une propriété, d'un bien mobilier)* seizure, distraint, distress; *(de produits d'une infraction)* seizure, confiscation; *(d'un bien pour non-paiement des traites)* repossession; **saisie conservatoire** sequestration *or* seizure of goods *(to prevent sale)*; **saisie conservatoire de droit commun** seizure of movable goods; **saisie des droits incorporels** seizure of incorporeal rights; **saisie immobilière** seizure of property; **saisie mobilière** seizure *or* distraint of goods; **saisie des rémunérations** seizure of salary; **faire** *ou* **opérer une saisie** to levy a distress **4** *Naut* seizure, embargo

saisie-appréhension [seziapʀeɑ̃sjɔ̃] *(pl* **saisies-appréhensions) NF** *Jur* = seizure of goods belonging to a creditor from the debtor

saisie-arrêt [seziaʀɛ] *(pl* **saisies-arrêts) NF** *Anciennement Jur* garnishment

saisie-attribution [seziatʀibysjɔ̃] *(pl* **saisies-attributions) NF** *Jur* garnishment

saisie-brandon [sezibʀɑ̃dɔ̃] *(pl* **saisies-brandons) NF** *Anciennement Jur* = distraint by seizure of crops

saisie-contrefaçon [sezikɔ̃tʀəfasɔ̃] *(pl* **saisies-contrefaçons) NF** *Jur* = seizure of counterfeit goods

saisie-exécution [sezigzekysjɔ̃] *(pl* **saisies-exécutions) NF** *Anciennement Jur* distraint (for an auction)

saisie-gagerie [sezigaʒʀi] *(pl* **saisies-gageries) NF** *Jur* = seizure by a court of the property of a tenant who has not paid their rent

saisie-revendication [seziʀəvɑ̃dikasjɔ̃] *(pl* **saisies-revendications) NF** *Jur* seizure under a prior claim

saisie-vente [sezivɑ̃t] *(pl* **saisies-ventes) NF** *Jur* = seizure of movable goods for sale

saisine [sezin] **NF 1** *Jur (d'un héritier)* seisin; **la s. d'un tribunal** the referral of a case to a court **2** *Naut* lashing

saisir [32] [seziʀ] **VT 1** *(avec brusquerie)* to grab (hold of), to seize, to grasp; *(pour porter, déplacer)* to catch (hold of), to take hold of, to grip; *(pour s'approprier)* to snatch; **s. qch au vol** to catch sth in mid-air; **s. un outil par le manche** to take (hold of) a tool by the handle; **s. qn aux épaules** to grab *or* to grip sb by the shoulders; **il m'a saisi par la manche** he grabbed me by the sleeve; **elle saisit ma main** she gripped my hand **2** *(mettre à profit)* to seize, to grab; **s. le moment propice** to choose the right moment; **s. l'occasion de faire qch** to seize *or* to grasp the opportunity to do sth; **s. un prétexte pour faire qch** to seize on a pretext to do something; **s. sa chance** to seize an opportunity; **je n'ai pas su s. ma chance** I missed (out on) my chance, I didn't seize the opportunity; **à s.** *(achat)* a real bargain **3** *(envahir → sujet: colère, terreur, dégoût)* to take hold of, to seize, to grip; **elle a été saisie d'un malaise, un malaise l'a saisie** she suddenly felt faint; **saisi d'étonnement** startled, staggered; **saisie de terreur** terror-stricken; **elle fut saisie de panique** she suddenly panicked; **le froid me saisit** the cold hit me **4** *(impressionner)* to strike, to stun; **la ressemblance entre les deux frères nous a saisis** we were struck by the resemblance between the two brothers; **quand j'ai vu le mort, je suis resté saisi** when I saw the dead man, I was (quite) overcome **5** *Belg (faire sursauter)* to startle **6** *(percevoir → bribes de conversation, mot)* to catch, to get; **je n'ai pas bien saisi son nom** I didn't quite catch his/her name **7** *(comprendre → explications, sens d'une phrase)* to understand, to get, to grasp; **elle a tout de suite saisi de quoi il s'agissait** she immediately grasped *or* got what it was about; **s. la nuance** to see the difference; **as-tu saisi l'allusion?** did you get the hint? **8** *Jur (débiteur, biens)* to seize, to levy distress (upon); *(navire)* to seize, to attach; *(articles prohibés)* to seize, to confiscate; *(tribunal)* to submit *or* to refer a case to; **s. un tribunal d'une affaire** to refer a matter to a court, to lay a matter

before a court; **la justice, saisie de l'affaire, annonce que...** the judicial authorities, apprised of the case, have indicated that...; **la juridiction compétente a été saisie** the case was referred to the appropriate jurisdiction; **l'huissier a fait s. tous ses biens** the bailiff ordered all his/her goods to be seized **9** *Ordinat* to capture; **s. des données (sur clavier)** to keyboard data **10** *Culin* to seal, to sear **11** *Naut (arrimer)* to stow, to secure **USAGE ABSOLU** *(comprendre)* **je ne saisis pas bien** I don't quite get it; **il saisit vite** he's quick (on the uptake); **alors, tu saisis?** do you get it? ► **se saisir VPR 1 se s. de** *(prendre)* to grab (hold of), to grip, to seize; **saisissez-vous de votre arme** grab (hold of) your weapon; **se s. du pouvoir/d'une ville** to seize power/a town **2 se s. de** *(étudier)* to examine; **le conseil doit se s. du dossier** the council will put the file on its agenda **3** *Belg (s'émouvoir)* to feel upset **4** *Belg (sursauter)* to start, to jump, to give a start

saisissable [sezisabl] **ADJ 1** *Jur* distrainable **2** *(perceptible)* perceptible

saisissant, -e [sezisɑ̃, -ɑ̃t] **ADJ 1** *(vif → froid)* biting, piercing **2** *(surprenant → ressemblance)* striking, startling; *(→ récit, spectacle)* gripping; *(→ contraste)* startling **3** *Jur (qui opère ou fait opérer une saisie)* seizing □ **NM,F** *(opérant une saisie)* distrainer, distrainor

saisissement [sezismɑ̃] **NM 1** *(émotion)* shock, rush of emotion; *(surprise)* astonishment, amazement; **pâle de s.** pale with emotion; **je suis resté muet de s. devant tant de beauté** I was dumbfounded by so much beauty **2** *(sensation de froid)* sudden chill; **il éprouva un s. au contact de l'eau glacée** he shivered as he entered the icy water

saison [sɛzɔ̃] **NF 1** *(période de l'année)* season; **en cette s.** at this time of (the) year; **en toutes saisons** all year round; **la s. n'est pas très avancée cette année** the season's a bit late this year; **la belle s.** *(printemps)* the spring months; *(été)* the summer months; **la mauvaise s., la s. froide** the winter months; **à la belle/mauvaise s.** when the weather turns warm/cold; *Littéraire* **la nouvelle s.** springtime, springtide; **la s. sèche** the dry season; **la s. des pluies** the rainy season, the rains **2** *(pour certains travaux, certains produits)* **ce n'est pas encore la s. des jonquilles** the daffodils aren't out yet; **ce n'est pas encore la s. des aubergines** aubergines aren't in season yet; **des fraises! mais ce n'est pas la s.!** strawberries! but it isn't the right time of year *or* it isn't the season for them; **la s. des cerises** the cherry season; **la s. des vendanges** grape-harvesting time; **la s. des amours** the mating season; **la s. de la chasse** *(à courre)* the hunting season; *(à tir)* the shooting season; **la s. de la pêche** the fishing season; *Can* **la s. des sucres** the maple sugar season **3** *(temps d'activité périodique)* season; **la s. théâtrale** the theatre season; **la s. touristique** the tourist season; **une s. sportive** a season; **il a fait deux saisons à Nice** *(footballeur)* he played two seasons for Nice; **faire les saisons** *(barman, femme de chambre)* to do seasonal work **4** *Com* season; **les restaurateurs ont fait une bonne s.** restaurant owners had a good season; **ici la s. commence en juin** the season starts in June here; **en s.** during the season; **en basse** *ou* **en morte s.** off season; **en haute s.** during the high season; **la pleine s.** the busy season; **en pleine s.** at the height of the season; **moyenne s.** shoulder period; **s. creuse** off season, slack season **5** *(cure)* season; **le médecin lui a recommandé une s. dans une station thermale** the doctor recommended that he/she spend a season at a spa **6** *Littéraire (âge de la vie)* age, time of life; **quarante ans est une s. cruelle** forty is a cruel age □ **de saison ADJ 1** *(adapté à la saison)* seasonal;

ce n'est pas un temps de s. this weather's unusual for the time of the year; **être de s.** *(fruit)* to be in season; *(vêtement)* to be seasonable

2 *(opportun)* timely; **tes critiques ne sont pas de s.** this is not the time or place for your criticism

saisonnalité [sɛzɔnalite] NF seasonal nature

saisonnier, -ère [sɛzɔnje, -ɛr] ADJ seasonal, seasonable; **nous avons un temps bien s.** this is just the (right) sort of weather for the time of year

NM *(employé)* seasonal worker; **les saisonniers** seasonal staff

sait *etc voir* **savoir**

saïte [sait] ADJ *Hist* of/from Saïs

sajou [saʒu] NM *Zool* capuchin monkey, sapajou

saké [sake] NM sake

Sakhaline [sakalin] NF Sakhalin

saki [saki] NM *Zool* saki

sakieh [sakje] NF sakieh

sal, -als [sal] NM *Bot* sal (tree)

salace [salas] ADJ *(histoire, allusion)* lewd, *Sout* salacious, lascivious; *(individu)* lecherous, lewd, *Sout* salacious

salacité [salasite] NF *Littéraire* lewdness, salaciousness

salade [salad] NF **1** *Bot* **s. (verte)** lettuce; **acheter une s.** to buy a (head of) lettuce

2 *Culin* salad; **s. de concombre/de haricots** cucumber/bean salad; **champignons/haricots verts en s.** mushroom/green bean salad; *Belg* **s. de blé** lamb's lettuce, corn salad; **s. composée** mixed salad; **s. de fruits** fruit salad; **s. grecque** Greek salad; **s. niçoise** salade niçoise, niçoise salad; **s. russe** Russian salad; **s. verte** green salad

3 *Fam (situation embrouillée)* muddle, mess; **quelle s.!** what a muddle *or* mess!

4 *Fam* **vendre sa s.** to make a pitch▪, to try to sell an idea▪

❑ **salades** NFPL *Fam (mensonges)* tall stories, fibs; **raconter des salades** to tell fibs *or Br* porkies

saladier [saladje] NM **1** *(récipient)* (salad) bowl **2** *(contenu)* **un s. de haricots** a bowlful of beans

salage [salaʒ] NM *Culin & (en travaux publics)* salting

salaire [salɛr] NM **1** *Écon (gén)* pay; *(d'un ouvrier → journalier, hebdomadaire)* wages, pay; *(d'un cadre supérieur)* salary; **un s. de famine** starvation wages; **s. à la tâche** *ou* **aux pièces** pay for piece work, piece rate; **s. après impôts** after-tax salary; **s. de base** basic salary *or* pay; **s. brut** gross pay; **s. de départ, s. d'embauche** starting salary; **s. fixe** fixed salary; **s. hebdomadaire** weekly pay *or* wage; **s. horaire** hourly wage; **s. indexé** index-linked pay; **s. indirect** fringe benefits; **s. mensuel** monthly pay; **s. au mérite** performance-related pay; **s. minimal** minimum wage; **s. minimum** minimum wage; *Agr* **s. minimum agricole garanti** = guaranteed minimum agricultural wage; **s. minimum interprofessionnel de croissance** = index-linked guaranteed minimum wage; *Anciennement* **s. minimum interprofessionnel garanti** = index-linked guaranteed minimum wage; **s. net** take-home pay, net salary; **s. nominal** nominal wage; **s. plafonné** wage ceiling; **s. réel** actual wage; **à s. unique** single-income; **je n'ai pas droit au s. unique** I'm not entitled to *Br* income support *or Am* the welfare benefit for single-income families

2 *Fig (dédommagement)* reward (**de** for); *(punition)* retribution (**de** for); **nous touchons maintenant le s. des années d'inflation** this is the price we have to pay for years of inflation

---

'Le Salaire de la peur' *Clouzot* 'The Wages of Fear'

---

salaison [salɛzɔ̃] NF *(opération)* salting

❑ **salaisons** NFPL *(gén)* salted foods; *(viande, charcuterie)* salt *or* salted meat

salaisonnerie [salɛzɔnri] NF salting industry

salamalecs [salamalɛk] NMPL *Fam* bowing and scraping; **faire des s. à qn** to kowtow to sb, to bow and scrape before sb; **épargnez-moi tous ces s.** spare me the bowing and scraping

Salamandre® [salamɑ̃dr] NF *(poêle)* slow combustion stove

salamandre [salamɑ̃dr] NF *Zool* salamander

Salamanque [salamɑ̃k] NM Salamanca

salami [salami] NM salami

salangane [salɑ̃gan] NF salangane

salant [salɑ̃] ADJ M salt *(avant n)*; **puits s.** brine well

NM salt marsh

salarial, -e, -aux, -ales [salarjal, -o] ADJ *(politique, revendications)* pay *(avant n)*, wage *(avant n)*, salary *(avant n)*; **revenus salariaux** income from salaries

salariat [salarja] NM **1** *(personnes)* wage earners **2** *(mode de rémunération → à la semaine)* (weekly) wages; *(→ au mois)* (monthly) salary **3** *(état)* **le s. ne lui convient pas** being an employee doesn't suit him/her

salarié, -e [salarje] ADJ **1** *(travailleur → au mois)* salaried; *(→ à la semaine)* wage-earning; **êtes-vous s.?** *(non chômeur)* are you in paid employment?; *(non libéral)* are you paid a salary? **2** *(travail)* paid; *(emploi, poste)* salaried

NM,F *(au mois)* salaried employee; *(à la semaine)* wage-earner; **les salariés** the employees; **les salariés de ce pays** this country's workforce

salarier [9] [salarje] VT to put on one's salaried staff; **je voudrais me faire s.** I'd like to get a permanent (salaried) job; **nous préférons ne pas les s.** we'd rather they didn't go on the payroll

salaud [salo] *très Fam* NM bastard, *Am* son-of-a-bitch; **c'est un beau s.** he's a real bastard; **je pars à Tahiti – ben mon s.!** I'm off to Tahiti – you lucky bastard *or Br* sod!

ADJ M **un mec s.** a bastard; **c'est s. de faire/de dire ça** that's a really shitty thing to do/to say, that's a bastard of a thing to do/to say; **il a été s. avec elle** he's been a real bastard to her

salbande [salbɑ̃d] NF *Géol* clay gouge

salchow [salko] NM *Sport* salchow

sale [sal] ADJ **1** *(malpropre)* dirty; **les rues de la ville sont sales** the city streets are dirty; **blanc s.** dirty white; **la façade est blanc s.** the façade is dirty white; **oh que tu es s.!** *(à un enfant)* you dirty thing!; **elle est s. dans son travail** she's messy in her work, she's a messy worker; **il est s. comme un cochon** *ou* **un peigne** *ou* **un porc** he's filthy dirty

2 *(salissant)* dirty; **un travail s.** dirty work

3 *(obscène)* filthy, dirty; **raconter des histoires sales** to tell dirty stories

4 *(avant le nom) Fam (mauvais, désagréable)* nasty; **c'est une s. affaire** it's a nasty business; **c'est un s. boulot** it's a rotten *or* a lousy job; **faire le s. boulot** to do the dirty work; **elle a un s. caractère** she has a filthy *or* a rotten temper; **quel s. temps!** what rotten *or* foul weather!; **il m'a joué un s. tour** he played a dirty trick on me; **s. bête** *(insecte)* nasty creature, *Hum* creepy crawly; *(personne)* nasty character *or Br* piece of work; *très Fam* **avoir une s. tête** *ou* **gueule** *(à faire peur)* to look evil, to be nasty-looking; **il a une s. tête ce matin** *(malade)* he looks under the weather *or Br* off-colour this morning; *(renfrogné)* he's got a face like a thundercloud this morning; **quand je vais lui dire, il va faire une s. tête** he's not going to be very pleased when I tell him; **s. fasciste!** dirty Fascist!

5 *Fam* **pas s.** *(appréciable)* pretty good, not bad

NMF *(personne)* dirty person

NM *Fam* **au s.** in *or* with the dirty washing▪; **ton pantalon est au s.** your trousers are with the dirty washing

salé, -e[1] [sale] ADJ **1** *Culin (beurre, cacahuètes, gâteaux secs)* salted; *(non sucré → mets)* savoury; *(→ goût)* salty; *(conservé dans le sel → morue, porc)* salt *(avant n)*, salted; **ta soupe est trop salée** your soup's too salty

2 *(lac)* salt *(avant n)*; **eau salée** salt water

3 *Fam (exagéré → condamnation)* stiff, heavy; *(→ addition)* steep, stiff; **on a eu une addition salée** the bill was a bit steep

4 *Fam (osé → histoire, plaisanterie)* steamy, X-rated

NM **1 le s.** *(non sucré)* savoury food; *(avec adjonction de sel)* salty food; **il vaut mieux manger le s. avant le sucré** it's better to eat savoury dishes before sweet ones

2 *Culin* salt pork; **petit s.** salted (flank end of) belly pork

ADV **je ne mange pas très s.** I don't like too much salt in my food; **je mange s.** I like my food well salted

salée[2] [sale] NF *Suisse* tart *(consisting of a pastry base topped with cream, cheese sauce etc)*

salement [salmɑ̃] ADV **1** *(malproprement)* dirtily; **qu'il mange s.!** he's such a messy eater! **2** *Fam (beaucoup)* badly▪; *(très) Br* dead, *Am* real; **s. blessé** badly injured; **s. déçu** sorely disappointed; **il a s. vieilli** he's really aged

salep [salɛp] NM *Pharm* salep

saler [3] [sale] VT **1** *Culin (assaisonner)* to salt, to add salt to; *(en saumure)* to pickle, to salt (down)

2 *(chaussée)* to salt

3 *Fam (inculpé)* to throw the book at

4 *Fam (facture)* to inflate; **c'était bon, mais ils ont salé l'addition!** it was good but the bill was a bit steep!; **je me suis fait s.!** I paid through the nose!, I've been stung *or* fleeced!

USAGE ABSOLU *Culin* **je ne sale presque pas** I hardly use any salt

Salerne [salɛrn] NM Salerno

saleron [salrɔ̃] NM small saltcellar

salers [salɛrs] ADJ *(vache)* Salers

NMF Salers cow

NM *(fromage)* Salers *(variety of Cantal cheese)*

salésien, -enne [salezjɛ̃, -ɛn] ADJ Salesian

NM,F Salesian

saleté [salte] NF **1** *(manque de propreté)* dirtiness; **les rues sont d'une s. incroyable** the streets are incredibly dirty *or* filthy; **rajoutez de la lessive en fonction de la s. des vêtements** add more washing powder according to how dirty *or* soiled the clothes are

2 *(tache, crasse)* speck *or* piece of dirt; **il y a des petites saletés dans l'eau** there's some dirt in the water; **tu as une s. sur ta veste** you've got some dirt on your jacket; **il y a des saletés qui bloquent le tuyau** the pipe is blocked up with muck; **faire des saletés** to make a mess; **ne rentre pas avec tes bottes, tu vas faire des saletés** don't come in with your boots on, you'll get dirt everywhere

3 *Fam (chose de mauvaise qualité) Br* rubbish, *Am* trash; **c'est de la s.** it's *Br* rubbish *or Am* trash; **c'est de la vraie s., ces chaussures en plastique** these plastic shoes are total *Br* rubbish *or Am* trash; **à la récréation, ils ne mangent que des saletés** all they eat at break is junk food

4 *(chose nuisible)* foul thing, nuisance; **le liseron, c'est de la s., ça étouffe toutes les fleurs** bindweed is a damned nuisance, it chokes all the flowers; **j'ai attrapé cette s. à la piscine** I caught this blasted thing at the swimming pool; **je dois prendre cette s. avant chaque repas!** I have to take this horrible stuff before every meal!; **quelle s., cette grippe!** this flu is a real pain *or* nuisance!

5 *très Fam (en injure)* **s.!** *(à un homme)* swine!, bastard!; *(à une femme)* bitch!, *Br* cow!; **c'est une vraie s.** *(homme)* he's a real bastard; *(femme)* she's a real bitch; **s. de chien!** damned *or Br* bloody dog!; **quelle s. de temps!** what foul *or* lousy weather!; **cette s. de voiture ne veut pas démarrer** the damned *or Br* bloody car won't start

6 *(calomnie)* (piece of) dirt; **tu as encore raconté des saletés sur mon compte** you've been spreading filthy rumours about me again

7 *(acte)* dirty *or* filthy trick; **il m'a fait une s.** he played a dirty trick on me

❑ **saletés** NFPL *(grossièretés)* dirt, filth, smut; **raconter des saletés** to say dirty things; *Euph* **les chiens font leurs saletés dans les jardins publics** dogs do their business in the parks

saleur, -euse [salœr, -øz] NM,F *Culin* salter

❑ **saleuse** NF *(en travaux publics)* salt spreader

salicacée [salikase] *Bot* NF member of the Salicaceae family of trees

❑ **salicacées** NFPL Salicaceae

salicaire [salikɛr] NF *Bot* purple loosestrife

salicine [salisin] NF *Pharm* salicin

salicole [salikɔl] ADJ salt *(avant n)*

salicoque [salikɔk] NF *(en Normandie)* prawn

salicorne [salikɔrn] NF *Bot* glasswort

saliculture [salikyltyr] NF salt production

salicylate [salisilat] **NM** *Chim* salicylate

salicylé, -e [salisile] **ADJ** *Chim* containing salicylic acid

salicylique [salisilik] **ADJ** *Chim* salicylic

salien [saljɛ̃] *Antiq* **ADJ M** Salian

NM Salian priest

salière [saljɛr] **NF 1** *(petit bol)* saltcellar; *(avec trous)* saltcellar, *Am* salt shaker; *(à couvercle)* salt box, salt pot **2** *Fam (d'une personne maigre)* saltcellar

salifère [salifɛr] **ADJ** saliferous

salifiable [salifjabl] **ADJ** *Chim* salifiable

salification [salifikasjɔ̃] **NF** *Chim* salification

salifier [9] [salifje] **VT** to salify, to form into a salt

saligaud, -e [saligo, -od] **NM,F** *très Fam* **1** *(homme méprisable)* swine, bastard; *(femme méprisable)* bitch, *Br* cow **2** *Vieilli (homme sale)* filthy pig; *(femme sale)* slut

salignon [saliɲɔ̃] **NM** *Tech* cake of salt *(extracted from a salt-water fountain)*

salin, -e [salɛ̃, -in] **ADJ** saline

NM 1 *Géog* salt marsh **2** *Chim* saline

❑ **saline NF 1** *(établissement)* saltworks *(singulier)* **2** *(marais)* salt marsh

salinage [salinaʒ] **NM 1** *(établissement)* saltworks *(singulier)* **2** *(concentration)* concentrating of the brine

salingue [salɛ̃g] *très Fam* **ADJ** filthy

NMF filthy pig

salinier, -ère [salinje, -ɛr] **ADJ** salt *(avant n)*, salt-producing

NM,F salt producer

salinité [salinite] **NF 1** *(degré)* (degree of) salinity **2** *(fait d'être salé)* salinity

salique [salik] **ADJ** *Hist* salic

salir [32] [salir] **VT 1** *(eau, surface)* to (make) dirty; *(vêtements)* to (make) dirty, to mess up, to soil; **tu as sali beaucoup de vaisselle** you've dirtied a lot of dishes; *Euph* **s. ses draps** *ou* **son lit** to soil one's bed; **je ne veux pas te faire s. d'autres draps, nous dormirons dans ceux-là** I don't want to make more dirty washing for you, we'll sleep on these sheets

2 *(honneur, amitié)* to besmirch; *(réputation)* to smear, to besmirch, to sully; *(nom, mémoire)* to besmirch, to sully; **ils cherchent à s. le leader de l'opposition** they're trying to smear *or* to sully the reputation of the leader of the opposition

►**se salir VPR 1** *(emploi réfléchi)* to get dirty, to dirty oneself; *Fig* to lose one's reputation; *aussi Fig* **se s. les mains** to get one's hands dirty; **c'est lui qui décide des licenciements, à moi de me s. les mains** he decides who'll get fired and I do the dirty work

2 *(emploi passif)* to get soiled *or* dirty; **ne prends pas un manteau beige, ça se salit vite** don't buy a beige coat, it shows the dirt *or* it gets dirty very quickly

salissant, -e [salisɑ̃, -ɑ̃t] **ADJ 1** *(qui se salit)* **être s.** to show the dirt; **c'est une teinte salissante** this shade shows the dirt **2** *(qui salit → travail)* dirty, messy

salissure [salisyr] **NF** *(restée en surface)* speck of dirt, piece of grime; *(ayant pénétré le tissu)* dirty mark, stain; **le papier peint est couvert de salissures** the wallpaper's stained all over; **l'abat-jour est couvert de salissures** the lampshade is covered in dirt

salivaire [salivɛr] **ADJ** salivary

salivation [salivasjɔ̃] **NF** salivation

salive [saliv] **NF 1** *Physiol* saliva, spit

2 *Fam (locutions)* **gaspiller sa s.** to waste one's breath; **je ne vais pas gaspiller ma s. à lui expliquer tout cela** I won't waste my breath telling him/her all that; **n'usez pas** *ou* **ne gaspillez pas** *ou* **épargnez votre s.** save *or* don't waste your breath; **avant d'obtenir les subventions, j'ai dû dépenser** *ou* **user beaucoup de s.** before getting the subsidies, I had to do a lot of (fast) talking; **avaler** *ou* **ravaler sa s.** *(se taire)* to keep quiet

saliver [3] [salive] **VI 1** *Physiol* to salivate

2 *(avoir l'eau à la bouche)* **le menu me fait s.** the menu is making my mouth water; **j'en salive d'avance** my mouth is watering just thinking about it; **le chien salivait devant sa pâtée** the dog was drooling *or* dribbling at the sight of his food

3 *Fam (d'envie)* to drool; **il salivait devant les voitures de sport** he was drooling over the sports cars; **il me fait s. en me parlant de ses vacances aux Caraïbes** he makes me green with envy talking about his holidays in the Caribbean

salle [sal] **NF 1** *(dans une habitation privée)* room; **s. de bains** *(lieu)* bathroom; *(mobilier)* bathroom suite; **s. d'eau** shower room; **s. de jeu** *(d'une maison) Br* playroom, *Am* rumpus room; *(d'un casino)* gaming room; **s. à manger** *(lieu)* dining room; *(mobilier)* dining room suite; **s. de séjour** living room

2 *(dans un édifice public)* hall, room; *(dans un café)* room; *(dans un musée)* room, gallery; **s. d'accueil (de la clientèle)** reception room; **s. d'armes** *Mil* arms room; *Escrime* fencing hall; **s. d'attente** waiting room; **s. d'audience** courtroom; **s. de bal** ballroom; **s. des banquets** banqueting hall; **s. capitulaire** chapter house; *Bourse* **s. des changes** dealing room; **s. de classe** classroom; **s. des coffres** strongroom; **s. des commandes** control room; *Typ* **s. de composition** composing room; **s. de concert** concert hall, auditorium; **s. de conférences** *Univ* lecture *Br* theatre *or Am* hall; *(pour colloques)* conference room; *TV* **s. de contrôle de production** production control room; **s. de démonstration** showroom; *TV* **s. de détente** *(pour invités)* green room; **s. d'embarquement** departure lounge; **s. d'escalade** *Br* climbing wall, *Am* climbing gym; **s. d'études** *Br* prep room, *Am* study hall; **s. d'exposition** showroom; *(pour une foire)* exhibition hall; **s. des fêtes** village hall; **s. de garde** (hospital) staffroom; *Vieilli* **s. d'hôpital, s. commune** hospital ward; *TV* **s. de maquillage** make-up room; *Bourse* **s. des marchés** trading floor; *Cin* **s. de montage** cutting room; **s. d'opération** *(à l'hôpital)* operating *Br* theatre *or Am* room; *Mil* operations room; **s. paroissiale** church hall; **s. des pas perdus** *Rail* (station) concourse; *(au tribunal)* waiting room *or* hall; *Mil* **s. de police** guardroom; **s. des professeurs** *Scol* (school) staffroom; *Univ Br* staff common room, *Am* professors' lounge; **s. de projection** projection room; **s. de réanimation** resuscitation unit; **s. de rédaction** *(d'un journal)* newsroom; *TV* **s. de rédaction télévision** television news centre, television newsroom; **s. de restaurant** (restaurant) dining room; **s. de réception** *(dans un hôtel)* function room; *(dans un palais)* stateroom; **s. de réunion** boardroom, meeting room; **s. de shoot** *(pour les drogués)* injection room; **s. de spectacle** auditorium; **s. des tortures** torture chamber; **s. de travail** workroom; **s. du trône** stateroom, throne room; **s. des ventes** *Br* auction room, *Am* auction gallery

3 *(dans un hôpital) Br* ward, *Am* room; **s. des urgences** *Br* emergency ward, *Am* emergency room

4 *Cin & Théât (lieu)* theatre, auditorium; *(spectateurs)* audience; **faire s. comble** to pack the house; **le cinéma a cinq salles** it's a five-screen *Br* cinema *or Am* movie theater; **sa dernière production sort en s. en septembre** his/her latest production will be released *or* out in September; **dans les salles d'art et d'essai** *ou* **les petites salles** in arthouse *Br* cinemas *or Am* movie theaters; **dans les salles obscures** in the *Br* cinemas *or Am* movie theaters; **s. de cinéma** theatre, auditorium

5 *Sport* **athlétisme en s.** indoor athletics; **jouer en s.** to play indoors

salmanazar [salmanazar] **NM** *(bouteille)* salmanazar

salmigondis [salmigɔ̃di] **NM 1** *(embrouillamini)* mish-mash, *Br* hotchpotch, *Am* hodgepodge **2** *Arch Culin Br* hotchpotch, *Am* hodgepodge

salmis [salmi] **NM** salmi, salmis *(game part-cooked by roasting then stewed in a wine sauce)*; **s. de pintade, pintade en s.** salmi of guinea fowl

salmonelle [salmɔnɛl] **NF** *Biol* salmonella

salmonellose [salmɔneloz] **NF** *Méd* salmonellosis

salmoniculteur, -trice [salmɔnikyltœr, -tris] **NM,F** salmon farmer

salmoniculture [salmɔnikyltyr] **NF** salmon farming

salmonidé [salmɔnide] *Ich* **NM** salmonid

❑ **salmonidés NMPL** Salmonidae

saloir [salwar] **NM 1** *(récipient)* salting *or* brine tub **2** *(pièce)* salting room **3** *Vieilli (salière)* salt pot

salol [salɔl] **NM** *Pharm* salol

Salomé [salɔme] **NPR** Salome

salomé [salɔme] **NM** T-bar shoe

Salomon [salɔmɔ̃] **NPR** *Bible* (King) Solomon

NFPL *Géog* **les îles S.** the Solomon Islands; **vivre aux îles S.** to live in the Solomon Islands; **aller aux îles S.** to go to the Solomon Islands

salon [salɔ̃] **NM 1** *(chez un particulier → pièce)* living *or* sitting room, *Br* lounge; *(→ meubles)* living-room suite; **s. en cuir** leather suite; **grand s.** drawing room; **petit s.** morning room; **s. de jardin** garden set; **s. de réception** reception room

2 *(dans un hôtel, un aéroport)* lounge; *(pour réceptions, pour fêtes)* function room; *(d'un paquebot)* saloon, lounge; **s. d'attente** waiting room; **s. classe affaires** *(dans un aéroport)* business lounge

3 *(boutique)* **s. de beauté** beauty parlour *or* salon; **s. de coiffure** hairdressing salon; **s. de manucure** nail salon, nail bar; **s. de thé** tearoom; **s. d'essayage** fitting room, changing room

4 *Com (exposition)* exhibition, trade fair; **S. de l'Agriculture** = agricultural show; **S. des Arts ménagers** *Br* ≃ Ideal Home Exhibition; *Am* ≃ home crafts exhibition *or* show; **S. de l'Automobile** Car *or Br* Motor *or Am* Automobile Show; **le S. des industries du commerce et de l'organisation du bureau** = annual information technology trade fair in Paris; **S. du Livre** = annual book fair in Paris; **S. nautique** *ou* **de la navigation** Boat Show; **S. du Prêt-à-porter** ready-to-wear fashion show; **s. professionnel** trade show *or* fair

5 *Ordinat* **s. (de bavardage)** chat room

6 *Beaux-Arts* salon

7 *Littérature* salon; **tenir s.** to hold a salon; *Fig* **alors, mesdemoiselles, on fait** *ou* **tient s.?** having an important discussion, are we, ladies?; **conversation de s.** idle chatter

Salonique [salɔnik] = **Thessalonique**

salon-lavoir [salɔ̃lavwar] *(pl* **salons-lavoirs***)* **NM** *Belg & Suisse (lavomatique) Br* launderette, *Am* laundromat

salonnard, -e [salɔnar, -ard] **NM,F** *Péj* lounge lizard, socialite

salonnier [salɔnje] **NM** *Journ* society columnist

saloon [salun] **NM** saloon *(bar in the Wild West)*

salop [salo] **NM** *très Fam Vieilli* bastard, *Am* son-of-a-bitch

salopard [salɔpar] **NM** *très Fam* bastard, *Am* son-of-a-bitch

salope [salɔp] *Vulg* **NF 1** *(femme méprisable)* bitch, *Br* cow; *(femme aux mœurs légères)* tart, slut, *Br* slapper **2** *(homme méprisable)* bastard, *Am* son-of-a-bitch; **c'est vraiment une s., ce type!** he's a real bastard, that guy!

ADJ F tu as été s. avec moi you were a bitch to me

saloper [3] [salɔpe] **VT** *très Fam* **1** *(salir)* to dirty■, to mess up **2** *(mal exécuter)* to make a dog's breakfast *or Br* a pig's ear of **3** *(souiller → vêtements, mur)* to mess up

saloperie [salɔpri] **NF** *très Fam* **1** *(marchandise de mauvaise qualité)* garbage, junk, *Br* rubbish

2 *(chose désagréable, nuisible)* **c'est de la s. à poser, ce papier peint** this wallpaper's a real pain to put on; **quelles saloperies, ces taupes!** these moles are a damn nuisance!; **le chien a avalé une s.** the dog has eaten something nasty; **depuis que j'ai cette s. au poumon...** since I've had this blasted thing on my lung...; **il a attrapé une s. en vacances** he caught something nasty on holiday; **c'est une vraie s., ce nouveau virus** this new virus is really nasty; **s. de neige!** damn *or* blasted *or Br* bloody snow!; **s. de voiture, elle ne veut pas démarrer!** the damn *or* blasted *or Br* bloody car won't start!

3 *(chose sale)* **tu as une s. sur ta manche** you've got a dirty mark on your sleeve; **j'ai une s. dans mon verre** I've got some crap in my drink; **il y avait toutes sortes de saloperies par terre** there was a load of crud *or Br* muck on the floor

4 *(calomnie)* nasty *or* bitchy remark; *(action méprisable)* nasty *or* dirty trick; **faire une s. à qn** to play a dirty *or* a nasty trick on sb

□ **saloperies** NFPL **1** (*grossièretés*) filthy language (*UNCOUNT*); **dire des saloperies** to use filthy language
2 (*calomnies*) nasty *or* bitchy remarks; **elle a encore dit des saloperies sur moi** she made some more bitchy remarks about me
3 (*aliments malsains*) junk (food), garbage, *Br* rubbish; **il bouffe que des saloperies** he eats nothing but garbage *or* junk *or Br* rubbish
salopette [salɔpɛt] NF (*de ville*) *Br* dungarees, *Am* overalls; (*de ski*) salopette; (*d'un ouvrier*) *Br* overalls, *Am* overall
salopiaud [salɔpjo] NM *Fam* **c'est un s.** he's a bit of a bastard
Salouen [salwɛn] NM OU NF **le** *ou* **la S.** the (River) Salween
salpe [salp] NF *Zool* salpa
salpêtre [salpɛtr] NM saltpetre; **s. du Chili** Chile saltpetre
salpêtrer [4] [salpetre] VT **1** (*champ*) to treat with saltpetre; (*fromage*) to cover with saltpetre **2** (*humidité*) to treat with saltpetre **3** (*murs*) to rot
Salpêtrière [salpetrijɛr] NF = hospital in Paris
salpicon [salpikɔ̃] NM *Culin* salpicon (*diced meat, poultry, vegetables etc in sauce, used as a filling for vol-au-vents etc*)
salpingectomie [salpɛ̃ʒɛktɔmi] NF *Méd* salpingectomy
salpingite [salpɛ̃ʒit] NF *Méd* salpingitis
salsa [salsa] NF salsa
salse [sals] NF *Géol* salse, mud volcano
salsepareille [salsəparɛj] NF sarsaparilla
salsifis [salsifi] NM salsify
SALT [salt] NM *Mil* (*abrév* **Strategic Arms Limitations Talks**) SALT
saltation [saltasjɔ̃] NF saltation
saltationnisme [saltasjɔnism] NM saltationism
saltatoire [saltatwar] ADJ **1** *Zool* (*organe*) saltatorial; (*mouvement*) saltatory **2** art **s.** (*la danse*) dance
saltimbanque [saltɛ̃bɑ̃k] NMF **1** (*acrobate*) acrobat **2** (*forain*) fairground *or* travelling entertainer **3** (*professionnel du spectacle*) entertainer
salto [salto] NM *Sport* (*en gymnastique*) salto
salubre [salybr] ADJ **1** (*climat*) salubrious, hygienic, wholesome; (*logement*) salubrious **2** *Fig* (*mesures*) salubrious, hygienic
salubrité [salybrite] NF **1** (*d'un local*) salubrity; (*d'un climat*) salubriousness, salubrity, healthiness **2** *Jur* **s. publique** public health
saluer [7] [salɥe] VT **1** (*dire bonjour à*) to say hello to, to greet; (*dire au revoir à*) to say goodbye to; (*faire signe à* → *de la main*) to wave at; (→ *de la tête*) to nod to; **il est passé sans me s.** he walked past me without saying hello; **l'acteur salue le public** the actor bows to the audience *or* takes his bow; **il m'a demandé de vous s.** he asked me to give you his regards; **comment doit-on s. le pape?** how should one address the Pope?; **Messieurs, je vous salue (bien)!** good day (to you), gentlemen!; **s. qn bien bas** to take one's hat off to sb; *Hum* **au revoir, mes amis, je vous salue bien bas** goodbye, my friends, and a very good day to you
2 *Mil* to salute
3 *Rel* **je vous salue Marie** Hail Mary
4 (*accueillir*) to greet; **je voudrais tout d'abord s. tous ceux qui nous ont aidés à préparer cette conférence** first of all I'd like to welcome all those who have helped us prepare this conference; **son film a été unanimement salué par la presse** his/her movie *or Br* film was unanimously acclaimed by *or* met with unanimous acclaim from the press; **sa suggestion fut saluée par des cris de joie** his/her suggestion was greeted with cheers; **des protestations ont salué sa nomination** his/her appointment met with protests; **à sa descente d'avion, la reine se fit s. par des vivats** there was much cheering as the queen stepped out of the plane
5 (*rendre hommage à* → *courage, génie*) to salute, to pay homage *or* tribute to; (*reconnaître en tant que*) to hail; **on a salué en elle le chef de file du mouvement** she was hailed as the leader of the movement; **je salue en lui notre sauveur** I salute him as our saviour; **s. la mémoire** *ou* **le souvenir de qn** to salute sb's memory
VI *Naut* **s. du pavillon** *ou* **des pavillons** to dip a flag (in salute)
►**se saluer** VPR (*se dire bonjour*) to say hello

---

salure [salyr] NF (*état*) saltiness; (*teneur en sel*) salinity
salut [saly] NM **1** (*marque de politesse*) **faire un s. de la main à qn** to wave to sb; **faire un s. de la tête à qn** to nod to sb; **il lui retourna son s.** (*en paroles*) he returned his/her greeting; (*de la main*) he waved back at him/her; **répondre au s. de qn** to return sb's greeting; **en guise** *ou* **signe de s.** as a greeting
2 *Mil* salute; **faire le s. militaire** to (give the military) salute; **s. au drapeau** saluting the colours
3 (*survie* → *d'une personne, d'un pays*) salvation, safety; (→ *d'une entreprise, d'une institution*) salvation; **je dois mon s. à son arrivée** I was saved by his/her arrival, his/her arrival was my salvation; **chercher/trouver le s. dans la fuite** to seek/to find safety in flight
4 *Littéraire* (*sauveur*) saviour; **Jeanne d'Arc fut le s. de la France** Joan of Arc was the saviour of France
5 *Rel* (*rédemption*) salvation; (*du saint sacrement*) Benediction (of the Holy Sacrament); **prions pour le s. de son âme** let us pray for the salvation of his/her soul; **faire son s. (sur la terre)** to earn one's salvation on earth
6 *Naut* (*du pavillon*) dipping the flag
EXCLAM **1** *Fam* (*en arrivant*) hi *or* hello (there)!; (*en partant*) bye!, see you!; **s. la compagnie!** (*en partant*) bye, everybody!
2 *Littéraire* **s. à vous, noble ami!** hail to thee, noble friend!
salutaire [salytɛr] ADJ **1** (*physiquement* → *air*) healthy; (→ *remède*) beneficial; (→ *exercice, repos*) salutary, beneficial; **cette semaine dans les Alpes m'a été s.** that week in the Alps did my health a power of good **2** (*moralement* → *conseil, épreuve*) salutary; (→ *lecture, effet*) beneficial
salutations [salytasjɔ̃] NFPL greetings; **elle t'envoie ses s.** she sends you her regards, she sends her regards to you; **les s. d'usage** the usual greetings; **je vous prie d'agréer, Monsieur, mes s. distinguées** (*à quelqu'un dont on connaît le nom*) *Br* yours sincerely, *Am* sincerely (yours); (*à quelqu'un dont on ne connaît pas le nom*) *Br* yours faithfully, *Am* sincerely (yours)
salutiste [salytist] ADJ Salvationist
NMF Salvationist
Salvador [salvadɔr] NM **le S.** El Salvador; **vivre au S.** to live in El Salvador; **aller au S.** to go to El Salvador
salvadorien, -enne [salvadɔrjɛ̃, -ɛn] ADJ Salvadorian, Salvadorean
□ **Salvadorien, -enne** NM,F Salvadorian, Salvadorean
salvagnin [salvaɲɛ̃] NM *Suisse* = red wine from the Vaud region
salvateur, -trice [salvatœr, -tris] ADJ *Littéraire* saving (*avant n*); **mesures salvatrices** safeguards; **la mort salvatrice** the blessed release of death
salve [salv] NF **1** *Mil* salvo, volley; **tirer une s.** (**d'honneur**) to fire a salute **2** *Fig* **s. d'applaudissements** round *or* burst of applause
Salzbourg [salzbur] NM Salzburg
SAM [sam] NM (*abrév* **Sol-Air Missile**) surface-to-air missile, SAM

Sam [sam] NPR **Oncle S.** (*personnification des États-Unis*) Uncle Sam
samara [samara] NM (*en Afrique francophone*) = thong sandal
samare [samar] NF *Bot* samara, key *or* winged seed
Samarie [samari] NF **la S.** Samaria
samaritain, -e [samaritɛ̃, -ɛn] ADJ Samaritan
NM *Suisse* (*secouriste*) qualified first-aider
□ **Samaritain, -e** NM,F Samaritan; **le bon S.** the good Samaritan; *Fig* **faire le bon S., jouer les bons Samaritains** to be a Good Samaritan; **les Samaritains** the Samaritans
□ **Samaritaine** NF *Rel* **la Samaritaine** the Samaritan woman
samarium [samarjɔm] NM *Chim* samarium
samba [sɑ̃ba] NF samba
sambar [sɑ̃bar] NM *Zool* sambar
sambo [sɑ̃bo] NM *Sport* sambo wrestling
samboïste [sɑ̃boist] NMF *Sport* sambo wrestler
sambuque [sɑ̃byk] NF *Hist* **1** (*instrument de musique*) sambuca, sambuke **2** (*engin de guerre*) sambuca
same [sam] NM *Ling* Lapp
samedi [samdi] NM Saturday; **S. saint** Holy *or* Easter Saturday; *Belg & Suisse* **faire le** *ou* **son s.** to do the weekly clean; *voir aussi* **mardi**
samit [samit] NM samite
samizdat [samizdat] NM samizdat
samnite [samnit] NM *Antiq* Samnite
Samoa [samɔa] NFPL *Géog* **les S. américaines** American Samoa; **les S. occidentales/orientales** Western/Eastern Samoa; **aller aux S. occidentales/orientales** to go to Western/Eastern Samoa; **vivre aux S. occidentales/orientales** to live in Western/Eastern Samoa
samoan, -e [samɔã, -an] ADJ Samoan
□ **Samoan, -e** NM,F Samoan
samole [samɔl] NM *Bot* water pimpernel, brookweed
samossa [samɔsa] NM *Culin* samosa
Samothrace [samɔtras] NF Samothrace

'**La Victoire de Samothrace**' 'The Winged Victory'

---

samouraï [samuraj] NM samurai
samovar [samɔvar] NM samovar
samoyède [samɔjɛd] ADJ (*peuple, chien*) Samoyedic
NM **1** (*peuple, chien*) Samoyed **2** (*langue*) **le s.** Samoyed
□ **Samoyèdes** NMPL Samoyed, Samoyeds
sampan, sampang [sɑ̃pɑ̃] NM sampan
sample [sɑ̃pəl] NM *Mus* sample
sampler[1] [sɑ̃plœr] NM *Mus* sampler
sampler[2] [3] [sɑ̃ple] VT *Mus* to sample
sampling [sɑ̃pliŋ] NM *Mus* sampling
sampot [sɑ̃po] NM sampot
SAMR [ɛsaɛmɛr] NM *Méd* (*abrév* **staphylococcus aureus méticillino-résistant**) MRSA
samsara [samsara] NM *Rel* samsara
Samson [sɑ̃sɔ̃] NPR **S. et Dalila** Samson and Delilah
SAMU, Samu [samy] NM (*abrév* **Service d'aide médicale d'urgence**) = French ambulance and emergency service, *Br* ≃ ambulance service, *Am* ≃ Paramedics; **appelez le S.!** call an ambulance!; **le S. social** = mobile medical and support service for homeless people
Samuel [samɥel] NPR *Bible* Samuel; **les livres de S.** the Books of Samuel
samurai [samuraj] = **samouraï**
sana [sana] NM *Fam* (*abrév* **sanatorium**) *Br* sanatorium■, *Am* sanitarium■
Sanaa [sanaa] NM Sana'a
San Antonio [sãɑ̃tɔnjɔ] NPR = le nom de plume of the author, narrator and main character in a highly successful series of spicily written detective novels by Frédéric Dard (1921–2000)
sanatorium [sanatɔrjɔm] NM *Br* sanatorium, *Am* sanitarium
san-benito [sãbenito] (*pl* **san-benitos**) NM *Hist* (*casaque*) sanbenito
sancerre [sãsɛr] NM (*vin*) Sancerre
sanctifiant, -e [sãktifjã, -ãt] ADJ *Rel* sanctifying
sanctificateur, -trice [sãktifikatœr, -tris] ADJ sanctifying
NM,F sanctifier; **le S.** the Holy Ghost
sanctification [sãktifikasjɔ̃] NF sanctification

sanctificatrice [sãktifikatris] *voir* **sanctificateur**

sanctifier [9] [sãktifje] VT 1 *Rel (rendre sacré)* to sanctify; *(célébrer)* to hallow; **que Ton nom soit sanctifié** hallowed be thy name 2 *Fig (patrie, valeurs)* to hold sacred

sanction [sãksjɔ̃] NF 1 *(mesure répressive)* sanction; **imposer des sanctions à** to apply sanctions against, to impose sanctions on; **lever des sanctions (prises) contre** to raise (the) sanctions against; **prendre des sanctions contre** to take sanctions against; **s. administrative** administrative sanction; **sanctions diplomatiques/économiques** diplomatic/economic sanctions; **sanctions ciblées** smart sanctions

2 *Scol & Sport* punishment, disciplinary action *(UNCOUNT)*; **prendre des sanctions contre un élève** to punish a pupil; **prendre des sanctions contre un sportif** to take disciplinary action against an athlete

3 *Jur* sanction, penalty; **s. éducative** juvenile sanction; **s. pénale** penal sanction

4 *(approbation)* sanction, ratification; **l'expression a reçu la s. de l'usage** the expression has become generally accepted

5 *(conséquence)* result, outcome; **l'échec est la s. de la paresse** failure is the result of laziness; **c'est la s. du succès** that's the price of success

sanctionner [3] [sãksjɔne] VT 1 *(punir → délit, élève)* to punish; *(→ sportif, haut fonctionnaire)* to take disciplinary action against; *(→ pays)* to impose sanctions on; **il s'est fait s. pour sa grossièreté envers l'arbitre** he was penalized for being rude to the umpire

2 *(ratifier → loi)* to sanction, to ratify; *(→ décision)* to sanction, to agree with; **sa théorie a été sanctionnée par le temps** time has proved his/her theory to be correct; **sanctionné par l'usage** generally accepted

sanctuaire [sãktɥɛr] NM 1 *Rel* sanctuary 2 *(asile)* sanctuary; **l'île est un s. pour les oiseaux** the island is a favourite haunt for birds 3 *(foyer, centre vital)* hub, centre; **un s. de la civilisation inca** a centre of Inca civilization 4 *Littéraire (tréfonds)* innermost part; **dans le s. de mon cœur** in my innermost being 5 *Pol* territory under the nuclear umbrella

sanctuariser [3] [sãktɥarize] VT *(nature)* to preserve, to protect; *(territoire)* to protect, to safeguard; *(lieu, etablissement)* to make secure; *(budget, fonds, crédits)* to ring-fence

sanctus [sãktus] NM *Rel & Mus* Sanctus

sandale [sãdal] NF sandal

sandalette [sãdalɛt] NF *(light)* sandal

sandaraque [sãdarak] NF 1 *Vieilli (réalgar)* sandarac, realgar 2 *(résine)* sandarac

sanderling [sãdɛrliŋ] NM *Orn* **s. (des sables)** sanderling

sandiniste [sãdinist] ADJ Sandinista
   NMF Sandinista

sandjak [sãdʒak] NM *Hist* sanjak

Sandow® [sãdo] NM 1 *(tendeur)* elastic luggage strap 2 *Aviat* catapult 3 *Sport (en gymnastique)* chest expander

sandre [sãdr] NM *Ich* zander, pikeperch

sandwich [sãdwitʃ] NM *(pl* **sandwichs** *ou* **sandwiches)** NM 1 *(gén)* sandwich; **s. au fromage** cheese sandwich; *Fam* **prendre qn en s.** to sandwich sb; *Fam* **j'étais pris en s. entre eux** I was sandwiched between them 2 *Belg (pain au lait)* finger roll *(made with milk)*; **s. garni** sandwich

sandwicher [3] [sãdwiʃe, sãdwitʃe] VT *Fam* to sandwich; **les deux dames entre qui j'étais sandwiché** the two ladies I was sandwiched between

sandwicherie [sãdwiʃəri, sãdwitʃəri] NF sandwich bar

sanforisage [sãforizaʒ] NM *Tex* sanforizing, sanforization

San Francisco [sãfrãsisko] NM San Francisco

sang [sã] NM 1 *Biol* blood; **à s. froid/chaud** cold-/warm-blooded; **fais un garrot pour arrêter le s.** make a tourniquet to stop the bleeding; **ça se transmet par le s.** it's transmitted in the blood; **du s. à la une** gory front-page news; **s. artériel/veineux** arterial/venous blood; **donner son s.** *(pour transfusion)* to give blood; *Fig* **avoir du s. sur les mains** to have blood on one's hands;

répandre *ou* **verser** *ou* **faire couler le s.** to shed *or* to spill blood; **le s. a coulé** *ou* **a été répandu** blood was shed; **noyer une révolte dans le s.** to put down a revolt ruthlessly; **être en s., nager** *ou* **baigner dans son s.** to be covered in blood; **se mordre les lèvres jusqu'au s.** to bite one's lips until one draws blood; **il m'a griffé jusqu'au s.** he scratched me and drew blood; *Fig* **avoir du s. dans les veines** to have courage *or* guts; *Fam* **ne pas avoir de s. dans les veines, avoir du s. de poulet** *ou* **de navet** to have no guts, to be a complete wimp; *Fig* **avoir le s. chaud** *(colérique)* to be *or* to have a short fuse; *(impétueux)* to be hot-headed; *(sensuel)* to be hot-blooded; **avoir la chanson dans le s.** to be a born singer; **il a ça dans le s.** it's in his blood; **mon s. s'est glacé** *ou* **figé dans mes veines** my blood ran cold *or* turned to ice in my veins; **le s. lui est monté au visage** *ou* **à la tête** the blood rushed to his/her cheeks; *Fig* **mon s. n'a fait qu'un tour** *(d'effroi)* my heart missed *or* skipped a beat; *(de rage)* I saw red; *Fig* **se faire du mauvais s.** to worry; **se faire un s. d'encre, se manger** *ou* **se ronger les sangs** to worry oneself sick, to be worried stiff, to fret; **je me fais du mauvais s. pour lui** I'm worried sick about him; **ça m'a tourné le s.** *ou* **les sangs** it gave me quite a turn; *Fig* **du s. frais** *ou* **nouveau** *ou* **neuf** *(personnes)* new blood; *(argent)* new *or* fresh money; **l'affaire du s. contaminé** = highly controversial legal case in France in which four doctors received prison sentences, having been found responsible for the transfusion of haemophiliacs with HIV-infected blood

2 *Littéraire (vie)* (life)blood; **donner son s. pour son pays** to shed one's blood *or* to sacrifice one's life for one's country; **payer de son s.** to pay with one's life

3 *(race, extraction)* blood; **épouser qn de son s.** to marry sb of the same blood *or* a blood relative; **nous ne sommes pas du même s.** we're not of the same flesh and blood; **les liens du s.** blood ties; **de s. royal** of royal blood; **s. noble** noble *or* blue blood; **avoir du s. noble** to be of noble blood; **s. bleu** blue blood; **lorsque l'on a du s. bleu dans les veines...** when one is blue-blooded...; *Prov* **bon s. ne saurait mentir** blood is thicker than water

4 *Fam (locution)* **bon s. (de bonsoir)!** *(exprimant la surprise)* Br blimey!, Am gee (whiz)!; *(exprimant la colère)* blast it!, hell!

❑ **au sang** ADV *Culin (canard)* = served with a sauce incorporating its own blood

❑ **de sang** ADJ *(cheval)* blood *(avant n)*

❑ **du sang** ADJ *(princier)* of the blood *(royal)*

═══ 📖 ═══

'**Le Sang des autres**' *de Beauvoir* 'The Blood of Others'

═══ 📖 ═══

'**Sang noir**' *Guilloux* 'Bitter Victory'

Culture

L'AFFAIRE DU SANG CONTAMINÉ

This is one of the worst scandals of late 20th-century France. In the early 1980s, thousands of haemophiliacs were given blood transfusions from stocks of blood that were known to have been HIV-infected, ultimately causing the death of around 4,000 people. It was established that the authorities had decided against screening blood stocks for HIV using an American-made product in order to give a French company time to get its own HIV-testing product on the market. Four doctors linked to the French national blood transfusion centre and other sections of the health service were given custodial sentences in the early 90s. However, several high-ranking politicians in the Mitterrand government – including one-time Prime Minister Laurent Fabius – who were believed to have been involved in the scandal were tried but found not guilty of any wrongdoing. The case was eventually dropped for lack of evidence in 2002 among cries of protest and accusations of whitewash from a large section of the French public.

sang-dragon [sãdragɔ̃], **sang-de-dragon** [sãdədragɔ̃] NM INV 1 *(résine)* dragon's blood 2 *(plante)* bloodwort, bloody dock

sang-froid [sãfrwa] NM INV composure, calm, sang-froid; **garder** *ou* **conserver son s.** to stay calm, to keep one's cool; **perdre son s.** to lose one's self-control *or* one's cool
❑ **de sang-froid** ADV in cold blood, cold-bloodedly; **tuer qn de s.** to kill sb in cold blood *or* cold-bloodedly; **commis de s.** cold-blooded

sanglant, -e [sãglã, -ãt] ADJ 1 *(blessure, bataille, règne)* bloody; *(bras, mains)* covered in blood, bloody; *(linge)* bloody, blood-soaked; *(spectacle)* gory 2 *(blessant → critiques)* scathing; *(→ reproches)* bitter; *(→ affront)* cruel 3 *Littéraire (couleur de sang)* blood-red

sangle [sãgl] NF 1 *(lanière → gén)* strap; *(→ d'un lit, d'une chaise)* webbing; *(→ d'un cheval)* girth; **s. d'ouverture automatique** *(d'un parachute)* static line 2 *Anat* **s. abdominale** abdominal muscles

sangler [3] [sãgle] VT 1 *(cheval)* to girth 2 *(paquet, valise)* to strap up 3 *Fig (serrer)* **sanglée dans son corset** tightly corseted; **sanglé dans son uniforme** buttoned up tight in his uniform
► **se sangler** VPR *(dans un vêtement très étroit)* to do oneself up tight

sanglier [sãglije] NM *Zool* (wild) boar

sanglon [sãglɔ̃] NM girth strap

sanglot [sãglo] NM 1 *(hoquet, pleurs)* sob; **"non", dit-il dans un s.** ''no,'' he sobbed; **avec des sanglots dans la voix** with a sob in one's voice; **il pleurait à gros sanglots** he was sobbing his heart out 2 *Littéraire (bruit plaintif)* lamentation; **les sanglots de l'océan** the sighing of the deep; **les sanglots du vent** the moaning of the wind

sanglotement [sãglɔtmã] NM *Littéraire* sobbing

sangloter [3] [sãglɔte] VI 1 *(pleurer)* to sob; **elle s'endormit en sanglotant** she cried herself to sleep 2 *Littéraire (océan, vent)* to sob, to sigh; *(accordéon)* to sigh

sang-mêlé [sãmele] NMF INV *Vieilli* half-caste

sangria [sãgrija] NF sangria

sangsue [sãsy] NF 1 *Zool* leech 2 *Vieilli (profiteur)* bloodsucker 3 *Fam (importun)* leech; **son frère est une véritable s.!** his/her brother sticks *or* clings to you like a leech!

sanguin, -e [sãgɛ̃, -in] ADJ 1 *(groupe, plasma, transfusion, vaisseau)* blood *(avant n)*; *(système)* circulatory 2 *(rouge → visage, teint)* ruddy 3 *(humeur, tempérament)* sanguine
   NM,F fiery person
❑ **sanguine** NF 1 *Beaux-Arts (crayon)* red chalk, sanguine; *(dessin)* red chalk drawing, sanguine 2 *Géol* red haematite 3 *(orange)* blood orange

sanguinaire [sãginɛr] ADJ 1 *(assoiffé de sang)* bloodthirsty; **une foule s. réclamait la mort de l'accusé** a bloodthirsty crowd was screaming for the death of the accused 2 *Littéraire (féroce → bataille, conquête)* bloody, sanguinary
   NF bloodroot, *Spéc* sanguinaria

Sanguinaires [sãginɛr] NFPL **les (îles) S.** the Sanguinaires islands

sanguinolent, -e [sãginɔlã, -ãt] ADJ 1 *(sécrétion)* spotted *or* streaked with blood, *Spéc* sanguinolent; *(linge, pansement)* soiled *or* tinged with blood, *Spéc* sanguinolent; *(plaie)* oozing blood; *(personne)* covered in blood, blood-streaked 2 *Littéraire (rouge → lèvres)* blood-red

sanguisorbe [sãgisɔrb] NF *Bot* burnet

sanhédrin [sanedrɛ̃] NM Sanhedrin

Sanibroyeur® [sanibrwajœr] NM Saniflo® *(toilet with macerator unit)*

sanicle [sanikl] NF *Bot* sanicle

sanie [sani] NF *Vieilli Méd* pus and blood, *Spéc* sanies

sanieux, -euse [sanjø, -øz] ADJ *Méd* sanious

Sanisette® [sanizɛt] NF superloo

sanitaire [sanitɛr] ADJ 1 *Admin & Méd (conditions)* sanitary, health *(avant n)*; *(règlement, mesures)* health *(avant n)*; *(personnel)* medical, health *(avant n)*
2 *Constr* sanitary, plumbing *(UNCOUNT)*; **l'équipement s.** the plumbing; **système s.** sanitation (system)
   NM 1 *(installations)* plumbing (for bathroom and toilet)
2 *(profession)* sanitary ware (dealing)
❑ **sanitaires** NMPL (bathroom and) toilet; **les**

sanitaires du camp sont tout à fait insuffisants the sanitary arrangements in the camp are totally inadequate

San José [sanrɔze] NM San José

San Juan [sanrwan] NM San Juan

SANS [sɑ̃] PRÉP **1** *(indiquant l'absence, la privation, l'exclusion)* without; **il est parti s. argent** he left without any money; **avec ou s. sucre?** with or without sugar?; **le jus d'orange, avec de la glace ou s.?** do you want the orange juice with or without ice?; **j'ai trouvé s. problème** I found it without any difficulty *or* with no difficulty; **on ira s. elle** we'll go without her; **ne partez pas s. moi** don't leave without me; **je voudrais te parler s. témoins** I'd like to speak to you alone; **son comportement est s. reproche** his/her behaviour is beyond reproach; **être s. scrupules** to have no scruples, to be unscrupulous; **tu as oublié le rendez-vous? tu es s. excuse!** you forgot the appointment? that's unforgivable!; **homme s. cœur/s. pitié** heartless/pitiless man; **couple s. enfants** childless couple; **mur s. fenêtre** blind wall; **s. additif** additive-free; **essence s. plomb** unleaded *or* lead-free petrol; **bonbons s. sucre** sugar-free sweets; **régime s. sel** salt-free diet; **marcher s. but** to walk aimlessly; **s. commentaire!** no comment!; **c'est 20 euros s. les frais de transport** it's 20 euros, exclusive of transport charges; **la chambre fait 40 euros, s. le petit déjeuner** the room costs 40 euros, breakfast not included *or* exclusive of breakfast; **nous y sommes arrivés s. difficultés** ou **mal** we managed it without any difficulty; **il n'est pas s. charme** he's not without charm, he's not lacking in charm; **très Fam être s. un** to be broke *or Br* skint

2 *(exprimant la condition)* but for; **s. toi, je ne l'aurais jamais fait** if it hadn't been for you *or* but for you, I would never have done it; **s. la pluie, tout aurait été parfait** had it not been raining *or* but for the rain, everything would have been perfect; **s. son entêtement, l'affaire serait déjà réglée** if he were not so stubborn *or* but for his stubbornness, the matter would have been settled by now

3 *(avec un infinitif)* without; **elle a réussi s. travailler beaucoup** she passed without doing much work; **s. être vu** without being seen; **venir s. être invité** to come without being invited; **partons s. plus attendre** come on, let's not wait any more; **s. plus attendre, je passe la parole à M. Blais** without further ado, I'll hand you over to Mr Blais; **cette découverte n'est pas s. l'inquiéter** he's/she's somewhat worried by this discovery; **tu n'es pas s. savoir qu'il est amoureux d'elle** you must be aware that he's in love with her; **je ne suis pas s. avoir de craintes** I am somewhat anxious; **il est responsable s. l'être tout à fait** it's his responsibility, but only to a certain extent; **je comprends s. comprendre** I understand, but only up to a point

ADV without; **il faudra faire s.!** we'll have to go without!; **passe-moi mon manteau, je ne peux pas sortir s.** hand me my coat, I can't go out without it; **c'est un jour s.!** *(tout va mal)* it's one of those days!

□ **non sans** PRÉP not without; **il l'a persuadée, mais non s. mal** he persuaded her, but not without difficulty, he had quite a job persuading her; **on est arrivés non s. peine** we got there, not without difficulty; **non s. protester** not without protesting; **je suis parti non s. leur dire ma façon de penser** I didn't leave without telling them what I thought

□ **sans cela, sans ça** CONJ *Fam* otherwise▪; **je serai absente; s. cela, j'aurais accepté votre invitation** I won't be here, otherwise I would have accepted your invitation; **il a intérêt à le faire, s. ça...!** he'd better do it, otherwise...!

□ **sans que** CONJ **ils ont réglé le problème s. que nous ayons à intervenir** they dealt with the problem without us having to intervene; **le projet était passé s. que personne (ne) s'y opposât** the bill was passed without any opposition

□ **sans quoi** CONJ **soyez ponctuels, s. quoi vous ne pourrez pas vous inscrire** be sure to be on time, otherwise you won't be able to register

---

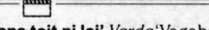

'Sans toit ni loi' *Varda* 'Vagabond'

---

sans-abri [sɑ̃zabri] NMF INV homeless person; **les s.** the homeless

sans-allure, sans allure [sɑ̃zalyr] NMF INV *Belg (personne négligée)* badly-dressed *or* badly-groomed person; *(personne incapable)* inept person

San Salvador [sɑ̃salvadɔr] NM San Salvador

sans-cœur [sɑ̃kœr] ADJ INV heartless; **ne sois pas s.!** have a heart!, don't be so heartless!

NMF INV heartless person; **donne-le-lui, espèce de s.!** give it to him/her, you heartless monster!

sanscrit, -e [sɑ̃skri, -it] = **sanskrit**

sans-culotte [sɑ̃kylɔt] *(pl* **sans-culottes***)* NM sans-culotte; *Hist* **les sans-culottes** the sans-culottes

Culture

LES SANS-CULOTTES

This was the name given to the Republican revolutionaries during the "Convention" (1792–95) because, instead of the short breeches ("culotte") worn by the upper classes, they adopted the trousers worn by the ordinary people. The term now has connotations of Republican extremism.

sans-dessein [sɑ̃desɛ̃] *Can Fam Péj* ADJ INV clueless, gormless

NMF INV clueless *or* gormless person

sans-emploi [sɑ̃zɑ̃plwa] NMF INV unemployed *or* jobless person; **les s.** the unemployed

sansevière [sɑ̃səvjɛr] NF *Bot* sansevieria

sans-façon [sɑ̃fasɔ̃] NM INV *Littéraire* casualness, offhandedness

sans-famille [sɑ̃famij] NMPL **les s.** people who have no families

sans-faute [sɑ̃fot] NM INV **faire un s.** *Sport* to do *or* to have a clear round; *Scol* not to make a single mistake; **pour l'instant, c'est un s.!** *(dans un jeu)* so far so good!

sans-fil [sɑ̃fil] NF INV *Vieilli* wireless (telegraphy) NM INV cordless telephone

sans-filiste [sɑ̃filist] *(pl* **sans-filistes***)* NMF radio ham

sans-gêne [sɑ̃ʒɛn] ADJ INV *(personne)* inconsiderate; *(manières)* bad; **qu'est-ce qu'il est s.!** he's got no consideration!

NM INV lack of consideration

NMF INV inconsiderate person; **en voilà une s.!** she's got no consideration!

sans-grade [sɑ̃grad] NMF INV underling, minion; **nous sommes les s. ici!** we're the small fry around here!

sanskrit, -e [sɑ̃skri, -it] ADJ Sanskrit NM *(langue)* Sanskrit

sanskritiste [sɑ̃skritist] NMF Sanskritist

sans-le-sou [sɑ̃lsu] NMF INV *Fam* pauper▪, penniless person▪; **les s.** the have-nots▪

sans-logis [sɑ̃lɔʒi] NMF INV homeless person; **les s.** the homeless

sansonnet [sɑ̃sɔnɛ] NM *Orn* starling

sans-papiers [sɑ̃papje] NMF INV illegal immigrant

sans-parti [sɑ̃parti] NMF INV *Pol (gén)* independent member *(of an assembly or a Parliament)*; *(dans un système de parti unique)* non-party member

sans-patrie [sɑ̃patri] NMF INV stateless person

sans-plomb [sɑ̃plɔ̃] NM INV *(essence)* unleaded

sans-souci [sɑ̃susi] ADJ INV carefree, happy-go-lucky

NMF INV *Littéraire* happy-go-lucky person

Santa Fé [sɑ̃tafe] NM Santa Fe

santal, -als [sɑ̃tal] NM *Bot* sandal; **bois de s.** sandalwood

santé [sɑ̃te] NF **1** *(de l'esprit, d'une économie, d'une entreprise)* health, soundness; *(d'une personne, d'une plante)* health; **avoir une bonne/mauvaise s.** to be healthy/unhealthy; **comment va la s.?** how are you keeping?; **c'est bon/mauvais pour la s.** it's good/bad for your health *or* for you; **en bonne s.** *(personne)* healthy, in good health; *(plante)* healthy; *(économie)* healthy, sound; *(monnaie)* strong; **je vous espère en bonne s.** I hope you're quite well, I hope you're in good health; **vous êtes en parfaite s.** you're perfectly healthy *or* there's

nothing the matter with you; **meilleure s.!** I hope you're better soon *or* you get well soon!; **en mauvaise s.** *(animal, personne)* in bad *or* poor health; *(plante)* unhealthy; *(économie, monnaie)* weak; **le bon air lui a rendu** ou **redonné la s.** the fresh air has restored him/her to health; **état de s.** health; **s. mentale** mental health; *Fam* **avoir la s.** *(être infatigable)* to be a bundle of energy; **avoir une s. de fer** to have an iron constitution, to be (as) strong as a horse; **avoir une petite s., ne pas avoir de s.** to be very delicate; *Fam* **avoir de la s.** *(avoir de l'audace)* to have a nerve *or Br* a brass neck

2 *Admin* **la s. publique** public health; **services de s.** health services

3 *Naut* **la s.** the quarantine service

4 *Mil* **service de s. des armées** medical corps

EXCLAM **1** *Fam (en trinquant)* cheers!

2 *Suisse (à vos souhaits)* bless you!

□ **Santé** NF **la S.** *(prison)* = men's prison in Paris

□ **à la santé de** PRÉP *(en portant un toast)* **à votre/ta s.!** cheers!, your (good) health!; **à la s. de ma femme!** (here's) to my wife!; **buvons à la s. des mariés!** let's drink to the bride and groom!; **je lève mon verre à la s. de la mariée!** I raise my glass to the bride!

Santiago [sɑ̃tjago] NM **S. (du Chili)** Santiago

santiags [sɑ̃tjag] NFPL *Fam* cowboy boots▪

santoline [sɑ̃tɔlin] NF *Bot* santolina, lavender cotton

santon [sɑ̃tɔ̃] NM crib *or* manger figurine *(in Provence)*

santonine [sɑ̃tɔnin] NF **1** *Bot* santonica, Levant wormseed **2** *Pharm* santonin

santonnier, -ère [sɑ̃tɔnje, -ɛr] NM,F maker of santons

Santorin [sɑ̃tɔrɛ̃] NM Santorini

sanve [sɑ̃v] NF *Bot* charlock, wild mustard

sanza [sɑ̃za] NF *Mus (en Afrique francophone)* thumb piano, mbira

saola [saɔla] NM *Zool* saola

Saône [son] NF **la S.** the (River) Saône

Saône-et-Loire [sonelwar] NF **la S.** Saône-et-Loire

São Paulo [saopolo] NM **1** *(ville)* Sao Paulo **2** *(État)* **l'État de S.** Sao Paulo (State)

São Tomé et Principe [saotɔmeeprɛ̃sip] NM São Tomé and Principe

saoudien, -enne [saudjɛ̃, -ɛn] ADJ Saudi (Arabian)

□ **Saoudien, -enne** NM,F Saudi (Arabian)

saoudite [saudit] ADJ Saudi (Arabian)

saoul, -e [su, sul] = **soûl**

saouler [sule] = **soûler**

sapajou [sapaʒu] NM **1** *Zool* capuchin monkey, sapajou **2** *Fam Vieilli (homme petit et laid)* troglodyte

sape [sap] NF **1** *Mil & (en travaux publics) (travaux)* sapping; *(tranchée)* sap; *très Fam Arg mil* **la s.** *(les hommes du génie)* sappers **2** *Fig* **travail de s.** *(insidieux)* undermining; **par un patient travail de s., ils ont fini par avoir raison de lui** they chipped away at him until he gave in **3** *(outil)* mattock

□ **sapes** NFPL *Fam* clothes▪, *Br* gear, clobber

sapement [sapmɑ̃] NM **1** *Mil & (en travaux publics)* sapping **2** *(de relief)* erosion

sapèque [sapɛk] NF *Anciennement* sapek, sapeque

saper [3] [sape] VT **1** *Mil & (en travaux publics)* to sap

2 *(nuire à)* to sap, to undermine; **ce travail lui a sapé la santé** this work undermined his/her health; **s. le moral à qn** to get sb down

3 *Fam (habiller)* to dress▪; **il est toujours bien sapé** he's always really smartly dressed

▶**se saper** VPR *Fam (s'habiller)* to get dressed▪; *(s'habiller chic)* to get all dressed up; **elle aime bien se s. pour sortir** she likes to get all dressed up to go out; **il sait pas se s.** he's got no dress sense; **elle se sape très seventies** she wears really seventies clothes, she dresses really seventies

saperde [sapɛrd] NF *Entom* saperda

saperlipopette [sapɛrlipɔpɛt] EXCLAM *Arch ou Hum* zounds!, strewth!

sapeur [sapœr] NM = young, well-dressed African man

sapeur-pompier [sapœrpɔ̃pje] *(pl* **sapeurs-pompiers***)* NM *Br* fireman, *Am* firefighter; **les**

sapeurs-pompiers *Br* the fire brigade, *Am* the fire department

saphène [safɛn] *Anat* **ADJ INV** **veine s.** saphena **NF** saphena; **grande s.** long *or* internal saphena; **petite s.** short *or* posterior *or* external saphena

saphique [safik] **ADJ** Sapphic; **vers s.** Sapphic metre

saphir [safir] **ADJ INV** *Littéraire* sapphire *(avant n)* **NM 1** *(pierre précieuse)* sapphire **2** *(d'un tourne-disque)* needle, stylus **3** *Littéraire (bleu)* sapphire

saphisme [safism] **NM** *Littéraire* sapphism, lesbianism

Sapho [safo] = **Sappho**

sapide [sapid] **ADJ** sapid

sapidité [sapidite] **NF** sapidity; **agent de s.** flavour enhancer

sapience [sapjãs] **NF** *Arch* wisdom, sapience

sapientiaux [sapjɛ̃sjo] **NMPL** *Rel* sapiential books

sapientiel, -elle [sapjɛ̃sjɛl] **ADJ** *Rel* sapiential

sapin [sapɛ̃] **NM 1** *Bot* fir (tree); **s. de Noël** Christmas tree; **faire un s. de Noël** *(chez soi)* to have a Christmas tree; *(dans une collectivité)* to have a Christmas party for the staff's children
2 *Menuis* fir, deal; **en s.** fir *(avant n)*, deal *(avant n)*; **s. blanc** *ou* **pectiné** (common) silver fir
3 *Fam Hum* **ça sent le s.** he's/she's/*etc* on his/her/*etc* last legs; **une toux qui sent le s.** a graveyard cough, a death-rattle of a cough

sapinages [sapinaʒ] **NMPL** *Can* fir branches

sapindacée [sapɛ̃dase] *Bot* **NF** member of the Sapindaceae family
□ **sapindacées** **NFPL** Sapindaceae

sapine [sapin] **NF 1** *(planche)* fir plank **2** *Constr* jib crane **3** *Naut* flat-bottomed deal boat

sapinette [sapinɛt] **NF 1** *Bot* **s. blanche/noire/rouge** white/black/red spruce **2** *Can (boisson)* spruce beer **3** *Naut* flat-bottomed deal boat

sapinière [sapinjɛr] **NF 1** *(plantation)* fir plantation **2** *(forêt)* fir forest

sapiteur [sapitœr] **NM** *Assur* claims adjuster *(in marine insurance)*

saponacé, -e [saponase] **ADJ** saponaceous

saponaire [saponɛr] **NF** *Bot* soapwort

saponase [saponaz] **NF** *Chim* lipase

saponifiable [saponifjabl] **ADJ** *Chim* saponifiable

saponifiant, -e [saponifjã, -ãt] *Chim* **ADJ** saponifying **NM** saponifier, saponifying agent

saponification [saponifikasjɔ̃] **NF** *Chim* saponification

saponifier [9] [saponifje] **VT** *Chim* to saponify

saponine [saponin] **NF** *Chim* saponin, saponine

saponite [saponit] **NF** saponite, bowlingite

sapotacée [sapotase] *Bot* **NF** member of the Sapotaceae, *Spéc* sapota
□ **sapotacées** **NFPL** Sapotaceae

sapote [sapot] **NF** sapota

sapotier [sapotje] **NM** *Bot* sapota

sapotille [sapotij] **NF** *Bot* sapodilla plum

sapotillier [sapotije] **NM** *Bot* sapodilla

Sappho [safo] **NPR** Sappho

sapristi [sapristi] **EXCLAM** *Vieilli (exprimant l'étonnement)* heavens!; *(exprimant la colère)* Great Scott!

saprogène [saprɔʒɛn] **ADJ** *Biol & Méd* saprogenic

sapropèle [sapropɛl] **NM** *Géol* sapropel

saprophage [saprofaʒ] *Biol* **ADJ** saprophagous **NM** *(insecte)* saprophagous insect

saprophyte [saprofit] *Biol* **ADJ** saprophytic **NM** saprophyte

saprophytisme [saprofitism] **NM** *Biol* saprophytism

saprozoïte [saprozoit] **ADJ** *Biol* saprozoic

saquer [sake] = **sacquer**

S.A.R. *(abrév écrite* Son Altesse Royale*)* HRH

sar [sar] **NM** *Ich* sea bream

Sara [sara] **NPR** *Bible* Sarah

sarabande [sarabãd] **NF 1** *Mus & (danse)* saraband **2** *Fam (tapage)* racket, *Br* row; **les enfants font la s. dans la salle de jeux** the children are making a racket in the playroom **3** *(ribambelle)* string, succession

Saragosse [saragɔs] **NM** Saragossa

Sarah [sara] **NPR** *Bible* Sarah

Sarajevo [sarajevo] **NM** Sarajevo

sarangi [sarãgi] **NM** *Mus* sarangi

Sarawak [sarawak] **NM** Sarawak

sarbacane [sarbakan] **NF** *(arme)* blowpipe; *(jouet)* peashooter

sarcasme [sarkasm] **NM 1** *(ironie)* sarcasm; **tu n'arriveras à rien par le s.** being sarcastic won't get you anywhere **2** *(remarque)* sarcastic remark; **essuyer les sarcasmes de qn** to put up with sb's sarcasm

sarcastique [sarkastik] **ADJ** sarcastic; **d'un ton s.** sarcastically

sarcastiquement [sarkastikmã] **ADV** sarcastically

sarcelle [sarsɛl] **NF** *Orn* **s. (d'hiver)** teal; **s. d'été** garganey; **s. marbrée** marbled teal; **s. soucrourou** blue-winged teal

sarcine [sarsin] **NF** *Biol* sarcina

sarclage [sarklaʒ] **NM** weeding

sarcler [3] [sarkle] **VT 1** *(mauvaises herbes → à la main)* to pull up, to weed out; *(→ avec une houe)* to hoe; *(→ avec une bêche)* to spud **2** *(betteraves, champ → à la main)* to weed; *(→ avec une houe)* to hoe

sarclette [sarklɛt] **NF** (weeding) hoe

sarcleur, -euse [sarklœr, -øz] **NM,F** weeder

sarcloir [sarklwar] **NM** (Dutch) hoe, spud

sarcoïde [sarkɔid] **NF** *Méd* sarcoid

sarcoïdose [sarkɔidoz] **NF** *Méd* sarcoidosis

sarcomateux, -euse [sarkɔmatø, -øz] **ADJ** *Méd* sarcomatous

sarcomatose [sarkɔmatoz] **NF** *Méd* sarcomatosis

sarcome [sarkom] **NM** *Méd* sarcoma; **s. de Kaposi** Kaposi's sarcoma

sarcophage [sarkofaʒ] **NM 1** *(cercueil)* sarcophagus **2** *Entom* fleshfly

sarcopte [sarkɔpt] **NM** itch mite, *Spéc* sarcoptid

Sardaigne [sardɛŋ] **NF** **la S.** Sardinia

sardane [sardan] **NF** sardana

sarde [sard] **ADJ** Sardinian **NM** *(langue)* Sardinian
□ **Sarde** **NMF** Sardinian

sardine [sardin] **NF 1** *Ich* sardine; **sardines à l'huile/à la tomate** sardines in oil/in tomato sauce **2** *très Fam Arg mil* stripe **3** *(de tente)* tent peg

sardinelle [sardinɛl] **NF** *Ich* sardinella

sardinerie [sardinri] **NF** sardine cannery

sardinier, -ère [sardinje, -ɛr] **NM,F 1** *(pêcheur)* sardine fisher **2** *(ouvrier)* sardine canner **NM 1** *(bateau)* sardine boat *or* fisher **2** *(filet)* sardine net

sardoine [sardwan] **NF** sard; **s. rubanée** sardonyx

sardonique [sardɔnik] **ADJ** sardonic

sardoniquement [sardɔnikmã] **ADV** sardonically

sardonyx [sardɔniks] **NF** *Minér* sardonyx

sargasse [sargas] **NF** *Bot* sargasso, gulfweed

Sargasses [sargas] *voir* **mer**

sargue [sarg] **NM** *Ich* sea bream

sari [sari] **NM** sari, saree

sarigue [sarig] **NF** *Zool* possum, opossum

sarin [sarɛ̃] **NM** sarin

sarisse [saris] **NF** *Antiq* sarissa, Macedonian spear

SARL, Sarl [ɛsaɛrɛl] **NF** *(abrév* **société à responsabilité limitée***)* limited liability company; **Balacor S.** *Br* ≃ Balacor Ltd, *Am* ≃ Balacor Inc

sarment [sarmã] **NM** *(tige)* twining *or* climbing stem, bine; **s. de vigne** vine shoot

sarmenter [3] [sarmãte] **VI** *Agr* to gather up the shoots *(after pruning vines)*

sarmenteux, -euse [sarmãtø, -øz] **ADJ** climbing *(avant n)*, sarmentous

sarode [sarɔd] **NM** *Mus* sarod

sarodiste [sarɔdist] **NMF** *Mus* sarodist

saron [sarɔ̃] **NM** *Mus* saron

sarong [sarɔg] **NM** sarong

saros [sarɔs] **NM** *Astron* saros

saroual, -als [sarwal], **sarouel** [sarwɛl] **NM** = baggy trousers traditionally worn in North Africa

sarracénie [saraseni] **NF** *Bot* sarracenia

sarrancolin [sarãkɔlɛ̃] **NM** *Minér* sarrancolin *(dark-red marble from the Pyrenees)*

sarrasin¹ [sarazɛ̃] **NM** *Bot* buckwheat

sarrasin², -e¹ [sarazɛ̃, -in] **ADJ** Saracen
□ **Sarrasin, -e** **NM,F** Saracen

sarrasine² [sarazin] **NF** *(d'un château fort)* portcullis

sarrau, -s [saro] **NM 1** *(d'artiste)* smock **2** *(de paysan)* smock frock **3** *(d'écolier)* overalls

Sarre [sar] **NF 1** *(région)* **la S.** Saarland, the Saar **2** *(rivière)* **la S.** the (River) Saar

Sarrebruck [sarbryk] **NM** Saarbrücken

sarrette [sarɛt] **NF** *Bot* sawwort

sarriette [sarjet] **NF** *Bot & Culin* savory; **s. commune** wild basil

sarrois, -e [sarwa, -az] **ADJ** of/from the Saar
□ **Sarrois, -e** **NM,F** = inhabitant of or person from the Saar

Sarthe [sart] **NF 1** *(rivière)* **la S.** the (River) Sarthe **2** *(département)* **la S.** the Sarthe

sartrien, -enne [sartrijɛ̃, -ɛn] **ADJ** Sartrean

S.A.S. *(abrév écrite* **Son Altesse Sérénissime***)* HSH

sas [sas] **NM 1** *(pièce étanche → de sous-marin, d'engin spatial)* airlock; *(d'une banque)* security (double) door **2** *(d'écluse)* lock (chamber); *(entre deux écluses)* airlock **3** *(crible)* sieve, screen

sashimi [saʃimi] **NM** *Culin* sashimi

Saskatchewan [saskatʃewan] **NM** **le S.** Saskatchewan

sassafras [sasafra] **NM** sassafras

sassage [sasaʒ] **NM 1** *(de farine, de plâtre)* sifting, sieving; *(de grain)* winnowing **2** *(de bijoux)* polishing *(by rubbing in sand)*

sassanide [sasanid] *Hist* **ADJ** Sassanian **NMF** Sassanid

sassement [sasmã] **NM** *(de farine, de plâtre)* sifting, sieving; *(de grain)* winnowing

sassenage [sasnaʒ] **NM** Sassenage *(cow's milk cheese from the Isère area)*

sasser¹ [3] [sase] **VT** *(farine, plâtre)* to sift, to sieve; *(grain)* to winnow; *Littéraire* **s. (et ressasser)** *(preuves)* to sift, to scrutinize; *(le pour et le contre)* to examine minutely; *(sujet)* to go over again and again

sasser² [3] [sase] **VT** *Naut (bateau)* to lock, to sluice

Satan [satã] **NPR** Satan

satané, -e [satane] **ADJ** *(avant le nom) Fam* **1** *(détestable)* **faites donc taire ce s. gosse!** shut that blasted kid up!; **s. temps!** what rotten weather! **2** *(en intensif)* **c'est un s. menteur** he's an out-and-out liar

satanique [satanik] **ADJ 1** *(de Satan)* satanic **2** *(démoniaque, pervers)* fiendish, diabolical, satanic; **avoir l' œil s.** to have an evil glint in one's eye

satanisme [satanism] **NM 1** *(culte)* satanism **2** *(méchanceté)* fiendishness, evil

sataniste [satanist] **ADJ** satanist **NMF** satanist

satellisable [satelizabl] **ADJ** which can be put into orbit

satellisation [satelizasjɔ̃] **NF 1** *Astron (d'une fusée)* putting *or* launching into orbit; **programme de s.** space programme **2** *(d'une nation, d'une ville, d'une organisation)* satellization

satelliser [3] [satelize] **VT 1** *Astron* **s. qch** to put *or* to launch sth into orbit, to orbit sth; **fusée satellisée** orbiting rocket **2** *(nation, ville, organisation)* to satellize
▶**se satelliser** **VPR 1** *Astron* to go into orbit **2** *(nation, ville, organisation)* to become a satellite

satellitaire [satelitɛr] **ADJ** satellite *(avant n)*

satellite [satelit] **NM 1** *Astron & Tél* satellite; **en direct par s.** live via satellite; **s. artificiel/météorologique/de télécommunications** artificial/meteorological/telecommunications satellite; *Mil* **s. antisatellite** killer satellite; **s. de diffusion directe** direct broadcast satellite, DBS; **s. de distribution** distribution satellite; **s. espion** spy satellite; **s. géostationnaire** geostationary satellite; **s. lunaire/terrestre** moon-orbiting/earth-orbiting satellite; **s. d'observation** observation satellite; **s. pour l'observation de la Terre** earth observation satellite; **s. de radiodiffusion** broadcast satellite; **s. de reconnaissance** reconnaissance satellite; **s. de télédétection** spy satellite; **s. de télédiffusion** broadcast satellite; **s. de télédiffusion directe** direct-broadcast satellite; **s. de télévision** television satellite; **transmission par s.** satellite transmission; **émission retransmise par s.** satellite broadcast **2** *Pol (personne, pays, ville)* satellite; **les**

satellites du bloc socialiste the satellite countries of the socialist bloc

3 *(d'une aérogare)* satellite

4 *Tech* bevel (wheel); **engrenage à s.** planetary gear; **s. de différentiel** differential gear

5 *Biol* satellite

ADJ 1 *(ville, pays)* satellite *(avant n)*; **ordinateur s.** satellite computer

2 *Anat* **veines satellites** companion veins

sati [sati] NM INV suttee, sutteeism

NF INV suttee *(widow)*

satiation [sasjasjɔ̃] NF *Psy* satiation

satiété [sasjete] NF satiety; **manger à s.** to eat one's fill; **redire qch jusqu'à s.** to repeat sth ad nauseam

satin [satɛ̃] NM 1 *Tex* satin; **s. de coton** satin cotton, sateen; **de s.** satin *(avant n)*; *Fig* **une peau de s.** a satin-smooth skin 2 *(douceur → gén)* softness, silkiness; *(→ de la peau)* silky softness

satinage [satinaʒ] NM 1 *Tex* satining 2 *Typ* calendering 3 *(en peausserie)* (satin) glazing

satiné, -e [satine] ADJ *(tissu, reflets)* satiny, satin *(avant n)*; *(papier)* calendered; *(peau)* satin *(avant n)*, satin-smooth; **un fini s.** a satin finish; **peinture satinée** satin-finish paint

NM *(d'une peinture, d'un papier, d'un tissu)* satin finish; **la lumière mettait en valeur le s. de sa peau** the light showed off his/her satin complexion

satiner [3] [satine] VT *(tissu)* to give a satin finish to, to put a satin finish on; *(papier)* to calender; *(peau)* to make smooth

satinette [satinɛt] NF *(en coton)* sateen; *(en soie et coton)* (silk and cotton) satinet

satire [satir] NF 1 *Littérature* satire 2 *(critique)* satire, spoof, *Br* send-up; **faire la s. de son époque** to satirize one's times; **sa s. du Premier ministre est excellente** his/her take-off of the Prime Minister is excellent

satirique [satirik] ADJ satirical

NMF satirist

satiriquement [satirikmɑ̃] ADV satirically

satiriser [3] [satirize] VT to satirize

satiriste [satirist] NMF satirist

satis [satis] NF *Belg Fam Arg scol (abrév* **satisfaction**) = minimum pass (grade)

satisfaction [satisfaksjɔ̃] NF 1 *(plaisir)* satisfaction, gratification; **la s. du travail bien fait** the satisfaction of a job well done; **éprouver de la s./une grande s. à faire qch** to feel satisfaction/great satisfaction in doing sth; **il a la s. d'être utile** he has the satisfaction of being useful, he can rest assured that he's being useful; **donner (entière** *ou* **toute) s. à qn** *(personne)* to give sb (complete) satisfaction; *(travail)* to fulfil sb completely, to give sb a lot of (job) satisfaction; **mon travail me donne peu de s.** my work is not very satisfying *or* fulfilling *or* gratifying; **à ma grande s.** to my great satisfaction, to my gratification; **le problème fut résolu à la s. générale** the problem was solved to everybody's satisfaction; **je constate/je vois avec s. que...** I am pleased to note/to see that...; **s. de la clientèle** customer satisfaction; **s. du consommateur** consumer satisfaction

2 *(sujet de contentement)* source *or* cause for satisfaction; **j'ai eu une grande s. aujourd'hui** something really good happened today; **mon travail m'apporte de nombreuses satisfactions** my job gives me great satisfaction; **mon fils m'apporte de nombreuses satisfactions** my son is a great source of pride to me; **s. professionnelle** job satisfaction; **avoir des satisfactions professionnelles/financières** to be rewarded professionally/financially

3 *(assouvissement → d'un désir)* satisfaction, gratification, fulfilment; *(→ d'ambitions, d'un besoin)* satisfying, fulfilment; *(→ de la faim)* appeasement, satisfying; *(→ de la soif)* quenching; **c'est pour elle une s. d'amour-propre** it flatters her self-esteem

4 *(gain de cause)* satisfaction; **accorder** *ou* **donner s. à qn** to give sb satisfaction; **obtenir s.** to obtain satisfaction

5 *(réparation)* satisfaction; **exiger/obtenir s. (de qch)** to demand/to obtain satisfaction (for sth); **obtenir s. d'un affront** to obtain satisfaction for an affront

6 *Belg Univ* = minimum pass (grade)

7 *Rel* **s. sacramentelle** (penitential) satisfaction

satisfaire [109] [satisfɛr] VT 1 *(contenter → sujet: résultat, travail)* to satisfy, to give satisfaction to; *(→ sujet: explication)* to satisfy; *(sexuellement)* to satisfy; **rien ne le satisfait** nothing satisfies him, he's never satisfied; **elle est difficile à s.** she's hard to please; **votre rapport ne me satisfait pas du tout** I'm not satisfied at all with your report, I don't find your report at all satisfactory; **ce que j'ai me satisfait pleinement** I'm quite content with what I've got; **j'espère que cet arrangement vous satisfera** I hope (that) you'll find this arrangement satisfactory *or* to your satisfaction; **la réunion a été fixée au 3 mars pour s. tout le monde** the date for the meeting has been fixed for 3 March, so as to satisfy *or* to accommodate everybody

2 *(répondre à → attente)* to come *or* to live up to; *(→ désir)* to satisfy, to fulfil; *(→ besoin)* to satisfy, to answer; *(→ curiosité)* to satisfy; *(→ demande)* to meet, to satisfy, to cope with, to keep up with; *(→ faim)* to satisfy, to appease; *(→ soif)* to satisfy, to quench; **il reste des revendications non satisfaites** there are still a few demands which haven't been met; *Euph* **s. un besoin naturel** to answer a call of nature

▫ **satisfaire à** VT IND 1 *(conditions)* to meet, to satisfy, to fulfil; *(besoin, exigences)* to meet, to fulfil; *(désir)* to satisfy, to gratify; *(attente)* to live *or* to come up to; *(promesse)* to fulfil, to keep; *(goût)* to satisfy; *(norme)* to comply with, to satisfy; **avoir satisfait à ses obligations militaires** to have fulfilled one's national service commitments

2 *Arch* **s. à qn** *(dans un duel)* to give sb satisfaction

▸**se satisfaire** VPR 1 *(sexuellement)* to have one's pleasure

2 *(uriner)* to relieve oneself

3 **se s. de** to be satisfied *or* content with; **tu te satisfais de peu!** you're content with very little!, it doesn't take much to make you happy!; **il ne se satisfait pas de promesses** he's not content with promises, promises aren't good enough for him

satisfaisant, -e [satisfəzɑ̃, -ɑ̃t] ADJ 1 *(convenable → réponse, travail, devoir scolaire)* satisfactory; **de manière satisfaisante** satisfactorily; **en quantité satisfaisante** in sufficient quantities; **ce n'est pas une excuse/une raison satisfaisante** it's not a good enough excuse/reason; **peu s.** *(résultat, travail)* unsatisfactory; *Scol* poor; **cette solution n'était satisfaisante pour personne** this solution pleased nobody

2 *(gratifiant → métier, occupation)* satisfying

satisfaisons *etc voir* **satisfaire**

satisfait, -e [satisfɛ, -ɛt] PP *voir* **satisfaire**

ADJ *(air, personne, regard)* satisfied, happy; **être s. de qn** to be satisfied *or* happy with sb; **es-tu s. de ta secrétaire?** are you satisfied *or* happy with your secretary?; **j'espère que vous en serez entièrement s.** *(appareil ménager, ordinateur etc)* I trust it will give you complete satisfaction; **s. ou remboursé** *(sur un produit)* satisfaction or your money back, money-back guarantee; **être s. de soi** *ou* **de soi-même** to be satisfied with oneself, to be self-satisfied; **être s. de** *(arrangement, résultat)* to be satisfied with, to be happy with *or* about; *(voiture, service)* to be satisfied with; **je suis très s. de ma prestation** I'm quite satisfied *or* pleased with my performance; **elle est partie maintenant, tu es s.?** now she's gone, are you satisfied?; **d'accord, j'ai menti, tu es s.?** OK, I've lied, are you satisfied now?

satisfecit [satisfesit] NM INV 1 *Scol* star, credit 2 *(approbation)* full credit; **décerner un s. à qn pour avoir fait qch** to congratulate sb for having done sth

satisfera *etc voir* **satisfaire**

satisfiable [satisfjabl] ADJ *Ling* satisfiable

satisfont *voir* **satisfaire**

Satolas [satɔlas] NM = airport near Lyons

saton [satɔ̃] NM *Fam* **coup de s.** kick▪, boot; **donner des coups de s. à qn/dans qch** to boot sb/sth, to give sb/sth a kicking

satonner [3] [satɔne] VT *Fam* **s. qn/qch** to boot sb/sth, to give sb/sth a kicking

satori [satɔri] NM INV *Rel* satori

satrape [satrap] NM 1 *Hist* satrap 2 *Littéraire (tyran)* satrap, despot; *(homme riche)* nabob

satrapie [satrapi] NF *Hist* satrapy

saturabilité [satyrabilite] NF saturability

saturable [satyrabl] ADJ saturable

saturant, -e [satyrɑ̃, -ɑ̃t] ADJ saturating, saturant

NM saturant

saturateur [satyratœr] NM 1 *Chim* saturator, saturater 2 *(pour radiateur)* humidifier

saturation [satyrasjɔ̃] NF 1 *Biol & Phys* saturation; **s. en eau** water saturation; **s. magnétique** (magnetic) saturation

2 *TV* chroma; *TV & Rad* **s. acoustique** popping

3 *Fig (d'une autoroute, d'un aéroport)* saturation, paralysis, gridlocking; *(d'un circuit de communication)* saturation, overloading; *(d'un marché)* saturation (point); **arriver** *ou* **parvenir à s.** *(marché, aéroport)* to reach saturation point; *(marcheur, travailleur)* to reach saturation point, to be unable to take any more; **nous arrivons à la s. totale du réseau** the network has reached saturation point

saturé, -e [satyre] ADJ 1 *(imprégné → gén)* impregnated; *(→ d'un liquide)* saturated; **sol s. de sel** very salty soil

2 *(rassasié, écœuré)* **s. de** sated with; **des enfants saturés de télévision** children who have watched too much television; **ah non, assez de pub, j'en suis s.!** no more ads, I'm sick of them!

3 *(engorgé → autoroute, aéroport)* saturated, paralysed, gridlocked; *(→ circuit de communication)* saturated, overloaded; *(→ marché)* saturated

4 *Biol, Phys & Tech* saturated

saturer [3] [satyre] VT 1 *Biol & Phys* to saturate; **s. qch de** to saturate sth with

2 *(surcharger, remplir en excès)* to saturate, to glut; **s. un marché de produits agricoles** to glut *or* to saturate a market with agricultural products; **nous sommes saturés de publicités pour des lessives** we're swamped with washing powder adverts; **le professeur nous sature de travail** the teacher is overloading us with work; **être saturé de travail** to be up to one's eyes in work, to be swamped with work; **les appels de nos téléspectateurs ont saturé le standard** our viewers' calls have jammed the switchboards; **saturé d'eau/de sang** saturated with water/with blood; **le jardin est saturé d'eau** the garden is waterlogged *or* saturated with water

VI *Fam* 1 *(marché)* to become saturated; *(lignes téléphoniques)* to overload; **ça sature** *(sonorisation)* we're getting distortion

2 *(personne)* to have had enough, to have had as much as one can take

saturnales [satyrnal] NFPL 1 *Littéraire (débauche)* saturnalia, (wild) orgies 2 *Antiq* saturnalia

Saturne [satyrn] NF *Astron* Saturn

NPR *Myth* Saturn

saturne [satyrn] NM Saturn *(in alchemy)*

saturnie [satyrni] NF *Entom* emperor moth

saturnien, -enne [satyrnjɛ̃, -ɛn] ADJ 1 *Astron* Saturnian 2 *Littéraire (morose)* saturnine

saturnin, -e [satyrnɛ̃, -in] ADJ 1 *Chim* lead *(avant n)* 2 *Méd* saturnine

saturnisme [satyrnism] NM *Méd* (chronic) lead poisoning, *Spéc* saturnism

satyre [satir] NM 1 *Myth & Entom* satyr 2 *(homme lubrique)* lecher 3 *Bot* **s. puant** stinkhorn

satyresse [satirɛs] NF *Littéraire* she-satyr

satyriasis [satirjazis] NM *Psy* satyriasis

satyrique [satirik] ADJ satyric, satyrical

sauce [sos] NF 1 *Culin* sauce; *(de salade)* salad dressing; *(vinaigrette)* French dressing, vinaigrette; *(jus de viande)* gravy; **s. à la moutarde/aux câpres** mustard/caper sauce; **s. béarnaise/hollandaise** béarnaise/hollandaise sauce; **s. madère/piquante** Madeira/hot sauce; **s. béchamel** béchamel *or* white sauce; **s. bordelaise** sauce bordelaise; **s. mousseline** sauce mousseline; **s. de soja** soy sauce; **s. suprême** sauce suprême; **s. tartare** tartare sauce; **pâtes à la s. tomate** pasta with tomato sauce; *Fam* **mettre** *ou* **servir qch à toutes les sauces** to make sth fit every occasion; *Fam* **mettre une citation/une théorie à toutes les sauces** to make a quotation/a theory fit every (available *or* possible) occasion; *Fam* **une expression qui a été mise à**

sat–sau

toutes les sauces a hackneyed phrase■ ; *Fam* **je me demande à quelle s. nous allons être mangés** I wonder what lies in store for us■ *or* what they're going to do to us■ ; *Prov* **la s. fait passer le poisson** a spoonful of sugar helps the medicine go down; *Fam* **allonger** *ou* **rallonger la s.** *(à l'écrit)* to waffle on

2 *Fam (pluie)* rain■ ; **prendre** *ou* **recevoir la s.** to get drenched *or* soaked (to the skin)

3 *Fam (courant électrique)* juice; **il n'y a pas assez de s.** there's not enough juice *or* power; **envoie la s.!** turn on the power *or* juice!; *Fam* **mettre la s.** to pull out all the stops, to go all out

4 *Beaux-Arts* soft black crayon

5 *Vulg* **balancer la s.** *(éjaculer)* to shoot one's load *or* wad

❑ **en sauce** ADJ with a sauce; **viande/poisson en s.** meat/fish served in a sauce

saucée [sose] NF *Fam* downpour; **prendre** *ou* **recevoir la s.** to get drenched *or* soaked (to the skin); **il va y avoir une s.** it's going to bucket down

saucer [16] [sose] VT **1** *Vieilli (tremper)* **s. son pain** to dip one's bread in sauce **2** *(essuyer → assiette)* to wipe (off) **3** *Fam (locution)* **se faire s.** to get drenched *or* soaked (to the skin)

saucier [sosje] NM **1** *(employé)* sauce chef **2** *(appareil)* sauce-maker

saucière [sosjɛr] NF *(pour sauce)* sauce boat; *(pour jus)* gravy boat

sauciflard [sosiflar] NM *Fam* (dried) sausage■

saucisse [sosis] NF **1** *Culin* sausage; **s. de Francfort** frankfurter; **s. de Strasbourg** knackwurst; **s. de Toulouse** = type of pork sausage **2** *Fam Arg mil (ballon captif)* barrage balloon■ **3** *Fam (personne)* **grande s.** beanpole; **espèce de grande s.!** you great lump!, you numbskull! **4** *Fam Hum* **s. à pattes** *(chien)* sausage dog

saucisson [sosisɔ̃] NM **1** *Culin* **s. (sec)** (dry) sausage; **s. à l'ail** garlic sausage; **s. pur porc** 100 percent pork sausage **2** *(pain)* sausage-shaped loaf **3** *(charge de poudre)* powder hose **4** *Fam Hum* **s. à pattes** *(chien)* sausage dog

saucissonnage [sosisɔnaʒ] NM *Fam* dividing up■

saucissonner [3] [sosisɔne] *Fam* VI to picnic■ , to have a snack■

VT **1** *(attacher → personne)* to tie up■ ; **ils ont saucissonné le gardien sur la chaise** they trussed up the caretaker and tied him to a chair; *Fig* **saucissonnée dans son collant/dans sa robe** bulging out of her tights/dress

2 *(diviser)* **le film a été saucissonné** the movie *or Br* film was divided up into episodes; **un film saucissonné par des publicités** a movie *or Br* film with frequent commercial breaks

saucissonneur, -euse [sosisɔnœr, -øz] NM,F *Fam* picnicker

sauf[1] [sof] PRÉP **1** *(à part)* except, apart from, *Sout* save; **tout le monde s. Paul** everyone except (for) *or* apart from Paul; **ils y ont tous cru, s. moi** they all believed it except me; **nous avons parlé de tout, s. de ce point précis** we spoke about everything except *or* apart from this one particular point; **j'ai voyagé partout en Allemagne, s. en Bavière** I've been everywhere in Germany except (for) Bavaria; **il a pensé à tout, s. à ça** he thought of everything except that; **il sait tout faire s. cuisiner** he can do everything except *or* but cook; **il s'arrête toujours ici s. s'il n'a pas le temps** he always stops here except if *or* unless he's in a hurry; **j'y vais régulièrement s. quand il ne fait pas beau** I go there regularly except when the weather's bad

2 *(à moins de)* unless; **s. avis contraire** unless otherwise instructed; **s. indications contraires** unless otherwise stated; **s. erreur ou omission** errors and omissions excepted; *Jur* **s. accord ou convention contraire** unless otherwise agreed

❑ **sauf à** PRÉP *Littéraire* **il a pris cette décision, s. à changer plus tard** he took this decision, but reserved the right to change it later

❑ **sauf que** CONJ except (for the fact) that, apart from the fact that; **il n'a pas changé, s. que ses cheveux ont blanchi** he hasn't changed, except (for the fact) that he has gone grey

sauf[2], **sauve** [sof, sov] ADJ **1** *(indemne → personne)* safe; **elle est sauve** she's safe, she escaped unhurt *or* unharmed **2** *Fig (intact)* **au moins, les apparences sont sauves** at least appearances have been kept up *or* saved; **sa réputation est sauve** his/her reputation is intact *or* saved

sauf-conduit [sofkɔ̃dɥi] *(pl* **sauf-conduits***)* NM safe-conduct

sauge [soʒ] NF **1** *Bot* salvia; **s. officinale** sage; **s. des prés** meadow clary **2** *Culin* sage

saugrenu, -e [sogrəny] ADJ absurd, ridiculous

Saül [sayl] NPR *Bible* Saul

saulaie [solɛ] NF willow plantation

saule [sol] NM willow; **s. blanc** white willow; **s. cassant** crack willow; **s. marsault** goat willow; **s. pleureur** weeping willow

saulée [sole] NF row of willow trees

saumâtre [somatr] ADJ **1** *(salé)* brackish, briny **2** *Fam (désagréable)* bitter■ , nasty■ ; **il l'a trouvée s.!** he didn't appreciate it at all, he wasn't amused *or* impressed

saumon [somɔ̃] NM **1** *Ich* salmon; **s. de l'Atlantique** Atlantic salmon; **s. chinook** chinook salmon; **s. de fontaine** brook salmon; *Culin* **s. fumé** *Br* smoked salmon, *Am* lox; **s. rouge** nerka **2** *(couleur)* salmon, salmon-pink **3** *Métal* pig

ADJ INV salmon, salmon-pink

saumoné, -e [somɔne] ADJ *(couleur)* salmon, salmon-pink

saumoneau, -x [somɔno] NM young salmon, parr

saumonette [somɔnɛt] NF *Culin* rock salmon

Saumur [somyr] NM = town in western France with a military academy famous as a centre for cavalry training

saumur [somyr] NM *(vin)* Saumur

saumurage [somyraʒ] NM pickling (in brine)

saumure [somyr] NF brine; **conserver du poisson/des cornichons dans la s.** to pickle fish/gherkins (in brine)

saumurer [3] [somyre] VT to pickle (in brine)

sauna [sona] NM sauna

saunage [sonaʒ] NM **1** *(fabrication)* salt making **2** *(saison)* salt (making) season **3** *(vente)* salt trade

saunaison [sonɛzɔ̃] NF = **saunage**

sauner [3] [sone] VI to yield salt

saunier [sonje] NM **1** *(ouvrier)* salt worker **2** *(marchand)* salt merchant; *Hist* **faux s.** contraband salt merchant

saunière [sonjɛr] NF **1** *Hist* salt box **2** *Chasse* salt lick

saupe [sop] NF *Ich* saupe, salema

saupiquet [sopike] NM *Culin (au lapin, au lièvre, au canard)* = type of spicy stew made from rabbit, hare or duck; *(au jambon)* = fried ham served with a spicy sauce

saupoudrage [sopudraʒ] NM **1** *Culin* sprinkling, dusting **2** *Fin & Pol (de crédits)* = allocation of small amounts of funding to various beneficiaries

saupoudrer [3] [sopudre] VT **1** *Culin* to dust, to sprinkle (**de** with) **2** *Fin & Pol* **s. des crédits** = to allocate small amounts of funding to various beneficiaries **3** *Fig Littéraire (parsemer)* to scatter, to sprinkle (**de** with); **s. un discours de citations** to pepper a speech with quotations

▸**se saupoudrer** VPR **se s. les mains de talc** to dust one's hands with talcum powder

saupoudreuse [sopudrøz] NF sprinkler

saur [sɔr] *voir* **hareng**

saura *etc voir* **savoir**

saurage [sɔraʒ] NM *(des harengs)* kippering, smoking; *(du jambon)* smoking, curing

saurer [3] [sɔre] VT *(harengs)* to kipper, to smoke; *(jambon)* to smoke, to cure

sauret [sɔrɛ] NM *Belg* smoked herring, kipper

saurien [sɔrjɛ̃] *Zool* NM saurian

❑ **sauriens** NMPL saurians, *Spéc* Sauria

saurin [sɔrɛ̃] NM freshly smoked herring, bloater

sauris [sɔri] NM (pickling) brine

saurischien [sɔriskjɛ̃] NM *Zool* saurischian

saurissage [sɔrisaʒ] NM *(des harengs)* kippering, smoking; *(du jambon)* smoking, curing

saurisserie [sɔrisri] NF herring-curing establishment

saurisseur, -euse [sɔrisœr, -øz] NM,F herring curer

saurophidien [sɔrofidjɛ̃] *Zool* NM member of the Squamata order

❑ **saurophidiens** NMPL Squamata

sauropsidé [sɔropside] *Zool* NM sauropsidan

❑ **sauropsidés** NMPL Sauropsida

saussaie [sosɛ] NF willow plantation

saut [so] NM **1** *Sport* jump; **le s.** jumping; **championnat/épreuves de s.** jumping championship/events; **s. en hauteur/en longueur** high/*Br* long *or Am* broad jump; **s. de l'ange** *Br* swallow *or Am* swan dive; **s. de carpe** jack-knife dive; *Fig* **faire des sauts de carpe** to bounce around; **s. carpé** pike; **s. en chute libre** free-fall jump; **s. en ciseaux** scissors jump; **s. à la corde** skipping; **s. à l'élastique** bungee jumping; **s. groupé** tuck; **s. de haies** hurdling; **s. de la mort** death jump; **s. d'obstacles** showjumping; **s. en parachute** *(discipline)* parachuting, skydiving; *(épreuve)* parachute jump; **faire du s. en parachute** to go parachuting *or* skydiving; **s. à la perche** *(discipline)* pole vaulting; *(épreuve)* pole vault; **s. périlleux** somersault; **s. à pieds joints** standing jump; **s. en rouleau** western roll; **s. à skis** *(discipline)* ski-jumping; *(épreuve)* (ski-)jump

2 *(bond)* jump, leap; **faire un s.** to jump, to leap, to take a leap; **se lever d'un s.** to leap *or* to jump to one's feet; **s. de puce** step; **au s. du lit** *(en se levant)* on *or* upon getting up; *(tôt)* first thing in the morning; *Fig Arch* **par sauts et par bonds** in fits and starts

3 *(chute)* drop; **elle a fait un s. de cinq mètres dans le vide** she fell *or* plunged five metres into the void

4 *(brève visite)* flying visit; **elle a fait un s. chez nous hier** she dropped by (our house) yesterday; **je ne fais qu'un s.** *(quelques instants)* I'm only passing, I'm not staying; *(quelques heures)* I'm only on a flying visit; **fais un s. chez le boucher** pop over *or* along to the butcher's

5 *Fig (changement brusque)* leap; **faire un s. dans l'inconnu** to take a leap in the dark; **faire un s. dans le passé** to go back into the past; **faire un s. d'un siècle** to jump a century; **le grand s.** *(la mort)* the big sleep; **faire le s.** to take the plunge

6 *Géog* falls, waterfall; **le s. du Doubs** the Doubs falls

7 *Ordinat & Math* jump

8 *Typ* **s. de ligne** line break; **s. de ligne manuel** hard return; **s. de page** page break

9 *Cin & TV* **s. en avant** flash forward; **faire un s. en avant** to flash forward; *Cin & TV* **s. de montage** jump cut

❑ **sauts** NMPL *(en danse)* jumps

sautage [sotaʒ] NM *(d'une mine)* blowing up

saut-de-lit [sodli] *(pl* **sauts-de-lit***)* NM dressing gown, light robe

saut-de-loup [sodlu] *(pl* **sauts-de-loup***)* NM ha-ha

saut-de-mouton [sodmutɔ̃] *(pl* **sauts-de-mouton***)* NM *Br* flyover, *Am* overpass

saute [sot] NF **1** *Météo* **s. de vent** shift (of the wind); **s. de température** sudden change in temperature **2** *Fig* **s. d'humeur** mood swing; **sujet à de fréquentes sautes d'humeur** prone to frequent changes of mood

sauté, -e [sote] ADJ *(pommes de terre, viande)* sautéed, sauté

NM sauté; **s. de veau** sauté of veal

saute-au-paf [sotopaf] NF INV *très Fam (femme aux mœurs légères)* nympho, *Br* goer

sautelle [sotɛl] NF *(sarment recourbé)* layered vine shoot

saute-mouton [sotmutɔ̃] NM INV leapfrog; **jouer à s.** to play leapfrog; **il jouait à s. par-dessus les tréteaux** he was leapfrogging over the trestles

SAUTER [3] [sote]

> VI to jump **1–3, 6** ■ to leap **1** ■ to blow up **4** ■ to come off **5** ■ to flicker **5** ■ to snap **5** ■ to fall **8**
> VT to jump over **1** ■ to leave out **2**

VI **1** *(bondir → personne)* to jump, to spring up; *(→ chat)* to jump, to leap; *(→ oiseau, insecte)* to hop; *(→ grenouille, saumon)* to leap; *(→ balle, curseur)* to bounce, to jump; **s. dans une tranchée/dans un puits** to jump into a trench/down a well; **s. en selle** to jump *or* to leap into the saddle; **s. d'une branche/d'une falaise** to leap off a branch/a cliff; **s. par-dessus une corde/un ruisseau** to leap over a rope/across a stream; **il faut s. pour atteindre l'étagère** you've got to jump up to

sau–sau

reach the shelf; **s. par la fenêtre** to jump out of the window; **quand je pense que je la faisais s. sur mes genoux il n'y a pas si longtemps** when I think that not so long ago, I was bouncing *or* dandling her on my knee; *Fig* **s. de joie** to jump for joy; *Fam* **s. au plafond, s. en l'air** *(de colère)* to hit the roof; *(de joie)* to be thrilled to bits, to jump for joy; **s. comme un cabri** to frolic

2 *Sport & (jeux)* **s. à cloche-pied** to hop; **s. à la corde** *Br* to skip (with a rope), *Am* to skip *or* to jump rope; **s. en parachute** to (parachute) jump, to parachute; **s. en hauteur/en longueur** to do the high/the *Br* long *or Am* broad jump; **s. à la perche** to pole-vault; **s. à skis** to ski-jump; **s. en ciseaux** to do a scissors jump

3 *(se ruer)* to jump, to pounce; **s. (à bas) du lit** to jump *or* to spring out of bed; **s. dans un taxi** to jump *or* to leap into a taxi; **il sauta sur le malheureux passant** he pounced on the wretched passer-by; *Fam Fig* **je lui sauterai dessus dès qu'il reviendra** I'll grab him as soon as he gets back; *Fam* **s. sur l'occasion** to jump at the chance; **c'est une excellente occasion, je saute dessus** it's a great opportunity, I'll grab it; **se faire s. dessus** to be jumped on; **s. à la gorge** *ou* **au collet de qn** to jump down sb's throat; *Fam* **va te laver les mains, et que ça saute!** go and wash your hands and jump to it *or* make it snappy!; **ça saute aux yeux** it's plain for all to see *or* as the nose on your face

4 *(exploser)* to blow up, to explode, to go off; **faire s. un pont/un char** to blow up a bridge/a tank; **faire s. une mine** to explode a mine; *Élec* **les plombs ont sauté** the fuses have blown; *Élec* **faire s. les plombs** to blow the fuses; **la lampe/le circuit a sauté** *Br* the lamp/the circuit has fused, *Am* the lamp fuse/the circuit has blown

5 *(être projeté)* **les boutons ont sauté** the buttons flew off *or* popped off; **faire s. le bouchon d'une bouteille** to pop a cork; *Fam* **se faire s. la cervelle** *ou* **le caisson** to blow one's brains out; *aussi Fig* **faire s. la banque** to break the bank

6 *(changer sans transition)* to jump

7 *(cesser de fonctionner → chaîne, courroie)* to come off; *(→ image de télévision)* to flicker; *(→ serrure)* to snap; *Ordinat (→ réseau)* to crash

8 *Fam (être renvoyé)* to fall; **le gouvernement a sauté** the government has fallen; **le ministre a sauté** the minister got fired *or Br* got the sack; **faire s. un directeur** to kick out *or* to fire a manager

9 *Culin* **faire s. des pommes de terre** to sauté potatoes; **faire s. des crêpes** to toss pancakes

10 *Naut (vent)* to change

VT 1 *(obstacle)* to jump *or* to leap over; *Fig* **s. le pas** to take the plunge

2 *(omettre)* to skip, to leave out; **s. une ligne** to leave a line; **s. une danse** to sit out a dance

3 *Vulg (sexuellement)* **s. qn** to screw sb; **se faire s.** to get laid

4 *très Fam (locution)* **la s.** *(se passer de manger)* to skip a meal; *(avoir faim)* to be starving

sautereau, -x [sotro] **NM** *Mus (partie du clavecin)* jack

sauterelle [sotrɛl] **NF 1** *Entom* grasshopper; *(criquet)* locust **2** *Fam (fille, femme)* chick, *Br* bird; **grande s.** beanpole **3** *(en manutention)* travelling belt, conveyor (belt) **4** *Menuis* bevel (square)

sauterie [sotri] **NF** *Hum* party■, get-together, *Br* do; **donner une petite s.** to throw a party, to have a get-together *or Br* do

sauternes [sotɛrn] **NM** Sauternes (wine)

saute-ruisseau [sotrɥiso] **NM INV** *Vieilli* errand boy

sauteur, -euse [sotœr, -øz] **ADJ** jumping, hopping

NM,F *Sport* jumper; **s. en hauteur/en longueur** high/*Br* long *or Am* broad jumper; **s. à la perche** pole-vaulter

NM *Fam (homme sans sérieux)* unreliable sort

▫ **sauteuse NF 1** *Culin* high-sided *Br* frying *or Am* fry pan **2** *Menuis* jigsaw, scroll saw **3** *Fam Vieilli (femme de mœurs légères)* slut

sautier [sotje] **NM** *Suisse Admin* = head of the legislative assembly of the canton of Geneva

sautillant, -e [sotijɑ̃, -ɑ̃t] **ADJ 1** *(démarche, oiseau)* hopping, skipping; **d'un pas s.** with a dancing step **2** *Fig (style)* light; *(refrain)* gay, bouncy

sautillement [sotijmɑ̃] **NM 1** *(petit saut)* hop, skip, skipping *(UNCOUNT)* **2** *(changement constant)* jumping around, chopping and changing

sautiller [3] [sotije] **VI 1** *(faire de petits sauts)* to hop, to skip; **marcher en sautillant** to skip along; **s. sur un pied** to hop; **s. d'un pied sur l'autre** to hop from one foot to the other **2** *(papillonner)* to flit; **sa pensée sautille sans cesse** his/her mind flits from one thing to another

sautoir [sotwar] **NM 1** *(bijou)* chain; **en s.** on a chain; **s. de perles** string of pearls **2** *Sport* long-jump area **3** *Culin* high-sided frying pan **4** *Hér* saltire

sauvage [sovaʒ] **ADJ 1** *Zool (non domestique)* wild; *(non apprivoisé)* untamed; **il est redevenu s.** *(chat)* he's gone feral *or* wild; *(jeune fauve)* he's gone back to the wild; **à l'état s.** wild

2 *(non cultivé)* wild; **le jardin est redevenu s. depuis leur départ** since they left the garden has become overgrown

3 *(peu fréquenté → lieu)* wild, remote; **les régions sauvages du nord de l'Écosse** the wilds *or* the remote regions of northern Scotland

4 *(réservé, timide)* shy; *(peu sociable)* unsociable

5 *Vieilli & (en anthropologie)* savage, uncivilized; **une peuplade s.** an uncivilized people; **retourner à la vie s.** to go back to the wild

6 *(barbare → personne, geste, violence)* savage, brutal; *(→ mœurs)* uncivilized

7 *(illégal → camping, vente)* unauthorized; *(→ urbanisation)* unplanned; *(→ immigration)* illegal

NMF 1 *Vieilli & (en anthropologie)* savage; **leurs premiers contacts avec les sauvages des îles** their first contacts with the island savages; **le bon s.** the noble savage

2 *(personne fruste, grossière)* boor, brute; **il se conduit comme un s.** he's a real brute; *Fam* **on n'est pas des sauvages!** we're not savages!; *Fam* **bande de sauvages!** you bunch of savages!

3 *(personne farouche)* unsociable person, recluse

sauvagement [sovaʒmɑ̃] **ADV** savagely, viciously; **s. assassiné** savagely *or* brutally murdered

sauvageon, -onne [sovaʒɔ̃, -ɔn] **NM,F** wild child

NM *(arbre)* wildling

sauvagerie [sovaʒri] **NF 1** *(méchanceté)* viciousness, brutality **2** *(misanthropie)* unsociability

sauvagin, -e [sovaʒɛ̃, -in] **ADJ** *Chasse (odeur, goût)* gamey

NM *Chasse (odeur)* gamey smell; *(goût)* gamey taste

▫ **sauvagine NF 1** *Chasse* wildfowl *(UNCOUNT)*; **chasse à la sauvagine** wildfowling **2** *(fourrure)* common pelts, fur skins

sauvaginier [sovaʒinje] **NM** *Chasse* wildfowler

sauve [sov] *voir* **sauf**[2]

sauvegarde [sovgard] **NF 1** *(protection)* safeguard, safeguarding *(UNCOUNT)*; **s. des ressources naturelles** conservation of natural resources; **sous la s. de qn** under sb's protection; *Jur* **sous la s. de la justice** under the protection of the Court

2 *(sécurité)* safety

3 *Ordinat* backup; **faire une s.** to save; **faire la s. d'un fichier** to save a file; **s. automatique** autosave, automatic backup; **s. sur bande** tape backup

4 *Naut* safety rope

sauvegarder [3] [sovgarde] **VT 1** *(protéger → bien)* to safeguard, to watch over; *(→ honneur, réputation)* to protect **2** *Ordinat* to save, to back up; **s. un fichier sur disquette** to save a file to disk; **s. automatiquement** to autosave

sauve-qui-peut [sovkipø] **NM INV** stampede; **ce fut un s. général** there was a general stampede

sauver [3] [sove] **VT 1** *(personne → gén)* to save, to rescue (**de** from); *(→ dans un accident, dans une catastrophe)* to rescue; **s. la vie à qn** to save sb's life; **s. qn de la noyade/de la faillite** to rescue sb from drowning/from bankruptcy; *Fig* **tu me sauves!** you're a lifesaver!; **être sauvé** *(sain et sauf)* to be safe; *(par quelqu'un)* to have been saved *or* rescued; **ils ont atteint la côte, ils sont sauvés!** they've reached the shore, they're safe!; **le malade est sauvé** the patient is out of danger; *Fig* **il y a une banque ouverte, je suis sauvé!** there's a bank open, saved again!; **tout est prêt pour la kermesse demain, nous sommes sauvés!** everything is ready for tomorrow's fete, we're home free *or Br* home and dry *Fam* **s. sa peau** to save one's skin *or* hide

2 *(protéger)* **s. les apparences** to keep up appearances; **pour s. l'honneur** so that honour may be saved; **s. la face** to save face; **s. la situation** to save *or* to retrieve the situation; **la musique sauve le film** the music saves the movie *or Br* film; **ce qui le sauve, c'est que...** his saving grace is that...; *Fam* **je lui ai sauvé la mise** I've got him/her out of trouble, I've bailed him/her out

3 *(préserver)* to salvage, to save; **on n'a pu s. qu'un morceau du toit** only part of the roof survived *or* could be salvaged; **s. qch de l'oubli** to rescue sth from oblivion; *Fam* **s. les meubles** to salvage something from the situation

4 *Rel* to save

▫ **sauve qui peut EXCLAM** run for your life!, every man for himself!

►**se sauver VPR 1** *Rel* to be saved

2 *(animal)* to escape (**de** from); *(pensionnaire)* to run away (**de** from); *(prisonnier)* to escape, to break out (**de** from); *(matelot)* to jump ship; **se s. à toutes jambes** to take to one's heels (and run)

3 *Fam (lait)* to boil over■

4 *Fam (s'en aller)* to leave, *Am* to split; **il est l'heure, il faut que je me sauve** it's time, I must get going; **sauve-toi!** run along now!; **bon, je me sauve!** right, I'm off *or* on my way!

'Boudu sauvé des eaux' *Renoir* 'Boudu Saved from Drowning'

---

sauvetage [sovtaʒ] **NM 1** *(d'un accidenté)* rescue; **opérer** *ou* **effectuer le s. d'un équipage** to rescue a crew; **il a fait plusieurs sauvetages en mer** he has been involved in several sea rescues; **mission de s.** rescue mission; *Fig* **s. d'une entreprise** financial rescue of a company; **s. aérien/en montagne** air/mountain rescue; **s. aérien en mer** air-sea rescue

2 *Naut (de l'équipage)* life saving, sea rescue; *(de la cargaison)* salvage

▫ **de sauvetage ADJ** life *(avant n)*

sauveté [sovte] **NF 1** *Hist* = medieval village serving as a hiding place for fugitives **2** *(en apiculture)* **cellule de s.** queen cell; **reine de s.** replacement queen

sauveterrien, -enne [sovterjɛ̃, -ɛn] *Archéol* **ADJ** Sauveterrian

NM Sauveterrian

sauveteur [sovtœr] **NM** rescuer

sauvette [sovɛt] **à la sauvette ADJ marchand** *ou* **vendeur à la s.** (illicit) street peddler *or* hawker; **vente à la s.** (illicit) street peddling *or* hawking **ADV 1** *(illégalement)* **vendre qch à la s.** to hawk *or* to peddle sth (without authorization) **2** *(discrètement)* stealthily; **il m'a glissé un mot à la s.** he slipped me a note

sauveur [sovœr] **NM 1** *(bienfaiteur)* saviour; *Hum* **tu es mon s.!** you've saved my life! **2** *Rel* **le S.** Our Saviour

ADJ M saving *(avant n)*

sauvignon [soviɲɔ̃] **NM 1** *Bot* Sauvignon plant **2** *(vin)* Sauvignon *(wine)*

SAV [ɛsave] **NM** *(abrév* **service après-vente)** after-sales service

savamment [savamɑ̃] **ADV 1** *(avec érudition)* learnedly; **elle expose s. ses connaissances** she presents her knowledge in a learned manner **2** *(habilement)* cleverly, cunningly; **des tresses s. enroulées** cleverly arranged tresses **3** *(par expérience)* **j'en parle s.** I know what I'm talking about, I have first-hand experience (in this matter)

savane [savan] **NF 1** *(dans les pays chauds)* bush, savanna, savannah **2** *Can (marécage)* bog

savant, -e [savɑ̃, -ɑ̃t] **ADJ 1** *(érudit → livre, moine, société)* learned; *(→ traduction, conversation)* scholarly; *(→ mot, terme)* specialist, technical; **être s. en peinture/en grec** to be well-versed in

painting/in Greek; **c'est trop s. pour lui!** that's (totally) beyond his grasp!; **faire de savants calculs** to work things out in complex detail

2 *(habile)* skilful, clever; **un s. édifice de paquets de lessive** a cleverly constructed tower of soap powder packs

3 *(dressé → chien, puce)* performing

NM,F *(lettré)* scholar

NM *(scientifique)* scientist; **Marie Curie fut un grand s.** Marie Curie was a great scientist

savarin [savarɛ̃] NM savarin (cake)

savart [savar] NM *Mus* savart

savate [savat] NF **1** *(chaussure)* worn-out (old) shoe; *(pantoufle)* old slipper; **il est en savates toute la journée** he pads around in his old slippers all day long; *Fam* **comme une s.** appallingly badly; **il chante comme une s.** he can't sing to save his life, *Br* he can't sing for toffee; *Fam* **traîner la s.** *(être sans le sou)* to be completely broke; *(être oisif)* to hang around, to bum around

2 *Sport* **la s.** French boxing

3 *Tech* sole (plate)

savater [3] [savate] VT *Fam* to kick▪, to boot

savetier [savtje] NM *Arch (cordonnier)* cobbler

saveur [savœr] NF **1** *(goût)* savour, flavour; **ce fruit est sans s.** this fruit is tasteless *or* has no flavour; **une poire pleine de s.** a tasty pear; **quelle s.!** very tasty! **2** *(trait particulier)* fragrance, savour; **il y a toute la s. de l'Italie dans son accent** there is all the flavour of Italy in his accent **3** *(piment → d'une remarque, d'un récit)* spice, pungency; **la s. du péché** the sweet taste of sin

Savoie [savwa] NF **la S.** Savoy, Savoie

SAVOIR [59] [savwar]

> NM knowledge
> VT to know **1–3, 5, 7, 8, 10** ▪ to know how to **6** ▪ to be aware of **7**
> USAGE ABSOLU to know
> VPR to become known **1**
> ADV namely

NM knowledge; **un homme d'un grand s.** a very knowledgeable *or* learned man, a man of great learning; **savoirs comportementaux** soft skills

VT **1** *(connaître → donnée, réponse, situation)* to know; **nous ne savons toujours pas le nom du vainqueur** we still don't know the winner's name; **que savez-vous de lui?** what do you know about *or* of him?; **tu sais la nouvelle?** have you heard the news?; **on le savait malade** we knew *or* we were aware (that) he was ill; **on le savait alcoolique** he was known to be an alcoholic, he was a known alcoholic; *Littéraire* **je lui savais une grande fortune** I knew him/her to be wealthy; *Littéraire* **on lui sait des parents** he/she is known to have relatives; **je ne te savais pas si susceptible** I didn't know *or* I didn't realize *or* I never thought you were so touchy; **je sais un moyen d'y parvenir** I know a way to do it; **je ne sais rien de plus apaisant que la musique** I don't know anything more soothing than music

2 *(être informé de)* **comment sais-tu que j'habite ici?** how do you know I live here?; **que va-t-il arriver à Tintin? pour le s., lisez notre prochain numéro!** what's in store for Tintin? find out in our next issue!; **c'est toujours bon à s.** it's (always) worth knowing; *Fam* **je sais des choses...** *(sur un ton taquin)* I know a thing or two; **c'est sa maîtresse – tu en sais des choses!** she's his mistress – you seem well informed!; *Fam* **je sais ce que je sais!** I know what I know!; **je sais ce que j'ai vu** I know what I saw; *Littéraire* **je ne sais** I do not know; **je n'en sais pas plus que toi** I don't know any more than you do; **pour en s. plus, composez le 34 15** *(sur Minitel®)* for more information *or* (if you want) to know more, dial 34 15; **il en savait trop** he knew too much; **ce n'est pas elle qui l'a dénoncé – qu'en savez-vous?** she wasn't the one who turned him in – what do you know about it *or* how do you know?; **je n'en sais rien du tout** I don't know anything about it, I haven't got a clue; **après tout, tu n'en sais rien!** after all, what do YOU know about it!; **il est venu ici, mais personne n'en a rien su** he came here, but nobody found out about it; **chercher à en s. davantage** to try and find out more; **en s. long sur qn/qch** to know a great deal about sb/sth; **j'en sais long sur lui** I know a lot about him; **on n'en sait pas long sur son enfance** we don't know much about his/her childhood; **en s. quelque chose** to have some knowledge (of a subject); **oh oui ça fait mal, j'en sais quelque chose!** yes, it's very painful, I can tell you!; **il n'aime pas les cafardeurs – tu dois en s. quelque chose!** he doesn't like sneaks – you'd know all about that!; **pour ce que j'en sais** for all I know; **je sais à quoi m'en tenir sur lui** I know what kind of (a) person he is; **je ne sais pas si elle a eu mon message** I don't know whether she got my message; **sais-tu où/pourquoi il est parti?** do you know where/why he went?; **je crois s. qu'ils ont annulé la conférence** I have reason *or* I'm led to believe that they called off the conference; **tout le monde sait que...** it's a well-known fact *or* everybody knows that...; **je ne sais combien, on ne sait combien** *(d'argent)* who knows how much; **ça a coûté je ne sais combien** it cost who knows *or* I don't know how much; **il y a je ne sais combien de temps** a very long time ago; **il a fallu je ne sais combien de soldats** God knows how many soldiers were needed; **je ne sais comment, on ne sait comment** God knows how; **elle y est arrivée on ne sait comment** she managed God knows how *or* somehow or other; **je ne sais où, on ne sait où** God knows where; **il est je ne sais où** God knows where he is; **je ne sais pourquoi, on ne sait pourquoi** God *or* who knows why; **sans (trop) s. pourquoi** *(agir, parler)* without really knowing why; *(marcher)* aimlessly; **sans trop s. quoi faire** *(attendre, marcher)* aimlessly; **je ne sais quel/quelle...** some... or other; **retenu par je ne sais quelle affaire** held up by some business or other; **je ne sais qui, on ne sait qui** somebody or other; **il y a je ne sais quoi de bizarre chez lui** there's something a bit weird about him; **il vendait des tapis, des bracelets et que sais-je encore** he was selling carpets, bracelets and goodness *or* God knows what else; *Math* **sachant que x = y, démontrez que...** if x = y, show that...; *Sout ou Hum* **je ne sache pas qu'on ait modifié le calendrier, on n'a pas modifié le calendrier, que je sache** the calendar hasn't been altered that I know of *or* as far as I know; **a-t-elle la permission? – pas que je sache** has she got permission? – not to my knowledge *or* not as far as I know; **Napoléon, qu'on sache, n'avait pas demandé leur reddition** Napoleon had not asked them to surrender, as far as is known; **va s. ce qui lui a pris!** who knows what possessed him/her?; **pourquoi est-elle partie? – allez s.?** why did she leave? – who knows?

3 *(être convaincu de)* to know, to be certain *or* sure; **je savais bien que ça ne marcherait pas!** I knew it wouldn't work!; **je sais parfaitement qu'il est innocent** I know for sure he's innocent; **je ne sais pas si ça en vaut la peine** I don't know if it's worth it; **je n'en sais trop rien** I'm not too sure, I don't really know

4 *(apprendre)* **s. qch par qn** to hear sth from sb; **je l'ai su par son frère** I heard it from his/her brother; **on a fini par s. qu'un des ministres était compromis** it finally leaked out that one of the ministers was compromised; **faire s. qch à qn** to inform sb *or* to let sb know of sth; **si elle arrive, faites-le moi s.** if she comes, let me know

5 *(se rappeler)* to know, to remember; **je ne sais plus la fin de l'histoire** I can't remember the end of the story; **le jour de l'examen, je ne savais plus rien** on the day of the exam I'd forgotten everything; **est-ce que tu sais ton rôle?** *Théât* do you know your lines?; *Fig* do you know what you are supposed to do?

6 *(pouvoir)* to know how to, to be able to; **s. faire qch** to know how to *or* to be able to do sth; **tu sais plonger/conduire?** can you dive/drive?; **elle ne sait ni lire ni écrire** she can't read or write; **j'ai su danser le charleston** I used to know how to *or* I used to be able to dance the charleston; **elle sait (parler) cinq langues** she can speak *or* she knows five languages; **il ne sait pas/il sait bien faire la cuisine** he's a bad/good cook; **si je sais bien compter/lire** if I count/read right; **il sait parler/vendre** he's a good talker/salesman; **quand on lui a demandé qui était président à l'époque, il n'a pas su répondre** when asked who was President at the time, he didn't know (what the answer was); **je ne sais pas mentir** I can't (tell a) lie; **il ne sait pas se faire obéir de ses enfants** he can't get his children to do as they are told; **il sait se contenter de peu** he can make do with very little; **je n'ai pas su la réconforter** I wasn't able to comfort her; **il faut s. écouter le patient** you have to be able to listen to your patient; **je sais être discret** I can be *or* I know when to be discreet; **elle ne sait pas se reposer** *(elle travaille trop)* she doesn't know when to stop; **il a su rester jeune/modeste** he's managed to remain young/modest; **s. s'y prendre avec les enfants** to know how to handle children, to be good with children; **je n'ai jamais su m'y prendre avec les filles** I've never known how to behave with girls!; **laisse-moi découper le poulet, tu ne sais pas y faire** let me carve the chicken, you don't know how to do it; **s. y faire avec qn** to know how to handle sb; **elle sait y faire avec le patron!** she knows how to get round *or* to handle the boss!; **il sait y faire avec les filles!** he knows how to get his (own) way with girls!; **on ne saurait tout prévoir** you can't think of everything; **je ne saurais te le dire** I couldn't tell you; **on ne saurait être plus aimable/déplaisant** you couldn't be nicer/more unpleasant

7 *(être conscient de)* to know, to be aware of; **si tu savais combien j'ai souffert!** if you knew how much I've suffered!; **je sais que c'est un escroc** I know he's a crook; **sachez-le bien** make no *or* let there be no mistake about this; **il faut s. que le parti n'a pas toujours suivi Staline** you've got to remember that the party didn't always toe the Stalinist line; **sache qu'en fait, c'était son idée** you should know that in fact, it was his/her idea; **sachez que je le fais bénévolement** for your information, I do it for nothing; **elle ne sait plus ce qu'elle fait ni ce qu'elle dit** *(à cause d'un choc, de la vieillesse)* she's become confused; *(sous l'effet de la colère)* she's beside herself (with anger); **il est tellement soûl qu'il ne sait plus ce qu'il dit** he's so drunk he doesn't know what he's saying; **je sais ce que je dis** I know what I'm saying; **elle sait ce qu'elle veut** she knows (exactly) what she wants; **tu ne sais pas ce que tu rates** you don't know what you're missing; **tu ne sais pas ce que tu veux/tu dis** you don't know what you want/what you're talking about; **il faudrait s. ce que tu dis!** make up your mind!; **il faudrait s. ce que tu dis, c'est demain ou c'est après-demain?** (come on), which is it to be, tomorrow or the day after?; **laisse-la, elle sait ce qu'elle fait** let her be, she knows what she's doing; **sais-tu au moins pourquoi tu pleures?** do you even know why you're crying?

8 *(imaginer)* **ne (plus) s. que** *ou* **quoi faire** to be at a loss as to what to do, not to know what to do; **elle ne savait que faire pour le rassurer** she didn't know what to do to reassure him; **les médecins ne savent plus quoi faire pour la sauver** the doctors don't know what to do to save her; **je ne sais (plus) que faire avec ma fille** I just don't know what to do with my daughter; **il ne sait plus quoi faire pour se rendre intéressant** he'd stop at nothing *or* there's nothing he wouldn't do to attract attention to himself; *Fam* **je ne savais plus où me mettre** *ou* **me fourrer** *(de honte)* I didn't know where to put myself

9 *Belg* **il ne sait pas venir demain** he can't make it tomorrow; **je ne sais pas l'attraper** I can't reach it; **ses résultats ne sont pas brillants, savez-vous?** *(n'est-ce pas)* his/her results aren't very good, are they *or* am I right?; **sais-tu, cette petite fête était charmante** it was a delightful little party, wasn't it?

10 *(pour prendre l'interlocuteur à témoin)* **ce**

n'est pas toujours facile, tu sais! it's not always easy, you know!; **tu sais, je ne crois pas à ses promesses** to tell you the truth, I don't believe in his/her promises; *Fam* **tu sais que tu commences à m'énerver?** you're getting on my nerves, you know that *or* d'you know that?

USAGE ABSOLU **ceux qui savent** informed people *or* sources; **oui, oui, je sais!** yes, yes, I'm aware of that *or* I know *or* I realize!; *Fam* **où est-elle? – est-ce que je sais, moi?** where is she? – don't ask me *or* how should I know?; **si j'avais su, je ne t'aurais rien dit** if I'd known, I wouldn't have said a word (to you); **comment s.?** how can you tell *or* know?; **qui sait?** who knows?; **peut-être guérira-t-il, qui sait?** he might recover, who knows? *or* you never can tell!; **on ne sait jamais, sait-on jamais** you never know; **prends un parapluie, on ne sait jamais** take an umbrella, just in case *or* you never know; **faudrait s.!** make up your mind!

ADV namely, specifically, i.e.; **le personnel se compose de 200 hommes, s. 160 employés et 40 cadres** the staff is made up of 200 people: 160 employees and 40 executives

□ **à savoir** ADV namely, that is, i.e.; **son principal prédateur, à s. le renard** its most important predator, namely the fox

□ **à savoir que** CONJ meaning *or* Sout to the effect that; **il nous a donné sa réponse, à s. qu'il accepte** he's given us his answer, that is, he accepts *or* Sout to the effect that he accepts

□ **savoir si** CONJ *Fam* but who knows whether; **elle a bien affirmé que oui, s. si elle était réellement informée** she did say yes, but who knows whether *or* but it remains to be seen whether she really knew what she was talking about

▸ **se savoir** VPR **1** (*emploi passif*) (*nouvelle*) to become known; **tout se sait dans le village** news travels fast in the village; **ça finira par se s.** people are bound to find out; **je ne veux pas que ça se sache** I don't want it to be publicized *or* to get around; *Fam* **cela** *ou* **ça se saurait s'il était si doué que ça** if he was that good, you'd know about it

2 (*personne*) **il se sait malade** he knows he's ill

Allusion

Si j'aurais su, j'aurais pas venu

This expression comes from a novel by Louis Pergaud, *La Guerre des boutons* ("The War of the Buttons") (1912), adapted for the screen in 1961 by Yves Robert. It tells the story of two gangs of village urchins who go about snatching each other's buttons off and keeping them as trophies. One of the boys, known as Petit Gibus, keeps saying **Si j'aurais su, j'aurais pas venu.** By this he means "I wouldn't have come if I'd known" but the grammar is wildly inaccurate; it should read **Si j'avais su, je ne serais pas venu.** The phrase is used humorously and allusively today to express one's disappointment.

---

savoir-faire [savwarfɛr] NM INV know-how; **elle a du s.** she's got the know-how

savoir-vivre [savwarvivr] NM INV good manners, breeding, *Sout* savoir-vivre; **avoir du s.** to have (good) manners; **manquer de s.** to have no manners; **manque de s.** bad manners, ill-breeding; **quel manque de s.!** how rude!

savoisien, -enne [savwazjɛ̃, -ɛn] ADJ of/from Savoy

□ **Savoisien, -enne** NM,F = inhabitant of or person from Savoy, Savoyard

savon [savɔ̃] NM soap; **un (morceau de) s.** a bar of soap; **s. blanc** white soap; **s. à barbe** shaving soap; **s. doux** mild soap; **s. liquide** liquid soap; **s. de Marseille** household soap (*traditionally used both for washing and for laundry*); **s. noir** soft soap; **s. en paillettes** soap flakes; **s. en poudre** soap powder; **s. de toilette** toilet soap; *Fam* **passer un s. à qn** to give sb a roasting, to bawl sb out; *Fam* **se faire passer** *ou* **prendre un s.** to get a roasting, to get bawled out; *Fam* **tu vas encore recevoir** *ou* **te faire passer un s.!** you'll get it in the neck again!

savonnage [savɔnaʒ] NM **1** (*de linge*) washing (with soap) **2** *Tech* (*du verre*) grinding

savonnée [savɔne] NF *Belg* soapy water

savonner [3] [savɔne] VT **1** (*linge, surface*) to soap; *Littéraire* **la pente savonnée** the slippery slope; *Fig* **la planche à qn** to make things difficult for sb **2** (*barbe*) to lather; **s. le dos à qn** to soap sb's back **3** *Tech* (*verre*) to grind **4** *Fam* (*locution*) **s. la tête à qn** to give sb the rough edge of one's tongue

▸ **se savonner** VPR to soap oneself (down); **se s. le visage/les mains** to soap (up) one's face/one's hands

savonnerie [savɔnri] NF **1** (*usine*) soap factory **2** (*fabrication*) soap manufacture **3** (*tapis*) Savonnerie (carpet); **la S.** = historic carpet manufacturing centre (now part of the "Manufacture des Gobelins")

savonnette [savɔnɛt] NF **1** (*savon*) (small) bar of soap, bar of toilet soap **2** *Fam* (*pneu usagé*) bald tyre **3** (*montre*) hunter **4** *Fam Arg drogue* (*de cannabis*) = 250-gram block of hashish

savonneux, -euse [savɔnø, -øz] ADJ soapy

savonnier, -ère [savɔnje, -ɛr] ADJ soap (*avant n*) ▸ NM *Bot* soapberry (tree)

savourer [3] [savure] VT **1** (*vin, mets, repas*) to enjoy, to savour **2** *Fig* (*moment, repos etc*) to relish, to savour; **elle savoure sa vengeance** she's savouring her vengeance

savoureuse [savurøz] *voir* **savoureux**

savoureusement [savurøzmɑ̃] ADV **1** (*préparé*) tastily **2** (*raconté*) with relish

savoureux, -euse [savurø, -øz] ADJ **1** (*succulent*) tasty, flavoursome, full of flavour **2** *Fig* (*anecdote, détails*) juicy; (*plaisanterie*) good; **je vais te raconter une histoire savoureuse** here's a juicy little story for you

savoyard, -e [savwajar, -ard] ADJ of/from Savoie

□ **Savoyard, -e** NM,F = inhabitant of or person from Savoie; *Arch* **petit S.** boy chimney sweep (*from Savoie*)

saxatile [saksatil] ADJ *Bot* saxicolous

Saxe [saks] NF **la S.** Saxony; **la Basse-S.** Lower Saxony

saxe [saks] NM **1** (*matière*) Dresden china (*UNCOUNT*), Meissen porcelain (*UNCOUNT*) **2** (*objet*) piece of Dresden china *or* of Meissen porcelain

Saxe-Anhalt [saksanalt] NF **la S.** Saxony-Anhalt

saxhorn [saksɔrn] NM saxhorn; **s. basse** euphonium

saxicole [saksikɔl] ADJ *Bot* saxicolous

saxifragacée [saksifragase] *Bot* NF member of the Saxifragaceae

□ **saxifragacées** NFPL Saxifragaceae

saxifrage [saksifraʒ] NF *Bot* saxifrage; **s. granulée** meadow saxifrage; **s. à trois doigts** rue-leaved saxifrage

saxo [sakso] NM *Fam* **1** (*abrév* **saxophone**) sax **2** (*abrév* **saxophoniste**) sax (player)

saxon, -onne [saksɔ̃, -ɔn] ADJ Saxon ▸ NM (*langue*) Saxon

□ **Saxon, -onne** NM,F Saxon

saxophone [saksɔfɔn] NM saxophone

saxophoniste [saksɔfɔnist] NMF saxophone player, saxophonist

Sayda [saida] = **Saïda**

saynète [sɛnɛt] NF playlet, sketch

sayon [sɛjɔ̃] NM *Hist* battle helmet

SBF [ɛsbeɛf] NF (*abrév* **Société des bourses françaises**) = company which runs the Paris Stock Exchange, *Br* ≃ LSE, *Am* ≃ NYSE; **le S. 120** = broad-based French stock exchange index

SBS [ɛsbeɛs] NF *Méd* (*abrév* **syndrome du bébé secoué**) SBS

sbire [sbir] NM henchman

sbrinz [sbrints] NM Sbrinz (*type of Swiss cheese made from cow's milk*)

SCA [ɛssea] NF *Com* (*abrév* **société en commandite par actions**) partnership limited by shares

scabieux, -euse [skabjø, -øz] ADJ *Méd* scabious

□ **scabieuse** NF *Bot* scabious

scabinal, -e, -aux, -ales [skabinal, -o] ADJ *Belg* (*d'un échevin*) of a deputy burgomaster

scabreux, -euse [skabrø, -øz] ADJ **1** (*indécent*) obscene **2** *Littéraire* (*dangereux*) risky, tricky

scaferlati [skafɛrlati] NM (*semi-fine*) cut tobacco

scalaire [skalɛr] ADJ *Math* scalar ▸ NM **1** *Math* scalar **2** *Ich* angelfish, *Spéc* scalare

scalde [skald] NM *Hist* scald, skald

scaldien, -enne [skaldjɛ̃, -ɛn] ADJ *Géog* of/from the Scheldt region

scaldique [skaldik] ADJ skaldic

scalène [skalɛn] ADJ **1** *Anat* scalene **2** *Math* scalene ▸ NM *Anat* scalenus (muscle)

scalp [skalp] NM **1** (*chevelure*) scalp **2** (*action*) scalping (*UNCOUNT*)

scalpel [skalpɛl] NM scalpel

scalper [3] [skalpe] VT to scalp; **se faire s.** to get scalped

scampi [skɑ̃pi] NMPL *Culin* scampi

scandale [skɑ̃dal] NM **1** (*indignation*) scandal; **au grand s. de...** to the indignation of...; **faire s.** to cause a scandal

2 (*scène*) scene, fuss; **il va encore faire (tout) un s.** he's going to make a (tremendous) fuss again

3 (*honte*) **c'est un s.!** (it's) outrageous!, it's an outrage!

4 *Jur* **pour s. sur la voie publique** for causing a public disturbance, for disturbing the peace

□ **à scandale** ADJ (*journal, presse*) sensationalist

scandaleuse [skɑ̃daløz] *voir* **scandaleux**

scandaleusement [skɑ̃daløzmɑ̃] ADV scandalously, outrageously; **s. riche** outrageously rich

scandaleux, -euse [skɑ̃dalø, -øz] ADJ (*attitude, mensonge*) disgraceful, outrageous, shocking; (*article, photo*) sensational, scandalous; (*prix*) outrageous, shocking; **vie scandaleuse** life of scandal, scandalous life; **les loyers ont atteint des prix s.** rents have reached outrageously high levels

scandaliser [3] [skɑ̃dalize] VT to shock, to outrage; **elle a scandalisé tout le monde par sa grossièreté** she shocked everyone with her vulgarity; **son cynisme a scandalisé la classe politique** his/her cynicism scandalized the politicians; **Picasso a scandalisé le public de son époque** Picasso shocked the public of his day

▸ **se scandaliser** VPR **se s. de qch** to be shocked *or* scandalized by sth; **elle ne se scandalise de rien** nothing shocks her, she's unshockable

scander [3] [skɑ̃de] VT **1** *Littérature* to scan **2** (*slogan*) to chant; (*mots, phrases, phrase musicale*) to stress

scandinave [skɑ̃dinav] ADJ Scandinavian ▸ NM (*langue*) Scandinavian, Northern Germanic

□ **Scandinave** NMF Scandinavian

Scandinavie [skɑ̃dinavi] NF **la S.** Scandinavia

scandium [skɑ̃djɔm] NM *Chim* scandium

Scanie [skani] NF *Géog* **la S.** Scandia

scanner¹ [skanɛr] NM **1** *Ordinat* scanner; **insérer qch par s., capturer qch au s.** to scan sth in; **s. à main** hand-held scanner; **s. optique** optical scanner; **s. à plat** flatbed scanner **2** *Méd* scanner; **passer au s.** (*sujet: personne*) to have a scan (done)

scanner² [3] [skane] VT to scan

scannérisation [skanerizasjɔ̃] NF scanning

scannériser [3] [skanerize] VT to scan

scanneur [skanœr] NM = **scanner¹**

scanographe [skanɔgraf] NM = **scanner¹**

scanographie [skanɔgrafi] NF **1** (*technique*) scanning (*UNCOUNT*), *Spéc* computerized (axial) tomography **2** (*image*) scan, scanner image, *Spéc* tomogram

scansion [skɑ̃sjɔ̃] NF *Littérature* scanning (*UNCOUNT*), scansion

scaphandre [skafɑ̃dr] NM **1** *Naut* diving suit; **s. autonome** aqualung **2** *Astron* spacesuit

---

'**Le Scaphandre et le papillon**' Bauby 'The Diving-bell and the Butterfly'

---

scaphandrier [skafɑ̃drije] NM *Naut* (deep-sea) diver

scaphite [skafit] NM scaphite

scaphoïde [skafɔid] *Anat* ADJ scaphoid, boat-shaped ▸ NM scaphoid

scaphopode [skafopod] NM *Zool* (*mollusque*) scaphopod

scapula [skapyla] NF *Anat* scapula

scapulaire [skapylɛr] *Anat* ADJ scapular ▸ NM scapular

scapulectomie [skapylɛktɔmi] NF *Méd* scapulectomy

scapulo-huméral, -e [skapylɔymeral] (*mpl* **scapulo-huméraux** [-o], *fpl* **scapulo-humérales**) ADJ *Anat* scapulohumeral

scarabée [skarabe] NM **1** *Entom* scarab (beetle), *Spéc* scarabaeid **2** *Archéol* scarab

scarabéidé [skarabeide] *Entom* NM scarabaeid
□ **scarabéidés** NMPL Scarabaeidae

Scaramouche [skaramuʃ] NPR Scaramouche

scare [skar] NM *Ich* parrot fish, *Spéc* scar, scarus

scarieux, -euse [skarjø, -øz] ADJ *Bot* scarious

scarifiage [skarifjaʒ] NM *Agr & Hort* scarifying

scarificateur [skarifikatœr] NM **1** *Méd* scarificator **2** *Agr & Hort* scarifier

scarification [skarifikasjɔ̃] NF **1** *Méd* scarring (UNCOUNT), *Spéc* scarification **2** (*d'un arbre*) scarifying

scarifier [9] [skarifje] VT to scarify

scarlatine [skarlatin] NF *Méd* scarlet fever, *Spéc* scarlatina

scarlatineux, -euse [skarlatinø, -øz] *Méd* ADJ suffering from scarlet fever *or Spéc* scarlatina
NM,F scarlet-fever *or Spéc* scarlatina patient

scarole [skarɔl] NF endive (*broad-leaved variety*)

scat [skat] NM *Mus* scat

scato [skato] ADJ *Fam* (*blague*) disgusting▪; **humour s.** toilet humour

scatol, scatole [skatɔl] NM skatol, skatole

scatologie [skatɔlɔʒi] NF scatology

scatologique [skatɔlɔʒik] ADJ (*goûts, écrit*) scatological; (*humour*) lavatory

scatophage [skatɔfaʒ] ADJ scatophagous

scatophile [skatɔfil] ADJ coprophilous

scavée [skave] = **cavée**

sceau, -x [so] NM **1** (*cachet*) seal; **apposer** *ou* **mettre son s. sur un document** to affix one's seal on *or* to a document; **sous le s. du secret** under the seal of secrecy; *Hist* **Grand S.** Great Seal, Broad Seal **2** *Littéraire* (*empreinte*) mark; **le s. du génie** the mark *or* the stamp of genius

sceau-de-Salomon [sodəsalomɔ̃] (*pl* **sceaux-de-Salomon**) NM *Bot* Solomon's seal

scélérat, -e [selera, -at] *Littéraire* ADJ heinous, villainous
NM,F villain, scoundrel, rogue

scélératesse [seleratɛs] NF *Littéraire* **1** (*caractère*) villainy, wickedness **2** (*action*) villainy, evil *or* wicked deed, heinous crime

scellage [sɛlaʒ] NM embedding, setting

scellé [sele] NM seal; **mettre** *ou* **apposer/lever les scellés** to put on/to remove the seals; **mettre** *ou* **apposer les scellés sur qch** to seal sth off
□ **sous scellés** ADV under seal

scellement [sɛlmɑ̃] NM embedding, sealing

sceller [4] [sele] VT **1** (*officialiser → acte, document*) to seal; **s. un pacte** to set the seal on an agreement; **le mariage scella leur alliance** the marriage set the seal on their alliance **2** (*fermer*) to put seals on, to seal up **3** (*fixer*) to fix, to set, to embed; **une fenêtre aux barreaux solidement scellés** a heavily barred window; **s. une couronne sur une dent** to crown a tooth

scénarimage [senarimaʒ] NM *Offic* storyboard

scénario [senarjo] (*pl* **scénarios** *ou* **scenarii** [senarii]) NM **1** *Cin* (*histoire, trame*) screenplay, scenario; (*texte*) (shooting) script, scenario; *Fig* **tout s'est déroulé selon le s. prévu** everything went as scheduled *or* according to plan; **s. d'auteur** writer's script; **s. dialogué** continuity script; *TV & Cin* **s.-maquette** storyboard; *Cin* **s. de répétition** rehearsal script; *Fig* **elle a encore perdu ses clés, c'est décidément un s. à répétition!** she's lost her keys again, she's making a habit of it *or* it's becoming a habit with her!; **un s. catastrophe** a nightmare scenario
2 *Théât* scenario
3 (*d'une bande dessinée*) story, storyboard, scenario
4 *Écon* (*cas de figure*) case, scenario; *Mktg* **s. d'achat** buying situation

scénariser [3] [senarize] VT **1** (*écrire le scénario de*) to script, to write the screenplay for **2** (*adapter pour l'écran*) to adapt for the screen

scénariste [senarist] NMF scriptwriter; **s. de réécriture** script editor

scène [sɛn] NF **1** (*plateau d'un théâtre, d'un cabaret etc*) stage; **la s. de l'Opéra de Paris** the stage of the Paris Opera; **être en s.** (*acteur*) to be on (stage); **(tout le monde) en s., s'il vous plaît!** the whole cast on stage, please!; **monter sur s.** to go on the stage; **remonter sur s.** to go back on the stage; **sortir de s.** to come off stage, to exit; **Arlequin sort de s.** exit Harlequin; **il sera sur la s. du Palladium à partir du 3 mars** (*chanteur, comique*) he'll be appearing at the Palladium from 3 March onwards; **scènes nationales** national stages; **s. tournante** revolving stage; **entrer en s.** to come on stage; *Fig* to come *or* to step in; **le Duc entre en s.** enter the Duke; *Fig* **c'est là que tu entres en s.** that's where you come in

2 (*art dramatique*) **la s.** the stage; **il a beaucoup écrit pour la s.** he's written a lot of plays *or* pieces for the stage; **quitter la s.** to retire from the stage *or* from acting; **adapter un livre pour la s.** to adapt a book for the stage *or* the theatre; **porter qch à la s.** to adapt sth for the stage; **mettre 'Phèdre' en s.** (*monter la pièce*) to stage 'Phèdre'; (*diriger les acteurs*) to direct 'Phèdre'; **la façon dont il met Polonius en s.** the way he directs Polonius; *Fig* **l'écrivain met en s. deux personnages hauts en couleur** the writer portrays two colourful characters

3 *Cin & Théât* (*séquence*) scene; **la première s.** the first *or* the opening scene; **la s. finale** the last *or* the closing scene; **acte II, s. trois** act two, scene three; **dans la s. d'amour/du balcon** in the love/balcony scene; **s. de foule** crowd scene; **s. de poursuite** chase scene; **s. de transparence** glass shot; **la s. se passe à Montréal** the action takes place in *or* the scene is set in Montreal; *Fig Hum* **jouer la grande s. du II** to make a big scene

4 (*décor*) scene; **la s. représente une clairière** the scene represents a clearing

5 (*moment, événement*) scene; **ce fut une s. déchirante** it was a heartbreaking scene; **une s. de la vie quotidienne** a scene of everyday life; **s. de violence** scene of violence; **imagine la s.!** imagine *or* picture the scene!, just imagine *or* picture it!

6 (*dispute*) scene; **faire une s.** to make a scene; **il m'a fait une s.** he made a scene; **s. de ménage** row; **s. de rupture** break-up scene

7 *Beaux-Arts* scene; **le tableau représente une s. de chasse** the painting represents a hunting scene; **s. de genre** genre painting

8 (*univers*) scene; **la s. internationale/politique** the international/political scene; **un nouveau venu sur la s. politique** a newcomer on the political scene

9 *Psy* **s. primitive** *ou* **originaire** primal scene

'**Scènes de la vie conjugale**' Bergman 'Scenes from a Marriage'

scéner [18] [sene] VI *Can Fam* **1** (*jouer la comédie*) to act▪; *Fig* to put on an act▪ **2** (*observer*) to watch **3** (*déambuler*) to stroll (along)▪; **elle aime bien s. dans les centres d'achats** she likes strolling around shopping *Br* centres *or Am* malls

scène-raccord [sɛnrakɔr] (*pl* **scènes-raccords**) NF *Cin & TV* link scene

scénique [senik] ADJ (*éclairage, décor*) stage (*avant n*); **l'art s.** stage design

scéniquement [senikmɑ̃] ADV theatrically

scénographe [senograf] NMF *Théât* **1** (*qui aménage la scène*) stage designer **2** (*peintre*) scenographer

scénographie [senografi] NF *Théât* **1** (*aménagement de la scène*) stage design **2** (*peinture*) scenography

scénographique [senografik] ADJ *Théât* **1** (*relatif à l'aménagement de la scène*) stage design (*avant n*) **2** (*relatif à la peinture en perspective*) scenographic

scénologie [senɔlɔʒi] NF stage design

scepticisme [sɛptisism] NM scepticism; **avec s.** sceptically

sceptique [sɛptik] ADJ (*incrédule*) sceptical
NMF (*personne qui doute*) sceptic; *Phil* Sceptic

sceptiquement [sɛptikmɑ̃] ADV sceptically

sceptre [sɛptr] NM **1** (*d'un roi*) sceptre **2** *Littéraire* (*autorité*) authority, royalty; **disputer son s. à qn** to try to usurp sb's authority; **un s. de fer** a rod of iron

SCH *Anciennement* (*abrév écrite* **schilling**) S, Sch

schabraque [ʃabrak] = **chabraque**

Schaffhouse [ʃafuz] NM *Géog* Schaffhausen; **le canton de S.** Schaffhouse

schako [ʃako] NM shako

schappe [ʃap] NF *Tex* schappe

schapska [ʃapska] NM *Hist & Mil* lancer cap

Schéhérazade [ʃeerazad] NPR Scheherazade

scheidage [ʃedaʒ] NM *Mines* hand-sorting, cobbing

scheider [3] [ʃede] VT *Mines* to hand-sort, to cob

scheik [ʃɛk] NM sheik

schelem [ʃlɛm] NM *Cartes & Sport* slam; **grand s.** grand slam; **petit s.** small *or* little slam

schéma [ʃema] NM **1** *Tech* diagram; (*dessin*) sketch; **faire un s.** to make *or* to draw a diagram; **comme le montre le s.** as shown in the diagram; **s. de câblage/de montage** wiring/set-up diagram
2 *Admin & Jur* **s. directeur** urban development plan
3 (*aperçu*) (broad) outline
4 (*système*) pattern; **il se comporte selon un s. relativement simple** his behaviour follows a relatively simple pattern
5 *Phys* **s. fonctionnel** block diagram
6 *Ling* schema
7 *Ordinat* **s. de clavier** keyboard map

schématique [ʃematik] ADJ **1** *Tech* diagrammatical, schematic **2** (*simplificateur*) schematic, simplified; **présenter un projet de façon s.** to present a project in a simplified form; **un peu trop s.** oversimplified, simplistic

schématiquement [ʃematikmɑ̃] ADV **1** *Tech* diagrammatically, schematically **2** (*en simplifiant*) to give the basic outline of a project/an operation; **s., voici comment nous allons nous y prendre** in broad outline, this is how we're planning to handle it

schématisation [ʃematizasjɔ̃] NF **1** *Tech* schematization, presenting as a diagram **2** (*simplification*) simplification, simplifying (UNCOUNT); *Péj* oversimplification

schématiser [3] [ʃematize] VT **1** *Tech* to schematize, to present in diagram form **2** (*simplifier*) to simplify; *Péj* to oversimplify
USAGE ABSOLU **il schématise à l'extrême** he's being much too oversimplistic

schématisme [ʃematism] NM **1** *Phil* schema **2** (*simplification*) simplification

schème [ʃɛm] NM **1** *Phil & Psy* schema **2** *Beaux-Arts* scheme

schéol [ʃeɔl] NM *Rel* Sheol

scherzando [skɛrtsando, skɛrdzãdo] ADV *Mus* scherzando

scherzo [skɛrdzo] *Mus* NM scherzo
ADV scherzando

schiedam [skidam] NM (*dans le Nord*) Hollands (gin)

schilling [ʃiliŋ] NM *Anciennement* schilling

schinder [3] [ʃɛ̃de] VI *Suisse* **1** (*dans le jeu du yass*) to bluff (*by laying a low card and keeping a higher one in one's hand*) **2** *Fam* (*tricher*) to cheat▪

schismatique [ʃismatik] ADJ schismatic
NMF schismatic

schisme [ʃism] NM **1** *Rel* schism; **le grand s. d'Occident** the Great (Western) Schism; **faire s.** to break away *or* (*religion*) schism, split

schiste [ʃist] NM **1** *Minér* schist; **s. bitumineux** oil shale **2** *Mines* (*déchets*) deads

schisteux, -euse [ʃistø, -øz] ADJ schistose, schistous

schistosité [ʃistozite] NF schistosity; **plan de s.** schistosity plane

schistosomiase [ʃistozomjaz] NF *Méd* schistosomiasis

schizo [skizo] *Fam* ADJ schizo, *Am* schiz
NMF schizo, *Am* schiz

schizogamie [skizogami] NF *Biol* schizogamy

schizogonie [skizogoni] NF *Biol* schizogony

schizoïde [skizoid] *Psy* ADJ schizoid
NMF schizoid

schizomycète [skizomisɛt] NM *Biol* schizomycete

schizophasie [skizofazi] NF *Psy* schizophasia

schizophrène [skizofrɛn] ADJ schizophrenic
NMF schizophrenic

schizophrénie [skizofreni] NF schizophrenia

schizophrénique [skizɔfrenik] ADJ schizophrenic

schizothyme [skizɔtim] *Psy* ADJ schizothymic NMF schizothyme

schizothymie [skizɔtimi] NF *Psy* schizothymia

schizothymique [skizɔtimik] *Psy* ADJ schizothymic
NMF schizothyme

schlague [ʃlag] NF **1** *Hist* flogging **2** *Fam (autorité brutale)* **elle mène son monde à la s.** she rules everybody with a rod of iron■

schlamms [ʃlam] NMPL *Tech* sludge, tailings

schlass¹ [ʃlas] NM *très Fam (couteau)* knife■, blade, *Am* shiv

schlass², schlasse [ʃlas] ADJ *très Fam (ivre)* sozzled, wasted; *(fatigué) Br* knackered, *Am* beat

Schleswig-Holstein [ʃlɛsviɡɔlstɛn] NM **le S.** Schleswig-Holstein

schleu [ʃlø] *Fam Péj Hist* ADJ = offensive term used to refer to German people
NM = offensive term used to refer to German people; **les schleus** ≃ the Jerries, ≃ the Boche

schlinguer [ʃlɛ̃ɡe] = **chlinguer**

schlittage [ʃlitaʒ] NM transporting by sledge

schlitte [ʃlit] NF sledge *(for transporting lumber)*

schlitter [3] [ʃlite] VT to transport by sledge

schlitteur [ʃlitœr] NM = worker who transports timber by sledge

schlof [ʃlɔf] NM *Fam* bed■, *Br* pit; **se mettre au s.** to hit the *Br* sack *or Am* hay

schmilblick [ʃmilblik] NM *Fam* **faire avancer le s.** to make progress■, to get somewhere; **tout ça, ça fait pas avancer le s.** that's not getting us any further forward

---

Allusion

Faire avancer le schmilblick

In the early 1970s there was a popular radio quiz show presented by Guy Lux, in which contestants had to try and identify the **schmilblick**, a mystery object, by asking questions about it. **Faire avancer le schmilblick** means literally "to get the schmilblick moving", ie to ask a question which takes the contestant closer to identifying the object. The phrase is used today to mean "to make progress". A sketch by the famous comedian Coluche, making fun of the radio show, helped to fix the expression in people's minds.

---

schmitt [ʃmit] NM *Fam* cop

schmolitz [ʃmɔlits] NM *Suisse* **faire s.** = to agree to use the "tu" form of address to one another *(often after the ritual draining of a glass of alcohol)*

schnaps [ʃnaps] NM schnapps

schnauzer [ʃnozɛr, ʃnawzœr] NM *(chien)* schnauzer

schnock, schnoque [ʃnɔk] *très Fam* ADJ INV *(cinglé)* nuts, loopy
NM *(imbécile)* halfwit, dope; **un vieux s.** an old fogey, an old codger; **espèce de vieux s.!** you old fogey *or* codger!; **alors, tu viens, du s.?** are you coming, dumbo?

schnorchel, schnorkel [ʃnɔrkɛl] NM snorkel

schnouf, schnouffe [ʃnuf] NF *Fam Arg drogue (héroïne)* junk, horse; *(cocaïne)* snow, charlie, coke

schofar [ʃɔfar] NM *Rel* schofar

schol, schole [skɔl] NF *Belg* dried plaice

scholiaste [skɔljast] NM scholiast

scholie [skɔli] NF *Littérature* scholium
NM *Math* scholium

scholle [skɔl] = **schol**

schooner [ʃunœr] NM *Naut* schooner

schorre [ʃɔr] NM salt meadow

schproum [ʃprum] NM *Fam* argument■, quarrel■; **ça va faire du s.!** there's going to be trouble!

schtarbé, -e [ʃtarbe] = **chtarbé**

Schtroumpf [ʃtrumf] NM Smurf; **les Schtroumpfs** the Smurfs

Schubert [ʃubɛr] NPR Schubert

schublig [ʃyblik] NM *Suisse* = long lightly smoked pork sausage

schuss [ʃus] NM schuss; **descendre en s.** to schuss down
ADV **descendre tout s.** to schuss down

schwa [ʃwa] NM *Ling* schwa

Schweppes® [ʃwɛps] NM tonic (water)

Schwyz [ʃwis] NM Schwyz; **le canton de S.** Schwyz

SCI [ɛssei] NF **1** *(abrév* **société civile immobilière***)* property investment partnership **2** *Écon (abrév* **société de commerce international***)* international trading corporation

sciable [sjabl] ADJ that can be sawed *or* sawn

sciage [sjaʒ] NM sawing; **(bois de) s.** sawn timber

Scialytique® [sjalitik] NM operating light

sciant, -e [sjɑ̃, -ɑ̃t] ADJ *Fam (étonnant)* staggering; *(drôle)* hilarious

sciatique [sjatik] ADJ *Anat* sciatic; **nerf petit/grand s.** small/great sciatic nerve
NF *Méd* sciatica

scie [si] NF **1** *Tech* saw; **s. à bois** wood saw; **s. à chaîne** chainsaw; **s. à chantourner** fretsaw; **s. circulaire** *Br* circular saw, *Am* buzz saw; **s. égoïne** (carpenter's) handsaw; **s. électrique** power saw; **s. à guichet** compass *or* keyhole saw; **s. mécanique** *ou* **à main** hand saw; **s. à métaux** hacksaw; *Can* **s. ronde** *Br* circular saw, *Am* buzz saw; **s. à ruban** bandsaw, ribbon saw; **s. sabre** *ou* **sauteuse** jigsaw, scroll saw; **s. universelle** *ou* **à refendre** frame *or* bow *or* turning saw
2 *Mus* **s. musicale** musical saw
3 *Fam (chanson)* song played to death; *(message)* message repeated again and again■
4 *Fam Péj (personne ou chose ennuyeuse)* bore, drag

sciemment [sjamɑ̃] ADV **1** *(consciemment)* knowingly **2** *(délibérément)* deliberately, on purpose

science [sjɑ̃s] NF **1** *(connaissances)* **la s.** science; **dans l'état actuel de la s.** in the current state of (our) knowledge; *Presse* **S. et Vie** = monthly science magazine
2 *(gén pl) (domaine spécifique)* science; **les sciences appliquées/physiques** the applied/physical sciences; **s. dure/molle** hard/soft science; **les sciences économiques** economics; **les sciences exactes** the exact sciences; **les sciences expérimentales** experimental science; **les sciences humaines** *(gén)* human sciences, the social sciences; *Univ* ≃ Arts; **les sciences mathématiques, la s. mathématique** mathematics, the mathematical sciences; **les sciences naturelles** *(gén)* the natural sciences; *Scol* biology; **la s. occulte, les sciences occultes** the occult (sciences); **les sciences politiques** politics, political sciences; *Univ* **les sciences sociales** social studies; *Scol* **les sciences de la vie** the life sciences
3 *(technique)* science, art; *(habileté)* skill; **la s. militaire** *ou* **de la guerre** the art *or* the science of war; **sa s. des effets dramatiques** his/her skill in producing dramatic effects
4 *(érudition)* knowledge; **il croit avoir la s. infuse** he thinks he's a fount of knowledge; **je n'ai pas la s. infuse!** I don't know everything!; **il faut toujours qu'il étale sa s.** he's always trying to impress everybody with his knowledge
5 *Rel* **S. chrétienne** Christian Science
□ **sciences** NFPL *Univ (par opposition aux lettres)* science, sciences; **être bon en sciences** to be good at science *or* at sciences; **une université réputée pour les sciences** a university famous for its science departments *or* for science
□ **de science certaine** ADV *Littéraire* **savoir qch de s. certaine** to know sth for certain *or* for a fact

---

Allusion

Science sans conscience n'est que ruine de l'âme

This famous maxim comes from Rabelais' *Pantagruel*, chapter 8, in which Pantagruel receives a letter from Gargantua, his father, on the subject of education. Gargantua says that learning should ideally go hand in hand with faith, reason and kindness to one's fellow-men. Today, this expression (which means literally "Knowledge without conscience is nothing but ruination of the soul") is used in support of the idea that there must be ethical constraints in the application of scientific discovery. For example, in the current controversy about genetically modified foods or cloning, this maxim might well be quoted today.

---

science-fiction [sjɑ̃sfiksjɔ̃] *(pl* **sciences-fictions***)* NF science fiction; **livre/film de s.** science-fiction book/film

Sciences-Po [sjɑ̃spo] NF = "grande école" for political science; **faire S.** to study at "Sciences-Po"

sciène [sjɛn] NF *Ich* sciaenid

scientificité [sjɑ̃tifisite] NF scientificity, scientific quality

scientifique [sjɑ̃tifik] ADJ scientific; **une importante découverte s.** an important scientific discovery; **une expédition s. au pôle Sud** a scientific expedition to the South Pole; **de manière s.** scientifically
NMF **1** *(savant)* scientist **2** *(personne douée pour les sciences)* **ce n'est pas un s.** he's not very scientifically-minded

scientifiquement [sjɑ̃tifikmɑ̃] ADV scientifically

scientisme [sjɑ̃tism] NM **1** *Phil* scientism **2** *Rel* Christian Science

scientiste [sjɑ̃tist] ADJ *Phil & Rel* scientistic
NMF **1** *Phil* proponent of scientism **2** *Rel* (Christian) Scientist

scientologie [sjɑ̃tɔlɔʒi] NF Scientology

scientologue [sjɑ̃tɔlɔg] NMF Scientologist

scier [9] [sje] VT **1** *(couper)* to saw; **s. une planche en deux** to saw through a plank, to saw a plank in two; **s. la branche d'un arbre** to saw a branch off a tree; **s. un tronc en rondins** to saw up a tree trunk (into logs); *Suisse Fam* **s. du bois** to snore like a pig
2 *(blesser)* to cut into; **la ficelle du paquet me scie les doigts** the string around the parcel is cutting into my fingers
3 *Fam (surprendre)* to amaze■, to flabbergast; **ça m'a scié d'apprendre que...** I was flabbergasted *or Br* gobsmacked to find out that...; **quand elle lui a raconté ce qui s'était passé, il était complètement scié** when she told him what had happened, he was flabbergasted *or Br* gobsmacked
VI *Naut* to row backwards, to back water

scierie [siri] NF sawmill

scieur [sjœr] NM **1** *(ouvrier)* sawyer; **s. de long** pit sawyer; *Can Fig Péj* **s. de bois** drudge **2** *(patron)* sawmill owner

scieuse [sjøz] NF *(machine)* mechanical saw

scille [sil] NF *Bot* scilla

Scilly [sili] = **Sorlingues**

scinder [3] [sɛ̃de] VT *(gén)* to divide, to split (up) (**en** into); *(société)* to break up, to split; **s. qch en deux** to divide *or* to split sth (up) into two
▸ **se scinder** VPR to split (**en** into); **le parti s'est scindé en deux tendances** the party split into two

scinque [sɛ̃k] NM *Zool* skink

scintigramme [sɛ̃tigram] NM *Méd* scintigram

scintigraphie [sɛ̃tigrafi] NF *Méd* scintigraphy

scintillant, -e [sɛ̃tijɑ̃, -ɑ̃t] ADJ *(yeux)* sparkling, twinkling; *(bijoux, reflet)* glittering, sparkling, scintillating; *(étoile)* twinkling
NM tinsel decoration(s)

scintillateur [sɛ̃tijatœr] NM scintillator

scintillation [sɛ̃tijasjɔ̃] NF **1** *(éclat lumineux)* scintillation **2** *Nucl* **compteur** *ou* **détecteur à s.** scintillation counter

scintillement [sɛ̃tijmɑ̃] NM **1** *(des yeux)* sparkling *(UNCOUNT)*, twinkling *(UNCOUNT)*; *(d'une lumière, de bijoux, de l'eau, d'un reflet)* glittering *(UNCOUNT)*, scintillating *(UNCOUNT)*; *(d'une étoile)* twinkling *(UNCOUNT)* **2** *Cin & TV* flicker, flickering, shimmer; **écran sans s.** flicker-free screen

scintiller [3] [sɛ̃tije] VI *(yeux)* to sparkle, to twinkle; *(lumière, bijoux, eau, reflet)* to sparkle, to glitter; *(étoile)* to twinkle; *Littéraire* **le ciel tout entier scintillait** the whole of the sky was aglitter

scintillogramme [sɛ̃tijɔgram] = **scintigramme**

scintillographie [sɛ̃tijɔgrafi] = **scintigraphie**

scintillomètre [sɛ̃tijɔmɛtr] NM scintillometer

scion [sjɔ̃] NM **1** *Bot (pousse)* (year's) shoot; *(à greffer)* scion **2** *Pêche* tip (of rod)

sciotte [sjɔt] NF *(stonecutter's)* hand saw

Scipion [sipjɔ̃] NPR Scipio; **S. l'Africain** Scipio Africanus

scirpe [sirp] NM *Bot* club rush, bulrush

scission [sisjɔ̃] NF **1** *Pol & Rel* scission, split, rent; **faire s.** to split off, to secede **2** *Biol & Phys*

---

fission, splitting **3** *(d'une société)* demerger; *Fin* **s. d'actifs** divestment of assets, hive-off of assets

scissionniste [sisjɔnist] **ADJ** secessionist **NMF** secessionist

scissipare [sisipar] **ADJ** *Biol* fissiparous

scissiparité [sisiparite] **NF** *Biol* fissiparousness, scissiparity, schizogenesis

scissure [sisyr] **NF** *Anat (du cerveau)* fissure, sulcus; *(du foie)* scissura, scissure; **s. de Sylvius** fissure of Sylvius

sciure [sjyr] **NF** **s. (de bois)** sawdust; **s. de marbre** marble dust

sciuridé [sjyride] *Zool* **NM** sciurine (rodent), member of the Sciuridae
❑ **sciuridés NMPL** Sciuridae

scléral, -e, -aux, -ales [skleral, -o] **ADJ** *Anat* sclerotic

scléranthe [sklerɑ̃t] **NM** *Bot* scleranth, scleranthus

sclère [sklɛr] **NF** *Anat* sclera

sclérenchyme [sklerɑ̃ʃim] **NM** *Bot* sclerenchyma

scléreux, -euse [sklerø, -øz] **ADJ 1** *Méd* sclerous **2** *Bot* sclerotic

scléroderme [sklerɔdɛrm] **NM** *Bot* scleroderm; *Culin* false truffle

sclérodermie [sklerɔdɛrmi] **NF** *Méd* scleroderma

sclérogène [sklerɔʒɛn] **ADJ** *Méd* sclerogenic

scléromètre [sklerɔmɛtr] **NM** sclerometer

sclérophylle [sklerɔfil] **ADJ** *Bot* sclerophyllous

scléroprotéine [sklerɔprɔtein] **NF** *Biol & Chim* scleroprotein

sclérosant, -e [sklerozɑ̃, -ɑ̃t] **ADJ 1** *Méd* sclerosing, sclerosis-causing **2** *Fig* paralysing; *(mode de vie, travail)* mind-numbing; **c'est en grande partie à cause de la politique sclérosante du Parti que la Chine s'est si peu ouverte sur le monde** the dead hand of party politics is the main reason for China's failure to open up to the rest of the world

sclérose [skleroz] **NF 1** *Méd* sclerosis; **s. artérielle** arteriosclerosis; **s. en plaques** multiple sclerosis, MS **2** *Fig* ossification

sclérosé, -e [skleroze] **ADJ 1** *Méd* sclerotic **2** *Fig* antiquated, ossified, creaky (with age); **avoir l'esprit s.** to have become set in one's ways **NM,F** *Méd* sclerosis sufferer

scléroser [skleroze] **VT 1** *Méd* to cause sclerosis of; **molécule qui sclérose les tissus** tissue-sclerosing molecule
2 *Fig (système)* to ossify, to paralyse; *(esprit)* to make rigid; **le parti a été sclérosé par des années d'inactivité** years of inertia have brought the party to a political standstill
▸ **se scléroser VPR 1** *Méd* to sclerose
2 *Fig (se figer)* to ossify, to become paralysed; **se s. dans ses habitudes** to become set in one's ways

sclérote [sklerɔt] **NM** *Biol* sclerotium

sclérothérapie [sklerɔterapi] **NF** *Méd* sclerotherapy

sclérotique [sklerɔtik] **NF** sclerotic, sclera

scolaire [skɔlɛr] **ADJ 1** *(de l'école)* school *(avant n)*; *(du cursus)* school *(avant n)*, academic; **le milieu s.** the school environment; **niveau/succès s.** academic standard/achievement; **livre** *ou* **manuel s.** (school) textbook
2 *Péj (écriture, raisonnement)* dry, scholastic; **il est très s.** his work is very unoriginal; **à l'université, il faut être moins s. et organiser soi-même son travail** university students shouldn't expect to be spoon-fed like they were at school **NMF** *(enfant)* schoolchild; **les scolaires rentrent demain** schoolchildren go back tomorrow

scolairement [skɔlɛrmɑ̃] **ADV** *Péj (réciter)* mechanically; *(écrire)* in a dry *or* scholastic way

scolarisable [skɔlarizabl] **ADJ** **population s.** school-age population

scolarisation [skɔlarizasjɔ̃] **NF 1** *Admin & Jur* school attendance, schooling; **la s. est obligatoire à partir de six ans** (attendance at) school is compulsory from the age of six; **je suis pour la s. des enfants à partir de l'âge de cinq ans** I'm in favour of children going to *or* starting school at the age of five; **taux de s.** percentage of children in full-time education
2 *(d'une région, d'un pays)* school-building programme

scolariser [skɔlarize] [3] **VT 1** *(enfant)* to send to school, to provide with formal education; **l'enfant est-il déjà scolarisé?** is the child already at school *or* attending school? **2** *(région, pays)* to equip with schools

scolarité [skɔlarite] **NF 1** *Admin & Jur* school attendance, schooling; **la s. est gratuite et obligatoire** schooling is free and compulsory; **la s. a tendance à se prolonger** pupils are tending to leave school later, the school-leaving age is rising
2 *(études)* school career; *(période)* schooldays; **j'ai eu une s. difficile** I had a difficult time at school

scolasticat [skɔlastika] **NM 1** *(bâtiment)* theological college **2** *(études)* theological course

scolastique [skɔlastik] **ADJ 1** *Hist* scholastic **2** *(formaliste)* scholastic, *Péj* pedantic **NF** *Phil & Rel* scholasticism **NM 1** *Hist* Scholastic, Schoolman **2** *Rel* theology student

scolex [skɔlɛks] **NM INV** *Zool* scolex

scoliaste [skɔljast] **NM** scholiast

scolie [skɔli] **NF** *Littérature* scholium **NM** *Math* scholium

scoliose [skɔljoz] **NF** *Méd* scoliosis, lateral curvature of the spine

scoliotique [skɔljɔtik] *Méd* **ADJ** scoliotic **NMF** scoliosis sufferer

scolopacidé [skɔlɔpaside] *Orn* **NM** member of the Scolopacidae family
❑ **scolopacidés NMPL** Scolopacidae

scolopendre [skɔlɔpɑ̃dr] **NF 1** *Bot* hart's-tongue, *Spéc* scolopendrium **2** *Entom* scolopendra

scolyte [skɔlit] **NM** *Entom* bark beetle, *Spéc* scolytid

scombridé [skɔ̃bride] *Ich* **NM** scombroid
❑ **scombridés NMPL** Scombridae

sconse [skɔ̃s] **NM 1** *Zool* skunk **2** *(fourrure)* skunk (fur)

scoop [skup] **NM 1** *(exclusivité)* scoop; **faire un s.** to get a scoop **2** *Fam* **j'ai un s.!** I've got some hot news!; **ce n'est pas vraiment un s.!** it's not exactly headline news!

scooter [skutœr] **NM** (motor) scooter; **s. des mers** jet ski; **s. des neiges** snowmobile, skidoo

scooter [skɔtɛr, skutɛr] **NM** *Belg* bumper car, dodgem

scootériste [skuterist] **NMF** scooter rider

SCOP [skɔp] **NF** *(abrév* **Société coopérative ouvrière de production)** = manufacturing cooperative

scope [skɔp] **NM** *Fam* Cinemascope®▪

scopie [skɔpi] **NF** *Fam* X-ray▪

scopolamine [skɔpɔlamin] **NF** *Pharm* scopolamine, hyoscine

scops [skɔps] **NM** *Orn* scops owl

scorbut [skɔrbyt] **NM** *Méd* scurvy

scorbutique [skɔrbytik] *Méd* **ADJ** scorbutic **NMF** scurvy sufferer

score [skɔr] **NM 1** *Sport* score; **où en est** *ou* **quel est le s.?** what's the score? **2** *(résultat)* **faire un bon s. aux élections** to get a good result in the election **3** *Mktg* score; **s. d'agrément** approval rating *or* score; **s. d'attribution** attribution score; **s. de mémorisation** recall score; **s. de reconnaissance** recognition score

scoriacé, -e [skɔrjase] **ADJ** scoriaceous

scorie [skɔri] **NF 1** *Métal* **s., scories** slag; *(laitier)* cinders; *(de fer)* (iron) clinker *or* dross; **s. de déphosphoration** basic slag **2** *Géol* **scories (volcaniques)** scoria **3** *Fig Littéraire* **scories** *(déchet)* waste, dregs

scorpène [skɔrpɛn] **NF** *Ich* scorpion fish

scorpénidé [skɔrpenide] *Ich* **NM** scorpaenid
❑ **scorpénidés NMPL** Scorpaenidae

Scorpion [skɔrpjɔ̃] **NM 1** *Astron* Scorpio **2** *Astrol* Scorpio; **être S.** to be Scorpio *or* a Scorpian

scorpion [skɔrpjɔ̃] **NM 1** *Entom* scorpion; **s. d'eau** water scorpion; *Ich* **s. de mer** sea scorpion **2** *Hist* scorpion

scorsonère [skɔrsɔnɛr] **NF 1** *Bot* scorzonera, **s. basse** viper's grass **2** *Culin* black salsify

Scotch® [skɔtʃ] **NM** adhesive tape, *Br* Sellotape®, *Am* Scotch tape

scotch [skɔtʃ] *(pl* **scotchs** *ou* **scotches)* **NM 1** *(whisky)* Scotch (whisky) **2** *Belg (bière)* Scotch

scotché, -e [skɔtʃe] **ADJ 1** *(collé)* taped, *Br* sellotaped, *Am* scotchtaped; *Fam Fig* **être s. devant la télé** to be glued to the TV **2** *Fam (stupéfait)* **je suis resté s.** I was staggered *or Br* gobsmacked

scotcher [skɔtʃe] [3] **VT 1** *(coller)* to tape, *Br* to sellotape, *Am* to scotchtape **2** *Fam (stupéfaire)* to flabbergast, to knock sideways; **ça m'a vraiment scotché!** I was staggered *or Br* gobsmacked!

scotch-terrier [skɔtʃtɛrje] *(pl* **scotch-terriers)* **NM** Scottish terrier, Scottie

scotie [skɔti] **NF** *Archit* scotia

scotisme [skɔtism] **NM** *Rel* Scotism

scotiste [skɔtist] *Rel* **ADJ** Scotist **NMF** Scotist, follower of Duns Scotus

scotome [skɔtom] **NM** *Méd* scotoma, scotomy

scotomisation [skɔtɔmizasjɔ̃] **NF** *Psy* scotomization

scotomiser [skɔtɔmize] [3] **VT** *Psy* to scotomize

scotopique [skɔtɔpik] **ADJ** *Méd* scotopic

scottish-terrier [skɔtiʃtɛrje] *(pl* **scottish-terriers)* **NM** Scottish terrier, Scottie

scoumoune [ʃkumun] **NF** *très Fam* rotten luck; **avoir la s.** to be jinxed

scoured [skawrɛd, skurɛd] **NM** *Tex* scoured

scout, -e [skut] **ADJ 1** *(relatif au scoutisme)* scout *(avant n)*; **camp/mouvement s.** scout camp/movement **2** *Fig* boy scout *(avant n)*; **il a un petit côté s.** he's a boy scout at heart **NM,F** *(personne)* (Boy) Scout, *f Br* (Girl) Guide, *Am* Girl Scout; **des scouts** (a troop of) Boy Scouts; **des scoutes** (a troop of) *Br* Girl Guides *or Am* Girl Scouts; **s., toujours prêt!** *(devise des scouts)* be prepared!; *Hum* always at your service!

scout-car [skutkar] *(pl* **scout-cars)* **NM** *Mil* scout-car

scoutisme [skutism] **NM 1** *(activité)* scouting **2** *(association → pour garçons)* Boy Scout movement; *(→ pour filles)* Br Girl Guide *or Am* Girl Scout movement

SCP [ɛssepe] *(abrév écrite* **société civile professionnelle)** professional *or* non-trading partnership

SCPI [ɛssepei] **NF** *(abrév* **Société civile de placement immobilier)** = company which owns and manages rented accommodation

Scrabble® [skrabl] **NM** Scrabble®

scrabbler [skrable] [3] **VI** to play Scrabble®

scrabbleur, -euse [skrablœr, -øz] **NM,F** Scrabble® player

scraper [skrapœr] **NM** scraper

scratch [skratʃ] **ADJ INV** *Sport (course, joueur)* scratch *(avant n)*
NM 1 *Sport (course)* scratch race **2** *Mus (en rap)* scratching; **faire un s.** to scratch

scratcher [skratʃe] [3] **VT** *Sport* to scratch, to withdraw
VI *Mus* to scratch
▸ **se scratcher VPR** *Fam* to go off the road; **il s'est scratché avec la moto de son frère** he went off the road on his brother's motorbike

scratching [skratʃiŋ] **NM** *Mus* scratching

scratch vidéo [skratʃvideo] **NM** scratch video

scriban [skribɑ̃] **NM** = **scribanne**

scribanne [skriban] **NF** bureau-cabinet

scribe [skrib] **NM 1** *Antiq & Rel* scribe **2** *(écrivain public)* copyist, public writer **3** *Péj Vieilli (gratte-papier)* pen-pusher

scribouillard, -e [skribujar, -ard] **NM,F** *Fam Péj* pen-pusher

scribouilleur, -euse [skribujœr, -øz] **NM,F** *Fam Péj* hack, scribbler

scripophilie [skripɔfili] **NF** scripophily

script [skript] **NM 1** *(écriture)* script; **écrire en s.** to write in block letters, to print (in block letters) **2** *Cin & Rad* script **3** *Bourse* scrip

scripte [skript] **NMF** continuity man, *f* girl

scripteur [skriptœr] **NM 1** *Rel* composer of Papal Bulls **2** *Ling* writer

script-girl [skriptgœrl] *(pl* **script-girls)* **NF** continuity girl

scripturaire [skriptyrɛr] **ADJ** *Rel* scriptural; **exégèse s.** scriptural exegesis

scriptural, -e, -aux, -ales [skriptyral, -o] **ADJ 1** *(relatif à l'écriture)* written **2** *Fin* cashless

scrofulaire [skrɔfylɛr] **NF** *Bot* figwort, *Spéc* scrophularia; **s. noueuse** common figwort

scrofulariacée [skrɔfylarjase] *Bot* **NF** member of the Scrophulariaceae family
❑ **scrofulariacées NFPL** Scrophulariaceae

scrofule [skʁɔfyl] NF *Méd* scrofula

scrofuleux, -euse [skʁɔfylø, -øz] *Méd* ADJ scrofulous
NM,F scrofulous person

scrogneugneu, -x [skʁɔɲøɲø] *Vieilli* NM cantankerous old soldier, Colonel Blimp
EXCLAM *Hum* damme, sir!

scrotal, -e, -aux, -ales [skʁɔtal, -o] ADJ scrotal

scrotum [skʁɔtɔm] NM *Anat* scrotum

scrub [skʁœb] NM *Bot* scrub

scrubber [skʁœbœʁ] NM *Chim* scrubber, gas-scrubbing apparatus

scrupule [skʁypyl] NM **1** *(cas de conscience)* scruple, qualm (of conscience); **avoir des scrupules** to have scruples; **n'aie pas de scrupules** don't have any qualms; **elle n'a aucun s.** she has no scruples; *Fam* **ce ne sont pas les scrupules qui l'étouffent** he's completely unscrupulous▪; **se faire s. de qch** to have scruples or qualms about doing sth; **il ne s'est pas embarrassé de scrupules pour le renvoyer** he didn't have any scruples about firing him; **avoir s. à faire qch** to have scruples or qualms about doing sth; **je n'aurai aucun s. à le lui dire** I'll have no scruples or qualms about telling him/her so; **n'ayez aucun s. à faire appel à moi** don't hesitate to ask for my help; **vos scrupules vous honorent** your scruples do you credit
2 *(minutie)* punctiliousness; **exact jusqu'au s.** scrupulously or punctiliously exact
3 *Arch (unité de poids)* scruple
□ **sans scrupules** ADJ *(individu)* unscrupulous, unprincipled, without scruples; **il est vraiment sans scrupules** he's totally unprincipled

scrupuleuse [skʁypyløz] *voir* **scrupuleux**

scrupuleusement [skʁypyløzmɑ̃] ADV scrupulously, punctiliously

scrupuleux, -euse [skʁypylø, -øz] ADJ **1** *(honnête)* scrupulous, scrupulously honest; **peu s.** unscrupulous; **il est très s. dans le remboursement de ses dettes** when it comes to paying off his debts, he's scrupulously honest; **d'une honnêteté scrupuleuse** scrupulously honest
2 *(minutieux)* scrupulous, meticulous; **sa secrétaire est très scrupuleuse** his/her secretary is very meticulous in all she does

scrutateur, -trice [skʁytatœʁ, -tʁis] ADJ searching *(avant n)*; **d'un air s.** searchingly
NM,F *Admin Br* scrutineer, *Am* teller

scruter [3] [skʁyte] VT **1** *(pour comprendre)* to scrutinize, to examine; **il scruta son visage** he searched his/her face **2** *(en parcourant des yeux)* to scan, to search; **elles scrutaient l'horizon** they scanned or they searched the horizon; **tous les matins, il scrute les petites annonces** every morning he scans or he scours the small ads

scrutin [skʁytɛ̃] NM **1** *(façon d'élire)* vote, voting *(UNCOUNT)*, ballot; **procéder au s.** to take a ballot; **dépouiller le s.** to count the votes; **s. de liste** list system; **s. d'arrondissement** district election system; **s. à deux tours** second ballot; **s. majoritaire** election on a majority basis, *Br* first-past-the-post election; **s. majoritaire plurinominal** first-past-the-post system *(voting for as many candidates/parties as there are seats)*; **s. majoritaire uninominal** first-past-the-post system *(voting for a single candidate)*; **s. plurinominal** = voting for more than one candidate; **s. proportionnel** ou **à la proportionnelle** *(voting using the system of)* proportional representation; **s. secret** secret ballot; **voter au s. secret** to have a secret ballot; **s. uninominal** voting for a single candidate; **s. uninominal préférentiel avec report de voix** single transferable vote system
2 *(fait de voter)* ballot; **par (voie de) s.** by ballot; **s. de ballottage** second ballot, *Am* runoff election
3 *(consultation électorale)* election; **le dernier s. a été favorable à la gauche** the last election showed a swing to the left

SCS [ɛssɛɛs] NF *(abrév* **société en commandite simple)** limited partnership

SCSI [ɛsɛsi] NF *(abrév* **small computer systems interface)** SCSI

SCT [ɛssete] NM *Méd (abrév* **syndrome du choc toxique)** TSS

---

scull [skyl, skœl] NM *Sport* scull

sculpter [3] [skylte] VT **1** *(pierre, marbre)* to sculpt; **s. qch dans le marbre** to sculpt sth out of marble; **escalier sculpté** sculptured staircase **2** *(bois)* to carve; *(bâton)* to scrimshaw **3** *Fig (façonner)* to sculpt, to carve, to fashion; **la mer a sculpté la falaise** the cliff has been sculpted by the sea
USAGE ABSOLU *(faire de la sculpture)* to sculpt

sculpteur, -trice [skyltœʁ, -tʁis] NM,F sculptor; **femme s.** sculptor, sculptress; **s. sur bois** woodcarver

sculptural, -e, -aux, -ales [skyltyʁal, -o] ADJ **1** *(relatif à la sculpture)* sculptural **2** *(beauté, formes)* statuesque

sculpture [skyltyʁ] NF **1** *(art)* sculpture *(UNCOUNT)*, sculpting *(UNCOUNT)*; **faire de la s.** to sculpt; **il fait de la s.** he's a sculptor; **s. sur bois** woodcarving **2** *(œuvre)* sculpture, piece of sculpture
□ **sculptures** NFPL *Aut (d'un pneu)* tread pattern

scutellaire [skytelɛʁ] NF *Bot* skullcap, *Spéc* scutellaria

scutum [skytɔm] NM *Antiq & Entom* scutum

scyphozoaire [sifɔzɔɛʁ] *Zool* NM scyphozoan
□ **scyphozoaires** NMPL Scyphozoa

scythe [sit] ADJ Scythian
□ **Scythe** NMF Scythian

Scythie [siti] NF *Géog* **la S.** Scythia

sdb *(abrév écrite* **salle de bains)** bathroom

SDECE [sdɛk] NM *Anciennement (abrév* **Service de documentation extérieure et de contre-espionnage)** = French Intelligence Service

SDF [ɛsdeɛf] NMF INV *(abrév* **sans domicile fixe)** homeless person; **les S.** the homeless

SDN [ɛsdeɛn] NF *(abrév* **Société des Nations)** **la S.** the League of Nations

SE [sə]

s' is used before a word beginning with a vowel or h mute.

PRON PERSONNEL **1** *(avec un verbe pronominal réfléchi)* **se salir** to get dirty; **s'exprimer** to express oneself; **elle se coiffe** she's doing her hair; **le chat s'est brûlé** the cat burnt itself; **elles s'en sont persuadées** they've convinced themselves of it; **il s'écoute parler** he listens to his own voice; **il s'est acheté une voiture** he bought himself a car; **elle s'est donné une heure pour le faire** she gave herself one hour to do it; **il s'attribuera tout le mérite de l'affaire** he'll take all the credit for it
2 *(se substituant à l'adjectif possessif)* **elle se lave les mains** she's washing her hands; **il s'est fracturé deux côtes** he broke two ribs; **se mordre la langue** to bite one's tongue
3 *(avec un verbe pronominal réciproque)* **pour s'aider, ils partagent le travail** to help each other or one another, they share the work; **ils ne se supportent pas** they can't stand each other or one another; **ils s'aiment profondément** they love each other deeply; **ils se rendent des services** they help each other; **elles se sont envoyé des lettres** they sent letters to each other, they exchanged letters
4 *(avec un verbe pronominal passif)* **cette décision s'est prise sans moi** this decision has been taken without me; **ce modèle se vend bien** this model sells well; **le champagne se sert frappé** champagne should be served well chilled; **ça se mange?** can you eat it?; **ça se mange froid** you eat it cold; **ça se trouve où?** where can you find that?
5 *(avec un verbe pronominal intransitif)* **ils s'en vont** they're leaving; **ils s'enfuient** they're running away; **elle s'est évanouie** she fainted; **ils s'en sont emparés** they grabbed or snatched it; **il se sentit défaillir** he felt himself becoming faint; **ils s'y voient contraints** they find themselves forced to do it; **il se laisse convaincre trop facilement** he is too easily persuaded; *Fam* **il s'est fait avoir!** he's been had!; **il se croyait lundi** he thought it was Monday today; **elle se croyait en sécurité** she thought she was safe; **elle se sait perdue** she knows (that) she's incurable; **il se dit médecin** he claims to be a doctor

---

6 *(dans des tournures impersonnelles)* **il s'en est vendu plusieurs millions d'exemplaires** several million copies have been sold; **il se fait tard** it's getting late; **il s'est mis à neiger** it started to snow; **il se peut qu'ils arrivent plus tôt** it's possible that they'll arrive earlier, they might arrive earlier; **il s'est glissé une erreur dans la dernière page** a mistake slipped into the last page
7 *Fam (emploi expressif)* **il se fait 5000 euros par mois** he's got 5,000 euros coming in per month; **elle se l'est écouté au moins 30 fois, ce disque** she listened to this record at least 30 times▪

S-E *(abrév écrite* **Sud-Est)** SE

S.E. *(abrév écrite* **Son Excellence)** HE

seaborgium [seabɔʁʒɔm] NM *Chim* seaborgium

sea-line [silajn] *(pl* **sea-lines)** NM undersea pipeline

séamment [seamɑ̃] ADV *Arch & Littéraire* becomingly, fittingly

séance [seɑ̃s] NF **1** *(réunion)* session; **être en s.** *(comité, Parlement)* to be sitting or in session; *(tribunal)* to be in session; **lever la s.** *(groupe de travail)* to close the meeting; *(comité)* to end or to close the session; *(Parlement)* to adjourn; **la s. est levée!** *(au tribunal)* the court will adjourn!; *Fam* **on lève la s.?** *(après une période de travail)* shall we call it a day?; **suspendre la s.** *(au Parlement, au tribunal)* to adjourn; **je déclare la s. ouverte** I declare the meeting open; **la s. est ouverte!** *(au tribunal)* this court is now in session!; **en s. publique** *(au tribunal)* in open court; **s. de concertation** *(au Parlement)* policy meeting; *Mktg* **s. de créativité** brainstorming session; **s. d'information** briefing (session); **s. plénière** *(au Parlement)* plenary (session); **s. publique** *(au Parlement)* public sitting
2 *Bourse* **ce fut une bonne/mauvaise s. aujourd'hui à la Bourse** it was a good/a bad day today on the Stock Exchange; **en début/en fin de s., les actions Roman étaient à 40 euros** the Roman shares opened/closed at 40 euros; **s. de clôture** closing session; **s. d'ouverture** opening session
3 *(période → d'entraînement, de traitement)* session; **s. de photo** photocall, photo opportunity; **s. de pose** sitting; **s. de projection** slide show; **s. de rééducation** session of physiotherapy; **s. de spiritisme** seance; **s. de travail** working session
4 *Cin* showing; **s. à 19h 10, film à 19h 30** programme 7:10, film starts 7:30; **je vais à la s. de 20 heures** I'm going to the 8 o'clock showing; **la dernière s.** the last showing; **s. privée** private showing
5 *Fam (crise)* scene, fuss, tantrum; **il nous a fait une de ces séances!** he made such a scene!; **il nous a fait une s. de larmes** he turned on the waterworks
6 *Belg* **s. académique** ceremony
□ **séance tenante** ADV forthwith, right away, without further ado; **il l'épousa s. tenante** he married her without further ado
□ **à la séance** ADJ *TV (film, programme)* pay-per-view

séancier [seɑ̃sje] NM *(parlementaire)* parliamentary reporter

séant, -e [seɑ̃, -ɑ̃t] ADJ **1** *Littéraire (convenable)* becoming, seemly; **il n'est pas s. de partir sans un mot de remerciement** it's not done to leave without a word of thanks **2** *Arch (flatteur)* becoming (à to)
NM *(postérieur)* **se mettre sur son s.** to sit up; **tomber sur son s.** to fall on one's behind

Seattle [siatəl] NM Seattle

seau, -x [so] NM **1** *(récipient)* bucket, pail; **s. à champagne** champagne bucket; **s. à charbon** coal scuttle; **s. d'enfant** child's bucket; **s. à glace** *Br* ice bucket, *Am* ice-pail; **s. hygiénique** slop pail
2 *(contenu)* bucketful; **un s. de lait** a bucket of milk
3 *(sac)* bucket bag
□ **à seaux** ADV *Fam* **il pleut à seaux, la pluie tombe à seaux** it's pouring or *Br* bucketing down

sébacé, -e [sebase] ADJ *Méd* sebaceous

sébacique [sebasik] ADJ *Chim* sebacic

sébaste [sebast] NM *Ich* Norway haddock, rose-

fish

Sébastopol [sebastɔpɔl] **NM** Sebastopol

SEBC [ɛsəbese] **NM** *Fin & Écon (abrév* **Système Européen de Banques Centrales**) ESCB

sébile [sebil] **NF** *Littéraire* begging bowl

sebka, sebkha [sɛpka], **sebkra** [sɛpkra] **NF** *Géog* sebka, sebkha

séborrhée [sebɔre] **NF** *Méd* seborrhoea

séborrhéique [sebɔreik] **ADJ** *Méd* seborrhoeic

sébum [sebɔm] **NM** sebum

SEC, SÈCHE[1] [sɛk, sɛʃ]

> **ADJ** dry **1, 3–6** ■ dried **2** ■ neat **2** ■ curt **4**
> **NM** dry feed
> **ADV** dry **1** ■ hard **2**

ADJ 1 *(air, bois, endroit, vêtement etc)* dry; **il fait un froid s.** it's cold and dry, there's a crisp cold air; **avoir l'œil s.** *ou* **les yeux secs** *Méd* to have dry eyes; *Fig* to be dry-eyed; **ma jupe n'est pas tout à fait sèche** my skirt isn't quite dry

2 *(légume, fruit)* dried; *(alcool)* neat; **shampooing s.** dry shampoo

3 *(non gras → cheveux, peau, mine de crayon)* dry; *(maigre → personne)* lean; *Fam* **être s. comme un coup de trique** to be all skin and bone *or* as thin as a rake

4 *(désagréable → ton, voix, explication, refus, remarque)* curt, terse; *(→ rire)* dry; **...dit-elle d'un ton s.** ...she said curtly *or* tersely; **il est très s. au téléphone** he's very curt on the phone; **un bruit s.** a snap, a crack; **ouvrir/fermer qch avec un bruit s.** to snap sth open/shut; **d'un coup s.** smartly, sharply; **casser qch d'un coup s.** to snap sth; **retire le sparadrap d'un coup s.** pull the sticking plaster off smartly; *Fam* **l'avoir s.** *(être déçu)* to be miffed

5 *Beaux-Arts (graphisme, style)* dry

6 *(champagne, vin)* dry

7 *Cartes* **atout/roi s.** singleton trump/king; **ma dame était sèche** my queen was a singleton

NM *Agr* dry feed

ADV 1 *Météo* **il fera s. toute la semaine** the weather *or* it will be dry for the whole week

2 *(brusquement)* hard; **démarrer s.** *(conducteur)* to shoot off at top speed; *(course)* to get a flying start; **il a pris son virage assez s.** he took the bend rather sharply

3 *Fam (beaucoup)* a lot■; **il boit s.** he can really knock it back; **ils ont dérouillé s. pendant la guerre** they went through total hell during the war

❑ **à sec ADJ 1** *(cours d'eau, source etc)* dry, dried-up; *(réservoir)* empty; **le ruisseau est à s.** the brook has dried up *or* is dry **2** *Fam (sans argent → personne)* broke, *Br* skint; *(→ caisse)* empty■ **3** *Constr* **maçonnerie à s.** dry-stone (work) **ADV 1** *(sans eau)* **on met la piscine à s. chaque hiver** the pool's drained (off) every winter; **le réservoir a été mis à s.** the reservoir has been drained; **le soleil a mis le marais à s.** the sun has dried up the marsh **2** *Fam (financièrement)* **mettre une entreprise à s.** to ruin a company **3** *Naut* **filer** *ou* **courir** *ou* **fuir à s. (de toile)** to run under bare poles

❑ **au sec ADV garder** *ou* **tenir qch au s.** to keep sth in a dry place, to keep sth dry; **rester au s.** to stay dry

sécable [sekabl] **ADJ 1** *Pharm* breakable, divisible **2** *Géom* divisible

SECAM, Secam [sekam] *TV (abrév* **séquentiel couleur à mémoire**) **ADJ INV** SECAM
NM INV SECAM

sécant, -e [sekɑ̃, -ɑ̃t] **ADJ** intersecting, secant
❑ **sécante NF** secant

sécateur [sekatœr] **NM un s.** *(pour les fleurs)* (a pair of) secateurs; *(pour les haies)* pruning shears

secco [seko] **NM** *(en Afrique francophone)* = fence made from interwoven branches, or the land enclosed within it

sécession [sesesjɔ̃] **NF** secession; **faire s.** to secede

sécessionniste [sesesjɔnist] **ADJ** secessionist
NMF secessionist

séchage [seʃaʒ] **NM 1** *(du linge, des cheveux, du foin)* drying **2** *(du bois)* seasoning

sèche[1] [sɛʃ] **ADJ F** *voir* **sec**

sèche[2] **NF** *Fam (cigarette)* smoke, *Br* fag, *Am* cig

sèche-cheveux [sɛʃʃəvø] **NM INV** hairdryer

sèche-linge [sɛʃlɛ̃ʒ] **NM INV** *(à tambour)* tumble-drier; *(placard)* airing cupboard

sèche-mains [sɛʃmɛ̃] **NM INV** hand-dryer

sèchement [sɛʃmɑ̃] **ADV 1** *(durement → parler, répondre)* dryly, curtly, tersely; **"ne comptez pas sur moi", répondit-elle s.** "don't count on me," she snapped back **2** *(brusquement → taper)* sharply; **prendre un virage un peu s.** to take a bend rather sharply **3** *(sans fioritures)* dryly; **il expose toujours ses arguments un peu s.** he always sets out his arguments rather unimaginatively

sécher [18] [seʃe] **VT 1** *(gén)* to dry; *(avec un torchon, avec une éponge)* to wipe dry; **sèche tes larmes** *ou* **tes yeux** dry your tears *or* your eyes; **s. les larmes** *ou* **les pleurs de qn** to console sb

2 *(vêtement)* to dry; **s. ses vêtements devant le feu** to dry one's clothes in front of the fire; **ne pas s. près d'une source de chaleur** *(sur étiquette de vêtement)* dry away from direct heat; **ne pas s. en machine** *(sur étiquette de vêtement)* do not tumble-dry

3 *(sujet: chaleur, soleil → terrain, plante)* to dry up; *(déshydrater → fruits)* to dry (up); **le vent sèche la peau** wind dries (out) the skin; **figues séchées au soleil** sun-dried figs

4 *Fam Arg scol (cours) Br* to bunk off, *Am* to skip

5 *Fam (boire)* to knock back; **il a séché trois cognacs** he knocked back three brandies

VI 1 *(surface)* to dry (off); *(linge)* to dry; *(éponge)* to dry (out); *(sol, puits)* to dry up; *(cours d'eau)* to dry up, to run dry

2 faire s. du linge to leave clothes to dry; **mettre le linge à s.** to put the washing out to dry; **faire s. sans essorer** *(sur l'étiquette d'un vêtement)* do not spin dry; **faire s. à plat** *(vêtement)* dry flat; **laisser s. les peintures** to leave the paintwork to dry

3 *(plante)* to dry up *or* out; *(bois)* to dry out; *(fruits, viande)* to dry; **faire s. du bois** to season wood; **faire s. du poisson/des haricots** to dry fish/beans; **s. sur pied** *(plante)* to wilt, to wither; *Fam* **on a séché sur pied tout l'été** we've been bored out of our minds all summer; *Littéraire* **s. d'impatience/d'ennui** to be consumed with impatience/with boredom

4 *Fam Arg scol (ne pas aller en classe) Br* to bunk off, *Am* to play hookey

5 *Fam (ne pas connaître la réponse)* to be completely stumped; **j'ai séché en physique/sur la deuxième question** the physics exam/the second question had me completely stumped

▶**se sécher VPR** to dry oneself; **se s. avec une serviette/au soleil** to dry oneself with a towel/in the sun; **sèche-toi bien derrière les oreilles** dry (yourself) carefully behind your ears; **se s. les mains/les cheveux** to dry one's hands/hair

sécheresse, sècheresse [sɛʃrɛs] **NF 1** *(d'un climat, d'un terrain, d'un style)* dryness; *(d'un trait)* dryness, harshness; *(d'une réplique, d'un ton)* abruptness; **répondre avec s.** to answer curtly *or* abruptly *or* tersely; **la s. de sa remarque** the curtness *or* the terseness of his/her remark; **montrer une grande s. de cœur** to show great heartlessness

2 *Météo* drought; **pendant la** *ou* **les mois de s.** during the dry months

sécherie, sècherie [sɛʃri] **NF 1** *(lieu)* drying room; *(d'une machine)* dryer; *(industrie)* drying plant **2** *Typ* dry end

sécheur [seʃœr] **NM** *(à tabac)* dryer

sécheuse [seʃøz] **NF** *(de linge)* tumble-drier

séchoir [seʃwar] **NM 1** *Agr & Tech (salle)* drying room; *(hangar)* drying shed; *(râtelier)* drying rack **2** *(à usage domestique)* dryer; **s. à cheveux** hairdryer; **s. à linge** *(à tambour)* tumble-drier; *(pliant)* clotheshorse; *(suspendu)* ceiling airer **3** *Typ* **s. à plat** sheet dryer

second, -e[1] [səgɔ̃, -ɔ̃d] **ADJ 1** *(dans l'espace, dans le temps)* second; **c'est la seconde rue à droite** it's the second street on the right; **pour la seconde fois** for the second time; **en s. lieu** secondly, in the second place; *Hist* **le S. Empire** the French Second Empire; **meubles/style S. Empire** (French) Second Empire furniture/style

2 *(dans une hiérarchie)* second; *(éclairagiste, maquilleur)* assistant *(avant n)*; **la seconde ville de France** France's second city; *Com* **s. associé** junior partner; *Transp* **seconde classe** second class; *Naut* **s. maître** petty officer; *Bourse* **s. marché** unlisted securities market, secondary market; *Littéraire* **sans s., à nul autre s.** *(sans pareil)* second to none, unparalleled; *Com* **s. œuvre** finishing (jobs); *Jur* **s. original** = second original copy of a document; *Cin* **s. rôle** secondary *or* supporting role; **meilleur s. rôle masculin/féminin** best supporting actor/actress

3 *(autre → chance, jeunesse, vie)* second; **l'Angleterre, c'est une seconde patrie pour elle** England's a second home for her; **c'est une seconde nature chez lui** it's second nature to him; **elle a été une seconde mère pour moi** she was like a mother to me; **seconde vue** clairvoyance, second sight; **don de seconde vue** clairvoyancy, second sight; **être doué de seconde vue** to be clairvoyant, to have second sight

4 *Math* **a seconde** a double point, a''

NM,F 1 *(dans l'espace, dans le temps)* second; **je lis le premier paragraphe, et toi le s.** I read the first paragraph, and you the second one *or* the next one

2 *(dans une hiérarchie)* second; **la seconde de ses filles** his/her second daughter; **mon s.** *(enfant)* my second child; **arriver (le) s.** *(dans une course, à une élection)* to come second

NM 1 *(assistant → d'un directeur)* right arm; *(→ dans un duel)* second; *Naut* first mate; *Mil* second in command; **s. de cuisine** senior sous chef; *TV & Cin* **s. assistant** best boy

2 *(dans une charade)* **mon s. est...** my second is...

3 *(étage) Br* second floor, *Am* third floor; **les voisins du s.** the neighbours on the *Br* second *or Am* third floor

❑ **seconde NF 1** *Aut* second gear; **passe en seconde** change into *or* to second gear

2 *Transp (classe)* second class; **(billet de) seconde** second-class ticket; **les secondes, les wagons de seconde** second-class carriages; **voyager en seconde** to travel second class

3 *Scol Br* ≃ fifth year, *Am* ≃ tenth grade

4 *Escrime* seconde

5 *(en danse)* second position

6 *Mus* second; **seconde majeure/mineure** major/minor second

❑ **secondes NFPL** *Typ* second proofs

❑ **en second ADJ capitaine en s.** first mate **ADV** second, secondly; **passer en s.** to be second

secondaire [səgɔ̃dɛr] **ADJ 1** *(question, personnage, route)* secondary; **c'est s.** it's of secondary importance *or* of minor interest; *Théât & Littérature* **intrigue s.** subplot

2 *Scol* secondary

3 *Géol* **ère s.** Mesozoic era

NM 1 *Géol* **le s.** the Mesozoic

2 *Scol* **le s.** *Br* secondary *or Am* high school *(UNCOUNT)*

3 *Élec* secondary winding; *Rad (du transformateur)* secondary

4 *Écon* **le s.** secondary production

secondairement [səgɔ̃dɛrmɑ̃] **ADV** secondarily

seconde[2] [səgɔ̃d] **NF 1** *(division horaire)* second; **s. intercalaire** leap second

2 *(court instant)* **(attendez) une s.!** just a second!; **j'en ai pour une s.** I'll only be a second *or* a moment; **je reviens dans une s.** I'll be back in a second, I'll be right back; **une s. d'inattention** a momentary lapse in concentration; **à une s. près, je ratais le train** I was within a second of missing the train; **à la s.** instantly, there and then; **avec lui, il faut que ce soit fait à la s.** he wants things done instantly

secondement [səgɔ̃dmɑ̃] **ADV** second, secondly

seconder [3] [səgɔ̃de] **VT 1** *(assister)* to assist, to back up **2** *(action, dessein)* to second

sécot [seko] **ADJ** *Fam* **1** *(sec)* dry■ **2** *(maigre)* skinny■, lanky

secoué, -e [skwe] **ADJ** *Fam (fou)* crazy, *Br* off one's nut *or* rocker

secouement [səkumɑ̃] **NM** *Littéraire* shaking

secouer [6] [səkwe] **VT 1** *(arbre, bouteille, personne)* to shake; *(tapis, vêtement)* to shake (out); *(coussin, oreiller)* to plump up, to shake

up; **il/le vent secouait l'arbre** he/the wind was shaking the tree; **la tempête secouait le bateau** the storm was buffeting the boat; **nous avons été secoués pendant la traversée/le vol** we were shaken about during the crossing/the flight, we had a rough crossing/flight; **l'explosion secoua l'immeuble** the explosion shook *or* rocked the building; **de violents spasmes secouaient son corps tout entier** violent spasms shook his/her whole body; **s. la tête** *(acquiescer)* to nod one's head; *(refuser)* to shake one's head; *Fam* **s. qn comme un prunier** to shake sb like a rag doll; *Fig* **s. le cocotier** to get rid of the dead wood

2 *(se débarrasser de → poussière, sable, miettes)* to shake off; *Fig (→ paresse, torpeur etc)* to shake off; **s. le joug de l'oppresseur** to shake off the yoke of the oppressor; *Fam* **s. les puces à qn** *(le gronder) Br* to tick sb off, *Am* to chew sb out

3 *Fam (houspiller → personne)* to shake up; **il a besoin d'être secoué pour travailler** he needs a good shake before he gets down to work

4 *(bouleverser → personne)* to shake up, to give a jolt *or* a shock to; **la nouvelle l'a beaucoup secoué** the news really shook him up

5 *très Fam* **j'en ai rien à s.** I don't give a damn *or Br* toss

USAGE ABSOLU ça secoue *(en avion, en train)* it's bumpy; *(en bateau)* it's rough

▸**se secouer VPR** *Fam* to shake oneself up, to snap out of it; **il serait grand temps de te s.!** it's high time you pulled yourself together!

secoueur [səkwœr] **NM 1** *Métal* form-breaker **2** *Agr* **s. de paille** straw shaker

secourable [səkurabl] **ADJ** helpful; **un automobiliste s.** a helpful driver; **peu s.** unhelpful

secourir [45] [səkurir] **VT 1** *(blessé)* to help; *(personne en danger)* to rescue; **les skieurs avaient perdu tout espoir d'être secourus** the skiing party had lost all hope of being rescued *or* of rescue **2** *(pauvre, affligé)* to aid, to help **3** *Littéraire (misères)* to relieve, to ease

secourisme [səkurism] **NM** first aid

secouriste [səkurist] **NMF 1** *(d'une organisation)* first-aid worker **2** *(personne qualifiée)* qualified first-aider

secourra *etc voir* **secourir**

secours [səkur] **NM 1** *(assistance)* help, assistance, aid; **appeler** *ou* **crier au s.** to call out for help; **au s.!** help!; **appeler qn à son s.** *(blessé, entreprise)* to call upon sb for help, to call sb to the rescue; **allez chercher du s.!** go and get (some) help!; **porter** *ou* **prêter s. à qn** to give sb assistance; **porter s. à un blessé** to give first aid to an injured person; **personne ne s'est arrêté pour me porter s.** nobody stopped to (come and) help me; **aller** *ou* **se porter au s. de qn** to go to sb's assistance; **venir au s. de qn** to come to sb's aid; **venir au s. d'une entreprise** to rescue a company; **le S. catholique, le S. populaire (français)** = charity organizations giving help to the poor; **société de s. mutuels** friendly *or Am* benefit society

2 *(sauvetage)* aid, assistance; **le** *ou* **les s. aux brûlés** aid *or* assistance for burn victims; **envoyer des s. à qn** to send relief to sb; **les s. ne sont pas encore arrivés** aid *or* help hasn't arrived yet; **le s. en montagne/en mer** mountain/sea rescue; **le** *ou* **les s. d'urgence** emergency aid

3 *(appui)* help; **être d'un grand s. à qn** to be of great help to sb; **la calculette ne m'a pas été d'un grand s.** the calculator was of (very) little help *or* use to me; **avec le s. du dictionnaire, je devrais me débrouiller** with the help *or* with the aid of the dictionary, I should be able to get by

4 *Jur* emergency payment *or* allowance

NMPL *Mil (troupes)* relief troops, relieving force

▫ **de secours ADJ** *(équipement, éclairage, porte, sortie)* emergency *(avant n)*; *(équipe, poste)* rescue *(avant n)*; *(locomotive, train)* relief *(avant n)*; *Ordinat (copie, fichier, disquette)* backup

secouru, -e [səkury] **PP** *voir* **secourir**

secousse [səkus] **NF 1** *(saccade)* jerk, jolt; **la s. du train qui démarrait la réveilla** she was woken by the jolt when the train started; **elle se dégagea d'une s.** she shook *or* jerked herself free; **elle réussit à déplacer la malle par secousses** she managed to jerk the trunk along; **le train avançait par secousses** the train jolted forwards; **s. (électrique)** electric shock

2 *Fig (bouleversement)* jolt, shock, upset; **toutes ces secousses ont fini par ébranler sa santé** all these upsets ended up weakening his/her health

3 *Géol* **s. (sismique** *ou* **tellurique)** (earth) tremor

secret, -ète [səkrɛ, -ɛt] **ADJ 1** *(inconnu → accord, code, document etc)* secret; **cela n'a rien de s.** it's no secret; **garder** *ou* **tenir qch s.** to keep sth secret

2 *(caché → escalier, passage, tiroir)* secret; **une vie secrète** a secret life

3 *(intime → ambition, désir, espoir, pensée)* secret, innermost; **ses sentiments les plus secrets** his/her innermost feelings

4 *(personne)* secretive, reserved; **il est assez s.** he's fairly reserved, he keeps himself to himself

NM 1 *(confidence)* secret; **c'est un s.!** it's a secret!; **ce n'est un s. pour personne** it's no secret, everybody knows about it; **elle n'en fait pas un s.** she makes no secret of the fact; **c'est un bien lourd s.** it's a weighty secret indeed; **confier un s. à qn** to let sb into a secret; **être dans le s.** to be in on the secret; **mettre qn dans le s.** to let sb in on the secret; **ne pas avoir de secrets pour qn** *(sujet: personne)* to have no secrets from sb; *(sujet: question, machine)* to hold no secret for sb; **faire un s. de tout** to be secretive about everything; **s. d'État** state secret; *Fig* **ce n'est pas un s. d'État!** it's not a state secret!; **être dans le s. des dieux** to have privileged information; **c'est un s. de Polichinelle** it's an open secret *or* not much of a secret

2 *(mystère → d'un endroit, d'une discipline)* secret; **les secrets du cœur/de la nature** secrets of the heart/of nature

3 *(recette)* secret, recipe; **le s. du bonheur** the secret of *or* the recipe for happiness; **ses secrets de beauté** his/her beauty secrets *or* tips; **trouver le s. pour faire qch** to find the knack of doing sth; **un soufflé dont lui seul a le s.** a soufflé for which he alone knows the secret; *Com* **s. de fabrication** *ou* **de fabrique** trade secret

4 *(discrétion)* secrecy *(UNCOUNT)*; **exiger/promettre le s. (absolu)** to demand/to promise (absolute) secrecy; **je vous demande le s. sur cette affaire** I want you to keep silent about this matter; **s. bancaire** banking secrecy; **s. professionnel** professional confidentiality; *Journ* obligation to respect the confidentiality of sources; **enfreindre le s. professionnel** to commit a breach of confidentiality; *Journ* to betray a confidential source

5 *Rel* **le s. de la confession** the seal of confession

▫ **secrète NF 1 la secrète** *(police)* the secret police

2 *Rel (oraison)* secret

▫ **à secret ADJ** *(cadenas)* combination *(avant n)*; *(tiroir)* with a secret lock; *(meuble)* with secret drawers

▫ **au secret ADV être au s.** to be (detained) in solitary confinement; **mettre qn au s.** to detain sb in solitary confinement

▫ **en secret ADV 1** *(écrire, économiser)* in secret, secretly

2 *(croire, espérer)* secretly, privately

secrétage [səkretaʒ] **NM** carroting

secrétaire [səkretɛr] **NMF 1** *(dans une entreprise)* secretary; **s. bilingue/trilingue** bilingual/trilingual secretary; **s. du conseil d'administration** secretary to the Board of Directors; **s. de direction** executive secretary, personal assistant; **s. d'édition** *(dans l'édition)* assistant editor; *Journ* subeditor; **s. général** *(dans une entreprise)* company secretary; *(d'un syndicat)* general secretary; **s. général adjoint** *(d'un syndicat)* deputy general secretary; **s. juridique** legal secretary; **s. médical** medical secretary; **s. particulier** private secretary; *Cin & TV* **s. de plateau** script supervisor; **s. de production** production secretary; **s. de rédaction** *(dans l'édition)* desk *or* assistant editor; *Presse* subeditor; **s. de séance** meetings secretary

2 *Pol* **s. d'ambassade** secretary; **s. général** *(auprès d'un ministre)* ≃ permanent secretary; *(dans un parti)* general secretary; **s. général de l'ONU** Secretary-General of the UN; **s. général de l'Assemblée** ≃ Clerk of the House; **s. général du Sénat** ≃ Clerk of the House; **s. d'État** *(en France)* ≃ Junior Minister; *(en Grande-Bretagne)* Secretary of State; *(aux États-Unis)* State Secretary; *Rel (au Vatican)* Secretary of State; **s. d'État à la santé/aux transports** *(en France)* ≃ Junior Minister for Health/Transport; *(en Grande-Bretagne)* Secretary of State for Health/Transport; **s. perpétuel** Permanent Secretary *(of a learned society)*

3 *Admin* **s. d'administration** *(fonctionnaire)* administrative officer, administrator; **s. de mairie** ≃ chief executive

NM 1 *(meuble)* writing desk, *Sout* secrétaire

2 *Orn* secretary bird

secrétairerie [səkretɛrəri] **NF** *Rel* **s. d'État** Secretariate of State

secrétariat [səkretarja] **NM 1** *(fonction)* secretaryship; **pendant son s.** during his/her term of office as secretary; **s. de rédaction** *(dans l'édition)* desk *or* assistant editorship; *Journ* post of subeditor

2 *(employés)* secretarial staff; **tout le s. est en grève** all the secretarial staff are on strike; **le budget du s.** budgeting for secretarial services; **faire partie du s.** to be a member of the secretariat

3 *(bureau)* secretariat; **aller au s.** to go to the secretariat *or* secretary's office; *Journ* **s. de rédaction** copy desk

4 *(tâches administratives)* secretarial work; **apprendre le s.** to learn to be a secretary, to do a secretarial course; **le s. est assuré par dix personnes** the administrative *or* secretarial work is carried out by ten people

5 *Pol* **s. d'État** *(fonction en France)* post of Junior Minister; *(ministère français)* Junior Minister's Office; *(fonction en Grande-Bretagne)* post of Secretary of State; *(ministère britannique)* Secretary of State's Office; *(fonction aux États-Unis)* post of State Secretary; **s. général de l'ONU** UN Secretary-Generalship

6 *Admin* **s. de mairie** *(fonction)* ≃ function of chief executive; *(bureau)* ≃ chief executive's office

secrétariat-greffe [səkretarjagrɛf] *(pl* **secrétariats-greffes)** **NM** clerk's office, clerk of the court's office

secrète [səkrɛt] *voir* **secret**

secrètement [səkrɛtmɑ̃] **ADV 1** *(en cachette)* secretly, in secret; **elle avait vendu ses bijoux s.** she had secretly sold her jewels **2** *(intérieurement)* secretly; **je souhaite s. qu'il échoue** I secretly hope that he'll fail

secréter [18] [səkrete] **VT** *(peaux de lapin)* to carrot

sécréter [18] [sekrete] **VT 1** *Biol & Physiol* to secrete **2** *Fig (ennui)* to exude, to ooze; *(passion, désir)* to cause, to release

sécréteur, -euse *ou* **-trice** [sekretœr, -øz, -tris] **ADJ** *Biol & Physiol* secretory

sécrétine [sekretin] **NF** *Biol & Physiol* secretin

sécrétion [sekresjɔ̃] **NF** *Biol & Physiol* secretion; **glande à s. externe/interne** exocrine/endocrine gland

sécrétoire [sekretwar] **ADJ** *Biol & Physiol* secretory

sectaire [sɛktɛr] **ADJ** sectarian

NMF sectarian

sectarisme [sɛktarism] **NM** sectarianism

sectateur, -trice [sɛktatœr, -tris] **NM,F 1** *Littéraire (partisan d'une doctrine)* partisan **2** *(membre d'une secte)* follower, adept

secte [sɛkt] **NF** sect

secteur [sɛktœr] **NM 1** *Écon* sector; **s. d'activité** area of activity; **s. d'affaires** business sector; **s. de croissance** growth sector; **s. économique** economic sector; **le s. de l'élevage** the livestock breeding sector; **s. en expansion** growth sector; **s. de la grande distribution** mass distribution sector; **s. industriel** branch *or* sector of industry; **s. primaire** primary sector; **s. privé** private sector *or* enterprise; **s. privé à but non lucratif** private non-profit-making sector; **s. public** public sector; **s. sanitaire** health sector; **s. secondaire** secondary sector; **s. des services** service sector; **s. tertiaire** tertiary sector

2 *(zone d'action → d'un policier) Br* beat, *Am*

patch; (→ *d'un représentant*) area, patch; (→ *de l'urbanisme*) district, area; *Mil & Naut* sector; *Admin* = local area covered by the French health and social services department; **le s. français de Berlin** the French sector of Berlin; **s. sauvegardé** area of listed buildings, buildings zoned for preservation; **s. de vente** sales area, sales territory

3 *Fam (quartier)* **c'est dans le s.** it's around here■ ; **ça fait longtemps que je ne l'ai pas vu dans le s.** I haven't seen him around here for ages■ ; **changer de s.** to make oneself scarce; **tu ferais mieux de changer de s.** *(partir)* you'd better make yourself scarce

4 *Fam (domaine)* **ce n'est pas mon s.** that's not my line

5 *Élec* **le s.** the mains (supply); **branché sur le s.** plugged into the mains; **ça se branche sur le s.** it runs off the mains

6 *Math & Astron* sector; **s. (angulaire)** sector; **s. sphérique** sector of a sphere

7 *Ordinat* sector; **s. endommagé** bad sector; **s. d'initialisation** boot sector

8 *Aut* **s. de direction** steering sector

section [sɛksjɔ̃] **NF 1** *(d'une autoroute, d'une rivière)* section, stretch; *(de ligne de bus, de tramway)* fare stage; *(d'un livre)* part, section; *(d'une bibliothèque)* section; *(d'un service)* branch, division, department

2 *Univ (département)* department; **il a changé de s.** *(enseignant)* he has transferred to another department

3 *Scol* = one of the groups into which "baccalauréat" students are divided, depending on their chosen area of specialization, *Br* ≃ stream, *Am* ≃ track; **s. économique/scientifique/littéraire** ≃ economics/science/arts *Br* stream *or Am* track; **au lycée, j'étais en s. économique** my main subject at school was economics

4 *(d'un parti)* local branch; **s. syndicale** = local branch of a union; *(dans l'industrie de la presse et du livre)* (union) chapel; **S. française de l'Internationale ouvrière** = the French Socialist Party between 1905 and 1969

5 *Math & Géom* section; **un câble de 12 mm de s.** a 12 mm (section) cable; **dessiner la s. de qch** to draw the section of sth *or* sth in section; **s. conique/plane** conic/plane section; **point de s.** point of intersection

6 *Nucl* **s. efficace** cross section

7 *(coupure)* cutting *(UNCOUNT)*, severing *(UNCOUNT)*; *Méd* amputation

8 *Biol (groupe, coupe)* section

9 *Élec* **s. morte** dummy coil

10 *Mil* section; **s. de bombardiers** bomber flight

11 *Mus* **s. rythmique** rhythm section

12 *Naut* **s. mouillée** wetted section

13 *Pol* **s. électorale** ward

14 *Pol* **s. administrative** administrative division *(of the "Conseil d'État")*; **s. du contentieux** Judicial Division *(of the "Conseil d'État")*; **s. du rapport et des études** Report and Research Division *(of the "Conseil d'État")*

sectionnement [sɛksjɔnmɑ̃] **NM 1** *(coupure)* cutting *(UNCOUNT)*, severing *(UNCOUNT)* **2** *(division)* division into sections **3** *Élec* sectioning (and isolation)

sectionner [3] [sɛksjɔne] **VT 1** *(tendon, câble, ligne)* to sever, to cut; *Méd* to amputate; **la lame avait sectionné le ligament** the blade had cut through the ligament **2** *(diviser)* to section, to divide *or* to split (into sections)
► **se sectionner** **VPR** *(être coupé)* to be severed

sectionneur [sɛksjɔnœr] **NM** section switch

sectoriel, -elle [sɛktɔrjɛl] **ADJ** sector-based; **revendications sectorielles** sector-based demands; **l'application sectorielle d'une mesure** the application of a measure to a certain sector (only)

sectorisation [sɛktɔrizasjɔ̃] **NF** *(gén)* sectorization, division into sectors; *(des services de santé)* = division into areas of responsibility for health and social services

sectoriser [3] [sɛktɔrize] **VT** *(gén)* to sector, to divide into areas *or* sectors; *(services de santé)* to divide into areas of health and social services responsibility

Sécu [seky] **NF** *Fam Admin (abrév* **Sécurité so-**

ciale*) (système) Br* ≃ Social Security■ , *Am* ≃ welfare■ ; *(organisme de remboursement) Br* ≃ DWP■ , *Am* ≃ Social Security■

séculaire [sekylɛr] **ADJ 1** *(vieux → tradition)* age-old; *(→ arbre)* ancient **2** *(de cent ans)* a hundred years old; **un arbre plusieurs fois s.** a tree several hundred years old **3** *(qui a lieu tous les cent ans)* centennial; **année s.** last year of the century **4** *Astron* secular

sécularisation [sekylarizasjɔ̃] **NF** secularization, secularizing *(UNCOUNT)*

séculariser [3] [sekylarize] **VT** to secularize

sécularité [sekylarite] **NF** secularity

séculier, -ère [sekylje, -ɛr] **ADJ** secular
   NM secular

secundo [səgɔ̃do] **ADV** in the second place, second, secondly

sécurisant, -e [sekyrizɑ̃, -ɑ̃t] **ADJ 1** *(qui rassure)* reassuring **2** *Psy* security *(avant n)*

sécurisation [sekyrizasjɔ̃] **NF la s. des citoyens est du ressort de la police** it is the responsibility of the police to make the public feel safe

sécuriser [3] [sekyrize] **VT 1** *(rassurer)* **s. qn** to make sb feel secure *or* safe, to reassure sb, to give sb a feeling of security **2** *(stabiliser)* to (make) secure; **des mesures visant à s. l'emploi** employment-conserving measures **3** *Fin* **s. un financement** to guarantee a loan; **s. un paiement** *(sur l'Internet)* to guarantee *or* to ensure the security of a transaction

Securit® [sekyrit] **NM (verre)** S. Triplex® glass

sécuritaire [sekyritɛr] **ADJ programme s.** security-conscious programme; **mesures sécuritaires** drastic security measures; **idéologie s.** law-and-order ideology

sécurité [sekyrite] **NF 1** *(protection d'une personne → physique)* safety, security; *(→ matérielle, affective etc)* security; **assurer la s. de qn** to ensure the safety of sb; **veiller à la s. de qn** to make sure sb is safe; **l'installation offre une s. totale** the plant is completely safe; **un bon contrat d'assurance, c'est une s.** a good insurance policy makes you feel safe *or* puts your mind at rest *or* gives you peace of mind; **mon travail m'apporte une s. matérielle** my job gives me financial security; **s. active** active security; **s. affective** emotional security; **s. civile** civil defence; *Ordinat* **s. des données** data security; **la s. de l'emploi** job security; **s. juridique** legal security; **s. nationale/internationale** national/international security; **s. passive** passive security; **s. préventive** preventive security; **s. publique** public safety; **s. routière** road safety

2 *(surveillance → de bâtiments, d'installations)* security

3 *(dispositif → gén)* safety catch; *(→ d'un tank, d'un navire)* safety catch *or* mechanism; **une porte munie d'une s. enfants** a door with a childproof lock
❑ **de sécurité** **ADJ** *(dispositif, mesure, règles)* safety *(avant n)*; *(services)* security *(avant n)*
❑ **en sécurité** **ADJ** safe; **être/se sentir en s.** to be/ to feel safe in a safe place; **mettre qch en s. dans un coffre** to keep sth in a safe
❑ **en toute sécurité** **ADV** in complete safety
❑ **Sécurité sociale** **NF** *Admin (système)* = French social security system providing public health benefits, pensions, maternity leave etc, *Br* ≃ Social Security, *Am* ≃ welfare; *(organisme de remboursement) Br* ≃ DWP, *Am* ≃ Social Security

sedan [sədɑ̃] **NM** *Tex* sedan cloth

sédatif, -ive [sedatif, -iv] **ADJ** sedative
   NM sedative

sédation [sedasjɔ̃] **NF** sedation, sedating *(UN-*

COUNT)

sédative [sedativ] *voir* **sédatif**

sédentaire [sedɑ̃tɛr] **ADJ 1** *(travail, habitude)* sedentary; *(employé)* desk-bound **2** *(population)* settled, non-nomad, sedentary; *(oiseau)* non-migrant; *(troupes)* garrison(ed)
   NMF *(personne)* sedentary person

sédentairement [sedɑ̃tɛrmɑ̃] **ADV vivre s.** to live a sedentary life

sédentarisation [sedɑ̃tarizasjɔ̃] **NF la s. d'une population** a people's adoption of a sedentary lifestyle

sédentariser [3] [sedɑ̃tarize] **VT** *(tribu)* to make sedentary, to settle
► **se sédentariser** **VPR** to become sedentary, to settle

sédentarité [sedɑ̃tarite] **NF** sedentary lifestyle

sédiment [sedimɑ̃] **NM 1** *Géol* sediment, deposit **2** *Méd & (en œnologie)* sediment

sédimentaire [sedimɑ̃tɛr] **ADJ** sedimentary

sédimentation [sedimɑ̃tasjɔ̃] **NF** sedimentation

sédimenter [3] [sedimɑ̃te] **VI** to form a deposit
► **se sédimenter** **VPR** to form a deposit

sédimentologie [sedimɑ̃tɔlɔʒi] **NF** sedimentology

sédimentologue [sedimɑ̃tɔlɔg] **NMF** sedimentologist

séditieux, -euse [sedisjø, -øz] **ADJ 1** *(propos, écrit)* seditious **2** *(troupe, armée)* insurrectionary, insurgent
   NM,F insurgent, rebel

sédition [sedisjɔ̃] **NF** rebellion, revolt, sedition

séducteur, -trice [sedyktœr, -tris] **ADJ** *(personne, sourire etc)* seductive
   NM,F seducer, *f* seductress; **c'est un grand s.** he's a real charmer; **c'est une grande séductrice** she's a real seductress

séduction [sedyksjɔ̃] **NF 1** *(charme → d'une personne)* charm; *(→ d'une musique, d'un tableau)* appeal, captivating power; *Mktg (→ d'un produit)* appeal; **elle ne manque pas de s.** she's very seductive; *Mktg* **s. du client** customer appeal

2 *(action)* seduction; **pouvoir de s.** powers of seduction; **exercer une s. mystérieuse/irrésistible sur qn** to exercise a mysterious/an irresistible attraction over sb

3 *Jur* **s. de mineur** corruption of a minor; **s. dolosive** = obtaining sexual favours by deceit

4 *(d'une chose)* attraction, attractiveness; **le pouvoir de s. de l'argent** the seductive power of money

séductrice [sedyktris] *voir* **séducteur**

séduire [98] [seduir] **VT 1** *(charmer → sujet: personne)* to attract, to charm; *(→ sujet: beauté, gentillesse, sourire)* to win over; *(→ sujet: livre, tableau)* to appeal to; **la ferme m'a tout de suite séduit** I immediately fell in love with the farmhouse

2 *(tenter → sujet: idée, projet, style de vie)* to appeal to, to be tempting to; **sa proposition ne me séduit pas beaucoup** his/her proposal doesn't tempt me *or* appeal to me very much; **j'ai été séduite du premier coup** it took my fancy *or* attracted me *or* appealed to me right away

3 *(tromper → sujet: politicien, promesses, publicité)* to lure, to seduce; **j'ai envie de me laisser s.** I'm very *or* sorely tempted; **ne vous laissez pas s. par leurs beaux discours!** don't let yourselves be led astray by their fine words!

4 *(attirer → client)* to attract

5 *(sexuellement)* to seduce
   USAGE ABSOLU *(charmer)* **il aime s.** he's a real charmer; **le secret pour s., c'est de ne pas trop en faire** the secret of seduction is not to overdo it

séduisant, -e [seduizɑ̃, -ɑ̃t] **ADJ 1** *(charmant → personne)* attractive; *(→ beauté)* seductive, enticing; *(→ sourire, parfum, mode etc)* appealing, seductive; **de manière séduisante** seductively **2** *(alléchant → offre, idée, projet)* attractive, appealing; **la proposition était séduisante** the offer was appealing

séduisit *etc voir* **séduire**

séduit, -e [sedɥi, -it] **PP** *voir* **séduire**

sedum [sedɔm] **NM** *Bot* sedum

seersucker [sirsœkœr] **NM** *Tex* seersucker

séfarade [sefarad] **ADJ** Sephardic
   NMF Sephardi; **les séfarades** the Sephardim

sefardi [sefardi] *(pl* **sefardim** [-dim]*)* **ADJ** Sephar-

dic
  NMF Sephardi; **les sefardim** the Sephardim
ségala [segala] **NM** *(dans le Massif central)* land planted *or* sown with rye
séghia [segja] = **seguia**
segment [sεgmᾶ] **NM 1** *Anat & Math* segment
  2 *Tech* ring; **s. de piston** piston ring; **s. racleur** scraper ring; *Aut* **s. de frein** (segmental) brake shoe; *Aut* **s. primaire** primary *or* leading shoe; *Aut* **s. secondaire** secondary shoe, trailing shoe
  3 *Mktg* segment; **s. démographique** demographic segment; **s. de marché** market segment
  4 *Ordinat* segment; **s. de programme** program segment
segmentaire [sεgmᾶtεr] **ADJ** segmental
segmentation [sεgmᾶtasjɔ̃] **NF 1** *Biol & Physiol* segmentation
  2 *Ordinat* segmentation
  3 *Mktg* segmentation; **s. par avantages recherchés** benefit segmentation; **s. comportementale** behaviour segmentation; **s. démographique** demographic segmentation; **s. fondée sur les besoins** needs-based segmentation; **s. du marché** market segmentation; **s. psychographique** psychographic segmentation; **s. stratégique** strategic segmentation; **s. par styles de vie** lifestyle segmentation
segmenter [3] [sεgmᾶte] **VT** *(diviser)* to segment
  ▸ **se segmenter VPR** to segment, to break into segments
Ségovie [segɔvi] **NF** Segovia
ségrairie [segrεri] **NF 1** *(possession)* joint ownership of woodland **2** *(bois)* woodland which is owned jointly
ségrais [segrε] **NM** isolated woodland *(exploited separately)*
ségrégabilité [segregabilite] **NF** *Constr* tendency to segregation
ségrégatif, -ive [segregatif, -iv] **ADJ** segregative; **lois ségrégatives** laws aimed at maintaining segregation
ségrégation [segregasjɔ̃] **NF 1** *(discrimination)* segregation; **une s. au niveau des salaires** a discriminatory wage policy; **s. raciale/sociale** racial/social segregation **2** *Biol, Métal & Tech* segregation
ségrégationnisme [segregasjɔnism] **NM** racial segregation
ségrégationniste [segregasjɔnist] **ADJ** *(personne)* segregationist; *(politique)* segregationist, segregational, discriminatory
  NMF segregationist
ségrégative [segregativ] *voir* **ségrégatif**
ségrégé, -e [segreʒe] **ADJ** *Métal* segregated
séguedille [segədij], **seguidilla** [segidija] **NF** seguidilla
seguia [segja] **NF** open channel *(for bringing water to Saharan oases)*
sehtar [setar] = **setar**
seiche [sεʃ] **NF 1** *Zool (mollusque)* cuttlefish **2** *Géog* seiche
séide [seid] **NM** *Littéraire (partisan)* zealot, fanatically dedicated henchman
seigle [sεgl] **NM** rye
seigneur [sεɲœr] **NM 1** *Hist* feudal lord *or* overlord
  2 *(maître)* lord; **le s. du château** the lord of the manor; *aussi Hum* **le s. de ces lieux** the lord of the manor; *Hum* **mon s. et maître** my lord and master; **agir en grand s.** to play the fine gentleman; **vivre en grand s.** to live like a lord; **comme un s., en grand s.** *(avec luxe)* like a lord; *(avec noblesse)* nobly; **être grand s., faire le grand s.** to spend money like water *or* as if there were no tomorrow; *Prov* **à tout s. tout honneur** give honour where honour is due
  3 *(magnat)* tycoon, baron; **les seigneurs de l'industrie** captains of industry; **les seigneurs de la guerre** the war lords
  4 *Rel* **le S.** the Lord; **Notre-S. Jésus-Christ** Our Lord Jesus Christ; *Littéraire* **S. (Dieu)!** Good Lord!; **le jour du S.** the Lord's Day

≡≡≡📖🎬≡≡≡
  '**Le Seigneur des anneaux**' *Tolkien, Jackson* 'The Lord of the Rings'

seigneuriage [sεɲœrjaʒ] **NM** seignorage, seigniorage
seigneurial, -e, -aux, -ales [sεɲœrjal, -o] **ADJ 1** *Hist* seigniorial, seigneurial **2** *Littéraire (digne d'un seigneur)* stately, lordly
seigneurie [sεɲœri] **NF 1** *Hist (propriété)* seigneury, lord's domain *or* estate; *(pouvoir, droits)* seigneury **2** *(titre)* **Votre S.** Your Lordship; *Hum* **Sa S.** his lordship **3** *Belg (maison de retraite)* retirement home, old people's home
seille [sεj] **NF** *Vieilli ou Suisse & (dans l'est de la France)* large (wooden) bucket *(with two handles)*
seillon [sεjɔ̃] **NM** *Vieilli ou Suisse & (dans l'est de la France)* **1** *(baquet)* small wooden tub **2** *(pour le vin)* = tub for catching drips of wine under the spigot
seime [sεm] **NF** *Vét* cracked hoof
sein [sε̃] **NM 1** *(partie du corps)* breast; **elle se promène les seins nus** she walks about topless; **danseuse aux seins nus** topless dancer; **le s.** *(pour allaiter)* the breast; **donner le s. à** to breast-feed; **être nourri au s.** to be breast-fed; **prendre le s.** to take the breast; *Méd* **cancer du s.** breast cancer; *Littéraire* **il présenta son s. à l'épée** he bared his breast to the sword
  2 *Littéraire (ventre)* womb; **porter un enfant dans son s.** to carry a child in one's womb
  3 *Littéraire (buste)* bosom; **serrer qn/qch contre son s.** to press sb/sth against one's bosom; **s'épancher dans le s. d'une amie** *(auprès de)* to open one's heart to a friend; **le s. de l'Église** the bosom of the Church
  4 *Littéraire (centre)* **le s. de la terre** the bowels of the earth; **dans le s. de** *(au centre de)* in or at the heart of, in the bosom of
  ◻ **au sein de PRÉP** within; **au s. du parti** within the party; **au s. de la famille** in the bosom *or* midst of the family

Couvrez ce sein que je ne saurais voir
In Molière's *Tartuffe* (1669) Act III scene 2, Tartuffe says to Dorine, Mariane's maid, **Couvrez ce sein que je ne saurais voir. Par de pareils objets les âmes sont blessées, Et cela fait venir de coupables pensées** ("Cover that breast I cannot look upon. Such objects wound the soul and foster guilty thoughts"). The first sentence here is used allusively today, jokingly addressed to someone who is accidentally revealing rather more flesh than intended.

Seine [sεn] **NF la S.** the (River) Seine
seine [sεn] **NF** *Pêche* seine
Seine-et-Marne [sεnemarn] **NF la S.** Seine-et-Marne
Seine-Maritime [sεnmaritim] **NF la S.** Seine-Maritime
Seine-Saint-Denis [sεnsε̃dni] **NF la S.** Seine-Saint-Denis
seing [sε̃] **NM** *(signature)* signature
  ◻ **sous seing privé ADJ** **acte sous s. privé** private agreement, simple contract
séismal, -e, -aux, -ales [seismal, -o] **ADJ** seismic
séisme [seism] **NM 1** *Géol* earthquake, *Spéc* seism; **le s. a atteint sept degrés sur l'échelle de Richter** the earthquake reached seven on the Richter scale **2** *Fig Littéraire (bouleversement)* upheaval
séismicité [seismisite] **NF** seismicity
séismique [seismik] **ADJ** seismic
séismographe [seismɔgraf] **NM** seismograph
séismologie [seismɔlɔʒi] **NF** seismology
SEITA, Seita [seita] **NF** *(abrév* **Société nationale d'exploitation industrielle des tabacs et allumettes)** = French government tobacco and matches monopoly
seize [sεz] **ADJ 1** *(gén)* sixteen **2** *(dans des séries)* sixteenth; **page/numéro s.** page/number sixteen
  PRON sixteen
  NM INV 1 *(gén)* sixteen **2** *(numéro d'ordre)* number sixteen **3** *(chiffre écrit)* sixteen; *voir aussi* **cinq**
seizième [sεzjεm] **ADJ** sixteenth
  NMF 1 *(personne)* sixteenth
  2 *(objet)* sixteenth (one)
  NM 1 *(partie)* sixteenth
  2 *(étage) Br* sixteenth floor, *Am* seventeenth floor
  3 *(arrondissement de Paris)* sixteenth (arrondissement)
  NF *Mus* sixteenth; *voir aussi* **cinquième**
  ◻ **seizièmes NMPL** *Sport* **les seizièmes de finale** the first round *(of a four-round knockout competition)*, the second round *(of a five-round knockout competition)*

SEIZIÈME
This term often refers to the upper-class social background, lifestyle, way of dressing etc associated with the sixteenth arrondissement in Paris: "elle est très seizième".

seizièmement [sεzjεmmᾶ] **ADV** in sixteenth place
séjour [seʒur] **NM 1** *(durée)* stay, sojourn; *Littéraire* delay; **s. 2 semaines en Martinique: 950 euros tout compris** 14 nights in Martinique: all-inclusive price 950 euros; **il a fait un s. de deux mois à la mer** he spent two months at the seaside; **il fait un s. linguistique aux États-Unis** he is spending some time in the United States learning the language; **je te souhaite un bon s. à Venise** I hope you have a nice time *or* I hope you enjoy your stay in Venice; **il a fait plusieurs séjours en hôpital psychiatrique** he's been in a psychiatric hospital several times; *Fam Fig* **il a fait un s. à l'ombre** he's been inside, he's done time
  2 *(pièce)* **(salle de) s.** living *or* sitting room, *Br* lounge
  3 *Littéraire (habitation)* abode, dwelling place; **l'Olympe, s. des dieux** Mount Olympus, home of the gods
séjourner [3] [seʒurne] **VI 1** *(habiter)* to stay, to sojourn; **s. à l'hôtel/chez un ami** to stay at a hotel/with a friend **2** *(eau, brouillard)* to lie; **les neiges séjournent longtemps en altitude** the snow stays for a long time at high altitude
SEL [εsəεl] **NF** *(abrév* **société d'exercice libérale)** = company practising a liberal profession
sel [sεl] **NM 1** *Culin* salt; **mettre du s. dans une sauce** to add salt to a sauce; **vous devriez supprimer le s.** you should cut out salt altogether; **gros s.** coarse salt; **s. de céleri** celery salt; **s. de cuisine** kitchen salt; **s. de table, s. fin** table salt; **s. marin** *ou* **de mer** sea salt
  2 *Chim* salt; **s. acide/basique** acid/basic salt; **s. double** double salt
  3 *Géol* salt; **s. gemme** rock salt; *Bible & Littéraire* **le s. de la terre** the salt of the earth
  4 *Pharm* salt; **s. d'Epsom** *ou* **d'Angleterre** Epsom salts; **s. de Vichy** sodium bicarbonate
  5 *(piquant)* wit (UNCOUNT); *Littéraire* **s. attique** Attic salt, wit; **une remarque pleine de s.** a witty remark; **la situation ne manque pas de s.!** the situation is not without a certain piquancy!
  ◻ **sels NMPL** *Pharm* (smelling) salts; **respirer des sels** to smell salts; **sels de bain** bath salts
  ◻ **sans sel ADJ** *(régime, biscotte)* salt-free; *(beurre)* unsalted
sélacien [selasjε̃] *Ich* **NM** selachian
  ◻ **sélaciens NMPL** Selachii
sélaginelle [selaʒinεl] **NF** *Bot* selaginella
sélect, -e [selεkt] **ADJ** *Fam* select, high-class
sélecter [3] [selεkte] **VT** *Tech* to select
sélecteur [selεktœr] **NM 1** *Rad & Tél* selector; **s. de programmes** programme selector **2** *Tech* gear shift; *(d'une moto)* (foot) gearshift control **3** *Ordinat* chooser
sélectif, -ive [selεktif, -iv] **ADJ 1** *(mémoire, herbicide, poste de radio)* selective **2** *Ordinat* **en mode s.** in veto mode
sélection [selεksjɔ̃] **NF 1** *(fait de choisir)* selection; **opérer une s. parmi 200 candidats** to make a selection *or* to choose from 200 candidates; **épreuve de s.** selection trial; *Cin* **s. cannoise** = films selected for nomination for the Palme d'or prize at the Cannes film festival; *Univ* **s. à l'entrée** selective *Br* entry *or* *Am* admission; *Mktg* **s. au hasard** random selection; *Cin* **s. officielle** = films selected for nomination for the Palme d'or prize at the Cannes film festival; **s. professionnelle** professional recruitment; *Presse* **S. (du Reader's Digest)** = French edition of the Reader's Digest
  2 *(échantillon)* selection, choice; **une s. des meilleurs fromages de la région** a choice or

selection of local cheeses
3 *Sport (choix)* selection; *(équipe)* team, squad; **match de s.** trial game; **Sandy Campbell a 51 sélections en équipe nationale** Sandy Campbell has been capped 51 times *or* has 51 caps
4 *Biol* **s. naturelle** natural selection; **s. artificielle** artificial selection
5 *Rad (signal)* separation
6 *Bourse* **s. d'actions** sharepicking; **s. de titres** stockpicking; **s. de portefeuille** portfolio selection

sélectionné, -e [selɛksjɔne] ADJ *(choisi)* selected; **s. pour les jeux Olympiques** selected for the Olympics; **s. en équipe nationale** capped; **des vins sélectionnés** selected *or* choice wines
NM,F **1** *(candidat)* selected candidate *or* contestant **2** *Sport* selected player

sélectionner [3] [selɛksjɔne] VT **1** *(gén)* to select **2** *Ordinat (texte)* to block, to select; **s. qch par défaut** to default to sth
  USAGE ABSOLU **ils sélectionnent à l'entrée** they have a selection process for admission

sélectionneur, -euse [selɛksjɔnœr, -øz] NM,F *Sport* selector

sélective [selɛktiv] *voir* **sélectif**

sélectivement [selɛktivmɑ̃] ADV selectively

sélectivité [selɛktivite] NF *Élec, Opt & Rad* selectivity

Selené [selene] NPR *Myth* Selene

sélène [selɛn] ADJ selenic

sélénhydrique [selenidrik] ADJ M **acide s.** hydroselenic acid, hydrogen selenide

séléniate [selenjat] NM selenate

sélénieux [selenjø] ADJ M selenious

sélénique [selenik] ADJ M selenic

sélénite¹ [selenit] ADJ of the moon
NMF *(habitant de la Lune)* moon-dweller

sélénite² [selenit] NM *Chim* selenite

séléniteux, -euse [selenitø, -øz] ADJ selenitic

sélénium [selenjɔm] NM *Chim* selenium

séléniure [selenjyr] NM *Chim* selenide

sélénographie [selenɔgrafi] NF selenography

sélénographique [selenɔgrafik] ADJ selenographic

sélénologie [selenɔlɔʒi] NF selenology

self [sɛlf] NF *Élec* self inductance
NM *Psy* self
NM INV *Fam (restaurant)* self-service (restaurant)⸱, cafeteria⸱

self-control [sɛlfkɔ̃trol] *(pl* **self-controls***)* NM self-control, self-command

self-défense [sɛlfdefɑ̃s] NF self-defence

self-government [sɛlfgɔvɛrnmɑ̃t] *(pl* **self-governments***)* NM self-government

self-inductance [sɛlfɛ̃dyktɑ̃s] *(pl* **self-inductances***)* NF self-inductance

self-induction [sɛlfɛ̃dyksjɔ̃] *(pl* **self-inductions***)* NF self-induction

self-made-man [sɛlfmɛdman] *(pl* **self-made-men** [-mɛn]*)* NM self-made man

self-média [sɛlfmedja] NM self-media

self-service [sɛlfsɛrvis] *(pl* **self-services***)* NM **1** *(restaurant)* self-service (restaurant), cafeteria **2** *(service)* self-service; **beaucoup de pompes à essence sont en s.** a lot of *Br* petrol *or* *Am* gas pumps are self-service

selle [sɛl] NF **1** *(de cheval)* saddle; **monter sans s.** to ride bareback; **monter en s.** to mount, to get into the saddle; **aider qn à monter en s.** to help sb into the saddle; *aussi Fig* **être bien en s.** to be firmly in the saddle; *aussi Fig* **mettre qn en s.** to give sb a leg up; *Fig* **remettre qn en s.** to put sb back on the rails; **se mettre en s.** to mount, to get into the saddle; *Fig* to get down to the job; *aussi Fig* **se remettre en s.** to get back in *or* into the saddle
2 *(de bicyclette)* saddle
3 *Culin* saddle; **s. de mouton/de chevreuil** saddle of mutton/of venison
4 *(escabeau de sculpteur)* turntable
5 *Anat* **s. turcique** sella turcica
6 *Méd* **aller à la s.** to have a bowel movement; **allez-vous à la s. régulièrement?** are you regular?
7 *Rail* bearing *or* sole plate
8 *Zool (d'un lombric)* saddle
❑ **selles** NFPL *(excréments)* faeces, stools

seller [4] [sele] VT to saddle (up)

sellerie [sɛlri] NF **1** *(équipement)* saddlery; *(pour voitures)* upholstery **2** *(lieu)* saddle room, tack-room **3** *(commerce)* saddlery trade

sellerie-bourrellerie [sɛlriburɛlri] *(pl* **selleries-bourrelleries***)* NF manufacture and repair of saddlery

sellerie-garnissage [sɛlrigarnisaʒ] *(pl* **selleries-garnissages***)* NF *Aut* upholstery and trim

sellerie-maroquinerie [sɛlrimarɔkinri] *(pl* **selleries-maroquineries***)* NF **1** *(articles)* (fine) leather goods **2** *(magasin)* leather-goods *Br* shop *or Am* store

sellette [sɛlɛt] NF **1** *Hist (siège)* (high) stand *or* table; *Fig* **mettre qn sur la s.** to put sb in the hot seat; *Fig* **être sur la s.** *(critiqué)* to be in the hot seat, to come under fire; *(examiné)* to be undergoing reappraisal **2** *Constr* slung cradle **3** *(pour sculpteur)* turntable **4** *(de cheval de trait)* saddle **5** *Aut* fifth wheel

sellier [selje] NM *(fabricant, marchand)* saddler; **façon s.** hand-stitched

sellier-maroquinier [seljemarɔkinje] *(pl* **selliers-maroquiniers***)* NM **1** *(fabricant)* fine leather goods manufacturer **2** *(commerçant)* dealer in fine leather goods

selon [səlɔ̃] PRÉP **1** *(conformément à)* in accordance with; **agir s. les vœux de qn** to act in accordance with sb's wishes; **agir s. les règles** to act *or* to go by the rules; **s. toute apparence** by *or* from *or* to all appearances; **s. toute vraisemblance** in all probability
2 *(en fonction de)* according to; **dépenser s. ses moyens** to spend according to one's means; **à chacun s. ses besoins** to each according to his/her needs; **s. le cas** as the case may be; **s. les circonstances/les cas** depending on the circumstances/each individual case; **ils varient s. les saisons** they vary from season to season; *Fam* **on se reverra? – c'est s.!** shall we see each other again? – it all depends!; **elle y allait à pied ou en voiture, c'était s.** she went on foot or used the car, depending
3 *(d'après)* according to; **s. les experts** according to the experts; **s. moi/vous** in my/your opinion, to my/your mind; **l'Évangile s. saint Matthieu** the Gospel according to Saint Matthew; **s. vos propres termes** in your own words; **s. l'expression consacrée** as the hallowed expression has it
❑ **selon que** CONJ **s. qu'on est étudiant ou non** depending on whether one is a student or not; **s. qu'il fera beau ou qu'il pleuvra** depending on whether it's fine or rainy

Seltz [sɛls] NPR **eau de S.** *Br* soda water, *Am* club soda

selva [sɛlva], **selve** [sɛlv] NF *Géog* selva

SEM [sɛm] NF *Écon (abrév* **société d'économie mixte***)* = company financed by state and private capital

Sem [sɛm] NPR *Bible* Shem

S.Em. *(abrév écrite* **Son Éminence***)* HE

semailles [səmaj] NFPL **1** *(action)* sowing **2** *(graines)* seeds **3** *(période)* sowing season; **les s. d'automne** autumn sowing

semaine [səmɛn] NF **1** *(sept jours)* week; **toutes les semaines** *(nettoyer, recevoir)* every *or* each week; *(publier, payer)* weekly, on a weekly basis; **deux visites par s.** two visits a week *or* per week; **dans une s.** in a week's time; **je serai de retour dans une s.** I'll be back in a week *or* in a week's time; **une s. de vacances** a week's holiday; **faire des semaines de 50 heures** to work a 50-hour week; **qui est de s.?** who's on duty this week?; **officier de s.** duty officer for the week; **la s. anglaise** the five-day (working) week; **faire la s. anglaise** to work a five-day week; **la s. de 35 heures** the 35-hour working week; **il te remboursera la s. des quatre jeudis** he'll never pay you back in a month of Sundays
2 *Rel* **la s. sainte** Holy Week; **la s. pascale** Easter week
3 *Com* **la s. du tapis d'Orient** Oriental carpet week; **la promotion de la s.** this week's special offer; **la s. de la photo** photography week; **s. commerciale** week-long promotion *or* sale; *Hum* **c'est sa s. de bonté** he's/she's been overcome by a fit of generosity
4 *(salaire)* week's pay *or* wages; **il est allé demander sa s. à son père** *(argent de poche)*

he went to ask his father for his pocket money; **je lui donne dix euros pour sa s.** I give him/her ten euros a week pocket money
5 *(bracelet)* seven-band bangle; *(bague)* seven-band ring
❑ **à la petite semaine** *Fam* ADJ *(politique)* short-sighted, day-to-day ADV **prêter à la petite s.** to make short-term loans *(with high interest)*; **vivre à la petite s.** to live from day to day *or* from hand to mouth
❑ **à la semaine** ADV *(payer)* weekly, on a weekly basis, by the week
❑ **en semaine** ADV during the week, on weekdays, on a weekday

semainier, -ère [səmenje, -ɛr] NM,F *(personne)* worker on duty for the week
NM **1** *(calendrier)* page-a-week diary **2** *(meuble)* semainier *(seven-drawer chest)* **3** *Ind* weekly time sheet **4** *(bracelet)* seven-band bangle

sémantème [semɑ̃tɛm] NM *Ling* semanteme

sémanticien, -enne [semɑ̃tisjɛ̃, -ɛn] NM,F semanticist

sémantique [semɑ̃tik] ADJ semantic
NF semantics *(singulier)*; **s. générative** generative semantics

sémantiquement [semɑ̃tikmɑ̃] ADV semantically

sémaphore [semafɔr] NM **1** *Rail* semaphore signal **2** *Naut (poste)* signal station

sémasiologie [semazjɔlɔʒi] NF *Ling* semasiology

sématique [sematik] ADJ *Biol* sematic

semblable [sɑ̃blabl] ADJ **1** *(comparable)* similar; **nous avons un cas s.** we have a similar case; **ils sont semblables** they are similar *or* alike; **s. à** similar to, like
2 *(tel)* **je n'ai rien dit de s.** I said nothing of the sort *or* no such thing; **je n'avais jamais rien vu de s.** I had never seen anything like it *or* the like of it; **de semblables projets/propos** such plans/remarks, plans/remarks like that
3 *Géom & Math* similar
NMF *(avec possessif)* **1** *(être humain)* **vous et vos semblables** you and your kind; **partager le sort de ses semblables** to share the lot of one's fellow man; **il n'a pas son s. dans l'art occidental** there's no one like him in western art
2 *(animal)* related species

semblablement [sɑ̃blabləmɑ̃] ADV similarly, likewise

semblant [sɑ̃blɑ̃] NM **1** *(apparence)* **un s. d'intérêt/d'affection** a semblance of interest/affection; **offrir un s. de résistance** to put on a show of *or* to put up a token resistance; **j'ai un s. de bronzage** I have a semblance of a tan *or* an apology for a tan
2 **faire s.** *(feindre)* to pretend; **il ne dort pas, il fait s.** he's not asleep, he's just pretending; **ne fais pas s. d'avoir oublié** don't pretend to have forgotten *or* (that) you've forgotten; **faire s. d'être malade** to sham illness, to malinger; **ne faire s. de rien** to pretend not to notice

sembler [3] [sɑ̃ble] VI to seem, to appear; **son histoire semble (être) vraie** his/her story seems *or* appears to be true; **elle semble plus âgée que lui** she seems (to be) *or* she looks older than him; **ils semblaient bien s'entendre** they seemed *or* appeared to be getting on well; **tu sembles préoccupé** you look *or* you seem worried; **ça peut s. drôle à certains** this may seem *or* sound funny to some
V IMPERSONNEL **1** **il semble que...** *(on dirait que)* it seems...; **il semble qu'il y a ou ait eu un malentendu** it seems that *or* it looks as if there's been a misunderstanding, there seems to have been a misunderstanding; **il semblait pourtant que tout allait bien** and yet everything seemed to be all right; **il semblerait qu'il ait décidé de démissionner** reports claim *or* it has been reported that he intends to resign
2 *(pour exprimer l'opinion)* **cela ne te semble-t-il pas injuste?** don't you find this unfair?, doesn't this strike you as being unfair?; **c'est bien ce qu'il m'a semblé** I thought as much; **il ne me semblait pas te l'avoir dit** I didn't think I'd told you about it; **il était, me semblait-il, au courant de tout** it seemed *or* it appeared to me that he was aware of everything; **il me semble**

qu'on s'est déjà vus I think we've met before; **je vous l'ai déjà dit, il me semble** ou **me semble-t-il** I'm sure I've already told you that; **faites comme bon vous semble** do as you think fit or best, do as you please; **il le fera si bon lui semble** he'll do it if he wants to; **je sors quand/avec qui bon me semble** I go out whenever/with whoever I please

❑ à ce qu'il semble, semble-t-il ADV seemingly, apparently; **ils sont blessés, semble-t-il** it seems (as though) they're hurt, apparently, they're hurt

sème [sɛm] NM *Ling* seme

séméiologie [semejɔlɔʒi] NF *Méd* semiology, semeiology

séméiologique [semejɔlɔʒik] ADJ *Méd* semiological, semeiological

semelage [səmlaʒ] NM sole section

semelle [səmɛl] NF **1** (d'une chaussure, d'un ski) sole; **bottes à semelles fines/épaisses** thin-soled/thick-soled boots; **chaussures à semelles compensées** platform shoes; **s. intérieure** insole, inner sole
2 *Fam* (viande dure) **c'est de la s., ce steak!** this steak is like (shoe) leather or Br is as tough as old boots
3 *Constr* (de plancher) sill or sole plate; (de poutre) flange; (de toiture) inferior (roof) purlin; (d'une marche) tread; **s. filante** (wall) footing
4 *Mines* (élément) sole (piece); (banc) sole
5 *Rail* **s. de frein** brake shoe (insert); **s. de crosse** crosshead slipper or shoe
6 *Tech* (d'une machine, d'un tour) bedplate
7 (d'un fer à repasser) base, sole
8 *Naut* **s. de dérive** leeboard
9 (locutions) **ne la lâchez** ou **quittez pas d'une s.** don't let her out of your sight; **on n'a pas avancé** ou **bougé d'une s.** we haven't moved an inch, we haven't made any progress whatsoever; **je ne reculerai pas d'une s.** I won't give an inch

sémème [semɛm] NM *Ling* sememe

semence [səmãs] NF **1** (graine) seed; **pomme de terre/blé de s.** seed potato/corn **2** *Littéraire* (germe) **les semences d'une révolte** the seeds of a revolt **3** *Littéraire* (sperme) semen, seed **4** (en joaillerie) **s. de perles** seed pearls; **s. de diamants** diamond sparks **5** (clou) tack; **s. de tapissier** upholstery tack

semencier, -ère [səmãsje, -ɛr] ADJ seed (avant n)
NM (vendeur) seedsman

semen-contra [semɛnkɔ̃tra] NM INV *Pharm* santonica

semer [19] [səme] VT **1** *Agr & Hort* to sow; **s. un champ** to sow a field
2 *Fig* (disperser → fleurs, paillettes) to scatter, to strew; **semé de** scattered or strewn with; **parcours semé d'embûches** course littered with obstacles; **il sème ses affaires partout** he leaves his things everywhere
3 *Fam* (laisser tomber) to drop■; **il a semé tous ses papiers dans l'escalier** he dropped all his papers on the stairs
4 (distancer) to lose, to shake off; **s. le peloton** to leave the pack behind
5 (propager) to bring; **s. le désordre** ou **la pagaille** to wreak havoc; **s. la discorde** to sow the seeds of discord; **s. la terreur/la mort** to bring terror/death; **s. le doute dans l'esprit de qn** to sow or to plant a seed of doubt in sb's mind
USAGE ABSOLU *Agr & Hort* **s. à la volée** to sow broadcast; **s. en ligne** to drill

semestre [səmɛstr] NM **1** (dans l'année civile) half-year, six-month period; **pour le premier s.** for the first half of the year or six months of the year **2** *Univ* half-year, semester **3** (rente) half-yearly pension; (intérêt) half-yearly interest

semestriel, -elle [səmɛstrijɛl] ADJ **1** (dans l'année civile) half-yearly **2** *Univ* semestral

semestriellement [səmɛstrijɛlmã] ADV **1** (dans l'année civile) half-yearly, every six months **2** *Univ* per year or every semester

semeur, -euse [səmœr, -øz] NM,F **1** *Agr* sower **2** *Fig* (propagateur) **s. de trouble** troublemaker; **s. de discorde** sower of discord
❑ Semeuse NF (sur les pièces) = symbol of the

French Republic on stamps and coins

semi- [səmi] PRÉF semi-

semi-aride [səmiarid] (pl **semi-arides**) ADJ semi-arid

semi-automatique [səmiotomatik] (pl **semi-automatiques**) ADJ semi-automatic

semi-auxiliaire [səmioksiljɛr] (pl **semi-auxiliaires**) *Gram* ADJ semi-auxiliary
NM semi-auxiliary verb

semi-chenillé, -e [səmiʃənije] (mpl **semi-chenillés**, fpl **semi-chenillées**) ADJ half-tracked
NM half-track

semi-circulaire [səmisirkylɛr] (pl **semi-circulaires**) ADJ semicircular

semi-coke [səmikɔk] (pl **semi-cokes**) NM semi-coke, Coalite®

semi-conducteur, -trice [səmikɔ̃dyktœr, -tris] (mpl **semi-conducteurs**, fpl **semi-conductrices**) ADJ semiconducting
NM semiconductor

semi-conductivité [səmikɔ̃dyktivite] NF semi-conductivity

semi-conductrice [səmikɔ̃dyktris] voir **semi-conducteur**

semi-conserve [səmikɔ̃sɛrv] (pl **semi-conserves**) NF = foodstuff which has a limited life and must be refrigerated

semi-consonantique [səmikɔ̃sɔnãtik] (pl **semi-consonantiques**) ADJ *Ling* semiconsonantal

semi-consonne [səmikɔ̃sɔn] (pl **semi-consonnes**) NF *Ling* semiconsonant, semivowel

semi-convergente [səmikɔ̃vɛrʒãt] (pl **semi-convergentes**) ADJ F *Math* semi-convergent

semi-déponent, -e [səmidepɔnã, -ãt] (mpl **semi-déponents**, fpl **semi-déponentes**) ADJ *Gram* semideponent

semi-dressant [səmidresã] (pl **semi-dressants**) NM *Mines* flat lying zone

semi-durable [səmidyrabl] (pl **semi-durables**) ADJ semi-perishable

semi-fini, -e [səmifini] (mpl **semi-finis**, fpl **semi-finies**) ADJ semi-finished, semi-manufactured

semi-grossiste [səmigrosist] (pl **semi-grossistes**) NMF = wholesaler who also deals in retail

semi-hebdomadaire [səmiɛbdɔmadɛr] (pl **semi-hebdomadaires**) ADJ half-weekly, bi-weekly

semi-liberté [səmilibɛrte] NF *Jur* temporary release (from prison); **être en s.** to be out on temporary release

semi-liquide [səmilikid] (pl **semi-liquides**) ADJ semifluid

sémillant, -e [semijã, -ãt] ADJ sprightly, spirited

sémillon [semijɔ̃] NM Sémillon (variety of white wine from the Bordeaux region)

semi-logarithmique [səmilɔgaritmik] (pl **semi-logarithmiques**) ADJ *Math* semi-logarithmic

semi-lunaire [səmilynɛr] (pl **semi-lunaires**) ADJ half-moon shaped, semilunar; **os s.** semilunar bone

semi-mensuel, -elle [səmimãsɥɛl] (mpl **semi-mensuels**, fpl **semi-mensuelles**) ADJ bi-monthly, Br fortnightly

semi-métal [səmimetal] (pl **semi-métaux** [-o]) NM *Chim* metalloid

séminaire [seminɛr] NM **1** (réunion) seminar, workshop **2** *Rel* seminary; **grand s.** seminary; **petit s.** Roman Catholic boys' school (staffed by priests)

séminal, -e, -aux, -ales [seminal, -o] ADJ seminal

séminariste [seminarist] NM seminarist, Am seminarian

séminifère [seminifɛr] ADJ seminiferous; **conduits séminifères** seminiferous tubules

Séminoles [seminɔl] NMPL **les S.** the Seminole

semi-nomade [səminomad] (pl **semi-nomades**) ADJ semi-nomadic
NMF semi-nomad

semi-nomadisme [səminomadism] (pl **semi-nomadismes**) NM semi-nomadism

séminome [seminom] NM *Méd* seminoma

semi-occlusif, -ive [semiɔklyzif, -iv] (mpl **semi-occlusifs**, fpl **semi-occlusives**) ADJ **1** *Méd* (pansement) semi-occlusive **2** *Ling* (consonne) semi-occlusive

semi-officiel, -elle [səmiɔfisjɛl] (pl **semi-officiels**, fpl **semi-officielles**) ADJ semi-official

sémiologie [semjɔlɔʒi] NF semiology, semeiology

sémiologique [semjɔlɔʒik] ADJ semiological, semeiological

sémiologue [semjɔlɔg] NMF semiologist

sémioticien, -enne [semjɔtisjɛ̃, -ɛn] NM,F semiotician

sémiotique [semjɔtik] ADJ semiotic
NF semiotics (singulier)

semi-ouvert, -e [səmiuvɛr, -ɛrt] (mpl **semi-ouverts**, fpl **semi-ouvertes**) ADJ *Math* **intervalle s.** half-open interval

semi-ouvré, -e [səmiuvre] (mpl **semi-ouvrés**, fpl **semi-ouvrées**) ADJ semi-manufactured, semi-finished

semi-palmé, -e [səmipalme] (mpl **semi-palmés**, fpl **semi-palmées**) ADJ *Zool* semipalmated, semipalmate

semi-peigné [səmipeɲe] (pl **semi-peignés**) ADJ M half-worsted

semi-perméable [səmipɛrmeabl] (pl **semi-perméables**) ADJ semipermeable

semi-polaire [səmipɔlɛr] (pl **semi-polaires**) ADJ semi-polar

semi-précieux, -euse [səmipresjø, -øz] (mpl **semi-précieux**, fpl **semi-précieuses**) ADJ semi-precious

semi-présidentiel, -elle [səmiprezidãsjɛl] (mpl **semi-présidentiels**, fpl **semi-présidentielles**) ADJ *Pol* semi-presidential

semi-produit [səmiprodɥi] (pl **semi-produits**) NM semi-finished product

semi-professionnel, -elle [səmiprɔfɛsjɔnɛl] (mpl **semi-professionnels**, fpl **semi-professionnelles**) ADJ semi-professional

semi-public, -ique [səmipyblik] (mpl **semi-publics**, fpl **semi-publiques**) ADJ semi-public

sémique [semik] ADJ semic

Sémiramis [semiramis] NPR *Myth* Semiramis

semi-remorque [səmirəmɔrk] (pl **semi-remorques**) NF semi-trailer
NM Br articulated lorry, Am trailer truck

semi-rigide [səmiriʒid] (pl **semi-rigides**) ADJ semi-rigid

semis [səmi] NM **1** (action) sowing; **s. à la volée** broadcast sowing **2** (terrain) seedbed **3** (jeune plante) seedling **4** *Fig* **c'était un tissu à fond blanc avec un s. de petites fleurs bleues** the material had a pattern of small blue flowers on a white background

semi-solide [səmisɔlid] (pl **semi-solides**) ADJ semisolid

semi-submersible [səmisybmɛrsibl] (pl **semi-submersibles**) ADJ semisubmersible

sémite [semit] ADJ Semitic
❑ Sémite NMF Semite; **les Sémites** the Semites

sémitique [semitik] ADJ Semitic

sémitisant, -e [semitizã, -ãt] NM,F Semitist

sémitisme [semitism] NM (études) Semitics (singulier); (phénomène) Semitism

semi-ton [səmitɔ̃] (pl **semi-tons**) NM *Mus* semi-tone

semi-transparence [səmitrãsparãs] NF semi-transparency

semi-transparent, -e [səmitrãsparã, -ãt] (mpl **semi-transparents**, fpl **semi-transparentes**) ADJ semi-transparent

semi-tubulaire [səmitybylɛr] (pl **semi-tubulaires**) ADJ semi-tubular

semi-voyelle [səmivwajɛl] (pl **semi-voyelles**) NF *Ling* semivowel, semiconsonant

semnopithèque [sɛmnopitɛk] NM *Zool* semno-pithecus

semoir [səmwar] NM **1** (panier) seed-bag **2** (machine) sower, seeder

semonce [səmɔ̃s] NF **1** (réprimande) reprimand, rebuke **2** *Naut* (navire) order to stop; *Naut & Fig* **coup de s.** warning shot

semoncer [16] [səmɔ̃se] VT **1** *Littéraire* (réprimander) to reprimand, to rebuke **2** *Naut* (navire) to order to stop

semoule [səmul] NF semolina; **s. de riz** rice flour; **s. de maïs** cornflour; **s. blanche** rice flour; **s. de blé dur** durum wheat flour

semoulerie [səmulri] NF **1** (usine) semolina processing factory **2** (commerce) semolina industry

semoulier, -ère [səmulje, -ɛr] NM,F **1** (fabricant) semolina manufacturer **2** (ouvrier) worker in a semolina factory

semper virens [sɛ̃pɛrvirɛ̃s] *Bot* ADJ INV evergreen

NM INV evergreen honeysuckle

sempervirent, -e [sɛ̃pɛrvirã, -ãt] *ADJ Bot* evergreen

sempervivum [sɛ̃pɛrvivɔm] **NM INV** *Bot* sempervivum, houseleek

sempiternel, -elle [sãpitɛrnɛl] *ADJ* neverending, endless

sempiternellement [sãpitɛrnɛlmã] *ADV* eternally, forever

semple [sãpl] **NM** *Tex* simple

sen [sɛn] **NM** *(monnaie)* sen

sénat [sena] **NM 1** *(assemblée)* senate; **le S.** the (French) Senate **2** *(lieu)* senate (house)

Culture

SÉNAT

The Sénat is the upper house of the French Parliament. Its members are elected for a nine-year mandate by the Deputies of the "Assemblée nationale" and certain other government officals. The President of the Senate may deputize for the President of the Republic in the case of incapacity or death. The powers of the Senate are almost as extensive as those of the "Assemblée nationale", although the latter is empowered to override the decisions of the Senate in cases where the two houses disagree.

'Mr Smith au Sénat' *Capra* 'Mr Smith Goes to Washington'

sénateur [senatœr] **NM** senator

sénatorial, -e, -aux, -ales [senatɔrjal, -o] *ADJ* senatorial, senate *(avant n)*
 □ **sénatoriales NFPL** senatorial elections

sénatus-consulte [senatyskɔ̃sylt] *(pl* **senatus-consultes**) **NM** *Antiq* senatus consult, senatus consultum

senau, -s [sano] **NM** *Hist & Naut* snow *(ship)*

séné [sene] **NM** *Bot & Pharm* senna

sénéchal, -aux [seneʃal, -o] **NM** *Hist* seneschal

sénéchaussée [seneʃose] **NF** *Hist (juridiction)* seneschalsy; *(tribunal)* seneschal's court

séneçon [sɛnsɔ̃] **NM** *Bot* **s. commun** groundsel; **s. cinéraire** ragwort

Sénégal [senegal] **NM** **le S.** Senegal; **vivre au S.** to live in Senegal; **aller au S.** to go to Senegal

sénégalais, -e [senegalɛ, -ɛz] *ADJ* Senegalese
 □ **Sénégalais, -e NM,F** Senegalese; **les S.** the Senegalese

sénégali [senegali] **NM** *Orn* waxbill

senellier [sənelje] **NM** *Can Bot* hawthorn

Sénèque [senɛk] **NPR** Seneca

sénescence [senesãs] **NF** senescence

sénescent, -e [senesã, -ãt] *ADJ* senescent

sénestre [senɛstr] *ADJ* **1** *Zool* sinistral **2** *Hér* sinister

senestrochère [senɛstrɔkɛr] **NM** *Hér* sinister arm *(starting from the dexter side of the shield)*

senestrorsum [senɛstrɔrsɔm] *ADJ INV* sinistrorse, sinistrorsal
 ADV sinistrorsely, sinistrorsally

sénevé [sɛnve] **NM** *Bot* (wild) mustard, charlock; *(graine)* mustard seed

sénile [senil] *ADJ* senile

sénilisme [senilism] **NM** premature senility

sénilité [senilite] **NF** senility

senior [senjɔr] *ADJ* **1** *(relatif aux plus de 50 ans)* mature, *Am* seniors'; **le marché s. est en pleine expansion** the mature *or Am* seniors' market is booming **2** *(confirmé)* senior; **ingénieur s.** senior engineer **3** *Sport* senior
 NMF 1 *(personne de plus de 50 ans)* older person, *Am* senior; **le marché des seniors** the mature market, *Am* the seniors' market **2** *Sport* senior

seniorie, séniorie [senjɔri] = **seigneurie 3**

séniorité [senjɔrite] **NF** seniority

senne [sɛn] **NF** *Pêche* seine

senneur [senœr] **NM** *Pêche* trawler

sénologie [senɔlɔʒi] **NF** *Méd* mastology

sénonais, -e [senɔnɛ, -ɛz] *ADJ* of/from Sens
 NM,F = person from or inhabitant of Sens

señorita [seɲɔrita] **NM** *(cigare)* = French-made cigarillo

---

SENS [sɑ̃s]

> **NM** sense **1, 2, 4** ▪ meaning **4** ▪ direction **5** ▪ line **6**
> **NMPL** senses

voir **sentir**

NM 1 *Physiol* sense; **le s. du toucher** the sense of touch; **sixième s.** sixth sense; **reprendre ses s.** to come to; *Fig* to come to one's senses

2 *(instinct)* sense; **s. moral/pratique** moral/practical sense; **avoir le s. pratique** to be practical; **avoir le s. de la mesure** to have a sense of proportion; **avoir le s. de la nuance** to be subtle; **elle n'a pas le s. de la nuance** she's rather unsubtle; **avoir le s. de l'humour** to have a (good) sense of humour; **avoir le s. de l'orientation** to have a good sense of direction; **avoir le s. des affaires** to have a good head for business; **ne pas avoir le s. des réalités** to have no grasp of reality; **avoir le s. du rythme** to have natural rhythm *or* a natural sense of rhythm; **bon s., s. commun** common sense; **plein de bon s.** very sensible; **faire preuve de bon s.** to be sensible; **manquer de bon s.** to lack common sense; **gros bon s.** horse sense, (sound) common sense; **avec son gros bon s., il avait tout de suite vu que...** he had the good sense to see straight away that...; **ça tombe sous le s.** it's obvious, it stands to reason

3 *(opinion)* **à mon/son s.** according to me/him/her; **à mon s., c'est impossible** as I see it *or* to my mind, it's impossible

4 *(signification → d'un mot, d'une phrase)* meaning, sense; *(→ d'une allégorie, d'un symbole)* meaning; *Ling* **le s.** meaning *(UNCOUNT)*, signification; **quel est le s. de ce mot?** what does this word mean?; **le mot a plusieurs s.** the word has several senses *or* meanings; **ce que tu dis n'a pas de s.** *(c'est inintelligible ou déraisonnable)* what you're saying doesn't make sense; **porteur de s.** meaningful; **lourd** *ou* **chargé de s.** meaningful; **vide de s.** meaningless; **au s. propre/figuré** in the literal/figurative sense; **au s. strict** strictly speaking; **le s. caché des choses** the hidden meaning of things; **chercher/trouver un s. à la vie** to look for/to find a meaning to life

5 *(direction)* direction; **dans tous les s.** in all directions, all over the place; *Fig* **chercher dans tous les s.** to look everywhere; **arrête de t'agiter dans tous les s.!** keep still for a minute!; **en s. inverse** the other way round *or* around; **le train qui venait en s. inverse** the oncoming train; **pose l'équerre dans ce s.-là/dans l'autre s.** lay the set square down this way/the other way round; **scier une planche dans le s. de la largeur/la longueur** to saw a board widthwise/lengthwise; **dans le s. nord-sud/est-ouest** in a southerly/westerly direction; **installer qch dans le bon s.** to fix sth the right way up; **fais demi-tour, on va dans le mauvais s.!** turn round, we're going the wrong way *or* in the wrong direction!; **il n'y a plus de trains dans le s. Paris–Lyon** there are no more trains from Paris to Lyons; **la circulation est bloquée dans le s. Paris–province** traffic leaving Paris is at a standstill; **dans le s. de la marche** facing the front *(of a vehicle)*; **dans le s. contraire de la marche** facing the rear *(of a vehicle)*; **dans le s. du courant** with the current; **dans le s. des aiguilles d'une montre** clockwise; **dans le s. inverse des aiguilles d'une montre** *Br* anticlockwise, *Am* counterclockwise; **dans le s. du bois** with the grain (of the wood); **dans le s. du tissu** along the weave (of the cloth); *Transp* **s. giratoire** *Br* roundabout, *Am* traffic circle; **s. interdit** *(panneau)* no-entry sign; *(rue)* one-way street; **être** *ou* **rouler en s. interdit** to be going the wrong way up/down a one-way street; **(rue à) s. unique** one-way street; *Fig* **à s. unique** *(amour)* unrequited; *(décision)* unilateral, one-sided

6 *Fig (orientation)* line; **nous agirons dans le même s.** we'll move along the same lines, we'll take the same sort of action; **des mesures allant dans le s. d'une plus grande justice** measures directed at greater justice; **nous avons publié une brochure dans ce s.** we have published a brochure along those (same) lines *or* to that effect; **leur politique ne va pas dans le bon s.** their policy's going down the wrong road
 NMPL *(sensualité)* (carnal) senses; **pour le plaisir des s.** for the gratification of the senses
 □ **dans le sens où CONJ** in the sense that, in so far as
 □ **dans un certain sens ADV** in a way, in a sense, as it were
 □ **en ce sens que CONJ** in the sense that, in so far as
 □ **sens dessus dessous ADV** upside down; **la maison était s. dessus dessous** *(en désordre)* the house was all topsy-turvy
 □ **sens devant derrière ADV** back to front, the wrong way round

sensas, sensass [sãsas] *ADJ INV Fam* sensational, terrific, *Br* fab

sensation [sãsasjɔ̃] **NF 1** *(impression)* sensation, feeling; **s. de fraîcheur** feeling of freshness, fresh sensation; **j'avais la s. qu'on reculait** I had the feeling we were going backwards; **privé de s.** numb, insensate; **les amateurs de sensations fortes** people who like thrills
 2 *(impact)* **faire s.** to cause a stir *or* a sensation
 3 *Physiol* sensation
 □ **à sensation ADJ** *(roman, titre)* sensational; **un reportage à s.** a shock *or* a sensation-seeking report

sensationnalisme [sãsasjɔnalism] **NM** sensationalism

sensationnel, -elle [sãsasjɔnɛl] *ADJ* **1** *(spectaculaire → révélation, image)* sensational
 2 *Fam (remarquable)* sensational, terrific, *Br* fab
 NM le s. the sensational; **un journal qui donne dans le s.** a sensationalist newspaper

sensé, -e [sãse] *ADJ* sensible, well-advised, wise; **dire des choses sensées** to talk sense; **ce qu'il a dit n'est pas très s.** what he said doesn't make much sense

sensément [sãsemã] *ADV Littéraire* sensibly, wisely

senseur [sãsœr] **NM** *Tech* sensor

sensibilisable [sãsibilizabl] *ADJ Phot* sensitizable

sensibilisant, -e [sãsibilizã, -ãt] *ADJ* priming
 NM primer

sensibilisateur, -trice [sãsibilizatœr, -tris] *ADJ* **1** *Chim* sensitizing **2** *(campagne)* consciousness-raising
 NM *Phot* sensitizer
 □ **sensibilisatrice NF** *Biol* sensitizer

sensibilisation [sãsibilizasjɔ̃] **NF 1** *(prise de conscience)* awareness; **il y a une grande s. des jeunes aux dangers du tabagisme** young people are alert to *or* are aware of the dangers of smoking; **la s. de l'opinion publique à l'environnement** raising public awareness of the environment; **campagne/techniques de s.** consciousness-raising campaign/techniques
 2 *Méd & Phot* sensitization

sensibilisatrice [sãsibilizatris] *voir* **sensibilisateur**

sensibiliser [3] [sãsibilize] *VT* **1** *(gén)* **s. qn à qch** to make sb conscious *or* aware of sth; **il faudrait essayer de s. l'opinion** we'll have to try and make people aware **2** *Méd & Phot* to sensitize
 ▸**se sensibiliser VPR** **se s. à qch** to become aware of sth

sensibilité [sãsibilite] **NF 1** *(physique)* sensitiveness, sensitivity; **s. à la douleur/au soleil** sensitivity to pain/to the sun
 2 *(intellectuelle)* sensibility; *(émotive)* sensitivity; **avoir une s. littéraire** to have a literary sensibility; **la s. romantique** the Romantic sensibility; **elle est d'une s. maladive** she's painfully *or* excruciatingly sensitive; **tu manques totalement de s.** you're utterly insensitive; *Mktg* **s. compétitive** competitive awareness; *Mktg* **s. aux marques** brand sensitivity; *Mktg* **s. aux prix** price sensitivity
 3 *Écon* **la s. du marché des changes** the sensitivity of the foreign exchange market
 4 *Phot, Physiol & Rad* sensitivity

sensible [sãsibl] *ADJ* **1** *(physiquement, émotivement)* sensitive; **avoir l'ouïe s.** to have sensitive hearing; **s. à** sensitive to; **trop s.** oversensitive;

être s. à la chaleur to be sensitive to *or* to feel the heat; **être s. aux souffrances d'autrui** to be sensitive to other people's sufferings; **cet enfant est très s. à la musique** this child has a great feeling for music; **sera-t-il s. à cette preuve d'amour?** will he be touched by this proof of love?; **s. à la beauté de qn** susceptible to sb's beauty; **nous avons été très sensibles à son geste** we really appreciated what he/she did; **c'est une nature s.** he's/she's the sensitive kind, he's/she's easily affected by things; **personnes sensibles s'abstenir** not recommended for people of a nervous disposition; *Mktg* **s. aux marques** brand-sensitive; *Mktg* **s. aux prix** price-sensitive

2 *(délicat → peau, gencive)* sensitive; *(→ endroit douloureux)* tender; **s. au toucher** tender *or* painful to the touch; **être s. du dos/des oreilles** to be prone to backaches/to earache

3 *(qui réagit → balance, microphone)* sensitive, responsive; *(→ direction de voiture)* responsive

4 *(phénomène → perceptible)* perceptible; *(→ notable)* noticeable, marked, *Sout* sensible; **s. à l'ouïe** perceptible to the ear; **la crise est le plus s. dans le Nord** the crisis is most acutely felt in the North; **hausse/baisse s.** marked rise/fall; **il n'y a pas eu de progrès s.** there's been no appreciable *or* noticeable progress; **d'une manière s.** noticeably

5 *Phil* sensory; **un être s.** a sentient being; **le monde s.** the world as perceived by the senses

6 *Mus (note)* leading

7 *Phot* sensitive; **papier s. à la lumière** light-sensitive paper

NMF **c'est un grand s.** he's very sensitive

NF *Mus* leading note, subtonic

sensiblement [sɑ̃sibləmɑ̃] ADV **1** *(beaucoup)* appreciably, noticeably, markedly; **il fait s. plus chaud dans ton bureau** it's distinctly warmer in your office **2** *(à peu près)* about, approximately, more or less, roughly

sensiblerie [sɑ̃sibləri] NF oversensitiveness, squeamishness

sensille [sɑ̃sil] NF *Entom* sensillum

sensitif, -ive [sɑ̃sitif, -iv] ADJ **1** *Anat* sensory **2** *(hypersensible)* oversensitive

NM,F *(hypersensible)* oversensitive subject; **c'est un s.** he's oversensitive

▫ **sensitive** NF *Bot* sensitive plant

sensitomètre [sɑ̃sitɔmɛtr] NM *Phot* sensitometer

sensitométrie [sɑ̃sitɔmetri] NF *Phot* sensitometry

sensoriel, -elle [sɑ̃sɔrjɛl] ADJ *(organe, appareil)* sense *(avant n)*; *(nerf, cortex)* sensory

sensorimétrique [sɑ̃sɔrimetrik] ADJ sensorimetric

sensorimoteur, -trice [sɑ̃sɔrimɔtœr, -tris] ADJ sensorimotor, sensomotor

sensualisme [sɑ̃sɥalism] NM *Phil* sensualism

sensualiste [sɑ̃sɥalist] *Phil* ADJ sensual

NMF sensualist

sensualité [sɑ̃sɥalite] NF sensuality

sensuel, -elle [sɑ̃sɥɛl] ADJ **1** *(plaisir, personne)* sensual, sybaritic **2** *(lèvres, voix)* sensuous; *(musique)* sensual

NM,F sensualist, sybarite

sentant, -e [sɑ̃tɑ̃, -ɑ̃t] ADJ sentient

sent-bon [sɑ̃bɔ̃] NM INV *Fam* scent■

sente [sɑ̃t] NF *Littéraire* path, footpath, track

sentence [sɑ̃tɑ̃s] NF **1** *(jugement)* sentence; **prononcer une s.** to pass *or* to give *or* to pronounce sentence; **s. arbitrale** arbitral sentence; **s. arbitrale motivée** = award stating the reasons on which it is based **2** *(maxime)* maxim, saying

sentencieuse [sɑ̃tɑ̃sjøz] *voir* **sentencieux**

sentencieusement [sɑ̃tɑ̃sjøzmɑ̃] ADV sententiously, moralistically

sentencieux, -euse [sɑ̃tɑ̃sjø, -øz] ADJ sententious, moralistic, moralizing

senteur, -euse [sɑ̃tœr] ADJ *Can Péj (indiscret)* nosy, prying

NF *Littéraire* fragrance, scent, aroma

senti, -e [sɑ̃ti] ADJ **bien s.** *(lecture, interprétation)* appropriate, *Sout* apposite; **c'était une repartie bien sentie** it was a retort that struck home; **une vérité bien sentie** a home truth

NM *Phil* sense datum

sentier [sɑ̃tje] NM **1** *(allée)* path, footpath

2 *Sport* **s. de grande randonnée** long-distance hiking path

3 *Fig Littéraire* path, way; **les sentiers de la gloire** the paths of glory; **être sur le s. de la guerre** to be on the warpath; **suivre les sentiers battus** to keep to well-trodden paths; **sortir des sentiers battus** to get *or* to wander off the beaten track

4 le S. = predominantly Jewish district of Paris famous as a centre for the clothing trade

5 *Pol* **le S. lumineux** the Shining Path, the Sendero Luminoso

sentiment [sɑ̃timɑ̃] NM **1** *(émotion)* feeling; **un s. de honte** a feeling of shame; **ses sentiments vis-à-vis de moi** his/her feelings towards me; **je ne doute pas de ses sentiments pour moi** I have no doubt that he/she loves me; **prendre qn par les sentiments** to appeal to sb's feelings; *Hum* **si tu me prends par les sentiments!** if you go for the heartstrings!

2 *(sensibilité)* feeling *(UNCOUNT)*; **le s. religieux** religious feeling *or* fervour; **chanter avec s.** to sing with feeling; **avoir le s. du tragique** to have a feeling for tragedy; **avoir le s. de la beauté** to have a sense of the aesthetic

3 *(sensiblerie)* (silly) sentimentalism; **ce n'est pas le moment de faire du s.** this is no time to get sentimental; **en affaires, je ne fais jamais de s.** I don't let emotions get in the way of business; *Fam* **avoir qn au s.** to get around sb; **n'essaie pas de m'avoir** *ou* **de me la faire au s.** don't try to get around me by appealing to my better nature

4 *(opinion)* feeling, opinion; **quel est votre s. sur la question?** what is your feeling about the matter?; **si vous voulez savoir mon s.** if you want to know what I think *or* I feel; **mon s. est que la guerre ne va pas durer** my feeling is that the war won't last; **j'ai ce s.-là aussi** my feelings exactly

5 *(conscience)* **avoir le/un s. de** to have the/a feeling of; **avoir le s. de sa solitude** to have a feeling of loneliness; **il avait le s. de sa mort prochaine** he sensed he would die soon; **j'ai le s. très net de m'être trompé/qu'il m'a menti** I have a distinct feeling that I made a mistake/that he lied to me

6 *Chasse* scent

7 *Arch (sensibilité physique)* consciousness; **être sans s.** to be unconscious

▫ **sentiments** NMPL **1** *(disposition)* **faire appel aux bons sentiments de qn** to appeal to sb's better *or* finer feelings; **ramener qn à de meilleurs sentiments** to bring sb round to a more generous point of view; **revenir à de meilleurs sentiments** to be in a better frame of mind

2 *(dans la correspondance)* **veuillez agréer l'expression de mes sentiments distingués** *(à quelqu'un dont on connaît le nom) Br* yours sincerely, *Am* sincerely (yours); *(à quelqu'un dont on ne connaît pas le nom) Br* yours faithfully, *Am* sincerely (yours); **nos sentiments les meilleurs** kindest regards

sentimental, -e, -aux, -ales [sɑ̃timɑ̃tal, -o] ADJ **1** *(affectif)* sentimental; **la valeur sentimentale d'une broche** the sentimental value of a brooch; **vie sentimentale** love life; **la pièce ne compte que pour l'intrigue sentimentale** the play is only saved by its love interest

2 *Péj* sentimental, mawkish

NM,F **c'est un grand s.** he's a great romantic; **pourtant, je ne suis pas une sentimentale** yet I'm not given to sentimentality

sentimentalement [sɑ̃timɑ̃talmɑ̃] ADV sentimentally; *Péj* mawkishly

sentimentalisme [sɑ̃timɑ̃talism] NM *Péj* sentimentality, mawkishness; **faire du s.** to be overly sentimental

sentimentaliste [sɑ̃timɑ̃talist] ADJ sentimentalist

NMF sentimentalist

sentimentalité [sɑ̃timɑ̃talite] NF *Péj* sentimentality, mawkishness

sentine [sɑ̃tin] NF **1** *Naut* bilge **2** *Littéraire (cloaque)* pigsty; **s. de tous les vices** sink of iniquity

sentinelle [sɑ̃tinɛl] NF *Mil* sentinel, sentry; *Vieilli* **faire s.** to keep watch, to stand guard, to be on the lookout; **en s.** on guard; **être en s.** to stand sentinel *or* sentry, to be on sentry duty; **les cambrioleurs ont mis un homme en s. à la sortie de la banque** the robbers have put a lookout in front of the bank

SENTIR [37] [sɑ̃tir]

> **VT** to smell **A1** ■ to taste **A2** ■ to feel **A3–6** ■ to sense **A4** ■ to be aware of **A4** ■ to have a feel for **A8** ■ to smell of **B1** ■ to smack of **B3**
> **VI** to smell **1, 2**
> **VPR** to show **2** ■ to feel **3, 4**

VT **A.** *AVOIR UNE IMPRESSION DE* **1** *(par l'odorat)* to smell; **avec mon rhume, je ne sens rien** with this cold, I can't smell anything *or* I've no sense of smell (left); *Fam* **sens-moi cette soupe!** just smell this soup!■; **je sens une odeur de gaz** I can smell gas

2 *(par le goût)* to taste; **as-tu senti le goût du romarin?** could you taste the rosemary?

3 *(par le toucher)* to feel; **s. un caillou dans sa chaussure** to feel a stone in one's shoe; **il marche sur les braises sans paraître rien s.** he walks on burning coals without showing any sign of pain; **je n'ai rien senti!** I didn't feel a thing!; **je ne sens plus mon nez** *(de froid)* my nose has gone numb; **je ne sens plus ma main** *(d'ankylose)* my hand's gone numb *or* dead; **je ne sens plus mes jambes** *(de fatigue)* my legs are killing me; *Fam* **quand je monte l'escalier, je sens mon genou** *(douleur ancienne)* my knee plays up when I walk up the stairs; **je sens une lourdeur dans mes jambes** my legs feel heavy; **elle commence à s. son âge** she's starting to feel her age; **s. son visage s'empourprer** to feel oneself blushing; **il sentit les larmes lui monter aux yeux** he could feel tears coming to his eyes; **elle sentait le sommeil la gagner** she felt sleepier and sleepier; **je sentais battre mon cœur** I could feel my heart beating; **je n'ai pas senti l'après-midi/les années passer** the afternoon/years just flashed by; **j'ai senti qu'on essayait de mettre la main dans ma poche** I was aware *or* I felt that someone was trying to reach into my pocket; *Fam* **je l'ai sentie passer!** *(douleur, claque, facture)* I knew all about it!; *Fam* **je l'ai sentie passer, la piqûre!** I really felt that jab!; **vous allez la s. passer, l'amende!** you'll certainly know all about it when you get the fine!; **c'est lui qui a payé le repas, il a dû le s. passer!** he paid for the meal, it must have cost him an arm and a leg!

4 *(avoir l'intuition de → mépris, présence, réticence)* to feel, to sense, to be aware of; *(→ danger, menace)* to be aware *or* conscious of, to sense; **on ne m'a pas dit qu'il était mort, mais je l'ai senti** I wasn't told he was dead but I sensed it *or* I had a feeling he was; **tu ne sens pas ta force** you don't know your own strength; *Fam* **ça devait arriver, je le sentais venir de loin** I could see it coming a mile off; *Fam* **je le sentais venir (de loin) avec son petit air innocent!** I could see him coming (a mile off) with that innocent look on his face!; **ils n'ont pas senti venir le danger** they didn't smell *or* sense (the) danger; **elle sentait le pouvoir lui échapper** she could feel (that) power was slipping away from her; **je le sentais prêt/résolu** I could feel *or* tell he was ready/determined; **je sens bien qu'il m'envie** I can feel *or* tell that he envies me; **j'ai senti qu'on me suivait** I felt *or* sensed (that) I was being followed; **sens-tu à quel point il t'aime?** do you realize how much he loves you?; **faire s. qch à qn** to make sb aware of sth, to show sb sth; **il m'a fait s. que j'étais de trop** he made me understand *or* he hinted that I was in the way; *Fam* **elle nous le fait s. qu'elle est le chef!** she makes sure we know who's the boss!; **les conséquences de votre décision se feront s. tôt ou tard** the implications of your decision will be felt sooner or later; *Fam Hum* **tu fais comme tu sens, coco!** just do your own thing, pal!

5 *(éprouver → joie, chagrin, remords)* to feel; **je ne sens rien pour lui** I feel nothing for him

6 *(apprécier → art, musique)* to feel, to have a feeling for

7 *Fam (être convaincu par)* **je ne la sens pas pour le rôle** my feeling is that she's not right for the part; **je ne le sens pas, ton projet** I'm not convinced by your plan

8 *(maîtriser → instrument, outil)* to have a feel for; *(→ rôle, mouvement à exécuter)* to feel at ease

sen–sen

with; **s. sa monture** to feel good in the saddle; **je ne sentais pas bien mon service aujourd'hui** *(au tennis)* my serve wasn't up to scratch today; **tu ne pourras pas sculpter tant que tu ne sentiras pas la pierre** you won't become a sculptor until you have the right feeling for stone; **cet acteur n'est pas convaincant, il ne sent pas son texte** this actor isn't very convincing, he doesn't get inside the role

9 *Fam (tolérer)* **je ne peux pas la s.** I can't stand *or Br* stick her; **je le sens pas bien, ce mec-là** there's something about that guy I don't like; **je ne peux pas s. ses blagues sexistes** I can't stomach *or* I just can't take his/her sexist jokes

B. *EXHALER, DONNER UNE IMPRESSION* **1** *(dégager → odeur, parfum)* to smell of, to give off a smell of; **qu'est-ce que ça sent?** what's that smell?; **s. le gaz** to smell of gas; **ça sent le poisson** it smells fishy *or* of fish; **les roses ne sentent rien** the roses don't smell (of anything) *or* have no smell; **ça sent bon le lilas, ici** there's a nice smell of lilac in here

2 *(annoncer)* **ça sent l'automne** there's a hint *or* a trace of autumn in the air; **ça sent la pluie/la neige** it feels like rain/snow; **ça sentait la mutinerie** there was mutiny in the air; **ses propositions sentent le traquenard** there's something a bit suspect about his/her proposals; **se faire s.** *(devenir perceptible)* to be felt, to become obvious; **la fatigue se fait s. chez les concurrents** the contestants are showing signs of tiredness; **l'hiver commençait à se faire s.** the first signs of winter were appearing

3 *(laisser deviner)* to smack of, to savour of; **son livre sent la morale catholique** his/her book smacks of Catholic morality; **son interprétation/son style sent un peu trop le travail** his/her performance/style is rather too laborious; *Fam* **il sent le policier à des kilomètres** you can tell he's a policeman a mile off; *Fam* **ce n'est pas un acte de vandalisme, ça sentirait plutôt la vengeance** it's not pure vandalism, it feels more like revenge■; *Fam* **ça sent sa province/les années trente!** it smacks of provincial life/the thirties!; **son accent sentait bon le terroir** he/she had a wonderful rural *or* country accent

VI 1 *(avoir une odeur)* to smell; **le fromage sent fort** the cheese smells strong; **ça sent bon** *(fleur, parfum)* it smells nice; *(nourriture)* it smells good *or* nice; **tu sens bon** you smell nice *or* lovely; **ça sent mauvais** it doesn't smell very nice; *Fam Fig* **ça commence à s. mauvais, filons!** things are beginning to turn nasty, let's get out of here!

2 *(puer)* to smell, to stink, to reek; **la viande commence à s.** the meat is starting to smell; **il sent des pieds** his feet smell, he's got smelly feet

3 *Can (être indiscret)* to snoop, to stick one's nose into other people's business

▶**se sentir VPR 1** *(se supporter) Fam* **ils ne peuvent pas se s.** they can't stand *or Br* stick each other

2 *(être perceptible)* to show; **lorsqu'elle est déprimée, cela se sent dans ses lettres** when she's depressed, you can sense it *or* it shows in her letters; **il ne l'aime pas – ça se sent** he doesn't like him/her – you can tell (he doesn't) *or* you can sense it; **il était de langue maternelle russe, mais cela ne se sent pas dans ses romans** his mother tongue was Russian but you wouldn't know it from his novels

3 *(suivi d'un adjectif ou d'un infinitif)* to feel; **se s. fatigué/bafoué** to feel tired/the object of ridicule; **est-ce que tu te sens visé?** do you feel this was meant for you?; **je me sens rajeuni de 20 ans** I feel 20 years younger; **se s. en sécurité/en danger** to feel safe/threatened; **elle se sentait revivre** she felt (she'd been) born again; **je me sentais glisser** I could feel myself slipping; **se s. mal** *(s'évanouir)* to feel faint; *(être indisposé)* to feel ill; **se s. bien** to feel good *or* all right; **je me sens mieux maintenant** I feel better now; **je ne m'en sens pas capable** I don't feel up to it *or* equal to it; *Fam* **non mais, tu te sens bien?** have you gone mad?, are you off your rocker?; *Hum* **ne plus se s.** *(se comporter de façon étrange)* to have taken leave of one's senses; *Fam* **ne plus se s. (pisser)** *(être vaniteux)* to be too big for one's *Br* boots *or Am* britches; *Fam* **elle ne se sent plus depuis qu'elle a eu le rôle** she's been really full of it since she landed the part; *Fam* **du caviar? tu te sens plus, toi!** caviar? hey, steady on!; **ne plus se s. de joie** to be bursting *or* beside oneself with joy

4 *Fam* **se s. de faire qch** *(avoir le courage)* to feel up to doing sth; **tu te sens d'y aller?** do you feel up to going?; **je ne me sens pas de le lui dire** I don't feel like telling him/her; **je ne me sens pas le courage/la force de marcher** I don't feel up to walking/have the strength to walk; **te sens-tu le cœur d'y aller?** do you feel up to going?

SEO [ɛsəo] *Compta (abrév* **sauf erreur ou omission)** E & OE

seoir [67] [swar] **seoir à VT IND** *Littéraire* **1** *(aller à)* to become, to suit; **le noir ne te sied pas** black doesn't become you **2** *(convenir à)* to suit; **cet air de gravité seyait à sa personne** this solemn air suited him/her *or* went well with his/her personality **V IMPERSONNEL** *Littéraire* **il sied de** *(il convient de)* it is right *or* proper to; **il sied d'envoyer un mot de remerciement** it is proper *or* fitting to send a note of thanks; **il sied à qn de...** it is proper for sb to..., *Sout* it behoves sb to...; **il ne vous sied pas** *ou* **il vous sied mal de protester** it ill becomes *or* befits you to complain; **comme il sied** as is proper *or* fitting

Séoul [seul] **NM** Seoul

SEP [ɛsəpe] **NF** *Méd (abrév* **sclérose en plaques)** MS

sep [sɛp] **NM** *Agr* (plough)share

sépale [sepal] **NM** *Bot* sepal

séparable [separabl] **ADJ s. de** separable from; **l'intelligence n'est pas s. de la sensibilité** intelligence cannot be separated *or* divorced from the emotions; **deux théories difficilement séparables** two theories which are difficult to separate

séparateur, -trice [separatœr, -tris] **ADJ** separating, separative; *Opt* **pouvoir s.** resolving power **NM 1** *Élec & Tech* separator; **s. d'eau et de vapeur** water trap; *TV* **s. de faisceau** beam splitter; **s. d'huile** oil separator **2** *Ordinat* separator

séparation [separasjɔ̃] **NF 1** *(éloignement)* separation, parting; **elle n'a pas supporté la s. d'avec ses enfants** she couldn't bear to be parted *or* separated from her children; **quand arriva le jour de notre s.** when the day of our separation arrived, when the day came for us to part

2 *(rupture)* break-up, split-up; **leur s. est imminente** they are on the brink of splitting up *or* breaking up

3 *Jur* separation (agreement); **s. amiable** *ou* **de fait** voluntary separation; **le régime de la s. de biens** (marriage settlement based on) separate ownership of property; **s. de biens (judiciaire)** judicial separation of property; **s. de corps** legal separation; **s. des patrimoines** separation of inheritance

4 *Pol* **la s. des pouvoirs** the separation of powers; **la s. de l'Église et de l'État** the separation of Church and State

5 *(cloison)* partition, division; **mur de s.** dividing wall

6 *Chim* separating, isolating

7 *Nucl* **s. isotopique** isotope separation

8 *Ordinat* **s. automatique des pages** automatic pagination

9 *Typ* **s. des couleurs** colour separation; **s. quadrichromique** four-colour separation

séparatisme [separatism] **NM** separatism

séparatiste [separatist] **ADJ** separatist **NMF** separatist

séparatrice [separatris] *voir* **séparateur**

séparé, -e [separe] **ADJ 1** *(éléments, problèmes, courrier)* separate **2** *(époux)* separated; **nous sommes séparés depuis un an** we've been separated for a year; **il vit s. de sa femme** he's separated (from his wife); **époux séparés de biens** couple living under a judicial separation order; **époux séparés de corps** legally separated couple

séparément [separemɑ̃] **ADV** separately; **vivre s.** to live apart *or* separately; **c'est un problème à traiter s.** this problem must be dealt with separately

séparer [3] [separe] **VT 1** *(isoler)* to separate (**de** from); **s. des gaz/des isotopes** to separate gases/isotopes; **s. le blanc et le jaune d'un œuf** to separate the yolk and *or* from the white; **s. les raisins gâtés des raisins sains** to separate the bad grapes from the good ones, to pick the bad grapes out from amongst the good ones; *Bible & Fig* **s. le bon grain de l'ivraie** to separate the wheat from the chaff

2 *(éloigner → gens)* to part, to separate, to pull apart; **rien ne peut nous s., mon amour** nothing can come between us, my love; **des milliers de kilomètres nous séparent** we are thousands of miles apart, we are separated by thousands of miles; **la guerre a séparé beaucoup de familles** many families were separated *or* broken up by the war; **jusqu'à ce que la mort nous sépare** till death do us part; **séparez-les, ils vont se tuer!** you have to separate them or they'll kill each other!; **on les a séparés de leur père** they were separated from *or* taken away from their father

3 *(différencier)* **s. l'amour et l'amitié amoureuse** to distinguish between love and a loving friendship; **leurs opinions politiques les séparent** their political opinions divide them; **tout les sépare** they're worlds apart, they have nothing in common

4 *(diviser → gén)* to separate, to divide; *(→ cheveux)* to part; **la piste de ski est séparée en deux** the ski slope is divided into two; **le coin travail est séparé du lit par un paravent** a screen provides a partition between the work area and the bed; **le Nord est séparé du Sud** *ou* **le Nord et le Sud sont séparés par un désert** the North is separated from the South by a desert; **deux heures/cinq kilomètres nous séparaient de la frontière** we were two hours/five kilometres away from the border

▶**se séparer VPR 1** *(se quitter → amis, parents)* to part; *(→ époux, amants)* to break up; **les Beatles se sont séparés en 1970** the Beatles split up *or* broke up in 1970; **nous devons nous s. maintenant** we'll have to say goodbye now; **on se sépara sur le pas de la porte** we parted on the doorstep

2 *(bifurquer)* to divide, to branch (off); **le fleuve se sépare en plusieurs bras** the river divides *or* splits into several channels; **c'est ici que nos chemins se séparent** this is where we go our separate ways *or* where our paths diverge

3 se s. de *(se priver de)* to part with; **j'ai dû me s. de mes disques de jazz/de mon jardinier** I had to part with my jazz records/let my gardener go; **je ne me sépare jamais de mon plan de Paris** I'm never without my street map of Paris; **il ne se sépare pas si facilement de son argent** he and his money are not so easily parted

4 se s. de *(quitter)* to separate from

sépharade [sefarad] = **séfarade**

sépia [sepja] **ADJ INV** sepia, sepia-coloured **NF 1** *Ich* cuttlefish ink **2** *Beaux-Arts (couleur)* sepia; *(dessin)* sepia (drawing)

sépiole [sepjɔl] **NF** *Zool (mollusque)* little cuttlefish, *Spéc* sepiola

sépiolite [sepjɔlit] **NF** *Minér* sepiolite, meerschaum

seps [sɛps] **NM** *Zool* seps

sept [sɛt] **ADJ 1** *(gén)* seven; **les S. Merveilles du monde** the Seven Wonders of the World

2 *(dans des séries)* seventh; **page/numéro s.** page/number seven

3 *Cartes* **le jeu des s. familles** Happy Families **PRON** seven

NM INV 1 *(gén)* seven

2 *(numéro d'ordre)* number seven

3 *(chiffre écrit)* seven

4 *Cartes* seven

5 *TV* **les S. d'or** = annual French television awards, *Br* ≃ BAFTAs, *Am* ≃ Emmys

NF INV la S. = former French television channel; *voir aussi* **cinq**

'Les Sept mercenaires' *Sturges* 'The Magnificent Seven'

'Les Sept péchés capitaux' *Bosch* 'The Seven Deadly Sins'

'Les Sept samouraïs' *Kurosawa* 'The Seven Samurai'

septain [sɛtɛ̃] **NM** *Littérature* seven-line stanza

septal, -e, -aux, -ales [sɛptal, -o] **ADJ** *Anat* septal

septantaine [sɛptɑ̃tɛn] **NF** *Belg & Suisse* **1** *(quantité)* **une s.** around *or* about seventy, seventy or so; **une s. de voitures** around *or* about seventy cars; **elle a une s. d'années** she's around *or* about seventy (years old)
  2 *(âge)* **avoir la s.** to be around *or* about seventy; **quand on arrive à** *ou* **atteint la s.** when you hit seventy

Septante [sɛptɑ̃t] **NF** *Bible* **la (version des) S.** the Septuagint

septante [sɛptɑ̃t] *Belg & Suisse* **ADJ 1** *(gén)* seventy **2** *(dans des séries)* seventieth; **page/numéro s.** page/number seventy
  PRON seventy
  NM INV 1 *(gén)* seventy **2** *(numéro d'ordre)* number seventy **3** *(chiffre écrit)* seventy; *voir aussi* **cinquante**

septantième [sɛptɑ̃tjɛm] *Belg & Suisse* **ADJ** seventieth
  NMF 1 *(personne)* seventieth **2** *(objet)* seventieth (one)
  NM 1 *(partie)* seventieth **2** *(étage) Br* seventieth floor, *Am* seventy-first floor; *voir aussi* **cinquième**

septantièmement [sɛptɑ̃tjɛmmɑ̃] **ADV** *Belg & Suisse* in seventieth place

septembre [sɛptɑ̃br] **NM** September; *voir aussi* **mars**

septemvir [sɛptɛmvir] **NM** *Antiq* septemvir

septemvirat [sɛptɛmvira] **NM** *Antiq* septemvirate

septénaire [sɛptenɛr] **NM** *Méd* septenary

septennal, -e, -aux, -ales [sɛptenal, -o] **ADJ 1** *(qui a lieu tous les sept ans)* septennial **2** *(qui dure sept ans)* septennial, seven-year *(avant n)*

septennalité [sɛptenalite] **NF** septenniality

septennat [sɛptena] **NM 1** *Pol* (seven-year) term of office; **pendant son premier s.** during his/her first term of office **2** *(période)* seven-year period

septentrion [sɛptɑ̃trijɔ̃] **NM** *Arch ou Littéraire* septentrion

septentrional, -e, -aux, -ales [sɛptɑ̃trijɔnal, -o] **ADJ** septentrional, northern

septicémie [sɛptisemi] **NF** *Méd* blood poisoning, *Spéc* septicaemia

septicémique [sɛptisemik] **ADJ** *Méd* septicaemic

septicité [sɛptisite] **NF** *Méd* sepsis, septicity

septicopyohémie [sɛptikɔpjɔemi] **NF** *Méd* septicopyaemia

septidi [sɛptidi] **NM** *Hist* seventh day of a ten-day period in the Republican calendar

septième [sɛtjɛm] **ADJ** seventh; **le s. art** cinema, the seventh art; **être au s. ciel** to be in seventh heaven
  NMF 1 *(personne)* seventh
  2 *(objet)* seventh (one)
  NM 1 *(partie)* seventh
  2 *(étage) Br* seventh floor, *Am* eighth floor
  3 *(arrondissement de Paris)* seventh (arrondissement)
  NF 1 *Anciennement Scol Br* = last year of primary school, *Am* ≃ fifth grade
  2 *Mus* seventh; *voir aussi* **cinquième**

'Le Septième Sceau' *Bergman* 'The Seventh Seal'

septièmement [sɛtjɛmmɑ̃] **ADV** seventhly, in seventh place

septimo [sɛptimo] **ADV** seventhly

septique [sɛptik] **ADJ** septic

septmoncel [sɛmɔ̃sɛl] **NM** = type of blue cheese produced in the Jura region

septomycète [sɛptɔmisɛt] *Bot* **NM** septomycete
  ❑ **septomycètes NMPL** Septomycetes

septuagénaire [sɛptɥaʒenɛr] **ADJ** septuagenarian; **être s.** to be in one's seventies
  NMF person in his/her seventies; **un sémillant s.** a dashing seventy-year-old

septuagésime [sɛptɥaʒezim] **NF** *Rel* Septuagesima

septum [sɛptɔm] **NM 1** *Anat* septum **2** *(diaphragme)* membrane

septuor [sɛptɥɔr] **NM** septet, septette

septuple [sɛptypl] **ADJ** septuple, sevenfold
  NM septuple

septupler [3] [sɛptyple] **VT s. qch** to increase sth sevenfold, to septuple sth
  VI to increase sevenfold, to septuple

sépulcral, -e, -aux, -ales [sepylkral, -o] **ADJ** *Littéraire* sepulchral; **un silence s.** the silence of the grave; **une voix sépulcrale** a cavernous *or* sepulchral voice

sépulcre [sepylkr] **NM** *Littéraire* sepulchre; *Bible & Fig* **s. blanchi** whited sepulchre

sépulture [sepyltyr] **NF 1** *(lieu)* burial place **2** *Littéraire (enterrement)* burial, sepulture; **être privé de s.** to be refused burial

séquelle [sekɛl] **NF** *(d'une maladie)* after-effect; **sa bronchite n'a pas laissé de s.** he/she suffered no after-effects from his/her bronchitis
  ❑ **séquelles NFPL** *(d'un bombardement, d'une guerre)* aftermath

séquençage [sekɑ̃saʒ] **NM** *Biol & Chim* sequencing

séquence [sekɑ̃s] **NF 1** *Cin, Géol, Mus & Rel* sequence; *Cin* **s. d'archives** stock scene; *Cin* **s. filmique** film sequence; *Cin* **s. onirique** dream sequence **2** *Cartes* **s. de cartes** run, sequence of cards **3** *Ordinat* sequence; **s. d'appel** call sequence; **s. de caractères** character string, sequence of characters; **s. de commandes** command sequence

séquencer [16] [sekɑ̃se] **VT** *Biol* to sequence

séquenceur [sekɑ̃sœr] **NM** *Ordinat* sequencer

séquentiel, -elle [sekɑ̃sjɛl] **ADJ 1** *(ordonné)* sequential **2** *Ordinat (accès)* sequential, serial; *(traitement)* sequential

séquestration [sekɛstrasjɔ̃] **NF 1** *Jur (d'une personne)* illegal confinement *or* restraint; *(de biens)* sequestration (order) **2** *Chim & Méd* sequestration

séquestre [sekɛstr] **NM 1** *Jur (saisie)* sequestration; *Naut* embargo **2** *(personne)* sequestrator **3** *Méd* sequestrum
  ❑ **sous séquestre ADJ** *(biens)* sequestrated **ADV** **mettre** *ou* **placer des biens sous s.** to sequestrate property

séquestrer [3] [sekɛstre] **VT 1** *(personne)* **s. qn** to keep sb locked up; *Jur* to confine sb illegally **2** *Jur (biens)* to sequestrate; *(navire)* to lay an embargo upon

sequin [səkɛ̃] **NM** *(monnaie)* sequin

séquoia [sekɔja] **NM** *Bot* sequoia wellingtonia, giant sequoia

sera *etc voir* **être¹**

sérac [serak] **NM** *Géog & Culin* serac

sérail [seraj] **NM 1** *(harem)* seraglio, harem **2** *(palais d'un sultan)* seraglio; *Fig* **fils de ministre, il a été élevé** *ou* **nourri dans le s. (politique)** as a cabinet minister's son, he grew up in a political atmosphere; **c'est un homme du s.** *(homme politique)* he's an establishment figure *or* an insider; *(commercial)* he's a company *or* organization man

sérançage [serɑ̃saʒ] **NM** *Tex* hackling, heckling

sérancer [16] [serɑ̃se] **VT** *Tex* to hackle, to heckle

serapeum [serapeɔm] **NM** *Archéol* serapeum

Séraphin, -e [serafɛ̃, -in] **NM,F** *Can Péj* scrooge

séraphin [serafɛ̃] **NM** seraph

séraphique [serafik] **ADJ** seraphic, seraphical

serbe [sɛrb] **ADJ** Serbian
  NM *(langue)* Serb
  ❑ **Serbe NMF** Serb

Serbie [sɛrbi] **NF** **la S.** Serbia; **vivre en S.** to live in Serbia; **aller en S.** to go to Serbia

serbo-croate [sɛrbɔkrɔat] *(pl* **serbo-croates)** **ADJ** Serbo-Croat, Serbo-Croatian
  NM *(langue)* Serbo-Croat, Serbo-Croatian

Sercq [sɛrk] **NF** (isle of) Sark

serdab [sɛrdab] **NM** *Archéol* serdab

séré [sere] **NM** *Suisse* fromage frais

serein, -e [sərɛ̃, -ɛn] **ADJ 1** *(esprit, visage)* serene, peaceful **2** *Littéraire (eau, ciel)* serene, clear,

tranquil **3** *(jugement)* unbiased, dispassionate; *(réflexion)* undisturbed, unclouded
  NM *Littéraire* evening dew

sereinement [sərɛnmɑ̃] **ADV 1** *(tranquillement)* serenely, peacefully **2** *(impartialement)* dispassionately

sérénade [serenad] **NF 1** *Mus* serenade; *(concert)* serenade; **donner la s. à qn** to serenade sb **2** *Fam (tapage)* racket; **le bébé nous a fait une drôle de s. toute la nuit** the baby wailed at the top of his lungs the whole night

sérénissime [serenisim] **ADJ** **la S. République** La Serenissima, the Venetian Republic

sérénité [serenite] **NF 1** *(d'une personne)* serenity, peacefulness; *(d'un jugement)* dispassionateness; *(des pensées)* clarity; **il envisage avec s. l'approche de la vieillesse** he has a serene attitude towards growing old **2** *Littéraire (du ciel)* serenity, tranquillity, clarity

séreux, -euse [serø, -øz] **ADJ** *Physiol* serous
  ❑ **séreuse NF** *Anat* serous membrane

serf, serve [sɛrf, sɛrv] **ADJ 1** *Littéraire (soumis)* serflike, servile **2** *Hist* **la condition serve** serfdom
  NM,F *Hist* serf; **le s. attaché à la glèbe** the serf bound to the land

serfouage [sɛrfwaʒ] **NM** *Agr* hoeing

serfouette [sɛrfwɛt] **NF** *Agr* hoe-fork

serfouir [32] [sɛrfwir] **VT** *Agr* to hoe

serfouissage [sɛrfwisaʒ] **NM** *Agr* hoeing

serge [sɛrʒ] **NF** *Tex* serge; **tailleur en s.** serge suit

sergé [sɛrʒe] **NM** *Tex* cotton serge

sergent [sɛrʒɑ̃] **NM 1** *Mil* sergeant; **s. fourrier** quartermaster sergeant; **s. instructeur** drill sergeant; **s. recruteur** recruiting sergeant **2** *Vieilli (agent de police)* **s. de ville** police officer, *esp Br* police constable **3** *Tech* cramp, clamp

sergent-chef [sɛrʒɑ̃ʃɛf] *(pl* **sergents-chefs)** **NM** *(dans l'armée de terre) Br* ≃ staff sergeant, *Am* ≃ master sergeant; *(dans l'armée de l'air) Br* ≃ flight sergeant, *Am* ≃ master sergeant

sergent-major [sɛrʒɑ̃maʒɔr] *(pl* **sergents-majors)** **NM** quartermaster sergeant, sergeant major; *Belg* **premier s.** *(dans l'armée de l'air) Br* ≃ flight sergeant, *Am* ≃ master sergeant

serial, -als [serjal] **NM** *TV* serial

sérialisme [serjalism] **NM** serialism

sériation [serjasjɔ̃] **NF** seriation

séricicole [serisikɔl] **ADJ** silkworm-breeding *(avant n)*, *Spéc* sericultural

sériciculteur, -trice [serisikyltœr, -tris] **NM,F** silkworm breeder, *Spéc* sericulturist

sériciculture [serisikyltyr] **NF** silkworm breeding, *Spéc* sericulture

séricigène [serisiʒɛn] **ADJ** *(insecte)* silk-producing; *(glande)* silk *(avant n)*

séricine [serisin] **NF** *Tex* sericin

série [seri] **NF 1** *(suite → de questions, de changements, de conférences)* series *(singulier)*; *(→ d'attentats)* series, spate, string; *(→ d'échecs)* series, run, string; *(→ de tests)* series, battery; **il y a eu récemment une s. de descentes de police** there's been a spate of police raids recently
  2 *(ensemble → de clefs, de mouchoirs)* set; *(→ de poupées russes, de tables gigognes)* nest; *Com & Ind (production)* batch; **elle en a toute une s.** she has a whole collection of them; **s. limitée** limited run; **s. de prix** rates, list of charges
  3 *(catégorie)* class, category; **classé dans la s. des récidivistes/des chefs-d'œuvre** belonging to the class of recidivists/of masterpieces; *Hum* **dans la s. "scandales de l'été", tu connais la dernière?** have you heard the latest in the series of summer scandals?
  4 *TV* **s. dramatique** drama series; **s. policière** crime series; **s. (télévisée)** television series
  5 *(au lycée)* = one of the groups into which baccalaureat students are divided, depending on their chosen area of specialization, *Br* ≃ stream, *Am* ≃ track
  6 *Sport (classement)* series; *(épreuve)* qualifying heat *or* round; *(au billard)* break
  7 *Géol, Chim, Math, Mus & Nucl* series *(singulier)*
  ADJ INV *Ordinat* serial
  ❑ **de série ADJ 1** *Ind* mass-produced
  2 *Com (numéro)* serial *(avant n)*
  3 *Aut (modèle)* production *(avant n)*

❏ **en série** ADJ **1** *Ind (fabrication)* mass *(avant n)* **2** *Élec (couplage, enroulement)* series *(avant n)* ADV **1** *Ind* **fabriquer qch en s.** to mass-produce sth **2** *Élec* **monté en s.** connected in series **3** *(à la file)* one after the other; **en ce moment, les malheurs arrivent en s.** it's just one disaster after another at the moment

❏ **série B** NF **(film de) s. B** B-movie

❏ **série noire** NF **1** *Littérature* crime thriller; **c'est un vrai personnage de s. noire** he's/she's like something out of a detective novel **2** *Fig* catalogue of disasters

sériel, -elle [serjɛl] ADJ serial; **musique sérielle** serial music

sérier [9] [serje] VT to arrange, to classify, to grade; **commençons par s. les problèmes** let's prioritize our problems

sérieuse [serjøz] *voir* **sérieux**

sérieusement [serjøzmã] ADV **1** *(consciencieusement)* seriously; **as-tu étudié la question s.?** have you looked at the matter thoroughly? **2** *(sans plaisanter)* seriously, in earnest; **tu ne dis pas ça s.?** you don't actually mean it?, you're not saying this in earnest?; **je pense me présenter aux élections – s.?** I think I'll stand in the election – seriously or really? **3** *(gravement)* seriously, gravely; **s. blessé** seriously or severely injured **4** *(vraiment)* **ça commençait à bouchonner s.** traffic was really building up; **il en a s. besoin** he's seriously in need of it

sérieux, -euse [serjø, -øz] ADJ **1** *(grave → ton, visage)* serious, solemn; **être s. comme un pape** to look as solemn as a judge; **ne prends pas cet air s.!** don't look so serious!; **vous n'êtes pas s.!** you can't be serious!, you must be joking! **2** *(important → lecture, discussion)* serious; **on a discuté de choses sérieuses** we discussed serious topics, we had a serious discussion; **entre elle et moi, c'est s.** we have a serious relationship; **tu n'as aucune raison sérieuse de refuser** you don't have any good reason to refuse **3** *(consciencieux → employé)* serious, responsible; *(→ élève)* conscientious; *(→ travail)* conscientious; **c'est du travail s.** it's good work; **être s. dans son travail** to be serious about one's work, to take one's work seriously; **être s. pour son âge** to be serious for one's age; **ça ne fait pas très s.** it won't make a very good impression; **arriver au bureau à midi, ça ne fait pas très s.** turning up at the office just before lunchtime isn't very responsible **4** *(digne de foi → partenaire, offre, candidature, revue)* serious, reliable, dependable; *(→ analyse, enquête)* serious, thorough, in-depth; **c'est l'ouvrage le plus s. sur la question** it's the most thorough work on the subject; **il me faut quelqu'un de s.** I need someone reliable; **peu s.** *(personne)* unreliable **5** *(dangereux → situation, maladie)* grave, serious; *(→ blessure)* severe **6** *(sincère, vrai)* serious; **pas s. s'abstenir** no time-wasters; **c'est s., cette histoire?** it's all true?; **c'est s., tu pars?** it's true that you are leaving?; **c'est s., cette histoire d'augmentation?** is this talk about getting a rise serious? **7** *(avant le nom) (important → effort)* real; *(→ dégâts, difficultés)* serious; *(→ risques)* great, considerable; *(→ somme d'argent)* sizeable; **il a de sérieuses chances de gagner** he stands a good chance of winning; **on a de sérieuses raisons de le penser** we have good reasons to think so; **de s. progrès techniques** considerable technical advances; **ils ont une sérieuse avance sur nous** they are well ahead of us

❏ **sérieux** NM **1** *(gravité → d'une personne)* seriousness; *(→ d'une situation)* gravity; **garder son s.** to keep a straight face **2** *(application)* seriousness, serious-mindedness; **elle fait son travail avec s.** she's serious about her work; **manque de s.** unreliability **3** *(fiabilité → d'une intention)* seriousness, earnestness; *(→ d'une source de renseignements)* reliability, dependability **4** *(chope de bière)* litre of beer ADV *Fam (sérieusement)* seriously; **ils se sont foutus sur la gueule s.** they seriously went for each other; **s.?** seriously?

❏ **au sérieux** ADV **prendre qn/qch au s.** to take sb/sth seriously; **se prendre (trop) au s.** to take oneself (too) seriously

serif [serif] NM *Typ* serif

sérigraphie [serigrafi] NF **1** *(procédé)* silk-screen or screen process printing **2** *(ouvrage)* silk-screen print, *Spéc* serigraph

sérigraphié, -e [serigrafje] ADJ silk-screen printed

serin, -e [sərɛ̃, -in] NM,F **1** *Orn* canary; **s. cini** serin **2** *Fam (personne)* nitwit
ADJ *Fam (personne)* silly*, idiotic*
ADJ M INV *(couleur)* **jaune s.** bright or canary yellow

sérine [serin] NF *Biol & Chim* serine

seriner [3] [sərine] VT **1** *Fam (répéter)* **s. qch à qn** to drill or to drum sth into sb; **il m'a seriné ça toute la soirée** he kept banging on about it all evening; **s. à qn que...** to tell sb time after time that... **2** *(instruire)* **s. un oiseau** to teach a bird to sing *(using a bird-organ)*

serinette [sərinɛt] NF *(boîte à musique)* bird-organ

seringa [sərɛ̃ga] NM *Bot* mock orange, syringa

seringage [sərɛ̃gaʒ] NM *Vieilli* syringing

seringat [sərɛ̃ga] = **seringa**

seringue [sərɛ̃g] NF **1** *Méd* needle, syringe; **s. hypodermique** hypodermic needle or syringe; **s. à injections** hypodermic needle or syringe; **s. jetable** disposable syringe **2** *Hort* garden syringe, (garden) pump spray **3** *Culin* syringe **4** *Aut* **s. de graissage** grease gun **5** *Fam Vieilli (pistolet)* pistol*, Am* gat

seringuer [3] [sərɛ̃ge] VT *Vieilli* to syringe

sériole [serjɔl] NF *Ich* amberjack

sérique [serik] ADJ *Méd* serous

serlienne [sɛrljen] NF *Archit* Venetian window, *Spéc* Serliana

serment [sɛrmã] NM **1** *(parole solennelle)* oath; **témoigner sous s.** to testify under oath; **déclaration sous s.** sworn statement, statement under oath; **déclarer sous la foi du s.** to declare on or upon oath; **faire un s. sur l'honneur** to pledge one's word of honour; **s. d'allégeance** oath of allegiance; *Jur* **s. décisoire** decisive oath; *Méd* **s. d'Hippocrate** Hippocratic oath; **s. judiciaire** oath or affirmation *(in a court of law)*; **s. politique** oath of allegiance; *Jur* **s. probatoire** oath; **s. professionnel** *(des magistrats, des policiers etc)* oath of office; *Jur* **s. promissoire** promissory oath; *Hist* **le s. du Jeu de paume** the Tennis Court Oath **2** *(promesse)* pledge; **des serments d'amour** pledges or vows of love; **on a fait le s. de ne pas se quitter** we've pledged or sworn never to part; **j'ai fait le s. de ne rien dire** I'm pledged or sworn to secrecy; **s. d'ivrogne** ou **de joueur** vain promise; *Fam* **tout ça, c'est des serments d'ivrogne!** I'll believe that when I see it!

'**Le Serment des Horaces**' *David* 'The Oath of the Horatii'

'**Le Serment du Jeu de Paume**' *David* 'The Tennis Court Oath'

sermon [sɛrmɔ̃] NM **1** *Rel* sermon; **faire un s.** to deliver or to preach a sermon; *Bible* **le s. sur la montagne** the Sermon on the Mount **2** *Fig Péj* lecture; **épargne-moi tes sermons** spare me the lecture

sermonnaire [sɛrmɔnɛr] NM *Rel* **1** *(recueil)* collection of sermons **2** *(auteur)* writer of sermons

sermonner [3] [sɛrmɔne] VT *(morigéner)* to lecture, to sermonize, to preach at

sermonneur, -euse [sɛrmɔnœr, -øz] ADJ sermonizing, lecturing
NM,F sermonizer

SERNAM®**, Sernam**® [sɛrnam] NM *(abrév* **Service national des messageries)** = rail delivery service, *Br* ≃ Red Star®

séroconversion [serɔkɔ̃vɛrsjɔ̃] NF *Méd* seroconversion

sérodiagnostic [serɔdjagnɔstik] NM *Méd* serodiagnosis, serum diagnosis

sérogroupe [serɔgrup] NM *Méd* serogroup

sérologie [serɔlɔʒi] NF *Méd (science)* serology; **faire une s.** to be screened for antibodies

sérologique [serɔlɔʒik] ADJ *Méd* serologic, serological

sérologiste [serɔlɔʒist] NMF *Méd* serologist

séronégatif, -ive [serɔnegatif, -iv] *Méd* ADJ *(gén)* seronegative; *(HIV)* HIV-negative
NM,F **les séronégatifs** HIV-negative people

séronégativité [serɔnegativite] NF *Méd (gén)* seronegativity; *(HIV)* HIV-negative status

séropo [seropo] *Fam Méd* ADJ HIV-positive*
NMF HIV-positive person*

séropositif, -ive [serɔpozitif, -iv] *Méd* ADJ *(gén)* seropositive; *(HIV)* HIV-positive
NM,F HIV-positive person

séropositivité [serɔpozitivite] NF *Méd (gén)* seropositivity; *(HIV)* HIV infection; **il a été renvoyé à cause de sa s.** he was dismissed for being HIV-positive

sérosité [serozite] NF *Physiol* serous fluid

sérothérapie [serɔterapi] NF *Méd* serotherapy

sérothérapique [serɔterapik] ADJ *Méd* serotherapeutic

sérotonine [serɔtɔnin] NF *Biol & Chim* serotonin

sérotype [serɔtip] NM *Méd* serotype

sérovaccination [serɔvaksinasjɔ̃] NF *Méd* serovaccination

serpe [sɛrp] NF bill, billhook; **un visage taillé à la s. ou à coups de s.** a rough-hewn face

serpent [sɛrpã] NM **1** *Zool* snake; *(dans la Bible)* serpent; **avec la ruse du s.** with fox's cunning; **s. corail** coral snake; **s. cracheur** spitting cobra; **s. d'eau** water snake; **s. à lunettes** Indian cobra; **s. marin** sea snake; **s. de mer** *Myth* sea monster or serpent; *Presse Br* silly-season story, *Am* flupp story; **le vieux s. de mer de la nationalisation** the old chestnut of nationalization; *Antiq* **s. à plumes** plumed serpent; **s. ratier** rat snake; **s. à sonnette** rattlesnake; **s. de verre** glass snake; **c'est (comme) le s. qui se mord la queue** it's a vicious circle **2** *Littéraire (personne)* viper; **réchauffer un s. dans son sein** to nourish a viper in one's bosom **3** *(forme sinueuse)* **s. de fumée** ribbon of smoke; **le long s. des véhicules sur la route** the long trail of vehicles winding up the road **4** *Fin* **s. monétaire** currency snake; **le s. monétaire européen** the European currency snake **5** *Mus* serpent

serpentaire [sɛrpɑ̃tɛr] NM *Orn* secretary bird
NF *Bot* snakeroot

serpenteau, -x [sɛrpɑ̃to] NM **1** *Zool* young snake **2** *(feu d'artifice)* serpent

serpentement [sɛrpɑ̃təmã] NM *Littéraire* meandering, winding course

serpenter [3] [sɛrpɑ̃te] VI to wind along, to meander; **le chemin monte/descend en serpentant** the road winds or snakes or meanders up/down

serpentiforme [sɛrpɑ̃tiform] ADJ twisting, serpentine

serpentin, -e [sɛrpɑ̃tɛ̃, -in] ADJ *Littéraire* twisting, winding, sinuous
NM **1** *(de papier)* (paper) streamer **2** *Phys* coil; **s. de réchauffage** heating coil
❏ **serpentine** NF *Minér* serpentine

serpent-roi [sɛrpɑ̃rwa] NM *Zool* king snake

serpette [sɛrpɛt] NF pruning hook or knife

serpigineux, -euse [sɛrpiʒinø, -øz] ADJ serpiginous

serpigo [sɛrpigo] NM *Méd* serpigo

serpillière [sɛrpijɛr] NF *(torchon)* floorcloth; **il faudrait passer la s. dans la cuisine** the kitchen floor needs cleaning

serpolet [sɛrpɔlɛ] NM *Bot & Culin* wild thyme

serpule [sɛrpyl] NF *Zool* serpula

serra [sera] NF serra

serrage [seraʒ] NM *(d'une vis)* screwing down, tightening; *(d'un joint)* clamping

serran [serã] NM *Ich* comber

serranidé [seranide] *Ich* NM serranid
❏ **serranidés** NMPL Serranidae

serrate [serat] ADJ *(pièce de monnaie)* serrated

serratule [seratyl] NF *Bot* sawwort

serratus [seratys] = **serrate**

serre [sɛr] NF **1** *Hort & Agr (en verre)* greenhouse, *Br* glasshouse; *(en plastique)* greenhouse; **cultures en** ou **de s.** greenhouse plants; **légumes poussés en** ou **sous s.** vegetables grown under glass; *Fig* **ils élèvent leurs enfants en** ou **sous s.** they wrap their children in cotton wool; **s.**

chaude hothouse; *Écol* **effet de s.** greenhouse effect
2 *Orn* claw, talon
3 *Tech (d'une substance)* pressing, squeezing
4 *Métal* ramming
5 *Naut* stringer

serré, -e [sere] ADJ **1** *(nœud, ceinture, vêtement)* tight; **s. à la taille** *(volontairement)* fitted at the waist, tight-waisted
2 *(contracté)* **les lèvres/les dents serrées** with set lips/clenched teeth; **la gorge serrée** with a lump in one's throat; **c'est le cœur s. que j'y repense** when I think of it, it gives me a lump in my throat
3 *(dense → style)* tight, concise; *(→ réseau)* dense; *(→ débat)* closely-conducted, closely-argued; *(→ écriture)* cramped; *(→ pluie)* teeming; **deux pages d'une écriture serrée** two closely written pages
4 *(délimité → emploi du temps)* tight, busy; *(→ budget)* tight
5 *(café)* strong; **je bois mon café très s.** I like my coffee very strong
6 *Sport (arrivée, peloton)* close; *(match)* tight, close-fought; **on a eu une fin de course serrée** it was a close finish; **jouer** *ou* **mener un jeu s.** to play a tight game
ADV **écrire s.** to have cramped handwriting; **tricoter s.** to knit a tight stitch; **jouer s.** to play a tight game

serre-file [sɛrfil] *(pl* **serre-files***)* NM **1** *Mil* serrefile
2 *Naut* rear ship *(of a line ahead)*

serre-fils [sɛrfil] NM INV *(vis)* binding screw; *(pince)* wire grip

serre-frein [sɛrfrɛ̃] *(pl* **serre-freins***)* NM *Rail* brakeman

serre-joint [sɛrʒwɛ̃] *(pl* **serre-joints***)* NM (builder's) clamp

serre-la-piasse [sɛrlapjas], **serre-la-piastre** [sɛrlapjastr] NM INV *Can Fam Péj* scrooge, stingy person

serre-livres [sɛrlivr] NM INV bookend; **deux s.** a pair of bookends

serrement [sɛrmɑ̃] NM **1** *(action)* **s. de cœur** pang, tug at the heartstrings; **avoir un s. de cœur** to feel a pang *or* a tug at the heartstrings; **s. de main** handshake **2** *Mines* dam

serre-patte [sɛrpat] *(pl* **serre-pattes***)* NM *Fam* sergeant■

SERRER [4] [sere]

> VT to hold tight **1** ■ to be too tight for **2** ■ to tighten **3** ■ to clench **4** ■ to put away **8** ■ to arrest **9**
> VPR to squeeze up **1**

VT **1** *(presser)* to hold tight; **il serrait la clé dans sa main** he was holding the key tight *or* he was clutching the key in his hand; **serre-moi fort dans tes bras** hold me tight in your arms; **s. qch contre son cœur** to clasp sth to one's breast; **s. qn contre son cœur** to clasp sb to one's bosom; **s. qn à la gorge** to grab sb by the throat; *Fam* **s. le kiki à qn** to try to strangle sb■; *Fam* **s. la main** *ou* **la pince à qn** to shake hands with sb■, to shake sb's hand■
2 *(sujet: vêtement, chaussure)* to be too tight for; **la chaussure droite/le col me serre un peu** the right shoe/the collar is a bit tight; **ton jean te serre trop aux cuisses** your jeans are too tight round the thighs
3 *(bien fermer → nœud, lacets)* to tighten, to pull tight; *(→ joint)* to clamp; *(→ écrou)* to tighten (up); *(→ frein à main)* to put on tight; *Fam* **s. la vis à qn** to crack down (hard) on sb
4 *(contracter)* to clench; **s. les lèvres** to set *or* to tighten one's lips; **s. les dents** to clench *or* to set *or* to grit one's teeth; **s. les mâchoires** to clench one's jaws; **en serrant les poings** clenching one's fists; *Fig* barely containing one's anger; **des images qui vous serrent le cœur** heartrending images; **avoir la gorge serrée par l'émotion** to be choked with emotion; **le chagrin lui serrait la gorge** he/she was choked with grief; *Fam* **s. les fesses** to have the jitters
5 *(rapprocher)* **en les serrant bien, une boîte suffira** if we pack them in tight, one box will do; *Typ* **s. une ligne** to close up a line; *Fig* **s. les rangs** to close ranks; *Sport* **s. le jeu** to play a tight game; **être serrés comme des sardines** *ou* **des harengs** to be squashed up like sardines
6 *(suivre) Aut* **s. le trottoir** to hug the kerb; **s. qn de près** to follow close behind sb, to follow sb closely; *Fig* **s. une femme de près** to be all over a woman; **s. un problème de plus près** to study a problem more closely
7 *Naut* **s. la côte** to hug the coast; **s. le vent** to sail close to *or* to hug the wind; **s. une voile** to take in (and reef) a sail
8 *(enfermer, ranger)* to put away; **serrez bien vos bijoux** put your jewellery away in a safe place
9 *Fam (arrêter) Br* to nick, to lift, *Am* to bust
VI *Aut* **s. à droite/à gauche** to keep to the right/left
▸**se serrer** VPR **1** *(se rapprocher)* to squeeze up; **si on se serre un peu, on pourra tous entrer** if we squeeze up a bit, we can all get in; **se s. contre qn** *(par affection)* to cuddle *or* to snuggle up to sb; *(pour se protéger)* to huddle up against sb; **se s. les uns contre les autres** to huddle together; **se s. contre un mur** to hug a wall
2 *(se contracter)* **je sentais ma gorge se s.** I could feel a lump in my throat; **mon cœur se serra en les voyant** my heart sank when I saw them
3 *(pour se saluer)* **se s. la main** to shake hands

serre-tête [sɛrtɛt] NM INV **1** *(accessoire)* headband, hairband **2** *Sport (d'athlète)* headband; *(de rugbyman)* scrum cap **3** *(d'aviateur)* helmet

serrette [sɛrɛt] NF *Bot* saw-wort

serriculture [serikyltyr] NF hothouse growing

serriste [serist] NMF greenhouse gardener

serrure [seryr] NF lock; **laisser la clef dans la s.** to leave the key in the lock *or* in the door; **s. à carte perforée** card-operated lock; **s. à combinaison** combination lock; **s. électronique** electronic lock; **s. encastrée** mortise lock; **s. magnétique** magnetic lock; **s. à pompe** high security spring lock *(with pump action mechanism)*; *Aut* **s. de sécurité** childproof lock; **s. de sûreté** safety lock

serrurerie [seryrri] NF **1** *(métier)* locksmithing, locksmithery **2** *(magasin)* locksmith's (*Br* shop *or Am* store) **3** *(ferronnerie)* ironwork; **grosse s.** heavy ironwork; **s. d'art** decorative ironwork

serrurier [seryrje] NM **1** *(qui pose des serrures)* locksmith **2** *(en ferronnerie)* iron manufacturer

sert *etc voir* **servir**

sertão [sɛrtɑ̃, sertao] NM sertão

serte [sɛrt] NF *(d'une pierre précieuse)* setting

serti [sɛrti] NM *(d'une pierre précieuse)* setting

sertir [32] [sɛrtir] VT **1** *(pierre précieuse)* to set; **couronne sertie de diamants** crown set with diamonds **2** *Métal (tôles)* to crimp over; *(rivet)* to clinch; *(boîte de conserve)* to crimp **3** *(cartouche)* to crimp

sertissage [sɛrtisaʒ] NM **1** *(d'une pierre précieuse)* setting **2** *Métal (de tôles)* crimping together; *(d'un rivet)* clinching; *(d'une cartouche, d'une boîte de conserve)* crimping

sertisseur, -euse [sɛrtisœr, -øz] NM,F **1** *(en joaillerie)* (jewel) setter **2** *Métal* crimper
NM *(appareil)* closing *or* sealing *or* double seaming machine

sertissure [sɛrtisyr] NF **1** *(sertissage)* setting **2** *(partie du chaton)* setting

sérum [serɔm] NM **1** *Physiol* **s. (sanguin)** (blood) serum **2** *Pharm* serum; **s. antivenimeux** antivenin serum; **s. antilymphocytaire** antilymphocytic serum, ALS; **s. physiologique** saline; **s. de vérité** truth drug **3** *(du lait)* whey

sérumalbumine [serɔmalbymin] NF *Biol* serum albumin

servage [sɛrvaʒ] NM **1** *Hist* serfdom **2** *Littéraire (esclavage)* bondage, thraldom

serval, -als [sɛrval] NM *Zool* serval (cat)

servant [sɛrvɑ̃] ADJ M *Rel* **frère s.** lay brother *(with domestic tasks)*
NM **1** *Rel* **s. (de messe)** server **2** *Mil* **s. (de canon)** gunner

servante [sɛrvɑ̃t] NF **1** *(domestique)* servant, maidservant; *Littéraire Ironique* **(je suis votre) s.** I would rather not *or* no, thank you **2** *Menuis* vice; **s. d'établi** bench vice **3** *(table)* serving table, *Br* dumbwaiter **4** *Théât (éclairage)* small lamp

serve [sɛrv] *voir* **serf**

serveur, -euse [sɛrvœr, -øz] NM,F **1** *(de restaurant)* waiter, *f* waitress; *(de bar)* barman, *f* barmaid
2 *Sport* server
3 *Cartes* dealer
4 *Ind (ouvrier)* feeder (worker)
NM *Ordinat* server; **(centre) s.** information retrieval centre; **s. de données** on-line data service; **s. de fichiers** file server; **s. FTP** FTP server; **s. mandataire** proxy server; **s. Minitel®** Minitel® service provider; **s. de réseau** network server; **s. sécurisé** secure server; **s. télématique** bulletin board (system); **s. Web** Web server

serviabilité [sɛrvjabilite] NF helpfulness, obligingness, willingness to help

serviable [sɛrvjabl] ADJ helpful, obliging, willing to help

serviablement [sɛrvjabləmɑ̃] ADV helpfully, obligingly

SERVICE [sɛrvis]

> NM duty **1, 8, 15** ■ service **2, 3, 7, 8, 10–14** ■ sitting **4** ■ favour **5** ■ department **6** ■ servicing **9** ■ set **12**
> NMPL services **1–3**

NM **1** *(travail)* duty, shift; **mon s. commence à 18 heures** I go on duty *or* I start my shift *or* I start work at 6 p.m.; **l'alcool est interdit pendant le s.** drinking is forbidden while on duty; **il n'a pu assurer son s.** he wasn't able to go to work; **qui est de s. ce soir?** who's on duty tonight?; **les pompiers de service** the *Br* firemen *or Am* fire fighters on duty; *Fam Fig* **le plaisantin/le râleur de service** the resident joker/grouch; **s. de jour** day duty; **s. de nuit** night duty; **il n'est pas de s.** he's off-duty; **elle a 22 ans de s. dans l'entreprise** she's been with the company for 22 years; **finir son s.** to come off duty; **prendre son s.** to go on *or* to report for duty; **il ne plaisante pas avec le s.** he sticks to the rule book; **reprendre du s.** to be employed for a supplementary period; *Fam Hum* **mon vieux manteau a repris du s.** my old coat has been saved from the bin
2 *(pour la collectivité)* service, serving; **le s. de l'État** public service, the service of the state; **ses états de s.** his/her service record; *Méd* **s. médical rendu** = assessment of the medical benefits of a drug or treatment
3 *(pour un client, pour un maître)* service; **prendre qn à son s.** to take sb into service; **elle a deux ans de s. comme femme de chambre** she's been in service for two years as a chambermaid; **à votre s.** at your service; **elle a passé sa vie au s. des autres** she spent her life helping others; **il a mis son savoir-faire au s. de la société** he put his expertise at the disposal of the company; **je ne suis pas à ton s.!** I'm not your slave!; **qu'y a-t-il pour votre s.?** what can I do for you?; **entrons ici, le s. est rapide** let's go here, the service is quick; **le s. laissait plutôt à désirer** the service left a lot to be desired; **demander 15 pour cent pour le s.** to impose a 15 percent service charge; **s. compris/non compris** *(dans un restaurant)* service included/not included; **prends ces cacahuètes et fais le s.** take these peanuts and hand them round; **après dix ans de bons et loyaux services** after ten years of good and faithful service; **s. après-vente** *(prestation)* after-sales service; **s. d'assistance** *(téléphonique)* help desk, help line; **s. clientèle** *ou* **clients** *(prestation)* customer service; **s. consommateurs** *(prestation)* customer service; **s. de livraison** delivery service; **s. de messageries** courier service; **services à la personne** personal services; *Mktg* **s. perçu** perceived service; *Mktg* **s. premier** premium service; **s. de relation clientèle** customer service; **escalier/porte/entrée de s.** service staircase/door/entrance
4 *(série de repas)* sitting; **nous irons au premier/au deuxième s.** we'll go to the first/second sitting
5 *(aide)* favour; **puis-je te demander un petit/un grand s.?** could I ask you to do me a small/a big favour?; **rendre un s. à qn** *(sujet: personne)* to help sb out, to do sb a favour; **elle n'aime pas rendre s.** she's not very helpful; **tu m'as bien rendu s.** you were a great help to me; **tu m'as bien rendu s. en me le prêtant** you did me a

great favour by lending it to me; **rendre un mauvais s. à qn** to do sb a disservice; **te faire tous tes devoirs, c'est un mauvais s. à te rendre!** it won't do you any good if I do all your homework for you!; **le congélateur me rend de grands services** I find the freezer very useful; **ton dictionnaire m'a bien rendu s.** your dictionary was very useful; **ça peut encore/toujours rendre s.** it can still/it'll always come in handy

6 (département → d'une entreprise, d'un hôpital) department; **s. des achats** purchasing department; **s. d'action commerciale** marketing department; **s. après-vente** after-sales department; **s. clientèle** ou **clients** customer service department; **s. des commandes** order department; **s. commercial** sales department; **s. commercial export** export department; **les services commerciaux** the sales department or division; **s. de (la) comptabilité** accounts department; **s. consommateurs** customer service department; **s. du contentieux** (département) legal department; (personnes) legal experts; **s. contrôle qualité, s. de contrôle de qualité** quality control department; **s. du courrier** mail room; Anciennement **S. de documentation extérieure et de contre-espionnage** French Intelligence Service; **s. d'études** research department; **s. d'étude marketing** market research department; **s. des expéditions** dispatch department; **s. export** ou **des exportations** export department; **s. du feu** Br fire brigade, Am fire department; **s. informatique** computer or IT department; Mil **S. d'information et de relations publiques des armées** = French army public information service; **s. juridique** legal department; **s. du marketing** marketing department; **S. médical d'urgence et de réanimation** = French ambulance and emergency unit; **S. national des messageries** = rail delivery service, Br ≃ Red Star®; **s. du personnel** personnel department or division; **s. de presse** (département) press office; (personnes) press officers, press office staff; **je les ai eus par le s. de presse** (livres) I got them free as review copies; (places de spectacle) they're complimentary tickets I got for reviewing purposes; **s. de publicité** advertising or publicity department; **S. régional de la police judiciaire** = regional crime unit; **s. de relation clientèle** customer service department; **s. des renseignements** information office; **s. du travail obligatoire** = compulsory labour service during the Second World War, when French workers were sent to Germany; **s. des urgences** Br casualty or A&E department, Am emergency room; **s. des ventes** sales department; **s. ventemarketing** sales and marketing department

7 Transp service; **s. de nuit des autobus** the night bus service; **s. d'été/d'hiver** summer/winter timetable; **s. non assuré le dimanche** no service on Sundays, no Sunday service; **le s. a été interrompu** the service has been suspended; Tél **services voix et données** rich voice

8 Mil **le s. de l'aide technique** ou **de la coopération** = organization providing technical assistance to developing countries; **s. actif** active service; **s. civil** = community work done by conscientious objectors instead of military service; **s. militaire** ou **national** military service; **faire son s. (militaire)** to do one's military service; **bon pour le s.** fit for military duties; Fig Hum **allez, bon/bons pour le s.!** it'll/they'll do!; **en s. commandé** on an official assignment; **tué en s. commandé** killed in action or whilst on active duty; **le s. de santé** the (army) medical corps; **le s. des transmissions** signals

9 Fin servicing; **s. de la dette extérieure** servicing the foreign debt; **assurer le s. de la dette** to service the debt

10 Rel **s. (divin)** service; **s. funèbre** funeral service

11 Admin **s. des douanes** customs service; **s. postal** ou **des postes** postal service(s); **s. public** public service; (gaz, eau, électricité) Br public utility, Am utility; **le s. public de l'audiovisuel** the publicly-owned channels (on French television)

12 (assortiment → de linge, de vaisselle) set; **un s. (de table) de 20 pièces** a 20-piece dinner set or service; **acheter un s. de six couverts en argent** to buy a six-place canteen of silver cutlery; **s. à café/à thé** coffee/tea set; Fam Hum **s. trois pièces** (sexe de l'homme) wedding tackle

13 Sport serve, service; **avoir un bon/mauvais s.** to have a good/poor serve, to serve well/badly; **Pichot au s.!, s. Pichot!** Pichot to serve!; **prendre le s. de qn** to break sb's serve

14 Naut **s. à la mer** service before the mast

15 Élec duty; **facteur de s.** duty factor

16 (d'un étalon) serving, mating

EXCLAM Suisse (je vous en prie) don't mention it!, you're welcome!

❑ **services** NMPL **1** Écon (secteur) services, service industries, tertiary sector; **biens et services** goods and services; **services aux entreprises, services du secteur tertiaire** business services

2 (collaboration) services; **se passer des services de qn** to do without sb's help; Euph (le licencier) to dispense with sb's services; **offrir ses services à qn** to offer one's services to sb, to offer to help sb out

3 Pol **services de renseignements** intelligence services; **services secrets** ou **spéciaux** secret service

4 Suisse (couverts) knives and forks (for laying at table)

❑ **en service** ADJ in service, in use ADV **mettre un appareil en s.** to put a machine into service; **cet hélicoptère/cette presse entrera en s. en mai** this helicopter will be put into service/this press will come on stream in May

❑ **service d'ordre** NM **1** (système) policing; **assurer le s. d'ordre dans un périmètre** to police a perimeter; **mettre en place un s. d'ordre dans un quartier** to establish a strong police presence in an area

2 (gendarmes) police (contingent); (syndiqués, manifestants) stewards

---

serviette [sɛrvjɛt] NF **1** (linge) **s. de bain** bath towel; **s. hygiénique** sanitary Br towel or Am napkin; **s. en papier** paper napkin; **s. de plage** beach towel; **s. (de table)** table napkin; **s. (de toilette)** towel; (pour s'essuyer les mains) (hand) towel **2** (cartable) briefcase

serviette-éponge [sɛrvjɛtepɔ̃ʒ] (pl **serviettes-éponges**) NF (terry) towel

servile [sɛrvil] ADJ **1** (personne, esprit, attitude) servile, subservient, Sout sycophantic; (manières) servile, cringing, fawning **2** (imitation, traduction) slavish **3** Vieilli (d'esclave) servile

servilement [sɛrvilmɑ̃] ADV **1** (bassement) obsequiously, subserviently **2** (sans originalité) slavishly

servilité [sɛrvilite] NF **1** (bassesse) obsequiousness, subservience **2** (manque d'originalité) slavishness

---

SERVIR [38] [sɛrvir]

VT to serve 1, 2, 4, 5, 7–9 ■ to give 3 ■ to work to the advantage of 5 ■ to pay (out) 6
USAGE ABSOLU to serve
VI to serve 3, 4 ■ to be useful 1
VPR to help oneself 1 ■ to be served 3 ■ to use 4

VT 1 (dans un magasin) to serve; **on vous sert?** (dans un café, dans une boutique) are you being

attended to?; **s. qn de** ou **en qch** to serve sb with sth, to serve sth to sb; **c'est une bonne cliente, sers-la bien** (en poids) be generous, she's a good customer; (en qualité) give her the best, she's a good customer; **c'est difficile de se faire s. ici** it's difficult to get served here; **il y a une cliente, allez la s.** here comes a customer, go and see or attend to her; Fig **tu voulais du changement, tu es** ou **te voilà servi!** you wanted some changes, now you've got more than you bargained for or now how do you like it?; **s. qn en qch** (approvisionner) to supply sb with sth; **c'est toujours lui qui me sert en huîtres** I always get my oysters from him

2 (donner → boisson, mets) to serve; (dans le verre) to pour (out); (dans l'assiette) to dish out or up, to serve up; **sers le café** pour the coffee; **puis-je te s. du poulet?** can I serve you some chicken?; **elle nous a servi un très bon cassoulet** she gave us or served up a delicious cassoulet; **le dîner est servi!** dinner's ready or served!; **Monsieur est servi** (au dîner) dinner is served, Sir; **une collation sera servie dans le hall** light refreshments will be served in the hall; **s. qch à qn** to serve sb with or to help sb to sth; **sers-moi à boire** give or pour me a drink; **faites-vous s. à boire** get the waiter to bring you a drink; **on nous a servi le petit déjeuner dans la chambre** our breakfast was brought up to or served in our room; **vous nous servirez le thé au salon** we'll take tea in the drawing room

3 Fam (raconter) to give ■; **si tu avais entendu les injures qu'il nous a servies!** you should have heard the way he insulted us! ■; **si tu n'as que cette excuse à lui s., tu ferais mieux de ne rien dire** if that's the only excuse you can give him/her or come up with, you'd better keep quiet; **ils nous servent toujours les mêmes histoires aux informations** they always dish out the same old stories on the news

4 (travailler pour → famille) to be in service with; (→ communauté, pays, parti) to serve; (→ justice) to be at the service of; (→ patrie, cause) to serve; **à la fin de la guerre, la grande bourgeoisie dut renoncer à se faire s.** by the end of the war the upper classes had to give up having servants; **j'aime bien me faire s.** I like to be waited on; **vous avez bien/mal servi votre entreprise** you have served your company well/haven't given your company good service; **s. l'intérêt public** (sujet: loi, mesure) to be in the public interest; (sujet: personne) to serve the public interest; **s. l'État** Pol to serve the state; (être fonctionnaire) to be employed by the state; **s. Dieu** to serve God, to be a servant of God; Hum **Charles Albert, pour vous s.** Charles Albert, at your service; Prov **on n'est jamais si bien servi que par soi-même** if you want something done, do it yourself

5 (aider → sujet: circonstances) to be of service to, to be or to work to the advantage of; **s. les ambitions de qn** to serve or to aid or to further sb's ambitions; **le mauvais temps l'a servi** the bad weather served him well or worked to his advantage or was on his side; **si la chance nous sert, nous réussirons** if our luck is in or if luck is on our side, we'll succeed; **sa mémoire la sert beaucoup** her memory's a great help to her; Littéraire **il m'a servi auprès du roi** he was of service to me with the king; Fam **finalement, son culot ne l'a pas servi** his cheek didn't get him anywhere in the end

6 (payer → pension, rente) to pay (out); **s. les intérêts d'une dette** to service a debt

7 Sport to serve; **s. une deuxième balle** to serve a second ball, to second-serve; **s. un ace** to serve an ace

8 (préparer → arme) to serve

9 Rel **s. la messe** to serve mass

10 Cartes (cartes) to deal (out); (joueur) to serve, to deal to; **c'est à toi de s.** it's your turn to deal; **servi!** (au poker) stick!

11 Chasse to dispatch

12 Vét & Zool (saillir) to cover, to serve

13 Suisse (utiliser) to use; **c'est un manteau que je ne sers plus** I don't wear this coat any more

USAGE ABSOLU nous ne servons plus après 23 heures we don't take orders after 11 p.m., last orders are at 11 p.m.; **servez chaud** serve hot; **démoulez juste avant de s.** turn out just before serving; **(à) s. frais/frappé** *(sur emballage)* serve cool/chilled

VI 1 *(être utile → outil, vêtement, appareil)* to be useful *or* of use, to come in handy; **garde la malle, ça peut toujours s.** keep the trunk, you might need it *or* it might come in handy one day; **le radiateur électrique peut encore s.** the electric heater can still be of use; **ça me servira pour ranger mes lettres** I can use it to put my letters in; **il a servi, ce manteau!** I got a lot of use out of this coat!; **cet argument a beaucoup servi** this argument has been put forward many times; **cela fait longtemps que cette gare ne sert plus** this station has been out of use *or* been disused for a long time; **ça n'a jamais servi** it's never been used

2 *(travailler)* **elle sert au château depuis 40 ans** she's worked as a servant *or* been in service at the castle for 40 years; **s. comme cuisinière/comme jardinier** to be in service as a cook/a gardener; **s. dans un café/dans un restaurant** *(homme)* to be a waiter in a café/restaurant; *(femme)* to be a waitress in a café/restaurant

3 *Mil* to serve; **être fier de s.** to be proud to serve (one's country); **s. dans l'artillerie** to serve in the artillery; **il a servi sous MacArthur** he served under MacArthur; **il a servi sous l'Empire/sous la République** he served under the Empire/the Republic

4 *Sport* to serve; **à toi de s.!** your serve *or* service!; **elle sert bien** *(gén)* she has a good service *or* serve; *(dans ce match)* she's serving well; **à Dancy de s.** Dancy to serve

▫ **servir à VT IND 1** *(être destiné à)* to be used for; **ça sert à quoi, cette machine?** what's this machine (used) for?; **le sonar sert à repérer les bateaux** the sonar is used to locate ships

2 *(avoir pour conséquence)* **ça ne sert à rien de lui en parler** it's useless *or* of no use talking to him/her about it; **ne pleure pas, ça ne sert à rien** don't cry, it won't make any difference; **crier ne sert à rien** there's no point in shouting; **à quoi servirait de lui en parler?** what would be the good *or* point of telling him/her?; *Fam* **à quoi ça sert que je parle si personne ne m'écoute?** what's the point *or* the use of me talking if nobody listens?; **tu vois bien que ça a servi à quelque chose de faire une pétition!** as you see, getting up a petition did serve some purpose!; **ça n'a servi qu'à le rendre encore plus furieux** it only served to make him *or* it only made him even more furious

3 *(être utile à)* **merci, ça m'a beaucoup servi** thanks, it was really useful; **ma connaissance du russe m'a servi dans mon métier** my knowledge of Russian helped me in my job; **les circonstances m'ont beaucoup servi** the circumstances were in my favour; **ce recoin sert la nuit aux clochards du quartier** this corner is used at night by the local tramps; **ça me servira à couper la pâte** I'll use it to cut the dough

▫ **servir de VT IND** *(sujet: article, appareil)* to be used as; *(sujet: personne)* to act as, to be; **le coffre me sert aussi de table** I also use the trunk as a table; **et qu'est-ce qui te sert de lit?** and what do you use for a bed?; **un vieux sac lui servait de manteau** he/she was wearing an old sack as a coat; **le proverbe qui sert d'exergue au chapitre** the proverb which heads the chapter; **les principes qui me servent de règles de conduite** the principles which dictate my conduct; **je lui ai servi d'interprète** I acted as *or* was his/her interpreter; **il lui a servi de père** he was like a father to him/her

▸**se servir VPR 1** *(emploi réfléchi) (à table, dans un magasin)* to help oneself; **servez-vous de** *ou* **en légumes** help yourself to vegetables; **elle se servit de la soupe** she helped herself to (some) soup; **je me suis servi un verre de lait** I poured myself a glass of milk; **sers-toi!** help yourself!; *Euph* **il s'est servi dans la caisse** he helped himself to (the money in) the till; **je l'ai surpris à se s. dans la caisse** I caught him with his fingers in the till

2 *(s'approvisionner)* **je me sers chez le boucher de l'avenue** I buy my meat at the butcher's on the avenue; **où te sers-tu en fromage?** where do you shop for *or* buy your cheese?

3 *Culin (emploi passif)* to be served; **ça se sert chaud ou froid** it can be served *or* you can serve it either hot or cold; **le vin rouge se sert chambré** red wine should be served at room temperature

4 se s. de qch to use sth; **il ne peut plus se s. de son bras droit** he can't use his right arm anymore; **c'est une arme dont on ne se sert plus** it's a weapon which is no longer used *or* in use; **quand tu auras fini de te s. du sèche-cheveux** when you've finished using *or* with the hairdryer; **je ne sais pas me s. de la machine à coudre** I don't know how to work *or* to use the sewing machine; **j'ai appris le chinois, mais je ne m'en sers jamais** I learnt Chinese but I never use it *or* put it to any use; **elle se sert toujours des mêmes arguments** she always uses the same old arguments; **l'opportunisme est l'art de se s. des circonstances** opportunism is the art of turning circumstances to one's own advantage; **se s. de qch comme qch** to use sth as sth; **il s'est servi de sa grippe comme prétexte** he used flu as an excuse; *Hum* **tu te sers de ta raquette comme d'une poêle à frire!** you hold *or* you handle your racket like a *Br* frying *or Am* fry pan!; **se s. de qn** to make use of *or* to use sb; **on s'est servi de vous (comme appât)!** you've been used (as bait)!

---

servite [sɛrvit] **NM** *Rel* servite

serviteur [sɛrvitœr] **NM** (male) servant; *Arch* **votre très humble s.** *(dans une lettre)* your obedient servant; *Hum* **votre (humble) s.!** your (humble) servant!, at your service!; *Littéraire Ironique* **(je suis votre) s.** I would rather not *or* no, thank you; **si vous n'êtes pas satisfait, adressez-vous à votre s.!** if you're not happy, please complain to yours truly!

servitude [sɛrvityd] **NF 1** *(soumission)* servitude **2** *(contrainte)* constraint; **se plier aux servitudes de la mode** to be a slave to fashion **3** *Jur* easement; **s. d'affouage** estovers; **s. altius non tollendi** prohibition to build above a certain height; **s. de drainage** aquaeductus; **s. non aedificandi** prohibition to build; **s. de passage** right of way; **s. de vue** easement of light

servocommande [sɛrvɔkɔmɑ̃d] **NF** servocontrol, power-assisted control, *Am* power booster

servodirection [sɛrvɔdirɛksjɔ̃] **NF** *Aut* servo steering, power steering

servofrein [sɛrvɔfrɛ̃] **NM** *Aut* servo brake, servo-assisted brake

servomécanisme [sɛrvɔmekanism] **NM** servomechanism, servosystem

servomoteur [sɛrvɔmɔtœr] **NM** servomotor

ses [se] *voir* **son**[3]

sésame [sezam] **NM 1** *Bot & Culin* sesame; **graine de s.** sesame seed; **huile de s.** sesame oil **2** *(locutions)* **S., ouvre-toi!** open, Sesame!; **le s. (ouvre-toi) de la réussite** the key to success

> *Allusion*
>
> **Sésame, ouvre-toi**
>
> In English as in French, this quotation from *Ali Baba and the Forty Thieves*, "Open, Sesame", is eternally familiar. In the tale from the *Thousand and One Nights*, it is the password used to gain admission to the thieves' den with all its treasure. In French, however, **Le sésame, ouvre-toi** is used as a noun, meaning "the key to success" and can be applied to a person, thing or act.

sésamoïde [sezamɔid] *Anat* **ADJ** sesamoid
NM sesamoid (bone)

sesbania [sɛsbanja] **NM** *Bot* sesban

sesbanie [sɛsbani] **NF** *Bot* sesban

sessile [sesil] **ADJ** *Bot & Méd* sessile

session [sesjɔ̃] **NF 1** *(réunion → d'une assemblée)* session, sitting; **pendant la s. de printemps du Parlement** during Parliament's spring session **2** *Univ* exam period; **il a été collé à la s. de juin** he failed the June exams; **elle a eu son DEUG à la deuxième s.** she passed her DEUG in the resits; **la s. de repêchage** *ou* **de rattrapage** the repeat examinations, *Br* the resits

sesterce [sɛstɛrs] **NM** *Antiq* sestertius, sesterce

SET® [ɛsəte] **NF** *Ordinat* (*abrév* **secure electronic transaction**) SET®

set [sɛt] **NM 1** *(objet)* **s. (de table)** *(individuel)* table mat; *(ensemble)* set of table mats **2** *Sport* set; **gagner en deux sets** to win in two sets; **balle de s.** set point **3** *Can (danse)* set (dance) **4** *Can (meubles)* **s. de chambre** bedroom suite; **s. de cuisine** set of kitchen furniture; **s. à dîner** dining-room suite; **s. de table** *(mobilier)* dining-room suite; *(pour mettre sous une assiette)* table mat

sétacé, -e [setase] **ADJ** *Biol* setaceous

setar [setar] **NM** *Mus* setar

setier [sətje] **NM** *Anciennement* setier

séton [setɔ̃] *Méd* **NM** seton
▫ **en séton ADJ blessure** *ou* **plaie en s.** seton wound

setter [setɛr] **NM** *(chien)* setter; **s. anglais/irlandais** English/Irish setter

seuil [sœj] **NM 1** *(dalle)* doorstep; *(entrée)* doorway, threshold; **franchir le s.** to cross the threshold; **il était debout sur le s.** he was standing in the doorway

2 *(début)* threshold, brink; **être au s. d'une ère nouvelle** to be on the brink of a new era; **être au s. de la mort** to be on the verge of death

3 *(limite)* threshold; **la population a atteint le s. critique d'un milliard** population has reached the critical level *or* threshold of one billion; *Écon* **le s. de pauvreté** the poverty line

4 *Biol & Phys* threshold; **s. d'émission** *(des gaz d'échappement)* emission limit; **s. de tolérance** threshold of tolerance

5 *Psy* threshold, *Spéc* limen

6 *Physiol* **s. absolu/différentiel** absolute/difference threshold; **s. d'élimination** renal threshold; **s. de sensibilité** threshold of sensitivity *or* of response

7 *Bourse* **s. d'annonce obligatoire** disclosure threshold; **s. d'imposition** tax threshold; **s. de performance** performance hurdle; *Com* **s. de prix** price threshold; **s. de rentabilité/de saturation** break-even/saturation point; **atteindre le s. de rentabilité** to break even, to reach break-even point

8 *Géog* sill

SEUL, SEULE [sœl]

> **ADJ** alone **1, 3, 5** ▪ on one's own **1, 3** ▪ lonely **2** ▪ only **4, 6** ▪ mere **7**
> **NM,F** only one

ADJ 1 *(sans compagnie)* alone, on one's own; **s. au monde** *ou* **sur la terre** (all) alone in the world; **laissons-le s.** let's leave him alone *or* on his own *or* by himself; **il n'est bien que s.** he prefers his own company; **enfin seuls!** alone at last!; **nous nous sommes retrouvés seuls** we found ourselves alone (together *or* with each other); **s. à s.** *(en privé)* in private, privately; **je voudrais te parler s. à s.** I'd like to talk to you in private; **se retrouver s. à s. avec qn** to find oneself alone with sb; **elle vit seule avec sa mère** she lives alone with her mother; **un homme s. a peu de chances de réussir** *(sans aucune aide)* it's unlikely that anybody could succeed on their own; **je dois d'abord y aller seule, tu entreras après** I must go in alone *or* on my own first and then you can come in; **agir s.** to act alone *or* on one's own; **tu seras s. à défendre le budget** you'll be the only one speaking for the budget; **prends donc un verre, je n'aime pas boire s.** have a drink, I don't like drinking on my own; **je préfère me promener s.** I prefer solitary walks *or* to walk on my own; **elle parle toute seule** she's talking to herself; **il a bâti sa maison tout s.** he built his house all by himself; **leur entrevue ne s'est pas passée toute seule!** their meeting didn't go smoothly!; **le dîner ne se préparera pas tout s.!** dinner isn't going to make itself!; *Fam* **laisse des pommes de terre, t'es pas tout s.!** leave some potatoes, you're not the only one eating!

2 *(abandonné, esseulé)* lonely, *Am* lonesome; **se sentir s.** to feel lonely; **on se sent si s. dans le**

ser–seu

phare it's so lonely *or* you're so cut off in the lighthouse

3 *(sans partenaire, non marié)* alone, on one's own; **un homme s.** *(non accompagné)* a man on his own; *(célibataire)* a single man, a bachelor; **elle s'est retrouvée seule à 30 ans** she found herself on her own at 30; **elle est seule avec trois enfants** she's bringing up three children on her own; **les personnes seules ne toucheront pas l'allocation** single *or* unmarried people will not be eligible for the allowance; **un club pour personnes seules** a singles club

4 *(avant le nom) (unique)* only, single, sole; **une seule pensée l'obsédait** he/she was obsessed by one idea (and one idea alone) *or* by one sole idea; **c'est l'homme d'une seule passion** he's a man with one overriding *or* ruling passion; **c'est l'homme d'une seule femme** he's a one-woman man; **une seule erreur et tout est à refaire** a single *or* one mistake and you have to start all over again; **un s. mot et tu es mort** one word and you're dead; **il n'a qu'un s. défaut** he's only got one fault; **je n'ai été en retard qu'une seule fois** I was late only once; **pas un s..../pas une seule...** not one..., not a single...; **pas un s. élève ne l'a oublié** not one pupil has forgotten him; **un s. et même.../une seule et même...** one and the same...; **il s'agit d'une seule et même personne** they are one and the same person; **un s. et unique.../une seule et unique...** only one (and one only)...; **vous avez droit à un s. et unique essai** you may have only one attempt; **je l'ai vue une seule et unique fois** I saw her only once; **le s. et unique exemplaire** the one and only copy; **le s. problème** *ou* **la seule chose, c'est que...** the only problem *or* thing is that...; **la seule fois que je l'ai vue** the only *or* one time I saw her; **c'est la seule possibilité** it's the only possibility, there's no other possibility; **c'est la seule clef qui ouvre cette porte** it's the one *or* only key that opens this door; **mon s. passe-temps** my only *or* sole *or* one hobby

5 *(sans autre chose)* **le numéro s.** *ou* **le s. numéro permet de retrouver le dossier** the number alone is enough to trace the file; **mon salaire s.** *ou* **mon s. salaire ne suffit pas à faire vivre ma famille** my salary alone is not enough to support my family; **le vase s. vaut combien?** how much is it for just the vase?; **la propriété à elle seule leur donne de quoi vivre** the property alone brings in enough for them to live on

6 *(comme adverbe)* only; **s. Pierre a refusé** only Pierre refused, Pierre was the only one to refuse; **s. l'écho lui répondit** only the echo answered him/her; **seuls les nouveaux n'ont pas été interrogés** only the newcomers weren't questioned

7 *(avant le nom) (simple)* mere; **la seule évocation de la scène lui donnait des frissons** the mere mention of *or* merely talking about the scene gave him/her goose pimples

NM,F **1** *(personne)* only one (person); **tu es la seule à qui je puisse me confier** you're the only one I can confide in; **je te crois mais je dois être la seule!** I believe you, thousands wouldn't!; **il est le s. en France qui connaisse encore cette recette** he's the only person in France who still knows this recipe; *Fam* **tu voudrais t'arrêter de travailler? t'es pas le s.!** you'd like to stop work? you're not the only one!; *Littéraire* **tout dépend des caprices d'un s.** everything hinges on one person's whims; **pas un s. (de ses camarades) n'était prêt à l'épauler** not a single one (of his/her friends) was prepared to help him/her; **pas un s. n'a survécu** not one (of them) lived; **pas une seule n'a voté pour lui** not one (of them) voted for him

2 *(animal, objet)* only one; **prends le chaton noir, c'est le s. qui me reste** have the black kitten, it's the only one I've got left

'Seul contre tous' *Noé* 'I Stand Alone'

seulement [sœlmɑ̃] ADV **1** *(uniquement)* only; **il y avait s. deux personnes** there were only two people; **j'ai dit ça s. pour rire** I only meant it as a joke; **il y va s. pour vous faire plaisir** he is only going to please you; **elle m'a donné s. les plus mûres** she gave me only *or* she only gave me the ripest ones; **je te demande s. un peu de patience** I'm only asking you to be a bit patient; **il ne s'agit pas s. d'argent** it's not only *or* just a question of money; **non s.... mais aussi, non s.... mais encore** not only... but also; **nous voulons conquérir non s. le marché européen, mais aussi** *ou* **encore des parts du marché mondial** we want not only to capture the European market, but also part of the world market (too); **non s.... mais en plus...** not only... but also...; **non s. il refuse de travailler, mais en plus il distrait les autres** not only does he refuse to do any work, but he also distracts the others

2 *(dans le temps)* **il arrive s. ce soir** he won't arrive before this evening; **il est arrivé s. ce matin** he only arrived this morning; **je viens s. de finir** I've only just finished; **le télex vient s. de partir** the telex has (only) just been sent; **et c'est s. maintenant que tu me le dis!** and you're only telling me about it now!

3 *(même)* even; **sais-tu s. de quoi tu parles?** do you even know what you're talking about?; **il est parti sans s. dire au revoir à ses hôtes** he left without even saying goodbye to his hosts

4 *(mais)* only, but; **je viendrais bien, s....** I'd like to come but... *or* only...; **je veux y aller, s. voilà, avec qui?** I'd love to go, but *or* only the problem is who with?

5 *Fam (pour renforcer)* **essaie s.!** just (you) try!

6 *Belg & Suisse (pour atténuer un impératif)* **faites s.** please do; **entrez s.** please, come in; **restez s.** why don't you stay

seulet, -ette [sœlɛ, -ɛt] ADJ *Vieilli ou Hum* (all) on one's own; **j'étais toute seulette ce jour-là** I was all by myself *or* all alone that day

sève [sɛv] NF **1** *Bot* sap; **sans s.** sapless; **plein de s.** full of sap, sappy; **s. ascendante** *ou* **brute** rising *or* ascending *or* crude sap; **s. descendante** *ou* **élaborée** falling *or* descending *or* elaborated sap **2** *(énergie)* **la s. de la jeunesse** the vigour of youth

sévère [sevɛr] ADJ **1** *(strict → personne, caractère, règlement)* strict, severe

2 *(dur → critique, verdict)* severe, harsh; **ne sois pas trop s. avec lui** don't be too hard on him

3 *(austère → visage)* stern; *(→ style, uniforme)* severe, austere, unadorned; **une coiffure trop s.** a rather severe hairstyle

4 *(important → pertes, dégâts)* severe

ADV *Fam (gravement)* something rotten; **je déprime s. en ce moment** I'm depressed something rotten at the moment

sévèrement [sevɛrmɑ̃] ADV **1** *(strictement)* strictly, severely **2** *(durement)* severely, harshly **3** *(gravement)* severely, seriously; **s. atteint** severely affected

sévérité [severite] NF **1** *(d'une personne, d'un caractère, d'un règlement)* strictness, severity **2** *(d'une critique, d'un verdict)* severity, harshness **3** *(d'un visage)* sternness; *(d'un style, d'un uniforme)* severity, austerity

sévices [sevis] NMPL **exposer qn à des s.** to expose sb to ill-treatment *or* physical cruelty; **être victime de s.** to suffer cruelty, to be ill-treated; **faire subir des s. à qn** to ill-treat sb; **s. sexuels** sexual abuse

sévillan, -e [sevijɑ̃, -an] ADJ of/from Seville

❑ **Sévillan, -e** NM,F = inhabitant of or person from Seville

Séville [sevij] NM Seville

sévir [32] [sevir] VI **1** *(personne)* **si tu continues à tricher, je vais devoir s.** if you keep on cheating, I'll have to do something about it; **s. contre la fraude fiscale** to deal ruthlessly with tax evasion

2 *(fléau, épidémie)* to rage, to be rampant *or* rife, to reign supreme; *(vandales)* to wreak havoc; **la crise qui sévit actuellement** the present crisis; *Hum* **Morin ne sévira pas longtemps comme directeur à la comptabilité** Morin won't reign long as head of accounts; **c'est une idée qui sévit encore dans les milieux économiques** unfortunately the idea still has currency among economists

sevrage [səvraʒ] NM **1** *(d'un bébé)* weaning **2** *(d'un drogué)* coming off (drugs); **quand je me suis retrouvé en prison, le s. a été brutal** when I found myself in prison, I had to come off drugs suddenly **3** *Hort* separation

sevrer [19] [səvre] VT **1** *(bébé)* to wean **2** *(drogué)* **s. qn** to get sb off drugs **3** *Fig* **s. qn de qch** to deprive sb of sth; **nous avons été sevrés de musique/de liberté** we were deprived of music/of freedom **4** *Hort* to separate *(a layer)*

sèvres [sɛvr] NM **1** *(matière)* Sèvres (china); **un service de s.** a Sèvres china service **2** *(objet)* piece of Sèvres china

sévrienne [sevrijɛn] NF *Univ* = student or ex-student of the "École Normale Supérieure de Jeunes Filles" (formerly situated in Sèvres)

sexage [sɛksaʒ] NM *(des poussins)* sexing

sexagénaire [sɛksaʒenɛr] ADJ sexagenarian; **être s.** to be in one's sixties

NMF person in his/her sixties; **un sémillant s.** a dashing sixty-year-old

sexagésimal, -e, -aux, -ales [sɛgzaʒezimal, -o] ADJ sexagesimal

sexagésime [sɛgzaʒezim] NF Sexagesima (Sunday)

sex-appeal [sɛksapil] *(pl* **sex-appeals)** NM sex appeal; **avoir du s.** to be sexy, to have sex appeal

S.Exc. *(abrév écrite* **Son Excellence)** HE

sexe [sɛks] NM **1** *(caractéristique)* sex; **enfant du s. masculin/féminin** male/female child; **le s. opposé** the opposite sex; **changer de s.** to have a sex change; **le beau s.** the fair *or* the gentle sex; *Arch* **le s.** *(les femmes)* the ladies; **le s. fort/faible** the stronger/weaker sex **2** *(parties sexuelles)* sex (organs), genitals **3 le s.** *(sexualité)* sex; **il ne pense qu'au s.** all he ever thinks about is sex

'Sexe, mensonge et vidéo' *Soderbergh* 'Sex, Lies and Videotape'

sexisme [sɛksism] NM **1** *(idéologie)* sexism **2** *(politique)* sexual discrimination; **ici nous ne faisons pas de s.** we don't believe in sexual discrimination here

sexiste [sɛksist] ADJ sexist

NMF sexist

sexologie [sɛksɔlɔʒi] NF sexology

sexologue [sɛksɔlɔg] NMF sexologist

sexothérapeute [sɛksoterapøt] NMF sex therapist

sexothérapie [sɛksɔterapi] NF sex therapy

sexpartite [sɛkspartit] ADJ *Archit* sexpartite

sex-ratio [sɛksrasjo] *(pl* **sex-ratios)** NM sex ratio

sex-shop [sɛksʃɔp] *(pl* **sex-shops)** NM sex shop

sexsomnie [sɛkssɔmni] NF *Méd* sexsomnia

sex-symbol [sɛkssɛ̃bɔl] *(pl* **sex-symbols)** NM sex symbol

sextant [sɛkstɑ̃] NM sextant

sexte [sɛkst] NF *Rel* sext

sextet [sɛkstɛt] NM *Ordinat* six-bit byte

sextidi [sɛkstidi] NM *Hist* sixth day of a ten-day period in the Republican calendar

sextillion [sɛkstiljɔ̃] NM *Br* sextillion, *Am* undecillion

sextine [sɛkstin] NF *Littérature* sestina

sexto [sɛksto] ADV sixthly, in the sixth place

sextolet [sɛkstɔlɛ] NM *Mus* sextuplet

sextuor [sɛkstɥɔr] NM sextet, sextette

sextuple [sɛkstypl] ADJ sextuple, six-fold

NM sextuple; **le s. (de)** *(quantité, prix)* six times as much (as); *(nombre)* six times as many (as); **le s. de sa valeur** six times its value; **120 est le s. de 20** 120 is six times 20

sextupler [3] [sɛkstyple] VT **s. qch** to sextuple sth, to increase sth sixfold

VI to sextuple, to increase sixfold

sextuplés, -ées [sɛkstyple] NM,F PL sextuplets

Sextus [sɛkstys] NPR *Antiq* Sextus

sexualisation [sɛksɥalizasjɔ̃] NF sexualization

sexualiser [3] [sɛksɥalize] VT to sexualize; **s. la publicité** to put sex into advertising

sexualité [sɛksɥalite] NF sexuality

sexué, -e [sɛksɥe] ADJ *(animal)* sexed; *(reproduction)* sexual

sexuel, -elle [sɛksɥɛl] ADJ *(comportement)* sexual; *(organes, éducation, hormone)* sex *(avant n)*; **l'acte s.** the sex *or* the sexual act

sexuellement [sɛksɥɛlmɑ̃] ADV sexually; **maladie s. transmissible** sexually transmitted disease

sexy [sɛksi] ADJ INV *Fam* sexy

seyait *etc voir* **seoir**

seyant, -e [sejɑ̃, -ɑ̃t] ADJ becoming; **peu s.** unbecoming; **sa nouvelle coiffure est peu seyante** his/her new hairstyle doesn't suit him/her

Seychelles [sɛʃɛl] NFPL **les (îles) S.** the Seychelles; **vivre aux S.** to live in the Seychelles; **aller aux S.** to go to the Seychelles

seychellois, -e [sɛʃelwa, -az] ADJ of/from the Seychelles
▪ NM,F = person from or inhabitant of the Seychelles

sézigue, sézig [sezig] PRON *Fam (soi)* his nibs

SF [ɛsɛf] NF *Fam (abrév* **science fiction***)* sci-fi, SF

SFI [ɛsɛfi] NF *Fin (abrév* **Société financière internationale***)* IFC

SFIO [ɛsɛfio] NF *Hist (abrév* **Section française de l'Internationale ouvrière***)* = the French Socialist Party between 1905 and 1969

sforzando [sfɔrzɑ̃do] ADV *Mus* sforzando

SFP [ɛsɛfpe] NF *TV (abrév* **Société française de production***)* = former state-owned television production company

SFS [ɛsɛfɛs] NM *TV (abrév* **service fixe par satellite***)* SFS

sfumato [sfumato] NM *Beaux-Arts* sfumato

SG [ɛsʒe] NM *Pol (abrév* **secrétaire général***)* GS

SGAO [ɛsʒeao] NM *Ordinat (abrév* **système de gestion assisté par ordinateur***)* computer-assisted management system

SGB [ɛsʒebe] NM *Med (abrév* **syndrome de Guillain-Barré***)* GBS

SGBD [ɛsʒebede] NM *Ordinat (abrév* **système de gestion de base de données***)* DBMS

SGBDR [ɛsʒebedeɛr] NM *Ordinat (abrév* **système de gestion de bases de données relationnelles***)* RDBMS

SGDG [ɛsʒedeʒe] ADJ *(abrév* **sans garantie du gouvernement***)* without government guarantee

SGEN [ɛsʒeɛn] NM *(abrév* **Syndicat général de l'Éducation nationale***)* = teachers' trade union

SGML [ɛsʒeɛmɛl] NM *Ordinat (abrév* **standard generalized mark-up language***)* SGML

sgraffite [sgrafit] NM *Beaux-Arts* sgraffitto

Shaba [ʃaba] NM Shaba

shabbat [ʃabat] NM *Rel* Shabbat

shah [ʃa] NM shah, Shah

shahnaï [ʃanaj] NM *Mus* shahnai

shake-hand [ʃɛkɑ̃d] NM INV *Arch & Hum* handshake

shaker [ʃɛkœr] NM (cocktail) shaker

shakespearien, -enne [ʃɛkspirjɛ̃, -ɛn] ADJ Shakespearean, Shakespearian

shako [ʃako] NM shako

shaktisme [ʃaktism] NM *Rel* Shaktism

shama [ʃama] NM *Orn* shama

shamisen [ʃamizɛn] NM *Mus* samisen, shamisen

shampoing [ʃɑ̃pwɛ̃] = **shampooing**

shampooiner [3] [ʃɑ̃pwine] VT to shampoo

shampooineur, -euse [ʃɑ̃pwinœr, -øz] NM,F **1** *(personne)* shampooer **2** *(machine)* carpet cleaner *or* shampooer

shampooing [ʃɑ̃pwɛ̃] NM **1** *(produit)* shampoo; **s. pour cheveux secs/gras** shampoo for dry/greasy hair; **s. crème/liquide** cream/liquid shampoo; **s. antipelliculaire** anti-dandruff shampoo; **s. aux œufs** egg shampoo; **s. sec** dry shampoo; **s. traitant** medicated shampoo; **s. pour moquettes** carpet shampoo
2 *(lavage)* shampoo; **se faire un s.** to shampoo *or* to wash one's hair; **faire un s. à qn** to shampoo sb('s hair), to wash sb's hair

shampouiner [ʃɑ̃pwine] = **shampooiner**

shampouineur, -euse [ʃɑ̃pwinœr, -øz] = **shampooineur**

shana [ʃana] NM *Mus* shahnai

Shanghai [ʃɑ̃gaj] NM Shanghai

Shannon [ʃanɔn] NM **le S.** the Shannon

shantoung, shantung [ʃɑ̃tuŋ] NM *Tex* shantung (silk)

shareware [ʃɛrwɛr] NM *Ordinat* shareware

sharia [ʃarja] = **charia**

shed [ʃɛd] NM *Constr* saw-toothed roof

Shéhérazade [ʃeerazad] = **Schéhérazade**

sheik [ʃɛk] NM sheik

shekel [ʃekɛl] NM *(monnaie)* shekel

shelf [ʃɛlf] NM *Géol* ice shelf

shéol [ʃeɔl] NM Sheol

shérardie [ʃerardi] NF *Bot* **s. des champs** field madder

shérardisation [ʃerardizasjɔ̃] NF *Métal* sherardization

shérif [ʃerif] NM **1** *(aux États-Unis)* sheriff **2** *(en Grande-Bretagne)* sheriff *(representative of the Crown)*

sherpa [ʃɛrpa] NM *(guide)* sherpa
□ **Sherpas** NMPL *(peuple)* Sherpas

sherry [ʃeri] *(pl* **sherrys** *ou* **sherries***)* NM sherry

Shetland [ʃɛtlɑ̃d] NFPL **les (îles) S.** the Shetland Islands, the Shetlands; **les (îles) S. du Sud** the South Shetland Islands; **vivre aux S.** to live in the Shetlands; **aller aux S.** to go to the Shetlands

shetland [ʃɛtlɑ̃d] NM **1** *Tex* Shetland (wool) **2** *(pullover)* Shetland jumper **3** *Zool* Shetland pony

shiatsu [ʃjatsu] NM shiatsu

shigelle [ʃigɛl] NF *Biol* shigella

shikhara [ʃikara] NM *Hist* shikhara

Shikoku [ʃikoku] NM *Géog* Shikoku

shilling [ʃiliŋ] NM shilling

shilom [ʃilɔm] NM chillum

shimmy [ʃimi] NM *Aut* shimmy

shingle [ʃiŋgl] NM *(roofing)* shingle

shinto [ʃinto], **shintoïsme** [ʃintɔism] NM Shinto, Shintoism

shintoïste [ʃintɔist] ADJ Shintoist
▪ NMF Shintoist

shipchandler [ʃipʃɑ̃dlœr] NM ship chandler

shirting [ʃœrtiŋ] NM *Tex* shirting *(material)*

shit [ʃit] NM *Fam Arg drogue* hash

shivaïsme [ʃivaism] NM *Rel* Shivaism, Sivaism

shivaïte [ʃivait] *Rel* ADJ Shivaistic, Sivaistic
▪ NMF Shivaite, Sivaite

shocking [ʃɔkiŋ] ADJ INV *Hum* shocking

shogoun [ʃɔgun] NM shogun

shogounal, -e, -aux, -ales [ʃɔgunal, -o] ADJ shogunal

shogounat [ʃɔguna] NM shogunate

shogun [ʃɔgun] = **shogoun**

shogunal, -e, -aux, -ales [ʃɔgunal, -o] = **shogounal**

shogunat [ʃɔguna] = **shogounat**

shoot [ʃut] NM **1** *Sport* shot **2** *très Fam Arg drogue (injection de drogue)* fix, shot; **se faire un s.** to shoot up, to jack up

shooté, -e [ʃute] *Fam* ADJ **1** *(drogué)* **être s.** to be a druggy *or* a junkie **2** *(fou)* crazy, *Br* barking (mad), *Am* wacko
▪ NM,F **1** *(drogué)* druggy, junkie **2** *(fou)* headcase, fruitcake

shooter [3] [ʃute] VI *Sport* to shoot
▪ VT *Sport* **s. un penalty** to take a penalty
► **se shooter** VPR *très Fam Arg drogue (drogué)* to shoot up, to jack up; **se s. à l'héroïne** to shoot *or* to mainline heroin; *Hum* **il se shoote au café** he has to have his fix of coffee

shooteuse [ʃutøz] NF *Fam Arg drogue* hype, hypo

shopping [ʃɔpiŋ] NM shopping; **faire du s.** to go shopping; **je fais toujours mon s. chez eux** I always shop there

short [ʃɔrt] NM (pair of) shorts; **être en s.** to be in *or* wearing shorts; **un petit garçon en s.** a little boy wearing shorts

shorthorn [ʃɔrtɔrn] NM shorthorn, Durham (breed)

short ton [ʃɔrttɔn] *(pl* **short tons***)* NF *(unité)* short *or* net ton, *Am* ton

short-track [ʃɔrttrak] *(pl* **short-tracks***)* NM *Sport* short-track speed skating

show [ʃo] NM **1** *(spectacle)* show; **s. aérien** air show **2** *(d'un homme politique)* performance; **le s. télévisé du Premier ministre** the Prime Minister's TV performance

show-biz [ʃobiz] NM INV *Fam* showbiz

show-business [ʃobiznɛs] NM INV show business

showroom [ʃorum] NM showroom

shrapnel, shrapnell [ʃrapnɛl] NM shrapnel

shudra [ʃudra] NM Sudra

shunt [ʃœ̃t] NM **1** *Élec* shunt; **moteur s.** shunt motor **2** *Méd* shunt

shunter [3] [ʃœ̃te] VT **1** *Élec* to shunt **2** *Fam Fig (court-circuiter → personne)* to bypass

SI [ɛsi] NM **1** *(abrév écrite* **syndicat d'initiative***)* tourist (information) office **2** *(abrév* **Système International***)* SI

si¹ [si] NM INV *Mus* B; *(chanté)* si, ti

SI² [si]

> | ADV | so 1 ▪ such 1 ▪ however 2 ▪ as 3 ▪ yes 4 |
> |---|---|
> | CONJ | if 1, 2, 5–10 ▪ what if 3 ▪ what about 4 ▪ whether 6 ▪ when 9 |

ADV **1** *(tellement → avec un adjectif attribut, un adverbe, un nom)* so; *(→ avec un adjectif épithète)* such; **elle est si belle** she's so beautiful; **il est si mignon!** he's (ever) so sweet!; **tout cela est si inattendu** all this is so unexpected; **ce n'est pas si facile que ça** it isn't as easy as (all) that; **il a un langage si vulgaire** his language is so crude; **elle est si femme** she's so womanly; **je la vois si peu** I see so little of her, I see her so rarely; **ça fait si mal!** it hurts so much!; **elle a de si beaux cheveux!** she has such beautiful hair!; *Ironique* **il est prétentieux – oh, si peu!** he's pretentious – oh isn't he just *or* I don't know what you mean!; **si... que...** so... that...; **c'est si petit qu'on ne peut le voir à l'œil nu** it's so small that it can't be seen with the naked eye; **tu n'es pas si timide que tu n'oses lui parler!** surely you're not so shy that you daren't talk to him/her!; **elle travaille si bien qu'on l'a augmentée** she works so well that she got a rise

2 *(exprimant la concession)* however; **si aimable soit-il...** however nice he may be...; **si occupé soit-il, il n'en reste pas moins aimable** however busy he is, he's always friendly; **si dur que ça puisse paraître, je ne céderai pas** however hard it may seem *or* hard as it may seem I won't give way; **si incroyable que ce soit, il nous a menti** however unbelievable it may be *or* unbelievable as it may be, he lied to us; **si vous le vexez si peu que ce soit, il fond en larmes** if you upset him even the slightest bit, he bursts into tears

3 *(dans une comparaison)* **si... que...** as... as...; **elle n'est pas si blonde que sa sœur** she's not as blonde as her sister; **il n'est pas si malin que tu le disais** he's not as sharp as you said; **il n'est pas si bête qu'il en a l'air** he's not as stupid as he seems

4 *(en réponse affirmative)* yes; **ce n'est pas fermé? – si** isn't it closed? – yes (it is); **tu ne me crois pas? – si(, je te crois)** don't you believe me? – yes (I do); **ça n'a pas d'importance – si, ça en a!** it doesn't matter – it DOES *or* yes it does!; **tu n'aimes pas ça? – si, si!** don't you like that? – oh yes I DO!; **je ne veux pas que tu me rembourses – si, si, voici ce que je te dois** I don't want you to pay me back – no, I insist, here's what I owe you; **si, si, acceptez!** DO accept!, oh but you MUST accept!; **je te dérange, si, si, je le vois bien!** I'm disturbing you, don't say I'm not, I can tell!; **tu ne l'as pas jeté tout de même? – eh si!** you didn't throw it away, did you? – yes I did!; **je n'y arriverai jamais – mais si!** I'll never manage – of course you will!; **le spectacle n'est pas gratuit – il paraît que si** the show isn't free – apparently it is; **vous n'allez pas me disqualifier? – que si!** you're not going to disqualify me, are you? – oh yes we are!; **tu ne vas quand même pas lui dire? – oh que si!** still, you're not going to tell him/her, are you? – oh yes I am!; *Littéraire* **ne voyez-vous pas un moyen de parvenir à vos fins? – si fait!** can you not see a way whereby you might succeed? – indeed I can!

CONJ **1** *(exprimant une condition)* if; **si tu veux, on y va** we'll go if you want; **si vous approchez, je crie** if you come near me I'll scream; **si tu l'as cru, tu as eu tort** if you believed him/it you were mistaken; **si vous avez joué le 4, vous avez gagné** if you played the 4 you've won; **si je m'en sors, je te revaudrai ça** if I get out of this, I'll repay you for it; **si tu ne réfléchis pas par toi-même et si** *ou* **que tu crois tout ce qu'on te dit...** if you don't think for yourself and you believe everything people tell you...; **je ne lui dirai que si tu es d'accord** I'll tell him/her only if you agree, I won't tell him/her unless you agree; **s'il est d'accord, qu'il signe** if he agrees, let him sign; **s'ils ont quelque chose à dire, qu'ils le disent** if they have something to say, let them

say it; **si tu oses...!** *(ton menaçant)* don't you dare!; **avez-vous des enfants? si oui, remplissez le cadre ci-dessous** do you have any children? if yes, fill in the box below

2 *(exprimant une hypothèse)* if; **si tu venais de bonne heure, on pourrait finir avant midi** if you came early we would be able to finish before midday; **s'il m'arrivait quelque chose, prévenez John** should anything happen to me *or* if anything should happen to me, call John; **si j'étais toi, je ne m'en vanterais pas** if I were you I wouldn't boast about it; **si j'avais le temps, je viendrais volontiers avec vous** if I had the time I'd love to come with you; **ah toi, si je ne me retenais pas...!** just count yourself lucky I'm restraining myself!; **si l'on croyait tout ce qu'on lit dans les journaux!** if we believed everything we read in the papers!; **si j'avais su, je me serais méfié** if I had known *or* had I known, I would have been more cautious; **si tu étais arrivé plus tôt, tu en aurais eu** had you arrived *or* if you'd arrived earlier, you would've got some; **s'il avait vécu** *ou Littéraire* **s'il eut vécu de notre temps, il eût été sénateur** if he had lived in our time, he would have been a senator

3 *(exprimant une éventualité)* what if; **et si tu te trompais?** what if you were wrong?

4 *(exprimant une suggestion)* what about; **et si on jouait aux cartes?** what about playing cards?

5 *(exprimant un souhait, un regret)* **ah, si j'étais plus jeune!** I wish *or* if only I were younger!; **si ça pouvait marcher!** if only it worked!; **si seulement il avait accepté!** if only he'd accepted!

6 *(dans l'interrogation indirecte)* if, whether; **dites-moi si vous venez** tell me if *or* whether you're coming; **je ne t'ai pas demandé si tu étais d'accord** I didn't ask you if *or* whether you agreed or not; **peux-tu me dire s'ils seront nombreux?** can you tell me if *or* whether there will be a lot of them?; *Littéraire* **est-ce bien lui? ou si mes yeux me trompent!** is it he, or do my eyes deceive me?

7 *(introduisant une complétive)* if, that; **je dois vérifier si tout est en ordre** I must check if *or* whether *or* that everything is in order; **ne sois pas surprise s'il a échoué** don't be surprised that *or* if he failed

8 *(introduisant une explication)* if; **si quelqu'un a le droit de se plaindre, c'est bien moi!** if anyone has reason to complain, it's me!; *Fam* **c'est de ta faute si ça a raté** it's your fault if it didn't work; **si ça ne répond pas, c'est qu'il n'est pas là** if there's no answer, it's because he's not there; **si je me répète, c'est pour que tu comprennes bien** if I'm repeating myself it's so that you understand properly *or* it's because I want you to understand properly

9 *(exprimant la répétition)* if, when; **si l'on excite le nerf, le muscle se contracte** if *or* when the nerve is stimulated, the muscle contracts; **si je prends une initiative, elle la désapprouve** whenever *or* every time I take the initiative, she disapproves (of it)

10 *(exprimant la concession, l'opposition)* **comment faire des économies si je gagne le salaire minimum?** how can I save if I'm only earning the minimum wage?; **si elle fut exigeante avec nous, elle l'était encore plus avec elle-même** if she was demanding with us, she was still more so with herself; **si son premier roman a été un succès, le second a été éreinté par la critique** though his/her first novel was a success, the second was slated by the critics

11 *(emploi exclamatif)* **tu penses s'il était déçu/heureux!** you can imagine how disappointed/happy he was!; **tu as l'intention de continuer? – si j'ai l'intention de continuer? bien sûr!** do you intend to go on? – of course I do *or* I certainly do *or* I do indeed!; **si ce n'est pas mignon à cet âge-là!** aren't they cute at that age!; **si je m'attendais à te voir ici!** well, I (certainly) didn't expect to meet you here, fancy meeting you here!

NM INV *Prov* **avec des si, on mettrait Paris en bouteille** if ifs and ands were pots and pans, there'd be no trade for tinkers

❑ **si bien que CONJ** *(de telle sorte que)* so; **elle travaille, si bien qu'elle est aujourd'hui indépendante** she works, and so she is now independent; **il ne sait pas lire une carte, si bien qu'on s'est perdus** he can't read a map, and so we got lost

❑ **si ce n'est PRÉP 1** *(pour rectifier)* if not; **ça a duré une bonne heure, si ce n'est deux** it lasted at least an hour, if not two

2 *(excepté)* apart from, except; **tout vous convient? – oui, si ce n'est le prix** is everything to your satisfaction? – yes, apart from *or* except the price; **si ce n'était sa timidité, c'est un garçon très agréable** he's a nice young man, if a little shy; **qui aurait pu écrire cela, si ce n'est elle?** who could have written that, apart from her?, who but her could have written that?

❑ **si ce n'est que CONJ** apart from the fact that, except (for the fact) that; **il n'a pas de régime, si ce n'est qu'il ne doit pas boire d'alcool** he has no special diet, except that he mustn't drink alcohol

❑ **si tant est que CONJ** provided that; **on se retrouvera à 18 heures, si tant est que l'avion arrive à l'heure** we'll meet at 6 p.m. provided (that) *or* if the plane arrives on time; **essaie, si tant est que tu en as le courage** try, if you've got the courage (that is); **si tant est qu'il nous ait** *ou* **a vus** if he saw us at all; **je l'aiderai, si tant est qu'il en ait besoin** I'll help him, that is *or* provided (that) *or* if he needs help

---

sial, -als [sjal] **NM** *Géol* sial

sialagogue [sjalagɔg] **ADJ** *Pharm* sialagogic, sialogogic

NM sialagogue, sialogogue

sialis [sjalis] **NM** *Entom* sialid

Sialkot [sialkɔt] **NM** *Géog* Sialkot

sialorrhée [sjalɔre] **NF** *Méd* sialorrhoea

Siam [sjam] **NM le S.** Siam; **au S.** in Siam

siamang [sjamɑ̃g] **NM** *Zool* siamang

siamois, -e [sjamwa, -az] **ADJ 1** *Géog* Siamese **2** *Méd* Siamese; **frères s.** (male) Siamese twins; **sœurs siamoises** (female) Siamese twins

NM 1 *(langue)* Siamese **2** *(chat)* Siamese (cat)

❑ **Siamois, -e NM,F** Siamese; **les S.** the Siamese

siau [sjo] **NM** *Can Fam* bucket■, pail■

Sibérie [siberi] **NF la S.** Siberia

sibérien, -enne [siberjɛ̃, -ɛn] **ADJ** Siberian; **il fait un froid s.** it's bitterly cold

❑ **Sibérien, -enne NM,F** Siberian

sibilance [sibilɑ̃s] **NF** *Méd* **s. respiratoire** wheezing

sibilant, -e [sibilɑ̃, -ɑ̃t] **ADJ** sibilant, hissing

sibylle [sibil] **NF** sibyl

sibyllin, -e [sibilɛ̃, -in] **ADJ 1** *Littéraire (mystérieux)* enigmatic, cryptic **2** *Myth* sibylic, sibyllic **3** *Antiq* **livres sibyllins** Sibylline Books; **oracles sibyllins** Sibylline Prophecies

sic [sik] **ADV** sic

SICAF, Sicaf [sikaf] **NF** *Bourse & Fin (abrév* **société d'investissement à capital fixe***)* closed-end investment company

sicaire [sikɛr] **NM** *Littéraire* hired assassin

SICAV, Sicav [sikav] **NF** *Bourse & Fin (abrév* **société d'investissement à capital variable***)* **1** *(société)* OEIC, *Br* ≃ unit trust, *Am* ≃ mutual fund; **S. actions** equity-based unit trust; **S. éthique** ethical investment fund; **S. mixte** split capital investment trust; **S. monétaire** money-based unit trust; **S. obligataire** bond-based unit trust **2** *(action)* = share in an open-ended investment trust

siccatif, -ive [sikatif, -iv] **ADJ** siccative

NM (paint) dryer, siccative

siccativité [sikativite] **NF** drying property

siccité [siksite] **NF** dryness

Sicile [sisil] **NF la S.** Sicily; **vivre en S.** to live in Sicily; **aller en S.** to go to Sicily

sicilien, -enne [sisiljɛ̃, -ɛn] **ADJ** Sicilian

NM *(langue)* Sicilian

❑ **Sicilien, -enne NM,F** Sicilian

❑ **sicilienne NF** *Mus* siciliano

sicle [sikl] **NM** *Hist* shekel

siclée [sikle] = **ciclée**

sicler [3] [sikle] = **cicler**

SICOB, Sicob [sikɔb] **NM** *(abrév* **Salon des industries du commerce et de l'organisation du bureau***)* **le S.** = annual information technology trade fair in Paris

SICOVAM, Sicovam [sikɔvam] **NF** *Bourse (abrév* **société interprofessionnelle pour la compensation des valeurs mobilières***)* = French central securities depository

SIDA, Sida [sida] **NM** *Méd (abrév* **syndrome immuno-déficitaire acquis***)* Aids, AIDS; **S. déclaré** full-blown Aids

side-car [sidkar, sajdkar] *(pl* **side-cars***)* **NM 1** *(habitacle)* sidecar **2** *(moto)* motorbike and sidecar

sidéen, -enne [sideɛ̃, -ɛn] **ADJ** suffering from Aids

NM,F Aids sufferer

sidéral, -e, -aux, -ales [sideral, -o] **ADJ** sidereal

sidérant, -e [siderɑ̃, -ɑ̃t] **ADJ** *Fam* staggering, amazing, stunning; **c'est s.!** it's mind-blowing!

sidération [siderasjɔ̃] **NF** sideration

sidéré, -e [sidere] **ADJ** *Fam (abasourdi)* flabbergasted, staggered

sidérer [18] [sidere] **VT 1** *Fam (abasourdir)* to stagger; **j'ai été sidéré d'apprendre cela** I was staggered to hear that, you could have knocked me down with a feather when I heard that **2** *Méd* to siderate

sidérite [siderit] **NF** *Géol & Minér* siderite

sidérographie [siderɔgrafi] **NF** siderography, steel engraving

sidérolithe, sidérolite [siderɔlit] **NF** *Vieilli* siderolite

sidérolithique, sidérolitique [siderɔlitik] **ADJ** siderolithic

sidérose [sideroz] **NF 1** *Minér* siderite **2** *Méd* siderosis

sidérostat [siderɔsta] **NM** *Astron* siderostat

sidéroxylon [siderɔksilɔ̃] **NM** *Bot* ironwood tree

sidérurgie [sideryrʒi] **NF 1** *(technique)* (iron and) steel metallurgy **2** *(industrie)* (iron and) steel industry

sidérurgique [sideryrʒik] **ADJ** (iron and) steel *(avant n)*; **usine s.** steelworks, steel factory

sidérurgiste [sideryrʒist] **NMF 1** *(ouvrier)* steel worker **2** *(industriel)* steelworks owner

sidologue [sidɔlɔg] **NMF** Aids specialist

Sidon [sidɔ̃] **NM** Sidon

siècle [sjɛkl] **NM 1** *(cent ans)* century; **l'église a plus de quatre siècles** the church is more than four centuries old; **au début du s.** at the turn of the century; **au IIème s. avant/après J.-C.** in the 2nd century BC/AD; **les écrivains du seizième s.** sixteenth-century writers

2 *(époque)* age; **vivre avec son s.** to keep up with the times, to be in tune with one's age; **c'est un homme de son s./d'un autre s.** he's a man of his time(s)/he belongs to another age *or* another century; **le s. de Périclès** the age of Pericles; *Fam* **ça fait des siècles que je ne suis pas allé à la patinoire** I haven't been to the ice rink for ages; **l'affaire du s.** the bargain of the century; **le s. des Lumières** the Enlightenment, the Age of Reason; **le Grand S., le s. de Louis XIV** the grand siècle, the age of Louis XIV; **de s. en s.** through the ages, from age to age, down the ages

3 *Rel* **le s.** worldly life, the world; **vivre dans le s.** to live in the world; **abandonner le s.** to leave one's worldly life behind; **pour les siècles des siècles** for ever and ever

sied *etc voir* **seoir**

siège [sjɛʒ] **NM 1** *(chaise → gén)* seat; *(→ de cocher)* box; **prenez donc un s.** (do) take a seat, do sit down; **une chaise à s. en cuir** a leather-seated chair; **le s. des W-C** the toilet seat; *Aut* **s. avant/arrière/baquet** front/back/bucket seat; *Aut* **s. basculant** tilting seat; *Aviat* **s. éjectable** ejector seat; **s. inclinable** reclining seat; **s. du passager** passenger seat; *Aut* **s. rehausseur** child booster seat; **s. de voiture pour bébé** baby car seat

2 *Pol* seat; **perdre/gagner des sièges** to lose/to win seats; **s. parlementaire** seat in Parliament; **s. vacant** *ou* **à pourvoir** vacant seat

3 *(centre → gén)* seat; *(→ d'un parti)* headquarters; **le s. du gouvernement** the seat of government; **localiser le s. de la douleur** to locate the seat of the pain; *Pol* **au s. du RPR** at (the) RPR headquarters; **s. administratif** administrative

headquarters; *Com* **s. d'exploitation** (company) works; **s. social** registered *or* head office; **la société a son s. (social) à Nanterre** the company's head office is in Nanterre

4 *Mil* siege; **faire le s. d'une ville, mettre le s. devant une ville** to lay siege to *or* to besiege a town; **lever le s.** to raise a siege; *Fig (partir)* to make tracks; **guerre de s.** siege warfare; **engin de s.** engine of war

5 *Méd* **l'enfant s'est présenté par le s.** it was a breech birth

6 *Jur* **le s.** the bench

7 *Rel* **s. épiscopal** (episcopal) see

8 *Tech (d'une valve)* seating

siéger [22] [sjeʒe] **VI 1** *(député)* to sit; **s. au Parlement** to have a seat *or* to sit in Parliament; **s. au tribunal** to be on the bench; **s. à un comité/au conseil d'administration** to sit on a committee/on the board

2 *(assemblée → tenir séance)* to be in session

3 *(avoir son siège)* to be based; **l'UNESCO siège à Paris** UNESCO's headquarters are in Paris

4 *(se trouver)* to be located; **chercher où siège la difficulté/l'infection** to seek to locate the difficulty/the infection

Siegfried [sigfrid] **NPR** *Myth* Siegfried

siemens [sjemɛ̃s] **NM** siemens

sien, sienne [sjɛ̃, sjɛn] *(mpl* **siens,** *fpl* **siennes) ADJ il a fait sienne cette maxime** he made this maxim his own; *Littéraire* **une sienne cousine** a cousin of his/hers

❑ **le sien, la sienne** *(mpl* **les siens,** *fpl* **les siennes) PRON** *(possesseur masculin)* his; *(possesseur féminin)* hers; *(en insistant)* his/her own; *(en se référant à un objet, à un animal)* its; **il préfère mon rôle au s.** he likes my part better than his (own); **j'ai pris ma voiture et lui la sienne** I took my car and he took his; **elle n'en a pas besoin, elle a le s.** she doesn't need it, she has her own; **chacun doit acheter la sienne** everyone must buy their own; **elle est partie avec une valise qui n'était pas la sienne** she left with a suitcase that wasn't hers *or* that didn't belong to her; **les deux siens** his/her two, the two *or* both of his/hers; *Fam* **le s. de bébé est plus intelligent!** his/her baby is more intelligent!▪ ; *Fam* **à la sienne!** *(en buvant)* let's drink to him/her!; **y mettre du s.** *(faire un effort)* to make an effort; *(être compréhensif)* to be understanding; **Jacques a encore fait des siennes** Jacques has (gone and) done it again; **ma voiture ne cesse de faire des siennes!** my car's always playing up!

❑ **les siens NMPL** one's family and friends

Sienne [sjɛn] **NM** Siena

siéra *etc voir* **seoir**

sierra [sjera] **NF** sierra; **la s. Madre** the Sierra Madre; **la s. Nevada** the Sierra Nevada

Sierra Leone [sjeraleɔn] **NF** *Géog* **la S.** Sierra Leone; **vivre en S.** to live in Sierra Leone; **aller en S.** to go to Sierra Leone

sieste [sjɛst] **NF** *(repos)* (afternoon) nap *or* rest; **faire la s.** to have *or* to take a nap (in the afternoon); **faire une petite s.** to have a little nap; **dans les pays chauds, à l'heure de la s.** in hot countries, at siesta time

sieur [sjœr] **NM 1** *Jur* **le s. Roux** Mr Roux **2** *Fam Hum* **le s. Dupond** old Dupond

sievert [sivœrt] **NM** sievert

sifflage [siflaʒ] **NM** *Vét* wheezing, whistling, roaring

sifflant, -e [siflɑ̃, -ɑ̃t] **ADJ 1** *(respiration)* hissing, whistling, wheezing **2** *Ling* sibilant

❑ **sifflante NF** *Ling* sibilant

sifflard [siflar] **NM** *Fam* (dried) sausage▪

sifflement [sifləmɑ̃] **NM 1** *(action → gén)* whistling *(UNCOUNT)*; *(→ d'un serpent, de la vapeur)* hiss, hissing *(UNCOUNT)*; *(→ d'un fouet)* swish, swishing *(UNCOUNT)*; *(→ d'un asthmatique)* wheezing *(UNCOUNT)*; **entendre le s. du vent dans les arbres** to hear the wind whistling through the trees; **les sifflements du public mécontent** the hissing *or* the booing of the angry crowd; **elle ignora les sifflements admiratifs des maçons** she ignored the builders' wolf whistles

2 *(bruit)* whistle; **s. d'oreilles** ringing in the ears

siffler [3] [sifle] **VI 1** *(serpent)* to hiss; *(oiseau)* to whistle; *Fig* **s. comme un merle** *ou* **comme un pinson** to sing like a lark

2 *(personne)* to whistle; *(gendarme, arbitre)* to blow one's whistle

3 *(respirer difficilement)* to wheeze

4 *(vent, train, bouilloire)* to whistle; **les balles sifflaient de tous côtés** bullets were whistling all around us

VT 1 *(chanson)* to whistle

2 *(chien, personne, taxi)* to whistle for; **s. les filles** to (wolf-)whistle at girls; *Fam* **je me suis fait s. (par la police)** I've been pulled up (by the police)

3 *(sujet: gendarme)* to blow one's whistle at; *(sujet: arbitre)* to whistle for; **s. la mi-temps** to blow the half-time whistle, to blow the whistle for half-time; **s. un penalty** to whistle for a penalty

4 *(orateur, pièce)* to hiss, to boo, to catcall

5 *Fam (boire)* to sink, to down, to knock back; **il a sifflé toute la bouteille** he knocked back the whole bottle

►**se siffler VPR il s'est sifflé un litre de rouge à lui tout seul** he sank *or* downed *or* knocked back a litre of red wine on his own

sifflet [siflɛ] **NM 1** *(instrument)* whistle; *Naut* pipe; **donner un coup de s.** to (blow the) whistle; **démarrez au coup de s.** start when you hear the whistle *or* when the whistle blows; *Sport* **donner le coup de s. final** to blow the final whistle; *Naut* **s. de brume** fog whistle; **s. à roulette** (pea) whistle; **s. à vapeur** steam whistle

2 *(sifflement)* whistle; **sifflets** *(huées)* hisses, catcalls; **quitter la scène sous les sifflets** to be booed off the stage

siffleur, -euse [siflœr, -øz] **ADJ** *(oiseau)* whistling; *(serpent)* hissing; **merle s.** whistling blackbird

NM,F *(à un spectacle)* catcaller, heckler

NM *Orn* wigeon, widgeon

siffleux [siflø] **NM** *Can (marmotte)* groundhog, woodchuck

sifflotement [siflɔtmɑ̃] **NM** whistling *(UNCOUNT)*

siffloter [3] [siflɔte] **VT s. qch** *(doucement)* to whistle sth to oneself; *(gaiement)* to whistle sth happily

VI *(doucement)* to whistle to oneself; *(gaiement)* to whistle away happily

sifilet [sifilɛ] **NM** *Orn* flagbird

sigillaire [siʒilɛr] **ADJ** sigillary; **anneau s.** signet ring

NF *Archéol & Bot* sigillaria

sigillé, -e [siʒile] **ADJ** *Archéol* sigillate, sigillated

sigillographie [siʒilɔgrafi] **NF** sigillography

sigillographique [siʒilɔgrafik] **ADJ** sigillographic

sigisbée [siʒizbe] **NM** *Littéraire* escort; **ses sigisbées** her gallant retinue

siglaison [siglezɔ̃] **NF** *(d'abréviations)* creation of abbreviations; *(d'acronymes)* creation of acronyms

sigle [sigl] **NM** *(abréviation)* abbreviation, initials; *(acronyme)* acronym

siglé, -e [sigle] **ADJ** designer *(avant n)*, with a designer label

sigma [sigma] **NM 1** *(lettre)* sigma **2** *Chim* sigma bond

sigmoïde [sigmɔid] **ADJ** *Anat* sigmoid

sigmoïdite [sigmɔidit] **NF** *Méd* sigmoiditis

signal, -aux [siɲal, -o] **NM 1** *(signe)* signal; **trois coups de pistolet servaient de s.** three pistol shots served as the signal; **au s., tous se levèrent** on the given signal *or* when the signal was given they all stood up; **à mon s., tous en rang!** when I give the signal, everybody line up!; **donner le s. du départ** to give the signal for departure; *Sport* to give the starting signal; **envoyer un s. de détresse** to send out a distress signal *or* an SOS

2 *(annonce)* signal; **cette loi a été le s. d'un changement de politique** this law signalled *or* was the signal for a shift in policy

3 *(dispositif)* signal; **s. acoustique** acoustic signal; **s. d'alarme/d'incendie** alarm/fire signal; **actionner le s. d'alarme** to pull the alarm cord; **s. d'alerte** warning (signal); *Tech* **s. d'appel** call *or* calling signal; **s. d'arrêt** stop sign; **s. audio** audio signal; **s. d'avertissement** *ou* **avertisseur** warning signal; *TV* **s. de chrominance** chrominance signal; **s. codé** coded signal; **s. de danger** warning sign; *Rad & TV* **s. de départ** in-cue; **s. de détresse** distress *or* SOS signal; *Rad & Tél* **s. horaire** time signal; *TV* **s. d'image** picture signal; **s. lumineux** light signal; **signaux lumineux** traffic lights; **s. optique** visible *or* visual signal; **s. radiophonique** radio signal; **signaux routiers** road signs; **s. son** audio signal; **s. sonore** tone, beep; *(pour avertir)* warning beep; *Rad & TV* **s. de sortie** out-cue; **s. stéréo** stereo signal; **s. de synchronisme** synchrony mark

4 *Naut* signal; **s. à bras** hand signal; **s. de brume** fog signal; **signaux de port** port *or* harbour signals

5 *Rail* signal; **s. à l'arrêt** signal at danger; **s. d'arrêt** danger signal; **s. avancé** *ou* **à distance** distant signal; **s. de chemin de fer** railway *or Am* railroad signal; **s. d'entrée** home signal; **s. ouvert/fermé** on/off signal

6 *Ordinat & Tél* signal; **s. analogique/numérique** analog/digital signal; **s. d'appel** call waiting function; **s. d'invitation à transmettre** proceed-to-send *or Am* start-dialing signal

7 *Écon* **s. du marché** market indicator

signalé, -e [siɲale] **ADJ** *Littéraire (remarquable)* signal, notable

signalement [siɲalmɑ̃] **NM 1** description, particulars; **donner le s. de son agresseur** to describe one's attacker **2** *Jur* reporting

signaler [3] [siɲale] **VT 1** *(faire remarquer → faute, détail)* to point out, to indicate, to draw attention to; *(→ événement important)* to draw attention to; *(→ accident, cambriolage)* to report; *(→ changement d'adresse)* to notify; **s. son changement d'adresse à qn** to notify sb of one's change of address; **la serrure est cassée, il faudra le s.** the lock's broken, we'll have to report it; **je l'ai signalé au directeur** I mentioned it to the manager; **s. qch à la police** to report sth to the police; **on signale des secousses telluriques dans la région** there are reports of earth tremors in the area; *TV & Rad* **on me signale que le ministre est à présent en ligne** I'm being told that the minister is now on air; **rien à s.** nothing to report; **à s. encore, une exposition à Beaubourg** another event worth mentioning is an exhibition at Beaubourg; **la qualité de la gravure est à s.** the quality of the print is well worth noting *or* worthy of note; **permettez-moi de vous s. qu'il est interdit de...** allow me to draw your attention to the fact that *or* to point out that it's forbidden to...; **il est déjà onze heures, je te signale!** for your information, it's already eleven o'clock!; **son ouvrage n'est signalé nulle part dans votre thèse** his/her book is not mentioned anywhere in your thesis; **c'est lui qui m'a signalé ce CD** it was he who told me about this CD

2 *(sujet: drapeau)* to signal; *(sujet: sonnerie)* to signal; *(sujet: panneau indicateur)* to signpost, to point to; **passage à niveau non signalé** unmarked level crossing; **le village n'est même pas signalé au croisement** the village is not even signposted *or* there's not even a signpost for the village at the junction; **la chapelle n'est pas signalée sur le plan** the chapel isn't indicated *or* marked *or* shown on the map; **il n'a pas signalé qu'il tournait** he didn't signal *or* indicate that he was turning

3 *(dénoter)* to indicate, to be the sign of; **c'est le symptôme qui nous signale la présence du virus** this symptom tells us that the virus is present

4 *Ordinat (marquer)* to flag up

►**se signaler VPR 1 se s. à l'attention de qn** to draw sb's attention to oneself; **je me permets de me s. à votre attention** I would like to draw your attention to my case

2 *(se distinguer)* **le mâle se signale par son long bec** the male is recognizable by its long beak; **elle ne s'est jamais signalée par quoi que ce soit** she's never done anything remarkable; **elle se signale surtout par son absence** she's remarkable mostly by her absence; **elle se signale surtout par sa bonne volonté** what sets her apart is her willingness to cooperate

signalétique [siɲaletik] **ADJ** *(plaque)* descriptive, identification *(avant n)*

NF 1 *(étude des signaux)* signaletics *(singulier)* **2** *(signalisation)* signals **3** *Mktg* signage

signaleur [siɲalœr] **NM 1** *Mil* signaller **2** *Rail* signalman

signalisateur, -trice [siɲalizatœr, -tris] ADJ signalling

signalisation [siɲalizasjɔ̃] NF **1** *(matériel → ferroviaire)* signals; **s. aérienne** markings and beacons; *Rail* **s. automatique** automatic signalling; **s. maritime** naval signalling; **s. routière** *(sur la chaussée)* (road) markings; *(panneaux et feux)* road signs and traffic lights

2 *(aménagement)* **faire la s. d'une section de route** to mark out and signpost a stretch of road; **faire la s. d'une section de voie ferrée** to put signals along a stretch of railway line; **faire la s. d'une piste aérienne** to mark out a runway

3 *Psy* signals

signalisatrice [siɲalizatris] *voir* **signalisateur**

signaliser [3] [siɲalize] VT *(route)* to provide with roadsigns and markings; *(voie ferrée)* to equip with signals; *(piste d'aéroport)* to provide with markings and beacons; **c'est bien/mal signalisé** *(route)* it's been well/badly signposted

signataire [siɲatɛr] ADJ signatory

NMF signatory; **les signataires du traité** the signatories of the treaty

NM *Belg (parafeur)* signature book

signature [siɲatyr] NF **1** *(signe)* signature; **elle a apposé sa s. au bas de la lettre** she signed the letter at the bottom of the page; **il ne manque plus que votre s. sur le contrat** it only remains for you to sign *or Sout* to put your signature to the contract; *Jur* **avoir la s.** to be an authorized signatory *(on behalf of a company)*; **pour s.** *(sur lettre)* for signature; **s. collective** joint signature; **s. électronique** *ou* **numérique** e-signature, digital signature; **s. sociale** signature of the company

2 *(marque distinctive)* signature; **cet attentat à la bombe porte leur s.** this bomb attack bears their mark *or* their imprint

3 *(artiste)* **les plus grandes signatures de la mode sont représentées dans le défilé** the biggest names in fashion are represented on the catwalk

4 *(acte)* signing; **le courrier est parti à la s.** the letters have been sent for signing *or* for signature; **vous serez payé à la s. du contrat** you'll be paid once the contract has been signed

5 *Phys* **s. spectrale** (characteristic) spectral signature; **s. thermique** thermal signature

6 *Typ* signature

7 *Mktg* **s. musicale publicitaire** (advertising) jingle

SIGNE [siɲ]

sign **1, 2, 4, 6** ▪ gesture **1** ▪ mark **3, 5**

NM **1** *(geste)* sign, gesture; **parler par signes** to communicate by sign language *or* by signs; **faire un s. à qn** to make a sign *or* to signal to sb; **faire un s. de tête à qn** *(affirmatif)* to nod to sb; *(négatif)* to shake one's head at sb; **faire un s. de la main à qn** *(pour saluer, pour attirer l'attention)* to wave to sb, to wave one's hand at sb; **agiter la main en s. d'adieu** to wave goodbye; **elle me fit approcher d'un s. du doigt** she beckoned to me to come nearer; **faire s. à qn** to signal to sb; **il m'a fait s. d'entrer** he beckoned me in; **il m'a fait s. de sortir** he signalled to me to go out; **le douanier nous a fait s. de passer** the customs officer waved us through; **fais-lui s. de se taire** signal (to) him/her to be quiet; **faire s. que oui** to nod (in agreement); **faire s. que non** *(de la tête)* to shake one's head (in refusal); *(du doigt)* to shake one's finger; *Fig* **quand vous serez à Paris, faites-moi s.** when you're in Paris, let me know; *Rel* **s. de la croix** sign of the cross; **faire un s. de croix** *ou* **le s. de la croix** to cross oneself, to make the sign of the cross

2 *(indication)* sign; **c'est un s.** *(mauvais)* that's ominous; *(bon)* that's a good sign; **c'est s. de pluie/de beau temps** it's a sign of rain/of good weather; **c'est s. de grands fléaux à venir** it portends *or* it signals evil days ahead; **c'est s. que...** it's a sign that...; **il ne nous a pas téléphoné, c'est s. que tout va bien** he hasn't phoned us, it means *or* it's a sign that everything's all right; **c'est s. qu'il est coupable** it shows *or* it's a sign that he's guilty; **c'est bon s.** it's a good sign, *Sout* it augurs well; **c'est mauvais s.** it's a bad sign, it's ominous; **il n'y a aucun s. d'amélioration** there's no sign of (any) improvement; **c'est un s. des temps/des dieux** it's a sign of the times/from the Gods; **il n'a pas donné s. de vie depuis janvier** there's been no sign of him since January; **présenter des signes d'essoufflement** to show signs of being out of breath; **donner des signes d'impatience** to give *or* to show signs of impatience; **la voiture donne des signes de fatigue** the car is beginning to show its age; **s. annonciateur** *ou* **avant-coureur** *ou* **précurseur** forerunner, portent; *Jur* **signes extérieurs de richesse** outward signs of wealth

3 *(marque)* mark; **s. cabalistique** cabalistic sign; *Admin* **signes particuliers** distinguishing marks; **signes particuliers: néant** *(sur carte d'identité, sur passeport)* distinguishing marks: none

4 *Ling, Math, Méd & Mus* sign; **s. d'égalité** *ou* **d'équivalence** equals sign; **le s. moins/plus** the minus/plus sign

5 *Typ* **s. de correction** proofreading mark *or* symbol; **s. diacritique** tittle; **s. d'insertion** insert mark; **s. de paragraphe** section mark; **s. de ponctuation** punctuation mark

6 *Astrol* **s. (du zodiaque)** sign (of the zodiac); **tu es de quel s.?** what sign are you?; **s. d'air/de terre/d'eau/de feu** air/earth/water/fire sign

▫ **en signe de** PRÉP as a sign *or* as a mark of; **en s. de respect** as a sign *or* as a mark of respect; **mettre un brassard en s. de deuil** to wear an armband as a sign of mourning

▫ **sous le signe de** PRÉP **1** *Astrol* under the sign of; **je suis né sous le s. du Cancer** I was born under the sign of Cancer

2 *Fig* **la réunion s'est tenue sous le s. de la bonne humeur** the atmosphere at the meeting was good-humoured

---

signé, -e [siɲe] ADJ *(exemplaire)* signed; *(argenterie, bijoux)* hallmarked

signer [3] [siɲe] VT **1** *(chèque, formulaire, lettre)* to sign; *(pétition)* to sign, to put one's name to; **s. son nom** to sign one's name; **c'est écrit "je reviens" et c'est signé Paul** it says "I'll be back" and it's signed Paul; **elle signe toujours "Julie B"** she always signs herself "Julie B"; **s. ici** (please) sign here; *Fig* **s. son arrêt de mort** to sign one's (own) death warrant

2 *(laisser sa marque personnelle sur)* to sign, to put one's signature to; **une veste signée Prada** a jacket by Prada, a Prada jacket; **en étranglant sa victime, il a signé son crime** by strangling his victim, he put his signature to the crime; **c'est signé!** no prizes for guessing who did that!; *Fam* **cette pagaille, c'est signé Maud!** this mess has Maud written all over it!

3 *(officialiser → contrat, traité)* to sign; **nous allons s. un accord commercial avec Dandy** we're going to sign a commercial agreement with Dandy; *Ftbl* **il a signé un contrat de deux ans avec Marseille** he's signed up with Marseilles for two years

4 *(être l'auteur de → argenterie)* to hallmark; *(→ pièce, film)* to be the author of; *(→ tableau)* to sign; *(→ ligne de vêtements)* to design; **elle a signé les meilleures chansons de l'époque** she wrote all the best songs of that era; **il a signé ses derniers tableaux d'un pseudonyme** he signed his latest pictures with a pseudonym; **c'est un bronze signé Degas** it's one of Degas' bronzes

5 *(dédicacer → livre)* to sign copies of; **elle signera son livre demain** tomorrow, she will be signing copies of her book

VI **1** *(tracer un signe)* to sign; **s. d'une croix/de son sang** to sign with a cross/in one's blood; **s. de son nom** to sign one's name

2 *(établir un acte officiel)* to sign; **nous signons demain pour la maison** we're signing (the papers) for the house tomorrow

3 *(s'exprimer par le langage des signes)* to sign

►**se signer** VPR to cross oneself, to make the sign of the cross

signet [siɲɛ] NM *(d'un livre, sur une page Web)* bookmark; *Ordinat* **créer un s. sur une page** to bookmark a page

signifiant [siɲifjɑ̃] ADJ *Littéraire (plein de sens)* meaningful

NM *Ling* **le s.** the signifier

significatif, -ive [siɲifikatif, -iv] ADJ **1** *(riche de sens → remarque, geste, symbole)* significant; *(→ regard)* significant, meaningful; **de façon significative** significantly; **il est s. que la radio n'en parle pas** it's significant that the radio's kept quiet about it

2 *(révélateur)* **s. de** revealing *or* suggestive of; **c'est très s. de son caractère/de ses goûts** it says a lot about his/her character/about his/her taste

3 *(important → écart, différence, changement)* significant

4 *Math* **chiffre s.** significant figure

signification [siɲifikasjɔ̃] NF **1** *(sens → d'un terme, d'une phrase, d'un symbole)* meaning, *Sout* signification; *(→ d'une action)* meaning; **lourd de s.** pregnant with meaning

2 *(importance → d'un événement, d'une déclaration)* import, significance; **il n'y a eu que des changements sans s.** there were only inconsequential changes; **c'est une mesure sans s. pour la suite du travail** this measure has no significance for the rest of the work

3 *Jur* (official) notification; **s. à domicile** service to an address

4 *Ling* **la s.** signifying, the signifying processes

significative [siɲifikativ] *voir* **significatif**

significativement [siɲifikativmɑ̃] ADV significantly

signifié [siɲifje] NM *Ling* **le s.** the signified

signifier [9] [siɲifje] VT **1** *(avoir tel sens → sujet: mot, symbole)* to mean, to signify; **que signifie ce dicton?** what does this saying mean?; **les statistiques ne signifient rien pour moi** figures don't mean anything *or* a thing to me; **le signe x signifie "multiplié par"** the x sign means "multiplied by"

2 *(indiquer → sujet: mimique, geste, acte)* to mean; **que signifie ce sourire?** what does that smile mean?; **il y a peu d'espoir de le retrouver, mais cela ne signifie pas que l'on va abandonner** there's little hope of finding him, but it doesn't mean *or* imply that we're giving up; **il ne m'a pas encore téléphoné – cela ne signifie rien** he hasn't phoned me yet – that doesn't mean anything; **de telles menaces ne signifient rien de sa part** such threats mean nothing coming from him

3 *(pour exprimer l'irritation)* **que signifie ceci?** what's the meaning of this?; **ils donnent de l'argent d'une main et le reprennent de l'autre, qu'est-ce que ça signifie?** what do they think they're doing giving out money with one hand and taking it back with the other?

4 *(être le signe avant-coureur de)* to mean; **les brumes matinales signifient que l'automne approche** the morning mists mean that autumn will soon be here; **cela signifierait sa ruine** that would spell ruin for him/her

5 *(impliquer)* to mean, to imply; **sa promotion signifie un surcroît de travail pour moi** his/her promotion means a lot more work for me

6 *(notifier)* to make known, to express; **s. ses intentions à qn** to make one's intentions known *or* to state one's intentions to sb; **il m'a signifié son départ/son accord** he has informed me that he is leaving/that he agrees; **il lui a signifié que...** he informed him/her that...; **j'ai écrit au ministre pour lui s. mon indignation** I've written to the Minister to express my indignation; **s. son congé à qn** to give sb his/her notice, *Sout* to give sb notice of dismissal

7 *Jur (jugement)* to notify; **s. à qn que...** to serve notice on *or* upon sb that...

signofile, signofil [siɲɔfil] NM *Suisse Aut (lampe) Br* indicator, *Am* turn signal; **mettre son s. (à droite/gauche)** *Br* to indicate (to the right/left), *Am* to put on one's turn signal (to turn right/left)

sika [sika] NM *Zool* **(cerf) s.** sika (deer)

sikh [sik] ADJ Sikh

NM Sikh

sikhisme [sikism] NM Sikhism

sil [sil] NM ochreous clay

silane [silan] NM *Chim* silane

silence [silɑ̃s] NM **1** *(absence de bruit)* silence; **un peu de s., s'il vous plaît!** *(avant un discours)*

(be) quiet please!; *(dans une bibliothèque, dans une salle d'étude)* quiet *or* silence, please!; **mais papa, je... – s.!** but Daddy, I... – (be) quiet *or* not another word (out of you)!; **demander** *ou* **réclamer le s.** to call for silence; **à son arrivée, tout le monde fit s.** there was a hush *or* everyone fell silent when he/she arrived; **garder le s.** to keep silent *or* quiet; **faire** *ou* **obtenir le s.** to make everyone keep quiet; *Cin* **s. on tourne!** quiet on the set, action!; **dans le s. de la nuit** in the still *or* in the silence of the night; **le s. de la mer** the stillness *or* the calm of the sea; **il régnait un s. de mort** it was as quiet *or* silent as the grave; **s. radio** radio silence; *Fam* **j'ai reçu quelques cartes postales peu après son départ, mais depuis, c'est le s. radio** I got a few postcards shortly after he/she left, but since then there's been total silence *or* I haven't heard a word

2 *(secret)* **acheter le s. de qn** to buy sb's silence, to pay sb to keep quiet; **garder le s. sur qch** to keep quiet about sth; **gardez le s. là-dessus** keep this very quiet; **imposer le s. à qn** to shut sb up; **passer qch sous s.** to pass over sth in silence, to keep quiet about sth

3 *(lacune)* **le s. de la loi en la matière** the absence of legislation regarding this matter

4 *(pause)* silence; **une lettre vint enfin rompre son s.** a letter came, thus breaking his/her silence; **après 15 ans de s., elle publia un roman** after a 15-year silence *or* break, she published a novel; **son récit était entrecoupé de nombreux silences** his/her story was interrupted by numerous pauses

5 *Mus* rest

6 *Biol & Méd* **mise sous s. des gènes** gene silencing

❑ **en silence** ADV *(se regarder)* in silence, silently; *(se déplacer)* silently, noiselessly; *(souffrir)* in silence, uncomplainingly

silencieuse [silɑ̃sjøz] *voir* **silencieux**

silencieusement [silɑ̃sjøzmɑ̃] ADV *(se regarder)* silently, in silence; *(se déplacer)* in silence, noiselessly; *(souffrir)* in silence, uncomplainingly

silencieux, -euse [silɑ̃sjø, -øz] ADJ **1** *(où règne le calme → trajet, repas, salle)* quiet, silent; **après la dispute, le reste de la soirée fut s.** after the quarrel the rest of the evening passed in silence

2 *(qui ne fait pas de bruit → pendule, voiture)* quiet, noiseless; *(→ mouvement)* noiseless; *(→ pas)* silent

3 *(qui ne parle pas)* silent, quiet; *(taciturne)* quiet, silent, *Péj* uncommunicative; **la majorité silencieuse** the silent majority

NM **1** *(arme)* silencer

2 *Aut Br* silencer, *Am* muffler

3 *Rad & Tél (pour supprimer les bruits de fond)* squelch

Silène [silɛn] NPR *Myth* Silenus

silène [silɛn] NM *Bot* campion; **s. acaule** bladder campion; **s. maritime** sea campion

Silentbloc® [silɛ̃ntblɔk] NM *Tech* Silentbloc®

siler [3] [sile] VI *Can* **1** *(siffler)* to whistle; *Fig* **j'ai les oreilles qui me silent** my ears are ringing **2** *(gémir)* to whine **3** *(respirer avec difficulté)* to wheeze

Silésie [silezi] NF **la S.** Silesia; **la basse/la haute S.** Lower/Upper Silesia

silex [silɛks] NM **1** *Géol* flint, flintstone **2** *Archéol (outil, arme)* flint

silhouette [silwɛt] NF **1** *(ligne générale → du corps)* figure; *(→ d'un véhicule)* lines; **elle a une jolie s.** she's got a nice *or* a good figure

2 *(contours)* silhouette, outline; *(forme indistincte)* (vague) form; **leurs silhouettes se détachaient sur le soleil couchant** they were silhouetted against the sunset; **je vis une s. dans le brouillard/derrière les rideaux** I saw a shape in the fog/behind the curtains

3 *Mil* **s. de tir** figure *or* silhouette target

4 *Beaux-Arts* silhouette

silhouetter [4] [silwete] VT *Beaux-Arts (dessiner les contours de)* to outline; *(découper dans du papier)* to silhouette

▸ **se silhouetter** VPR *Littéraire* **se s. sur** to stand out *or* to be silhouetted against

silicagel [silikaʒɛl] NM *Chim* silica gel

silicate [silikat] NM *Chim* silicate

silicaté, -e [silikate] ADJ *Chim* silicated

silice [silis] NF *Chim* silica; **verre de s., s. fondue** *ou* **vitreuse** silica glass, vitreous silica

siliceux, -euse [silisø, -øz] ADJ *Chim* siliceous; **roches siliceuses** siliceous deposits

silicicole [silisikɔl] ADJ *Bot* silicicolous

silicique [silisik] ADJ *Chim* silicic

silicium [silisjɔm] NM *Chim* silicon

siliciure [silisjyr] NM *Chim* silicide

silicone [silikon] NF *Chim* silicone

NM *(pour la cosmétologie, pour les prothèses)* silicone

siliconer [3] [silikɔne] VT **1** *(matériau)* to coat with silicone **2** *(poitrine)* **un mannequin siliconé** a model with silicone implants; **elle a la poitrine siliconée** she has silicone implants

silicose [silikoz] NF *Méd* silicosis

silicosé, -e [silikoze] *Méd* ADJ silicotic

NM,F silicosis sufferer

silicotique [silikɔtik] ADJ *Méd* silicotic

silicule [silikyl] NF *Bot* silicle, silicula, silicule

silionne [siljɔn] NF *Tech* silionne

silique [silik] NF *Bot* siliqua, silique

sillage [sijaʒ] NM **1** *Naut (trace)* wake; *(remous)* wash

2 *(d'une personne, d'un véhicule)* wake; **il y avait toujours deux ou trois gamins dans son s.** she always had two or three kids following her around; **les troupes n'avaient laissé que désolation dans leur s.** the troops had left total devastation in their wake; **cette mesure entraîne dans son s. une refonte de nos structures hospitalières** this decision brings with it *or* entails a restructuring of our hospital system; *aussi Fig* **marcher dans le s. de qn** to follow in sb's footsteps *or* in sb's wake

3 *Aviat (trace)* (vapour) trail; *(remous)* wake; **efffet de s.** wake effect

4 *Phys* wake

sillet [sijɛ] NM *Mus* nut

sillimanite [silimanit] NF *Minér* sillimanite

sillon [sijɔ̃] NM **1** *Agr (de gros labours)* furrow; *(petite rigole)* drill; *Littéraire* **sillons** *(champs)* fields, country; *Fig* **creuser** *ou* **tracer son s.** to plough one's furrow **2** *Littéraire (ride)* furrow **3** *(d'un disque)* groove **4** *(traînée)* **s. de lumière/de feu** *(d'une fusée)* streak of light/of fire **5** *Anat (du cerveau)* fissure, sulcus; **s. fessier** anal cleft

sillonner [3] [sijɔne] VT **1** *(parcourir → sujet: canaux, voies)* to cross, to criss-cross; **des éclairs sillonnaient le ciel** flashes of lightning were streaking the sky; **j'ai sillonné la Bretagne** I've visited every corner of *or* I've travelled the length and breadth of Brittany; **il sillonnait les mers depuis 20 ans** he'd been sailing the seas for 20 years; **le pays est sillonné de rivières** the country is criss-crossed by rivers

2 *(marquer)* to furrow, to groove; **son visage sillonné de rides** his/her furrowed *or* deeply lined face; **les torrents sillonnent le flanc de la montagne** the mountainside is grooved *or* scored by rushing streams

3 *Agr* to furrow

silo [silo] NM **1** *Agr* silo; **mettre en s.** to silo; **s. à blé** grain silo; **s. à ciment** cement silo **2** *Mil* **s. (de lancement)** (launching) silo

silo-cuve [silokyv] *(pl* **silos-cuves)** NM *Agr* pit silo

silo-meule [silomøl] *(pl* **silos-meules)** NM *Agr* stack silo

silotage [silɔtaʒ] NM ensilage

silo-tranchée [silotrɑ̃ʃe] *(pl* **silos-tranchées)** NM *Agr* trench silo

siloxane [silɔksan] NM *Chim* siloxane

silphe [silf] NM *Entom* carrion beetle

silt [silt] NM silt

silure [silyr] NM *Ich* silurid; **s. électrique** electric catfish

silurien, -enne [silyrjɛ̃, -ɛn] ADJ Silurian

NM Silurian

siluriforme [silyrifɔrm] NM *Ich* siluroid fish

SIM [ɛsiɛm] NM **1** *Mktg (abrév* **système d'information marketing)** MIS **2** *Tél (abrév* **subscriber identity module)** SIM; **carte S.** *(pour téléphone portable)* SIM card

sima [sima] NM *Anciennement Géol* sima

simagrées [simagre] NFPL **faire des s.** *(minauder)* to simper; *(faire des chichis)* to put on airs; **arrête tes s. et prends-le!** stop pretending you don't want it!

simarre [simar] NF **1** *Hist (vêtement long)* robe **2** *(soutane)* (bishop's) chimere **3** *Arch* magistrate's cassock *(as worn under gown)*; *Littéraire* **ambitionner la s.** to aim at high judicial office

simaroube [simarub], **simaruba** [simaruba] NM *Bot* simaruba, simarouba; *Pharm* **écorce de s.** simaruba *or* simarouba bark

simbleau, -x [sɛ̃blo] NM = cord for drawing circles

Siméon [simeɔ̃] NPR *Bible* Simeon

simien, -enne [simjɛ̃, -ɛn] *Zool* ADJ simian

NM simian, ape

simiesque [simjɛsk] ADJ monkey-like, ape-like, *Spéc* simian

similaire [similɛr] ADJ similar (**à** to)

similairement [similɛrmɑ̃] ADV similarly

similarité [similarite] NF similarity, likeness

simili [simili] PRÉF **s. marbre** imitation marble; **s. pierre** artificial stone

NM **1** *(imitation)* **c'est du s.** it's artificial *or* an imitation; **bijoux en s.** imitation *or* costume jewellery **2** *(cliché)* half-tone engraving

NF *(procédé)* half-tone process

similibois [similibwa] NM imitation wood

similicuir [similikɥir] NM imitation leather, leatherette

simili-écaille [similiekaj] NM INV imitation tortoiseshell

similigravure [similigravyr] NF **1** *(procédé)* half-tone process **2** *(cliché)* half-tone engraving

similisage [similizaʒ] NM *Tex* schreinering

similiser [3] [similize] VT *Tex* to schreiner

similiste [similist] NMF half-tone engraver

similitude [similityd] NF **1** *(d'idées, de style)* similarity, *Sout* similitude; *(de personnes)* similarity, likeness; **leur s.** the likeness between them **2** *Math* similarity

similor [similɔr] NM pinchbeck, imitation gold

SIMM [sim] NM *Ordinat (abrév* **single in-line memory module)** SIMM

simoniaque [simɔnjak] *Rel* ADJ simoniacal

NM simoniac, simonist

simonie [simɔni] NF *Rel* simony

simoun [simun] NM simoon

simple [sɛ̃pl] ADJ **1** *(facile → exercice, système)* simple, straightforward, easy; **pour aller à Paris, c'est tout ce qu'il y a de plus s.** the way to Paris is very straightforward *or* extremely simple; **ce n'est pas s. d'élever des enfants!** bringing up children isn't easy!; **c'est très s. à utiliser** it's very easy *or* simple to use; **c'est bien s., il accepte ou on part** it's quite simple, either he accepts or we go; **c'est s. comme bonjour** it's as easy as ABC *or* as pie

2 *(avant le nom) (avec une valeur restrictive)* mere, simple; **c'est une s. question d'argent** it's simply *or* only a matter of money; **pour la s. raison que...** for the simple reason that...; **réduit à sa plus s. expression** reduced to its simplest form; **il a été arrêté sur un s. soupçon** he was arrested on mere suspicion; **vous aurez une démonstration gratuite sur s. appel** all you need do is (to) *or* simply phone this number for a free demonstration; **ce n'est qu'une s. formalité** it's merely a *or* it's a mere formality; **ça s'ouvre d'une s. pression du doigt** it opens simply by pressing on it; **d'un s. bond, il franchit le fossé** with one leap, he was on the other side of the ditch; **ce n'est qu'un s. employé de bureau** he's just an ordinary office worker; **un s. particulier** an ordinary citizen; **s. soldat** private (soldier); **s. matelot** ordinary seaman

3 *(non raffiné → gens)* unaffected, uncomplicated; *(→ objets, nourriture, goûts)* plain, simple; **ils ont des goûts très simples** they have very simple tastes; *Hum* **elle est apparue dans le plus s. appareil** she appeared in her birthday suit

4 *(ingénu)* simple, simple-minded

5 *(non composé → mot, élément, fleur, fracture)* simple; *(→ chaînette, nœud)* single; **un cornet s. ou double?** *(de glace)* one scoop or two?

6 *Chim* **liaison s.** single bond

NM **1** *(ce qui est facile)* **aller du s. au complexe** to progress from the simple to the complex

2 *(proportion)* **augmenter du s. au double** to double; **les prix varient du s. au double** prices can double; **passer du s. au triple** to triple

3 *Sport* singles; **jouer en s.** to play a singles match; **s. messieurs/dames** men's/ladies' singles
□ **simples** NMPL medicinal herbs *or* plants
□ **simple d'esprit** NM simpleton, halfwit ADJ **il est un peu s. d'esprit** he's a bit simple

simplement [sɛ̃pləmɑ̃] ADV **1** *(seulement)* simply, merely, just; **je l'ai s. touchée et s'est mise à crier** I simply *or* I merely touched her and she started to scream; **je voulais s. te dire que...** I simply *or* just *or* merely wanted to tell you that...; **je te demande s. de me dire la vérité** I'm simply *or* just asking you to tell me the truth **2** *(sans apprêt → parler)* unaffectedly, simply; *(→ s'habiller)* simply, plainly; *(→ vivre)* simply; **elle nous a reçus très s.** she received us simply *or* without ceremony; **la chambre est décorée très s.** the room is plainly decorated; **nous avons déjeuné très s.** we had a very simple *or* plain lunch **3** *(clairement)* **expliquer qch s.** to explain sth in simple *or* straightforward terms

simplesse [sɛ̃plɛs] NF *Arch & Littéraire* simpleness, artlessness

simplet, -ette [sɛ̃plɛ, -ɛt] ADJ **1** *(personne → peu intelligente)* simple, simple-minded; *(→ ingénue)* naive; **elle est un peu simplette** she's a bit simple **2** *(sans finesse → jugement, réponse, scénario)* simplistic, black-and-white

simplex [sɛ̃plɛks] NM *Ordinat & Tél* simplex

simplexe [sɛ̃plɛks] NM *Math* simplex

simplicité [sɛ̃plisite] NF **1** *(facilité)* simplicity, straightforwardness; **l'exercice est d'une s. enfantine** the exercise is child's play; **l'opération est d'une grande s.** the operation is very straightforward; **cette machine est la s. même** this machine is simplicity itself **2** *(de vêtements, d'un décor, d'un repas)* plainness, simplicity; **avec s.** simply, plainly **3** *(naturel)* unaffectedness, lack of affectation; **j'aimais sa s.** his/her lack of affectation appealed to me; **elle manque de s.** she is pretentious *or* affected **4** *(naïveté)* naivety; **il fallait être d'une grande s. pour y croire** you would have to have been very naive to believe it
□ **en toute simplicité** ADV **nous avons dîné en toute s.** we had a very simple dinner; **elle l'a avoué en toute s.** she admitted it without making a big thing of it

simplifiable [sɛ̃plifjabl] ADJ **1** *Math* reducible **2** *(procédé)* which can be simplified *or* made simpler

simplificateur, -trice [sɛ̃plifikatœr, -tris] ADJ simplifying

simplification [sɛ̃plifikasjɔ̃] NF **1** *Math* reduction **2** *(d'un système)* simplification, simplifying

simplificatrice [sɛ̃plifikatris] *voir* **simplificateur**

simplifier [9] [sɛ̃plifje] VT **1** *(procédé)* to simplify; *(explication)* to simplify, to make simpler; **en simplifiant le texte à outrance** *ou* **à l'excès** by oversimplifying the text; **si tu me disais la vérité, cela simplifierait les choses** it would make things easier if you told me the truth; **cela me simplifie la vie** that simplifies my life, that makes life *or* things easier for me **2** *Math (fraction)* to reduce, to simplify; *(équation)* to simplify
▸ **se simplifier** VPR **1** to become simplified *or* simpler; **avec l'automatisation, les procédés de fabrication se simplifient** automation has simplified manufacturing processes **2** to simplify; **elle se simplifie l'existence en refusant de prendre des responsabilités** she makes her life simpler by refusing to take any responsibility

simplisme [sɛ̃plism] NM simplism

simplissime [sɛ̃plisim] ADJ dead easy

simpliste [sɛ̃plist] ADJ *(théorie, explication)* simplistic, oversimple; *(esprit)* simplistic, superficial
NMF simplistic person

Simplon [sɛ̃plɔ̃] NM **le S.** the Simplon Pass

simulacre [simylakr] NM **1** *(par jeu, comme méthode)* imitation **2** *(pour tromper)* **un s. de négociations** mock *or* sham negotiations; **un s. de résistance** a (poor) show of resistance; **ce n'était qu'un s. de procès** it was a mockery of a trial

simulateur, -trice [simylatœr, -tris] NM,F **1** *(imitateur)* simulator; *Hum* **s., va!** you're such a fraud! **2** *(faux malade)* malingerer
NM *Aviat, Ordinat & Mil* simulator; **s. de réalité virtuelle** virtual reality simulator; **s. de vol** flight simulator

simulation [simylasjɔ̃] NF **1** *(d'un sentiment)* feigning, faking, simulation; *(d'une maladie)* malingering **2** *(de bataille, de vol etc)* simulation; **s. d'entretien d'embauche** practice job interview; **s. sur ordinateur** computer simulation **3** *Jur* nondisclosure *or* concealment of contract

simulatrice [simylatris] *voir* **simulateur**

simulcasting [simylkastiŋ] NM *Rad & TV* simulcasting

simulé, -e [simyle] ADJ **1** *(pitié, douleur)* faked, feigned **2** *Aviat, Ordinat & Mil* simulated **3** *Jur* **acte s.** bogus deed *(concealing a contract)*

simuler [3] [simyle] VT **1** *(feindre → douleur, ivresse, folie)* to feign; **s. l'innocence** to put on an air *or* a show of innocence; **s. la folie** to pretend to be mad, to feign madness; **s. la cécité** to feign blindness; **s. la maladie** *(appelé, employé)* to malinger; *(enfant)* to pretend to be ill; **l'animal simule la mort** the animal is playing dead **2** *(imiter)* **la porte simule un rideau** the door is made to look like a curtain **3** *Mil & Tech* to simulate **4** *Jur (acte)* to deceive *(by nondisclosure of a contract)*
USAGE ABSOLU *(feindre)* **je ne pense pas qu'elle simule** I don't think she's pretending

simulie [simyli] NF *Entom* simulium

simultané, -e [simyltane] ADJ simultaneous
□ **simultanée** NF *Échecs* simultaneous game (of chess)

simultanéisme [simyltaneism] NM *Littérature* use of simultaneous narratives

simultanéité [simyltaneite] NF simultaneity, simultaneousness

simultanément [simyltanemɑ̃] ADV simultaneously

Sinaï [sinaj] NM **le S.** Sinai; **le mont S.** Mount Sinai

sinanthrope [sinɑ̃trɔp] NM Sinanthropus, Peking Man

sinapisé, -e [sinapize] ADJ **bain/cataplasme s.** mustard bath/poultice *or* plaster

sinapisme [sinapism] NM sinapism, mustard plaster

Sinbad [sinbad] NPR **S. le marin** Sinbad the Sailor

sincère [sɛ̃sɛr] ADJ **1** *(amitié, chagrin, remords)* sincere, genuine, true; *(personne)* sincere, genuine; *(réponse)* honest, sincere; **tu n'es pas s. quand tu dis cela** you're being insincere in saying that; **être s. avec soi-même** to be honest with oneself **2** *(dans les formules de politesse)* **nos vœux les plus sincères** our very best wishes; **je vous présente mes sincères condoléances** please accept my sincere *or* my heartfelt condolences; **veuillez agréer mes sincères salutations** *(à quelqu'un dont on connaît le nom)* Br yours sincerely, Am sincerely (yours); *(à quelqu'un dont on ne connaît pas le nom)* Br yours faithfully, Am sincerely (yours) **3** *Jur (acte)* genuine, authentic

sincèrement [sɛ̃sɛrmɑ̃] ADV **1** *(avec sincérité)* sincerely, genuinely, truly; **je crois s. en son repentir** I genuinely believe he/she has repented **2** *(à vrai dire)* honestly, frankly; **s., tu me déçois** honestly, you really disappoint me; **s., ça ne valait pas le coup** to tell you the truth, it wasn't worth it

sincérité [sɛ̃serite] NF **1** *(franchise)* sincerity; **je ne remets pas en cause sa s.** I'm not saying he/she wasn't sincere *or* genuine; **en toute s.** in all sincerity, to be quite honest; **manque de s.** lack of sincerity, disingenuousness **2** *(authenticité → d'une amitié, de remords)* genuineness; *(→ d'une réponse)* honesty **3** *(absence de truquage → d'une élection, d'un document)* honesty, genuineness

sincipital, -e, -aux, -ales [sɛ̃sipital, -o] ADJ *Anat* sincipital

sinciput [sɛ̃sipyt] NM *Anat* sinciput, calvarium

sinécure [sinekyr] NF sinecure; *Fam* **ce n'est pas une s.** it's no picnic

sine die [sinedje] ADV sine die; **remettre qch s.** to postpone sth indefinitely

sine qua non [sinekwanɔn] ADJ INV **condition s.** essential condition; **c'est la condition s. de ma participation** it's an essential condition if I am to take part at all

singalette [sɛ̃galɛt] NF *Tex* mull

Singapour [sɛ̃gapur] NF Singapore; **vivre à S.** to live in Singapore; **aller à S.** to go to Singapore

singapourien, -enne [sɛ̃gapurjɛ̃, -ɛn] ADJ Singaporean
□ **Singapourien, -enne** NM,F Singaporean

singe [sɛ̃ʒ] NM **1** *Zool (à longue queue)* monkey; *(sans queue)* ape; **les grands singes** the (great) apes; **s. araignée** spider monkey; **s. capucin** capuchin monkey; **s. hurleur** howler monkey; **s. laineux** woolly monkey; **s. de nuit** night *or* owl monkey; **s. patas, s. pleureur** patas *or* red *or* dancing monkey; **s. rhésus** rhesus monkey; **s. rouge** patas *or* red *or* dancing monkey; **s. vert** green monkey; **le s. imite l'homme!** copycat! **2** *(imitateur)* mimic; **quel s.!** isn't he a little comic!; **faire le s.** *(faire des grimaces)* to make faces; *(faire des pitreries)* to clown *or* to monkey around **3** *très Fam (chef)* boss▪ **4** *très Fam (bœuf en conserve)* corned beef▪

singer [17] [sɛ̃ʒe] VT **1** *(personne)* to ape, to mimic **2** *(manières distinguées, passion)* to feign, to fake

singerie [sɛ̃ʒri] NF *(section d'un zoo)* monkey *or* ape house
□ **singeries** NFPL *(tours et grimaces)* clowning; *(d'un clown)* antics; *Péj (manières affectées)* affectedness, airs and graces; **faire des singeries** to clown *or* to monkey around

single [siŋgəl] NM **1** *(disque)* single **2** *Rail* single sleeper **3** *Sport* singles (game) **4** *(dans un hôtel)* single (room)

singlet [sɛ̃glɛ] NM *Belg* singlet

singleton [sɛ̃glətɔ̃] NM **1** *Cartes* singleton **2** *Math* singleton (set)

singulariser [3] [sɛ̃gylarize] VT **s. qn** to make sb conspicuous, to set sb apart; **s. qn de** to set sb apart from, to make sb stand out from
▸ **se singulariser** VPR **1** *(se faire remarquer)* to make oneself conspicuous; **il faut toujours que tu te singularises!** you always have to be different from everyone else, don't you? **2** *(être remarquable)* **il s'est singularisé par son courage** he distinguished himself by his courage

singularité [sɛ̃gylarite] NF **1** *(étrangeté → d'un comportement, d'idées, d'une tenue)* oddness, strangeness **2** *(trait distinctif → d'une personne)* peculiarity; *(→ d'un système)* distinctive feature, peculiarity; **c'est une des singularités de son caractère** it's one of the strange *or* odd things about him/her; **la boîte présentait cette s. de s'ouvrir par l'arrière** the box was unusual in that it opened at the back **3** *Littéraire (unicité)* uniqueness **4** *Math & Phys* singularity

singulier, -ère [sɛ̃gylje, -ɛr] ADJ **1** *(étrange → comportement, idées)* odd, strange, *Sout* singular; **je trouve s. que...** I find it odd *or* strange that... **2** *(remarquable → courage, beauté)* remarkable, rare, unique **3** *Ling* singular **4** *(d'un seul)* singular, single
NM *Gram* singular; **au s.** in the singular

singulièrement [sɛ̃gyljɛrmɑ̃] ADV **1** *(beaucoup)* very much; **il m'a s. déçu** I was extremely disappointed in him; **s. beau** extremely *or* remarkably handsome; **s. réussi** hugely successful **2** *(étrangement)* oddly, in a strange *or* peculiar way **3** *(notamment)* especially, particularly

sinisant, -e [sinizɑ̃, -ɑ̃t] NM,F sinologue, sinologist

sinisation [sinizasjɔ̃] NF sinicization, sinification

siniser [3] [sinize] VT to sinicize, to sinify

sinistralité [sinistralite] NF *Assur* number of claims

sinistre [sinistr] ADJ **1** *(inquiétant → lieu, bruit)* sinister; *(→ personnage)* sinister, evil-looking; **un s. présage** an ill omen; **c'est s. ici!** it's spooky here!

2 (*triste* → *personne, soirée*) dismal; (→ *paysage*) bleak; *Fam* **comment c'était, Noël avec tes parents? – s.!** how was Christmas with your parents? – hideous!

3 (*avant le nom*) (*en intensif*) **c'est un s. imbécile/une s. canaille** he's a total idiot/crook

NM 1 (*incendie*) fire, blaze; (*inondation, séisme*) disaster; **les pompiers se sont rendus maîtres du s.** the firemen have the fire under control

2 *Assur* (*incendie*) fire; (*accident de la circulation*) accident; **déclarer un s.** to put in a claim; **évaluer un s.** to estimate a claim

sinistré, -e [sinistre] ADJ (*bâtiment, village, quartier* → *gén*) damaged, stricken; (→ *brûlé*) burnt-out; (→ *bombardé*) bombed-out; (→ *inondé*) flooded; **la ville est sinistrée** (*après un tremblement de terre*) the town has been devastated by the earthquake; **les personnes sinistrées** the disaster victims; (*après des inondations*) the flood victims; **population sinistrée** stricken population; *Admin* **région** *ou* **zone (déclarée) sinistrée** disaster area

NM,F disaster victim

sinistrement [sinistrəmɑ̃] ADV sinisterly, in a sinister way; **rire s.** to give a sinister laugh

sinistrose [sinistroz] NF **1** *Psy* post-traumatic stress disorder **2** *Fam* (*systematic*) pessimism■; **le pays est en proie à la s.** the country's morale is very low

sinité [sinite] NF Chinese character

Sinn Féin [sinfɛjn] NM Sinn Féin

sinn-feiner [sinfɛjnœr] (*pl* **sinn-feiners**) NMF Sinn Féiner

sinoc [sinɔk] = **sinoque**

sino-japonais, -e [sinoʒaponɛ, -ɛz] (*mpl* **sino-japonais**, *fpl* **sino-japonaises**) ADJ Sino-Japanese

sinologie [sinɔlɔʒi] NF sinology

sinologique [sinɔlɔʒik] ADJ sinological

sinologue [sinɔlɔg] NMF specialist in Chinese studies, sinologist

sinon [sinɔ̃] CONJ **1** (*sans cela*) otherwise, or else; **un jus d'orange, s. rien** an orange juice, otherwise nothing; **je ne peux pas te joindre à vous, s. je l'aurais fait avec plaisir** I can't join you, much as I would have liked to; **j'essaierai d'être à l'heure, s. partez sans moi** I'll try to be on time, but if I'm not go without me; **tiens-toi tranquille, s. je me fâche** keep still, or else *or* otherwise I'll get angry; **tais-toi, s....!** be quiet or else...!

2 (*si ce n'est*) if not; **elle était, s. jolie, du moins gracieuse** she was, if not pretty, at least graceful; **faites-le, s. avec plaisir, du moins de meilleure grâce** if you can't do it with pleasure, at least do it with better grace; **elle l'a, s. aimé, du moins apprécié** although *or* if she didn't like it she did at least appreciate it; **elle est une des rares, s. la seule, à y avoir cru** she was one of the few, if not the only one, who believed it

3 (*excepté*) except, other than; **que faire, s. attendre?** what can we do other than *or* except wait?

□ **sinon que** CONJ except that; **je ne sais rien, s. qu'il est parti** all I know is that he's left

sinople [sinɔpl] NM *Hér* sinople

sinoque [sinɔk] *Fam* ADJ crazy, nuts; **t'es s.!** you're off your rocker!

NMF nutcase, *Br* nutter

sino-tibétain, -e [sinotibetɛ̃, -ɛn] (*mpl* **sino-tibétains**, *fpl* **sino-tibétaines**) ADJ Sino-Tibetan

NM *Ling* Sino-Tibetan

sintérisation [sɛ̃terizasjɔ̃] NF *Tech* sinterization

sintériser [3] [sɛ̃terize] VT *Tech* to sinter

sinué, -e [sinɥe] ADJ *Bot* sinuate

sinuer [7] [sinɥe] VI *Littéraire* to wind

sinueux, -euse [sinɥø, -øz] ADJ **1** (*tracé, chemin*) winding, sinuous; (*fleuve*) winding, meandering; **rivière au cours s.** meandering *or* sinuous river **2** (*pensée*) convoluted, tortuous

sinuosité [sinɥozite] NF **1** (*fait d'être courbé* → *d'un tracé, d'un chemin*) winding; (→ *d'une rivière*) winding, meandering **2** (*courbe* → *d'un tracé*) curve; (→ *d'un chemin*) curve, bend; (→ *d'une rivière*) meander

□ **sinuosités** NFPL *Fig* (*d'un raisonnement*) tortuousness, convolutions

sinus [sinys] NM **1** *Anat* sinus; **s. du cœur** sinus venosus; **s. veineux** venous sinuses **2** *Math* sine

sinusal, -e, -aux, -ales [sinyzal, -o] ADJ *Anat* sinoauricular

sinusien, -enne [sinyzjɛ̃, -ɛn] ADJ *Méd* sinus (*avant n*), sinusal

sinusite [sinyzit] NF *Méd* sinusitis; **avoir une s.** to have sinusitis

sinusoïdal, -e, -aux, -ales [sinyzɔidal, -o] ADJ sinusoidal

sinusoïde [sinyzɔid] NM *Anat* sinusoid

NF *Math* sine curve

Sion [sjɔ̃] NF Zion, Sion

sionisme [sjɔnism] NM Zionism

sioniste [sjɔnist] ADJ Zionist

NMF Zionist

sioux [sju] ADJ **1** (*amérindien*) Sioux **2** *Fam* (*astucieux*) sharp

NM (*langue*) Sioux

□ **Sioux** NMF Sioux; **les S.** the Sioux (Indians)

siphoïde [sifɔid] ADJ siphon-shaped, siphonal

siphomycète [sifomisɛt] *Bot* NM phycomycete

□ **siphomycètes** NMPL Phycomycetes

siphon [sifɔ̃] NM **1** *Méd, Phys, Géol & Zool* siphon **2** (*d'appareils sanitaires*) trap, U-bend **3** (*carafe*) *Br* soda siphon, *Am* siphon bottle **4** (*en travaux publics*) (inverted) siphon

siphonage [sifonaʒ] NM *Méd* siphonage

siphonaptère [sifonaptɛr] *Entom* NM member of the Siphonaptera order

□ **siphonaptères** NMPL Siphonaptera

siphonnage [sifonaʒ] = **siphonage**

siphonné, -e [sifone] ADJ *Fam* (*fou*) crazy, nuts

siphonnement [sifonmɑ̃] NM siphonage

siphonner [3] [sifone] VT to siphon; **s. de l'eau/un réservoir** to siphon off water/a reservoir

siphonogamie [sifonogami] NF *Biol* siphonogamy

siphonophore [sifonofor] NM *Zool* siphonophore

sipo [sipo] NM *Bot* African mahogany

sir [sœr] NM sir

sirdar [sirdar] NM *Hist* sirdar

sire [sir] NM (*seigneur*) lord; **un triste s.** a dubious character

□ **Sire** NM (*à un roi*) Your Majesty, *Arch* Sire; (*à un empereur*) Your Imperial Majesty, *Arch* Sire

sirène [sirɛn] NF **1** (*des pompiers, d'une voiture de police, d'une ambulance, d'une usine*) siren; (*d'un navire*) siren, (fog) horn; **s. d'alarme** (*d'incendie*) fire alarm; (*en temps de guerre*) air-raid siren **2** *Myth* siren **3** (*femme séduisante*) siren

sirénien [sirenjɛ̃] *Zool* NM sea cow, *Spéc* sirenian

□ **siréniens** NMPL Sirenia

SIRET [sirɛt] NM **n° S.** company registration number

sirex [sirɛks] NM *Entom* sirex

Sirius [sirjys] NF *Astron* Sirius

sirli [sirli] NM *Orn* **s. du désert** hoopoe lark, bifasciated lark; **s. de Dupont** Dupont's lark

sirocco [sirɔko] NM sirocco

sirop [siro] NM **1** *Culin* (*concentré*) syrup, cordial; (*dilué*) (fruit) cordial *or* drink; **s. d'érable** maple syrup; **s. de fraise/de menthe** strawberry/mint cordial; **s. d'orgeat** barley water; **s. de sucre** golden syrup **2** *Pharm* syrup; **s. pour** *ou* **contre la toux** cough mixture **3** *Fig Péj* mawkishness, schmaltz; **son film, c'est du s.** his/her movie *or Br* film is pure schmaltz **4** *Belg Culin* = thick apple or pear syrup

siroperie [siropri] NF *Belg* = place where "sirop" is made

siroter [3] [sirɔte] VT to sip, to take sips of

VI *Fam* to booze; **il sirote bien** he likes a drop of the hard stuff

SIRPA, Sirpa [sirpa] NM *Mil* (*abrév* **Service d'information et de relations publiques des armées**) = French military services public information service

sirtaki [sirtaki] NM sirtaki

sirupeux, -euse [sirypø, -øz] ADJ **1** (*visqueux et sucré*) syrupy **2** *Péj* (*sentiment*) schmaltzy, syrupy

sis, -e [si, siz] ADJ *Jur* **s. à** located *or* situated at; **maison sise rue Saint-Honoré** house located *or* situated in the Rue Saint-Honoré

sisal, -als [sizal] NM *Bot* sisal

sismal, -e, -aux, -ales [sismal, -o] ADJ seismic

sismicité [sismisite] NF seismicity

sismique [sismik] ADJ seismic

sismogramme [sismogram] NM seismogram

sismographe [sismograf] NM seismograph

sismographie [sismografi] NF seismography

sismologie [sismɔlɔʒi] NF seismology

sismologique [sismɔlɔʒik] ADJ seismological

sismologue [sismɔlɔg] NMF seismologist

sismomètre [sismomɛtr] NM seismometer

sismométrie [sismometri] NF seismometry

sismothérapie [sismoterapi] NF *Psy* shock therapy

sister-ship [sistœrʃip] (*pl* **sister-ships**) NM *Naut* sister ship

sistre [sistr] NM *Mus* sistrum

sisymbre [sizɛbr] NM *Bot* sisymbrium; **s. officinal** hedge mustard

Sisyphe [sizif] NPR *Myth* Sisyphus; **le mythe de S.** the myth of Sisyphus; **le rocher de S.** the rock of Sisyphus; **un travail de S.** a never-ending task

SIT [ɛsite] NM (*Banque*) (*abrév* **système interbancaire de compensation**) = interbank automated clearing system, *Br* ≃ CHAPS

sitar [sitar] NM *Mus* sitar

sitariste [sitarist] NMF sitar player, sitarist

sitcom [sitkɔm] NM OU NF *TV* sitcom

site [sit] NM **1** (*panorama*) beauty spot; **il y a plusieurs sites touristiques par ici** there are several tourist spots *or* places of interest for tourists round here; *Admin* **s. classé** conservation area, *Br* ≃ National Trust area; **s. historique** historical site

2 (*environnement*) setting

3 (*emplacement*) site, siting; **le choix du s. de la centrale a posé problème** the siting of the power station has caused problems; **s. archéologique** (*gén*) archeological site; (*en cours d'excavation*) archeological dig; **s. de lancement** launch area

4 *Chim & Écon* site; *Mktg* **s. témoin** test site

5 *Ordinat* site; **s. de bavardage** chat room; **s. à consultation payante** pay-per-visit site; **s. FTP** FTP site; **s. marchand** e-commerce site; **s. miroir** mirror site; **s. sécurisé** secure site; **s. Web** Web site

6 *Transp* **s. propre** bus lane

□ **de site** ADJ *Mil* **angle/ligne de s.** angle/line of sight

sit-in [sitin] NM INV sit-in; **faire un s.** to stage a sit-in

sitogoniomètre [sitogonjomɛtr] NM *Tech* sitogoniometer

sitologie [sitolɔʒi] NF study of conservation

sitologue [sitolɔg] NMF conservation expert

sitostérol [sitosterol] NM *Biol* sitosterol

sitôt [sito] ADV **1** (*avec une participiale*) **s. levé, je me mettais au travail** no sooner was I up than I'd start work, I'd start work as soon as I was up; **s. le dîner fini, il partit** as soon as dinner was over, he left; **s. dit, s. fait** no sooner said than done

2 *Littéraire* (*aussitôt*) immediately; **s. après l'orage** immediately after the storm; **s. après la gare** just *or* immediately past the station

3 *Littéraire* (*si rapidement*) **une rose épanouie et s. fanée** a rose in full bloom and yet so quick to wither

PRÉP *Littéraire* **s. son élection...** as soon as he/she was elected..., no sooner was he/she elected...

□ **pas de sitôt** ADV **on ne se reverra pas de s.** we won't be seeing each other again for a while; **je n'y retournerai pas de s.!** I won't go back there *or* you won't catch me going back there in a hurry!; **la société idéale n'existera pas de s.** the ideal society is a long way off

□ **sitôt que** CONJ *Littéraire* as soon as; **s. qu'il la vit, il se mit à rire** as soon as he saw her he started to laugh

sittelle [sitɛl] NF *Orn* nuthatch

sittidé [sitide] *Orn* NM member of the Sittidae family

□ **sittidés** NMPL Sittidae

situation [sitɥasjɔ̃] NF **1** (*circonstances*) situation; **je lui ai exposé ma s.** I explained my situation *or* position to him/her; **s. économique/politique** economic/political situation; **quelle est votre s. financière exacte?** what is your precise *or* exact financial position?; **ma s. financière n'est pas brillante!** my financial situation is *or* my finances are none too healthy!; **se trouver dans une s. délicate** to find oneself in an awkward

situation *or* position; **je n'aimerais pas être dans ta s.** I wouldn't like to be in your position; *Vieilli Euph* **elle est dans une s. intéressante** *(enceinte)* she's in an interesting condition; **tu vois un peu la s.!** do you get the picture?; **c'est l'homme de la s.** he's the right man for the job; *Admin* **s. de famille** marital status; *Mktg* **s. d'achat** buying situation; *Mktg* **s. de nouvel achat** new-buy situation

2 *(emploi rémunéré)* job; **chercher/trouver une s.** to look for/to find a job; **avoir une bonne s.** *(être bien payé)* to have a well-paid job; *(être puissant)* to have a high-powered job; **elle s'est fait une belle s.** she worked her way up to a very good position; **être sans s.** to have no job; **s. sociale** *(d'une personne)* social position, standing in society

3 *(lieu)* situation, position, location; **le manoir jouit d'une magnifique s.** the manor house is beautifully situated

4 *Fin (d'une société)* report of assets; **s. en banque** financial position *or* situation; **s. de caisse** cash statement; **s. de compte** account position *or* balance; **s. financière** financial situation *or* position; **s. hebdomadaire** *(de la Banque de France)* weekly report; **s. nette** net assets, net worth; **s. de trésorerie** cash budget

5 *Littérature & Théât* situation; **comique de s.** situation comedy

❑ **en situation** ADV in real life; **voyons comment elle va aborder les choses en s.** let's see how she gets on in real life *or* when faced with the real thing; **mettre qn en s.** to give sb experience of a real-life situation

❑ **en situation de** PRÉP **être en s. de faire qch** to be in a position to do sth; **je ne suis pas en s. de décider** I'm not in a position to decide

situationnisme [sitɥasjɔnism] NM situationism

situationniste [sitɥasjɔnist] ADJ situationist NMF situationist

situé, -e [sitɥe] ADJ **maison bien/mal située** well-/poorly-situated house

situer [7] [sitɥe] VT **1** *(dans l'espace, dans le temps → gén)* to place; *(→ roman, film etc)* to set; **je connais la ville mais je ne saurais pas la s.** I know the name of the town but I wouldn't be able to place it *or* to say where it is; **à quelle époque situez-vous l'action de votre roman?** in what period have you set your novel?; **on situe l'apparition de l'écriture à cette époque** writing is believed to have appeared during this period; **je n'arrive pas à le s.** I'm afraid I can't place him

2 *(classer)* to place, to situate; **il est difficile de le s. dans l'architecture/dans la politique française** it's difficult to know where to place him in French architecture/politics; **je situerais plutôt ce groupe dans le courant trip-hop** I would describe the band as being more trip-hop; **sa prise de position le situe dans l'opposition** the stand he has taken places him amongst the opposition

3 *Fam (cerner → personne)* to define▪; **on a du mal à la s.** it's difficult to know what makes her tick

▸ **se situer** VPR **1** *(prendre position)* **se s. par rapport à qn/qch** to place oneself in relation to sb/sth; **où vous situez-vous dans ce conflit?** where do you stand in this conflict?

2 *(gén)* to be situated *or* located; *(scène, action)* to take place; **leur groupe se situe très à gauche** their group is on the far left; **où se situe-t-elle dans le mouvement expressionniste?** where would you place her in the expressionist movement?; **l'augmentation se situera aux alentours de 3 pour cent** the increase will be in the region of 3 percent

sium [sjɔm] NM *Bot* sium

sivaïsme [ʃivaism] NM *Rel* Shivaism, Sivaism

sivaïte [ʃivait] *Rel* ADJ Shivaistic, Sivaistic NMF Shivaite, Sivaite

sivapithèque [sivapitɛk] NM Sivapithecus

SIVOM, Sivom [sivɔm] NM *(abrév* **Syndicat intercommunal à vocation multiple)** = group of local authorities pooling public services

SIVP [ɛsivepe] NM *(abrév* **stage d'initiation à la vie professionnelle)** = training scheme for young unemployed people

six [sis] ADJ **1** *(gén)* six; *Sport* **les S. Jours** the Six Day Race; *Mus* **le groupe des S.** = group of French composers (Durey, Honegger, Milhaud, Poulenc, Auric and Tailleferre) founded in Paris in 1918

2 *(dans des séries)* sixth; **page/numéro s.** page/number six
   PRON six
   NM INV **1** *(gén)* six
   2 *(numéro d'ordre)* number six
   3 *(chiffre écrit)* six
   4 *Cartes* six; *voir aussi* **cinq**

sixain [sizɛ̃] NM **1** *Littérature* hexastich **2** *Cartes* set of six packs *or Am* decks of cards

six-huit [sisɥit] NM INV *Mus* six-eight time

sixième [sizjɛm] ADJ sixth
   NMF **1** *(personne)* sixth **2** *(objet)* sixth (one)
   NM **1** *(partie)* sixth **2** *(étage) Br* sixth floor, *Am* seventh floor **3** *(arrondissement de Paris)* sixth (arrondissement)
   NF **1** *Scol Br* ≃ first year, *Am* ≃ sixth grade **2** *Mus* sixth; *voir aussi* **cinquième**

sixièmement [sizjɛmmɑ̃] ADV sixthly, in sixth place

six-quatre-deux [siskatdø] **à la six-quatre-deux** ADV *Fam* **faire qch à la s.** to do sth any old how; **encore une dissertation faite à la s.** another slapdash *or* rushed essay

Sixte [sikst] NPR *(pape)* Sixtus

sixte [sikst] NF **1** *Mus* sixth **2** *Escrime* sixte

Sixtine [sikstin] NF **la chapelle S.** the Sistine Chapel

sizain [sizɛ̃] NM = **sixain**

sizerin [sizrɛ̃] NM *Orn* **s. blanchâtre** Arctic redpoll; **s. cabaret** lesser redpoll; **s. flammé** redpoll

Sjaelland [ʃelɑ̃d] NM *Géog* Sjælland, Zealand

ska [ska] NM *Mus* ska

Skagerrak [skagərak] NM *Géog* **le S.** the Skagerrak

Skaï® [skaj] NM imitation leather, Leatherette®

skate [skɛt] NM **le s.** skateboarding; **faire du s.** to skateboard, to go skateboarding

skateboard [skɛtbɔrd] NM skateboard; **faire du s.** to skateboard, to go skateboarding

skatepark [skɛtpark] NM skatepark

skeet [skit] NM *Sport* skeet shooting

skeleton [skəlɛtɔn] NM *(luge, sport)* skeleton

sketch [skɛtʃ] *(pl* **sketches)** NM sketch

skeud [skœd] NM *Fam (verlan de disque)* record▪

ski [ski] NM **1** *Sport (activité)* skiing; **faire du s.** to go skiing; **s. acrobatique** hot-dogging; **s. alpin/nordique** Alpine/Nordic skiing; **s. artistique** freestyle skiing; **s. de descente** downhill skiing; **s. évolutif** (graduated) short-ski method; **s. de fond** cross-country skiing; **s. nautique** water-skiing; **faire du s. nautique** to water-ski; **s. de randonnée** ski-touring; **s. sauvage** *ou* **hors piste** off-piste skiing

2 *(planche)* ski; **skis compacts** *ou* **courts** short skis; **skis paraboliques** parabolic skis, carving skis

3 *Aviat* landing skid

❑ **de ski** ADJ *(chaussures, lunettes, station)* ski *(avant n)*; *(vacances, séjour)* skiing *(avant n)*

skiable [skjabl] ADJ skiable; **la piste noire n'est plus s.** it's now impossible to ski down *or* to use the black run

skiascopie [skjaskɔpi] NF *Opt* skiascopy, sciascopy

skiatron [skjatrɔ̃] NM *Électron* skiatron

ski-bob [skibɔb] *(pl* **ski-bobs)** NM skibob; **faire du s.** to go skibobbing

skier [10] [skje] VI to ski; **je vais s. tous les dimanches** I go skiing every Sunday

skieur, -euse [skjœr, -øz] NM,F skier; **s. de fond** cross-country skier; **s. nautique** water-skier

skiff [skif] NM skiff; *(en aviron)* single scull

skin [skin] NM *(abrév* **skinhead)** skin, skinhead

skinhead [skinɛd] NM skinhead

skip [skip] NM *Ind* skip

skipper [skipœr] NM *Naut* skipper

skons [skɔ̃s] NM **1** *Zool* skunk **2** *(fourrure)* skunk (fur)

skooter [skɔtœr, skutɛr] NM = **scooter²**

Skopje [skɔpje] NM Skopje

skua [skya] NM *Orn* skua

skunks [skɔ̃s] NM **1** *Zool* skunk **2** *(fourrure)* skunk (fur)

Skydome® [skajdom] NM *(hublot)* sky-dome

skyscraper [skajskrɛpœr] NM *Mktg* skyscraper ad

skye-terrier [skajtɛrje] *(pl* **skye-terriers)** NM Skye terrier

sky-surf [skajsœrf], **sky-surfing** [skajsœrfiŋ] NM *Sport* sky surfing

slache [slaʃ] NF *Belg (savate)* worn-out (old) shoe; *(tong)* flip-flop

slalom [slalɔm] NM **1** *Sport (course)* slalom; **descendre une piste en s.** to slalom down a slope; **s. nautique** water-ski slalom; **s. spécial/géant** special/giant slalom **2** *Fam (zigzags)* zigzagging▪; **faire du s. entre** to zigzag between; **la moto faisait du s. entre les voitures** the motorbike was dodging in and out among the cars *or* dodging through the traffic

slalomer [3] [slalɔme] VI **1** *Sport* to slalom **2** *Fam (zigzaguer)* **s. entre** to zigzag▪ *or* to weave in and out of; **il est dangereux de s. entre les voitures** weaving in and out of the traffic is dangerous

slalomeur, -euse [slalɔmœr, -øz] NM,F slalom skier

slang [slãg] NM (English) slang

slash [slaʃ] *(pl* **slashs** *ou* **slashes)** NM *Ordinat* slash

slave [slav] ADJ Slavonic, *Am* Slavic NM *(langue)* Slavonic, Slavic ❑ **Slave** NMF Slav

slavisant, -e [slavizɑ̃, -ɑ̃t] NM,F Slavicist, Slavist

slaviser [3] [slavize] VT to submit to a Slavonic influence, to Slavonicize

slaviste [slavist] NMF Slavicist, Slavist

slavistique [slavistik] NF Slavistics *(singulier)*

slavon [slavɔ̃] NM Slavic, Slavonic

Slavonie [slavɔni] NF **la S.** Slavonia

slavophile [slavɔfil] ADJ Slavophil, Slavophile NMF Slavophil, Slavophile

SLBM [ɛsɛlbeɛm] NM *(abrév* **Submarine Launched Ballistic Missile)** SLBM

SLCM [ɛsɛlseɛm] NM *(abrév* **Submarine Launched Cruise Missile)** SLCM

sleeping [slipiŋ] NM *Vieilli* sleeping car

slibard [slibar] NM *très Fam Br* boxers, *Am* shorts, skivvies

slice [slajs] NM *(au tennis, au golf)* slice

slicer [16] [slajse] VT *(au tennis, au golf)* to slice

slikke [slik] NF *Géog* mud flat, tidal flat

slip [slip] NM **1** *(d'homme)* (pair of) (under)pants, *Am* shorts; *(de femme) Br* pants, *Am* panties; **où est mon s.?** where are my pants?; **s. de bain** *(d'homme)* bathing *or* swimming trunks; **s. kangourou** Y-fronts **2** *Naut* slip, slipway

s.l.n.d. *(abrév écrite* **sans lieu ni date)** = date and origin unknown

sloche [slɔʃ] NF *Can Joual* slush

slogan [slɔgã] NM slogan; **s. publicitaire** advertising slogan

sloop [slup] NM *Naut* sloop

sloughi [slugi] NM saluki

slovaque [slɔvak] ADJ Slovak, Slovakian NM *(langue)* Slovak ❑ **Slovaque** NMF Slovak, Slovakian

Slovaquie [slɔvaki] NF **la S.** Slovakia; **vivre en S.** to live in Slovakia; **aller en S.** to go to Slovakia

slovène [slɔvɛn] ADJ Slovene, Slovenian NM *(langue)* Slovene ❑ **Slovène** NMF Slovene, Slovenian

Slovénie [slɔveni] NF **la S.** Slovenia; **vivre en S.** to live in Slovenia; **aller en S.** to go to Slovenia

slow [slo] NM **1** *(gén)* slow number; **s. de l'été** the slow number everyone's dancing to this summer; **danser un s. avec qn** to slow-dance with sb **2** *(fox-trot)* slow fox trot

SM [ɛsɛm] NM *(abrév* **sado-masochisme)** S&M

S.M. *(abrév écrite* **Sa Majesté)** HM

smack [smak] NM *Fam Arg drogue* smack, scag

SMAG, Smag [smag] NM *Agr (abrév* **salaire minimum agricole garanti)** = guaranteed minimum agricultural wage

smala, smalah [smala] NF **1** *(d'un chef arabe)* retinue **2** *Fam (famille)* tribe; **avec toute sa s.** with his/her whole tribe

smalt [smalt] NM smalt

smaragdin, -e [smaragdɛ̃, -in] ADJ *Littéraire* emerald green, smaragdine

smaragdite [smaragdit] NF *Minér* smaragdite

smart [smart] ADJ INV *Fam Vieilli* chic, smart

smash [smaʃ] (*pl* **smashs** *ou* **smashes**) NM *Sport* smash; **faire un s.** to smash (the ball)

smasher [3] [smaʃe] *Sport* VI to smash
VT to smash

SMCT [ɛsɛmsete] NM *UE* (*abrév* **soutien monétaire à court terme**) STMS

SME [ɛsɛmø] NM *Écon* 1 (*abrév* **Système monétaire européen**) EMS 2 (*abrév* **Serpent monétaire européen**) European currency snake

smectique [smɛktik] ADJ *Chim & Phys* smectic; **argile s.** fuller's earth

smeerlap [smerlap] NM *Belg Fam Péj (homme méprisable)* swine

smegma [smɛgma] NM *Physiol* smegma

SMI [ɛsɛmi] NM *Écon* (*abrév* **Système monétaire international**) IMS

SMIC, Smic [smik] NM (*abrév* **salaire minimum interprofessionnel de croissance**) = index-linked guaranteed minimum wage

smicard, -e [smikar, -ard] NM,F *Fam* minimum-wage earner■ ; **les smicards** people earning *or* on the minimum wage■

SMIG [smig] NM *Anciennement* (*abrév* **salaire minimum interprofessionnel garanti**) = index-linked guaranteed minimum wage

smiley [smajli] NM *Ordinat* smiley, emoticon

smillage [smijaʒ] NM *Tech* spalling

smille [smij] NF *Tech* spalling hammer

smithsonite [smitsɔnit] NF *Minér* smithsonite

smocks [smɔk] NMPL smocking; **faire des s. sur une robe** to smock a dress

smog [smɔg] NM smog

smoke meat [smɔkmit] NM *Can* smoked meat

smoking [smɔkiŋ] NM *Br* dinner suit, *Am* tuxedo; **(veste de) s.** *Br* dinner jacket, *Am* tuxedo

smolt [smɔlt] NM *Ich* smolt

smorzando [smɔrtsãdo] *Mus* ADV smorzando
NM smorzando

smoutbol, smoutebol [smutbɔl] (*pl* **smoutbollen, smoutebollen** [smutbɔlən]) NF OU NM *Belg* fritter

SMP [ɛsɛmpe] NF *Mil* (*abrév* **société militaire privée**) PMC

SMR [ɛsɛmɛr] NM *Méd* (*abrév* **service médical rendu**) = assessment of the medical benefits of a drug or treatment

SMS [ɛsɛmɛs] NM *Tél* (*abrév* **short message service**) SMS

SMUR, Smur [smyr] NM *Méd* (*abrév* **Service médical d'urgence et de réanimation**) = French ambulance and emergency unit

smurf [smœrf] NM breakdancing; **faire du s.** to breakdance

smurfer [3] [smœrfe] VI to breakdance

Smyrne [smirn] NF Smyrna

snack [snak] NM 1 (*restaurant*) snack bar, self-service restaurant, cafeteria 2 (*collation*) snack

snack-bar [snakbar] (*pl* **snack-bars**) NM snack bar, self-service restaurant, cafeteria

SNALC [ɛsɛnaɛlse] NM (*abrév* **Syndicat national des lycées et collèges**) = teachers' union

SNC[1] [ɛsɛnse] NF *Écon* (*abrév* **société en nom collectif**) general partnership

SNC[2] (*abrév écrite* **service non compris**) service not included

SNCB [ɛsɛnsebe] NF *Belg* (*abrév* **Société nationale des chemins de fer belges**) = Belgian national railway company

SNCF [ɛsɛnseɛf] NF (*abrév* **Société nationale des chemins de fer français**) = French national railway company; **la S. est en grève** there's a (French) rail strike; **il travaille à la S.** he works for the (French) *Br* railways *or Am* railroads

SNE [ɛsɛne] NF (*abrév* **Syndicat national de l'édition**) = French publishers' union

SNECMA [snɛkma] NF *Aviat* (*abrév* **Société nationale d'études et de construction de moteurs d'avion**) = aeroplane engine manufacturer

SNES, Snes [snɛs] NM (*abrév* **Syndicat national de l'enseignement secondaire**) = secondary school teachers' union

Sne-sup, Snesup [snɛsyp] NM (*abrév* **Syndicat national de l'enseignement supérieur**) = university teachers' union

SNG [ɛsɛnʒe] NM (*abrév* **satellite news gathering**) SNG

SNI [sni] NM *Anciennement* (*abrév* **Syndicat national des instituteurs**) = primary school teachers' union

sniff [snif] EXCLAM (*bruit de pleurs*) boo hoo!
NM *très Fam Arg drogue (de cocaïne)* snort

sniffer [3] [snife] *très Fam Arg drogue* VI to snort
VT (*cocaïne*) to snort; (*colle*) to sniff■

SNJ [ɛsɛnʒi] NM (*abrév* **Syndicat national des journalistes**) = journalists' union

snob [snɔb] ADJ snobbish, snobby; **elle est un peu s.** she's a bit of a snob
NM,F snob

snober [3] [snɔbe] VT (*personne*) to snub; (*chose*) to turn one's nose up at; **certains libraires snobent les bandes dessinées** some booksellers think it beneath them to stock comics

snobinard, -e [snɔbinar, -ard] *Fam* ADJ stuck-up, snobby
NM,F snob■

snobisme [snɔbism] NM snobbery, snobbishness; **il joue au golf par s.** he plays golf out of snobbery *or* purely for the snob value; **du s. à rebours** inverted snobbery

snoreau, -aude, -aux, -audes [snɔro, -od] NM,F *Can Fam* little rascal *or* scamp

snow-boot [snobut] (*pl* **snow-boots**) NM snow boot

SNSM [ɛsɛnɛsɛm] NF (*abrév* **Société nationale de sauvetage en mer**) = national sea-rescue association

snul [snyl] NM *Belg Fam Péj* cretin, *Br* wally

S-O (*abrév écrite* **Sud-Ouest**) SW

s.o. (*abrév écrite* **sans objet**) n/a

soap opera [sopɔpera], **soap** [sop] (*pl* **soap operas** *ou* **soaps**) NM *Rad & TV* soap (opera)

sobre [sɔbr] ADJ 1 (*personne → tempérante*) sober, temperate, *Sout* abstemious; (*→ non ivre*) sober; **tu es s. maintenant?** have you sobered up?, are you sober now?; **être s. comme un chameau** to be as sober as a judge
2 (*modéré, discret → architecture, tenue, style*) sober, restrained; (*→ vêtement*) simple; **elle est toujours s. dans ses déclarations** she always speaks with restraint; *Littéraire* **s. de paroles/de louanges** sparing in one's words/one's praise

sobrement [sɔbrəmã] ADV 1 (*avec modération*) temperately, soberly 2 (*avec discrétion, avec retenue*) soberly

sobriété [sɔbrijete] NF 1 (*tempérance*) soberness, temperance 2 (*discrétion, retenue*) soberness; **il mit de la s. dans ses félicitations** he was restrained in his congratulations 3 (*dépouillement → d'un style, d'un décor*) bareness

sobriquet [sɔbrikɛ] NM nickname; **un petit s. affectueux** a pet name

soc [sɔk] NM ploughshare

soccer [sɔkœr] NM *Can* soccer

Sochaux [sɔʃo] NF = site of the Peugeot car factory

sociabiliser [3] [sɔsjabilize] VT to make sociable

sociabilité [sɔsjabilite] NF sociableness, sociability

sociable [sɔsjabl] ADJ 1 (*individu, tempérament*) sociable, gregarious; **j'ai été un enfant très s.** I was a very outgoing child; **je ne suis pas d'humeur s. ce soir** I don't feel very sociable this evening 2 (*vivant en société*) social

social, -e, -aux, -ales [sɔsjal, -o] ADJ 1 (*réformes, problèmes, ordre, politique*) social; **c'est une menace sociale** it represents a threat to society
2 *Admin* social (*avant n*), welfare (*avant n*); **avantages sociaux** welfare benefits; **logements sociaux** public housing; **services sociaux** social services
3 *Zool* social; **l'homme est un animal s.** man is a social animal
4 *Jur* company (*avant n*); **un associé peut être tenu responsable des dettes sociales** a partner may be liable for company debts
NM **le s.** social issues *or* matters; **le nouveau gouvernement s'intéresse beaucoup au s.** the new government takes a strong interest in social issues; **travailler dans le s.** to work in the social sector; *Fam Fig* **je ne suis pas là pour faire du s.** that's not my problem
□ **Sociale** NF *Vieilli* **la Sociale** socialism

social-chrétien, sociale-chrétienne [sɔsjalkretjɛ̃, -ɛn] (*mpl* **sociaux-chrétiens** [sɔsjokretjɛ̃], *fpl* **sociales-chrétiennes**) *Belg* ADJ Christian Socialist
NM,F Christian Socialist

social-démocrate, sociale-démocrate [sɔsjaldemɔkrat] (*mpl* **sociaux-démocrates** [sɔsjodemɔkrat], *fpl* **sociales-démocrates**) ADJ social democratic
NMF (*gén*) social democrat; (*adhérent d'un parti*) Social Democrat

social-démocratie [sɔsjaldemɔkrasi] (*pl* **social-démocraties**) NF social democracy

socialement [sɔsjalmã] ADV socially

social-impérialisme [sɔsjalɛ̃perjalism] (*pl* **social-impérialismes**) NM social imperialism

socialisant, -e [sɔsjalizã, -ãt] ADJ 1 *Pol* left-leaning, with left-wing tendencies 2 (*préoccupé de justice sociale*) socialistic
NM,F 1 *Pol* socialist sympathizer 2 (*contestataire social*) advocate of social equality

socialisation [sɔsjalizasjɔ̃] NF 1 *Écon* collectivization 2 *Pol* **depuis la s. du pays** since the country went socialist 3 *Psy* socialization

socialiser [3] [sɔsjalize] VT 1 *Écon* to collectivize 2 *Psy* to socialize

socialisme [sɔsjalism] NM socialism; **s. chrétien** Christian socialism; **s. d'État** State socialism

socialiste [sɔsjalist] ADJ socialist
NMF socialist

socialité [sɔsjalite] NF social instinct

socialo [sɔsjalo] *Fam* (*abrév* **socialiste**) ADJ socialist■ , leftie, lefty
NMF socialist■ , leftie, lefty

social-révolutionnaire, sociale-révolutionnaire [sɔsjalrevɔlysjɔnɛr] (*mpl* **sociaux-révolutionnaires** [sɔsjorevɔlysjɔnɛr], *fpl* **sociales-révolutionnaires**) ADJ social-revolutionary
NM,F social-revolutionary

sociétaire [sɔsjetɛr] NMF 1 (*d'une association*) member; **s. de la Comédie-Française** = actor co-opted as a full member of the Comédie-Française 2 *Fin* (*d'une société anonyme*) *Br* shareholder, *Am* stockholder

sociétal, -e, -aux, -ales [sɔsjetal, -o] ADJ societal

sociétariat [sɔsjetarja] NM membership

société [sɔsjete] NF 1 (*communauté*) society; **la s.** society; **problème de s.** social problem; **vivre en s.** to live in society; **les insectes qui vivent en s.** social insects; **la s. d'abondance** the affluent society; **la s. de consommation** the consumer society
2 *Littéraire* (*présence*) company, society; **rechercher la s. de qn** to seek (out) sb's company; **je me plais dans sa s.** I enjoy (being in) his/her company; **être dans la s. de qn** to be in company with *or* in the society of sb
3 *Fam* (*personnes réunies*) company, gathering
4 (*catégorie de gens*) society; **faire ses débuts dans la s.** to make one's debut in society; **cela ne se fait pas dans la bonne s.** it's not done in polite society; **la haute s.** high society
5 (*association → de gens de lettres, de savants*) society; (*→ de sportifs*) club; **s. littéraire/savante** literary/learned society; **s. secrète** secret society; **s. de tempérance** temperance society; **la S. des Amis** the Society of Friends, the Quakers; **la S. de Jésus** the Society of Jesus; **la S. de Marie** the Society of Mary; **la S. des Nations** the League of Nations; **la S. protectrice des animaux** = society for the protection of animals, *Br* ≃ RSPCA, *Am* ≃ ASPCA
6 *Com, Jur & Écon* (*entreprise*) company, firm; **le matériel appartient à la s.** the equipment belongs to the firm *or* to the company; **la S. Martin** Martin's; **s. par actions** joint-stock company, *Am* incorporated company; **s. affiliée** affiliated company, *Am* affiliate; *Agr* **S. d'aménagement foncier et d'établissement rural** = agency entitled to buy land and earmark it for agricultural use; **s. anonyme** (public) limited company; **s. d'assurance** insurance company; *Mus* **S. des auteurs, compositeurs et éditeurs de musique** = body responsible for collecting and distributing royalties, *Br* ≃ Performing Rights Society, *Am* ≃ Copyright Royalty Tribunal; **s. de Bourse** stockbroker, stockbroking firm; **s. de capital-risque** venture capital company; **s. à capital variable** company with variable capital; **s. de capitaux (à responsabilité limitée)** limited liability company; **s. civile immobilière** property investment partnership; **S. civile de placement immobilier** = company which owns and manages rented

accommodation; **s. civile professionnelle** professional *or* non-trading partnership; **s. en commandite** limited partnership; **s. en commandite par actions** partnership limited by shares; **s. en commandite simple** ≃ general partnership; **s. de commerce international** international trading corporation; **s. commerciale** company, firm; **s. de conseil en investissement** investment consultancy; **S. coopérative ouvrière de production** = manufacturing cooperative; **s. cotée en Bourse** listed company; **s. cotée à la Cote officielle** quoted company; **s. de crédit immobilier** *Br* ≃ building society, *Am* ≃ savings and loan association; **s. d'économie mixte** government-controlled corporation; **s. d'État** state-owned *or* public company; **s. d'études** research company; **s. d'exercice libéral** = company practising a liberal profession; **s. d'exploitation en commun** joint venture; **s. de fait** de facto partnership; **s. familiale** family business; **s. fictive** dummy company; **S. financière internationale** International Finance Corporation, IFC; **S. française d'enquêtes par sondages** = French market research company; *TV* **S. française de production** = former state-owned television company; **s. de gestion** holding company; **s. immobilière** real-estate company; **s. d'intérêt collectif agricole** agricultural cooperative; **s. Internet** dotcom; **s. d'investissement à capital fixe** closed-end investment company; **s. d'investissement à capital variable** open-ended investment trust, *Br* ≃ unit trust, *Am* ≃ mutual fund; **s. de location de voitures** *Br* car hire company, *Am* car rental company; **s. mère** parent company; *Mil* **s. militaire privée** private military company; **s. multinationale** multinational company *or* corporation, multinational; **s. de mutualité** mutual insurance company, *Br* friendly society; **s. nationale** state-owned *or* public company; *Belg Rail* **S. nationale des chemins de fer belges** = Belgian national railway company; *Rail* **S. nationale des chemins de fer français** = French national railway company; *Aviat* **S. nationale d'études et de construction de moteurs d'avion** = aeroplane engine manufacturer; **S. nationale d'exploitation industrielle des tabacs et allumettes** = French government tobacco and matches monopoly; **S. nationale de sauvetage en mer** = national sea-rescue association; **s. en nom collectif** general partnership; **s. en participation** joint venture; **s. de personnes** partnership; *Belg* **s. de personnes à responsabilité limitée** limited liability company; **s. de placement** investment trust; **s. à portefeuille** holding company; **s. de prévoyance** provident society; **S. de la propriété artistique et des dessins et modèles** = organization set up to defend the interests of designers, photographers, artists etc; **s. à responsabilité limitée** ≃ limited liability company; **s. de services** service company; **s. sœur** sister company; *Suisse TV* **S. suisse de Radiodiffusion et de Télévision** = French-speaking Swiss broadcasting company; **s. de transport** carrier, transport firm; **S. des transports intercommunaux de Bruxelles** = Brussels transport authority; **s. unipersonnelle** single-person company; **s. d'utilité publique** *Br* public utility company, *Am* utility; **s. de vente par correspondance** mail-order company *or* firm

7 *Banque* **s. financière/de crédit** finance/credit company; **la S. Générale** = large French bank

8 *Jur* **s. d'acquêts** joint (matrimonial) assets

9 *Ordinat* **s. de services et d'ingénierie informatique** services and software organization

société-écran [sɔsjeteekrɑ̃] (*pl* **sociétés-écrans**) **NF** shield company

socinianisme [sɔsinjanism] **NM** Socinianism

socinien, -enne [sɔsinjɛ̃, -ɛn] **ADJ** Socinian
NM,F Socinian

sociobiologie [sɔsjɔbjɔlɔʒi] **NF** sociobiology

sociocentrisme [sɔsjɔsɑ̃trism] **NM** sociocentrism

sociocritique [sɔsjɔkritik] **NF** sociocriticism

socioculturel, -elle [sɔsjɔkyltyrɛl] **ADJ** (*tendances, étude, groupe*) sociocultural; **centre s.** social and cultural centre

sociodramatique [sɔsjɔdramatik] **ADJ** sociodramatic

sociodrame [sɔsjɔdram] **NM** sociodrama

sociodémographique [sɔsjɔdemɔgrafik] **ADJ** sociodemographic

socio-économique [sɔsjɔekɔnɔmik] (*pl* **socio-économiques**) **ADJ** socioeconomic

socio-éducatif, -ive [sɔsjɔedykatif, -iv] (*mpl* **socio-éducatifs**, *fpl* **socio-éducatives**) **ADJ** socio-educational

sociogenèse [sɔsjɔʒənɛz] **NF** *Psy* sociogenesis

sociogramme [sɔsjɔgram] **NM** sociogram

sociolinguistique [sɔsjɔlɛ̃gɥistik] **ADJ** sociolinguistic
NF sociolinguistics (*singulier*)

sociologie [sɔsjɔlɔʒi] **NF** sociology; **s. religieuse** sociology of religion

sociologique [sɔsjɔlɔʒik] **ADJ** sociological

sociologiquement [sɔsjɔlɔʒikmɑ̃] **ADV** sociologically

sociologisme [sɔsjɔlɔʒism] **NM** sociologism

sociologiste [sɔsjɔlɔʒist] **ADJ** sociologistic

sociologue [sɔsjɔlɔg] **NMF** sociologist

sociométrie [sɔsjɔmetri] **NF** sociometry

sociométrique [sɔsjɔmetrik] **ADJ** sociometric

sociopathie [sɔsjɔpati] **NF** *Psy* sociopathy

sociopolitique [sɔsjɔpɔlitik] **ADJ** sociopolitical

socioprofessionnel, -elle [sɔsjɔprɔfɛsjɔnɛl] **ADJ** socio-professional

socio-style [sɔsjɔstil] (*pl* **socio-styles**) **NM** *Mktg* lifestyle group

sociothérapie [sɔsjɔterapi] **NF** sociotherapy

socket [sɔkɛ] **NM** *Belg* light socket

socle [sɔkl] **NM 1** *Archit* (*piédestal*) pedestal, base; (*stylobate*) stylobate **2** (*d'un vase, d'une lampe, d'un moniteur*) base; (*d'un appareil*) stand; **s. orientable** *ou* **pivotant** (*d'un moniteur*) swivel base **3** *Constr* (*d'un bâtiment*) plinth, socle; (*d'un mur*) footing; **s. de béton** base course, (concrete) sole **4** *Géol* shelf **5** *Menuis* (*de chambranle*) skirting, capping; (*de marche*) string, stairstring

socque [sɔk] **NM 1** *Antiq* sock; *Littéraire* **le s. et le cothurne** sock and buskin **2** (*chaussure*) clog, sock

socquet [sɔkɛ] = **socket**

socquette [sɔkɛt] **NF** ankle sock, *Am* bobby sock

Socrate [sɔkrat] **NPR** Socrates

socratique [sɔkratik] **ADJ** Socratic; *Littéraire* **mœurs socratiques** pederasty

soda [sɔda] **NM 1** (*boisson gazeuse*) fizzy drink, *Am* soda; **s. à l'orange** orangeade, *Am* orange soda **2** (*eau de Seltz*) soda (water); **whisky s.** whisky and soda

sodé, -e [sɔde] **ADJ** sodium (*avant n*)

sodique [sɔdik] **ADJ** sodic, sodium (*avant n*)

sodium [sɔdjɔm] **NM** sodium

sodoku [sɔdɔku] **NM** *Méd* sodoku, rat-bite fever

Sodome [sɔdɔm] **NF** *Bible* Sodom; **S. et Gomorrhe** Sodom and Gomorrah

'Salò ou les 120 journées de Sodome' *Pasolini* 'Salo, or the 120 Days of Sodom'

sodomie [sɔdɔmi] **NF** sodomy, buggery

sodomiser [3] [sɔdɔmize] **VT** to sodomize, to bugger

sodomite [sɔdɔmit] **NM** sodomite

sœur [sœr] **NF 1** (*parente*) sister; **c'est une vraie s. pour moi** she's like a sister to me; **nous étions comme des sœurs** we were like sisters; **l'envie et la calomnie sont sœurs** envy and slander are sisters; *Hum* **je n'ai qu'une chaussette, où est sa s.?** I've got only one sock, where's its partner?; **ma grande s.** my big sister; **ma petite s.** my little sister; **ma s. aînée** my elder *or* older sister; **ma s. cadette** my younger sister; **s. de lait** foster sister; **s. de sang** blood sister; **les sœurs filandières** the Fates; **les neuf sœurs** the nine Muses; *très Fam* **et ta s.!** mind your own damn business! **2** *Rel* sister, nun; **chez les sœurs** with the nuns, in a convent; **bien, ma s.** very well, sister; **s. Thérèse** Sister Theresa; *Fam* **bonne s.** nun▪; **les Petites Sœurs des pauvres** the Little Sisters of the Poor **3** *Fam* (*femme*) chick, *Br* bird

sœurette [sœrɛt] **NF** *Fam* (little) sister▪; **ça va, s.?** alright, sis?

sofa [sɔfa] **NM** sofa

soffite [sɔfit] **NM** *Archit* soffit

Sofia [sɔfja] **NM** Sofia

SOFRES, Sofres [sɔfrɛs] **NF** (*abrév* **Société française d'enquêtes par sondages**) **la S.** = French market research company

soft[1] [sɔft] **NM INV** *Fam* software▪

soft[2] [sɔft] *Fam* **ADJ INV** (*film, roman*) soft-porn
NM soft porn

softball [sɔftbol] **NM** *Sport* softball

soft-drink [sɔftdrink] (*pl* **soft-drinks**) **NM** soft drink

software [sɔftwɛr] **NM** software

soi [swa] **PRON 1** (*représentant un sujet indéterminé*) oneself; **n'aimer que s.** to love only oneself; **être content de s.** to be pleased with oneself; **il ne faut pas penser qu'à s.** one shouldn't think only of oneself; **marmonner qch pour s. seul** to mumble sth to oneself *or* under one's breath; **quand on marche, il faut regarder devant s.** you must keep looking in front of you when you walk; **ne pas regarder derrière s.** not to look back; **avoir de l'argent/ses papiers sur s.** to have some money/one's papers on one; **prendre sur s.** to get a grip on oneself; **prendre sur s. de faire qch** to take it upon oneself to do sth

2 (*représentant un sujet déterminé* → *homme*) himself; (→ *femme*) herself; (→ *être inanimé*) itself; **on ne pouvait lui reprocher de ne penser qu'à s.** he/she couldn't be accused of thinking only of himself/herself

3 (*locutions*) **en s.** in itself, *Sout* per se; **ce geste en s. n'est pas condamnable** the gesture is not blameworthy in itself; **cela va de s.** that goes without saying; **tu lui diras? – cela va de s.!** will you tell him/her? – of course *or* that goes without saying!; **ça paraît pourtant aller de s.** it seems obvious; **il va de s. que...** it goes without saying that...

NM *Phil* **le s.** the self; *Psy* the id

soi-disant [swadizɑ̃] **ADJ INV 1** (*qu'on prétend tel* → *liberté, gratuité*) so-called; (→ *coupable, responsable*) alleged

2 (*qui se prétend tel* → *aristocrate*) self-styled; (→ *ami, héritier, génie*) so-called; **ce s. plombier était en fait un espion** the so-called plumber turned out to be a spy

ADV *Fam* (*à ce qu'on prétend*) supposedly▪, allegedly▪; **elle l'a s. tué** they say she killed him▪ *or* she's alleged to have killed him▪; **tu étais s. absent!** you were supposed to be out!▪; **elle est sortie, s. pour acheter du fromage** she went out, supposedly to get some cheese▪ *or* to get some cheese, or so she said▪

❑ **soi-disant que CONJ** *Fam* apparently▪; **s. qu'il ne nous aurait pas vus!** he didn't see us, or so he said!▪

soie [swa] **NF 1** *Tex* silk; **s. grège/naturelle/sauvage** raw/natural/wild silk; **s. moirée** watered silk; *Fig* **dormir** *ou* **vivre dans la s.** to live in the lap of luxury

2 *Zool* (*de sanglier, de chenille*) bristle; (*de bivalves*) byssus; **blaireau en soies de sanglier** bristle shaving brush

3 (*d'un couteau, d'une épée*) tang

4 *Littéraire* (*douceur*) **la s. de sa peau** the silken texture of his/her skin

❑ **de soie ADJ** (*étoffe, tapis*) silk (*avant n*); (*peau*) silky

soierie [swari] **NF 1** (*étoffe*) silk **2** (*activité*) silk trade

soif [swaf] **NF 1** (*envie de boire*) thirst; **avoir s.** to be thirsty; **avoir grand s.** to be parched; **ça m'a donné s.** it made me thirsty; **ça donne s. de bêcher au soleil** digging away in the sun works up a thirst; *Fam* **il fait s.** I'd kill for a drink, *Br* I could murder a drink; **jusqu'à plus s.** (*boire*) till one's thirst is quenched; *Fig* to one's heart's content; *Fig* **rester sur sa s.** to remain unsatisfied

2 *Fig* (*désir*) **s. de pouvoir/de richesses** craving for power/for wealth; **s. de connaissances** thirst for knowledge; **avoir s. de sang** to thirst for blood

soiffard, -e [swafar, -ard] *Fam* **ADJ** (*personne*) boozy
NM,F boozer, alky

soignant, -e [swaɲɑ̃, -ɑ̃t] **ADJ personnel s.** nursing staff

soigné, -e [swaɲe] **ADJ 1** (*propre* → *apparence, personne*) neat, tidy, well-groomed; (→ *vêtements*) neat; (→ *ongles*) well-kept; (→ *mains*)

well-cared for; **être très s. de sa personne** to be very well-groomed; **peu s.** *(apparence, personne, tenue)* untidy; *(coiffure)* unkempt; **très peu s.** slovenly

2 *(fait avec soin → décoration)* carefully done; *(→ style)* polished; *(→ écriture, coiffure)* neat, tidy; *(→ travail)* neat, careful; *(→ dîner)* carefully prepared; *(→ jardin)* neat, well-kept; **peu s.** *(jardin)* badly kept; *(dîner)* carelessly put together; *(écriture)* untidy; *(travail)* careless, shoddy; **les acteurs évoluent dans des décors très soignés** the set for the play is highly sophisticated

3 *Fam (en intensif)* **une engueulade soignée** a hell of a telling-off, a telling-off and a half; **il lui a fichu une raclée, quelque chose de s.!** he thrashed him/her to within an inch of his/her life!; **j'ai un mal de tête s.!** I've got a splitting headache!; **le devoir de chimie était s.!** the chemistry paper was a real stinker!; **l'addition était soignée** the *Br* bill *or Am* check was a bit steep

soigner [3] [swaɲe] **VT** 1 *(malade)* to treat, to nurse, to look after; *(maladie)* to treat; **à l'hôpital où on la soignait pour une anorexie** at the hospital where she was being treated for anorexia; **il ne veut pas se faire s.** he refuses (any) treatment; **ils m'ont soigné aux antibiotiques** they treated me with antibiotics; **c'est le docteur Jean qui la soigne** *(d'habitude)* she's under *or* in the care of Dr Jean; **je n'arrive pas à s. mon rhume** I can't get rid of my cold; **il a dû aller se faire s. en Suisse** he had to go to Switzerland for treatment; *Fam* **il faut te faire s.!** you need (to get) your head examined!

2 *(bien traiter → ami, animal, plantes)* to look after, to take care of; *(→ jardin)* to look after; *Fam* **elle soigne son petit mari** she takes good care of *or* she looks after her hubby

3 *(être attentif à → apparence, tenue, présentation, prononciation)* to take care *or* trouble over; *(→ écriture, style)* to polish (up); *(→ image de marque)* to take good care of, to nurse; *(→ repas)* to prepare carefully, to take trouble over (the preparation of); **s. le moindre détail** to take care over every detail; **s. sa mise** to dress with care

4 *Fam (exagérer)* **ils ont soigné l'addition!** the *Br* bill's *or Am* check's a bit steep!

5 *Fam (frapper)* **tu aurais vu ses bleus, le mec l'a soigné!** you should've seen his bruises, the guy made mincemeat of him!

▸**se soigner VPR** 1 *(prendre des médicaments)* **tu devrais te s.** you should take something for it; **quand j'ai un rhume, je ne me soigne jamais** I never take anything for a cold; **il se soigne à l'homéopathie** he relies on homeopathic treatment when he's ill; *Hum* **je suis timide mais je me soigne!** I'm shy but I'm doing my best to overcome it!

2 *(pouvoir être soigné)* to be susceptible to treatment; **ça se soigne bien** it can be easily treated; **ça se soigne difficilement** it's difficult to treat (it); *Fam Hum* **ça se soigne, tu sais!** they have a cure for that these days, you know!

soigneur [swaɲœr] **NM** *(d'un boxeur)* second; *(d'un cycliste)* trainer; *(d'une équipe de football, de rugby)* *Br* physiotherapist, *Am* physical therapist

soigneuse [swaɲøz] *voir* **soigneux**

soigneusement [swaɲøzmɑ̃] **ADV** *(écrire, plier)* neatly, carefully; *(rincer, laver)* carefully; **elle ferma très s. la porte** she closed the door very carefully *or* with great care; **sa chambre est toujours rangée très s.** his/her room is always very neat (and tidy); **il a s. omis de me le dire** he was very careful not to tell me

soigneux, -euse [swaɲø, -øz] **ADJ** 1 *(propre et ordonné)* tidy; **il n'est pas du tout s. dans son travail** he's quite untidy *or* messy in his work; **tu n'es pas assez s. de tes habits** you're not careful enough with *or* you don't take enough care of your clothes

2 *(consciencieux → employé)* meticulous; *(→ recherches, travail)* careful, meticulous; **elle est très soigneuse dans ce qu'elle fait** she's very careful in what she does, she takes great care over her work

3 *(soucieux)* **s. de sa réputation** mindful of his reputation

soi-même [swamɛm] **PRON** oneself; **être/rester s.** to be/to remain oneself; **il faut tout faire s. ici** you have to do everything yourself around here; *Fam Hum* **c'est Antoine? – s.!** is it Antoine? – in person *or* none other!; **faire qch de s.** to do sth spontaneously; **par s.** by oneself, on one's own; **se replier sur s.** to withdraw into oneself

SOIN [swɛ̃]

> **NM** care **1, 2** ▪ concern **2** ▪ neatness **3** ▪ task **4**
> **NMPL** care **1, 2** ▪ treatment **1** ▪ attention **2**

NM 1 *(attention)* care; **avoir** *ou* **prendre s. de qch** to take care of sth; **ne vous en faites pas, j'aurai bien** *ou* **grand s. de vos plantes** don't worry, I'll take good care of your plants; **prendre s. de qn** to look after *or* to take care of sb; **avoir** *ou* **prendre s. de faire qch** to take care to do *or* to make a point of doing sth; **prends s. de fermer toutes les portes à clé** take care to *or* make sure that you lock all the doors; **elle a bien pris s. de lui cacher son identité** she took great care to conceal *or* went to a great deal of trouble concealing her identity from him/her; **on dirait qu'elle met un s. tout particulier à m'agacer** it's as if she was making a point of annoying me; **avec s.** carefully, with care; **nettoyez la plaie avec le plus grand s.** clean the wound very carefully; **être sans s. (dans son travail)** to be careless (in one's work); **faire qch sans s.** to do sth carelessly; **manque de s.** carelessness

2 *(souci)* care, concern; **mon premier s. fut de tout ranger** my first concern *or* the first thing I did was to put everything back into place

3 *(propreté)* neatness; **avoir beaucoup de s.** to be very tidy *or* orderly; **elle n'a aucun s.** she's totally untidy *or* messy; **avec s.** neatly, tidily; **sa maison est toujours rangée avec s.** his/her house is always very neat *or* tidy; **être sans s.** to be untidy; **il a peint le cadre sans aucun s.** he made a mess of painting the frame

4 *(responsabilité)* task; **je te laisse le s. de la convaincre** I'm leaving it (up) to you to convince her; **confier à qn le s. de faire qch** to entrust sb with the task of doing sth; **il lui a confié le s. de gérer son garage** he entrusted him/her with running his garage

▫ **soins NMPL** 1 *(prodigués à une personne → de routine)* care; *(→ médicaments)* treatment; **cela ne requiert pas de soins particuliers** it doesn't require any special medical attention *or* care; **donner** *ou* **dispenser des soins à** *(médicaux)* to give medical care to; **prodiguer des soins à qn** to lavish care on sb; **premiers soins, soins d'urgence** first aid; **soins de beauté** skin care *(for the face)*; **soins du corps** skin care *(for the body)*; **soins dentaires** dental treatment *or* care; **soins intensifs** intensive care; **soins (médicaux)** medical care *or* treatment; **soins post-hospitaliers** follow-up care; **soins prolongés** extended care; **soins du visage** skin care *(for the face)*

2 *(attention)* care, attention; **nous apporterons tous nos soins au règlement de cette affaire** we'll do our utmost to settle this matter; **confier qn aux (bons) soins de qn** to leave sb in the care of sb; **ils avaient confié l'enfant aux bons soins de sa tante** they had placed the child in the care of his/her aunt; **aux bons soins de** *(dans le courrier)* care of; *Fam* **sa grand-mère est aux petits soins pour lui** his grandmother waits on him hand and foot

soir [swar] **NM** 1 *(fin du jour)* evening; *(début de la nuit)* night; **les soirs d'été** summer evenings; **le s. tombe** night is falling, the evening is drawing in; **le s. de ses vingt ans** on the evening of her twentieth birthday; *Littéraire* **au s. de sa vie** in the evening of his/her life; **quand le grand s. sera arrivé** when the revolution comes

2 *(dans des expressions de temps)* **ce s.** tonight, this evening; **à ce s.!** see you tonight *or* this evening!; **lundi s.** Monday evening *or* night; **hier s.** yesterday evening, last night; **le onze au s.** on the eleventh in the evening, on the evening of the eleventh; **le s.** in the evening, in the evenings; **tous les soirs, chaque s.** every evening; **vers six heures du s.** around six (o'clock) in the evening, around six p.m.; **à dix heures du s.** at ten (o'clock) at night, at ten p.m.

3 *Presse* **Le S.** = main Belgian daily newspaper

▫ **du soir ADJ** 1 *(journal)* evening *(avant n)*; *(prière)* night *(avant n)*

2 *Fam (personne)* **il est du s.** he's a night owl

soirée [sware] **NF** 1 *(fin de la journée)* evening; **les longues soirées d'hiver** the long winter evenings; **viens dans la s.** *(aujourd'hui)* come this evening; *(un jour quelconque)* come in the evening; *Fam* **on s'est fait une s. télévision/théâtre** we spent the evening in front of the television/at the theatre; **bonne s.!** have a nice evening!, enjoy your evening!

2 *(fête, réunion)* party; **s. dansante** (evening) dance; **s. de gala** gala evening; **s. musicale** musical evening

3 *Théât* evening performance; *Cin* evening showing; **projeter un film en s.** to show a movie *or Br* film in the evening, to have an evening showing of a movie *or Br* film; **elle n'a pas joué en s.** she didn't play in the evening performance

sois *etc voir* **être**[1]

soit CONJ [swa] 1 *(c'est-à-dire)* that is to say; **il a perdu toute sa fortune, s. plusieurs millions d'euros** he has lost his entire fortune, that is to say several million euros; **ça fait 10 euros plus 8 euros, s. 18 euros** that's 10 euros plus 8 euros, that makes 18 euros

2 *(introduisant une hypothèse)* **s. une droite AB** let AB be a line, given a line AB

ADV [swat] **s., j'accepte vos conditions** very well then, I accept your conditions; **tu préfères cela? eh bien s.!** all right *or* very well then, if that's what you prefer!; **puisque vous y tenez, s., mais je vous aurai prévenu** very well, since you're so determined, but don't say I didn't warn you

▫ **soit que... ou que... CONJ** either... or...; **s. que le train ait eu du retard ou qu'il y ait eu des embouteillages, ils arrivèrent après minuit** either the train was late or they were held up in traffic, but they arrived after midnight

▫ **soit que..., soit que... CONJ** either... or...; **s. que vous veniez chez moi, s. que j'aille chez vous, nous nous retrouverons demain** either you come to my place or I'll go to yours, but we'll meet up tomorrow

▫ **soit... soit... CONJ** either... or...; **s. toi, s. moi** either you or me; **j'ai cet article s. en rouge, s. en bleu, s. en vert** I have this item (either) in red, blue or green; **c'est s. l'un, s. l'autre** it's (either) one or the other; **s. distraction, s. malveillance, il avait omis de les avertir** either through absent-mindedness or carelessness he had forgotten to warn them

soit-communiqué [swakɔmynike] **NM INV** *Jur* **ordonnance de s.** = order of an examining magistrate to send the papers relating to a case to the public prosecutor

soixantaine [swasɑ̃tɛn] **NF** 1 *(quantité)* **une s.** around *or* about sixty, sixty or so; **une s. de voitures** around *or* about sixty cars; **elle a une s. d'années** she's around *or* about sixty (years old) 2 *(âge)* **avoir la s.** to be around *or* about sixty; **quand on arrive à** *ou* **on atteint la s.** when you hit sixty

soixante [swasɑ̃t] **ADJ** 1 *(gén)* sixty 2 *(dans des séries)* sixtieth; **page/numéro s.** page/number sixty

PRON sixty

NM INV 1 *(gén)* sixty 2 *(numéro d'ordre)* number sixty 3 *(chiffre écrit)* sixty; *voir aussi* **cinquante**

soixante-dix [swasɑ̃tdis] **ADJ INV** 1 *(gén)* seventy 2 *(dans des séries)* seventieth; **page/numéro s.** page/number seventy

PRON INV seventy

NM INV 1 *(gén)* seventy 2 *(numéro d'ordre)* number seventy 3 *(chiffre écrit)* seventy; *voir aussi* **cinquante**

soixante-dix-huit tours [swasɑ̃tdizɥitur] **NM INV** 78 rpm, seventy-eight (record)

soixante-dixième [swasɑ̃tdizjɛm] *(pl* **soixante-dixièmes)** **ADJ** seventieth

NMF 1 *(personne)* seventieth 2 *(objet)* seventieth (one)

NM 1 *(partie)* seventieth 2 *(étage)* *Br* seventieth

floor, *Am* seventy-first floor; *voir aussi* **cinquième**

soixante-dixièmement [swasɑ̃tdizjɛmmɑ̃] **ADV** in seventieth place

soixante-huitard, -e [swasɑ̃tɥitar, -ard] *(mpl* **soixante-huitards,** *fpl* **soixante-huitardes)** **ADJ** *(réforme)* = brought about by the students' revolt of 1968; *(tendance)* anti-establishment
NM,F veteran of the 1968 students' revolt

soixante-neuf [swasɑ̃tnœf] **NM INV** *Fam (position sexuelle)* sixty-nine

soixantième [swasɑ̃tjɛm] **ADJ** sixtieth
NMF **1** *(personne)* sixtieth **2** *(objet)* sixtieth (one)
NM **1** *(partie)* sixtieth **2** *(étage) Br* sixtieth floor, *Am* sixty-first floor; *voir aussi* **cinquième**

soixantièmement [swasɑ̃tjɛmmɑ̃] **ADV** in sixtieth place

soja [sɔʒa] **NM** soya; **lait de s.** soya milk

sol [sɔl] **NM INV** *Mus* G; *(chanté)* sol, so, soh
NM **1** *Agr & Hort (terre)* soil; **s. calcaire** chalky soil; **le s. est détrempé par les pluies** the soil is soaked with rainwater
2 *(surface → de la Terre)* ground; *(→ d'une planète)* surface; **l'avion s'est écrasé au s.** the plane crashed; **le s. lunaire** the surface of the Moon
3 *(surface aménagée → à l'intérieur)* floor; **le s. du hangar** the floor of the shed; **pour l'entretien des sols** for cleaning floors; **spécialiste des sols** flooring specialist
4 *Littéraire (patrie)* soil; **sur le s. américain** on American soil; **son s. natal** his/her native soil
5 *Géol* soil, *Spéc* solum
6 *Sport* floor
7 *Chim* sol
8 *Arch (sou)* sol
❑ **au sol** **ADJ** **1** *Sport (exercice)* floor *(avant n)*
2 *Aviat (vitesse, ravitaillement, personnel)* ground *(avant n)*

solage [sɔlaʒ] **NM** *Can (d'une maison)* foundations

sol-air [sɔlɛr] **ADJ INV** ground-to-air; **S. Missile** surface-to-air missile, SAM

solaire [sɔlɛr] **ADJ** **1** *Astron* solar; **le rayonnement s.** the Sun's radiation **2** *(qui a trait au soleil)* solar; **les symboles solaires dans l'Égypte ancienne** the solar symbols of Ancient Egypt **3** *(qui utilise le soleil → capteur, four)* solar; *(→ habitat)* solar, solar-heated **4** *(qui protège du soleil)* sun *(avant n)*; **crème/huile s.** suntan lotion/oil **5** *Anat* **plexus s.** solar plexus
NM *Écol* **le s.** solar energy

solanacée [sɔlanase] *Bot* **NF** member of the Solanaceae
❑ **solanacées** **NFPL** Solanaceae

solarigraphe [sɔlarigraf] **NM** solarimeter, pyranometer

solarisation [sɔlarizasjɔ̃] **NF** solarization

solariser [3] [sɔlarize] *Phot* **VT** to solarize
►**se solariser** **VPR** to solarize

solarium [sɔlarjɔm] **NM** solarium

soldanelle [sɔldanɛl] **NF** *Bot* soldanella

soldat [sɔlda] **NM** **1** *Mil* soldier; *(grade)* private; **s. Dubois!** Private Dubois!; **se faire s.** to go into *or* to join the army; **simple s., s. de deuxième classe** *(dans l'armée de terre)* private; *(dans l'armée de l'air) Br* aircraftman, *Am* airman basic; **s. de première classe** *(dans l'armée de terre) Br* ≃ lance corporal, *Am* ≃ private first class; **le S. inconnu** the Unknown Soldier *or* Warrior
2 *(jeu)* **(petits) soldats de plomb** tin *or* lead *or* toy soldiers; **jouer aux petits soldats** to play with toy soldiers; *Fam* **jouer au petit s.** to swagger
3 *Entom* soldier (ant)

soldate [sɔldat] **NF** *Fam* woman soldier■, servicewoman■

soldatesque [sɔldatɛsk] *Littéraire* **ADJ** **des manières soldatesques** rough soldierly manners
NF *Péj* **la s.** army rabble

solde[1] [sɔld] **NF** **1** *Mil* pay
2 *(en Afrique francophone) (salaire)* salary, wages
❑ **à la solde de** **PRÉP** *Péj* in the pay of; **il était à la s. de l'ennemi** he was in the pay of the enemy; **avoir qn à sa s.** to be sb's paymaster

solde[2] [sɔld] **NM** **1** *Fin (d'un compte)* (bank) balance; *(à payer)* outstanding balance; **pour s. de tout compte** in full settlement; **régler le s.** to pay the balance; **vous serez remboursés du s. en janvier** you'll be paid the balance in January; **s. actif** credit balance; **s. bancaire, s. en banque** bank balance; **s. bénéficiaire** credit balance; **s. en caisse** cash balance; **s. commercial** balance of trade; **s. créditeur** credit balance; **s. cumulé** cumulative balance; **s. débiteur** *ou* **déficitaire** debit balance, balance owed; **s. à découvert** outstanding balance; **s. disponible** available balance; **s. de dividende** final dividend; **s. dû** balance due; **s. de fin de mois** end-of-month-balance; *Compta* **s. à nouveau** balance brought forward; *Compta* **s. nul** nil balance; **s. d'ouverture** opening balance; **s. passif** debit balance; *Compta* **s. reporté** balance brought forward; **s. à reporter** balance carried forward; **s. de trésorerie** cash balance; **pour s. de tout compte** in (full) settlement
2 *Com (vente)* sale; *(marchandise)* sale item *or* article; **en s.** *(marchandise) Br* in the sale, *Am* on sale; **acheter** *ou* **avoir qch en s.** to buy *or* to get sth *Br* in the sale *or Am* on sale; **le bonnet était en s.** the hat was reduced; **mettre** *ou* **vendre qch en s.** to sell sth off; **s. de fermeture** closing-down sale; **s. de fin de saison** end-of-season sale; **s. après inventaire** stocktaking sale
❑ **soldes** **NMPL** *(période)* sale, sales; **au moment des soldes** during the sales, when the sales are on; **il y a de belles affaires pendant les soldes chez eux** they have really good bargains in their sales; **faire les soldes** to go round the sales; **ils font des soldes toute l'année** they have sales *or* a sale on all year round

solder [3] [sɔlde] **VT** **1** *Com (stock)* to sell off, to discount; **toutes nos chemises sont soldées** all our shirts are at a reduced *or* at sale price; **elle me l'a soldé pour 30 euros** she knocked the price down to 30 euros, she let me have it for 30 euros; **tout est soldé à 10 euros** everything is reduced to 10 euros
2 *(dette)* to settle; **s. l'arriéré** to make up back payments
3 *Banque (compte)* to close
USAGE ABSOLU *Com* **on solde!** the sales are on!, there's a sale on!
►**se solder** **VPR** **1** **se s. par** *(se terminer par)* to result in; **se s. par un échec** to result in failure, to come to nothing; **encore une soirée qui se solde par une querelle** yet again, the party's ended in an argument; **leurs cinq derniers matches se sont soldés par une défaite** their last five matches ended in defeat
2 *Com, Écon & Fin* **se s. par un excédent/un déficit de qch** to show a surplus/a deficit of sth

solderie [sɔldəri] **NF** discount store

soldeur, -euse [sɔldœr, -øz] **NM,F** discount trader

sole [sɔl] **NF** **1** *(d'un four)* hearth **2** *Agr* break (field) **3** *Mines* sill, sole **4** *(d'un cheval)* sole **5** *Tech* sole piece **6** *Constr* (trowel) throw **7** *Naut (d'un navire)* flat bottom **8** *Ich* sole

soléaire [sɔleɛr] *Anat* **ADJ** soleus
NM soleus muscle

solécisor [3] [sɔlesize] **VT** *Littéraire* to solecize

solécisme [sɔlesism] **NM** *Gram* solecism

soleil [sɔlɛj] **NM** **1** *(étoile qui éclaire la Terre)* **le S.** the Sun; **se lever avec le s.** to be up with the lark; **le s. levant/couchant** the rising/setting sun; **au s. levant/couchant** at sunrise/sunset; **le s. de minuit** the midnight sun; **il n'y a rien de nouveau sous le s.** there is nothing new under the sun; *Prov* **le s. brille pour tout le monde** = the sun shines for everyone
2 *(étoile quelconque)* sun
3 *(chaleur)* sun, sunshine; *(clarté)* sun, sunlight, sunshine; **quelques brèves apparitions du s.** some sunny spells; **il y aura beaucoup de s. sur le sud de la France** it'll be very sunny in *or* over southern France; **une journée sans s.** a day with no sunshine; **un s. de plomb** a blazing sun; **ma chambre manque de s.** my room doesn't get enough sun *or* sunlight; **on a le s. sur le balcon jusqu'à midi** the balcony gets the sun until noon; **c'est une plante qui adore le s.** this plant thrives in sunlight; **au s.** in the sun; *Fig* **avoir des biens** *ou* **du bien au s.** to own property; **tu es en plein s.** you're right in the sun; **prendre le s.** to sunbathe
4 *Bot* sunflower
5 *Sport* (backward) grand circle
6 *(feu d'artifice)* Catherine wheel
7 *Hér* sol
8 *Presse* **le S.** = Quebec French-language daily newspaper

solen [sɔlɛn] **NM** *Br* razor shell, *Am* razor clam

solennel, -elle [sɔlanɛl] **ADJ** **1** *(obsèques, honneurs, silence)* solemn; **prendre des airs solennels** to adopt a solemn air **2** *(déclaration, occasion, personne, ton)* solemn, formal **3** *Jur (contrat)* solemn

solennellement [sɔlanɛlmɑ̃] **ADV** **1** *(en grande pompe)* formally, ceremoniously **2** *(cérémonieusement)* solemnly, in a solemn voice **3** *(officiellement)* solemnly; **je le jure s.** I solemnly swear

solenniser [3] [sɔlanize] **VT** to solemnize

solennité [sɔlanite] **NF** **1** *(d'une réception)* solemnity **2** *(d'un ton, d'une personne)* solemnity, formality; **avec s.** solemnly **3** *(fête)* solemn ceremony *or* celebration; **la s. de Pâques** the solemn celebration of Easter **4** *Jur* solemnity

solénoïdal, -e, -aux, -ales [sɔlenɔidal, -o] **ADJ** solenoidal

solénoïde [sɔlenɔid] **NM** solenoid

soleret [sɔlrɛ] **NM** *Hist* solleret, steel shoe

Soleure [sɔlœr] **NM** *Géog* Solothurn; **le canton de S.** Solothurn

Solex® [sɔlɛks] **NM** ≃ moped

solfatare [sɔlfatar] **NF** solfatara

solfège [sɔlfɛʒ] **NM** **1** *(notation)* music theory; *(déchiffrage)* sight-reading; **faire du s.** to study music theory; **s. chanté** sol-fa **2** *(manuel)* music primer

solfier [9] [sɔlfje] **VT** to sol-fa; **solfiez correctement le morceau suivant** sol-fa the following piece of music accurately

solicitor [sɔlisitɔr] **NM** solicitor

solidage [sɔlidaʒ] **NF** *Bot* goldenrod; **s. du Canada** Canadian goldenrod

solidago [sɔlidago] **NM** = **solidage**

solidaire [sɔlidɛr] **ADJ** **1** *(personnes)* **être solidaires** *(les uns des autres)* to stand *or* to stick together; *(l'un de l'autre)* to show solidarity with each other; **nous sommes solidaires de nos camarades** we support *or* we stand by our comrades; **ne cherchez pas à diviser les dockers, ils sont tous solidaires** don't try to split the dockers, they're in complete solidarity; **deux syndicats peu solidaires** two unions showing little solidarity
2 *(reliés → processus, pièces mécaniques)* interdependent; **être s. de** to interact with; **une roue s. d'une autre** a wheel integral with another
3 *(interdépendants)* interdependent; **ces deux questions sont solidaires (l'une de l'autre)** these two questions are interdependent
4 *Jur (responsabilité)* joint and several; *(personnes)* jointly liable; **obligation s.** obligation binding on all parties

solidairement [sɔlidɛrmɑ̃] **ADV** **1** *(conjointement)* jointly, in solidarity with each other **2** *Fig* **les processus fonctionnent s.** the processes are interdependent **3** *Tech (par engrenage)* in a mesh; *(directement)* locked (together) **4** *Jur* jointly and severally

solidariser [3] [sɔlidarize] **VT** **1** *(faire partager les mêmes intérêts)* to unify, to bring together **2** *(relier → processus)* to make interdependent **3** *Tech (par engrenage)* to mesh; *(directement)* to lock (together), to interlock
►**se solidariser** **VPR** **se s. (avec)** to make common cause (with), to show solidarity (with)

solidarité [sɔlidarite] **NF** **1** *(entre personnes)* solidarity; **par s. avec** out of fellow-feeling for, in order to show solidarity with; **s. ministérielle** ministerial responsibility **2** *(de processus)* interdependence **3** *Tech (engrenage)* meshing; *(entraînement)* locking, interlocking **4** *Jur* joint and several liability; **s. pénale** joint liability

SOLIDE [sɔlid]

ADJ solid **1, 2, 4, 5, 7** ■ sturdy **1, 3** ■ strong **1, 2** ■ sound **2, 3** ■ firm **2** ■ substantial **4** ■ resistant **6**
NM solid ground **2** ■ solid food **3** ■ solid **4**

ADJ **1** *(résistant → meubles, matériel)* solid, sturdy, strong; *(→ papier)* tough, strong; *(→ vêtements)* hard-wearing; *(→ bâtiment)* solid, strong; *(→ verrou, nœud)* secure; **peu s.** *(chaise, pont)* rickety;

attention, cette chaise n'est pas très s. careful, that chair's not very safe

2 *(établi, stable → formation, culture, technique)* sound; *(→ entreprise)* well-established; *(→ institution, argument, preuves)* solid, sound; *(→ garanties)* solid, reliable; *(→ professionnalisme, réputation)* solid; *(→ bases)* solid, sound, firm; *(→ amitié)* firm, strong; *(→ foi)* firm, staunch; *(→ principes, qualités)* staunch, sound, sterling *(avant n)*; *(→ liens)* strong, close; *(→ monnaie)* strong, firm; **j'ai de solides raisons de croire que...** I have good reasons for believing that...; **ça ne repose sur rien de s.** there is no sound *or* no solid basis for that; **attitude empreinte d'un s. bon sens** no-nonsense attitude, attitude based on sound common sense; **elle s'est entourée d'une s. équipe de chercheurs** she's surrounded herself with a reliable *or* a strong research team

3 *(robuste → personne, membre)* sturdy, robust; *(→ santé)* sound; **avoir une s. constitution** to have a strong constitution; **le poulain n'est pas encore très s. sur ses pattes** the foal isn't very steady on its legs yet; **le cœur n'est plus très s.** the heart's getting weaker; **la tête n'est plus très s.** his/her mind's going; **être encore s. comme un roc** *ou* **comme le Pont-Neuf** to be still hale and hearty

4 *(avant le nom) Fam (substantiel)* substantial■, solid■; **un s. petit déjeuner** a substantial *or* a solid breakfast; **un s. coup de poing** a mighty punch; **avoir une s. avance sur ses concurrents** to enjoy a secure *or* a comfortable lead over one's rivals■; **avoir un s. appétit** *ou* **coup de fourchette** to have a hearty appetite■

5 *(non liquide → aliments, corps, état)* solid; **la lave devient s. en refroidissant** lava solidifies *or* hardens as it cools down; **elle ne peut rien manger de s.** she can't eat solid foods *or* solids

6 *Tex (tissu)* resistant; *(teinture)* fast

7 *Math* solid

NM 1 *(ce qui est robuste)* **les voitures suédoises, c'est du s.** Swedish cars are built to last; *Fam* **son dernier argument, c'est du s.!** his/her last argument is rock solid!

2 *(sol ferme)* solid ground; **marcher sur du s.** to walk on solid ground

3 *(aliments solides)* solids, solid food

4 *Math & Phys* solid; **s. de révolution** solid of revolution

---

solidement [sɔlidmɑ̃] **ADV 1** *(fortement)* securely, firmly; **attache-le s. à cet arbre** tie it securely to this tree; **un homme s. bâti** a solidly *or* a sturdily built man **2** *(profondément)* firmly; **c'est une croyance s. ancrée** it's a deeply-rooted *or* a deep-seated belief **3** *Fam (en intensif)* seriously; **je l'ai s. grondé** I gave him a good talking-to

solidification [sɔlidifikasjɔ̃] **NF** solidification

solidifier [9] [sɔlidifje] **VT** to solidify, to harden

▸**se solidifier VPR** to solidify, to harden

solidité [sɔlidite] **NF 1** *(d'un meuble)* solidity, sturdiness; *(d'un vêtement)* sturdiness, durability; *(d'un bâtiment)* solidity; **c'est d'une s. à toute épreuve** it stands up to anything

2 *(d'une institution, de principes, d'arguments)* solidity, soundness; *(d'une amitié)* firmness, strength; *(d'une équipe)* reliability; *(d'une monnaie)* strength; **la s. technique de son jeu** the soundness of his/her playing technique

3 *(force d'une personne)* sturdiness, robustness

4 *Tex (d'un tissu)* resistance; *(d'une teinture)* colourfastness

soliflore [sɔliflɔr] **NM** bud vase

solifluxion [sɔliflyksjɔ̃] **NF** *Géol* solifluction, solifluxion

soliloque [sɔlilɔk] **NM** soliloquy

soliloquer [3] [sɔlilɔke] **VI** to soliloquize

Soliman [sɔlimɑ̃] **NPR S. Ier** *ou* **le Magnifique** Suleiman the Magnificent

solin [sɔlɛ̃] **NM** *Constr (espace)* space between joists; *(enduit)* plaster filling

solipède [sɔlipɛd] *Vieilli Zool* **ADJ** solidungulate, whole-hoofed

NM soliped

solipsisme [sɔlipsism] **NM** *Phil* solipsism

soliste [sɔlist] **NMF** soloist

solitaire [sɔlitɛr] **ADJ 1** *(personne, existence, activité)* solitary, lonely

2 *(isolé → île, quartier, retraite)* solitary, lone; **une maison s. dans la forêt** a solitary house in the forest; **passer des vacances solitaires** to spend one's holidays on one's own

3 *Archit (colonne)* isolated

4 *Bot & Zool* solitary; **ver s.** tapeworm

NMF 1 *(misanthrope)* loner; **c'est une s.** she is a loner, she enjoys her own company

2 *(navigateur, voyageur)* **c'est une course de solitaires** it's a single-handed race

NM 1 *(anachorète)* hermit, recluse

2 *(jeu, diamant)* solitaire

3 *Zool* solitary boar

❑ **en solitaire ADJ** *(course, vol)* solo *(avant n)*; *(navigation)* single-handed **ADV** *(vivre, travailler)* on one's own; *(naviguer)* single-handed; **il vit en s. dans sa vieille maison** he lives on his own in his old house

solitairement [sɔlitɛrmɑ̃] **ADV se promener s.** to walk alone; **vivre s.** to lead a solitary life

solitude [sɔlityd] **NF 1** *(d'une personne → momentanée)* solitude; *(→ habituelle)* loneliness; **rechercher la s.** to seek solitude; **la s. lui pèse** solitude weighs heavily upon him/her; **j'aime la s.** I like to be alone *or* on my own; **vivre dans la s.** to live alone *or* on one's own; **dans une grande s. morale** morally isolated; **la s. à deux** the loneliness of a couple *(when the two stop communicating with each other)* **2** *(d'une forêt, d'un paysage)* loneliness, solitude **3** *Littéraire (lieu solitaire)* **les grandes solitudes désertiques** the vast lonely expanses of the desert

solive [sɔliv] **NF** *Constr* joist; **s. apparente** exposed joist

soliveau, -x [sɔlivo] **NM** *Constr* small joist

Soljenitsyne [sɔlʒenitsin] **NPR** Solzhenitsyn

sollicitation [sɔlisitasjɔ̃] **NF 1** *(requête)* request, entreaty; **j'ai fini par céder à leurs sollicitations** I ended up giving in to their requests **2** *(tentation)* temptation **3** *(poussée, traction)* **les freins répondent à la moindre s.** the brakes are extremely responsive **4** *Constr* stress; **s. de compression/de torsion/de traction** compressive/torsion/tensile stress

solliciter [3] [sɔlisite] **VT 1** *(requérir → entrevue)* to request, to solicit, *Sout* to beg the favour of; *(→ aide, conseils)* to solicit, to seek (urgently); *(→ emploi)* to apply for; *(→ voix)* to canvass for; **s. qch de qn** to request sth from sb; **je me permets de s. votre bienveillance** may I appeal to your kindness

2 *(mettre en éveil → curiosité, attention)* to arouse; *(→ élève)* to spur *or* to urge on; **le problème qui nous sollicite** *ou* **qui sollicite notre attention actuellement** the problem currently before us

3 *(texte)* to overinterpret

4 *(faire appel à)* to approach, to appeal to; **être très sollicité** to be (very much) in demand; **sollicité par les chasseurs de tête** head-hunted; **on m'a déjà sollicité pour une séance de pose** I've already been approached for a photo-call; **ils nous ont souvent sollicités par téléphone** they often made cold calls to us; **s. qn de faire qch** to appeal to sb to do sth

5 *(faire fonctionner → mécanisme)* to put a strain on; **dès que les freins sont sollicités** as soon as you touch the brakes

6 *Équitation (cheval)* to spur *or* to urge on

solliciteur, -euse [sɔlisitœr, -øz] **NM,F** *(quémandeur)* suppliant, supplicant

sollicitude [sɔlisityd] **NF** *(intérêt → affectueux)* (excessive) care, *Sout* solicitude; *(→ soucieux)* concern, *Sout* solicitude; **il m'écoutait avec s.** he was listening to me with concern *or Sout* solicitude; **plein de s.** solicitous, attentive; **être plein de s. envers qn** to be very attentive to *or* towards sb

solo [sɔlo] *(pl* **solos** *ou* **soli** [-li]) **NM 1** *Mus* solo; **s. de piano/de harpe** piano/harp solo; **elle joue/chante en s.** she plays/sings solo; *Fig* **une escalade en s.** a solo climb **2** *Théât (spectacle → d'homme)* one-man show; *(→ de femme)* one-woman show

NMF *(pl* **solos**) *(célibataire)* single person; **les solos** singles

ADJ INV solo *(avant n)*; **violon/album s.** solo violin/album; *Théât* **spectacle s.** *(d'homme)* one-man show; *(de femme)* one-woman show

Sologne [sɔlɔɲ] **NF la S.** the Sologne

Solon [sɔlɔ̃] **NPR** Solon

sol-sol [sɔlsɔl] **ADJ INV** ground-to-ground; **s. balistique stratégique** ≃ medium-range ballistic missile, MRBM

solstice [sɔlstis] **NM** solstice; **s. d'été/d'hiver** summer/winter solstice

solsticial, -e, -aux, -ales [sɔlstisjal, -o] **ADJ** solsticial

solubilisation [sɔlybilizasjɔ̃] **NF** solubilization

solubiliser [3] [sɔlybilize] **VT** to solubilize, to make soluble

solubilité [sɔlybilite] **NF** solubility; **produit de s.** solubility product

soluble [sɔlybl] **ADJ 1** *Chim* soluble; **s. dans l'eau** water-soluble **2** *(problème)* solvable, soluble

soluté [sɔlyte] **NM** *Chim* solute; **s. physiologique** saline solution, (artificial) serum

solution [sɔlysjɔ̃] **NF 1** *(résolution, clé)* solution, answer (**de** to); *Scol* **la s. d'un exercice** the solution *or* the answer to an exercise; **la s. d'une énigme** the key to an enigma *or* to a mystery; **l'envoyer en prison ne serait pas une s.** sending him/her to prison wouldn't solve anything *or* wouldn't be a solution; **apporter une s. à un problème** to find a solution to *or* to solve a problem; **une s. de facilité** an easy way out; **s. de principe** standard solution

2 *(terme → d'une crise)* resolution, settling; *(→ d'une situation complexe)* resolution

3 *Hist* **la s. finale** the Final Solution

4 *Math* solution

5 *Méd* **s. de continuité** solution of continuity; *Fig* **sans s. de continuité** without interruption

6 *Chim & Pharm* solution; **en s.** dissolved, in (a) solution; *Phot* **s. de fixage** fixing solution; **s. de rinçage** wetting solution; **s. saline** saline solution; **s. saturée** saturated solution

solutionner [3] [sɔlysjɔne] **VT** to solve, to resolve

Solutré [sɔlytre] **NM** = prehistoric site in Burgundy where François Mitterrand traditionally used to take a much-publicized annual walk

solutréen, -enne [sɔlytreɛ̃, -ɛn] **ADJ** Solutrean

❑ **Solutréen NM** Solutrean (period)

solvabilité [sɔlvabilite] **NF** solvency; **degré de s.** credit rating

solvable [sɔlvabl] **ADJ** solvent

solvant [sɔlvɑ̃] **NM** *Chim* solvent

solvatation [sɔlvatasjɔ̃] **NF** *Chim* solvation

solvate [sɔlvat] **NM** *Chim* solvate

solvatisation [sɔlvatizasjɔ̃] **NF** *Chim* solvation

solvatisé [sɔlvatize] **ADJ** *Chim* solvated

solvens [sɔlvɛ̃s] **NM** *Jur* = person who pays a sum owed

soma [sɔma] **NM** *Biol* soma

somali, -e [sɔmali] **ADJ** Somalian, Somali

NM *(langue)* Somali

❑ **Somali, -e NM,F** Somali; **les Somalis** the Somalis *or* Somali

Somalie [sɔmali] **NF 1 la S.** *(république)* Somalia; **vivre en S.** to live in Somalia; **aller en S.** to go to Somalia **2** *(bassin)* Somaliland; *Hist* **la S. britannique/italienne** British/Italian Somaliland

somalien, -enne [sɔmaljɛ̃, -ɛn] **ADJ** Somalian, Somali

NM *(langue)* Somali

❑ **Somalien, -enne NM,F** Somali; **les Somaliens** the Somalis *or* Somali

somatique [sɔmatik] **ADJ** somatic; **affection s.** somatic disorder

somatisation [sɔmatizasjɔ̃] **NF** somatization

somatiser [3] [sɔmatize] **VT** *Psy* to somatize

USAGE ABSOLU mais non, tu n'es pas malade, tu somatises you're not really ill, it's all in your head

somatogène [sɔmatɔʒɛn] **ADJ** *Biol* somatogenic

somatologie [sɔmatɔlɔʒi] **NF** somatology

somatotrope [sɔmatɔtrɔp] **ADJ** *Physiol* somatotropic, somatotrophic; **hormone s.** growth *or* somatotrophic hormone

somatotrophine [sɔmatɔtrɔfin], **somatotropine** [sɔmatɔtrɔpin] **NF** *Physiol* somatotropin, somatotrophin

sombre [sɔ̃br] **ADJ 1** *(pièce, ruelle, couleur, robe)* dark; **il fait très s.** it's very dark

2 *(personne, caractère, humeur, regard)* gloomy,

melancholy, sombre; *(avenir, perspectives)* gloomy; **de sombres réflexions** sombre *or* gloomy thoughts; **les jours les plus sombres de notre histoire** the darkest days of our history

3 *(avant le nom) Fam (en intensif)* **c'est une s. crapule/un s. crétin** he's the scum of the earth/a total idiot; **il m'a raconté une s. histoire de fraude fiscale** he told me some murky story about tax evasion; **ils se sont fâchés pour une s. histoire d'argent** they quarrelled over some sordid little business of money; **ce s. individu reparut deux jours plus tard** that unsavoury character was seen again two days later

4 *Ling (voyelle)* dark

sombrement [sɔ̃brəmɑ̃] **ADV** gloomily, sombrely; **"rien", fit-il s.** "nothing," he said gloomily

sombrer [3] [sɔ̃bre] **VI 1** *(bateau)* to sink, to founder

2 *(être anéanti → civilisation)* to fall, to decline, to collapse; *(→ entreprise)* to go bankrupt, to fail, to collapse; *(→ projet)* to collapse, to fail; *(→ espoir)* to fade, to be dashed; **sa raison a sombré** he/she lost his/her reason

3 **s. dans** *(s'abandonner à)* to sink into; **s. dans le sommeil/le désespoir** to sink into sleep/despair; **s. dans la folie/l'alcoolisme** to sink into insanity/alcoholism; **ça l'a fait s. dans l'alcool/la dépression** it drove him to drink/plunged him into depression

sombrero [sɔ̃brero] **NM** sombrero

somesthésie [sɔmɛstezi] **NF** *Physiol* somaesthesia

somite [sɔmit] **NM** *Biol* somite

sommable [sɔmabl] **ADJ** *Math* summable

sommaire [sɔmɛr] **ADJ 1** *(succinct)* brief, succinct; **voici une description s. des lieux** here is a brief description of the premises

2 *(rudimentaire → réparation)* makeshift; *(→ repas)* scanty; **il n'a reçu qu'une éducation s.** his education was rudimentary, to say the least

3 *(superficiel → analyse)* summary, basic; *(→ examen)* cursory, perfunctory; **son analyse est trop s.** his/her analysis is too superficial *or* doesn't go far enough; **faire une toilette s.** to have a quick wash

4 *(expéditif → procès, exécution)* summary; **après un jugement s.** after a summary trial

NM *(d'un magazine)* summary; *(d'un livre)* summary, synopsis; **au s. de notre journal ce soir** our main news stories tonight

sommairement [sɔmɛrmɑ̃] **ADV 1** *(brièvement)* briefly; **analysez s. ce texte** make a brief analysis of this text

2 *(rudimentairement)* basically; **leur appartement est très s. meublé** their *Br* flat *or Am* apartment is very basic *or* very sparsely furnished

3 *(rapidement)* hastily, rapidly; **il a s. inventorié le contenu des poches de la victime** he made a rapid inventory of the contents of the victim's pockets

4 *(expéditivement)* summarily; **les prisonniers ont été s. exécutés** the prisoners were summarily executed

sommation [sɔmasjɔ̃] **NF 1** *Mil (avant de tirer)* warning, challenge; **faire une s.** to challenge; **tirer sans s.** to fire without warning; **après les sommations d'usage** after the standard warning (had been given)

2 *Jur* notice, demand; **avoir s. de payer une dette** to receive notice *or* a demand to pay a debt; **s. de se présenter au tribunal** summons to appear (in court); **s. sans frais** (tax) reminder

3 *(requête)* demand; **je me rendis à ses sommations courtoises mais pressantes** I gave in to his/her polite but insistent demands

4 *Math* summation

5 *Physiol* convergence

Somme [sɔm] **NF 1** *(fleuve)* **la S.** the (River) Somme **2** *(département)* **la S.** the Somme **3** *Hist* **la bataille de la S.** the (battle of the) Somme

somme¹ [sɔm] **NM** nap; **faire un (petit) s.** to have a nap

somme² [sɔm] **NF 1** *Fin* **s. (d'argent)** sum *or* amount (of money); **pour la s. de 50 euros** for (the sum of) 50 euros; **elle me doit une s. importante** she owes me a lot of money; **j'ai dépensé des sommes folles** I spent huge amounts of money; **c'est une s.!** that's a lot of money!; **le papier peint, la peinture, ça fait des sommes tout ça!** wallpaper, paint, it all adds up!; **s. due** amount *or* total due; **s. forfaitaire** lump sum; **s. nette** net amount; *Compta* **sommes payables** sums payable; **s. totale** total amount, sum total

2 *Math* sum; **la s. totale** the grand total; **faire une s.** to add up (figures); **faire la s. de 15 et de 16** to add (up) 15 and 16; **s. algébrique** algebraic sum

3 *(quantité)* amount; **s. de travail/d'énergie** amount of work/of energy; **ça représente une s. de sacrifices/d'efforts importante** it means great sacrifices/a lot of effort; **quand on fait la s. de tout ce que j'ai remué comme archives** when you add up the number of archive documents I've handled

4 *(œuvre)* general survey; **son 'Histoire de France', c'est une s.** his/her 'French History' is an essential reference work; **s. philosophique** general survey of philosophy; *Rel* **la S. Théologique** the Summa Theologica

❑ **en somme ADV 1** *(en bref)* in short; **en s., tu refuses** in short, your answer is no

2 *(en définitive)* all in all; **c'est assez simple en s.** all in all, it's quite easy

❑ **somme toute ADV** all things considered, when all is said and done; **s. toute, tu as eu de la chance** all things considered, you've been lucky

sommeil [sɔmɛj] **NM 1** *(repos)* sleep; **je manque de s.** I haven't been getting enough sleep; **il cherchait le s.** he was trying to sleep; **j'en perds le s.** I'm losing sleep over it; **j'ai le s. léger/profond** I'm a light/a heavy sleeper; *Fam* **tu as les yeux pleins de s.** your eyes are all sleepy *or* full of sleep; **une nuit sans s.** a sleepless night, a night without sleep; **trois jours sans s.** three days without sleep; **avoir s.** to be *or* to feel sleepy; **donner s. à qn** to make sb sleepy; **tomber de s.** to be ready to drop, to be falling asleep (on one's feet); **s. lent/paradoxal** NREM/REM sleep; **s. partagé** co-sleeping; **le premier s.** the first hours of sleep; *Littéraire* **le s. éternel, le dernier s.** eternal rest; **dormir d'un s. de plomb** *(d'habitude)* to be a heavy sleeper, to sleep like a log; *(ponctuellement)* to be sleeping like a log *or* fast asleep

2 *Fig (inactivité)* inactivity, lethargy, sluggishness; **il a tiré l'artisanat de son profond s.** he's given the stagnant arts and crafts market a new lease of life *or* impetus

❑ **en sommeil ADJ** *(volcan, économie)* inactive, dormant **ADV rester en s.** to remain dormant *or* inactive; **laisser une affaire en s.** to put a matter on the back burner; **mettre un secteur économique en s.** to put an economic sector in abeyance

sommeiller [4] [sɔmeje] **VI 1** *(personne)* to doze; **je commençais à s. au volant** I was falling asleep at the wheel **2** *(affaire, passion, volcan)* to lie dormant

sommeilleux, -euse [sɔmɛjø, -øz] **ADJ** *Littéraire* sleepy

NM,F = person suffering from sleeping sickness

sommelier, -ère [sɔməlje, -ɛr] **NM,F 1** *(caviste)* cellarman; *(qui sert les vins)* sommelier, wine waiter, *f* wine waitress **2** *Suisse (serveur)* waiter, *f* waitress

sommellerie [sɔmɛlri] **NF 1** *(métier)* sommelier's *or* wine waiter's job **2** *(cave)* wine cellar

sommer [3] [sɔme] **VT 1** *Jur* **s. qn de faire qch** to summon sb to do sth **2** *(ordonner à)* **s. qn de faire qch** to order sb to do sth **3** *Archit* to crown, to top **4** *Math* to add up

sommes *voir* **être¹**

sommet [sɔmɛ] **NM 1** *(plus haut point → d'un mont)* summit, highest point, top; *(→ d'un bâtiment, d'un arbre)* top

2 *(partie supérieure → d'un arbre, d'une colline)* crown; *(→ d'une montagne)* top, summit; *(→ d'une vague)* crest; *(→ de la tête)* crown, *Spéc* vertex; **les sommets neigeux** the snowy heights *or* summits *or* mountain tops; *Fig* **leurs émissions n'atteignent pas des sommets** their programmes don't aim very high *or* aren't exactly intellectually ambitious; *Méd* **présentation d'un bébé par le s.** head presentation of a baby

3 *(degré suprême → d'une hiérarchie)* summit, top; *(→ d'une carrière)* top, summit, *Sout* acme; **une décision prise au s.** a decision taken from the top; **le s. de la perfection** the acme of perfection; **le s. de la gloire** the pinnacle of fame; **elle est au s. de son talent** she's at the height of her talent

4 *Élec* node

5 *Math (d'un angle, d'une hyperbole)* vertex

6 *Pol* summit (meeting); **conférence** *ou* **réunion** *ou* **rencontre au s.** summit meeting *or* conference

sommier [sɔmje] **NM 1** *(de lit)* (bed) base; **s. à lattes** slatted base; **s. métallique** wire mattress; **s. tapissier (à ressorts)** (sprung) bed base

2 *Archit (d'une voûte → poutre)* springer, skewback; *(→ pierre)* impost; *(d'un clocher)* stock

3 *Constr (d'une porte)* lintel; *(d'une grille)* crossbar

4 *Mus (d'un orgue)* windchest; *(d'un piano)* frame; **s. de chevilles** pinblock

5 *(de comptabilité)* register, ledger; **s. de police technique** central register of criminal records

sommital, -e, -aux, -ales [sɔmital, -o] **ADJ** summit *(avant n)*

sommité [sɔmite] **NF 1** *(personnage)* authority; **les sommités de la médecine** leading medical experts; **sommités du monde de l'art** leading figures *or* lights in the art world; **ce n'est pas une s.!** he's no genius! **2** *Bot* head

somnambule [sɔmnɑ̃byl] **ADJ être s.** to sleepwalk, to be a sleepwalker *or Spéc* somnambulist

NMF sleepwalker, *Spéc* somnambulist; **parler comme un s.** to speak like a zombie; **des gestes de s.** trance-like movements

somnambulique [sɔmnɑ̃bylik] **ADJ** sleepwalking, *Spéc* somnambulistic

somnambulisme [sɔmnɑ̃bylism] **NM** sleepwalking, *Spéc* somnambulism

somnifère [sɔmnifɛr] *Pharm* **ADJ** soporific, sleep-inducing

NM *(substance)* soporific; *(comprimé)* sleeping pill *or* tablet

somniloque [sɔmnilɔk] **ADJ** somniloquous, somniloquent

NMF somniloquist, sleep talker

somniloquie [sɔmnilɔki] **NF** somniloquy, sleep talking

somnolence [sɔmnɔlɑ̃s] **NF 1** *(d'une personne)* drowsiness, sleepiness, *Sout* somnolence; **ce médicament peut provoquer des états de s.** this medicine may cause drowsiness; **la chaleur nous plonge dans un état de s.** the heat makes us drowsy *or* lethargic **2** *(d'une économie)* lethargy, sluggishness

somnolent, -e [sɔmnɔlɑ̃, -ɑ̃t] **ADJ 1** *(personne)* drowsy, sleepy, *Sout* somnolent **2** *(village)* sleepy; *(voix)* droning; *(esprit)* dull, lethargic, apathetic; *(économie)* lethargic, sluggish; *(faculté intellectuelle)* dormant

somnoler [3] [sɔmnɔle] **VI 1** *(personne)* to doze **2** *(ville)* to be sleepy; *(économie)* to be lethargic *or* in the doldrums; *(faculté intellectuelle)* to lie dormant, to slumber

somptuaire [sɔ̃ptɥɛr] **ADJ 1** *(dépenses)* extravagant **2** *Beaux-Arts* **arts somptuaires** decorative arts **3** *Antiq & Hist* sumptuary

somptueuse [sɔ̃ptɥøz] *voir* **somptueux**

somptueusement [sɔ̃ptɥøzmɑ̃] **ADV** *(décorer, illustrer)* sumptuously, lavishly, richly; *(vêtir)* sumptuously, magnificently

somptueux, -euse [sɔ̃ptɥø, -øz] **ADJ 1** *(luxueux → vêtements, cadeau)* sumptuous, splendid; *(→ décor, salon, palais)* magnificent, splendid **2** *(superbe → banquet)* sumptuous, lavish; *(→ illustration)* lavish; **la pièce a une somptueuse distribution** the play has a glittering cast

somptuosité [sɔ̃ptɥozite] **NF** *Littéraire (d'une toilette)* sumptuousness, magnificence; *(d'un décor, d'une pièce, d'illustrations)* sumptuousness, splendour, lavishness

son¹ [sɔ̃] **NM 1** *Ling, Mus & Phys* sound; **un s. pur** a pure sound; **un s. étouffé** a muffled sound; **un s. sourd** a thump, a thud; **un s. strident** *(de Klaxon®, de trompette)* a blast; **émettre** *ou* **produire un s.** to give out a sound; **les sons inarticulés qui sortaient de sa bouche** the inarticulate sounds he/she was uttering; **le mur rend un s. creux** the wall has a hollow sound;

le s. du tambour/de la trompette the beat of the drum/blare of the trumpet; **ça ressemble au s. de la harpe** it sounds like a harp; **c'est un autre s. de cloche** that's (quite) another story; **j'ai entendu plusieurs sons de cloche** I've heard several variants *or* versions of that story; **clamer** *ou* **annoncer qch à s. de trompe** to trumpet sth abroad; **(spectacle) s. et lumière** son et lumière

2 *(volume)* sound, volume; **baisser/monter le s.** to turn the sound up/down; **le niveau du s.** the sound level; **on a le s. mais pas l'image** we've got sound but no picture; **s. seul** sound only, wild track; *Cin* **le s. était épouvantable** the soundtrack was terrible; **au s., Marcel Blot** sound (engineer), Marcel Blot; **s. ambiant** ambient sound; **s. asynchrone** wild sound, asynchronous sound; **s. direct** actual sound; **s. naturel** natural sound; **s. non synchrone** wild sound, asynchronous sound; **s. numérique** digital sound; **s. optique** optical sound; **s. stéréo** stereo sound; **s. synchrone** synchronous sound; **s. 3D** surround sound

❑ **au son de** PRÉP to the sound of; **danser au s. de l'accordéon** to dance to the music *or* to the sound *or* to the sounds of the accordion; **ils défilèrent aux sons** *ou* **au s. des tambours** they marched to the beat *or* to the sound *or* to the sounds of drums; **ils se lèvent tous les matins au s. du clairon** every morning, they wake to the sound *or* to the call of the bugle

son² [sɔ̃] NM *Agr* bran; **s. d'avoine** oat bran; **flocons de s.** bran flakes; **pain au s.** bran loaf

son³, sa, ses [sɔ̃, sa, se]

> **sa** becomes **son** before a word beginning with a vowel or mute h.

ADJ POSSESSIF **1** *(d'un homme)* his; *(d'une femme)* her; *(d'une chose)* its; *(d'un bateau, d'une nation)* its, her; **s. frère et sa sœur, ses frère et sœur** his/her brother and sister; **il a mis s. chapeau et ses gants** he put on his hat and (his) gloves; **un de ses amis** a friend of his/hers, one of his/her friends; **donne-lui s. biberon** give him/her his/her bottle; **le bébé, dès ses premiers contacts avec le monde** the baby, from its first experience of the world; **ce n'est pas s. genre** he/she isn't like that, that's not his/her style; **ce n'est pas s. travail** it's not his/her job; **la police est à sa recherche** the police are looking for him/her/it; **à sa vue, elle s'évanouit** on seeing him/her, she fainted; **s. propre fils** his/her own son; *Fam* **dans sa maison à lui** in HIS house, in his own house; *Fam* **s. imbécile de frère** his/her idiot of a brother

2 *(d'un sujet indéfini)* **il faut faire ses preuves** you have to show your mettle, *Sout* one has to show one's mettle; **tout le monde a ses problèmes** we all have our problems; **chacun a pris s. sac** everybody took their bags; **ici, on passe s. temps à bavarder** everybody spends their time chatting here; **en Alsace, on prend s. café en même temps que le dessert** in Alsace, they have their coffee along with their dessert

3 *(dans des titres)* **S. Altesse Royale** His/Her Royal Highness; **Sa Majesté** His/Her Majesty; **Sa Sainteté le Pape** His Holiness the Pope

4 *(d'une abstraction)* **avant de prendre une décision, il faut penser à ses conséquences** before taking a decision, you *or Sout* one must think about the consequences (of it); **dans cette affaire, tout a s. importance** in this affair everything is of importance

5 *(emploi expressif)* **ça a s. charme** it's got its own charm *or* a certain charm; *Fam* **il fait s. intéressant** he's trying to draw attention to himself; *Fam* **elle fait sa timide** she's being all shy; *Fam* **elle se fait ses 3000 euros par mois** she brings in 3,000 euros a month; **il va encore piquer sa colère!** he's going to have another one of his outbursts!; *Fam* **il a réussi à avoir s. samedi** he managed to get Saturday off

sonagramme [sɔnagram] NM sonogram

sonagraphe [sɔnagraf] NM sonograph

sonal, -als [sɔnal] NM *Offic* jingle

sonar [sɔnar] NM sonar

sonate [sɔnat] NF sonata; **s. pour violon** violin sonata

'Sonate d'automne' *Bergman* 'Autumn Sonata'

sonatine [sɔnatin] NF sonatina

sondage [sɔ̃daʒ] NM **1** *(enquête)* poll, survey; *(activité)* sampling; **faire un s. (sur qch)** to carry out a poll *or* a survey (on sth); **faire un s. auprès d'un groupe** to poll a group, to carry out a survey among a group; **j'ai fait un petit s. parmi mes amis** I sounded out some of my friends; **s. aléatoire** random sampling; **s. Gallup** Gallup poll; **s. d'opinion** opinion poll; **s. par quotas** quota sampling; **s. par téléphone** telephone interviewing

2 *(d'un terrain)* sampling, sounding

3 *Méd* probe, probing; **s. vésical** urethral catheterization

4 *Mines & Pétr (processus)* boring; *(puits)* bore hole

5 *Naut* sounding; **faire des sondages** to take soundings

6 *Géol* **s. sismique** sonoprobing

Sonde [sɔ̃d] *voir* **archipel**

sonde [sɔ̃d] NF **1** *Astron & Météo* sonde; **s. aérienne** balloon sonde; **s. à fil chaud** hot-wire anemometer; *Aviat* **s. de réservoir** tank probe; *Astron* **s. spatiale** (space) probe

2 *Naut* **(ligne de) s.** lead (line), sounding line; **être sur les sondes** to be on soundings; **naviguer à la s.** to navigate by soundings

3 *Méd* probe, sound; **s. (d'alimentation)** feeding tube; **nourri à la s.** tube-fed; **s. (creuse)** catheter, can(n)ula; **s. œsophagienne** oesophageal probe, probang

4 *Com (pour les liquides, le beurre)* taster; *(pour les grains)* sampler; *(de douanier)* probe; **s. à fromage** cheese taster

5 *Tech* **s. pyrométrique** *ou* **thermométrique** thermometer probe

6 *Pétr* drill

sondé, -e [sɔ̃de] NM,F *Mktg* respondent, person polled

sonder [3] [sɔ̃de] VT **1** *(personne → gén)* to sound out; *(→ dans une enquête)* to poll; **je vais tâcher de la s. là-dessus** I'll try and sound her out on that; **nous n'avons sondé que des étudiants** we polled students only; **s. l'opinion** to carry out *or* conduct an opinion poll; **10 pour cent de la population sondée** 10 percent of those polled

2 *Naut* to sound; **s. la côte** to take soundings along the coast

3 *Météo* to probe; **s. l'atmosphère** to make soundings in the atmosphere

4 *Méd (plaie)* to probe; *(malade, vessie)* to catheterize

5 *Pétr* to bore, to drill; *Fig* **s. le terrain** to test the ground *or* the waters

6 *(bagages)* to probe; *(fromage, liquides)* to taste; *(grains)* to sample

7 *(intentions)* to sound out; **s. l'âme/le cœur de qn** to try to penetrate sb's soul/sb's heart

sondeur, -euse [sɔ̃dœr, -øz] NM,F *(pour une enquête)* pollster

NM **1** *Naut* depth finder, sounder **2** *Météo* **s. acoustique** echo sounder; **s. ionosphérique** ionosonde; **s. par ultrasons** echo sounder **3** *Géol* probe

❑ **sondeuse** NF *Pétr* boring *or* drilling machine

songe [sɔ̃ʒ] NM *Littéraire* **1** *(rêve)* dream; **faire un s.** to have a dream; **voir qn/qch en s.** to see sb/sth in one's dreams; *Prov* **songes, mensonges** *ou* **s. est mensonge** = dreams never tell the truth **2** *(chimère)* dream, daydream, illusion

'Le Songe d'une nuit d'été' *Shakespeare* 'A Midsummer Night's Dream'

songé, -e [sɔ̃ʒe] ADJ *Can Fam (réfléchi)* reflective, thoughtful; **il est très s. comme garçon** he's the sort of boy who thinks about things very deeply

songe-creux [sɔ̃ʒkrø] NM INV *Littéraire* dreamer, daydreamer; **air de s.** dreamy look

songer [17] [sɔ̃ʒe] VT to muse, to reflect, to think; **il est charmant, songeait-elle** he's charming, she mused *or* reflected; **comment aurais-je pu s. qu'ils nous trahiraient?** how could I have imagined that they'd betray us?

VI *(rêver)* to dream

❑ **songer à** VT IND **1** *(penser à)* to think about; *(en se souvenant)* to muse over, to think back to; **à quoi songes-tu?** what are you thinking about?, what's on your mind?; **je songeais aux Noëls passés** I was musing over *or* thinking back to Christmases past

2 *(prendre en considération → carrière, personne)* to think of, to have regard for; **songe un peu plus à toi-même!** think of yourself a bit more!; **songe un peu plus aux autres!** be a bit more considerate (of others)!; **songez à ce que vous faites!** think about what you're doing!

3 *(envisager)* to contemplate, to think of; **voyons, vous n'y songez pas!** come now, you can't mean it *or* be serious!; **il ne faut pas y s.** that's quite out of the question; **songez donc!** just think!, just imagine!; **s. au mariage** to consider *or* to contemplate marriage; **la seule issue à laquelle nous n'avions pas songé** the only outcome we never expected; **il songe sérieusement à se remarier** he's seriously considering *or* contemplating remarriage; **il ne songe qu'à gagner de l'argent** making money is all he thinks about

4 *(s'occuper de)* to remember; **as-tu songé aux réservations?** did you remember to make reservations?

5 *(réfléchir à → offre, suggestion)* to think over, to consider

songerie [sɔ̃ʒri] NF *Littéraire* daydreaming

songeur, -euse [sɔ̃ʒœr, -øz] ADJ *(rêveur)* dreamy; *(pensif)* pensive, thoughtful; **d'un air s.** dreamily; **d'un ton s.** dreamily; **ça laisse s.** it makes you wonder

sonie [sɔni] NF loudness

sonique [sɔnik] ADJ sonic; **mur s.** sonic wall, sound barrier; **détonation** *ou* **gong s.** supersonic boom *or* bang, sonic boom; **avion s.** supersonic aircraft

sonnaille [sɔnaj] NF **1** *(pour le bétail)* cowbell **2** *(bruit)* jangling

sonnailler [sɔnaje] NM *(animal)* bellwether

sonnant, -e [sɔnɑ̃, -ɑ̃t] ADJ sharp; **à trois heures sonnantes** at three (o'clock) sharp, at three on the dot, at the stroke of three (o'clock); *Littéraire* **l'airain s.** the blare of the brass

sonné, -e [sɔne] ADJ **1** *(annoncé par la cloche)* gone, past; **il est midi s.** it's past *or Br* gone twelve **2** *Fam (révolu)* **elle a la cinquantaine bien sonnée** she's on the wrong side of fifty **3** *Fam (fou)* crazy, nuts **4** *Fam (assommé)* groggy; **un boxeur s.** a punch-drunk boxer

sonner [3] [sɔne] VI **1** *(téléphone, cloche)* to ring; *(minuterie, réveil)* to go off; *(carillon, pendule)* to chime; *(glas, tocsin)* to toll, to sound; **la cloche n'a pas encore sonné** *(à l'école)* the bell hasn't gone *or* rung yet; **j'ai mis le réveil à s. pour** *ou* **à huit heures** I've set the alarm for eight o'clock; **s. à toute volée** to peal *or* to ring (out)

2 *(avoir un son → instrument en cuivre)* to sound; *(→ clefs, pièces métalliques)* to jingle, to jangle; *(→ pièces de monnaie)* to jingle, to chink; *(→ enclume, marteau)* to ring, to resound; *(→ rire)* to ring, to peal (out); *(→ voix)* to resound, to ring; **s. du clairon/du cor** to sound the bugle/the horn; **il faisait s. des pièces dans sa poche** he was jingling coins in his pocket; **s. bien/mal** to sound good/bad; **l'italien sonne bien à l'oreille** Italian is a pleasant-sounding language; **s. clair** *(monnaie)* to ring true; *(marteau)* to give *or* to have a clear ring; **s. creux** to sound hollow, to give a hollow sound; *Fig* to have a hollow ring; **s. faux** to ring false; *Fig* not to ring true

3 *(heure)* to strike; **quatre heures ont sonné** it has struck four o'clock, four o'clock has struck; **attendez que la fin du cours sonne!** wait for the bell!, wait till the bell goes *or* rings!; *Fig* **l'heure de la vengeance a sonné** the time for revenge has come

4 *(à la porte)* to ring; **on a sonné** there's someone at the door; **s. chez qn** to ring sb's doorbell; **j'ai sonné plusieurs fois (à ta porte)** I rang your doorbell *or* at your door several times; **(prière de) s. ici** *(sur panneau)* ring here (for attention); **s. avant d'entrer** *(sur panneau)* please ring before entering; **entrez sans s.** *(sur panneau)* go (straight) in

5 *(accentuer)* **faire s. une consonne** to sound a consonant; **"pour la gloire", dit-il en faisant s. le dernier mot** "for glory," he said, making the

last word ring out; **faire s. ses bottes sur le parquet** to stamp one's boots on the floor; *Littéraire* **faire s. (haut) une action** to praise *or* to extol a deed

VT 1 *(cloche)* to ring, to chime; *(glas, toscin)* to sound, to toll; *Fam* **s. les cloches à qn** to bawl sb out, *Br* to give sb what-for; **tu vas te faire s. les cloches!** you'll catch it!

2 *(pour faire venir → infirmière, valet)* to ring for; *Fam* **toi, on t'a pas sonné!** nobody asked you!

3 *(pour annoncer → messe, vêpres)* to ring (the bells) for; *Mil (→ charge, retraite, rassemblement)* to sound; **sonnez le dîner** ring the bell for dinner, ring the dinner-bell; *Mil* **s. le réveil** to sound the reveille

4 *(sujet: horloge)* to strike; **l'horloge sonne les heures/les demi-heures** the clock strikes the hours/every half-hour; **la pendule vient de s. deux heures** the clock has just struck two

5 *Fam (assommer)* to knock out, to stun; *(abasourdir)* to stun, to stagger, to knock (out); **ça l'a sonné!** he was reeling under the shock!

6 *Tech (sonder → installation, monnaie)* to sound

7 *Belg (appeler)* to telephone, to call

USAGE ABSOLU **Madame a sonné?** you rang, Madam?

sonnerie [sɔnri] NF **1** *(son)* ring; **la s. du téléphone/du réveil la fit sursauter** the telephone/the alarm clock gave her a start; **s. de clairon** bugle call **2** *(mélodie)* ringtone; **télécharger des sonneries** *(sur un téléphone portable)* to download ringtones; **s. polyphonique** polyphonic ringtone **3** *Mil* call; **la s. du réveil** the sounding of reveille **4** *(cloches)* (set of) bells *or* chimes **5** *(mécanisme → d'un réveil)* alarm, bell; *(→ d'une pendule)* chimes; *(→ d'une sonnette)* bell **6** *(alarme)* alarm (bell)

sonnet [sɔnɛ] NM sonnet

sonnette [sɔnɛt] NF **1** *(avertisseur)* bell; **s. d'alarme** alarm bell; **tirer la s. d'alarme** *Rail* to pull the communication cord; *Fig* to sound the alarm **2** *(son)* **(coup de) s.** ring; **personne ne répondit à mon coup de s.** no one answered the bell; **as-tu entendu la s.?** did you hear the bell? **3** *(en travaux publics)* pile-driver

sonneur [sɔnœr] NM **1** *(de cloches)* bellringer; **dormir comme un s.** to sleep like a log **2** *Mus* player **3** *Tech* pile-driver operator

sono [sɔno] NF *Fam (abrév* **sonorisation***)* *(d'un groupe, d'une discothèque)* sound system■, sound; *(d'une salle de conférences)* public-address system■, PA (system)■

sonomètre [sɔnɔmɛtr] NM sound-level meter

sonore [sɔnɔr] ADJ **1** *(signal)* acoustic, sound *(avant n)*; *(onde, effets, niveau)* sound *(avant n)* **2** *(bruyant → rire, voix)* loud, ringing, resounding; *(→ claque, baiser)* loud, resounding **3** *(résonnant → escalier, voûte)* echoing; **le vestibule est s.** sound reverberates *or* echoes in the hall **4** *Ling (phonème)* voiced; **le "d" est s.** the "d" is voiced

NF *Ling* voiced consonant

sonorisation [sɔnɔrizasjɔ̃] NF **1** *(d'un lieu → action)* wiring for sound **2** *(équipement → d'une salle de conférences)* public-address system, PA system; *(→ d'une discothèque)* sound system **3** *Cin (d'un film)* dubbing **4** *Ling* voicing

sonoriser [3] [sɔnɔrize] VT **1** *(salle de conférences)* to fit with a public-address *or* PA system; *(discothèque)* to fit with a sound system **2** *Cin (film)* to dub, to add the soundtrack to **3** *Ling* to voice

sonorité [sɔnɔrite] NF **1** *(d'un instrument de musique)* tone; *(de la voix)* tone, *Sout* sonority; *(d'une langue)* sonority **2** *(résonance → de l'air)* resonance, *Sout* sonority; *(→ d'une pièce)* acoustics *(singulier)*; *(→ d'un lieu)* sonority **3** *Ling* voicing

sonothèque [sɔnɔtɛk] NF sound (effects) library

sonotone® [sɔnɔtɔn] NM miniature hearing aid

sont *voir* **être¹**

Sopalin® [sɔpalɛ̃] NM kitchen paper

Sophia-Antipolis [sɔfjaãtipɔlis] NM = "technopôle" near Nice

sophisme [sɔfism] NM sophism

sophiste [sɔfist] NMF **1** *(raisonneur)* sophist **2** *Antiq* Sophist

sophistication [sɔfistikasjɔ̃] NF **1** *(raffinement)*

refinement, sophistication **2** *(affectation)* affectation, sophistication **3** *(complexité technique)* sophistication, complexity **4** *Vieilli (action de frelater)* adulteration

sophistique [sɔfistik] ADJ sophistic

NF sophistry

sophistiqué, -e [sɔfistike] ADJ **1** *(raffiné)* sophisticated, refined **2** *(affecté)* affected, sophisticated **3** *(complexe)* complex, sophisticated **4** *Vieilli (frelaté)* adulterated

sophistiquer [3] [sɔfistike] VT **1** *(raffiner à l'extrême)* to refine **2** *(perfectionner)* to make more sophisticated, to perfect **3** *Vieilli (frelater)* to adulterate

Sophocle [sɔfɔkl] NPR Sophocles

sophora [sɔfɔra] NM *Bot* sophora; **s. du Japon** Japanese pagoda tree

sophrologie [sɔfrɔlɔʒi] NF sophrology *(form of autogenic relaxation)*

sophrologue [sɔfrɔlɔg] NMF sophrologist

SOPK [ɛsopeka] NM *Méd (abrév* **syndrome des ovaires polykystiques***)* PCOS

sopor [sɔpɔr] NM *Méd* sopor

soporifique [sɔpɔrifik] ADJ **1** *Pharm* soporific **2** *(ennuyeux)* boring, soporific

NM *Vieilli* soporific; **ce livre est un vrai s.** this book is terribly boring

soprane [sɔpran] NMF soprano

sopraniste [sɔpranist] NM male soprano

soprano [sɔprano] *(pl* **sopranos** *ou* **soprani** [-ni]*)* NM *(voix → de femme)* soprano; *(→ d'enfant)* soprano, treble

NMF soprano

soquet [sɔkɛ] = **socket**

sorbe [sɔrb] NF sorb (apple)

sorbet [sɔrbɛ] NM *Br* sorbet, *Am* sherbet; **s. au cassis** blackcurrant *Br* sorbet *or Am* sherbet

sorbetière [sɔrbətjɛr] NF *(de glacier)* ice-cream churn; *(de ménage)* ice-cream maker

sorbier [sɔrbje] NM *Bot* sorb, service tree; **s. des oiseleurs** *ou* **des oiseaux** rowan tree, mountain ash

sorbique [sɔrbik] ADJ *Chim* sorbic

sorbitol [sɔrbitɔl] NM sorbitol

sorbonnard, -e [sɔrbɔnar, -ard] *Fam* ADJ *(esprit)* niggling, pedantic

NM,F *(professeur)* Sorbonne academic■; *(étudiant)* Sorbonne student■

Sorbonne [sɔrbɔn] NF **la S.** the Sorbonne

LA SORBONNE

The Sorbonne, founded in the thirteenth century, is the oldest university in Paris. Its headquarters are in the heart of the Latin Quarter (so-called because scholars originally spoke Latin there), and the institution has a highly prestigious international reputation.

sorcellerie [sɔrsɛlri] NF **1** *(pratique)* sorcery, witchcraft **2** *Fam (effet surprenant)* magic; **c'est de la s.!** it's magic!

sorcier, -ère [sɔrsje, -ɛr] NM,F **1** *(magicien)* wizard, *f* witch; *Fam* **il ne faut pas être (grand) s. pour comprendre cela** you don't need to be a genius to understand that; *Can Fam* **être en s.** to be fuming, to be hopping mad

2 *(en anthropologie)* sorcerer, *f* sorceress

ADJ M *Fam* **ce n'est pourtant pas s.** it's not exactly rocket science

□ **sorcière** NF *(mégère)* witch, harpy

'Les Sorcières de Salem' *Miller* 'The Crucible'

sordide [sɔrdid] ADJ **1** *(misérable → vêtements)* filthy; *(→ pièce, quartier)* squalid, sordid **2** *(vil → égoïsme)* petty; *(→ crime)* foul, vile **3** *(mesquin → motif)* squalid, sordid; **de sordides bagarres autour de l'héritage** sordid arguments over the legacy

sordidement [sɔrdidmã] ADV *(agir)* sordidly; **vivre s.** to live in squalor

sordidité [sɔrdidite] NF *Littéraire* sordidness

sore [sɔr] NM *Bot* sorus

Sorel [sɔrɛl] NPR **Julien S.** = the hero of Stendhal's 'le Rouge et le Noir', a working-class intellectual exasperated with the bourgeois mediocrity around him

sorgho [sɔrgo] NM sorghum

sorite [sɔrit] NM *Ling* sorites

Sorlingues [sɔrlɛ̃g] NFPL **les (îles) S.** the Scilly Isles

sornettes [sɔrnɛt] NFPL balderdash *(UNCOUNT)*, twaddle *(UNCOUNT)*; **débiter** *ou* **raconter des sornettes** to talk nonsense

sororal, -e, -aux, -ales [sɔrɔral, -o] ADJ sororal

sororat [sɔrɔra] NM sororate

sororité [sɔrɔrite] NF sorority

Sorrente [sɔrãt] NM Sorrento

sors *etc voir* **sortir²**

sort [sɔr] NM **1** *(condition)* fate, lot; **être content de son s.** to be happy with one's lot; **tu n'es jamais content de ton s.!** you're never happy with your lot *or* what you've got!; **des mesures ont été prises pour améliorer le s. des immigrés** steps were taken to improve the lot *or* the status of immigrants; **je n'envie pas son s.!** I wouldn't like to be in his/her shoes!; **tu m'abandonnes à mon triste s.!** you've left me to my fate!; *Fam* **faire un s. à** *(plat)* to make short work of, to polish off; *(bouteille)* to polish off, to drink up

2 *(destin)* fate, destiny; **mon s. est entre vos mains** my future depends on you, *Sout* my fate is in your hands; **toutes les demandes d'emploi subissent le même s.** all letters of application meet with the same fate *or* receive the same treatment

3 *(puissance surnaturelle)* **le s.** Fate, Fortune, Destiny; **le s. lui fut enfin favorable** Fate *or* Fortune smiled upon him/her at last; **je me demande ce que le s. nous réserve** I wonder what fate has in store for us; **mais le s. en a décidé autrement** but fate decided otherwise; **le mauvais s.** misfortune; **le s. en est jeté** the die is cast

4 *(sortilège → gén)* spell; *(→ défavorable)* curse; **jeter un s. à qn** to cast a spell on sb

sortable [sɔrtabl] ADJ **tu n'es vraiment pas s.!** I can't take you anywhere!

sortant, -e [sɔrtã, -ãt] ADJ **1** *Pol* outgoing; **le maire s.** the outgoing mayor **2** *(au jeu)* **les numéros sortants** the numbers chosen **3** *Ordinat* output *(avant n)*

NM,F **1** *Pol* incumbent; **tous les sortants ont été réélus au premier tour** all the incumbents were re-elected in the first round **2** *(personne qui sort)* **on contrôle également les sortants** those leaving are also screened

sorte [sɔrt] NF **1** *(genre)* sort, kind, type; **vous n'avez que cette s. de jupes?** is that the only style of skirt you have?; **on a souvent cette s. de temps en automne** we often get this kind *or* this sort of weather in autumn; **pour moi, il y a deux sortes de gens** in my opinion, there are two kinds *or* sorts *or* types of people; **toutes sortes de** all kinds *or* sorts of; **des gens de toute s.** *ou* **toutes sortes** all sorts *or* kinds of people

2 *(pour exprimer une approximation)* **une s. de** a sort *or* a kind of; **c'est une s. de gelée** it's a sort of jelly; *Péj* **une s. de grand dadais** a big clumsy oaf

3 *Typ* sort

□ **de la sorte** ADV that way; **comment osez-vous me traiter de la s.?** how dare you treat me in that way *or* like that!; **je n'ai rien dit/rien fait de la s.** I said/did no such thing, I said/did nothing of the kind *or* sort; **je n'ai jamais été humiliée de la s.!** I've never been so humiliated!

□ **de sorte à** CONJ in order to, so as to

□ **de (telle) sorte que** CONJ **1** *(suivi du subjonctif) (de manière à ce que)* so that, in such a way that; **disposez vos plantes de (telle) s. qu'elles reçoivent beaucoup de lumière** arrange your plants so that they receive maximum light

2 *(suivi de l'indicatif) (si bien que)* so that; **elle m'a montré la ville, de (telle) s. que le temps a passé très vite** she showed me round the town, so the time just flew by

□ **en aucune sorte** ADV *Littéraire* not in the least; **en avez-vous parlé à quelqu'un? – en aucune s.** did you tell anyone? – not at all *or* by no means

□ **en quelque sorte** ADV as it were, in a way, somewhat; **immobile, pétrifié en quelque s.** motionless, as it were paralysed; **alors, on repart à zéro? – oui, en quelque s.** so, we're

back to square one? – yes, in a manner of speaking

❑ **en sorte de** CONJ so as to; **fais en s. d'arriver à l'heure** try to be there on time

❑ **en sorte que 1 faites en s. que tout soit prêt à temps** see to it that everything is ready in time

2 *Littéraire* = **de (telle) sorte que**

sorteur, -euse[1] [sɔrtœr, -øz] *Belg* ADJ **ils sont très sorteurs** they like to party *or* to live it up

NM,F reveller, partygoer

NM *(videur)* bouncer

sorteux, -euse[2] [sɔrtø, -øz] *Can Fam* ADJ sociable▪, who likes going out▪

NM,F sociable person▪

SORTIE [sɔrti]

exit **1, 6, 7** ▪ end **3** ▪ outing **4, 12** ▪ evening out **4** ▪ sortie **5** ▪ entrance **6** ▪ export **8** ▪ outgoings **8** ▪ release **2, 9** ▪ launch **9** ▪ output **10**

NF **1** *(action) & Théât* exit; **sa s. fut très remarquée** his/her exit *or* departure did not go unnoticed; **essaie de faire une s. discrète** try to make a discreet exit *or* to leave discreetly; *Théât* **faire sa s.** to leave the stage, to exit; **faire une fausse s.** to make as if to leave

2 *(moment)* **à ma s. de prison/d'hôpital** on my release from prison/discharge from hospital; **les journalistes l'ont assaillie dès sa s. de l'hôtel** the journalists thronged round her as soon as she stepped *or* came out of the hotel; **à la s. des bureaux/des usines, la circulation est infernale** when the offices/factories come out, the traffic is hell; **retrouvons-nous à la s. du travail/du spectacle** let's meet after work/the show; **le voilier a heurté la bouée à la s. du port** the yacht hit the buoy as she was leaving port; **il s'est retourné à la s. du virage** he rolled (his car) over just after *or* as he came out of the bend

3 *(fin)* end; **à la s. de l'hiver** when winter was (nearly) over; **à ma s. de l'école** *(à la fin de mes études)* when I left school

4 *(excursion, promenade)* outing; *(soirée en ville)* evening *or* night out; **on a organisé une petite s. en famille/à vélo** we've organized a little family outing/cycle ride; **priver qn de s.** to confine sb to quarters; **ils m'ont privé de s. trois dimanches de suite** they kept me in for three Sundays in a row; **s. éducative** *ou* **scolaire** school outing

5 *Aviat & Mil* sortie; **faire une s.** to make a sortie; **les pompiers font jusqu'à 20 sorties par semaine** the firemen are called out up to 20 times a week; **s. offensive** sally

6 *(porte, issue → d'une école, d'une usine)* entrance, gates; *(→ d'une salle de spectacles)* exit, way out; **par ici la s.!** this way out, please!; **poussé vers la s.** pushed towards the exit; **attends-moi à la s.** wait for me outside; **gagner la s.** to reach the exit; **il gagna la s. sans encombre** he made his way out unimpeded; **le supermarché se trouve à la s. de la ville** the supermarket is on the outskirts of the town; **attention, s. de garage/de véhicules** *(sur panneau)* caution, garage entrance/vehicle exit; **s. de secours** emergency exit; **s. de service** service entrance; **s. des artistes** stage door

7 *(sur route)* exit; **j'ai raté la s.** I've missed the exit; **à toutes les sorties de Paris** at every major exit from Paris; **s. (de route)** turnoff

8 *Banque & Écon (de produits, de devises)* export; *(de capital)* outflow; *(sujet de dépense)* item of expenditure; *(dépense)* outgoing; **la s. de devises est limitée à 1000 euros par personne** currency export is limited to 1,000 euros per person

9 *(d'un disque, d'un film)* release; *(d'un roman)* publication; *(d'un modèle)* launch; **au moment de sa s. dans les salles parisiennes** when released in Parisian cinemas; **à sa s., cette voiture paraissait révolutionnaire** when first launched, this car seemed revolutionary; **s. générale** general release

10 *Ordinat (de données)* output, readout; *(option sur programme)* exit; **s. sur imprimante** printout; **s. papier** output

11 *Sport (en gymnastique)* exit; **préparer sa s.** to prepare one's exit; *(aux jeux de ballon)* **s. en touche** going out of play *or* into touch; **il y a s. en touche!** the ball's gone into touch!; **faire une s.** *(gardien de but)* to come out of goal, to leave the goalmouth

12 *(d'un cheval)* outing; **c'est sa première s. de la saison** it's his/her first race *or* outing of the season

13 *Fam (remarque)* quip, sally; *(emportement)* outburst; **elle a parfois de ces sorties!** you don't know what she's going to come out with next!

14 *(d'eau, de gaz)* outflow, outlet

15 *Can Élec (prise de courant)* socket

16 *Beaux-Arts (gravure)* fading, tailing off

17 *Typ (des presses)* delivery

❑ **sorties** NFPL *Fin* outgoings; **sorties de fonds** expenses, outgoings; **sorties de trésorerie** cash outflow

❑ **de sortie** ADJ **c'est son jour de s.** *(domestique)* it's his/her day off; **être de s.** *(domestique)* to have one's day off; **la cuisinière est de s. le lundi** Monday is the cook's day off; *Fam* **je suis de s. demain** *(au restaurant, au spectacle)* I'm going out tomorrow

sortie-de-bain [sɔrtidbɛ̃] *(pl* **sorties-de-bain***)* NF bathrobe

sortie-de-bal [sɔrtidbal] *(pl* **sorties-de-bal***)* NF evening wrap, opera cloak

sortilège [sɔrtilɛʒ] NM charm, spell

sortir[1] [sɔrtir] *Littéraire* NM *(fin)* **dès le s. de l'enfance, il dut apprendre à se défendre** he was barely out of his childhood when he had to learn to fend for himself

❑ **au sortir de** PRÉP **1** *(dans le temps)* at the end of; **au s. de l'hiver** as winter draws to a close; **au s. de la guerre** at the end of the war

2 *(dans l'espace)* **je vis la cabane au s. du bois** as I was coming out of the woods, I saw the hut

SORTIR[2] [32] [sɔrtir]

VI to go out **1, 3, 13** ▪ to come out **1, 5, 7, 10** ▪ to come through **4** ▪ to come up **4, 8** ▪ to get out **6** ▪ to exit **11, 14**
VT to take out **1, 3, 4** ▪ to put out **2** ▪ to bring out **2, 6** ▪ to throw out **5** ▪ to say **7**
VPR to get out of

VI *(aux être)* **1** *(quitter un lieu → vu de l'intérieur)* to go out; *(→ vu de l'extérieur)* to come out; **ne sors pas sans manteau** don't go out without a coat (on); **il vient de s.** *(d'ici)* he's just gone out; **vous trouverez la boîte aux lettres en sortant** you'll find the letter box on your way out; **s. par la fenêtre** to get out *or* to leave by the window; **sors!** get out (of here)!; **fais s. la guêpe** get the wasp out (of here); **Madame, je peux s.?** please Miss, may I leave the room?; **une méchante grippe l'empêche de s.** a bad bout of flu is keeping him/her indoors *or* at home; **le médecin lui a dit de ne pas s.** the doctor told him/her to stay indoors *or* not to go out; **je commence à pouvoir s. un peu** I can go out *or* outdoors a little now; **vivement que je puisse s.!** I can't wait to get out!; **elle est sortie déjeuner/se promener** she's gone (out) for lunch/for a walk; **être sorti** *(ne pas être chez soi)* to be out; **si elle se présente, dites-lui que je suis sorti** if she calls, tell her I'm out *or* I've gone out *or* I'm not in; **il était si mauvais que le public est sorti** he was so bad that the audience walked out (on him); **il y a trop d'encombrements, on va essayer de s. par le pont Bouvier** there's too much traffic, we'll try to get out via Bouvier bridge; **s. d'une pièce** to leave a room; **il est sorti de son examen avant la fin** he left his exam before the end; **les gens sortaient du théâtre** people were coming out of *or* leaving the theatre; **s. d'une voiture** to get out of a car; **je l'ai vu qui sortait de l'hôpital/l'école vers seize heures** I saw him coming out of the hospital/school at about four p.m.; **fais s. ce chien de la voiture** get that dog out of the car; **faites-les s.!** send them out!; **il faisait s. des lapins de son chapeau** he pulled rabbits out of his hat; **sors de ta cachette!** come out wherever you are!; **s. de l'eau** to emerge from the water; **sors de l'eau!** get out of the water!; **s. du lit** to get out of bed; **s. du bain** to get out of the bath; **alors que l'express sortait de la gare** as the express train was pulling out of *or* leaving the station; **les bolides sortent du virage à 150 km/h** the racing cars come out of the bend at 150 km/h; **il est sorti de sa vie** he's out of his/her life; *Fam* **ça me sort par les yeux** I'm sick and tired of it, I've had it up to here; *Fam* **d'où tu sors?** where have you been?, what planet have you been on?

2 *(marquant la fin d'une activité, d'une période)* **s. de table** to leave the table; **elle sort de l'hôpital demain** she's getting out of hospital tomorrow; **laisser qn s. de l'hôpital** to let sb out of *or* to discharge sb from hospital; **s. de l'école/du bureau** *(finir sa journée)* to finish school/work; **à quelle heure sors-tu?** *(du bureau, du lycée)* what time do you finish?; **s. de prison** to come out of *or* to be released from prison

3 *(pour se distraire)* **je sors très peu** I hardly ever go out; **ils sortent au restaurant tous les soirs** they eat out every night; **s. avec qn** to go out with sb; **tu sors avec quelqu'un demain?** are you going out with someone tomorrow?; *Fam* **je ne sors plus avec lui** I'm not going out with him *or* I'm not seeing him any more; *Fam* **ils sortent ensemble depuis trois ans** they've been going out together for three years

4 *(apparaître → dent, bouton)* to come through; *(→ pousse)* to come up, to peep through; **l'antenne sort quand on appuie sur le bouton** the *Br* aerial *or Am* antenna comes out when you press the button

5 *(se répandre)* to come out; **le son sort par là** the sound comes out here; **des flammes sortaient de la gueule du dragon** flames were coming out of the dragon's mouth; **c'est pour que la fumée sorte** it's to let the smoke out *or* for the smoke to escape

6 *(s'échapper)* to get out; **des pensionnaires réussissaient parfois à s.** some boarders would manage to get out *or* to escape from time to time; **aucun dossier ne doit s. de l'ambassade** no file may be taken out of *or* leave the embassy; **faire s. qn/des marchandises d'un pays** to smuggle sb/goods out of a country; **je vais te confier quelque chose mais cela ne doit pas s. d'ici** I'm going to tell you something, but it mustn't go any further than these four walls

7 *(être mis en vente → disque, film)* to be released, to come out; *(→ livre)* to be published, to come out; **s. sur le marché** *(produit)* to come onto the market; **le film sortira (sur les écrans) en septembre** the film will be released *or* will be out in September; **à l'heure où les journaux sortent** when the papers come off the presses; **ce nouveau type de revêtement devrait bientôt s.** this new type of flooring material should be on the market fairly soon; **ça vient de s.!** it's just (come) out!, it's (brand) new!

8 *(être révélé au public → sujet d'examen)* to come up; *(→ numéro de loterie)* to be drawn; *(→ numéro à la roulette)* to turn or to come up; *(→ tarif, barème)* to be out; *Fam* **je ne révise pas la crise de 29, ça ne sortira pas** I'm not going to revise the Wall Street crash, it won't come up

9 *(être promulgué)* **la loi a été votée mais le décret d'application ne sortira qu'en septembre** the bill has been passed, but it won't become law until September

10 *Fam (être dit)* to come out; **il fallait que ça sorte!** it had to come out *or* to be said!; **c'est sorti comme ça, je n'ai pas pu m'en empêcher** I just came out with it *or* blurted it out, I couldn't help myself

11 *Ordinat* **s. (d'un système)** to exit (from a system); **s. d'un programme** to exit a program

12 *Naut & Aviat* **s. du port** to leave harbour; **s. en mer** to put out to sea; **aujourd'hui, les avions/les bateaux ne sont pas sortis** the planes were grounded/the boats stayed in port today

13 *Sport (balle)* to go out; **la balle est sortie (du court)** the ball was out; **le ballon est sorti en**

corner/en touche the ball went out for a corner/ went into touch; **on a fait s. le joueur (du terrain)** *(pour faute)* the player was sent off; *(il est blessé)* the player had to go off because of injury; **et voilà le dernier Français qui sort du tournoi!** now the last Frenchman's out of the tournament!

14 *Théât* **le roi sort** exit the King; **les sorcières sortent** exeunt (the) witches

15 *Typ* **faire s. une ligne** to run on a line

VT *(aux avoir)* **1** *(mener dehors → pour se promener, se divertir)* to take out; **s. un enfant** to take a child out for a walk; **sors le chien** take the dog out (for a walk); **il faut s. les chiens régulièrement** dogs have to be walked regularly; **viens avec nous au concert, ça te sortira** come with us to the concert, that'll get you out (of the house)

2 *(mettre dehors → vu de l'intérieur)* to put out *or* outside; *(→ vu de l'extérieur)* to bring out *or* outside; **s. la poubelle** to take out *Br* the rubbish *or Am* the trash

3 *(présenter → crayon, outil)* to take out; *(→ pistolet)* to pull out; *(→ papiers d'identité)* to produce; **on va bientôt pouvoir s. les vêtements d'été** we'll soon be able to get out our summer clothes; **sors le jeu d'échecs** take *or* get the chess set out; **l'escargot sort ses cornes** the snail is putting out its horns; *Fam* **il a toujours du mal à les s.** he's never too keen to put his hand in his pocket

4 *(extraire)* **s. qch de qch** to take *or* to get sth out of sth; **sors un verre du placard** get a glass out of *or* from the cupboard; **il a sorti quelque chose de sa poche** he drew *or* took *or* got something out of his pocket; **sors les mains de tes poches!** take *or* get your hands out of your pockets!; **ils ont eu du mal à s. le car du lac** they had problems getting *or* pulling *or* hauling the coach out of the lake; **des mesures ont été prises pour s. le pays de la crise** measures have been taken to get the country out of *or* to rescue the country from the present crisis; **s. qn de qch** to get *or* to pull sb out of sth; **ils ont sorti les blessés des décombres** they pulled the injured out of the rubble; **s. qn du sommeil** to wake sb; **j'ai eu du mal à le s. de son lit** *(le faire lever)* I had trouble getting him out of bed; **je vais te s. d'affaire** *ou* **d'embarras** *ou* **de là** I'll get you out of it

5 *Fam (expulser)* to get *or* to throw out; **sortez-le ou je fais un malheur!** get him out of here before I do something I'll regret!; **sortez l'arbitre!** get off, ref!; **elle a sorti la Suédoise en trois sets** she disposed of *or* beat the Swedish player in three sets

6 *(mettre sur le marché)* to launch, to bring out; **s. un disque/un film** *(auteur)* to bring out a record/a movie *or Br* film; *(distributeur)* to release a record/a movie *or Br* film; **s. un livre** to bring out *or* to publish a book; **nous devons s. un produit nouveau chaque mois** we have to bring out a new product every month

7 *Fam (dire)* to say▪, to come out with; **elle n'a sorti que des banalités** she just came out with a load of clichés; **tu sais ce qu'elle m'a sorti?** you know what she came out with?; **il m'a sorti que j'étais trop vieille!** he told me I was too old, just like that!; **vas-y, sors tout ce que tu as sur le cœur!** come on, out with it, what's bothering you?

8 *(roue, train d'atterrissage)* to drop; *(volet)* to raise

❑ **sortir de VT IND 1** *(emplacement, position)* to come out of, to come off; **la porte coulissante est sortie de la rainure** the sliding door has come out of the groove; **s. des rails** to go off *or* to jump the rails; **s. de la piste** *(voiture)* to come off *or* to leave the track; *(skieur)* to come off the piste; **ça m'était complètement sorti de la tête** *ou* **de l'esprit** it had gone right out of my head *or* mind; **l'incident est sorti de ma mémoire** *ou* **m'est sorti de la mémoire** I've forgotten the incident

2 *(venir récemment de)* to have (just) come from *or* left; **elle sort de chez moi** she's just left my place; **je sortais de chez le coiffeur** I was just coming out of the hairdresser's; **il sort de son entretien/de son examen** he has just got out of his interview/exam; **je sors d'une grippe** I'm just recovering from a bout of flu; *Fam* **s. de faire qch** to have just done sth▪; *Fam* **je sors de lui parler** I was just this minute talking to him/her; *Fam* **je sors d'en prendre** I've had quite enough of that, thank you

3 *(venir à bout de)* to come out of; **nous avons eu une période difficile mais heureusement nous en sortons** we've had a difficult time but fortunately we're now emerging from it *or* we're seeing the end of it now; *Fam* **est-ce qu'on va enfin en s.?** when are we going to see an end to all this?; *Fam* **on n'en sortira pas** we'll be there till kingdom come *or* till the cows come home

4 *(se tirer de, se dégager de)* **elle est sortie indemne de l'accident** she came out of the accident unscathed; **le président n'est pas sorti indemne de ce face à face** the president didn't emerge unscathed from this encounter; **elle est sortie première de sa promotion** she came out first in her class; **qui sortira victorieux de ce match?** who will win this match?; **s. de sa rêverie** to emerge from one's reverie; **s. du sommeil** to emerge from *or* to wake from sleep; **lorsqu'on sort de l'adolescence pour entrer dans l'âge adulte** when one leaves adolescence (behind) to become an adult

5 *(se départir de)* **il est sorti de sa réserve après quelques verres de vin** he opened up *or* loosened up after a few glasses of wine; **elle est sortie de son silence pour écrire son second roman** she broke her silence to write her second novel

6 *(s'écarter de)* **attention à ne pas s. du sujet!** be careful not to get off *or* to stray from the subject!; **cela sort de mes compétences** that's not my field; **s. de l'ordinaire** to be out of the ordinary; **enfin une collection de mode qui sort de l'ordinaire!** at last a fashion show with a difference!; **il ne veut pas s.** *ou* **il ne sort pas de là** he won't budge; **il n'y a pas à s. de là** *(c'est inévitable)* there's no way round it, there's no getting away from it

7 *(être issu de)* **s. d'une bonne famille** to come from *or* to be of a good family; **pour ceux qui sortent des grandes écoles** for those who have studied at *or* are the products of the "grandes écoles"; **il ne faut pas être sorti de Polytechnique pour savoir ça** you don't need a PhD to know that; **mais d'où sors-tu?** *(tu es mal élevé)* where did you learn such manners?, where were you brought up?; *(tu ne connais rien)* where have you been?, what planet have you been on?

8 *(être produit par)* to come from; **la veste sortait de chez un grand couturier** the jacket was made by a famous designer; **mes personnages sortent tout droit de mon imagination** my characters are straight out of my imagination

9 *(tournure impersonnelle) (résulter de)* **que sortira-t-il de tout cela?** what will come of all this?; **il n'est rien sorti de son interrogatoire** his/her interrogation revealed nothing; **il ne sortira rien de bon de toutes leurs manigances** no good will come of all their schemes

▶**se sortir VPR se s. de** to get out of; **j'ai du mal à me s. du lit le matin** I find it difficult to get out of bed in the morning; **se s. d'une situation embarrassante** to get (oneself) out of *or Sout* to extricate oneself from an embarrassing situation; *Fam* **aide-moi à finir, je ne m'en sortirai jamais seul!** give me a hand, I'll never get this finished on my own; **donne-lui une fourchette, il ne s'en sort pas avec des baguettes** give him a fork, he can't manage with chopsticks; **tu t'en es très bien sorti** you did very well; **la voiture a fait un tonneau mais il s'en est sorti sans une égratignure** his car turned right over but he escaped without a scratch; **elle s'en est sortie avec quelques bleus** she escaped with a few bruises; **il s'en est finalement sorti** *(il a survécu)* he pulled through in the end; *(il a réussi)* he won through in the end; **s'en s. à peu près** *(financièrement)* to get by; **s'en s. très bien** to manage very well; **on ne s'en sort pas avec une seule paie** it's impossible to manage on *or* to get by on a single wage; **malgré les allocations, on ne s'en sort pas** in spite of the allowance, we're not making ends meet; *Fam* **s'en s. pour** *(avoir à payer)* to be stung for; **tu t'en es sorti pour combien?** how much were you stung for?; **on s'en est sortis pour 150 euros à quatre** we had to cough up 150 euros among the four of us

---

SOS [ɛsoɛs] **NM** *(abrév* **save our souls) 1** *(signal de détresse)* SOS; **lancer un S.** to put *or* to send out an SOS

2 *Fam (demande d'argent)* **envoyer un S. à ses parents** to send an urgent request for money to one's parents

3 *(dans des noms de sociétés)* **S.-Amitié** = charity providing support for people in despair, *Br* ≃ the Samaritans; **S. médecins/dépannage** emergency medical/repair service; **S.-Racisme** = voluntary organization set up to combat racism in French society

sosie [sɔzi] **NM** double, doppelganger; **c'est ton s.!** he's/she's the spitting image of you!

sostenuto [sɔstenuto] **ADV** *Mus* sostenuto

sot, -otte [so, sɔt] **ADJ 1** *(idiot)* stupid; **il n'est pas s.** he's no fool; *Fam Hum* **aussi s. que grenu** as mad as a hatter **2** *Littéraire (embarrassé)* dumbfounded **3** *Belg (fou)* mad, crazy

NM,F 1 *(idiot)* fool, idiot; **petite sotte!** little fool! **2** *Belg (fou)* madman, *f* madwoman

sotch [sɔtʃ] **NM** *Géol* uvala

sotie [sɔti] **NF** *Littérature* medieval farce

sot-l'y-laisse [solilɛs] **NM INV** oyster *(in poultry)*

sotte [sɔt] *voir* **sot**

sottement [sɔtmɑ̃] **ADV** foolishly, stupidly

sottie [sɔti] **NF** *Littérature* medieval farce

sottise [sɔtiz] **NF 1** *(caractère)* stupidity, silliness; **a-t-on idée d'une pareille s.!** how can anyone be so silly?; **cette fille est d'une s. rare** that girl is exceptionally stupid

2 *(acte)* stupid *or* foolish action; **arrête de faire des sottises** *(à un enfant)* stop messing about; **je viens de faire une grosse s.** I've just done something very stupid *or* silly

3 *(parole)* stupid remark; **ne dis pas de sottises, le soleil se couche à l'ouest** don't be silly *or* talk nonsense, the sun sets in the west; **ai-je dit une s.?** have I said something stupid?

❑ **sottises NFPL** *(injures)* insults; **elle m'a dit des sottises** she insulted me

sottisier [sɔtizje] **NM** collection of howlers

sou [su] **NM 1** *Hist (sol)* sol, sou; *(cinq centimes)* five centimes; **cent sous** five francs

2 *Fam (argent)* penny, *Am* cent; **tu n'auras pas un s.!** you won't get a *Br* penny *or Am* cent!; *Fam* **ça ne vaut pas un s.** it's not worth *Br* tuppence *or Am* a red cent; **économiser s. à** *ou* **par s.** to save every spare penny; **il a dépensé jusqu'à son dernier s.** he's spent every last penny he had; **ils n'ont pas le s.** they haven't got a penny (to their name); **être sans le s.** to be broke; **je suis sans un s.** I haven't got any money (on me); **elle n'a jamais eu un s. vaillant** she never had two pennies to rub together; **un s. est un s.** a penny saved is a penny gained

3 *(locutions) Fam* **elle n'a pas (pour) un s.** *ou* **deux sous de jugeote** she hasn't an ounce of sense; **elle n'est pas méfiante pour un s.** *ou* **deux sous** she's not in the least suspicious▪; **être propre comme un s. neuf** to be as clean as a new pin

4 *Can (cent)* cent *(of a dollar)*; **un cinq sous** a nickel; **un dix sous** a dime

❑ **sous NMPL** *Fam (argent)* cash; **donne-moi des sous pour les courses** give me some cash to do the shopping; **des sous, toujours des sous!** money for this, money for that!; **c'est une affaire** *ou* **une histoire de gros sous** there's a lot of cash involved

Souabe [swab] **NF la S.** Swabia

souahéli, -e [swaeli] **ADJ** Swahili

NM *(langue)* Swahili

❑ **Souahéli, -e NM,F** Swahili; **les S.** the Swahilis *or* Swahili

soubassement [subasmɑ̃] **NM 1** *Archit & Constr* foundation **2** *Géol* bedrock **3** *(base → d'une théorie)* basis, underpinnings **4** *Can (sous-sol)* basement

soubresaut [subrəso] NM 1 *(secousse)* jerk, jolt 2 *(haut-le-corps)* shudder; **avoir un s.** to shudder 3 *(saccade)* **les derniers soubresauts de la bataille** the last throes of the battle

soubrette [subrɛt] NF 1 *Théât* soubrette, maid; **jouer les soubrettes** to play minor roles 2 *Littéraire (servante)* lady's maid

soubreveste [subrəvɛst] NF *Hist* surcoat

souçaille [susaj] NM *Fam (souci)* worry■; **no s.!** *Br* no worries!, *Am* no sweat!

souche [suʃ] NF 1 *Bot (d'un arbre en terre)* stock, bole; *(d'un arbre coupé)* stump; *(d'une vigne)* stock; **ne reste pas là planté comme une s.!** don't just stand there like *Br* a lemon *or Am* a turkey! 2 *(d'un carnet)* stub, counterfoil; **carnet de tickets à s.** book of tickets with counterfoils 3 *(origine)* descent, stock; **de s. paysanne** of peasant stock; **mot de s. saxonne** word with a Saxon root *or* of Saxon origin; **faire s.** *(ancêtre)* to found *or* to start a line; **un mot de s. indo-européenne** a word with an Indo-European root 4 *Fam (crétin)* idiot, dumbo 5 *Constr* base; **s. de cheminée** chimney stack 6 *Biol* strain 7 *Jur* stock 8 *Belg (ticket de caisse, reçu)* receipt ▫ **de souche** ADJ **ils sont français de s.** they're of French extraction *or* origin ▫ **de vieille souche** ADJ of old stock

souchet [suʃɛ] NM 1 *Bot* cyperus; **s. long/odorant** sweet cyperus, sweet sedge, galingale; **s. comestible** rush nut, tiger nut; **s. d'Amérique** rattan (cane); **s. des Indes** turmeric, curcuma 2 *Orn* shoveller

souchetage [suʃtaʒ] NM 1 *(des arbres pour la coupe)* marking 2 *(des arbres coupés)* verification

souchette [suʃɛt] NF *Bot* spindle shank

sou-chong [suʃɔ̃, suʃɔ̃g] NM souchong

souci [susi] NM 1 *(inquiétude)* worry; **se faire du s.** to worry, to fret; **se faire du s. pour qn/qch** to worry *or* to be worried about sb/sth; **elle n'a pas le moindre s. à se faire quant à son avenir** she needn't worry in the slightest about her future; **ne te fais donc pas tant de s.!** don't worry so much!; **donner du s. à qn** to worry sb; **mon fils me donne bien du s.!** my son is a great worry to me; **eh oui, tout ça c'est bien du s.!** oh dear, what a worry it all is!; *Littéraire* **soucis rongeurs** gnawing anxiety 2 *(préoccupation)* worry; **avoir des soucis** to have worries; **cet enfant est un perpétuel s.** this child is a perpetual (source of) worry; **c'est un s. de moins!** that's one thing less to worry about!; **des soucis d'argent/de santé** money/health worries; **c'est le dernier** *ou* **le cadet de mes soucis!** that's the least of my worries!; *Fam* **il n'y a pas de soucis!** *Br* no worries!, *Am* no sweat! 3 *(soin)* concern; **avoir le s. de la vérité/de l'exactitude** to be meticulously truthful/accurate; **avoir le s. de bien faire** to be concerned *or* to care about doing things well 4 *Bot* marigold; **s. d'eau** marsh marigold; **s. des jardins** garden marigold ▫ **dans le souci de** CONJ **je l'ai fait dans le s. de t'aider** I was (only) trying to help you when I did it ▫ **dans un souci de** PRÉP **je me suis limité à deux auteurs dans un s. de clarté** I limited myself to two authors in order to keep things clear ▫ **sans souci** ADJ *(vie, personne → insouciant)* carefree; **être sans s.** *(sans tracas)* to be free of worries ▫ **sans s.** ADV **vivre sans s.** *(de façon insouciante)* to live a carefree life; *(sans tracas)* to live a life free of worries

soucier [9] [susje] VT *Arch (causer de l'inquiétude à)* to trouble, to worry ▸ **se soucier** VPR **1 se s. de** *(s'inquiéter de)* to worry about; *(s'intéresser à)* to care about; **je ne m'en soucie guère** I don't worry much about it; **pars en vacances et ne te soucie de rien** go on holiday and don't worry about a thing; *Fam* **il s'en soucie comme d'une guigne** *ou* **de sa première chemise** *ou* **de l'an quarante** he doesn't give a damn about it

Littéraire **je ne me soucie pas qu'il vienne** I am not anxious that he should come

soucieuse [susjøz] *voir* **soucieux**

soucieusement [susjøzmã] ADV anxiously, worriedly

soucieux, -euse [susjø, -øz] ADJ 1 *(inquiet)* worried, preoccupied; **elle m'a regardé d'un air s.** she looked at me worriedly; **assis devant le feu, le front s.** sitting in front of the fire with a worried look on his face *or* with a furrowed brow 2 **s. de** *(attaché à)* concerned about, mindful of; **peu s. du qu'en dira-t-on** indifferent to *or* unconcerned about what people (may) say; **peu s. de la rencontrer** unconcerned about meeting her; **elle a toujours été soucieuse de ne pas les décevoir** she has always been anxious not to let them down; **s. que** *(attentif à)* anxious that; **elle était soucieuse que tout se passe bien** she was anxious that everything should go well

soucoupe [sukup] NF saucer; **s. volante** flying saucer; **faire** *ou* **ouvrir des yeux comme des soucoupes** to have eyes like saucers

soudabilité [sudabilite] NF *(par soudage → hétérogène)* solderability; *(→ autogène)* weldability

soudable [sudabl] ADJ *(par soudage → hétérogène)* solderable; *(→ autogène)* weldable

soudage [sudaʒ] NM **s. à l'arc/au gaz** arc/gas welding; **s. autogène** welding; **s. par fusion/ par pression** fusion/pressure welding; **s. hétérogène** soldering

soudain, -e [sudɛ̃, -ɛn] ADJ sudden, unexpected; **un revirement s. de la situation** an unexpected reversal of the situation ADV all of a sudden, suddenly; **s. la porte s'ouvrit** all of a sudden *or* suddenly, the door opened

soudainement [sudɛnmã] ADV suddenly, all of a sudden; **pourquoi est-il parti si s.?** why did he leave so hurriedly?

soudaineté [sudɛnte] NF suddenness; **la s. de son départ** his/her hurried *or* sudden departure

Soudan [sudã] NM **le S.** (the) Sudan; **vivre au S.** to live in (the) Sudan; **aller au S.** to go to (the) Sudan

soudanais, -e [sudanɛ, -ɛz], **soudanien, -enne** [sudanjɛ̃, -ɛn] ADJ Sudanese ▫ **Soudanais, -e, Soudanien, -enne** NM,F Sudanese (person); **les S.** the Sudanese

soudant, -e [sudã, -ãt] ADJ welding *(avant n)*

soudard [sudar] NM 1 *Hist* ill-disciplined soldier 2 *Littéraire (individu grossier et brutal)* brute 3 *Belg (soldat)* soldier; *(conscrit)* conscript

soude [sud] NF 1 *Chim* soda; **s. caustique** caustic soda; **s. du commerce** washing soda 2 *Bot* barilla

souder [3] [sude] VT 1 *Tech (par soudure → hétérogène)* to solder; *(→ autogène)* to weld; **s. à l'arc** to arc-weld; **s. au cuivre** *ou* **au laiton** to braze; **s. à l'étain** to soft-solder; **s. par points** to spot-weld 2 *(unir)* to bring together, to unite; **le malheur les avait soudés** misfortune had united them; **communautés soudées par la religion** communities solidly linked by religion ▸ **se souder** VPR 1 *(vertèbres, mots)* to become fused 2 *(s'unir → personnes, groupe)* to unite

soudeur, -euse [sudœr, -øz] NM,F *(par soudure → hétérogène)* solderer; *(→ autogène)* welder; **s. au chalumeau** lamp *or* torch welder ▫ **soudeuse** NF *(machine)* welder, welding machine

soudier, -ère [sudje, -ɛr] ADJ soda *(avant n)*

soudoyer [13] [sudwaje] VT 1 *(acheter)* to bribe; **s. qn pour qu'il fasse qch** to bribe sb into doing sth; **on a su par la suite que le gardien s'était fait s.** we discovered later that the guard had been bribed 2 *Arch (mercenaire)* to pay

soudure [sudyr] NF 1 *(soudage → hétérogène)* soldering; *(→ autogène)* welding; **s. au cuivre** *ou* **au laiton** brazing; **s. à l'étain** soft-soldering; **s. par points** spot weld 2 *(résultat → hétérogène)* soldered joint; *(→ autogène)* weld 3 *(jonction)* join; **ça s'est cassé à (l'endroit de) la s.** it broke along the join; **assurer** *ou* **faire la s. (entre)** to bridge the gap (between); **elle fera la**

s. entre les deux directeurs she'll be acting manager 4 *(alliage → hétérogène)* solder; *(→ autogène)* weld 5 *Anat & Bot* suture

soue [su] NF *Can ou Vieilli* pigsty

souffert, -e [sufɛr, -ɛrt] PP *voir* **souffrir**

soufflage [suflaʒ] NM 1 *(modelage → du verre)* blowing; *(→ des polymères)* inflation 2 *Rail* **s. mesuré** measured shovel packing 3 *Naut* sheathing 4 *Mines* heave 5 *Métal* blow 6 *Élec* **s. magnétique** magnetic blowout (phenomenon)

soufflant, -e [suflã, -ãt] ADJ 1 *(appareil)* machine **soufflante** blowing *or* blast engine; **radiateur s.** fan heater 2 *Fam (étonnant)* staggering, amazing; **ça alors, c'est s.!** well I never! NM *très Fam (pistolet)* gun■ ▫ **soufflante** NF 1 *(dans un haut fourneau)* blower 2 *(dans un turboréacteur)* turbofan; **soufflante de sustentation** *(d'un aéroglisseur)* lift fan

soufflard [suflar] NM *Géol* fumarole (jet)

souffle [sufl] NM 1 *(air expiré → par une personne)* blow; **elle dit oui dans un s.** she breathed her assent; *Littéraire* **dernier s.** last breath; **jusqu'à mon dernier s.** as long as I live and breathe, to my dying day 2 *(respiration)* breath; *(rythme respiratoire)* breathing; **je sentis un s. sur ma nuque** I felt a breath on my neck; **on la renverserait d'un s.** you could knock her over with a feather; **il a éteint toutes les bougies d'un s.** he blew out all the candles in one go; **exhaler son dernier s.** to breathe one's last; **avoir du s.** to have a lot of breath; **avoir le s. court, manquer de s.** to be short of breath; **être à bout de s., n'avoir plus de s.** *(haletant)* to be out of breath; *Fig* **l'entreprise est à bout de s.** the company is on its last legs; **reprendre son s.** to get one's breath *or* wind back; *aussi Fig* **retenir son s.** to hold one's breath; **trouver un deuxième** *ou* **un second s.** to get *or* to find one's second wind; *Fig* to get a new lease of life 3 *(courant d'air)* **s. d'air** *ou* **de vent** breath of air; **il n'y a pas un s. de vent** there isn't a breath of air, the air is completely still; **un s. de vent agita les roseaux** a puff of wind blew through the reeds 4 *Littéraire (force)* breath, spirit; **un s. épique traverse le poème** the poem is imbued with an epic spirit; **le s. vital** the breath of life 5 *(d'une explosion)* blast; **le magasin a été détruit par le s.** the *Br* shop *or Am* store was destroyed by the blast; **le s. d'un sèche-cheveux/d'un ventilateur** warm air blown by a hairdryer/a fan 6 *Tél* (thermal) noise; **s. du signal** modulation noise 7 *Méd* murmur; **s. au cœur** heart murmur 8 *Zool (d'un cétacé)* blow

‖═══📽═══‖

'**Le Souffle au cœur**' *Malle*'Murmur of the Heart' *or* 'Dearest Love'

soufflé, -e [sufle] ADJ 1 *Tech* blown 2 *Fam (étonné)* amazed, staggered, dumbfounded; **j'étais s.!** I was speechless!, you could have knocked me down with a feather! 3 *Culin* soufflé *(avant n)*; **pommes de terre soufflées** soufflé potatoes 4 *(boursouflé → visage, main)* puffy, swollen NM 1 *Culin* soufflé; **s. au fromage** cheese soufflé 2 *Tech* blowing

soufflement [sufləmã] NM *Littéraire* blowing

SOUFFLER [3] [sufle]

VI	to breathe out 1 ■ to blow 2, 3, 6 ■ to get one's breath back 4 ■ to have a break 5
VT	to blow out 1 ■ to whisper 3, 4 ■ to flabbergast 5 ■ to blow up 8 ■ to blow 9
USAGE ABSOLU	to whisper

VI 1 *(expirer → personne)* to breathe out; **inspirez, soufflez!** breathe in, breathe out!; **soufflez dans le ballon** *(Alcootest®)* blow into the bag; **ils m'ont fait s. dans le ballon** they gave me a breath test; **s. dans un cor/dans un trombone** to blow (into) a horn/a trombone; **il soufflait sur ses mains/sur ses doigts** he was blowing

on his hands/fingers; **souffle sur ton potage si c'est trop chaud** blow on your soup if it's too hot; *Fam* **ça ne se fait pas en soufflant dessus!** you can't do it just like that!; **s. sur le feu** to blow on the fire; *Fig* to add fuel to the flames; *Fam* **s. dans les bronches à qn** to bawl sb out

2 *Météo (vent)* to blow; **le vent soufflera sur tout le pays** it'll be windy all over the country; **le vent soufflait en rafales** *ou* **en bourrasques** there were gusts of wind, the wind was gusting; **le vent souffle à plus de 120 km/h par endroits** there are gusts of wind reaching 120 km/h in places; **quand le vent souffle de l'ouest** when the wind blows *or* comes from the west

3 *(respirer avec difficulté)* to blow, to puff, to breathe hard; **suant et soufflant** puffing and blowing; *Fam* **s. comme un bœuf** *ou* **un cachalot** *ou* **une forge** *ou* **une locomotive** *ou* **un phoque** to wheeze like a pair of old bagpipes

4 *(retrouver sa respiration → personne)* to get one's breath back; *(→ cheval)* to get its breath back; **souffle un peu, avant de soulever l'armoire** get your breath back before you move the cupboard; **laisser s. son cheval** to blow *or* to wind one's horse

5 *(se reposer)* to have a break *or* a breather; **ça fait trois semaines que je travaille sans arrêt, j'ai besoin de s. un peu** I've been working for three weeks non-stop, I need a break *or* a breather; **au bureau, on n'a pas le temps de s.!** it's all go at the office!; **tu ne prends donc jamais le temps de s.?** don't you ever let up *or* give yourself a break?

6 *Zool (cétacé)* to blow

VT 1 *(bougie)* to blow out; **elle a soufflé toutes les bougies d'un seul coup** she blew all the candles out in one go

2 *(exhaler)* **va s. ta fumée de cigarette ailleurs** go and blow your smoke elsewhere; *Fig* **s. le chaud et le froid** to blow hot and cold

3 *(murmurer → mot, réponse)* to whisper; *Théât* to prompt; **s. qch à qn** to whisper sth to sb; **il a fallu qu'on lui souffle son rôle** he/she had to have a prompt; **évidemment qu'il a gagné, il s'est fait s. toutes les réponses** of course he won, somebody was whispering all the answers to him!; **ne pas s. mot (de qch)** not to breathe a word (about sth); **il a juré de n'en s. mot à personne** he swore not to breathe a word about it to anyone

4 *(suggérer → idée, conseil)* to whisper, to suggest; **et qui t'a soufflé cette brillante idée?** who did you get that bright idea from?

5 *Fam (époustoufler → sujet: événement, personne)* to stagger, to flabbergast; **son insolence m'a vraiment soufflé!** I was quite staggered at his/her rudeness!; **ça t'a soufflé, hein, qu'il refuse?** him saying no stumped you, didn't it?

6 *Fam (dérober)* **s. qch à qn** to pinch sth from sb; **je me suis fait s. ma place** someone's pinched my seat

7 *(dans un jeu → pion)* to huff; **s. n'est pas jouer!** to huff doesn't count as a move!

8 *(sujet: bombe, explosion)* to blow up; **l'explosion a soufflé la toiture** the blast blew the roof off

9 *Métal & Tech* to blow

USAGE ABSOLU *(murmurer)* **on ne souffle pas!** no whispering!, don't whisper (the answer)!

---

soufflerie [sufləri] **NF 1** *Aviat* wind tunnel; **en s.** in a wind tunnel **2** *Ind* blower; *(d'une forge)* bellows **3** *Mus (d'un orgue)* bellows

soufflet [suflɛ] **NM 1** *(instrument)* (pair of) bellows; **s. de forge** (forge *or* blacksmith's) bellows **2** *(d'un cartable)* extendible pocket **3** *Littéraire (gifle)* slap; *(affront)* snub; **sa remarque lui fit l'effet d'un s.** his/her remark was like a slap in the face **4** *Couture* (pocket) gusset **5** *Phot* bellows **6** *Rail* (wagon) communication bellows **7** *Mus (d'un orgue)* bellows

souffleter [27] [suflәte] **VT** *Littéraire (gifler)* to slap in the face; *(insulter)* to insult

soufflette [suflɛt] **NF** *Belg (ampoule)* blister; *(boursouflure)* swelling

souffleur, -euse [suflœr, -øz] **NM,F 1** *Théât* prompter **2** *Tech* **s. de verre** glassblower

NM *Zool* **(dauphin) s.** bottlenosed dolphin

❑ **souffleuse NF 1** *Agr* blower container **2** *Can* **souffleuse (à neige)** snowblower, snow thrower, snow sweeper

soufflure [suflyr] **NF 1** *Métal (à la surface)* blister; *(à l'intérieur)* blowhole **2** *(dans un enduit, dans une peinture)* blister **3** *(dans le verre)* blister, bubble

souffrance [sufrɑ̃s] **NF 1** *(fait de souffrir)* suffering **2** *(mal → physique)* pain; *(→ psychologique)* pain, torment; **abréger les** *ou* **mettre fin aux souffrances de qn** to put an end to sb's suffering

❑ **en souffrance ADV** *(dossier)* pending; *(factures)* overdue, outstanding; *(colis)* held up in transit, awaiting delivery; **être** *ou* **rester en s.** to be held up

---

'Les Souffrances du jeune Werther' *Goethe*
'The Sorrows of Young Werther'

---

souffrant, -e [sufrɑ̃, -ɑ̃t] **ADJ 1** *(malade)* **être s.** to be unwell **2** *(malheureux)* suffering; **l'humanité souffrante** the downtrodden masses

souffre-douleur [sufrədulœr] **NM INV** scapegoat; **à l'école, c'était toujours lui le s.** at school, he was always the one who got bullied

souffreteux, -euse [sufrətø, -øz] **ADJ 1** *(malingre)* sickly, *Péj* puny; **un enfant s.** a sickly *or* a delicate child **2** *(maladif → air)* sickly; **une mine souffreteuse** an unhealthy *or* a sickly complexion **3** *(rabougri → plante)* stunted, scrubby

souffrir [34] [sufrir] **VT 1** *(endurer → épreuves)* to endure, to suffer; **si tu avais souffert ce que j'ai souffert!** if you'd suffered as much as I have!, if you had gone through what I have!; **s. le martyre** to go through *or* to suffer agonies; **son dos lui fait s. le martyre** he/she has terrible trouble with his/her back; **j'ai souffert mille morts** I felt I was dying a thousand deaths

2 *Littéraire (tolérer)* **elle ne souffre pas d'être critiquée** *ou* **qu'on la critique** she can't stand *or* take criticism; **il ne souffrait pas la contradiction** he couldn't stand being contradicted; **je ne peux pas s. cet homme/cette odeur** I can't bear *or* stand that man/smell

3 *Littéraire (admettre → sujet: personne)* to allow, to tolerate; *(→ sujet: règlement)* to allow (for), to admit of; **souffrez au moins que je vous accompagne** at least allow me to accompany you; **le règlement de son dossier ne peut s. aucun délai** the settlement of his/her case simply cannot be postponed; **cette règle ne souffre aucune exception** the rule admits of no exception

4 *Fam (supporter)* **elle ne peut pas le s.** she can't stand him

USAGE ABSOLU les récoltes n'ont pas trop souffert the crops didn't suffer too much *or* weren't too badly damaged; **seule la carrosserie a souffert** only the bodywork was damaged; **c'est le sud du pays qui a le plus souffert** the southern part of the country was the worst hit

VI 1 *(avoir mal)* to be in pain, to suffer; **tu souffres?** are you in pain?, does it hurt?; **souffre-t-il beaucoup?** is he in much pain?, is he suffering a lot?; **où souffrez-vous?** where is the pain?, where does it hurt?; **elle a beaucoup souffert lors de son accouchement** she had a very painful delivery; **c'est une intervention bénigne, vous ne souffrirez pas** it's a very minor operation, you won't feel any pain; **s. en silence** to suffer in silence; **il est mort sans s.** he felt no pain when he died; *Euph* **elle a cessé de s., elle ne souffrira plus** she's out of pain (now); *Hum* **il faut s. pour être belle!** one must suffer to be beautiful!; **faire s. qn** to cause pain to sb, to hurt sb; **mon dos me fait s. ces temps-ci** my back's been hurting (me) lately; **si ça vous fait encore s., revenez me voir** if it starts hurting again, come back and see me

2 *(moralement)* to suffer; **elle l'a fait terriblement s.** she's caused him/her a lot of pain

3 *Fam (peiner)* to toil, to have a hard time (of it); **notre équipe a souffert pendant la première mi-temps** our team had a rough time *or* was put through the mill during the first half

❑ **souffrir de VT IND** *(avoir mal à cause de)* **s. de la hanche** to have trouble with one's hip; **pour tous les gens qui souffrent du diabète/du dos** for all diabetes sufferers/people with back problems; **s. de la faim/de la soif** to suffer from hunger/thirst; **s. de la chaleur** *(être très sensible à)* to suffer in the heat; *(être atteint par)* to suffer from the heat; **s. de la solitude** to feel lonely; **ils souffrent de son indifférence** they're hurt by his/her indifference; **elle souffre de le savoir si loin** it pains her to know he's so far away; **sa renommée a souffert du scandale** his/her reputation suffered from the scandal; **la crédibilité de l'intrigue en souffre** it makes the plot less plausible; **dût ton amour-propre en s.** even though your pride may be hurt by it

▸**se souffrir VPR** *Littéraire* **ils ne peuvent pas se s.** they can't stand *or* bear each other

soufi [sufi] **NM** *Rel* Sufi

soufisme [sufism] **NM** *Rel* Sufism

soufrage [sufraʒ] **NM 1** *(des allumettes)* sulphuring **2** *Agr & Tex* sulphuration

soufre [sufr] **NM 1** *Chim* sulphur; **s. octaédrique/prismatique** monoclinic/rhombic sulphur **2** *(locution)* **sentir le s.** to be highly unorthodox

ADJ INV sulphur (yellow)

soufrer [3] [sufre] **VT 1** *(allumettes)* to sulphur **2** *Agr* to (treat *or* spray with) sulphur **3** *Tex* to sulphurate

soufreur, -euse [sufrœr, -øz] **NM,F** *Agr* = person who treats vines etc with sulphur

❑ **soufreuse NF** sulphurator, sulphur sprayer

soufrière [sufrijɛr] **NF** sulphur mine

souhait [swɛ] **NM** wish; **faire un s.** to make a wish; **si je pouvais formuler un s.** if I had one wish; **tous nos souhaits de bonheur** all our best wishes for your future happiness; **envoyer ses souhaits de bonne année** to send New Year greetings; **à tes souhaits!, à vos souhaits!** bless you! *(after a sneeze)*

❑ **à souhait ADV** *Littéraire* extremely well, perfectly; **tout marche à s.** everything's going well *or* perfectly; **rôti à s.** cooked to perfection, done to a turn; **doré à s.** beautifully golden

souhaitable [swɛtabl] **ADJ** desirable; **ce n'est guère s.** this is not to be desired; **il serait s. que vous n'en parliez à personne** it would be better if you didn't mention this to anybody

souhaiter [4] [swete] **VT 1** *(espérer)* to wish *or* to hope for; **il ne reviendra plus – souhaitons-le** *ou* **c'est à s.!** he won't come back – let's hope not!; **ce n'est pas à s.!** it's not something we would wish for!; **s. la mort/la ruine/le bonheur de qn** to wish sb dead/for sb's ruin/for sb's happiness; **s. que...** to hope that...; **souhaitons que tout aille bien** let's hope everything goes all right; **il est à s. que...** it's to be hoped that...

2 *(formuler un vœu de)* to wish; **en vous souhaitant un prompt rétablissement/un bon anniversaire** wishing you a swift recovery/a happy birthday; **nous vous souhaitons un joyeux Noël** with our best wishes for a happy Christmas; **s. sa fête/son anniversaire à qn** to wish sb a happy saint's day/a happy birthday; **je te souhaite beaucoup de réussite/d'être heureux** I wish you every success/happiness; **je vous souhaite de réussir** I hope you will succeed; **souhaite-moi bonne chance!** wish me luck!; **je ne leur ai pas encore souhaité la bonne année** *(par écrit)* I haven't sent them my wishes for the New Year yet; *(oralement)* I haven't wished them a happy New Year yet; **je vous souhaite bonne nuit** I'll say good night to you; **je ne le souhaite à personne** I wouldn't wish that on anyone; *Fam Ironique* **je te souhaite bien du plaisir!, je t'en souhaite!** best of luck to you!; *Fam* **je te la souhaite bonne et heureuse!** all my best wishes for a happy New Year!

3 *(désirer)* to wish; **je souhaite qu'on me tienne au courant** I wish to be kept informed; **je souhaiterais parler au responsable** I'd like to speak to the person in charge; **je souhaiterais pouvoir t'aider** I wish I could help (you), I'd like to be able to help (you)

▸**se souhaiter VPR nous nous sommes souhaité la bonne année** we wished each other a happy New Year

souillard [sujar] **NM** *Constr (trou)* sinkhole; *(dalle)* sink-stone

souille [suj] **NF 1** *Chasse* (boar's) wallow, soil **2** *(trace d'un projectile)* strike **3** *Naut (d'un navire)* bed, impression

souiller [3] [suje] **VT** *Littéraire* **1** *(maculer)* to soil; **des vêtements souillés de boue** mudstained clothes **2** *(polluer)* to contaminate, to pollute, to taint **3** *(entacher → réputation)* to ruin, to sully, to tarnish; *(→ innocence)* to defile, to taint

souillon [sujɔ̃] **NMF** *(homme)* slob; *(femme)* slob, slut; *(servante)* slovenly maid

souillure [sujyr] **NF** **1** *Littéraire (tache)* stain **2** *Littéraire (flétrissure)* blemish, taint; **la s. du péché** the stain of sin **3** *Chasse* (boar's) wallow

souimanga [swimɑ̃ga] **NM** *Orn* sunbird

souk [suk] **NM** **1** *(marché)* souk **2** *Fam (désordre)* shambles; **c'est le s. dans sa piaule!** his/her room's an absolute bombsite *or* pigsty!; **foutre le s. (dans)** to make a mess (of)■ ; **il fout le s. en classe** he creates havoc in the classroom■

soul [sul, sol] *Mus* **ADJ INV** soul *(avant n)*
NM *(jazz)* hard bop
NF *(pop)* soul (music)

soûl, -e [su, sul] **ADJ** **1** *(ivre)* drunk; *Fam* **s. comme une bourrique** *ou* **un cochon** *ou* **une grive** *ou* **un Polonais** *Br* (as) drunk as a lord, *Am* stewed to the gills
2 *Fig Littéraire* **s. de** *(rassasié de)* sated with; *(étourdi par)* drunk *or* intoxicated with
NM **tout son s.** to one's heart's content; **manger/boire tout son s.** to eat/to drink one's fill *or* to one's heart's content; **en avoir tout son s.** to have one's fill; **dormir tout son s.** to sleep as much as one wants

soulagement [sulaʒmɑ̃] **NM** relief, *Sout* solace; **éprouver un sentiment de s.** to feel relieved; **c'est un s. de le savoir sain et sauf** it's a relief to know he's safe and sound; **c'est un s. de t'avoir ici** it helps *or* it's a comfort to have you around; **le s. se lisait sur son visage** you could see from his/her face how relieved he/she was; **à mon grand s., il partit enfin** I was greatly relieved when he left at last

soulager [17] [sulaʒe] **VT** **1** *(personne → physiquement)* to relieve, to bring relief to; **les comprimés ne me soulagent plus** the pills don't bring me relief any more; **cela devrait vous s. de votre mal de tête** this should relieve *or* help your headache
2 *(personne → moralement)* to relieve, to soothe; **pleure, ça te soulagera** have a good cry, you'll feel better afterwards; **ça me soulage de savoir qu'il est bien arrivé** it's a relief to know he got there safely; **je suis soulagé de l'apprendre** I'm relieved to hear it; **si ça peut te s., sache que je suis dans la même situation** if it makes you feel any better, I'm in the same situation; **s. la conscience de qn** to ease sb's conscience
3 *(diminuer → misère, souffrances)* to relieve; *(→ douleur)* to relieve, to soothe; **j'aimerais pouvoir s. ta peine** I wish I could relieve your sorrow *or* bring you some comfort
4 *(décharger)* to relieve; **nous allons réduire certains impôts pour s. les entreprises** some taxes will be reduced to relieve companies; **mon collègue me soulage parfois d'une partie de mon travail** my colleague sometimes relieves me of part of my work; *Hum* **s. qn de son portefeuille** to relieve sb of his/her *Br* wallet *or Am* billfold
5 *Constr (étayer)* to shore up
6 *Naut (ancre)* to weigh
▶**se soulager VPR** **1** *(d'une charge de travail)* to lessen the strain on oneself; **prends un collaborateur pour te s.** take somebody on to take some of the pressure of work off you
2 *(moralement)* to get *or* to find relief, to take comfort; **il m'arrive de crier pour me s.** sometimes I shout to let *or* to blow off steam
3 *Fam (uriner, déféquer)* to relieve oneself
4 *très Fam (se masturber)* to give oneself relief

soulane [sulan] **NF** *(dans les Pyrénées)* sunny side *(of a valley)*

soûlant, -e [sulɑ̃, -ɑ̃t] **ADJ** *Fam* exhausting■ , *Br* knackering; **elle parle, elle parle, c'en est s.!** she goes on and on, it makes your head spin!

soûlard, -e [sular, -ard], **soûlaud, -e** [sulo, -od] **NM,F** *Fam* boozer, alky; **c'est une vieille soûlarde** she's an old soak; **c'était un fameux s.!** he was a renowned boozer!

soûler [3] [sule] **VT** **1** *Fam (rendre ivre)* **s. qn** to get sb drunk■
2 *(étourdir)* to make dizzy *or* giddy; **tu me soûles, avec tes questions!** you're making me dizzy with all these questions!; **le grand air m'a soûlé** the fresh air made me dizzy
▶**se soûler VPR** **1** *Fam (s'enivrer)* to get drunk■ ; **je vais me s. à mort pour oublier!** I'm going to get dead drunk so that I forget all about it!; *très Fam* **se s. la gueule** *Br* to get pissed, *Am* to tie one on
2 *Fig (s'étourdir)* **se s. de** to get intoxicated with; **il se soûle de paroles** he talks so much that it goes to his head

soûlerie [sulri] **NF** *Fam* **1** *(beuverie)* bender, drinking session■ **2** *(ivresse)* drunkenness■

soulèvement [sulɛvmɑ̃] **NM** **1** *(mouvement)* lifting; **déclenché par le s. du clapet** triggered by the lifting of the valve **2** *(insurrection)* uprising **3** *Géol* **s. de terrain** upheaval *or* uplift (of the ground)

soulever [19] [sulve] **VT** **1** *(pour porter, pour élever → charge, personne debout)* to lift (up); *(→ couvercle, loquet, voile)* to lift; *(→ capot)* to lift, to open; *(→ personne allongée)* to raise (up); *(→ chapeau)* to raise; *(→ voiture)* to lift; *(→ voiture sur cric)* to jack up; *(→ avec effort)* to heave; **s. le couvercle d'une casserole** to lift (up) the lid of a saucepan; **de gros sanglots soulevaient sa poitrine** his/her chest was heaving with sobs; **s. qn/qch de terre** to lift sb/sth off the ground; **le vent m'a presque soulevée de terre!** the wind nearly lifted me off the ground *or* off my feet!; *Littéraire* **s. le voile qui cache l'avenir** to raise a corner of the veil that hides the future
2 *(remuer → poussière, sable)* to raise; **le vent soulevait les feuilles mortes** the wind was stirring up dead leaves
3 *(provoquer → protestations, tollé)* to raise; *(→ enthousiasme, émotion)* to arouse; *(→ difficulté)* to bring up, to raise; **son imitation souleva une tempête de rires** his/her impersonation caused gales of laughter; **sa déclaration souleva un tonnerre d'applaudissements** his/her announcement met with thunderous applause
4 *(poser → question, objection)* to raise, to bring up; **je voudrais s. le point suivant** I'd like to raise the following point
5 *(pousser à se révolter → population)* to stir up; **ils ont tout fait pour s. le peuple contre la monarchie** they did everything they could to stir up the people against the monarchy; **une vague de protestation a soulevé le pays tout entier** a wave of protest swept the country
6 *(retourner)* **ça m'a soulevé le cœur** it turned my stomach, it made me sick; **une puanteur à vous s. le cœur** a sickening stench
7 *très Fam (prendre → chose)* to pinch; *(→ mari, maîtresse)* to steal; **elle lui a soulevé une bonne partie de sa clientèle** she took most of his/her customers away from him/her
▶**se soulever VPR** **1** *(se redresser)* to lift *or* to raise oneself up; **il l'aida à se s.** he helped him/her to sit up
2 *(mer)* to swell (up), to heave; *(poitrine)* to heave; **sa jupe se soulevait au moindre souffle de vent** the slighest puff of wind blew her skirt up
3 *(peuple)* to rise up, to revolt

soulier [sulje] **NM** **1** *(chaussure)* shoe **2** *Fam (locution)* **être dans ses petits souliers** to feel (very) small

soulignage [suliɲaʒ], **soulignement** [suliɲəmɑ̃] **NM** underlining

souligner [3] [suliɲe] **VT** **1** *(mettre un trait sous)* to underline; **s. qch deux fois** to underline sth twice
2 *(accentuer)* to enhance, to emphasize; **s. son regard d'un trait de khôl** to enhance *or* to emphasize one's eyes with a touch of kohl; **une robe qui souligne la taille** a dress which emphasizes the waist; **volant souligné d'un liséré bleu** flounce trimmed with blue ribbon
3 *(faire remarquer)* to emphasize, to stress; **je souligne que je n'y suis pour rien** let me stress that I have nothing to do with it; **soulignons que l'auteur a lui-même connu la prison** let's note *or* let's not forget that the author himself spent some time in prison

soûlographe [sulɔgraf] **NMF** *Fam* lush, soak

soûlographie [sulɔgrafi] **NF** *Fam (ivrognerie)* drunkenness■

soûlon [sulɔ̃] **NM** *Suisse & Can Fam* lush, soak

soûlot, -e [sulo, -ɔt] = **soûlard**

soulte [sult] **NF** *Fin & Jur* compensation *or* equalization payment

soumaintrain [sumɛ̃trɛ̃] **NM** Soumaintrain *(cheese)*

soumettre [84] [sumɛtr] **VT** **1** *(se rendre maître de → nation)* to subjugate; *(→ mutins)* to take control of, to subdue, to bring to heel; *(→ passion)* to control, to tame
2 *(à une épreuve, à un règlement)* **s. qn à** to subject sb to; **s. qn à sa volonté** to subject *or* to bend sb to one's will; **être soumis à des règles strictes** to be bound by strict rules; **s. qch à un examen** to subject sth to an examination; **nos voitures sont soumises à des tests très stricts** our cars have to go through *or* are subjected to stringent tests; **s. un malade à un régime strict** to put a patient on a strict diet; **s. qn/qch à l'impôt** to subject sb/sth to tax
3 *(présenter → loi, suggestion, texte)* to submit; **je lui soumettrai votre demande** I'll refer your request to him/her; **je voulais d'abord le s. à votre approbation** I wanted to submit it for your approval first; **s. une lettre à la signature** to present a letter for signature; **le projet de loi sera ensuite soumis au Sénat** the bill will then be brought before the Senate *or* be submitted to the Senate (for approval)
▶**se soumettre VPR** to give in, to submit, to yield; **les rebelles ont fini par se s.** the rebels finally gave in; **se s. à** *(se plier à)* to submit *or* to subject oneself to; *(s'en remettre à)* to abide by; **se s. à la décision de qn** to abide by sb's decision; **dans une telle situation, il faut se s. ou se démettre** it's the kind of situation where you either comply with the rules or you give up

soumis, -e [sumi, -iz] **ADJ** **1** *(docile)* submissive, obedient, dutiful **2** *(astreint)* subject (**à** to); **s. à l'impôt sur le revenu** liable to income tax; **s. au (droit de) timbre** subject to stamp duty; **s. aux fluctuations du marché** subject to fluctuations in the market

soumission [sumisjɔ̃] **NF** **1** *(obéissance → à un pouvoir)* submission, submitting; *(→ à une autorité)* acquiescence, acquiescing; **faire acte de s.** to submit; **il exigeait une totale s. au règlement** he demanded rigid adherence to the rules
2 *(asservissement)* submissiveness; **vivre dans la s.** to live a submissive life, to live one's life in a state of submission
3 *Com* tender; **par (voie de) s.** by tender; **faire une s. pour un travail** to tender for a piece of work; **s. cachetée** sealed-bid tender; **s. d'offre** tender proposal
4 *Jur* **s. cautionnée** customs bond

soumissionnaire [sumisjɔnɛr] **NMF** tenderer

soumissionner [3] [sumisjɔne] **VT** to bid *or* to tender for

soumit *etc voir* **soumettre**

soundcheck [saundtʃɛk] **NM** *Mus* sound check

soupape [supap] **NF** **1** *Aut & Tech* valve; **s. d'admission** inlet valve; **s. automatique** automatic control; **s. d'échappement** exhaust *or* outlet valve; **soupapes latérales** side valves; **s. à papillon** butterfly valve; *aussi Fig* **s. de sécurité** *ou* **de sûreté** safety valve; **soupapes en tête** overhead valves **2** *(bonde)* plug **3** *Élec* valve, tube **4** *Mus* pallet

soupçon [supsɔ̃] **NM** **1** *(suspicion)* suspicion; **de graves soupçons pèsent sur lui** grave suspicions hang over him; **éveiller les soupçons** to arouse *or* to excite suspicion; **avoir des soupçons sur qn/qch** to be suspicious of sb/sth; **j'ai eu des soupçons dès le début** I suspected something from the beginning; **être à l'abri** *ou* **au-dessus de tout s.** to be free from *or* above all suspicion
2 *(idée, pressentiment)* suspicion, inkling; **je n'en avais pas le moindre s.** I didn't have the slightest suspicion, I never suspected it for a moment
3 *(petite quantité)* **un s. de crème** a touch *or* a dash of cream; **un s. de maquillage** a hint *or* a touch of make-up; **un s. d'ironie** a touch *or* a hint of irony; **un s. de rhum** a dash *or* a (tiny) drop of rum

soupçonnable [supsɔnabl] ADJ open to suspicion, suspicious

soupçonner [3] [supsɔne] VT **1** (*suspecter*) to suspect; **s. qn de meurtre/de trahison** to suspect sb of murder/of treason; **soupçonné d'avoir fait de l'espionnage** suspected of having been a spy *or* of espionage

2 (*pressentir → piège*) to suspect; **je ne lui aurais jamais soupçonné autant de talent** I would never have suspected *or* thought that he was so talented; **s. que...** to have a feeling *or* to suspect that...; **comment pouvais-je s. qu'il ferait une fugue?** how could I possibly have foreseen *or* predicted that he'd run away?

3 (*douter de*) to doubt; **il n'y a aucune raison de s. sa bonne foi** there's no reason to doubt his/her good faith

4 (*imaginer*) to imagine, to suspect

soupçonneuse [supsɔnøz] *voir* **soupçonneux**

soupçonneusement [supsɔnøzmɑ̃] ADV suspiciously, with suspicion

soupçonneux, -euse [supsɔnø, -øz] ADJ suspicious; **un mari s.** a suspicious husband; **il la regarda d'un air s.** he looked at her suspiciously

soupe [sup] NF **1** *Culin* soup; **s. aux choux/au crabe** cabbage/crab soup; **s. au lait** bread and milk; *Fig* **c'est une s. au lait, elle est très s. au lait, elle monte comme une s. au lait** she flies off the handle easily; *Fam* **faire la s. à la grimace** to sulk ▪, to be in the huff; **il est rentré tard hier soir et a eu droit à la s. à la grimace** he got home late last night, so now he's in the doghouse; *Fig* **s. la s.** to have an eye to the main chance; *Fam* **par ici la bonne s.!** that's the way to make money!

2 *Fam* (*repas*) grub, nosh; **s. populaire** soup kitchen; *Hum* **je suis bon pour la s. populaire!** I might as well go and beg on the streets!; **à la s.!** grub's up!, come and get it!

3 *Fam* (*neige*) slushy snow

4 *Fam* (*musique*) supermarket *or* elevator music

5 *Arch* (*tranche de pain*) sop, soaked slice of bread

▫ **soupe de lait** ADJ (*couleur de la robe d'un cheval*) cream-coloured

'**Soupe au canard**' *McCarey* 'Duck Soup'

soupente [supɑ̃t] NF **1** (*dans un grenier*) loft; (*sous un escalier*) *esp Br* cupboard, *Am* closet (*under the stairs*) **2** *Tech* (*barre de soutien*) supporting bar

souper¹ [supe] NM **1** *Vieilli ou Can, Belg, Suisse, & (en français régional)* (*dîner*) dinner, supper **2** (*après le spectacle*) (late) supper

souper² [3] [supe] VI **1** *Vieilli ou Can, Belg, Suisse & (en français régional)* (*dîner*) to have dinner; **s. de qch** to dine on sth; **nous avons soupé d'un peu de pain et de fromage** we dined on a morsel of bread and cheese **2** (*après le spectacle*) to have a late supper (*after a show*) **3** *Fam* **en avoir soupé de qch** to have had enough of sth, to be fed up (to the back teeth) of sth

soupeser [19] [supəze] VT **1** (*en soulevant*) to feel the weight of, to weigh in one's hand *or* hands **2** (*juger*) to weigh up

soupeur, -euse [supœr, -øz] NM,F diner (*after a show*)

soupière [supjɛr] NF (*soup*) tureen

soupir [supir] NM **1** (*expiration*) sigh; **un gros s.** a heavy *or* a deep sigh; **s. de soulagement** sigh of relief; **pousser des soupirs** to sigh; "**oui**", **murmura-t-elle dans un s.** "yes," she sighed; *Littéraire* **dernier s.** last breath; **rendre le dernier s.** to breathe one's last; **elle a recueilli son dernier s.** she was with him/her when he/she breathed his/her last

2 *Mus Br* crotchet rest, *Am* quarter *or* quarternote rest

▫ **soupirs** NMPL *Littéraire* (*désirs*) **l'objet de mes soupirs** the one I yearn for

soupirail, -aux [supiraj, -o] NM (*d'une cave*) (cellar) ventilator; (*d'une pièce*) basement window

soupirant [supirɑ̃] NM suitor

soupiraux [supiro] *voir* **soupirail**

soupirer [3] [supire] VI (*pousser un soupir*) to sigh; **s. d'aise** to sigh with contentment; "**eh oui**", **dit-il en soupirant** "I'm afraid so," he sighed

VT (*dire*) to sigh; "**c'est impossible**", **soupira-t-elle** "it's impossible," she sighed

▫ **soupirer après** VT IND *Littéraire* to long *or* to sigh *or* to yearn for

▫ **soupirer pour** VT IND *Littéraire* (*être amoureux de*) to sigh for

souple [supl] ADJ **1** (*lame*) flexible, pliable, supple; (*branche*) supple; (*plastique*) non-rigid

2 (*malléable*) **argile s.** plastic clay

3 (*agile → athlète, danseur, corps*) supple; (→ *démarche*) fluid, flowing

4 (*doux → cuir, peau, brosse à dents*) soft; **pour rendre votre linge plus s.** to make your washing softer; **gel fixation s.** light hold hair gel; **une voiture dotée d'une suspension s.** a car with smooth suspension

5 (*aménageable*) flexible, adaptable; **la réglementation/l'horaire est s.** the rules/the hours are flexible

6 (*qui sait s'adapter*) flexible, adaptable

7 (*docile*) docile, obedient; **à cet âge-là, ils sont encore assez souples** they're still quite docile at that age; **être s. comme un gant** to be very docile

8 (*écriture, style*) flowing

9 (*en œnologie*) smooth

10 *Aut* (*moteur*) flexible

11 *Aviat* non-rigid

souplement [supləmɑ̃] ADV smoothly; **le chat retomba s. sur ses pattes** the cat landed smoothly on its feet

souplesse [suplɛs] NF **1** (*d'une personne, d'un félin, d'un corps*) suppleness; (*d'une démarche*) suppleness, springiness; **admirez la s. du trait chez Degas** observe the easy flow of Degas' lines

2 (*douceur → d'un cuir, d'un tissu*) softness; (→ *de la peau*) smoothness

3 (*malléabilité → d'une matière*) flexibility, pliability

4 (*d'un horaire, d'une méthode, d'une personne*) flexibility, adaptability; **s. d'esprit** (*agilité*) nimble-mindeness; (*adaptabilité*) versatility; *Péj* (*servilité*) servility

▫ **en souplesse** ADV smoothly; **retomber en s. sur ses jambes** (*après une chute*) to land nimbly on one's feet; (*en gymnastique*) to make a smooth landing; **on recommence, et cette fois en s.!** one more time, and smoothly now!; **une transition en s.** a smooth transition

souquenille [suknij] NF *Vieilli* smock

souquer [3] [suke] VT **1** (*amarrage*) to pull taut **2** (*bateau*) to push to its limits

VI to pull at the oars, to stretch out; **s. ferme** to pull hard at the oars

sourate [surat] NF *sura*

source [surs] NF **1** (*point d'eau*) spring; **la s. est tarie** the spring has dried up; **s. chaude** *ou* **thermale** hot spring

2 (*origine*) spring, source; **où la Seine prend-elle sa s.?** where is the source of the Seine?, where does the Seine originate?; **remonter jusqu'à la s.** (*d'un fleuve*) to go upriver until one finds the source; (*d'une habitude, d'un problème*) to go back to the root; **à la s.** (*au commencement*) at the source, in the beginning; **retenir les impôts à la s.** to deduct tax at source; **il nous faut aller à la s.** (*même*) **du mal** we must go to the very root *or* heart of the trouble; **une tradition qui prend sa s. dans une culture ancienne** a tradition originating in *or* springing from an ancient culture

3 (*cause*) source; **une s. de revenus** a source of income; **cette maison n'a été qu'une s. d'ennuis** this house has been nothing but trouble; **être s. de qch** to give rise to sth; **cette formulation peut être s. de malentendus** the way it's worded could give rise to misinterpretations

4 *Presse* **tenir ses renseignements de bonne s.** *ou* **de s. sûre** *ou* **de s. bien informée** to have information on good authority; **nous savons** *ou* **nous tenons de s. sûre que...** we have it on good authority that..., we are reliably informed that...; **de s. officielle/officieuse, on apprend que...** official/unofficial sources reveal that...; **quelles sont vos sources?** what sources did

you use?; **citer ses sources** to cite one's sources

5 *Astron* **s. de rayonnement** radiation source

6 *Élec* **s. de courant** power supply

7 *Ordinat* source; **s. de données** data source

8 *Ling* (*comme adj*) source (*avant n*)

9 *Métal* **coulée en s.** bottom casting

10 *Nucl* **s. radioactive** radioactive source

11 *Phys* **s. lumineuse** *ou* **de lumière** light source; **s. de chaleur/d'énergie** source of heat/energy, heat/energy source

12 *Pétr* oil deposit

13 *Jur* **s. du droit** source of law

sourcer [16] [surse] VT **1** (*citation*) to source, to acknowledge the source of **2** *Journ* (*information*) to check the source of

sourcier, -ère [sursje, -ɛr] NM,F dowser, water-diviner

sourcil [sursi] NM eyebrow; **il a des sourcils bien fournis** he's beetle-browed

sourcilier, -ère [sursilje, -ɛr] ADJ superciliary

sourciller [3] [sursije] VI to frown; **sans s.** without batting an eyelid *or* turning a hair; **elle n'a pas sourcillé** she didn't bat an eyelid *or* turn a hair

sourcilleux, -euse [sursijø, -øz] ADJ **1** (*pointilleux*) pernickety, finicky **2** *Littéraire* (*hautain*) haughty, supercilious

sourd, -e [sur, surd] ADJ **1** (*personne*) deaf; **être s. de naissance** to be born deaf; **s. de l'oreille gauche** deaf in the left ear; **arrête de crier, je ne suis pas s.!** stop shouting, I'm not deaf *or* I can hear (you)!; **grand-père devient s./est un peu s.** grandpa is losing his hearing/is a bit deaf; **faire la sourde oreille** to pretend not to hear; *Fam* **être s. comme un pot** to be as deaf as a post; *Fam* **il vaut mieux entendre ça que d'être s.!** I've heard it all now!, what a load of *Br* rubbish *or Am* hogwash!

2 (*indifférent*) **le gouvernement est resté s. à leurs revendications** the government turned a deaf ear to their demands

3 (*atténué → son, voix*) muffled, muted; **il y eut trois coups sourds à la porte** there were three muffled knocks on the door; **la poire tomba avec un bruit s.** the pear fell with a (dull) thud

4 (*mal défini → douleur, teinte*) dull; (→ *sentiment*) muted, subdued; **j'éprouvais une sourde inquiétude** I felt vaguely worried

5 (*clandestin*) hidden, secret

6 (*en acoustique*) **chambre** *ou* **salle sourde** dead room

7 *Ling* unvoiced, voiceless

NM,F deaf person; **les sourds** the deaf; **c'est comme si on parlait à un s.** it's like talking to a brick wall; **crier** *ou* **hurler comme un s.** to scream *or* to shout at the top of one's voice; **frapper** *ou* **taper comme un s.** to bang with all one's might

▫ **sourde** NF *Ling* unvoiced *or* voiceless consonant

sourdement [surdəmɑ̃] ADV *Littéraire* **1** (*sans bruit*) dully, with a muffled noise **2** (*secrètement*) secretly; **intriguer s.** to engage in silent intrigue

sourdine [surdin] NF *Mus* (*d'une trompette, d'un violon*) mute; (*d'un piano*) soft pedal; *Fig* **mettre une s. à qch** (*critiques, démonstrations de joie*) to tone sth down; *Fig* **mettre la s.** to tone it down ▫ **en sourdine** ADJ muted ADV **1** *Mus* (*jouer*) quietly, softly; *Fam Fig* **mets-la en s.!** put a sock in it! **2** (*en secret*) quietly, on the quiet

sourdingue [surdɛ̃g] *Fam* ADJ cloth-eared NM,F cloth-ears

sourd-muet, sourde-muette [surmɥɛ, surdmɥɛt] (*mpl* **sourds-muets**, *fpl* **sourdes-muettes**) ADJ deaf and dumb

NM,F deaf-mute, deaf-and-dumb person

sourdre [73] [surdr] VI *Littéraire* **1** (*liquide*) to rise (up) **2** (*idée, sentiment*) to well up; **le mécontentement commençait à s. dans la population** discontent was beginning to make itself felt among the population; **que verra-t-on s. de ces événements?** what will arise from these events?

souri [suri] PP *voir* **sourire²**

souriant, -e [surjɑ̃, -ɑ̃t] ADJ **1** (*regard, visage*) smiling, beaming; (*personne*) cheerful **2** (*agréable → paysage*) pleasant, welcoming; (→ *pensée*) agreeable; **un avenir s.** a bright future

souriceau, -x [suriso] NM baby mouse

souricière [surisjɛr] NF **1** *(ratière)* mousetrap **2** *(piège)* trap; **dresser une s.** to set a trap; **se jeter dans la s.** to fall into a trap

sourire¹ [surir] NM smile; **il a un beau s.** he's got a nice smile; **elle esquissa un s.** she smiled faintly; **il entra, le s. aux lèvres** he came in with a smile on his lips *or* face; **avec un grand** *ou* **large s.** beaming, with a broad smile; **faire un s. à qn** to smile at sb; **fais-moi un petit s.** give me a smile!; **elle était tout s.** she was wreathed in *or* all smiles; **avoir le s.** to have a smile on one's face; **elle n'a pas le s. aujourd'hui** she doesn't look very happy today; **il a toujours le s.!** he's always smiling!; **il a pris la nouvelle avec le s.** he took the news cheerfully; **quand vous répondez aux clients, faites-le avec le s.** when you answer the customers, do it with a smile; **il faut savoir garder le s.** you have to learn to keep smiling

sourire² [95] [surir] VI to smile; **souriez!** *(pour une photo)* smile!; **je vais lui faire passer l'envie de s.!** I'll knock *or* wipe the smile off his/her face!; **la remarque peut faire s.** this remark may bring a smile to your face *or* make you smile; **les dialogues m'ont à peine fait s.** the dialogue hardly even made me smile; **quand tu vois la manière dont ils agissent, ça fait s.** it is rather amusing to see the way they behave; **s. à qn** to smile at sb, to give sb a smile; **elle lui sourit poliment** she gave him/her a polite smile, she smiled at him/her politely

  ❑ **sourire à** VT IND **1** *(être favorable à)* to smile on; **la fortune lui sourit enfin** fortune is smiling on him/her at last; **la chance ne te sourira pas toujours!** you won't always be (so) lucky! **2** *(plaire à → sujet: idée, perspective)* to appeal to; **passer le jour de l'an en famille ne me sourit guère!** the idea of spending New Year's Day with my family doesn't really appeal to me!, I don't relish (the thought of) spending New Year's Day with my family!

  ❑ **sourire de** VT IND *(se moquer de)* to smile *or* to laugh at; **il souriait de mon entêtement** my stubbornness made him smile; **ne souris pas de sa naïveté** don't laugh at his/her naivety

souris¹ *voir* **sourire²**

souris² [suri] NF **1** *Zool* mouse; **s. blanche** white mouse; **s. à poche** pocket mouse; *Fig* **j'aurais aimé être une petite s.!** I'd like to have been a fly on the wall!; *Fig* **on entendrait trotter une s.** you could hear a pin drop
  2 *très Fam (femme)* chick, *Br* bird
  3 *Culin (de gigot)* knuckle-joint
  4 *Ordinat* mouse; **s. à infrarouge** infrared mouse; **s. optique** optical mouse; **s. sans fil** cordless *or* wireless mouse; **s. tactile** touchpad mouse; **s. à trois boutons** three-button mouse
  5 *(poisson)* **s. de mer** dragonet
  ADJ INV mousy, mouse-coloured
  ❑ **souris d'hôtel** NF (female) hotel thief

sournois, -e [surnwa, -az] ADJ **1** *(personne, regard)* cunning, shifty, sly **2** *(attaque, procédé)* underhand **3** *(douleur)* dull, gnawing
  NM,F sly person

sournoisement [surnwazmã] ADV slyly; **regarder s. qn** to look shiftily at sb; **il approcha s. sa main du tiroir** he slyly reached out his hand towards the drawer

sournoiserie [surnwazri] NF **1** *(caractère)* shiftiness, slyness, underhand manner **2** *(acte)* sly piece of work; *(parole)* sly remark

---

SOUS [su]

under **1, 2, 5, 8** ■ underneath **1** ■ beneath **1, 2** ■ behind **2** ■ during **3** ■ within **4**	

PRÉP **1** *(dans l'espace)* under, underneath, beneath; **le plancher grinçait s. ses pieds** the floor creaked beneath *or* under his/her feet; **se mettre un oreiller s. la nuque** to put a pillow under one's head; **son journal s. le bras** (with) his/her newspaper under his/her arm; **être s. la douche** to be in the *or* having a shower; **se promener s. la pluie** to walk in the rain; **un paysage s. la neige** a snow-covered landscape; **Londres s. les bombes** London during the air raids; **nager s. l'eau** to swim underwater; **s. terre** underground, below ground; **assis s. le**

parasol sitting under *or* underneath *or* beneath the parasol; **il venait chanter s. sa fenêtre** he'd come and sing under his/her window; *Fam* **enlève ça de s. la table** get it out from under the table; **s. l'Équateur** at the Equator; **s. les tropiques** in the Tropics; **ça s'est passé s. nos yeux** it took place before our very eyes; **les expressions figées sont données s. le premier mot** set phrases are given under the first word; **s. quel numéro est enregistré son dossier?** what number is his/her file (registered) under?

2 *Fig (derrière)* behind, under, beneath; **il cache beaucoup de bienveillance s. des airs indifférents** he hides a lot of goodwill behind a cold exterior; **s. des dehors taciturnes** behind a stern exterior; **s. son air calme...** beneath his/her calm appearance...

3 *(à l'époque de)* **s. Louis XV** during the reign of *or* under Louis XV; **s. sa présidence/son ministère** under his/her presidency/ministry; **s. la Commune** during *or* at the time of the Paris Commune

4 *(dans un délai de)* within; **s. huitaine/quinzaine** within a week/two weeks *or Br* a fortnight

5 *(marquant un rapport de dépendance)* under; **s. ses ordres** under his/her command; **il est placé s. ma responsabilité** I'm in charge of him; **le festival est placé s. l'égide de l'UNESCO** the festival is held under the auspices of UNESCO; **s. contrat** under contract; **s. serment** under oath; **s. surveillance** under surveillance; **s. escorte** under escort; **s. caution** on bail; **tomber s. le coup de la loi** to be within the law

6 *Méd* **être s. anesthésie** to be under anaesthetic; **être s. antibiotiques/s. perfusion** to be on antibiotics/a drip

7 *(marquant la manière)* **emballé s. vide** vacuum-packed; **emballé s. plastique** plastic-wrapped; **s. verre** under glass; **s. globe** in a glass case; **s. pli scellé** in a sealed envelope; **elle a acheté le billet s. un faux nom** she bought the ticket under an assumed name; **elle se présente aux élections s. l'étiquette libérale** she's running as a candidate on the liberal ticket; **vu s. cet angle** seen from this angle; **vu s. cet éclairage nouveau** considered in this new light; **parfait s. tous rapports** perfect in every respect

8 *(avec une valeur causale)* under; **s. la torture/ la canonnade** under torture/fire; **s. le coup du choc...** with the shock...; **s. le coup de l'émotion** in the grip of the emotion; **s. l'influence de l'alcool** under the influence of alcohol; **elle le tient s. son charme** she has him under her spell; **s. le poids de** under the weight of; **s. la pression des événements** under the pressure of events

---

📖🎬

'Sous le soleil de Satan' *Bernanos, Pialat* 'Under Satan's Sun'

SOUS- [su] PRÉF

This is a very productive prefix in French.

● When added to nouns, **sous-** can convey the idea of a LOWER POSITION IN SPACE. Its English equivalent is often *under-* or *sub-*, eg:
  sous-sol subsoil/cellar/basement; **sous-marin** submarine; **sous-bois** undergrowth; **sous-vêtement** piece of underwear, undergarment

● When added to nouns or verbs, **sous-** can suggest a relation of SUBORDINATION. Although the translation can vary, several job titles in English include the prefix *sub-* or *under-*, eg:
  sous-directeur assistant manager/deputy head; **sous-lieutenant** second lieutenant/sublieutenant; **sous-préfet** subprefect; **sous-secrétaire d'État** undersecretary of State; **sous-traitant** subcontractor; **sous-traiter** to subcontract

● **Sous-** is also used to prefix nouns to convey an idea of SUBDIVISION. The usual English equivalent in this case is *sub-*, eg:
  sous-continent subcontinent; **sous-catégorie** subcategory; **sous-ensemble** subset; **sous-ordre** suborder

● **Sous-** is particularly productive when describing INSUFFICIENCY or POOR QUALITY. The idea of insufficiency is usually conveyed by the prefix *under-* in English, whereas *sub-* tends to be used more pejoratively to imply poor quality.
The more established variations on this theme are prefixed nouns, verbs or adjectives, but it is also possible to use **sous-** before a proper noun when referring to a work of art, a book, a film, etc which is deemed to be a pale imitation of a better author's work, or even to a person considered a *second-rate...*, eg:
  sous-peuplement underpopulation; **sous-peuplé** underpopulated; **sous-utiliser** to underuse, to underutilize; **sous-exploiter** to underexploit; **sous-payé** underpaid; **sous-humanité** subhumanity; **une sous-merde** a nobody, a non-entity; **il fait du sous-Picasso** he paints like a second-rate Picasso; **un sous-Marlon Brando** a second-rate Marlon Brando

---

sous-acquéreur [suzakerœr] *(pl* **sous-acquéreurs)** NM *Jur* subpurchaser

sous-administré, -e [suzadministre] *(mpl* **sous-administrés,** *fpl* **sous-administrées)** ADJ under-managed

sous-affrètement [suzafrɛtmã] *(pl* **sous-affrètements)** NM *Transp* sub-chartering

sous-affréter [18] [suzafrete] VT *Transp* to sub-charter

sous-alimentation [suzalimãtasjɔ̃] NF malnutrition, undernourishment

sous-alimenté, -e [suzalimãte] *(mpl* **sous-alimentés,** *fpl* **sous-alimentées)** ADJ undernourished, underfed; **des enfants sous-alimentés** children suffering from malnutrition

sous-alimenter [3] [suzalimãte] VT to undernourish

sous-amendement [suzamãdmã] *(pl* **sous-amendements)** NM amendment to an amendment

sous-arbrisseau [suzarbriso] *(pl* **sous-arbrisseaux)** NM chin-strap

sous-assurer [3] [suzasyre] VT to underinsure

sous-bail [subaj] *(pl* **sous-baux)** NM sublease

sous-barbe [subarb] *(pl* **sous-barbes)** NF chin strap

sous-bas [suba] NM INV understocking

sous-bibliothécaire [subibliɔtekɛr] *(pl* **sous-bibliothécaires)** NMF sub-librarian, assistant librarian

sous-bock [subɔk] *(pl* **sous-bocks)** NM beer mat

sous-bois [subwa] NM INV **1** *(végétation)* undergrowth, underwood; **se promener dans les s.** to walk in the undergrowth **2** *Beaux-Arts* picture of a forest interior

sous-brigadier [subrigadje] *(pl* **sous-brigadiers)** NM deputy sergeant

sous-calibré, -e [sukalibre] *(mpl* **sous-calibrés,** *fpl* **sous-calibrées)** ADJ undersize, undersized

sous-capitalisation [sukapitalizasjɔ̃] NF *Écon* under-capitalization, underfunding

sous-capitalisé, -e [sukapitalize] *(mpl* **sous-capitalisés,** *fpl* **sous-capitalisées)** ADJ *Écon* under-capitalized, underfunded

sous-catégorie [sukategɔri] *(pl* **sous-catégories)** NF subcategory

sous-cavage [sukavaʒ] *(pl* **sous-cavages)** NM *Mines* undercutting

sous-caver [3] [sukave] VT *Mines* to undercut

sous-chef [suʃɛf] *(pl* **sous-chefs)** NM **1** *(gén)* second-in-command **2** *(de bureau)* deputy chief clerk **3** *(dans un restaurant)* sous-chef, underchef **4** *Rail* **s. de gare** assistant station master

sous-chemise [suʃmiz] *(pl* **sous-chemises)** NF folder

sous-classe [suklas] *(pl* **sous-classes)** NF subclass

sous-clavier, -ère [suklavje, -ɛr] *(mpl* **sous-claviers,** *fpl* **sous-clavières)** ADJ *Anat* subclavian

sous-comité [sukɔmite] *(pl* **sous-comités)** NM subcommittee

sous-commissaire [sukɔmisɛr] *(pl* **sous-commissaires)** NM sub-commissioner; *(dans la marine)* assistant paymaster

sous-commission [sukɔmisjɔ̃] *(pl* **sous-commissions)** NF subcommittee

sous-compte [sukɔ̃t] *(pl* **sous-comptes)** NM sub-account

sous-consommation [sukɔ̃sɔmasjɔ̃] NF underconsumption, underconsuming (UNCOUNT)

sous-continent [sukɔ̃tinɑ̃] (pl **sous-continents**) NM subcontinent; **le s. indien** the Indian subcontinent

sous-contractant, -e [sukɔ̃traktɑ̃, -ɑ̃t] (mpl **sous-contractants**, fpl **sous-contractantes**) NM,F subcontractor

sous-contrat [sukɔ̃tra] (pl **sous-contrats**) NM subcontract

sous-cortical, -e [sukɔrtikal, -o] (mpl **sous-corticaux** [-o], fpl **sous-corticales**) ADJ Méd subcortical

souscoté, -e [sukɔte] ADJ Fin (action, marché, monnaie) undervalued

sous-couche [sukuʃ] (pl **sous-couches**) NF 1 (de peinture, de vernis) undercoat 2 Géol underlayer 3 Nucl subshell 4 Phot subbing, substratum; **s. antihalo** antihalation backing 5 Phys **s. laminaire** lower boundary layer

souscripteur [suskriptœr] NM 1 Fin (d'un emprunt) subscriber 2 (d'une assurance) policy holder 3 (d'une publication) subscriber

souscription [suskripsjɔ̃] NF 1 (engagement) subscription, subscribing (UNCOUNT) 2 (somme) subscription; **lancer** ou **ouvrir une s.** to start a fund; **verser une s.** to pay a subscription 3 (signature) signing (UNCOUNT) 4 Fin application, subscription 5 (d'une police d'assurance) taking out
　□ **en souscription** ADV **publier une revue en s.** to publish a journal on a subscription basis; **uniquement en s.** available to subscribers only

souscrire [99] [suskrir] VT 1 Jur (signer → acte) to sign, to put one's signature to, Sout to subscribe; (→ billet, chèque) to draw, to sign
　2 (abonnement, police d'assurance) to take out
　3 Fin (actions) to apply for
　USAGE ABSOLU **pour combien souscrivez-vous?** how much will you subscribe?; **s. pour 50 euros** to subscribe 50 euros
　□ **souscrire à** VT IND 1 (approuver) to approve, to subscribe to, to go along with; **je souscris entièrement à ce qui vient d'être dit** I go along totally with what's just been said
　2 (sujet: lecteur) to take out a subscription to
　3 Fin (emprunt) to subscribe to; (actions) to apply for

sous-culture [sukyltyr] (pl **sous-cultures**) NF subculture

sous-cutané, -e [sukytane] (mpl **sous-cutanés**, fpl **sous-cutanées**) ADJ subcutaneous

sous-déclarer [3] [sudeklare] VT 1 (revenus) to underdeclare 2 (bien) to declare less than the value of

sous-délégation [sudelegasjɔ̃] (pl **sous-délégations**) NF subdelegation

sous-délégué, -e [sudelege] (mpl **sous-délégués**, fpl **sous-déléguées**) ADJ subdelegated

sous-développé, -e [sudevlɔpe] (mpl **sous-développés**, fpl **sous-développées**) ADJ 1 (pays, région) underdeveloped 2 (usine) underequipped

sous-développement [sudevlɔpmɑ̃] (pl **sous-développements**) NM underdevelopment

sous-diaconat [sudjakɔna] (pl **sous-diaconats**) NM Rel subdiaconate

sous-diacre [sudjakr] (pl **sous-diacres**) NM subdeacon

sous-directeur, -trice [sudirɛktœr, -tris] (mpl **sous-directeurs**, fpl **sous-directrices**) NM,F 1 (de société) assistant manager 2 (d'une école) Br deputy head, Am assistant principal

sous-diviser [3] [sudivize] VT to subdivide

sous-division [sudivizjɔ̃] (pl **sous-divisions**) NF subdivision

sous-dominant, -e [sudɔminɑ̃, -ɑ̃t] (mpl **sous-dominants**, fpl **sous-dominantes**) ADJ Biol subdominant
　□ **sous-dominante** NF Mus subdominant

sous-effectif [suzefɛktif] (pl **sous-effectifs**) NM understaffing; **être en s.** to be understaffed

sous-embranchement [suzɑ̃brɑ̃ʃmɑ̃] (pl **sous-embranchements**) NM Biol sub-branch

sous-emploi [suzɑ̃plwa] (pl **sous-emplois**) NM underemployment

sous-employé, -e [suzɑ̃plwaje] (mpl **sous-employés**, fpl **sous-employées**) ADJ (travailleur) underemployed; (appareil) underused

sous-employer [13] [suzɑ̃plwaje] VT (travailleur) to underemploy; (appareil) to underuse

sous-ensemble [suzɑ̃sɑ̃bl] (pl **sous-ensembles**) NM subset

sous-entendre [73] [suzɑ̃tɑ̃dr] VT to imply; **que sous-entendez-vous par là?** what are you hinting or driving at?, what are you trying to imply?; **sous-entendu, je m'en moque!** meaning I don't care!

sous-entendu [suzɑ̃tɑ̃dy] (pl **sous-entendus**) NM innuendo, hint, insinuation; **en fixant sur moi un regard lourd de sous-entendus** giving me a meaningful look

sous-entrée [suzɑ̃tre] (pl **sous-entrées**) NF (dans un dictionnaire) sub-entry

sous-entrepreneur [suzɑ̃trəprənœr] (pl **sous-entrepreneurs**) NM subcontractor

sous-équipé, -e [suzekipe] (mpl **sous-équipés**, fpl **sous-équipées**) ADJ underequipped

sous-équipement [suzekipmɑ̃] (pl **sous-équipements**) NM underequipment

sous-espace [suzɛspas] (pl **sous-espaces**) NM Math subspace

sous-espèce [suzɛspɛs] (pl **sous-espèces**) NF subspecies

sous-estimation [suzɛstimasjɔ̃] (pl **sous-estimations**) NF 1 (jugement) underestimation, underestimating, underrating 2 Fin (d'un revenu) underestimation, underassessment; (d'un bien) undervaluation

sous-estimer [3] [suzɛstime] VT 1 (qualité, bien) to underestimate, to underrate 2 Fin to undervalue
　▸ **se sous-estimer** VPR to underestimate oneself

sous-évaluation [suzevalɥasjɔ̃] (pl **sous-évaluations**) NF undervaluation

sous-évaluer [7] [suzevalɥe] VT to undervalue

sous-exploitation [suzɛksplwatasjɔ̃] (pl **sous-exploitations**) NF underexploitation, underexploiting (UNCOUNT), underuse

sous-exploiter [3] [suzɛksplwate] VT to underexploit

sous-exposé, -e [suzɛkspoze] (mpl **sous-exposés**, fpl **sous-exposées**) ADJ Phot underexposed

sous-exposer [3] [suzɛkspoze] VT Phot to underexpose

sous-exposition [suzɛkspozisjɔ̃] (pl **sous-expositions**) NF Phot underexposure

sous-faîte [sufɛt] (pl **sous-faîtes**) NF Constr ridge-piece

sous-famille [sufamij] (pl **sous-familles**) NF subfamily

sous-fifre [sufifr] (pl **sous-fifres**) NM Fam underling■, minion■

sous-garde [sugard] (pl **sous-gardes**) NF gunlock

sous-genre [suʒɑ̃r] (pl **sous-genres**) NM subgenus

sous-glaciaire [suglasjɛr] (pl **sous-glaciaires**) ADJ subglacial

sous-gorge [sugɔrʒ] NF INV Équitation throat latch

sous-gouverneur [suguvɛrnœr] (pl **sous-gouverneurs**) NM deputy governor, vice-governor

sous-groupe [sugrup] (pl **sous-groupes**) NM subgroup

sous-homme [suzɔm] (pl **sous-hommes**) NM Péj subhuman

sous-humanité [suzymanite] NF Péj subhumanity

sous-industrialisé, -e [suzɛ̃dystrjalize] (mpl **sous-industrialisés**, fpl **sous-industrialisées**) ADJ underindustrialized

sous-inspecteur, -trice [suzɛ̃spɛktœr, -tris] (mpl **sous-inspecteurs**, fpl **sous-inspectrices**) NM,F assistant inspector

sous-intendance [suzɛ̃tɑ̃dɑ̃s] (pl **sous-intendances**) NF Hist under-stewardship, junior intendance

sous-intendant [suzɛ̃tɑ̃dɑ̃] (pl **sous-intendants**) NM 1 Mil = Assistant Quartermaster-General 2 Hist under-steward, junior intendant

sous-jacent, -e [suʒasɑ̃, -ɑ̃t] (mpl **sous-jacents**, fpl **sous-jacentes**) ADJ 1 (caché) underlying; **l'urbanisation et les problèmes sous-jacents** urbanization and its underlying problems 2 Géol subjacent

Sous-le-Vent [suləvɑ̃] NFPL **les îles S.** (en Polynésie) the Leeward Islands, the Western Society Islands; (aux Antilles) the Netherlands (and Venezuelan) Antilles

sous-lieutenant [suljøtnɑ̃] (pl **sous-lieutenants**) NM (dans l'armée de terre) ≃ second lieutenant; (dans l'armée de l'air) Br ≃ pilot officer, Am ≃ second lieutenant; (dans la marine) Br ≃ sublieutenant, Am ≃ lieutenant junior grade

souslik [suslik] NM Zool suslik, ground squirrel

sous-locataire [sulɔkatɛr] (pl **sous-locataires**) NMF subtenant

sous-location [sulɔkasjɔ̃] (pl **sous-locations**) NF 1 (action → par le propriétaire) subletting; (→ par le locataire) subrenting 2 (bail) subtenancy

sous-louer [6] [sulwe] VT (sujet: propriétaire) to sublet; (sujet: locataire) to subrent

sous-main [sumɛ̃] NM INV 1 (buvard) desk blotter 2 (carton, plastique) pad
　□ **en sous-main** ADV secretly; **il y a eu des tractations en s.** some underhand deals were struck

sous-maîtresse [sumetrɛs] (pl **sous-maîtresses**) NF Arch madam (in brothel)

sous-marin, -e [sumarɛ̃, -in] (mpl **sous-marins**, fpl **sous-marines**) ADJ (câble, plante) submarine, underwater; (navigation) submarine; (courant) submarine, undersea; (photographie) underwater, undersea
　NM 1 Naut submarine; **s. nucléaire** nuclear(-powered) submarine; **s. de poche** pocket submarine
　2 Fam (espion) mole
　3 Fam (véhicule de surveillance) = converted van used for police surveillance
　4 (boisson) = cocktail consisting of a pint of beer with a shot glass of tequila in the bottom of the beer glass, served with a straw
　5 Can (sandwich) submarine, sub

sous-marinier [sumarinje] (pl **sous-mariniers**) NM submariner

sous-marque [sumark] (pl **sous-marques**) NF sub-brand

sous-maxillaire [sumaksilɛr] (pl **sous-maxillaires**) ADJ Anat submaxillary

sous-médicalisé, -e [sumedikalize] (mpl **sous-médicalisés**, fpl **sous-médicalisées**) ADJ with insufficient medical facilities

sous-mentionné, -e [sumɑ̃sjɔne] (mpl **sous-mentionnés**, fpl **sous-mentionnées**) ADJ undermentioned

sous-mentonnière [sumɑ̃tɔnjɛr] (pl **sous-mentonnières**) NF chin strap

sous-menu [sum(ə)ny] (pl **sous-menus**) NM Ordinat submenu

sous-merde [sumɛrd] (pl **sous-merdes**) NF très Fam nobody■, nonentity■; **traiter qn comme une s.** to treat sb like shit

sous-ministre [suministr] (pl **sous-ministres**) NM Can Br undersecretary (of state), Am deputy minister

sous-multiple [sumyltipl] (pl **sous-multiples**) NM submultiple

sous-munitions [sumynisjɔ̃] NFPL Mil submunition

sous-nappe [sunap] (pl **sous-nappes**) NF undercloth

sous-normale [sunɔrmal] (pl **sous-normales**) NF Géom subnormal

sous-nutrition [sunytrisjɔ̃] NF malnutrition

sous-occipital, -e [suzɔksipital] (mpl **sous-occipitaux** [-o], fpl **sous-occipitales**) ADJ Anat suboccipital

sous-œuvre [suzœvr] **en sous-œuvre** ADV **reprendre un bâtiment en s.** to underpin a building; **reprise en s.** underpinning

sous-off [suzɔf] (pl **sous-offs**) NM Fam Arg mil (abrév **sous-officier**) non-commissioned officer■

sous-officier [suzɔfisje] (pl **sous-officiers**) NM non-commissioned officer

sous-ongulaire [suzɔ̃gylɛr] (pl **sous-ongulaires**) ADJ Anat subungual

sous-orbitaire [suzɔrbitɛr] (pl **sous-orbitaires**) ADJ Anat suborbital

sous-orbital, -e [suzɔrbital] (mpl **sous-orbitaux** [-o], fpl **sous-orbitales**) ADJ Astron suborbital

sous-ordre [suzɔrdr] (pl **sous-ordres**) NM 1 Biol suborder 2 (subordonné) subordinate, underling, minion
　□ **en sous-ordre** ADJ (opposant, créancier) subsidiary

sous-palan [supalɑ̃] **en sous-palan** ADV Com ready for delivery

sous-payer [11] [supeje] **VT** to underpay

sous-peuplé, -e [supœple] (*mpl* **sous-peuplés**, *fpl* **sous-peuplées**) **ADJ** underpopulated

sous-peuplement [supœpləmɑ̃] **NM** underpopulation

sous-pied [supje] (*pl* **sous-pieds**) **NM** stirrup (*on trousers*)

sous-plat [supla] (*pl* **sous-plats**) **NM** *Belg* table mat

sous-poutre [suputr] (*pl* **sous-poutres**) **NF** *Constr* under girder, bolster

sous-préfectoral, -e [suprefɛktɔral] (*mpl* **sous-préfectoraux** [-o], *fpl* **sous-préfectorales**) **ADJ** subprefectorial

sous-préfecture [suprefɛktyr] (*pl* **sous-préfectures**) **NF** subprefecture

sous-préfet [suprefɛ] (*pl* **sous-préfets**) **NM** subprefect

sous-préfète [suprefɛt] (*pl* **sous-préfètes**) **NF** 1 (*fonctionnaire*) (*female*) subprefect 2 (*épouse*) subprefect's wife

sous-pression [supresjɔ̃] (*pl* **sous-pressions**) **NF** *Tech* uplift

sous-production [suprɔdyksjɔ̃] (*pl* **sous-productions**) **NF** underproduction

sous-produit [suprɔdɥi] (*pl* **sous-produits**) **NM** 1 *Ind & Com* by-product 2 (*ersatz*) poor imitation, (*inferior*) derivative

sous-programme [suprɔgram] (*pl* **sous-programmes**) **NM** *Ordinat* subroutine, subprogram; **s. ouvert** open subroutine *or* subprogram

sous-prolétaire [suprɔletɛr] (*pl* **sous-prolétaires**) **NMF** member of the urban underclass

sous-prolétariat [suprɔletarja] (*pl* **sous-prolétariats**) **NM** urban underclass

sous-pull [supyl] (*pl* **sous-pulls**) **NM** thin polo-neck sweater

sous-refroidi, -e [surəfrwadi] (*mpl* **sous-refroidis**, *fpl* **sous-refroidies**) **ADJ** supercooled

sous-répertoire [suprepɛrtwar] (*pl* **sous-répertoires**) **NM** *Ordinat* subdirectory

sous-représentation [suprəprezɑ̃tasjɔ̃] **NF** *Pol* under-representation

sous-représenté, -e [suprəprezɑ̃te] (*mpl* **sous-représentés**, *fpl* **sous-représentées**) **ADJ** *Pol* under-represented

soussaille [susaj] = **souçaille**

sous-saturé, -e [susatyre] (*mpl* **sous-saturés**, *fpl* **sous-saturées**) **ADJ** *Géol* undersaturated

sous-scapulaire [suskapylɛr] (*pl* **sous-scapulaires**) **ADJ** *Anat* subscapular

sous-secrétaire [susəkretɛr] (*pl* **sous-secrétaires**) **NM** **s. (d'État)** undersecretary (of State), junior minister

sous-secrétariat [susəkretarja] (*pl* **sous-secrétariats**) **NM** 1 (*bureau*) undersecretary's office 2 (*poste*) undersecretaryship

sous-secteur [susɛktœr] (*pl* **sous-secteurs**) **NM** subsection

sous-section [susɛksjɔ̃] (*pl* **sous-sections**) **NF** (*au Conseil d'État*) section; **sous-sections réunies** combined sections

sous-seing [susɛ̃] **NM INV** *Jur* private agreement *or* contract

soussigné, -e [susiɲe] **ADJ** undersigned; **je s. Robert Brand, déclare avoir pris connaissance de l'article 4** I, the undersigned Robert Brand, declare that I have read clause 4
  NM,F **le s. déclare/les soussignés déclarent que...** the undersigned declares/declare that...

sous-sol [susɔl] (*pl* **sous-sols**) **NM** 1 *Géol* subsoil 2 (*d'une maison*) cellar; (*d'un magasin*) basement, lower ground floor; **allez voir notre grand choix d'affaires au s.** visit our bargain basement!

sous-solage [susɔlaʒ] (*pl* **sous-solages**) **NM** *Agr* subsoiling

sous-soleuse [susɔløz] (*pl* **sous-soleuses**) **NF** *Agr* subsoil plough

sous-station [sustasjɔ̃] (*pl* **sous-stations**) **NF** *Élec* substation

sous-système [sustʃsistɛm] (*pl* **sous-systèmes**) **NM** subsystem

sous-tangente [sutɑ̃ʒɑ̃t] (*pl* **sous-tangentes**) **NF** subtangent

sous-tasse [sutas] (*pl* **sous-tasses**) **NF** saucer

sous-tendre [73] [sutɑ̃dr] **VT** 1 *Géom* to subtend 2 (*être à la base de*) to underlie, to underpin

sous-tension [sutɑ̃sjɔ̃] (*pl* **sous-tensions**) **NF** undervoltage

sous-titrage [sutitraʒ] (*pl* **sous-titrages**) **NM** subtitling; **le s. est excellent** the subtitles are very good

sous-titre [sutitr] (*pl* **sous-titres**) **NM** 1 *Presse* subtitle, subheading, subhead 2 *Cin* subtitle

sous-titré, -e [sutitre] (*mpl* **sous-titrés**, *fpl* **sous-titrées**) **ADJ** subtitled, with subtitles; **un film s. en anglais** a film with English subtitles

sous-titrer [3] [sutitre] **VT** 1 (*article de journal*) to subtitle, to subhead; (*livre*) to subtitle 2 (*film*) to subtitle

sous-total [sutɔtal] (*pl* **sous-totaux** [-to]) **NM** subtotal

soustracteur [sustraktœr] **NM** subtracter

soustractif, -ive [sustraktif, -iv] **ADJ** subtractive

soustraction [sustraksjɔ̃] **NF** 1 *Math* subtraction; **il ne sait pas encore faire les soustractions** he can't subtract yet 2 *Jur* (*vol*) removal, removing (UNCOUNT), *Sout* purloining (UNCOUNT); **s. de documents** abstraction of documents

soustractive [sustraktiv] *voir* **soustractif**

soustraire [112] [sustrɛr] **VT** 1 *Math* to subtract, to take away; **s. 10 de 30** to take 10 away from 30
  2 (*enlever*) **s. qn/qch à** to take sb/sth away from; **s. qn à la justice** to shield sb from justice, to protect sb from the law; **s. qn/qch aux regards indiscrets** to hide sb/sth from prying eyes; **on dut s. ces tableaux à la vue du public** these pictures have had to be withdrawn from public view
  3 (*subtiliser*) to remove; **de grosses sommes ont été soustraites du fonds d'entraide** large sums of money have gone missing from the charity fund; **s. un dossier aux archives** to remove a file from the archives
  ►**se soustraire VPR se s. à l'impôt/à une obligation/à un devoir** to evade tax/an obligation/a duty; **se s. à la justice** to escape the law

sous-traitance [sutrɛtɑ̃s] (*pl* **sous-traitances**) **NF** subcontracting; **donner un travail en s.** to subcontract a job; **faire de la s.** to subcontract; **je fais ce travail en s.** I'm on this job as subcontractor

sous-traitant, -e [sutrɛtɑ̃, -ɑ̃t] (*mpl* **sous-traitants**, *fpl* **sous-traitantes**) **ADJ** subcontracting; **des entreprises sous-traitantes** subcontracting firms
  NM subcontractor; **donner un travail à un s.** to farm out a piece of work

sous-traité [sutrɛte] (*pl* **sous-traités**) **NM** subcontract

sous-traiter [4] [sutrete] **VT** **s. un travail** (*entrepreneur principal*) to subcontract a job, to contract a job out; (*sous-entrepreneur*) to contract into *or* to subcontract a job

soustrayait *etc voir* **soustraire**

sous-unguéal, -e [suzɔ̃gɥeal] (*mpl* **sous-unguéaux** [-o], *fpl* **sous-unguéales**) **ADJ** *Anat* subungual

sous-utiliser [3] [suzytilize] **VT** to underuse, to underutilize

sous-variété [suvarjete] (*pl* **sous-variétés**) **NF** *Biol & Math* subvariety

sous-ventrière [suvɑ̃trijɛr] (*pl* **sous-ventrières**) **NF** girth (*for a horse*); *Fam Fig* **manger à s'en faire péter la s.** to pig out, to stuff oneself

sous-verge [suvɛrʒ] **NM INV** (*unridden*) off horse

sous-verre [suvɛr] **NM INV** (*pour encadrer*) glass mount; (*photo, image*) photograph *or* picture mounted under glass
  NM *Belg* (*dessous-de-verre*) coaster

sous-vêtement [suvɛtmɑ̃] (*pl* **sous-vêtements**) **NM** piece of underwear, undergarment; **en sous-vêtements** in one's underwear *or* underclothes

sous-virer [3] [suvire] **VI** *Aut* to understeer

sous-vireur, -euse [suvirœr, -øz] (*mpl* **sous-vireurs**, *fpl* **sous-vireuses**) **ADJ** *Aut* which understeers

soutache [sutaʃ] **NF** *Couture* braid

soutacher [3] [sutaʃe] **VT** *Couture* to braid

soutane [sutan] **NF** cassock; **porter (la) s.** to be in Holy Orders; **prendre la s.** to enter the Church, to take (Holy) Orders; *Fam* **la s.** (*prêtres*) men of the cloth

soute [sut] **NF** hold; **s. à bagages** luggage hold;

Aviat **s. à bombes** bomb bay; **s. à charbon** coal bunker, *Br* coal hole; **s. à essence** fuel bunker; **s. à mazout** oil tank; **s. à munitions** magazine; **s. à voiles** sail locker
  ❏ **soutes NFPL** (*combustible*) fuel oil

soutenable [sutnabl] **ADJ** 1 (*défendable*) defensible, tenable 2 (*supportable*) bearable

soutenance [sutnɑ̃s] **NF** *Univ* **s. (de thèse)** = oral examination for thesis, *Br* viva

soutenant, -e [sutnɑ̃, -ɑ̃t] **ADJ** sustaining (power)
  NM,F *Univ* = student defending his/her thesis

soutènement [sutɛnmɑ̃] **NM** 1 *Constr* support 2 *Mines* timbering
  ❏ **de soutènement ADJ** support (*avant n*), supporting

souteneur [sutnœr] **NM** 1 (*proxénète*) pimp 2 *Littéraire* (*d'une cause, d'une idée*) defender, upholder

---

SOUTENIR [40] [sutnir]

> **VT** to hold up 1 ■ to support 1–4, 6 ■ to uphold 4 ■ to assert 5 ■ to withstand 6 ■ to keep up 7 ■ to sustain 7, 8
> **VPR** to stand by each other 1 ■ to hold oneself up 2 ■ to be kept up 3

VT 1 (*maintenir → sujet: pilier, poutre*) to hold up, to support; (*→ sujet: attelle, gaine, soutien-gorge*) to support; **il lui tendit la main pour la s.** he gave her his hand for support; **un médicament pour s. le cœur** a drug to sustain the heart *or* to keep the heart going
  2 (*réconforter*) to support, to give (moral) support to; **sa présence m'a beaucoup soutenue dans cette épreuve** his/her presence was a great comfort to me in this ordeal
  3 (*être partisan de → candidature, cause, politique etc*) to support, to back (up), to stand by; **nous vous soutiendrons!** we'll be right with *or* we'll stand by you!; **tu soutiens toujours ta fille contre moi!** you always stand up for *or* you're always siding with your daughter against me!; **s. une équipe** to be a fan of *or* to support a team; **s. qn comme la corde soutient le pendu** to be more of a hindrance than a help to sb
  4 (*faire valoir → droits*) to uphold, to defend; (*→ argument, théorie*) to uphold, to support
  5 (*affirmer*) to assert, to claim; **je pense que nous sommes libres mais elle soutient le contraire** I think that we are free but she claims (that) the opposite is true; **il soutient que tu mens** he keeps saying that you're a liar; *Fam* **elle m'a soutenu mordicus qu'il était venu ici** she swore blind *or* she insisted that he'd been here
  6 (*résister à → attaque*) to withstand; (*→ regard*) to bear, to support; **ils ont soutenu l'assaut des produits japonais** they were able to bear the onslaught of Japanese products; **s. la comparaison avec** to stand *or* to bear comparison with; **les champignons de culture ne soutiennent pas la comparaison** cultivated mushrooms just don't compare; *Mil* **s. un siège** to last out *or* to withstand a siege
  7 (*prolonger → attention, discussion, suspense etc*) to keep up, to sustain; (*→ réputation*) to maintain, to keep up; **il est difficile de s. une conversation lorsque les enfants sont présents** it's difficult to keep a conversation going *or* to keep up a conversation when the children are around
  8 *Mus* (*note*) to sustain, to hold
  9 *Univ* **s. sa thèse** to defend one's thesis, *Br* to take one's viva
  ►**se soutenir VPR** 1 (*personnes*) to stand by each other, to stick together; **entre amis, il faut bien se s.!** friends must stick together!
  2 (*se tenir*) to hold oneself up, to support oneself; **le vieillard n'arrivait plus à se s. sur ses jambes** the old man's legs could no longer support *or* carry him; **elle se soutenait avec peine** she could hardly stay upright; **se s. dans l'eau** to keep (oneself) afloat
  3 (*se prolonger → attention, intérêt, suspense*) to be kept up *or* maintained

soutenu, -e [sutny] **ADJ** 1 (*intense → couleur*) intense, deep; (*→ note de musique*) sustained;

(→ *attention, effort*) unfailing, sustained, unremitting; (→ *rythme*) steady, sustained **2** *Ling* formal; **en langue soutenue** in formal speech

souterrain, -e [sutɛrɛ̃, -ɛn] ADJ **1** (*sous la terre*) underground, subterranean; **câble s.** underground cable; **des eaux souterraines** ground water **2** (*dissimulé*) hidden, secret **3** *Mines* deep, underground

NM **1** (*galerie*) underground *or* subterranean passage **2** (*en ville*) *Br* subway, *Am* underpass

soutien [sutjɛ̃] NM **1** (*soubassement*) supporting structure, support

2 (*aide*) support; **apporter son s. à qn** to support sb, to back sb up; **s. financier** financial backing; **mesures de s. à l'économie** measures to bolster the economy

3 (*défenseur*) supporter; **c'est l'un des plus sûrs soutiens du gouvernement** he's one of the mainstays of the government

4 *Scol* **cours de s.** remedial class

5 *Jur* **s. de famille** (main) wage earner; **être s. de famille** to have dependents (*and receive special treatment as regards French National Service*)

6 *Écon* **s. des prix** price support; *Mktg* **s. commercial** sales support; *UE* **s. monétaire à court terme** short-term monetary support

7 *Mil* support; **s. logistique** logistic support; **unité de s.** support unit

soutien-gorge [sutjɛ̃gɔrʒ] (*pl* **soutiens-gorge**) NM bra; **s. d'allaitement** nursing bra

soutient *etc voir* **soutenir**

soutier [sutje] NM **1** *Naut* stoker **2** *Fig* (*personne qui occupe une fonction ingrate*) toiler

soutif [sutif] NM *Fam* bra ▪

soutint *etc voir* **soutenir**

soutirage [sutiraʒ] NM **1** (*action*) decanting, decantation **2** (*vin*) decanted wine

soutirer [3] [sutire] VT **1** (*vin*) to draw off, to decant **2** (*extorquer*) **s. qch à qn** to get sth from *or* out of sb; **s. une promesse à qn** to extract a promise from sb; **s. des renseignements à qn** to get *or* to squeeze some information out of sb; **il s'est fait s. pas mal d'argent par ses petits-enfants** his grandchildren managed to squeeze a lot of money out of him

soutra [sutra] *Rel* sutra

soutrage [sutraʒ] NM clearing of undergrowth

souvenance [suvnɑ̃s] NF *Littéraire* **à ma s.** as far as I can recall *or* recollect; **je n'ai pas s. de cela** I don't recall this, I have no recollection of this; **je n'ai pas s. que nous ayons signé** I don't recall our having signed

souvenir¹ [suvnir] NM **1** (*impression*) memory, recollection; **l'été 1999 m'a laissé un s. impérissable** the summer of 1999 has left me with lasting memories; **votre opération ne sera bientôt plus qu'un mauvais s.** your operation will soon be nothing but a bad memory; **je garde un excellent s. de ce voyage** I have excellent memories of that trip; **n'avoir aucun s. de** to have no remembrance *or* recollection of; **elle n'en a qu'un vague s.** she has only a dim *or* vague recollection of it; **cela n'éveille donc aucun s. en toi?** doesn't it remind you of anything?; **mes souvenirs d'enfance** my childhood memories; **au s. de ces événements, il se mit à pleurer** when he thought back to the events, he started to cry; **avoir le s. de** to have a memory of, to remember; **j'ai le s. d'un homme grand et fort** I remember a tall strong man; **je garderai jusqu'à ma mort le s. de cette journée** I'll remember that day until I die

2 (*dans des formules de politesse*) **avec mon affectueux s.** yours (ever); **mes meilleurs souvenirs à votre sœur** (my) kindest regards to your sister; **meilleurs souvenirs de Rome** greetings from Rome

3 (*objet* → *donné par une personne*) keepsake; (→ *rappelant une occasion*) memento; (→ *pour touristes*) souvenir; **cette broche est un s. de ma grand-mère** this brooch is a keepsake from my grandmother; **s. de Lourdes** souvenir of Lourdes; *Hum* **il m'a laissé ses dettes comme s.** he left me his debts to remember him by

4 (*comme adj; avec ou sans trait d'union*) souvenir (*avant n*); **poser pour la photo-s.** to pose for a commemorative photograph

❑ **en souvenir de** PRÉP (*afin de se remémorer*)

prenez ce livre en s. de cet été/de moi take this book as a souvenir of this summer/as something to remember me by

souvenir² [40] [suvnir] V IMPERSONNEL *Littéraire* **il me souvient un détail/de l'avoir aperçu** I remember a detail/having seen him; **du plus loin qu'il m'en souvienne** as far back as I can remember

▶ **se souvenir** VPR **se s. de** (*date, événement*) to remember, to recollect, to recall; (*personne, lieu*) to remember; **on se souviendra d'elle comme d'une grande essayiste** she'll be remembered as a great essay-writer; **je ne me souviens jamais de son adresse** I keep forgetting *or* I can never remember his/her address; **je ne me souviens pas de l'avoir lu** I can't remember *or* I don't recall *or* I don't recollect having read it; *Fam Ironique* **je m'en souviendrai, de ses week-ends reposants à la campagne!** I won't forget his/her restful weekends in the countryside in a hurry!; **je ne veux pas te le prêter – je m'en souviendrai!** I don't want you to borrow it – I'll remember that!

USAGE ABSOLU **mais si, souviens-toi, elle était toujours au premier rang** come on, you must remember her, she was always sitting in the front row; **je me souviens que j'ai crié en la voyant** I remember (that) I shouted when I saw her

souvenir-écran [suvnirekrɑ̃] (*pl* **souvenirs-écrans**) NM *Psy* screen memory

souvent [suvɑ̃] ADV often; **il va s. au théâtre** he often goes to the theatre; **il va très s. au théâtre** he goes to the theatre very often; **on se voit de moins en moins s.** we see less and less of each other; **pas** *ou* **peu s.** not often, seldom; **il ne vient pas s. nous voir** he doesn't often come and see us, he seldom comes to see us; **le plus s., c'est elle qui conduit** most often *or* more often than not *or* usually, she's the one who does the driving; **c'est (bien) s. ce qui arrive si l'on va trop vite** it's what (very) often happens when you go too fast; **plus s. qu'à son tour** far too often; *Fam Vieilli* **plus s.!** no fear!, not likely!

Allusion

Souvent femme varie

This expression is attributed to François I of France who is alleged to have scratched the words on a window at the Château de Chambord after a disappointment in love. The full phrase is: **Souvent femme varie, et bien fol qui s'y fie** ("Woman is fickle, and only a fool puts his faith in her"). The saying is used allusively in modern French in a modified form to refer to anything that you believe to be unreliable. For example, in a newspaper one might read **Souvent sondages varient, bien fol qui s'y fie** ("Opinion polls vary, and only a fool puts his faith in them").

---

souvenu, -e [suvny] PP *voir* **souvenir²**

souverain, -e [suvrɛ̃, -ɛn] ADJ **1** (*efficace* → *remède*) excellent, sovereign; **c'est s. contre les maux de gorge** it works like a charm on sore throats, it's perfect for sore throats

2 *Pol* (*pouvoir, peuple*) sovereign; *Jur* (*tribunal*) supreme; **la Chambre est souveraine** the House is a sovereign authority

3 (*suprême*) supreme; **avoir un s. mépris pour qch** to utterly despise sth; **avec une souveraine méconnaissance des faits** supremely ignorant of the facts

4 *Phil* **le s. bien** the sovereign good

5 *Rel* **le s. pontife** the Pope, the Supreme Pontiff

NM,F monarch, sovereign; **notre souveraine** our Sovereign; **s. absolu** absolute monarch; **s. fantoche** puppet monarch

NM (*monnaie*) sovereign (coin)

souverainement [suvrɛnmɑ̃] ADV **1** (*suprêmement*) utterly, totally, intensely; **être s. indifférent à** to be utterly *or* supremely indifferent to **2** (*sans appel*) with sovereign power

souveraineté [suvrɛnte] NF sovereignty; **s. populaire** popular sovereignty

souverainisme [suvrɛnism] NM **1** (*doctrine des défenseurs d'une Europe des nations*) (European) sovereignism *or* pro-sovereignty **2** *Can* (*doctrine des partisans d'un Québec indépendant*) (Quebec) separatism

souverainiste [suvrɛnist] ADJ **1** (*favorable à une Europe des nations*) (European) sovereignist *or* pro-sovereignty **2** *Can* (*favorable à l'indépendance du Québec*) (Quebec) separatist

NMF **1** (*personne favorable à une Europe des nations*) (European) sovereignist **2** *Can* (*personne favorable à l'indépendance du Québec*) (Quebec) separatist

souvient *etc voir* **souvenir²**

souvint *etc voir* **souvenir²**

souvlaki [suvlaki] NM *Culin* souvlaki

soviet [sɔvjɛt] NM (*assemblée*) soviet; **le S. Suprême** the Supreme Soviet

soviétique [sɔvjetik] ADJ Soviet

❑ **Soviétique** NMF Soviet

soviétisation [sɔvjetizasjɔ̃] NF sovietization, sovietizing (*UNCOUNT*)

soviétiser [3] [sɔvjetize] VT to sovietize

soviétologue [sɔvjetɔlɔg] NMF Sovietologist

sovkhoze [sɔvkoz] NM sovkhoz

Soweto [sɔwɛto] NM Soweto

soyeux, -euse [swajø, -øz] ADJ silky

NM (*dans la région de Lyon*) (*fabricant*) silk manufacturer; (*négociant*) silk merchant

soyons *voir* **être¹**

SPA [ɛspea] NF (*abrév* **Société protectrice des animaux**) = society for the protection of animals, *Br* ≃ RSPCA, *Am* ≃ ASPCA

spa [spa] NM **1** (*bain à remous bouillonnant*) spa bath **2** (*centre d'hydrothérapie*) (health) spa

space opera [spɛsopera] (*pl* **space operas**) NM space opera

spacieuse [spasjøz] *voir* **spacieux**

spacieusement [spasjøzmɑ̃] ADV **ils sont très s. installés** they've got a very roomy *or* spacious place

spacieux, -euse [spasjø, -øz] ADJ spacious, roomy

spadassin [spadasɛ̃] NM **1** *Arch* swordsman **2** *Littéraire* (*tueur*) (hired) killer; **un mafioso et ses spadassins** a Mafia boss and his hit men

SPADEM [spadɛm] NF (*abrév* **Société de la propriété artistique et des dessins et modèles**) = organization set up to defend the interests of designers, photographers, artists etc

spadice [spadis] NM *Bot* spadix

spadiciflores [spadisiflɔr] NFPL *Bot* Spadiciflorae

spaetzli [ʃpɛtsli] NM *Suisse Culin* = small strips of pasta often served with game

spaghetti [spageti] (*pl inv ou* **spaghettis**) NM **des s., des spaghettis** spaghetti; **un s.** a strand of spaghetti; **spaghetti bolognaise/carbonara** spaghetti bolognese/carbonara

spahi [spai] NM spahi (*native member of the Algerian, Moroccan or Tunisian cavalry in the French army*)

spalax [spalaks] NM *Zool* mole rat

spallation [spalasjɔ̃] NF *Phys* spallation

spalter [spaltɛr] NM graining brush

spam [spam] NM *Ordinat* spam e-mail

spammer [3] [spame] VT *Ordinat* to spam

spammeur [spamœr] NM *Ordinat* spammer

spamming [spamiŋ] NM *Ordinat* spamming

spanioménorrhée [spanjomenɔre] NF *Méd* oligomenorrhoea

sparadrap [sparadra] NM *Br* (sticking) plaster, *Am* Band-Aid

sparages [sparaʒ] NM *Can Fam* big *or* expansive gestures ▪; **il parlait en faisant de grands s.** he gestured expansively as he spoke ▪

spardeck [spardɛk] NM *Naut* spar deck

sparidé [sparide] *Ich* NM sparid, sparoid

❑ **sparidés** NMPL Sparidae

sparring-partner [spariŋpartnɛr] (*pl* **sparring-partners**) NM *Boxe* sparring partner

spart [spart] NM esparto (grass)

Spartacus [spartakys] NPR Spartacus

spartakisme [spartakism] NM Spartacism

spartakiste [spartakist] ADJ Spartacist

NMF Spartacist

Sparte [spart] NF Sparta

sparte [spart] = **spart**

sparterie [spartri] NF esparto goods

spartiate [sparsjat] ADJ **1** (*de Sparte*) Spartan **2** *Fig* (*austère*) spartan, ascetic

❑ **Spartiate** NMF Spartan

❑ **spartiates** NFPL (*sandales*) (Roman) sandals

❑ **à la spartiate** ADV austerely; **élever ses enfants**

à la s. to give one's children a spartan upbringing

spasme [spasm] NM spasm

spasmodique [spasmɔdik] ADJ spasmodic, spastic

spasmolytique [spasmɔlitik] ADJ spasmolytic NM spasmolytic

spasmophile [spasmɔfil] *Méd* ADJ suffering from spasmophilia, spastic
NMF = person suffering from spasmophilia, spastic

spasmophilie [spasmɔfili] NF *Méd* spasmophilia

spasmophilique [spasmɔfilik] *Méd* ADJ spasmophilic
NMF spasmophile

spastique [spastik] ADJ spastic, spasmodic

spatangue [spatɑ̃g] NM spatangoid

spath [spat] NM *Minér* spar; **s. calcaire** *ou* **d'Islande** Iceland spar; **s. fluor** fluor spar, fluorite; **s. pesant** barytes, barite

spathe [spat] NF *Bot* spathe

spatiabiliser [3] [spasjabilize] VT to prepare for operation in space

spatial, -e, -aux, -ales [spasjal, -o] ADJ 1 *(de l'espace)* spatial; *Math* **coordonnées spatiales** spatial coordinates 2 *Astron & Mil* space *(avant n)*
NM space industry

spatialisation [spasjalizasjɔ̃] NF 1 *(du temps, des sons)* spatialization 2 *(d'un engin)* sending into space

spatialiser [3] [spasjalize] VT *(lancer dans l'espace)* to send into space

spatialisme [spasjalism] NM *Beaux-Arts* Spatialism

spatialiste [spasjalist] *Beaux-Arts* ADJ Spatialist
NMF Spatialist

spatialité [spasjalite] NF spatiality

spationaute [spasjonot] NMF spaceman, f spacewoman

spationef [spasjonɛf] NM spaceship

spatio-temporel, -elle [spasjɔtɑ̃pɔrɛl] *(mpl* **spatio-temporels**, *fpl* **spatio-temporelles**) ADJ spatio-temporal

spatule [spatyl] NF 1 *Culin* spatula 2 *(d'un ski)* tip 3 *Beaux-Arts* (pallet) knife 4 *Constr* jointer 5 *Ich* paddlefish 6 *Orn* spoonbill

spatulé, -e [spatyle] ADJ spatulate

speaker, speakerine [spikœr, spikrin] NM,F announcer
NM *Pol (en Grande-Bretagne, aux États-Unis)* **le s.** the Speaker

spécial, -e, -aux, -ales [spesjal, -o] ADJ 1 *(d'une catégorie particulière)* special, particular, specific, distinctive; **une clef spéciale** a special key; **des caractéristiques spéciales** distinctive features; **savon s. peaux grasses** soap for greasy skin; *Littéraire* **privilège s. aux militaires** privilege reserved for *or* restricted to military men
2 *(exceptionnel → gén)* special, extraordinary, exceptional; *(→ numéro, édition)* special; **rien de s.** nothing special; **instituer une procédure spéciale** to set up a special procedure; **bénéficier d'une faveur spéciale** to be especially favoured
3 *(bizarre)* peculiar, odd; **ils ont une mentalité spéciale** they're a bit eccentric *or* strange; **ce livre est s., on aime ou on n'aime pas** this book is very particular, either you like it or you don't; **toi, t'es s.!** you're a bit weird!
4 *Écon* **commerce s.** import-export trade (balance)
5 *Sport (slalom)* special
NM *Fam* (special) slalom
◻ **spéciale** NF 1 *Scol* = second year of a two year entrance course for a "grande école"
2 *(huître)* = type of cultivated oyster
3 *Sport* (short) off-road rally

spécialement [spesjalmɑ̃] ADV 1 *(à une fin particulière)* specially, especially; **je me suis fait faire un costume s. pour le mariage** I had a suit made specially for the wedding; **parlez-nous de l'Italie et (plus) s. de Florence** tell us about Italy, especially Florence
2 *(très)* particularly, especially; **ça n'a pas été s. drôle** it wasn't particularly *or* especially amusing; **tu veux lui parler? – pas s.** do you want to talk to him/her? – not particularly *or* especially

spécialisation [spesjalizasjɔ̃] NF specialization, specializing

spécialisé, -e [spesjalize] ADJ *(gén)* specialized; *(école, hôpital)* special; *Ordinat* dedicated, special-purpose; **notre personnel hautement s.** our highly specialized staff; **des chercheurs spécialisés dans l'intelligence artificielle** researchers specializing in artificial intelligence

spécialiser [3] [spesjalize] VT 1 *(étudiant, travailleur)* to turn *or* to make into a specialist; **nous spécialisons des biochimistes** we train specialists in biochemistry
2 *(usine, activité)* to make more specialized; **on a décidé de s. les usines de la région** it was decided to make the factories in the area more specialized
► **se spécialiser** VPR to specialize; *Scol* **quatorze ans, c'est trop tôt pour se s.** fourteen is too young to start specializing in certain subjects; **se s. dans la dermatologie** to specialize in dermatology

spécialiste [spesjalist] NMF 1 *(gén)* & *Méd* specialist; **un s. en maladies respiratoires** a specialist in respiratory illnesses; **c'est un s. du marketing** he's an expert in marketing; **s. produit** product specialist; *Fin* **s. en valeurs du Trésor** primary dealer
2 *Fam (habitué)* **c'est un s. des gaffes** he's an expert at putting his foot in it
ADJ 1 *(médecin)* specialist
2 *Fam (habitué)* **elle est s. de ce genre de gaffes** she's an expert at putting her foot in it like that

spécialité [spesjalite] NF 1 *Culin* speciality; **spécialités de la région** local specialities *or* products; **fais-nous une de tes spécialités** cook us one of your special recipes *or* dishes; **la s. du chef** *(sur la carte d'un restaurant)* (the) chef's speciality
2 *Pharm* **s. pharmaceutique** branded pharmaceutical *or* (patented) pharmaceutical product
3 *Scol & Univ* field, area; **s. médicale** area of medicine; **quelle est votre s.?** what area do you specialize in?; **ma s., c'est la botanique** I specialize in botany; **le meilleur dans** *ou* **de sa s.** the best in his field
4 *(manie, habitude)* **le vin, c'est sa s.** he's/she's the wine expert; **encore en retard? c'est ta s., ma parole!** late again? you seem to be making a habit of it!
5 *Fin* **s. budgétaire** budgetary speciality

spéciation [spesjasjɔ̃] NF *Biol* speciation

spécieuse [spesjøz] *voir* **spécieux**

spécieusement [spesjøzmɑ̃] ADV speciously, fallaciously

spécieux, -euse [spesjø, -øz] ADJ specious, fallacious

spécification [spesifikasjɔ̃] NF specification; **sans s. de** without specifying, without mention of; **une réunion a été décidée sans s. d'heure ni de lieu** a meeting was arranged, but the time and place were not specified; **s. de la fonction** job specification

spécificité [spesifisite] NF distinctiveness, distinctive nature; **s. culturelle** cultural specificity; **le pays cherche à faire reconnaître sa s. culturelle** the country wants its distinctive cultural identity to be acknowledged; **ce type d'institution est une s. française** this kind of institution is a specifically French phenomenon *or* is a distinctive feature of France

spécifier [9] [spesifje] VT to specify, to state, to indicate; **s. les conditions d'un prêt** to specify *or* to indicate the conditions of a loan; **je lui ai bien spécifié l'heure du rendez-vous** I made sure I told him/her the time of the appointment; **j'avais pourtant bien spécifié que je voulais une peinture mate!** I had quite specifically asked for matt paint!; **elle a tenu à faire s. ce point dans le contrat** she wanted this point to be specified in the contract

spécifique [spesifik] ADJ specific

spécifiquement [spesifikmɑ̃] ADV specifically

spécimen [spesimɛn] NM 1 *(exemple)* specimen, example; **ce poème est un très beau s. de l'art pour l'art** this poem is a fine example of art for art's sake; *Fam* **le type était un parfait s. d'avocat véreux** the man was a perfect example of a

corrupt lawyer■ *or* your typical corrupt lawyer; **s. de signature** specimen signature
2 *Typ* specimen; **s. (gratuit)** *(d'un livre)* desk copy
3 *Fam (individu bizarre)* *Br* queer fish, *Am* odd duck; **méfie-toi, c'est un drôle de s.!** be careful, he's a *Br* queer fish *or Am* an odd duck!

spéciosité [spesjozite] NF speciosity, speciousness

spectacle [spɛktakl] NM 1 *(représentation)* show; **aller au s.** to go to (see) a show; **faire un s.** to do a show; **monter un s.** to put on a show; **consulter la page (des) spectacles** to check the entertainment *or* entertainments page; **le s.** *(activité)* showbusiness; *Cin* **s.** permanent continuous performances; **s. solo** one-man show; **s. télévisé** televised show, television show; **s. de variétés** variety show; **le s. est dans la salle** the real show's in the auditorium; **le s. continue** the show must go on
2 *(ce qui se présente au regard)* sight, scene; **le s. qui s'offrait à nous** the sight before our eyes; **sur le port nous attendait un s. affligeant** on the quayside, a heart-breaking scene met our eyes; **elle présentait un bien triste/curieux s.** she looked a rather sorry/odd sight; **au s. de** at the sight of; **au s. de sa mère blessée, il s'évanouit** at the sight of *or* on seeing his injured mother, he fainted
◻ **à grand spectacle** ADJ film à grand s. epic
◻ **en spectacle** ADV on nous les donne en s. they are paraded in front of us; **se donner** *ou* **s'offrir en s.** to make an exhibition *or* a spectacle of oneself

spectaculaire [spɛktakylɛr] ADJ 1 *(exceptionnel, frappant)* spectacular, impressive; **de manière s.** dramatically; **elle a fait une chute s.** she had a spectacular fall 2 *(notable)* spectacular; **des progrès spectaculaires** spectacular progress

spectateur, -trice [spɛktatœr, -tris] NM,F 1 *au théâtre, au cinéma)* spectator, member of the audience; *Sport* spectator; **les spectateurs** *(au théâtre, au cinéma)* the audience; *Sport* the crowd; **plusieurs spectateurs ont quitté la salle** several people in *or* members of the audience walked out
2 *(d'un accident, d'un événement)* spectator, witness; **les spectateurs finirent par se disperser** the crowd eventually began to disperse
3 *(simple observateur)* onlooker; **il a participé à nos réunions en s.** he just came to our meetings as an onlooker

spectral, -e, -aux, -ales [spɛktral, -o] ADJ 1 *Littéraire (fantomatique)* ghostly, ghostlike, spectral
2 *Phys* spectral; **analyse spectrale** spectrum *or* spectroscopic analysis

spectre [spɛktr] NM 1 *(fantôme)* ghost, phantom, spectre; *Littéraire* **le s. rouge** the ghost of revolution
2 *Fam (personne maigre)* ghostly figure, apparition
3 *(représentation effrayante)* **le s. de** the spectre of; **le s. de la famine** the spectre of famine; **agiter le s. de la révolution** to invoke the spectre of rebellion
4 *Chim, Élec & Phys* spectrum; **s. solaire** solar spectrum; **s. visible** visible spectrum; **s. électrique/magnétique** electric/magnetic spectrum
5 *Pharm (d'un antibiotique)* spectrum; **à large s.** broad-spectrum

spectrochimique [spɛktrɔʃimik] ADJ spectrochemical

spectrogramme [spɛktrɔgram] NM spectrogram

spectrographe [spɛktrɔgraf] NM spectrograph; **s. de masse** mass spectrograph

spectrographie [spɛktrɔgrafi] NF spectrography; **s. d'absorption** absorption spectrography; **s. d'émission** emission spectrography; **s. de masse** mass spectrography

spectrographique [spɛktrɔgrafik] ADJ spectrographic

spectrohéliographe [spɛktrɔeljɔgraf] NM spectroheliograph

spectromètre [spɛktrɔmɛtr] NM spectrometer

spectrométrie [spɛktrɔmetri] NF spectrometry; **s. de masse** mass spectrometry

spectrométrique [spɛktrɔmetrik] ADJ spectrometric

spectrophotomètre [spɛktrɔfɔtomɛtr] NM spectrophotometer

spectrophotométrie [spɛktrɔfɔtometri] NF spectrophotometry

spectroscope [spɛktrɔskɔp] NM spectroscope

spectroscopie [spɛktrɔskɔpi] NF spectroscopy

spectroscopique [spɛktrɔskɔpik] ADJ spectroscopic

spéculaire [spekylɛr] ADJ 1 *(minéral)* specular 2 *(produit par un miroir → image, écriture)* mirror *(avant n)*
▪ NF *Bot* Venus's looking glass

spéculateur, -trice [spekylatœr, -tris] NM,F speculator; **s. à la baisse** bear; **s. à la hausse** bull; **s. sur devises** currency speculator; **s. à la journée** scalper; **s. sur plusieurs positions** position trader

spéculatif, -ive [spekylatif, -iv] ADJ speculative

spéculation [spekylasjɔ̃] NF speculation; **s. à la baisse** bear operations; **s. à la hausse** bull operations; **s. immobilière** property speculation; **s. à la journée** day trading

spéculative [spekylativ] *voir* **spéculatif**

spéculativement [spekylativmã] ADV speculatively

spéculatrice [spekylatris] *voir* **spéculateur**

spéculaus [spekylos] = **spéculoos**

spéculer [3] [spekyle] VI 1 *Bourse* to speculate; **s. à la baisse** to go a bear, to speculate for a fall *or* on a falling market; **s. à la hausse** to go a bull, to speculate for a rise *or* on a rising market; **s. en Bourse** to speculate on the stock exchange; **s. sur l'or** to speculate in gold
2 *Littéraire (méditer)* to speculate
▪ **spéculer sur** VT IND *(compter sur)* to count *or* to bank *or* to rely on; **le gouvernement spécule sur une hausse de la natalité** the government is banking *or* relying on a rise in the birthrate

spéculoos [spekylos] NM *Belg* = ginger biscuit

spéculum [spekylɔm] NM *Méd* speculum

speech [spitʃ] *(pl* **speechs** *ou* **speeches)** NM *Fam* (short) speech ▪; **il nous a refait son s. sur l'importance des bonnes manières** he made the same old speech about the importance of good manners

speed [spid] *Fam* ADJ *(nerveux)* hyper
▪ NM *(amphétamines)* speed

speedé, -e [spide] ADJ *Fam* 1 *(nerveux)* hyper 2 *(drogué aux amphétamines)* **être s.** to be speeding

speeder [3] [spide] VI *Fam* 1 *(être sous l'effet d'amphétamines)* to be speeding 2 *(se dépêcher)* to get a move on, *Am* to get it in gear

spéléologie [speleɔlɔʒi] NF *(science et étude)* speleology; *(sport) Br* potholing, *Am* spelunking

spéléologique [speleɔlɔʒik] ADJ speleologic

spéléologue [speleɔlɔg] NMF *(savant, chercheur)* speleologist; *(sportif) Br* potholer, *Am* spelunker

spencer [spɛnsœr] NM *(veste → d'homme)* monkey jacket; *Mil* mess jacket; *(→ de femme)* spencer

spéos [speos] NM *Antiq* speos

spergulaire [spɛrgylɛr] NF *Bot* **s. rouge** sand spurrey

spergule [spɛrgyl] NF *Bot* spurrey

spermaceti [spɛrmaseti] NM spermaceti, sperm oil

spermaphyte [spɛrmafit] *Bot* NM spermatophyte, spermophyte
▪ **spermaphytes** NMPL Spermatophyta

spermatide [spɛrmatid] NM *Zool* spermatid

spermatie [spɛrmati] NF *Bot* spermatium

spermatique [spɛrmatik] ADJ *(du sperme)* spermatic

spermatocyte [spɛrmatosit] NM *Bot & Zool* spermatocyte

spermatogenèse [spɛrmatoʒenɛz] NF spermatogenesis

spermatogonie [spɛrmatogoni] NF spermatogonium

spermatophore [spɛrmatofɔr] NM *Zool* spermatophore

spermatophyte [spɛrmatofit] *Bot* NM spermatophyte
▪ **spermatophytes** NMPL Spermatophyta

spermatozoïde [spɛrmatozɔid] NM 1 *Biol* sperm (cell), spermatozoon 2 *Bot* spermatozoid

---

sperme [spɛrm] NM sperm

spermète [spɛrmɛt] NM *Orn* mannikin

spermicide [spɛrmisid] ADJ spermicidal
▪ NM spermicide

spermogramme [spɛrmogram] NM sperm count

spermophile [spɛrmofil] NM *Zool* ground squirrel, *Spéc* spermophile

spet [spɛ] NM *Ich* spet

sphacèle [sfasɛl] NM *Méd* sphacelus, gangrene

sphaigne [sfɛɲ] NF *Bot* sphagnum (moss), peat moss

sphène [sfɛn] NM *Minér* sphene

sphéniscidé [sfeniside] *Orn* NM member of the Spheniscidae
▪ **sphéniscidés** NMPL Spheniscidae

sphénodon [sfenɔdɔ̃] NM *Zool* tuatara, *Spéc* sphenodon

sphénoïdal, -e, -aux, -ales [sfenɔidal -o] ADJ *Anat* sphenoidal

sphénoïde [sfenɔid] *Anat* ADJ sphenoid
▪ NM sphenoid, sphenoidal bone

sphère [sfɛr] NF 1 *Astron & Géom* sphere; **s. céleste** celestial sphere; **s. terrestre** globe 2 *(zone)* field, area, sphere; **nous n'évoluons pas dans les mêmes sphères** we don't move in the same circles; **s. d'activité** field *or* sphere of activity; **s. d'influence** sphere of influence; *Littéraire* **les hautes sphères** the higher realms

sphéricité [sferisite] NF sphericity

sphérique [sferik] ADJ spherical, spheric

sphéroïdal, -e, -aux, -ales [sferɔidal, -o] ADJ spheroidal

sphéroïde [sferɔid] NM spheroid

sphéromètre [sferɔmɛtr] NM *Phys* spherometer

sphérule [sferyl] NF spherule

sphincter [sfɛktɛr] NM *Anat* sphincter

sphinctérien, -enne [sfɛkterjɛ̃, -ɛn] ADJ sphincteral, sphincter *(avant n)*

sphinge [sfɛ̃ʒ] NF *Myth* female sphinx

sphingidé [sfɛ̃ʒide] NM *Entom* hawk moth, *Spéc* sphingid

sphinx [sfɛ̃ks] NM 1 *Beaux-Arts & Myth* sphinx; **le S.** the Sphinx 2 *(personne énigmatique)* sphinx; **son impassibilité de s. me déroutait** his/her sphinx-like inscrutability disconcerted me 3 *Entom* hawk moth; **s. bélier** burnet moth

sphygmogramme [sfigmogram] NM *Méd* sphygmogram

sphygmographe [sfigmograf] NM *Méd* sphygmograph

sphygmomanomètre [sfigmomanomɛtr] NM *Méd* sphygmomanometer

sphyrène [sfirɛn] NF *Ich* Sphyraena; **s. barracuda** becuna, great barracuda

SPI [ɛspei] NMPL *(abrév* **Secrétariats professionnels internationaux)** ITS

spi [spi] NM *Naut* spinnaker, balloon sail

spic [spik] NM *Bot* spike lavender

spicilège [spisilɛʒ] NM *(recueil)* spicilege

spicule [spikyl] NM 1 *Zool (d'éponge)* spicule, spiculum 2 *Astron* spicule

spider [spidɛr] NM *Aut Br* dickey (seat), *Am* rumble seat

spiegel [ʃpigœl] NM *Métal* spiegeleisen

spiering [spiriŋ] NM *Belg (échine de porc)* pork loin chop; *(collier de bœuf)* neck of beef; *(collet de mouton)* neck of mutton

spin [spin] NM *Phys* spin

spina-bifida [spinabifida] NM INV spina bifida

spinal, -e, -aux, -ales [spinal, -o] ADJ spinal

spinelle [spinɛl] NM *Minér* spinel

spinnaker [spinɛkœr] NM *Naut* spinnaker, balloon sail

spinosisme [spinozism] NM *Phil* Spinozism

spinosiste [spinozist] *Phil* ADJ Spinozistic
▪ NMF Spinozist

spinozisme [spinozism] = **spinosisme**

spinoziste [spinozist] = **spinosiste**

spinule [spinyl] NF *Biol* spinule

spioncelle [spjɔ̃sɛl] NF *Orn* water pipit

spiral, -e, -aux, -ales [spiral, -o] ADJ spiral, helical
▪ NM *(ressort)* spiral, spring; *(d'une montre)* hairspring
▪ **spirale** NF 1 *(circonvolution)* spiral; **des spirales de fumée** coils of smoke 2 *(hausse rapide)* spiral; **la spirale inflationniste** the inflationary spiral; **la spirale des prix et des salaires** the

---

wage-price spiral 3 *Journ* **spirale du silence** spiral of silence
▪ **à spirale** ADJ *(cahier)* spiral, spiralbound
▪ **en spirale** ADJ *(escalier, descente)* spiral ADV in a spiral, spirally; **s'élever/retomber en spirale** to spiral upwards/downwards

spiralé, -e [spirale] ADJ spiral, helical

spire [spir] NF *(d'un coquillage)* whorl; *(d'une spirale, d'une hélice)* turn, spire

spirée [spire] NF *Bot* spiraea

spirifer [spirifɛr] NM *Archéol* spirifer

spirille [spirij] NM spirillum

spirillose [spiriloz] NF *Méd* spirillosis

spiring [spiriŋ, spirɛ̃g], **spiringue** [spirɛ̃g] = **spiering**

spiritain [spiritɛ̃] NM *Rel* member of the order of Saint-Esprit

spirite [spirit] ADJ spiritualistic
▪ NMF spiritualist

spiritisme [spiritism] NM spiritualism, spiritism

spiritual, -als [spiritɥol, -olz] NM *(Negro)* spiritual

spiritualisation [spiritɥalizasjɔ̃] NF spiritualization, spiritualizing *(UNCOUNT)*

spiritualiser [3] [spiritɥalize] VT to give a spiritual dimension to, to spiritualize

spiritualisme [spiritɥalism] NM spiritualism

spiritualiste [spiritɥalist] ADJ spiritualistic
▪ NMF spiritualist

spiritualité [spiritɥalite] NF spirituality

spirituel, -elle [spiritɥɛl] ADJ 1 *Phil* spiritual; **la nature spirituelle de l'âme** the spiritual nature of the soul
2 *(non physique)* spiritual; **père s.** spiritual father
3 *(plein d'esprit)* witty; **elle est très spirituelle** she's very witty; **une repartie spirituelle** a witty reply; **comme c'est s.!** how clever!
4 *Rel* spiritual; **chef s.** spiritual head; **pouvoir s.** spiritual power; **concert s.** concert of sacred music
▪ NM *Rel* 1 *Hist (Franciscain dissident)* spiritual
2 **le s.** things spiritual; **le s. et le temporel** the spiritual and the temporal; **le retour du s.** the revival of interest in the spiritual *or* in things spiritual

spirituellement [spiritɥɛlmã] ADV 1 *Phil & Rel* spiritually 2 *(brillamment)* wittily

spiritueux, -euse [spiritɥø, -øz] ADJ *(boisson)* strong, *Spéc* spirituous
▪ NM spirit; **vins et s.** wines and spirits

spirling [spirlɛg, spirlɛ̃], **spirlingue** [spirlɛ̃g] = **spiering**

spirochète [spirɔkɛt] NM *Biol* spirochaete

spirochétose [spirɔketoz] NF *Méd* spirochaetosis

spirographe [spirɔgraf] NM *Méd* spirograph

spirogyre [spirɔʒir] NF *Biol* spirogyra

spiroïdal, -e, -aux, -ales [spirɔidal, -o] ADJ spiroid; **fracture spiroïdale** spiral fracture

spiromètre [spiromɛtr] NM *Méd* spirometer

spirométrie [spirometri] NF *Méd* spirometry

spirorbe [spirɔrb] NM *Zool* spirorbis

Spirou [spiru] NM *Presse* = popular weekly cartoon magazine

spiruline [spirylin] NF spirulina

spitant, -e [spitã, -ãt] ADJ *Belg* 1 *(personne)* lively 2 *(gazeux)* **eau spitante** carbonated water

spiter [3] [spite] VT *Belg* 1 *(faire gicler)* to spray, to squirt 2 *(éclabousser)* to splash, to splatter

Spitsberg [spidzbɛrg] NM Spitsbergen, Spitzbergen

spitz [spitz] NM *(chien)* spitz

Spitzberg [spidzbɛrg] = **Spitsberg**

splanchnique [splãknik] ADJ *Anat* splanchnic

spleen [splin] NM *Littéraire* spleen, melancholy; **avoir le s.** to be melancholic

splendeur [splãdœr] NF 1 *(somptuosité)* magnificence, splendour
2 *(merveille)* **son collier est une s.** her necklace is splendid *or* magnificent; **les splendeurs des églises baroques** the magnificence of baroque churches
3 *(prospérité, gloire)* grandeur, splendour; *Littéraire* **Rome, au temps de sa s.** Rome at her apogee; *Hum* **voilà le macho dans toute sa s.** that's macho man in all his glory
4 *Littéraire (du soleil)* brilliance, splendour

📖

'Splendeurs et misères des courtisanes' *Balzac* 'A Harlot High and Low'

🎬

'La Splendeur des Amberson' *Welles* 'The Magnificient Ambersons'

Allusion

Splendeurs et misères des courtisanes

This is the title of the sequel to Balzac's *Illusions perdues* published in 1843 and 1847. In it, we meet again the daughters of Père Goriot, a materialistic pair who have their ups and downs, both social and romantic. The title is used allusively in modern French, usually replacing **courtisanes** with another word, to refer to anyone or anything that has a sudden decline after a period of success.

---

splendide [splɑ̃did] ADJ **1** *(somptueux → décor, fête, repas)* splendid, magnificent **2** *(beau → gén)* magnificent, wonderful, splendid; *(→ journée, temps)* splendid; **une s. créature entra** a gorgeous *or* magnificent creature entered; **tu es s. aujourd'hui** you look wonderful today; **elle avait une mine s.** she was radiant **3** *(rayonnant → soleil)* radiant **4** *Littéraire (glorieux)* splendid

splendidement [splɑ̃didmɑ̃] ADV splendidly, magnificently

splénectomie [splenɛktɔmi] NF *Méd* splenectomy

splénique [splenik] ADJ *Méd* splenic

splénite [splenit] NF *Méd* splenitis

splénomégalie [splenomegali] NF *Méd* splenomegaly

splif [splif] NM *Fam Arg drogue* spliff, joint

split [split] NM *Bourse* split

spoiler [spɔjlœr] NM *Aut & Aviat* spoiler

spoliateur, -trice [spɔljatœr, -tris] *Littéraire* ADJ spoliatory, despoiling
   NM,F spoliator, despoiler

spoliation [spɔljasjɔ̃] NF *Littéraire* spoliation, despoilment

spoliatrice [spɔljatris] *voir* **spoliateur**

spolier [9] [spɔlje] VT *Littéraire* to spoliate, to despoil; **spoliés de leurs droits/possessions** stripped of their rights/possessions

spondée [spɔ̃de] NM *Ling* spondee

spondias [spɔ̃djas] NM *Bot* hog plum

spondylarthrite [spɔ̃dilartrit] NF spondylitis; **s. ankylosante** ankylosing spondylitis

spondyle [spɔ̃dil] NM *Zool* spondylus

spondylite [spɔ̃dilit] NF *Méd* spondylitis

spongiaire [spɔ̃ʒjɛr] *Zool* NM sponge, poriferan
   ❑ **spongiaires** NMPL Porifera

spongieux, -euse [spɔ̃ʒjø, -øz] ADJ **1** *Anat* spongy **2** *(sol, matière)* spongy, sponge-like

spongiforme [spɔ̃ʒifɔrm] ADJ *Méd* spongiform

spongille [spɔ̃ʒil] NF *Zool* spongilla, freshwater sponge

spongiosité [spɔ̃ʒjozite] NF sponginess

sponsor [spɔ̃sɔr, spɔnsɔr] NM sponsor

sponsoring [spɔ̃sɔriŋ, spɔnsɔriŋ], **sponsorat** [spɔ̃sɔra, spɔnsɔra] NM sponsorship

sponsorisation [spɔ̃sɔrizasjɔ̃] NF sponsoring

sponsoriser [3] [spɔ̃sɔrize] VT to sponsor

spontané, -e [spɔ̃tane] ADJ spontaneous; *(aveux)* unprompted

spontanéisme [spɔ̃taneism] NM *Pol* belief in spontaneous political action

spontanéiste [spɔ̃taneist] NMF *Pol* believer in spontaneous political action

spontanéité [spɔ̃taneite] NF spontaneity, spontaneousness

spontanément [spɔ̃tanemɑ̃] ADV spontaneously; **elle a avoué s.** she owned up of her own accord

Sporades [spɔrad] NFPL **les S.** the Sporades

sporadicité [spɔradisite] NF sporadic nature *or* character

sporadique [spɔradik] ADJ *(attaque, effort)* sporadic, occasional; *(symptôme, crise)* sporadic, isolated; *(averse)* scattered

sporadiquement [spɔradikmɑ̃] ADV sporadically

sporange [spɔrɑ̃ʒ] NM *Bot* sporangium

spore [spɔr] NF *Biol* spore

sporifère [spɔrifɛr] ADJ *Biol* spore-bearing, sporiferous

sporogone [spɔrɔgɔn] NM *Bot* sporogonium

sporophyte [spɔrɔfit] NM *Bot* sporophyte

sporotrichose [spɔrɔtrikoz] NF *Méd* sporotrichosis

sporozoaire [spɔrɔzɔɛr] *Zool* NM sporozoan, sporozoon
   ❑ **sporozoaires** NMPL Sporozoa

sport [spɔr] ADJ INV **1** *(pratique, de détente)* casual; **manteau/chaussures s.** casual coat/shoes **2** *Vieilli (fair-play)* sporting
   ADV **habillé s.** casually dressed
   NM **1** *(ensemble d'activités, exercice physique)* sport; *(activité de compétition)* (competitive) sport; **faire du s.** to do *Br* sport *or Am* sports; **un peu de s. te ferait du bien** some physical exercise would do you good; **il y a trop de s. à la télé** there's too much sport on TV; **sports aquatiques** water sports; **s. cérébral** *ou* **intellectuel** brainteasers; *Fam Hum* **s. en chambre** *(rapports sexuels)* bedroom sports; **s. de combat** combat sport; **s. de contact** contact sport; **s. équestre** equestrian sport, equestrianism; **sports d'équipe** team sports; **sports d'hiver** winter sports; **aller aux sports d'hiver** to go skiing, to go on a winter sports *Br* holiday *or Am* vacation; **s. individuel** individual sport; **sports nautiques** water sports; *TV* **le journal des sports** the sports news; **la page des sports** the sports page
   2 *Fam (locutions)* **c'est du s.** it's no picnic; **c'est du s. de faire démarrer la tondeuse!** getting the mower started is no picnic *or* is the devil's own job!; **il va y avoir du s.!** now we're going to see some fun!; **faire qch pour le s.** to do sth for the fun *or* the hell of it
   ❑ **de sport** ADJ *(terrain, vêtement, voiture)* sports *(avant n)*

sport-études [spɔretyd] NM *Scol* = secondary-school curriculum with special emphasis on sport

sportif, -ive [spɔrtif, -iv] ADJ **1** *(association, club, magazine, reportage)* sports *(avant n)*; **reporter s.** sports reporter, sportscaster **2** *(événement, exploit)* sporting **3** *(personne → qui aime le sport)* sporty; **elle est très sportive** she does a lot of sport; **je ne suis pas très s.** I'm not very sporty; **avoir une allure sportive** to look athletic **4** *(loyal → public)* sporting, fair; *(→ attitude, geste)* sporting, sportsmanlike; **avoir l'esprit s.** to show sportsmanship; **ce n'était pas très s. de sa part** it wasn't very sporting of him/her
   NM,F sportsman, *f* sportswoman; *Hum* **c'est un s. en chambre** he's an armchair sportsman

sportivement [spɔrtivmɑ̃] ADV sportingly; **très s., il l'a aidé à se relever** he helped him up, which was very sporting of him; **il a pris les choses très s.** he was very sporting about things

sportivité [spɔrtivite] NF *(d'une personne)* sportsmanship; **le match a manqué de s.** it wasn't a very sporting match

sport-nature [spɔrnatyr] *(pl* **sports-nature***)* NM outdoor sports

sportsman [spɔrtsman] *(pl* **sportsmen** [-mɛn]*)* NM *Vieilli* **1** *(qui s'occupe de sport)* sportsman **2** *(amateur de courses de chevaux)* racegoer

sportswear [spɔrtswɛr] NM sportswear, casual wear

sportule [spɔrtyl] NF *Antiq* sportula

sportwear [spɔrtwɛr] = **sportswear**

sporulation [spɔrylasjɔ̃] NF *Biol* sporulation, sporulating *(UNCOUNT)*

sporuler [3] [spɔryle] VI *Biol* to sporulate

SPOT, Spot [spɔt] NM *(abrév* **satellite pour l'observation de la Terre***)* earth observation satellite

spot [spɔt] NM **1** *(projecteur, petite lampe)* spotlight; **s. à pince** clip lamp **2** *Phys* light spot **3** *Électron* spot **4** *(publicité)* **s. publicitaire** advert, commercial; **s. télé** *ou* **TV** TV advert, TV commercial

spouleur [spulœr] NM *Ordinat* spooler

Spoutnik [sputnik] NM Sputnik

sprat [sprat] NM *Ich* sprat

spray [sprɛ] NM spray; **parfum/peinture en s.** spray *or* spray-on perfume/paint

spread [sprɛd] NM *Bourse* spread; **s. horizontal** horizontal spread; **s. vertical** vertical spread

springbok [spriŋbok] NM **1** *Zool* springbok, springbuck **2** *Sport* **les Springboks** the Springboks

springer [spriŋœr, spriŋɛr] NM springer *(spaniel)*

sprinkler [sprinklœr] NM sprinkler

sprint [sprint] NM *Sport (course)* sprint (race); *(pointe de vitesse → gén)* spurt; *(→ en fin de parcours)* final spurt *or* sprint; **elle m'a battu au s.** she beat me in the final sprint; **il est bon au s.** he's got a good sprint finish; **piquer un s.** to put on a spurt, to sprint; *Fam* **j'ai dû piquer un s. pour avoir mon train** I had to sprint to catch my train

sprinter[1] [sprintœr] NM sprinter

sprinter[2] [3] [sprinte] VI to sprint; *(en fin de parcours)* to put on a spurt

SPRL [ɛspeɛrɛl] NF *Belg (abrév* **société de personnes à responsabilité limitée***)* limited liability company

sprue [spry] NF *Méd* sprue

spume [spym] NF foam, froth; *Méd (sang)* foamy blood; *(expectorations)* frothy expectoration

spumescent, -e [spymesɑ̃, -ɑ̃t] ADJ spumescent, foaming

spumeux, -euse [spymø, -øz] ADJ *Méd* foamy; **cellules spumeuses** foam cells; **rétrovirus s.** foamy virus, spumaretrovirus

spumosité [spymozite] NF *Méd* spumescence

sq *(abrév écrite* **sequiturque***)* f

sqq *(abrév écrite* **sequunturque***)* ff

squale [skwal] NM shark

squamate [skwamat] *Zool* NM member of the Squamata order
   ❑ **squamates** NMPL Squamata

squame [skwam] NF *Méd* scale, *Spéc* squama

squameux, -euse [skwamø, -øz] ADJ *Méd* scaly, *Spéc* squamous

squamifère [skwamifɛr] ADJ *Zool* squamate

squamule [skwamyl] NF *Entom* squamula

square [skwar] NM **1** *(jardin)* (small) public garden *or* gardens **2** *(place)* square; **il habite s. Blériot** he lives in Blériot Square

squarreux, -euse [skwarø, -øz] ADJ *Bot* squarrose

squash [skwaʃ] NM squash; **jouer au s.** to play squash

squat [skwat] NM *(habitation)* squat

squatine [skwatin] NM OU NF *Ich* squatina, angelfish

squatter[1] [skwatœr] NM squatter

squatter[2] [3] [skwate], **squattériser** [3] [skwaterize] VT **1** *(bâtiment)* to squat in **2** *Fam (monopoliser)* to take over■, to hog; **il squatte toujours la télécommande quand on regarde la télé** he always hogs the remote control when we're watching TV; **arrête de s. le joint, fais tourner!** stop bogarting that joint, pass it round!
   VI to squat; **ça fait trois semaines qu'il squatte chez moi** he's been squatting *or* camping out at mine for three weeks now

squatteur, -euse [skwatœr, -øz] NM,F squatter

squaw [skwo] NF squaw

squeeze [skwiz] NM *Cartes (au bridge)* squeeze

squeezer [3] [skwize] VT **1** *Cartes* to squeeze **2** *Fam (mettre en difficulté)* to put the squeeze on

squelette [skəlɛt] NM **1** *Anat* skeleton; **c'est un s. ambulant** he's nothing but skin and bone, he's a walking skeleton **2** *(d'un discours)* skeleton, broad outline **3** *Chim* skeleton **4** *Constr & Naut* carcass, skeleton

squelettique [skəletik] ADJ **1** *(animal, enfant)* skeleton-like, skeletal; *(plante)* stunted; **elle a des jambes squelettiques** she's got legs like matchsticks; **il est devenu s.** he's become emaciated **2** *(troupes)* decimated; *(équipe)* skeleton *(avant n)* **3** *Anat* skeletal

squille [skij] NF *Zool* squilla; **s.-mante** mantis shrimp

squirre, squirrhe [skir] NM *Méd* scirrhus

SR [ɛsɛr] NM *Journ (abrév* **sécrétaire de rédaction***)* subeditor

SRAS [sras] NM *Méd (abrév* **syndrome respiratoire aigu sévère***)* SARS

Sri Lanka [srilɑ̃ka] NM **le S.** Sri Lanka; **vivre au S.** to live in Sri Lanka; **aller au S.** to go to Sri Lanka

sri lankais, -e [srilɑ̃kɛ, -ɛz] ADJ Sri Lankan
   ❑ **Sri Lankais, -e** NM,F Sri Lankan

SRPJ [εsεrpeʒi] NM (abrév **Service régional de la police judiciaire**) = French regional crime unit

SRS [εsεrεs] NM Rad & TV (abrév **service de radiodiffusion par satellite**) SBS

SS [εsεs] Hist (abrév **SchutzStaffel**) NFSS
   NM **un SS** a member of the SS; **les SS** the SS

S/S Naut (abrév écrite **steamship**) S/S

S.S. 1 Admin (abrév écrite **Sécurité sociale**) SS, Br ≃ DWP, Am ≃ SSA **2** (abrév écrite **Sa Sainteté**) HH

SSBS [εsεsbeεs] NM (abrév **sol-sol balistique stratégique**) ≃ MRBM

S-S-E (abrév écrite **sud-sud-est**) SSE

SSII [εsεsii] NF (abrév **société de services et d'ingénierie en informatique**) = software and computing services company

S-S-O (abrév écrite **sud-sud-ouest**) SSW

SSR [εsεsεr] NF Suisse TV (abrév **Société suisse de Radiodiffusion et de Télévision**) = French-speaking Swiss broadcasting company

St (abrév écrite **saint**) St., St

st (abrév écrite **stère**) st

stabat mater [stabatmatεr] NM INV Rel & Mus Stabat Mater

stabilisant, -e [stabiliză, -ăt] ADJ stabilizing
   NM stabilizing agent, stabilizer

stabilisateur, -trice [stabilizatœr, -tris] ADJ stabilizing
   NM **1** (de vélo) stabilizer **2** Aviat (horizontal) tail plane, Am horizontal stabilizer; (vertical) fin, Am vertical stabilizer **3** Aut antiroll or torsion bar **4** Chim stabilizer **5** Élec **s. de tension** voltage regulator or stabilizer **6** Écon **s. automatique** automatic stabilizer

stabilisation [stabilizasjɔ̃] NF **1** Aviat & Astron stabilization, stabilizing (UNCOUNT) **2** Chim stabilization **3** Écon supporting (UNCOUNT) **4** Métal & (en travaux publics) stabilizing (UNCOUNT)

stabilisatrice [stabilizatris] voir **stabilisateur**

stabiliser [3] [stabilize] VT **1** (échafaudage → donner un équilibre à) to stabilize; (→ maintenir en place) to hold steady
   2 (consolider → situation) to stabilize, to normalize; **le traité devrait s. les relations entre les deux pays** the treaty should stabilize relations between the two countries
   3 (personne) **son mariage va le s.** marriage will make him settle down
   4 (monnaie, devise, prix) to stabilize
   5 (malade, maladie) to stabilize
   ►**se stabiliser** VPR **1** (monnaie, prix, ventes) to stabilize, to level out; (situation) to stabilize; (objet) to steady; (athlète) to regain one's balance; **la situation militaire semble se s.** the military situation seems to be stabilizing
   2 (personne) to settle down; **elle s'est stabilisée depuis qu'elle a un emploi** she's settled down since she got a job

stabilité [stabilite] NF **1** (d'un véhicule, d'un échafaudage, d'une structure) steadiness, stability **2** (d'une monnaie, d'un marché, des prix) & Pol stability **3** (psychologique) stability **4** Chim, Météo & Phys stability

Stabilo® [stabilo] NM highlighter (pen)

stable [stabl] ADJ **1** (qui ne bouge pas → véhicule, échafaudage, structure) steady, stable; **la table n'est pas très s.** the table's a bit unsteady or wobbly; **tu n'as pas l'air d'être dans une position très s.** you look a bit precarious
   2 (constant → marché, emploi) stable, steady; (→ monnaie, prix, ventes) stable; (→ situation politique) stable; **l'état du malade est s.** the patient's condition is stable
   3 (psychologiquement) stable
   4 Chim, Météo & Phys stable

stabulation [stabylasjɔ̃] NF **1** (entretien) stalling (of cattle); **s. libre** loose housing **2** (bâtiment) stalls

staccato [stakato] Mus ADV staccato
   NM staccato

stade [stad] NM **1** Sport stadium; **le S. de France** = stadium in Saint-Denis (north of Paris) built for the 1998 football World Cup, used for international football and rugby matches
   2 (étape, phase) stage; **à ce s. de l'enquête** at this stage of the investigation; **j'en suis arrivé au s. où...** I've reached the stage where...
   3 Antiq stadium

4 Psy stage; **le s. du miroir** the mirror stage; **le s. anal/oral/génital** the anal/oral/genital stage

stadhouder [stadudεr] NM Hist stadtholder

stadia [stadja] NF Tech stadia

stadier, -ère [stadje, -εr] NM,F steward (at sports stadium)

staff [staf] NM **1** Constr staff **2** (personnel) staff

staffer [3] [stafe] VT Constr to construct in staff

staffeur [stafœr] NM Constr = mason specializing in decorative staff work

stage [staʒ] NM **1** (cours) training course; (sur le temps de travail) in-service training; (expérience professionnelle) Br work placement, Am internship; **un s. de trois mois** a three-month Br work placement or Am internship; **faire un s.** (cours) to go on a training course; (expérience professionnelle) to go on Br a work placement or Am an internship; **être en s.** (cours) to be on a course; (expérience professionnelle) to be on Br a work placement or Am an internship; **s. en entreprise** Br work experience or placement, Am internship; **faire un s. en entreprise** to do Br a work placement or Am an internship; **s. de formation** training course; **s. d'initiation ou d'insertion à la vie professionnelle** = training scheme for young unemployed people; **s. pédagogique** teaching practice; **s. de perfectionnement** advanced training course; **s. de recyclage** retraining period
   2 faire un s. de plongée (cours) to have scuba diving lessons; (vacances) to go on a scuba diving holiday; **faire un s. d'espagnol/de traitement de texte** to go on a Spanish/word-processing course

stagflation [stagflasjɔ̃] NF stagflation

stagiaire [staʒjεr] ADJ (en entreprise, dans l'armée) trainee (avant n); (avocat) pupil (avant n); (journaliste) cub (avant n); **un instituteur s.** a student teacher
   NMF Br = person on work experience or a work placement, Am intern; **il est s.** Br he's doing work experience or a work placement, Am he's an intern; **un s. en comptabilité** a trainee accountant (gaining work experience)

stagnant, -e [stagnã, -ãt] ADJ **1** (eau) stagnant; Littéraire **les mares stagnantes de la littérature** literary backwaters **2** (affaires) sluggish

stagnation [stagnasjɔ̃] NF stagnation, stagnating

stagner [3] [stagne] VI **1** (liquide) to stagnate; **des bancs de brume stagnaient dans la vallée** patches of mist were lying in the valley **2** (économie, affaires) to stagnate, to be sluggish; **l'industrie du textile stagne** the textile industry is stagnating **3** (personne) to stagnate, to get into a rut; **s. dans son ignorance** to be bogged down in one's own ignorance

stakhanovisme [stakanɔvism] NM Stakhanovism

stakhanoviste [stakanɔvist] ADJ Stakhanovite
   NMF Stakhanovite

stakning [staknin] NM Ski double poling

stalactite [stalaktit] NF stalactite

stalag [stalag] NM stalag

stalagmite [stalagmit] NF stalagmite

stalagmomètre [stalagmɔmεtr] NM Phys stactometer, stalagmometer

Staline [stalin] NPR Stalin

Stalingrad [stalingrad] NM Stalingrad

stalinien, -enne [stalinjɛ̃, -εn] ADJ Stalinist
   NM,F Stalinist

stalinisme [stalinism] NM Stalinism

stalle [stal] NF (de cheval, d'église) stall

staminal, -e, -aux, -ales [staminal, -o] ADJ Bot staminal

staminé, -e [stamine] ADJ staminate

staminifère [staminifεr] ADJ Bot staminiferous

stamm [ʃtam] NM Suisse (d'une association) meeting room; (lieu de rencontre) hang-out

stance [stɑ̃s] Littérature NF stanza
   ❑ **stances** NFPL = lyrical poem composed of stanzas

stand [stɑ̃d] NM **1** (d'exposition) stand; (de fête foraine, de kermesse) stall; **s. d'exposition** exhibition stand **2** Mil & (loisir) **s. (de tir)** (shooting) range **3** Sport **s. (de ravitaillement)** pit **4** (de machine à écrire, de calculatrice) stand, rest

standard [stɑ̃dar] ADJ **1** (normalisé → modèle, pièce, prix, taille) standard (avant n) **2** (non original → discours, goûts) commonplace, unoriginal, standard **3** Ling standard

NM **1** Com & Ind standard **2** Écon **s. de vie** living standard **3** Tél switchboard **4** Mus (jazz) standard

standardisation [stɑ̃dardizasjɔ̃] NF standardization, standardizing

standardiser [3] [stɑ̃dardize] VT (normaliser, uniformiser) to standardize

standardiste [stɑ̃dardist] NMF (switchboard) operator

stand-by [stɑ̃dbaj] ADJ INV **1** Aviat (billet, passager, siège) standby (avant n) **2** Fin standby (avant n); **crédit s.** standby credit
   NM INV **(ticket/passager en) s.** standby (ticket/passenger)

standing [stɑ̃diŋ] NM **1** (d'une personne → position sociale) social status or standing; (→ réputation) (good) reputation, standing **2** (confort) **appartement (de) grand s.** luxury Br flat or Am apartment

stanneux, -euse [stanø, -øz] ADJ Chim stannous

stannifère [stanifεr] ADJ Chim (gén) staniferous; (alluvion) tin-bearing

stannique [stanik] ADJ Chim stannic

staphisaigre [stafizεgr] NF Bot stavesacre

staphylier [stafilje] NM Bot bladdernut

staphylin [stafilɛ̃] NM Entom rove beetle

staphylococcie [stafilɔkɔksi] NF staphylococcia

staphylocoque [stafilɔkɔk] NM staphylococcus; **s. doré** staphylococcus aureus

star [star] NF **1** Cin (film) star; Mus & Théât star; **en une semaine, elle était devenue une s.** within a week, she'd risen to stardom **2** (du monde politique, sportif) star; **la s. du football français** the star of French football **3** (favorite) number one; **la s. des routières de la décennie** the top touring car of the decade **4** Mktg (produit) star

Stara Planina [staraplanina] NF **la S.** the Stara Planina, the Balkan Mountains

starets [starεts] NM Hist starets

starie [stari] NF Naut **jours de s.** lay days

starisation [starizasjɔ̃] NF **la s. de qn** making sb into a star

stariser [3] [starize] VT to make a star of, to bring to stardom

starking [starkin] NF starking (apple)

starlette [starlεt] NF starlet

staroste [starɔst] NM Hist starosta

starsky [starski] NM Fam cop, Am flatfoot

star-system [starsistεm] (pl **star-systems**) NM Cin, Mus & Théât star system

starter [startεr] NM **1** Aut choke; **mettre le s.** to pull the choke out; **enlever le s.** to push in the choke; **j'ai roulé avec le s.** I drove with the choke out **2** Sport starter; **les chevaux sont sous les ordres du s.** the horses are under starter's orders

starting-block [startinblɔk] (pl **starting-blocks**) NM starting block

starting-gate [startingεt] (pl **starting-gates**) NM ou NF starting gate

start-up [startœp] (pl **start-ups**) NF start-up

stase [staz] NF Méd stasis

statère [statεr] NM Antiq stater

stathouder [statudεr] NM Hist stadtholder

statice [statis] NM ou NF Bot statice

statif [statif] NM (de microscope, d'accessoires de laboratoire) stand

statine [statin] NF Pharm statin

station [stasjɔ̃] NF **1** Transp **s. d'autobus** bus stop; **s. de métro** Br underground or Am subway station; **s. de taxis** taxi Br rank or Am stand
   2 (centre) **s. agronomique** agricultural research station; **s. d'épuration** sewage treatment plant; **s. de lavage** carwash; **s. météorologique** weather station; **s. de pompage** (de pétrole) pumping station
   3 Rad, TV & Tél station; **s. de base** base station; **s. d'écoute** monitoring station; **s. émettrice** broadcasting station, transmitting station; **s. d'émission** broadcasting station, transmitting station; **s. extérieure** outstation; **s. généraliste** general-interest station; **s. musicale** music station; **s. périphérique** private radio station; **s. de radio** radio station; **s. de radio locale** local radio station; **s. satellite** satellite station, outstation; **s. de télévision** television station; **s. terrestre** ground or earth station
   4 (lieu de séjour) resort; **s. d'altitude** mountain resort; **s. balnéaire** seaside resort; **s. de ski** ou

de sports d'hiver ski resort; **s. thermale** (thermal) spa; **s. verte** = rural tourist centre

5 *Ordinat (d'un réseau)* station, node; **s. d'accueil** docking station; **s. de travail** workstation

6 *(position)* posture; **s. verticale** upright position; **la s. debout est déconseillée** standing is not advisable

7 *(pause)* stop; **j'ai dû faire de longues stations avant d'arriver au sommet** I had to make long rest stops before reaching the summit; **faire de longues stations devant les magasins** to stop for long periods in front of shops; **les stations du chemin de croix** the Stations of the Cross

8 *Astron (d'une planète)* stationary point

9 *Astron (engin spatial)* **s. orbitale** orbital station; **s. spatiale** space station

10 *Belg (gare)* station

station-aval [stasjɔaval] *(pl* **stations-aval)** NF *(en astronautique)* down-range station

stationnaire [stasjɔnɛr] ADJ **1** *Math & Biol* stationary; *Astron* **théorie de l'état** *ou* **de l'Univers s.** steady-state theory **2** *Méd (état)* stable **3** *Phys (phénomène)* stable; *(onde)* stationary, standing; *(état)* stationary
▪ NM *Naut* station ship

stationnement [stasjɔnmã] NM **1** *(arrêt)* parking; **s. bilatéral** parking on both sides of the road; **s. en double file** double-parking; **s. unilatéral** parking on one side (only); **s. payant** parking fee payable; **s. interdit** *(sur panneau → gén)* no parking; *(→ devant une gare)* no waiting; **s. gênant** *(sur panneau)* ≃ restricted parking

2 *Can (parc de stationnement)* Br car park, Am parking lot

▫ **en stationnement** ADJ **1** *(véhicule)* parked
2 *Mil* stationed

stationner [3] [stasjɔne] VI **1** *(véhicule)* to be parked; **une voiture stationnait en double file** a car was double-parked

2 *Mil* **les troupes stationnées en Allemagne** troops stationed in Germany

3 *(rester sur place → personne)* to stay, to remain; **ne pas s. devant la sortie** *(sur panneau)* keep exit clear; **défense de s.** *(sur panneau → gén)* no parking; *(→ devant une gare)* no waiting; **la police empêche les manifestants de s. devant l'ambassade** the police are making the demonstrators move on from outside the embassy

station-service [stasjɔsɛrvis] *(pl* **stations-service)** NF service station, filling station, Br petrol station, Am gas station

station-sol [stasjɔsɔl] *(pl* **stations-sol)** NF *Rad* ground station

statique [statik] ADJ **1** *(immobile)* static; **tu es trop s. dans cette scène** you don't move around enough during the scene **2** *(inchangé)* static, unimaginative; **une politique s.** an unimaginative policy **3** *Élec* static
▪ NF statics *(singulier)*

statiquement [statikmã] ADV statically

statisme [statism] NM static state *or* character

statisticien, -enne [statistisjɛ̃, -ɛn] NM,F statistician

statistique [statistik] ADJ statistical
▪ NF **1** *(étude)* statistics *(singulier)* **2** *(donnée)* statistic; **des statistiques** statistics, a set of figures; **statistiques corrigées des variations saisonnières** seasonally adjusted statistics; **statistiques démographiques** demographics; **statistiques désaisonnalisées** seasonally adjusted statistics

statistiquement [statistikmã] ADV statistically

statocyste [statɔsist] NM *Anat* statocyst

stator [statɔr] NM stator

statoréacteur [statɔreaktœr] NM *Aviat* ramjet (engine)

statthalter [statalter, ʃtatalter] NM *Hist* = governor of Alsace-Lorraine from 1879 to 1918

statuaire [statɥɛr] ADJ statuary
▪ NMF sculptor, f sculptress
▪ NF statuary

statue [staty] NF *Beaux-Arts* statue; **la s. de la Liberté** the Statue of Liberty; **s. équestre** equestrian statue; **s. en pied** *ou* **pédestre** standing *or* pedestrian statue; **droit** *ou* **raide comme une s.** stiff as a poker; *Fig* **s. de sel** pillar of salt; **la réponse de son père l'a changée en s. de sel** her father's reply rooted her to the spot

statue-colonne [statykɔlɔn] *(pl* **statues-colonnes)** NF *Beaux-Arts* pillar-statue

statuer [7] [statɥe] VT to rule; **le tribunal a statué qu'il y avait eu faute** the court ruled that misconduct had taken place

▫ **statuer sur** VT IND **s. sur un litige** to rule on a lawsuit; **la cour n'a pas statué sur le fond** the court pronounced no judgement *or* gave no ruling on the merits of the case

statuette [statɥɛt] NF statuette

statufier [9] [statyfje] VT **1** *(représenter en statue)* to erect a statue of *or* to **2** *(faire un éloge excessif de)* to lionize **3** *Littéraire (pétrifier)* to petrify; **statufié par la peur** transfixed with fear, petrified

statu quo [statykwo] NM INV *(état actuel des choses)* status quo; **maintenir le s.** to maintain the status quo

stature [statyr] NF **1** *(carrure)* stature; **de haute s.** very tall **2** *(envergure)* stature, calibre; **son frère est d'une autre s.** his/her brother is in a different league (altogether)

staturo-pondéral, -e, -aux, -ales [statyrɔpɔ̃deral, -o] ADJ with regard to height and weight

statut [staty] NM *(état)* status; **mon s. de femme mariée** my status as a married woman; **avoir le s. de cadre/de fonctionnaire** to have executive/civil servant status; **s. juridique** *ou* **légal** legal status; **s. personnel** personal status; **s. réel** real status; **s. social** social status; **il réclame le s. de réfugié politique** he is asking for political refugee status

▫ **statuts** NMPL *(règlements)* statutes, articles of association, Am bylaws; **statuts et règlements** rules and regulations

statutaire [statytɛr] ADJ **1** *(conforme aux statuts)* statutory **2** *(désigné par les statuts → gérant)* registered

statutairement [statytɛrmã] ADV statutorily

staurotide [stɔrɔtid] NF *Minér* staurolite

Stavisky [staviski] NPR **l'affaire S.** the Stavisky case

stayer [stɛjœr] NM *Cyclisme (derrière une moto)* long-distance cyclist; *Courses de chevaux* stayer

St Christophe [sɛ̃kristɔf] N *Géog* St Kitt's

Ste *(abrév écrite* **sainte)** St., St

Sté *(abrév écrite* **société)** Co; **S. Leroux** Leroux

Steadicam® [stɛdikam] NM *Cin & TV* Steadicam®

steak [stɛk] NM steak; **s. frites** steak and chips; **un s. haché** a burger, Am a hamburger, Br a beefburger; **s. au poivre** pepper steak; **s. tartare** steak tartare

steamer [stimœr] NM *Vieilli Naut* steamer

stéarate [stearat] NM *Chim* stearate

stéarine [stearin] NF *Chim* stearin

stéarique [stearik] ADJ *Chim* stearic; **acide s.** stearic *or* stearin *or* stearine acid

stéatite [steatit] NF *Minér* steatite, soapstone

stéatopyge [steatɔpiʒ] ADJ steatopygic

stéatopygie [steatɔpiʒi] NF steatopygia

stéatose [steatoz] NF *Méd* steatosis

steenbok [stɛnbɔk] NM *Zool* steenbok, steinbok

steeple [stipl], **steeple-chase** [stipəltʃɛz] *(pl* **steeple-chases)** NM steeplechase

stéganographie [steganografi] NF *Tech* steganography

stégocéphale [stegosefal] NM stegocephalian

stégomyie [stegɔmii] NF *Entom* aedes

stégosaure [stegozɔr] NM stegosaurus

steinbock [stɛnbɔk] = **steenbok**

stèle [stɛl] NF stele

stellage [stelaʒ] NM *Bourse* put and call option, double option

stellaire [steler] ADJ **1** *Astron* stellar **2** *Anat (ganglion)* stellate
▪ NF *Bot* stitchwort, starwort

Stellite® [stelit] NM Stellite

stem, stemm [stɛm] NM *Ski* stem (turn)

stemmate [stemat] NM *Entom* stemma

stencil [stɛnsil] NM stencil

stendhalien, -enne [stɛ̃daljɛ̃, -ɛn] ADJ Stendhalian

sténo [steno] NMF shorthand note-taker, Am stenographer
▪ NF shorthand; **prendre une lettre en s.** to take down a letter in shorthand

sténodactylo [stenɔdaktilo] NMF *(personne)* Br shorthand typist, Am stenographer
▪ NF *(activité)* Br shorthand typing, Am stenography

sténodactylographie [stenɔdaktilɔgrafi] NF Br shorthand typing, Am stenography

sténogramme [stenɔgram] NM logogram, logograph

sténographe [stenɔgraf] NMF shorthand note-taker, Am stenographer; **s. judiciaire** court reporter

sténographie [stenɔgrafi] NF shorthand

sténographier [9] [stenɔgrafje] VT to take down in shorthand; **notes sténographiées** shorthand notes, notes in shorthand

sténographique [stenɔgrafik] ADJ shorthand *(avant n)*

sténographiquement [stenɔgrafikmã] ADV stenographically

sténohalin, -e [stenɔalɛ̃, -in] ADJ *Écol* stenohaline

sténopé [stenope] NM *Phot* pinhole

sténose [stenoz] NF *Méd* stricture, stenosis

sténotherme [stenɔtɛrm] ADJ *Écol* stenothermal, stenothermic

sténotype [stenɔtip] NF Stenotype®

sténotyper [3] [stenɔtipe] VT to take down on a Stenotype®

sténotypie [stenɔtipi] NF stenotypy

sténotypiste [stenɔtipist] NMF stenotypist

Stentor [stãtɔr] NPR *Myth* Stentor

stentor [stãtɔr] NM *Zool* stentor

step [stɛp] NM step (aerobics)

stéphanois, -e [stefanwa, -az] ADJ of/from Saint-Étienne
▫ **Stéphanois, -e** NM,F = inhabitant of or person from Saint-Étienne

steppage [stepaʒ] NM *Méd* steppage

steppe [stɛp] NF steppe

stepper, steppeur [stɛpœr] NM *(matériel de gymnastique)* stepper

steppique [stepik] ADJ steppe *(avant n)*

stéradian [steradjã] NM *Géom* steradian

stercoraire [stɛrkɔrɛr] ADJ *Méd* stercoraceous
▪ NM **1** *Entom* dung beetle **2** *Orn* skua

stercoral, -e, -aux, -ales [stɛrkɔral, -o] ADJ *Méd* stercoral

sterculiacée [stɛrkyljase] NF *Bot* sterculia
▫ **sterculiacées** NFPL Sterculiaceae

stère [stɛr] NM stere *(cubic metre of wood)*

stéréo [stereo] ADJ INV stereo
▪ NF **1** *(procédé)* stereo **2** *Fam (récepteur)* stereo
▫ **en stéréo** ADJ stereo *(avant n)* ADV in stereo

stéréochimie [stereɔʃimi] NF *Chim* stereochemistry

stéréochimique [stereɔʃimik] ADJ *Chim* stereochemical

stéréocomparateur [stereɔkɔ̃paratœr] NM stereocomparator

stéréognosie [stereɔgnozi] NF stereognosis

stéréogramme [stereɔgram] NM stereogram

stéréographique [stereɔgrafik] ADJ stereographic, stereographical

stéréo-isomère [stereɔizɔmɛr] *(pl* **stéréo-isomères)** *Chim* ADJ stereoisometric
▪ NM stereoisomer

stéréo-isomérie [stereɔizɔmeri] *(pl* **stéréo-isoméries)** NF *Chim* stereoisomerism

stéréométrie [stereɔmetri] NF stereometry

stéréométrique [stereɔmetrik] ADJ stereometric

stéréophonie [stereɔfoni] NF stereophony
▫ **en stéréophonie** ADJ stereo *(avant n)* ADV in stereo, in stereophonic sound

stéréophonique [stereɔfonik] ADJ stereophonic

stéréophotographie [stereɔfotografi] NF 3-D photography, stereophotography

stéréorégularité [stereɔregylarite] NF *Chim* stereoregularity

stéréorégulier, -ère [stereɔregylje, -ɛr] ADJ *Chim* stereoregular

stéréoscope [stereɔskɔp]ɴᴍ stereoscope
stéréoscopie [stereɔskɔpi]ɴꜰ stereoscopy
stéréoscopique [stereɔskɔpik]ᴀᴅᴊ stereoscopic
stéréospécificité [stereɔspesifisite]ɴꜰ Chim stereospecificity
stéréospécifique [stereɔspesifik] ᴀᴅᴊ stereospecific
stéréotaxie [stereɔtaksi]ɴꜰ stereotaxis
stéréotaxique [stereɔtaksik]ᴀᴅᴊ stereotaxic
stéréotomie [stereɔtɔmi]ɴꜰ stereotomy
stéréotomique [stereɔtɔmik]ᴀᴅᴊ stereotomic
stéréotype [stereɔtip]ɴᴍ **1** (formule banale) stereotype, cliché **2** Typ stereotype
stéréotypé, -e [stereɔtipe] ᴀᴅᴊ (comportement) stereotyped; (tournure) clichéd, hackneyed
stéréotypie [stereɔtipi]ɴꜰ stereotypy
stéréovision [stereɔvizjɔ̃]ɴꜰ stereovision
stérer [18] [stere] ᴠᴛ **1** (mesurer) to divide into steres **2** (entasser) to stack in steres
stéride [sterid]ɴᴍ Chim sterid, steroid
stérile [steril] ᴀᴅᴊ **1** (femme) infertile, sterile, barren; (homme) sterile; (mariage) childless; (sol) barren; (végétal) sterile
  2 (improductif → artiste) unproductive; (→ imagination) barren, infertile; (→ hypothèse) unproductive, vain; (→ rêve) vain, hopeless; (→ discussion, effort) vain, fruitless
  3 Méd (aseptique) sterile, sterilized
  4 Mines & Minér dead
  ɴᴍ Mines & Minér dead ground
  ❑ **stériles** ɴᴍᴘʟ Géol deads, waste rock
stérilement [sterilmɑ̃] ᴀᴅᴠ Littéraire (vainement) fruitlessly
stérilet [sterilɛ]ɴᴍ Méd IUD, coil; **se faire poser/enlever un s.** to have a coil put in/taken out
stérilisant, -e [steriliză, -ɑ̃t] ᴀᴅᴊ **1** (procédure, technique) sterilizing **2** (idéologie, mode de vie) numbing, brain-numbing
  ɴᴍ sterilant
stérilisateur [sterilizatœr]ɴᴍ sterilizer
stérilisation [sterilizasjɔ̃] ɴꜰ **1** (action de rendre infécond) sterilization **2** (désinfection) sterilization **3** Littéraire (de la créativité) stifling
stérilisé, -e [sterilize]ᴀᴅᴊ sterilized
stériliser [3] [sterilize] ᴠᴛ **1** (rendre infécond) to sterilize **2** (rendre aseptique) to sterilize **3** (appauvrir, tuer → créativité) to stifle
stérilité [sterilite] ɴꜰ **1** (d'une femme) sterility, infertility, barrenness; (d'un homme) infertility, sterility; (d'un sol) barrenness **2** (de l'imagination) barrenness; (d'une discussion, d'efforts) fruitlessness, futility **3** Méd (asepsie) sterility
stérique [sterik]ᴀᴅᴊ Chim steric
Stéristrip® [steristrip]ɴᴍ Méd Steristrip®
sterlet [stɛrlɛ]ɴᴍ sterlet
sterling [stɛrliŋ]ᴀᴅᴊ ɪɴᴠ sterling
  ɴᴍ ɪɴᴠ sterling
sternal, -e, -aux, -ales [stɛrnal, -o] ᴀᴅᴊ Anat sternal
sterne [stɛrn]ɴꜰ Orn tern; **s. arctique** Arctic tern; **s. caugek** sandwich tern; **s. de Dougall** roseate tern; **s. naine** little tern; **s. pierregarin** common tern
sternite [stɛrnit]ɴᴍ Zool sternite
sterno-claviculaire [stɛrnɔklavikylɛr] (pl **sterno-claviculaires**) ᴀᴅᴊ Anat sterno-clavicular
sterno-cléido-mastoïdien [stɛrnɔkleidɔmastɔidjɛ̃] (pl **sterno-cléido-mastoïdiens**) Anat ᴀᴅᴊ sternocleidomastoid
  ɴᴍ sternocleidomastoid muscle
sterno-costal, -e [stɛrnɔkɔstal] (mpl **sterno-costaux** [-o], fpl **sterno-costales**) ᴀᴅᴊ Anat sterno-costal
sternum [stɛrnɔm] ɴᴍ **1** Anat breastbone, Spéc sternum **2** Orn sternum
sternutation [stɛrnytasjɔ̃]ɴꜰ Physiol sternutation
sternutatoire [stɛrnytatwar] ᴀᴅᴊ sternutatory; **poudre s.** sneezing powder
stéroïde [sterɔid] Pharmᴀᴅᴊ steroidal
  ɴᴍ steroid; **stéroïdes anabolisants** anabolic steroids
stéroïdien, -enne [sterɔidjɛ̃, -ɛn], **stéroïdique** [sterɔidik] Pharm steroid (avant n), steroidal
stérol [sterɔl]ɴᴍ Chim sterol
stertoreux, -euse [stɛrtɔrø, -øz] ᴀᴅᴊ Méd stertorous
stéthoscope [stetɔskɔp]ɴᴍ Méd stethoscope
stéthoscopie [stetɔskɔpi]ɴꜰ Méd stethoscopy

stéthoscopique [stetɔskɔpik] ᴀᴅᴊ Méd stethoscopic
steward [stiwart] ɴᴍ (à bord d'un avion, d'un paquebot) steward
St George's [sɛ̃dʒɔrʒiz]ɴᴍ Géog St George's
sthénique [stenik]ᴀᴅᴊ Méd sthenic
St-Kitts-et-Nevis [sɛ̃kitsenɛvis] ɴᴍ St Kitts and Nevis
Stib [stib] ɴꜰ Belg (abrév **Société des transports intercommunaux de Bruxelles**) = Brussels transport authority
stibié, -e [stibje] ᴀᴅᴊ Pharm impregnated with antimony, stibiated; **tartre s.** tartrate emetic, tartar emetic
stibine [stibin]ɴꜰ Pharm **1** (nom générique) stibine **2** (sulfure d'antimoine) stibnite
stick [stik]ɴᴍ **1** (de colle) stick; **déodorant en s.** stick deodorant **2** Sport (au hockey) (hockey) stick; (de cavalier) (riding) stick; (de parachutistes) stick **3** Fam Arg drogue (de marijuana) (thin) joint or Br spliff
sticker [stikœr]ɴᴍ sticker
stigma [stigma]ɴᴍ Zool (tache) eyespot, stigma
stigmate [stigmat]ɴᴍ **1** Méd mark, Spéc stigma **2** (marque) **porter les stigmates de la guerre** to bear the cruel marks of war; **porter les stigmates de la débauche** to bear the signs of debauchery **3** Hist (châtiment) brand **4** Bot (tache) eyespot, stigma **5** Entom (respiratory) stigma
  ❑ **stigmates** ɴᴍᴘʟ Rel stigmata
stigmatique [stigmatik]ᴀᴅᴊ stigmatic
stigmatisation [stigmatizasjɔ̃] ɴꜰ stigmatization, stigmatizing
stigmatisé, -e [stigmatize] Relᴀᴅᴊ stigmatized
  ɴᴍ,ꜰ stigmatized person
stigmatiser [3] [stigmatize] ᴠᴛ **1** (dénoncer) to stigmatize, to condemn, to pillory **2** Littéraire (marquer → condamné) to brand, to stigmatize
stigmatisme [stigmatism]ɴᴍ stigmatism
stigmomètre [stigmɔmɛtr]ɴᴍ Phot stigmometer
stilbène [stilbɛn]ɴᴍ Chim stilbene
stilbœstrol [stilbøstrɔl]ɴᴍ Biol & Chim stilboestrol
stilligoutte [stiligut]ɴᴍ dropper
stilton [stiltɔn]ɴᴍ Stilton
stimulant, -e [stimylă, -ɑ̃t] ᴀᴅᴊ **1** (fortifiant → climat) bracing, stimulating; (→ boisson) stimulant (avant n) **2** (encourageant → résultat, paroles) encouraging
  ɴᴍ **1** (remontant, tonique) stimulant **2** (pour relancer) stimulus, spur **3** (pour encourager) incentive; **stimulants de la production** production incentives; Mktg **stimulants de vente** sales incentives
stimulateur, -trice [stimylatœr, -tris]ᴀᴅᴊ stimulative
  ɴᴍ Méd stimulator; **s. (cardiaque)** pacemaker
stimulation [stimylasjɔ̃] ɴꜰ **1** Chim, Physiol & Psy stimulation, stimulus; **stimulations sensorielles** sensory stimulation or stimuli
  2 (d'une fonction organique) stimulation; **pour la s. de leur appétit** to stimulate or to whet their appetite
  3 (incitation) stimulus; (encouragement) incentive; **s. financière** cash incentive; **une parole gentille peut être une s. efficace** a kind word can work wonders
  4 Méd **s. électrique fonctionnelle** functional electrical stimulation, FES
stimulatrice [stimylatris] voir **stimulateur**
stimuler [3] [stimyle] ᴠᴛ **1** (activer → fonction organique) to stimulate; **s. l'appétit** to stimulate or to whet the appetite; **s. la croissance des plantes** to encourage or to stimulate the growth of plants
  2 (enflammer → sentiment) to stimulate; **les difficultés stimulent l'imagination** difficulties stimulate the imagination
  3 (encourager → personne) to encourage, to motivate; **s. les élèves par des récompenses** to motivate pupils by a system of rewards; **il faut sans arrêt le s.** you have to keep prodding him
  4 (intensifier → activité) to stimulate; **s. l'industrie/l'économie/la demande** to stimulate industry/the economy/demand
stimuline [stimylin]ɴꜰ stimulin
stimulus [stimylys] (pl inv ou **stimuli** [-li]) ɴᴍ

stimulus; Psy **s. conditionnel** conditioned stimulus; **s. inconditionnel** unconditioned stimulus
stipe [stip]ɴᴍ Bot stipe
stipendié, -e [stipɑ̃dje] ᴀᴅᴊ Littéraire Péj venal, corrupt
stipendier [9] [stipɑ̃dje] ᴠᴛ Littéraire Péj (mercenaire, tueur) to hire; (homme politique, fonctionnaire) to bribe, to buy
stipulant, -e [stipylă, -ɑ̃t] Jurᴀᴅᴊ stipulatory
  ɴᴍ,ꜰ stipulator
stipulation [stipylasjɔ̃] ɴꜰ **1** (spécification) stipulation, stipulating **2** Jur stipulation; **s. pour autrui** third-party provision; **s. particulière** special provision
stipule [stipyl]ɴꜰ Bot stipule
stipuler [3] [stipyle] ᴠᴛ **1** Jur to stipulate
  2 (spécifier) to stipulate, to specify; **la circulaire stipule que l'augmentation sera appliquée à partir du mois prochain** the circular stipulates that the rise will be applicable as from next month; **j'avais bien stipulé que j'en voulais deux** I'd made it clear I wanted two of them; **ils ont bien fait s. cette condition dans l'accord** they made very sure that this condition was clearly stated in the agreement
St John's [sɛ̃dʒɔnz]ɴᴍ Géog St John's
St Martin, St Maarten [sɛ̃martɛ̃] ɴᴍ Géog St Martin, St Maarten
STO [ɛsteo] ɴᴍ Hist (abrév **service du travail obligatoire**) = compulsory labour service during the Second World War for which French workers were sent to Germany
stochastique [stɔkastik]ᴀᴅᴊ Math stochastic
stock [stɔk]ɴᴍ **1** Com stock; Écon stock, supply; Compta **stocks** stock, Am inventory; **dans la limite des stocks disponibles** while stocks last, subject to availability; **constituer des stocks** to build up stocks; **épuiser les stocks** to deplete or exhaust stocks; **s. d'alerte** minimum stock level; **stocks excédentaires** surplus stock; **s. existant** stock in hand; **s. final** closing stock; **s. d'or** (d'une banque d'État) gold reserve; **s. d'ouverture** opening stock; **stocks de réserve** stockpile; **s. de sécurité** safety stock; **s. stratégique** perpetual inventory; **s. tampon** buffer stock
  2 (réserve personnelle) stock, collection, supply; **tu peux prendre des confitures, j'en ai tout un s.** you can take some jam, I've got plenty of it or a whole stock of it; **faire des stocks (de)** to stock up (on)
  3 Biol stock
  ❑ **en stock** ᴀᴅᴊ (marchandise) in stockᴀᴅᴠ **avoir qch en s.** to have sth in stock; **nous n'avons plus de shampooing en s.** we're out of shampoo, Com shampoo is out of stock
stockage [stɔkaʒ]ɴᴍ **1** (constitution d'un stock → gén) stocking (up); (→ en grande quantité) stockpiling, building up of stocks **2** (conservation → d'énergie, d'informations, de liquides, d'armes) storage **3** Tech storage; **s. dynamique** flow storage **4** Ordinat storage; **s. de données** data storage
stock-car [stɔkkar] (pl **stock-cars**) ɴᴍ (voiture) stock car; (course) stock car racing; **faire du s.** to go stock car racing
stocker [3] [stɔke] ᴠᴛ **1** (s'approvisionner en) to stock up on; (avoir → en réserve) to (keep in) stock; (→ en grande quantité) to stockpile **2** Ordinat to store
stockfisch [stɔkfiʃ] ɴᴍ **1** (poisson) stockfish **2** (morue) dried cod
Stockholm [stɔkɔlm]ɴᴍ Stockholm
stockiste [stɔkist] ɴᴍꜰ Com stockist, Am dealer; Aut dealer, agent
stock-option [stɔkɔpsjɔ̃] (pl **stock-options**) ɴꜰ stock option
stock-outil [stɔkuti] (pl **stocks-outils**)ɴᴍ running stock or stocks
stock-shot [stɔkʃɔt] (pl **stock-shots**) ɴᴍ archive footage
stœchiométrie [stekjɔmetri] ɴꜰ Chim stoichiometry
stœchiométrique [stekjɔmetrik] ᴀᴅᴊ Chim stoichiometric
stoeffer[1] [stufœr]ɴᴍ Belg show-off
stoeffer[2] [3] [stufe]ᴠɪ Belg to show off
stoemelin [stuməliŋ], **stoemeling** [stuməliŋk],

stoemelings [stuməliŋks] **en stoemelin** ADV *Belg* on the sly *or* quiet

stoemp [stump] NM*Belg Culin* = mashed potatoes and vegetables

stoïcien, -enne [stɔisjɛ̃, -ɛn] ADJ **1** *Phil* Stoic **2** *Littéraire (impassible)* stoic, stoical NM,F*Phil* Stoic

stoïcisme [stɔisism] NM**1** *(impassibilité)* stoicism **2** *Phil* Stoicism

stoïque [stɔik] ADJstoical NM,Fstoic

stoïquement [stɔikmɑ̃] ADVstoically

stoker [stɔkɛr, stɔkœr] NM*Rail* (mechanical) stoker

stokes [stɔks] NM*Arch Phys* stokes

stol [stɔl] NM INV *Aviat (abrév* **short take-off and landing**) STOL

stolon [stɔlɔ̃] NM**1** *Bot* runner, *Spéc* stolon **2** *Zool* stolon

stolonifère [stɔlɔnifɛr] ADJ*Bot* stoloniferous

stomacal, -e, -aux, -ales [stɔmakal, -o] ADJ stomach *(avant n)*, gastric

stomachique [stɔmaʃik] ADJ stomachic, stomachical

stomate [stɔmat] NM*Bot* stoma

stomatite [stɔmatit] NF*Méd* stomatitis

stomatogastrique [stɔmatɔgastrik] ADJstomatogastric

stomatologie [stɔmatɔlɔʒi] NFstomatology

stomatologiste [stɔmatɔlɔʒist], **stomatologue** [stɔmatɔlɔg] NMFstomatologist

stomatoplastie [stɔmatɔplasti] NFstomatoplasty

stomie [stɔmi] NF*Méd* ostomy

stomisé, -e [stɔmize] *Méd* ADJostomy *(avant n)* NM,Fostomate

stomocordé [stɔmɔkɔrde] *Zool* NMmember of the Hemichordata
◻ **stomocordés** NMPLHemichordata

stomoxe [stɔmɔks] NM*Entom* stable fly

stonba [stɔba] NF*Fam* scuffle, *Br* punch-up, *Am* slugfest

stone [stɔn], **stoned** [stɔnd] ADJ*Fam* stoned

stop [stɔp] NM**1** *(panneau)* stop sign
2 *(lumière)* brake light, stoplight
3 *Fam (auto-stop)* hitching, hitchhiking ■; **faire du s.** to hitch, to thumb *Br* a lift *or Am* ride; **je suis descendu à Nice en s.** I hitched *or* hitchhiked to Nice
4 *(dans un télégramme)* stop
EXCLAMstop!; **j'ai dit s.!** I said that's enough!; **il faut savoir dire s.** you have to learn to say enough is enough; **tu me diras s. – s.!** *(en versant à boire)* say when – when!

stop-and-go [stɔpɛndgo] NM INV *Écon* stop-and-go method

stoppage [stɔpaʒ] NM*Tex* invisible mending

stopper[1] [stɔpɛr] NM *Belg Ftbl* stopper, centre back

stopper[2] [stɔpe] VT**1** *(train, voiture)* to stop, to bring to a halt; *(engin, maladie)* to stop; *(développement, processus, production)* to stop, to halt; *(pratique)* to put a stop to, to stop **2** *Tex* to mend *(using invisible mending)*
VI *(marcheur, véhicule, machine, processus, production)* to stop, to come to a halt *or* standstill; **la voiture a stoppé net** the car stopped dead

stoppeur, -euse [stɔpœr, -øz] NM,F**1** *Fam (en voiture)* hitcher, hitchhiker ■ **2** *Ftbl* stopper, centre back **3** *Tex* invisible mender

stop-vente [stɔpvɑ̃t] NF*Bourse* stop-loss selling

storax [stɔraks] NM*Bot* storax

store [stɔr] NM*(intérieur)* blind; *(extérieur → d'un magasin)* awning; **s. vénitien** Venetian blind

storiste [stɔrist] NMF**1** *(fabricant)* blind manufacturer **2** *(commerçant)* blind seller

story-board [stɔribɔrd] *(pl* **story-boards**) NM*TV & Cin* storyboard

stot [stɔt] NM *Mines (de surface)* crown pillar; *(de fond)* barrier pillar

stouffer [stufɔr] NM*Belg* show-off

stoupa [stupa] NM*Rel* stupa

stout [stawt] NM*(bière)* stout

stp *(abrév écrite* **s'il te plaît**) please

strabique [strabik] ADJ *Opt* strabismic, strabismal, strabismical

strabisme [strabism] NM*Opt* squint, *Spéc* strabismus; **elle a un léger s.** she has a slight squint; **s.**

convergent esotropia, convergent strabismus; **s. divergent** exotropia, divergent strabismus

stradiot [stradjo] NM*Hist & Mil* Estradiot

stradivarius [stradivarjys] NMStradivarius

stramoine [stramwan] NF *Bot* thorn apple, *Spéc* stramonium

strangulation [strɑ̃gylasjɔ̃] NF strangulation, strangling *(UNCOUNT)*; **il est mort par s.** he died by strangulation, he was strangled to death

strangurie [strɑ̃gyri] NF*Méd* strangury

strapontin [strapɔ̃tɛ̃] NM**1** *(siège)* jump *or* folding seat **2** *(locutions)* **avoir un s.** to hold a minor position; **elle n'a obtenu qu'un s. au conseil** she was given only minor responsibilities on the board

strapping [strapiŋ] NM*Méd* strapping

stras [stras] = **strass**

Strasbourg [strazbur] NMStrasbourg

strasbourgeois, -e [strazburʒwa, -az] ADJ of/ from Strasbourg
◻ **Strasbourgeois, -e** NM,F = inhabitant of or person from Strasbourg

strass [stras] NM paste *(UNCOUNT)*, strass; **en s.** *(bijou)* paste

strasse [stras] NF *Tex* waste silk

stratagème [strataʒɛm] NMstratagem, ruse

strate [strat] NF **1** *Géol* stratum **2** *(niveau)* layer; **les strates de la personnalité** the layers *or* strata of the personality **3** *Bot* zone

stratège [strateʒ] NM**1** *Mil* strategist **2** *Fig* **un fin s.** a cunning strategist

stratégie [strateʒi] NF strategy; **s. de campagne** campaign strategy; **s. commerciale** business strategy; **s. de croissance** growth strategy; **s. de l'entreprise** corporate strategy; **s. d'imitation** imitation strategy, me-too strategy; **s. marketing** game plan, marketing strategy; **s. de la marque** brand strategy; **s. de pénétration** market penetration strategy; **s. de positionnement** positioning strategy; **s. publicitaire** advertising strategy; **s. pull** pull strategy; **s. push** push strategy; **s. de recrutement** recruitment strategy; **s. de retrait** exit strategy

stratégique [strateʒik] ADJ **1** *Mil* strategic, strategical **2** *Fig* **un repli s.** a strategic retreat; **matières premières stratégiques** strategic raw materials

stratégiquement [strateʒikmɑ̃] ADVstrategically

stratification [stratifikasjɔ̃] NFstratification, stratifying *(UNCOUNT)*; **la s. sociale** social stratification

stratifié, -e [stratifje] ADJ*(roches, société)* stratified; *Tech (papier, tissu)* laminated
NMlaminate

stratifier [9] [stratifje] VTto stratify

stratiforme [stratifɔrm] ADJstratiform

stratigraphie [stratigrafi] NF*Géol* stratigraphy

stratigraphique [stratigrafik] ADJ *Géol* stratigraphic, stratigraphical

stratiome [stratjɔm] NM *Entom* soldier fly, *Spéc* stratiomyid

strato-cumulus [stratɔkymylys] NM INVstratocumulus

stratoforteresse [stratɔfɔrtərɛs] NFflying fortress

stratopause [stratɔpoz] NFstratopause

stratosphère [stratɔsfɛr] NFstratosphere

stratosphérique [stratɔsferik] ADJstratospheric

stratus [stratys] NMstratus

Stravinski [stravinski] NPRStravinsky

streamé, -e [strime] ADJ*Ordinat* streamed

streamer [strimœr] NM*Ordinat* tape streamer

streaming [strimiŋ] NM *Ordinat* streaming; **s. audio/vidéo** streaming audio/video

strelitzia [strelitzja] NM*Bot* strelitzia

strepsiptère [strɛpsiptɛr] *Entom* NM member of the Strepsiptera order
◻ **strepsiptères** NMPLStrepsiptera

streptococcie [strɛptɔkɔksi] NF*Méd* streptococcicosis

streptococcique [strɛptɔkɔksik] ADJstreptococcic, streptococcal

streptocoque [strɛptɔkɔk] NMstreptococcus

streptomycine [strɛptɔmisin] NFstreptomycin

stress [strɛs] NMstress; **les maladies liées au s.** stress-related illnesses

stressant, -e [strɛsɑ̃, -ɑ̃t] ADJ stressful, stress-inducing

stressé, -e [strɛse] ADJstressed

stresser [4] [strɛse] VTto put under stress; **elle me stresse** I find her very stressful; **vivre à Paris me stresse** I find living in Paris very stressful
▸ **se stresser** VPRto get stressed

Stretch® [strɛtʃ] ADJ INV stretch *(avant n)*, stretchy; **une jupe en S.** a stretch skirt
NMstretch material

stretching [strɛtʃiŋ] NM stretching; **cours de s.** stretch class; **faire du s.** to do stretching exercises

strette [strɛt] NF*Mus* stretto

striation [strijasjɔ̃] NFstriation

strict, -e [strikt] ADJ **1** *(astreignant, précis → contrôle, ordre, règle, principe)* strict; **la loi est très stricte à ce sujet** the law's very strict on that
2 *(minimal)* strict; **le s. nécessaire** *ou* **minimum** the bare minimum; **il a le s. nécessaire pour vivre** he lives on the bare minimum; **faire le s. minimum** to do only what is strictly necessary; **les obsèques seront célébrées dans la plus stricte intimité** the funeral will take place strictly in private
3 *(sévère → éducation, personne)* strict; *(→ discipline)* strict, rigorous; **tu es trop s. avec les enfants** you're too hard on *or* too strict with the children; **ils sont très stricts sur la politesse** they're very strict about politeness
4 *(austère → intérieur, vêtement)* severe, austere; **elle est coiffée de manière très stricte** she wears her hair in a very severe style
5 *(rigoureux, absolu)* strict, absolute; **c'est ton droit le plus s.** it's your lawful right; **c'est la stricte vérité!** it's absolutely true!

strictement [striktəmɑ̃] ADV **1** *(rigoureusement)* strictly, scrupulously; **vous devez observer s. le règlement** you must obey the rules to the letter
2 *(absolument)* strictly, absolutely; **c'est s. confidentiel** it's strictly *or* highly confidential
3 *(sobrement)* severely; **sa robe s. boutonnée jusque sous le cou** her dress severely buttoned right up to the neck

striction [striksjɔ̃] NF **1** *Méd* stricture **2** *Métal* contraction, necking (down)

stricto sensu [striktosɛ̃sy] ADVstrictly speaking, *Sout* stricto sensu

stridence [stridɑ̃s] NF*Littéraire* stridence, stridency

strident, -e [stridɑ̃, -ɑ̃t] ADJ *(son, voix)* strident, shrill, piercing

strideur [stridœr] NF*Arch & Littéraire* piercing *or* strident noise

stridor [stridɔr] NM*Méd* stridor

stridulant, -e [stridylɑ̃, -ɑ̃t] ADJstridulous, stridulant

stridulation [stridylasjɔ̃] NF stridulation, stridulating

striduler [3] [stridyle] VIto stridulate

striduleux, -euse [stridylø, -øz] ADJstridulous

strie [stri] NF**1** *(sillon)* (thin) groove, *Spéc* stria **2** *(ligne de couleur)* streak **3** *Archit* stria, fillet **4** *Géol & Minér* stria

strié, -e [strije] ADJ **1** *(cannelé → roche, tige)* striated **2** *(veiné → étoffe, marbre)* streaked **3** *Anat* striated; **muscles striés** striated muscles; **corps s.** (corpus) striatum

strier [10] [strije] VT **1** *(creuser)* to striate, to groove **2** *(veiner)* to streak; **strié de bleu** streaked with blue

strige [striʒ] NFghoul

strigidé [striʒide] *Orn* NMmember of the Strigidae
◻ **strigidés** NMPLStrigidae

strigile [striʒil] NM**1** *Antiq* strigil **2** *Archéol* strigil

string [striŋ] NMG-string

strioscopie [strijɔskɔpi] NF schlieren photography

strioscopique [strijɔskɔpik] ADJschlieric

strip [strip] NM*Fam* striptease ■

stripage [stripaʒ] NM*Nucl* stripping

strip-line [striplajn] *(pl* **strip-lines**) NM *Électron* stripline

stripping [stripiŋ] NM*Méd & Pétr* stripping

strip-poker [strippɔkɛr] *(pl* **strip-pokers**) NMstrip poker

strip-tease [striptiz] *(pl* **strip-teases**) NM striptease act; **faire un s.** to do a strip-tease

strip-teaseur, -euse [striptizœr, øz] *(mpl* **strip-teaseurs**, *fpl* **strip-teaseuses**) NM,F *(homme)* male stripper; *(femme)* stripper

striure [strijyr] NF striation

strobile [strɔbil] NM **1** *Zool* strobila **2** *Bot* strobilus

stroboscope [strɔbɔskɔp] NM stroboscope, strobe (light)

stroboscopie [strɔbɔskɔpi] NF stroboscopy

stroboscopique [strɔbɔskɔpik] ADJ stroboscopic

stroma [strɔma] NM *Biol* stroma

strombe [strɔ̃b] NM *Zool (mollusque)* stromb

Stromboli [strɔ̃bɔli] NM Stromboli

strombolien, -enne [strɔ̃bɔljɛ̃, -ɛn] ADJ Strombolian

strongle [strɔ̃gl], **strongyle** [strɔ̃ʒyl] NM *Zool* strongyle

strongylose [strɔ̃ʒyloz] NF *Vét* strongyloidiasis

strontiane [strɔ̃sjan] NF *Chim* strontia

strontium [strɔ̃sjɔm] NM *Chim* strontium

strophantus [strɔfɑ̃tys] NM *Bot* strophanthus

strophe [strɔf] NF **1** *(d'un poème)* stanza **2** *(de tragédie grecque)* strophe

structurable [stryktyrabl] ADJ which can be structured

structural, -e, -aux, -ales [stryktyral, -o] ADJ structural

structuralisme [stryktyralism] NM structuralism

structuraliste [stryktyralist] ADJ structuralist
  NMF structuralist

structurant, -e [stryktyrɑ̃, -ɑ̃t] ADJ structuring

structuration [stryktyrasjɔ̃] NF *(action)* structuring; *(résultat)* structure

structure [stryktyr] NF **1** *(organisation → d'un service, d'une société, d'un texte)* structure; **votre devoir manque de s.** your essay is badly organized or structured; **réformes de s.** structural reforms; **s. de l'entreprise** corporate or company structure; **s. hiérarchique** line organization; **s. du marché** market structure; **s. des salaires** wage structure
  2 *(institution)* system, organization; **structures administratives/politiques** administrative/political structures
  3 *(ensemble de services)* facility; **structures d'accueil** reception facilities *(for recently arrived tourists, refugees etc)*
  4 *Constr* building, structure
  5 *Ling* structure; **s. profonde/superficielle** deep/surface structure
  6 *Ordinat* structure; **s. en anneau** ring structure; **s. arborescente** directory or tree structure; **s. en arbre** tree structure; **s. en étoile** star structure; **s. de fichier** file structure

structuré, -e [stryktyre] ADJ structured, organized

structurel, -elle [stryktyrɛl] ADJ structural

structurellement [stryktyrɛlmɑ̃] ADV structurally

structurer [3] [stryktyre] VT to structure, to organize; **c'est une ébauche de scénario qu'il faudrait s.** it's the idea for a scenario which needs to be given some shape
  ► **se structurer** VPR to take shape; **un parti politique qui se structure** a political party taking shape

strudel [strydɛl, ʃtrudœl] NM *Culin* **s. (aux pommes)** (apple) strudel

strume [strym] NF *Vieilli Méd* struma, goitre

strychnine [striknin] NF strychnine

strychnisme [striknism] NM *Méd* strychninism

strychnos [striknos] NM *Bot* strychnos

stryge [striʒ] = **strige**

STS [ɛstɛes] NF *(abrév* **section de technicien supérieur***)* = two-year advanced vocational course, taken after the "baccalauréat"

stuc [styk] NM stucco
  ❑ **en stuc** ADJ stucco *(avant n)*

stucage [stykaʒ] NM stucco work

stucateur [stykatœr] NM stucco worker

stud [styd] NM *Belg Ftbl (crampon)* stud; *(chaussure)* boot

stud-book [stœdbuk] *(pl* **stud-books***)* NM stud-book

student [stydɛnt] NM *Belg Fam* student▪

studette [stydɛt] NF small studio *Br* flat or *Am* apartment, *Br* bedsit

studieuse [stydjøz] *voir* **studieux**

studieusement [stydjøzmɑ̃] ADV studiously

studieux, -euse [stydjø, -øz] ADJ **1** *(appliqué → élève)* hard-working, studious **2** *(consacré à l'étude)* **une soirée studieuse** an evening of study, a studious evening; **une retraite studieuse** *(endroit)* a place of study

studio [stydjo] NM **1** *(appartement) Br* studio flat, *Am* studio apartment
  2 *Cin, TV, Mus & Rad* studio; **s. de cinéma** film studio; **s. de doublage** dubbing suite; **s. d'enregistrement** recording studio; **s. insonorisé** sound stage; **s. de postproduction** postproduction studio; **s. de télévision** television studio
  3 *(atelier → de peintre, de photographe)* studio; **s. de danse** dance studio
  4 *Belg (chambre dans un hôtel de passe)* = room rented out by prostitutes; *(hôtel de passe)* = hotel used for prostitution
  ❑ **en studio** ADV **tourné en s.** shot in studio; **scène tournée en s.** studio scene

stuka [ʃtuka] NM *Hist & Aviat* Stuka

stupa [stupa] NM *Rel* stupa

stupéfaction [stypefaksjɔ̃] NF amazement, astonishment, stupefaction; **je constate avec s. que…** I am amazed to note that…; **à ma (grande) s.** to my utter amazement

stupéfaire [109] [stypefɛr] VT to amaze, to astound, to stun

stupéfait, -e [stypefɛ, -ɛt] ADJ *(personne)* amazed, astounded, stupefied; **je suis s. de voir qu'il est revenu** I'm amazed to see he came back

stupéfiant, -e [stypefjɑ̃, -ɑ̃t] ADJ **1** *(nouvelle, réaction)* amazing, astounding, stupefying **2** *Pharm* narcotic
  NM *(drogue)* drug, narcotic

stupéfier [9] [stypefje] VT **1** *(abasourdir)* to amaze, to astound, to stun; **sa décision a stupéfié sa famille** his/her family was stunned by his/her decision **2** *Littéraire (sujet: froid, peur)* to stupefy

stupeur [stypœr] NF **1** *(ahurissement)* amazement, astonishment; **le public était plongé dans la s.** the audience was dumbfounded or stunned; **je constate avec s. que…** I am amazed to note that… **2** *Méd & Psy* stupor

stupide [stypid] ADJ **1** *(inintelligent → personne, jeu, initiative, réponse, suggestion)* stupid, silly, foolish; *(→ raisonnement)* stupid; **il eut un rire s.** he laughed stupidly **2** *(absurde → accident, mort)* stupid; **ce serait trop s. de rater le début** it'd be stupid or a shame to miss the beginning **3** *(ahuri)* stunned, dumbfounded; **je restai s. devant son aveu** his/her confession left me speechless

stupidement [stypidmɑ̃] ADV stupidly, foolishly; **rire s.** to give a stupid laugh; **mourir s.** to die a stupid death

stupidité [stypidite] NF **1** *(d'une action, d'une personne, d'un propos)* stupidity, foolishness **2** *(acte)* piece of foolish behaviour **3** *(parole)* stupid or foolish remark; **arrête de dire des stupidités!** stop talking nonsense!; **répondre par une s.** to give a stupid answer

stuporeux, -euse [stypɔrø, -øz] ADJ *Psy* stuporous

stupre [stypr] NM *Littéraire* depravity

stups [styp] NMPL *Fam* **la brigade des s., les s.** the Drug Squad

stuquer [3] [styke] VT to stucco

sturnidé [styrnide] *Orn* NM member of the Sturnidae family
  ❑ **sturnidés** NMPL Sturnidae

Stuttgart [ʃtutgart] NM Stuttgart

St-Vincent-et-les-Grenadines [sɛ̃vɛ̃sɑ̃elegrɛnadin] NM St Vincent and the Grenadines

style [stil] NM **1** *(d'un écrivain, d'un journal)* style; **dans un s. très pompeux** in a highly pompous or bombastic style; **c'est écrit dans le plus pur s. administratif/journalistique** it's written in purest bureaucratic jargon/journalese; **en s. télégraphique** in a telegraphic style; **s. maison** *(dans l'édition, le journalisme)* house style
  2 *(d'un artiste, d'un sportif)* style; **son s. de jeu** his (particular) way of playing, his style; **ce skieur a un beau s.** this skier has (a) good style
  3 *Beaux-Arts* style; **un opéra (de) s. italien** an opera in the Italian style; **s. gothique/Régence** Gothic/Regency style
  4 *(genre, ordre d'idée)* style; **dis-leur que tu vas réfléchir, ou quelque chose dans ou de ce s.** tell them you'll think about it, or something along those lines or in that vein; **une veste un peu dans le s. de la tienne** a jacket the same sort of style as yours
  5 *Fam (manière d'agir)* style; **tu aurais pu**

l'avoir dénoncé – ce n'est pas mon s. you could have informed on him – it's not my style or that's not the sort of thing I'd do; **serait-il parti sans nous prévenir? – ce n'est pas son s.** he may have gone without telling us – it's not like him; **ça serait bien son s.!** that would be just like him/her or just his/her style!
  6 *(élégance)* style, class; **avoir du s.** to have style; **elle a beaucoup de s.** she's very stylish or chic; **leur maison manque de s./a du s.** their house lacks/has style; **elle s'habille avec beaucoup de s.** she dresses very stylishly
  7 *Bot & Zool* style
  8 *(d'un cadran solaire)* style, gnomon; *(d'un cylindre enregistreur)* needle, stylus; *Antiq & Hist (poinçon)* style, stylus
  9 *(système chronologique)* **vieux/nouveau s.** Old/New Style
  10 *Zool (d'une antenne)* style, seta
  11 s. de vie lifestyle
  12 *Ling* **s. direct/indirect** direct/indirect speech; **s. indirect libre** free indirect speech
  ❑ **de style** ADJ *(meuble, objet)* period *(avant n)*; **un fauteuil de s.** a period chair

stylé, -e [stile] ADJ *(personnel)* well-trained

styler [3] [stile] VT to train

stylet [stilɛ] NM **1** *Méd* stilet, stylet **2** *(dague)* stiletto **3** *Zool* stylet

stylicien, -enne [stilisjɛ̃, -ɛn] NM,F designer

styliforme [stiliform] ADJ *Zool* styliform, stylus-shaped

stylique [stilik] NF design

stylisation [stilizasjɔ̃] NF stylization

styliser [3] [stilize] VT to stylize; **oiseau stylisé** stylized (drawing of a) bird

stylisme [stilism] NM **1** *(de mode)* fashion design; *(dans l'industrie)* industrial design **2** *(en littérature)* attention to style

styliste [stilist] NMF **1** *(de mode, dans l'industrie)* designer **2** *(auteur)* stylist

stylisticien, -enne [stilistisjɛ̃, -ɛn] NM,F expert in stylistics

stylistique [stilistik] ADJ stylistic
  NF stylistics *(singulier)*

stylite [stilit] NM *Rel* stylite; **saint Siméon S.** Saint Simeon Stylites

stylo [stilo] NM pen; **s. (à bille)** ballpoint (pen), *Br* Biro®; **s. à encre/cartouche** fountain/cartridge pen; **s. correcteur** eraser pen; *Ordinat* **s. optique** light pen

stylobate [stilɔbat] NM *Archit* stylobate

stylo-feutre [stiloføtr] *(pl* **stylos-feutres***)* NM felt-tip pen

stylographe [stilɔgraf] NM *Vieilli* fountain pen

styloïde [stilɔid] *Anat* ADJ styloid
  NF styloid process

stylo-mastoïdien, -enne [stilomastoidjɛ̃, -ɛn] *(mpl* **stylo-mastoïdiens**, *fpl* **stylo-mastoïdiennes***)* ADJ *Anat* stylomastoid

stylo-maxillaire [stilomaksilɛr] *(pl* **stylo-maxillaires***)* ADJ *Anat* stylo-maxillary

Stylomine® [stilomin] NM propelling pencil

styrax [stiraks] NM *Bot* storax, styrax; **s. benjoin** benzoin tree, benjamin tree

styrène [stirɛn] NM *Chim* styrene

Styrie [stiri] NF la S. Styria

styrolène [stirɔlɛn] NM *Chim* styrene

Styx [stiks] NM le S. the Styx

su, -e [sy] PP *voir* **savoir**
  NM **au su de qn** to the knowledge of sb; **au vu et au su de tout le monde** in front of everybody, quite openly

suage [sɥaʒ] NM sweating, oozing

suaire [sɥɛr] NM shroud

suant, -e [sɥɑ̃, -ɑ̃t] ADJ **1** *Fam (ennuyeux)* dull▪, boring▪; *(énervant)* annoying▪; **ce que tu peux être s.!** you're a pain (in the neck)! **2** *(en sueur)* sweaty

suave [sɥav] ADJ *(manières, ton)* suave, sophisticated; *(senteur)* sweet; *(teintes)* subdued, mellow; *Hum* **de sa voix s.** in his suave voice, in dulcet tones

suavement [sɥavmɑ̃] ADV suavely, smoothly

suavité [sɥavite] NF *(de manières, d'un ton)* suaveness, suavity, smoothness; *(d'une musique, de senteurs)* sweetness; *(de teintes)* mellowness

subaérien, -enne [sybaerjɛ̃, -ɛn] ADJ subaerial

subaigu, -ë [sybegy] ADJ *Méd* subacute

subalcalin [sybalkalɛ̃] NM *Chim & Géol* subalkaline

subalpin, -e [sybalpɛ̃, -in] ADJ subalpine

subalterne [sybaltɛrn] ADJ **1** *(position)* secondary; **un rôle s.** a secondary *or* minor role **2** *(personne)* subordinate, junior *(avant n)*; **j'ai eu affaire à un fonctionnaire s.** I saw a junior clerk ◾ NMF subordinate, subaltern; *Péj* underling; *Mil* subaltern (officer)

subaquatique [sybakwatik] ADJ subaquatic

subaride [sybarid] ADJ subarid

subatomique [sybatɔmik] ADJ subatomic

subcarence [sybkarɑ̃s] NF *Méd* mild deficiency

subcaudal, -e, -aux, -ales [sybkodal, -o] ADJ *Zool* subcaudal

subclaquant, -e [sybklakɑ̃, -ɑ̃t] ADJ *Fam* **être s.** to be on one's last legs, to have one foot in the grave

subconsciemment [sybkɔ̃sjamɑ̃] ADV subconsciously

subconscience [sybkɔ̃sjɑ̃s] NF subconsciousness

subconscient, -e [sybkɔ̃sjɑ̃, -ɑ̃t] ADJ subconscious ◾ NM subconscious

subculture [sybkyltyr] NF subculture

subdéléguer [18] [sybdelege] VT to subdelegate

subdésertique [sybdezɛrtik] ADJ semi-desert *(avant n)*

subdiviser [3] [sybdivize] VT to subdivide; **chapitre subdivisé en deux parties** chapter subdivided into two parts
  ▸**se subdiviser** VPR **se s. (en)** to subdivide (into)

subdivisible [sybdivizibl] ADJ subdivisible

subdivision [sybdivizjɔ̃] NF **1** *(processus)* subdivision, subdividing **2** *(catégorie)* subdivision

subdivisionnaire [sybdivizjɔnɛr] ADJ subdivisional

subduction [sybdyksjɔ̃] NF *Géol* subduction

subéquatorial, -e, -aux, -ales [sybekwatɔrjal, -o] ADJ subequatorial

suber [sybɛr] NM *Bot* suber

subérate [syberat] NM *Chim* suberate

subéreux, -euse [syberø, -øz] ADJ *Bot* cork *(avant n)*, *Spéc* subereous

subérine [syberin] NF *Chim* suberin

subérique [syberik] ADJ *Chim* suberic

subintrant, -e [sybɛ̃trɑ̃, -ɑ̃t] ADJ *Méd* subintrant

subir [32] [sybir] VT **1** *(dommages, pertes)* to suffer, to sustain; *(conséquences, défaite)* to suffer; *(attaque, humiliation, insultes, sévices)* to be subjected to, to suffer; **la maison a subi quelques dégâts pendant les orages** the house sustained some storm damage; **faire s. une punition à qn** to inflict a punishment on sb; **faire s. une torture à qn** to subject sb to torture; **après tout ce qu'elle m'a fait s.** after all she inflicted on me *or* made me go through; **il lui a fait s. les pires humiliations** he made him/her suffer *or* endure the most terrible humiliations; *Hum* **nous allons encore s. ses histoires de guerre!** we'll be subjected to his war stories yet again!
  2 *(situation, personne)* to put up with; **s. l'influence de qn** to be under sb's influence; **je ne pouvais que s. son envoûtement** I could not free myself of his/her spell; **il a l'air de s. le match** he looks as though he's just letting the match go on around him
  3 *(opération, transformation)* to undergo; **le métal subit un traitement avant d'être laminé** the metal undergoes *or* is subjected to treatment before it's laminated

subit, -e [sybi, -it] ADJ sudden

subitement [sybitmɑ̃] ADV suddenly, all of a sudden

subito [sybito] ADV **1** *Fam (tout à coup)* suddenly▪, all of a sudden▪ **2** *(locutions)* **s. presto** *Mus* subito presto; *Fam (tout de suite)* at once▪, immediately▪; **va me chercher le journal, allez, s. presto!** go and get me the paper, and make it snappy!

subjacent, -e [sybʒasɑ̃, -ɑ̃t] ADJ *Littéraire* subjacent

subjectif, -ive [sybʒɛktif, -iv] ADJ subjective

subjectile [sybʒɛktil] NM substrate

subjective [sybʒɛktiv] *voir* **subjectif**

subjectivement [sybʒɛktivmɑ̃] ADV subjectively

subjectivisme [sybʒɛktivism] NM subjectivism

subjectiviste [sybʒɛktivist] ADJ subjectivistic ◾ NMF subjectivist

subjectivité [sybʒɛktivite] NF subjectivity, subjectiveness

subjonctif, -ive [sybʒɔ̃ktif, -iv] ADJ subjunctive ◾ NM subjunctive; **au s.** in the subjunctive

subjuguer [3] [sybʒyge] VT **1** *(sujet: discours, lecture)* to enthral, to captivate; *(sujet: beauté, charme, regard)* to enthral, to beguile; *(sujet: éloquence)* to enthral; **elle le subjuguait** she held him spellbound; **je restai subjugué devant tant de grâce** I was enthralled by so much grace **2** *Vieilli Littéraire (asservir → esprits, peuple)* to subjugate

sublimable [syblimabl] ADJ *Chim* sublimable

sublimation [syblimasjɔ̃] NF **1** *(élévation morale)* sublimation, sublimating **2** *Chim & Psy* sublimation

sublimatoire [syblimatwar] ADJ sublimatory

sublime [syblim] ADJ **1** *(noble, grand)* sublime, elevated; **une beauté s.** sublime beauty **2** *(exceptionnel, parfait)* sublime, wonderful, magnificent; **tu as été s.** you were magnificent; **un repas s.** a wonderful meal; **un tableau s.** a sublime painting ◾ NM **le s.** the sublime

sublimé, -e [syblime] ADJ sublimated ◾ NM *Chim* sublimate

sublimement [syblimmɑ̃] ADV sublimely

Sublime-Porte [syblimpɔrt] NF **la S.** the (Sublime) Porte

sublimer [3] [syblime] VT **1** *Psy* to sublimate **2** *Chim* to sublimate, to sublime

subliminal, -e, -aux, -ales [sybliminal, -o], **subliminaire** [syblyminɛr] ADJ subliminal

sublimité [syblimite] NF *Littéraire* sublimeness

sublingual, -e, -aux, -ales [syblɛ̃gwal, -o] ADJ *Anat* sublingual; **comprimé s.** tablet to be placed under the tongue

sublunaire [syblynɛr] ADJ **1** *Astron* sublunary **2** *Littéraire ou Hum* pertaining to this world, mundane

subluxation [syblyksasjɔ̃] NF subluxation

submergé, -e [sybmɛrʒe] ADJ **1** *(rochers)* submerged; *(champs)* submerged, flooded **2** *(surchargé, accablé)* inundated; **s. de travail** snowed under with work; **s. de réclamations** inundated with complaints **3** *(incapable de faire face)* swamped, up to one's eyes; **depuis que ma secrétaire est partie, je suis s.** since my secretary left, I've been up to my eyes in work

submerger [17] [sybmɛrʒe] VT **1** *(inonder)* to flood, to submerge; **des villages entiers sont submergés** entire villages have been flooded *or* are under water
  2 *(envahir → sujet: angoisse, joie)* to overcome, to overwhelm; *(→ sujet: réclamations)* to inundate, to swamp; *(→ sujet: dettes)* to overwhelm, to swamp; **notre standard est submergé d'appels** our switchboard's swamped with *or* jammed by calls; **je suis submergé de travail** I'm snowed under with work; **se laisser s.** to allow oneself to be overcome
  3 *(écraser → défenseur)* to overwhelm, to overrun; **le service d'ordre fut rapidement submergé par les manifestants** the police were soon unable to contain the demonstrators

submersibilité [sybmɛrsibilite] NF submersibility

submersible [sybmɛrsibl] ADJ **1** *(bateau, moteur)* submersible **2** *Bot (plante)* submersed ◾ NM submersible

submersion [sybmɛrsjɔ̃] NF *Littéraire* submersion, submerging; **mort par s.** death by drowning

submillimétrique [sybmilimetrik] ADJ submillimetric

subodorer [3] [sybɔdɔre] VT *Hum (danger)* to smell, to sense; **je subodore un canular** I can smell a hoax

suborbital, -e, -aux, -ales [sybɔrbital, -o] ADJ *Astron* suborbital

subordination [sybɔrdinasjɔ̃] NF **1** *(dans une hiérarchie)* subordination, subordinating; **il a refusé sa s. au directeur commercial** he refused to work under the sales manager **2** *Gram* subordination
  ❑ **de subordination** ADJ **relation de s.** relation of subordination; **complément/conjonction de s.** subordinating complement/conjunction

subordonnant [sybɔrdɔnɑ̃] *Gram* ADJ subordinating ◾ NM subordinating word

subordonné, -e [sybɔrdɔne] ADJ **1** *(subalterne)* subordinate **2** *Gram* subordinate, dependent ◾ NM,F *(subalterne)* subordinate, subaltern
  ❑ **subordonnée** NF *Gram* subordinate *or* dependent clause

subordonner [3] [sybɔrdɔne] VT **1** *(hiérarchiquement)* **s. qn à** to subordinate sb to; **les statuts subordonnent le directeur au conseil d'administration** the director is answerable to the board **2** *(faire dépendre)* **s. qch à** to subordinate sth to, to make sth dependent on; **il fallait tout s. à ses désirs** his/her wishes had to come before everything else; **l'admission est subordonnée à l'obtention de la moyenne au concours** admission is subject to passing the entrance exam **3** *(faire passer après)* **s. qch à** to subordinate sth to; **je ne subordonnerai jamais mes devoirs de père à ma carrière** I'll never allow my career to come before my duties as a father **4** *Ling (proposition)* to subordinate

subornation [sybɔrnasjɔ̃] NF subornation; **s. de témoins** subornation of witnesses

suborner [3] [sybɔrne] VT **1** *Jur (témoin)* to suborn **2** *Vieilli (avec des pots-de-vin)* to bribe **3** *Littéraire (jeune fille)* to seduce

suborneur, -euse [sybɔrnœr, -øz] NM,F *Jur* suborner ◾ NM *Littéraire (séducteur)* seducer

subpolaire [sybpɔlɛr] ADJ sub-polar

subrécargue [sybrekarg] NM *Naut* supercargo

subreptice [sybrɛptis] ADJ **1** *Littéraire (manœuvre)* surreptitious, stealthy **2** *Jur* **acte s.** subreption

subrepticement [sybrɛptismɑ̃] ADV *Littéraire* surreptitiously, stealthily

subrogateur [sybrɔgatœr] ADJ M **acte s.** subrogation

subrogatif, -ive [sybrɔgatif, -iv] ADJ subrogate

subrogation [sybrɔgasjɔ̃] NF subrogation, subrogating *(UNCOUNT)*

subrogative [sybrɔgativ] *voir* **subrogatif**

subrogatoire [sybrɔgatwar] ADJ *(acte)* of subrogation; *(action)* subrogation *(avant n)*

subrogé, -e [sybrɔʒe] ADJ **1** *(remplaçant)* surrogate **2** *Jur* **s. tuteur** deputy *or* surrogate guardian ◾ NM,F *Jur* surrogate, deputy

subroger [17] [sybrɔʒe] VT to subrogate

subsaharien, -enne [sypsaarjɛ̃, -ɛn] ADJ sub-Saharan ◾ NM,F sub-Saharan

subséquemment [sypsekamɑ̃] ADV subsequently, later on

subséquent, -e [sypsekɑ̃, -ɑ̃t] ADJ **1** *Littéraire (qui suit)* subsequent **2** *Géog* **affluent s.** subsequent stream

subside [sypsid] NM *(de l'État)* grant, subsidy; **il vivait des subsides de ses parents** he lived on the allowance he received from his parents; **s. de l'État** state subsidy

subsidence [sypsidɑ̃s, sybzidɑ̃s] NF *Géol* subsidence

subsidiaire [sybzidjɛr] ADJ *(motif, ressources)* subsidiary, additional

subsidiarité [sybzidjarite] NF subsidiarity

subsidiation [sybzidjasjɔ̃] NF *Belg* subsidization

subsidier [9] [sybzidje] VT *Belg* to subsidize

subsistance [sybzistɑ̃s] NF **1** *(existence matérielle)* subsistence; **pourvoir à ou assurer la s. de qn** to support *or* to maintain *or* to keep sb; **elle arrive tout juste à assurer sa s.** she just manages to survive, she has just enough to keep body and soul together; **moyen de s.** means of support **2** *Mil* **mise en s.** secondment

subsistant, -e [sybzistɑ̃, -ɑ̃t] ADJ remaining, subsisting ◾ NM,F *(assuré social)* transferred (benefit) claimant ◾ NM *Mil (soldat)* seconded soldier; *(officier)* seconded officer

subsister [3] [sybziste] VI **1** *(demeurer → doute, espoir, rancœur, traces)* to remain, to subsist; *(→ tradition)* to live on; **plus rien ne subsiste de ces magnifiques monuments** nothing is left *or* remains of those magnificent buildings;

quelques questions subsistent auxquelles on n'a pas répondu there are still a few questions which remain unanswered
2 *(survivre)* to survive; **ces nomades trouvent à peine de quoi s. dans le désert** these nomads can barely eke out an existence in the desert; **je n'ai que 50 euros par semaine pour s.** I only have 50 euros a week to live on
subsonique [sypsɔnik] **ADJ** subsonic
substance [sypstɑ̃s] **NF** 1 *(matière)* substance; **plaie avec perte de s.** wound with loss of tissue; **s. active** active ingredient; **s. biodégradable/solide/liquide** biodegradable/solid/liquid substance; **s. organique/vivante** organic/living matter; **s. alimentaire** food; *Anat* **s. grise** grey matter; *Anat* **s. blanche** white matter;
2 *(essentiel → d'un texte)* substance, gist; *(→ d'une idéologie)* substance; **je ne peux pas traduire toute la lettre – donne-nous-en juste la s.** I can't translate the whole letter – just give us the gist of it
3 *(profondeur, signification)* substance; **quelques exemples auraient donné un peu plus de s. à votre exposé** a few examples would have given more substance to your talk; **des mots vides de toute s.** words empty of substance, meaningless words
4 *Phil & Rel* substance; *(matérialité)* substance, reality; **des créatures sans s.** insubstantial *or* ghostly beings
❑ **en substance ADV** in substance; **c'est, en s., ce qu'elle m'a raconté** that's the gist of what she told me
substantialisme [sypstɑ̃sjalism] **NM** *Phil* substantialism
substantialiste [sypstɑ̃sjalist] *Phil* **ADJ** substantialist
NMF substantialist
substantialité [sypstɑ̃sjalite] **NF** *Phil* substantiality, substantialness
substantiel, -elle [sypstɑ̃sjɛl] **ADJ** 1 *(nourriture, repas)* substantial, filling 2 *(argument)* substantial, sound; **je cherche des lectures un peu plus substantielles** I'm looking for books with a bit more substance (to them) 3 *(avantage, différence)* substantial, significant, important; *(somme)* substantial, considerable
substantiellement [sypstɑ̃sjɛlmɑ̃] **ADV** substantially
substantif, -ive [sypstɑ̃tif, -iv] **ADJ** substantive
NM noun, *Spéc* substantive
substantification [sypstɑ̃tifikasjɔ̃] **NF** substantification
substantifique [sypstɑ̃tifik] **ADJ F** **la s. moelle** the pith, the very substance
substantivation [sypstɑ̃tivasjɔ̃] **NF** turning into a noun, *Spéc* substantivizing
substantive [sypstɑ̃tiv] *voir* **substantif**
substantivement [sypstɑ̃tivmɑ̃] **ADV** as a noun, *Spéc* substantively
substantiver [3] [sypstɑ̃tive] **VT** to turn into a noun *or Spéc* substantive
substituant [sybstitɥɑ̃] **NM** *Chim* substituent
substituable [sypstitɥabl] **ADJ** substitutable
substituer [7] [sypstitɥe] **VT** 1 **s. qch à qch** to substitute sth for sth, to replace sth by sth; **le mot "sournois" a été substitué à "rusé"** the word "sly" was substituted for "cunning", "cunning" was replaced by the word "sly"
2 *Chim* to substitute
3 *Jur* **s. un héritier** to appoint an heir in succession to another *or* failing another; **s. un héritage** to entail an estate
▸**se substituer VPR se s. à** *(pour aider, représenter)* to substitute for, to stand in for, to replace; *(de façon déloyale)* to substitute oneself for; **personne ne peut se s. à la mère** no one can take the place of the mother
substitut [sypstity] **NM** 1 *(produit, personne)* substitute (**de** for); **un s. de la graisse de baleine** a substitute for whale fat; *Mktg* **s. rapproché** close substitute 2 *Jur* deputy *or* assistant public prosecutor; **s. général** ≃ Assistant Primary State Counsel 3 *Psy* surrogate
substitutif, -ive [sypstitytif, -iv] **ADJ** substitutive
substitution [sypstitysjɔ̃] **NF** 1 *(d'objets, de personnes)* substitution; **il y a eu s. de documents** documents have been substituted; **il y a eu s. d'enfant** the babies were switched round 2 *Chim, Ling & Math* substitution 3 *Jur* **s. fidéicommissaire** = creation of a life estate and a remainder; **s. de motifs** substitution of motives; **s. vulgaire** = substitution *(appointment of a second legatee when the first does not accept an inheritance)*
❑ **de substitution ADJ** *(réaction)* substitution *(avant n)*; *(père, mère)* surrogate; **produit de s.** substitute
substitutive [sypstitytiv] *voir* **substitutif**
substrat [sypstra] **NM** 1 *Chim & Électron* substrate 2 *Géol, Ling & Phil* substratum
substratum [sypstratɔm] **NM** subsoil, substratum
substruction [sypstryksjɔ̃] **NF** *Archéol & Archit* substruction
substructure [sypstryktyr] **NF** substructure
subsumer [3] [sypsyme] **VT** *Phil* to subsume
subterfuge [syptɛrfyʒ] **NM** piece of subterfuge, ruse, trick; **user de subterfuges** to resort to subterfuge
subtil, -e [syptil] **ADJ** 1 *(argument, esprit, raisonnement, personne)* subtle, discerning; **ses plaisanteries ne sont pas très subtiles** his/her jokes aren't very subtle *or* are a bit heavy-handed
2 *(allusion, différence)* subtle; *(nuance, distinction)* subtle, fine, nice
3 *(arôme, goût, parfum)* subtle, delicate
4 *(alambiqué)* subtle, over-fine; **il recourt toujours à de subtiles arguties** he always splits hairs
5 *Arch (fluide)* tenuous, thin
subtilement [syptilmɑ̃] **ADV** subtly
subtilisation [syptilizasjɔ̃] **NF** spiriting away
subtiliser [3] [syptilize] **VT** 1 *(voler)* to steal, to spirit away; *Hum* **ils lui ont subtilisé sa montre** they relieved him/her of his/her watch 2 *Arch (raffiner)* to refine
VI *Littéraire Péj (être trop subtil)* to subtilize
subtilité [syptilite] **NF** 1 *(d'un raisonnement, d'un parfum, d'une nuance)* subtlety, subtleness, delicacy; **les subtilités de la langue** the subtleties of the language 2 *(argutie)* hairsplitting; **je ne comprends rien à ces subtilités** all these fine distinctions are beyond me
subtropical, -e, -aux, -ales [syptrɔpikal, -o] **ADJ** subtropical
suburbain, -e [sybyrbɛ̃, -ɛn] **ADJ** suburban
suburbicaire [sybyrbikɛr] **ADJ** *Rel* suburbicarian
subvenir [40] [sybvənir] **subvenir à VT IND** *(besoins)* to provide for; *(dépenses)* to meet
subvention [sybvɑ̃sjɔ̃] **NF** subsidy; **subventions en capital** capital grants; **notre troupe reçoit une s. de la mairie** our company gets a subsidy from *or* is subsidized by the city council; **s. d'État** government subsidy; **s. d'exploitation** operating subsidy; **s. à l'exportation** export subsidy; **s. de fonctionnement** operational subsidy; **s. d'investissement** investment grant
subventionné, -e [sybvɑ̃sjɔne] **ADJ** *(cinéma, théâtre, recherches)* subsidized; **école privée subventionnée** ≃ grant-aided *or* state-aided private school
subventionner [3] [sybvɑ̃sjɔne] **VT** *(entreprise, théâtre)* to subsidize, to grant funds to; *(recherche)* to subsidize, to grant funds towards
subvenu, -e [sybvəny] **PP** *voir* **subvenir**
subversif, -ive [sybvɛrsif, -iv] **ADJ** subversive
subversion [sybvɛrsjɔ̃] **NF** subversion, subverting *(UNCOUNT)*
subversive [sybvɛrsiv] *voir* **subversif**
subvertir [32] [sybvɛrtir] **VT** *Littéraire* to overthrow, to subvert
subvient *etc voir* **subvenir**
subvint *etc voir* **subvenir**
subwoofer [sœbwufœr] **NM** subwoofer
suc [syk] **NM** 1 *Physiol* juice; **sucs gastriques** gastric juices 2 *Bot* sap 3 *Littéraire* **le s. de la science** the essence of scientific knowledge
succédané [syksedane] **NM** 1 *(ersatz)* substitute; **un s. de café** coffee substitute, ersatz coffee 2 *(personne ou chose de second ordre)* **un s. de Rembrandt/comédie musicale** a second-rate Rembrandt/musical 3 *Pharm* substitute, *Spéc* succedaneum
succéder [18] [syksede] **succéder à VT IND** 1 *(remplacer dans une fonction)* to succeed, to take over from; **qui lui succédera?** who will take over from him/her?, who will be his/her successor?; **tous ceux qui lui ont succédé** all his/her successors, all those who came after him/her; **s. à qn sur le trône** to succeed sb to the throne
2 *(suivre)* to follow; **un épais brouillard a succédé au soleil** the sun gave way to thick fog; **les pleurs avaient succédé aux rires** laughter had given way to tears; **puis les défaites succédèrent aux victoires** after the victories came defeats; **le désert succéda à la steppe** the steppe gave way to desert
3 *Jur (hériter de → personne)* to inherit from; *Arch* **s. au trône** to succeed to the throne; *Arch* **s. à une fortune** to inherit a fortune
▸**se succéder VPR** 1 *(se suivre)* to follow each other; **les journées se succédaient, toutes pareilles** one uneventful day followed another; **les crises se succèdent** it's just one crisis after another; **les hypothèses les plus folles se succédaient dans ma tête** the wildest suppositions ran through my head
2 *(alterner)* **les Ravit se sont succédé à la tête de l'entreprise depuis 50 ans** the Ravit family has been running the company for 50 years
succenturié, -e [syksɑ̃tyrje] **ADJ** *Orn* succenturiate
succès [syksɛ] **NM** 1 *(heureux résultat, réussite personnelle)* success; **il lui en veut de son s.** he resents him/her for being successful *or* for his/her success; **être couronné de s.** to be crowned with success, to be successful; **cette voix qui a fait le s. de Maria Petit** the voice which has made Maria Petit so successful
2 *(exploit, performance)* success, achievement; *(en amour)* conquest; **l'opération est un s. total** the operation is a complete success; **aller** *ou* **voler de s. en s.** to go from one success to another; **leurs nombreux s. en coupe d'Europe** their many victories in the European Cup
3 *(approbation → du public)* success, popularity; *(→ d'un groupe)* success; **son film a toutes les chances de s.** his/her movie *or Br* film has every chance of succeeding *or* being a success; **remporter un immense s.** to achieve great success; **avoir du s.** *(œuvre, artiste)* to be successful; *(suggestion)* to be very well received; **avoir un s. fou** *(artiste, film)* to be hugely successful; **les casquettes de baseball ont un s. fou auprès des jeunes** baseball caps are big *or* a big hit with young people; **sa pièce a eu beaucoup de s. auprès des critiques mais peu auprès du public** his/her play was acclaimed by the critics but the public was less than enthusiastic; **il a beaucoup de s. auprès des femmes/jeunes** he's very popular with women/young people; **je n'ai pas eu de s. avec ma proposition** I was unsuccessful *or* had no success with my proposal; **eh bien, il a du s., mon soufflé!** well, I see you like my soufflé *or* my soufflé appears to be a success!
4 *(chanson)* hit; *(film, pièce)* (box-office) hit *or* success; *(livre)* success, bestseller; **s. d'estime** succès d'estime; **l'ouvrage a été un s. d'estime** the book was well-received by the critics (but not by the public); **s. de librairie** bestseller; **sa comédie musicale a été un immense s. commercial** his/her musical was a box office hit *or* a runaway success; **un gros s.** *(film)* a big success; *(livre)* a best-seller; *(disque)* a hit
❑ **à succès ADJ** *(auteur, chanteur)* popular; **chanson à s.** hit record *or* song; **romancier à s.** popular *or* best-selling novelist
❑ **avec succès ADV** successfully, with success; **il a tenté avec s. d'escalader la face nord** he was successful in his attempt to climb the north face; **passer un examen avec s.** to pass an exam
❑ **sans succès ADV** *(essayer)* unsuccessfully, without (any) success; **elle s'est présentée plusieurs fois sans s. à ce poste** she made several unsuccessful applications for this job
successeur [syksesœr] **NM** 1 *(remplaçant)* successor; **ses successeurs** his/her successors, the people who succeeded him/her 2 *Jur* heir 3 *Math* successor
successibilité [syksesibilite] **NF** 1 *(droit de succéder)* right to inherit 2 *(ordre de succession)* order of inheriting
successible [syksesibl] **ADJ** 1 *(qui a droit à la succession)* entitled to inherit 2 *(qui donne droit*

à la succession) **à défaut de parents au degré s.** in the absence of relations close enough to inherit the estate

NMF eventual heir, *Spéc* remainderman

successif, -ive [syksesif, -iv] ADJ successive; **trois essais successifs** three successive attempts

succession [syksesjɔ̃] NF **1** *Jur (héritage)* succession, inheritance; *(biens)* estate; **liquider une s.** to settle a succession; **elle a laissé une s. énorme** she left a large estate; **s. vacante** estate in abeyance

2 *(remplacement)* succession; **prendre la s. d'un directeur** to take over from *or* to succeed a manager; **prendre la s. d'un monarque** to succeed a monarch (to the throne)

3 *(suite → gén)* succession, series *(singulier)*; *(→ de visiteurs, d'admirateurs)* stream, succession; **la s. des événements est difficile à suivre** the succession of events is difficult to follow; **cet hiver-là, il y eut une s. d'accidents aériens** that winter, there was a succession *or* series of air disasters

successive [syksesiv] *voir* **successif**

successivement [syksesivmɑ̃] ADV successively, one after the other

successivité [syksesivite] NF successiveness, successivity

successoral, -e, -aux, -ales [syksesɔral, -o] ADJ *(accroissement, loi)* successoral; **droit s.** right of succession

succin [syksɛ̃] NM *Géol* yellow amber

succinct, -e [syksɛ̃, -ɛ̃t] ADJ **1** *(bref, concis)* brief, concise, succinct; **un rapport s.** a brief *or* concise report **2** *(laconique)* brief, laconic; **soyez s., nous n'avons pas beaucoup de temps** be brief, we haven't much time **3** *(sommaire, réduit)* **un auditoire s.** a sparse audience; **un repas s.** a light meal

succinctement [syksɛ̃tmɑ̃] ADV **1** *(brièvement)* briefly, succinctly; **résumer s. une discussion** to sum up a discussion briefly **2** *(sommairement)* frugally; **déjeuner s.** to have a light lunch

succinique [syksinik] ADJ *Chim* succinic

succion [sy(k)sjɔ̃] NF **1** *(aspiration)* suction; **l'instinct de s. chez le nouveau-né** the sucking instinct of the newborn baby; **des bruits de s.** sucking noises **2** *Bot & Tech* suction

succombance [sykɔ̃bɑ̃s] NF *Jur* = loss of a case, resulting in the party concerned having to pay legal costs

succomber [3] [sykɔ̃be] VI **1** *(décéder)* to die, *Sout* to succumb

2 *(céder → personne)* to succumb; **il a succombé sous le nombre** he was forced to yield to greater numbers *or* because he was outnumbered; **s. sous un fardeau** to collapse under a burden; **l'entreprise a succombé sous la concurrence** the company couldn't hold out against the competition; **le nounours était si adorable, j'ai succombé** the teddy bear was so cute I couldn't resist it; **s. à** *(désir)* to yield to, *Sout* to succumb to; *(désespoir, émotion)* to give way to, *Sout* to succumb to; *(fatigue, sommeil)* to succumb to; *(blessures)* to die from, *Sout* to succumb to; **j'ai succombé à ses charmes** I fell victim *or* I succumbed to his/her charms; *Bible* **ne nous laisse pas s. à la tentation** let us not yield to temptation

succube [sykyb] NM succubus

succulence [sykylɑ̃s] NF *Littéraire* succulence, succulency

succulent, -e [sykylɑ̃, -ɑ̃t] ADJ **1** *(savoureux → mets, viande)* succulent; *Fig* **son autobiographie est remplie d'anecdotes succulentes** his/her autobiography is full of juicy anecdotes **2** *Bot* **plante succulente** succulent

succursale [sykyrsal] NF **1** *Com* branch **2** *Rel* succursal church

succursalisme [sykyrsalism] NM retail chain

succursaliste [sykyrsalist] ADJ chain *(avant n)*

NMF retail (chain) outlet

succussion [sykysjɔ̃] NF *Méd* succussion

sucement [sysmɑ̃] NM sucking

sucer [16] [syse] VT **1** *(liquide)* to suck; *(bonbon, glace, sucette)* to eat, to suck; **s. le venin d'une blessure** to suck the venom out of a wound; **pastilles à s.** lozenges to be sucked

2 *(doigt, stylo)* to suck (on); **s. son pouce** to suck one's thumb; *Vieilli* **s. qch avec le lait** to take sth in with one's mother's milk; *Fam* **s. la pomme** *ou* **la couenne** *ou* **la poire** *ou* **le museau à qn** *Br* to snog sb, *Am* to make out with sb

3 *Vulg* **s. qn** *(pratiquer la fellation sur)* to go down on sb, to suck sb off; *(pratiquer le cunnilingus sur)* to go down on sb, to give sb head

4 *Fam (boisson)* to knock back; **qu'est-ce qu'il suce, son frère!** his/her brother's a real boozer!; **il suce pas que de la glace** he drinks like a fish

▸ **se sucer** VPR **1 se s. les doigts** to suck one's fingers

2 *très Fam (l'un l'autre)* **se s. la pomme** *ou* **la couenne** *ou* **la poire** *ou* **le museau** *Br* to snog, *Am* to make out

3 *(emploi passif)* **ces cachets se sucent** these tablets are (meant) to be sucked

sucette [sysɛt] NF **1** *(friandise)* lollipop, *Br* lolly; *Fam* **partir en s.** to go down the tubes *or* pan **2** *(tétine) Br* dummy, *Am* pacifier

suceur, -euse [sysœr, -øz] ADJ sucking

NM,F *Littéraire* **s. de sang** bloodsucker

NM **1** *(d'aspirateur)* nozzle **2** *Entom* sucking insect **3** *très Fam (flatteur) Br* arse-licker, *Am* ass-licker

❑ **suceuse** NF *Agr* suction dredger

suçoir [syswar] NM *Bot & Entom* sucker

suçon [sysɔ̃] NM *Br* lovebite, *Am* hickey; **faire un s. à qn** to give sb a *Br* lovebite *or Am* hickey

suçotement [sysɔtmɑ̃] NM sucking

suçoter [3] [sysɔte] VT to suck (slowly); **il suçotait sa pipe** he was sucking at his pipe

sucrage [sykraʒ] NM **1** *(gén)* sugaring **2** *(en œnologie)* chaptalization

sucrant, -e [sykrɑ̃, -ɑ̃t] ADJ sweetening; **agent s.** sweetener; **avoir un grand pouvoir s.** to be a strong sweetener

sucrase [sykraz] NF sucrase, invertase

sucrate [sykrat] NM sucrate, saccharate

sucre [sykr] NM **1** *(produit de consommation)* sugar; **enrobé de s.** sugar-coated; **je prends toujours mon thé sans s.** I don't take sugar in my tea; **confiture sans s.** sugar-free jam; **s. de betterave** beet sugar; **s. brun** brown sugar; **s. candi** candy sugar; **s. de canne** cane sugar; **s. cristallisé** (coarse) granulated sugar; **s. d'érable** maple sugar; *Belg* **s. fin** (fine) caster sugar; **s. glace**, *Belg* **s. impalpable** *Br* icing sugar, *Am* confectioner's *or* powdered sugar; **s. en morceaux** lump *or* cube sugar; **s. d'orge** *(produit)* barley sugar; *(bâton)* stick of barley sugar; *Can* **s. du pays** maple sugar; **s. en poudre** (fine) caster sugar; **s. roux** brown sugar; **s. semoule** (fine) caster sugar; *Belg* **s. ultrafin** (fine) caster sugar; **s. vanillé** vanilla sugar

2 *(sucreries)* **évitez le s.** avoid sugar *or* sweet things

3 *(morceau)* sugar lump *or* cube; **tu prends ton café avec un ou deux sucres?** do you take your coffee with one or two sugars?

4 *Biol, Chim & Méd* sugar; **s. d'amidon** starch sugar

5 *(comme adj)* **confiture pur s.** jam made with pure sugar; **il est tout s. tout miel** he's all sweetness and light

6 *Can (bonbon)* **s. à la crème** maple fudge

❑ **au sucre** ADJ *(fruits, crêpes)* (sprinkled) with sugar

❑ **en sucre** ADJ **1** *(confiserie, décoration)* sugar *(avant n)*, made with sugar

2 *Fam Fig* **mon bébé en s.** my sweetie pie; **ne touche pas au bébé – il n'est pas en s.!** don't touch the baby – don't worry, he's not made of glass!

sucré, -e [sykre] ADJ **1** *(naturellement)* sweet; *(artificiellement)* sweetened; **mon thé est trop s.** my tea is too sweet, there's too much sugar in my tea; **je n'aime pas le café s.** I don't like sugar in my coffee; **un verre d'eau sucrée** a glass of sugar water; **non s.** unsweetened

2 *(doucereux → paroles)* sugary, sweet, honeyed; *(→ voix)* suave, sugary; **il a son petit air s.** he looks as if butter wouldn't melt in his mouth

NM,F **faire le s./la sucrée** to go all coy

NM **le s.** sweet things; **j'ai envie de s.** I'd like something sweet to eat; **c'est une sauce qui combine le s. et le salé** it's a sauce which is sweet and savoury at the same time; **aimer le s.** to have a sweet tooth

sucrer [3] [sykre] VT **1** *(avec du sucre → café, thé)* to sugar, to put sugar in; *(→ vin)* to add sugar to, to chaptalize; *(→ fruits)* to sprinkle with sugar; **sucrez à volonté** add sugar to taste; **je ne sucre jamais mon thé** I never put sugar in my tea; *Fam* **s. les fraises** *(trembler)* to have shaky hands; *(être gâteux)* to be doddery

2 *(avec une matière sucrante)* to sweeten; **il sucre son lait avec du miel** he sweetens his milk with honey

3 *très Fam (supprimer → permis, licence)* to take away▪; *(→ permission, prime)* to cancel▪; *(→ argent de poche)* to stop▪; **on lui a sucré son permis de conduire après son accident** they took his/her *Br* driving licence *or Am* driver's license away after the accident

VI **le miel sucre moins que le sucre** sugar is a better sweetener than honey

▸ **se sucrer** VPR *Fam* **1** *(prendre du sucre)* to help oneself to sugar▪

2 *(s'octroyer un bénéfice)* to line one's pockets

sucrerie [sykrəri] NF **1** *(friandise)* sweet thing, sweetmeat; **vous devez éviter les sucreries** you must avoid eating sweet things; **elle adore les sucreries** she has a sweet tooth *or* loves sweet things **2** *(raffinerie)* sugar refinery; *(usine)* sugar house **3** *Can (forêt d'érables)* maple plantation **4** *(en Afrique francophone) (boisson)* soft drink

Sucrette® [sykrɛt] NF (artificial) sweetener

sucrier, -ère [sykrje, -ɛr] ADJ *(industrie, betterave)* sugar *(avant n)*; *(région)* sugar-producing

NM **1** *(pot)* sugar basin *or* bowl; **s. verseur** sugar shaker **2** *(producteur)* sugar producer

sucrin [sykrɛ̃] *Bot* ADJ M **melon s.** sugary melon

NM sugary melon

sucrine [sykrin] NF = variety of lettuce similar to cos

sud [syd] NM INV **1** *(point cardinal)* south; **au s.** in the south; **où est le s.?** which way is south?; **la partie la plus au s. de l'île** the southernmost part of the island; **le vent vient du s.** it's a south *or* southerly wind, the wind is coming from the south; **un vent du s.** a southerly wind; **le vent du s.** the south wind; **aller au** *ou* **vers le s.** to go south *or* southwards; **les trains qui vont vers le s.** trains going south, southbound trains; **rouler vers le s.** to drive south *or* southwards; **aller droit vers le s.** to head due south; **la cuisine est plein s.** *ou* **exposée au s.** the kitchen faces due south *or Sout* has a southerly aspect

2 *(partie d'un pays, d'un continent)* south, southern area *or* regions; *(partie d'une ville)* south; **le s. de l'Italie** southern Italy, the south of Italy; **dans le s. de l'Espagne** in southern Spain, in the south of Spain; **elle habite dans le S.** she lives in the South; **il habite dans le s. de Paris** he lives in the south of Paris; **elle est du S.** she's from the South; **les gens du S.** people who live in the South

ADJ INV south *(avant n)*, southern; *(→ côte, face)* south; *(→ banlieue, partie, région)* southern; **la façade s. d'un immeuble** the south-facing wall of a building; **la chambre est côté s.** the bedroom faces south; **dans la partie s. de la France** in the South of France, in southern France; **suivre la direction s.** to head *or* to go southward

❑ **Sud** ADJ INV South; **le Pacifique S.** the South Pacific NM *Géog* **le S.** the South

❑ **au sud de** PRÉP (to the) south of; **il habite au s. de Paris** he lives to the south of Paris

sud-africain, -e [sydafrikɛ̃, -ɛn] *(mpl* **sud-africains**, *fpl* **sud-africaines)** ADJ South African

❑ **Sud-Africain, -e** NM,F South African

sud-américain, -e [sydamerikɛ̃, -ɛn] *(mpl* **sud-américains**, *fpl* **sud-américaines)** ADJ South American

❑ **Sud-Américain, -e** NM,F South American

sudation [sydɑsjɔ̃] NF sweating, *Spéc* sudation

sudatoire [sydatwar] ADJ sudatory

sud-coréen, -enne [sydkɔreɛ̃, -ɛn] *(mpl* **sud-coréens**, *fpl* **sud-coréennes)** ADJ South Korean

❑ **Sud-Coréen, -enne** NM,F South Korean

sud-est [sydɛst] ADJ INV south-east

NM INV **1** *(point cardinal)* south-east; **au s. de Lyon** south-east of Lyons; **vent de s.** south-east

or south-easterly wind **2** *Géog* **le S. asiatique** South East Asia

Sudètes [sydɛt] **NMPL les S.** *(région)* the Sudeten, *Formerly* Sudetenland; *(montagnes)* the Sudetes, the Sudeten Mountains

sudiste [sydist] *Hist* **ADJ** Confederate
NMF Confederate

sudoral, -e, -aux, -ales [sydɔral, -o] **ADJ** sudoral

sudorifère [sydɔrifɛr] **ADJ** sudoriferous; **glande s.** sweat gland

sudorifique [sydɔrifik] **ADJ** sudorific
NM sudorific

sudoripare [sydɔripar] **ADJ** sudoriferous; **glande s.** sweat gland

sud-ouest [sydwɛst] **ADJ INV** south-west
NM INV south-west; **au s. de Tokyo** south-west of Tokyo; **vent de s.** south-west *or* south-westerly wind
❑ **Sud-Ouest NM** *Presse* = daily newspaper published in Bordeaux; *Hist* **le S. africain** South West Africa

SUD-PTT [sydpetete] **NM** *(abrév* **solidaires, unitaires et démocratiques-postes, télécommunications et télédiffusion**) = French post office and telecommunications trade union

sudra [ʃudra] **NM INV** Sudra

sud-sud-est [sydsydɛst] **ADJ INV** south-south-east
NM INV south-south-east

sud-sud-ouest [sydsydwɛst] **ADJ INV** south-south-west
NM INV south-south-west

Sud Viêt-nam [sydvjɛtnam] **NM** *Hist* **le S.** South Vietnam

sud-vietnamien, -enne [sydvjɛtnamjɛ̃, -ɛn] *(mpl* **sud-vietnamiens,** *fpl* **sud-vietnamiennes**) **ADJ** South Vietnamese
NM,F South Vietnamese

Suède [sɥɛd] **NF la S.** Sweden; **vivre en S.** to live in Sweden; **aller en S.** to go to Sweden

suède [sɥɛd] **NM** suede; **des gants en s.** suede *or* kid gloves

suédé, -e [sɥede] **ADJ** imitation suede
NM suede cloth, imitation suede

suédine [sɥedin] **NF** suedette

suédois, -e [sɥedwa, -az] **ADJ** Swedish
NM *(langue)* Swedish
❑ **Suédois, -e NM,F** Swede; **les S.** the Swedish

suée [sɥe] **NF** *Fam (transpiration)* sweat■ ; **attraper** *ou* **prendre une (bonne) s.** *(en faisant un effort)* to work up quite a sweat; **j'en ai encore des suées** I still break out in a cold sweat when I think about it

suer [7] [sɥe] **VI 1** *(transpirer → personne)* to sweat, to get sweaty; **s. à grosses gouttes** to be pouring with sweat, to be sweating profusely
2 *(bois, plâtres)* to ooze, to sweat; *Culin* **faire s. des oignons** to sweat onions
3 *Fam (fournir un gros effort)* to slave (away), *Br* to slog; **j'en aurai sué toute ma vie pour rien** I'll have slogged all my life for nothing; **j'en ai sué pour faire démarrer la tondeuse!** I had the devil's own job trying to get the mower started!; *Fam* **faire s. le burnous** to be a real slave-driver
4 *Fam (locutions)* **faire s. qn** *(l'embêter)* to bug sb, *Br* to get up sb's nose; **il nous fait s.!** he's a pain in the neck!; **ça me ferait s. de devoir y retourner** I'd hate to have to go back there; **elle m'a fait s. toute la matinée pour que je joue avec elle** she pestered me all morning to play with her; **se faire s.** *(s'ennuyer)* to get bored stiff *or* to death; **je me suis fait s. toute la journée** I was bored stiff all day long
VT 1 *(sueur)* to sweat; **s. sang et eau** *(faire de grands efforts)* to sweat blood; **ils ont sué sang et eau pour restaurer la maison** they sweated blood over the renovation of the house; *Fam* **en s. une** *(danser au bal)* to have a bop
2 *(humidité)* to ooze
3 *Littéraire (laisser paraître → bêtise, ennui, égoïsme)* to exude, to reek of; **cette banlieue sue la tristesse** this suburb positively exudes dreariness

suet [sɥɛt] **NM INV** *Naut* south-east

Suétone [sɥetɔn] **NPR** Suetonius

suette [sɥɛt] **NF** *Méd* **s. miliaire** miliaria, miliary fever, prickly heat

sueur [sɥœr] **NF 1** *(transpiration)* sweat; **sa chemise était mouillée par la s.** his/her shirt was sweaty *or* was damp with sweat; **sueurs froides** cold sweat; **j'en ai eu des sueurs froides** I was in a cold sweat; **donner des sueurs froides à qn** to put sb in a cold sweat
2 *(effort intense)* sweat; **vivre de la s. du peuple** to live off the sweat of the people; **à la s. de son front** by the sweat of one's brow; **gagner qch à la s. de son front** to earn sth with the sweat of one's brow
❑ **en sueur ADJ** in a sweat; **être en s.** to be in a sweat, to be sweating

Suez [sɥɛz] **NM** Suez

suffète [syfɛt] **NM** *Antiq* suffete

suffire [100] [syfir] **VI 1** *(en quantité)* to be enough, to be sufficient, *Sout* to suffice; **quelques gouttes suffisent** a few drops are enough *or* sufficient; **deux bouteilles pour cinq, ça ne suffira pas** two bottles for five people won't be enough; **une cuillerée, ça te suffit?** is one spoonful enough for you?; **mon salaire ne nous suffit plus** we can no longer survive on my salary; **la fessée ne semble pas t'avoir suffi!** you obviously want your bottom smacked again!; **deux minutes suffisent pour le cuire** it just takes two minutes to cook; **une heure me suffira pour tout ranger** one hour will be enough for me to put everything away; **je ne lui rendrai plus service, cette expérience m'a suffi** I won't help him/her again, I've learned my lesson; **il faut doubler l'effectif – le budget n'y suffira jamais** the staff has to be doubled – the budget won't cover it; **je n'y suffis plus** *(je suis débordé)* it's too much for me, I can't cope
2 *(en qualité)* to be (good) enough; **parler ne suffit pas, il faut agir** words aren't enough, we must act; **des excuses ne me suffisent pas** I'm not satisfied with an apology; **ma parole devrait vous s.** my word should be good enough for you; **l'amitié ne lui suffisait pas** he/she wanted more than friendship; **pas besoin de tralala, un sandwich me suffit** there's no need for anything fancy, a sandwich will do; **s. aux besoins de qn** to meet sb's needs; **ça suffit à mon bonheur** it's enough to make me happy
3 *(tournure impersonnelle)* **je n'avais jamais volé – il suffit d'une fois!** I've never stolen before – once is enough!; **il suffit d'une heure pour tout nettoyer** it only takes an hour to clean everything; **il suffit d'une erreur pour que tout soit à recommencer** one single mistake means starting all over again; **il a suffi de quelques mots pour le persuader** a few words were enough to persuade him; **il suffirait de quelques euros** a few euros would be enough; **il suffirait de peu pour que le régime s'écroule** it wouldn't take much to bring down the regime; **il suffit de l'écouter parler deux minutes pour saisir sa personnalité** you only have to listen to him/her for two minutes to know what sort of person he/she is; **s'il suffisait de travailler pour réussir!** if only work was enough to guarantee success!; **il te suffit de dire que nous arriverons en retard** just say we'll be late; **il suffit qu'on me dise ce que je dois faire** I just have *or* need to be told what to do; **il suffisait que tu passes un coup de téléphone** all you had to do was phone; **il suffit que je tourne le dos pour qu'elle fasse des bêtises** I only have to turn my back and she's up to some mischief; *Fam* **(ça) suffit!** (that's) enough!; **ça suffit comme ça!** that's enough now!; **il suffit!** it's enough!
►**se suffire VPR 1** *(emploi réciproque)* **ils se suffisent l'un à l'autre** they've got each other and that's all they need
2 se s. à soi-même *(matériellement)* to be self-sufficient; *(moralement)* to be quite happy with one's own company

suffisamment [syfizamɑ̃] **ADV** sufficiently, enough; **le travail n'est pas s. rémunéré** the work isn't sufficiently well paid, the pay isn't adequate; **je t'ai s. prévenu** I've warned you often enough; **s. de** enough; **il n'y a pas s. de couverts pour tout le monde** there aren't enough places set for all these people; **ah non, j'ai s. de soucis comme ça!** I've got enough problems as it is, for goodness' sake!

suffisance [syfizɑ̃s] **NF 1** *(vanité)* self-importance, conceit; **c'est un homme plein de s.** he's very self-important **2** *Littéraire* **avoir sa s. de qch, avoir qch à s.** to have plenty of sth; **manger à sa s.** to eat one's fill
❑ **en suffisance ADV** *Littéraire* **de l'argent en s.** plenty of *or* sufficient money

suffisant, -e [syfizɑ̃, -ɑ̃t] **ADJ 1** *(en quantité)* sufficient; **ma retraite est suffisante pour deux** my pension's sufficient *or* enough for two; **trois bouteilles pour cinq, c'est bien** *ou* **amplement s.** three bottles for five, that's plenty *or* that's quite enough
2 *(en qualité)* sufficient, good enough; **votre accord n'est pas s., nous avons aussi besoin de celui de son père** your consent isn't enough, we also need his/her father's; **des excuses ne seront pas suffisantes, il veut un démenti** apologies won't be sufficient *or* won't do, he wants a denial; **tes résultats à l'école sont tout juste suffisants** your school results are just about satisfactory; **il n'a pas l'envergure suffisante pour diriger l'entreprise** he isn't of a high enough calibre to run the company; **c'est une raison suffisante pour qu'il accepte** it's a good enough reason *or* it's reason enough to make him accept
3 *(arrogant → air, personne)* self-important, conceited; **d'un air s.** smugly
NM,F faire le s. to give oneself airs

suffisons *etc voir* **suffire**

suffixal, -e, -aux, -ales [syfiksal, -o] **ADJ** suffixal

suffixation [syfiksasjɔ̃] **NF** suffixation, suffixing *(UNCOUNT)*

suffixe [syfiks] **NM** suffix

suffixer [3] [syfikse] **VT** to suffix; **mot suffixé** word with a *or* that has a suffix

suffocant, -e [syfɔkɑ̃, -ɑ̃t] **ADJ 1** *(atmosphère, chaleur, odeur)* suffocating, stifling **2** *(ahurissant)* astounding, staggering, stunning

suffocation [syfɔkasjɔ̃] **NF** suffocation; **j'ai des suffocations** I feel as if I am choking

suffoquer [3] [syfɔke] **VI** *(étouffer)* to suffocate, to choke; **on suffoque ici!** it's stifling in here!; **s. de** to choke *or* to suffocate with; **s. de colère** to be choking with anger; **s. de joie** to be overcome with happiness
VT 1 *(sujet: atmosphère, fumée, odeur)* to suffocate, to choke; **la chaleur nous suffoquait** the heat was suffocating, it was stiflingly hot; **le fou rire la suffoquait** she was choking with laughter
2 *(causer une vive émotion à)* to choke; **la colère le suffoquait** he was choking with anger
3 *(ahurir → sujet: attitude, prix)* to stagger, to stun, to confound; **ma réponse l'avait suffoqué** my answer left him speechless *or* fairly took his breath away
4 *Arch (tuer)* to suffocate

suffragant [syfragɑ̃] *Rel* **ADJ M** suffragan
NM suffragan (bishop)

suffrage [syfraʒ] **NM 1** *Pol (système)* suffrage; *Hist* **s. censitaire** suffrage with property qualification *or* for householders (only); **s. direct** direct suffrage; **s. indirect** indirect suffrage; **être élu au s. direct/indirect** to be elected by direct/indirect suffrage; **s. restreint** restricted suffrage; **s. universel** universal suffrage; **s. universel direct** direct universal suffrage; **s. universel indirect** indirect universal suffrage;
2 *(voix)* vote; **obtenir beaucoup/peu de suffrages** to poll heavily/badly; **c'est leur parti qui a eu le plus de suffrages** their party headed the poll
3 *Littéraire (approbation)* approval, approbation; **avoir le s. de qn** to win sb's approval; **sa dernière pièce a enlevé** *ou* **remporté tous les suffrages** his last play was an unqualified success; **accorder son s. à** to give one's approval to

suffragette [syfraʒɛt] **NF** suffragette

suffusion [syfyzjɔ̃] **NF** *Méd* suffusion

suggérer [18] [sygʒere] **VT 1** *(conseiller, proposer → acte)* to suggest; *(→ nom, solution)* to suggest, to put forward, to propose; **que suggères-tu?** what do you suggest?; **nous lui avons suggéré de renoncer** we suggested he/she should give up; **je suggère que nous partions tout de suite** I suggest that we go right away
2 *(évoquer)* to suggest, to evoke; **que vous suggèrent ces images?** what do these pictures suggest to you?; **sa peinture suggère plus qu'elle ne représente** his/her painting is more evocative than figurative

suggestibilité [sygʒɛstibilite] **NF** suggestibility

suggestible [sygʒɛstibl] **ADJ** suggestible

suggestif, -ive [sygʒɛstif, -iv] **ADJ 1** *(évocateur)* suggestive, evocative; **de façon suggestive** suggestively **2** *(érotique → pose)* suggestive, provocative; *(décolleté)* revealing, plunging

suggestion [sygʒɛstjɔ̃] **NF 1** *(conseil, proposition)* suggestion; **faire une s.** to make a suggestion; **je vais te faire une s.** let me make a suggestion **2** *Psy* suggestion **3** *(influence)* suggestion, incitement; *Littéraire* **les suggestions du démon** the suggestions of the Evil One

suggestionner [3] [sygʒɛstjɔne] **VT s. qn** to put an idea/ideas into sb's head; **elle s'est laissé s. par lui** she allowed him to put ideas into her head

suggestive [sygʒɛstiv] *voir* **suggestif**

suggestivité [sygʒɛstivite] **NF 1** *(évocation)* evocativeness **2** *(érotisme)* suggestiveness

suicidaire [sɥisidɛr] **ADJ 1** *(instinct, personne, tendance)* suicidal **2** *(qui conduit à l'échec)* suicidal; **de si gros investissements, ce serait s.!** such large investments would be suicidal *or* courting disaster!

NMF suicidal person, potential suicide

suicidant, -e [sɥisidɑ̃, -ɑ̃t] **ADJ** who has attempted suicide

NM,F = person who has attempted suicide

suicide [sɥisid] **NM 1** *(mort)* suicide; **faire une tentative de s.** to try to commit suicide, to attempt suicide; **s. assisté** assisted suicide **2** *(désastre)* suicide; **s. politique** political suicide; **ce serait un s. politique** it would be political suicide; *Fig* **n'y va pas, c'est du s.!** don't go, it would be madness *or* it's suicide!

ADJ INV suicide *(avant n)*; **une mission s.** a suicide mission

suicidé, -e [sɥiside] **ADJ** who has committed suicide

NM,F suicide

suicider [3] [sɥiside] **se suicider VPR 1** *(se tuer)* to commit suicide, to kill oneself; **tenter de se s.** to attempt suicide, to try to commit suicide **2** *Fig (causer sa propre perte)* to commit suicide

suidé [sɥide] *Zool* **NM** suid

◻ **suidés NMPL** Suidae

suie [sɥi] **NF** soot; **être couvert** *ou* **noir de s.** to be all sooty *or* black with soot

suif [sɥif] **NM 1** *(de bétail)* fat; *Culin* suet; *(pour chandelles)* tallow **2** *Fam (bagarre)* **chercher du s. à qn** to try to pick a fight with sb; **faire du s.** to kick up a fuss; **il va y avoir du s.** there's going to be a scrap

suiffer [3] [sɥife] **VT** *(cuir)* to tallow; *(gond)* to grease

suiffeux, -euse [sɥifø, -øz] **ADJ** fatty

suiforme [sɥifɔrm] **NM** *Zool* suidian

sui generis [sɥiʒeneris] **ADJ INV** sui generis, unique; *Euph* **une odeur s.** a rather distinctive smell

suint [sɥɛ̃] **NM** suint

suintant, -e [sɥɛ̃tɑ̃, -ɑ̃t] **ADJ** *(gén)* sweating, oozing; *(plaie)* running, weeping; **des murs suintants** damp walls

suintement [sɥɛ̃tmɑ̃] **NM 1** *(écoulement → gén)* sweating *(UNCOUNT)*, oozing *(UNCOUNT)*; *(de blessure)* running *(UNCOUNT)*, weeping *(UNCOUNT)* **2** *Pétr* oozing (forth) *(UNCOUNT)*

suinter [3] [sɥɛ̃te] **VI 1** *(s'écouler)* to ooze, to seep; **l'humidité suinte des murailles** the walls are dripping with moisture **2** *(laisser échapper un liquide → plaie)* to weep; **ce mur suinte** this wall is running with moisture **3** *Littéraire (se manifester)* to ooze; **l'ennui suinte dans cette petite ville** this little town has a pervasive atmosphere of boredom

VT *Littéraire (l'ennui, la haine)* to ooze

suintine [sɥɛ̃tin] **NF** *Tex* suint

suis 1 *voir* **être**[1] **2** *voir* **suivre**

Suisse [sɥis] **NF la S.** Switzerland; **vivre en S.** to live in Switzerland; **aller en S.** to go to Switzerland; **la S. allemande** *ou* **alémanique/romande** the German-speaking/French-speaking part of Switzerland

suisse [sɥis] **ADJ** Swiss; **s. allemand/romand** Swiss German/French

NM 1 *(au Vatican)* Swiss guard **2** *(bedeau)* beadle **3** *Can* chipmunk

◻ **Suisse NMF** Swiss (person); **S. allemand/romand** German-speaking/French-speaking Swiss; **les Suisses** the Swiss

◻ **en suisse ADV boire/manger en s.** to drink/to eat on one's own

Suissesse [sɥisɛs] **NF** Swiss woman

suit *etc voir* **suivre**

SUITE [sɥit]

> continuation **1** ▪ sequel **1** ▪ follow-up **1** ▪ series **2** ▪ retinue **3** ▪ suite **4, 9** ▪ consequence **5** ▪ coherence **6**

NF 1 *(prolongation → gén)* continuation; *(→ d'un film, d'un roman)* sequel; *(→ d'une émission)* follow-up; **elle a écrit une s. à 'Autant en emporte le vent'** she wrote a sequel to 'Gone with the Wind'; **s. page 17** continued on page 17; **la s. au prochain numéro** to be continued (in our next issue); **ceci n'est qu'un préambule, lis la s.** *(le reste)* this is just a preamble, read what comes afterwards; **s. et fin** final instalment; **apportez-moi la s.** *(pendant un repas)* bring me the next course; **écoute la s.** *(du discours)* listen to what comes next; *(de mon histoire)* listen to what happened next; **je n'ai pas pu entendre la s.** I couldn't hear the rest; **on entendra demain la s. des témoignages** further *or* more evidence will be heard tomorrow; **attendons la s. des événements** let's wait to see what happens next; **faire s. à** to follow; **de violents orages ont fait s. à la sécheresse** the drought was followed by violent storms; **le logement fait s. à l'arrière-boutique** the *Br* flat *or Am* apartment is connected to the back of the shop; **prendre la s. de qn** to take over from sb, to succeed sb

2 *(série)* series, succession; **une s. de malheurs** a run *or* series of misfortunes

3 *(cortège)* retinue

4 *(dans un hôtel)* suite; **la s. présidentielle/royale** the presidential/royal suite

5 *(répercussion)* consequence; **la s. logique/naturelle de mon adhésion au parti** the logical/natural consequence of my joining the party; **donner s. à qch** *(lettre, réclamation)* to follow sth up; *(commande)* to deal with sth; *(projet)* to carry on with sth; **avoir des suites** to have repercussions; **elle est morte des suites de ses blessures** she died as a result of her injuries

6 *(lien logique)* coherence; **ses propos n'avaient guère de s.** what he/she said wasn't very logical; **avoir de la s. dans les idées** to be coherent *or* consistent; *Hum* **tu as de la s. dans les idées!** you certainly know what you want!

7 *Jur* pursuit; **droit de s.** *(d'un belligérant)* right of (hot) pursuit; *(d'un créancier)* right to follow property

8 *Ling & Math* sequence

9 *Mus* suite

◻ **à la suite ADV 1** *(en succession)* one after the other; **nous avons fait plusieurs voyages à la s.** we made several trips one after the other

2 *(après)* **un nom avec plusieurs chiffres inscrits à la s.** a name followed by a string of numbers

◻ **à la suite de PRÉP 1** *(derrière → dans l'espace)* behind; *(→ dans un écrit)* after; **il entra et nous à sa s.** he went in and we followed; **cinq chambres les unes à la s. des autres** five rooms in a row

2 *(à cause de)* following; **à la s. de son discours télévisé, sa cote a remonté** following his/her speech on TV, his/her popularity rating went up

◻ **de suite ADV 1** *Fam (immédiatement)* straightaway, right away; **il revient de s.** he'll be right back

2 *(à la file)* in a row, one after the other, in succession; **il a mangé dix œufs durs de s.** he ate ten hard-boiled eggs in a row; **elle est restée de garde 48 heures de s.** she was on duty for 48 hours on end; **on n'a pas eu d'électricité pendant cinq jours de s.** we didn't have any electricity for five whole days *or* five days running

◻ **par la suite ADV** *(dans le passé)* afterwards, later; *(dans le futur)* later; **il se l'est beaucoup reproché par la s.** he very much blamed himself for it afterwards *or* later; **ils se sont mariés par la s.** they eventually got married

◻ **par suite ADV** therefore; **c'est encore une enfant, et par s., elle est impulsive** she's still a child and therefore impulsive

◻ **par suite de PRÉP** due to, owing to; **par s. d'un arrêt de travail des techniciens** due to industrial action by technical staff

◻ **sans suite ADJ 1** *(incohérent)* disconnected; **il tenait des propos sans s.** his talk was incoherent

2 *Com* discontinued; **produit sans s.** discontinued product

◻ **suite à PRÉP** *Admin* **s. à votre lettre** further to *or* in response to *or* with reference to your letter; **s. à votre appel téléphonique** further to your phone call

suitée [sɥite] **ADJ F** *Zool (femelle)* followed by its young; **biche s.** hind with calf; **laie s.** sow with young

suivait *etc voir* **suivre**

suivant[1] [sɥivɑ̃] **PRÉP 1** *(d'après)* according to; **s. son habitude, elle s'est levée très tôt** as is her habit *or Sout* wont, she got up very early; **s. leurs indications, ça devrait être à gauche** according to their directions, it should be on the left; **s. vos instructions** *(dans une lettre)* as per your instructions

2 *(en fonction de)* according to, depending on; **vous donnerez s. vos possibilités** you'll give according to your means; **s. votre âge/vos besoins** depending on your age/your needs; **cela varie s. le jour/la température** it varies from day to day/with the temperature

3 *(le long de)* **découper s. le pointillé** cut along the dotted line

◻ **suivant que CONJ** according to whether; **s. que vous parlez avec l'un ou l'autre** according to which one you talk to

◻ **en suivant ADV** *Belg (d'affilée → gén)* in a row; *(→ dans le temps)* at a stretch

suivant[2]**, -e** [sɥivɑ̃, ɑ̃t] **ADJ 1** *(qui vient après → chapitre, mois, semaine)* following, next; *(→ échelon, train)* next; **les trois jours suivants** the next three days; **quel est le chiffre s.?** what's the next number?, what number comes next?; **quelle est la personne suivante?** *(dans une file d'attente)* who's next?

2 *(pour introduire)* following; **il m'a raconté l'histoire suivante** he told me the following story; **procédez de la manière suivante** follow these instructions

NM,F 1 *(dans une succession)* next one; **(au) s., s'il vous plaît** next, please; **son premier roman, et même les suivants** his/her first novel and even the following ones *or* the ones that followed; **pas mardi prochain mais le s.** not this coming Tuesday but the next one *or* the one after; **voir page 6 et suivantes** see page 6 and following *or Sout* et seq

2 *(pour introduire)* **la raison est la suivante** here is why; **les résultats sont les suivants** here are the results, the results are as follows

3 *Mktg* follower; *(sur le marché)* market follower; **s. immédiat** early follower

NM *(membre d'une escorte)* attendant

◻ **suivante NF** *Théât* lady's maid

suiveur, -euse [sɥivœr, -øz] **ADJ voiture suiveuse** = car following a cycle race

NM 1 *(de femmes → gén)* skirt-chaser; *(→ en voiture)* kerb-crawler **2** *Mktg* follower; *(sur le marché)* market follower **3** *Sport* **les suiveurs** = officials and back-up squads following a cycle race **4** *(inconditionnel, imitateur)* slave, uncritical follower

suivi, -e [sɥivi] **PP** *voir* **suivre**

ADJ 1 *(ininterrompu → effort)* sustained, consistent; *(→ correspondance)* regular; *(→ qualité)* consistent; *(→ activité)* steady; *Com (→ demande)* steady, persistent; **nous avons eu une correspondance très suivie pendant des années** we wrote to each other very regularly for years; *Com* **article s.** stock item

2 *(logique → propos, raisonnement)* coherent; *(→ politique)* consistent

3 *(qui a la faveur du public)* **mode/émission très suivie** very popular fashion/programme; **conférence peu/très suivie** poorly attended/well-attended conference; **la grève a été peu/très suivie** there was little/a lot of support for the strike

NM *(d'un cas, d'un dossier)* follow-up; **assurer le s. de qch** *(cas, dossier)* to follow sth through; *(commande)* to deal with sth; *Com (article)* to

continue to stock sth; **je m'occuperai personnellement du s. de votre dossier** I'll deal with your case personally; **le travail en petits groupes assure un meilleur s.** working in small groups means that individual participants can be monitored more successfully; *Jur* **s. socio-judiciaire** = social and judicial supervision of sex offenders following release from custody

suivisme [sɥivism] **NM** *(attitude d'imitation servile)* herd instinct

suiviste [sɥivist] **ADJ** sheep-like
NMF sheep-like follower

SUIVRE [89] [sɥivr]

> **VT** to follow **A1–3, B1, 4, C1, 3** ■ to come after **A2, 3** ■ to walk/drive/sail along **B2** ■ to undergo **B3** ■ to comply with **B4** ■ to keep up (with) **C1** ■ to pay attention to **C2** ■ to deal with **C4** ■ to follow the progress of **C4**
> **USAGE ABSOLU** to follow suit **4**
> **VI** to follow **2, 3** ■ to keep up (with) **1**
> **VPR** to follow one another **1** ■ to be in the right order **2** ■ to be coherent **4**

VT A. *DANS L'ESPACE, LE TEMPS* **1** *(pour escorter, espionner, rattraper)* to follow; **les enfants suivaient leurs parents en courant** the children were running behind their parents; **suivez-moi** follow me; **suivez le guide** this way (for the guided tour), please; **ils sont entrés, suivis de leur chien** they came in followed by their dog; **la police les a suivis sur plusieurs kilomètres** the police chased them for several kilometres; **il l'a fait s. par un détective privé** he had him/her followed by a private detective; **tu t'es fait s. en venant ici?** were you followed on your way here?; **s. qn de près** *(gén)* to follow close behind sb; *(pour le protéger)* to stick close to sb; **le coureur anglais, suivi de très près par le Belge** the English runner, with the Belgian close on his heels; **s. la piste de qn** to follow sb's trail; **s. qn à la trace** to follow sb's tracks; **s. qn comme son ombre** to follow sb like a shadow; **s. qn des yeux** *ou* **du regard** to follow sb with one's eyes; **il suivait des yeux ses moindres gestes** he was watching his/her every move; **certaines personnes, suivez mon regard, n'ont pas fait leur travail** certain people, who shall be *or* remain nameless, haven't done their work

2 *(se dérouler après)* to follow (on from), to come after; **la réunion sera suivie d'une collation** refreshments will be served after the meeting; **pendant l'heure qui a suivi** during the hour that followed; **le jour qui suivit** (the) next day, the following day; **il suit de** it follows from; **il suit de votre déclaration que le témoin ment** it follows from your statement that the witness is lying

3 *(être placé après)* to follow, to come after; **votre nom suit le mien sur la liste** your name is right after mine on the list; **les conjonctions toujours suivies du subjonctif** the conjunctions always followed by *or* that always govern the subjunctive; **suit un résumé du roman précédent** then comes a summary of the previous novel; **dans les pages qui suivent** in the following pages

B. *ADOPTER, OBÉIR À* **1** *(emprunter → itinéraire, rue)* to follow; **en suivant un long couloir, on arrive au cloître** at the end of a long corridor, one comes to the cloister; **il vous suffit de s. la grande avenue** just follow the main avenue

2 *(longer → à pied)* to walk along; *(→ en voiture)* to drive along; *(→ en bateau)* to sail along; **la route suit la rivière sur plusieurs kilomètres** the road runs along *or* follows (the course of) the river for several kilometres; **le circuit suit ce tracé** here is the outline of the course; **découper en suivant les pointillés** cut along the dotted line

3 *(se soumettre à → traitement)* to undergo; **s. des cours de cuisine** to attend a cookery course; **s. un régime** to be on a diet

4 *(se conformer à → conseil, personne, instructions)* to follow; *(→ règlement)* to comply with; **vous n'avez qu'à s. les panneaux** just follow the signs; **son exemple n'est pas à s.** he's/she's not a good example; **j'ai toujours suivi la même ligne de conduite** I always followed the same line of conduct; **je préfère s. mon idée** I prefer to do it my way; **je ne te suivrai jamais sur cette voie** I'll never follow you down that road; *Fam* **s. le mouvement** to go with the flow

5 *Cartes* **je suis** I'm in

6 *Com (stocker)* to stock; *(produire)* to produce

C. 1 *(observer → carrière, progrès, feuilleton)* to follow; *(→ actualité)* to keep up with; **il suit le feuilleton à la radio tous les jours** he tunes in to the serial every day; **je ne suis pas les sports** I don't follow sport

2 *(se concentrer sur → exposé, messe)* to listen to, to pay attention to; **maintenant, suivez-moi bien** now, listen to me carefully *or* pay close attention; **suis bien mes gestes** watch my gestures closely

3 *(comprendre → explications, raisonnement)* to follow; **il est difficile parfois de le s. dans ses divagations** it's sometimes difficult to follow his train of thought; **je ne te suis plus** I'm not with you any more, I don't follow you

4 *(s'occuper de → dossier, commande)* to deal with; *(→ élève)* to follow the progress of; **elle suit ses patients de près** she follows her patients' progress closely; **je suis suivie par un très bon médecin** I'm with *or* under a very good doctor

USAGE ABSOLU 1 *(être derrière)* **ils ne suivent plus** they're not behind us any more

2 *(prêter attention)* **encore un qui ne suivait pas!** *(distrait)* so, someone else wasn't paying attention!; **je vais s. avec Pierre** *(sur son livre)* I'll share Pierre's book

3 *(garder le rythme)* **marche moins vite, je ne peux pas s.** slow down, I can't keep up

4 *(faire la même chose)* to follow suit; **l'Égypte a condamné Israël mais les autres pays arabes n'ont pas suivi** Egypt condemned Israel but the other Arab countries didn't follow suit

VI 1 *Scol (assimiler le programme)* to keep up; **il a du mal à s. en physique** he's having difficulty keeping up in physics; **elle suit très bien en classe** *ou* **à l'école** she keeps up well with her schoolwork; **il n'arriverait pas à s. dans la classe supérieure** he wouldn't be able to keep up if he was put in the next class

2 *(être acheminé après)* **les bagages vont s.** luggage follows; **lettre suit** *(correspondance administrative)* will write soon, letter follows; **faire s.** *(lettre)* to forward, to send on; *(sur enveloppe ou colis)* please forward; **faire s. son courrier** to have one's mail forwarded; **veux-tu que je fasse s. les factures?** do you want me to send the bills on to you?

3 *(être ci-après)* to follow; **sont reçus les candidats dont les noms suivent** the names of the successful candidates are as follows; **procéder comme suit** proceed as follows

❑ **à suivre ADJ c'est une affaire à s.** it's something we should keep an eye on **ADV** *(dans une série télévisée)* to be continued

▸**se suivre VPR 1** *(être l'un derrière l'autre → personnes, lettres)* to follow one another; **par temps de brouillard, ne vous suivez pas de trop près** in foggy conditions, keep your distance (from other vehicles); **les trois coureurs se suivent de très près** the three runners are very close behind one another *or* are tightly bunched

2 *(être dans l'ordre → pages)* to be in the right order, to follow on from one another

3 *(se succéder dans le temps) Prov* **les jours se suivent et ne se ressemblent pas** every day is a new dawn

4 *(s'enchaîner logiquement → raisonnement)* to be coherent

sujet, -ette [syʒɛ, -ɛt] **ADJ 1 s. à** *(susceptible de → migraine, attaques)* subject to; **s. au mal de mer** liable to become seasick, prone to seasickness; **s. à des crises de larmes** liable to burst into tears; **nous sommes tous sujets à l'erreur** anyone can make a mistake; **nos prix sont sujets à révision** our prices are subject to revision; **s. à oublier** apt *or* liable to forget; **s. à mentir** given to lying

2 s. à caution *(franchise, honnêteté, moralité)* questionable; **leurs informations sont sujettes à caution** their information should be taken warily

3 *Littéraire (assujetti)* subjugated, enslaved; **peuple s. de Rome** people subject to Rome

NM,F *(citoyen)* subject

NM 1 *(thème → d'une discussion, d'une pièce, d'un roman, d'un exposé, d'une recherche)* subject; **le s. de notre débat ce soir est...** the question we'll be debating tonight is...; **quel est le s. du livre?** what's the book about?; **je tiens le s. d'une pièce** I have an idea *or* a subject for a play; **tu tiens là un bon s. de thèse** you have a good subject for your PhD; **nos avis s'accordent sur le s. de la nourriture** we have the same opinions on the subject of food; **s. de conversation** topic (of conversation); **changeons de s.** let's change the subject; **s. de plainte** grievance; **c'est devenu un s. de plaisanterie** it has become a standing joke; **s. d'examen** examination question

2 *(motif)* **s. de** cause of, ground for, grounds for; **ils ont de nombreux sujets de discorde** they have many reasons to disagree; **leur salaire est leur principal s. de mécontentement** the main cause of their dissatisfaction is their salary; **sa santé est devenue un gros s. de préoccupation** his/her condition is now giving serious grounds for concern *or* has become a great source of anxiety; **tu n'as pas s. de te plaindre** you have no cause *or* grounds for complaint; **se mettre en colère sans s.** to lose one's temper for no good reason

3 *Beaux-Arts & Mus* subject; **peindre des sujets allégoriques** to paint allegorical subjects

4 *(individu)* **mauvais s.** bad lot, ne'er-do-well; **brillant s.** *(élève)* brilliant pupil

5 *(figurine)* figurine; **des petits sujets en porcelaine** little china figures *or* figurines

6 *Gram (fonction)* subject; *Ling* **le s. parlant** the speaker

7 *Méd, Phil & Psy* subject; **s. d'expérience** experimental subject

8 *Jur* **s. de droit** possessor of a right

9 *Hort* stock

❑ **au sujet de PRÉP** about, concerning; **c'est au s. de Martha?** is it about Martha?; **la décision qu'ils ont prise au s. du projet** the decision they made about *or* concerning the project; **j'aimerais vous faire remarquer, à ce s., que...** concerning this matter, I'd like to point out to you that...; **je voudrais parler au directeur – c'est à quel s.?** I'd like to talk to the manager – what is it about?; **éprouver des craintes au s. de qch** to have misgivings about sth

sujétion [syʒesjɔ̃] **NF 1** *Pol (d'un peuple)* subjection, enslavement (**à** to); **vivre dans la s.** to live in subjection; **tenir en s.** to hold *or* to have in one's power **2** *(à une règle)* subjection, subjecting *(UNCOUNT)* (**à** to); **une habitude devient vite une s.** we soon become slaves to a habit **3** *(contrainte)* constraint; **c'est une vraie s. d'avoir des animaux domestiques** having pets is a real tie

sulciforme [sylsifɔrm] **ADJ** sulcate, sulcated

sulfacide [sylfasid] **NM** *Chim* sulpho-acid, thio-acid

sulfadiazine [sylfadjazin] **NF** *Pharm* sulfadiazine

sulfamide [sylfamid] **NM** *Pharm* sulphonamide

sulfanilamide [sylfanilamid] **NM OU NF** *Pharm* sulphanilamide

sulfatage [sylfataʒ] **NM** *Agr* copper sulphate treatment

sulfatation [sylfatɑsjɔ̃] **NF** *Agr* sulphation

sulfate [sylfat] **NM** *Chim* sulphate; **s. d'ammonium** ammonium sulphate

sulfaté, -e [sylfate] **ADJ 1** *Chim* sulphated, sulphate *(avant n)* **2** *Agr* treated with copper sulphate

sulfater [3] [sylfate] **VT 1** *Agr* to treat with copper sulphate **2** *Élec* to sulphate

sulfateur, -euse [sylfatœr, -øz] **NM,F** *Agr* = person who treats vines with copper sulphate

❑ **sulfateuse NF 1** *Agr* copper sulphate sprayer **2** *très Fam (mitrailleuse)* submachine *or* machine gun■, *Br* typewriter

sulfhydrique [sylfidrik] **ADJ M** *Chim* **acide s.** hydrogen sulphide

sulfhydryle [sylfidril] **NM** *Chim* sulphhydryl

sulfinisation [sylfinizɑsjɔ̃] **NF** *Métal* case hardening

sulfitage [sylfitaʒ] NM*Agr* sulphidizing

sulfite [sylfit] NM*Chim* sulphite

sulfonation [sylfɔnasjɔ̃] NF*Chim* sulphonation

sulfone [sylfɔn] NF*Chim* sulphone

sulfoné, -e [sylfɔne] ADJ*Chim* sulphonated

sulfosel [sylfɔsɛl] NM*Chim* sulphosalt

sulfoxyde [sylfɔksid] NM*Chim* sulphoxide

sulfurage [sylfyraʒ] NM*Agr* sulphuration

sulfure [sylfyr] NM *Chim* sulphide; **s. de fer** iron pyrites

sulfuré, -e [sylfyre] ADJ *Chim* sulphuretted; **hydrogène s.** hydrogen sulphide

sulfurer [3] [sylfyre] VT 1 *Chim* to sulphuret, to sulphurate 2 *Agr* to treat with sulphide

sulfureux, -euse [sylfyrø, -øz] ADJ 1 *Chim* sulphurous; (*eau, source*) sulphur (*avant n*) 2 *Fig* (*charme*) fiendish, infernal; (*écrit, discours, thèse*) heretical, subversive; **il a toujours eu une réputation sulfureuse** there's always been a whiff of scandal *or* of sulphur about him

sulfurique [sylfyrik] ADJ*Chim* sulphuric

sulfurisé, -e [sylfyrize] ADJ *Chim* sulphurized; **papier s.** greaseproof *or Spéc* sulphurized paper

sulky [sylki] NMsulky

sultan [syltɑ̃] NMsultan

sultanat [syltana] NMsultanate

sultane [syltan] NF 1 (*titre*) sultana, sultaness 2 (*canapé*) sultana

sumac [symak] NM*Bot* sumach (tree)

Sumatra [symatra] NMSumatra; **à S.** in Sumatra

Sumer [symɛr] NMSumer

sumérien, -enne [symerjɛ̃, -ɛn] ADJSumerian

 NM*(langue)* Sumerian

 ▫ **Sumérien, -enne** NM,FSumerian

summum [sɔmɔm] NM 1 (*d'une carrière*) peak, *Sout* zenith; (*d'une civilisation*) highest point; (*de l'élégance, du luxe, de l'arrogance*) height; **au s. de sa puissance** at the peak of its power; **elle était au s. de son art quand elle peignit ce tableau** her talent was at its peak *or* height when she painted this picture

 2 *Fam* (*locution*) **c'est le s.!** (*on ne peut faire mieux*) it's the tops!; (*on ne peut faire pire*) it's the pits!

sumo [symo, sumo] NMsumo (wrestling); **lutteur de s.** sumo wrestler

sumotori [symɔtɔri, sumɔtɔri] NMsumo wrestler

sunlight [sœnlajt] NM*Cin* (artificial) sunlight

sunna [suna, syna] NFSunna

sunnisme [synism] NMSunnism

sunnite [synit] ADJSunni

 NMFSunnit, Sunnite

sup [syp] ADJ INV *Fam* **faire des heures s.** to work overtime▪; **cadre s.** senior exec

super [sypɛr] *Fam* ADJ INVgreat, terrific, fantastic; **ce serait s. si tu pouvais venir!** it'd be great if you could come!; **c'est de la s. qualité** it's fantastic quality; **s. réductions sur tout le stock!** massive reductions on the whole stock!

 ADV (*compliqué, bon, cher, propre, gentil*) *Br* dead, *Am* real; **un bouquin s. chiant** a *Br* dead *or Am* real boring book; **elle est s. organisée** she's incredibly well-organized; **on s'est s. bien marrés** we had a great time

 EXCLAMgreat!, terrific!

 NM (*essence*) *Br* four-star (petrol), *Am* premium

 NF *Belg* (*essence*) *Br* four-star (petrol), *Am* premium

super- [sypɛr] PRÉF 1 (*en intensif*) super; **des collants super-fins** extra-sheer tights; **super-rapide** superfast 2 *Fam* (*exceptionnel*) super; **super-flic** supercop; **une super-voiture** a supercar; **un super-cerveau** a superbrain

super-8 [sypɛrɥit] ADJ*Cin & TV*Super 8

superacide [sypɛrasid] NM*Chim*superacid

superalliage [sypɛraljaʒ] NMsuperalloy

superamas [sypɛrama] NM*Astron* **s. local** supergalaxy

superbe [sypɛrb] ADJ 1 (*magnifique → yeux, bijou, ville*) superb, beautiful, magnificent; (→ *bébé, femme*) beautiful, gorgeous; (→ *homme*) good-looking, handsome; (→ *voix*) superb, beautiful; (→ *journée*) glorious, beautiful; (→ *temps*) wonderful; **tu as une mine s. aujourd'hui** you look radiant today; **il a fait un temps s.** the weather was wonderful

 2 **s. de** (*sublime*) superbly; **il a été s. de**

cynisme/d'indifférence he was superbly cynical/indifferent

 3 *Littéraire* (*altier → air*) haughty

 NF *Littéraire* haughtiness; **cela va lui faire perdre de sa s.** he/she won't be quite so proud after this

superbement [sypɛrbəmɑ̃] ADV 1 (*splendidement*) superbly, magnificently, beautifully 2 *Littéraire* (*arrogamment*) arrogantly, haughtily

superbénéfice [sypɛrbenefis] NM excess profit, surplus profit

superbombe [sypɛrbɔ̃b] NFsuperbomb

supercagnotte [sypɛrkaɲɔt] NF superjackpot (*in the "Loto"*)

supercalculateur [sypɛrkalkylatœr] NM supercomputer

supercarburant [sypɛrkarbyrɑ̃] NM*Br* four-star *or* high-octane petrol, *Am* premium

superchampion, -onne [sypɛrʃɑ̃pjɔ̃, -ɔn] NM,F sports superstar

supercherie [sypɛrʃəri] NFhoax

supercritique [sypɛrkritik] ADJsupercritical

superdividende [sypɛrdividɑ̃d] NM *Fin* surplus dividend

supère [sypɛr] ADJ*Bot* superior

superétatique [sypɛretatik] ADJsuprastate

supérette [sypɛrɛt] NFmini-market, *Am* superette

superfamille [sypɛrfamij] NF*Biol* superfamily

superfétation [sypɛrfetasjɔ̃] NF *Littéraire* superfluity, redundancy, supererogation; **ce serait une s. de...** it would be superfluous *or* supererogatory to...

superfétatoire [sypɛrfetatwar] ADJ *Littéraire* superfluous, unnecessary, redundant

superficialité [sypɛrfisjalite] NFsuperficiality

superficie [sypɛrfisi] NF 1 (*d'un champ*) acreage, area; (*d'une maison*) surface area, floor space; **l'entrepôt fait 3000m² de s.** *ou* **a une s. de 3000m²** the warehouse has a surface area of 3,000m²

 2 *Littéraire* (*apparence*) superficial *or* external appearance; **s'arrêter à la s. des choses** to do no more than skim the surface of things; **il ne connaît le problème qu'en s.** he has only a superficial knowledge of the problem

 3 *Agr* **s. agricole utile** *ou* **utilisée** utilized agricultural area

superficiel, -elle [sypɛrfisjɛl] ADJ 1 (*brûlure*) superficial, surface (*avant n*); *Géog* **eau superficielle** surface water 2 (*connaissances, personne*) shallow, insubstantial; (*étude, travail*) superficial, perfunctory; (*contrôle*) superficial, cursory

superficiellement [sypɛrfisjɛlmɑ̃] ADV 1 (*blesser*) superficially 2 (*inspecter, corriger*) cursorily, superficially; **répondre s.** to give a superficial answer

superfin, -e [sypɛrfɛ̃, -in] ADJ (*produit*) top-quality, of superior quality; (*qualité*) superior

superfinition [sypɛrfinisjɔ̃] NFsuperfinishing

superflu, -e [sypɛrfly] ADJ 1 (*non nécessaire →biens, excuse, recommandation*) superfluous, unnecessary

 2 (*en trop → détails, exemple*) redundant, superfluous; **un grand lessivage ne serait pas s.** a good scrub wouldn't do any harm *or* wouldn't go amiss; **pour vous débarrasser de vos kilos/poils superflus** to get rid of that excess weight/unwanted hair

 NM**le s.** = that which is superfluous; **se passer du s.** to do without non-essentials

superfluide [sypɛrflyid] ADJsuperfluid

 NMsuperfluid

superfluidité [sypɛrflyidite] NFsuperfluidity

superfluité [sypɛrflyite] NF*Littéraire* superfluity

superforme [sypɛrfɔrm] NF*Fam* **être en s., tenir la s.** to be in great form *or* on top form *or* bursting with health; **une équipe en s.** a team in peak condition

super-g [sypɛrʒe] NM INV*Ski* super-g

super-géant [sypɛrʒeɑ̃] (*pl* **super-géants**) NM *Ski* super-giant (slalom)

supergéante [sypɛrʒeɑ̃t] NF*Astron* supergiant

supergrand [sypɛrgrɑ̃] NM*Fam* superpower

super-huit [sypɛrɥit] ADJ INVsuper eight

 NM INV (*format*) super eight; (*caméra*) super-eight (film) camera

supérieur, -e [sypɛrjœr] ADJ 1 (*plus haut que le reste → étagère, étage*) upper, top; (→ *ligne*) top;

(*juste au-dessus → étagère, ligne*) above; **le bord s. droit de la page** the top right-hand corner of the page; **le cours s. d'un fleuve** the upper reaches of a river; **la partie supérieure de l'immeuble** the top *or* upper part of the building; **les jouets sont à l'étage s.** toys are on the next floor *or* the floor above

 2 (*quantitativement → efficacité*) higher, greater (**à** than); (→ *prix, rendement, vitesse*) higher (**à** than); (→ *volume*) bigger, greater (**à** than); **j'ai fait une offre supérieure** I bid more *or* made a higher bid; **un nombre s.** a higher number; **troupes supérieures en nombre** troops superior in number; **leurs joueurs se retrouvent maintenant supérieurs en nombre** their players now outnumber the opposition; **donne-moi un chiffre s. à 8** give me a number higher than 8; **taux légèrement s. à 8 pour cent** rate slightly over 8 percent; **une note supérieure à 10** a *Br* mark *or Am* grade above 10; **d'une longueur/largeur supérieure à...** longer/wider than...; **il est d'une taille supérieure à la moyenne** he's taller than average

 3 (*au sommet de la hiérarchie → échelons*) upper, topmost; (→ *classes sociales*) upper; (→ *enseignement*) higher; (*juste au-dessus → niveau*) next; (→ *grade, rang*) senior; **les autorités supérieures** the powers above; **vous passerez à l'échelon s. dans deux mois** you'll move up to the next grade in two months' time; *Scol* **passer dans la classe supérieure** to move up one class; **je lui suis hiérarchiquement s.** I'm his/her superior *or* senior

 4 (*dans une échelle de valeurs → intelligence, esprit, être*) superior; (→ *intérêts*) higher; (→ *produit, marchandises*) of superior quality, top-quality; **de qualité supérieure** of superior quality, top-quality; **intelligence supérieure à la moyenne** above-average intelligence; **leur lessive est-elle vraiment supérieure à toutes les autres?** is their washing powder really better than all the others?; *Sport* **il est techniquement s. au Suédois** his technique is superior to *or* better than that of the Swedish player; **il se croit s. à tout le monde** he thinks he's above everyone else, he thinks he's superior; **se montrer s. aux événements** to rise above events; **être s. à la tâche** to be more than equal to the task

 5 (*hautain → air, ton*) superior; **ne prends pas cet air s.!** don't look so superior!

 6 *Anat* (*membre, mâchoire*) upper

 7 *Astron* (*planète*) superior

 8 *Biol* (*animal, espèce, végétal*) higher

 9 *Géog* (*en amont*) upper

 10 *Math* superior; **s. ou égal à** superior or equal to, greater than or equal to

 11 *Rel* **le Père s.** the father superior; **la Mère supérieure** the mother superior

 NM,F (*dans une hiérarchie*) **s. (hiérarchique)** superior

 NM*Univ* **le s.** higher education

 ▫ **Supérieur, -e** NM,F*Rel* father, *f* mother superior ADJ**le lac S.** Lake Superior

supérieurement [sypɛrjœrmɑ̃] ADV exceptionally; **elle est s. douée** she's exceptionally gifted

superinfection [sypɛrɛ̃fɛksjɔ̃] NF *Méd & Vét* superinfection

superintendant [sypɛrɛ̃tɑ̃dɑ̃] NM *Anciennement* superintendent

supériorité [sypɛrjɔrite] NF 1 (*en qualité*) superiority; **ils vantent la s. des transports en commun** they praise the superiority of public transport; **découvrez la s. de notre nouvelle lessive!** see for yourself how much better our new washing powder is!; **c'est indubitablement une s. que vous avez sur elle** that's definitely one area where you're better than she is

 2 (*en quantité*) superiority; **s. militaire** military superiority; **s. numérique** superiority in numbers; **la s. que donne l'argent** the power that money confers

 3 (*arrogance*) patronizing attitude, superiority; **un air de s.** a superior air

superlatif, -ive [sypɛrlatif, -iv] ADJsuperlative

 NM*Ling* superlative; **s. relatif/absolu** relative/absolute superlative

 ▫ **au superlatif** ADV 1 *Ling* in the superlative 2 (*très*) extremely; **il est paresseux au s.** he's extremely lazy

superlativement [sypɛrlativmɑ̃] ADV *Fam Vieilli* superlatively▪

superléger [sypɛrleʒe] NM *Boxe* light welterweight

superlourd [sypɛrlur] NM *Boxe* super heavyweight

superman [sypɛrman] (*pl* **supermans** *ou* **supermen** [-mɛn]) NM *Fam* superman; **jouer les supermen** to play at being superman

supermarché [sypɛrmarʃe] NM supermarket

supermolécule [sypɛrmɔlekyl] NF supermolecule

supernova [sypɛrnɔva] (*pl* **-ae**) NF *Astron* supernova

superordinateur [sypɛrɔrdinatœr] NM supercomputer

superordre [sypɛrɔrdr] NM superorder

superoxyde [sypɛrɔksid] NM *Chim* superoxide

superpactole [sypɛrpaktɔl] NM *Fam* bumper jackpot

superpétrolier [sypɛrpetrɔlje] NM supertanker

Superphénix [sypɛrfeniks] NM *Nucl* Superphenix (*controversial fast-breeder reactor*)

superphosphate [sypɛrfɔsfat] NM superphosphate

superplasticité [sypɛrplastisite] NF superplasticity

superplastique [sypɛrplastik] ADJ superplastic

superposable [sypɛrpozabl] ADJ **1** *Géom* superposable **2** (*chaise, lit*) stacking (*avant n*)

superposé, -e [sypɛrpoze] ADJ (*images, couleurs*) superimposed; **des couches superposées de chocolat et de chantilly** layers of chocolate and whipped cream one on top of the other; **lits superposés** bunk beds, bunks

superposer [3] [sypɛrpoze] VT **1** (*meubles*) to stack (up); (*images, couleurs, sons*) to superimpose (**à** *on or* upon); **cette année la mode superpose les épaisseurs** layered fabrics are fashionable this year **2** *Géom* to superpose **3** *Ordinat* **s. une écriture** to overwrite
▸**se superposer** VPR **1** (*emploi passif*) (*étagères*) to stack; **les plateaux se superposent facilement** the trays are easy to stack **2** (*se mêler → images, couleurs, sons*) to be superimposed; **leurs deux visages se superposent dans ma mémoire** their two faces have become indistinguishable in my memory **3** *Géom* to be superposed

superposition [sypɛrpozisjɔ̃] NF **1** (*d'étagères, de plats*) stacking **2** *Géom* superposition **3** (*d'images, de couleurs, de sons*) superimposition, superimposing (UNCOUNT); **la s. de deux images** the superimposing of two images **4** *Géol* **principe de s.** principle of superposition

superproduction [sypɛrprɔdyksjɔ̃] NF *Cin* big-budget movie *or Br* film

superprofit [sypɛrprɔfi] NM enormous profit

superpuissance [sypɛrpɥisɑ̃s] NF superpower

supersonique [sypɛrsɔnik] ADJ supersonic
NM supersonic aircraft

superstar [sypɛrstar] NF superstar

superstitieuse [sypɛrstisjøz] *voir* **superstitieux**

superstitieusement [sypɛrstisjøzmɑ̃] ADV superstitiously

superstitieux, -euse [sypɛrstisjø, -øz] ADJ superstitious; **ils ont un attachement s. aux traditions** they have an exaggerated respect for tradition
NM,F superstitious person

superstition [sypɛrstisjɔ̃] NF superstition; **j'évite les échelles par pure s.** I walk round ladders simply because I'm superstitious; **la s. religieuse** religious superstition; **avoir la s. du passé** to be excessively attached to the past

superstructure [sypɛrstryktyr] NF superstructure

supertanker [sypɛrtɑ̃kœr] NM supertanker

superviser [3] [sypɛrvize] VT to supervise, to oversee

superviseur [sypɛrvizœr] NM **1** (*personne*) supervisor **2** *Ordinat* supervisor, scheduler

supervision [sypɛrvizjɔ̃] NF supervision; **être sous la s. de qn** to be supervised by sb, to be under sb's supervision

superwelter [sypɛrwɛltɛr] NM *Boxe* light middleweight

superwoman [sypɛrwuman] (*pl* **superwomans**) NF *Fam* superwoman

---

supin [sypɛ̃] NM *Ling* supine

supinateur [sypinatœr] *Anat* ADJ M supinator NM supinator muscle

supination [sypinasjɔ̃] NF *Anat* supination

supion [sypjɔ̃] NM small cuttlefish

supplantation [syplɑ̃tasjɔ̃] NF supplanting, supplantation

supplanter [3] [syplɑ̃te] VT **1** (*rival*) to supplant, to displace, to supersede; **un autre l'avait supplanté dans son cœur** another man had supplanted him in his/her affections; **il s'est fait s. à la tête de la société** he was replaced at the head of the company **2** (*machine, système*) to supplant, to take over from; **la machine va-t-elle s. l'homme?** will machines take the place of people?

suppléance [sypleɑ̃s] NF **1** *Scol* (*poste de remplaçant*) *Br* supply post, *Am* substitute post; (*poste d'adjoint*) assistantship; (*activité → de remplaçant*) *Br* supply *or Am* substitute teaching; (*→ d'adjoint*) assistantship; **assurer la s. de qn** (*le remplacer*) to deputize for sb; (*l'assister*) to assist sb **2** *Jur & Pol* deputy **3** *Ling* suppletion

suppléant, -e [sypleɑ̃, -ɑ̃t] ADJ **1** *Scol* (*remplaçant*) *Br* supply (*avant n*), *Am* substitute (*avant n*); (*adjoint*) assistant (*avant n*) **2** (*médecin*) locum (*avant n*) **3** *Jur & Pol* deputy (*avant n*) **4** *Gram* (*verbe, terme*) substitute (*avant n*)
NM,F **1** *Scol* (*remplaçant*) *Br* supply teacher, *Am* substitute teacher; (*adjoint*) assistant teacher **2** (*médecin*) locum **3** *Jur & Pol* deputy

suppléer [15] [syplee] VT **1** *Littéraire* (*remédier à → manque*) to make up for, to compensate for; (*→ lacune*) to fill in **2** *Littéraire* (*ajouter → réponse manquante*) to provide, to supply **3** (*compléter*) to complement, to supplement; **là où l'intelligence artificielle peut s. l'intelligence humaine** the areas where artificial intelligence can take over from human intelligence; **s. qch par** to complete sth with **4** *Scol* (*remplacer*) to replace, to stand in for **5** *Jur & Pol* (*remplacer*) to deputize for
❑ **suppléer à** VT IND **1** (*remédier à → insuffisance*) to make up for, to compensate for; **sa curiosité suppléait à son manque de formation** his/her curiosity made up for his/her lack of training **2** (*remplacer → sujet: personne*) to replace; **l'énergie nucléaire a peu à peu suppléé aux énergies traditionnelles** nuclear energy has gradually taken over from *or* replaced traditional forms of energy

supplément [syplemɑ̃] NM **1** (*coût*) extra *or* additional charge; **ils demandent un s. de 8 euros pour le vin** they charge 8 euros extra for wine; **payer un s.** to pay extra; **prévoyez un s. pour les valises de plus de 20 kilos** please note that there is a charge for luggage weighing over 20 kilos; **s. chambre individuelle** single room supplement **2** *Rail* supplement; **s. couchette** sleeper charge; **un train à s.** a train with a fare surcharge *or* supplement **3** (*de nourriture*) extra portion; *Fin* (*de crédits*) additional facility; **un s. d'informations** additional *or* further information; **s. d'enquête** further investigation; **le juge a demandé un s. d'enquête** the judge asked that the investigation be pursued further; **je lui ai donné un s. d'argent de poche** I gave him/her extra pocket money; **un s. d'âme** a little extra **4** (*à un livre, un journal*) supplement; **le s. du dimanche** the Sunday supplement; **s. détachable** pullout; **s. illustré** *ou* **en couleurs** colour supplement; **s. éducation** education supplement **5** *Jur* **s. de revenu familial** ≃ family income supplement **6** *Math* supplement
❑ **en supplément** ADV extra; **c'est en s.** it comes as an extra, it's an extra; **menu 15 euros, boisson en s.** menu 15 euros, drinks extra

supplémentaire [syplemɑ̃tɛr] ADJ **1** (*crédit, dépense*) additional, supplementary, extra; **un délai s.** an extension (of deadline); **nous avons obtenu des rations supplémentaires** we got extra rations; **nous attendons des informations supplémentaires** we are awaiting further information; **ce sera une charge s. pour les**

---

contribuables it will mean even more of a burden to the taxpayer **2** *Rail* (*train*) relief (*avant n*) **3** *Math* supplementary **4** *Mus* **lignes supplémentaires** ledger *or* added lines

supplémentation [syplemɑ̃tasjɔ̃] NF **s.** *ou* **s. nutritionnelle** nutritional supplementation, taking nutritional supplements

supplétif, -ive [sypletif, -iv] ADJ **1** (*gén*) auxiliary, additional **2** *Jur* (*loi*) supplementary **3** *Mil* auxiliary **4** *Ling* suppletive
NM *Mil* auxiliary

supplétoire [sypletwar] ADJ **serment s.** suppletory oath

suppliant, -e [syplijɑ̃, -ɑ̃t] ADJ begging, imploring, beseeching; **d'un air s.** pleadingly; **d'un ton s.** imploringly, pleadingly; **d'une voix suppliante** pleadingly
NM,F supplicant

supplication [syplikasjɔ̃] NF **1** (*demande*) entreaty, *Sout* supplication; **malgré toutes mes supplications** despite all my pleading **2** *Rel* supplication

supplice [syplis] NM **1** *Hist* torture; **conduire** *ou* **mener un prisonnier au s.** to take a prisoner to his place of execution; **il va à l'école comme au s.** when he goes to school, it's as if he was going to his own funeral; **s. chinois** Chinese water torture; *Fig* extreme torment; **subir le s. de la roue** to be broken on the wheel; **le s. de Tantale** the punishment of Tantalus; **le dernier s.** (*la peine de mort*) execution **2** (*douleur physique*) agony, torture; (*douleur morale*) torment, torment, agony; **ce mal de tête est un vrai s.** this headache is absolute agony; **la conversation était devenue un s.** the conversation had become sheer torture; **être au s.** to be in agonies; **je suis au s., quand rentrera-t-il?** this is sheer torture, when will he be back?; **mettre qn au s.** to torture sb **3** *Rel* **les supplices éternels** the torments of the damned

supplicié, -e [syplisje] NM,F (*personne → qui a subi la peine de mort*) execution victim; (*→ qui a été torturée*) torture victim; **les corps des suppliciés étaient entassés dans des charrettes** the bodies of those executed were piled onto carts

supplicier [9] [syplisje] VT *Littéraire* **1** (*exécuter*) to execute; (*torturer*) to torture **2** (*tourmenter*) to torment, to rack, to plague; **les remords la suppliciaient** she was racked by remorse

supplier [10] [syplije] VT to beg, to implore, to beseech; **s. qn (à genoux) de faire qch** to beg sb (on bended knee) to do sth; **épargnez-le, je vous en supplie** spare him, I beg you *or Sout* I beseech you

supplique [syplik] NF *Jur & Rel* petition; **présenter une s. à qn** to petition sb; *Littéraire* **ayez égard à ma s.** hear my prayer

support [sypɔr] NM **1** (*de colonne, de meuble*) base, support; (*de statuette*) stand, pedestal; (*pour un échafaudage*) support; (*pour outils*) rest; (*pour une lampe, un tube à essai*) stand; **s. mural** wall bracket; **s. de tasse** (*dans une voiture*) cup holder **2** (*de communication*) medium; **le gouvernement se sert de la télévision comme s. pour la campagne électorale** the government is using television to get its election campaign across; **supports audiovisuels** audiovisual aids, audiovisuals; **s. de publicité** *ou* **publicitaire** publicity *or* advertising medium; **supports visuels** visual aids, visuals **3** (*en acoustique*) **s. magnétique** magnetic tape **4** *Culin* base **5** *Hér* supporter **6** *Typ* support; **s. d'impression** = material on which printing is done **7** *Ordinat* medium; **s. de données** data carrier; **s. d'information** data support; **s. individuel d'information** smart card, individual data support; **sur s. papier** hard copy; **s. de sortie** output medium; **s. de stockage** storage medium; **s. technique** technical support **8** *Math & Phot* support

supportable [sypɔrtabl] ADJ **1** (*douleur*) bearable; **il fait froid, mais c'est s.** it's cold but not

unbearably so **2** *(conduite, personne)* tolerable; **tu n'es plus s.!** I can't take any more of this from you!

supportablement [sypɔʀtabləmɑ̃] **ADV** bearably

supporter[1] [sypɔʀtɛʀ] **NM** *Sport* supporter

SUPPORTER[2] [3] [sypɔʀte]

> **VT** to support **1, 8, 9** ■ to hold up **1** ■ to assume **2** ■ to bear **2, 5, 6** ■ to be subject to **3** ■ to withstand **4, 7** ■ to put up with **5** ■ to stand **6**
> **VPR** to bear each other **2** ■ to be bearable **3**

VT 1 *(servir d'assise à)* to support, to hold up; **cinq piliers supportent la voûte** the roof is held up by five pillars

2 *(assumer → responsabilité, obligation)* to assume; *(prendre en charge → dépense)* to bear; **l'acheteur supporte les frais** the fees are borne by the purchaser; **tu apprendras à s. les conséquences de tes actes** you'll learn to take responsibility for what you do

3 *(être assujetti à → impôt)* to be subject to; **les articles de luxe supportent de lourdes taxes** luxury goods are subject to heavy taxes

4 *(résister à)* to stand up to, to withstand; **la porcelaine fine ne supporte pas la chaleur excessive** fine china will not withstand excessive heat; **des plantes qui supportent/ne supportent pas le froid** plants that do well/badly in the cold; **elle a bien supporté la route** *(personne)* she came through the journey all right; *(voiture)* it stood up to the journey all right; **bien s. une opération** to come through an operation in good shape; **mal s. une opération** to have trouble recovering from an operation; **je ne supporte pas l'alcool/la pilule** drink/the pill doesn't agree with me; **on supporterait bien une petite laine** it's cold enough to wear a sweater or *Br* jumper

5 *(subir sans faillir → épreuve, privation)* to bear, to endure, to put up with; *(→ insulte, menace)* to bear; **elle supporte tout de lui** she puts up with anything from him; **elle supporte bien la douleur** she bears pain well, she has a high pain threshold; **elle supporte mal la douleur** she can't cope with pain, she has a low pain threshold; **je ne supporte pas son départ** I can't bear or *Sout* endure his/her leaving; **comment s. tant de misère/d'ineptie?** how can one possibly put up with such poverty/nonsense?

6 *(tolérer, accepter)* to bear, to stand; **je ne supporte pas la fumée** I can't bear or stand cigarette smoke; **je ne supporte pas de perdre** I can't stand losing; **c'est plus que je ne peux s.** it's more than I can bear; **décidément, je ne la supporte pas!** I just can't stand her!; **il faudra le s. encore deux jours** we'll have to put up with him for two more days; **j'arrive tout juste à les s.** I can just about tolerate them

7 *(résister à)* to withstand; **leur nouvelle voiture supporte la comparaison avec la concurrence** their new car will bear or stand comparison with anything produced by their competitors; **sa théorie ne supporte pas une critique sérieuse** his theory won't stand up to serious criticism

8 *(en Afrique francophone)* *(personne, famille)* to support

9 *Sport (encourager)* to support

▸**se supporter** **VPR 1** *(emploi réfléchi)* **je ne me supporte plus en blonde/en noir** blonde hair/black just isn't right for me any more

2 *(emploi réciproque)* to bear or to stand each other

3 *(emploi passif)* to be bearable; **le froid sec se supporte plus facilement** when it's cold and dry, it's more bearable

supporteur, -trice [sypɔʀtœʀ, -tʀis] **NM,F** supporter

supposable [sypozabl] **ADJ** imaginable

supposé, -e [sypoze] **ADJ 1** *(faux → testament)* false, forged; *(→ nom)* assumed

2 *(admis)* **la vitesse est supposée constante** the speed is assumed to be constant

3 *(présumé → vainqueur)* supposed, presumed; *(→ père)* putative; *(→ dimension)* estimated; **l'auteur s. du pamphlet** the supposed author of

the pamphlet; **le nombre s. des victimes** the presumed number of casualties

4 *Can (censé)* supposed to

◻ **supposé que** **CONJ** supposing (that), assuming that

supposer [3] [sypoze] **VT 1** *(conjecturer, imaginer)* to suppose, to assume; **je suppose qu'il t'a emprunté de l'argent** I suppose or I assume he borrowed money from you; **je suppose que tu n'es pas prêt** I take it or I suppose you're not ready; **on le suppose à Paris, on suppose qu'il est à Paris** he is supposed to be in Paris; **cela laisse s. que...** this suggests that...; **sa réponse laisse s. qu'il était au courant** his answer leads one to assume he knew all about it; **tout laisse s. qu'il avait été contacté par la CIA** everything points to his having been contacted by the CIA; **en supposant que tu échoues** suppose (that) or supposing (that) or let's suppose (that) you fail; **à s. que** assuming that, supposing

2 *(estimer, penser)* **et tu la supposes assez bête pour se laisser faire?** so you think she's stupid enough to let it happen?; **s. qch à qn** to credit sb with sth; **vous lui supposez une grandeur d'âme qu'il n'a pas** you credit him with a magnanimity he doesn't possess

3 *(impliquer)* to imply, to require, to presuppose; **une mission qui suppose de la discrétion** an assignment where discretion is required or is a must; **la liberté de parole suppose le pluralisme** freedom of speech implies pluralism; **cela suppose la connaissance des mathématiques** it presupposes a knowledge of mathematics

4 *Jur (imposteur)* to put forward; *(faux testament)* to present

supposition [sypozisjɔ̃] **NF 1** *(hypothèse)* supposition, assumption; **des suppositions gratuites** mere or gratuitous suppositions; **je n'en suis pas sûr, c'est une s.** I'm not sure, I'm only assuming; **faire des suppositions** to speculate; **dans cette s.** if this is the case; *Fam* **une s.: il s'enfuit** suppose he runs away■; *Fam* **une s. qu'elle dise la vérité** supposing (that) she's telling the truth■

2 *Jur* **s. de nom** false personation; **s. d'enfant** *ou* **de part** setting up of a suppositious child

suppositoire [sypozitwaʀ] **NM** suppository

suppôt [sypo] **NM** *Littéraire* henchman; **s. de Satan** *ou* **du diable** fiend

suppresseur [sypʀesœʀ] **ADJ M** *Méd* **gène s.** suppressor gene

suppression [sypʀesjɔ̃] **NF 1** *(abrogation)* abolition; *(annulation → service d'autobus, d'un train)* cancellation; **la s. de la peine de mort** the abolition of the death penalty

2 *(dans un texte)* deletion

3 *(élimination)* elimination; **s. de la douleur par piqûres** elimination of pain by injections

4 *(assassinat)* elimination, liquidation; **la s. des témoins gênants** the elimination of awkward witnesses

5 *Écon* **il y a eu beaucoup de suppressions d'emploi dans la région** there were many job losses in the area

6 *Jur* **s. d'enfant** *ou* **de part** concealment of birth; **s. d'état** = destruction of proof of somebody's civil status

supprimable [sypʀimabl] **ADJ** that can be got rid of

supprimer [3] [sypʀime] **VT 1** *(faire cesser → cause, effet)* to do away with; *(→ habitude, obstacle)* to get rid of; *(→ pauvreté, racisme)* to put an end to, to do away with; *(→ douleur)* to kill, to stop; *(→ fatigue)* to eliminate

2 *(démolir → mur, quartier)* to knock or to pull down, to demolish

3 *(annuler → loi)* to repeal, to annul; *(→ projet)* to do away with; *(→ service d'autobus, train)* to cancel; *(→ allocation, prime)* to withdraw, to stop; *(→ concurrence)* to cut out

4 *(retirer)* **s. des emplois** to axe jobs; **on va te s. ton permis de conduire** they'll take away your *Br* driving licence or *Am* driver's license; **j'ai partiellement supprimé le sel** I cut down on salt; **j'ai totalement supprimé le sel** I cut out salt (altogether); **ils vont s. des trains dans les zones rurales** train services will be cut in rural areas; **le médecin lui a supprimé le tabac** the doctor told him/her to stop smoking

5 *(enlever → opération, séquence)* to cut (out), to take out; *(→ mot, passage)* to delete; **s. les étapes/intermédiaires** to do away with the intermediate stages/the middlemen

6 *(tuer)* to do away with; **il s'est fait s. par la mafia** the mafia did away with him

▸**se supprimer** **VPR** to take one's own life

suppurant, -e [sypyʀɑ̃, -ɑ̃t] **ADJ** suppurating

suppuration [sypyʀasjɔ̃] **NF** suppuration

suppuré, -e [sypyʀe] **ADJ** suppurating

suppurer [3] [sypyʀe] **VI** to suppurate

supputation [sypytasjɔ̃] **NF** calculation, estimation

supputer [3] [sypyte] **VT** *(quantité)* to estimate; *(possibilités)* to assess; **s. les possibilités d'aboutir à un accord** to assess the likelihood of reaching an agreement; **s. ses chances** to calculate one's chances

supra [sypʀa] **ADV** supra; **voir s.** supra, see above

supraconducteur, -trice [sypʀakɔ̃dyktœʀ, -tʀis] **ADJ** superconductive **NM** superconductor

supraconduction [sypʀakɔ̃dyksjɔ̃] **NF** superconduction

supraconductivité [sypʀakɔ̃dyktivite] **NF** supraconductivity

supraconductrice [sypʀakɔ̃dyktʀis] *voir* **supraconducteur**

supraliminaire [sypʀaliminɛʀ] **ADJ** supraliminal

supramoléculaire [sypʀamɔlekylɛʀ] **ADJ** supramolecular

supranational, -e, -aux, -ales [sypʀanasjɔnal, -o] **ADJ** supranational

supranationalité [sypʀanasjɔnalite] **NF** supranationality

suprasegmental, -e, -aux, -ales [sypʀasɛgmãtal, -o] **ADJ** *Ling* suprasegmental

suprasensible [sypʀasɑ̃sibl] **ADJ** supersensible

supraterrestre [sypʀatɛʀɛstʀ] **ADJ** superterrestrial

suprématie [sypʀemasi] **NF** supremacy

suprématisme [sypʀematism] **NM** *Beaux-Arts* Suprematism

suprême [sypʀɛm] **ADJ 1** *(supérieur)* supreme; **le pouvoir s.** the supreme power; *Rel* **l'Être s.** the Supreme Being

2 *(extrême → importance, bonheur, plaisir)* extreme, supreme; *(→ ignorance)* utter, blissful, sublime; *(→ mépris)* sublime; **au s. degré** to the highest or greatest degree

3 *(dernier)* supreme, final; **dans un s. effort** in a final attempt; **à l'heure** *ou* **au moment s.** at the hour of reckoning, at the moment of truth

4 *Culin* supreme

NM *Culin* suprême; **s. de volaille** chicken suprême

suprêmement [sypʀɛmmã] **ADV** supremely

SUR[1] [syʀ]

> on **1, 9, 11** ■ over **1, 3, 13** ■ on top of **1** ■ against **1** ■ in **1** ■ for **3** ■ towards **4** ■ around **4** ■ after **7** ■ upon **7** ■ out of **12** ■ by **12**

PRÉP 1 *(dans l'espace → dessus)* on; *(→ par-dessus)* over; *(→ au sommet de)* on top of; *(→ contre)* against; **s. la table** on the table; **étendu s. le lit/le sol** lying on the bed/the floor; **dormir s. le dos** to sleep on one's back; **un visage est dessiné s. le sable** a face has been drawn in the sand; **elle avait des bleus s. tout le visage** she had bruises all over her face, her face was covered in bruises; **s. la place du village** on the village green; **s. le continent** on the continent; **s. l'île** on the island; **s. le bateau** on the boat; **il a jeté ses affaires s. le lit** he threw his things onto the bed; **monter s. un escabeau** to climb (up) a stepladder; **monter s. un manège/une bicyclette** to get on a roundabout/bicycle; **marcher s. les mains** to walk on one's hands; **mets un châle s. tes épaules** put a shawl round or over your shoulders; **versez le rhum s. le gâteau** pour the rum over the cake; *Fam* **retire tes pieds de s. la chaise** take your feet off the chair; **jeter une passerelle s. une rivière** to build a footbridge over or across a river; **demain, du soleil s. le nord** tomorrow there will

be sunshine in the north; **ouragan s. la ville** hurricane over the city; **une chambre avec vue s. la mer** a room with a view of *or* over the sea; **des fenêtres qui donnent s. la rue** windows giving onto *or* overlooking the street; **s. le toit** on the roof; **s. pilotis** on stilts; **s. la pile de livres** on (top of) the pile of books; **s. la colline** on the top of the hill; **s. la cime de l'arbre** at the top of the tree; **je lui ai mis les mains s. les yeux** I put my hands over his/her eyes; **mettre un doigt s. sa bouche** to put a finger to one's lips; **il y a des graffiti partout s. le mur** there's graffiti all over the wall; **la peinture est appliquée directement s. le plâtre** the paint is applied directly onto the plaster; **sa silhouette se détachait s. le ciel** he/she was silhouetted against the sky; **j'ai toujours mon agenda s. moi** I always have my diary with *or* on me; **je n'ai pas d'argent s. moi** I haven't got any money on me; **s'appuyer s. un mur** to lean against a wall; **il y avait un monde fou, on était tous les uns s. les autres** there was a huge crowd, we were all crushed up together *or* one on top of the other; **vivre les uns s. les autres** to live in overcrowded conditions *or* on top of one another; **s. la page de garde** on the flyleaf; **je l'ai lu s. le journal** I read it in the paper; **s. la photo** in the photo; **les données sont s. disquette** the data is on disk; **la ville n'est pas s. la carte** the town isn't on the map; **la clef est s. la porte** the key's in the door; **je n'ai plus d'argent s. mon compte** I haven't any money left in my account; *Beaux-Arts* **sculpture s. bois** wood carving; *Beaux-Arts* **sculpture s. marbre** marble sculpture; **il est s. le chantier** he's on the (building) site; **je cherche un logement s. Paris** I'm looking for somewhere to live in Paris

2 *(indiquant la direction)* **s. votre gauche, le Panthéon** on *or* to your left, the Pantheon; **en allant s. Rennes** going towards Rennes; **ils avançaient s. Moscou** they were advancing towards *or* on Moscow; **obliquer s. la droite** to turn *or* to bear right; **diriger son regard s. qn** to look in sb's direction; **tirer s. qn** to shoot at sb; **les policiers se sont jetés s. eux** the police charged (at) them; **le malheur s'est abattu s. cette famille** unhappiness has fallen upon this family; **la porte s'est refermée s. elle** the door closed behind *or* after her

3 *(indiquant une distance)* over, for; **virages s. 3 km** *(sur panneau)* bends for 3 km; **il est le plus rapide s. 400 mètres** he's the fastest over 400 metres; **la foire s'étend s. 3000m^2** the fair covers 3,000m^2; **s. toute la longueur du parcours** over the whole *or* entire length of the course

4 *(dans le temps → indiquant l'approximation)* towards, around; **s. les 4 heures, quelqu'un a téléphoné** (at) around 4, somebody phoned; **s. le soir, un orage éclata** a thunderstorm broke towards evening

5 *(indiquant la proximité)* **s. le moment** *ou* **le coup, je me suis étonné** at the time *or* at first, I was surprised; **être s. le départ** to be about to leave; **il va s. ses 40 ans** he's approaching *or* nearly 40

6 *(indiquant la durée)* **c'est un contrat s. cinq ans** it's a five-year contract, the contract runs for five years; **les versements sont étalés s. plusieurs mois** the instalments are spread over several months

7 *(indiquant la répétition)* after, upon; **il commet gaffe s. gaffe** he makes blunder after *or* upon blunder; **je lui ai envoyé lettre s. lettre** I sent him/her letter after *or* upon letter; **elle écrit roman s. roman** she writes one novel after another; **entasser pierre s. pierre** to pile stone upon stone

8 *(indiquant la cause)* **condamné s. faux témoignage** condemned on false evidence; **juger qn s. ses propos/son apparence** to judge sb by his/her words/appearance; **j'ai agi s. vos ordres** I acted on your orders; **il est venu s. votre invitation** he came at your invitation

9 *(indiquant la manière, l'état, la situation)* **jurer qch s. la Bible** to swear sth on the Bible; **prendre modèle s. qn** to model oneself on sb; **faire pression s. qn** to put pressure on sb; **avoir un effet s. qn/qch** to have an effect on sb/sth; **être s. ses gardes/la défensive/le qui-vive** to be on one's guard/the defensive/the look-out; **être s. des charbons ardents** to be on tenterhooks; **s. la base de 1000 euros par mois** on the basis of 1,000 euros per month; **danser s. un air connu** to dance to a well-known tune; *Mus* **s. le mode majeur/mineur** in the major/minor key; **c'est s. la première chaîne/France Inter** it's on channel one/France Inter; **s. 100,4 Khz** on 100.4 Khz

10 *(indiquant le moyen)* **vivre s. ses économies/un héritage** to live off one's savings/a legacy; **je n'aime pas choisir s. catalogue** I don't like choosing from a catalogue; **on peut tailler deux jupes s. le même patron** you can make two skirts out of *or* from the same pattern; **ça s'ouvre s. simple pression** you open it just by pressing it; **vous obtiendrez le renseignement s. (un) simple coup de téléphone** just phone for information; **fait s. traitement de texte** done on a word-processor; **le film se termine s. une vue du Lido** the film ends with *or* on a view of the Lido

11 *(indiquant le domaine, le sujet)* **on a un dossier s. lui** we've got a file on him; **je sais peu de choses s. elle** I don't know much about her; **s. ce point, nous sommes d'accord** we agree on that point; **travailler s. qch** to work on sth; **30 personnes sont s. le projet** there are 30 people on *or* involved in the project; **faire des recherches s. qch** to do some research into sth; **un essai s. la métaphysique** an essay on metaphysics; **un poème s. la solitude** a poem about solitude; **questionner qn s. ses projets** to ask sb about his/her plans; **elle s'est expliquée s. ses choix politiques** she explained her political choices; **médite s. ce qu'elle t'a dit** think about what she told you; **elle pleurait s. ses jeunes années** she was crying over her lost youth; **s'apitoyer s. soi-même** to feel sorry for oneself; **il y a des réductions s. les meubles** there are discounts on furniture; **impôt s. le tabac/l'alcool** tax on tobacco/alcohol; **je prends une commission de 12 pour cent s. les ventes** I take a 12 percent commission on sales; **prélever un pourcentage s. une somme** to deduct a percentage from a sum; **les cotisations sont prises s. le salaire** contributions are deducted from one's salary

12 *(indiquant → une proportion)* out of; *(→ une mesure)* by; **un homme s. deux** one man in two, every second man; **un jour s. deux** every other day; **un lundi s. trois** every third Monday; **s. 100 candidats, 15 ont été retenus** 15 out of 100 candidates were shortlisted; **99 fois s. 100** 99 times out of 100; **tu as une chance s. deux de gagner** you've got a fifty-fifty chance of winning; **5 mètres s. 3** 5 metres by 3; *Math* **12 s. 3 égale 4** 12 divided by *or* over 3 equals 4; **noter s. 20** to *Br* mark *or Am* grade out of 20; **j'ai eu 12 s. 20** I got 12 out of 20; **faire une enquête s. 1000 personnes** to do a survey of *or* involving 1,000 people

13 *(indiquant une relation de supériorité)* over; **régner s. un pays** to rule over a country; **avoir de l'autorité s. qn** to have authority over sb; **son emprise s. moi** his/her influence over me; **c'est une victoire s. la maladie** it's a victory over illness; **l'emporter s. qn** to defeat sb; **son pouvoir s'exerce s. tous** he/she has power over everybody; **avoir des droits s. un héritage** to have rights over *or* on an inheritance

'Sur mes lèvres' *Audiard* 'Read My Lips'

'Sur les quais' *Kazan* 'On the Waterfront'

SUR- [syr] **PRÉF**

This prefix has two main uses, one of which is still generating new coinages today.

• **Sur-** can mean HIGHER or ABOVE when coupled with a noun or a verb. The word *over*, used as an adverb or a prefix, often features in the English translation, eg:

surchemise overshirt; **surtitre** strapline/surtitle; **surligner** to highlight (with a fluorescent pen); **surligneur** highlighter (pen); **survoler** to fly over; **surnager** to float; **surplomber** to overhang

• **Sur-** can suggest SUPERIORITY or EXCESS when added to nouns, verbs or adjectives. The English translation usually includes an equivalent prefix *(over-, super-)* or expression of abundance, eg:

surhomme superman; **surhumain** superhuman; **surabondance** overabundance, profusion, wealth; **des... en surnombre** too many...; **suralimenté(e)** overfed/supercharged; **surcharger** to overload/to overburden; **surchauffé(e)** overheated

The use of **sur-** in connection with the idea of excess has been quite productive in recent years, mostly in media-speak, which is often the way in which new coinages enter the language, eg:

aujourd'hui les gens sont surinformés today people are bombarded with too much information; **la surmédicalisation de la grossesse** excessive medical intervention during pregnancy; **surbooking, surréservation** overbooking, double booking; **être surlooké(e)** to be a fashion victim; **surjouer** to overact, to ham

sur^2, -e [syr] **ADJ** sour

SÛR, -E [syr] **ADJ 1** *(certain, convaincu)* sure, certain; **j'en suis tout à fait s., j'en suis s. et certain** I'm absolutely sure, I'm positive; **c'est s. et certain** it's a hundred percent sure; **j'en étais s.!** I knew it!; **n'en sois pas si s.** don't be so sure; **il l'a oublié, c'est s.** he has forgotten it, that's for certain *or* sure; **c'est s. qu'il pleuvra** it's bound to rain; **c'est s. qu'ils ne viendront pas** it's certain that they won't come; **une chose est sûre** one thing's for sure; **tu viendras? – ce n'est pas s.** are you coming? – I don't know for sure; **rien n'est moins s.** nothing is less certain; **être s. de** to be sure of; **être s. de son fait** to be positive; **le public est s. du dénouement** the audience can (confidently) predict the outcome; **elle est sûre de réussir** she's sure she'll succeed; **je suis s. d'avoir raison** I'm sure I'm right; **je ne suis pas s. d'avoir gardé un double** *(d'un document)* I'm not sure (whether) I kept a copy

2 *(confiant)* sure, confident; **être s. de qn** to have (every) confidence in sb; **le général n'était plus s. de ses hommes** the general had lost confidence in his men; **être s. de soi** *(en général)* to be self-assured *or* self-confident; *(sur un point particulier)* to be confident; **il n'est plus s. de ses réflexes** he has lost confidence in his reflexes; **être s. de son coup** to be sure of success

3 *(fiable → personne, ami)* trustworthy, reliable; *(→ données, mémoire, raisonnement)* reliable, sound; *(→ alarme, investissement)* safe; *(→ goût)* reliable; **avoir le coup d'œil/de crayon s.** to be good at sizing things up/at capturing a likeness *(in drawing)*; **avoir la main sûre** to have a steady hand; **avoir le pied s.** to be surefooted; **avoir l'oreille sûre** to have a keen ear; **le temps n'est pas s.** the weather is unreliable

4 *(sans danger)* safe; **l'avion est plus s. que la voiture** flying is safer than travelling by car; **des rues peu sûres** unsafe streets; **le plus s. est de...** the safest thing is to...; **cache l'argent, c'est plus s.** it's safer to hide the money; **appelle-moi, c'est plus s.!** call me, just to be on the safe side!

ADV *Fam* **s. qu'il va gagner!** he's bound to win!; *Fam* **il va accepter – pas s.!** he'll accept – don't count on it!

❑ **à coup sûr ADV** definitely, no doubt; **elle sera à coup s. en retard** she's sure to be late

❑ **pour sûr ADV** *Fam* for sure

surabondamment [syrabɔ̃damɑ̃] **ADV** overabundantly, profusely

surabondance [syrabɔ̃dɑ̃s] **NF** overabundance, profusion, wealth; *(de marchandises)* surfeit, glut; **une s. de** a wealth of; **une s. de céréales** an overabundance of cereals

surabondant, -e [syrabɔ̃dɑ̃, -ɑ̃t] **ADJ** overabundant, profuse

surabonder [3] [syʀabɔ̃de] **VI les minéraux surabondent dans la région** the region is rich in minerals; **les activités culturelles surabondent dans cette ville** the town offers a wide range of cultural activities; **les campeurs surabondent dans la région** the area is overrun with campers ❑ **surabonder de, surabonder en VT IND** to abound with *or* in

suraccumulation [syʀakymylasjɔ̃] **NF** overaccumulation

suractivé, -e [syʀaktive] **ADJ** superactivated

suractivité [syʀaktivite] **NF** overactivity

surah [syʀa] **NM** syrah

suraigu, -ë [syʀegy] **ADJ 1** (*voix, son*) very shrill **2** (*douleur*) intense, acute

surajouter [3] [syʀaʒute] **VT** to add; **il surajoute toujours des détails inutiles** he always adds unnecessary details
▶ **se surajouter VPR** to come on top (**à** of)

sural, -e, -aux, -ales [syʀal, -o] **ADJ** *Anat* sural

suralcoolisation [syʀalkɔlizasjɔ̃] **NF** (*de vin*) fortifying

suralimentation [syʀalimɑ̃tasjɔ̃] **NF 1** (*d'une personne* → *consommation excessive*) overeating; (→ *par quelqu'un d'autre*) overfeeding; (*d'un animal*) overfeeding **2** *Tech* boosting, supercharging **3** *Méd* superalimentation

suralimenté, -e [syʀalimɑ̃te] **ADJ 1** (*personne, animal*) overfed **2** *Tech* (*moteur*) supercharged

suralimenter [3] [syʀalimɑ̃te] **VT 1** (*personne, animal*) to overfeed **2** *Tech* (*moteur*) to supercharge

suramplificateur [syʀɑ̃plifikatœʀ] **NM** booster

suranné, -e [syʀane] **ADJ 1** (*style, idées*) old-fashioned, outmoded; **une mode surannée** an outdated fashion **2** *Arch* (*qui a expiré*) expired

surarbitre [syʀaʀbitʀ] **NM** *Jur* (independent) arbitrator

surarmement [syʀaʀməmɑ̃] **NM** stockpiling of weapons

surate [syʀat] **NF** sura

surbaissé, -e [syʀbese] **ADJ 1** (*plafond*) lowered; (*arc, voûte*) surbased **2** *Aut* **voiture (à carrosserie) surbaissée** underslung *or* low-slung car

surbaissement [syʀbɛsmɑ̃] **NM** (*d'un arc, d'une voûte*) surbasement

surbaisser [4] [syʀbese] **VT 1** (*plafond*) to lower; (*arc, voûte*) to surbase **2** *Aut* to underslung

surbau, -x [syʀbo] **NM** *Naut* (hatchway) coaming

surbooké, -e [syʀbuke] **ADJ** overbooked

surbooker [3] [syʀbuke] **VT** to overbook

surbooking [syʀbukiŋ] **NM** overbooking, double-booking

surboum [syʀbum] **NF** *Vieilli* party (*for teenagers*)

surbrillance [syʀbʀijɑ̃s] **NF** highlighting; **apparaître en s.** to be highlighted

surcapacité [syʀkapasite] **NF** overcapacity

surcapitalisation [syʀkapitalizasjɔ̃] **NF** overcapitalization, overcapitalizing (UNCOUNT)

surcapitalisé, -e [syʀkapitalize] **ADJ** overcapitalized

surcharge [syʀʃaʀʒ] **NF 1** (*excédent de poids*) overload, overloading; **s. de bagages** excess luggage; **la s. de la voiture est à l'origine de l'accident** the accident occurred because the car was overloaded; *Méd* **s. pondérale** excess weight
2 (*excès*) overabundance, surfeit; **s. de travail** extra work; **les parents se plaignent de la s. des programmes scolaires** parents are complaining that the school curriculum is overloaded
3 (*sur un mot*) alteration; **un acte public ne doit comporter ni rature ni s.** official documents must include neither deletions nor alterations
4 (*sur un timbre*) surcharge, overprint
5 *Constr* (*d'un enduit*) overthick coat; (*ornementation*) frills, over-embellishment
6 *Élec* overload
7 (*d'un cheval de course*) (weight) handicap
❑ **en surcharge ADJ** excess (*avant n*), extra (*avant n*) **ADV** **prendre des passagers en s.** to take on excess passengers

surcharger [17] [syʀʃaʀʒe] **VT 1** (*véhicule*) to overload **2** (*accabler*) to overburden (**de** with); **surchargé de travail** overworked **3** (*alourdir*) to weigh down **4** (*raturer*) to alter; **un rapport surchargé de ratures** a report containing too many deletions **5** (*marché*) to glut, to overload **6** (*timbre*) to surcharge, to overprint

surchauffe [syʀʃof] **NF 1** *Phys* superheating **2** (*d'un moteur, d'un appareil*) overheating **3** *Écon* overheating **4** *Métal* (*technique*) superheating; (*défaut*) overheating

surchauffé, -e [syʀʃofe] **ADJ 1** (*trop chauffé*) overheated; **l'air était toujours s. dans l'atelier** the air in the workshop was always too hot **2** (*surexcité*) overexcited; **un public s.** an overexcited audience; **des esprits surchauffés** reckless individuals **3** *Phys* **vapeur surchauffée** superheated steam

surchauffer [3] [syʀʃofe] **VT 1** (*pièce, appareil*) to overheat **2** *Phys* to superheat

surchauffeur [syʀʃofœʀ] **NM** *Phys* superheater

surchemise [syʀʃəmiz] **NF** overshirt

surchoix [syʀʃwa] **ADJ** (*produit*) top-quality (*avant n*) **NM** top quality

surclasser [3] [syʀklase] **VT** to outclass

surcollage [syʀkɔlaʒ] **NM** *Belg* postering over

surcoller [3] [syʀkɔle] **VT** *Belg* to poster over

surcompensation [syʀkɔ̃pɑ̃sasjɔ̃] **NF** overcompensation

surcompenser [3] [syʀkɔ̃pɑ̃se] **VT** to overcompensate

surcomplémentaire [syʀkɔ̃plemɑ̃tɛʀ] **ADJ** *Assur* **assurance s.** = optimal extra health insurance to cover large medical bills

surcomposé, -e [syʀkɔ̃poze] **ADJ** *Gram* = which uses an auxiliary twice

surcompression [syʀkɔ̃pʀesjɔ̃] **NF** (*procédé*) supercharging; (*état*) supercharge

surcomprimé, -e [syʀkɔ̃pʀime] **ADJ** **moteur s.** supercharged engine

surcomprimer [3] [syʀkɔ̃pʀime] **VT** to supercharge

surcongélation [syʀkɔ̃ʒelasjɔ̃] **NF** deep freezing

surconsommation [syʀkɔ̃sɔmasjɔ̃] **NF** overconsumption, excess *or* excessive consumption

surcontre [syʀkɔ̃tʀ] **NM** *Cartes* redouble

surcontrer [3] [syʀkɔ̃tʀe] **VT** *Cartes* to redouble

surcot [syʀko] **NM** *Hist* surcot

surcote [syʀkɔt] **NF** *Bourse* higher value

surcoté, -e [syʀkɔte] **ADJ** (*action, marché, monnaie*) overvalued

surcoupe [syʀkup] **NF** *Cartes* overtrumping

surcouper [3] [syʀkupe] **VT** *Cartes* to overtrump

surcoût [syʀku] **NM** (*supplément prévu*) surcharge, overcharge; (*dépense*) overspend, overexpenditure

surcreusement [syʀkʀøzmɑ̃] **NM** *Géol* overdeepening

surcroît [syʀkʀwa] **NM un s. de travail** extra *or* additional work
❑ **de surcroît ADV** moreover, what's more; **il est beau, et intelligent de s.** he's handsome, and moreover *or* what's more, he's bright
❑ **en surcroît ADV** (*en plus*) in addition; **venir** *ou* **être donné en s.** to come on top; **il y a cinq jours de vacances, le lundi de Pentecôte vient en s.** there are five days' holiday, plus Whit Monday
❑ **par surcroît** = **de surcroît**

surcuit [syʀkɥi] **NM** overburnt lime

surdent [syʀdɑ̃] **NF** wolf tooth

surdétermination [syʀdetɛʀminasjɔ̃] **NF** overdetermination

surdéterminer [3] [syʀdetɛʀmine] **VT** to overdetermine

surdéveloppé, -e [syʀdevlɔpe] **ADJ** *Écon* (*très développé*) highly developed; (*excessivement développé*) overdeveloped

surdéveloppement [syʀdevlɔpmɑ̃] **NM** *Écon* (*haut niveau*) high state of development; (*excès*) overdevelopment

surdévelopper [3] [syʀdevlɔpe] **VT** *Écon* (*beaucoup*) to develop to a high degree; (*excessivement*) to overdevelop

surdimensionné, -e [syʀdimɑ̃sjɔne] **ADJ** oversized

surdimutité [syʀdimytite] **NF** deaf-muteness, deaf-mutism

surdiplômé, -e [syʀdiplome] **ADJ** overqualified

surdité [syʀdite] **NF** deafness; **s. de perception/transmission** perceptive/conductive deafness; **s. verbale** word-deafness

surdon [syʀdɔ̃] **NM 1** (*compensation*) = compensation allowable to purchaser for damage to goods **2** (*droit*) = right to non-acceptance of damaged goods

surdorer [3] [syʀdɔʀe] **VT** to double-gild

surdorure [syʀdɔʀyʀ] **NF** double-gilding

surdos [syʀdo] **NM** loin strap

surdosage [syʀdozaʒ] **NM** overdosage, overdosing

surdose [syʀdoz] **NF** overdose

surdoué, -e [syʀdwe] **ADJ** gifted, *Spéc* hyperintelligent
NM,F gifted *or* *Spéc* hyperintelligent child

sureau, -x [syʀo] **NM** *Bot* elder, elderberry tree

sureffectif [syʀefɛktif] **NM** overstaffing; **être en s.** to be overstaffed

surélévation [syʀelevasjɔ̃] **NF** *Constr* (*action*) heightening; (*état*) additional *or* extra height

surélever [19] [syʀelve] **VT** *Constr* (*mur*) to heighten, to raise; **s. un immeuble de deux étages** to add two floors to a building; **on a surélevé la voie ferrée** the railway has been raised above ground level

surelle [syʀɛl] **NF** *Bot & Culin* sorrel

sûrement [syʀmɑ̃] **ADV 1** (*en sécurité*) safely
2 (*efficacement*) efficiently, with a sure hand; **conduire s. ses affaires** to run one's affairs with a sure hand
3 (*certainement*) certainly, surely; **ce que tu as dit l'a condamné plus s. que s'il avait été pris sur le fait** what you said condemned him even more surely than if he'd been caught red-handed; **il sera s. en retard** he's bound to *or* sure to be late; **ils ont s. été pris dans les embouteillages** they must have been caught in the traffic; **oui, s., il vaudrait mieux le prévenir** yes, no doubt, it would be better to warn him; *Fam* **s. qu'il vaudrait mieux attendre, mais...** sure, it's better to wait, but...
4 (*oui*) certainly; **s. pas!** certainly not!

suréminent, -e [syʀeminɑ̃, -ɑ̃t] **ADJ** very eminent, egregious

surémission [syʀemisjɔ̃] **NF** overissue

suremploi [syʀɑ̃plwa] **NM** overemployment

surenchère [syʀɑ̃ʃɛʀ] **NF 1** (*prix*) higher bid, overbid; **faire une s.** to make a higher bid; **faire une s. sur qn** to bid higher than sb; **une s. de 100 euros à ma droite** another 100 euros on my right
2 *Fig* **la s. électorale** exaggerated political promises (*during an election campaign*); **la s. publicitaire/médiatique** advertising/media overkill; **une s. de violence** an increase in violence; **faire de la s.** to go one better; *Fam* **d'accord, il a été courageux, pas besoin de faire de la s.** OK, so he was brave, there's no need to lay it on so thick

surenchérir [32] [syʀɑ̃ʃeʀiʀ] **VI 1** (*offrir de payer plus*) to overbid, to raise one's bid, to make a higher bid; **si personne ne vient s.** if nobody makes a higher bid; **il y aura un délai pour s.** a period of time will be set aside for any higher bids; **s. sur qn** to bid higher than sb **2** *Fig* **s. sur** to go one better than; **s. sur une offre** to make a better offer

surenchérissement [syʀɑ̃ʃeʀismɑ̃] **NM** fresh rise *or* increase (in price)

surenchérisseur, -euse [syʀɑ̃ʃeʀisœʀ, -øz] **NM,F** higher bidder

surendetté, -e [syʀɑ̃dete] **ADJ** heavily in debt

surendettement [syʀɑ̃dɛtmɑ̃] **NM** excessive debt

surentraînement [syʀɑ̃tʀɛnmɑ̃] **NM** overtraining

surentraîner [4] [syʀɑ̃tʀene] **VT** to overtrain

surépaisseur [syʀepɛsœʀ] **NF** extra thickness

suréquipement [syʀekipmɑ̃] **NM** (*action*) overequipping; (*état*) overequipment; (*excès*) excess equipment

suréquiper [3] [syʀekipe] **VT** to overequip

surestarie [syʀestaʀi] **NF** *Naut* demurrage

surestimation [syʀɛstimasjɔ̃] **NF 1** (*action*) overestimation; *Com* overvaluing **2** (*résultat*) overestimate; *Com* overvaluation

surestimer [3] [syʀɛstime] **VT 1** *Com* (*objet*) to overvalue **2** (*valeur, difficultés, personne*) to overestimate
▶ **se surestimer VPR** to think too highly of oneself

suret, -ette [syʀɛ, -ɛt] **ADJ** sourish, slightly tart; **un petit vin s.** a wine with a hint of tartness

sûreté [syʀte] **NF 1** (*sécurité*) safety; **la s. de l'État** state security; **s. nucléaire** nuclear safety; **s. publique** public safety; **par mesure de s., pour plus de s.** as a precaution

2 *(fiabilité → de la mémoire, d'une méthode, d'un diagnostic, des freins)* reliability; *(→ de la main)* sureness, steadiness; *(→ de la vision, du goût, du jugement)* soundness; *(→ d'une serrure)* security

3 *(système de protection)* safety device; **équiper sa porte d'une s.** to fit one's door with a security system

4 *Jur* **s. personnelle** guarantee, surety; **s. individuelle** (rights of) personal security *(against arbitrary detention)*; **s. réelle** (valuable) security; **la S. (nationale)** = the French criminal investigation department; *Br* ≃ CID, *Am* ≃ FBI

❏ **de sûreté** ADJ *(épingle, serrure etc)* safety *(avant n)*

❏ **en sûreté être en s.** to be safe *or* out of harm's way ADV **mettre qch en s.** to put sth in a safe place *or* away for safekeeping

surévaluation [syrevalɥasjɔ̃] NF overvaluation, overestimation

surévaluer [7] [syrevalɥe] VT **1** *(donner une valeur supérieure à)* to overvalue; **le conseil municipal a surévalué les terrains** the council overvalued the land **2** *(accorder une importance excessive à)* to overestimate

surexcitable [syrɛksitabl] ADJ **1** *(gén)* overexcitable **2** *Psy* hyperexcitable

surexcitant, -e [syrɛksitɑ̃, -ɑ̃t] ADJ overexciting

surexcitation [syrɛksitasjɔ̃] NF overexcitement

surexcité, -e [syrɛksite] ADJ overexcited

surexciter [3] [syrɛksite] VT **1** *(personne)* to overexcite **2** *(sentiment, faculté)* to overexcite, to overstimulate, to inflame; **s. l'imagination de qn** to overexcite *or* to overstimulate sb's imagination

surexploitation [syrɛksplwatasjɔ̃] NF **1** *(d'une terre, de ressources)* overexploitation **2** *(de la main-d'œuvre)* exploitation

surexploiter [3] [syrɛksplwate] VT **1** *(terre, ressources)* to overexploit **2** *(ouvrier)* to exploit **3** *(idée)* to overuse

surexposer [3] [syrɛkspoze] VT to overexpose

surexposition [syrɛkspozisjɔ̃] NF overexposure

surf [sœrf] NM **1** *(planche)* surfboard **2** *(sport)* surfing; **faire du s.** to go surfing; **s. des neiges** snowboarding; **faire du s. des neiges** to snowboard, to go snowboarding

surfaçage [syrfasaʒ] NM **1** *Tech* surfacing **2** *Méd (en chirurgie dentaire)* **s. (radiculaire)** root planing

surface [syrfas] NF **1** *(aire)* (surface) area; **calculer la s. d'une pièce** to calculate the (surface) area of a room; **quelle est la s. de l'entrepôt?** how big is the warehouse?; *Ordinat* **s. d'affichage** display area; *Jur* **s. corrigée** surface area *(used in the evaluation of a reasonable rent)*; *Mktg* **s. d'exposition** *ou* **de présentation** display space; **s. au sol** floor space; **s. de travail** work surface; **s. utile** floor space; **s. de vente** sales area;

2 *(partie extérieure)* surface, outside; **la s. de la Terre** the Earth's surface; **la s. de l'étang est gelée** the surface of the pond is frozen, the pond is frozen over; **une peau se forme à la s. du lait** skin forms on the surface *or* on top of the milk; **remonter à la s., faire s.** *(sous-marin, nageur)* to surface; **refaire s., revenir à la s.** *(après évanouissement)* to come to *or* round; *(après anesthésie)* to come out of anaesthetic, to come round; *(après une dépression)* to pull out of it; *(après une absence)* to reappear; **le corps du mineur a été remonté à la s.** the miner's body was brought up to the surface

3 *(apparence)* surface, (outward) appearance; **la s. des choses** the surface of things; **il reste à la s. des choses** he doesn't go into things in any depth

4 *Fam (position sociale)* status■; **avoir de la s.** to be influential

5 *Aviat* **s. portante** *Br* aerofoil, *Am* airfoil

6 *Élec* **s. d'onde** wavefront

7 *Géog, Ling & Math* surface

8 *Phot* **s. sensible** sensitized surface

9 *Sport* **s. de réparation** penalty area

10 *Tech* **s. de chauffe** heating surface

11 *Fin* **s. financière** financial standing

❏ **de surface** ADJ **1** *Naut & Phys* surface *(avant n)* **2** *(amabilité, regrets)* superficial

❏ **en surface** ADV **1** *(à l'extérieur)* on the surface

2 *(superficiellement)* on the face of things, superficially

surfacer [16] [syrfase] VT **1** *Tech* to surface **2** *Méd (en chirurgie dentaire)* to plane

surfaceuse [syrfasøz] NF surfacer

surfacique [syrfasik] ADJ *Phys* surface *(avant n)*

surfacturation [syrfaktyrasjɔ̃] NF overbilling, overcharging

surfacturer [syrfaktyre] VT to overbill, to overcharge

surfaire [109] [syrfɛr] VT *Littéraire* **1** *(marchandise)* to overprice **2** *(ouvrage, talent)* to overrate, to overvalue

surfait, -e [syrfɛ, -ɛt] ADJ **1** *(auteur, œuvre)* overrated; *(réputation)* inflated; **c'est un peu s.** it's not all it's cracked up to be, it's a bit overrated **2** *(surévalué)* overvalued; **leurs prix sont surfaits** their prices are too high

surfaix [syrfɛ] NM *Équitation* surcingle

surfer [3] [sœrfe] VI to surf; **s. sur l'Internet** to surf the net *or* the Internet

surfeur, -euse [sœrfœr, -øz] NM,F surfer; **s. des neiges** snowboarder

surfil [syrfil] NM *(technique)* whipping; *(point)* overcasting stitch

surfilage [syrfilaʒ] NM *Couture* whipping

surfiler [3] [syrfile] VT **1** *Couture* to whip, to whipstitch **2** *Tex (fil)* to give an extra twist to

surfin, -e [syrfɛ̃, -in] ADJ *(produit)* top-quality, of superior quality; *(qualité)* superior

surfondu, -e [syrfɔ̃dy] ADJ superfused, supercooled

surfréquentation [syrfrekɑ̃tasjɔ̃] NF *(d'un lieu)* overvisiting; **les problèmes de pollution sont dus à la s. touristique** the pollution problems are caused by too many tourists

surfréquenté, -e [syrfrekɑ̃te] ADJ *(lieu touristique)* attracting too many visitors

surfusion [syrfyzjɔ̃] NF superfusion, supercooling

surgé [syrʒe] NMF *Fam Arg scol* head supervisor■ *(person in charge of school discipline)*

surgélateur [syrʒelatœr] NM *(industrial)* deep freeze *or* freezer

surgélation [syrʒelasjɔ̃] NF *(industrial)* deep-freezing

surgelé, -e [syrʒele] ADJ frozen, deep-frozen
    NM **j'ai acheté un s. pour ce soir** I've bought a frozen dinner for tonight; **surgelés** frozen food

surgeler [25] [syrʒəle] VT to deep-freeze *(industrially)*

surgénérateur, -trice [syrʒeneratœr, -tris] *Nucl* ADJ fast breeder *(avant n)*
    NM breeder reactor; **s. à neutrons rapides** fast breeder reactor

surgénération [syrʒenerasjɔ̃] NF *Nucl* breeding

surgénératrice [syrʒeneratris] *voir* **surgénérateur**

surgeon [syrʒɔ̃] NM *Bot* sucker

surgir [32] [syrʒir] VI **1** *(personne, animal, objet)* to appear *or* to materialize suddenly, to loom up; *(hors du sol et rapidement)* to shoot *or* to spring up; **des gens, surgis d'on ne sait où** people who had sprung from nowhere; **l'eau surgit du sol entre deux rochers** the water springs *or* gushes out of the ground between two rocks
    2 *(conflit)* to arise; *(difficultés)* to crop up, to arise; **la situation a fait s. un certain nombre de problèmes annexes** the situation gave rise to a number of related problems

surgissement [syrʒismɑ̃] NM *Littéraire* sudden appearance, looming up; *(hors du sol et rapide)* shooting *or* springing up

surhaussé, -e [syrose] ADJ *Constr* stilted

surhaussement [syrosmɑ̃] NM *Constr* raising

surhausser [3] [syrose] VT *Constr* to raise

surhomme [syrɔm] NM **1** *(gén)* superman **2** *Phil* übermensch, superman

surhumain, -e [syrymɛ̃, -ɛn] ADJ superhuman; **ce qu'on me demande est s.** I'm being asked to do something beyond human endurance

suricate [syrikat] NM *Zool* suricate

surimi [syrimi] NM surimi

surimposer [3] [syrɛ̃poze] VT *Fin* to overtax

surimposition [syrɛ̃pozisjɔ̃] NF **1** *Fin* overtaxation **2** *Géog* superimposition

surimpression [syrɛ̃presjɔ̃] NF superimposition
    ❏ **en surimpression** ADJ superimposed; **les deux images sont en s.** the two pictures are superimposed

surin [syrɛ̃] NM **1** *Bot* young appletree stock **2** *Fam Arg crime (couteau)* knife■, blade

Surinam, Suriname [syrinam] NM **le S.** Surinam, Suriname; **vivre au S.** to live in Surinam; **aller au S.** to go to Surinam

suriner [3] [syrine] VT *Fam Arg crime (blesser avec un couteau)* to knife■, to cut; *(tuer avec un couteau)* to stab to death■

surinfecté, -e [syrɛ̃fɛkte] ADJ *Méd* **plaie surinfectée** wound with a secondary infection

surinfection [syrɛ̃fɛksjɔ̃] NF *Méd* secondary infection

surinformation [syrɛ̃fɔrmasjɔ̃] NF information overload

surinformé, -e [syrɛ̃fɔrme] ADJ **les gens sont surinformés** people are bombarded with too much information

surinformer [3] [syrɛ̃fɔrme] VT to overload with information

surintendance [syrɛ̃tɑ̃dɑ̃s] NF superintendency

surintendant, -e [syrɛ̃tɑ̃dɑ̃, -ɑ̃t] NM,F (in-house) social worker
    NM *Hist* **s. général des finances** ≃ Lord High Treasurer; **s. général des bâtiments du roi** ≃ Surveyor General of the King's Works
    ❏ **surintendante** NF *Hist* First Lady-in-Waiting

surintensité [syrɛ̃tɑ̃site] NF (current) overload

surinvestissement [syrɛ̃vɛstismɑ̃] NM *Fin & Psy* overinvestment

surir [32] [syrir] VI to (become *or* turn) sour

surjalée [syrʒale] ADJ F *Naut* fouled by the stock

surjaler [3] [syrʒale] VI *Naut* to become unstocked

surjectif, -ive [syrʒɛktif, -iv] ADJ surjective

surjection [syrʒɛksjɔ̃] NF surjection

surjective [syrʒɛktiv] *voir* **surjectif**

surjet [syrʒɛ] NM *(point)* overcast stitch; *(couture)* overcast seam

surjeter [27] [syrʒəte] VT to overcast

surjouer [6] [syrʒwe] VT *(rôle)* to overact
    VI to overact

sur-le-champ [syrləʃɑ̃] ADV immediately, at once, straightaway

surlendemain [syrlɑ̃dmɛ̃] NM **le s. de la fête** two days after the party; **il m'a appelé le lendemain, et le s.** he called me the next day, and the day after; **et le s., j'étais à Paris** and two days later, I was in Paris

surligner [3] [syrliɲe] VT to highlight *(with a fluorescent pen)*

surligneur [syrliɲœr] NM highlighter

surliure [syrljyr] NF *Naut* serving, whipping

surlonge [syrlɔ̃ʒ] NF middle rib and chuck; **bifteck de s.** sirloin steak

surlouer [6] [syrlwe] VT *(donner ou prendre en location)* to rent at an unreasonable *or* excessive price

surloyer [syrlwaje] NM additional rental expenses

surmarquage [syrmarkaʒ] NM overpricing, overcharging

surmarquer [3] [syrmarke] VT to overprice

surmédiatisation [syrmedjatizasjɔ̃] NF excessive media coverage

surmédiatiser [3] [syrmedjatize] VT to give excessive media coverage to

surmédicalisation [syrmedikalizasjɔ̃] NF overmedicalization

surmédicaliser [3] [syrmedikalize] VT to overmedicalize

surmenage [syrmənaʒ] NM *(nerveux)* overstrain, overexertion; *(au travail)* overwork, overworking; **souffrir de s.** to be overworked, to suffer from overwork; **s. intellectuel** mental strain

surmené, -e [syrməne] ADJ *(nerveusement)* in a state of nervous exhaustion; *(par le travail)* overworked
    NM,F *(nerveusement)* person suffering from nervous exhaustion; *(par le travail)* overworked person

surmener [19] [syrməne] VT **1** *(bête de somme, cheval)* to overwork, to drive too hard **2** *(personne → physiquement)* to overwork; *(→ nerveusement)* to overtax
    ► **se surmener** VPR to overtax oneself, to overdo it

sur-mesure [syrməzyr] NM INV made-to-measure tailoring

surmoi [syrmwa] NM INV *Psy* superego

surmontable [syrmɔ̃tabl] ADJ surmountable, which can be overcome, *Sout* superable

surmonter [3] [syrmɔ̃te] VT 1 *(être situé sur)* to surmount, to top; **un dôme surmonte l'édifice** the building is crowned by a dome; **une colonne surmontée d'une croix** a column surmounted *or* topped by a cross; **une église surmontée d'un clocher** a church with a steeple 2 *(triompher de → difficulté)* to get over, to surmount, to overcome; *(→ peur, émotion)* to overcome, to get the better of, to master; *(→ fatigue)* to overcome; *Littéraire* **s. ses ennemis** to overcome one's enemies

▸**se surmonter** VPR to master *or* control one's feelings

surmontoir [syrmɔ̃twar] NM *Mktg* = advertising item placed above product advertised

surmortalité [syrmɔrtalite] NF comparatively high death rate

surmoulage [syrmulaʒ] NM 1 *(action)* casting into a working mould 2 *(objet)* casting from a working mould

surmoule [syrmul] NM working mould

surmouler [3] [syrmule] VT **s. qch** to cast sth into a working mould

surmulet [syrmylɛ] NM *Ich* red mullet, *Am* surmullet

surmulot [syrmylo] NM *Zool* **(rat) s.** brown *or* common *or* Norway *or* sewer rat

surmultiplication [syrmyltiplikasjɔ̃] NF overdrive (device)

surmultiplié, -e [syrmyltiplije] ADJ **vitesse surmultipliée** overdrive

❑ **surmultipliée** NF overdrive

surnager [17] [syrnaʒe] VI 1 *(flotter)* to float; **le pétrole surnage à la surface de la mer** oil is floating on the sea 2 *(subsister → ouvrage)* to remain; *(→ souvenir)* to linger on; **seuls quelques noms surnagent dans ma mémoire** only a few names linger on in my memory

surnatalité [syrnatalite] NF comparatively high birth rate

surnaturel, -elle [syrnatyrɛl] ADJ 1 *(d'un autre monde)* supernatural 2 *(fabuleux, prodigieux)* uncanny; **le clair de lune donnait au paysage une beauté surnaturelle** the landscape was uncannily beautiful in the moonlight 3 *(divin)* spiritual; **la vie surnaturelle** the spiritual life

NM **le s.** the supernatural

surnom [syrnɔ̃] NM 1 *(appellation)* nickname; **on lui a donné le s. de Rick** he was given the nickname of Rick, he was nicknamed Rick; **Cœur de Lion était le s. du roi Richard** King Richard was known as the Lionheart 2 *Antiq* agnomen

surnombre [syrnɔ̃br] NM excessive numbers

❑ **en surnombre** ADJ redundant, excess *(avant n)*; **des ouvriers en s.** too many workers; **nous étions en s.** there were too many of us

surnommer [3] [syrnɔme] VT to nickname; **elles l'ont surnommé "le Tombeur"** they nicknamed him ''Ladykiller''; **dans sa famille, on la surnomme "Rosita"** her family's pet name for her is ''Rosita''; **ce n'est pas pour rien qu'il se fait s. "l'homme invisible"!** they don't call him ''the invisible man'' for nothing!

surnuméraire [syrnymerɛr] ADJ supernumerary

NMF supernumerary

surocclusion [syrɔklyzjɔ̃] NF *Méd* overbite

suroffre [syrɔfr] NF 1 *(offre plus avantageuse)* higher bid *or* offer 2 *Écon* oversupply

suroît [syrwa] NM 1 *(vent)* southwester, southwesterly 2 *(chapeau)* sou'wester

suros [syro, syrɔs] NM *Vét* splint

suroxyder [3] [syrɔkside] VT *(peroxyder)* to peroxidize; *(par erreur)* to overoxidize

suroxygéné, -e [syrɔksiʒene] ADJ *Chim* hyperoxygenated

suroxygéner [18] [syrɔksiʒene] VT *Chim* to hyperoxygenate

surpaie *etc voir* **surpayer**

surpassable [syrpasabl] ADJ surpassable; **difficilement s.** hard to beat

surpassement [syrpasmɑ̃] NM **le s. de soi** *ou* **de soi-même** excelling oneself

surpasser [3] [syrpase] VT 1 *(surclasser)* to surpass, to outdo; **il a surpassé ses concurrents** he outdid his competitors; **s. qn en habileté** to be more skilful than sb

2 *(aller au-delà de)* to surpass, to go beyond; **leur enthousiasme surpasse toutes mes espérances** their enthusiasm is beyond all my expectations, they're far more enthusiastic than I expected

▸**se surpasser** VPR to excel oneself; **quel gâteau, tu t'es surpassé!** what a cake, you've really surpassed yourself!

surpâturage [syrpatyraʒ] NM overgrazing

surpaye [syrpɛj] NF overpayment

surpayé, -e [syrpɛje] ADJ overpaid

surpayer [11] [syrpeje] VT 1 *(employé)* to overpay 2 *(marchandise)* to be overcharged for

surpêche [syrpɛʃ] NF overfishing

surpeuplé, -e [syrpœple] ADJ *(pays, région)* over-populated; *(bar, plage)* overcrowded

surpeuplement [syrpœpləmɑ̃] NM *(d'un pays, d'une région)* overpopulation; *(d'un bar, d'une plage)* overcrowding

surpiquer [3] [syrpike] VT to oversew

surpiqûre [syrpikyr] NF oversewn seam

surplace [syrplas] NM **faire du s.** *(à vélo)* to do a track stand; *(en voiture)* to be stuck; *Fig* **l'économie fait du s.** the economy is marking time *or* treading water; **en allemand, je fais du s.** I'm not getting anywhere with German

surplis [syrpli] NM surplice

surplomb [syrplɔ̃] NM overhang

❑ **en surplomb** ADJ overhanging

surplombant, -e [syrplɔ̃bɑ̃, -ɑ̃t] ADJ overhanging

surplombement [syrplɔ̃bmɑ̃] NM overhang

surplomber [3] [syrplɔ̃be] VT to overhang; **des falaises qui surplombent la mer** overhanging cliffs; **de chez elle on surplombe tout Paris** from her window you have a bird's-eye view of the whole of Paris

VI to overhang

surplus [syrply] NM 1 *(excédent)* surplus, extra; **le s. de la récolte** the surplus crop

2 *(supplément → à une quantité)* supplement; *(→ à un prix)* surcharge; **vous paierez le s. le mois prochain** you'll pay the extra next month

3 *Écon (stock excédentaire)* surplus (stock); *(gain)* surplus; *Fin* **surplus exceptionnels, surplus extraordinaires** excess profits; **s. d'importation** import surplus; *Fin* **s. monétaire** monetary surplus

4 *(boutique)* (army) surplus (store); **les s. américains** US army surplus

5 *(revenu)* disposable income

❑ **au surplus** ADV moreover, what's more

surpoids [syrpwa] NM excess weight

surpopulation [syrpɔpylasjɔ̃] NF overpopulation

surpositionnement [syrpozisjɔnmɑ̃] NM *Mktg* over-positioning

surpositionner [3] [syrpozisjɔne] VT *Mktg* to over-position

surprenait *etc voir* **surprendre**

surprenant, -e [syrprənɑ̃, -ɑ̃t] ADJ 1 *(inattendu, étonnant)* surprising; **ça n'a rien de s.** that's hardly surprising 2 *(exceptionnel)* astonishing, amazing; **un film s. de lyrisme** an astonishingly lyrical film

surprendre [79] [syrprɑ̃dr] VT 1 *(dans un acte délictueux)* **s. qn** to catch sb in the act; **on l'a surprise à falsifier la comptabilité** she was caught (in the act of) falsifying the accounts

2 *(prendre au dépourvu)* **ils sont venus nous s. à la maison** they paid us a surprise visit at home; **ils réussirent à s. la sentinelle** they managed to take the sentry by surprise; **s. qn au saut du lit** to catch sb when he/she has just got up; **la mort l'a surpris dans son sommeil** he died in his sleep; **se laisser s. par** *(orage)* to get caught in; *(marée)* to get caught by; *(crépuscule)* to be overtaken by; **il s'est fait s. en train de regarder** *ou* **à regarder par le trou de la serrure** he was caught looking through the keyhole

3 *(conversation)* to overhear; *(secret)* to find out; **j'ai surpris leur regard entendu** I happened to see the knowing look they gave each other

4 *(déconcerter)* to surprise; **être surpris de qch** to be surprised at sth; **ça a l'air de vous s.** you seem surprised; **cela ne surprendra personne** this will come as a surprise to nobody; **cela ne vous surprendra pas d'apprendre que je pars** you won't be surprised *or* it will come as no surprise to you to hear that I'm leaving; **cela me**

surprendrait qu'il revienne *ou* **s'il revenait** I should be surprised if he came back; **là, vous me surprenez!** well, you astound me!

5 *Littéraire (tromper)* **s. la confiance de qn** to violate sb's trust; **votre bonne foi a été surprise** your good faith was taken advantage of

▸**se surprendre** VPR **se s. à faire qch** to find *or* to catch oneself doing sth; **je me surprends à en douter** I catch myself having doubts about it

surpression [syrpresjɔ̃] NF very high pressure

surprime [syrprim] NF extra *or* additional premium

surpris, -e [syrpri, -iz] PP *voir* **surprendre**

ADJ 1 *(pris au dépourvu)* surprised; **l'ennemi, s., n'opposa aucune résistance** caught off their guard, the enemy put up no resistance

2 *(déconcerté)* surprised; **en apercevant son père, elle parut extrêmement surprise** when she saw her father, she looked extremely surprised; **je suis s. de son absence/de ne pas la voir/qu'elle ne réponde pas/de ce qu'elle ne réagisse pas** I'm surprised (that) she's not here/not to see her/(that) she doesn't reply/(that) she hasn't reacted; **être agréablement/désagréablement s.** to be pleasantly/unpleasantly surprised; **je serais bien s. si elle ne demandait pas une augmentation** I'd be surprised if she didn't ask for a *Br* rise *or* *Am* raise; **quand on m'a dit que ma fille se mariait, j'ai été le premier s.** when I heard that my daughter was getting married, it came as a real surprise

3 *(vu, entendu par hasard)* **quelques mots s. entre deux portes** a snatch of overheard conversation

❑ **surprise** NF 1 *(étonnement, stupéfaction)* surprise; **cette information causa une grande surprise** this information was received with amazement *or* caused much surprise; **à la grande surprise de** to the great surprise of; **à la grande surprise de toute la famille, il s'est marié** to his family's great surprise, he got married; **à ma grande surprise** to my great surprise, much to my surprise; **à la surprise générale** to everybody's surprise; **regarder qn avec surprise** to look at sb in surprise; **on va de surprise en surprise avec eux** with them it's just one surprise after another

2 *(événement inattendu)* surprise; **quelle (bonne) surprise!** what a (nice *or* pleasant) surprise!; **avoir une surprise** to be surprised; **tout le monde a eu la surprise d'avoir une prime** everyone was surprised to get a bonus; **faire une surprise à qn** to spring a surprise on sb; **ne lui dis pas, je veux lui faire la surprise** don't tell him/her, I want it to be a surprise; **on a souvent de mauvaises surprises avec lui** you often have unpleasant surprises with him; **attaque surprise** surprise attack; **visite surprise** surprise *or* unexpected visit; **voyage surprise** unplanned trip

3 *(cadeau)* surprise; *(pour les enfants)* lucky bag; **j'ai une petite surprise pour toi** I brought you a little surprise

4 *Mil* surprise; **ce qui compte dans une offensive, c'est la surprise** surprise *or* the element of surprise is the most important thing in an attack

❑ **par surprise** ADV *Mil* **prendre une ville par surprise** to take a town by surprise

❑ **sans surprise(s)** ADJ **ce fut un voyage sans surprise** it was an uneventful trip; **son père est sans surprise** his/her father is very predictable

surprise-partie [syrprizparti] (*pl* **surprises-parties**) NF *Vieilli* party

surprit *etc voir* **surprendre**

surprix [syrpri] NM excess price

surproducteur, -trice [syrprɔdyktœr, -tris] ADJ overproducing

surproduction [syrprɔdyksjɔ̃] NF overproduction

surproductrice [syrprɔdyktris] *voir* **surproducteur**

surproduire [98] [syrprɔdɥir] VT to overproduce

surprofit [syrprɔfi] NM abnormally high profit

surprotection [syrprɔtɛksjɔ̃] NF *(d'un enfant)* over-protection, coddling

surprotéger [22] [syrprɔteʒe] VT *(enfant)* to over-protect, to coddle

surpuissant, -e [syrpɥisɑ̃, -ɑ̃t] ADJ 1 *Tech* ultra-powerful 2 *(personne)* too powerful

surqualifié, -e [syrkalifje] ADJ overqualified

surréaction [syrreaksjɔ̃] NF *Écon* overshooting

surréalisme [syrrealism] NM surrealism

surréaliste [syrrealist] ADJ **1** *Beaux-Arts & Littérature* surrealist **2** *(magique)* surreal
    NMF surrealist

surrection [syrrɛksjɔ̃] NF *Géol* uplift

surréel [syrreɛl] ADJ surreal, surrealistic
    NM **le s.** the surreal

surrégénérateur, -trice [syrreʒeneratœr, -tris] ADJ fast breeder *(avant n)*
    NM breeder reactor; **s. à neutrons rapides** fast breeder reactor

surrégénération [syrreʒenerasjɔ̃] NF *Nucl* breeding

surrégénératrice [syrreʒeneratris] *voir* **surrégénérateur**

sur-régime [syrreʒim] NM *Aut* overspeeding

surremise [syrrəmiz] NF bulk discount

surrénal, -e, -aux, -ales [syrrenal, -o] ADJ suprarenal, adrenal
    ❑ **surrénale** NF suprarenal *or* adrenal gland

surrénalien, -enne [syrrenaljɛ̃, -ɛn] ADJ of the suprarenal *or* adrenal gland

surréservation [syrrezɛrvasjɔ̃] NF overbooking

sursalaire [syrsalɛr] NM bonus

sursaturation [syrsatyrasjɔ̃] NF **1** *Écon* oversaturation **2** *Phys* supersaturation

sursaturé, -e [syrsatyre] ADJ **1** *Géol* oversaturated **2** *Fam* **s. de** *(information, sensations)* flooded with

sursaturer [3] [syrsatyre] VT **1** *Écon* to oversaturate **2** *Phys* to supersaturate

sursaut [syrso] NM **1** *(tressaillement)* start, jump; **elle eut un s. de peur** she jumped in alarm **2** *(regain subit)* burst; **un s. d'énergie** a burst of energy
    ❑ **en sursaut** ADV *(brusquement)* with a start; **elle se réveilla en s.** she woke up with a start

sursauter [3] [syrsote] VI to start, to jump; **faire s. qn** to give sb a start, to make sb start *or* jump

surseoir [66] [syrswar] **surseoir à** VT IND **1** *Littéraire (différer → publication, décision)* to postpone, to defer. **2** *Jur* **s. à statuer, s. à un jugement** to defer a judgment; **s. à une exécution** to stay an execution

sursimulation [syrsimylasjɔ̃] NF **s. d'une maladie** exaggerating one's symptoms

sursis [syrsi] PP *voir* **surseoir**
    NM **1** *(délai)* reprieve, extension; **ils bénéficient d'un s. pour payer leurs dettes** they've been granted an extension of the time limit for paying their debts
    2 *Jur* reprieve; **bénéficier d'un s.** to be granted *or* given a reprieve; **s. assorti de l'obligation d'un travail d'intérêt général** = suspension combined with a community service order; **s. avec mise à l'épreuve** ≃ probation order; **s. probatoire** probation order; **s. simple** ≃ conditional discharge
    3 *(ajournement)* deferment, extension; **s. à exécution** stay of execution; **s. à statuer** stay of proceedings; *Mil* **s. d'incorporation** deferment *or* deferral of call-up
    ❑ **avec sursis** ADJ suspended; **il est condamné à (une peine de) cinq ans avec s.** he's been given a five-year suspended (prison) sentence
    ❑ **en sursis** ADJ **1** *Jur* in remission
    2 *(en attente)* **c'est un mort en s.** he's living on borrowed time

sursitaire [syrsitɛr] *Mil* ADJ provisionally exempted
    NM provisionally exempted conscript

sursoit *etc voir* **surseoir**

surtaux [syrto] NM excessively high rate

surtaxe [syrtaks] NF **1** *(taxe supplémentaire)* surcharge; **s. à l'importation** import surcharge **2** *(taxe excessive)* excessive tax

surtaxer [3] [syrtakse] VT *(frapper d'une taxe → supplémentaire)* to surcharge; *(→ excessive)* to overcharge

surtension [syrtɑ̃sjɔ̃] NF *(voltage)* overload, overvoltage

surtitrage [syrtitraʒ] NM **1** *Journ* provision of a strapline **2** *(traduction)* surtitling

surtitre [syrtitr] NM **1** *Journ* strapline **2** *(traduction)* surtitle

surtitrer [3] [syrtitre] VT **1** *Journ* to provide a strapline for **2** *(traduire)* to surtitle

surtout¹ [syrtu] ADV **1** *(avant tout, par-dessus tout)* above all; *(plus particulièrement)* particularly, especially; **il leur faut naturellement de l'argent, mais s. de l'aide** they obviously need money, but above all *or* but most important of all, they need help; **il y avait s. des touristes dans la salle** most of the audience were tourists; **elle aime s. l'art moderne** she particularly likes modern art; **j'adore la viande, s. bien cuite** I love meat, especially when it's well done; **c'est un endroit merveilleux, s. l'été** it's a wonderful place, especially in summer; **ils sont pingres, s. lui!** they're tight-fisted, especially him!; **il est agréable s. quand il a besoin d'aide!** he's very nice, especially when he needs help!
    2 *(renforçant un conseil, un ordre)* **s., téléphonez-moi dès que vous serez arrivé** you MUST ring *or* call me as soon as you get there; **s., dis au médecin que tu as de l'asthme** be sure to tell the doctor that you've got asthma; **s., pas de panique!** whatever you do, don't panic!; **ne faites s. pas de bruit** don't you make ANY noise; **je vais lui dire – s. pas!** I'll tell him/her – you'll do nothing of the sort!
    ❑ **surtout que** CONJ *Fam* especially as; **il ne devrait pas fumer, s. qu'il a les poumons fragiles** he shouldn't smoke, especially as he has weak lungs

surtout² [syrtu] NM **1** *(décor de table)* centrepiece, epergne **2** *Vieilli* overcoat

survaleur [syrvalœr] NF *Compta* goodwill

survécu, -e [syrveky] PP *voir* **survivre**

surveillance [syrvɛjɑ̃s] NF **1** *(contrôle → de travaux)* supervision, overseeing; *(→ médical)* monitoring; *(→ des prix)* monitoring; **c'est Jane qui est chargée de la s. des enfants ce matin** Jane's looking after the children this morning; **exercer une s. discrète sur** to keep a discreet watch on; **tromper** *ou* **déjouer la s. de qn** to give sb the slip; **être chargé de la s. de qch** to be responsible for supervising sth; **chargé de la s. des travaux/de l'examen** responsible for overseeing the work/*Br* invigilating *or Am* proctoring the examination; **cet appareil est destiné à la s. des contractions/du rythme cardiaque** this machine monitors contractions/the heartbeat; **s. électronique** electronic surveillance
    2 *Admin & Jur* surveillance; **s. légale** sequestration (by the courts); **s. de la pêche** fisheries protection service; **s. du territoire** counterespionage *or* counterintelligence section
    ❑ **de surveillance** ADJ **1** *(service, salle)* security *(avant n)*; *(avion, équipe)* surveillance *(avant n)*; *(appareil)* supervisory; *(caméra)* surveillance *(avant n)*, closed-circuit *(avant n)*
    2 *Méd* monitoring
    ❑ **en surveillance** ADV **le malade est en s. à l'hôpital** the patient is under observation in hospital
    ❑ **sans surveillance** ADV unattended, unsupervised
    ❑ **sous la surveillance de** PRÉP under the surveillance of, under observation by; **sous la s. de la police** under police surveillance
    ❑ **sous surveillance** ADV **1** *(par la police)* under surveillance; **mettre** *ou* **placer qch sous s.** to put sth under surveillance; **banque sous s. électronique** bank under electronic surveillance
    2 *Méd* under observation

surveillant, -e [syrvɛjɑ̃, -ɑ̃t] NM,F **1** *(de prison)* prison guard; *(d'hôpital)* supervisor; *(de magasin)* store detective; *(de chantier)* supervisor, overseer **2** *Scol* monitor; *(d'examen) Br* invigilator, *Am* proctor; **s. d'internat** boarders' supervisor; *Vieilli* **s. général** head supervisor *(person in charge of school discipline)*

surveiller [4] [syrveje] VT **1** *(épier)* to watch; **s. un prisonnier** to guard a prisoner; **il fait s. sa femme par un détective privé** he's having his wife watched by a private detective; **le commissaire faisait s. l'entrepôt** the superintendent placed the warehouse under surveillance; **on nous surveille** we're being watched

    2 *(contrôler → travaux, ouvriers, études)* to oversee, to supervise; *(→ cuisson)* to watch; *(→ examen) Br* to invigilate, *Am* to proctor; *(→ prix)* to monitor; **surveille le lait, il ne doit pas bouillir** watch that the milk doesn't boil; **vous devriez s. les fréquentations de vos enfants** you should keep an eye on the company your children keep; **voilà ce qui arrive aux adolescents que leurs parents ne surveillent pas** that's what happens to unsupervised adolescents
    3 *(observer)* to watch, to keep watch on *or* over; **s. les mouvements de troupes à la frontière** to keep watch on enemy troop movements along the border; **s. un territoire** to keep watch over a territory; **l'ambassade est surveillée de près** *(gén)* the embassy is closely watched; *(exceptionnellement)* the embassy is under strict surveillance; **la situation est à s. de près** the situation should be very closely monitored
    4 *(veiller sur → bébé, bagages)* to watch, to keep an eye on; **s. un malade** *(personne)* to watch over a patient; *(avec une machine)* to monitor a patient; **vas-y, je surveille tes affaires** go ahead, I'll keep an eye on your things; **j'aurais dû le s. davantage** I should have kept a closer watch on him
    5 *(prendre soin de → santé, ligne)* to watch; **s. son langage** to watch *or* mind one's language
    USAGE ABSOLU to keep watch; **je surveille, vous pouvez y aller** go ahead, I'm keeping watch
    ►**se surveiller** VPR **1** *(se contrôler)* to be careful what one does; **dans ce pays, il faut sans cesse se s.** you have to be very careful in this country
    2 *(se restreindre)* to watch oneself, to keep a watch on oneself; **tu as grossi, tu devrais te s.** you've put on weight, you should watch yourself

survenance [syrvənɑ̃s] NF *Jur* unexpected arrival *or* appearance; **s. d'enfant** unforeseen childbirth

survenant, -e [syrvənɑ̃, -ɑ̃t] ADJ *Littéraire* coming unexpectedly, supervening
    NM,F *Littéraire* chance comer
    NM *Can* = person who shows up unexpectedly

survendre [73] [syrvɑ̃dr] VT *Com* to overcharge for

survenir [40] [syrvənir] VI **1** *(problème, complication)* to arise, to crop up; *(événement, incident)* to happen, to occur, to take place **2** *Littéraire (personne)* to appear *or* to arrive unexpectedly
    V IMPERSONNEL **s'il ne survient pas de complications** if no complications arise; *Littéraire* **s'il survient un visiteur** if a visitor happens to come

survente [syrvɑ̃t] NF **1** *Com* overcharging **2** *Naut* increase of wind force

survenu, -e [syrvəny] PP *voir* **survenir**
    ❑ **survenue** NF *Littéraire* **1** *(d'une personne)* unexpected arrival *or* appearance **2** *(d'une complication)* appearance

survêt [syrvɛt] NM *Fam* tracksuit■

survêtement [syrvɛtmɑ̃] NM tracksuit

survie [syrvi] NF **1** *(continuation de la vie)* survival; **quelques jours de s.** a few more days to live; **donner à un malade quelques mois de s.** to prolong a patient's life for a few more months; **la s. d'une tradition** the continuance *or* survival of a tradition; **nous luttons pour la s. de notre entreprise** we are fighting for the survival of our company; **équipement de s.** *(d'astronaute)* life support equipment; **expérience de s.** survival experiment
    2 *(au-delà de la mort)* afterlife
    3 *Jur* **droits** *ou* **gains de s.** (stipulated *or* contractual) rights of survivorship
    4 *Écol* survival

survient *etc voir* **survenir**

survint *etc voir* **survenir**

survirage [syrviraʒ] NM *Aut* oversteer

survirer [3] [syrvire] VI *Aut* to oversteer

survireur, -euse [syrvirœr, -øz] ADJ *Aut* that tends to oversteer

survit *etc voir* **survivre**

survitesse [syrvitɛs] NF excessive speed

survitrage [syrvitraʒ] NM double glazing; **poser un s.** to fit double glazing

survivabilité [syrvivabilite] NF survivability

survivable [syrvivabl] ADJ survivable

survivance [syrvivɑ̃s] NF **1** *(d'une coutume)* trace, survival; **c'est une s. des rites païens** it's a relic *or* a survival from pagan rites **2** *Littéraire (survie)* survival; **s. de l'âme** the survival of the soul after death **3** *Ling* archaicism

survivant, -e [syrvivɑ̃, -ɑ̃t] ADJ *(conjoint, coutume)* surviving *(avant n)*

NM,F **1** *(rescapé)* survivor; **les survivants du tremblement de terre** the survivors of the earthquake; **il est le seul s.** he is the sole survivor **2** *Fig* survivor; **un s. du surréalisme** a survivor from the surrealist era

survivre [90] [syrvivr] VI **1** *(réchapper)* to survive, to live on; **ceux qui ont survécu** those who survived, the survivors

2 *(continuer à exister)* to survive; **une coutume qui a survécu à travers les siècles** a custom that has survived *or* endured through the ages; **dans le monde des affaires, il faut lutter pour s.** in business, it's a struggle for survival; **s. à** *(accident)* to survive; *(personne)* to survive, to outlive; **elle a survécu à tous ses enfants** she has survived *or* outlived all her children; **il a survécu à sa femme** he has outlived his wife; **je ne veux pas lui s.** I don't want to live on after his/her death; **l'association n'a pas survécu à son créateur** the association did not outlive its founder; **le régime a survécu au putsch** the government survived the putsch; **la statue a survécu aux bombardements** the statue has survived the bombing

▶**se survivre** VPR **1** *(artiste, célébrité)* to outlive one's fame *or* success

2 *Littéraire* **se s. dans qn/qch** to live through sb/sth; **se s. dans ses enfants** to live on through one's children

survol [syrvɔl] NM **1** *Aviat* **l'Espagne a refusé le s. de son territoire** Spain refused to allow the aircraft to fly over *or* to overfly its territory **2** *(d'un texte)* skimming through; *(d'une question)* skimming over; **un s. du roman montre que...** a quick look at the novel shows that...

survoler [3] [syrvɔle] VT **1** *Aviat* to overfly, to fly over **2** *(texte)* to skim through; *(question)* to skim over; **vous ne faites que s. la question** your treatment of the question is (too) cursory *or* superficial **3** *Ordinat* to browse through

survoltage [syrvɔltaʒ] NM (voltage) overload, overvoltage

survolté, -e [syrvɔlte] ADJ *Fam (surexcité)* hyper, worked up

survolter [3] [syrvɔlte] VT **1** *Élec* to boost **2** *Fam (exciter)* to work up, to overexcite▪

survolteur [syrvɔltœr] NM *Élec (transformateur)* booster, step-up transformer

survolteur-dévolteur [syrvɔltœrdevɔltœr] *(pl* **survolteurs-dévolteurs***)* NM *Élec* reversible booster

sus [sy(s)] ADV *Littéraire* **courir s. à qn** to give chase to sb

EXCLAM *Arch* **s., mes amis!** come, my friends!; **s. à l'ennemi!** have at them!

▫ **en sus** ADV in addition

▫ **en sus de** PRÉP in addition to

sus-caudal, -e [syskodal] *(mpl* **sus-caudaux** [-o], *fpl* **sus-caudales***)* ADJ *Orn* **plumes sus-caudales** upper tail-coverts

susceptibilité [sysɛptibilite] NF **1** *(sensibilité)* touchiness, sensitiveness; **il est d'une grande s.** he's very touchy *or* sensitive; **blesser la s. de qn** to hurt sb's feelings; **ménager la s. de qn** to humour sb **2** *Phys* **s. magnétique** magnetic susceptibility

susceptible [sysɛptibl] ADJ **1** *(sensible)* touchy, oversensitive, thin-skinned; **trop s.** oversensitive; **ne sois pas si s.** don't be so ready to take offence

2 *(exprime la possibilité)* **ce cheval est s. de gagner** that horse is capable of winning; **votre offre est s. de m'intéresser** I might be interested in your offer; **une situation s. de se produire** a situation likely to occur; **projet s. d'être amélioré** project open to improvement; **texte s. de plusieurs interprétations** text open to a number of interpretations; **c'est la seule personne s. de nous aider** he's the only person who might be able to help us

susciter [3] [sysite] VT **1** *(envie, jalousie, haine, intérêt, sympathie)* to arouse; *(mécontentement, incompréhension, étonnement)* to cause, to give rise to; *(problèmes)* to give rise to, to create **2** *(déclencher* → *révolte)* to stir up; *(*→ *dispute)* to provoke; *(*→ *malveillance)* to incite

suscription [syskripsjɔ̃] NF **1** *(adresse)* address, *Sout* superscription **2** *(sur un acte diplomatique)* superscription **3** *Jur* **acte de s.** (testamentary) superscription

sus-dénommé, -e [sysdenɔme] *(mpl* **sus-dénommés**, *fpl* **sus-dénommées***)* *Jur* ADJ above-named, aforenamed

NM,F above-named, aforenamed

susdit, -e [sysdi, -it] *(mpl* **susdits**, *fpl* **susdites***)* *Jur* ADJ aforesaid

NM,F aforesaid

sus-dominante [sysdɔminɑ̃t] *(pl* **sus-dominantes***)* NF *Mus* submediant, sixth

sus-hépatique [syzepatik] *(pl* **sus-hépatiques***)* ADJ suprahepatic

sushi [suʃi] NM sushi

sus-jacent, -e [syʒasɑ̃, -ɑ̃t] *(mpl* **sus-jacents**, *fpl* **sus-jacentes***)* ADJ *Géol* overlying

sus-maxillaire [sysmaksilɛr] *(pl* **sus-maxillaires***)* ADJ supramaxillary

susmentionné, -e [sysmɑ̃sjɔne] ADJ *Jur* abovementioned, aforementioned

susnommé, -e [sysnɔme] *Jur* ADJ above-named, aforenamed

NM,F above-named, aforenamed

suspect, -e [syspɛ, -ɛkt] ADJ **1** *(attitude, objet)* suspicious, suspect; *(aliment)* suspect; **un individu s.** a suspicious-looking person; **se rendre s. à qn** to arouse sb's suspicions; **cela m'est s.** it looks suspicious *or* suspect to me, I don't like the look of it

2 *(dont on peut douter)* **je trouve ses progrès soudains très suspects** I'm rather suspicious of his/her sudden progress

3 *(suspecté)* **être s. de qch** to be suspected *or* under suspicion of sth

4 *(susceptible)* **elle était peu suspecte de sympathie envers le terrorisme** she was hardly likely to approve of terrorism

NM,F suspect

suspecter [4] [syspɛkte] VT **1** *(soupçonner)* to suspect **(de qch/de faire qch** of sth/of doing sth); **on le suspecte d'avoir commis un meurtre** he's suspected of murder, he's under suspicion of murder; **je le suspecte de ne pas me dire la vérité** I suspect he's not telling me the truth, I suspect him of not telling me the truth; **je suspecte un mauvais coup** I suspect there's some foul play going on

2 *(douter de)* to doubt, to have doubts about; **je suspecte la véracité de son témoignage** I doubt the truth of his testimony; **s. la sincérité de qn** to doubt sb's sincerity

suspendre [73] [syspɑ̃dr] VT **1** *(accrocher* → *lustre, vêtement)* to hang; **suspends ta veste à la patère** hang your jacket (up) on the hook; **on suspend les poulets par les pattes** chickens are hung (up) by the feet; **suspendu dans le vide** hanging *or* suspended in mid-air

2 *Fig* **être suspendu à** *(dépendre de)* to depend *or* to be dependent on; **l'avenir de l'entreprise est suspendu à votre décision** the future of the firm depends entirely on your decision, your decision holds the key to the future of the firm

3 *(interrompre* → *hostilités, paiements)* to suspend; *(*→ *négociations)* to break off; *(*→ *séance, audience)* to adjourn; *(*→ *récit)* to interrupt; **la séance est suspendue** we will now adjourn; *Banque* **s. le paiement d'un chèque** to stop a cheque; *Ordinat* **s. l'exécution d'un programme** to abort a program

4 *(différer* → *décision)* to defer, to postpone; **s. son jugement** to suspend *or* to reserve judgement

5 *(interdire* → *émission, journal)* to ban; *(révoquer* → *fonctionnaire, prêtre, juge)* to suspend; **l'administration l'a suspendu** he's been suspended

▶**se suspendre** VPR to hang **(à/par** from/by)

suspendu, -e [syspɑ̃dy] ADJ **1** *Constr* hanging *(avant n)* **2** *(en travaux publics* → *pont)* suspension *(avant n)* **3** *Aut* **voiture bien/mal suspendue** car with good/bad suspension **4** *Bot* suspended **5** *Géog* **vallée suspendue** hanging valley

suspens [syspɑ̃] ADJ M *Rel* suspended

▫ **en suspens** ADJ **1** *(affaire, dossier)* pending, unfinished; *(problème, question)* unresolved; *(lecteur)* uncertain **2** *(flocons, planeur)* suspended, hanging ADV **tenir qn en s.** to keep sb in suspense; **laisser un dossier en s.** to keep a file pending; **laisser une question en s.** to leave a question unanswered *or* unresolved

suspense[1] [syspɑ̃s] NF *Rel* suspension

suspense[2] [syspɛns] NM suspense; **il y a un s. terrible dans le livre** the book's full of suspense; **prolonger** *ou* **faire durer le s.** to prolong the suspense; **ne fais pas durer le s., raconte-nous la fin!** the suspense is killing us, do tell us the ending!

▫ **à suspense** ADJ suspense *(avant n)*; **film à s.** thriller; **roman à s.** thriller, suspense story

suspenseur [syspɑ̃sœr] ADJ M *Anat* suspensory

NM *Bot* suspensor

suspensif, -ive [syspɑ̃sif, -iv] ADJ *Jur* suspensive

suspension [syspɑ̃sjɔ̃] NF **1** *(d'un objet)* hanging

2 *(interruption)* suspension; *Mil* **s. d'armes** suspension of hostilities; *Jur* **s. d'audience** adjournment (of hearing); *Ordinat* **s. d'exécution** *(d'un programme)* abort; *Jur* **s. d'instance** deferment of proceedings; **s. de paiement** suspension *or* withholding of payment; *Jur* **s. de peine** ≃ deferred sentence; **s. provisoire des poursuites** suspension of proceedings; **s. de séance** adjournment; **demander une s. de séance** to ask for an adjournment

3 *Admin (sanction)* suspension; **s. de permis de conduire** suspension of *Br* driving licence, *Am* driver's license; **sous peine d'un an de s. du permis de conduire** the penalty being a one-year driving ban

4 *Aut* suspension; **s. avant à roues indépendantes** independent front suspension; **s. hydraulique** hydraulic suspension; **s. hydroélastique** hydroelastic suspension; **s. hydropneumatique** hydropneumatic suspension; **s. à roues indépendantes** independent suspension; **s. triangulée** wishbone suspension

5 *Chim, Géog, Mus & Rail* suspension; *Méd* **s. buvable** oral suspension

6 *Typ* **points de s.** suspension points

7 *Mines* **s. dense** dense *or* heavy medium

8 *(luminaire)* ceiling light fitting

▫ **en suspension** ADJ **1** *(poussière)* hanging; **en s. dans l'air** hanging in the air

2 *Chim* in suspension

suspensive [syspɑ̃siv] *voir* **suspensif**

suspensoir [syspɑ̃swar] NM athletic support *or* supporter, jockstrap

suspente [syspɑ̃t] NF **1** *Naut* sling **2** *(de parachute)* suspending ropes **3** *Constr* (wire) support **4** *(en travaux publics)* suspender

suspicieux, -euse [syspisjø, -øz] ADJ *Littéraire* suspicious, suspecting

suspicion [syspisjɔ̃] NF **1** *(défiance)* suspicion, suspiciousness; *Littéraire* **avoir de la s. à l'égard de qn** to have one's suspicions about sb; **jeter la s. sur qn** to cast suspicion on sb **2** *Jur (supposition d'un délit)* suspicion; **s. de fraude** suspicion of fraud; **s. légitime** = reasonable suspicion that a fair trial will not be given

sustentation [systɑ̃tasjɔ̃] NF **1** *Aviat* lift **2** *Phys* sustentation; **base** *ou* **polygone de s.** basis of support

sustenter [3] [systɑ̃te] VT **1** *Vieilli (nourrir* → *personne)* to sustain **2** *Aviat* to lift

▶**se sustenter** VPR *Hum* to feed, to take sustenance; **nous nous sustentions de quelques morceaux de pain** we fed on a few pieces of bread

sus-tonique [systɔnik] *(pl* **sus-toniques***)* NF *Mus* supertonic

susurrant, -e [sysyrɑ̃, -ɑ̃t] ADJ *Littéraire* susurrant, whispering; *(mer)* murmuring; *(vent)* soughing; *(arbres)* rustling

susurration [sysyrasjɔ̃] NF *Littéraire* susurration, whispering; *(de la mer)* murmuring; *(du vent)* soughing; *(des arbres)* rustling

susurrement [sysyrmɑ̃] NM *Littéraire* susurration, whispering; *(de la mer)* murmuring; *(du vent)* soughing; *(des arbres)* rustling

susurrer [3] [sysyre] *Littéraire* VT *(chuchoter)* to whisper; **s. des mots doux à l'oreille de qn** to whisper sweet nothings in sb's ear

vi to whisper; *(mer)* to murmur; *(vent)* to sough; *(arbres)* to rustle

susvisé, -e [sysvize] **ADJ** *Jur* abovementioned, aforementioned

sut *etc voir* **savoir**

sutra [sutra] **NM** sutra

sutural, -e, -aux, -ales [sytyral, -o] **ADJ** sutural

suture [sytyr] **NF 1** *Bot, Géol & Zool* suture **2** *Anat & Méd* suture; **point de s.** stitch; **on lui a fait cinq points de s.** he/she had five stitches (put in)

suturer [3] [sytyre] **VT** *Méd* to stitch up, *Spéc* to suture

Suze® [syz] **NF** = flavoured liqueur drunk as an aperitif

suzerain, -e [syzrɛ̃, -ɛn] **ADJ** suzerain

NM,F suzerain, (feudal) overlord

suzeraineté [syzrɛnte] **NF** suzerainty

svastika [svastika] **NM** swastika

svelte [svɛlt] **ADJ** *(bras, jambes)* slender; *(personne)* slender, svelte

sveltesse [svɛltɛs] **NF** *Littéraire* svelteness, slenderness, slimness

SVP [ɛsvepe] *(abrév* **s'il vous plaît***)* please

swahili, -e [swaili] **ADJ** Swahili

NM *(langue)* Swahili

❑ **Swahili, -e NM,F** Swahili; **les S.** the Swahilis *or* Swahili

swap [swap] **NM** *Bourse* swap; *Fin* **s. d'actifs** asset swap; *Fin* **s. de change** exchange rate swap; *Bourse* **s. vanilla** vanilla swap

swastika [swastika] **NM** swastika

Swazi [swazi] **NMF** Swazi

Swaziland [swazilɑ̃d] **NM** **le S.** Swaziland; **vivre au S.** to live in Swaziland; **aller au S.** to go to Swaziland

sweater [swetœr] **NM** sweater

sweat-shirt [switʃœrt] *(pl* **sweat-shirts***)* **NM** sweatshirt

sweepstake [swipstɛk] **NM** sweepstake

swing [swiŋ] **NM 1** *Mus (rythme)* swing, swinging; *(style)* swing **2** *Sport* swing

swinguer [3] [swiŋge] **VI** to swing; **quel orchestre, ça swingue!** that band really swings!

sybarite [sibarit] **ADJ** *Littéraire* sybaritic

NMF *Littéraire (hédoniste)* hedonist, sybarite, pleasure-seeker

❑ **Sybarite NMF** *Antiq* Sybarite

sybaritique [sibaritik] **ADJ** *Littéraire* sybaritic

sybaritisme [sibaritism] **NM** *Littéraire* sybaritism

sycomore [sikɔmɔr] **NM** sycamore

sycophante [sikɔfɑ̃t] **NM 1** *Littéraire (dénonciateur)* informer; *(calomniateur)* scandal-monger **2** *Antiq* sycophant

sycosis [sikozis] **NM** *Méd* sycosis

Sydney [sidnɛ] **NM** Sydney

syénite [sjenit] **NF** *Géol* syenite

syllabaire [silabɛr] **NM 1** *(livre)* (syllabic) spelling-book **2** *Ling* syllabary

syllabation [silabasjɔ̃] **NF** syllabification

syllabe [silab] **NF 1** *Ling* syllable; **s. ouverte/fermée** open/closed syllable **2** *(parole)* **elle n'a pas prononcé une s.** she never opened her mouth; **je n'ai pas pu lui arracher une seule s.** I couldn't get a single word out of him/her

syllabique [silabik] **ADJ** syllabic

syllabus [silabys] **NM 1** *(pl inv)* *Rel* syllabus **2** *(pl* **syllabi***)* *Belg (polycopié)* handout *(for a university class)*

syllepse [silɛps] **NF** *Gram* sense agreement, syllepsis

sylleptique [silɛptik] **ADJ** *Gram* sylleptic

syllogisme [silɔʒism] **NM** syllogism

syllogistique [silɔʒistik] **ADJ** syllogistic, syllogistical

NF syllogistic, syllogistics *(singulier)*

sylphe [silf] **NM** *Myth* sylph

sylphide [silfid] **NF** *Myth & Littéraire* sylph

❑ **de sylphide ADJ** *(corps, taille)* sylph-like

Sylvain [silvɛ̃] **NPR** *Myth* Silvanus, Sylvanus

sylvain [silvɛ̃] **NM** *Myth* sylvan, silvan

sylvaner [silvanɛr] **NM 1** *Bot* Sylvaner grape **2** *(vin)* Sylvaner

sylve [silv] **NF** *Géog* rainforest

sylvestre [silvɛstr] **ADJ** *Littéraire* sylvan, forest *(avant n)*

sylvicole [silvikɔl] **ADJ** forestry *(avant n)*, *Spéc* silvicultural

sylviculteur, -trice [silvikyltœr, -tris] **NM,F** forester, *Spéc* silviculturist

sylviculture [silvikyltyr] **NF** forestry, *Spéc* silviculture

sylviidé [silvide] *Orn* **NM** warbler, *Spéc* sylvia

❑ **sylviidés NMPL** Sylviidae

sylvinite [silvinit] **NF** *Minér* sylvinite

sylvite [silvit] **NF** *Minér* sylvite

symbiose [sɛ̃bjoz] **NF** *Biol & Fig* symbiosis

❑ **en symbiose ADV** symbiotically, in symbiosis; *Fig* **ils vivent en s.** they're inseparable; **vivre en s. avec la nature** to live in harmony with nature

symbiote [sɛ̃bjɔt] **NM** *Biol* symbiont, symbiote

symbiotique [sɛ̃bjɔtik] **ADJ** *Biol* symbiotic

symbole [sɛ̃bɔl] **NM 1** *(signe)* symbol; **le drapeau est le s. de la nation** the flag is the symbol of the nation **2** *(personnification)* symbol, embodiment; **il est le s. du respect filial** he's the embodiment of filial duty, he's filial duty personified **3** *Rel* **S.** Creed; **le S. des Apôtres/de Nicée** the Apostles'/Nicene Creed **4** *Chim, Ordinat & Math* symbol

symbolique [sɛ̃bɔlik] **ADJ 1** *(fait avec des symboles)* symbolic; **langage/logique s.** symbolic language/logic; **écriture s.** writing in symbols **2** *(sans valeur réelle)* token, nominal; **une somme s.** a nominal amount; **un geste s.** a symbolic *or* token gesture

NM le s. the symbolic

NF 1 *(ensemble des symboles)* symbolic system, symbolism

2 *(étude des symboles)* interpretation of symbols, symbology

symboliquement [sɛ̃bɔlikmɑ̃] **ADV** symbolically; **on leur a donné s. un euro à chacun** they each got a token one-euro piece

symbolisation [sɛ̃bɔlizasjɔ̃] **NF 1** *(mise en symboles)* symbolization **2** *Math* symbolization

symboliser [3] [sɛ̃bɔlize] **VT** to symbolize; **on symbolise la justice par une balance** justice is symbolized by a pair of scales; **la colombe symbolise la paix** the dove symbolizes peace *or* is the symbol of peace

symbolisme [sɛ̃bɔlism] **NM 1** *(système)* symbolism **2** *Beaux-Arts & Littérature* Symbolism

symboliste [sɛ̃bɔlist] **ADJ 1** *(relatif aux symboles)* symbolistic **2** *Beaux-Arts & Littérature* Symbolist

NMF Symbolist

symétrie [simetri] **NF 1** *(gén)* symmetry; **la parfaite s. des fenêtres sur la façade** the perfect symmetry of the windows on the front of the building; **son visage manque de s.** his/her face lacks symmetry *or* isn't very symmetrical **2** *Géom* **s. de révolution/d'axes** rotational/axial symmetry; **s. à droite/gauche** right/left inverse

symétrique [simetrik] **ADJ 1** *(gén)* symmetrical; **deux parties symétriques** two symmetrical parts; **une rangée s. de l'autre** one row symmetrical to the other **2** *Géom* symmetrical; *Math* symmetric **3** *Électron (circuit)* balanced

NM *(point)* symmetrical point; *(élément)* symmetrical element

NF *(figure)* symmetrical figure; **x est un s. de y** x and y are symmetrical

symétriquement [simetrikmɑ̃] **ADV** symmetrically

sympa [sɛ̃pa] **ADJ** *Fam* nice■ ; **merci, c'était une soirée super s.** thank you, that was a really great evening

sympathectomie [sɛ̃patɛktɔmi], **sympathicectomie** [sɛ̃patisɛktɔmi] **NF** *Méd* sympathectomy

sympathie [sɛ̃pati] **NF 1** *(cordialité)* friendship, fellow feeling; **il y a une grande s. entre eux** they get on very well; **être en s. avec qn** to be on friendly terms with sb

2 *(penchant)* liking; **avoir** *ou* **éprouver de la s. pour qn** to like sb, to have a liking for sb; **je n'ai aucune s. pour lui** I don't like him at all, I have no liking for him at all; **inspirer la s.** to be likeable

3 *(bienveillance)* sympathy *(UNCOUNT)*; **témoigner de la s. à qn** to be friendly towards sb; **croyez à notre s.** our deepest sympathy; **recevoir des témoignages de s.** to receive expressions of sympathy

4 *(pour une idée)* sympathy; **je n'ai pas beaucoup de s. pour ce genre d'attitude** I don't have much time for that kind of attitude

5 *Méd* sympathy

❑ **sympathies NFPL** *(tendances)* sympathies;

ses sympathies vont vers les républicans his sympathies are *or* lie with the Republicans

sympathique [sɛ̃patik] **ADJ 1** *(personne)* nice, pleasant; **elle m'est très s.** I like her very much **2** *(visage)* friendly; *(idée)* good; *(lieu)* pleasant, nice; *(plat)* appetizing; *(ambiance, soirée, spectacle)* pleasant; *(attitude)* pleasant, friendly; **ce n'est pas très s. de sa part** that's not very nice of him/her; **il est bien s., ce petit vin/fromage!** nice little wine/cheese, this! **3** *Physiol* sympathetic

NM *Anat* sympathetic nervous system

sympathiquement [sɛ̃patikmɑ̃] **ADV** nicely, in a kindly way

sympathisant, -e [sɛ̃patizɑ̃, -ɑ̃t] **ADJ** sympathizing

NM,F sympathizer; **un s. du New Labour** a New Labour sympathizer

sympathiser [3] [sɛ̃patize] **VI 1** *(s'entendre)* **s. avec** *esp Br* to get on with, *esp Am* to get along with; **il n'a pas sympathisé avec les autres enfants** he didn't get on with the other children; **nous avons tout de suite sympathisé** we took to *or* liked each other right away **2** *Pol* **elle sympathise avec les communistes** she's a communist sympathizer

sympatholytique [sɛ̃patɔlitik] *Biol* **ADJ** sympatholytic

NM sympatholytic

sympathomimétique [sɛ̃patɔmimetik] **ADJ** sympathomimetic

NM sympathomimetic

symphonie [sɛ̃fɔni] **NF 1** *Mus* symphony; **les symphonies de Mozart** Mozart's symphonies; **s. concertante** sinfonia concertante **2** *Littéraire (harmonie)* symphony; **le paysage offrait toute une s. de verts** the countryside was a harmonious blend of greens

'**La Symphonie inachevée**' *Schubert* 'The Unfinished Symphony'

'**La Symphonie fantastique**' *Berlioz* 'Symphony fantastique'

symphonique [sɛ̃fɔnik] **ADJ** *(œuvre, poème)* symphonic; *(orchestre)* symphony *(avant n)*

symphoniste [sɛ̃fɔnist] **NMF 1** *(auteur)* symphonist **2** *(musicien)* orchestral player, symphonist

symphorine [sɛ̃fɔrin] **NF** *Bot* snowberry, waxberry

symphyse [sɛ̃fiz] **NF 1** *Anat* symphysis; **s. mentonnière** symphisis mandibulae **2** *Méd* **s. cardiaque** cardiac symphisis; **s. pleurale** adherent pleura

symplésiomorphie [sɛ̃plezjɔmɔrfi] **NF** *Biol* symplesiomorphy

symposium [sɛ̃pozjɔm] **NM** *(colloque)* symposium

symptomatique [sɛ̃ptɔmatik] **ADJ 1** *Méd* symptomatic **2** *(caractéristique)* symptomatic, indicative *(de* of); **c'est s. de leurs relations** it's symptomatic of *or* it tells you something about their relationship

symptomatologie [sɛ̃ptɔmatɔlɔʒi] **NF** symptomatology

symptôme [sɛ̃ptom] **NM 1** *Méd* symptom; **quand avez-vous ressenti les premiers symptômes?** when did you first notice the symptoms? **2** *(signe)* symptom, sign; **les premiers symptômes de qch** the forerunners *or* first signs of sth

synagogue [sinagɔg] **NF** synagogue

synalèphe [sinalɛf] **NF** *Ling* synaloepha

synallagmatique [sinalagmatik] **ADJ** *Jur* synallagmatic

synapomorphie [sinapɔmɔrfi] **NF** *Biol* synapomorphy

synapse [sinaps] **NF 1** *Anat* synapse **2** *Biol* synapsis

synaptique [sinaptik] **ADJ** synaptic

synarchie [sinarʃi] **NF** synarchy

synarthrose [sinartroz] **NF** synarthrosis

synchrocyclotron [sɛ̃krɔsiklɔtrɔ̃] **NM** synchrocyclotron

synchrone [sɛ̃kron] **ADJ** synchronous *(avec* with)

synchronie [sɛ̃kʀɔni] NF synchrony

synchronique [sɛ̃kʀɔnik] ADJ synchronic

synchroniquement [sɛ̃kʀɔnikmɑ̃] ADV synchronically

synchronisateur [sɛ̃kʀɔnizatœʀ] NM synchronizer

synchronisation [sɛ̃kʀɔnizasjɔ̃] NF synchronization

synchroniser [3] [sɛ̃kʀɔnize] VT to synchronize (**avec** with)

synchroniseur [sɛ̃kʀɔnizœʀ] NM **1** *Aut* synchromesh (device) **2** *Cin, Élec & Phot* synchronizer **3** *Écol* biorhythm trigger *or* signal

synchroniseuse [sɛ̃kʀɔnizøz] NF *Cin* film synchronizer

synchronisme [sɛ̃kʀɔnism] NM synchronism

synchrotron [sɛ̃kʀɔtʀɔ̃] NM *Phys* synchrotron

syncinésie [sɛ̃sinezi] NF syncinesis, synkinesis

syncitium [sɛ̃sitjɔm] NM *Biol* syncytium

synclinal, -e, -aux, -ales [sɛ̃klinal, -o] ADJ synclinal

    NM syncline

syncopal, -e, -aux, -ales [sɛ̃kɔpal, -o] ADJ *Méd* syncopal

syncope [sɛ̃kɔp] NF **1** *Méd* faint, blackout, *Spéc* syncope; **tomber en s., avoir une s.** to faint **2** *Ling* syncope **3** *Mus* syncopation

syncopé, -e [sɛ̃kɔpe] ADJ syncopated

syncoper [3] [sɛ̃kɔpe] *Mus* VT to syncopate

    VI to syncopate

syncrétique [sɛ̃kʀetik] ADJ syncretic

syncrétisme [sɛ̃kʀetism] NM syncretism

syncrétiste [sɛ̃kʀetist] ADJ syncretist

    NMF syncretist

syncytial, -e, -aux, -ales [sɛ̃sitjal, -o] ADJ *Biol* syncytial

syncytium [sɛ̃sitjɔm] NM *Biol* syncytium

syndactyle [sɛ̃daktil] ADJ syndactyl

syndactylie [sɛ̃daktili] NF syndactyly, syndactylism

synderme [sɛ̃dɛʀm] NM synthetic leather, leather substitute

syndic [sɛ̃dik] NM **1** *Admin* **s. (d'immeuble)** managing agent **2** *Anciennement Jur* **s. (de faillite)** (official) receiver (*before 1985*) **3** *Hist* syndic **4** *Bourse* president **5** *Suisse* (*président de commune*) = high-ranking civic official, similar to a mayor, in certain Swiss cantons

Culture

SYNDIC

A "syndic" is an administrative body which represents the interests of the owners of all the flats in a building, collectively known as the "syndicat de copropriété". The role of the "syndic" is to ensure the upkeep of the building and to organize meetings during which a vote is taken on any repairs, improvements etc that are deemed necessary. The services of the "syndic" are paid for by the owners of the flats.

syndical, -e, -aux, -ales [sɛ̃dikal, -o] ADJ **1** *Pol* (*Br* trade *or Am* labor) union (*avant n*) **2** *Admin* management (*avant n*); **droit s.** right of association

syndicalisation [sɛ̃dikalizasjɔ̃] NF unionization; **le taux de s. dans l'industrie est en chute libre depuis 20 ans** union membership in this industry has been plummeting for the last 20 years; **ils ont monté une campagne de choc pour essayer de relancer la s. dans les grandes entreprises** they launched a hard-hitting campaign to try to boost union membership in large companies

syndicaliser [3] [sɛ̃dikalize] VT to unionize

syndicalisme [sɛ̃dikalism] NM **1** (*mouvement*) (*Br* trade *or Am* labor) unionism **2** (*ensemble des syndicats*) (*Br* trade *or Am* labor) unions **3** (*action*) union activities; **faire du s.** to be active in a union **4** (*doctrine*) unionism

syndicaliste [sɛ̃dikalist] ADJ **1** (*mouvement*) (*Br* trade *or Am* labor) union (*avant n*) **2** (*doctrine*) unionist

    NMF (*Br* trade *or Am* labor) unionist

syndicat [sɛ̃dika] NM **1** *Pol* (*travailleurs*) (*Br* trade *or Am* labor) union; **se former** *ou* **se regrouper en s.** to form a union; **S. général de l'Éducation nationale** = teachers' union; **S. national de** l'enseignement **secondaire** = secondary school teachers' union; **S. national de l'enseignement supérieur** = university teachers' union; **S. national des instituteurs** = primary school teachers' union; **S. national des journalistes** = journalists' union; **S. national des lycées et collèges** = teachers' union; **s. ouvrier** (*Br* trade *or Am* labor) union; **s. patronal** employers' confederation *or* association; **s. professionnel** trade *or* professional association, trade body; **s. des typographes** print union

    2 *Jur* (*association*) association; **s. de communes** association of communes; **s. intercommunal à vocation multiple** = group of local authorities pooling public services; **s. interdépartemental** association of regional administrators; **s. de copropriétaires** co-owners' association

    3 *Fin* **s. d'émission/de garantie** issuing/underwriting syndicate; **s. d'enchères** tender pool; **s. financier** financial syndicate; **s. de placement** selling group; **s. de prise ferme** underwriting syndicate

    ❑ **syndicat d'initiative** NM tourist (information) office

syndicataire [sɛ̃dikatɛʀ] ADJ **1** (*d'un syndicat de copropriétaires*) = of a co-owners' association **2** *Fin* syndicate (*avant n*)

    NMF **1** (*copropriétaire*) member of a co-owners' association **2** *Fin* underwriter

syndication [sɛ̃dikasjɔ̃] NF *Banque* syndication

syndiqué, -e [sɛ̃dike] ADJ **1** (*membre d'un syndicat financier*) belonging to a syndicate **2** (*membre d'un syndicat de travailleurs*) belonging to a (*Br* trade *or Am* labor) union; **être s.** to be a member of a (*Br* trade *or Am* labor) union

    NM,F (*Br* trade *or Am* labor) union member

syndiquer [3] [sɛ̃dike] VT to unionize, to organize; **s. les travailleurs d'un atelier** to organize the workers in a workshop

    ► **se syndiquer** VPR **1** (*se constituer en syndicat*) to form a (*Br* trade *or Am* labor) union **2** (*adhérer à un syndicat*) to join a (*Br* trade *or Am* labor) union

syndrome [sɛ̃dʀom] NM *Méd* syndrome; **s. d'alcoolisme fœtal** foetal alcohol syndrome, FAS; **s. d'Asperger** Asperger's syndrome; **s. du bébé secoué** shaken baby syndrome; *Fam* **s. de la blouse blanche** white coat syndrome; **s. cervical traumatique** whiplash injury; **s. du choc toxique** toxic shock syndrome; **s. du côlon irritable** irritable bowel syndrome, IBS; **s. de Cushing** Cushing's syndrome; **s. de déficience immune combinée sévère** severe combined immunodeficiency, SCID; **s. de Down** Down's syndrome; **s. d'Edwards** Edwards' syndrome; **s. d'enfermement** locked-in syndrome; **s. de fatigue chronique** chronic fatigue syndrome; **s. des faux souvenirs** false memory syndrome; **s. de Gilles de la Tourette** Tourette's syndrome; **s. de Guillain-Barré** Guillain-Barré syndrome; **s. immunodéficitaire acquis** acquired immunodeficiency syndrome, Aids; **s. inflammatoire pelvien** pelvic inflammatory disease, PID; **s. métabolique** metabolic syndrome; **s. de Münchhausen** Münchhausen syndrome; **s. de Münchhausen par procuration** Münchhausen (syndrome) by proxy; **s. des ovaires polykystiques** polycystic ovary syndrome; **s. de Pfeiffer** Pfeiffer syndrome, Pfeiffer's syndrome; **s. postviral** postviral syndrome; **s. prémenstruel** premenstrual tension *or* syndrome; **s. du QT long** long QT syndrome; **s. de Stockholm** Stockholm syndrome; **s. de stress post-traumatique** post-traumatic stress disorder; **s. de la tête plate** flat head syndrome; **s. d'Usher, s. de Usher** Usher syndrome

synecdoque [sinɛkdɔk] NF *Ling* synecdoche

synéchie [sineʃi] NF *Méd* synechia

synécologie [sinekɔlɔʒi] NF *Biol* synecology

synectique [sinɛktik] NF synectics (*singulier*)

synérèse [sinerɛz] NF *Chim & Ling* synaeresis

synergide [sinɛrʒid] NF *Bot* synergid

synergie [sinɛrʒi] NF synergy, synergism

synergique [sinɛrʒik] ADJ *Physiol & Fig* synergic, synergetic

synergisme [sinɛrʒism] NM synergism

synergiste [sinɛrʒist] ADJ synergist, synergistic

synesthésie [sinɛstezi] NF synaesthesia

syngnathe [sɛ̃gnat] NM *Ich* pipefish

syngnathidé [sɛ̃gnatide] *Ich* NM pipefish, *Spéc* member of the Syngnathidae

    ❑ **syngnathidés** NMPL pipefish(es), *Spéc* Syngnathidae

synodal, -e, -aux, -ales [sinodal, -o] ADJ *Rel* synodal, synodical

synode [sinod] NM *Rel* synod

synodique [sinodik] ADJ *Astron & Rel* synodic

    NM *Rel* synodal

synonyme [sinɔnim] ADJ synonymous (**de** with)

    NM synonym; **cherchez un s. de "beau"** find another word *or* a synonym for "beautiful"

synonymie [sinɔnimi] NF synonymy

synonymique [sinɔnimik] ADJ synonymic, synonymous

synopse [sinɔps] NF synoptic table of the Gospels

synopsie [sinɔpsi] NF *Méd* synopsia, colour hearing

synopsis [sinɔpsis] NF (*bref aperçu*) synopsis

    NM *Cin* synopsis

synoptique [sinɔptik] ADJ synoptic, synoptical; **les Évangiles synoptiques** the Synoptic Gospels

    ❑ **synoptiques** NMPL **les synoptiques** the Synoptic Gospels

synostose [sinɔstoz] NF *Anat* synostosis

synovectomie [sinɔvɛktɔmi] NF *Méd* synovectomy

synovial, -e, -aux, -ales [sinɔvjal, -o] *Anat* ADJ synovial

    ❑ **synoviale** NF synovium, synovial membrane

synovie [sinɔvi] NF *Physiol* synovia, synovial fluid

synoviorthèse [sinɔvjɔʀtɛz] NF *Méd* synoviorthesis

synovite [sinɔvit] NF *Méd* synovitis

syntacticien, -enne [sɛ̃taktisjɛ̃, -ɛn] NM,F *Ling* syntactician

syntactique [sɛ̃taktik] ADJ *Chim & Ling* syntactic

syntagmatique [sɛ̃tagmatik] *Ling* ADJ syntagmatic

    NF syntagmatic analysis, syntagmatics (*singulier*)

syntagme [sɛ̃tagm] NM phrase, *Spéc* syntagm; **s. nominal/verbal/adjectival** noun/verb/adjectival phrase

syntaxe [sɛ̃taks] NF *Ordinat & Ling* syntax

syntaxique [sɛ̃taksik] ADJ **1** *Ling* syntactic **2** *Ordinat* syntax (*avant n*)

synthé [sɛ̃te] NM *Fam* synthesizer ∎

synthèse [sɛ̃tɛz] NF **1** (*structuration de connaissances*) synthesis; **faire la s. d'un récit** to summarize the main elements of a story

    2 (*exposé, ouvrage*) summary, résumé; **écrire une s. sur l'histoire de l'après-guerre** to write a brief history of the post-war years

    3 *Biol, Chim & Phil* synthesis

    4 *Ordinat* synthesis; **s. des images** image synthesis; **s. de la parole** speech synthesis

    ❑ **de synthèse** ADJ **1** (*non analytique*) **avoir l'esprit de s.** to be able to see the overall picture

    2 (*fibre, parole*) synthetic

synthétase [sɛ̃tetaz] NF *Biol* synthetase

synthétique [sɛ̃tetik] ADJ **1** (*raisonnement, approche*) all-encompassing; (*bilan*) summary; **une vue s. des choses** an overall *or* all-encompassing view of things; **avoir un esprit s.** to be able to see the overall picture **2** *Chim* (*fibre*) synthetic, man-made, artificial **3** *Ling & Phil* synthetic

    NM (*matière*) synthetic *or* man-made fibres

synthétiquement [sɛ̃tetikmɑ̃] ADV synthetically

synthétisable [sɛ̃tetizabl] ADJ which can be synthesized

synthétiser [3] [sɛ̃tetize] VT **1** (*idées, résultats, relevés*) to synthesize, to bring together **2** *Biol & Chim* to synthesize

synthétiseur [sɛ̃tetizœʀ] NM synthesizer; **s. de paroles** speech *or* voice synthesizer

synthétisme [sɛ̃tetism] NM *Beaux-Arts* Synthetism

syntone [sɛ̃tɔn] ADJ *Psy* syntonic

syntonie [sɛ̃tɔni] NF *Psy & Rad* syntony

syntonine [sɛ̃tɔnin] NF *Biol & Chim* syntonin

syntonisateur [sɛ̃tɔnizatœʀ] NM *Rad* tuner

syntonisation [sɛ̃tɔnizasjɔ̃] NF *Rad* syntonization

syntoniser [3] [sɛ̃tɔnize] **vт** *Rad* to syntonize

syntoniseur [sɛ̃tɔnizœr] **NM** tuner

syphilide [sifilid] **NF** *Méd* syphilid, syphilide

syphilis [sifilis] **NF** syphilis

syphilitique [sifilitik] **ADJ** syphilitic
NMF syphilitic

syphilo [sifilo] **NMF** *Fam* (*abrév* **syphilitique**) = person suffering from syphilis

Syracuse [sirakyz] **NM** Syracuse

syrah [sira] **NF** (*cépage*) Syrah

syriaque [sirjak] **ADJ** Syriac
NM Syriac

Syrie [siri] **NF** la S. Syria; **vivre en S.** to live in Syria; **aller en S.** to go to Syria

syrien, -enne [sirjɛ̃, -ɛn] **ADJ** Syrian
NM (*langue*) Syrian
❏ **Syrien, -enne NM,F** Syrian

syringe [sirɛ̃ʒ] **NF** *Archéol* rock-cut tomb

syringomyélie [sirɛ̃gɔmjeli] **NF** *Méd* syringomyelia

syrinx [sirɛ̃ks] **NF 1** (*flûte de Pan*) pan's pipes **2** *Orn* lower larynx

syrphe [sirf] **NM** *Entom* hoverfly

syrphidé [sirfide] *Entom* **NM** hoverfly, *Spéc* syrphid
❏ **syrphidés NMPL** Syrphidae

syrte [sirt] *Géog* **NF** syrtis
❏ **syrtes NFPL** *Vieilli* syrtes

sysop [sizɔp] **NM** *Ordinat* (*abrév* **Systems Operator**) SYSOP

systématicien, -enne [sistematisjɛ̃, -ɛn] **NM,F** taxonomist, systematist

systématique [sistematik] **ADJ 1** (*méthodique*) methodical, orderly, systematic; **de façon s.** systematically
2 (*invariable → réaction*) automatic, invariable; (*→ refus*) automatic; **c'est s., quand je dis oui, il dit non** when I say yes, he invariably *or* automatically says no; **je le fais parfois mais ce n'est pas s.** I do it sometimes but not as a matter of course *or* not automatically
3 (*inconditionnel → soutien*) unconditional, solid
4 *Méd* systemic
NF *Biol & Phys* systematics (*singulier*)

systématiquement [sistematikmɑ̃] **ADV** systematically

systématisation [sistematizasjɔ̃] **NF** systematization

systématisé, -e [sistematize] **ADJ** *Psy* systematized

systématiser [3] [sistematize] **vт** (*organiser en système*) to systemize, to systematize
USAGE ABSOLU (*être de parti pris*) to systemize, to systematize; **il a trop tendance à s.** he's too inclined to reduce everything to a system; **il ne faut pas s.** we mustn't generalize

système [sistɛm] **NM 1** (*structure*) system; **s. philosophique** philosophical system; **le s. éducatif/de santé français** the French educational system/health services; **s. de production** system of production; **s. scolaire** school system; **s. de valeurs** system of values; **il refuse d'entrer dans le s.** he refuses to be part of the system; **avoir l'esprit de s.** to have a systematic mind; **s. bancaire** bank *or* banking system; *Banque* **s. de changes** exchange rate regime; *Banque* **s. de compensation** clearing system; **s. comptable** accounting system; *Compta* **s. de contrôle de stocks** stock control system; *Fin* **s. déclaratif** = system under which people must file tax returns; **s. de direction** management system; *Com* **s. de distribution** distribution system; *Fin* **s. fiscal** tax system; *Com* **s. de gestion des performances** performance management system; **s. d'information marketing** marketing information system; *Bourse* **s. informatique de cotation** computerized trading system; **s. d'intelligence marketing** marketing information system; *Com* **s. d'inventaire** inventory method; *Jur* **s. du juge unique** single judge system; *Écon* **s. monétaire européen** European Monetary System; **s. de participation aux bénéfices** profit-sharing scheme; **s. de retraite** pension scheme; **s. de retraite par répartition** contributory pension plan; **s. solaire** solar system
2 (*méthode*) way, means; **il faut trouver un s. pour sortir de là** we've got to find a way of getting out of here; **je connais un bon s. pour faire fortune** I know a good way of making a fortune; **il a trouvé le s. pour ne pas être dérangé** he's found a way to avoid being disturbed; **s. D** resourcefulness■; **recourir au s. D** to use one's wits; **comment tu as fait pour avoir**

toutes les places gratuitement? – s. D! how did you manage to get all the tickets for nothing? – I used my wits!
3 (*appareillage*) system; **s. de chauffage/d'éclairage** heating/lighting system; **s. de fermeture/de freinage** locking/braking system; **s. de navigation** navigation system
4 (*réseau → de routes, de canaux*) system, network
5 *Anat & Méd* system; **s. nerveux/digestif/immunitaire** nervous/digestive/immune system; **s. nerveux central** central nervous system; **s. osseux** bone structure; **s. pileux** hair (*on body and head*); **s. végétatif** vegetative system
6 (*armement*) **s. d'arme** weapon *or* weapons system
7 *Constr* **s. de construction** system
8 *Géol* system
9 *Ordinat* system; **s. expert** expert system; **s. d'exploitation** operating system; **s. d'exploitation ou à disques** disk operating system; **s. d'exploitation réseau** network operating system; **s. de gestion de bases de données** database management system; **s. de gestion de fichiers** file management system; **s. d'information** information system; **s. informatique** computer system; **s. informatisé** computerized information system; **s. multi-utilisateur** multi-user system; **s. de sauvegarde sur bande** tape backup system; **s. de secours** backup system; **s. serveur** host system; **s. à tour** tower system; **s. de traitement de l'information** data processing system
10 *Math* **s. décimal** decimal system; **s. d'équations** simultaneous equations
11 *Météo* **s. nuageux** cloud system
12 *Phys* **s. international d'unités** SI unit; **s. métrique** metric system
13 *Fam* (*locution*) **taper sur le s. à qn** to get on sb's nerves *or* *Br* wick
❏ **par système ADV** as a matter of principle

systémique [sistemik] **ADJ** systemic
NF systems analysis

systole [sistɔl] **NF** *Physiol* systole

systolique [sistɔlik] **ADJ** *Physiol* systolic

syzygie [siziʒi] **NF** *Astron* syzygy; **les marées de s.** the spring tides

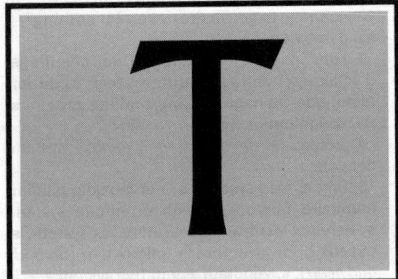

T¹, t¹ [te] NM INV **1** (*lettre*) T, t; **T comme Thérèse** ≃ T for Tommy **2** (*forme*) T (shape)

❏ **en T** ADJ T-shaped; **bandages en T** T bandage

ADV **mettre les bureaux en T** to arrange the desks so that they form a T

T² 1 (*abrév écrite* **tesla**) T **2** (*abrév écrite* **téra**) T

t² 1 (*abrév écrite* **tonne**) t.

t. (*abrév écrite* **tome**) vol.

t' [t] *voir* **te, tu²**

T9 [tenœf] NM *Tél* predictive text (input), T9

ta [ta] *voir* **ton³**

TAA [teaɑ] NM *Transp* (*abrév* **train autos accompagnées**) *Br* Motorail train, *Am* Auto Train

taal [tal] NM *Mus* tala

TAB [teabe] NM *Méd* TAB (vaccine)

tabac [taba] ADJ INV (*couleur*) buff

NM **1** *Bot* tobacco plant

2 (*produit*) tobacco; **elle a les doigts jaunis par le t.** she's got tobacco-stained fingers; **le t. peut provoquer le cancer** smoking can cause cancer; **campagne contre le t.** anti-smoking campaign; **t. blond/brun** mild/dark tobacco; **t. à chiquer** *ou* **à mâcher** chewing tobacco; **t. à priser, t. râpé** snuff

3 (*magasin*) *Br* tobacconist's, *Am* tobacco store (*which also sells stamps, phonecards and lottery tickets*); **si tu passes devant un t....** if you pass a *Br* tobacconist's *or Am* tobacco store...; **un bar t., un bar-t.** = bar where tobacco, stamps and lottery tickets are also sold over the counter

4 *Hist & Admin* **les Tabacs** the Tobacco Department

5 *Météo* **coup de t.** squall, gale

6 *Fam* (*locutions*) **faire un t.** to be a big hit; **passer qn à t.** to beat sb up, to give sb a hammering; **passage à t.** beating (up), hammering; **c'est le même t.** it's the same difference, it amounts to the same thing; **c'est toujours le même t.** it's always the same old thing *or* story

❏ **du même tabac** ADJ *Fam* of the same kind ■; **ils sont du même t.** they're tarred with the same brush; **et autres ennuis du même t.** and troubles of that ilk

tabagie [tabaʒi] NF **1** *Fam* (*lieu enfumé*) **c'est une vraie t. ici** you can't see for smoke around here **2** *Can* (*magasin*) *Br* tobacconist's, *Am* tobacco store

tabagique [tabaʒik] ADJ tobacco (*avant n*), nicotine-related

NMF tobacco addict, chain-smoker

tabagisme [tabaʒism] NM tobacco addiction, *Spéc* nicotinism; **t. passif** passive smoking; **lutter contre le t. dans les lycées** to campaign against smoking in secondary schools

tabard [tabar] NM *Hist* tabard

tabarnouche [tabarnuʃ], **tabarouette** [tabarwɛt]

EXCLAM *Can Fam* damn!

Tabaski [tabaski] NF (*en Afrique francophone*) = Muslim festival when sheep are sacrificed to commemorate the sacrifice made by Abraham

tabassage [tabasaʒ] NM *Fam* beating, hammering

tabassée [tabase] NF *Fam* beating, hammering

tabasser [3] [tabase] *Fam* VT **t. qn** to beat sb up, to give sb a hammering; **se faire t.** to be *or* get beaten up

▸ **se tabasser** VPR to beat each other up

tabatière [tabatjɛr] NF **1** (*boîte*) snuffbox **2** *Constr* skylight (opening), roof light **3** *Anat* **t. anatomique** (anatomical) snuffbox **4** *Archit* (*rosace*) (double) rosette

TABDT [teabedete] NM *Méd* = vaccine against typhoid, paratyphoid A & B, diphtheria and tetanus

tabellaire [tabelɛr] ADJ xylographic, xylographical

tabelle [tabel] NF *Suisse* register, list

tabellion [tabeljɔ̃] NM **1** *Hist* scrivener, tabellion **2** *Littéraire Péj* (*notaire*) lawyer

tabernacle NM [tabɛrnakl] **1** *Naut & Rel* tabernacle **2** *Constr* (*tap*) chamber

EXCLAM [tabɛrnak] *Can Vulg* fucking hell!

tabès [tabɛs] NM *Méd* tabes

tabétique [tabetik] *Méd* ADJ tabetic

NMF tabetic

tabla [tabla] NM *Mus* tabla

tablar, tablard [tablar] NM *Suisse* shelf

tablature [tablatyr] NF tablature

table [tabl] NF **1** (*pour les repas*) table; **dresser** *ou* **mettre la t.** to set the table; **débarrasser** *ou* **desservir la t.** to clear the table; **sortir** *ou* **se lever de t.** to leave the table, to get up from the table; **nous nous sommes levés de t. à minuit** we finished dinner at midnight; **qui sera mon voisin de t.?** who will I be sitting next to (for the meal)?; **retenir une t.** (**pour quatre personnes**) to book *or* to reserve a table (for four people); **une t. de six couverts** a table set for six; **dîner à la t. des officiers** to dine at the officers' table; **propos de t.** table talk; **t. d'hôte** table d'hôte; **faire t. d'hôte** = to provide a meal where all paying guests eat at the same table; **nous avons pris notre repas à la t. d'hôte** we ate with the other guests in the hotel dining room; **tenir t. ouverte** to keep open house; *Littéraire* **la t. du festin** the festive board

2 (*nourriture*) **la t.** food; **avoir une bonne t.** to keep a good table; **sa t. et sa cave sont bonnes** he/she serves good food and wine; **aimer la t.** to enjoy *or* to like good food; **une des meilleures tables de Paris** (*restaurant*) one of the best restaurants in Paris

3 (*tablée*) table, tableful; **présider la t.** to preside over the guests (*at a meal*); **il a fait rire toute la t.** he made the whole table laugh

4 (*meuble à usages divers*) table; **t. de chevet** *ou* **de nuit** bedside table; **t. de cuisine/de salle à manger** kitchen/dining-room table; **t. anglaise** gate-leg table; **t. basse** coffee table; **t. de billard** billiard table; **t. de cuisson** hob; **t. à découper** carving table; **t. à dessin** drawing board; **t. de jeu** card table; **t. à langer** baby-changing table; **t. de lecture** turntable; **t. de mixage** TV mixing console; *Rad* sound mixer; **t. de montage** *Typ & Phot* light table; *Cin* cutting table; *TV* editing desk *or* table; *Journ* light table; **t. des négociations** negotiating table; **s'asseoir à la t. des négociations** to get round the negotiating table; **t. d'opération** operating table; **t. d'orientation** panoramic table, viewpoint indicator; **t. à ouvrage** work table; **t. de ping-pong** table-tennis table; **t. à rallonges** extension *or* draw table; **t. à repasser** ironing board; *Littérature* **la T. ronde** the Round Table; *aussi Fig* **t. ronde** round table; (*débat*) debate; **t. roulante** *ou* **à roulettes** trolley; *Am* tea wagon; **t. de toilette** washstand; **t. tournante** = table used for séances; **faire tourner les tables** to hold a séance; **t. de travail** work table; **t. à volets** drop-leaf table; **tables gigognes** nest of tables

5 (*liste, recueil*) table; **t. de logarithmes/mortalité/multiplication** log/mortality/multiplication table; **t. alphabétique** alphabetical table *or* list; **t. des matières** (table of) contents, contents page; *Écon* **t. des parités** parity table; *Phil* **t. de**

vérité truth table; *Bible* **les Tables de la Loi** the Tables of the Law; *Phil* **t. rase** tabula rasa; *Fig* **faire t. rase** to wipe the slate clean, to make a fresh start; *Fig* **faire t. rase de qch** to make a clean sweep of sth; *Fig* **faire t. rase du passé** to wipe the slate clean; *Assur* **t. de survie** mortality table

6 *Astron* **t. de lancement** launch pad, launching pad *or* platform

7 *Constr* (*plaque*) panel; (*panneau*) panel, table; *Tech* (*de marteau, de valve*) face; (*de poutre métallique*) flange

8 (*de pierre*) slab; (*d'un dolmen*) cap stone

9 *Géol* table, mesa

10 *Typ* table; **t. de réception** delivery table

11 *Tél* switchboard

12 *Électron* table, board

13 *Ordinat* table; **t. traçante** plotter; **t. de corrélation/correspondance/décision** correlation/function/decision table; **t. des fichiers** file allocation table, FAT; **t. de recherche** *ou* **de référence** look-up table; **t. de vérité** truth table; **t. à digitaliser** digitizing pad

14 (*en joaillerie*) table; **diamant en t.** table (diamond)

15 *Mus* (*d'un violon*) sounding board, belly; **t. d'harmonie** soundboard

16 *Rail* **t. de roulement** running *or* rail surface; (*d'un rail*) tread

17 *Rel* **t. d'autel** (altar) table; **la t. de communion, la sainte t.** the communion *or* the Lord's table

18 *Hér* **t. d'attente** field

❏ **à table** ADV at table; **passer à** *ou* **se mettre à t.** to sit down to a meal; **nous pouvons passer à t.** the meal is ready now; **être à t.** to be at (the) table *or* at dinner/lunch/*etc*; **je te rappelle plus tard, je suis à t.** I'll call you later, I'm eating; **nous serons dix à t.** there will be ten of us at table; **il se tient mieux à t. qu'à cheval** he's a hearty eater; *très Fam Arg crime* **se mettre** *ou* **passer à t.** (*parler*) to spill the beans

EXCLAM it's ready!

❏ **table d'écoute** NF wiretapping set *or* equipment; **elle est sur t. d'écoute** her phone is tapped; **mettre qn sur t. d'écoute** to tap sb's phone

TABLEAU, -X [tablo]

board 1-3 ■ painting 4 ■ picture 4-6 ■ scene 5,18 ■ table 7, 8, 12, 14 ■ chart 7 ■ list 8 ■ statement 9

NM **1** *Scol* board, blackboard; **aller au t.** to go up to the board *or* to the front of the class; **Paul, au t.!** Paul, please come up to the blackboard *or* to the front of the class!; **t. noir** blackboard; **t. blanc** whiteboard; *Ordinat* **t. interactif** interactive whiteboard

2 (*support mural*) rack, board; **mettre ses clés au t.** to hang one's keys on the rack; **t. pour fusibles** fuseboard

3 (*panneau d'information*) board; **t. d'affichage** *Br* notice *or Am* bulletin board; **t. des arrivées/départs** arrivals/departures board; **t. des publications de mariage** = board where banns are posted

4 *Beaux-Arts* painting, picture; **un t. de Goya** a painting by Goya; **un t. ancien** an old master

5 *Fig* (*spectacle*) scene, picture; **ils formaient un t. touchant** they were a touching sight; *Fam* **tu imagines le t.!** you can picture *or* imagine

the scene!; *Fam* **je vois d'ici le t.!** I can just picture it!; *Fam* **vieux t.** *(vieille coquette)* (painted) old hag

6 *Fig (description)* picture; **vous nous faites un t. très alarmant de la situation** you've painted an alarming picture of the situation; **pour achever le t.** to cap it all

7 *(diagramme)* table; *(graphique)* chart; **remplir un t.** to fill in a table; **mettre qch sous forme de t.** to tabulate sth; **trois tableaux illustrent le texte** the text is illustrated with three tables; **tableaux d'activité économique** economic activity tables; **t. d'avancement de commandes** order flowchart; *Gram* **t. de conjugaison** conjugation table; **t. de conversion** conversion table; **t. des réservations** reservations chart; *Com* **t. de service** rota; **t. synoptique** synopsis, summary

8 *(liste → gén)* list, table; *(→ d'une profession)* roll; **t. des avocats** roll of lawyers; **être rayé** *ou* **se faire rayer du t.** to be struck off the rolls; **se faire inscrire au t.** *(avocat)* to be called to the bar; **t. d'avancement** promotions roster *or* list; *Chim* **t. des éléments** periodic table; **t. de gonflage** tyre-pressure table; *Scol* **t. d'honneur** board of honour; **t. horaire** *(des trains)* timetable; *Chim* **t. de Mendeleïev** periodic table

9 *Compta* **t. d'amortissement** depreciation schedule; **t. comptable** (financial) statement; **t. des emplois et ressources de fonds** statement of sources and applications of funds; **t. de financement** statement of sources and uses of funds, cashflow statement; *(planning)* finance plan; **t. de roulement** statement of changes in working capital

10 *Constr* reveal

11 *Élec* **t. de commande** *(d'appareil électroménager)* control panel, panel of switches; *Élec & Tél* **t. commutateur** switchboard, distribution board *or* panel; **t. de contrôle** control board; **t. de distribution** distribution board *or* switchboard; **t. d'éclairage** lighting panel; **t. de manœuvre** instrument board *or* panel; **t. de raccordement** patchboard

12 *Typ* table

13 *Ordinat* array; **t. de connexions** plugboard

14 *Math* table

15 *Méd* **t. clinique** overall clinical picture

16 *Naut* transom

17 *Pharm* (French) drugs classification; **t. A** toxic drugs (list); **t. B** narcotics (list); **t. C** dangerous drugs (list)

18 *Théât* scene; **premier t. du troisième acte** act three, scene one; **t. de service** *(répétitions)* rehearsal roster; *(représentations)* performances roster; **t. vivant** tableau vivant

19 *(locutions)* **gagner sur les deux/tous les tableaux** to win on both/all counts; **perdre sur tous les tableaux** to lose on all counts; **jouer** *ou* **miser sur plusieurs tableaux** to hedge one's bets

❑ **tableau de bord** NM 1 *Aut* dashboard

2 *Aviat & Naut* instrument panel

3 *Écon* (list of) indicators; *Com* management control data

4 *Ordinat* control panel; **t. de connexions** plugboard

❑ **tableau de chasse** NM 1 *Chasse* bag

2 *Aviat* list of kills

3 *Fig (conquêtes amoureuses)* conquests; **tu pourras la mettre à ton t. de chasse!** that's another notch on your gun!

---

tableautin [tablotɛ̃] NM *(peinture)* small painting

tablée [table] NF table; **toute la t. s'est levée** the whole table *or* company stood up; **une t. de jeunes** a tableful *or* party of youngsters; **une joyeuse t.** a merry gathering (around a table)

tabler [3] [table] **tabler sur** VT IND to bank *or* to count on; **ne table pas sur une augmentation** don't bank on getting a *Br* rise *or Am* raise

tabletier, -ère [tablətje, -ɛr] NM,F = maker of chessboards, fancy articles of ebony, ivory, bone etc, and inlaid ware

tablette [tablɛt] NF 1 *(petite planche)* shelf; *(dans un avion)* table; *Aut* **t. arrière** rear parcel shelf, back shelf; **t. à coulisse** *(d'un bureau)* pull-out flap; **t. de piano** music rest

2 *Culin (de chewing-gum)* stick; *(de chocolat)* bar; *Fam Hum* **avoir les abdos en t. de chocolat** to have a six-pack

3 *Constr* slab; *(de radiateur)* top; *(de cheminée)* mantelpiece; *(d'une maçonnerie)* coping; **t. de fenêtre** windowsill

4 *Ordinat* **t. graphique** graphics tablet

5 *Pharm* tablet

6 *Élec* **t. à bornes** terminal plate

❑ **tablettes** NFPL *Antiq* tablets; *Fig* **je vais l'inscrire** *ou* **le noter dans mes tablettes** I'll make a note of it

tabletter [3] [tablɛte] VT *Can* 1 *(ne pas tenir compte de)* to ignore, to leave aside 2 *Fam (employé)* to sideline

tabletterie [tablɛtri] NF 1 *(objets)* = chessboards, fancy articles of ebony, ivory, bone etc, and inlaid ware 2 *(fabrication)* = manufacturing of chessboards, fancy articles of ebony, ivory, bone etc, and inlaid ware 3 *(métier)* = trade in chessboards, fancy articles of ebony, ivory, bone etc, and inlaid ware

tableur [tablœr] NM *Ordinat* spreadsheet; **t. de graphiques** graphics spreadsheet

tablier [tablije] NM 1 *(de cuisine)* apron; *(blouse) Br* overall, *Am* work coat; *(d'enfant)* smock; **je mets toujours un t. pour faire la cuisine** I always put on an apron to do the cooking; **rendre son t.** *(démissionner)* to hand in one's resignation; *(domestique)* to give notice; *Fig* to give up, to throw in the towel; *Fam* **ça lui va comme un t. à une vache** it looks like a sack on him/her

2 *(rideau → de cheminée)* register; *(→ d'un magasin)* shutter

3 *(en travaux publics)* deck and beams, superstructure; *(de pont)* roadway

4 *Aut (d'une voiture)* cowl; *(d'un scooter)* footrest; *Mil (d'avant-train)* footboard; **t. de pare-chocs** bumper apron

5 *Rail* foot plate

6 *Tech (de machine-outil, de tour)* apron; *(de laminoir)* table; *(de forge)* hearth; *Ind* **t. sans fin** apron feed

7 *Vieilli (damier, échiquier)* board

tabloïd, tabloïde [tablɔid] NM 1 *(journal)* tabloid

2 *Pharm* tablet

ADJ **format t.** tabloid format

tabloïdisation [tablɔidizasjɔ̃] NF *Journ* tabloidization

tabor [tabɔr] NM *Hist* = corps of Moroccan troops

taborite [tabɔrit] NMF *Hist* Taborite

tabou, -e [tabu] ADJ 1 *Rel & (en anthropologie)* taboo 2 *(à ne pas évoquer)* forbidden, taboo; **c'est un sujet t.** that's taboo, that's a taboo subject 3 *(à ne pas critiquer)* untouchable

NM *Rel & (en anthropologie)* taboo; **ce sont des tabous** these are taboo subjects

tabouiser [3] [tabuize] VT to taboo, to declare taboo

taboulé [tabule] NM tabbouleh

tabouret [taburɛ] NM 1 *(siège)* stool; **t. de bar/cuisine/piano** bar/kitchen/piano stool; **t. à traire** milking stool 2 *(pour les pieds)* foot stool

Tabriz [tabriz] NM Tabriz

tabulaire [tabylɛr] ADJ tabular

tabulateur [tabylatœr] NM tabulator; **régler les tabulateurs** to set tabs (**à** at)

tabulation [tabylasjɔ̃] NF 1 *(positionnement)* tabulation 2 *(taquets)* tabs; **poser des tabulations dans** to tab; **délimité par des tabulations** tab-delimited

tabulatrice [tabylatris] NF tabulator

tabuler [3] [tabyle] VT to tabulate, to tab

TAC [teɑse] NM *Transp (abrév* **train autocouchettes**) car sleeper (train), *Br* Motorail train *(with sleeping accommodation)*

tac [tak] ONOMAT *(bruit sec)* tap, rat-a-tat; **et t.!** so there!

NM *(locutions)* **du t. au t.** tit for tat; **répondre du t. au t.** to answer tit for tat; **je lui ai répondu du t. au t. que...** I retorted quick as a flash that..., I came back quick as lightning that...

tacaud [tako] NM *Ich* bib, pout

tacca [taka] NM *Bot* tacca

tacet [tasɛt] NM *Mus* tacet

tachant, -e [taʃɑ̃, -ɑ̃t] ADJ 1 *(qui tache)* staining 2 *(qui se tache)* easily soiled

tache [taʃ] NF 1 *(marque)* stain; **t. d'encre** ink-stain; *Psy* inkblot; **t. de graisse** grease stain *or* mark; **t. de sang** bloodstain; **t. de suie** fleck of soot, smut; **t. de vin** wine stain; **faire une t./des taches** to make a mess; **tu as fait une t. à ta chemise** you've got a stain on your shirt; **je me suis fait une t.** I've stained my clothes; **je n'ai pas pu faire partir la t.** I couldn't remove the stain; **la t. ne partira pas** the stain won't come out; *Fam* **faire t.** *(jurer)* to stand *or* stick out like a sore thumb; **le piano moderne fait t. dans le salon** the modern piano looks out of place in the living room; **faire t. d'huile** to spread

2 *(partie colorée)* patch, spot; *(de couleur, de lumière)* splash; **des taches bleues dans un ciel gris** patches of blue in a grey sky; **le soleil faisait des taches de lumière sur le sol** the sun dappled the ground with light; **t. de lumière** *Théât & Cin* hot spot; *TV* shading

3 *(sur un fruit)* mark, blemish; *(dans une pierre précieuse)* flaw, blemish; **les pommes sont pleines de taches** the apples are all marked

4 *(sur la peau)* mark, spot; **la rougeole donne des taches rouges sur la peau** measles causes the skin to come out in red spots; **t. de rousseur** *ou* **de son** freckle; **t. de vin** strawberry mark *(birthmark)*

5 *Fig (souillure morale)* blot, stain, blemish; **cette fraude est une t. à sa réputation** this fraud has stained his/her reputation; *Rel* **t. originelle** stain of original sin

6 *Astron* **t. solaire** sunspot; **(Grande) T. rouge** Red Spot

7 *Beaux-Arts* patch, tache

8 *Méd (sur une radiographie)* opacity; *(coloration anormale)* spot; **taches auditives** auditory spots, *Spéc* maculae acusticae; **t. jaune** yellow spot, *Spéc* macula lutea; **taches lenticulaires** rose *or* typhoid spots; **t. de Mariotte** blind *or* Mariotte's spot

9 *Zool* patch, spot, mark; **chien blanc à taches feu** white dog with reddish markings *or* patches *or* spots

10 *Fam (personne)* nonentity, loser, no-hoper; **quelle t. ce mec-là!** what a total non-entity *or* loser *or* no-hoper that guy is!

❑ **sans tache** ADJ 1 *(fruit)* unblemished

2 *Fig (réputation)* spotless

taché, -e [taʃe] ADJ 1 *(vêtement, tissu)* stained; **t. d'encre/de sang/de graisse** ink-/blood-/grease-stained 2 *(fruit)* bruised 3 *(animal)* spotted; **un chien à la robe noire tachée de blanc** a dog with a black coat with white markings

tâche [tɑʃ] NF 1 *(travail)* task, job; **remplir une t.** to fulfil a task; **assigner une t. à qn** to give sb a task *or* a job *or* a piece of work to do; **faciliter/compliquer la t. à qn** to make things easier/more complicated for sb; **tâches ménagères** housework

2 *(mission, rôle)* task, mission; **faire régner la paix, voilà la t. qu'il s'est fixée** the task he has set for himself is to bring peace; **la t. des scientifiques d'aujourd'hui** the mission of today's scientists; *Littéraire* **prendre à t. de faire qch** to undertake to do sth

3 *Ordinat* task; **t. d'arrière-plan** *ou* **de fond** background task *or* job

❑ **à la tâche** ADJ *Ind* **travail à la t.** piece-work ADV *Ind* **travailler à la t.** to be on piecework; **il est à la t.** he's a pieceworker; *Fam* **on n'est pas à la t.!** what's the rush?; **mourir à la t.** to die in harness

tachéomètre [takeɔmɛtr] NM *Géog* tacheometer, tachymeter

tachéométrie [takeɔmetri] NF *Géog* tacheometry, tachymetry

tacher [3] [taʃe] VT 1 *(salir → vêtement, tapis)* to stain; **t. de sang/chocolat** to stain with blood/chocolate

2 *(colorer)* to spot, to dot; **le soleil tache de rose les cimes neigeuses** the sun tints the snowy mountain tops a rosy hue

3 *Fig (ternir → réputation, nom, honneur)* to stain

VI *(encre, sauce, vin)* to stain

▶**se tacher** VPR 1 *(emploi réfléchi)* to get oneself dirty, to stain one's clothes

2 *(emploi passif) (tissu)* to stain; *(bois, peinture, moquette)* to mark; *(fruit)* to become marked; **le blanc se tache facilement** white soils *or* gets dirty easily; **le noir ne se tache pas** black doesn't show the dirt

tâcher [3] [tɑʃe] VT **t. que...** to make sure that...;

tâche qu'elle ne l'apprenne pas make sure she doesn't hear about it

◻ **tâcher de** VT IND to try to; **tâchez de ne pas oublier** try not to forget; **tâche d'être à l'heure** try to be on time

tâcheron [tɑʃʀɔ̃] NM **1** *(petit entrepreneur)* jobber; *(ouvrier agricole)* hired hand **2** *Péj (travailleur)* drudge, workhorse; *(écrivaillon)* hack; **les tâcherons d'Hollywood** Hollywood hacks; **j'en ai assez de faire ce métier de t.!** I've had enough of this drudgery or skivvying!

tacheté, -e [taʃte] ADJ *(papier, plumage)* speckled, mottled; *(chat)* tabby; **une robe blanche tachetée de vert** a white dress spotted with green; **chat noir t. de blanc** black cat with white spots or markings; **des champs tachetés de lumière** fields flecked or dappled with sunlight

tacheter [27] [taʃte] VT to spot, to speckle, to fleck

tacheture [taʃtyʀ] NF spot, speckle

tachina [takina] NM *Entom* tachina (fly), tachinid fly

tachine [takin] NF *Entom* tachina (fly), tachinid fly

tachisme [taʃism] NM *Beaux-Arts* tachism, tachisme

tachiste [taʃist] *Beaux-Arts* ADJ tachist, tachiste NMF tachist, tachiste

tachistoscope [takistɔskɔp] NM tachistoscope

Tachkent [taʃkɛnt] NM Tashkent

tachyarythmie [takiaritmi] NF *Méd* tachyarrhythmia

tachycardie [takikaʀdi] NF *Méd* tachycardia

tachycardique [takikaʀdik] ADJ *Méd* tachycardiac

tachygraphe [takigʀaf] NM tachograph

tachymètre [takimɛtr] NM tachometer; *Aut* speedometer

tachyon [takjɔ̃] NM *Phys* tachyon

tachyphémie [takifemi] NF *Physiol* tachyphemia, tachyphrasia

tachypnée [takipne] NF *Méd* tachypnoea

tachypsychie [takipsiʃi] NF tachypsychia

Tacite [tasit] NPR Tacitus

tacite [tasit] ADJ tacit; **c'était un aveu t.** it was a tacit admission; **(par) t. reconduction** (by) tacit agreement to renew

tacitement [tasitmɑ̃] ADV tacitly

taciturne [tasityʀn] ADJ taciturn, silent, uncommunicative

tacle [takl] NM *Ftbl* tackle; **t. glissé** sliding tackle; **faire un t. à qn** to tackle sb

tacler [3] [takle] VT *Ftbl* to tackle

taco [tako] NM *Culin* taco

tacon [takɔ̃] NM *Suisse (pièce en tissu)* leather patch *(for repairing clothes)*

taconeos [takɔneɔs] NMPL *(dans la danse flamenca)* = rhythmic hammering of the heels on the floor

tacot [tako] NM *Fam* **1** *(vieille voiture)* (old) heap, *Br* banger **2** *(taxi)* taxi■, cab, *Am* hack

TacOTac® [takɔtak] NM = public lottery with a weekly prize draw

tact [takt] NM **1** *Vieilli Physiol* (sense of) touch **2** *(délicatesse)* tact, delicacy; **être plein de t.** to be very tactful; **avoir du t.** to be tactful; **manquer de t.** to be tactless; **manque de t.** tactlessness; **quel manque de t.!** how tactless!; **annoncer la nouvelle avec/sans t.** to break the news tactfully/tactlessly

tacticien, -enne [taktisjɛ̃, -ɛn] NM,F **1** *Mil* (military) tactician **2** *Fig (stratège)* strategist; **en fine tacticienne, elle a laissé parler tout le monde avant d'intervenir** she very cleverly allowed everyone else to speak before intervening

tacticité [taktisite] NF *Chim* tacticity

tactile [taktil] ADJ tactile

tactique [taktik] ADJ tactical NF **1** *Mil* tactics *(singulier)* **2** *(moyens)* tactics; **t. commerciale** marketing tactics; **je vais devoir changer de t.** I'm going to have to change my tactics; **ce n'est pas la meilleure t. pour le convaincre** it's not the best way of convincing him

tactiquement [taktikmɑ̃] ADV tactically

tactisme [taktism] NM tropism, taxis

tadjik [tadʒik] ADJ Tadzhiki NM *(langue)* Tadzhiki ◻ **Tadjik** NMF Tadzhik; **les T.** the Tadzhik

Tadjikie [tadʒiki] NF = **Tadjikistan**

Tadjikistan [tadʒikistɑ̃] NM **le T.** Tadzhikistan; **vivre au T.** to live in Tadzhikistan; **aller au T.** to go to Tadzhikistan

Tadj Mahall [tadʒmaal] = **Taj Mahal**

tadorne [tadɔrn] NM *Orn* sheldrake; **t. de Belon** shelduck

taekwondo [taekwɔ̃do, tɛkwɔ̃do] NM taekwondo

tael [taɛl] NM *Hist* tael

tænia [tenja] NF = **ténia**

taf [taf] NM *Fam (travail)* work■; *(emploi)* job■; **j'ai du t.** *(travail)* I've got work to do; *(emploi)* I've got a job

taffe [taf] NF *Fam (de cigarette)* drag

taffer [3] [tafe] VI *Fam (travailler)* to work■

taffetas [tafta] NM **1** *Tex* taffeta; **une robe en** *ou* **de t.** a taffeta dress **2** *Pharm* **t. gommé** *ou* **anglais** adhesive bandage

tafia [tafja] NM tafia

tafiard, -e [tafjaʀ, -aʀd], **tafieux, -euse** [tafjø, -øz] *Belg* ADJ boastful NM,F boaster

tag [tag] NM tag *(piece of graffiti)*

tagal [tagal] NM **1** *(langue)* Tagalog **2** *Bot* abaca, manila hemp

Tage [taʒ] NM **le T.** the (River) Tagus

tagetes [taʒetɛs], **tagète, tagette** [taʒet] NM *Bot* marigold, *Spéc* tagetes

tagine [taʒin] = **tajine**

tagliatelle [tagljatɛl, taljatɛl] *(pl inv ou* **tagliatelles)** NF piece of tagliatelle; **des t.** *ou* **tagliatelles** tagliatelle

tagme [tagm] NM *Zool* tagma

taguer [3] [tage] VT to cover in graffiti■

tagueur, -euse [tagœʀ, -øz] NM,F graffiti artist■, tagger

Tahiti [taiti] NF Tahiti; **à T.** in Tahiti

tahitien, -enne [taisjɛ̃, -ɛn] ADJ Tahitian NM *(langue)* Tahitian ◻ **Tahitien, -enne** NM,F Tahitian

TAI [teai] NM *(abrév* **temps atomique international)** IAT

taïaut [tajo] EXCLAM *Chasse* tally-ho!

Taibei [tajbɛj] NM Taipei, T'ai-pei

tai-chi [tajʃi] NM INV T'ai Chi

tai-chi-chuan [tajʃiʃwan] NM INV T'ai Chi Ch'uan

taie [tɛ] NF **1** *(enveloppe)* **t. d'oreiller** pillowcase, pillow slip; **t. de traversin** bolster case **2** *Méd* leucoma; *Fig Littéraire* **avoir une t. sur l'œil** to be blinkered, to have tunnel vision

taïga [tajga] NF taiga

taiji [tajtʃi, tajʃi] NM Taiji

taïkonaute [tajkonot] NMF taikonaut, Chinese astronaut

taillable [tajabl] ADJ **1** *Hist* subject to tallage **2** *(locution)* **être t. et corvéable à merci** *(sujet à l'impôt)* to be subject to tallage; *(soumis à des travaux)* to be a drudge; *Fig* **je ne suis pas t. et corvéable à merci, moi!** I won't be treated like a drudge!

taillade [tajad] NF **1** *(estafilade)* slash, gash; **se faire une t. au doigt** to gash one's finger **2** *Hort (sur un arbre)* gash **3** *Couture (ouverture)* slash

tailladé, -e [tajade] ADJ *Couture* slashed

taillader [3] [tajade] VT to gash or to slash (through)

▶ **se taillader** VPR **se t. le doigt/le menton** to gash one's finger/chin; **se t. les poignets** *ou* **les veines** to slash one's wrists

taillage [tajaʒ] NM *Ind* milling, cutting

taillanderie [tajɑ̃dʀi] NF **1** *(fabrication, commerce)* edge-tool industry **2** *(outils)* edge-tools

taillandier [tajɑ̃dje] NM edge-tool maker

taillant [tajɑ̃] NM **1** *(tranchant)* (cutting) edge **2** *Mines & (en travaux publics)* bit

taillaule [tajol] NF *Suisse* = sweet pastry roll

taille [taj] NF **1** *(hauteur → d'une personne, d'un animal)* height; **une femme de haute t.** a tall woman; **un homme de petite t.** a short man; **un enfant de t. moyenne** a child of average height; **ils ont à peu près la même t.** they're about the same height; **de la t. de** as big as, the size of; **atteindre sa t. adulte** to reach one's full height

2 *(grandeur → d'un endroit, d'un objet)* size; **une pièce de t. moyenne** an average-sized room; **une lettre de la t. d'une affiche** a letter the size of a poster, a poster-sized letter; **des avocats de la t. du poing** avocados the size of your fist; **il te**

faudrait un plat d'une t. plus grande you need a larger(-sized) dish

3 *(importance)* size; **une erreur de cette t. est impardonnable** a mistake of this magnitude is unforgivable

4 *(de vêtement)* size; **quelle est votre t.?, quelle t. faites-vous?** what size are you or do you take?; **ce n'est pas ma t.** it's not my size; **deux tailles au-dessus/en dessous** two sizes bigger/smaller; **avez-vous la t. au-dessus/en dessous?** do you have the next size up/down?; **donnez-moi la t. en dessous/au-dessus** give me one size down/up; **les grandes/petites tailles** the large/small sizes; **pour les grandes tailles** outsize; **elles font toutes deux la même t.** they both wear the same size; **t. XL** size XL; **t. unique** one size; **je n'ai plus votre t.** I'm out of your size; **elle a la t. mannequin** she's got a real model's figure

5 *(partie du corps)* waist; **avoir la t. longue/courte** to be long-/short-waisted; **avoir la t. fine** to be slim-waisted or slender-waisted; **sa robe est serrée/trop serrée à la t.** her dress is fitted/too tight at the waist; **elle avait la t. prise dans une robe de soie violette** her slim waist was set off by a purple silk dress; **elle n'a pas de t.** she's got no waist; **avoir une t. de guêpe** *ou* **de nymphe** to have an hourglass figure; **avoir la t. bien prise** to have a nice or good figure; **prendre qn par la t.** *(d'un bras)* to put an arm round sb's waist; *(des deux mains)* to take sb by the waist, to seize sb round the waist

6 *(partie d'un vêtement)* waist; **robe à t. haute/basse** high-/low-waisted dress; **un jean (à) t. basse** low-waisted or low-rise or *Br* hipster or *Am* hip-hugger jeans

7 *Ordinat* **t. de disque dur** hard disk size; **t. de champ** field size; **t. (de) mémoire** storage capacity

8 *Typ* **t. de corps** body size; **t. de fonte** font size; **t. des caractères** typesize

9 *Hort (d'un arbre → gén)* pruning; *(→ importante)* cutting back; *(→ légère)* trimming; *(d'une haie)* trimming, clipping; *(de la vigne)* pruning; **la t. de la vigne commence en février** the pruning of the vines begins in February; **t. longue** pinching, light pruning

10 *(tranchant)* edge; **frapper de t.** to strike or to slash with the edge of one's sword

11 *Beaux-Arts (du bois, du marbre)* carving; *(en gravure)* etching; **t. au burin** chiselling; **l'art de la t.** carving

12 *Constr (à la carrière)* hewing, cutting; *(sur le chantier)* dressing

13 *Hist (impôt)* taille, tallage

14 *Ind (d'un engrenage)* milling, cutting; **t. bâtarde/croisée/simple** bastard/crosscut/float cut

15 *(en joaillerie)* cutting; **t. à angles** step-cut

16 *Vieilli Méd* cystotomy, lithotomy

17 *Mines* longwall, working face

18 *Mus* tenor (line)

19 *Can Joual (jeu de chat)* tag, tig

◻ **à la taille de** PRÉP in keeping with; **ses moyens ne sont pas à la t. de ses ambitions** his/her ambitions far exceed his/her means

◻ **à ma/sa/leur/etc taille** ADV *(de même envergure)* **trouver un adversaire à sa t.** to meet one's match; **trouver un collaborateur à sa t.** to find a colleague who is one's equal or who has an equal level of skills

◻ **de taille** ADJ **1** *(énorme)* huge, great; **le risque est de t.** the risk is considerable; **une fraude de t.** a major fraud; **un mensonge de t.** a whopper; **le mensonge était de t.** it was a thumping great lie; **une surprise de t.** a huge surprise

2 *(capable)* **être de t. à** to measure up; **face à un adversaire comme lui, tu n'es pas de t.** you're no match for an opponent like him; **de t. à** capable of, able to; **elle n'est pas de t. à se défendre** she's not capable of defending herself; **je ne suis pas de t. à écrire une thèse** I'm not up to writing a thesis; **il est de t. à vous battre** he is big enough or strong enough to beat you; **il n'est pas de t. à être chef** he's not cut out to be a leader, he's not the stuff that leaders are made of; **je ne suis pas de t. à vous prouver le contraire** I'm not in a position to prove you wrong; **il n'est pas de t. à lutter contre vous** he is no match for you, he stands no chance

against you; **rien à craindre, il n'est pas de t.** there's nothing to be afraid of, he's not up to it

taillé, -e [taje] **ADJ 1** *(coupé → arbre)* trimmed, pruned; *(→ haie)* trimmed, clipped; *(→ cristal)* cut; *(→ crayon)* sharpened; *(→ barbe, moustache, ongles)* trimmed; **bien/mal t.** *(haie, barbe, moustache, ongles)* neatly/badly trimmed; *(crayon)* sharp/blunt; **un costume bien/mal t.** a well-cut/badly-cut suit; **un crayon t. en pointe** a sharp pencil; **une barbe taillée en pointe** a goatee (beard); **avoir les cheveux taillés en brosse** to have a brush cut; **t. dans le roc** carved out of the rock

2 *(bâti)* **un homme bien t.** a well-built man; **un gaillard t. en hercule** a great hulk of a man

3 *Fig (apte à)* **t. pour** cut out for; **tu n'es pas t. pour ce métier** you're not cut out for this job; **être t. pour faire qch** to be cut out to do sth

taille-crayon [tajkrɛjɔ̃] *(pl* **inv** *ou* **taille-crayons)** **NM** pencil sharpener

taille-douce [tajdus] *(pl* **tailles-douces)** **NF** intaglio; **gravure** *ou* **impression en t.** copper-plate engraving

taille-haie [tajɛ] *(pl* **taille-haies)** **NM** hedge trimmer

tailler [3] [taje] **VT 1** *(ciseler → pierre)* to cut, *Sout* to hew; *(→ verre)* to engrave; *(→ bois, marbre)* to carve; *(→ diamant)* to cut; *Fig* **t. en pièces une armée** to cut an army to pieces; *Fig* **la critique l'a taillé en pièces** the reviewers made mincemeat out of him; *Vieilli* **t. des croupières à qn** to put difficulties in sb's way; *Fam* **t. la route** *(parcourir beaucoup de chemin)* to eat up the miles; *(partir)* to beat it, *Br* to scarper, *Am* to book it

2 *(couper → barbe, moustache)* to trim; *(→ crayon)* to sharpen; *(→ bifteck)* to cut; **t. sa barbe en pointe** to trim one's beard into a goatee; *Fam* **t. une bavette** to have a chat *or Br* a chinwag

3 *(façonner)* to cut, *Sout* to hew; **il a taillé un escalier dans la pente** he cut some steps into the hillside

4 *Couture (vêtement)* to cut (out); **t. une jupe dans du velours** to cut a skirt out of a piece of velvet; *Fam* **t. une veste** *ou* **un costard à qn** to badmouth sb, *Br* to slag sb off; *Fam* **il a failli se faire t. un short en traversant la rue** he almost got run over crossing the street■

5 *Hort (arbre)* to prune, to cut back; *(haie)* to trim, to clip; *(vigne)* to prune

6 *Ind (engrenage)* to mill, to cut

VI 1 *(inciser)* to cut; **t. dans les chairs avec un scalpel** to cut into the flesh with a scalpel

2 *(vêtement)* **cette robe taille grand/petit** this dress *Br* is cut *or Am* runs large/small

3 *Vieilli & (dans un jeu)* to keep the bank, to be banker

▶**se tailler VPR 1** *Fam (partir)* to beat it, *Br* to scarper, *Am* to book it; **allez, on se taille!** come on, let's beat it!; **taille-toi!** scram!, beat it!

2 *(se couper)* **se t. la barbe** to trim one's beard; **se t. un chemisier dans un vieux drap** to make a blouse for oneself from *or* out of an old sheet

3 *(se faire)* **se t. un chemin à travers les ronces** to hack one's way through the brambles; **se t. un chemin à travers la foule** to force one's way through the crowd; **se t. un (beau) succès** to be a great success; **se t. un empire** to carve out an empire for oneself

taillerie [tajri] **NF 1** *(art)* gem-cutting **2** *(atelier)* gem-cutting workshop

tailleur [tajœr] **NM 1** *(couturier)* tailor; **t. pour dames** ladies' tailor; **t. à façon** *Br* bespoke *or Am* custom tailor

2 *(ouvrier)* **t. de diamants** diamond *or* gem cutter; **t. de pierres/de pavés/de marbre** stone/paving stone/marble cutter; **t. de verre** glass engraver

3 *(vêtement)* (lady's) suit; **un t. sur mesure** a tailor-made suit; **un t. Chanel** a Chanel suit *(the expression is often used to evoke a wealthy, conservative but fashionable lifestyle)*

❑ **en tailleur ADV** cross-legged; **s'asseoir en t.** to sit cross-legged

tailleur-pantalon [tajœrpɑ̃talɔ̃] *(pl* **tailleurs-pantalons)** **NM** *Br* trouser suit, *Am* pantsuit

tailleuse [tajøz] **NF** *Vulg* **c'est une sacrée t. de pipes** *ou* **de plumes** she gives a great blow-job, she gives great head

taillis [taji] **NM** coppice, copse, thicket; **dans les t.** in the copse *or* coppice; **t. sous futaie** coppice with standards

ADJ bois t. copsewood, brushwood

tailloir [tajwar] **NM** *Archit* abacus

taillole [tajɔl] **NF** *Arch* = long, wide belt made of wool, worn by men in Provence

tain [tɛ̃] **NM 1** *(pour miroir)* silvering; **refaire le t. d'une glace** to resilver a mirror; **glace** *ou* **miroir sans t.** two-way mirror **2** *Métal (bain)* tin bath

taipan [tajpɑ̃] **NM** *Zool* taipan

Taipei, T'ai-pei [tajpɛ] = **Taibei**

taire [111] [tɛr] **VT 1** *(passer sous silence → raisons)* to conceal, to say nothing about; *(→ information)* to hush up; *(→ plan, projet)* to keep secret, to say nothing about, to keep quiet about; **une personne dont je tairai le nom** a person who shall remain nameless; **il a préféré t. ses projets** he preferred to keep his plans secret; **à quoi bon t. la vérité maintenant?** what's the use of concealing *or* not telling the truth now?; **t. qch à qn** to keep *or* hide *or* conceal sth from sb

2 *Littéraire (cacher → sentiment)* **elle sait t. ses émotions** she's able to keep her emotions to herself

3 faire t. qn *(adversaire)* to silence sb, to force sb to be quiet; **faire t. la critique** to silence the critics; **faites t. les enfants** make the children be quiet; **mais faites-le t.!** somebody shut him up, for goodness' sake!; **faire t. qch** to stifle sth; **faire t. sa conscience** to stifle one's conscience; **fais t. tes scrupules** forget your scruples

▶**se taire VPR 1** *(être silencieux)* to be quiet *or* silent; *(cesser de parler)* to stop talking, to fall silent; *(décider de ne rien dire)* to keep quiet *or* silent; **tais-toi!** be quiet!; **elle sait se t. et écouter les autres** she knows when to be silent and listen to others; *Hum* **elle a perdu une occasion de se t.** she would have done better to say nothing *or* to keep her mouth shut

2 *(cesser de s'exprimer)* to fall silent; **l'opposition s'est tue** the opposition has gone very quiet

3 *Littéraire (cesser de faire du bruit)* to fall *or* to become silent; *(bruit)* to stop, to cease; **les oiseaux/canons se turent** the birds/cannon fell silent

4 *Fam (locutions)* **tais-toi!, taisez-vous!** (oh) don't!; **et quand il t'a invitée à danser? – tais-toi, je ne savais plus où me mettre!** and when he asked you to dance? – don't, I felt so embarrassed!

taiseux, -euse [tezø, -øz] *Belg* **ADJ** taciturn

NM,F taciturn person

taisons *etc voir* **taire**

Taïwan [tajwan] **NF** Taiwan; **vivre à T.** to live in Taiwan; **aller à T.** to go to Taiwan

taïwanais, -e [tajwanɛ, -ɛz] **ADJ** Taiwanese

❑ **Taïwanais, -e NM,F** Taiwanese; **les T.** the Taiwanese

Taizé [tɛze] **NM** = home of a Protestant monastic community in Saône-et-Loire

tajine [taʒin] **NM** *Culin* tagine, tajine

Taj Mahal [taʒmaal] **NM le T.** the Taj Mahal

takahé [takahe] **NM** *Orn* takahe

take-off [tɛkɔf] **NM INV** *Écon* takeoff

tala [tala] **NM** *Mus* tala

talbin [talbɛ̃] **NM** *Fam (billet de banque) Br* note■, *Am* greenback

talc [talk] **NM** *Minér* talc; *(produit)* talcum powder, talc

talé, -e [tale] **ADJ** *(fruit)* bruised

taleggio [taledʒjo] **NM** *(fromage)* taleggio

talent[1] [talɑ̃] **NM 1** *(capacité artistique)* **le t.** talent; **avoir du t.** to have talent, to be talented; **son second album est plein de t.** his/her second album is quite inspired

2 *(don, aptitude particulière)* talent, skill, gift; **essaie de la raisonner – je n'ai jamais eu ce t.!** try to make her see reason – that's a skill I've never had!; **son t. de pianiste** his/her talent as a pianist; **ses talents de communicateur** his/her talents as a communicator; **exploiter ses talents de cuisinier** to make use of one's talents as a cook; **elle exerçait ses talents de dentiste dans une ville de province** she practised as a dentist in a provincial town; **votre fille a vraiment tous les talents** your daughter is extremely talented; *Fam* **montrer ses talents à qn** to show sb what one can do

3 *(personne)* talent; **il est à la recherche de jeunes/nouveaux talents** he's looking for young/fresh talent; **faire appel à tous les talents** to call in the best talent *or* brains

❑ **de talent ADJ** talented; **un jeune écrivain de t.** a talented young writer; **un styliste de grand t.** a designer of great talent, a highly talented designer

❑ **sans talent ADJ** untalented; **chanteur sans t.** untalented singer

talent[2] [talɑ̃] **NM** *Hist (unité de poids, monnaie)* talent

talentueuse [talɑ̃tɥøz] *voir* **talentueux**

talentueusement [talɑ̃tɥøzmɑ̃] **ADV** with talent

talentueux, -euse [talɑ̃tɥø, -øz] **ADJ** talented, gifted

taler [3] [tale] **VT** to bruise

talet, taleth [talɛt] **NM** *Rel* tallith

taliban [talibɑ̃] **NM** Taliban

talibé [talibe] **NM** *(en Afrique francophone) (dans une école coranique)* = student of a Koranic school; *(disciple d'un marabout)* = disciple of a marabout

talion [taljɔ̃] **NM** talion; *Hist* **la loi du t.** lex talionis, an eye for an eye (and a tooth for a tooth); **appliquer la loi du t.** to demand an eye for an eye; *Fig* **dans ce cas-là, c'est la loi du t.** in that case, it's an eye for an eye (and a tooth for a tooth)

talisman [talismɑ̃] **NM 1** *(amulette)* talisman **2** *Littéraire (sortilège)* spell, charm

talismanique [talismanik] **ADJ** talismanic

talitre [talitr] **NM** *Zool* sand flea, sandhopper

talkie-walkie [tɔkiwɔki] *(pl* **talkies-walkies)** **NM** walkie-talkie

talk-show [tɔkʃo] *(pl* **talk-shows)** **NM** talk-show

tallage [talaʒ] **NM** *Agr* tillering

talle [tal] **NF 1** *Agr* tiller **2** *Can (touffe)* cluster, clump; **t. de framboisiers** cluster of wild raspberry bushes; *Fig* **sors de ma t.!** get off my patch!

taller [3] [tale] **VI** *Agr* to tiller

Tallinn [talin] **NM** Tallinn

tallipot [talipo] **NM** *Bot* talipot

tallith [talɛt] **NM** *Rel* tallith

talmouse [talmuz] **NF** *Vieilli Culin* cheese turnover

Talmud [talmyd] **NM le T.** the Talmud

talmudique [talmydik] **ADJ** Talmudic

talmudiste [talmydist] **NMF** Talmudist

taloche [talɔʃ] **NF 1** *Constr* float **2** *Fam (gifle)* clout, cuff; **filer** *ou* **flanquer une t. à qn** to clout sb; **il s'est pris une belle t.!** he got a real clout!

talocher [3] [talɔʃe] **VT** *Fam* **t. qn** to clout *or* to cuff sb

talon [talɔ̃] **NM 1** *Anat* heel; **accroupi sur ses talons** crouching (on his haunches *or* heels); **son t. d'Achille** his Achilles' heel; **donner du t. à son cheval** to give one's horse the spur; **être** *ou* **marcher sur les talons de qn** to follow close on sb's heels; **montrer** *ou* **tourner les talons** *(s'enfuir)* to show a clean pair of heels; **tourner les talons** *(faire demi-tour)* to turn on one's heel

2 *(d'une chaussure)* heel; **mettre un t. à une chaussure** to put a heel on *or* to heel a shoe; **talons aiguilles** spike *or Br* stiletto heels; **(chaussures à) talons aiguilles** spike heels, *Br* stilettos; **talons bottiers** medium heels; **talons compensés** built-up heels; **(chaussures à) talons hauts** high-heeled shoes; **porter des talons hauts** *ou* **des hauts talons** to wear high heels; **(chaussures à) talons plats** flat-heeled shoes, flats; **porter des talons plats** to wear flat heels; **t. rouge** *Hist* = elegant 17th-century nobleman who wore red-heeled shoes; *Fig Littéraire (personne raffinée)* aristocrat

3 *(d'une chaussette)* heel; **tes chaussettes sont trouées au t.** your socks have got holes in the heels

4 *(d'un fromage, d'un jambon)* heel

5 *(d'un chèque)* stub, counterfoil; *(d'un carnet à souches)* counterfoil; **t. à retourner** reply slip; **t. et volant** *(de chèque)* counterfoil and leaf

6 *(de queue de billard)* butt; *(de lame d'épée, de baïonnette, de palan, d'essieu)* shoulder

7 *Archit (moulure)* talon *or* ogee moulding

8 *Cartes* stock, talon

9 *Mus* heel, nut

10 *Rail* heel

11 *Tech (de quille, de serrure, de ski)* heel

talonnade [talɔnad] NF *Ftbl* backheel

talonnage [talɔnaʒ] NM **1** *Sport* heeling (*UNCOUNT*); **faire un t.** to heel (the ball) **2** *Naut* touching (*UNCOUNT*)

talonnement [talɔnmɑ̃] NM (*de cheval*) spurring on; *Fig* (*harcèlement*) hounding

talonner [3] [talɔne] VT **1** (*poursuivre*) **t. qn** to follow on sb's heels; **le coureur marocain, talonné par l'Anglais** the Moroccan runner, with the Englishman close on his heels

2 (*harceler* → *sujet: créancier*) to hound; (→ *sujet: gêneur*) to pester; **le directeur me talonne pour que je remette mon rapport** the manager's after me to get my report in; **se faire t. par le fisc** to be hounded by the *Br* tax man *or Am* IRS, to have the *Br* tax man *or Am* IRS breathing down one's neck

3 (*tourmenter* → *sujet: faim*) to gnaw at; **être talonné par la mort** to be pursued by death

4 (*cheval*) to spur with one's heels

5 *Sport* to heel, to hook

VI 1 *Naut* (*navire*) to touch the bottom

2 *Sport* to heel

talonnette [talɔnɛt] NF **1** (*d'une chaussure*) counter; (*à l'intérieur de la chaussure*) heel pad **2** (*d'un pantalon*) binding strip

talonneur [talɔnœr] NM (*au rugby*) hooker

talonnière [talɔnjɛr] NF **1** *Beaux-Arts* block (*placed under the heel during a pose*) **2** *Myth* talaria

talpack [talpak] NM *Hist* busby

talquer [3] [talke] VT to put talcum powder *or* talc on

talqueux, -euse [talkø, -øz] ADJ *Minér* talcose, talcous

talure [talyr] NF bruise

talus¹ [taly] NM **1** (*d'un chemin*) (side) slope; **en t.** sloping; **couper** *ou* **tailler qch en t.** to cut sth at an angle; **la voiture est tombée dans le t.** the car fell down the slope

2 (*d'une voie ferrée, d'un canal*) embankment

3 *Constr* (*de mur*) batter, talus

4 *Mil* talus

5 *Géol* **t. d'éboulis** scree, talus; **t. continental** continental slope

6 *Typ* beard; **t. de pied** shoulder

7 (*en travaux publics*) **t. de déblai/remblai** excavation/embankment slope

talus² [taly] ADJ **M pied t.** talipes calcaneus (*sort of club foot*)

talweg [talvɛg] NM *Géol & Météo* talweg, thalweg

tamandua [tamɑ̃dɥa] NM *Zool* tamandua, collared *or* lesser anteater

Tamanghasset [tamɑ̃gasɛt] = **Tamanrasset**

tamanoir [tamanwar] NM *Zool* (great) anteater

Tamanrasset [tamɑ̃rasɛt] NM Tamanrasset

tamarin [tamarɛ̃] NM **1** *Zool* tamarin **2** *Bot* (*tamarinier, fruit du tamarinier*) tamarind **3** *Bot* (*tamaris*) tamarisk

tamarinier [tamarinje] NM *Bot* tamarind (tree)

tamaris [tamaris], **tamarix** [tamariks] NM *Bot* tamarisk

tamazight [tamazig] NM (*langue*) Tamazight

tambouille [tɑ̃buj] NF *Fam* **1** (*cuisine*) cooking ◾; **faire la t.** to do the cooking **2** (*nourriture*) food ◾, grub; **on s'est fait une bonne petite t.** we made ourselves some great grub

tambour [tɑ̃bur] NM **1** *Mus* (*instrument*) drum; **jouer du t.** to play the drum; **on entendait les tambours de la fanfare** we could hear the drumming of the band; **t. de basque** tambourine; *Fig* **au son du t.** (*bruyamment*) noisily; *Fig* **sans t. ni trompette** discreetly, unobtrusively; **il a quitté le parti sans t. ni trompette** he left the party quietly *or* without making any fuss; *Fig* **t. battant** briskly; **elle a mené l'affaire t. battant** she didn't waste any time getting it done

2 (*son*) drumbeat; **le matin, on les réveille au t.** they're woken in the morning by the sound of a drum

3 (*joueur*) drummer; **les tambours battent la retraite** the drummers are beating the retreat; *Hist* **t. de ville** town crier

4 *Archit, Aut & Électron* drum; *Élec* (*d'une bobine*) cylinder; **t. de frein** brake drum

5 *Constr* (*sas*) tambour (door); (*tourniquet*) revolving door; (*d'église*) vestibule

6 *Couture* (*à broder*) tambour, hoop

7 *Ordinat* **t. magnétique** magnetic drum

8 *Pêche* **t. fixe** fixed reel

9 *Tech* (*de lave-linge*) drum; (*en horlogerie*) barrel; **t. de photocopie** photocopier drum; *Typ* **t. d'impression** print drum

'Le Tambour' *Grass* 'The Tin Drum'

tambourin [tɑ̃burɛ̃] NM (*de basque*) tambourine; (*provençal*) = small drum used in Provençal folk music

tambourinage [tɑ̃burinaʒ] NM drumming

tambourinaire [tɑ̃burinɛr] NM **1** (*musicien*) "tambourin" player **2** *Hist* (*annonceur*) town crier

tambourinement [tɑ̃burinmɑ̃] NM drumming

tambouriner [3] [tɑ̃burine] VI **1** (*frapper*) to drum (on); (*avec les doigts*) to drum one's fingers; **il est venu t. à notre porte à six heures du matin** he came beating *or* hammering on our door at six in the morning; **la grêle tambourinait à la fenêtre** hailstones were drumming on *or* beating against the window pane

2 *Mus & Vieilli* to drum

VT 1 *Mus* (*air, cadence*) to drum (out); (*avec les doigts*) to tap out

2 *Hist* (*proclamer*) to announce; *Fig Vieilli* to shout from the rooftops

tambourineur, -euse [tɑ̃burinœr, -øz] NM,F tambourine player

tambour-major [tɑ̃burmaʒɔr] (*pl* **tambours-majors**) NM drum major

Tamerlan [tamɛrlɑ̃] NPR **T. le Grand** Tamerlane *or* Tamburlaine the Great

tamia [tamja] NM *Zool* chipmunk, ground squirrel

tamier [tamje] NM *Bot* black bryony

tamil [tamil] ADJ Tamil

◻ NM (*langue*) Tamil

◻ Tamil, -e NM,F Tamil; **les Tamils** the Tamils *or* Tamil

tamis [tami] NM **1** (*à farine*) sieve; (*en fil de soie, de coton*) tammy (cloth), tamis; **passer au t.** (*farine, sucre*) to put through a sieve, to sift, to sieve; *Fig* (*dossier, témoignage*) to go through with a fine-tooth comb **2** *Chim* **t. moléculaire** molecular sieve **3** *Constr* (*à sable*) sifter, *Spéc* riddle; **passer au t.** (*sable*) to sift **4** *Sport* (*d'une raquette*) strings

tamisage [tamizaʒ] NM (*de farine*) sifting, sieving; (*de sable*) sifting, *Spéc* riddling

Tamise [tamiz] NF **la T.** the Thames

tamisé, -e [tamize] ADJ **1** (*farine, terre*) sifted, sieved **2** (*éclairage*) soft, subdued; (*lumière naturelle*) subdued

tamiser [3] [tamize] VT **1** (*farine, poudre*) to sift, to sieve **2** (*éclairage*) to subdue; (*lumière naturelle*) to filter **3** *Constr* (*sable*) to sift, *Spéc* to riddle

tamiserie [tamizri] NF **1** (*fabrique*) sieve factory **2** (*commerce*) sieve trade

tamiseur, -euse [tamizœr, -øz] NM,F (*personne*) sifter

NM cinder sifter

◻ **tamiseuse** NF sifting machine

tamisier, -ère [tamizje, -ɛr] NM,F **1** (*fabricant*) maker of sieves **2** (*commerçant*) dealer in sieves

tamoul, -e [tamul] ADJ Tamil

NM (*langue*) Tamil

◻ **Tamoul, -e** NM,F Tamil; **les Tamouls** the Tamils *or* Tamil

tamouré [tamure] NM tamure

tampico [tɑ̃piko] NM Tampico fibre

tampon [tɑ̃pɔ̃] NM **1** (*pour absorber*) wad

2 (*pour imprégner*) pad; **t. encreur** ink pad

3 (*pour nettoyer*) pad; **t. Jex** ≃ Brillo pad®; **t. à récurer** scouring pad, scourer

4 (*pour obturer*) plug, bung; (*d'un tonneau*) bung; **il a bouché la fissure avec un t. de papier** he stopped up the crack with a wad of paper

5 (*plaque gravée*) rubber stamp; (*oblitération*) stamp; **donner à qch un coup de t.** to stamp sth; **faites apposer le t. de la mairie sur votre certificat** have the town hall stamp your certificate; **le t. de la poste** the postmark; **t. dateur** date stamp

6 *Fig* buffer; **il sert de t. entre la direction et le personnel** he acts as a buffer between the management and the staff

7 *Beaux-Arts* dabber, dauber

8 *Constr* (*dalle*) cover; (*cheville*) wall plug; **t. d'égout** manhole cover

9 *Ordinat & Rail* buffer; **coup de t.** collision (*between buffers*)

10 *Tech* plug gauge

11 *Méd & Pharm* (*pour nettoyer*) swab; (*pour boucher*) pad, plug; **t. (périodique** *ou* **hygiénique)** tampon

12 (*comme adj*) *Pol* **État/zone t.** buffer state/zone; *Chim* **substance t.** buffer

tampon-buvard [tɑ̃pɔ̃byvar] (*pl* **tampons-buvards**) NM blotter

tamponnade [tɑ̃pɔnad] NF *Méd* **t. du cœur** (*cardiac*) tamponade

tamponnage [tɑ̃pɔnaʒ] NM **1** *Méd* dabbing **2** *Chim* buffering

tamponne [tɑ̃pɔn] NF *Belg Fam* (drinking) binge; **prendre une t.** to get plastered

tamponnement [tɑ̃pɔnmɑ̃] NM **1** (*accident*) collision **2** *Méd* tamponage **3** (*obturation*) plugging

tamponner [3] [tɑ̃pɔne] VT **1** (*document, passeport*) to stamp; (*lettre timbrée*) to postmark; **faire t. un document** to have a document stamped

2 (*télescoper*) to collide with, to hit, to bump into; (*violemment*) to crash into

3 (*sécher* → *front, lèvres, yeux*) to dab (at)

4 (*enduire* → *meuble*) to dab

5 *Chim* to buffer

6 *Constr* (*mur*) to plug

7 *Méd* (*plaie*) to tampon, to plug

8 *Vieilli* (*boucher*) to plug, to stop (up)

▶ **se tamponner** VPR **1** (*emploi réciproque*) to collide, to bump into one another; **ils se sont tamponnés** they collided

2 (*emploi réfléchi*) **se t. le front** to mop one's brow; **se t. les yeux** to dab one's eyes; *très Fam* **je m'en tamponne (le coquillard)!** I don't give a damn!

3 *Belg Fam* to get plastered

tamponneur, -euse [tɑ̃pɔnœr, -øz] ADJ colliding; **le train t.** the train which crashed into the back of the other one

tamponnoir [tɑ̃pɔnwar] NM pin *or* wall bit

tam-tam [tamtam] (*pl* **tam-tams**) NM **1** *Mus* (*d'Afrique*) tom-tom; (*gong*) tam-tam **2** *Fam* (*publicité tapageuse*) hype; (*vacarme*) fuss, to-do; **faire du t. autour de qch** to make a great fuss *or* to-do about sth

tan [tɑ̃] NM tanbark

tanagra [tanagra] NM *ou* NF *Antiq* Tanagra figurine

tanaisie [tanezi] NF *Bot* tansy

Tananarive [tananariv] NM Antananarivo

tancer [16] [tɑ̃se] VT *Littéraire* to scold; **t. vertement qn** to berate sb

tanche [tɑ̃ʃ] NF **1** *Ich* tench **2** *Fam Br* pillock, plonker, *Am* meathead

tandem [tɑ̃dɛm] NM **1** (*vélo*) tandem **2** (*couple*) duo, pair; **le t. qu'ils forment est redoutable** together, they make a formidable pair

◻ **en tandem** ADJ (*attelage*) tandem (*avant n*); *Tech* **cylindres en t.** tandem cylinders ADV (*agir, travailler*) in tandem, as a pair; **chevaux attelés en t.** horses driven tandem

tandis que [tɑ̃dikə]

---

tandis qu' is used before a word beginning with a vowel or h mute.

CONJ **1** (*pendant que*) while, *Sout* whilst; (*au même moment que*) as; **il l'observait tandis qu'elle parlait** he watched her while she was talking *or* as she talked; **le téléphone sonna tandis qu'il ouvrait la porte** the phone rang as he opened the door **2** (*alors que*) whereas; **elle aime l'opéra t. lui préfère le jazz** she likes opera whereas he prefers jazz

'Tandis que j'agonise' *Faulkner* 'As I Lay Dying'

tandoori [tɑ̃dɔri, tɑ̃duri] NM *Culin* tandoori

tanga [tɑ̃ga] NM thong, tanga

tangage [tɑ̃gaʒ] NM *Aviat & Naut* pitching; **il y avait du t.** the boat was pitching

Tanganyika [tɑ̃ganika] *voir* lac

tangara [tɑ̃gara] NM *Orn* tanager; **t. rouge** scarlet tanager

tangence [tɑ̃ʒɑ̃s] NF tangency; **point de t.** point of contact *or Spéc* tangency

tangent, -e [tɑ̃ʒɑ̃, -ɑ̃t] ADJ **1** *Géom & Math* tangent, tangential; **t. à** at a tangent to

2 *Fam* (*limite* → *cas, candidat*) borderline; **ses**

notes sont tangentes her *Br* marks *or Am* grades put her on the borderline; **je ne l'ai pas renvoyé, mais c'était t.** I didn't fire him but it was touch and go *or* it was a close thing

❑ **tangente** NF **1** *Géom & Math* tangent; **une tangente à la courbe** a tangent to the curve

2 *Fam (locution)* **prendre la tangente** *(se sauver)* to slip off *or* away, to make oneself scarce; *(esquiver une question)* to dodge the issue

tangentiel, -elle [tɑ̃ʒɑ̃sjɛl] ADJ tangential

tangentiellement [tɑ̃ʒɑ̃sjɛlmɑ̃] ADV tangentially

Tanger [tɑ̃ʒe] NM Tangier, Tangiers

tangerine [tɑ̃ʒrin] NF tangerine

tangibilité [tɑ̃ʒibilite] NF tangibility, tangibleness

tangible [tɑ̃ʒibl] ADJ **1** *(palpable)* tangible, *Sout* palpable; **la réalité t.** tangible reality **2** *(évident)* tangible, real; **l'amélioration des résultats est t.** there has been a real improvement in the results

tangiblement [tɑ̃ʒibləmɑ̃] ADV *Littéraire* tangibly, palpably

tango[1] [tɑ̃go] ADJ INV *(couleur)* bright orange

tango[2] [tɑ̃go] NM *(danse)* tango; **danser le t.** to tango

tango[3] [tɑ̃go] *(boisson)* = cocktail consisting of beer and grenadine

tangon [tɑ̃gɔ̃] NM *Naut (mobile)* swinging boom; *(de spi)* spinnaker boom

tangue [tɑ̃g] NF sea sand

tanguer [3] [tɑ̃ge] VI **1** *Naut* to pitch; **la tempête faisait t. le navire** the storm was tossing the boat around, the boat was tossed about in the storm **2** *Fam (tituber)* to reel, to sway **3** *Fam (vaciller → décor)* to spin; **tout tanguait autour d'elle, elle sentit qu'elle allait s'évanouir** everything around her was spinning and she felt she was going to faint

tanière [tanjɛr] NF **1** *(d'un animal)* den, lair **2** *(habitation)* retreat; **il ne sort jamais de sa t.** he never leaves his den **3** *(habitation sordide)* hovel

tanin [tanɛ̃] NM tannin

tanisage [tanizaʒ] NM *(en œnologie)* adding of tannin

taniser [3] [tanize] VT **1** *(poudre)* to add tan to **2** *(en œnologie)* to add tannin to

tank [tɑ̃k] NM *Ind, Mil & Hum (voiture)* tank

tanka [tɑ̃ka] NM **1** *Littérature* tanka **2** *Rel* thang-ka, tanka

tanker[1] [tɑ̃kœr] NM *Naut* tanker

tanker[2] [3] [tɑ̃ke] VI *Can Joual (faire le plein)* to tank up; *Fig (boire beaucoup)* to knock it back

tankini [tɑ̃kini] NM *(maillot)* tankini

tankiste [tɑ̃kist] NM *Mil* soldier with a tank unit

tannage [tanaʒ] NM tanning

tannant, -e [tanɑ̃, -ɑ̃t] ADJ **1** *(produit)* tanning **2** *Can Fam (remuant)* boisterous■ **3** *Fam (importun)* annoying■; *(énervant)* maddening■; **ce que tu peux être t. avec tes questions!** you're a real pain with all these questions!

NM,F *Can Fam (enfant turbulent)* little devil, scamp

❑ **tannante** NF *Can Fam* **une tannante de tempête** a hell of a storm; **j'ai attrapé une tannante de grippe** I've caught an awful dose of (the) flu

tanne [tan] NF **1** *(sur le cuir)* spot **2** *(sur le visage)* blackhead

tanné, -e [tane] ADJ **1** *(traité → peaux, cuir)* tanned

2 *(hâlé → peau)* weathered, weather-beaten

3 *Can Fam* **être t.** *(en avoir assez)* to be fed up; **je suis tannée à faire le ménage** I'm fed up *or* I've had it up to here doing housework; **être t. de qn/qch** to be sick of sb/sth

NM **1** *(couleur)* tan (colour)

2 gants en t. tan *or* tanned leather gloves

❑ **tannée** NF **1** *(écorce)* tanbark

2 *très Fam (correction)* hiding, thrashing; **prendre une tannée** to get a hiding

3 *très Fam (défaite humiliante)* drubbing, trouncing; **il a pris** *ou* **s'est ramassé une tannée aux présidentielles** he got well and truly thrashed in the presidential election

tanner [3] [tane] VT **1** *(traiter → peaux, cuir)* to tan

2 *(hâler → peau)* to tan

3 *Fam (harceler)* to pester, to badger; **son fils le tanne pour avoir une moto** his son keeps pestering him for a motorbike; **je me suis fait t. pour acheter ce ping-pong et maintenant personne ne s'en sert!** they pestered the life out of me to buy this ping-pong table, and now nobody uses it!

4 *très Fam* **t. (le cuir à) un enfant** to thrash a child, to tan a child's hide; **il s'est fait t. le cuir par des voleurs** he was beaten up by thieves

tannerie [tanri] NF **1** *(établissement)* tannery **2** *(industrie, opérations)* tanning

tanneur, -euse [tanœr, -øz] NM,F tanner

tannin [tanɛ̃] = **tanin**

tannique [tanik] ADJ tannic

tannisage [tanizaʒ] = **tanisage**

tanniser [tanize] = **taniser**

tanrec [tɑ̃rɛk] NM *Zool* tenrec

tan-sad [tɑ̃sad] *(pl* **tan-sads)** NM pillion(-seat)

TANT [tɑ̃] ADV **1** *(avec un verbe) (tellement, à tel point)* so much; **il l'aime t.** he loves her so much; **ne fume pas t.!** don't smoke so much!; **il a t. travaillé sur son projet!** he's worked so hard on his project!; **j'en ai t. rêvé** I've dreamt about it so much *or* often; **ce n'est pas la peine de t. vous presser** you needn't be in such a hurry

2 *(avec un verbe, en corrélation avec "que")* **j'ai t. crié que je suis enroué** I shouted so much that I've lost my voice; **ils ont t. fait qu'ils ont obtenu tout ce qu'ils voulaient** they worked so hard that they ended up getting everything they wanted; **t. était grande sa discrétion que…** so great was his/her discretion that…; *Prov* **t. va la cruche à l'eau qu'à la fin elle se casse** the pitcher will go to the well once too often

3 *(avec un participe passé)* **le jour t. attendu arriva enfin** the long-awaited day arrived at last

4 *(introduisant la cause)* so, to such a degree; **les plantes ont gelé t. il a fait froid** it was so cold the plants froze; **deux personnes se sont évanouies t. il faisait chaud** it was so hot (that) two people fainted; **il ne peut pas se lever t. il est malade** he's too ill to get up

5 *(exprimant une quantité imprécise)* so much; **ce sera t. par mois** that will be so much per month; **tu lui dis simplement "ça fait t."** just tell him/her "it costs so much"; **il gagne t. de l'heure** he earns so much per hour

6 *(introduisant une comparaison)* **le spectacle peut plaire t. aux enfants qu'aux parents** the show is aimed at children as well as adults; **pour des raisons t. économiques que politiques** for economic as well as political reasons; **elle n'est pas t. sotte que naïve** she's not so much stupid as naive; **ce n'est pas t. leur colère qui me fait mal que leur mépris** it is not so much their anger that hurts me as their contempt; **t. aux Indes qu'ailleurs** both in India and elsewhere; **t. pour vous que pour moi** for your sake as much as mine, for you as much as for me; **il est sévère t. avec ses enfants qu'avec ses élèves** he is as strict with his children as he is with his pupils; **je suis à l'aise t. avec lui qu'avec elle** I get on with him AND with her

7 *(locutions)* **une maison de banlieue comme il y en a t.** one of those suburban houses that you come across so often; *Fam* **tu m'en diras t.!** you don't say!

NM **suite à votre lettre du t.** with reference to your letter of such and such a date; **vous serez payé le t. de chaque mois** you'll be paid on such and such a date every month

❑ **en tant que** CONJ **1** *(en qualité de)* as; **en t. que directeur, la décision vous revient** as director, the decision is yours; **en t. que père, tu dois prendre tes responsabilités** you must face up to your responsibilities as a father

2 *(dans la mesure où)* as long as; **il ne s'intéresse à nous qu'en t. que nous lui rendons service** he's only interested in us as long as *or* while we can be of use to him; **l'homme en t. qu'il diffère des animaux** man, as distinct from animals

❑ **tant bien que mal** ADV after a fashion; **je l'ai repassé t. bien que mal** I've ironed it after a fashion *or* as best I could; **le moteur est reparti, t. bien que mal** somehow, the engine started up again

❑ **tant de** DÉT **1** *(tellement de → suivi d'un nom non comptable)* so much, such; *(→ suivi d'un nom comptable)* so many; **t. de bonheur** such *or* so much happiness; **elle s'est donné t. de mal** she went to such (a lot of) *or* so much trouble; **il y a t. de livres à lire** there are so many books to read; **t. de gens** so many people; **t. de fois** so many times, so often

2 *(en corrélation avec "que")* **elle a t. de travail qu'elle n'a même plus le temps de faire les courses** she has so much work that she doesn't even have the time to go shopping any more; **vous m'avez reçu avec t. de générosité que je ne sais quoi dire** you've made me so welcome that I'm lost for words; **t. d'années ont passé que j'ai oublié** it was so many years ago that I've forgotten

3 *(exprimant une quantité imprécise)* **il y a t. de lignes par page** there are so many lines to a page; **t. de centimètres** so many centimetres; **t. de grammes** so many grammes

❑ **tant et plus** ADV **1** *(à maintes reprises)* over and over again, time and time again; **j'ai insisté t. et plus** I insisted over and over again *or* time and time again; **ils tiraient t. et plus** they were pulling for all they were worth

2 *(nombreux)* **il a des amis t. et plus** he has plenty of friends

❑ **tant et plus de** DÉT **il a t. et plus d'argent** he has any amount of money

❑ **tant et si bien que** CONJ so much so that; **t. et si bien que je ne lui parle plus** so much so that we're no longer on speaking terms; **ils ont fait t. et si bien qu'ils ont réussi** they worked so hard that they succeeded

❑ **tant et tant que** CONJ **j'ai crié t. et t. qu'il est parti** I shouted so much that he went (away); **on a attendu t. et t. que…** we waited so long that…

❑ **tant il est vrai que** CONJ **il s'en remettra, t. il est vrai que le temps guérit tout** he'll get over it, for it's true that time is a great healer

❑ **tant mieux** ADV good, fine, so much the better; **vous n'avez rien à payer – t. mieux!** you don't have anything to pay – good *or* fine!; **il est parti et c'est t. mieux** he's left and just as well *or* and a good thing too; **t. mieux pour lui** good for him

❑ **tant pis** ADV never mind, too bad; **il n'est pas là – t. pis!** he isn't in – never mind!; **je reste, t. pis s'il n'est pas content** I'm staying, too bad if he doesn't like it; **t. pis pour lui** too bad (for him)

❑ **tant que** CONJ **1** *(autant que)* as *or* so much as; **elle ne travaille pas t. que les autres** she doesn't work as much *or* as hard as the others; **il sort t. qu'il peut** he goes out as much *or* often as he can; **j'ai couru t. que j'ai pu** I ran as hard as I could; **manges-en t. que tu veux** have as many *or* much as you like; **n'aimer rien t. que…** to like nothing more than…; **elle dit n'aimer rien t. que l'automne** she says there is nothing she likes more than the autumn; **elle gagne plus de 3000 euros par mois – t. que ça!** she earns over 3,000 euros a month – as much as that *or* that much!; **il y en a déjà plus de cent – t. que ça?** there are already more than a hundred (of them) – as many as that *or* that many?; **tu l'aimes t. que ça?** do you love him/her that much?; **ça fait mal! – t. que ça?** it hurts! – that much?; **il y a 15 ans – t. que ça?** that was 15 years ago – that long ago?; **il peut espérer gagner dans les 5000 euros – non, pas t. que ça** he can expect to earn about 5,000 euros – no, not as much as that *or* not that much; **il souffre? – non, pas t. que ça** is he in pain? – no, not really; **il en faudra combien, une centaine? – pas t. que ça** how many (of them) will we need, about a hundred? – no, not as many as that *or* not that many; **elle est jolie – pas t. que ça** she's pretty – not really; **vous irez, tous t. que vous êtes** every last one of you will go; **tous t. que nous sommes** all of us, every single *or* last one of us; *Fam* **il pleut t. que ça peut** it's raining like anything

2 *(aussi longtemps que)* as long as; *(pendant que)* while; **t. que je vivrai** as long as I live; **tu peux rester t. que tu veux** you can stay as long as you like; **rien ne peut être décidé t. qu'il n'a pas donné son avis** nothing can be decided until (such time as) he makes his opinion known; **t. qu'il y aura des hommes** as long as there are men; **t. que j'y pense, as-tu reçu ma carte?** while I think of it *or* before I forget, did you get my card?; **sois grossier t. que tu y es!** be rude (as well) while you're at it!; **pourquoi pas un château avec piscine t. que tu y es!** why not a castle with a swimming pool while

you're at it!; **t. qu'il y a de la vie, il y a de l'espoir** where there's life there's hope; *Fam* **t. que ce n'est pas grave!** as long as it's not serious!

3 *(quelque)* however; **t. aimable qu'il soit** however pleasant he may be

4 *Belg* **t. que maintenant** up to now, until now, till now

▫ **tant qu'à** CONJ **1** *(quitte à)* **t. qu'à partir, autant partir tout de suite** if I/you/*etc* must go, I/you/*etc* might as well do it right away; **t. qu'à m'expatrier, j'aime mieux que ce soit dans un beau pays** if I have to go and live abroad, I'd rather go somewhere nice; **t. qu'à faire** *ou Can* **t. qu'à y être, je préférerais du poisson** I'd rather have fish if I have the choice; **t. qu'à faire** *ou Can* **t. qu'à y être, sortons maintenant** we might as well go out now; **t. qu'à faire** *ou Can* **t. qu'à y être, autant en acheter deux** you/we/*etc* might as well buy two

2 *Can Fam (quant à)* as for■; **t. qu'à moi/lui** as for me/him

3 *Belg* **t. qu'à présent** up to now, until now, till now

▫ **tant s'en faut** ADV far from it

▫ **tant soit peu** ADV **s'il est t. soit peu intelligent, il comprendra** if he is even the slightest bit intelligent, he'll understand

▫ **un tant soit peu** ADV a little, somewhat; **si tu étais un t. soit peu observateur** if you were the least bit observant; **si elle avait un t. soit peu de bon sens** if she had the slightest bit of common sense; **s'il voulait être un t. soit peu plus aimable** if he would only be just the slightest *or* tiniest bit more friendly

---

tant-à-faire [tɑ̃tafɛr] NMF *Belg* busybody

Tantale [tɑ̃tal] NPR *Myth* Tantalus

tantale [tɑ̃tal] NM **1** *Orn* **t. (d'Amérique)** tantalus, wood stork **2** *Chim* tantalum

tantalique [tɑ̃talik] ADJ *Chim* tantalic

tante [tɑ̃t] NF **1** *(dans une famille)* aunt; **t. Marie** Aunt Marie **2** *très Fam (mont-de-piété)* **chez ma t.** at my uncle's, at the pawnshop■ **3** *très Fam (homosexuel)* fairy, = offensive term used to refer to a male homosexual

tantième [tɑ̃tjɛm] ADJ **la t. partie des bénéfices** so much of the profits

NM *(part proportionnelle)* proportion; *(quote-part de bénéfice)* director's fee *or* percentage

tantine [tɑ̃tin] NF *Fam* aunty

tantinet [tɑ̃tinɛ] NM tiny bit; **un t. stupide** a tiny bit stupid; **un t. plus long** a tiny bit *or* a shade *or* a fraction longer

tantôt [tɑ̃to] ADV **1** *Fam (cet après-midi)* this afternoon■; **je dois le voir t.** I have to see him this afternoon

2 *Belg & (régional) (plus tard)* later; **à t.** see you later

3 *Belg & (régional) (plus tôt)* earlier; **je l'ai vu t.** I saw him earlier

4 *Vieilli (régional) (bientôt)* soon, presently; **voici t. deux mois qu'il est parti** it will soon be two months since he left

▫ **tantôt..., tantôt...** sometimes..., sometimes...; **nous passons le week-end t. chez mes parents, t. chez les siens** sometimes we spend the weekend with my parents, sometimes with his/hers; **t. triste, t. gai** now sad, now cheerful

tantouse, tantouze [tɑ̃tuz] NF *très Fam* fairy, = offensive term used to refer to a male homosexual

tantra [tɑ̃tra] NMPL *Rel* Tantras

tantrique [tɑ̃trik] ADJ Tantric

tantrisme [tɑ̃trism] NM Tantrism

Tanzanie [tɑ̃zani] NF **la T.** Tanzania; **vivre en T.** to live in Tanzania; **aller en T.** to go to Tanzania

tanzanien, -enne [tɑ̃zanjɛ̃, -ɛn] ADJ Tanzanian

▫ **Tanzanien, -enne** NM,F Tanzanian

TAO [teao] NF *(abrév* **traduction assistée par ordinateur***)* CAT

tao [tao] NM Tao

taoïsme [taɔism] NM Taoism

taoïste [taɔist] ADJ Taoist

NMF Taoist

taon [tɑ̃] NM *Entom* horsefly

tapa [tapa] NM *(en Polynésie)* tapa, bark cloth

tapage [tapaʒ] NM **1** *(bruit)* din, racket; **faire du t.** to make a racket **2** *(scandale)* scandal, fuss; **ça a fait tout un t.** there was quite a fuss about it; **faire du t. autour de qch** to make a great fuss *or* a great ballyhoo *or* a song and dance about sth **3** *Jur* **t. nocturne** breach of the peace *(at night)*

tapageur, -euse [tapaʒœr, -øz] ADJ **1** *(bruyant)* noisy, rowdy; **les enfants sont un peu tapageurs** the children are a bit rowdy **2** *(voyant → vêtement, couleur)* loud, flashy; *(→ publicité)* obtrusive **3** *(dont on parle beaucoup)* **une liaison tapageuse** a much talked-about affair

tapageusement [tapaʒøzmɑ̃] ADV flashily, showily

tapant, -e [tapɑ̃, -ɑ̃t] ADJ **je serai là à dix heures tapantes** I'll be there at ten o'clock sharp *or* on the dot; **il est rentré à minuit t.** he came home on the stroke of midnight

tapas [tapas] NFPL *Culin* tapas

tape [tap] NF **1** *(pour punir)* (little) slap, tap; **je lui ai donné une petite t. sur les fesses** I gave him/her a little smack *or* slap on the bottom **2** *(amicale)* pat; **donner une petite t. sur le dos/bras de qn** to pat sb's back/arm **3** *(pour attirer l'attention)* tap; **donner une petite t. sur l'épaule de qn** to tap sb's shoulder

tapé, -e [tape] ADJ **1** *Fam (fou)* nuts, crackers **2** *(fruit → abîmé)* bruised; *(→ séché)* dried **3** *Fam (juste et vigoureux → réplique)* smart; **ça, c'est une réponse bien tapée!** that's really hit the nail on the head! **4** *Fam (marqué par l'âge → visage)* aged■

▫ **tapée** NF *Fam (multitude)* **une tapée** *ou* **des tapées de...** masses *or* heaps *or* loads of...; **une tapée de dossiers** heaps of files; **il y avait une tapée de photographes** there was a swarm of photographers

tape-à-l'œil [tapalœj] *Fam* ADJ INV *(couleur, bijoux, toilette)* flashy, showy

NM INV **c'est du t.** *(objets, toilette)* it's all show; **il aime le t.** he likes showy things

tape-cul *(pl* **tape-culs***)*, **tapecul** [tapky] NM **1** *(tilbury)* gig **2** *Fam Équitation* **faire du t.** to do a sitting trot **3** *Fam (voiture)* boneshaker **4** *Fam (balançoire) Br* seesaw■, *Am* teeter-totter■ **5** *(voile)* jigger■; *(mât)* jigger mast■

tapée [tape] *voir* **tapé**

tapement [tapmɑ̃] NM **1** *(action)* tapping, drumming **2** *(bruit)* tapping

tapenade [tapənad] NF tapenade

TAPER¹ [3] [tape]

> **VT** to hit **1** ■ to tap **2** ■ to hammer **2** ■ to bang **2** ■ to knock **3** ■ to type **4** ■ to key **5** ■ to dial **6** ■ to thump out **7**
> **VI** to bang **1** ■ to hit **1, 2** ■ to type **3** ■ to beat down **4**
> **VPR** to hit each other **1** ■ to bang **2**

VT **1** *(personne → gén)* to hit; *(→ gifler)* to smack; **ne tape pas ton petit frère** don't hit your little brother; **arrête ou je te tape!** stop or I'll smack you!

2 *(marteler → doucement)* to tap; *(→ fort)* to hammer, to bang; **elle tapait rageusement le sol avec son pied** she was stamping her foot angrily; *Fam* **t. le carton** to play cards■, to have a game of cards■

3 *(heurter)* **t. un coup à une porte** to knock once on a door; **il est venu t. plusieurs coups sur ma vitre** he came and knocked (several times) on my window

4 *(dactylographier)* to type; **t. un document à la machine** to type (out) a document; **un devoir tapé à la machine** a typed *or* typewritten piece of homework; **je préfère que les devoirs soient tapés à la machine** I prefer the homework to be typed (out) *or* typewritten; **t. 40 mots à la minute** to type 40 words per minute

5 *Ordinat* to key; **tapez entrée ou retour** select enter or return; **t. qch sur ordinateur** to key sth (on the computer)

6 *Tél (code)* to dial; **tapez le 36 15** dial 36 15

7 *Fam (jouer → air de musique)* to thump *or* to hammer out; **il tapait une valse sur le piano** he was hammering out a waltz on the piano

8 *Fam* **t. qch à qn** *(emprunter → objet)* to borrow sth from sb■; *(→ argent)* to bum *or* cadge sth off sb, to hit *or Br* tap sb for sth; **il est encore venu me t.** he came to scrounge off me again; **il m'a tapé de 50 euros** he bummed *or* cadged 50 euros off me

9 *Fam (atteindre)* **t. le cent/le deux cents** to hit a hundred/two hundred (kilometres an hour)

10 *Fam* **la petite veste rose m'avait tapé dans l'œil** I took quite a fancy to the little pink jacket; *Fam* **elle lui a tapé dans l'œil** he was really taken with her, he took quite a shine to her

VI **1** *(donner un coup à quelque chose)* **t. sur** *(clavier)* to bang *or* to thump away at; *(clou, pieu)* to hit; *(avec un marteau)* to hammer (away at); **elle a tapé (du poing) sur la table** she banged *or* thumped her fist on the table; *Fam Mil* **t. sur un objectif** to strafe a target; **t. à la porte** to bang on the door; **t. au carreau** to knock on *or* at the window; **t. au plafond** *(avec un balai etc)* to bang *or* to knock on the ceiling; **t. dans une balle** *(lui donner un coup)* to kick a ball; *(s'amuser avec)* to kick a ball around; **t. avec un marteau (contre le mur)** to hammer (the wall); **t. à côté** to miss the target; *Fig* **alors là, tu as tapé à côté** you're way off beam, *Am* you're way out in left field; **la bôme est venu t. contre le mât** the boom hit the *or* banged into the mast; **t. du pied** *ou* **des pieds** to stamp one's foot *or* feet; **t. des mains** to clap one's hands

2 *(battre, frapper)* **t. sur qn** *(une fois)* to hit sb; *(à coups répétés)* to beat sb up; **c'est un bon boxeur et il tape dur** he's a good boxer and he hits hard *or* packs a powerful punch; *Fam* **t. sur le ventre à qn** to give sb a dig in the ribs *(as a mark of familiarity)*; *Fam* **t. sur la gueule à qn** to belt sb; **se faire t. sur les doigts** to get rapped over the knuckles

3 *(dactylographier)* **t. (à la machine)** to type; **t. au toucher** to touch-type; **il tape bien/mal** he types well/badly, he's a good/bad typist; **tape sur cette touche** *(de machine à écrire, d'ordinateur)* press *or* hit this key

4 *Fam (soleil)* to beat down; **le soleil tapait** the sun was beating down; **ça tape** *(il fait chaud)* it's scorching; **ça tapait sur la plage cet après-midi** it was scorching hot on the beach this afternoon; **le vin rouge m'a tapé sur la tête** the red wine knocked me out

5 *Fam (critiquer)* **t. sur** *(personne, film)* to run down, to knock; **elle s'est fait t. dessus dans la presse** *ou* **par les journaux** the newspapers really slated her

6 *Fam* **t. sur un piano** *(mal jouer)* to bash away *or* to thump away on a piano

7 *Fam (puiser)* **t. dans** *(réserves, économies)* to dig into; *(tiroir-caisse)* to help oneself from; *(nourriture)* to help oneself to, to dig into; **voilà la viande, tapez dedans!** here's the meat, dig *or esp Br* tuck in!; **elle ne pouvait pas s'empêcher de t. dans la caisse** she couldn't keep her fingers out of the till

8 *très Fam (sentir mauvais)* to reek, to stink; **ça tape dans ta chambre!** your room stinks!

9 *Fam (en Afrique francophone) (aller à pied)* to walk■; **elle a manqué le car et a dû t.** she missed the coach and had to walk

▸**se taper** VPR **1** *(emploi réciproque)* to hit each other; **ils ont fini par se t. dessus** eventually they came to blows; *très Fam* **se t. sur le ventre** *(être en bonnes relations)* to be very close■; **lui et le ministre se tapent sur le ventre** he and the minister are great buddies

2 *(se cogner)* **se t. le front** to bang one's forehead; **se t. la tête contre qch** to bang one's head against sth

3 *Fam (consommer → dîner, petits fours)* to guzzle, *Br* to scoff; *(→ boisson)* to sink, to lower; **je me taperais bien une bière** I'd kill for *or Br* I could murder a beer

4 *très Fam (sexuellement)* to screw, *Br* to shag

5 *Fam (subir → corvée, travail, gêneur)* to get stuck *or Br* landed *or* lumbered with; **je me suis tapé les cinq étages à pied** I had to walk up the five floors■; **on s'est tapé les embouteillages** we got stuck in the traffic jams■; **il a fallu que je me tape tout Proust pour l'examen** I had to devour the entire works of Proust for the exam

6 *très Fam (s'en moquer)* **elle s'en tape** she doesn't give a shit *or Br* a toss *or Am* a rat's ass;

si tu savais comme je m'en tape! I don't give a shit!

7 *(locutions) Fam* **se t. (sur) les cuisses** *(de satisfaction, de rire)* to slap one's thighs; *très Fam* **tu peux (toujours) te t.!** you can whistle for it!; **c'était à se t.** *Fam* **le derrière** *ou très Fam* **le cul par terre** it was hysterical *or* side-splitting; *Fam* **c'est à se t. la tête contre les murs** it's enough to drive you crazy; *Fam* **se t. la cloche** to pig out, *Br* to have a blow-out; *Fam* **se t. la honte** *ou* **la zone** to make a fool *or Br* a prat *or Am* a jerk of oneself

taper[2] [3] [tape] **VT** *Tech & Naut (boucher → trou)* to plug, to stop up

tapette [tapɛt] **NF 1** *(petite tape)* pat, tap **2** *(piège à souris)* mousetrap **3** *Fam (bagou)* **il a une bonne** *ou* **fière t.** he's a real chatterbox!, can HE talk! **4** *très Fam (homosexuel)* queer, fairy, *Am* fag, = offensive term used to refer to a male homosexual **5** *(contre les mouches)* flyswatter; *(pour les tapis)* carpet beater **6** *(petit marteau)* mallet

7 *Beaux-Arts (de graveur)* dauber, dobber

tapeur, -euse [tapœr, -øz] **NM,F** *Fam* sponger, scrounger

taphophobie [tafofɔbi] **NF** *Psy* taphephobia

tapi, -e [tapi] **ADJ 1** *(accroupi)* crouching, hunched up; *(en embuscade)* lurking **2** *Littéraire (blotti, dissimulé)* lurking, skulking, lying low; **une chaumière tapie au cœur de la forêt** a cottage hidden *or* lying in the heart of the forest **3** *(retiré)* buried, shut away; **tapie chez elle, elle tente de finir son roman** she's shut herself away at home in an attempt to finish her novel

tapin [tapɛ̃] **NM 1** *très Fam* **faire le t.** *(se prostituer)* to walk the streets, *Br* to be on the game **2** *Fam Vieilli (joueur de tambour)* drummer■

tapiner [3] [tapine] **VI** *très Fam* to walk the streets, *Br* to be on the game

tapineur, -euse [tapinœr, -øz] **NM,F** *très Fam* streetwalker

tapinois [tapinwa] **en tapinois ADV** *(entrer, se glisser)* sneakily, furtively; **s'approcher en t.** to creep up

tapioca [tapjɔka] **NM** tapioca; **potage au t.** tapioca soup

tapir[1] [tapir] **NM** *Zool* tapir

tapir[2] [32] [tapir] **se tapir VPR 1** *(se baisser)* to crouch (down); *(se dissimuler → par peur)* to hide; *(→ en embuscade)* to lurk; **il se tapit derrière un buisson et l'attendit** he lay in wait for her behind a bush **2** *(se retirer)* to hide away; **depuis son accident, elle se tapit dans un petit village à la montagne** since her accident, she's been hiding away in a small mountain village

tapis [tapi] **NM 1** *(recouvrant le sol)* carpet; *(de petite taille)* rug; *(pour la gymnastique)* mat; **recouvrir le plancher d'un t.** to carpet the floor; **t. chinois/persan** Chinese/Persian carpet; **t. de bain, t. de salle de bains** bath mat; **t. de haute laine** deep-pile carpet; **t. de laine rase** short-pile carpet; **t. d'Orient** oriental carpet; **t. de prière** prayer mat; *aussi Fig* **t. rouge** red carpet; *Fig* **dérouler le t. rouge pour qn** to roll out the red carpet for sb, to give sb the red carpet treatment; *Hum* **tu ne veux pas le t. rouge aussi?** what do you want, the red-carpet treatment?; **t. de selle** saddlecloth; **t. de sol** *(sol de tente)* ground sheet; *(petit matelas)* sleeping mat *(underneath sleeping bag)*; *(pour la gymnastique)* floor mat; *Ordinat* **t. de souris** mouse mat; **t. volant** flying *or* magic carpet; **t. de yoga** yoga mat; *Fig* **se prendre les pieds dans le t.** to get into a mess

2 *(recouvrant un meuble)* cloth, cover; *(de billard, d'une table de jeu)* cloth, baize; **t. de table** table cover; **t. vert** *(table de jeu)* green baize; *(de conférence)* baize; **T. Vert** = game of chance organized by the French national lottery; *Fig* **le t. brûle** *ou* **crie** there's a stake missing

3 *Littéraire (couche → de feuilles, de neige)* carpet; **un t. d'aiguilles de pin/de fleurs** a carpet of pine needles/of flowers; **le sol était recouvert d'un t. de neige** the ground was covered with a carpet of snow

4 *Géog* **t. végétal** plant cover

5 *Hort* **t. de gazon** smooth, even lawn; **t. de verdure** (large) lawn

6 *Sport (dans une salle de sport)* mat; *(à la boxe)* canvas; **aller au t.** *(boxeur)* to be knocked down; **envoyer son adversaire au t.** to floor one's opponent; *Fig* **entreprise mise au t. par la concurrence** company knocked for six *or* KO'd by the competition; **il est resté au t.** he stayed down, he didn't get up

7 *Tech* **t. roulant** *(pour piétons)* travelator, moving *Br* pavement *or Am* sidewalk; *(pour marchandises, pour bagages)* conveyor belt; **t. transporteur** *(pour bagages, pièces de montage)* conveyor (belt); **t. de livraison des bagages** baggage carousel *or* conveyor (belt)

8 *(en travaux publics)* (bituminous) carpet

9 *Belg* **t. plain** carpet

❑ **sur le tapis ADV 1** *(dans un jeu)* on the table; **il y avait plus de 1000 euros sur le t.** there were more than 1,000 euros on the table

2 *Fig* **mettre qch sur le t.** to bring sth up for consideration *or* for discussion; **l'affaire est de nouveau sur le t.** the matter is being discussed again; **à quoi bon remettre toutes nos vieilles querelles sur le t.?** what's the use of bringing up *or* raking over all our old quarrels again?; **ce genre d'argument revient toujours sur le t.** this sort of argument keeps cropping up

tapis-brosse [tapibrɔs] *(pl* **tapis-brosses***)* **NM** doormat

tapisser [3] [tapise] **VT 1** *(mur → avec du papier peint)* to wallpaper; *(→ avec du tissu)* to hang with material; *(→ avec des tentures)* to hang with *Br* curtains *or Am* drapes; *(fauteuil)* to upholster; *(étagères)* to cover; **mur tapissé d'affiches** wall covered *or* plastered with posters; **t. une cloison de posters** to cover a partition with posters; **les murs sont tapissés de jaune** the walls are papered in yellow

2 *(l'intérieur d'une armoire)* to line *or* to cover (**de** with); *Culin (garnir)* to line; **tapissez votre moule de papier d'aluminium** line your *Br* tin *or Am* pan with foil

3 *Littéraire (sujet: bruyère, neige → sol)* to carpet; *(sujet: lierre → mur)* to cover; **le trèfle tapissait le champ** the field was carpeted with clover; **un banc tapissé de mousse/neige** a moss-/snow-covered bench; **un nid tapissé de feuilles** a nest lined with leaves

4 *Anat & Bot* to line

tapisserie [tapisri] **NF 1** *(art, panneau)* tapestry; **les tapisseries des Gobelins** the Gobelins tapestries; **la t. de Bayeux** *ou* **de la reine Mathilde** the Bayeux tapestry; *Hum* **faire t.** *(dans une réunion)* to be left out; *(au bal)* to be a wallflower

2 *(petit ouvrage)* tapestry; **t. au** *ou* **sur canevas** tapestry *or* crewel work; **faire de la t.** to do tapestry *or* tapestry-work; **point de t.** canvas stitch; **chaise en t.** chair upholstered with tapestry, tapestry chair

3 *(papier peint)* wallpaper *(UNCOUNT)*; **refaire les tapisseries d'une chambre** to repaper a bedroom

4 *(métier)* tapestry-making

tapissier, -ère [tapisje, -ɛr] **NM,F 1** *(fabricant)* tapestry-maker **2** *(vendeur)* upholsterer **3** *(décorateur)* interior decorator

tapissier-garnisseur [tapisjegarnisœr] *(pl* **tapissiers-garnisseurs***)* **NM** *Belg* interior decorator

tapocher [3] [tapɔʃe] **VT** *Can Fam (frapper)* to thump; *(battre)* to hammer

tapon [tapɔ̃] **NM** *Vieilli (bouchon)* plug, bung; **rouler qch en t.** to roll sth into a ball

taponner [3] [tapɔne] *Can Fam* **VT** *(tâter)* to touch■, to feel■; *(sexuellement)* to fondle, to grope

VI *(ne rien faire)* to waste time■

tapotement [tapɔtmɑ̃] **NM** *(avec les doigts)* tapping; *(avec la main)* patting; *(au piano)* plonking

tapoter [3] [tapɔte] **VT 1** *(dos, joue)* to pat; *(surface)* to tap; **elle lui a tapoté amicalement la joue** she gave him/her cheek a friendly pat; **il tapota son pupitre avec sa baguette** he tapped the rostrum with his baton

2 *(air de musique)* to bang out

VI 1 *(tambouriner)* to tap; *(en signe d'énervement)* to drum; **elle tapotait sur la table avec un crayon** she was drumming (on) the table with a pencil

2 *(jouer médiocrement)* **il tapotait sur le vieux piano** he was banging out a tune on the old piano

tapure [tapyr] **NF** *Métal* shrinkage crack, cooling crack

tapuscrit [tapyskri] **NM** typescript

taquage [takaʒ] **NM** *Typ* jolting

taque [tak] **NF 1** *Constr* fireback (plate) **2** *Tech* cast-iron plate **3** *Belg (plaque → d'égout, de soupirail)* cover; *(→ de cuisinière)* hotplate; *(→ de four)* baking tray

taquer [3] [take] **VT** *Typ* **1** *(forme)* to plane, to plane down **2** *(feuilles de papier)* to jolt, to jog

taquet [takɛ] **NM 1** *(cale → de meuble)* wedge; *(→ de porte)* wedge, stop; **t. de sûreté** safety stop

2 *Constr (coin en bois)* (wood) angle block; *(d'une porte)* catch; **t. d'échelle** ladder jack

3 *(d'arpenteur) & Agr* (small) picket, peg

4 *Typ* jogger

5 *Naut* **t. (de tournage)** (belaying) cleat; *(en aviron)* button, collar

6 *Rail* **t. d'arrêt** Scotch block

7 *Tech (d'une machine à écrire, d'un ordinateur)* tabulator stop; **poser un t. (de tabulateur)** to set a tab *or* a tabulator stop

8 *Tex* picker

taquin, -e [takɛ̃, -in] **ADJ** teasing; **d'un air t.** teasingly, playfully; **il est un peu t. par moments** he's a bit of a tease sometimes; **elle est très taquine** she's a great one for teasing

NM,F *(personne)* teaser, tease

NM *(jeu)* = puzzle consisting of sliding plates in a frame which have to be arranged in a set order

taquiner [3] [takine] **VT 1** *(faire enrager)* to tease; **cesse de la t.** stop teasing her; **se faire t.** to get teased **2** *(être légèrement douloureux)* to bother; **j'ai une dent qui me taquine** one of my teeth is bothering me *or* giving me a bit of bother **3** *Fam (locutions)* **t. le piano/violon** to play the piano/violin a bit; **t. le goujon** to do a bit of fishing

▶**se taquiner VPR** to tease each other

taquinerie [takinri] **NF 1** *(action)* teasing; **il m'a dit que j'étais gros – c'était par t.** he said I was fat – he was just teasing (you) **2** *(parole)* **cesse tes taquineries** stop teasing

taquoir [takwar] **NM** *Typ* planer

tar [tar] **NM** *Mus* = type of lute used in Iranian and Azerbaijani scholarly music

tara [tara] **NM** *(en Afrique francophone)* = low seat made of intertwined branches

tarabiscot [tarabisko] **NM** *Archit & Menuis* **1** *(rainure)* groove, channel *(between mouldings)* **2** *(rabot)* moulding plane

tarabiscoté, -e [tarabiskɔte] **ADJ 1** *(bijou)* overornate **2** *(style, phrases)* fussy, affected **3** *(explication, récit)* complicated, involved, convoluted; **ton histoire est bien tarabiscotée!** your story is pretty complicated!

tarabuster [3] [tarabyste] **VT 1** *(houspiller → personne)* to pester, to badger; **elle m'a tarabusté jusqu'à ce que j'accepte** she just wouldn't leave me alone until I said yes **2** *(tracasser)* to bother; **elle doit se faire opérer et ça la tarabuste** she's got to have an operation and it's preying on her mind

taraf [taraf] **NM** *Mus* = small group of Hungarian gypsies who play especially stringed instruments

tarage [taraʒ] **NM** *Com* taring

tarama [tarama] **NM** taramasalata

tararage [tararaʒ] **NM** *Agr* winnowing

tarare [tarar] **NM** *Agr* winnowing machine

tarasque [tarask] **NF** *Myth* = amphibious monster, said to have haunted the Rhône near Tarascon, where its effigy is still carried in feast-day processions

taratata [taratata] **EXCLAM** *Fam (pour exprimer la méfiance, l'incrédulité)* nonsense!, *Br* rubbish!; *(pour exprimer la contrariété)* fiddlesticks!; **t., tu as dit que tu viendrais, tu viendras!** no, no, you said you'd come, so come you will!

taraud [taro] **NM** *(pour filetage)* tap, screw tap

taraudage [tarodaʒ] **NM 1** *(action)* tapping **2** *(trou)* female thread

tarauder [3] [tarode] **VT 1** *Tech (acier)* to tap, to thread **2** *Fig Littéraire (obséder → personne)* to gnaw at

taraudeuse [tarodøz] **NF** tapping machine, tapper

tarbouch, tarbouche [tarbuʃ] NM tarboosh

tard [tar] ADV **1** *(à la fin de la journée, d'une période)* late; **il se couche/lève t.** he goes to bed/gets up late; **il est t.** it's late; **il se fait t.** it's getting late; **t. dans la matinée/l'après-midi** late in the morning/afternoon; **il a fait chaud t. dans la saison** *(en retard)* the hot weather came late in the season; *(longtemps)* the weather remained hot until late in the season

2 *(après le moment fixé ou opportun)* late; **j'ai déjeuné t. aujourd'hui** I had a late lunch *or* had lunch late today; **les magasins restent ouverts t.** the shops stay open late *or* keep late opening hours; **il est un peu t. pour changer d'avis** it's a little late to change your mind; **tu arrives bien t. aujourd'hui** you're very late today; **c'est trop t.** it's too late; **il ne fallait pas attendre si t. pour m'en parler** you shouldn't have left it so late before talking to me about it; **elle est venue t. à la danse classique** she was a latecomer to ballet; **se marier t.** to marry late (in life)

3 plus t. *(après un certain temps)* later (on); **je reviendrai plus t.** I'll come back later; **il est arrivé encore plus t. que moi** he came in even later than I did; **je m'en occuperai un peu plus t.** I'll deal with it a little later; **nous parlions de lui pas plus t. que ce matin** we were talking about him only *or* just this morning; **je le ferai et pas plus t. que ce soir** I'll do it this very evening; **pas plus t. qu'hier** as recently as yesterday, only yesterday; **deux minutes plus t. et je manquais le bateau** another two minutes and I would have missed the boat; **remettre qch à plus t.** to put sth off until later

▫ **au plus tard** ADV at the latest; **donnez-moi votre réponse lundi au plus t.** give me your answer on Monday at the latest

▫ **sur le tard** ADV late (on) in life; **elle s'est mariée sur le t.** she married late in life

tarder [3] [tarde] VI **1** *(être lent à se décider → personne)* to delay; **je n'aurais pas dû tant t.** I shouldn't have left it so late *or* have put it off so long; **ne pars pas maintenant – j'ai déjà trop tardé** don't go now – I should be gone already

2 *(être long à venir → événement)* to be a long time coming, to take a long time to come; **leur décision n'a pas tardé** their decision wasn't long (in) coming, they didn't take long to decide; **ça ne tardera plus maintenant** it won't be long now; **cela n'a pas tardé** it wasn't long (in) coming; **je t'avais dit qu'on le reverrait, ça n'a pas tardé!** I told you we'd see him again, we didn't have to wait long!; **et cela n'a pas tardé, il s'est cassé la cheville** and as expected he duly broke his ankle; **tu vas recevoir une gifle, cela ne va pas t.** you're going to get smacked before long *or* in a minute or two, you've got a smack coming to you; **la réponse tardait à venir** the answer took a long time to come; **aujourd'hui, le soleil tarde à se montrer** it's taking a long time for the sun to come out today; **un conflit ne tardera pas à éclater entre les deux pays** it won't be long before the two countries enter into conflict

3 *(mettre du temps → personne)* **t. en chemin** to loiter on the way; **elle devrait être rentrée, elle ne va pas t.** she should be back by now, she won't be long; **pourquoi tarde-t-il?** why is he (taking) so long?; **nous ne tarderons pas à le savoir** we'll soon know; **nous ne tardâmes pas à avoir de ses nouvelles** it wasn't long before we heard from him/her, we didn't have to wait too long for news of him/her; **elle n'a pas tardé à se rendre compte que...** it didn't take her long to realize that..., she soon realized that...; **t. à faire qch** to take a long time doing sth; **il a trop tardé à donner son accord** he waited too long before giving his approval; **excusez-moi si j'ai tardé à vous répondre** I apologize for not answering sooner

V IMPERSONNEL **il lui tarde de partir** he/she is longing to get away; **il nous tarde tant que tu reviennes** we long so much for you to return; **il me tarde que tu sois grand/aies 18 ans** I can't wait until you're grown up/18

▫ **sans (plus) tarder** ADV without delay; **partons sans plus t.** let's leave without further delay

tardif, -ive [tardif, -iv] ADJ **1** *(arrivée, fruit, récolte)* late; *(remords, excuses)* tardy, belated; **l'arrivée tardive des secours sur le lieu de l'accident** the late arrival of the emergency services at the scene of the accident; **tes regrets sont trop tardifs pour être sincères** your regrets are too late to be sincere

2 *(heure)* late, *Sout* advanced; **à cette heure tardive** at this late hour

3 *Agr* late, late-developing

tardiflore [tardiflɔr] ADJ *Bot* late-blooming, late-flowering

tardigrade [tardigrad] *Zool* NM water bear, *Spéc* tardigrade

▫ **tardigrades** NMPL Tardigrada

tardillon, -onne [tardijɔ̃, -ɔn] NM,F *Fam Vieilli* = last-born child in a family, arriving some time after siblings

tardive [tardiv] *voir* **tardif**

tardivement [tardivmɑ̃] ADV **1** *(à une heure tardive)* late **2** *(trop tard)* belatedly, tardily **3** *(se marier, s'établir)* late in life

tardiveté [tardivte], **tardivité** [tardivite] NF **1** *Littéraire (d'un développement)* lateness; *(d'un regret)* tardiness, belatedness **2** *Agr* lateness

tare [tar] NF **1** *(défectuosité → physique)* (physical) defect; *(→ psychique)* abnormality; **tous les chiots de la portée sont sans t.** all of the puppies in the litter are perfectly normal

2 *Fig* defect, flaw; **l'agressivité est la t. de la société moderne** aggressiveness is the ugliest feature of modern society; *Hum* **ça n'est pas une t.!** it's not a crime!

3 *Com (perte de valeur)* loss, shrinkage

4 *Vét (tumeur du cheval)* **cheval sans t.** sound horse

5 *(d'une balance, d'un poids brut, d'un prix)* tare; **faire la t.** to allow for the tare

taré, -e [tare] ADJ **1** *(gâté → fruit)* imperfect

2 *(atteint d'une tare)* abnormal

3 *(corrompu)* corrupt; **un politicien t.** a corrupt politician

4 *Fam (fou)* crazy, off one's head *or* rocker; *(imbécile) Br* thick, *Am* dumb; **il faut être t. pour faire cela!** you have to be mad *or* to have a screw loose to do that!

5 *Vét* unsound

NM,F **1** *Méd* imbecile

2 *(vicieux)* pervert

3 *Fam (fou)* nutcase, headcase; *(imbécile)* moron, idiot

tarentais, -e [tarɑ̃tɛ, -ɛz] ADJ = relating to a breed of cows originally from the Tarentaise region of France

NM,F = one of a breed of cows originally from the Tarentaise region of France

Tarente [tarɑ̃t] NM Taranto

tarentelle [tarɑ̃tɛl] NF tarantella

tarentisme [tarɑ̃tism] NM *Méd* tarentism

tarentule [tarɑ̃tyl] NF *Entom* (European) tarantula

tarentulisme [tarɑ̃tylism] NM *Méd* tarentism

tarer [3] [tare] VT *Com* to tare

taret [tarɛ] NM *Zool* shipworm, teredo

targe [tarʒ] NF *Hist* targe, buckler

TARGET [targɛt] NM *Banque & UE (abbr* **Trans-European Automated Real-Time Gross Settlement Transfer System**) TARGET

targette [tarʒɛt] NF small bolt

▫ **targettes** NFPL *Fam* **1** *(pieds)* feet■, *Br* plates, *Am* dogs **2** *(chaussures)* shoes■

targuer [3] [targe] **se targuer** VPR **se t. de qch** *(se vanter de)* to boast about *or* of sth; *(s'enorgueillir de)* to pride oneself on sth; **se t. de faire qch** *(se vanter de)* to boast about doing sth; *(s'enorgueillir de)* to pride oneself on doing sth; **il se targue de connaître plusieurs langues** he boasts that he knows several languages; **un risque que je me targue d'avoir pris** a risk I'm proud to have taken *or* I pride myself on having taken

targui, -e [targi] ADJ Tuareg

▫ **Targui, -e** NM,F Tuareg

targum [targum] NM *Rel* Targum

tarière [tarjɛr] NF **1** *Agr* drill; *Mines* borer **2** *Entom* terebra, ovipositor **3** *Menuis* (centre) auger

tarif [tarif] NM **1** *(liste de prix)* price list; *(barème)* rate, rates; **t. douanier** customs rate; **t. lettres** letter rate; **tarifs postaux** postal *or* postage rates; **t. progressif** increasing rate; **il est payé au t. syndical** he's paid the union rate; **augmentation du t. horaire** increase in *or* of the hourly rate

2 *(prix pratiqué)* rate; *(d'un billet d'avion ou de train)* fare; **tarifs aériens/ferroviaires** air/rail fares; **quel est votre t.?, quels sont vos tarifs?** *(femme de ménage, baby-sitter, mécanicien, professeur particulier)* how much do you charge?; *(conseiller, avocat)* what fee do you charge?, what are your fees?; **les compagnies d'assurances ne communiquent pas leurs tarifs au téléphone** insurance companies don't quote premiums over the phone; **quel est le t. courant pour une traduction?** what's the usual *or* going rate for translation?; **t. normal** standard rate; **t. heures creuses/pleines** *(gaz, électricité)* off-peak/full tariff rate; **à plein t.** *Transp* full-fare; *(au cinéma, au musée)* full-price; **billet (à) plein t.** full-fare ticket; **payer plein t.** *(passagers)* to pay full fare; *(pour marchandises)* to pay the full rate; **à t. réduit** *Transp* reduced-fare; *(au cinéma, au musée)* reduced-price; **t. réduit le lundi** reduced price on Mondays; **t. réduit pour étudiants** *(au cinéma, au musée)* student discount; **t. d'abonnement** *(gén)* subscription charge; *(au gaz, à l'électricité)* standing charge; *Tél* rental; **t. affaires** business rate; *(transport)* business fare; **t. APEX** APEX fare; **t. de base** basic rate; **t. des chambres** room rate; **t. en chambre double** *(dans un hôtel)* double occupancy rate; *Aviat* **t. commun** common rated fare, joint fare; **t. couplage** *(en publicité)* combination rate; **t. du distributeur** dealer list price; *Com* **t. d'entrée** import list; **t. étudiant** student rate; *(d'un voyage)* student fare; **le t. étudiant est de 6 euros** the price for students is 6 euros; **t. excursion** excursion fare, APEX fare; **t. export** export tariff; **t. famille** family rate; *(d'un voyage)* family fare; *Mktg* **t. des insertions** advertising rates; **t. jeunes** youth fare; **t. journalier** daily *or* day rate; **t. minimum** minimum charge; **t. promotionnel** promotional rate; *(d'un voyage)* promotional fare; **t. de la publicité** advertising rates; **t. de référence** basing fare; **t. des salaires** salary scale; **t. social** reduced train fare for the general public; **t. société** commercial *or* corporate rate; **t. standby** standby fare; **t. d'urgence** = first-class rate; **t. uniforme** flat rate

3 *Fam (sanction)* fine, penalty; **100 euros d'amende? – c'est le t.!** a 100-euro fine? – that's how much it is!; **dix jours de prison, c'est le t.** ten days in the cooler is what it's usually worth *or* what you usually get

4 *Jur* **t. criminel** fines bracket

tarifaire [tarifɛr] ADJ *(disposition, réforme)* tariff *(avant n)*; *Com* **politique t.** pricing policy

tarifé, -e [tarife] ADJ fixed-price

tarifer [3] [tarife] VT *(marchandises)* to fix the price of

tarification [tarifikasjɔ̃] NF pricing; **t. au coût-plus-marge** mark-up pricing; **t. différentielle** differential pricing; **t. discriminatoire** discriminatory pricing; **t. en fonction de la valeur perçue** perceived value pricing; **t. géographique** geographical pricing; **t. de pénétration du marché** market penetration pricing

tarin [tarɛ̃] NM **1** *Orn* **t. (des aulnes)** siskin **2** *Fam (nez) Br* hooter, conk, *Am* schnozzle

tariqa [tarika] NF *Rel* tariqa

tarir [32] [tarir] VI **1** *(cesser de couler)* to dry up, to run dry; **les torrents de montagne ne tarissent jamais** mountain streams never run dry; **le puits de pétrole a tari** the oil well has run dry

2 *(pleurs)* to dry (up)

3 *Fig (s'épuiser → conversation)* to dry up; *(→ enthousiasme, inspiration)* to dry up, to run dry; **la discussion n'a pas tari pendant deux heures** the discussion has been flowing freely for two hours; **une fois lancé sur ce sujet, il ne tarit pas** once he's started on the subject he never shuts up *or* stops; **ne pas t. de** to be full of, to bubble with; **ne pas t. d'éloges sur qn** to be full of praise for sb; **elle ne tarissait pas de détails** she gave a wealth of detail; **il ne tarit pas sur le sujet** he never stops talking *or* shuts up about the subject; **les journaux ne tarissent pas sur la jeune vedette** the papers are full of stories about the young star

VT **1** *(assécher → puits, source)* to dry up; **la source est tarie** the spring is dry

2 *(faire cesser → pleurs)* to dry

3 *Fig (épuiser → fortune, inspiration)* to dry up; **son imagination est tarie** his/her imagination has dried up on him/her

▸**se tarir** VPR **1** *(mare, puits)* to dry up; *(rivière)* to run dry; **son lait s'est tari** her milk dried up

2 *Fig (inspiration, enthousiasme, fortune)* to dry up, to peter out

tarissable [tarisabl] ADJ **une source t.** a spring which can dry up

tarissement [tarismɑ̃] NM **1** *(d'une source, d'un puits)* drying up; **le t. des ressources minières a accéléré le déclin de la région** the gradual exhaustion of mining resources hastened the decline of the region **2** *Fig (d'une conversation, de l'imagination)* running dry, drying up **3** *Vét (d'une vache)* petering out

tarlatane [tarlatan] NF tarlatan

tarmac [tarmak] NM tarmac

tarmacadam [tarmakadam] NM tarmacadam

Tarn [tarn] NM **1** *(fleuve)* **le T.** the (River) Tarn **2** *(département)* **le T.** the Tarn

Tarn-et-Garonne [tarnegarɔn] NM **le T.** Tarn-et-Garonne

taro [taro] NM *Bot* taro

tarot [taro] NM **1** *Cartes (carte, jeu)* tarot; **jouer au t.** to play tarot; **faire un t.** *ou* **une partie de t.** to have a game of tarot **2** *(cartomancie)* Tarot, tarot

taroté, -e [tarɔte] ADJ *(carte)* = with a grilled or chequered back

tarpan [tarpɑ̃] NM tarpan

tarpé [tarpe] NM *Fam* (*verlan de* **pétard**) joint, spliff

Tarpéienne [tarpejɛn] *voir* **roche**

tarpon [tarpɔ̃] NM *Ich* tarpon

Tarquin [tarkɛ̃] NPR Tarquin

Tarragone [taragɔn] NM Tarragona

tarse [tars] NM tarsus

tarsien, -enne [tarsjɛ̃, -ɛn] ADJ tarsal

tarsier [tarsje] NM *Zool* tarsier

tarsiiforme [tarsiifɔrm] NM *Zool* tarsiiform

Tarsus [tarsys] NM *Géog* Tarsus

Tartan® [tartɑ̃] NM Tartan

tartan [tartɑ̃] NM tartan

tartane [tartan] NF *Naut* tartan, tartane, tartana

tartare [tartar] ADJ **1** *Hist* Tatar, Tartar **2** *Culin* tartar, tartare

NM *Culin* steak tartare

❑ **Tartare** NMF *Hist* Tartar

tartarin [tartarɛ̃] NM *Fam* braggart; **quel t.!** he's so full of himself!

❑ **Tartarin** NPR = character created by Alphonse Daudet, a braggart with a heart of gold

tarte [tart] NF **1** *Culin* tart; **t. aux pommes** apple tart *or* pie; **t. aux prunes/fraises** plum/strawberry tart; **t. Tatin** tarte Tatin, = caramelized apples covered in shortcrust pastry and turned out upside down; **t. à la crème** *Culin* custard pie *or* tart; *Fig (cliché)* stock reply, cliché; **humour t. à la crème** slapstick, *Br* custard pie humour

2 *très Fam (gifle)* clout, wallop; **flanquer une t. à qn** to clout *or* wallop sb

3 *Fam (locutions)* **c'est pas de la t.** *(c'est difficile)* it's no walkover, it's no picnic; **gagner chez eux, ça n'a pas été de la t.!** winning the away match wasn't exactly a walkover!

ADJ *Fam* **1** *(ridicule → personne) Br* plain-looking, plain, *Am* homely; *(→ chapeau, robe)* stupid-looking, *Br* naff; **ce que tu as l'air t.!** you look a (real) idiot!

2 *(stupide → personne) Br* dim, *Am* dumb; *(→ film, histoire, roman) Br* daft, *Am* dumb

tartelette [tartəlɛt] NF tartlet, little tart

Tartempion [tartɑ̃pjɔ̃] NPR *Fam* thingy, what's-his-name, *f* what's-her-name

tartiflette [tartiflɛt] NF *Culin* = Savoyard dish of potatoes and melted reblochon cheese

tartignol, tartignolle [tartiɲɔl] ADJ *Fam* ridiculous▪, *Br* naff

tartine [tartin] NF **1** *Culin* slice of bread; **t. grillée** slice *or* piece of toast; **une t. de beurre** *ou Belg* **au beurre** a slice of bread and butter; **une t. de confiture** *ou Belg* **à la confiture** a slice of bread and jam; **une t. de pâté** *ou Belg* **au pâté** a slice of bread and pâté; **faire des tartines** to butter (some) bread

2 *Fam Fig (tirade)* long-winded speech; *(article de journal, lettre)* screed; **en mettre une t.** *ou* **des tartines** to write screeds, to waffle on; **c'est juste une carte postale, pas la peine d'en mettre une t.** *ou* **des tartines** it's only a postcard, there's no need to write your life story; **pourquoi en mettre toute une t.?** why go on *or Br* bang on about it?

3 *Fam (pied)* foot▪, *Br* plate, *Am* dog; *(chaussure)* shoe▪

tartiner [3] [tartine] VT **1** *Culin* to spread; **t. du pain de** *ou* **avec du beurre** to butter bread, to spread bread with butter; **commence à t. les canapés** start getting the canapés ready; **sors le beurre et tartine les toasts** take the butter out and spread it on the toast

2 *Fam (enduire en grande quantité)* **t. qn/qch de qch** to cover sb/sth in sth▪

3 *Fam Fig (écrire)* to churn out; **il a fallu qu'elle (en) tartine des pages et des pages** she had to write page after page

▸**se tartiner** VPR *Fam* **se t. de qch** to cover oneself in sth▪

tartir [32] [tartir] VI *très Fam* **se faire t.** to be bored shitless

tartrate [tartrat] NM *Chim* tartrate

tartre [tartr] NM **1** *(dans une bouilloire, une machine à laver)* fur, scale **2** *(des dents, du vin)* tartar **3** *(sur un tonneau)* tartar, argol **4** *Chim* **crème de t.** cream of tartar

tartré, -e [tartre] ADJ tartarized

tartreux, -euse [tartrø, -øz] ADJ tartarous

tartrique [tartrik] ADJ *Chim* tartaric

tartufe [tartyf] = **tartuffe**

tartuferie [tartyfri] = **tartufferie**

tartuffe [tartyf] ADJ *Littéraire (hypocrite)* **il est un peu t.** he's a bit of a hypocrite *or* Tartuffe

NM hypocrite, Tartuffe

> *Allusion*
>
> **Tartuffe**
>
> Molière's play of 1669, originally banned as immoral, tells the story of a religious hypocrite named Tartuffe, who manages to worm his way into people's good graces. To call someone a Tartuffe is to call him a sanctimonious hypocrite.

tartufferie [tartyfri] NF **1** *(caractère)* hypocrisy **2** *(parole, acte)* piece of hypocrisy

Tarzan [tarzɑ̃] NPR Tarzan

tas [tɑ] NM **1** *(amoncellement → de dossiers, de vêtements)* heap, pile; *(→ de sable, de cailloux)* heap; *(→ de planches, de foin)* stack; **mettre en t.** *(feuilles, objets)* to pile *or* to heap up; **faites des petits t. de pâte** shape the dough into small mounds; **t. de fumier** dung heap; **t. d'ordures** *Br* rubbish *or Am* garbage heap; *Mines* **t. de déblais** dump; *Fam* **son vieux t. de boue** *ou* **ferraille** his/her rusty old heap; *Fam Péj* **un gros t.** *(gros individu mou)* a big fat lump; *(grosse fille laide)* a fat cow

2 *Fam* **un t.** *ou* **des t. de** *(un grand nombre de, une grande quantité de)* loads of, tons of; **un t. de mensonges** a pack of lies; **tout un t. de vieilleries** masses *or* heaps *or* a whole pile of old things; **tout un t. de gens** a whole gang (of people), a whole load of people; **elle nous a donné des t. de détails** she gave us a ton of details; **elle a fait un t. de choses dans sa vie** she has done masses of things in her life; **il y a des t. de vieilleries à la cave** there are piles of old things in the cellar; **il y en a des t. (et des t.)** there are heaps *or* masses of them; **t. de paresseux/menteurs!** you bunch of lazybones/liars!, *Br* you lazy/lying lot!

3 *Constr* constructed fabric; *(construction)* building under construction; *(chantier)* building site; **t. de charge** springing stones

4 *Métal (enclume)* (stake) anvil; *(pour embouti, former)* dolly

❑ **dans le tas** ADV *Fam* **1** *(dans un ensemble)* **il y aura bien quelqu'un dans le t. qui pourra me renseigner** there must be someone around who can tell me; **dans le t., il doit y en avoir un ou deux que tu connais** there must be one or two out of that lot that you know; **l'armoire est pleine de vêtements, tu en trouveras bien un ou deux qui t'iront dans le t.** the wardrobe's full of clothes, you're bound to find something there that will fit you

2 *(au hasard)* **la police a tiré/tapé dans le t.** the police fired into the crowd/hit out at random

❑ **sur le tas** *Fam* ADJ **1** *(formation)* on-the-job **2** *Constr* on-site ADV **1** *(se former)* on the job; **il a appris son métier sur le t.** he learned his trade as he went along **2** *Constr (tailler)* on site

Tasman [tasman] *voir* **mer**

Tasmanie [tasmani] NF **la T.** Tasmania

tasmanien, -enne [tasmanjɛ̃, -ɛn] ADJ Tasmanian

❑ **Tasmanien, -enne** NM,F Tasmanian

Tass [tas] NF *Anciennement* **l'agence T.** TASS

tassage [tɑsaʒ] NM *Sport* boxing in, crowding

Tasse [tas] NPR **le T.** Tasso

tasse [tɑs] NF **1** *(récipient)* cup; **t. à café** coffee cup; **t. à thé** teacup

2 *(contenu)* cup, cupful; **t. de café/thé** cup of coffee/tea; **ajouter deux tasses de farine** add two cupfuls of flour; **je t'en ressers une t.?** would you like another cup?, shall I fill you up again?; **voulez-vous une t. de thé?** would you like a cup of tea?; *Fig* **ce n'est pas ma t. de thé** it's not my cup of tea; *Fam* **boire la t.** *(avaler de l'eau)* to get a mouthful of water

❑ **tasses** NFPL *Fam (urinoirs)* street urinals▪

tassé, -e [tɑse] ADJ **1** *(serrés → voyageurs)* packed *or* crammed in

2 *(ratatiné, voûté → personne)* wizened

❑ **bien tassé, -e** ADJ *Fam* **1** *(café)* strong; *(scotch, pastis)* stiff; *(verre)* full (to the brim), well-filled

2 *(dépassé → âge)* **elle a 60 ans bien tassés** she's 60 if she's a day

3 *(féroce → remarque)* choice▪, well-chosen▪; **il lui a envoyé quelques remarques bien tassées** he came out with a few choice *or* well-chosen remarks

4 *(grave → maladie)* nasty; **je tenais une grippe bien tassée** I had a nasty bout of flu

tasseau, -x [tɑso] NM **1** *Menuis (de lattis)* brace, strut; *(de tiroir)* batten, strip **2** *Constr (d'une couverture métallique)* roll **3** *Métal* (stake) anvil

tassement [tɑsmɑ̃] NM **1** *(affaissement → de neige, de terre)* packing down

2 *(récession)* slight drop, downturn (**de** in); **l'augmentation de la TVA a provoqué un léger t. de nos ventes** the rise in VAT has caused a slight drop in our sales; **un t. des voix de gauche aux dernières élections** a slight fall in the numbers of votes for the left in the last elections

3 *Bourse* easing, falling back

4 *Constr* subsidence

5 *Méd* **t. de vertèbres** spinal compression

tasser [3] [tɑse] VT **1** *(neige, terre)* to pack down, to tamp down

2 *(entasser)* to cram, to squeeze (**dans** into); **tasse les vêtements dans le sac** press the clothes down in the bag; **ils nous ont tassés dans une cellule** they crammed *or* packed us into a cell

3 *(faire paraître plus petit)* to shrink; **cette robe la tasse** that dress makes her look dumpy

4 *Sport* to box in, to crowd

VI *Hort* to thicken

▸**se tasser** VPR **1** *(s'effondrer → fondations, terrain)* to subside

2 *(se voûter → personne)* to shrink

3 *(s'entasser → voyageurs, spectateurs)* to cram, to squeeze up; **tout le monde s'est tassé dans la salle à manger** everybody crammed into the dining room; **en se tassant, on peut tenir à quatre à l'arrière (de la voiture)** if we squeeze up, four of us can get in the back (of the car)

4 *Fam (s'arranger → situation)* to settle down; **je crois que les choses vont se t.** I think things will settle down

5 *(ralentir → demande, vente)* to fall, to drop; *(→ production)* to slow down; **le marché des valeurs s'est tassé** the securities market has levelled off

6 *très Fam (aliment, boisson)* to down; **ils se sont tassé tous les gâteaux** they've guzzled all the cakes

tassergal [tasɛrgal] NM *Ich* bluefish

tassette [tasɛt] NF tasse, tasset

tassili [tasili] NM sandstone massif *(in the Sahara)*

taste-vin [tastəvɛ̃] NM INV *(tasse)* taster (cup), tastevin

TAT [teate] NM *Psy & Mktg (abrév* **thematic apperception test** *ou* **test d'aperception thématique***)* TAT

tata [tata] NF **1** *(en langage enfantin → tante)* aunty,

auntie; **T. Jacqueline** aunty *or* auntie Jacqueline **2** *très Fam (homosexuel)* queer, fairy, = offensive term used to refer to a male homosexual

tatami [tatami] NM tatami

tatane [tatan] NF *Fam* shoe ■

tataner [3] [tatane] VT *Fam* **t. qn/qch** to give sb/sth a kicking; **se faire t.** to get a kicking

Tataouine-les-Bains [tatawinlebɛ̃] NF *Fam* **à T.** in the middle of nowhere

tataouiner [3] [tatawine] VI *Can Fam (ne rien faire)* to loaf about

tatar, -e [tatar] ADJ Tatar, Tartar

NM *(langue)* Tatar, Tartar

❑ **Tatar, -e** NM,F Tatar, Tartar

Tatarie [tatari] NF **la T.** Tartary

tâter [3] [tɑte] VT **1** *(fruit, membre, tissu)* to feel; **t. la porte pour trouver la poignée** to feel for the door handle; **ne tâtez pas les tomates** don't handle *or* squeeze the tomatoes; **elle avançait en tâtant les objets de la chambre** she was groping her way across the room; **tâte l'eau avec ton coude** test (the temperature of) the water with your elbow

2 *Fig (sonder)* **t. le terrain** to see how the land lies; **tâte le terrain avant de leur faire une proposition** put some feelers out before making them an offer; **tu lui as demandé une augmentation? – non, mais j'ai tâté le terrain** did you ask him/her for a *Br* rise *or Am* raise? – no, but I tried to sound him/her out

3 *(tester → personne)* to sound out; **t. l'opinion** to sound out attitudes, to put out feelers

❑ **tâter de** VT IND **1** *Hum (nourriture, vin)* to try, to taste

2 *(faire l'expérience de)* **elle a déjà tâté de la prison** she's already had a taste of prison; **il a tâté de plusieurs métiers** he's tried his hand at several jobs; *Littéraire* **t. du chagrin/dégoût** to experience sorrow/disgust

▸**se tâter** VPR **1** *(après un accident)* to feel oneself; **se t. la jambe/le bras** to feel one's leg/one's arm

2 *Fam (être indécis)* to be *Br* in *or Am* of two minds; **je ne sais pas si je vais accepter, je me tâte encore** I don't know whether I'll accept, I'm still *Br* in *or Am* of two minds

tâteur [tɑtœr] NM *Agr* control device

tâte-vin [tɑtvɛ̃] NM INV *(tasse)* taster (cup), taste-vin

Tati® [tati] NM = name of a chain of cut-price stores, specializing mainly in clothes

tatie [tati] NF *Fam* aunty, auntie; **T. Sonia** aunty *or* auntie Sonia

tatillon, -onne [tatijɔ̃, ɔn] *Fam* ADJ *(vétilleux)* fussy, pernickety; **son côté t. m'exaspère** his/her fussiness really gets on my nerves

NM,F *(personne)* nitpicker, fusspot

tâtonnant, -e [tɑtɔnɑ̃, -ɑ̃t] ADJ **1** *(personne)* groping **2** *Fig (style)* hesitant; **nos recherches sont encore tâtonnantes** we're still proceeding by trial and error

tâtonnement [tɑtɔnmɑ̃] NM **avancer par tâtonnements** to grope one's way along; *Fig* to proceed by trial and error; *Fig* **nous n'en sommes encore qu'aux tâtonnements** we're still trying to find our way; *Fig* **les tâtonnements de la science/recherche** the tentative progress of science/research

tâtonner [3] [tɑtɔne] VI **1** *(pour marcher)* to grope *or* to feel one's way (along); *(à la recherche de quelque chose)* to grope about *or* around; **t. pour retrouver la porte** to grope about for the door; **se diriger en tâtonnant vers qch** to grope *or* feel one's way towards sth

2 *Fig (hésiter)* to grope around; *(expérimenter)* to proceed by trial and error; **nous avons beaucoup tâtonné avant de trouver l'explication** we groped around a lot before finding the solution

tâtons [tɑtɔ̃] **à tâtons** ADV **1** *(à l'aveuglette)* **avancer/entrer/sortir à t.** to grope *or* to feel one's way along/in/out; **elle chercha l'interrupteur à t.** she felt *or* groped around for the switch **2** *Fig* **c'est un domaine nouveau, nous devons avancer à t.** it's a new field, we have to feel our way (along)

tatou [tatu] NM armadillo

tatouage [tatwaʒ] NM **1** *(action)* tattooing; **se faire faire un t.** to get a tattoo *or* tattooed **2** *(dessin, numéro d'identification)* tattoo; **il est couvert de tatouages** he's tattooed all over

tatouer [6] [tatwe] VT to tattoo; **se faire t.** to get a tattoo *or* tattooed; **se faire t. le bras** to have one's arm tattooed; **faire t. un chien/chat** to have a dog/cat tattooed *(for identification)*

tatoueur [tatwœr] NM tattoo artist, tattooist

tau [to] NM INV **1** *(lettre grecque)* tau **2** *Hér* tau cross, Saint Anthony's cross

taud [to] NM *Naut* (rain) awning

taude [tod] NF *Naut* (rain) awning

taudis [todi] NM slum, hovel; *Fig* dump; **c'est un vrai t. chez lui!** his place is a real dump *or* pigsty!

taulard, -e [tolar, -ard] NM,F *très Fam Arg crime* jailbird

taule [tol] *Fam* NF **1** *(prison)* clink, slammer, *Br* nick; **sortir de t.** to come out of the clink *or* the slammer *or Br* the nick; **faire de la t.** to do time *or* a stretch; **elle a fait un an de t.** she did a one-year stretch (inside)

2 *(lieu de travail)* workplace ■

3 *(chambre)* room ■

❑ **en taule** ADV inside; **je ne veux pas me retrouver en t.** I don't want to wind up inside; **on l'a foutu en t.** he was put inside

taulier, -ère [tolje, -ɛr] NM,F *Fam* **1** *(d'un hôtel)* boss **2** *(logeur)* landlord ■, *f* landlady ■

tauon [toɔ̃] NM *Phys* tau

taupe [top] NF **1** *Zool (mammifère)* mole; *(poisson)* porbeagle; *Fam* **vieille t.** old hag *or* bat **2** *(fourrure)* moleskin **3** *très Fam Arg scol* = second year of a two-year entrance course for the Science sections of the "grandes écoles" **4** *très Fam Arg mil* sapper **5** *Fam (agent secret)* mole **6** *(en travaux publics)* mole

taupé, -e [tope] ADJ **feutre t.** velour(s) felt

NM **1** *(feutre)* velour(s) felt **2** *(chapeau)* velour(s) hat

taupe-grillon [topgrijɔ̃] *(pl* **taupes-grillons***)* NM *Entom* mole cricket

tauper [3] [tope] VT *Suisse Fam* **t. qch à qn** *(emprunter)* to bum *or* to cadge sth from sb; *(soustraire indûment)* to do *or* to con sb out of sth

taupier [topje] NM mole catcher

taupière [topjɛr] NF *(piège)* mole trap

taupin [topɛ̃] NM **1** *très Fam Arg scol* = pupil preparing for entry to the Science sections of the "grandes écoles" **2** *très Fam Arg mil Arch* sapper **3** *Entom* click beetle, skipjack

taupinière [topinjɛr], **taupinée** [topine] NF molehill

taure [tɔr] NF *Can & (régional)* heifer

Taureau [tɔro] NM **1** *Astron* Taurus **2** *Astrol* Taurus; **être T.** to be Taurus *or* a Taurean

taureau, -x [tɔro] NM bull; **t. de combat** fighting bull; **il a un cou de t.** he's got a neck like a bull; **son frère a une force de t.** his/her brother is as strong as an ox; *Fam* **prendre le t. par les cornes** to take the bull by the horns

taurides [tɔrid] NFPL *Astron* taurides

taurillon [tɔrijɔ̃] NM bull calf

taurin, -e [tɔrɛ̃, -in] ADJ bullfighting; **jeux taurins** bullfights

❑ **taurine** NF *Biol & Chim* taurine

taurobole [tɔrɔbɔl] NM *Antiq* taurobolium

tauromachie [tɔrɔmaʃi] NF bullfighting, *Spéc* tauromachy

tauromachique [tɔrɔmaʃik] ADJ bullfighting, *Spéc* tauromachian

Taurus [tɔrys] NM **le T.** the Taurus Mountains

tautisme [totism] NM = confusion between the reality of an event and how it is represented in the media, often described as an excess of communication leading to the communication being lost altogether

tautochrone [totɔkron] ADJ *Math* **courbe t.** tautochrone

tautologie [totɔlɔʒi] NF tautology

tautologique [totɔlɔʒik] ADJ tautological

tautomère [totɔmɛr] ADJ **1** *Anat* tautomeral **2** *Chim* tautomeric

tautomérie [totɔmeri] NF *Chim* tautomerism

taux [to] NM **1** *(tarif)* rate

2 *(proportion)* rate; *Scol* **t. d'absentéisme** truancy rate; **t. d'audience** *ou* **d'écoute** *TV* ratings, viewing figures; *Rad* ratings; **t. de chômage** unemployment rate; **t. de chômage naturel** natural rate of unemployment; **t. d'échec/de réussite** failure/success rate; **t. de fécondité** reproduction *or* fertility rate; **t. de fréquentation** attendance rate; *(de chambres d'hôtel)* sleeper occupancy; **t. de mortalité/natalité** death/birth rate; **t. de participation** *(d'élection)* (voter) turnout; **t. de scolarisation** = percentage of children attending school

3 *Aut* **t. de compression** compression ratio

4 *Fin, Banque & Com* rate; **à quel t. prêtent-ils?** what is their lending rate?; **à t. fixe** fixed-rate; **t. de 8 pour cent** rate of 8 percent; **emprunter à un t. de 7 pour cent** to borrow at 7 percent (interest); **t. d'accroissement** rate of increase *or* of growth; **t. d'activité** participation rate; **t. actuariel annuel** annual equivalent rate, AER; **t. annualisé** annual percentage rate, APR; **t. de l'argent au jour le jour** overnight rate; **t. d'attribution** attribution rate; **t. de base bancaire** bank base lending rate; **t. de change** exchange rate; **t. de change à l'achat** bank buying rate; **t. de change à la vente** bank selling rate; **t. de change en cours** current rate of exchange; **t. de change effectif** effective exchange rate; **t. de change flottant** floating exchange rate; **t. de conversion** conversion rate; **t. court** short-term rate; **t. de couverture** coverage rate; **t. de crédit** lending rate; **t. de croissance** growth rate; **t. directeur** intervention rate; **t. d'échange** rate of exchange, exchange rate; **t. effectif global** annual percentage rate, APR; **t. d'emprunt** borrowing rate; **t. d'épargne** savings rate; **t. d'escompte** discount rate; **t. d'exclusivité à la marque** brand exclusivity rate; **t. hypothécaire** mortgage rate; **t. d'imposition** tax rate, rate of taxation; **t. d'inflation** inflation rate, rate of inflation; **t. interbancaire offert à Paris** Paris Inter-Bank Offer Rate; **t. d'intérêt** interest rate, rate of interest; **t. d'intérêt à court terme/à long terme** short-term/long-term interest rate; **t. d'intérêt réel** real interest rate; **t. linéaire** straight-line rate; *Banque* **t. Lombard** Lombard rate; **t. long** long-term rate; **t. long obligataire** long-term bond rate; **t. du marché monétaire** money market rate; *Bourse* **t. de marge** *ou* **de marque** mark-up (percentage); *Mktg* **t. de mémorisation** recall rate; *Mktg* **t. de notoriété** *(d'un produit)* awareness rating; *Mktg* **t. de pénétration** *(d'un marché)* penetration rate, rate of penetration; **t. plafonné** cap; *Can Banque* **t. préférentiel** prime rate; *Banque* **t. de prêt** lending rate; **t. de prévalence** prevalence rate; **t. privé** market rate; **t. proportionnel** *(d'un crédit)* proportional interest rate; *Mktg* **t. de réachat** rebuy *or* repurchase rate; *Fin* **t. réduit** reduced rate; *Banque* **t. de référence** reference *or* benchmark rate; **t. de refus** refusal rate; **t. de renouvellement** rate of renewal; **t. de rentabilité** rate of return; **t. de répétition** frequency rate; **t. de réponse** response rate; *Fin* **t. des repos** repo rate; *Com* **t. de rotation** *(des stocks)* turnover rate; **t. de TVA** VAT rate, rate of VAT; **t. uniforme** uniform *or* flat rate; *Fin* **t. d'usure** penal rate

5 *Compta* **t. d'actualisation** net present value rate, NPV rate; **t. d'amortissement** rate of depreciation, depreciation rate; **t. de capitalisation** price/earnings ratio, p/e ratio

6 *Ind* **t. horaire** hourly rate; *Tech & Ind* **t. de rendement** coefficient of efficiency, utilization factor

7 *Méd (d'albumine, de cholestérol)* level; **t. d'invalidité** degree of disability; **son t. d'invalidité est de 50 pour cent** he's/she's 50 percent disabled

8 *Ordinat* ratio, rate; **t. d'actualisation** refresh rate; **t. de cliquage** *(sur Internet)* click rate; **t. de compression** compression rate; **t. de rafraîchissement** refresh rate; **t. de transfert** transfer rate

9 *Jur* **t. de compétence** = value of a case determining which court will hear it; **t. de responsabilité** degree of responsibility; **t. de ressort** = value of a case determining the possibility of appeal

tauzin [tozɛ̃] NM *Bot* Pyrenean oak

tavaïolle [tavajɔl] NF *Rel* chrisom cloth

tavel [tavɛl] NM Tavel (wine)

tavelé, -e [tavle] ADJ **1** *(fruit)* marked **2** *(peau)* spotted, speckled (**de** with)

taveler [24] [tavle] VT **1** *(fruit)* to mark **2** *(peau)* to speckle (**de** with)

▸**se taveler** VPR *(fruit)* to become marked

tavelure [tavlyr] NF 1 *(d'un fruit)* mark 2 *(sur la peau)* speckle, (old-age) freckle 3 *Agr (maladie)* scab

taverne [tavɛrn] NF 1 *Hist* inn, public house 2 *Can (bistrot)* beer parlour, tavern 3 *(restaurant)* restaurant

tavernier, -ère [tavɛrnje, -ɛr] NM,F *Hist* innkeeper

tavillon [tavijɔ̃] NM *Suisse (bardeau)* = thin, rounded wooden slat used for covering walls and roofs in Switzerland

taxable [taksabl] ADJ *Écon* taxable, liable to duty

taxacée [taksase] *Bot* NF taxad
 □ **taxacées** NFPL Taxaceae

taxateur, -trice [taksatœr, -tris] ADJ *(fonctionnaire)* taxing; *(juge)* assessing
 NM taxer, assessor

taxation [taksasjɔ̃] NF 1 *Fin* taxation, taxing *(UNCOUNT)*; **t. d'office** estimation of tax *(in the case of failure to file a tax return)*; *Com* **t. au poids** tax on weight; **t. différentielle** differential taxation; **t. à la valeur** tax on value
 2 *Jur (réglementation → des prix)* statutory price fixing; *(→ des salaires)* statutory wage fixing; *(→ des dépens)* assessment
 3 *Tél* **zone de t.** charging area; *Ordinat* **période de t.** charging period

taxatoire [taksatwar] ADJ *Belg* tax *(avant n)*

taxatrice [taksatris] *voir* **taxateur**

taxe [taks] NF 1 *Fin & Admin* tax; **toutes taxes comprises** inclusive of tax; **hors taxes** exclusive of tax; **t. à l'achat** purchase tax; **t. d'aéroport** airport tax; **t. d'apprentissage** = tax paid by businesses to fund training programmes; **t. d'atterrissage** airport landing tax; **t. sur le chiffre d'affaires** sales or turnover tax; **t. de départ** *(à l'aéroport)* departure tax; **t. de douane** customs duty; **t. écologique** ecotax; **t. d'entrée** *(à l'aéroport)* entry tax; **t. à l'exportation** export tax; **t. foncière** property tax; **t. forfaitaire** flat rate; **t. d'habitation** = tax paid on residence, *Br* ≃ council tax; **t. à l'importation** import tax; **t. locale** *(pour une entreprise)* uniform business *Br* rate or *Am* tax; *(pour un particulier)* local (property) tax; **t. de luxe** tax on luxury goods, luxury tax; **t. parafiscale** additional levy; **t. de port** harbour dues; **t. professionnelle** = tax paid by businesses and self-employed people; **t. régionale** local tax; **t. de séjour** visitor's or tourist tax; **t. supplémentaire** surcharge; **t. Tobin** Tobin tax; **t. à la** *ou* **sur valeur ajoutée** *Br* value-added tax, *Am* sales tax
 2 *Jur (des dépens)* assessment
 3 *(prix fixé)* controlled price; **vendre des marchandises à la t.** to sell goods at the controlled price

taxer [3] [takse] VT 1 *Écon & Fin* to tax; **t. les disques à 10 pour cent** to tax records at 10 percent, to put a 10 percent tax on records
 2 *Jur* **t. les dépens** to fix or to assess or to tax costs
 3 *Tél (appel)* to charge for
 4 *(accuser)* **t. qn de** to accuse sb of, *Sout* to tax sb with; **vous m'avez taxé d'hypocrisie** you accused me of being a hypocrite
 5 *(qualifier)* **on l'a taxé d'opportuniste** he's been called an opportunist; **une politique que je taxerais de rétrograde** a policy I would describe as backward-looking; **se faire t. d'égoïste** to be accused of selfishness or being selfish, to be called selfish
 6 *Fam (emprunter)* to scrounge, to sponge, to bum; **il m'a taxé une cigarette** he scrounged a cigarette off me
 7 *Fam (voler)* to pinch, *Br* to nick; **je me suis fait t. mon blouson en cuir par une bande de skins** I got my leather jacket pinched or *Br* nicked by a bunch of skinheads

taxi [taksi] NM 1 *(voiture)* taxi, cab; **prendre un t.** to take a taxi or a cab 2 *Fam (conducteur)* cabby, taxi or cab driver▪; **faire le t.** to be a taxi or cab driver; **il en a marre de faire le t.** he's fed up driving everyone about 3 *Hist* **les taxis de la Marne** = taxis commandeered by Gallieni, governor of Paris, to transport reinforcements to the front line in 1914 *(see box at entry* **Marne***)*

taxiarque [taksiark] NM *Antiq* taxiarch

taxi-brousse [taksibrus] *(pl* **taxis-brousse***)* NM *(en Afrique francophone)* bush taxi

taxidermie [taksidɛrmi] NF taxidermy

taxidermiste [taksidɛrmist] NMF taxidermist

taxie [taksi] NF *Biol* taxis

taxi-girl [taksigœrl] *(pl* **taxi-girls***)* NF taxi-dancer, hostess *(hired for dancing)*

taximan [taksiman] *(pl* **taximans** *ou* **taximen** [-mɛn])* NM *Belg (en Afrique francophone)* taxi driver

taximètre [taksimɛtr] NM taximeter

taxinomie [taksinɔmi] NF taxonomy

taxinomique [taksinɔmik] ADJ taxonomic

taxinomiste [taksinɔmist] NMF taxonomist, taxonomer

Taxiphone® [taksifɔn] NM *Vieilli* public phone, pay-phone

taxis [taksis] NM *Méd* taxis

taxiway [taksiwɛ] NM taxiway, taxi strip or track

taxodium [taksɔdjɔm] NM *Bot* Taxodium

taxol [taksɔl] NM *Bot & Méd* taxol

taxon [taksɔ̃] NM taxon

taxonomie [taksɔnɔmi] NF taxonomy

taxonomique [taksɔnɔmik] ADJ taxonomic

taxonomiste [taksɔnɔmist] NMF taxonomist, taxonomer

tayaut [tajo] = **taïaut**

taylorisation [tɛlɔrizasjɔ̃] NF Taylorization

tayloriser [3] [tɛlɔrize] VT to Taylorize

taylorisme [tɛlɔrism] NM Taylorism

TB, tb *Scol (abrév écrite* **très bien***)* vg

TBE, tbe *(abrév écrite* **très bon état***)* vgc

TBF [tebeɛf] NM *Banque (abrév* **transferts Banque de France***)* = French automated clearing system

Tbilissi [tbilisi] NM Tbilisi

TCA [teseɑ] NF *Fin (abrév* **taxe sur le chiffre d'affaires***)* sales or turnover tax

TCF [teseɛf] NM *Aut (abrév* **Touring Club de France***)* = French motorists' club

Tchad [tʃad] NM **le T.** Chad; **vivre au T.** to live in Chad; **aller au T.** to go to Chad; **le lac T.** Lake Chad

tchadien, -enne [tʃadjɛ̃, -ɛn] ADJ Chadian
 NM *(langue)* Chadic
 □ **Tchadien, -enne** NM,F Chadian

tchador [tʃadɔr] NM chador, chuddar

tchadri [tʃadri] NM chadri, burka

Tchaïkovski [tʃajkɔfski] NPR Tchaikovsky

Tchang Kaï-chek [tʃɑ̃ŋkajtʃɛk] NPR Chiang Kai-shek

tchao [tʃao] = **ciao**

tchapalo [tʃapalo] NM *(en Afrique francophone)* = beer made from pearl millet or sorghum

tcharchaf [tʃarʃaf] NM = black veil worn by Turkish women to hide their faces

tchatche [tʃatʃ] NF *Fam* **avoir la t.** to have the gift of the gab; **tout ça c'est de la t.** that's just a lot of talk

tchatcher [3] [tʃatʃe] VI *Fam* to chat

tchatcheur, -euse [tʃatʃœr, -øz] NM,F *Fam* smooth talker

tchater [3] [tʃate] VI to chat online

tchécoslovaque [tʃekɔslɔvak] *Anciennement* ADJ Czechoslovakian, Czechoslovak
 □ **Tchécoslovaque** NMF Czechoslovakian, Czechoslovak

Tchécoslovaquie [tʃekɔslɔvaki] *Anciennement* NF **la T.** Czechoslovakia

Tchekhov [tʃekɔf] NPR Chekhov

tchèque [tʃɛk] ADJ Czech
 NM *(langue)* Czech
 □ **Tchèque** NMF Czech

tchéquer [3] [tʃeke] VT *Can Joual* to check▪

Tchernenko [tʃɛrnɛnko] NPR Chernenko

Tchernobyl [tʃɛrnɔbil] NM Chernobyl

tchernozem [tʃɛrnɔzɛm], **tchernoziom** [tʃɛrnozjɔm] NM *Géol* chernozem

tchétchène [tʃetʃɛn] ADJ Chechen
 □ **Tchétchène** NMF Chechen

Tchétchénie [tʃetʃeni] NF **la T.** Chechenya; **vivre en T.** to live in Chechenya; **aller en T.** to go to Chechenya

tchi [tʃi] **que tchi** ADV *Fam* zilch, sweet FA; **il y comprend que t.** he doesn't understand a damn or *Br* bloody thing

tchin-tchin [tʃintʃin] EXCLAM *Fam* cheers!

tchitola [tʃitɔla] NM *Bot* tchitola

TCI [tesei] NM *Com (abrév* **terme commercial international***)* incoterm

TCP/IP [tesepeipe] NF *Ordinat (abrév* **transmission control protocol/Internet protocol***)* TCP-IP

TCS [tesees] NM *Aut (abrév* **Touring Club de Suisse***)* = Swiss motorists' club

TD [tede] NMPL *Univ (abrév* **travaux dirigés***)* seminars

TdF [tedeɛf] NF *TV (abrév* **Télédiffusion de France***)* = French broadcasting authority which controls both radio and TV networks

TDM [tedeɛm] NF *Méd (abrév* **tomodensitométrie***)* CT

te [tə]

 t' is used before a word beginning with a vowel or h mute.

PRON 1 *(avec un verbe pronominal)* **tu te lèves tard** you get up late; **tu te fatigues** you're tiring yourself; **tu vas te faire mal** you'll hurt yourself; **arrête de te ronger les ongles** stop biting your nails; **à quelle heure t'es-tu levé?** what time did you get up (at)?; **tu te dépêches un peu?** hurry up, will you?; **tu te prends pour qui?** who do you think you are?; **va-t'en** go away

 2 *(complément)* you; **je te crois** I believe you; **elle t'a envoyé un colis** she's sent you a parcel; **je te l'ai donné** I gave you it, I gave it to you; **le film t'a-t-il plu?** did you like the movie or *Br* film?; **elle t'est devenue indispensable** she has become indispensable to you; *Fam* **il te court après** he's after you; **ne te laisse pas faire** don't let yourself be pushed around

 3 *Fam (emploi expressif)* **je te l'ai envoyé balader, celui-là!** I sent HIM packing!; **je vais te le mater, celui-là!** I'll sort HIM out!; **je vais te lui dire ce que je pense!** I'm going to give HIM/HER a piece of my mind!; **et je te range, et je te fais la cuisine** and I tidy up AND I do the cooking

 4 *(en s'adressant à Dieu)* You, Thee

té [te] NM 1 *(équerre)* T-square 2 *Menuis* tee
 EXCLAM *(dans le Midi)* **té! voilà Martin!** hey, here comes Martin!
 □ **en té** ADJ T-shaped; **règle en té** T-rule

teaser [tizœr] NM teaser *(in advertising)*

teasing [tizin] NM *Mktg* teaser advertising

TEC [tɛk] NF *Belg (abrév* **société de transport en commun***)* = Walloon public transport authority

tec [tɛk] NF INV *(abrév* **tonne d'équivalent charbon***)* TCE

techi [təʃi] NM *Fam (verlan de* **shit***)* hash, *Br* blow

technétium [tɛknesjɔm] NM *Chim* technetium

technicien, -enne [tɛknisjɛ̃, -ɛn] ADJ *(esprit, civilisation)* technically-oriented
 NM,F 1 *(en entreprise)* technician, engineer; **il est t. en informatique** he's a computer technician; *Cin & TV* **t. en chef** key grip; **t. du froid** refrigeration engineer; **t. de laboratoire** laboratory technician; **t. de maintenance** maintenance or service engineer; **t. de surface** cleaner
 2 *(dans un art, dans un sport)* **c'est une excellente technicienne mais elle gagne peu de matchs** she's got an excellent technique or technically speaking, she's excellent but she doesn't win many matches

techniciser [3] [tɛknisize] VT *(processus)* to make technical

technicité [tɛknisite] NF 1 *(d'un mot, d'un texte)* technical nature or quality, *Sout* technicality; **la t. d'une expression/d'un article de journal** the technical nature of an expression/of a newspaper article
 2 *(avance technologique)* technological sophistication; **matériel d'une haute t.** hi-tech equipment
 3 *(savoir-faire)* skill; **les ingénieurs ont mis leur t. au service de l'entreprise** the engineers have contributed their knowhow to the company

technico-commercial, -e [tɛknikokɔmɛrsjal] *(mpl* **technico-commerciaux** [-o], *fpl* **technico-commerciales**) ADJ **notre personnel t.** our technical sales staff; **agent t.** sales technician, sales engineer; **service t.** technical sales (department)

NM,F sales technician, sales engineer

Technicolor® [tɛknikɔlɔr] NM Technicolor®; **en T.** Technicolor® *(avant n)*

technique [tɛknik] ADJ **1** *(pratique)* technical, practical; **elle a une certaine habileté t.** she's got a certain knack of doing things

2 *(mécanique)* technical; **incident t.** technical hitch; **ce n'est qu'un problème t.** it's only a technical problem

3 *(technologique)* technical; **les progrès techniques en informatique** technical advances in computer science

4 *(spécialisé)* technical; **le sens t. d'un mot** the technical sense *or* meaning of a word

NM *Scol* **le t.** vocational education; **élèves du t.** pupils taking technical subjects; **professeurs du t.** teachers of technical subjects; **enseigner dans le t.** to teach technical subjects, to be a technical teacher

NF **1** *(d'un art, d'un métier)* technique; **la t. de l'aquarelle** the technique of watercolour painting

2 *(savoir-faire)* technique; **un très jeune joueur de tennis qui doit améliorer sa t.** a very young tennis player who has to improve his technique; **ce pianiste a une bonne t./manque de t.** this pianist has good technique/lacks technique; **t. de vente** sales technique

3 *(méthode)* technique; **c'est toute une t. d'ouvrir les huîtres** there's quite an art to opening oysters; **répondre à une question par une autre question, c'est sa t.** answering a question by another question is his/her speciality; **ce n'est pas la bonne t.** that's not the right way to go about it; **avec lui, j'ai ma t.** I have my own way of dealing with him; *Fam* **tu n'as pas la t.!** you haven't got the knack!; *Méd* **t. Alexander** Alexander technique; **techniques commerciales** marketing techniques; **techniques marchandes** merchandising techniques; **techniques promotionnelles** promotional techniques; **t. de sondage d'opinion** opinion measurement technique

4 *(de production)* technique; **de nouvelles techniques industrielles** new industrial techniques; **t. de pointe** state-of-the-art technique

5 *(applications de la science)* **la t.** applied science

techniquement [tɛknikmɑ̃] ADV technically; **t. faisable** technically feasible

techno [tɛkno] ADJ techno

NF techno

technobureaucratique [tɛknɔbyrɔkratik] ADJ technobureaucratic

technocentre [tɛknɔsɑ̃tr] NM ≃ R & D centre

technocrate [tɛknɔkrat] NMF technocrat

technocratie [tɛknɔkrasi] NF technocracy

technocratique [tɛknɔkratik] ADJ technocratic

technocratisation [tɛknɔkratizasjɔ̃] NF **combattre la t. de notre société** to fight against the spread of technocracy in our society

technocratiser [3] [tɛknɔkratize] VT *(pays)* to turn into a technocracy; *(système, processus)* to make technocratic

technocratisme [tɛknɔkratism] NM technocratism

technologie [tɛknɔlɔʒi] NF **1** *Scol* technology, applied science

2 *(technique)* technology; **de haute t.** high tech; **la t. de l'informatique** computer technology; **t. de substitution** alternative technology; **technologies avancées** advanced technology, high technology; **nouvelles technologies** new technologies; *Ordinat* **t. du push de données** push technology

3 *(théorie)* technology, technological theory, technologies

technologique [tɛknɔlɔʒik] ADJ technological

technologue [tɛknɔlɔg], **technologiste** [tɛknɔlɔʒist] NMF technologist

technophile [tɛknɔfil] ADJ technophile

technophobe [tɛknɔfɔb] ADJ technophobe

technopole [tɛknɔpɔl] NF = large urban centre

with teaching and research facilities to support development of hi-tech industries

technopôle [tɛknɔpol] NM = area specially designated to accommodate and foster hi-tech industries

technoscience [tɛknɔsjɑ̃s] NF technoscience

technostructure [tɛknɔstryktyr] NF technostructure

teck [tɛk] NM teak

□ **en teck** ADJ teak *(avant n)*

teckel [tekɛl] NM dachshund; **t. à poil ras/long** short-haired/long-haired dachshund

tectibranche [tɛktibrɑ̃ʃ] *Zool* ADJ tectibranch

NM tectibranch

□ **tectibranches** NMPL Tectibranchia

tectite [tɛktit] NF *Minér* tektite

tectonique [tɛktɔnik] ADJ tectonic

NF tectonics *(singulier)*; **t. des plaques** plate tectonics

tectonophysique [tɛktɔnɔfizik] NF tectonophysics *(singulier)*

tectrice [tɛktris] NF tectrix

teddy-bear [tedibɛr] *(pl teddy-bears)* NM **1** *Vieilli (ours)* teddy bear **2** *(fourrure synthétique)* plush

Te Deum [tedeɔm] NM INV Te Deum

TEE [teəə] NM *Rail (abrév* **Trans-Europ-Express)** TEE

tee [ti] NM *Golf* tee; **poser la balle sur le t.** to tee up; **partir du t.** to tee off

teenager [tinedʒœr] NMF teenager; **vêtements pour teenagers** teenage clothes

tee-shirt [tiʃœrt] *(pl tee-shirts)* NM tee-shirt, T-shirt

tefillin [tefilin] NMPL *Rel* tefillin, tephillin

Téflon® [teflɔ̃] NM Teflon®; **poêle en T.** Teflon® frying pan

téflonisé, -e [teflɔnize] ADJ Teflon® *(avant n)*

TEG [teəʒe] NM *Fin (abrév* **taux effectif global)** APR

tégénaire [teʒenɛr] NF *Entom* house spider, *Spéc* Tegenaria

Tegucigalpa [tegusigalpa] NM Tegucigalpa

tégument [tegymɑ̃] NM *Bot & Zool* tegument, integument

tégumentaire [tegymɑ̃tɛr] ADJ tegumental, tegumentary

Téhéran [teerɑ̃] NM Tehran, Teheran

teignait *etc voir* **teindre**

teigne [tɛɲ] NF **1** *Entom* moth, *Spéc* tineid

2 *Méd* ringworm, *Spéc* tinea; **t. tondante** ringworm of the scalp, *Spéc* tinea captis

3 *Bot* burdock

4 *Fam (homme)* louse; *(femme)* vixen■; **quelle t., celle-là!** wretched woman!; **être mauvais** *ou* **méchant comme une t.** *Br* to be a nasty piece of work, *Am* to be real ornery

teigneux, -euse [tɛɲø, -øz] ADJ **1** *Méd* suffering from ringworm **2** *Fam (hargneux)* nasty■, *Am* ornery

NM,F **1** *Méd* ringworm sufferer **2** *Fam (homme)* bastard■; *(femme)* bitch, *Br* cow

teillage [tejaʒ] NM *Tex* stripping, scutching

teille [tɛj] NF **1** *(du tilleul)* bast, bass; **paillasson de t.** bass(-mat) **2** *(de chanvre)* harl

teiller [4] [teje] VT *Tex* to strip, to scutch

teilleur, -euse [tejœr, -øz] *Tex* NM,F flax stripper, flax scutcher

□ **teilleuse** NF scutching machine, scutcher

teindre [81] [tɛdr] VT **1** *(soumettre à la teinture)* to dye; **t. qch en rouge** to dye sth red; **j'ai fait t. mon tee-shirt en bleu** I had my T-shirt dyed blue; **se faire t. les cheveux** to have one's hair dyed

2 *Littéraire (colorer)* to tint; **la lumière du soleil teignait la mer en vert émeraude** the sunlight turned the sea to emerald green

▶**se teindre** VPR **1** *(emploi passif)* **c'est une étoffe qui se teint facilement** it's a material which is easy to dye *or* which takes dye well *or* which dyes well

2 *(emploi réfléchi)* **se t. (les cheveux)** to dye one's hair; **se t. les cheveux/la barbe en roux** to dye one's hair/beard red

3 *Littéraire (se colorer)* **la neige se teignit du sang des soldats blessés** the snow turned red with the blood of the wounded soldiers; **au coucher du soleil, les cimes se teignent de rose et d'or** at sunset, the mountaintops are tinted pink and gold

4 *Fig Littéraire* **se t. de** *(se mêler de)* to be tinged

with; **sa grande courtoisie se teignait d'un peu de condescendance** his/her excessive politeness smacked somewhat of condescension

teint [tɛ̃] NM *(habituel)* complexion; *(momentané)* colour, colouring; **avoir le t. pâle/jaune/mat** to have a pale/sallow/matt complexion; **avoir un t. de rose** to have a rosy complexion; **un homme au t. jaune** a man with a sallow complexion

□ **bon teint** ADJ INV **1** *Tex* colour-fast

2 *Fig (pur)* staunch; **des royalistes bon t.** staunch *or* dyed-in-the-wool royalists

□ **grand teint** ADJ INV *(couleur)* fast; *(tissu)* colour-fast

teintant, -e [tɛ̃tɑ̃, -ɑ̃t] ADJ *(produit)* dyeing *(avant n)*

teinte [tɛ̃t] NF **1** *(couleur franche)* colour; *(ton)* shade, tint, hue; **une t. grise** a greyish tinge; **plusieurs teintes de bleu** several shades of blue; **du tissu aux teintes vives** brightly coloured material **2** *Fig (petit quantité → de libéralisme, de sadisme)* tinge; *(→ d'ironie, de mépris)* hint; **avec une t. de mépris dans la voix** with a hint *or* touch of scorn in his/her voice

teinté, -e [tɛ̃te] ADJ **1** *(lunettes)* tinted; *(verre)* tinted, stained **2** *(bois)* stained

teinter [3] [tɛ̃te] VT **1** *(verre)* to tint, to stain; *(lunettes, papier)* to tint; *(boiseries)* to stain

2 *(colorer)* to tint; **le soleil couchant teintait le lac de rose** the setting sun gave the lake a pinkish tinge

3 *Fig (mêler)* to tinge; **son amitié était teintée de pitié** his/her friendship was tinged with pity, there was a hint of pity in his/her friendship

▶**se teinter** VPR **1** *(se colorer)* **se t. d'ocre/de rose** to take on an ochre/a pink tinge *or* hue

2 *Fig* **se t. de** *(être nuancé de)* to be tinged with; *(se nuancer de)* to become tinged with; **son intérêt se teinte de condescendance** there's a hint of condescension in the interest he's/she's showing

teinture [tɛ̃tyr] NF **1** *(action)* dyeing; **se faire faire une t.** to have one's hair dyed

2 *(produit)* dye; **t. pour coton** cotton dye; **tissu qui prend bien la t.** material that dyes well

3 *Pharm* tincture; **t. d'arnica** (tincture of) arnica; **t. d'iode** (tincture of) iodine

4 *Fig Littéraire (connaissance superficielle)* smattering; **avoir une vague t. d'allemand** to have a smattering of German; **elle a une t. d'histoire** she has a vague knowledge of history

teinturerie [tɛ̃tyrri] NF **1** *(activité)* dyeing **2** *(boutique)* dry cleaner's

teinturier, -ère [tɛ̃tyrje, -ɛr] NM,F **1** *(qui nettoie)* dry cleaner **2** *(qui colore)* dyer

téju [teʒy] NM *Zool* teju (lizard)

tek [tɛk] = **teck**

ADJ INDÉFINI such and such **A1** ■ such **A2, 3, 5, B3** ■ like **A4, B2** ■ so **A5, B3** ■ such as **B2**	
PRON INDÉFINI so-and-so **2**	

ADJ INDÉFINI A. *EMPLOYÉ SEUL* **1** *(avec une valeur indéterminée)* **t. jour, t. endroit, à telle heure** on such and such a day, at such and such a place, at such and such a time; **il m'a demandé de lui acheter t. et t. livres** he asked me to buy him such and such books; **pourrais-tu me conseiller t. ou t. plat?** could you recommend any particular dish?; **selon que telle ou telle méthode est choisie** depending on whether this or that method is chosen; **cela peut se produire dans telle ou telle circonstance** it can happen under certain circumstances

2 *(semblable)* such; **je n'ai rien dit de t.** I never said such a thing, I said nothing of the sort; **un t. homme peut être dangereux** a man like that can be dangerous; **tu ne retrouveras jamais une telle occasion** you'll never have such an opportunity *or* an opportunity like that again; **de telles gens sont rares** such people are few and far between; **pourquoi un t. aveu?** why this confession?; **comme t./telle** as such; **il était médecin et comme t.**, **il avait des passe-droits** he was a doctor and as such he enjoyed special rights and privileges; **il n'est pas avare, mais il passe pour t.** he's not mean, but people

think he is; **en tant que t.** as such; **elle est médecin, en tant que telle elle saura te conseiller** she's a doctor, as such she'll be able to advise you

3 (ainsi) **telle fut l'histoire qu'il nous raconta** such was the story he told us; **t. fut son langage** those were his/her words; **telle avait été sa vie, telle fut sa fin** as had been his/her life, such was his/her death; Hum **pourquoi ça? – parce que t. est mon bon plaisir!** and why is that? – because I say so!

4 (introduisant un exemple, une énumération, une comparaison) like; **des métaux tels le cuivre et le fer** metals such as copper and iron; **les révolutionnaires qui, t. Danton, croyaient à la démocratie** the revolutionaries who, like Danton, believed in democracy; **elle a filé t. l'éclair** she shot off like a bolt of lightning; **il allait et venait telle une bête en cage** he paced to and fro like a caged animal; **il pleurait, t. un enfant** he was crying like a child; Prov **t. père, t. fils** like father, like son; Ordinat **t. écran-t. écrit** WYSIWYG

5 (en intensif) such; **c'est un t. honneur pour nous...** it is such an honour for us...; **un t. génie/une telle gentillesse est rare** such a genius/such kindness is rare; **c'est un t. pianiste!** he's such a wonderful pianist!; **une telle insolence dépasse les bornes** such insolence is intolerable; **elle est d'une telle générosité!** she's so generous!; **c'est d'un t. ennui!** it's so boring!

B. EN CORRÉLATION AVEC "QUE" **1** (introduisant une comparaison) **il est t. que je l'ai toujours connu** he's just the same as when I knew him; **un homme t. que lui** a man like him; **la maison était telle qu'il l'avait décrite** the house was exactly how he had described it; **la clause telle qu'elle est** the clause as it stands; **voir les hommes/les choses tels qu'ils/telles qu'elles sont** to see men/things as they are; **telle que je la connais, elle va être en retard** knowing her, she's bound to be late; **telle que vous me voyez, je reviens de chez lui** I've just been to see him this very minute; **t. que tu me vois, je viens de décrocher un rôle** the person you see before you has just got a part; Fam **tu prends le lot t. que** take the batch as it is; Fam **il me l'a dit t. que!** he told me just like that!

2 (introduisant un exemple ou une énumération) **t. que** such as, like; **les fauves, tels que le lion et le tigre** big cats like or such as lions and tigers; **un philosophe t. que Descartes** a philosopher such as or like Descartes

3 (avec une valeur intensive) **son bonheur était t. qu'il ne pouvait y croire** he was so happy that he could hardly believe it; **la douleur fut telle que je faillis m'évanouir** the pain was so bad that I nearly fainted; **il a fait un t. bruit qu'il a réveillé toute la maisonnée** he made such a noise or so much noise that he woke the whole house up; **elle n'en a pas un besoin t. qu'il faille le lui rendre aujourd'hui** she doesn't need it so badly that we have to give it back to her today; **(il n'y a) rien de t. qu'un bon cigare** there's nothing like or you can't beat a good cigar; **il n'est rien de t. que d'être jeune** there's nothing like being young

PRON INDÉFINI **1** (désignant des personnes ou des choses non précisées) **t. ou t. vous dira que...** some people will tell you that...; **telle ou telle de ses idées aurait pu prévaloir** one or other of his/her ideas might have prevailed; **c'est en manœuvrant t. et t. qu'il a réussi à se faire élire** he managed to get himself elected by manipulating various people; Prov **t. est pris qui croyait prendre** it's the biter bitten; Prov **t. qui rit vendredi dimanche pleurera** = you can be laughing one day and crying the next

2 (en remplacement d'un nom propre) **a-t-il rencontré Un t.?** did he meet so-and-so?; **Une telle m'a dit que...** so-and-so told me that...

□ **tel quel, telle quelle** ADJ **tout est resté t. quel depuis son départ** everything is just as he/she left it; **il me l'a rendu t. quel** that's how he gave it back to me; **tu peux manger les huîtres telles quelles ou avec du citron** you can eat oysters on their own or with lemon; Presse **T.**

Quel = literary review which published articles by influential avant-garde writers and critics from 1960 to 1982

tél. (abrév écrite **téléphone**) tel

télamon [telamɔ̃] NM Archit telamon

télangiectasie [telɑ̃ʒjɛktazi] NF Méd telangiectasis, telangiectasia

Tel-Aviv [tɛlaviv] NM Tel Aviv; **T.-Jaffa** Tel Aviv-Jaffa

télé [tele] Fam NF (poste, émissions) TV, Br telly; **regarder la t.** to watch TV or Br the telly; **réaliser des documentaires pour la t.** to make TV documentaries or documentaries for TV; **travailler à la t.** to work in TV; **passer à la t.** (personne) to be or to appear on TV or Br the telly; **c'est passé à la t.** it was on TV or Br the telly; **il n'y a rien ce soir à la t.** there's nothing on TV or Br the telly tonight; Presse **T. 7 Jours** = weekly TV, radio and entertainments listings magazine
□ **de télé** ADJ (chaîne, émission) TV (avant n)

tèle [tɛl] NF Belg (terrine) dish

téléachat [teleaʃa] NM **1** (d'articles présentés à la télévision) teleshopping (where articles are offered on television and ordered by telephone or Minitel®) **2** (par l'Internet) on-line shopping; **ce nouveau logiciel améliore la sécurité des téléachats** this new software makes on-line shopping or on-line transactions safer

téléacheteur, -euse [teleaʃtœr, -øz] NM,F television shopper (who orders articles offered on television by telephone or Minitel®)

téléacteur, -trice [teleaktœr, -tris] NM,F telesalesperson

téléaffichage [teleafiʃaʒ] NM telecontrolled signboarding

téléalarme [telealarm] NF telemonitored alarm (system)

téléassistance [teleasistɑ̃s] NF Ordinat remote help

téléaste [teleast] NMF TV television producer

téléavertisseur [teleavɛrtisœr] NM Can pager

télébenne [telebɛn] NF cable car

Téléboutique® [telebutik] NF Br telephone shop, Am telephone store

télécabine [telekabin] NF **1** (cabine) cable car; **les skieurs montent en t.** skiers go up in a cable car **2** (installation) cableway

Télécarte® [telekart] NF phonecard

téléchargeable [teleʃarʒabl] ADJ Ordinat downloadable

téléchargement [teleʃarʒəmã] NM Ordinat downloading

télécharger [17] [teleʃarʒe] VT Ordinat to download; (vers un gros ordinateur) to upload

télécinéma [telesinema] NM **1** (procédé) telecine **2** (appareil) telecamera

télécommandable [telekɔmãdabl] ADJ **t. (à distance)** remote-controlled

télécommande [telekɔmãd] NF **1** (procédé, appareil) remote control; **t. à infrarouge** infra-red remote control; **t. universelle** universal remote control **2** (par radio) radio-control **3** Ordinat telecommand

télécommandé, -e [telekɔmãde] ADJ **1** Tech (engin, mise à feu) remote-controlled; **la porte du garage est télécommandée** the garage door is remote-controlled or works by remote control **2** Fig (ordonné de loin) masterminded or manipulated from afar

télécommander [3] [telekɔmãde] VT **1** (engin, mise à feu, télévision) to operate by remote control **2** Fig (ordonner de loin) to mastermind, to manipulate; **ces mouvements ont été télécommandés depuis l'Europe** these movements have been masterminded from Europe; **sa décision était télécommandée par des agents ennemis** his/her decision was dictated by enemy agents

télécommunication [telekɔmynikasjɔ̃] NF telecommunication; **les télécommunications** telecommunications

télécomposition [telekɔ̃pozisjɔ̃] NF Typ teletypesetting

télécoms [telekɔm] NFPL Fam **les t.** telecom, telecoms

téléconférence [telekɔ̃ferɑ̃s] NF **1** (procédé) teleconferencing **2** (conférence) teleconference

téléconseil [telekɔ̃sɛj] NM teleconsulting

téléconseiller, -ère [telekɔ̃seje, -jɛr] NM,F teleconsultant

télécopie [telekɔpi] NF fax; **envoyer qch par t.** to fax sth; **t. sur papier ordinaire** plain paper fax

télécopier [9] [telekɔpje] VT to fax

télécopieur [telekɔpjœr] NM fax (machine), Spéc facsimile machine

télécran [telekrɑ̃] NM large-sized television screen

tel écran-tel écrit [tɛlekrɑ̃tɛlekri] ADJ INV Ordinat WYSIWYG

télédémarchage [teledemarʃaʒ] NM Mktg telephone canvassing or prospecting

télédépannage [teledepanaʒ] NM Ordinat remote troubleshooting

télédétection [teledetɛksjɔ̃] NF remote sensing; **satellite de t.** spy satellite

télédiagnostic [teledjagnɔstik] NM telediagnosis

télédiffuser [3] [teledifyze] VT to broadcast (on television), to televise

télédiffuseur [teledifyzœr] NM television broadcaster

télédiffusion [teledifyzjɔ̃] NF televising, (television) broadcasting; **t. directe par satellite** direct broadcasting by satellite; **T. de France** = French broadcasting authority

télédistribution [teledistribysjɔ̃] NF cable television

téléécriture [teleekrityr] NF telewriting

téléenseignement, télé-enseignement [teleɑ̃sɛɲmɑ̃] (pl **télé-enseignements**) NM distance learning

Téléfax® [telefaks] NM fax (machine)

téléférique [teleferik] = **téléphérique**

téléfilm [telefilm] NM TV movie, movie made for television

téléga [telega] NF telega

télégénique [teleʒenik] ADJ telegenic; **être t.** to look good on television

télégestion [teleʒɛstjɔ̃] NF teleprocessing, telecomputing

télégramme [telegram] NM telegram, cable; **envoyer un t. à qn** to send a telegram to sb; **t. téléphoné** = telegram delivered over the phone, Br ≃ Telemessage®; Presse **le T. de Brest** = daily newspaper published in Morlaix

télégraphe [telegraf] NM telegraph

télégraphie [telegrafi] NF telegraphy; **t. optique** visual signalling; Vieilli **t. sans fil** (appareil) wireless; (procédé) wireless telegraphy

télégraphier [9] [telegrafje] VT to cable, to telegraph; **t. qch à qn** to cable sb sth

télégraphique [telegrafik] ADJ **1** Tél (poteau) telegraph (avant n); (message) telegraphic; **dépêche t.** telegram **2** Fig (en) langage ou style t. (in) telegraphic language or style

télégraphiquement [telegrafikmɑ̃] ADV by telegram, by cable, by wire

télégraphiste [telegrafist] NMF (technicien) telegrapher, telegraphist; Vieilli **(petit) t.** (porteur de dépêches) telegraph boy

télègue [telɛg] NF telega

téléguidage [telegidaʒ] NM radio control

téléguidé, -e [telegide] ADJ **1** (piloté à distance → avion) radio-controlled; **engin t.** guided missile **2** Fig (manipulé) manipulated; **sa décision était téléguidée** his/her decision was dictated by outside forces

téléguider [3] [telegide] VT **1** Tech (maquette) to control by radio **2** Fig (inspirer) to manipulate; **c'est lui qui a téléguidé la campagne de presse** he's the one who masterminded the press campaign from behind the scenes

téléimpression [teleɛ̃presjɔ̃] NF teleprinting

téléimprimeur [teleɛ̃primœr] NM teleprinter

téléinformatique [teleɛ̃fɔrmatik] NF teleprocessing

téléjournal, -aux [teleʒurnal, -o] NM Can television news

téléjournaliste [teleʒurnalist] NMF television journalist

télékinésie [telekinezi] NF telekinesis

télémaintenance [telemɛ̃tnɑ̃s] NF remote maintenance; Astron housekeeping; Ordinat remote access

télémanipulateur [telemanipylatœr] NM remote manipulator

Télémaque [telemak] NPR *Myth* Telemachus

télémarché [telemarʃe] NM telemarket

télémark [telemark] NM *Vieilli Ski* telemark

télémarketing [telemarkətiŋ] NM telemarketing

télématique [telematik] ADJ telematic; **par voie t.** using data comms (technology)
NF data communications, telematics *(singulier)*

télématiser [3] [telematize] VT to provide with telematic facilities
▶ **se télématiser** VPR to equip oneself with telematic facilities

télémédecine [telemedsin] NF telemedicine, remote medicine

télémercatique [telemɛrkatik] NF telemarketing

télémessage [telemesaʒ] NM *Tél* text message

télémessagerie [telemesaʒri] NF electronic messaging

télémesure [telemɔzyr] NF telemetry, telemetering

télémètre [telemɛtr] NM telemeter; *Mil & Phot* rangefinder

télémétrie [telemetri] NF telemetry; *Mil & Phot* range finding

télencéphale [telãsefal] NM telencephalon

télénomie [telenɔmi] NF *Phil* teleonomy

téléobjectif [teleɔbʒɛktif] NM telephoto (lens), long lens; **photographie au t.** telephotography

téléologie [teleɔlɔʒi] NF *Phil* teleology

téléologique [teleɔlɔʒik] ADJ teleological

téléonomie [teleɔnɔmi] NF *Phil* teleonomy

téléostéen [teleɔsteɛ̃] *Ich* NM teleost
❑ **téléostéens** NMPL Teleostei

télépaiement [telepɛmã] NM *(par téléphone)* telephone payment; *(par Internet)* electronic payment

télépathe [telepat] ADJ telepathic; *Hum* **je ne suis pas t.!** I'm not psychic!
NMF telepathist, telepath

télépathie [telepati] NF telepathy; **communiquer par t.** to communicate via telepathy

télépathique [telepatik] ADJ telepathic

télépéage [telepeaʒ] NM = toll system using electronic tagging of cars

téléphérage [teleferaʒ] NM *Tech* telpherage, overhead cable transport

téléphérique [teleferik] ADJ *Tech (câble)* telpher
NM *(dispositif, cabine)* cable car

téléphone [telefɔn] NM 1 *(instrument)* phone, telephone; **appeler qn au t.** to (tele)phone sb, to call sb; **repose le t.** put down the receiver; **t. à bâtiment-terre** ship to shore (tele)phone; **t. à carte** cardphone; **t. cellulaire** cellular phone, Cell-phone®; **t. de courtoisie** courtesy phone; **t. intelligent** smart phone; **t. intérieur** internal telephone; **t. Internet** Internet telephone; **t. à manivelle/sans fil/à touches** magneto/cordless/touch-tone telephone; **t. mobile** *Br* mobile phone, *Am* cellphone; **t. à pièces** payphone, coin-operated telephone; **t. portable** *ou* **portatif** *Br* mobile phone, *Am* cellphone; **t. public** public telephone, payphone; **le t. rouge** *(entre présidents)* the hot line; **t. de voiture** carphone; **t. WAP** WAP phone
2 *(installation)* phone, telephone; **il a/n'a pas le t.** *Br* he's/he isn't on the phone, *Am* he has a/has no phone; **j'ai demandé à avoir le t.** I asked to have a phone put in; **installer le t.** to connect the phone; **combien payes-tu de t. par mois?** what's your monthly phone bill?
3 *(service)* **le t. marche plutôt mal chez nous** we have a rather bad telephone service
4 *Fam (numéro)* (phone) number; **donne-moi ton t.** give me your phone number
❑ **au téléphone** ADV **parler à qn au t.** to speak to sb on the phone; **je suis au t.** I'm on the phone; **je l'ai eu au t.** I talked to him on the phone; **je ne peux pas te le dire au t.** I can't tell you over the phone
❑ **de téléphone** ADJ *(facture, numéro)* phone *(avant n)*, telephone *(avant n)*; **coup de t.** (tele)phone call; **donner** *ou* **passer un coup de t.** to make a phone call; **passer un coup de t. à qn** to phone sb, to give sb a call *or Br* a ring
❑ **par téléphone** ADV **il a réservé par t.** he phoned (in) his booking; **réservation possible par t.** phone booking available; **faites vos achats par t.** do your shopping by phone; **commander qch par t.** to order sth by phone

❑ **téléphone arabe** NM grapevine; **j'ai appris par le t. arabe qu'il était rentré** I heard on the grapevine that he was back

téléphoné, -e [telefɔne] ADJ 1 *Tél voir* **message, télégramme** 2 *Fam (prévisible)* predictable ■, obvious ■; **des gags téléphonés** jokes that you can see coming (a mile off); **c'était t.** you could see it coming (a mile off) 3 *Sport* **sa passe était téléphonée** he/she telegraphed his/her pass

téléphoner [3] [telefɔne] VI to make a phone call; **puis-je t.?** can I make a phone call?, may I use the phone?; **combien est-ce que ça coûte pour t. en Angleterre?** how much does it cost to call England?; **ne me dérangez pas quand je téléphone** please do not disturb me when I'm on the phone; **je passe tout mon temps à t.** I spend all my time on the phone; **t. à qn** to phone sb, to call sb
VT to phone; **je te téléphonerai tes résultats** I'll call and let you know your results, I'll call you with your results; **je te téléphonerai la nouvelle dès que je la connaîtrai** I'll phone and tell you the news as soon as I get it; **t. à qn de venir** to (tele)phone for sb; **elle m'a téléphoné de venir les rejoindre pour dîner** she called to ask me to join them for dinner
▶ **se téléphoner** VPR to call each other; **on se téléphone, d'accord?** I'll talk to you later, OK?

téléphonie [telefɔni] NF telephony; **t. fixe** landline services; **t. sans fil** wireless telephony, wireless services; **la t. mobile** *ou* **portable** mobile telephony, the mobile phone sector; **t. sur l'Internet** Internet telephony, Internet phone services

téléphonique [telefɔnik] ADJ *(message, ligne, réseau)* telephone *(avant n)*, phone *(avant n)*; **commande t.** order by telephone, telephone order; **nous avons eu un entretien t.** we had a discussion over the phone

téléphoniquement [telefɔnikmã] ADV by telephone

téléphoniste [telefɔnist] NMF *Br* telephonist, *Am* (telephone) operator

téléphotographie [telefɔtɔgrafi] NF 1 *Tél* phototelegraphy 2 *Phot* telephotography; *(cliché)* telephotograph

télépointage [telepwɛ̃taʒ] NM *Mil* = directing of gunfire by means of a director theodolite

téléport [telepɔr] NM teleport

téléportation [telepɔrtasjɔ̃] NF teleportation

téléporter [3] [telepɔrte] VT to teleport

télé-poubelle [telepubɛl] *(pl* **télé-poubelles***)* NF *Fam* trash television

téléprésence [teleprezãs] NF telepresence

téléprompteur [teleprɔ̃ptœr] NM Teleprompter®, *Br* Autocue®

téléprospecteur, -trice [teleprɔspɛktœr, -tris] NM,F telesalesperson

téléprospection [teleprɔspɛksjɔ̃] NF telemarketing, teleprospecting

téléprospectrice [teleprɔspɛktris] *voir* **téléprospecteur**

téléradar [teleradar] NM = combined use of radar and television

téléradio [teleradio], **téléradiographie** [teleradjɔgrafi] NF teleradiography

Télérama [telerama] NM = French weekly TV and entertainments magazine

télé-réalité, téléréalité [telerealite] NF *TV* reality TV

téléréglage [teleregglaʒ] NM remote control

téléreportage [telerəpɔrtaʒ] NM 1 *(émission)* television report 2 *(activité)* television reporting

téléreporter [telerəpɔrtɛr] NM television reporter

téléréunion [telereynjɔ̃] NF teleconference

téléroman [telerɔmã] NM *Can* TV series, soap opera

télescopage [teleskɔpaʒ] NM 1 *(de véhicules)* collision; *(de trains etc)* telescoping; **t. (en série)** *(de véhicules)* pile-up 2 *Fig (d'idées, de souvenirs)* intermingling 3 *Ling* telescoping, blending

télescope [teleskɔp] NM telescope; **t. coudé** coudé telescope; **t. électronique** electron telescope

télescoper [3] [teleskɔpe] VT *(véhicule)* to collide with, to crash into; *(train)* to crash into
▶ **se télescoper** VPR 1 *(véhicules, trains)* to concertina 2 *Fig (idées, souvenirs)* to intermingle

télescopique [teleskɔpik] ADJ *(antenne, volant)* telescopic

téléscripteur [teleskriptœr] NM teleprinter; *Bourse* ticker tape; **une nouvelle vient de tomber sur nos téléscripteurs** some news has just come through on our teleprinters

télésecrétariat [telesəkretarja] NM remote secretarial services

téléservice [teleservis] NM 1 *Ordinat* on-line service 2 *(fourni par un télétravailleur)* teleservicing

télésiège [telesjɛʒ] NM chair *or* ski lift; **on y monte en t.** you get there by chair lift, you take the chair lift up

télésignalisation [telesiɲalizasjɔ̃] NF telesignalling

téléski [teleski] NM drag lift, ski tow

télésouffleur [telesuflœr] NM Teleprompter®, *Br* Autocue®

téléspectateur, -trice [telespɛktatœr, -tris] NM,F television *or* TV viewer; **la majorité des téléspectateurs** the majority of viewers *or* of the viewing audience

télésurveillance [telesyrvɛjãs] NF (security) telemonitoring

Télétel® [teletɛl] NM = computerized information network available through Minitel®

Télétex® [teletɛks] NM teletex

télétexte [teletɛkst] NM teletext

téléthérapie [teleterapi] NF *Méd* teletherapy

téléthon [teletɔ̃] NM telethon

télétraitement [teletrɛtmã] NM teleprocessing

télétransmission [teletrãsmisjɔ̃] NF *(gén)* remote transmission; *(de données informatiques)* teletransmission

télétravail, -aux [teletravaj, -o] NM teleworking, telecommuting

télétravailleur, -euse [teletravajœr, -øz] NM,F teleworker

Télétype® [teletip] NM Teletype®

téleutospore [teløtɔspɔr] NF *Bot* teleutospore, teliospore

télévangéliste [televãʒelist] NMF televangelist

télévendeur, -euse [televãdœr, -øz] NM,F = specialist in selling goods on shopping channels

télévente [televãt] NF = selling goods on shopping channels *(where articles are offered on television and ordered by telephone or Minitel®)*

télé-vérité [televerite] NF *TV* reality TV

télévidéothèque [televideɔtɛk] NF *TV* = on-demand film service available through cable or digital TV

télévisé, -e [televize] ADJ *(discours, match)* televised

téléviser [3] [televize] VT to broadcast on television, to televise

téléviseur [televizœr] NM television *or* TV (set); **t. couleur** colour television (set); **t. à écran plat** flat-screen television (set); **t. grand écran** widescreen television (set); **t. numérique** digital television (set)

télévision [televizjɔ̃] NF 1 *(entreprise, système)* television; **il regarde trop la t.** he watches too much television; **les télévisions européennes** European television companies; **la t. à accès conditionnel** conditional access television; **t. à antenne maîtresse** Master Antenna Television, MATV; **t. câblée** *ou* **par câble** cable television; **t. à la carte** pay-per-view television; **t. en circuit fermé** closed circuit television; **t. (en) couleur** colour television; **t. cryptée** *Br* coded *or Am* scrambled television; **t. haute définition** high-definition TV, hi-def TV; **t. hertzienne** terrestrial television; **t. interactive** interactive television; **t. locale** local television; **t. du matin** breakfast television; **t. numérique** digital television; **t. numérique par satellite** digital satellite television; **t. numérique terrestre** digital terrestrial television; **t. ouverte** access broadcasting; **la t. à péage** pay-TV, pay television; **t. à plasma** plasma television; **t. par satellite** satellite television; **t. scolaire** schools *or* educational television, television for schools; **t. de service public** public television
2 *(appareil)* television; **allumer la t.** to turn the television on; **regarder la t.** to watch television
❑ **à la télévision** ADV on television *or* TV; **à la t. ce soir** *(annonce orale)* tonight on television; *(comme titre)* tonight's television; **passer à la t.** to go on television; **travailler à la t.** to work in television

télévision-réalité [televisjɔ̃realite] **NF** *TV* reality television

télévisuel, -elle [televizɥɛl] **ADJ** televisual

télex [telɛks] **NM** telex; **envoyer un t.** to (send a) telex; **envoyer qch par t.** to telex sth

télexer [4] [telɛkse] **VT** to telex

télexiste [telɛksist] **NMF** telex operator

tell [tɛl] **NM** *Archéol* tell

tellement [tɛlmɑ̃] **ADV 1** *(avec un adverbe, un adjectif) (si)* so; **c'est t. loin** it's so far; **il parle t. doucement** he speaks so softly; **elle en parle t. souvent** she talks about it so often; **je n'ai pas t. mal** it doesn't hurt that *or* so much; **il est t. têtu** he's so stubborn; **c'est t. facile** it's so (very) easy; **ce serait t. plus simple** it would be so much simpler; **c'est t. mieux comme ça** it's so much better like that; **tu es t. plus jolie quand tu souris!** you're so much prettier when you smile!; **ce ne sera pas t. pire** it won't be so much worse; **ce n'est pas t. beau** it's not all that beautiful

2 *(avec un verbe)* **il l'aime t.** he loves her so much; **j'ai t. pleuré!** I cried so much!

3 *(en corrélation avec "que")* **il est t. sourd qu'il faut crier** he is so deaf that you have to shout; **j'en ai t. rêvé que j'ai l'impression d'y être déjà allée** I've dreamt about it so much *or* so often that I feel I've been there already; **il en sait déjà t. que...** he knows so much about it that...; **elle n'est pas t. malade qu'elle ne puisse se lever** she's not so ill that she can't get up

4 *(introduisant la cause)* **personne ne l'invite plus t. il est ennuyeux** he's so boring (that) nobody invites him any more; **j'ai mal aux yeux t. j'ai lu** my eyes hurt from reading so much; **elle ne peut pas se lever t. elle est malade** she can't get up, she is so ill

5 *Fam (locutions)* **pas t.** not really; **je n'aime pas t. me presser** I don't really like to hurry; **ça te plaît? – pas t.** do you like it? – not very much *or* not really; **je n'ai pas t. envie de le revoir** I'm not all that keen on seeing him again; **plus t.** not really any more; **je n'aime plus t. ça** I don't really like that any more

❑ **tellement de DÉT 1** *(nombre)* so many; *(quantité)* so much; **j'ai t. de travail/de soucis en ce moment** I've got so much work/so many worries at the moment; **j'ai t. de choses à faire!** I've got so many things *or* so much to do!; **des jeunes au chômage, comme on en voit t. dans la rue** young people on the dole such as you often come across on the street

2 *(en corrélation avec "que")* **il y avait t. de bruit que l'on ne s'entendait plus** there was so much noise that we could no longer hear ourselves speak; **il y a t. d'hôtels que je ne sais lequel choisir** there are so many hotels that I don't know which one to choose

tellière [teljɛr] **ADJ** foolscap

NM foolscap (paper)

tellurate [telyrat] **NM** *Chim* tellurate

tellure [telyr] **NM** *Chim* tellurium

tellureux, -euse [telyrø, -øz] **ADJ** *Chim* tellurous

tellurhydrique [telyridrik] **ADJ** *Chim* **acide t.** hydrogen telluride, tellurated hydrogen

tellurien, -enne [telyrjɛ̃, -ɛn] **ADJ** tellurian

tellurique [telyrik] **ADJ** telluric; **courants telluriques** telluric currents

telluromètre [telyrɔmɛtr] **NM** tellurometer

tellurure [telyryr] **NM** *Chim* telluride

Telnet [tɛlnɛt] **NM** *Ordinat* Telnet

téloche [telɔʃ] **NF** *Fam* TV, *Br* telly

télolécithe [telɔlesit] **ADJ** *Biol* telolecithal

télomère [telɔmɛr] **NM** *Biol* telomere

télophase [telɔfɑz] **NF** *Biol* telophase

télougou [telugu] *Ling* **ADJ INV** Telugu

NM Telugu

telson [tɛlsɔ̃] **NM** *Zool* telson

tel-tel [tɛltɛl] **ADJ INV** *Ordinat* WYSIWYG

telugu [telugu] = **télougou**

témazépam [temazepam] **NM** *Pharm* temazepam

temenos [temenɔs] **NM** *Antiq* temenos

téméraire [temerɛr] **ADJ 1** *(imprudent → personne)* foolhardy, rash, reckless; **c'est un jeune homme t.** he is a foolhardy young man **2** *(aventuré → tentative)* rash, reckless; **l'entreprise est t., mais elle peut réussir** it's a reckless *or* foolhardy venture, but it may (just) succeed **3** *(fait à la légère)* rash; **voici une remarque bien t.** this is an extremely rash comment

témérairement [temerɛrmɑ̃] **ADV** *(imprudemment)* rashly, recklessly

témérité [temerite] **NF 1** *(hardiesse)* boldness, *Littéraire* temerity **2** *(imprudence → d'une initiative, d'une personne)* foolhardiness, recklessness; *(→ d'un jugement)* rashness

témoignage [temwaɲaʒ] **NM 1** *Jur (action de témoigner)* testimony, evidence; **porter t.** to give evidence; **porter t. en faveur de qn** to give evidence *or* to testify on sb's behalf; *Fig* **ce livre se contente de porter t. sur l'époque** the book is content to describe the era; **porter t. de qch** to bear witness to sth; **rendre t. de qch** to give evidence about sth; **recueillir des témoignages** to collect evidence; **les témoignages ont duré toute la journée** the hearing went on all day; **faux t.** perjury, false evidence, false witness; **faire un faux t.** to commit perjury, to give false evidence; **condamné pour faux t.** found guilty of perjury *or* of giving false evidence; **rendre t. à qch** *(rendre hommage)* to pay tribute to *or* to salute *or Sout* to hail sth; **je rends t. à son courage** I salute his courage; **rendre t. à qn** *(témoigner publiquement en sa faveur)* to testify in sb's favour; **la presse unanime a rendu t. au Premier ministre** all the newspapers came out in support of the Prime Minister

2 *(contenu des déclarations)* deposition, (piece of) evidence; **d'après** *ou* **selon son t.** according to his/her statement; **le t. du chauffeur de taxi est accablant pour elle** the taxi driver's statement is conclusive evidence against her; **un t. de bonne conduite** a statement of (good) character, a character reference; *Fig* **t. des sens** evidence of the senses

3 *(preuve)* gesture, expression, token; **un t. d'amitié** a token of friendship; **leur comportement est un t. vivant de leur foi** their conduct is a living expression of *or* a living testimony to their faith; **recevoir des témoignages de sympathie** *(après un deuil)* to receive messages of sympathy; *(pendant une épreuve)* to receive messages of support; **en t. de qch** as a token *or* sign of sth

4 *(récit → d'un participant, d'un observateur)* (eyewitness) account; **des témoignages sur les conditions de vie des paysans** accounts of the living conditions of peasants; **cette pièce sera un jour considérée comme un t. sur la vie des années 80** this play will one day be considered as an authentic account of life in the 80s

5 *Mktg (publicité)* testimonial advertising

témoigner [3] [temwaɲe] **VI** *Jur* to testify, to give evidence; **t. en faveur de/contre l'accusé** to give evidence for/against the defendant; **t. contre ses complices** *Br* to turn King's *or* Queen's evidence, *Am* to turn State's evidence; **t. par oral/écrit** to give oral/written evidence; **nous ferons t. la personne qui a filmé la scène** we'll get the person who filmed the scene to testify

VT 1 *Jur (certifier)* **t. que...** to testify that...; **j'irai t. que je ne l'ai pas vu ce soir-là** I'll go and testify that I didn't see him that night; **il a témoigné avoir passé la soirée avec l'accusé** he testified to spending the evening with the defendant

2 *(montrer → sympathie, dégoût, goût, intérêt)* to show, *Sout* to evince; **il ne m'a témoigné que du mépris** he showed me nothing but contempt; **sa réaction témoigne qu'il s'y attendait** his reaction shows *or* is proof that he was expecting it

❑ **témoigner de VT IND 1** *Jur* to testify to; **je suis prêt à t. de son innocence** I'm ready to testify *or* to swear to his/her innocence

2 *(indiquer → bonté, générosité, intérêt)* to show, to indicate; **cela témoigne de leur intérêt pour les problèmes sociaux** this shows their interest in social problems; **sa réponse témoigne d'une grande maturité** his/her answer shows great maturity

3 *(prouver)* to show, to bear witness *or* to testify to, *Sout* to attest; **le problème ne fait qu'empirer, comme en témoignent ces statistiques** the problem is only getting worse, witness these statistics *or* as these statistics show

témoin [temwɛ̃] **NM 1** *Jur (qui fait une déposition)* witness; **citer qn comme t.** to call sb as a witness; **il a été cité comme t.** he was called as a witness; **être entendu comme t.** to be a witness; **le t. est à vous** your witness; **t. assisté** = material witness who benefits from legal representation like the defendant, but who has not been formally charged; **t. auriculaire** ear witness; **t. à charge/décharge** witness for the prosecution/defence; **t. de fait** material witness; **t. instrumentaire** witness to a deed; **t. de mauvaise foi** untruthful witness; **t. de moralité** character reference; **t. oculaire** eyewitness; **faux t.** perjurer

2 *(à un mariage, à la signature d'un contrat)* witness; *(à un duel)* second; **il était t. au mariage de sa sœur** he was a witness at his sister's wedding; **c'est le t. du marié** he's the best man; **devant témoins** in front of witnesses

3 *(spectateur)* witness, eyewitness; **faire qch devant t.** to do sth before a witness; **l'accident s'est passé sans témoins** there were no witnesses to the accident; **ils se sont vus sans témoins** they saw each other in private, there were no witnesses present when they saw each other; **elle m'a arraché mon sac – vous avez des témoins?** she grabbed my bag – have you any witnesses?; **être t. de qch** to be witness to *or* to witness sth; **j'ai été un t. involontaire de leur dispute** I was an unwitting witness to their quarrel; **j'en suis t.** I'm a witness; **mes yeux en sont témoins** I saw it with my own eyes; **Stendhal, t. de son temps** Stendhal, a witness of his time; **prendre qn à t.** to call upon sb as a witness; **je vous prends tous à t. que...** I call on you all to witness that...; **Dieu/le ciel m'est t. que j'ai tout fait pour l'en empêcher** as God/heaven is my witness, I did all I could to stop him

4 *(preuve)* witness; **les témoins d'une civilisation perdue** the evidence of a lost civilization; **elle a bien mené sa carrière, t. sa réussite** she has managed her career well, her success is a testimony to that; **... t. les coups que j'ai reçus** ... witness the blows which I received

5 *(borne)* boundary mark

6 *Constr* (plaster) telltale

7 *Aut* **t. d'alerte de pression d'huile moteur** oil-pressure warning light; **t. d'allumage** ignition light; **t. de baisse du niveau d'essence** petrol-low warning light; **t. de charge** *ou* **de contrôle de la batterie** battery-charge warning light; **t. de frein parking** handbrake-on light

8 *Rel* **T. de Jéhovah** Jehovah's Witness

9 *Sport* baton; **passer le t.** to hand over *or* to pass the baton

10 *Can Ordinat* cookie

11 *(comme adj)* **appartements témoins** *Br* show flats, *Am* model apartments; **groupe/sujet t.** control group/subject; *Phot* **plaque** *ou* **épreuve t.** pilot print; **voici les bilans de quatre entreprises témoins** here are the balance sheets from four sample companies

tempe [tɑ̃p] **NF** temple; **un coup à la t.** a blow to the side of the head; **ses tempes commencent à grisonner** he's going grey at the temples

TEMPÉ [teɑɛmpe] **NM** *Bourse (abrév* **taux moyen pondéré en euros)** EONIA

tempera [tɑ̃pera] *Beaux-Arts* **NF** tempera

❑ **à tempera, à la tempera ADJ** *(peinture)* tempera *(avant n)* **ADV** *(peindre)* in tempera

tempérage [tɑ̃peraʒ] **NM** *(de chocolat)* tempering

tempérament [tɑ̃peramɑ̃] **NM 1** *(caractère)* temperament, disposition, nature; **ce n'est pas dans mon t.** it's not like me, it's not in my nature; **il est d'un t. plutôt anxieux** he's the worrying kind; **il est d'un t. plutôt instable** he's got a rather unstable character; **elle est violente de t., elle a un t. violent** she is of *or* has a violent disposition; **il a un t. de vendeur** he's commercially-minded; **elle a un t. d'artiste** she has an artistic temperament, she's of an artistic disposition

2 *(disposition physique)* temperament, constitution; **t. bilieux/sanguin** bilious/sanguine temperament; **t. lymphatique/nerveux** lymphatic/nervous disposition; *Fam* **s'abîmer** *ou* **s'esquinter** *ou très Fam* **se crever le t. à faire qch** to wreck one's health doing sth

3 *Fam (sensualité)* sexual nature■; **être d'un t. fougueux/exigeant** to be an ardent/a demanding lover■; *Euph* **il a du t.!** he's hot-blooded!

4 *Fam (forte personnalité)* strong-willed person■; **avoir du t.** to have character; **alors elle, c'est un t.!** she's a force to be reckoned with!

5 *Arch (modération)* moderation, restraint

6 *Mus* temperament; **t. égal/inégal** equal/unequal temperament

7 *Com* **vente** *ou* **achat à t.** hire purchase, *Am* installment plan; **acheter qch à t.** to buy sth on hire purchase *or Am* on the installment plan

❑ **par tempérament** ADV naturally, by nature; **plus musicien que son frère par t.** more musical than his brother by nature

tempérance [tɑ̃perɑ̃s] NF **1** *Rel* temperance **2** *(sobriété)* temperance, moderation; **société de t.** temperance society

tempérant, -e [tɑ̃perɑ̃, -ɑ̃t] ADJ temperate, sober

NM,F temperate person

température [tɑ̃peratyr] NF **1** *Méd & Physiol* temperature; **t. du corps humain** temperature of the human body, blood heat; *Fam* **avoir** *ou* **faire de la t.** to have a temperature; **prendre la t. de** *(patient)* to take the temperature of; *Fig (assemblée, public)* to gauge (the feelings of); **la méthode des températures** *(de contraception)* the rhythm method

2 *Météo* temperature; **il y eut une brusque chute de la t.** *ou* **des températures** there was a sudden drop in temperature; **on a atteint des températures de -17° C/40° C** temperatures went down to -17° C/reached 40° C

3 *(d'une pièce, d'une serre, d'un bain)* temperature; **avant d'aller nager, je prends la t. de l'eau** before going swimming, I test the water

4 *Phys* temperature; **t. absolue/critique/thermodynamique** absolute/critical/thermodynamic temperature; **t. d'ébullition** boiling point

tempéré, -e [tɑ̃pere] ADJ **1** *Géog (climat, région)* temperate **2** *Mus (gamme)* tempered

tempérer [18] [tɑ̃pere] VT **1** *Littéraire (température excessive)* to temper, to ease

2 *(atténuer → colère)* to soften, to appease; *(→ ardeurs, passion, sévérité)* to soften, to temper; *(→ enthousiasme)* to moderate; **tempère ton enthousiasme, je n'ai pas encore dit oui** don't get too excited, I haven't said yes yet

3 *(chocolat)* to temper

▸**se tempérer** VPR **1** *(se modérer)* to restrain oneself; **apprends à te t.** learn to restrain yourself

2 se t. de *(être mêlé de)* to be softened *or* tempered with; **sa colère se tempérait d'un peu de pitié** a hint of pity softened his/her anger

tempéreuse [tɑ̃perøz] NF *(machine)* temperer

tempête [tɑ̃pɛt] NF **1** *Météo* storm, *Littéraire* tempest; **le vent souffle en t.** it's blowing a gale, a gale force wind is blowing; **t.** *(sur un baromètre)* stormy; **t. magnétique** magnetic storm; **t. de neige** snowstorm; **t. de sable** sandstorm

2 *Fig (troubles)* storm; **son livre a provoqué une véritable t. dans les milieux politiques** his/her book caused quite a stir in political circles; **nous avons traversé la t.** we've managed to weather the storm; **une t. dans un verre d'eau** *Br* a storm in a teacup, *Am* a tempest in a teapot

3 *Fig (déferlement)* wave, tempest, storm; **t. d'applaudissements/de critiques/de protestations** storm of applause/criticism/protest; **t. d'insultes** hail of abuse; **nous avons eu droit à une t. d'insultes** insults rained down on us; **une t. de rires accueillait chaque réplique** each line unleashed gales of laughter

'La Tempête' *Shakespeare* 'The Tempest'

tempêter [4] [tɑ̃pete] VI to rage, to rant (and rave); **il a eu beau t., elle a maintenu son refus** despite his raging at her, she kept saying no; **ils ne cessent de t. contre les syndicats** they're always railing against the unions

tempétueux, -euse [tɑ̃petɥø, -øz] ADJ *Littéraire* **1** *(côte, mer)* tempestuous, stormy; *(courant)* turbulent **2** *Fig (amour, passion)* tempestuous, stormy; *(accueil)* boisterous, tempestuous; *(vie)* turbulent, stormy

temple [tɑ̃pl] NM **1** *Rel (gén)* temple; *(chez les protestants)* church; **le T.** *(ordre)* the Order of the Temple, the Knights Templar; *(à Paris)* = densely-populated district in the 3rd arrondissement of Paris, well known for the gardens and covered market built on the site of the old stronghold of the Knights Templar **2** *Fig (haut lieu)* temple; **le t. de la mode/musique** the Mecca of fashion/music

templier [tɑ̃plije] NM *Hist* (Knight) Templar

tempo [tɛmpo] NM **1** *Mus* tempo **2** *Fig (rythme → d'un film, d'un roman)* tempo, pace; *(→ de la vie)* pace

temporaire [tɑ̃pɔrɛr] ADJ **1** *(provisoire)* temporary; **c'est une employée t.** she's a temporary worker **2** *Mus* **valeur t. d'une note** time value of a note

temporairement [tɑ̃pɔrɛrmɑ̃] ADV temporarily

temporal, -e, -aux, -ales [tɑ̃pɔral, -o] *Anat* ADJ temporal

NM temporal bone

temporalité [tɑ̃pɔralite] NF *Littéraire* temporality, temporalness

temporel, -elle [tɑ̃pɔrɛl] ADJ **1** *Rel (autorité, pouvoir)* temporal; *(bonheur)* temporal, earthly; *(biens)* worldly, temporal **2** *(qui concerne le temps)* time **3** *Ling* temporal

temporellement [tɑ̃pɔrɛlmɑ̃] ADV temporally

temporisateur, -trice [tɑ̃pɔrizatœr, -tris] ADJ *(politique, tendance)* delaying, *Sout* temporizing; *(stratégie, tactique)* delaying

NM,F *Sout* temporizer; **c'est un t.** *(qui attend pour agir)* he doesn't make hasty decisions; *(qui fait traîner les choses)* he's always stalling *or* playing for time

NM **1** *Phys* retarder **2** *Ordinat* timer **3** *Élec* (automatic) time switch

temporisation [tɑ̃pɔrizasjɔ̃] NF **1** *(fait de retarder)* delaying tactics, *Sout* temporization **2** *Élec* delay time

temporisatrice [tɑ̃pɔrizatris] *voir* **temporisateur**

temporiser [3] [tɑ̃pɔrize] VI to use delaying tactics, *Sout* to temporize; **notre équipe devrait t. pour conserver son but d'avance** our team should now play for time to retain its one-goal lead

TEMPS [tɑ̃]

> **NM** weather **A** ▪ time **B1-7, B9, 10, 15, 16, 18** ▪ season **B7** ▪ stage **B8** ▪ tense **B11** ▪ stroke **B12** ▪ beat **B13**
> **NMPL** times

NM **A.** *CLIMAT* weather; **le t. s'améliorera lundi** there will be an improvement in the weather on Monday; **quel t. fait-il à Nîmes?** what's the weather like in Nîmes?; **avec le t. qu'il fait, par ce t.** in this weather; **vous sortez par un pareil t.** *ou* **par le t. qu'il fait!** you're going out in weather like this *or* in this weather!; **si le t. le permet** weather permitting; **demain, le t. sera variable** tomorrow, the weather will be changeable *or* unsettled; **vous nous amenez le beau/mauvais t.** you've brought the fine/bad weather with you; **il fait beau/mauvais t.** the weather's fine/bad; **il fait un t. gris** it's overcast, the weather's gloomy *or Br* dull; **par beau t.** *ou* **par t. clair, on voit la côte anglaise** when it's fine *or* on a clear day, you can see the English coast; **par t. humide** in wet weather; **par t. de pluie/neige/brouillard** in wet/snowy/foggy weather; **par t. froid** in cold weather, when it's cold; **par gros t.** in rough weather at sea, in rough seas; **par tous les t.** in all weathers

B. *DURÉE* **1** *(écoulement des jours)* **le t.** time; **la fuite** *ou* **course du t.** the passing of time; **comme le t. passe!, comme** *ou* **que le t. passe vite!** how time flies!; *Prov* **le t., c'est de l'argent** time is money; **le T.** Old Father Time

2 *(durée indéterminée)* time (UNCOUNT); **c'est du t. perdu** it's a waste of time; **nous avons gâché un t. précieux** we've wasted a lot of precious time; **mettre du t. à faire qch** to take time to do sth; **mettre du t. à se décider** to take a long time deciding *or* to decide; **je passe mon t. à lire** I spend (all) my time reading; **pour passer le t.** to while away *or* to pass the time; **prendre du t.** to take time; **cela ne m'a pas pris beaucoup de t. pour apprendre la chanson** it didn't take me long to learn the song; **chercher une maison prend beaucoup de t.** househunting is very time-consuming; **cela ne prendra pas beaucoup de t.** it won't take long; *Fam* **ça prendra le t. qu'il faudra** *ou* **que ça prendra** it'll take as long as is needed *or* as it takes; **pour passer le t.** to pass the time, to while away the time; **trouver le t. long,** *Belg* **avoir le t. long** to feel time dragging by; **je commençais à trouver le t. long** *(d'impatience)* I was growing impatient *or* restless; *(d'ennui)* I was getting bored; **un (certain) t., quelque t.** for a while, for a time; **après quelque t., au bout d'un certain t.** after a time; **pendant ce t.** meanwhile, in the meantime; **il y a peu de t.** not long ago, a little while ago, a short time ago; **peu de t. après** shortly *or* a short time *or* not long after; **d'ici quelque t.** soon, shortly, in a short while; **au bout de très peu de t.** in a very short space of time; **tout le t.** all the time; **il est tout le t. en train de se plaindre** he is constantly *or* he keeps complaining; **c'est ce que je lui dis tout le t.** that's what I keep telling him/her; *Belg* **tout un t.** quite a while, quite a long time; *Belg* **un petit t.** (for) a while

3 *(durée nécessaire)* time; **calculer le t. que met la lumière pour aller du Soleil à la Terre** to compute the time that light takes to go from the Sun to the Earth; **va chercher du lait, le t. que je fasse du thé** go and get some milk while I make some tea; **le t. de faire qch** (the) time to do sth; **je voudrais prendre un peu de t. pour y réfléchir** I'd like to have some time to think about it; **elle a pris/trouvé le t. de nous l'expliquer** she took/found the time to explain it to us; **donner à qn le t. de faire qch** to give sb time to do sth; **(donnez-moi) le t. de signer** *ou* **que je signe et je suis à vous** just give me time *or* a minute to sign this and I'll be with you; **laissez-lui le t. de répondre/de réfléchir** give him/her time to answer/to think; **le t. d'enfiler un manteau et j'arrive** just let me put on a coat and I'll be with you; **juste le t. de les entendre** just long enough to hear them; **avoir le t. de faire qch** to have (the) time to do sth; **nous n'avons pas le t. à présent** we don't have time *or* there's no time now; **je n'ai même pas eu le t. de lui dire au revoir** I didn't even have time to say goodbye to him/her; **auras-tu le t. de venir me chercher?** will you have time to come and collect me?; **elle voudrait venir te voir mais elle n'a pas le t.** she'd like to come and see you but she hasn't got (the) time; **fais-le quand tu en auras le t.** do it at your leisure *or* when you've got (the) time; **prendre (tout) son t.** to take one's time; **je dois étudier le dossier – prenez votre t.** I have to take a close look at the file – take your time (over it); *Ironique* **surtout prends ton t.!** take your time, won't you?, don't hurry, will you?; **prendre le t. de faire qch** to take the time to do sth; **prends le t. de manger** take the time to eat; **il faut prendre le t. de vivre** you should take time to enjoy life; *Culin* **t. de cuisson/préparation** cooking/preparation time; **un t. partiel** a part-time job; **un t. plein** *ou* **plein t.** a full-time job; **être** *ou* **travailler à t. partiel** to work part-time, to have a part-time job; **être** *ou* **travailler à plein t.** *ou* **à t. plein** to work full-time, to have a full-time job; **travailler à t. complet** to work full-time; **faire un trois quarts (de) t.** ≃ to work 30 hours per week; *Mktg* **t. d'accès au marché** time to market; *Phot* **t. de pose** exposure time; *Belg* **t. de midi** lunchtime; **t. de repos** break; *Psy* **t. de réaction** response latency, reaction time; **le t. de la réflexion** time to think; *Astron* **le t. de révolution d'une planète** the period of a planet's orbit; **diminuer le t. de travail** to shorten working hours

4 *(loisir)* time; **maintenant qu'elle est à la retraite, elle ne sait plus quoi faire de son t.** now that she's retired, she doesn't know how to fill her time; **les enfants prennent tout mon t.** the children take up all my time; **pour aller à la pêche, il trouve toujours le t.!** he can always find time to go fishing!; **avoir du t.** *ou* **le t.** to have time; **je n'ai pas beaucoup de/j'ai besoin d'un peu plus de t.** I haven't got much/I need a bit more time; **mon train est à 7 heures, j'ai grandement** *ou* **tout le t.** my train is at 7, I've plenty of time (to spare); **avoir tout son t.** to have all the time in the world; *Ironique* **ne nous pressons pas, on a tout notre t.!** couldn't you

go (just) a little bit slower?; **avoir du t. devant soi** to have time to spare *or* on one's hands; **t. libre** free time; **avoir du t. libre** to have some spare time

5 *(moment favorable)* **il est (grand) t.!** it's high time!, it's about time!; **la voilà – il était t.!** here she is – it's about time *or* and not a minute too soon *or* and about time too!; **il était t., le bol allait tomber** that was close, the bowl was about to fall; **il n'est plus t.** time's run out, it's too late; **je voulais tout recopier mais il n'est plus t.** I wanted to write it all out again but there's no time for that now; **cours vite prendre ton train, il n'est que t.** run and catch your train, there's not much time; **il est t. de** now's the time for; *Belg* **il devient t. de faire qch** it's time to do sth; **il est t. d'y penser** now's the time to think about it; **il n'est plus t. de discuter, il faut agir** the time for discussion is past *or* enough talking, we must act; **il est t. que tu t'inscrives** you'd better enrol soon, it's time you enrolled; **le t. est venu de nous ressaisir** it's time *or* the time has come for us to pull ourselves together; **le t. était venu pour moi de partir** the time had come for me to *or* it was time for me to leave

6 *(époque déterminée)* time; **le t. n'est plus aux querelles** we should put quarrels behind us, the time for quarrelling is past; **ce fut un grand homme dans son t.** he was a great man in his day *or* time; **elle a eu son t. de beauté** she was a beauty in her day; **du t. ou au t. de Napoléon** in Napoleon's time; **du t. de ma jeunesse, du t. où j'étais jeune** when I was young, in my youth; **il fut un t. où...** there was a time when...; **le t. n'est plus où...** gone are the days when...; **la plus grande découverte de notre t.** the biggest discovery of our time; **être en avance/en retard sur son t.** to be ahead of/behind one's time; **aller** *ou* **marcher avec son t.** to keep up *or* to move with the times; **être de son t., vivre avec son t.** to move with the times; **tu es bien de ton t., toi!** you really are a child of the times!; **il n'était pas de son t.** *(en retard)* he was out of step with his time; *(en avance)* he was ahead of his time; **dans mon jeune t.** when I was young, in my younger days; **un t.** for a (short) while; **j'ai cru, un t., que...** I thought, for a while, that...; **il y a un t. pour tout** there's a time for everything; **n'avoir** *ou* **ne durer qu'un t.** to last but a short time; **elle est fidèle – ça n'aura** *ou* **ne durera qu'un t.** she's faithful – it won't last; **cela ne durera qu'un t.** it won't last for ever; **un tel chagrin n'aura qu'un t.** such sorrow can't last (for ever); **tout n'a qu'un t.** everything must come to an end; **faire son t.** to do *or* to serve one's time; *(détenu)* to serve one's sentence; *Fam* **la cafetière/mon manteau a fait son t.** the coffee machine's/my coat's seen better days; **des idées qui ont fait leur t.** outmoded ideas; **les diligences ont fait leur t.** the days of stagecoaches are gone; **en t. normal** *ou* **ordinaire** usually, in normal circumstances; **en t. opportun** at an appropriate time, *Sout* in due season; **en t. voulu** in good time; **en t. utile** in due time *or* course; **en son t.** in due course; **chaque chose en son t.** there's a right time for everything; **le bon vieux t.** the good old days; **dans le t.** in the old days; *Arch* **au t. jadis** in times past, in days gone by; **de tout t.** always

7 *(saison, période de l'année)* time, season; **le t. des moissons** harvest (time); **le t. des cerises/pêches** the cherry/peach season

8 *(phase → d'une action, d'un mouvement)* stage; **faire un t. de galop** to gallop for a while; **l'épaulé-jeté s'exécute en trois t.** the clean and jerk is done in three stages *or* movements; **dans un premier t.** first; **dans un deuxième t.** secondly; **dans un troisième t.** thirdly

9 *Astron* **t. astronomique/sidéral** astronomical/sidereal time; **t. absolu** absolute time; **t. atomique international** international atomic time; **t. solaire** solar time, Greenwich Mean Time

10 *Jur* **t. civil/légal** civil/standard time

11 *Ling* tense; **t. composé/simple/du passé** compound/simple/past tense; **t. primitifs** *(d'un verbe)* principal parts

12 *Tech* stroke; **moteur à quatre t.** four-stroke

engine; *Aut* **t. compression** *(d'un moteur)* compression stroke; *Aut* **t. détente** *(d'un moteur)* power stroke; *Aut* **t. explosion** *(d'un moteur)* power stroke; **t. de fonctionnement** *(d'une machine)* running time; **t. d'immobilisation** *(d'une machine)* down time; *Aut* **t. d'immobilité du piston** piston dwell; **t. mort** *(d'une machine)* idle time *or* period, down time; *Aviat* **t. mort au sol** turn-round time; **t. moteur** engine *or* power *or* working stroke; *Ind* **étude des t. et ordonnancements** time and motion study; *Élec & Électron* **t. d'ouverture** on period; **t. moyen entre deux pannes** *(d'une machine)* mean time between failures, MTBF; *Aut* **t. de réaction** thinking distance; **t. à vide** *(d'une machine)* off-load period

13 *Mus* beat; **valse à trois t.** waltz in three-four time

14 *Rel* **le t. de l'avent/du carême** (the season of) Advent/Lent; **le t. pascal** Easter time, Eastertide

15 *Sport (d'une course)* time; *Escrime (durée → d'une action)* time, temps; *(→ d'un combat)* bout; **quel est son t. sur 100 mètres?** what's his/her time over 100 metres?; **elle a fait le meilleur t. aux essais** hers was the best time *or* she was the fastest in the trials

16 *Ordinat* **base de t.** time base; **t. d'accès** access time; **t. d'accès disque** disk access time; **t. d'adressage** address speed; **t. d'amorçage** start-up time; **t. d'attente** wait state; **t. critique** critical time; **en t. différé** off-line; **t. écoulé** elapsed time; **t. d'exécution** execution *or* execute time; **t. de libération** clearing time; **t. machine** machine time; **t. de montée** rise time; **t. partagé** time sharing; **utilisation** *(d'un ordinateur)* **en t. partagé** time sharing; **t. réel** real time; **horloge t. réel** real-time clock; **travailler en t. réel** to work in real time; **t. de rémanence** afterglow time; **t. de réponse** response time; **t. de retournement** turn-around time; **t. de sortie** output time; **t. total** elapsed time; **t. de traitement** processing time

17 *Com* **t. de cycle** business cycle

18 *Psy* **t. de latence** latent time

NMPL *(époque)* times, days; **les t. sont durs** *ou* **difficiles!** times are hard!; **les t. modernes/préhistoriques** modern/prehistoric times; **les t. anciens** ancient times *or* days; **signe des t.** sign of the times; **par les t. qui courent** in this day and age, these days, nowadays; **en d'autres t., je n'aurais pas hésité** once upon a time I wouldn't have hesitated; **ces t.-ci** these days

❑ **à temps** ADV in time; **se ressaisir à t.** to pull oneself together just in time; **ils m'ont fait payer le billet, je ne me suis pas décommandé à t.** I had to pay for the ticket since I didn't cancel it early enough; **je n'arriverai/je ne finirai jamais à t.!** I'll never make it/I'll never finish in time!

❑ **à temps perdu** ADV in one's spare time, in a spare moment

❑ **au même temps** = en même temps

❑ **au même temps que** = en même temps que

❑ **au temps de** PRÉP in *or* at the time of, in the days of; **au t. de Voltaire** in Voltaire's time *or* day; **au t. du cinéma muet** in the days of silent movies

❑ **au temps jadis** ADV in times past, in the old days

❑ **au temps où, au temps que** CONJ in the days when, at the time when

❑ **avec le temps** ADV with the passing of time; **avec le t., tout s'arrange** time is a great healer

❑ **ces temps-ci** ADV these days, lately; **il était malade ces t.-ci** he's been ill lately

❑ **dans ce temps-là** = en ce temps-là

❑ **dans le même temps** = en même temps

❑ **dans le même temps que** = en même temps que

❑ **dans le temps** ADV before, in the old days

❑ **dans les temps** ADV on time; **être dans les t.** *(pour un travail)* to be on schedule *or* time; *(pour une course)* to be within the time (limit); **vous devez finir dans les t.** you must finish on time

❑ **de temps à autre, de temps en temps** ADV from time to time, occasionally, (every) now and then

❑ **de temps immémorial** ADV from time immemorial

❑ **du temps de** PRÉP **du t. de Louis XIV** in the days of Louis the 14th; **du t. de notre père, tu n'aurais pas osé** when our father was (still) alive, you wouldn't have dared; **de mon t., ça n'existait pas** when I was young *or* in my day, there was no such thing

❑ **du temps où, du temps que** = au temps où

❑ **en ce temps-là** ADV at that time, then

❑ **en même temps** ADV at the same time; **en même t. mère et sœur** both mother and sister, mother and sister at the same time

❑ **en même temps que** CONJ at the same time as

❑ **en temps de** PRÉP **en t. de crise** in a crisis, at a time of crisis; **en t. de guerre/paix** in wartime/peacetime; **en t. de prospérité/récession** in times of prosperity/recession

❑ **en temps et lieu** ADV in due course *or* time, at the proper time and place

❑ **en un temps où** CONJ at a time when

❑ **par les temps qui courent** ADV *Fam* (things being as they are) these days *or* nowadays

❑ **tout le temps** ADV all the time, always; **elle est tout le t. là** she's always there, she's there all the time; **ne me harcèle pas tout le t.!** don't keep on pestering me!

❑ **temps fort** NM *Mus* strong beat; *Fig* high point, highlight; **les t. forts de l'actualité/de l'année 2001** the main points of the news/the main events of 2001; **un des t. forts du festival** one of the high points *or* highlights of the festival; **ce fut un des t. forts de ma vie/de la représentation** it was one of the high points of my life/of the performance

❑ **temps mort** NM **1** *Sport (au basket-ball et au volley-ball)* time-out

2 *Fig* lull, slack period; **pendant les t. morts** *(dans une période de travail)* when things are quiet; *(dans une conversation)* lull, pause

3 *Phys* time-out (interval)

'Les Temps modernes' Chaplin 'Modern Times'

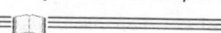

'Le Temps retrouvé' Proust 'Time Regained'

tenable [tənabl] ADJ **1** *(supportable)* bearable; **la situation n'est plus t., il faut agir** the situation's become untenable *or* unbearable, we must take action; **la chaleur/le froid est à peine t.** the heat/the cold is hardly bearable **2** *(contrôlable)* **à l'approche de Noël, les enfants ne sont plus tenables** as Christmas gets nearer, the children are going wild **3** *Mil (position)* tenable, defensible

tenace [tənas] ADJ **1** *(obstiné → travailleur)* tenacious, obstinate; *(→ chercheur)* tenacious, dogged; *(→ ennemi)* relentless; *(→ résistance, volonté)* tenacious; *(→ refus)* dogged; *(→ vendeur)* tenacious, insistent; **tu es t. toi!** you don't give up easily!

2 *(durable → fièvre, grippe, toux)* persistent, stubborn; *(→ douleur, souvenir, parfum)* persistent, lingering; *(→ tache)* stubborn; *(→ couleur)* fast; *(→ préjugé, impression, superstition)* deep-rooted, stubborn, tenacious; *(→ espoir)* stubborn, tenacious

tem-ten

3 *(qui adhère fortement* → *colle)* strong; *(→ plante, lierre)* clinging

tenacement [tənasmɑ̃] **ADV** tenaciously, persistently, stubbornly, doggedly

ténacité [tenasite] **NF 1** *(d'une personne, d'une volonté)* tenacity, tenaciousness; **avec t.** doggedly; **faire preuve de t.** to be persistent **2** *(d'une fièvre, d'une toux, d'une odeur, d'une douleur, d'un souvenir)* persistence; *(d'une tache)* stubbornness; *(d'un préjugé, d'une superstition)* deep-rootedness, persistence **3** *Tech* resilience

tenaille [tənɑj] **NF 1** *(de charpentier, de menuisier)* pincers; *(de cordonnier)* pincers, nippers; *(de forgeron)* tongs; **t. à vis** hand vice **2** *(fortification)* tenaille

❑ **en tenaille, en tenailles ADV prendre qn en t.** *ou* **tenailles** to catch *or* to trap sb in a pincer movement

tenaillement [tənɑjmɑ̃] **NM** *Littéraire (du doute, du remords)* tormenting, gnawing, nagging

tenailler [3] [tənɑje] **VT 1** *(faim, soif)* to gnaw; *(doute, inquiétude, remords)* to gnaw (at), to rack, to torment; *(douleur)* to grip; **tenaillé par la faim** to be racked with hunger; **être tenaillé par le remords** to be tormented by remorse; **être tenaillé par la douleur** to be gripped with pain **2** *Hist* to torture

tenancier, -ère [tənɑ̃sje, -ɛr] **NM,F 1** *(d'un café, d'un hôtel, d'une maison de jeu)* manager; *(d'une maison close)* keeper **2** *(fermier)* tenant farmer **3** *Hist* (feudal) tenant

tenant, -e [tənɑ̃, -ɑ̃t] **ADJ chemise à col t.** shirt with a collar attached

NM,F *Sport* **t. (du titre)** holder, titleholder

NM 1 *(d'une doctrine, d'une idéologie, d'un principe)* supporter, upholder **2** *Hér* supporter

❑ **tenants NMPL** *(d'une terre)* adjacent parts, *Jur* abuttals; **les tenants et les aboutissants** *(d'une affaire)* the ins and outs, the full details; **je suis seul à connaître les tenants et les aboutissants de leur accord** only I know all the ins and outs of their agreement

❑ **d'un (seul) tenant ADJ** all in one block; **trois hectares d'un seul t.** three adjoining hectares

tendance [tɑ̃dɑ̃s] **NF 1** *(disposition, propension)* tendency, propensity, leaning; **avoir t. à** to tend to, to have a tendency to; **ayant t. à l'autoritarisme** tending towards authoritarianism; **elle a t. à se laisser aller** she has a tendency *or* she's inclined to let herself go; **tu as un peu trop t. à croire que tout t'est dû** you're too inclined to think that the world owes you a living; **avoir t. à s'enrhumer facilement** to be prone to catching colds

2 *(orientation, évolution* → *gén)* trend; *(→ d'un créateur)* leanings; *(→ d'un livre, d'un discours)* drift, tenor; **les nouvelles tendances de l'art/la mode** the new trends in art/fashion; **tendances de l'automne** *(mode)* the autumn fashions

3 *(position, opinion)* allegiance, leaning, sympathy; **un parti de t. libérale** a party with liberal tendencies; **la t. centriste au sein du parti** the middle-of-the-road tendency within the party; **des partis de toutes tendances étaient représentés** the whole spectrum of political opinion was represented; **le groupe a décidé, toutes tendances réunies** *ou* **confondues, de voter l'amendement** all the factions within the group voted in favour of supporting the amendment; **à quelle t. appartiens-tu?** what are your political leanings?, where do your (political) sympathies lie?

4 *Bourse & Écon* trend; **une t. baissière** *ou* **à la baisse** a downward trend, a downswing; *Bourse* a bearish tendency; **tendances conjoncturelles** economic trends; **tendances de la consommation** consumer trends; **t. de croissance** growth trend; **t. de l'économie, t. économique** economic trend; **t. générale à la hausse/baisse** general upward/downward trend; **une t. haussière** *ou* **à la hausse** an upward trend, an upswing; *Bourse* a bullish tendency; **t. inflationniste** inflationary trend; **t. du marché** market trend; **quelle est la t. du marché?** what's the market trend?

5 *Psy* tendency; **tendances affectives/vitales** affective/vital tendencies

6 *(résultat d'une étude)* trend; **t. générale** (general) trend

7 *(comme adj) Fam (à la mode)* trendy

tendanceur [tɑ̃dɑ̃sœr] **NM** *Mktg* trendspotter

tendanciel, -elle [tɑ̃dɑ̃sjɛl] **ADJ une évolution tendancielle** a trend-setting development

tendancieuse [tɑ̃dɑ̃sjøz] *voir* **tendancieux**

tendancieusement [tɑ̃dɑ̃sjøzmɑ̃] **ADV** tendentiously, tendenciously

tendancieux, -euse [tɑ̃dɑ̃sjø, -øz] **ADJ** *(film, récit, interprétation)* tendentious, tendencious; *(question)* loaded

tendelle [tɑ̃dɛl] **NF** *Chasse* thrush snare

tender [tɑ̃dɛr] **NM** *Pétr & Rail* tender

tenderie [tɑ̃dri] **NF** *Chasse (pièges)* bird traps and snares

tendeur [tɑ̃dœr] **NM 1** *(pour tendre* → *câble)* tensioner; *(→ toile de tente)* guy rope; *(→ chaîne de bicyclette)* chain adjuster; *(de machine à coudre)* tension (device); *(pour chaussure)* shoe tree; *Aut* **t. de courroie** belt tensioner; **t. de sangle** belt tensioner; **t. à vis** turnbuckle

2 *(courroie élastique)* bungee (cord); *(pour porte-bagages)* luggage strap

3 *Rail* **t. d'attelage** coupling screw

tendineux, -euse [tɑ̃dinø, -øz] **ADJ 1** *Anat* tendinous **2** *(viande)* stringy

tendinite [tɑ̃dinit] **NF** *Méd* tendinitis

tendoir [tɑ̃dwar] **NM** *Tex* drying-pole

tendon [tɑ̃dɔ̃] **NM** tendon, sinew; **t. d'Achille** Achilles' tendon

tendre[1] [tɑ̃dr] **ADJ 1** *(aimant* → *personne)* loving, gentle, tender; *(→ voix)* gentle; *(→ yeux)* gentle, loving; *(→ regard, geste)* loving, affectionate, tender; *(affectueux* → *lettre)* loving, affectionate; **chanson t.** love song; **il n'a jamais un geste t. envers sa femme** he never shows his wife any affection; **elle n'est pas t. avec lui** she's hard on him; **les critiques n'ont pas été tendres pour son film** the reviewers were very hard on his/her movie *or Br* film; **la presse n'est pas t. pour elle ce matin** she's been given a rough ride in the papers this morning; **dire à qn des mots tendres** to say tender *or* loving things to sb; **avoir le cœur t.** to be soft-hearted; **il a le vin t.** drink makes him sentimental

2 *(moelleux* → *viande, légumes)* tender; **je voudrais quatre steaks bien tendres** I'd like four nice tender steaks; **t. comme la rosée** (as) fresh as the morning dew

3 *(mou* → *roche, mine de crayon, métal)* soft; **bois t.** softwood

4 *Littéraire (délicat* → *feuillage, bourgeons)* tender, delicate; *(→ herbe)* soft; **de tendres boutons de rose** tender rosebuds

5 *(doux* → *teinte)* soft, delicate; **un tissu rose/vert t.** a soft pink/green material

6 *(jeune)* early; **nos tendres années** our early years; **âge t., t. enfance** early childhood; **dès sa plus t. enfance** since his/her earliest childhood

NMF softhearted person; **c'est un t.** he's softhearted

NM 1 *Arch* **avoir un t. pour qn** to have a soft spot for sb

2 *Culin* **t. de tranche** topside (of beef)

❑ **Tendre NM** *Littérature* **la Carte du T.** the Map of the Human Heart, the Map of the Land of Love

TENDRE[2] [73] [tɑ̃dr]

VT to tighten **1** ■ to tauten **1** ■ to stretch **1** ■ to hang **2** ■ to cover **3** ■ to tense **4** ■ to stretch out **4** ■ to hold out **4, 5** ■ to offer **5**
VPR to tighten **1** ■ to tauten **1** ■ to stretch out **2** ■ to become strained **3**

VT 1 *(étirer* → *câble, corde de raquette, de violon)* to tighten, to tauten; *(→ élastique, ressort)* to stretch; *(→ corde d'arc)* to draw back; *(→ arc)* to bend; *(→ arbalète)* to arm; *(→ peau d'un tambour)* to pull, to stretch; **t. fortement une corde** to strain a rope

2 *(disposer* → *hamac, fil à linge, tapisserie)* to hang; *(→ voile)* to spread; *(→ collet, souricière)* to set (**à** for); **ils ont tendu une corde en travers de la route** they stretched *or* tied a rope across the road; **t. des lignes** to put out (fishing) lines; **t. une embuscade** *ou* **un piège à qn** to set an ambush *or* a trap for sb; **t. ses filets** to set one's nets; *Fig* to set a trap

3 *(revêtir* → *mur)* to cover; **t. une pièce de toile de jute** to cover the walls of a room with *or* in hessian; **les murs étaient tendus de papier peint à fleurs** there was flowered paper on the walls

4 *(allonger* → *muscles)* to tense; *(→ bras, jambe)* to stretch out, to hold out; **t. le cou** to crane *or* to stretch one's neck; **il tendit un doigt accusateur vers l'enfant** he pointed an accusing finger at the child; **elle tendit son front/sa joue à sa mère pour qu'elle l'embrasse** she offered her forehead/her cheek for her mother to kiss; **t. les bras** *(en signe de bienvenue)* to stretch one's arms wide, to throw one's arms out; **t. les bras vers qn** to stretch out one's arms towards sb; **il m'a tendu les bras en signe de pardon** he held out his arms to me in forgiveness; **assieds-toi, il y a un fauteuil qui te tend les bras** sit down, there's an armchair waiting for you; **vas-y, le poste de directeur te tend les bras** go ahead, the director's job is yours for the taking; **t. la main** *(pour recevoir quelque chose)* to hold out one's hand; *(mendier)* to beg; **t. la main à qn** *(pour dire bonjour)* to hold out one's hand to sb; *(pour aider)* to offer a helping hand to sb; *(pour se réconcilier)* to extend a *or* the hand of friendship to sb; **t. l'autre joue** to turn the other cheek; **tout ce qu'il sait faire, c'est t. le dos** all he does (in time of trouble) is to lie back and take it all

5 *(offrir)* to offer; *(présenter)* to hold out; **t. qch à qn** *(offrir)* to offer sth to sb *or* sb sth; *(présenter)* to hold sth out to sb; **il lui tendit la boîte de chocolats/un miroir** he offered him/her the box of chocolates/held out the mirror to him/her; **elle tendit une pomme à l'enfant** she offered the child an apple

6 *(concentrer)* **t. sa volonté vers la réussite** to strive for success; **t. ses efforts vers un but** to strive to achieve an aim

❑ **tendre à VT IND 1** *(avoir tendance à)* **c'est une pratique qui tend à disparaître** it's a custom which is dying out; **les douleurs tendent à disparaître** the pain is starting to go

2 *(contribuer à)* **cela tendrait à prouver que j'ai raison** this would seem to prove that I'm right

3 *(viser à)* **t. à la perfection** to aim for perfection; **t. à un idéal** to aim at an ideal

4 *(arriver à)* **t. à sa fin** to near an end; **la période de crise tend à sa fin** the end of the crisis is in sight, the crisis is nearing its end

❑ **tendre vers VT IND 1** *(viser à)* **t. vers la perfection** to aim for perfection, to strive towards perfection

2 *(approcher de)* **le rythme de la production tend vers son maximum** maximum output is close to being reached

3 *Math* **t. vers zéro/l'infini** to tend to zero/infinity

▸**se tendre VPR 1** *(courroie, câble)* to tighten (up), to become taut, to tauten

2 *(main)* to stretch out; **pas une main ne s'est tendue vers moi** not a hand was stretched out towards me

3 *Fig (atmosphère, relations)* to become strained

tendrement [tɑ̃drəmɑ̃] **ADV** *(embrasser, regarder, sourire)* tenderly, lovingly; **ils s'aiment t.** they love each other dearly

tendresse [tɑ̃drɛs] **NF 1** *(attachement* → *d'un amant)* tenderness; *(→ d'un parent)* affection, tenderness; **t. maternelle** maternal affection *or* love; **une enfance sans t.** a childhood deprived of affection, a loveless childhood; **avec t.** tenderly; **aimer qn avec t.** to feel great affection for sb; **avoir de la t. pour qn** to feel affection for sb

2 *(inclination, penchant)* **je n'ai aucune t. pour les menteurs** I have no love for liars, I don't think much of liars; **avoir des tendresses royalistes** to have royalist sympathies

❑ **tendresses NFPL** *(témoignages d'affection)* **se dire des tendresses** to exchange sweet nothings; **je vous envoie mille tendresses ainsi qu'aux enfants** much love to you and to the children

tendreté [tɑ̃drəte] **NF** *(d'un légume, d'une viande)* tenderness

tendron [tɑ̃drɔ̃] **NM 1** *Culin* **t. de veau** middle-cut

breast of veal **2** *Bot* shoot **3** *Fam (jeune fille)* **un t.** a slip of a girl

tendu, -e [tɑ̃dy] PP *voir* **tendre**

ADJ **1** *(nerveux → de tempérament)* tense; *(→ dans une situation)* tense, strained, fraught; *(→ avant un événement, un match)* keyed up, tense; **elle est très tendue nerveusement** she's very tense, she's under a lot of strain; **"jamais", dit-il d'une voix tendue** ''never,'' he said in a strained voice

2 *(atmosphère)* strained; *(rapports)* strained, *Br* fraught; *(situation, climat politique)* tense, *Br* fraught

3 *(partie du corps, muscle)* tensed up; *(visage)* strained; **avoir les nerfs tendus** *(habituellement)* to be tense; *(momentanément)* to be tense or on edge

4 *(étiré → corde, courroie)* tight, taut; *(→ corde d'arc)* drawn; *(→ arc)* drawn, bent; *(→ voile, peau de tambour)* stretched; *Sport (tir)* straight; **la chaîne est mal tendue** *ou* **n'est pas assez tendue** the chain isn't tight enough *or* is a bit slack; **ma raquette de tennis est trop tendue/ n'est pas assez tendue** my tennis racket strings are too tight/too slack; *Bourse* **prix tendus** hard *or* firm prices

5 *(allongé)* **avancer le doigt t./le poing t./les bras tendus** to advance with pointed finger/ raised fist/outstretched arms; **il est venu la main tendue** he came with his hand held out

6 *Ling* tense

7 *(tapissé)* **t. de** *(tapisseries, tissu)* hung with; *(papier peint)* covered with

Tène [tɛn] NF *Archéol* **La T.** the La Tène (period)

ténèbres [tenɛbr] NFPL **1** *(nuit, obscurité)* darkness *(UNCOUNT)*, dark *(UNCOUNT)*; **être plongé dans les t.** to be in total darkness; **les t. de la nuit** the darkness of the night; **dans les t. de la mort** in the shades of death **2** *Fig (de l'ignorance, de l'inconscient)* depths; **les t. de la superstition** the dark age of superstition **3** *Rel* Tenebrae

ténébreux, -euse [tenebrø, -øz] ADJ *Littéraire* **1** *(forêt, maison, pièce)* dark, gloomy, tenebrous; *(recoin, cachot)* dark, murky

2 *(inquiétant → intrigue, complot)* dark; *(→ époque, situation)* obscure, murky; **une ténébreuse affaire** a murky *or* obscure affair; **de t. projets** devious plans

3 *(incompréhensible)* mysterious, unfathomable; **une ténébreuse affaire** a shady business; **le t. langage de la loi** the obscure language of the legal profession

4 *(personne, caractère)* melancholic, *Littéraire* saturnine

5 *Rel* **l'Ange t.** the dark angel, the devil; **le t. séjour** the shades, the realm of the dead

NM,F **1** *Littéraire (personne mélancolique)* melancholic

2 *Hum* **un beau t.** a tall, dark, handsome stranger

'**Une ténébreuse affaire**' *Balzac* 'A Murky Business'

ténébrion [tenebrijɔ̃] NM *Entom* tenebrio, mealworm

ténébrisme [tenebrism] NM *Beaux-Arts* tenebrism

tènement [tɛnmɑ̃] NM **1** *Hist* holding **2** *(copropriété)* jointly-owned property

Tenerife, Ténériffe [tenerif] NF Tenerife

ténesme [tenɛsm] NM *Méd* tenesmus

teneur[1] [tənœr] NF **1** *(contenu → d'un document)* content; *(→ d'un traité)* terms; **quelle est exactement la t. de son article?** what exactly is his/ her article about?; **je vais vous résumer la t. de ses propos** I'll give you the general tenor *or* gist of what he/she said; **la t. du marché** the market trend *or* maker

2 *Chim* content; **t. en eau/fer** water/iron content; **t. en alcool** alcohol content, alcoholic strength

3 *Mines* content, grade, tenor; **t. en carbone** percentage of carbon, carbon content; **minerai à faible/forte t. en plomb** ore with a low/high lead content

4 *Nucl* **t. isotopique** abundance ratio, isotopic abundance

teneur[2], **-euse** [tənœr, -øz] NM,F **1** *Com* **t. de livres**

bookkeeper **2** *Typ* **t. de copie** copyholder **3** *Bourse* **t. de marché** market maker

ténia [tenja] NM tapeworm, *Spéc* taenia

ténicide [tenisid] *Méd* ADJ taeniacide

NM taeniacide

ténifuge [tenifyʒ] *Méd* ADJ **médicament t.** taeniafuge

NM taeniafuge

TENIR [40] [tənir]

VT ■ to hold **A, B1, 2, D1, 3, E2, G** ■ to keep **B1, 3, C5, D2** ■ to get **C1** ■ to have caught **C2** ■ to have **C3, D3-5** ■ to control **D1** ■ to run **D2** ■ to give **D4** ■ to play **D5** ■ to take up **E1, F2** ■ to take **F1** ■ to keep to **F2** ■ to consider **G**

VI ■ to hold **1, 4** ■ to last **2, 3** ■ to hold out **2, 3** ■ to stand **4** ■ to fit **5**

VPR ■ to take place **2** ■ to hold on **4** ■ to stand **5** ■ to sit **5** ■ to behave **6** ■ to hold together **7**

VT **A.** *AVOIR DANS LES MAINS* **1** *(retenir)* to hold (on to); **t. la main de qn** to hold sb's hand; **il tenait sa casquette sous le bras** he was holding his cap under his arm; **tiens mon sac deux minutes** can you hold my bag for a moment?; **tiens bien le livre** hold on tight to the book; **je tenais mal la bouteille et elle m'a échappé** I wasn't holding the bottle tightly enough and it slipped

2 *(manier)* to hold; **tu tiens mal ta raquette/ ton arc** you're not holding your racket/your bow properly; **tiens mieux ton verre/pinceau** hold your glass/brush properly; **apprendre à t. le ciseau** to learn the correct way to hold a chisel; **tenez la lime horizontale** hold the file flat *or* horizontal *or* horizontally; **tenez la bouteille verticale** hold the bottle upright *or* vertical *or* vertically

B. *CONSERVER* **1** *(maintenir → dans une position)* to hold, to keep; *(→ dans un état)* to keep; **enlève les vis qui tiennent le panneau** undo the screws which hold the panel in place; **l'amarre qui tient le bateau** the cable tying up the boat; **tiens-lui la porte, il est chargé** hold the door open for him, he's got his hands full; **il tenait les yeux baissés** he kept his eyes lowered; **cette étoffe ne tient pas le pli** this material won't hold its crease; **tenez-lui la tête hors de l'eau** hold his/her head above the water; **t. les fenêtres fermées/ouvertes** to keep the windows shut/open; **elle tient ses chiens attachés** she keeps her dogs tied up; **t. chaud** to keep warm; **je veux une robe qui tienne chaud** I'd like a warm dress; **t. un plat au chaud** to keep a dish hot; **tenez le bois au sec** keep the wood in a dry place; **t. une chambre en ordre** to keep a room tidy; **tenez-le prêt (à partir)** make sure he's ready (to leave); **ils tiennent le pont sous le feu de leurs mitraillettes** they're keeping the bridge under machine-gun fire

2 *(garder → note)* to hold; **t. l'accord** to stay in tune; **tenez votre droite** *(panneau sur la route)* keep (to the) right; *(sur un escalator)* keep to the right

3 *Vieilli (conserver → dans un lieu)* to keep; **où tenait-il les bijoux?** where did he keep the jewels?; **dans nos nouveaux locaux, nous tenons une plus grande sélection d'articles** we keep a larger selection of goods on our new premises

4 *Belg (collectionner)* to collect

C. *POSSÉDER* **1** *(avoir reçu)* **t. qch de qn** *(par hérédité)* to get sth from sb; **je tiens mes yeux bleus de mon père** I get my blue eyes from my father; **une passion pour les affaires qu'elle tient de famille** a taste for business which she inherited from her family; **les propriétés que je tenais de ma mère** *(par héritage)* the properties I'd inherited from my mother

2 *(avoir capturé)* to have caught, to have got hold of; *(avoir à sa merci)* to have got; **nous tenons son chien, qu'il vienne le chercher** we've got his dog, let him come and fetch it; **je tiens une truite!** I've caught *or* I've got a trout!; **c'est un cul-de-sac, nous le tenons** it's a dead end, he's trapped *or* we've got him; **ah, ah, petit**

coquin, je te tiens! got you, you little devil!; **si je tenais celui qui a défoncé ma portière!** just let me get *or* lay my hands on whoever smashed in my car door!; **la police tient un des coupables** the police have caught one of the culprits; **vous avez trouvé un nouveau collaborateur? – oui, je tiens mon homme** have you found a new assistant? – yes, I've found the very man; **elle m'a tenu une heure avec ses histoires de divorce** I had to listen to her going on about her divorce for a whole hour; **pendant que je vous tiens (au téléphone), pourrais-je vous demander un service?** since I'm speaking to you (on the phone), may I ask you a favour?

3 *(détenir → indice, information, preuve)* to have; *(→ contrat)* to have, to have won; *(→ réponse, solution)* to have found *or* got; **ça y est, je tiens la solution!** hurrah, I've found *or* got the answer!; **je crois que je tiens un scoop!** I think I've got a scoop!; **je tiens enfin l'édition originale** I've finally got my hands on the original edition; **t. qch de** *(l'apprendre)* to have (got) sth from; *(le tirer de)* to derive sth from; **il a eu des troubles psychologiques – de qui tenez-vous cela?** he's had psychological problems – who told you that?; **nous tenons de source sûre/soviétique que...** we have it on good authority/we hear from Soviet sources that...; **je tiens mon autorité de l'État** I derive my power from the state; *Fam* **qu'est-ce que je tiens comme rhume!** I've got a horrible *or Br* stinking cold!; *Fam* **elle en tient une couche!** *Br* she's as thick as two short planks!, *Am* she's got rocks in her head!; *Fam* **il en tient une bonne ce soir** he's three sheets to the wind *or Br* he's had a skinful tonight; *Fam* **t. une bonne cuite** *(être ivre)* to be totally wasted *or Br* legless

4 *(transmettre)* **nous vous ferons t. une copie des documents** we will make sure you receive a copy of the documents; **faites-le-lui t. en mains propres** make sure it's handed to him/ her personally

5 *Belg (élever → volaille, animaux)* to keep

D. *CONTRÔLER, AVOIR LA RESPONSABILITÉ DE* **1** *(avoir prise sur, dominer)* to hold; *Mil* to control; *(avoir de l'autorité sur → classe, élève)* to (keep under) control; **quand la colère le tient, il peut être dangereux** he can be dangerous when he's angry; **la jalousie le tenait** jealousy had him in its grip, he was gripped by jealousy; **ce rhume me tient depuis deux semaines** I've had this cold for two weeks; **les Anglais tenaient la mer** the English ruled the seas; **qui tient la presse tient le pays** whoever controls the press controls the country; **quand Noël approche, on ne peut plus les t.** when Christmas is near, you just can't control them

2 *(diriger, s'occuper de → commerce, maison, hôtel)* to run; *(→ comptabilité, registre)* to keep; **t. la caisse** to be at the cash desk, to be the cashier; **t. les livres** to keep the books; **je tiens la maison pendant son absence** I look after *or* I mind the house while he's/she's away; **elle tient la rubrique artistique à 'Madame'** she has a regular arts column in 'Madame'; **le soir, il tenait le bar** at night he used to serve behind the bar; **je tiens l'orgue de l'église** I'm the church organist; *Sport & (dans un jeu)* **t. la marque** to keep score

3 *(donner → assemblée, conférence, séance)* to hold, to have; **elle va t. une conférence de presse** she is going to hold *or* to have a press conference; **le tribunal tiendra audience dans le nouveau bâtiment** the court hearings will be held in the new building

4 *(prononcer → discours)* to give; *(→ raisonnement)* to have; *(→ langage)* to use; **elle m'a tenu tout un discours sur la ponctualité** she gave me a lecture about being on time; **il me tint à peu près ce langage** here's roughly what he said to me; **t. des propos désobligeants/élogieux** to make offensive/appreciative remarks; **comment peux-tu t. un tel raisonnement?** how can you possibly think this way?

5 *Théât (rôle)* to play, to have; **t. des emplois secondaires** to play minor parts; *Fig* **t. un rôle dans** to play a part in; **il a bien tenu son rôle de fils** he acted as a son should

6 *Équitation (cheval)* to keep in hand; **t. un cheval serré** to keep a tight rein on a horse; **t. un cheval court** to ride a horse on a short rein

E. *EXPRIME UNE MESURE* **1** *(occuper)* to take up, to occupy; **le fauteuil tient trop de place** the armchair takes up too much room; **la barricade tenait toute la rue** the barricade took up the whole width of the street; **t. une place importante** to have *or* to hold an important place

2 *(contenir)* to hold; **le réservoir ne tient pas plus de 40 litres** the tank doesn't hold more than 40 litres

F. *ÊTRE CONSTANT DANS* **1** *(résister à)* (to be able) to take; **il tient l'alcool** he can hold *or esp Br* take his drink; **je ne tiens pas le vin** wine doesn't agree with me; *Fam* **t. le coup** *(assemblage, vêtements)* to hold out; *(digue)* to hold (out); *(personne)* (to be able) to take it; **le soir, je ne tiens pas le coup** I can't take late nights; **elle travaillait trop et n'a pas tenu le coup longtemps** she was overworked and couldn't cope *or* take it for long; **sa foi l'a aidé à t. le coup** his faith helped him to keep going; **t. la mer** to keep the sea (well); **t. la route** *(véhicule)* to hold the road well, *Br* to have good road-holding; *Fig* **ton raisonnement ne tient pas la route** your argument doesn't stand up to scrutiny

2 *(respecter → promesse)* to keep to, to stand by, to uphold; *(s'engager dans → pari)* to take up; **t. (sa) parole** to keep one's word; **t. une promesse** to keep *or* to fulfil a promise; **je tiens la gageure** *ou* **le pari!** I'll take up the challenge!; **tenu!, je tiens!** *(dans un jeu)* you're on!

G. *CONSIDÉRER* to hold, to consider; **je tiens que les romanciers sont les historiens du présent** it is my belief *or* I hold that novelists are the chroniclers of our time; **t. qn/qch pour** to consider sb/sth to be, to look upon sb/sth as; **on la tenait pour une divinité** she was considered to be *or* as a deity; **nous tenons ce procès/cette élection pour une supercherie** we consider this trial/this election (to be) a sham

VI **1** *(rester en position → attache)* to hold; *(→ chignon)* to stay up, to hold; *(→ bouton, trombone)* to stay on; *(→ empilement, tas)* to stay up; **t. en place** to stay in place; **mets du gel, tes cheveux tiendront mieux** use gel, your hair'll hold its shape better; **la porte du placard ne tient pas fermée** the cupboard door won't stay shut; **tout ça tient avec de la colle** all this is held together with glue; **ces sandales ne tiennent pas aux pieds** these sandals keep slipping off *or* won't stay on; **le porridge vous tient au corps** *ou* **à l'estomac** porridge keeps you going; **faire t. qch avec de la colle/des clous** to glue/to nail sth into position; **t. à** *(être fixé à)* to be fixed on *or* to; *(être contigu à)* to be next to; **assurez-vous que les ventouses tiennent bien au mur** make sure that the suction pads are securely fixed to the wall; **les bureaux tenant à l'atelier** the offices next to *or* adjoining the workshop; **essaie de t. le plus longtemps possible sur un pied** try to remain standing on one foot as long as possible; **il ne tient pas encore bien sur sa bicyclette/ses skis/ses jambes** he's not very steady on his bike/his skis/his legs yet; **je ne tiens plus sur mes jambes** *(de fatigue)* I can hardly stand; **cet enfant ne tient pas sur sa chaise** this child can't sit still *or* is always fidgeting in his chair; **elle ne tient pas en place** she can't sit still

2 *(résister → union)* to last, to hold out; *(→ chaise, vêtements)* to hold *or* to last out; *(→ digue)* to hold out; *(→ personne)* to hold *or* to last out; **leur mariage n'a pas tenu deux ans** their marriage didn't even last two years; **ce manteau a bien tenu** that coat lasted well; **je ne tiens plus au soleil, je rentre** I can't stand the sun any more, I'm going in; **je ne tiendrais pas longtemps sous la torture** I wouldn't hold out very long under torture; **on peut t. plusieurs jours sans manger** you can survive several days without eating; **le cœur ne tiendra pas** his/her/*etc* heart won't take it; **il n'a pas tenu longtemps au gouvernement** he didn't stay *or* last long in office; **tes arguments ne tiendront pas longtemps face à la réalité** your arguments won't hold water for very long in a real-life situation; **malgré une deuxième vague de bombardements, l'armée a tenu** despite a second bombing raid, the troops held out *or* stood their ground; **t. bon** *ou* **ferme** *(s'agripper)* to hold firm *or* tight; *(ne pas céder)* to hold out; **tenez bon, les secours arrivent** hold *or* hang on, help's on its way; **il me refusait une augmentation, mais j'ai tenu bon** he wouldn't give me a *Br* rise *or Am* raise but I held out *or* stood my ground; **la défense lyonnaise tient bon** the Lyons defence is holding fast *or* is standing firm; **le dollar tient toujours bon** the dollar is still holding firm; **n'y tenant plus, je l'appelai au téléphone** unable to stand it any longer, I phoned him/her; **soudain, elle n'y tint plus et se jeta dans ses bras** suddenly she couldn't contain herself any longer and threw herself in his arms; **ça sent si bon le chocolat, je ne vais pas pouvoir y t.** there's such a gorgeous smell of chocolate, I just won't be able to resist it; **c'est à n'y pas t.!** *(mauvaise odeur, mauvaise ambiance)* it's unbearable *or* intolerable!

3 *(durer, ne pas s'altérer → fleurs)* to keep, to last; *(→ tissu)* to last (well); *(→ beau temps)* to last, to hold out; *(→ bronzage)* to last; *(→ neige)* to settle, to stay; **les coquelicots ne tiennent pas dans l'eau** poppies don't last in water; **aucun parfum ne tient sur moi** perfumes don't last on me; **pour que votre rouge à lèvres tienne plus longtemps** so that your lipstick stays on longer

4 *(être valable, être d'actualité → offre, pari, rendez-vous)* to stand; *(→ promesse)* to hold; **l'invitation tient pour samedi** the invitation for Saturday is still on *or* still stands; **ça tient toujours pour demain?** is it still on for tomorrow?; **il n'y a pas de congé qui tienne** there's no question of having leave; **il n'y a pas de "mais ma tante" qui tienne, tu vas te coucher!** there's no "but Auntie" about it, off to bed with you!

5 *(pouvoir être logé)* to fit; **une fois plié, le sac tient dans la poche** when folded up, the bag fits in your pocket; **il ne tiendra pas sur cette chaise** he'll never fit in *or* get into that chair; **le compte rendu tient en une page** the report takes up one page; **t. en hauteur/largeur (dans)** to fit vertically/widthwise (in); **quatre enfants peuvent t. sur la banquette arrière** four children can fit on the back seat; **on tient facilement à cinq dans la barque** the boat sits five in comfort; **on ne tiendra jamais à trente dans ton salon** you'll never get thirty people into your living-room; **on n'arrivera jamais à tout faire t. dans cette valise** we'll never get everything into this suitcase; **il faudrait arriver à faire t. tous les meubles dans la camionnette pour ne faire qu'un voyage** if we only want to make one journey, we'll have to get all the furniture to fit into the van at once; **ma conclusion tiendra en deux mots** I will conclude in just two words; **son histoire tient en peu de mots** his/her story can be summed up in a few words

6 *(locutions) Fam* **en t. pour qn** to have a crush on sb; *Fam* **en t. pour qch** *(aimer)* to be hooked on sth; *(ne considérer que)* to stick to sth; **il en tient pour la varappe** he's really hooked on *or* mad about rock climbing; **elle en tient vraiment pour l'hypothèse de l'assassinat** she seems convinced it was murder; *Prov* **un tiens vaut mieux que deux tu l'auras** a bird in the hand is worth two in the bush

7 tiens, tenez *(en donnant quelque chose)* here; **tiens, reprends ta bague** here, have your ring back; **tu me passes le sel? – tiens** can you pass me the salt? – here you are

8 tiens, tenez *(pour attirer l'attention, pour insister)* listen, look; **tiens, le tonnerre gronde** listen, it's thundering; **tenez, les voilà justement** look, here they come; **tenez, je vais tout vous raconter** look *or* listen, I'll tell you everything; **tiens, rends-toi utile** here, make yourself useful; **tiens, je préférerais le jeter que de lui donner!** see, I'd rather throw it away than give it to him/her!; **tenez, je ne vous ferai même pas payer l'électricité** look, I won't even charge you for the electricity; **s'il est intéressé par le salaire? tiens, bien sûr que oui!** is he interested in the salary? you bet he is!

9 tiens, tenez *(exprime la surprise, l'incrédulité)* **tiens, Bruno! que fais-tu ici?** (hello) Bruno, what are you doing here?; **tiens, je n'aurais jamais cru ça de lui** well, well, I'd never have expected it of him; **tiens, c'est bizarre** hmm, that's strange; **tiens, tiens, ça serait bien dans son style** hmm, that's just the sort of thing he'd/she'd do; *Fam Ironique* **elle a refusé? tiens donc!** she said no? you amaze me! *or* surprise, surprise!

❑ **tenir à** **VT IND** **1** *(être attaché à → personne)* to care for, to be very fond of; *(→ objet)* to be attached to; *(→ réputation)* to care about; *(→ indépendance, liberté)* to value; **je tiens énormément à sa confiance** I set great store by *or* I greatly value his/her trust; **je ne ferai pas la grève, je tiens à mon emploi** I won't go on strike, I want to keep my job; **si tu tiens à la vie...** if you value your life...

2 *(vouloir)* **t. à faire qch** to be eager to do *or* to be keen on doing sth; **je tiens à être présent à la signature du contrat** I insist on being there when the contract is signed; **il tenait tellement à monter cette pièce** he was so keen on the idea of staging this play; **tu veux lui parler? – je n'y tiens pas vraiment** would you like to talk to him/her? – not really *or* not particularly; **je tiens à ce qu'ils aient une bonne éducation** I'm determined that they should have a good education; **je ne tiens pas à ce qu'on me reconnaisse** I don't want to be recognized; **tiens-tu à ce que cela se sache?** do you really want it to become known?; **je voudrais t'aider – je n'y tiens pas** I'd like to help you – I'd rather you didn't; **venez dîner, j'y tiens absolument!** come and have dinner, I insist!

3 *(résulter de)* to stem *or* to result from, to be due to, to be caused by; **ses erreurs tiennent surtout à son manque d'expérience** his/her mistakes are mainly due to *or* stem mainly from his/her lack of experience; **à quoi tient son charisme?** what's the secret of his/her charisma?; **sa défaite aux élections a tenu à trois voix** he/she was defeated in the election by just three votes; **le bonheur tient parfois à peu de chose** sometimes it's the little things that give people the most happiness; *Fam* **à quoi ça tient?** what's the reason for it?, what's it due to?; **qu'à cela ne tienne** never mind, *Hum* fear not; **vous n'avez pas votre voiture? qu'à cela ne tienne, je vais vous reconduire** you haven't got your car? never mind, I'll give you a lift

4 *(tournure impersonnelle) (être du ressort de)* **il ne tient qu'à toi de mettre fin à ce désordre** it's entirely up to you to sort out this shambles; **il ne tient qu'à vous de choisir** the choice rests *or* lies with you, it's entirely up to you; **il tenait à lui seul que ma nomination fût effective** it was entirely up to him to validate my appointment; **s'il ne tenait qu'à moi** if it was up to me *or* my decision; **il a tenu à peu de chose que je ne rate mon train** I very nearly missed my train

❑ **tenir de** **VT IND** **1** *(ressembler à)* to take after; **elle tient de moi** she takes after me; **ce chien tient à la fois de l'épagneul et du setter** this dog is a cross between a spaniel and a setter; **elle est vraiment têtue/douée – elle a de qui t.!** she's so stubborn/gifted – it runs in the family!

2 *(relever de)* **sa guérison tient du miracle** his/her recovery is something of a miracle; **ça tient de l'exploit** it's something of *or* quite a feat; **des propos qui tiennent de l'injure** remarks verging on the insulting; **le paysage tenait de la féerie** the scenery was like something out of a fairytale

►**se tenir** **VPR** **1** *(emploi réciproque)* **ils marchaient en se tenant la main** they were walking hand in hand; **ils se tenaient par le cou/la taille** they had their arms round each other's shoulders/waists

2 *(se dérouler → conférence)* to be held, to take place; *(→ festival, foire)* to take place; **la réunion se tiendra dans la salle de bal** the meeting will be held in the ballroom; **le festival se tient en plusieurs endroits** there are several venues for

the festival; **le congrès des sidologues se tient deux fois par an** the Aids specialists' convention is held twice a year

3 se t. la tête à deux mains to hold *or* to clutch one's head in one's hands

4 *(se retenir)* to hold on (tight); **tenez-vous bien, on démarre!** hold on tight *or* fast, here we go!; **se t. à** to hold on to; *(fortement)* to cling to, to clutch, to grip; **tiens-toi à la rampe pour descendre** hold on to the rail on the way down

5 *(se trouver → en position debout)* to stand, to be standing; *(→ en position assise)* to sit, to be sitting *or* seated; **il se tenait sur le seuil/dans l'embrasure de la porte** he was standing on the doorstep/in the doorway; **ne te tiens pas si près de la cheminée** don't stand so close to the fireplace; **se t. (légèrement) en retrait** to stand back (slightly); **se t. debout** to be standing (up); **se t. droit** *(debout)* to stand up straight; *(assis)* to sit up straight; **tiens-toi droit** straighten up; **tenez-vous droits!** *(à des personnes assises)* sit up straight *or* properly!; *(à des personnes debout)* stand up straight!; **tiens-toi mieux sur ta chaise** sit properly on your chair; **c'est parce que tu te tiens mal que tu as mal au dos** you get backaches because of bad posture; **se t. aux aguets** to be on the lookout, to watch out; **se t. coi** to remain silent; **se t. immobile** to remain *or* to be still

6 *(se conduire)* to behave; **elle ne sait pas se t. quand il y a des invités** she doesn't know how to behave when there are guests; **bien se t.** to behave oneself; **mal se t.** to behave oneself badly; *Fam* **Superman est là, les méchants n'ont qu'à bien se t.!** Superman is around, watch out, all you baddies!

7 *(être cohérent)* to hold together, to stand up; *(coïncider → indices, événements)* to hang together, to be linked; **se t. (bien)** *(argumentation, intrigue)* to hold together, to stand up; *(raisonnement)* to hold water, to hold together; **l'intrigue du roman ne se tient pas** the plot doesn't stand up *or* hang together; **je voudrais trouver un alibi qui se tienne** I'm looking for a plausible excuse; **ça se tient, elle servait au bar et lui était client, c'est comme ça qu'ils se sont rencontrés!** but of course, she was a barmaid and he was a customer, that's how they met!

8 *(se considérer)* **je ne me tiens pas encore pour battu** I don't reckon I'm *or* I don't consider myself defeated yet; **se t. pour satisfait** to feel satisfied; **je ne me tiens pas pour un génie** I don't regard myself as *or* think of myself as *or* consider myself a genius

9 *(locutions)* **tenez-vous-en aux ordres** confine yourself to carrying out orders; **d'abord ingénieur puis directrice d'usine, elle ne s'en est pas tenue là** she started out as an engineer, then became a factory manager, but she didn't stop there; **tenons-nous-en là pour aujourd'hui** let's leave it at that for today, let's call it a day; **je ne m'en tiendrai pas à ses excuses** I won't be content with a mere apology from him/her; **ne pas se t. de** *(joie, impatience)* to be beside oneself with; **la presse ne se tenait plus de curiosité** the newspapers were beside themselves with curiosity; **on ne se tenait plus de rire** we were in absolute fits (of laughter); **ils ont détourné, tiens-toi bien, 10 millions d'euros!** they embezzled, wait for it, 10 million euros!; **elle a battu le record, tenez-vous bien, de plus de deux secondes!** she broke the previous record and by over two seconds, would you believe!; **et, tiens-toi bien, elle voulait en plus que je lui paie ses frais!** and would you believe, she wanted me to pay her expenses as well!

10 *(locutions)* **je ne supporterai pas tes insolences, tiens-toi-le pour dit!** I'll say this only once, I won't put up with your rudeness!; **on lui a ordonné de ne plus revenir et il semble qu'il se le soit tenu pour dit** he was told never to come back and he seems to have got the message

Tennessee [tenesi] NM **le T.** Tennessee; **dans le T.** in Tennessee

tennis [tenis] NM **1** *(activité)* tennis; **jouer au t.** to play tennis; **t. sur gazon** lawn tennis; **jouer au t. sur terre battue** to play (tennis) on clay; **t. en salle** indoor tennis; **t. de table** table tennis **2** *(court)* (tennis) court

NMPL OU NFPL *(chaussures → pour le tennis)* tennis shoes; *(→ pour la marche) Br* trainers, *Am* sneakers

tennis-elbow [tenisɛlbo] *(pl* **tennis-elbows***)* NM tennis elbow

tennisman [tenisman] *(pl* **tennismans** *ou* **tennismen** [-men]) NM (male) tennis player

tennistique [tenistik] ADJ *(exploit, magazine, tournoi)* tennis *(avant n)*

tenon [tənɔ̃] NM **1** *Tech* tenon **2** *(d'une couronne dentaire)* pivot

❑ **à tenon** ADJ **assemblage à t.** tenon joint ADV **assembler à t.** to tenon

tenonner [3] [tənɔne] VT *Menuis* to tenon

tenonneuse [tənɔnøz] NF *Menuis* tenoning machine, tenoner

ténor [tenɔr] NM **1** *Mus* tenor; **t. léger** light tenor; **fort t.** operatic tenor **2** *Fig (vedette)* big name; **tous les (grands) ténors de la politique seront là** all the big political names will be there

ADJ *Mus* **saxophone t.** tenor saxophone

ténorino [tenɔrino] NM *Mus* tenorino, falsetto tenor

ténoriser [3] [tenɔrize] VI *Mus* to sing like a tenor *or* in the tenor register

ténorite [tenɔrit] NF *Minér* tenorite, melaconite

ténosynovite [tenɔsinɔvit] NF *Méd* tenosynovitis

ténotomie [tenɔtɔmi] NF *Méd* tenotomy

tenrec [tɑ̃rɛk] NM *Zool* tenrec

tenseur [tɑ̃sœr] ADJ M *Anat* tensor

NM **1** *Anat & Math* tensor **2 = tendeur**

tensif, -ive [tɑ̃sif, -iv] ADJ *Méd* tensive

tensioactif, -ive [tɑ̃sjɔaktif, -iv] *Chim* ADJ surface-active, surfactant

NM surface-active *or* wetting agent, surfactant

tensioactivité [tɑ̃sjɔaktivite] NF *Chim* surface activity

tensiomètre [tɑ̃sjɔmɛtr] NM **1** *Tech* tensometer, tensiometer **2** *Méd* sphygmomanometer **3** *Phys & Tex* tensiometer

tension [tɑ̃sjɔ̃] NF **1** *(étirement)* tension, tightness; **ça sert à régler la t. de la courroie** it's for adjusting the tension of the drive belt; *Tech* **t. de courroie** belt tension; *Tech* **t. de cisaillement** shear stress; *Tech* **t. de rupture** breaking strain *or* stress

2 *(état psychique)* **t. (nerveuse)** tension, strain, nervous stress; **elle est dans un tel état de t. qu'un rien la met en colère** she's so tense that the slightest thing makes her lose her temper

3 *Fig (désaccord, conflit, difficulté)* tension; **la t. monte entre les deux pays** tension is mounting between the two countries; **des tensions au sein de la majorité** tension *or* strained relationships within the majority

4 *Fig (effort intellectuel intense)* **t. d'esprit** mental effort; **t. intellectuelle** mental stress

5 *Élec* voltage, tension; **t. de coupure/grille** cut-off/grid voltage; **t. de 2000 volts** tension of 2,000 volts; **t. nulle** zero voltage *or* potential; **basse/haute t.** low/high voltage; **danger, haute t.** *(sur panneau)* beware, high voltage; **sans t.** dead; **montage de piles en t.** connection of batteries in series

6 *Méd* **t. artérielle** *ou* **vasculaire** blood pressure; **prendre la t. de qn** to check sb's blood pressure; *Fam* **avoir** *ou* **faire de la t.** to have high blood pressure▪; *Fam* **avoir deux de t.** to be all sluggish

7 *Ling* tenseness

8 *Phys (d'un liquide)* tension; *(d'un gaz)* pressure; **t. de vapeur** (saturated) vapour pressure; **t. superficielle** surface tension

❑ **à basse tension** ADJ *Élec* low-voltage, low-tension

❑ **à haute tension** ADJ *Élec* high-voltage, high-tension; **câbles à haute t.** high-tension cables

❑ **sous tension** ADJ **1** *Élec (fil)* live; **être sous t.** to be switched on, to be powered up; **la télécommande s'utilise quand le récepteur est sous t.** use the remote control switch when the set is in standby mode; **mettre sous t.** *(circuit)* to apply the voltage to, to switch on; *(appareil)* to switch on

2 *(nerveux)* tense, under stress; **tout le monde était sous t.** everybody was under stress

ADV **mettre un appareil sous t.** to switch on an appliance

tensive [tɑ̃siv] *voir* **tensif**

tenson [tɑ̃sɔ̃] NF *Littérature* tenson

tensoriel, -elle [tɑ̃sɔrjɛl] ADJ **calcul t.** tensor calculus

tentaculaire [tɑ̃takylɛr] ADJ **1** *Zool* tentacular **2** *Fig (ville)* sprawling; *(industrie, structure)* gigantic; *(organisme)* octopus-like; **traverser des banlieues tentaculaires** to cross the vast sprawl of the suburbs; **une entreprise t.** a massive *or* gigantic organization

tentacule [tɑ̃takyl] NM *Zool* tentacle

tentant, -e [tɑ̃tɑ̃, -ɑ̃t] ADJ *(nourriture)* tempting; *(projet, pari, idée)* tempting; *(offre, suggestion)* tempting, attractive; **il est très t. de penser que...** it is very tempting to think that...; **ce que tu me proposes est très t.** I'm very tempted by your offer

tentateur, -trice [tɑ̃tatœr, -tris] ADJ *(propos)* tempting; *(sourire, charme)* alluring

NM tempter; *Rel* **le T.** the Tempter

❑ **tentatrice** NF temptress

tentation [tɑ̃tasjɔ̃] NF **1** *(attrait, désir)* temptation; **céder** *ou* **succomber à la t.** to yield to temptation; **ne cède pas à la t. de l'humilier en public** don't give in to temptation and humiliate him/her in public; **avoir** *ou* **éprouver la t. de faire qch** to be tempted to do sth; **et si vous aviez la t. de nous rejoindre...** and if you felt tempted to join us...

2 *Rel* **induire qn en t.** to lead sb into temptation

tentative [tɑ̃tativ] NF **1** *(essai)* attempt; **faire une t.** to make an attempt; **une t. d'évasion** an escape attempt, an attempted escape; **une t. de suicide** a suicide attempt, an attempted suicide; **faire une t. de suicide** *ou Fam* **une t.** to try to commit suicide; **faire une nouvelle t. de suicide** to make another suicide attempt; **faire une t. de conciliation** to make an attempt at reconciliation, to attempt reconciliation

2 *Jur* **t. d'assassinat** *ou* **de meurtre** attempted murder; **il a été accusé de t. d'assassinat** he has been charged with attempted murder

tentatrice [tɑ̃tatris] *voir* **tentateur**

tente [tɑ̃t] NF **1** *(de camping)* tent; *(à une garden-party)* marquee; **monter une t.** to put up *or* to pitch a tent; **coucher sous la t.** to sleep under canvas; **passer une semaine sous la t.** to go camping for a week; *Fig* **se retirer sous sa t.** to retire into splendid isolation; **t. conique** bell tent; **t. igloo** igloo tent

2 *(chapiteau de cirque)* (circus) tent; **la grande t.** the big top

3 *Anat* **t. du cervelet** tentorium (cerebelli)

4 *Méd* **t. à oxygène** oxygen tent

5 *Naut* awning

tente-abri [tɑ̃tabri] *(pl* **tentes-abris***)* NF shelter tent

tenter [3] [tɑ̃te] VT **1** *(risquer, essayer)* to try, to attempt; **tentons une dernière démarche** let's make a last attempt; **t. d'inutiles efforts pour...** to make useless attempts to...; **t. une expédition de secours** to mount a rescue attempt; **t. une ascension difficile** to attempt a difficult climb; **je vais tout t. pour la convaincre** I'll try everything to convince her; **t. le tout pour le tout** to go for broke; **c'est une expérience à t.** it's worth having a go *or* giving it a try; **t. de faire qch** to try *or* to attempt *or Sout* to endeavour to do sth; **t. de se suicider** to attempt (to commit) suicide, to try to commit suicide, to make a suicide attempt; **elle s'est blessée en tentant de se dégager** she was hurt while trying to free herself; **il a tenté de battre le record/de se donner la mort** he tried to beat the record/to kill himself

2 *(soumettre à une tentation)* to tempt; **le serpent tenta Ève** the serpent tempted Eve; **le gâteau me tentait** the cake looked very tempting; **cela m'a toujours tenté de partir là-bas** I've always been tempted to go there; **une petite jupe noire m'avait tentée** a little black skirt had caught my eye; **le mariage, cela ne te tente pas?** don't you ever feel like getting married?; **se laisser t.** to give in to temptation; **j'ai envie de me laisser t.** *(accepter)* I'm tempted to say yes; *(faire quelque chose)* I'm tempted to do it; **laisse-toi t.** be a devil; **il te propose une sortie,**

laisse-toi t. he's offering to take you out, so why not accept?; **être tenté de faire qch** to be tempted *or* to feel inclined to do sth; **je suis tenté de tout abandonner** I feel like dropping the whole thing; **je dois dire que je suis très tenté** I'm very tempted *or* it's very tempting I must say; **je serais tenté de croire qu'il est responsable, lui aussi** I'm tempted to believe that he is responsible too; **t. (la) fortune** *ou* **la chance** *ou* **le sort, t. sa chance** to try one's luck; *Fam* **t. le coup** to give it a try *or* go, to have a try *or* go; *Fig* **t. Dieu** to embark on a superhuman enterprise; *Fig* **t. le diable** to tempt fate; *Fig* **t. la Providence** to tempt Providence

tente-roulotte [tɑ̃trulɔt] (*pl* **tentes-roulottes**) NF *Can* folding camper

tenthrède [tɑ̃trɛd] *Entom* NF sawfly
□ **tenthrèdes** NFPL sawflies, *Spéc* Tenthredae

tenture [tɑ̃tyr] NF **1** *(tapisserie)* hanging; *(ensemble de tapisseries)* hangings; **t. murale** wall-covering **2** *(rideaux)* Br curtain, *Am* drape **3** *Belg (double rideau)* (thick) Br curtain *or Am* drape **4** *(pour un service funèbre)* funeral hanging

tenu, -e[1] [təny] PP *voir* **tenir**
ADJ **1** *(soigné, propre)* **bien t.** *(maison, cahier, registres)* well-kept, tidy; *(jardin)* neat, trim; **une maison mal tenue** an untidy *or* a badly kept house; **des enfants bien/mal tenus** well/poorly turned-out children; **des comptes bien tenus** well-kept accounts
2 *(soumis à une stricte surveillance)* **les élèves sont très tenus** the pupils are kept on a tight rein
3 *(astreint)* **être t. de faire qch** to be obliged to do sth; **les passants sont tenus de marcher sur le trottoir** pedestrians must walk on the pavement; **le médecin est t. au secret professionnel** doctors are bound by professional confidentiality; **nous sommes tenus à la discrétion** we're obliged to be very discreet; **être t. de faire qch** to have to do sth; **le conseil n'est pas t./est t. de respecter la recommandation du comité** the committee's recommendation is not/is binding on the council; **je me sens t. de la prévenir** I feel morally obliged *or* duty-bound to warn her
4 *(pari)* **t.!** done!, you're on!
5 *Bourse (actions)* firm
6 *Mus* sustained, held
7 *Ling* tense
NM *Ftbl & Boxe* holding

ténu, -e [təny] ADJ **1** *(mince → fil, pointe)* fine, slender; *(→ voix, air, brume)* thin; *(→ espoir)* slender, slight, slim **2** *(subtil → raison, distinction)* tenuous; *(→ nuance)* subtle, fine; *(→ lien)* tenuous

---

TENUE² [təny]

holding **A1, 3, 7, 8** ▪ running **A2** ▪ firmness **A4** ▪ posture **B1** ▪ behaviour **B2** ▪ appearance **B3** ▪ clothes, outfit **B4** ▪ quality **B5**

NF **A. 1** *(d'une séance, d'un rassemblement)* **ils ont interdit la t. de la réunion dans nos locaux** they banned the meeting from being held on our premises; **pendant la t. du concile** while the council was in session
2 *(gestion → d'une maison, d'un établissement)* running; **je ne peux pas m'occuper en plus de la t. de la maison** I can't look after the running of the house as well; **l'école est réputée pour sa t.** the school is renowned for being well-run
3 *Aut* **t. de route** road holding; **avoir une bonne t. de route** to hold the road well, to have good road holding; **avoir une mauvaise t. de route** to have poor road holding
4 *Bourse (fermeté)* firmness; **la bonne/mauvaise t. des valeurs** the strong/poor performance of the stock market
5 *Compta* **t. de caisse** petty cash management; *Compta* **t. des comptes, t. des livres** bookkeeping
6 *Équitation (d'un cheval)* stamina
7 *Mus* holding
8 *Naut (qualité de mouillage)* hold, holding
9 *Ling* tenseness
B. 1 *(attitude corporelle)* posture, position; **trop**

---

d'élèves ont une mauvaise t. lorsqu'ils écrivent too many pupils adopt a bad posture when writing
2 *(comportement, conduite)* behaviour; **manquer totalement de t.** to behave appallingly; **voyons, un peu de t.!** come now, behave yourself!; **puni pour sa mauvaise t.** punished for his/her bad behaviour *or* his/her misbehaviour
3 *(aspect extérieur d'une personne)* appearance; **sa t. négligée/stricte** his/her slovenly/austere appearance; **ils exigent de leurs employés une t. correcte** they require their employees to be smartly dressed
4 *(habits → gén)* clothes, outfit, dress; *(→ de policier, de militaire, de pompier)* uniform; **une t. de sport** sports gear *or* kit; **dans ma t. de travail** in my work clothes; **t. correcte exigée** *(à l'entrée d'un restaurant)* dress code; **t. de cérémonie, grande t.** full-dress *or* dress uniform; **t. de soirée** evening dress
5 *(rigueur intellectuelle)* quality; **un roman d'une haute t.** a fine novel; **un magazine d'une haute t.** a quality magazine
6 *Équitation (d'un cavalier)* seat
7 *Tex* firmness
□ **en grande tenue** ADJ *Mil* in full-dress *or* dress uniform; **officiers en grande t.** officers in dress uniform; *Fig Hum* **en grande t. de demandeur d'emploi** all dressed up for a job interview
□ **en petite tenue** ADJ scantily dressed *or* clad, in one's underwear; **se promener en petite t.** to walk around with hardly a stitch on
□ **en tenue** ADJ *(militaire, policier)* uniformed; **ce jour-là, je n'étais pas en t.** *(militaire)* I was in civilian clothes that day; *(policier)* I was in plain clothes that day
□ **en tenue légère** = **en petite tenue**

ténuirostre [tenyirɔstr] ADJ *Orn* tenuirostrate
ténuité [tenyite] NF *Littéraire* **1** *(minceur)* slenderness, thinness **2** *(subtilité)* tenuousness
tenure [tənyr] NF *Hist (système)* tenure; *(terre)* holding
tenuto [tenuto] ADV *Mus* tenuto
teocalli [teɔkali] NM *Archéol* teocalli
téorbe [teɔrb] NM *Mus* theorbo
TEP [teəpe] NM **1** *Théât (abrév* **Théâtre de l'Est parisien***)* = theatre in Paris **2** *Com (abrév* **terminal électronique de paiement***)* electronic payment terminal, PDQ
NF *Méd (abrév* **tomographie à émission de positrons***)* PET
tep [tɛp] NF INV *(abrév* **tonne d'équivalent pétrole***)* TOE
tépale [tepal] NM *Bot* tepal
tephillin [tefilin] NMPL *Rel* tefillin, tephillin
téphra [tefra] NM *Géol* tephra
téphrite [tefrit] NF *Minér* tephrite
téphrosie [tefrozi] NF *Bot* tephrosia
tepidarium [tepidarjɔm] NM *Antiq* tepidarium
tépide [tepid] ADJ *Littéraire* tepid
tequila [tekila] NF tequila
TER [teœr] NM *Transp (abrév* **transport express régional***)* = French regional network of trains and coaches
ter [tɛr] ADV **1** *(dans des numéros de rue)* ≃ b **2** *(à répéter trois fois)* three times; *Mus* ter
teraoctet [teraɔktɛ] NM *Ordinat* terabyte
téraspic [teraspik] NM *Bot* candytuft
tératogène [teratɔʒɛn] ADJ *Méd* teratogenic
tératogenèse [teratɔʒənɛz], **tératogénie** [teratɔʒeni] NF *Méd* teratogenesis, teratogeny
tératoïde [teratɔid] ADJ *Méd* teratoid
tératologie [teratɔlɔʒi] NF *Méd & Biol* teratology
tératologique [teratɔlɔʒik] ADJ *Méd & Biol* teratological
tératome [teratɔm] NM *Méd* teratoid, teratoma
terbium [tɛrbjɔm] NM *Chim* terbium
tercer [16] [tɛrse] VT *Agr* to plough for the third time
tercet [tɛrsɛ] NM *Littérature* tercet
térébelle [terebɛl] NF *Zool* terebella
terebellum, térébellum [terebɛlɔm] NM *Zool* terebellum
térébenthine [terebɑ̃tin] NF turpentine
térébinthacée [terebɛ̃tase] *Bot* NF member of the Terebinthaceae family
□ **térébinthacées** NFPL Terebinthaceae

térébinthe [terebɛ̃t] NM *Bot* terebinth, turpentine tree
térébique [terebik] ADJ *Chim* terebic
térébrant, -e [terebrɑ̃, -ɑ̃t] ADJ **1** *(insecte)* boring, *Spéc* terebrant **2** *Méd (douleur)* piercing; *(ulcération)* deep
térébratule [terebratyl] NF *Zool* lamp shell, *Spéc* Terebratula
téréphtalique [tereftalik] ADJ *Chim* terephthalic
Teresa [tereza] NPR **Mère T.** Mother Teresa
terfès, terfesse [tɛrfɛs], **terfèze** [tɛrfɛz] NF *Bot* terfez
Tergal® [tɛrgal] NM *Tex Br* Terylene®, *Am* Dacron®
tergite [tɛrʒit] NM *Entom* tergite
tergiversations [tɛrʒiversasjɔ̃] NFPL prevarication; **après bien des t.** after a lot of prevarication; **cessez vos t.** stop prevaricating
tergiverser [3] [tɛrʒiverse] VI to prevaricate
termaillage [tɛrmajaʒ] NM *Écon* leads and lags
terme [tɛrm] NM **1** *(dans l'espace)* end, *Sout* term; **ils arrivèrent enfin au t. de leur voyage** they finally reached the end of their journey; **le t. de la course est une île du Pacifique** the race ends on the shores of a Pacific island
2 *(dans le temps)* end, *Sout* term; **parvenir** *ou* **toucher à son t.** *(aventure, relation)* to reach its conclusion *or Sout* term; **sa convalescence touche à son t.** his/her convalescence will soon be over; **la restructuration doit aller jusqu'à son t.** the restructuring must be carried through to its conclusion; **quel est le t. de leur mandat?** when does their mandate end?; **mettre un t. à qch** to put an end to sth; **mets un t. à tes récriminations** stop complaining; **mettre un t. à l'injustice** to put an end to injustice
3 *(date butoir)* term, deadline; **passé ce t., vous devrez payer des intérêts** after that date, interest becomes due; **t. de livraison** delivery deadline
4 *(échéance d'un loyer)* date for payment of rent; *(montant du loyer)* rent; **l'augmentation prendra effet au t. de janvier** the increase applies to rent paid as from January; **avoir plusieurs termes de retard** to be several months behind (with one's rent); **t. de bail** term of lease
5 *(date d'un accouchement)* **le t. est prévu pour le 16 juin** the baby is due on 16 June; **elle a dépassé le t. de deux semaines** she is (two weeks) overdue
6 *(versement)* instalment; **payable en deux termes** payable in two instalments
7 *Banque & Bourse* date for payment; *Compta* **t. de liquidation** account *or* settlement period
8 *Jur* term; **t. de rigueur** latest due date; **t. de grâce** days of grace; **demander un t. de grâce** *(délai)* to ask for time to pay; **t. de préavis** notice period
9 *(mot)* term, word; **employer le t. propre** to use the right word; **il utilise trop de termes étrangers** he uses too many foreign terms; **ce furent ses propres termes** those were his/her very words; **choisissez les termes propres** choose the right words; **en termes simples** in plain *or* simple terms; **il commenta la pièce en termes peu flatteurs** he commented on the play in rather unflattering terms; **s'exprimer en termes orduriers** to use filthy language; **parler de qn en bons/mauvais termes** to speak well/ill of sb; **je ne me suis pas exprimé en ces termes** that's not (quite) what I said; **puis, elle s'exprima en ces termes** then she said this; **il ne l'a pas dit en ces termes mais…** he didn't put it in quite those terms *or* words but…; **en d'autres termes** in other words; **t. argotique** slang expression; **termes commerciaux** commercial terms; **termes commerciaux internationaux** incoterms; **un t. de médecine/droit** a medical/legal term; **t. de métier** professional *or* technical term; **t. technique** technical term
10 *Beaux-Arts, Phil & Math* term
□ **termes** NMPL **1** *(sens littéral d'un écrit)* wording (UNCOUNT), terms; **les termes de la loi sont indiscutables** the wording of the law leaves no room for doubt
2 *(relations)* terms; **être en bons/mauvais termes avec qn** to be on friendly/bad terms with sb; **nous sommes en très bons termes** we

get along splendidly; **en quels termes êtes-vous?** what kind of terms are you on?; **en quels termes l'a-t-il quittée?** what terms were they on when he left her?

3 *(conditions → d'un contrat)* terms, terms and conditions; **termes de paiement** terms of payment; *Écon* **termes de l'échange** commodity terms of trade

❑ **à court terme** ADJ *(prêt, projet)* short-term; *(prévisions)* short-term, short-range; *Fin (factures)* short-dated ADV in the short term *or* run

❑ **à long terme** ADJ *(prêt, projet)* long-term; *(prévisions)* long-term, long-range; *Fin (factures)* long-dated ADV in the long term *or* run; **il faut prévoir à long t.** you have to look to the long term

❑ **à terme** ADJ **1** *Banque* **compte à t.** = deposit account requiring notice for withdrawals, *Am* time deposit; **compte à t. de 30 jours** 30-days account; **assurance à t.** term insurance; **à t. fixe** fixed-term **2** *Bourse* **marché à t.** forward market; *(change)* futures market; **opérations à t.** forward transactions; **valeurs à t.** securities dealt in for the account ADV **1** *(à la fin)* to the end, to its conclusion; **arriver à t.** *(délai)* to expire; *(travail)* to reach completion; *(paiement)* to fall due; **conduire** *ou* **mener à t. une entreprise** to bring an undertaking to a successful conclusion, to carry an undertaking through successfully **2** *(tôt ou tard)* sooner or later, in the end, in the long run; **leur politique est condamnée à t.** their policy is doomed to failure in the long run **3** *Com (à la date prévue)* on credit **4** *Fin* **acheter à t.** to buy forward; **vendre à t.** to sell forward **5** *Méd* at term; **bébé né à t.** baby born at full term; **être à t.** *(femme enceinte)* to have reached term

❑ **au terme de** PRÉP *(à la fin de)* at the end of, in the final stage of; **parvenir au t. de son existence/aventure** to reach the end of one's life/adventure

❑ **aux termes de** PRÉP *(selon)* under the terms of; **aux termes de la loi/du traité** under the terms of the law/of the treaty

❑ **avant terme** ADV prematurely; **bébé né avant t.** premature baby; **il est né six semaines avant t.** he was six weeks premature

terminaison [tɛrminɛzɔ̃] NF **1** *(dénouement, fin)* end; **la t. de difficiles négociations** the end of difficult negotiations **2** *Jur (action → de procès)* termination **3** *Anat* **terminaisons nerveuses** nerve endings **4** *Ling* ending; **mot à t. en "al"** word ending in "al"

terminal, -e, -aux, -ales [tɛrminal, -o] ADJ **1** *(qui forme l'extrémité)* terminal; **un bourgeon t.** a terminal bud

2 *(final)* last, final

3 *Méd (phase, malade)* terminal; **cancer en phase terminale** terminal cancer; **être en phase terminale** *(malade)* to be terminally ill

4 *Scol* **classe terminale** *Br* ≃ final year, upper sixth (form), *Am* ≃ senior year, twelfth grade

NM **1** *Ordinat* terminal; **t. bancaire/industriel** bank/manufacturing terminal; **t. de consultation** look-up terminal; **t. distant** remote terminal; *Com* **t. électronique de paiement** electronic payment terminal, PDQ; **t. éloigné** remote terminal; **t. graphique** graphic terminal, graphic display device; **t. intelligent** smart terminal, remote station; **t. lourd** high-speed terminal; *TV* **t. de montage** editing terminal; **t. de paiement électronique** pinpad; **t. de paiement en ligne** on-line terminal; **t. passif** dumb terminal; **t. de pilotage** control terminal; **t. point de vente** point-of-sale terminal; **t. portable/vocal** portable/voice terminal

2 *Pétr* **t. pétrolier** oil terminal

3 *Transp* terminal; **t. d'aérogare** air terminal; **t. maritime** shipping terminal; **t. urbain** *(d'une ligne aérienne)* city terminal

❑ **terminale** NF *Scol Br* ≃ final year, upper sixth (form), *Am* ≃ senior year, twelfth grade; **élève de terminale** *Br* ≃ upper sixth former, *Am* ≃ twelfth grader

terminateur [tɛrminatœr] NM *Astron* terminator

terminer [3] [tɛrmine] VT **1** *(mener à sa fin → repas, tâche, lecture, lettre)* to finish (off), to end; *(travail)* to complete, to finish (off); **c'est terminé, rendez vos copies** time's up, hand in your papers

2 *(stopper → séance, débat)* to end, to close, to bring to an end *or* a close

3 *(être le dernier élément de)* to end; **le volume qui termine la série comprend un index** the last volume in the series includes an index; **un clip termine l'émission** the programme ends with a pop video

4 *(finir → plat, boisson)* to finish (off), to eat up; **termine tes tomates!** eat up your tomatoes!

5 *Tél* **t. une session** to log off, to log out

USAGE ABSOLU *(finir)* **j'ai presque terminé** I've nearly finished; **pour t., je remercie tous les participants** finally, let me thank all those who took part; **je terminerai en vous demandant encore une fois d'être très prudents** finally, I'd like to ask you once again to be very careful; *Rad* **terminé!** out!

❑ **(en) terminer avec** VT IND to finish with; **je termine avec M. Dubois et je suis à vous** I'll just finish with Mr Dubois and then I'll be with you; **je suis bien soulagé d'en avoir terminé avec cette affaire** I'm really glad to have seen the end of this business; **il faut en t.** we must finish; **il faut en t. avec cette histoire** we have to put an end to this; **j'en ai terminé avec cette fille!** I'm *or* I've finished with that girl!

►**se terminer** VPR **1** *(arriver à sa fin → durée, période, saison)* to draw to a close; **la chanson/guerre vient de se t.** the song/war has just finished; **heureusement que ça se termine, j'ai hâte de retrouver ma maison** thank God the end is in sight, I can't wait to get back home

2 *(se conclure → soirée, film etc)* to end (**par** with); *(→ rue, mot)* to end (**par** in); **se t. bien/mal** *(film, histoire)* to have a happy/an unhappy ending; *(équipée, menée)* to turn out well/disastrously; **comment tout cela va-t-il se t.?** where's it all going to end?; **leur aventure s'est terminée au poste** the whole affair ended up with them being taken to the police station; **se t. en** to end in; **se t. en pointe/spirale/v** to end in a point/spiral/v; **ça s'est terminé en drame** it ended in tragedy; **les verbes qui se terminent en -er** verbs which end in -er; **la queue du scorpion se termine par un dard** the scorpion's tail has a sting at the end; **l'histoire se termine par la mort du héros** the story ends with the death of the hero; **les mots qui se terminent par une voyelle** words which end in a vowel

terminisme [tɛrminism] NM terminism, nominalism

terminologie [tɛrminɔlɔʒi] NF terminology

terminologique [tɛrminɔlɔʒik] ADJ terminological

terminologue [tɛrminɔlɔg] NMF terminologist

terminus [tɛrminys] NM terminus; **t.! tout le monde descend!** last stop! all change!

ADJ INV **gare t.** terminus

termite [tɛrmit] NM *Entom* termite; *Fig* **faire un travail de t.** to work secretly and destructively

termitière [tɛrmitjɛr] NF termite mound, *Spéc* termitarium

ternaire [tɛrnɛr] ADJ ternary; *Mus* **mesure t.** triple time

terne [tɛrn] ADJ **1** *(sans éclat → cheveux, regard)* dull; *(→ teint)* sallow; **les dorures sont devenues ternes avec le temps** the gilt has become tarnished over the years; **mes cheveux sont ternes en ce moment** my hair's lost its shine

2 *(ennuyeux)* dull, drab, dreary; *(voix)* dull, flat; **il a eu une vie bien t.** he led a very dull *or* dreary life; **son style est t.** his/her style is dull *or* lacklustre

3 *(inintéressant)* dull; **un élève t.** a slow pupil; **une intelligence t.** a slow mind

NM **1** *(à la loterie)* tern

2 *(au loto)* three numbers (on one line)

3 *(aux dés)* two treys *or* threes

4 *Élec* three-phase transmission line

ternir [32] [tɛrnir] VT **1** *(métal, argenterie)* to tarnish; *(glace)* to dull

2 *Fig (honneur, réputation, mémoire)* to tarnish, to stain, to smear; *(souvenir, beauté)* to cloud, to dull; **la nouvelle vint t. l'éclat de cette belle soirée d'été** the news cast a shadow *or* a cloud over that fine summer's evening; **un amour que les ans n'ont pu t.** a love undimmed by the passing years

►**se ternir** VPR **1** *(métal)* to tarnish; *(miroir)* to dull; **l'argenterie se ternit si on ne l'entretient pas** silverware loses its shine *or* becomes tarnished unless it is regularly cleaned

2 *Fig (honneur, réputation)* to become tarnished *or* stained; *(beauté, nouveauté)* to fade; *(souvenir)* to fade, to grow dim

ternissement [tɛrnismɑ̃] NM *(d'un métal)* tarnishing; *(d'une glace)* dulling

ternissure [tɛrnisyr] NF **1** *(condition)* tarnish, tarnished appearance **2** *(tache)* tarnished *or* dull spot

terpène [tɛrpɛn] NM *Chim* terpene

terpénique [tɛrpenik] ADJ *Chim* terpenic

terpine [tɛrpin] NF *Chim* terpin, terpinol

terpinéol [tɛrpineɔl], **terpinol** [tɛrpinɔl] NM *Chim* terpineol

Terpsichore [tɛrpsikɔr] NPR *Myth* Terpsichore

terrafungine [tɛrafɔ̃ʒin] NF *Pharm* oxytetracycline, Terramycin®

terrage [tɛraʒ] NM *Hist* champart, seigneurial tithe

TERRAIN [tɛrɛ̃]

soil **A1, 2** ▪ ground **1, 3, B3, 5, C3, 4** ▪ (plot of) land **B1, 2** ▪ field **B3, 4, C1**

NM **A.** *SOL, TERRE* **1** *Géol* soil, ground; **terrains alluviaux** alluvial land; **terrains calcaires** limestone soil *or* areas; **terrains crétacés** Cretaceous formations; **t. sédimentaire/volcanique** sedimentary/volcanic formations

2 *Agr* soil; **t. argileux/fertile** clayey/fertile soil; **t. gras/humide/sec** sticky/damp/dry soil; **t. meuble** loose soil

3 *(relief)* ground, terrain; **t. accidenté** uneven terrain; **t. en pente** sloping ground

B. *LIEU À USAGE SPÉCIFIQUE* **1** *Constr* piece *or* plot of land; **le t. coûte cher à Genève** land is expensive in Geneva; **t. à bâtir** development land *(UNCOUNT)*, building plot; **t. loti** developed site; **t. vague** piece of waste ground *or* land, *Am* empty lot

2 *Agr* land; **t. cultivé/en friche** cultivated/uncultivated land

3 *Sport & (loisirs) (lieu du jeu)* field, *Br* pitch; *(moitié défendue par une équipe)* half; *(installations)* ground; *Sport* **notre correspondant sur le t.** our correspondent on the spot; **t. d'aventure** adventure playground; **t. de boules** = ground for playing boules; **t. de camping** campsite, campground; **t. de football/rugby** football/rugby field *or Br* pitch; **t. de golf** golf course *or* links; **t. de jeux** playground; **t. de sports** sports field *or* ground

4 *Aviat* field; **t. (d'aviation)** airfield; **t. d'atterrissage** landing field

5 *Mil* ground; *(d'une bataille)* battleground; *(d'une guerre)* war *or* combat zone; **t. d'exercice** *ou* **militaire** training ground; **t. miné** minefield; **l'armée occupe le t. conquis** the army is occupying the captured territory; **la prochaine offensive nous permettra de gagner du t.** the next offensive will enable us to gain ground

6 *(lieu d'un duel)* duelling place

C. *SENS ABSTRAIT* **1** *(lieux d'étude)* field; **vous n'êtes pas allé sur le t., vous ne savez pas de quoi vous parlez** you've not been in the field *or* you've no practical experience, you don't know what you're talking about; **les jeunes députés n'hésitent pas à aller sur le t.** young MPs are always ready to go out and meet people; **un homme de t.** a man with practical experience

2 *(domaine de connaissances)* **être sur son t.** to be on familiar ground; **ils discutent de chiffres et je ne peux pas les suivre sur ce t.** they're discussing figures, so I'm out of my depth; **tu n'as pas intérêt à porter le débat sur le t. financier** it would be unwise of you to bring the debate around to financial matters; **situons la discussion sur le t. juridique/psychologique** let's discuss this from the legal/psychological angle

3 *(ensemble de circonstances)* **il a trouvé là un t. favorable à ses idées** he found there a breeding ground for his ideas; **elle connaît le t., laissons-la décider** she knows the situation, let her decide; **sonde le t. avant d'agir** see how the

land lies before making a move; **se placer sur un bon/mauvais t.** to argue from a position of strength/weakness; **je ne te suis pas sur ce t.** I'm not with you there; **être en t. neutre/sur un t. glissant** to be on neutral/on a dangerous ground; **être sur un t. mouvant** to be on shaky ground; **trouver un t. d'entente** to find common ground; **t. brûlant** dangerous ground; **perdre/gagner du t.** *(monnaie, entreprise)* to lose/to gain ground; **l'entreprise regagne du t. sur le marché français** the company is making up lost ground on the French market

4 *Méd* ground; **l'enfant présente un t. favorable aux angines** the child is susceptible to throat infections; **quand le virus trouve un t. favorable** when the virus finds its ideal breeding conditions

terramare [tɛramar] **NF** *Agr* terramare (fertilizer)

terraqué, -e [terake] **ADJ** *Littéraire* composed of earth and water

terrarium [tɛrarjɔm] **NM** terrarium

terrassant, -e [tɛrasɑ̃, -ɑ̃t] **ADJ 1** *(nouvelle, révélation)* staggering, stunning, crushing **2** *(coup)* staggering, crushing

terrasse [tɛras] **NF 1** *(balcon)* balcony; *(entre maison et jardin)* terrace, (raised) patio; *(sur le toit)* (roof) terrace

2 *(d'un café, d'un restaurant)* **être assis à la t.** to sit outside; **elle attendait à la t. d'un café** she was waiting at a table outside a café

3 *(d'un jardin, d'un parc)* terrace, terraced garden

4 *(d'une pierre, d'un marbre)* terrace

❑ **en terrasse ADJ 1** *Agr* terrace *(avant n)*; **jardin en t.** terraced garden; **cultures en terrasses** terrace cultivation **2** *(à l'extérieur d'un café)* outside; **les clients en t.** the customers sitting outside; **prix des consommations en t.** price of drinks served outside **ADV** *(consommer)* outside; **nous prendrons le café en t.** we'll have our coffee at one of the outside tables

terrassement [tɛrasmɑ̃] **NM 1** *(action)* excavation

2 *(remblai)* earthwork, excavation

❑ **de terrassement ADJ** *(travail)* excavation *(avant n)*; *(engin)* earth-moving; *(outil)* digging *(avant n)*

terrasser [3] [tɛrase] **VT 1** *(jeter à terre, renverser)* to bring *or* to strike down; **on y voit un homme terrassant un taureau** it shows a man striking down a bull

2 *(foudroyer)* to strike down; *(sujet: maladie)* to lay low; **être terrassé par une crise cardiaque** to be struck down by a heart attack

3 *(atterrer, accabler)* to crush, to shatter; **l'annonce de leur mort l'a terrassé** he was shattered by the news of their death; **terrassé par le chagrin** prostrate *or* overcome with grief

4 *(en travaux publics)* to excavate, to dig

5 *Agr (vignoble)* to work the soil of

terrassier [tɛrasje] **NM** workman *(employed for excavation work)*

TERRE [tɛr]

> **NM** Earth **A1** ▪ earth **A2, B8, C** ▪ ground **B1, 8** ▪ land **B2-6** ▪ country **B4** ▪ estate **B5** ▪ soil **B6, C1** ▪ clay **C2**
> **NMPL** estate

NF A. *GLOBE* **1** *(planète)* **la T.** the Earth; **la T. est ronde/tourne autour du Soleil** the Earth is round/moves around the Sun; **sciences de la T.** earth sciences

2 *(monde terrestre)* earth; **le bonheur existe-t-il sur la t.?** is there such a thing as happiness on this earth *or* in this world?; **si je suis encore sur cette t.** if I am still alive; **sur le point de quitter cette t.** about to give up the ghost

B. *SOL* **1** *(surface du sol)* ground; **j'avais l'impression que la t. se dérobait sous moi** I felt as if the ground was giving way beneath me; **la neige couvrait la t.** the ground was covered in snow; **elle souleva l'enfant de t.** she picked the child up (from the ground); **t. battue** *(dans une habitation)* earth *or* hard-earth *or* mud floor; *(dans une cour)* bare ground; *(sur un court de tennis)* clay (surface); **mettre qn plus bas que t.** *(en actes)* to treat sb like dirt; *(en paroles)* to tear sb to shreds

2 *(élément opposé à la mer)* land *(UNCOUNT)*; **on les transporte par voie de t.** they are transported overland *or* by land; **nous sommes en vue de la t.** we are in sight of land; **nous avons navigué sans nous éloigner des terres** we sailed close to the coast; *Naut* **t.!** land ahoy!; **prendre t.** to make land; **sur la t. ferme** on dry land, on terra firma

3 *(région du monde)* land; **les terres arctiques** the Arctic regions; **les terres australes** the Southern lands; **il reste des terres inexplorées** there are still some unexplored regions

4 *(pays)* land, country; **la t. de France** French soil; **(la) t. Adélie** Adelie Land; **la t. d'Arnhem** Arnhem Land; **la t. de Baffin** Baffin Island; **t. d'accueil** host country; **t. d'exil** place of exile; **t. natale** native land *or* country; **la T. promise** the Promised Land; **la T. sainte** the Holy Land

5 *(terrain)* land *(UNCOUNT)*, estate; **acheter une t.** to buy a piece of land

6 *(symbole de la vie rurale)* **la t.** the land, the soil; **homme de la t.** man of the soil; **revenir à/quitter la t.** to return to/to leave the land

7 *Beaux-Arts* **ligne de t.** ground line

8 *Élec Br* earth, *Am* ground; **mettre** *ou* **relier qch à la t.** *Br* to earth *or Am* to ground sth

C. *MATIÈRE* **1** *(substance → gén)* earth, soil; **ne joue pas avec la t.** don't play in the dirt; **l'odeur de la t. fraîchement retournée** the smell of freshly-dug earth *or* soil; **mettre** *ou* **porter qn en t.** to bury sb; **t. à vigne/à blé** soil suitable for wine-growing/for wheat; **t. arable** farmland; **t. de bruyère** peaty soil; **t. grasse** heavy *or* clayey soil; **t. noire** chernozem, black earth; **t. végétale** topsoil; **t. vierge** virgin soil

2 *(matière première)* clay, earth; **t. cuite** earthenware; **en t. cuite** earthenware *(avant n)*; **des terres cuites** earthenware *(UNCOUNT)*; **t. à foulon** fuller's earth; **t. glaise** (brick) clay, *Br* brickearth; **t. de pipe** pipeclay; **t. à polir** earth tripolite; **t. rouge** terracotta

3 *(pigment)* **t. de Cassel** Cassel earth; **t. d'ombre** terra ombra, raw umber; *Chim* **terres rares** rare earths; **t. de Sienne** sienna; **t. verte** green earth, terra verde

❑ **terres NFPL** *(domaine, propriété)* estate, estates; **vivre sur/de ses terres** to live on/off one's estates

❑ **à terre ADV 1** *(sur le sol)* on the ground; **poser un fardeau à t.** to put a load down (on the ground); **frapper qn à t.** to strike sb when he's down

2 *Naut* on land; **descendre à t.** to land; **vous pourrez rester à t. deux heures** you may stay ashore for two hours

3 *Can Fam (déprimé)* down, depressed▪; **être à t.** to be *or* feel down

❑ **en pleine terre ADV** *Agr* in the open, in open ground

❑ **par terre ADJ** *(ruiné, anéanti)* spoilt, wrecked; **avec la pluie, notre promenade est par t.** the rain has ruined our plans for a walk *or* put paid to our walk **ADV** *(sur le plancher)* on the floor; *(sur le sol)* on the ground; **pose-le par t.** put it (down) on the floor; **tomber par t.** to fall down; *Fam* **j'ai lavé par t.** I've washed the floor

❑ **sous terre ADV 1** *(sous le sol)* underground; **ils durent établir des abris sous t.** they had to build shelters underground *or* underground shelters

2 *(locutions)* **j'aurais voulu être à cent pieds sous t.** *ou* **rentrer sous t.** I wished the earth would swallow me up; **je l'ai fait rentrer sous t.** I made him eat humble pie

❑ **sur terre ADV 1** *(ici-bas)* on (this) earth; **pourquoi sommes-nous sur t.?** why were we put on this earth?

2 *(locutions)* **revenir** *ou* **redescendre sur t.** to come back to earth (with a bump)

'Terre des hommes' *Saint-Exupéry* 'Wind, Sand and Stars'

terre à terre [tɛratɛr] **ADJ INV** *(esprit, personne)* down-to-earth, matter-of-fact; *(pensée, occupation, vie)* mundane

terreau, -x [tɛro] **NM** compost *(UNCOUNT)*; **t. de couche** garden mould; **t. de feuilles** leaf mould

terreautage [tɛrotaʒ] **NM** spreading with compost, composting

terreauter [3] [tɛrote] **VT** to compost

Terre de Feu [tɛrdəfø] **NF la T.** Tierra del Fuego; **en T.** in Tierra del Fuego

Terre François Joseph [tɛrfrɑ̃swaʒozɛf] **N la T.** Franz-Josef Land

terre-neuvas [tɛrnœva] **NM INV** = **terre-neuvier**

Terre-Neuve [tɛrnœv] **NF** Newfoundland; **à T.** in Newfoundland

terre-neuve [tɛrnœv] **NM INV 1** *(chien)* Newfoundland **2** *(personne dévouée)* **avoir une mentalité de t.** to be a Good Samaritan

terre-neuvien, -enne [tɛrnœvjɛ̃, -ɛn] *(mpl* **terre-neuviens,** *fpl* **terre-neuviennes) ADJ** from Newfoundland

❑ **Terre-Neuvien, -enne NM,F** Newfoundlander

terre-neuvier [tɛrnœvje] *(pl* **terre-neuviers) NM 1** *(navire)* fishing boat (from Newfoundland) **2** *(marin)* fisherman (from Newfoundland)

terre-plein [tɛrplɛ̃] *(pl* **terre-pleins) NM 1** *(sur route)* **t. central** *Br* central reservation, *Am* center divider strip; **t. circulaire** *(dans un rond-point)* central island **2** *Constr* earth platform **3** *Mil* terreplein

terrer [4] [tɛre] **VT 1** *Agr & Hort (arbre, plante)* to earth up; *(recouvrir de terre)* to cover over with soil; *(semis)* to earth over **2** *Tex* to full

▸**se terrer VPR 1** *(se mettre à l'abri, se cacher)* to go to ground *or* to earth, to lie low; *(se retirer du monde)* to hide away; **être terré dans** to have gone to earth in, to be holed up in **2** *(dans un terrier)* to go to ground *or* to earth, to burrow; **être terré dans** to have gone to earth in

terrestre [tɛrɛstr] **ADJ 1** *(qui appartient à notre planète)* earth *(avant n)*, earthly, terrestrial; **la croûte** *ou* **l'écorce t.** the Earth's crust; **le globe t.** the terrestrial globe

2 *(qui se passe sur la terre)* earthly, terrestrial; **durant notre vie t.** during our life on earth

3 *(vivant sur la terre ferme)* land *(avant n)*; **animaux/plantes terrestres** land animals/plants

4 *(établi au sol → transport)* land *(avant n)*; *Mil* **effectifs terrestres** land forces

5 *(d'ici-bas → joie, plaisir)* worldly, earthly

terreur [tɛrœr] **NF 1** *(effroi)* terror, dread; **être fou de t.** to be wild with fear; **être glacé de t.** to be terror-stricken; **vivre dans la t.** to be terrified *or* in (a state of) terror; **vivre dans la t. de qch** to live in dread of sth; **avoir la t. de faire qch** to have a terror of doing sth; **le tremblement de terre a provoqué la t. dans la population** the earthquake caused terror among the population

2 *(terrorisme)* **la t.** terror (tactics); *Hist* **la T.** the (Reign of) Terror; **gouverner par la t.** to rule by terror; **faire régner la t.** to instil terror; **un régime de t.** a reign of terror

3 *(voyou → d'une ville, d'une école)* terror; **jouer les terreurs** to act the bully; **celui-là, c'est une t.** he's a terror *or* a horror

4 *(personne ou chose effrayante)* **le patron est sa t.** he's/she's terrified of the boss; **le bac est sa t.** the baccalaureat exam is his/her greatest fear

5 *Psy* **terreurs nocturnes** night terrors

> *Culture*
> **LA TERREUR**
> "La Terreur", 1793–4, refers to a period of numerous political arrests, summary trials and executions under the regime of the Montagnards led by Robespierre. The "Grande Terreur" started on 10 June 1794 and ended with the fall of Robespierre, on 9 Thermidor (27 July 1794).

terreux, -euse [tɛrø, -øz] **ADJ 1** *(couvert de terre → chaussure, vêtement)* muddy; *(→ mains)* dirty; *(→ légume)* caked with soil; *(→ laitue)* gritty **2** *(brun → couleur, teint, ciel)* muddy; **avoir le visage t.** to be ashen faced **3** *(qui rappelle la terre → odeur, goût)* earthy

terri [tɛri] **NM** slag heap

terrible [tɛribl] **ADJ 1** *(affreux → nouvelle, accident, catastrophe)* terrible, dreadful; **ce n'est qu'une coupure, rien de (bien) t.** it's just a cut, nothing serious *or* major

2 *(insupportable → chaleur, douleur)* terrible, unbearable; *(→ déception, conditions de vie)* terrible; **elle est t. avec sa façon de bouder sans raison** it's awful the way she sulks for no reason; **ces enfants sont terribles** those children are little terrors; **vous êtes t.!** you really are the limit!

3 *(en intensif → bruit, vent, orage)* terrific, tremendous; **elle a eu une chance t.** she's been incredibly lucky

4 *(terrifiant → colère, cri, rage)* terrible; **il est t. quand il s'énerve** he's awful *or* terrible when he loses his temper

5 *(pitoyable)* terrible, awful, dreadful; **c'est t. de penser que...** how dreadful *or* it is terrible to think that...; **ce qui est t., c'est de dire que...** the terrible thing about it is saying that...; **le plus t., c'est de savoir que...** the worst thing *or* part of it is knowing that...

6 *Fam (fantastique)* terrific, great; **t.!** great!, smashing!; **son concert? pas t.!** his/her concert? it was nothing to write home about!

ADV *Fam (très bien)* great; **son nouveau spectacle marche t.** his/her new show is a big success; **ça ne va pas t.** things aren't too great

terriblement [tɛribləmɑ̃] **ADV** terribly, dreadfully

terricole [tɛrikɔl] **ADJ** terricolous

terrien, -enne [tɛrjɛ̃, -ɛn] **ADJ 1** *(qui possède des terres)* landowning; **noblesse terrienne** landed aristocracy; **propriétaire t.** landowner **2** *(rural)* rural; **les habitudes terriennes** rural customs **3** *(de la Terre)* of the Earth

NM,F 1 *(habitant de la Terre)* inhabitant of the Earth; *(dans un récit de science-fiction)* earthling **2** *(paysan)* countryman **3** *(opposé au marin)* landsman, *Péj* landlubber

terrier[1] [tɛrje] **NM** *(abri → d'un lapin)* (rabbit) hole *or* burrow; *(→ d'un renard)* earth, hole, foxhole; *(→ d'un blaireau)* set; *(→ d'une taupe)* hole

terrier[2] [tɛrje] **NM** *(chien)* terrier

terrifiant, -e [tɛrifjɑ̃, -ɑ̃t] **ADJ 1** *(effrayant)* terrifying **2** *Fam (extraordinaire)* amazing; **c'est t. ce qu'il a grandi en quelques mois!** it's amazing how much he's grown in just a few months!

terrifier [9] [tɛrifje] **VT** to terrify; **absolument terrifié** absolutely terrified

terrigène [tɛriʒɛn] **ADJ** terrigenous

terril [tɛril] **NM** slag heap

terrine [tɛrin] **NF 1** *(récipient)* terrine dish **2** *Culin* terrine; **t. de lapin** rabbit terrine *or* pâté

terrir [32] [tɛrir] **VI** *Pêche* **poissons qui terrissent** fish living in coastal waters

territoire [tɛritwar] **NM 1** *Géog* territory; **sur le t. français** on French territory; **en t. ennemi** in enemy territory; **le T. du Nord** Northern Territory; *Can* **les Territoires du Nord-Ouest** Northwest Territories; *Pol* **les territoires occupés** the occupied territories; **le T. de Belfort** Territoire de Belfort; *Pol* **t. sous mandat** mandate

2 *Admin* area; **territoires d'outre-mer** (French) overseas territories

3 *(de juge, d'évêque)* jurisdiction

4 *Zool* territory; **les animaux marquent leur t.** animals mark (out) their territory

5 *(secteur, fief)* territory; **sa chambre, c'est son t.** his/her room is his/her kingdom; **défendre son t.** to defend one's patch

6 *Com & Mktg (d'un représentant)* territory; **t. exclusif** exclusive territory; **t. de vente** sales territory

territorial, -e, -aux, -ales [tɛritɔrjal, -o] **ADJ** territorial

NM *Mil* territorial

❑ **territoriale NF** *Mil* territorial army

territorialement [tɛritɔrjalmɑ̃] **ADV** territorially

territorialité [tɛritɔrjalite] **NF** *Jur* territoriality; **t. des lois/de l'impôt** = laws/tax regulations applying to people in a given territory

terroir [tɛrwar] **NM 1** *Agr* soil; **goût de t.** *(d'un vin)* tang of the soil, native tang

2 *(région agricole)* region; **le t. de la Beauce** the Beauce region; **le t. de Vosne-Romanée** the Vosne-Romanée region

3 *(campagne, ruralité)* country; **il a gardé l'accent du t.** he has kept his rural accent; **c'est un écrivain du t.** he's a regional author; *Fig* **avoir un goût de t.** to be evocative *or* redolent of the soil; **ses livres ont un goût de t.** his/her books are evocative of rural *or* country life; **toute son œuvre sent le t.** his/her entire work is richly evocative of his/her native soil

terrorisant, -e [tɛrɔrizɑ̃, -ɑ̃t] **ADJ** terrorizing

terroriser [3] [tɛrɔrize] **VT 1** *(martyriser)* to terrorize; **il terrorisait ses camarades de classe** he terrorized his classmates **2** *(épouvanter)* to terrify; **l'idée de la mort la terrorise** the idea of death terrifies her

terrorisme [tɛrɔrism] **NM** terrorism; **t. écologique** eco-terrorism

terroriste [tɛrɔrist] **ADJ** terrorist

NMF terrorist

terser [3] [tɛrse] = **tercer**

tersiops [tɛrsjɔps] **NM** *Zool* bottlenosed dolphin

tertiaire[1] [tɛrsjɛr] **ADJ 1** *Chim & Méd* tertiary; *Géol* **ère t.** Tertiary era **2** *Admin & Écon* **secteur t.** tertiary sector, service industries

NM 1 *Géol* **le t.** the Tertiary era **2** *Admin & Écon* **le t.** the tertiary sector

tertiaire[2] [tɛrsjɛr] **NMF** *Rel* tertiary

tertiairisation [tɛrsjɛrizasjɔ̃], **tertiarisation** [tɛrsjarizasjɔ̃] **NF** *Écon* expansion of the tertiary sector; **la t. de l'économie** the tertiarization of the economy

tertio [tɛrsjo] **ADV** third, thirdly; **t., je n'ai pas le temps** thirdly, I haven't got time

tertre [tɛrtr] **NM 1** *(monticule)* hillock, mound **2** *(sépulture)* **t. (funéraire)** burial mound

Tertullien [tɛrtyljɛ̃] **NPR** Tertullian

tervueren [tɛrvyrɛn] **NM** *Zool* Belgian Tervuren

Térylène® [terilɛn] **NM** Terylene®

terza rima [tɛrzarima] *(pl* **inv** *ou* **terze rime)** **NF** *Littérature* terza rima

terzetto [tɛrdzɛto] **NM** *Mus* terzetto

tes [te] *voir* **ton**[3]

tesla [tɛsla] **NM** tesla

tesselle [tesɛl] **NF** tessera *(of mosaic)*

tessère [tesɛr] **NF** *Antiq* tessera

Tessin [tesɛ̃] **NM** *Géog* **1** *(rivière)* **le T.** the (River) Ticino **2** *(canton)* **le T.** Ticino

tessiture [tesityr] **NF** tessitura; *(d'un instrument)* range

tesson [tesɔ̃] **NM** *(de verre, de poterie)* shard; **un mur hérissé de tessons de bouteille** a wall with broken glass all along the top

test[1] [tɛst] **NM 1** *(essai individuel)* test; *(procédé)* testing; **soumettre qn à un t., faire passer un t. à qn** to give sb a test; **t. d'aptitude professionnelle** aptitude test; *Aut* **t. de choc** impact test; **t. comparatif** comparative test; **t. de conformité** compliance test; **t. d'hypothèse** statistical test; *Aut* **t. de roulage** road testing; **un t. de roulage** a road test; **t. à sec** dry run; **t. statistique** statistical test; **t. technique** engineering test; *Aut* **t. de tonneaux** roll-over test

2 *(épreuve)* test; **sa réponse sera un t. de sa bonne volonté** his/her answer will be a test of his/her goodwill

3 *Ordinat* test; **t. automatique** automatic testing

4 *Méd* test; **t. allergologique** allergy test; **t. cutané** cutaneous reaction test; **t. de dépistage du SIDA** Aids test; **t. de grossesse** pregnancy test

5 *Psy* test; **t. d'aperception thématique** thematic apperception test; **t. projectif** projective test; **t. de Rorschach** Rorschach *or* ink blot test

6 *Sport (test-match)* (rugby) test (match)

7 *Mktg* test; **tests** *(procédure)* testing; **t. auprès des consommateurs** consumer test; **t. d'acceptabilité auprès des consommateurs** customer-acceptance test; **t. aveugle** blind test; **t. de la bande dessinée** *ou* **de la bulle** balloon test; **t. comparatif** comparison test; **t. de concept** concept test; **tests d'emballage** package testing; **t. d'enquête** enquiry test; **t. de frustration** balloon test; **t. du lendemain** (day-after) recall test; **t. de marché** market test; *(d'un produit)* test marketing, market test; **t. de média** media test; **t. de mémoire** *ou* **de mémorisation** memory *or* recall test; **t. monadique** monadic test; **tests de nom** name testing; **t. de performance** performance test; **t. de performance du produit** product performance test; **t. sur place** field test; **t. de préférence** preference test; **t. de produit** product test; **t. de rappel** recall test; **t. de reconnaissance** recognition test; **t. de support** media test; **t. de vente** market test

8 *(comme adj; avec ou sans trait d'union)* test *(avant n)*; **population t.** test population; **région t.** test region; *Mktg* **ville-t.** test city

test[2] [tɛst] **NM** *Zool* test

testable [tɛstabl] **ADJ** testable

testacé, -e [tɛstase] **ADJ** *Biol* shelled, *Spéc* testaceous

testacelle [tɛstasɛl] **NF** *Zool* shelled slug, *Spéc* testacella

testage [tɛstaʒ] **NM** progeny-test

testament [tɛstamɑ̃] **NM 1** *Jur* will, testament; **faire son t.** to make one's will; **léguer qch à qn par t.** to leave sth to sb in one's will; **ceci est mon t.** this is my last will and testament; **tu ne seras pas dans mon t.** you'll be cut out of my will; **elle l'a mis** *ou* **couché sur son t.** she put him in her will; *Fam Fig* **il peut faire son t.!** he'd better make (out) his will!; **t. authentique** *ou* **public** executed will; **t. mystique** *ou* **secret** sealed will; **t. olographe** holograph will; **t. de vie** living will

2 *(ultime message d'un artiste)* legacy

'Testament à l'anglaise' *Coe* 'What a Carve up!'

'Le Testament de l'orange' *Burgess* 'A Clockwork Testament'

'Le Testament du Docteur Mabuse' *Lang* 'The Testament of Doctor Mabuse'

testamentaire [tɛstamɑ̃tɛr] **ADJ** testamental

testateur, -trice [tɛstatœr, -tris] **NM,F** testator, *f* testatrix

tester[1] [3] [tɛste] **VT 1** *(déterminer les aptitudes de → élèves)* to test; **nous testerons tous les candidats** we will be testing all the candidates

2 *(vérifier le fonctionnement de → appareil, produit)* to test; *Mktg* to test, to test-market; **ils testent le nouveau produit auprès des médecins** they're testing the new product with doctors; **t. qch sur le marché** to test-market sth; **t. un questionnaire** to pilot a questionnaire; **testé en laboratoire** laboratory-tested

3 *(mettre à l'épreuve)* to put to the test; **elle a voulu t. ma loyauté/sa collègue** she wanted to put my loyalty/her colleague to the test

tester[2] [3] [tɛste] **VI** *Jur* to make out one's will

testeur [tɛstœr] **NM** *(personne, machine)* tester

testiculaire [tɛstikylɛr] **ADJ** testicular

testicule [tɛstikyl] **NM** testicle, *Spéc* testis

testimonial, -e, -aux, -ales [tɛstimɔnjal, -o] **ADJ** testimonial

test-match [tɛstmatʃ] *(pl* **test-match(e)s)** **NM** (rugby) test (match)

teston [tɛstɔ̃] **NM** *Hist* teston, testoon

testostérone [tɛstɔsterɔn] **NF** testosterone

têt [tɛ] **NM t. à gaz** beehive shelf; **t. à rôtir** roasting crucible

tétanie [tetani] **NF** *Méd* tetany; **avoir une crise de t.** to go into spasms

tétanique [tetanik] **ADJ** tetanic; **bacille t.** tetanus bacillus; **malade t.** person with tetanus

NMF tetanus sufferer

tétanisation [tetanizasjɔ̃] **NF** tetanization

tétaniser [3] [tetanize] **VT 1** *Méd* to tetanize **2** *Fig* **être tétanisé** *(de peur)* to be petrified; *(d'étonnement)* to be stunned; *(de froid)* to be frozen stiff; **être tétanisé de peur/de froid** to be petrified/frozen stiff; **la vue des rats l'a tétanisée** she was petrified by the sight of the rats

tétanisme [tetanism] **NM** *Physiol* tetanic state

tétanos [tetanos] **NM** lockjaw, *Spéc* tetanus; *(contraction de muscle)* tetanus

têtard [tɛtar] **NM 1** *Zool* tadpole **2** *Hort* pollard **3** *Fam (enfant)* kid, brat

TÊTE [tɛt]

head **A1, 2, 4, 5, B, C2-4, D4, 5, 7-11** ■ face **A3** ■ mind **B1** ■ person **C1** ■ leader **C3** ■ top **D1, 4** ■ front end **D2**

NF A. *PARTIE DU CORPS* **1** *Anat* head; **dresser** *ou* **redresser la t.** to raise one's head; **la t. haute** with (one's) head held high; **marcher la t. haute** to walk with (one's) head held high; **la t. la première** head first; **de la t. aux pieds** from head to

foot *or* toe; **avoir mal à la t.** to have a headache; **avoir la t. lourde** to feel fuzzy, *Br* to have a thick head; **j'ai la t. qui tourne** *(malaise)* my head is spinning; **la t. me tourne** *(panique)* I'm in a spin; **ne tourne pas la t., elle nous regarde** don't look round, she's watching us; **dès qu'il m'a vu, il a tourné la t.** as soon as he saw me, he looked away; **tenir t. à qn** to stand up to sb; *Fam* **en avoir par-dessus la t.** to be sick (and tired) of it; **avoir la t. sur les épaules** to have a good head on one's shoulders; *Fam* **faire une (grosse) t.** *ou* **une t. au carré à qn** to smash sb's face in; **j'en donnerais** *ou* **j'en mettrais ma t. à couper** I'd stake my life on it; *Fam* **tomber sur la t.** to go off one's rocker, to lose it; *Fam* **non mais t'es tombé sur la t. ou quoi?** you must be out of your mind!; *Fam* **ça va pas la t.?** are you mad?; **il ne réfléchit jamais, il fonce t. baissée** he always charges in *or* ahead without thinking; *Fig* **se cogner** *ou* **se taper la t. contre les murs** to bang one's head against a (brick) wall; **se jeter à la t. de qn** to throw oneself at sb

2 *(en référence à la chevelure, à la coiffure)* **se laver la t.** to wash one's hair; **t. nue** bareheaded; **nos chères têtes blondes** *(les enfants)* our little darlings; *Hist* **têtes rondes** Roundheads

3 *(visage, expression)* face; **avoir une bonne t.** to look like a nice person; **ne fais pas cette t.!** don't make *or Br* pull such a long face!; **tu en fais une t.!** what's that look for?; **il a fait une de ces têtes quand je lui ai dit!** you should have seen his face when I told him!; **elle ne savait plus quelle t. faire** she didn't know how to react; **il a une t. à se faire rouler** he looks like he could be conned easily; **elle n'a pas une t. à se laisser faire** she doesn't look the sort to be pushed around; **jeter** *ou* **lancer qch à la t. de qn** to throw sth in sb's face; *Fam* **il a** *ou* **c'est une t. à claques** he's got a face you want to slap; *très Fam* **t. de con, t. de nœud** dickhead; **faire la t.** to sulk; **faire la t. à qn** to ignore sb; **avec lui, c'est à la t. du client** *(restaurant)* he charges what he feels like; *(professeur)* he gives you a good *Br* mark *or Am* grade if he likes your face

4 *(mesure)* head; **il a une t. de plus que son frère** he's a head taller than his brother; **le favori a été battu d'une courte t.** the favourite was beaten by a short head

5 *Culin* head; **de la t. de veau** calf's head; *Belg* **t. pressée** *(fromage de tête) Br* pork brawn, *Am* headcheese

6 *Sport* header; **faire une t.** to head the ball

7 *Zool* **t. de lion** lionhead

B. *SIÈGE DE LA PENSÉE* **1** *(siège des pensées, de l'imagination, de la mémoire)* mind, head; **il a la t. bourrée de chiffres/dates** his head is stuffed with figures/dates; **il a des rêves plein la t.** he's a dreamer; **une drôle d'idée m'est passée par la t.** a strange idea came into my head; **se mettre qch dans la t.** to get sth into one's head; **se mettre dans la t. que...** to get it into one's head that...; **se mettre dans la t.** *ou* **en t. de faire qch** to make up one's mind to do sth; **elle s'est mis en t. de terminer son livre avant l'automne** she's made up her mind to finish her book before the autumn; **une t. bien faite** a good mind; *Fam* **être une t.** to be brainy, to have brains; *Fam* **avoir** *ou* **attraper la grosse t.** to have a big head, to be big-headed; **avoir toute sa t.** to have all one's faculties; **faire sa mauvaise t.** to dig one's heels in; *Fam* **ce qu'il a dans la t. il ne l'a pas aux pieds** *ou* **aux talons** when he's made up his mind he wants something there's no stopping him; **avoir la t. chaude, avoir la t. près du bonnet** to be quick-tempered; **monter la t. à qn** to give sb big ideas; **monter à la t. de qn** *(succès)* to go to sb's head; *(chagrin)* to unbalance sb; **se monter la t.** to get carried away; **tourner la t. à qn** to turn sb's head; *Fam* **prendre la t. à qn** *Br* to get up sb's nose, to get on sb's wick, *Am* to tick sb off; *Fam* **prise de t.** pain (in the neck); **avoir la t. vide/dure** to be empty-headed/stubborn; **il est t. en l'air** he's got his head in the clouds; **excuse-moi, j'avais la t. ailleurs** sorry, I was thinking about something else *or* I was miles away; **il n'a pas de t.** *(il est étourdi)* he's scatterbrained *or* a scatterbrain; **ça m'est sorti de la t.** I forgot, it slipped my mind; **il ne sait plus où donner de la t.** he doesn't know whether he's coming or going; **n'en faire qu'à sa t.** to do exactly as one pleases; **je le lirai à t. reposée** I'll take the time to read it in a quiet moment; *Can* **être une t. de Papineau** to be extremely bright▪; **ce n'est pas une t. de Papineau** he's no rocket scientist

2 *(sang-froid, présence d'esprit)* head; **elle a gardé toute sa t. devant le danger** she kept her head in the face of danger; **avoir** *ou* **garder la t. froide** to keep a cool head

C. *PERSONNE, ANIMAL* **1** *(individu)* person; **plusieurs têtes connues** several familiar faces; **prendre un viager sur deux têtes** to buy a property in return for a life annuity for two people; **prendre une assurance sur la t. de qn** to take out an insurance policy on sb; *Fam* **être une t. de lard** *ou* **de mule** *ou* **de pioche** to be as stubborn as a mule, to be pig-headed; **t. de linotte** *ou* **d'oiseau** *ou* **sans cervelle** scatterbrain; *Can Fam* **t. carrée** = pejorative term used to refer to an English Canadian; **t. de cochon** bloody-minded individual; **t. couronnée** crowned head; **forte t.** rebel; *Fam* **une grosse t.** a brain; *Fam* **petite t.** pinhead; *Fam* **avoir ses têtes** to have one's favourites

2 *(vie d'une personne)* head, neck; **le procureur réclame la t. de l'accusé** the prosecution is demanding the prisoner's execution; **jouer** *ou* **risquer sa t.** to risk one's skin; **sauver sa t.** to save one's skin *or* neck

3 *(meneur, leader)* head, leader; **il est la t. du mouvement** he's the leader of the movement; **les têtes pensantes du comité** the brains of the committee

4 *(animal d'un troupeau)* head *inv*; **un cheptel de plusieurs centaines de têtes** several hundred head of cattle; **cinquante têtes de bétail** fifty head of cattle

D. *PARTIE HAUTE, PARTIE AVANT, DÉBUT* **1** *(faîte)* top; **la t. d'un arbre** a treetop; **la t. d'un mât** the top of a mast

2 *(partie avant)* front end; **la t. du train** the front of the train; **t. de lit** bedhead; **mets la t. du lit vers le nord** turn the head of the bed towards the north; **prendre la t. du défilé** to head *or* to lead the march; **prendre la t.** *(marcher au premier rang)* to take the lead; *(commander, diriger)* to take over; **elle prendra la t. de l'entreprise** she'll take over the (running of the) firm; **t. de ligne** *(gén)* terminus, end of the line; *Rail* railhead

3 *(début)* **faites ressortir les têtes de chapitres** make the chapter headings stand out

4 *(dans un classement)* top, head; **les dix élèves qui forment la t. de la classe** the ten best pupils in the class; **t. d'affiche** top of the bill; **être en t. d'affiche** to top the bill; *Pol* **t. de liste** *Br* leading candidate, *Am* head of the ticket; *Sport* **t. de série** seeded player; **t. de série numéro 8** number 8 seed

5 *(extrémité → d'un objet, d'un organe)* head; *(→ d'un os)* head, caput; **la t. d'un clou** the head of a nail; **t. d'ail** head of garlic; **t. de bielle** big end; **t. de cylindre** cylinder head; **t. d'épingle** pinhead; **gros comme une t. d'épingle** the size of a pinhead

6 *Can* **t. d'oreiller** pillow case

7 *(en audiovisuel)* head; **t. d'effacement** erase head; **t. d'enregistrement** recording head; **t. de lecture** head; **t. magnétique** magnetic head

8 *Typ* head, top

9 *Ordinat* head; **t. de lecture-écriture** read-write head; **t. d'impression** print head

10 *Mil* head; **t. de pont** *(sur rivière)* bridgehead; *(sur plage)* beachhead

11 *Nucl* head; **t. chercheuse** homing device; **t. nucléaire** warhead

12 *Pétr* **t. d'injection** swivel; **t. de puits** well head

13 *Mktg* **t. de gondole** aisle end display, gondola end

▫ **à la tête de** **PRÉP** **1** *(en possession de)* **elle s'est trouvée à la t. d'une grosse fortune** she found herself in possession of a great fortune

2 *(au premier rang de)* at the head *or* front of; **à la t. du cortège** at the head of the procession; **à la t. d'un groupe de mécontents** heading a group of protesters

3 *(à la direction de)* in charge of, at the head of; **être à la t. d'une société** to head a company; **il est à la t. d'un cabinet d'assurances** he runs an insurance firm

▫ **de tête** **ADJ** **1** *(femme, homme)* able **2** *(convoi, voiture)* front *(avant n)* **3** *Typ* head *(avant n)* **ADV** *(calculer)* in one's head; **de t., je dirais que ça fait 600** working it out in my head, I'd say it comes to 600; **de t., je dirais que nous étions 20** at a guess I'd say there were 20 of us

▫ **en tête** **ADV** **1** *(devant)* **monter en t.** to go to the front; **être en t.** *(gén)* to be at the front; *(dans une course, une compétition)* to (be in the) lead

2 *(à l'esprit)* **avoir qch en t.** to have sth in mind; **j'ai encore en t. le souvenir de notre dernière rencontre** I can still remember our last meeting; **je ne l'ai plus en t.** I can't remember it

▫ **en tête à tête** **ADV** alone together; **nous avons passé deux heures en t. à t.** we spent two hours alone together; **dîner en t. à t. avec qn** to have a quiet dinner (alone) with sb

▫ **en tête de** **PRÉP** **1** *(au début de)* at the beginning *or* start of; **tous les mots placés en t. de phrase** the first word of every sentence

2 *(à l'avant de)* at the head *or* front of; **les dirigeants syndicaux marchent en t. du défilé** the union leaders head *or* lead the march

3 *(au premier rang de)* at the top of; **en t. du palmarès** at the top of the hit-parade; **en t. des sondages** leading the polls

▫ **par tête** **ADV** per head, a head, apiece; *Fin* per capita; **ça coûtera 40 euros par t.** it'll cost 40 euros a head *or* per head *or* apiece

▫ **par tête de pipe** *Fam* = **par tête**

▫ **sur la tête de** **PRÉP** **1** *(sur la personne de)* **le mécontentement populaire s'est répercuté sur la t. du Premier ministre** popular discontent turned towards the Prime Minister

2 *(au nom de)* in the name of; **il a mis tous ses biens sur la t. de sa femme** he's put all his possessions in his wife's name

3 *(en prêtant serment)* **je le jure sur la t. de mes enfants** I swear on my mother's grave

▫ **tête brûlée** **NF** hothead

▫ **tête croche** **NF** *Can* stubborn person, diehard

▫ **tête de mort** **NF** **1** *(crâne)* skull

2 *(emblème)* death's head, skull and crossbones

▫ **tête de nègre** = **tête-de-nègre** **NF**

▫ **tête de Turc** **NF** whipping boy, scapegoat

Allusion

Une tête bien faite vaut mieux qu'une tête bien pleine

This famous maxim comes from Montaigne's *Essais* (1580–95). It means "A mind that has been taught how to think is better than a mind crammed with facts". Montaigne was speaking of the education of young people, and the ideal qualities for a teacher. The expression is still used in debates about educational methods and goals.

tête-à-queue [tɛtakø] **NM INV** **1** *(de voiture)* (180°) spin; **faire un t.** to spin round, to spin 180° **2** *(de cheval)* (sudden) turn; **faire un t.** to whip round

tête-à-tête [tɛtatɛt] **NM INV** **1** *(réunion)* tête-à-tête, private talk; **avoir un t. avec qn** to have a tête-à-tête with sb **2** *(sofa)* tête-à-tête, vis-à-vis **3** *(service → à thé)* tea set for two; *(→ à café)* coffee set for two

tête-bêche [tɛtbɛʃ] **ADV** **1** *(lits, personnes)* head to foot *or* to tail; **dormir t.** to sleep head to foot; **ranger des bouteilles t.** to store bottles alternate ways up **2** *(timbres)* tête-bêche

tête-de-clou [tɛtdəklu] *(pl* **têtes-de-clou***)* **NF** *Archit* nail-head(ed) moulding

tête-de-loup [tɛtdəlu] *(pl* **têtes-de-loup***)* **NF** ceiling brush

tête-de-Maure [tɛtdəmɔr] *(pl* **têtes-de-Maure***)* **NF** = type of Dutch cheese with a dark brown rind

tête-de-nègre [tɛtdənɛgr] *(pl* **têtes-de-nègre***)* **ADJ INV** dark brown, chocolate-brown

NM INV *(couleur)* dark brown

NF **1** *Culin* chocolate-coated meringue **2** *Bot* Boletus aereus

tête-de-rivière [tɛtdəʀivjɛʀ] (*pl* **têtes-de-rivière**) NF (*en aviron*) head race

tétée [tete] NF **1** (*action de téter*) feeding, breast-feeding **2** (*repas*) *Br* feed, *Am* feeding; **six tétées par jour** six *Br* feeds *or Am* feedings a day; **l'heure de la t.** *Br* feeding time, *Am* nursing time; **pendant les tétées** during feeds, while feeding; **donner la t. à un enfant** to feed a child

téter [18] [tete] VT **1** (*sein, biberon*) to suck (at); **t. sa mère** to suck (at) one's mother's breast, to feed *or* to breast-feed from one's mother **2** (*crayon*) to suck on; (*pouce*) to suck; **il m'écoutait en tétant sa pipe** he puffed at his pipe as he listened to me
▪ USAGE ABSOLU **donner à t. à un enfant** to feed *or* suckle a child; **il tète encore** he's still being breast-fed, *Am* he's still nursing
VI *Fam* (*boire avec excès*) to knock it back, to drink like a fish

téterelle [tetʀɛl] NF breast reliever

têtière [tɛtjɛʀ] NF **1** (*d'un fauteuil, d'un sofa*) antimacassar **2** (*d'un cheval*) headstall, crownpiece **3** *Naut* (*d'une voile*) head **4** (*d'une serrure*) faceplate

tétin [tetɛ̃] NM **1** *Zool* teat **2** *Vieilli* (*d'une femme*) nipple

tétine [tetin] NF **1** *Zool* (*mamelle*) teat **2** (*d'un biberon*) *Br* teat, *Am* nipple **3** (*sucette*) *Br* dummy, *Am* pacifier

téton [tetɔ̃] NM **1** *Fam* (*sein*) tit, boob **2** *Tech* stud, nipple; **t. de positionnement** spigot, dowel; **t. de purge** bleed nipple

tétrachlorométhane [tetʀaklɔʀometan] NM *Chim* tetrachloromethane

tétrachlorure [tetʀaklɔʀyʀ] NM tetrachloride; **t. de carbone** carbon tetrachloride

tétracorde [tetʀakɔʀd] NM *Mus* tetrachord

tétracycline [tetʀasiklin] NF *Chim* tetracycline

tétradactyle [tetʀadaktil] ADJ four-toed, *Spéc* tetradactyl, tetradactylous

tétrade [tetʀad] NF *Biol* tetrad

tétradrachme [tetʀadʀakm] NM *Antiq* tetradrachm

tétradyname [tetʀadinam] ADJ *Bot* tetradynamous

tétraèdre [tetʀaɛdʀ] NM tetrahedron

tétraédrique [tetʀaedʀik] ADJ tetrahedral

tétragone [tetʀagɔn] NF *Bot* tetragonia

tétrahydrogestrinone [tetʀaidʀoʒɛstʀinɔn] NF *Chim* tetrahydrogestrinone

tétraline [tetʀalin] NF *Chim* tetralin, tetrahydronaphthalene

tétralogie [tetʀalɔʒi] NF *Littérature, Théât & Mus* tetralogy

♪

'La Tétralogie' Wagner '(The) Ring Cycle' *or* 'The Ring of the Nibelung'

tétramère [tetʀamɛʀ] ADJ *Entom & Biol* tetramerous
▪ NM *Biol & Chim* tetramer

tétramètre [tetʀamɛtʀ] NM *Littérature* tetrameter

tétraplégie [tetʀapleʒi] NF quadriplegia, tetraplegia

tétraplégique [tetʀapleʒik] ADJ quadriplegic, tetraplegic
▪ NMF quadriplegic

tétraploïde [tetʀaplɔid] *Biol* ADJ tetraploid
▪ NM tetraploid

tétraploïdie [tetʀaplɔidi] NF *Biol* tetraploidy

Tétrapode® [tetʀapɔd] NM (*en travaux publics*) tetrapod

tétrapode [tetʀapɔd] *Zool* ADJ tetrapod
▪ NM tetrapod

tétraptère [tetʀaptɛʀ] *Entom* ADJ tetrapterous
▪ NM tetrapteron

tétrarchat [tetʀaʀka] NM *Antiq* tetrarchate

tétrarchie [tetʀaʀʃi] NF *Antiq* tetrarchy

tétrarque [tetʀaʀk] NM *Antiq* tetrarch

tétras [tetʀa] NM *Orn* grouse; **grand t.** capercaillie

tétras-lyre [tetʀaliʀ] (*pl* **tétras-lyres**) NM *Orn* black grouse

tétrastyle [tetʀastil] *Archit* ADJ tetrastyle
▪ NM tetrastyle

tétrasyllabe [tetʀasilab] *Littérature* ADJ tetrasyllabic
▪ NM tetrasyllable

tétrasyllabique [tetʀasilabik] ADJ tetrasyllabic

tétratomique [tetʀatɔmik] ADJ tetratomic

tétravalent, -e [tetʀavalɑ̃, -ɑ̃t] ADJ *Chim* tetravalent

tétrode [tetʀɔd] NF *Électron* tetrode (valve)

tétrodon [tetʀɔdɔ̃] NM *Ich* globefish, *Spéc* Tetrodon, Tetraodon

tétrodotoxine [tetʀɔdɔtɔksin] NF *Méd* tetrodotoxin

têtu, -e [tety] ADJ stubborn, obstinate; **il a un air t.** he has a stubborn look about him; **t. comme une mule** *ou* **un âne** *ou* **une bourrique** stubborn as a mule
▪ NM *Tech* sledgehammer

teuch [tœʃ] NM *Fam* (*verlan de shit*) hash, *Br* blow, draw

teuf [tœf] NF *Fam* (*verlan de fête*) party ▪

teufer [3] [tœfe] VI *Fam* (*verlan de fêter*) (*faire la fête*) to party

teufeur [tœfœʀ] NM *Fam* **1** (*dans une soirée*) party animal **2** (*dans une rave*) raver

teuf-teuf [tœftœf] (*pl* **teufs-teufs**) *Fam* NM (*train*) choo-choo train
▪ NM OU NF (*vieille voiture*) jalopy, *Br* old banger
▪ ONOMAT (*bruit du train*) puff-puff, choo-choo

-TEUR, -TEUSE/-TRICE [tœʀ, tøz, tʀis] SUFF

The suffix **-teur, -teuse** *or* **-teur, -trice** appears in adjectives and nouns derived from a verb and gives the idea of a person WHO PERFORMS THE ACTION described by the verb. It mostly refers to occupations or social activities, as well as character traits. The English suffixes *-er* and *-or* are common equivalents, e.g.

un acheteur, une acheteuse a buyer; **un éditeur, une éditrice** a publisher/an editor; **un lecteur, une lectrice** a reader; **un conducteur, une conductrice** a driver; **un menteur, une menteuse** a liar; **elle est très rouspéteuse** she's very grumpy

The recent trend for systematically feminizing names of occupations has highlighted the difficulty in deciding between the **-teuse** and **-trice** forms when trying to come up with a new feminine equivalent. The general rule is to use **-trice** in most cases. However, **-teuse** is to be used
(i) when there is a verb which is directly linked to the noun from a semantic point of view and which has a **-t-** in its ending, and/or
(ii) when there is no correlated noun ending in **-tion, -ture** or **-torat**

A few examples of newly feminized names of occupations following this model are:

ajusteuse (masc. *ajusteur*) fitter; **apparitrice** (masc. *appariteur*) usher/porter; **arpentrice** (masc. *arpenteur*) (land) surveyor; **metteuse en scène** (masc. *metteur en scène*) director; **reportrice** (masc. *reporter*) reporter

---

teuton, -onne [tøtɔ̃, -ɔn] ADJ Teutonic
▪ **Teuton, -onne** NM,F **1** *Hist* Teuton **2** *Fam* (*Allemand*) Jerry, = offensive term used to refer to a German

teutonique [tøtɔnik] ADJ Teutonic; **les chevaliers teutoniques** the Teutonic knights

tex [tɛks] NM *Tex* tex

texan, -e [tɛksɑ̃, -an] ADJ Texan
▪ **Texan, -e** NM,F Texan

Texas [tɛksas] NM le T. Texas; **au T.** in Texas

texte [tɛkst] NM **1** (*écrit*) text; **reportez-vous au t. original** consult the original; **ce n'était pas dans le t.** it was not in the text *or* in the original; **commenter/résumer un t.** to do a commentary on/to do a précis of a text
2 (*œuvre littéraire*) text; **les grands textes classiques** the great classical texts *or* works
3 (*extrait d'une œuvre*) passage; **textes choisis** selected passages
4 *Mus* (*paroles d'une chanson*) lyrics; (*d'une pièce de théâtre*) script; (*d'un acteur*) lines; **un jeune chanteur qui écrit lui-même ses textes** a young singer who writes his own lyrics; **apprendre/savoir son t.** to learn/to know one's lines
5 *Jur* (*teneur d'une loi, d'un traité*) text, terms, wording; (*la loi elle-même*) law, act; (*le traité lui-même*) treaty; **selon le t. de la loi/du traité** according to the terms of the law/treaty; **le t. est paru au Journal officiel** the act was published in the official gazette

6 *Typ* (*opposé aux marges, aux illustrations*) text; **il y a trop de t. et pas assez de photos** there's too much text and not enough pictures; **gravure hors t.** plate, full-page engraving; **t. courant** running text; **t. en habillage** text wrap; **t. de présentation** (*d'un livre*) blurb
7 *Ling* (*corpus, énoncé*) text
8 *Littérature* text, work; **elle a proposé son t. à plusieurs éditeurs** she sent her work to several publishers; **t. de présentation** introduction; **écrire un court t. d'introduction** to write a short introduction
9 *Scol & Univ* (*sujet de devoir*) question (for work in class or homework); **je vais vous lire le t. de la dissertation** I'll give you the essay question; **t. libre** free composition; **vous avez t. libre pour la rédaction** you can write about anything you like
10 *Mktg* **t. publicitaire** advertising copy
▪ **dans le texte** ADV in the original; **lire Platon dans le t.** to read Plato in the original; **en français dans le t.** in French in the original; *Fig* to quote the very words used

texteur [tɛkstœʀ] NM *Ordinat* word *or* text processor

textile [tɛkstil] ADJ textile; **fibre/verre t.** textile fibre/glass
▪ NM (*tissu*) fabric, material; **elle s'y connaît dans les textiles** she knows her fabrics; **les textiles synthétiques** *ou* **artificiels** synthetic *or* man-made fibres **2** (*industrie*) **le t., les textiles** the textile industry

texto¹ [tɛksto] ADV *Fam* word for word ▪, verbatim ▪; **il m'a dit t.: fous le camp** get the hell out of here, those were his exact *or* very words

texto² [tɛksto] NM *Tél* text (message)

textuel, -elle [tɛkstɥɛl] ADJ **1** (*conforme → à ce qui est écrit*) literal, word-for-word; (*→ à ce qui a été dit*) verbatim **2** *Littérature* textual; **analyse textuelle** textual analysis
▪ ADV *Fam* quote unquote; **elle m'a dit qu'elle s'en fichait, t.!** she told me she didn't care, those were her exact *or* very words!

textuellement [tɛkstɥɛlmɑ̃] ADV word for word; **je reprends t. ses mots** those were his/her exact *or* very words

texturant [tɛkstyʀɑ̃] NM texturizer

texturation [tɛkstyʀasjɔ̃] NF *Tex* texturizing

texture [tɛkstyʀ] NF **1** (*d'un bois, de la peau*) texture **2** *Géol, Métal & Tex* texture **3** *Littéraire* (*structure*) structure; **la t. du roman est dense/lâche** it's a tightly-structured/loosely-structured novel

texturer [3] [tɛkstyʀe] VT *Tex* to texturize

tézigue [tezig] PRON *Fam* you ▪

TF1 [teɛf1] NF *TV* (*abrév* **Télévision Française 1**) = French independent television company

TG [teʒe] NF **1** *Fin* (*abrév* **trésorerie générale**) paymaster's office (in a "département") **2** *Mktg* (*abrév* **tête de gondole**) aisle end display, gondola end

TGB [teʒebe] NF (*abrév* **très grande bibliothèque**) = the new French national library in the Tolbiac area of Paris

TGI [teʒei] NM *Jur* (*abrév* **tribunal de grande instance**) = court of first instance in civil and criminal matters

TGP [teʒepe] NM *Cin & TV* (*abrév* **très gros plan**) BCU

TGV [teʒeve] NM *Rail* (*abrév* **train à grande vitesse**) = French high-speed train

th (*abrév écrite* **thermie**) 10^6 calories

Thada [tada] NM *Méd* (*abrév* **trouble d'hyperactivité avec déficit de l'attention**) ADHD

thaï, -e [taj] ADJ Thai
▪ NM (*langue*) Thai
▪ **Thaï, -e** NM,F Thai; **les Thaïs** the Thais *or* Thai

thaïlandais, -e [tajlɑ̃dɛ, -ɛz] ADJ Thai; **un restaurant t.** a Thai restaurant; **un ressortissant t.** a Thai (national)
▪ **Thaïlandais, -e** NM,F Thai; **j'ai rencontré un T.** I met someone from Thailand

Thaïlande [tajlɑ̃d] NF **la T.** Thailand; **vivre en T.** to live in Thailand; **aller en T.** to go to Thailand; **le golfe de T.** the Gulf of Siam

thalamique [talamik] ADJ thalamic

thalamus [talamys] NM *Anat* thalamus

thalassémie [talasemi] NF *Méd* thalassaemia

thalasso [talaso] NF *Fam* (*abrév* **thalassothérapie**) seawater therapy ▪, thalassotherapy ▪

thalassocratie [talasɔkrasi] NF *Hist* thalassocracy, thalattocracy
thalassothérapie [talasɔterapi] NF seawater therapy, thalassotherapy
thaler [talɛr] NM *Hist* thaler; **t. de Marie-Thérèse** Maria Theresa thaler *or* dollar
Thalès [talɛs] NPR Thales
thalidomide [talidɔmid] NF thalidomide
thalle [tal] NM thallus
thallium [taljɔm] NM *Chim* thallium
thallophyte [talɔfit] NF thallophyte
thalweg [talvɛg] NM *Arch* talweg, thalweg
thameng [tamɛŋ], **thamin** [tamɛ̃] NM *Zool* thamin (deer), Eld's deer
thanatologie [tanatɔlɔʒi] NF *Méd* thanatology
thanatopraxie [tanatɔpraksi] NF thanatopraxy
thanatos [tanatɔs] NM Thanatos
thatchérien, -enne [tatʃerjɛ̃, -ɛn] ADJ Thatcherite
NM,F Thatcherite
thatchérisme [tatʃerism] NM Thatcherism
thaumaturge [tomatyrʒ] NMF thaumaturge, thaumaturgist
thaumaturgie [tomatyrʒi] NF thaumaturgy
thé [te] NM **1** *(boisson)* tea; **faire du t.** to make (a pot of) tea; **prendre le t.** to have tea; **boire du t.** to drink tea; **t. de Chine/Ceylan** China/Ceylon tea; **t. (au) citron** tea with lemon, *Br* lemon tea; **t. glacé** iced tea; **t. des jésuites** *ou* **du Paraguay** maté; **t. au lait** tea with milk; **t. à la menthe** mint tea; **t. nature** tea without milk; **t. noir** black (leaf) tea; **t. vert** green tea
2 *(feuilles)* tea, tea leaves; **une cuillerée de t.** a spoonful of tea
3 *(réception)* tea party; *(repas)* (afternoon) tea; **t. dansant** tea dance, thé dansant; **inviter qn pour le t.** to invite sb to *or* for tea
4 *Bot* tea, tea plant; **arbre à t.** tea tree
5 *Belg & Suisse (infusion)* herbal tea
6 *Can Bot* **t. des bois** wintergreen
théatin [teatɛ̃] NM *Hist & Rel* Theatine
théâtral, -e, -aux, -ales [teɑtral, -o] ADJ **1** *(relatif au théâtre)* theatrical, stage *(avant n)*, theatre *(avant n)*; **une représentation théâtrale** theatrical production; **production théâtrale** stage production
2 *(scénique)* stage *(avant n)*; **l'adaptation théâtrale du roman** the stage adaptation of the novel; **il aurait fallu utiliser une écriture théâtrale** it should have been written in a style more suitable for the stage
3 *(spectaculaire → geste, action)* dramatic, theatrical; **faire une entrée théâtrale** to make a dramatic *or* grand entrance; **avec de grands gestes théâtraux** with a lot of histrionics *or* drama
théâtralement [teɑtralmɑ̃] ADV *(avec affectation)* theatrically
théâtraliser [3] [teɑtralize] VT to theatricalize
théâtralisme [teɑtralism] NM *Psy* histrionism
théâtralité [teɑtralite] NF *Littérature* stageworthiness
théâtre [teɑtr] NM **A. 1** *(édifice → gén)* theatre, *Antiq* amphitheatre; **aller au t.** to go to the theatre; **elle va souvent au t.** she's a regular theatregoer; **t. d'eau** ornamental fountains; **le T.-Français** the Comédie Française; **t. lyrique** opera house; **t. d'ombres** shadow theatre; **t. de poche** small theatre; **t. en rond** theatre-in-the-round; **t. de verdure** open-air theatre
2 *(compagnie théâtrale)* theatre company; **t. municipal** local theatre; **t. national** national theatre; **théâtres subventionnés** state-subsidized theatres; **le T.-Libre** = theatre company set up in 1887 by André Antoine, famous for its naturalistic staging; **le T. du Soleil** = theatre company directed by Ariane Mnouchkine; **le T. national populaire** the French National Theatre *(based at the Palais de Chaillot in Paris until 1972 and at Villeurbanne near Lyons since then)*
3 *(art, profession)* drama, theatre; **elle veut faire du t.** she wants to go on the stage *or* to become an actress *or* to act; **je vis pour le t.** *(acteur)* I live for the theatre *or* stage; **quand j'étais étudiant j'ai fait un peu de t.** when I was a student I did some acting; **t. filmé** film of a play
4 *(genre)* drama, theatre; **je préfère le t. au cinéma** I prefer theatre *or* plays to films; **le t. dans le t.** a play within a play; **le t. élisabéthain/romantique** Elizabethan/Romantic theatre *or* drama; **le t. de l'absurde** the theatre of the absurd; **le t. de boulevard** mainstream popular theatre *(as first played in theatres on the Paris boulevards)*; **t. musical** musicals; **le t. de rue** street theatre; **t. total** total theatre
5 *(œuvres d'un auteur)* works, plays; **le t. complet d'Anouilh** the complete plays *or* dramatic works of Anouilh
6 *(attitude pleine d'outrance)* histrionics; **tout ça c'est du t.** it's all just histrionics *or* a show; **le voilà qui fait son t.** there he goes, putting on his usual act
7 *(en Afrique francophone) (représentation)* play; **les étudiants de première année présenteront un t.** the first-year students will put on a play
B. 1 *(lieu d'un événement)* scene; **le juge a demandé à se rendre sur le t. du crime** the magistrate asked to go to the scene of the crime; **notre région a été le t. de nombreuses mutations** our part of the country has seen a lot of changes; **une entreprise en perte de vitesse n'était pas le t. qui convenait à ses ambitions** he/she was too ambitious to stay in a company on the decline
2 *Mil* **t. d'opérations** *ou* **des opérations** the theatre of operations; **t. d'opérations extérieur** = theatre of operations situated outside home territory
❑ **de théâtre** ADJ *(critique, troupe)* drama *(avant n)*, theatre *(avant n)*; *(cours)* drama *(avant n)*; *(agence)* booking *(avant n)*; *(jumelles)* opera *(avant n)*; *(accessoire, décor)* stage *(avant n)*; **une femme de t.** a woman of the stage *or* theatre; **écrivain de t.** playwright; **metteur en scène de t.** (stage) director

'Le Théâtre et son double' *Artaud* 'Theatre and its Double'

théâtreux, -euse [teɑtrø, -øz] NM,F *Péj ou Hum* luvvie, thespian
thébaïde [tebaid] NF *Littéraire* solitary retreat
thébain, -e [tebɛ̃, -ɛn] ADJ Theban
❑ **Thébain, -e** NM,F Theban
thébaïne [tebain] NF *Pharm* thebaine
thébaïque [tebaik] ADJ thebaic
Thèbes [tɛb] NM Thebes
thecla [tɛkla], **thècle** [tɛkl] NM *Entom* hairstreak butterfly
théier, -ère [teje, -ɛr] ADJ tea *(avant n)*; **la production théière** tea production
NM tea plant
❑ **théière** NF teapot
théine [tein] NF theine
théisme [teism] NM **1** *(consommation excessive)* excessive tea drinking; *(empoisonnement)* tea poisoning **2** *Rel* theism
théiste [teist] ADJ theist, theistic
NMF theist
Thélème [telɛm] NM *voir* **abbaye**
thématique [tematik] ADJ thematic; **index/catalogue t.** subject index/catalogue
NF **1** *Littérature* themes; **la t. des contes de fées** the themes developed in fairy tales; **la t. de Kafka** themes in Kafka **2** *Mus* themes
thème [tɛm] NM **1** *(sujet)* theme; **choisissons un t. de discussion** let's choose a subject for discussion; **sur le t. de** on the theme of
2 *Scol (traduction)* translation into a foreign language, prose; **t. latin/allemand** translation into Latin/German *(from one's native language)*; **faire du t.** to translate into a foreign language
3 *Beaux-Arts, Littérature & Mus* theme
4 *Ling* stem, theme
5 *Astrol* **t. astral** birth chart; **faire son t. à qn** to draw up sb's birth chart
Thémis [temis] NPR *Myth* Themis; *Littéraire* **le temple de T.** the law courts
Thémistocle [temistɔkl] NPR Themistocles
thénar [tenar] *Anat* ADJ **éminence t.** thenar eminence, ball of the thumb
NM thenar eminence, ball of the thumb
théobromine [teɔbrɔmin] NF *Chim & Pharm* theobromine
théocentrisme [teɔsɑ̃trism] NM theocentrism
théocratie [teɔkrasi] NF theocracy
théocratique [teɔkratik] ADJ theocratic
Théocrite [teɔkrit] NPR Theocritus
théodicée [teɔdise] NF *Phil* theodicy
théodolite [teɔdɔlit] NM theodolite
théogonie [teɔgɔni] NF theogony
théogonique [teɔgɔnik] ADJ theogonic
théologal, -e, -aux, -ales [teɔlɔgal, -o] ADJ theological; **les trois vertus théologales** the three theological virtues
théologie [teɔlɔʒi] NF theology; **docteur en t.** doctor of divinity, DD; **faire sa t.** to study theology, to be a divinity student; **t. de la libération** liberation theology
théologien, -enne [teɔlɔʒjɛ̃, -ɛn] NM,F theologian
théologique [teɔlɔʒik] ADJ theological
théologiquement [teɔlɔʒikmɑ̃] ADV theologically
théomaniaque [teɔmanjak] NMF *Méd* theomaniac
théomanie [teɔmani] NF *Méd* theomania
théophanie [teɔfani] NF *Rel* theophany
théophilanthrope [teɔfilɑ̃trɔp] NMF *Hist* theophilanthropist
théophilanthropie [teɔfilɑ̃trɔpi] NF *Hist* theophilanthropy
théophilanthropisme [teɔfilɑ̃trɔpism] NM *Hist* theophilanthropism
Théophraste [teɔfrast] NPR Theophrastus
théophylline [teɔfilin] NF *Chim & Pharm* theophylline
théorbe [teɔrb] NM *Mus* theorbo
théorématique [teɔrematik] ADJ theorematic
théorème [teɔrɛm] NM theorem; **le t. de Pythagore** Pythagoras' theorem; **le t. de Newton** the binomial theorem; **le t. de Thalès** Thales' theorem
théorétique [teɔretik] *Phil* ADJ theoretical
NF theoretics *(singulier)*
théoricien, -enne [teɔrisjɛ̃, -ɛn] NM,F **1** *(philosophe, chercheur etc)* theorist, theoretician; **un t. de la mécanique quantique** an expert in quantum theory **2** *(adepte → d'une doctrine)* theorist; **les théoriciens du libéralisme/marxisme** the theorists of the free market/of Marxism
théorie[1] [teɔri] NF **1** *(en science)* theory; **t. des ensembles** set theory; *Math* **t. des catastrophes** catastrophe theory; *Phys* **t. cinétique des gaz** kinetic theory of gases; *Math & Ordinat* **t. des probabilités** theory of probability; **la t. de la relativité** the theory of relativity; *Biol* **t. de Weissmann** Weismannism
2 *(ensemble de concepts)* theory; **la t. du surréalisme** the theory of surrealism
3 *(ensemble des règles)* theory; **avant de commencer le piano, il faut faire un peu de t.** before playing the piano you have to study a bit of theory; **il possède bien la t. des échecs** he has a good theoretical knowledge of chess
4 *(opinion)* theory; **bâtir une t.** to construct a theory; **c'est la t. du gouvernement** that's the government's theory *or* that's what the government claims
5 *(connaissance spéculative)* theory; **le fossé qui existe entre la t. et la pratique** the gap between theory and practice; **tout cela, c'est de la t.** this is all purely theoretical
6 *Mktg* **t. de la décision** decision theory; *Écon* **t. de la dépendance** dependency theory; **t. des jeux** game theory; **t. des prix** price theory; **t. quantitative** quantity theory
7 *Mil* theoretical instruction
❑ **en théorie** ADV in theory, theoretically; **en t., tu as raison, en fait le système est inapplicable** in theory you're right, but in actual fact the system is unworkable
théorie[2] [teɔri] NF **1** *Antiq* theory **2** *Littéraire (défilé)* procession; **une longue t. de fidèles progressait vers le sanctuaire** a long procession of worshippers was moving towards the sanctuary
théorique [teɔrik] ADJ theoretical; *Fin* **profits théoriques** paper profits
théoriquement [teɔrikmɑ̃] ADV **1** *(d'un point de vue spéculatif)* theoretically, in theory; **le principe est t. acceptable** the principle is acceptable in theory **2** *(en toute hypothèse)* in theory; **t., je devrais arriver à 21 heures** in theory, I ought to arrive at 9 p.m.
théorisation [teɔrizasjɔ̃] NF theorization, theorizing
théoriser [3] [teɔrize] VT to theorize
VI to theorize, to speculate

théosophe [teɔzɔf] NMF theosophist

théosophie [teɔzɔfi] NF theosophy

théosophique [teɔzɔfik] ADJ theosophic

thèque [tɛk] NF Zool theca

-thèque [tɛk] SUFF **bibliothèque** library; **cinémathèque** movie or Br film library; (personnelle) movie or Br film collection; **vidéothèque** video library; (personnelle) video collection

thérapeute [terapøt] NMF 1 (spécialiste des traitements) therapist 2 Littéraire (médecin) doctor, physician 3 (psychothérapeute) therapist

thérapeutique [terapøtik] ADJ therapeutic; **les avancées thérapeutiques sont remarquables dans ce domaine** remarkable medical advances have been made in this field; **acte t.** invasive treatment; **aléa t.** risk attached to treatment; **accident t.** accident in the course of treatment NF 1 (traitement) therapy, treatment; **le choix entre plusieurs thérapeutiques** the choice between several courses of treatment
2 (discipline médicale) therapeutics (singulier)

thérapie [terapi] NF 1 (traitement) therapy, treatment; Méd **t. par électrochocs** electroconvulsive therapy 2 Psy therapy; **commencer une t.** to start a course of therapy, to start therapy; **être en t.** to be in therapy; **t. cognitive** cognitive therapy; **t. de couple** couples therapy; **t. familiale** family therapy; **t. génique** gene therapy; **t. de groupe** group therapy; **t. primale** primal scream therapy

theravada [teravada] ADJ M INV Rel Theravadin

thériaque [terjak] NF Arch Méd theriac

théridion [teridjɔ̃], **theridium** [teridjɔm] NM Entom tangled-web spider, Spéc Theridion

thermal, -e, -aux, -ales [tɛrmal, -o] ADJ (eau) thermal, -e; (source) thermal, hot; **ville thermale** spa town

thermalisme [tɛrmalism] NM 1 (science) balneology 2 (thérapie) hydrotherapy, water cures; **l'argent de la commune provient du t.** the commune derives its revenue from its spa facilities

thermalité [tɛrmalite] NF characteristics of hot springs

thermes [tɛrm] NMPL 1 (établissement de cure) thermal baths 2 Antiq thermae

thermicien, -enne [tɛrmisjɛ̃, -ɛn] NM,F heat engineer

thermicité [tɛrmisite] NF heat balance

thermidor [tɛrmidɔr] NM = 11th month of the French Revolutionary calendar (from 19 July to 17 August)

THERMIDOR AN II
This refers to the three days during which Robespierre attacked his enemies before the "Convention". He was arrested on the second day and executed together with his supporters on the third day.

thermidorien, -enne [tɛrmidɔrjɛ̃, -ɛn] ADJ Thermidorian, of the 9th Thermidor
❑ **Thermidoriens** NMPL revolutionaries of the 9th Thermidor, Thermidorians

thermie [tɛrmi] NF (ancienne unité de mesure) 10^6 calories

thermique [tɛrmik] ADJ (réacteur, équilibre, signature, papier) thermal; (énergie) thermic; (moteur, écran, traitement) heat (avant n)
NF heat sciences
NM thermal

thermiquement [tɛrmikmɑ̃] ADV thermally

thermistance [tɛrmistɑ̃s] NF Élec thermistor

thermisteur [tɛrmistœr], **thermistor** [tɛrmistɔr] NM Élec thermistor

thermite [tɛrmit] NF Métal thermit, thermite

thermobarique [tɛrmɔbarik] ADJ (bombe) thermobaric

thermocautère [tɛrmɔkotɛr] NM thermocautery

thermochimie [tɛrmɔʃimi] NF thermochemistry

thermochimique [tɛrmɔʃimik] ADJ thermochemical

thermoclastie [tɛrmɔklasti] NF Géol thermoclasty

thermocline [tɛrmɔklin] NF (en océanologie) thermocline

thermocollage [tɛrmɔkɔlaʒ] NM Tech heat sealing

thermocollant, -e [tɛrmɔkɔlɑ̃, -ɑ̃t] ADJ Tech heat-sealing

thermoconduction [tɛrmɔkɔ̃dyksjɔ̃] NM Phys heat conduction

thermocontact [tɛrmɔkɔ̃takt] NM Élec thermal or temperature switch

thermocouple [tɛrmɔkupl] NM thermocouple

thermodurcissable [tɛrmɔdyrsisabl] ADJ thermosetting
NM thermoset (substance)

thermodynamicien, -enne [tɛrmɔdinamisjɛ̃, -ɛn] NM,F thermodynamics specialist

thermodynamique [tɛrmɔdinamik] ADJ thermodynamic
NF thermodynamics (singulier)

thermoélectricité [tɛrmɔelɛktrisite] NF thermoelectricity

thermoélectrique [tɛrmɔelɛktrik] ADJ thermoelectric; **pince t.** thermocouple; **couple t.** thermoelectric couple; **pile t.** thermopile

thermoélectronique [tɛrmɔelɛktrɔnik] ADJ thermoelectronic

thermoformage [tɛrmɔfɔrmaʒ] NM thermoforming

thermogène [tɛrmɔʒɛn] ADJ thermogenous, thermogenetic

thermogenèse [tɛrmɔʒɛnɛz], **thermogénèse** [tɛrmɔʒenɛz] NF Physiol thermogenesis

thermographe [tɛrmɔgraf] NM Phys thermograph

thermographie [tɛrmɔgrafi] NF Phys thermography

thermoïonique [tɛrmɔjɔnik] ADJ **effet t.** thermionic emission

Thermolactyl® [tɛrmɔlaktil] NM = thermal clothing fabric

thermoluminescence [tɛrmɔlyminesɑ̃s] NF thermoluminescence

thermolyse [tɛrmɔliz] NF thermolysis

thermomagnétisme [tɛrmɔmaɲetism] NM Phys thermomagnetism

thermomécanique [tɛrmɔmekanik] ADJ thermomechanical

thermomètre [tɛrmɔmɛtr] NM 1 (appareil) thermometer; **le t. indique 5°** the thermometer stands at or registers 5°; **le t. monte/descend** the temperature (on the thermometer) is rising/falling; **t. digital** digital thermometer; **t. à gaz** (constant volume) gas thermometer; **t. médical** clinical thermometer; **t. à mercure** mercury thermometer; **t. à maximum et minimum** maximum and minimum thermometer
2 Fig (indice) barometer, gauge; **la Bourse est le t. de l'activité économique et financière** the Stock Exchange is a barometer of economic and financial activity

thermométrie [tɛrmɔmetri] NF thermometry

thermométrique [tɛrmɔmetrik] ADJ thermometric

thermonucléaire [tɛrmɔnykleɛr] ADJ thermonuclear

thermophile [tɛrmɔfil] Biol ADJ thermophil, thermophile
NM thermophil, thermophile

thermopile [tɛrmɔpil] NF Élec thermopile

thermoplastique [tɛrmɔplastik] ADJ thermoplastic

thermoplongeur [tɛrmɔplɔ̃ʒœr] NM portable immersion heater

thermopompe [tɛrmɔpɔ̃p] NF heat pump

thermopropulsé, -e [tɛrmɔprɔpylse] ADJ thermopropulsion (avant n)

thermopropulsif, -ive [tɛrmɔprɔpylsif, -iv] ADJ thermopropulsive

thermopropulsion [tɛrmɔprɔpylsjɔ̃] NF thermopropulsion

thermopropulsive [tɛrmɔprɔpylsiv] voir **thermopropulsif**

Thermopyles [tɛrmɔpil] NMPL **les T.** Thermopylae

thermorécepteur [tɛrmɔresɛptœr] NM thermoreceptor

thermorégulateur, -trice [tɛrmɔregylatœr, -tris] ADJ thermoregulator

thermorégulation [tɛrmɔregylasjɔ̃] NF thermoregulation

thermorégulatrice [tɛrmɔregylatris] voir **thermorégulateur**

thermorésistant, -e [tɛrmɔrezistɑ̃, -ɑ̃t] ADJ heat-resistant, thermoresistant

Thermos® [tɛrmɔs] NM OU NF Thermos®

thermoscope [tɛrmɔskɔp] NM thermoscope

thermosiphon [tɛrmɔsifɔ̃] NM thermosiphon

thermosphère [tɛrmɔsfɛr] NF thermosphere

thermosphérique [tɛrmɔsferik] ADJ thermospheric

thermostat [tɛrmɔsta] NM thermostat; **t. 7** (dans recette) gas mark 7; **réglage par t.** thermostatic control

thermostatique [tɛrmɔstatik] ADJ thermostatic

thermotactisme [tɛrmɔtaktism] NM thermotaxis

thermothérapie [tɛrmɔterapi] NF Méd deep-heat treatment, Spéc thermotherapy

théromorphes [terɔmɔrf] NMPL Zool Theromorpha, Pelycosauria

théropsidé [terɔpside] NM Zool therapsid

thésard, -e [tezar, -ard] NM,F Fam research student■, PhD student■

thésaurisation [tezɔrizasjɔ̃] NF (gén) & Écon hoarding

thésauriser [3] [tezɔrize] VI to hoard money
VT to hoard (up)

thésauriseur, -euse [tezɔrizœr, -øz] ADJ hoarding
NM,F hoarder

thésaurus, thesaurus [tezɔrys] NM 1 (lexique) lexicon 2 (outil de classement) thesaurus

thèse [tɛz] NF 1 Scol thesis; **t. de doctorat d'État** ≃ PhD, Br ≃ doctoral thesis, Am ≃ doctoral or PhD dissertation; **t. de troisième cycle** (en lettres) Br ≃ MA, Am ≃ master's thesis; (en sciences) Br ≃ MSc, Am ≃ master's thesis
2 (théorie) argument, thesis, theory; **t., antithèse, synthèse** thesis, antithesis, synthesis; **il défend la t. suivante:...** he argues that...; **la t. de l'accident n'est pas écartée** the possibility that it may have been an accident hasn't been ruled out; **la famille rejette la t. du suicide** the family rejects the idea of suicide; Littéraire **voilà qui change la t.!** that alters the case, that makes all the difference
❑ **à thèse** ADJ **pièce à t.** problem play, drama of ideas; **roman à t.** novel of ideas

THÈSE, ANTITHÈSE, SYNTHÈSE
This is the conventional structure of a rhetorical argument (especially in an essay or "dissertation") as traditionally taught to French pupils. Students are traditionally instructed to adhere to this format when presenting written work during the academic year and at examinations.

Thésée [teze] NPR Myth Theseus

thesmophories [tɛsmɔfɔri] NFPL Antiq Thesmophoria

thesmothète [tɛsmɔtɛt] NM Antiq thesmothete

Thessalie [tesali] NF **la T.** Thessaly

thessalien, -enne [tesaljɛ̃, -ɛn] ADJ Thessalian
❑ **Thessalien, -enne** NM,F Thessalian

Thessalonique [tesalɔnik] NF Thessalonika

thêta [teta] NM INV theta

thétique [tetik] ADJ Phil thetic

théurgie [teyrʒi] NF theurgy

THG [teaʒe] NF Chim (abrév **tétrahydrogestrinone**) THG

thiamine [tjamin] NF thiamin

thiazole [tjazɔl] NM thiazole

thibaude [tibod] NF carpet underlay felt

thier, thiers [tjɛr] NM Belg slope, hill

Thimbu [timbu] NM Géog Thimphu

thinocore [tinɔkɔr] NM Orn seedsnipe

thioacide [tjɔasid] NM thioacid

thioalcool [tjɔalkɔl] NM thioalcohol

thiocarbonate [tjɔkarbɔnat] NM thiocarbonate

thiodiphénylamine [tjɔdifenilamin] NF Chim phenothiazine

thiofène [tjɔfɛn] = **thiophène**

thiol [tjɔl] NM thioalcohol

thionate [tjɔnat] NM Chim thionate

thionine [tjɔnin] NF Chim thionine

thionique [tjɔnik] ADJ Chim thionic

thiophène [tjɔfɛn] NM Chim thiophene

thiosulfate [tjɔsylfat] NM Chim thiosulphate

thiosulfurique [tjɔsylfyrik] ADJ Chim thiosulphuric

thio-urée [tjɔyre] (pl **thio-urées**) NF Chim thiourea

thixotropie [tiksɔtrɔpi] NF Chim thixotropy

thlaspi [tlaspi] NM Bot pennycress, Spéc thlaspi

tholos [tɔlɔs] NF Archit & Archéol tholos

thomas [tɔma] NM *Fam Vieilli (pot de chambre)* chamberpot■, *Br* jerry

thomise [tɔmiz] NM *Entom* crab spider, *Spéc* thomisid

thomisme [tɔmism] NM Thomism

thomiste [tɔmist] ADJ Thomistic, Thomistical
NMF Thomist

thon [tɔ̃] NM **1** *(poisson)* tuna, *Br* tunny; *Culin* tuna (fish); **t. blanc** *Ich* long-fin tuna *or Br* tunny; *Culin* white-meat tuna; *Ich* **t. rouge** bluefin tuna, *Br* (red) tunny; *Culin* **t. en boîte** tinned tuna; *Culin* **t. à l'huile** tuna in oil; *Culin* **t. au naturel** tuna in brine; *Ich* **t. obèse** bigeye tuna **2** *Fam (femme laide)* dog, *Br* boot, *Am* beast

thonaire [tɔnɛr] NM *Pêche* tuna *or Br* tunny net

thonier [tɔnje] NM tuna *or Br* tunny boat

thonine [tɔnin] NF *Ich* little tunny

Thor [tɔr] NPR *Myth* Thor

Thora [tɔra] = **Tora**

thoracentèse [tɔrasɛ̃tɛz] NF thoracentesis, thoracocentesis, pleurocentesis

thoracique [tɔrasik] ADJ thoracic

thoracoplastie [tɔrakɔplasti] NF *Méd* thoracoplasty

thoracoscopie [tɔrakɔskɔpi] NF *Méd* thoracoscopy

thoracotomie [tɔrakɔtɔmi] NF *Méd* thoracotomy

thorax [tɔraks] NM *Anat* thorax

thorianite [tɔrjanit] NF *Minér* thorianite

thorine [tɔrin] NF *Chim* thoria, thorium oxide

thorite [tɔrit] NF *Minér* thorite

thorium [tɔrjɔm] NM *Chim* thorium

thoron [tɔrɔ̃] NM *Chim* thoron

Thoune [tun] NM Thun

Thrace [tras] NF **la T.** Thrace

thrace [tras] NM *Antiq* = gladiator equipped with a helmet, a small round shield and a scimitar

thrène [trɛn] NM *Antiq* threnody

thréonine [treɔnin] NF *Biol & Chim* threonine

thridace [tridas] NF *Pharm* thridace, lactucarium

thriller [srilœr, trilœr] NM thriller

thrips [trips] NM *Entom* thrips, *Spéc* thysanopter

thrombine [trɔ̃bin] NF *Biol & Chim* thrombin

thrombocyte [trɔ̃bɔsit] NM *Physiol* thrombocyte

thromboembolique [trɔ̃bɔ̃ãbɔlik] ADJ *Méd* thromboembolic

thrombokinase [trɔ̃bɔkinaz] NF *Méd* thrombokinase, thromboplastin

thrombolyse [trɔ̃bɔliz] NF *Méd* thrombolysis

thrombopénie [trɔ̃bɔpeni] NF *Méd* thrombocytopenia

thrombophlébite [trɔ̃bɔflebit] NF *Méd* thrombophlebitis

thromboplastine [trɔ̃bɔplastin] NF *Méd* thrombokinase, thromboplastin

thromboplastique [trɔ̃bɔplastik] ADJ *Méd* thromboplastic

thrombopoïèse [trɔ̃bɔpɔjɛz] NF *Méd* thrombopoiesis

thrombose [trɔ̃boz] NF *Méd* thrombosis; **t. veineuse profonde** deep-vein thrombosis

thrombosé, -e [trɔ̃boze] ADJ *Méd* thrombosed

thrombotique [trɔ̃bɔtik] ADJ *Méd* thrombotic

thrombus [trɔ̃bys] NM *Méd* thrombus

THS [teaʃɛs] NM *Méd (abrév* **traitement hormonal substitutif***)* HRT

Thucydide [tysidid] NPR Thucydides

thug [tyg] NM *Hist* thug

thulium [tyljɔm] NM *Chim* thulium

thune [tyn] NF *Fam* **1** *Vieilli* five-franc coin **2** *Suisse* Swiss five-franc coin **3** *(argent)* cash, *Br* dosh, *Am* bucks; **je n'avais pas une t.** I was broke, I hadn't a bean; **mon père me filera de la t.** my father will give me some cash *or Br* a few quid; **gagner de la t.** *ou* **des thunes** to be raking it in, to be making megabucks; **être pété de thunes** to be loaded

Thurgovie [tyrgɔvi] NF **la T.** Thurgau

thuriféraire [tyriferɛr] NM **1** *Rel* thurifer **2** *Littéraire* flatterer, sycophant

Thuringe [tyrɛ̃ʒ] NF **la T.** Thuringia

thuya [tyja] NM *Bot* thuja; **t. occidental** white cedar

thyade [tjad] NF *Myth* thyiad

thylacine [tilasin] NM *Zool* Tasmanian wolf, *Spéc* thylacine

thym [tɛ̃] NM thyme

thymie [timi] NF *Psy* thymia

thymine [timin] NF *Biol & Chim* thymine

thymique [timik] ADJ *Méd & Psy* thymic

thymoanaleptique [timɔanalɛptik] *Pharm* ADJ thymoanaleptic
NM thymoanaleptic

thymol [timɔl] NM *Chim* thymol

thymus [timys] NM thymus

thyratron [tiratrɔ̃] NM *Électron* thyratron

thyréostimuline [tireɔstimylin] NF *Physiol* thyrotropin, thyrotrophin, thyroid-stimulating hormone

thyréotrope [tireɔtrɔp] ADJ *Physiol* thyreotropic, thyrotropic, thyrotrophic

thyristor [tiristɔr] NM *Élec* thyristor

thyroïde [tirɔid] ADJ thyroid
NF thyroid (gland)

thyroïdectomie [tirɔidɛktɔmi] NF *Méd* thyroidectomy

thyroïdien, -enne [tirɔidjɛ̃, -ɛn] ADJ thyroid *(avant n)*

thyroïdite [tirɔidit] NF *Méd* thyroiditis

thyrotoxicose [tirɔtɔksikoz] NF *Méd* Graves' disease

thyroxine [tirɔksin] NF *Biol* thyroxin, thyroxine

thyrse [tirs] NM *Myth & Bot* thyrsus

thysanoptère [tizanɔptɛr] *Entom* NM thysanopter, thysanopteron
□ **thysanoptères** NMPL Thysanoptera

thysanoure [tizanur] *Entom* NM thysanuran
□ **thysanoures** NMPL Thysanura

TI [tei] NM *Jur (abrév* **tribunal d'instance***)* = lowest-level court in French legal system, having limited jurisdiction

tiaffe [tjaf] NF *Suisse Fam* **1** *(chaleur)* heatwave■ **2** *(neige fondante)* slush■

tiags [tjag] NFPL *Fam (abrév* **santiags***)* cowboy boots■

tian [tjã] NM *(grand plat)* tian, = large, shallow earthenware dish; *(gratin)* tian, = vegetable gratin cooked in a "tian"

tiare [tjar] NF **1** *(coiffure)* tiara **2** *(dignité papale)* **la t.** the Papal tiara; **coiffer la t.** to become Pope

tiaré [tjare] NM *Bot* tiaré, tiare

Tibère [tibɛr] NPR Tiberius

Tibériade [tiberjad] NF **le lac de T.** Lake Tiberias, the Sea of Galilee

Tibesti [tibɛsti] NM **le T.** the Tibesti (Massif)

Tibet [tibɛ] NM **le T.** Tibet; **au T.** in Tibet

tibétain, -e [tibetɛ̃, -ɛn] ADJ Tibetan
NM *(langue)* Tibetan
□ **Tibétain, -e** NM,F Tibetan

tibéto-birman [tibetɔbirmã] NM *Ling* Tibeto-Burman

TIBEUR *Fin (abrév écrite* **taux interbancaire européen***)* EURIBOR

tibia [tibja] NM **1** *Anat (os)* shinbone, *Spéc* tibia; *(devant de la jambe)* shin; **donner à qn un coup de pied dans les tibias** to kick sb in the shins **2** *Zool* tibia

tibial, -e, -aux, -ales [tibjal, -o] ADJ *Anat* tibial

tibio-tarsien, -enne [tibjɔtarsjɛ̃, -ɛn] *(mpl* **tibio-tarsiens***, fpl* **tibio-tarsiennes***)* ADJ *Anat* tibiotarsal

Tibre [tibr] NM **le T.** the (River) Tiber

tic [tik] NM **1** *(au visage)* tic, (nervous) twitch; **il a un t.** he has a twitch *or* a tic, his face twitches; **il a un t. à la bouche/à l'œil** he has a twitch at the corner of his mouth/in his eye; **son visage était agité de tics** his/her face twitched nervously; **t. nerveux** nervous tic *or* twitch; **t. douloureux** facial neuralgia, *Spéc* tic douloureux **2** *(manie gestuelle)* (nervous) tic, twitch; *Fam* **il est bourré de tics** he's got a lot of nervous tics **3** *(répétition stéréotypée)* habit; **il a un t., il répète toujours le dernier mot de ses phrases** he has a habit of always repeating the last word of his sentences; **un t. de langage** a (speech) mannerism **4** *Vét (avec déglutition d'air)* wind-sucking

tichodrome [tikɔdrom] NM *Orn* **t. des murailles** wallcreeper

ticket [tikɛ] NM **1** *(de bus, de métro)* ticket; *(de vestiaire, de consigne)* slip, ticket; **les tickets, s'il vous plaît!** tickets please!; **t. de caisse** *Br* till receipt, *Am* sales slip; **t. de quai** platform ticket **2** *(coupon →de rationnement, de pain)* coupon **3** *Anciennement Fam (dix francs)* ten-franc note■; **cette montre m'a coûté 100 tickets** this watch set me back a thousand francs **4** *Pol (aux États-Unis)* ticket **5** *Can Joual (contravention) Br* parking *or Am* traffic ticket■

6 *Mktg* **t. d'entrée** = cost of entering the market **7** *Fam (locution)* **avoir un** *ou* **le t. (avec qn)** to have made a hit (with sb); **tu as le t.** *Br* he/she fancies you, *Am* he's/she's sweet on you; **il a un t. avec elle** *Br* she fancies him, *Am* she's sweet on him
□ **ticket modérateur** NM *(pour la Sécurité sociale)* = proportion of medical expenses payable by the patient

ticket-repas [tikɛrɛpa] *(pl* **tickets-repas***)* NM = voucher given to employees to cover part of luncheon expenses, *Br* luncheon voucher, *Am* ≃ meal ticket

Ticket-Restaurant® [tikɛrɛstɔrã] *(pl* **Tickets-Restaurant***)* NM = voucher given to employees to cover part of luncheon expenses, *Br* ≃ luncheon voucher, *Am* ≃ meal ticket

tickson [tiksɔ̃] NM *Fam* ticket■

ticoune [tikun] NMF *Can Fam* moron, cretin, idiot■

tic-tac [tiktak] NM INV *(d'une pendule, d'une bombe)* ticking *(UNCOUNT)*, tick-tock; **faire t.** to tick (away), to go tick-tock
ONOMAT tick-tock

tictaquer [3] [tiktake] VI *(horloge)* to tick (away), to go tick-tock

tie-break [tajbrɛk] *(pl* **tie-breaks***)* NM tie break

tiédasse [tjedas] ADJ lukewarm, tepid

tiède [tjɛd] ADJ **1** *(ni chaud ni froid)* lukewarm, warm, tepid; **délayez la poudre dans de l'eau t.** mix the powder with warm water; **un vent t. et agréable** a nice warm breeze; **salade t.** warm salad **2** *(pas suffisamment chaud)* lukewarm, not hot enough; **le thé va être t., bois-le vite** drink your tea before it gets cold *or* while it's hot **3** *Fig (peu enthousiaste →accueil, réaction)* lukewarm, unenthusiastic, half-hearted; *(→sentiment, foi, défenseur)* half-hearted; **les syndicalistes sont tièdes** the union members lack conviction *or* are apathetic **4** *(avant le nom) (doux, calme)* pleasant, sweet
NMF *Fam (indifférent, mou)* wimp, *Br* wet
ADV **je préfère boire/manger t.** I don't like drinking/eating very hot things; **il fait t. aujourd'hui** it's mild *or* warm today; **la tarte Tatin doit se manger t.** tarte Tatin should be eaten warm
NF *Suisse* heatwave

tièdement [tjɛdmã] ADV *(accueillir)* coolly, unenthusiastically; *(soutenir)* half-heartedly

tiédeur [tjedœr] NF **1** *(d'un liquide)* lukewarmness; *(d'un solide)* warmth; *(de l'air)* mildness; **la t. d'un matin de juin** the mildness of a June morning **2** *Fig (d'un accueil)* lukewarmness, coolness; *(d'un sentiment, d'un défenseur)* half-heartedness; **avec t.** half-heartedly, without any great enthusiasm; **la t. de ses paroles** his/her unenthusiastic *or* half-hearted words **3** *(agréable douceur)* warmth; **il se réfugia dans la t. de la vie familiale** he took refuge in the warmth of family life

tiédir [32] [tjedir] VI **1** *(se refroidir →boisson, métal, air)* to cool (down); **laisser t. le gâteau/lait** leave the cake/milk to cool down **2** *(se réchauffer)* to grow warmer; **faire t. du lait** to warm up some milk **3** *Fig (faiblir →conviction, sentiment)* to wane, to weaken, to cool
VT **1** *(refroidir légèrement)* to cool (down); **le vent du soir a tiédi l'air** the evening breeze has cooled the air **2** *(réchauffer légèrement)* to warm (up); **posele un instant sur le radiateur pour le t.** put it on the radiator for a minute to warm it up; **passez la tarte au four une minute pour la t.** put the tart in the oven for a minute to warm it through *or* up

tiédissement [tjedismã] NM **1** *(refroidissement)* cooling (down *or* off) **2** *(réchauffement)* warming up

tien, tienne [tjɛ̃, tjɛn] *(mpl* **tiens***, fpl* **tiennes***)* ADJ *Littéraire* yours; *Vieilli* **un t. cousin** a cousin of yours; **tu feras tiens ses principes** you will adopt his/her principles as your own; **feras-tu tiennes les félicitations qu'ils m'adressent?** will you join them in congratulating me?; **je suis tienne pour toujours** I am yours forever
□ **le tien, la tienne** *(mpl* **les tiens***, fpl* **les tiennes***)*
PRON yours; *Rel & Arch* thine; **prends ma voiture,**

si la tienne est au garage use my car, if yours is at the garage; **il n'a qu'à prendre la tienne** he can just take yours; **il ressemble au t.** it looks like yours; **tu veux bien me donner du t.?** can I have some of yours?; **de toutes ces solutions, tu préfères la tienne?** out of those possible solutions, do you prefer your own?; **tu n'en as pas besoin, tu as le t.** you don't need it, you've got your own; **je n'en ai pas besoin, j'ai le t.** I don't need it, I've got yours; **mes enfants sont plus âgés que les tiens** my children are older than yours (are); **ce parapluie n'est pas le t.** this is not your umbrella, this umbrella is not yours *or* doesn't belong to you; **je me mêle de mes affaires, mêle-toi des tiennes** I'll mind my business and you mind yours; **les deux tiens** your two, the two *or* both of yours; *(en insistant)* your own two; **tu lui as laissé deux des tiens** you gave him/her two of yours; *Fam* **le t. de bébé est plus intelligent** your baby is more intelligent

NM le t. *(ce qui t'appartient)* yours; **ne cherchons pas à distinguer le t. du mien** let's not waste time arguing about who owns what; **ici, il n'y a pas de t. et de mien** it's share and share alike here; *Fam* **à la tienne!** *(à ta santé)* good health!, cheers!; *(bon courage)* all the best!; **tu comptes la convaincre? eh bien, à la tienne!** so you think you can convince her? well all I can say is, good luck to you *or* rather you than me!; **mets-y du t.** *(fais un effort)* make an effort; *(sois compréhensif)* try to be understanding; *Fam* **tu as encore fait des tiennes!** you've (gone and) done it again!

NMPL les tiens *(ta famille)* your family, *Am* your folks; *(tes partisans)* your followers; *(tes coéquipiers)* your team-mates

tienne [tjɛn] **1** *voir* **tien**
2 = **thier**

tient *etc voir* **tenir**

tiento [tjɛnto] **NM** *Mus* tiento

tierce [tjɛrs] *voir* **tiers**[2]

tiercé[1], **-e** [tjɛrse] **ADJ 1** *Agr* third ploughed **2** *Hér* tierced, en tierce **3** *Littérature* **rimes tiercées** terza rima

tiercé[2] [tjɛrse] **ADJ M pari t.** triple forecast
NM triple forecast; **jouer au t.** = to put money on horses; **gagner le t. (dans l'ordre/le désordre)** to win on three horses (with the right placings/without the right placings); **toucher un gros t.** = to win a lot of money on the horses; **le t. gagnant** the first three horses

tiercefeuille [tjɛrsəfœj] **NF** *Hér* trefoil

tiercelet [tjɛrsəlɛ] **NM** *Orn* tercel, tiercel

tiercer [16] [tjɛrse] **VT** *Agr* to plough for the third time

tierceron [tjɛrsərɔ̃] **NM** *Archit* tierceron (rib)

tierne [tjɛrn] = **thier**

tiers[1] [tjɛr] **NM 1** *(partie d'un tout divisé en trois)* third; **elle en a lu un t.** she's a third of the way through (reading it); **tu as droit aux deux t. de la somme** you're entitled to two thirds of the sum; **cinq est le t. de quinze** five is a third of fifteen, five goes into fifteen three times; **la maison était brûlée aux deux t.** two thirds of the house had been destroyed by fire; **une remise d'un t. (du prix)** a discount of a third, a third off

2 *(troisième personne)* third person; *(personne étrangère à un groupe)* stranger, outsider, third party; **elle l'a dit devant des t.** she said it in front of people it had nothing to do with; *Fam* **le t. et le quart** everybody, anybody; *Fam* **il se fiche** *ou* **se moque du t. comme du quart** he couldn't care less

3 *Jur* third party; **les dommages causés à un t.** third party damages; **t. acquéreur** subsequent purchaser; **t. détenteur** third party holder; **t. opposant** (opposing) third party; **t. possesseur** third party owner; **t. saisi** garnishee

4 *Com* **t. bénéficiaire** *(d'un chèque, d'un effet)* beneficiary; **t. porteur** *(d'un effet de commerce)* second endorser; *(d'un effet)* holder in due course

5 *Fin* **t. provisionnel** = thrice-yearly income tax payment based on estimated tax due for the previous year

6 *Hist* **le t.** the Third Estate

7 *(pour la Sécurité sociale)* **t. payant** = system by which a proportion of the fee for medical treatment is paid directly to the hospital, doctor or pharmacist by the patient's insurer; **t. responsable** third party (responsible)

▫ **au tiers ADJ** *Jur* third-party *(avant n)*; **assurance au t.** third-party insurance

▫ **en tiers ADV** *(en tant qu'étranger à un groupe)* as an outsider; **assister en t. à un entretien** to attend an interview as an outside observer

tiers[2], **tierce** [tjɛr, tjɛrs] **ADJ 1** *(étranger à un groupe)* third; **tierce personne** third party; **je n'en parlerai pas devant une tierce personne** I will not speak of it in front of a third party

2 *UE* **pays t.** third *or* non-EU country; **produits t.** non-community products

3 *Jur* **tierce collision** third-party *(avant n)*

4 *Scol* **t. temps pédagogique** = in French nursery and primary schools before 1985, division of the weekly timetable into three parts, each corresponding to a different educational field

5 *Hist* **le t. état** the Third Estate

6 *Math* **a tierce** "a" triple dash

7 *Rel* **t. ordre** third order

8 *Ordinat* **tierce partie de confiance** trusted third party

▫ **tierce NF 1** *Cartes* tierce; **tierce à la dame** = three-card run with queen as the highest card; **tierce majeure** tierce major

2 *Escrime & Hér* tierce

3 *Typ* press proof

4 *Mus* third; **tierce majeure/mineure** major/minor third

5 *Astron & Math* = sixtieth part of a second

6 *Rel* terce, tierce

tiers-arbitre [tjɛrarbitr] *(pl* **tiers-arbitres**) **NM** *Jur* (independent) arbitrator

tiers-monde [tjɛrmɔ̃d] *(pl* **tiers-mondes**) **NM** Third World; **les pays du t.** Third World countries

tiers-mondialisation [tjɛrmɔ̃djalizasjɔ̃], **tiers-mondisation** [tjɛrmɔ̃dizasjɔ̃] **NF la t. du pays** the country's economic decline to Third World levels

tiers-mondisme [tjɛrmɔ̃dism] *(pl* **tiers-mondismes**) **NM** = support for the Third World

tiers-mondiste [tjɛrmɔ̃dist] *(pl* **tiers-mondistes**)
ADJ 1 *(du tiers-mondisme)* pro-Third World **2** *(du tiers-monde)* Third World *(avant n)*
NMF 1 *(spécialiste du tiers-monde)* Third World expert **2** *(idéologue du tiers-mondisme)* Third Worldist

tiers-point [tjɛrpwɛ̃] *(pl* **tiers-points**) **NM 1** *Archit* **arc en t.** pointed equilateral arch **2** *(lime)* triangular file, three-cornered file

tifoso [tifozo] *(pl* **tifosi** [-zi]) **NM** fan

tifs, tiffes [tif] **NMPL** *Fam* hair■; **il faut que j'aille me faire couper les t.** I have to go and get my hair cut

TIG [teiʒe] **NM** *Jur (abrév* **travail d'intérêt général**) ≃ community service

tige [tiʒ] **NF 1** *Bot (d'une feuille)* stem, stalk; *(de blé, de maïs)* stalk; *(d'une fleur)* stem; **tulipe à longue t.** long-stemmed tulip; **rosier sur t.** standard rose; **t. aérienne/souterraine** aerial/underground stem; **arbre de haute/basse t.** tall/half standard

2 *(axe → d'une épingle, d'une aiguille, d'un clou, d'un candélabre, d'une flèche)* shaft; *(→ d'un cadran solaire)* finger, pointer; *(→ d'un guéridon)* pedestal; **une t. de bois** a wooden shaft, a dowel; **une t. de fer** an iron rod; **clef à t. creuse/pleine** key with a hollow/solid shank; **t. de selle** *(de bicyclette)* saddle pillar

3 *Fam (cigarette) Br* fag, *Am* cig

4 *(d'une chaussure)* upper; **la t. est doublée** the upper is lined; **bottes à tiges** top boots; **bottes à t. basse** ankle boots; **baskets à t. haute** high tops

5 *Fig Littéraire (origine d'une famille)* stock, line; **la t. des Bourbon-Parme** the Bourbon-Parma line; **faire t.** to found a line

6 *Archit (de colonne)* shaft

7 *Aut* rod; *(sur le volant)* stalk; **t. de crémaillère** rack link; *(de la direction)* control rod; **t. de culbuteur/piston** push/piston rod; **t. de frein** brake rod; **t. de jauge** dipstick; **t. (de maintien) de capot** *Br* bonnet strut, *Am* hood strut; **t. de poussée** thrust pin, pushrod; **t. poussoir** pushrod; **t. à vis du frein** brake screw

8 *Pétr* **t. de forage** drill pipe

9 *Tech (d'une valve)* stem; *(d'une pompe, d'un piston, d'un paratonnerre)* rod; *(d'un rivet, d'une clé, d'une ancre, d'une lettre)* shank; *Mus (d'un archet)* stick; *Typ* **t. à caractères** type bar

10 *Vulg (pénis)* dick, prick, cock

11 *Belg (d'une montagne)* crest

tigelle [tiʒɛl] **NF** *Bot* tigelle, tigella, tigel

tigette [tiʒɛt] **NF** *Archit* caulicole, caulicolo

tiglon [tiglɔ̃] = **tigron**

tignasse [tiɲas] **NF** *Fam* **1** *(chevelure mal peignée)* mop *or* mane (of hair) **2** *(chevelure)* hair■; **il l'a attrapée par la t.** he grabbed (hold of) her by the hair

Tigre [tigr] **NM 1** *Géog* **le T.** the (River) Tigris **2** *Hist* **le T.** = nickname of Georges Clemenceau

tigre [tigr] **NM 1** *Zool* tiger; **t. du Bengale** Bengal tiger; **t. blanc** white tiger; **t. de Mandchourie** Manchurian *or* Amur *or* Siberian tiger; **t. royal** Bengal tiger; **t. de Sibérie** Siberian *or* Amur *or* Manchurian tiger **2** *Littéraire (homme cruel)* **c'est un vrai t.** he's a real ogre; **t. de papier** paper tiger

tigré, -e [tigre] **ADJ 1** *(pelage)* striped, streaked; *(chat)* tabby *(avant n)*, tiger *(avant n)* **2** *(moucheté)* **bananes tigrées** (dessert) bananas

tigresse [tigrɛs] **NF 1** *Zool* tigress **2** *Littéraire (femme très jalouse)* tigress; **jalouse comme une t.** madly *or* wildly jealous

tigridie [tigridi] **NF** *Bot* tiger flower

tigron [tigrɔ̃] **NM** tigon, tiglon

ti-jos-connaissant [tiʒɔkɔnɛsɑ̃] **NM** *Can Fam Péj Br* know-all, *Am* know-it-all

Tiki [tiki] **NM** Tiki

tiki [tiki] **NM** tiki *(statue representing a Polynesian god)*; **t. bar** tiki bar *(Polynesian-themed bar)*

tilapia [tilapja], **tilapie** [tilapi] **NM** *Ich* tilapia

tilbury [tilbyri] **NM** tilbury

tilde [tild, tilde] **NM** *(en espagnol)* tilde; *(en phonétique, pour remplacer un mot)* swung dash

tillac [tijak] **NM** *Naut & Hist* upper deck

tillage [tijaʒ] **NM** *Tex* stripping, scutching

tillandsia [tijɑ̃dsja, tilɑ̃dsja] **NF** *Bot* tillandsia

tille [tij] **NF 1** *(du tilleul)* bast, bass; **paillasson de t.** bass(-mat) **2** *(de chanvre)* harl

tiller [3] [tije] **VT** *Tex* to strip, to scutch

tilleul [tijœl] **NM 1** *Bot* lime (tree) **2** *(feuilles séchées)* lime blossom *(UNCOUNT)*; *(infusion)* lime *or* lime-blossom tea **3** *(bois)* limewood; **en t.** *(coffret, boîte)* limewood
ADJ INV (vert) t. lime green

tilleur, -euse [tijœr, -øz] *Tex* **NM,F** flax stripper, flax scutcher

▫ **tilleuse NF** scutching machine, scutcher

tilsit [tilsit] **NM** *Suisse* = hard cheese from the canton of Saint-Gall

tilt [tilt] **NM 1** *(dans un jeu)* tilt signal **2** *Fam (locutions)* **le mot a fait t.** *(je me suis souvenu)* the word rang a bell; **et soudain, ça a fait t.** *(j'ai compris)* and suddenly it clicked *or* the penny dropped

timbale [tɛ̃bal] **NF 1** *(gobelet)* (metal) cup; **t. en argent** *(donnée aux enfants baptisés)* silver christening cup **2** *Culin (moule)* timbale mould; *(préparation)* timbale; **t. de saumon** salmon timbale; **t. milanaise** = timbale of macaroni, veal sweetbreads and truffles **3** *Mus* kettledrum; **une paire de timbales** timpani, a set of kettledrums; **les timbales** *(d'un orchestre)* the timpani

timbalier [tɛ̃balje] **NM** timpanist

timbrage [tɛ̃braʒ] **NM 1** *(action de timbrer)* stamping **2** *(procédé d'impression)* embossing

timbre[1] [tɛ̃br] **NM 1** *(pour lettre)* stamp; **mettre un t. sur une lettre** to stamp a letter, to put a stamp on a letter; **t. de collection** collector's stamp

2 *(vignette → au profit d'une œuvre)* sticker *(given in exchange for a donation to charity)*; *(→ attestant un paiement)* stamp *(certifying receipt of payment)*

3 *(sceau, marque)* stamp; **apposer son t. sur un document** to put one's stamp on *or* to rubber-stamp a document

4 *(instrument marqueur)* stamp; **t. dateur** date stamp; **t. en caoutchouc** rubber stamp; **t. sec** embossing stamp

5 *Jur* **t. fiscal** tax stamp

6 *Méd* patch; **t. tuberculinique** tuberculosis patch

TIMBRE FISCAL

These stamps are sold at most tobacconists and are used to pay fees due for obtaining official documents, such as identity papers, vehicle documents and legal certificates.

timbre[2] [tɛ̃br] **NM 1** (qualité sonore → d'un instrument) tone, timbre, colour; (→ d'une voix) tone, resonance; **un beau t. de voix** beautiful mellow tones, a beautiful rich voice; **une voix au t. argentin** a silvery voice; **"ce n'est pas moi", dit-elle d'une voix sans t.** "it wasn't me," she said tonelessly

2 (sonnette) bell; (de porte) doorbell; **t. de bicyclette** bicycle bell; Fam Arch **avoir le t. fêlé** to be cracked or daft, to have a screw loose

3 Mus (instrument) (small) bell; (de tambour) snare

timbré, -e [tɛ̃bre] **ADJ 1** Fam (fou) nuts, crazy

2 (document, enveloppe) stamped; **une enveloppe timbrée portant vos nom et adresse** a stamped addressed envelope; **lettre timbrée de Paris** letter with a Paris postmark, letter postmarked Paris

3 papier t. au chiffre de qn paper stamped with sb's arms

4 (d'une bonne sonorité) **une voix joliment** ou **agréablement timbrée** a pleasant voice; **de sa voix bien timbrée** in his/her mellow or rich tones

timbre-amende [tɛ̃bramɑ̃d] (pl **timbres-amendes**) **NM** = stamp purchased to certify payment of a fine

timbre-poste [tɛ̃brəpɔst] (pl **timbres-poste**) **NM** (postage) stamp

timbre-prime [tɛ̃brəprim] (pl **timbres-primes**) **NM** trading (discount) stamp

timbre-quittance [tɛ̃brəkitɑ̃s] (pl **timbres-quittances**) **NM** receipt stamp

timbrer [3] [tɛ̃bre] **VT 1** (lettre, colis) to stamp, to stick or to put a stamp on; **je n'ai pas assez timbré la lettre** I didn't put enough stamps or I put insufficient postage on the letter **2** Jur (document) to stamp, to put a stamp on, to affix a stamp to

VI Suisse (au chômage) to sign on

timbre-ristourne [tɛ̃brəristurn] (pl **timbres-ristournes**) **NM** trading (discount) stamp

timbre-taxe [tɛ̃brətaks] (pl **timbres-taxes**) **NM** postage-due stamp

time code [tajmkod] **NM** Cin time code

Timée [time] **NPR** Timaeus

time-sharing [tajmʃɛriŋ] (pl **time-sharings**) **NM** Ordinat time sharing

timide [timid] **ADJ 1** (embarrassé → sourire, air, regard) timid, shy; (→ personne) bashful, diffident; **il est t. avec les femmes** he's shy of or he shrinks away from women; **faussement t.** coy

2 (faible) slight, feeble, tiny; **une critique t.** hesitant criticism; **une t. amélioration du dollar** a slight improvement in the position of the dollar; **l'auteur de quelques timides réformes** the author of a handful of half-hearted or feeble reforms

NMF shy person; **c'est un t.** he's a shy person, he's shy of people; **c'est un grand t.** he's very shy

timidement [timidmɑ̃] **ADV 1** (avec embarras) timidly, shyly, diffidently; (gauchement) self-consciously, bashfully **2** (de façon peu perceptible) slightly, feebly, faint-heartedly; **le dollar remonte t.** the dollar is rising slightly

timidité [timidite] **NF 1** (manque d'assurance) timidity, shyness, diffidence; (gaucherie) self-consciousness, bashfulness **2** (d'un projet, d'une réforme) feebleness, half-heartedness

timing [tajmiŋ] **NM** timing (of a technical process)

timon [timɔ̃] **NM 1** Agr (d'une charrette) shaft; (d'une charrue) (draught) beam **2** Aut trailing arm **3** Vieilli Naut tiller

timonerie [timɔnri] **NF 1** Naut (abri) wheelhouse; (service) wheelhouse, steering; (personnel) wheelhouse crew; **kiosque de t.** wheelhouse, pilot house **2** Aut steering and braking gear

timonier [timɔnje] **NM 1** Naut helmsman; (aux signaux) signalman, wheelhorse, wheeler **2** Agr wheelhorse, wheeler **3** Hist **le grand t.** the Great Helmsman; Hum **le grand t. du Parti**

républicain the Grand Panjandrum of the Republican party

Timor [timɔr] **NM le T.** Timor; **le T. Oriental** East Timor

timorais, -e [timɔrɛ, -ɛz] **ADJ** Timorese

□ **Timorais, -e NM,F** Timorese; **les T.** the Timorese

timoré, -e [timɔre] **ADJ** timorous, fearful, unadventurous; Rel & Littéraire (conscience) overscrupulous

NM,F timorous or fearful or unadventurous person

Timothée [timɔte] **NPR** Bible Timothy

tin [tɛ̃] **NM** Naut (en cale sèche) keel block

tinamou [tinamu] **NM** Orn tinamou

tincal [tɛ̃kal] **NM** Minér tincal

tine [tin] **NF** Belg basin, tub

tinéidés [tineide] **NMPL** Entom Tineidae

tinette [tinɛt] **NF** (récipient) mobile latrine

□ **tinettes NFPL** Fam (toilettes) Br lav, Am john

tint etc voir **tenir**

tintamarre [tɛ̃tamar] **NM 1** (vacarme) racket, din; **écoute-moi ce t.!** listen to this racket or din!; **faire du t.** to make a din or racket; Fig **on a fait du t. autour de son livre** there was a lot of hooha or a big to-do about his/her book **2** Can (en acadien) = noisy street parade which takes place every year in Acadia on 15 August, the Acadians' national holiday

tintement [tɛ̃tmɑ̃] **NM 1** (d'une cloche, d'une sonnette) ringing (UNCOUNT); (d'un lustre) tinkling (UNCOUNT); (de grelots, de clefs, de pièces de monnaie) jingle, jingling (UNCOUNT); (de verres, de bouteilles) chink, clink, clinking (UNCOUNT) **2** Méd **t. d'oreilles** ringing in the ears, Spéc tinnitus; **avoir des tintements d'oreilles** to have a ringing or buzzing (noise) in one's ears

tinter [3] [tɛ̃te] **VI 1** (sonner lentement) to ring (out), to peal; **minuit tinte au clocher** the church bell is ringing midnight

2 (produire des sons clairs) to tinkle, to jingle; **les verres tintaient sur le plateau** the glasses were clinking on the tray; **le lustre en cristal tintait doucement** the crystal chandelier was tinkling softly; **faire t. des pièces de monnaie** to jingle coins

3 (oreilles) to ring, to buzz; **les oreilles me tintaient** my ears were ringing or buzzing; Fig **les oreilles doivent lui t.** his/her ears must be burning

VT 1 (sonner → cloche) to chime

2 (coup) **la cloche du village tintait les coups de midi** the church bell was striking twelve

3 (annoncer → glas, messe) to toll the bell for; **t. le tocsin** to sound the tocsin; **t. l'angélus** to toll the bell for the Angelus

tintin [tɛ̃tɛ̃] **EXCLAM** Fam no way(, José)!, no chance!, nothing doing!; **les cadres ont eu une augmentation, et nous t.!** the management got a Br rise or Am raise, but we got zilch!; **faire t.** to go without

tintinnabuler [3] [tɛ̃tinabyle] **VI** Littéraire to tinkle, to jingle, to tintinnabulate

Tintoret [tɛ̃tɔrɛ] **NPR le T.** Tintoretto; **un tableau du T.** a painting by Tintoretto

tintouin [tɛ̃twɛ̃] **NM** Fam **1** (inquiétude, souci) grief, hassle; **les gosses, ça vous donne bien du t.!** kids can be such a hassle or headache!; **se faire du t.** to get all worked up **2** (vacarme) racket, din; **quel t. à côté!** what a racket they're making next door! **3** (locution) **sa canne à pêche, ses bottes, son chapeau et tout le t.** his/her fishing rod, boots, hat and all the rest of it

TIOP [tjɔp] **NM** Banque (abrév **taux interbancaire offert à Paris**) PIBOR

TIP [tip] **NM** Banque (abrév **titre interbancaire de paiement**) = payment slip for bills

tiper [3] [tipe] **VT** Suisse (achat) to ring up; **est-ce que vous l'avez tipé?** have you counted that?, have you rung that up?

tipi [tipi] **NM** tepee, teepee

TIPP [teipɛp] **NF** (abrév **taxe intérieure sur les produits pétroliers**) domestic tax on petroleum products

tipper [tipe] = **tiper**

tipule [tipyl] **NF** Entom crane fly

tique [tik] **NF** tick; **collier anti-tiques** tick collar

tiquer [3] [tike] **VI 1** Fam (réagir) to wince■; **le prix l'a fait** ou baulked when he saw the price; **il n'a pas tiqué** he didn't turn a hair or bat an eyelid; **t. sur qch** to baulk at sth; **j'ai tiqué sur la somme** I baulked at the sum **2** Vét to wind-suck

tiqueté, -e [tikte] **ADJ** speckled, mottled, dotted

tiqueture [tiktyr] **NF** speckles, mottling (UNCOUNT)

tiqueur, -euse [tikœr, -øz] **ADJ 1** (personne) with a nervous tic **2** Vét wind-sucking

NM,F 1 (personne) person with a nervous tic **2** Vét wind-sucker

TIR [teiɛr, tir] **NM** Transp (abrév **transport international routier**) TIR

tir [tir] **NM 1** Mil (action de lancer au moyen d'une arme) shooting, firing; (projectiles envoyés) fire; **les tirs cessèrent** the firing stopped; **un t. bien/mal ajusté** a well-aimed/badly-aimed launch or shot; **un t. intense/nourri/sporadique** heavy/sustained/sporadic fire; **il y eut des tirs sporadiques puis plus rien** there were occasional bursts of gunfire then the firing stopped altogether; **il a un t. précis** he's a good shot or marksman; **il a un t. rapide** he shoots quickly; **allonger/raccourcir le t.** to increase/reduce the range; **adresse** ou **habileté au t.** marksmanship; Fig **rectifier le t.** to change one's angle of attack, to change one's approach to a problem; **t. d'accompagnement** cover (fire); **tirs amis** friendly fire; **t. d'artillerie** artillery fire; **t. automatique** automatic fire; **arme à t. automatique** automatic weapon; **t. de barrage** barrage fire; **t. de batterie** battery fire; **t. au but** precision firing; **t. courbe** high-angle fire; **t. direct/indirect** direct/indirect fire; **tirs fratricides** friendly fire; **t. instinctif** firing at random; **t. précis** ou **groupé** grouped fire; **t. par rafales** firing in bursts; **t. rasant/plongeant** raking/downward fire

2 (endroit → pour l'entraînement) rifle or shooting range; **t. (forain)** shooting gallery

3 Mines & (en travaux publics) blasting

4 Sport **le t.** (discipline olympique) shooting; **t. à l'arbalète** crossbow archery; **t. à l'arc** archery; **t. à la carabine** ou **au fusil** rifle-shooting; **t. aux pigeons (d'argile)** clay pigeon shooting; **t. au pistolet** pistol-shooting

5 Chasse **chasse à t.** shooting; **chasse à t. aux chiens courants** shooting with hounds

6 Ftbl shot; **faire un t. du pied gauche** to shoot with the left foot; **t. (au but)** shot at goal; (penalty) penalty; **les tirs au but, l'épreuve** ou **la séance des tirs au but** the penalty shootout

7 (aux boules) throw; **apprendre la technique du t.** to learn how to throw

8 (au basket-ball) shot; **t. en suspension** jump shot

□ **de tir ADJ** (concours, champion) shooting; (position, vitesse) firing; **angle/ligne de t.** angle/line of fire

tirade [tirad] **NF 1** Cin & Théât monologue, speech **2** Péj (discours) speech, tirade

tirage [tiraʒ] **NM 1** Typ (action) printing; (ensemble d'exemplaires) print run, impression; (d'une gravure, d'un enregistrement) edition; **un t. de 50 000 exemplaires** a print run of 50,000; **un mille de t.** a (print) run of a thousand; **écrivain qui fait de gros tirages** bestselling author; **édition à t. limité** limited edition; **t. défectueux** batter; **t. héliographique** arc print; **t. de luxe** edition; **t. numéroté** numbered edition; **t. à part** offprint

2 Presse (action) printing, running; (exemplaires mis en vente) circulation; **un t. de 50 000** circulation figures or a circulation of 50,000; **le t. a baissé** circulation is down or has fallen or has dropped; **à fort** ou **grand t.** with large circulation figures; **la presse à grand t.** the popular press

3 Ordinat (sur imprimante) printout

4 Phot (action) printing; (copies) prints; **deux tirages sur papier brillant** two sets of prints on gloss paper

5 Banque drawing; (d'un prêt) drawdown; **t. en blanc** ou **en l'air** drawing of a dud cheque, Spéc kiting; Écon **droits de t. spéciaux** special drawing rights; Compta **tirages annuels** annual drawings

6 *(d'une carte)* taking, picking; *(d'une tombola)* draw; **t. au sort** drawing of lots; **procéder à un t. au sort** to draw lots; **être désigné par voie de t. au sort** to be chosen by drawing lots; **nous t'avons désigné par t. au sort** we drew lots and your name came up; *Sport* **le t. au sort des quarts de finale de la Coupe a eu lieu ce matin** the draw for the quarter finals of the Cup took place this morning; *Sport* **on connaît maintenant le t. au sort des demi-finales** we now have the results of the draw for the semifinals

7 *(d'une cheminée, d'un poêle)* draught; **le t. est bon/mauvais** it draws well/doesn't draw well; **t. renversé** *ou* **inverti** back draught; *Aut* **carburateur à t. en bas** down-draught carburettor

8 *(action de → traîner)* dragging; *(→ haler)* hauling

9 *Métal* drawing

10 *(de rochers)* quarrying, extraction; **t. à la poudre** blasting

11 *Tex* reeling; *(de la soie)* spinning

12 *Cin* copying; **t. en surimpression** overprint

13 *(d'un disque)* pressing

14 *Fam (locution)* **il y a du t. entre eux** there's some friction between them

tiraillement [tirɑjmɑ̃] **NM 1** *(sur une corde)* tugging, pulling

2 *(d'estomac)* gnawing pain; *(de la peau, d'un muscle)* tightness; **quand on m'a enlevé les fils, je n'ai senti qu'un t.** when they removed the stitches, I only felt a slight pulling *or* tugging; **sentir les tiraillements de la faim** to feel pangs of hunger; **avoir des tiraillements d'estomac** to have gnawing pains in one's stomach *or* pangs of hunger

❑ **tiraillements NMPL** *(conflit)* struggle, conflict; **il y a des tiraillements dans la famille/le syndicat** there is friction within the family/the union

tirailler [3] [tirɑje] **VT 1** *(tirer sur)* to tug at, to pull on, to give little pulls on; **il tiraillait nerveusement sa moustache** he was pulling nervously at his moustache

2 *(faire souffrir légèrement)* to prick; **la faim lui tiraillait l'estomac** he/she felt pangs of hunger

3 *(solliciter)* to dog, to plague; **être tiraillé entre l'espoir et l'inquiétude** to be torn between hope and anxiety; **être tiraillé entre ses parents** to be torn between one's parents

VI 1 *(avec une arme)* to fire at random; **on entendait t. dans les bois** random fire could be heard in the woods, people could be heard firing away in the woods

2 *(peau)* to feel tight; **j'ai la peau qui (me) tiraille** my skin feels tight

tiraillerie [tirɑjri] **NF 1** *Mil* wild firing **2** *(friction)* wrangling, friction

tirailleur [tirɑjœr] **NM 1** *(éclaireur)* scout **2** *Hist & Mil* skirmisher; **les tirailleurs algériens/sénégalais** the Algerian/Senegalese (Infantry) corps **3** *Fig (personne qui agit isolément)* **dans une grève, il y a toujours quelques tirailleurs** during a strike, there are always some who don't play by the book

❑ **en tirailleurs ADV** *(avancer)* in skirmishing order

tiramisu [tiramisu] **NM** *Culin* tiramisu

Tirana [tirana] **NM** Tirana, Tiranë

tirant [tirɑ̃] **NM 1** *Naut* **t. d'eau** draught; **avoir 5 pieds de t. d'eau** to draw 5 feet (of water); **barque à faible t. d'eau** shallow draught barge; **échelle de t. d'eau** draught marks *or* numbers

2 *(d'une botte)* (boot) strap; *(d'une chaussure)* (heel) strap

3 *(d'une bourse)* purse string

4 *Constr (entrait)* tie beam; *(fer plat)* rod

5 *Mines* strap, tie beam

6 *Tech* stay, brace; **t. de frein** brake rod

7 *(en travaux publics)* **t. d'air** (maximum) headroom

tirasse [tiras] **NF 1** *Chasse* draw net, clap net **2** *Mus* pedal coupler

tire [tir] **NF 1** *très Fam (voiture)* car■, *Br* motor **2** *Can (friandise)* maple toffee *or Am* taffy; **t. d'érable** maple candy; **t. Sainte Catherine** molasses candy *(traditionally eaten in Quebec on St Catherine's Day, 25 November)*

tiré, -e [tire] **ADJ 1** *(fatigué et amaigri → visage)* drawn, pinched; **avoir les traits tirés** to look drawn

2 *(tendu)* **broderie à fils tirés** drawn-thread work; **aux cheveux tirés** with his/her hair drawn *or* pulled back

3 *Banque* **chèque t. sur qn** cheque drawn on sb

4 *(locution)* **t. par les cheveux** contrived, far-fetched; **tes arguments sont complètement tirés par les cheveux** your arguments are terribly far-fetched

NM 1 *Banque* drawee

2 *Presse* **t. à part** off-print

3 *Mus* down-bow

❑ **tirée NF** *Fam* **1** *(trajet)* haul, trek; **ça fait une tirée d'ici à là-bas** it's a bit of a haul *or* trek from here

2 une tirée de qch *(grande quantité)* loads of sth

tire-au-cul [tiroky] **NM INV** *très Fam Br* skiver, *Am* goldbrick

tire-au-flanc [tiroflɑ̃] **NM INV** *Fam Br* skiver, *Am* goldbrick

tire-bonde [tirbɔ̃d] *(pl* **tire-bondes***)* **NM** bung drawer

tire-botte [tirbɔt] *(pl* **tire-bottes***)* **NM 1** *(pour mettre)* boot hook **2** *(pour enlever)* bootjack

tire-bouchon [tirbuʃɔ̃] *(pl* **tire-bouchons***)* **NM** corkscrew

❑ **en tire-bouchon ADJ** corkscrew *(avant n)*; **cochon à la queue en t.** pig with a corkscrew tail; **elle a toujours ses chaussettes en t.** her socks are always twisted round her ankles

tire-bouchonnage [tirbuʃɔnaʒ] **NM** *(d'un fil)* corkscrewing; *(d'un vêtement)* = twisting of the seams after washing

tire-bouchonner [3] [tirbuʃɔne] **VT** *(mèche)* to twiddle *or* to twist (round and round); *(fil de fer)* to twist; **chaussettes tire-bouchonnées** socks twisted round the ankles

VI to twist round and round; *(pantalon)* to be crumpled; **mes chaussettes tire-bouchonnent** my socks are all twisted round my ankles

tire-bouton [tirbutɔ̃] *(pl* **tire-boutons***)* **NM** *Vieilli* buttonhook

tire-braise [tirbrɛz] *(pl* **inv** *ou* **tire-braises)** **NM** (baker's) oven rake

tire-clou [tirklu] *(pl* **tire-clous***)* **NM** nail puller

tire-d'aile [tirdɛl] **à tire-d'aile ADV 1** *(en volant)* **s'envoler à t.** to fly swiftly away; **les corbeaux passèrent au-dessus de la maison à t.** the crows flew over the house with strong, regular wingbeats **2** *Fig (à toute vitesse)* **partir** *ou* **s'éloigner à t.** to fly off; **il s'est enfui à t.** he took to his heels

tire-fesses [tirfɛs] **NM INV** *Fam* ski tow, T-bar; **monter en t.** to go up by the T-bar, to take the T-bar up

tire-fond [tirfɔ̃] **NM INV 1** *Constr (vis)* long screw; *(anneau)* eye bolt **2** *Rail* sleeper screw

tire-jus [tirʒy] **NM INV** *très Fam* snotrag

tire-laine [tirlɛn] **NM INV** *Littéraire Vieilli* highwayman

tire-lait [tirlɛ] **NM INV** breast-pump

tire-larigot [tirlarigo] **à tire-larigot ADV** *Fam* **boire à t.** to drink like a fish; **il y en a à t.** there's loads *or* tons of them

tire-ligne [tirliɲ] *(pl* **tire-lignes***)* **NM** drawing pen

tirelire [tirlir] **NF 1** *(en forme de cochon)* piggy bank; *(boîte)* moneybox; *Fig* **casser sa t.** to break into one's piggy bank **2** *très Fam (estomac)* belly, gut **3** *Fam (tête)* head■, nut, *Br* bonce; *(visage)* face■, mug

tire-moelle [tirmwal] **NM INV** *très Fam* snotrag

tire-nerf [tirnɛr] *(pl* **tire-nerfs***)* **NM** broach *(for extracted tooth)*

tire-pognon [tirpɔɲɔ̃] *(pl* **tire-pognons***)* **NM** *Fam Vieilli* one-arm(ed) bandit, fruit machine

TIRER [3] [tire]

> **VT** to pull **A1-3, B1** ■ to drag **A1** ■ to draw **A1, 4, B1, 4, 8, E1** ■ to fire **C1** ■ to set off **C2** ■ to shoot **C3** ■ to throw **C4** ■ to print **E2, 3**
> **VI** to pull **4, 7** ■ to draw **5, 6** ■ to fire **1** ■ to shoot **1-3**
> **VPR** to get going **2** ■ to draw to a close **3** ■ to get out of **4**

VT A. *DÉPLACER* **1** *(traîner → avec ou sans effort)* to pull, to drag; *(→ en remorquant)* to draw, to tow; **tire la table au milieu de la pièce** pull the table out to the centre of the room; **un cheval tirait la péniche le long du canal** a horse was towing *or* pulling the barge along the canal; **tiré par un cheval** horse-drawn; **tiré par des bœufs** ox-drawn; **le skieur est tiré par un hors-bord** a speed boat pulls *or* tows the skier (along); **t. qn par le bras/les cheveux/les pieds** to drag sb by the arm/hair/feet

2 *(amener à soi)* to pull; *(étirer → vers le haut)* to pull (up); *(→ vers le bas)* to pull (down); **je sentis que quelqu'un tirait ma veste** I felt a tug at my jacket; **elle me tira doucement par la manche** she tugged *or* pulled at my sleeve; **tirez doucement le levier de vitesse** pull the gear lever gently (back); **t. les cheveux à qn** to pull sb's hair; **t. ses cheveux en arrière** to draw *or* to pull one's hair back; **tire bien le drap** stretch the sheet (taut); **t. un fil** *(accidentellement)* to pull a thread; *(pour faire un jour)* to draw a thread; *Can & (régional)* **t. une vache** to milk a cow; **t. la couverture à soi** *(s'attribuer le mérite)* to take all the credit; *(s'attribuer le profit)* to take the lion's share; *Can* **t. la pipe à qn** to pull sb's leg, to tease sb

3 *(pour actionner → cordon d'appel, élastique)* to pull; *(→ tiroir)* to pull (open *or* out); **t. les rideaux** to pull *or* to draw the curtains; **tire le portail derrière toi** close the gates behind you, pull the gates to; **t. un verrou** *(pour ouvrir)* to slide a bolt open; *(pour fermer)* to slide a bolt to, to shoot a bolt; **t. la chasse d'eau** to flush the toilet

4 *Naut* to draw; **t. 5 mètres** to draw 5 metres of water

B. *EXTRAIRE, OBTENIR* **1** *(faire sortir)* **t. qch de** to pull *or* to draw sth out of; **t. des billets/un revolver de son sac** to pull banknotes/a gun out of one's bag; **la valise dont il tirait des jouets** the suitcase from which he pulled out toys; **t. de l'eau d'un puits** to draw water (out of a well); **t. le vin/cidre (du tonneau)** to draw wine/cider (off from the barrel); **t. qn de** *(le faire sortir de)* to get sb out of; **t. qn d'un asile/de prison** to get sb out of an asylum/prison; **t. qn d'une voiture en feu** to drag *or* to pull sb out of a blazing car; **va le t. du lit** go and get *or* drag him out of bed; *Fig* **t. qn d'un cauchemar** to rouse sb from a nightmare; **t. qn du sommeil** to wake sb up; **t. qn du coma** to pull sb out of a coma; **t. qn de sa rêverie** to rouse sb from his/her daydream; **t. qn de son silence** to draw sb out (of his/her silence); **t. une œuvre de l'oubli** to rescue a work from oblivion; **t. qn d'une situation difficile** to get sb out of a difficult situation; **tire-moi de là** help me out

2 *(fabriquer)* **t. qch de** to derive *or* to get *or* to make sth from; **les produits que l'on tire du pétrole** oil-based products; **t. des sons d'un instrument** to get *or* to draw sounds from an instrument; **t. un film d'une pièce de théâtre** to adapt a play for the screen; **photos tirées d'un film** movie stills

3 *(percevoir → argent)* **elle tire sa fortune de ses terres** she makes her money from her land; **elle savait ce qu'on peut t. d'un placement judicieux** she knew what could be gained from a wise investment; **il a bien tiré 5 millions de la vente de la maison** he must have made at least 5 million from the sale of the house; **tu ne tireras pas grand-chose de ta vieille montre** you won't get much (money) for your old watch

4 *(retirer → chèque, argent liquide)* to draw; **t. de l'argent d'un compte** to draw money out of *or* to withdraw money from an account

5 *(extraire, dégager)* **t. la morale/un enseignement de qch** to learn a lesson from sth; **ce vers est tiré d'un poème de Villon** this line is (taken) from a poem by Villon; **ce que j'ai tiré de ce livre/cet article** what I got out of this book/article; **t. sa force de sa foi** to derive *or* to draw one's strength from one's faith; **ce roman tire son titre d'une chanson populaire** the title of this novel is taken from a popular song; **les mots que le français a tirés du latin** French words taken from Latin; **t. satisfaction de qch** to derive satisfaction from sth; **t. vanité de qch** to be proud of sth; **t. fierté de qch** to pride oneself on *or* in sth; **t. vengeance de qch** to avenge sth

6 *(obtenir, soutirer)* **t. de l'argent de qn** to extract money from sb, to get money out of sb; **la police n'a rien pu t. de lui** the police couldn't get anything out of him; **tu auras du mal à lui t. des excuses** you'll be hard pressed to get an apology out of him/her; **tu auras du mal à lui t. des remerciements** you'll get no thanks from him/her; **j'ai réussi à lui t. un sourire** I managed to get a smile out of him/her; **t. des larmes à qn** to make sb cry; *Fam* **t. les vers du nez à qn** to worm *or* drag it out of sb; **il est rebelle à l'apprentissage, mais je suis sûr qu'on peut en t. quelque chose** he's a poor learner but I'm sure we can make something of him; *Fam* **on n'en tirera jamais rien, de ce gosse** *(il n'est bon à rien)* we'll never make anything out of this kid; *(il ne parlera pas)* we'll never get this kid to talk, we'll never get anything out of this kid; **je n'ai pas pu en t. davantage** I couldn't get any more out of him/her

7 *Fam (voler)* **je me suis fait t. mon portefeuille au cinéma!** somebody pinched *or Br* nicked my wallet at the *Br* cinema *or Am* movie theater!

8 *(billet, numéro)* to draw, to pick; *(loterie)* to draw, to carry out the draw for; *(carte)* to draw, to take; **tirez une carte postale au hasard** pick any postcard; **qui va t. le nom du gagnant?** who will draw (out) the name of the winner?; **le gagnant sera tiré au sort** there will be a draw to decide the winner

C. *PROJETER* **1** *Mil (coup de fusil, missile)* to fire; *(balle, flèche)* to shoot; **t. un coup de feu** to fire a shot; **ils tiraient les passants comme des lapins** they were picking off passers-by one by one

2 *(feu d'artifice)* to set off; **ce soir, on tirera un feu d'artifice** there will be a fireworks display tonight

3 *Chasse (lapin, faisan)* to shoot; **t. un animal** to shoot an animal

4 *(à la pétanque → boule en main)* to throw; *(→ boule placée)* to knock out; *Ftbl* to take; *(au tennis → passing-shot, volée)* to hit; *(en haltérophilie)* to lift; **t. un corner** to take a corner; **t. un coup franc** to take a free kick; **le penalty va être tiré par le capitaine** the penalty will be taken by the captain; **il tire 150 kilos à l'épaulé-jeté** he can clean and jerk 150 kilos; *Escrime* **t. des armes** to fence

5 *Vulg (posséder sexuellement)* to screw, *Br* to shag; **t. un coup** to get laid, to have a screw *or Br* a shag

D. *PASSER Fam* to spend■ **il est en train de t. dix piges pour vol à main armée** he's doing a ten-year stretch for armed robbery; **encore deux mois à t. avant les vacances** another two months to get through before the *Br* holidays *or Am* vacation

E. *TRACER, IMPRIMER* **1** *(dessiner → ligne)* to draw; *(→ plan)* to draw up; **tirez deux traits sous les verbes** underline the verbs twice

2 *Phot* to print; **je voudrais que cette photo soit tirée sur du papier mat** I'd like a mat print of this picture

3 *Typ (livre)* to print; *(estampe, lithographie)* to print, to draw; *(tract)* to print, to run; *(gravure)* to strike, to pull, to print; **t. un tract à 5000 exemplaires** to print 5,000 copies of a tract; **ce magazine est tiré à plus de 200 000 exemplaires** this magazine has a print run *or* a circulation of 200,000; **"bon à t."** "passed for press"; **un bon à t.** *(épreuve)* a press proof; **signer le bon à t.** to pass for press

4 *Belg (locution)* **tu es assez grand, tu tires ton plan** you're old enough to look after yourself

VI 1 *Mil (faire feu)* to fire, to shoot; **ne tirez pas, je me rends!** don't shoot, I surrender!; **ne tirez plus!** hold your fire!, stop shooting!; **tirez dans les jambes** shoot at *or* aim at the legs; **il tire mal** he's a bad shot; **t. à la cible** to aim *or* to shoot at the target; **t. à balles/à blanc** to fire bullets/blanks; **t. en l'air/à vue** to shoot in the air/on sight; **t. sur qn** to take a shot *or* to shoot *or* to fire at sb; **ils ont l'ordre de t. sur tout ce qui bouge** they've been ordered to shoot *or* to fire at anything that moves; **on m'a tiré dessus** I was fired *or* shot at; **cette carabine tire juste** this rifle shoots straight

2 *Sport* **t. à l'arc/l'arbalète** *(activité sportive)* to do archery/crossbow archery; *(action ponctuelle)* to shoot a bow/crossbow; **t. à la carabine/au pistolet** *(activité sportive)* to do rifle/pistol shooting; *(action ponctuelle)* to shoot with a rifle/pistol

3 *Ftbl & Golf* to shoot; *Escrime* to fence; **il a tiré dans le mur/petit filet** he sent the ball against the wall/into the side netting

4 *(exercer une traction)* to pull; **à mon signal, tirez tous dans le même sens** when I give the signal, all pull in the same direction; **tire!** pull!, heave!; *Fam* **ça tire dans les genoux à la montée** going up is tough on the knees; *Fam* **elle tire bien, ta voiture!** it runs well, your car!; **la moto tire à droite** the motorbike pulls to the right; **la direction tire d'un côté** the steering pulls to one side; **t. sur un câble** to pull *or* to heave on a cable; **t. sur un levier** to pull (back) a lever; **t. sur les rênes** to pull on the reins; **t. sur un élastique** to stretch *or* to pull on an elastic band; **ne tire pas sur ton gilet** don't pull your cardigan out of shape; **ne tire pas (sur la laisse), Rex!** stop pulling (on your lead), Rex!; **il tira violemment sur le fil du téléphone** he gave the phone wire a sharp pull; *Fig* **t. sur** *(délais, budget)* to stretch; **elle tire un peu sur sa permission de minuit** she's stretching it a bit with her midnight curfew; **t. sur la ficelle** to go a bit far; *Suisse* **t. sur la même corde** to pull together

5 *(aspirer → fumeur)* **t. sur une pipe** to draw on *or* to pull at a pipe; **t. sur une cigarette** to puff at *or* to draw on a cigarette

6 *(avoir un bon tirage → cheminée, poêle)* **t. (bien)** to draw (well); **la cheminée/pipe tire mal** the fireplace/pipe doesn't draw properly

7 *(peau)* to feel tight; *(points de suture)* to pull; *Fam* **ma peau me tire** my skin feels tight; **aïe, ça tire!** ouch, it's pulling!

8 *(dans un jeu)* **t. au sort** to draw *or* to cast lots

9 *Typ* **t. à 50 000 exemplaires** to have a circulation of *or* to have a (print) run of 50,000 (copies); **à combien le journal tire-t-il?** what are the paper's circulation figures?

10 *Suisse (thé)* to brew

11 *Belg & Suisse (locution)* **ça tire** there's a draught

12 *Banque* **t. à découvert** to overdraw; **t. à vue** to draw at sight

❑ **tirer à VT IND 1** *Presse* **t. à la ligne** to pad out an article *(because it is being paid by the line)*

2 *Naut* **t. au large** to make for the open sea

3 *Fam* **t. au flanc** *ou* **cul** to shirk, *Br* to skive

4 *(locution)* **t. à sa fin** to come to an end

❑ **tirer sur VT IND** *(couleur)* to verge *or* to border on; **ses cheveux tirent sur le roux** his/her hair is reddish *or* almost red

▸**se tirer VPR 1** *(emploi passif)* **le store se tire avec un cordon** the blind pulls down with a cord

2 *Fam (partir, quitter un endroit)* to hit the road, to get going; *(s'enfuir) Br* to clear off, *Am* to book it; **s'il n'est pas là dans cinq minutes, je me tire** if he's not here in five minutes I'm off; **tire-toi!** *(ton menaçant)* beat it!; **on se tire, voilà les flics!** it's the cops, let's get out of here!; **il s'est tiré de chez lui** he's left home; **dès que je peux, je me tire de cette boîte** as soon as I can, I'll get out of this dump

3 *Fam (toucher à sa fin → emprisonnement, service militaire)* to draw to a close■; **plus qu'une semaine, ça se tire quand même!** only a week to go, it's nearly over!

4 **se t. de** *(se sortir de)* to get out of; **elle sait se t. de situations délicates** she knows how to get out of *or* to extricate herself from tricky situations; **il s'est bien/mal tiré de l'entrevue** he did well/badly at the interview

5 *Fam* **s'en t.** *(s'en sortir)* **avec son culot, elle s'en tirera toujours** with her cheek, she'll always come out on top; **si tu ne m'avais pas aidé à finir la maquette, je ne m'en serais jamais tiré** if you hadn't given me a hand with the model, I'd never have managed; **les débuts furent difficiles, mais elle s'en tire très bien maintenant** it was difficult for her in the beginning, but she's getting along fine now; **on n'avait qu'un seul salaire, mais on s'en est tirés** we had just the one salary, but we got by *or* scraped by; **rien à faire, je ne m'en tire pas!** *(financièrement)* it's impossible, I just can't make ends meet!; **il y a peu de chances qu'il s'en tire** *(qu'il survive)* the odds are against him pulling through; **je m'en suis tiré avec une suspension de permis** I got away with my licence being suspended; **il s'en tire avec des égratignures** he came through with just a few scratches; **tu ne t'en tireras pas avec de simples excuses** *(être quitte)* you won't get away *or* off with just a few words of apology; **s'en t. à** *ou* **avec** *ou* **pour** *(devoir payer)* to have to pay; **je m'en suis tiré avec** *ou* **pour 500 euros de réparations** I had to cough up *or* fork out 500 euros for the repairs; **à quatre, on ne s'en tirera pas à moins de 150 euros le repas** the meal will cost at least 150 euros for the four of us; **il ne s'en tirera pas comme ça** he won't get off so lightly, he won't get away with it; **on n'a encaissé qu'un seul but, on ne s'en est pas trop mal tirés** they scored only one goal against us, we didn't do too badly; **je n'aime pas faire de discours – tu t'en es très bien tiré** I don't like to make speeches – you did very well

Tirésias [tirezjas] **NPR** *Myth* Tiresias

tiret [tirɛ] **NM 1** *Typ (de dialogue)* dash; *(en fin de ligne)* rule; **t. cadratin** em dash; **t. demi-cadratin** en dash; **t. de fin de ligne** line-end hyphen **2** *(trait d'union)* hyphen; *Ordinat & Typ* **t. conditionnel/insécable** soft/hard hyphen

tiretaine [tirtɛn] **NF** *Vieilli Tex* linsey-woolsey, wincey

tirette [tirɛt] **NF 1** *Vieilli (cordon → de sonnette)* bellpull; *(→ de stores)* cord; *(→ de rideaux)* draw string **2** *Tech* pull handle, pull knob; *(d'un fourneau)* flue damper; *Aut* (pull-out) knob; *Élec* pull knob **3** *(d'un meuble)* (sliding) leaf; *(d'un bureau)* pull-out shelf **4** *Belg (fermeture Éclair®) Br* zip, *Am* zipper; *Hum (entaille suturée)* stitched wound

tireur, -euse [tirœr, -øz] **NM,F 1** *(criminel, terroriste)* gunman; *(de la police)* marksman; **bon/mauvais t.** good/bad shot; **t. isolé** *ou* **embusqué** sniper; **t. d'élite** sharpshooter

2 *(aux boules)* thrower

3 *Banque* drawer

4 *Escrime* fencer

5 *Ftbl* shooter

6 *Phot* printer

7 **t. de cartes, tireuse de cartes** fortune-teller *(who reads cards)*

❑ **tireuse NF 1** *Phot (machine)* printer

2 *(pour le vin)* bottle-filling machine

tire-veille [tirvɛj] **NM INV** *Naut (rampe)* ladder rope; *(de gouvernail)* yoke line

tire-veine [tirvɛn] *(pl* **tire-veines)** **NM** (surgical) stripper

tiroir [tirwar] **NM 1** *(de meuble)* drawer **2** *Rail* siding **3** *Tech* slide valve; **t. rond** *ou* **à pistons** piston valve **4** *Fam (ventre)* stomach■, belly

❑ **à tiroirs ADJ 1** *(à épisodes)* = containing episodes independent of the main action; **roman/comédie à tiroirs** episodic novel/play **2** *Fam (à rallonge)* **un nom à tiroirs** a double-barrelled name

tiroir-caisse [tirwarkɛs] *(pl* **tiroirs-caisses)** **NM** till

tisane [tizan] **NF 1** *(infusion)* herb tea, herbal tea **2** *très Fam (raclée, volée)* thrashing, hiding

tisanière [tizanjɛr] **NF** teapot *(for herbal tea)*

tiser [3] [tize] *Fam* **VT** to knock back

VI to booze, to knock it back

tison [tizɔ̃] **NM** brand

tisonné, -e [tizɔne] **ADJ** *(robe d'un cheval)* with black spots

tisonner [3] [tizɔne] **VT** to poke

tisonnier [tizɔnje] **NM** poker; **donner un coup de t. dans le feu** to give the fire a poke

tissage [tisaʒ] **NM 1** *(procédé)* weaving; *(entrecroisement de fils)* weave; **un t. serré/lâche** a close/loose weave; **t. à la main** *ou* **à bras** handloom weaving; **t. mécanique** power-loom weaving **2** *(bâtiment)* cloth mill

tisser [3] [tise] **VT 1** *Tex (laine, coton, tissu)* to

weave; **t. le lin/une nappe** to weave linen/a tablecloth; *Fig* **l'habitude tisse des liens** *(entre des personnes)* the more you get to know someone, the closer you feel to them

2 *(toile d'araignée)* to spin

3 *Fig (élaborer)* to weave, to construct; **l'auteur a subtilement tissé son intrigue** the playwright subtly wove *or* constructed the plot

▸**se tisser** VPR *Fig (lien, intrigue)* to be woven; **l'intrigue qui se tissait autour de cette disparition** the web of intrigue which was being woven around the disappearance

tisserand, -e [tisʀɑ̃, -ɑ̃d] NM,F weaver

tisserin [tisʀɛ̃] NM **1** *(artisan)* weaver **2** *Orn* weaverbird; **t. à capuchon** village weaver

tisseur, -euse [tisœʀ, -øz] NM,F **1** *(artisan)* weaver **2** *(industriel)* mill owner

tissu [tisy] NM **1** *Tex* fabric, material, cloth; **une longueur de t.** a length of fabric; **du t. pour faire des vêtements** dressmaking material *or* fabric; **du t. d'ameublement** furnishing fabric *or* material; **le rayon des tissus d'ameublement** the soft furnishings department; **t. matelassé** quilted material; **t. métallique** wire gauze

2 *Fig (enchevêtrement)* **un t. de mensonges** a pack *or Sout* tissue of lies; **un t. d'absurdités** one absurdity after another; **un t. d'incohérences** a mass of contradictions; **c'est un t. d'incohérences** it's full of inconsistencies

3 *(en sociologie)* fabric, make-up; **le t. culturel de la nation** the cultural make-up *or* fabric of our country; **le t. social** the social fabric; **le t. urbain** the urban infrastructure

4 *Biol* tissue; **t. conjonctif** connective tissue; **t. musculaire** muscle tissue

5 *Bot* tissue

❑ **de tissu, en tissu** ADJ fabric *(avant n)*, cloth *(avant n)*

tissu-éponge [tisyepɔ̃ʒ] *(pl* **tissus-éponges***)* NM terry, terry-towelling, *Am* terry cloth; **en t.** terry *(avant n)*, terry-towelling *(avant n)*, *Am* terry cloth; **peignoir en t.** towelling robe; **serviette en t.** terry towel

tissulaire [tisylɛʀ] ADJ tissual, tissue *(avant n)*

tissu-pagne [tisypaɲ] *(pl* **tissus-pagnes***)* NM *(en Afrique francophone)* = cotton material used to make loincloths

Titan [titɑ̃] NM **1** *Astron* Titan **2** *Mil* **(missile) T.** Titan missile

NMPL *Myth* **les Titans** the Titans

titan [titɑ̃] NM *Littéraire (colosse)* titan; **c'est un t.** he's got superhuman strength

❑ **de titan** ADJ *(travail)* Herculean; **travail de t.** Herculean task; **un combat de titans** an epic battle

titane [titan] NM titanium

titanesque [titanɛsk] ADJ *Littéraire (force)* massive, superhuman; *(travail)* Herculean; *(ouvrage)* monumental

titaneux, -euse [titanø, -øz] ADJ *Chim* titanous

titanique[1] [titanik] = **titanesque**

titanique[2] [titanik] ADJ *Chim* titanic

Tite [tit] NPR Titus

Tite-Live [titliv] NPR Livy

titi [titi] *Fam* NM **t. parisien** Parisian street urchin▪

❑ **en titi** *Can* ADJ **être en t.** to be fuming, to be hopping mad ADV damn, *Br* bloody; **il fait froid en t.** it's damn *or Br* bloody cold

Titicaca [titikaka] NM **le lac T.** Lake Titicaca

Titien [tisjɛ̃] NPR **(le) T.** Titian

titillation [titijasjɔ̃] NF **1** *(léger chatouillement)* tickling, tickle **2** *Fig (excitation de l'esprit)* titillation

titiller [3] [titije] VT **1** *(chatouiller agréablement)* to tickle; **le champagne me titillait le palais** the champagne tickled my palate **2** *Fig (exciter légèrement)* to titillate; **la curiosité me titillait** the curiosity was killing me **3** *(énerver)* to pester, to aggravate; **arrête de t. ta sœur!** stop pestering your sister!

titisme [titism] NM Titoism

titiste [titist] ADJ Titoist

NMF Titoist

titrage [titʀaʒ] NM **1** *(d'un film)* titling; *Journ* **t. à cheval** spread head **2** *Chim* titration, titrating **3** *Mines (d'un minerai)* assaying **4** *(d'un alcool, d'un vin)* determination of the strength **5** *Tex* counting

titraille [titʀaj] NF *Journ* coverline

TITRE [titʀ]

title **A1, 2,** ■ **B1, 3, C5** ■ headline **A3** ■ track **A4** ■ qualification **B2** ■ credentials **C1** ■ security **C3, 4** ■ certificate **C4**

NM **A. 1** *(d'un roman, d'un poème)* title; *(d'un chapitre)* title, heading; **je n'ai pas encore trouvé de t. pour mon roman** I haven't come up with a title for my novel yet; **il a proposé un t. pour une nouvelle émission de télévision** he suggested a title for a new television programme

2 *Typ* **t. courant** running title; **faux t.** half-title; **grand t.** full title; **(page de) t.** title page

3 *Journ* headline; **t. sur cinq colonnes à la une** five-column front-page headline; **les gros titres** the main headlines; **faire les gros titres des quotidiens** to hit *or* to make the front page of the daily newspapers

4 *(chanson, morceau)* track; **le CD comporte onze titres** there are eleven tracks on the CD; **un CD deux/trois titres, un deux/trois titres** two-track/three-track CD

B. 1 *(désignation d'un rang, d'une dignité)* title; **le t. de roi/d'empereur** the title of king/emperor; **porter un t.** to have a title, to be titled; **porter le t. de duc** to have the title of duke; *Fig* **il revendique le t. de libérateur** he insists on being called a liberator; **un t. de noblesse** *ou* **nobiliaire** a title; **avoir des titres de noblesse** to be titled

2 *(nom de charge, de grade)* qualification; **conférer le t. de docteur à qn** to confer the title of doctor on *or* upon sb

3 *Sport* title; **mettre son t. en jeu** to risk one's title; **le boxeur défendra son t.** the boxer will defend his title; **disputer le t. de champion du monde à qn** *(boxeur)* to fight sb for the world championship title

C. 1 *(certificat)* credentials; **il a produit des titres authentiques** he produced genuine credentials; **voici les titres à présenter à l'appui de votre demande** the following documents must accompany your application; **décliner ses titres universitaires** to list one's academic *or* university qualifications; **recruter sur titres** to recruit on the basis of (paper) qualifications; **t. de pension** pension book; **t. de permission** (leave) pass; **t. de transport** ticket; **les voyageurs doivent présenter leur t. de transport à la sortie** passengers must show their tickets at the exit

2 *Fig* **il s'est acquis des titres de reconnaissance du peuple** he won the people's gratitude; **son t. de gloire est d'avoir introduit l'informatique dans l'entreprise** his/her proudest achievement is to have computerized the company

3 *Banque* (transferable) security; **avance sur titres** advance on *or* against securities; **t. universel de paiement** universal payment order; **t. de crédit** proof of credit; **titres déposés en nantissement** securities lodged as collateral

4 *Bourse (certificat)* certificate; *(valeur)* security; **les titres** securities, bonds; **t. d'action** share certificate; **t. nominatif** registered bond; **titres en portefeuille** securities (in portfolio); **t. au porteur** *(action)* bearer share; *(obligation)* floater *or* bearer security; **t. de rente** government bond; **titres à terme** futures

5 *Jur* title; **t. exécutoire** writ of execution; **t. de propriété** title deed, document of title; **t. putatif** putative deed; **juste t.** good title

6 *Fin* **t. budgétaire** ≃ budget item *(one of the seven categories into which public spending is divided in the French budget)*

D. 1 *(en joaillerie)* fineness, *Spéc* titre; **le t. des monnaies d'or et d'argent est fixé par la loi** the precious metal content of gold and silver coins is determined by law

2 *Pharm* titre; **t. d'une solution** titre of a solution

3 *Tex* count

E. *(locutions)* **à t. amical** as a friend; **consulter qn à t. d'ami** to consult sb as a friend; **demander une somme à t. d'avance** to ask for some money by way of an advance; **à t. consultatif** in an advisory capacity; **à t. d'essai** on a trial basis; **à t. exceptionnel** exceptionally; **à t. d'exemple** by way of an example, as an example; **à t. privé/professionnel** in a private/professional capacity; **décoration attribuée à t. posthume** posthumous award; **à t. provisoire** on a provisional basis; **présidence accordée à t. honorifique** honorary title of president; **à t. gracieux** free of charge, without charge; **à t. onéreux** for a fee *or* consideration; **à t. de journaliste, vous pourrez entrer** you will be allowed in because you are from the press; **à t. indicatif** for information only; **à quel t.?** *(en vertu de quel droit)* in what capacity?; *(pour quelle raison)* on what grounds?; **à quel t. vous occupez-vous de ses affaires?** *(gén)* in what capacity are you looking after his/her affairs?; *(avec irritation)* who told you you could *or* who gave you permission to look after his/her affairs?; **à quel t. lui fais-tu ces reproches?** on what grounds do you criticize him/her?

❑ **à aucun titre** ADV on no account; **il n'est à aucun t. mon ami** he is no friend of mine

❑ **à ce titre** ADV *(pour cette raison)* for this reason, on this account; **l'accord est signé et à ce t. je suis satisfait** the agreement has been signed and for this reason I am satisfied

❑ **à de nombreux titres, à divers titres** ADV for several reasons, on more than one account; **je me félicite à plus d'un t. du résultat de ces négociations** I have more than one reason to be pleased with the outcome of these negotiations

❑ **à juste titre** ADV *(préférer)* understandably, rightly; *(croire)* correctly, justly, rightly; **elle s'est emportée, (et) à juste t.** she lost her temper and understandably *or* rightly so

❑ **à plus d'un titre** = **à de nombreux titres**

❑ **au même titre** ADV for the same reasons; **elle a obtenu une prime, j'en réclame une au même t.** she got a bonus, I think I should have one too for the same reasons

❑ **au même titre que** CONJ for the same reasons as; **je proteste au même t. que mon voisin** I protest for the same reasons as my neighbour

❑ **en titre** ADJ **1** *Admin* titular

2 *(officiel → fournisseur, marchand)* usual, appointed; **le fournisseur en t. de la cour de Hollande** the official *or* appointed supplier to the Dutch Court; *Hum* **son amant en t.** her official lover

titré, -e [titʀe] ADJ **1** *(anobli)* titled **2** *Pharm (liqueur, solution)* standard *(avant n)*

titrer [3] [titʀe] VT **1** *Presse* **t. qch** to run sth as a headline; **le journal titrait sur trois colonnes: France 3 Brésil 0** the newspaper ran a three-column headline: France 3 Brazil 0 **2** *Pharm* to titrate **3** *Mines* to assay **4** *(alcool, vin)* to determine the strength of **5** *Tex & Tech (coton, fil de fer)* to size, to number **6** *(anoblir)* to confer a title upon **7** *(œuvre d'art, roman)* to give a title to, to entitle

titreur, -euse [titʀœʀ, -øz] NM,F *Journ* headline writer

❑ **titreuse** NF **1** *Cin (appareil)* titler **2** *Typ (pour gros titres)* headliner

titrier, -ère [titʀije, -ɛʀ] NM,F *Journ* headline writer; *Typ* headline setter

titrimétrie [titʀimetʀi] NF titrimetry

titrisation [titʀizasjɔ̃] NF *Bourse & Fin* securitization

titriser [titʀize] VT *Bourse & Fin* to securitize

titubant, -e [titybɑ̃, -ɑ̃t] ADJ *(démarche)* unsteady, weaving, wobbly; **un ivrogne t.** a drunkard staggering about

titubation [titybasjɔ̃] NF titubation

tituber [3] [titybe] VI *(ivrogne)* to stagger *or* to reel (along); *(malade)* to stagger (along); **marcher/entrer/sortir en titubant** to stagger *or* lurch along/in/out; **t. de fatigue** to reel *or* stagger *or* totter with exhaustion

titulaire [titylɛʀ] ADJ **1** *(enseignant)* tenured; *(évêque)* titular; **être t.** *(professeur d'université)* to have tenure; *(sportif)* to be under contract; **devenir t.** to get tenure

2 *(détenteur)* **être t. de** *(permis, document,*

passeport) to hold; **être t. d'un compte en banque** to be an account holder

3 *Jur* **être t. d'un droit** to be entitled to a right

NMF 1 *Admin & Rel* incumbent

2 *(détenteur → d'un permis)* holder; *(→ d'un passeport)* bearer, holder; **t. d'action** shareholder

3 *Jur* **le t. d'un droit** the person entitled to a right

4 *Sport* player under contract, team member; **il a plus de sélections comme remplaçant que comme t.** he has made the squad (as a sub) more often than he has made the team

titularisation [titylarizasjɔ̃] NF **la t. de qn** *(gén)* giving a permanent contract to sb; *(professeur d'université)* granting tenure to sb; *(enseignant)* appointing sb to a permanent post; *(sportif)* giving a contract to sb, signing sb up (as a full member of the team)

titulariser [3] [titylarize] VT *(gén)* to give a permanent contract to; *(professeur d'université)* to grant tenure to; *(enseignant)* to appoint to a permanent post; *(sportif)* to give a contract to, to sign up (as a full member of the team)

titulature [titylatyr] NF (set of) titles

tjaële, tjäle [tjɛl] NM *Géog* tjaele, taele

TJJ [teʒiʒi] NM *Fin (abrév* **taux d'argent au jour le jour***)* overnight *or* call rate

TLJ *(abrév écrite* **tous les jours***)* every day

tmèse [tmɛz] NF *Ling* tmesis

TMM [teɛmɛm] NM *Fin (abrév* **taux moyen du marché monétaire***)* money-market rate

TMT [teɛmte] NM *(abrév* **technology, media and telecommunications***)* TMT

TNP [teɛnpe] NM *Théât (abrév* **Théâtre national populaire***)* **le T.** the French National Theatre *(based at the Palais de Chaillot in Paris until 1972 and at Villeurbanne near Lyons since then)*

TNT [teɛnte] NM *Chim (abrév* **trinitrotoluène***)* TNT

NF *TV (abrév* **télévision numérique terrestre***)* digital television, DTT

TO *Aut (abrév écrite* **toit ouvrant***)* sunroof

toast [tost] NM **1** *(en buvant)* toast; **t. de bienvenue** welcome toast; **porter un t.** to propose a toast; **porter un t. à qn** to drink (a toast) to sb, to toast sb **2** *(pain grillé)* piece of toast; **des toasts** toast, toasted bread; **des toasts au saumon** salmon canapés

toaster, toasteur [tostœr] NM toaster

toboggan [tɔbɔgɑ̃] NM **1** *(glissière → sur terre)* slide; *(→ dans l'eau)* chute, flume; *(→ dans un parc d'attractions)* helter-skelter; *(→ pour marchandises)* chute; **les enfants qui font du t.** the children going down the slide; **tu veux faire du t.?** do you want to go on the slide?; **t. de secours** escape chute

2 *(luge)* toboggan; **faire du t.** to go tobogganing

3 *Aut (armature de pneu)* (type) casing reinforcement

4 *Can (traîneau)* toboggan; **faire du t.** to go tobogganing; **piste de t.** toboggan run

▫ **Toboggan®** NM *(pont) Br* flyover, *Am* overpass

Tobrouk [tɔbruk] NM Tobruk

toby [tɔbi] NM *Ich* Moorish idol

TOC [teose] NM *(abrév* **trouble obsessionnel compulsif***)* OCD

toc [tɔk] NM *Fam* **1** *(imitation sans valeur → d'un matériau)* fake■, worthless imitation■; *(→ d'une pierre)* rhinestone■, paste■; *(→ d'un bijou)* fake■; **en t.** fake■, imitation■; **sa bague, c'est du t.** his/her ring is fake■

2 *Fig (ce qui est factice)* sham■; **sa culture/son amitié, c'est du t.** his/her so-called education/friendship is just a sham *or* is all on the surface

ADJ INV *Fam* **1** *(faux)* trashy, tacky, *Br* rubbishy; **ça fait t.** it looks tacky

2 **être un peu t. t.** *(fou)* to be a bit crazy *or* cracked; **il est un peu t. t.** he's not all there

EXCLAM **1** *(coups à la porte)* **t. t.!** knock knock!

2 *Fam (après une remarque)* **et t.!** so there!, put that in your pipe and smoke it!; **et t., bien fait pour toi/lui/eux!** and (it) serves you/him/them right!

tocade [tɔkad] = **toquade**

tocante [tɔkɑ̃t] NF *Fam* watch■

tocard, -e [tɔkar, -ard] *Fam* ADJ *(tableau, décor)* tacky, *Br* naff

NM,F *(personne)* dead loss, (born) loser

NM *(cheval de course)* mediocre racehorse

toccata [tɔkata] NF *Mus* toccata

tock [tɔk] NM *Orn* **t. à bec rouge** red-billed hornbill

tocologie [tɔkɔlɔʒi] NF *Méd* tocology

tocophérol [tɔkɔferɔl] NM *Chem* tocopherol

tocsin [tɔksɛ̃] NM alarm bell, *Sout* tocsin; **sonner le t.** to ring the alarm, *Sout* to sound the tocsin

tof, toffe[1] [tɔf] ADJ *Belg Fam* great, fantastic

toffe[2] [tɔf] ADJ *Can Joual* tough

tofu [tɔfu] NM *Culin* tofu

toge [tɔʒ] NF **1** *Antiq* toga; **t. prétexte/virile** toga praetexta/virilis **2** *(de magistrat)* gown

Togo [tɔgo] NM **le T.** Togo; **vivre au T.** to live in Togo; **aller au T.** to go to Togo

togolais, -e [tɔgɔlɛ, -ɛz] ADJ Togolese

▫ **Togolais, -e** NM,F Togolese; **les T.** the Togolese

tohu-bohu [tɔybɔy] NM INV **1** *(désordre et confusion)* confusion, chaos **2** *(bruit → de voitures, d'enfants)* racket, din; *(→ d'un marché, d'une gare)* hustle and bustle; *(→ d'une foule)* hubbub; *(→ d'une foire)* hurly-burly

toi [twa] PRON **1** *(après un impératif)* **dis-t. bien que...** bear in mind that...; **réveille-t.!** wake up!; **habille-t.!** get dressed!; **rappelle-t.!** remember!; **assieds-t.!** sit down!; **dis-le-lui, t.** YOU tell him/her

2 *(sujet)* you; **moi, je reste, et t., tu pars** I'll stay and you go; **qui va le faire? – t.** who's going to do it? – you (are); **t. parti, il ne restera personne** when you're gone there'll be nobody left; **tu en veux, t.?** do you want some?; **qu'est-ce que tu en sais, t.?** what do YOU know about it?; **t., tu l'as vu!** you saw it/him!; **tu t'amuses, t., au moins** at least YOU'RE having fun; **et t. qui lui faisais confiance!** and you trusted him/her!; **viendrez-vous, Pierre et t.?** will you and Pierre come?; **t. et moi** you and I; **t. et moi, nous irons ensemble** you and I will go together; **t. et les tiens êtes les bienvenus** you and your family are welcome; **t. seul peux la convaincre** you're the only one who can persuade her

3 *(avec un présentatif)* you; **c'est t.?** is it you?; **je veux que ce soit t. qui y ailles** I want it to be you who goes; **c'est t. qui le dis!** that's what YOU say!; **ah c'est bien t., ça!** that's typical of you!, that's just like you!

4 *(complément)* you; **il vous a invités, Pierre et t.** he's invited you and Pierre; **t., je te connais!** I know you!

5 *(après une préposition)* **avec/sans/pour/***etc* **t.** with/without/for/*etc* you; **on lui a parlé de t.** he's/she's heard about you; **c'est à t. qu'on l'a demandé** you were the one who was asked, YOU were asked; **qui te l'a dit, à t.?** who told YOU about it?; **je te fais confiance, à t.** I trust you; **eh, je te parle, à t.!** hey, I'm talking to you!; **à t., je peux le dire** I can tell YOU; *Fam* **un ami à t.** a friend of yours; **c'est à t.?** is this yours?; **ce livre est à t.** this book is yours *or* belongs to you; **à t. de jouer!** your turn!; **il est plus âgé que t.** he is older than you; **j'ai d'aussi bonnes raisons que t.** I've got just as good reasons as you; **il n'aime que t.** he loves only you

6 *(pronom réfléchi)* yourself; **alors, tu es content de t.?** I hope you're pleased with yourself, then!

toilage [twalaʒ] NM *Couture* ground

toile [twal] NF **1** *Tex (matériau brut)* canvas, (plain) cloth; **t. de coton/lin** cotton/linen cloth; **t. d'amiante** asbestos; **t. anglaise** binding cloth; **t. à bâches** tarpaulin; **t. de Jouy** toile de Jouy; **t. de jute** gunny, (jute) hessian; **t. à matelas** ticking; **t. métis** cotton-linen mix; **t. à sac** sackcloth, sacking; **t. de tente** canvas; **t. à voiles** sailcloth; **grosse t.** rough *or* coarse canvas

2 *(tissu apprêté)* cloth; **t. caoutchoutée** rubberized cloth; **t. cirée** waxcloth; **nappe en t. cirée** waxed tablecloth; **t. émeri** emery cloth; **t. plastifiée** plastic-coated cloth; **t. métallique** wire gauze; **t. de tente** tent canvas

3 *Fam (film)* **se payer** *ou* **se faire une t.** to go to the movies *or Br* the pictures

4 *Beaux-Arts (vierge)* canvas; *(peinte)* canvas, painting; **quelques toiles du jeune peintre** some paintings by the young artist; **faire une t.** to do a painting

5 *Couture* cloth; **t. à patron** toile

6 *Naut (ensemble des voiles d'un navire)* sails; *Arch* **bien porter la t.** to bear sail; **réduire la t.** to take in sail

7 *(couverture d'un livre)* cloth

8 *Théât* (painted) curtain; *aussi Fig* **t. de fond** backdrop; *Fig* **avec la guerre en t. de fond** with the war as a backdrop, against the backdrop of the war

9 *Zool* web; **t. d'araignée** cobweb, spider's web

10 *Ordinat* **la T.** the Web

11 *Littéraire* **tendre sa t.** *ou* **ses toiles** to lay one's snares

▫ **toiles** NFPL *Fam (draps de lit)* sheets■; **se mettre dans les toiles** to hit the sack *or* the hay

▫ **de toile, en toile** ADJ *(robe, pantalon)* cotton *(avant n)*; *(sac)* canvas *(avant n)*; **reliure en t.** cloth binding

toilé, -e [twale] ADJ **1** *Beaux-Arts* **huile sur carton/papier t.** oil on canvas board/paper **2** *Typ (couverture)* cloth-bound, cloth *(avant n)*

toilerie [twalri] NF **1** *(atelier)* canvas mill **2** *(commerce)* canvas trade; *(fabrication)* canvas manufacturing, canvas making

toilettage [twalɛtaʒ] NM *(d'un chat, d'un chien)* grooming

toilette [twalɛt] NF **1** *(soins de propreté)* washing, *Sout* toilet; **faire sa t.** to have a wash, to get washed; **faire une t. rapide** to have a quick wash; **faire une t. de chat** to give oneself a lick and a promise *or Br* a cat's lick; **être à sa t.** *(se laver)* to be having a wash, to be getting washed; *Fam Vieilli (s'apprêter)* to be making one's toilet; **faire la t. d'un malade** to wash a sick person; **faire la t. d'un mort** to lay out a corpse; **produits pour la t. de bébé** baby care products; **articles** *ou* **produits de t.** toiletries

2 *(lustrage du pelage, des plumes)* grooming; **le chat fait sa t.** the cat's washing *or* grooming itself

3 *(tenue vestimentaire)* clothes, outfit, *Sout* toilette; **changer de t.** to change (one's outfit *or* clothes); **encore une nouvelle t.!** ANOTHER new outfit!; **elle est en grande t.** she is (dressed) in all her finery

4 *(table)* dressing-table; *(avec vasque)* washstand

5 *Tech* reed packaging

6 *Culin* veal caul

7 *Belg & Can* = **toilettes**

▫ **toilettes** NFPL *(chez un particulier) Br* toilet, *Am* bathroom; *(dans un café)* toilet, *Br* toilets, *Am* restroom; **toilettes publiques** *Br* toilets, *Am* restroom; **aller aux toilettes** to go to the toilet; **je cherche les toilettes** *(pour dames)* I'm looking for *Br* the ladies *or Am* the ladies' room; *(pour hommes)* I'm looking for *Br* the gents *or Am* the men's room

toiletter [4] [twalete] VT **1** *(chien, chat)* to groom; **je fais t. le chien au moins une fois par mois** I take the dog to be groomed at least once a month **2** *Fam (modifier légèrement → texte)* to amend■, to doctor

▸**se toiletter** VPR *Can* to dress up (smartly)

toilier, -ère [twalje, -ɛr] ADJ cloth *(avant n)*

NM,F **1** *(fabricant)* cloth manufacturer **2** *(commerçant)* cloth dealer

toi-même [twamɛm] PRON yourself; *Rel & Arch* thyself; **tu l'as vu t.** you saw it yourself; **il faut que tu le comprennes de t.** you must understand it (for) yourself; **vérifie par t.** check for yourself; *Fam* **imbécile t.!** same to you!, look who's talking!; **menteur – t.!** liar – liar yourself!

toise [twaz] NF **1** *(règle graduée)* height gauge; **passer qn à la t.** to measure sb's height; **se mettre sous la t.** to have one's height measured **2** *Arch* = former French unit of measurement equal to 1.949 metres

toisé [twaze] NM *Tech* measuring (up), measurement

toiser [3] [twaze] VT **1** *Vieilli (personne)* to measure sb's height **2** *Fig* **t. qn** to look sb up and down, to eye sb from head to foot

▸**se toiser** VPR *(se regarder)* to look each other up and down, to take each other's measure

toison [twazɔ̃] NF **1** *Zool* fleece; *(de lion, de*

tit–toi

cheval) mane **2** *(chevelure)* mane **3** *Fam (poils)* bushy (tuft of) hair **4** *Myth* **la T. d'or** the Golden Fleece

toit [twa] **NM 1** *Archit & Constr* roof; **habiter sous les toits** *(dans une chambre)* to live in an attic room *or* in a garret; *(dans un appartement)* to live in a *Br* top-floor flat *or Am* top-story apartment with a sloping ceiling; **t. plat/en pente** flat/sloping roof; **t. d'ardoises** slate roof; **t. de chaume** thatched roof; **une maison au t. de chaume** a thatched cottage; **t. en terrasse** terrace roof; **t. de tuiles** tiled roof; **t. vert** green roof; **double t.** *(de tente)* flysheet; **le t. du monde** the Roof of the World

2 *Fig (demeure)* roof; **avoir un t.** to have a roof over one's head; **je n'ai plus de t.** I've no longer got a roof over my head, I haven't got anywhere to live anymore; **chercher un t.** to look for somewhere to live; **se retrouver sans t.** to find oneself without a roof over one's head; **sous le t. de qn** under sb's roof, in sb's house; **sous le t. conjugal** in the marital home; **accueillir qn sous son t.** to take sb in; **vivre sous le même t.** to live under the same roof

3 *Aut* **t. ouvrant** sunroof; **t. ouvrant coulissant** sliding sunroof; **une voiture à t. ouvrant** a car with a sunroof; **t. à arceau en T** T-bar roof

4 *Mines* roof

5 *Suisse* **mettre sous t.** *(bâtiment)* to complete; *Fig (loi, projet)* to see through; **mis sous t.** *(bâtiment)* completed; *Fig (loi, projet, négociations)* successfully completed; **mise sous t.** completion

toiture [twatyr] **NF 1** *(ensemble des matériaux)* roofing; *(couverture)* roof; **toute la t. du manoir** all the roofs of the manor house; **refaire la t.** to repair the roof **2** *Archit* **t. à redents** sawtooth roof

toiture-terrasse [twatyrtɛras] *(pl* **toitures-terrasses***)* **NF** cut *or* terrace roof

tokaj [tɔkaj] **NM** (Hungarian) Tokay

tokamak [tɔkamak] **NM** *Nucl* tokamak

tokay [tɔkɛ] **NM 1** *(vin)* (Alsatian) Tokay **2** *Zool* tokay

tokharien, -enne [tɔkarjɛ̃, -ɛn] **ADJ** Tocharian, Tokharian

NM *(langue)* Tocharian, Tokharian

Tokyo [tɔkjo] **NM** Tokyo

tokyoïte [tɔkjɔit], **tokyote** [tɔkjɔt] **ADJ** of/from Tokyo

NMF = inhabitant of or person from Tokyo

tolar [tɔlar] **NM** tolar

tôlard, -e [tolar, -ard] = **taulard**

tôle[1] [tol] **NF 1** *Métal (non découpée)* sheet metal; *(feuille)* metal sheet; **t. d'acier/d'aluminium** sheet steel/aluminium; **t. de cuivre** copper sheeting; **t. galvanisée/laminée** galvanized/laminated iron; **t. ondulée** corrugated iron; **toit en t. ondulée** corrugated iron roof **2** *Fam (mauvais revêtement de route)* uneven surface **3** *Élec* **t. magnétique** magnetized strip

tôle[2] [tol] = **taule**

tôlé, -e [tole] **ADJ** *Aut* metal-panelled

❑ **tôlée ADJ F neige tôlée** crusted snow **NF** crusted snow

Tolède [tɔlɛd] **NM** Toledo

tolérable [tɔlerabl] **ADJ** *(bruit, chaleur, douleur)* bearable, tolerable; *(attitude, entorse à une règle)* tolerable, permissible; **ça n'est pas t.** that is intolerable *or* cannot be tolerated; **son impertinence n'est plus t.** his/her impertinence can no longer be tolerated

NM à la limite du t. barely *or* scarcely tolerable

tolérance [tɔlerɑ̃s] **NF 1** *(à l'égard d'une personne)* tolerance; **faire preuve de t. (à l'égard de qn)** to be tolerant (with *or* towards sb); **manquer de t.** to lack tolerance, to be intolerant; **sans t., pas de convivialité** without (a measure of) tolerance, people cannot live in harmony

2 *(à l'égard d'un règlement)* tolerance, latitude; **ce n'est pas un droit, c'est une simple t.** this is not a right, it is merely something which is tolerated; **il y a une t. d'un litre d'alcool par personne** each person is allowed to bring in a litre of spirits free of duty; **t. orthographique** permitted variation in spelling; **t. zéro (vis-à-vis de qch)** zero tolerance (towards *or* regarding sth)

3 *Bot & Physiol* tolerance; **t. au bruit/à la chaleur/à une drogue** tolerance to noise/to heat/to a drug; **pour étudier la t. du sujet aux glucides** to study the tolerance of an individual to glucides; **t. des greffes tissulaires** acceptance *or* tolerance of tissue grafts; **t. congénitale/acquise** congenital/acquired tolerance; **t. immunitaire** immunological tolerance

4 *Fin (d'une monnaie)* tolerance

5 *(à la douane)* **t. (permise)** allowance; **il y a une t. d'un demi-litre** you are allowed to bring in half a litre duty-free

6 *Tech* tolerance; **affecter une t. à une cote** to allow a margin of tolerance *(when determining dimensions)*; **t. nulle** zero allowance; **t. sur l'épaisseur/la longueur** thickness/length margin; **t. de fonctionnement** operational tolerance; *Électron* **t. de fréquence** frequency tolerance; **à t. de pannes** fault-tolerant

7 *Rel* toleration; **la loi institue une t. alors presque unique en Europe** the law established a form of toleration which was almost unique in Europe at that time

tolérant, -e [tɔlerɑ̃, -ɑ̃t] **ADJ 1** *(non sectaire)* tolerant, broad-minded; **il est t. et éloigné de tout fanatisme** he is tolerant and a stranger to all forms of extremism **2** *(indulgent)* lenient, indulgent, easy-going; **une mère trop tolérante** an overindulgent *or* excessively lenient mother

tolérer [18] [tɔlere] **VT 1** *(permettre → infraction)* to tolerate, to allow; **ils tolèrent le stationnement bilatéral à certaines heures** you're allowed to park on both sides of the street at certain times of the day; **nous tolérons un petit excédent de bagages** we allow a small amount of excess luggage

2 *(admettre → attitude, personne)* to tolerate, to put up with; **je ne tolérerai pas son insolence** I won't stand for *or* put up with *or* tolerate his/her rudeness; **je ne tolère pas qu'on me parle sur ce ton!** I won't tolerate being spoken to like that!; **le directeur ne tolère pas les retards** the manager will not have people arriving late; **la loi peut-elle t. l'injustice?** can the law tolerate injustice?; **elle ne l'aimait pas, elle tolérait juste sa présence à ses côtés** she didn't like him, she just put up with having him around; **ici, on la tolère, c'est tout** we put up with her and that's about all

3 *(supporter → médicament, traitement)* to tolerate; **son foie ne tolère plus l'alcool** his/her liver can no longer tolerate alcohol; **les femmes enceintes tolèrent bien ce médicament** pregnant women can take this drug without adverse effects

►**se tolérer VPR** *(l'un l'autre)* to put up with *or* tolerate each other

tôlerie [tolri] **NF 1** *(fabrique)* sheet-metal workshop; *Aut* body shop **2** *(technique)* sheet-metal manufacture **3** *(commerce)* sheet-metal trade **4** *(d'un véhicule)* panels, bodywork; *(d'un réservoir)* plates, (steel) cladding

tolet [tɔlɛ] **NM** *Naut* oarlock, rowlock, swivel

toletière [tɔltjɛr] **NF** *Naut* strengthening plate

tôlier, -ère [tolje, -ɛr] **NM,F** = **taulier**

NM *Ind* **1** *(marchand)* sheet-iron merchant **2** *(ouvrier)* sheet-metal worker; *Aut* panel beater

ADJ M ouvrier t. sheet-metal worker

tolite [tɔlit] **NF** tolite

tollé [tɔle] **NM** general outcry; **soulever un t. général** to provoke a general outcry

Tolstoï [tɔlstɔj] **NPR Léon T.** Leon Tolstoy

tolu [tɔly] **NM** Tolu balsam

toluène [tɔlɥɛn] **NM** *Chim* toluene

toluidine [tɔlɥidin] **NF** *Chim* toluidine

toluol [tɔlɥɔl] **NM** *Chim* toluol, toluene

TOM [tɔm] **NM INV** *Admin (abrév* **territoire d'outre-mer***)* French overseas territory; *voir encadré à* **DOM-TOM**

tomahawk [tɔmaok] **NM** tomahawk

tomaison [tɔmɛzɔ̃] **NF** *Typ* volume numbering

toman [tɔmɑ̃] **NM** toman

tomate [tɔmat] **NF 1** *Bot (plante)* tomato (plant); *(fruit)* tomato; **la sauce a un goût de t. très prononcé** the sauce tastes strongly of tomatoes; **t. cerise** cherry tomato; *Culin* **tomates farcies** stuffed tomatoes; *Fig* **envoyer des tomates (pourries) à qn** *(conspuer)* to boo sb **2** *Fam (boisson)* = pastis with grenadine

❑ **à la tomate ADJ** tomato-flavoured

tombac [tɔ̃bak] **NM** tombac

tombal, -e, -als *ou* **-aux, -ales** [tɔ̃bal, -o] **ADJ** funerary, tomb *(avant n)*, tombstone *(avant n)*; **inscription tombale** funerary *or* tomb *or* tombstone inscription

tombant, -e [tɔ̃bɑ̃, -ɑ̃t] **ADJ 1** *(oreille, moustache)* drooping; *(seins, fesses)* sagging; *(épaules)* sloping; *(tentures)* hanging; **des yeux aux paupières tombantes** hooded eyes **2** *(jour)* failing, dwindling

tombe [tɔ̃b] **NF** *(fosse)* grave; *(dalle)* tombstone; *(monument)* tomb; *Can (cercueil) Br* coffin, *Am* casket; **aller sur la t. de qn** *(pour se recueillir)* to visit sb's grave; **prier sur la t. de qn** to pray at sb's grave(side); **muet** *ou* **silencieux comme une t.** as silent *or* quiet as the grave; *Can* **être une t.** to be the soul of discretion, to be well able to keep a secret; **sa femme est morte, il la suivra sans doute d'ici peu dans la t.** his wife has died, he probably won't outlive her long

tombé [tɔ̃be] **NM 1** *(en danse)* tombé **2** *Sport* fall; **coup de pied t.** drop kick

tombeau, -x [tɔ̃bo] **NM 1** *(sépulcre)* grave, tomb, sepulchre; **suivre qn au t.** to follow sb to the grave; **descendre au t.** to go to one's grave; **conduire** *ou* **mettre qn au t.** to entomb sb, to commit sb to the grave; *Fig (causer sa mort)* to send sb to his/her grave; **mise au t.** entombment

2 *Fig Littéraire (endroit)* morgue; *(fin)* death, end; **la guerre fut le t. de la dictature** the war spelt the end for the dictatorship

3 *(personne discrète)* **parle sans crainte, c'est un t.** you can speak freely, he's/she's the soul of discretion

4 *(locution)* **à t. ouvert** at breakneck speed

tombée [tɔ̃be] **NF 1 à la t. du jour** *ou* **de la nuit** at nightfall *or* dusk **2** *Journ (pour la remise d'un travail)* copy deadline; *(pour la sortie d'une édition)* edition time

tombelle [tɔ̃bɛl] **NF** *Archéol* = grave covered with a small mound of earth

TOMBER[1] [3] [tɔ̃be]

VI to fall **A1, 3, 5, 6, 8, 10** ■ to get nabbed **A2** ■ to die **A3** ■ to fall off/out **A4** ■ to hang **A5** ■ to droop **A5** ■ to drop **A8** ■ to subside **A8** ■ to disappear **A9** ■ to fall on **B1** ■ to come out **B3**
VT to defeat **1** ■ to pick up **2** ■ to take off **3**

VI *(aux être)* **A.** *CHANGER DE NIVEAU* **1** *(personne)* to fall (down); *(meuble, pile de livres)* to fall over, to topple over; *(cloison)* to fall down, to collapse; *(avion, bombe, projectile)* to fall; **il l'a entraînée en tombant** he pulled her with him when he fell; **j'ai buté contre la racine et je suis tombé** I tripped over the root and fell; **t. par terre** to fall on the floor, to fall down; **t. à plat ventre** to fall flat on one's face; **t. dans l'eau** to fall into the water; **t. sous les coups de qn** to fall under sb's blows; **t. dans un fauteuil** to fall *or* to collapse into an armchair; **t. de fatigue** to be ready to drop (from exhaustion); *Belg Fam* **t. dans l'œil de qn** to take *or* catch sb's fancy; **t. de sommeil** to be asleep on one's feet; **ne monte pas à l'échelle, tu vas t.** don't go up the ladder, you'll fall off; **la tuile tomba à ses pieds** the tile fell at his/her feet; **le jupon tomba à ses pieds** the petticoat fell round her ankles; **des cascades qui tombent de plusieurs dizaines de mètres** waterfalls dropping hundreds of feet; **t. d'un échafaudage** to fall off some scaffolding; **t. dans l'escalier** to fall down the stairs; **t. dans un ravin** to fall into a ravine; **t. de cheval** to fall off *or* from a horse; **t. de moto** to fall off a motorbike; **t. d'un arbre** to fall out of a tree *or* from a tree; **faire t. qn** *(en lui faisant un croche-pied)* to trip sb up; *(en le bousculant)* to knock *or* to push sb over; **le vent a fait t. des arbres** the wind blew some trees over *or* down; **elle l'a fait t. de la table** she made him fall off the table; **faire t. qch** *(en poussant)* to push sth over; *(en renversant)* to knock sth over; *(en lâchant)* to drop sth; *(en donnant un coup de pied)* to kick sth over; **j'ai fait t. mes lunettes** I've dropped my glasses; **le vent a fait t. mon chapeau** the wind blew my hat off; *Fig* **tu es tombé bien bas** you've sunk

very low; **es-tu tombé si bas que tu réclames cet argent?** have you really sunk so low as to ask for this money back?

2 *Fam (être arrêté)* to get *Br* nabbed *or Am* busted

3 *(mourir)* to fall, to die; **t. sur le champ de bataille** to fall on the battlefield; **ceux qui sont tombés au champ d'honneur** those killed in action; **ceux qui sont tombés pour la France** those who died for France

4 *(se détacher → feuille, pétale, fruit)* to fall off, to drop off; *(→ cheveu, dent)* to fall out, to come out; **ne ramasse pas les cerises qui sont tombées** don't pick the cherries which are on the ground; **on a le droit de prendre les pommes qui sont tombées** we're allowed to collect windfalls; **du plâtre tombait du plafond** plaster was falling *or* peeling off the ceiling; **une boule est tombée du sapin de Noël** a bauble has come *or* fallen off the Christmas tree; *Fig* **des paroles méprisantes tombaient de ses lèvres** words of contempt fell from his/her lips

5 *(pendre → cheveux, tentures)* to fall, to hang; *(→ moustaches)* to droop; *(→ seins)* to sag, to droop; **ses longs cheveux lui tombaient dans le dos** his/her long hair hung down his/her back; **une mèche lui tombait sur un œil** a lock of hair hung over one eye; **de lourdes grappes de raisin tombaient de la tonnelle** heavy bunches of grapes were hanging from the bower; **il a les épaules qui tombent** he's got sloping shoulders; **bien t.** *(vêtement)* to hang well *or* nicely; **la robe tombe bien sur toi** the dress hangs well *or* nicely on you

6 *(s'abattre, descendre → rayon de soleil, radiations, nuit)* to fall; *(→ brouillard, gifle, coup)* to come down; **la neige/pluie tombait** it was snowing/raining; **une petite bruine tombait** it was drizzling; **une goutte est tombée dans mon cou** a drop trickled *or* rolled down my neck; **quand la pluie aura fini de t.** when it stops raining, when the rain has stopped; **il tombe en moyenne 3 mm d'eau par jour** the average daily rainfall is 3 mm; *Fam* **qu'est-ce qu'il est tombé hier soir!** it was absolutely pouring *or Br* bucketing down *or* chucking it down last night!; **il tombera de la neige sur l'Est** there will be snow in the east; **il tombe quelques gouttes** it's spitting; **il tombe de grosses gouttes/gros flocons** big drops/flakes are falling; **il tombe de la grêle** it's hailing; **il tombera de la grêle** hail is expected; *Fam* **toi, tu as ta paie qui tombe tous les mois** you have a regular salary coming in (every month); *Fam* **il lui tombe au moins 3000 euros par mois** he has at least 3,000 euros coming in every month; *Fam* **il m'est tombé deux factures/amendes hier** I was landed with a couple of bills/fines yesterday; *Fam* **ça va t.!** *(il va pleuvoir)* it's going to pour (with rain)!; *(il va y avoir des coups)* you're/we're/*etc* going to get it!; *Fam* **son père s'est mis en colère et c'est tombé!** his/her father got angry and *Br* he/she didn't half cop it *or Am* he/she caught hell!; **des têtes vont t.!** heads will roll!; **t. sous les yeux de qn** to come to sb's attention

7 *(déboucher)* **là où la rue Daneau tombe dans le boulevard Lamain** at the point where Rue Daneau joins *or* meets Boulevard Lamain; **continuez tout droit et vous tomberez sur le marché** keep going straight on and you'll come to the market

8 *(diminuer → prix, température, voix, ton)* to fall, to drop; *(→ fréquentation)* to drop (off); *(→ fièvre)* to drop; *(→ colère)* to die down, to subside; *(→ inquiétude)* to melt away, to vanish; *(→ enthousiasme, agitation, intérêt)* to fall away, to fade away, to subside; *(→ tempête)* to subside, to abate, to die away; *(→ vent)* to drop, to fall, to die down; *(→ jour)* to draw to a close; **la température est tombée de 10 degrés** the temperature has dropped *or* fallen (by) 10 degrees; **sa cote de popularité est tombée très bas/à 28 pour cent** his/her popularity rating has plummeted/has dropped to 28 percent; **faire t. la fièvre** to bring down *or* to reduce the fever

9 *(disparaître → obstacle)* to disappear, to vanish; *(→ objection, soupçon)* to vanish, to fade; **sa**

réticence est tombée devant mes arguments he/she gave way in the face of my arguments; **sa joie tomba brusquement** his/her happiness suddenly vanished *or* evaporated; **ses défenses sont tombées** he/she dropped his/her guard

10 *(s'effondrer → cité)* to fall; *(→ dictature, gouvernement, empire)* to fall, to be brought down, to be toppled; *(→ record)* to be broken; *(→ concurrent)* to go out, to be defeated; *(→ plan, projet)* to fall through; **les candidats de droite sont tombés au premier tour** the right-wing candidates were eliminated in the first round; **le chef du gang est tombé hier** the ringleader was arrested yesterday; **le dernier joueur français est tombé en quart de finale** the last French player was knocked out in the quarter final; **faire t.** *(cité)* to bring down; *(gouvernement)* to bring down, to topple; *(record)* to break; *(concurrent)* to defeat

11 *(devenir)* **t. amoureux,** *Can* **t. en amour** to fall in love; **t. enceinte** to become pregnant; **t. malade** to become *or* to fall ill; *Fam* **t. fou** to go mad; **t. (raide) mort** to drop dead, to fall down dead

12 *Cartes* **tous les atouts sont tombés** all the trumps have been played; **le roi n'est pas encore tombé** the king hasn't been played yet; **faire t. la dame** to make one's opponent to play the queen

B. *SE PRODUIRE, ARRIVER* **1** *(événement)* to fall on, to be on; **mon anniversaire tombe un dimanche** my birthday is *or* falls on a Sunday; **t. juste** *(calcul)* to work out exactly; **bien t.** to come at the right moment *or* at a convenient time; **l'héritage n'aurait pas pu mieux t.!** the legacy couldn't have come at a better moment *or* more convenient time!; **ton bureau l'intéresse – ça tombe bien, je voulais m'en débarrasser** he's interested in your desk – that's lucky, I was just about to get rid of it; **mal t.** to come at the wrong moment *or* at an inconvenient time; **les jours chômés tombent mal cette année** public holidays fall badly this year; **cette grossesse tombe vraiment mal** this pregnancy has come at a very inconvenient time; **le mardi tombe assez mal pour moi** Tuesday's not a good day *or* very convenient for me

2 *(personne)* **je tombe toujours aux heures de fermeture** I always get there when it's closed; **on est tombés en plein pendant la grève des trains** we got there right in the middle of the rail strike; **t. juste** *(deviner)* to guess right; **bien t.** *(opportunément)* to turn up at the right moment; *(avoir de la chance)* to be lucky *or* in luck; **ah, vous tombez bien, je voulais justement vous parler** ah, you've come at just the right moment, I wanted to speak to you; **tu ne pouvais pas mieux t.!** you couldn't have come at a better time!; **il est excellent, ce melon, je suis bien tombé** this melon's excellent, I was lucky; **elle est bien tombée avec Hugo, c'est le mari parfait** she was lucky to meet Hugo, he's the perfect husband; **mal t.** *(inopportunément)* to turn up at the wrong moment; *(ne pas avoir de chance)* to be unlucky *or* out of luck; **tu tombes mal, on doit partir cet après-midi** you've picked a bad time, we're leaving this afternoon; **il ne pouvait pas plus mal t.** he couldn't have picked a worse time; **travailler pour Fanget? tu aurais pu plus mal t.** working for Fanget? it could have been a lot worse; **tu tombes à point!** you've timed it perfectly!, perfect timing!

3 *(nouvelles)* to be out, to come out; **l'édition du soir tombe à cinq heures** the evening edition comes out at five; **les dernières nouvelles qui viennent de t. font état de 143 victimes** news just out *or* released puts the number of victims at 143; **à 20 heures, la nouvelle est tombée** the news came through at 8 p.m.

VT *(aux avoir)* **1** *(triompher de → candidat, challenger)* to defeat

2 *Fam (séduire)* to pick up, *Br* to pull; **il les tombe toutes** he's got them falling at his feet

3 *Fam (enlever)* to take off■; **il a tombé la veste** he took his jacket off

□ **tomber dans** VT IND *(se laisser aller à → découragement, désespoir)* to sink into, to lapse into; **elle tombe souvent dans la vulgarité** she often lapses into vulgarity; **comment en parler sans t. dans le jargon scientifique?** how can we talk about it without lapsing into scientific jargon?; **sans t. dans l'excès inverse** without going to the other extreme; **des traditions qui tombent dans l'oubli** traditions which are falling into oblivion; **t. dans la dépression** to become depressed; **t. dans l'erreur** to commit an error

□ **tomber en** VT IND **t. en lambeaux** to fall to bits *or* pieces; **t. en décadence** to fall into decline; **t. en ruine** to go to rack and ruin; **t. en morceaux** to fall to pieces

□ **tomber sur** VT IND *Fam* **1** *(trouver par hasard → personne)* to come across, to run *or* to bump into; *(→ objet perdu, trouvaille)* to come across *or* upon, to stumble across; **je suis tombé sur ton article dans le journal** I came across your article in the newspaper; **je suis tombé sur une arête** I bit on a fishbone; **on a tiré au sort et c'est tombé sur elle** lots were drawn and her name came up

2 *(avoir affaire à → examinateur, sujet d'examen)* to get; **quand j'ai téléphoné, je suis tombé sur sa mère/un répondeur** when I phoned, it was his/her mother who answered (me)/I got an answering machine

3 *(assaillir → personne)* to set about, to go for; **il tombe sur les nouveaux pour la moindre erreur** he comes down on the newcomers (like a ton of bricks) if they make the slightest mistake; **la cavalerie est tombée sur l'ennemi** the cavalry swooped down on the enemy; **il a fallu que ça tombe sur moi!** it had to be me!

4 *(se porter sur → regard, soupçon)* to fall on; *(→ conversation)* to turn to; **les soupçons sont tombés sur la nièce** suspicion fell on the niece; **la conversation est tombée sur la religion** the conversation turned to religion; **mes yeux sont tombés sur un objet qui brillait** my eyes fell on a shiny object

---

Allusion

Être tombé dedans quand on était petit

This is a very famous expression from the cartoon-strip *Astérix*, created by René Goscinny and Albert Uderzo in 1959. There is a magic potion which makes people invincible, and fortunately for Astérix's companion Obélix, **Il est tombé dedans quand il était petit** ("He fell into it when he was little"), thus acquiring its benefits by accident. The expression is used today of someone who is either naturally very talented, at music for example, or who has grown up in a certain environment from a young age, for example his/her parents were musicians. Thus, if one says of someone **Il est tombé dedans quand il était petit** it means "He's been doing it all his life, it's hardly surprising he's good at it".

---

tomber² [tɔ̃be] NM **1** *Littéraire* **au t. du jour** *ou* **de la nuit** at nightfall *or* dusk **2** *Sport (de lutte)* fall

tombereau, -x [tɔ̃bro] NM **1** *(benne)* dumper, dump truck; **t. à ordures** *Br* bin lorry, dustcart; *Am* garbage truck **2** *(contenu)* truckload; *Fig* **des tombereaux de** masses of **3** *Rail* = high-sided open wagon

tombeur [tɔ̃bœr] NM *Fam* **1** *(séducteur)* womanizer **2** *(lutteur)* killer **3** *Sport* **le t. du champion d'Europe** the man who defeated the European champion

tombola [tɔ̃bola] NF raffle, tombola

tombolo [tɔ̃bolo] NM *Géog* tombolo

Tombouctou [tɔ̃buktu] NM Timbuktu

tome [tɔm] NM *(section d'un ouvrage)* part; *(volume entier)* volume

     NF = **tomme**

tomenteux, -euse [tɔmɑ̃tø, -øz] ADJ *Bot* tomentose, tomentous

tomer [3] [tɔme] VT *Typ (ouvrage)* to divide into volumes

tomette [tɔmɛt] = **tommette**

tomien, -enne [tɔmjɛ̃, -ɛn] ADJ of/from a French overseas territory
□ **Tomien, -enne** NM,F = inhabitant of or person from a French overseas territory

tomme [tɔm] NF Tomme (cheese)

tommette [tɔmɛt] NF = red hexagonal floor tile

tommy [tɔmi] (pl **tommies**) NM Fam Br Tommy (soldier), Am doughboy

tomodensitomètre [tɔmɔdɑ̃sitɔmɛtr] NM Méd tomodensitometer

tomodensitométrie [tɔmɔdɑ̃sitɔmetri] NF Méd tomodensitometry

tomographie [tɔmɔgrafi] NF Méd & Géol tomography; **t. par émission de positrons** positron emission tomography

tom-pouce [tɔmpus] NM INV **1** Fam (nain) dwarf, midget **2** (petit parapluie) stumpy umbrella

ton¹ [tœn] NF (mesure de masse) ton

ton² [tɔ̃] NM **A. 1** (qualité de la voix) tone; **t. monocorde** drone; **sur un t. monocorde** monotonously
  2 (hauteur de la voix) pitch (of voice); **t. nasillard** twang
  3 (intonation) tone, intonation; **t. arrogant/ amical/implorant** arrogant/friendly/pleading tone; **je voudrais que le t. reste à la courtoisie** I'd like the (tone of the) discussion to remain courteous; **le t. des entretiens est resté cordial** the atmosphere of the talks remained cordial; **d'un t. sec** curtly; **hausser le t.** to up the tone; **pas la peine de prendre un t. ironique/méchant pour me répondre!** there's no need to be so ironic/spiteful when you answer me!; **ne me parle pas sur ce t.!** don't speak to me like that or in that tone of voice!; **ne le prends pas sur ce t.!** don't take it like that!
  4 (style → d'une lettre, d'une œuvre artistique) tone, tenor; **j'aime le t. badin de ses lettres** I like the playful tone of his/her letters; **le t. de ses plaisanteries ne me plaît guère** I don't much like the tone of his/her jokes; **le t. général de la pièce est assez optimiste** the overall tone of the play is fairly optimistic
  5 (manière de se comporter) **le t. des milieux artistiques** the lifestyle of artistic circles; **un t. provincial** a small-town flavour; **le bon t.** good form; **de bon t.** the thing to do; **il est de bon t. de se moquer de l'astrologie** making fun of astrology is what's expected
  6 Ling (en phonétique) tone, pitch; (dans une langue tonale) pitch; **les langues à t.** tonal languages
  B. 1 (tonalité) tone
  2 Mus (d'une voix, d'un instrument) tone; (tube) crook, shank; (mode musical) key; **le t. d'une sonate** the tone of a sonata; **prendre le t.** to tune (up); **baisser/élever le t. en chantant** to lower/ to raise the pitch while singing; **le t. majeur/ mineur** major/minor key; **donner le t.** Mus to give the chord; Fig to set the tone; **elle a très vite donné le t. de la conversation** she quickly set the tone of the conversation; **ils donnent le t. de la vie dans notre petite ville** they set the tone in our little town
  C. 1 (couleur) tone, shade; **dans les tons verts** in shades or tones of green; **les verts sont en tons dégradés** the greens are shaded (from dark to light); **être dans le même t. que** to tone in with
  2 Beaux-Arts shade; **les tons chauds/froids** warm/cool tones; **tons rompus** broken tones
□ **dans le ton** ADV **tu crois que je serai dans le t.?** do you think I'll fit in?; **ici on ne fait pas de manières, il faudra te mettre dans le t.** we don't stand on ceremony here, you'll just have to take us as you find us; **se mettre dans le t. de qn** to take on sb's ways
□ **de bon ton** ADJ in good taste; **il est de bon t. de mépriser l'argent** it's quite the thing or good form to despise money
□ **sur le ton de** PRÉP **sur le t. de la conversation** conversationally, in a conversational tone; **sur le t. de la plaisanterie** jokingly, in jest, in a joking tone
□ **sur tous les tons** ADV in every possible way; **on nous répète sur tous les tons que...** we're being told over and over again that..., it's being drummed into us that...
□ **ton sur ton** ADJ (en camaïeu) in matching tones or shades

ton³ [tɔ̃]

> **ta** becomes **ton** before a word beginning with a vowel or h mute.

ADJ POSSESSIF **1** (indiquant la possession) your; **t. ami/amie** your friend; **t. meilleur ami/ta meilleure amie** your best friend; **t. oncle et ta tante** your aunt and (your) uncle; **t. père et ta mère**, Littéraire **tes père et mère** your father and mother; **tes frères et sœurs** your brothers and sisters; **j'ai mis t. chapeau et tes gants** I put on your hat and (your) gloves; **un de tes amis** one of your friends, a friend of yours; **un professeur de tes amis** a teacher friend of yours
  2 Fam (emploi expressif) **eh bien regarde-la, t. émission!** all right then, watch your (damned) programme!; **arrête de faire t. intéressant!** stop trying to draw attention to yourself!; **il pleut souvent dans ta Bretagne!** it rains a lot in your beloved Brittany!; **tu auras ta chambre à toi** you'll have your own room; **t. imbécile de frère** your idiot of a brother; **t. artiste de mari** your artist husband; **alors, je peux le rencontrer, t. artiste?** so, can I meet this artist of yours?; **alors, tu l'as eu, t. vendredi?** so you managed to get Friday off, then?; **alors, c'était ça, tes vacances de rêve!** so much for your dream holiday!
  3 Rel & Arch Thy

-TON [tɔ̃] SUFF

This is an ARGOT suffix, that is one that was used in the language of the underworld. Although this type of slang is now largely outdated, some of its words are still in use today. This is the case for several words ending in **-ton**, eg:
> **biffeton, bifton** (from billet) note/ticket; **fiston** (from fils) son, sonny; **frometon** (from fromage) cheese; **mecton** (from mec, itself a slang word) guy, bloke; **cureton** (from curé) priest

tonal, -e, -als, -ales [tɔnal] ADJ **1** Ling pitch (avant n) **2** Mus tonal

tonalisme [tɔnalism] NM Beaux-Arts tonalism

tonalité [tɔnalite] NF **1** Beaux-Arts & Phot tonality; (de paysage) key
  2 Mus (organisation) tonality; (d'un morceau) key; **j'aime la t. de cet instrument/de sa voix** I like the way the instrument/his/her voice sounds, I like the timbre of the instrument/his/ her voice
  3 (atmosphère) tone; **le film prend vite une t. tragique** the movie soon becomes tragic in tone
  4 Élec tonality; (d'une radio) tone
  5 Tél **t. (continue ou d'invitation à numéroter)** dial or Br dialling tone; **attendez d'avoir la t.** wait for the dial tone; **je n'ai pas de t.** I'm not getting a or there's no dial tone; **il n'y a plus de t.** there's no dial tone; **t. d'appel** ringing tone; **t. de sonnerie** ringtone

tondage [tɔ̃daʒ] NM Tex shearing, cropping

tondaison [tɔ̃dɛzɔ̃] NF shearing time

tondeur, -euse [tɔ̃dœr, -øz] NM,F shearer; **t. de moutons** sheepshearer
□ **tondeuse** NF **1** Hort **tondeuse (à gazon)** (lawn) mower; **tondeuse électrique/à main ou mécanique** electric/hand mower; **passer la tondeuse à gazon** to mow the lawn, to give the lawn a mow **2** (de coiffeur) (pair of) clippers **3** (pour moutons) (pair of) sheep shears **4** Tex (pair of) shears

tondre [75] [tɔ̃dr] VT **1** (cheveux → couper très court) to crop; (→ raser) to shave off; (laine de mouton) to shear (off); **il a les cheveux tondus** he's got close-cropped hair or a crew cut
  2 (mouton) to shear; (chien) to clip; **t. un caniche** to clip a poodle; **t. qn** to shave sb's head
  3 (pelouse) to mow, to cut; (haie) to clip
  4 Tex to shear, to crop
  5 Fam (dépouiller, voler) to fleece; (exploiter) to fleece, to take to the cleaners; **t. qn** (au jeu) to clean sb out; **ils se sont laissé t. sans protester** they got taken to the cleaners and they didn't say a word; Fig **il tondrait un œuf** he's a real skinflint or Scrooge or Am tightwad

tondu, -e [tɔ̃dy] ADJ **1** (cheveux → coupés très court) closely cropped; **avoir le crâne t.** ou les

cheveux tondus (être rasé) to have a shaven head
  2 (mouton) shorn; (chien) clipped
  3 (pelouse) mowed, mown; (haie) clipped
  NM,F (personne → aux cheveux coupés très court) = person with close-cropped hair; (→ aux cheveux rasés) = person with a shaven head; Hist **les tondues** = French women whose heads were shaved at the end of World War II for fraternizing with Germans
  NM **1** Fam Vieilli (moine) monk▪
  2 Hist **le Petit T.** = nickname of Napoleon (Bonaparte)

toner [tɔnɛr] NM toner

tonétique [tɔnetik] NF Ling tonetics (singulier); **la t. anglaise** the laws of stress in English

tong [tɔg] NF flip-flop, Am thong; **des tongs** (a pair of) flip-flops or Am thongs

Tonga [tɔ̃ga] NFPL **les (îles) T.** Tonga; **vivre aux T.** to live in Tonga; **aller aux T.** to go to Tonga

tonicardiaque [tɔnikardjak] ADJ cardiotonic
  NM cardiotonic

tonicité [tɔnisite] NF **1** Physiol muscle tone, Spéc tonicity **2** (de l'air, de la mer) tonic or bracing effect

tonie [tɔni] NF Physiol pitch

tonifiant, -e [tɔnifjɑ̃, -ɑ̃t] ADJ **1** (air, climat) bracing, invigorating; (promenade) invigorating; (crème, exercice, massage) tonic, toning **2** (influence, conseils) stimulating, inspiring

tonifier [9] [tɔnifje] VT (corps, peau) to tone up; (cheveux) to give new life to; (esprit) to stimulate; **une marche au grand air tonifie l'organisme** a walk in the open air does wonders for the constitution

tonique [tɔnik] ADJ **1** (air, climat) bracing; (médicament) tonic, fortifying; (lotion) toning, tonic; (boisson) tonic; (activité) stimulating, invigorating **2** Physiol tonic **3** Ling (syllabe) tonic, stressed
  NM **1** Méd tonic **2** (lotion) toner
  NF Mus tonic, keynote

tonitruant, -e [tɔnitryɑ̃, -ɑ̃t] ADJ thundering, resounding, stentorian; **..., dit-il d'une voix tonitruante ...**, he thundered

tonitruer [3] [tɔnitrye] VI to thunder, to resound

tonka [tɔ̃ka] NM Bot tonka bean (plant); **fève t.** tonka bean

Tonkin [tɔ̃kɛ̃] NM Anciennement **le T.** Tonkin

tonlieu [tɔ̃ljø] NM Hist **1** (droit d'étalage) = tax levied on stallholders at fairs **2** (sur les marchandises transportées) = tax on goods transported by land or water

tonnage [tɔnaʒ] NM **1** (d'un bateau) tonnage; **t. brut/net** gross/net tonnage; **t. port en lourd** deadweight tonnage **2** (d'un port) tonnage **3** (droit de) t. duty based on) tonnage

tonnant, -e [tɔnɑ̃, -ɑ̃t] ADJ (voix) thundering; **voix tonnante** voice of thunder, thunderous voice

tonne [tɔn] NF **1** (unité de masse) ton, tonne; **un bateau de mille tonnes** a thousand-ton ship; **t. (métrique)** (metric) ton or tonne; **un (camion de) deux tonnes** a two-ton Br lorry or Am truck; **t. américaine** short ton; **t. d'arrimage** measurement ton; **t. courte** short ton (= 907.185 kg); Naut **t. de déplacement** ton of displacement, displacement ton; **t. d'encombrement** measurement ton; **t. d'équivalent charbon** tonne of coal equivalent; **t. d'équivalent pétrole** ton oil equivalent; **t. forte** long or gross ton (= 1016.06 kg); Naut **t. fret** rate of freight; **t. de jauge** gross or register ton; **t. kilométrique** ton kilometre
  2 Fam **des tonnes** (beaucoup) tons, heaps, loads; **j'ai des tonnes de choses à vous raconter** I've got tons or loads of things to tell you; **en faire des tonnes** (en rajouter) to lay it on (really) thick
  3 Agr (réservoir) tank; (grand tonneau) large cask or barrel; (son contenu) cask, barrel; Can Fam Fig **sentir la t.** ou **le fond de t.** to stink of booze

tonneau, -x [tɔno] NM **1** (contenant pour liquide) cask, barrel; **vin au t.** wine from the barrel or cask; **vin en t.** wine in the barrel or cask; **mettre du vin en t.** to pour wine in or into barrels; **t. d'arrosage** water cart; **t. à mortier** mortar mixer; **c'est le t. des Danaïdes** (travail

interminable) it's an endless task; *(gouffre financier)* it's a bottomless pit; **le t. de Diogène** Diogenes' tub

2 *(quantité de liquide)* caskful, barrelful

3 *(accident)* somersault; **faire un t.** to roll over, to somersault; **la voiture a fait quatre tonneaux** the car rolled over *or* turned over four times

4 *Aviat* roll; **faire un t.** to do a barrel roll

5 *Naut* ton; **t. d'affrètement** measurement ton; *Vieilli* **t. de jauge** ton, tonnage

6 *Hist (voiture à cheval)* governess cart

▫ **du même tonneau** ADJ *Fam* of the same ilk

tonnelage [tɔnlaʒ] NM **marchandises de t.** goods in barrels

tonnelet [tɔnlɛ] NM keg, small cask

tonnelier [tɔnəlje] NM cooper

tonnelle [tɔnɛl] NF **1** *(abri)* bower, arbour; *Littéraire* **déjeuner sous la t.** to lunch al fresco **2** *Archit* barrel *or* tunnel vault **3** *Chasse* tunnel net *(for partridges)*

tonnellerie [tɔnɛlri] NF *(fabrication)* cooperage

tonner [3] [tɔne] VI *(artillerie)* to thunder, to roar, to boom; **on entendait t. les canons** you could hear the thunder *or* roar of the cannons

  V IMPERSONNEL **il tonne** it's thundering; **il a tonné plusieurs fois aujourd'hui** it's been thundering quite a bit today

▫ **tonner contre** VT IND *(sujet: personne)* to fulminate against

tonnerre [tɔnɛr] NM **1** *(bruit de la foudre)* thunder; **le t. gronda dans le lointain** there was a rumble of thunder in the distance; **une voix de t.** a thunderous voice; **un bruit** *ou* **fracas de t.** a racket, a din; **coup de t.** thunderclap; *Fig* bombshell; *Fig* **ses révélations ont eu l'effet d'un coup de t. dans l'assemblée** the meeting was thunderstruck by his/her revelations

2 *Fig (tumulte soudain)* storm, tumult, commotion; **un t. d'applaudissements** thunderous applause; **il quitta l'estrade sous un t. d'applaudissements** he left the platform to *or* amidst thunderous applause

  EXCLAM *Fam* **t. (de Dieu)!** hell and damnation!; **t. de Brest!, mille tonnerres!** hang *or* damn it all!

▫ **du tonnerre (de Dieu)** *Fam Vieilli* ADJ *(voiture, fille, repas, spectacle)* terrific, fantastic; **un solo de batterie du t.** a really mean drum solo; **il fera un marin du t. de Dieu** he'll make a thundering good sailor ADV tremendously *or* terrifically well; **ça a marché du t.** it went like a dream

tonographie [tɔnɔɡrafi] NF tonography

tonologie [tɔnɔlɔʒi] NF tonology

tonomètre [tɔnɔmɛtr] NM *Méd & Mus* tonometer

tonométrie [tɔnɔmetri] NF *Méd & Mus* tonometry

tonométrique [tɔnɔmetrik] ADJ *Méd & Mus* tonometric

tonsure [tɔsyr] NF **1** *Rel (partie rasée)* tonsure; *(cérémonie)* tonsuring; **porter la t.** to be tonsured **2** *Fam (calvitie)* bald patch; **il commence à avoir une petite t.** he's going a bit thin on top

tonsuré [tɔsyre] ADJ M tonsured

  NM monk, cleric

tonsurer [3] [tɔsyre] VT to tonsure

tonte [tɔt] NF **1** *(de moutons → activité)* shearing; *(→ époque)* shearing time **2** *(laine tondue)* fleece **3** *(d'une pelouse)* mowing

tontine [tɔtin] NF **1** *Jur* tontine **2** *Hort* = covering placed around soil ball of plant

tontiner [3] [tɔtine] VT *Hort* to ball and burlap

tontisse [tɔtis] ADJ *Tex* **bourre t.** cropping flock; **papier t.** flock paper

tonton [tɔtɔ] NM **1** *Fam (oncle)* uncle▪; **T. Jules** Uncle Jules **2** *Hist* **t. macoute** Tonton Macoute, Haitian secret policeman *(under the Duvalier regime)*

▫ **Tonton** NPR = one of the nicknames of François Mitterrand

tonture[1] [tɔtyr] NF *Tex (action)* shearing, cropping; *(résultat)* shearings, croppings, flock

tonture[2] [tɔtyr] NF *Naut (courbure)* sheer, camber

tonus [tɔnys] NM **1** *Fig (dynamisme)* dynamism, energy; **avoir du t.** to be full of energy; **elle a un sacré t.** she's got an incredible amount of energy, she's incredibly energetic **2** *Physiol* tonus; **t. musculaire** muscle tone

top [tɔp] NM **1** *(signal sonore)* pip, beep; **au quatrième t., il sera exactement une heure** at the fourth stroke, it will be one o'clock precisely;

Électron **t. d'écho** blip, *Am* pip; *Électron* **t. de synchronisation** synchronizing signal

2 *(dans une course)* **t., partez!** ready, steady, go!; **donner le t. de départ** to give the starting signal

3 *Fam* **c'est le t. (du t.)!** it's the best of stuff!, *Br* it's the business!

  ADJ INV *Fam* great, *Br* fab, *Am* awesome

topaze [tɔpaz] NF topaz; **couleur t.** topaz

toper [3] [tɔpe] VI *Fam* **tope là!** it's a deal!, you're on!

topette [tɔpɛt] NF small bottle

tophacé, -e [tɔfase] ADJ *Méd* tophaceous, tophous

tophus [tɔfys] NM *Méd* tophus, chalkstone

topiaire [tɔpjɛr] ADJ topiary

  NF topiary

topinambour [tɔpinɑ̃bur] NM Jerusalem artichoke

topique [tɔpik] ADJ **1** *(argument)* relevant; *(remarque)* pertinent, apposite, relevant **2** *Pharm* topical

  NM **1** *Ling* topic **2** *Pharm* topical remedy

  NF *Phil* topics *(singulier)*

topless [tɔplɛs] ADJ INV topless

  NM **faire du t.** to go topless

top management [tɔpmanaʒmɛnt] NM *Com* top management, top-level management

top model [tɔpmɔdɛl] *(pl* **top models)**, **top-modèle** *(pl* **top-modèles)** [tɔpmɔdɛl] NM top model, supermodel

top niveau [tɔpnivo] *(pl* **top niveaux)** NM *Fam* **elle est au t.** *(sportive)* she's a top-level sportswoman; *(cadre)* she's a top-flight executive

topo [tɔpo] NM *Fam* **1** *(discours)* lecture▪; *(exposé)* rundown; **faire un t. à qn sur qch** to give sb the rundown on sth, *Am* to hip sb to sth; **c'est toujours le même t.!** it's always the same old story!; **tu vois (d'ici) le t.!** (you) see what I mean? **2** *Vieilli (croquis)* sketch▪, draft▪ **3** *(en escalade)* topo▪

topographe [tɔpɔɡraf] NMF topographer

topographie [tɔpɔɡrafi] NF **1** *(technique, relief)* topography **2** *(représentation)* map, plan

topographique [tɔpɔɡrafik] ADJ topographic, topographical

topographiquement [tɔpɔɡrafikmɑ̃] ADV topographically

topo-guide [tɔpɔɡid] *(pl* **topo-guides)** NM topographical guide

topologie [tɔpɔlɔʒi] NF topology

topologique [tɔpɔlɔʒik] ADJ topologic(al)

topométrie [tɔpɔmetri] NF land surveying

toponyme [tɔpɔnim] NM place name, *Spéc* toponym

toponymie [tɔpɔnimi] NF toponymy; **elle s'intéresse à la t.** she's interested in place names

toponymique [tɔpɔnimik] ADJ toponymical

top secret [tɔpsəkrɛ] ADJ INV top secret, highly confidential

toquade [tɔkad] NF *Fam* **1** *(lubie)* fad, whim; **les casquettes, c'est sa dernière t.!** baseball caps are his/her latest fad!; **ça lui passera, ce n'est qu'une t.** he'll/she'll get over it, it's just a passing fancy **2** *(passade)* crush; **avoir une t. pour qn** to have a crush on sb

toquante [tɔkɑ̃t] = **tocante**

toquard, -e [tɔkar, -ard] = **tocard**

toque [tɔk] NF **1** *(de femme)* pill-box hat, toque; **t. de fourrure** (pill-box shaped) fur hat **2** *(de liftier, de jockey, de magistrat)* cap; **t. (blanche) de cuisinier** chef's hat **3** *(cuisinier dans un restaurant)* chef

toqué, -e [tɔke] *Fam* ADJ **1** *(cinglé)* crazy, nuts; **un vieil oncle un peu t.** a slightly dotty old uncle **2** **être t. de qn** *(passionné de)* to be mad *or* nuts about sb **3** *(têtu)* stubborn▪, pigheaded

  NM,F **1** *(fou)* headcase, *Br* nutter, *Am* wacko; **un t. d'écologie** an ecology freak **2** *Can (personne têtue)* **c'est un t.** he's as pigheaded as they come

toquer [3] [tɔke] **toquer à** VT IND *Vieilli* **t. à la porte** to tap on *or* to knock on the door

  ▸**se toquer** VPR *Fam* **se t. de qn** to become besotted with sb; **se t. de qch** to have a sudden passion for sth

Tora, Torah [tɔra] NF **la T.** the Torah

torailler [3] [tɔraje] VI *Suisse (fumer beaucoup)* to puff away

torana [tɔrana] NM *Archit* toran, torana

torball [tɔrbal] NM goalball

torche [tɔrʃ] NF **1** *(bâton résineux)* torch; **à la lumière des torches** by torchlight; **elle n'était plus qu'une t. vivante** *ou* **vive** she'd become a human torch, her whole body was ablaze

2 *Élec & Tech* **t. électrique** flashlight, *Br* (electric) torch; **t. de soudage** soldering torch

3 *Aviat* **le parachute s'est mis en t.** the parachute didn't open properly

4 *Pétr* flare

5 *Can Fam Péj (femme)* fat slob *(of a woman)*

torché, -e [tɔrʃe] ADJ *Fam* **1** **bien t.** *(réponse, devoir, travail)* well put-together **2** *(bâclé → travail)* botched

torche-cul [tɔrʃky] NM INV *très Fam* **1** *(papier)* *Br* bog roll, *Am* TP **2** *(texte)* trash, *Br* rubbish **3** *(journal)* rag

torchée [tɔrʃe] NF *Fam (correction)* thrashing, hammering; **filer une t. à qn** to thrash *or* hammer sb

torcher [3] [tɔrʃe] VT **1** *Fam (essuyer → plat, casserole)* to wipe clean

2 *Fam (vider entièrement)* **ils avaient torché leurs assiettes** they'd scraped their plates clean

3 *très Fam (nettoyer → fesses)* to wipe; *Vulg* **t. (le cul de) qn** to wipe sb's *Br* arse *or* *Am* ass; **j'ai envie de faire autre chose que de t. des mômes** I don't want to spend my life cleaning up after kids

4 *Fam (bâcler → lettre, exposé)* to knock off, to dash off; *(→ réparation)* to make a pig's ear of, to botch

5 *Constr* to cob

  ▸**se torcher** VPR *très Fam* **1** *(se nettoyer)* **se t. (le derrière)**, *Vulg* **se t. le cul** to wipe one's *Br* arse *or* *Am* ass; **je m'en torche (de tes problèmes)!** I don't give a shit *or* *Am* a rat's ass (about your problems)!

2 *(s'enivrer)* to get shit-faced *or* *Br* pissed

torchère [tɔrʃɛr] NF **1** *Pétr* flare stack **2** *(candélabre)* candle-stand, torchère

torchis [tɔrʃi] NM *Constr* cob

torchon [tɔrʃɔ̃] NM **1** *(pour essuyer)* **t. (à vaisselle)** dish towel, *Br* tea towel; **donner un coup de t. à qch** *(verre, table)* to give sth a wipe; *Fam* **coup de t.** *(querelle)* dust-up; *(épuration)* shake-up; *Fam* **le t. brûle** *(dans un parti, un gouvernement, une entreprise)* tempers are getting frayed; *(dans un couple, entre des collègues, des amis)* there's a bit of friction between them

2 *Fam (écrit mal présenté)* mess; *(devoir scolaire)* dog's breakfast *or* dinner; **qu'est-ce que c'est que ce t.?** do you call that mess homework?

3 *Fam (mauvais journal)* rag

4 *Belg (serpillière)* floorcloth

torchonner [3] [tɔrʃɔne] VT **1** *Fam (travail)* to make a mess of, to foul up **2** *Belg* to mop, to clean (with a floorcloth)

torcol [tɔrkɔl] NM *Orn* wryneck

torda [tɔrda] NM *Orn* razorbill

tordage [tɔrdaʒ] NM *Tex* twisting

tordant, -e [tɔrdɑ̃, -ɑ̃t] ADJ *Fam (amusant)* hysterical, side-splitting; **elle est tordante, ta fille** your daughter's a scream *or* riot *or* hoot

tord-boyaux [tɔrbwajo] NM INV *Fam* rotgut, *Am* alky

tordeur, -euse [tɔrdœr, -øz] NM,F *Tex* twister

▫ **tordeuse** NF **1** *(machine)* cable-twisting machine **2** *Entom* leaf-roller, *Spéc* tortrix; **tordeuse du chêne** oak moth

tord-nez [tɔrne] NM INV *Vét* twitch *(for keeping horse under control during operation)*

tordoir [tɔrdwar] NM **1** *(bâton)* rope tightener, rack stick **2** *(machine à tordre les fils)* cable-twisting machine **3** *(pour le linge)* mangle, wringer

tordre [76] [tɔrdr] VT **1** *(déformer → en courbant, en pliant)* to bend; *(→ en vrillant)* to twist; **tu as tordu le clou en tapant de travers** you've bent the nail by not hitting it straight

2 *(linge mouillé)* to wring (out); **elle tordait nerveusement son mouchoir** she was playing with *or* twiddling her handkerchief nervously

3 *(membre)* to twist; **t. le bras à qn** to twist sb's arm; **t. le cou à une volaille** to wring a bird's neck; *Fam* **t. le cou à qn** to wring sb's neck; **t.**

l'estomac à qn *(sujet: peur)* to churn up sb's insides; *Fam* **t. les boyaux à qn** *(sujet: alcool)* to rot sb's insides

4 *(défigurer)* **le dégoût lui tordait la bouche** he/she screwed up his/her mouth in disgust; **un rictus de douleur tordait sa bouche** his/her mouth was twisted *or* contorted in a grimace of pain; **les traits tordus par la douleur** his/her features twisted *or* his/her face contorted with pain

5 *(faire mal à)* **les brûlures qui lui tordaient l'estomac** the burning pains which were knotting his/her stomach; *Fam* **la peur lui tordait les boyaux** his/her stomach was churning with fear

6 *Tex* to twist

▶**se tordre** VPR **1** *(ver)* to twist; *(pare-chocs)* to buckle; *(branches)* to become gnarled; **se t. sur son siège** to squirm in one's seat; **se t. de douleur** to be doubled up with pain; **se t. (de rire)** to be in stitches, to kill oneself (laughing), to be doubled up (with laughter); **tout le monde se tordait derrière moi** they were doubled up with laughter behind me; **c'était à se t. de rire, il y avait de quoi se t.** it was a scream, it was hilarious

2 se t. la cheville to sprain *or* to twist one's ankle; **se t. le pied** to sprain *or* to twist one's foot; **se t. les mains (de désespoir)** to wring one's hands (in despair)

tordu, -e [tɔrdy] ADJ **1** *(déformé → bouche)* twisted; *(→ doigt)* crooked; **un vieil homme tout t.** a crooked old man; **avoir les jambes tordues** to have crooked legs; *très Fam* **avoir la gueule tordue** to be as ugly as sin

2 *(plié, recourbé → clef)* bent; *(→ roue de vélo, pare-chocs)* buckled; *(vrillé)* twisted

3 *Fam (extravagant → idée, logique)* twisted, weird; *(→ esprit)* twisted, warped; **tu es complètement t.!** you're off your head!; **c'est un plan t.** it's a crazy idea

4 *Fam (vicieux)* **coup t.** *(acte malveillant)* mean *or* nasty *or* dirty trick; **c'est la spécialiste des coups tordus** she's always playing dirty tricks on people

NM,F *Fam (personne bizarre ou folle)* nutcase, headcase; **où il va, l'autre t.?** where's that idiot off to?

tore [tɔr] NM **1** *Archit & Math* torus **2** *Ordinat* **t. magnétique** magnetic core

toréador [tɔreadɔr] NM *Vieilli* toreador, torero

toréer [15] [tɔree] VI *(professionnel)* to be a bullfighter; **il doit t. demain** he'll be bullfighting tomorrow

torero [tɔrero] NM bullfighter, torero

toreutique [tɔrøtik] NF toreutics *(singulier)*

torgnole [tɔrɲɔl] NF *très Fam* clout, wallop; **je vais lui filer** *ou* **flanquer une t.** I'll clout *or* wallop *or* land him/her one; **recevoir** *ou* **prendre une t.** to get clouted *or* walloped

tories [tɔriz] *voir* **tory**

torii [tɔrii] NM INV *Archit* torii

toril [tɔril] NM toril, bull pen

torique [tɔrik] ADJ toric; *Tech* **joint t.** O-ring

tormentille [tɔrmɑ̃tij] NF *Bot* tormentil

tornade [tɔrnad] NF **1** *Météo* tornado; **entrer comme une t.** to come in like a whirlwind **2** *Littéraire (tourmente, catastrophe)* catastrophe, disaster; **sa fortune fut engloutie dans la t. boursière** his/her fortune was swallowed up in the stock market crash

tornate [tɔrnat] NF *Can Fam* head■, *Br* bonce

toroïdal, -e, -aux, -ales [tɔrɔidal, -o] ADJ toroidal

toron [tɔrɔ̃] NM strand

toronneuse [tɔrɔnøz] NF stranding machine

Toronto [tɔrɔ̃to] NM Toronto

torpédo [tɔrpedo] NF *Aut Br* open tourer, *Am* open touring car

torpeur [tɔrpœr] NF torpor; **sortir de sa t.** to shake oneself up, to rouse oneself; **tirer qn de sa t.** to shake sb out of his/her torpor, to rouse sb

torpide [tɔrpid] ADJ *Littéraire* torpid

torpillage [tɔrpijaʒ] NM **1** *Mil* torpedoing **2** *Fig (sabotage)* sabotage, *Br* scuppering; **le t. de la négociation** the wrecking of the negotiations

torpille [tɔrpij] NF **1** *Mil (projectile sous-marin)* torpedo; **t. aérienne** aerial torpedo **2** *Ich* torpedo (ray), electric ray

torpiller [3] [tɔrpije] VT **1** *Mil* to torpedo **2** *(projet)* to torpedo, to scupper

torpilleur [tɔrpijœr] NM torpedo boat

torque [tɔrk] NM *(collier)* torque

NF *Tech* coil of wire

torr [tɔr] NM torr

torrée [tɔre] NF *Suisse* = open-air meal where food is cooked beneath the ashes of a large fire

torréfacteur [tɔrefaktœr] NM **1** *(machine → pour le café)* roaster, coffee-roaster; *(→ pour le tabac)* (tobacco) toaster **2** *(commerçant)* coffee merchant

torréfaction [tɔrefaksjɔ̃] NF *(du café, du cacao)* roasting; *(du tabac)* toasting

torréfier [9] [tɔrefje] VT *(café, cacao)* to roast; *(tabac)* to toast; **grains torréfiés** roasted beans

torrent [tɔrɑ̃] NM **1** *(ruisseau de montagne)* torrent, (fast) mountain stream

2 *(écoulement abondant)* torrent, stream; **un t. de lave** a torrent *or* stream of lava; **des torrents d'eau** *(inondation)* a flood; *(pluie)* torrential rain, a torrential downpour; **des torrents de larmes** floods of tears; **un t. d'injures** a stream *or* torrent of abuse; **des torrents de lumière** a flood of light; **des torrents de musique jaillissaient des haut-parleurs** loud music was booming from the loudspeakers

❑ **à torrents** ADV **il pleut à torrents** it's pouring down

torrentiel, -elle [tɔrɑ̃sjɛl] ADJ **1** *(d'un torrent → eau, allure)* torrential **2** *(très abondant)* **des pluies torrentielles** torrential rain

torrentiellement [tɔrɑ̃sjɛlmɑ̃] ADV torrentially, like a torrent

torrentueux, -euse [tɔrɑ̃tɥø, -øz] ADJ *Littéraire* **1** *(rivière)* rushing, onrushing, fast **2** *Fig (rythme)* frantic; *(vie)* hectic

torride [tɔrid] ADJ *(chaleur, après-midi)* torrid, scorching; *(soleil)* scorching; *(été)* scorching (hot); *(région, climat, érotisme)* torrid; **il fait une chaleur t.** it's scorching

torrieux, -euse [tɔrjø, -øz] *Can Fam* NM,F **c'est un t. de beau garçon!** he's one hell of a good-looking guy; **c'est une torrieuse de belle fille!** she's one hell of a good-looking girl!

NM **sors de là, mon t.!** beat it, you wretch!

❑ **en torrieux** ADV **il fait froid en t.!** it's damn *or Br* bloody cold!

tors, -e[1] [tɔr, tɔrs] ADJ **1** *(laine, soie)* twisted **2** *(colonne)* wreathed; *(pied de meuble)* twisted **3** *(membre)* crooked, bent **4** *Menuis (bois)* spiral grained

NM *Tex* twist

torsade [tɔrsad] NF **1** *(de cordes)* twist; **t. de cheveux** twist *or* coil of hair; **cheveux en torsades** braided *or* twisted hair **2** *(en tricot)* **(point) t.** cable stitch; **aiguille à t.** cable needle **3** *Archit* cabling, cable moulding

❑ **à torsades** ADJ **1** *Archit* cabled **2** *(vêtement)* **pull à torsades** cablestitch sweater

torsadé, -e [tɔrsade] ADJ **1** *(cheveux)* coiled **2** *Archit* **colonne torsadée** cabled column **3** *Élec* **paire torsadée** twisted pair; **raccord t.** twist joint **4** *Biol & Chim* stranded

torsader [3] [tɔrsade] VT *(fil)* to twist; *(cheveux)* to twist, to coil

torse[2] [tɔrs] ADJ F *voir* **tors**

NM **1** *Anat* trunk, torso; **se mettre t. nu** to strip to the waist; **il était t. nu** he was bare-chested **2** *Beaux-Arts* torso

torseur [tɔrsœr] NM torque

torsion [tɔrsjɔ̃] NF **1** *(d'un cordage, d'un bras)* twisting **2** *Math, Phys & Tech* torsion **3** *Tex* twist (level)

tort [tɔr] NM **1** *(sans article)* **avoir t.** *(se tromper)* to be wrong; **j'ai t., je le reconnais** I admit that I'm (in the) wrong; **c'est elle qui a t., pas toi** she's the one who's wrong *or* (who's) in the wrong, not you; **tout de même, il n'a pas toujours t.!** he can't be wrong all the time!; **tu as t. de ne pas la prendre au sérieux** you're making a mistake in not taking her seriously, you're wrong not to take her seriously; **tu n'avais pas tout à fait t./pas t. de te méfier** you weren't entirely wrong/you were quite right to be suspicious; **il n'est pas d'accord, et il n'a pas t.** he doesn't agree and he's right (not to); **donner t. à qn** *(rendre quelqu'un responsable)* to blame sb, to lay the blame on sb; *(désapprouver)* to disagree with sb; **elle me donne toujours t. contre son fils** she always sides with her son against me; **les faits lui ont donné t.** events proved him/her (to be) wrong *or* showed that he/she was (in the) wrong

2 *(défaut, travers)* fault, shortcoming; **je reconnais mes torts** I admit I was wrong; **c'est son seul t.** it's his/her only fault; **elle a le t. d'être trop franche** the trouble *or* problem with her is (that) she's too direct; **il a eu le t. de ne pas demander de reçu** he made the mistake of not asking for a receipt; **c'est un t. (de)** it's a mistake (to); **tu ne fais pas de sport? c'est un t.** don't you do any exercise? you definitely ought to *or* should; **c'est un t. d'agir sans réfléchir** it's a mistake to act without due reflection; **c'est un t. de le lui avoir dit** it was wrong *or* a mistake to tell him/her; **avoir le t. de** to make the mistake of; **il a eu le t. de lui faire confiance** he made the mistake of trusting him/her

3 *(dommage)* wrong; **réparer le t. qu'on a causé** to right the wrong one has caused, to make good the wrong one has done; **réparer un t.** to make amends; **faire du t. à qn** to do harm to sb, to wrong sb, to harm sb; **ça lui a fait beaucoup de t.** that did him/her a lot of harm; **cette loi a fait beaucoup de t. aux petits épargnants** this law penalized the small saver heavily; **faire du t. à une cause** *(personne)* to harm a cause; *(initiative)* to be detrimental to a cause

4 *(part de responsabilité)* fault; **avoir tous les torts** *(gén)* to be entirely to blame; *(dans un accident)* to be fully responsible; *(dans un divorce)* to be the guilty party; **les torts sont partagés** both parties are equally to blame; **j'ai des torts envers eux** I have done them wrong; *Jur* **prononcer un jugement au t. d'une des parties** to find against one of the parties

❑ **à tort** ADV **1** *(faussement)* wrongly, mistakenly; **croire/affirmer qch à t.** to believe/to state sth wrongly

2 *(injustement)* wrongly; **condamner qn à t.** to blame sb wrongly

❑ **à tort ou à raison** ADV right or wrong, rightly or wrongly; **on croit à t. ou à raison que c'est contagieux** it is believed, rightly or wrongly, to be contagious

❑ **à tort et à travers** ADV **tu parles à t. et à travers** you're talking nonsense; **elle dépense son argent à t. et à travers** money burns a hole in her pocket, she spends money like water

❑ **dans mon/son/***etc* **tort** ADV **être dans son t.** to be in the wrong; **mettre qn dans son t.** to make sb appear to be in the wrong; **se mettre dans son t.** to put oneself in the wrong; **en ne la prévenant pas, tu t'es mis dans ton t.** you put yourself in the wrong by not warning her

❑ **en tort** ADV in the wrong; **dans cet accident, c'est lui qui est en t.** he is to blame for the accident

torticolis [tɔrtikɔli] NM stiff neck, *Spéc* torticollis; **avoir un t.** to have a stiff neck

tortil [tɔrtil] NM *Hér* baron's coronet

tortilla [tɔrtija] NF *Culin* tortilla

tortillage [tɔrtijaʒ] NM **1** *(fait de tortiller)* twisting **2** *(fait de se tortiller)* wriggling, squirming

tortillard [tɔrtijar] NM *Fam* slow (local) train■

tortille [tɔrtij] NF winding path

tortillement [tɔrtijmɑ̃] NM *(d'un ver)* wriggling *(UNCOUNT)*, squirming *(UNCOUNT)*; *(des hanches)* wiggling *(UNCOUNT)*

tortiller [3] [tɔrtije] VT **1** *(mèche, mouchoir, fil, papier, ruban)* to twist; *(doigts)* to twiddle; *(moustache)* to twirl

2 *(fesses)* to wiggle

VI **1** *(onduler)* **t. des fesses/hanches** to wiggle one's bottom/hips; **marcher en tortillant du postérieur** to walk with a wiggle

2 *très Fam* **y a pas à t.**, *Vulg* **y a pas à t. du cul pour chier droit** there's no getting away from it, there are no two ways about it

▶**se tortiller** VPR *(ver)* to wriggle, to squirm; *(personne → par gêne, de douleur)* to squirm; *(→ d'impatience)* to fidget, to wriggle; *(→ en dansant)* to wriggle about; **se t. sur sa chaise comme un ver** to wriggle in one's chair like a worm

tortillon [tɔrtijɔ̃] NM **1** *(de papier)* twist; **des tortillons de pâte à choux** choux pastry twists **2**

Beaux-Arts (estompe) tortillon, stump **3** *(pour porter une charge)* pad

tortionnaire [tɔrsjɔnɛr] **ADJ policier t.** police torturer

NMF torturer

tortore [tɔrtɔr] **NF** *Fam* cooking■; **elle fait de la vachement bonne t.** she makes really great food *or Br* scran

tortorer [3] [tɔrtɔre] **VT** *Fam Vieilli* to wolf down, to gobble up

tortricidés [tɔrtriside] **NMPL** *Entom* Tortricidae

tortu, -e[1] [tɔrty] **ADJ** *Littéraire* **1** *(nez, jambes)* crooked **2** *(esprit)* warped

tortue[2] [tɔrty] **NF 1** *Zool (reptile)* tortoise; **t. alligator** alligator (snapping) turtle; **t. d'eau douce** terrapin; **t. à écailles** hawksbill (turtle); **t. éléphantine** giant tortoise; **t. franche** green turtle; **t. géante** giant tortoise; **t. happante** snapping turtle; **t. luth, fausse t.** leatherback, leathery turtle; **t. marine** sea turtle; **t. olivâtre** olive Ridley turtle; **t. terrestre** tortoise; **t. verte** green turtle

2 *Entom* tortoiseshell (butterfly)

3 *Fam (traînard) Br* slowcoach, *Am* slowpoke; **avancer comme une t.** to go at a snail's pace, to crawl along

4 *Antiq & Mil* testudo

5 *Can (poêle à bois)* potbellied wood-burning stove

tortueuse [tɔrtyøz] *voir* **tortueux**

tortueusement [tɔrtɥøzmɑ̃] **ADV 1** *(en lacets)* tortuously; **la route se déroule t. jusqu'au col** the road winds *or* twists its way (tortuously) up to the col

2 *(se conduire, manœuvrer)* deviously

tortueux, -euse [tɔrtɥø, -øz] **ADJ 1** *(en lacets → sentier)* winding, *Sout* tortuous; *(→ ruisseau)* meandering, winding

2 *(compliqué → raisonnement, esprit)* tortuous; *(→ style)* convoluted, involved; *(retors → moyens)* devious, crooked

torturant, -e [tɔrtyrɑ̃, -ɑ̃t] **ADJ** *(pensée)* tormenting, agonising

torture [tɔrtyr] **NF 1** *(supplice infligé)* torture; **t. indienne** *(jeu)* Chinese burn; **instrument de t.** instrument of torture

2 *Fig (souffrance)* torture, torment; **l'attente des résultats fut pour lui une véritable t.** he suffered agonies waiting for the results

□ **à la torture ADV être à la t.** to suffer agonies; **mettre qn à la t.** to put sb through hell

□ **sous la torture ADV** under torture; **elle n'a pas parlé, même sous la t.** she refused to talk, even under torture

torturé, -e [tɔrtyre] **ADJ** *(marqué par la souffrance)* tortured, tormented; **les traits torturés** tortured *or* tormented features; **un regard t.** a tormented look

torturer [3] [tɔrtyre] **VT 1** *(supplicier → sujet: bourreau)* to torture

2 *Fig (tourmenter → sujet: angoisse, faim)* to torture, to torment, to rack; *(→ sujet: personne)* to put through torture, to torture; **la jalousie le torturait** he was tortured by jealousy; **torturé par sa conscience** tormented by his conscience

3 *Fig (style, texte)* to labour

▸**se torturer VPR** to torture oneself, to worry oneself sick; **ne te torture pas, ce n'est pas ta faute** don't torture yourself, it isn't your fault; **ne te torture pas l'esprit!** don't rack your brains (too much)!

torve [tɔrv] **ADJ il m'a lancé un regard t.** he shot me a murderous sideways look

tory [tɔri] *(pl* **torys** *ou* **tories)** **ADJ** Tory

NMF Tory

torysme [tɔrism] **NM** toryism

tos [tos] **NMF** *très Fam* Dago, = offensive term used to refer to a Portuguese person

toscan, -e [tɔskɑ̃, -an] **ADJ** Tuscan

NM *(dialecte)* Tuscan

□ **Toscan, -e NM,F** Tuscan

Toscane [tɔskan] **NF la T.** Tuscany

tosser [3] [tɔse] **VI 1** *Naut* to bump **2** *Fam (fumer de la drogue)* to get stoned

tôt [to] **ADV 1** *(de bonne heure)* early; **se lever t.** *(ponctuellement)* to get up early; *(habituellement)* to be an early riser; **elle part t. le matin** she leaves early in the morning; **je prendrai l'avion t. demain** I'll catch an early plane tomorrow *or* a plane early tomorrow; **se coucher t.** to go to bed early

2 *(au début d'une période)* **t. dans l'après-midi** early in the afternoon, in the early afternoon; **t. dans la saison/le mois** early in the season/month

3 *(avant le moment prévu ou habituel)* soon; **il est trop t. pour le dire** it's too early *or* soon to say that; **arrive suffisamment t. ou il n'y aura pas de place** be there in good time or there won't be any seats left; **il fallait y penser plus t.** you should have thought about it earlier *or* before; **vous auriez dû me le dire plus t.** you should have told me sooner *or* earlier *or* before this; **je voudrais passer les prendre plus t.** I would like to come and collect them sooner *or* earlier; **je suis arrivée plus t. que toi** I arrived earlier than you; **elle a dû partir plus t. que prévu** she had to leave earlier than expected; **ce n'est pas trop t.!** at last!, (it's) about time too!

4 *(rapidement)* soon; **je ne m'attendais pas à le revoir si t.** I didn't expect to see him again so soon; **le plus t. possible** as early *or* as soon as possible; **le plus t. sera le mieux** the sooner, the better; **plus t. tu commenceras plus vite tu auras fini** the sooner you begin the sooner you'll finish; **je n'avais pas plus t. raccroché qu'il me rappela** no sooner had I put the receiver down than he phoned me back; **avoir t. fait de** to be quick to; **ils eurent t. fait de s'emparer du sac** they lost no time in seizing the bag; **elle a eu t. fait de changer d'avis** she soon changed her mind, it wasn't long before she changed her mind; **je n'y retournerai pas de si t.!** I won't go back there in a hurry!; **on ne le reverra pas de si t.** we won't see him for a long time; *(il est parti fâché, ruiné etc)* we won't see him again in a hurry

□ **au plus tôt ADV 1** *(rapidement)* as soon as possible; **partez au plus t.** leave as soon as possible *or* as soon as you can

2 *(pas avant)* at the earliest; **samedi au plus t.** on Saturday at the earliest, no earlier than Saturday

□ **tôt ou tard ADV** sooner or later; **t. ou tard, quelqu'un se plaindra** sooner or later *or* one of these days, someone's bound to complain

total, -e, -aux, -ales [tɔtal, -o] **ADJ 1** *(entier → liberté, obscurité)* total, complete; *(→ grève)* all-out; *(→ guerre)* full-scale, full-blown; **un silence t.** complete *or* total *or* absolute silence; **j'ai une confiance totale en elle** I trust her totally *or* implicitly; **la surprise fut totale** we/they were completely taken aback

2 *(généralisé → destruction, échec)* total, utter, complete

3 *(global → hauteur, poids, dépenses)* total; **somme totale** total (amount)

4 *Astron (éclipse)* total

5 *Théât* **spectacle t.** total theatre

ADV *Fam* the net result is that; **t., j'ai perdu mon boulot/il a fallu que je recommence** the upshot is, I lost my job/I had to start again; **et t. on l'a renvoyé** and, to cut a long story short, he got the sack; **tu voulais jouer les femmes indépendantes, et t., tu es toute seule, maintenant** you wanted to be independent and look where it's got you, you're all alone now

NM total (amount); **le t. s'élève à 130 euros** the total comes to 130 euros; **faire le t.** to work out the total; **faire le t. de** to total up, to add up, to reckon up; **fais le t. de ce que je te dois** work out everything I owe you; *Fig* **le t. d'une vie** the sum total of one's experiences; **t. général** sum total, grand total; **t. global** grand total; **t. partiel** subtotal; *Compta* **t. des recettes** total receipts; **t. à payer** total payable; *Fin* **t. de l'actif** total assets; *Fin* **t. du passif** total liabilities

□ **totale NF** *Fam* **1** *Méd* (total) hysterectomy■

2 *(ensemble)* **on a eu droit à la totale, verglas, embouteillages, barrages de routiers** black ice, traffic jams, lorry drivers' road blocks, you name it, we had it; **quand il m'a demandée en mariage, il m'a fait la totale** when he proposed to me, he really went all out

□ **au total ADV 1** *(addition faite)* in total; **au t., il vous revient 2000 euros** in total you are entitled to 2,000 euros

2 *(tout bien considéré)* all in all, all things (being) considered, on the whole

totalement [tɔtalmɑ̃] **ADV** *(ignorant, libre, ruiné)* totally, completely; *(détruit)* utterly; **il est t. incapable de gagner sa vie** he is totally *or* quite incapable of earning a living

totalisant, -e [tɔtalizɑ̃, -ɑ̃t] **ADJ** *Phil* synthetic

totalisateur, -trice [tɔtalizatœr, -tris] **ADJ** totalizing; *(machine)* adding

NM 1 *(appareil)* adding machine, totalizer; *Ordinat* accumulator; *Aut* **t. kilométrique journalier** trip recorder **2** *(au turf)* totalizator

totalisation [tɔtalizasjɔ̃] **NF** adding up, addition, totalizing

totalisatrice [tɔtalizatris] *voir* **totalisateur**

totaliser [3] [tɔtalize] **VT 1** *(dépenses, recettes)* to add up, to total up, to reckon up, to totalize **2** *(atteindre le total de)* to have a total of, to total; **il totalise 15 victoires** he has won a total of 15 times; **qui totalise le plus grand nombre de points?** who has the highest score?

totaliseur [tɔtalizœr] **NM 1** *(appareil)* adding machine, totalizer **2** *(au turf)* totalizator

totalitaire [tɔtalitɛr] **ADJ** totalitarian

totalitarisme [tɔtalitarism] **NM** totalitarianism

totalité [tɔtalite] **NF 1** *(ensemble)* **la t. des marchandises** all the goods; **la presque t. des tableaux** almost all the paintings; **l'entreprise exporte la t. de sa production** the company exports its entire production; **les marchandises seront livrées dans leur t. avant le 20 décembre** all the goods will be delivered before 20 December

2 *(intégralité)* whole; **la t. de la somme** the whole (of the) sum; **elle dit ne pas pouvoir payer la t. de son loyer** she says she can't pay all her rent; **la somme sera remise dans sa t. à la fondation** the whole *or* entire sum will be given back to the foundation; **ce concept, pris dans sa t., n'a rien de surprenant** this concept, (taken) as a whole, is not at all surprising

3 *Phil* totality, wholeness

□ **en totalité ADV** in full; **somme remboursée en t.** sum paid back in full; **le navire a été détruit en t.** the ship was completely destroyed, the whole ship was destroyed

totem [tɔtɛm] **NM** totem

totémique [tɔtemik] **ADJ** totemic; **mât** *ou* **poteau t.** totem (pole)

totémisme [tɔtemism] **NM** totemism

tôt-fait [tofɛ] *(pl* **tôt-faits)** **NM** = cake that can be made quickly

totipotence [tɔtipɔtɑ̃s] **NF** *Biol* totipotency

totipotent, -e [tɔtipɔtɑ̃, -ɑ̃t] **ADJ** *Biol* totipotent

toto [toto] **NM** *Fam (pou)* louse■, *Am* cootie

toton [tɔtɔ̃] **NM** teetotum

touage [twaʒ] **NM** *Naut* chain-towing

touareg, -ègue [twarɛg] **ADJ** Tuareg

NM *(langue)* Tuareg

□ **Touareg, -ègue NM,F** Tuareg; **les Touaregs** *ou* **T.** the Tuaregs *or* Tuareg

toubab [tubab] **NM** *Fam (en Afrique francophone)* = French person of native stock, as opposed to immigrants or their descendants

toubib [tubib] **NM** *Fam* doctor■, doc

toucan [tukɑ̃] **NM** *Orn* toucan

touchant[1] [tuʃɑ̃] **PRÉP** *Littéraire (concernant)* concerning, about

touchant[2], **-e** [tuʃɑ̃, -ɑ̃t] **ADJ** *(émouvant)* touching, moving; **une scène touchante** a sight to melt the heart; **de façon si touchante** in such a touching *or* moving way; **être t. de maladresse/sincérité** to be touchingly awkward/earnest

touchau, -x, touchaud [tuʃo] **NM** touch needle, test needle *(for testing precious metals)*

TOUCHE [tuʃ]

key **A1, 3, 4** ■ button **A1** ■ touch **B2, C1-3** ■ stroke **C1** ■ look **C4** ■ touchline **D1**

NF A. 1 *(gén)* key; *(d'un téléviseur)* button; *(d'un téléphone)* key, button

2 *Élec (plot de contact)* contact

3 *Mus (de clavier)* key; *(d'instrument à cordes)* fingerboard, fretboard

4 *Ordinat & (d'une machine à écrire)* key; **t. de curseur** cursor key; **t. de défilement** scroll key; **t. de déplacement du curseur** cursor

tor–tou

movement key; **t. d'échappement** escape key; **t. d'effacement** delete key; **t. d'espacement arrière** backspace (key); **t. fin** end (key); **t. fléchée, t. (à) flèche** arrow key; **t. flèche vers le bas** down arrow key; **t. flèche vers la droite** right arrow key; **t. flèche vers la gauche** left arrow key; **t. flèche vers le haut** up arrow key; **t. majuscule** shift key; **t. numérique** number key; **t. page précédente** page up key; **t. page suivante** page down key; **t. retour** return *or* enter key; **t. de tabulation** tab key; **t. de verrouillage du clavier numérique** number lock key; **t. de verrouillage des majuscules** caps lock key

B. 1 *Escrime* hit

2 *(en joaillerie)* touch

3 *Pêche* bite; **j'ai eu des touches mais je n'ai rien pris** I've had some bites but I haven't caught anything

4 *Fam (personne séduite)* **avoir une t. avec qn** to be in with sb; **je crois que j'ai fait une t.** I think I'm in there

5 *très Fam Vieilli (locution)* **la sainte t.** *(le jour de la paie)* payday▪

6 *Can Fam (fumer)* **tirer** *ou* **prendre une t.** to have a smoke▪

C. 1 *(coup de pinceau)* touch, (brush) stroke; **du vert en touches légères** light strokes of green; **quelle finesse de t.!** what delicate brushwork!; **en quelques touches** using just a few brush strokes; **mettre la t. finale à qch** to put the finishing touches to sth

2 *(cachet, style)* touch; **il était loin d'avoir la t. d'un Dickens** he lacked the Dickens touch

3 *(trace)* note, touch; **une t. de couleur** a touch of colour; **une t. de cynisme** a touch *or* tinge *or* hint of cynicism

4 *Fam (apparence)* look▪; **il a une de ces touches avec sa veste à franges!** he looks like something from another planet with that fringed jacket of his!; **on avait une de ces touches avec nos cheveux mouillés!** we looked really funny with our hair all wet!; **quelle t.!** what a sight!; **ton prof a une drôle de t.!** your teacher looks a bit weird!; **il a la t. d'un ancien militaire** he looks like an ex-army man, he has the look of an ex-army man (about him)

D. *Sport* **1** *(ligne)* touchline

2 *(remise en jeu → au rugby)* line-out; *(→ au football)* throw-in; **il y a t.** *(sortie de ballon)* the ball is out; **jouer la t.** to play for time *(by putting the ball into touch)*

❑ **en touche** ADV *Sport* into touch; **envoyer le ballon en t.** to kick the ball into touch; **il a mis le ballon en t.** he kicked the ball into touch; **ils ne prennent aucune balle en t.** they never win a line-out

❑ **sur la touche** ADV *Sport* **rester sur la t.** to stay on the bench; *Fam Fig* **être** *ou* **rester sur la t.** to be left out; **quand il a eu 50 ans, ils l'ont mis sur la t.** when he was 50, they put him out to grass *or* they threw him on the scrap heap

touche-à-tout [tuʃatu] *Fam* ADJ INV **il est t.** *(enfant)* he's into everything

NMF INV **1** *(importun)* meddler; **c'est un t.** *(adulte)* he can't keep his hands off anything; *(enfant)* he's into everything **2** *(dilettante)* dabbler, Jack-of-all-trades (and master of none); **il écrit, il peint, c'est un peu un t.** he writes, he paints, he does a bit of everything

toucheau, -x [tuʃo] = **touchau**

touche-pipi [tuʃpipi] NM INV *Fam* **jouer à t.** to play at doctors and nurses

toucher¹ [tuʃe] NM **1** *(sens)* (sense of) touch; *(palpation)* touch

2 *(sensation)* feel; **le t. rugueux de l'écorce** the rough feel of bark; **le t. onctueux de l'argile** the smooth feel of clay

3 *(gén) & Mus (manière de toucher)* touch; **avoir un t. délicat/vigoureux** to have a light/energetic touch

4 *Méd* examination, *Spéc* (digital) palpation; **t. buccal/rectal/vaginal** oral/rectal/vaginal examination

5 *Sport* touch; **il a un bon t. de balle** he's got a nice touch

❑ **au toucher** ADV to the touch *or* feel; **doux/rude au t.** soft/rough to the touch; **c'est facile à reconnaître au t.** it's easy to tell what it is by touching it *or* by the feel of it

TOUCHER² [3] [tuʃe]

> VT to touch **A1, 2, 6, B1, 2, 5, 6** ▪ to feel **A1** ▪ to contact **A3** ▪ to reach **A3** ▪ to examine **A4** ▪ to hit **B3, 4** ▪ to concern **B4, C2** ▪ to affect **B4, 5** ▪ to receive **B7** ▪ to be adjacent (to) **C1** ▪ to be related to **C3**
> VPR to touch **1** ▪ to (be in) contact **1**

VT **A. 1** *(pour caresser, saisir)* to touch; *(pour examiner)* to feel; **tu m'as fait mal – je t'ai à peine touché** you hurt me – I hardly touched you; **ne touchez pas les fruits!** don't touch *or* handle the fruit!; **ne me touche pas!** get your hands off me!, don't touch me!; **le parchemin s'effrite dès qu'on le touche** the parchment crumbles as soon as you touch it; **t. qch du pied** to touch sth with one's foot; **prière de ne pas t.** *(dans un magasin)* please do not touch; *Fam* **pas touche!** hands off!; **touchez avec les yeux!** don't touch, just look!

2 *(entrer en contact avec)* to touch; **il a touché le filet avec sa raquette** he touched the net with his racket, his racket touched *or* hit the net; **ma main a touché sa main** my hand brushed (against) his/hers; **sa robe touchait presque le sol** her dress reached almost to the ground; **au moment où la navette spatiale touche le sol** when the space shuttle touches down *or* lands; **les ailes de la libellule touchaient à peine l'eau** the wings of the dragonfly barely skimmed the water

3 *Fam (joindre → sujet: personne)* to contact, to reach, to get in touch with; *(→ sujet: lettre)* to reach; **où peut-on vous t. en cas d'urgence?** where can you be contacted *or* reached in an emergency?; **si notre message l'avait touché** if our message had got (through) to him *or* reached him

4 *Méd* to examine, *Spéc* to palpate

5 *Naut (port)* to put in at, to call at; *(rochers, fonds)* to hit, to strike; **nous toucherons Marseille lundi** we'll put in at *or* reach Marseilles on Monday

6 *(en joaillerie)* to touch

B. 1 *(se servir de → accessoire, instrument)* to touch; **il n'a pratiquement pas touché le ballon pendant la première mi-temps** he hardly touched the ball during the first half; **cela fait des années que je n'ai pas touché une guitare** I haven't touched a guitar for years; *Fam* **son service est si puissant que je ne touche pas une balle** his/her serve is so powerful I can't get anywhere near the ball

2 *(consommer)* to touch; **il n'a même pas touché son repas/la bouteille** he never even touched his meal/the bottle

3 *(blesser)* to hit; **la balle l'a touché à la jambe** the bullet hit him in the leg; **touché à l'épaule** hit in the shoulder; *Escrime* **touché!** touché!; **touché, coulé!** *(à la bataille navale)* hit, sunk!; *Fig* **t. juste** to hit the target

4 *(atteindre → sujet: mesure)* to concern, to affect, to apply to; *(→ sujet: crise, krach boursier, famine)* to affect, to hit; *(→ sujet: incendie, épidémie)* to spread to; **la marée noire a touché tout le littoral** the oil slick spread all along the coast; **reste-t-il un secteur que l'informatique n'ait pas touché?** are there still any areas untouched by computerization?; **les personnes touchées par l'impôt sur les grandes fortunes** people in the top tax bracket

5 *(émouvoir → sujet: film, geste, gentillesse, spectacle)* to move, to touch; *(affecter → sujet: décès)* to affect, to shake; *(→ sujet: critique, propos désobligeants)* to affect, to have an effect on; **ses chansons ne me touchent pas** his/her songs leave me cold; **vos compliments me touchent beaucoup** I'm very touched by your kind words; **ses prières avaient touché mon cœur** his/her entreaties had moved *or* stirred me; **elle a été très touchée par sa disparition** she was badly shaken by his/her death

6 *Fam (s'en prendre à → personne)* to touch; **c'est le plus gros notable du pays, on ne peut pas le t.** he's the most important public figure in the region, we can't touch him

7 *(percevoir → allocation, honoraires, pension, salaire)* to receive, to get, to draw; *(→ indemnité, ration)* to receive, to get; *(→ chèque)* to cash (in); **combien touches-tu par an?** how much do you get a year?, what's your yearly salary?; **t. beaucoup d'argent** *(salarié)* to earn a good wage; *(artiste, médecin)* to earn large fees; **les saisonniers ne touchent presque rien** seasonal workers don't get paid much; **elle touche 100 000 euros par an** she earns 100,000 euros a year; *Fam* **t. gros** to line one's pockets, to make a packet; **touchez-vous les allocations familiales?** do you get child benefit?; **t. des droits d'auteur** to get royalties; *Fam* **il a dû t. pas mal d'argent** he must've been slipped a tidy sum; **t. le tiercé** to win the "tiercé"; **t. le chômage** *Br* to be on the dole, *Am* to be on welfare

C. 1 *(être contigu à)* to join onto, *Sout* to adjoin, to be adjacent to; **ma maison touche la sienne** my house is adjacent to his/hers

2 *(concerner)* **il s'occupe de tout ce qui touche le financement** he deals with all matters connected with financing *or* with all finance-related matters; **une affaire qui touche la Défense nationale** a matter related to defence, a defence-related matter; **en ce qui touche les vacances** concerning *or* as regards the holidays

3 *(être parent avec)* to be related to; **elle ne nous touche ni de loin ni de près** she is not related to us in any way at all

VI **1** *Naut* to touch bottom

2 *Pêche* to bite

3 *très Fam (exceller)* to be brilliant (**en/à** at); **elle touche en informatique!** she's a wizard at *or* she knows a thing or two about computers!; **ça y est, au saxo, je commence à t.!** I'm beginning to get the hang of the sax now!

4 *Fam (recevoir de l'argent)* to collect

5 *(locution)* **touchez là!** it's a deal!, (let's) shake on it!

❑ **toucher à** VT IND **1** *(porter la main sur → objet)* to touch; **évitez de t. aux fruits** try not to handle the fruit; **que je ne te reprenne pas à t. aux allumettes!** don't let me catch you playing with matches again!

2 *Fam (frapper → adversaire, élève)* to touch, to lay hands *or* a finger on; **si tu touches à un seul cheveu de sa tête...!** if you so much as lay a finger on him/her...!

3 *(porter atteinte à)* to interfere with, to harm, to touch; **ils ne veulent pas vraiment t. au gouvernement** their aim isn't really to harm the government; **ne touchez pas aux parcs nationaux!** hands off the national parks!

4 *(modifier → appareil, documents, législation)* to tamper *or* to interfere with; **quelqu'un a dû t. aux freins** someone must have tampered with the brakes; **ton dessin est parfait, n'y touche plus** your drawing is perfect, leave it as it is

5 *(utiliser → aliment, instrument)* to touch; *(→ somme d'argent)* to touch, to break into; **je n'ai jamais touché à la drogue** I've never touched drugs; **et la drogue? – elle n'y touche plus** what about drugs? – she's given them up; **tu n'as pas touché à ton repas/assiette?** you haven't touched your meal/what was on your plate, have you?; *Fam* **il ne touche plus à la bouteille** he never touches a drop now; **cela fait longtemps que je n'ai pas touché à un volant/piano** I haven't touched a steering wheel/a piano for a long time; **t. à tout** to fiddle with *or* to touch everything; *Fig* to dabble (in everything); **je touche un peu à tout** *(artisan)* I'm a Jack-of-all-trades, I do a little bit of everything; *(artiste)* I'm a man of many parts

6 *(être proche de → sujet: pays, champ)* to border (upon), *Sout* to adjoin; *(→ sujet: maison, salle)* to join on to, *Sout* to adjoin; **notre propriété touche aux salines** our property borders on the salt marsh; *Fig* **t. à la perfection** to be close to perfection; *Fig* **sa prudence touche à la lâcheté** his/her caution borders on cowardice

7 *(concerner, se rapporter à → activité, sujet)* to have to do with, to concern; **les questions touchant à l'environnement** questions related to

the environment, environment-related questions; **tout ce qui touche au sexe est tabou** everything connected *or* to do with sex is taboo

8 *(aborder → sujet, question)* to bring up, to come onto, to broach; **vous venez de t. au point essentiel du débat** you've put your finger on the key issue in the debate

9 *(atteindre → un point dans l'espace, dans le temps)* to reach; **nous touchons au terme du voyage/aux portes de la ville** we've reached the end of our trip/the city gates; **le navire touche au port ce soir** the ship will enter *or* reach harbour tonight; **le projet touche à son terme** the project is nearing its end; **notre séjour touche à sa fin** our stay is nearing its end; *Littéraire* **il ne touche pas à terre** he is treading on air, he is in seventh heaven

►**se toucher** **VPR** **1** *(être en contact)* to touch, to be in contact; *(entrer en contact)* to touch, to come into contact; *(jardins, communes)* to touch, to be adjacent (to each other), *Sout* to adjoin each other; **à l'endroit où les deux lignes se touchent** where the two lines meet; **leurs corps se touchèrent à peine** their bodies (merely) brushed against each other *or* barely touched; **ils se touchèrent de l'épaule** their shoulders touched

2 *très Fam Euph (se masturber)* to play with oneself

3 *Fam* **se t. (la nuit)** to fool oneself, to kid oneself on

touche-touche [tuʃtuʃ] **à touche-touche** **ADV** *Fam* **être à t.** to be nose to tail *or* bumper to bumper

touchette [tuʃɛt] **NF** fret

toucheur, -euse [tuʃœr, -øz] **NM,F** *(qui conduit les bœufs)* (cattle) drover

touée [twe] **NF** *Naut* **1** *(câble)* warp, (warping) cable **2** *(longueur)* scope

touer [6] [twe] **VT** *Naut* to chain-tow

toueur [twœr] **NM** *Naut* tug *(using chain-towing)*

touffe [tuf] **NF** **1** *(de cheveux, de poils)* tuft **2** *(d'arbustes)* clump, cluster **3** *(de fleurs)* clump; **t. d'herbe** tussock **4** *Vulg (toison pubienne)* bush; **une jupe ras la t.** a micro mini-skirt, *Br* a bum-freezer

touffeur [tufœr] **NF** *Littéraire* sultry *or* sweltering heat

touffu, -e [tufy] **ADJ** **1** *(bois, feuillage, haie)* thick, dense; *(barbe, sourcils)* thick, bushy; *(arbre)* thickly covered, with dense foliage **2** *Fig (texte)* dense

touillage [tujaʒ] **NM** *Fam (d'une sauce)* stirring▪; *(d'une salade)* tossing▪

touille [tuj] **NF** *Ich* porbeagle, mackerel shark

touiller [3] [tuje] **VT** *Fam (sauce, soupe)* to stir▪; *(salade)* to toss▪

toujours [tuʒur] **ADV** **1** *(exprimant la continuité dans le temps)* always; **je l'ai t. dit/cru** I've always said/thought so; **elle regrettera t. d'avoir dit non** she will always regret having said no; **ça ne durera pas t.** it won't last forever; **ils n'ont pas t. été aussi riches** they haven't always been so rich; **depuis t.** always; **je t'aime depuis t.** I've always loved you, I've been in love with you for as long as I can remember; *Fam* **il est t. à se plaindre** he's always *or* he never stops complaining; **le ciel t. bleu** the eternally blue sky; **la t. charmante Sophie** the ever charming Sophie; **Sophie, t. plus belle** Sophie, ever more beautiful; **t. plus haut, t. plus vite, t. plus loin** ever higher, ever faster, ever farther; **influence t. plus étendue** ever-increasing influence; **t. plus** more and more, still more; **ils sont t. plus exigeants** they are more and more demanding

2 *(marquant la fréquence, la répétition)* always; **elle est t. en retard** she is always late; **il termine t. à 5 heures** he always finishes at 5 o'clock; **c'est t. moi qu'on punit** I'm always the one who gets punished; **cette expérience ne réussit pas t.** this experiment is not always successful; **les erreurs ne sont pas t. où on les attend** mistakes sometimes occur where we least expect them; **elle trouve t. un bon prétexte** she always finds a good excuse; **on a presque t. habité la même ville** we have almost always lived in the same town; **tu as t. raison, enfin presque t.!** you're always right, well, nearly always!

3 *(encore)* still; **tu travailles t.?** are you still working?; **il travaillait t. quand je suis arrivée** he was still working when I arrived; **tu écris t. des poèmes?** do you still write poems?; **es-tu t. décidé à le faire?** are you still determined to do it?; **il est t. fâché** he's still cross; **il fait t. aussi chaud** it is as hot as ever; *Ironique* **tu es t. aussi serviable!** you're just *or* still as helpful as ever(, I see)!; **t. pas** still not; **je ne suis t. pas satisfait** I'm still not satisfied; **ta leçon n'est t. pas sue** you still don't know your lesson; **elle n'a t. pas téléphoné** she hasn't phoned yet, she still hasn't phoned; **alors, il est rentré? – t. pas** he's back then? – not yet

4 *(dans des emplois expressifs)* **on peut t. y aller, on verra ce qu'il se passera** we can always go and see what happens; **on peut t. lui demander** we can always ask him/her; **tu peux t. essayer** you can always try, you might as well try; **tu peux t. chercher** look as much as you like, look by all means; **elle peut t. attendre!** she'll have a long wait!; **entrez t. mais je ne vous promets rien** come in anyway, but I'm not promising anything; **prends-le, tu peux t. en avoir besoin** take it, you may *or* might need it (some day); **ça peut t. servir** it might come in handy *or* useful; **c'est t. mieux que rien** still, it's better than nothing; **c'est t. ça (de pris)** (at any rate) it's better than nothing, at least it's something; **on trouvera t. un moyen** we're sure *or* bound to find a way; **tu peux t. pleurer, je ne céderai pas** (you can) cry as much as you like, I won't give in; **tu trouveras t. quelqu'un à qui demander** you're bound to find somebody you can ask; **tu lui fais confiance? – pas dans le travail, t.!** do you trust him/her? – not when it comes to work, anyway!; **tu la connais? – pas sous cet angle, t.!** do you know her? – not that side of her, anyway!

▫ **comme toujours** **ADV** as always, as ever; **il a été charmant, comme t.** he was charming as always; **comme t., il est en retard** as always *or* as ever, he's late; **optimiste comme t., il...** ever the optimist, he...

▫ **de toujours** **ADJ** **elle se retrouvait face à son public de t.** she found herself before her faithful audience of old; **une amitié de t.** a lifelong friendship; **ces coutumes sont de t.** these customs date from time immemorial

▫ **pour toujours** **ADV** for ever; **tu me le donnes pour t.?** can I keep it for ever *or* for good?; *Littéraire* **adieu pour t.!** farewell for ever!

▫ **toujours est-il que** **CONJ** the fact remains that; **j'ignore pourquoi elle a refusé, t. est-il que le projet tombe à l'eau** I don't know why she refused, but the fact remains that the plan has had to be abandoned

touladi [tuladi] **NM** *Can Ich* lake char, lake trout

toulonnais, -e [tulɔnɛ, -ɛz] **ADJ** of/from Toulon

▫ **Toulonnais, -e** **NM,F** = inhabitant of or person from Toulon

touloupe [tulup] **NF** = sheepskin coat worn by Russian peasants

toulousain, -e [tuluzɛ̃, -ɛn] **ADJ** of/from Toulouse

▫ **Toulousain, -e** **NM,F** = inhabitant of or person from Toulouse

toundra [tundra] **NF** tundra

toune [tun] **NF** *Can Fam* **1** *(terme d'affection)* sweetie, sweetheart **2** *(chanson)* tune **3** *Péj (grosse femme)* fat cow

toungouse, toungouze [tunguz] **ADJ** Tungus

NM *(langue)* Tungus

▫ **Toungouse, Toungouze** **NMF** Tungus; **les Toungouses** the Tungus

toupaye [tupaj] **NM** *Zool* tree shrew

toupet [tupɛ] **NM** **1** *Fam (audace)* nerve, *Br* cheek; **avoir du t.** to have a nerve *or Br* a cheek; **elle a un sacré t.!, elle ne manque pas de t.!** she's got some nerve *or Br* cheek!; **il a eu le t. de...** he had the nerve *or Br* cheek to... **2** *(de cheveux)* tuft of hair, *Br* quiff; **faux t.** toupee, hairpiece **3** *Zool (d'un cheval)* forelock

toupie [tupi] **NF** **1** *(jeu)* (spinning) top; **t. d'Allemagne** humming top; **tourner comme une t.** to spin like a top **2** *(de meuble)* moulded foot *(Louis XVI style)* **3** *Menuis* spindle moulder **4** *(en plomberie)* turnpin, reamer **5** *Fam* **une vieille t.** *(harpie)* an old crone *or* bag

toupiller [3] [tupije] **VT** *Menuis* to shape with a spindle moulder

toupilleur [tupijœr] **NM** *Menuis* spindle moulder operator

toupilleuse [tupijøz] **NF** *Menuis* spindle moulding machine

toupillon [tupijɔ̃] **NM** *(de poils, de plumes)* small tuft

toupin [tupɛ̃] **NM** *Suisse* cowbell

toupine [tupin] **NF** *(en Suisse et dans le sud de la France)* stoneware jar

toupiner [3] [tupine] **VI** to spin like a top

touque [tuk] **NF** (metal) drum

tour[1] [tur] **NF** **1** *Archit & Constr* tower; *Bible* **la t. de Babel** the Tower of Babel; **le palais de l'Unesco est une vraie t. de Babel** you can hear a real mixture of languages at UNESCO headquarters; *Aviat* **t. de contrôle** control tower; **la t. Eiffel** the Eiffel Tower; **t. de guet** observation tower; *Fig* **t. d'ivoire** ivory tower; *Fig* **s'enfermer dans une t. d'ivoire** to remain aloof; **t. de lancement** launch tower; **la t. de Londres** the Tower of London; **t. d'observation** watchtower, observation tower; **la t. (penchée) de Pise** the Leaning Tower of Pisa; *Ind* **t. de refroidissement** *ou* **de réfrigération** cooling tower; **t. de remplissage** *(pour fusée)* umbilical tower

2 *(immeuble)* high-rise building; **t. d'habitation** tower *or* high-rise block; **t. de bureaux** office (tower) block; **immeuble t.** tower block

3 *Fam (personne grande et corpulente)* **c'est une vraie t.** he's/she's like the side of a house

4 *Échecs* castle, rook

5 *Chim* **t. de fractionnement** fractionating column; **t. de Gay-Lussac/Glover** Gay-Lussac/Glover tower

6 *Pétr* **t. de forage** drilling rig; **t. de sondage** derrick, rig

7 *Ordinat* tower

8 *TV & Cin* camera tower

9 **t. à CD** CD tower

TOUR[2] [tur]

> girth **A1** ▪ circumference **A1** ▪ measurement **A2** ▪ tour **A4** ▪ walk **A5** ▪ drive **A5** ▪ ride **A5** ▪ turn **B1, D1, E1** ▪ round **B2** ▪ trick **C1, 2** ▪ expression **D2** ▪ revolution **E1, 2** ▪ lathe **E5**

NM **A.** CERCLE **1** *(circonférence → d'un fût, d'un arbre)* girth; *(→ d'un objet, d'une étendue)* circumference; **mesurer le t. d'une piscine** to measure round a swimming pool, to measure the circumference of a swimming pool; **le t. de ses yeux était souligné d'un trait** she'd drawn a line round her eyes; **le t. du lac est planté d'arbres** trees have been planted all round *or* around the lake

2 *(mensuration)* **t. de taille/hanches** waist/hip measurement; **elle fait 55 cm de t. de taille** her waist (measurement) is 55 cm; **prends ton t. de taille** measure (round) your waist; **quel est votre t. de taille/hanches?** what size waist/hips are you?; **t. de cou** collar size; **il fait (un) 42 de t. de cou** he takes a size 42 collar; **t. de poitrine** *(d'une femme)* bust measurement *or* size; *(d'un homme)* chest measurement *or* size; **t. de tête** head measurement

3 *(parure)* **t. de cou** *(collier)* choker; *(en fourrure)* fur collar; **t. de lit** (bed) valance

4 *(circuit)* tour, circuit; **j'ai fait le grand t. pour venir ici** I came here the long way round; **faire le t. d'un parc** to go round a park; *(à pied)* to walk round a park; *(en voiture)* to drive round a park; **nous avons fait le t. du vieux quartier** we went round the old part of the town; **faire le t. du monde** to go round the world; **faire le t. du monde en auto-stop/en voilier** to hitch-hike/to sail round the world; **une jeune Américaine faisant son t. d'Europe** a young American travelling round Europe; **t. de circuit** lap; **le T. de France** *(cycliste)* the Tour de France; *(des compagnons)* the Tour de France *(carried out by an apprentice to become a journeyman)*; **t. d'honneur** lap of honour; **t. d'horizon** overview; **faire un t. d'horizon** to take stock; **t. de piste** *(en athlétisme)* lap; *Équitation* round; **faire un t. de piste** *(en athlétisme)* to run a lap; *Équitation* **faire**

un t. de piste sans faute to have a clear round; **on a fait le t. du propriétaire** we went *or* looked round the property; **fais-moi faire le t. du propriétaire** show me round your property; *Fam* **j'ai fait le t. du cadran** I slept round the clock; *Fig* **l'anecdote a fait le t. des bureaux** the story went round the offices *or* did the rounds of the offices; **faire le t. d'une question** to consider a problem from all angles; **j'ai fait le t. de toutes les options** I've explored all the possibilities; **je sais ce qu'il vaut, j'en ai vite fait le t.** I know what he's worth, it didn't take me long to size him up

5 (*promenade* → *à pied*) walk, stroll; (→ *en voiture*) drive, ride; (→ *à bicyclette, à cheval, en hélicoptère*) ride; (*court voyage*) trip, outing; **faire un t.** (*à pied*) to go for a walk; (*en voiture*) to go for a drive *or* ride; (*à vélo*) to go for a ride; **faire un t. en ville** to go into town; **je vais faire un petit t. près de la rivière** I'm going for a short walk near the river; **nous irons faire un t. dans les Pyrénées** we'll go for a trip in the Pyrenees

B. *PÉRIODE, ÉTAPE* **1** (*moment dans une succession*) turn; (*dans un jeu* → *gén*) move, go; **c'est (à) ton t.** (*gén*) it's your turn *or* go; *Échecs* it's your move; **à qui le t.?** whose turn is it?, who's next?; **chacun son t.** everyone will have his turn; **prendre le t. de qn** to take sb's turn; **laisser passer son t.** to miss one's turn; **attendre son t.** to wait one's turn; **tu attendras ton t. pour poser une question** you'll have to wait until it's your turn to ask a question; **c'est à ton t. de mettre la table** it's your turn to lay *or* to set the table; **tu parleras à ton t.** you'll have your chance to say something; **nous veillons chacun à notre t.** we take turns to be on watch; **t. de garde** (*d'un médecin*) spell *or* turn of duty; *Pol* **t. de scrutin** ballot; **au premier t.** in the first ballot *or* round

2 *Sport* (*série de matches*) round; **le second t. de la coupe d'Europe** the second round of the European Cup

C. *ACTION HABILE OU MALICIEUSE* **1** (*stratagème*) trick; **elle prépare un mauvais t.** she's up to some mischief; **j'en ai fait, des tours, quand j'étais petit!** I was always up to no good when I was a child!; **jouer un t. à qn** to play a trick on sb; **jouer un sale** *ou* **mauvais t. à qn** to play a nasty *or* dirty trick on sb; **jouer un t. pendable à qn** to play a really nasty trick on sb; **ça vous jouera un mauvais** *ou* **vilain t.!** you'll be sorry for it!, it'll catch up with you (one day)!; **ma mémoire/vue me joue des tours** my memory/sight is playing tricks on me; **et le t. est joué!** and there you have it!; **avoir plus d'un t. dans son sac** to have more than one trick up one's sleeve

2 (*numéro, technique*) **t. d'adresse** skilful trick, feat of skill; **t. de cartes** card trick; **t. de passe-passe** sleight of hand; **t. de prestidigitation** conjuring trick

D. *ASPECT* **1** (*orientation*) turn; **cette affaire prend un très mauvais t.** this business is going very wrong; **la discussion prend un très mauvais t.** the discussion is taking a nasty turn; **je n'aime pas le t. qu'a pris la situation** I don't like the turn the situation has taken *or* the way the situation is developing; **la manifestation prit un t. tragique** the demonstration took a tragic turn; **t. d'esprit** turn *or* cast of mind; **ce n'était pas dans son t. d'esprit** this wasn't the way his/her mind worked; *Suisse* **donner le t.** (*maladie*) to take a turn for the better; (*personne*) to wrap up

2 *Ling* (*expression*) expression, phrase; (*en syntaxe*) construction; **un t. de phrase maladroit** an awkward turn of phrase

E. *ROTATION* **1** (*d'une roue, d'un cylindre*) turn, revolution; (*d'un outil*) turn; *Astron* revolution; **la Terre fait un t. sur elle-même en 24 heures** the Earth completes a revolution in 24 hours *or* revolves on its axis once every 24 hours; **faire un t./trois tours sur soi-même** to spin round once/three times (on oneself); **il n'y a qu'un t. de clef** the key's only been turned once; **donner deux tours de clef** to give a key two turns, to turn a key twice; **n'oublie pas de donner un t.**

de clef (à la porte) don't forget to lock the door; **t. de manège** ride on a merry-go-round *or* Br a roundabout; **t. de vis** (turn of the) screw; **il suffit de donner un seul t. de vis** all it needs is one turn of the screw

2 *Aut* revolution, rev

3 *Méd* **attraper** *ou* **se donner un t. de reins** to put one's back out, to rick one's back

4 *Culin* folding (*UNCOUNT*); **donner trois tours à la pâte** fold the pastry over three times

5 *Tech* lathe; **t. parallèle** centre lathe; **t. de potier** potter's wheel; **t. revolver** turret lathe; **t. vertical** vertical milling machine; *Fig* **fait au t.** beautifully made

6 (*disque*) **un 33 tours** an LP; **un 45 tours** a single, a 45

❑ **à tour de bras** ADV (*frapper*) with all one's strength *or* might

❑ **à tour de rôle** ADV in turn; **ils président la réunion à t. de rôle** they chair the meeting in turn *or* turns, they take turns at chairing the meeting; **on peut le faire à t. de rôle si tu veux** we can take (it in) turns if you like

❑ **tour à tour** ADV alternately, by turns; **t. à t. charmant et odieux** alternately *or* by turns charming and obnoxious

❑ **tour de chant** NM (song) recital; **au programme de mon t. de chant ce soir** among the songs I'm going to sing tonight

❑ **tour d'échelle** NM *Jur* = the right to place ladders on a neighbour's property in order to repair a party wall

❑ **tour de force** NM tour de force, (amazing) feat; **il a réussi le t. de force de la convaincre** he achieved the impossible and managed to convince her

❑ **tour de main** NM **1** (*savoir-faire*) knack; **avoir/prendre le t. de main** to have/to pick up the knack; **c'est un t. (de main) à prendre** it's just a knack one has to pick up

2 (*locution*) **en un t. de main** in no time (at all), in the twinkling of an eye

❑ **tour de table** NM **1** *Fin* (*réunion*) = meeting of shareholders or investors to decide a course of action; (*ensemble de partenaires*) pool, backers; **deux nouveaux actionnaires sont entrés dans le t. de table du groupe** two new shareholders have joined the group's pool

2 (*débat*) **faisons un t. de table** I'd like each of you in turn to give his or her comments; **réunir un t. de table** to organize a brainstorming session

---

'Le Tour du monde en quatre-vingts jours' Verne, Anderson 'Around the World in Eighty Days'

TOUR DE FRANCE
This world-famous annual cycle race starts in a different town each year, but the home stretch is always the Champs-Élysées in Paris. The widespread excitement caused by the race, along with the heroic status of many "coureurs cyclistes", reflects the continuing fondness of the French for cycling in general.

touraillage [turajaʒ] NM kilning
touraille [turaj] NF malt kiln
touraillons [turajɔ̃] NMPL malt comes
Touraine [turɛn] NF **la T.** the Touraine (region)
tourangeau, -elle [turãʒo, -ɛl] ADJ **1** (*de la Touraine*) of/from the Touraine **2** (*de Tours*) of/from Tours
❑ **Tourangeau, -elle** NM,F **1** (*de la Touraine*) = inhabitant of or person from the Touraine **2** (*de Tours*) = inhabitant of or person from Tours
touranien, -enne [turanjɛ̃, -ɛn] ADJ Turanian
NM,F Turanian
tourbe [turb] NF (*matière*) peat, turf
tourber [3] [turbe] VI to cut peat
tourbeux, -euse [turbø, -øz] ADJ (*sol*) peat (*avant n*), peaty, boggy
tourbier, -ère [turbje, -ɛr] ADJ **1** (*gén*) peat (*avant n*) **2** (*sol*) peaty

NM,F **1** (*ouvrier*) peat worker **2** (*propriétaire*) peat-bog owner
❑ **tourbière** NF peat bog
tourbillon [turbijɔ̃] NM **1** *Météo* (*vent tournoyant*) whirlwind, vortex
2 (*masse d'air, de particules*) **t. de poussière/sable** eddy of dust/sand; **t. de fumée** twist *or* coil *or* eddy of smoke; **t. de feuilles** flutter of whirling leaves; **t. de neige** snow flurry
3 (*dans l'eau* → *important*) whirlpool; (→ *petit*) swirl; **l'eau faisait des tourbillons** the water was eddying *or* swirling
4 (*rotation rapide*) whirling, spinning; **les tourbillons de la valse** the whirling motion of a waltz
5 *Littéraire* (*vertige, griserie*) whirl; **le t. de la vie moderne** the whirl of modern life; **un t. de plaisirs** a giddy round of pleasures; **emporté par un t. de souvenirs** carried away by a rush of memories
6 *Tech & Phys* vortex
7 *Aut* (*dans un moteur*) rotary *or* barrel swirl, swirl
❑ **en tourbillons** ADV **monter/descendre en tourbillons** to swirl up/down
tourbillonnaire [turbijɔnɛr] ADJ vortical
tourbillonnant, -e [turbijɔnɑ̃, -ɑ̃t] ADJ **1** (*vent, poussière*) whirling; (*feuilles, flocons*) swirling, whirling, fluttering **2** (*existence*) whirlwind (*avant n*), hectic
tourbillonnement [turbijɔnmɑ̃] NM (*de feuilles, de flocons*) whirling, swirling
tourbillonner [3] [turbijɔne] VI **1** (*eau, rivière*) to swirl, to make eddies; **l'eau tourbillonnait autour des piles du pont** the water swirled around the bridge supports
2 (*tournoyer* → *flocons, feuilles, sable*) to whirl, to swirl, to flutter; (→ *fumée*) to whirl, to eddy; (→ *danseur, patineur*) to spin *or* to whirl *or* to twirl (round); **les tracts tombaient en tourbillonnant** the pamphlets were fluttering *or* spiralling down (to the ground); **le vent faisait t. les feuilles mortes** the dead leaves were fluttering in the wind
3 (*défiler rapidement* → *pensées*) **les idées tourbillonnaient dans sa tête** ideas were whirling *or* dancing around in his/her head
tourd [tur] NM *Ich* Mediterranean wrasse
tourde [turd] NF *Vieilli Orn* thrush
tourelle [turɛl] NF **1** *Archit* turret, tourelle; **à tourelles** turreted **2** *Mil* (*abri*) (gun) turret; (*d'un bateau*) conning tower **3** *Cin* (*lens*) turret **4** *Tech* (*d'un tour*) turret
touret [turɛ] NM **1** (*machine-outil*) lathe; **t. à polir** polishing lathe **2** (*tour de graveur*) wheel **3** *Naut* (*dévidoir*) reel
Tourgueniev [turgenjɛf] NPR Turgenev
tourie [turi] NF carboy
tourière [turjɛr] ADJ F **sœur t.** = sister responsible for a convent's external relations
NF = sister responsible for a convent's external relations
tourillon [turijɔ̃] NM **1** *Tech* (*d'une pièce*) pivot, trunnion; (*d'axe*) journal; (*axe*) (wheel) spindle **2** (*d'un canon*) trunnion **3** *Menuis* (*fixing*) dowel
tourillonner [3] [turijɔne] *Tech* VT (*pièce*) to put a pivot on
VI to swivel, to pivot
tourin [turɛ̃] NM = garlic soup thickened with egg yolks
Touring Club de France [turiŋklœbdəfrɑ̃s] NM = French motoring organization
tourismatique [turismatik] NF computerized reservation systems
tourisme [turism] NM **1** (*fait de voyager*) touring; **faire du t.** (*dans un pays*) to go touring; (*dans une ville*) to go sightseeing; **t. d'affaires** business tourism; **t. agricole** agricultural tourism, agritourism; **t. balnéaire** seaside tourism; **t. blanc** winter sports tourism; **t. écologique** ecotourism; **t. émetteur** outbound tourism; **t. à la ferme** farm tourism; **t. de loisirs** leisure *or* holiday tourism; **t. ludique** leisure tourism; **t. de masse** mass tourism; **t. morbide** dark tourism; **t. national** national *or* domestic tourism; **t. organisé** package tourism; **t. récepteur** inbound tourism; **t. sexuel** sex tourism; **t. spatial** space tourism; **t. vert** green tourism

2 *(commerce)* **le t.** tourism, the tourist industry; **notre région vit du t.** we are a tourist area

3 *Aut* **(voiture) grand t.** tourer, touring car

❑ **de tourisme** ADJ **1** *(ville)* tourist *(avant n)*; *(agence)* travel *(avant n)*

2 *(à usage personnel → avion, voiture)* private

touriste [turist] NMF **1** *(gén)* tourist; *(pour la journée)* day-tripper; **il y a trop de touristes ici** there are too many tourists around here; **t. sexuel** sex tourist

2 *Fam Péj (dilettante, amateur)* (outside) observer; **faire qch en t.** to do sth amateurishly; **suivre un cours en t.** to do a course in a half-hearted kind of way; **vous allez participer au débat? – non, je suis là en t.** are you going to take part in the discussion? – no, I'm just watching *or* just an observer *or* just sitting in

ADJ *Naut & Aviat* **classe t.** tourist class

touristique [turistik] ADJ **1** *(pour le tourisme → brochure, guide)* tourist *(avant n)*; **route t.** scenic route; **pendant la saison t.** in season, during the tourist season

2 *(qui attire les touristes)* tourist *(avant n)*; **c'est un village très t.** this village is very popular with tourists *or* is a very popular spot; **cette ville est beaucoup trop t. à mon goût** there are too many tourists in this town for my taste

tourmaline [turmalin] NF tourmaline

tourment [turmɑ̃] NM **1** *Littéraire (physique)* intense suffering, agony; **dans les tourments de la soif** suffering the pangs of thirst; **les tourments de la maladie** the torments *or* throes of illness

2 *(moral)* agony, torment; **les tourments de l'incertitude** torments of uncertainty; **en proie aux tourments de la création** in the throes of creation; **endurer mille tourments** to go through torment, to suffer agonies; **mon fils me donne bien du t.** my son's giving me a lot of worry

3 *Arch (supplice)* torture

tourmentant, -e [turmɑ̃tɑ̃, -ɑ̃t] ADJ *Littéraire* tormenting

tourmente [turmɑ̃t] NF *Littéraire* **1** *(tempête)* tempest, storm; **t. de neige** blizzard; **le vent soufflait en t.** the wind was gusting from all quarters

2 *Fig (bouleversements)* turmoil; **pris dans une t. judiciaire** caught up in a legal turmoil; **nous fûmes pris sous une t. de feu** *(à la guerre)* we were caught in a hail of gunfire

tourmenté, -e [turmɑ̃te] ADJ **1** *(angoissé → personne)* tormented, troubled, anguished; *(→ conscience)* tormented, troubled

2 *(visage)* tormented; **les traits tourmentés** tormented features; **un regard t.** a haunted *or* tormented look

3 *(agité → époque)* troubled; **la période tourmentée des guerres de Religion** the troubled period of the Wars of Religion; **une époque tourmentée de ma vie** a turbulent time in my life

4 *(accidenté → paysage, côte)* wild, rugged, craggy; *(changeant → ciel)* changing, shifting; **un paysage d'orage sous un ciel t.** a stormy landscape under a shifting sky

5 *Littérature & Beaux-Arts* tortuous; **un bâtiment aux sculptures tourmentées** a building with contorted *or* convoluted sculptures

6 *Météo & Naut* **mer tourmentée** rough *or* heavy sea

tourmenter [3] [turmɑ̃te] VT **1** *(martyriser → animal, personne)* to torment, to ill-treat; **veux-tu cesser de t. cette pauvre bête!** will you stop tormenting *or* baiting that poor animal!

2 *(harceler)* to harass; **tourmenté par ses héritiers** plagued *or* harassed by his heirs

3 *(sujet: faim, soif, douleur)* to torment, to plague, to rack; *(sujet: incertitude, remords)* to torment, to haunt, to rack; *(sujet: jalousie)* to plague, to torment; *(sujet: obsession)* to torment, to haunt; **ses rhumatismes le tourmentent** he's plagued by rheumatism; **les souvenirs le tourmentent** he's tormented by his memories; **le remords/la douleur le tourmente** he's racked with remorse/pain; **tourmenté par la douleur** racked with pain

4 *Arch (torturer)* to torture

5 *Littérature & Beaux-Arts* to overelaborate; **t. son style** to write in an unnatural *or* overelaborate style

▸**se tourmenter** VPR *(s'inquiéter)* to worry oneself, to fret, to be anxious; **elle se tourmente pour son fils** she's worried sick about her son; **ne vous tourmentez pas!** don't worry!; **ne vous tourmentez pas, nous la raccompagnerons** there's no need to be anxious, we'll take her home

tourmentin [turmɑ̃tɛ̃] NM **1** *Naut* storm jib **2** *Orn* storm petrel

tournage [turnaʒ] NM **1** *Cin* shooting, filming; **sur le t.** during filming; **sur les lieux du t.** on the set; **le t. de son nouveau film commence la semaine prochaine** shooting starts on his/her new movie next week; **t. en décor naturel** *ou* **en extérieur** location filming **2** *Banque* inter-bank loan **3** *Tech* turning **4** *Rail* turntabling **5** *Naut* belaying

tournailler [3] [turnɑje] VI *Fam* to wander round and round▪; **t. autour de** to hang *or* to prowl around; **les gamins tournaillaient devant l'entrée du bar** the kids were loitering outside the bar

tournant[1] [turnɑ̃] NM **1** *(virage)* bend, turn; **une série de tournants dangereux** a series of dangerous bends; **la voiture s'est renversée dans un t.** the car overturned on a bend

2 *Fig* turning point, watershed; **le t. du match** the turning point in *or* the decisive moment of the match; **elle est à un t. de sa carrière** she is at a turning point in her career; **la Révolution est un t. de notre histoire** the Revolution was a turning point in our history; **marquer un t.** to indicate *or* to mark a change of direction; **son discours marque un t. dans la politique du gouvernement** his/her speech marks a watershed *or* the beginning of a new direction in government policy; **cette décision constitue un t. décisif** this decision marked a turning point *or* a watershed; **prendre le** *ou* **un t.** to adapt to changing circumstances; **quand la société s'est informatisée, il a su prendre le t.** when they computerized the company, he took to it really well; *Fam* **attendre qn au t.** to be waiting for a chance to get even with sb, to have it in for sb; *Fam* **avoir** *ou* **attraper qn au t.** to get one's own back on sb, to get even with sb

tournant[2], **-e** [turnɑ̃, -ɑ̃t] ADJ **1** *(dispositif, siège)* swivel *(avant n)*, swivelling; *(pont)* swing *(avant n)*; *Tech (essieu)* live **2** *(scène)* revolving; *(escalier, route)* winding **3** *Mil (manœuvre)* outflanking

❑ **tournante** NF **1** *Belg* rotation system **2** *Fam (viol collectif)* gang rape

tourne [turn] NF **1** *(du lait)* turning, going sour; *(du vin)* souring **2** *Journ (d'un article)* continuation

tourné, -e [turne] ADJ **1** *(façonné au tour)* turned; **un pied de lampe en bois t.** a hand-turned wooden lamp base

2 *Culin (altéré → produits laitiers)* sour, curdled; *(→ vin)* sour; **ce lait est t.** this milk is *Br* off *or Am* bad *or* has gone *Br* off *or Am* bad; **ce bouillon est t.** this soup has gone bad *or Br* off

3 *(locutions)* **bien t.** *(taille)* neat; *(lettre, réponse)* well-phrased; **mal t.** *(lettre, réponse)* badly phrased; **avoir l'esprit mal t.** to have a dirty mind; *Belg* **être bien/mal t.** to be in a good/bad mood

tourne-à-gauche [turnagoʃ] NM INV **1** *(porte-outil)* wrench **2** *(pour donner de la voie aux scies)* saw set

tourneboular [3] [turnəbule] VT *Fam (troubler)* to confuse▪, to mix up; **il était tout tourneboulé** he was in a real dither

tournebroche [turnəbrɔʃ] NM **1** *(gén)* roasting jack *or* spit; *(d'un four)* rotisserie; **canard/agneau au t.** spit-roasted duck/lamb **2** *Arch (marmiton, chien)* turnspit

tourne-disque [turnədisk] *(pl* **tourne-disques***)* NM record player

tournedos [turnədo] NM tournedos

tournée [turne] ADJ F *voir* **tourné**

NF **1** *(d'un facteur, d'un commerçant)* round; **faire sa t.** *(facteur, livreur)* to do *or* to make one's round; *(représentant)* to be on the road; **faire une t. électorale** *(candidat, député)* to canvass one's constituency; *(dans une élection présidentielle)* to go on the campaign trail; **t. de conférences** lecture tour; **en t. de conférences aux États-Unis** on the American (lecture) circuit; **t. d'inspection** tour of inspection; *Com* **t. de présentation** roadshow

2 *(d'un artiste, d'une troupe)* tour; **faire une t.** to go on tour; **il achèvera sa t. à Biarritz** his tour will finish (up) in Biarritz; **faire une t. en Europe** to go on a European tour

3 *(visite)* **faire la t. des galeries** to do the rounds of *or* to go round the art galleries; **faire la t. des grands ducs** to go out on the town

4 *Fam (au bar)* round; **t. générale!** drinks all round!; **c'est ma t.** it's my round; **c'est la t. du patron** drinks are on the house

5 *Fam (volée de coups)* hiding

❑ **en tournée** ADV **être en t.** *(facteur, représentant)* to be off on one's rounds; *(chanteur)* to be on tour; **acteur qui passe la plus grande partie de l'année en t.** actor who spends most of the year touring *or* on tour

tournemain [turnəmɛ̃] **en un tournemain** ADV in no time at all

tourné-monté [turnemɔ̃te] *(pl* **tournés-montés***)* NM *TV & Cin* sequential shooting

tourne-pierre [turnəpjɛr] *(pl* **tourne-pierres***)* NM *Orn* turnstone

TOURNER [3] [turne]

> VI to turn **A1, B1, 2** ▪ to go round **A1, 2, C1** ▪ to spin (round) **A1** ▪ to rotate **A1, B3** ▪ to tour **A3** ▪ to turn out **B4** ▪ to go bad **B6**
> VT to turn **A1, 3, C1, 2** ▪ to stir **A2** ▪ to turn over **A4** ▪ to shoot **B** ▪ to phrase **C2**
> VPR to turn round **1** ▪ to turn **2**

VI **A.** *DÉCRIRE DES CERCLES* **1** *(se mouvoir autour d'un axe → girouette)* to turn, to revolve; *(→ disque)* to revolve, to spin; *(→ aiguille de montre, manège)* to turn, to go round; *(→ objet suspendu, rouet, toupie)* to spin (round); *(→ aile de moulin)* to turn *or* to spin round; *(→ clef, pédale, poignée)* to turn; *(→ hélice, roue, tour)* to spin, to rotate; **t. sur soi-même** to turn round; *(vite)* to spin (round and round); **la Terre tourne sur elle-même** the Earth spins on its axis; **tourne pour que je voie si l'ourlet est droit** turn round, so I can see whether the hem's straight; **je voyais tout t.** everything was spinning *or* swimming; **faire t.** *(pièce de monnaie, manège, roue)* to spin; *(clef)* to turn; **le croupier fit t. la roulette** the croupier spun the roulette wheel; **ça me fait t. la tête** it makes my head spin; *Fam* **t. de l'œil** to pass out▪, to keel over

2 *(se déplacer en cercle → personne)* to go round; *(→ oiseau)* to fly *or* to wheel round, to circle (round); *(→ insecte)* to fly *or* to buzz round; *(→ avion)* to fly round (in circles), to circle (round); *(→ astre, satellite)* to revolve, to go round; **les prisonniers tournaient dans la cour** the prisoners were walking round (and round) the yard; **l'avion a tourné plusieurs fois au-dessus de la piste** the plane circled the runway several times; **j'ai tourné dix minutes avant de trouver à me garer** I drove round (and round) for ten minutes before I found a parking space; **les voiliers ont tourné autour de la bouée** the yachts went round *or* rounded the buoy

3 *Fam (être en tournée → chanteur)* to (be on) tour▪; **notre représentant tourne dans votre région en ce moment** our representative is in your area at the moment▪

B. *CHANGER D'ORIENTATION, D'ÉTAT* **1** *(changer de direction → vent)* to turn, to veer, to shift; *(→ personne)* to turn (off); *(→ véhicule)* to turn (off), to make a turn; *(→ route)* to turn, to bend; **si le vent tourne, il pleuvra** if there's a change in the wind *or* if the wind turns, it'll rain; **tournez à droite** turn (off to the) right; **la rue tourne légèrement après le parc** the road turns *or* bends slightly beyond the park; **tourne dans l'allée** turn into the drive; **t. au coin de la rue** to turn the corner (of the street); **la chance** *ou* **la fortune a tourné (pour eux)** their luck has changed

2 *(faire demi-tour)* to turn (round); **tourne dans le parking** turn round in the *Br* car park *or Am* parking lot

3 *Fam (se succéder → équipes)* to rotate▪; **les médecins tournent pour assurer les urgences** the doctors operate a rota system to cover emergencies▪

4 *(évoluer)* to go, to turn out; **la course aurait tourné autrement si...** the race would've had a different outcome if...; **attends de voir comment les choses vont t.** wait and see how things turn out *or* go; **bien t.** *(situation, personne)* to turn out well *or* satisfactorily; **mal t.** *(initiative, plaisanterie)* to turn out badly, to go wrong; **la révolution est en train de mal t.** the revolution's going badly wrong; **tout ça va mal t.!** no good will come of (all) that!; **la conversation a très mal tourné** the discussion took a very nasty turn; **un jeune qui a mal tourné** a youngster who turned out badly *or* went off the rails

5 *Fam (devenir)* **t. homo** to turn gay; **t. hippie** to become *or* turn into a hippy■

6 *(s'altérer → lait)* to turn (sour), to go *Br* off *or Am* bad; *(→ viande)* to go bad *or Br* off; *(→ crème, mayonnaise)* to curdle; **faire t. du lait/une mayonnaise** to curdle milk/mayonnaise

7 *Belg* **t. fou** *ou* **sot** *(personne)* to go mad; *(machine)* to act up

C. *MARCHER, RÉUSSIR* **1** *(fonctionner → compteur)* to go round; *(→ taximètre)* to tick away; *(→ programme informatique)* to run; **le moteur tourne** the engine's running *or* going; **faire t. un moteur (à plein régime)** to run an engine (at full throttle); **l'heure** *ou* **la pendule tourne** time passes; **l'heure tourne et vous ne faites rien** time's marching on and you're not doing anything; **l'usine tourne à plein (rendement)** the factory's working at full capacity; **faire t. une entreprise** *(directeur)* to run a business; **ce sont les commandes étrangères qui font t. l'entreprise** orders from abroad keep the business going; *Ordinat* **je ne peux pas sauvegarder pendant que mon programme tourne** I can't save while my program's running

2 *(réussir → affaire, entreprise, économie)* to be running well; *Fam* **alors, les affaires, ça tourne?** so, how's business (going)?; *Fam* **ça ne tourne pas très bien entre eux** it's not going too well between them

VT A. *FAIRE CHANGER D'ORIENTATION* **1** *(faire pivoter → bouton, clé, poignée, volant)* to turn; **tourne le bouton jusqu'au 7** turn the knob to 7; **il faut t. le couvercle pour ouvrir le bocal** it's a jar with a twist-off top

2 *(mélanger → sauce, café)* to (give a) stir; *(→ salade)* to toss; **ajoutez la farine tout en tournant** add the flour while stirring

3 *(diriger → antenne, visage, yeux)* to turn; **t. qch vers la droite/gauche** to turn sth to the right/left; **tourne la télévision vers moi** turn the set towards me; **t. son regard** *ou* **les yeux vers** to turn one's eyes *or* to look towards; **t. ses pensées vers** to turn one's thoughts to *or* towards; **t. son attention vers** to focus one's attention on

4 *(retourner → carte)* to turn over *or* up; *(→ page)* to turn (over); *(→ brochette, grillade)* to give a turn, to turn (over); **tournez la page, s'il vous plaît** please turn (over) the page; **il tournait sa casquette entre ses mains** he was turning his cap round and round in his hands; **t. qch contre un mur** to turn sth to face a wall; **t. et retourner, t. dans tous les sens** *(boîte, gadget)* to turn over and over; *(problème)* to turn over and over (in one's mind), to mull over; *Sport* **t. la mêlée** to wheel the scrum (round)

5 *(contourner → cap)* to round; *(→ coin de rue)* to turn; *(→ ennemi)* to get round; **ils ont réussi à t. la cavalerie** they managed to outflank the cavalry; *Fig* **t. la difficulté/le règlement/la loi** to get round the problem/the regulations/the law

6 *(locution)* **t. le cœur à qn** to nauseate sb, to turn sb's stomach; *Fig* to break sb's heart; **ça m'a tourné le cœur quand je l'ai entendu pleurer** my heart went out to him when I heard him crying

B. *Cin & TV* **t. un film** *(cinéaste)* to shoot *or* to make a movie *or Br* film; *(acteur)* to make a movie *or Br* film; **t. une scène** *(cinéaste)* to shoot *or* to film a scene; *(acteur)* to play *or* to act a scene; **la dramatique a été tournée au Kenya/en studio/en extérieur** the TV play was shot in Kenya/in the studio/on location; **on a tourné la scène du départ plus de dix fois** the farewell scene was shot over ten times, there were over ten takes of the farewell scene

C. *METTRE EN FORME* **1** *Menuis & Métal* to turn; **t. le bois** to work wood on the lathe, to turn wood

2 *(formuler → compliment)* to turn; *(→ critique)* to phrase, to express; **je ne sais pas comment t. cela** I don't know how to put it; **il tourne bien ses phrases** he's got a neat turn of phrase; **sa demande était bien tournée** his/her request was well phrased

3 *(transformer)* **elle tourne tout au tragique** she's always making a drama out of everything; **t. qch à son avantage/désavantage** to turn sth to one's advantage/disadvantage; **t. qn/qch en ridicule** to ridicule sb/sth, to make fun of sb/sth

USAGE ABSOLU **elle a tourné plusieurs fois avec Pasolini** she's been in several of Pasolini's movies *or Br* films; **silence, on tourne!** quiet please, action!

❑ **tourner à VT IND t. au burlesque/drame** to take a ludicrous/tragic turn; **t. à la catastrophe** to take a disastrous turn; **t. au ridicule** to become ridiculous; **la retraite a vite tourné à la débâcle** the retreat rapidly turned into a rout; **ça tourne à la farce!** it's turning into a farce!; **le temps tourne à la pluie/neige** it looks like rain/snow; **le ciel commençait à t. au rouge** the sky was beginning to turn red

❑ **tourner autour de VT IND 1** *(axe)* to move *or* to turn round; **les planètes qui tournent autour du Soleil** the planets revolving round the Sun; **l'escalier tourne autour de l'ascenseur** the staircase spirals *or* winds round the lift

2 *(rôder)* **t. autour de qn** *(gén)* to hang *or* to hover round sb; *(pour le courtiser)* to hang round sb; **les enfants tournaient autour du magasin depuis un moment** *(par désœuvrement)* the children had been hanging around outside the shop for a while; *(avec de mauvaises intentions)* the children had been loitering outside the shop for a while

3 *(valoir environ)* to be around *or* about, to be in the region of; **les réparations devraient t. autour de 80 euros** the repairs should cost around *or* should cost about *or* should be in the region of 80 euros

4 *(concerner → sujet: conversation)* to revolve round, to centre on, to focus on; *(→ sujet: enquête policière)* to centre on; **tout le poème tourne autour de ce souvenir** the whole poem revolves round this memory

❑ **tourner en VT IND** to turn *or* to change into; **la neige tourne en gadoue** the snow's turning into slush

►**se tourner VPR 1** *(faire un demi-tour)* to turn round; **tourne-toi, que je voie si l'ourlet est droit** turn round, so that I can see whether the hem's straight; **tourne-toi, je me déshabille** turn round *or* turn your back, I'm getting undressed

2 *(changer de position)* to turn; **il se tournait et se retournait dans son lit** he was tossing and turning in his bed; **tourne-toi sur le ventre** turn over onto your belly; *Fig* **de quelque côté qu'on se tourne** wherever you turn; **je ne sais plus de quel côté me t.** I don't know which way to turn any more

3 *Fam* **se t. les pouces, se les t.** to twiddle one's thumbs

4 se t. contre to turn against; **le peuple ne tarda pas à se t. contre lui** the people soon turned against him

5 *Littéraire* **se t. en** to turn into; **leur amertume se tourna en sédition** their bitterness turned into sedition

6 se t. vers *(s'orienter vers)* to turn towards; **les feuilles se tournent vers la lumière** the leaves turn towards *or* follow the light; **tous les regards se tournèrent vers elle** all eyes turned to look at her

7 *Fig* **se t. vers qn/Dieu** to turn to sb/God; **se t. vers une carrière** to take up a career; **se t. vers la religion** to turn to religion

tournerie [turnəri] **NF** wood turning

tournesol [turnəsɔl] **NM 1** *Bot* sunflower; **graine de t.** sunflower seed **2** *Chim (colorant)* litmus; **(papier de) t.** litmus (paper)

'Tournesols' *Van Gogh* 'Sunflowers'

tournette [turnɛt] **NF** *(pour couper le verre)* circular glass cutter

tourneur, -euse [turnœr, -øz] **NM,F** turner; *Cér* thrower; **t. sur bois/métal** wood/metal turner; **t. de vis** screwcutter

tourne-vent [turnəvɑ̃] **NM INV** chimney cowl, chimney jack

tournevis [turnəvis] **NM** screwdriver; **t. à choc** impact screwdriver; **t. cruciforme** Phillips screwdriver®; **t. d'électricien** electrician's screwdriver; **t. à embout** bit screwdriver; **t. à lame plate** flat blade screwdriver; **t. plat** bit screwdriver

tournicoter [3] [turnikɔte] **VI** *Fam* to wander around aimlessly■; **t. autour de qn** *(courtiser quelqu'un)* to hang around sb; **une idée qui me tournicote dans la tête** an idea that keeps running through my mind

tourniole [turnjɔl] **NF** *Fam* whitlow■

tourniquer [3] [turnike] = **tournicoter**

tourniquet [turnikɛ] **NM 1** *(à l'entrée d'un établissement)* turnstile; *(porte à tambour)* revolving door **2** *(présentoir)* revolving stand, spinner **3** *(pour arroser)* rotary sprinkler **4** *Méd* tourniquet **5** *(de volet)* (shutter) fastener **6** *Naut* roller **7** *Entom* whirligig beetle **8** *très Fam Arg mil* **passer au t.** to be court-martialled■

tournis [turni] **NM 1** *Vét* gid, sturdy, *Spéc* coenuriasis **2** *(locutions)* **avoir le t.** to feel giddy *or* dizzy; **donner le t. à qn** to make sb (feel) giddy

tournisse [turnis] **NF** *Constr* stud (post)

tournoi [turnwa] **NM 1** *Sport & (jeux)* tournament; **t. de tennis de table** table tennis tournament; **t. open** open (tournament); *Anciennement* **T. des Cinq Nations** Five Nations Tournament; **T. des Six Nations** Six Nations Tournament **2** *Hist* tournament, tourney **3** *Littéraire (compétition)* challenge; **t. d'éloquence** contest of eloquence

tournoie *etc voir* **tournoyer**

tournoiement [turnwamɑ̃] **NM** *(de feuilles, de papiers)* whirling, swirling; *(de l'eau)* eddying, swirling; *(d'un danseur)* twirling, swirling, whirling

tournois [turnwa] **ADJ INV** *Hist* minted at Tours, tournois

tournoyant, -e [turnwajɑ̃, -ɑ̃t] **ADJ** *(feuilles, fumée, flocons)* whirling, swirling; *(eau)* eddying, swirling; *(oiseau)* wheeling; *(danseur)* swirling, twirling, whirling

tournoyer [13] [turnwaje] **VI** *(feuilles, fumée, flocons)* to whirl, to swirl; *(eau)* to eddy, to swirl; *(oiseau)* to wheel *or* to circle round; *(danseur)* to swirl *or* to twirl *or* to whirl (round); **le radeau tournoyait dans les rapides** the raft was tossed round (and round) in the rapids; **descendre en tournoyant** to come whirling down; **faire t. qch** to whirl *or* to swing sth

tournure [turnyr] **NF 1** *(allure, aspect)* demeanour; **elle avait une t. un peu gauche** she was of a somewhat awkward demeanour

2 *(évolution, tendance)* trend, tendency; **attendons de voir quelle t. prennent les événements** let's wait and see how the situation develops; **d'après la t. que prend la situation** from the way the situation is developing *or* going; **prendre t.** to take shape; **les choses prennent (une) meilleure/une mauvaise t.** things are taking a turn for the better/the worse; **t. d'esprit** turn *or* cast of mind

3 *Ling (expression)* turn of phrase, expression; *(en syntaxe)* form, construction; **t. de phrase** turn of phrase; **t. impersonnelle/interrogative** impersonal/interrogative form; **t. fautive** incorrect construction

4 *Métal* turning, turnings

5 *(faux-cul)* bustle

tournus [turnys] **NM** *Suisse* schedule, rota

touron [turɔn, turɔ̃] **NM** = kind of nougat of Spanish origin, containing almonds

tour-opérateur [turɔperatœr] *(pl* **tour-opérateurs)** **NM** tour operator

tourte [turt] **NF 1** *(tarte)* pie; **t. aux poires/épinards** pear/spinach pie **2** *(pain rond)* round loaf **3** *Fam Vieilli (balourd)* dumbo, *Br* thicko

tourteau, -x [turto] **NM 1** *(crabe)* edible crab **2** *Agr*

oil-cake, cattle cake **3** *Culin* **t. fromagé** ≃ baked cheesecake

tourtereau, -x [turtəro] **NM** *Orn* young turtledove ▫ **tourtereaux NMPL** *Hum* lovebirds; **où sont les tourtereaux?** *(à un mariage)* where's the happy couple?

tourterelle [turtərɛl] **NF** *Orn* turtledove; **t. triste** mourning dove; **t. turque** collared dove

tourtière [turtjɛr] **NF 1** *(plat)* piedish, pie plate **2** *Can Culin* pork pie *(traditional dish)*

tous ADJ [tu] *voir* **tout**

PRON [tus] *voir* **tout**

touselle [tuzɛl] **NF** *Bot* beardless wheat

Toussaint [tusɛ̃] **NF** *Rel* **(le jour de) la T.** All Saints' Day; **la veille de la T.** Hallowe'en; **un temps de T.** miserable weather

Culture

TOUSSAINT

All Saints' Day is a public holiday in France. It is the traditional occasion for a visit to the cemetery to lay flowers (usually chrysanthemums) on the graves of family and loved ones.

tousse [tus] **NF** *Belg* cough

tousser [3] [tuse] **VI 1** *Méd* to cough; **tu tousses?** do you have a cough?; **je tousse beaucoup/un peu** I have a bad/slight cough; **il toussa pour m'avertir** he coughed *or* gave a cough to warn me **2** *(moteur)* to splutter; **le moteur toussa plusieurs fois puis démarra** the engine spluttered several times then came to life

tousseur, -euse [tusœr, -øz] **NM,F** *Fam* cougher

toussotement [tusɔtmɑ̃] **NM** (slight) coughing *(UNCOUNT)*, (slight) cough

toussoter [3] [tusɔte] **VI 1** *Méd* to have a bit of a cough *or* a slight cough **2** *(pour prévenir)* to give a little *or* a discreet cough

TOUT, -E [tu, tut]

ADJ all (the) **1, 2** ▪ the whole (of the) **1** ▪ completely **5** ▪ only **6** ▪ everything **7**
ADJ INDÉFINI any **A** ▪ all (the) **A, B1** ▪ every **A, B4**
PRON INDÉFINI everything **A** ▪ anything **A** ▪ all **A, B1-3**
ADV very **1** ▪ completely **1** ▪ right **2**
NM whole **1**

When **tous** is a pronoun, it is pronounced [tus].

(pl **tous, toutes)** **ADJ 1** *(entier)* all (the), the whole (of the); **toute la nuit** all night; **elle a parcouru toute la distance en deux heures** she covered the full distance in two hours; **pendant t. le concert** throughout the concert, during the whole concert; **il se plaint toute la journée** he complains all the time *or* the whole day long; **t. le village a participé** the whole village took part; **t. le pays était à l'écoute** the whole country was listening; **t. l'intérêt de la pièce réside dans la mise en scène** the whole *or* the sole interest of the play is in the production; **la grève a duré t. un mois** the strike lasted a whole month; **toute une journée** a whole day; **t. ceci/cela** all (of) this/that; **toute cette histoire** this whole story; **t. ce travail pour rien!** all this work for nothing!; **j'ai t. mon temps** I've plenty of time *or* all the time in the world; **t. mon courage/enthousiasme a disparu** all my courage/enthusiasm has gone; **toute ma fortune** my whole fortune; **il doit venir avec toute sa famille** he's supposed to be coming with his whole family; **ils se sont aimés toute leur vie** they loved each other all their lives; **avec lui, c'est t. l'un ou t. l'autre** with him, it's either (all) black or (all) white

2 *(devant un nom propre)* all; **t. Vienne l'acclamait** he/she was the toast of all Vienna; **j'ai visité t. Paris en huit jours** I saw all *or* the whole of Paris in a week; **il a lu t. Racine** he's read the whole *or* the complete works of Racine; **il a lu t. 'les Misérables'/tous les 'Mémoires' de Saint-Simon** he's read the whole of 'Les Misérables'/all of Saint-Simon's 'Mémoires'

3 *(devant un nom sans article)* **on a t. intérêt à y aller** it's in our every interest to go; **c'est en toute liberté que j'ai choisi** I made the choice completely of my own free will; **rouler à toute vitesse** to drive at full *or* top speed; **en toute franchise/simplicité** in all sincerity/simplicity; **c'est de toute beauté** it's extremely beautiful; *Littéraire* **le fait est faux et de toute fausseté** the statement is a downright lie

4 *(avec une valeur emphatique)* **c'est toute une affaire!** it's quite a to-do!; **c'est toute une expédition pour y aller!** getting there involves quite a trek!; **c'est t. un travail de le nourrir!** feeding him's quite a job!

5 *(comme adv) (entièrement)* completely; **elle était toute à son travail** she was completely absorbed in her work; **elle était toute de bleu vêtue** she was dressed completely in blue

6 *(unique, seul)* only; **c'est t. l'effet que ça te fait?** is that all it means to you?; **ma fille est t. mon bonheur** my daughter is my sole *or* only source of happiness; **pour t. remerciement on m'a renvoyé** by way of thanks I got fired; **pour toute indemnité, j'ai reçu 100 euros** 100 euros was the only compensation I got; **pour toute famille il n'avait qu'une cousine éloignée** one distant cousin was all the family he had

7 *(suivi d'une relative)* **t. ce qu'on dit** everything people say; **il représente t. ce que je déteste** he embodies all the things *or* everything I hate; **t. ce qui me gêne, c'est la différence d'âge** the only thing *or* all I'm worried about is the age difference; **t. ce que l'entreprise compte de personnel qualifié** the company's entire qualified workforce; **ils s'amusaient t. ce qu'ils savaient** they were having a whale of a time; **ses enfants sont t. ce qu'il y a de bien élevés** his children are very well-behaved *or* are models of good behaviour; **t. ce qu'il y a de gens honnêtes a signé la pétition** all decent and upright people signed the petition; **ce projet est t. ce qu'il y a de plus sérieux** this project couldn't be more serious

ADJ INDÉFINI A. *AU SINGULIER (chaque, n'importe quel)* any, all, every; **t. citoyen a des droits** every citizen has rights, all citizens have rights; **toute personne ayant vu l'accident** anyone who witnessed the accident; **t. changement les inquiète** the slightest change worries them; **toute faute sera pénalisée** all mistakes will be penalized without exception; **pour t. renseignement, écrivez-nous** for further information, write to us; **pour éviter t. tracas** to avoid any worries; **à t. âge** at any age; **à toute heure** at any hour, at any time; **à toute heure du jour et de la nuit** at any hour of the day or night; **sandwiches à toute heure** sandwiches available at all times; **de t. temps** since time immemorial, from the beginning of time; **en toute occasion, il cherche à rendre service** he takes any opportunity to be of service, he is always eager to be of service; **en t. temps** throughout *or* all through history; **t. autre** anybody else; **t. autre que lui aurait refusé** anyone other than him *or* anybody else would have refused; *Prov* **toute peine mérite salaire** the labourer is worthy of his hire

B. *AU PLURIEL* **1** *(exprimant la totalité)* all; **tous les hommes** all men, the whole of mankind; **tous les gens** everybody, everyone; **pour toutes les personnes concernées** for all (the people) concerned; **je veux tous les détails** I want all the details *or* the full details; **nous avons essayé tous les traitements** we've tried all the treatments *or* every (single) treatment available; **tous vos commentaires et remarques seront publiés** all your comments and remarks will be published; **ça se vend maintenant à tous les coins de rue** it's now sold on every street corner; **tous ceux-ci/ceux-là** all (of) these/those

2 *(devant un numéral)* **ils viennent tous les deux** both of them *or* the two of them are coming; **quand nous sommes tous les deux** when we're on our own, when there's just the two of us; **ils nous ont invitées toutes les quatre** they've invited the *or* all four of us; **toutes deux iront** both of them will go; **nous avons tous deux les mêmes goûts** we both have the same tastes; **tous (les) trois** all three of them

3 *(devant un nom sans article)* **ils étaient 150 000, toutes disciplines/races confondues** there were 150,000 of them, taking all disciplines/races together; **champion toutes catégories** overall champion; **il roulait tous feux éteints** he was driving with his lights off; **je dois le rencontrer toutes affaires cessantes** I must meet him forthwith; **Munich, Mexico, Séoul, toutes villes qui ont reçu les jeux Olympiques** Munich, Mexico City, Seoul, all (of them) cities which have hosted the Olympic Games; **il est mon préféré à tous égards** I like him best in every respect

4 *(exprimant la périodicité)* every; **tous les jours** every day; **tous les lundis** every Monday; **le magazine paraît toutes les semaines/tous les mois** the magazine comes out every week/every month; **toutes les deux semaines** every other week, every second week, every two weeks; **à prendre toutes les quatre heures** *(sur médicament)* to be taken every four hours *or* at four-hourly intervals; **toutes les fois qu'on s'est rencontrés** every time we've met; **tous les 100 mètres** every 100 metres

PRON INDÉFINI A. *AU SINGULIER* everything, all; *(n'importe quoi)* anything; **j'ai t. jeté** I threw everything away; **c'est moi qui ai t. fait** I did it all; **il se plaint toujours de t.** he's always complaining about everything; **il me dit t.** he tells me everything, he has no secrets from me; **dis-moi t.** tell me all about it; *Fam* **t'as t. compris!** that's it!, that's right!; **c'est t. dire** that says it all; **elle est bonne en t.** she's good at everything, she's a good all-rounder; **il mange de t.** he eats anything; **il est prêt à t.** he's ready for anything; **capable de t.** capable of anything; **pour lui t. était prétexte à plaisanter** he would make a joke out of anything; **c'est t.** that's all; **ce sera t. pour aujourd'hui** that will be all for today; **ce sera t.?** *(dans un magasin)* will that be all?, anything else?; **ce n'est pas t.** that's not all; **il a du culot! – attendez, ce n'est pas t.!** he's got some nerve! – wait, there's more to come *or* that's not all!; **ce n'est pas t. de faire des enfants, il faut les élever ensuite** having children is one thing, but then you've got to bring them up; **être t. pour qn** to be everything for sb, to mean everything to sb; *Fam* **et t. et t.** and all that (sort of thing); **elle t'envoie ses amitiés et t. et t.** she sends her regards and all that sort of thing; **il y avait des bougies, de la musique et t. et t.** there were candles, music and all that sort of thing *or* and the whole works; **on aura t. vu!** now I've *or* we've seen everything!; **t. est là** *(objets)* that's everything; *(problème)* that's the whole point *or* the crux of the matter; **t. ou partie** all or part; **vous serez remboursé t. ou partie** you'll get all or part of your money back; **t. ou rien** all or nothing; **avec toi c'est t. ou rien** with you, it's all or nothing *or* one extreme or the other; **c'est t. sauf du foie gras** it's anything but foie gras; **il est t. sauf un génie** he's far from being a genius; **t. se passe comme si...** it's as though...; **à t. faire** *(produit)* all-purpose; **t. bien considéré, t. bien réfléchi** all things considered; **t. bien pesé** after weighing up the pros and the cons; **il a t. de l'escroc** he's your typical crook; **il a t. de son père** he's the spitting image of his father

B. *AU PLURIEL* **1** *(désignant ce dont on a parlé)* **il y a plusieurs points de vue, tous sont intéressants** there are several points of view, they are all interesting; **j'adore les prunes – prends-les toutes** I love plums – take them all *or* all of them

2 *(avec une valeur récapitulative)* all; **Jean, Pierre, Jacques, tous voulaient la voir** Jean, Pierre, Jacques, they all wanted to see her; **ce sont tous banquiers et gens de finance** they're all bankers and financiers; *Fam* **c'est tous feignants et compagnie!** they're just a bunch of idlers!

3 *(tout le monde)* **vous m'entendez tous?** can you all hear me?; **à vous tous qui m'avez aidé, merci** to all of you who helped me, thank you; **écoutez-moi tous!** listen to me, all of you!; **des émissions pour tous** programmes

suitable for all (audiences); **jeu pour tous** game suitable for all ages *or* any age group; **tous ensemble** all together; **tous tant** *ou* **autant que nous sommes** all of us, every (single) one of us

ADV

> The adverb agrees in gender and number before a feminine noun beginning with a consonant or aspirate h.

1 *(entièrement, tout à fait)* very, completely; **ils étaient t. seuls** they were quite *or* completely alone; **la ville t. entière** the whole town; **t. neuf** brand new; **t. nu** stark naked; **t. cru** (totally) raw; **un t. jeune homme** a very young man; **elle était t. émue** she was very moved; **sa chevelure était toute hérissée** his/her hair was all messy; **elle est rentrée toute contente** she came back very happy; **ses t. premiers mots** his/her very first words; **les t. premiers temps** at the very beginning; **une robe t. en dentelle** a dress made of lace; **être t. en sueur** to be running with *or* bathed in sweat, to be all sweaty; **le jardin est t. en longueur** the garden is just one long strip; **le porche est t. en marbre** the porch is all in marble *or* made entirely of marble; **un de nos t. meilleurs acteurs** one of our very best actors; **arriver parmi les t. premiers** to be among the very first to arrive; **j'étais t. gêné** I was most *or* very embarrassed; **t. mouillé** wet *or* soaked through, drenched; **être t. occupé à faire qch** to be very busy doing sth; **elles étaient toutes surprises de le voir** they were most *or* very surprised to see him; **je t'aime t. autant qu'autrefois** I love you just as much as I did before; **t. simplement/autrement** quite simply/differently; **téléphone-moi, t. simplement** just phone me, that's the easiest (way); **une toile t. coton** a 100 percent cotton cloth, an all-cotton material; **elle était t. efficacité** she was the very model of efficiency; **il est toute bonté/générosité** he is goodness/generosity itself; **ça, c'est t. lui!** that's typical of him *or* just like him!

2 *(en intensif)* **t. en haut/bas** right at the top/bottom; **t. au début** right at the beginning; **c'est t. près** it's very close; **il roulait t. doucement** he was driving very *or* extremely slowly; **t. à côté de moi** right next to me; **c'est t. près d'ici** it's very close to here, it's a stone's throw (away) from here; **t. contre le mur** right up against the wall; **c'est t. le contraire!** it's quite the opposite!

3 *(déjà)* **t. prêt** *ou* **préparé** ready-made; **t. bébé, elle dansait déjà** even as a baby, she was already dancing; **on verra – c'est t. vu!** we'll see – it's already decided!

4 *(avec un gérondif) (indiquant la simultanéité)* **on mangera t. en marchant** we'll eat while we're walking; **t. en tricotant** while knitting

5 *(avec un gérondif) (indiquant la concession)* **t. en avouant son ignorance dans ce domaine, il continuait à me contredire** although he'd confessed his ignorance in that field, he kept on contradicting me

NM 1 *(ensemble)* whole; **former un t.** to make up a whole; **je vous vends le t. pour 50 euros** you can have the whole lot for 50 euros; **versez le t. dans un bol** put the whole mixture into a bowl; **mon t. est un instrument de musique** *(dans une charade)* my whole *or* all is a musical instrument

2 le t. *(l'essentiel)* the main *or* the most important thing; **le t., c'est de ne pas bafouiller** the most important thing is not to stutter; *Fam* **ce n'est pas le t., mais je dois partir** that's all very well, but I've got to go now; **ce n'est pas le t. de critiquer, il faut pouvoir proposer autre chose** it's not enough to criticize, you've got to be able to suggest something else; **jouer** *ou* **risquer le t. pour le t.** to risk (one's) all; **tenter le t. pour le t.** to make a (final) desperate attempt *or* a last-ditch effort; **c'est un t.** it's all the same, it makes no difference; **partir ou rester, pour moi c'est un t.** go or stay, it's all the same to me; **à quand le t. informatique?** when will everything be computerized?; **s'engager dans le t. nucléaire** to go all-nuclear; **la politique du t.**

ou rien an all-or-nothing policy; **changer du t. au t.** to change completely

□ **du tout** ADV not at all; **je vous dérange? – du t., du t.!** am I disturbing you? – not at all *or* not in the least!; **elle finissait son café sans du t. se soucier de notre présence** she was finishing her coffee without paying any attention to us at all *or* whatsoever

□ **en tout** ADV **1** *(au total)* in total, in all; **cela fait 95 euros en t.** that comes to 95 euros in all *or* in total

2 *(exactement)* exactly, entirely; **la copie est conforme en t. à l'original** the copy matches the original exactly

□ **en tout et pour tout** ADV (all) in all; **en t. et pour t., nous avons dépensé 600 euros** all in all, we've spent 600 euros

□ **tout à coup** ADV all of a sudden, suddenly

□ **tout à fait** ADV **1** *(complètement)* quite, fully, absolutely; **je suis t. à fait rassuré** I'm fully *or* quite reassured; **en es-tu t. à fait conscient?** are you fully aware of it?; **je vous comprends t. à fait** I understand you perfectly well; **ce n'est pas t. à fait exact** it's not quite correct; **n'ai-je pas raison? – t. à fait!** am I right? – absolutely!

2 *(exactement)* exactly; **c'est t. à fait ce que je cherche** it's exactly what I've been looking for; **c'est t. à fait le même** it's exactly the same

3 *(oui)* certainly; **vous faites les retouches? – t. à fait** do you do alterations? – certainly (we do)

□ **tout de bon** EXCLAM *Suisse* take care!

□ **tout de même** ADV **1** *(malgré tout)* all the same, even so; **j'irai t. de même** all the same, I'll still go

2 *(en intensif)* **t. de même, tu exagères!** steady on!, that's a bit much!

□ **tout de suite** ADV **1** *(dans le temps)* straight away, right away, at once; **apporte du pain – t. de suite!** bring some bread – right away!

2 *(dans l'espace)* immediately; **tournez à gauche t. de suite après le pont** turn left immediately after the bridge

□ **tout le même** *Belg* = **tout de même**

□ **tout... que** CONJ **t. directeur qu'il est** *ou* **qu'il soit,...** although he's/I don't care if he is the boss,...; **t. policier qu'il est, je n'ai pas peur de lui** I don't care if he is a policeman, I'm still not afraid of him; **toute enthousiaste qu'elle soit, elle n'en devra pas moins attendre** however enthusiastic she is, she'll still have to wait

═══ ✿ ═══

'Tout est bien qui finit bien' *Shakespeare* 'All's Well That Ends Well'

tout-à-l'égout [tutalegu] NM INV main *or* mains drainage, main sewer; **avoir le t.** to be connected to the main sewer

Toutankhamon [tutãkamõ] NPR Tutankhamen, Tutankhamun

toute [tut] *voir* **tout**

toute-épice [tutepis] *(pl* **toutes-épices** [tutepis]*)* NF allspice

toutefois [tutfwa] ADV however, nevertheless; **t., j'ai omis** *ou* **j'ai t. omis un détail important** I have, however *or* nevertheless, omitted an important detail; **c'est un homme généreux, t. peu l'apprécient** he's a generous man, yet he's disliked by many; **je lui parlerai, si t. il veut bien me recevoir** I'll talk to him, that is, if he'll see me; **elle n'est guère patiente, sauf, t., avec ses enfants** she's not exactly patient, except, of course, with her own children

toute-puissance [tutpµisãs] NF INV omnipotence, all-powerful influence; *Fig (d'un désir)* overwhelming nature

toute-puissante [tutpµisãt] ADJ F *voir* **tout-puissant**

toutes [tut] *voir* **tout**

toutes-boîtes [tutbwat] NM INV *Belg* free paper, freesheet

tout-fou [tufu] *(pl* **tout-fous)** *Fam* ADJ M crazy NM idiot, nut

toutim, toutime [tutim] NM *Fam* **et tout le t.** the works, the whole enchilada, *Br* the full monty

tout-info [tutɛ̃fo] NM INV **le t.** round-the-clock news broadcasting

tout-ménage [tumenaʒ] *(pl* **tous-ménages)** NM *Suisse* leaflet

toutou [tutu] NM *Fam* **1** *(chien)* doggy, doggie **2** *(personne docile)* lapdog; **filer** *ou* **obéir comme un (petit) t.** to be a lapdog

Tout-Paris [tupari] NM INV **le T.** the Parisian smart set; **le T. y était** everyone who's anyone in Paris was there

tout-petit [tupəti] *(pl* **tout-petits)** NM *(qui ne marche pas)* infant; *(qui marche)* toddler; **un livre/une émission pour les tout-petits** a book/a programme for the very young

tout-puissant, toute-puissante [tupµisã, tutpµisãt] *(mpl* **tout-puissants,** *fpl* **toutes-puissantes)** ADJ **1** *(influent)* omnipotent, all-powerful; *Fig (désir)* overwhelming **2** *Rel* almighty

□ **le Tout-Puissant** NM the Almighty

tout-terrain [tutɛrɛ̃] ADJ INV cross-country *(avant n)*, off-road *(avant n)*

  NM INV off-road driving

  NM *ou* NF INV off-road vehicle, off-roader

tout-va, tout va [tuva] **à tout-va, à tout va** ADV like mad, like nobody's business; **le gouvernement privatise à t.** the government are privatizing things like nobody's business ADV galore; **pour attirer le client, le magasin proposait des réductions à t.** the shop was offering discounts galore to attract customers

tout-venant [tuvnã] NM INV **1** *(choses)* everyday things; *(personnes)* ordinary people; **des places d'opéra qui ne sont pas pour le t.** opera tickets that are beyond the means of ordinary people **2** *Minér* ungraded product; *(houille)* unsorted coal

toux [tu] NF cough; **t. grasse/nerveuse/sèche** loose/nervous/dry cough

touzepar [tuzpar] NF *Fam (verlan de* **partouze)** orgy█

township [tawnʃip] NM *ou* NF township

toxémie [tɔksemi] NF *Méd* toxaemia

toxicité [tɔksisite] NF toxicity; **coefficient de t.** toxicity rating

toxico [tɔksiko] NMF *Fam* junkie, addict█

toxicodépendance [tɔksikodepãdãs] NF drug dependence *or* dependency

toxicologie [tɔksikɔlɔʒi] NF toxicology

toxicologique [tɔksikɔlɔʒik] ADJ toxicological

toxicologue [tɔksikɔlɔg] NMF toxicologist

toxicomane [tɔksikɔman] ADJ drug-addicted

  NMF drug addict

toxicomaniaque [tɔksikɔmanjak] ADJ drug-addiction-related, *Spéc* toxicomaniac *(avant n)*

toxicomanie [tɔksikɔmani] NF drug addiction

toxicomanogène [tɔksikɔmanɔʒɛn] ADJ *Méd* addictive

toxicose [tɔksikoz] NF *Méd* toxicosis

toxidermie [tɔksidɛrmi] NF *Méd* toxicodermatitis

toxi-infectieux, -euse [tɔksiɛ̃fɛksjø, -øz] *(mpl inv, fpl* **toxi-infectieuses)** ADJ toxi-infectious

toxi-infection [tɔksiɛ̃fɛksjõ] *(pl* **toxi-infections)** NF *Méd* toxi-infection

toxine [tɔksin] NF toxin

toxique [tɔksik] ADJ toxic, poisonous

  NM poison, toxin

toxocarose [tɔksɔkaroz] NF *Méd* toxocariasis

toxoïde [tɔksɔid] NM *Méd* toxoid

toxoplasme [tɔksɔplasm] NM *Méd* toxoplasma

toxoplasmose [tɔksɔplasmoz] NF *Méd* toxoplasmosis

TP [tepe] NMPL **1** *Scol & Univ (abrév* **travaux pratiques)** **avoir un TP de chimie** to have a practical chemistry lesson *or* a chemistry lab; **être en TP** to be in the lab **2** *(abrév* **travaux publics)** civil engineering

  NM *Fin (abrév* **Trésor public)** **le TP** *Br* ≃ the Treasury, *Am* ≃ the Treasury Department

TPC [tepese] NF *Ordinat (abrév* **tierce partie de confiance)** TTP

TPE [tepeə] NF *Écon (abrév* **très petite entreprise)** very small business *(employing fewer than 20 people)*

  NM *(abrév* **terminal de paiement électronique)** pinpad

TPG [tepeʒe] NM *Fin (abrév* **trésorier-payeur général)** paymaster *(for a "département" or "région")*

TPIR [tepeiɛr] NM *Jur (abrév* **Tribunal pénal international pour le Rwanda)** ICTR

TPIY [tepeiigrɛk] **NM** *Jur (abrév* **Tribunal pénal international pour l'ex-Yougoslavie**) ICTY
tpm [tepeɛm] **NMPL** *Tech (abrév* **tours par minute**) rpm
TPS [tepeɛs] **NF** *Can Fin (abrév* **taxe sur les produits et services**) GST
tps *(abrév écrite* **temps**) time
TPV [tepeve] **NM** *Mktg (abrév* **terminal point de vente**) point-of-sale terminal, POST
tr *(abrév écrite* **tour**) rev
trabe [trab] **NF** *Hér* anchor-stock
trabée [trabe] **NF** *Antiq* trabea
trabendiste [trabɑ̃dist] **NMF** *(en Algérie → petit trafiquant)* small-time smuggler
trabendo [trabɑ̃do] **NM** *(en Algérie → marché noir, contrebande)* black market
traboule [trabul] **NF** *(à Lyon)* alleyway
trabouler [3] [trabule] **VI** *(à Lyon)* to cut through
trac[1] [trak] **NM** *Fam (devant un public)* stage fright■; *(à un examen)* exam nerves■; **avoir le t.** to have the jitters; **il a le t. avant d'entrer en scène** he gets very nervous before going on stage■; **j'avais le t. avant mon entretien** I had butterflies before the interview; **elle cherche un remède contre le t.** she's looking for a remedy to stop herself getting so nervous■
trac[2] [trak] **tout à trac ADV** *Vieilli* out of the blue, just like that; **elle a dit ça tout à t.** she just came out with it, she blurted it out all of a sudden
traçabilité [trasabilite] **NF** traceability
traçage [trasaʒ] **NM 1** *(d'un trait, d'une figure)* drawing; *(d'une inscription)* writing *or* tracing (out); *(d'une route)* laying out; *(d'un itinéraire)* plotting (out) **2** *Mines* horizontal working **3** *Tech* marking, scribing
traçant, -e [trasɑ̃, -ɑ̃t] **ADJ 1** *Mil (projectile)* tracer *(avant n)* **2** *Bot* running, creeping
tracas [traka] **NM 1** *(soucis)* worry, upset; **cette affaire lui cause un grand t.** *ou* **bien du t.** this business is causing him/her a lot of worry *or* upset
2 *(efforts)* trouble, bother; **tu t'es donné bien du t.** you've gone to a great deal of trouble *or* bother; **ne te donne pas tant de t.** don't go to such trouble *or* bother
NMPL *(soucis matériels ou financiers)* troubles; **tous les t. engendrés par le chômage** all the worries caused by being unemployed
tracasser [3] [trakase] **VT** *(sujet: situation)* to worry, to bother; *(sujet: enfant)* to worry; **son état de santé actuel me tracasse** I'm worried about the current state of his/her health
▶**se tracasser VPR** to worry (**pour qch** about sth); **ne te tracasse plus pour cela** don't give it another thought
tracasserie [trakasri] **NF** *(souvent pl)* petty annoyance; **faire face à des tracasseries administratives** to put up with a lot of frustrating red tape; **être en butte aux tracasseries de la police** to be subjected to police harassment
tracassier, -ère [trakasje, -ɛr] **ADJ** *(administration, fonctionnaire)* pettifogging; *(personne)* nitpicking
NM,F nitpicker
tracassin [trakasɛ̃] **NM** *Fam Vieilli* state of worry■
trace [tras] **NF 1** *(empreinte → d'un animal)* track, trail, spoor; *(→ d'un fugitif)* trail; **des traces de pas** footprints, footmarks; **des traces de pneus** tyre *or* wheel marks; **retrouver la t. de qn** to pick up the trail of sb; **perdre la t. de qn** to lose trace *or* track of sb; *Fig* **suivre la t.** *ou* **les traces de qn, marcher sur les traces de qn** to follow in sb's footsteps
2 *(d'un coup, d'une maladie)* mark; **une t. de brûlure/piqûre** a burn/needle mark; **il portait des traces de coups** his body showed signs of having been beaten; **elle a quelques traces de varicelle** she's got some chickenpox scars; **déceler chez qn quelques traces de fatigue** to notice sb is showing signs of tiredness
3 *(marque, indice)* trace, smear; **mon manteau a des traces d'usure** my coat is showing signs of wear; **il y a des traces de doigts sur la vitre** there are fingermarks on the windowpane; **des traces de peinture** paint marks; **des traces de sang sur le sol** traces of blood on the ground; **quelques traces de lutte** some signs of fighting; **on dirait des traces de préparatifs** it looks as if preparations are being made for something; **on ne retrouve aucune t. de cet événement dans les journaux** there is no trace *or* mention of the event in the newspapers; **toute t. de cet événement semble avoir été effacée** all traces of the event seem to have been wiped out; **ses larmes n'avaient laissé aucune t. sur son visage** his/her face bore no trace of the tears he/she had shed; **elle a laissé des traces de son passage** you can see she's been here; **sans laisser de traces** without (a) trace; **disparaître sans laisser de t.** to disappear without trace; **pas la moindre t. d'effraction** no sign *or* evidence *or* trace of a break-in; **il n'y a pas t. d'elle** *ou* **aucune t. d'elle** no sign of her (anywhere); **ne pas trouver t. de qch** to find no trace of sth; **on ne trouve pas t. de votre dossier** your file cannot be traced, there's no trace of your file
4 *(quantité infime)* trace; **on a retrouvé des traces d'arsenic dans le thé** traces of arsenic have been found in the tea; **elle parle sans la moindre t. d'accent** she speaks without the slightest trace *or* hint of an accent
5 *(vestige)* trace; **on y a retrouvé les traces d'une civilisation très ancienne** traces of a very ancient civilization have been discovered there
6 *(marque psychique)* mark; **la mort de son père a laissé en lui des traces profondes** his father's death deeply affected him; **cela a laissé en elle des traces profondes** it affected her deeply *or* made a profound impression on her; **une telle épreuve laisse forcément des traces** such an ordeal is bound to take its toll
7 *(comme adj) Chim* **élément t.** trace element
8 *Électron* **t. acoustique** soundtrack; **t. du spot** trace *(in cathode-ray tube)*
9 *Math & Psy* trace
10 *Sport* trail; **faire la t.** to break a trail; **t. directe** direct descent
▫ **à la trace ADV 1** *(d'après les empreintes)* **suivre à la t.** *(fuyard, gibier)* to track (down); **il était blessé, ils l'ont suivi à la t.** he was wounded and they followed his trail
2 *Fam Fig* **on peut le suivre à la t., il sème ses stylos partout** he's easy to track down, he leaves his pens lying around all over the place
▫ **sur la trace de PRÉP** *(à la recherche de)* on the trail of *or* track of; **ils sont sur la t. du bandit** they are on the bandit's trail; **ils sont sur la t. d'un manuscrit** they're tracking down a manuscript
tracé [trase] **NM 1** *(représentation → d'une ville, d'un réseau)* layout, plan; **faire le t. d'une route** to lay out *or* to plan a road *(on paper)* **2** *(chemin suivi → par un fleuve)* course; *(→ par une voie)* route; **suivre le t. du fleuve** to follow the river **3** *(ligne → dans un graphique)* line; *(→ dans un dessin)* stroke, line; *(contour → d'un littoral)* outline **4** *(en travaux publics)* tracing, marking out *(on site)*
tracement [trasmɑ̃] **NM 1** *(d'un trait, d'une figure)* drawing; *(d'une inscription)* writing *or* tracing (out); *(d'une route)* laying out; *(d'un itinéraire)* plotting (out) **2** *Mines* horizontal working **3** *Tech* marking, scribing
tracéologie [traseɔlɔʒi] **NF** *Archéol* traceology
tracer [16] [trase] **VT 1** *(trait, cercle, motif)* to draw; **t. une circonférence/ligne** to draw a circumference/line; *Fig* **vous nous tracez un tableau pessimiste de l'avenir** you're painting a less than rosy picture of our future
2 *(inscription, lettre, mot)* to write; **à cinq ans, ils ont encore du mal à t. les chiffres et les lettres** at five years old they still have difficulty forming numbers and letters; **au bas du tableau, il avait tracé quelques mots** he had written a few words at the bottom of the blackboard
3 *(marquer l'emplacement de → itinéraire)* to trace, to plot; *(→ chemin, terrain)* to mark *or* to stake *or* to lay out; *(→ sillon)* to mark out; *(→ chemin dans la jungle)* to open up; **t. les allées d'un parc** to lay out the paths in a park; **t. une route à travers la brousse** to plot the course of a road through the bush; **t. les lignes d'un court de tennis** to mark out a tennis court
4 *Fig (indiquer)* to map out, to plot; **t. une ligne de conduite pour qn** to plot a course of action for sb; **t. le chemin** *ou* **la route** *ou* **la voie à qn** to mark out *or* to pave the way for sb; **sa voie est toute tracée** his/her career is mapped out (for him/her); **t. les grandes lignes de qch** to outline sth, to indicate the general outlines of sth
5 *Math (courbe)* to plot; **t. le graphe d'une fonction** to plot the graph of a (mathematical) function
6 *Mines* to open up
7 *Tech* to mark, to scribe
8 *Suisse (rayer)* to delete, to cross off
VI 1 *Fam (aller très vite)* to belt along, to bomb along; *(déguerpir)* to beat it, *Br* to clear off; **elle trace, ta bagnole!** your car goes like a bomb!
2 *Suisse* **t. après qn** *(le poursuivre)* to chase sb
3 *Bot (racine)* to run out, to creep
traceret [trasrɛ] **NM** scriber, tracing awl
traceur, -euse [trasœr, -øz] **ADJ** *Phys* tracer *(avant n)*
NM,F *Tech* scriber
NM 1 *Chim, Nucl & Phys* tracer **2** *(pour dessins)* tracer; *(d'un appareil enregistreur)* pen **3** *Ordinat* **t. (de courbes)** graph plotter; **t. à plat** flatbed plotter; **t. à plumes** pen plotter; **t. à tambour** drum plotter
trachéal, -e, -aux, -ales [trakeal, -o] **ADJ** tracheal
trachée [traʃe] **NF 1** *Anat* windpipe, *Spéc* trachea **2** *Zool* trachea **3** *Bot* tracheary elements, trachea
trachée-artère [traʃeartɛr] *(pl* **trachées-artères**) **NF** *Anat* trachea
trachéen, -enne [trakeɛ̃, -ɛn] **ADJ** *Zool* tracheal
trachéide [trakeid] **NF** *Bot* tracheid
trachéite [trakeit] **NF** *Méd* tracheitis *(UNCOUNT)*
trachéo-bronchite [trakeɔbrɔ̃ʃit] *(pl* **trachéo-bronchites**) **NF** *Méd* tracheobronchitis
trachéoscopie [trakeɔskɔpi] **NF** *Méd* tracheoscopy
trachéostomie [trakeɔstɔmi] **NF** *Méd* tracheostomy
trachéotomie [trakeɔtɔmi] **NF** *Méd* tracheotomy
trachomateux, -euse [trakɔmatø, -øz] **ADJ** *Méd* trachomatous
trachome [trakom] **NM** *Méd* trachoma
trachyte [trakit] **NM** *Minér* trachyte
traçoir [traswar] **NM** scriber, tracing awl
tract [trakt] **NM** pamphlet, leaflet, tract; **distribuer des tracts (à)** to leaflet
tractable [traktabl] **ADJ** towable
tractage [traktaʒ] **NM** towing, pulling
tractations [traktasjɔ̃] **NFPL** *Péj* dealings, negotiations; **des t. eurent lieu et l'affaire fut étouffée** negotiations took place and the whole business was hushed up
tracté, -e [trakte] **ADJ** motor-drawn
tracter [3] [trakte] **VT** to tow, to pull
VI *Fam* to leaflet■
tracteur, -trice [traktœr, -tris] **ADJ 1** *Aut* towing *(avant n)* **2** *(en hydrologie)* **force** *ou* **puissance tractrice** transport capacity
NM 1 *Agr* tractor **2** *Aut* **t. routier** tractor; **t. et semi-remorque** articulated vehicle **3** *(d'imprimante)* **t. de papier** paper tractor; **t. à picots** tractor drive
tractif, -ive [traktif, -iv] **ADJ** *Tech (force)* tractive
traction [traksjɔ̃] **NF 1** *(mode de déplacement)* traction, haulage; **t. animale/mécanique** animal/mechanical traction, animal/mechanical haulage
2 *Aut* **une t.** a vintage Citroën, an old front-wheel drive Citroën; **t. avant/arrière** *(système)* front-wheel/rear-wheel drive
3 *Méd* traction
4 *Phys* traction; **force de t.** tractive force; **résistance à la t.** tensile strength; **t. magnétique** magnetic pull; *Aut* **exercer une t. sur qch** to exercise traction on sth
5 *Rail (force)* traction; **la t.** = department dealing with the maintenance and driving of engines; **t. électrique/à vapeur** electric/steam traction; **t. en unité multiple** multiple-unit traction
6 *Sport (sur une barre, aux anneaux)* pull-up; *(au sol)* push-up, *Br* press-up; **faire des tractions** *(en tirant)* to do pull-ups; *(en poussant)* to do push-ups *or Br* press-ups
tractive [traktiv] *voir* **tractif**
tractopelle [traktɔpɛl] **NF** backhoe loader
tractoriste [traktɔrist] **NMF** tractor driver
tractrice [traktris] *voir* **tracteur**
tractus [traktys] **NM** *Anat* tract, tractus; **t. digestif** digestive tract

trad. **1** (*abrév écrite* **traduction**) trans. **2** (*abrév écrite* **traducteur**) translator **3** (*abrév écrite* **traduit par**) translated by

trade marketing [trɛdmarketiŋ] **NM** trade marketing

trader [trɛdœr] **NM** *Bourse* trader

tradescantia [tradɛskɑ̃sja] **NM** *Bot* tradescantia

trade-union [trɛdjunjɔn] (*pl* **trade-unions**) **NF** (*Br* trade *or Am* labor) union

traditeur [traditœr] **NM** *Hist* traditor

tradition [tradisjɔ̃] **NF 1** (*ensemble des coutumes*) tradition; **la t. veut que l'on attende minuit** tradition dictates that we wait till midnight; **la t. veut qu'elle soit née ici** tradition has it that she was born here; **faire qch selon la t.** to do sth in the traditional way; **selon la t. bretonne** according to Breton tradition; **dans la plus pure t. française** in true French tradition; **c'est dans la plus pure t. écossaise** it's in the best Scottish tradition; **il est bien dans la t. musulmane/juive/***etc* **de faire ceci** it is very much in the Muslim/Jewish/*etc* tradition to do this; **t. populaire** folk tradition

2 (*usage*) tradition, custom; **dans notre famille, c'est une t.** it's a family tradition; **il existe une longue t. de liens culturels entre ces pays** there is a long history of cultural links between the countries

3 *Jur* tradition, transfer

4 *Rel* **la T.** Tradition

❑ **de tradition ADJ** traditional; **un peuple de t. orthodoxe** a traditional orthodox people; **c'est de t.** it's traditional *or* a tradition; **il est de t. de/que...** it's a tradition to/that...

traditionalisme [tradisjɔnalism] **NM 1** (*gén*) traditionalism **2** *Rel* Traditionalism

traditionaliste [tradisjɔnalist] **ADJ** traditionalist

NMF traditionalist

traditionnel, -elle [tradisjɔnɛl] **ADJ 1** (*fondé sur la tradition*) traditional; **une interprétation traditionnelle d'un texte** a conventional interpretation of a text **2** (*passé dans les habitudes*) usual, traditional; **la date traditionnelle de la remise des prix** the traditional *or* usual date for the prize-giving; **le t. baiser de la mariée** the time-honoured tradition of kissing the bride

traditionnellement [tradisjɔnɛlmɑ̃] **ADV 1** (*selon la tradition*) traditionally; **se marier t.** to have a traditional wedding **2** (*comme d'habitude*) as usual, as always; **un secteur industriel t. déficitaire** an industrial sector which usually *or* traditionally runs at a loss

traduc [tradyk] **NF** *Fam* translation■

traducteur, -trice [tradyktœr, -tris] **NM,F** translator

NM 1 *Tech* transducer **2** *Ordinat* translator

❑ **traductrice NF** translating *or* translation machine

traduction [tradyksjɔ̃] **NF 1** (*processus*) translating, translation; **la t. n'est pas une discipline facile** translating is not easy; **son roman perd beaucoup à la t.** his/her novel loses a lot in translation; **c'est un mot qui a plusieurs traductions** it's a word which can be translated in several different ways; **t. de l'espagnol en allemand** translation from Spanish into German; **t. assistée par ordinateur** computer *or* machine (assisted) translation; **t. automatique** automatic translation; **t. littérale** literal *or* word-for-word translation; **t. simultanée** simultaneous translation

2 (*texte*) translation; **acheter une t. de 'Guerre et Paix'** to buy a translation of 'War and Peace'; **elle ne lit que des traductions** she only ever reads translations *or* in translation

3 (*transposition*) expression; **la t. musicale de sa passion** the expression of his/her passion in music, the musical expression of his/her passion

4 *Ordinat* **t. des informations** data reduction

traductrice [tradyktris] *voir* **traducteur**

traduire [98] [tradɥir] **VT 1** (*écrivain, roman, terme*) to translate (**de/en** from/into); **livre traduit de l'anglais** book translated from (the) English; **t. qch du russe en chinois** to translate sth from Russian *or* out of Russian into Chinese; **la première phrase est mal traduite** the first sentence is mistranslated *or* badly translated; **elle est peu traduite en Europe** very few of her works are translated in Europe

2 (*exprimer* → *pensée, sentiment*) to express, to reflect, to convey; (→ *colère, peur*) to reveal, to indicate; **vous traduisez mal ma pensée** you're misinterpreting me *or* my thoughts; **cette réaction traduit une grande sensibilité** this reaction is indicative of *or* points to great sensitivity; **ce genre de comportement traduit un manque d'affection** this kind of behaviour is symptomatic of *or* a sign of a lack of affection

3 *Jur* **t. qn en justice** to bring sb before the courts, to prosecute sb

4 *Ordinat (carte)* to interpret

VI *Ling* to translate (**de/vers** from/into); **t. mot à mot** to translate word for word

▸**se traduire VPR 1** (*emploi passif*) to be translated; **la phrase peut se t. de différentes façons** the sentence can be translated *or* rendered in different ways

2 se t. par (*avoir pour résultat*) to result in; **cela se traduit par des changements climatiques profonds** it results in *or* entails radical changes in the climate; **le ralentissement de l'activité économique s'est traduit par de nombreux licenciements** the slowdown in economic activity resulted in numerous redundancies; **la sécheresse s'est traduite par une baisse de la production agricole** agricultural production fell as a result of the drought

3 se t. par (*être exprimé par*) to be expressed in; **son émotion se traduisit par des larmes** his/her emotion was expressed in tears

traduisible [tradɥizibl] **ADJ 1** (*mot, expression, texte*) translatable; **difficilement t.** difficult to translate; **ce proverbe n'est pas t.** this proverb cannot be translated *or* is untranslatable **2** *Jur* **t. en justice** liable to prosecution

traduisons *etc voir* **traduire**

traduit, -e [tradɥi, -it] **PP** *voir* **traduire**

Trafalgar [trafalgar] **NM** *Fig* **coup de T.** underhand trick

trafic [trafik] **NM 1** (*commerce illicite*) traffic, trafficking; **t. d'armes** arms dealing, gunrunning; **le t. de drogue** *ou* **de stupéfiants** drug trafficking; **faire du t. de drogue** (*gén*) to be involved in drug trafficking; (*organisateur*) to traffic in drugs; (*revendeur*) to deal in *or* to push *or* to peddle drugs; *Fig* **faire t. de son corps** *ou* **de ses charmes** to sell one's body

2 *Fam* (*manigance*) fishy business; **il y a tout un t. dans le recrutement des cadres** executive recruitment is a real racket; **il y a un drôle de t. dans cette boutique** there's something very odd *or* funny going on in that shop

3 *Jur* **t. d'influence** influence peddling; **il a obtenu ce marché grâce à un véritable t. d'influence** he landed the deal thanks to a fair amount of string-pulling

4 *Transp (circulation)* traffic; **t. aérien/ferroviaire/maritime/portuaire/routier** air/rail/sea/port/road traffic; **t. de voyageurs** passenger traffic; **le t. est dense/fluide sur l'autoroute** traffic is heavy/light on the motorway; **le t. est ralenti sur la nationale 7** traffic is moving slowly on route 7; **t. interrompu sur les lignes 2, 3 et 9** (*du métro*) there are delays on lines 2, 3 and 9

5 *Électron* traffic; *Ordinat* **t. de réseau** network traffic

6 *Vieilli (commerce)* trading, trade

traficoter [3] [trafikɔte] *Fam Péj* **VI** to be on the fiddle; **il traficote** he's a small-time crook, he's into petty dealing

VT (*manigancer*) to be up to; **qu'est-ce que tu traficotes dans ma chambre?** what do you think you're up to in my room?

trafiquant, -e [trafikɑ̃, -ɑ̃t] **NM,F** dealer, trafficker; **t. de drogue** drug dealer *or* trafficker; **t. d'armes** gunrunner, arms dealer

trafiquer [3] [trafike] **VI** (*faire du commerce illicite*) to traffic, to racketeer; **il a fait fortune en trafiquant pendant la guerre** he made a fortune on the black market during the war; *Littéraire* **t. de sa fonction/de ses relations** to make corrupt use of one's position/of one's relationships

VT *Fam* **1** (*falsifier, altérer* → *comptabilité, résultats électoraux*) to fiddle, to doctor■; (→ *vin*) to adulterate■; (→ *compteur électrique, freins*) to tamper with■; (→ *compteur kilométrique*) to rig■; (*moteur de voiture, Mobylette®*) to tinker with

2 *Fam* (*manigancer*) to be up to; **qu'est-ce que tu trafiques là-dedans?** what are you doing *or* what are you up to in there?; **je me demande ce qu'ils trafiquent** I wonder what they're up to

tragédie [traʒedi] **NF 1** *Littérature* tragedy; **les tragédies d'Euripide** the tragedies of Euripides

2 *Théât* tragedy; **c'est dans la t. qu'elle a atteint au sublime** she gave her finest performances in tragic roles; **c'est dans la t. qu'elle a créé ses plus beaux rôles** her greatest roles were tragic ones

3 *Fig (événement funeste)* tragedy, disaster, calamity; **l'émeute a tourné à la t.** the riot had a tragic outcome; **c'est une véritable t.** it's a real tragedy, it's really tragic; **ce n'est pas une t.!** it's not the end of the world!

tragédien, -enne [traʒedjɛ̃, -ɛn] **NM,F** tragedian, *f* tragedienne, tragic actor, *f* actress

tragi-comédie [traʒikɔmedi] (*pl* **tragi-comédies**) **NF 1** *Littérature* tragicomedy **2** *Fig* tragicomic saga; **leur liaison est une perpétuelle t.** their love affair is one long series of ups and downs

tragi-comique [traʒikɔmik] (*pl* **tragi-comiques**) **ADJ** *Littérature & Fig* tragicomic; **un incident t.** an incident that inspires both laughter and tears *or* that makes you laugh and cry

NM *Littérature* **le t.** the tragicomic

tragique [traʒik] **ADJ 1** *Littérature* tragic; **un auteur t.** a tragic author, an author of tragedies, a tragedian

2 *Fig (dramatique)* tragic; **un sort t.** a tragic destiny; **elle a eu une fin t.** she came to a sad *or* tragic end; **ce n'est pas t.** it's not the end of the world; **ce n'est qu'une chute de vélo, ce n'est pas t.!** it's only a fall from a bicycle, nothing to worry about!; **ce qu'il y avait de vraiment t., c'est que...** what was really tragic *or* the real tragedy was that...

3 *Fig (angoissé* → *regard)* anguished; **d'une voix t., elle commença son récit** she began her story in a doom-laden voice

NM 1 *Littérature* **le t.** tragedy, tragic art

2 (*auteur de tragédies*) tragic author, tragedian; **les tragiques grecs** the Greek tragedians

3 *Fig* tragedy; **le t. de sa situation** the tragic side *or* the tragedy of his/her situation; **prendre qch au t.** to make a tragedy out of sth; **elle ne prend jamais rien au t.** she never looks on the dark side of things, she never makes a drama out of things; **tourner au t.** to take a tragic turn, to go tragically wrong

tragiquement [traʒikmɑ̃] **ADV** tragically; **finir t.** to end tragically *or* in tragedy

tragus [tragys] **NM** *Anat* tragus

trahir [32] [trair] **VT 1** (*son camp*) to betray; **il a trahi son pays** he was a traitor to *or* he betrayed his country

2 (*renier* → *idéal, foi*) to betray; **elle a trahi la cause de notre jeunesse/la cause de notre parti** she has betrayed the ideals of our youth/the cause of our party

3 *Littéraire (tromper* → *ami, amant)* **t. qn** to deceive sb, to be unfaithful to sb

4 (*manquer à*) to break, to go against; **t. sa promesse/ses engagements** to break one's promise/one's commitments; **t. sa foi** to go against *or* to betray one's faith; **t. la vérité** to distort *or* to twist the truth

5 (*décevoir*) to betray; **t. l'attente de qn** to fail to live up to sb's expectations; **t. les intérêts de qn** to betray sb's interests; **les résultats ont trahi nos espoirs** the results failed to live up to our hopes *or* betrayed our hopes

6 (*dénaturer* → *pensée*) to misinterpret, to distort, to do an injustice to; (→ *en traduisant*) to give a false rendering of; **je ne crois pas t. votre pensée en disant cela** I don't think I'm misinterpreting your ideas by saying that

7 (*ne pas correspondre à*) **mes paroles ont trahi ma pensée** my words failed to express my true thoughts

8 (*faire défaut à* → *sujet: forces, mémoire*) to fail; **si ma mémoire ne me trahit pas** if my memory serves me right; **mes yeux m'auraient-ils trahi?** could my eyes have deceived me?

9 (*révéler*) to betray, to give away; **je faillis t. mes sentiments** I almost revealed my feelings; **t. un secret** to give away a secret

10 (*démasquer*) to give away; **les empreintes qu'ils ont laissées les ont trahis** the fingerprints they left gave them away; **son silence l'a trahie** her silence gave her away

11 *(exprimer)* to betray; **son visage ne trahit aucun émoi** he/she remained stony-faced; **elle s'efforçait de sourire pour ne pas t. son inquiétude** she did her best to smile so as not to betray her anxiety; **un léger tremblement trahissait sa nervosité** a slight tremble betrayed his/her nervousness

USAGE ABSOLU **ceux qui trahissent** *(patrie)* traitors, those who betray their country

▶**se trahir** VPR **1** *(se révéler)* **l'angoisse se trahissait dans sa voix** his/her voice betrayed his/her anxiety

2 *(laisser voir une émotion)* to betray oneself, to give oneself away; **en apprenant la nouvelle elle s'est trahie** when she heard the news she gave herself away

3 *(se faire découvrir)* to give oneself away; **il s'est trahi en faisant du bruit** he gave himself away by making a noise

trahison [traizɔ̃] NF **1** *Jur* treason; *Mil & Pol* **haute t.** high treason; **c'est lui, mesdames et messieurs les jurés, que j'accuse de cette t.** he's the one *or* it's him I accuse of this treachery, ladies and gentlemen of the jury

2 *(infidélité)* infidelity, unfaithfulness; **elle me soupçonne des pires trahisons** she thinks I'm always being unfaithful to her

3 *(déloyauté)* betrayal, disloyalty; **acte de t.** betrayal; **c'est (une) pure t. de ta part de ne pas l'avoir soutenu** you have totally betrayed him by not supporting him; **je l'ai vécu comme une t.** I took it as a betrayal

'La Trahison des clercs' *Benda* 'The Betrayal of the Clerks'

trail [trɛjl] NM trail bike

traille [trɑj] NF **1** *(câble)* ferry cable **2** *(bac)* ferry

TRAIN [trɛ̃]

> train **A1-3, 8, 10, 13, 15** ▪ rail **A2** ▪ line **A4** ▪ set **A5, 12** ▪ stream **A11** ▪ pace **B1** ▪ pacemaker **B4** ▪ din **B5** ▪ quarters **C1** ▪ backside **C2**

NM **A. 1** *(convoi)* train; **j'irai t'attendre au t.** I'll wait for you at the station; **le t. de 9h 40** the 09:40 train; **il y a beaucoup de trains pour Lyon** there's a very good train service to Lyons; **je prends le t. à Arpajon** I catch the train at Arpajon; **être dans le t.** to be on the train; **attention, un t. peut en cacher un autre** *(sur panneau)* beware of oncoming trains; **t. autos accompagnées** *Br* Motorail train, *Am* Auto Train; **t. autocouchette** car-sleeper train; **t. automoteur** motorcoach train; **t. de banlieue** suburban *or* commuter train; **t. direct** non-stop *or* through train; **t. électrique** *(jeu)* train set; **t. express** express train; **t. de grande ligne** long-distance train, *Br* intercity train; **t. à grande vitesse** high-speed train; **t. de marchandises** freight *or Br* goods train; **t. mixte** freight *or Br* goods and passenger train; **les trains de neige** = trains taking holidaymakers to ski resorts; **t. omnibus** slow *or* local train; **ce t. est omnibus entre Paris et Vierzon** this train stops *or* calls at all stations between Paris and Vierzon; **t. postal** mail train; **t. rapide** fast train; **t. supplémentaire** relief train; **t. de voyageurs** passenger train; *Fig* **prendre le t. en marche** to climb onto *or* to jump on the bandwagon; *Can Fam* **manquer le t.** *(rester célibataire)* to be left on the shelf; *(rater une occasion)* to miss the boat

2 *(moyen de transport)* **le t.** rail (transport), train; **j'irai par le** *ou* **en t.** I'll go (there) by train; **elle voyage beaucoup en t.** she travels by train a great deal; **j'aime (prendre) le t.** I like rail travel *or* travelling by train

3 *(voyageurs)* train; **tout le t. s'est mis à chanter** the whole train started to sing

4 *(file de véhicules)* line (of cars); **t. de camions** convoy *or* line of *Br* lorries *or Am* trucks; **t. de flottage** timber raft; **t. de péniches** train *or* string of barges; **t. routier** convoy (of *Br* articulated lorries *or Am* semi-trailers)

5 *(ensemble, série)* set, batch; **t. de réformes** set of reforms; **t. de mesures économiques/fiscales** set of economic/tax measures

6 *Aviat* **t. d'atterrissage** landing gear *(UNCOUNT)*, undercarriage

7 *Agr* **t. de bois** logging raft

8 *Astron* **t. spatial** space train

9 *Aut* **t. avant/arrière** front/rear wheel-axle unit; **t. de pneus** set of tyres

10 *Mil* **t. des équipages** ≃ the Army Service Corps; **t. de combat** (combat *or* unit) train; **t. régimentaire** supply train; **t. sanitaire** hospital train

11 *Ordinat (de travaux)* stream

12 *Tech* **t. baladeur** sliding gear; **t. d'engrenages** gear train *or* set; **t. de roulement** set of bearings

13 *Métal* **t. de laminoirs** (mill) train

14 *Pétr* **t. de forage** *ou* **de sonde** (set of) drilling pipes

15 *Phys* **t. d'ondes** wave train

16 *Suisse* **t. (de campagne)** farm

17 *Can Vieilli* **faire le t.** *(s'occuper du bétail)* to look after the animals; *(traire les vaches)* to milk the cows; *(nettoyer l'étable)* to clean out the cowshed

B. 1 *(allure)* pace; **accélérer le t.** *(marcheur, animal)* to quicken the pace; *(véhicule)* to speed up; **aller à un t. soutenu** to go at a brisk pace; **au** *ou* **du t. où vont les choses** the way things are going, at this rate; **aller à fond de t.** *ou* **à un t. d'enfer** to speed *or* to race along; **nous sommes rentrés à un t. d'enfer** we sped *or* raced home; **aller à un t. de sénateur** to have a stately gait; **aller bon t.** *(en marchant)* to walk at a brisk pace; **les négociations ont été menées bon t.** the negotiations made good progress; **aller son petit t.** *(marcher)* to jog along; *(agir posément)* to do things at one's own pace; **aller son t.** to carry on (as normal)

2 *(manière de vivre)* **t. de vie** lifestyle, standard of living; **t. de maison** (retinue of) servants; **mener grand t.** to live in grand style; **on menait grand t. chez les Duparc** the Duparcs had a lavish lifestyle *or* lived like kings

3 *Littéraire (enchaînement de faits)* **le t. de la vie quotidienne** the daily grind *or Br* round

4 *Sport (dans une course → de personnes, de chevaux)* pacemaker; **gagner au t.** to win after setting the pace throughout the race; **mener le t.** to set the pace

5 *Can Fam (vacarme)* din, racket; **ne faites pas tant de t.!** stop making such a racket!

C. 1 *Zool* quarters; **t. avant** *ou* **de devant** forequarters; **t. arrière** *ou* **de derrière** hindquarters

2 *Fam (fesses)* backside; **il nous faisait avancer à coups de pied dans le t.** he pushed us on with the occasional kick up the backside; **courir** *ou* **filer au t. de qn** *(suivre partout)* to stick to sb like glue; *(prendre en filature)* to tail *or* to shadow sb

▫ **en train** ADJ **1** *(en cours)* **être en t.** *(ouvrage, travaux)* to be under way; **j'ai un tricot en t.** I'm knitting something **2** *(personne)* **être en t.** *(plein d'allant)* to be full of energy; *(de bonne humeur)* to be in good spirits *or* in a good mood; **je ne me sens pas vraiment en t. en ce moment** I don't feel my usual perky self, I'm not feeling especially perky at the moment ADV **1** *(en route)* **mettre un projet en t.** to get a project started *or* under way; **mettre un roman en t.** to start a novel; **se mettre en t.** to warm up **2** *(en forme)* **le repas m'avait mis en t.** the meal had put me in good spirits

▫ **en train de** PRÉP **être en t. de faire qch** to be (busy) doing sth; **il est toujours en t. de taquiner sa sœur** he's always teasing his sister; **l'opinion publique est en t. d'évoluer** public opinion is changing

'Le train sifflera trois fois' *Zinnemann* 'High Noon'

traînage [trɛnaʒ] NM **1** *(transport par traîneaux)* transport by *Br* sledge *or Am* sled, *Br* sledging *(UNCOUNT)*, *Am* sledding *(UNCOUNT)* **2** *(action de traîner)* dragging; *Rail (de trains)* haulage; **câble de t.** haulage rope

traînailler [3] [trɛnɑje] VI *Fam* **1** *(être lent)* to dawdle **2** *(perdre son temps)* to hang about, *Br* to faff about

traînant, -e [trɛnɑ̃, -ɑ̃t] ADJ **1** *(lent → élocution, voix)* drawling, lazy; *(→ démarche, pas)* shuffling, dragging; **"je m'en moque", dit-elle d'une voix traînante** "I don't care," she drawled **2** *(qui traîne à terre)* trailing; **une robe traînante** a dress that drags along the floor

traînard, -e [trɛnar, -ard] NM,F *Fam* **1** *(lambin) Br* slowcoach, *Am* slowpoke **2** *(dans une marche)* straggler

NM *Tech* saddle

traînasser [3] [trɛnase] VI *Fam* **1** *(errer paresseusement)* to loaf *or* to hang about; **elle est toujours à t. dans les rues** she's always hanging around the streets **2** *(être lent)* to dawdle, to drag one's feet; *(n'avoir aucune énergie)* to drag oneself around **3** *(lambiner dans son travail)* to fall behind **4** *(élocution)* to drawl; **sa voix traînassait** his/her voice drawled on

train-auto [trɛ̃oto] *(pl* **trains-autos)** NM car-sleeper train

train-couchettes [trɛ̃kuʃɛt] NM INV *Rail* sleeper

traîne [trɛn] NF **1** *(bas d'un vêtement)* train **2** *Météo* **ciel de t.** cloudy sky *(after a storm)* **3** *Naut* tow; **à la t.** in tow **4** *Pêche* dragnet; **pêche à la t.** trolling **5** *Can (traîneau)* sleigh; **t. sauvage** toboggan

▫ **à la traîne** ADJ **être** *ou* **rester à la t.** *(coureur, pays, élève)* to lag *or* to drag behind; **j'ai beaucoup de travail à la t.** I've got a big backlog of work

traîneau, -x [trɛno] NM **1** *(tiré par des chevaux)* sleigh; *(tiré par des chiens) Br* sledge, *Am* sled **2** *Pêche* dragnet

traîne-bûches [trɛnbyʃ] NM INV *Fam Pêche* bait▪

traîne-buisson [trɛnbɥisɔ̃] *(pl* **inv** *ou* **traîne-buissons)** NM *Orn* dunnock, hedge sparrow

traînée [trɛne] NF **1** *(trace → au sol, sur un mur)* trail, streak; *(→ dans le ciel)* trail; **une t. de sable** a trail of sand; **une t. de sang/peinture** a streak of blood/paint; **une t. de fumée** a trail of smoke; **l'escargot a laissé une t. visqueuse derrière lui** the snail has left a slimy trail behind it; **se propager** *ou* **se répandre comme une t. de poudre** to spread like wildfire

2 *très Fam Péj (femme)* tart, *Br* slapper, scrubber

3 *Aviat* **t. de condensation** (vapour) trail

4 *Phys (force)* drag

traînement [trɛnmɑ̃] NM *(des pieds)* dragging

traîne-misère [trɛnmizɛr] NMF INV *Fam* down-and-out

TRAÎNER [4] [trene]

> VT to pull **1** ▪ to drag (along/about/around) **1-3**
> VI to drag (on) **1, 6** ▪ to lie around **2** ▪ to dawdle **3** ▪ to hang around **4** ▪ to drawl **7**
> VPR to crawl (along) **1, 4** ▪ to drag on **3**

VT **1** *(tirer → gén)* to pull; *(→ avec effort)* to drag, to haul; *(→ wagon)* to pull, to haul; **elle descendait les escaliers en traînant le sac derrière elle** she was dragging the sack down the stairs (behind her); **elle traînait cinq enfants après elle** she was trailing *or* dragging five children after her; **t. qn par les pieds** to drag sb (along) by the feet; **t. les pieds** to shuffle along, to drag one's feet; *Fig* to drag one's feet; *Fam* **t. la jambe** *ou* **patte** to hobble *or* to limp along; *Fig* **t. qn dans la boue** *ou* **la fange** to drag sb's name through the mud; *Fig* **t. un boulet** to have a millstone round one's neck; *Fam* **t. ses guêtres** *ou* **ses bottes** to loaf *or* to hang about

2 *(emmener → personne réticente)* to drag along; *(→ personne non désirée)* to trail, to drag about; **t. qn en prison** to drag sb off to prison; **t. qn chez le dentiste** to drag sb along to the dentist's; **j'ai dû le t. au concert** I had to drag him with me to the concert

3 *(garder avec soi → fétiche, jouet)* to drag around; **elle traîne son nounours partout** she never goes anywhere without her teddy bear

4 *(avoir)* **t. son ennui** to be constantly bored; **t. un rhume** to have a nagging cold; **ça fait des semaines que je traîne cette angine** this sore throat has been with *or* plaguing me for weeks; **toute ma jeunesse, j'ai traîné ce sentiment**

de culpabilité throughout my youth I carried around this sense of guilt; *Fam* **je traîne ce prof depuis trois ans!** I've had to put up with this teacher for three years!

VI **1** *(pendre)* **t. (par terre)** to drag on the floor *or* ground; **la perdrix traînait de l'aile** the partridge was dragging a wing

2 *Fam (ne pas être rangé → documents, vêtements)* to lie around, to be scattered around; **tes vêtements traînent partout dans la maison** your clothes are scattered all over the house; **laisser t. qch** to leave sth lying around

3 *(s'attarder, flâner)* to dawdle; *(rester en arrière)* to lag *or* to drag behind; **ne traîne pas, Mamie nous attend** stop dawdling *or* do hurry up, Grandma's expecting us; **t. en chemin** *ou* **en route** to dawdle on the way; *Fam* **j'aime bien t. sur les quais** I like strolling along the banks of the river; *Fam* **on a traîné dans les musées toute la journée** we've been wandering around the museums all day long

4 *Péj (errer)* to hang about *or* around; **t. dans la rue** *ou* **par les rues** to hang *or* to knock around the streets; **il traîne dans tous les bistrots** he hangs around in all the bars; **des chiens traînent dans le village** dogs roam around the village; *Fam* **fais attention, il y a toujours des flics qui traînent par ici** be careful, there are always cops hanging around here; **qu'est-ce que tu fais? – je traîne** what are you doing? – I'm just hanging about

5 *Fig Péj (maladie, idée)* **elle attrape toutes les maladies qui traînent** she catches every bug that's going around; **des statistiques périmées qui traînent dans tous les livres** outdated statistics still found in every book

6 *Fam Péj (s'éterniser → affaire, conversation, procédure)* to drag on; *(→ superstition, maladie)* to linger *or* to drag on; **t. en longueur** *(discours, négociations)* to drag on; **les choses commencent à t. en longueur!** things are beginning to drag on!; **ça n'a pas traîné!** it didn't take long!, it wasn't long coming!; **...et que ça ne traîne pas!** ...and don't take forever about it!, ...and be quick about it!; **déjà mariés? vous n'avez pas traîné!** married already? you didn't hang around, did you?; **faire t. des pourparlers/un procès** to drag out negotiations/a trial

7 *(ralentir → voix)* to drawl (out); **elle a la voix qui traîne** she drawls

►**se traîner** VPR **1** *(blessé)* to crawl; **se t. par terre** to crawl on the floor *or* ground; **il se traîna jusqu'au fossé** he dragged himself *or* crawled to the ditch; *Fig* **je me suis traînée jusque chez le docteur** I dragged myself to the doctor's

2 *(manquer d'énergie)* **depuis sa mort, elle se traîne** she's been moping around the place since he/she died

3 *(aller lentement → conversation, soirée)* to drag on; **les journées se traînent** the days are dragging (by), the days are passing slowly; **les heures se traînent lourdement** time drags, time hangs heavy

4 *Fam (conducteur, véhicule)* to crawl along, to go at a crawl; **on se traîne!** we're just crawling along!

5 *Fam (subir)* **je me suis traîné cette sale grippe tout l'hiver** I've had this rotten cold hanging around all winter; **je me suis traîné ces vieilles chaussures tout l'hiver** I've had to wear *or* put up with these old shoes all winter

traînerie [trɛnri] NF *Can Fam* **1 ramasse les traîneries dans ta chambre!** *(objets en désordre)* clear away all the junk that's lying around your bedroom! **2 pas de t.!** *(dépêche-toi)* look sharp!, be quick about it!

traîne-savates [trɛnsavat] NMF INV *Fam Br* dosser, *Am* bum

traîneur, -euse [trɛnœr, -øz], **traîneux, -euse** [trɛnø, -øz] *Can Fam* ADJ slovenly■

NM,F slob

train-ferry [trɛ̃feri] *(pl* **trains-ferries**) NM train ferry

trainglot [trɛ̃glo] NM *Fam Arg mil* = soldier in the French Army Service Corps

training [trɛniŋ] NM **1** *(chaussure)* sports shoe, trainer; *(survêtement)* tracksuit **2** *Sport (entraînement)* training **3** *Psy* **t. autogène** self-induced relaxation

train-parc [trɛ̃park] *(pl* **trains-parcs**) NM = train providing accommodation for men working on a railway track

train-poste [trɛ̃pɔst] *(pl* **trains-poste**) NM mail train

train-train, traintrain [trɛ̃trɛ̃] NM INV *Fam* routine■; **il est venu interrompre mon t.** he came and disrupted my (daily) routine; **le t. quotidien** the daily grind

traire [112] [trɛr] VT *(vache)* to milk; *(lait)* to draw; **machine à t.** milking machine

TRAIT [trɛ]

NM	line **1** ■ feature **2** ■ act **3** ■ shaft **4-6**
NMPL	features

NM **1** *(ligne)* line; *(en Morse)* dash; *Typ* **t. de coupe** crop mark; **t. discontinu** broken line; *Typ* **t. double** double line; **t. ondulé** wavy line; **t. plein** continuous line; *Typ* **t. en pointillé** dotted underline; *Typ* **t. simple** single line; *Typ* **t. de soulignement** underscore; **d'un t. de plume** with a stroke of the pen; **signer d'un t. de plume** to sign with a flourish; **tout l'esprit de l'affiche est dans le t.** the whole effect of the poster lies in the use of line; **tirer** *ou* **tracer un t. (à la règle)** to draw a line (with a ruler); *Fig* **tirer un t. sur ses vacances** to say goodbye to one's holidays, to kiss one's holidays goodbye; *Fig* **cela fait longtemps que j'ai tiré un t. sur notre relation** I gave up all hope for our relationship long ago; *Fig* **tirer un t. sur le passé** to turn over a new leaf, to make a complete break with the past; *Fig* **tirons un t. sur cette dispute** let's forget this argument, let's put this argument behind us; **allez, on tire un t. là-dessus** come on, let's forgive and forget

2 *(marque distinctive → d'un système, d'une œuvre, d'un style)* (characteristic) feature; **t. de caractère** (character) trait; *Biol* **t. génétique** genetic trait; *Ling* **t. pertinent** significant feature; **c'est l'un de ses traits distinctifs** it's one of his/her peculiarities *or* distinctive traits; **les grands traits de qch** the main features of sth

3 *(acte)* **t. de bravoure** act of bravery, brave deed; **t. d'esprit** witticism, flash of wit; **t. de générosité** act of generosity; **t. de génie** stroke of genius

4 *(de lumière)* beam, shaft

5 *Littéraire (projectile)* shaft, spear; **partir** *ou* **filer comme un t.** to set off like a shot

6 *Fig (repartie)* shaft; **un t. mordant** a sarcastic remark; **t. satirique** shaft of satire; **t. railleur** taunt, gibe; **envoyer** *ou* **lancer un t. à qn** to get a dig in at sb

7 *Mus (psaume)* tract; *(passage)* virtuosic passage

8 *Échecs* **avoir le t.** to have first move

9 *(locution)* **avoir t. à** *(avoir un rapport avec)* to have to do *or* to be connected with; **tout ce qui a t. à la psychanalyse** everything connected *or* to do with psychoanalysis; **ayant t. à** regarding, concerning

❑ **traits** NMPL *(du visage)* features; **il a des traits fins/grossiers** he has delicate/coarse features; **avoir des** *ou* **les traits réguliers** to be (classically) good-looking, to have classical good looks; **avoir les traits tirés** to look drawn; *Fig* **on l'a présenté sous les traits d'un maniaque** he was portrayed as a maniac

❑ **à grands traits** ADV *(dessiner, esquisser)* roughly, in broad outline; **voici l'intrigue, résumée à grands traits** here's a broad *or* rough outline of the plot

❑ **à longs traits** ADV *(boire)* in long draughts

❑ **de trait** ADJ *(bête, cheval)* draught *(avant n)*

❑ **d'un (seul) trait** ADV *(avaler)* in one gulp, in one go; *(réciter)* (all) in one breath; *(lire)* without stopping, at a single sitting; *(dormir)* uninterruptedly

❑ **trait pour trait** ADV *(exactement)* exactly; **c'est sa mère t. pour t.** she's the spitting image of her mother

❑ **trait d'union** NM hyphen; *Fig* link; **ce mot prend un t. d'union** this word is hyphenated, this is a hyphenated word; **mettre un t. d'union à un mot** to hyphenate a word; *Fig* **servir de t. d'union entre** to bridge the gap between, to link; *Ordinat* **t. d'union conditionnel** soft hyphen; *Ordinat* **t. d'union insécable** hard hyphen

traitable [trɛtabl] ADJ **1** *(sujet, question)* treatable; *(problème)* manageable; **la question n'est pas t. en une demi-heure** the question cannot be dealt with in half an hour **2** *Littéraire (accommodant)* amenable, helpful

traitant, -e [trɛtɑ̃, -ɑ̃t] ADJ *(shampooing)* medicated

traite [trɛt] NF **1** *Com, Fin & Jur* draft, bill; *(lettre de change)* bill of exchange; **tirer une t. sur** to draw a bill *or* draft on; **escompter une t.** to discount a bill *or* draft; **présenter une t. à l'acceptation** to present a bill for acceptance; **t. du Trésor** bill issued by public bodies; **t. bancaire** bank draft, banker's draft; **t. de complaisance** accommodation bill; **t. contre acceptation** acceptance bill; **t. à courte échéance** short-dated bill; **t. à date fixe** time bill; **t. documentaire** documentary bill; **t. libre** clean bill; **t. à longue échéance** long-dated bill; **t. pro forma** pro forma bill; **t. "sans frais"** bill "without protest"; **t. à terme** term draft; **t. à vue** sight draft

2 *(versement)* instalment, payment; **on n'arrive plus à payer les traites de la maison** we can't pay the mortgage (on the house) any longer

3 *(commerce, trafic)* **t. d'êtres humains** people smuggling; **la t. des Noirs** the slave trade; **la t. des Blanches** the white slave trade

4 *Agr (action)* milking *(UNCOUNT)*; *(lait)* milk (yield); **t. manuelle** hand milking; **t. mécanique** machine milking

5 *(chemin)* stretch; **j'ai fait une longue t.** I've come a long way

6 *Can* **payer la t.** *(gén)* to pay for everybody, to treat everybody; *(dans un bar)* to buy a round

❑ **de traite** ADJ *(poste, salle)* milking *(avant n)*

❑ **d'une (seule) traite, tout d'une traite** ADV *(voyager)* in one go, without stopping; *(avaler)* at one go, in one gulp; *(lire, réciter)* in one stretch *or* breath; *(dormir)* uninterruptedly; *(travailler)* without interruption, at a stretch; **faire le chemin d'une t.** to do the journey nonstop *or* without stopping

traité [trete] NM **1** *(accord)* treaty; **t. d'adhésion** membership treaty; **t. d'alliance** treaty of alliance; **t. de commerce** commercial treaty; *Assur* **t. facultatif obligatoire** open cover; **t. de Maastricht** Maastricht Treaty; **t. de non-prolifération nucléaire** Nuclear Non-Proliferation Treaty; **t. de paix** peace treaty; **le t. de Rome** the Treaty of Rome; **t. sur l'Union européenne** Treaty on European Union

2 *(ouvrage)* treatise; **t. de philosophie sur** philosophical treatise on *or* upon

traitement [trɛtmɑ̃] NM **1** *Méd & Pharm* treatment; **un bon t. contre les poux** a cure for lice; **prescrire un t.** to prescribe treatment; **donner un t. à qn** to prescribe (a treatment) for sb; **suivre le t. d'un médecin** to follow the treatment prescribed by a doctor; **t. par la chaleur** heat treatment; **t. chirurgical** surgery; **t. par électrochocs** electroconvulsive therapy; **un t. homéopathique** a course of homeopathic treatment; **t. hormonal substitutif** hormone replacement therapy

2 *(d'un fonctionnaire)* salary, wage, wages; **t. de base** basic pay *or* salary; **t. fixe** fixed salary; **t. initial** starting salary; **sans t.** *(secrétaire)* honorary; *(magistrat)* unsalaried

3 *(façon d'agir envers quelqu'un)* treatment *(UNCOUNT)*; **mauvais traitements** ill-treatment *(UNCOUNT)*; **faire subir de mauvais traitements à qn** to ill-treat sb; **t. de choc** shock treatment; **t. dégradant** degrading treatment; **t. de faveur** special *or* preferential treatment; **avoir un** *ou* **bénéficier d'un t. de faveur** to enjoy preferential treatment; **t. inhumain** inhumane treatment

4 *Ordinat* processing; **t. différé** off-line processing; **t. différé par lots** batch processing; **t. à distance** teleprocessing; **t. de données** data processing, DP; **t. d'images** image processing;

t. de l'information *ou* **des informations** data processing, DP, information processing; **t. automatique de l'information** *ou* **des informations** automatic data processing; **t. électronique de l'information** electronic data processing, EDP; **t. en temps réel** real-time processing; **t. de texte** word processing; *(logiciel)* word-processing package; *(machine)* word processor; **réaliser qch par t. de texte** to word-process sth; **t. de texte à balises** word processing with embedded tags; **t. vectoriel** vector processing; **capacité** *ou* **débit de t., données en t.** throughput; **unité de t.** task, job

5 *Ind* treatment, processing; **le t. des matières premières/des aliments** the processing of raw materials/of foodstuffs; **le t. des récoltes** the treating of crops; *(par avion)* the spraying of crops; *Com* **t. des commandes** order processing; **le t. d'une lentille/surface** the coating of a lens/surface; **t. superficiel** *(en travaux publics)* surfacing; **capacité de t.** processing *or* handling capacity

6 *(d'un problème, d'une question)* treatment, presentation; **le t. de l'information dans la presse** the way the news is presented in the press

▫ **en traitement, sous traitement** ADJ under treatment; **être en** *ou* **sous t.** to be being treated *or* having treatment *or* under treatment

traiter [4] [trete] VT **1** *(se comporter avec)* to treat; **t. qn avec égard** to treat sb with consideration, to show consideration to sb; **t. qn avec douceur** to treat *or* to handle sb gently; **t. qn avec condescendance** to be condescending towards sb, to patronize sb; **t. qn durement/complaisamment** to be harsh/accommodating towards sb; **t. qn en ami/enfant** to treat sb like *or* as a friend/a child; *Fam* **il me traite comme un ami/gamin** he treats me like a friend/kid; **tout dépend de la façon dont tu traites les élèves** it all depends on how you treat the pupils; **bien t. qn** to treat sb well; **mal t. qn** to treat sb badly, to ill-treat sb; **t. qn d'égal à égal** to treat sb as an equal; **tous les actionnaires sont traités de la même façon** all shareholders are treated equally *or* get the same treatment; **nous avons été très bien traités** we were very well looked after, we had very good service; **ils l'ont plutôt mal traitée dans son nouveau service!** she got a rather raw deal in her new department!; **je ne supporterai pas de me faire t. comme cela!** I won't take being treated like this!, I won't take this treatment!

2 *Fam (insulter)* to bad-mouth, *Br* to slag off; **t. qn d'imbécile** to call sb an idiot; **se faire t. de menteur** to be called a liar; **t. qn de tous les noms** to call sb all the names under the sun

3 *(soigner → patient, maladie)* to treat; **se faire t. pour** to undergo treatment *or* to be treated for; **on me traite à l'homéopathie** I'm having homeopathy; **je le traite à l'aspirine** *(patient)* I prescribe him aspirin; *(mal)* I treat it with aspirin, I use aspirin for it

4 *Ind* to treat, to process; *(aliments, minerai, matière première)* to process; *(bois)* to treat; *(lentille)* to coat

5 *Agr (récoltes → gén)* to treat; *(→ par avion)* to spray; **oranges non traitées** unsprayed oranges

6 *Com (affaire, demande, dossier)* to deal with, to handle; *(marché)* to negotiate

7 *(étudier → thème)* to treat, to deal with; **vous ne traitez pas le sujet** you're not addressing the question

8 *Ordinat (données, texte, images)* to process; **t. qch par lots** to batch-process sth; **données non traitées** raw data

9 *Littéraire Vieilli (régaler)* to entertain

▫ **traiter avec** VT IND to negotiate *or* to deal with; **nous ne traiterons pas avec des terroristes** we won't bargain *or* negotiate with terrorists

▫ **traiter de** VT IND *(sujet: roman, film, thèse)* to deal with, to be about; *(sujet: auteur)* to deal with

▸**se traiter** VPR **1** *(maladie)* **ça se traite aux antibiotiques** it can be treated with antibiotics; **cela se traite très bien, maintenant** it can be treated now, there's treatment for it now

2 *(sujet, écrivain)* to be dealt with; **c'est un sujet qui se traite facilement** it's a subject that can be easily dealt with

3 *(affaire)* to be dealt with; **l'affaire s'est traitée assez rapidement** the matter was dealt with quite quickly

4 *(emploi réciproque) (personne)* **ils se traitaient de menteurs** they were calling each other liars

traiteur [trɛtœr] NM **1** *(qui livre)* caterer; **chez le t.** *(magasin)* at the delicatessen **2** *Arch (restaurateur)* restaurateur

traître, -esse [trɛtr, -ɛs] ADJ **1** *(déloyal → personne)* traitorous, treacherous; **être t. à sa patrie** to be a traitor to *or* to betray one's country; *Littéraire* **t. à l'honneur** false to honour

2 *(trompeur → visage, sourire)* deceptive; *(→ paroles)* treacherous

3 *(dangereux → escalier, crevasse, virage)* dangerous, treacherous; *(→ soleil)* treacherous, strong; *(→ vin)* deceptively strong; **il est t., ce petit vin de pays!** this local wine is stronger than you'd think!

4 *(locution)* **pas un t. mot** not a single word; **elle n'a pas dit un t. mot** she didn't breathe *or* say a (single) word; **je n'ai pas compris un t. mot de ce qu'il a dit** I didn't understand a single word of what he said

NM,F **1** *(gén) & Pol* traitor, *f* traitress; *Hum* **ah, le t., il ne nous disait rien!** the sly devil, he didn't tell us!

2 *Théât* villain

▫ **en traître** ADV **prendre qn en t.** to play an underhand trick on sb; **agir en t.** to act treacherously

traîtreusement [trɛtrøzmɑ̃] ADV treacherously, traitorously, *Sout* perfidiously

traîtrise [trɛtriz] NF **1** *(caractère)* treacherousness, treachery **2** *(acte → perfide)* (piece of) treachery; *(→ déloyal)* betrayal

Trajan [traʒɑ̃] NPR Trajan

Trajane [traʒan] ADJ F **la colonne T.** Trajan's column

trajectographie [traʒɛktɔgrafi] NF trajectory calculation

trajectoire [traʒɛktwar] NF **1** *(d'une balle, d'un missile)* trajectory, path; *(d'une planète, d'un avion)* path; **t. de vol** flight path **2** *(carrière professionnelle)* career path

trajet [traʒɛ] NM **1** *(chemin parcouru)* distance; *(voyage)* journey; *(d'un car, d'un autobus)* route; **j'ai beaucoup de t. de chez moi au bureau** I have a long journey from home to the office; **je fais tous les jours le t. Paris–Egly** I commute every day between Paris and Egly; **il y a bien deux heures de t.** it takes a good two hours; **elle a deux heures de t. pour aller au bureau** she has a two-hour journey to the office; **il a fait le t. en huit heures** he covered the distance in eight hours; **j'ai fait une partie du t. en avion** I flew part of the way; **j'ai dû faire le t. à pied** I had to walk all the way; **faire le t. en voiture** to do the journey by car; **un t. en voiture/autobus** a car/bus journey *or* ride; **t. par mer** crossing

2 *Anat* course

3 *(d'un projectile)* path

4 *Élec (d'un courant)* path

5 *Ordinat* **t. de papier** *(d'une imprimante)* paper path

tralala [tralala] *Fam* NM fuss■, frills; **pas besoin de tant de t.** no need to make so much fuss; **se marier en grand t.** to get married with all the works *or* trimmings; **(et) tout le t.** the (full) works, *Br* the full monty; **il y avait des petits-fours, du champagne, tout le t.!** there were petits fours, champagne, the (whole) works!

EXCLAM **c'est moi qui l'ai eu, t.!** ha-ha, I got it!

trâlée [trɑle] NF *Can Fam (d'enfants)* flock, brood; **elle était accompagnée de sa t. d'enfants** she had her entire brood of children with her

traluire [97] [tralɥir] VI *Suisse (raisin)* to change skin colour *(when ripening)*

tram [tram] NM **1** *(moyen de transport) Br* tram, *Am* streetcar **2** *(véhicule) Br* tram, tramcar, *Am* streetcar

tramage [tramaʒ] NM weaving

tramail [tramaj] NM *Pêche* trammel (net)

trame [tram] NF **1** *Tex (base)* weft, woof; *(fil)* weft, weft thread **2** *Fig (d'un livre, d'un film)* thread, basic outline *or* framework; **la t. du récit** the storyline; *Littéraire* **la t. de la vie** the web *or* thread of life **3** *Archit & Typ* screen; **t. de maquette** layout sheet; **t. optique** half-tone screen **4** *TV (lignes)* raster; *(ensemble)* field; *(pour lignes paires et impaires)* frame; **t. double** frame **5** *Arch (complot)* plot, conspiracy

tramelot [tramlo] NM *Suisse Br* tram *or Am* streetcar worker

tramer [3] [trame] VT **1** *(conspiration)* to hatch; *(soulèvement)* to plot; *Fig* **elle trame quelque chose!** she's plotting something!

2 *Tex* to weave

3 *Typ & Phot* to screen; **t. un cliché** to take a negative through a screen; **phototype tramé** screened phototype

▸**se tramer** VPR to be afoot; **un complot se tramait contre l'empereur** a plot was being hatched against the emperor; **qu'est-ce qui se trame?** what's going on?; **il se trame quelque chose** something's afoot

traminot [tramino] NM *Br* tram *or Am* streetcar worker

tramontane [tramɔ̃tan] NF **1** *(vent)* **la t.** the tramontana **2** *Arch (étoile)* north star; *Fig* **perdre la t.** to lose one's bearings; *(devenir fou)* to go off one's head

tramp [trɑ̃p] NM tramp (steamer)

tramping [trɑ̃piŋ] NM *Naut* tramping

trampoline [trɑ̃pɔlin] NM **1** *(appareil)* trampoline **2** *(sport)* trampolining; **faire du t.** to do trampolining

tram-train [tramtrɛ̃] *(pl* **trams-trains***)* NM *Transp* tram-train *(tram which can run on railways as well as traditional tramways)*

tramway [tramwɛ] NM **1** *(moyen de transport)* tramway (system) **2** *(véhicule) Br* tram, tramcar, *Am* streetcar

'Un Tramway nommé Désir' *Williams, Kazan*
'A Streetcar Named Desire'

tranchage [trɑ̃ʃaʒ] NM *(gén) & Menuis* slicing, cutting

tranchant, -e [trɑ̃ʃɑ̃, -ɑ̃t] ADJ **1** *(lame)* sharp, keen, cutting; *(outil)* cutting; *(bord)* sharp, cutting **2** *Fig (personne, réponse, ton)* curt, sharp

NM **1** *(d'une lame)* sharp *or* cutting edge; *(d'une cale)* thin end; **le t. de la main** the edge of the hand **2** *(d'apiculteur)* hive tool **3** *(de tanneur)* fleshing knife, flesher

tranche [trɑ̃ʃ] NF **1** *(de pain, de viande, de pastèque)* slice; **t. de bacon** *(à frire)* rasher (of bacon); **t. de saumon** *(darne)* salmon steak; *(fumée)* slice *or* leaf of (smoked) salmon; **une t. fine** a sliver, a thin slice; **une t. de rôti** a slice cut off the joint; **coupez-moi une t. près de l'entame, s'il vous plaît** slice off a piece near the end for me, please; *Culin* **t. napolitaine** Neapolitan ice cream; *Fig* **une t. de vie** a slice of life; *Fam* **s'en payer une t.** to have a ball *or Am* a blast

2 *(en boucherie)* **la t. (grasse)** top rump; **t. au petit os** *Br* middle of silverside; **morceau coupé dans la t.** = piece of topside

3 *(subdivision → d'un programme de construction)* stage, phase; *Admin* **t. horaire** period of time; **t. d'âge** age bracket; *(dans une étude de marché)* age group; **t. de salaires/de revenus** salary/income bracket; **elle est dans la t. des 50 000 euros par an** she's in the 50,000 (euros a year) bracket; **t. d'imposition** tax bracket; *Fam* **j'ai sauté de t. (d'impôts)** I've moved up into the next tax bracket■

4 *Bourse & Fin (d'actions)* block, tranche; *(d'emprunt)* instalment; *(d'assistance financière internationale)* tranche; **t. d'émission** *(de loterie)* issue

5 *Élec (unité de production)* tranche

6 *Rail* portion

7 *Rad & TV* slot; **t. horaire** (time) slot

8 *(outil)* chisel

9 *(de marbre)* slab

10 *(bord → d'un livre)* edge; *(→ d'une médaille, d'une pièce)* edge, rim; **doré sur t.** gilt-edged

11 *Tech (coupe)* section; **t. verticale** vertical section

12 *Ordinat* wafer; **microprocesseur en tranches** bit-slice microprocessor

▫ **en tranches** ADJ *(pain, saucisson)* sliced ADV **débiter** *ou* **couper qch en tranches** to slice sth

(up), to cut sth into slices; **je vous le coupe en tranches?** would you like it sliced?

tranché, -e [trɑ̃ʃe] ADJ **1** *(sans nuances → couleurs)* distinct, clear, sharply contrasted

2 *(distinct → catégories)* distinct; *(→ caractères)* distinct, well-defined, clear-cut

3 *(péremptoire → position)* clear-cut, uncompromising, unequivocal

4 *Hér* tranché, party per bend

NM *Hér* tranché, party per bend

❑ **tranchée** NF **1** *Mil & (en travaux publics)* trench; *Agr* drain; **creuser une tranchée** to (dig a) trench; **il était dans les tranchées pendant la guerre** he fought in the trenches

2 *(en forêt)* cutting *(UNCOUNT)*; *(pare-feu)* firebreak

❑ **tranchées** NFPL *Méd* colic *(UNCOUNT)*, gripe *(UNCOUNT)*, gripes; **tranchées utérines** afterpains

tranchée-abri [trɑ̃ʃeabri] *(pl* **tranchées-abris)** NF *Mil* dugout

tranchefile [trɑ̃ʃfil] NF *(en reliure)* headband

trancher [3] [trɑ̃ʃe] VT **1** *(couper → pain, jambon)* to slice, to cut; **t. la gorge à qn** to cut *or* to slit sb's throat; **t. la tête à qn** to cut off *or* chop off sb's head; **qu'on lui tranche la tête!** off with his head!; **la hache lui a tranché le doigt** the axe sliced *or* chopped his/her finger off, the axe severed his/her finger; *Littéraire* **la Parque a tranché ses jours** fate cut the thread of his/her life

2 *(différend)* to settle; *(difficulté)* to solve; *(question)* to decide; **je ne peux pas t. ce problème** I can't be the judge in this matter

3 *(discussion)* to bring to a sudden end, to cut short

VI *(décider)* to make *or* to take a decision, to decide; **qui va t.?** who's going to decide?; **t. dans le vif** to take drastic action

❑ **trancher avec, trancher sur** VT IND *(sujet: couleur)* to stand out against, to contrast sharply with; *(sujet: attitude)* to be in sharp contrast *or* to contrast strongly with; **sa déclaration tranche avec les propos apaisants du gouvernement** his/her remarks are in sharp contrast to the pacifying words of the government

▶ **se trancher** VPR **se t. le doigt/la main** to chop one's finger/hand off

tranchet [trɑ̃ʃɛ] NM **1** *(de cordonnier)* leather *or* skiving knife; **t. à parer** paring knife **2** *(de forgeron)* hardy; *(de serrurier)* anvil cutter

trancheur [trɑ̃ʃœr] NM *Tech & Mines* cutter; *Pêche* cod gutter

trancheuse [trɑ̃ʃøz] NF **1** *(à jambon, à pain)* slicer **2** *Menuis* veneer saw **3** *(en travaux publics)* trench excavator, trencher, ditcher

tranchoir [trɑ̃ʃwar] NM *(planche)* chopping board

tranquille [trɑ̃kil] ADJ **1** *(sans agitation → quartier, rue)* quiet; *(→ campagne)* quiet, peaceful, tranquil; *(→ soirée)* calm, quiet, peaceful; *(→ sommeil, vie)* peaceful, tranquil; *(→ air, eau, mer)* still, quiet, tranquil; **je cherche un endroit t. où je pourrai travailler** I'm looking for a quiet place where I'll be able to work; **aller** *ou* **marcher d'un pas t.** to stroll unhurriedly; **dormir d'un sommeil t.** to sleep peacefully; *Fig* **vous pouvez dormir t.** you can sleep in peace, you can rest easy; *Fig* **alors, on ne peut pas dormir t. ici!** (come on now,) people are trying to sleep here!

2 *(en paix)* **on ne peut même plus être t. chez soi!** you can't even get peace and quiet at home any more!; **allons dans mon bureau, nous y serons plus tranquilles pour discuter** let's go into my office, we can talk there without being disturbed; **laisser qn t.** to leave sb alone *or* in peace; **elle veut qu'on la laisse t. quand elle travaille** she wants to be left in peace *or* she doesn't want to be disturbed when she's working; **le bébé ne la laisse jamais t.** the baby gives her no peace; **laisse-le t. avec tes problèmes!** stop bothering him with your problems!; **laisse-moi t., je suis assez grand pour ouvrir la boîte tout seul!** leave me alone, I'm old enough to open the box on my own!; *Fam* **laisser qch t.** *(ne pas y toucher)* to leave sth alone■; **laisse ma maquette t.!** hands off my model!, leave my model alone!; **laisse ma vie de famille t.!** leave my family life out of it!

3 *(calme, sage)* quiet; **se tenir** *ou* **rester t.** to keep quiet *or* still; *(ne pas se faire remarquer)* to keep a low profile; **il n'y a que la télé pour les faire tenir tranquilles** TV's the only thing that keeps them quiet; **il a été un enfant t. jusqu'à l'âge de onze ans** he was a very placid child until the age of eleven

4 *(serein → personne, foi)* calm, serene; **t. comme Baptiste** perfectly calm; **il affirma avec une conviction t. que...** he said with quiet conviction that...

5 *(rassuré)* **je suis parti t.** I left with my mind at rest *or* at ease; **être t.** to feel *or* to be easy in one's mind; **soyez t.** don't worry, set your mind at rest *or* at ease; **sois t., elle va bien** don't worry *or* set your mind at rest, she's all right; **fais-le maintenant, comme ça tu seras t.** do it now, that way you won't have to worry about it; **avec ce plan d'épargne, je suis t.** with this savings scheme I don't need to worry; **je serais plus t. s'il n'était pas seul** I'd feel easier in my mind knowing that he wasn't on his own; **je ne suis pas** *ou* **ne me sens pas t. quand il est sur les routes** I worry when he's on the road; **elle ne m'a pas rappelé, je ne suis pas t.** she hasn't phoned me back, I'm anxious *or* worried *or* not easy in my mind; **je ne suis pas t. dans cette grande maison** I get nervous in this big house

6 *(sûr)* **tu peux être t. (que)...** you can rest assured (that)...; **ils n'auront pas mon argent, sois t.!** they won't get my money, that's for sure!

tranquillement [trɑ̃kilmɑ̃] ADV **1** *(calmement → dormir, jouer)* quietly, peacefully; *(→ répondre, regarder)* calmly, quietly **2** *(sans se presser → marcher, travailler)* unhurriedly; **on est allés t. jusqu'à l'église avec grand-mère** we walked slowly to the church with grandma

tranquillisant, -e [trɑ̃kilizɑ̃, -ɑ̃t] ADJ *(paroles, voix, présence)* soothing, reassuring; *Pharm* **avoir un effet t.** to act as a sedative

NM *Pharm* tranquillizer; *Fam* **bourré de tranquillisants** doped up to the eyeballs (with tranquillizers)

tranquilliser [3] [trɑ̃kilize] VT **t. qn** to set sb's mind at rest, to reassure sb

▶ **se tranquilliser** VPR to stop worrying, to be reassured; **tranquillise-toi, je ne rentrerai pas en auto-stop** don't worry, I won't hitch-hike home

tranquillité [trɑ̃kilite] NF **1** *(calme → d'un lieu)* quietness, peacefulness, *Sout* tranquillity; *(→ d'une personne)* peace, *Sout* tranquillity; *(→ de sommeil)* peacefulness; **les enfants ne me laissent pas un seul moment de t.** the children don't give me a single moment's peace; **elle a besoin d'une parfaite t. pour écrire** she needs (complete) peace and quiet to write; **troubler la t. publique** *Br* to cause a breach of the peace, *Am* to disturb the peace

2 *(sérénité)* **t. d'esprit** peace of mind

❑ **en toute tranquillité** ADV *(sereinement)* with complete peace of mind

tranquillos [trɑ̃kilos] ADV *Fam (tranquillement)* **vas-y t., inutile de faire des excès de vitesse** take your time, there's no need to break the speed limit; **ils étaient dans le canapé en train de siroter mon whisky, t.** they were on the sofa sipping away at my whisky, without a care in the world

transaction [trɑ̃zaksjɔ̃] NF **1** *Bourse, Com & Écon* transaction, deal; **transactions** transactions, dealings; **transactions bancaires** bank transactions; **transactions boursières** Stock Exchange transactions; *Banque* **t. par carte** card transaction; *Bourse* **t. de clôture** closing trade; **transactions commerciales** business transactions; *Bourse* **t. au comptant** cash *or* spot transaction; **t. à crédit** credit transaction; **transactions hors Bourse** after-hours dealing, street dealing; **transactions invisibles** invisible trade; *Bourse* **transactions à terme** futures; *Banque* **t. valeur jour** value today trade

2 *Jur* (formal) settlement, compromise

3 *Ordinat* transaction

transactionnel, -elle [trɑ̃zaksjɔnɛl] ADJ **1** *Jur (formule, règlement)* compromise *(avant n)*; **solution transactionnelle** compromise **2** *Psy* transactional

transafricain, -e [trɑ̃zafrikɛ̃, -ɛn] ADJ transafrican, cross-Africa

transalpin, -e [trɑ̃zalpɛ̃, -in] ADJ transalpine; *(italien)* Italian

transaméricain, -e [trɑ̃zamerikɛ̃, -ɛn] ADJ transamerican

transaminase [trɑ̃zaminɑz] NF *Biol* transaminase

transandin, -e [trɑ̃sɑ̃dɛ̃, -in] ADJ trans-Andean

transantarctique [trɑ̃zɑ̃tarktik] ADJ transantarctic

transat [trɑ̃zat] NM *Fam* deckchair■

NF *Sport* transatlantic race; **la t. en solitaire** the single-handed transatlantic race

transatlantique [trɑ̃zatlɑ̃tik] ADJ transatlantic

NM **1** *Naut* (transatlantic) liner **2** *(chaise longue)* deckchair

NF *Sport* transatlantic race

transatmosphérique [trɑ̃satmɔsferik] ADJ *Astron* transatmospheric

trans-avant-garde [trɑ̃savɑ̃gard] *(pl* **trans-avant-gardes)** NF *Beaux-Arts* trans-avant-garde; **la t. italienne** the transavanguardia

transbahuter [3] [trɑ̃sbayte] *Fam* VT to shift, to hump, to lug; **les bagages ont été transbahutés dans une autre voiture** the luggage was shoved into another car

▶ **se transbahuter** VPR to shift oneself

transbordement [trɑ̃sbɔrdəmɑ̃] NM *(de marchandises)* transshipment; *Rail* transfer; *(de voyageurs)* transferring *(of passengers to another vessel or vehicle)*

transborder [3] [trɑ̃sbɔrde] VT *(marchandises)* to tranship, to transfer; *(voyageurs)* to transfer

transbordeur [trɑ̃sbɔrdœr] NM *(navire)* transporter bridge

ADJ M **pont t.** transporter bridge

transcanadien, -enne [trɑ̃skanadjɛ̃, -ɛn] ADJ trans-Canadian, trans-Canada *(avant n)*

❑ **Transcanadienne** NF **la Transcanadienne** *(autoroute)* the Trans-Canada Highway

Transcaucasie [trɑ̃skokazi] NF **la T.** Transcaucasia

transcaucasien, -enne [trɑ̃skokazjɛ̃, -ɛn] ADJ transcaucasian

transcendance [trɑ̃sɑ̃dɑ̃s] NF **1** *Phil* transcendence, transcendency **2** *Math* transcendence

transcendant, -e [trɑ̃sɑ̃dɑ̃, -ɑ̃t] ADJ **1** *Fam (génial)* brilliant; **ce n'est pas t.!** *(livre, film)* it's not exactly brilliant!; **il n'est pas t.!** he's no genius!

2 *Math & Phil* transcendental

transcendantal, -e, -aux, -ales [trɑ̃sɑ̃dɑ̃tal, -o] ADJ transcendental

transcendantalisme [trɑ̃sɑ̃dɑ̃talism] NM transcendentalism

transcender [3] [trɑ̃sɑ̃de] VT to transcend

▶ **se transcender** VPR to transcend oneself

transcodage [trɑ̃skɔdaʒ] NM *(gén)* transcoding, code translation; *Ordinat* compiling; *TV* transcoding, standards conversion

transcoder [3] [trɑ̃skɔde] VT *(gén)* to transcode; *Ordinat* to compile; *TV* to transcode

transcodeur [trɑ̃skɔdœr] NM *(gén)* transcoder; *Ordinat* compiler; *TV* transcoder, standards converter

transconteneur [trɑ̃skɔ̃tənœr] NM transcontainer; *(navire)* transcontainer ship

transcontinental, -e, -aux, -ales [trɑ̃skɔ̃tinɑ̃tal, -o] ADJ transcontinental

transcriptase [trɑ̃skriptɑz] NF *Biol* **t. inverse** *ou* **reverse** reverse transcriptase

transcripteur [trɑ̃skriptœr] NM transcriber

transcription [trɑ̃skripsjɔ̃] NF **1** *(fait d'écrire → gén)* transcription, transcribing, noting (down); *(→ des notes)* copying out (in longhand); *(→ un document officiel)* recording

2 *(copie)* copy, transcript; *(document officiel)* record; **t. à l'état civil** = certified copy of registry office document

3 *Ling & Mus (gén)* transcribing, transcription; *(translittération)* transliteration; **la t. de mon nom russe/chinois en caractères romains** the Romanization of my Russian/Chinese name; **t. phonétique** phonetic transcription; **faire une t. phonétique** to transcribe a word into phonetic symbols

4 *Biol* **t. génétique** (genetic) transcription

transcrire [99] [trɑ̃skrir] VT **1** *(conversation)* to transcribe, to note *or* to take down; *(notes)* to copy *or* to write out (in longhand); *(dans un registre)* to record; *Jur (divorce)* to register; *Com* to post; **je transcris tout ce que vous dites** I'm taking down everything you're saying

2 *Ling (dans un autre alphabet)* to transcribe, to

transliterate; **t. un livre en braille** to copy a book in Braille; **t. un mot d'un alphabet dans un autre** to transliterate a word; **t. un nom russe/ chinois en caractères romains** to Romanize a Russian/Chinese name

3 *Mus* to transcribe

transculturel, -elle [trɑ̃skyltyrɛl] **ADJ** transcultural, cross-cultural

transcutané, -e [trɑ̃skytane] **ADJ** transcutaneous

transdermique [trɑ̃sdɛrmik] **ADJ** transdermal; **timbre t.** skin patch, transdermal patch

transdisciplinaire [trɑ̃sdisiplinɛr] **ADJ** interdisciplinary

transducteur [trɑ̃sdyktœr] **NM** transducer

transduction [trɑ̃sdyksjɔ̃] **NF** transduction

transe [trɑ̃s] **NF 1** *(état d'hypnose)* trance

2 *(exaltation)* trance, exaltation

▫ **transes NFPL 1** *(mouvements)* convulsions; **être pris de transes** to go into convulsions

2 *Vieilli ou Littéraire (anxiété)* fear; **être dans les transes** to be sick with worry, to be out of one's mind with anxiety

▫ **en transe ADJ être en t.** to be in a trance; *Fig* to be beside oneself **ADV entrer en t.** *(médium)* to go *or* to fall into a trance; *Fig Hum* to get all worked up; **faire entrer qn en t.** to put sb into a trance

transept [trɑ̃sɛpt] **NM** transept

transfection [trɑ̃sfɛksjɔ̃] **NF** *Biol & Méd* transfection

transférable [trɑ̃sferabl] **ADJ** transferable

transférase [trɑ̃sferaz] **NF** *Biol* transferase

transfèrement [trɑ̃sfɛrmɑ̃] **NM** transfer, transferring; **t. cellulaire** transfer by police van

transférentiel, -elle [trɑ̃sferɑ̃sjɛl] **ADJ** *Psy* transferential, transference *(avant n)*

transférer [18] [trɑ̃sfere] **VT 1** *(prisonnier, sportif)* to transfer; *(diplomate)* to transfer, to move; *(évêque)* to translate; **t. qn de... à...** to transfer sb from... to...; **être transféré** *(sportif)* to be transferred; *(diplomate)* to move, to be moved

2 *(magasin, siège social)* to transfer, to move; *(fonds)* to transfer; *(reliques)* to translate; **il a transféré son argent sur un compte suisse** he's transferred *or* switched his money to a Swiss account; **succursale transférée au n° 42** *(sur écriteau)* our branch is now at no. 42

3 *Ordinat (information)* to transfer

4 *Jur (droits)* to transfer, to convey **(à** to); *(propriété →* gén**)** to transfer, to convey **(à** to); *(→ par legs)* to demise **(à** to); *(pouvoirs)* to transfer, to pass on **(à** to)

5 *Psy* **t. qch sur qn** to transfer sth onto sb

6 *Beaux-Arts* **t. un motif sur** to transfer a design on *or* onto; **t. un motif au pochoir** to stencil a motif

transfériste [trɑ̃sferist] **NMF** tour rep *(responsible for greeting tourists at the airport and coordinating travel to their destination)*

transfert [trɑ̃sfɛr] **NM 1** *(gén)* & *Com* transfer; *(de population)* resettlement **(dans** in); **t. d'actions** transfer of shares; *Banque* **transferts Banque de France** = French automated clearing system; **t. de capitaux** transfer of capital, capital transfer; **t. par CCP** giro transfer; *Compta* **t. de charges** expense transfer, transfer of charges; *Compta* **t. de compte à compte** book entry transfer; *Compta* **t. de créances** assignment of accounts receivable *or* of debts; **t. de devises** currency transfer; **t. de fonds** transfer of funds; **t. de fonds électronique, t. électronique de fonds** electronic funds transfer, EFT; **t. de fonds électronique sur point de vente** electronic funds transfer at point of sale; **t. télégraphique** telegraphic transfer

2 *Rel (d'un évêque, de reliques)* translation

3 *Ordinat* transfer; **t. de données** data transfer; **t. de fichiers** file transfer

4 *Jur (de propriété)* transfer, conveyance; *(de droits, de pouvoirs)* transfer; **t. par legs** demise

5 *Psy* transference; **elle fait un t. sur toi** she's using you as the object of her transference

6 *Tél* **t. d'appel** call diversion

7 *Can Joual Transp (correspondance)* connection■, transfer■

transfiguration [trɑ̃sfigyrasjɔ̃] **NF 1** *(changement profond)* transfiguration **2** *Rel* **la T.** the Transfiguration

transfigurer [3] [trɑ̃sfigyre] **VT** to transfigure

---

transfiler [3] [trɑ̃sfile] **VT** *Naut* **1 t. deux voiles** to lace two sails together **2** *(cordage)* to snub

transfini, -e [trɑ̃sfini] **ADJ** transfinite

transfixion [trɑ̃sfiksjɔ̃] **NF** *Méd* transfixion

transfo [trɑ̃sfo] **NM** *Fam Élec* adapter■, adaptor■

transformable [trɑ̃sfɔrmabl] **ADJ 1** *(modifiable)* changeable, alterable; **des décors transformables** flexible sets **2** *Sport* convertible

transformante [trɑ̃sfɔrmɑ̃t] **ADJ F** *Géol* **faille t.** transform fault

transformateur, -trice [trɑ̃sfɔrmatœr, -tris] **ADJ** *(influence)* transforming; *(station)* transformer *(avant n)*

NM *Élec* transformer; *(prise)* adapter, adaptor; **t. de traversée** bushing (current) transformer

transformation [trɑ̃sfɔrmasjɔ̃] **NF 1** *(d'une personnalité, d'un environnement)* transformation; *(d'une matière première, d'énergie)* conversion; *(d'une maison, d'un vêtement)* change, alteration; **la t. de l'eau en glace** the transformation of water to ice; **subir une t.** *(personne)* to undergo a transformation; *(matière première)* to be converted; **c'est celle que nous avions achetée ensemble, mais nous lui avons fait subir quelques transformations** it's the one we bought together, but we've made a few changes or alterations to it

2 *(résultat d'un changement)* transformation, alteration, change; **nous avons fait des transformations dans la maison** *(travaux)* we've made some alterations to the house; *(décor, ameublement)* we've made some changes in the house

3 *(au rugby)* conversion; **réussir une t.** to make a conversion

4 *Ling & Math* transformation

5 *Élec* **rapport de t.** transformer ratio; *Électron* **t. de signaux** signal transformation

transformationnel, -elle [trɑ̃sfɔrmasjɔnɛl] **ADJ** transformational

transformatrice [trɑ̃sfɔrmatris] *voir* **transformateur**

transformé [trɑ̃sfɔrme] **NM** *Math* transform

transformer [3] [trɑ̃sfɔrme] **VT 1** *(faire changer →* bâtiment, personnalité, institution, paysage*)* to transform, to change, to alter; *(→ matière première)* to transform, to convert; *(→ vêtement)* to make over, to alter; **sa maternité l'a complètement transformée** motherhood has completely transformed her; **t. qch en** *(faire devenir)* to convert sth into; **t. une pièce en bureau** to convert a room into an office; **la sorcière l'a transformé en souris** the witch turned him into a mouse

2 *Ling & Math* to transform

3 *(au rugby)* to convert

4 *Électron* to transform, to map

▸**se transformer VPR** *(quartier, personnalité, paysage, institution)* to change; **l'environnement se transforme lentement/rapidement** the environment is changing slowly/rapidly; **se t. en** to turn into; **elle se transforma en cygne** she turned *or* changed into a swan; **ce voyage se transformait en cauchemar** the trip was turning into a nightmare

transformisme [trɑ̃sfɔrmism] **NM** transformism

transformiste [trɑ̃sfɔrmist] **ADJ** *(évolutionniste)* transformist *(avant n)*

NMF *(évolutionniste)* transformist

NM *(travesti)* drag artist; **spectacle de transformistes** drag show

transfrontalier, -ère [trɑ̃sfrɔ̃talje, -ɛr] **ADJ** cross-border *(avant n)*

transfuge [trɑ̃sfyʒ] **NMF** *Mil & Pol* renegade, turncoat; *(qui change de camp)* defector

transfusé, -e [trɑ̃sfyze] **ADJ** **sang t.** transfused blood

NM,F = person receiving/having received a (blood) transfusion; **le nombre des transfusés** the number of people receiving (blood) transfusions

transfuser [3] [trɑ̃sfyze] **VT 1** *Méd (sang)* to transfuse; *(malade)* to give a (blood) transfusion to, to transfuse; **elle se fait t. régulièrement à cause de sa maladie** she has regular blood transfusions because of her illness **2** *Littéraire (sentiment)* to instil, to communicate, to pass on

transfusion [trɑ̃sfyzjɔ̃] **NF t. sanguine** *ou* **de sang**

---

blood transfusion; **centre de t. sanguine** blood transfusion centre; **t. d'échange** exchange transfusion; **faire une t. à qn** to give sb a (blood) transfusion

transfusionnel, -elle [trɑ̃sfyzjɔnɛl] **ADJ** transfusional

transgène [trɑ̃sʒɛn] **NM** *Biol* transgene

transgenèse [trɑ̃sʒɔnɛz] **NF** *Biol* transgenosis

transgénique [trɑ̃sʒenik] **ADJ** *Biol* transgenic

transgénose [trɑ̃sʒenoz] = **transgenèse**

transgresser [4] [trɑ̃sgrese] **VT** *(règle)* to break, *Sout* to infringe, to contravene; *(ordre)* to disobey, to go against; **t. la loi** to break the law; **t. les interdits** to break the taboos

transgresseur [trɑ̃sgresœr] **NM** *Littéraire* transgressor, contravener **(de** of)

transgressif, -ive [trɑ̃sgresif, -iv] **ADJ** boundary-breaking, controversial

transgression [trɑ̃sgresjɔ̃] **NF 1** *(d'une règle, d'une loi)* infringement, contravention, breaking; *(d'un ordre)* disobeying **2** *Géol* transgression

transgressive [trɑ̃sgresiv] *voir* **transgressif**

transhorizon [trɑ̃sɔrizɔ̃] **ADJ INV** forward-scatter

transhumance [trɑ̃zymɑ̃s] **NF 1** *(de troupeaux)* seasonal migration, *Spéc* transhumance; **au moment de la t.** when the herds are moved to the grazing grounds **2** *(d'abeilles)* migratory beekeeping

transhumant, -e [trɑ̃zymɑ̃, -ɑ̃t] **ADJ** transhumant

transhumer [3] [trɑ̃zyme] **VI** *(vers les pâturages)* to move up to (summer) grazing grounds; *(vers la vallée)* to move down to the wintering grounds

VT 1 *(troupeaux)* to move **2** *Hort* to transplant

transi, -e [trɑ̃zi] **ADJ être t. (de froid)** to be chilled to the bone *or* to the marrow; **être t. de peur** to be paralysed *or* transfixed by fear

transiger [17] [trɑ̃ziʒe] **VI 1** *(composer)* to (come to a) compromise; **il n'a pas voulu t.** he refused all compromise; **t. avec qn** to seek a compromise *or* to bargain with sb; **nous ne transigerons pas avec les terroristes** we will not bargain with the terrorists; **t. avec sa conscience** to make a deal with one's conscience; **je ne transigerai pas avec le règlement** I refuse to compromise *or* I am intransigent when it comes to the rules; **t. sur ses principes** to compromise one's principles; **ne pas t. sur la ponctualité** to be uncompromising in matters of punctuality, to be a stickler for punctuality; **il ne transige pas sur l'honnêteté** he is uncompromisingly honest, he makes no compromises when it comes to honesty; **les circonstances m'ont fait t. en sa faveur** the circumstances led me to compromise in his/her favour

2 *Can (négocier)* to negotiate

Transilien® [trɑ̃siljɛ̃] **NM** *(abrév* **transport francilien** *)* = Paris suburban train network

transillumination [trɑ̃silyminasjɔ̃] **NF** *Méd* transillumination

transir [32] [trɑ̃zir] **VT** *Littéraire (sujet: peur)* to paralyse; **le froid m'avait transi** the cold had gone right through me

VI *Arch (de froid)* to be chilled to the bone; *(de peur)* to be paralysed with fear

transistor [trɑ̃zistɔr] **NM 1** *Rad* transistor (radio) **2** *Électron* transistor; **t. à effet de champ** field-effect transistor, FET; **t. en couche mince** thin film transistor, TFT

▫ **à transistors ADJ** transistorized

transistorisation [trɑ̃zistɔrizasjɔ̃] **NF** *Électron* transistorization

transistoriser [3] [trɑ̃zistɔrize] **VT** *Électron* to transistorize

transit [trɑ̃zit] **NM 1** *Com (de marchandises, de touristes)* transit; **t. communautaire** Community transit; **t. douanier** Customs transit; *Aut* **t. temporaire (autorisé)** = registration for vehicles bought in France for tax-free export by non-residents

2 *Physiol* **t. intestinal** intestinal transit; **favorise le t. intestinal** *(sur emballage)* relieves constipation

3 *Électron* **t. par bande perforée** tape relay

▫ **de transit ADJ** transit *(avant n)*; **maison de t.** forwarding agency; **marchandises de t.** goods for transit; **salle de t.** *(dans un aéroport)* transit lounge

▫ **en transit** ADJ in transit, transiting; **passagers en t.** (*dans un aéroport*) passengers in transit, transfer passengers

transitaire [trãziter] ADJ (*commerce, port*) transit (*avant n*); **pays t.** country of transit

NM forwarding agent; **t. aéroportuaire** airfreight forwarder; **t. portuaire** maritime freight forwarder

transitaire-groupeur [trãzitergrupœr] (*pl* **transitaires-groupeurs**) NM forwarder and consolidator

transiter [3] [trãzite] VT (*marchandises*) to forward

VI 1 (*voyageurs, marchandises*) **t. par** to pass through; **t. par Anchorage** to transit *or* to go via Anchorage; **ces dossiers transitent par mon service** those files come through my department 2 *Ordinat* (*signaux*) to flow

transitif, -ive [trãzitif, -iv] ADJ transitive

NM *Ling* transitive verb

transition [trãzisjɔ̃] NF 1 (*entre deux états*) transition; *Archit* **style de t.** transitional style

2 (*entre deux paragraphes, deux scènes*) transition, link; *TV & Rad* **t. musicale** segue

3 (*entre deux gouvernements*) interim; **assurer la t.** to make sure there is no hiatus, to make sure there is a seamless transition

4 *Phys* transition

▫ **de transition** ADJ 1 (*administration, gouvernement*) interim (*avant n*); **période** *ou* **phase de t.** period of transition, transition *or* transitional period

2 *Aviat & Chim* transition (*avant n*)

▫ **sans transition** ADV without transition; **le journaliste est passé sans t. de l'accident d'avion à la météo** the newsreader went from the plane crash to the weather forecast without any transition *or* a break; **sans t., nous passons aux nouvelles sportives** and now for something completely different, over to the sports news; **elle passait sans t. de l'enthousiasme à la fureur** her mood used to change *or* to switch abruptly from enthusiasm to rage

transitionnel, -elle [trãzisjɔnɛl] ADJ 1 (*gén*) transitional 2 *Psy* **objet t.** transitional object

transitive [trãzitiv] *voir* **transitif**

transitivement [trãzitivmã] ADV transitively

transitivité [trãzitivite] NF transitivity

transitoire [trãzitwar] ADJ 1 (*administration, dispositions, régime*) interim (*avant n*), transitional; (*mesure*) transitional, temporary; (*charge*) temporary 2 (*situation*) transitory, transient

Transjordanie [trãzɔrdani] NF *Hist* **la T.** Transjordan

Transkei [trãskɛj] NM **le T.** Transkei

translatif, -ive [trãslatif, -iv] ADJ *Jur* conveyance (*avant n*)

translation [trãslasjɔ̃] NF 1 *Rel* (*de cendres, de reliques*) translation; (*d'une fête*) transfer 2 *Jur* (*d'une juridiction, d'un dignitaire*) transfer; (*de propriété*) conveyance, transfer 3 *Ordinat* **t. dynamique** dynamic relocation 4 *Math & Phys* translation; **mouvement de t.** translating movement 5 *Tél* (*de message*) retransmission, relaying

translative [trãslativ] *voir* **translatif**

translittération [trãsliterasjɔ̃] NF transliteration; (*en braille*) copying

translittérer [18] [trãslitere] VT to transliterate; (*en braille*) to copy

translocation [trãslɔkasjɔ̃] NF *Biol* translocation

transloquer [3] [trãslɔke] VT *Biol* to translocate

translucide [trãslysid] ADJ translucent

translucidité [trãslysidite] NF translucence, translucency

transluminal, -e, -aux, -ales [trãslyminal, -o] ADJ *Méd* transluminal

transmanche [trãsmãʃ] ADJ INV cross-Channel

transmet *etc voir* **transmettre**

transmetteur [trãsmetœr] NM 1 *Tél, Ordinat & Biol* transmitter 2 *Naut* **t. d'ordres** telegraph, transmitter 3 *Mil* ≃ soldier in the Signals Corps 4 *Méd* (*d'une maladie, d'un virus*) carrier

transmettre [84] [trãsmetr] VT 1 *Tél* to transmit

2 *Rad & TV* (*émission*) to transmit, to relay, to broadcast; (*information*) to send, to transmit

3 *Phys* to transmit; **t. un mouvement à qch** to set sth in motion

4 (*de la main à la main*) to hand (on), to pass on; **transmettez-lui ce colis** give him/her this parcel; **l'ailier transmet le ballon à l'avant-centre** the winger passes the ball to the centre-forward

5 (*de génération en génération → gén*) to pass on, to hand down; (*→ recette, don*) to hand on; (*→ connaissances*) to hand on, to pass on

6 (*communiquer → information, ordre, remerciement*) to pass on, *Sout* to convey; (*→ pli*) to send on, to forward; (*→ secret*) to pass on; **transmettez mes amitiés à votre frère** (*à l'oral*) please remember me to your brother; (*dans une lettre*) please send my regards to your brother; **transmettez mes respects à votre frère** (*à l'oral*) please convey my respects to your brother; (*dans une lettre*) please send my respects to your brother; **avez-vous fait t. le message au Président?** have you made sure that the President has been given the message?; **qui vous a transmis la nouvelle?** who gave *or* told you the news?, who passed the news on to you?

7 (*faire partager → goût, émotion*) to pass on, to put over; **il m'a transmis son enthousiasme pour l'art abstrait** he communicated his enthusiasm for abstract art to me

8 *Méd* to transmit, to pass on

9 *Jur* (*propriété*) to pass on, to transfer; (*pouvoirs*) to pass on, to hand over, to transfer; (*actions*) to assign; **t. ses pouvoirs à qn** to hand over to sb

USAGE ABSOLU (*communiquer*) **laissez-moi un message et je transmettrai** leave me a message and I'll pass it on; **écrire au journal, qui transmettra** write care of the newspaper

►**se transmettre** VPR to be transmitted; (*message, maladie*) to be passed on; (*coutume*) to be handed down, to be passed on; **le virus se transmet par contact/par la salive** the virus is transmitted by (direct) contact/through saliva; **la vibration se transmet à la membrane** the vibration spreads *or* is transmitted to the membrane; **le savoir se transmet de la mère à la fille** knowledge is handed down *or* passed on from mother to daughter

transmigration [trãsmigrasjɔ̃] NF 1 *Littéraire* (*émigration*) migration 2 (*réincarnation*) transmigration

transmigrer [3] [trãsmigre] VI 1 *Littéraire* (*émigrer*) to migrate 2 (*âme*) to transmigrate

transmis, -e [trãsmi, -iz] PP *voir* **transmettre**

transmissibilité [trãsmisibilite] NF transmissibility

transmissible [trãsmisibl] ADJ 1 *Méd* transmittable, transmissible; **sexuellement t.** sexually transmitted; **c'est t. par contact/par la salive** it can be transmitted by (direct) contact/through saliva 2 *Jur* (*biens, droit*) transferable, transmissible; *Fin* **t. par endossement** transferable by endorsement

transmission [trãsmisjɔ̃] NF 1 *Aut & Tech* (*pièces*) organes de **t.** transmission (system); *Tech* **t. du mouvement** transmission of movement; *Aut* power flow; *Aut* **t. automatique** automatic transmission; *Aut* **t. finale** final drive; *Tech* **t. flexible** flexible shaft(ing); *Aut* **t. intégrale** all-wheel drive system; *Aut* **t. manuelle** manual transmission; *Aut* **t. à variation continue** continuously variable transmission

2 *Phys* (*de chaleur, de son*) transmission

3 *Tél* transmission; *Rad & TV* (*d'une émission*) transmission, relaying, broadcasting; **erreur de t.** (*d'un message*) error in transmission; *Rad & TV* **t. différée** *ou* **en différé** recorded broadcast *or* programme; **t. directe** *ou* **en direct** live broadcast *or* programme; *Rad & TV* **t. par satellite** satellite broadcast

4 *Méd* passing on, transmission, transmitting; *Biol* (*de caractères génétiques*) transmission, handing on

5 (*d'une information, d'un ordre*) passing on, conveying; (*d'un secret*) passing on; (*d'une lettre*) forwarding, sending on; **t. de pensée** telepathy, thought transference; **c'est de la t. de pensée!** we/they/etc can read each other's minds!

6 (*d'une tradition*) handing down *or* on; (*du savoir*) handing on, passing on

7 (*legs → d'un bijou, d'une histoire*) handing down, passing on; (*→ d'un état d'esprit*) passing on

8 *Jur* (*de pouvoirs, de biens*) transfer; (*d'actions*) assignment; **t. de données** data transmission *or* transfer; *Admin* **t. des pouvoirs** (*d'un ministre à un autre, d'un président à un autre*) handover; **t. à titre particulier** transfer of particular goods; **t. à titre universel** transfer of a share of an estate; **t. universelle** transfer of an estate

9 *Ordinat* transmission; **t. de données** data transmission *or* transfer; **voie de t.** transmission channel; **t. par modem** modem transmission; **la t. d'un document par modem** the transmission of a document by modem, the modeming of a document; **t. de paquets** packet transmission

▫ **transmissions** NFPL *Mil* les **transmissions** ≃ the Signals Corps; **officier de transmissions** signal(s) officer; **centre de transmissions** signal centre

transmit *etc voir* **transmettre**

transmodulation [trãsmɔdylasjɔ̃] NF cross modulation

transmuable [trãsmɥabl] ADJ transmutable

transmuer [7] [trãsmɥe] VT to transmute; **t. qch en** to transmute sth into

►**se transmuer** VPR to be transmuted

transmutabilité [trãsmytabilite] NF transmutability

transmutable [trãsmytabl] ADJ transmutable

transmutation [trãsmytasjɔ̃] NF transmutation (**en** into)

transmuter [3] [trãsmyte] VT to transmute; **t. qch en** to transmute sth into

►**se transmuter** VPR to be transmuted

transnational, -e, -aux, -ales [trãsnasjɔnal, -o] ADJ transnational

transocéanique [trãzɔseanik] ADJ transoceanic

Transpac® [trãspak] NM = the French packet-switching network

transpalette [trãspalɛt] NM pallet truck, stacker

transparaître [91] [trãsparɛtr] VI (*lumière, couleur, sentiment*) to show *or* to filter through; **le doute transparaît sous son calme** doubt is showing (through) beneath his/her calm; **son visage ne laissa rien t.** he/she remained impassive, his/her face showed no emotion; **l'auteur laisse t. son désenchantement** the author allows his/her disenchantment to show *or* to filter through

transparence [trãsparãs] NF 1 (*propriété → d'une porcelaine, d'une surface*) transparence, transparency; (*→ d'une peau*) clearness, transparence, transparency; (*→ d'un regard, d'un liquide*) transparency, clearness; **la t. de son teint** his/her clear complexion; **regarder qch par t.** to look at sth against the light; **on peut le lire par t.** you can read it by holding it up to the light; **on voit son soutien-gorge par t.** her bra is showing through; **on voit ses jambes par t.** you can see her legs against the light

2 *Fig* (*caractère d'évidence → d'un dessein, d'une personnalité*) transparency, obviousness

3 *Fig* (*caractère public → de transactions, d'une comptabilité*) public accountability; (*d'un parti politique*) transparency, openness; **dans notre pays, la t. des revenus n'est pas de règle** in our country, it is not usual for people to reveal what they earn

4 *Jur* **t. fiscale** open taxation

5 *Cin* back projection

transparent, -e [trãsparã, -ãt] ADJ 1 (*translucide → porcelaine, papier, surface*) transparent; (*→ regard, eau*) transparent, limpid; (*→ vêtement*) transparent, see-through; **ta robe est très transparente** your dress is very transparent *or* see-through

2 (*lumineux, clair → peau*) transparent, clear

3 *Fig* (*évident → dessein, motif*) obvious, transparent; **c'était un homme t.** it was easy to read his mind *or* to know what he was thinking

4 *Fig* (*public → comptabilité, transaction*) open

NM 1 (*de projection*) transparency, OHP slide 2 (*pour écrire droit*) ruled sheet

transparu [trãspary] PP *voir* **transparaître**

transpercement [trãspɛrsəmã] NM *Méd* transfixion

transpercer [16] [trãspɛrse] VT 1 (*sujet: flèche, épée*) to pierce (through), to transfix; (*sujet: balle*) to go through, to pierce; **t. qn d'un coup d'épée** to run sb through with a sword; **il a eu le**

pied transpercé par la flèche the arrow went (right) through his foot; **la balle l'a transpercé** the bullet went right through him/it

2 (pénétrer → sujet: pluie) to get through; **un froid qui transperce** piercing cold; **le froid/la pluie transperçait les badauds** the bystanders were chilled to the bone/soaked to the skin; **la pluie a transpercé ses vêtements** the rain went or soaked right through his/her clothes

transpersonnel, -elle [trãspɛrsɔnɛl] ADJ Psy transpersonal

transphrastique [trãsfrastik] ADJ Ling transphrastic

transpirant, -e [trãspirã, -ãt] ADJ perspiring, sweating

transpiration [trãspirasjɔ̃] NF **1** Physiol (sudation) perspiration; (sueur) perspiration, sweat; **humide de t.** (vêtement) sweaty **2** Bot transpiration

transpirer [3] [trãspire] VI **1** Physiol to perspire, to sweat; **t. des mains/pieds** to have sweaty hands/feet; **se mettre à t.** to start to sweat, to break into a sweat; **je transpirais à grosses gouttes** great drops or beads of sweat were rolling off my forehead

2 Fig (faire des efforts) to sweat blood, to be hard at it; Fam **t. sur qch** to sweat over sth

3 Fig (être divulgué) to leak out, to come to light; **la nouvelle a transpiré** the news has got or leaked out

4 Bot to transpire

transplant [trãsplã] NM (avant l'opération) organ for transplant; (après l'opération) transplant, transplanted organ

transplantable [trãsplãtabl] ADJ transplantable

transplantation [trãsplãtasjɔ̃] NF **1** Méd (d'un organe → méthode) transplantation; (→ opération) transplant; **t. cardiaque/rénale/hépatique** heart/kidney/liver transplant; **t. embryonnaire** surgical transplantation of an embryo

2 Agr & Hort transplantation, transplanting; **faire des transplantations** to do some transplanting

3 (déplacement → de personnes) moving, resettling; (→ d'animaux) transplantation

transplanté, -e [trãsplãte] NM,F receiver (of a transplant); **les transplantés du cœur/du foie** people who have had heart/liver transplants; **le nombre des transplantés** the number of people receiving transplants

transplanter [3] [trãsplãte] VT **1** Méd (organe) to transplant; (embryon) to implant; **t. un cœur/un rein** to perform a heart/a kidney transplant (operation); **un malade transplanté** a transplant patient

2 Agr & Hort to transplant

3 (populations) to move, to transplant, to uproot

▸ **se transplanter** VPR (dans un autre milieu) to transplant oneself; **se t. en France/aux États-Unis** to resettle in France/in the United States

transplantoir [trãsplãtwar] NM trowel

transpolaire [trãspɔler] ADJ transpolar

transpondeur [trãspɔ̃dœr] NM Tél transponder

transport [trãspɔr] NM **1** (acheminement → de personnes, de marchandises) Br transport, Am transportation; (→ d'énergie) conveyance, conveying; **assurer le t. des blessés** to be responsible for transporting the wounded; **engagé pour le t. du matériel** hired to carry the equipment; **cela permet de faire les transports urgents par avion** this enables urgent freight to be sent by air; **abîmé pendant le t.** damaged in transit; **t. d'acheminement** transfer transport; **t. aérien, t. par air** ou **avion** air transport, airfreight; **t. par chemin de fer** rail transport; **le t. civil aérien** civil aviation; **t. ferroviaire** rail transport; **t. fluvial** inland waterway transport; **t. international routier** TIR; **t. de marchandises** transport of goods; **t. maritime** ou **par mer** shipping; **t. par route** road transport or haulage; **t. terrestre** land transport; Mil **t. de troupes** (acheminement) troop transportation; (navire, avion) (troop) carrier, troop transport

2 Littéraire (émotion) transport, burst; **t. de joie** transport or burst of joy; **t. d'enthousiasme** burst or gush of enthusiasm; **t. de colère** burst or outburst of anger; **dans un t. d'admiration, elle me dit...** fairly carried away or transported with admiration, she said to me...; Littéraire ou Hum **transports amoureux** amorous transports

3 Jur (cession) **t.(-cession)** (de biens, de droits) transfer, conveyance; **t. sur les lieux, t. de justice** visit to the scene of the accident or crime

4 Banque (de fonds) transfer (from one account to another)

5 Compta transfer

◻ **transports** NMPL Admin transport network; **les transports (publics** ou **en commun)** public transport (UNCOUNT); **je passe beaucoup de temps dans les transports pour aller au travail** I spend a lot of time commuting; **prendre les transports en commun** to use public transport; **les transports aériens** (the) airlines; **les transports ferroviaires** the rail (transport) network; **les transports fluviaux** the waterways (transport) network; **les transports maritimes** the shipping lines; **les transports routiers** road transport (UNCOUNT); **les transports urbains** the urban transport system

◻ **de transport** ADJ Br transport (avant n), Am transportation (avant n)

transportable [trãspɔrtabl] ADJ (denrées) transportable; (blessé) fit to be moved; **elle n'est pas t.** she's not fit to be moved, she can't be moved

transportation [trãspɔrtasjɔ̃] NF Hist transportation

transporté, -e [trãspɔrte] ADJ Fig carried away, transported; **t. de joie** beside oneself with joy, transported with joy

NM,F Hist transported convict, transport

transporter [3] [trãspɔrte] VT **1** (faire changer d'endroit → cargaison, passager, troupes) to carry, to transport, Sout to convey; (→ blessé) to move; **t. une caisse à la cave** to move a crate to the cellar; **t. qch dans une brouette** to cart sth in a wheelbarrow; **t. des vivres par avion/par bateau** to fly/to ship food supplies; **t. qch par avion** to air-freight sth, to transport sth by air; **t. qch par camion** to send sth Br by lorry or Am by truck; **t. qch par mer** to transport sth by sea; **t. qch par train** to transport sth by rail; **le camion transporte des explosifs** the truck is carrying explosives; **t. qn à l'hôpital** to take sb to hospital; **t. qn d'urgence à l'hôpital** to rush sb to hospital; **les personnes transportées** (passagers) passengers

2 Fig (par l'imaginaire) to take; **le premier acte nous transporte en Géorgie/nous transporte au XVIIème siècle** the first act takes us to Georgia/takes us back to the 17th century

3 (porter) to carry; **les alluvions transportées par le fleuve** the sediment carried (along) by the river

4 Phys to convey

5 Littéraire (enthousiasmer) to carry away, to send into raptures; **cette bonne nouvelle l'a transporté** he was overjoyed by the good news; **je me sentais transporté par la musique** the music sent me into raptures; **être transporté de joie** to be overjoyed or in transports of delight

6 Fin (fonds) to transfer

7 Jur (céder → biens, droits) to transfer (à to)

8 Hist (condamné) to transport

▸ **se transporter** VPR **1** (se déplacer) to move

2 Fig (en imagination) to imagine oneself; **se t. (par la pensée) dans un pays lointain** to let one's imagination carry one to a distant country; **transportez-vous maintenant au Moyen Âge** now let your imagination take you back to the Middle Ages

3 Jur **se t. sur les lieux** to visit the scene of the accident or crime

transporteur, -euse [trãspɔrtœr, -øz] ADJ carrying (avant n); **benne transporteuse** skip; **hélice/courroie transporteuse** spiral/belt conveyor

NM **1** (entreprise) haulage contractor, Br haulier, Am hauler; (en langage juridique) carrier; **t. routier** road haulage contractor, road Br haulier or Am hauler

2 (outil) conveyor; **(chariot) t.** travelling crane or platform; **t. élévateur** elevator

3 Naut **t. de vrac** bulk carrier

4 Pétr **t. de gaz** gas transporter (ship)

transposable [trãspɔzabl] ADJ transposable; **difficilement t.** difficult to transpose; **t. à l'écran** that can be adapted for the screen

transposée [trãspoze] NF Math **t. d'une matrice** transpose of a matrix

transposer [3] [trãspoze] VT **1** (intervertir → mots) to switch (round), to transpose **2** (adapter) **t. un sujet antique à l'époque moderne** to adapt an ancient subject to a contemporary setting; **t. un roman à l'écran/à la scène** to adapt a novel for the screen/for the stage **3** Mus to transpose

transpositeur [trãspozitœr] ADJ M Mus transposing; **piano t.** transposing piano

transposition [trãspozisjɔ̃] NF **1** (commutation) transposition **2** (adaptation) adaptation; **t. d'un roman à l'écran/à la scène** screen/stage adaptation **3** Élec, Typ, Math, Méd & Mus transposition

transposon [trãspozɔ̃] NM Biol transposon

transpyrénéen, -enne [trãspireneɛ̃, -ɛn] ADJ **1** (qui traverse) trans-Pyrenean **2** (venant de l'autre côté) from across the Pyrenees

transsaharien, -enne [trãssaarjɛ̃, -ɛn] ADJ trans-Saharan

transsexualisme [trãssɛksɥalism] NM transsexualism

transsexuel, -elle [trãssɛksɥɛl] ADJ transsexual

transsibérien, -enne [trãssiberjɛ̃, -ɛn] ADJ trans-Siberian

NM le T. the Trans-Siberian (Railway)

transsonique [trãssɔnik] ADJ trans-sonic

transstockeur [trãstɔkœr] NM stacker-retriever (crane)

transsubstantiation [trãssypstãsjasjɔ̃] NF Rel transubstantiation

transsudat [trãssyda] NM Méd transudate

transsudation [trãssydasjɔ̃] NF transudation

transsuder [3] [trãssyde] VI to transude

transuranien [trãsyranjɛ̃] Chim ADJ M transuranic

NM transuranic

Transvaal [trãsval] NM le T. the Transvaal; **au T.** in the Transvaal

transvasement [trãsvazmã] NM **1** (d'un liquide) decanting **2** (d'abeilles) transferral

transvaser [3] [trãsvaze] VT to decant; **transvasez le bouillon dans un verre gradué** pour the stock into a measuring jug

transversal, -e, -aux, -ales [trãsvɛrsal, -o] ADJ (coupe, fil, poutre, trait) cross (avant n), transverse, transversal; (onde, axe, moteur) transverse; (voie) which runs or cuts across; **rue transversale** side road; Constr **mur t.** partition (wall); Anat **muscle t.** transverse (muscle); Naut **soutes transversales** cross bunkers; Géog **vallée transversale** transverse valley

◻ **transversale** NF **1** Ftbl (barre) crossbar; (passe) cross

2 Géom transversal

3 (route) cross-country Br trunk road or Am highway

4 Rail (entre régions) cross-country line; (de ville à ville) Br intercity or Am interurban line

5 Naut & Pétr transverse (frame)

transversalement [trãsvɛrsalmã] ADV transversally, across

transversalité [trãsvɛrsalite] NF transversality

transverse [trãsvɛrs] ADJ Anat & Géom transverse

transvestisme [trãsvɛstism] NM transvestism

transvider [3] [trãsvide] VT to decant; **t. qch dans qch** to pour sth into sth, to transfer sth to sth

transylvain, -e [trãsilvɛ̃, -ɛn] ADJ Transylvanian

◻ **Transylvain, -e** NM,F Transylvanian

Transylvanie [trãsilvani] NF la T. Transylvania

transylvanien, -enne [trãsilvanjɛ̃, -ɛn] ADJ Transylvanian

◻ **Transylvanien, -enne** NM,F Transylvanian

trapèze [trapɛz] NM **1** Géom Br trapezium, Am trapezoid; **t. rectangle** right-angled trapezium **2** Anat (muscle) trapezius **3** (activité) trapeze; **faire du t.** to perform on the trapeze; **t. volant** flying trapeze

ADJ **1** Anat **muscle t.** trapezius; **os t.** trapezium **2** (jupe, robe) A-line

trapéziste [trapezist] NMF trapezist, trapeze artist

trapézoïdal, -e, -aux, -ales [trapezɔidal, -o] ADJ trapezoidal

trapézoïde [trapezɔid] ADJ trapezoid (avant n)

NM trapezoid (bone)

trapillon [trapijɔ̃] NM **1** (d'une trappe) catch **2** Théât (sur le plancher de la scène) slot

trappage [trapaʒ] NM Can trapping

Trappe [trap] NF **1** (abbaye) Trappist monastery **2** (ordre) la T. the Trappist order

trappe [trap] NF **1** (piège) trap **2** (sur le sol → porte)

trapdoor; *(→ ouverture)* hatch; *(d'une scène de théâtre)* trap opening; *(pour parachutiste)* exit door; *Tech* hatch; **passer à la t.** to be whisked away (without trace); **t. de visite** inspection hatch; *Aut* **t. à essence** petrol tank flap **3** *Can Fam (bouche)* trap, *Br* gob **4** *Can (chasse)* trapping

trapper [3] [trape] *Can* **VT** to trap
VI to trap

trappeur [trapœr] **NM** trapper

trappillon [trapijɔ̃] = **trapillon**

trappiste [trapist] **NM** *(moine)* Trappist monk
NF *Belg (bière)* beer *(made by Trappist monks)*

trappistine [trapistin] **NF 1** *(religieuse)* Trappistine, Trappist nun **2** *(liqueur)* Trappistine

trapu, -e [trapy] **ADJ 1** *(personne)* stocky, thickset **2** *(bâtiment)* squat **3** *Fam (difficile → devoir, exercice)* tough, tricky; **l'examen était vraiment t.!** the exam was a real stinker! **4** *Fam (savant)* brainy; **il est t. en chimie** he's brilliant at chemistry

traque [trak] **NF** *Chasse* **la t.** beating (game)

traquenard [traknar] **NM 1** *(machination)* snare, trap; **tomber dans un t.** to fall into a trap **2** *(pour les oiseaux)* bird trap; *(pour les souris)* trap **3** *Équitation (trot)* rack; *(cheval)* racker

traquer [3] [trake] **VT 1** *(criminel, fuyard)* to track *or* to hunt down; *(vedette)* to hound; *(erreur)* to track down; **en le traquant, ils ont découvert où il habitait** they tracked him down to his home; **se faire t.** to be tracked down *or* hunted down **2** *Chasse (rechercher)* to track down; *(rabattre)* to drive; **animal traqué** hunted animal

traquet [trakɛ] **NM 1** *(battant)* (mill) clapper *or* clack **2** *Orn* **t. (motteux)** wheatear; **t. (pâtre)** stonechat; **t. noir** black wheatear; **t. oreillard** black-eared wheatear; **t. rieur** black wheatear; **t. tarier** whinchat

traqueur, -euse [trakœr, -øz] **NM,F** *Chasse* beater, driver

trash [traʃ] *Fam* **ADJ INV** *(musique, film, esthétique)* trash
NM *(style)* trash

trattoria [tratɔrja] **NF** trattoria

trauma [troma] **NM** trauma

traumatique [tromatik] **ADJ** traumatic

traumatisant, -e [tromatizɑ̃, -ɑ̃t] **ADJ** traumatic

traumatiser [3] [tromatize] **VT** to traumatize; *Fam* **il ne faut pas que ça te traumatise** you mustn't let it traumatize you, you mustn't be traumatized by it

traumatisme [tromatism] **NM** trauma, traumatism; **t. crânien** cranial trauma

traumatologie [tromatɔlɔʒi] **NF** traumatology

traumatologique [tromatɔlɔʒik] **ADJ** traumatological

traumatologiste [tromatɔlɔʒist] **NMF** traumatologist

travail[1], -s [travaj] **NM** *Vét* trave

TRAVAIL[2], -AUX [travaj, -o]

NM work **A1, 2, 4, 5, 10-12, B2, C** ▪ job **A3, 7** ▪ working **A6** ▪ labour **A8, 10** ▪ action **A9** ▪ piece **B1** ▪ workplace **C**
NMPL work **1-3** ▪ working **1**

NM A. *ACTION* **1** *(occupation)* **le t.** work; **le t. de bureau** office work; **le t. de jour/nuit** day/night work; **alterner t. et repos** to alternate between work and rest *or* working and resting; **je finis le t. à cinq heures** I stop *or* finish work at five; **je fais des vitraux – et vous vivez de votre t.?** I make stained-glass windows – and can you earn a living from your work?; **être lent au t.** to be slow in one's work, to be a slow worker; **écrire un dictionnaire est un t. collectif** writing a dictionary involves working as a team; **un corps usé par le t.** a work-weary body; **t. de force** hard physical work; **un t. de longue haleine** a long-term project; **le t. scolaire/universitaire** school/academic work; **le t. posté** *ou* **par roulement** shift work; *Aviat* **t. aérien** aerial work; **t. complémentaire** follow-up work; **le t. à domicile** outwork; **faire** *ou* **prendre du t. à domicile** to take work in; **t. d'équipe** teamwork; *Jur* **t. d'intérêt général** community service; **le t. manuel** manual work *or* labour; **le t. au noir** *(occasionnel)* undeclared casual work, moonlighting; *(comme pratique généralisée)* the black economy; **t. à la pièce** piecework; **le t. saisonnier** seasonal work; **le t. salarié** paid work; **le t. temporaire** *(gén)* temporary work; *(dans un bureau)* temping; **t. sur le terrain** fieldwork; **t. à plein temps** full-time work; **t. à temps partiel** part-time work

2 *(tâches imposées)* work; **son t.** his/her work *or* workload; **avoir beaucoup de t.** to have a lot of work; **cela me fait du t. en plus** it's extra work for me; **donner du t. à qn** to give sb (some) work to do; **leur professeur leur donne trop de t.** their teacher gives *or* sets them too much work *or* homework

3 *(tâche déterminée)* job; **faire un t. de recherche/un t. de traduction** to do a piece of research/a translation; **c'est un t. de bagnard** it's backbreaking work *or* a backbreaking job; **c'est un t. de bénédictin** it's painstaking work; **c'est un t. de forçat** it's backbreaking work *or* a backbreaking job; **c'est un t. de fourmi** it's a painstaking task; **c'est un t. de Romain** *ou* **de titan** it's a colossal job

4 *(efforts)* (hard) work; **c'est du t. d'élever cinq enfants!** bringing up five children is a lot of (hard) work!; **tout ce t. pour rien!** all this (hard) work for nothing!; **c'est tout un t., de vous réunir tous les huit!** it's quite a job, getting the eight of you together!; **il a encore du t. s'il veut devenir champion** he's still got a lot of work to do if he wants to be champion

5 *(exécution)* work; **en électronique, le t. doit être minutieux** electronics work calls for extreme precision; **admirez le t. du pinceau** admire the brushwork; **une dentelle d'un t. très délicat** a very delicate piece of lacework; **on lui a confié les peintures et elle a fait du bon/mauvais t.** she was responsible for doing the painting and she made a good/bad job of it; **regarde-moi ce t.!** just look at this mess!; **je ne retrouve pas un seul stylo bleu, qu'est-ce que c'est que ce t.?** I can't find a single blue pen, what's going on here?; *Fam* **et voilà le t.!** and that's all there is to it!, *Br* and Bob's your uncle!

6 *(façonnage)* working; **elle est attirée par le t. du bois/de la soie** she's interested in working with wood/with silk; **t. au tour** lathework

7 *(poste)* job, occupation, post; *(responsabilité)* job; **chercher du** *ou* **un t.** to be job-hunting, to be looking for a job; **trouver un t. à mi-temps/plein temps** to find a part-time/full-time job; **sans t.** unemployed, jobless, out of work; **le suivi des commandes, c'est son t.** following up orders is his/her job; **je n'aurais pas à m'en occuper si tu faisais ton t.** I wouldn't have to worry about it if you did your job (properly)

8 *(dans le système capitaliste)* labour; **le t. et le capital** labour and capital; **cherchons une nouvelle organisation du t.** let's devise a new organization *or* a different distribution of labour

9 *(contrainte exercée → par la chaleur, l'érosion)* action

10 *Physiol (accouchement)* labour; *(activité)* work; **le t. n'est pas commencé/est commencé** the patient has not yet gone/has gone into labour; **réduire le t. du cœur/des reins** to lighten the strain on the heart/on the kidneys

11 *Tech & Phys* work; **l'unité de t. est le joule** the joule is the unit of work; **évaluer le t. d'une machine** to measure the work done by a machine

12 *Psy* work, working through; **t. du deuil** grieving process; **t. du rêve** dreamwork

B. *RÉSULTAT, EFFET* **1** *(écrit)* piece; **il a publié un t. très intéressant sur Proust** he published a very interesting piece on Proust

2 *(transformation → gén)* work; *(modification interne → dans le bois)* warping; *(→ dans le fromage)* maturing; *(→ dans le vin)* working; *Naut* **t. des liaisons** working, labouring

C. *LIEU D'ACTIVITÉ PROFESSIONNELLE* work, workplace; **aller à son t.** to go to (one's) work; **je te téléphone du t.** I'm phoning you from work

▫ **travaux NMPL 1** *(tâches)* work *(UNCOUNT)*, working *(UNCOUNT)*; **gros travaux** heavy work; **petits travaux** odd *or* small jobs; **j'ai fait des petits travaux** I did some odd jobs; **faire des travaux** to have some work carried out *or* done; **ils font des travaux après le pont** there are roadworks after the bridge; **nous sommes en travaux à la maison** we're having some work done on the house, we've got (the) workmen in; **fermé pendant les travaux** *(sur la vitrine d'un magasin)* closed for refurbishment *or* alterations; **travaux** *(sur panneau) Br* roadworks ahead, *Am* roadwork ahead; **attention, travaux** *(sur panneau)* caution, work in progress; **travaux domestiques** *ou* **ménagers** housework; **travaux agricoles** *ou* **des champs** farm *or* agricultural work; *Couture* **travaux d'aiguille** needlework; **travaux d'aménagement** alterations; **travaux d'approche** *Mil* approaches; *Fig* manoeuvring; **tout le monde a remarqué ses travaux d'approche pour obtenir le poste** everyone noticed how he was lining himself up for the job; **travaux d'assainissement** drainage work; **travaux de construction** building work; **travaux d'entretien** maintenance work; *Scol* **travaux d'éveil** learning exercises; **travaux forcés** hard labour; **travaux d'Hercule** *Myth* labours of Hercules; *Fig* herculean tasks; **travaux manuels** *(gén)* arts and crafts; *Scol* handicraft; **travaux d'utilité collective** ≃ YTS; **grands travaux** large-scale public works; **les Travaux publics** civil engineering; **entrer aux Travaux publics** to become a civil engineer

2 *(d'une commission)* work; **nous publierons le résultat de nos travaux** we'll publish our findings; **l'Assemblée nationale reprendra ses travaux le mois prochain** the new session of the National Assembly begins next month

3 *Univ* **travaux scientifiques** research (work); **travaux sociologiques** sociology research; **travaux universitaires** academic research; **travaux dirigés** tutorial, seminar; **travaux pratiques** *(gén)* practical work; *(en laboratoire)* lab work; **on nous l'a donné à faire en travaux pratiques** we had to do it for our practical

4 *Jur* **travaux préparatoires** *(à un projet de loi)* preliminary documents

▫ **au travail ADV 1** *(en activité)* at work, working; **se mettre au t.** to get down *or* to set to work; **se remettre au t.** to start work again, to get down to one's work again; **allez, au t.!** come on, get to work!

2 *(sur le lieu d'activité)* at work, in the workplace; **je vous donne mon numéro au t.** I'll give you my work number

▫ **de travail ADJ 1** *(horaire, séance)* working *(avant n)*; *(vêtement, camarade, permis)* work *(avant n)*; **mes instruments de t.** the tools of my trade; **contrat de t.** employment contract

2 *(d'accouchement → période)* labour *(avant n)*; *(→ salle)* labour *(avant n)*, delivery *(avant n)*

▫ **du travail ADJ** *(accident, sociologie, législation)* industrial; **conflit du t.** employment dispute; **droit du t.** employment law

▫ **en travail ADV** *Physiol* in labour; **alors que j'étais en plein t.** when I was in the middle of labour; **entrer en t.** to go into *or* to start labour

travaillant, -e [travajɑ̃, -ɑ̃t] *Can* **ADJ** hardworking
NM,F hard worker

travaillé, -e [travaje] **ADJ 1** *(de travail)* **jours travaillés** (number of) days worked; **heures travaillées** (number of) hours worked **2** *(élaboré → style)* polished; *(→ façade, meuble)* finely *or* elaborately worked; *(→ fer)* wrought **3** *Sport* **des balles très travaillées** balls with a lot of spin **4** *(préoccupé)* **être t. par qch** to be tormented by sth

travailler [3] [travaje] **VI 1** *(être actif)* to work; **tu as le temps de t. avant dîner** you've got time to do some work *or* to get some work done before dinner; **elle travaille beaucoup trop!** she's working (herself) too hard!; **t. dur** to work hard; **elle travaille vite** she's a fast worker; **le maçon a bien travaillé** the bricklayer made a good job of it; **t. 40 heures par semaine** to work a 40-hour week; **une femme qui travaille** a working woman; **t. à** *ou* **sur une chanson** to work at *or* on a song; **j'y travaille** I'm working on it; **t. sur ordinateur** to work on a computer; **t. comme un bœuf** *ou* **forçat** to slave away, to work like a Trojan; *Vieilli* **t. comme un nègre** to work like a

nigger; *Fam* **t. du chapeau** *ou* **de la touffe** to have a screw loose

2 *(avoir une profession)* to work; **vous travaillez?** do you work?, do you have a job?; **où travailles-tu?** where do you work?; **j'ai arrêté de t. à 55 ans** I stopped work *or* retired at 55; **t. pour payer ses études** to work one's way *or* to put oneself through college/university; **aller t.** to go to work; **elle n'est pas venue t. hier** she didn't come to work yesterday; **t. en free-lance** to do freelance work, to be a freelancer; **t. en indépendant** to be self-employed; **t. en usine** to work in a factory; **t. dans un bureau** to work in an office; **t. dans le privé** to work in the private sector; **elle travaille dans l'informatique** she works with computers; **elle travaille dans la maroquinerie** she's in the leather trade; **les enfants travaillaient dans les mines dès l'âge de six ans** children were put to work in the mines at the age of six; **t. à la télévision** to work for a television company; **t. à la mairie** to work at the town hall; **les marins syndiqués refusent de t. sur les navires de la compagnie** union seamen are refusing to handle the company's vessels; **t. comme chauffeur de taxi** to work as a taxi driver; **t. à son compte** to have one's own business; **t. pour qn/une société** *(être employé par)* to work for sb/a company; **j'ai travaillé pour le roi de Prusse!** I got nothing whatsoever for it!; **t. au ralenti** to go slow

3 *(faire des affaires)* to do (good) business; **entreprise qui travaille bien/mal/à perte** thriving/stagnating/lossmaking firm

4 *(pratiquer son activité → artiste, athlète)* to practise, to train; *(→ boxeur)* to work out, to train; *(→ animaux de cirque)* to go through their performance; **faire t. ses muscles** to make one's muscles work; **faire t. ses jambes** to make one's legs work, to exercise one's legs; **faire t. une machine** to work *or* run a machine; **fais t. ton imagination** use your imagination; **c'est ton imagination qui travaille** your imagination's working overtime, you're imagining things; *Fig* **faire t. son argent** to make one's money work

5 *(changer de forme, de nature → armature, poutre)* to warp; *(→ fondations, vin)* to work; *(→ mur)* to crack; *(→ navire, câble)* to strain

6 *(œuvrer)* **t. à** *(succès)* to work *or* to strive for; **t. à la perte de qn** *ou* **à perdre qn** to try to ruin sb; **t. contre/pour** to work against/for; **le temps travaille contre nous/travaille pour nous** time is working against us/is on our side

VT 1 *(façonner → bois, bronze, glaise)* to work; *Culin (mélange, sauce)* to stir; *Culin* **t. la pâte** to knead *or* to work the dough; *(peintre)* to work the paste; **t. la terre** to work *or Sout* to till the land; **t. une balle** *(au tennis)* to put spin on a ball

2 *(perfectionner → discours, style)* to work on, to polish up, to hone; *(→ concerto, scène)* to work on, to rehearse; *Sport (→ mouvement)* to practise, to work on; *(étudier → matière scolaire)* to work at *or* on, to go over; *(→ texte, auteur)* to study; **cet élève devra t. la trigonométrie** this pupil should work (harder) at trigonometry; **tu ferais mieux d'aller t. ton piano** you'd be better to go and do your piano practice; **travaillez votre revers** work on your backhand

3 *(préoccuper)* to worry; **ça m'a travaillé toute la journée** it's been preying on my mind all day; **ça me travaille de le savoir malheureux** it worries me to know that he's unhappy; **l'idée de la mort le travaillait** (the idea of) death haunted him; **être travaillé par le remords/l'angoisse** to be tormented by remorse/anxiety

4 *(tenter d'influencer)* to work on; **t. les délégués pour les convaincre** to work on *or* to lobby the delegates in order to persuade them

5 *Équitation* to work

6 *Pêche* to work, to play

7 *Boxe* **t. qn au corps** to punch sb around the body

travailleur, -euse [travajœr, -øz] **ADJ** hardworking, industrious

NM,F 1 *(exerçant un métier)* worker; **t. intellectuel** white-collar worker; **t. manuel** manual *or esp Am* blue-collar worker; **les travailleurs** *(gén)* working people, the workers; *(ouvriers)* labour *(UNCOUNT)*; *(prolétariat)* the working classes; **t. agricole** agricultural *or* farm worker; **t. à domicile** outworker, homeworker; **t. immigré** migrant worker; **travailleurs immigrés** immigrant workers *or* labour; **t. indépendant** self-employed person, freelance worker; **t. au noir** = worker in the black economy; **t. occasionnel** casual worker; **les travailleurs pauvres** the working poor; **t. posté** shift worker; **t. saisonnier** seasonal worker; **t. à plein temps/à mi-temps** full-time/part-time worker

2 *Admin* **t. social** social worker; **travailleuse familiale** home help

3 *(personne laborieuse)* hard worker; **c'est un gros t.** he's very hardworking

NM *Orn* quelea; **t. à bec rouge** red-billed quelea

❑ **travailleuse NF** work table *(for needlework)*

travaillisme [travajism] **NM** Labour doctrine *or* philosophy

travailliste [travajist] **ADJ** Labour *(avant n)*; **être t.** to be a member of the Labour Party *or* party; **le parti t.** the Labour Party *or* party

NMF member of the Labour Party; **les travaillistes se sont opposés à cette mesure** Labour opposed the move

travailloter [3] [travajɔte] **VI** *Fam* to potter around

travée [trave] **NF 1** *(rangée de sièges, de personnes assises)* row **2** *Archit & Constr (d'une voûte, d'une nef)* bay; *(solivage)* girder; *(d'un pont)* span **3** *Aviat (d'aile)* rib

travelage [travlaʒ] **NM** *Rail* **1** *(sur toute la voie)* sleepers **2** *(par kilomètre)* number of sleepers per kilometre

traveller's cheque, traveller's check [travlœrʃɛk, travlœrstʃɛk] *(pl* **traveller's cheques** *ou* **checks)** **NM** *Br* traveller's cheque, *Am* traveler's check

travelling [travliŋ] **NM** *Cin* **1** *(déplacement → gén)* tracking; *(→ sur plate-forme)* dollying; **faire un t.** *(caméra, cameraman)* to track; *(sur plate-forme)* to dolly; **t. avant/arrière/latéral** tracking in/out/sideways; *(sur plate-forme)* dollying in/out/sideways **2** *(plate-forme)* dolly, travelling platform **3** *(prise de vue)* tracking shot

travelo [travlo] **NM** *très Fam* drag queen, *Br* tranny; **habillé en t.** in drag

travers [travɛr] **NM 1** *(largeur)* breadth; **sa voiture m'a heurté par le t.** his/her car hit me broadside on

2 *(viande)* **t. (de porc)** spare rib

3 *Naut* **par le t.** abeam, on the beam; **collision par le t.** collision broadside on

4 *(défaut)* fault, shortcoming, failing; **elle tombait dans les mêmes t. que ses prédécesseurs** she displayed the same shortcomings as her predecessors; **un petit t.** a minor fault; **tous les t. de son père** all the shortcomings of his/her father's character; *Arch* **t. (d'esprit)** eccentricity

❑ **à travers PRÉP** through, across; **à t. la fenêtre/le plancher/les barreaux** through the window/the floor/the bars; **à t. la forêt** across *or* through the forest; **à t. la foule** through the crowd; **à t. les âges** throughout the centuries; **à t. les siècles** down (through) the centuries; **on voit à t. sa robe** you can see through her dress; **regarde, on voit à t.** look, you can see through it; **il jeta les livres à t. la chambre** he flung the books across the room; **on entend tout à t. les cloisons** you can hear everything through these partitions; **prendre** *ou* **passer à t. champs** to go through the fields *or* across country; **couper à t. bois** to cut across *or* through the woods; **ils ont prêché à t. tout le pays** they went preaching throughout the length and breadth of the country; *Pêche & Fig* **passer à t. les mailles du filet** to slip through the net; **j'ai réussi à passer à t. le contrôle fiscal** I managed to escape the tax inspection

❑ **au travers ADV elle n'a pas réussi à passer au t.** she didn't manage to escape; **si tu crois passer au t., tu te trompes!** if you think you're going to get away with it you're mistaken

❑ **au travers de PRÉP 1** *(en franchissant)* through; **passer au t. des dangers** to escape danger

2 *(par l'intermédiaire de)* through, by means of; **son idée se comprend mieux au t. de cette comparaison** his/her idea is easier to understand by means of this comparison

❑ **de travers ADJ** crooked; *Naut* **vent de t.** wind on the beam **ADV 1** *(en biais → couper)* askew, aslant; *(→ accrocher)* askew; **la remorque du camion s'est mise de t.** the truck jack-knifed; **votre chapeau est de t.** your hat is (on) crooked; **il a la bouche/le nez de t.** he's got a crooked mouth/nose; *très Fam* **elle a la gueule de t.** her face is all twisted; **j'ai avalé de t.** it went down the wrong way; **j'ai avalé mon pain de t.** the bread went down the wrong way; **marcher de t.** *(ivrogne)* to stagger *or* to totter along **2** *(mal)* **tu fais tout de t.!** you do everything wrong!; **comprendre de t.** to misunderstand; **elle comprend tout de t.!** she gets everything wrong!, she always gets the wrong end of the stick!; **regarder qn de t.** to give sb a funny look; **tout va** *ou* **marche de t.** everything's going wrong; **répondre de t.** to give the wrong answer; **il prend tout ce qu'on lui dit de t.** he takes everything the wrong way; **il a des idées tout(es) de t.** his ideas are all wrong

❑ **en travers ADV 1** *(en largeur)* sideways, across, crosswise; **autobus avec places disposées en t.** bus with seats arranged crosswise; **le wagon s'est mis en t.** the carriage ended up sideways (across the tracks); **la remorque du camion s'est mise en t.** the truck jack-knifed

2 *Naut* abeam

❑ **en travers de PRÉP** across; **le couteau posé en t. de l'assiette** the knife laid crosswise on the plate *or* across the plate; **l'arbre était tombé en t. du chemin** the tree had fallen across the path; *Fig* **s'il se met en t. de mon chemin** *ou* **de ma route** if he stands in my way; *Naut* **en t. (du navire)** athwart (ships)

traversable [travɛrsabl] **ADJ** which can be crossed; **la rivière est t.** *(à gué)* the river is fordable; *(en bateau)* the river can be crossed by boat

traversant [travɛrsɑ̃] **NM** *Suisse* through *Br* flat *or Am* apartment

travers-banc [travɛrbɑ̃] *(pl* **travers-bancs)** **NM** *Mines* crosscut

traverse [travɛrs] **NF 1** *Rail Br* sleeper, *Am* crosstie **2** *Constr (de charpente)* crossbeam, crosspiece; *(entre deux montants)* (cross) strut; *(d'échelle)* rung; **(barre de) t.** crossbar, crosspiece **3** *Aut (du châssis)* cross member; **t. de suspension avant** front suspension cross **4** *Littéraire (obstacle)* setback

traversée [travɛrse] **NF 1** *(d'une route, d'un pont, d'une frontière, d'un cours d'eau, d'une mer)* crossing; *(d'une agglomération, d'un pays)* going *or* getting through, going *or* getting across; **combien de temps dure la t.?** how long is the crossing *or* does it take to get across?; **il a fait la t. du canyon en deltaplane** he flew across the canyon on a hang-glider; **ils ont fait la t. en yacht jusqu'à Cherbourg** they sailed across *or* went over to Cherbourg in a yacht; **faire une bonne t.** to have a good crossing; **faire la t. de Douvres à Calais** to cross from Dover to Calais; **la t. de l'Atlantique en solitaire** crossing the Atlantic single-handed; *Fig* **après une longue t. du désert…** *(politicien)* after a long time spent in the political wilderness…; *(écrivain, artiste)* after a long lean spell *or* period…; *(entreprise, secteur)* after a long period in the doldrums…; **il a fait sa t. du désert** *(politicien)* he spent his period in the political wilderness

2 *(en alpinisme → épreuve)* through route; *(→ passage)* traverse; *Ski* traverse; **faire une t.** to traverse

3 *Rail* crossing point

traversée-jonction [travɛrseʒɔ̃ksjɔ̃] *(pl* **traversées-jonctions)** **NF** *Rail* slip switch; **t. simple/double** single/double slip switch

traverser [3] [travɛrse] **VT 1** *(parcourir → mer, pièce, route)* to go across, to cross, *Sout* to traverse; *(→ pont)* to go over, to go across; *(→ tunnel, forêt)* to go through, to pass through; *(→ ville, région, pays)* to go through, to pass through, to cross; **t. qch à la nage/à cheval/en voiture/en bateau/en avion** to swim/to ride/to drive/to sail/to fly across sth; **t. l'Europe en vélo** to cross *or* go across Europe on a bike, to bike across Europe; **t. une rivière à gué** to ford a river; **t. une pièce en courant/en sautillant** to run/to skip through a room; **c'est une rue difficile à t. aux heures de pointe** it's difficult to get across this street in the rush hour; **aider qn à t. la route** to help sb across the road; **faire t.**

une vieille dame to help an old lady across the road; **tu m'as fait t. Paris pour ça?** you mean you made me come from the other side of Paris for this?; *Fig* **il n'a fait que t. ma vie** he only passed through my life; **t. la foule** to make one's way *or* pass through the crowd

2 *(s'étirer d'un côté à l'autre de → sujet: voie)* to cross, to run across, to go across; *(→ sujet: pont)* to cross, to span; *(→ sujet: tunnel)* to cross, to run under, to go under; **pont/route qui traverse la rivière** bridge/road that crosses *or* goes across the river

3 *(vivre → époque)* to live through, to go through; *(→ difficultés)* to go through; **t. les siècles** to come down through the ages; **son nom a traversé l'histoire** his/her name lived (on) through history; **son divorce lui a fait t. une période difficile** he/she went through a difficult period because of the divorce; **elle traverse une période heureuse** she's having a spell of happiness

4 *(transpercer → sujet: épée)* to run through, to pierce; *(→ sujet: balle)* to go through; *(→ sujet: pluie, froid)* to come through, to go through; **la balle lui traversa le bras** the bullet went through *or* pierced his/her arm; **pour empêcher la pluie de t. la toile** to stop the rain soaking through the canvas; **t. l'esprit** *(idée, doute)* to cross one's mind; **une image me traversa l'esprit** an image passed *or* flashed through my mind; **mon cœur fut traversé d'une joie soudaine** my heart was filled with a sudden feeling of joy

5 *Arch (contrarier → quelqu'un, les intentions de quelqu'un)* to cross, to thwart

traversier, -ère [travɛrsje, -ɛr] ADJ **rue traversière** cross street

NM *Can* ferry

traversin [travɛrsɛ̃] NM **1** *(oreiller)* bolster **2** *Menuis* crosspiece **3** *Naut* crosstree **4** *(de tonneau)* head

traversine [travɛrsin] NF crossbar *(of fence etc)*

travertin [travɛrtɛ̃] NM travertine

travesti, -e [travɛsti] ADJ **1** *(pour tromper)* in disguise, disguised; *(pour s'amuser)* dressed up (in fancy dress)

2 *Théât (comédien)* playing a female part; **rôle t.** = female part played by a man

3 *(vérité)* distorted; *(propos)* twisted, misrepresented

NM **1** *Théât* actor playing a female part; *(dans un cabaret)* female impersonator, drag artist; *(rôle)* female part (for an actor); **numéro** *ou* **spectacle de t.** drag act

2 *(homosexuel)* transvestite

3 *(vêtement → d'homosexuel)* drag *(UNCOUNT)*; *(→ de bal)* fancy dress *(UNCOUNT)*

travestir [32] [travɛstir] VT **1** *(pour une fête)* to dress up; *(comédien)* to cast in a female part; **t. qn en** to dress sb up as

2 *(pensées)* to misrepresent; *(vérité)* to distort; *(propos)* to twist

3 *Littérature (pièce, poème)* to parody, to burlesque; *(auteur)* to parody

▸**se travestir** VPR **1** *(homme)* to dress as a woman, to put on drag; *(femme)* to dress as a man

2 *(pour une fête)* to dress up (in fancy dress), to put fancy dress on; **se t. en punk** to dress up as a punk

travestisme [travɛstism] NM transvestism

travestissement [travɛstismɑ̃] NM **1** *(pour une fête → action)* dressing up, wearing fancy dress; *(→ déguisement)* disguise; *Théât* **rôle à travestissements** quick-change part **2** *Psy* cross-dressing **3** *(de propos, de la vérité)* twisting, distortion, distorting; *(de pensées)* misrepresentation

traviole [travjɔl] **de traviole** *Fam* ADJ *(tableau)* lopsided, skew-whiff; *(dents)* crooked▪, wonky

ADV **1** *(en biais)* **marcher de t.** *(ivrogne)* to be staggering all over the place; **j'écris de t.** my handwriting's all crooked; **tu as mis ton chapeau de t.** you've put your hat on crooked *or Br* skew-whiff

2 *(mal)* **il fait tout de t.** he can't do anything right; **tout va de t.** everything's going wrong▪; **tu comprends toujours tout de t.** you always get hold of the wrong end of the stick

trax [traks] NM *Suisse* bulldozer

trayait *etc voir* **traire**

trayeur, -euse [trɛjœr, -øz] NM,F milker, *Am* milkman, *f* milkwoman

❑ **trayeuse** NF milking machine

trayon [trɛjɔ̃] NM teat

trébuchant, -e [trebyʃɑ̃, -ɑ̃t] ADJ *(ivrogne, allure)* staggering, stumbling; *(diction)* stumbling, halting

trébucher [3] [trebyʃe] VI **1** *(perdre l'équilibre)* to stumble, to stagger; **t. sur une pierre** to stumble on a stone; **t. contre une marche** to trip over a step; **faire t. qn** to trip sb up **2** *(achopper)* to stumble; **t. sur un mot** to stumble over a word **3** *(balance)* to turn

VT *Tech* to weigh

trébuchet [trebyʃɛ] NM **1** *(piège)* bird trap **2** *(petite balance)* assay balance

trécheur [treʃœr] NM *Hér* tressure

tréfilage [trefilaʒ] NM wiredrawing

tréfiler [3] [trefile] VT to wiredraw, to draw *(a wire)*

tréfilerie [trefilri] NF drawing *or* wiredrawing mill

tréfileur, -euse [trefilœr, -øz] NM,F *(ouvrier)* wiredrawer, wire maker; *(industriel)* wire manufacturer

tréflé, -e [trefle] ADJ trefoil *(avant n)*, trefoiled; *Archit* **arc t.** trefoil arch

trèfle [trɛfl] NM **1** *Bot* clover, trefoil; **t. blanc** white *or* Dutch clover; **t. d'eau** bogbean; **t. rouge** red clover; **t. à quatre feuilles** four-leaf clover **2** *Cartes* **du t.** clubs; **la dame de t.** the queen of clubs; **jouer à** *ou* **du t.** to play clubs **3** *Archit & Hér* trefoil **4** *(en travaux publics)* **carrefour en t.** cloverleaf (junction) **5** *(emblème irlandais)* shamrock **6** *Fam (argent)* cash, *Br* dosh, *Am* bucks

tréflière [treflijɛr] NF clover field

tréfoncier, -ère [trefɔ̃sje, -ɛr] ADJ *Jur & Mines* **redevance tréfoncière** royalty

tréfonds [trefɔ̃] NM **1** *Littéraire (partie profonde)* **être ému jusqu'au t. de son être** to be moved to the depths of one's soul; **atteint jusqu'au t.** very deeply hurt; **dans le t. de son âme** in the (innermost) depths of his/her soul; **au t. de mon cœur** in my heart of hearts **2** *Jur* subsoil

tréhalose [trealoz] NM *Chim* trehalose

treillage [trɛjaʒ] NM *Hort* **1** *(assemblage)* trellis *or* lattice (work); *(d'une vigne)* wire trellis **2** *(clôture)* trellis fencing; **t. métallique** *ou* **en fil de fer** wire fencing

treillager [17] [trɛjaʒe] VT *(plante, vigne)* to trellis; *(fenêtre)* to lattice; **fenêtre treillagée** lattice window

treillageur [trɛjaʒœr] NM = maker of trellis and wire fencing

treille [trɛj] NF **1** *(vigne)* climbing vine **2** *(tonnelle)* arbour

treillis [treji] NM **1** *Tex* canvas **2** *Mil* (usual) outfit **3** *(en lattes)* trellis; *(en fer)* wire-mesh

treillisser [3] [trejise] VT to trellis

treize [trɛz] ADJ **1** *(gén)* thirteen; **acheter/vendre des huîtres t. à la douzaine** to buy/to sell thirteen oysters for the price of twelve; **il y en a t. à la douzaine** it's a baker's dozen; *Fig Péj* **des informaticiens, il y en a t. à la douzaine** computer scientists are *Br* ten a penny *or Am* a dime a dozen

2 *(dans des séries)* thirteenth; **page/numéro 13** page/number13

PRON thirteen

NM INV **1** *(gén)* thirteen; **le t. porte malheur** thirteen is unlucky *or* is an unlucky number

2 *(numéro d'ordre)* number thirteen

3 *(chiffre écrit)* thirteen; *voir aussi* **cinq**

treizième [trɛzjɛm] ADJ thirteenth; **t. mois** = extra month's salary paid as an annual bonus

NMF **1** *(personne)* thirteenth **2** *(objet)* thirteenth (one)

NM **1** *(partie)* thirteenth **2** *(étage) Br* thirteenth floor, *Am* fourteenth floor; *voir aussi* **cinquième**

treizièmement [trɛzjɛmmɑ̃] ADV in thirteenth place

treiziste [trɛzist] NM rugby league player

trek [trɛk] NM trekking *(UNCOUNT)*; **faire un t.** to go on a trek; **faire du t. en Inde** to go trekking in India

trekkeur, -euse [trɛkœr, -øz] NM,F trekker

trekking [trɛkiŋ] = **trek**

tréma [trema] NM diaeresis; **e t.** e (with) diaeresis

trémail [tremaj] NM *Pêche* trammel (net)

trématage [trematаʒ] NM *Naut* **1** *(dépassement)* passing **2** **droit de t.** priority of passage *(at a lock)*

trémater [3] [tremate] VT *Naut* to pass, to overtake

trématode [trematɔd] *Zool* NM trematode, *Spéc* member of the Trematoda

❑ **trématodes** NMPL trematodes, *Spéc* Trematoda

tremblaie [trɑ̃blɛ] NF aspen plantation, aspen grove

tremblant, -e [trɑ̃blɑ̃, -ɑ̃t] ADJ **1** *(qui tremble → flamme)* trembling, flickering; *(→ feuilles)* fluttering, quivering; *(→ main, jambes)* shaking, trembling, wobbly; *(→ lèvres)* trembling, quivering; *(→ voix)* tremulous, quavering, shaky; **t. de peur** trembling *or* shaking *or* shuddering with fear; **t. de froid** trembling *or* shivering with cold; **écrire d'une main tremblante** to write shakily; **répondre d'une voix tremblante** to answer tremulously

2 *(peu solide → pont, chaise etc)* shaky, wobbly

❑ **tremblante** NF *Vét* **la tremblante du mouton** scrapie

tremble [trɑ̃bl] NM *Bot* aspen

tremblé, -e [trɑ̃ble] ADJ **1** *(écriture)* shaky, wobbly; *(trait)* wobbly, wavy **2** *Mus* **sons tremblés** quavering **3** *Typ* **filet t.** wavy rule

NM *Typ* wavy rule

tremblement [trɑ̃bləmɑ̃] NM **1** *(d'une personne → de froid)* shiver; *(→ de fièvre)* shivering *(UNCOUNT)*; *(→ de peur)* tremor, shudder; **être pris de tremblements** to start to shake; **son corps était secoué** *ou* **parcouru de tremblements** his/her whole body was shaking *or* trembling

2 *(de la main)* shaking *(UNCOUNT)*, trembling *(UNCOUNT)*, tremor; *(de la voix)* trembling *(UNCOUNT)*, quavering *(UNCOUNT)*, tremor; *(des paupières)* twitch, twitching *(UNCOUNT)*; *(des lèvres)* trembling *(UNCOUNT)*, tremble; **avoir des tremblements** to shake; **avec un t. dans la voix** with a tremor in his/her voice, in a tremulous voice; *Fam* **et tout le t.** the (full) works, *Br* the full monty; *Fam* **l'église, la robe blanche et tout le t.** the church, the white dress, the whole works

3 *(du feuillage)* trembling *(UNCOUNT)*, fluttering *(UNCOUNT)*; *(d'une lueur, d'une flamme)* trembling *(UNCOUNT)*, flickering *(UNCOUNT)*

4 *(d'un édifice)* trembling *(UNCOUNT)*, shaking *(UNCOUNT)*; *(d'une cloison, de vitres)* shaking *(UNCOUNT)*, rattling *(UNCOUNT)*

❑ **tremblement de terre** NM earthquake

trembler [3] [trɑ̃ble] VI **1** *(personne)* **t. de peur** to tremble *or* to shake with fear; **t. de froid** to shiver *or* to tremble with cold; **t. de rage** to tremble *or* to quiver with anger; **t. de tout son corps** *ou* **de tous ses membres** to be shaking *or* to be trembling all over, to be all of a tremble; **t. comme une feuille** to be shaking like a leaf

2 *(main, jambes)* to shake, to tremble; *(voix)* to tremble, to shake, to quaver; *(menton, lèvres)* to tremble, to quiver; *(paupière)* to twitch; **j'ai la main/voix qui tremble** my hand/voice is trembling

3 *(feuillage)* to tremble, to quiver, to flutter; *(flamme, lueur)* to flicker; *(gelée)* to wobble

4 *(édifice, mur)* to shake; *(cloison, vitre)* to shake, to rattle; *(terre)* to quake, to shake; **faire t. les vitres** to make the windows shake *or* rattle; **les trains font t. la maison** the trains are shaking the house; **la terre a tremblé** there's been an earthquake *or* an earth tremor; **il sentait le sol t. sous ses pas** he felt the ground tremble *or* shake beneath him

5 *(avoir peur)* to tremble (with fear); **l'armée faisait t. tout le pays** the whole country lived in fear of the troops; **t. devant qn/qch** to stand in fear of sb/sth, to be terrified of sb/sth; **t. pour (la vie de) qn** to fear for sb *or* sb's life; **t. à la pensée de/que** *(de crainte)* to tremble at the thought of/that; *(d'horreur)* to shiver at the thought of/that; **je tremble de le rencontrer** I tremble *or* I am terrified at the thought of meeting him; **je tremblais de le réveiller** I was terrified of wakening him; **il tremblait d'apprendre la vérité** he feared the truth, he was afraid to learn the truth; **elle**

tremble qu'il ne s'en rende compte she is terrified that he might find out

trembleur [trɑ̃blœr] NM Élec trembler; Tél buzzer

tremblotant, -e [trɑ̃blɔtɑ̃, -ɑ̃t] ADJ (personne) trembling (slightly); (corps) quivering, shivering; (main) shaking, trembling; (voix) tremulous, quavering, shaking; (lueur) flickering, trembling

tremblote [trɑ̃blɔt] NF Fam **avoir la t.** (de peur) to have the jitters; (de froid, à cause de la fièvre) to have the shivers; (à cause d'une maladie) to have the shakes; (vieillard) to be shaky

tremblotement [trɑ̃blɔtmɑ̃] NM 1 (d'une personne → gén) shaking (UNCOUNT); (→ de fièvre, de froid) shivering (UNCOUNT); (→ de peur) shivering (UNCOUNT), shuddering (UNCOUNT); **être pris de tremblotements** to start to shake 2 (d'une main) (faint) shaking or trembling; (d'une voix) slight tremor, slight quavering (UNCOUNT); (d'une lueur) flickering (UNCOUNT)

trembloter [3] [trɑ̃blɔte] VI (gén) to tremble; (vieillard, main) to shake; (voix) to quaver; (lueur) to flicker; (de froid) to shiver; (de peur) to shudder (with fear); **j'ai les mains qui tremblotent** my hands are shaky

trémelle [tremɛl] NF Bot tremella

trémie [tremi] NF 1 (pour les raisins, les betteraves) hopper; (pour le blé) tank; (pour les volailles) feed hopper 2 Constr (pour béton) trémie; **t. d'ascenseur** Br lift or Am elevator shaft; **t. de cheminée** hearth cavity; **t. d'escalier** stairwell 3 (de sel) pyramid salt formation 4 (accès à un tunnel) mouth, well, entrance 5 Belg (tunnel routier) road tunnel

trémière [tremjɛr] voir rose

trémolite [tremɔlit] NF Minér tremolite, grammatite

trémolo [tremɔlo] NM 1 Mus tremolo 2 (d'un orgue) tremolo stop 3 Fig (de la voix) **avec des trémolos dans la voix** with a tremor in his/her voice

trémoussement [tremusmɑ̃] NM jigging up and down (UNCOUNT); (en se dandinant) wiggling (UNCOUNT)

trémousser (se) [3] [tremuse] se trémousser VPR (enfant) to jig up and down; (pour séduire) to wiggle; **elle marchait en se trémoussant** she wiggled her hips as she walked; **arrête de te t. sur ta chaise** stop wriggling round or fidgeting on your chair

trempabilité [trɑ̃pabilite] NF quenchability

trempage [trɑ̃paʒ] NM 1 (de l'orge, de vêtements) soaking 2 Typ damping, wetting

trempe [trɑ̃p] NF 1 (caractère) **une femme de sa t.** a woman with such moral fibre; **son frère est d'une autre t.** his/her brother is cast in a different mould

2 Fam (correction) thrashing, pasting; **recevoir une bonne t.** to get a good thrashing or pasting; **si tu continues, je vais te filer une t.** if you don't stop, you'll get a thrashing

3 (immersion) soaking, steeping; **mettre qch en t.** to put sth in to soak

4 Métal (traitement) quenching; (résultat) temper; **de bonne t.** well-tempered; **acier/atelier de t.** hardening steel/plant; **t. à l'air** air hardening; **t. à l'eau/à l'huile** water/oil quenching; **t. par cémentation, t. de ou en surface** case hardening; **bain de t.** hardening or quenching bath

ADJ Can, Suisse & (régional en France) (personne, vêtements) soaked, drenched; (chaussures, jardin) waterlogged; **t. de sueur** soaked with sweat

trempé, -e [trɑ̃pe] ADJ 1 (personne, vêtements) soaked, drenched; (chaussures, jardin) waterlogged; **t. de sueur** soaked with sweat; **t. de larmes** (mouchoir) tear-stained; **être tout t.** to be soaked or wet through, to be soaking wet; Fam **être t. jusqu'aux os** ou **comme une soupe** to be soaked to the skin, to be wet through

2 (vin, lait) watered-down

3 (énergique) **avoir le caractère bien t.** to be resilient

4 Métal hardened, tempered

5 (verre) toughened

tremper [3] [trɑ̃pe] VT 1 (plonger → chiffon) to dip, to soak; (→ sucre, tartine, pain) to dip, to dunk;

(→ linge, vaisselle) to soak; (→ écrevisses, moules, escargots) to plunge; **t. sa plume dans l'encrier** to dip one's pen in the ink; **t. les mains dans l'eau** to dabble one's hands in the water; **je n'ai fait que t. mes lèvres dans le champagne** I just had a taste or took a sip of the champagne; **j'y ai à peine trempé les lèvres** I've hardly touched it; **je n'ai fait que t. mes pieds dans l'eau** I only dipped my feet in the water; Typ **t. le papier** to wet or damp the paper

2 Vieilli **t. la soupe** (la verser) to pour soup over bread

3 (mouiller) **j'ai trempé ma chemise tellement je transpirais** I sweated so much (that) my shirt got soaked; **tu as trempé la nappe!** you've made the tablecloth (all) wet!; **se faire t. (par la pluie)** to get soaked

4 Métal to quench; (fonte de fer) to chill; **t. par induction** to induction harden

5 Littéraire (affermir → personnalité, caractère) to steel, to toughen, to harden; **cela va lui t. le caractère** this'll toughen him/her up

VI (vêtement, vaisselle, lentilles) to soak; **mettre du linge à t.** to put the washing to soak; **j'ai fait t. les draps** I put the sheets in to soak; **faire t. des haricots** to soak beans, to leave beans to soak; **les clichés trempent dans un bain spécial** the photographs (are left to) soak in a special solution; **attention, tes manches trempent dans la soupe** careful, you've got your sleeves in the soup

□ **tremper dans** VT IND Fam (être impliqué dans) to be mixed up in; **elle a trempé dans une sordide affaire** she was involved in a sordid affair■

▸se tremper VPR 1 (se baigner) to have a quick dip

2 (baigner) to soak; **elle s'est trempé les pieds dans une bassine d'eau** she soaked her feet in a bowl of water

3 (mouiller) **il s'est trempé les pieds en marchant dans l'eau** he stepped into a puddle and got his feet wet

trempette [trɑ̃pɛt] NF 1 Fam **faire t.** (se baigner) to have a (quick) dip; **les enfants font t. dans le bassin** the children are splashing about in the pool 2 **faire t.** (tremper son pain etc) to dip or dunk one's bread/etc; Can (dans du sirop d'érable) to dip one's bread in maple syrup

trempeur [trɑ̃pœr] NM 1 Métal temperer, hardener 2 Typ wetter

tremplin [trɑ̃plɛ̃] NM 1 Sport (de gymnastique) springboard; (de plongeon) diving board, springboard; (de ski nautique, de planche à roulettes) ramp; **t. de ski** ski jump; (de ski nautique) ski ramp

2 Fig (impulsion initiale) springboard, stepping stone, launching pad; **servir de t. à qn** to be a springboard for sb; **cet opéra a servi de t. à sa carrière** the opera was a springboard for his/her career or launched his/her career

trémulant, -e [tremylɑ̃, -ɑ̃t] ADJ Littéraire tremulant, tremulous

trémulation [tremylasjɔ̃] NF Méd tremor

trémuler [3] [tremyle] Littéraire VI to tremble

VT **t. les doigts** to twiddle one's fingers

trenail [trɛnaj] NM Rail trenail, treenail

trench-coat [trɛnʃkot] (pl trench-coats), **trench** [trɛnʃ] (pl trenchs) NM trench coat

trend [trɛnd] NM Écon trend

trentain [trɑ̃tɛ̃] NM Rel **t. (grégorien)** trental

trentaine [trɑ̃tɛn] NF 1 (quantité) **une t.** around or about thirty, thirty or so; **une t. de voitures** around or about thirty cars; **elle a une t. d'années** she's around or about thirty (years old) 2 (âge) **avoir la t.** to be around or about thirty; **quand on arrive à ou atteint la t.** when you hit thirty

Trente [trɑ̃t] NM Trent, Trento

trente [trɑ̃t] ADJ 1 (gén) thirty 2 (dans des séries) thirtieth; **page/numéro t.** page/number thirty 3 (au tennis) **t. à** thirty all

PRON thirty

NM INV 1 (gén) thirty 2 (numéro d'ordre) number thirty 3 (chiffre écrit) thirty; voir aussi **cinquante**

'37°2 le matin' Djian, Beineix 'Betty Blue'

LES TRENTE-CINQ HEURES

In an attempt to create new jobs and reduce the relatively high unemployment rate in France, the socialist government of Prime Minister Lionel Jospin (1997–2002) decided to phase in a reduction of the average working week from 39 to 35 hours (see entry "RTT"). There was a great deal of flexibility in the implementation of the law and many exemptions were allowed, especially for small and medium-sized companies. In many cases, the shift to the 35-hour week was negotiated at company level between management and trade unions. Initially, employers were very hostile to the idea but the fact that by way of compensation their national insurance contributions were significantly reduced brought most of them round. Overall, results have been mixed, with not as many new jobs being created as first expected. Some people feel the law has made their situation worse, as they have to do the same amount of work in fewer hours, while many others enjoy the extra leisure time. The centre-right government elected in 2002 has been moving towards introducing even more flexibility to the law.

trente-et-quarante [trɑ̃tekarɑ̃t] NM INV (jeu) (game of) trente-et-quarante

trente-et-un [trɑ̃teœ̃] ADJ thirty-one

NM INV thirty-one; Fam **être sur son t.** to be dressed up to the nines; **se mettre sur son t.** to get all dressed up

trentenaire [trɑ̃tnɛr] ADJ 1 (qui dure trente ans) thirty-year (avant n) 2 (personne) in his/her thirties; (bâtiment) over thirty years old

NMF person in his/her thirties, thirtysomething

trente-six [trɑ̃tsis] ADJ 1 (gén) thirty-six

2 Fam (pour exprimer la multitude) umpteen, dozens of; **il y en a pas t.** there aren't that many of them; **des raisons, je pourrais t'en citer t.** I could give you umpteen reasons; **il y a pas t. solutions** there's no getting away from it, there are no two ways about it; **j'ai t. mille choses à faire** I've a hundred and one things to do; **voir t. chandelles** to see stars; Can Fam **faire t. métiers** to be a Jack-of-all-trades

NM INV thirty-six; Fam **tous les t. du mois** once in a blue moon; Can Fam **être sur son t.** to be dressed up to the nines; Fam **se mettre sur son t.** to get all dressed up■

trente-sixième [trɑ̃tsizjɛm] ADJ 1 (gén) thirty-sixth 2 Fam (locution) **être dans le t. dessous** to be in a tight spot

trente-sous [trɑ̃tsu] NM INV Can quarter, twenty-five-cent piece

trentième [trɑ̃tjɛm] ADJ thirtieth

NMF 1 (personne) thirtieth 2 (objet) thirtieth (one)

NM 1 (partie) thirtieth 2 (étage) Br thirtieth floor, Am thirty-first floor; voir aussi **cinquième**

trentièmement [trɑ̃tjɛmmɑ̃] ADV in thirtieth place

Trentin-Haut-Adige [trɑ̃tɛ̃notadiʒ] NM **le T.** Trentino-Alto Adige

trépan [trepɑ̃] NM 1 Méd trephine 2 Pétr & Tech trepan

trépanation [trepanasjɔ̃] NF Méd & Tech trephination, trepanning

trépané, -e [trepane] NM,F Méd trephined or trepanned patient

trépaner [3] [trepane] VT Méd & Tech to trephine, to trepan

trépang [trepɑ̃] NM Écon trend = **tripang**

trépas [trepa] NM Littéraire **le t.** death

trépassé, -e [trepase] NM,F Littéraire deceased; **les trépassés** the departed, Sout the dead 2 Rel **le jour** ou **la fête des Trépassés** All Souls' Day

trépasser [3] [trepase] VI Littéraire to depart this life, Euph to pass away

tréphine [trefin] NF Méd trephine

tréphone [trefɔn] NF Biol trephone

trépidant, -e [trepidɑ̃, -ɑ̃t] ADJ 1 (animé → époque) frantic, hectic; (→ vie) hectic; (→ danse, rythme) wild, frenzied 2 (véhicule) vibrating, throbbing

trépidation [trepidasjɔ̃] NF 1 (d'un moteur) vibration 2 Méd tremor 3 (agitation) bustle, whirl

trépider [3] [trepide] VI (moteur) to vibrate, to throb; (surface) to vibrate

trépied [trepje] NM **1** *(support → d'appareil photo)* tripod; *(→ pour cuisiner)* trivet **2** *(tabouret)* three-legged stool

trépignement [trepiɲmɑ̃] NM stamping (of feet); **dès qu'on lui refuse quelque chose, ce sont des trépignements** when he/she can't get his/her own way, he/she throws a tantrum

trépigner [3] [trepiɲe] VI to stamp one's feet; **t. de colère** to stamp one's feet in anger; **t. d'impatience** to be hopping up and down with impatience; *Fig* **il trépignait à l'idée de partir** he was itching to start

trépointe [trepwɛ̃t] NF *(de chaussure)* welt

tréponématose [treponematoz] NF *Méd* treponematosis

tréponème [treponɛm] NM *Biol* treponema; **t. pâle** Treponema pallidum

très [trɛ] ADV **1** *(avec un adjectif, un adverbe, une préposition)* very; **c'est t. bon** it's very good; **c'est t. aimable à vous** that's very kind of you; **il est t. connu** he is very well known; **elle est t. estimée** she is greatly *or* highly respected; **elle est t. aimée** she is much *or* greatly liked; **il est t. snob** he's a real snob; **la soirée fut t. réussie** the evening was very successful *or* a huge success; **être d'une intelligence t. supérieure à la moyenne** to be of much higher than average intelligence; **une entreprise t. compétitive** a highly competitive company; **un poste t. convoité** a much *or* highly coveted job; **un auteur t. lu** a very popular author; **c'est t. à la mode** it's very fashionable *or* very much in fashion; **c'est t. très douloureux/cher** it's extremely painful/expensive; **un produit t. peu vendu** a product for which there is very little demand; **t. peu utilisé** rarely used; **je ne l'ai pas vu depuis t. longtemps** I haven't seen him for ages *or* for a very long time; **il travaille t. bien** he works very well; **t. bien payé** very well *or* highly paid; **tu comprends ce que je veux dire? – non, pas t. bien** do you see what I mean? – not very well *or* not really; **t. bien, je m'en vais** all right (then) *or* very well (then) *or* OK (then), I'm going; **vivre t. au-dessus de ses moyens** to live way beyond one's means; **prendre qch t. au sérieux** to take sth very seriously; **il est t. enfant** he's such a child; **elle est t. femme** she is very feminine *or* very much a woman; **nous sommes tous t. famille** we're all very much into family life; **ce sont des gens t. comme il faut** they are very *or* highly respectable people; **faire des heures supplémentaires? t. peu pour moi!** me, do overtime? not likely!

2 *(dans des locutions verbales)* **avoir t. peur/faim** to be very frightened/hungry; **il fait t. froid** it's very cold, it's freezing; **avoir t. envie de faire qch** to really feel like doing sth; **j'ai t. envie de sortir** I really feel like going out, I would really like to go out, I would love to go out; **j'ai t. envie de lui dire ses quatre vérités** I very much want to tell him/her a few home truths

3 *(employé seul, en réponse)* very; **fatigué? – oui, t.** tired? – yes, very; **il y a longtemps qu'il est parti? – non, pas t.** has he been gone long? – no, not very

trésaille [trezaj] NF crosspiece, upper rail

trescheur [treʃœr] NM *Hér* tressure

Très-Haut [treo] NM **le T.** God, the Almighty

trésor [trezɔr] NM **1** *(objets précieux, argent)* treasure *(UNCOUNT)*; **trouver un t.** to find treasure; *Fig* **elle a dû dépenser des trésors pour l'acheter** it must have cost her a fortune (to buy); **t. de guerre** war chest

2 *Jur* treasure trove

3 *(chose précieuse)* treasure; **son grenier est plein de trésors** his/her attic is full of treasures *or* is a real treasure-house; **les trésors du Prado** the treasures of the Prado

4 *(d'une cathédrale)* (collection of) relics and ornaments; *(lieu)* treasure-house, treasury

5 *Archéol (d'un sanctuaire)* treasure, treasury

6 *(gén pl) (grande quantité)* **ce livre est un t. d'informations** this book is a treasure trove *or* a mine of information, this book contains a wealth of information; **des trésors de bienfaits/de patience** a wealth of good/patience

7 *Fam (terme d'affection)* **mon (petit) t.** my treasure *or* darling *or* pet; **tu es un t.** you're a treasure *or* a darling *or* an angel

8 *Fin* **le T. (public)** *(service) Br* ≃ the Treasury, *Am* ≃ the Treasury Department; *(moyens financiers)* state finances

9 *Hist* exchequer

trésorerie [trezɔrri] NF **1** *(argent → gén)* treasury, finances; *(→ d'une entreprise)* liquid assets; *(→ d'une personne)* budget; **ses problèmes de t.** his/her cash (flow) problems; **t. nette** net cash position

2 *(gestion)* accounts

3 *(bureaux → gouvernementaux)* public revenue office; *(→ privés)* accounts department; *Fin* **T. générale** paymaster's office

4 *(fonction → gén)* treasurership; *(→ d'un trésorier-payeur)* paymastership

trésorier, -ère [trezɔrje, -ɛr] NM,F **1** *Admin* treasurer; **commis t.** treasury clerk; **t. de banque** bank treasurer **2** *Mil* paymaster

trésorier-payeur [trezɔrjepɛjœr] *(pl* **trésoriers-payeurs**) NM **t. général** paymaster *(for a "département" or "région")*

tressage [trɛsaʒ] NM *(de rotin)* weaving; *(de cheveux)* plaiting, braiding

tressaillement [tresajmɑ̃] NM *(de joie)* thrill; *(de plaisir)* quiver; *(de peur)* shudder, quiver, quivering *(UNCOUNT)*; *(de surprise)* start, jump; *(de douleur)* wince

tressaillir [47] [tresajir] VI **1** *(personne, animal → de surprise, de peur)* to (give a) start; *(→ de douleur)* to flinch, to wince; *(→ de plaisir)* to quiver; **t. de joie** to thrill **2** *Littéraire (feuillage)* **un souffle soudain vint faire t. les peupliers** a sudden breeze set the leaves of the poplars rustling

tressautement [tresotmɑ̃] NM **1** *(sursaut)* start, jump **2** *(secousse)* jolting *(UNCOUNT)*; **les tressautements du vieux tramway** the jolting *or Br* juddering of the old tram

tressauter [3] [tresote] VI **1** *(sursauter)* to jump, to start; **la sonnette m'a fait t.** the bell made me jump *or* startled me **2** *(être cahoté → passager)* to be tossed about; **les cahots du chemin faisaient t. les voyageurs** the passengers were thrown *or* jolted around by the bumps in the road

tresse [trɛs] NF **1** *(de cheveux, de fils)* plait, *esp Am* braid; **se faire des tresses** to plait *or esp Am* braid one's hair; **porter des tresses** to have (one's hair in) plaits; **des cheveux noués dans une t.** hair done up in a plait **2** *Archit* strapwork *(UNCOUNT)* **3** *Élec* braid *(UNCOUNT)*, braiding *(UNCOUNT)*; **fil conducteur sous t.** braided conductor wire **4** *Naut* vinnet **5** *Suisse (pain)* plaited loaf

tresser [4] [trese] VT *(cheveux, rubans, fils)* to plait, to braid; *(paille, osier)* to plait; *(corbeille)* to weave; *(câble)* to twist; *(guirlande)* to wreathe; *Fig* **t. des couronnes à qn** to praise sb to the skies; **je ne veux pas lui t. des couronnes, mais...** I don't want to praise him/her unduly, but...

tresseur, -euse [trɛsœr, -øz] NM,F *(de corbeilles)* weaver

tréteau, -x [treto] NM trestle; **table à tréteaux** trestle table; *Fig Vieilli* **monter sur les tréteaux** to become an actor, to tread the boards

treuil [trœj] NM winch, windlass; *(d'ascenseur)* winding gear *(UNCOUNT)*; **t. à chaîne** chain hoist

treuillage [trœjaʒ] NM winching

treuiller [5] [trœje] VT to winch; **t. une charge** *(vers le haut)* to winch up a load; *(vers le bas)* to winch down a load

trêve [trɛv] NF **1** *Mil* truce; *Hist* **la t. de Dieu** the Truce of God

2 *Fig (repos)* rest, break; **mes rhumatismes ne me laissent aucune t.** my rheumatism gives me no respite; **elle s'est accordée une t. dans la rédaction de sa thèse** she took a break from writing her thesis; **faire t. à** to suspend; **la t. des confiseurs** = the lull in political activities between Christmas and the New Year in France; **c'est la t. des confiseurs** it's the seasonal truce in political activity

❑ **sans trêve** ADV unceasingly, without respite, never-endingly

❑ **trêve de** ADJ enough; **t. de bavardages!** we must stop chatting!, enough of this chatting!; **allez, t. de plaisanteries, où est la clef?** come on, stop messing about, where's the key?

Trèves [trɛv] NM Trier

trévire [trevir] NF parbuckle

trévirer [3] [trevire] VT to parbuckle

trévise [treviz] NF radicchio lettuce

tri [tri] NM **1** *(de fiches)* sorting out, sorting, classifying; *(de renseignements)* sorting out, selecting; *(de candidats)* selection; *(de propositions)* screening; **faire le t. dans qch** to sort sth out; **faire du t. dans ses vêtements/papiers** to sort through *or* go through one's clothes/papers; **il faut faire le t. dans ce qu'il dit** you have to sift out the truth in what he says; **il va falloir faire le t.** we'll have to sort through them; **t. sélectif** sorting of *Br* rubbish *or Am* garbage *(for recycling purposes)*

2 *(de lettres)* sorting; **t. postal** mail sorting; **bureau de t.** *(de la Poste)* sorting office; **le (service du) t.** *(d'une entreprise)* the mail room

3 *Ordinat* sort; **effectuer un t.** to do a sort; **t. alphabétique** alphabetic sort, alpha sort; **t. en ordre croissant/décroissant** ascending/reverse *or* descending sort

4 *Mktg* **t. croisé** *(de statistiques)* cross tabulation; **t. à plat** *(de statistiques)* simple tabulation

triacide [triasid] NM *Chim* triacid

triade [trijad] NF *(groupe de trois)* triad

triadique [triadik] ADJ triadic

triage [trijaʒ] NM **1** *(pour répartir)* sorting (out); **t. à la main** hand sorting; **nous devons faire un t. à la main** we have to sort them by hand **2** *(pour choisir)* grading, selecting, sifting **3** *Mines* picking *(UNCOUNT)* **4** *(en papeterie)* assorting, sorting **5** *Rail* marshalling *(UNCOUNT)*

trial, -als [trijal] NM (motorbike) trial *or* trials
NF trial motorbike

trialcool [trialkɔl] NM *Chim* trialcohol

trialle [trijal] NF *Zool* donax (clam)

triandrie [triɑ̃dri] NF *Bot* Triandria

triangle [trijɑ̃gl] NM **1** *Géom* triangle; **triangles semblables** similar triangles

2 *Géog* **le t. des Bermudes** the Bermuda Triangle; **le T. d'or** the Golden Triangle

3 *Mus* triangle

4 *Aut* **t. de présignalisation** hazard warning triangle; **t. de sécurité** warning triangle

5 *Naut (pavillon)* triangular flag

6 *Suisse (chasse-neige)* snowplough

❑ **en triangle** ADV in a triangle; **le jardin se termine en t.** the garden ends in a triangle

triangulaire [trijɑ̃gylɛr] ADJ **1** *(gén) & Géom* triangular; *(tissu, salle)* triangular, triangular-shaped **2** *(à trois éléments)* triangular; **élection t.** three-cornered election; *Hist* **commerce t.** triangular trade
NF *Pol* three-cornered contest *or* fight

triangulation [trijɑ̃gylasjɔ̃] NF triangulation, triangulating

trianguler [3] [trijɑ̃gyle] VT *(en arpentage)* to triangulate

Trianon [trijanɔ̃] NM = the name of two châteaux in the grounds of the Palace of Versailles, "le Grand Trianon" (1687) and "le Petit Trianon" (1766), later the favourite residence of Marie-Antoinette

trias [trijas] NM *Géol* **le t.** the Triassic *or* Trias

triasique [trijazik] ADJ *Géol* Triassic

triathlète [trijatlɛt] NMF triathlete

triathlon [trijatlɔ̃] NM triathlon

triathlonien, -enne [trijatlɔnjɛ̃, -ɛn] NM,F triathlete

triatome [triatɔm] NM *Entom* assassin bug

triatomique [triatɔmik] ADJ *Chim* triatomic

tribade [tribad] NF *Littéraire* tribade

tribadisme [tribadism] NM *Littéraire* tribadism

tribal, -e, -aux *ou* **als, -ales** [tribal, -o] ADJ tribal

tribalisme [tribalism] NM tribalism

triballe [tribal] NF tilt hammer

triballer [3] [tribale] VT *(peaux)* to stock

tri-bande [tribɑ̃d] ADJ *Tél* tri-band

tribart [tribar] NM yoke, poke *(attached to animal's neck to prevent it from going through fences)*

triboélectricité [tribɔelɛktrisite] NF *Phys* triboelectricity

triboélectrique [tribɔelɛktrik] ADJ *Phys* triboelectric

tribologie [tribɔlɔʒi] NF *Tech* tribology

triboluminescence [tribɔlyminɛsɑ̃s] NF *Phys* triboluminescence

tribométrie [tribɔmetri] NF *Phys* tribometry

tribord [tribɔr] NM *Naut* starboard; **à t.** (to) starboard, on the starboard side

tribordais [tribɔrdɛ] NM *Naut* member of the starboard watch

triboulet [tribulɛ] NM *(de bijoutier)* ring gauge

tribu [triby] NF **1** *Antiq & (en anthropologie)* tribe **2** *Fam (groupe nombreux)* **toute la t.** *(famille)* the entire clan; *(amis)* the (whole) crowd *or* gang **3** *(d'animaux)* tribe, swarm

tribulations [tribylasjɔ̃] NFPL (trials and) tribulations; **après toutes ces t.** after all these trials and tribulations; **tu n'es pas au bout de tes t.!** you're not out of the woods yet!

tribun [tribœ̃] NM **1** *(orateur)* eloquent (public) speaker **2** *Antiq* tribune

❑ **de tribun** ADJ *(éloquence)* spellbinding; **il a un talent de t.** he's very good at public speaking

tribunal, -aux [tribynal, -o] NM **1** *Jur (édifice)* court, courthouse; *(magistrats)* court, bench; **en plein t.** in open court; **porter une affaire devant le t.** *ou* **les tribunaux** to take a matter to court *or* before the Courts; **comparaître devant le t.** to appear before the Court; **traîner qn devant les tribunaux** to take sb to court; **prendre la voie des tribunaux** to take legal action, to go to court; **nous irons au t. s'il le faut** we'll go as far as the Courts if necessary; **t. administratif** = court which deals with internal French civil service matters; **t. des affaires de sécurité sociale** social-security appeal tribunal; **t. arbitral** court of arbitration; **t. de commerce** *(pour litiges)* commercial court; *(pour liquidations)* bankruptcy court; **T. des conflits** = tribunal which settles jurisdictional disputes between the civil and administrative courts; **t. correctionnel** criminal court; **t. de droit commun** court of general jurisdiction; **t. pour enfants** juvenile court; **t. d'exception** special court *(with limited jurisdiction)*; **t. de grande instance** = court of first instance in civil and criminal matters; **t. d'instance** = lowest-level court in French legal system, having limited jurisdiction; **t. paritaire** = court comprising a mixture of judicial and lay officers; **t. paritaire des baux ruraux** agricultural land tribunal; **t. de police** = name given to a "tribunal d'instance" when a criminal case is being heard; *UE* **T. de première instance** European Court of First Instance; **t. prévôtal** provostal court; **t. révolutionnaire** revolutionary tribunal

2 *Mil* **t. aux armées** military court, court martial; **t. militaire** court martial; **traduire qn devant le t. militaire** to court-martial sb; **passer devant le t. militaire** to be court-martialled; **t. territorial des forces armées** = military tribunal set up during wartime

3 *Fig Littéraire* tribunal; **le t. de l'histoire jugera** History will judge

tribunat [tribyna] NM **1** *Antiq* tribunate, tribuneship **2** *Hist (en France)* **le T.** the Tribunate *(1800–1807)*

tribune [tribyn] NF **1** *(places → assises)* grandstand, stand; *(→ debout dans un stade de football) Br* terraces, *Am* bleachers; **t. d'honneur** VIP stand; **t. des journalistes** commentary box; **t. officielle** VIP stand; **t. de la presse** press gallery; **t. du public** public gallery

2 *(estrade)* rostrum, platform, *Sout* tribune; **monter à la t.** *(gén)* to go to the rostrum; *(au Parlement)* to address the House

3 *(lieu de discussions)* forum; **notre émission offre une t. aux écologistes** our programme provides a platform for the Green Party; **à la t. de ce soir, le racisme** racism is the subject of our discussion tonight

4 *Journ* **t. libre** *(colonne)* opinion column; *(page)* opinions page; **s'exprimer dans les tribunes d'une émission de radio** to put one's point of view in an open radio programme; *Presse* **La T. de Genève** = Swiss French-language daily newspaper

5 *Archit* gallery, tribune

6 *Mus* **t. d'orgues** organ loft

tribunitien, -enne [tribynisjɛ̃, -ɛn] ADJ *Antiq* tribunitial, tribunitian

tribut [triby] NM **1** *Littéraire* tribute; **payer t.** to pay tribute; **payer t. à la nature** to pay one's debt to nature; **le pays a payé un lourd t. à la guerre** the war cost the country dearly; **la population a payé un lourd t. à l'épidémie** the epidemic took a heavy toll of the population **2** *Hist* tribute

tributaire [tribytɛr] ADJ **1** *(dépendant)* **t. de** reliant *or* dependent on; **mon invalidité m'empêchant de sortir, je suis t. du téléphone** I depend on *or* I rely heavily on the telephone, as my disability keeps me at home **2** *Géog* **être t. de** to be a tributary of, to flow into **3** *Hist* tributary

NM *Géog* tributary

tric [trik] = **trick**

tricalcique [trikalsik] ADJ *Chim* tricalcic, tricalcium *(avant n)*

tricard, -e [trikar, -ard] *Fam Arg crime* ADJ = prohibited from entering a certain area

NM,F = ex-convict prohibited from entering a certain area

-trice SUFF *voir* **-teur**

tricennal, -e, -aux, -ales [trisenal, -o] ADJ thirty-year-long *(avant n)*, *Sout* tricennial

tricentenaire [trisɑ̃tnɛr] ADJ three-hundred-year-old *(avant n)*

NM tercentenary

tricéphale [trisefal] ADJ three-headed

triceps [trisɛps] NM *Anat* triceps (muscle); **t. brachial** triceps brachii

tricératops [triseratɔps] NM triceratops

triche [triʃ] NF *Fam* **c'est le roi de la t.** he's a total cheat; **c'est de la t.!** that's cheating!

tricher [3] [triʃe] VI to cheat; **il triche** he's cheating, he's not playing by the rules; **t. aux cartes/à un examen** to cheat at cards/in an exam; **t. sur** to cheat on; **t. sur le poids** to give short weight; **t. sur les prix** to overcharge; **il triche sur son âge** he lies about his age; **t. avec** to play around with; **on ne peut pas t. avec la maladie** you can't fool around with illness; **je n'aime pas t. avec les gens** I don't like being dishonest with people; **je n'avais plus assez de tissu alors j'ai triché un peu** I didn't have enough material left so I cheated a bit

tricherie [triʃri] NF cheating *(UNCOUNT)*; **j'en ai assez de toutes tes tricheries!** I've had enough of your cheating!

tricheur, -euse [triʃœr, -øz] NM,F *(au jeu, aux examens, en amour)* cheat; *(en affaires)* trickster, con man

'Le Tricheur à l'as de carreaux' *La Tour* 'The Cheat with the Ace of Diamonds'

trichiasis [trikjazis] NM *Méd* trichiasis

trichine [trikin] NF *Zool* trichinella, trichina

trichiné, -e [trikine] ADJ *Méd* trichinated, trichinous

trichineux, -euse [trikinø, -øz] ADJ *Méd* trichinous

trichinose [trikinoz] NF *Méd* trichinosis

trichlo [triklo] NM *Fam (abrév* **trichloréthylène***)* trichlorethylene▪ *(used as a drug)*

trichloréthylène [triklɔretilɛn] NM *Chim* trichlorethylene, trichloroethylene

trichocéphale [trikɔsefal] NM *Zool* whipworm, *Spéc* trichocephalus

trichogramme [trikɔgram] *Entom* NM member of the Trichogrammidae

❑ **trichogrammes** NMPL Trichogrammidae

tricholome [trikɔlom] NM *Bot* tricholoma; **t. de la Saint-Georges** St George's mushroom

trichoma [trikɔma], **trichome** [trikom] NM *Méd* plica, trichoma

trichomonas [trikɔmɔnas] NM *Zool* trichomonad, Trichomonas

trichomonase [trikɔmɔnaz], **trichomonose** [trikɔmɔnoz] NF *Méd* trichomoniasis

trichophyton [trikɔfitɔ̃] NM *Biol* trichophyte, trichophyton

trichoptère [trikɔptɛr] *Entom* NM caddis fly, *Spéc* trichopteran, member of the Trichoptera order

❑ **trichoptères** NMPL caddis flies, *Spéc* trichopterans, Trichoptera

trichose [trikoz] NF *Méd* trichosis

trichrome [trikrom] ADJ three-colour, *Spéc* trichromatic

trichromie [trikromi] NF **1** *Typ* three-colour printing, *Spéc* trichromatism **2** *Tex* trichrome printing **3** *TV* three-colour process

trick [trik] NM *(au bridge)* odd trick

trickster [trikstœr] NM *Myth* trickster

triclinique [triklinik] ADJ *Minér* triclinic; **système t.** triclinic *or* anorthic system

triclinium [triklinjɔm] NM *Antiq* triclinium

tricoises [trikwaz] NFPL **1** *(de maréchal-ferrant)* (blacksmith's) pincers **2** *(de pompier)* (fireman's) wrench

tricolore [trikɔlɔr] ADJ **1** *(à trois couleurs)* three-coloured **2** *(aux couleurs françaises)* red, white and blue **3** *(français)* French; **l'équipe t.** the French team

NMF French player; **les tricolores** the French (team)

tricône [trikon] NM *Pétr* tricone

tricorne [trikɔrn] NM tricorn, cocked hat

tricorps [trikɔr] *Aut* ADJ notchback *(avant n)*

NM notchback vehicle

tricot [triko] NM **1** *(technique)* knitting *(UNCOUNT)*; **apprendre le t.** to learn to knit; **faire du t.** to knit, to do some knitting; **commencer/finir un t.** to cast on/off; **t. plat** flat knitting; **t. rond** circular knitting

2 *(étoffe)* knitted *or* worsted fabric

3 *(ouvrage)* knitting *(UNCOUNT)*; *Com* knitwear *(UNCOUNT)*; **j'ai commencé un t.** I've started to knit something; **où ai-je mis mon t.?** where did I put my knitting?

4 *(vêtement → gén)* knitted garment; *(→ pull)* pullover, sweater; *(→ gilet)* cardigan; **t. de corps** *ou* **de peau** *Br* vest, *Am* undershirt

❑ **en tricot** ADJ *(cravate, bonnet)* knitted

tricotage [trikɔtaʒ] NM knitting

tricoter [3] [trikɔte] VT **1** *(laine, maille)* to knit; *(vêtement)* to knit (up); **je lui tricote des gants** I'm knitting him/her some gloves; **tricotez une maille à l'endroit, une maille à l'envers** knit one, purl one; **tricoté (à la) main** hand-knitted; *Can Fig* **connaître qn comme si on l'avait tricoté** to know sb inside out

2 *Fig (mettre en forme, élaborer)* to work out; **l'auteur a tricoté une intrigue très intéressante** the author has woven a very interesting plot

VI **1** *Tex* to knit; **apprendre à t.** to learn to knit; **t. à la machine/main** to machine-/hand-knit

2 *Fam (s'activer → coureur)* to scramble▪; *(→ danseur, cheval)* to prance▪; *(→ cycliste)* to pedal hard▪; **t. des jambes** *ou* **des gambettes** *(marcher vite)* to leg it, to belt along; *(pédaler)* to pedal like mad, to go like the clappers

3 *Can Sport (au hockey)* = to control the puck skilfully with one's hockey stick in order to outplay an opponent

❑ **à tricoter** ADJ *(aiguille, laine, machine)* knitting *(avant n)*

tricoteur, -euse [trikɔtœr, -øz] NM,F knitter

NM knitting worker

❑ **tricoteuse** NF **1** *(machine à tricoter)* knitting machine **2** *(table à ouvrage)* small worktable

trictrac [triktrak] NM *(jeu)* tric-trac, trick-track *(game similar to backgammon)*; *(partie)* game of tric-trac *or* trick-track; *(damier)* tric-trac *or* trick-track board

tricuspide [trikyspid] ADJ *Anat* tricuspid

tricycle [trisikl] NM tricycle; **faire du t.** to go tricycling

ADJ *Aviat* tricycle *(avant n)*

tricyclique [trisiklik] ADJ tricyclic

tridacne [tridakn] NM *Zool* giant clam

tridactyle [tridaktil] ADJ tridactyl, tridactylous

NM *Orn* button quail

trident [tridɑ̃] NM **1** *Pêche* three-pronged fish spear, trident **2** *Agr* three-pronged (pitch)fork **3** *Géom & Myth* trident

tridenté, -e [tridɑ̃te] ADJ three-pronged, *Spéc* tridentate, tridental

tridi [tridi] NM *Hist* = third day of a ten-day period in the Republican calendar

tridimensionnel, -elle [tridimɑ̃sjɔnɛl] ADJ *(gén) & Chim* three-dimensional

trièdre [triɛdr] *Géom* ADJ trihedral

NM trihedron, trihedral

triennal, -e, -aux, -ales [trijenal, -o] ADJ **1** *(ayant lieu tous les trois ans)* three-yearly, *Sout* triennial **2** *(qui dure trois ans)* three-year *(avant n)*, three-year-long *(avant n)*, *Sout* triennial; **comité t.** committee appointed for three years **3** *Agr* three-yearly

triennat [triena] NM three-year mandate *or* period of office

trier [10] [trije] VT **1** *(sortir d'un lot → fruits)* to pick

(out); (→ *photos, candidats*) to select; **triez les plus beaux fruits** pick out the best fruit; **triez les grains pour en extraire les cailloux** separate the grit from the grain; **ses amis sont triés sur le volet** his/her friends are hand-picked

2 (*répartir par catégories* → *lettres*) to sort (out); (→ *vêtements*) to sort or go through; (→ *œufs*) to grade; (→ *lentilles*) to pick over

3 *Rail* (*wagons*) to marshal

4 *Ordinat* to sort; **t. par ordre alphabétique** to sort in alphabetical order, to alphasort

▸**se trier** VPR *Ordinat* to sort

triérarque [trierark] NM *Antiq* trierarch

trière [trijɛr] NF *Antiq* trireme

Trieste [trijɛst] NM Trieste

triester [trijɛstɛr] NM *Chim* triester

trieur, -euse [trijœr, -øz] NM,F sorter, grader

  NM **1** *Agr* sorting or grading machine **2** *Mines* picker (machine); **t. magnétique** magnetic separator

  ❏ **trieuse** NF (*machine*) sorter, sorting machine; *Ordinat* sorter; (*logiciel*) sort program

trieur-calibreur [trijœrkalibrœr] (*pl* **trieurs-calibreurs**) NM *Ind* grading machine

trieuse [trijøz] *voir* **trieur**

trifide [trifid] ADJ *Biol* trifid, three-cleft

trifolié, -e [trifɔlje] ADJ *Bot* three-leafed, *Spéc* trifoliate, trifoliated

trifoliolé, -e [trifɔljɔlje] ADJ *Bot* trifoliolate

trifonctionnel, -elle [trifɔ̃ksjɔnɛl] ADJ trifunctional

triforium [trifɔrjɔm] NM *Archit* triforium

trifouiller [3] [trifuje] *Fam* VT **1** (*fouiller*) to rummage through **2** (*toucher à*) to fiddle with, to tinker with

  VI **qu'est-ce que tu trifouilles?** what are you up to?; **je ne sais pas ce que j'ai trifouillé mais ça ne marche plus** I don't know what I've done but it's not working

  ❏ **trifouiller dans** VT IND **1** (*fouiller dans* → *papiers, vêtements*) to rummage around in **2** (*tripoter* → *moteur*) to tinker with

Trifouillis-les-Oies [trifujilɛzwa] N *Fam* = fictional name for the archetypal isolated village; **il vit à T.** he lives in the back of beyond

trigémellaire [triʒemɛlɛr] ADJ **grossesse t.** triplet pregnancy

trigéminé, -e [triʒemine] ADJ *Méd* (*pouls*) trigeminal, intermittent

trigle [trigl] NM *Ich* gurnard; **t. cardina** piper gurnard; **t. hirondelle** sapphirine gurnard; **t. lyre** piper gurnard; **t. pin** red gurnard

triglycéride [trigliserid] NM *Chim* triglyceride

triglyphe [triglif] NM *Archit* triglyph

trigo [trigo] NF *Fam Math* (*abrév* **trigonométrie**) trig, trigonometry▪

trigone [trigon] ADJ trigonal, triquetrous

  NM *Astrol* trigon

trigonelle [trigɔnɛl] NF *Bot* fenugreek, trigonella

trigonocéphale [trigɔnɔsefal] NM trigonocephalus

trigonométrie [trigɔnɔmetri] NF *Math* trigonometry

trigonométrique [trigɔnɔmetrik] ADJ *Math* trigonometric, trigonometrical

trigonométriquement [trigɔnɔmetrikmɑ̃] ADV *Math* trigonometrically

trigramme [trigram] NM **1** (*mot de trois lettres*) trigram **2** (*groupe de trois caractères*) trigraph, trigram **3** (*dans la divination chinoise*) trigram

trihebdomadaire [triɛbdɔmadɛr] ADJ three-times-weekly (*avant n*), thrice-weekly (*avant n*)

  NM thrice-weekly publication

trijumeau, -x [triʒymo] *Anat* ADJ m trigeminal

  NM trigeminal nerve

trilatéral, -e, -aux, -ales [trilateral, -o] ADJ *Géom* trilateral, three-sided

trilingue [trilɛ̃g] ADJ trilingual

  NMF trilingual person

trilitère [trilitɛr] ADJ *Ling* triliteral

trille [trij] NM trill; **les trilles des oiseaux** the trilling of the birds; **faire des trilles** to trill

triller [3] [trije] VT to trill

  VI to trill

trillion [triljɔ̃] NM (10^{18}) *Br* trillion, *Am* quintillion

trilobe [trilɔb] NM trefoil

trilobé, -e [trilɔbe] ADJ **1** *Archit* trefoil (*avant n*) **2** *Bot* trilobate

trilobite [trilɔbit] *Zool* NM trilobite, *Spéc* member of the Trilobita class

  ❏ **trilobites** NMPL trilobites, *Spéc* Trilobita

triloculaire [trilɔkylɛr] ADJ *Bot* trilocular

trilogie [trilɔʒi] NF **1** (*groupe de trois*) triad **2** *Antiq & Littérature* trilogy; **le roman est une t.** the novel is a trilogy

trilogique [trilɔʒik] ADJ *Littérature* trilogic, trilogical

trim. *Scol & Univ* (*abrév écrite* **trimestre**) term

trimaran [trimarɑ̃] NM *Naut* trimaran

trimard [trimar] NM *Fam Vieilli* road▪

trimarder [3] [trimarde] VI *Fam Vieilli* to be on the road

trimardeur, -euse [trimardœr, -øz] NM,F *Fam Vieilli* tramp, *Am* hobo

trimbalage [trɛ̃balaʒ], **trimbalement** [trɛ̃balmɑ̃] NM *Fam* lugging or dragging or carting around; **le t. du matériel a duré toute la nuit** it took all night to shift the equipment

trimbaler [3] [trɛ̃bale] *Fam* VT **1** (*porter*) to hump, to lug around; **il trimbale sa famille partout où il va** he has his family in tow everywhere he goes

  2 (*emmener*) to take▪; **il nous y a trimbalés dans sa nouvelle voiture** he ran us there in his new car; **elle trimbale son fils partout** she trails her son around or drags her son with her everywhere she goes; **qui les trimbale chaque jour à l'école?** who ferries them to and from school every day?; **le pauvre gosse s'est fait t. toute la journée de musée en musée** the poor kid was dragged about from museum to museum all day long

  3 (*locution*) **qu'est-ce qu'il trimbale!** what a total halfwit!

▸**se trimbaler** VPR **1** (*aller et venir*) to trail around; **t'as pas honte de te t. en short?** I don't know how you can prance about in your shorts like that

  2 (*se déplacer*) to go▪; **elle se trimbale toujours avec son frère** she drags that brother of hers around with her everywhere

trimballage [trɛ̃balaʒ] = **trimbalage**

trimballement [trɛ̃balmɑ̃] = **trimbalement**

trimballer [trɛ̃bale] = **trimbaler**

trimer [3] [trime] VI *Fam* to slave away; **il a trimé toute sa vie** he's spent his entire life slaving away or working his fingers to the bone; **faire t. qn** to keep sb hard at it, to keep sb's nose to the grindstone

trimère [trimɛr] ADJ *Biol & Bot* trimerous

  NM *Chim* trimer

trimestre [trimɛstr] NM **1** *Scol & Univ* term; **premier t.** autumn term; **deuxième t.** spring term; **troisième t.** summer term; **passer un test tous les trimestres** to sit a test every term

  2 (*trois mois*) quarter; **payer tous les trimestres** ou **par t.** to pay on a quarterly basis

  3 (*somme payée ou reçue*) quarterly instalment; (*salaire*) quarter's salary; (*loyer*) quarter's rent; *Scol* (*frais*) term fees; (*d'une assurance, une bourse*) quarterly instalment or payment

trimestriel, -elle [trimɛstrijɛl] ADJ **1** *Scol* (*bulletin*) end-of-term (*avant n*); (*réunion*) termly **2** (*réunion, magazine, loyer*) quarterly; **fonction trimestrielle** position lasting for three months

trimestriellement [trimɛstrijɛlmɑ̃] ADV **1** *Scol & Univ* once a term, on a termly basis **2** (*payer, publier*) quarterly, on a quarterly basis, every three months

trimétal, -aux [trimetal, -o] NM trimetal

trimètre [trimɛtr] NM *Littérature* trimeter

trimmer [trimœr] NM *Pêche & Rad* trimmer

trimorphisme [trimɔrfism] NM *Biol* trimorphism

trimoteur [trimɔtœr] ADJ M three-engined

  NM three-engined aircraft

trimurti [trimurti] NF *Rel* Trimurti

trin, -e [trɛ̃, trin] ADJ **1** *Rel* triune **2** *Astrol* **t. aspect** trine aspect

trinervé, -e [trinɛrve] ADJ *Bot* trinervate

tringle [trɛ̃gl] NF **1** (*pour pendre*) rail; **t. à rideaux** curtain rail **2** (*pour tenir*) rod; **t. de tapis d'escalier** stair rod; **t. à rideau** curtain rod **3** *Tech* control rod **4** (*d'une crémone*) rod **5** *Archit* square moulding

tringler [3] [trɛ̃gle] VT **1** *Tech* (*avec une ficelle crayeuse*) to mark with a line **2** *Vulg* to screw; **se faire t.** to get laid

tringlerie [trɛ̃glǝri] NF *Tech* rod system, linkage

tringlot [trɛ̃glo] NM *Fam Arg mil* = soldier in the French Army Service Corps

trinidadien, -enne [trinidadjɛ̃, -ɛn] ADJ Trinidadian

  ❏ **Trinidadien, -enne** NM,F Trinidadian

trinitaire [trinitɛr] ADJ *Rel* Trinitarian

Trinité [trinite] NF (**l'île de**) **la T.** Trinidad

trinité [trinite] NF **1** *Rel* **la (sainte) T.** the (Holy) Trinity; **la (fête de la) T.** Trinity Sunday; **à la T.** on Trinity Sunday **2** *Littéraire* (*trois éléments*) trinity

Trinité-et-Tobago [triniteetɔbago] NF Trinidad and Tobago; **vivre à T.** to live in Trinidad and Tobago; **aller à T.** to go to Trinidad and Tobago

trinitrine [trinitrin] NF *Chim* nitroglycerine, trinitrin; *Pharm* trinitrine

trinitrotoluène [trinitrɔtɔlɥɛn] NM *Chim* TNT, trinitrotoluene

trinôme [trinom] *Math* ADJ trinomial

  NM trinomial

trinquart [trɛ̃kar] NM herring boat

trinqueballe [trɛ̃kǝbal] = **triqueballe**

trinquer [3] [trɛ̃ke] VI **1** (*choquer les verres*) to clink glasses; **t. à qn/qch** to drink (a toast) to sb/sth; **t. à la santé de qn** to drink a toast to sb; **trinquons!** let's drink to that!

  2 *Fam* (*subir un dommage*) to be the one who suffers▪, to pay the price; **c'est ma voiture qui a trinqué** my car got the worst of it; **c'est lui qui va t.** he'll be the one who suffers; **les parents divorcent, les enfants trinquent** when the parents get a divorce, it's the children that suffer

  3 *Fam* (*boire avec excès*) to booze; **on a trinqué ensemble** we had a few drinks together

trinquet[1] [trɛ̃kɛ] NM *Naut* foremast

trinquet[2] [trɛ̃kɛ] NM (*dans le sud-ouest de la France*) = hall fitted out for playing pelota

trinquette [trɛ̃kɛt] NF *Naut* forestaysail

trio [trijo] NM **1** (*trois personnes*) trio, threesome; **notre t. n'en eut pas pour longtemps à résoudre le mystère** our three heroes solved the mystery in no time **2** *Mus* trio

triode [trijɔd] *Électron* ADJ triode (*avant n*)

  NF triode

triol [trijɔl] NM *Chim* triol

triolet [trijɔlɛ] NM *Mus & Littérature* triolet

triolisme [trijɔlism] NM troilism

triomphal, -e, -aux, -ales [trijɔ̃fal, -o] ADJ (*entrée, accueil*) triumphant; (*victoire, succès*) resounding; (*élection*) resoundingly successful; (*arc, procession*) triumphal; (*geste*) triumphant, of triumph

triomphalement [trijɔ̃falmɑ̃] ADV (*sourire, dire*) triumphantly; (*traiter, recevoir*) in triumph; **être accueilli t.** to be received in triumph or triumphantly; **descendre t. les Champs-Élysées** to parade down the Champs-Élysées in triumph

triomphalisme [trijɔ̃falism] NM triumphalism; **dans un moment de t.** in a moment of self-congratulation; **sans faire de t., il me semble que...** while I don't want to crow, it seems to me that...

triomphaliste [trijɔ̃falist] ADJ (*discours, vainqueur*) self-congratulatory, gloating; (*attitude*) overconfident

  NMF crower

triomphant, -e [trijɔ̃fɑ̃, -ɑ̃t] ADJ triumphant; **un sourire t.** a triumphant smile; **d'un ton t.** triumphantly; **il est sorti t. de l'épreuve** he came out the winner; **il est arrivé t., avec la preuve qu'il avait raison** he came back cock-a-hoop with the proof that he was right

triomphateur, -trice [trijɔ̃fatœr, -tris] ADJ triumphant

  NM,F winner, victor

  NM *Antiq* conquering hero

triomphe [trijɔ̃f] NM **1** (*d'une armée, d'un groupe*) triumph, victory; (*d'un artiste, d'une idée*) triumph; **remporter un t.** (*chose*) to be a resounding success; (*personne*) to be hugely successful; **remporter un t. sur un parti adverse** to win a sweeping victory over the opposing party; **l'album est un t.** the album is a great success; **la pièce a fait un t. à Paris** the play was a great or a triumphant success in Paris; **c'est le t. de la démocratie/de la bêtise** it's a triumph for democracy/of stupidity

  2 (*jubilation*) triumph; **son t. fut de courte**

durée his/her triumph was short-lived; **avoir le t. modeste** to be modest in victory; **sourire/cri de t.** smile/shout of triumph, triumphant smile/ shout; **pousser un cri de t.** to give a shout of triumph, to shout triumphantly

3 *(ovation)* **faire un t. à qn** to give sb a triumphant welcome; **ils m'ont fait un t. à la fin de mon discours** they gave me a standing ovation at the end of my speech; **porter qn en t.** to carry sb in triumph *or* shoulder-high

triompher [3] [trijɔ̃fe] VI 1 *(armée)* to triumph; *(parti)* to win (decisively)

2 *(idée)* to triumph, to prevail; *(bêtise, corruption, racisme)* to be rife; **son point de vue a fini par t.** his/her point of view finally won the day *or* prevailed; **la vérité finit toujours par t.** truth will prevail; **faire t. une idée** to win recognition for an idea

3 *(artiste)* to be a great success; **elle triomphe dans le rôle d'Orlando** she's a great success in the role of Orlando; **il triomphe à l'Apollo tous les soirs** he's playing to packed houses at the Apollo every night

4 *(jubiler)* to gloat; **elle triomphe maintenant que tu es parti!** she's gloating now that you've gone!; **gardons-nous de t. trop vite** let's not celebrate too quickly

5 *Antiq* to triumph

□ **triompher de** VT IND *(ennemi, rival)* to triumph over, to beat; *(malaise, obstacle)* to triumph over, to overcome; **sa persévérance l'a fait t. de toutes ces épreuves** his/her perseverance helped him/her through all these ordeals

trionyx [triɔniks] NM *Zool* soft-shell *or* soft-shelled turtle

trioxyde [triɔksid] NM *Chim* trioxide

trip [trip] NM 1 *Fam Arg drogue* trip; **être en plein t.** to be on a trip, to be tripping; **faire un t.** to trip; **faire un mauvais t.** to have a bad trip; *Fig* to have a rough time

2 *Fam (centre d'intérêt)* kick

3 *Fam (locutions)* **il est en plein t. écolo en ce moment** he's on some environmental kick at the moment; **c'est vraiment pas mon t., ce genre de truc** I'm not really into that kind of thing, it's not my scene, that kind of thing; **le jazz, c'est plutôt son t.** jazz is his/her thing

tripaille [tripaj] NF *Fam* innards, guts

tripale [tripal] ADJ *(hélice)* three-bladed

tripang [tripɑ̃] NM *Zool* trepang, sea cucumber

tripant, -e [tripɑ̃, -ɑ̃t] ADJ *Can Fam* great, fantastic

triparti, -e [triparti] ADJ *(traité)* tripartite; *(négociations)* three-way; *(alliance électorale)* three-party *(avant n)*

tripartisme [tripartism] NM three-party government

tripartite [tripartit] ADJ *(traité)* tripartite; *(négociations)* three-way; *(alliance électorale)* three-party *(avant n)*

NF *Belg* tripartite coalition

tripartition [tripartisjɔ̃] NF tripartition, splitting into three

tripatouillage [tripatujaʒ] NM *Fam* 1 *(malaxage)* messing around 2 *(truquage → d'un document)* tampering (**de** with); *(→ des chiffres, des résultats)* fixing (**de** of); **t. des comptes** cooking the books; **il y a eu t. des résultats** the results were a fix

tripatouiller [3] [tripatuje] *Fam* VT 1 *(truquer → document)* to tamper with; *(→ chiffres, résultats)* to fix; **t. les comptes** to cook the books; **t. les statistiques** to massage the figures

2 *(modifier → textes)* to alter■

3 *(toucher → personne)* to paw, to feel up; *(→ cheveux)* to play *or* fiddle with; *(→ bouton)* to pick at; *(→ nourriture)* to play with

VI **les enfants adorent t. dans le sable** children love messing around in the sand

tripatouilleur, -euse [tripatujœr, -øz] NM,F *Fam* **c'est un t.** *(mauvais bricoleur)* he's a botcher; *(mauvais écrivain)* he's a hack, he just cobbles other people's ideas together

triper [3] [tripe] VI *Fam* to trip *(after taking drugs)*

triperie [tripri] NF 1 *Br (boutique)* tripe and offal shop, *Am* variety meat store 2 *(activité) Br* tripe (and offal) trade, *Am* variety meat trade 3 *(abats) Br* offal *(UNCOUNT)*, *Am* variety meat

tripes [trip] NFPL 1 *Culin* **des t.** tripe *(UNCOUNT)*; **t. à la mode de Caen** tripe à la mode de Caen *(tripe braised with onions, carrots and cider)* 2 *Fam (entrailles)* guts, insides 3 *Fam Fig* **une histoire qui vous prend aux t.** a story that gets you in the guts *or* right there; **la peur m'a pris aux t.** I was petrified with fear; **ce film m'a remué les t.** that movie really got me going; **jouer avec ses t.** to give it one's all; **dans ce film, elle joue vraiment avec ses t.** she gives a powerful performance in this movie■; **parler avec ses t.** to speak from the heart■ 4 *(de cigare)* core, filling

tripette [tripɛt] NF *Fam* **ça ne vaut pas t.** it's a load of tripe *or* dross, *Am* it's not worth diddly

triphasé, -e [trifaze] *Élec* ADJ three-phase

NM three-phase current; **installation en t.** three-phase wiring

triphénylméthane [trifenilmetan] NM *Chim* triphenylmethane

triphosphate [trifɔsfat] NM *Biol* triphosphate

triphtongue [triftɔ̃g] NF *Ling* triphthong

tripier, -ère [tripje, -ɛr] NM,F tripe (and offal) butcher

triplace [triplas] ADJ three-seater *(avant n)*

NM *Aviat* three-seater (plane)

triplan [triplɑ̃] NM *Aviat* triplane

triple [tripl] ADJ 1 *(à trois éléments)* triple; **une t. collision ferroviaire** a crash involving three trains; **une t. semelle** a three-layer sole; **un t. menton** a triple chin; **un t. rang de perles** three rows *or* a triple row of pearls; **en t. exemplaire** in triplicate; **t. saut** triple jump; **t. saut périlleux** triple somersault; *Hist* **la T. Alliance** the Triple Alliance; *Hist* **la T. Entente** the Triple Entente

2 *(trois fois plus grand)* treble, triple; **ton jardin est t. du mien** your garden is treble the size of mine; **une t. dose** three times the usual amount

3 *Fam (en intensif)* **un t. sot** a prize idiot; **t. imbécile!** you stupid idiot!; **t. buse!** you stupid nit!

4 *Mus* **t. croche** *Br* demi-semiquaver, *Am* thirty-second note

NM **le t. (de)** *(quantité, prix)* three times as much (as); *(nombre)* three times as many (as); **neuf est le t. de trois** nine is three times three; **il fait le t. de travail** he does three times as much work; **le t. de poids/longueur** three times as heavy/long; **ça a pris le t. de temps** it took three times as long; **on a payé le t.** we paid three times that amount; **ça coûte le t.** it's three times the price; **je l'ai acheté le t. de toi/de sa valeur** I paid three times as much as you did/as much as it was worth

□ **en triple** ADV *(copier, signer)* in triplicate

triplé, -e [triple] NM,F triplet; **des triplées** (girl) triplets

NM 1 *(aux courses)* treble, = bet on the first three horses in a race; **gagner le t.** to win a treble 2 *(d'un athlète)* triple win; *(d'une équipe)* hat trick; **faire** *ou* **réussir le t.** *(athlète)* to come first in three events; *(footballeur)* to score a hat trick

triplement[1] [tripləmɑ̃] ADV in three ways, on three counts; **t. déçu** disappointed on three counts

triplement[2] [tripləmɑ̃] NM trebling, tripling; **le t. de mes ressources** the threefold increase in *or* the trebling of my income

tripler [3] [triple] VT 1 *(dépenses, dose)* to treble, to triple 2 *Scol* **t. une classe** to repeat a *Br* year *or Am* class for a second time, to do a *Br* year *or Am* class for a third time

VI to treble, to triple; **la population a triplé** the population has tripled *or* has increased threefold

triplet [triplɛ] NM 1 *Math* triplet 2 *Opt & Phot* triple lens 3 *Archit* triplet

triplette [triplɛt] NF 1 *(d'hommes)* three-man team; *(de femmes)* three-woman team; *(mixte)* three-person team 2 *(aux boules)* threesome

'Les Triplettes de Belleville' *Chomet* 'Belleville Rendezvous'

Triplex® [triplɛks] NM Triplex® (glass)

triplex [triplɛks] NM 1 *(carton)* triplex 2 *(papier)* three-sheet paper 3 *(appartement) Br* three-storey flat, *Am* triplex (apartment) 4 *Can* triplex *(three-storey house divided into three self-contained flats)*

triplicata [triplikata] *(pl* **triplicatas** *ou* **inv***)* NM triplicate

triplique [triplik] NF *Jur* surrejoinder

triploblastique [triplɔblastik] ADJ *Biol* triploblastic

triploïde [triplɔid] ADJ *Biol* triploid

triploïdie [triplɔidi] NF *Biol* triploidy

triplure [triplyr] NF *Couture* buckram, stiffening

tripode [tripɔd] ADJ 1 *Naut* tripod *(avant n)* 2 *(meuble)* three-legged, *Spéc* tripod *(avant n)*

NM automatic ticket barrier *(in Paris métro)*

tripodie [tripɔdi] NF *Littérature* tripody

Tripoli [tripɔli] NM Tripoli

triporteur [tripɔrtœr] NM delivery tricycle

tripot [tripo] NM *Péj* 1 *(lieu mal famé)* = disreputable bar, nightclub etc 2 *(maison de jeu)* gambling den

tripotage [tripɔtaʒ] NM *Fam* 1 *(de fruits)* handling *(UNCOUNT)*; *(d'une breloque)* fiddling *(UNCOUNT)* 2 *(attouchements)* fondling *(UNCOUNT)*, groping *(UNCOUNT)* 3 *(pratique louche)* scam, *Br* fiddle; **le t. électoral est monnaie courante** election rigging is common; **tripotages** *(magouilles)* scheming *(UNCOUNT)*, dirty tricks, skulduggery *(UNCOUNT)*

tripotée [tripɔte] NF *Fam* 1 *(grand nombre)* **une t. de** tons of, loads of; **ils ont toute une t. d'enfants** they've got loads of kids 2 *(correction, défaite)* thrashing, hammering; **filer une t. à qn** to thrash *or* hammer sb, to give sb a thrashing *or* a hammering; **prendre une t.** to get thrashed *or* hammered

tripoter [3] [tripɔte] VT *Fam* 1 *(toucher distraitement → crayon, cheveux)* to twiddle, to play *or* to fiddle with

2 *(palper → fruit, objet)* to handle, to finger; **arrête de t. tes boutons** stop touching *or* keep your hands off your spots

3 *(personne)* to feel up, to grope

VI *Fam* 1 *(fouiller)* to rummage *or* to root around, to root about; **t. dans les affaires de qn** to rummage *or* root about in sb's things

2 *(en affaires)* to be up to some funny *or Br* dodgy business; **t. dans qch** to be mixed up *or* involved in sth■; **t. dans la caisse** to tamper with the cash

▸**se tripoter** VPR *très Fam* 1 *(se masturber)* to play with oneself

2 *(deux personnes)* to paw *or* to grope each other, to feel each other up

3 *(toucher)* **se t. le nez/le menton** to fiddle with one's nose/chin

tripoteur, -euse [tripɔtœr, -øz] NM,F *Fam* 1 *(qui trafique)* shady dealer, crook 2 *(qui caresse)* fondler, groper

ADJ *(mains)* groping; **avoir les mains tripoteuses** to be a bit of a groper

tripous, tripoux [tripu] NMPL *Culin* = dish of sheep innards cooked with sheep's trotters

triptane [triptan] NM *Chim* triptane

triptyque [triptik] NM 1 *Beaux-Arts, Littérature & Mus* triptych 2 *Aut & Admin* triptyque

trique [trik] NF 1 *(bâton)* cudgel; **des coups de t.** cudgel blows; **donner des coups de t. à qn** to thrash sb; *Fig* **mener qn à la t.** to rule sb with a rod of iron; *Fig* **mener son monde à la t.** to rule with a rod of iron, to rule by fear 2 *Vulg (érection)* hard-on, boner; **avoir la t.** to have a hard-on *or* a boner

triqueballe [trikbal] NM timber cart

trique-madame [trikmadam] NF INV *Bot* white stonecrop

triquer [3] [trike] VI *Vulg* to have a hard-on *or* a boner

triquet [trikɛ] NM 1 *(échelle)* pair of steps 2 *(de jeu de paume)* (real-tennis) racket

trirectangle [trirɛktɑ̃gl] ADJ *Géom* trirectangular

trirème [trirɛm] NF *Antiq* trireme

trisaïeul, -e [trizajœl] NM,F great-great-grandfather, *f* great-great-grandmother; **trisaïeuls** great-great-grandparents

trisannuel, -elle [trizanɥɛl] ADJ 1 *(qui a lieu tous les trois ans)* three-yearly, *Sout* triennial 2 *(qui dure trois ans)* three-year-long *(avant n)*, *Sout* triennial

trisecteur, -trice [trisɛktœr, -tris] ADJ trisecting *(avant n)*

trisection [trisɛksjɔ̃] NF trisection

trisectrice [trisɛktris] *voir* **trisecteur**

triskaïdékaphobie [triskaidɛkafɔbi] NF triskaide-kaphobia

triskèle [triskɛl] NM OU NF triskele

trisme [trism], **trismus** [trismys] NM *Méd* lockjaw, *Spéc* trismus

triso [trizo] *Fam Péj* (*abrév* **trisomique**) ADJ spazzy, *Br* mong
▪ NMF spaz, *Br* mong

trisoc [trizɔk] NM *Agr* triple-furrow *or* three-shared plough

trisomie [trizɔmi] NF *Méd* trisomy; **t. 18** Edwards' syndrome; **t. 21** Down's syndrome, trisomy 21; **enfant atteint de t. 21** child with Down's syndrome

trisomique [trizɔmik] *Méd* ADJ **enfant t.** Down's syndrome child; **être t.** to have Down's syndrome
▪ NMF child with Down's syndrome

trisser [3] [trise] VI *Fam* to hightail it, to scoot, *Am* to split
▪ VT *Belg Scol* **t. une classe** to repeat a *Br* year *or* Am class for a second time, to do a *Br* year *or Am* class for a third time
▶**se trisser** VPR *Fam* to hightail it, to scoot, *Am* to split

Tristan [tristɑ̃] NPR Tristan

📖

'Tristan et Iseut' 'Tristram *or* Tristan and Iseult'

🎵

'Tristan et Isolde' *Wagner* 'Tristan and Isolde'

triste [trist] ADJ **1** (*déprimé* → *personne*) sad; (→ *sourire, visage*) sad, unhappy, sorrowful; (→ *mine, air*) sad, forlorn; **d'un air t.** bleakly; **ne prends pas cet air t.** don't look so glum; **être tout t.** to be (very) dejected *or* in low spirits; **je fus (bien) t. d'apprendre que...** I was (very) sorry to hear that...; **un clown t.** a sad-looking clown; **t. comme un bonnet de nuit** as miserable as sin; **t. comme la mort** utterly dejected; *Littéraire* **faire t. figure** *ou* **mine** to look pitiful; **faire t. figure** *ou* **mine à qn** to give sb a cold reception
2 (*pénible*) sad, unhappy; **tel est mon t. devoir** such is my painful duty; **son t. sort** his/her sad *or* unhappy fate
3 (*attristant*) sad; **un film t.** a sad film; **c'est t. à dire** it's sad to say; **c'est vraiment t. à voir** it's really sad to see; **t. comme un lendemain de fête** a real anticlimax
4 *Fam* **c'est pas t.!** what a hoot *or* laugh!; **il est pas t., avec sa chemise à fleurs** he's a scream in his flowery shirt; **il est pas t., son frère!** his/her brother is quite a character!; **tu as vu son gâteau, il est pas t.!** have you seen that masterpiece of a cake?; **ils font voter les réformes sans avoir le financement, ça va pas être t.!** they're pushing the reforms through without funds, what a farce!
5 (*terne* → *couleur*) drab, dull; (*morne* → *rue, saison*) bleak; (→ *campagne*) bleak, depressing; (→ *vie, pièce*) dreary, dismal, depressing; **être t. à mourir** (*gens, ambiance, lieu*) to be thoroughly depressing *or* dreary; **une ville t. à pleurer** a dreadfully bleak town
6 (*avant le nom*) (*déplorable*) deplorable, sorry, sad; **elle était dans un t. état** she was in a sorry state; **nous vivons une bien t. époque** we're living through pretty grim times; **c'est la t. réalité** that's the way things are; **c'est une t. affaire** it's a sorry *or* bad business; **c'est tout de même t.!** it's pretty pathetic!; **c'est quand même t. de voir ça dans notre pays!** it's dreadful to see that type of thing in our own country!
7 *Péj* (*méprisable* → *repas, excuse*) poor, sorry, wretched; (→ *morceau de pain*) sad- *or* sorry-looking; **un t. sire** an unsavoury character
▪ NMF (*personne sombre*) gloomy *or* miserable person; **ce n'est pas un t.!** he's a lot of fun!

═📖

'Tristes Tropiques' *Lévi-Strauss* 'A World on the Wane'

tristement [tristəmɑ̃] ADV **1** (*en étant triste*) sadly; **nous avons t. appris la nouvelle** we heard the news with great sadness, we were sad *or* sorry to hear the news

2 (*de façon terne*) drearily; **la maison est t. décorée** the house is decorated in a dreary *or* depressing fashion
3 (*de manière pénible*) sadly, regrettably; **faire t. défaut** to be sadly lacking; **t. célèbre** notorious; **le t. célèbre Barbe-Bleue** the infamous *or* notorious Bluebeard

tristesse [tristɛs] NF **1** (*sentiment*) sadness; **sourire avec t.** to smile sadly; **un sourire plein de t.** a very sad smile; **ressentir une grande t.** to feel very sad; **dans un moment de t.** in a moment of sadness; **c'est avec t. que je quitte ce pays** I am very sorry to be leaving this country; **quelle t. de voir une telle déchéance!** how sad to see such decrepitude!
2 (*d'un livre, d'une vie*) sadness; **la t. du paysage** the bleakness of the landscape; **la t. de son regard** the sad look *or* expression in his/her eyes
3 (*manque de vitalité*) dreariness, dullness; **ma vie est d'une grande t.** my life is very dreary
4 tristesses (*moments*) sorrows

tristounet, -ette [tristunɛ, -ɛt] ADJ *Fam* **1** (*triste*) sad▪; **il est un peu t. aujourd'hui** he's a bit low today; **une petite figure tristounette** a sad little face **2** (*qui rend triste*) gloomy▪, dreary▪, depressing▪ **3** (*terne*) dull▪; **un peu t. comme pull** that pullover is a bit drab

trisyllabe [trisilab] ADJ trisyllabic
▪ NM trisyllable

trisyllabique [trisilabik] ADJ trisyllabic

trithérapie [triterapi] NF *Méd* combination therapy

triticale [tritikal] NM *Agr* triticale

tritium [tritjɔm] NM *Chim* tritium

Triton [tritɔ̃] NPR *Myth* Triton

triton [tritɔ̃] NM **1** *Zool* (*amphibien*) newt, *Spéc* triton; (*gastropode*) triton, Triton's shell **2** *Mus* tritone **3** *Phys* triton

triturateur [trityratœr] NM (*en papeterie*) triturator, triturating machine

trituration [trityrasjɔ̃] NF grinding up, *Spéc* trituration

triturer [3] [trityre] VT **1** (*pétrir* → *bras, corps, pâte*) to knead **2** (*manipuler* → *gants, breloque*) to fiddle with **3** (*influencer*) to manipulate, to distort; **les grands groupes de presse triturent l'opinion publique** the big newspaper groups distort public opinion **4** *Pharm* (*médicament*) to crush, to grind, *Spéc* to triturate
▶**se triturer** VPR *Fam* **se t. les méninges** *ou* **la cervelle** to rack one's brains

triumvir [trijɔmvir] NM triumvir

triumviral, -e, -aux, -ales [trijɔmviral, -o] ADJ triumviral

triumvirat [trijɔmvira] NM **1** (*groupe*) triumvirate, troika **2** *Antiq* triumvirate

trivalent, -e [trivalɑ̃, -ɑ̃t] ADJ trivalent

trivalve [trivalv] ADJ trivalvular, trivalve (*avant n*)

trivial, -e, -aux, -ales [trivjal, -o] ADJ **1** (*grossier*) crude, offensive **2** (*banal*) trivial, trite; **un détail t.** a minor detail; **une remarque triviale** a commonplace, a mundane remark **3** *Math* trivial

trivialement [trivjalmɑ̃] ADV **1** (*vulgairement*) crudely, coarsely **2** (*banalement*) trivially, tritely

trivialité [trivjalite] NF **1** (*caractère vulgaire*) crudeness, coarseness **2** (*parole vulgaire*) crude remark; (*expression*) vulgar *or* coarse expression **3** (*caractère banal*) triviality, banality; **des idées d'une t. affligeante** incredibly trivial *or* banal ideas

tr/mn, tr/min *Tech* (*abrév écrite* **tours par minute**) rpm

troc [trɔk] NM **1** (*système économique*) barter; (**économie de**) **t.** barter economy; **faire du t.** to barter **2** (*échange*) swap; **je ne l'ai pas acheté, j'ai fait le t.** avec quelqu'un I didn't buy it, I bartered for it *or* I did a swap

Trocadéro [trɔkadero] NM **le T., la place du T.** = public square opposite the Eiffel Tower

trocart [trɔkar] NM *Méd* trocar

trochaïque [trɔkaik] ADJ *Littérature* trochaic

trochanter [trɔkɑ̃tɛr] NM *Anat & Zool* trochanter; **le grand t.** the great trochanter, trochanter major; **le petit t.** the lesser trochanter, trochanter minor

troche [trɔʃ] NF = **troque**

trochée [trɔʃe] NM *Littérature* trochee

trochet [trɔʃɛ] NM *Bot* cluster

trochilidé [trɔkilide] *Orn* NM hummingbird, *Spéc* trochilus, member of the Trochilidae
❑ **trochilidés** NMPL hummingbirds, *Spéc* Trochilidae

trochin [trɔʃɛ̃] NM *Anat* lesser tuberosity

trochiter [trɔkitɛr] NM *Anat* great tuberosity

trochlée [trɔkle] NF *Anat* trochlea

trochophore [trɔkɔfɔr], **trochosphère** [trɔkɔsfɛr] NF *Zool* trochophore, trochosphere

trochure [trɔʃyr] NF *Zool* fourth tine

troène [trɔɛn] NM *Bot* privet

troglobie [trɔglɔbi] *Biol* ADJ troglobiotic
▪ NM troglobiont

troglodyte [trɔglɔdit] NM **1** (*en anthropologie*) cave dweller, *Spéc* troglodyte **2** *Orn* wren; **t. familier** house wren

troglodytique [trɔglɔditik] ADJ (*population*) cave-dwelling, *Spéc* troglodytic; **habitations troglodytiques** cave dwellings

trogne [trɔɲ] NF *Fam* face▪, mug; **il avait une t. d'ivrogne** he had the look of a wino about him

trognon [trɔɲɔ̃] NM **1** (*de pomme*) core; (*de chou, salade etc*) stalk; *très Fam* **il t'exploitera jusqu'au t.** he'll bleed you dry; *très Fam* **on s'est fait avoir jusqu'au t.** we were well and truly ripped off **2** *Fam* (*terme d'affection*) sweetie
▪ ADJ (*invariable en genre*) *Fam* cute; **elles sont vraiment trognons** they're so cute

trogonidé [trɔgɔnide] *Orn* NM trogon, *Spéc* member of the Trogonidae
❑ **trogonidés** NMPL trogons, *Spéc* Trogonidae

Troie [trwa] NM Troy; **le cheval/la guerre de T.** the Trojan Horse/War

troïka [trɔika] NF **1** (*traîneau*) troika **2** (*trois personnes*) troika; **la t. qui dirige maintenant le journal** the newspaper's new management trio; **t. européenne** European troika

trois [trwa] ADJ **1** (*gén*) three; *Théât* **frapper les t. coups** = to announce the beginning of a theatre performance by knocking three times; *Théât* **la salle a dû être évacuée avant même les t. coups** the auditorium had to be cleared before the performance had even started; **maquette en t. dimensions** three-dimensional model; **reproduire qch en t. dimensions** to produce a three-dimensional model of sth; *Mus* **à t. temps** in triple *or* three-four time; **les t. quarts du temps** most of the time; **les t. Grâces** the (three) Graces; *Anciennement Mil* **les t. jours** (*à l'armée*) = in France, induction course preceding military service (now lasting one day); *Fam* **haut comme t. pommes** knee-high to a grasshopper; **Les T. Suisses** = French mail-order company
2 (*dans des séries*) third; **page/numéro t.** page/number three
3 (*exprimant une approximation*) **dans t. minutes** in a couple of minutes; **il n'a pas dit t. mots** he hardly said a word; **deux ou t., t. ou quatre** a few, a handful; **prends t. ou quatre prunes** take a few plums
▪ PRON three
▪ NM INV **1** (*gén*) three **2** (*numéro d'ordre*) number three **3** (*chiffre écrit*) three **4** *Cartes* three; *voir aussi* **cinq**

═📖

'Les Trois mousquetaires' *Dumas* 'The Three Musketeers'

═🎵

'Trois morceaux en forme de poire' *Satie* 'Three Pear-shaped Pieces'

trois-étoiles [trwazetwal] ADJ INV three-star
▪ NM INV (*hôtel*) three-star hotel; (*restaurant*) three-star restaurant

3G [trwaʒe] NF *Ordinat & Tél* (*abrév* **troisième génération**) 3G

trois-huit [trwaɥit] NM INV *Mus* three-eight (time)
▪ NMPL *Ind* **les t.** = shift system based on three eight-hour shifts; **faire les t.** to work in shifts of eight hours

troisième [trwazjɛm] ADJ third; *Cin* **t. cinéma** Third Cinema; **t. dimension** third dimension; *Ordinat & Tél* **t. génération** third generation, 3G; *Gram* **la t. personne du singulier/pluriel** the third person singular/plural; **il était le t. larron dans cette affaire** he took advantage of the

tri-tro

quarrel the other two were having; **de t. ordre** third-rate; *Pol* **la t. voie** the Third Way

NMF 1 *(personne)* third **2** *(objet)* third (one)

NM 1 *(partie)* third **2** *(étage) Br* third floor, *Am* fourth floor **3** *(arrondissement de Paris)* third (arrondissement)

NF 1 *Scol Br* ≃ fourth year, *Am* ≃ ninth grade **2** *Aut* third gear **3** *Mus* third **4** *(en danse)* third position **5** *(édition)* **t. de couverture** inside back cover; *voir aussi* **cinquième**

troisièmement [trwazjɛmmɑ̃] **ADV** thirdly, in third place

trois-mâts [trwama] **NM INV** *Naut* three-master

trois-pièces [trwapjɛs] **NM INV 1** *(appartement)* three-room(ed) *Br* flat *or Am* apartment; **t. cuisine** *Br* three-room flat with kitchen, *Am* three and a half **2** *(costume)* three-piece suit

trois-ponts [trwapɔ̃] **NM INV** *Naut* three-decker

trois-quarts [trwakar] **ADJ INV** three-quarter

NM INV 1 *(manteau)* three-quarter (length) coat **2** *Sport* three-quarter; **t. aile/centre** wing/centre (three-quarter); **la ligne des t.** the three-quarter line **3** *Mus (violon)* three-quarter violin

trois-quatre [trwakatr] **NM INV** *Mus* three-four time

troll [trɔl] **NM 1** *Myth* troll **2** *Fam Ordinat (message, personne)* troll

trolle[1] [trɔl] **NM** *Bot* globe flower

trolle[2] [trɔl] **NF** *Chasse* casting

troller [trɔle] **VI** *Fam Ordinat* to troll

trolley [trɔlɛ] **NM 1** *Transp* trolleybus **2** *(chariot)* truck *(on cableway)* **3** *Élec* trolley; **perche de t.** trolley pole

trolleybus [trɔlɛbys] **NM** *Transp* trolleybus

trom [trɔm] **NM** *Fam (verlan de* **métro***) Br* underground▪, *Am* subway▪

trombe [trɔ̃b] **NF** *Météo (sur mer)* waterspout; *(sur terre)* whirlwind; **t. d'eau** downpour; **sous des trombes d'eau** in the torrential rain; **il pleuvait des trombes** it was pouring down

❑ **en trombe ADV** *Fam* briskly and noisily▪; **elle entra en t.** she burst in; **la voiture passa en t.** the car shot past; **partir en t.** to shoot off

trombidion [trɔ̃bidjɔ̃] **NM** *Entom* trombidium

trombidiose [trɔ̃bidjoz] **NF** *Méd* trombidiasis

trombine [trɔ̃bin] **NF** *Fam (visage)* mug; *(physionomie)* look▪; **si tu avais vu sa t.!** you should have seen his/her face!▪

trombiner [3] [trɔ̃bine] **VT** *Vulg (posséder sexuellement)* to fuck, to screw, *Br* to shag

trombinoscope [trɔ̃binɔskɔp] **NM** *Fam* rogues' gallery

tromblon [trɔ̃blɔ̃] **NM 1** *(fusil)* blunderbuss **2** *(cylindre)* grenade sleeve

trombone [trɔ̃bɔn] **NM 1** *Mus (instrument)* trombone; *(musicien)* trombonist, trombone (player); **t. à coulisse/pistons** slide/valve trombone **2** *(agrafe)* paper clip

tromboniste [trɔ̃bɔnist] **NMF** trombonist, trombone (player)

tromé [trome] = **trom**

trommel [trɔmɛl] **NM** revolving screen, trommel

trompe [trɔ̃p] **NF 1** *Zool (d'éléphant)* trunk, *Spéc* proboscis; *(de papillon)* proboscis; *(de tapir)* snout, *Spéc* proboscis **2** *Mus* horn; *Naut* **t. de brume** foghorn; *Chasse* **t. de chasse** (French) hunting horn; *Chasse* **sonner de la t.** to sound the horn; *Fig* **publier qch à son de t.** to trumpet sth abroad **3** *Aut (avertisseur)* horn **4** *Anat* **t. d'Eustache** Eustachian tube; **t. utérine** *ou* **de Fallope** Fallopian tube **5** *Archit* squinch **6** *Tech* **t. à eau** water pump

trompe-la-mort [trɔ̃plamɔr] **NMF INV** daredevil

trompe-l'œil [trɔ̃plœj] **NM INV 1** *Beaux-Arts (style)* trompe l'œil **2** *Fig (faux-semblant)* window dressing; **son discours antiraciste n'était qu'un t.** his antiracist speech was mere window-dressing

❑ **en trompe-l'œil** *Beaux-Arts* **ADJ peinture en t.** trompe l'œil painting **ADV peindre en t.** to do a trompe l'œil painting, to use trompe l'œil techniques

tromper [3] [trɔ̃pe] **VT 1** *(conjoint)* to be unfaithful to, *Sout* to deceive, to betray; **il trompe sa femme avec sa secrétaire** he's having an affair with his secretary; **elle le trompe avec Thomas** she's having an affair with Thomas behind his back

2 *(donner le change à)* to fool, to trick, to deceive; **elle nous a trompés avec son doux sourire** she fooled us with her sweet smile; **mais si, tu y étais, tu cherches à nous t.!** of course you were there, you're trying to mislead us!; **cela ne trompe personne** nobody's taken in, nobody's fooled; **avec ses airs affables, il trompe bien son monde** everybody is taken in by his kindly manner

3 *(berner, flouer)* to dupe, to cheat; **il m'a trompé dans la vente de la maison** he cheated me on the sale of the house

4 *(induire en erreur)* to mislead; **t. qn sur qn/qch** to deceive *or* mislead sb about sb/sth; **t. qn sur ses intentions** to mislead sb as to one's intentions; **on m'a trompé sur la qualité** I was misinformed as to the quality; **mon instinct ne me trompe jamais** my instincts never let me down *or* fail me; **sa bonne mine a trompé ses proches** his/her healthy appearance fooled *or* deceived his/her relatives; **ne te laisse pas t. par les apparences** don't be taken in by appearances; **c'est ce qui nous a trompés** that's what misled *or* fooled *or* deceived us

5 *(échapper à)* **t. la vigilance de qn** to elude sb; **tu ne pourras pas t. la vigilance du percepteur** you won't hoodwink *or* outwit the *Br* taxman *or Am* IRS; **t. l'ennui** to stave off boredom; **pour t. le temps** to pass the time, to kill time

6 *(apaiser →* *faim)* to appease

7 *Littéraire (décevoir)* **t. l'espoir de qn** to disappoint sb; **je ne voulais pas t. son attente** I didn't want to disappoint him/her; **l'amour l'avait trompée dans son attente** love had fallen short of her expectations

USAGE ABSOLU c'est un signe qui ne trompe pas it's a sure sign; **il a rougi, cela ne trompe pas!** his blushing said it all!

►**se tromper VPR 1** *(commettre une erreur)* to make a mistake; **je dois me t.** I must be mistaken, I must be wrong; **j'ai dû me t.** I must have made a mistake; **si je ne me trompe** if I'm not mistaken; **c'était en 1989 si je ne me trompe** it was in 1989, correct me if I'm wrong; **je ne m'étais pas trompé de beaucoup** I wasn't far wrong *or* far off; **c'est justement ce en quoi tu te trompes** that's just where you're wrong; **tout le monde peut se t.** anybody can make a mistake, we all make mistakes; **se t. dans une addition/dictée** to get a sum/dictation wrong; **je me suis trompé de 3 euros** I was 3 euros *Br* out *or Am* off; **vous m'avez fait me t.** you made me make a mistake

2 *(prendre une chose pour une autre)* **se t. de jour** to get the day wrong; **se t. de bus** to get on the wrong bus; **se t. d'adresse** to go to the wrong address; *Fam Fig* **si c'est un complice que tu cherches, tu te trompes d'adresse** if it's an accomplice you want, you've come to the wrong address; **je me suis trompé de direction/de maison** I went the wrong way/to the wrong house; **vous devez vous t. de numéro** *(au téléphone)* you must have the wrong number; **elle ressemble à sa sœur à s'y t.** you can't tell her and her sister apart

3 *(s'illusionner)* to make a mistake, to be wrong; **je le croyais intelligent mais je me suis trompé** I thought he was intelligent, but I was wrong; **se t. sur les motifs de qn** to misunderstand sb's motives; **ou je me trompe fort ou c'était bien lui** I'm pretty sure it was him; **je ne m'y trompe pas, du reste** I'm not fooled *or* taken in; **que l'on ne s'y trompe pas** let there be no misunderstanding about that; **au fond, elle était malheureuse et ses amis ne s'y trompaient pas** deep down she was unhappy and her friends could tell

tromperie [trɔ̃pri] **NF** *(supercherie)* deception; **il y a t. sur la qualité** the quality hasn't been described accurately; **j'en ai assez de tes tromperies** I've had enough of your deceit *or* deceitfulness

trompeter [27] [trɔ̃pete] **VT** *(fait)* to trumpet, to shout from the rooftops

VI *Vieilli (musicien)* to play the trumpet, to trumpet; *(aigle)* to scream

trompette [trɔ̃pɛt] **NF 1** *(instrument)* trumpet; **t. basse** bass trumpet; **t. bouchée** muted trumpet; **t. de cavalerie** bugle; *Bible* **les trompettes de Jéricho** the trumpets of Jericho; **la t. du Jugement dernier** (the sound of) the Last Judgment; **t. marine** marine trumpet, trumpet marine; **t. à pistons** valve trumpet; *Littéraire* **les trompettes de la Renommée** the trumpet blast of Fame; **t. simple** bugle

2 *Aut* rear axle tube

3 *Ich* **t. de mer** trumpet fish

NM *(musicien →* *gén)* trumpet player, trumpet, trumpeter; *Mil* trumpeter

❑ **en trompette ADJ** *(nez)* turned up, upturned; **avoir le nez en t.** to have a turned up *or* upturned nose

trompette-des-morts [trɔ̃pɛtdemɔr] *(pl* **trompettes-des-morts**), **trompette-de-la-mort** [trɔ̃pɛtdəlamɔr] *(pl* **trompettes-de-la-mort**) **NF** *Bot* horn of plenty

trompettiste [trɔ̃petist] **NMF** trumpet player, trumpet, trumpeter

trompeur, -euse [trɔ̃pœr, -øz] **ADJ 1** *(personne)* lying, deceitful **2** *(signe, air, apparence)* deceptive, misleading; *(publicité)* misleading; **de belles fraises d'un rouge t.** luscious strawberries of a deceptive red; **le vent faiblit mais c'est t.** the wind's dropping but you can't rely on that

NM,F deceiver; *Prov* **à t., t. et demi** it's the biter bit

trompeusement [trɔ̃pøzmɑ̃] **ADV** *(en apparence)* deceptively; *(traîtreusement)* deceitfully

tronc [trɔ̃] **NM 1** *Bot* trunk

2 *Anat (d'un être humain)* trunk, torso; *(d'un animal)* trunk, barrel; *(d'un nerf, d'une artère)* trunk, *Spéc* truncus

3 *(boîte pour collectes)* offertory box; **t. des pauvres** alms box

4 *Géom* **t. de cône/pyramide** truncated cone/pyramid

5 *Fam* **se casser le t.** to strain oneself; **il ne s'est pas cassé le t.** he didn't kill himself, he didn't overexert himself▪

6 *(comme adj; avec ou sans trait d'union)* limbless; **homme-/femme-t.** armless and legless man/woman

❑ **tronc commun NM** *(d'une famille)* common stock, ancestry; *Scol* compulsory subjects, core curriculum

troncation [trɔ̃kasjɔ̃] **NF** *Ling* truncation, abbreviation

troncature [trɔ̃katyr] **NF** *Minér, Ordinat, Math & (gén)* truncation

tronche [trɔ̃ʃ] **NF** *Fam* **1** *(visage)* face▪, mug; *(expression)* look▪; **il a une sale t.** he's an ugly-looking customer; **il a une t. qui ne me revient pas** I don't like the look of him; **il a une drôle de t.** he looks really odd, he's really odd-looking; **il se l'est pris en plein dans la t.** he got it smack in the face; **t'en fais une t., qu'est-ce qu'il t'arrive?** you look really down, what's up?; **t'aurais vu la t. qu'il faisait!** you should have seen the look on his face!▪; **faire la t.** *(bouder)* to sulk▪, to be in a *or* the huff

2 *(personne intelligente)* brain, brainy person; **ce mec-là, c'est une t.!** that guy's a real brain *or* so brainy!

troncher [3] [trɔ̃ʃe] **VT** *Vulg* to screw, *Br* to shag

tronchet [trɔ̃ʃɛ] **NM** (cooper's) block

tronçon [trɔ̃sɔ̃] **NM 1** *(morceau coupé)* segment, section; *(de mât, de lance, d'épée)* (broken) stump; **un tuyau divisé en tronçons** a pipe divided into segments **2** *Transp (de voie)* section; *(de route)* section, stretch **3** *(d'un texte)* part, section **4** *Archit* frustum **5** *Menuis* log, block

tronconique [trɔ̃kɔnik] **ADJ** truncated

tronçonnage [trɔ̃sɔnaʒ], **tronçonnement** [trɔ̃sɔnmɑ̃] **NM 1** *Menuis* sawing *or* chopping (into sections) **2** *Métal* sectioning

tronçonner [3] [trɔ̃sɔne] **VT** to cut *or* to chop (into sections); **t. un arbre** to saw a tree (into sections)

tronçonneuse [trɔ̃sɔnøz] **NF** motor saw; **t. à chaîne** chainsaw

tronculaire [trɔ̃kylɛr] **ADJ** *Anat* truncal; **anesthésie t.** block anaesthesia, conduction anaesthesia

trône [tron] **NM 1** *(siège, pouvoir)* throne; **monter sur le t.** to ascend *or* to come to the throne; **placer** *ou* **mettre qn sur le t.** to put sb on the throne **2** *Fam Hum* **être sur le t.** *(aux toilettes)* to be on the throne

❑ **trônes NMPL** *Rel* thrones

trôner [3] [trone] VI **1** *(personne)* to sit enthroned *or* in state **2** *(bouquet, œuvre d'art)* to sit prominently *or* imposingly; **son portrait trônait dans le salon** his/her portrait was displayed in a prominent position in the drawing room; **son diplôme trône sur la cheminée** his/her diploma occupies a place of honour on the mantelpiece **3** *Péj (faire l'important)* to lord it

tronqué, -e [trɔ̃ke] ADJ *(colonne, pyramide)* truncated; *(mât)* stub *(avant n)*; *(texte)* cut, truncated; *(citation)* shortened, truncated

tronquer [3] [trɔ̃ke] VT **1** *(phrase, récit)* to shorten; *(citation)* to shorten, to truncate **2** *(pilier, statue)* to truncate

TROP [tro] ADV **1** *(excessivement → devant un adjectif, un adverbe)* too; **c'est t. difficile** it's too difficult; **les fraises sont t. chères** the strawberries are too expensive; **il est t. gros** he's overweight *or* too fat; **un plat t. riche** an excessively rich dish; **de la viande t. cuite** overcooked meat; **être t. attaché à qn** to be too attached to sb, to be overfond of sb; **être t. fatigué (pour faire qch)** to be too tired (to do sth); **être t. habillé** *(porter trop de vêtements)* to have too many clothes on; *(porter des vêtements trop chic)* to be overdressed; **et en plus, c'est moi qui paye, c'est t. fort!** and what's more I'm the one who's paying, it really is too much!; **il habite t. loin** he lives too far away; **j'ai dormi t. longtemps** I slept too long; **elle sort t. peu** she doesn't go out enough; **son t. peu de confiance en elle lui nuit** her lack of self-confidence works against her

2 *(excessivement → avec un verbe)* too much; **boire t., t. boire** to drink to excess *or* too much; **manger t., t. manger** to overeat, to eat too much; **tu manges (beaucoup) t.** you eat (far) too much; **avoir t. faim/soif** to be too hungry/thirsty; **t. fumer provoque des maladies graves** too much smoking can lead to serious illness; **on a t. chargé la voiture** we've overloaded the car; **il allait t. en dire** *ou* **en dire t.** he was going to say too much; **j'en ai déjà t. dit, j'en ai déjà dit t.** I've already said more than I should have *or* too much; **je ne l'ai que t. dit** I've said it time and time again; **cela n'a que t. duré** it's been going on far too long; **je ne la connais que t.** I know her all *or* only too well; **il ne le sait que t.** he knows (it) only too well; **on ne saurait t. le répéter** it cannot be repeated too often; **il n'y tient pas t.** he's not too bothered (about it); **ne vous y fiez pas t., il ne faut pas t. vous y fier** don't count on it too much; **ne fais pas t. le difficile** don't be too awkward

3 *(en corrélation avec "pour")* **tu es t. intelligent pour croire cela** you're too intelligent to believe that; **le trou était t. étroit pour qu'un rat entrât par là** the hole was too narrow for a rat to get in by; **elle est t. belle pour toi** she's too beautiful for you; **ne soulève pas l'armoire, c'est t. lourd pour toi tout seul** don't (try to) lift the cupboard, it's too heavy for you on your own; **il est t. fier pour accepter** he's too proud to accept; **c'est t. beau pour être vrai** it's too good to be true; **il a t. tardé à répondre pour qu'elle lui écrive encore** he has taken too long in replying for her to write to him again; **c'est t. important pour que vous ne vous en occupiez pas vous-même** it's too important for you not to deal with it yourself

4 *(emploi nominal) (quantité)* too much; *(nombre)* too many; **ne demande pas t.** don't ask for too much; **prends la dernière part – non, c'est t.** have the last slice – no, it's too much; **je dépense t.** I'm overspending, I'm spending too much; **c'est t.!, c'en est t.!** that's it!, I've had enough!; **t. c'est t.!** enough is enough!; **je sors, t. c'est t.** I'm leaving, I've had enough!

5 *(très, beaucoup)* so; **ce bébé est t. mignon!** this baby is so cute!; **il est t. drôle!** he's so funny!; **c'était t. drôle** it was too funny for words *or* just too funny; **c'est t. bête!** how stupid!; **vous êtes t. aimable** how very kind of you, you're very *or* too kind; *Fam* **j'étais t. dégoûté** I was so bummed *or Br* gutted; *Fam* **il est t. mortel, son plan** his/her plan's so *or* too brilliant; *Fam* **j'étais t. mort de rire** I was absolutely killing myself

6 *(dans des phrases négatives)* **il n'est pas t. content** he's not too *or* very happy; **je ne sais t.** I'm not sure; **je ne sais t. que dire/penser** I hardly know *or* I don't quite know what to say/think; **je n'aime pas t. le chocolat** I don't like chocolate very *or* that much, I'm not very *or* that keen on chocolate; **je ne le connais pas t.** I don't know him very *or* that well; **on ne se voit plus t.** we don't see much of each other any more; **je ne me sens pas t. à l'aise** I'm not overly comfortable, I'm none too comfortable; **sans t. savoir pourquoi** without really knowing why; **ça va? – pas t. mal** how are things? – not bad at all *or* not too bad; **ça te plaît? – pas t.** do you like it? – not (very) much; **c'est bien fait? – pas t. mal** is it good? – it's not bad at all

ADJ INV *Fam (incroyable)* too much, unreal; **il est t., lui!** he really is too much!

❑ **de trop** ADV **j'ai une carte de t.** I have one card too many; **j'ai payé 5 euros de t.** I paid 5 euros too much; **il y a une assiette de t.** there's one plate too many; **c'est une fois de t.** that's once too often; **votre remarque était de t.** that remark of yours was uncalled for; **je suis de t., peut-être?** are you telling me I'm in the way *or* not wanted?; **se sentir de t.** to feel that one is in the way; *Fam* **tu fumes/bois de t.** you smoke/drink too much▪; *Fam* **travailler de t.** to work too hard *or* too much▪, to overwork▪; *Fam* **quand j'ai du temps de t.** when I have time to spare▪; *Fam* **deux jours ne seront pas de t. pour tout terminer** two days should just about be enough to finish everything; *Fam* **un rafraîchissement ne serait pas de t.!** a drink wouldn't go amiss!

❑ **en trop** ADV **j'ai une carte en t.** I have one card too many; **tu as des vêtements en t. à me donner?** have you got any spare clothes to give me?; **j'ai payé 5 euros en t.** I paid 5 euros too much; **il y a de l'argent en t.** there's too much money; **il y a un verre en t.** there's a *or* one glass too many; **se sentir en t.** to feel in the way

❑ **par trop** ADV *Littéraire* much too, far too; **il est par t. méfiant** he's much *or* far too distrustful; **c'est par t. injuste** it's simply too unfair (for words)

❑ **trop de** DÉT **1** *(suivi d'un nom non comptable)* too much; *(suivi d'un nom comptable)* too many; **ils ont t. d'argent** they've got too much money; **j'ai acheté t. de lait** I've bought too much milk; **il y a beaucoup t. de monde** there are far too many people; **tu veux des bonbons? – non, merci, j'en ai déjà t. mangé** do you want some sweets? – no thanks, I've already eaten too many; **je n'aurai pas t. d'une heure pour le faire** it will take me a good hour; **nous ne serons pas t. de cinq pour soulever le piano** it'll take at least five of us to lift the piano; **elle n'a fait preuve que de t. de patience** she has shown far too much patience

2 *(en corrélation avec "pour")* **il a t. d'expérience pour se tromper** he is too experienced to make a mistake; **j'ai t. de soucis pour me charger des vôtres** I've too many worries of my own to deal with yours

3 *(comme nom)* **le t. d'énergie des enfants** the children's excess *or* surplus energy

4 *(locution)* **en faire t.** *(travailler)* to overdo things; *(pour plaire)* to overdo it

trope [trɔp] NM trope

trophallaxie [trɔfalaksi] NF *Zool* trophallaxis

trophée [trɔfe] NM trophy

trophique [trɔfik] ADJ *Biol* trophic

trophoblaste [trɔfɔblast] NM *Anat* trophoblast

trophoblastique [trɔfɔblastik] ADJ *Anat* trophoblastic

tropical, -e, -aux, -ales [trɔpikal, -o] ADJ tropical

tropicalisation [trɔpikalizasjɔ̃] NF tropicalization

tropicaliser [3] [trɔpikalize] VT to tropicalize

tropique [trɔpik] ADJ tropical

NM *Astron & Géog* tropic; **le t. du Cancer/Capricorne** the tropic of Cancer/Capricorn

❑ **tropiques** NMPL *Géog* **les tropiques** the tropics; **sous les tropiques** in the tropics

tropisme [trɔpism] NM *Biol* tropism; *Fig* pull, (strong) attraction; **le t. des marchés envers la stabilité des prix** the way the markets are gravitating towards price stability

tropopause [trɔpɔpoz] NF tropopause

troposphère [trɔpɔsfɛr] NF troposphere

troposphérique [trɔpɔsferik] ADJ tropospheric

trop-perçu [trɔpɛrsy] *(pl* **trop-perçus***)* NM overpayment, excess payment

trop-plein [trɔplɛ̃] *(pl* **trop-pleins***)* NM **1** *(de forces, d'émotion)* overflow, surplus; **ton t. d'énergie** your surplus energy; **laisser déborder le t. de son cœur** to give vent to one's overflowing emotions; **elle épancha le t. de son âme** she poured out her soul **2** *(d'eau, de graines)* overflow; *(de vin)* surplus **3** *Tech* overflow; *(tuyau)* overflow pipe

troque [trɔk] *Zool* NM top-shell, *Spéc* trochus, member of the Trochidae

❑ **troques** NMPL top-shells, *Spéc* Trochidae

troquer [3] [trɔke] VT **1** *(échanger)* to exchange, to swap; **je troquerais bien mon manteau contre le tien** I wouldn't mind swapping coats with you **2** *Com* to barter, to trade; **ils troquent les fruits contre de la soie** they trade fruit for silk

troquet [trɔkɛ] NM *Fam* bar▪, *Br* boozer

trot [tro] NM *Équitation* trot, trotting *(UNCOUNT)*; **prendre le t.** to break into a trot; **course de t.** trotting *or* harness race; **t. assis** sitting trot; **t. attelé** trotting (with a sulky); **t. enlevé** rising trot; **t. monté** saddle-trot, saddle-trotting

❑ **au trot** ADV **1** *Équitation* at a trot *or* trotting pace; **aller au t.** to trot; **partir au t.** to set off at a trot; **au grand t.** at a brisk trot; **au petit t.** at a jogging pace

2 *Fam (vite)* on the double; **allez, et au t.!** come on, jump to it!

Trotski [trɔtski] NPR Trotsky

trotskisme [trɔtskism] NM Trotskyism

trotskiste [trɔtskist] ADJ Trotskyist

NMF Trotskyist

trotte [trɔt] NF *Fam* hike, stretch; **ils en ont fait une t.!** they've covered quite a distance!▪; **tout d'une t.** without stopping▪

trotte-menu [trɔtmәny] ADJ INV *Littéraire* **la gent t.** mice

trotter [3] [trɔte] VI **1** *(cheval, cavalier)* to trot

2 *(marcher vite → enfant)* to trot *or* to run along; *(→ souris)* to scurry along; **à cet âge-là, ils ont envie de t.** at that age, they want to run around; **on entendrait t. une souris** you could have heard a pin drop

3 *Fam (marcher beaucoup)* to do a lot of walking▪, to cover quite a distance on foot▪

4 *Fig* **j'ai une idée qui me trotte dans la tête** *ou* **la cervelle** I have an idea in my head; **cet air me trotte dans la tête!** I can't get that tune out of my head!

5 *Can Fam (vadrouiller)* to be gallivanting about; **il trotte du matin au soir** he's forever out gallivanting

►**se trotter** VPR *Fam* to take off, *Br* to scarper

trotteur, -euse [trɔtœr, -øz] ADJ **1** *Équitation* **cheval t.** trotter **2** *(chaussure)* **talon t.** low heel

NM,F *(cheval)* trotter

NM *(pour bébé)* baby-walker

❑ **trotteurs** NMPL *(chaussures)* flat shoes

❑ **trotteuse** NF **1** *(d'une montre)* second hand **2** *Can (pour bébés)* baby-walker

trottin [trɔtɛ̃] NM *Fam Vieilli* errand girl▪

trottinement [trɔtinmɑ̃] NM *(marche rapide)* trotting, scurrying; *(d'un enfant)* toddling; *(d'une souris)* scampering; *(bruit de pas)* patter

trottiner [3] [trɔtine] VI **1** *(souris)* to scurry, to scamper; *(cheval)* to jog-trot (along) **2** *(personne)* to trot along; **la petite trottinait près de son père** the little girl trotted along next to her father

trottinette [trɔtinɛt] NF **1** *(patinette)* scooter; **faire de la t.** to ride one's scooter; **t. à moteur** motorized scooter **2** *Fam (petite voiture)* little car▪

trotting [trɔtiŋ] NM *Équitation* breeding of trotting horses

trottoir [trɔtwar] NM **1** *(bord de chaussée) Br* pavement, *Am* sidewalk; **heurter le t.** *(en conduisant)* to hit the kerb; **il peint sur les trottoirs** he's a pavement artist; *Fam* **faire le t.** to be on the game, *Am* to hook **2** *Tech* **t. roulant** travelator, travolator, moving walkway

trou [tru] NM **1** *(cavité → gén)* hole; *(→ sur la route)* pothole; **faire un t. dans les économies de qn** to make a hole in sb's savings; **t. de mémoire** memory lapse, lapse of memory; **j'ai eu un t. (de mémoire)** my mind went blank *or* was a blank; **j'ai eu un t. (de mémoire) en scène** I dried up on stage; **j'ai un t.** my mind has gone blank *or* is a

blank; *Fam* **boire comme un t.** to drink like a fish; **un t. de souris** a mouse hole; **un studio ça? plutôt un t. de souris!** a studio? it's more like a hole in the wall!; **j'étais tellement gêné que j'aurais voulu disparaître dans un t. de souris** I was so embarrassed I wished the earth would swallow me up; **je ne veux pas déménager, j'ai fait mon t. ici** I don't want to move, I've settled down here; **parti de rien, il a fait son t.** he made his way in the world from very humble beginnings; **elle a fait son t. dans l'édition** she has made a nice little niche for herself in publishing; *Sport* **faire le t.** to break away from the field; **sortir de son t.** to go out into the big wide world; **t. d'aération** air vent; *Aut* **t. d'alimentation** supply port; *Naut* **t. du chat** lubber's hole; *Aut* **t. d'évacuation** drain hole; *Tech* **t. de graissage** oil hole; **t. d'homme** manhole; *Mines* **t. de mine** blast-hole, drillhole; **t. noir** *Astron* black hole; *Fig* depths of despair; **après la mort de mon mari, ça a été le t. noir** after my husband died I was in a black hole of depression; **t. normand** = glass of Calvados taken between courses of a meal; **faire le t. normand** = to take a break between courses with a glass of Calvados; *Mines & Constr* **t. de sondage** *ou* **de sonde** borehole; *Théât* **t. du souffleur** prompter's box

2 *(ouverture → dans une clôture, dans les nuages)* hole, gap; *(→ d'une aiguille)* eye; *(→ dans du cuir)* eyelet; **le maçon a fait un t. dans le mur** the builder knocked a hole in the wall; **le t. de la serrure** the keyhole; **regarder par le t. de la serrure** to watch through the keyhole; **le t. de la couche d'ozone** the hole in the ozone layer

3 *(déchirure)* hole, tear, rip; **avoir des trous à ses chaussettes** to have holes in one's socks; **faire un t. dans une membrane** to puncture *or* to perforate a membrane; **faire un t. à son collant** to make a hole in *or* to rip one's tights; **il a fini par faire un t. à son pull à l'endroit du coude** he finally wore a hole in the elbow of his jumper; **j'ai laissé tomber une allumette sur la nappe et ça a fait un t.** I dropped a match on the tablecloth and it burned a hole in it; **drap plein de trous** tattered sheet, sheet full of holes

4 *(moment)* gap; **un t. dans son emploi du temps** *(élève)* a free period; *(dans la reconstitution d'un crime)* = a period of time during which one's movements cannot be accounted for; *Fam* **il y a un t. dans ton CV** there's a gap in your *Br* CV *or Am* résumé; **la coiffeuse a un t. à 11 heures** the hairdresser can fit you in at 11 o'clock

5 *Fam (endroit isolé)* hole; **il n'est jamais sorti de son t.** he's never been out of his own backyard; **habiter un petit t. (perdu)** to live at the back of beyond; **je ne resterai pas dans ce t.** I won't stay in this hole; **pas même un café, quel t.!** not even a café, what a dump!

6 *Fam (tombe)* grave▪; **quand je serai dans le t.** when I've kicked the bucket *or* I'm six feet under

7 *Fam Arg crime (prison)* slammer, clink, *Br* nick; **être au t.** to be inside; **on l'a mis au t.** he was sent down

8 *Fam (déficit)* deficit▪; **il est parti en laissant un t. de 50 000 euros** he went off leaving us/the company/*etc* 50,000 euros worse off; **un t. dans le budget** a budget deficit; **le t. de la Sécu** the deficit in the French Social Security budget

9 *Anat* hole, *Spéc* foramen; **t. occipital** occipital foramen; **t. de l'oreille** earhole; **trous vertébraux** vertebral foramina; *Fam* **trous de nez** nostrils; *Fam* **s'en mettre jusqu'aux trous de nez** to stuff one's face; *Fam* **ça me sort par les trous de nez** I've had it up to here; *Vulg* **t. du cul** *ou* **de balle** *Br* arsehole, *Am* asshole; *Fam* **il n'a pas les yeux en face des trous** *(il n'est pas observateur)* he never sees what's going on right in front of him; *(il est à moitié endormi)* he hasn't come to yet, his brain isn't in gear yet; *Fam* **avoir un t. sous le nez** to drink like a fish

10 *Fam* **il a fait un t. dans l'eau** he's gone for a Burton

11 *Aviat* **t. d'air** air pocket; **des trous d'air** turbulence *(UNCOUNT)*

12 *Golf* hole; **le t. est partagé** the hole is halved; **envoyer la balle dans le t.** to hole out; **réussir t. en un** to get a hole in one; **faire un t.** to get the ball in the hole; **partie par trous** match play

troubadour [trubadur] **NM** troubadour

troublant, -e [trublɑ̃, -ɑ̃t] **ADJ 1** *(événement)* disturbing, unsettling, disquieting; *(question, ressemblance)* disconcerting **2** *(sensuel)* disturbing, provocative; *(déshabillé, sourire)* thrilling, arousing; *(parfum)* heady; **une femme troublante** a desirable woman

trouble[1] [trubl] **ADJ 1** *(eau)* cloudy, murky; *(vin)* cloudy; *(image)* blurred; *(photo)* blurred, out-of-focus; *(regard, verre)* misty, dull; *(lumière)* dim; **avoir la vue t.** to have blurred vision

2 *(confus)* vague, unclear, imprecise; **une vision t. du problème** a muddled view of the problem; **un désir t.** a vague desire

3 *(équivoque)* equivocal, ambiguous; **elle aime les situations un peu troubles** she likes slightly ambiguous situations

4 *(peu honnête)* dubious; **une affaire t.** a murky business; **personnage t.** suspicious character; **période t. de l'histoire** murky period of history; **il y a quelque chose de t. dans cette affaire** there's something shady *or* fishy *or* not kosher about this business

ADV through a blur; **je vois t.** everything *or* my vision is blurred

trouble[2] [trubl] **NM 1** *(sentiment → de gêne)* confusion, embarrassment; *(→ de perplexité)* confusion; *(→ de peine)* distress, turmoil; *(→ d'amour)* agitation; **il ne put cacher son t. en la voyant** he couldn't hide his embarrassment when he saw her; **la nouvelle sema** *ou* **jeta le t. dans les esprits** the news sowed confusion in people's minds *or* threw people's minds into confusion; *Littéraire* **c'est un t. si doux que l'amour** love is such sweet turmoil

2 *Méd* disorder; **t. de l'adaptation** adjustment disorder; **t. caractériel** emotional disorder; **troubles circulatoires** circulation problems, trouble with one's circulation; **t. cognitif léger** mild cognitive impairment *(UNCOUNT)*; **un t. du comportement** a behaviour problem; **troubles gastriques/intestinaux** stomach/intestinal disorder; **elle souffre de troubles digestifs** she has trouble with her digestion; **t. d'hyperactivité avec déficit de l'attention** attention deficit hyperactivity disorder; **troubles du langage** speech disorders; **troubles mentaux** mental disorders; **t. obsessionnel compulsif** obsessive compulsive disorder; **troubles de la personnalité** personality problems; *Psy* personality disorders; **troubles respiratoires** respiratory disorders; **troubles visuels** *ou* **de la vue** eye trouble *(UNCOUNT)*

3 *(désaccord)* discord, trouble; **jeter** *ou* **semer le t. dans une famille** to sow discord within a family; **ne viens pas jeter** *ou* **semer le t. ici!** don't you come stirring up trouble (around here)!

4 *Jur* disturbance (of rights); **t. de jouissance** disturbance of possession

5 *Pétr* **point de t.** cloud *or* turbidity point

❑ **troubles NMPL 1** *(agitation sociale)* unrest *(UNCOUNT)*, disturbances; **période de troubles** period of unrest; **les troubles s'étendent** the rioting is spreading

2 *(d'un cours d'eau)* suspended matter *(UNCOUNT)*

trouble[3] [trubl] = **truble**

troubleau, -x [trublo] **NM** = **truble**

trouble-fête [trubləfɛt] *(pl inv ou* **trouble-fêtes***)* **NMF** killjoy, spoilsport; **jouer les t.** to be a killjoy *or* spoilsport; **je ne veux pas jouer les t., mais...** I don't want to be a spoilsport *or* to put a damper on the proceedings, but...

troubler [3] [truble] **VT 1** *(eau)* to cloud

2 *(rendre moins net)* to blur, to dim, to cloud; **t. la vue de qn** to blur *or* to cloud sb's vision

3 *(sommeil)* to disturb; *(paix)* to disturb, to disrupt; *(silence)* to break; *(digestion)* to upset; *(bonheur)* to spoil

4 *(fête, réunion)* to disrupt; *(plan)* to upset, to disrupt; **un incident est venu t. notre soirée** an unfortunate incident cast a cloud over our evening; **une époque troublée** troubled times; **période troublée par la guerre** period disrupted by war; **t. l'ordre public** *Br* to cause a breach of the peace, *Am* to disturb the peace; **discours propre à t. l'ordre public** inflammatory speech

5 *(déconcerter)* to confuse, to disconcert; **un détail nous trouble encore** one detail is still baffling us; **ses remarques m'avaient troublé** his/her remarks had unsettled me; **la question semble te t.** you seem put out *or* disconcerted by the question; **ce qui me trouble dans cette affaire** what bothers *or* disturbs me about this matter

6 *(mettre en émoi → personne)* to thrill, to arouse; *(→ imagination)* to stir; **t. qn** to make sb nervous, to fluster sb; **ce film m'a vraiment troublé** I found the movie quite disturbing; **sa présence le troublait profondément** her presence aroused *or* excited him profoundly

7 *Jur* **t. qn dans la jouissance d'un bien** to disturb sb's enjoyment of possession

▸**se troubler VPR 1** *(eau)* to become cloudy *or* turbid; *(vue)* to become blurred, to grow dim; *(mémoire)* to fade; *(voix)* to break (with emotion); *(idées)* to become confused

2 *(perdre contenance)* to get confused; **dès qu'on le regarde, il se trouble** as soon as somebody looks at him he goes to pieces; **sans se t.** *(répondre)* unruffled, without turning a hair; **continuez sans vous t.** carry on and don't let yourself get ruffled

trouduc [trudyk], **trou-du-cul** [trudyky] **NM** *Vulg (imbécile) Br* arsehole, *Am* asshole

troué, -e[1] [true] **ADJ un vieux châle t.** a *Br* tatty *or Am* raggedy old shawl; **la chaussette est trouée** the sock's got a hole in; **des chaussettes toutes trouées** socks full of holes; **avoir des bas troués** to have holes in one's stockings; **t. comme une écumoire** *ou* **une passoire** full of *or* riddled with holes

trouée[2] [true] **NF 1** *(ouverture)* gap; **une t. de ciel bleu** a patch of blue sky; **une t. dans les nuages** a break in the clouds; **la t. du chemin** the opening formed by the path **2** *Géog* gap **3** *Mil* breach; **effectuer une t.** to break through

trouer [3] [true] **VT 1** *(percer → carton, tissu)* to make a hole in; *(→ tôle)* to pierce; *Tech (→ zinc)* to perforate; *(→ cloison)* to make *or* to bore a hole in; **la pointe a troué le caoutchouc** the tip made a hole in the rubber; **la balle lui a troué le corps** the bullet pierced his/her body; *Fam* **t. la peau à qn** *(tuer quelqu'un)* to shoot sb▪, to put a bullet in sb; *Fam* **se faire t. la peau** to get shot▪, to be pumped full of lead

2 *(traverser)* to pierce; *(lignes ennemies)* to breach; **le soleil trouait les nuages** the sun was breaking through the clouds

3 *(cribler)* to pit; **des météorites ont troué le fond du canyon** meteorites have pitted the bottom of the canyon; **des immeubles troués par des bombes** buildings pockmarked with shell holes; **surface trouée de balles** surface pitted with bullet holes

▸**se trouer VPR** *(d'un seul trou)* to get a hole; *(de plusieurs trous)* to get holes, *Br* go into holes; **mes chaussures se sont trouées au bout d'une semaine** there was a hole in my shoes after a week

troufignon [trufiɲɔ̃] **NM** *très Fam (anus) Br* arsehole, *Am* asshole; *(derrière) Br* arse, *Am* ass

troufion [trufjɔ̃] **NM 1** *Fam (simple soldat) Br* squaddie, *Am* grunt **2** *très Fam (postérieur) Br* arse, *Am* ass

trouillard, -e [trujar, -ard] *très Fam* **ADJ** lily-livered, chicken

NM,F chicken *(person)*

trouille [truj] **NF** *très Fam* fear▪, fright▪; **ça va lui flanquer** *ou* **ficher la t.** it'll scare the living daylights out of him/her; **avoir la t.** to be petrified, to be scared stiff; **j'avais une t. bleue** I was scared stiff *or* to death; **je n'ai jamais eu une telle t. de ma vie** I've never been so petrified in my life

trouillomètre [trujɔmɛtr] **NM** *très Fam* **avoir le t. à zéro** to be scared stiff *or* to death

trouilloter [3] [trujɔte] **VI** *très Fam* **1** *(avoir peur)* to be scared shitless, to be shit-scared **2** *(sentir mauvais)* to stink, *Br* to pong

trouilloteuse [trujɔtøz] **NF** = machine for punching holes in banknotes to render them invalid

trou-madame [trumadam] *(pl* **trous-madame***)* **NM** nineholes *(singulier)*

troupe [trup] **NF 1** *(de touristes, d'enfants)* troop; **ils se déplacent toujours en t.** they always go round as a group

2 *Mil (formation, régiment)* troop; **la t., les troupes** the troops *or* men; **officier de t.** regimental officer; **officiers et t.** officers and men *or*

and other ranks; **on fit donner** *ou* **intervenir la t., on envoya la t.** the army was *or* troops were sent in; **troupes de choc** shock troops

3 *Théât* **t. (de théâtre** *ou* **de comédiens)** company, troupe; **t. d'amateurs** amateur company *or* troupe; **monter une t.** to set up a company; **final avec toute la t.** grand finale (with all the cast)

4 *(de scouts)* troop

5 *(d'éléphants)* herd; *(de sangliers)* sounder, herd; **ces animaux vivent en t.** these animals live in herds *or* are gregarious

troupeau, -x [trupo] **NM 1** *(de vaches, d'éléphants, de girafes)* herd; *(de moutons)* flock; *(d'oies)* gaggle; **il garde le t.** *(de vaches)* he's tending the herd; *(de moutons)* he's tending the flock **2** *Rel* **le t. des fidèles** the flock **3** *Péj (multitude passive)* herd; **quel t. d'imbéciles!** what a load of idiots!

troupiale [trupjal] **NM** *Orn* troopial, troupial

troupier [trupje] **ADJ M** *voir* **comique**

NM *Fam* soldier▪

troussage [trusaʒ] **NM 1** *Culin* trussing **2** *Métal* strickling

trousse [trus] **NF 1** *(étui)* case; *(d'écolier)* pencil case; **t. de maquillage** make-up bag; **t. de médecin** medical bag; **t. à ongles** manicure set; **t. à outils** toolkit; **t. de secours** first-aid kit; **t. de toilette** spongebag

2 *(pour un acrobate)* tights

3 *Mines* **t. coupante** cutting *or* drum curb; **t. de cuvelage** curb, crib

❑ **aux trousses de PRÉP être aux trousses de qn** to be after *or* chasing sb, to be (hot) on sb's heels; **le fisc est à nos trousses** we've got the taxman after us; **il a la police aux trousses** the police are after him, the police are on his tail *or* hot on his heels; **comme s'il avait le diable à ses trousses** *ou* **le feu aux trousses** like a bat out of hell

troussé, -e [truse] **ADJ** *Fam* **bien t.** *(objet, compliment)* neat▪; **un petit refrain bien** *ou* **joliment t.** a catchy little tune; **un petit slogan bien t.** a snappy slogan

trousseau, -x [truso] **NM 1** *(assortiment)* **t. (de clés)** bunch of keys **2** *(de mariée)* trousseau *(including linen)* **3** *(de pensionnaire)* clothes, outfit

trousse-pied [truspje] **NM INV** leg strap *(for animal)*

trousse-queue [truskø] **NM INV** tail case *(for horse)*

troussequin [truskɛ̃] **NM 1** *(de selle)* cantle **2** *(outil)* marking gauge

trousser [3] [truse] **VT 1** *Culin* to truss (up) **2** *(rédiger avec brio)* **en deux minutes, il troussait un poème** he could dash off a poem in a couple of minutes; **t. un compliment à qn** to pay sb a neat compliment **3** *très Fam (posséder sexuellement)* to hump, *Br* to shag **4** *Vieilli (retrousser → vêtement)* to hitch up

►**se trousser VPR** *Vieilli* to hitch up one's skirts

trousseur [trusœr] **NM** *Fam Vieilli* **t. de jupons** womanizer, philanderer▪

trou-trou [trutru] *(pl* **trou-trous***)* **NM** = embroidery of ribbon-leading eyelets; **jupon/corsage à trou-trous** broderie anglaise petticoat/blouse, frilly petticoat/blouse

trouvable [truvabl] **ADJ** possible to find

trouvaille [truvaj] **NF** *(objet, lieu)* find; *(idée, méthode)* brainwave; *(expression)* coinage; **une émission pleine de trouvailles** a programme full of good ideas

trouvé, -e [truve] **ADJ 1** *(découvert) voir* **enfant 2** *(locutions)* **bien t.** *(original)* well-chosen, apposite; **voilà une réponse bien trouvée!** that's a (pretty) good answer!; **tout t.** ready-made; **voici un moyen tout t. de gagner de l'argent** here's a ready-made way of making money

TROUVER [3] [truve]

> **VT** to find **A1-3, B, C, D1** ▪ to discover **A1, 2** ▪ to catch **B2** ▪ to think **D**
> **V IMPERSONNEL** there is/are **1**
> **VPR** to be found **2** ▪ to be (situated) **3** ▪ to find oneself **5, 7** ▪ to feel **6** ▪ to happen **8**

VT A. *APRÈS UNE RECHERCHE* **1** *(objet perdu, personne, emploi)* to find; *(empreintes, trésor)* to find, to discover; *(pétrole)* to strike, to find; **je n'ai toujours pas de secrétaire – patiente, tu finiras par t. quelqu'un** I still haven't got a secretary – be patient, you'll find someone in the end; **ah, je te trouve enfin!** so I've found you at last!; **où pourrais-je la t. mardi?** where could I find *or* contact her on Tuesday?; **je sais où on trouve des champignons** I know where you can find mushrooms; **t. un village sur une carte** to find *or* to locate a village on a map; **d'après ce que les archéologues ont trouvé** from the archaeologists' findings, from what the archaeologists have found; **là, vous allez t. la route Paris–Lyon** that's where you'll join up with the Paris–Lyons road; **as-tu trouvé où il se cache?** have you found where he's hiding *or* his hiding-place?; **j'ai trouvé où faire reproduire des cartes postales anciennes** I've found a place where they do reproductions of old postcards; **il faut que je trouve 200 euros avant demain** I must get hold of *or* find 200 euros before tomorrow; **j'ai trouvé en elle la sœur/l'amie que je cherchais** in her I found the sister/the friend I'd been looking for

2 *(détecter)* to find, to discover; **je ne trouve plus son pouls** I can't feel his/her pulse any more; **je ne trouve rien (d'anormal) à la radiographie** I can't find *or* I haven't detected anything wrong on the X-ray; **ils lui ont trouvé quelque chose au sein** they found a lump in her breast; **des traces de sang ont été trouvées sur ses vêtements** blood stains were found *or* discovered on his/her clothes; **ils ont trouvé beaucoup de coquilles dans le texte** they found *or* spotted a lot of misprints in the text; *Ordinat* **t. et remplacer** to find and replace

3 *(acheter)* to find, to get; **je n'ai pas trouvé de crème fraîche, alors j'ai mis du yaourt** I couldn't find *or* get any cream so I used yoghurt instead; **du safran, on en trouve dans les épiceries fines** you can get *or* find saffron in good delicatessens

4 *(rendre visite à)* **aller t. qn** to go to sb, to go and see sb; **il faut que tu ailles t. un spécialiste** you should go and see a specialist; **venir t. qn** to come to sb, to come and see sb; **on vient souvent me t. pour me demander conseil** people often come to me for advice

B. *INVOLONTAIREMENT* **1** *(tomber sur → personne, lettre, trésor)* to find; **j'ai trouvé ce livre en faisant du rangement** I found *or* came across this book while I was tidying up; **j'ai trouvé ce bouquet de roses en rentrant chez moi** I found this bunch of roses waiting for me when I got home; **en abattant la cloison, ils ont trouvé un coffret** when they pulled down the partition they discovered *or* found a casket; **à notre grande surprise, nous avons trouvé le beau temps en arrivant** when we got there we were surprised to find that the weather was good; **si je m'attendais à te t. là!** fancy meeting you here!; **si je trouve celui qui m'a cabossé ma portière!** just let me lay my hands on whoever dented my car door!; **t. qch par hasard** to chance *or* to stumble upon sth; **j'ai trouvé ma maison cambriolée** I found my house burgled *or* that my house had been burgled; **on l'a trouvé mort dans la cuisine** he was found dead in the kitchen; **t. à qui parler** *(un confident)* to find a friend; *Fam* **s'il continue comme ça, il va t. à qui parler!** if he goes on like that, I'll give him what for!

2 *(surprendre)* to find, to catch; **que personne ne te trouve ici!** don't let anyone find *or* catch you here!; **je l'ai trouvé fouillant** *ou* **qui fouillait dans mes tiroirs** I found *or* I caught him searching through my drawers

C. *PAR L'ESPRIT, LA VOLONTÉ* **1** *(inventer → prétexte, méthode etc)* to find; **où as-tu trouvé cette idée?** where did you get that idea from?; **tu trouveras bien un prétexte** you'll find some excuse (or other); **tu n'as rien trouvé de mieux à faire?** couldn't you find anything better to do?; **je ne savais pas ce que je faisais – c'est tout ce que tu as trouvé?** I didn't know what I was doing – is that the best you can come up with?; **t. qch à répondre** to find an answer; **je n'ai rien trouvé à répondre** I was stuck for an answer

2 *(deviner → solution)* to find; *(→ réponse, mot de passe)* to find (out), to discover; *(→ code)* to break, to crack; **je n'ai pas pu t. la raison de son refus** I was unable to find out why he refused; **j'ai trouvé!** I've got it!, I know!; **39 moins 7, il fallait t. 32** 39 take away 7, the correct result was 32

3 *(parvenir à)* to find; **t. la force/le courage de faire qch** to find the strength/the courage to do sth; **il a trouvé son équilibre dans la peinture** he found peace of mind in painting; **ça y est, j'ai trouvé ce que je voulais te dire!** I know what I wanted to tell you!; **je n'arrivais pas à t. mes mots** I couldn't find the right words, I was lost for words; **là, tu as trouvé le mot juste!** you've said it!; *Hum* **tu as trouvé ça tout seul?** did you come up with that all on your own?; **t. à se loger** to find accommodation *or* somewhere to live; **je trouverai à me faire remplacer** I'll find someone to stand in for me; **t. à vendre sa voiture** to find a buyer for one's car; **on ne trouve jamais à se garer par ici** you can never find anywhere to park around here; **le chien a encore trouvé à s'échapper** the dog's managed to run away again

4 *(se ménager)* to find; **t. le temps de lire** to find time to read; **je n'ai pas le temps – trouve-le!** I haven't got time – (then you must) make time!; **t. l'occasion de faire qch** to find the opportunity to do sth

5 *(ressentir)* to find; **t. du plaisir à qch/à faire qch** to take pleasure in sth/in doing sth, to enjoy sth/doing sth; **nous trouvions de la satisfaction à remplir notre devoir** we used to find it satisfying to do our duty

D. *AVOIR COMME OPINION* **1** *(juger, estimer)* to find, to think; **t. qch remarquable** to find sth remarkable, to think that sth is remarkable; **tu ne trouves rien de bizarre à cette demande?** don't you find that request somewhat strange?; **je la trouve déprimée en ce moment** I find her depressed at the moment; **tu vas me t. vieilli** you'll think *or* find I've aged; **comment me trouves-tu dans cette robe?** how do you like me in this dress?; **t. que** to think *or* to find that; **je trouve que ça en vaut la peine** I think *or* I reckon it's worth it; **je trouve qu'il change beaucoup en ce moment** he seems to me to be going through a lot of changes at the moment; **il est prétentieux – je ne trouve pas** he's pretentious – I don't think so; **la soupe manque de sel, tu ne trouves pas?** the soup needs more salt, don't you think?; **tu trouves?** do you think so?

2 *(reconnaître)* **je lui trouve du charme** I think he's/she's got charm; **tu ne lui trouves pas une petite ressemblance avec ta sœur?** don't you think *or* wouldn't you say that she looks a bit like your sister?; *Fam* **mais enfin, qu'est-ce que tu lui trouves, à ce type?** for goodness' sake, what do you see in this guy?; **je lui trouve mauvais goût, à ce vin** I don't think this wine tastes very nice; **je lui ai trouvé mauvaise mine hier** he/she didn't look very well to me yesterday

►**se trouver V IMPERSONNEL 1 il se trouve** *(suivi d'un singulier)* there is; *(suivi d'un pluriel)* there are; **il se trouvera toujours quelqu'un pour te renseigner** you'll always find somebody *or* there'll always be someone you can ask; **il s'est trouvé peu de gens pour accepter** only a few people said yes *or* accepted

2 il se trouve que... *(le hasard fait que)* as it happens,...; **il se trouve que quelqu'un vous a vu dans mon bureau** as it happens, somebody saw you in my office; **il s'est trouvé que je les ai entendus** I chanced to overhear them, by chance I overheard them; **il s'est trouvé que c'était lui le fautif** it turned out that HE was to blame

VPR 1 *(s'estimer)* **je me trouve trop mince** I think I'm too thin; **et tu te trouves drôle?** so you think you're (being) funny?; **il se trouve génial** he thinks he's great, he really fancies himself

2 *(emploi passif)* to be found, to exist; **cette fleur ne se trouve qu'en montagne** this flower

is only (to be) found *or* only grows in the mountains; **de bons artisans, cela se trouve difficilement** it's not easy to find *or* to get good craftsmen; *aussi Hum* **des hommes galants, ça ne se trouve plus!** real gentlemen are a dying breed!; **ça ne se trouve pas sous le pas d'un cheval** *(argent)* it's hard to come by

3 *(en un lieu, une circonstance → personne)* to be; *(→ bâtiment, ville)* to be, to be situated, to be located; *(résider → intérêt, problème)* to be, to lie; **je me trouvais là par hasard** I just happened to be there; **qu'est-ce que tu dirais si tu te trouvais face à face avec lui?** what would you say if you suddenly found yourself face to face with him?; **ma main s'est trouvée coincée dans la porte** my hand got caught in the door; **trouve-toi devant la gare à 18 heures** make sure you're outside the station at 6 p.m.; **où se trouve la gare?** where's the station?; **Senlis se trouve au nord de Paris** Senlis is to the north of Paris, Senlis is situated *or* located north of Paris; **A se trouve à égale distance de B et de C** B and C are equidistant from A; **se t. sur** *(figurer)* to appear *or* to be shown on; **mon nom ne se trouve pas sur la liste** my name doesn't feature *or* figure on the list, my name isn't listed; **c'est là que se trouve la difficulté/le dilemme** that's where the difficulty/dilemma lies

4 *(arriver)* **quand vous vous trouverez sur la place, tournez à droite** when you arrive at the square, turn right

5 *(dans une situation)* to find oneself, to be; **je me trouve devant un choix** I'm faced with a choice; **se t. dans l'impossibilité de faire qch** to find oneself *or* to be unable to do sth; **se t. dans l'obligation de faire qch** to have no option but to do sth

6 *(se sentir)* to feel; **je me suis trouvé bête d'avoir crié** I felt stupid for having screamed; **se t. bien/mieux** *(du point de vue de la santé)* to feel good/better; *(dans un siège)* to feel comfortable/more comfortable; *(avec quelqu'un)* to feel at ease/more at ease; *(dans un vêtement élégant)* to feel (that one looks) good/better; **se t. mal** *(s'évanouir)* to pass out, to faint; **elle a suivi mes conseils et s'en est bien/mal trouvée** she followed my advice, and benefited from it/ and lived to regret it; **qu'il parte, je ne m'en trouverai que mieux!** let him leave, see if I care!

7 *(se réaliser)* to find oneself; **en tant qu'écrivain, elle ne s'est pas encore trouvée** as a writer, she hasn't found her individual voice *or* style yet

8 *(exprime la fortuité d'un événement, d'une situation)* to happen; **ils se trouvaient appartenir au même club** it turned out that they belonged to the same club; **je me trouve être libre ce jour-là** it so happens that I'm free that day; *Fam* **si ça se trouve** maybe; **on l'a abandonné, ce gamin, si ça se trouve!** maybe the kid's been abandoned(, who knows)!; **si ça se trouve, il y a une fuite** maybe there's a leak

trouvère [truvɛr] NM *Littérature* trouvère

trouveur, -euse [truvœr, -øz] NM,F *Littéraire* discoverer, inventor

troyen[1], -enne[1] [trwajɛ̃, -ɛn] ADJ *(de Troie)* Trojan
□ **Troyen, -enne** NM,F Trojan

troyen[2], -enne[2] [trwajɛ̃, -ɛn] ADJ *(de Troyes)* of/ from Troyes
□ **Troyen, -enne** NM,F = inhabitant of or person from Troyes

tr/s *Tech* (*abrév écrite* **tours par seconde**) revs/s

truand [tryɑ̃] NM **1** *(escroc)* crook; *(gangster)* gangster, hood; *Fig* **les commerçants du coin sont tous des truands!** the local shopkeepers are all crooks! **2** *Arch (mendiant)* beggar

truander [3] [tryɑ̃de] VT *Fam (escroquer)* to con, to swindle■; *(faire payer trop cher)* to rip off; **se faire t.** to be *or* get conned; *(payer trop cher)* to get ripped off

VI **1** *Fam (tricher)* **t. (à un examen)** to cheat■ (in

an exam) **2** *Fam (resquiller)* to sneak in■ **3** *Arch (vivre en truand)* to live a beggar's life

truanderie [tryɑ̃dri] NF *Fam Vieilli* con, scam

truble [trybl] NF *Pêche* hoop net

trublion [tryblijɔ̃] NM troublemaker

truc[1] [tryk] NM *Fam* **1** *(astuce)* trick■; **un t. tout bête et qui marche à tous les coups** a simple little trick that works every time; **tu ne le prendras pas en défaut, il connaît tous les trucs** you won't catch him out, he knows all the tricks; **connaître (tous) les trucs du métier** to know the tricks of the trade; **j'ai trouvé le t.!** I've got the hang of it!; **elle a toujours pas pigé le t.!** she still hasn't got the hang of it!; **il y a un t.!** there's a trick in it!; **il doit y avoir un t., c'est trop beau** there's bound to be a catch, it's too good to be true; **je te donne un t. pour enlever les taches** here's a trick for *or* a clever way of removing stains; **j'ai un t. pour rentrer sans payer** I know a way of getting in without paying■

2 *Cin & Théât* (special) effect■, trick■; **pièce à trucs** play with elaborate stage effects■

3 *(chose)* thing■; **je pense à un t.** I've just thought of something; **il faudrait que tu me dises un t....** tell me something...; **j'ai plein de trucs à faire** I've got lots to do; **je voudrais lui offrir un petit t.** I'd like to give him/her a little something; **tu devrais t'acheter un t. pour nettoyer ton four** you ought to buy something to clean your oven with; **elle a encore acheté des trucs** she's been shopping again■; **mange pas de ce t.-là!** don't eat any of that (stuff)!; **sa maladie, c'est un sale t.** his/her illness is a nasty business■

4 *(objet dont on ne connaît pas le nom)* thing, whatchamacallit, *Br* thingy; **tu sais, ce t. dont on se sert pour couper la pâte** you know, the thing you use to cut the pastry with; **qu'est-ce que c'est que ce t.-là?** what's that (thingumajig)?

5 *(intérêt)* **ce n'est pas/c'est mon t.** it's not/it's my cup of tea; **le rock, c'est pas mon t.** rock music is not my (kind of) thing; **l'écologie, c'est vraiment son t.** he's/she's really into environmental issues; **c'est tout à fait son t.** it's just his/ her sort of thing, *Br* it's right up his/her street

6 *(personne dont on a oublié le nom)* **T.** what's-his-name, *f* what's-her-name, *Br* thingy

truc[2] [tryk] = **truck**

trucage [trykaʒ] = **truquage**

truchement [tryʃmɑ̃] NM **1** **par le t. de son ami** through *or* via his/her friend **2** *Arch (interprète)* interpreter

trucider [3] [tryside] VT *Fam* to bump off, to waste; *Hum* **une heure de retard, on va se faire t.!** we're an hour late, they'll kill us!

truck [tryk] NM *Rail* truck, *Am* freight car

truckman [trykman] (*pl* **truckmen** [trykmɛn]) NM *TV & Cin* special effects person

trucmuche [trykmyʃ] NM *Fam* **1** *(chose)* thingumajig, thingamabob, *Br* thingy **2 T.** *(personne)* what's-his-name, *f* what's-her-name, *Br* thingy

truculence [trykylɑ̃s] NF colourfulness

truculent, -e [trykylɑ̃, -ɑ̃t] ADJ colourful

truelle [tryɛl] NF **1** *(du maçon)* trowel **2** *(pour servir)* **t. à poisson** fish slice **3 travailler à la t.** *(peintre)* to work with a trowel

truellée [tryɛle] NF trowelful

truffe [tryf] NF **1** *(champignon)* truffle; **omelette aux truffes** truffle omelette **2** *(friandise)* **t. (au chocolat)** (chocolate) truffle **3** *(de chien, de chat)* nose **4** *Fam (nez)* snout **5** *Fam (imbécile)* *Br* divvy, *Am* lamebrain, schmuck

truffer [3] [tryfe] VT **1** *Culin* to garnish with truffles; **pâté truffé** truffled pâté, pâté with truffles; **poularde truffée** truffled chicken **2** *Fig (emplir)* to fill; **ils l'ont truffé de balles** they pumped him full of bullets; **truffé de mines** riddled with mines; **truffé d'anecdotes/de citations** peppered with anecdotes/with quotations; **truffé de fautes** riddled with mistakes

trufficulture [tryfikyltyr] NF truffle cropping

truffier, -ère [tryfje, -ɛr] ADJ **chien t.** truffle hound; **chêne t.** = oak on whose roots truffles grow
□ **truffière** NF truffle-bed, trufflery

truie [tryi] NF **1** *Zool* sow **2** *Mil* ballista **3** *Ich* **t. de mer** hog-fish

truisme [tryism] NM truism; **c'est un t.!** it's obvious!, it goes without saying!

truite [tryit] NF trout; **t. arc-en-ciel** rainbow trout, steelhead; **t. fario** river trout; **t. de lac** lake trout; **t. de mer** sea trout; *Culin* **t. meunière** = trout sautéed in butter and served with parsley and lemon juice; **t. de rivière** river trout; **t. saumonée** salmon trout

truité, -e [tryite] ADJ **1** *(tacheté → gén)* speckled; *(→ chien, cheval)* spotted **2** *Cér* crackled

trullo [trulo] (*pl* **trullos** *ou* **trulli**) NM *Archit* trullo

trumeau, -x [trymo] NM **1** *(entre des fenêtres)* (window) pier **2** *(panneau de lambris, de peinture, de glace)* pier glass; *(d'une cheminée)* overmantel **3** *Archit* pier **4** *Culin* leg of beef **5** *Fam (femme laide)* dog, *Br* boot, *Am* beast

truquage [trykaʒ] NM **1** *Cin (action)* (use of) special effects; *(résultat)* special effect; *(de photographie)* faking; **c'est un t.** it's all faked **2** *(d'élections, de résultats)* rigging; *(de match)* fixing, rigging; *(de comptes)* fiddling

truquer [3] [tryke] VT **1** *(élection, statistiques)* to rig; *(match)* to fix, to rig; *(comptes)* to fiddle; *(entretien)* to set up; *(tableau)* to fake; *(dés)* to load; **les dés sont truqués** the dice are loaded **2** *(photographie)* to fake, to rig; *Cin* **une scène truquée** the scene contains *or* has special effects **3** *Mines (mine, minerai, échantillon)* to salt

truqueur, -euse [trykœr, -øz] NM,F **1** *(escroc)* cheat **2** *Cin* special effects person *or* generator

truquiste [trykist] NMF *Cin* special effects man, *f* woman

trusquin [tryskɛ̃] NM marking gauge

trusquiner [3] [tryskine] VT to mark with a gauge

trust [trœst] NM **1** *Écon* trust; **t. commercial** commercial monopoly; **t. industriel** industrial monopoly; **t. de placement** investment trust; **t. de valeurs** holding company; **t. vertical** vertical trust **2** *(entreprise)* corporation

truste [tryst] NF *Hist* = group of men forming the entourage of a Frankish king

trustee [trœsti] NM *Banque & Admin* trustee

truster [3] [trœste] VT **1** *(marché)* to corner, to monopolize **2** *Fam (monopoliser)* to monopolize■, to hog; **t. les médailles** *(athlète)* to carry off all the medals; **il truste les premiers rôles du cinéma français** he gets all the leading roles in French cinema■

VI *Com* to form a monopoly

trutticulture [trytikyltyr] NF trout breeding

trypanosome [tripanozom] *Zool* NM trypanosome, *Spéc* member of the Trypanosoma genus
□ **trypanosomes** NMPL trypanosomes, *Spéc* Trypanosoma

trypanosomiase [tripanɔzɔmjaz] NF *Méd* trypanosomiasis

trypsine [tripsin] NF *Biol & Chem* trypsin

trypsinogène [tripsinɔʒɛn] NM *Biol & Chem* trypsinogen

tryptophane [triptɔfan] NM *Biol & Chem* tryptophan

ts (*abrév écrite* **tous**) all

tsar [tsar, dzar] NM tsar, czar

tsarévitch [tsarevitʃ, dzarevitʃ] NM tsarevitch, czarevitch

tsarine [tsarin, dzarin] NF tsarina, czarina

tsarisme [tsarism, dzarism] NM tsarism, czarism

tsariste [tsarist, dzarist] ADJ tsarist, czarist
NMF tsarist, czarist

tsé-tsé [tsetse] NF INV *Entom* tsetse (fly)

TSF [teɛsɛf] NF *Vieilli Tél* (*abrév* **télégraphie sans fil**) *(appareil)* wireless; *(procédé)* wireless telegraphy

T-shirt [tiʃœrt] = **tee-shirt**

tsigane [tsigan] ADJ Gypsyish
□ **Tsigane** NMF (Hungarian) Gypsy

tsuba [tsuba] NM tsuba

tsunami [tsynami] NM tsunami

TSVP (*abrév écrite* **tournez s'il vous plaît**) PTO

TT [tete] NM *Aut* (*abrév* **transit temporaire (autorisé)**) = registration for vehicles bought in France for tax-free export by non-residents

tt *(abrév écrite* **tout)** **ADJ** all
ADV everything
TTA [teteɑ] = **TT**
TTC [tetese] **ADJ** *Com (abrév* **toutes taxes comprises)** inclusive of all tax, including tax
tt conf *(abrév écrite* **tout confort)** with all mod cons
tte *(abrév écrite* **toute)** all
ttes *(abrév écrite* **toutes)** all
TTL [teteɛl] **ADJ** *Phot (abrév* **through the lens)** TTL
TTX *Ordinat (abrév écrite* **traitement de texte)** WP
TU [tey] **NM** *(abrév* **temps universel)** UT, GMT; **à 0h TU** at 0h UT *or* GMT
tu¹, -e [ty] **PP** *voir* **taire**
tu² [ty] **PRON PERSONNEL 1** *(sujet d'un verbe)* you; **tu as raison** you're right; **qui es-tu?** who are you?; *Fam* **qu'est-ce que t'as?** what's up (with you)?▪; *Fam* **t'en veux?** do you want some?▪; *Fam* **t'es bête!** you're stupid!▪
2 *Rel* thou; *(en s'adressant à Dieu)* **Tu** Thou; **tu ne tueras point** thou shall not kill
3 *(emploi nominal)* **dire tu à qn** to use the familiar form *or* the "tu" form with *or* to sb; **allez, on va se dire tu** ≃ come on, let's not stand on ceremony; **vous vous dites tu?** ≃ are you on first-name terms with each other?; **être à tu et à toi avec qn** ≃ to be on first-name terms with sb

> *Allusion*
> **Tu quoque, fili!**
> According to Latin historians, these are the words (meaning "you too, my son!") spoken by Caesar when he was stabbed to death as he recognized his friend Brutus amongst his assassins. The phrase is used in literary French with somewhat facetious overtones to express surprised disappointment at the discovery that a friend has let you down. Sometimes the friend's name is used instead of "fili". The English equivalent, also in Latin, is "Et tu, Brute!", from Shakespeare's *Julius Caesar.*

tuable [tɥabl] **ADJ** *(animal)* fit for slaughter
tuage [tɥaʒ] **NM** slaughter(ing), killing
Tuamotu [twamotu] **NFPL les T.** the Tuamotu Archipelago
tuant, -e [tɥɑ̃, -ɑ̃t] **ADJ** *Fam* **1** *(épuisant)* exhausting▪ **2** *(insupportable)* exasperating▪; **c'est t., ce bruit** this noise is driving me up the wall; **les enfants sont vraiment tuants aujourd'hui** the kids are being a real pain today **3** *(ennuyeux)* deadly dull▪ *or* boring▪
tub [tœb] **NM 1** *(objet)* tub, bathtub **2** *(bain)* bath; **prendre un t.** to take *or* have a bath
tuba [tyba] **NM 1** *Mus* tuba **2** *(pour nager)* snorkel
tubage [tybaʒ] **NM 1** *Méd* intubation, cannulation; **t. gastrique** gastric intubation **2** *Pétr* casing
tubaire [tybɛr] **ADJ** *Anat* tubal
tubard, -e [tybar, -ard] *Fam* **ADJ** suffering from TB▪
NM,F TB sufferer▪
tube [tyb] **NM 1** *(conduit)* tube, pipe; *Mines* **t. carottier** core barrel; **t. de condenseur** *ou* **à condensation** condenser tube; *Aut* **t. de direction** steering column; **tubes d'exploitation** tubing; **t. à flamme** *(d'un moteur à réaction)* flame tube; **t. à gaz** gas-filled tube *or* valve; **t. de graissage** oil duct *or* way; **t. lance-torpilles** torpedo tube; **t. de niveau d'eau** water-gauge column; *Aviat* **t. de Pitot** Pitot tube; **tubes de pompage** tubing; **t. raccord** pipe connection; **t. de selle** *(d'un vélo)* saddle post
2 *Élec* **t. amplificateur** amplifier tube; *TV* **t. analyseur** camera tube; **t. cathodique** cathode-ray tube; *TV* **t. image** picture tube; **t. au néon** neon tube; **t. à vide** vacuum tube
3 *(contenant)* tube; **t. d'aspirine** = packet of aspirin; **t. pour dosage, t. doseur** measuring tube; **t. à essai** test tube; **t. gradué** graduated tube; **t. de peinture** tube of paint; **t. de rouge à lèvres** (stick of) lipstick; **en t.** in a tube; **acheter de la mayonnaise en t.** to buy a tube of mayonnaise
4 *Anat & Bot* tube; **t. bronchique** bronchial tube; **t. capillaire** capillary (tube); **t. digestif** digestive tract
5 *Fam (chanson)* (smash) hit, chart-topper; **le t. de l'été** this summer's chart-topper
6 *Fam Courses de chevaux (indication)* tip

tubeless [tyblɛs] **ADJ INV** tubeless
tuber [3] [tybe] **VT 1** *Pétr* to line, to case **2** *(en travaux publics)* to tube
tubéracé, -e [tyberase] *Bot* **ADJ** tuberaceous
▫ **tubéracée NF** member of the Tuberaceae family
▫ **tubéracées NFPL** Tuberaceae
tubérale [tyberal] *Bot* **NF** member of the Tuberales order
▫ **tubérales NFPL** Tuberales
tubercule [tybɛrkyl] **NM 1** *Bot* tuber **2** *Anat & Méd* tubercle
tuberculeux, -euse [tybɛrkylø, -øz] **ADJ 1** *(malade)* tuberculous; *(symptôme)* tuberculous, tubercular; **être t.** to have tuberculosis **2** *Bot* tuberous
NM,F tuberculosis sufferer, tubercular patient
tuberculination [tybɛrkylinasjɔ̃] **NF** *Méd* tuberculin-testing
tuberculine [tybɛrkylin] **NF** *Méd* tuberculin
tuberculinique [tybɛrkylinik] **ADJ** *Méd* tuberculin *(avant n)*
tuberculinisation [tybɛrkylinizasjɔ̃] **NF** *Méd* tuberculin-testing
tuberculisation [tybɛrkylizasjɔ̃] **NF** *Méd* tuberculization, tuberculation
tuberculoïde [tybɛrkylɔid] **ADJ** *Méd* tuberculoid
tuberculose [tybɛrkyloz] **NF** *Méd* tuberculosis, TB; **avoir la t.** to have tuberculosis; **t. pulmonaire** pulmonary tuberculosis; **t. résistante (aux médicaments)** multi-drug resistant tuberculosis, MDR tuberculosis
tubéreux, -euse [tyberø, -øz] **ADJ** tuberous
▫ **tubéreuse NF** tuberose
tubériforme [tyberifɔrm] **ADJ** truffle-shaped, *Spéc* tuberiform
tubérisation [tyberizasjɔ̃] **NF** tuberization
tubérisé, -e [tyberize] **ADJ** tuberous
tubérosité [tyberɔzite] **NF** *Anat* tuberosity
tubicole [tybikɔl] *Zool* **ADJ** tubicolous
NM *(ver)* tube worm
tubifex [tybifɛks] **NM** *Zool* tubifex
tubing [tybiŋ] **NM** *Sport* tubing
tubipore [tybipɔr] **NM** *Zool* tubipore
tubiste¹ [tybist] **NM 1** *(qui travaille sous l'eau)* = worker in a caisson **2** *Métal* = worker making metal tubes **3** *Électron* = worker making electronic tubes
tubiste² [tybist] **NMF** *Mus* tuba player
tubulaire [tybylɛr] **ADJ 1** *Anat & Constr* tubular **2** *(chaudière)* tubulous **3** *(en travaux publics)* **pont t.** tubular bridge
tubule [tybyl] **NM** *Anat* tubule
tubulé, -e [tybyle] **ADJ** *Bot* tubulate
tubuleux, -euse [tybylø, -øz] **ADJ** *Bot* tubulous
tubulidenté [tybylidɑ̃te] *Zool* **NM** member of the Tubulidentata order
▫ **tubulidentés NMPL** Tubulidentata
tubuliflore [tybyliflɔr] **ADJ** *Bot* tubuliflorous
tubulure [tybylyr] **NF 1** *(ouverture d'un flacon)* tubulure **2** *(tuyauterie)* piping; *(tube)* pipe **3** *Aut* **t. d'admission/d'échappement** inlet/exhaust manifold
TUC, Tuc [tyk] *(abrév* **travaux d'utilité collective)** **NM** = community work for unemployed young people; **faire un T.** to do community work
NMF *(employé)* = person involved in a "TUC" scheme
tuciste [tysist] **NMF** = person involved in a "TUC" scheme
tudesque [tydɛsk] **ADJ** *Vieilli* Teutonic, Germanic
tudieu [tydjø] **EXCLAM** *Fam Arch* zounds!
TUE [teyə] **NM** *EU (abrév* **traité sur l'Union européenne)** TEU
tué, -e [tɥe] **NM,F 1** *(dans un accident)* **11 tués et 25 blessés** 11 dead *or* 11 people killed and 25 injured **2** *Mil* **t. à l'ennemi** killed in action
tue-chien [tyʃjɛ̃] **NM INV** *Bot* **1** *(colchique d'automne)* autumn crocus **2** *(morelle noire)* black nightshade
tue-diable [tydjabl] **NM INV** *Pêche* wobbler
tue-mouches [tymuʃ] **ADJ INV 1** *(insecticide)* **papier t.** flypaper **2** *Bot* **amanite t.** fly agaric
NM INV *Can* fly swatter
tuer [7] [tɥe] **VT 1** *(personne)* to kill; **t. qn d'un coup de couteau** *ou* **de poignard** to stab sb to death; **t. qn d'un coup de revolver** to shoot and kill sb (with a revolver); **t. qn à coups de couteau** to stab sb *or* to knife sb to death; **t. qn à coups de pierres** to stone sb to death; **se faire t.** to be *or* get killed; **un coup à t. un bœuf** a blow to fell an ox; **il a reçu une gifle à t. un bœuf** he got an almighty slap, he got a slap that made his ears ring; **ce week-end, la route a encore tué des centaines d'automobilistes** this weekend, road accidents have again claimed hundreds of victims; **c'est la solitude/le chagrin qui l'a tué** he died of loneliness/grief; *Fig* **je t'assure, il est à t.!** *(exaspérant)* honestly, I could (cheerfully) strangle him!; *Fig* **ta fille me tuera!** *(dit par énervement)* your daughter will be the death of me!; **ce voyage m'a tué** *(épuisé)* this trip's worn me out *or* killed me; **tous ces déplacements m'ont tué** *(épuisé)* I'm dead *or* done for after all that travelling; **ces escaliers me tuent** these stairs will be the death of me; *Fam* **qu'il ne comprenne pas, ça me tue** *(ça me sidère)* it amazes me he doesn't understand▪; *Fam* **ça m'a tué d'apprendre qu'il se remariait** *(sidéré)* I was staggered to hear that he was getting married again; *Fam* **ça me tue d'entendre des âneries pareilles!** *(ça me révolte)* it really gets me when I hear such nonsense!; **ça tue!** it's a killer!
2 *(plante)* to kill (off); *(animal de boucherie)* to kill, to slaughter; *(gibier)* to shoot; *Fig* **t. le veau gras** to kill the fatted calf; *Fig* **t. la poule aux œufs d'or** to kill the goose that lays the golden eggs; *Fig* **t. qch dans l'œuf** to nip sth in the bud
3 *(anéantir → tourisme, espoir)* to ruin, to spoil, to kill; **la misère peut t. l'amour** poverty can prove fatal to romance; **t. l'enthousiasme** to kill *or* to deaden enthusiasm; **cette musique va t. l'ambiance** that music is going to kill the atmosphere stone dead *or* totally destroy the atmosphere
4 *(locution)* **t. le temps** to kill time
USAGE ABSOLU le tabac tue tobacco kills *or* is a killer; **la route tue tous les ans** people die on the roads every year
▸**se tuer VPR 1** *(se suicider)* to kill oneself
2 *(par accident)* to die, to be killed; **se t. au volant** to be killed in a road accident
3 *(s'entre-tuer)* to kill one another
4 *(s'épuiser)* **elle se tue à la tâche** *ou* **à la peine** *ou* **au travail** she's working herself to death; **comme je me tue à te le répéter** as I keep telling you again and again; **c'est ce que je me tue à vous dire!** that's what I've been trying to TELL you!
tuerie [tyri] **NF** slaughter, massacre, bloodbath
tue-tête [tytɛt] **à tue-tête ADV** at the top of one's voice; **elle criait à t.** she was shouting at the top of her voice; **chantant l'hymne national à t.** bellowing out the national anthem
tueur, -euse [tɥœr, -øz] **ADJ** *(fauves, cellule, virus)* killer *(avant n)*
NM,F 1 *(meurtrier)* killer; **t. fou** psychopath; **t. professionnel** *ou* **à gages** hired assassin; **t. en série** serial killer **2** *Chasse* pothunter **3** *(aux abattoirs)* slaughterer
tuf [tyf] **NM 1** *Géol* **t. calcaire** tufa; **t. volcanique** tuff **2** *Fig Littéraire* bedrock, foundation
tufeau, -x, tuffeau, -x [tyfo] **NM** *Minér* calcareous tufa, micaceous chalk
tufier, -ère [tyfje, -ɛr] **ADJ** *Minér* tufaceous
tuile [tɥil] **NF 1** *Constr* (roofing) tile; **toit en tuiles** tiled roof; **t. canal** *ou* **creuse** curved tile; **t. faîtière** ridge tile; **t. mécanique** interlocking tile; **t. plate** plain tile; **t. romaine** curved tile; **t. solaire** solar tile
2 *Culin Br* biscuit, *Am* cookie *(in the shape of a curved tile)*; **tuiles aux amandes** almond biscuits
3 *Fam (problème)* hassle; **il m'arrive une t.** I'm in a bit of a mess; **on n'a plus de gaz, la t.!** we're out of gas, what a pain!
4 *(au mah-jong)* tile
tuileau, -x [tɥilo] **NM** piece of broken tile, fragment of tile
tuiler [3] [tɥile] **VT** to tile
tuilerie [tɥilri] **NF 1** *(industrie)* tile industry **2** *(fabrique)* tilery **3** *(four)* tile kiln **4 les Tuileries** = a formal royal residence in Paris, now the site of the Tuileries Gardens, near the Louvre
tuilier, -ère [tɥilje, -ɛr] **ADJ** tile *(avant n)*
NM,F tiler
tularémie [tylaremi] **NF** *Vét & Méd* tularaemia

tulipe [tylip] NF **1** *Bot* tulip **2** *(abat-jour)* tulip-shaped lampshade; *(verre)* tulip glass **3** *Tech (d'une imprimante)* thimble

tulipier [tylipje] NM *Bot* tulip tree

tulle [tyl] NM **1** *Tex* tulle; **t. de soie/de coton** silk/cotton tulle; **robe de t.** tulle dress **2** *Pharm* **t. gras** tulle gras

tullerie [tylri] NF **1** *(industrie)* tulle making **2** *(fabrique)* tulle factory

tullier, -ère [tylje, -ɛr] ADJ tulle *(avant n)*

tulliste [tylist] NMF tulle maker

tumbling [tœbliŋ] NM *Sport* tumbling

tuméfaction [tymefaksjɔ̃] NF **1** *(fait d'enfler)* swelling, *Spéc* tumefaction **2** *(partie enflée)* swelling, swollen area *or* part

tuméfié, -e [tymefje] ADJ swollen, *Spéc* tumid

tuméfier [9] [tymefje] VT to cause to swell, *Spéc* to tumefy
▸**se tuméfier** VPR to swell up, *Spéc* to tumefy

tumescence [tymesɑ̃s] NF tumescence

tumescent, -e [tymesɑ̃, -ɑ̃t] ADJ tumescent

tumeur [tymœr] NF **1** *Méd* tumour; **t. bénigne/maligne/blanche** benign/malignant/white tumour; **t. au cerveau** brain tumour; **t. secondaire** secondary tumour **2** *Bot* tumour

tumoral, -e, -aux, -ales [tymɔral, -o] ADJ tumorous, tumoral

tumulaire [tymylɛr] ADJ sepulchral; **pierre t.** tombstone

tumulte [tymylt] NM *(activité → soudaine)* commotion, tumult; *(→ incessante)* hurly-burly, turmoil; *Littéraire* **le t. des flots** the tumult of the waves; **le t. des passions** the turmoil *or* tumult of passions; **dans le t.** *(dans la confusion)* in an uproar, in confusion; **dans le t. de la fusillade** in the confusion *or* commotion of the shooting; **dans un t. d'applaudissements** to thunderous applause

tumultueuse [tymyltɥøz] *voir* **tumultueux**

tumultueusement [tymyltɥøzmɑ̃] ADV stormily, tumultuously

tumultueux, -euse [tymyltɥø, -øz] ADJ *(discussion)* stormy, turbulent, tumultuous; *(foule)* boisterous, turbulent; *(vie)* stormy, turbulent; *(passion)* tumultuous, turbulent; *(relation)* stormy; *(flots)* turbulent

tumulus [tymylys] NM tumulus

tune [tyn] = **thune**

tuner [tynɛr] NM *Rad* tuner

tungar [tœgar] NM *Électron* tungar rectifier

tungstate [tœgstat] NM *Chim* tungstate

tungstène [tœkstɛn, tœgstɛn] NM *Chim* tungsten

tungstique [tœkstik, tœgstik] ADJ *Chim* tungstic

tunicelle [tynisɛl] NF *Rel* tunicle

tunicier [tynisje] *Zool* NM tunicate, *Spéc* member of the Tunicata subphylum
❑ **tuniciers** NMPL tunicates, *Spéc* Tunicata

tunique [tynik] NF **1** *(vêtement)* tunic **2** *Anat* tunic, tunica **3** *Bot* tunic

tuniqué, -e [tynike] ADJ *Bot* tunicate, tunicated

Tunis [tynis] NM Tunis

Tunisie [tynizi] NF **la T.** Tunisia; **vivre en T.** to live in Tunisia; **aller en T.** to go to Tunisia

tunisien, -enne [tynizjɛ̃, -ɛn] ADJ Tunisian
❑ **Tunisien, -enne** NM,F Tunisian

tunisois, -e [tynizwa, -az] ADJ of/from Tunis
❑ **Tunisois, -e** NM,F = inhabitant of *or* person from Tunis

tunnel [tynɛl] NM **1** tunnel; **percer un t. (sous)** to tunnel (under); **t. aérodynamique** wind tunnel; **t. routier** road tunnel; **le t. sous la Manche** the Channel Tunnel; **le t. du Simplon** the Simplon Tunnel **2 t. de publicités** extended commercial break

tunnelier [tynəlje] NM tunneller *(machine)*

TUP [typ] NM *Banque (abrév* **titre universel de paiement)** universal payment order

tupaïa, tupaja [typaja] NM *Zool* tree shrew

tupi [typi] NM *Ling* Tupi

tupi-guarani [typigwarani] NM INV *Ling* Tupi-Guarani

tupinambis [typinɑ̃bis] NM *Zool* tegu

Tupperware® [typɛrwar] NM Tupperware® container

tuque [tyk] NF *Can* wool *or* fur hat, tuque

turban [tyrbɑ̃] NM **1** *(couvre-chef)* turban; *Littéraire* **prendre le t.** to go over to Islam **2** *Culin* ring-shaped mould

türbe [tyrbe] NM *Rel & Archit* = Islamic mausoleum comprising a single high tower with a conical roof

turbellarié [tyrbelarje] *Zool* NM turbellarian, *Spéc* member of the Turbellaria class
❑ **turbellariés** NMPL turbellarians, *Spéc* Turbellaria

turbide [tyrbid] ADJ *Littéraire* cloudy, turbid

turbidimètre [tyrbidimɛtr] NM turbidimeter

turbidité [tyrbidite] NF **1** *(d'un liquide)* cloudiness, *Spéc* turbidity **2** *(d'un cours d'eau)* turbidity, turbidness **3** *(en océanologie)* **courant de t.** turbidity current

turbin [tyrbɛ̃] NM *très Fam* work■; **aller au t.** to go off to the daily grind; **après le t.** after work■, after a day's grind

turbinage [tyrbinaʒ] NM *Tech (du sucre)* treatment by centrifugal turbine action

turbine [tyrbin] NF turbine; *(d'une pompe à eau)* impeller; **t. à air** air *or* wind turbine; *Tech* **t. centrifuge** centrifugal blower; **t. à gaz** gas turbine; **t. hydraulique** water turbine; **t. à impulsion** impulse turbine; *Tech* **t. moteur** power turbine; **t. à réaction** reaction turbine; **t. à vapeur** steam turbine; *Tech* **t. de ventilation** blower
❑ **à turbine** ADJ turbine-powered

turbiné, -e [tyrbine] ADJ *Biol* turbinate, turbinated

turbiner [3] [tyrbine] VI *très Fam* **1** *(travailler)* to slog away, to slave away **2** *(se livrer à la prostitution)* to turn tricks, *Br* to be on the game
VT *Tech (sucre)* to treat by centrifugal turbine action

turbith [tyrbit] NM *Bot & Pharm* turpeth

turbo [tyrbo] ADJ INV turbine-driven, turbo *(avant n)*
NM **1** *Aut* turbo; *Fam* **mettre le t.** to get a move on **2** *Ordinat* turbo
NF turbo *(car)*

turboalternateur [tyrbɔaltɛrnatœr] NM turboalternator

turbocompressé, -e [tyrbɔkɔ̃prese] ADJ turbocharged

turbocompresseur [tyrbɔkɔ̃presœr] NM turbocharger; **t. de suralimentation** turbosupercharger

turbodiesel [tyrbodjezɛl] NM *(moteur)* turbo diesel
NF *(voiture)* turbo diesel

turboforage [tyrbɔfɔraʒ] NM turbodrilling

turbomachine [tyrbɔmaʃin] NF turbine

turbomoteur [tyrbɔmɔtœr] NM turboshaft engine

turbopompe [tyrbɔpɔ̃p] NF turbopump, turbine pump

turbopropulseur [tyrbɔprɔpylsœr] NM turboprop; **avion à t.** turboprop aircraft

turboréacteur [tyrbɔreaktœr] NM turbojet (engine); **t. à double flux** by-pass turbojet

turbosoufflante [tyrbɔsuflɑ̃t] NF turboblower

turbot [tyrbo] NM *Ich* turbot

turbotière [tyrbɔtjɛr] NF fish kettle *(especially for cooking turbot)*

turbotin [tyrbɔtɛ̃] NM *Ich* small turbot

turbotrain [tyrbɔtrɛ̃] NM turbotrain

turbulence [tyrbylɑ̃s] NF **1** *(d'un enfant)* boisterousness, unruliness **2** *Littéraire (d'une foule, d'une fête)* rowdiness; *(de l'océan)* turbulence **3** *Météo* turbulence, turbulency; **nous traversons une zone de turbulences** we're encountering some turbulence

turbulent, -e [tyrbylɑ̃, -ɑ̃t] ADJ **1** *(enfant)* boisterous, unruly; *(élèves)* rowdy, disruptive; *(classe)* boisterous, noisy **2** *Littéraire (foule, fête)* rowdy; *(époque)* stormy; *(eaux)* turbulent **3** *Phys* turbulent; **régime t.** turbulent flow

turc, turque [tyrk] ADJ Turkish
NM *(langue)* Turkish
❑ **Turc, Turque** NM,F Turk; *Hist* **le Grand T.** the Grand Turk; *Hist* **les Jeunes-Turcs** the Young Turks; *Pol* **jeunes turcs** young radicals; **fort comme un T.** as strong as a horse
❑ **à la turque** ADJ **1** *(cabinets)* seatless, hole-in-the-ground *(avant n)* **2** *Beaux-Arts* Turkish ADV *(s'asseoir)* cross-legged

turcique [tyrsik] ADJ *Ling* Turkish-speaking

turcophone [tyrkɔfɔn] ADJ Turkish-speaking
NMF Turkish speaker

turdidé [tyrdide] *Orn* NM thrush, *Spéc* member of the Turdidae family
❑ **turdidés** NMPL thrushes, *Spéc* Turdidae

turf [tœrf] NM **1** *(activité)* horseracing **2** *(terrain)* turf, racecourse **3** *très Fam (travail)* work■; *(lieu de travail)* workplace■; **aller au t.** to go to work■ **4** *très Fam (prostitution)* prostitution■; **faire le t.** to turn tricks, *Br* to be on the game

turfiste [tœrfist] NMF racegoer

turgescence [tyrʒesɑ̃s] NF turgescence

turgescent, -e [tyrʒesɑ̃, -ɑ̃t] ADJ turgescent

turgide [tyrʒid] ADJ *Littéraire* turgid, swollen

Turin [tyrɛ̃] NM Turin

turinois, -e [tyrinwa, -az] ADJ of/from Turin
❑ **Turinois, -e** NM,F = inhabitant of *or* person from Turin

turion [tyrjɔ̃] NM *Bot* turion

turista [turista] NF *Fam* **la t.** Montezuma's revenge, Delhi belly

Turkestan [tyrkɛstã] NM **le T.** Turkestan, Turkistan

turkmène [tyrkmɛn] ADJ Turkoman
NM *(langue)* Turkmen
❑ **Turkmène** NMF Turkoman; **les Turkmènes** the Turkomans *or* Turkomen

Turkménistan [tyrkmenistã] NM **le T.** Turkmenistan; **vivre au T.** to live in Turkmenistan; **aller au T.** to go to Turkmenistan

Turks et Caicos [tyrksekaikos] NFPL **les T.** the Turks and Caicos (Islands); **vivre aux T.** to live in the Turks and Caicos (Islands); **aller aux T.** to go to the Turks and Caicos (Islands)

turlupiner [3] [tyrlypine] VT *Fam* to bother■, to bug; **c'est ce qui me turlupine** that's what's bugging me *or* what's on my mind

turlute [tyrlyt] NF *très Fam* blowjob; **faire une t. à qn** to give sb a blowjob, to go down on sb

turluter [3] [tyrlyte] VI *Can Fam (chantonner)* to trill, to sing tra-la-la; *(fredonner)* to hum■

turlutte [tyrlyt] NF *Pêche* jig

turlututu [tyrlytyty] EXCLAM fiddlesticks!; **t. chapeau pointu!** yah boo, sucks to you!

turne [tyrn] NF *Fam (chambre d'étudiant)* room■; *(logement d'étudiant)* digs; *(taudis)* dive

turnep [tyrnɛp], **turneps** [tyrnɛps] NM kohlrabi

turnix [tyrniks] NM *Orn* button quail

turnover [tœrnɔvœr] NM turnover *(of personnel)*

turonien, -enne [tyrɔnjɛ̃, -ɛn] *Géol* ADJ Turonian
NM Turonian

turpide [tyrpid] ADJ *Littéraire (caractère)* depraved; *(acte)* base, vile, depraved; *(paroles)* vile

turpitude [tyrpityd] NF *Littéraire* **1** *(caractère vil)* turpitude, depravity **2** *(acte)* base *or* vile *or* depraved act **3** *(parole)* vile remark

turque [tyrk] *voir* **turc**

turquerie [tyrkəri] NF *Beaux-Arts* Turkish-style work

turquette [tyrkɛt] NF *Bot* smooth *or* glabrous rupturewort

Turquie [tyrki] NF **la T.** Turkey; **vivre en T.** to live in Turkey; **aller en T.** to go to Turkey

turquin [tyrkɛ̃] ADJ M **bleu t.** dark blue; **marbre t.** dark blue marble

turquoise [tyrkwaz] NF turquoise
ADJ INV turquoise (blue)

turriculé, -e [turikyle] ADJ *Zool* turriculate(d), turreted

turritelle [tyritɛl] NF *Zool* screw shell, *Spéc* turritella

tussah [tysa] = **tussor**

tussilage [tysilaʒ] NM *Bot* coltsfoot, *Spéc* tussilago

tussor [tysɔr] NM *Tex* tussore (silk)

tut *etc voir* **taire**

tutélaire [tytelɛr] ADJ **1** *Littéraire (divinité, rôle)* guardian *(avant n)*, tutelary **2** *Jur* tutelary; **gestion t.** guardianship; **puissance t.** power of guardianship

tutelle [tytɛl] NF **1** *Jur* guardianship, tutelage; **il est en** *ou* **sous t.** he has a guardian, he's under tutelage; **placer** *ou* **mettre qn en** *ou* **sous t.** to put sb into the care of a guardian; **t. légale, t. d'État** wardship (order)
2 *Admin* **t. administrative** administrative supervision
3 *Pol* trusteeship; **territoire sous t.** trust territory **4** *(protection)* care, protection; *(contrainte)* control; **sous la t. de** *(famille, loi)* under the protection of; **prendre qn sous sa t.** to take sb under one's wing; **tenir un pays en t.** *ou* **sous sa t.** to hold sway over a country

tuteur, -trice [tytœr, -tris] NM,F **1** *Jur* guardian; **t. datif** = guardian appointed by a court; **t. légal** legal guardian; **t. ad hoc** = specially appointed guardian (ad litem) **2** *Littéraire (appui, protection)* guardian, guarantee; **la loi est la tutrice de nos libertés** the law is the guardian or guarantee of our liberty

 NMprop, support, *Hort* stake; **mettre un t. à une plante** to stake a plant

tuteurage [tytœraʒ] NM*Hort* staking
tuteurer [5] [tytœre] VT*Hort* to stake (up)
tuthie, tutie [tyti] NF*Métal* tutty, crude zinc oxide
tutoie *etc voir* **tutoyer**
tutoiement [tytwamã] NM = use of the familiar "tu"; **le t. est de rigueur** everybody says "tu" to each other

TUTOIEMENT ET VOUVOIEMENT
Traditionally, non-native French speakers waited until they were addressed using the informal "tu" form before using it themselves, except when speaking to young children. However, in the past twenty or thirty years, people in France have become much more casual about using "tu", and it is now commonly used among colleagues in the workplace, while the "vous" form tends to be used when talking to people from an older generation or to hierarchical superiors (see also entries **tu** and **vous**).

tutorat [tytɔra] NMguardianship, tutelage
tutoriel [tytɔrjɛl] NMtutorial
tutoyer [13] [tytwaje] VT**1** *(personne)* = to use the familiar "tu" form with; **elle tutoie son professeur** ≃ she's on first-name terms with her teacher; **moi, je me fais t. par tous mes employés** all my employees call me "tu" **2** *Équitation* **t. l'obstacle** to brush against the fence *(without knocking it)* **3** *Fig (être proche de)* to come close to; **il a tutoyé la mort plus d'une fois** he's had more than one brush with death

▶**se tutoyer** VPRto address each other as "tu", = to be on familiar terms (with each other)

tutrice [tytris] *voir* **tuteur**
tutti [tuti] NM INV*Mus* tutti
tutti frutti [tutifruti] ADJ INVtutti-frutti *(avant n)*
tutti quanti [tutikwãti] ADV**et t.** and the rest; **la grand-mère, le cousin et t.** the grandmother, the cousin and the whole brood
tutu [tyty] NMtutu
Tuvalu [tyvaly] NMTuvalu
tuyau, -x [tɥijo] NM **1** *(conduit)* pipe; *(flexible)* tube; **t. d'arrosage** (garden) hose, hosepipe; **t. de cheminée** (chimney) flue; **t. de chute, t. vertical** standpipe; **t. de descente** downpipe; **t. d'eau/de gaz** water/gas pipe; **t. d'échappement** exhaust (pipe); **t. d'écoulement** drainpipe; *Aut* **t. d'essence** petrol pipe; *Mus* **t. d'orgue** organ pipe; **t. de pipe** stem of a pipe; **t. de poêle** stovepipe; **en t. de poêle** *(pantalon)* drainpipe *(avant n)*; *(chapeau)* stovepipe *(avant n)*; *Fam* **la famille t. de poêle** = family whose members have an incestuous relationship; *Aut* **t. de pression** pressure hose; *Aut* **t. de reniflard** breather pipe; *Aut* **t. de trop-plein** overflow pipe; *Fam* **il le lui a dit** *ou* **glissé dans le t. de l'oreille** he whispered it in her ear; *Fam* **être dans les tuyaux** *(être en cours de réalisation)* to be in the pipeline

2 *Bot (d'une tige)* stalk
3 *(d'une plume)* quill
4 *Fam (conseil)* tip ■, hint ■; *(aux courses)* tip ■; *(information)* tip-off; **avoir un t.** to have a tip-off; **qui est-ce qui t'a filé le t.?** who tipped you off?, who put you on to it?; **c'est lui qui m'a filé les tuyaux** I got the info or *Br* gen from him; **un t. percé** a useless tip-off; **c'est un t. increvable** it's straight from the horse's mouth
5 *Couture* flute

tuyautage [tɥijotaʒ] NM**1** *Fam (fait de renseigner)* tipping off **2** *Couture* fluting **3** *Tech* plumbing
tuyauté [tɥijote] NMfluting *(UNCOUNT)*, flutes
tuyauter [3] [tɥijote] VT**1** *Fam (conseiller)* to give a tip to ■ **(sur** about); *(informer)* to tip off **(sur** about); **je me suis fait t. pour la prochaine**

course, on ne peut pas perdre someone's given me a tip for the next race, we can't lose **2** *(plisser)* to flute; **fer à t.** goffering tongs
tuyauterie [tɥijotri] NF **1** *(canalisations)* pipes, piping *(UNCOUNT)* **2** *(d'un orgue)* pipes **3** *Aut* **t. de carburant** fuel pipe or line; *Aut* **t. de frein** brake pipe or line **4** *Fam (organes de la digestion)* innards, guts; *(poumons)* lungs ■
tuyauteur, -euse [tɥijotœr, -øz] NM,F**1** *Fam (aux courses)* tipster ■ **2** *(ouvrier)* pipe fitter
tuyère [tyjɛr] NF**1** *(d'une turbine)* nozzle; *Aviat* **t. d'échappement** jet pipe; **t. de propulsion** thrust nozzle **2** *(d'un haut-fourneau)* tuyère
TV [teve] NF*(abrév* **télévision**) TV
TVA [teve] NF*Fin (abrév* **taxe sur la valeur ajoutée)** *Br* ≃ VAT, *Am* ≃ sales tax; **exempt de T.** zero-rated; **soumis à la T.** ≃ subject to *Br* VAT or *Am* sales tax; **T. encaissée** output tax; **T. récupérée** input tax
TVHD [tevea ʃde] NF*(abrév* **télévision haute définition)** HDTV
TVP [tevepe] NF*(abrév* **thrombose veineuse profonde)** DVT
tweed [twid] NMtweed; **veste de t.** tweed jacket
tweeter [twitœr] NM*(haut-parleur)* tweeter
twin-set [twinsɛt] *(pl* **twin-sets)** NMtwinset
twist [twist] NMtwist *(dance)*
twister [3] [twiste] VIto (dance the) twist
tylenchus [tilɛkys] NM*Zool* tylench, tylenchid
tympan [tɛpɑ̃] NM **1** *Anat* eardrum, *Spéc* tympanum; **un bruit à crever** *ou* **à déchirer les tympans** an ear-splitting noise; **arrête, tu nous déchires les tympans!** stop that ear-splitting noise! **2** *Archit* tympanum **3** *Tech* pinion
tympanal, -aux [tɛpanal, -o] *Anat* ADJ **M os t.** tympanic bone

 NMtympanic (bone)
tympanique [tɛpanik] ADJ*Anat* tympanic
tympanisme [tɛpanism] NM*Méd* tympanites
tympanite [tɛpanit] NF*Méd* tympanitis
tympanon [tɛpanɔ̃] NM*Mus* dulcimer
tympanoplastie [tɛpanɔplasti] NF*Méd* tympanoplasty
tyndallisation [tɛdalizasjɔ̃] NFtyndallization
type [tip] NM **1** *(genre)* kind, type; **c'est le t. d'homme à partir sans payer** he's the type or sort of man who would leave without paying; **avoir le t. latin/nordique** to have Latin/Nordic looks; **elle a le t. indien** she looks Indian; **c'est tout à fait mon t.** *(homme)* he's just my type (of man) or my sort of man, he's exactly the kind of man I find attractive; **c'est pas mon t.** he's/ she's not my type; **c'est le t. même du romantique** he's the typical romantic; **c'est le t. même de la mère abusive** she's the classic example of the possessive mother; **voilà un produit qui conviendra mieux à votre t. de peau** here's a product which is more suitable for your skin type; **un écrou du t. X** a type X nut; **plusieurs types de canapés** different types or models of sofas; **ce t. de repas** that sort or kind of meal; **quatre types de tournures** four types of set phrases

2 *(comme adj; avec ou sans trait d'union)* typical; **intellectuel t.** typical intellectual; **contrat t.** model contract; **erreur t.** typical or classic mistake; **lettre t.** standard letter
3 *Bot* type
4 *Typ (ensemble de caractères)* type; *(empreinte)* typeface
5 *Fam (homme)* guy, *Br* bloke; **un pauvre t.** a sad individual ■; **pauvre t.!** you're/he's/*etc* pathetic or sad!; **c'est un drôle de t.!** *(bizarre)* he's a pretty weird bloke!; *(louche)* he's a shady character!; **un sale t.** a bad egg, a nasty piece of work; **c'est un chic t.** he's a nice guy or *Am* a mensch or a good Joe

typé, -e [tipe] ADJ**elle est indienne mais pas très typée** she's Indian but doesn't have typical Indian features; **une femme brune très typée** a dark-haired woman with very distinctive looks
typer [3] [tipe] VT**1** *(donner des caractéristiques à)* to give the relevant characteristics to **2** *Tech* to stamp, to mark

typesse [tipɛs] NF*Péj* female ■
typha [tifa] NM*Bot* typha
typhacée [tifase] *Bot* NF member of the Typhaceae family

❑ **typhacées** NFPLTyphaceae
typhique [tifik] ADJtyphous, typhoid *(avant n)*

 NMtyphoid sufferer
typhlite [tiflit] NF*Méd* typhlitis
typhoïde [tifɔid] *Méd* ADJtyphoid *(avant n)*

 NFtyphoid
typhoïdique [tifɔidik] ADJ*Méd* typhoidal; **bacille t.** typhoid bacillus
typhon [tifɔ̃] NM*Météo* typhoon
typhose [tifoz] NF*Vét* **t. aviaire** fowl pest
typhus [tifys] NM **1** *Méd* typhus (fever) **2** *Vét* typhus; **t. du chat** (infectious) feline gastroenteritis
typicité [tipisite] NFtypicalness, typicality
typique [tipik] ADJ **1** *(caractéristique)* typical, characteristic; **un cas t. de delirium tremens** a typical or classic case of delirium tremens; **c'est t. d'elle d'être en retard** it's typical of or just like her to be late **2** *(musique)* Latin-American
typiquement [tipikmã] ADVtypically
typo[1] [tipo] NF*Fam* typography ■
typo[2]**, -ote** [tipo, -ɔt] NM,F*Fam* typographer ■
typographe [tipɔgraf] NMF *(compositeur → sur machine)* typographer; *(→ à la main)* hand compositor
typographie [tipɔgrafi] NF **1** *(technique)* letterpress (printing) **2** *(présentation)* typography; **la t. est confuse** the page is badly set out
typographique [tipɔgrafik] ADJ*(procédé)* letterpress *(avant n)*; *(caractère)* typographic
typographiquement [tipɔgrafikmã] ADV**1** *(imprimer)* by letterpress **2** *(présenter, représenter)* typographically
typologie [tipɔlɔʒi] NFtypology
typologique [tipɔlɔʒik] ADJtypological
typomètre [tipɔmɛtr] NMtype gauge
typon [tipɔ̃] NM*Typ* offset film
typosquatting [tiposkwatiŋ] NM *Ordinat* typosquatting
typothèque [tipotɛk] NF*Ordinat* type library
typtologie [tiptɔlɔʒi] NFtyptology
Tyr [tir] NMTyre
tyran [tirɑ̃] NM **1** *(despote)* tyrant; **faire le t.** to tyrannize or to bully people **2** *Orn* kingbird; **t. écarlate** vermilion flycatcher; **t. occidental** western kingbird; **t. savana** eastern kingbird
tyranneau, -x [tirano] NMpetty tyrant, bully
tyrannicide [tiranisid] NMFtyrannicide
tyrannie [tirani] NF tyranny; **la t. de la mode/de l'amour** the tyranny of fashion/of love; **exercer sa t. sur** to exercise one's tyranny over, to tyrannize
tyrannique [tiranik] ADJtyrannical
tyranniquement [tiranikmã] ADVtyrannically
tyranniser [3] [tiranize] VT*(peuple)* to tyrannize, to bully; *(frère, sœur)* to bully; **se faire t.** to be bullied
tyrannosaure [tiranozɔr] NMtyrannosaurus
tyrien, -enne [tirjɛ̃, -ɛn] ADJTyrian

 NM,FTyrian
Tyrol [tirɔl] NM**le T.** the Tyrol or Tirol; **vivre au T.** to live in the Tyrol or Tirol; **aller au T.** to go to the Tyrol or Tirol
tyrolien, -enne [tirɔljɛ̃, -ɛn] ADJTyrolean, Tyrolese

❑ **Tyrolien, -enne** NM,FTyrolean, Tyrolese
❑ **tyrolienne** NF**1** *(air)* Tyrolienne, yodel; **chanter une tyrolienne** to yodel **2** *(danse)* Tyrolienne
tyrosinase [tirɔzinaz] NF*Biol & Chem* tyrosinase
tyrosine [tirɔzin] NF*Biol & Chem* tyrosine
tyrothricine [tirɔtrisin] NF*Pharm* tyrothricin
Tyrrhénienne [tirenjɛn] *voir* **mer**
tzar [tsar, dzar] = **tsar**
tzarévitch [tsarevitʃ, dzarevitʃ] = **tsarévitch**
tzarine [tsarin, dzarin] = **tsarine**
tzigane [dzigan] = **tsigane**

U, u [y] NM INV **1** *(lettre)* U, u; **U comme Ursule** ≃ U for umbrella **2** *(forme)* U (shape)
❑ **en U** ADJ U-shaped; **fer en U** channel iron; **virage en U** U-turn; **tables (disposées) en U** tables arranged in a horseshoe

-U, -UE [y] SUFFIX

> The suffix **-u, -ue** appears at the end of adjectives with the meaning of WHICH/WHO HAS the quality of what is described by the noun radical. It is most commonly added to nouns referring to parts of the human body, sometimes with an informal or very informal effect. A possible English equivalent for this suffix is -ed, eg:
>
> **pointu(e)** sharp, pointed; **pentu(e)** steep, sloping; **pêchu(e)** (from *pêche*, as in *avoir la pêche*) on top form, full of go; **barbu** bearded; **moustachu** with a moustache; **têtu(e)** stubborn; **fessu(e)** big-bottomed; **bossu(e)** humpbacked; **couillu(e)** ballsy

UAP [yape] NF *Ind (abrév* **unité autonome de production**) autonomous production unit

UAS [yɑs] NF *Mktg (abrév* **unité d'activité stratégique**) SBU

ubac [ybak] NM = northern side of a valley

ubiquinone [ybikinɔn] NM *Biol & Chim* ubiquinone

ubiquiste [ybikuist] ADJ **1** *(personne)* ubiquitous **2** *Écol* ubiquitous
NMF ubiquitous person

ubiquité [ybikuite] NF ubiquity, ubiquitousness; *Hum* **avoir le don d'u.** to be ubiquitous *or* everywhere at once; **je n'ai pas le don d'u.** I can't be everywhere at once

Ubu [yby] NPR **le père U.** = the grotesque and disreputable character in a number of plays by Alfred Jarry, especially 'Ubu roi' (1896), from which the adjective ''ubuesque'' derives

ubuesque [ybyɛsk] ADJ **1** *Littérature* Ubuesque **2** *(grotesque)* grotesque, farcical

UCE [ysea] NF *Aut (abrév* **unité de contrôle** *ou* **de commande électronique**) ECU

uchronie [ykrɔni] NF *Littérature Br* alternative history, *Am* alternate history, *Spéc* uchronia

UDF [ydeɛf] NF *Pol (abrév* **Union pour la démocratie française**) = right-of-centre French political party

UDR [ydeɛr] NF *Anciennement Pol (abrév* **Union pour la défense de la République**) = right-wing French political party

UE [yə] NF *(abrév* **Union européenne**) EU

-ue SUFF *voir* **-u**

UEAPME [yəapɛɛmə] NF *Écon (abrév* **Union européenne de l'artisanat et des petites et moyennes entreprises**) UEAPME, European Association of Craft, Small and Medium-sized Enterprises

UEFA [yəfa] NF *Ftbl (abrév* **Union of European Football Associations**) UEFA; **la coupe de l'U.** the UEFA cup

UEM [yəɛm] NF *Écon (abrév* **Union économique et monétaire**) EMU

UEMOA [yəɛmoa] NF *Écon (abrév* **Union économique et monétaire ouest-africaine**) WAEMU

UEO [yəo] NF *(abrév* **Union de l'Europe occidentale**) WEU

UER [yəɛr] NF **1** *Anciennement Univ (abrév* **unité d'enseignement et de recherche**) = former name for a university department **2** *Rad (abrév* **Union européenne de radiodiffusion**) EBU

UFC [yɛfse] NF *(abrév* **Union fédérale des consommateurs**) = French consumers' association

ufologie [yfolɔʒi] NF ufology

UFR [yɛfɛr] NF *Univ (abrév* **unité de formation et de recherche**) = university department

UFT [yɛfte] NF *Pol (abrév* **Union française du travail**) = French association of independent trade unions

UHF [yaʃɛf] NF *Phys (abrév* **ultra-haute fréquence**) UHF

uhlan [ylɑ̃] NM *Hist* uhlan

UHT [yaʃte] ADJ *(abrév* **ultra-haute température**) UHT; **lait stérilisé U.** UHT sterilized milk

UIT [yite] NF *Tél (abrév* **Union internationale des télécommunications**) ITU

UJP [yʒipe] NF *Pol (abrév* **Union des jeunes pour le progrès**) = French political party

ukase [ykaz] NM *Hist & Fig* ukase; *Fig* **u. paternel** paternal fiat

Ukraine [ykrɛn] NF **l'U.** (the) Ukraine; **vivre en U.** to live in (the) Ukraine; **aller en U.** to go to (the) Ukraine

ukrainien, -enne [ykrɛnjɛ̃, -ɛn] ADJ Ukrainian
NM *(langue)* Ukrainian
❑ **Ukrainien, -enne** NM,F Ukrainian

ukulélé [jukulele] NM ukulele

ulcératif, -ive [ylseratif, -iv] ADJ *Méd* ulcerative

ulcération [ylserasjɔ̃] NF *Méd* ulceration

ulcéré, -e [ylsere] ADJ **1** *Méd* ulcerated **2** *Fig* **u. par tant d'ingratitude** appalled *or* sickened by such ungratefulness; **elle en était ulcérée** it rankled with her

ulcère [ylsɛr] NM *Méd* ulcer; **u. à** *ou* **de l'estomac** stomach ulcer

ulcérer [18] [ylsere] VT **1** *Méd* to ulcerate **2** *Fig (indigner)* to appal, to sicken; **sa réaction m'a ulcéré** I resented his/her reaction, his/her reaction rankled with me
▶ **s'ulcérer** VPR *Méd* to ulcerate, to form an ulcer; **la plaie commence à s'u.** the wound is beginning to ulcerate *or* to fester

ulcéreux, -euse [ylserø, -øz] ADJ *Méd (couvert d'ulcères)* ulcerous; *(de la nature d'un ulcère)* ulcer-like; *(plaie)* ulcerated, festering

ulcérogène [ylserɔʒɛn] ADJ *Méd* ulcerogenic

ulcéroïde [ylserɔid] ADJ *Méd* ulcer-like

uléma [ylema] NM ulema

uligineux, -euse [yliʒinø, -øz] ADJ *(plante)* uliginous; *(terrain)* swampy

ullucu [ylyky], **ulluque** [ylyk] NM *Bot* ullucu, olluco

ULM [yɛlɛm] NM *Aviat (abrév* **ultraléger motorisé**) microlight

ulmacée [ylmase] *Bot* NF member of the Ulmaceae family
❑ **ulmacées** NFPL Ulmaceae

ulmaire [ylmɛr] NF *Bot* meadowsweet *(UNCOUNT)*

ulmiste [ylmist] NMF *Aviat (pilote)* microlight pilot; *(passager)* microlight passenger

ulna [ylna] NF *Anat* ulna

ulnaire [ylnɛr] ADJ *Anat* ulnar

Ulster [ylstɛr] NM **l'U.** Ulster

ulstérien, -enne [ylsterjɛ̃, -ɛn] ADJ Ulster *(avant n)*
❑ **Ulstérien, -enne** NM,F Ulsterman, *f* Ulsterwoman)

ultérieur, -e [ylterjœr] ADJ later, subsequent (**à** to); **à une date ultérieure** at a later date; **notre voyage est remis à une date ultérieure** our trip has been postponed; **la parution de ce livre est ultérieure à celle du vôtre** this book came out after yours did

ultérieurement [ylterjœrmɑ̃] ADV later (on), subsequently; **nous déciderons u.** we'll make up our minds at a later stage

ultimatum [yltimatɔm] NM ultimatum; **adresser un u. à qn** to present sb with an ultimatum

ultime [yltim] ADJ *(dernier)* ultimate, final; *(paroles, moment)* (very) last; *(préparatifs)* final; **ce furent là ses ultimes paroles** those were his/her last *or* final words; **l'u. sacrifice** the ultimate sacrifice

ultimo [yltimo] ADV lastly, finally

ultra [yltra] ADJ extremist, reactionary
NMF **1** *(extrémiste)* extremist, reactionary **2** *Hist* ultra-royalist

ultrabasique [yltrabazik] ADJ *Géol* ultrabasic

ultracentrifugation [yltrasɑ̃trifygasjɔ̃] NF ultracentrifugation

ultracentrifugeuse [yltrasɑ̃trifyʒøz] NF ultracentrifuge

ultracompétitif, -ive [yltrakɔ̃petitif, -iv] ADJ *(société, prix)* very highly competitive

ultra-confidentiel, -elle [yltrakɔ̃fidɑ̃sjɛl] *(mpl* **ultra-confidentiels**, *fpl* **ultra-confidentielles**) ADJ top secret, highly confidential

ultraconservateur, -trice [yltrakɔ̃sɛrvatœr, -tris] ADJ ultraconservative

ultracourt, -e [yltrakur, -kurt] ADJ ultrashort

ultrafiltration [yltrafiltrasjɔ̃] NF *Chim* ultrafiltration

ultrafiltre [yltrafiltr] NM *Chim* ultrafilter

ultra-haute fréquence [yltraotfrekɑ̃s] NF *Phys* ultra-high frequency

ultraléger, -ère [yltraleʒe, -ɛr] ADJ superlight, extralight
NM *Aviat* microlight
❑ **ultralégère** NF *(cigarette)* superlight, ultra low

ultralibéralisme [yltraliberalism] NM ultra-liberalism

ultramicroscope [yltramikrɔskɔp] NM ultramicroscope

ultramoderne [yltramɔdɛrn] ADJ ultramodern, state-of-the-art *(avant n)*

ultramontain, -e [yltramɔ̃tɛ̃, -ɛn] ADJ **1** *Géog & Rel* ultramontane **2** *(par rapport à la France)* beyond the Alps
NM,F *Rel* ultramontanist

ultramontanisme [yltramɔ̃tanism] NM *Rel* ultramontanism

ultraorthodoxe [yltraɔrtɔdɔks] NMF *Rel* ultraorthodox

ultra-perfectionné, -e [yltrapɛrfɛksjɔne] *(mpl* **ultra-perfectionnés**, *fpl* **ultra-perfectionnées**) ADJ ultra-high performance *(avant n)*

ultra-petita [yltrapetita] *Jur* NM INV excessive award
ADV **statuer u.** to award more than is asked for

ultraportatif [yltraportatif] NM notebook computer

ultrapropre [yltrapropr] ADJ ultraclean

ultrapropreté [yltraproprəte] NF ultracleanliness

ultrarapide [yltrarapid] ADJ high-speed

ultraroyaliste [yltrarwajalist] *Hist* ADJ ultraroyalist
NMF ultraroyalist

ultrasensible [yltrasɑ̃sibl] ADJ **1** *(instrument)* ultrasensitive; *(peau)* highly sensitive **2** *Phot* high-speed *(avant n)*

ultrason [yltrasɔ̃] NM ultrasound *(UNCOUNT)*, ultrasonic sound

ultrasonique [yltrasɔnik], **ultrasonore** [yltrasɔnɔr] ADJ ultrasonic

ultrastructure [yltrastryktyr] NF *Biol* ultrastructure

ultravide [yltravid] NM ultra-high vacuum

ultraviolet, -ette [yltravjɔlɛ, -ɛt] ADJ ultraviolet
NM ultraviolet ray; *Fam* **faire une séance d'ultraviolets** to have a sunbed session ■

ultra-vires [yltravirɛs] ADJ INV*Jur* ultra vires

ultravirus [yltravirys] NM*Vieilli* ultravirus

ululation [ylylasjɔ̃] NF*(d'un hibou)* hooting *(UN-COUNT)*

ululement [ylylmɑ̃] NM*(d'un hibou)* hooting *(UN-COUNT)*

ululer [3] [ylyle] VI*(hibou)* to hoot

ulve [ylv] NF*Bot* sea lettuce, ulva

Ulysse [ylis] NPR*Myth* Ulysses

═══📖═══

'Ulysse' *Joyce* 'Ulysses'

UMA [yema] NF *Écon* (*abrév* **Union du Maghreb arabe**) AMU

U-Matic® [ymatik] NM*TV* U-Matic®

umbanda [umbɑ̃da] NM*Rel* Umbanda

UME [yema] NF *UE* (*abrév* **Union monétaire européenne**) EMU

umlaut [umlawt] NM*Typ* umlaut

UMP [yɛmpe] NF *Pol* **1** (*abrév* **Union pour un Mouvement Populaire**) = centre-right French political party, formed mainly from members of the former RPR party **2** *Anciennement* (*abrév* **Union pour la Majorité Présidentielle**) = former centre-right coalition, now renamed ''Union pour un Mouvement Populaire''

UMTS [yɛmtɛes] NM *Tél* (*abrév* **Universal Mobile Telecommunications System**) UMTS

UN, UNE [œ̃, yn]

ARTICLE INDÉFINI ▪ a/an **1, 2, 4, 5** ▪ such a/an **3**
PRONOM INDÉFINI ▪ one **1-4** ▪ one person **5** ▪ someone **5**
ADJ ▪ one **1, 3** ▪ first **2**
NM INV ▪ one **1, 3** ▪ number one **2**

ART INDÉFINI 1 (*avec une valeur indéterminée → en général*) a; (*devant une voyelle ou un h muet*) an; **un jour/une pomme/une heure** a day/an apple/an hour; **un père et une mère** a father and mother; **un père de famille** the father of a family; **un homme a appelé ce matin** a man called this morning; **j'ai reçu une lettre d'Italie** I received a letter from Italy; **il doit y avoir une erreur** there must be a *or* some mistake; **un jour, ce sera permis** one day *or* someday, it will be allowed; **on a sonné, ça doit être un démarcheur** there goes the doorbell *or* there's somebody at the door, it's probably a salesman; **il y a des enfants qui jouent dans la rue** there are (some) children playing in the street; **des filles et des garçons** (some) girls and boys; **des fruits et légumes** fruit and vegetables; **voici des fleurs** here are some flowers; **as-tu des livres à me prêter?** do you have any books you can lend me?

2 (*avec une valeur particularisante → en général*) a; (*devant une voyelle ou un h muet*) an; **c'est une erreur** it's a mistake; **des nuages passèrent devant la lune** clouds drifted across the moon; **venez me voir un lundi** come and see me one Monday *or* some Monday; **cela tombe un mardi** it falls on a Tuesday; **un jour de la semaine dernière** one day last week; **faites venir un médecin** get a doctor; **joue-moi un ré** play a D for me; **ce fut un soulagement pour toute la famille** it was a relief for the whole family; **c'est avec un grand plaisir que...** it's with great pleasure that...; **tu es une idiote** you're an idiot; **un marbre d'Italie** an Italian marble; **elle a fait preuve d'une réelle gentillesse** she showed real kindness; **un triangle a trois côtés** a triangle has three sides; **un homme peut-il se conduire aussi bassement?** can a *or* any man behave in such a vile way?; **un grand voyage se prépare des mois à l'avance** a *or* any long journey needs months of preparation

3 (*avec une valeur emphatique*) **il est d'une bêtise/d'un drôle!** he's SO stupid/funny!; **il parle avec une éloquence!** he is SO eloquent!; **j'ai eu un monde aujourd'hui!** I've had such a lot of visitors today!; *Fam* **j'ai eu une frousse, mais une frousse!** I was absolutely terrified!; **il y avait une foule!** there was such a crowd!; **il y a un de ces mondes en ville!** the town is incredibly busy, there are an incredible lot of people in

town; **j'ai une de ces migraines!** I've got a splitting headache!; **elle a poussé un de ces cris** she gave such a shout!; **j'ai attendu des heures!** I waited for hours!; **il est resté des mois et des mois sans rien faire** he didn't do anything for months (and months); **il travaille jusqu'à des trois heures du matin** he works as late as three in the morning; **il gagne des 5000 ou 6000 euros par mois** he makes up to 5,000 *or* 6,000 euros a month; **on était inondés, avec des un mètre, un mètre cinquante d'eau** we were flooded, there was at least a metre or a metre and a half of water in the house

4 (*avec un nom propre*) **un M. Baloi vous demande au téléphone** there's a Mr Baloi for you (on the phone); **tout le monde ne peut pas être un Rimbaud** we can't all be Rimbauds; **c'est une future Callas** she will be another *or* she's the next Callas; **c'est un Apollon** he's a real Adonis; **c'est un McEnroe en état de grâce que l'on a vu jouer ce jour-là** it was an inspired McEnroe that we saw on court that day; **j'ai trouvé un Boisseau souriant, optimiste et décontracté** I found a smiling, optimistic and relaxed Boisseau

5 (*désignant une œuvre*) **faire l'acquisition d'un Picasso/d'un Van Gogh** to acquire a Picasso/a Van Gogh; **et si on allait voir un vieux Truffaut?** how about going to see an oldTruffaut movie *or Br* film?; **des Renoir seront mis en vente chez Sotheby's** some Renoirs will be put on sale at Sotheby's

PRON INDÉFINI 1 (*dans un ensemble*) one; **il n'y en a pas un qui parle anglais** not one of them speaks English; **pas un n'était au courant** not a (single solitary) soul *or* absolutely nobody knew about it; *Fam* **être menteur/hypocrite comme pas un** to be a dreadful liar/hypocrite ▪; *Fam* **il fait du bruit comme pas un** he's unbelievably noisy ▪; *Fam* **il danse comme pas un** he's a great dancer ▪

2 (*en corrélation avec "de"*) **un des seuls** one of the few; **un de nous, un d'entre nous** one of us; **appelle-le un de ces jours** give him a call one of these days; **c'est encore un de ces westerns stupides** it's another one of those stupid westerns; **un des événements qui a le plus retenu mon attention** one of the events that really grabbed my attention

3 (*avec l'article défini*) **c'est l'un des concerts les plus réussis de ma carrière** it's one of the most successful concerts of my career; **l'une des voitures les plus vendues d'Europe** one of the biggest selling cars in Europe; **l'un de mes amis** one of my friends, a friend of mine; **l'un des deux** one of the two; **l'un de vous deux est de trop** one of you is not needed; **l'un d'entre nous ira** one of us will go; **l'une d'entre vous est-elle volontaire?** does one of you want to volunteer?; **les uns disent que...** some say that...; **les uns et les autres** people, everybody

4 (*en corrélation avec "en"*) one; **on demanda un médecin, il y en avait un dans la salle** they called for a doctor, there was one in the room; **parmi les enfants, il y en a un qui...** one of the children...; **je t'en ai acheté un** I bought you one; **il n'en reste qu'un** there's only one left; *Fam* **mais bien sûr que j'en ai une, de voiture!** of course I've got a car! ▪; *Fam* **il n'en loupe** *ou* **rate pas une** he's forever screwing up

5 (*quelqu'un*) one person, someone; **une qui n'a pas du tout changé, c'est Jeanne** one person *or* someone who hasn't changed at all is Jeanne; **un qui a de la chance, c'est Pierre, il est parti à la Réunion** Pierre's one of the lucky ones, he's gone off to Réunion; **ce n'est pas comme un que je connais...** (it's) not like someone (else) I know...; **j'en connais une qui va être surprise!** I know someone who's going to get a surprise!; **en voilà une qui sait ce qu'elle veut!** there's somebody who knows what she wants!

ADJ 1 (*gén*) one; **à une condition** on one condition; **un café et deux chocolats, s'il vous plaît** one coffee and two hot chocolates, please; **les enfants de un à sept ans** children (aged) from one to seven; **une femme sur cinq** one woman

out of *or* in five; **il vient un jour sur deux** he comes every other *or* second day; **il y a un problème, un seul** there's just one problem; **ils n'ont même pas marqué un (seul) but** they didn't even score one *or* a single goal; **il rentre dans une ou deux semaines** he'll be back in a week or two *or* in a couple of weeks; **je ne resterai pas une minute de plus ici** I won't stay here another minute; **j'ai fait plus d'une erreur dans ma jeunesse** I made many mistakes *or* more than one mistake in my youth; **une à une, les lumières s'éteignaient** the lights were going out one by one *or* one after the other; **vingt et un ans** twenty-one years; **deux heures une** one minute past two; **la cuisine ne fait qu'un avec le salon** there is an open-plan kitchen-cum-living room; **il ne faisait qu'un avec sa monture** horse and rider were as one; **et d'un, et de deux!** that's one, and another (one)!

2 (*dans des séries*) first; **numéro un** number one; **page un** *ou* **une** page one; **dans l'acte III scène un** in Act III, scene 1; **l'an I de la République** (*calendrier républicain*) year one of the Republic; **une, deux! une, deux!** left, right! left, right!; **un(e), deux, trois, partez!** one, two, three, go!; *Fam* **et d'une** for a start, for starters; **et d'une, je ne t'ai jamais rien promis** first of all, I never promised you anything; *Fam* **ne faire ni une ni deux** not to think twice

3 **Dieu est un** God is one; **dans l'œuvre dramatique, l'action doit être une** the plot of a play must have a degree of unity; **ils ne font qu'un** (*ils sont très proches*) they are as one; **la maison et l'atelier ne font qu'un** the house and workshop are one and the same

NM INV 1 (*gén*) one; **donnez-moi deux chiffres entre un et dix** give me two numbers between one and ten; **un et un** [œ̃eœ̃] **font deux** one and one are two

2 (*numéro d'ordre*) number one; **la clef du un est perdue** the key for number one has been lost; **le un est sorti** (*au jeu*) number one came up; *Théât* **on répète la dernière scène du un** we're rehearsing the last scene of act one

3 (*chiffre écrit*) one; **tu fais mal tes un** your ones don't look right

❏ **un à un, un par un** ADVone by one, one at a time; **avale les cachets un par un** swallow the tablets one by one *or* one at a time

❏ **l'un dans l'autre** ADV*Fam* all in all ▪, by and large ▪

---

unanime [ynanim] ADJ **1** (*commun, général → vote, décision*) unanimous **2** (*du même avis*) **la presse u. a condamné ce geste** the press unanimously condemned this gesture; **ils sont unanimes à vous accuser** they are unanimous in accusing you; **nous sommes unanimes à le soutenir** we're unanimous in our support for him

unanimement [ynanimmɑ̃] ADVunanimously

unanimisme [ynanimism] NM*Littérature* unanimism

unanimiste [ynanimist] *Littérature* ADJunanimist NMFunanimist

unanimité [ynanimite] NF unanimity; **voter à l'u. pour qn** to vote unanimously for sb; **élu à l'u. moins une voix** elected with only one dissenting vote; **faire l'u.** to win unanimous support; **un candidat qui fait l'u. contre lui** a candidate who has no support from anyone; **sa politique n'a pas fait l'u.** his/her policy failed to win unanimous support

unau, -s *ou* **-x** [yno] NM*Zool* unau, two-toed sloth

unciforme [ɔ̃sifɔrm] ADJ*Anat* unciform, uncinate

unciné, -e [ɔ̃sine] ADJ **1** *Bot* uncinate, uncinated **2** *Psy* **crise uncinée** uncinate fit *or* seizure

underground [œndœrgrawnd] ADJ INV underground

NM INVunderground (culture), counter-culture

une [yn] ART INDÉFINI*voir* **un**

NF **1** *Journ* **la u.** page one, the front page; **faire la u.** to make the headlines; **la naissance de la princesse fait la** *ou* **est à la u. de tous les quotidiens** the birth of the princess is on the front page of all the dailies; **ce sujet sera à la u. de notre dernier journal télévisé ce soir** this will be one of the main items in our late news

bulletin; **tu es à la u. de tous les journaux** you've made the front page, you're front-page news *or* in the headlines

2 *TV* **la U.** = private French TV channel

3 *Fam (histoire, nouvelle)* one; **je vais t'en raconter u. qui se passe dans une maison hantée** let me tell you the one about the haunted house; **j'en ai u. (bonne) à t'apprendre** wait till you hear this

4 *Fam (fessée, claque)* **tu vas en recevoir u.!** you're going to get a slap!; **j'en ai pris u. en pleine poire** I got one right across the face

5 *Fam* scene one; **on répète la u. du trois** we're rehearsing scene one of act three

UNEDIC [ynedik] **NF** *(abrév* **Union nationale interprofessionnelle pour l'emploi dans l'industrie et le commerce***)* = the department controlling the "ASSEDIC"

UNEF, Unef [ynɛf] **NF** *(abrév* **Union nationale des étudiants de France***)* ≃ National Union of Students

UNESCO, Unesco [ynɛsko] **NF** *(abrév* **United Nations Educational, Scientific and Cultural Organization***)* UNESCO, Unesco

unetelle [yntɛl] *voir* **untel**

unguéal, -e, -aux, -ales [ɔ̃gɥeal, -o] **ADJ** nail *(avant n)*, *Spéc* ungual; **infection unguéale** nail *or Spéc* ungual infection

unguifère [ɔ̃gɥifɛr] **ADJ** *Zool* unguiferous

unguis [ɔ̃gɥis] **NM** *Anat* unguis, lachrymal bone

Uni [yni] **NF** *Suisse Fam* uni; **aller à l'U.** to go to uni

uni, -e [yni] **ADJ 1** *(d'une seule couleur)* plain, *Br* self-coloured, *Am* solid; *(sans motif)* plain

2 *(sable)* smooth, fine; *(terrain)* even, level, smooth; *(mer)* smooth, unruffled

3 *(soudé → couple)* close; *(→ famille, société)* close-knit; **ils sont très unis** they are very close; **unis derrière le chef** united behind the leader; **tous unis face aux pollueurs!** let's unite (in the fight) against pollution!

NM *(étoffe)* plain fabric

uniate [ynjat] *Rel* **ADJ** Uniat, Uniate

NMF Uniat, Uniate

uniaxe [yniaks] **ADJ** *Bot & Minér* uniaxial

unicaméral, -e, -aux, -ales [ynikameral, -o] **ADJ** *Pol* unicameral

unicaule [ynikol] **ADJ** *Bot* uniaxial

UNICEF, Unicef [ynisɛf] **NF** *(abrév* **United Nations International Children's Emergency Fund***)* **l'U.** UNICEF, Unicef

unicellulaire [yniselylɛr] **ADJ** *Biol* unicellular, single-celled

unicité [ynisite] **NF** uniqueness

unicolore [ynikɔlɔr] **ADJ** plain, *Br* self-coloured, *Am* solid

unicorne [ynikɔrn] **ADJ** one-horned, single-horned

NM *Myth* unicorn

unidimensionnel, -elle [ynidimɑ̃sjɔnɛl] **ADJ** unidimensional

unidirectionnel, -elle [ynidirɛksjɔnɛl] **ADJ** unidirectional

unidose [ynidoz] **NF** single-dose sachet; **ce médicament est disponible en u.** this medicine is available in single-dose sachets

unième [ynjɛm] **ADJ** first; **quarante et u.** forty-first; **cent u.** hundred and first

unièmement [ynjɛmmɑ̃] **ADV** **vingt et u.** in the twenty-first place

unif [ynif] **NF** *Belg Fam* uni

unifamilial, -e, -aux, -ales [ynifamiljal, -o] *Belg & Can* **ADJ** *(logement)* for a single family

❑ **unifamiliale NF** detached house *(for a single family)*

unificateur, -trice [ynifikatœr, -tris] **ADJ** unifying, uniting

NM,F unifier

unification [ynifikasjɔ̃] **NF 1** *(d'un pays)* unification **2** *(uniformisation)* standardization, standardizing **3** *Fin & Com (des crédits)* consolidation; *(fusion d'entreprises)* merger

unificatrice [ynifikatris] *voir* **unificateur**

unifié, -e [ynifje] **ADJ** unified; *(crédits)* consolidated

unifier [9] [ynifje] **VT 1** *(réunir → provinces)* to unify, to unite **2** *(uniformiser → tarifs)* to standardize, to bring into line with each other **3** *Fin (crédits)* to consolidate

▸**s'unifier VPR** *(parti, pays)* to become united

unifilaire [ynifilɛr] **ADJ** *Élec* unifilar, single-wire

uniflore [ynifl ɔr] **ADJ** *Bot* uniflorous, unifloral

unifolié, -e [ynifɔlje] **ADJ** *Bot* one-leafed, *Spéc* unifoliate

NM *Can* = name given to the Canadian national flag, because of its maple leaf emblem

uniforme [ynifɔrm] **ADJ 1** *(régulier → vitesse)* uniform, regular, steady; *(→ surface)* even, smooth, level; *(→ mouvement)* regular

2 *(identique)* **horaire u. pour tout le personnel** the same timetable for all members of staff

3 *(monotone)* uniform, unvarying, unchanging; **une vie u.** a humdrum existence; **un paysage u.** an unchanging *or* a monotonous landscape

NM uniform; **endosser/quitter l'u.** *(de l'armée)* to join/to leave the forces

❑ **en uniforme ADJ** in uniform; **un policier en u.** a uniformed policeman; **en grand u.** in full uniform *or* regalia

uniformément [ynifɔrmemɑ̃] **ADV 1** *(sans aspérités)* uniformly, evenly; **étendre la colle u.** spread paste evenly; **paysage u. plat** uniformly flat landscape

2 *(identiquement)* **des femmes u. vêtues de noir** women all dressed in the same black clothes

3 *(sans changement)* regularly, steadily, uniformly; **la vie s'écoulait u.** life went on in its usual way

4 *Phys* **vitesse u. accélérée** uniform change of speed

uniformisation [ynifɔrmizasjɔ̃] **NF** standardization, standardizing

uniformiser [3] [ynifɔrmize] **VT** to standardize

uniformité [ynifɔrmite] **NF 1** *(régularité)* uniformity, evenness; *(de couleurs)* uniformity **2** *(monotonie)* monotony; **l'u. de sa vie** the monotony of his/her life

unijambiste [yniʒɑ̃bist] **ADJ** one-legged

NMF one-legged person

unilatéral, -e, -aux, -ales [ynilateral, -o] **ADJ** *(désarmement, décision)* unilateral; *(contrat, accord)* one-sided

unilatéralement [ynilateralmɑ̃] **ADV** unilaterally

unilatéralisme [ynilateralism] **NM** *Pol* unilateralism

unilatéraliste [ynilateralist] *Pol* **ADJ** unilateralist

NMF unilateralist

unilinéaire [ynilineɛr] **ADJ** unilinear

unilingue [ynilɛ̃g] **ADJ** unilingual, monolingual

uniloculaire [ynilɔkylɛr] **ADJ** *Bot* unilocular

uniment [ynimɑ̃] **ADV** *Littéraire* **1** *(régulièrement)* smoothly, evenly **2** *(franchement)* **dire qch (tout) u.** to say sth (quite) plainly *or* frankly

uninominal, -e, -aux, -ales [yninɔminal, -o] *voir* **scrutin**

union [ynjɔ̃] **NF 1** *(fait de mélanger)* union, combination; *(mélange)* union, integration

2 *(solidarité)* union, unity; *Presse* **L'U.** = daily newspaper published in Reims; *Hist* **l'U. sacrée** = unity of all Frenchmen in the face of the enemy *(called for by Poincaré on the outbreak of the First World War)*; **faire l'u. sacrée** *(être solidaires)* to show *or* to present a united front; *Hist* to unite in the face of the aggressor *(in 1914)*; *Prov* **l'u. fait la force** unity is strength

3 *(harmonie → dans un groupe)* harmony; *(→ dans une famille, un couple)* closeness; **resserrer encore davantage l'u. qui existe entre deux personnes** to strengthen the bond between two people

4 *(liaison entre un homme et une femme)* union; *Littéraire* **u. charnelle** union of the flesh; **u. civile** civil union; **u. conjugale** marital union; **u. libre** cohabitation; **vivre en u. libre** to cohabit

5 *Zool & (en anthropologie)* **u. monogame** pair-bonding

6 *(regroupement)* union, association; **U. africaine** African Union; *Mktg* **U. des annonceurs** = organization which defends the interests of advertisers; **u. de consommateurs** consumer association; *Anciennement Pol* **U. pour la défense de la République** = right-wing French political party; *Pol* **U. pour la démocratie française** = right-of-centre French political party; **u. douanière** customs union; *UE* **U. douanière européenne** European Customs Union; **u. économique** economic union; **U. économique et monétaire** Economic and Monetary Union; **U. européenne** European Union; **réaliser l'u. européenne** to make European union a reality; *Rad* **U. européenne de radiodiffusion** European Broadcasting Union; **U. de l'Europe occidentale** Western Europe Union; **U. fédérale des consommateurs** = French consumers' association; **l'U. de la gauche** = union of left-wing parties; *Tél* **U. internationale des télécommunications** International Telecommunications Union; *Anciennement Pol* **U. des jeunes pour le progrès** = French political party; *Anciennement Pol* **U. pour la Majorité Présidentielle** = former centre-right coalition, now renamed "Union pour un Mouvement Populaire"; *UE* **U. monétaire européenne** European Monetary Union; *Pol* **U. pour un Mouvement Populaire** = centre-right French political party; **u. nationale** national coalition; **U. nationale des étudiants de France** ≃ National Union of Students; **U. nationale interprofessionnelle pour l'emploi dans l'industrie et le commerce** = the department controlling the "ASSEDIC"; *Hist* **U. pour la nouvelle République** = former Gaullist political party; **U. postale universelle** Universal Postal Union; *Admin* **U. pour le recouvrement des cotisations de Sécurité sociale et d'allocations familiales** = French administrative body responsible for collecting social security payments; *Sport* **u. sportive** sports club *or* association; *Aviat* **U. des transporteurs aériens** = French airline company

7 *Anciennement* **l'U. soviétique** *ou* **des républiques socialistes soviétiques** the Soviet Union, the Union of Soviet Socialist Republics; **l'ex-U. soviétique** the former Soviet Union; **l'U. sud-africaine** the Union of South Africa

unionisme [ynjɔnism] **NM 1** *Arch (syndicalisme)* unionism **2** *Hist* Unionism

unioniste [ynjɔnist] **ADJ 1** *Arch (syndicaliste)* unionist **2** *Hist* Unionist

NMF 1 *Arch (syndicaliste)* unionist **2** *Hist* Unionist

uniovulé, -e [yniɔvyle] **ADJ** uniovular

unipare [ynipar] **ADJ** *Bot & Zool* uniparous

unipersonnel, -elle [ynipɛrsɔnɛl] **ADJ 1** *Ling* impersonal **2** *Com* **entreprise** *ou* **société unipersonnelle** one-person business, sole proprietorship

unipolaire [ynipɔlɛr] **ADJ** unipolar

unique [ynik] **ADJ 1** *(seul)* (one and) only, one; *(parti, prix)* single; *(candidat)* sole; **c'est mon u. exemplaire** it's my only *or* one copy; **c'est mon u. recours** it's the only recourse I have, it's my sole recourse; **l'u. porte de sortie était verrouillée** the only *or* one exit was locked; **mon u. souci est que tu sois heureux** my only *or* one *or* sole concern is that you should be happy; **l'u. explication possible** the only possible explanation; **un même et u. problème** one and the same problem; **c'est son seul et u. défaut** it's his/her one and only fault; **la seule et l'u. Arletty** the one and only Arletty

2 *(exceptionnel)* unique; **j'en possède l'u. exemplaire** I own the only (existing) copy of it; **il a des pièces uniques dans sa collection de porcelaine** he has several unique pieces in his porcelain collection; **il est u. au monde** it's unique, there's only one of its kind in the world

3 *Fam (étonnant)* priceless; **il est vraiment u., lui!** he's priceless, he is!

4 *(dans une famille)* **être fils/fille/enfant u.** to be an only son/daughter/child; **les enfants uniques** only children

uniquement [ynikmɑ̃] **ADV** only, solely; **elle mange u. des légumes** she eats just *or* only vegetables, she eats nothing but vegetables; **on le trouve u. dans les régions du nord** it is found only in northern areas; **je viens u. pour vous voir** I've come just to see you, the only reason I've come is to see you; **il pense u. à ton bien** he's only thinking of what's good for you; **nous nous occupons u. de prêts à court terme** we deal only *or* solely *or* exclusively in short-term loans; **je l'ai fait u. pour te faire plaisir** I only did it to please you; **tu penses à l'argent? – pas u.** are you thinking of the money? – not only that; **vous faites des dictionnaires? – pas u., nous faisons aussi des traductions** you

compile dictionaries, don't you? – not just that, we do translations as well

unir [32] [ynir] **VT 1** *(lier)* to unite, to bring together; **l'amitié qui nous unit** the friendship that unites us; **u. deux pays** to unite two countries; **u. une province à un pays** to unite a province with a country

2 *(marier)* to join in marriage *or* matrimony; **le Père Patrick les unira** Father Patrick will marry them *or* will officiate at their wedding; **être uni par le mariage à...** to be joined in matrimony *or* marriage to...; **vous voilà unis par les liens du mariage** I now pronounce you man and wife

3 *(villes)* to link, to connect; **le canal qui unissait Orville à Lorgeac** the canal which used to run between Orville and Lorgeac; **le pont qui unit les deux rives** the bridge which links *or* connects the two banks

4 *(combiner)* to combine; **son style unit l'aisance à** *ou* **et la rigueur** his/her style combines both ease and precision; **un homme qui unit des qualités de décideur à un sens de l'humour** a man who combines decision-making abilities with a sense of humour

5 *(aplanir → sol, surface)* to smooth, to level

▸**s'unir VPR 1** *(se regrouper)* to unite; **s'u. à qn** to join forces with sb; **s'u. contre un ennemi commun** to unite against a common enemy

2 *(se marier)* to become joined in marriage *or* matrimony; **s'u. à qn** to marry sb

3 *(être compatible)* to match

unisexe [yniseks] **ADJ** unisex

unisexué, -e [ynisɛksɥe], **unisexuel, -elle** [ynisɛksɥɛl] **ADJ** *Biol* unisexual

unisson [ynisɔ̃] **NM** unison

❑ **à l'unisson ADV** in unison; **nos cœurs battaient à l'u.** our hearts were beating as one *or* in unison

❑ **à l'unisson de PRÉP** at one with; **se mettre à l'u. des critiques** to be of one mind with the critics

unitaire [ynitɛr] **ADJ 1** *(principe, slogan)* uniting; *(politique)* unitarian; *(système)* unitary **2** *Math (matrice, vecteur)* unit *(avant n)* **3** *Com* **prix u.** unit price; **tarification u.** tariff based on the price per unit **4** *Rel* Unitarian

NMF *Rel* Unitarian

unitarien, -enne [ynitarjɛ̃, -ɛn] **ADJ** *Pol* unitarian; *Rel* Unitarian

NM,F *Pol* unitarian; *Rel* Unitarian

unité [ynite] **NF 1** *(cohésion)* unity; *(de style)* consistency; **cela manque d'u.** *(projet, texte)* it doesn't hang together very well; **l'u. et la pluralité** unity and plurality; **arriver à une certaine u. de pensée** *ou* **vues** to reach a certain consensus; *Fin* **u. budgétaire** yearly budget *(presented before Parliament)*; *Pol* **l'u. nationale** national unity; *Hist & Théât* **les trois unités, l'u. d'action, l'u. de temps et l'u. de lieu** the three unities, unity of action, unity of time and unity of place

2 *(étalon)* unit, measure; *Écon* **u. de compte** unit of account; **u. de compte européenne** European unit of account; **u. de compte monétaire** money of account; **u. de longueur** unit of length; **u. de masse** weight; **u. de mesure** unit of measurement; **u. monétaire** monetary unit; *Anciennement* **u. monétaire européenne** European currency unit; **u. de poids** unit of weight; **u. de temps** unit for measuring time *or* time measure

3 *(élément, module)* unit, item; **2 euros l'u.** 2 euros each; **les ventes ont dépassé les 3000 unités** sales have passed the 3,000 mark; *Com* **u. d'activité stratégique** strategic business unit; *Ind* **u. autonome de production** autonomous production unit; *Com* **u. de chargement** load unit; *Pétr* **u. de craquage** cracking unit; *Anciennement Univ* **u. d'enseignement et de recherche** = former name for a university department; *Univ* **u. de formation et de recherche** = university department; **u. d'intervention chirurgicale** field surgical unit; *TV & Rad* **u. mobile (de tournage)** OB unit, outside broadcast vehicle; **u. pilote** experimental unit; *Ind* **u. de production** production unit; *TV* **u. de programme** programme production team; *Mktg* **u. de sondage** sampling unit; *Bourse* **u. de transaction** lot size; *Univ* **u. de valeur** course credit *or* unit; *TV* **u. de voix hors champ automatique** automatic voice-over unit, ducker

4 *Ling* (distinctive) feature; **une u. linguistique/phonétique** a linguistic/phonetic feature; **u. lexicale** lexeme

5 *Math* unit; **dans 243, le chiffre 3 est celui des unités** in the number 243, 3 represents the units; **le chiffre des unités** the units figure; **la colonne des unités** the units column

6 *Mil* unit; **rejoindre son u.** to go back to *or* rejoin one's unit; *Naut* to go back to *or* rejoin one's ship; **grande u.** major unit; **petite u.** minor unit; **u. de combat** *Br* fighting unit, *Am* combat unit; **u. de choc** shock unit

7 *(dans un hôpital)* unit; **u. de soins coronariens** coronary care unit; **u. de soins intensifs** intensive care unit

8 *Pharm* unit

9 *Ordinat* unit; *(de disque)* drive; **u. d'affichage** display unit; **u. de bande** tape unit; **u. centrale** central processing unit, CPU; **u. centrale (de traitement)** central processor unit, mainframe; **u. de commande** control unit; *Aut* **u. de contrôle** *ou* **de commande électronique** electronic control unit; **u. de destination** target drive; **u. de disque** disk drive; **u. de disque dur** hard drive; **u. de disquettes** floppy drive; **u. d'entrée** input device; **u. logique** logical drive; **u. d'origine** source drive; **u. périphérique** peripheral; **u. de sauvegarde** backup device; **u. de sortie** output device; **u. de stockage** storage device; **u. de télécommande** remote control unit, RCU; **u. de traitement** processing unit; **u. de traitement de texte** text processor; **u. de visualisation** visual display unit, VDU

10 *Fam Anciennement (10 000 francs)* 10,000 francs▪

❑ **à l'unité ADJ prix à l'u.** unit price **ADV** *(acheter, vendre)* by the unit, singly, individually; **vendu à l'u.** sold singly

unitif, -ive [ynitif, -iv] **ADJ 1** *Rel* unitive; **vie unitive** unitive life, life of perpetual communion with God **2** *Anat* unitive

univ [ynif] **NF** *Belg Fam* uni

univalent, -e [ynivalɑ̃, -ɑ̃t] **ADJ** *Biol & Chim* univalent, monovalent

univalve [ynivalv] **ADJ** univalve *(avant n)*

univers [ynivɛr] **NM 1** *Astron* **l'U.** the Universe; **l'u.** *(notre planète)* the world; **l'u. entier a salué cet exploit** people all over the world admired this exploit

2 *Fig (domaine)* world, universe; **l'u. du rêve** the world *or* realm of dreams; **l'u. mathématique** the field of mathematics; **mes chats et mes roses, c'est là tout mon u.** my cats and my roses are my whole world; **le monde de l'argent ce n'est pas vraiment mon u.** big money isn't really my thing *or* line; **l'u. très particulier du cirque** the strange world of the circus; **l'u. poétique de Mallarmé** Mallarmé's poetic world; **l'u. carcéral** life in prison; *Ling* **u. du discours** universe of discourse

3 *Mktg (nombre de personnes dans un groupe, dans un segment)* universe

universalisation [ynivɛrsalizasjɔ̃] **NF** universalization

universaliser [3] [ynivɛrsalize] **VT** to universalize, to make universal

▸**s'universaliser VPR** to become universal

universalisme [ynivɛrsalism] **NM 1** *Phil* universalism **2** *Rel* Universalism

universaliste [ynivɛrsalist] **ADJ 1** *Phil* universalist **2** *Rel* Universalist

NMF 1 *Phil* universalist **2** *Rel* Universalist

universalité [ynivɛrsalite] **NF** universality; *Jur* **u. de droits** = set of rights and obligations under a particular legal regime

universaux [ynivɛrso] **NMPL** *Phil & Ling* **les u.** the universals, the five predictables

universel, -elle [ynivɛrsɛl] **ADJ 1** *(mondial)* universal; **produit de réputation universelle** world-famous product; **faire l'objet d'une adoration universelle** to be universally adored; **paix universelle** world peace

2 *(partagé par tous → sentiment)* universal, general; **la jalousie est universelle** jealousy is universal; **rechercher les règles universelles qui régissent les langues** to look into the general rules which govern languages

3 *(à usages multiples)* **remède u.** panacea, universal remedy; *Tech* **joint u.** universal joint

4 *(personne)* of wide knowledge; *(savoir)* all-embracing; **un érudit au talent u.** a multi-talented scholar

NM l'u. the universal

universellement [ynivɛrsɛlmɑ̃] **ADV** universally; **u. reconnu** recognized by all; **u. admiré** universally admired

universitaire [ynivɛrsitɛr] **ADJ** *(carrière, études)* academic, university *(avant n)*; *(année, centre, titre)* academic; *(ville)* university *(avant n)*; *(restaurant)* university *(avant n)*

NMF 1 *(enseignant)* academic, university teacher **2** *Belg & Suisse (étudiant)* university student; *(diplômé)* graduate

université [ynivɛrsite] **NF 1** *(institution, bâtiment)* university; **aller à l'u.** to go to university; **enseigner à l'u.** to be a university teacher, *Am* to teach college; *Univ* **u. d'été** summer school; **u. du troisième âge** post-retirement *or* senior citizens' university; **l'U. (de France)** = the teaching profession *(including university staff, schoolteachers, inspectors)* **2** *Pol* **les universités d'été du parti socialiste** socialist party summer school *(during which party leaders meet younger members)*

univitellin, -e [ynivitɛlɛ̃, -in] **ADJ** *Biol* monovular, monozygotic; **jumeaux univitellins** identical twins

univocité [ynivɔsite] **NF** unequivocalness

univoque [ynivɔk] **ADJ 1** *Ling* unequivocal **2** *(relation, rapport)* one-to-one

Unix® [yniks] **NM** *Ordinat (abrév* **Uniplexed Information and Computing System***)* Unix®

unnilennium [ynilɛnjɔm] **NM** *Chim* unnilennium

unnilhexium [ynilɛksjɔm] **NM** *Chim* unnilhexium

unniloctium [ynilɔktjɔm] **NM** *Chim* unniloctium

unnilpentium [ynilpɛ̃tjɔm] **NM** *Chim* unnilpentium

unnilquadium [ynilkwadjɔm] **NM** *Chim* unnilquadium

unnilseptium [ynilsɛptjɔm] **NM** *Chim* unnilseptium

UNR [yɛnɛr] **NF** *Hist (abrév* **Union pour la nouvelle République***)* = former Gaullist political party

UNSA [ynsa] **NF** *Pol (abrév* **Union nationale des syndicats autonomes***)* = French trade union representing civil servants and other workers

untel, unetelle, Untel, Unetelle [œ̃tɛl, yntɛl] **NM,F** Mr So-and-so, *f* Mrs So-and-so; **tu dis "bonjour, Mademoiselle Unetelle, puis-je parler au directeur?"** you say "good morning, Miss so-and-so *or* Miss Whatever-her-name-is, may I speak to the manager?"

UPA [ypea] **NF** *Pol (abrév* **Union professionnelle artisanale***)* = French employers' organization for craft industries

upas [ypas] **NM** *(arbre, poison)* upas

upérisation [yperizasjɔ̃] **NF** uperization

upériser [3] [yperize] **VT** to uperize

UPI [ypei] **NF** *Presse (abrév* **United Press International***)* UPI

uppercut [ypɛrkyt] **NM** uppercut; **u. du droit** right uppercut

Uppsala [ypsala] **NM** Uppsala

upsilon [ypsilɔn] **NM INV** upsilon

UPU [ypey] **NF** *(abrév* **Union postale universelle***)* UPU

upwelling [œpwɛliŋ] **NM** *Géol* upwelling

Ur [yr] **NF** *Antiq* Ur

uracile [yrasil] **NM** *Biol & Chim* uracil

uraète [yraɛt] **NM** *Orn* eagle-hawk, wedge-tailed eagle

uræus [yreys] **NM** *Antiq* uraeus

uranate [yranat] **NM** *Chim* uranate

urane [yran] **NM** *Chim* uranium oxide

uraneux [yranø] **ADJ M** *Chim* uranous

uranie [yrani] **NF** *Entom* = large, brilliantly-coloured moth belonging to the Uraniidae family

uranifère [yranifɛr] **ADJ** uranium-bearing

uraninite [yraninit] **NF** *Minér* uraninite

uranique [yranik] **ADJ** *Chim* uranic

uranisme [yranism] **NM** *Littéraire* uranism, male homosexuality

uranite [yranit] **NF** *Minér* uranite

uranium [yranjɔm] **NM** *Chim* uranium; **u. enrichi/appauvri** enriched/depleted uranium

uranoscope [yranɔskɔp] **NM** *Ich* stargazer

Uranus [yranys] **NF** *Astron* Uranus

NPR *Myth* Uranus

uranyle [yranil] NM *Chim* uranyl

urate [yrat] NM *Chim* urate

urbain, -e [yrbɛ̃, -ɛn] ADJ **1** *(de la ville)* urban, city *(avant n)*; **un grand centre u.** a big city; **vivre en milieu u.** to live in an urban environment **2** *Littéraire (courtois)* urbane, worldly
  NM,F *(personne qui habite une ville)* urbanite, city dweller
  ▫ **urbaine** NF *Aut* urban car, *Fam* runabout

urbanisation [yrbanizasjɔ̃] NF urbanization; **plan d'u.** urban development plan

urbaniser [3] [yrbanize] VT to urbanize; **zone urbanisée** built-up area
  ▶**s'urbaniser** VPR to become urbanized *or* built-up; **c'est une région qui s'est urbanisée trop rapidement** it is an area that has become urbanized *or* built-up too quickly

urbanisme [yrbanism] NM town planning; **cabinet d'u.** firm of town-planning consultants

urbaniste[1] [yrbanist] NMF town planner

urbaniste[2] [yrbanist], **urbanistique** [yrbanistik] ADJ town planning *(avant n)*

urbanité [yrbanite] NF *Littéraire* urbanity

urbi et orbi [yrbiɛtɔrbi] ADJ *Rel (bénédiction)* Urbi et Orbi
  ADV *Rel* urbi et orbi; *Fig* far and wide, to all and sundry

urcéolé, -e [yrseɔle] ADJ *Bot* urceolate

urdu [urdu] NM Urdu

ure [yr] = **urus**

uréase [yreaz] NF *Biol & Chim* urease

urédinale [yredinal] *Bot* NF rust fungus, *Spéc* member of the Uredineae order
  ▫ **urédinales** NFPL rust fungi, *Spéc* Uredineae

urédospore [yredɔspɔr] NF *Bot* uredospore, urediospore

urée [yre] NF *Biol & Chim* urea; **avoir de l'u.** to have excess urea

urée-formaldéhyde [yreformaldeid] NF *Chim* urea-formaldehyde

uréide [yreid] NM *Chim* ureide

urémie [yremi] NF *Méd* uraemia

urémique [yremik] *Méd* ADJ uraemic
  NMF uraemic

urétéral, -e, -aux, -ales [yreteral, -o] ADJ *Anat* ureteral

uretère [yrtɛr] NM *Anat* ureter

urétérite [yreterit] NF *Méd* ureteritis

urétérostomie [yreterɔstɔmi] NF *Méd* ureterostomy

uréthane, uréthanne [yretan] NM *Chim* urethan, urethane

urétral, -e, -aux, -ales [yretral, -o] ADJ *Anat* urethral

urètre [yrɛtr] NM *Anat* urethra

urétrite [yretrit] NF *Méd* urethritis; **u. non spécifique** non-specific urethritis

urétroscope [yretrɔskɔp] NM *Méd* urethroscope

urétroscopie [yretrɔskɔpi] NF *Méd* urethroscopy

urgemment [yrʒamɑ̃] ADV urgently

urgence [yrʒɑ̃s] NF **1** *(caractère pressant)* urgency; **l'u. d'une décision** the urgent need for a decision; **ces mesures ont été prises dans l'u.** these measures were taken in a great hurry; **il y a u.** it's a matter of urgency, it's an emergency; **il n'y a pas u.** it's not urgent, there's no urgency; *Fam* **bois ton café tranquillement, il n'y a pas u.** drink your coffee, there's no (desperate) rush; **il y a u. à ce que vous preniez une décision** it's urgent for you to come to a decision; **en cas d'u.** in case of *or* in an emergency
  2 *(incident)* emergency
  3 *Méd (cas)* emergency case; *(malade)* emergency patient
  ▫ **urgences** NFPL *Méd Br* casualty department, *Am* emergency room; **salle des urgences** emergency ward
  ▫ **de toute urgence** ADV most urgently; **faire qch de toute u.** to give sth (top) priority, to treat sth as a matter of (top) priority
  ▫ **d'urgence** ADJ **1** *(mesures, soins)* emergency *(avant n)*; **c'est un cas d'u.** it's an emergency; **n'oubliez pas d'emporter une trousse d'u.** don't forget to take a first-aid kit **2** *Pol* **état d'u.** state of emergency; **procédure d'u.** emergency *or* special powers ADV as a matter of emergency; **opérer qn d'u.** to perform an emergency operation on sb; **il fut opéré d'u.** he had an emergency operation; **on l'a transporté d'u. à l'hôpital** he

was rushed (off) to hospital; **on l'a appelé d'u. de l'hôpital** he received an urgent call from the hospital; **faites-le venir d'u.** ask him to come straightaway; **réunir les ministres d'u.** to call an emergency Cabinet meeting; **convoquer d'u. les actionnaires** to call an extraordinary meeting of the shareholders; **à envoyer/payer d'u.** to be sent/paid immediately

urgent, -e [yrʒɑ̃, -ɑ̃t] ADJ urgent; **c'est u.** it's urgent; **ce n'est pas u.** it's not urgent, there's no (desperate) rush; **la situation est urgente** this is an emergency; **il devient u. de trouver une solution** a solution must be found urgently, a solution is urgently required; **avoir un besoin d'argent u.** to be in urgent need *or* badly in need of money; **commençons par le plus u.** let's start with the most urgent thing; **il est u. que je le voie** I must see him urgently; **pli u.** urgent letter

urgentiste [yrʒɑ̃tist] *Méd* ADJ emergency *(avant n)*
  NMF emergency doctor *or Am* physician

urgentologue [yrʒɑ̃tɔlɔg] *Can Méd* ADJ emergency *(avant n)*
  NMF emergency doctor *or Am* physician

urger [17] [yrʒe] VI *Fam* to be urgent[*]; **ça urge?** is it urgent?, how urgent is it?; **je veux faire pipi – ça urge?** I want a pee – how desperate are you?; **j'ai du travail, mais ça urge pas** I do have some work to do, but it's not urgent *or* but there's no rush; **il n'y a rien qui urge** there's no desperate hurry

Uri [uri] NM **le canton d'U.** Uri canton

uricémie [yrisemi] NF *Méd* uricaemia

uridine [yridin] NF *Biol & Chim* uridine

urinaire [yrinɛr] ADJ urinary

urinal, -aux [yrinal, -o] NM (bed) urinal

urine [yrin] NF u., **urines** urine *(UNCOUNT)*; **dans les urines du patient** in the patient's urine

uriner [3] [yrine] VI to urinate, to pass water

urineux, -euse [yrinø, -øz] ADJ urinous

urinifère [yrinifɛr] ADJ uriniferous

urinoir [yrinwar] NM (public) urinal

urinomètre [yrinɔmɛtr] NM *Méd* urinometer

urique [yrik] ADJ uric

URL [yɛrɛl] NF *Ordinat (abrév* **uniform resource locator)** URL

urne [yrn] NF **1** *Pol* ballot box; **se rendre aux urnes** to go to the polls **2** *(vase)* urn; **u. funéraire** (funeral) urn

urobiline [yrɔbilin] NF *Chim* urobilin

urobilinurie [yrɔbilinyri] NF *Méd* urobilinuria

urochrome [yrɔkrom] NM urochrome

urocordé [yrɔkɔrde] *Zool* NM urochord, *Spéc* member of the Urochorda subphylum
  ▫ **urocordés** NMPL urochords, *Spéc* Urochorda

urocyon [yrɔsjɔ̃] NM *Zool* grey fox, tree fox

urodèle [yrɔdɛl] *Zool* NM urodele, tailed amphibian, *Spéc* member of the Urodela order
  ▫ **urodèles** NMPL urodeles, tailed amphibians, *Spéc* Urodela

uro-génital, -e [yrɔʒenital] *(mpl* **uro-génitaux,** *fpl* **uro-génitales)** ADJ *Méd* urogenital, urinogenital

urographie [yrɔgrafi] NF *Méd* urography

urokinase [yrɔkinaz] NF *Pharm* urokinase

urolagnie [yrɔlaɲi] NF *Méd* urolagnia

urologie [yrɔlɔʒi] NF *Méd* urology

urologique [yrɔlɔʒik] ADJ *Méd* urological

urologue [yrɔlɔg] NMF *Méd* urologist

uromètre [yrɔmɛtr] NM *Méd* ureameter, ur(e)ometer

uropode [yrɔpɔd] NM *Zool* uropod

uropygial, -e, -aux, -ales [yrɔpiʒjal, -o] ADJ *Orn* uropygial

uropygien, -enne [yrɔpiʒjɛ̃, -ɛn] ADJ *Orn* **glande uropygienne** uropygial gland

uroscopie [yrɔskɔpi] NF *Méd* uroscopy

ursidé [yrside] *Zool* NM ursid, *Spéc* member of the Ursidae family
  ▫ **ursidés** NMPL ursids, *Spéc* Ursidae

URSS [yrs, yɛrɛsɛs] NF *Anciennement (abrév* **Union des républiques socialistes soviétiques)** l'U. the USSR; **l'ex-U.** the former USSR

URSSAF, Urssaf [yrsaf] NF *Admin (abrév* **Union pour le recouvrement des cotisations de Sécurité sociale et d'allocations familiales)** l'U. = French administrative body responsible for collecting social security payments

ursuline [yrsylin] NF *Rel* Ursuline

urticacée [yrtikase] *Bot* NF urticaceous plant, *Spéc* member of the Urticaceae family
  ▫ **urticacées** NFPL urticaceous plants, *Spéc* Urticaceae

urticaire [yrtikɛr] NF *Méd* nettle rash, hives, *Spéc* urticaria; **crise d'u.** attack of hives; **avoir une crise d'u.** to come out *or* break out in hives; **avoir de l'u.** to have nettle rash; **les huîtres me donnent de l'u.** oysters bring me out in spots; *Fig Hum* **cette musique, ça me donne de l'u.** that music makes my skin crawl

urticale [yrtikal] NF *Bot* member of the Urtica genus

urticant, -e [yrtikɑ̃, -ɑ̃t] ADJ *Bot & Zool* urticating

urtication [yrtikasjɔ̃] NF *Méd* skin rash *or* irritation, *Spéc* urtication

urubu [yryby] NM *Orn* buzzard

Uruguay [yrygwɛ] NM **1** *(pays)* l'U. Uruguay; **vivre en U.** to live in Uruguay; **aller en U.** to go to Uruguay **2** **le fleuve U.** the Uruguay (River)

uruguayen, -enne [yrygwejɛ̃, -ɛn] ADJ Uruguayan
  ▫ **Uruguayen, -enne** NM,F Uruguayan

urus [yrys] NM *(aurochs)* ure, urus

US [yɛs] NF *Sport (abrév* **union sportive)** sports club *or* association; **l'US (de) Liévin** the Liévin Sports Association *or* SA

us [ys] NMPL *Littéraire* customs; **les us et coutumes** (the) habits and customs

USA [yɛsa] NMPL *(abrév* **United States of America)** **les U.** the USA, the US, the States

usage [yzaʒ] NM **1** *(utilisation)* use; **l'u. de la porte latérale est réservé au personnel** only staff members are authorized to use the side door; **faire u. de qch** to use sth; **faire u. de la force** to use *or* employ force; **faire u. de ses privilèges** to exercise one's privileges; **faire bon u. de qch** to put sth to good use; **faire mauvais u. de qch** to misuse sth; **faire un u. abusif du pouvoir** to abuse one's power; **faire un u. excessif des virgules** to use too many commas; **faire un u. immodéré de l'alcool** to drink too much *or* to excess; **faire de l'u.** to stand up to a lot of use; **ce manteau vous fera de l'u.** you'll get a lot of wear out of this coat; **mon imperméable a fait de l'u.** I've had a lot of wear out of my raincoat; **avoir l'u. de** to have the use of; **nous avons l'u. de la piscine** we have access to *or* the use of the pool; *Jur* **une maison dont elle n'a pas la propriété mais l'u.** a house which she doesn't own, but which she is legally entitled to use; **je n'en aurai pas l'u.** I won't be needing it, I won't have any use for it; **je n'en ai aucun u.** I have no use for it; **à mon u. personnel** for my private *or* own personal use; **être d'u. courant** to be in common *or* everyday use; **c'est un mot d'u. courant** it's a common *or* everyday word; **j'en fais un u. courant** I often use it; *Jur* **u. de faux** use of forged documents; *Jur* **droit d'u.** right of use

  2 *(contrôle)* use; **il a encore l'u. de son bras** he can still use his arm; **perdre l'u. des yeux/l'u. d'un bras** to lose one's sight/the use of an arm; **perdre l'u. de la parole** to lose one's power of speech; **perdre l'u. de la vue/de l'ouïe** to lose one's sight/hearing; **garder l'u. de sa** *ou* **la vue** to retain one's sight

  3 *(fonction)* use, purpose; **avoir plusieurs usages** to have various uses; **appareil d'u. courant** household appliance; **à divers usages** multipurpose; **à u. intensif** heavy-duty; **à u. unique** *(seringue, produit)* single-use; **locaux à u. administratif** office space; **à usages multiples** multipurpose; **locaux à u. commercial** business *or* commercial premises; *Pharm* **à u. interne** *(sur emballage)* for internal use, to be taken internally; *Pharm* **à u. externe** *(sur emballage)* for external use only, not to be taken internally

  4 *Ling* (accepted) usage; **u. écrit/oral** written/spoken usage; **le mot est entré dans l'u.** the word is now in common use; **le mot est sorti de l'u.** the word has become obsolete *or* is no longer used; **c'est un mot que l'on trouve uniquement dans l'u. écrit** the word is found only in written documents; **les mots se modifient par l'u.** words are changed by *or* through use; *Arch* **le bon u., le bel u.** correct usage

  5 *(coutume)* habit, habitual practice; **selon** *ou* **suivant l'u.** according to custom; **selon un u.**

bien établi following a well-established habit; **suivant les usages bancaires** according to normal banking practice; **l'u., les usages** accepted *or* established custom, (the rules of) etiquette; **c'est l'u.** it's the done thing; **ce n'est pas l'u. d'applaudir au milieu d'un air** it's not done to clap *or* you just don't clap in the middle of an aria; **c'est conforme à l'u.** *ou* **aux usages** it's in accordance with the rules of etiquette; **c'est contraire à l'u.** *ou* **aux usages, c'est contre l'u.** *ou* **les usages** it's not the done thing, it's contrary to the rules of etiquette

6 *Littéraire (civilité, politesse)* **avoir de l'u.** to be well-bred; **manquer d'u.** to be uncouth, to lack breeding, to be lacking in the social graces

❑ **à l'usage** ADV with use; **le cuir fonce à l'u.** leather turns darker with use; **c'est un excellent outil, je l'ai bien vu à l'u.** it's an excellent tool, I saw it was when I used it; **c'est à l'u. qu'on s'aperçoit des défauts d'une cuisine** you only realize what the shortcomings of a kitchen are after you've used it for a while; **nous verrons à l'u.!** let's wait and see!

❑ **à l'usage de** PRÉP **à l'u. des écoles/des étudiants** for use in schools/by students; **un livre de cuisine à l'u. des enfants** a cookery book aimed at *or* intended for children

❑ **d'usage** ADJ **1** *(habituel)* customary, usual; **finir une lettre avec la formule d'u.** to end a letter in the usual *or* accepted manner; **j'ai fait modifier la formule d'u.** I had the standard wording altered; **échanger les banalités d'u.** to exchange the customary platitudes; **il est d'u. de laisser un pourboire** it is customary to leave a tip; **comme il est d'u.** as is customary; **les conditions d'u.** the usual terms

2 *Ling* **l'orthographe d'u.** the generally accepted spelling; **faute d'u.** misuse

❑ **en usage** ADJ in use; **cette technique n'est plus en u.** this technique is now obsolete *or* is no longer in use

usagé, -e [yzaʒe] ADJ **1** *(usé → costume)* worn, old; *(→ verre)* used, old; *(ticket)* used **2** *(d'occasion)* used, second-hand

usager [yzaʒe] NM **1** *(utilisateur)* user; **les usagers du téléphone/de la route** telephone/road users; **les usagers du train** rail travellers; **les usagers du métro parisien** Parisian underground users; **les usagers de la Poste** post office users *or* customers **2** *(locuteur)* **les usagers de l'espagnol** Spanish language speakers, speakers of the Spanish language

usance [yzɑ̃s] NF usance

usant, -e [yzɑ̃, -ɑ̃t] ADJ *(tâche)* gruelling, wearing; *(enfant)* wearing, tiresome; **c'est u.** it really wears you down; **il est u.** he wears you out

USB [yɛsbe] NM *Ordinat* (*abrév* **universal serial bus**) USB

usé, -e [yze] ADJ **1** *(vieux → habit)* worn, worn-out; *(→ pile)* worn, old; *(→ lame)* blunt; *(→ pneu)* worn, bald; *(→ corde)* frayed; **u. jusqu'à la corde** *ou* **trame** threadbare; **u. par l'eau** worn away by water; **u. par le frottement** worn(-out) by rubbing; **u. par le temps** timeworn

2 *(rebattu → sujet)* hackneyed, well-worn; *(→ plaisanterie)* old; **c'est u.! essaye une autre excuse** I've heard that one before! try another excuse

3 *(affaibli → vieillard)* worn-out, weary; **cheval u.** old nag; **terre usée** exhausted land; **u. par les épreuves** careworn; **u. par le travail** worn-out by work; **u. par le pouvoir** *(homme politique, monarque)* worn-out *or* jaded by too many years in power

user [3] [yze] VT **1** *(détériorer → terrain, métal)* to wear away; *(→ pneu)* to wear smooth; *(→ veste, couverture)* to wear out; **l'érosion use la roche** erosion wears away *or* eats away the rock; **u. un pull aux coudes** to wear out a pullover at the elbows; **u. un jean jusqu'à la corde** *ou* **trame** to wear out a pair of jeans; *Fig* **on avait usé nos fonds de culottes sur les mêmes bancs** we'd been at school together; *Fig* **cela finit par u. la passion/l'intérêt** in the end it kills off passion/interest

2 *(utiliser → eau, poudre)* to use; *(→ gaz, charbon)* to use, to burn; *(→ réserves)* to use, to go through; **cette machine use trop d'électricité** this machine uses too much electricity; **j'use un tube de rouge à lèvres tous les six mois** I go through a lipstick every six months; **je ne vais pas u. mon énergie à essayer de te persuader** I'm not going to waste my energy trying to persuade you

3 *(fatiguer)* to wear out; **usé par des années de vie politique** worn out by years in politics; **tu uses tes yeux à lire dans le noir** you'll ruin your eyesight reading in the dark; **son pessimisme m'a usé le moral** his/her pessimism wore down *or* sapped my morale; **le petit dernier m'use (complètement)** my youngest child really wears me out; *Fam* **tu m'uses la santé!** you'll be the death of me!

VI *Littéraire* **en u. bien avec qn** to treat sb well, to do well by sb; **en u. mal avec qn** to treat sb badly, to mistreat sb; **en u. trop familièrement avec ses supérieurs** to be overfamiliar with one's superiors; **comme vous en usez, jeune homme!** don't you use that tone of voice with me, young man!

❑ **user de** VT IND *(utiliser → autorité)* to exercise; *(→ mot, tournure, outil)* to use; *(→ audace, diplomatie)* to use, to employ; **u. de son influence (pour faire qch)** to use one's influence (to do sth); **u. de son droit** to exercise one's right; **u. de violence** to use violence; **u. de patience** to exercise patience; **n'hésitez pas à u. de sévérité** don't hesitate to be strict; **u. de douceur avec qn** to handle sb gently; **l'alcool? j'en ai usé et abusé** alcohol? I've used and abused it

▶ **s'user** VPR **1** *(se détériorer → gén)* to wear out; *(→ pile)* to run down; *(→ lame)* to go blunt; *(→ talons, semelles)* to wear out, to wear down; **c'est un tissu qui s'use vite** this material wears (out) quickly; **les semelles en cuir ne s'usent pas vite** there's a lot of wear in leather soles; **les pneus se sont usés très vite** the tyres wore smooth very rapidly

2 *Fig (s'affaiblir)* **leur amour s'est usé** their love has grown cold; **ma patience commence à s'u.** my patience is wearing thin; **sa résistance finira bien par s'u.** his/her resistance will wear down *or* break down in the end

3 *Fig (se fatiguer)* to wear oneself out; **je me suis usé à le lui dire** I'm tired of telling him/her, I've told him/her till I'm blue in the face; **mais c'est ce que je m'use à te dire depuis hier!** that's what I've been trying to tell you since yesterday!; *Fam* **s'u. la santé** to exhaust oneself, to wear oneself out; **elle s'est usée** *ou* **usé la santé à élever dix enfants** she wore herself out bringing up ten children; **s'u. les yeux** *ou* **la vue** to strain one's eyes; **je ne vais pas m'u. la vue à lire vos pattes de mouche!** I don't intend to strain my eyes trying to read your scrawl!

usinabilité [yzinabilite] NF suitability for machining

usinage [yzinaʒ] NM machining

usine [yzin] NF **1** *Ind* factory, plant, mill; **u. d'armement** arms factory; **u. d'assemblage** assembly plant; **u. de fabrication** manufacturing plant; **u. à gaz** gasworks; *Fig* overly complicated system; **u. métallurgique** ironworks; **u. de montage** assembly plant; **u. à papier** paper mill; **u. de production** production plant; **l'U. de la Rance** = large tidal power station in Brittany; **u. sidérurgique** steel mill, steelworks

2 *Fig Péj* **on peut pas souffler cinq minutes, c'est l'u. ici!** you can't get a minute's peace in here, it never stops!; **ce restaurant, c'est une vraie u.!** this restaurant is like a conveyor belt!; **cette école est une usine à bureaucrates** the school is a production line for bureaucrats

usiner [3] [yzine] VT **1** *Métal (moulages)* to machine, to tool; *(pièces)* to machine(-finish); **pièce à u.** part to be machined; **parties usinées** bright parts **2** *(fabriquer)* to manufacture

VI *Fam (travailler dur)* to slog *or* slave away, to be hard at it; **ça usinait dans la cuisine** they were slogging away *or* hard at it in the kitchen

usinier, -ère [yzinje, -ɛr] ADJ *(industrie)* factory *(avant n)*; **faubourg u.** industrial suburb

Usinor-Sacilor [yzinɔrsasilɔr] NM = state-owned steelmaking firm

usité, -e [yzite] ADJ *(terme)* commonly used; **l'expression n'est plus usitée** the phrase has gone out of use *or* is no longer in common use; **c'est le temps du passé le plus u.** it's the most commonly used past tense; **mot très u.** very common word; **mot peu u.** little-used word

usnée [ysne] NF *Bot* tree moss

ustensile [ystɑ̃sil] NM utensil, implement; **ustensiles de cuisine** cooking *or* kitchen utensils; **ustensiles de jardinage** garden tools

ustilaginale [ystilaʒinal] *Bot* NF member of the Ustilaginales order

❑ **ustilaginales** NFPL Ustilaginales

usucapion [yzykapjɔ̃] NF *Jur* usucapion, usucaption

usuel, -elle [yzɥɛl] ADJ *(ustensile, vêtement)* everyday *(avant n)*; *(vocabulaire, terme)* common, everyday *(avant n)*; *(dénomination)* common; **l'anglais u.** everyday English; **il est u. d'accepter des pots-de-vin** accepting bribes is common practice; **le procédé u. est de...** it's common practice to...

NM **les usuels** *(de bibliothèque)* reference works; **cet ouvrage est un u., vous ne pouvez pas l'emprunter** this book is for reference only, you may not borrow it

usuellement [yzɥɛlmɑ̃] ADV ordinarily, commonly

usufructuaire [yzyfryktɥɛr] ADJ *Jur* usufructuary

usufruit [yzyfrɥi] NM *Jur* usufruct; **laisser qch en u. à qn** to leave sb the life tenancy of sth

usufruitier, -ère [yzyfrɥitje, -ɛr] *Jur* ADJ usufructuary

NM,F *(gén)* usufructuary; *(d'un bien immobilier)* tenant for life

usuraire [yzyrɛr] ADJ usurious

usure¹ [yzyr] NF **1** *(action de s'user)* wear (and tear); *(du sol, de roches)* erosion, wearing away; **tissu qui résiste à l'u.** material that wears well; **matière résistante à l'u.** material that stands up to wear (and tear), material that wears well, hard-wearing material; **organes sujets à l'u.** *(d'une machine)* wearing parts; **u. des pneus** tyre wear; **l'u. des roches** erosion suffered by the rock; **u. par frottement** abrasion; **l'u. normale** normal wear and tear; *Tech* **surface d'u.** wearing surface

2 *(affaiblissement)* **l'u. des forces/sentiments** the erosion of one's strength/feelings; **victime de l'u. du pouvoir** worn down by the exercise of power; **notre mariage a résisté à l'u. du temps** our marriage has stood the test of time; *Fam* **avoir qn à l'u.** to wear *or* to grind sb down (until he/she gives in)

usure² [yzyr] NF *(intérêt de prêt)* usury; **pratiquer l'u.** to practise usury; **prêter à u.** to lend upon usury *or* at usurious rates of interest; *Fig* **je vous revaudrai ce service avec u.** I'll repay you for this service with interest

usurier, -ère [yzyrje, -ɛr] NM,F usurer

usurpateur, -trice [yzyrpatœr, -tris] ADJ *Littéraire* usurping *(avant n)*

NM,F usurper

usurpation [yzyrpasjɔ̃] NF usurpation, usurping; *Ordinat* **u. d'adresse IP** spoofing; **u. d'état civil** usurpation of civil status; **u. de pouvoir** usurpation *or* usurping of power; **u. de titre** usurpation of title

usurpatoire [yzyrpatwar] ADJ usurpatory

usurpatrice [ysyrpatris] *voir* **usurpateur**

usurper [3] [yzyrpe] VT *(droit, identité)* to usurp; *Fig* **sa gloire est usurpée** his/her fame isn't rightfully his/hers

❑ **usurper sur** VT IND *Littéraire* to encroach on *or* upon

usus [yzys] NM *Jur* usus

ut [yt] NM INV **1** *Mus* C; **ut dièse** C sharp; **clef d'ut** C clef; **clef d'ut quatrième ligne** tenor clef **2** *Jur* **ut singuli** considered individually; **ut universi** considered universally

UTA [ytea] NF *Aviat* (*abrév* **Union des transporteurs aériens**) = French airline company

Utah [yta] NM **l'U.** Utah; **dans l'U.** in Utah

utérin, -e [yterɛ̃, -in] ADJ **1** *Anat* uterine **2** *(de la même mère)* **frères utérins** uterine brothers; **sœurs utérines** uterine sisters

utero [yterɔ] *voir* **in utero**

utérus [yterys] NM *Anat* womb, *Spéc* uterus

utile [ytil] ADJ **1** *(qui sert beaucoup)* useful; **il est bien u., ton petit couteau** that little knife of yours comes in very handy *or* is very useful; **ça peut (toujours) être u.** it might come in handy; **être u. à qn/à qch** to be useful to sb/for sth; **les notes sont utiles à la compréhension du texte** the notes are helpful for understanding the text;

cela m'a été bien u. *(cet objet)* it came in very handy, I found it very helpful; *(ce renseignement)* it was very helpful; **cela m'a été u. de connaître la langue** my knowledge of the language was very useful to me; **elle nous a été très u.** she was a lot of help, she was very helpful to us

2 *(nécessaire)* necessary; **prenez toutes les dispositions utiles** make all the necessary arrangements; **il n'est pas u. d'avertir la police** there's no need to notify the police; **il n'était pas u. que tu t'en occupes** there was no point in you dealing with it

3 *(serviable)* useful; **se rendre u.** to make oneself useful; **il cherche toujours à se rendre u.** he always tries to make himself useful; **rends-toi u., emporte ces caisses à la cave** make yourself useful, take these crates down to the cellar; **puis-je t'être u. à quelque chose?** can I be of any help to you?, can I help you with anything?; **en quoi puis-je vous être u.?** what can I do for you?, how can I help you?; **si je puis vous être u.** if I can be of any use *or* help *or* service *or* assistance to you; **elle peut t'être u. un jour** she may be of help to you *or* useful one day

4 *Mktg (marché, audience)* addressable

NM l'u. that which is useful; **joindre l'u. à l'agréable** to combine business with pleasure

utilement [ytilmɑ̃] **ADV** usefully, profitably; **conseiller/renseigner u. qn** to give sb useful *or* helpful advice/information; **employer son temps u.** to spend one's time profitably, to make good use of one's time

utilisable [ytilizabl] **ADJ 1** *(objet, appareil)* usable; *(crédit)* available; **ce vieux réveil est encore u.?** is this old alarm clock still working?; **les vieux bocaux ne sont plus utilisables** the old jars are no longer usable; **facilement u.** easy to use **2** *(billet)* valid

utilisateur, -trice [ytilizatœr, -tris] **NM,F** *(d'un appareil)* user; *(d'un service)* user, consumer; *Mktg* **u. final** end-user; *Ordinat* **pour utilisateurs multiples** multi-user; *Mktg* **u. pilote** lead user; *Mktg* **u. tardif** late adopter

utilisation [ytilizasjɔ̃] **NF** use, utilization; **la sorbetière est d'u. simple** the ice-cream maker is

simple *or* easy to use; **pour une bonne u. de ce produit…** in order to make correct use of this product…; **notice d'u.** instructions for use; *Écon* **u. du potentiel de production** capacity utilization

utilisatrice [ytilizatris] *voir* **utilisateur**

utiliser [3] [ytilize] **VT 1** *(appareil, carte, expression)* to use; *(moyens, tactique)* to use, to employ; **utilise le moins possible de farine** use as little flour as possible; **u. l'avion pour traiter les récoltes** to use a plane to treat the crops; **je n'ai pas su u. les possibilités qui m'étaient offertes** I didn't make the most of the opportunities I was given; **bien/mal u. qch** *(compétences, ressources)* to make/not to make good use of sth; *(mot, expression)* to use sth correctly/incorrectly; **le peu d'espace disponible a été bien utilisé** they have made good use of what little space there is; *Péj* **avoir l'impression qu'on vous utilise** to have the feeling you're being used; *Péj* **il sait u. son monde** he knows how to make the best use of his connections; **tu vas te faire u.** they'll use you

2 *Ordinat* to run; **il peut être utilisé sur…** it can run on…

utilitaire [ytiliter] **ADJ 1** *(utile)* utilitarian **2** *Ordinat* utility *(avant n)*; **programme u.** utility (program)

NM *Ordinat* utility (program); **u. de conversion** conversion utility; **utilitaires de programmation** utilities

utilitarisme [ytilitarism] **NM** utilitarianism

utilitariste [ytilitarist] **ADJ** utilitarian

NMF utilitarian

utilité [ytilite] **NF 1** *(caractère utile)* use, usefulness; **chaque ustensile a son u.** every implement has its specific use; **c'est un appareil qui a son u.** it's an apparatus that has its uses; **des objets sans u.** useless objects; **être d'une u. à qn** to be of use to sb; **ça ne t'est plus d'aucune u.** it's no longer of any use to you, you no longer need it; **la carte de la région m'a été de peu d'u./d'une grande u.** the map of the area was of little/of great use to me; **un appareil sans grande u.** an appliance that's not much use;

quelle est l'u. d'avoir une voiture dans Paris? what's the use of having a car in Paris?; **avoir l'u. de qch** (to be able) to make use of sth; **en as-tu l'u.?** can you make use of it?, do you need it?; **pourquoi garder des choses dont on n'a pas l'u.?** why keep things you have no use for?; **je ne vois pas l'u. de lui en parler** I don't see any point in mentioning it to him/her; **reconnu d'u. publique** = officially recognized as beneficial to the public at large

2 *Écon* utility; **u. collective** collective utility; **u. marginale** marginal utility; **u. marginale décroissante** diminishing marginal utility

☐ **utilités NFPL** **jouer les utilités** *Théât* to play minor *or* small parts; *Fig* to play second fiddle

utopie [ytɔpi] **NF 1** *Phil* Utopia, Utopian ideal **2** *(chimère)* Utopian idea; **c'est de l'u.!** that's all pie in the sky!; **votre programme politique relève de l'u.** your political programme is rather Utopian

utopique [ytɔpik] **ADJ** Utopian

utopisme [ytɔpism] **NM** Utopianism

utopiste [ytɔpist] **ADJ** Utopian

NMF *(rêveur)* & *Phil* Utopian

utraquiste [ytrakist] **NM** *Rel* Utraquist, Calixtine

Utrecht [ytrɛkt] **NM** Utrecht

utriculaire [ytrikyler] **NF** *Bot* bladderwort

utricule [ytrikyl] **NM** *Anat & Bot* utricle

UV [yve] **NF** *Univ* *(abrév* **unité de valeur**) course credit *or* unit

NM INV *(abrév* **ultraviolet**) UV; **faire des UV** to go to a solarium

UVA [yvea] **NM INV** *(abrév* **ultraviolet A**) UVA; **bronzage U.** sunbed tan

uval, -e, -aux, -ales [yval, -o] **ADJ** grape *(avant n)*; **cure uvale** grape cure

uva-ursi [yvayrsi] **NM INV** *Bot* uva-ursi, bearberry

uvée [yve] **NF** *Anat* uvea

uvéite [yveit] **NF** *Méd* uveitis

uvulaire [yvyler] **ADJ** *Anat & Ling* uvular

uvule [yvyl] **NF** *Anat* uvula

uxorilocal, -e, -aux, -ales [yksɔrilɔkal, -o] **ADJ** uxorilocal

uzbek [yzbɛk] = **ouzbek**

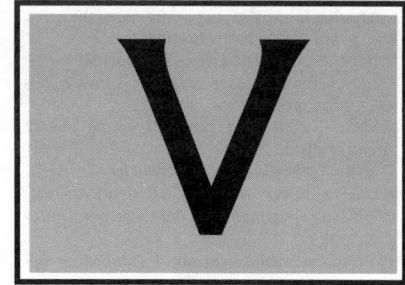

V¹, v [ve] NM INV **1** *(lettre)* V, v; **V comme Victor** ≃ V for Victor; **double v** W, w **2** *(forme)* V (shape); **faire le V de la victoire** to make the victory sign

◊ en V ADJ V-shaped; **un pull (à col) en V** a V-necked sweater; **décolleté en V** plunging neckline

V² *(abrév écrite* **volt***)* V

V. *(abrév écrite* **voir***)* see

v. 1 *(abrév écrite* **vers***)* v *(verse)* **2** *(abrév écrite* **verset***)* v *(verse)* **3** *(abrév écrite* **vers***)* towards **4** *(abrév écrite* **voir***)* see

V1 [veœ̃] NM *Mil* V-1

V2 [vedø] NM *Mil* V-2

VA *(abrév écrite* **voltampère***)* VA

va [va] *voir* **aller²**

vacance [vakɑ̃s] NF **1** *(d'un emploi)* vacancy; **il y a une v. à la comptabilité** the accounts department has a vacancy

2 *(d'une fonction politique)* **pendant la v. du siège** while the seat is empty; **élection provoquée par la v. du siège** election made necessary because the seat became vacant; **pendant la v. du pouvoir** while there is no one officially in power; **dû à la v. du pouvoir** because there is no one officially in power; **il n'y aura pas de v. du pouvoir** there will be a smooth transition of control

3 *Jur* **v. de succession** abeyance of succession **4** *Littéraire (de l'esprit)* emptiness

◊ **vacances** NFPL **1** *(période de loisirs)* *Br* holidays, *Am* vacation; **avoir besoin de vacances** to be in need of a holiday; **prendre des vacances** to take a holiday, to go on holiday; **prendre quelques jours de vacances** to take a few days' holiday; **prendre deux mois de vacances** to take two months off, to have a two-month holiday; **quand prends-tu tes vacances?** when are you going to take your holiday?; **rentrer de vacances** to come back from one's holiday; **quand rentre-t-il de vacances?** when is he back from holiday?; **en rentrant de vacances, ils ont trouvé la maison cambriolée** when they came back from their holiday, they found that the house had been *Br* burgled *or Am* burglarized; **un jour de vacances** a (day's) holiday; **les départs/retours de vacances** going away on/coming back from holiday; **automobilistes: attention aux retours de vacances** drivers: watch out for the end-of-holiday rush; **vous pourrez continuer à recevoir le journal sur votre lieu de vacances** the newspaper can be sent to your holiday address, you can continue to receive the newspaper while you are on holiday; *Fam* **il part? très bien, ça me fera des vacances!** he's going? great, that will be just like a holiday for me!; *Fam* **fais-moi des vacances!** give me a break!; **vacances actives** adventure holiday; **vacances de neige** skiing holidays *or* vacation; **vacances à thème** special-interest holiday

2 *(période du calendrier)* **vacances judiciaires** recess (of the Courts); **vacances parlementaires** Parliamentary recess; **vacances scolaires** school *Br* holidays *or Am* break; **vacances universitaires** *Br* vacation, *Am* university recess; **pendant les vacances (universitaires)** during the vacation; **un job pendant les vacances (universitaires)** a summer job; **les vacances de Noël** *Scol & Univ* the Christmas *Br* holidays *or Am* break; *(pour les salariés)* the Christmas break; **les grandes vacances** *Br* the summer holidays, *Am* the long vacation

◊ **en vacances** ADV on *Br* holiday *or Am* vacation; **pendant que nous étions en vacances en Italie** while we were *Br* holidaying *or Am* vacationing in Italy; **partir en vacances** to go (off) on holiday; **aller** *ou* **partir en vacances en Espagne** to go on holiday to Spain, to go to Spain on holiday; **je l'ai rencontré en vacances** I met him (when I was) on holiday

vacancier, -ère [vakɑ̃sje, -ɛr] NM,F *Br* holidaymaker, *Am* vacationist, vacationer

vacant, -e [vakɑ̃, -ɑ̃t] ADJ **1** *(libre → logement)* vacant, unoccupied; *(→ siège, trône)* vacant; **poste v.** vacancy; **il y a un poste d'ingénieur v.** there's a vacancy for an engineer; *Jur* **succession vacante** estate in abeyance **2** *Littéraire (vague → regard)* vacant, empty; *(mains)* idle

vacarme [vakarm] NM racket, din, row; **les enfants faisaient un v. infernal** the children were making a terrible racket *or* an awful din; **le v. des radios sur la plage** the blaring of radios on the beach

vacataire [vakatɛr] NMF *(remplaçant)* stand-in, temporary replacement; *Univ* part-time lecturer; **avoir un poste de v. à l'Unesco** to be under temporary contract to UNESCO; **c'est une v.** she's on a short-term *or* temporary contract

vacation [vakasjɔ̃] NF **1** *Scol & Univ* supply work; **être payé à la v.** to be paid on a sessional basis; **faire des vacations** to work on a short-term basis **2** *Jur* session, sitting **3** *(de vente aux enchères)* day's sale

◊ **vacations** NFPL **1** *Jur* recess **2** *(honoraires)* fees

vacature [vakatyr] NF *Belg Admin* vacancy

vaccaire [vakɛr] NF *Bot* vaccaria

vaccin [vaksɛ̃] NM **1** *(produit)* vaccine; **v. antivariolique** smallpox vaccine; **v. contre le tétanos/l'hépatite** tetanus/hepatitis vaccine; **v. préventif** preventive vaccine; **v. de Salk** Salk vaccine; **v. TAB** TAB vaccine; **v. thérapeutique** curative vaccine; *Fig* **le meilleur v. contre la paresse** the best antidote to laziness **2** *(injection)* vaccination; **faire un v. à qn** to vaccinate sb **3** *Ordinat* **v. informatique** computer vaccine

vaccinable [vaksinabl] ADJ **à quel âge sont-ils vaccinables?** how old do they have to be before they can be vaccinated?

vaccinal, -e, -aux, -ales [vaksinal, -o] ADJ vaccinal; **complications vaccinales** complications following vaccination; **contamination d'origine vaccinale** contamination originating in a vaccine; **essais vaccinaux** vaccine tests; **préparation vaccinale** vaccine

vaccinateur, -trice [vaksinatœr, -tris] ADJ vaccinating *(avant n)*

NM,F vaccinator

vaccination [vaksinasjɔ̃] NF vaccination, inoculation; **v. curative** curative inoculation; **v. préventive** protective inoculation; **la v. contre la rage est obligatoire** vaccination *or* inoculation against rabies is compulsory

vaccinatrice [vaksinatris] *voir* **vaccinateur**

vaccine [vaksin] NF **1** *Vét* cowpox, *Spéc* vaccinia **2** *Méd* inoculated cowpox; **fausse v.** vaccinella, false vaccinia

vaccinelle [vaksinɛl] NF *Méd* vaccinella, false vaccinia

vacciner [3] [vaksine] VT **1** *Méd* to vaccinate, to inoculate; **se faire v. (contre)** to get vaccinated (against); **être vacciné (contre)** to be vaccinated (against)

2 *Fam Fig* **être vacciné** to have learnt one's lesson; **je suis vacciné contre ce genre de remarque** I've become immune to that kind of remark; **plus de ski, je suis vacciné pour un moment** no more skiing, I've had my fill of that for the time being; **être vacciné au vinaigre** to be in a foul mood; *très Fam* **être vacciné à la merde** to be in a shit mood

vaccinide [vaksinid] NF *Méd* vaccinid

vaccinifère [vaksinifɛr] ADJ *Méd & Vét* vacciniferous

vaccinostyle [vaksinɔstil] NM *Arch Méd* scarificator

vaccinothérapie [vaksinɔterapi] NF vaccine therapy

vachard, -e [vaʃar, -ard] ADJ *Fam (coup)* rotten, mean■, nasty■; *(question)* nasty■; **il était v., l'examen!** the exam was a real stinker!

vache [vaʃ] ADJ *Fam* **1** *(méchant)* rotten, mean■, nasty■; **faire un coup v. à qn** to play a dirty trick on sb; **c'est v. de ta part** it's rotten of you; **allez, ne sois pas v.** come on, don't be rotten; **ce qu'elle peut être v.!** she can be so bitchy *or* such a bitch!; **elle a été v. pour les notes d'oral** she *Br* marked *or Am* graded the orals really strictly■

2 *(remarquable)* **il a un v. (de) coquard** he's got a hell of a black eye; **il a eu une v. d'idée** he had a hell of an idea

NF **1** *Zool* cow; **v. marine** sea cow; **v. sacrée** sacred cow; **v. laitière** *ou* **à lait** milker, dairy cow; *Fig* **v. à lait** milch cow; *Mktg (produit)* cash cow; *Fam* **dans la famille, c'est moi qui suis la v. à lait** I have to fork out for everybody in this family; *Fam* **traverser une période de vaches maigres** to go *or* to live through lean times; *Fam* **finies, les vaches grasses!** the good days are over!; *Fam* **manger** *ou* **bouffer de la v. enragée** to have a hard time of it; *Fam* **parler français comme une v. espagnole** to murder the French language; *Fam* **comme une v. qui regarde passer les trains** with a vacant look on one's face **2** *(cuir)* cowhide

3 *(récipient)* **v. à eau** water bag

4 *Fam (homme)* swine; *(femme)* cow; **ah les vaches, ils ne m'ont pas invité!** the swines didn't invite me!; **ah les vaches, ils sont partis sans moi!** the rotten lot, they left without me!; *très Fam* **cette v. de bagnole!** that damn *or Br* bloody car!; *très Fam* **une v. de moto** one hell of a motorbike

5 *très Fam Arg crime (policier)* cop, pig

6 *Fam* **(ah) la v.!** *(pour exprimer la surprise)* God!; *(pour exprimer l'admiration)* wow!; *(pour exprimer l'indignation, la douleur)* oh hell!; **la v., qu'est-ce qu'il fait froid!** God, it's so cold!; **la v., tu as vu à quelle vitesse il va!** wow! have you seen the speed he's going at?

◊ **en vache** ADV *Fam* on the sly; **faire un coup en v. à qn** to stab sb in the back; **elle a dit ça en v.** she just said that to be bitchy *or* a bitch

vachement [vaʃmɑ̃] ADV *Fam* really■, *Br* dead, *Am* real; **c'est v. difficile** it's *Br* dead *or Am* real difficult; **c'est v. une bonne idée** that's a really good idea; **elle est v. belle, ta robe** that's a great dress you're wearing; **il a v. vieilli** he's got a hell of a lot older looking; **elle a v. changé** she's changed a hell of a lot; **ça fait une sacrée différence? – oui, v.!** it makes a difference!; you can say that again!; *Ironique* **mais je t'assure qu'il t'aime – oui, v.!** but I'm telling you he loves you – like hell he does!

vacher, -ère [vaʃe, -ɛr] NM,F cowboy, f cowgirl

vacherie [vaʃri] NF *Fam* **1** *(caractère méchant)* meanness■, nastiness■

2 *(acte)* dirty *or* rotten trick; **faire une v. à qn** to play a dirty *or* rotten trick on sb; **ils m'ont fait une v.** they played a rotten trick on me; **cette v. de tache ne veut pas partir** this damn *or* blasted stain just won't come out; **quelle v. de temps!** what rotten *or* lousy weather!

3 *(propos)* nasty remark▪ ; **il me disait des vacheries** he was saying really nasty things to me, he was being really horrible to me

vacherin [vaʃrɛ̃] NM **1** *(dessert)* v. **(glacé)** = meringue with cream, ice cream and fruit **2** *(fromage)* vacherin cheese

vachette [vaʃɛt] NF **1** *(animal)* young cow **2** *(peau)* calfskin
▫ **en vachette** ADJ calfskin *(avant n)*

vaché [vaʃte] ADV *Fam* really▪ , *Br* dead, *Am* real

vacieu [vasjø] NM *Agr* = all the ewes not producing milk

vacillant, -e [vasijã, -ãt] ADJ **1** *(titubant → démarche)* unsteady, shaky; **avec une démarche vacillante d'ivrogne** staggering drunkenly; **v. de fatigue** staggering or reeling with tiredness **2** *(qui bouge → flamme)* flickering **3** *(courage)* faltering, wavering; *(mémoire)* failing, faltering; *(santé)* failing; **sa raison vacillante** his/her failing reason **4** *(caractère)* wavering, irresolute, indecisive

vacillation [vasijasjɔ̃] NF **1** *(d'une lueur, d'une flamme)* flickering *(UNCOUNT)* **2** *Littéraire (irrésolution)* hesitations, hesitating *(UNCOUNT)*; **après bien des vacillations, j'ai pris ma décision** after changing my mind several times, I made a decision

vacillement [vasijmã] NM **1** *(d'un poteau, d'une pile de livres)* wobbling; *(d'une flamme)* flickering **2** *Fig (indécision, doute)* indecision, vacillating

vaciller [vasije] VI **1** *(tituber → bébé)* to totter; *(→ ivrogne)* to sway, to stagger; **sortir d'une/ entrer dans une pièce en vacillant** to stagger out of/into a room; **il s'avança en vacillant jusqu'à la porte** he staggered as far as the door; **v. sur ses jambes** to be unsteady on one's legs; **elle vacilla sur ses jambes** her legs nearly gave way under her **2** *(chaise, pile de livres)* to wobble; **faire v. un tabouret** to make a stool wobble; **tout vacillait autour de moi** everything was swimming around me **3** *(flamme)* to flicker; **une lueur vacillait à la fenêtre** a light flickered at the window **4** *(raison, courage)* to falter, to waver; *(voix)* to falter, to shake; *(mémoire)* to be failing, to falter; **sa santé vacille** his/her health is failing or faltering **5** *(hésiter)* to vacillate, to waver; **elle n'a jamais vacillé dans ses prises de position** she has never wavered in her attitude; **v. dans ses réponses** to reply hesitantly

vacive [vasiv] *(dans le Berry)* ADJ F **brebis v.** = two-year-old ewe not yet having borne young
   NF = two-year-old ewe not yet having borne young

va-comme-je-te-pousse [vakɔmʃtəpus] à la **va-comme-je-te-pousse** ADV *Fam* any old how; **ça a été fait à la v.** *(ouvrage, repas)* it was just thrown together; *(lit)* it was made in a hurry▪ ; *(réforme)* it was just pushed through; **on a été élevés à la v.** we weren't brought up, we were dragged up

vacuité [vakɥite] NF *Littéraire* **1** *(vide)* vacuity, emptiness; **la v. de mon existence après ton départ** the emptiness of my life after you left **2** *(inanité)* vacuity, vacuousness, inanity; **un roman d'une effrayante v.** a dreadfully inane novel

vacuolaire [vakɥɔlɛr] ADJ **1** *Biol* vacuolar, vacuolate **2** *Géol* vesicular

vacuole [vakɥɔl] NF **1** *Biol* vacuole **2** *Géol* vesicle

vacuum [vakɥɔm] NM vacuum

vade-mecum [vademekɔm] NM INV *Littéraire* vade mecum

vadrouille [vadruj] NF **1** *Fam (excursion)* ramble▪ , jaunt▪ ; **faire une v. en Italie** to go off for a jaunt in Italy; **une v. de trois jours en montagne** a three-day ramble or hike in the mountains▪ **2** *Can (balai)* long-handled mop *(used for dusting or washing floors)* **3** *Naut* (deck) swab
▫ **en vadrouille** ADV *Fam* **être en v.** to be wandering or roaming around▪ ; **il est rarement à son bureau, il est toujours en v.** he's hardly ever at his desk, he's always wandering around somewhere; **partir en v.** to go (off) on a jaunt▪ ;

il est encore parti en v. he's out gallivanting again

vadrouiller [3] [vadruje] VI *Fam* to wander or roam around▪ ; **v. de par le monde** to rove▪ or to knock about the world

vadrouilleur, -euse [vadrujœr, -øz] NM,F *Fam* rover▪ ; **j'ai toujours été un v.** I've always been a bit of a rover

Vaduz [vadyz] NM Vaduz

va-et-vient [vaevjɛ̃] NM INV **1** *(circulation)* comings and goings, toings and froings; **il y a eu trop de v. ce week-end** there was too much coming and going this weekend; **le continuel v. des voitures de police** the endless toing and froing of police cars **2** *(aller et retour)* **faire le v.** to go back and forth or backwards and forwards; **ils font le v. entre le navire et la côte** they go back and forth between the ship and the coast; **ils font le v. entre l'Allemagne et la Belgique** they go back and forth between Germany and Belgium; **l'avion qui fait le v. entre Londres et Édimbourg** the air shuttle service between London and Edinburgh; **le navire qui fait le v. entre Boulogne et Douvres** the boat that sails between Boulogne and Dover **3** *Tech (latéral)* to-and-fro motion; *(vertical)* up-and-down movement; **dispositif de v.** reciprocating device **4** *Élec* **(interrupteur de) v.** two-way switch; **circuit de v.** two-way wiring **5** *(charnière de porte)* helical hinge; **porte/battant à v.** swing door/panel **6** *(bac)* small ferry or ferryboat **7** *Naut (cordage)* hauling line

vagabond, -e [vagabɔ̃, -ɔ̃d] ADJ **1** *(mode de vie, personne)* wandering *(avant n)*, roving *(avant n)* **2** *Fig (pensée)* wandering *(avant n)*, roaming *(avant n)*; **avoir l'humeur vagabonde** to be in a restless mood
   NM,F *Péj* tramp, vagabond, vagrant; *Littéraire (voyageur)* wanderer, vagabond

vagabondage [vagabɔ̃daʒ] NM **1** *(errance)* roaming, roving, wandering **2** *Littéraire (rêveries)* **les vagabondages de l'esprit/l'imagination** the wanderings of the mind/the imagination **3** *Jur* vagrancy **4** *Admin* **v. spécial** living on immoral earnings

vagabonder [3] [vagabɔ̃de] VI to wander, to roam; **j'ai toujours voulu v.** I've always wanted to be on the road; **v. par monts et par vaux** to roam up hill and down dale; *Fig* **mon esprit/imagination vagabondait vers des pays lointains** my mind/imagination strayed to thoughts of faraway lands; *Fig* **ses pensées vagabondent sans parvenir à se fixer** his/her thoughts wander or drift without any focus

vagal, -e, -aux, -ales [vagal, -o] ADJ *Anat* vagal

vagile [vaʒil] ADJ *Zool* vagile

vagin [vaʒɛ̃] NM *Anat* vagina

vaginal, -e, -aux, -ales [vaʒinal, -o] ADJ *Anat* vaginal

vaginisme [vaʒinism] NM *Méd* vaginismus

vaginite [vaʒinit] NF *Méd* vaginitis *(UNCOUNT)*

vagir [32] [vaʒir] VI *(crier → nouveau-né)* to cry, to wail; *(→ lièvre)* to squeal; *(→ crocodile)* to bark

vagissant, -e [vaʒisã, -ãt] ADJ *(bébé)* crying, wailing; *(lièvre)* squealing; *(crocodile)* barking

vagissement [vaʒismã] NM *(d'un bébé)* cry, wail; *(d'un lièvre)* squeal; *(d'un crocodile)* bark; **attiré par de faibles vagissements** alerted by the sound of whimpering

vagolytique [vagolitik] *Méd* ADJ vagolytic
   NM vagolytic

vagotomie [vagotomi] NF *Méd* vagotomy

vagotonie [vagotoni] NF *Méd* vagotony, vagotonia

vagotonique [vagotonik] ADJ *Méd* vagotonic

vague¹ [vag] NF **1** *(dans la mer)* wave; **grosse v.** roller; **plonger dans les vagues** to dive into the waves; **courir dans les vagues** to run into the waves or surf; *aussi Fig* **v. de fond** groundswell; *aussi Fig* **faire des vagues** to make waves; *Fig* **je ne veux pas de vagues** I don't want any scandal; *Fig* **arriver par vagues** to come in waves **2** *Littéraire (des blés, des cheveux)* wave, ripple; *(de dunes)* wave; *(motif décoratif)* wavy pattern; **effet de v.** ripple effect; *Archit* waved motif **3** *Fig (manifestation)* wave; **v. de colère** wave

or surge of anger; **v. de tendresse** wave or surge of tenderness; **v. de violence** wave or surge of violence **4** *(série)* wave; *(de publicités)* run, series; **v. d'arrestations** wave of arrests; **v. d'attentats** wave of bombings; **v. de criminalité** crime wave; **la première v. de départs** the first wave of departures; **v. d'immigrants** wave of immigrants; **v. de protestations/grèves** wave of protest/strikes **5** *Météo* **v. de chaleur** heatwave; **v. de froid** cold spell **6** *Mil* **v. d'assaut** wave of assault **7** *Écon* **v. de prospérité** boom

vague² [vag] ADJ **1** *(peu marqué → sourire, détail)* vague; *(→ souvenir, connaissances)* vague, hazy; *(→ contour, sensation)* vague, indistinct; *(→ forme)* undefined, indistinct; *(vacant → regard, expression)* vacant, abstracted; **avoir l'air v.** to look vague, to have a vacant expression (on one's face); **esquisser un v. sourire** to smile faintly; **regarder qn d'un air v.** to look vacantly at sb; **il eut un geste v.** he gestured vaguely, he made a vague gesture; **elle est restée très v. sur ses intentions** she was very vague about her intentions **2** *(avant le nom)(non précisé)* vague; **un v. cousin à moi** some distant cousin of mine; **quelque v. écrivain** some writer or other; **il avait écrit un v. roman** he had written a novel of sorts, he had written some kind of a novel; **il m'a raconté une v. histoire de migraine** he told me some vague story about a migraine; **elle dit avoir un v. diplôme en comptabilité** she claims to have some sort or kind of diploma in accounting; **ils ont eu une v. liaison** they had some sort or kind of an affair; **il habite du côté de la Grande Place – c'est plutôt v.!** he lives somewhere near the Grande Place – that's a bit vague! **3** *(large, ample → vêtement)* loose, loose-fitting, generously cut **4** *Anat (nerf)* vagal
   NM **1** *(flou)* vagueness, indistinctness; *(imprécision)* vagueness; **laisser une question dans le v.** to be vague about a matter; **rester dans le v.** to be (as) vague (as possible), to avoid giving any details; **essaye de rester dans le v.** try to keep it vague or to be as vague as possible; **elle m'a bien parlé d'un projet de départ mais elle est restée dans le v.** she did mention something about going away but she never went into any detail **2** *(vide)* **regarder dans le v.** to gaze vacantly into space or the blue; **le regard perdu dans le v.** with a faraway or a far-off or a distant look (in his/her eyes)
▫ **vague à l'âme** NM melancholy; **avoir du v. à l'âme** to be melancholy

vaguelette [vaglɛt] NF wavelet

vaguement [vagmã] ADV **1** *(de façon imprécise)* vaguely; **je me sentais v. coupable** I felt vaguely guilty, I felt in some vague way that I was to blame; **ils se ressemblent v.** they look vaguely alike, there is a vague resemblance between them; **j'avais v. cru qu'il devait venir ici** I had the vague idea he was supposed to come here; **c'est ce que j'ai v. compris** that's what I more or less understood; **il a été v. question de lui offrir le poste** there was some vague talk of offering him/her the position; **il indiqua v. la sortie** he waved his arm in the general direction of the exit; **on la reconnaît v. sur la photo** you can just make her out in the photo; **on distinguait v. les bateaux dans l'ombre du quai** the boats were just discernible in the shadow of the wharf; **tu as prévu le repas de ce soir? – v.!** have you thought of what to cook tonight? – sort of!; *Péj* **elle est v. actrice** she's some kind of actress **2** *(un peu)* vaguely, mildly; **il avait l'air v. intéressé** he seemed vaguely interested; **v. inquiet** mildly anxious

vaguemestre [vagmɛstr] NM *Mil* post orderly; *Naut* postman

vaguer [3] [vage] VI *Littéraire (vagabonder → personne)* to wander, to roam; *(→ pensée)* to rove, to wander; **laisser v. son imagination** to allow one's imagination free rein; **laisser v. ses pensées** to let one's thoughts wander

vahiné [vaine] NF Tahitian woman

vaigrage [vεgraʒ] NM*Naut (en métal)* ceiling; *(en bois)* inner planking

vaigre [vεgr] NF*Naut (en métal)* ceiling plate; *(en bois)* inner plank

vaillamment [vajamɑ̃] ADVvaliantly, bravely, gallantly; **se défendre v.** to put up stout resistance; **elle a v. fait front** she valiantly *or* gallantly stood up to the situation

vaillance [vajɑ̃s] NF *(courage → moral)* courage, bravery, stout-heartedness; *(→ physique)* valiance; *(→ de soldat)* gallantry; **supporter une épreuve avec v.** to face an ordeal with courage; **elle a beaucoup de v.** she's very brave

vaillant, -e [vajɑ̃, -ɑ̃t] ADJ 1 *(courageux → moralement)* courageous, brave, stout-hearted; *(→ physiquement)* valiant; *(→ soldat)* gallant 2 *(bien portant)* strong, healthy; **il est encore v.** he's still in good health; **elle n'est plus bien vaillante** she's not very strong these days

vaille *etc voir* **valoir**

vain, -e [vɛ̃, vεn] ADJ 1 *(inutile)* vain, fruitless, pointless; *(démarche, entreprise)* futile; **tous nos efforts ont été vains** all our efforts were fruitless *or* in vain; **il est v. de continuer** it is pointless to continue

2 *Littéraire (superficiel)* shallow, superficial; *(vaniteux)* vain, conceited; **un homme v.** a vain *or* self-important man

3 *(avant le nom) (serment, espérance)* empty, vain; *(promesse)* empty, hollow, worthless; **ce n'étaient pas là de vaines paroles** these were no empty *or* no idle words; **je te dis qu'elle est dangereuse, et ce n'est pas un v. mot!** I tell you she's dangerous, and it's no empty claim *or* and I know what I'm talking about! **"socialisme" n'est pas un v. mot pour moi** to me, "socialism" is not an empty *or* idle word

4 *Jur* **vaine pâture** common grazing land

❑ **en vain** ADV in vain, vainly, fruitlessly; **il a essayé de me consoler, mais en v.** he tried to console me, but all in vain *or* to no avail; **c'est en v. qu'elle a tenté de m'en dissuader** she tried in vain to talk me out of it

vaincre [114] [vɛ̃kr] VT 1 *(équipe, adversaire)* to beat, to defeat; *(armée)* to defeat; **la vérité vaincra!** the truth will out!; **la justice vaincra!** justice will be done!; **nous vaincrons!** we shall overcome!

2 *Fig (peur, douleur, inhibition)* to overcome, to conquer, to master; *(mal de tête, maladie)* to overcome; *(hostilité, réticences)* to overcome, to triumph over; **v. une résistance** to overcome resistance; **v. toutes les résistances** to carry all before one; **être vaincu par le sommeil/la fatigue** to be overcome with sleep/exhaustion

USAGE ABSOLU **il faut v. ou mourir** we must do or die; *Prov* **à v. sans péril, on triomphe sans gloire** triumph without peril does not bring glory

vaincu, -e [vɛ̃ky] ADJbeaten, defeated; **s'avouer v.** to admit defeat; **les joueurs partaient vaincus d'avance** the players felt beaten *or* defeated before they began; **tu es toujours v. d'avance!** you always start off with the idea you're going to lose!

NM,F defeated man, *f* woman; **les vaincus** the defeated, the vanquished; **les vaincus ne participeront pas aux demi-finales** the losers will not take part in the semi-finals; **attitude/comportement de v.** defeatist attitude/behaviour

vainement [vεnmɑ̃] ADV in vain, vainly, fruitlessly; **on l'a v. cherché** we looked for him in vain

vainquait *etc voir* **vaincre**

vainqueur [vɛ̃kœr] ADJ M winning *(avant n)*, victorious, triumphant, conquering *(avant n)*; **air/sourire v.** triumphant look/smile; **sortir v. d'une épreuve** to emerge (as) the winner of a contest

NM 1 *(gagnant) & Sport* winner; *Boxe* **être v. par K.-O./aux points** to win by a knockout/on points; **le v. de l'Annapurna** the conqueror of Annapurna 2 *Mil* victor

vair [vεr] NMvair; **la pantoufle de v. de Cendrillon** Cinderella's glass slipper

vairé, -e [vεre] *Hér* ADJvairy

NMvairy

vairon[1] [vεrɔ̃] ADJ M **aux yeux vairons** *(de couleurs différentes)* with different-coloured eyes; *(avec un anneau blanc)* wall-eyed; **avoir les**

---

yeux vairons *(de couleurs différentes)* to have different-coloured eyes; *(avec un anneau blanc)* to have wall-eyes, to be wall-eyed

vairon[2] [vεrɔ̃] NM*Ich* minnow

vais [vε] *voir* **aller[2]**

vaishya [vaiʃja] NM INV Vaisya, Vaishya

vaisseau, -x [vεso] NM 1 *(navire)* ship, *Sout* vessel; **v. amiral** flagship; **v. fantôme** ghost ship; **v. de guerre** warship, man-of-war

2 *Anat* vessel; **v. capillaire/lymphatique/sanguin** capillary/lymphatic/blood vessel

3 *Bot* vessel; **plantes à vaisseaux** vascular plants

4 *Astron* **v. spatial** spacecraft; **v. spatial habité** spaceship, manned spacecraft

5 *Archit (de cathédrale)* nave; *(d'un édifice)* body, hall

6 *Arch (récipient)* vessel, receptacle

7 *Bible* **v. d'élection** chosen vessel

♫

'Le Vaisseau fantôme' *Wagner* 'The Flying Dutchman'

vaisselier [vεsəlje] NM*Br* dresser, *Am* buffet

vaisselle [vεsεl] NF 1 *(service)* crockery; **acheter de la belle v.** to buy some nice tableware; **v. plate** (gold/silver) plate; **v. de porcelaine** china tableware; **v. de terre** earthenware plates and dishes; *Fam* **liquide v.** *Br* washing-up liquid, *Am* dish soap

2 *(ustensiles sales)* (dirty) dishes; **la v. empilée dans l'évier** the dishes piled up in the sink; **faire** *ou* **laver la v.** to do *or* to wash the dishes, *Br* to do the washing-up

vaissellerie [vεsεlri] NF manufacture of kitchenware and tableware

vajrayana [vadʒrajana] NM*Rel* vajrayana

Val [val] NM *Rail (abrév* **véhicule automatique léger)** automatic urban train service

val, -als *ou* **-aux** [val, vo] NM*(vallée)* valley; **le V. d'Aoste** Valle d'Aosta; **le V. de Loire** the Loire Valley, the Val de Loire

valable [valabl] ADJ 1 *(valide → ticket, acte)* valid; **au-delà de cette limite, votre billet n'est plus v.** tickets are not valid beyond this point; **non v.** invalid

2 *(acceptable → schéma, argument)* valid, good; *(→ excuse, raison)* valid, good, legitimate; **le jury a considéré le témoignage comme v.** the jury accepted the testimony as valid; **cela reste v.** that still stands; **ce qui est v. pour l'un est v. pour l'autre** what goes for one goes for the other

3 *(excellent → musicien, athlète)* decent, serious; **c'est pas v. comme idée** that idea's worthless *or* no good

valablement [valabləmɑ̃] ADV 1 *(à bon droit)* validly, justifiably, legitimately; **peut-on v. invoquer la légitime défense?** can we justifiably plead self-defence?; **c'est ce qu'on lui a v. reproché** this is what he/she was accused of, and rightly so; **être v. autorisé à qch/à faire qch** to have the necessary authority for sth/to do sth

2 *(efficacement)* usefully; **l'art d'investir son argent v.** the art of making a worthwhile investment; **pour être à même de traiter v. ce problème** in order to be able to deal with this problem satisfactorily

Valachie [valaki] NF*Anciennement* Valachia

Valais [valε] NM le V. Valais; **le canton de V.** the Valais canton, the canton of Valais

valaisan, -anne [valεzɑ̃, -an] ADJof/from Valais

❑ **Valaisan, -anne** NM,F = inhabitant of or person from Valais

valaque [valak] ADJof/from Valachia

❑ **Valaque** NMF = inhabitant of or person from Valachia

valda [valda] NF*Fam (balle d'arme à feu)* bullet ■, slug

Val-de-Grâce [valdəgras] NM le V. = military hospital in Paris

Val-de-Marne [valdəmarn] NM le V. Val-de-Marne

valdinguer [3] [valdɛ̃ge] VI *Fam (tomber)* to go flying; **il est allé v. contre le parcmètre** he went sprawling against the parking meter; **la bouilloire est allée v. contre le placard** the kettle went flying against the cupboard; **envoyer v. qn/qch** to send sb/sth flying; **envoyer v. une**

---

assiette/un livre to send a plate/a book flying; *Fig* **tout envoyer v.** to pack or to jack it all in

valdisme [valdism] NM*Rel* Waldensian doctrine, Vaudism

Val-d'Oise [valdwaz] NM le V. Val-d'Oise

valdôtain, -e [valdotɛ̃, -εn] ADJ of/from Valle d'Aosta

❑ **Valdôtain, -e** NM,F = inhabitant of or person from Valle d'Aosta

valençay [valɑ̃sε] NM goat's cheese *(from the Berry area)*

Valence [valɑ̃s] NM 1 *(ville d'Espagne)* Valencia 2 *(ville de France)* Valence

valence [valɑ̃s] NF*Chim Br* valency, *Am* valence

valence-gramme [valɑ̃sgram] *(pl* **valences-grammes)** NF*Phys* gram-equivalent

Valenciennes [valɑ̃sjεn] NFValenciennes

valenciennes [valɑ̃sjεn] NF(Valenciennes) lace

valentin, -e [valɑ̃tɛ̃, -in] NM,F*(personne)* valentine NM *Can (carte de vœux)* valentine's card, valentine

valentinite [valɑ̃tinit] NF*Minér* valentinite

valentinois, -e [valɑ̃tinwa, -az] ADJ of/from Valence

❑ **Valentinois, -e** NM,F= inhabitant of or person from Valence

valérianacée [valerjanase] *Bot* NF member of the Valerianaceae family

❑ **valérianacées** NFPLValerianaceae

valériane [valerjan] NF*Bot* valerian; **v. grecque** Jacob's ladder

valérianelle [valerjanεl] NF *Bot* lamb's lettuce, corn salad

Valérien [valerjɛ̃] NPR*Antiq* Valerian

valérique [valerik] ADJ*Chim* valeric

valet [valε] NM 1 *(serviteur)* servant, valet; *Théât* **jouer les valets de comédie** to play servants' parts; *Péj* **les valets de l'impérialisme occidental** the lackeys of Western imperialism; **v. de chambre** manservant, valet; **v. de chiens** *(à la chasse)* whipper-in; **v. d'écurie** groom, stable boy; **v. de ferme** farm hand; **v. de limier** *(à la chasse)* harbourer; **v. de pied** footman

2 *Hist* varlet, page

3 *Cartes* jack, knave; **v. de pique** jack *or* knave of spades

4 *(cintre)* **v. (de nuit)** valet

5 *Menuis* clamp

valetaille [valtaj] NF*Littéraire Péj* flunkeys; **toute une v. s'empressait autour de nous** a whole crowd of flunkeys was fussing around us

Valette [valεt] NF*La V.* Valetta, Valletta

valétudinaire [valetydinεr] *Littéraire* ADJ valetudinarian, valetudinary

NMFvaletudinarian

VALEUR [valœr]

| value 1, 2, 4, 6, 8, 11 ■ worth 1, 7 ■ time 3 ■ meaning 5 |

NF 1 *(prix)* value, worth; **avoir de la v.** to be of value; **cette statue a-t-elle une quelconque v.?** is this statue worth anything?; **la v. en a été fixée à 500 euros** its value has been put at 500 euros, it's been estimated to be worth 500 euros; **prendre/perdre de la v.** to increase/to decrease in value, to go up/down in value; **cet appartement ne cesse de prendre de la v.** this flat keeps going up in value, the value of this flat is constantly increasing; **estimer qch au-dessus/au-dessous de sa v.** to overvalue/to undervalue sth; **des objets de peu de v.** objects of little value; **être sans v.** to be of no value; **bijoux sans v.** *ou* **qui n'ont aucune v.** worthless jewels; **bijou de grande v.** jewel of great value, very valuable jewel; **manuscrit d'une v. inestimable** invaluable manuscript; **des marchandises d'une v. de 5000 euros** goods to the value of 5,000 euros; **v. de vérité** truth value; **mettre en v.** *(terre)* to exploit; *(capital)* to get the best return out of; *(connaissances)* to put to good use; *(taille, minceur)* to enhance; *(talent, qualités)* to bring out, to highlight; **une bordure vert tendre met en v. le rose de l'abat-jour** a soft green border sets off the pink in the lampshade; **mettre en v. les meilleures qualités de qn** to bring out the best in sb; **le noir est la couleur qui me met le plus en v.** black is the colour

vai-val

that suits me best; **elle sait se mettre en v.** she knows how to show herself off to the best advantage; **bien mis en v.** *(objet d'art, tableau)* well-displayed; **mal mis en v.** *(objet d'art, tableau)* poorly displayed; **mise en v. d'un terrain** development of a site

2 *Com, Écon, Fin & Math* value; **v. absolue** absolute value; **en v. absolue** in absolute terms; **v. d'achat** purchase value; **v. de l'actif** asset value; **v. actionnariale** shareholder value; *Compta* **v. actualisée** present value; *Compta* **v. actuelle** current value; *Compta* **v. actuelle nette** current net value; **v. ajoutée** added value, value added; **à haute v. ajoutée** high value-added; **v. approchée** approximate value; **v. assurable** insurable value; **v. assurée** insured value; **v. de bilan** book value; *Compta* **v. bilantielle** balance-sheet value; **v. en bourse** *ou* **boursière** market value; **v. brute** gross value; **v. en capital** capital assets; *Fin* **v. compensée** cleared value; **v. comptable** book value; **v. comptable nette** net book value; **v. en compte** value in account; **v. déclarée** declared value; **colis chargé avec v. déclarée 50 euros** parcel insured for 50 euros; *Mktg* **v. distinctive** distinctive value; **v. en douane** customs value, value for customs purposes; **v. d'échange** exchange value; *Fin* **v. à l'échéance** maturity value; *Fin* **v. d'émission** issue price; *Fin* **v. à l'encaissement** value for collection; *Compta* **v. d'inventaire** balance sheet value, break-up value; *Banque* **v. jour** same-day value; **v. locative** rental value; **v. marchande** market value; **v. marginale** marginal value; *Bourse* **v. nominale** *(d'une obligation)* par value; *(d'une action)* face *or* nominal value; *Bourse* **v. non cotée** unlisted security; *Bourse* **v. au pair** parity *or* par value; *Mktg* **v. perçue** perceived value; **v. de rachat** *(d'une police)* surrender value; **v. refuge** *(gén)* sound *or* safe investment; *Bourse* currency-safe investment; **v. de remboursement** redemption value; **v. de rendement** *(d'une entreprise)* profitability value; **v. de reprise** trade-in allowance; **v. à la revente** resale value; **v. d'usage** use value; **v. vénale** monetary value

3 *Mus (d'une note)* time (value), length

4 *(d'une carte)* value

5 *(sens)* meaning; **c'est là que le terme prend toute sa v.** that's when the term takes on its full meaning

6 *(importance subjective)* value; **attacher** *ou* **accorder une grande v. à qch** to prize sth; **attacher** *ou* **accorder de la v. aux traditions** to value *or* to set store by traditions; **j'attache beaucoup de v. à la présentation** I set great store by presentation; **tu sais la v. que j'accorde à ton avis** you know how much I value your opinion; **ton opinion n'a aucune v. pour moi** as far as I'm concerned, your opinion is worthless; **ce document n'a aucune v. légale** this document is not legally binding *or* has no standing in law; **n'avoir qu'une v. sentimentale** to be of *or* to have purely sentimental value; **estimer qn à sa juste v.** to judge sb at his/her true value *or* worth; **cette découverte a redonné une v. à ma vie** this discovery has given my life new meaning

7 *(mérite)* worth, merit; **livre de grande v.** book of considerable merit; **voilà un ouvrage qui n'a pas grande v.** this book is of little merit; **votre argument n'est pas sans v.** your argument is not without its merits; **avoir conscience de sa v.** to know one's own worth

8 *(notion morale)* value; **valeurs sociales/morales/familiales** social/moral/family values; **avoir le sens des valeurs** to have a sense of values; **lui et moi, nous n'avons pas les mêmes valeurs** he and I don't have *or* share the same values

9 *Littéraire (bravoure)* valiance, bravery; **la v. n'attend pas le nombre des années** there is no age for courage

10 *Littéraire (personne de mérite)* **une v.** a great name; **une v. sûre de la sculpture française** one of the top French sculptors

11 *(validité → d'une méthode, d'une découverte)* value; **sa déposition enlève toute v. à la vôtre**

his/her testimony renders yours invalid *or* worthless

12 *(équivalent)* **donnez-lui la v. d'une cuillère à soupe de sirop** give him/her the equivalent of a tablespoonful of syrup

❏ **valeurs NFPL** *Bourse* **valeurs (boursières)** securities, shares, stock; **valeurs (mobilières) de placement** marketable securities; **valeurs bancaires** bank shares; **valeurs cotées** *ou* **de bourse** quoted securities; **valeurs défensives** defensive shares; **valeurs disponibles** liquid *or* tangible assets; **valeurs émises** securities issued; **valeurs en espèces** cash *(UNCOUNT)*, bullion *(UNCOUNT)*; **valeurs immobilières** real property shares; **valeurs minières** mining shares; **valeurs mobilières** stocks and shares, transferable securities; **valeurs négociables** marketable securities; **valeurs nominatives** registered securities; **valeurs passives** liabilities; **valeurs de père de famille** blue chip stock; **valeurs pétrolières** oil shares; **valeurs de portefeuille** portfolio securities; **valeurs de premier ordre** blue chip stock; **valeurs réalisables** realizable *or* marketable securities; **valeurs à revenu fixe/variable** fixed/variable income securities; **valeurs du second marché** unlisted securities; **valeurs des sociétés industrielles** industrials; **valeurs spéculatives** *ou* **de spéculation** speculative securities; **valeurs stannifères** tin shares; **valeurs à terme** futures; **valeurs de tout repos** gilt-edged securities; **valeurs vedettes** leading shares; **les valeurs françaises sont en baisse/en hausse** French securities *or* stocks are down/up

❏ **de valeur ADJ 1** *Com & Fin (bague, tableau)* valuable; **des objets de v.** valuables, items of value, valuable items

2 *(personne)* **homme de v.** *(doué)* man of real ability, talented man; *(de mérite)* man of merit; **un collaborateur de v.** a prized colleague

3 *Can Fam (dommage)* **c'est de v. qu'il pleuve/qu'elle ne puisse pas venir** it's too bad that it's raining/that she can't come

valeureuse [valœrøz] *voir* **valeureux**

valeureusement [valœrøzmɑ̃] ADV *Littéraire* bravely, gallantly, valiantly

valeureux, -euse [valœrø, -øz] ADJ *Littéraire (vaillant)* brave, gallant, valiant

valeur-or [valœrɔr] NF *Fin* value in gold currency

valgus [valgys] *Méd* ADJ M INV valgus
　　　　　　　　 NM INV valgus

validation [validasjɔ̃] NF *(d'un billet, d'une élection)* validation; *(d'un document)* authentication; *(d'une loi)* ratification

valide [valid] ADJ **1** *(permis, titre de transport)* valid; **votre carte n'est plus v.** your card has run out *or* is out of date *or* has expired; **non v.** invalid **2** *(bien portant)* fit, (well and) strong; *(non blessé)* able-bodied; *(membre)* functioning; **il n'avait qu'un bras v.** he had only one good arm; **je ne suis plus bien v.** I'm not as strong as I used to be

validement [validmɑ̃] ADV validly

valider [3] [valide] VT **1** *(traité)* to ratify; *(document)* to authenticate; *(testament)* Br to prove, Am to probate; *(billet, passeport, élection)* to validate; **(faire) v. son titre de transport** *(par un contrôleur)* to have one's ticket stamped; *(dans une machine)* to stamp one's ticket; **il faut faire v. le bulletin de Loto dans un bureau de tabac** you have to get the Loto ticket stamped in a newsagent's

2 *Ordinat (option)* to confirm; *(cellule, case)* to select

valideuse [validøz] NF *(Loto)* = machine used for endorsing Loto tickets

validité [validite] NF **1** *Admin & Transp* validity; **durée de v.** period of validity; **proroger la v. d'un visa** to extend a visa; **établir la v. d'un document** to authenticate a document; **établir la v. d'un testament** to prove *or* to probate a will; **date (limite) de v.** expiry date **2** *(bien-fondé → d'un argument, d'un témoignage)* validity

valine [valin] NF *Biol* valine

valise [valiz] NF **1** *(bagage)* suitcase, bag; **mes valises** my suitcases *or* bags *or* luggage; **défaire ses valises** to unpack (one's bags); **faire ses valises** to pack (one's bags); **mes valises sont**

faites I've packed; *Fig* **faire sa v.** *ou* **ses valises** *(partir)* to pack one's bags and go; *Fam* **tu cesses de parler sur ce ton à ta mère ou tu fais tes valises!** either you stop speaking to your mother like that or you're out on your ear!

2 *Fam (sous les yeux)* **avoir des valises (sous les yeux)** to have bags under one's eyes

3 *Jur* **la v. diplomatique** the diplomatic bag *or* Am pouch; **expédier du courrier par la v. diplomatique** to send mail via the diplomatic bag

4 *Can Joual (coffre d'une voiture)* Br boot■, Am trunk■

5 *Can Fam (personne crédule)* sucker, Br mug; *(personne naïve)* simpleton■

Valium® [valjɔm] NM Valium®

valkyrie [valkiri] = **walkyrie**

vallée [vale] NF **1** *Géog* valley; **les gens de la v.** people who live in the valley; *(pour les montagnards)* lowlanders; **descendre dans la v.** to go down into the valley; **v. d'effondrement** rift valley; **v. glaciaire** *ou* **en U** glaciated *or* U-shaped valley; **v. (à profil) en V** V-shaped valley; **v. sèche** *ou* **morte** dried-up valley; **v. suspendue** hanging valley; **dans la V. de la Loire/du Rhône** in the Loire/Rhône valley; **la V. de la Mort** Death Valley; **la V. des Rois** Valley of the Kings

2 *Bible* **la v. de Josaphat** the Valley of Jehoshaphat; *Littéraire* **cette v. de larmes** this vale of tears

valleuse [valøz] NF *Géog* = small dry (hanging) valley between cliffs

vallisnérie [valisneri] NF *Bot* eelgrass, tape grass

vallon [valɔ̃] NM small valley; *(en Écosse)* glen

vallonné, -e [valɔne] ADJ undulating, hilly

vallonnement [valɔnmɑ̃] NM undulation, hilliness *(UNCOUNT)*

valoche [valɔʃ] NF *Fam (valise)* suitcase■, case■; *Fig (sous les yeux)* **avoir des valoches (sous les yeux)** to have bags (under one's eyes); **faire ses valoches** to pack (up); *Fig* to pack up and go

VALOIR [60] [valwar]

VI to be worth **1, 3** ■ to cost **2** ■ to apply **5** ■ to emphasize **7** ■ to assert **7** ■ to put forward **7**
V IMPERSONNEL it is/would be better to…
VT to earn **1** ■ to be worth **2, 3** ■ to be equivalent (to) **2** ■ to be as good as **4**
VPR to be equivalent

VI 1 *(avoir tel prix)* to be worth; **une maison qui vaut 200 000 euros** a house worth 200,000 euros; **un bijou pareil vaut bien 10 000 euros** a piece of jewellery like that must cost a good 10,000 euros; **sa maison vaut le double maintenant** his/her house is worth twice that now *or* has doubled its value now; **combien vaut cette statuette, à votre avis?** how much is this statuette worth, do you think?; **as-tu une idée de ce que peut v. ce guéridon?** have you any idea how much this little table might be worth?; **ma vieille cuisinière ne vaut plus rien** my old stove isn't worth anything now, I wouldn't get anything for my old stove now; *Fam* **une famille qui vaut plusieurs milliards de dollars** a family worth several billion dollars; *Fam* **après sa promotion, elle vaut 80 000 euros par an** now she's been promoted, she's worth 80,000 euros a year

2 *(coûter)* to cost; **le ruban vaut 3 euros le mètre** the ribbon costs *or* is 3 euros a metre; **v. cher** *(objet en vente)* to be expensive; *(objet précieux)* to be worth a lot; **ne pas v. cher** to be cheap *or* inexpensive; **le bureau ne vaut pas cher** the desk isn't expensive *or* is fairly cheap; **c'est tout ce que ça vaut** that's all it's worth; **ne pas v. grand-chose** not to be worth much; *Fig* **ces gens-là ne valent pas cher** *ou* **pas grand-chose** those people are just worthless *or* contemptible

3 *(avoir telle qualité)* to be worth; **que vaut ton jeune élève?** how good is your young pupil?; **je sais ce que je vaux** I know my worth *or* what I'm worth; **que vaut une vie d'artiste sans la reconnaissance du public?** what's the point of being an artist without public recognition?; **ils verront à l'usage ce que vaut leur nouvelle organisation** in time, they'll see how good their

new organization is; **prends mon avis, pour ce qu'il vaut** take my advice, for what it's worth; **il ne vaut rien, ton marteau** your hammer's no good or useless; **son idée/projet ne vaut rien** his/her idea/project is worthless; **son explication ne vaut rien** his/her explanation is worthless or useless; **quand je manque de sommeil, je ne vaux rien** if I haven't had enough sleep, I'm useless; **c'est une excellente scientifique, mais elle ne vaut rien en tant que professeur** she's a brilliant scientist but a hopeless teacher; **il ne vaut pas mieux que son frère** he's no better than his brother; **mes premières chansons ne valaient pas grand-chose** my early songs weren't particularly good; **l'émission d'hier ne valait pas grand-chose** yesterday's programme wasn't up to much; **elle vaut mieux que la réputation qu'on lui fait** she's much better than her reputation would suggest; **vous ne valez pas mieux l'un que l'autre** you're as bad as each other; **et il t'a quittée? tu vaux mieux que ça** and he left you? you deserve better than that

4 (tirer sa valeur) **ma bague ne vaut que par les souvenirs qu'elle représente** my ring has only sentimental value; **son livre vaut essentiellement par le style** his/her book's main strength is its style; **son initiative vaut surtout par son audace** the main merit of his/her initiative is its boldness

5 (être valable, applicable) **v. pour** to apply to, to hold for; **le règlement vaut pour tout le monde** the rules hold for everyone; **et ça vaut pour tout le monde** and that goes for everyone; **cette critique vaut pour toutes ses pièces** that criticism is true of or is valid for or applies to all his/her plays; **l'embargo ne vaut que pour les armes** the embargo only applies to weapons; **mes compliments/reproches valent pour toute la classe** my praise/criticism applies to the whole class

6 Com **il y a 5 euros à v. sur votre prochain achat** you'll get 5 euros off your next purchase; **à v. sur (une somme)** on account of (a sum); **verser un acompte à v. sur une somme** to pay a deposit to be set off against a sum; **à v. sur qn** on or for account of sb; **payer 10 euros à v.** to pay 10 euros on account

7 (locutions) **faire v.** (argument) to emphasize, to put forward; (opinion, raisons) to put forward; (droit) to assert, to enforce; (qualité) to highlight, to bring out; **faire v. son bon droit** to assert or to vindicate one's rights; **faire v. ses droits à la retraite** to provide evidence for one's entitlement to a pension; **elle a fait v. le coût de l'opération pour justifier sa réticence** she cited the cost of the operation as justification for her reluctance; **pour avoir le poste, il a fait v. ses dix ans d'expérience** to get the job, he stressed his ten years' experience; **j'ai fait v. que...** I pointed out or urged that...; **j'ai fait v. qu'il y avait des circonstances atténuantes** I pointed out or stressed that there were extenuating circumstances; **elle fait v. sa fille** she pushes her daughter forward; **la monture fait v. la pierre** the setting shows off the stone (to (good) advantage); **se faire v.** to show oneself off to advantage; **elle ne sait pas se faire v. dans les entrevues** she doesn't know how to sell herself at interviews; Écon **faire v. un capital** to turn a sum of money to (good) account, to make a sum of money yield a good profit; **faire v. des terres/une propriété** to derive profit from land/a property

V IMPERSONNEL il vaut mieux ou **il vaudrait mieux rester à la maison** it's or it would be better to stay at home; **dans ce cas, mieux vaut s'abstenir** in that case, it's better to do nothing; **mieux vaut tard que jamais** better late than never; **il vaut mieux se taire que de dire des bêtises** it's better to keep quiet than to talk nonsense; **il vaut mieux ne pas répondre** it's best or better not to answer; **il vaudrait mieux que tu y réfléchisses** you'd do better to or you should think about it; **il vaudrait mieux te faire oublier pendant un certain temps** you'd better keep a low profile for a while; **il aurait mieux**

valu pour elle qu'elle meure it would have been better for her if she'd died; **appelle le médecin, ça vaut mieux** it would be better or safer if you called the doctor; **je vais lui dire – je crois que ça vaut mieux** I'm going to tell him/her – I think that would be the best thing to do; **ça vaut mieux ainsi** ou **comme ça** it's better that way; **ça vaut mieux pour lui** it's better for him; **je vais te rembourser – ça vaudrait mieux pour toi!** I'll pay you back – you'd better!; **des choses qu'il vaut autant ne pas rappeler** things best forgotten

VT **1** (procurer) **v. qch à qn** to earn sb sth, to bring sth to sb; **leurs efforts leur ont valu une médaille aux jeux Olympiques** their efforts earned them a medal at the Olympic Games; **cela ne m'a valu que des soucis** all it brought me was trouble; **tous les soucis que m'a valus ce club** all the worries that club cost me; **ça lui a valu trois jours de mise à pied** that earned him/her three days' suspension; **il n'a valu que des malheurs à ses parents** all he ever brought his parents was unhappiness; **qu'est-ce qui m'a valu votre mépris?** what did I do to deserve your contempt?; **voilà ce que ça m'a valu de l'aider** that's all I got for helping him/her!; **qu'est-ce qui me vaut l'honneur/le plaisir de ta visite?** to what do I owe the honour/the pleasure of your visit?; **l'émission d'hier soir nous a valu une avalanche de coups de téléphone** we were deluged with telephone calls after last night's programme; **cette action lui a valu d'être décoré** this act won him a decoration; **ne rien v. à qn** (ne pas lui convenir) to be no good for sb, not to agree with sb, not to suit sb; **le mariage ne lui vaut rien, il est devenu exécrable!** marriage doesn't agree with him, he's become unbearable!; **décidément, la Bretagne ne me vaut rien!** Brittany is decidedly no or not good for me!; **les pays chauds ne me valent rien, j'en rentre toujours épuisé** hot countries don't suit me, I always come back exhausted; **ce climat ne vous vaut rien** this climate is bad for you or doesn't suit you; **son exploit lui a valu d'être admiré par tous** his achievement earned him widespread admiration

2 (représenter) to be equivalent to, to be worth; **une dame vaut 10 points** a queen is worth 10 points; **un essai vaut trois points** a try is worth three points; **un euro vaut cent centimes** a euro is equivalent or is equal to a hundred cents; **une livre vaut 1,60 euros** a pound is worth or is equivalent to or is equal to 1.60 euros; **chaque faute de grammaire vaut quatre points** you lose four points for each grammatical mistake

3 (mériter) to be worth; **le village vaut le détour/déplacement** the village is worth the detour/journey; **voilà un service qui vaut au moins un remerciement, non?** surely a favour like that deserves some form of thanks?; **sa cuisine vaut d'être goûtée** his/her cooking's worth sampling; **son livre vaudrait d'être traduit** his/her book deserves to be translated; **le livre vaut d'être lu** the book is worth reading; **l'expérience vaut d'être tentée** it's worth trying the experiment, the experiment is worth trying; **rien ne vaut d'être obtenu au prix d'une trahison** nothing is worth betraying for; **l'enjeu de l'affaire vaut que l'on prenne le temps de la réflexion** it's worth taking time to reflect when you see what's at stake in the deal; **un service en vaut un autre** one good turn deserves another; **cela ne vaut pas le voyage** it's not worth the journey, it's not worth a special trip; **ça vaut le coup d'œil** it's worth seeing; Fam **v. la peine** ou **le coup** to be worth it, to be worthwhile; **je viendrai si cela en vaut la peine** I'll come if it's worth (my) while or worth the trouble or worth it; **cela ne vaut pas la peine de s'y arrêter** there's no point (in) dwelling on it; **ça vaut le coup** it's worth a try; **ça ne vaut pas le coup** it isn't worth the trouble; **ça vaut le coup d'essayer** it's worth trying or a try; **on pourrait essayer de le raccommoder – ça n'en vaut pas la peine** we could try to mend it – it's not worth it or worth the trouble; **quand je paie 50 euros pour un**

spectacle, je veux que ça en vaille la peine if I spend 50 euros on a show I like to get my money's worth; **j'ai gagné 1000 euros – dis donc, ça vaut le coup!** I won 1,000 euros – well, that was certainly worth it!; **à ce prix-là, ça vaut le coup** at that price, you can't go wrong

4 (dans une comparaison) to be as good as, to match up (to); **c'est bon, mais ça ne vaut pas le repas de la dernière fois** it's good, but not as good as the meal we had last time; **c'est moins cher, mais ça ne vaut pas le cuir!** it's cheaper, but there's no comparison with real leather!; **son idée en vaut une autre** his/her idea is as good as any other; **tu la vaux largement** you're every bit as good as her; **toutes les explications de la terre ne valent pas un bon croquis** no amount of explanation can take the place of a good diagram; **ah, rien ne vaut les confitures de grand-mère!** there's nothing like grandma's jam!; **rien ne vaut un bon grog pour guérir une grippe** there's nothing like a good hot toddy to cure flu; **pour moi, rien ne vaut Mozart!** give me Mozart any day!; **ça ne vaut pas ce qui m'est arrivé l'autre jour** that's nothing to what happened to me the other day; Fam **ça ne vaut pas Éric, tu sais ce qu'il m'a dit?** that's nothing, do you know what Éric told me?

❑ **vaille que vaille** ADV somehow (or other); **vaille que vaille, elle est arrivée au sommet** somehow she made it to the top; **on essaiera vaille que vaille de l'aider** we'll try as best we can to help him/her

▶**se valoir** VPR to be equivalent; **les deux traitements se valent** there's nothing to choose between the two treatments; **tous les métiers se valent** one job is as good as another; **ils se valent tous** there's not much to choose between them, they're all pretty much the same; **nous nous valons au sprint** we're both equally good (as) sprinters; **le père et le fils se valent, aussi têtus l'un que l'autre!** father and son are two of a kind, they're so stubborn!; **vous vous valez bien!** you're both as bad as each other!; **tu vas voter Dupond ou Dufort? – tout ça se vaut!** are you going to vote Dupond or Dufort? – it's six of one and half a dozen of the other or it's all the same thing!

valorisant, -e [valɔrizɑ̃, -ɑ̃t] ADJ (satisfaisant moralement) rewarding; **il fait un travail v.** he has a rewarding job; **la situation des femmes au foyer n'est guère valorisante** being a housewife can hardly be considered a fulfilling occupation

valorisation [valɔrizasjɔ̃] NF **1** Écon (mise en valeur) economic development; (valeur) enhanced value; Compta (d'un inventaire) valuation; **...ce qui permettra une v. de vos investissements** ...which will increase or enhance the value of your investments

2 Fig **on observe une v. des tâches manuelles** manual work is becoming more highly valued; **la v. des diplômes techniques** increasing the prestige of technical diplomas

valoriser [3] [valɔrize] VT **1** Écon (région) to develop the economy of; (bien, monnaie) to increase the value of; **une nouvelle gare valorisera les terrains avoisinants** a new railway station will enhance the value of local land

2 (augmenter le prestige de) **son succès l'a valorisé aux yeux de ses amis** his success has increased his standing in the eyes of his friends; **cherchez un travail qui vous valorise** look for a job which will give you personal satisfaction

▶**se valoriser** VPR Com & Fin to increase in value; **région/secteur qui se valorise** region/industry which is going through a period of growth, up-and-coming region/industry

valpolicella [valpɔlitʃɛla] NM Valpolicella (wine)

valse [vals] NF **1** (danse) waltz; **v. musette** waltz (played on the accordion); **v. viennoise** Viennese waltz

2 Fam (succession rapide) (game of) musical chairs; **la v. des ministres** ministerial musical chairs, constant changes of the ministerial merry-go-round

3 Fam (modification) **la v. des prix** ou **des étiquettes** spiralling prices■

4 *Fam (correction)* hammering, thrashing; **foutre une v. à qn** to give sb a hammering *or* a thrashing
5 *(boisson)* = beer with a dash of mint-flavoured syrup

▬▬▬ 🎬 ▬▬▬
'La Valse des pantins' *Scorsese* 'The King of Comedy'

valse-hésitation [valsezitasjɔ̃] *(pl* **valses-hésitations)** NF *(tergiversation)* shilly-shallying, dithering (about); **après une interminable v.** after much shilly-shallying

valser [3] [valse] VI **1** *(danser)* to waltz; **faire v. qn** to waltz with sb; **invite-la à v.** ask her for a waltz **2** *Fam (tomber)* to career▪, to hurtle▪; **la lampe a valsé dans la cheminée** the lamp went flying into the fireplace; **la voiture est allée v. contre le mur** the car went careering *or* hurtling into the wall; **envoyer v. qch** to send sth flying; **envoyer v. qn** *(le faire tomber)* to send sb flying; *(l'éconduire)* to send sb packing, to show sb the door; **il m'a envoyé v. contre le mur** he sent me flying into the wall; **faire v. l'argent** *ou* **les billets** to throw money around *or* around
3 *Fam* **faire v. le personnel** *(déplacer, congédier)* to play musical chairs with the staff
4 *Fam (abandonner)* **j'ai envie de tout envoyer v.** I feel like packing it all in

valseur, -euse [valsœr, -øz] NM,F waltzer
◽ NM *très Fam Br* bum, *Am* fanny
◻ **valseuses** NFPL *Vulg* balls

▬▬▬ 🎬 ▬▬▬
'Les Valseuses' *Blier* 'Making it' (UK), 'Going Places' (US)

valu, -e [valy] PP *voir* **valoir**
valvaire [valvɛr] ADJ valvate
valve [valv] NF **1** *Anat, Bot & Zool* valve; **v. cardiaque** cardiac valve
2 *Tech (clapet)* valve; *(soupape à clapet)* valve; **v. de compensation** compensating valve; **v. à** *ou* **de dépression** vacuum valve; **v. à glissement** slide valve; **v. modulatrice** modulator valve; **v. papillon** butterfly valve; **v. de purge** bleed valve; **v. à tiroir** slide valve
3 *Aut* **v. de chambre à air** inner-tube valve; **v. à clapet** throttle valve; **v. de gonflage** tyre valve
4 *Électron* valve; **v. redresseuse** rectifying valve
◻ **valves** NFPL *Belg* noticeboard; **aux valves** on the noticeboard

valvé, -e [valve] ADJ *Bot* valvate
valvulaire [valvylɛr] ADJ *Anat* valvular
valvule [valvyl] NF **1** *Anat* valve; **v. mitrale** mitral valve **2** *Bot* valve, valvule
valvulite [valvylit] NF *Méd* valvulitis
vamp [vãp] NF vamp; **prendre des airs de v.** to put on a vampish look; **elle se prend pour une v.** she thinks she's some kind of vamp
◽ ADJ vampish; **habillée très v.** dressed very vampishly
vamper [3] [vãpe] VT *Fam* to vamp
vampire [vãpir] NM **1** *(suceur de sang)* vampire **2** *Littéraire Péj (parasite)* vampire, vulture, bloodsucker; *(assassin)* mass murderer **3** *Zool* vampire bat
vampirique [vãpirik] ADJ vampiric
vampiriser [3] [vãpirize] VT **1** *(sujet: vampire)* to suck the blood of **2** *Fam (dominer)* to have under one's sway, to subjugate; **ayant vampirisé la presse écrite, il s'attaque maintenant à la télévision** having taken over the print media, he's now preparing for an assault on television
vampirisme [vãpirism] NM **1** *(croyance, pratique)* vampirism **2** *Littéraire (rapacité)* vampirism
VAN [veaɛn] NF *Compta (abrév* **valeur actuelle nette)** NPV, net present value
van[1] [vã] NM *Agr (corbeille)* winnowing basket, fan
van[2] [vã] NM *(véhicule pour chevaux)* horse *Br* box *or Am* trailer
van[3] [van] NM *(camionnette)* van
vanadinite [vanadinit] NF *Minér* vanadinite
vanadique [vanadik] ADJ *Chim* vanadic
vanadium [vanadjɔm] NM *Chim* vanadium
Vancouver [vãkuvɛr] NM Vancouver
vanda [vãda] NF *Bot* vanda

vandale [vãdal] NM **1** *(voyou)* vandal; **et mon parquet, bande de vandales!** look what you've done to my floor, you vandals! **2** *Hist* Vandal
vandaliser [3] [vãdalize] VT to vandalize
vandalisme [vãdalism] NM vandalism; **commettre des actes de v.** to commit acts of vandalism; **les anciens arrêts d'autobus étaient très exposés au v.** the old bus stops were very prone to being vandalized
vandoise [vãdwaz] NF *Ich* dace
vanesse [vanɛs] NF *Entom* vanessid; **v. tortue** tortoiseshell (butterfly)
vanille [vanij] NF vanilla
◻ **à la vanille** ADJ vanilla *(avant n)*, vanilla-flavoured
vanillé, -e [vanije] ADJ vanilla-flavoured
vanillier [vanije] NM vanilla plant
vanilline [vanilin] NF vanillin
vanillon [vanijɔ̃] NM vanillon
vanisage [vanizaʒ] NM *Tricot* mixed-yarn knitting
vanité [vanite] NF **1** *(orgueil)* vanity, pride, conceit; **blesser** *ou* **toucher qn dans sa v.** to hurt sb's pride; **tirer v. de qch** to pride oneself on sth, to take pride in sth; **tirer v. de son origine ouvrière** to pride oneself on one's working-class background; **elle avait été championne régionale mais elle n'en a jamais tiré v.** she'd been a local champion but she never boasted about the fact; **il est d'une v. incroyable** he's so incredibly vain, he's so conceited; **sans v., je crois pouvoir faire mieux** with all due modesty *or* without wishing to boast, I think I can do better; **agir par v.** to act out of vanity
2 *(futilité)* pointlessness, futility; **la v. de l'existence humaine** the futility of human existence; *Littéraire* **tout est v.** all is vanity
3 *Beaux-Arts* vanitas *(singulier)*
vaniteuse [vanitøz] *voir* **vaniteux**
vaniteusement [vanitøzmã] ADV vainly, conceitedly, self-importantly
vaniteux, -euse [vanitø, -øz] ADJ *(orgueilleux)* vain, conceited, self-important
◽ NM,F conceited man, *f* woman
vanity-case [vanitikɛz] *(pl* **vanity-cases)** NM vanity case
vannage [vanaʒ] NM *Agr* winnowing
vanne[1] [van] NF **1** *(d'une écluse)* sluicegate; *(d'un moulin)* hatch; **v. de décharge** floodgate; **v. glissante** slide gate; **v. levante** lift gate; **v. manuelle** manual valve; **v. à tiroir** slide valve; **v. de vidange** sluicegate; **ouvrir les vannes** to open the sluicegates; *Fig* to open the floodgates **2** *(robinet)* stopcock
vanne[2] [van] NF *Fam (remarque désobligeante)* snide remark▪, dig, jibe; **envoyer des vannes à qn** to make digs at sb **2** *(plaisanterie)* joke▪, crack
vanné, -e [vane] ADJ *Fam* dead beat, *Br* knackered, *esp Am* pooped; **je suis v.!** I've had it!, I'm beat!
vanneau, -x [vano] NM **1** *Orn* **v. (huppé)** lapwing, peewit; *Culin* **œufs de v.** plovers' eggs **2** *(mollusque)* queen scallop
vannée [vane] ADJ F *voir* **vanné**
◽ NF *Agr* winnowings
vannelle [vanɛl] NF sluicegate, paddle
vanner[1] [3] [vane] VT *Agr* to winnow
vanner[2] [3] [vane] VT *Fam (se moquer de)* to make digs at; *(épuiser)* to wear out
vannerie [vanri] NF **1** *(activité)* basketwork, basketry; **faire de la v.** to weave baskets **2** *(objets)* basketwork, wickerwork
◻ **en vannerie** ADJ wicker, wickerwork *(avant n)*
vannet [vanɛ] NM *Pêche* = kind of net spread on a beach at low tide
vanneur, -euse [vanœr, -øz] NM,F *Agr* winnower
vannier [vanje] NM basket maker
vannure [vanyr] NF *Agr* winnowings
vantail, -aux [vãtaj, -o] NM *(de porte)* leaf; *(de fenêtre)* casement; **porte à double v.** *ou* **à vantaux** *Br* stable *or Am* Dutch door
vantard, -e [vãtar, -ard] ADJ boastful, boasting *(avant n)*, bragging *(avant n)*
◽ NM,F bragger, braggart
vantardise [vãtardiz] NF **1** *(glorification de soi)* boastfulness, bragging **2** *(remarque)* boast
vantaux [vãto] *voir* **vantail**
vantelle [vãtɛl] NF *Naut* sluicegate, paddle
vanter [3] [vãte] VT *(louer, exalter)* to praise, to

extol; **v. l'élégance de qn** to praise sb's elegance; **v. les mérites de qch** to sing the praises of sth; **v. les mérites de qn** to sing sb's praises; *Fam* **une pub vantant les mérites d'une lessive** an ad singing the praises of a washing powder; **un magazine qui vante les charmes de l'Écosse** a magazine which sings the praises of Scotland; *Hum* **v. sa marchandise** to boast
▸ **se vanter** VPR to boast, to brag **(de qch** about sth); **elle n'arrête pas de se v.** she's always singing her own praises *or* bragging; **elle se vante de connaître six langues** she boasts *or* brags that she knows *or* about knowing six languages; **il s'est vanté de gagner la course** he boasted that he would win the race; **il s'est vanté d'avoir gagné la course** he bragged that he had won the race; **elle l'a fait renvoyer mais elle ne s'en vante pas** she had him fired, but she keeps quiet about it; **tu ne t'en es pas vanté!** you kept that quiet *or* under your hat!; **il n'y a pas de quoi se v.** this is nothing to be proud of *or* to boast about; **ce n'est pas pour me v. mais...** I don't mean to boast, but...; **sans (vouloir) me v., je suis plutôt bon au tennis** I'm rather good at tennis, though I say so myself; **sans (vouloir) me v., j'avais déjà compris** I don't wish to boast, but I'd got the idea already; **soit dit sans (vouloir) me v.** without wishing to boast *or* to brag *or Br* to blow my own trumpet
Vanuatu [vanwaty] NM **le V.** Vanuatu; **vivre au V.** to live in Vanuatu; **aller au V.** to go to Vanuatu
va-nu-pieds [vanypje] NMF INV *Péj (clochard)* tramp, beggar
vapes [vap] NFPL *Fam* **être dans les v.** *(évanoui)* to be out of it; *(rêveur)* to be miles away; **je suis encore un peu dans les v.** I'm still a bit out of it; **elle est constamment dans les v.** her head is always in the clouds; **quoi? j'étais complètement dans les v.** what? I was miles away; **tomber dans les v.** *(s'évanouir)* to pass out▪, to keel over
vapeur [vapœr] NF **1** *(gén)* steam; **v. (d'eau)** steam, (water) vapour; **v. atmosphérique** atmospheric vapour; **mettre la v.** to put steam on; *Fig* **nous avons dû mettre la v. pour finir à temps** we had to pull out all the stops to finish on time
2 *Chim & Phys* vapour; **densité/pression de la v.** vapour density/pressure; **v. sèche/saturante** dry/saturated vapour; **vapeurs d'essence** *Br* petrol *or Am* gas fumes; **vapeurs d'alcool** alcoholic fumes
3 *Littéraire (brouillard)* haze, vapour
◽ NM *Naut* steamship, steamer
◻ **vapeurs** NFPL *Vieilli* **avoir des** *ou* **ses vapeurs** to have a fit of the vapours
◻ **à la vapeur** ADV **ça marche à la v.** it's steam-driven; **cuit à la v.** steam-cooked; **cuire des légumes à la v.** to steam vegetables; **cuisiner à la v.** to steam food; **repassage à la v.** steam ironing; **ouvrir une enveloppe à la v.** to steam open an envelope
◻ **à toute vapeur** ADV *Fam* **aller à toute v.** *(navire)* to sail full steam ahead; *(train)* to go full steam ahead, to go at full speed▪; *Fig* to go as fast as one can▪; **va chez le boulanger, et à toute v.!** go to the *Br* baker's *or Am* bakery, and be quick about it!
◻ **à vapeur** ADJ steam *(avant n)*, steam-driven; **machine à v.** steam engine; **bateau à v.** steamboat, steamer; **locomotive à v.** steam locomotive; **train à v.** steam train; **marine à v.** steamers, steamships
vapocraquage [vapokrakaʒ] NM *Pétr* steam cracking
vapocraqueur [vapokrakœr] NM *Pétr* steam reformer
vapocuiseur [vapokɥizœr] NM *Culin* pressure cooker
vaporeuse [vaporøz] *voir* **vaporeux**
vaporeusement [vaporøzmã] ADV *Littéraire* vaporously
vaporeux, -euse [vaporø, -øz] ADJ **1** *(voilé → lumière, paysage)* hazy, misty; *(atmosphère)* steamy; **une brume vaporeuse** hazy mist **2** *(léger → tissu)* filmy, diaphanous; *(→ robe)* flimsy; *Fig (idées)* hazy
vaporisage [vaporizaʒ] NM *Tex* steaming process

◻ **val-vap** (side tab)

vaporisateur [vapɔrizatœr] NM **1** *(pulvérisateur)* spray; *(atomiseur)* spray, atomizer; **parfum en v.** spray perfume **2** *Tech (échangeur)* vaporizer

vaporisation [vapɔrizasjɔ̃] NF **1** *(pulvérisateur)* spraying **2** *Tech (volatilisation)* vaporization; *Aut* **v. (du carburant)** (fuel) atomization

vaporiser [3] [vapɔrize] VT **1** *(pulvériser)* to spray; **ne pas v. vers une flamme** *(sur emballage)* do not spray onto a naked flame **2** *Tech (volatiliser)* to vaporize

►**se vaporiser** VPR to vaporize, to turn to vapour

vaquer [3] [vake] VI *Admin* **1** *(parlement, tribunal)* to be on vacation **2** *Vieilli (poste)* to be vacant
□ **vaquer à** VT IND to attend to, to see to; **v. à ses occupations** to attend to or to go about one's business; **v. aux tâches ménagères** to see to or to attend to the household chores

Var [var] NM **le V.** the Var

var [var] NM *Élec (abrév* **volt-ampère-réactif)** var

vara [vara] ADJ F INV *Méd* inturned

varaigne [varɛɲ] NF tide gate

varan [varɑ̃] NM *Zool* monitor lizard; **v. géant** Komodo dragon or lizard

varangue [varɑ̃g] NF *Naut* floor timber or frame

varappe [varap] NF *(activités)* rock-climbing; *(course)* rock-climb; **faire de la v.** to go rock-climbing

varapper [3] [varape] VI to rock-climb, to go rock-climbing

varappeur, -euse [varapœr, -øz] NM,F rock-climber

varech [varɛk] NM *Bot* kelp, varec

vareuse [varøz] NF **1** *Naut* fisherman's smock **2** *Couture* loose-fitting jacket **3** *Mil* uniform jacket

varheure [varœr] NM *Élec* reactive volt-ampere-hour

varia [varja] NMPL **1** *Littéraire (recueil)* (literary) miscellany, varia **2** *Presse* = article on various subjects

variabilité [varjabilite] NF variability, changeableness; **la v. du temps** the changeableness of the weather

variable [varjabl] ADJ **1** *(changeant* → *temps)* unsettled; *(*→ *taux)* variable; *(*→ *vitesse)* varying; **être d'humeur v.** to be moody
2 *Gram* **mot v.** inflected or inflectional word; **mot v. en genre/nombre** word inflected in gender/number
3 *(varié* → *composition, forme)* varied, diverse; **être v.** to vary; **c'est très v.** it's very variable, it varies a lot
4 *Astron (étoile)* variable
NF *Écon, Math, Ordinat & Phys* variable; **v. aléatoire/discrète/continue** random/discrete/continuous variable; *Écon* **v. endogène** endogenous variable; **v. liée/libre** dependent/independent variable; *Ordinat* **v. de mémoire** memory variable
NM *Météo* **le baromètre est au "v."** the barometer is at or reads "change"

variance [varjɑ̃s] NF variance; **analyse de v.** analysis of variance; **v. de l'échantillon** sample variance

variant, -e [varjɑ̃, -ɑ̃t] ADJ variable
NM *Méd* **nouveau v. de la maladie de Creutzfeldt-Jakob** new variant CJD
□ **variante** NF **1** *(gén) & Ling* variant; **il existe trois variantes du chapitre 12** there are three variant versions of chapter 12; **la 305 est une variante du modèle précédent** the 305 is a variation on the previous model **2** *(aux échecs)* opening move

variateur [varjatœr] NM **1** *Tech* **v. de vitesse** speed variator **2** *Élec* **v. (de lumière** *ou* **d'intensité)** dimmer (switch)

variation [varjasjɔ̃] NF **1** *(fluctuation)* variation, change (**de** in); **v. d'intensité/de poids** variation in intensity/in weight; **pour vos plantes, attention aux variations de température** your plants do not like changes in temperature; **v. du compas** compass error
2 *Mus* variation; **v. sur un thème de Paganini** variation on a theme by Paganini; *Fig* **une v. sur le thème de...** a variation on the theme of...
3 *Astron* variation
4 *Biol* variation
□ **variations** NFPL *(modifications)* changes, modifications; **subir des variations** to undergo

change or changes; *Écon* **variations saisonnières** seasonal variations; **corrigé des variations saisonnières** seasonally adjusted

varice [varis] NF *Méd* varicose vein, *Spéc* varix; **avoir des varices** to have varicose veins; **se faire enlever les varices** to have one's varicose veins removed

varicectomie [varisɛktɔmi] NF *Méd* varicotomy

varicelle [varisɛl] NF *Méd* chickenpox, *Spéc* varicella

varicocèle [varikɔsɛl] NF *Méd* varicocele

varié, -e [varje] ADJ **1** *(non uniforme* → *style, répertoire, alimentation)* varied; *(*→ *vocabulaire)* wide; **une gamme variée de papiers peints** a wide range of wallpapers; **proposer un menu v.** to offer a varied menu; **programme de musique variée** programme of varied music; **un travail très peu v.** a monotonous job, a job with little variety
2 *(au pluriel) (différents)* various, diverse, miscellaneous; **objets divers et variés** various or miscellaneous objects; **des sujets aussi variés que la musique et la chimie** subjects as diverse as music and chemistry; *Culin* **hors-d'œuvre variés** selection of hors d'oeuvres
3 *Mus* **thème v.** theme and variations
4 *Phys (mouvement)* variable

varier [9] [varje] VT *(diversifier* → *cursus, menu, occupations)* to vary, to diversify; **les accessoires permettent de v. une tenue** accessories allow one to vary an outfit; **il faut v. la présentation de votre argument principal** you must present your main argument in different ways; **pour v. les plaisirs** just for a change; **v. son alimentation** to vary one's diet; **v. le menu** to vary the (basic) menu; *Fig* **v. ring the changes;** *Fam* **on prend les mêmes idées, mais on varie la sauce** you take the same ideas, only you dress them up differently or you make them look different
VI **1** *(changer* → *temps, poids, humeur)* to vary, to change; **les produits varient en qualité** products vary in quality; **les prix varient de 50 à 150 euros** prices vary or range from 50 to 150 euros; **les prix peuvent v. du simple au double** prices can vary by a factor of two; **je vous sers du poisson, pour v. un peu** I'm giving you fish, just for a change
2 *Fin (marchés)* to fluctuate
3 *Math* **faire v. une fonction** to vary a function
4 *(différer)* to differ; **leurs opinions varient sur ce point** they differ or they don't see eye to eye on this point; **il n'a jamais varié sur ce point** he's never changed his mind about it; **les médecins varient dans le choix du traitement** doctors differ in or are at variance on the choice of the treatment; **v. dans ses réponses** to be inconsistent in one's replies

variétal, -e, -aux, -ales [varjetal, -o] ADJ *Biol* varietal

variété [varjete] NF **1** *(diversité)* variety, diversity (**de** of); **son œuvre manque de v.** his/her work lacks variety or is not varied enough; **nos châles existent dans une v. de coloris** our shawls come in a variety or a wide range of colours; **j'apprécie surtout la v. des articles qu'on y trouve** I especially like the variety or range of articles you get there; **la v. du paysage** the varying nature of the landscapes; *Com* **grande v. de rayons** wide range of departments
2 *(sorte, genre)* variety, kind, sort, type; **toutes les variétés possibles et imaginables d'escroquerie** every conceivable type of swindle
3 *Bot* variety; *(de maïs, de blé)* (crop) strain; **une nouvelle v. de fleur/pomme** a new variety of flower/apple; **les variétés cultivées** cultivars
4 *Mus* **la v.** *(industrie)* the commercial music business; *(genre)* commercial music
□ **variétés** NFPL *Littérature* miscellanies; *Mus* easy listening; *TV* light entertainment, variety; **regarder les variétés à la télévision** to watch variety shows on television
□ **de variétés** ADJ *(spectacle, émission)* variety *(avant n)*; *(musique)* light; **disque de variétés** easy listening record

variétoche [varjetɔʃ] NF *Fam* middle-of-the-road music

variolaire [varjɔlɛr] ADJ *Méd* variolar

variole [varjɔl] NF *Méd* smallpox, *Spéc* variola;

avoir la v. to have smallpox; *Vét* **v. des vaches** cowpox

variolé, -e [varjɔle] ADJ pockmarked

varioleux, -euse [varjɔlø, -øz] *Méd* ADJ **1** *(patient)* suffering from smallpox, *Spéc* variolous **2** *(boutons)* variolous
NM,F smallpox sufferer

variolique [varjɔlik] ADJ *Méd* smallpox *(avant n)*, *Spéc* variolous

variolisation [varjɔlizasjɔ̃] NF *Arch Méd* variolation

variomètre [varjɔmɛtr] NM *Élec* variometer

variqueux, -euse [varikø, -øz] ADJ varicose

varistance [varistɑ̃s] NF *Électron* varistor

varlet [varlɛ] NM *Hist* varlet, page

varlope [varlɔp] NF *Menuis* trying plane

varloper [3] [varlɔpe] VT *Menuis* to try up

Varna [varna] NM Varna

varois, -e [varwa, -az] ADJ of/from the Var
□ **Varois, -e** NM,F = inhabitant of or person from the Var

varon [varɔ̃] NM = **varron**

varroa [varɔa] NM *Zool* varroa

varron [varɔ̃] NM *Entom & Vét* warble

Varsovie [varsɔvi] NM Warsaw; **le pacte de V.** the Warsaw Pact

varsovien, -enne [varsɔvjɛ̃, -ɛn] ADJ of/from Warsaw
□ **Varsovien, -enne** NM,F = inhabitant of or person from Warsaw

varus [varys] *Méd* ADJ M inturned
NM varus

varve [varv] NF *Géol* varve; **argile à varves** varved clay

vas [va] *voir* **aller²**

vasard, -e [vazar, -ard] ADJ sludgy
NM sludgy bottom

vasculaire [vaskylɛr] ADJ *Anat & Bot* vascular

vascularisation [vaskylarizasjɔ̃] NF **1** *Méd* vascularization **2** *Anat* vascularity

vascularisé, -e [vaskylarize] ADJ *Anat & Bot* vascular

vasculariser [3] [vaskylarize] VT *Méd* to vascularize

vasculo-nerveux, -euse [vaskylonɛrvø, -øz] *(mpl inv, fpl* **vasculo-nerveuses)** ADJ *Anat* composed of vessels and nerves

vase¹ [vaz] NF *(boue)* mud, silt; **banc de v.** mudbank

vase² [vaz] NM **1** *(récipient décoratif)* vase
2 *Chim & Phys* vessel; **v. à bec** beaker; **vases communicants** connecting vessels; *Fig* **c'est le principe des vases communicants** there's been a knock-on effect; **v. Dewar** Dewar flask; **v. d'un élément de pile** battery jar; **v. d'expansion** expansion tank
3 v. de nuit chamberpot
□ **vases** NMPL *Rel* **vases sacrés** sacred vessels
□ **en vase clos** ADV **nous vivions en v. clos** we led an isolated existence; **la recherche ne peut se faire en v. clos** research cannot be carried out in isolation or in a vacuum

---

Allusion

Souviens-toi du vase de Soissons

This sentence is used with reference to a famous episode in French history. It is said that, while in Soissons (a city in northern France), Clovis – King of the Franks – ordered one of his soldiers to return a vase that had been given to him following the looting of a church, at the request of the Bishop of Reims. Rather than give the vase back, the aggrieved soldier broke it with his axe. Some time later, during an inspection of his troops, Clovis spotted the soldier, snatched his axe from his hands and threw it to the ground. As the soldier bent over to pick it up, Clovis smashed his head with his own axe, saying the words **Souviens-toi du vase de Soissons** ("Remember the vase of Soissons"). The sentence is used allusively when someone gets their revenge on someone who has wronged them.

---

vasectomie [vazɛktɔmi] NF *Méd* vasectomy

vasectomiser [3] [vazɛktɔmize] VT *Méd* to perform a vasectomy on

vaseline [vazlin] NF petroleum jelly, Vaseline®

vaseliner [3] [vazline] VT to smear with petroleum

jelly *or* Vaseline®, to put petroleum jelly *or* Vaseline® on
vaser [3] [vɑze] **V IMPERSONNEL** *Fam* to rain cats and dogs, *Br* to bucket down
vaseux, -euse [vazø, -øz] **ADJ 1** *(boueux)* muddy, silty, sludgy **2** *Fam (confus → idée, plan)* hazy, woolly **3** *Fam (malade)* **se sentir tout v.** *(affaibli)* to feel under the weather, to feel off-colour; *(étourdi)* to feel woozy **4** *Fam (médiocre)* pathetic; **ses blagues vaseuses** his/her pathetic jokes
vasière [vazjɛr] **NF** *(étendue couverte de vase)* mudflats; *(d'un marais salant)* tidal reservoir
vasistas [vazistas] **NM** fanlight, *Am* transom
vasoconstricteur, -trice [vazɔkɔ̃striktœr, -tris] *Physiol & Méd* **ADJ** vasoconstrictor *(avant n)*
NM vasoconstrictor
vasoconstriction [vazɔkɔ̃striksjɔ̃] **NF** *Anat & Méd* vasoconstriction
vasoconstrictrice [vazɔkɔ̃striktris] *voir* **vasoconstricteur**
vasodilatateur, -trice [vazɔdilatatœr, -tris] *Physiol & Méd* **ADJ** vasodilator *(avant n)*
NM vasodilator
vasodilatation [vazɔdilatasjɔ̃] **NF** *Physiol & Méd* vasodilation
vasodilatatrice [vazɔdilatatris] *voir* **vasodilatateur**
vasomoteur, -trice [vazɔmɔtœr, -tris] **ADJ** *Physiol & Méd* vasomotor *(avant n)*
vasomotricité [vazɔmɔtrisite] **NF** *Physiol* vasomotion
vasopresseur [vazɔprɛsœr] **NM** *Méd* vasopressor
vasopressine [vazɔprɛsin] **NF** *Physiol* vasopressin
vasotomie [vazɔtɔmi] = **vasectomie**
vasouillard, -e [vazujar, -ard] **ADJ** *Fam* **1** *(mauvais)* **plaisanterie/excuse v.** feeble *or* pathetic joke/excuse; **raisonnement v.** woolly *or Br* dodgy argument **2** *(mal-en-point)* under the weather, out of sorts
vasouiller [3] [vazuje] **VI** *Fam* to flounder; **et votre projet? – ça vasouille** what about your project? – we're struggling
vasque [vask] **NF 1** *(bassin)* basin *(of fountain)* **2** *(coupe)* bowl **3** *(lavabo)* hand basin
vassal, -e, -aux, -ales [vasal, -o] **ADJ** vassal *(avant n)*
NM vassal
vassalique [vasalik] **ADJ** vassal *(avant n)*
vassaliser [3] [vasalize] **VT** to vassalize
vassalité [vasalite] **NF** *Hist* vassalage; *Fig (soumission)* vassalage, bondage
vasselage [vaslaʒ] **NM** *Hist* vassalage
vassiveau, -x [vasivo] **NM** *(dans le Berry)* yearling lamb
vaste [vast] **ADJ 1** *(immense → vêtement)* enormous, huge; *(→ domaine, sujet)* vast, far-reaching; *(→ savoir)* vast, extensive; *(→ palais, gouffre)* vast, huge, immense; **de par le v. monde** the world over **2** *(de grande ampleur)* huge; **victime d'une v. supercherie** victim of a huge hoax; **ce procès a été une v. farce** this trial has been a huge farce
vastement [vastəmɑ̃] **ADV** *Littéraire* vastly
va-t-en-guerre [vatɑ̃gɛr] **NMF INV** warmonger
ADJ INV warmongering
Vatican [vatikɑ̃] **NM le V.** the Vatican; **l'État de la cité du V.** the Vatican City; **travailler au V.** to work in the Vatican City; **le premier/deuxième concile du V.** the first/second Vatican Council
vaticane [vatikan] **ADJ F** of the Vatican; **la bibliothèque V.** the Vatican Library
❑ **Vaticane NF la V.** the Vatican Library
vaticinateur, -trice [vatisinatœr, -tris] *Péj* **ADJ** vaticinal, prophetic
NM vaticinator, prophet
vaticination [vatisinasjɔ̃] **NF** *Littéraire* vaticination
vaticiner [3] [vatisine] **VI** *Littéraire* to vaticinate
va-tout [vatu] **NM INV jouer son v.** to risk *or* to stake one's all
Vauban [vobɑ̃] **NPR barrière V.** security barrier
vauchérie [voʃeri] **NF** *Bot* vaucheria
Vaucluse [voklyz] **NM le V.** the Vaucluse
vauclusien, -enne [voklyzjɛ̃, -ɛn] **ADJ** of/from the Vaucluse
❑ **Vauclusien, -enne NM,F** = inhabitant of or person from the Vaucluse
Vaud [vo] **NM** *Géog* **le V.** Vaud; **le canton de V.** Vaud canton, the canton of Vaud
vaudaire [vodɛr] **NF** = south-east wind which blows over Lake Geneva
vaudeville [vodvil] **NM 1** *(comédie)* vaudeville, light comedy; *(avant le XIXème siècle)* light comedy with songs and dances, vaudeville; *Fig* **tourner au v.** to become farcical **2** *Vieilli (chanson)* topical *or* satirical song *(with refrain)*
vaudevillesque [vodvilɛsk] **ADJ 1** *Théât* vaudeville *(avant n)* **2** *(grotesque)* farcical, ludicrous, preposterous
vaudevilliste [vodvilist] **NMF** writer of vaudeville
vaudois, -e [vodwa, -az] **ADJ 1** *Géog* of/from the canton of Vaud **2** *Rel* Waldensian
❑ **Vaudois, -e NM,F 1** *Géog* = person from or inhabitant of the canton of Vaud **2** *Rel* Waldensian
vaudou, -e [vodu] **ADJ** voodoo *(avant n)*
NM le v. voodoo, voodooism
vaudra *etc voir* **valoir**
vau-l'eau [volo] **à vau-l'eau ADV aller à v.** *(barque)* to go with the stream *or* current; *(affaire, projet)* to be going downhill *or* to the dogs
Vaulx-en-Velin [voɑ̃vəlɛ̃] **NF** = suburb of Lyon where youth riots broke out in 1990
vaurien, -enne [vorjɛ̃, -ɛn] **NM,F 1** *(voyou)* good-for-nothing, scoundrel, rogue **2** *(enfant)* **petit v.!** you little devil!
vaut *etc voir* **valoir**
vaute [vot] **NF** *Belg Culin* = type of thick pancake
vautour [votur] **NM 1** *Orn* vulture; **v. aura** turkey vulture *or* buzzard; **v. griffon** griffon vulture **2** *(personne cupide)* vulture, shark
vautrait [votrɛ] **NM** *Chasse* pack of boar hounds
vautrer [3] [votre] **se vautrer VPR 1** *(se rouler)* to wallow; **se v. par terre** to grovel; **des porcs se vautrant dans la boue** pigs wallowing in mud; *Fig* **se v. dans le vice** to wallow *or* revel in vice **2** *(s'affaler)* to sprawl, to be sprawled; **se v. dans un fauteuil** to loll in an armchair; **être vautré dans un fauteuil** to be lolling in an armchair; **il était vautré sur son lit** he was sprawling on his bed **3** *Fam (tomber)* to go flying
Vautrin [votrɛ̃] **NPR** = a character in several novels by Balzac who, beginning as an escaped convict at war with society, ends as head of the "Sûreté"
vauvert [vovɛr] **ADJ** *Fam* **c'est au diable v.** it's miles from anywhere, it's out in the wilds, it's in the middle of nowhere
vaux *etc voir* **valoir**
Vaux-le-Vicomte [voləvikɔ̃t] **NM** = château near Melun, built for the superintendent Fouquet in 1661
vavasseur [vavasœr] **NM** *Hist* vavasour, valvassor
va-vite [vavit] **NM INV** *Can Fam* **avoir le v.** to have the runs *or* the trots
❑ **à la va-vite ADV** in a rush *or* hurry; **travail fait à la v.** slapdash work; **on a fait nos valises à la v.** we packed in a rush
vd *(abrév écrite* **vend)** **particulier vd...** for sale...
VDQS [vedekyɛs] **NM** *(abrév* **vin délimité de qualité supérieure)** = label indicating quality of wine
vds *(abrév écrite* **vends)** for sale
vé [ve] **NM** *Tech* V-block
veau, -x [vo] **NM 1** *Zool* calf; **v. marin** common *or* harbour seal; *Bible* **le v. d'or** the golden calf; *Fig* **adorer le v. d'or** to worship Mammon
2 *Culin* veal; **escalope/côtelette de v.** veal escalope/cutlet; **rôti de v.** roast veal; **v. marengo** veal Marengo
3 *(cuir)* calf, calfskin
4 *Fam Péj (personne)* lump, *Br* clot; **espèce de gros v.!** you great fat lump!
5 *Fam (voiture)* **cette voiture est un v.** this car is a real heap
6 *Constr* V-block
❑ **veaux NMPL** *Belg* **veaux de mars** (April) showers
❑ **en veau ADJ** calf *(avant n)*, calfskin *(avant n)*
vécés [vese] **NMPL** *Fam (toilettes) Br* loo, *Am* john
vecteur [vɛktœr] **NM 1** *Géom* vector; **v. lié/libre** localized/free vector **2** *Méd* carrier, vector **3** *Mil* carrier **4** *(pour charge nucléaire)* vehicle; *Fig* **v. d'information/de progrès** vehicle for information/for progress; **v. de croissance économique** growth driver
vectoriel, -elle [vɛktɔrjɛl] **ADJ** vector *(avant n)*, vectorial; **espace v.** vector space; **fonction vectorielle** vector function; *Ordinat* **police vectorielle** outline font
vectorisation [vɛktɔrizasjɔ̃] **NF** *Ordinat* **v. d'images** image vectoring
vécu, -e [veky] **PP** *voir* **vivre²**
ADJ 1 *(réel)* real, real-life, true; **c'est une histoire vécue** it's a true story; **ce qu'il raconte là sont des choses vécues** there he talks about things that have actually happened *or* about actual experience; **bien/mal v.** easy/hard *or* difficult to come to terms with
2 *Phil* **temps v., durée vécue** time as experienced
NM le v. de qn sb's (real-life) experiences; **le livre m'a intéressé parce que c'était du v.** I found the book interesting because it was based on a real-life experience
vedettariat [vədɛtarja] **NM** stardom; **accéder au v.** to achieve stardom *or* star status
vedette [vədɛt] **NF 1** *(artiste)* star; **v. de la chanson** singing star; **v. de cinéma** movie *or Br* film star; **v. du petit écran** TV star *or* personality; **v. de la télévision** television star *or* personality; **chanter devant un parterre de vedettes** to sing to a star-studded audience; **elle a tout pour devenir une v.** she's got star quality; **v. américaine** warm-up act; **passer en v. américaine** to be the warm-up act, to get second billing
2 *(célébrité)* star, celebrity; **une v. de la politique/du rugby** a big name in politics/in rugby; **une v. du barreau** a big name at the bar; **présentateur-v.** star presenter
3 *(première place)* **avoir** *ou* **tenir la v.** *Théât* to top the bill, to have star billing; *Fig* to be in the limelight; **ce problème tient la v. depuis longtemps dans ce pays** the problem has long been a major concern in this country; **partager la v. avec qn** *Théât* to share star billing with sb; *Fig* to share the limelight with sb; *Fig* **ravir** *ou* **souffler** *ou* **voler la v. à qn** to upstage sb
4 *Mktg (produit)* star
5 *Naut* launch; **v. de croisière** cabin cruiser; **v. de la douane** customs patrol boat; **v. lance-torpilles** *ou* **de combat** motor torpedo boat
6 *Mil* sentinel; **en v.** on vedette duty
7 *(dans un texte)* heading; *(dans un dictionnaire)* headword
❑ **en vedette ADV être en v.** to be in the limelight, to (have) hit the headlines; **mettre qn/qch en v.** to put the spotlight on sb/sth; **mettre un nom/mot en v.** to highlight *or* emphasize a name/word **ADJ mots en v.** words in bold type
vedettisation [vədɛtizasjɔ̃] **NF la v. de qn** turning sb into a celebrity
vedettiser [3] [vədɛtize] **VT** to turn into a celebrity
vedika [vedika] **NF** = balustrade around a stupa
védique [vedik] **ADJ** *Rel* Vedic
védisme [vedism] **NM** *Rel* Vedaism
végétal, -e, -aux, -ales [veʒetal, -o] **ADJ** *(fibre)* plant *(avant n)*; *(huile)* vegetable *(avant n)*; **règne v.** plant kingdom; **sol v.** humus
NM plant, vegetable
végétalien, -enne [veʒetaljɛ̃, -ɛn] **ADJ** vegan
NM,F vegan
végétalisation [veʒetalizasjɔ̃] **NF** covering with plants
végétalisé, -e [veʒetalize] **ADJ** *(toiture)* covered with plants
végétaliser [3] [veʒetalize] **VT** to cover with plants
végétalisme [veʒetalism] **NM** veganism
végétaliste [veʒetalist] **ADJ** vegan
NMF vegan
végétarien, -enne [veʒetarjɛ̃, -ɛn] **ADJ** vegetarian
NM,F vegetarian
végétarisme [veʒetarism] **NM** vegetarianism
végétatif, -ive [veʒetatif, -iv] **ADJ 1** *Anat, Bot & Méd* vegetative **2** *(inactif)* **mener une vie végétative** to sit around all day
végétation [veʒetasjɔ̃] **NF** *Bot* vegetation; **des arbres en pleine v.** trees in full growth
❑ **végétations NFPL** *Méd* **végétations (adénoïdes)** adenoids; **opérer qn des végétations** to take out sb's adenoids
végétative [veʒetativ] *voir* **végétatif**
végéter [18] [veʒete] **VI 1** *Péj (personne)* to vegetate, to stagnate; **je végète ici!** I'm stagnating here!; **son affaire végète** his/her business is

sluggish; **le marché végète** trading is slow **2** *Arch (plante)* to vegetate, to grow
véhémence [veemɑ̃s] NF vehemence
□ **avec véhémence** ADV vehemently, passionately
véhément, -e [veemɑ̃, -ɑ̃t] ADJ *(plaidoyer)* vehement, passionate; *(dénégation)* vehement, vociferous
véhémentement [veemɑ̃tmɑ̃] ADV *Littéraire* vehemently, passionately
véhiculaire [veikylɛr] *voir* **langue**
véhicule [veikyl] NM **1** *Transp* vehicle; **v. automobile** motor vehicle; **v. sur coussin d'air** air-cushion vehicle; **v. à deux roues** two-wheeler; **v. hippomobile** horse-drawn vehicle; **v. lent** slow vehicle; **v. lourd** heavy-goods vehicle; **v. multifonction** multipurpose vehicle, MPV; **v. de remplacement** courtesy car; **v. sanitaire** ambulance; **v. spatial** spacecraft, spaceship; **v. de tourisme** private car; **v. tout-terrain** off-road vehicle, off-roader; **v. de transport de marchandises** heavy goods vehicle, HGV; **v. de transport de troupe** armoured troop-carrier; **v. à usages multiples** multipurpose vehicle, MPV; **v. utilitaire** commercial vehicle
2 *(moyen de transmission)* vehicle; **le v. du son/de la lumière** the medium *or* the vehicle of sound/of light; **la parole est le v. de la pensée** speech is the vehicle of thought; **la radio est un des véhicules de l'information** radio is one of the vehicles for information *or* one of the news media
3 *Beaux-Arts & Pharm* vehicle
4 *Rel* **petit v.** Hinayana; **grand v.** Mahayana
véhiculer [3] [veikyle] VT **1** *Transp* to convey, to transport **2** *(transmettre → idée, message)* to convey, to serve as *or* to be a vehicle for; **v. une maladie/un virus** to transmit a disease/a virus
véhiculeur [veikylœr] NM *Tex* carrier
veille [vɛj] NF **1** *(jour d'avant)* **la v.** the previous day, the day before; **la v., je lui avais dit...** the day before, I'd said to him/her...; **la v. au soir** the night before; **faites mariner la v. au soir** marinate overnight; **la v. de** the eve of, the day before; **la v. de la bataille** the day before the battle, the eve of the battle; **la v. de Noël** Christmas Eve; **la v. du jour de l'an** New Year's Eve; **la v. de son départ** the day before he/she left; **la v. de sa mort** the day before he/she died; **à la v. des présidentielles/de la visite du pape** on the eve of the presidential elections/of the Pope's visit; **le pays est à la v. d'un tournant historique** the country is on the eve *or* brink of a historic change; **on était à la v. d'entrer en guerre** we were on the brink of war *or* on the point of declaring war; **nous étions à la v. de nous séparer** we were on the brink *or* verge of splitting up; **être à la v. de se marier** to be on the point of getting married, to be about to get married
2 *(absence de sommeil)* wakefulness; **état de v.** waking state; **entre la v. et le sommeil** between waking and sleeping
3 *(absence de sommeil volontaire)* sitting up, staying up; *(auprès d'un malade)* watching, keeping watch; **de longues heures de v. consacrées à la poésie** long sleepless nights devoted to poetry
4 *(surveillance)* vigil; *Mil* night watch; *Naut* **homme de v.** lookout; *Naut* **chambre de v.** chart house; **prendre la v.** to take one's turn on watch; **v. marketing** marketing intelligence; **v. technologique** monitoring of technological development
5 *Ordinat* standby mode
□ **en veille** ADJ *(appareil, ordinateur)* on standby
ADV **se mettre en v.** to go on standby
veillée [veje] NF **1** *(soir)* evening; **pendant les longues veillées d'hiver** during the long winter evenings; **prolonger la v. jusqu'aux petites heures du matin** to stay up until the small hours
2 *(réunion)* evening gathering; *Can (fête)* party; **faire une v. autour d'un feu** to spend the evening round a fire; **les histoires que l'on se racontait à la v.** the stories people used to tell at evening gatherings; *Can* **v. du jour de l'an** New Year's Day party
3 *(en colonie de vacances)* evening activities
4 *(d'un malade)* night nursing; *(d'un mort)* watch, vigil; *Hist* **v. d'armes** knightly vigil; *Fig* **c'est notre v. d'armes avant le concours** it's the last night before our exam
veiller [4] [veje] VT *(un malade)* to watch over, to sit up with; *(un mort)* to keep watch *or* vigil over
VI **1** *(rester éveillé)* to sit *or* to stay up; **je n'ai pas l'habitude de v.** I'm not used to staying up late; **v. jusque tard dans la nuit** to sit up *or* stay awake till late into the night; **ne veille pas trop tard** don't stay up too late
2 *(être de garde)* to keep watch, to be on watch
3 *(être sur ses gardes)* to be watchful *or* vigilant
4 *(entre amis)* to spend the evening in company
□ **veiller à** VT IND to see to; **v. aux intérêts du pays** to attend to *or* to see to *or* to look after the interests of the country; **je veillais au bon déroulement des opérations** I saw to it that everything was running smoothly; **veillez à ce qu'il ne tombe pas** be careful *or* watch that he doesn't fall; **je veillerai à ce qu'elle arrive à l'heure** I'll see (to it) *or* make sure that she gets there on time; **veillez à ne pas refaire la même faute** take care *or* be careful not to make the same mistake again; *Fig* **v. au grain** to keep one's weather eye open
□ **veiller sur** VT IND *(surveiller → enfant)* to watch (over), to look after, to take care of; *(→ santé)* to watch, to take care of
▸**se veiller** VPR *Suisse Fam* to be careful ▪
veilleur [vejœr] NM **1** *Mil (soldat)* lookout **2** *(gardien)* **v. de nuit** night watchman
veilleuse [vejøz] NF **1** *(lampe)* night-light; *(flamme)* pilot light; *(de TV, de chaîne hi-fi)* standby; **mettre en v.** *(lumière)* to dim, to turn down low; *Fam Fig (projet)* to put on the back burner, to shelve; *très Fam* **la mettre en v.** to shut up, to put a sock in it; **mets-la en v.!** just shut up, will you! **2** *Bot* meadow saffron
□ **veilleuses** NFPL *Aut* sidelights
veilleuses-codes [vejøzkɔd] NFPL *Aut* dim-dip
veinard, -e [vɛnar, -ard] *Fam* ADJ *(chanceux)* lucky ▪, *Br* jammy
NM,F lucky devil; **c'est un v.** he has all the luck; **sacré v., va!** you lucky devil!
veine [vɛn] NF **1** *Anat* vein; **s'ouvrir les veines** to slash one's wrists; **v. cave** vena cava; **v. porte** portal vein; **v. pulmonaire** pulmonary vein
2 *(d'un minerai)* vein, lode; *(de charbon)* seam; *(du bois)* grain; *(d'une feuille)* vein
3 *(inspiration)* vein, inspiration; **les deux récits sont de la même v.** the two stories are in the same vein
4 *Fam (chance)* luck ▪; **avoir de la v.** to be lucky ▪; **elle n'a pas eu de v.** she's been unlucky ▪; **quel coup de v.!** what a stroke of luck!, what a fluke!; **pas de v.!** hard *or* tough luck!; *Ironique* **c'est bien ma v.!** just my luck!; **avoir une v. de cocu** *ou* **de pendu** to have the luck of the devil
5 *(locutions)* **être en v. de générosité** to be in a generous mood; **je suis en v. d'inspiration ce matin** I'm feeling inspired this morning
veiné, -e [vene] ADJ *(bras, main)* veiny; *(bois)* grained; *(feuille, marbre)* veined; **v. de rose** pink-veined
veiner [4] [vene] VT to vein
veineux, -euse [venø, -øz] ADJ **1** *Anat* venous **2** *(strié → bois)* grainy
veinosité [venozite] NF *Anat* = veinlet which is visible beneath the skin
veinule [venyl] NF *Anat* venule, veinlet
veinure [venyr] NF veining; **le bois présente des veinures** the wood is veined
vêlage [vɛlaʒ] NM calving
vélaire [velɛr] ADJ velar
NF velar
vélani [velani] NM *Bot* valonia oak
vélar [velar] NM *Bot* hedge mustard
vélarium [velarjɔm] NM *Antiq* velarium
velche [vɛlʃ] = **welche**
Velcro® [vɛlkro] NM Velcro®; **(fermeture) V.** Velcro® (fastening); **fermé par un V.** fastened with Velcro®, with a Velcro® fastening
veld [vɛlt] NM veldt
Vél'd'Hiv, Vel'd'Hiv [vɛldiv] NM *voir* **rafle**
veldt [vɛlt] = **veld**
vêlement [vɛlmɑ̃] NM calving
vêler [4] [vele] VI to calve
vêleuse [veløz] NF = apparatus used to ease calving
vélideltiste [velidɛltist] NMF *Suisse* hang-glider *(person)*
vélie [veli] NF *Entom* water flea
velimeux [velimø] *Can Fam* NM **1** *(chanceux)* lucky devil; **le petit v.!** (the) lucky devil! **2** *(intrigant)* crafty devil **3** *(coquin)* (little) rascal *or* devil
□ **en velimeux** ADV **être fort/riche en v.** to be very strong/rich ▪ ADJ **être en v.** to be fuming *or* livid
vélin [velɛ̃] NM vellum; *voir* **papier**
véliplanchiste [veliplɑ̃ʃist] NMF windsurfer
vélique [velik] ADJ *Naut* **point v.** centre of effort
vélite [velit] NM **1** *Antiq* velite, light-armed soldier **2** *Hist* light infantryman *(belonging to a unit created by Napoleon)*
vélivole [velivɔl], **vélivoliste** [velivɔlist] ADJ glider *(avant n)*
NMF glider pilot
vellave [velav] ADJ of/from Velay
□ **Vellave** NMF = inhabitant of or person from Velay
velléitaire [veleitɛr] ADJ indecisive
NMF **c'est une v.** she has ideas but never carries them through
velléité [veleite] NF vague desire *or* impulse; **il lui vient des velléités de repeindre la cuisine** he/she sometimes gets the urge to redecorate the kitchen (but never gets round to it); **des velléités littéraires** a vague desire to write; **j'ai acheté toutes ces pelotes de laine quand j'avais des velléités de tricot** I bought all these balls of wool when I was in my knitting phase
vélo [velo] NM **1** *(bicyclette)* bike, bicycle; **faire du v., monter à v.** to ride a bike; **une fois qu'on a appris à faire du v....** once you've learned to ride a bike...; **aller à** *ou* **en v.** to go by bike, to cycle; **je vais au travail en** *ou* **à v.** I cycle to work, I go to work on my bike, I ride my bike to work; **on a fait un tour à v.** we went for a ride (on our bikes); **v. d'appartement** exercise bike; **v. de course** racing bike; **v. de (cyclo-)cross/de piste** cyclo-cross/racing bike; **v. tout chemin** hybrid (bike); **v. tout-terrain** mountain bike; *Fam Hum* **avoir un petit v. (dans la tête)** to be off one's rocker, to be not all there
2 *Sport* **le v.** cycling
véloce [velɔs] ADJ *Littéraire (rapide)* swift, fleet; *(agile)* nimble, deft
vélocimètre [velɔsimɛtr] NM velocimeter
vélocimétrie [velɔsimetri] NF velocimetry
vélocipède [velɔsipɛd] NM *Hum* velocipede
vélociste [velɔsist] NMF *(vendeur)* cycle dealer; *(réparateur)* cycle mechanic
vélocité [velɔsite] NF **1** *Littéraire (rapidité)* velocity, speed, swiftness; **avec v.** swiftly; *Mus* **exercice de v.** finger exercise **2** *Phys* velocity **3** *Écon* velocity
vélocross [velɔkrɔs] NM cyclo-cross; **faire du v.** to go cross-country cycling
vélodrome [velɔdrom] NM velodrome
vélomoteur [velɔmɔtœr] NM lightweight motorcycle, *Br* moped
véloski [velɔski] NM skibob
velot [vɔlo] NM = skin of stillborn calf
velours [vəlur] NM **1** *Tex* velvet; **veste/rideaux en v.** velvet jacket/curtains; **v. bouclé** uncut velvet, loop pile fabric; **v. côtelé, v. à côtes** corduroy; **pantalons en v. côtelé** *ou* **v. à côtes** corduroy trousers, cords; **v. de coton** cotton velvet, velveteen; **v. façonné** figured velvet; **v. de laine** velour(s); **v. milleraies** needlecord; **v. de soie** silk velvet; **v. uni** plain velvet
2 *Fig* **ce vin/sa peau est comme du v.** this wine/her skin is as smooth as velvet; **goûte ce vin, c'est du v.** taste this wine, it's sheer velvet; **des yeux de v.** soft *or* velvet eyes; **elle lui fait ses yeux de v.** she's making eyes at him, she's giving him the eye; **une voix de v.** a velvety *or* silky voice; **le v. de ses joues** his/her velvety cheeks; *Fig* **là on joue sur du v.** we can't go wrong there; *Littéraire* **le chemin de v.** the primrose path
3 *(liaison incorrecte)* incorrect liaison (eg **j'ai été** [ʒezete])
4 *Zool* velvet; **bois de v.** velvet antlers
velouté, -e [vəlute] ADJ **1** *(doux → peau)* velvet *(avant n)*, silky; *(→ pêche)* velvety, downy; *(→ vin)* smooth, mellow **2** *Tex (tissu)* raised-nap *(avant n)*; *(papier peint)* flocked

NM 1 *Culin (potage)* cream soup; *(sauce)* velouté (sauce); **v. d'asperges** cream of asparagus (soup) **2** *(douceur → de la peau)* velvetiness, silkiness; *(→ d'une pêche)* bloom

veloutement [vəlutmɑ̃] NM *Littéraire* velvetiness

velouter [3] [vəlute] VT **1** *Tex* to raise, to nap **2** *(papier peint)* to flock **3** *(rendre doux)* to make velvety

▸**se velouter** VPR *(voix)* to soften

velouteux, -euse [vəlutø, -øz] ADJ velvety, soft, silky

veloutier [vəlutje] NM velvet maker

veloutine [vəlutin] NF *Tex* velveteen

Velpeau® [vɛlpo] *voir* **bande**

velte [vɛlt] NF **1** *(ancienne mesure)* = unit of measure of approximately 7.5 litres **2** *(règle)* gauging stick *(for casks)*

velu, -e [vəly] ADJ **1** *(homme, poitrine)* hairy **2** *Bot* hairy, downy, *Spéc* villous **3** *Tex* raised-nap *(avant n)*

vélum [velɔm] NM **1** *(protection)* awning **2** *Antiq* velarium **3** *Anat, Zool & Bot* velum

Vélux® [velyks] NM roof light

velvet [vɛlvɛt] NM *Tex* velvet

velvote [vɛlvɔt] NF *Bot* toadflax

venaison [vənɛzɔ̃] NF venison

vénal, -e, -aux, -ales [venal, -o] ADJ **1** *(corrompu)* venal, corrupt **2** *Péj (intéressé)* venal, mercenary; **un amour v.** a venal love affair **3** *Écon voir* **valeur**

vénalité [venalite] NF venality

venant [vənɑ̃] NM **à tout v., à tous venants** *(au premier venu)* to all and sundry; **à tout v.** *(à tout propos)* constantly; **s'occuper du tout v.** to deal with the everyday *or* run-of-the-mill stuff

Venceslas [vɛ̃sɛslas] NPR Wenceslas

vendable [vɑ̃dabl] ADJ saleable, sellable; **ma voiture n'est pas v.** my car has no market value

vendange [vɑ̃dɑ̃ʒ] NF **1** *(cueillette)* grape-picking, grape-harvesting, grape harvest; **faire la v.** *ou* **les vendanges** *(vigneron)* to harvest the grapes; *(journalier)* to go grape-picking; **pendant les vendanges** during the grape-harvesting *or* grape-picking season

2 *(quantité récoltée)* grape harvest, grape yield; *(qualité récoltée)* vintage; **la v. de l'année sera bonne** this year's vintage will be good, this year will be a good vintage

▫ **vendanges** NFPL *(saison)* grape-harvesting time

vendangeoir [vɑ̃dɑ̃ʒwar] NM grape basket

vendanger [17] [vɑ̃dɑ̃ʒe] VT *(raisin)* to harvest, to pick; *(vigne)* to pick the grapes from

VI to harvest grapes; **ils sont partis v. dans le Midi** they went to pick grapes in the South of France

vendangerot [vɑ̃dɑ̃ʒəro] NM *(en Bourgogne)* wicker grape basket

vendangeur, -euse [vɑ̃dɑ̃ʒœr, -øz] NM,F grape-picker

NM *Entom* harvest mite, chigger

▫ **vendangeuse** NF **1** *(machine)* grape-picker **2** *Bot* aster

Vendée [vɑ̃de] NF **la V.** the Vendée; **en V.** in the Vendée area; **les guerres de V.** the Wars of the Vendée

vendéen, -enne [vɑ̃deɛ̃, -ɛn] ADJ Vendean

▫ **Vendéen, -enne** NM,F Vendean

vendémiaire [vɑ̃demjɛr] NM = 1st month in the French Revolutionary calendar (from 22/23/24 September to 21/22/23 October)

vendetta [vɑ̃deta] NF vendetta

vendeur, -euse [vɑ̃dœr, -øz] ADJ selling *(avant n)*; **être v.** to be willing to sell; **j'allais vendre ma voiture mais je ne suis plus v.** I was going to sell my car but I've decided not to *or* but I've taken it off the market; **commissionnaire v.** selling agent

NM,F **1** *(dans un magasin) Br* sales assistant, shop assistant, *Am* (sales) clerk; **recherche vendeurs** *(petite annonce)* sales staff wanted

2 *(dans une entreprise)* (sales) representative; **il est bon v.** he's a good salesman; *Mktg* **v. représentant placier** sales representative

3 *(marchand)* seller, salesman, *f* saleswoman; **v. de chaussures** shoe seller; *Bourse* **v. à découvert** short seller; **v. à domicile** door-to-door salesman; *Fig* **les vendeurs d'évasion** dream merchants, the dream industry; **v. export** exporter; **vendeuse de glaces** ice-cream lady; **v. de journaux** newsman, newspaperman; **v. par téléphone** telesales person

4 *(non professionnel)* seller

NM *Jur* vendor, seller

vendition [vɑ̃disjɔ̃] NF *Belg* auction

Vendôme [vɑ̃dom] *voir* **place**

vendre [73] [vɑ̃dr] VT **1** *(céder → propriété, brevet, marchandise)* to sell; **il vend ses melons (à) 2 euros** he sells his melons at *or* for 2 euros each; **v. qch à la pièce/à la douzaine/au poids** to sell sth by unit/by the dozen/by weight; **v. (qch) comptant** to sell (sth) for cash; **v. (qch) au détail** to retail (sth), to sell (sth) retail; **v. (qch) en gros** to sell (sth) wholesale; **v. qch au prix fort** to price sth high; **v. (qch) à perte** to sell (sth) at a loss; **v. moins cher que qn** to undercut sb; **v. qch aux enchères** *(gén)* to auction sth; *(pour s'en débarrasser)* to auction sth off; **elle a tout vendu et elle a fait ses valises** she sold *Br* up *or Am* out and packed her bags; **v. qch à qn** to sell sb sth, to sell sth to sb; *Bourse* **v. à découvert** to sell short, to go a bear; *Bourse* **v. à terme** to sell forward; **elle m'a vendu sa montre (pour) 30 euros** she sold me her watch for 30 euros; **tu me la vendrais combien?** how much would you sell it (to me) for?; **cette maison n'est pas à v.** this house is not for sale; **à v.** *(sur panneau)* for sale; *Fam* **v. chèrement sa peau** to fight for one's life; *Fam* **v. sa salade** to sell one's line *or* oneself; *Prov* **il ne faut jamais v. la peau de l'ours avant de l'avoir tué** don't count your chickens before they're hatched; **v. son silence** to be paid for one's silence; *Euph* **v. ses charmes** to sell one's body; **il vendrait père et mère** he'd sell his own grandmother; *Fig* **v. de l'évasion** *ou* **du rêve** to sell dreams

2 *(commercialiser)* to market

3 *(trahir → secret)* to sell; *(→ personne)* to sell out; *(→ associé, confident)* to sell down the river; **v. son âme au diable** to sell one's soul to the devil; **v. la mèche** *(exprès)* to give the game away, to spill the beans; *(par accident)* to let the cat out of the bag

USAGE ABSOLU *Com* **ils vendent cher/ne vendent pas cher chez Zapp** Zapp's is expensive/cheap; **ce qui les intéresse, c'est de v.** they're interested in selling *or* sales; **nous vendons beaucoup à l'étranger** we sell a lot abroad, we get a lot of sales abroad; **la publicité fait v.** advertising sells

▸**se vendre** VPR **1** *(emploi passif)* to sell; **ça se vend bien/mal actuellement** it is/isn't selling well at the moment; **se v. comme des petits pains** to sell *or* to go like hot cakes

2 *(se mettre en valeur)* to sell oneself; **une société qui sait se v.** a company that knows how to sell *or* market itself; **il faut savoir se v.** you must be able to sell yourself *or* to show yourself off to your best advantage

3 *(traître)* to sell oneself; **se v. à l'ennemi** to sell oneself to *or* to sell out to the enemy

Vendredi [vɑ̃drədi] NPR *(dans 'Robinson Crusoé')* Man Friday; **j'ai été son V.** I was his/her Man Friday

vendredi [vɑ̃drədi] NM Friday; **le v. saint** Good Friday; **v. treize** Friday the thirteenth; *voir aussi* **mardi**

vendu, -e [vɑ̃dy] PP *voir* **vendre**

ADJ *(vénal)* corrupt

NM,F *Péj* turncoat, traitor

'La Fiancée vendue' *Smetana* 'The Bartered Bride'

venelle [vənɛl] NF lane, alleyway

vénéneux, -euse [venenø, -øz] ADJ **1** *(toxique)* poisonous, toxic; **champignon v.** toadstool **2** *Littéraire (pernicieux)* **elle nourrissait des pensées vénéneuses** malignant thoughts were going through her mind

vénérable [venerabl] ADJ venerable; **d'un âge v.** ancient

NM *(d'une loge maçonnique)* worshipful master

vénération [venerasjɔ̃] NF **1** *Rel* reverence **2** *(admiration)* veneration, reverence, respect; **avoir de la v. pour qn** to revere sb

vénère [venɛr] *Fam* ADJ *(verlan de* **énervé***)* *Br* wound up, *Am* ticked off

VT *(verlan de* **énerver***)* **v. qn** to bug sb, *Br* to wind sb up, *Am* to tick sb off

vénérer [18] [venere] VT **1** *Rel* to worship, to revere **2** *(admirer)* to revere, to worship, to venerate

vénéricarde [venerikard] NF *Zool* heart cockle, heart shell

vénerie [vɛnri] NF hunting; **la grande v.** = hunting with hounds; **la petite v.** = hunting with small dogs

vénérien, -enne [venerjɛ̃, -ɛn] ADJ venereal

vénérologie [venerɔlɔʒi] NF *Méd* venereology

vénérologue [venerɔlɔg] NMF *Méd* venereologist

venet [vənɛ] NM *Pêche* semicircular moored tide net

vénète [venɛt] *Antiq* ADJ Venetic

NM Venetic

Vénètes [venɛt] NMPL *Antiq* **les V.** the Veneti

Vénétie [venesi] NF **la V.** the Veneto

venette [vənɛt] NF *Vieilli* fear

veneur [vənœr] NM **1** *(chasseur)* hunter **2** *(maître des chiens)* master of hounds **3** *Hist* **le Grand v.** ≃ the Master of the Royal Hunt

Venezuela [venezɥela] NM **le V.** Venezuela; **vivre au V.** to live in Venezuela; **aller au V.** to go to Venezuela

vénézuélien, -enne [venezɥeljɛ̃, -ɛn] ADJ Venezuelan

▫ **Vénézuélien, -enne** NM,F Venezuelan

vengeance [vɑ̃ʒɑ̃s] NF revenge, vengeance; **crier** *ou* **demander** *ou* **réclamer v.** to cry out for revenge; **tirer v. d'une injustice** to avenge an injustice; **tirer v. d'une injure** to be revenged for an insult; **avoir sa v.** to have one's revenge *or* vengeance; **exercer sa v. sur qn** to have one's revenge *or* vengeance on sb; **par v., par esprit de v.** out of revenge *or* vengeance; **soif** *ou* **désir de v.** revengefulness, vengefulness; *Hum* **c'est la v. divine** *ou* **du ciel** it's divine retribution; *Prov* **la v. est un plat qui se mange froid** revenge is a dish best eaten cold

venger [17] [vɑ̃ʒe] VT **1** *(réparer)* to avenge; **v. un affront** to avenge an insult

2 *(dédommager)* **v. qn de qch** to avenge sb for sth; **cela le venge de son échec** it makes up for his failure

▸**se venger** VPR **1** *(tirer réparation)* to revenge *or* to avenge oneself, to take vengeance; **je me vengerai!** I'll get my own back!; **il s'est vengé brutalement** he retaliated brutally; **se v. de qn/de qch** to take one's revenge on sb/for sth; **elle m'a menti pour se v. de ma cruauté** she lied to me in revenge for my cruelty; **il s'est vengé de l'assassin de sa sœur** he took his revenge on his sister's murderer; **se v. sur qn (de qch)** to take (one's) revenge on sb (for sth)

2 *Fam (calmer sa colère)* **ne te venge pas sur moi** don't take it out on me

vengeresse [vɑ̃ʒrɛs] *voir* **vengeur**

vengeron [vɑ̃ʒrɔ̃] NM *Suisse Ich* roach

vengeur, -eresse [vɑ̃ʒœr, vɑ̃ʒrɛs] ADJ avenging, revengeful, vengeful; **..., dit-elle d'un ton v.** ..., she said, vindictively; **une petite remarque vengeresse** a vengeful little remark

NM,F avenger

véniel, -elle [venjɛl] ADJ **1** *(excusable)* minor, slight **2** *Rel* venial

venimeux, -euse [vənimø, -øz] ADJ **1** *(toxique)* venomous, poisonous **2** *Fig (méchant)* venomous, malevolent; **il m'a lancé un regard v.** he looked daggers at me, he shot me a murderous glance; **des commentaires v.** barbs, barbed remarks

venin [vənɛ̃] NM **1** *(poison)* venom **2** *Littéraire (malveillance)* **cracher** *ou* **jeter son v.** to vent one's spleen; **répandre son v. contre qn/qch** to speak viciously about sb/sth

VENIR [40] [vənir]

> **V AUX** to come and/to + infinitive **1** ▪ to have just done **2** ▪ to happen to **3**
> **VI** to come **A1, C1-3** ▪ to reach **B** ▪ to come along well **C4**
> **V IMPERSONNEL** to come **1**

V AUX **1** *(se rendre quelque part pour)* to come and *or* to; **Roger viendra me chercher** Roger will come and collect me; **viens t'asseoir près de moi** come and sit down near me; **je suis venu m'excuser** I've come to apologize; **venez manger!**

dinner's ready!; **v. voir qn** to come and see *or* to visit sb, *Am* to visit with sb; **ils ne viennent plus nous voir** *(après une querelle)* we're not on visiting terms any more; **v. voir qch** to come and see sth; **beaucoup de gens sont venus voir notre pièce** a lot of people turned out *or* came to see our play; **si tu tombes, ne viens pas pleurer!** if you fall, don't come crying to me!; **tu l'as bien cherché, alors ne viens pas te plaindre!** you asked for it, so don't come moaning to me about it!; **il est venu raconter qu'elle avait des dettes** he came telling tales about her being in debt; *Fam* **qu'est-ce que tu viens nous raconter** *ou* **chanter là?** what on earth are you talking about *or Br* on about?

2 v. de *(avoir fini de)* **v. de faire qch** to have just done sth; **je viens de laver les vitres et il pleut!** I've just finished cleaning the windows and now it's raining!; **je viens de l'avoir au téléphone** I was on the phone to him/her just a few minutes *or* a short while ago; **elle vient de terminer son premier album** *(il y a quelques jours)* she's just *or* she recently finished her first album; **je venais de terminer mes devoirs** I had just finished my homework

3 v. à *(exprime un hasard)* to happen to; **si son pied venait à glisser** should his/her foot slip, if his/her foot slipped; **si les vivres venaient à manquer** should food supplies run out, if food supplies were to run out

VI A. *AVEC IDÉE DE MOUVEMENT* **1** *(se déplacer, se rendre)* to come; **viens plus près** come closer; **je ne suis pas venu pour parler de la pluie et du beau temps!** I didn't come here to talk about the weather!; **faut-il v. déguisé?** do we have to come in *or* to wear fancy dress?; **il y aura un orchestre et du champagne, il faut v.!** there will be a band and champagne, you must come along!; **venez nombreux!** do come along!; **ils sont venus nombreux** they came in droves; **il est reparti** *ou* **il s'en est allé comme il était venu** he left just as he had come; *(il est mort)* he died without having made his mark; **comment êtes-vous venus?** how did you get here?; **ma mère disparue, il a commencé à v. chez nous** after my mother passed away, he took to visiting us; **je l'ai rencontrée en venant ici** I met her on my way here; **il vient au collège en planche à roulettes/en taxi** he comes to college on a skateboard/in a taxi; **il ne vient plus au collège** he never comes to college now; **viens au lit** come to bed; **on ne peut v. au chalet qu'à pied** the only way to reach the chalet is on foot; **quand il est venu en Australie** when he came to Australia; **comment est-elle venue sur l'île?** how did she get to *or* reach the island?; **v. avec qn** to come with *or* to accompany sb; **alors, tu viens?** are you coming?; **on va au restaurant, tu viens avec nous?** we're off to the restaurant, are you coming with us *or* along?; **à la piscine? d'accord, je viens avec toi** the swimming pool? OK, I'll come *or* go with you; **d'où viens-tu?** where have you been?; **je viens de Paris et je repars à New York** I've just been in Paris and now I'm off to New York; **v. sur** *(sujet: prédateur, véhicule)* to move in on, to bear down upon; **la moto venait droit sur nous** the motorbike was heading straight for us; **v. vers qn** *(s'approcher)* to come up to *or* towards sb; **v. à qn** *(s'adresser à qn)* to come to sb; *(atteindre qn)* to reach sb; **il vient toujours à moi quand il a besoin d'argent** he always comes to me when he needs money

2 faire v. *(médecin, police, réparateur)* to send for, to call; *(parasites, touristes)* to attract; **faire v. une personne chez soi** to have somebody come round; **faites v. le prévenu chez le juge** bring the accused to the judge's office; **je fais v. mon foie gras directement du Périgord** I have my foie gras sent straight from Périgord; **faire v. les larmes aux yeux de qn** to bring tears to sb's eyes

3 *Naut* **v. sur bâbord/tribord** to alter course to port/starboard; **v. au vent** *ou* **lof** to come round (into the wind)

B. *SANS IDÉE DE MOUVEMENT* **v. à** *ou* **jusqu'à** *(vers le haut)* to come up to, to reach (up to); *(vers le bas)* to come down to, to reach (down to); *(en largeur, en longueur)* to come out to, to stretch to, to reach; **la vigne vierge vient jusqu'à ma fenêtre** the Virginia creeper reaches up to my window; **l'eau vient jusqu'à la cheville/jusqu'au genou** the water is ankle-deep/knee-deep

C. *SURGIR, SE MANIFESTER* **1** *(arriver → moment, saison)* to come; **le moment est venu de** the time has come to; **quand vient l'hiver** when winter comes; **quand vint le jour du mariage** when the wedding day came; **l'aube vint enfin** dawn broke at last; **voici v. la nuit** it's nearly night *or* night-time; **puis la guerre est venue** then came the war; **la retraite vient vite!** retirement isn't long in coming!; **puis il vient un âge/un moment où...** then comes an age/a time when...; **je ne suis jamais tombé amoureux – non, mais ça va v.!** I've never fallen in love – (no, but) you will one day!; **alors, elle vient cette bière?** am I getting that beer or not?, how long do I have to wait for my beer?; **alors, ça vient?** hurry up!; **ça vient, ça vient!** all right, it's coming!

2 *(apparaître → inspiration, idée, boutons)* to come; **mon nouveau roman commence à v.** my new novel is coming along (nicely); **la prudence vient avec l'âge** wisdom comes with age; **prendre la vie comme elle vient** *ou* **les choses comme elles viennent** *ou* **les événements comme ils viennent** to take things in one's stride *or* as they come, to take life as it comes; **l'envie m'est soudain venue d'aller me baigner** I suddenly felt like going swimming, *Br* I suddenly fancied a swim; **une idée géniale m'était venue** a great idea had dawned on me; **le remords m'est venu peu à peu** remorse crept up on me; **les mots ne me viennent pas facilement en russe** my Russian isn't fluent, I'm not fluent in Russian; **les mots semblaient lui v. si facilement!** his/her words seemed to flow so effortlessly!; **les mots ne me venaient pas** I was at a loss for words, I couldn't find the words; **les idées me viennent mais pas les mots** I've got ideas but I can't find words to express them; **des rougeurs me sont venues sur tout le corps** I came out in red blotches all over; **v. à l'esprit de qn** *ou* **à l'idée de qn** to come to *or* to dawn on sb; **rien ne lui venait à l'esprit** *ou* **l'idée** his/her mind was a blank; **une solution m'est venue à l'esprit** a solution dawned on me

3 *(dans une chronologie, un ordre, une hiérarchie)* to come; **le mois/l'année/la décennie qui vient** the coming month/year/decade; **le trimestre qui vient** next term; **fais tes devoirs, la télé viendra après** do your homework, we'll see about TV later on; **dans ce jeu, l'as vient après le valet** in this game, the ace is worth less than the jack

4 *(se développer)* to come along *or* up (well), to do well; **les rosiers viennent mieux dans un terrain glaiseux** rosebushes do better in a clayey soil; **les capucines ne sont pas bien venues** the nasturtiums didn't come up *or* do well; **v. à fruit** to (go into) fruit; **v. à maturité** to reach maturity, to ripen

5 *Typ & Phot* **les verts viennent bien sur la photo** the green shades come out beautifully in the photograph

6 *Can & Suisse Fam (devenir)* to get; **v. vieux/fatigué** to get old/tired; **il est venu médecin** he became a doctor■

V IMPERSONNEL 1 *(se déplacer)* **il vient des amateurs de jazz des quatre coins de l'Europe** jazz lovers come from all over Europe; **il vient peu de touristes en hiver** few tourists come in winter

2 il me vient une idée I've got an idea; **il m'est venu à l'idée de faire** I suddenly thought of doing, it dawned on me to do; **il me vient à l'idée que nous pourrions l'interroger aussi** come to think of it, we could ask him as well; **soudain il m'est venu un doute** I suddenly wasn't so sure; **il m'est venu une envie de tout casser** I suddenly felt like smashing the place up

3 *(exprime un hasard)* **s'il venait à pleuvoir** should it (happen to) rain

□ **à venir ADJ dans les jours/semaines/mois à v.** in the days/weeks/months to come; **les années à v.** the coming years, the years to come; **les générations à v.** future *or* coming generations; **mes amours à v.** my future loves

□ **venir à VT IND 1** *(choisir)* to come to; **elle est venue tard à la musique** she was a latecomer to music; **vous êtes venu tôt à la politique** you started your political career early

2 en v. à *(thème, problème)* to come *or* to turn to; *(conclusion)* to come to, to reach; *(décision)* to come to; **venons-en aux statistiques** (now) let's turn to *or* look at the figures; **en v. au fait** *ou* **à l'essentiel** to come *or* to go straight to the point; **j'en viens au détail croustillant!** I'm coming to the juicy bit!; **la discussion en était venue à la politique** the discussion had turned to politics; **je sais certaines choses... – où veux-tu en v.?** I know a thing or two... – what do you mean by that?, what are you getting at *or* driving at?; **pourquoi a-t-elle exigé cela? – je crois savoir où elle veut en v.** why did she make that particular demand? – I think I know what she's after; **en v. aux mains** *ou* **coups** to come to blows; **en v. à faire qch** *(finir par faire)* to come to do sth; *(en dernière extrémité)* to resort *or* to be reduced to doing sth; **ils en étaient venus à douter de son talent** they'd come to question his/her talent; **j'en viens à me demander si...** I'm beginning to wonder whether...; **j'en viendrais presque à souhaiter sa mort** I've reached the stage where I almost wish he/she were dead; **si j'en suis venu à voler, c'est que...** I resorted to stealing because...; **et l'argent? – j'y viens** what about the money? – I'm coming to that; **y v.** *(s'y résoudre)* to come round to it; **je ne prendrai jamais de médicaments – vous y viendrez** I'll never take any medicine – you'll come round to it; *Fam* **je vais te casser la figure – viens-y un peu!** I'm going to smash your face in – come on then *or* just you try!

□ **venir de VT IND 1** *(être originaire de → sujet: personne)* to come from, to be from, to be a native of; *(→ sujet: plante, fruit, animal)* to come *or* to be *or* to originate from; **sa femme vient du Chili** his wife comes from *or* is from Chile; **je boycotte tout ce qui vient de leur pays** I boycott everything that comes from *or* is produced in their country; **la perle vient de la famille de mon père** the pearl has been passed down from my father's family; **une mode qui vient d'Espagne** a fashion which comes from *or* originated in Spain; **le mot vient du latin** the word comes *or* derives from Latin

2 *(provenir de → sujet: marchandise)* to originate from; *(→ sujet: bruit, vent)* to come from; **ces images nous viennent de Tokyo** these pictures come to us from Tokyo

3 *(être issu de)* to come from; **les produits qui viennent du pétrole** oil-based products; *Sout* **d'où vient la conscience?** where does consciousness spring from?; **les ordres viennent de beaucoup plus haut** the orders come from much higher up; **la suggestion doit v. de toi, il l'acceptera mieux** he'll accept the suggestion more readily if it comes from you; **venant de lui, rien ne m'étonne** nothing he says or does can surprise me; **venant d'elle, c'est presque un compliment** coming from her it's almost a compliment

4 *(être dû à → sujet: problème)* to come *or* to stem from, to lie in *or* with; **le problème vient de la prise** it's the plug; **ça ne peut v. que du carburateur** it can only be the carburettor; **quand il y a des problèmes au bureau, tu peux être sûr que ça vient d'elle** when there's trouble at the office, you can be sure she's had a hand in it; **il y a une grosse erreur dans la comptabilité – ça ne vient pas de moi** there's a big discrepancy in the books – it's got nothing to do with me; **c'est de là que vient le mal/problème** this is the root of the evil/problem; **de là vient son indifférence** hence his/her indifference, that's why he's/she's indifferent; **les travaux sont finis, de là vient que tout est calme** the building work is over, hence the peace and quiet; **je dois terminer pour demain, d'où vient que je n'ai pas de**

temps à vous consacrer my deadline is tomorrow, that's why I can't give you any of my time; **d'où vient que...?** how is it that...?
▸**s'en venir** VPR *Littéraire* to come; **un cavalier s'en venait** a rider was coming *or* approaching

Allusion
Si tu ne viens pas à Lagardère, Lagardère ira à toi
This expression comes from the swashbuckling novel *Le Bossu* by 19th-century writer Paul Féval and has been popularized by several film adaptations of the book. In it, a character called Lagardère vows to avenge the Duke of Nevers, who has been killed by a mysterious assassin when both men were set upon. As Lagardère slashes the hand of his friend's murderer, he says **Qui que tu sois, ta main gardera ma marque. Je te reconnaîtrai. Et, quand il sera temps, si tu ne viens pas à Lagardère, Lagardère ira à toi!** ("Whoever you are, your hand will bear my mark and, sooner or later, if you don't find me first, rest assured that I will find you!"). This expression is used in a wide variety of contexts, with the word "Lagardère" replaced to suit the situation. For instance, when writing about a travelling science show aimed at a wide public, commentators might use the slogan **Si tu ne viens pas à la science, la science ira à toi** ("If you don't come to science, science will come to you").

Venise [vəniz] NM Venice; **point de V.** Venetian lace; **carnaval de V.** Venice carnival
vénitien, -enne [venisjɛ̃, -ɛn] ADJ Venetian
❑ **Vénitien, -enne** NM,F Venetian
vent [vɑ̃] NM **1** *Météo* wind; **un v. du nord/nord-est** a north/north-east wind; **le v. du nord/sud** the north/south wind; **v. de terre/mer** land/sea breeze; **le v. souffle/tourne** the wind is blowing/changing; **le v. tombe/se lève** the wind is dropping/rising; **il y a** *ou* **il fait du v.** it's windy *or* breezy; **être ouvert** *ou* **exposé aux quatre vents** to be exposed to the four winds; **elle courait les cheveux au v.** she ran with her hair streaming in the wind; **une journée sans v.** a still day; **une journée de grand v.** a windy day; **plante de plein v.** outdoor plant; **coup de v.** gust of wind, squall; **entrer/sortir en coup de v.** to dash in/out; **il fait un v. à décorner les bœufs** there is a fierce wind blowing, it's a blustery day
2 *Naut & Aviat* **au v. (de)** windward (of); *Naut* **remonter au v.** to beat, to sail upwind; *Naut* **venir au v.** to luff; *Naut* **mettre la barre au v.** to put the helm up; **aller contre le v.** *Naut* to head into the wind; *Aviat* to go up the wind; *Naut* **sous le v. (de)** leeward (of), downwind (of); *Naut* **venir sous le v.** to come alee; **côté du v.** weather side; **côté sous le v.** lee side; **v. arrière** *Aviat* tail wind; *Naut* rear wind; *Naut* **aller** *ou* **faire v. arrière** to sail *or* run before the wind; **v. contraire** adverse wind; **v. debout** head wind; **v. fort, grand v.** high wind, gale; **v. frais** strong breeze; **v. de travers** crosswind; **avoir le v. en poupe** *Naut* to sail before the wind, to have the wind astern; *Fig* to have the wind in one's sails, to be riding high; *Fam* **avoir du v. dans les voiles** to be three sheets to the wind; **avoir bon v.** to have a fair wind; **quel bon v. vous amène?** to what do we owe the pleasure (of your visit)?; *Fam* **bon v.!** good riddance!; **il a réussi contre vents et marées** he managed against all the odds; **je le ferai contre vents et marées** I'll do it come hell or high water; **aller** *ou* **filer comme le v.** to fly *or* to hurtle along; **(éparpillés) à tous les vents** *ou* **à tout v.** (scattered) far and wide; *Fig* **tourner à tous les vents** to be a weathercock
3 *(courant d'air)* **du v.** *(de l'air)* some air, a breeze; *Fig (des paroles vaines)* hot air; *(des actes vains)* empty posturing; **mettre qch au v.** to hang sth out to dry; **il lui a fait un peu de v. avec son journal** he fanned him/her with his newspaper; *Fig Péj* **ce n'est que du v.!** it's just hot air!; *Fig* **elle fait beaucoup de v.** she just makes a lot of noise; *Fam* **du v.!** clear off!, get lost!; **v. coulis** draught
4 *Méd & Physiol* **des vents** wind *(UNCOUNT)*; **avoir des vents** to have wind; **lâcher des vents** to break wind
5 *Chasse* wind; **avoir le v. de son gibier** to have the wind of one's game; **chasser au v.** to keep the wind; *Fig* **avoir v. de qch** to (get to) hear of sth; **je n'ai pas eu v. de la rumeur** the rumour didn't come my way; **elle a eu v. de l'affaire** she heard about *or* she got wind of the story
6 *(d'un soufflet, d'une balle)* blast; *Aviat* **v. de l'hélice** propeller slipstream
7 *Fig (atmosphère)* **un v. de panique a soufflé sur la foule** a ripple of panic ran through the crowd; **le v. est à la révolte** there is unrest in the air; **prendre le v.** to test the water, to gauge the situation; **sentir** *ou* **voir d'où vient le v.** to see which way the wind blows *or* how the land lies; **sentir le v. tourner** to feel the wind change, to realize that the tide is turning; **le v. tourne** the wind is changing, the tide is turning
8 *Astron* **v. solaire** solar wind
9 *Géog* **les îles du V.** the Windward Isles
❑ **vents** NMPL *Mus* wind instruments; **les vents jouent trop fort** the wind section is playing too loud
❑ **dans le vent** ADJ *Fam* up-to-date▪
❑ **en plein vent** ADJ *(exposé)* exposed (to the wind) ADV *(dehors)* in the open (air)
ventage [vɑ̃taʒ] NM *Agr* winnowing
ventail, -aux [vɑ̃taj, -o] NM, **ventaille** [vɑ̃taj] NF ventail
vente [vɑ̃t] NF **1** *(opération)* sale; **la v. ne s'est pas faite** the sale fell through; **nous déménagerons après la v. de la maison** we'll move after the house is sold *or* after the sale of the house; **autoriser/interdire la v. de** to authorize/to prohibit the sale of; **retiré de la v.** withdrawn from sale; **ici, v. de tomates** *(sur une pancarte dans un marché)* tomatoes on *or* for sale here; **réaliser une v.** to make a sale; **acte de v.** bill of sale; **bureau de v.** sales agency; **lettre/promesse de v.** sales letter/agreement; **v. action** bargain offer; *Com* **v. à l'arrivée** sale at arrival; **ventes de base** baseline sales, market minimum; **v. pour cause d'inventaire** stocktaking sale; **v. à la cheville** wholesale butchery trade; **v. à (la) commission** commission sale; **v. (au) comptant** cash sale; **v. au comptoir** over-the-counter sales; **v. au déballage** warehouse sale; *Bourse* **v. à découvert** short sale; *Com* **v. au départ** sale at departure; **v. sur description** sale by description; **v. directe** direct sale; **v. de droits** sale of rights; **v. sur échantillon** sale by sample; **v. à l'essai** sale on approval; **v. en l'état** sale as seen; **ventes export, ventes à l'exportation** export sales; *Com* **v. avec faculté de retour** sale or return; **v. d'immeuble à construire** = sale of a property which is yet to be built on a particular plot of land; **v. indirecte** indirect sale; **v. jumelée** tie-in sale; **v. en ligne** e-tail; **v. pour** *ou* **de liquidation** closing-down sale; **v. et marketing** sales and marketing; **v. et marketing assistés par ordinateur** computer-aided sales and marketing; **v. à perte** sale at a loss; **v. promotionnelle** promotional sale; **v. de référence** reference sale; **v. à réméré** sale with option of repurchase; **v. répétée** repeat sale; **v. en semi-gros** small wholesale sales; *Bourse* **v. spéculative** speculative selling; **ventes par téléphone** telephone sales, telesales
2 *(activité)* selling; *(secteur)* sales; **elle est dans la v.** she's in sales; **l'art de la v.** the art of selling; **technique de v.** selling technique; **v. à la boule de neige** snowball selling; **v. par catalogue** catalogue selling; **v. au comptant** cash selling; **v.-conseil** sales consultancy; **v. en coopération** co-operative selling; **v. par correspondance** mail-order (selling); **v. à crédit** credit selling; *(à tempérament)* hire purchase, *Am* installment plan; **v. au détail/en demi-gros** *(par le négociant)* retailing/small wholesaling; *(profession)* retail/small wholesale trade; **v. directe** direct selling; **v. directe en B to B** back-to-back direct selling; **v. à distance** distance selling; **v. à domicile** door-to-door selling; **v. domiciliaire** home selling; *Ordinat* **v. électronique** on-line selling; **v. forcée** inertia selling; **v. à froid** cold selling; **v. en gros** *(par le négociant)* wholesaling; *(profession)* wholesale trade; **v. indirecte** indirect selling; **v. sans intermédiaire** direct selling; *Ordinat* **v. en ligne** on-line selling; *(transaction)* on-line sale; **v. par lot** banded pack selling; **v. parallèle** parallel selling; **v. personnelle** personal selling; **v. avec prime** premium selling; **v. de prospection** missionary selling; **v. pyramidale** pyramid selling; *Mktg* **v. par réseau coopté** multi-level marketing; **v. par téléphone** telesales, telemarketing; **v. à tempérament** hire purchase, *Am* installment plan; *Bourse* **v. à terme** forward sale
3 *Jur* **v. (par adjudication) forcée/judiciaire** compulsory sale, sale by order of the court
4 *(réunion, braderie)* sale; **v. à la criée** auction (sale) *(especially of fish or meat)*; **v. à l'encan** *ou* **aux enchères** auction (sale); **v. paroissiale** church bazaar; **v. publique** public sale
5 *Bourse* **le dollar vaut 2 livres à la v.** the selling rate for the US dollar is 2 pounds
6 *Can (soldes)* sale
7 *(part de bois)* fellable stand; *(arbres)* **asseoir les ventes** to mark trees *(before felling them)*; **jeunes ventes** saplings
❑ **ventes** NFPL *Com* selling, sales; *Compta* sales, turnover; **achats et ventes** buying and selling; **le responsable des ventes** the sales manager; **un pourcentage sur les ventes** a percentage on sales; **ventes d'armes** arms sales
❑ **en vente** ADJ & ADV *(à vendre)* for sale; *(disponible)* available, on sale; **en v. en pharmacie** on sale at *or* available from the chemist's; **en v. dans toutes les bonnes librairies** on sale in all good bookshops; **en v. libre** *(gén)* freely available; *(médicaments)* sold without a prescription; **en v. sur/sans ordonnance** obtainable on prescription/without a prescription; **mettre qch en v.** to put sth up for sale, to offer sth for sale; *(commercialiser)* to put sth on the market
venté, -e [vɑ̃te] ADJ **1** *(où le vent souffle)* windswept, windy **2** *(exposé)* windswept
vente-marketing [vɑ̃tmarketiŋ] NF INV sales and marketing
venter [3] [vɑ̃te] V IMPERSONNEL **il vente** it's windy, the wind is blowing
venteux, -euse [vɑ̃tø, -øz] ADJ **1** *(où le vent souffle)* windswept, windy **2** *(à courants d'air)* draughty
ventilateur [vɑ̃tilatœr] NM **1** *(pour rafraîchir)* fan; *TV & Cin* wind machine; **v. électrique** electric fan; **v. à pales/de plafond** blade/ceiling fan; *Ordinat* **v. de refroidissement** cooling fan; **v. rotatif** fan **2** *Aut* cooling fan
ventilation [vɑ̃tilasjɔ̃] NF **1** *(système)* ventilation (system); *(appareil)* fan; **faire marcher la v.** to turn on the fan; *Constr* **v. mécanique contrôlée** mechanical ventilation system
2 *(aération)* supply of (fresh) air
3 *Méd & Physiol* ventilation; **v. assistée** respiratory assistance; **v. maxima** maximum breathing capacity; **v. en pression expiratoire positive** continuous positive airway pressure, CPAP
4 *(d'une comptabilité)* breakdown; **la v. des frais généraux** the breakdown of overheads
5 *(répartition)* allocation, apportionment; **la v. des revenus** the allocation of income *or* allocating income
6 *Jur (d'un domaine)* separate valuation
ventiler [3] [vɑ̃tile] VT **1** *(aérer)* to air, to ventilate; **mal ventilé** stuffy, airless
2 *Méd* to ventilate, to give respiratory assistance to
3 *(diviser → données)* to explode, to scatter; *(→ élèves, emplois)* to distribute, to spread; **ils ont ventilé les postes sur trois régions différentes** they allocated posts in three different areas
4 *Fin* to break down; *(crédits, équipements)* to allocate; *Com* **v. un lot** to break bulk
5 *Jur (domaine)* to value separately
ventileuse [vɑ̃tiløz] NF *Entom* fanning bee
ventilo [vɑ̃tilo] NM *Fam* fan▪ ; **faire marcher le v.** to turn on the fan
ventis [vɑ̃ti] NMPL = trees blown down by the wind
ventôse [vɑ̃toz] NM = 6th month in the French Revolutionary calendar (from 20 February to 21 March)
ventouse [vɑ̃tuz] NF **1** *(en caoutchouc)* suction cup; **fléchettes à v.** rubber-tipped darts
2 *Méd* cup, cupping glass; **poser des ventouses à qn** to cup sb; **application de ventouses**

cupping; **v. eutocique** suction extractor; **v. obstétricale** *ou* **suédoise** vacuum extractor

3 *Zool* sucker

4 *(déboucheur)* plunger; **faire v.** to adhere *or* to hold fast (through suction)

5 *Constr (pour l'aération)* air valve, air vent

ventral, -e, -aux, -ales [vɑ̃tral, -o] **ADJ** *Anat, Bot & Zool* front *(avant n)*, *Spéc* ventral

ventre [vɑ̃tr] **NM 1** *(estomac)* stomach; *(d'animal)* belly, underbelly; *Anat* abdomen; **être couché sur le v.** to be lying down *or* flat on one's stomach; **mettez-vous sur le v.** *(de la position debout)* lie on your stomach; *(de la position couchée)* roll over onto your stomach; **rentrer le v.** to hold one's stomach in; **avoir du v.** to have a paunch, to be pot-bellied; **il commence à prendre** *ou* **avoir du v.** he's starting to get a paunch *or* a belly; *Fig* **il leur marcherait** *ou* **passerait sur le v.** he'd trample all over them; **avoir mal au v.** to have (a) stomachache; *Fam* **lui, professeur? ça me ferait mal au v.!** a professor, him? like hell he is!; **avoir le v. creux** *ou* **vide** to have an empty stomach; **avoir le v. plein** to be full, to have a full stomach; **il ne pense qu'à son v.** all he ever thinks about is his stomach; **ne rien avoir dans le v.** to have nothing in one's stomach; *Fig* to have no guts; **je n'ai rien dans le v. depuis trois jours** I haven't had anything to eat for three days, I've had to go hungry for the last three days; *Fig* **il n'a rien dans le v.** he's got no guts; *Fig* **elle a quelque chose dans le v.** she's got guts, she's got what it takes; *Fig* **je voudrais bien savoir ce qu'elle a dans le v.** *(de manière générale)* I'd like to know what makes her tick; *(sur un point précis)* I'd like to know what she's up to; **v. à terre** *(cheval)* at full speed, flat out; **il s'est sauvé v. à terre** you couldn't see him for dust; **rentrer/partir v. à terre** to get back/to go off on the double; *Fig* **le v. mou de qch** the soft underbelly of sth; *Prov* **v. affamé n'a point** *ou* **pas d'oreilles** = there is no reasoning with a starving man

2 *(contenu → d'un appareil, d'un véhicule)* innards

3 *(utérus)* womb; **un bébé dans le v. de sa mère** a baby in its mother's womb

4 *(renflement → d'un vase, d'un tonneau, d'un pot)* bulge, belly; *(→ d'un bateau)* bilge; *(→ d'une voile)* belly, sag; *(→ d'un avion)* belly

5 *Constr* **faire (du) v.** to bulge (out), to jut out; *(pendre)* to sag

6 *Phys* loop, antinode; **v. de tension** potential loop, voltage loop

ventrebleu [vɑ̃trəblø] **EXCLAM** *Arch* gadzooks!, zounds!

ventrèche [vɑ̃trɛʃ] **NF** *(dans le sud de la France)* streaky bacon

ventrée [vɑ̃tre] **NF** *Fam (de nourriture)* bellyful; **on s'est mis une v. (de saucisses)** we stuffed ourselves (with sausages)

ventriculaire [vɑ̃trikylɛr] **ADJ** *Anat* ventricular

ventricule [vɑ̃trikyl] **NM** *Anat* ventricle

ventriculographie [vɑ̃trikylɔgrafi] **NF** *Méd* ventriculography

ventrière [vɑ̃trijɛr] **NF 1** *(sangle → ventrale)* girth; *(→ de levage)* sling **2** *Constr* crosspiece, purlin **3** *Naut* bilge block

ventriloque [vɑ̃trilɔk] **NMF** ventriloquist

ventriloquie [vɑ̃trilɔki] **NF** ventriloquism

ventripotent, -e [vɑ̃tripɔtɑ̃, -ɑ̃t] **ADJ** potbellied, rotund

ventru, -e [vɑ̃try] **ADJ 1** *(personne)* potbellied, paunchy **2** *(potiche)* potbellied; *(colonne)* bulbous; *(voile)* bulging, swelling

venturi [vɑ̃tyri] **NM** *Phys* Venturi tube

venturon [vɑ̃tyrɔ̃] **NM** *Orn* **v. montagnard** citril finch

venu, -e [vəny] **PP** *voir* **venir**

ADJ 1 bien v. *(enfant, plante, animal)* strong, sturdy, robust; *(conseil, remarque)* timely, apposite; *(attitude)* appropriate; *(roman)* mature; **mal v.** *(enfant, animal)* sickly; *(plante)* stunted; *(remarque, attitude)* uncalled for, unwarranted, ill-advised; *(conseil)* untimely, unwelcome

2 être bien v. de *(être bien inspiré de)* **tu serais bien v. de t'excuser** you'd be well-advised to apologize, it would be a good idea for you to apologize; **tu serais mal v. de critiquer!** *(tu n'es pas qualifié en la matière)* it's not for you to criticize!; *(tu n'en as fait autant)* you're hardly in a position to criticize!; **il serait mal v. de la critiquer** it wouldn't be appropriate to criticize her; **il serait mal v. d'insister** it would be ill-mannered to insist

NM,F le premier v. the first to arrive; *(n'importe qui)* anybody; **c'est à la portée du premier v.** anybody can do it; **le dernier v.** the last to arrive; **les nouveaux venus/les nouvelles venues** the newcomers

❑ **venue NF 1** *(d'une personne)* arrival; **la venue de ma sœur** my sister's arrival; **attendre la venue de qn** to wait for sb to arrive; **annoncer la venue de qn** to announce sb's arrival; **c'est ce qui explique ma venue** that's why I'm here

2 *(d'une saison)* approach; **la venue du printemps** the approach of spring

3 *(apparition → d'ordinateurs)* advent

4 *(naissance)* birth; **la venue (au monde) d'un enfant** the arrival *or* birth of a child

5 *Tech* **venue d'eau/de gaz** water/gas inrush

6 *Littéraire (locutions)* **d'une belle venue** *(arbre)* well-grown, sturdy, lush; **des pages d'une belle venue** beautifully written pages; **d'une seule venue, tout d'une venue** grown all in one spurt

Vénus [venys] **NPR** *Myth* Venus

NF 1 *Astron* Venus **2** *(belle femme)* Venus; **ce n'est pas une V.** she's no (great) beauty

---

'Vénus anadyomène' *Titien* 'Venus Rising from the Sea'

'Vénus au miroir' *Velázquez* 'The Rokeby Venus'

'Vénus d'Urbin' *Titien* 'Venus of Urbino'

---

vénus [venys] *Zool* **NF** Venus-shell, *Spéc* member of the Veneridae

❑ **vénus NFPL** Venus-shells, *Spéc* Veneridae

vénusien, -enne [venyzjɛ̃, -ɛn] **ADJ** Venusian

NM,F Venusian

vénusté [venyste] **NF** *Littéraire* graceful beauty

vépéciste [vepesist] **NM** *Com* mail-order organization

vêpres [vɛpr] **NFPL** *Rel* vespers; **aller aux v.** to go to vespers; **sonner les v.** to ring the bell for vespers

ver [vɛr] **NM** *(gén)* worm; *(de viande)* maggot; *(de fruit)* grub, maggot; *(asticot)* maggot; *(larve)* larva; *Méd* **avoir des vers** to have worms; **il y a des vers dans la viande** the meat is maggoty; **cette pomme est pleine de vers** worms have been at this apple; **meuble mangé aux** *ou* **rongé aux** *ou* **piqué des vers** worm-eaten piece of furniture; **v. blanc** grub; **v. à bois** woodworm *(UNCOUNT)*; **v. de farine** mealworm; *Ordinat* **v. informatique** worm; **v. luisant** glow-worm; **v. des pêcheurs** lug(worm); **v. plat** flatworm; **v. rond** roundworm; **v. rongeur** canker(worm); **v. de sable** sandworm, lug(worm); **v. à soie** silkworm; *Méd* **v. solitaire** tapeworm; **v. de terre** earthworm; **v. de vase** bloodworm; *Fam* **tirer les vers du nez à qn** to worm it out of sb; *Fam* **pas moyen de lui tirer les vers du nez** he/she won't give anything away; **j'ai fini par lui tirer les vers du nez** I finally wormed it out of him/her; *Fig* **le v. est dans le fruit** the rot's set in

véracité [verasite] **NF 1** *Littéraire (habitude de dire vrai)* veracity, truthfulness **2** *(authenticité)* truth; **la v. de ce témoignage est évidente** this statement is obviously true; **une histoire dont la v. n'est pas garantie** an unauthenticated story

véraison [verɛzɔ̃] **NF** ripening, *Spéc* veraison

véranda [verɑ̃da] **NF 1** *(galerie)* veranda, verandah, *Am* porch **2** *(pièce)* conservatory

vératre [veratr] **NM** *Bot & Pharm* veratrum

vératrine [veratrin] **NF** *Pharm* veratrine

verbal, -e, -aux, -ales [vɛrbal, -o] **ADJ 1** *(dit de vive voix)* verbal; **il y a eu un contrat v.** a verbal contract was established

2 *(s'exprimant par les mots)* **violence verbale** angry words; **la violence verbale d'une description** the violence of the language used in a description; **c'est un merveilleux délire v.** it's a wonderful feast of words; *Péj* **elle est en plein délire v.** she can't stop talking

3 *Ling (adjectif, système)* verbal; *(phrase, forme, groupe)* verb *(avant n)*

verbalement [vɛrbalmɑ̃] **ADV** verbally, orally

verbalisateur [vɛrbalizatœr] **ADJ M agent v.** policeman *(in charge of reporting petty offences)*

verbalisation [vɛrbalizasjɔ̃] **NF 1** *(par un agent)* reporting offences **2** *Psy* verbalization, verbalizing

verbaliser [3] [vɛrbalize] **VI** to report an offender; **je suis obligé de v.** I'll have to report you

VT to express verbally, to put into words, to verbalize

verbalisme [vɛrbalism] **NM** verbalism

verbatim [vɛrbatim] **NM INV** verbatim account

verbe [vɛrb] **NM 1** *Gram* verb; **v. actif** active verb; **v. auxiliaire** auxiliary verb; **v. défectif** defective verb; **v. à particule** phrasal verb

2 *(ton de voix)* **avoir le v. facile** to find it easy to talk; **avoir le v. haut** to speak loudly; *Fig* to take a haughty tone, *Br* to lord it; **il n'a plus le v. si haut depuis que sa protectrice est partie** now that his protector's gone, he's had to quieten down

3 *Littéraire (expression de la pensée)* words, language; **la magie du v.** the magic of words *or* language

4 *Bible* **le V.** the Word; **le V. fait chair** the Word made flesh

verbénacée [vɛrbenase] *Bot* **NF** verbena, *Spéc* member of the Verbenaceae

❑ **verbénacées NFPL** verbenas, *Spéc* Verbenaceae

verbeuse [vɛrbøz] *voir* **verbeux**

verbeusement [vɛrbøzmɑ̃] **ADV** verbosely

verbeux, -euse [vɛrbø, -øz] **ADJ** verbose, wordy, long-winded

verbiage [vɛrbjaʒ] **NM** verbiage; **votre v. ne m'intéresse pas** your meaningless chatter is of no interest to me

verbicruciste [vɛrbikrysist] **NMF** crossword compiler

verbigération [vɛrbiʒerasjɔ̃] **NF** *Psy* verbigeration

verbomanie [vɛrbɔmani] **NF** *Psy* verbomania

verboquet [vɛrbokɛ] **NM** *Vieilli* guy, guide rope

verbosité [vɛrbozite] **NF** verbosity, wordiness

ver-coquin [vɛrkɔkɛ̃] *(pl* **vers-coquins)** **NM 1** *Agr (parasite)* vine grub **2** *Vét* stagger worm

verdage [vɛrdaʒ] **NM** *Agr* manure crop

verdâtre [vɛrdatr] **ADJ** greenish

verdelet, -ette [vɛrdəlɛ, -ɛt] **ADJ** *(vin)* slightly acid *or* tart

verdeur [vɛrdœr] **NF 1** *(vigueur)* vitality, vigour **2** *(crudité)* raciness, boldness, sauciness **3** *(acidité → d'un vin, d'un fruit)* slight tartness *or* acidity

verdict [vɛrdikt] **NM 1** *Jur* verdict; **rendre** *ou* **prononcer son v.** to pass sentence, to return a verdict; **le juge a rendu un v. sévère** the judge brought in a stiff sentence; **rendre un v. de culpabilité** *ou* **positif** to return a verdict of guilty; **rendre un v. d'acquittement** *ou* **négatif** to return a verdict of not guilty; **quel est votre v.?** how do you find?

2 *(opinion)* verdict, pronouncement; **le v. du médecin n'était pas très encourageant** the doctor's prognosis wasn't very hopeful; **seul compte le v. du consommateur** the only thing that matters is the verdict of the consumer

verdier [vɛrdje] **NM** *Orn* greenfinch

verdir [32] [vɛrdir] **VI 1** *(devenir vert)* to turn green **2** *Fig (de peur)* to blanch; **elle a verdi en apprenant la nouvelle** the blood drained out of her face when she heard the news; **v. (de jalousie)** to go *or* to turn green with envy **3** *(plante, arbre)* to have green shoots

VT to add green *or* a green tinge to

verdissant, -e [vɛrdisɑ̃, -ɑ̃t] **ADJ les cerisiers verdissants** the cherry trees covered in green shoots

verdissement [vɛrdismɑ̃] **NM** turning green

verdoie *etc voir* **verdoyer**

verdoiement [vɛrdwamɑ̃] **NM 1** *(couleur verte)* greenness; **le v. des arbres dans le lointain** the green hue of trees in the distance **2** *(action de se couvrir de verdure)* **le v. des arbres annonçait l'arrivée du printemps** the green leaves on the trees heralded the arrival of spring; **le rapide v. printanier de la campagne/de la forêt** the way the countryside/the forest suddenly turns green in the spring

verdoyant, -e [vɛrdwajɑ̃, -ɑ̃t] ADJ **1** *(vert)* green, verdant **2** *(vivace)* lush; **les champs verdoyants** the lush pastures

verdoyer [13] [vɛrdwaje] VI to be green *or* verdant

Verdun [vɛrdœ̃] NM Verdun; **la bataille de V.** the Battle of Verdun

Culture

VERDUN

Verdun is a strategic town of great importance in French history. It saw the signing of the treaty in 843 establishing the existence of what is now France, two occupations by Prussian forces, in 1792 and 1870, and Pétain's ten-month resistance to the German siege of 1916, a hard-won victory involving enormous loss of life which etched itself deeply into the memory of the French people.

verdunisation [vɛrdynizasjɔ̃] NF chlorination *(of drinking water)*

verduniser [3] [vɛrdynize] VT to chlorinate

verdure [vɛrdyr] NF **1** *(couleur)* greenness *(UNCOUNT)*, verdure *(UNCOUNT)*
2 *(végétation)* greenery *(UNCOUNT)*, verdure *(UNCOUNT)*; *(dans un bouquet)* greenery *(UNCOUNT)*, (green) foliage *(UNCOUNT)*; **rideau de v.** curtain of greenery; **tapis de v.** carpet of green, greensward
3 *Culin (salade)* salad *(UNCOUNT)*; *(légumes verts)* greens; **je vous le sers avec un peu de v.?** shall I serve it with some salad?
❑ **de verdure** ADJ *(tapisserie)* verdure *(avant n)*; *(théâtre)* open-air; **salle de v.** green arbour

verdurier, -ère [vɛrdyrje, -ɛr] NM,F *Belg Br* greengrocer, *Am* vegetable seller

vérécondieux, -euse [verekɔ̃djø, -øz] ADJ *Littéraire* reserved, discreet

vérétille [veretij] NM *Zool* veretillum

véreux, -euse [verø, -øz] ADJ **1** *(plein de vers → fruit, viande)* wormy, maggoty **2** *Fig (malhonnête → affaire, avocat, architecte, policier)* shady

verge [vɛrʒ] NF **1** *(barre)* rod; **v. du balancier d'une horloge** pendulum rod; *Fig Littéraire* **être sous la v. de qn** to be ruled by sb, to be under sb's thumb
2 *(insigne)* rod, wand, staff
3 *Anat* penis
4 *(mesure)* yard; **v. d'arpenteur** measuring stick; *Can* yard
5 *Naut* **v. de l'ancre** anchor shank
6 *(en acoustique)* bar
7 *Bot* **v. d'or** goldenrod
❑ **verges** NFPL *Vieilli (badine)* birch (rod); **donner les verges à qn** to birch sb; *Fig* **donner des verges à qn pour se faire fouetter** to give sb a stick to beat one with, to make a rod for one's own back

vergé, -e [vɛrʒe] ADJ **1** *Tex* ribbed, corded **2** *(papier)* laid
NM laid paper

vergence [vɛrʒɑ̃s] NF *Opt* vergence

vergeoise [vɛrʒwaz] NF brown sugar; *(autrefois)* low-grade beet sugar

verger [vɛrʒe] NM (fruit) orchard

vergerette [vɛrʒərɛt] NF *Bot* erigeron

vergeté, -e [vɛrʒəte] ADJ **1** *(peau, cuisse)* stretch-marked **2** *Hér* paly
NM paly escutcheon

vergette [vɛrʒɛt] NF **1** *(bâtonnet)* small cane, switch **2** *(de vitrail)* lead came **3** *Hér* pallet

vergetures [vɛrʒətyr] NFPL stretchmarks; **avoir des v.** to have stretchmarks; **c'est la crème que j'ai utilisée contre les v.** here's the cream I used to prevent stretchmarks

vergeure [vɛrʒyr] NF **1** *(fils de laiton)* wires *(of the mould for laid paper)* **2** *(marque)* wire mark

verglacé, -e [vɛrglase] ADJ **une route verglacée** a road covered in *Br* black ice *or Am* glare ice; **attention, les routes sont verglacées** careful, there's *Br* black ice *or Am* glare ice on the roads; *Can* **pluie verglacée** freezing rain

verglacer [16] [vɛrglase] V IMPERSONNEL **il verglace** the roads are icing over

verglas [vɛrgla] NM *Br* black ice, *Am* glare ice; **danger v.** *(sur panneau) Br* black ice, *Am* glare ice; **il y a du v.** it's icy *or* slippery; **il y a du v. dans l'allée** the drive is iced over; **plaques de v.** patches of *Br* black ice *or Am* glare ice, icy patches

vergne [vɛrɲ] = **verne**

vergobret [vɛrgobre] NM *Hist* = head of some Gallic towns, appointed annually by the druids

vergogne [vɛrgɔɲ] **sans vergogne** ADJ shameless
ADV shamelessly; **mentir sans v.** to lie shamelessly *or* without compunction

vergue [vɛrg] NF *Naut* yard; **v. de hunier** topsail yard; **v. de misaine** foreyard; **grande v.** mainyard; **bout de v.** yardarm

véridicité [veridisite] NF *Littéraire* veracity, accuracy

véridique [veridik] ADJ **1** *Littéraire (sincère → témoin)* truthful, veracious **2** *(conforme à la vérité)* genuine, true; **c'est une histoire absolument v.** it's a true story; **tout cela est parfaitement v.** there's not a word of a lie in all this; *Fam* **elle les a renvoyés, v.!** she fired them, it's true![■]
3 *(qui ne trompe pas)* genuine, authentic

véridiquement [veridikmɑ̃] ADV truthfully, *Sout* veraciously

vérif [verif] NF *Fam* check[■]

vérifiable [verifjabl] ADJ verifiable; **son témoignage n'est pas v.** there's no way of checking *or* verifying his/her testimony; **votre hypothèse n'est pas v.** your hypothesis can't be tested

vérificateur, -trice [verifikatœr, -tris] ADJ testing *(avant n)*, checking *(avant n)*; **appareil v.** testing machine; **instrument v.** gauge, callipers; **mesure vérificatrice** checking measurement
NM,F inspector, controller; *Fin* **v. de comptes** auditor; *Fin* **v. externe/interne** external/internal auditor; **v. des poids et mesures** *Br* weights and measures inspector, *Am* sealer
NM *(contrôleur → de courant, de réseau)* tester; *(→ de l'altimètre, de filetage)* gauge; *Ordinat* **v. orthographique** spellchecker
❑ **vérificatrice** NF *(personne)* verifier operator; *(machine)* verifier; **vérificatrice de bande** tape verifier; **vérificatrice de cartes** card verifier

vérificatif, -ive [verifikatif, -iv] ADJ verificatory; **faire une étude vérificative** to carry out a check

vérification [verifikasjɔ̃] NF **1** *(d'identité)* check; *(d'un témoignage, d'un déplacement)* check, verification; *(d'un dossier)* examination, scrutiny; *(d'un travail)* inspection, examination, checking; *(de votes)* checking; **v. faite auprès du percepteur** having checked with the tax office
2 *(d'une hypothèse, d'une preuve)* checking, verification; *(d'un pronostic)* confirmation; **faire la v. d'une hypothèse** to test a hypothesis
3 *Fin* checking; **v. des comptes** *(service)* audit; *(activité)* auditing; **v. fiscale** tax audit; *Compta* **v. à rebours** audit trail
4 *Tech* test, check; *Aut* **v. sur place** spot check
5 *Ordinat* check, control; **v. antivirale** antiviral check; **v. orthographique** spellcheck
6 *Jur* **v. des dépens** verification of expenses; **v. d'écriture** handwriting identification; **vérifications personnelles du juge** view *(of a place or object)*

vérificationnisme [verifikasjonism] NM *Ling* verificationism

vérificative [verifikativ] *voir* **vérificatif**

vérificatrice [verifikatris] *voir* **vérificateur**

vérifier [9] [verifje] VT **1** *(examiner → mécanisme)* to check, to verify; *(→ dossier)* to check, to go through; *(→ travail)* to inspect, to check; **v. que la quantité indiquée est la même sur les deux recettes** check that the amount shown is the same in both recipes
2 *(preuve, témoignage)* to check; **vérifie son adresse** check that his/her address is correct, check his/her address; **v. que** *ou* **si...** to check *or* to make sure that..., to check whether...; **je vais v. que** *ou* **si ce que vous dites est vrai** I'll make sure that you're telling the truth
3 *(confirmer → hypothèse)* to confirm, to bear out; **la chute du dollar a vérifié nos prévisions** the drop in the dollar bore out our predictions
4 *Math (calcul)* to check, to verify; **v. un calcul par total de contrôle** to check a sum
5 *(comptes)* to audit
USAGE ABSOLU **v. plutôt deux fois qu'une** to check and double-check; **il doit être là, je vais v.** he must be there, I'll check *or* make sure
►**se vérifier** VPR *(affirmation)* to prove correct, to be confirmed; *(craintes, supposition)* to be borne out *or* confirmed; **mes soupçons se sont vérifiés par la suite** my suspicions were subsequently confirmed

vérifieur, -euse [verifjœr, -øz] NM,F verifier operator

vérin [verɛ̃] NM jack; **v. à air comprimé** thruster; **v. à châssis** tripod jack; **v. à cliquet** ratchet jack; **v. de fermeture** closing thruster *or* cylinder; **v. à gaz** gas strut; **v. hydraulique** hydraulic jack; **v. pneumatique** pneumatic jack; **v. de réglage de plinthe** levelling screw; **v. à vis** screw jack

vérine [verin] NF *Naut* hook rope

vérisme [verism] NM *Beaux-Arts & Littérature* verism

vériste [verist] *Beaux-Arts & Littérature* ADJ verist
NMF verist

véritable [veritabl] ADJ **1** *(d'origine)* real, true; **son v. nom est inconnu** nobody knows his/her real *or* true name
2 *(authentique → or, cuir)* real, genuine; *(→ amitié, sentiment, ami)* true; **c'est de la soie v.** it's real silk; **du v. sirop d'érable** genuine maple syrup
3 *(avant le nom) (absolu)* real; **une v. idée de génie** a really brilliant idea; **un v. cauchemar** a real nightmare; **une v. montagne de papiers** a veritable mountain of papers; *très Fam* **une v. ordure** a real shit; **se montrer sous son v. jour** to show one's true colours, to show oneself in one's true light; **ce fut une v. surprise** it was a real surprise; **nous assistons là à une v. révolution** we are witnessing a real revolution

véritablement [veritabləmɑ̃] ADV **1** *(réellement)* genuinely; **il est v. malade** he's genuinely ill; **nous nous sommes v. compris** we understood each other perfectly
2 *(exactement)* really, exactly; **ce n'est pas v. ce que j'avais prévu** it's not exactly *or* quite what I expected
3 *(en intensif)* truly, really, absolutely; **je suis v. désolé de ne pas vous avoir trouvé chez vous** I'm very sorry indeed (that) I didn't find you at home

vérité [verite] NF **1** *(ce qui est réel ou exprimé comme réel)* **la v.** the truth; **dire la v.** to tell *or* speak the truth; **dire la v. à qn** to tell sb the truth; **dis-moi la v.** tell me the truth; **la v. pure et simple** the plain unvarnished truth; **c'est la v.** it's true, it's a fact; *Fam* **c'est la v. vraie!** it's true, honest it is!; **l'heure de v.** the moment of truth; **récit conforme à la v.** true *or* factual account; **s'écarter de la v. historique** to take liberties with history; **je sais que c'est la v.** I know it for a fact; **la v., c'est que ça m'est égal** actually *or* in fact, I don't care, the truth is I don't care; **je finirai bien par savoir la v.** I'll get at the truth eventually; **être loin de la v.** to be wide of the mark; **12 millions? vous n'êtes pas loin de la v.** 12 million? you're not far from the truth; **à chacun sa v.!** each to his own!; **la v. toute nue** the plain *or* naked truth; *Jur* **la v., toute la v., rien que la v.** the truth, the whole truth and nothing but the truth; **la v. n'est pas toujours bonne à dire, toute v. n'est pas bonne à dire** the truth is sometimes better left unsaid; **il n'y a que la v. qui blesse** nothing hurts like the truth; **prends ça pour toi si tu veux, il n'y a que la v. qui blesse!** if the *Br* cap *or Am* shoe fits, wear it!; *Prov* **la v. sort de la bouche des enfants** out of the mouths of babes and sucklings (comes forth the truth); **v. en deçà des Pyrénées, erreur au-delà** = what is considered true in one country may be thought of as false in the next
2 *(chose vraie)* **une v.** a true fact
3 *(principe)* truth; **une v. première** a basic truth; **les vérités éternelles** undying truths, eternal verities; **les vérités essentielles** fundamental truths
4 *(ressemblance)* **ses tableaux sont d'une grande v.** his/her paintings are very true to life
5 *(sincérité)* truthfulness, candidness; **air/accent de v.** ring of truth; **son récit avait un accent de v.** his/her story rang true
❑ **à la vérité** ADV to tell the truth
❑ **en vérité** ADV really, actually

verjus [vɛrʒy] NM **1** *(suc)* verjuice **2** *(vin)* sour wine

verjuté, -e [vɛrʒyte] **ADJ** *(acide)* acid *(avant n)*, sour

verlan [vɛrlɑ̃] **NM** ≃ back-slang; **parler en v.** to speak in back-slang

> *Culture*
>
> **VERLAN**
>
> This form of slang, mostly used among young French people, particularly in the impoverished areas of large cities, involves inverting the syllables of words and making any spelling changes necessary to facilitate pronunciation. The word "verlan" is itself the inverted form of "l'envers", meaning "the other way round". Some "verlan" terms are used or understood by a great many speakers, eg "laisse béton!" ("laisse tomber!" = "forget it!"), "ripou" ("pourri", used to refer to corrupt policemen), "meuf" ("femme") and "beur" ("arabe"). It is, however, an extremely generative form of slang and new words are constantly being made up.

vermée [vɛrme] **NF** *Pêche* worms

Vermeer [vɛrmir] **NPR V. (de Delft)** Vermeer

vermeil, -eille [vɛrmɛj] **ADJ** *(rouge → pétale, tenture)* vermilion; *(→ teint, joue)* ruddy, rosy; *(→ lèvres)* rosy
NM vermeil, gilded silver

vermet [vɛrmɛ] **NM** *Zool* vermetid, worm shell

vermicelle [vɛrmisɛl] **NM v., vermicelles** vermicelli *(UNCOUNT)*; **vermicelles chinois** Chinese noodles; **soupe aux vermicelles** noodle soup

vermicide [vɛrmisid] **ADJ** vermicidal
NM vermicide

vermiculaire [vɛrmikylɛr] **ADJ 1** *(en forme de ver)* wormlike, *Sout* vermicular **2** *Anat* **appendice v.** vermiform appendix; **mouvement v.** vermiculation

vermiculé, -e [vɛrmikyle] **ADJ** *Archit* vermiculate, vermiculated

vermiculure [vɛrmikylyr] **NF** *Archit* vermiculation *(UNCOUNT)*

vermidien [vɛrmidjɛ̃] *Zool* **NM** member of the Phoronida phylum
□ **vermidiens NMPL** Phoronida

vermiforme [vɛrmifɔrm] **ADJ** wormlike, *Sout* vermiform

vermifuge [vɛrmifyʒ] **ADJ** vermifuge, *Spéc* anthelmintic; **poudre v.** worming powder
NM vermifuge, *Spéc* anthelmintic

vermille [vɛrmij] **NF** ground line *(for eel fishing)*

vermiller [3] [vɛrmije] **VI** *(sanglier, cochon)* to root; *(blaireau)* to burrow

vermillon [vɛrmijɔ̃] **ADJ INV** vermilion, bright red
NM 1 *(cinabre)* vermilion, cinnabar **2** *(couleur)* vermilion

vermillonner [3] [vɛrmijɔne] **VI** *(blaireau)* to burrow, to grub

vermine [vɛrmin] **NF 1** *(parasites)* vermin *(UNCOUNT)*; **couvert** *ou* **grouillant de v.** verminous, crawling with vermin **2** *Fig Péj* **fréquenté par la v.** frequented by lowlife characters *or* members of the underworld; **ces gens-là, c'est de la v.** those people are vermin

vermineux, -euse [vɛrminø, -øz] **ADJ** verminous

verminose [vɛrminoz] **NF** *Méd* verminosis

vermis [vɛrmis] **NM** *Anat* vermis (cerebelli)

vermisseau, -x [vɛrmiso] **NM** small worm

vermivore [vɛrmivɔr] **ADJ** worm-eating, *Spéc* vermivorous

Vermont [vɛrmɔ̃] **NM le V.** Vermont; **dans le V.** in Vermont

vermouler [3] [vɛrmule] **se vermouler VPR** to get woodworm

vermoulu, -e [vɛrmuly] **ADJ 1** *(piqué des vers)* worm-eaten; **la plupart des poutres sont vermoulues** most of the beams are worm-eaten, there's woodworm in most of the beams **2** *Fig (vieux)* antiquated, age-old; **des institutions vermoulues** antiquated institutions

vermoulure [vɛrmulyr] **NF 1** *(trou)* wormhole **2** *(poussière)* woodworm dust

vermouth [vɛrmut] **NM** vermouth

vernaculaire [vɛrnakylɛr] **ADJ** vernacular; **nom v.** vernacular *or* common name; **langue v.** vernacular
NM vernacular

vernal, -e, -aux, -ales [vɛrnal, -o] **ADJ** vernal

vernalisation [vɛrnalizasjɔ̃] **NF** *Agr* vernalization

vernation [vɛrnasjɔ̃] **NF** *Bot* vernation, prefoliation

verne [vɛrn] **NM** *Bot* alder; *(bois)* alder(wood)

verni, -e [vɛrni] **ADJ 1** *(meuble, ongle)* varnished; *(acajou)* French-polished; *(brique, poterie)* enamelled, glazed; **parquet v.** varnished *or* polished floor; **cuir v.** patent leather; **des souliers vernis** patent leather shoes
2 *(brillant)* glossy, shiny
3 *Fam (chanceux)* lucky■, *Br* jammy; **tu es encore malade, tu n'es vraiment pas v.** you're sick again, you poor thing
NM,F *Fam* lucky thing
NM patent leather

vernier [vɛrnje] **NM** vernier, sliding gauge

vernir [32] [vɛrnir] **VT 1** *(enduire → bois, tableau, ongle)* to varnish; *(→ acajou)* to French-polish; *(→ cuir)* to japan; *(→ céramique)* to enamel, to glaze; **v. au tampon** to French-polish **2** *Littéraire (faire luire)* **le soleil vernissait les feuilles** the sun gave a glossy shine to the leaves

vernis [vɛrni] **NM 1** *(enduit → sur bois)* varnish; *(→ sur métal)* polish; **v. à l'alcool** spirit varnish; **v. à l'asphalte** asphalt varnish, black japan; **v. cellulosique** cellulose varnish; **v. à l'essence** turpentine varnish; **v. japonais** japan; **v. au tampon** French polish
2 *(enduit → sur céramique)* enamel; **v. au plomb** lead glazing; **v. de potier** glaze
3 *Typ* varnish; **v. UV** UV varnish
4 *Élec* **v. conducteur** conductive lacquer *or* varnish; **v. isolant** isolac, enamel
5 *(cosmétique)* **v. à ongles** nail polish; **se mettre du v. à ongles** to varnish *or* paint one's nails
6 *Beaux-Arts* **v. à l'huile** oil varnish; **v. gras** long-oil varnish; **v. maigre** short-oil varnish
7 *Bot* **v. du Japon** varnish tree, lacquer tree, tree of heaven
8 *Fig Péj* veneer; **avoir un v. de culture** to have a smattering of culture; **il suffit de gratter le v. pour comprendre qui il est** you only have to scratch the surface to find out who he really is; **le v. d'éducation ne cache pas sa vulgarité** a veneer of good manners does nothing to hide his/her vulgarity

vernissage [vɛrnisaʒ] **NM 1** *(d'un tableau, d'un meuble)* varnishing; *(d'une céramique)* glazing; *(du métal)* enamelling; **v. électrophorétique** immersion electrophoretic enamelling, electro-dipcoat **2** *(d'une exposition)* private viewing, opening

vernissé, -e [vɛrnise] **ADJ 1** *(céramique, tuile)* glazed **2** *(luisant → feuilles)* glossy

vernisser [3] [vɛrnise] **VT** to glaze, to enamel

vernisseur, -euse [vɛrnisœr, -øz] **NM,F** *(de carrosserie)* body painter; *(à la laque)* lacquerer; *(de meuble)* furniture varnisher; *(au pistolet)* spray painter; *(de céramique)* glazer

vernix caseosa [vɛrnikskazeoza] **NM INV** vernix caseosa

vérole [verɔl] **NF 1** *Fam (syphilis)* pox; **avoir la v.** to have the pox; **ils se sont jetés sur le buffet comme la v. sur le bas clergé** they descended on the buffet like there was no tomorrow **2** *Méd (variole)* **petite v.** smallpox; **avoir la petite v.** to have smallpox **3** *Fam* **quelle v.!** what a pain!

vérolé, -e [verɔle] **ADJ** *Fam* poxy

Véronal® [verɔnal] **NM** *Pharm* Veronal®, barbital, barbitone

Vérone [verɔn] **NM** Verona

Véronèse [verɔnɛz] **NPR** Veronese

véronique[1] [verɔnik] **NF** *Bot* speedwell, *Spéc* veronica; **v. des champs** wall speedwell; **v. en épi** spiked speedwell; **v. à feuilles de lierre** ivy-leaved speedwell; **v. des montagnes** wood speedwell; **v. officinale** heath speedwell; **v. petit-chêne** germander speedwell

véronique[2] [verɔnik] **NF** *(passe de tauromachie)* veronica

véroter [3] [verɔte] **VI** *Orn* to probe for worms

verra *etc voir* **voir**

verranne [vɛran] **NF** *Tech* verranne

verrat [vera] **NM 1** *(porc)* breeding boar **2** *Can très Fam (homme méprisable)* swine, bastard
EXCLAM *Can très Fam* **(maudit) v.!** shit!, *Br* bloody hell!
□ **en verrat ADV** *Can Fam* **1** *(en intensif)* very■; **un beau film en v.** a damn *or Br* bloody good movie *or Br* film **2** *(en colère)* **être en (beau) v.** to be fuming, to be in a foul temper■

verre [vɛr] **NM 1** *(matériau)* glass; **se casser** *ou* **se briser comme du v.** to be as brittle as glass; **v. antiballes** bulletproof glass; **v. armé** wired glass; **v. blanc** white glass; **v. cathédrale** cathedral glass; **v. coloré** stained glass; **v. dépoli** frosted *or* ground glass; **v. double** plate glass; **v. feuilleté** laminated glass; **v. filé** spun glass; **v. flotté** float glass; **v. fumé** smoked glass; **v. à glaces** plate glass; **v. grillagé** wire(d) glass; **v. incassable** shatterproof glass; **v. moulé** pressed glass; **v. neutre** neutral glass; **v. optique** optical glass; **v. organique** organic glass; **v. pilé** spun glass; **v. de sécurité** safety glass; **v. soluble** water glass; **v. soufflé** blown glass; **v. trempé** tempered *or* toughened glass; **v. à vitre** window glass
2 *(protection)* glass; **v. de lampe** lamp glass; **v. de montre** watch glass
3 *(récipient)* glass; **lever son v. à qn** to raise one's glass to sb; **v. ballon** round wine glass; **v. à dents** tooth glass; **v. doseur** measuring glass; **v. à eau** *(droit)* tumbler; **v. gradué** *(en chimie)* graduated vessel; *(pour la cuisine)* measuring glass; **v. à liqueur** liqueur glass; **v. à moutarde** mustard jar *(that can be used as a glass when empty)*; **v. à pied** stemmed glass; **v. à vin** wine-glass; **v. à whisky** whisky glass
4 *(contenu)* glass(ful); **boire un v.** to have a drink; **je bois** *ou* **prends juste un petit v.** I'll just have a quick one; **tu restes prendre un v.?** are you staying for a drink?, would you like to stay for a drink?; **allez viens, on va prendre un v.** come on, let's go for a drink; **un v. et je suis ivre** it only takes one drink to get me drunk; **v. de** glass of, glassful of; **mettez un v. de vin rouge** add a glass of red wine; **il but** *ou* **vida deux grands verres d'eau pour étancher sa soif** he drank two large glasses of water to quench his thirst; *Fam* **avoir un v. dans le nez** to have had one too many; **il a pris** *ou* **a bu un v. de trop** he's had one too many, he's had a drop too much
5 *Géol* **v. volcanique** volcanic glass
□ **verres NMPL 1** *Opt* glasses; **elle a besoin de ses verres pour lire** she needs her glasses to read; **verres de contact** contact lenses; **verres correcteurs** correcting lenses; **verres fumés** tinted lenses; **verres polarisés** polaroid lenses
2 *(bouteilles)* bottles; **ici on reprend les verres vides** hand back your empty bottles here
3 verres dalles pavement lights
□ **de verre ADJ** glass *(avant n)*; **objets de v.** glassware *(UNCOUNT)*
□ **en verre ADJ** *(bibelot)* glass *(avant n)*; **ce n'est pas en v.** it won't break; **n'aie pas peur de sauter, tu n'es pas en v.!** jump, you won't break!
□ **sous verre ADJ** *(photo, fleurs)* glass-framed; **une photo sous v.** a glass-mounted photograph
ADV mettre qch sous v. to put sth in a frame

verré, -e [vɛre] **ADJ** coated with powdered glass

verrée [vɛre] **NF** *Suisse (tournée)* round (of drinks); *(rencontre)* drinks party

verrerie [vɛrri] **NF 1** *(usine)* glassworks *(singulier)* **2** *(technique)* glasswork, glassmaking **3** *(objets)* glassware **4** *(industrie)* glass trade

verrier, -ère [vɛrje, -ɛr] **ADJ** glass *(avant n)*
NM 1 *(souffleur de verre)* glassblower **2** *(artisan → en verrerie)* glassmaker; *(→ en vitraux)* stained-glass maker **3** *(casier)* glass rack
□ **verrière NF 1** *(toit)* glass roof **2** *(baie → à hauteur de plafond)* glass wall *or* partition; *(→ à mi-hauteur)* glass screen **3** *(de protection)* glass casing **4** *(vitrail)* stained-glass window **5** *Aviat* canopy

verrine [vɛrin] **NF 1** *(de lampe)* glass globe **2** *Naut* hook rope

verroterie [vɛrɔtri] **NF** *(bibelots)* glass trinkets; *(bijoux)* glass jewels; *(perles)* glass beads; **collier de v.** string of glass beads, glass necklace

verrou [veru] **NM 1** *(fermeture)* bolt; **mettre** *ou* **pousser les verrous** to slide the bolts home, to bolt the door; **on ne peut pas entrer, elle a mis le v.** we can't get in, she's bolted the door; **fermer une porte au v.** to bolt a door; **s'enfermer au v.** to bolt oneself in; **tirer le v.** to unbolt the door; **v. de sûreté** safety latch, night bolt; **v. trois points** multilock; *Fig* **faire sauter un v.** to get over an obstacle

2 *Rail* lock; **v. d'aiguille** facing point lock; **v. d'enclenchement** track slide bar
3 *Géol* glacial cross cliff
4 *Mil* breechblock, bolt
5 *Mil* blockade
6 *Sport* **jeu de v.** defensive game *(in football)*
❑ **sous les verrous** ADV **être sous les verrous** to be behind bars; **mettre qn sous les verrous** to put sb behind bars; *Fam* **on va te mettre sous les verrous pour un bon bout de temps** they're going to put you away for a long stretch

verrouillage [veruja3] NM **1** *(d'une porte)* locking, bolting; *(d'une portière)* locking; **v. automatique** central locking; **à v. automatique** self-locking; **v. central** central locking; *Aut* **v. central** *ou* **centralisé des portes** central door-locking; *Aut* **v. à distance** remote-control locking; **v. de sécurité enfants** childproof lock; *Aut* **v. du volant** steering lock
2 *Mil* blockade
3 *Aviat* **v. du train d'atterrissage** *(procédé)* up-and-down locking; *(dispositif)* up-and-down lock
4 *Rail* **v. électrique** electric interlocking
5 *Électron (procédé)* clamping; *(dispositif)* clamping device
6 *Ordinat (du clavier)* locking; *(de l'accès)* lockout; **v. du clavier numérique** numbers lock; **v. des fichiers** file lock; **v. en lecture seule** read-only lock; **v. en majuscule(s)** caps lock

verrouiller [3] [veruje] VT **1** *(clore → porte)* to lock, to bolt
2 *(empêcher l'accès de)* to close off; **la police a verrouillé le quartier** the police have cordoned off *or* sealed off the area
3 *(enfermer → personne)* to lock in
4 *Ordinat (clavier)* to lock; *(capitales)* to lock on; **v. en écriture** *(fichier)* to lock; **verrouillé en majuscules** *(clavier)* with caps lock on
5 *Mil (ville)* to blockade; *(passage, brèche)* to block
6 *Fam (contrôler → système, équipe)* to control; *(→ marché)* to block; **v. un prix** to freeze a price; **avant d'envoyer le contrat, assure-toi que tout est verrouillé** before you send off the contract, make sure that everything is in order
▸ **se verrouiller** VPR **se v. (chez soi)** to shut *or* to lock oneself in

verrouilleur [verujœr] NM *Ftbl* sweeper

verrucosité [verykozite] NF *Méd* warty growth

verrue [very] NF wart; **v. plantaire** verruca, plantar wart

verruqueux, -euse [verykø, -øz] ADJ warty, *Spéc* verrucose

vers[1] [ver] NM *Littérature* **1** *(genre)* verse; **v. blancs** blank verse; **v. héroïques** heroic verse; **v. libres** free verse; **v. métriques/syllabiques/rythmiques** quantitative/syllabic/accentual-syllabic verse
2 *(unité)* line; **le dernier v. est faux** *ou* **boiteux** the last line doesn't scan; **les v. obéissent à certaines règles** lines of verse *or* verse lines follow a given pattern
NMPL *(poème)* lines of poetry, poetry *(UNCOUNT)*, verse *(UNCOUNT)*; **écrire** *ou* **faire des v.** to write poetry *or* verse; **v. de circonstance** occasional verse; **des v. de mirliton** doggerel *(UNCOUNT)*
❑ **en vers** ADJ **conte/lettre en v.** tale told/letter written in verse ADV **mettre qch en v.** to put sth into verse

vers[2] [ver] PRÉP **1** *(dans la direction de)* to, towards; **il regarde v. la mer** he's looking towards the sea; **ma chambre regarde v. le nord** my bedroom looks *or* faces north; **un kilomètre v. le sud** one kilometre to the south; **v. la gauche** to the left; **en route v. la Californie** on the way to California; **le village v. lequel nous nous dirigions** the village we were heading for; *Fam* **v. où tu vas?** which way are you going?; **se précipiter v. la sortie** to hurry towards *or* to make for the exit; **v. les quais** *(sur panneau)* to the trains; **il s'est tourné v. moi** he turned to *or* towards me; *(pour que je l'aide)* he turned *or* came to me; **v. une solution au problème du chômage** towards a solution to the problem of unemployment; **un pas v. la paix** a step towards peace
2 *(indiquant l'approximation → dans le temps)* around; *(→ dans l'espace)* near; **v. midi** around midday; **v. la mi-juillet** around mid-July; **v. 1830** in about 1830; **il a neigé v. six heures** it snowed at about *or* around six o'clock; *Fam* **v. (les) trois heures** about *or* around three (o'clock); **v. la fin de qch** towards the end of sth; **v. la fin du siècle** at the turn of the century; **v. les années 30** in the 30s or thereabouts; **l'accident a eu lieu v. Ambérieu** the accident happened somewhere near Ambérieu; **v. les 1800 mètres, la végétation se raréfie** around 1,800 metres, the vegetation becomes sparse; **on a trouvé des jonquilles v. la rivière** we found some daffodils near the river

versage [versa3] NM *Belg (de déchets)* dumping

versaillais, -e [versajε, -εz] ADJ **1** of/from Versailles **2** *Hist* **l'armée versaillaise** the Versailles army *(loyal to the Thiers government in 1871)*
❑ **Versaillais, -e** NM,F **1** = inhabitant of or person from Versailles **2** *Hist* soldier in the Versailles army *(loyal to the Thiers government in 1871)*; **les V.** the loyalists

Versailles [versaj] NM Versailles; **le château de V.** (the Palace of) Versailles

> *Culture*
> **VERSAILLES**
> Versailles is France's greatest palace, designed by Le Vau and Mansart, with gardens laid out by Le Nôtre. Built at enormous cost by Louis XIV and added to in the 18th century, it was the home of the French court until the Revolution. Numerous treaties were signed there, including that of 1919 marking the end of the First World War.

versant, -e [versã, -ãt] ADJ *Can (qui renverse facilement)* unsteady
NM **1** *Géog (côté → d'une montagne, d'une vallée)* side, slope; *(→ de colline)* hillside; **un v. abrupt** a steep slope *or* hillside; **le v. suisse du Jura** the Swiss side of the Jura **2** *(aspect → d'une position, d'un argument)* side, aspect; **notre politique a deux versants** there are two sides *or* aspects to our policy

versatile [versatil] ADJ **1** *(esprit, caractère, personne)* fickle; *(homme politique)* mercurial; **elle est v.** she's always changing her mind **2** *Biol* versatile

versatilité [versatilite] NF **1** *(inconstance)* fickleness **2** *Biol* versatility

verse [vers] NF **1** *Agr* lodging, laying **2** *Mines (tas)* slag heap; *(déversement)* dumping
❑ **à verse** ADV **il pleut à v.** it's pouring (with rain), it's pouring down; **la pluie tombait à v.** the rain was coming down in torrents

versé, -e [verse] ADJ versed; **être très/peu v. dans la politique** to be well-versed/not particularly well-versed in politics; **être v./peu v. dans l'art contemporain** to be conversant with/ignorant of contemporary art

Verseau [verso] NM **1** *Astron* Aquarius **2** *Astrol* Aquarius; **être V.** to be Aquarius *or* an Aquarian

versement [versəmã] NM **1** *(paiement)* payment; **v. annuel** yearly payment; **v. à la commande** down payment; **versements compensatoires** compensatory payments, compensation *(UNCOUNT)*; **v. comptant** cash payment; **v. d'espèces** cash payment; **v. en numéraire** payment in cash
2 *(paiement partiel)* instalment; **effectuer un v.** to pay an instalment; **un premier v.** a down payment; **versements échelonnés** staggered payments; **en plusieurs versements, par versements échelonnés** by *or* in instalments; **v. libératoire** final instalment; **v. partiel** instalment
3 *(dépôt)* deposit; **effectuer** *ou* **faire un v. à la banque** to pay money into a bank account; **quand avez-vous fait le v.?** when did you pay the money in?; **v. en espèces** cash deposit; **bulletin de v.** paying-in *or Am* deposit slip

verser [3] [verse] VT **1** *(répandre → sang, larmes)* to shed; **v. des larmes** *ou* **pleurs** to cry; **sans qu'une goutte de sang n'ait été versée** without a drop of blood being spilt; **il irait jusqu'à v. son sang pour défendre ses idées** he'd be willing to sacrifice his life for his ideas
2 *(servir → liquide)* to pour out; **verse-lui-en un peu plus** pour him/her a bit more; **v. à boire à qn** to pour sb a drink, to pour a drink for sb; **v. du vin dans une cruche** to pour wine into a jug; *Fig Littéraire* **v. ses chagrins dans le cœur de qn** to pour out one's troubles to sb
3 *(faire basculer → sable, gravier, chargement)* to tip; **verse la farine dedans** pour the flour in; **verse le trop-plein dans le seau** tip *or* pour the overflow out into the bucket
4 *(coucher à terre → céréales)* to lay *or* to beat down
5 *(affecter)* to assign, to transfer; **elle vient d'être versée à la comptabilité** she's just been assigned to accounts; *Mil* **v. des hommes à un régiment/dans une armée** to draft *or* assign *or* transfer men to a regiment/to an army
6 *Mil (provisions)* to issue
7 *(payer)* to pay; *(sur un compte)* to deposit; **combien faut-il v.?** how much should one pay?; **v. de l'argent sur un compte** to put money into an account; **v. qch au crédit de qn** to credit sb with sth; **v. un acompte** to make a down payment; **on vous versera une retraite** you will receive a pension
8 *(apporter)* to add, to append; **v. une pièce au dossier** to add a new item to the file; *Fig* to bring further information to bear on the case
9 *Belg (déchets)* to dump
VI **1** *(véhicule)* to overturn; **la charrette a versé** the cart tipped over *or* overturned; **sa voiture est allée v. dans le ravin** his/her car tipped over into the ravine
2 *(cultures)* to be beaten down, to be laid flat
❑ **verser dans** VT IND to lapse into; **nous versons dans le mélodrame** this is becoming melodramatic; **v. dans le ridicule** *(personne, film)* to become ridiculous

verset [versε] NM **1** *(d'un livre sacré, d'un poème)* verse **2** *Rel* versicle

'Les Versets sataniques' *Rushdie* 'The Satanic Verses'

verseur, -euse [versœr, -øz] ADJ **bec v.** *(d'une théière)* spout; *(d'une casserole, d'une tasse)* lip; **camion v.** dump truck
NM,F *(personne)* pourer
NM *Mines* tipper
❑ **verseuse** NF *(cafetière)* coffee pot

versicolore [versikolor] ADJ **1** *(de couleur changeante)* versicoloured **2** *(multicolore)* variegated, many-coloured

versificateur [versifikatœr] NM *Péj* versifier, poetaster, rhymester

versification [versifikasjõ] NF versification, versifying

versifier [9] [versifje] VT to versify, to turn into verse, to write in verse
VI **1** *(faire des vers)* to versify, to write *or* to compose verse **2** *Péj* to versify

version [versjõ] NF **1** *(variante → d'une œuvre, d'un logiciel)* version; *(→ d'une automobile)* model, version; **la v. cinématographique du livre** the movie *or Br* film (version) of the book; **v. longue** uncut version; **v. originale** version in the original language; **en v. originale** in the original language; **en v. originale sous-titrée** with subtitles; **en v. française** dubbed in French; **un film américain en v. française** an American movie *or Br* film dubbed into French; **v. du réalisateur** director's cut; *Aut* **v. bâchée** soft top
2 *Scol & Univ* translation *(from a foreign language into one's mother tongue)*; **v. anglaise** *(pour un Français)* translation from English into French; **v. latine** translation from Latin
3 *(interprétation)* version; **voici ma v. des faits** this is my version of the facts, this is how I see what happened; **c'est la v. officielle des faits** that's the official version of what happened
4 *Méd* version, turning
5 *Ordinat* **v. alpha** alpha version; **v. bêta** beta version; **v. brouillon** draft version

vers-libriste [verlibrist] *(pl* **vers-libristes***)* NMF writer of free verse

verso [verso] NM **1** *(envers)* verso, other side; **je n'ai pas lu le v.** I haven't read the back of the page **2** *Ordinat* back
❑ **au verso** ADV **voir au v.** see overleaf; **la suite au v.** continued overleaf; **l'adresse est au v.** the address is overleaf *or* on the back

versoir [verswar] NM mouldboard

verste [verst] NF verst *(1,067 metres)*

versus [vɛrsys] **PRÉP** *Ling* versus

vert, -e [vɛr, vɛrt] **ADJ 1** *(couleur)* green; **v. de rage** livid; **être v. de peur** to be white with fear; **être v. de jalousie** to be green with envy

2 *(vin)* tart, acid; *(fruit)* green, unripe; *Fig (débutant, apprenti)* inexperienced; **ce vin est encore v.** this wine isn't ready for drinking yet

3 *(bois)* green

4 *(à préparer)* **cuir v.** untanned leather

5 *(vigoureux)* sprightly

6 *(agricole, rural)* green, agricultural, rural; **l'Europe verte** farming within the EU; **la livre verte** the green pound; **faire de la moto verte** to go cross-country motorcycling; **station verte** rural tourist centre

7 *(écologiste)* green *(avant n)*; **produit v.** green *or* environmentally friendly product; **les candidats verts** the green candidates

8 *(osé)* risqué, raunchy; **avoir un langage v.** to be rather bold in one's language

9 *(avant le nom) (violent)* **une verte semonce** a good dressing-down

NM 1 *(couleur)* green; **peint/teint en v.** painted/tinted green; **tu t'es mis du v. sur ton pantalon** *(en t'asseyant dans l'herbe)* you've got a grass stain on your trousers; **v. amande** almond green; **v. bouteille** bottle green; **v. cendré** sage green; **v. de chrome** chrome green; **v. d'eau** sea green; **v. émeraude** emerald green; **v. jade** jade; **v. Nil** Nile green; **v. olive** olive green; **v. pomme** apple green; **v. tendre** soft green

2 *Transp* green light; **les voitures doivent passer au v.** motorists must wait for the light to turn green; **le feu est passé au v.** the lights have turned (to) green

3 *(locutions)* **mettre un cheval au v.** to turn a horse out to grass; *Fam* **mettre qn au v.** to put sb out to grass; **se mettre au v.** *(pour se reposer)* to go to the countryside; *(pour se cacher)* to hide out *or* to lie low *or* to hole up in the country; **cet été, je me mets au v. et je lis** I'm going to spend this summer tucked away in the countryside reading

❑ **Verts NMPL** *Pol* **les Verts** = the French Green Party

❑ **vertes NFPL** *Fam* **en dire/en avoir entendu des vertes et des pas mûres** to tell/to have heard some pretty raunchy jokes; **en avoir vu des vertes et des pas mûres** to have been through a lot; **il lui en a fait voir des vertes et des pas mûres!** he's really put him/her through it!

❑ **vert galant NM** old charmer

> *Allusion*
>
> **Ils étaient trop verts**
>
> La Fontaine's fable *The Fox and the Grapes* tells of how a fox sees some grapes which are too high for him to reach. Rather than admit defeat, he tells himself "They were too green, nobody civilized would touch them." The usage of **Ils étaient trop verts** in French is exactly like the expression "It's a case of sour grapes" in English.

vert-de-gris [vɛrdəgri] **NM INV** verdigris; **les v.** = German soldiers during the Second World War

ADJ INV blue-green

vert-de-grisé, -e [vɛrdəgrize] *(mpl* **vert-de-grisés,** *fpl* **vert-de-grisées)** **ADJ** verdigrised

vertébral, -e, -aux, -ales [vɛrtebral, -o] **ADJ** vertebral *(avant n)*, spinal *(avant n)*

vertébré, -e [vɛrtebre] **ADJ** vertebrate

NM vertebrate

vertèbre [vɛrtɛbr] **NF** vertebra; **v. cervicale/dorsale/lombaire** cervical/dorsal/lumbar vertebra; **se déplacer une v.** to slip a disc; **avoir une v. déplacée** to have a slipped disc

vertébrothérapie [vɛrtebrɔterapi] **NF** *Méd* vertebrotherapy, ≃ chiropractic

vertement [vɛrtəmɑ̃] **ADV** harshly, sharply; **répondre v.** to retort sharply, to give a sharp answer; **se faire v. recevoir** to get a frosty welcome; *Littéraire ou Hum* **se faire tancer v.** to get a good dressing-down

vertex [vɛrtɛks] **NM** *Anat & Zool* vertex

vertical, -e, -aux, -ales [vɛrtikal, -o] **ADJ** *(droit → position, corps, arbre)* vertical, upright; *(→ écriture, ligne)* vertical; **éclairage v.** overhead lighting

NM *Astron* vertical circle

❑ **verticale NF** vertical line; *Tech* plumb line

❑ **à la verticale ADJ** vertical; **un versant à la verticale** a sheer drop **ADV** vertically; **monter à la verticale** to go up vertically, to go straight up; **descendre/tomber à la verticale** to go/to fall straight down *or* down vertically; **la falaise tombe à la verticale dans la mer** there is a sheer drop from the cliff to the sea; **s'élever à la verticale** to rise vertically, to go vertically upwards; **se mettre à la verticale** to stand vertically *or* upright

verticalement [vɛrtikalmɑ̃] **ADV 1** *(tout droit)* vertically; **tomber/monter v.** to fall down/to come up in a straight line **2** *(dans les mots croisés)* down

verticalité [vɛrtikalite] **NF** *(d'une ligne, d'un mur)* verticality; *(d'une falaise)* sheerness

verticille [vɛrtisil] **NM** *Bot* verticil, whorl

verticillé, -e [vɛrtisile] **ADJ** *Bot* verticillate, whorled

verticité [vɛrtisite] **NF** *Phys* verticity

vertige [vɛrtiʒ] **NM 1** *(peur du vide)* vertigo; **avoir le v.** to suffer from vertigo; **il a facilement le v.** he has no head for heights; **je n'ai jamais le v.** I'm not scared of heights

2 *(malaise)* dizzy spell; **avoir un v.** to feel dizzy *or* faint; **avoir des vertiges** to have dizzy spells; **elle a souvent des vertiges** she often feels dizzy *or* faint; **donner le v. à qn** to make sb's head swim; **cela me donne le v.** it's making my head swim, it's making me (feel) dizzy; *Fig* **des sommes astronomiques qui donnent le v.** huge amounts of money that make one's head swim *or* that don't bear thinking about

3 *Fig (égarement)* giddiness; **céder/résister au v. de la spéculation** *(tentation)* to give in to/to resist the temptations of speculation

vertigineuse [vɛrtiʒinøz] *voir* **vertigineux**

vertigineusement [vɛrtiʒinøzmɑ̃] **ADV** dizzily, *Sout* vertiginously; **une route v. escarpée** a breathtakingly steep road; **grimper v.** to rocket; **plonger v.** to plummet

vertigineux, -euse [vɛrtiʒinø, -øz] **ADJ 1** *(effrayant → altitude)* vertiginous, dizzy *(avant n)*, giddy *(avant n)*; *(→ vitesse)* terrifying, breakneck *(avant n)*; **une baisse vertigineuse des cours** a spectacular collapse on the stock exchange; **une hausse vertigineuse des prix** a staggering increase in prices; **des sommes vertigineuses** absurdly large sums of money **2** *Méd* vertiginous

vertigo [vɛrtigo] **NM** *Vét* (blind) staggers

vertiport [vɛrtipɔr] **NM** *Aviat* heliport

vertisol [vɛrtisɔl] **NM** *Géol* regur (soil), black cotton soil

vertu [vɛrty] **NF 1** *Littéraire (conduite morale)* virtue, virtuousness; **je n'ai aucune v. à ne pas fumer, je n'aime pas ça** I can't claim any credit for not smoking *or Sout* there is nothing admirable in my not smoking, I just don't like it; **le chemin de la v.** the path of righteousness

2 *(qualité)* virtue; **les vertus cardinales** the cardinal virtues; **les vertus théologales** the theological virtues

3 *(propriété)* virtue, property, power; **la camomille a de nombreuses vertus** camomile has many beneficial uses; **avoir des vertus calmantes** to have calming *or* soothing properties; **les vertus thérapeutiques des plantes** the healing properties of plants; *Fig* **réapprenons les vertus de la vie à la campagne** let us rediscover the virtues of country life

4 *Hum (chasteté)* virtue; **défendre/perdre sa v.** to defend/to lose one's virtue

❑ **vertus NFPL** *Rel* Virtues

❑ **en vertu de PRÉP** according to; **en v. des bons principes** following accepted moral principles; **en v. des pouvoirs qui me sont conférés, je...** in accordance with the powers vested in me, I...; **en v. de la loi** according to the law, in accordance with the law, under the law; **en v. de cet arrangement** under (the terms of) this agreement; **en v. de ce contrat, vous nous devez...** under the terms of this contract, you owe us...; **en v. de quoi...** for which reason...; **en v. de quoi il passe d'abord** that's the reason for his going first; **en v. de quoi est-il intervenu?** what gave him the right to intervene?

vertubleu [vɛrtyblø], **vertuchou** [vɛrtyʃu], **vertudieu** [vɛrtydjø] **EXCLAM** *Arch* oddsbodikins!

vertueuse [vɛrtyøz] *voir* **vertueux**

vertueusement [vɛrtɥøzmɑ̃] **ADV** virtuously; **vivre v.** to live virtuously

vertueux, -euse [vɛrtɥø, -øz] **ADJ 1** *(qui a des qualités morales)* virtuous, righteous; *(intentions)* honourable **2** *Vieilli (chaste)* virtuous

vertugadin [vɛrtygadɛ̃] **NM** *Hist* farthingale

verve [vɛrv] **NF 1** *(fougue)* verve, gusto; *(esprit)* wit; **avec v.** with gusto *or* verve; **exercer sa v. contre qn** to use one's wit against sb **2** *Littéraire (créativité)* inspiration; **la v. poétique** poetic talent *or* inspiration

❑ **en verve ADJ être en v.** to be particularly witty; **elle était en v. ce soir-là** she was on top form that night

verveine [vɛrvɛn] **NF 1** *Bot* vervain, verbena; **v. odorante** lemon verbena; **v. officinale** verbena officinalis **2** *(tisane)* verbena tea **3** *(liqueur)* vervain liqueur

vervelle [vɛrvɛl] **NF** *Chasse* varvel, vervel

vervet [vɛrvɛ] **NM** *Zool* vervet (monkey), green monkey

verveuse [vɛrvøz] *voir* **verveux[2]**

verveux[1] [vɛrvø] **NM** *Pêche* hoop net

verveux[2], -euse [vɛrvø, -øz] **ADJ** *Littéraire* animated, lively, spirited

vésanie [vezani] **NF** *Littéraire* vesania, insanity

vesce [vɛs] **NF** *Bot* vetch, tare

vésical, -e, -aux, -ales [vezikal, -o] **ADJ** *Méd* vesical; **calcul v.** bladder stone, *Spéc* vesical calculus

vésicant, -e [vezikɑ̃, -ɑ̃t] **ADJ** *Méd & Pharm* vesicant, vesicatory; **gaz v.** blister gas

vésication [vezikasjɔ̃] **NF** *Méd* vesication

vésicatoire [vezikatwar] *Méd* **ADJ** vesicatory

NM vesicatory; **appliquer un v. à qn** to blister sb

vésiculaire [vezikylɛr] **ADJ** bladder-like, *Spéc* vesicular

vésicule [vezikyl] **NF 1** *Méd (ampoule)* blister, vesicle; *Anat (cavité)* bladder; **v. biliaire/cérébrale** gall/brain bladder; **v. séminale** seminal vesicle **2** *Bot* vesicle, bladder-like cavity *or* cell

vésiculeux, -euse [vezikylø, -øz] **ADJ** *Méd* vesicular, vesiculate

vesou [vəzu] **NM** cane juice

Vespa® [vɛspa] **NF** Vespa®

Vespasien [vɛspazjɛ̃] **NPR** *Antiq* Vespasian

vespasienne [vɛspazjɛn] **NF** *Vieilli* street urinal

vespéral, -e, -aux, -ales [vɛsperal, -o] **ADJ** *Littéraire* evening *(avant n)*, vespertine; **les lueurs vespérales** evening lights, the lights at eventide; **les étoiles vespérales** the vespertine stars

NM *Rel* vesperal

vespertilion [vɛspɛrtiljɔ̃] **NM** *Zool* vespertilio

vespidé [vɛspide] *Entom* **NM** vespid, *Spéc* member of the Vespidae

❑ **vespidés NMPL** vespids, *Spéc* Vespidae

vesprée [vɛspre] **NF** *Belg ou Arch* dusk

vesse [vɛs] **NF** *Fam Vieilli* silent but deadly fart

vesse-de-loup [vɛsdəlu] *(pl* **vesses-de-loup)** **NF** *Bot* puffball

vesser [4] [vese] **VI** *Fam Vieilli* to release a silent but deadly fart

vessie [vesi] **NF 1** *Anat & Zool* bladder; **v. natatoire** air *or* swim bladder, sound; *Fig* **prendre des vessies pour des lanternes** to be easily hoodwinked; **il voudrait nous faire prendre des vessies pour des lanternes** he's trying to pull the wool over our eyes **2** *(sac)* bladder

vessigon [vɛsigɔ̃] **NM** *Vét* wind gall

vestale [vɛstal] **NF 1** *(prêtresse)* vestal virgin **2** *Littéraire (femme chaste)* vestal; *Hum* **ce n'est pas une v.** she's no paragon of virtue *or* no saint

veste [vɛst] **NF** jacket; **v. de bûcheron** lumberjacket; **v. de pyjama** pyjama jacket *or* top; **v. de tailleur** suit jacket; **v. de tweed** tweed jacket; *Fig* **retourner sa v.** to be a turncoat; **tomber la v.** to take off one's jacket; *Fig* to get down to work *or* business; *Fam Fig* **ramasser** *ou* **(se) prendre une v.** *(échouer)* to come unstuck; *(être rejeté)* to get turned down

vestiaire [vɛstjɛr] **NM 1** *(placard)* locker **2** *(dépôt)* cloakroom; **vous avez un v.?** did you have a coat or anything?; **prendre** *ou* **récupérer son v.** to collect one's things *or* belongings from the cloakroom **3** *(pièce)* changing room, *Am* locker room; *(de tribunal)* robing room; **l'arbitre, au v.!** get off, ref!; *Fig* **laisser sa fierté/ses principes au v.** to forget one's pride/one's principles

vestibulaire [vɛstibylɛr] ADJ vestibular

vestibule [vɛstibyl] NM **1** *(d'un bâtiment public, d'une maison)* (entrance) hall, vestibule; *(d'un hôtel)* lobby **2** *Méd* vestibule

vestige [vɛstiʒ] NM *(d'une armée)* remnant; *(d'une ville, d'une société)* vestige; *(d'une croyance, du passé, d'une coutume)* remnant, vestige; *(d'une idée, d'un sentiment)* remnant, trace, vestige; **les derniers vestiges de l'impérialisme** the last remnants *or* traces of imperialism; **quelques vestiges du passé** a few relics of the past; **il ne reste que des vestiges de sa grandeur** only a shadow of his/her former greatness remains; *Archéol* **vestiges humains** human traces

vestimentaire [vɛstimɑ̃tɛr] ADJ clothing *(avant n)*; **dépenses vestimentaires** clothes expenditure, money spent on clothing; **élégance v.** sartorial elegance

veston [vɛstɔ̃] NM jacket

Vésuve [vezyv] NM *Géog* **le V.** (Mount) Vesuvius

vétéciste [vetesist] NMF hybrid biker

vêtement [vɛtmɑ̃] NM **1** *(habit)* piece *or* article *or* item of clothing, *Sout* garment; *(costume distinctif)* dress, garb; **je ne trouve pas mon v.** *(manteau)* I can't find my coat; *(veste)* I can't find my jacket; *(pull)* I can't find my sweater *or Br* jumper; **tu devrais mettre** *ou* **passer un v.** you should put something on; **il fait froid, mets un v. chaud** it's cold, put something warm on; **vêtements** clothes, clothing *(UNCOUNT)*; **des vêtements en loques** tattered clothes, rags; **ils vendent des vêtements ravissants** they sell lovely clothes; **il portait ses vêtements de tous les jours** he was wearing his everyday clothes; **vêtements de détente** leisurewear *(UNCOUNT)*; **vêtements ecclésiastiques** clerical garb *or* dress; **vêtements d'été** summer clothes; **vêtements pour femme** ladieswear *(UNCOUNT)*; **vêtements habillés** formal dress *(UNCOUNT)*; **vêtements d'hiver/d'été** winter/summer clothes; **vêtements pour homme** menswear *(UNCOUNT)*; **vêtements de nuit** nightwear *(UNCOUNT)*; **vêtements de pluie** rainwear *(UNCOUNT)*; **vêtements sacerdotaux** vestments; **vêtements de ski** skiwear *(UNCOUNT)*; **vêtements de sport** sportswear *(UNCOUNT)*; **vêtements de travail** work *or* working clothes; **vêtements de ville** informal clothes

2 *(profession)* **l'industrie du v.** the clothing industry; *Fam* **être dans le v.** to be in the *Br* rag trade *or Am* garment industry

3 *Com* **vêtements dames** *ou* **femmes** ladieswear; **vêtements enfants** childrenswear; **vêtements hommes** menswear

vétéran [veterɑ̃] NM **1** *(soldat)* veteran, old campaigner; *(ancien combattant)* (war) veteran **2** *Fig (personne expérimentée)* veteran, old hand; **un v. de la politique** a veteran political campaigner **3** *Sport* veteran

vétérance [veterɑ̃s] NF veterancy

vétérinaire [veterinɛr] ADJ veterinary; **faire des études vétérinaires** to study veterinary medicine *or* science

NMF vet, *Br* veterinary surgeon, *Am* veterinarian

vététiste [vetetist] NMF mountain biker

vétillard, -e [vetijar, -ard] ADJ *Vieilli* fussy, hair-splitting

vétille [vetij] NF trifle; **perdre son temps à des vétilles** to waste time over trivial details; **se disputer pour des vétilles** to argue over trivialities *or* trivial details; **ce n'est qu'une v.** it's just a trivial detail

vétiller [3] [vetije] VI **1** *(s'occuper à des riens)* to occupy oneself with trifles **2** *(chicaner)* to quibble

vétilleux, -euse [vetijø, -øz] ADJ *Littéraire* fussy, hair-splitting, quibbling

vêtir [44] [vetir] VT **1** *(habiller → enfant, malade)* to dress (**de** in) **2** *(prisonnier, malade)* to clothe, to provide with clothes, *Br* to kit out **3** *Littéraire (revêtir)* to put on, to don

▸**se vêtir** VPR **1** *(emploi réfléchi)* to dress (oneself) (**de** in); **trouver de quoi se v.** to find something to put on **2 en hiver, la campagne se vêt de neige** in winter, the countryside is clothed in snow

vétiver [vetivɛr] NM *Bot* vetiver

veto [veto] NM INV **1** *Pol* veto; **mettre** *ou* **opposer son v. à une mesure** to veto a measure; **exercer son droit de v.** to use one's power of veto; **v. absolu** absolute veto; **v. suspensif** suspensive veto **2** *(interdiction)* **opposer son v. à qch** to forbid *or* to prohibit *or* to veto sth

véto [veto] NM *Fam (vétérinaire)* vet■

vêtu, -e [vety] PP *voir* **vêtir**

ADJ dressed; **être bien/mal v.** to be well/badly dressed; **être chaudement v.** to be warmly dressed; **elle était court vêtue** she was wearing a short skirt; **à demi-v.** half-dressed; **v. de** dressed in, wearing; **un enfant v. d'un blouson** a child wearing a jacket; **une femme toute vêtue de blanc** a woman all in white; **un homme v. de haillons** a man in rags; **professeurs vêtus de leurs toges** professors wearing *or* in their gowns; **toute de soie/noir vêtue** all dressed in silk/black; *Littéraire* **mur v. de lierre** ivy-clad wall, wall covered in ivy

vêture [vetyr] NF **1** *Rel (prise d'habit)* taking of the habit; *(prise de voile)* taking of the veil **2** *Littéraire (vêtements)* clothing*(UNCOUNT)*

vétuste [vetyst] ADJ dilapidated, decrepit; **la pompe était v.** the pump had fallen into disrepair

vétusté [vetyste] NF *(d'un bâtiment)* dilapidated state; *(d'une loi)* obsolescence; **la v. de l'installation électrique est en cause** the poor state of the wiring is to blame

veuf, veuve [vœf, vœv] ADJ **1** *(personne)* **devenir v.** to be widowed, to become a widower; **devenir veuve** to be widowed, to become a widow; **je m'occupe de ma tante qui est veuve** I look after my widowed aunt; **il est v. de plusieurs femmes** he's a widower several times over; *Fig Littéraire* **v. de son innocence** deprived *or* bereft of his innocence

2 *Typ* **ligne veuve** widow

NM,F widower, *f* widow; *Admin* **Madame veuve Dupont** Mrs Dupont *(term of address used on official correspondence to widows)*; **la veuve Dupont** Mrs Dupont *(slightly informal way of referring to a widow)*; *Fig* **veuve joyeuse** merry widow; **veuve de guerre** war widow

❑ **veuve** NF **1** *Orn* widow bird, whydah (bird)

2 *Entom* **veuve d'Australie** redback (spider); **veuve noire** black widow (spider)

3 *Typ* widow

4 *Fam Arch* **la Veuve** the guillotine■

5 *très Fam Hum* **la veuve Poignet** masturbation■

veuille *etc voir* **vouloir**[2]

veule [vøl] ADJ *Littéraire (personne)* spineless, cowardly; *(visage, traits)* weak

veulent *voir* **vouloir**[2]

veulerie [vølri] NF *Littéraire* spinelessness

veut *voir* **vouloir**[2]

veuvage [vœvaʒ] NM *(perte d'un mari)* widowhood; *(perte d'une femme)* widowerhood

veuve [vœv] *voir* **veuf**

veux *voir* **vouloir**[2]

vexant, -e [vɛksɑ̃, -ɑ̃t] ADJ **1** *(blessant → personne)* hurtful; *(→ remarque)* cutting, slighting, hurtful **2** *(contrariant)* annoying; **c'est v.!** how infuriating!

vexateur, -trice [vɛksatœr, -tris] ADJ *Littéraire* hurtful

vexation [vɛksasjɔ̃] NF **1** *(humiliation)* snub, slight, humiliation; **essuyer des vexations** to be snubbed; **être en proie aux vexations de qn** to be constantly being snubbed *or* put down by sb **2** *Vieilli (mauvais traitement)* vexation

vexatoire [vɛksatwar] ADJ vexatious, harassing

vexatrice [vɛksatris] *voir* **vexateur**

vexer [4] [vɛkse] VT **v. qn** to hurt sb's feelings; **je ne voulais pas le v.** I didn't mean to hurt his feelings; **être vexé** to be hurt *or* offended; **être vexé comme un pou** to be extremely upset; **elle est horriblement vexée** she's cut to the quick; **il est vexé de n'avoir pas compris** he's cross because he didn't understand; **elle est vexée que tu ne la croies pas** she feels hurt because you don't believe her

▸**se vexer** VPR to be hurt *or* offended *or* upset, to take offence; **ne te vexe pas, mais...** no offence meant, but...; **se v. facilement** to be easily offended, to be oversensitive; **se v. de qch** to feel hurt *or* to be upset by sth; **il se vexe de tout/pour un rien** he gets upset over everything/over the slightest thing

vexillaire [vɛksilɛr] ADJ *Naut* **signaux vexillaires** flag signals

NM *Antiq* vexillary, standard bearer

vexille [vɛksil] NM **1** *Antiq* vexillum **2** *Orn* vexillum

vexillologie [vɛksilɔlɔʒi] NF vexillology

vexillum [vɛksilɔm] NM *Antiq* vexillum

VF [veɛf] *Cin* NF *(abrév* **version française***)* = indicates that a film is dubbed in French

❑ **en VF** ADJ dubbed in French; **voir un film en VF** to see a film dubbed in French

VGE [veʒeə] NPR *(abrév* **Valéry Giscard d'Estaing***)* Valéry Giscard d'Estaing

VHD [veaʃde] NF *(abrév* **vidéo haute définition***)* HDV

VHF [veaʃɛf] NF *TV & Rad (abrév* **very high frequency***)* VHF

VHS [veaʃɛs] NM *TV (abrév* **video home system***)* VHS

VI [vei] NF *Compta (abrév* **valeur d'inventaire***)* balance sheet value, break-up value

via [vja] PRÉP via, through; **Paris, v. Calais** Paris, via Calais

viabilisation [vjabilizasjɔ̃] NF installation of water, gas and electricity *(for building purposes)*

viabiliser [3] [vjabilize] VT to service; **terrain viabilisé** piece of land with water, gas and electricity installed *(for building purposes)*; **v. une entreprise** to make a business viable

viabilité [vjabilite] NF **1** *(aménagements)* utilities, services **2** *(état d'une route)* practicability **3** *(d'un organisme, d'un projet, d'un fœtus)* viability

viable [vjabl] ADJ **1** *Biol* viable; **avant 24 semaines de gestation, le fœtus n'est pas v.** if born before 24 weeks' gestation the foetus is not viable **2** *(entreprise, projet)* viable, practicable, feasible

viaduc [vjadyk] NM viaduct

via ferrata [vjaferata] NF INV *Sport* via ferrata

viager, -ère [vjaʒe, -ɛr] ADJ life *(avant n)*

NM (life) annuity

❑ **en viager** ADV **placer son argent en v.** to buy an annuity; **acheter/vendre une maison en v.** to buy/to sell a house so as to provide the seller with a life annuity

Viagra® [vjagra] NM *Pharm* Viagra®

viande [vjɑ̃d] NF **1** *Culin* meat; **v. blanche** white meat; **v. de bœuf** beef; **v. de boucherie** fresh meat *(as sold by the butcher)*; **v. de cheval** horsemeat; **v. crue** raw meat; **v. cuite** cooked meat; **v. froide** dish of cold meat; **v. fumée** smoked meat; **v. hachée** minced meat, *Br* mince, *Am* ground meat; **v. de porc** pork; **v. rouge** red meat; **v. salée** cured *or* salted meat; **v. de veau** veal

2 *très Fam (corps)* **amène ta v.!** get your butt *or* carcass over here!; **montrer sa v.** to bare one's flesh; **il y a de la v. soûle dans les rues** the streets are full of drunken bodies; **de la v. froide** *(un cadavre)* a stiff; *(des cadavres)* stiffs

3 *Littéraire (aliment)* nourishment, sustenance; **v. creuse** meagre nourishment

viander [3] [vjɑ̃de] VI *(cerf, daim, chevreuil)* to graze, to feed

▸**se viander** VPR *très Fam* to get smashed up; **ils se sont viandés contre un mur** they smashed into a wall

viandeux, -euse [vjɑ̃dø, -øz] ADJ *Belg* **1** *(charnu → animal)* fleshy **2** *(boucher)* **bovin/bétail v.** beef cow/cattle

viandis [vjɑ̃di] NM *Zool* feeding; **faire son v.** *(cerf, daim, chevreuil)* to graze, to feed

Viandox® [vjɑ̃dɔks] NM = liquid seasoning containing meat essences, ≃ Bovril®

viatique [vjatik] NM **1** *Rel* viaticum

2 *Littéraire (atout)* asset; **il n'a que son savoir pour tout v.** his knowledge is his only asset, his only means to success is his knowledge; **j'avais pour seul v. cette lettre de recommandation** this letter was all I had to recommend me

3 *(soutien)* help; **ces paroles furent pour moi un v.** those words were of invaluable help to me throughout my life

4 *Arch (pour un voyage)* provisions and money (for the journey); **on leur a donné un v. de 200 euros pour leur voyage** we gave them 200 euros for their trip

vibices [vibis] NFPL *Méd (purpura)* vibices

vibord [vibɔr] NM *Naut* sheer strake

vibrage [vibraʒ] NM vibrating; **v. du béton** vibrating of concrete

vibrant, -e [vibrã, -ãt] ADJ **1** (corde, lamelle) vibrating; Ling **consonne vibrante** vibrant consonant **2** (fort → voix, cri) vibrant **3** (émouvant → accueil, discours) stirring; (→ voix) tremulous; **v. de** ringing or echoing with; **il lui a rendu un hommage v.** he paid him/her a warm tribute **4** (sensible → nature, personne, caractère) sensitive
  ◻ **vibrante** NF Ling vibrant

vibraphone [vibrafɔn] NM vibraphone, Am vibraharp

vibraphoniste [vibrafɔnist] NMF vibraphonist

vibrateur [vibratœr] NM **1** Tech vibration generator **2** Constr vibrator

vibratile [vibratil] voir cil

vibration [vibrasjõ] NF **1** (tremblement → d'un moteur, d'une corde, du sol) vibration; (→ d'une voix) quaver, tremor **2** Phys & Électron vibration
  ◻ **vibrations** NFPL vibrations; Fam **il y a de bonnes vibrations ici** you get a good feeling or good vibes from this place

vibrato [vibrato] NM Mus vibrato

vibratoire [vibratwar] ADJ vibratory

vibrer [3] [vibre] VI **1** (trembler → diapason, vitre, plancher, voix) to vibrate; **v. d'émotion** to quiver or to quaver with emotion; **sa voix vibrait de colère** his/her voice was quivering with anger; **faire v. qch** to vibrate sth
  2 Fig **faire v. le cœur de qn** to make sb's heart pound; **faire v. qn** (l'intéresser) to thrill or to stir sb; Fam Hum **la musique expérimentale, ça ne me fait pas v.** I don't really get off on experimental music
  VT to vibrate; **béton vibré** vibrated concrete

vibreur [vibrœr] NM (sonnerie) buzzer; (dispositif) vibrator; (interrupteur de courant) chopper

vibrion [vibrijõ] NM **1** Biol vibrio, bacillus; **v. septique** gas bacillus **2** Fam (personne) fidget

vibrionner [3] [vibrijone] VI Fam to fidget

vibrisse [vibris] NF **1** (chez l'homme) nostril hair **2** (du chat) whisker, Spéc vibrissa

vibromasseur [vibromasœr] NM vibrator

vicaire [vikɛr] NM Rel (auxiliaire → d'un curé) assistant priest; (→ d'un évêque, du pape) vicar; **Grand V., V. général** vicar-general; **v. apostolique** vicar apostolic; **le v. du Christ** the Vicar of Christ

vicarial, -e, -aux, -ales [vikarjal, -o] ADJ Rel (fonction) of a curate

vicariance [vikarjãs] NF vicariousness

vicariant, -e [vikarjã, -ãt] ADJ vicarious

vicariat [vikarja] NM Rel **1** (fonction) curacy **2** (territoire) vicariate

vice [vis] NM **1** (le mal) vice; **le v. et la vertu** vice and virtue; Fam Hum **mais c'est du v.!** it's sheer perversion!
  2 (sexuel) **le v.** perverse tendencies; **un v. contre nature** an unnatural tendency; **vivre dans le v.** to lead a life of vice
  3 (moral) vice; **avoir tous les vices** to have all the vices; **on ne lui connaît aucun v.** he/she has no known vice; **il a le v. de la boisson** drinking is his vice; **v. solitaire** masturbation, self-abuse; Littéraire **bourbier du v.** sink of iniquity
  4 Hum (travers) vice
  5 (défaut) & Com & Jur defect, flaw; **v. apparent** conspicuous defect; **v. caché** hidden or latent defect; Jur **v. du consentement** defect of consent; **v. de construction** structural fault; Jur **v. dirimant** nullifying defect; **v. de fabrication** manufacturing defect; Jur **v. de forme** legal technicality; (dans un contrat) flaw; Jur **annulé pour v. de forme** annulled because of a mistake in the drafting; Com **v. inhérent** inherent vice; **v. de prononciation** faulty pronunciation; Com **v. rédhibitoire** material defect
  6 Anat **v. de conformation** congenital defect

vice- [vis] PRÉF vice-

vice-amiral [visamiral] (pl **vice-amiraux** [-o]) NM vice-admiral

vice-chancelier [visʃãsəlje] (pl **vice-chanceliers**) NM vice-chancellor

vice-consul [viskõsyl] (pl **vice-consuls**) NM vice-consul

vice-consulat [viskõsyla] (pl **vice-consulats**) NM vice-consulate

vice-gerant, -e [visʒerã, -ãt] (mpl **vice-gérants,** fpl **vice-gérantes**) NM,F deputy manager

vicelard, -e [vislar, -ard] très Fam ADJ **1** (dépravé) kinky, Br pervy **2** (perfide) crafty▪, sneaky▪; **une question vicelarde** a devious question▪
  NM,F **1** (personne cruelle) crafty or sneaky person▪ **2** (pervers) perv; **un vieux v.** a dirty old man, an old lecher; **petite vicelarde!** you little tramp!

Vicence [visãs] NM Vicenza

vicennal, -e, -aux, -ales [visɛnal, -o] ADJ vicennial

vice-présidence [visprezidãs] (pl **vice-présidences**) NF (d'un État) vice-presidency; (d'un congrès, d'une entreprise) vice-chairmanship

vice-président, -e [visprezidã, -ãt] (mpl **vice-présidents,** fpl **vice-présidentes**) NM,F (d'un État) vice-president; (d'un congrès, d'une entreprise) vice-chairman, f vice-chairwoman, vice-chairperson

vice-recteur [visrɛktœr] (pl **vice-recteurs**) NM Br ≃ pro-vice-chancellor, Am ≃ vice-president

vice-roi [visrwa] (pl **vice-rois**) NM viceroy

vice-royauté [visrwajote] (pl **vice-royautés**) NF viceroyalty

vicésimal, -e, -aux, -ales [visezimal, -o] ADJ vigesimal, vicenary

vice versa [vis(e)vɛrsa] ADV vice versa

Vichy [viʃi] NM **le gouvernement de V.** the Vichy government; **la France de V.** Vichy France

Culture
VICHY
Vichy was the seat of the French government under Maréchal Pétain from 1940 to 1944, during the German occupation. Pétain's right-wing traditionalist and authoritarian regime extolled the virtues of a "new order" and a "National Revolution" which would bring back the values of "Work, Family and Fatherland". The Vichy government collaborated with the Germans and deported French Jews after 1942. Reduced to a puppet regime after the German invasion of the free zone in November 1942, the government collapsed after the Allied victory.

vichy [viʃi] NM **1** Tex gingham; **une jupe en v. rouge et blanc** a red and white gingham skirt **2** (eau) Vichy (water); **un v. fraise** = a glass of Vichy water with strawberry syrup **3** Culin vichy; **carottes v.** carrots vichy (glazed with butter and sugar)
  NF bottle of Vichy water

vichyssois, -e [viʃiswa, -az] ADJ of/from Vichy
  ◻ **Vichyssois, -e** NM,F **1** = inhabitant of or person from Vichy **2** Hist Vichyist
  ◻ **vichyssoise** NF Culin vichyssoise (soup)

vichyste [viʃist] ADJ of the Vichy government
  NMF Vichy government supporter, Vichyist

viciable [visjabl] ADJ Littéraire vitiable

viciateur, -trice [visjatœr, -tris] ADJ Littéraire corrupting

viciation [visjasjõ] NF (de principes moraux etc) corruption, Sout vitiation; (de l'air) pollution, contamination; (du sang) thinness; Jur (d'un contrat) vitiation, invalidation

viciatrice [visjatris] voir **viciateur**

vicié, -e [visje] ADJ **1** (pollué → air, sang) polluted, contaminated **2** Littéraire (faussé → raisonnement, débat) warped, vitiated **3** Jur vitiated

vicier [9] [visje] VT **1** (polluer → air, sang) to pollute, to contaminate **2** Littéraire (dénaturer → esprit, qualité) to corrupt, to taint; (→ goût) to corrupt; (→ relation, situation) to make worse **3** Jur to vitiate, to invalidate

vicieuse [visjøz] voir **vicieux**

vicieusement [visjøzmã] ADV **1** (lubriquement) lecherously, licentiously **2** (incorrectement) faultily, wrongly **3** (méchamment) maliciously, nastily

vicieux, -euse [visjø, -øz] ADJ **1** (pervers → livre, film) obscene; (→ regard) depraved; (→ personne) lecherous, depraved; **il faut vraiment être v. pour trouver ça drôle** you have to have a pretty warped sense of humour to find that funny
  2 (trompeur → personne) underhand, sly; (→ coup, balle) nasty, treacherous; (→ calcul) misleading
  3 (animal) vicious

4 (incorrect → expression, prononciation, position) incorrect, wrong
  NM,F (homme) lecher, pervert; **un vieux v.** a dirty old man, an old lecher; **petite vicieuse!** you little slut or tramp!

vicinal, -e, -aux, -ales [visinal, -o] ADJ voir **chemin**
  NM Belg suburban tram

vicinalité [visinalite] NF **1** (d'une route) local status **2** (réseau routier) network of local byroads

vicissitude [visisityd] NF Littéraire (succession) vicissitude
  ◻ **vicissitudes** NFPL **1** (difficultés) tribulations; **après bien des vicissitudes** after many trials and tribulations, after many hard knocks **2** (événements) vicissitudes, ups and downs; **les vicissitudes de la vie** ou **de l'existence** the ups and downs or trials and tribulations of life

vicomtal, -e, -aux, -ales [vikõtal, -o] ADJ (d'un vicomte) of a viscount; (d'une vicomtesse) of a viscountess; (d'une vicomté) of a viscountcy or viscounty

vicomte [vikõt] NM viscount

vicomté [vikõte] NF **1** (titre) viscountcy, viscounty **2** (terrain) viscounty

vicomtesse [vikõtɛs] NF viscountess

victime [viktim] NF **1** (d'un accident, d'un meurtre) victim, casualty; **les victimes du crash** the victims of the crash; **les victimes de la route** the road accident victims; **accident de la route, trois victimes** car crash, three casualties; **l'accident a fait trois victimes** three people died in the accident; **les victimes ont été emmenées à l'hôpital** the victims were taken to (the) hospital; **un nouveau meurtre porte à 15 le nombre des victimes** a new killing brings the number of victims to 15; **les victimes du Sida** Aids victims; **les victimes de la dictature** the victims of the dictatorship
  2 Rel (sacrificial) victim
  3 (bouc émissaire) scapegoat, victim
  4 (d'un préjudice) victim; **être la v. d'un escroc** to fall prey to or to be the victim of a con man; **être la v. d'un système d'imposition** to be badly hit by a system of taxation; **être v. d'un malentendu** to labour under a misconception; **être v. d'hallucinations** to suffer from delusions; **v. par ricochet** indirect victim

victimisation [viktimizasjõ] NF victimization

victimiser [viktimize] VT to victimize

victimologie [viktimolɔʒi] NF victimology

victoire [viktwar] NF **1** (fait de gagner → bataille, compétition) victory, winning; (→ dans une entreprise) victory, success (UNCOUNT); **chanter** ou **crier v.** to claim victory
  2 (résultat → militaire) victory; (→ sportif) victory, win; (→ dans une entreprise) victory, success; **v. aux points** win on points; **après leurs deux victoires en Coupe du monde** after their two wins or after winning twice in the World Cup; **remporter une v. (sur qn)** to gain a victory (over sb); Fig **remporter une v. sur soi-même** to triumph over oneself; **une v. à la Pyrrhus** a Pyrrhic victory
  3 (déesse) **V.** Victory, Victoria

Victoria [viktɔrja] NPR (reine) **la reine V.** Queen Victoria
  NM **1** (État d'Australie) **le V.** Victoria **2** **le lac V.** Lake Victoria

victoria [viktɔrja] NM Bot victoria
  NF Transp victoria

victorien, -enne [viktɔrjɛ̃, -ɛn] ADJ Victorian

victorieuse [viktɔrjøz] voir **victorieux**

victorieusement [viktɔrjøzmã] ADV victoriously

victorieux, -euse [viktɔrjø, -øz] ADJ Sport victorious, winning (avant n); Pol victorious, winning (avant n), successful; Mil victorious; (air) triumphant; **sortir v. d'un combat** to come out victorious

victuailles [viktɥaj] NFPL food (UNCOUNT), provisions, Sout victuals

vidage [vidaʒ] NM **1** (d'un récipient) emptying **2** (de poissons) gutting, cleaning; (de volailles) drawing **3** Fam (d'une personne) kicking out **4** Ordinat term (→ to (take a) dump; **v. sur disque/de la mémoire** disk/core dump; **v. de mémoire** storage or memory dump; **bande de v.** dump tape; **gestionnaire de v.** dumper; **v. d'écran (sur imprimante)** screen dump

Vidal [vidal] NM le 'V.' = dictionary used by doctors as a reference book on medicines

vidame [vidam] NM Hist vidame, = secular deputy of bishop or abbot

vidamé [vidame] NM Hist vidameship

vidamie [vidami] NF Hist vidameship

vidange [vidãʒ] NF **1** (d'un récipient, d'un réservoir) emptying; (d'un carter à huile, d'une fosse septique) draining, emptying; (d'une chaudière) blowing off

2 (dispositif) drain, (waste) outlet; **v. du carter** oil-pan drain or outlet

3 Aut oil change; **faire la v.** to change the oil; **v.-graissage** oil change and lubrication

4 Agr timber hauling or skidding

5 Belg (verre consigné) returnable empties

◻ **vidanges** NFPL **1** (eaux usées) sewage (UNCOUNT), liquid waste (UNCOUNT)

2 Can (ordures ménagères) refuse (UNCOUNT), Br rubbish (UNCOUNT), Am garbage (UNCOUNT)

◻ **de vidange** ADJ (huile, système, tuyau) waste (avant n); **bouchon de v.** sump plug; (de radiateur) draining plug

◻ **en vidange** ADJ **tonneau en v.** broached cask

vidanger [17] [vidãʒe] VT **1** (huile, eaux) to empty (out), to drain off; (fosse septique, radiateur, carter à huile) to drain; (chaudière) to blow off **2** Aut (huile) to change **3** Aviat to defuel

vidangeur [vidãʒœr] NM **1** (qui vidange les fosses septiques) septic tank emptier **2** Can Fam (éboueur) Br dustman■, Am garbage collector■

vidangeuse [vidãʒøz] NF sewage tanker

vide [vid] ADJ **1** (sans contenu) empty; (case de document) blank; **tasse à demi v.** half-empty cup; **bouteilles vides** empty bottles, empties; **un espace v.** (entre deux objets) an empty space; (sur un document) a blank space; **une pièce v.** an empty or unfurnished room; **un regard v.** a vacant stare; **des phrases vides** empty or meaningless words; **v.** devoid of; **des rues vides de gens** empty streets; **la ville est v. de ses habitants** the town is empty (of its inhabitants); **des remarques vides de sens** meaningless remarks, remarks devoid of meaning; Com **v. en retour** empty on return

2 (sans occupant) empty; **une maison v.** an empty house

3 (sans intérêt → vie) empty

4 (dénudé → mur) bare, empty; **l'appartement est encore très v.** (peu meublé) the Br flat or Am apartment is still very bare

NM **1** Astron le v. (empty) space, the void; **un astronaute qui évolue dans le v.** an astronaut floating in the void

2 (néant) space; **regarder dans le v.** to stare into space; **c'est comme si je parlais dans le v.** it's like talking to a brick wall; **faire des promesses dans le v.** to make empty promises

3 Phys vacuum; **faire le v.** (dans un vase clos) to create a vacuum; **faire le v. dans une ampoule** to evacuate air from a bulb; Fig **faire le v.** (se ressourcer) to switch off; **faire le v. dans son esprit** to make one's mind go blank; **faire le v. autour de soi** to drive all one's friends away; **faire le v. autour de qn** to isolate sb

4 (distance qui sépare du sol) (empty) space; **la maison est construite, en partie, au-dessus du v.** part of the house is built over a drop; **avoir peur du v.** to be scared of heights; **être attiré par le v.** to feel the urge to jump; **pendre dans le v.** to hang in mid-air; **tomber dans le v.** to fall into (empty) space

5 (trou → entre deux choses) space, gap; (→ entre les mots ou les lignes d'un texte) space, blank; (→ dans un emploi du temps) gap

6 Fig (lacune) void, gap, blank; **son départ a laissé un grand v. dans ma vie** he/she left a gaping void in my life when he/she went; Jur **v. juridique** legal vacuum; **il y a un v. juridique en la matière** the law is not specific on this matter

7 Fig (manque d'intérêt) emptiness, void; **le v. de l'existence** the emptiness of life; **le v. de sa conversation** the inanity of his/her conversation

8 Constr **v. d'air** airspace; **v. sanitaire** ventilation or crawl space

◻ **à vide** ADJ **1** (hors fonctionnement) no-load (avant n); (batterie) discharged; **courant/pertes à v.** no-load current/losses; **poids à v.** unladen

weight **2** (sans air) **cellule/tube/cuve à v.** vacuum photocell/tube/tank **3** Mus **corde à v.** open string ADV **marcher à v.** (machine) to run light or without load; **le moteur tourne à v.** the engine's ticking over or idling; **les usines tournent à v.** the factories are running but not producing; **rouler à v.** (bus) to have no passengers; **le train est parti à v.** the train left empty; **camion revenant à v.** truck returning empty; **il est difficile de réfléchir à v.** it's not easy to think without any data or with nothing to go on

◻ **sous vide** ADJ vacuum (avant n); **condensateur/interrupteur sous v.** vacuum capacitor/switch ADV **emballé sous v.** vacuum-packed

vidé, -e [vide] ADJ **1** (volaille) drawn, cleaned; (poisson) gutted; **vendre des poulets vidés** to sell chickens without giblets **2** Fam (épuisé) drained, dead beat; **après le tournage, toute l'équipe était vidée** when the filming was over, the whole crew felt drained

NM Belg Culin chicken vol-au-vent

vidéaste [videast] NMF video maker

vide-bouteille [vidbutɛj] (pl **vide-bouteilles**) NM **1** (siphon) siphon (for emptying bottles) **2** (pavillon de jardin) ≃ gazebo, summer house

vide-cave [vidkav] (pl **vide-caves**) NM pump (for pumping water out of cellars)

vide-grenier [vidgrənje] NM INV second-hand goods sale, Br ≃ car boot sale, Am ≃ yard sale

videlle [vidɛl] NF **1** Naut darn **2** (dénoyauteur) fruit stoner

vidéo [video] ADJ INV video (avant n); **caméra/cassette v.** video camera/cassette

NF **1** (technique) video (recording); (cassette) video, videotape; **faire de la v.** to make videos; **v. à la demande** video-on-demand, VOD; **v. de démonstration** demo (video); **v. d'entreprise** corporate video; **v. fixe** video still; **v. institutionnelle** corporate video; **v. numérique** digital video; **v. pirate** pirate video; **v. presque à la demande** near video-on-demand, NVOD; **v. promotionnelle** promotional video **2** Ordinat **v. inverse** ou **inversée** reverse video

vidéocassette [videokasɛt] NF video cassette, video

vidéoclip [videoklip] NM (music) video

vidéoclub [videoklœb] NM videoclub

vidéocommunication [videokɔmynikasjɔ̃] NF video communication

vidéocomposite [videokɔ̃pozit] ADJ Électron **signal v.** videocomposite signal

vidéoconférence [videokɔ̃ferãs] NF (concept) videoconferencing; (conférence) videoconference

vidéodiagnostic [videodjagnɔstik] NM Méd video diagnostics (singulier)

vidéodisque [videodisk] NM videodisc

vidéofréquence [videofrekãs] NF video frequency

vidéogramme [videogram] NM videogram

vidéographie [videografi] NF videography; **v. interactive** Videotex®; **v. diffusée** ≃ Teletext®; **v. interactive** ≃ Viewdata®

vidéographique [videografik] ADJ videographic

vidéolecteur [videolɛktœr] NM videoplayer

vidéophone [videofɔn] NM videophone, viewphone

vidéoprojecteur [videoprɔʒɛktœr] NM video projector

vidéoprojection [videoprɔʒɛksjɔ̃] NF video projection

vidéoquestionnaire [videokɛstjɔnɛr] NM (par Minitel®) video questionnaire

vide-ordures [vidɔrdyr] NM INV Br rubbish or Am garbage chute

vidéosurveillance [videosyrvejãs] NF video surveillance

vidéotex [videotɛks] NM Videotex®, Viewdata®; **v. diffusé** Teletext®

vidéothèque [videotɛk] NF video library; (personnelle) video collection

vidéotransmission [videotrãsmisjɔ̃] NF video transmission

vidéovente [videovãt] NF video selling

vide-poches [vidpɔʃ] NM INV **1** (meuble) tidy **2** (de voiture) storage tray; (dans la porte) door pocket, map pocket

vide-pomme [vidpɔm] (pl **vide-pommes**) NM apple corer

vide-poubelles [vidpubɛl] NM INV Belg Br rubbish or Am garbage chute

vider [3] [vide] VT **1** (le contenu de → seau, verre, sac) to empty (out); (→ poche, valise) to empty (out); (→ pièce, tiroir) to empty, to clear out; (→ baignoire) to let the water out of, to empty; (→ tonneau, étang) to empty, to drain; (→ chaudière) to blow off; **v. les ordures** to put out the Br rubbish or Am garbage; **v. un sac de riz dans un pot** to empty a bag of rice into a pot; **il vida le tiroir par terre** he emptied the contents of the drawer (out) onto the floor; **vide le vase dans l'évier** empty the vase into the sink; **v. son chargeur** to empty one's magazine; **la chaleur a entièrement vidé la ville** the heat has completely emptied the city; **partir en vidant la caisse** to make off with the takings; **v. les poches de qn** to empty sb's pockets; (sujet: voleur) to pick sb's pockets; **v. une maison de ses meubles** to empty a house of its furniture, to clear the furniture from a house; **v. les lieux** to vacate the premises; **le juge a fait v. la salle** the judge ordered the court (to be) cleared; Fig **v. l'abcès** to clear the air, to make a clean breast of things; Fig **v. son cœur** to pour out one's feelings; Fig **v. son sac** to get things off one's chest, to unburden oneself

2 (le milieu de → pomme) to core; (→ carcasse) to eviscerate; (→ volaille) to empty, to clean (out); (→ poisson) to gut

3 (boire) to drain; **v. son verre** to drain one's glass; **vide ton verre!** (finis de boire) drink up!; **v. une bouteille** to empty a bottle; **nous avons vidé une bouteille à deux** we downed a bottle between the two of us; **v. les fonds de bouteille** to drink the dregs

4 Fam (épuiser) to drain, to wipe out; **ce cross m'a vidé** that cross-country race has just about finished me off

5 (mettre fin à) to settle (once and for all); **v. une vieille querelle** to settle an old dispute

6 Jur **v. un délibéré** to give a verdict after deliberation

7 Fam (renvoyer) to throw or to kick out; **v. qn** (employé) to fire or Br to sack sb; (client) to throw sb out, Am to bounce sb; (élève) to throw or to chuck sb out; **se faire v.** (d'une pièce) to be sent out■; (d'un bar) to be chucked or thrown out; (d'un collège) to be expelled■; (être renvoyé) to get fired, Br to get the sack

8 Ordinat to dump; **v. la corbeille** to empty the waste basket or Am the trash; **v. l'écran** to clear the screen

9 Équitation **v. les arçons** ou **étriers** to take a tumble (off one's horse); **se faire v.** to be thrown

▸**se vider** VPR **1** (contenu) to empty or to drain (out); **la baignoire est en train de se v.** the bath is emptying out, the bathwater is draining away; **l'eau du réservoir se vide ensuite dans une fosse** the water in the reservoir then drains or flows out into a ditch; **la locution s'est peu à peu vidée de son sens** the expression has gradually lost its meaning

2 (salle, ville) to empty; **le stylo s'est vidé dans mon sac** the pen has leaked inside my bag; **se v. de son sang** to bleed to death

videur, -euse [vidœr, -øz] NM,F (de volaille) cleaner

NM (de boîte de nuit) bouncer

vide-vite [vidvit] NM INV emergency draining device

vidicon [vidikɔ̃] NM TV Vidicon®

vidimer [3] [vidime] VT Admin to attest, to authenticate

vidimus [vidimys] NM Admin (acte certifié conforme) vidimus, attested copy

vidoir [vidwar] NM (d'un vide-ordures) mouth

viduité [vidɥite] NF Jur viduity; (d'une femme) widowhood; (d'un homme) widowerhood; **délai de v.** = time a widow or widower must wait before remarrying

vidure [vidyr] NF **1** (de volaille) entrails; (de poisson) guts **2 vidures de poubelle** Br dustbin rubbish, Am garbage-can trash

vie [vi] NF **1** Biol life; **la v. animale/végétale** animal/plant life; **durée de v.** lifespan

2 (existence) life; **il a eu la v. sauve** he has been spared; **laisser la v. sauve à qn** to spare sb's life; **je lui dois la v.** I owe him/her my life; **donner la v. à un enfant** to give birth to a child; **mettre sa v. en danger** to put one's life in

danger; **risquer sa v.** to risk one's life; **perdre la v.** to lose one's life; **ôter la v. à qn** to take sb's life; **revenir à la v.** to come back to life; **ramener qn à la v.** to bring sb back to life; **sauver la v. de qn** to save sb's life; **Fig tu me sauves la v.!** you're a life-saver!; **au début de sa v.** at the beginning of his/her life; **à la fin de sa v.** at the end of his/her life, late in life; **une fois dans sa v.** once in a lifetime; **de sa v., elle n'avait vu un tel sans-gêne** she'd never seen such a complete lack of consideration; **de toute ma v., je n'ai jamais entendu chose pareille!** I've never heard such a thing in all my life!; **l'œuvre de toute une v.** a lifetime's work; **il promit de lui rester fidèle pour la v.** he promised to be faithful to her for life; **à Julie, pour la v.** to Julie, forever or for ever; **avoir la v. devant soi** (ne pas être pressé) to have all the time in the world; (être jeune) to have one's whole life in front of one; **être entre la v. et la mort** to be hovering between life and death, to be at death's door; **c'est une question de v. ou de mort** it's a matter of life and death; **il y va de sa v.** his/her life is at stake; **passer de v. à trépas** to pass away, to depart this life; **la v. continue** life goes on; **à la v. à la mort** for life (and beyond the grave); **entre eux, c'est à la v., à la mort** they'd die for each other; **Presse La V.** = weekly Catholic magazine

3 (personne) life; **son rôle est de sauver des vies** he/she is there to save lives

4 (entrain) life; **mettre un peu de v. dans** to liven up; **donner de la v. à une conversation/une réunion** to liven up or enliven or animate a conversation/a meeting; **plein de v.** (ressemblant) true to life, lifelike; (énergique) lively, full of life; **un enfant, c'est plein de v.!** children are so full of life!

5 (partie de l'existence) life; **v. privée** private life; **la v. affective/intellectuelle/sexuelle** love/intellectual/sex life; **v. politique/professionnelle** political/professional life; **entrer dans la v. active** to start working; **la v. associative** community life

6 (façon de vivre → d'une personne, d'une société) life, lifestyle, way of life; (→ des animaux) life; **la v. des abeilles/de l'entreprise** the life of bees/of the company; **la v. des volcans** the evolution of volcanoes; **la v. en Australie** the Australian lifestyle or way of life; **dans la v., l'important c'est de...** the important thing in life is to...; **faire sa v. avec qn** to settle down with sb; **avoir la v. dure** (sujet: personne, mauvaise herbe) to be tough (as old boots), to be hard to kill or to get rid of; (sujet: superstitions, préjugés) to be hard to kill off or to get rid of; **faire ou mener la v. dure à qn, rendre la v. dure à qn** to make life difficult for sb; **il lui a fait une de ces vies!** he gave him/her hell!; **rater sa v.** to make a mess of one's life; **refaire sa v.** to start afresh or all over again; **changer de v.** to change one's (way of) life; (faire amende honorable) to mend one's ways, to turn over a new leaf; Fam **sa v. est fichue** he's/she's finished; **c'est la v.!, ainsi va la v.!, la v. est ainsi faite!** such is or that's life!; **je connais la v.** I've seen something of life; **regarder la v. en face** to look life in the face; **elle veut mener sa v. comme elle l'entend** she wants to lead her life as she sees fit; Fam Fig **mener une v. de bâton de chaise** ou **de patachon** to lead a riotous life; **v. de bohème** bohemian life; Fig **mener une v. de chanoine** to live the life of Riley; **avoir une v. sédentaire** to have a sedentary lifestyle or (way of) life; Fam **une v. de chien** a dog's life; **ce n'est pas une v.!** I don't call that living!; **c'est la belle v.** ou **la v. de château!** this is the life!; Fam **faire la v.** to live it up; **mener joyeuse v.** to lead a merry life; **femme de mauvaise v.** loose woman

7 (biographie) life; **il a écrit une v. de Flaubert** he wrote a life or biography of Flaubert; **raconter sa v.** to tell one's life story

8 (conditions économiques) (cost of) living; **dans ce pays, la v. n'est pas chère** prices are very low in this country; **le coût de la v.** the cost of living

9 Rel life; **la v. éternelle** everlasting life; **la v. ici-bas** this life; **la v. terrestre** life on earth; **dans cette v. comme dans l'autre** in this life as in the next

10 Tech life; **à courte v.** short-lived; **à longue v.** long-lived; **v. d'un neutron** neutron lifetime; Mktg **v. économique** (d'un produit) economic life; **v. moyenne** mean life; Électron **v. de surface** surface lifetime; **v. utile** service life

□ **à vie** ADJ for life, life (avant n); **amis à v.** friends for life; **président à v.** life president; **membre à v.** life member ADV for life; **nommé à v.** appointed for life

□ **en vie** alive, living; **être toujours en v.** to be still alive or breathing

□ **sans vie** ADJ (corps) lifeless, inert; (œuvre) lifeless, dull

'La Vie, mode d'emploi' Perec 'Life: A User's Manual'

'Une Vie' Maupassant 'A Woman's Life'

'Vie des hommes illustres' Plutarque 'Plutarch's Lives' or 'Parallel Lives'

'La Vie est un long fleuve tranquille' Chatiliez 'Life Is a Long, Quiet River'

Allusion

La vie est un long fleuve tranquille

This enormously successful French film, made by Étienne Chatilliez (1987), tells the story of a respectable, churchgoing bourgeois French family. They would like to feel that, as the title says, "Life is a long quiet river", but instead they are subjected to all sorts of comical shocks and dramas. The film title is used ironically, to comment on a frenzied situation where we are at the mercy of circumstances. The expression can be varied, and different words substituted.

---

vieil [vjɛj] voir **vieux**

vieillard [vjɛjar] NM old man; **les vieillards** old people, the old, the aged

'Suzanne et les vieillards' Tintoretto 'Susanna and the Elders'

vieillarde [vjɛjard] NF Littéraire old woman

vieille [vjɛj] voir **vieux**

Vieille-Castille [vjɛjkastij] NF **la V.** Old Castile

vieillerie [vjɛjri] NF **1** (objet) old thing **2** (idée) **qui s'intéresse à ces vieilleries?** who's interested in those stale ideas?

vieillesse [vjɛjɛs] NF **1** (d'une personne) old age; **avoir une v. heureuse** to be happy in old age; **pendant sa v.** in his/her old age; **mourir de v.** to die of old age **2** Littéraire (d'un bijou, d'un vase) age **3** (personnes) **la v.** old people, the old, the aged

vieilli, -e [vjeji] ADJ **1** (démodé) old-fashioned; (mot, expression) old-fashioned, dated **2** (vieux) **je l'ai trouvé très v.** I thought he'd aged a lot

vieillir [32] [vjejir] VI **1** (personne) to age, to be getting old; **tout le monde vieillit** we all grow old; **je veux v. dans cette maison** I want to spend my old age in this house; **bien v.** to grow old gracefully; **il a mal vieilli** he hasn't aged well; **les soucis l'ont fait v. de dix ans** anxiety has put ten years on him

2 (paraître plus vieux) **il a vieilli de vingt ans** he looks twenty years older; **tu ne vieillis pas** you never seem to look any older

3 (vin, fromage) to age, to mature; **faire v. du fromage en cave/du vin en fût** to mature cheese in a cellar/wine in a cask; **l'argent vieillit bien** silver ages well

4 (usage, mot) to become obsolete or antiquated or out of date; (technique) to become outmoded; **ce mot a vieilli** this word is obsolescent; **cette chanson/construction n'a pas vieilli** this song/building has stood the test of time or hasn't dated; **la pièce a beaucoup vieilli** the play seems very dated; **ce film vieillit mal** the movie doesn't stand the test of time

VT **1** (rendre vieux → personne) to make old, to

age; **les soucis l'ont vieilli** worry has aged him

2 (vin, fromage) to age, to mature; (métal) to age-harden

3 (meubles) to distress; **pour v. un peu la photo** to age the photo a little

4 v. qn (sujet: vêtement, couleur) to make sb seem older; (sujet: personne) **vous me vieillissez!** you're making me older than I am!; **le noir te vieillit** black makes you look older; **c'est fou ce que les cheveux longs la vieillissent!** long hair makes her look a lot older!

►**se vieillir** VPR (en apparence) to make oneself look older; (en mentant) to lie about one's age (by pretending to be older)

vieillissant, -e [vjejisã, -ãt] ADJ ageing; **des techniques vieillissantes** techniques that are being superseded

vieillissement [vjejismã] NM **1** (naturel) ageing, the ageing process; **le v. d'un réacteur/d'un vin/d'une population** the ageing of a reactor/of a wine/of a population; **les signes qui trahissent le v.** the telltale signs of age or of the ageing process; **retarder le v. de la peau** to slow down the ageing process of the skin

2 (technique) ageing; (de meubles) distressing; **v. au four/naturel/rapide** furnace/natural/quick ageing

3 (d'un fromage, d'un vin) ageing, maturing

vieillot, -otte [vjejo, -ɔt] ADJ old-fashioned

vièle [vjɛl] NF Mus = any stringed instrument sounded by a bow or wheel

vielle [vjɛl] NF **v. (à roue)** hurdy-gurdy

vieller [4] [vjele] VI to play the hurdy-gurdy

vielleur, -euse [vjɛlœr, -øz], **vielleux, -euse** [vjɛlø, -øz] NM,F hurdy-gurdy player

'Le Vielleur au chien' La Tour 'The Hurdy-Gurdy Player with a Dog'

viendra etc voir **venir**

Vienne [vjɛn] NM **1** (en Autriche) Vienna; **le congrès de V.** the Congress of Vienna **2** (en France → ville) Vienne

NF **la V.** (rivière) the (River) Vienne; (département) Vienne

vienne etc voir **venir**

viennois, -e [vjɛnwa, -az] ADJ **1** (d'Autriche) Viennese **2** (de France) of/from Vienne

□ **Viennois, -e** NM,F **1** (en Autriche) = inhabitant of or person from Vienna **2** (en France) = inhabitant of or person from Vienne

viennoiserie [vjɛnwazri] NF **1** (gâteaux) = pastries made with sweetened dough (croissant, brioche etc) **2** (magasin) = shop selling pastries made with sweetened dough (croissant, brioche etc)

vient etc voir **venir**

Vierge [vjɛrʒ] NF **1** Rel **la (Sainte) V., la V. (Marie)** the Virgin (Mary), the Blessed Virgin **2** Astron Virgo **3** Astrol Virgo; **être V.** to be Virgo or a Virgoan

vierge [vjɛrʒ] ADJ **1** (personne) virgin; **il/elle est encore v.** he's/she's still a virgin; **une fille v.** a virgin

2 (vide → cahier, feuille) blank, clean; (→ casier judiciaire) clean; (→ pellicule, film) unexposed; (→ cassette, ligne, espace) blank; (→ disquette) blank

3 (inexploité → sol, terre) virgin; **de la neige v.** fresh snow

4 (sans additif) **minerai v.** native ore; **métal v.** virgin metal

5 Littéraire (pur) pure, unsullied, uncorrupted; **un cœur v.** a pure heart; **v. de** devoid of, innocent of

NF (femme) virgin; Fam **jouer les vierges effarouchées** to go all squeamish; Beaux-Arts **une V. à l'enfant** a Madonna and child

'Vierge en majesté' 'Virgin in Majesty'

Viêt-nam [vjɛtnam] NM **le V.** Vietnam; **vivre au V.** to live in Vietnam; **aller au V.** to go to Vietnam; **le Nord/Sud V.** North/South Vietnam; **un ancien du V.** a Vietnam veteran

vietnamien, -enne [vjɛtnamjɛ̃, -ɛn] ADJ Vietnamese

NM (langue) Vietnamese

▫ **Vietnamien, -enne** NM,F Vietnamese; **les Vietnamiens** the Vietnamese; **V. du Nord/Sud** North/South Vietnamese

VIEUX, VIEILLE [vjø, vjɛj]

vieil is used before masculine singular nouns beginning with a vowel or h mute.

ADJ **1** *(âgé)* old; **sa vieille mère** her old *or* aged mother; **un vieil homme** an old *or* elderly man; **une vieille femme** an old *or* elderly woman; **les vieilles gens** old people, elderly people, the elderly; **un v. cheval/chêne** an old horse/oak; **être v.** to be old; **il n'est pas bien v.** he's not very old, he's still young; **50 ans, ce n'est pas v.!** 50 isn't old!; **devenir v.** to grow old, to get old; **vivre v.** *(personne, animal)* to live to be old, to live to a ripe old age; **se faire v.** to be getting on (in years), to be getting old; **ma voiture commence à se faire vieille** my car's starting to get a bit old; **pour ses v. jours** for one's old age; **je deviens frileux sur mes v. jours** I feel the cold more with age; **être moins/plus v. que** to be younger/older than; **le plus v. des deux** the older *or* elder (of the two); **le plus v. des trois** the eldest *or* oldest of the three; **faire v.** to look old; **elle fait moins vieille que ça** she looks younger than that; **elle fait plus vieille que son âge** she looks older than she really is; **je me sens v.** I feel old; **être v. avant l'âge** to be old before one's time; *Rel* **vieil homme** unredeemed Man

2 *(avant le nom) (de longue date → admirateur, camarade, complicité, passion)* old, long-standing; *(→ famille, tradition)* old, ancient; *(→ dicton, recette, continent, montagne)* old; **la vieille ville** the old (part of the) town; **connais-tu le v. Nice?** do you know the old part of Nice?; **l'une des plus vieilles institutions de notre pays** one of the most ancient *or* oldest institutions of our country; **un vieil ami** an old friend, a friend of long standing; **nous sommes de v. amis** we're old friends; **c'est un v. célibataire** he's an old bachelor; **le V. Monde** the Old World

3 *(ancien → bâtiment)* old, ancient; **c'est v. comme Hérode** *ou* **le Pont-Neuf** *ou* **le monde** it's as old as the hills, it goes back to the year dot

4 *(désuet → instrument, méthode)* old; **c'est un tissu un peu v. pour une robe de fillette** this material is a bit old-fashioned for a little girl's dress; **une vieille expression** *(qui n'est plus usitée)* an obsolete turn of phrase; *(surannée)* an old-fashioned turn of phrase; *Ling* **le v. français** Old French

5 *(usé, fané)* old; **de v. vêtements** old clothes; **une malle pleine de vieilles photos et de vieilles lettres** a trunk full of old pictures and letters; **recycler les v. papiers** to recycle waste paper; **un v. numéro** *(de magazine)* a back copy *or* issue *or* number; **vieil or** old gold; **v. rose** old rose

6 *(précédent)* old; **sa vieille moto était plus belle** his/her old bike was nicer

7 *Fam (à valeur affectueuse)* **alors, mon v. chien?** how's my old doggy, then?; **mes vieilles mains tremblent** my old hands are shaking; **le v. père Davril** old Davril; **v. farceur!** you old devil!

8 *Fam (à valeur dépréciative)* **il doit bien rester un v. bout de fromage** there must be an odd bit of cheese left over; **t'aurais pas une vieille enveloppe?** got an envelope lying around?; **qu'est-ce que c'est que ce v. tas de ferraille?** what's that old heap?; **espèce de vieille folle!** you crazy old woman!; **v. dégoûtant!** you disgusting old man!

9 *Fam (à valeur intensive)* **j'ai une vieille faim!** I'm starving!; **ta voiture a pris un v. coup** your car got a nasty bash; **j'ai eu un v. coup de cafard** I felt really low

10 *(en œnologie) voir* **vin**

NM **1** *Fam Péj (homme âgé)* old man; **le v. ne vendra jamais** the old man will never sell; **un v. de la vieille** *(soldat de Napoléon)* an old veteran of Napoleon's guard; *(personne d'expérience)* an old hand

2 *très Fam (père)* old man; **mon/son v.** my/his old man

3 *Fam (à valeur affective → entre adultes)* pal, *Br* mate, *Am* buddy; **comment ça va, v.?** how are you doing, pal *or Br* mate *or Am* buddy?; **allez, (mon) v., ça va s'arranger** come on *Br* mate *or Am* buddy, it'll be all right; **tu vas sur cinquante ans – eh oui, mon (petit) v.!** so it's the big fifty next – (it) sure is, *Br* mate *or Am* buddy!; **débrouille-toi, mon (petit) v.!** you sort it out yourself, pal *or Br* mate *or Am* buddy!; **alors là, mon v., ce n'est pas mon problème** that's not my problem, pal *or Br* mate *or Am* buddy!; **j'en ai eu pour 500 euros – ben mon v.!** it cost me 500 euros – good heavens!

4 *(ce qui est ancien)* old things; **faire du neuf avec du v.** to turn old into new; **le vin sent le** *ou* **a un goût de v.** the wine tastes as though it's past its best

5 *Fam (locutions)* **elle a pris un sacré coup de v.** she's looking a lot older▪ ; **le film a pris un coup de v.** the film has dated▪

ADV **ça fait v.!** it's really old-fashioned!; **s'habiller v.** to wear old-fashioned clothes; **elle s'habille plus v. que son âge** she dresses too old for *or* older than her age

NMPL *Péj* **1** *Fam (personnes âgées)* **les v.** old people▪ ; **les petits v.** old folk; *très Fam* **elle dit qu'elle ne veut pas aller chez les v.** she says she doesn't want to go to an old people's *or* folk's home▪

2 *très Fam (parents)* **les** *ou* **mes v.** my folks, my *Br* mum *or Am* mom and dad

▫ **vieille** NF **1** *Fam Péj (femme âgée)* old woman *or* girl; **une petite vieille** a little old lady

2 *très Fam (mère)* old lady, *Br* old dear; **la vieille, ma/ta vieille** my/your old lady

3 *Fam (à valeur affective → entre adultes)* **salut, ma vieille!** hi there!; **il est trop tard, ma vieille!** it's too late, darling!; **t'es gonflée, ma vieille!** *(exprime l'indignation)* you've got some nerve, you!

4 *Ich* **vieille (de mer)** wrasse; **vieille commune** Ballan wrasse; **vieille coquette** cuckoo wrasse

▫ **de vieux, de vieille** ADJ old-fashioned, antiquated; **tu as des idées de v.** you're so old-fashioned (in your ideas); **ce sont des hantises de v.** those are old people's obsessions

▫ **vieux, vieille de** ADJ *(qui date de)* **c'est un manteau v. d'au moins 30 ans** it's a coat which is at least 30 years old; **une amitié vieille de 20 ans** a friendship that goes back 20 years

▫ **vieille fille,** *Belg* **vieille jeune fille** NF *Vieilli ou Péj* spinster, old maid; **rester vieille fille** to remain unmarried; **c'est une manie de vieille fille** it's an old-maidish thing to do

▫ **vieux beau** NM ageing Adonis, old roué

▫ **vieux garçon,** *Belg* **vieux jeune homme** NM *Vieilli ou Péj* bachelor; **rester v. garçon** to remain single *or* a bachelor; **des manies de v. garçon** bachelor ways

▫ **vieux jeu** ADJ *(personne, attitude)* old-fashioned; *(vêtements, idées)* old-fashioned, outmoded; **ce que tu peux être v. jeu!** you're so behind the times!

'Le Vieil Homme et la mer' *Hemingway, Sturges* 'The Old Man and the Sea'

vieux-catholique, vieille-catholique [vjøkatɔlik, vjɛjkatɔlik] *(mpl* **vieux-catholiques,** *fpl* **vieilles-catholiques)** *Hist & Rel* ADJ Old Catholic
NM,F Old Catholic

vieux-croyant [vjøkrwajɑ̃] *(pl* **vieux-croyants)** NM *Rel* Old Believer

vieux-lille [vjølil] NM INV = matured Maroilles cheese with a very distinctive flavour

vieux-pays [vjøpei] NMPL *Can* **les v.** Europe, the Old World, the old countries

VIF, VIVE [vif, viv]

ADJ lively **1, 9** ▪ sharp **2, 4, 5** ▪ quick **2** ▪ biting **3, 4** ▪ brusque **3** ▪ bright **4** ▪ strong **4** ▪ deep **4** ▪ keen **4** ▪ alive **6**
NM quick **1**

ADJ **1** *(plein d'énergie → personne)* lively, vivacious; *(→ musique, imagination, style)* lively; **d'un geste v., il saisit le revolver sur la table** he snatched the gun off the table; **avoir le regard v.** to have a lively look in one's eye; **marcher d'un pas v.** to walk briskly; **rouler à vive allure** to drive at great speed

2 *(intelligent → élève)* sharp; *(→ esprit)* sharp, quick; **être v. (d'esprit)** to be quick *or* quick-witted *or* sharp; **ce qu'elle est vive!** she's quick on the uptake!; *Euph* **il n'est pas très v.** he's not the sharpest knife in the drawer

3 *(emporté → remarque, discussion, reproche)* cutting, biting; *(→ geste)* brusque, brisk; **tu as été un peu trop v. avec elle** you were a bit curt *or* abrupt with her; **excusez-moi de ces mots un peu vifs** I apologize for having spoken rather sharply; **il y a eu un échange de paroles vives** there was a sharp exchange of words

4 *(très intense → froid)* biting; *(→ couleur)* bright, vivid; *(→ désir, sentiment)* strong; *(→ déception, intérêt)* keen; *(→ félicitations, remerciements)* warm; *(→ regret, satisfaction)* deep, great; *(→ douleur)* sharp; **porter un v. intérêt à** to be greatly *or* keenly interested in; **avec un v. soulagement** with a profound sense of relief; **c'est avec un v. plaisir que...** it's with great pleasure that...; **éprouver un v. plaisir à faire qch** to take great pleasure in doing sth; **à feu v.** over a brisk heat; **l'air v. de la montagne** the sharp *or* bracing mountain air; **l'air est v. au bord de la mer** the sea air is bracing; **l'air est v. ce matin** it's chilly this morning; **une flambée vive brûlait dans la cheminée** a fire was blazing away merrily in the hearth

5 *(nu → angle, arête)* sharp; *(→ joint)* dry; *(→ pierre)* bare

6 *(vivant)* **être brûlé/enterré v.** to be burnt/buried alive

7 *Hort (arbre, bois, haie)* quickset *(avant n)*

8 *Géog* **marée de vive eau** spring tide

9 *(vin)* lively

10 *Chasse (forêt, vallée)* rich in *or* teeming with game

NM **1** *(chair vivante)* **le v.** the living flesh, the quick; **tailler dans le v.** to cut into the flesh; **piquer qn au v.** to cut sb to the quick; **être piqué au v.** to be cut to the quick

2 *Fig (centre)* **trancher** *ou* **tailler dans le v.** to take drastic measures; **entrer dans le v. du sujet** to get to the heart of the matter

3 *Pêche* **le v.** live bait; **pêcher au v.** to fish with live bait

4 *Jur* living person; **donation entre vifs** donation inter vivos

5 *Constr* sharp edge

6 *Géog* **le v. de l'eau** new moon and full moon tides

▫ **à vif** ADJ *(blessure)* open; **la chair était à v.** the flesh was exposed; **j'ai les nerfs à v.** my nerves are on edge ADV **éplucher une orange à v.** = to peel an orange and remove all the pith round the segments

▫ **de vive voix** ADV personally; **je le lui dirai de vive voix** I'll tell him/her personally

▫ **sur le vif** ADV *(peindre)* from life; *(commenter)* on the spot; **une photo prise sur le v.** an action shot *or* photo; **ces photos ont été prises sur le v.** these photos were unposed

vif-argent [vifarʒɑ̃] *(pl* **vifs-argents)** NM quicksilver; **c'est du** *ou* **un v.** he's a bundle of energy

vigie [viʒi] NF **1** *Rail* observation box; **v. de frein/signaux** brake/signal cabin **2** *Naut (balise)* danger-buoy; *Vieilli (guetteur)* look-out; *(poste)* look-out post; *(panier)* crow's nest; **être de** *ou* **en v.** to be on look-out (duty) *or* on watch, to keep watch

vigil, -e [viʒil] ADJ *Méd* **coma v.** semi-comatose state; **en coma v.** in a semi-comatose state

vigilamment [viʒilamɑ̃] ADV *Littéraire* vigilantly

vigilance [viʒilɑ̃s] NF vigilance, watchfulness; **avec v.** watchfully; **redoubler de v.** to increase one's vigilance; **surprendre la v. de qn** to catch sb napping; **sa v. s'est relâchée** he's/she's become less vigilant

vigilant, -e [viʒilɑ̃, -ɑ̃t] ADJ *(personne, regard)* vigilant, watchful; *(soins)* vigilant; **soyez v.!** watch out!; **sous l'œil v. de leur mère** under the (ever) watchful eye of their mother

vigile[1] [viʒil] NM **1** *(d'une communauté)* vigilante;

(veilleur de nuit) night watchman; *(surveillant)* guard **2** *Antiq* watch

vigile² [viʒil] **NF** *Rel* vigil

vigne [viɲ] **NF 1** *Agr* vine, grapevine; *(vignoble)* vineyard; **la v. pousse bien par ici** it's easy to grow vines around here; **une région de vignes** a wine-producing region; *Fig* **être dans les vignes du Seigneur** to be drunk; *Fig Littéraire* **travailler à la v. du Seigneur** to work in the Lord's vineyard **2** *Bot* **v. vierge** Virginia creeper

vigneau, -x [viɲo] **NM** winkle

vigneron, -onne [viɲərɔ̃, -ɔn] **NM,F** wine-grower, wine-producer

vignetage [viɲtaʒ] **NM** *Phot* vignetting

vigneter [27] [viɲəte] **VI** *Phot* to cause vignetting

vignette [viɲɛt] **NF 1** *Com* (manufacturer's) label; *(sur un médicament)* label *or* sticker *(for reimbursement within the French Social Security system)* **2** *Anciennement Admin & Aut* **v. (auto** *ou* **automobile)** *Br* ≃ (road) tax disc, *Am* ≃ (car) registration sticker; **tu as pensé à acheter la v.?** did you remember to pay the road tax? **3** *Beaux-Arts (sur un livre, une gravure)* vignette **4** *Ordinat* thumbnail

vignettiste [viɲetist] **NMF** vignettist

vigneture [viɲətyr] **NF** = decorative border of vine leaves on miniatures

vignoble [viɲɔbl] **NM** vineyard; **le v. italien/alsacien** the vineyards of Italy/Alsace; **une région de vignobles** a wine-growing area

ADJ région v. wine(-growing) area

vignot [viɲo] = **vigneau**

vigogne [vigɔɲ] **NF 1** *Zool* vicuna, vicuña **2** *(laine)* vicuna *or* vicuña (wool)

vigoureuse [vigurøz] *voir* **vigoureux**

vigoureusement [vigurøzmɑ̃] **ADV** *(frapper, frictionner)* vigorously, energetically; *(se défendre)* vigorously; *(protester)* forcefully

vigoureux, -euse [vigurø, -øz] **ADJ 1** *(fort → homme)* vigorous, sturdy; *(→ membres)* strong, sturdy; *(→ corps)* vigorous, robust; *(→ arbre, plante)* sturdy; *(→ santé)* robust; *(→ poignée de main, répression)* vigorous; **il est encore v.!** he's still hale and hearty *or* going strong!; **un coup de poing v. le renversa sur le trottoir** a hefty punch knocked him flat on the pavement

2 *(langage, argument)* forceful; *(opposition, soutien)* strong; *(défense)* vigorous, spirited; *(contestation, effort)* vigorous, forceful, powerful; *(mesures)* energetic; **opposer une résistance vigoureuse à** *(projet, réforme)* to put up strong opposition to; **elle opposa une résistance vigoureuse à son assaillant** she put up a strong fight against her attacker, she tried to fight her attacker off

vigousse [vigus] **ADJ** *Suisse Fam (personne)* lively▪, bouncy; *(plante)* sturdy▪; **être v.** *(personne)* to be full of beans

viguerie [vigri] **NF** *Hist* provostship *(in the South of France)*

vigueur [vigœr] **NF 1** *(d'une personne, d'une plante)* strength, vigour; *(d'un coup)* vigour, strength, power; **avec v.** vigorously, energetically; **le bon air lui a rendu un peu de sa v.** the fresh air has perked him/her up a bit; **reprendre de la v.** to get some strength back

2 *(d'un style, d'une contestation)* forcefulness, vigour; *(d'un argument)* forcefulness; **se défendre avec v.** to defend oneself vigorously; **protester avec v.** to object forcefully; **admirez la v. du trait** look at how firmly drawn the lines are

❑ **en vigueur ADJ** *(décret, loi, règlement)* in force; *(tarif, usage)* current; **cesser d'être en v.** *(loi)* to lapse; *(règlement)* to cease to apply **ADV entrer en v.** *(décret, tarif)* to come into force *or* effect; **cette mesure entrera en v. le 7 juillet** this measure will come into effect on 7 July; **cesser d'être en v.** to lapse

viguier [vigje] **NM 1** *Hist (dans le Midi)* provost **2** *(en Andorre)* magistrate

VIH [veiaʃ] **NM** *Méd (abrév* **virus de l'immunodéficience humaine**) HIV

vihara [viara] **NM INV** *Rel* vihara

viking [vikiŋ] **ADJ** Viking

❑ **Viking NMF** Viking; **les Vikings** the Vikings

vil, -e [vil] **ADJ 1** *Littéraire (acte, personne, sentiment)* base, vile, despicable; **de viles calomnies** foul calumnies **2** *(avant le nom) Littéraire (métier, condition)* lowly, humble **3** *(métal)* base *(avant n)* **4** *(locution)* **à v. prix** extremely cheap; **il me l'a cédé à v. prix** he let me have it for next to nothing

vilain, -e [vilɛ̃, -ɛn] **ADJ 1** *(laid → figure, personne)* ugly; *(→ quartier)* ugly, sordid; *(→ décoration, bâtiment, habit)* ugly, hideous; **ils ne sont pas vilains du tout, tes dessins** your drawings aren't bad at all; **elle n'est pas vilaine** she's not bad looking, she's not what you'd call ugly; **un v. petit canard** an ugly duckling

2 *(méchant)* naughty; **tu es un v. petit garçon!** you're a naughty boy!; **c'est un v. monsieur** he's a bad man; **la vilaine bête, elle m'a mordu!** that nasty beast has bitten me!; **ce sont de vilaines gens** they're a bad *or* nasty lot; **ne dis pas ces vilains mots** don't say those bad words; **jouer un v. tour à qn** to play a rotten *or* dirty trick on sb

3 *(sérieux → affaire, coup, maladie)* nasty; **une vilaine blessure** a nasty *or* an ugly wound

4 *(désagréable → odeur)* nasty, bad; *(→ temps)* nasty, awful; **la matinée s'annonce vilaine** it looks like really foul weather this morning

NM,F bad *or* naughty boy, *f* girl; **oh le v./la vilaine!** you naughty boy/girl!

NM 1 *Hist* villein

2 *Fam (situation désagréable)* **il va y avoir du v.!** there's going to be trouble!; **ça tourne au v.!** things are getting nasty!

vilainement [vilɛnmɑ̃] **ADV v. habillé** shabbily dressed

vilayet [vilajɛ] **NM** *Hist* vilayet

vile [vil] *voir* **vil**

vilebrequin [vilbrəkɛ̃] **NM 1** *Tech* (bit) brace; **v. à cliquet** ratchet brace **2** *Aut* crankshaft

vilement [vilmɑ̃] **ADV** vilely, basely

vilenie [vileni] **NF** *Littéraire* **1** *(caractère)* baseness, villainy **2** *(action)* base *or* vile deed, villainous act

vilipender [3] [vilipɑ̃de] **VT 1** *Littéraire* to disparage, to revile; **il a été vilipendé dans la presse** he was pilloried in the press **2** *Suisse (gaspiller)* to waste, to squander

villa [vila] **NF 1** *(résidence secondaire)* villa **2** *(pavillon)* (detached) house **3** *Antiq & Hist* villa **4** *(rue)* private road

village [vilaʒ] **NM 1** *(agglomération, personnes)* village; **v. de pêcheurs** fishing village; *Écon* **le v. global** *ou* **mondial** *ou* **planétaire** the global village **2** *(centre de vacances)* **v. (de vacances), v.-vacances** *Br* holiday *or Am* vacation village; **v. vacances famille** = state-subsidized holiday village; **v. de toile** (*Br* holiday *or Am* vacation) camp (under canvas)

villageois, -e [vilaʒwa, -az] **ADJ** village *(avant n)*, country *(avant n)*

NM,F villager, village resident

villanelle [vilanɛl] **NF** *Littérature* villanelle, pastoral poem; *Mus* villanella

ville [vil] **NF 1** *(moyenne)* town; *(plus grande)* city; **dans les grandes villes** in big cities; **il n'aime pas les grandes villes** he doesn't like big cities; **la seconde v. de France** France's second city; **la v. a voté à droite** the town voted for the right; **toute la v. en parle** it's the talk of the town; **à la v. comme à la scène** in real life as (well as) on stage; **v. d'eaux** spa (town); **la V. éternelle** the Eternal City; **v. industrielle** industrial town; **la V. lumière** the City of Light; **v. nouvelle** new town; **v. ouverte** open city; *Rel* **la V. sainte** the Holy City; *Mktg* **v. test** test city; **v. universitaire** university town

2 *(quartier)* **v. haute/basse** upper/lower part of town

3 *Admin* **la v.** *(administration)* the local authority; *(représentants)* the (town) council; **financé par la v.** financed by the local authority; **la V. de Paris** the City of Paris

4 *(milieu non rural)* **la v.** towns, cities; **les gens de la v.** city-dwellers, townspeople; **la vie à la v.** town *or* city life; **habiter à la v.** to live in a town/city; **partir à la v.** to go and live in a town/city; **je viens profiter un peu de la v.** I've come to sample the delights of city life

❑ **de ville ADJ 1** *(vêtements, chaussures)* **chaussures de v.** shoes for wearing in town; **tenue de v.** town clothes; *(sur une invitation)* lounge suit **2** *Typ* **travaux de v.** jobbing work

❑ **en ville ADV aller en v.** *Br* to go to *or* into town, *Am* to go downtown; **aller habiter en v.** *(venant de la campagne)* to move to the city; *(venant de la banlieue)* to move *Br* to the town centre *or Am* downtown; **et si nous dînions en v.?** let's eat out tonight; **trouver un studio en v.** to find a *Br* flat *or Am* studio apartment in town

ville-champignon [vilʃɑ̃piɲɔ̃] *(pl* **villes-champignons)** **NF** fast-expanding town

ville-dortoir [vildɔrtwar] *(pl* **villes-dortoirs)** **NF** dormitory town

villégiature [vileʒjatyr] **NF** *Br* holiday, *Am* vacation; **être en v.** to be on *Br* holiday *or Am* vacation; **partir en v.** to go on *Br* holiday *or Am* vacation; **être en v. à la campagne** to be on *Br* holiday *or Am* vacation in the countryside; **(lieu de) v.** *Br* holiday resort, *Am* vacation resort; **avez-vous trouvé un lieu de v.?** have you found somewhere to spend your holidays?

villégiaturer [3] [vileʒjatyre] **VI** *Fam Vieilli* to be on *Br* holiday▪ *or Am* vacation▪

Villejuif [vilʒɥif] **NF** = Paris suburb famous for its cancer treatment centre

Villers-Cotterêts [vilɛrkɔtərɛ] **NM** *Hist* **l'ordonnance de V.** = Francis I's edict (1539) ordering that all decrees and judgements be drawn up in French

ville-satellite [vilsatelit] *(pl* **villes-satellites)** **NF** satellite town

Villette [vilɛt] **NF la V.** = cultural complex in the north of Paris (including a science museum, several theatres and a park)

villeux, -euse [vilø, -øz] **ADJ** *Bot, Méd & Zool* villous

villosité [vilozite] **NF 1** *Anat* villosity; **prélèvement des villosités choriales** chorionic villus sampling **2** *(état)* hairiness; *(poils)* hair

Vilnius [vilnjys] **NM** Vilnius

vimana [vimana] **NM INV** *Archit* vimana

vin [vɛ̃] **NM 1** *(boisson)* wine; *(ensemble de récoltes)* vintage; **ce sera une bonne année pour le v.** it'll be a good vintage this year; **le v. de 1959** the 1959 vintage; **grand v., v. de grand cru** vintage wine; *Prov* **quand le v. est tiré, il faut le boire** you've made your bed and now you must lie in it; **v. d'appellation d'origine contrôlée** "appellation contrôlée" wine; **v. blanc** white wine; **v. de Bordeaux** *(rouge)* claret; *(blanc)* white Bordeaux; **v. de Bourgogne** Burgundy; **v. bourru** new wine; **v. chaud** mulled wine; **v. de consommation courante** table wine; **v. de coupage** blended wine; **v. du cru** local wine; **v. cuit** fortified wine; **v. délimité de qualité contrôlée** medium-quality wine; **v. délimité de qualité supérieure** = label indicating quality of wine; **v. de fruits** fruit wine; **v. gris** pale rosé, *Am* blush wine; **v. de messe** altar *or* communion wine; **v. mousseux** sparkling wine; **v. nouveau** new wine; **v. ordinaire** table wine; **v. de paille** straw wine; **v. de pays** local wine; **v. pétillant** sparkling wine; **v. de presse** press wine, pressings; **v. (de) primeur** new wine; **v. du Rhin** hock; **v. rosé** rosé wine; **v. rouge** red wine; **v. de table** table wine; **v. vieux** aged wine; **avoir le v. gai/triste/mauvais** to get merry/depressed/nasty after a few drinks; **être entre deux vins** to be tiddly *or* tipsy

2 *(liqueur)* **v. de canne/riz** cane/rice wine

❑ **vin d'honneur NM** reception *(where wine is served)*

vina [vina] **NF INV** *Mus* vina

vinage [vinaʒ] **NM** fortifying, fortification *(of wine)*

vinaigre [vinɛgr] **NM 1** *(condiment)* vinegar; **cornichons/oignons au v.** pickled gherkins/onions; **v. d'alcool** spirit vinegar; **v. balsamique** balsamic vinegar; **v. blanc** distilled vinegar; **v. de cidre** cider vinegar; **v. à l'estragon** tarragon vinegar; **v. de framboise** raspberry vinegar; **v. de vin** wine vinegar

2 *Fam (locutions)* **tourner au v.** *(vin)* to turn sour▪; *(discussion, relation)* to turn sour; *(expédition, opération)* to go wrong▪; **les choses ont tourné au v.** things went wrong; **faites v.** hurry up, get a move on; **faire v.** *(à la corde à sauter)* to go very fast *(with a skipping rope)*

vinaigrer [4] [vinegre] **VT** to add vinegar to; **ce n'est pas assez vinaigré** there's not enough vinegar in it; **de l'eau vinaigrée** water with a touch of vinegar added

vinaigrerie [vinɛgrəri] NF **1** *(fabrique)* vinegar factory **2** *(production)* vinegar making **3** *(commerce)* vinegar trade

vinaigrette [vinɛgrɛt] NF vinaigrette, French dressing; **haricots à la** *ou* **en v.** beans with vinaigrette *or* French dressing

vinaigrier [vinɛgrije] NM **1** *(bouteille)* vinegar bottle **2** *(fabricant)* vinegar maker *or* manufacturer

vinaire [vinɛr] ADJ wine *(avant n)*

vinasse [vinas] NF **1** *Fam Péj (vin)* cheap wine■, *Br* plonk **2** *(résidu)* vinasse

vinblastine [vɛ̃blastin] NF *Méd* vinblastine

vincamine [vɛ̃kamin] NF *Physiol* vincamine

vindas [vɛ̃da, vɛ̃das] NM *(treuil)* windlass, winch; *(cabestan)* capstan

vindicatif, -ive [vɛ̃dikatif, -iv] ADJ vindictive

vindicte [vɛ̃dikt] NF **1** *Jur* **la v. publique** prosecution and punishment; **désigner** *ou* **livrer qn à la v. populaire** to expose sb to trial by the mob **2** *Littéraire (punition)* **exercer des vindictes** to punish crimes

vinée [vine] NF *(branche à fruits)* fruit branch

viner [3] [vine] VT to fortify, to add alcohol to

vineux, -euse [vinø, -øz] ADJ **1** *(rappelant le vin → couleur)* wine-coloured; *(→ visage)* blotchy; *(→ goût)* wine-like; *(→ haleine)* which reeks of wine; *(→ melon)* wine-flavoured; **d'une couleur vineuse** wine-coloured; **une odeur vineuse** a winy smell **2** *(en œnologie)* **vin v.** wine with a high alcohol content; **région vineuse** a rich wine-producing area

vingt [vɛ̃] ADJ **1** *(gén)* twenty; *Fig* **je te l'ai dit v. fois!** I've told you a hundred times!; **il n'a pas encore v. ans** he's not yet twenty, he's still in his teens; **je n'ai plus v. ans, je n'ai plus mon cœur de v. ans** I'm not as young as I used to be; **ah, si j'avais encore mes jambes/mon cœur de v. ans!** if only I still had the legs/the heart of a twenty-year-old!; *Vieilli* **v. dieux, la belle fille!** Lord *or Br* strewth, what a beauty!; *Vieilli* **ne touche pas à ça, v. dieux!** leave that alone, for God's sake!

2 *(dans des séries)* twentieth; **page/numéro v.** page/number twenty

PRON twenty

NM INV **1** *(gén)* twenty

2 *(numéro d'ordre)* number twenty; **il a joué trois fois le v.** he played three times on number twenty

3 *(chiffre écrit)* twenty; *voir aussi* **cinquante**

vingtaine [vɛ̃tɛn] NF **1** *(quantité)* **une v.** around *or* about twenty, twenty or so; **une v. de voitures** around *or* about twenty cars; **elle a une v. d'années** she's around *or* about twenty (years old) **2** *(âge)* **avoir la v.** to be around *or* about twenty; **quand on arrive à** *ou* **atteint la v.** when you hit twenty

vingt-deux [vɛ̃tdø] ADJ twenty-two

NM INV twenty-two; *très Fam* **v. v'là les flics!** watch out, here come the cops!

vingt-et-un [vɛ̃teœ̃] ADJ twenty-one

NM INV twenty-one; *(jeu)* vingt-et-un, twenty-one, *Br* pontoon

vingtième [vɛ̃tjɛm] ADJ twentieth

NMF **1** *(personne)* twentieth **2** *(objet)* twentieth (one)

NM **1** *(partie)* twentieth **2** *(étage) Br* twentieth floor, *Am* twenty-first floor **3** *(arrondissement de Paris)* twentieth (arrondissement); *voir aussi* **cinquième**

vingtièmement [vɛ̃tjɛmmɑ̃] ADV in twentieth place

vingt-quatre [vɛ̃tkatr] ADJ twenty-four; **v. heures sur v.** round the clock; **surveillé v. heures sur v.** under round-the-clock surveillance; **ouvert v. heures sur v.** open all day *or* round the clock, open twenty-four hours (a day)

NM INV twenty-four

vinicole [vinikɔl] ADJ *(pays)* wine-growing *(avant n)*; *(industrie, production)* wine *(avant n)*; **entreprise v.** *Br* wine-making firm, *Am* winery

viniculture [vinikyltyr] NF viniculture

vinifère [vinifɛr] ADJ wine-producing *(avant n)*, *Sout* viniferous

vinificateur, -trice [vinifikatœr, -tris] NM,F wine-producer, wine-maker

vinification [vinifikasjɔ̃] NF *(de jus de fruits)* vinification; *(pour l'obtention de vin)* wine-making process

vinificatrice [vinifikatris] *voir* **vinificateur**

vinifier [9] [vinifje] VT to make into wine

vinosité [vinozite] NF vinosity

vint *etc voir* **venir**

vintage[1] [vɛ̃taʒ] NM *(porto)* vintage

vintage[2] [vintɛdʒ] ADJ INV *(vêtements)* vintage *(avant n)*

NM *(mode)* vintage

Vintimille [vɛ̃timij] NM Ventimiglia

vinyle [vinil] NM vinyl; *Fam (disque)* record■; **c'est sorti sur v.** it came out on vinyl; **il rachète tous les vieux vinyles qu'il trouve** he buys all the old records he can find

vinylique [vinilik] ADJ vinyl *(avant n)*

vioc, vioque [vjɔk] NM,F *très Fam* **1** *(vieille personne)* old fossil, *Br* wrinkly, *Am* geezer **2** *(père, mère)* **la** *ou* **ma vioque** my old lady; **le** *ou* **mon v.** my old man; **les** *ou* **mes viocs** *Br* my old dears, *Am* my rents

viol [vjɔl] NM **1** *(d'une personne)* rape; **v. collectif** gang rape **2** *(d'un sanctuaire)* violation, desecration

violacé, -e [vjɔlase] ADJ purplish-blue; **un rouge v.** a purplish red; **les mains violacées par le froid** hands blue with cold; **prendre un teint v.** *(à cause du froid)* to go blue

❑ **violacée** NF *Bot* member of the Violaceae family

❑ **violacées** NFPL *Bot* Violaceae

violacer [16] [vjɔlase] **se violacer** VPR *(visage)* to turn *or* to go *or* to become purple; *(mains)* to turn *or* to go *or* to become blue

violat [vjɔla] ADJ M *Pharm* containing essence of violet

violateur, -trice [vjɔlatœr, -tris] NM,F *(d'une loi, d'une constitution)* transgressor; *(d'un sanctuaire, d'une sépulture)* violator, desecrator

violation [vjɔlasjɔ̃] NF **1** *(d'une loi, d'une règle)* violation; *(d'un serment)* breach; *(d'un accord)* violation, breach; **agir en v. d'une règle** to act in contravention of a rule; **v. du droit à l'image** violation of privacy *(by publicizing images taken for private use)* **2** *(d'un sanctuaire, d'une sépulture)* violation, desecration; **v. de domicile** forcible entry *(into somebody's home)*; **v. de sépulture** desecration of graves

violâtre [vjɔlatr] ADJ *Littéraire* purplish-blue

violatrice [vjɔlatris] *voir* **violateur**

viole [vjɔl] NF *Mus* viol, viola; **v. d'amour** viola d'amore; **v. de bras** viola da braccio; **v. de gambe** bass viol, viola da gamba

violemment [vjɔlamɑ̃] ADV *(frapper)* violently; *(protester, critiquer)* vehemently; *(désirer)* passionately; **il se jeta v. sur moi** he hurled himself at me

violence [vjɔlɑ̃s] NF **1** *(brutalité → d'un affrontement, d'un coup, d'une personne)* violence; *(→ d'un sport)* roughness, brutality; **avec v.** with violence, violently; **scène de v.** violent scene; **quand il est ivre, il est d'une grande v.** he gets very violent when he's drunk; **pour mesurer la v. de l'attaque** to realize how violent *or* brutal the attack was; **il tomba sous la v. du choc** the violence of the blow threw him to the ground; **le choc fut d'une v. inouïe** the impact was incredibly violent; **obliger qn à faire qch par la v.** to force sb to do sth by violent means; **répondre à la v. par la v.** to meet violence with violence; *Arch* **faire v. à une femme** to violate a woman; *Fig* **faire v. à** *(principes, sentiments)* to do violence to, to go against; *(texte)* to do violence to, to distort the meaning of; **se faire v.** to force oneself

2 *(acte)* assault, violent act; **subir des violences** to be the victim of assault; **v. à** *ou* **sur agent** assault on (the person of) a police officer

3 *(intensité → d'un sentiment, d'une sensation)* intensity; *(→ d'un séisme, du vent)* violence, fierceness; *(→ d'une confrontation)* fierceness; **le vent soufflait avec v.** the wind was raging

violent, -e [vjɔlɑ̃, -ɑ̃t] ADJ **1** *(brutal → sport, jeu)* rough, brutal; *(→ attaque, affrontement)* fierce, violent, brutal; *(→ personne)* violent, brutal; *(→ tempérament)* violent, fiery; **se montrer v. avec qn** to be violent with sb; **..., dit-il d'un ton v.** ..., he said violently

2 *(intense → pluie)* driving *(avant n)*; *(→ vent, tempête)* violent, raging; *(→ couleur)* harsh, glaring; *(→ parfum)* pungent, overpowering; *(→ effort)* huge, strenuous; *(→ besoin, envie)* intense, uncontrollable, urgent; *(→ douleur)* violent; **un v. mal de tête** a splitting headache; **une violente douleur au côté** a shooting pain in one's side

3 *Fam (qui scandalise)* **c'est un peu v.!** that's a bit much!

NM,F violent person

violenter [3] [vjɔlɑ̃te] VT **1** *(femme)* to assault sexually; **elle a été violentée** she was sexually assaulted **2** *Littéraire (désir, penchant)* to do violence to, to go against; *(morale)* to do violence to; *(texte)* to distort

violer [3] [vjɔle] VT **1** *(personne)* to rape; **se faire v.** to be raped **2** *(loi, règle)* to violate; *(serment, promesse)* to break; *(accord, secret professionnel)* to violate, to break; *(secret)* to betray **3** *(sanctuaire, sépulture)* to violate, to desecrate; *Jur* **v. le domicile de qn** to force entry into sb's home; *Fig* **v. les consciences** to violate people's consciences

violet, -ette [vjɔlɛ, -ɛt] ADJ purple; **ses mains violettes de froid** his/her hands blue with cold

NM purple

❑ **violette** NF *Bot* violet; **violette odorante/de Parme** sweet/Parma violet

violeter [27] [vjɔlte] VT **v. qch** to dye sth violet

violette [vjɔlɛt] *voir* **violet**

violeur, -euse [vjɔlœr, -øz] NM,F rapist

violier [vjɔlje] NM *Bot* stock

violine [vjɔlin] ADJ dark purple

violiste [vjɔlist] NMF *Mus* violist, viol *or* viola player

violon [vjɔlɔ̃] NM **1** *Mus (instrument → d'orchestre)* violin; *(→ de violoneux)* fiddle; **v. d'Ingres** hobby; *Fam* **accordez vos violons** make up your minds

2 *(artiste)* violin (player); **premier v. (solo)** first violin; **second v.** second violin; *Fig* **jouer les seconds** *ou* **troisièmes violons** to play second fiddle

3 *Fam Arg crime (prison)* slammer, clink; **il s'est retrouvé au v.** he wound up in the slammer *or* clink

4 *Tech* **(poulie à) v.** fiddle block

5 *Naut* **violons de mer** *(contre le roulis)* fiddles

violoncelle [vjɔlɔ̃sɛl] NM **1** *(instrument)* cello, *Spéc* violoncello **2** *(musicien)* cello (player), cellist

violoncelliste [vjɔlɔ̃selist] NMF cellist, cello player, *Spéc* violoncellist

violoné, -e [vjɔlɔne] ADJ *(dossier de fauteuil, objet chantourné)* violin-shaped *(characteristic of Louis XV style)*

violoneux [vjɔlɔnø] NM **1** *Péj* mediocre violinist **2** *(de musique traditionnelle)* fiddler

violoniste [vjɔlɔnist] NMF violinist, violin player

vioque [vjɔk] *voir* **vioc**

viorne [vjɔrn] NF *Bot* viburnum

VIP [viajpi, veipe] NMF *(abrév* **very important person)** VIP

vipère [vipɛr] NF *Zool* adder, viper; **v. ammodyte** ammodyte, sand viper; **v. aspic** asp; **v. cornue** *ou* **à cornes** horned viper; **v. du Gabon** gaboon viper; **v. heurtante** puff adder; **v. de Russell** Russell's viper; **v. des sables** sand viper; *Fig Péj* **c'est une vraie v.** she's really vicious

'Vipère au poing' *Bazin* 'Viper in the Fist'

vipereau, -x [vipro], **vipéreau, -x** [vipero] NM young viper

vipéridé [viperide] *Zool* NM viperid, *Spéc* member of the Viperidae

❑ **vipéridés** NMPL viperids, *Spéc* Viperidae

vipérin, -e [viperɛ̃, -in] ADJ **1** *Zool* viperine; **couleuvre vipérine** viperine grass snake **2** *Littéraire (méchant)* viperish, vicious

❑ **vipérine** NF **1** *Bot* viper's bugloss **2** *Zool* viperine snake

virage [viraʒ] NM **1** *(d'une route)* bend, curve, *Am* turn; **elle allait à 110 km/h dans les virages** she was taking the bends at 110 km/h; **prendre** *ou* **aborder un v.** to take a bend, to go round a bend; **prendre le v. à la corde** to hug the bend; **prendre un v. sur les chapeaux de roue** to take a bend *or* a turn on two wheels; **v. en épingle à**

cheveux hairpin bend; **v. en S** *Br* S-bend, *Am* S-curve; **v. sans visibilité** blind corner; **v. relevé** banked corner; **virages sur 5 km** *(sur panneau)* bends for 5 km

2 *(d'une piste de vitesse)* banked corner, bank

3 *(mouvement → d'un véhicule, au ski)* turn; *Aviat* **faire un v. incliné** *ou* **sur l'aile** to bank; **faire faire un v. sur l'aile à un avion** to bank an aeroplane; *Aviat* **angle de v.** angle of bank; *Ski* **v. parallèle** parallel turn

4 *Fig (changement → d'attitude, d'idéologie)* (drastic) change *or* shift; *Pol* **v. à droite/gauche** shift to the right/left

5 *Phot* toning *(UNCOUNT)*

6 *Chim* change in colour

7 *Méd* **v. de cuti-réaction** positive reaction to a skin test

8 *Can* **v. ambulatoire** = Quebec government's policy of increasingly providing ambulatory care rather than hospitalization

virago [virago] **NF** *Péj* virago, shrew

viral, -e, -aux, -ales [viral, -o] **ADJ** viral; **maladie virale** viral infection *or* illness

vire [vir] **NF** ledge *(on mountain)*

virée [vire] **NF** *Fam* **1** *(promenade)* **faire une v. à vélo/en voiture** to go for a bicycle ride■ /a drive■ ; **faire une v. dans les bars** *Br* to go on a pub crawl, *Am* to barhop; **si on faisait une v. dans les bars du coin?** let's hit the local bars **2** *(court voyage)* trip■ , tour■ , jaunt■ ; **on a fait une petite v. en Bretagne** we went for a little jaunt to Brittany

virelai [virlɛ] **NM** *Littérature* virelay

virement [virmɑ̃] **NM** **1** *Banque* transfer; **faire un v. de 200 euros sur un compte** to transfer 200 euros to an account; **v. automatique** automatic transfer; **v. bancaire** bank transfer; **v. par courrier** mail transfer; **v. de crédit** credit transfer; *Admin* **v. de fonds** = transfer (often illegal) of funds from one article of the budget to another; **v. interbancaire** interbank transfer; **v. postal** post office transfer; **v. SWIFT** SWIFT transfer; **v. télégraphique** cable transfer; **v. par télex** telex transfer

2 *Naut* **v. de bord** tacking

virémie [viremi] **NF** *Méd* viraemia

virer [3] [vire] **VI** **1** *(voiture)* to turn; *(vent)* to veer; *(grue)* to turn round; *(personne)* to turn *or* to pivot round; *Can Fig (changer d'allégeance)* to change sides; *Aut* **v. court** to corner sharply; *Aut* **v. sur place** to turn in one's own length; *Aviat* **v. sur l'aile** to bank; *Naut* **v. de bord** *(gén)* to veer; *(voilier)* to tack; *Fig* to take a new line *or* tack; *Naut* **faire v. un bateau** to veer a boat; *Naut* **v. vent arrière** to wear; *Naut* **v. au cabestan** to heave at the capstan; *Naut* **paré à v.!** ready about!

2 *Chim (liquide)* to change colour; **encre qui vire au noir en séchant** ink that dries black; **la couleur est en train de v.** the colour is changing

3 *Méd (cuti-réaction)* to come up positive

4 *Phot* to tone

5 *Fam (devenir)* **v. homo** to turn gay; **v. voyou** to become *or* to turn into a thug

VT **1** *Banque* to transfer; **v. 300 euros sur un compte** to transfer 300 euros to an account

2 *Fam (jeter → meuble, papiers)* to chuck (out), to ditch; **vire-moi ces journaux de là** get those papers out of there

3 *Fam (renvoyer → employé)* to fire, *Br* to sack; *(→ importun)* to kick out, to chuck out; **se faire v.** *(employé)* to get *Br* the sack *or Am* the bounce; **je me suis fait v. de chez moi** I got kicked *or* thrown out of my place

4 *Méd* **il a viré sa cuti** his skin test was positive; *Fig* he changed radically; *Fam (est devenu homosexuel)* he turned gay

5 *Naut* to veer; **virez l'ancre!** weigh the anchor!

6 *Phot* to tone

❑ **virer à VT IND v. à l'aigre** *(vin)* to turn sour; **v. au vert/rouge** to turn green/red

▶**se virer VPR** *Fam* **vire-toi de là!** shift yourself!

virescence [virɛsɑ̃s] **NF** *Bot* virescence

vireton [virtɔ̃] **NM** = type of crossbow bolt that rotates in flight

vireur [virœr] **NM** *Tech* turning gear

vireux, -euse [virø, -øz] **ADJ** *Bot* noxious, poisonous

virevolte [virvɔlt] **NF** **1** *(pirouette)* pirouette, twirl; **faire des virevoltes** to pirouette **2** *Fig (changement)* volte-face; **faire des virevoltes** to chop and change; **les virevoltes de la fortune** the sudden changes of fortune; **je m'attends à une v. de sa part** I expect he'll/she'll change his/her mind

virevolter [3] [virvɔlte] **VI** **1** *(tourner sur soi)* to pirouette, to spin round; **il l'a fait v.** he spun him/her around **2** *(s'agiter)* to dance around; **elle virevoltait gaiement dans la maison** she was flitting happily about the house; **j'ai des taches qui virevoltent devant les yeux** I've got spots before my eyes

Virgile [virʒil] **NPR** Virgil

virginal, -e, -als *ou* **-aux, -ales** [virʒinal, -o] **ADJ** virginal, maidenly; *Littéraire* **d'une blancheur virginale** virgin white, lily-white

NM *Mus* virginals

❑ **virginale NF** *Mus* virginals

Virginie [virʒini] **NM** Virginia (tobacco)

NF *Géog* **la V.** Virginia; **vivre en V.** to live in Virginia; **aller en V.** to go to Virginia; **la V.-Occidentale** West Virginia; **en V.-Occidentale** in West Virginia

virginité [virʒinite] **NF** **1** *(d'une personne)* virginity; **perdre sa v.** to lose one's virginity; *Fig* **le parti devra se refaire une v.** the party will have to forge itself a new reputation **2** *Littéraire (d'un lys, de la neige)* purity

virgule [virgyl] **NF** **1** *(dans un texte)* comma; *Fig* **copier qch sans y changer une v.** to copy sth out without a single alteration; **c'est ce qu'il a dit à la v. près** that's word for word what he said **2** *Math* (decimal) point; **4 v. 9** 4 point 9; **v. flottante** floating comma; *Ordinat* **v. fixe** fixed point

viril, -e [viril] **ADJ** **1** *(propre à l'homme)* male; *(force, langage)* manly, virile; *(allure, démarche)* masculine **2** *(sexuellement)* virile

virilement [virilmɑ̃] **ADV** in a manly way

virilisant, -e [virilizɑ̃, -ɑ̃t] **ADJ** causing the development of male sexual characteristics

virilisation [virilizasjɔ̃] **NF** *Biol* virilization

viriliser [3] [virilize] **VT** **1** *Biol (sujet: médicament)* to cause the development of male sexual characteristics in **2** *(en apparence → sujet: sport)* to make more masculine in appearance

virilisme [virilism] **NM** *Méd* virilism

virilité [virilite] **NF** **1** *(gén)* virility, manliness; **se sentir menacé/attaqué dans sa v.** to feel that one's manhood is being threatened/attacked **2** *(vigueur sexuelle)* virility

virilocal, -e, -aux, -ales [virilɔkal, -o] **ADJ** virilocal

virion [virjɔ̃] **NM** *Biol* virion

virocide [virɔsid] = **virucide**

viroïde [virɔid] **NM** *Biol* viroid

virole [virɔl] **NF** **1** *(d'une canne, d'un manche)* ferrule **2** *Tech (moule)* ring die

viroler [3] [virɔle] **VT** **1** *(canne, manche)* to fit with a ferrule **2** *Tech (mouler)* to place in the ring die

virolo [virɔlo] **NM** *Fam* bend■ *(in road)*

virologie [virɔlɔʒi] **NF** *Biol & Méd* virology

virologiste [virɔlɔʒist], **virologue** [virɔlɔg] **NMF** *Biol & Méd* virologist

virose [viroz] **NF** *Méd* virus disease, virosis

virtualité [virtɥalite] **NF** **1** *(gén)* potentiality **2** *Ordinat, Opt & Phys* virtuality

virtuel, -elle [virtɥɛl] **ADJ** **1** *(fait, valeur)* potential **2** *Ordinat, Opt & Phys* virtual

virtuellement [virtɥɛlmɑ̃] **ADV** **1** *(potentiellement)* potentially **2** *(très probablement)* virtually, to all intents and purposes, practically

virtuose [virtɥoz] **NMF** *Mus* virtuoso; **v. du violon** violin virtuoso; **c'est une v. du tennis/de l'aiguille** she's a brilliant tennis player/needlewoman

virtuosité [virtɥozite] **NF** virtuosity; **elle a joué la fugue avec une grande v.** she gave a virtuoso rendering of the fugue; **manier le pinceau avec v.** to be a brilliant painter

virucide [virysid] *Biol* **ADJ** virucidal, viricidal

NM virucide, viricide

virulence [virylɑ̃s] **NF** **1** *(d'un reproche, d'un discours)* virulence, viciousness, venom **2** *Méd* virulence

virulent, -e [virylɑ̃, -ɑ̃t] **ADJ** **1** *(critique, discours)* virulent, vicious, venomous; *(haine)* burning, bitter; **faire une critique virulente de qch** to criticize sth venomously **2** *Méd (agent, poison)* virulent

virulicide [virylisid] **ADJ** *Biol* virucidal, viricidal

virure [viryr] **NF** *Naut* strake

virus [virys] **NM** **1** *Biol & Méd* virus; **v. Ebola** Ebola virus; **v. ECHO** echovirus; **v. d'Epstein–Barr** Epstein–Barr virus; **v. filtrant** filterable virus; **v. de la grippe** flu virus; **v. d'immunodéficience humaine** human immunodeficiency virus; **v. Marburg** Marburg virus; **v. du Nil occidental** West Nile virus; *Fam* **il y a un v. qui traîne** *ou* **dans l'air** there's a virus going around

2 *Fig* **tout le pays était atteint par le v. du loto** the whole country was gripped by lottery fever; *Fam* **elle a attrapé le v. du deltaplane** she's completely hooked on hang-gliding, she's got the hang-gliding bug; **pour ceux qui ont le v. de la photo** for photography enthusiasts

3 *Ordinat* virus; **désactiver un v.** to disable a virus

vis [vis] **NF** **1** *Tech* screw; **v. à ailettes** wing screw; **v. d'Archimède** Archimedes' screw; **v. d'arrêt** stop screw; **v. autotaraudeuse** self-tapping screw; **v. de blocage** stop screw; **v. à bois** woodscrew; **v. de direction** worm; **v. à droite** right-handed screw *or* thread; **v. sans fin** worm *or* endless screw; **v. à gauche** left-handed screw *or* thread; **v. hexagonale** hexagon screw; **v. à métaux** metal screw; **v. micrométrique** micrometer screw; **v. à oreilles** wing screw; *Aut* **v. platinée** contact point; **v. à pointe ronde** ball-ended screw; **v. de purge** bleeder screw, bleed screw; **v. de réglage** adjuster screw, adjusting screw; **v. de serrage** setscrew; **v. sans tête** grub screw; **v. à tête cylindrique** cheese-head(ed) screw; **v. à tête fraisée** countersunk (head) screw; **v. à tête ronde** round-head(ed) screw; **tige à v.** screwed *or* threaded rod

2 *(spirale) voir* **escalier**

Visa® [viza] **NF** **la (carte) Visa** Visa® (card)

visa [viza] **NM** **1** *(sur un passeport)* visa; **demander/obtenir un v.** to apply for/to obtain a visa; **un v. pour l'Australie** a visa for Australia; **v. d'entrée/de sortie** entry/exit visa; **v. de touriste** *ou* **de visiteur** *Br* tourist *or Am* non-immigrant visa; **v. de transit** transit visa

2 *(sur un document)* stamp; **apposer un v. sur** to stamp; *Cin* **v. de censure** (censor's) certificate; **v. d'exploitation** exploitation licence

3 *(paraphe → d'un supérieur)* initials

visage [vizaʒ] **NM** **1** *(d'une personne)* face; **au v. rond** round-faced; **au v. ovale** with an oval-shaped face; **homme au v. agréable** pleasant-faced man; **frapper qn au v.** to hit sb in the face; **elle a un v. de bébé** *ou* **d'enfant** she has a baby face; **il n'avait plus v. humain** he was completely disfigured; **j'aime voir de nouveaux visages** I like to see new faces *or* to meet new people; **il y avait des visages connus** there were some familiar faces; **je n'arrive pas à mettre un nom sur ce v.** I can't put a name to that face; **elle a changé de v. depuis l'opération** her face looks different since the operation; **il a soudain changé de v.** his expression suddenly changed; *Fig* **faire bon v. à qn** to put on a show of friendliness for sb; *Fig* **à v. découvert** *(sans masque)* unmasked; *(sans voile)* unveiled; *(ouvertement)* openly; *Fig* **à deux visages** two-faced; *Fig* **sans v.** faceless

2 *(aspect)* aspect; **l'Afrique aux multiples visages** the many faces of Africa; **enfin une ville à v. humain!** at last a town made for people to live in!; **pour un socialisme à v. humain** for socialism with a human face; **le vrai v. de** *(la nature de)* the true nature *or* face of; **elle révélait enfin son vrai v.** she was revealing her true self *or* nature at last; **il nous montre le vrai v. du fascisme** he shows us the true face of fascism; **présenter un pays sous un autre** *ou* **nouveau v.** to present a country in a new light

❑ **Visage pâle NM** paleface

visagisme [vizaʒism] **NM** facial therapy

visagiste [vizaʒist] **NMF** facialist; **coiffeur-v.** hairstylist

vis-à-vis [vizavi] **NM INV** **1** *(personne en face)* **mon v.** the person opposite me; **au dîner, j'avais le président pour v.** at dinner, I was seated opposite the president; **faire v. à qn** to be opposite

sb, to face sb; **le passager qui lui faisait v.** the passenger who was sitting opposite him/her

2 *(lieu, immeuble qui fait face)* **nous avons le lac pour v.** we look out on to *or* face the lake; **nous n'avons pas de v.** there are no buildings directly opposite

3 *(canapé)* tête-à-tête

4 *(entretien)* tête-à-tête, meeting

▫ **vis-à-vis de** PRÉP **1** *(en face de)* **être v. de qn** to be opposite sb; **les statues sont v. l'une de l'autre** the statues are opposite *or* facing one another

2 *(envers)* towards, vis-à-vis; **ce n'est pas très juste v. du reste de la famille** it's not very fair to the rest of the family; **mes sentiments v. de lui** my feelings towards *or* for him; **être sincère v. de soi-même** to be truthful with oneself; **quelle position avez-vous v. de ce problème?** what is your position on this problem?

3 *(par rapport à)* by comparison with, next to, against; **le dollar se tient bien v. des autres monnaies** the dollar is firm against the other currencies

▫ **en vis-à-vis** ADV **être en v.** to be opposite each other, to be facing each other; **assis en v.** sitting opposite each other *or* face-to-face

viscache [viskaʃ] NF *Zool* viscacha, vizcacha

viscéral, -e, -aux, -ales [viseral, -o] ADJ **1** *Anat* visceral **2** *Fig (dégoût)* profound; *(peur)* deep-rooted, profound; *(jalousie)* pathological; *(réaction)* gut *(avant n)*; *(répulsion)* instinctive; **je ne l'aime pas, c'est v.** I don't like him/her, it's a gut feeling

viscéralement [viseralmɑ̃] ADV *(jaloux)* pathologically

viscère [visɛr] NM *Anat* viscus; **viscères** viscera

viscoélasticité [viskoelastisite] NF *Phys* viscoelasticity

viscoélastique [viskoelastik] ADJ *Phys* viscoelastic

viscoplasticité [viskoplastisite] NF *Phys* viscoplasticity

viscoplastique [viskoplastik] ADJ *Phys* viscoplastic

viscose [viskoz] NF viscose; **robe en v.** viscose dress

viscosimètre [viskozimɛtr] NM *Phys* viscometer, viscosimeter

viscosité [viskozite] NF *(gén) & Phys* viscosity

visé [vize] NM aimed shot; **tirer au v.** to aim and fire

visée [vize] NF **1** *(gén pl) (intention)* design, aim; **avoir des visées sur qn/qch** to have designs on sb/sth **2** *Mil* aiming *(UNCOUNT)*, taking aim *(UNCOUNT)*, sighting; **ligne de v.** line of sight; **point de v.** target **3** *Cin & Phot* viewfinding

viser[1] [3] [vize] VT **1** *Mil (cible)* to (take) aim at; *(jambe, tête)* to aim for; **bien visé!** good shot!

2 *(aspirer à → poste)* to set one's sights on, to aim for; *(→ résultats)* to aim at *or* for; **il vise ce poste depuis longtemps** he's had his eye on this job for a long time

3 *Com (cibler → clientèle, public)* to target

4 *(concerner → sujet: réforme)* to be aimed *or* directed at; *(→ sujet: critique)* to be aimed *or* directed at, to be meant for; **cette loi vise plusieurs catégories de gens** this law is directed at several categories of people; **les denrées alimentaires ne sont pas visées par ce décret** foodstuffs are not affected by this order; **qui visais-tu par cette remarque?** who was your remark aimed *or* directed at?; **vous parlez de licenciements, qui exactement est visé?** you're talking about lay-offs *or Br* redundancies, who exactly do you have in mind?; **je ne vise personne!** I don't mean anybody in particular!; **se sentir visé** to feel one is being got at

5 *Fam (regarder)* to check out; **dis donc, vise un peu la chemise!** wow, check out the shirt!; **vise un peu la fille!** have a look at her!, get a load of her!

6 *Golf* **v. la balle** to address the ball

VI **1** *Mil* to (take) aim; **v. juste/trop bas** to aim accurately/too low

2 *Fig* **v. (trop) haut** to set one's sights *or* to aim (too) high; **tu as visé juste en lui disant cela!** you didn't miss the mark when you said that to him/her!

▫ **viser à** VT IND *(sujet: politique, personne)* to aim at; **v. à faire qch** to aim at doing sth; **mesures visant à faire payer les pollueurs** measures aimed at making the polluters pay

viser[2] [3] [vize] VT *Admin (passeport)* to visa; *(document → gén)* to stamp; *(→ avec ses initiales)* to initial; *Compta* **v. les livres de commerce** to certify the books; *Fin* **v. un effet** to stamp a bill

viseur [vizœr] NM **1** *(gén)* sight, sights; *(à lunette)* telescopic sight; *Aviat* **v. de lancement** bomb sight(s) **2** *Opt* telescopic sight **3** *Cin & Phot* viewfinder; **v. à cadre lumineux** collimator viewfinder

Vishnou [viʃnu] NPR *Rel* Vishnu

vishnouisme [viʃnuism] NM *Rel* Vishnuism

visibilité [vizibilite] NF visibility; **la v. est très réduite par le brouillard** visibility has been greatly reduced by the fog; *Aviat* **vol sans v.** instrument flying; **atterrir sans v.** to make a blind landing, to land blind; **v. nulle** zero visibility; *Aut* **v. panoramique** all-round visibility; *Aut* **v. de trois-quarts** three-quarter vision

visible [vizibl] ADJ **1** *(objet)* visible; **v. à l'œil nu** visible to the naked eye; **v. au microscope** visible under a microscope; **la tache est encore bien v.** the stain is still visible, you can still see the stain; **à peine v.** barely visible

2 *(évident → gêne, intérêt, mépris)* obvious, visible; *(→ amélioration, différence)* visible, perceptible; **elle m'en veut, c'est v.** she resents me, it's obvious; **il est v. que...** it's obvious *or* clear that...; **prendre un v. plaisir à faire qch** to take obvious pleasure in doing sth

3 *(prêt à recevoir)* **elle est v. de midi à quatre heures** she receives visitors between twelve and four; *Hum* **je ne serai pas v. demain** I won't be available to callers tomorrow; *Hum* **n'entre pas, je ne suis pas v.** don't come in, I'm not decent

4 *(pouvant être visité)* **l'appartement est v. le matin** the *Br* flat *or Am* apartment can be viewed in the morning

NM **le v.** that which is visible

visiblement [viziblәmɑ̃] ADV *(gêné, mécontent)* obviously, visibly; *(amélioré)* perceptibly, visibly; **v., ils se connaissaient déjà** they'd obviously met before

visière [vizjɛr] NF *(gén) Br* eyeshade, *Am* vizor; *(d'un casque)* visor, vizor; *(d'une casquette)* peak; **mettre sa main en v.** to shade one's eyes with one's hand; **v. de protection** faceguard

visigoth, -e [vizigo, -ɔt] = **wisigoth**

visiocasque [visjokask] NM cyberhelmet

visioconférence [vizjokɔ̃ferɑ̃s] NF *(conférence)* videoconference; *(concept)* videoconferencing

vision [vizjɔ̃] NF **1** *(idée)* view, outlook; **nous n'avons pas la même v. des choses** we see things differently; **nous partageons la même v. de la vie/du monde** we see *or* view life/the world in the same way; **sa v. idéaliste du mariage** his/her idealistic view of married life; **sa v. du monde** his/her world view

2 *(d'un créateur)* vision, imagination

3 *(image)* vision; *(hallucination)* vision, apparition; **v. momentanée de qch** momentary glimpse of sth; **une épouvantable v. de notre avenir** a nightmarish vision of our future; **avoir des visions** *(hallucinations)* to have visions *or* hallucinations, to see things; *Fam Hum* **tu as des visions!** you're seeing things!

4 *Physiol* vision; **la v. chez l'homme comprend quatre fonctions** human vision consists of four functions; *Tech* **système de v. de nuit** night vision system

visionique [visjɔnik] NF *Ordinat* computer vision

visionnage [vizjɔnaʒ] NM viewing *(of film, programme)*

visionnaire [vizjɔnɛr] ADJ visionary

NMF visionary, dreamer

visionnement [vizjɔnmɑ̃] NM *TV & Cin* screening; **v. préalable** preview

visionner [3] [vizjɔne] VT *(film, émission)* to view; *(diapositives)* to look at

visionneuse [vizjɔnøz] NF viewer

Visiopass® [vizjɔpɑs] NM *TV* = decoding card for French pay channels

visiophone [vizjɔfɔn] NM videophone, viewphone

visiophonie [vizjofɔni] NF video teleconferencing

visitandine [vizitɑ̃din] NF **1** *(religieuse)* nun of the Order of the Visitation, Visitandine **2** *(gâteau)* = cake made of beaten egg whites, butter and ground almonds

Visitation [vizitasjɔ̃] NF *Rel & Beaux-Arts* **la V.** the Visitation

visite [vizit] NF **1** *(chez quelqu'un → gén)* visit; *(→ courte)* call; *(→ d'un représentant)* call; **avoir** *ou* **recevoir la v. de qn** to have a visit from sb; **avoir la v. de la police** to receive a visit from the police; **avoir la v. d'un représentant** to be called on by a rep; **nous avons eu la v. de Marc** Marc called in to see us; **je m'attendais à sa v.** I was expecting him/her to call; **rendre v. à qn** to pay sb a visit, to call on sb, to visit sb; **rendre sa v. à qn** to return sb's visit *or* call; **faire une petite v. à qn** to pop round and see sb; **être en v. chez qn** to be paying sb a visit, to be visiting sb *or Am* with sb; **v. d'affaires** business call; **v. éclair** flying visit; *Com* **v. à froid** cold call; **v. officielle** official visit; **v. de politesse** courtesy call *or* visit; **v. privée** private visit; *Com* **v. de relance** follow-up visit

2 *(à l'hôpital, auprès d'un détenu)* visit; **heures de v.** visiting hours

3 *(visiteur)* **avoir de la v.** to have a visitor; *Fam* **tu attends de la** *ou* **une v.?** are you expecting a visitor *or* somebody?

4 *(exploration → d'un lieu)* visit, tour; *(→ d'une ville)* sightseeing tour; **v. guidée** guided tour; **v. pédagogique** educational visit

5 *(d'un médecin → chez le patient)* visit, call; *(→ dans un hôpital)* (ward) round; **le chirurgien fait sa v. tous les matins** the surgeon does his (ward) round every morning; **le docteur ne fait pas de visites** the doctor doesn't make house calls; **v. de contrôle** follow-up examination; **v. à domicile** house call *or* visit; **v. médicale** medical *or Am* physical examination, medical, *Am* physical; **passer une v. médicale** to undergo a medical examination, *Am* to take a physical examination; **tu as passé la v.?** did you have your medical *or Am* physical?; *Mil* have you seen the MO?

6 *(inspection → pour acheter)* viewing; *(→ pour surveiller)* inspection; **v. domiciliaire** house search; **v. de douane** customs inspection; **v. d'inspection** visitation, visit; **faire une v. d'inspection de** to visit

7 *Rel* **v. pastorale** *ou* **de l'évêque** pastoral visit, visitation *(by bishop)*

visiter [3] [vizite] VT **1** *(se promener dans → région, monument)* to visit; *(→ caves, musée)* to go round, to visit; *(→ pour acheter)* to view; *(→ par curiosité)* to look round; **v. une cathédrale** to visit *or* to tour a cathedral; **on nous a fait v. l'usine** we were shown round *or* over the factory, we were given a tour of the factory; **une personne de l'agence vous fera v. l'appartement** somebody from the agency will show you round *or Am* through the *Br* flat *or Am* apartment; **c'est joli ici, je peux v.?** it's nice here, can I have a look around *or* can I look around?; **elle m'a fait v. sa maison** she showed me around her house; *Hum* **nous avons déjà été visités une fois** *(on nous a déjà cambriolés)* we've been burgled once already

2 *(rendre visite à → détenu)* to visit; *(→ malade, indigent)* to visit, to call on; *(→ client)* to call on

3 *(inspecter → matériel, valise)* to examine, to inspect; *(→ bateau)* to inspect

4 *Rel (diocèse)* to visit; *(sujet: Saint-Esprit)* to visit

5 *Tex* to perch

▸**se visiter** VPR to be open to visitors; **le musée se visite en deux heures** it takes two hours to go round the museum

visiteur, -euse [vizitœr, -øz] NM,F **1** *(invité)* visitor, caller; *(d'un musée)* visitor; *Hum* **ils ont eu des visiteurs la nuit dernière** *(voleurs, souris)* they had visitors last night

2 *(professionnel)* **v. des douanes** customs inspector; **v. de prison** prison visitor; **visiteuse scolaire** *ou* **sociale** = social worker who specializes in visiting schools in the interests of child welfare

3 *Com* representative, rep; **v. médical** representative in pharmaceutical products, medical

representative; **v. en soies** representative *or* traveller in silks

4 *Tex* percher

5 *Mktg* **v. unique** unique visitor

❑ **visiteurs** NMPL *Sport* visiting *or* away team

'Les Visiteurs du soir' *Carné* 'The Devil's Envoys'

visnage [visnaʒ]NM *Bot* bishop's weed

vison [vizɔ̃] NM **1** *Zool* mink **2** *(fourrure)* mink **3** *(manteau)* mink (coat)

visonnière [vizɔnjɛr]NF mink farm

visqueux, -euse [viskø, -øz]ADJ **1** *Phys (matière)* viscous; *(surface)* viscid **2** *Fig (personne)* slimy

vissage [visaʒ] NM *(d'un écrou, d'un couvercle, d'un bouchon)* screwing on; *(d'une planche sur un support)* screwing down

vissé, -e [vise]ADJ *Fam* **être bien/mal v.** to be in a good/foul mood■

visser [3] [vise]VT **1** *(fixer → planche, support)* to screw on; *(→ couvercle)* to screw on *or* down; **le miroir est vissé au mur** the mirror is screwed to the wall; *Fig* **le monocle vissé à l'œil** his monocle screwed into his eye socket; **un chapeau vissé sur la tête** with a hat clamped on his/her head; **être vissé sur son siège** to be glued to one's chair

2 *(en tournant → bouchon, embout, écrou)* to screw on; *(→ robinet)* to turn off

3 *Fam (personne)* to crack down on, to put the screws on; **il a toujours vissé ses gosses** he always kept a tight rein on his kids

▶**se visser** VPR to screw on *or* in; **ampoule qui se visse** screw-in bulb; **la lance se visse au bout du tuyau** the nozzle screws on to the end of the hose; **le couvercle se visse facilement/se visse mal** the lid screws on easily/doesn't screw on properly

visserie [visri] NF **1** *(vis et boulons)* screws and bolts **2** *(usine)* screw-cutting factory

visseuse [visøz]NF screwing machine

Vistule [vistyl]NF **la V.** the River Vistula

visu [vizy] *voir* **de visu**

visualisation [vizɥalizasjɔ̃]NF **1** *(mentale)* visualization, visualizing **2** *Ordinat* display; **console** *ou* **écran de v.** visual display terminal *or* unit, VDU; **v. de la page à l'écran** page preview; **v. sur écran** soft copy; **v. de vidéo** video playback

visualiser [3] [vizɥalize] VT **1** *(mentalement)* to visualize **2** *(rendre visible)* to make visible to the eye; *Ordinat* to display

visualiseur [vizɥalizœr]NM *Ordinat* viewer

visuel, -elle [vizɥɛl]ADJ *(mémoire, support)* visual

NM **1** *Ordinat* visual display unit *or* terminal, VDU **2** *(d'une affiche)* artwork **3** *(publicité)* visual

visuellement [vizɥɛlmɑ̃]ADV visually

vit 1 *voir* **vivre**[2] **2** *voir* **voir**

vitacée [vitase] *Bot* NF member of the Vitaceae family

❑ **vitacées** NFPL Vitaceae

vital, -e, -aux, -ales [vital, -o]ADJ **1** *Biol & Physiol* vital **2** *(indispensable)* vital, essential; **l'agriculture est vitale pour notre région** agriculture is vital to this region; **il est v. que...** it's vital *or* essential that...; *Fam* **il faut que tu viennes, c'est v.!** you must come, it's vital!, you absolutely must come! **3** *(fondamental → problème, question)* vital, fundamental

vitalisme [vitalism]NM *Phil* vitalism

vitaliste [vitalist] *Phil* ADJ vitalistic, vitalist

NMF vitalist

vitalité [vitalite] NF *(d'une personne)* vitality, energy; *(d'une économie)* dynamism, vitality, buoyancy; *(d'une expression, d'une théorie)* vitality; **être plein de v.** to be full of energy

vitamine [vitamin]NF vitamin; **la v. A/B12** vitamin A/B12; **alimentation riche/pauvre en vitamines** food with a high/low vitamin content, food that is high/low in vitamins; **enfant qui manque de vitamines** child with a vitamin deficiency; **as-tu pris tes vitamines?** have you taken your vitamins?

vitaminé, -e [vitamine]ADJ with added vitamins, vitaminized

vitaminique [vitaminik]ADJ vitamin *(avant n)*

vitaminothérapie [vitaminɔterapi] NF vitamin therapy

vite [vit]ADV **1** *(rapidement → courir, marcher)* fast, quickly; *(→ se propager)* rapidly, quickly; **roule moins v.** slow down, don't drive so fast; **va plus v.** speed up, go faster; **plus v.!** faster!; **ne va pas si v.!** *(en voiture)* not so fast!, slow down a bit!; **tout s'est passé si v. que je n'ai pas eu le temps de voir** everything happened so quickly that I didn't see a thing; **comme le temps passe v.!** doesn't time fly!; **elle apprend/travaille v.** she's a quick learner/worker; **il calcule v.** he's quick at calculations; **on fait faire des travaux, mais ça ne va pas v.** we're having some alterations done, but it's taking a long time *or* it's a long job; **prenons un taxi, ça ira plus v.** let's take a taxi, it'll be quicker; **les exercices vont trop v. pour moi** I can't keep up *or* keep pace with the exercises; **ça a été v. réglé** it was settled in no time at all, it was soon settled; **je me suis v. rendu compte que...** I soon *or* quickly *or* swiftly realized that...; **fais v.!** hurry up!, be quick (about it)!; **tu retournes en ville? – je fais v.** are you going back into town? – I won't be long; **v., il arrive!** quick *or* hurry up, he's coming!; **prends l'argent, v.!** take the money, quick *or* quickly!; **et plus v. que ça!** and be quick about it!; **va faire tes devoirs, et plus v. que cela!** go and do your homework, and get a move on *or* and be quick about it!; *Fam* **v. fait** quickly■; **avoir v. fait de faire qch** to be quick (about) doing sth; **tu auras v. fait de t'en apercevoir** you'll soon realize■; **il eut v. fait de s'habiller** he was dressed in no time; **boire un coup v. fait** to have a quick drink■; **range-moi ta chambre v. fait!** tidy up your room and be quick about it!; **il est parti v. fait** he cleared off without wasting too much time; **tu vas aller au lit v. fait si tu continues à pleurer!** you'll be in bed in no time at all if you carry on crying!; **ça a été du v. fait!** it didn't take long!■, that was quick work!; *Péj* it's slapdash work!■; *Fam* **faire qch v. fait, bien fait** to do sth in next to no time; **on lui a repeint sa grille v. fait, bien fait** we gave his/her gate a nice new coat of paint in no time; *très Fam* **je vais l'envoyer se faire voir v. fait, bien fait!** I'll send him/her packing once and for all!; *Fig* **aller plus v. que la musique** *ou* **les violons** to jump the gun

2 *(à la hâte)* quickly, in a hurry *or* rush; **manger v.** to bolt one's food (down); **manger trop v.** to eat too fast *or* too quickly; **je vais v. faire une course** I'm going to do one quick errand; **aller v.** *(dans ses conclusions)* to be hasty; **tu vas un peu v.!** you're a bit hasty!; **ne conclus pas trop v.** don't jump *or* rush to conclusions; **ils vont gagner – c'est v. dit!** they're going to win – I wouldn't be so sure!; **il est assez efficace – il faut le dire v.!** he's quite efficient – well, that's one way of putting it!; **parler trop v.** to speak too soon; **ne parle pas trop v.!** don't speak too soon!

3 *(sans tarder)* quickly, soon; **il faut agir v.** we must do something quickly *or* very soon; **vous serez v. guéri** you'll soon be better; **réponds-moi aussi v. que tu peux** answer me as quickly as you can *or* as soon as possible; **envoyez v. votre bulletin-réponse!** send your entry form now!; **viens v. nous retrouver au bord de la mer!** come and join us at the seaside soon!; **lève-toi v., on sonne!** get up quick, there's someone at the door!; **j'ai v. compris de quoi il s'agissait** I soon realized what it was all about, it didn't take me long to realize what it was all about

4 *(facilement)* quickly, easily; **elle s'énerve v.** she loses her temper easily; **méfie-toi, il a v. fait de s'énerver** be careful, he loses his temper easily; **on a v. fait de dire...** it's easy to say...; **on a v. fait de se brûler avec ça!** it's easy to burn yourself on that thing!

5 *(locution)* **aller v. en besogne** *(être rapide)* to be a quick worker; *(être trop pressé)* to be over-hasty; **tu vas l'épouser? tu vas v. en besogne!** so you're marrying him/her? you didn't waste any time!; **vous allez un peu v. en besogne, je ne vous accuse pas!** don't jump to conclusions, I haven't accused you of anything!

ADJ *(en langage journalistique → coureur)* fast

❑ **au plus vite** ADV as soon as possible

vitellin, -e [vitɛlɛ̃, -in] ADJ *Biol* vitelline; **membrane vitelline** vitelline membrane; **cellule vitelline** vitelline cell; **vésicule vitelline, sac v.** yolk sac

vitellus [vitɛlys]NM *Biol* vitellus, yolk

vitelotte [vitlɔt]NF kidney potato

vitesse [vitɛs] NF **1** *(d'un coureur, d'un véhicule)* speed; **à la v. de 180 km/h** at (a speed of) 180 km/h; **la v. est limitée à 90 km/h** the speed limit is 90 km/h; **à quelle v. rouliez-vous?** what speed were you driving at *or* doing?; **rouler à une v. folle** to drive at breakneck speed; **faire de la v.** to drive *or* to go fast; **la route est dégagée, tu peux faire un peu de v.** the road's clear, you can speed up a bit; **prendre de la v.** to pick up speed, to speed up; **gagner/perdre de la v.** to gather/to lose speed; *Aviat* **v. ascensionnelle** rate of climb; *aussi Fig* **v. de croisière** cruising speed; **nous avons atteint notre v. de croisière qui est de 750 km/h** *(en avion)* we're now cruising at (a speed of) 750 km/h; **le projet a maintenant atteint sa v. de croisière** the project is now running smoothly along; **v. de pointe** top *or* maximum speed; *Aviat* **v. relative** airspeed; *Arch Rail* **grande/petite v.** fast/slow goods service; **gagner** *ou* **prendre qn de v.** *(à pied)* to walk faster than sb; *(en voiture)* to go *or* to drive faster than sb; *Fig* to beat sb to it

2 *Phys (d'un corps)* speed, velocity; *(de la lumière)* speed; **v. acquise** momentum; **v. aréolaire** areal velocity; **v. initiale** *(gén)* initial speed; *Mil* muzzle speed; **v. de libération** escape velocity *or* speed; **v. moyenne** average speed; **v. de réaction** reaction velocity *or* speed; **la v. du son** the speed of sound; **à la v. du son** at the speed of sound

3 *(rythme → d'une action)* speed, quickness, rapidity; *(→ d'une transformation)* speed, rapidity; **ses cheveux poussent à une v. incroyable!** his/her hair grows so fast!; **il travaille à la v. d'un escargot!** he works at a snail's pace!; **à la v. de deux pages par jour** at the rate of two pages per day

4 *Aut & Tech* gear; **première/deuxième/troisième v.** first/second/third gear; **changer de v.** to change gear; **passer les vitesses** to go up through the gears; *(en rétrogradant)* to go down through the gears; *Fam* **les vitesses ne veulent pas passer** the gearbox is sticking; **passer à la v. supérieure** to change up *(to next gear)*; *Fig* **à deux vitesses** two-tier; **médecine/sécurité sociale à deux vitesses** two-tier medical/social security system; **une Europe à deux vitesses** a two-speed Europe; *Fam* **à la v. grand V** at the double, *Br* at a rate of knots; **et ramène-le-moi à la v. grand V!** and bring it back to me PDQ!; **il est parti à la v. grand V** you couldn't see him for dust

5 *Ordinat* **v. d'accès** access speed; **v. d'affichage** display speed; **v. de calcul** processing *or* computing speed; **v. de clignotement** blink rate; **v. d'écriture** write speed; **v. d'exécution** execution speed; **v. de frappe** keying speed; **v. de frappe à la minute/à l'heure** keystrokes per minute/per hour; **v. d'horloge** clock rate *or* speed; **v. d'impression** print speed; **v. du processeur** processor speed; **v. de traitement** processing speed; **v. de transfert** transfer speed

6 *Écon* **v. de circulation de la monnaie** velocity of circulation of money; **v. de transformation des capitaux** income velocity of capital

7 *Physiol* **v. de sédimentation** erythrocyte sedimentation rate

❑ **à toute vitesse** ADV in double-quick time; **aller à toute v.** to go at full *or* top speed, to rush along, **il est revenu à toute v.** he was back double quick; **passer à toute v.** *(temps, moto)* to fly by

❑ **en vitesse** ADV *(rapidement)* quickly; *(à la hâte)* in a rush *or* hurry; **déjeuner/se laver en v.** to have a quick lunch/wash; **écrire une lettre en v.** to dash off a letter; **un petit mot en v. pour vous dire...** just a quick line to let you know...; **je peux venir te voir en v.?** can I pop in for a minute?; **on prend un verre en v.?** shall we have a quick drink?; **sors d'ici, et en v.!** get out of here and be sharp about it!; **fais ton lit, et en v.!** make your bed and do it quickly!; **il a déguerpi en v.!** he left at the double!, he didn't hang around!

viticole [vitikɔl] ADJ **région** v. wine-growing or wine-producing region; **entreprise** v. Br wine-making company, Am winery; **culture** v. wine-growing, Spéc viticulture; **industrie** v. wine industry

viticulteur, -trice [vitikyltœr, -tris] NM,F wine-grower, wine-producer, Spéc viticulturist

viticulture [vitikyltyr] NF vine-growing, Spéc viticulture

vitiligo [vitiligo] NM Méd vitiligo, leucoderma

vitivinicole [vitivinikɔl] ADJ relating to vine-growing and wine-making

vitiviniculture [vitivinikyltyr] NF vine-growing and wine-making

vitoulet [vitulɛ] NM Belg = veal meatball

vitrage [vitraʒ] NM 1 (vitres) windows; (panneau) glass partition 2 (verre) window glass 3 (installation) glazing 4 (rideau) net curtain

vitrail, -aux [vitraj, -o] NM 1 (gén) stained-glass window; (non coloré) leaded glass window; **les vitraux de Chartres** the stained-glass windows of Chartres 2 (technique) **le** v. stained-glass window making

vitrain [vitrɛ̃] NM Géol vitrain

vitraux [vitro] voir **vitrail**

vitre [vitr] NF 1 (plaque de verre) (window) pane 2 (fenêtre) window; **produit pour les vitres** glass-or window-cleaning product; **faire les vitres** to clean the windows; Fam **casser les vitres** to get angry■, to kick up a fuss; Aut v. **arrière** rear window

vitré, -e [vitre] ADJ 1 (porte → complètement) glass (avant n); (→ au milieu) glazed; (panneau, toit) glass (avant n) 2 (parchemin) vitreous 3 Anat (corps, humeur) vitreous

vitrer [3] [vitre] VT (fenêtre, porte) to glaze; (verrière) to fit with glass

vitrerie [vitrəri] NF 1 (fabrique) glaziery 2 (commerce) window glass trade or industry 3 (vitres) window glass

vitreux, -euse [vitrø, -øz] ADJ 1 (terne → œil, regard) glassy, glazed; **regard** v. glassy stare, glazed look 2 Géol & Phys vitreous 3 (porcelaine) vitreous

vitrier [vitrije] NM glazier; Fam **ton père n'est pas** v.! I can't see through you, you know!

vitrière [vitrijɛr] NF metal framing (for windows)

vitrifiable [vitrifjabl] ADJ 1 Nucl vitrifiable 2 (parquet) sealable

vitrificateur [vitrifikatœr] NM sealant

vitrification [vitrifikasjɔ̃] NF 1 (d'un parquet) sealing; (de tuiles) glazing 2 (de sable, de déchets nucléaires) vitrification

vitrifier [9] [vitrifje] VT 1 (parquet) to seal; (tuiles) to glaze; **brique vitrifiée** glazed brick 2 (déchets nucléaires, sable) to vitrify 3 (ville) to destroy with nuclear weapons

vitrine [vitrin] NF 1 (devanture) display window, Br shop or Am store window; (vitre) shop window; (objets exposés) window display; **faire une** v. to dress a window; **refaire la** v. to change the window display; **mettre qch en** v. to display or to put sth in the window; **des articles en** v. articles (on display) in the window; Fam **faire ou lécher les vitrines** to do some window-shopping; Fig **Paris est la** v. **de la France** Paris is the showcase of France
2 (meuble → de maison) display cabinet; (→ de musée) display cabinet, showcase; (→ de magasin) showcase, display case

vitriol [vitrijɔl] NM 1 Chim vitriol; **(huile de)** v. oil of vitriol; Fig **des propos au** v. caustic or vitriolic remarks; Fig **une attaque au** v. a vitriolic or devastating attack 2 Fam (mauvais vin) cheap wine■, Br plonk; (mauvais alcool) gutrot

vitriolage [vitrijɔlaʒ] NM (sur quelqu'un) acid attack

vitrioler [3] [vitrijɔle] VT 1 (traiter) to vitriolize 2 (blesser) v. **qn** to attack sb with acid; **se faire** v., **être vitriolé** to have acid thrown in one's face, to be the victim of an acid attack

vitrioleur, -euse [vitrijɔlœr, -øz] NM,F acid thrower

vitro [vitro] voir **in vitro**

vitrocéramique [vitroseramik] ADJ **plaque** v. ceramic hob

vitrophanie [vitrofani] NF window sticker

vitulaire [vitylɛr] ADJ Vét **fièvre** v. puerperal fever, milk fever

vitupérations [vityperasjɔ̃] NFPL Littéraire vituperation (UNCOUNT), vilification (UNCOUNT), verbal abuse (UNCOUNT)

vitupérer [18] [vitypere] VI Littéraire to vituperate; v. **contre qn/qch** to inveigh against sb/sth; **elle passe son temps à** v. **contre les transports en commun** she spends her time ranting and raving about public transport
VT to inveigh against, Sout to vituperate

vivable [vivabl] ADJ (situation) bearable; (habitation) fit for living in; Fam (personne) **elle n'est pas** v. she's impossible to live with; **cette situation n'est plus** v. this situation is intolerable; **ce n'est plus** v. **au bureau!** it's unbearable in the office now!

vivace[1] [vivas] ADJ 1 Bot hardy 2 (qui dure → croyance, opinion, tradition) deep-rooted; (→ souvenir) abiding; (→ foi) steadfast; **une région où le sentiment socialiste est très** v. a staunchly socialist region; **son souvenir est encore** v. his/her memory is still very much alive

vivace[2] [vivatʃe] Mus ADJ INV vivace
ADV vivace

vivacité [vivasite] NF 1 (promptitude → d'une attaque, d'une démarche, d'un geste) briskness; (→ d'une intelligence) sharpness, acuteness; **elle s'est retournée avec** v. she turned round sharply; v. **d'esprit** quick-wittedness; (humour) sparkling wit
2 (brusquerie → d'une personne, de propos) brusqueness; v. **d'humeur** hotness of temper, quick-temperedness; **la** v. **de sa réplique** the sharpness of his/her reply
3 (entrain → d'une personne, d'un style) vivaciousness, vivacity, liveliness; (→ d'un marché) liveliness, buoyancy; (→ d'une description) vividness, vivacity; (→ d'un regard) vivacity; **une femme âgée pleine de** v. a sprightly old woman; **parler avec** v. to speak animatedly; **la** v. **de la conversation** the lively pace of the conversation
4 (force → d'une douleur) sharpness, intensity; (→ du froid) bitterness, sharpness; (→ d'une impression) vividness, keenness; (→ d'une couleur) brightness, vividness; (→ d'une lumière) brightness

vivandier [vivɑ̃dje] NM Hist sutler

vivandière [vivɑ̃djɛr] NF Hist vivandière, sutler

vivaneau, -x [vivano] NM Ich snapper

vivant, -e [vivɑ̃, -ɑ̃t] ADJ 1 Biol (organisme) living; (personne, animal) alive; **enterré** v. buried alive; **il est encore** v. he's still alive; **je suis** v.! I'm alive!; **j'en suis sorti** v. I lived to tell the tale, I survived; **cuire un homard** v. to cook a live lobster or a lobster alive; **lui** v., **personne n'allait là-bas** while he was alive, nobody went there
2 (existant → croyance, tradition, souvenir) living; **l'emploi du mot est resté très** v. the term is still very much in use
3 (animé → enfant, conférence, présentation) lively, spirited; (→ bourg, rue) lively, bustling, full of life; **c'est une classe très vivante** it's a very lively class; **il a laissé en nous un souvenir très** v. he left us with a very vivid memory of him
4 (réaliste → description, style) vivid
5 (constitué d'humains → rempart) human
6 (incarné, personnifié → preuve, exemple, témoignage) living
NM 1 (période) **de son** v. (dans le passé) when he/she was alive; (dans le présent) as long as he/she lives; **je ne verrai pas ça de mon** v.! I won't live to see it!; **du** v. **de mon frère, j'y allais souvent** when my brother was alive, I used to go there often
2 (personne) **un bon** v. a bon viveur, a connoisseur of the good things in life
□ **vivants** NMPL Rel **les vivants** the living; **les vivants et les morts** (gén) the living and the dead; Bible the quick and the dead

vivarium [vivarjɔm] NM vivarium

vivaro-alpin [vivaroalpɛ̃] NM = langue d'oc dialect spoken in the Ardèche and Drôme

vivat [viva] NM cheer; **s'avancer sous les vivats** to walk forth through a hail of applause
EXCLAM Arch hurrah!, bravo!

vive[1] [viv] ADJ voir **vif**

vive[2] [viv] EXCLAM v. **le roi!** long live the King!; v. **le Canada/la République!** long live Canada/the

Republic!; v. **ou vivent les vacances!** three cheers for holidays!; Fam Hum v. **moi!** hurrah for me!

vive[3] [viv] NF Ich weever

vive-eau [vivo] (pl **vives-eaux** [vivzo]) NF spring tide

vivement [vivmɑ̃] ADV 1 (exprime un souhait) v. **le week-end!** I can't wait for the weekend!, Br roll on the weekend!, Am bring on the weekend!; v. **qu'il s'en aille!** I'll be glad when he's gone!
2 (extrêmement → ému, troublé) deeply, greatly; (→ intéressé) greatly, keenly; **je souhaite** v. **que...** I sincerely wish that...; **féliciter/remercier/recommander qn** v. to congratulate/thank/recommend sb warmly; **s'intéresser** v. **à qch** to take a keen interest in sth
3 (intensément → éclairé, coloré) brightly; **contraster** v. **avec** to contrast sharply with
4 (brusquement → interpeller) sharply; v. **rabroué** told off in no uncertain terms
5 (vite → marcher) briskly; **se tourner** v. to turn round quickly; **il se dirigea** v. **vers la sortie** he walked briskly towards the exit

vivent [viv] 1 voir **vive**[2] 2 voir **vivre**[2]

viverridé [vivɛride] Zool NM viverrid, Spéc member of the Viverridae
□ **viverridés** NMPL viverrids, Spéc Viverridae

viverrin, -e [vivɛrɛ̃, -in] ADJ Zool viverrine

viveur, -euse [vivœr, -øz] NM,F Vieilli bon viveur

vividité [vividite] NF Psy vividness

vivier [vivje] NM 1 (d'un commerce) fish tank 2 Pêche (enclos → pour poissons) fishpond; (→ pour homards) crawl; (→ d'un bateau) fish tank or well; v. **de capture** box trap 3 Fig **un véritable** v. **d'acteurs** a breeding ground for actors

vivifiant, -e [vivifjɑ̃, -ɑ̃t] ADJ (air, climat) bracing, invigorating; (expérience) invigorating; (atmosphère) enlivening

vivificateur, -trice [vivifikatœr, -tris] ADJ Littéraire (air, climat) invigorating; (expérience, atmosphère) revivifying

vivifier [9] [vivifje] VT (personne) to revivify, to invigorate; (industrie, région) to bring life to; (imagination, sentiments) to quicken, to sharpen
VI Rel to give life

vivipare [vivipar] Zool ADJ viviparous
NMF member of the Vivipara

viviparité [viviparite] NF Zool viviparity, viviparousness

vivisection [vivisɛksjɔ̃] NF vivisection; **être contre la** v. to be an antivivisectionist, to be against live experiments

vivo [vivo] voir **in vivo**

vivoir [vivwar] NM Can Vieilli living room

vivoter [3] [vivɔte] VI (personne) to get by or along (with little money); **il vivotait de ses tableaux** he scraped a living from his paintings

vivre[1] [vivr] NM **le** v. **et le couvert** bed and board
□ **vivres** NMPL food (UNCOUNT), foodstuffs, provisions; **couper les vivres à qn** to stop sb's allowance

vivre[2] [90] [vivr] VI 1 Biol (personne, animal) to live, to be alive; (cellule, plante) to live; **elle vivait encore quand ils l'ont emmenée** she was still alive when they took her away; v. **vieux ou longtemps** to live to a great age or a ripe old age; **cesser de** v. to die; **elle a vécu jusqu'à 95 ans** she lived to be 95; **qu'aurait-elle pensé si elle avait vécu?** what would she have thought if she'd lived?; **à l'époque où il vivait** at the time when he was alive; **il ne lui reste plus longtemps à** v. he/she hasn't got much time left (to live); **il lui reste deux mois à** v. he's/she's got two months to live; **les plantes/animaux qui vivent dans l'eau** plants/animals which live in water; **Mil qui vive?** who goes there?; **avoir vécu** to have had one's day; **le Front populaire a vécu** the Popular Front has had its day or is finished; Fam **ma pauvre télé a vécu** my poor old TV is on its last legs; Prov **qui vivra verra** time will tell
2 (mener une existence) to live; v. **en paix** to live in peace; v. **en honnête homme** to lead an honest life; v. **heureux** to live happily; v. **libre et indépendant** to lead a free and independent life; **mes personnages vivent indépendamment de moi** my characters have a life of their own; v. **malhonnêtement/pieusement** to lead a dishonest/pious life; v. **au jour le jour** to take

each day as it comes; **v. à l'heure de l'Europe/du XXIème siècle** to live in the world of the European community/of the 21st century; **v. dans le luxe/l'angoisse** to live in luxury/anxiety; **v. dans le péché** to lead a sinful life; **on voit que tu n'as jamais vécu dans la misère** it's obvious you've never experienced poverty; **ne v. que pour la musique/sa famille** to live only for music/one's family; **une rue qui vit la nuit** a street that comes alive at night; **se laisser v.** to take life easily *or* as it comes; **prendre le temps de v.** to take the time to enjoy life; **il fait bon v. ici** life is good *or* it's a good life here; **une maison où il fait bon v.** a house that's good to live in; **elle a beaucoup vécu** she's seen life; *Littéraire* **il a vécu** he is dead; **on ne vit plus** *(on est inquiet)* we're worried sick; *(on est harassé)* this isn't a life, this isn't what you can call living; **il ne sait pas v.** *(il est impoli)* he has no manners; *(il est trop nerveux)* he doesn't know how to enjoy life; *Fam* **je vais t'apprendre à v.!** I'll teach you some manners!; **ils vécurent heureux et eurent beaucoup d'enfants** (and) they lived happily ever after; *Prov* **pour v. heureux, vivons cachés** = the happiest people are those who keep themselves to themselves

3 *(résider)* to live; **ils sont venus v. ici** they came to live *or* to settle here; **v. au Brésil/dans un château** to live in Brazil/in a castle; **v. à Paris/en province/à la campagne/à l'étranger** to live in Paris/in the provinces/in the country/abroad *or* overseas; **v. dans une** *ou* **en communauté** to live communally *or* in a community; **v. à la campagne ne m'a jamais attiré** country life has never appealed to me; **v. avec qn** *(maritalement)* to live with sb; *(en amis)* to share *or* to live with sb; **v. ensemble** *(couple non marié)* to live together; **être facile à v.** to be easy-going *or* easy to get on with; **être difficile à v.** to be difficult to get on with; **son mari est difficile à v.** her husband makes her life very difficult

4 *(subsister)* to live; **travailler pour v.** to work for a living; **les sommes que tu m'envoies m'aident à v.** the money you send me keeps me going; **avoir de quoi v.** to have enough to live on; **ils ont tout juste de quoi v.** they've just enough to live on; **de quoi vit-il?** what does he live on?; *(que fait-il dans la vie?)* what does he do for a living?; **v. sur un seul salaire** to live *or* to exist on just one salary; **faire v. une famille** *(personne)* to provide a living for *or* to support a family; *(commerce)* to provide a living for a family; **v. bien/chichement** to have a good/poor standard of living; **v. de** to live on; **v. de fruits/de ses rentes** to live on fruit/on one's private income; **ils vivaient de la cueillette et de la chasse** they lived on what they gathered and hunted *or* off the land; **v. de sa plume** to live by one's pen; **v. de chimères** to live a life of illusion; **v. d'espérances** to live in hope; *Littéraire* **v. d'industrie** to live by one's wits; **l'espoir fait v.!** we all live in hope!; **il faut bien v.!** one's got to keep the wolf from the door *or* to live (somehow)!; **v. aux crochets de qn** to sponge off sb; **v. de l'air du temps** to live on thin air; **v. d'amour et d'eau fraîche** to live on love alone

5 *(se perpétuer* → *croyance, coutume)* to be alive; **pour que notre entreprise vive** so that our company may continue to exist

6 *(donner l'impression de vie* → *sculpture, tableau)* **voici une description qui vit** here is a description that is full of life

VT 1 *(passer par* → *époque, événement)* to live through; **elle a vécu la guerre** she lived through *or* went through the war; **v. des temps difficiles** to live through *or* to experience difficult times; **v. des jours heureux/paisibles** to spend one's days happily/peacefully; **v. une expérience unique/inoubliable** to go through *or* to have a unique/an unforgettable experience; **v. une passion** to live out a passion

2 *(assumer* → *divorce, grossesse, retraite)* to experience; **elle a mal/bien vécu mon départ** she couldn't cope/she coped well after I left

3 *(locutions)* **v. sa vie** to live one's own life; **v. sa foi** to live intensely through one's faith; **il faut v. l'instant présent** one must live for the moment

►**se vivre VPR la maladie se vit mal quand on est seul** it's difficult being ill when you're on your own

vivré, -e [vivre] **ADJ** *Hér* dancetté, dancetty

vivrier, -ère [vivrije, -ɛr] **ADJ cultures vivrières** food crops

vizir [vizir] **NM** vizier; **le Grand v.** the Grand Vizier

vizirat [vizira] **NM** *Hist* vizierate, viziership

VL [veɛl] **NM** *Transp (abrév* **véhicule lourd**) HGV

v'là [vla] **PRÉP** *Fam* **le v.!** here he is!; **et juste à ce moment-là, v. t-y pas qu'il se met à pleuvoir!** and just then, would you believe it, it starts raining!

Vladivostok [vladivɔstɔk] **NM** Vladivostok

vlan, v'lan [vlɑ̃] **EXCLAM** *(bruit* → *de porte)* bang!, wham!, slam!; *(*→ *de coup)* smack!, thud!, wallop!; **et v.! il est tombé** and bang, he fell over!

VLF [veɛlɛf] **NF** *TV & Rad (abrév* **very low frequency**) VLF

vlimeux [vlimø] *Can Fam* **NM 1** *(chanceux)* lucky devil; **le petit v.!** (the) lucky devil! **2** *(intrigant)* crafty devil **3** *(coquin)* (little) rascal *or* devil

▫ **en vlimeux ADV être fort/riche en v.** to be very strong/rich▪ **ADJ être en v.** to be fuming, to be in a temper

vlog [velɔg] **NM** *Ordinat* vlog, video blog

VMC [veɛmse] **NF** *Constr (abrév* **ventilation mécanique contrôlée**) mechanical ventilation system

vMCJ *Méd (abrév écrite* **variant de la maladie de Creutzfeldt-Jakob**) vCJD

VMP [veɛmpe] **NFPL** *Bourse (abrév* **valeurs mobilières de placement**) marketable securities

VNO [veɛno] **NM** *Méd (abrév* **virus du Nil occidental**) West Nile virus

VO [veo] *Cin* **NF** *(abrév* **version originale**) = indicates that a film is in the original language and not dubbed

▫ **en VO ADJ** in the original version; **en VO sous-titrée** in the original version with subtitles; **voir un film en VO** to see a film in the original (language) version

vo *(abrév écrite* **verso**) vo.

vocable [vɔkabl] **NM 1** *Ling* term **2** *Rel* name, patronage; **sous le v. de** dedicated to

vocabulaire [vɔkabylɛr] **NM 1** *Ling* vocabulary; **v. argotique/philosophique** slang/philosophical vocabulary; **v. administratif/juridique/technique** administrative/legal/technical vocabulary; **le v. d'un enfant de six ans** the vocabulary of a six-year-old (child); **enrichir son v.** to enlarge one's vocabulary; **avoir du v.** to have a wide vocabulary; **surveiller son v.** to watch *or* to mind one's language; **ce mot n'est pas dans mon v.** it's not a word that I use; **quel v.!** *(réprimande)* language!; **un junkie, pour employer le v. à la mode** a junkie, to use the in *or* fashionable word

2 *(lexique)* lexicon, (specialized) dictionary

vocal, -e, -aux, -ales [vɔkal, -o] **ADJ** vocal

vocalement [vɔkalmɑ̃] **ADV** vocally

vocalique [vɔkalik] **ADJ** vocalic, vowel *(avant n)*

vocalisateur, -trice [vɔkalizatœr, -tris] **NM,F** *Mus* vocalizer

vocalisation [vɔkalizasjɔ̃] **NF** *Ling & Mus* vocalization, vocalizing

vocalisatrice [vɔkalizatris] *voir* **vocalisateur**

vocalise [vɔkaliz] **NF** *Mus* singing exercise, *Spéc* vocalise; **faire des vocalises** to do singing exercises

vocaliser [3] [vɔkalize] **VI** *Mus* to practise scales, *Spéc* to vocalize

VT *Ling* to vocalize

►**se vocaliser VPR** to become vocalized

vocalisme [vɔkalism] **NM** *Ling* vocalism

vocatif [vɔkatif] **NM** *Gram* vocative (case); **au v.** in the vocative (case)

vocation [vɔkasjɔ̃] **NF 1** *(d'une personne)* vocation, calling; **avoir une v. musicale/théâtrale** to have a musical/theatrical vocation; **ne pas avoir/avoir la v. (de)** to feel no/to feel a vocation (for); **pour être assistante sociale, il faut avoir la v.** to be a social worker, one has to feel a vocation for it; **faire qch par v.** to do sth as a labour of love; **j'ai manqué** *ou* **raté ma v., j'aurais dû être architecte** I've missed my vocation, I should have been an architect; **voilà un pansement bien fait, tu as manqué** *ou* **raté ta v.** what a professional-looking bandage, you missed your vocation

2 *(rôle, mission)* **la v. industrielle de l'Allemagne** Germany's long industrial tradition; **grâce à la v. touristique de notre région** because our area is dedicated to tourism; **la v. du nouveau musée est d'éduquer les jeunes** the new museum is designed to be of educational value to young people; **région à v. agricole/industrielle** agricultural/industrial region

3 *Admin* **avoir v. à** *ou* **pour faire** to be empowered to do

voceratrice [vɔtʃeratritʃe] **NF** *Mus* vocero singer

vocero [vɔtʃero] *(pl* **voceros** *ou* **voceri**) **NM** *Mus* Corsican funeral chant

vociférateur, -trice [vɔsiferatœr, -tris] **NM,F** *Littéraire* vociferant, shouter

vocifération [vɔsiferasjɔ̃] **NF** vociferation; **des vociférations** an outcry, a clamour; **pousser des vociférations** to shout and bawl; **sous les vociférations du public** met by boos and hisses from the audience

vocifératrice [vɔsiferatris] *voir* **vociférateur**

vociférer [18] [vɔsifere] **VI** to yell, to shout, *Sout* to vociferate; **v. contre** to inveigh against, to berate

VT *(injures)* to scream, to shout (**contre** at)

vocodeur [vɔkɔdœr] **NM** *Ordinat* vocoder

VOD [veode] **NF** *(abrév* **video-on-demand**) VOD

vodka [vɔdka] **NF** vodka; **une v. orange** a vodka and orange

vœu, -x [vø] **NM 1** *(souhait)* wish; **faire un v.** to (make a) wish; **tu peux faire trois vœux** you may have three wishes; **si je n'avais qu'un v. à faire, ce serait celui de...** if I could have just one wish, it would be to...; **la première cerise! fais un v.!** it's the first cherry, you must make a wish!; **faire le v. que...** to wish *or* to pray that...; **je fais le v. qu'elle revienne** I pray (that) she may come back; **je fais des vœux pour qu'il ne pleuve pas dimanche** I'm praying it won't rain on Sunday; **former le v. que qch se réalise** to express a *or* the wish that sth should be done; **il faut tenir compte des vœux de la nation** the nation's wishes must be taken into account; **exaucer un v.** to grant a wish; **faire un v. pieux** to make a vain wish

2 *(serment)* vow; **faire v. de tempérance** to take a vow of temperance, to take the pledge; **faire (le) v. de faire qch** to (make a) vow to do sth; **j'ai fait le v. de ne plus y retourner** I vowed never to go back (there again); **il a fait le v. de se venger** he vowed revenge

3 *Rel* **faire v. de pauvreté/de chasteté/d'obéissance** to take a vow of poverty/of chastity/of obedience; **vœux du baptême** baptismal vows; **vœux (de religion)** (religious) vows; **prononcer ses vœux** to take one's vows

▫ **VŒUX NMPL 1** *(de fin d'année)* **meilleurs vœux** *(sur une carte)* Season's Greetings; **envoyer ses vœux à qn** to send sb one's best wishes; **nous vous adressons nos meilleurs vœux** *ou* **nos vœux les plus sincères pour la nouvelle année** our best wishes for the New Year; **elle est venue nous présenter ses vœux** she came to wish us a happy New Year; **le président a présenté ses vœux télévisés** the president made his New Year speech *or* address on TV

2 *(dans une grande occasion)* wishes; **tous nos vœux pour...** our best wishes for..., with all good wishes for...; **meilleurs vœux de la part de...** with all good wishes from...; **tous nos vœux de bonheur** our very best wishes for your happiness; **tous mes vœux de prompt rétablissement** hope you get well soon; *Sout* (my) best wishes for a speedy recovery; **tous nos vœux de succès** all the best, good luck; **je fais** *ou* **forme des vœux pour ta réussite** I wish you every success

vogelpik [vogəlpik] **NM** *Belg (jeu de fléchettes)* darts; *Fig (jeu de hasard)* game of chance

vogue [vɔg] **NF 1** *(mode)* vogue, fashion, trend; **c'est la v. des bas résille** fishnet stockings are in vogue *or* fashion; **c'est la grande v.** *(vêtement)* it's the latest fashion; *(sport)* it's the latest craze

2 *(popularité)* vogue, popularity; **connaître une grande v.** *(style, activité, sport)* to be very fashionable; **la v. que connaissent actuellement les jeux vidéo** the current vogue *or* craze for video games

3 *Suisse (dans le canton de Genève) (kermesse)* village fête

❑ **en vogue** ADJ fashionable; **une tenue très en v.** an extremely fashionable outfit; **c'est la coiffure en v.** it's the latest hairstyle; **être en v.** *(vêtement)* to be fashionable *or* in vogue; *(activité, personne)* to be fashionable

voguer [3] [vɔge] VI **1** *Naut* to sail; **v. vers** *(navire)* to sail towards; *(personne)* to sail for; *Vieilli* **et vogue la galère!** whatever will be will be! **2** *Littéraire (nuage, image)* to drift *or* to be floating by

voici [vwasi] PRÉP **1** *(désignant ce qui est proche dans l'espace → suivi d'un singulier)* here is, this is; *(→ suivi d'un pluriel)* here are, these are; **v. mes neveux** *(en les présentant)* these are my nephews; *(ils arrivent)* here are my nephews; **v. notre nouvelle voiture** this is our new car; **le v.** here he/it is; **la v.** here she/it is; **les v.!** here they are!; **j'ai perdu mon crayon – en v. un** I've lost my pencil – here's one; **du riz? en v.!** rice? here you are *or* there you are!; **en v. une qui sera plus à ta taille** here's one which will be more your size; *Fam* **en v. un qui n'a pas peur!** HE's certainly got guts!; **en v. une surprise!** what a surprise!; **ah, te v. enfin** so here *or* there you are at last; **nous y v.!** here we are!; *(dans une discussion)* now...; **l'homme que v.** this man (here); **les fleurs que v.** these flowers (here); **mon ami que v. vous le dira** my friend here will tell you; **Monsieur/l'objet que v.** this gentleman/object; **la petite histoire que v.** the following little story; **as-tu un timbre? – v.!** do you have a stamp? – here (you are)!; **vous voulez la clef? – v.!** do you want the key? – here!; **v., madame, ce sera tout?** here you are, madam, will there be anything else?; **v. pour vous** *(en donnant un pourboire)* this is for you; **v. ma sœur et voilà mon fils** this is my sister and that's my son

2 *(caractérisant un état)* **le v. endormi** he's gone to sleep; **vous v. rassuré, j'espère** I hope that's reassured you; **me v. prêt** I'm ready now; **nous v. riches!** we're rich!; **la v. cassée** now it's broken; **vous v. installés** here you are all settled in; **nous v. à Paris** here we are in Paris; **les v. enfin partis!** at last they've gone!; **nous v. enfin seuls** alone at last; **nous v. enfin arrivés!** here we are at last!; **la v. qui vient** here she comes, that's her (coming) now; **la v. qui recommence à pleurer** she's starting to cry again, that's her starting to cry again; **le v. qui veut faire du karaté maintenant!** now he wants to take up karate!; *Fam Ironique* **me/te/nous/***etc* **v. bien!** what a mess!; *Fam* **il lui a tout dit, me v. bien!** he told him/her everything, now what am I going to do?

3 *(introduisant ce dont on va parler → suivi d'un singulier)* this *or* here is; *(→ suivi d'un pluriel)* these *or* here are; **v. ce qui s'est passé** this *or* here is what happened; **v. ce dont il s'agit** this is *or* here's what it's all about; **v. nos intentions** these *or* here are our plans; **v. ce que je pense** this is what I think; **v. comment on fait des crêpes** here *or* this is how you make pancakes; **v. comment je vois les choses** this is *or* here's how I see things; **je le ferai et v. comment** I'll do it and here's how, *Sout* I shall do it in the following manner; **j'irai seul et v. pourquoi** I'll go alone and this is why; **v., je crains que ma demande ne vous surprenne beaucoup** now, I'm afraid my request may come as a big surprise to you; **v., c'est l'histoire d'une princesse qui...** so, it's the story of a princess who...; **voilà ce que j'ai dit devant les autres, v. maintenant ce que j'ai à te dire** that was what I said in front of the others, now this is what I have to say to you

4 *(pour conclure)* **v. qui m'étonne!** that's a surprise!; **v. qui est bien joué!** (now that's) well played!; **v. où mène la paresse** this *or* that is what you get for being lazy; **v. pourquoi je ne lui fais pas confiance** this *or* that is why I don't trust him/her; **v. ce que c'est que de mentir!** this *or* that is where lying gets you!

5 *(désignant une action proche dans le temps)* **et me v. à pleurer** and here I am crying; **v. l'heure du départ** it's time to go now; **v. l'orage** here comes the storm; **v. venir le printemps** spring is coming; **v. venir Noël, v. Noël qui arrive** Christmas is coming; **v. que la nuit tombe** (now) it's getting dark; **v. qu'il se met à pleuvoir** that's the rain on; **v. qu'arrive le mois de mai** (now) the month of May is upon us; *Littéraire* **v. venir Jeanne** here comes Jeanne; **comme je rentrais, v. un livreur qui arrive** just as I was arriving home a delivery man turned up; **v. le train qui arrive** here's the train coming now; **v. qu'ils recommencent avec leur musique!** their music's started (up) again!

6 *(exprimant la durée)* **j'y suis allé v. trois mois** I went there three months ago; **elle est partie v. cinq minutes** she left five minutes ago; **je l'ai rencontrée v. quelques années** I met her some years ago; **v. une heure qu'il est au téléphone** he's been on the phone for an hour; **v. trois mois que j'habite ici** I have been living here for (the last) three months; **v. deux ans que nous nous sommes perdus de vue** it's been two years (now) since we lost touch with each other

VOIE [vwa]

road **1** ▪ lane **2** ▪ way **3, 5, 6** ▪ route **3** ▪ track **4, 7, 11, 14** ▪ tract, duct **9** ▪ channel **14**

NF **1** *(rue)* road; **v. d'accès** access road; **la v. Appienne** the Appian Way; **les voies sur berges** *(à Paris)* = expressway running along the Seine in Paris; **v. de dégagement** *(en agglomération)* relief road; *(sur une autoroute) Br* slip road, *Am* ramp; **v. à double sens** two-way road; **v. express** expressway; **v. express urbaine** urban expressway; **v. de passage** major road; **v. piétonne** pedestrian street; **v. prioritaire** main road; **v. privée** private road; *Admin* **v. publique** (public) highway *or* thoroughfare; **v. de raccordement** access road; **v. rapide** expressway; **v. rapide urbaine** urban expressway; *Antiq* **v. romaine** Roman way *or* road; **v. sacrée** sacred way; **v. sans issue** no through road, cul-de-sac; **v. à sens unique** one-way road; *Fig* **être par voies et par chemins** to be always on the move

2 *(pour une file de voitures)* lane; **(route à) trois voies** three-lane road; **(route à) quatre voies** *(gén)* fourlane road; *(séparée en deux)* dual *Br* carriageway *or Am* highway; **v. d'accélération** acceleration lane; **v. de décélération** deceleration lane, exit lane

3 *(moyen d'accès)* way; *(itinéraire)* route; **par la v. des airs** by air; **par v. de terre** overland, by land; **par v. de mer** by sea; **dégagez la v.!** get out of *or* clear the way!; *Fig* **la v. est libre** the road is clear; *aussi Fig* **laisser la v. libre à qn** to make way for sb; *Fig* **ouvrir la v. à qn** to pave the way for sb; *Fig* **ouvrir la v. à qch** to make way for sth; *Fig* **trouver sa v.** to find one's niche in life; **la v. du devoir** the path of duty; **la v. de la réussite** the road to success; *Fig* **ta v. est toute tracée** your career is mapped out for you; **v. aérienne** air route, airway; **v. de communication** communication route; **voies d'eau** watercourses; **v. fluviale** (inland) waterway; **v. maritime** sea route, seaway; **la V. maritime du Saint-Laurent** the St Lawrence Seaway; **v. navigable** (inland) waterway; **entrer dans l'Administration par la v. royale** to take the most prestigious route into the Civil Service

4 *Rail* track; **v. (ferrée)** *Br* (railway) track *or* line, *Am* railroad; **ne pas traverser les voies** *(sur panneau)* do not cross the tracks; **le train pour Lausanne? v. 2, Mademoiselle** the train to Lausanne? platform 2; **le train 242 est attendu v. 9** train 242 is due to arrive on platform 9; **v. de dégagement** siding; **v. descendante** down line; **v. étroite** narrow-gauge line; **v. de garage** siding; *Fig* **mettre sur une v. de garage** *(projet)* to shelve, *Am* to table; *(employé)* to push aside, to put on the sidelines; **pour moi, la direction commerciale serait une v. de garage** becoming head of sales would be a dead end for me; **v. impaire** down line; **v. montante** *ou* **paire** up line; **v. principale** main line; **v. de service** siding; **v. de triage** siding; **v. unique** single track

5 *(procédure, moyen)* **la v. la plus simple/rapide** the easiest/quickest way; **suivre la v. hiérarchique/diplomatique/normale** to go through the official/diplomatic/usual channels; **la v. des armes** recourse to arms; **par des voies détournées** by devious means, by a circuitous route; **par v. de conséquence** consequently

6 *Rel* **la v. étroite** the narrow way; **les voies du Seigneur sont impénétrables** the Lord works in mysterious ways

7 *Chasse (chemin parcouru par le gibier)* track, trail; *(odeurs qui trahissent son passage)* scent; **mettre qn sur la v.** to put sb on the right scent; *Fig (en devinant)* to give sb a clue; *(dans une enquête)* to put sb on the right track; **être sur la bonne v.** to have the scent; *Fig* to be on the right track *or* lines; *Fig* **être sur la mauvaise v.** to be barking up the wrong tree; **v. chaude** *ou* **de bon temps** *(du cerf)* warm scent; *(du renard)* fresh line; **v. de hautes erres** *ou* **de vieux temps** *(du cerf)* cold scent; *(du renard)* stale line

8 *Pharm* **par v. orale** *ou* **buccale** orally; **par v. nasale/rectale** through the nose/the rectum, nasally/rectally

9 *Anat & Physiol* tract, duct; **par les voies naturelles** naturally; **voies biliaires** biliary ducts; **voies digestives** digestive tracts; **voies respiratoires** airways, respiratory tracts; **voies urinaires** urinary tracts

10 *Chim* **v. humide/sèche** wet/dry process; **essai par la v. sèche** dry test

11 *Tech (largeur → entre deux essieux)* track; *(→ des roues de véhicule)* gauge; *(→ d'un outil)* kerf, clearance; *(→ d'un trait de scie)* set; **donner de la v. à une scie** to set a saw

12 *Mines* **v. d'aérage** airway

13 *Fin* **voies et moyens** ways and means

14 *Ordinat & Tél (sur bande)* track; *(de communication)* channel; **v. d'accès** path; **v. bidirectionnelle simultanée** full duplex; **v. d'entrée** input channel; **v. de transmission** transmission channel; **v. de transmission de données** data link

15 *Naut* **v. d'eau** leak; **avoir une v. d'eau** to have sprung a leak

16 *Astron* **la V. lactée** the Milky Way

17 *Jur* **v. de fait** *(action illégale)* blatantly unlawful act; *(violence)* act of violence; **v. parée** foreclosure

❑ **voies** NFPL *Jur* **voies de fait** *(coups)* assault and battery; **se livrer à des voies de fait sur qn** to assault sb; **voies de droit** recourse to legal proceedings; **voies d'exécution** execution; **voies de recours** possibilities of review

❑ **en bonne voie** ADJ **être en bonne v.** to be going well; **maintenant, les affaires sont en bonne v.** business is looking up; **votre dossier est en bonne v.** your file is being processed

❑ **en voie de** PRÉP **en v. d'achèvement** on the way to completion; **en v. de cicatrisation** healing over; **en v. de construction** being built, under construction; **espèces en v. de disparition** endangered species; **en v. de guérison** getting better, on the road to recovery; **être en v. de développement** *(pays)* to be developing; **pays en v. de développement** developing country; **être en v. de faire qch** to be (well) on the way to doing sth; **être en (bonne) v. de réussir** to be (well) on the way *or* road to success

❑ **par la voie de** PRÉP through, via; **régler un litige par la v. de la négociation** to settle a conflict through negotiation

VOILÀ [vwala] PRÉP **1** *(désignant ce qui est éloigné → suivi d'un singulier)* there *or* that is; *(→ suivi d'un pluriel)* there *or* those are; **v. leur maison** there *or* that is their house; **le monument que v.** that monument (there); **les v., là-bas, au bout du jardin** there they are, down at the bottom of the garden; **v. Henri** *(qu'on cherchait)* there's Henri; *(qui arrive)* there's Henri (now), that's Henri (now); *(dont je te parlais)* that's Henri; **voici mon lit, v. le tien** here's *or* this is my bed and there's *or* that's yours

2 *(désignant ce qui est proche → suivi d'un singulier)* here *or* this is; *(→ suivi d'un pluriel)* here *or* these are; **v. mes parents** here are my parents; *(dans des présentations)* these are my parents; **v. Paul et Henri** *(en les présentant)* this is Paul and this is Henri; *(sur une photo)* this is Paul and this *or* that is Henri; **v. l'homme dont je vous ai parlé** here *or* this is the man I spoke to you about; **v. ma démission** here's my resignation;

le v. there he/it is; **la v.** there she/it is; **tiens, les v.!** look, here *or* there they are!; **ah, te v. enfin!** so here *or* there you are at last!; **nous y v.!** here we are!; *(dans une discussion)* now...; **je l'avoue, j'étais jaloux – nous y v.!** I admit it, I was jealous – now the truth's coming out!; **l'homme que v.** this man (here); **du riz? en v.!** rice? here *or* there you are!; **en v. pour cent euros** there's a hundred euros' worth; **je ne trouve pas de marteau – en v. un** I can't find a hammer – here's one; **tu voulais un adversaire à ta mesure? en v. un!** you wanted an opponent worthy of you? well, you've got one!; *Fam* **en v. un qui fera son chemin!** there's a man who will get on!; *Fam* **en v. un qui n'a pas peur!** HE's certainly got guts!; *Fam* **en v. une qui sait ce qu'elle veut** there's someone who knows what she wants; **en v. une surprise/des manières!** what a surprise/a way to behave!; **vous vouliez la clef, v.** you wanted the key, here it is *or* here you are; **v. pour vous** *(en donnant un pourboire)* this is for you; **v., madame, ce sera tout?** here you are, madam, will there be anything else?

3 *(caractérisant un état)* **le v. endormi** he's gone to sleep; **la v. recousue/cassée** now it's sewn up again/broken; **la v. rassurée** she's calmed down now; **me v. prêt** I'm ready now; **les v. enfin partis!** at last they've gone!; **nous v. enfin seuls!** alone at last!; **comme te v. changé!** you've changed so much!, how you've changed!; **dire que te v. marié!** to think you're married now!; **vous v. content maintenant?** (are you) happy now?; **les v. comme deux ennemis** and now they're like enemies; **le v. qui entre, v. qu'il entre** there he is coming in; **les v. qui arrivent** there they are (now); **le v. qui veut faire du karaté maintenant!** now he wants to take up karate!; *Fam* **nous v. frais** *ou* **beaux!** now we're in a fix *or* mess!; *Ironique* **te v. beau, que t'est-il arrivé?** you're in a fine state, what's happened to you?; *Fam Ironique* **me/te/nous/***etc* **v. bien!** now what a mess!; **il lui a tout dit, me v. bien!** he told him/her everything, now what am I going to do?

4 *(introduisant ce dont on va parler → suivi d'un singulier)* this *or* here is; *(→ suivi d'un pluriel)* these *or* here are; **v. ce que je lui dirai** this *or* here is what I'll say to him/her; **v. ce qui arrivera si...** this is what will happen if...; **v. comment il faut faire** this is *or* here's how you do it; **alors v., c'est l'histoire d'une princesse qui...** so, it's the story of a princess who...; **la petite histoire que v.** the following little story; **que veux-tu dire par là? – eh bien v....** what do you mean by that? – well...; **v. ce que j'ai fait jusqu'ici, voici ce que j'ai décidé maintenant** that's what I've been doing up to now, this is what I have decided to do from now on; **v. les temps difficiles qu'elle a connus, et voici, j'espère, une période plus heureuse** those were difficult days she went through, and now, I hope, she'll have a happier time

5 *(pour conclure → suivi d'un singulier)* that's; *(→ suivi d'un pluriel)* those are; **c'est lâche, v. mon avis** it's cowardly, that's what I think; **c'est cher, v. le hic!** it's expensive, that's the only snag!; **v. ce que j'ai fait jusqu'ici** that's what I've been doing up to now; **v. ce que j'en pense** that's what I think of *or* about it; **v. ce qui s'est passé** that's what happened; **v. bien les hommes!** how typical of *or* how like men!; **v. ce que c'est, la jalousie!** that's jealousy for you!; **v. ce que c'est que de mentir!** that's where lying gets you!; **v. ce que c'est que de mentir à ses parents/ d'être trop honnête** that's what happens *or* that's what you get when you lie to your parents/when you're too honest; **v. ce qui s'appelle danser!** now that's what I call dancing!; **v. où je voulais en venir** that's what I was getting *or* driving at; **v. où mène la paresse** that's what you get for being lazy; **un hypocrite, v. ce que tu es!** you're nothing but a hypocrite!; **v. comment il conçoit la vie!** that's his idea of life!; **v. qui est étrange!** (now) that's strange!; **v. qui est bien joué!** (now that's) well played!; **quelques jours de repos, v. qui devrait te remettre sur pied** a few day's rest, THAT should set you right again; **et v. pourquoi je ne lui fais pas confiance** that's why I don't trust him/her; **on lui paiera les réparations et v.!** we'll pay him/her for the repairs and that's all (there is to it)!; **et v., il a encore renversé son café!** I don't believe it, he spilt his coffee again!; **et v., ça devait arriver!** what did I tell you!; **ah v., c'est parce qu'il avait peur!** so, that explains it, he was frightened!; **à vrai dire, je ne veux pas le faire – ah, v.!** to be quite frank, I don't want to do it – so that's it *or* that's what it is!; **v.! vous avez tout compris** that's it! you've got it; **v. tout** that's all; **elle était déçue, v. (tout)** she was disappointed, that's all; **on s'est quittés, v. tout** we split up, that's all (there is to say); **en v. une idée!** *(bizarre)* what a ridiculous idea!; *(excellente)* now THERE'S an idea!; **en v. assez!** that's enough!, that will do!

6 *(introduisant une objection, une restriction)* **j'en voudrais bien un, seulement v., c'est très cher** I'd like one, but the problem is *or* but you see, it's very expensive; **c'est facile, seulement v., il fallait y penser** it's easy once you've thought of it; **j'aurais dû lui dire, mais v., je n'ai pas osé** I should've told him/her, but (when it came to it) I didn't dare; **tu t'excuses, d'accord, mais v., il est trop tard!** fine, you're apologizing, but the thing is, it's too late!; **v., j'hésitais à vous en parler, mais...** well, yes, I wasn't going to mention it, but...

7 *(désignant une action proche dans le temps)* **v. la pluie** *(il ne pleut pas encore)* here comes the rain; *(il pleut)* it's raining; **v. venu le moment de s'expliquer** now's the moment to explain; **v. que la nuit tombe** (now) it's getting dark; *Fam* **v. qu'ils remettent ça avec leur musique!** they're at it again with their music!; **v. que vous allez l'obliger à sortir, maintenant** now you're going to make him/her go out; **v., Monsieur, je suis à vous dans un instant** yes, sir, I'll be with you in a minute; **il y a quelqu'un? – v., v.** anybody in? – hang on, I'm coming!; **il vient mon dessert? – v., v.** is my dessert ready yet? – just coming!; *Fam* **ne v.-t-il pas que je descends de voiture et ne v.-t-il pas qu'une contractuelle arrive!** I get out of my car and guess what, a traffic warden turns up!; *Fam* **(ne) v.-t-il pas qu'on deviendrait coquette!** vain, now, are we?

8 *(exprimant la durée)* **en juin v. trois ans** three years ago in June; **il est rentré v. une heure** he's been home for an hour, he came home an hour ago; **quand il est né, v. près de soixante-trois ans** when he was born, nearly sixty-three years ago; **v. longtemps/deux mois qu'il est parti** he's been gone a long time/two months; **v. trois ans que je n'y suis pas retourné** I haven't been back there for three years; **v. cinq minutes que je t'appelle!** I've been calling you for five minutes!

---

voilage [vwalaʒ] NM **1** *(gauchissement → du métal)* buckling; *(→ d'une roue)* warping **2** *(tissu)* net *(UNCOUNT)*; *(rideau)* net curtain

voile[1] [vwal] NM **1** *(d'une toilette, d'un monument)* veil; **porter le v.** to wear the veil; **v. de deuil** mourning veil; **v. de mariée** marriage veil; *Rel* **prendre le v.** to take the veil

2 *Tex (pour rideau)* net *(UNCOUNT)*, piece of netting, netting *(UNCOUNT)*; *(pour chapeau)* piece of gauze, gauze *(UNCOUNT)*, veil

3 *Fig* veil; **ils ont enfin levé le v. sur ce mystère** they have at last lifted the curtain on this mystery; **jeter** *ou* **mettre** *ou* **tirer un v. sur** to throw a veil across, to draw a veil over; **jetons un v. sur cet épisode** let's just forget that whole incident

4 *Littéraire (opacité)* **un v. de brume/fumée** a veil of mist/smoke; **un v. de larmes devant les yeux** eyes misted up *or* blurred with tears; **un v. de tristesse vint assombrir son regard** his/her eyes veiled over with sadness

5 *Méd* **v. au poumon** shadow on the lung; **j'ai un v. devant** *ou* **sur les yeux** my vision *or* sight is blurred

6 *Aviat & Astron* **v. gris** greyout; **v. noir** blackout; **v. rouge** redout

7 *Phot* fog *(UNCOUNT)*

8 *Anat* **v. du palais** soft palate, *Spéc* velum

9 *Bot* veil

10 *Aut (flanc de roue)* spider

❑ **sous le voile de** PRÉP in the guise of; **c'est la xénophobie sous le v. du patriotisme** it's xenophobia in the guise of patriotism; **on voit là l'hypocrisie sous le v. de la respectabilité** here we have hypocrisy under a cloak of respectability

voile[2] [vwal] NM *(déformation → du métal)* buckle, buckling; *(→ du plastique, du bois)* warp, warping

voile[3] [vwal] NF **1** *Naut* sail; **un bateau à voiles** *Br* a sailing boat, *Am* a sailboat; *Hist* a clipper; **déployer** *ou* **établir une v.** to set a sail; **faire v. vers** to sail towards; **faire force de voiles** to crowd on *or* to cram on all sail; **être sous voiles** to be under sail; **mettre à la v.** to set sail; **aller à la v.** to sail; **faire le tour du monde à la v.** to sail around the world; **nous sommes rentrés à la v.** we sailed back; **v. aurique** gaff-sail; **v. d'avant** foresail; **v. carrée/latine** square/lateen sail; *Fam* **mettre les voiles** to clear off

2 *Littéraire (bateau)* sail, sailing boat

3 *Sport* **la v.** sailing, yachting; **faire de la v.** to sail, to go yachting

❑ **à voile** ADJ **1** *Naut* **la marine à v.** sailing ships

2 *très Fam (locution)* **marcher à v. et à vapeur** to be AC/DC, to swing both ways

❑ **toutes voiles dehors** ADV **1** *Naut* in full sail, all sail *or* sails set; **mettre toutes voiles dehors** to put on full sail *or* canvas

2 *Fam (rapidement)* like a bat out of hell

voilé[1], **-e**[1] [vwale] ADJ **1** *(monument, visage, personne)* veiled; **femme voilée** woman wearing the veil; **des femmes voilées de noir** women veiled in black

2 *(couvert → lune, soleil, horizon)* hazy; *(→ ciel)* overcast; *(lumière → par le brouillard)* hazy; *(→ par les nuages)* dim; **le ciel est v.** it's hazy; **le mourant avait le regard v.** the dying man had a glazed expression; **des yeux voilés de larmes** eyes dimmed *or* blurred with tears

3 *(voix)* hoarse, husky; *(tambour)* muffled

4 *Fig (dissimulé → signification)* obscure; **une allusion à peine voilée** a thinly veiled *or* a transparent hint; **s'exprimer en termes voilés** to express oneself in oblique *or* veiled terms; **leur déception à peine voilée** their thinly veiled disappointment

5 *Phot* fogged, veiled

voilé[2], **-e**[2] [vwale] ADJ *(déformé → métal)* buckled; *(→ bois, plastique)* warped

voilement [vwalmɑ̃] NM *Tech (de métal)* buckling; *(de bois, plastique)* warping

voiler[1] [3] [vwale] VT **1** *(couvrir → femme, statue)* to veil, to hide, to cover; **v. sa nudité** to hide one's nakedness

2 *(rendre moins net → contours)* to veil; *(→ lumière)* to dim; **des nuages voilèrent le ciel** the sky clouded over; **le regard voilé par les larmes** his/her eyes misty *or* blurred with tears

3 *(enrouer → voix)* to make husky; *(son, tambour)* to muffle; **la voix voilée par l'émotion/ l'alcool** his/her voice husky with emotion/thick with drink

4 *Littéraire (dissimuler → fautes)* to conceal, to veil; *(→ motifs, vérité)* to mask, to veil, to disguise; *(→ trouble, émotion)* to hide, to conceal; **sans v. leurs intentions** without disguising their intentions

5 *Phot* to fog

6 *Naut (navire)* to rig with sails

▸**se voiler** VPR **1 se v. le visage** *(le couvrir)* to wear a veil (over one's face); *Fig* **se v. la face** to bury one's head in the sand, to hide from the truth

2 *(lune, soleil)* to become hazy; *(ciel → de nuages)* to cloud over; *(→ de brume)* to mist over, to become hazy *or* misty; **son regard s'était voilé** *(mouillé de larmes)* his/her eyes had misted over *or* become blurred (with tears); *(terni par la mort)* his/her eyes had become glazed

3 *(voix)* to grow *or* to become husky

4 *Phot* to fog

voiler[2] [3] [vwale] VT *(déformer → métal)* to buckle; *(→ bois, plastique)* to warp

▸**se voiler** VPR *(métal)* to buckle; *(bois, plastique)* to become warped

voilerie [vwalri] NF *Naut* sail loft

voilette [vwalɛt] NF (hat) veil

voilier[1] [vwalje] NM **1** *Naut* **v. (de plaisance)** sailing boat, *Am* sailboat; *(navire à voiles)* sailing ship; **navire bon/mauvais v.** good/bad sailer *(ship)* **2** *(ouvrier)* sailmaker; **maître v.** master

sailmaker **3** *Ich* sailfish **4** *Orn* **grand v.** long-flight bird

voilier[2], **-ère** [vwalje, -ɛr] **ADJ** *Vieilli (bateau)* sailing *(avant n)*; *(oiseau)* long-flight

voilure[1] [vwalyr] **NF1** *Naut* sail, sails; **changer de/réduire la v.** to change/to shorten sail; **dans la v.** aloft, in the rigging **2** *Aviat Br* aerofoil, *Am* airfoil; **v. tournante** rotary wing; *(de parachute)* canopy; **appareil à v. fixe/tournante** fixed/rotary wing aircraft

voilure[2] [vwalyr] **NF** *(du métal, d'une roue)* buckling

VOIR [62] [vwar]

> **VT** to see **A1-8, B1-7** ▪ to find **A3** ▪ to look at **A4** ▪ to notice **A4** ▪ to visit **A5** ▪ to imagine **B1** ▪ to think of **B2** ▪ to realize **B4** ▪ to consider **B5** ▪ to check **B6**
> **VI** to see **A1**
> **VPR** to see oneself **1, 2** ▪ to picture oneself **2** ▪ to see each other **3** ▪ to be visible **4** ▪ to happen **5** ▪ to find oneself **6**

VT A. *PERCEVOIR AVEC LES YEUX* **1** *(distinguer)* to see; *Physiol* to (be able to) see; **il ne voit rien de l'œil gauche** he can't see anything with his *or* he's blind in the left eye; **grand-mère ne voit plus rien** grandma's lost her sight; **on n'y voit pas grand-chose dans la cave** you can hardly see a thing in the cellar; **tu vois cette étoile?** can you see that star?; **je voyais ses cartes** I could see his/her cards; **excusez-moi, je suis passé sans vous v.** sorry, I walked right past without seeing you; **on ne voit presque pas la reprise** the mend hardly shows; **d'ici, on voit chez le monsieur d'en face** from here, you can see into the man opposite's house; **il faut le v. pour le croire!** you have to see it to believe it!; **je voudrais la v. en mariée** I'd like to see her as a bride; **à les v., on ne dirait pas qu'ils roulent sur l'or** to look at them, you wouldn't think they were rolling in it; **à la v. si souriante, on ne dirait pas qu'elle souffre** when you see how cheerful she is, you wouldn't think she's in pain; **v. qn faire** *ou* **qui fait qch** to see sb do *or* doing sth; **on t'a vu l'embrasser** you were seen kissing her, someone saw you kiss her; **je l'ai vu qui descendait d'avion** I saw him get *or* getting off the plane; **on en a vu qui pleuraient** some were seen crying; **elle m'a fait v. sa robe de mariée** she showed me her wedding dress; **fais v.!** let me see!; *Littéraire* **que vois-je?** what is this (that I see)?; **v. le jour** *(bébé)* to be born; *(journal)* to come out; *(théorie, invention)* to appear; **je les ai vus comme je vous vois** I saw them with my own eyes; *Fam* **il était habillé, faut v.!** you should have seen what he was wearing!; *Fam* **elle chante, faut v.!** she can't sing to save her life!; **il faut la v. lui répondre, il faut v. comment elle lui répond** you should see the way she speaks to him/her; *Fam* **il faut v. comme il fait la mayonnaise!** you should see how he makes mayonnaise!; *Fam* **tu repasses tes pantalons il faut v. comme!** you have a funny way of ironing your trousers!; *Fam* **elle parle à ses parents il faut v. comme!** you should hear how she talks to her parents!; **cela a fait scandale – le gouvernement n'avait rien vu venir** there was a big scandal – the government hadn't seen it coming *or* hadn't anticipated that; *Sport* **il voit venir les coups** he anticipates the shots; *Fam* **je te vois venir, tu veux de l'argent!** I can see what you're leading up to *or* getting at, you want some money!; *Fam* **le garagiste m'a fait payer 500 euros – il t'a vu venir!** the mechanic charged me 500 euros – he saw you coming!; **Noël n'est que dans trois semaines, on a le temps de v. venir!** Christmas isn't for another three weeks, we've got plenty of time!; *Fam* **j'ai mis de l'argent de côté, pour v. venir** I've put some money away for a rainy day

2 *(assister à → accident, événement)* to witness, to see; *(→ film, spectacle)* to see; **personne n'a vu l'accident** there were no witnesses to *or* nobody saw the accident; **c'est vrai, je l'ai vue le faire** it's true, I saw her do it; **vas-y, que je te voie faire** go ahead, let me see you do it; **je l'ai vu faire des erreurs** I saw him making *or* make mistakes; **pourrais-tu v. maltraiter un animal?** could you bear to see an animal being ill-treated?; **à v.** well worth seeing; **c'est un film à v. absolument** that movie is a must; **à v., l'exposition Rouault à la galerie Moersch** well worth seeing, the Rouault exhibition at the Moersch gallery; **ici, les terrains ont vu leur prix doubler en cinq ans** land prices here doubled over five years; **les deux-roues ont vu leur vignette augmenter** road tax has been increased for motorcycles; **avoir beaucoup vu** to have seen life; **tu n'as encore rien vu** you haven't seen anything yet; *Fig* **n'avoir rien vu** to be wet behind the ears, to be green; **on aura tout vu!** that beats everything!; **j'en ai vu, des choses pendant la guerre!** I saw quite a few things in the war!; **j'en ai vu d'autres!** I've seen worse!, I've been through worse!; **ils en ont vu, avec leur aînée!** their oldest girl really gave them a hard time!; *Fam* **j'en ai jamais vu la couleur** I haven't seen hide nor hair of it; *Fam* **en v. (de toutes les couleurs** *ou* **des vertes et des pas mûres** *ou* **de drôles)** to go through hell, to have a hellish time of it; **il en a vu de toutes les couleurs** *ou* **des vertes et des pas mûres** *ou* **de drôles** he's been through quite a lot; **avec lui, elle en a vu de toutes les couleurs** *ou* **des vertes et des pas mûres!** she's had a hard *or* a rough time (of it) with him!, she's been through a lot with him!; **j'en ai vu de drôles avec lui quand il était petit!** he nearly drove me up the wall when he was little!; *Fam* **en faire v. (de toutes les couleurs** *ou* **des vertes et des pas mûres** *ou* **de drôles) à qn** to make sb's life a misery, to put sb through hell; **mets de l'eau dessus pour v.** pour some water on it, just to see what happens; **j'ai fait du chinois pendant un an pour v.** I studied Chinese for a year just to see how I got on; **répète un peu, pour v.!** don't (you) DARE say that again!; **je voudrais bien, pour v., qu'il lui raconte tout!** I'd just LOVE him to tell him/her everything!; *très Fam* **va te faire v. (chez les Grecs)!** go to hell!, *Br* bugger off!, piss off!

3 *(trouver → spécimen)* to see, to find, *Sout* to encounter; *(→ qualité)* to see; **il faut aller très haut pour v. des bouquetins** you have to climb very high to see ibex; **je n'ai jamais vu tant d'assurance/tant de talent chez un enfant** I've never seen so much self-confidence/so much talent in a child; **les téléphones portables, on en voit partout!** you see mobile phones everywhere!; **j'ai vu la recette dans un magazine** I saw *or* found the recipe in a magazine; **un homme galant comme on n'en voit plus** the kind of gentleman they don't make any more

4 *(inspecter → appartement)* to see, to view; *(→ rapport)* to see, to (have a) look at; *(→ leçon)* to go *or* to look over; *(remarquer)* to see, to notice; **j'aimerais que tu voies le plan du bateau** I'd like you to have a look at the plan of the boat; **j'ai vu deux erreurs dans l'article** I saw two mistakes in the article; **il préfère ne pas v. ses infidélités** he prefers to turn a blind eye to *or* to shut his eyes to her affairs; **elle me regarde mais ne me voit pas** she stares at me but doesn't see me

5 *(visiter)* to see, to visit; **je n'ai pas encore vu le nord de l'Espagne** I've not yet been to *or* seen *or* visited northern Spain; **qui n'a pas vu l'Égypte n'a rien vu** unless you've seen Egypt, you haven't lived

6 *(consulter, recevoir → ami, médecin)* to see; **puis-je vous v. quelques minutes?** may I see you a minute?; **j'aimerais te v. plus souvent** I'd like to see you more often *or* to see more of you; **le médecin va vous v. dans quelques instants** the doctor will be with *or* will see you in a few minutes; *Fam Fig* **il faut v. un psychiatre, mon vieux!** you need your head examined, pal!; **dans l'attente de vous v.** looking forward to seeing you; **aller v.** to go to; **je dois aller v. le médecin** I've got to go to the doctor's; **je vais aller v. mes amis** I'm going to go and see my friends; **je vois toujours Pascale, ma vieille amie de classe** I still see *or* I'm still in touch with Pascale, my old school friend; **nous avons rompu, je ne le vois plus** we split up, I don't go out with *or* I'm not seeing him any more

7 *(être en présence de)* to see; **je la vois chaque jour** I see her every day; **je les ai vus hier par hasard** I saw them yesterday by chance; *Fam* **va-t'en, je t'ai assez vu!** go away, I've seen *or* had enough of you!; **quand je le vois, je pense à son père** whenever I see him I'm reminded of his father

8 *(se référer à)* **v. illustration p. 7** see diagram p. 7; **pour la conjugaison de "acquérir", v. ce mot** for the conjugation of "acquérir" see that word; **v. ci-dessus** see above; **voyez l'horaire des trains** check *or* consult the train timetable

B. *PENSER, CONCEVOIR* **1** *(imaginer)* to see, to imagine, to picture; **tu me vois déguisé en évêque?** can you imagine *or* see *or* picture me dressed up as a bishop?; **je voyais le jardin plus grand** I'd imagined the garden to be bigger; **le pull est trop large – je te voyais plus carré que cela** the jumper is too big – I thought you had broader shoulders; **je nous vois mal gagner le match** I can't see us winning the match; **je vois sa tête/réaction d'ici** I can just imagine his/her face/reaction; **lui confier le budget? je vois ça d'ici!** ask him/her to look after the budget? I can just see it!

2 *(concevoir → méthode, solution)* to see, to think of; **je ne vois pas comment je pourrais t'aider** I can't see how I could help you; **je ne vois pas qui tu veux dire/comment faire/quel parti prendre** I don't see who you mean/how to proceed/which side to take; **vous voyez quelque chose à ajouter?** can you think of anything else (which needs adding)?; **certains ne voient dans sa sculpture que des fils de fer** some consider his/her sculptures to be just a load of wires; **les juges n'ont vu en lui qu'un malade** to the judges, he was clearly a sick man; **je ne vois pas de** *ou* **je ne vois aucune honte à être pauvre** I don't see any shame in being poor; **je ne vois pas de mal à cela** I don't see any harm in it; **v. qch d'un mauvais œil, ne pas v. qch d'un bon œil** to be displeased about sth; **elle voit d'un mauvais œil mon amitié avec sa fille** she's none too pleased about *or* she doesn't look very kindly on my friendship with her daughter; **organiser un carnaval? les autorités ne voient jamais cela d'un très bon œil** organizing a carnival? that's never very popular with the authorities; **elle le voit avec les yeux de l'amour** she sees him through a lover's eyes

3 *(comprendre → danger, intérêt)* to see; **tu vois ce que je veux dire?** do you see *or* understand what I mean?; **je ne vois pas ce qu'il y a de drôle!** I can't see what's so funny!, I don't get the joke!; **je n'en vois pas l'utilité** I can't see the point of it; **elle m'a fait v. que la vengeance était inutile** she made me realize that revenge was futile; **un jour, tu verras que j'avais raison** one day, you'll realize *or* see that I was right; **ne vois-tu pas qu'elle ne t'aime plus?** can't you see *or* don't you realize that she doesn't love you any more?; **il est directeur de banque – je vois!** he's a bank manager – I see!

4 *(constater)* to see, to realize; **tu vois que mes principes n'ont pas changé** as you can see, my principles haven't changed; **elle ne nous causera plus d'ennuis – c'est** *ou* **ça reste à v.!** she won't trouble us any more – that remains to be seen *or* that's what YOU think!

5 *(considérer, prendre en compte)* to see, to consider, to take into account; **ils ne voient que leur intérêt** they only consider their own interest; **elle ne voit que les avantages à court terme** she only sees the short-term advantages; **il n'a vu que son devoir** he only considered his duty

6 *(examiner)* to see, to check; **je n'ai pas eu le temps de v. vos copies** I didn't have time to look at your essays; **nous prenons rendez-vous? – voyez cela avec ma secrétaire** shall we make an appointment? – arrange that with my secretary; **voyez si l'on peut changer l'heure du vol** see *or* check whether the time of the flight can be changed; **je voudrais que tu voies si ma robe te va** I'd like you to see *or* whether my dress fits you; **il faut v. si c'est rentable** we must see whether it's profitable; **j'irai peut-être,**

c'est à v. I might go, I'll have to see; **les photos seraient mieux en noir et blanc – hum, il faut v.** the pictures would look better in black and white – mm, maybe(, maybe not)

7 *(juger)* to see; **voilà comment je vois la chose** that's how I see it; **essaie de v. les choses de mon point de vue** try to see things my way *or* from my point of view; **tu n'es pas sur place, tu vois mal la situation** you're not on the spot, your view of the situation is distorted; **se faire bien v. de qn** to make oneself popular with sb; **se faire mal v. de qn** to make oneself unpopular with sb; **ne te fais pas mal v. de Luc, c'est le fils du directeur** don't make yourself unpopular with Luc *or* don't rub Luc up the wrong way, he's the boss's son

8 *(locutions)* **avoir à v. avec** *(avoir un rapport avec)* to have to do with; **vous aurez peu à v. avec les locataires du dessus** you'll have very little to do with the upstairs tenants; **je voudrais vous parler: ça a à v. avec notre discussion d'hier** I would like to speak to you: it's to do with what we were talking about yesterday; **n'avoir rien à v. avec** *(n'avoir aucun rapport avec)* to have nothing to do with; **l'instruction n'a rien à v. avec l'intelligence** education has nothing to do with intelligence; **je n'ai rien à v. avec la famille des Bellechasse** I'm not related at all to the Bellechasse family; **cela n'a rien à v. avec le sujet** that's irrelevant; *Fam* **on parle beaucoup de Yann et toi – nous n'avons rien à v. ensemble!** there's a lot of talk about you and Yann – there's nothing between us!; **tu parles de grèves, mais ça n'a rien à v.!** you talk about strikes but that has nothing to do with it!; **l'amour et l'argent sont deux choses qui n'ont rien à v.!** love and money have nothing to do with each other!; **tu vois, je préférais ne rien savoir** I preferred to remain in the dark, you see; **je te l'avais dit, tu vois!** what did I tell you!; **vous voyez, je crois qu'il a raison** you see, I think he's right; **elle est si jeune, voyez-vous!** she's so young, you see!; **essaie de recommencer et tu verras!** just (you) try it again and see!; **tu verrais, si j'avais encore mes jambes!** if my legs were still up to it, there'd be no holding *or* stopping me!; *Fam* **attendez v.** hang on, wait a sec; *Fam* **dis v., où est le calendrier?** tell me, where's the calendar?; *Fam* **écoute v., on va y aller ensemble, d'accord?** listen, let's go together, OK?; *Fam* **essaie v.!** *(encouragement)* go on, have a try!; *(défi)* (you) just try!, don't you dare!; *Fam* **regardez v.** (just) look at that; *Fam* **la viande ne me paraît pas bonne, sens v.** the meat seems off to me, you have a smell (of it); *Fam* **voyons v.** *ou* **regardons v. ce que tu as comme note** let's just have a look and see what mark you got; **une moto à 14 ans, voyez-vous ça!** a motorbike at 14, whatever next!; **un rendez-vous avec sa secrétaire, voyez-vous cela!** a date with his secretary, well, well, well *or* what do you know!; **voyons!** come (on) now!; **un peu de courage, voyons!** come on, be brave!; **ne pleure pas, voyons!** come on, don't cry!; **voyons, voyons, un peu de tenue!** come on now, behave yourselves!; **voyons, tu n'espères pas que je vais te croire!** you don't seriously expect me to believe you, do you?

USAGE ABSOLU *(concevoir)* **pose-moi n'importe quelle question – bon, je vais v.** ask me anything – let's see *or* let me think; **il faut trouver un moyen! – je ne vois pas** we must find a way! – I can't think of one *or* anything

VI A. *PERCEVOIR LA RÉALITÉ, SENS PROPRE ET FIGURÉ* **1** *Physiol* to (be able to) see; **il ne voit que d'un œil** he can only see out of one eye; **elle ne** *ou* **n'y voit plus** she can't see *or* she's blind now; **il ne sait pas v.** he just doesn't use his powers of observation; **v. bien** to see clearly, to have good eyesight; **v. mal** to have poor eyesight; **v. double** to have double vision

2 *(juger)* **v. bien** *ou* **juste** to have sound judgement; **encore une fois, tu as vu juste** you were right, once again; **v. faux** to have poor judgement; **ne v. que par les yeux de qn** to see everything through sb's eyes

B. *Cartes* **aller** *ou* **jouer** *ou* **mettre sans v.** to play *or* to bet blind; **10 euros, pour v.** 10 euros, and I'll see you

❑ **voir à VT IND** *(veiller à)* **v. à faire qch** to see to it *or* to make sure *or* to ensure that sth is done; **voyez à la prévenir** see to it that she is told; **voyons à la préparer à leur décision** let's see to it that she's prepared for their decision; **il faudrait v. à ranger ta chambre/payer tes dettes** you'd better tidy up your room/clear your debts; **v. à ce que qch soit fait** to see to it *or* to make sure *or* to ensure that sth is done; **voyez à ce que le colis parte ce soir** see to it that the parcel is sent tonight; *Fam* **un jour tu dis ça, le lendemain tu dis autre chose, faudrait v. à v.!** one day you say one thing, the next something different, what IS this?; *Fam* **tu vas m'obéir, non mais, faudrait v. à v.!** will you do as I say, or do I have to get really angry?

▶**se voir VPR 1** *(se contempler)* to (be able to) see oneself; **mes carreaux brillent tellement que je me vois dedans** my tiles are so shiny that I can see my reflection in them; **en rêve, je me voyais flotter au-dessus de mon lit** in my dream I could see myself floating above my bed; *Fig* **il s'est vu mourir** he knew he was dying

2 *(s'imaginer)* to see *or* to imagine *or* to picture oneself; **elle se voyait déjà championne!** she thought the championship was hers already!; **je me vois bien diva** I can see myself as an opera singer; **voici comment je me vois** this is how I see myself; **je me vois encore entrant** *ou* **entrer dans mon bureau** I can still see myself walking into my office; **je me vois mal grimper aux arbres à mon âge!** I can't see myself climbing trees at my age!; **elle se voyait mal lui faire faux-bond maintenant** she couldn't see how she could possibly let him/her down now; **je ne me vois pas lui demander une augmentation** I (just) can't see myself asking him/her for a rise

3 *(se rencontrer)* to see each other; **tu ne peux pas les empêcher de se v.** you can't keep them from seeing each other

4 *(être visible, évident → défaut)* to show, to be visible; *(→ émotion, gêne)* to be visible, to be obvious, to be apparent; **la cicatrice ne se voit presque plus** the scar hardly shows any more, you can hardly see the scar now; **ton slip se voit sous ta jupe** your pants show through your skirt; **il porte une perruque, ça se voit bien** you can tell he wears a wig; **leurs opinions ne se voient pas dans leurs chansons** their opinions don't show in their lyrics

5 *(se manifester → événement)* to happen; *(→ attitude, coutume)* to be seen *or* found; **ça se voit couramment** it's commonplace

6 *(se trouver)* **se v. dans l'impossibilité de faire qch** to find oneself unable to do sth; **se v. dans l'obligation de...** to find oneself obliged to...; **je ne voudrais pas me v. forcé de sévir!** I wouldn't like to find myself forced *or* having to use harsh methods!; **il s'est vu cité comme témoin** he was asked to testify as a witness; **leur équipe s'est vue reléguée à la quinzième place** their team saw themselves drop to fifteenth position; **les crédits se verront affectés à la rénovation des locaux** the funds will be used to renovate the building

7 *(suivi d'un infinitif)* **se v. interdire l'inscription à un club** to be refused membership to a club; **il s'est vu retirer son permis de conduire sur-le-champ** he had his driving licence taken away from him on the spot

voire [vwar] **ADV v. (même)** (or) even; **certains, v. la majorité** some, or *or* perhaps even most; **la nourriture est mauvaise, v. immangeable** the food's bad, not to say inedible; **vexé, v. offensé** upset, not to say offended

voirie [vwari] **NF 1** *(entretien des routes)* road maintenance; *Admin* **le service de la v.** road maintenance and cleaning department (of the local council); **travaux de v.** roadworks **2** *(réseau)* public road network **3** *(décharge)* *Br* refuse dump, *Am* garbage dump

voisé, -e [vwaze] **ADJ** *Ling* voiced

voisement [vwazmɑ̃] **NM** *Ling* voicing

voisin, -e [vwazɛ̃, -in] **ADJ 1** *(d'à côté)* next, adjoining; *(qui est à proximité)* neighbouring; **la chambre voisine est inoccupée** there's nobody in the next room; **deux maisons voisines** two houses next to each other, two adjoining houses; **il habite la maison voisine** he lives next door; **nos jardins sont voisins** our gardens are next to each other, we've got adjoining gardens; **une rue voisine des Champs-Élysées** a street adjoining the Champs-Élysées; **pays voisins** neighbouring countries; **les pays voisins de l'équateur/voisins de notre territoire** the countries near the equator/bordering on our territory; **un prix v. du million** a price approaching *or* around one million

2 *(dans le temps)* **v. de** *(antérieur à)* preceding, before; *(postérieur à)* after, following; *(autour de)* around; **les années voisines de 1968** the years around 1968; **cela aura lieu à une date voisine de la rentrée** it'll be sometime around the start of the new term; *Littéraire* **Noël était tout v.** Christmas was (close) at hand

3 *(similaire → idées, langues, expérience)* similar; *(→ espèces)* closely related; **v. de** akin to; **des pratiques voisines du charlatanisme** practices akin to *or* bordering on quackery; **émotion voisine de la terreur** emotion akin to *or* bordering on terror

NM,F 1 *(habitant à côté)* neighbour; **v. d'à côté** next-door neighbour; **mes voisins du dessus/dessous** the people upstairs/downstairs from me; **essayons d'être bons voisins!** let's try to act in a neighbourly way!; **v. de palier** neighbour (across the landing)

2 *(placé à côté)* neighbour; **mon v. de table** the person next to me *or* my neighbour at table; **mon v. dans le train** the person (sitting) next to me on the train; **nos voisins belges** our Belgian neighbours

3 le v. *(autrui)* the next man, one's fellow (man)

voisinage [vwazinaʒ] **NM 1** *(proximité)* vicinity, proximity, nearness; **les maisons dans le v. des montagnes** the houses in the vicinity of *or* near the mountains; **apprécier le v. de la nature** to enjoy the proximity *or* closeness of nature; **le v. de la gendarmerie les rassure** they are comforted by the fact that there is a police station nearby

2 *(quartier)* vicinity, neighbourhood; **il rôde dans le v.** he hangs around the neighbourhood; **il n'y avait personne dans le v.** there was nobody in the vicinity, there was nobody about; **les hôtels du v.** the nearby hotels, the hotels in the vicinity

3 dans le v. de in the vicinity of; **ils habitent dans le v. d'une centrale nucléaire** they live near a nuclear plant

4 *(dans le temps)* **au v. de Noël** *(avant)* just before Christmas; *(après)* just after Christmas; *(avant et après)* around Christmas (time)

5 *(personnes)* neighbours; **tout le v. est au courant** the whole neighbourhood knows about it

6 *(rapports)* **relations de bon v.** (good) neighbourliness; **être** *ou* **vivre en bon v. avec qn, entretenir des relations de bon v. avec qn** to be on neighbourly terms with sb

7 *Math* neighbourhood

voisiner [3] [vwazine] **VI 1 v. avec** *(être près de)* to be near **2** *Littéraire (fréquenter ses voisins)* to be on friendly terms with one's neighbours; **à Paris, on voisine peu** in Paris you don't see much of your neighbours

voiturage [vwatyraʒ] **NM** *(de marchandises)* carriage, conveyance, cartage

voiture [vwatyr] **NF 1** *(de particulier)* car, *Am* automobile; **on y va en v.?** shall we go (there) by car?, shall we drive (there)?; **il y a trop de voitures à Paris** there are too many cars in Paris; **prendre sa** *ou* **la v.** to take the car; **v. à combustible mixte** dual-fuel car; **v. de compétition** competition car; **v. de course** racing car; **v. décapotable** convertible; **v. (de) deux places** two-seater; **v. à double commande** dual-controlled car; *Vieilli* **v. d'enfant** *(landau)* *Br* pram, *Am* baby carriage; *(poussette)* *Br* pushchair, *Am* stroller; **v. de fonction** company car; **v. de grand tourisme** *Br* GT (saloon) car, *Am* 4-door sedan; **v. hybride** hybrid car; *Vieilli* **v. d'infirme** wheelchair; *Mil* **v. de liaison** radio car; **v. de livraison** delivery van; **v. de location**

ou **de louage** rental car, *Br* hire car; **v. d'occasion** second-hand car, used car; **v. particulière** private car; **v. à pédales** pedal car; **v. de police** police car; **v. des pompiers** fire engine, *Am* fire truck; **v. (de) quatre places** four-seater; *TV & Rad* **v. de reportage** outside broadcasting vehicle; **v. de service** company car; **v. de société** company car; **v. de sport** sports car; **v. de tourisme** private car; **v. tout-terrain** all-terrain vehicle; **v. ventouse** illegally parked car, abandoned car; **v. de ville** urban car, *Fam* runabout; **petite v.** *(d'enfant)* toy car; *(d'infirme)* wheelchair

2 *Rail* coach, *Br* carriage, *Am* car; **en v.!** all aboard!; **v. de tête/queue** front/rear *Br* carriage *or Am* car

3 *(véhicule sans moteur → pour personnes)* carriage, coach; *(→ pour marchandises)* cart; **v. à bras** handcart; **v. à cheval** *ou* **hippomobile** horsedrawn carriage; **v. à deux/quatre chevaux** carriage and pair/and four; **v. de louage** *ou* **place** hackney carriage

4 *Arch (mode de transport)* conveyance, transport

voiture-balai [vwatyrbalɛ] *(pl* **voitures-balais***)* **NF** *Sport* = car that follows a cycle race to pick up competitors who drop out; *Fig* **faire la v.** to go round picking up the stragglers

voiture-bar [vwatyrbar] *(pl* **voitures-bars***)* **NF** *Rail* buffet car

voiture-couchette [vwatyrkuʃɛt] *(pl* **voitures-couchettes***)* **NF** *Rail* sleeping compartment

voiturée [vwatyre] **NF** *Littéraire ou Arch (de passagers → d'une voiture à cheval)* carriageful, coachload; *(→ d'une automobile)* carload; *(de marchandises)* cartload

voiture-école [vwatyrekɔl] *(pl* **voitures-écoles***)* **NF** driving-school car

voiture-lit [vwatyrli] *(pl* **voitures-lits***)* **NF** *Rail* sleeper, *Am* Pullman

voiture-poste [vwatyrpɔst] *(pl* **voitures-poste***)* *Rail Br* mail van, *Am* mail truck

voiturer [3] [vwatyre] **VT** *Hum ou Arch (transporter → gén)* to convey; *(→ dans une charrette)* to cart; *Fam* **je vais te v.** I'll drive you■

voiture-restaurant [vwatyrrɛstɔrɑ̃] *(pl* **voitures-restaurants***)* **NF** *Rail* restaurant *or* dining car

voiture-salon [vwatyrsalɔ̃] *(pl* **voitures-salon***)* **NF** *Rail Br* saloon *or Am* parlor car

voiturette [vwatyrɛt] **NF 1** *(charrette)* trap **2** *(auto)* small car

voiturier [vwatyrje] **NM 1** *(d'hôtel)* porter *(who parks the guests' cars)*; **service de v.** valet parking **2** *Com & Jur* carrier

voix [vwa] **NF 1** *Physiol* voice; **avoir une jolie v.** to have a nice voice; **avoir une v. grave/chaude** to have a deep/warm voice; **parler par la v. de qn** to speak through sb; **prendre une grosse/petite v.** to put on a gruff/tiny voice; **une v. intérieure me disait que...** a voice in my head was telling me that...; *Littéraire* **la v. des flots/cloches** the voice of the ocean/bells; *Ordinat* **v. artificielle** synthesized speech; *TV & Cin* **v. in** voice in; *TV & Cin* **v. dans le champ** in-frame voice; *TV & Cin* **v. hors champ** voice-over; **v. de mêlé-cassis** husky voice; *TV & Cin* **v. off** voice-over; **commentaire en v. off** voice-over commentary; *TV & Cin* **v. en surimpression** voice-over; **une v. de stentor** a stentorian voice; **faire la grosse v.** to raise one's voice; *Fam* **attention, Papa va faire la grosse v.!** watch out, Daddy's going to get very cross!; **donner de la v.** *(chien)* to bay; *(personne)* to shout, to bawl; *Fig* **donner de la v. contre qch** *(protester)* to protest vehemently against sth; **de la v. et du geste** with much waving and shouting; **ils encourageaient les cyclistes de la v. et du geste** they were shouting and waving the riders on; *Fig* **d'une commune v.** by common consent, with one voice

2 *Mus (de chanteur)* voice; *(partition)* part; **chanter d'une v. juste** to sing in tune; **avoir de la v.** to have a strong voice; **poser sa v.** to train one's voice; **chanter à plusieurs/cinq v.** to sing in parts/five parts; **fugue à deux/trois v.** fugue for two/three voices; *Fig* **la v. chaude du saxophone** the mellow tones *or* voice of the saxophone; **v. de basse/soprano/ténor** bass/soprano/tenor voice; **v. céleste** *(d'un orgue)* voix céleste, vox angelica; **v. de fausset** falsetto voice; **v. humaine** *(d'un orgue)* vox humana; **v. de poitrine/tête** chest/head voice

3 *(personne)* voice; **nous accueillons ce soir une des plus belles v. du monde** tonight we welcome one of the finest voices in the world; **"c'est faux", dit une v. au premier rang** "it's not true", said a voice from the front row; **une grande v. de la radio s'éteint** one of the great voices of radio has disappeared

4 *(message)* voice; **la v. de la conscience** the voice of one's conscience; **écouter la v. de la raison/de la sagesse/de Dieu** to listen to the voice of reason/of wisdom/of God; **la v. du peuple** the voice of the people; *Presse* **La V. du Nord** = daily newspaper published in Lille; **je ne sais ce qui m'a alerté, sans doute la v. du sang** I don't know what alerted me, my family instinct probably; **entendre des v.** to hear voices; **avoir v. au chapitre** to have a *or* one's say in the matter; **tu n'as pas v. au chapitre** you have no say in the matter

5 *Pol* vote; **un homme, une v.** one man, one vote; **v. pour/contre** vote for/against; **obtenir 1500 v.** to win *or* to get 1,500 votes; **recueillir** *ou* **remporter 57 pour cent des v.** to win 57 percent of the vote *or* votes; **le parti qui a le plus grand nombre de v.** the party which heads the poll *or* with the largest number of votes; **élu à la majorité des v.** elected by a majority; **donner sa v. à** to give one's vote to, to vote for; **mettre qch aux v.** to put sth to the vote; **où iront les v. du Parti radical?** how will the Radical Party vote?; **v. consultative** advisory vote; **avoir v. consultative** to have an advisory role; **v. délibérative** deliberative vote; **avoir v. délibérative** to have the right to vote; **avoir v. prépondérante** to have the casting vote

6 *Gram* voice; **v. active/passive** active/passive voice; **à la v. active** in the active voice; **à la v. passive** in the passive (voice)

▫ **à haute voix ADV 1** *(lire)* aloud

2 *(parler)* loud, loudly, in a loud voice; **à haute (et intelligible) v.** loudly and clearly

▫ **à voix basse ADV** in a low voice; **les élèves parlaient à v. basse** the pupils were whispering; **les deux hommes discutaient à v. basse dans un coin** the two men spoke in lowered tones in a corner

▫ **à voix haute = à haute voix**

▫ **en voix ADJ être en v.** to be in good voice; **elle n'est pas en v. ce soir** she's not in very good voice *or* singing well tonight

▫ **sans voix ADJ être** *ou* **rester sans v.** *(d'épouvante)* to be speechless, to be struck dumb; *(d'émotion, de chagrin)* to be speechless

Vojvodine [vɔjvɔdin] **NF la V.** Vojvodina

vol[1] [vɔl] **NM 1** *Jur* theft, robbery; **commettre un v.** to commit a theft, to steal; **v. aggravé** robbery with violence; **v. à l'américaine** confidence trick; **v. à l'arraché** bag snatching; **v. avec effraction** breaking and entering; **v. à l'étalage** shoplifting; **v. de grand chemin** highway robbery; *Ordinat* **v. d'identité** identity theft; **v. à main armée** armed robbery; **v. à la portière** = act of theft whereby the thief opens the door of a vehicle waiting at traffic lights etc and steals any available valuable item before the driver has time to react; **v. qualifié** aggravated theft; **v. à la roulotte** theft from parked cars; **v. simple** common theft; **v. à la tire** pickpocketing; **v. de voiture** car theft

2 *(vente à un prix excessif)* **c'est du v. (manifeste)!** it's daylight robbery!; **à ce prix-là, c'est du v.!** that's daylight robbery!; **c'est du v. organisé!** it's a racket!

vol[2] [vɔl] **NM 1** *Aviat & Astron* flight; **prendre son v.** to take off; **il y a quarante minutes de v.** it's a forty-minute flight; **à trois heures de v. de Paris** three hours' flying time from Paris; *Fam Hum* **elle a pas mal d'heures de v.** she's no spring chicken; **on annonce le retard du v. 804** flight 804 will be delayed; **avion en v.** aircraft in flight; **v. d'affaires** business flight; **v. aller-retour** *Br* return flight, *Am* round-trip flight; **v. d'apport** feeder flight; **v. en ballon** *(excursion)* balloon trip; *(activité)* ballooning; **v. (en) charter** charter flight; **v. avec escale** flight with stopover; **v. d'essai** trial flight; **v. habité** manned flight; **v. inaugural** inaugural flight; **v. aux instruments** instrument flight; **v. libre** hang-gliding; **pratiquer le** *ou* **faire du v. libre** to hang-glide, to go hang-gliding; **v. en rase-mottes** hedge-hopping flight; **v. régulier** scheduled flight; **v. sec** flight only; **v. à voile** gliding; **pratiquer le** *ou* **faire du v. à voile** to glide, to do gliding; **v. à vue** sight flight

2 *Zool* flight; **prendre son v.** to fly away, to take wing; **faire un v. plané** to glide; *Fam Fig* **j'ai fait un v. plané!** I went flying!

3 *(groupe → d'oiseaux)* flight, flock; *(→ d'insectes)* swarm; **v. d'oies sauvages** flight *or* flock of wild geese; **v. de perdreaux** flock *or* covey of partridges; **v. de pigeons** flight of pigeons

▫ **au vol ADV 1** *(en passant)* **saisir au v.** *(ballon, clés)* to catch in midair; **attraper** *ou* **prendre un bus au v.** to jump on to a moving bus; **saisir une occasion au v.** to jump at *or* to seize an opportunity; **saisir un nom au v.** to (just) catch a name

2 *Chasse* **tirer/tuer un oiseau au v.** to shoot/to kill a bird on the wing; *Arch* **(chasse au) v.** hawking, falconry

▫ **à vol d'oiseau ADV** as the crow flies; **c'est à 10 kilomètres à v. d'oiseau** it's 10 kilometres as the crow flies

▫ **de haut vol ADJ** *(artiste, spécialiste)* top *(avant n)*; *(projet)* ambitious, far-reaching; *Littéraire* **âme de haut v.** lofty soul

---

'Vol de nuit' *Saint-Exupéry* 'Night Flight'

'Vol au-dessus d'un nid de coucou' *Kesey, Forman* 'One Flew Over the Cuckoo's Nest'

---

vol. *(abrév écrite* **volume***)* vol

volable [vɔlabl] **ADJ** likely to be stolen

volage [vɔlaʒ] **ADJ** fickle; *Fig* **le public est v.** audiences are fickle *or* unpredictable

volaille [vɔlaj] **NF 1 une v.** *(oiseau de basse-cour)* a fowl; **de la v.** poultry **2** *Fam Péj* **la v.** *(police)* the cops, the pigs

volailler [vɔlaje] **NM 1** *(éleveur)* poultry *or* chicken farmer **2** *(marchand)* poultryman, *Br* poulterer

volant[1] [vɔlɑ̃] **NM 1** *Aut* steering wheel; **être au v.** to be at the wheel, to be behind the wheel, to be driving; **prendre le** *ou* **se mettre au v.** to take the wheel, to get behind the wheel; **je te recommande la prudence au v.** take care when driving; **peux-tu prendre le v. après Évreux?** could you take over the driving after Évreux?; **qui tenait le v.?** who was driving?; **donner un coup de v.** to pull on the wheel (sharply)

2 *Tech (manuel)* handwheel; **v. d'inertie** flywheel; **v. magnétique** *(d'un cyclomoteur)* magneto

3 *(d'horloge)* fly

4 *(garniture de vêtement)* flounce; **robe à volants** flounced dress

5 *(jeu → objet)* shuttlecock; *(→ activité)* battledore and shuttlecock; **jeu de v.** (game of) battledore and shuttlecock

6 *(feuille)* tear-off portion

7 *Écon & Fin* **v. de main-d'œuvre** labour reserve; **v. de sécurité** *(financier)* reserve funds; *(en personnel)* reserve; **v. de trésorerie** cash reserve

8 *Aviat* member of the cabin crew, crew member

volant[2], **-e** [vɔlɑ̃, -ɑ̃t] **ADJ 1** *Aviat & Zool* flying *(avant n)*; *Aviat* **personnel v.** cabin crew; *Naut* **escadre volante** flying squadron

2 *(mobile → câble, camp, échafaudage, pont, service)* flying *(avant n)*; **on mettra une table volante devant le fauteuil** we'll put an occasional table in front of the armchair; *Sport* **gardien de but v.** rush goalkeeper

volapük [vɔlapyk] **NM** *Ling* Volapük; *Fig Péj* **dans un effroyable v.** in gobbledygook

volatil, -e[1] [vɔlatil] **ADJ 1** *Chim* volatile **2** *(fluctuant → électorat)* fickle; *(→ situation, sentiment)* volatile

volatile[2] [vɔlatil] **NM 1** *Hum (oiseau)* bird, (feathered) creature; **le malheureux v. se retrouva dans la casserole** the wretched bird ended up in the pot **2** *(oiseau de basse-cour)* fowl, chicken

volatilisable [vɔlatilizabl] **ADJ** volatilizable

volatilisation [vɔlatilizasjɔ̃] **NF** volatilization

volatiliser [3] [vɔlatilize] **VT** *Chim* to volatilize

▸**se volatiliser VPR 1** *(disparaître)* to vanish

(into thin air); **elles ne se sont pourtant pas volatilisées, ces clefs!** those keys can't just have vanished into thin air!; **en une soirée au club, mes 300 euros s'étaient volatilisés** one evening at the club and my 300 euros had gone up in smoke **2** *Chim* to volatilize

volatilité [vɔlatilite] **NF** volatility

vol-au-vent [vɔlovɑ̃] **NM INV** *Culin* vol-au-vent

volcan [vɔlkɑ̃] **NM 1** *Géog & Géol* volcano; **v. en activité/dormant/éteint** active/dormant/extinct volcano **2** *Fig* **c'est un vrai v.** he's/she's likely to explode at any moment; **être assis** *ou* **danser** *ou* **dormir sur un v.** to be sitting on a powder keg

volcanique [vɔlkanik] **ADJ 1** *Géog & Géol* volcanic **2** *Littéraire (passion)* fiery, volcanic, blazing; *(imagination)* vivid; *(tempérament)* fiery, impetuous

volcaniser [3] [vɔlkanize] **VT** to volcanize

volcanisme [vɔlkanism] **NM** *Géol* volcanism

volcanologie [vɔlkanɔlɔʒi] **NF** *Géol* volcanology, vulcanology

volcanologique [vɔlkanɔlɔʒik] **ADJ** *Géol* volcanological, vulcanological

volcanologue [vɔlkanɔlɔg] **NMF** *Géol* volcanologist, vulcanologist

vole [vɔl] **NF** *Cartes* vole, all the tricks

volé, -e[1] [vɔle] **ADJ** *(argent, bijou)* stolen
NM,F victim of theft

volée[2] [vɔle] **NF 1** *(ce qu'on lance)* **v. d'obus/de pierres** volley of shells/of stones; **v. de flèches** volley *or* flight of arrows; **v. de coups** shower of blows; *Fig* **v. d'insultes** shower of insults; *Fig* **une v. de bois vert** a barrage of fierce criticism; **son dernier disque a reçu une v. de bois vert** his/her last record was panned

2 *Fam (correction)* thrashing, hiding; **tu vas recevoir la v.!** you're really going to get it!; **elle a reçu une bonne v.** she got a sound thrashing *or* a good hiding

3 *Fam (défaite)* beating, hammering; **je lui ai flanqué sa v. au ping-pong** I licked him/her at table tennis; **il a pris une sacrée v. en demi-finale** he got trounced *or* thrashed in the semi-finals

4 *Sport* volley; **reprendre une balle de v.** to volley a ball, to hit the ball on the volley; **monter à la v.** to come to the net; **il n'est pas/il est très bon à la v.** he's a bad/he's a good volleyer; **v. amortie/de coup droit/de revers** *(au tennis)* drop/forehand/backhand volley; **coup de v.** punt; **envoyer une balle d'un coup de v.** to punt a ball

5 *Orn (formation)* flock, flight; *(de perdrix)* covey; *(distance)* flight; *Fig Littéraire* **une v. de fillettes** a crowd of little girls; **prendre sa v.** *(oiseau)* to fly away, to take wing; *Fig (débutant, adolescent)* to spread one's wings

6 *(son de cloche)* peal (of bells), pealing bells

7 *Constr* **v. d'escaliers** flight of stairs

8 *(en travaux publics)* (crane) jib

9 *Suisse (promotion)* **on était de la même v.** we were in the same year

❑ **à la volée ADV 1** *(en passant)* **attraper** *ou* **saisir à la v.** *(clés, balle)* to catch in mid-air; **relancer une balle à la v.** *(au tennis)* to volley a return; **saisir un nom à la v.** to (just) catch a name

2 *Agr* **semer à la v.** to (sow) broadcast

3 *Chasse* **tirer à la v.** to shoot without aiming first

❑ **à toute volée ADV** *(frapper, projeter)* vigorously, with full force; **il a lancé le vase à toute v. contre le mur** he hurled the vase at *or* flung the vase against the wall; **claquer une porte à toute v.** to slam *or* to bang a door shut; **sonner à toute v.** *(cloches)* to peal (out); *(carillonneur)* to peal all the bells

❑ **de haute volée ADJ** *(spécialiste)* top *(avant n)*; *(projet)* ambitious, far-reaching

voler[1] [3] [vɔle] **VI 1** *Aviat & Zool* to fly; **faire v. un cerf-volant** to fly a kite; **nous volons à une vitesse de...** we are flying at a speed of...; *Fig* **v. de ses propres ailes** to stand on one's own two feet, to fend for oneself

2 *(étincelles, projectile)* to fly; **il faisait v. ses adversaires** he was throwing his opponents around; **il faisait v. les assiettes** he was throwing the plates in the air; **v. en éclats** to be smashed to bits *or* to pieces; *Fam* **ça vole bas!, ça ne vole pas haut!** VERY funny!; *Fam* **chez eux, ça ne vole pas bien haut** they've got a rather crude sense of humour▪

3 *Littéraire (nuages, flocons)* to fly (along)

4 *(se précipiter)* **v. vers qn/qch** to fly to sb/towards sth; **il a volé à sa rencontre** he rushed to meet him/her; **v. au secours de qn** to fly to sb's assistance; **v. au secours de la victoire** to show up when the battle has been won; *Fam* **v. dans les plumes à qn** to let fly at sb, to have a go at sb; *Fam* **elle lui a volé dans les plumes** she had a real go at him/her

voler[2] [3] [vɔle] **VT 1** *(objet, idée)* to steal; **v. qch à qn** to steal sth from sb; **on m'a volé ma montre!** my watch has been stolen!; **il volait de l'argent dans la caisse** he used to steal money from the till; *Littéraire* **v. un baiser à qn** to steal a kiss from sb; **je n'ai pas volé mon argent/dîner/week-end** I've certainly earned my money/earned myself some dinner/earned myself a weekend; **c'est un repos que tu n'as pas volé** it's a well-deserved rest, you've earned your rest; **tu ne l'as pas volé!** *(tu le mérites)* you've earned it!; *(tu es bien puni)* you (certainly) asked for it!, it serves you right!; *Prov* **qui vole un œuf vole un bœuf** = there's no such thing as a petty thief

2 *(personne)* to rob; **se faire v. qch** to have sth stolen; **il s'est fait v. son portefeuille/tout son matériel hi-fi** his wallet/all his stereo equipment was stolen

3 *(léser)* to cheat, to swindle; **on s'est fait v.** we were ripped off, we were really stung; **je me suis fait v. de 10 euros** I've been swindled out of 10 euros; **elle ne t'a pas volé sur le poids de la viande** she gave you a good weight of meat; *Fam* **le spectacle était super, on n'a pas été volés!** the show was just great, it was worth every penny *or* we really got our money's worth!

USAGE ABSOLU to steal; **ce n'est pas bien de v.** it's wrong to steal, stealing is wrong; *Bible* **tu ne voleras point** thou shalt not steal

volerie [vɔlri] **NF** *Hist* hawking; **haute v.** hawking with long-winged *or* noble hawks; **basse v.** hawking with short-winged *or* ignoble hawks

volet [vɔlɛ] **NM 1** *(d'une maison)* shutter

2 *(d'un document → section)* section; *Beaux-Arts (d'un polyptyque)* wing, *Spéc* volet; *(d'un chèque)* tear-off portion

3 *(d'une politique, d'un projet de loi)* point, part; *(d'une émission)* part; **une politique sociale en trois volets** a social policy in three points *or* parts; **le v. social** *(de la Communauté européenne)* the social chapter

4 *Aviat* flap; **sortir/rentrer les volets** to lower/raise flaps; **v. de freinage/d'intrados** brake/split flap; **v. de courbure** *(de parachute)* flap

5 *Aut* **v. de départ** throttle *or* butterfly valve

6 *Tech (d'une roue à eau)* paddle; *(de carburateur)* throttle *or* butterfly valve

voletant, -e [vɔltɑ̃, -ɑ̃t] **ADJ 1** *(oiseau, papillon)* fluttering **2** *Littéraire (flammèche)* fluttering, dancing

voleter [27] [vɔlte] **VI 1** *(oiseau, papillon)* to flutter *or* to flit (about) **2** *Littéraire (flammèche)* to flutter, to dance

voleur, -euse [vɔlœr, -øz] **ADJ être v.** *(enfant)* to be a (bit of a) thief; *(marchand)* to be a crook *or* a cheat; **la souris voleuse qui avait visité mon garde-manger** the mouse which had pilfered my larder; **il est v. comme une pie** he's got sticky fingers

NM,F *(escroc)* thief, robber; *(marchand)* crook, cheat; *(cambrioleur)* burglar; **v. de bétail** cattle thief; **v. d'enfants** kidnapper; **v. à l'étalage** shoplifter; *Hist* **v. de grand(s) chemin(s)** highwayman, footpad; **v. d'idées** plagiarist; **v. de moutons** sheep stealer; **v. à la tire** pickpocket; **au v.!** stop thief!; **partir** *ou* **se sauver comme un v.** *(en courant)* to take to one's heels; *(discrètement)* to slip away

❑ **voleuse NF** *Fam* **voleuse de santé** nympho, *Br* goer

'Le Voleur de bicyclette' *De Sica* 'Bicycle Thieves' (UK), 'The Bicycle Thief' (US)

Volga [vɔlga] **NF la V.** the (River) Volga

Volgograd [vɔlgɔgrad] **NM** Volgograd

volière [vɔljɛr] **NF** *(enclos)* aviary; *(cage)* birdcage; *Fig* **c'est une vraie v. dans cette classe!** it's like a zoo in this class!

volige [vɔliʒ] **NF** *Constr* batten; *(pour tuiles)* slate lath; **caisse en voliges** crate

voligeage [vɔliʒaʒ] **NM** *Constr* battening; *(pour tuiles)* lathing

voliger [17] [vɔliʒe] **VT** *Constr* to batten; *(pour tuiles)* to lath

volis [vɔli] **NM** broken treetop

volitif, -ive [vɔlitif, -iv] **ADJ** *Phil* volitional

volition [vɔlisjɔ̃] **NF** *Phil* volition

volitive [vɔlitiv] *voir* **volitif**

volley [vɔlɛ] **NM** *Fam* volleyball▪ ; **v. de plage** beach volleyball▪

volley-ball [vɔlɛbol] *(pl* **volley-balls***)* **NM** volleyball

volleyer [12] [vɔlɛje] **VI** to volley

volleyeur, -euse [vɔlɛjœr, -øz] **NM,F 1** *(au volleyball)* volleyball player **2** *(au tennis)* volleyer; **c'est un bon/mauvais v.** he volleys/doesn't volley well

volnay [vɔlnɛ] **NM** Volnay (wine)

volontaire [vɔlɔ̃tɛr] **ADJ 1** *(déterminé)* determined, self-willed; *(têtu)* headstrong, wilful; **avoir le menton/front v.** to have a firm *or* determined chin/a set forehead

2 *(voulu → engagement)* voluntary; *(→ oubli)* intentional

3 *(qui agit librement → engagé, travailleur)* volunteer *(avant n)*; **se porter v. pour** to volunteer for; **quand il s'agit de m'aider, il est toujours v.** when it comes to helping me, he's always willing (to do so) *or* he always volunteers

4 *Physiol (muscle, nerf)* voluntary *(avant n)*

NMF volunteer; *Anciennement Mil* **v. du service national** = before national service was abolished, a recruit who chose to carry out his national service by doing voluntary service overseas; **v. international** = young person who does a voluntary work placement overseas, working for a French-run organization or promoting French interests

volontairement [vɔlɔ̃tɛrmɑ̃] **ADV 1** *(sans y être obligé)* voluntarily, of one's own free will **2** *(intentionnellement)* on purpose, intentionally, deliberately; **c'est v. que j'ai supprimé ce passage** I deleted this passage on purpose

volontariat [vɔlɔ̃tarja] **NM le v.** *(gén)* voluntary work; *Mil* voluntary service; **faire du v.** to do voluntary service

volontarisme [vɔlɔ̃tarism] **NM** *Phil* voluntarism, voluntaryism

volontariste [vɔlɔ̃tarist] **ADJ** voluntaristic; *(politique)* aggressive
NMF voluntarist

volonté [vɔlɔ̃te] **NF 1** *(détermination)* will, willpower; **avoir de la v./beaucoup de v.** to have willpower/a strong will; **avoir une v. de fer** to have a will of iron *or* an iron will; **il n'a aucune v.** he has no willpower; **elle n'a pas assez de v. pour...** she hasn't got enough willpower to...; **il manque de v.** he lacks willpower, he doesn't have enough willpower; **faire un effort de v.** to make an effort of willpower; **arriver à qch à force de v.** to achieve sth by sheer willpower

2 *(désir)* will, wish; **la v. de l'électorat** the will of the electorate; **accomplir la v. de qn** to carry out sb's wish; **faire qch/aller contre la v. de qn** to do sth/to go against sb's will; **la v. de gagner/de survivre** the will to win/to survive; **dire sa v. de réussir/de progresser** to express a wish to succeed/to advance; **montrer sa v. de faire qch** to show one's determination to do sth; **faire qch de sa propre v.** to do sth of one's own accord *or* spontaneously; **la v. divine** *ou* **de Dieu** God's will; *Phil* **v. de puissance** will-to-power; **les dernières volontés de qn** *(document)* sb's last will and testament; *(vœux)* sb's last wishes; *Rel* **que Ta/Votre v. soit faite** Thy will be done

3 *(disposition)* **bonne v.** willingness; **faire preuve de bonne v.** to show willing; **être plein de bonne v.** to be full of goodwill; **il est plein de bonne v. mais il n'arrive à rien** he tries hard but doesn't achieve anything; **faire appel aux bonnes volontés** to appeal for volunteers to come forward; **personne de bonne v.** willing person; **avec la meilleure v. du monde** with the

best will in the world; **mauvaise v.** unwillingness; **faire preuve de mauvaise v.** to be grudging; **elle y met de la mauvaise v.** she's doing it with very bad grace; **allez, lève-toi, c'est de la mauvaise v.!** come on, get up, you're not really trying!

❑ **à volonté** ADJ **café à v.** as much coffee as you want, unlimited coffee; *Mil* **feu à v.** fire at will ADV *(arrêter, continuer)* at will; **poivrez à v.** add pepper to taste; **servez-vous à v.** take as much as you want; *Fin* **billet payable à v.** promissory note payable on demand

volontiers [vɔlɔ̃tje] ADV **1** *(de bon gré)* gladly, willingly; *(avec plaisir)* with pleasure; **elle en parle v.** she will happily talk about it; **je prendrais v. un verre de vin** I could do with *or* I'd love a glass of wine; **un café? – très v.** a coffee? – yes please *or* I'd love one

2 *(souvent)* willingly, readily; **on croit v. que...** we are apt to think *or* ready to believe that...; **elle est v. cynique** she tends to be cynical; **il ne sourit pas v.** he's not very generous with his smiles

volt [vɔlt] NM volt

Volta [vɔlta] NF **la V.** the Volta; **la V. Blanche** the White Volta; **la V. Noire** the Black Volta

voltage [vɔltaʒ] NM voltage

voltaïque[1] [vɔltaik] ADJ *Élec* voltaic, galvanic

voltaïque[2] [vɔltaik] ADJ **1** *Géog* Voltaic, of Burkina-Faso **2** *Ling* Gur, Voltaic

voltaire [vɔltɛr] NM Voltaire chair

voltairianisme [vɔltɛrjanism] NM *Phil* Voltairism, Voltairianism

voltairien, -enne [vɔltɛrjɛ̃, -ɛn] ADJ Voltairean, Voltairian

NM,F Voltairean, Voltairian

voltamètre [vɔltamɛtr] NM *Élec* voltameter

voltampère [vɔltɑ̃pɛr] NM *Élec* volt-ampere

volte [vɔlt] NF **1** *Équitation* volt, volte **2** *Naut (changement de cap)* turn

volte-face [vɔltəfas] NF INV **1** *(fait de pivoter)* about-turn, *Am* about-face; **faire v.** to turn round **2** *Fig (changement → d'opinion, d'attitude)* volte-face, about-turn; **le parti a fait une v.** the party did a 180-degree turn *or* a U-turn

volter [3] [vɔlte] VI *Équitation* to execute a volt *or* volte; **faire v. un cheval** to make a horse execute a volt *or* volte

voltige [vɔltiʒ] NF **1** *(au trapèze)* **la haute v.** acrobatics, flying trapeze exercises **2** *Équitation* mounted gymnastics, voltige **3** *Aviat* **v. (aérienne)** aerobatics; **pilote de v.** stunt pilot **4** *Fig (entreprise difficile)* **la Bourse, c'est de la v.** speculating on the Stock Exchange is a highly risky business

voltigement [vɔltiʒmɑ̃] NM fluttering

voltiger [17] [vɔltiʒe] VI **1** *(libellule, oiseau)* to fly about, to flutter (about); *(abeille, mouche)* to buzz about **2** *(flocon, papier)* to float around in the air, to flutter (about) **3** *(sur un trapèze)* to do acrobatics, to perform on the flying trapeze; *(sur un cheval)* to do acrobatics, to perform on horseback

voltigeur, -euse [vɔltiʒœr, -øz] NM,F acrobat

NM **1** *Hist* light infantryman **2** *(au base-ball)* **v. gauche/droit** left/right fielder; **v. du centre** centre fielder

voltmètre [vɔltmɛtr] NM voltmeter

volubile [vɔlybil] ADJ **1** *(qui parle → beaucoup)* garrulous, voluble; *(→ avec aisance)* fluent **2** *Bot* voluble

volubilis [vɔlybilis] NM *Bot* morning glory, convolvulus

volubilité [vɔlybilite] NF volubility, volubleness, garrulousness; **parler avec v.** to be a voluble talker, to talk volubly

volucelle [vɔlysɛl] NF *Entom* syrphid fly, flower fly

volucompteur [vɔlykɔ̃tœr] NM *Br* petrol pump *or Am* gas pump indicator

volume [vɔlym] NM **1** *(tome)* volume; **une encyclopédie en deux volumes** an encyclopedia in two volumes, a two-volume encyclopedia; *Fam Fig* **elle m'en écrit toujours des volumes** she always writes me reams (and reams)

2 *(du son)* volume; **augmente** *ou* **monte le v.** turn the sound up; **baisse** *ou* **descends le v.** turn the sound down; **v. sonore** sound level

3 *(quantité globale)* volume, amount; **v. d'achats** purchase volume, volume of purchases; **le v. d'une affaire** the size of a business; **v. annuel de production** annual (volume of) production; **le v. des échanges commerciaux** the volume of trade; **le v. des exportations** the volume of exports; **le v. des importations** the volume of imports; *Com* **v. de point mort** break-even quantity; **v. des ventes** sales volume, volume of sales

4 *Beaux-Arts & Géom* volume; **v. de révolution** volume of revolution

5 *(poids, épaisseur)* volume; **faire du v.** *(chose)* to take up a lot of space; *Fam (personne)* to show off, to throw one's weight about; *Fam* **il a pris du v.** he's put on weight■; **une permanente donnerait du v. à vos cheveux** a perm would give your hair more body; **v. atomique/moléculaire** atomic/molecular volume

6 *(cubage)* volume; *(de réservoirs)* capacity; **v. (d'eau) du fleuve** volume of water in the river; **eau oxygénée (à) 20 volumes** 20-volume hydrogen peroxide

7 *Ordinat (unité)* volume; **v. mémoire** storage capacity

8 *Bourse* **v. d'affaires** trading volume

9 *Naut* **chargé en v.** laden in bulk

volumétrie [vɔlymetri] NF volumetry

volumétrique [vɔlymetrik] ADJ volumetric

volumineux, -euse [vɔlyminø, -øz] ADJ *(sac)* bulky, voluminous; *(dossier)* bulky; *(correspondance)* voluminous, massive; **très peu v.** taking up little space

volumique [vɔlymik] ADJ volumic

volupté [vɔlypte] NF **1** *(plaisir)* sensual *or* voluptuous pleasure; *Littéraire* **la v.** the pleasures of the flesh **2** *(caractère sensuel)* voluptuousness

voluptueuse [vɔlyptɥøz] *voir* **voluptueux**

voluptueusement [vɔlyptɥøzmɑ̃] ADV voluptuously

voluptueux, -euse [vɔlyptɥø, -øz] ADJ voluptuous

volute [vɔlyt] NF **1** *(de fumée)* coil; *(de lianes)* curl, scroll; *(en arts décoratifs)* volute, helix; **la fumée s'élève en v.** the smoke is spiralling upwards; **ressort en v.** helical spring **2** *Zool (mollusque)* volute, *Spéc* member of the Volutidae

❑ **volutes** NFPL *Zool* volutes, *Spéc* Volutidae

volvaire [vɔlvɛr] NF *Bot* rice straw mushroom, volvaria; **v. soyeuse** silky agaric

volve [vɔlv] NF *Bot* volva

volvocales [vɔlvɔkal] NFPL *Bot* Volvocales

volvoce [vɔlvɔs], **volvox** [vɔlvɔks] NM *Bot* volvox

volvulus [vɔlvylys] NM *Méd* volvulus

vomer [vɔmɛr] NM *Anat* vomer

vomérien, -enne [vɔmerjɛ̃, -ɛn] ADJ *Anat* vomerine

vomi [vɔmi] NM vomit

vomique [vɔmik] ADJ *Bot* **noix v.** nux vomica

vomiquier [vɔmikje] NM *Bot* nux vomica (tree)

vomir [32] [vɔmir] VT **1** *Physiol (repas)* to bring up, to vomit; *(sang, bile)* to bring *or* to cough up

2 *Fig (fumée)* to spew, to vomit; *(foule)* to spew forth; *(insultes)* to spew out

3 *Fig (rejeter avec dégoût)* to have no time for, to feel revulsion for; *(personne)* to loathe, *Sout* to abhor; **un article qui vomit le postmodernisme** an article pouring venom on post-modernism

VI to be sick, to vomit; **sucré à (faire) v.** sickeningly sweet; **une odeur à vous faire v.** a nauseating smell; **avoir envie de v.** to feel sick *or Am* nauseous; **elle est riche à faire v.** she's so rich it makes you sick; **une telle hypocrisie me donne envie de v.** such hypocrisy makes me sick; **ça me fait v.!** it makes me sick!

vomissement [vɔmismɑ̃] NM **1** *(action)* vomiting *(UNCOUNT)*; **si l'enfant est pris de vomissements** if the child starts to vomit **2** *(substance)* vomit *(UNCOUNT)*

vomissure [vɔmisyr] NF vomit *(UNCOUNT)*

vomitif, -ive [vɔmitif, -iv] ADJ **1** *Méd* emetic, vomitive **2** *Fam Fig (dégoûtant)* revolting■, gross

NM *Méd* emetic, vomitive

vomitoire [vɔmitwar] NM *Antiq* vomitorium, vomitory

vomito negro [vɔmitonegro] *(pl* **vomitos negros***)* NM *Méd* black vomit *(UNCOUNT)*

vont [vɔ̃] *voir* **aller**[2]

vorace [vɔras] ADJ **1** *(mangeur)* voracious; *(appétit)* insatiable, voracious; *(lecteur)* voracious, avid; **se sentir d'un appétit v.** to feel ravenously hungry; *Ordinat* **application v. en mémoire** memory-intensive application **2** *Bot* **plantes voraces** plants which exhaust the soil

voracement [vɔrasmɑ̃] ADV voraciously

voracité [vɔrasite] NF voracity, voraciousness

vortex [vɔrtɛks] NM vortex

vorticelle [vɔrtisɛl] *Zool* NF vorticella, vorticellid

vorticisme [vɔrtisism] NM *Beaux-Arts* Vorticism

vos [vo] *voir* **votre**

Vosges [voʒ] NFPL **les V.** the Vosges; **dans les V.** in the Vosges

vosgien, -enne [voʒjɛ̃, -ɛn] ADJ of/from the Vosges

❑ **Vosgien, -enne** NM,F = inhabitant of or person from the Vosges

votant, -e [vɔtɑ̃, -ɑ̃t] NM,F voter

votation [vɔtasjɔ̃] NF *Suisse* vote

vote [vɔt] NM **1** *(voix, suffrage)* vote; **le v. noir/des femmes** the black/women's vote; **v. blanc** blank ballot paper; **v. de confiance** vote of confidence; **v. défavorable** "no" vote; **v. de défiance** vote of no confidence; **v. favorable** "yes" vote; **v. nul** spoilt ballot paper; **v. de protestation** protest vote; **v. réactionnaire** reactionary vote; **v. sanction** sanction vote; **v. utile** tactical vote

2 *(élection)* vote; *(action)* voting; **prendre part au v.** to go to the polls, to vote; **procédons** *ou* **passons au v.** let's have *or* take a vote; **v. par acclamation** voice vote; **v. à bulletin secret** secret ballot; **v. par correspondance** *Br* postal vote *or* ballot, *Am* absentee ballot; **v. direct/indirect** direct/indirect vote; **v. libre** free vote; **v. à main levée** vote by show of hands; **v. majoritaire** majority vote; **v. obligatoire** compulsory vote; **v. pondéré** weighted vote; **v. préférentiel** preferential voting; **v. par procuration** proxy vote; **v. secret** secret ballot; **v. unique transférable** single transferable vote

3 *(d'une loi)* passing; *(de crédits)* voting; *(d'un projet de loi)* vote; **v. bloqué** = enforced vote on a text containing only government amendments

voter [3] [vɔte] VI to vote; **v. à droite/à gauche/au centre** to vote for the right/left/centre; **v. pour qn** to vote for sb; **v. pour les conservateurs, v. conservateur** to vote Conservative; **v. à main levée** to vote by show of hands; **v. par procuration** to vote by proxy; **v. contre/pour qch** to vote against/for sth; **on leur a demandé de v. pour ou contre la grève** they were balloted about the strike; **v. utile** to vote tactically; **votons sur la dernière motion présentée** let's (take a) vote on the last motion before us; **v. (pour) Thomas!** vote for Thomas!

VT *(crédits)* to vote; *(loi)* to pass; *(projet de loi)* to vote for; *(budget)* to approve; **être voté** *(projet de loi)* to go through; **v. la peine de mort** to pass a vote in favour of capital punishment; **v. des remerciements à qn** to offer sb a vote of thanks

votif, -ive [vɔtif, -iv] ADJ votive

votre [vɔtr] *(pl* **vos** [vo]*)* ADJ POSSESSIF **1** *(indiquant la possession)* your; **v. livre et vos crayons** *(d'une personne)* your book and your pencils; *(de plusieurs personnes)* your books and your pencils; **v. père et v. mère,** *Littéraire* **vos père et mère** your father and mother; **un de vos amis** one of your friends, a friend of yours; **un professeur de vos amis** a teacher friend of yours; *Fam* **vous aurez v. chambre à vous** *(chacun aura sa chambre)* you will have your own rooms■; *Fam* **vous avez v. vendredi** you've got Friday off■; **dans v. deuxième chapitre...** in your second chapter...

2 *(dans des titres)* **V. Majesté** Your Majesty; **V. Altesse** Your Highness; **V. Excellence** Your Excellency

3 *(emploi expressif)* your; **comment va v. cher Victor?** how is your dear Victor?; **alors, vous l'avez achetée, v. petite maison?** so did you buy your little house?; *Fam* **v. imbécile de frère** your idiot of a brother; *Fam* **v. artiste de mari** your artist husband; *Fam* **alors, c'était ça vos vacances de rêve!** so much for your dream holiday!

4 *Rel* Thy

vôtre [votr] ADJ yours; *Littéraire* **un v. cousin** a cousin of yours; **cette maison qui fut v.** this house which was yours *or* which belonged to you; **mes ambitions, vous les avez faites vôtres** you espoused my ambitions; **vous ferez v. nos principes** you will adopt our principles as your own; **ferez-vous vôtres les félicitations qu'ils nous adressent?** will you join them in congratulating us?; **bien sincèrement v.** with kindest regards; **amicalement v.** best wishes

NMPL **les vôtres** *(votre famille)* your family, *Am* your folks; *(vos partisans)* your followers; *(vos coéquipiers)* your team-mates; **nos intérêts et ceux des vôtres** our interests and those of your family; **vous et les vôtres** you and yours; **dans la lutte, je suis des vôtres** I'm with you *or* I'm on your side in the struggle; **je ne pourrai pas être des vôtres ce soir** I will not be able to join you tonight

❑ **le/la vôtre, les vôtres** PRON POSSESSIF **nos intérêts sont les vôtres** our interests are yours; **un père comme le v....** a father like yours...; **ma voiture est garée à côté de la v.** my car is parked next to yours; **il ressemble au v.** it looks like yours; **vous voulez bien nous donner du v.?** can we have some of yours?; **de toutes ces solutions, préférez-vous la v.?** out of those possible solutions, do you prefer yours *or* your own?; **vous n'en avez pas besoin, vous avez le v.** you don't need it, you've got your own; **les deux vôtres** your two, the two *or* both of yours; *(en insistant)* your own two; **vous lui avez laissé deux des vôtres** you gave him/her two of yours; *(vous lui en avez sacrifié deux)* you gave him/her two of your own; **si au moins vous y mettiez du v.!** you could at least make an effort!; **vous avez encore fait des vôtres!** you've gone and done it again!; *Fam* **le v. de bébé est plus intelligent!** YOUR baby is more intelligent!; **à la (bonne) v.!** (your) good health!

votum mortis [votɔmmɔrtis] NM *Jur* = wish for the death of another

voudra *etc voir* **vouloir**[2]

vouer [6] [vwe] VT **1** *(dédier → vie, énergie)* to devote; *(→ admiration, fidélité, haine)* to vow; **v. sa vie à l'étude** to devote *or* dedicate *or* give up one's life to study; **toute l'affection que nous lui avons vouée** all the affection we gave him/her; **v. obéissance au roi** to pledge allegiance to the king

2 *(destiner)* **voué à l'échec** destined for failure, doomed to fail

3 *Rel (enfant)* to dedicate; *(temple)* to vow, to dedicate; **voué à la mémoire de...** sacred to the memory of...

►**se vouer** VPR **se v. à** to dedicate one's energies *or* oneself to; **se v. à la cause de** to take up the cause of

vouge [vuʒ] NM *(arme ancienne)* vouge, voulge

vouivre [vwivr] NF **1** *Myth* serpent **2** *Hér* serpent vorant a child

vouloir[1] [vulwar] NM **bon v.** goodwill; **mauvais v.** ill-will; **cela dépendra de son bon v.** it will depend on how he/she feels; **il s'exécuta avec un mauvais v. évident** he complied with obvious reluctance

VOULOIR[2] [57] [vulwar]

> **VT** to want **A1, 3, 6, B1-3** ■ to claim **A2** ■ to mean **A3, C6** ■ to expect **A5** ■ to wish **B1** ■ to require **C2** ■ to be willing **D**
> **USAGE ABSOLU** to want to
> **VPR** to be annoyed with oneself **2** ■ to have a grudge **3**

VT **A.** *AVOIR POUR BUT* **1** *(être décidé à obtenir)* to want; **ils veulent votre démission/une augmentation** they want your resignation/an increase; **il veut la présidence** he wants to be chairman; **lui au moins, il sait ce qu'il veut** he knows what he wants; **je le ferai, que tu le veuilles ou non** I'll do it, whether you like it or not; **v. absolument (obtenir) qch** to be set on (getting) sth; **vous voulez absolument ce modèle?** are you set on this model?; **quand elle veut quelque chose, elle le veut!** when she's decided she wants something, she's determined (to get it)!; **si tu veux mon avis** if you ask me; **lui, j'en fais (tout) ce que je veux** I've got him eating out of my hand; **l'argile, elle en fait (tout) ce qu'elle veut** she can do wonders *or* anything with clay; **je ne veux pas que tu lui dises** I don't want you to tell him/her; **v. absolument que** to insist (that); **je veux absolument que tu ranges ta chambre** I insist (that) you tidy up your bedroom; **v. faire qch** to want to do sth; **elle veut récupérer son enfant/être reçue par le ministre** she's determined to get her child back/that the Minister should see her; **arrangez-vous comme vous voulez, mais je veux être livré demain** I don't mind how you do it but I insist the goods are delivered tomorrow; **je veux récupérer l'argent qui m'est dû** I want to get back the money which I'm owed; **je ne veux pas entendre parler de ça!** I won't hear of it *or* such a thing!; **je ne veux plus en parler** I don't want to talk about it any more; **à ton âge, pourquoi v. faire le jeune homme?** at your age, why do you try to act like a young man?; **le peuple veut être gouverné** the people want a government; **il veut 10 000 euros de son studio** he wants 10,000 euros for his studio (*Br* flat *or Am* apartment); **v. qch de qn** to want sth from sb; **que voulez-vous de moi?, que me voulez-vous?** what do you want from me?; **que veux-tu de moi?, qu'est-ce que tu me veux?** what do you want from me?

2 *(prétendre → sujet: personne)* to claim; **si l'art est une religion, comme le veulent certaines personnes** if art is a religion, as some people would have it *or* claim

3 *(avoir l'intention de)* **v. faire qch** to want *or* to intend *or* to mean to do sth; **je voulais passer à la gare, mais je n'ai pas eu le temps** I wanted to drop in at the station, but I didn't have time; **je ne voulais pas te vexer** I didn't mean to offend you; **sans v. me mêler de tes affaires/te contredire...** I don't want to interfere/to contradict you but...; **je l'ai vexé sans le v.** I offended him unintentionally *or* without meaning to; **je ne voudrais surtout pas t'empêcher de voir ton match!** I wouldn't dream of preventing you from watching the match!; **si vous voulez finir le projet à temps, il faut recruter plus de personnel** if you want *or* intend to keep the project on schedule, you must take on more staff; **j'ai dit "attelle", je voulais dire "appelle"** I said "attelle", I meant "appelle"; **il ne s'est pas ennuyé ce soir-là – que veux-tu dire par là?** he had some fun that night – what do you mean by that *or* what are you getting at?; **vous voulez dire qu'on l'a tuée?** do you mean *or* are you suggesting (that) she was killed?

4 *(essayer de)* **v. faire** to want *or* to try to do; **en voulant la sauver, il s'est noyé** he drowned in his attempt *or* trying to rescue her; **tu veux me faire peur?** are you trying to frighten me?

5 *(s'attendre à)* to expect; **tu voudrais peut-être aussi que je te remercie!** you don't expect to be thanked into the bargain, do you?; **comment veux-tu que je te croie, maintenant?** how do you expect me to believe you now?; **comment veux-tu qu'elles s'en sortent avec des salaires si bas?** how do you expect them *or* how are they expected to survive on such low salaries?; **pourquoi voudrais-tu qu'on se fasse cambrioler?** why do you assume we might be burgled?; **que veux-tu que j'y fasse?** what do you want me to do about it?, what can I do about it?; **il est très malheureux – que veux-tu que j'y fasse?** he's very unhappy – what do you expect ME to do about it?; **que voulez-vous que je vous dise?** what can I say?, what do you want me to say?; **qu'est-ce que tu veux que je te dise, il ne fallait pas la provoquer** what can I say? you shouldn't have provoked her; **on va le faire réparer, que veux-tu que je te dise?** we'll get it fixed, what (else) can I say?

6 *Fam (sexuellement)* to want

B. *PRÉFÉRER, SOUHAITER* **1** *(dans un choix)* to want, to wish; **pour le premier, je voulais un garçon** I wanted the first baby to be a boy; **prends toutes les pommes que tu veux** have as many apples as you want; **j'en voudrais de plus mûres, de préférence** I'd rather have (some) riper ones, if possible; **jus d'ananas ou d'orange? – ce que tu veux!** pineapple or orange juice? – whatever *or* I don't mind!; **voulez-vous que nous prenions un thé ou préférez-vous marcher encore un peu?** would you like to stop for tea or would you prefer to walk on a bit?; **je préfère acheter des actions – comme vous voulez** I prefer to buy shares – as you wish; **on prend ma voiture ou la tienne? – c'est comme tu veux** shall we take my car or yours? – as you wish *or* please *or* like; **je me débrouillerai seul – comme tu voudras!** I'll manage on my own – suit yourself!; **où va-t-on? – où tu veux** where are we going? – wherever you want; **je pourrai revenir? – bien sûr, quand vous voulez!** may I come again? – of course, any time *or* whenever you want!; *Fam* **je vais vous chanter une chanson... – quand tu veux!** I'm going to sing you a song... – when you're ready!; *Fam* **je te prends quand tu veux au badminton** I'll give you a game of badminton any time; **viens avec nous si tu veux** come with us if you want; **tu peux dessiner une maison si tu veux** you could draw a house, if you like; **mets-en tant que tu veux** put in as much as you want; **on peut donner tant qu'on veut, cela ne résout pas le problème de la pauvreté** you can give as much as you want, it won't solve the problem of poverty; **tu peux rire tant que tu veux, ça m'est bien égal** you can laugh as much as you want, I don't care; **tu l'as** *ou* **l'auras voulu!** you asked for it!

2 *(dans une suggestion)* to want; **voulez-vous** *ou* **voudriez-vous du thé?** would you like some tea?; **veux-tu de l'aide?** do you want *or* would you like some help?; **tu veux une fessée?** do you want your bottom smacked?; **voulez-vous que je vous achète le journal?** would you like me to buy *or* shall I buy the newspaper for you?; **voudriez-vous vous joindre à nous?** would you care *or* like to join us?; **voudriez-vous essayer la robe bleue?** perhaps you might care to try on the blue dress?; **peut-être vouliez-vous que je m'en aille?** did you want me to go?

3 *(dans un souhait)* **je ne veux que ton bonheur** I only want you to be happy; **j'aurais tellement voulu être avec vous** I'd have so much liked *or* loved to have been with you; **quand tu me parles, je te voudrais un autre ton** please don't use that tone when you're talking to me; **comme je voudrais avoir des enfants!** how I'd love to have children!; **elle voudrait vous dire quelques mots en privé** she'd like a word with you in private; **je voudrais te voir à ma place** I'd like to see what you'd do if you were in my shoes; **je voudrais vous y voir!** I'd like to see how YOU'd cope with it!; **il faut tout terminer d'ici demain, je voudrais t'y voir!** it's all got to be finished by tomorrow, how'd YOU like to have to do it?; *Ironique* **aller au match sans avoir rangé ta chambre, je voudrais bien voir ça!** whatever gave you the idea (that) you could go to the match without tidying up your room first?

4 *(dans une demande polie)* **veuillez m'excuser un instant** (will you) please excuse me for a moment; **veuillez avoir l'obligeance de...** would you kindly *or* please...; **veuillez vous asseoir** please take a seat; **veuillez recevoir, Monsieur, mes salutations distinguées** yours *Br* sincerely *or Am* truly; **veuillez vous retirer, Marie** you may go now, Marie; **veuillez n'en rien dire à personne** would you kindly *or* please not mention anything to anyone; **voudriez-vous avoir l'amabilité de me prêter votre crayon?** would you be so kind as to lend me your pencil?; **nous voudrions une chambre pour deux personnes** we'd like a double room; **je vous serais reconnaissant de bien v. m'envoyer votre brochure** I should be glad to receive your brochure; **voulez-vous me suivre** please follow me

5 *(dans un rappel à l'ordre)* **veux-tu (bien) me répondre!** will you (please) answer me!; **veux-tu laisser le chat tranquille!** just leave the cat alone!, will you leave the cat alone!; **voulez-vous ne pas toucher à ça!** please don't touch that!; **ne m'interromps pas, tu veux!, veuille bien ne pas m'interrompre!** will you please

not interrupt me?, would you mind not interrupting me?; **un peu de respect, tu veux (bien)!** a bit less cheek, if you don't mind!

C. *SUJET: CHOSE* **1** *(se prêter à, être en état de)* **le rideau ne voulait pas se lever** the curtain wouldn't go up; **les haricots ne veulent pas cuire** the beans won't cook; *Hum* **la télé ne marche que quand elle veut** the TV only works when it feels like it

2 *(exiger)* to require; **la coutume veut que...** custom requires that...; **la tradition voulait que...** it was a tradition that...; **la dignité de notre profession veut que...** the dignity of our profession demands that...; **comme le veulent les usages** as convention dictates; **les lois le veulent ainsi** that is what the law says

3 *(prétendre)* **comme le veut une vieille légende** as an old legend has it

4 *(déterminer → sujet: destin, hasard, malheur)* **le sort voulut que le train fût en retard** as fate would have it, the train was late; **la chance a voulu que...** as luck would have it...; **le malheur voulut qu'il fût seul ce soir-là** unfortunately he was alone that night; **le calendrier a voulu que cela tombe un lundi** it fell on a Monday, as it so happened

5 *(s'efforcer de)* **le décor veut évoquer une ferme normande** the decor strives *or* tries to suggest a Normandy farmhouse

6 v. dire *(avoir comme sens propre)* to mean; *(avoir comme implication)* to mean, to suggest; **que veut dire "Arbeit"?** what does "Arbeit" mean?; **elle a fait un geste de la main qui voulait dire "peu importe"** she waved her hand to say "never mind"; **je me demande ce que veut dire ce changement d'attitude** I wonder what the meaning of this turnaround is *or* what this turnaround means; **cela ne veut rien dire** it doesn't mean anything; **être millionnaire, ça ne veut plus rien dire de nos jours** being a millionaire doesn't mean anything nowadays; **ça veut tout dire!** that says it all!; **ça veut bien dire ce que ça veut dire!** it's clear *or* plain enough!; *Fam* **tu vas m'obéir, non mais, qu'est-ce que ça veut dire?** for goodness' sake, will you do as I say!

7 *Gram* to take; **la conjonction "pourvu que" veut le subjonctif** the conjunction "pourvu que" takes the subjunctive

D. *LOCUTIONS* **bien v. faire qch** to be willing *or* to be prepared *or* to be quite happy to do sth; **nous voulons bien lui parler** we're prepared *or* quite willing to talk to him/her; **je veux bien me contenter d'un sandwich** I'm quite happy to make do with a sandwich; **je veux bien être patient, mais il y a des limites!** I can be patient, but there are limits!; **un petit café? – oui, je veux bien** fancy a coffee? – yes please; **poussons jusqu'à la prochaine ville – moi je veux bien, mais il est tard!** let's go on to the next town – I don't mind, but it IS late!; **allons-y, puisque ta mère veut bien garder les enfants** your mother's agreed to look after the children, so let's go; **je veux bien qu'il y ait des restrictions budgétaires, mais...** I understand (that) there are cuts in the budget, but...; **je veux bien avoir des défauts, mais pas celui-là** granted, I have some shortcomings, but that isn't one of them; **moi je veux bien!** (it's) fine by me!; **il a dit nous avoir soutenus, moi je veux bien, mais le résultat est là!** he said he supported us, OK *or* and that may be so, but look at the result!; *Fam* **il t'a cogné? – je veux!** did he hit you? – he sure did!; *Fam* **tu vas à la pêche demain? – je veux que j'y vais!** are you going fishing tomorrow? – you bet I am *or* I sure am!; **que veux-tu, j'ai pourtant essayé!** I tried, though!; **c'est ainsi, que voulez-vous!** that's just the way it is!; **j'accepte ses humeurs, que veux-tu!** I (just) put up with his/her moods, what can I do?; **j'ai dit que c'était ton idée, que veux-tu, sinon on m'aurait renvoyé** I said it was your idea, what could I do, otherwise they'd have sacked me; **que voulez-vous, ils se conduisent comme les jeunes de leur âge** they're just acting their age, what can you do?; **si tu veux, si vous voulez** more or less, if you like; **ça ressemble à un gros lapin, si tu veux** it looks a bit like a big rabbit

USAGE ABSOLU *(être décidé à obtenir)* **quand tu veux, tu fais très bien la cuisine** you can cook beautifully when you put your mind to it; **il peut être vraiment désagréable quand il veut** he can be a real nuisance when he wants to; *Prov* **v., c'est pouvoir** where there's a will, there's a way; *Prov* **quand on veut, on peut** where there's a will, there's a way

V AUX *Suisse (pour exprimer le futur proche)* to be going to; **il veut pleuvoir** it's going to rain; **ça veut aller** it will be all right

❑ **en veux-tu en voilà** ADV *Fam (en abondance)* **il y avait des glaces en veux-tu en voilà** there were ice creams galore; **on dirait qu'elle a de l'argent en veux-tu en voilà** she seems to have money to burn; **il leur faisait des compliments en veux-tu en voilà** he was showering them with compliments

❑ **si l'on veut** ADV **1** *(approximativement)* if you like; **on peut dire, si l'on veut, que...** if you like you can say that...

2 *(pour exprimer une réserve)* **c'est drôle/propre si l'on veut** I wouldn't say it's particularly funny/clean; **il est fidèle... si l'on veut!** he's faithful... after a fashion!

❑ **vouloir de** VT IND **1** *(être prêt à accepter)* **v. de qn/qch** to want sb/sth; **je ne veux plus de ces vieux journaux, jette-les** I don't want these old papers any more, throw them out; **je ne veux pas d'une relation sérieuse** I don't want a serious relationship

2 *(locutions) Fam* **elle en veut** *(elle a de l'ambition)* she wants to make it *or* to win; *(elle a de l'application)* she's dead keen; *Fam* **elle en veut, sur le court** she's out to win when she's on (the) court; *Fam* **il faut en v. pour réapprendre à marcher** you need a lot of determination to learn to walk again▪; **en v. à qn** *(éprouver de la rancune)* to bear *or* to have a grudge against sb; **je ne l'ai pas fait exprès, ne m'en veux pas** I didn't do it on purpose, don't be cross with me; **décidément, ton chien m'en veut** your dog's definitely got something against me; **tu m'en veux encore beaucoup pour l'autre soir?** are you still angry *or* cross with me about the other night?; **je n'en veux à personne, je demande simplement justice** I'm not after anyone's blood, all I want is justice; **tu ne m'en veux pas?** no hard feelings?; **vous ne m'en voudrez pas si je pars plus tôt, n'est-ce pas?** you won't mind *or* be cross if I leave earlier, will you?; **elle m'en voulait de mon manque d'intérêt pour elle** she resented my lack of interest in her; **mes frères m'en veulent de mon succès** my brothers hold my success against me; **elle m'en veut d'avoir refusé** she holds it against me that I said no; **il ne faut pas lui en v. d'exprimer son amertume** don't resent him/her for showing his/her bitterness; **j'ai l'impression qu'il en veut à ma cadette** I feel he has designs on my youngest daughter; **elle en veut à ma fortune** she's after my money; **en v. à qch** *(vouloir le détruire)* to seek to damage sth; **qui peut en v. à ma vie?** who could wish me dead?; **qui peut en v. à ma réputation** who would want to damage my reputation?

▶**se vouloir** VPR **1 je me voudrais plus audacieux** I'd like to be bolder; **les pièces qui se veulent intellectuelles** plays with intellectual pretensions; **le livre se veut une satire de l'aristocratie allemande** the book claims *or* is supposed to be a satire on the German aristocracy

2 *(emploi réfléchi)* **s'en v.** to be angry *or* annoyed with oneself; **je m'en veux de l'avoir laissé partir** I feel bad at having let him go; *Fam* **je m'en voudrais!** not likely!; **80 euros pour un match de football? je m'en voudrais!** 80 euros for a football match? not likely!

3 *(emploi réciproque)* **s'en v.** to bear each other a grudge, to have a grudge against each other; **elles s'en veulent à mort** they really hate each other

4 *Littéraire* **il se voulut** *ou* **s'est voulu défendre** he endeavoured to defend himself

voulu, -e [vuly] ADJ **1** *(requis)* required, desired, *Sout* requisite; **vous aurez toutes les garanties voulues** you'll have all the required guarantees; **ça a eu l'effet v.** it produced the desired effect

2 *(délibéré)* deliberate, intentional; **c'est v.** it's intentional *or* (done) on purpose

3 *(décidé d'avance)* agreed; **au moment v.** at the right time; **en temps v.** in due course, eventually; **terminé en temps v.** completed on schedule

vous [vu] PRON PERSONNEL **1** *(en s'adressant à une personne → sujet ou objet direct)* you; **si j'étais v.** if I were you; **c'est v.?** *(à la porte)* is that you?; **v. parti, je lui écrirai** once you've gone, I shall write to him/her; **eux m'ont compris, pas v.** they understood me, you didn't; **qui a fini? v.?** who's finished? have you?; **il nage mieux que v.** he swims better than you (do); **elle a fait comme v.** she did (the same) as you did; **et v. qui aviez toujours peur!** to think YOU're the one who was always scared!; **je v. connais, v.!** I know YOU!; **v., v. restez** as for you, you're staying

2 *(en s'adressant à une personne → objet indirect)* **c'est à v.** *(objet)* it belongs to you; **à v.!** *(dans un magasin, un jeu)* it's your turn!; **une maison bien à v.** a house of your very own, your very own house; **une plage rien qu'à v.** a beach to yourself; **elle ne parle qu'à v.** you're the only one she speaks to; **c'est à v. de juger** it's for you to judge; **pensez un peu à v.** think of yourself a bit; **un livre de v.** a book by you; **c'est de v. cette lettre?** is this one of your letters?; **de v. à moi** between (the two of) us *or* you and me; **chez v.** at your house, in your home; **faites comme chez v.** please make yourself at home; *Fam* **ça va, chez v.?** (are) things OK at home?

3 *(en s'adressant à une personne → dans des formes réfléchies)* **taisez-v.!** be quiet!; **cachez-v.!** hide!; **regardez-v.** look at yourself

4 *(en s'adressant à plusieurs personnes → sujet ou objet direct)* you; *(en renforcement)* you (people); **v. êtes témoins** you have all witnessed this; **v. partis, je lui écrirai** once you've all gone, I shall write to him/her; **elle v. a accusés tous les trois** she accused all three of you; **et v. qui aviez toujours peur!** to think YOU were the ones who were always scared!; **v., v. restez** as for you (people), you're staying; **v. (autres), les spécialistes, v. ne faites rien** YOU're the specialists and you're not doing anything; **v. (autres), les intellectuels, v. êtes tous pareils** you're all the same, you intellectuals; **v. autres, v. allez au cinéma?** you lot, are you going to the cinema?

5 *(après une préposition)* **c'est à v.** *(objet)* it belongs to you; *Rad & TV* **à v.** over to you; **à v. le studio!** I'm handing you back to the studio!; **pensez à v. et à vos amis** think of yourselves and of your friends; **à v. trois, v. finirez bien la tarte?** surely the three of you can finish the tart?; **l'un de v. trahira** one of you will be a traitor

6 *(dans des formes réfléchies)* **taisez-v. tous!** be quiet, all of you!; **cachez-v., tous les deux!** hide, you two!; **regardez-v.** look at yourselves

7 *(dans des formes réciproques)* one another, each other; **aidez-v.** help one another; **battez-v.** fight with each other

8 *Fam (valeur intensive)* **il v. mange tout un poulet** he can put away a whole chicken; **elle sait v. séduire une foule** she does know how to captivate a crowd▪; **ils v. démolissent une maison en trois quarts d'heure** they can demolish a house in three quarters of an hour, no trouble (at all)

NM **le v.** the "vous" form; **leurs enfants leur disent "v."** their children use the "vous" form to them; **nous pourrions arrêter de nous dire "v."** we could be less formal with each other, we could start using the "tu" form to each other

vous-même [vumɛm] *(pl* **vous-mêmes***)* PRON yourself; **vous-mêmes** yourselves; **avez-vous fait votre exercice v.?** did you do your exercise yourself?; **vous devriez comprendre de vous-mêmes** you ought to understand for yourselves; **vous pouvez vérifier par v.** you can check for yourself

vousoiement [vuzwamɑ̃] NM *Suisse* "vous" form of address

vousoyer [13] [vuzwaje] *Suisse* VT to address as "vous"; **les parents se faisaient v. par leurs enfants** the children addressed their parents as "vous"

▸**se vousoyer** VPR to address each other as "vous"

voussoir [vuswar] NM *Archit* voussoir, arch stone

voussure [vusyr] NF *Archit (d'une voûte)* spring; *(d'une baie)* arch; *(d'un plafond)* coving *(UNCOUNT)*

voûtain [vutɛ̃] NM *Archit (portion de voûte)* cell, segment

voûte [vut] NF **1** *Archit (construction)* vault; *(passage)* archway; **v. d'arête** groined vault; **v. en berceau** barrel vault; **v. (sur croisée) d'ogives** ribbed vault; **v. en éventail** fan *or* palm vaulting *(UNCOUNT)*; **v. en plein cintre** semicircular vault

2 *Littéraire* vault, canopy; **la v. céleste** *ou* **des cieux** the canopy of heaven; **la v. étoilée** the starry dome

3 *Anat* **v. crânienne** cranial vault; **v. palatine** *ou* **du palais** roof of the mouth; **v. plantaire** arch of the foot

❑ **en voûte** ADJ vaulted

voûté, -e [vute] ADJ **1** *(homme)* stooping, round-shouldered; *(dos)* bent; **avoir le dos v.** to stoop, to have a stoop; **marcher v.** to walk with a stoop; **ne te tiens pas v.** stand up straight **2** *(galerie)* vaulted, arched

voûter [3] [vute] VT **1** *Archit* to vault, to arch **2** *(courber)* to cause to stoop; **l'âge a voûté son dos** age has bowed his back *or* made him stoop

▸**se voûter** VPR to stoop, to become round-shouldered

vouvoie *etc voir* **vouvoyer**

vouvoiement [vuvwamɑ̃] NM "vous" form of address; **ici, le v. est de rigueur** people have to address each other as "vous" here

vouvoyer [13] [vuvwaje] VT to address as "vous"; **les parents se faisaient v. par leurs enfants** the children addressed their parents as "vous"

▸**se vouvoyer** VPR to address each other as "vous"

vouvray [vuvrɛ] NM Vouvray (wine)

vox populi [vɔkspɔpyli] NF INV *Littéraire* vox populi; **écouter la v.** to listen to what the people have to say

voyage [vwajaʒ] NM **1** *(excursion lointaine)* journey, trip; *(circuit)* tour, trip; *(sur la mer, dans l'espace)* voyage; **notre v. se fera en péniche/à dos de chameau** we will travel on a barge/on a camel; **v. en autocar** bus *or Br* coach trip; **les voyages en avion** air travel; **leur v. en Italie** their trip to Italy; **aimer les voyages** to like travel *or* travelling; *Littéraire* **mes voyages au pays de l'imaginaire** my imaginary travels; **faire un v.** to go on a trip; **faire un v. dans le temps** *(passé, futur)* to journey through time; **faire un v. autour du monde** to go round the world; **ils ont fait des voyages partout dans le monde** they have travelled the world; **j'ai fait de nombreux voyages en Méditerranée** I've travelled extensively throughout the Mediterranean; **faire le v. de Bangkok** to go to Bangkok; **partir en v.** to go on a trip; **nous partons en v.** we're off on a trip, we're going away; *Fam Fig* **être en v.** *(être en prison)* to be inside *or* behind bars; **elle est en v.** she's away; **vous serez du v.?** *(avec eux)* are you going on the trip?; *(avec nous)* are you coming on the trip?; **ils partent demain mais elle ne sera pas du v.** they're off tomorrow but she won't be going (with them) *or* be making the journey; **quelle merveille, cela valait le v.!** what a sight, it was well worth coming all this way to see it!; **cela représente deux jours/six mois de v.** it means a two-day/six-month trip; **vous avez fait bon v.?** did you have a good journey?; **bon v.!** have a nice trip!; **v. d'affaires** business trip; **être en v. d'affaires** to be away on business; **partir en v. d'affaires** to go (off) on a business trip; **v. d'agrément** (pleasure) trip; **v. d'études** field trip; **v. de familiarisation** familiarization trip; **v. à forfait** inclusive tour, package tour, all-expense tour, all-in tour; **v. en mer** sea voyage, journey by sea; **v. de noces** honeymoon; **être en v. de noces** to be honeymooning *or* on one's honeymoon; **nous sommes partis en v. de noces en Guadeloupe** we went to Guadeloupe on *or* for our honeymoon; **v. officiel** *(en un endroit)* official trip; *(en plusieurs endroits)* official tour; **v. organisé** package tour; **ils y sont allés en v. organisé** they went there on a package tour; **v. de presse** press visit; **v. scolaire** school trip; **v. de stimulation** incentive trip *or* tour; **v. (touristique) accompagné** conducted *or* guided tour; *(excursion)* escorted tour; *Euph Littéraire* **le grand v.** the last journey; **faire le grand v.** to go on one's last journey; **compagnon de v.** travelling companion; *(dans voiture etc)* fellow passenger; **livre de v.** travel book; **récit de v.** travel story; *Rad* travelogue; *Prov* **les voyages forment la jeunesse** travel broadens the mind; *Fam Ironique* **si il vient se plaindre à moi, il va pas être déçu du v.!** if he comes complaining to me, he'll wish he hadn't bothered!; *Can Fam* **j'ai mon v.!** *(j'en ai eu assez)* I've had enough!▪, I've had it up to here!; *(je n'y crois pas)* I can't get over it!, I can't believe it!▪

2 *(déplacement local)* journey; **tous les matins, je fais le v. en train** I do the journey by train every morning; **v. en train/avion** train/plane journey; **v. aller** outward journey; **v. aller et retour** return *or* round trip; **v. retour** return *or* homeward journey

3 *(allée et venue)* trip; **ça va t'obliger à faire deux voyages** that way you'll need to make two trips; **j'ai fait des voyages de la cave au grenier toute la matinée** I've been up and down from cellar to attic all morning

4 *Fam (sous drogue)* trip

'Les Voyages de Gulliver' *Jonathan Swift* 'Gulliver's Travels'

'Le Voyage dans la Lune' *Méliès, Cyrano de Bergerac* 'A Trip to the Moon' (film), 'A Voyage to the Moon' (book)

Allusion

Voyage au bout de la nuit

The writer Louis-Ferdinand Céline was a soldier in the 1914–18 war. Though decorated for his bravery, he could not subscribe to the heroic notion of war, and in his 1932 novel *Voyage au bout de la nuit* ("Journey to the End of Night") he recalled the true horror of his experiences. Today, the expression is used either in describing a situation where someone is pushed to an absolute extreme, perhaps staring death in the face, or, substituting another word for **nuit**, when a subject is treated in depth. For example, an in-depth TV documentary on drugs could be called **Voyage au bout de la drogue**.

voyageage [vwajaʒaʒ], **voyagement** [vwajaʒmɑ̃] NM *Can Fam* travelling (back and forth)▪

voyager [17] [vwajaʒe] VI **1** *(faire une excursion)* to travel; *(faire un circuit)* to tour; **elle a beaucoup voyagé** she has travelled widely *or* a lot, she's well travelled; **nous avons beaucoup voyagé en Grèce** we've travelled extensively throughout Greece; **aimer v.** to like travelling; **v. dans le temps** *(passé, futur)* to travel through time; **un film qui fait v.** a movie *or Br* film that takes you to far-off places

2 *(se déplacer)* to travel; **v. en bateau/en avion/en chemin de fer** to travel by sea/by air/by rail; **v. par mer** to travel by sea; **v. pour affaires** to travel on business; **v. en deuxième classe** to travel second-class; **la société fait v. ses cadres en première classe** the company pays for its executives to travel first-class

3 *(denrées, sacs)* to travel; **le vin voyage mal** wine doesn't travel well; **ce produit doit v. en wagon frigorifique** this product must be carried in refrigerated trucks

4 *Com* to travel; **v. pour une société** to travel for a firm

voyageur, -euse [vwajaʒœr, -øz] ADJ *Littéraire (caractère)* wayfaring, travelling

NM,F **1** *(dans les transports en commun)* passenger; *(dans un taxi)* fare **2** *(qui explore)* traveller; *Vieilli (aventurier)* voyager, explorer; **c'est une grande voyageuse** she travels extensively **3** *Com* **v. de commerce, v. représentant placier** commercial traveller, sales representative

voyageur-kilomètre [vwajaʒœrkilɔmɛtr] *(pl* **voyageurs-kilomètres)** NM passenger-kilometre

voyagiste [vwajaʒist] NM tour operator

voyait *etc voir* **voir**

voyance [vwajɑ̃s] NF clairvoyance

voyant, -e [vwajɑ̃, -ɑ̃t] ADJ *(couleur)* loud, gaudy, garish; *(robe)* showy, gaudy, garish; **peu v.** inconspicuous; **trop v.** obtrusive

NM,F **1** *(visionnaire)* visionary, seer; **v. (extralucide)** *(spirite)* clairvoyant

2 *(non aveugle)* sighted person; **les voyants** the sighted

NM **1** *(d'un signal nautique)* mark; *(d'arpenteur)* sighting board; *(d'un instrument scientifique)* sighting slit, aperture; *(d'un bateau-phare)* sphere

2 v. (lumineux) indicator *or* warning light; **v. de baisse de tension des piles** "battery low" warning light; **v. de charge** battery charge warning light; **v. de frein à main** "handbrake on" light; **v. d'huile/d'essence** oil/petrol indicator light; **v. de marche** activation light

voyelle [vwajɛl] NF vowel; **v. thématique** thematic vowel

voyeur, -euse [vwajœr, -øz] NM,F voyeur

voyeurisme [vwajœrism] NM voyeurism

voyeuse [vwajøz] *voir* **voyeur**

voyou, -oute [vwaju, -ut] ADJ loutish; **verve voyoute** vulgar wit

NM **1** *(jeune délinquant)* lout; *(escroc)* crook **2** *(ton affectueux ou amusé)* **petit v.!** you little rascal!

voyoucratie [vwajukrasi] NF = rule by crooks

voyoute [vwajut] *voir* **voyou**

VPC [vepese] NF *(abrév* **vente par correspondance)** mail-order (selling)

vrac [vrak] NM **1** *(mode de distribution)* bulk

2 *(marchandise)* material transported in bulk; **faire le v., transporter le v.** to transport goods in bulk

❑ **en vrac** ADJ & ADV **1** *(non rangé)* in a jumble; **outils jetés en v. sur le plancher** tools thrown higgledy-piggledy on the floor; **tout est posé en v. sur ma table** everything is lying higgledy-piggledy *or* in a jumble *or* jumbled together on my table; **elle a déposé ses affaires en v. sur la table** she dumped her things on the table; **ses idées sont en v. dans sa dissertation** the ideas are just jumbled together in his/her essay

2 *(non emballé)* loose; *(en gros)* in bulk; **marchandises en v.** loose goods; **vendu en v.** sold loose; **charger en v.** to load in bulk; *Fam Fig* **on invite toute la famille en v.** we're inviting the whole family in one go

VRAI, -E [vrɛ]

ADJ true **1, 2, 6-8** ▪ real **2-4** ▪ complete **4** ▪ straightforward **5**
NM truth
ADV realistic, true to life **2**

ADJ **1** *(exact)* true; **au négatif, la proposition reste vraie** if negated, the proposition remains true; **si ce que tu dis est v.** if you're telling the truth, if what you say is true; **vous maintenez votre déposition? – tout est v.** are you sticking to your statement? – it's all true; **il n'y a pas un mot de v. dans son témoignage** there's not a word of truth in his/her testimony; **ils n'ont aucune intégrité – cette observation n'est pas vraie de tous** they have no integrity – that isn't true of all of them *or* you can't say that of all of them; **Oslo est la capitale de la Norvège, v. ou faux?** Oslo is the capital of Norway, true or false?; **tu me l'avais promis, v. ou faux?** you'd promised me, yes or no?; **c'est v.** it's *or* that's true; **elle est gentille, c'est v., mais pas très fine** she's nice, I agree, but she's not very bright; **ce serait plus facile – c'est v., mais...** it would be easier – true *or* certainly *or* granted, but...; **tu ne fais jamais rien! – c'est v., ça!** you never do anything! – that's quite right *or* true!; **ma voiture peut monter jusqu'à 300 km/h – c'est v.?** my car can do up to 300 km/h – can it (really) *or* oh really?; *Fam* **c'est v. qu'on n'a pas eu de chance** true, we were a bit unlucky; *Fam* **c'est**

vou–vra

pas v.! *(pour nier)* it's *or* that's not true!; *(ton incrédule)* you're joking!; *(ton exaspéré)* I don't believe this!; *(ton horrifié)* my God, no!; **je pars en Chine – c'est pas v.!** I'm off to China – no!; **il est mort hier – c'est pas v.!** he died yesterday – never *or* I can't believe it!; **mais tu es agaçant ce matin, c'est pas v.!** God, you ARE being a pain this morning!; **et maintenant une coupure de courant, c'est pas v.!** and now there's a power cut, I don't believe it!; **elle va pas recommencer, c'est pas v.!** she's going to start again, I (just) don't believe it!, oh my God, she's not starting again!; **c'est si v. que...** so much so that...; **elle était furieuse, c'est si v. qu'elle a écrit au ministre** she was beside herself, to the point of writing to the minister; **il est v.** it's *or* that's true; **elle est un peu menteuse, il est v.** it's true that she's a bit of a liar, she's a bit of a liar, true; **la loi est dure, il est v.** the law is tough, true (enough); **il est v. que...** it's true (to say) that...; **il est très irritable, il est v. qu'il n'est pas encore habitué à eux** he's very irritable, true, he's not used to them yet; **il est bien v. que...** it's absolutely true *or* it can't be denied that...; **il est bien v. que la situation économique se dégrade** there's no denying that the state of the economy is getting worse

2 *(authentique → cuir, denrée)* genuine, real; *(→ or)* real; *(→ connaisseur)* real, true; *(→ royaliste, républicain)* true; **couleurs vraies** lifelike *or* realistic colours; *Littéraire* **je cherche l'amour v.** I'm looking for true love; **avec une simplicité vraie** with genuine simplicity; **c'est une copie, ce n'est pas un v. Modigliani** it's a copy, it's not a real Modigliani; **les vraies rousses sont rares** there are few genuine *or* real redheads; **ce ne sont pas mes vraies dents** they're not my own teeth; **la seule vraie religion** the only true religion; **nous prônons le v. socialisme** we want to promote real *or* genuine socialism; **le v. cricket, ça ne se joue pas comme ça!** that's not how you play proper cricket!; **le rôle est tenu par la vraie sœur de l'actrice** the part is played by the actress's real *or* real-life sister; **c'est un v. gentleman** he's a real gentleman; **il n'a jamais été un v. père** he was never (like) a real father; **où sont tes vrais amis, maintenant?** where are your true *or* real friends now?; *Fam Hum* **c'est v., ce mensonge?** are you fibbing?; **le soleil, il n'y a que ça de v.** give me sunshine any day; **pour enlever les taches, l'acétone, il n'y a que ça de v.** to remove stains, acetone's the thing

3 *(non fictif, non inventé → raison)* real; **c'est une histoire vraie** it's a true story; **quel est le v. motif de votre visite?** what's the real purpose of your visit?; **mon v. nom est Jacob** my real name is Jacob; **le v. problème n'est pas là** the real problem lies elsewhere

4 *(avant le nom) (à valeur intensive)* real, complete, utter; **c'est un v. désastre** it's a real *or* an utter disaster; **il a été un v. père pour moi** he was like a father to me; **c'est un v. casse-tête** it's a real headache; **c'est une vraie honte!** it's utterly disgraceful!; *très Fam* **t'es un v. salaud!** you're a real bastard!; **c'est une vraie folle!** she's completely crazy!

5 *(franc, naturel → personne, acteur)* straightforward; **pour les persuader, sois v.** to convince them, be straightforward; **je suis v. quand je joue ce personnage** I am *or* play myself when I play this character; **son style est toujours v.** he/she always writes naturally; **des dialogues vrais** dialogues that ring true; **des personnages vrais** characters that are true to life

6 *(avant le nom) (assigné)* true; **la statue n'est pas à sa vraie place** *(elle a été déplacée)* the statue is not in its right place; **un philosophe qui n'a jamais été mis à sa vraie place** a philosopher who was never granted true recognition *or* granted the recognition he deserved

7 *Astron* **temps v.** true time

8 *Anat* **vraie côte** true rib

NM,F **un homme, un v.** a real man; **c'est une infirmière, une vraie** she's a nurse, the real thing *or* the genuine article; *Fam* **ça c'est de la bière, de la vraie!** that's what I call beer!

NM **le v.** *(la vérité)* the truth; **il y a du** *ou* **un peu de v. dans ses critiques** there's some truth *or* an element of truth in his/her criticism; **il y a du v., là-dedans** there's some truth in it; **où est le v. dans ce qu'elle nous raconte?** where is the truth in what she's telling us?; **distinguer le v. du faux** to distinguish truth from falsehood; **être dans le v.** to be right; **ce n'est pas tout à fait cela mais tu es dans le v.** that's not quite true, but broadly speaking, you're correct *or* you're on the right lines

ADV **1** *(conformément à la vérité)* **elle dit v.** *(elle dit la vérité)* she's telling the truth; *(elle a raison)* she's right, what she says is right; **si tu as dit v.** if you were telling the truth, if what you said is true; **et s'il n'avait pas dit v.?** what if he was lying *or* wasn't telling the truth?; **tu n'en veux plus? – non, v., j'ai trop mangé** don't you want some more? – no, really, I've eaten too much already; *Littéraire* **de v.** truly, indeed, in truth

2 *(avec vraisemblance)* **des auteurs qui écrivent/acteurs qui jouent v.** authors whose writing/actors whose acting is true to life; **faire v.** *(décor, prothèse)* to look real; **avec des monstres qui font v.** with lifelike monsters

3 *Fam Vieilli (exprime la surprise, l'irritation)* **v., j'ai cru que je n'en verrais jamais la fin!** I thought I'd never see the back of it, I did!; **v., ce qu'il est drôle!** isn't he funny, though!; **il a été reçu au permis! – eh ben v.!** he passed his driving test! – you don't say!

▫ **à dire (le) vrai** = **à vrai dire**

▫ **au vrai** ADV to be specific; **au v., voici ce qui s'est passé** specifically, this is what took place

▫ **à vrai dire** ADV in actual fact, to tell you the truth, to be quite honest

▫ **pas vrai?** ADV *Fam* **il l'a bien mérité, pas v.?** he deserved it, didn't he?; **toi aussi, tu le penses, pas v.?** you think so too, don't you *or* right?; **on ira tous les deux, pas v.?** we'll go together, OK?

▫ **pour de vrai** ADV *Fam* really ■, truly ■; **cette fois-ci, je pars pour de v.** this time I'm really leaving; **elle ne le disait pas pour de v.** she wasn't (being) serious, she didn't (really) mean it; **c'est pour de v.** I'm serious, I (really) mean it; **cette fois, c'est pour de v.** this time it's serious *or* for real

▫ **vrai de vrai, vraie de vraie** ADJ *Fam* **je pars avec toi – v. de v.?** I'm going with you – really (and truly)?; **c'est un Italien v. de v.** he's an Italian born and bred; **ça c'est de la bière, de la vraie de vraie!** that's what I call beer!; **ça c'est un homme, un v. de v.!** that's (what I call) a real man!

---

vrai-faux, vraie-fausse [vrɛfo, -fos] *(mpl* **vrais-faux**, *fpl* **vraies-fausses)** ADJ *Hum* **de vrais-faux plombiers** professional cowboy plumbers; **de vrais-faux passeports** genuine false passports

vraiment [vrɛmɑ̃] ADV **1** *(réellement)* really; **il avait l'air v. ému** he seemed really *or* genuinely moved; **tu as v. fait ça?** did you really do that?; **il est v. médecin?** is he really a doctor?; **v., je n'y tiens pas** I'm really not that keen; **je ne savais v. pas quoi faire** I really didn't know what to do; **je vous assure, v., je dois y aller** no, really, I must go

2 *(en intensif)* really; **il a v. dépassé les bornes** he's really gone too far; **elle peint v. bien** she paints really well; **j'en ai v. assez** I've really had enough; **tu nous as v. bien aidés** you've been a real help to us; **vous êtes v. trop bon** you are really too kind; **ils voyagent v. beaucoup** they really travel a lot, *Am* they sure do a lot of traveling; **il est v. bête!** he's really *or* so stupid!; **tu n'as v. rien compris!** you haven't understood a thing!; **tu trouves que j'ai fait des progrès? – ah oui, v.!** do you think I've improved *or* made any progress? – oh yes, a lot!; **non merci, v.** no thank you, really; **v., il exagère!** he really has got a nerve!

3 *(exprimant le doute)* **v.?** really?, indeed?, is that so?; **v.? tu en es sûr?** really? are you sure?; *Ironique* **elle a dit que c'était moi le meilleur – v.?** she said I was the best – you don't say *or* really!

vraisemblable [vrɛsɑ̃blabl] ADJ *(théorie)* likely; *(dénouement, excuse)* convincing, plausible; **une fin peu v.** a rather implausible ending; **il est (très) v. qu'il ait oublié** he's forgotten, in all likelihood; **il n'est pas v. qu'elle avoue** it wouldn't be like her to own up

NM **le v.** the plausible

vraisemblablement [vrɛsɑ̃blabləmɑ̃] ADV in all likelihood *or* probability, very likely; **est-il là? – v. non** is he there? – it appears not; **les photos seront prêtes v. demain** the pictures will probably be ready tomorrow

vraisemblance [vrɛsɑ̃blɑ̃s] NF **1** *(d'une œuvre)* plausibility, *Sout* verisimilitude **2** *(d'une hypothèse)* likelihood

▫ **selon toute vraisemblance** ADV in all likelihood; **selon toute v., il est allé se plaindre** he very likely went and complained, in all likelihood, he went and complained

vraquier [vrakje] NM *Naut* bulk carrier

VRC [veɛrse] NF *Mktg* *(abrév* **vente par réseau coopté)** multilevel marketing, MLM

V/Réf *(abrév écrite* **Votre référence)** your ref

vreneli [frenəli] NM *Suisse* = gold coin worth 20 Swiss francs

vrillage [vrijaʒ] NM **1** *Tex* kinking, kink, snarl **2** *Aviat* twist **3** *Aut (de la transmission)* wind-up

vrille [vrij] NF **1** *Bot* tendril **2** *(outil)* gimlet **3** *Aviat* spin; **v. à plat** flat spin; **v. serrée** steep spin; **v. sur le dos** inverted spin

▫ **en vrille** ADJ **descente en v.** spin; **escalier en v.** spiral staircase ADV **descendre en v.** to spin downwards; **monter en v.** to corkscrew up; **se mettre en v.** to go into a (vertical) spin; *Fam* **partir en v.** to go down the tubes *or* pan

vrillé, -e[1] [vrije] ADJ **1** *Bot* tendrilled **2** *(tordu)* twisted **3** *(percé)* bored into, pierced into

vrillée[2] [vrije] NF *Bot* bindweed

vriller [3] [vrije] VI **1** *(avion, fusée)* to spiral, to spin **2** *(corde, fil)* to twist, to kink

VT to pierce, to bore into

vrillette [vrijɛt] NF *Entom* deathwatch beetle

vrombir [32] [vrɔ̃bir] VI *(avion, moteur)* to throb, to hum; *(insecte)* to buzz, to hum; **faire v. un moteur** to rev up an engine

vrombissement [vrɔ̃bismɑ̃] NM *(d'un avion, d'un moteur)* throbbing sound, humming *(UNCOUNT)*; *(d'un insecte)* buzzing *(UNCOUNT)*, humming *(UNCOUNT)*

vroum [vrum] EXCLAM vroom!

VRP [veɛrpe] NM *Com* *(abrév* **voyageur représentant placier)** sales rep; **V. multicarte** freelance rep *(working for several companies)*

vs *Ling (abrév écrite* **versus)** v, vs

VSAT [vesat] NM INV *Tél (abrév* **very small aperture terminal)** VSAT

VSD [veɛsde] NM *Presse* *(abrév* **vendredi samedi dimanche)** = French popular weekly news magazine

VSN [veɛsɛn] NM *Mil* *(abrév* **volontaire du service national)** = recruit who chooses to carry out his national service by doing voluntary service overseas

VTC [vetese] NM *(abrév* **vélo tout chemin)** hybrid (bike)

VTOL [veteoɛl] NM INV *Aviat* *(abrév* **vertical take-off and landing)** VTOL

VTT [vetete] NM *(abrév* **vélo tout-terrain)** mountain bike

vu[1] [vy] NM INV **1 au vu et au su de tous** openly; **au vu de son dossier...** looking at his case...

2 *Jur (d'un décret)* preamble

vu[2] [vy] PRÉP *(en considération de)* in view of, considering, given; **vu le temps qu'il fait, je pense qu'on ne va pas y aller** in view of *or* given the bad weather, I don't think we'll be going; **vu son rang** in view of his *or* considering *or* given his rank; *Jur* **vu l'article 317 du Code pénal...** in view of article 317 of the Penal Code...

▫ **vu que** CONJ *(étant donné que)* in view of the fact that, seeing that, considering that; **il lui faudra au moins deux heures pour venir, vu qu'il est à pied** he'll need at least two hours to get here, seeing that he's (coming) on foot

vu[3], **-e**[1] [vy] PP *voir* **voir**

ADJ **1** *(considéré)* **il est bien vu de travailler tard** it's the done thing *or* it's good form to work late; **il veut être bien vu** he wants to be well thought of; **fumer, c'est assez mal vu ici** smoking is disapproved of here; **j'ai toujours été parmi les élèves mal vus** I was always one of

the pupils the teachers disapproved of; **être bien vu de qn** to be well thought of by sb; **être mal vu de qn** to be not well thought of by sb

2 *(analysé)* **personnages bien/mal vus** finely observed/poorly-drawn characters; **un problème bien vu** an accurately diagnosed problem; **une situation bien vue** a finely judged situation; **bien vu!** well spotted!

3 *Fam (compris)* **(c'est) vu?** OK?, all right?, got it?; **tu es sage, vu?** you're to be good, understand?; **(c'est) vu!** OK!, got it!; **et l'eau froide arrive par là – vu!** and this is the cold water pipe – OK!

vue² [vy] NF **1** *(sens)* eyesight, sight; **recouvrer la v.** to get one's sight *or* eyesight back; **perdre la v.** to lose one's sight, to go blind; **avoir une bonne v.** to have good eyesight; **avoir une mauvaise v.** to have bad *or* poor eyesight; **avoir la v. basse** to have weak eyes; **ma v. baisse** my eyes are getting weaker; **avoir une v. perçante** to be hawk-eyed

2 *(regard)* **porter la v. sur qch** to take a look at sth; **se présenter** *ou* **s'offrir à la v. de qn** *(personne, animal, chose)* to appear before sb's eyes; *(spectacle, paysage)* to unfold before sb's eyes; **se tenir hors de v.** to keep out of sight

3 *(fait de voir)* sight; **je ne supporte pas la v. du sang** I can't stand the sight of blood; **la v. de ces malheureux me fend le cœur** seeing *or* the sight of these wretched people breaks my heart

4 *(yeux)* eyes; **tu vas t'abîmer la v.** you'll ruin your eyes; **ils ont vérifié ma v.** they checked my eyesight; *Fam* **en mettre plein la v. à qn** to knock sb dead, to blow sb away; **on va leur en mettre plein la v.!** let's really knock them dead!

5 *(panorama)* view; **quelle v. avez-vous de la chambre?** what can you see from the bedroom (window)?; **d'ici, vous avez une v. magnifique** the view (you get) from here is magnificent; **v. sur la mer** sea view; **une v. imprenable** an unobstructed view; **de ma cuisine, j'ai une v. plongeante sur leur chambre** from my kitchen I can see straight down into their bedroom; **avoir v. sur** to look out on; **le balcon a v. sur le lac** the balcony looks out over the lake, there's a view of the lake from the balcony; **chambre avec v. sur le jardin** room that looks out on(to) the garden; **je voudrais une chambre avec v., s'il vous plaît** I'd like a room with a view, please; **v. aérienne** aerial view; *Aut* **v. panoramique** all-round view

6 *(aspect)* view, aspect; **dessiner une v. latérale de la maison** to draw a side view *or* the side aspect of the house; **v. de face/de côté** *(d'objet, de personne)* front/side view; **v. en coupe** cross-section

7 *(image)* view; **acheter des vues de Cordoue** to buy (picture) postcards of Cordoba; *Phot* **prendre une v.** to take a shot; **v. du port** *(peinture, dessin, photo)* view of the harbour; **v. d'ensemble** *Phot* general view; *Fig* overview; *Phot* **v. fixe** slide

8 *(idée, opinion)* view, opinion; **avoir des vues bien arrêtées sur qch** to have firm opinions *or* ideas about sth

9 *(interprétation)* view, understanding, interpretation; **une v. pessimiste de la situation** a pessimistic view of the situation; *Péj* **v. de l'esprit** idle fancy; **c'est une v. de l'esprit** that's a very theoretical point of view

10 *Jur (d'une maison)* window, light; **droit de vues** ancient lights; **condamner les vues** to block up the windows

11 *(d'extralucide)* **seconde v.** second sight

❏ **vues** NFPL **1** *(desseins)* plans, designs; **contrarier les vues de qn** to hinder sb's plans; **cela n'était** *ou* **n'entrait pas dans nos vues** this was no part of our plan; **avoir des vues sur qn** to

have designs on sb; **avoir des vues sur qch** to covet sth; *Hum* **il a des vues sur mon blouson** he's got his eye on my jacket

2 *Can Fam* **les vues** the movies▪, *Br* the cinema▪; **aller aux (petites) vues** to go to the movies *or Br* cinema

❏ **à courte vue** ADJ *(idée, plan)* short-sighted

❏ **à la vue de** PRÉP **1** *(au spectacle de)* **à la v. de qn/qch** at the sight of sb/sth; **il s'évanouit à la v. du sang** he faints at the sight of blood; **elle poussa un hurlement à la v. du chien** she screamed at the sight of *or* when she saw the dog

2 *(sous les yeux de)* in front of; **à la v. de tous** in front of everybody, in full view of everybody; **s'exhiber à la v. de tous** to expose oneself in front of everybody

❏ **à première vue** ADV at first sight

❏ **à vue** ADJ **1** *Banque* **dépôt à v.** call deposit; **retrait à v.** withdrawal on demand **2** *Théât voir* **changement 3** *Aviat & Naut* **navigation à v.** visual navigation ADV *(atterrir, voler)* visually; *(tirer)* on sight; *(payable)* at sight; *Mus* **jouer un morceau à v.** to play a piece at sight

❏ **à vue de nez** ADV *Fam* roughly, approximately; **on lui donnerait 20 ans, à v. de nez** at a rough guess, he/she could be about 20

❏ **à vue d'œil** ADV **la grenouille grossissait à v. d'œil** the frog was getting bigger before our very eyes; **ton cousin grossit à v. d'œil** your cousin is getting noticeably *or* visibly fatter; **mes économies disparaissent à v. d'œil** my savings just disappear before my very eyes

❏ **de vue** ADV by sight; **je le connais de v.** I know his face, I know him by sight; **perdre qn de v.** to lose sight of sb; *(perdre contact)* to lose touch with sb; **nous nous sommes perdus de v. depuis cette période** since then, we've lost touch with each other

❏ **en vue** ADJ **1** *(célèbre)* prominent; **les gens en v.** people in the public eye *or* in the news; **les gens les plus en v.** people most in the public eye **2** *(escompté)* **avoir une solution en v.** to have a solution in mind; **j'ai quelqu'un en v. pour racheter ma voiture** I've got somebody who's interested in buying my car; **un auteur pour qui le Nobel est en v.** an author who is in the running for the Nobel prize ADV **mettre qch (bien) en v. dans son salon** to display sth prominently in one's lounge; **avoir qch en v.** to have sth in view *or* in mind

❏ **en vue de** PRÉP **1** *(tout près de)* within sight of; **le bateau a coulé en v. des côtes de Limassol** the boat sank within sight of Limassol

2 *(afin de)* so as *or* in order to; **j'y vais en v. de préparer le terrain** I'm going in order to prepare the ground; **travailler en v. de l'avenir** to work with an eye to the future

Vulcain [vylkɛ̃] NPR *Myth* Vulcan

vulcain [vylkɛ̃] NM *Entom* red admiral

vulcanien, -enne [vylkanjɛ̃, -ɛn] ADJ *Géol* vulcanian

vulcanisation [vylkanizasjɔ̃] NF *Chim* vulcanization, vulcanizing

vulcaniser [3] [vylkanize] VT *Chim* to vulcanize

vulcanologie [vylkanɔlɔʒi] = **volcanologie**

vulcanologique [vylkanɔlɔʒik] = **volcanologique**

vulcanologue [vylkanɔlɔg] = **volcanologue**

vulgaire [vylgɛr] ADJ **1** *(sans goût → meuble, vêtement)* vulgar, common, tasteless; *(→ couleur)* loud, garish; *(→ style)* crude, unrefined; *(→ plaisanterie)* vulgar; *(→ personne)* uncouth, vulgar; **ça la rend v.** it makes her look common

2 *(impoli)* crude, coarse; **ne sois pas v.!** no need for that sort of language!

3 *(avant le nom)* *(ordinaire)* ordinary, common, common-or-garden *(avant n)*; **ce n'est**

pas du caviar, mais de vulgaires œufs de lump it's not caviar, only common-or-garden lumpfish roe; **un v. employé** a common clerk

4 *(non scientifique)* **nom v.** common name; **"oseille" est le nom v. du "Rumex acetosa"** "sorrel" is the common *or* usual name of "Rumex acetosa"

5 *(non littéraire → langue)* vernacular, everyday *(avant n)*; *(→ latin)* vulgar

NM **1** *(vulgarité)* **le v.** vulgarity; **tomber dans le v.** to lapse into vulgarity; **la décoration de leur appartement est d'un v.!** the way they've decorated their *Br* flat *or Am* apartment is so vulgar *or* common!

2 *Vieilli (foule, masse)* **le v.** the common people

vulgairement [vylgɛrmɑ̃] ADV **1** *(avec mauvais goût)* coarsely, vulgarly, tastelessly **2** *(de façon impolie)* coarsely, rudely; **ses panards, pour parler v.** his/her plates of meat, to use a coarse expression **3** *(de façon non scientifique)* commonly; **"Papaver rhoeas", v. appelé "coquelicot"** "Papaver rhoeas", commonly called the "poppy"

vulgarisateur, -trice [vylgarizatœr, -tris] ADJ *(ouvrage)* popularizing; **l'auteur tente de n'être pas trop v.** the author attempts to avoid over-simplification

vulgarisation [vylgarizasjɔ̃] NF popularization; **un ouvrage de v.** a book for the layman; **la v. de la pensée d'Einstein** the simplification of Einstein's thought

vulgarisatrice [vylgarizatris] *voir* **vulgarisateur**

vulgariser [3] [vylgarize] VT **1** *(faire connaître → œuvre, auteur)* to popularize, to make accessible to a large audience **2** *Littéraire (rendre grossier)* to vulgarize, to debase, to make coarser

USAGE ABSOLU **il nous faut expliquer sans v.** we have to explain without over-simplifying

vulgarisme [vylgarism] NM *(tournure)* vulgarism

vulgarité [vylgarite] NF **1** *(caractère vulgaire)* vulgarity, coarseness **2** *(action)* vulgar behaviour; *(parole)* vulgar *or* coarse remark

Vulgate [vylgat] NF *Bible* **la V.** the Vulgate (version)

vulgate [vylgat] NF *Péj* = popularized ideology; **la v. marxiste** Marxism for the masses

vulgo [vylgo] ADV *Littéraire* vulgo

vulgos [vylgos] ADJ *Fam* vulgar▪, coarse▪

vulgum pecus [vylgɔmpekys] NM INV **le v.** the hoi polloi

vulnérabiliser [3] [vylnerabilize] VT to make more vulnerable

vulnérabilité [vylnerabilite] NF vulnerability, vulnerableness

vulnérable [vylnerabl] ADJ **1** *(fragile)* vulnerable; **ne l'attaque pas, il est v.** don't attack him, he's easily hurt **2** *(au bridge)* vulnerable

vulnéraire¹ [vylnerɛr] *Méd Vieilli* ADJ vulnerary NM vulnerary

vulnéraire² [vylnerɛr] NF *Bot* kidney vetch

vulnérant, -e [vylnerɑ̃, -ɑ̃t] ADJ *(organe animal ou végétal, projectile etc)* likely to cause injury

vulpin [vylpɛ̃] NM *Bot* foxtail (grass)

vultueux, -euse [vyltɥø, -øz] ADJ *Méd* red and puffy

vulvaire¹ [vylvɛr] NF *Bot* stinking goosefoot

vulvaire² [vylvɛr] ADJ *Anat* vulvar

vulve [vylv] NF *Anat* vulva

vulvite [vylvit] NF *Méd* vulvitis

vumètre [vymɛtr] NM volume unit meter

Vve *(abrév écrite* **veuve***)* widow

VVF [veveɛf] NM *(abrév* **village vacances famille***)* = state-subsidized holiday village

vx *(abrév écrite* **vieux***)* old

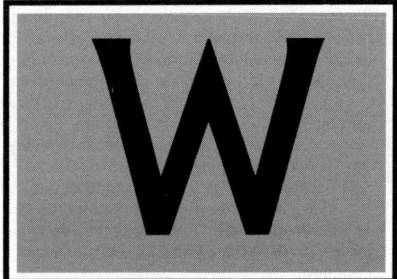

W¹, w [dubləve] NM INV *(lettre)* W, w; **W comme William** ≃ W for William

W² 1 *Phys (abrév écrite* **watt**) W **2** *(abrév écrite* **ouest**) W

W3 [trwadubləve] NM *Ordinat (abrév* **World Wide Web**) WWW

Wadden [wadɛn] *voir* **mer**

wading [wɛdiŋ] NM *Pêche* wading

wagage [wagaʒ] NM river mud *or* slime *(used as a fertilizer)*

Wagner [vagnɛr] NPR Wagner

wagnérien, -enne [vagnerjɛ̃, -ɛn] ADJ Wagnerian NM,F Wagnerian

wagnérisme [vagnerism] NM Wagnerism, Wagnerianism

wagon [vagɔ̃] NM **1** *(voiture)* w. **(de passagers)** coach, *Br* carriage, *Am* car; w. **(de marchandises)** *Br* wagon, truck, *Am* freight car, boxcar; w. **à bagages** *Br* luggage van, *Am* baggage car; w. **à bestiaux** cattle truck, *Am* stock car; w. **frigorifique** refrigerated van **2** *(contenu) Br* wagonload, truckload, *Am* carload; **des plaintes? on en a reçu tout un w.** complaints? they've been coming in by the truckload; *Fam* **des types sympas comme lui, il n'y en a pas des wagons** nice guys like him don't come by the truckload

wagon-bar [vagɔ̃bar] *(pl* **wagons-bars**) NM buffet car

wagon-citerne [vagɔ̃sitɛrn] *(pl* **wagons-citernes**) NM tank *Br* wagon *or Am* car

wagon-foudre [vagɔ̃fudr] *(pl* **wagons-foudres**) NM tank *Br* wagon *or Am* car *(for transporting wine and other drinks)*

wagon-lit [vagɔ̃li] *(pl* **wagons-lits**) NM sleeper, sleeping car, wagon-lit

wagonnée [vagɔne] NF *Br* wagonload, truckload, *Am* carload

wagonnet [vagɔnɛ] NM *Br* truck, *Am* cart

wagonnier [vagɔnje] NM *Br* wagon *or Am* car shunter

wagon-poste [vagɔ̃pɔst] *(pl* **wagons-poste**) NM *Br* mail van, *Am* mail truck

wagon-réservoir [vagɔ̃rezɛrvwar] *(pl* **wagons-réservoirs**) NM *Vieilli* tank *Br* wagon *or Am* car

wagon-restaurant [vagɔ̃rɛstɔrɑ̃] *(pl* **wagons-restaurants**) NM dining *or* restaurant car

wagon-tombereau [vagɔ̃tɔ̃bro] *(pl* **wagons-tombereaux**) *Rail* = high-sided open wagon

wagon-trémie [vagɔ̃tremi] *(pl* **wagons-trémies**) NM *Br* hopper wagon, *Am* hopper car

waguine [wagin] NF *Can* farm wagon

wahhabisme [waabism] NM *Rel & Pol* Wahabism, Wahabiism

wahhabite [waabit] *Rel & Pol* ADJ Wahabite NMF Wahhabi, Wahabi

wahoo [wau] NM *Ich* wahoo

WAIS [wɛjz] NM *Ordinat (abrév* **wide area information service** *or* **system**) WAIS

walé [wale] NM = popular African game using pebbles or seeds that are moved around a board with twelve holes

Walhalla [valala] NM *Myth* Valhalla

wali [wali] NM = government official at the head of a ''wilaya''

Walkman® [wɔkman] NM Walkman®, personal stereo

walk-over [wɔkɔvœr] NM INV *Sport* **1** *(compétition à un seul concurrent)* walkover **2** *Fam (victoire facile)* walkover

walkyrie [valkiri] NF Valkyrie, Walkyrie; *Fig Hum* **une w.** an Amazon

wallaby [walabi] *(pl* **wallabys** *ou* **wallabies**) NM *Zool* wallaby

wallingant, -e [walɛ̃gɑ̃, -ɑ̃t] ADJ *(manifestant, région)* in favour of Walloon autonomy NM,F *Belg Péj* Walloon autonomist

Wallis-et-Futuna [walisefutuna] NM Wallis and Futuna (Islands)

wallisien, -enne [walisjɛ̃, -ɛn] ADJ of/from the Wallis Islands
  ❑ **Wallisien, -enne** NM,F = inhabitant of or person from the Wallis Islands

wallon, -onne [walɔ̃, -ɔn] ADJ Walloon NM *(langue)* Walloon
  ❑ **Wallon, -onne** NM,F Walloon

Wallonie [walɔni] NF **la W.** southern Belgium *(where French and Walloon are spoken)*, Wallonia

wallonisme [walɔnism] NM Walloon expression

wallonne [walɔn] *voir* **wallon**

wampum [wampum] NM wampum

WAP [wap] NM *Tél (abrév* **wireless application protocol**) WAP; **W. lock** WAP lock

wapiti [wapiti] NM *Zool* North American elk, wapiti

warfarine [warfarin] NF *Pharm* warfarin

wargame [wargɛm] NM wargame

warning [warniŋ] NM *Aut* hazard warning light

warrant [warɑ̃] NM *Com* warrant; **w. cédule** warrant

warrantage [warɑ̃taʒ] NM *Com* securing goods by warrant

warranter [3] [warɑ̃te] VT *Com* to warrant; **marchandises warrantées** goods covered by a warehouse warrant

Washington [waʃiŋtɔn] NM **1** *(ville)* Washington DC **2** *(État)* Washington State; **dans l'État de W.** in Washington

wasserette [wasrɛt] NF *Belg Br* launderette, *Am* Laundromat®

wassingue [wasɛ̃g] NF floorcloth

water-ballast [watɛrbalast] *(pl* **water-ballasts**) NM water ballast tank

water-closet [watɛrklɔzɛt] *(pl* **water-closets**) NM *Vieilli* water closet

watergang [watɛrgɑ̃g] NM *(dans le Nord de la France) & Belg* polder channel

Watergate [watɛrgɛt] NM **le (scandale du) W.** (the) Watergate (scandal)

wateringue [watɛrɛ̃g] NF *(dans le Nord de la France) & Belg (travaux)* drainage works; *(zone)* drainage area; *(association)* = association in charge of drainage works

water-polo [watɛrpɔlo] *(pl* **water-polos**) NM water polo

waterproof [watɛrpruf] ADJ INV waterproof

waters [watɛr] NMPL toilet

waterzoï [watɛrzɔj], **waterzoui** [watɛrzui] NM *Belg Culin* = speciality made from fish or meat in cream sauce

watt [wat] NM *Phys* watt

wattheure [watœr] NM *Phys* watt-hour

wattman [watman] *(pl* **wattmen** [watmɛn]) NM *Fam Vieilli (d'un tramway électrique)* driver

wattmètre [watmɛtr] NM *Élec* wattmeter

wax [waks] NM *(en Afrique francophone)* = good-quality printed cotton

Wb *Phys (abrév écrite* **weber**) Wb

W-C [vese, dubləvese] NMPL *(abrév* **water closet**) WC

Web [wɛb] NM INV *Ordinat* **le W.** the Web

webcam [wɛbkam] NF *Ordinat* webcam

webcast [wɛbkast] NM *Ordinat* webcast

webcasting [wɛbkastiŋ] NM *Ordinat* webcasting

weber [vebɛr] NM *Phys* weber

weblog [wɛblɔg] NM *Ordinat* weblog

webmarchand [wɛbmarʃɑ̃] NM *Ordinat* online retailer

webmarketeur [wɛbmarketœr] NM *Ordinat* e-marketer

webmarketing [wɛbmarketiŋ] NM *Ordinat* e-marketing

webmaster [wɛbmastœr] NM *Ordinat* webmaster

webmestre [wɛbmɛstr] NM *Ordinat* webmaster

webphone [wɛbfɔn] NM *Ordinat* webphone

webradio [wɛbradjo] NF *Ordinat* web radio

webzine [wɛbzin] NM *Ordinat* webzine

week-end [wikɛnd] *(pl* **week-ends**) NM weekend; **partir en w.** to go away for the weekend; **on part en w.** we're going away for the weekend; **w. prolongé** long weekend

wehnelt [venɛlt] NM *Électron* Wehnelt cylinder

Weimar [vɛmar] NM Weimar; *Hist* **la république de Weimar** the Weimar Republic

welche [vɛlʃ] *Suisse* ADJ French-speaking Swiss NMF French-speaking Swiss *(person)*

Wellington [wɛliŋtɔn] NPR Wellington

wellingtonia [weliŋtɔnja] NM *Bot* giant sequoia, *Br* wellingtonia

welsche [vɛlʃ] = **welche**

welter [wɛltɛr] NM welter, welterweight

welwitschia [wɛlwitʃja] NM *Bot* welwitschia

wergeld [vɛrgɛld] NM *Hist* wergeld, wergild

western [wɛstɛrn] NM western

western-spaghetti [wɛstɛrnspageti] *(pl* **westerns-spaghettis**) NM spaghetti western

Westphalie [vɛsfali] NF **la W.** Westphalia

Wh *Phys (abrév écrite* **wattheure**) Wh

wharf [warf] NM wharf

whig [wig] *Hist* ADJ Whig NM Whig

whipcord [wipkɔrd] NM whipcord

whippet [wipɛt] NM *Zool (chien)* whippet

whisky [wiski] *(pl* **whiskys** *ou* **whiskies**) NM *(écossais)* whisky; *(irlandais ou américain)* whiskey; **un w.-coca** a whisky and Coke®

whist [wist] NM whist; **w. de Gand** solo (whist)

white-spirit [wajtspirit] *(pl* **inv** *ou* **white-spirits**) NM white spirit

Whitney [witnɛ] *voir* **mont**

wienerli [vinɛrli] NM *Suisse* = small sausage

WiFi [wifi] *Ordinat (abrév* **wireless fidelity**) NM WiFi
  ADJ WiFi

Wight [wajt] NF **l'île de W.** the Isle of Wight

wigwam [wigwam] NM wigwam

wiki [wiki] *Ordinat* NM wiki
  ADJ wiki

wilaya [vilaja] NF = administrative division in Algeria

Williamine® [wiljamin] NF *Suisse* = pear brandy made from Williams pears

williams [wiljams] NF Williams pear

winch [winʃ] *(pl* **winchs** *ou* **winches**) NM *Naut* winch

Windsurf® [windsœrf] NM Windsurf® (surfboard)

windsurfiste [windsœrfist] NMF windsurfer

Winnipeg [winipɛg] NM Winnipeg

wintergreen [wintœrgrin] NM **essence de w.** wintergreen oil, gaultheria oil

Wisconsin [wiskɔnsin] NM **le W.** Wisconsin; **dans le W.** in Wisconsin

wishbone [wiʃbon] NM *Naut* wishbone

wisigoth, -e [vizigo, -ɔt] ADJ Visigothic

❑ **Wisigoth, -e** NM,F Visigoth; **les Wisigoths** the Visigoths

wisigothique [vizigɔtik] ADJ Visigothic

witloof [witlɔf] NF = large-rooted Brussels chicory

witz [vits] NM *Suisse Fam* joke▪

wok [wɔk] NM wok

wolfram [vɔlfram] NM *Minér* wolfram

wolof [wɔlɔf] ADJ, NM *Ling* Wolof

wombat [wɔ̃ba] NM *Zool* wombat

won [wɔn] NM *(monnaie)* won

woofer [wufœr] NM woofer

world music [wœrldmjyzik] NF world music

World Wide Web [wœrldwajdwɛb] NM *Ordinat* le **W.** the World Wide Web

Wuppertal [vupərtal] NM Wuppertal

würm [vyrm] NM *Géol* Würm

würmien, -enne [vyrmjɛ̃, -ɛn] ADJ *Géol* Würmian

WW [dubləvedubləve] ADJ *(neuf)* brand new▪

WWW [dubləvedubləvedubləve] NM *Ordinat (abrév* **World Wide Web***)* WWW

wyandotte [vjãdɔt] ADJ F Wyandotte
NF Wyandotte chicken
NMF *(membre d'une tribu)* Wyandotte

Wyoming [wajɔmiŋ] NM le **W.** Wyoming; **dans le W.** in Wyoming

WYSIWYG [wiziwig] *Ordinat (abrév* **what you see is what you get***)* WYSIWYG

X, x [iks] NM INV **1** *(lettre)* X, x; **X comme Xavier** ≃ X for xylophone

2 *(personne inconnue, nombre inconnu)* X; **Madame X** Mrs X; **dans x années** in X number of years; **j'ai vu la pièce x fois** I've seen the play umpteen times; **ça fait x temps que je te demande de le faire** I've asked you to do it umpteen times

3 *Jur* **accoucher sous X** to give birth anonymously; **naître sous X** to be born to an unidentified mother

▸ NMF *Fam Arg scol* = student *or* ex-student of the ''École polytechnique''

▸ NF **1** *Fam Arg scol* **l'X** the ''École polytechnique''■

2 *Fam Arg drogue (ecstasy)* X, E

xanthélasma [gzãtelasma] NM *Méd* xanthelasma

xanthène [gzãtɛn] NM *Chim* xanthene

xanthie [gzãti] NF *Entom* **x. jaune tachetée** pink-barred sallow

xanthine [gzãtin] NF *Chim* xanthin, xanthine

xanthoderme [gzãtɔdɛrm] ADJ xanthoderm

xanthogénique [gzãtɔʒenik] ADJ *Chim* xanthogenic

xanthoma [gzãtɔma], **xanthome** [gzãtom] NM *Méd* fatty lump, *Spéc* xanthoma

xanthophycée [gzãtɔfise] *Bot* NF member of the Xanthophyceae

▫ **xanthophycées** NFPL Xanthophyceae

xanthophylle [gzãtɔfil] NF *Bot* xanthophyll

xantique [gzãtik] ADJ *Chim* xanthogenic

X-Dax [iksdaks] NM *Bourse* **(indice) X.** X-Dax (index)

xénarthre [gzenartr, ksenartr] *Zool* NM member of the Xenarthra order

▫ **xénarthres** NMPL Xenarthra

xénocristal, -aux [gzenɔkristal, -o] NM *Géol* xenocryst

xénogénique [gzenɔʒenik] ADJ *Méd* xenogenic

xénoglossie [gzenɔglɔsi] NF xenoglossia

xénogreffe [gzenɔgrɛf] NF *Méd* xenotransplant

xénolite [gzenɔlit] NF *Géol* xenolith

xénon [gzenɔ̃] NM *Chim* xenon

xénophile [gzenɔfil] ADJ xenophilous
▸ NMF xenophile

xénophilie [gzenɔfili] NF xenophilism

xénophobe [gzenɔfɔb] ADJ xenophobic
▸ NMF xenophobe

xénophobie [gzenɔfɔbi] NF xenophobia

Xénophon [gzenɔfɔ̃] NPR *Antiq* Xenophon

xénotransplantation [gzenɔtrãsplãtasjɔ̃] NF *Méd* xenotransplantation

xéranthème [gzerãtɛm, kserãtɛm] NM *Bot* xeranthemum

Xérès [gzerɛs, kserɛs] NM *(ville)* Jerez

xérès [gzerɛs, kserɛs] NM sherry

Xérocopie® [gzerɔkɔpi, kserɔkɔpi] NF Xerox® copy

xérodermie [gzerɔdɛrmi, kserɔdɛrmi] NF *Méd* xerodermia

Xérographie® [gzerɔgrafi, kserɔgrafi] NF xerography

xérophile [gzerɔfil, kserɔfil] ADJ *Bot* xerophilous

xérophtalmie [gzerɔftalmi, kserɔftalmi] NF *Méd* xerophthalmia

xérophyte [gzerɔfit, kserɔfit] *Bot* NF xerophyte
▸ ADJ xerophytic

xérophytique [gzerɔfitik, kserɔfitik] ADJ *Bot* xerophytic

xérus [gzerys, kserys] NM *Zool* palm squirrel

Xerxès [gzɛrksɛs] NPR *Antiq* Xerxes

Xetra-Dax [gzetradaks] NM *Bourse* **(indice) X.** Xetra-Dax (index)

ximénie [gzimeni, ksimeni] NF *Bot* ximenia

xipho [gzifo, ksifo] NM *Ich* swordtail

xiphoïde [gzifɔid, ksifɔid] ADJ *Anat* **appendice x.** xiphoid process

xiphoïdien, -enne [gzifɔidjɛ̃, -ɛn, ksifɔidjɛ̃, -ɛn] ADJ *Anat* xiphoidian, xiphisternal

xiphophore [gzifɔfɔr, ksifɔfɔr] = **xipho**

XMCL [iksɛmseɛl] NM *Ordinat (abrév* **Extensible Media Commerce Language**) XMCL

XML [iksɛmɛl] NM *Ordinat (abrév* **extensible markup language**) XML

xylème [gzilɛm, ksilɛm] NM *Bot* xylem

xylène [gzilɛn, ksilɛn] NM *Chim* xylene

xylidine [gzilidin, ksilidin] NF *Chim* xylidine

xylocope [gzilɔkɔp, ksilɔkɔp] NM *Entom* xylocopa, carpenter bee

xylographe [gzilɔgraf, ksilɔgraf] NMF wood-engraver, *Spéc* xylographer

xylographie [gzilɔgrafi, ksilɔgrafi] NF xylograph; *(procédé)* xylography

xylographique [gzilɔgrafik, ksilɔgrafik] ADJ xylographic

xylol [gzilɔl, ksilɔl] NM *Chim* xylol, raw commercial xylene

xylophage [gzilɔfaʒ, ksilɔfaʒ] ADJ xylophagous
▸ NMF xylophage

Xylophène® [gzilɔfɛn, ksilɔfɛn] NM wood preserver

xylophone [gzilɔfɔn, ksilɔfɔn] NM *Mus* xylophone

xylopia [gzilɔpia, ksilɔpia] NM *Bot* xylopia

xylose [gzilɔz, ksilɔz] NM *Chim* xylose

xyste [ksist] NM *Antiq* xystus, xyst

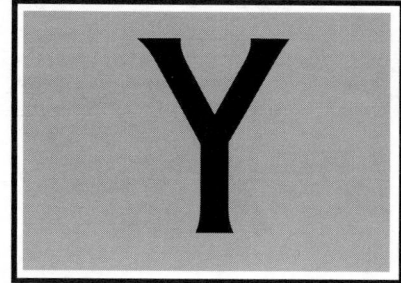

Y¹, y¹ [igrɛk] **NM INV 1** *(lettre)* Y, y; **Y comme Yvonne** ≃ Y for yellow **2** *(forme)* Y (shape)

Y² *(abrév écrite* **yen)** Y

y² [i] **PRON & ADV 1** *(représente le lieu)* there; **j'y vais souvent** I often go there; **on y entre comment?** how do you get in?; **on n'y voit rien** you can't see a thing (here); **passe chez elle, elle y est peut-être** go round *or Am* around to her place, maybe she's there; **j'y suis, j'y reste** here I am and here I stay; **je n'y suis pour personne** whoever it is, I'm not in

2 *(représente une chose)* it; **j'y pense sans cesse** I think about it constantly; **l'aider? tu n'y penses pas!** help him? what are you thinking of?; **je n'y manquerai pas** I certainly will; **j'y renonce** I give up; **je n'y comprends rien** I can't make head nor tail of it; **je m'y attendais** I expected as much; **ça, on pouvait s'y attendre** it was to be expected; **il a du charme mais je n'y suis pas sensible** he has charm, but it leaves me cold; **j'y ai trouvé une certaine satisfaction** I found it quite satisfying

3 *(représente une personne)* **elle est bizarre, ne t'y fie pas** she's strange, don't trust her; **les fantômes, j'y crois** I believe in ghosts; **les jeunes? elle n'y comprend rien** young people? she doesn't understand them; **pensez-vous encore à lui? – oui, j'y pense sans cesse** do you still think of him? – yes I do, all the time

4 *(avec un impératif)* **vas-y!** go there!; *(agis)* go on!, get on with it!; **vas-y, entre!** go on in!; **vas-y, saute!** go on, jump!; **penses-y** [pɑ̃szi] think about it; **pensez-y, à mon offre** do think about my offer; **n'y pensez plus** forget about it; **n'y comptez pas** don't count *or* bank on it

5 *(locutions)* **il y va de** it's a matter of; **il y va de ma dignité** my dignity's at stake; **il y va d'une vie humaine** a (human) life is at stake; **chacun y va de sa chansonnette** everyone comes out with a little song; **quand elle y va de ses grands mots** when she starts coming out with her big words; **j'y suis!** *(j'ai compris)* (I've) got it!; *(je t'ai compris)* I've got you!; **je n'y suis plus** *(je ne comprends plus)* I've lost track (of things); *(je ne te comprends plus)* I'm not with you any more, you've lost me; **excusez-moi, je n'y étais pas du tout** I'm sorry, I didn't get that at all; **vous n'y êtes pas du tout** you're way off the mark; **pendant que vous y êtes** while you're at *or* about it; *Ironique* **non mais fouille dans mes affaires pendant que tu y es!** just rummage through my things, why don't you!; **j'y suis pour un tiers** I'm in for a third; **il doit y être pour une bonne part** *(dans une décision)* he must have had a lot to do with it; **y être pour quelque chose** to have something to do with it; **je n'y suis pour rien, moi!** it's (got) nothing to do with me!, it's not my fault!; **laisse-le choisir, il s'y connaît** let him choose, he knows all about it; **ils s'y entendent pour faire des histoires** they're past masters at making a fuss; **tu as promis, tu dois t'y tenir** you made a promise, you must stick to it; **si tu veux un matériel de qualité, il faut y mettre le prix** if you want quality material, you have to pay for it; **avec les petits, il faut savoir s'y prendre** with little children you have to know how to handle them; **il est timide, il n'y peut rien** he's shy, he can't help it; **je vous y prends!** caught you!

y³ [i] *Fam* = **il, ils**

yacht [jɔt] **NM** yacht; **y. de course** racer; **y. de croisière** cruiser; **croisière en y.** yachting cruise

yacht-club [jɔtklœb] *(pl* **yacht-clubs)** **NM** yacht club

yachting [jɔtiŋ] **NM** *Vieilli* yachting; **faire du y.** to sail (yachts)

yachtman [jɔtman] *(pl* **yachtmen** [jɔtmɛn]), **yachtsman** [jɔtsman] *(pl* **yachtsmen** [jɔtsmɛn]) **NM** yachtsman

yack, yak [jak] **NM** *Zool* yak

yakusa [jakuza] **NM** yakuza

Yalta [jalta] **NM** Yalta; **la conférence de Y.** the Yalta Conference

Yamoussoukro [jamusukro] **NM** *Géog* Yamoussoukro

yang [jɑ̃g] **NM** yang

Yang-tseu-kiang [jɑ̃gtsekjɑ̃g], **Yangzi Jiang** [jɑ̃gzijɑ̃g] **NM le Y.** the Yangtze (River)

yankee [jɑ̃ki] **ADJ** Yankee

❑ **Yankee NMF** Yankee

Yaoundé [jaunde] **NM** Yaoundé, Yaunde

yaourt [jaurt] **NM 1** *(produit laitier)* yoghurt; **y. nature/aux fruits/aromatisé** plain/fruit/flavoured yoghurt; **y. bio** bio yoghurt; **y. maigre** low-fat yoghurt **2** *Fam (charabia)* = type of gibberish which imitates English sounds without forming actual words, used by people who want to sound as if they are talking or singing in English

yaourtière [jaurtjɛr] **NF** *(appareil)* yoghurt maker

yapock [japɔk] **NM** *Zool* yapok

yard [jard] **NM** yard *(measurement)*

yass [jas] = **jass**

yassa [jasa] **NM** *Culin* = dish of meat, fish or poultry, marinated and grilled, then cooked in a spicy sauce with lemon and onions

yasser [jase] = **jasser**

yasseur, -euse [jasœr, -øz] = **jasseur**

yawl [jol] **NM** yawl

yearling [jœrliŋ] **NM** yearling *(horse)*

yèble [jɛbl] **NF** *Bot* dwarf elder

Yellowstone [jeloston] **NM le parc national de Y.** the Yellowstone National Park

Yémen [jemɛn] **NM le Y.** Yemen; **vivre au Y.** to live in Yemen; **aller au Y.** to go to Yemen; **le Y. du Nord** North Yemen; **le Y. du Sud** South Yemen

yéménite [jemenit] **ADJ** Yemeni

❑ **Yéménite NMF** Yemeni

yen [jɛn] **NM** yen

yeoman [jɔman] *(pl* **yeomans** *ou* **yeomen** [jɔmɛn]) **NM** yeoman

yeomanry [jomanri] **NF** yeomanry

yeomen [jɔmɛn] *voir* **yeoman**

yersinia [jɛrsinja] **NF** *Méd* yersinia

yeshiva [jeʃiva] **NF** *Rel* yeshiva, yeshivah

yeti [jeti] **NM** yeti

Yeu [jø] **NF l'île d'Y.** the île d'Yeu

yeuse [jøz] **NF** *Bot* holm oak

yeux [jø] *pl de* **œil**

yé-yé [jeje] *Vieilli* **ADJ INV** pop *(in the sixties)*; *(mode)* sixties *(avant n)*

NMF INV *(chanteur)* (sixties) pop singer; *(garçon, fille)* sixties pop fan

yiddish [jidiʃ] **ADJ INV** Yiddish

NM INV Yiddish

yi-king [jikiŋ] **NM** I Ching

yin [jin] **NM** yin

yinque [jinkə] **ADV** *Can Joual* **je fais y. regarder** I'm just *or* only looking▪; **il y a y. dix spectateurs dans la salle** there are no more than *or* there are barely ten people in the cinema▪; **y. ça?** is that all?▪

ylang-ylang [ilɑ̃ilɑ̃] *(pl* **ylangs-ylangs)** **NM** *Bot* ylang-ylang, ilang-ilang

Yngling [iŋgliŋ] **NM** *(voilier)* Yngling

yo [jo] **EXCLAM** *Fam* yeah!

yod [jɔd] **NM** *Ling* yod

yodler [3] [jɔdle] **VI** to yodel

yoga [jɔga] **NM** yoga; **faire du y.** to do yoga; **cours/posture de y.** yoga class/position

yoghourt [jɔgurt] = **yaourt**

yogi [jɔgi] **NM** yogi

yogourt [jɔgurt] = **yaourt**

yohimbehe [jɔimbe] **NM** *Bot* yohimbe

yohimbine [jɔimbin] **NF** *Pharm* yohimbine

Yokohama [jɔkɔama] **NM** Yokohama

yole [jɔl] **NF** skiff

Yom Kippour [jɔmkipur] **NM INV** Yom Kippur

Yonne [ijɔn] **NF l'Y.** Yonne

yorkshire [jɔrkʃœr], **yorkshire-terrier** [jɔrkʃœrterje] *(pl* **yorkshire-terriers)** **NM** Yorkshire terrier

youde [jud] *très Fam* **ADJ** Jewish▪, yid

NMF yid, kike, *Am* hebe, = offensive term used to refer to a Jew

yougo [jugo] *très Fam* **ADJ** *(abrév* **yougoslave)** Yugoslav▪

❑ **Yougo NMF** *(abrév* **Yougoslave)** Yugoslav▪, = offensive term used to refer to a Yugoslav

yougoslave [jugoslav] **ADJ** Yugoslav, Yugoslavian

❑ **Yougoslave NMF** Yugoslav, Yugoslavian

Yougoslavie [jugoslavi] **NF la Y.** Yugoslavia; **vivre en Y.** to live in Yugoslavia; **aller en Y.** to go to Yugoslavia

youp [jup] **EXCLAM** hup!

youpala [jupala] **NM** baby bouncer

youpi [jupi] **EXCLAM** yippee!, hooray!

youpin, -e [jupɛ̃, -in] *très Fam* **ADJ** Jewish▪, yid

NM,F yid, kike, *Am* hebe, = offensive term used to refer to a Jew

yourte [jurt] **NF** yurt

youtre [jutr] *très Fam* **ADJ** Jewish▪, yid

NMF yid, kike, *Am* hebe, = offensive term used to refer to a Jew

youve [juv], **youvoi** [juvwa] **NM** *Fam* hood, hooligan, *Br* yob

youyou [juju] **NM** dinghy

Yo-Yo® [jojo] **NM INV** yo-yo

yoyoter [3] [jojote] **VI** *Fam* **1** *(mal fonctionner)* to be on the blink, *Am* to be on the fritz **2** *(déraisonner)* to be off one's trolley, to have a screw loose

ypérite [iperit] **NF** mustard gas

yponomeute [ipɔnɔmøt] **NM** *Entom* ermine moth

ypréau, -x [ipreo] **NM** *Bot (peuplier blanc)* white poplar

ysopet [izɔpɛt] **NM** *Hist* collection of fables

ytterbine [itɛrbin] **NF** *Chim* ytterbium oxide

ytterbium [itɛrbjɔm] **NM** *Chim* ytterbium

yttria [itrija] **NM** *Chim* yttria

yttrifère [itrifɛr] **ADJ** *Minér* yttriferous

yttrique [itrik] **ADJ** *Chim* yttric; **groupe y.** yttrium group; **terres yttriques** yttrium earths

yttrium [itrijɔm] **NM** *Chim* yttrium

yuan [jɥɑ̃] **NM** yuan

Yucatan [jukatan] **NM le Y.** Yucatan

yucca [juka] **NM** *Bot* yucca

yue [jɥe] **NM** *(langue)* Cantonese

Yukon [jukɔ̃] **NM le Y.** *(fleuve)* the Yukon River; *(territoire)* the Yukon (territory)

Yunnan [junan] **NM le Y.** Yunnan

yuppie [jupi] **NMF** yuppie

'**Yvain ou le Chevalier au lion**' *Chrétien de Troyes* 'Yvain, or the Knight with the Lion'

Yvelines [ivəlin] **NFPL les Y.** Yvelines

yvette [ivɛt] **NF** *Can Fam Péj* housewife▪, homemaker▪

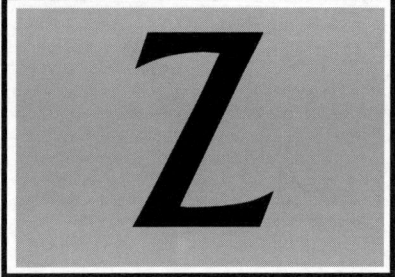

Z, z [zɛd] NM INV (lettre) Z, z; **Z comme Zoé** ≃ Z for zebra

ZA (abrév écrite **zone artisanale**) small industrial Br estate or Am park (for craft-based businesses)

zabre [zabr] NM Entom cereal beetle

ZAC, Zac [zak] NF (abrév **zone d'aménagement concerté**) = area earmarked for local government planning project

Zacharie [zakari] NPR Bible **1** (père de saint Jean-Baptiste) Zachariah, Zacharias, Zachary **2** (prophète) Zechariah

ZAD, Zad [zad] NF (abrév **zone d'aménagement différé**) = area earmarked for future development

Zagreb [zagrɛb] NM Zagreb

zain [zɛ̃] ADJ M (cheval, chien) = all of one colour and with no white hairs

Zaïre [zair] NM **1** Anciennement **le Z.** (pays) Zaïre; **vivre au Z.** to live in Zaïre; **aller au Z.** to go to Zaïre **2 le Z.** (fleuve) the (River) Zaïre

zaïrois, -e [zairwa, -az] ADJ Zairean
□ **Zaïrois, -e** NM,F Zairean

Zambèze [zɑ̃bɛz] NM **le Z.** the Zambese or Zambezi (River)

Zambie [zɑ̃bi] NF **la Z.** Zambia; **vivre en Z.** to live in Zambia; **aller en Z.** to go to Zambia

zambien, -enne [zɑ̃bjɛ̃, -ɛn] ADJ Zambian
□ **Zambien, -enne** NM,F Zambian

zamia [zamja], **zamier** [zamje] NM Bot zamia

zancle [zɑ̃kl] NM Ich zanclus

zani, zanni [dzani] NM Théât zany

zanzi [zɑ̃zi] NM = game played with three dice

Zanzibar [zɑ̃zibar] NM Zanzibar; **vivre à Zanzibar** to live in Zanzibar; **aller à Zanzibar** to go to Zanzibar

zanzibar [zɑ̃zibar] = **zanzi**

zaouïa [zauja] NF = Islamic religious establishment, situated near a venerated tomb

Zaporojie [zaporoʒi] NM Zaporozhye

Zapotèques [zapotɛk] NMPL **les Z.** the Zapotecs

zapper [3] [zape] VI to channel-hop, to channel-surf
▸ VT Fam **1** (supprimer) to scrap, to scratch **2** (oublier) to forget■; **excuse-moi, mais j'ai complètement zappé** I'm sorry, I completely forgot or it totally slipped my mind **3** (négliger) to neglect■; **je l'ai un peu zappé ces derniers temps** I've been neglecting him a bit lately

zappette [zapɛt] NF Fam remote control■, zapper

zappeur, -euse [zapœr, -øz] NM,F (compulsive) channel-hopper

zapping [zapiŋ] NM **le z.** zapping, (constant) channel-hopping; **faire du z.** to zap

zarabe [zarab] NMF (à la Réunion) Muslim Indian

Zarathoustra [zaratustra] NPR Zarathustra

'**Ainsi parlait Zarathoustra**' Nietzsche, Strauss 'Thus Spake Zarathustra'

zarbi [zarbi] ADJ Fam (verlan de **bizarre**) strange■, weird■

zarma [zarma] EXCLAM Fam wow!, God!

zarzuela [sarswela] NF Littérature zarzuela

zawiya [zawija] = **zaouïa**

zaydite [zaidit] Rel ADJ Zaydite
▸ NMF Zaydite

Zazie [zazi] NPR = main character in Queneau's novel 'Zazie dans le métro', a little girl who combines the mischievousness and impertinence of a child with the worldliness of an adult

zazou [zazu] Fam ADJ **1** Vieilli (dans les années 40) hep **2** Péj (fou) crazy

NMF **1** Vieilli (amateur de jazz) hepcat **2** Péj (fou) crazy man, f woman; **qu'est-ce qu'il fait, ce z.?** what's this crazy guy doing?

ZCIT [zɛdseit] NF Météo (abrév **zone de convergence intertropicale**) ITCZ

Zébédée [zebede] NPR Bible Zebedee

zèbre [zɛbr] NM **1** Zool zebra; **courir** ou **filer comme un z.** to go like greased lightning **2** Fam (individu) **c'est un (drôle de) z., celui-là!** (ton dépréciatif) he's a weirdo!; (ton amusé ou admiratif) he's quite something!; **arrête de faire le z.!** stop being silly!

zébré, -e [zebre] ADJ striped (**de** with), stripy; **un mur z. d'ombre et de lumière** a wall with stripes of or striped with shadow and light; **un ciel d'orage z. par les éclairs** a stormy sky streaked with lightning

zébrer [18] [zebre] VT (de lignes → irrégulières) to streak; (→ régulières) to stripe

zébrure [zebryr] NF **1** (du zèbre, du tigre) stripe **2** (marque de coup) weal **3** (d'éclair) streak

zébu [zeby] NM Zool zebu

ZEC [zɛk] NF Can (abrév **zone d'exploitation contrôlée**) = area in which hunting and fishing are restricted

zée [ze] NM Ich John Dory

Zeebrugge [zibryʒ] NM Zeebrugge

zef [zɛf] = **zeph**

zéine [zein] NF Chim zein

Zélande [zelɑ̃d] NF Zealand

zélateur, -trice [zelatœr, -tris] NM,F **1** Littéraire (adepte) devotee, partisan **2** Rel zealot

zélé, -e [zele] ADJ zealous; **trop z.** over-zealous

zèle [zɛl] NM zeal; **elle travaillait avec z.** she worked zealously; **fais pas de z.!** don't do more than you have to!, don't overdo it!

zellige [zeliʒ] NM (dans l'art maghrébin) = small element in enamelled ceramic inlaid work

zélote [zelɔt] NM **1** Hist Zealot **2** Péj (personne animée d'un zèle fanatique) zealot

zen [zɛn] ADJ INV **1** Rel Zen (avant n); **le bouddhisme z.** Zen Buddhism **2** Fam (serein) **être/ rester z.** to be/to stay cool; **après deux heures de yoga, je suis z.** after two hours of yoga my mind's completely relaxed; **c'est très z. chez toi** your place is very minimalist
▸ NM Rel Zen

zénana [zenana] NM **1** (appartement des femmes) zenana **2** (textile) zenana cloth

zend [zɛd] NM Ling Zend

zénith [zenit] NM **1** Fig (sommet) zenith, acme; **arrivé au z. de ses pouvoirs** having reached the zenith of his/her powers **2** Astron zenith; Littéraire **le soleil en son z.** the sun at its zenith

zénithal, -e, -aux, -ales [zenital, -o] ADJ Astron zenithal

Zénon [zenɔ̃] NPR Antiq Zeno

zéolite, zéolithe [zeolit] NF Minér zeolite

ZEP, Zep [zɛp] NF **1** Scol (abrév **zone d'éducation prioritaire**) = designated area with special educational needs **2** Écol (abrév **zone d'environnement protégé**) = environmentally protected zone

zeph [zɛf] NM Fam wind■

zéphyr [zefir] NM **1** (vent) zephyr, light breeze; Myth **Z.** Zephyrus **2** Tex zephyr

zéphyrien, -enne [zefirjɛ̃, -ɛn] ADJ Littéraire soft or light as a breeze, zephyrean

zeppelin [zeplɛ̃] NM zeppelin

zéro [zero] NM **1** Math zero, nought; (dans un numéro de téléphone) zero, Br O [əʊ]; (dans une gradation) zero; **z. zéro trente-cinq** double zero or Br O three-five; **l'option z.** the zero option

2 Phys zero (degrees centigrade), freezing (point); **z. absolu** absolute zero

3 Sport zero, Br nil; (au tennis) love; **deux buts à z.** two (goals to) zero or Br nil; **z. partout** no score; (au tennis) love all

4 Scol zero, Br nought; **j'ai eu z.** I got (a) nought; **collectionner les zéros** (élève) to get nothing but bad marks; **z. de conduite** black mark; **z. pointé** zero, Br nought

5 Fam (incapable) dead loss; **c'est un triple z. en bricolage** he's/she's a dead loss as far as do-it-yourself goes

6 Beaux-Arts **le groupe Z.** (Group) Zero

7 (comme adj) (sans intérêt) nil, worthless; **au niveau organisation, c'était z.** as far as organization goes it was useless; **ils ont de beaux tissus, mais pour la confection, c'est z.** they've got some nice fabrics but when it comes to making clothes they haven't a clue; **il est bien gentil, mais pour le travail, z.!** he's nice enough, but when it comes to work he's a dead loss; **le spectacle? z. et triple z.** the show? an absolute washout

ADJ **z. faute** no mistakes; **z. degré Celsius** zero degrees Celsius; **z. heure** midnight, Spéc zero hour; **à z. heure** at midnight, at twenty-four hundred hours; **z. heure quinze** zero hours fifteen; **ça te coûtera z. euro** it'll cost you nothing at all; **ça m'a coûté z. euro, z. centime** it didn't cost me a Br penny or Am cent; Com **z. défaut** zero defects
□ **à zéro** ADJ Fam **avoir le moral** ou **être à z.** to be at an all-time low; très Fam **les avoir à z.** to be scared stiff ADV Fam **être réduit à z.** to be reduced to nothing; **recommencer** ou **repartir à z.** (dans sa carrière, dans un raisonnement) to go back to square one or the drawing board; (sans argent, sans aide) to start again from scratch; **remettre le chronomètre à z.** to set the stopwatch back to zero; Fig to start from scratch again; Fam **avoir la boule à z.** to have a shaved head■

'**Le Zéro et l'Infini**' Koestler 'Darkness at Noon'

'**Zéro de conduite**' Vigo 'Zero for Conduct'

zérotage [zerotaʒ] NM calibration, fixing of the zero point

zérumbet [zerɔ̃bɛt] NM Bot shell ginger

zest [zɛst] NM Arch **être entre le zist et le z.** to be neither one thing nor the other, to be betwixt and between; (hésiter) to shillyshally, to waver

zeste [zɛst] NM **1** (d'un agrume) zest; **un z. de citron** a piece of lemon peel; **z. confit, z. d'Italie** candied peel **2** Fam (petite quantité) pinch; **un z. d'accent** a hint or faint trace of an accent; **un z. d'ironie/d'humour/de cynisme** a touch or a note of irony/humour/cynicism

zester [3] [zɛste] VT Culin to zest, to peel the zest off

zêta [dzɛta] NM zeta

zeugma [zøma], **zeugme** [zøgm] NM Ling zeugma

Zeus [dzøs] NPR Myth Zeus

zeuzère [zøzɛr] NF Entom leopard moth, Spéc zeuzera

zézaie etc voir **zézayer**

zézaiement [zezemɑ̃] NM lisp

zézayer [11] [zezeje] VI to (have a) lisp

zézette [zezɛt] NF Fam **1** (sexe de l'homme) Br willy, Am peter **2** (sexe de la femme) pussy, Br fanny

zgueg [zgɛg] NM *très Fam* (*penis*) dick, *Br* willy, *Am* peter

Zhejiang [zejɑ̃g] NM **le Z.** Chekiang

ZI (*abrév écrite* **zone industrielle**) industrial *Br* estate *or Am* park

zibeline [ziblin] NF (*fourrure, animal*) sable

zicmu [zikmy] NF *Fam* (*verlan de* **music**) music■, sounds, tunes

zidovudine [zidɔvydin] NF *Pharm* zidovudine

zieuter [3] [zjøte] VT *Fam* to check out, to eyeball; **t'as passé la soirée à z. ma femme** you've spent the whole evening eyeing up my wife

zievereer [zivərɛr] NM *Belg Fam Hum* drivelling fool

zieverer [3] [zivəre] VI *Belg Fam Hum* to talk drivel *or* rubbish

ZIF [zif] NF (*abrév* **zone d'intervention foncière**) = area earmarked for local government planning project

zig [zig] NM *très Fam* guy, *Br* bloke; **c'est un bon z.** he's a good guy *or Br* bloke; **c'est un drôle de z.!** he's a weird one!

ziggomar [zigurat] NF *Archéol* ziggurat

zigomar [zigɔmar], **zigoto** [zigɔto] NM *Fam* crackpot, crank, *Am* kook; **c'est un drôle de zigoto!** he's a weird one!; **faire le zigoto** to act the fool, to clown around; **n'essayez pas de faire les zigotos!** don't try it on!

zigouigoui [zigwigwi] NM *Fam Hum* **1** (*pénis*) *Br* willy, *Am* peter **2** (*sexe de la femme*) pussy, *Br* fanny **3** (*objet*) thingy, whatsit

zigouiller [3] [ziguje] VT *très Fam* to bump off, to ice; **se faire z.** to get done in

zigoune [zigun] NF *Can Fam* hand-rolled cigarette■

zigue [zig] NM *très Fam* guy, *Br* bloke

zigzag [zigzag] NM zigzag; **la route fait des zigzags dans la montée** the road zigzags up; **elle marchait en faisant des zigzags** she was zigzagging along
❑ **en zigzag** ADJ zigzagging, winding

zigzaguer [3] [zigzage] VI to zigzag; **il avançait en zigzaguant** he zigzagged along; **il sortit du bar en zigzaguant** he staggered out of the bar

zig-zig [zigzig] NM INV *Fam* **faire z.** to have a bit of nooky *or Br* rumpy-pumpy

Zimbabwe [zimbabwe] NM **le Z.** Zimbabwe; **vivre au Z.** to live in Zimbabwe; **aller au Z.** to go to Zimbabwe

zimbabwéen, -enne [zimbabweɛ̃, -ɛn] ADJ Zimbabwean
❑ **Zimbabwéen, -enne** NM,F Zimbabwean

zinc [zɛ̃g] NM **1** (*métal*) zinc **2** *Fam* (*comptoir*) bar■; **on prend un verre sur le z.?** shall we have a drink at the bar? **3** *Fam* (*café*) bar■ **4** *Fam* (*avion*) plane■

zincage [zɛ̃kaʒ] NM **1** (*du toit etc*) covering with zinc **2** *Métal* (*de l'acier*) galvanizing

zincate [zɛ̃kat] NM *Chim* zincate

zincifère [zɛ̃sifɛr] ADJ zinciferous

zincique [zɛ̃sik] ADJ zincic

zincographie [zɛ̃kɔgrafi] NF **1** (*procédé*) zincography **2** (*estampe*) zincograph

zingage [zɛ̃gaʒ] NM = **zincage**

zingaro [dzingaro] (*pl* **zingari** [dzingari]) NM *Arch* gipsy

zingibéracée [zɛ̃ʒiberase] *Bot* NF member of the Zingiberaceae family
❑ **zingibéracées** NFPL Zingiberaceae

zinguer [3] [zɛ̃ge] VT **1** (*toit*) to cover with zinc **2** *Métal* (*acier*) to galvanize

zingueur [zɛ̃gœr] NM zinc worker

zinjanthrope [zɛ̃ʒɑ̃trɔp] NM *Archéol* zinjanthropus

zinneke [zinəkə] *Belg* NMF = native of Brussels with mixed Franco-Flemish culture
NM mongrel

zinnia [zinja] NM *Bot* zinnia

zinzin [zɛ̃zɛ̃] *Fam* ADJ loopy; **elle est devenue complètement z.** she's gone completely off her rocker
NM **1** (*idiot*) nutcase **2** *Bourse* **les zinzins** institutional investors■ **3** (*truc*) thingamajig, thingamajig; **un z. pour peler les patates** a gadget for peeling spuds; **une espèce de z. au milieu du jardin** a weird contraption in the middle of the garden

zinzolin [zɛ̃zɔlɛ̃] ADJ M INV reddish-purple
NM reddish-purple

Zip® [zip] NM *Br* zip, *Am* zipper

zippé [zipe] ADJ with a *Br* zip *or Am* zipper, zip-up; **robe zippée dans le dos** dress that zips up at the back

zipper [3] [zipe] VT *Ordinat* to zip

zique [zik] NF *Fam* music■, sounds, tunes

zircon [zirkɔ̃] NM *Minér* zircon

zircone [zirkɔn] NF *Chim* zirconium oxide, zirconia

zirconite [zirkɔnit] NF *Minér* zirconite

zirconium [zirkɔnjɔm] NM *Chim* zirconium

zist [zist] NM *voir* **zest**

ziva [ziva] *Fam* EXCLAM (*verlan de* **vas-y**) no way!, get out of here!; **z.! je l'invite pas à ma teuf, ce gros nul!** no way *or* get out of here!, I'm not inviting that loser to my party!
NMF (*personne*) *Br* ≃ chav, *Am* ≃ trailer trash

zizania [zizanja] NM *Bot* zizania

zizanie [zizani] NF **1** *Bot* (*ivraie*) tare **2** *Fig* (*mésentente*) discord; **c'est la z. entre les frères** the brothers are at odds *or* loggerheads; **jeter** *ou* **mettre** *ou* **semer la z. dans un groupe** to stir things up in a group; **la mort de la tante a jeté la z. dans la famille** the aunt's death set the family at odds with each other

zizi[1] [zizi] NM *Orn* cirl bunting

zizi[2] [zizi] NM *Fam* **1** (*sexe de l'homme*) *Br* willy, *Am* peter **2** (*sexe de la femme*) pussy, *Br* fanny

zizique [zizik] NF = **zique**

ZLEA [zɑdɛlɔa] NF *Com* (*abrév* **Zone de libre-échange des Amériques**) FTAA

zloty [zlɔti] NM zloty

zoanthaire [zɔɑ̃tɛr] *Zool* NM zoantharian, *Spéc* member of the Zoantharia order
❑ **zoanthaires** NMPL zoantharians, *Spéc* Zoantharia

zob [zɔb] NM *Vulg* prick, knob

zoccoli, zoccolis [zɔkɔli] NMPL *Suisse* clogs

Zodiac® [zɔdjak] NM inflatable (dinghy)

zodiacal, -e, -aux, -ales [zɔdjakal, -o] ADJ **1** (*signe*) zodiac (*avant n*), zodiacal **2** *Astron voir* **lumière**

zodiaque [zɔdjak] NM *Astron & Astrol* zodiac; **signe du z.** sign of the zodiac

zoé [zɔe] NF *Zool* zoea, zoaea

zoécie [zɔesi] NF *Zool* bryozoan, polyzoan

zombie, zombi [zɔ̃bi] NM *aussi Fig* zombie

zona [zona] NM *Méd* shingles (*singulier*), *Spéc* herpes zoster; **avoir un z.** to have shingles

zonage [zonaʒ] NM *Géog & Ordinat* zoning

zonal, -e, -aux, -ales [zonal, -o] ADJ *Géog* zonal

zonalité [zonalite] NF *Géog* zonation

zonard, -e [zonar, -ard] NM,F *Fam* (*marginal*) dropout

zone [zon] NF **1** (*domaine*) zone, area; **z. de flou** *ou* **d'incertitude** *ou* **d'ombre** grey area; **la z. d'activité du directeur commercial** the commercial manager's area; **la z. d'influence de l'Asie** Asia's sphere of influence; **z. dangereuse** danger zone
2 *Anat* **z. érogène** erogenous zone
3 *Admin* (*surface délimitée*) area, zone; **z. d'aménagement concerté** = area earmarked for local government planning project; **z. d'aménagement différé** = area earmarked for future development; **z. artisanale** small industrial *Br* estate *or Am* park (*for craft-based businesses*); **z. bleue** restricted parking area; **z. de chalandise** catchment area; **le campus se trouve dans la z. de desserte des autobus** the campus is served by buses; **z. de développement** development area; **Can z. d'exploitation contrôlée** = area in which hunting and fishing are restricted; **z. frontière** frontier zone; **z. industrielle** industrial *Br* estate *or Am* park; **z. interdite** prohibited *or* restricted area; **z. d'intervention foncière** = area earmarked for local government planning project; **z. de pêche** fishing zone *or* ground; **z. piétonnière** *ou* **piétonne** pedestrian area *or Br* precinct; **z. postale** postal area; **z. résidentielle** residential area; **z. sous douane** customs zone; **z. de stationnement** parking zone; **z. de stationnement contrôlé** *ou* **réglementé** controlled parking zone; **z. de stationnement interdit** no parking area; **z. à urbaniser en priorité** = area earmarked for urgent urban development; *Admin & Fin* **abattement de z.** = band within which the minimum wage or family benefits are reduced by a prescribed percentage; **zones des salaires** = wage bands subject to the same percentage reduction
4 *Hist* **z. libre/occupée** unoccupied/occupied France
5 *Géog* **z. des alizés** trade-wind belt; **z. désertique** desert belt; **z. forestière** forest belt; **z. glaciale/tempérée/torride** frigid/temperate/torrid zone; **z. de végétation** vegetation zone; **z. verte** green belt
6 *Météo* **quelques zones pluvieuses demain** there'll be rain over some areas tomorrow; **z. de convergence intertropicale** Intertropical Convergence Zone; **z. de dépression, z. dépressionnaire** trough of low pressure; **z. de haute pression** area of high pressure
7 *Géol & Math* zone
8 **z. commerciale** retail park; **z. euro** euro area or zone; *Fin* **z. franc** = monetary zone in Africa where the franc is the principal currency; *Écon* **z. franche** free zone; *Com* **z. franchise** duty-free zone; **z. de libre-échange** free-trade area; **Z. de libre-échange des Amériques** Free-Trade Area of the Americas; **z. monétaire** monetary area; *Fin* **z. sterling** sterling area; *Mktg* **z. test** test area
9 *Ordinat* **z. d'affichage** display area, viewable area; **z. d'amorçage** boot sector; **z. chaude** = most visited area of a website; **z. de dialogue** dialog(ue) box; **z. de données** data field; **z. d'écriture** write area; **z. d'état** status box; **z. froide** = least visited area of a website; **z. de mémoire** storage area; **z. tampon (en mémoire)** (memory) buffer; **z. de travail** work area
10 *Électron* **z. de brouillage** interference zone; **z. de couverture** (*d'un satellite*) area of coverage; **z. de dégradé** (*d'un satellite*) shadow area; **z. d'ombre** (*d'un satellite*) shadow area
11 *Mil* **z. des armées** war zone, zone of operations; **z. des combats** combat zone; **z. démilitarisée** demilitarized zone; **z. d'exclusion aérienne** no-fly zone; **z. tampon** buffer zone
12 *Scol* **z. d'éducation prioritaire** = area targeted for special help in education
13 *Fam Péj* (*banlieue misérable*) slum area, rough area; (*endroit pauvre*) dump, hole, dive; (*endroit sale*) tip, pigsty, bombsite; **c'est la z.** (*quartier pauvre*) it's a really rough area; (*désordre*) it's a real mess *or* tip; (*c'est nul*) it sucks, it's the pits; **c'est la z., ta chambre!** your room looks as if a bomb hit it!; **cette famille, c'est vraiment la z.!** that family really is the pits!
❑ **de deuxième zone** ADJ second-rate, second-class
❑ **de troisième zone** ADJ third-rate; **un acteur de troisième z.** a third-rate actor

---

Culture

ZONE

The Paris area is divided into fare zones for public transport. Zones 1 and 2 cover metropolitan Paris and certain areas of the nearby suburbs. The remaining zones cover the outer suburbs: "j'habite en zone 3", "une carte orange quatre zones". France is divided into three "zones" (A, B and C), the schools in the different zones taking their mid-term breaks and Easter holidays at different times to avoid swamping the public transport system and tourist infrastructure.

---

zoné, -e [zone] ADJ zoned, zonate

zoner [3] [zone] VT *Géog & Ordinat* to zone
VI *Fam* **1** (*traîner*) to hang around, to bum around **2** (*faire*) **qu'est-ce que tu zones?** what are you up to?
▸**se zoner** VPR *Fam* to hit the sack *or* hay

zonga [zɔ̃ga] NM *Fam* (*verlan de* **gazon**) (*marijuana*) grass, weed, herb

zoning [zoniŋ] NM **1** *Géog & Ordinat* zoning **2** *Belg* (*zone*) area, zone; **z. artisanal** small industrial *Br* estate *or Am* park (*for craft-based businesses*); **z. commercial** retail park; **z. industriel** industrial *Br* estate *or Am* park

zonure [zonyr] NM *Zool* zonure

zonzon [zɔ̃zɔ̃] NF *Fam* slammer, clink

zoo [zo(o)] NM zoo; *Fig* **c'est le z. ici!** this place is like a madhouse!; **le Z. de Vincennes** = France's biggest zoo, in the Bois de Vincennes

zooflagellé [zooflaʒle] NM *Biol* zooflagellate

zoogamète [zoogamet] NM *Bot* zoogamete

zoogéographie [zoogeografi] NF zoogeography

zooglée [zoogle] NF *Biol* zoogloea

zoographique [zɔɔgrafik] ADJ zoographic, zoographical

zoolâtre [zɔɔlatr] ADJ zoolatrous
  NMF zoolater

zoolâtrie [zɔɔlatri] NF zoolatry

zoologie [zɔɔlɔʒi] NF zoology

zoologique [zɔɔlɔʒik] ADJ zoological; **jardin** *ou* **parc z.** zoo, zoological garden(s)

zoologiste [zɔɔlɔʒist] NMF zoologist

zoom [zum] NM *(objet)* zoom lens; *(procédé)* zoom; **faire un z. sur** to zoom in on; **z. arrière** zoom-out; **faire un z. arrière** to zoom out; **z. avant** zoom-in; **faire un z. avant** to zoom in (**sur** on)

zoomer [3] [zume] VI *(pour se rapprocher)* to zoom in; *(pour s'éloigner)* to zoom out

zoomorphe [zɔɔmɔrf] ADJ zoomorphic

zoomorphisme [zɔɔmɔrfism] NM zoomorphism

zoonose [zɔɔnoz] NF *Méd & Vét* zoonosis

zoopathie [zɔɔpati] NF *Psy* zoopathy

zoopathique [zɔɔpatik] ADJ zoopathic

zoophage [zɔɔfaʒ] ADJ zoophagous
  NMF zoophagan

zoophile [zɔɔfil] ADJ zoophilic
  NMF zoophile

zoophilie [zɔɔfili] NF zoophilia, bestiality

zoophobie [zɔɔfɔbi] NF zoophobia

zoophyte [zɔɔfit] NM *Zool* zoophyte

zooplancton [zɔɔplɑ̃ktɔ̃] NM *Zool* zooplankton

zoopsie [zɔɔpsi] NF *Psy* zoopsia

zoospore [zɔɔspɔr] NF *Biol* zoospore

zootechnicien, -enne [zɔɔtɛknisjɛ̃, -ɛn] NM,F specialist in animal husbandry

zootechnie [zɔɔtɛkni] NF animal husbandry, zootechnics *(singulier)*

zootechnique [zɔɔtɛknik] ADJ zootechnical

zoothèque [zɔɔtɛk] NF = collection of naturalized animals or animal skeletons

zoothéraphie [zɔɔterapi] NF animal therapy

zoreille [zɔrɛj] NMF *Fam (aux Antilles, en Nouvelle-Calédonie, à la Réunion)* = person from metropolitan France living or arriving in the overseas territories

zorille [zɔrij] NF *Zool* zorille, zorilla, striped polecat

Zoroastre [zɔrɔastr] NPR Zoroaster

zoroastrien, -enne [zɔrɔastrijɛ̃, -ɛn] *Rel* ADJ Zoroastrian
  NM,F Zoroastrian

zoroastrisme [zɔrɔastrism] NM *Rel* Zoroastrianism

zostère [zɔstɛr] NF *Bot* eel grass, *Spéc* zostera

zostérien, -enne [zɔsterjɛ̃, -ɛn] ADJ *Méd* relating to shingles

zou [zu] EXCLAM *(pour éloigner)* shoo!; *(pour marquer la rapidité)* whoosh!; **allez z., tout le monde dehors!** come on, everybody outside!; **allez, z. les enfants, au lit!** come on, off to bed, children!; **on ferme la maison et z., on part pour l'Italie** we'll shut up the house and whizz off to Italy

zouave [zwav] NM **1** *Mil & Hist* Zouave; **le z. du Pont de l'Alma** = the one surviving statue of the four built at water level on the Pont de l'Alma in Paris; it serves as a popular guide to the level of water in the Seine, which reached his beard in 1910 **2** *Fam (locution)* **faire le z.** *(faire le pitre)* to clown about; *(faire le malin)* to show off

Zoug [zug] NM *(ville)* Zug; **le canton de Z.** Zug canton, the canton of Zug

zouk [zuk] NM *Mus* = type of Caribbean music

zoulou, -e [zulu] ADJ Zulu
  NM *(langue)* Zulu
  ▫ **Zoulou, -e** NM,F Zulu; **les Zoulous** the Zulus *or* Zulu; *Fam* **un Z.** *(un jeune noir)* a young black man ▪

Zoulouland [zululɑ̃d] NM **le Z.** Zululand, Kwazulu

zourna [zurna] NM *Mus* zurna

zozo [zozo] NM *Fam* ninny, nitwit

zozotement [zozɔtmɑ̃] NM lisp

zozoter [3] [zozɔte] VI to lisp

Zululand [zululɑ̃d] = **Zoulouland**

ZUP, Zup [zyp] NF *(abrév* **zone à urbaniser en priorité)** = area earmarked for urgent urban development

Zurich [zyrik] NM *(ville)* Zürich; **le canton de Z.** Zürich canton; **le lac de Z.** Lake Zürich

zurichois, -e [zyrikwa, -az] ADJ of/from Zürich
  ▫ **Zurichois, -e** NM,F = inhabitant of or person from Zürich

zut [zyt] EXCLAM *Fam Br* blast!, *Am* shoot!; **z. alors, y a plus de sucre!** blast (it), there's no sugar

left!; **et puis z., tant pis, je l'achète!** what the hell, I'll buy it!; **et puis z., si tu n'es pas content, c'est pareil!** and if you don't like it, tough *or* hard cheese!; **dis-lui z.** tell him/her to get lost

zutique [zytik] ADJ = relating to the "zutistes"

zutiste [zytist] NMF = member of a group of late 19th-century French poets including Rimbaud, Verlaine and Charles Cros

zwanze [zwɑ̃z] NM OU NF *Belg Fam* joke ▪; **faire la z.** to live it up, to party ▪; **mettre de la z.** to liven things up ▪

zwanzer [3] [zwɑ̃ze] VI *Belg Fam (plaisanter)* to joke ▪; *(faire la fête)* to live it up, to party ▪

zwanzeur [zwɑ̃zœr] NM *Belg Fam (personne qui aime plaisanter)* joker ▪; *(personne qui fait la fête)* reveller ▪

zwieback [tsvibak] NM *Suisse (biscotte)* = piece of toasted bread sold in packets and often eaten for breakfast, *Am* zwieback

zwinglianisme [zwɛ̃glijanism] NM *Rel* Zwinglianism

zwinglien, -enne [zwɛ̃glijɛ̃, -ɛn] *Rel* ADJ Zwinglian
  NM,F Zwinglian

zwitterion [zviteriɔ̃] NM *Chim* zwitterion

zydeco [zideko] NM OU NF *Mus* zydeco

zyeuter [3] [zjøte] = **zieuter**

zygène [ziʒɛn] NF *Entom* zygaenid

zygodactyle [zigodaktil] ADJ *Orn* zygodactyl

zygoma [zigoma] NM *Anat* zygoma, zygomatic arch

zygomatique [zigomatik] ADJ *Anat* zygomatic

zygomorphe [zigomɔrf] ADJ *Bot* zygomorphic, zygomorphous

zygomycète [zigomisɛt] NM *Bot* zygomycete

zygopétale [zigopetal] NM *Bot* Zygopetalum

zygote [zigot] NM *Biol* zygote

zymase [zimaz] NF *Chim* zymase

zymogène [zimoʒɛn] NM *Biol & Chim* zymogen

zymologie [zimɔlɔʒi] NF *Chim* zymology

zymotique [zimɔtik] ADJ **1** *Chim* zymotic **2** *Vieilli Méd* zymotic

zythum [zitɔm] NM *Hist* zythum

zyva [ziva] = **ziva**

Supplement
Appendice

Chronology Chronologie	(3-28)
French Communication Guide	(29-58)
Nations of the World	(59-63)
Administrative Divisions (French)	(65-66)
French Legal System	(67-68)
Military Ranks Grades militaires	(69-71)
French Allusions	(73-80)
Abréviations français-anglais French-English Abbreviations	(81-98)

Chronology/Chronologie

Note: Historical events are marked with a solid lozenge (♦), cultural events are marked with an empty lozenge (◇).

Les événements historiques et culturels sont signalés respectivement par un losange noir (♦) et un losange blanc (◇).

English/Anglais	Français/French
♦ 55 av. J.-C. L'invasion romaine: Jules César (100 ou 101 – 44 av. J.-C.) conquiert l'île de Bretagne. ◇ Vers l'an 8 ap. J.-C. C'est à cette époque qu'est écrite l'épopée de *Beowulf*, vaillant héros et pourfendeur de dragon. Un manuscrit sur toile datant de la fin du 10ème siècle survit encore. ♦ 122 – 128 Construction du mur d'Hadrien dans le nord de l'Angleterre actuelle, destiné à repousser les invasions des Pictes et autres tribus venant de ce qui est maintenant l'Écosse. Ce mur marquait la frontière septentrionale de l'empire romain. ♦ 162 Les Romains ont perdu le contrôle de l'Écosse et se sont retranchés en deçà du mur d'Hadrien.	♦ 53 BC Vercingetorix (72 – 46 BC), chief of the Gauls, goes to war against the Romans. ♦ 52 BC Defeat of Vercingetorix by Caesar at Alésia. ◇ 50 AD The Pont du Gard and the Théâtre des Chorégies at Orange are built by the Romans. ♦ 352 Frankish invasions of Gaul.

400

♦ Vers 400 – 410 Le mur d'Hadrien cesse d'être un mur de défense.	♦ 406 Great invasion of Germanic tribes. 428 – 751 The Merovingians ♦ 476 Fall of the Roman Empire in the West. ♦ 481 Reign of Clovis, king of the Franks (466 – 511). ♦ 496 Conversion of Clovis to Christianity.

500

♦ Vers 500 Les envahisseurs nordiques (principalement Angles et Saxons) s'installent dans l'île de Bretagne et refoulent plusieurs tribus celtes vers le pays de Galles et la Cornouailles où leurs descendants sont encore très nombreux. ◇ 563 Le missionnaire irlandais St Columba fonde un monastère sur l'île écossaise d'Iona. Aujourd'hui encore cette île reste un lieu de pèlerinage.	♦ 507 Clovis beats back the Visigoths at Vouillé (Charentes). ◇ 507 Foundation by Clovis of the Basilica of the Apostles (later Sainte-Geneviève). ♦ 511 Clovis publishes the Salic Law (legal code of the Salian Franks) which included a clause preventing women from inheriting land. Death of Clovis. ◇ 543 Foundation of the Abbey of Saint-Germain-des-Prés (543 – 556). ♦ 558 Clotaire becomes king of the Franks (497 – 561). On his death, his sons divide up his kingdom. ♦ 579 The Bretons invade the regions of Rennes and Nantes.

600

◇ Vers 634 St Aidan d'Iona fonde un monastère sur l'île de Lindisfarne ou Holy Island (l'Île Sainte). Lindisfarne, qui compte St Cuthbert parmi ses évêques les plus célèbres, devient un foyer d'érudition et de christianisation. C'est là que sont enluminés les *Lindisfarne Gospels* (Évangiles de Lindisfarne) entre 690 et 700. ◇ Vers 650 Rédaction du *Book of Durrow* (Le Livre de Durrow). C'est le plus ancien exemple connu du nouvel art chrétien celte.	♦ 629 Dagobert I (ca. 600 – ca. 638) becomes king of the Franks. Saint-Eloi is his principal counsellor. ◇ 654 Foundation of the Abbey of Jumièges. ◇ 660 Foundation of the Abbey of Chelles.

700

	◇ ca. 700 Latin disappears as a spoken language in Gaul. ♦ 732 Charles Martel (688 – 741) checks Arab expansion at the Battle of Poitiers. ♦ 738 Saracen invasions in Provence. ♦ 742 – 743 Last great plague epidemic of the Early Middle Ages. 751 – 987 The Carolingians ♦ 751 Pepin the Short (Pépin le Bref) (741 – 768) is made king of the Franks at Soissons. ◇ 754 Pepin imposes the Latin liturgy on all the States of his Empire. Growth of Gregorian Chant. ♦ 771 Charlemagne (742 – 814) inherits the kingdom of the Franks. ♦ 778 Charlemagne is ambushed at Roncevaux in the Pyrenees. ◇ 782 Creation of the Palatine school of Aix-la-Chapelle (Aachen).

800

♦ Vers 800 Fin de la rédaction du *Book of Kells*, manuscrit des Évangiles somptueusement enluminé par des moines irlandais sur l'île écossaise d'Iona. ♦ 843 Kenneth MacAlpin bat les Pictes et devient le premier roi de toute l'Écosse. ♦ 871 Règne du roi Alfred the Great (Alfred le Grand) (849 – 899). Il bat les Pictes, organise une armée et une flotte. Il fait renaître la religion, favorise l'instruction et la littérature et traduit plusieurs ouvrages latins en anglais.	♦ 800 Charlemagne is anointed Emperor of the West (empereur d'Occident) in St Peter's Basilica in Rome. His kingdom includes Gaul, Germania, and parts of modern-day Spain and Italy. His reign witnesses a flowering of the arts and the spread of Christianity. ♦ 814 Reign of Louis the Pious (Louis le Pieux) (778 – 840). ◇ 842 The Strasbourg Oaths (Serments de Strasbourg), which seal the alliance between Charles the Bald (Charles le Chauve) and Louis the German (Louis le Germanique), written in 'Roman' and German, considered the oldest document in French. ♦ 843 The Treaty of Verdun formally divides the empire into three kingdoms; Francia Occidentalis, the future France, is given to Charles the Bald (823 – 877). Royal power begins to decline in favour of the nobility; creation of large duchies (Normandy, Burgundy, Flanders, Aquitaine) as the territory under the control of the King is gradually reduced to just the Île de France. ◇ 846 First Bible of Charles the Bald illuminated at the Abbey of Saint-Martin at Tours. ♦ 877 Charles signs the charter of Kiersy-sur-Oise, which promulgates the heredity of fiefs and seigneurial benefices. Reign of Louis II the Stammerer (Louis II le Bègue) (846 – 879). ♦ 879 Reigns of Louis III (863 – 882) and Carloman (867 – 884). ◇ 881 The *Séquence de Sainte Eulalie*, the first poem in langue d'oïl to be preserved, marks the beginnings of French literature.

[3]

English/Anglais	French/Français

English/Anglais

◇ Vers 909 Naissance du prélat anglo-saxon St Dunstan (mort en 988). Réformateur de la vie monastique, il fait de Glastonbury un centre de culture chrétienne.

◆924 – 939 Règne du roi anglo-saxon Athelstan (v. 895 – 939). Ce règne marque une période d'unification pour l'Angleterre. En 927 Athelstan envahit la Northumbrie et devient le premier roi de toute l'Angleterre. En 937, à la bataille de Brunanburh, il défait les Danois alliés aux Écossais et aux Gallois, renforçant ainsi son contrôle sur l'Angleterre.

◇975 *L'Exeter Book* (Le Livre d'Exeter), l'un des plus importants recueils de poèmes en vieil anglais, est copié et plus tard offert à la cathédrale d'Exeter.

◆978 Début du règne d'Ethelred II (the Unready) (968 – 1016). Il forge le premier lien dynastique entre la France et l'Angleterre par son mariage avec Emma, fille du duc de Normandie. Mais chassé de son trône par les Vikings en 1013, il doit s'exiler.

French/Français

◆898 Reign of Charles the Simple (Charles le Simple) (879 – 929), son of Louis the Stammerer (Louis le Bègue).

◇ ca. 910 Foundation of the monastery of Cluny by William I of Aquitaine (Guillaume d'Aquitaine).

◆911 Beginning of the Feudal period (10th–12th century). Viking invasions in Normandy. Creation of autonomous regions (notably Anjou, Maine and Toulouse).

◇ ca. 915 – 917 Building of the First Abbey Church of Cluny, centre for the spread of Benedictine reform across Europe.

◆936 Reign of Louis IV d'Outremer (921 – 954), son of Charles the Simple.

◇949 First written account of the pilgrimage to Santiago de Compostela (Saint-Jacques-de-Compostelle).

◆954 Reign of Lothaire (941 – 986).

◇966 Richard I of Normandy founds the abbey of Mont-Saint-Michel, entrusted to the Benedictines.

◆985 Reign of Louis V (967 – 987).

987 – 1328 The Capetians

◆987 Reign of Hugo Capet (Hugues Capet) (987 – 996).

◇990 Building of the keep of the château of Langeais.

English/Anglais

◆1009 Les Danois envahissent l'Angleterre.

◆1014 Défaite des Vikings à la bataille de Clontarf, en Irlande.

◆1016 Mort du roi Ethelred the Unready. Canut bat Edmond II Côte-de-Fer (Edmund Ironside) à la bataille d'Ashington; Edmond règne sur l'Écosse pendant une courte période, jusqu'à sa mort. Canute devient alors souverain de toute l'Angleterre.

◇ Vers 1020 Mort d'Aelfric dit 'the Grammarian' (le Grammairien), abbé et érudit anglo-saxon. Sa prose, écrite en langue vulgaire, en fait le plus grand écrivain de son époque. On lui doit entre autres les *Lives of the Saints* (Vies de saints).

◆1028 Canut, roi d'Angleterre et du Danemark, conquiert la Norvège.

◆1031 Canut oblige Malcolm, roi des Écossais, à reconnaître sa suzeraineté.

◆1040 Macbeth assassine Duncan Ier, roi des Écossais, et monte sur le trône.

◆1042 Fin de la période de domination danoise. Le Saxon Édouard le Confesseur (Edward the Confessor) devient roi. Fils d'Ethelred the Unready et d'Emma, il est le dernier souverain de la vieille lignée royale anglaise. C'est sa grande piété qui lui a valu son surnom.

◇1065 Consécration de l'abbaye de Westminster, abbaye de style roman construite sur les ordres d'Édouard le Confesseur.

1066 – 1154 L'Angleterre normande

◆1066 'La Conquête Normande' (The Norman Conquest): la victoire de Guillaume le Conquérant (William the Conqueror) (1028 – 1087), duc de Normandie, sur Harold II à Hastings, lui assure la couronne d'Angleterre.

◇1066 Début de la transformation radicale de la langue anglaise au contact du français, langue maternelle des Normands. Pendant les trois siècles qui suivront (les Angevins succédant aux Normands à la couronne d'Angleterre), le français sera la langue du droit, la langue du parlement, ainsi que la langue maternelle des rois d'Angleterre.

◇1067 Début des travaux de construction de la Tour de Londres, conçue pour être à la fois palais et forteresse.

◆1072 Guillaume le Conquérant étend sa conquête à l'Écosse.

◇1077 La tapisserie de Bayeux (tapisserie de la reine Mathilde, épouse de Guillaume le Conquérant), brodée en Angleterre, est terminée. Elle représente les événements qui ont précédé la conquête de l'Angleterre par les Normands ainsi que la bataille d'Hastings en 1066.

◇1086 *Domesday* ou *Doomsday Book* (t. orig. Livre du jugement dernier): ce recensement de toutes les terres d'Angleterre est réalisé sur l'ordre de Guillaume le Conquérant, probablement pour permettre au souverain d'estimer la capacité fiscale et militaire des nouveaux fiefs.

◆1087 Guillaume le Conquérant meurt. Son fils Guillaume II le Roux (William II) (v. 1056 – 1100) lui succède.

◆1091 Signature du Traité de Caen entre Guillaume II le Roux et son frère qui se disputaient la Normandie. Aux termes de ce traité, les terres du premier à décéder reviendront au survivant.

◆1093 Malcolm, roi d'Écosse, est tué au cours de l'invasion d'Alnwick dans le Northumberland.

◆1096 Le frère de Guillaume II le Roux, Robert, part pour la première croisade. Son départ expose la Normandie aux convoitises de Guillaume.

French/Français

◆1060 Reign of Philip I (1053 – 1108).

◇1060 Building of the abbey church of Sainte-Foy de Conques (on the pilgrims' route to Santiago de Compostela).

◆1066 William the Conqueror (Guillaume le Conquérant) (1028 – 1087), Duke of Normandy, lands in England and defeats Harold at the Battle of Hastings. He has himself crowned king.

◆1096 Peter the Hermit (Pierre l'Hermite) (1050 – 1115) advocates a crusade to aid the Christians of the East.

◇1098 Foundation of the Abbey of Cîteaux (Cistercian order) by Robert of Molesme.

◇ ca. 1098 – 99 Beginning of the *Chanson de Roland* (Song of Roland), the oldest chanson de geste. An historical event (the defeat of Charlemagne at Roncevaux in 778) is turned into an heroic epic.

◆1099 Under the leadership of Godfrey of Bouillon (Godefroy de Bouillon) (1061 – 1100), Duke of Lorraine, the crusaders take Jerusalem.

◇1099 Foundation in Jerusalem of the Hospitaliers de Saint-Jean.

English/Anglais

◆1100 Henri Ier Beauclerc (1068 – 1135) succède à son frère aîné Guillaume après la mort suspecte de ce dernier, tué par une flèche au cours d'une chasse.

◆1106 Henri Ier l'emporte sur son frère Robert II Courteheuse (Robert Curthose) à la bataille de Tinchebrai et devient duc de Normandie. Son but est de faire de l'Angleterre et de la Normandie un seul royaume.

French/Français

◆1108 Reign of Louis VI the Fat (Louis VI le Gros) (1081 – 1137).

◇1108 Abelard (1079 – 1142) disputes the 'querelle des Universaux' (doctrine of Universals).

◇1110 The Tympanum of the Apocalypse is sculpted on the portal of the church at Moissac.

English/Anglais	French/Français

English/Anglais column:

✦1124 David Ier, personnage influent, devient roi d'Écosse. Il compte de nombreux amis anglo-normands et de plus épouse une riche héritière normande. David est en position de force en Écosse et dans une partie du nord de l'Angleterre. Il établit une nouvelle aristocratie de langue française dans le sud de l'Écosse.
◊ Vers 1125 Adélard de Bath traduit le traité de géometrie d'Euclide, *Éléments*, de l'arabe en latin.
✦1128 Mathilde, fille d'Henri I, épouse Geoffroi le Bel (dit Plantagenêt), comte d'Anjou.

✦1135 À la mort du roi Henri I, son neveu Étienne de Blois (Stephen) (v.1090 – 1154) s'empare du trône à la place de Mathilde. Début de la guerre civile qui oppose ses partisans à ceux de Mathilde.
◊ Vers 1136 Geoffroi de Monmouth (Geoffrey of Monmouth) écrit son *Historia Regum Britanniae* (Histoire des Bretons). Cette œuvre fait entrer la légende d'Arthur dans la littérature européenne.

✦1141 Après une série d'attaques contre l'Angleterre, David Ier d'Écosse réussit à s'emparer d'une partie de la Northumbrie.

✦1147 – 1149 Deuxième croisade.

✦1153 Le roi Étienne (King Stephen), resté sans héritier, désigne comme successeur à la couronne d'Angleterre Henri Plantagenêt (1113 – 1189), (fils de Mathilde et de Geoffroi le Bel) alors duc de Normandie, comte d'Anjou, et duc d'Aquitaine (depuis son mariage avec Aliénor d'Aquitaine en 1152).

1154 – 1485 Les Plantagenêts

✦1154 Henri Plantagenêt est couronné roi d'Angleterre et devient Henri II d'Angleterre. Premier souverain de la dynastie des Plantagenêts, il règne sur le grand empire angevin.
◊1154 Adrien IV (Nicholas Breakspear) (v.1100 – 1159) devient pape. Il demeure le seul pape anglais.
◊1155 Le poète anglo-normand Robert Wace (v.1115 – 1183) termine son *Roman de Brut*, adaptation de l'Histoire des Bretons de Geoffroi de Monmouth.
◊ Entre 1155 et 1170 Le poète anglo-normand Thomas d'Angleterre compose sa version de *Tristan et Iseut* en français.
✦1164 Signature des Constitutions de Clarendon qui définissent les pouvoirs de l'Église et de l'État.
◊ Vers 1167 Henri II ayant interdit aux Anglais d'étudier à Paris, l'université d'Oxford se développe rapidement.
✦1170 Assassinat de Thomas Becket, archevêque de Cantorbéry, dans sa cathédrale. Il s'était opposé à la politique religieuse du roi qui voulait soumettre la justice ecclésiastique à la justice royale.
✦1171 Henri II mène une expédition victorieuse contre l'Irlande et annexe l'île.
✦1173 – 1174 Le fils d'Henri II, nommé lui aussi Henri, se révolte contre son père, soutenu par Guillaume Ier d'Écosse, Louis VII de France et le comte Philippe de Flandre.
◊1173 Thomas Becket est canonisé.
◊1176 Premier Eisteddfod (festival d'arts) au Pays de Galles.
◊ Vers 1187 Première mention de l'utilisation d'une boussole comme instrument de navigation dans *De utensilibus* d'Alexander Neckham.
✦1189 Les fils d'Henri II, Richard et Jean (John), s'emparent du Maine et de la Touraine. Henri accepte de reconnaître Richard comme son seul héritier. Richard Ier Cœur de Lion (the Lionheart) (1157 – 1199) devient roi d'Angleterre.
✦1189 – 1192 Troisième croisade, conduite par Richard Cœur de Lion et Philippe Auguste. Prise de Chypre et de Saint-Jean-d'Acre.
◊ Vers 1190 Le poète anglo-normand Béroul compose sa version de *Tristan et Iseut* en français.
✦1199 Jean sans Terre (John Lackland) (1167 – 1216) devient roi d'Angleterre.

1200

✦1200 Traité du Goulet : les Français reconnaissent les possessions françaises du roi Jean sans Terre.
◊ Vers 1200 L'arc de guerre est couramment utilisé par les forces anglaises.
✦1202 – 1204 Quatrième croisade et prise de Constantinople.

✦1204 La France reprend la Normandie à l'Angleterre.

✦1209 Jean sans Terre est excommunié par le pape.
◊1209 À la suite d'émeutes à Oxford, plusieurs membres de l'université quittent cette ville pour aller s'installer à Cambridge où ils fondent une nouvelle université.
Construction du premier pont en pierre de Londres.
◊ Vers 1214 Naissance du théologien et philosophe anglais Roger Bacon (mort en 1292). Il publie de nombreux ouvrages de mathématiques, de philosophie et de logique dont l'importance ne sera reconnue que beaucoup plus tard.
✦1215 Les barons imposent *The Magna Carta* (la Grande Charte) à Jean sans Terre à Runnymede. Garantie contre l'arbitraire royal, cette charte fondamentale marque le début de l'évolution de l'Angleterre vers un régime parlementaire. Elle servira de modèle à d'autres systèmes de gouvernement basés sur le système anglais.
✦1216 Plusieurs barons anglais abandonnent leur roi et invitent le futur Louis VIII de France à monter sur le trône d'Angleterre.
Mort soudaine de Jean sans Terre. Son fils Henri III lui succède.

French/Français column:

William of Aquitaine (Guillaume d'Aquitaine) (1071 – 1126), Count of Poitiers is the first troubadour; birth of the ideal of courtly love.
◊1115 Reform of the Cistercian order by Saint Bernard of Clairvaux (1090 – 1153).
◊1119 Foundation in Jerusalem of the Order of the Templars (Ordre des Templiers).

✦1132 Abbot Suger of Saint-Denis (1081 – 1151) is political and religious advisor to Louis VI the Fat, then to Louis VII the Young (Louis VII le Jeune).
✦1137 Reign of Louis VII the Young (1120 – 1180). He marries Eleanor of Aquitaine (Aliénor d'Aquitaine) (1122 – 1204).
◊1137 Rebuilding (1137 – 1144) of the chancel of the abbey church of Saint-Denis directed by abbot Suger: emergence of the Gothic style.

◊1145 The Royal Portal of Chartres Cathedral is built (1145 – 1150).
✦1146 Bernard of Clairvaux (1090 – 1153) argues for the second crusade (1147 – 1149), which fails at Damas.
✦1147 – 1149 Second crusade.
◊ ca. 1150 *Raoul de Cambrai*, chanson de geste on the feudal revolt and treachery between barons.
The court of Eleanor marks the apogee of courtly love, with the troubadours Bernard de Ventadour, Marcabru, Jaufre Rudel in residence.
✦1152 Eleanor of Aquitaine, repudiated by Louis VII, marries Henry Plantagenet (son of Geoffrey the Fair, and Duke of Normandy and Count of Anjou), which makes him Duke of Aquitaine.

✦1154 Henry Plantagenet is crowned Henry II, King of England, which becomes part of the possessions of the Angevins.

◊1162 – 1182 Chrétien de Troyes (1135 – 1183) writes various works.
◊1163 The building of Notre-Dame de Paris begins.
◊1168 *Lancelot ou le chevalier à la charrette* (Lancelot or the Knight of the Cart) by Chrétien de Troyes.

◊1170 *Le Roman de Renart* (1170 – 1205), an anonymous satirical romance, is started.

✦1180 Philippe II Augustus (Philippe Auguste) (1165 – 1223) accedes to the throne of France. He will strengthen the power of the monarchy and enlarge the territory under royal control.
◊1180 *Perceval ou le conte du Graal* (Percival or the Story of the Holy Grail) by Chrétien de Troyes.
✦1189 Beginning of the third crusade (1189 – 1192), led by Philippe II Augustus and Richard I (the Lionheart). Cyprus and Acre are taken.

◊ ca. 1200 *Aucassin et Nicolette*, first romance in prose and verse.

✦1202 Fourth crusade (1202 – 1204). The crusaders take Constantinople.

✦1204 England loses Normandy to France.

✦1209 Crusade (1209 – 1229) against the Albigenses (Cathar heretics).

✦1214 Victory of Philippe Augustus at the Battle of Bouvines against Otto IV (Otton IV) (Emperor of the Holy Roman Empire) and his allies including English King John Lackland.
◊1215 *Le Livre de Lancelot du Lac*, by Chrétien de Troyes. Prose romance.

English/Anglais	French/Français

English/Anglais

♦1217 Louis et ses partisans sont chassés d'Angleterre après leur défaite à la bataille de Douvres.
♦1217 – 1221 Cinquième croisade, contre l'Égypte.

♦1228 Sixième croisade (1228 – 1229) et prise de Jérusalem.

♦ Vers 1240 C'est vers cette date que l'on commence à utiliser le terme 'Parlement' pour désigner le Grand Conseil, réuni pour la première fois en 1224.
♦1242 Henri III tente vainement de reprendre le Poitou et autres fiefs français confisqués à son père, Jean sans Terre.
◇1245 Reconstruction de l'abbaye de Westminster dans le style gothique anglais.
♦1248 – 1254 Septième croisade, conduite par Louis IX de France (Saint-Louis).
◇1249 Fondation d'University College à Oxford.
♦1254 Le pape donne le contrôle du royaume de Sicile à Henri III.
♦1258 Traité de Paris: Henri III abandonne ses prétentions sur les provinces annexées par Philippe Auguste et reconnaît sa vassalité pour ses fiefs du sud-ouest de la France.
◇1259 Mort du chroniqueur et moine bénédictin Matthew Paris (né v. 1200). Ses *Chronica Majora*, qui relatent les événements survenus entre 1236 et 1259, en font le meilleur chroniqueur de son époque.
◇ Vers 1265 Naissance du théologien et philosophe franciscain John Duns Scotus (Duns Scot) (mort en 1308). Il est, avec Thomas d'Aquin, le plus grand théologien du Moyen Âge.
♦1266 'The Dictum of Kenilworth' (la paix de Kenilworth) met fin à la guerre des barons (menés par Simon de Montfort) dont la cause avait été le refus du roi d'appliquer les 'Provisions d'Oxford' qui demandaient une réunion périodique du 'Parlement'. Le roi recouvre le pouvoir mais doit s'engager à respecter les articles de la Grande Charte.

♦1270 – 1272 Huitième croisade.
♦1272 Mort d'Henri III. Son fils Édouard Ier (1239 – 1307) lui succède. Édouard reste en Sicile jusqu'en 1274. Pendant cette période le pays est gouverné par des régents.
♦ Vers 1274 Naissance de William Wallace, chef écossais et champion de l'indépendance de l'Écosse.
♦1276 Début de la première guerre galloise.

♦1284 Édouard Ier soumet les Gallois et annexe le pays de Galles.

♦1290 L'opinion publique se retourne contre les Juifs qui sont expulsés d'Angleterre.
♦1290 – 1292 Le trône d'Écosse est vacant pendant cette période.
♦1291 Édouard Ier impose sa suzeraineté sur l'Écosse.
♦1295 Formation d'une alliance franco-écossaise.
♦1296 Édouard Ier bat les Écossais à Dunbar et gouverne l'Écosse après l'abdication de John Balliol (John Bailleul) d'Écosse. Il fait transporter la pierre du couronnement des rois écossais ('the Stone of Destiny') du palais de Scone à l'abbaye de Westminster, marquant sa souveraineté par ce geste symbolique.
♦1297 Les Écossais, menés par William Wallace, battent les Anglais à Stirling Bridge.
♦1298 Édouard Ier bat William Wallace à Falkirk.

French/Français

♦1217 – 1221 Fifth crusade, against Egypt.

♦1223 Reign of Louis VIII (1187 – 1226).

♦1226 Reign of Louis IX (known as Saint-Louis) (1226 – 1270). During his reign he establishes the main bodies of central government.

♦1228 Sixth crusade (1228 – 1229). Jerusalem is taken.

♦1229 End of the crusade against the Albigenses.
◇ ca. 1235 First part of the *Roman de la Rose* (Romance of the Rose) by Guillaume de Lorris (1200 – 1240).

◇1241 Saint-Louis has the Sainte-Chapelle (1241 – 1248) built in Paris.

♦1248 – 1254 Seventh crusade, led by Louis IX (Saint-Louis).

◇1257 Foundation of the Sorbonne.
♦1258 The Treaty of Paris: Henry III renounces the French provinces he has lost and becomes a vassal of the French king for his remaining fiefs in the south-west of France.

♦1270 – 1272 Eighth crusade. Death of Saint-Louis near Tunis. Reign of Philip III the Bold (Philippe III le Hardi) (1245 – 1285).
◇ ca. 1275 Second part of the *Roman de la Rose*, by Jean de Meung (1240 – 1305).

♦1285 Reign of Philip IV the Fair (Philippe IV le Bel) (1268 – 1314).

◇1290 Beginning of the composition of *La Légende Dorée* (The Golden Legend), by Jacques de Voragine (1228 – 1298).

♦1295 Formation of an alliance between France and Scotland.

1300

♦1305 L'Écossais William Wallace est arrêté et pendu par les Anglais.
♦1306 Robert Bruce (Robert the Bruce) (1274 – 1329) est couronné roi d'Écosse à Scone mais, vaincu par les Anglais à la bataille de Methven, il est contraint de s'enfuir en Irlande.
♦1307 Robert Bruce revient d'exil et bat les Anglais à Loudoun Hill. Édouard Ier meurt. Son fils Édouard II (1284 – 1327) lui succède.
♦1314 Sous Robert Bruce les Écossais remportent une victoire décisive sur les forces anglaises d'Édouard II à la bataille de Bannockburn.
♦1314 – 1317 Une série de récoltes désastreuses entraîne une famine et une forte hausse des prix de la nourriture en Angleterre.
♦1319 Conclusion d'une trêve entre l'Angleterre et l'Écosse.
♦1327 Édouard II est assassiné dans sa prison. Son fils Édouard III lui succède et parvient à restaurer le pouvoir de la monarchie. Renouvellement de l'alliance franco-écossaise au traité de Corbeil.

♦1328 Le traité de Northampton reconnaît l'indépendance de l'Écosse et le droit de Robert Bruce à la couronne d'Écosse.
♦1331 Édouard III confirme qu'il doit hommage lige à la France pour ses fiefs continentaux et discute des termes d'une paix durable entre les deux pays.
♦1332 Première mention de la coupure du Parlement en deux chambres, les Lords et les Commoners (les Communes).

♦1337 Édouard III revendique la couronne de France. A la même époque Philippe VI s'empare de l'Aquitaine, alors possession anglaise. Ces événements déclenchent le long conflit auquel sera donné le nom de Guerre de Cent Ans (1337 – 1453).

♦1309 Pope Clement V (? – 1314) establishes the papacy in Avignon.
◇1309 *Livre des saintes paroles et des bon faits de notre roi Louis* (Life of Saint-Louis), by Jean de Joinville (1224 – 1317).
♦1314 Reign of Louis X the Stubborn (Louis X le Hutin) (1289 – 1316).
♦1316 Reign of Philip V the Tall (Philippe V le Long) (1293 – 1322).

♦1322 Reign of Charles IV the Fair (Charles IV le Bel) (1295 – 1328), last of the Capetian kings.

♦1327 Renewal of the alliance between France and Scotland with the treaty of Corbeil.
◇1327 The poet Petrarch (Pétrarque) (1304 – 1374) undertakes the writing of his *Canzoniere* at the court of the popes of Avignon.

1328 – 1589 The Valois

♦1328 Accession of Philip VI de Valois (1293 – 1350) to the throne of France, by virtue of the Salic Law, containing a clause which excluded women from succession to the throne of France.
♦1337 Philip VI confiscates Aquitaine from the king of England; at the same time Edward III lays claim to the French Crown. These events mark the beginning of the Hundred Years War (1337 – 1453).

English/Anglais	French/Français
◆1340 Édouard III détruit la flotte française à la bataille de Sluys. À Gand il revêt le blason de France et se proclame roi de ce pays. ◇ Vers 1342 Naissance de Julian of Norwich (Julienne de Norwich), mystique et recluse anglaise (morte en 1413). Son ouvrage *Sixteen Revelations of Divine Love* (Seize révélations de l'amour divin) influencera longtemps les théologiens. ◆1346 Édouard III défait les troupes françaises à la bataille de Crécy. C'est la première fois que les Anglais utlisent l'arc de guerre sur le continent. Les Écossais attaquent dans le nord de l'Angleterre et sont battus près de Durham. Leur roi, David II, est fait prisonnier.	◆1346 Edward III defeats the French troops at the battle of Crécy. Beginning of the Black Death ('la Peste noire' or 'Grande Peste'), which ravages the whole of Europe and decimates a third of the French population.
◆1347 Calais se rend aux Anglais. ◇ 1347 La première monnaie d'or anglaise est frappée pour célébrer la capitulation de Calais. ◆1348 – 1350 Une épidémie de peste noire ('The Black Death' ou 'Great Plague') se propage à travers l'Angleterre et l'Écosse. ◇ Vers 1349 Mort du philosophe et théologien anglais William of Ockham (Guillaume D'Occam) (né v.1285) dont la pensée exercera une profonde influence.	◆1347 Calais surrenders to the English troops. ◇ 1349 Guillaume de Machaut (1300 – 1377) composes the *Messe Notre-Dame*: advent of polyphony. ◆1350 Reign of John II the Good (Jean II le Bon) (1319 – 1364). ◆1356 The French are defeated by the English at the Battle of Poitiers, and the French king, John II, is captured. ◆1358 Etienne Marcel (1316 – 1358), provost of the merchants of Paris, leads an uprising against the Dauphin (future Charles V). Overburdened by taxes, the peasants (Jacques) rise up in Île-de-France, an episode known as the Jacquerie.
◆1356 Les Français sont vaincus par les Anglais à Poitiers et leur roi, Jean II le Bon, est fait prisonnier. ◆1360 Le traité de Brétigny entre la France et l'Angleterre met fin a la première phase de la Guerre de Cent Ans. Par ce traité, en plus d'une énorme rançon en échange de sa liberté, Jean II le Bon abandonne à l'Angleterre de nombreux territoires français. ◆1361 – 1362 Deuxième épidémie de peste en Angleterre. ◇ 1362 L'anglais remplace le français comme langue officielle au Parlement et dans les tribunaux ('The Statute of Pleading'). ◇ Vers 1375 Un auteur inconnu écrit l'un des plus grands poèmes de cette période *Sir Gawain and the Green Knight* (Sire Gauvain et le Chevalier Vert). ◆1376 Premier cas d'impeachment de l'histoire de l'Angleterre: au cours de la réunion du 'Good Parliament' (le Bon Parlement), certains individus sont nommés et mis en accusation. ◆1377 Édouard III meurt. Son petit-fils âgé de dix ans, Richard II (1367 – 1400), devient roi. La première capitation ('poll tax'), impôt levé sur chaque adulte, est introduite en Angleterre. Tout comme les futures capitations, cet impôt est fort mal accueilli par l'opinion et nombreux sont ceux qui se soustraient à son paiement. ◇ 1380 Geoffrey Chaucer (v. 1345 – 1400) entame les *Contes de Cantorbéry* (The Canterbury Tales). ◆1381 La mutiplication des impôts entre 1377 et 1381 provoque la Révolte des Paysans, menée par Wat Tyler, dans le sud de l'Angleterre. Cette révolte est rapidement réprimée. ◇ 1384 Mort du théologien et réformateur anglais John Wycliffe (né v. 1330). Précurseur de la Réformation, il prêche le retour à la Bible comme seule autorité en matière de foi. Il est l'auteur de la première traduction anglaise de la Bible. ◇ 1385 William Langland commence à écrire son poème allégorique *The Vision of Piers Plowman* (La Vision de Pierre le Laboureur). ◆1388 – 1399 Le règne de Richard II est marqué par une série de conflits avec le Parlement et se termine par son abdication.	◆1360 France and England sign the Treaty of Brétigny, which ends the first stage of the Hundred Years War. Under the Treaty, Edward III makes great territorial gains on France, and exacts a huge ransom for the French king's release. ◆1364 Charles V the Wise (Charles V le Sage) (1338 – 1380) succeeds John II the Good. ◆1367 Pope Urban V (1310 – 1370) leaves Avignon for Rome, then returns to Avignon (1370). ◆1369 Bertrand Du Guesclin (1320 – 1380), military commander, takes back the lands ceded by the Treaty of Brétigny as a ransom for the abduction of John the Good. ◇ 1378 Start of the Great Western Schism (1378 – 1417): Pope Clement VII (1342 – 1394) takes up residence in Avignon. ◆1380 Reign of Charles VI (1368 – 1422). His uncles the dukes of Anjou and Bourgogne act as regents (1380 – 1388). ◆1392 Charles VI is declared mad. His uncles take back power. Start of the war between the Armagnacs, on the side of the Dauphin (future Charles VII), and the Burgundians, on the side of the English.
1399 – 1461 Les Lancastres ◆1399 Richard abdique en faveur d'Henri IV (1366 – 1413) mettant ainsi la maison de Lancastre sur le trône. C'est seulement sous le règne de Henri IV que le roi d'Angleterre parle l'anglais comme langue maternelle et non plus le français (depuis Guillaume le Conquérant).	

━━━ 1400 ━━━

English/Anglais	French/Français
◆1400 Henri IV attaque l'Écosse mais est battu. ◆1401 Les Gallois, conduits par Owen Glendower, se révoltent contre Henri IV. ◆1403 Henri IV bat les Écossais, alliés aux Gallois et au comte Henry 'Hotspur' Percy, à Shrewsbury. ◆1404 Les Français s'allient au Gallois Owen Glendower. ◇ 1408 Mort de John Gower, le dernier des poètes anglo-normands, auteur de poèmes en latin, en français et en anglais. ◇ 1411 Fondation de l'université de St Andrews, la plus ancienne d'Écosse. ◆1413 Henri IV meurt. Son fils Henri V (1387 – 1422) lui succède. ◆1415 Henri V, qui veut reconquérir la couronne de France, bat les Français à Azincourt.	◆1407 Murder of Louis of Orléans (brother of King Charles VI) by the duke of Burgundy, John the Fearless (Jean sans Peur) (1371 – 1419). Start of the Civil War (1407 – 1435) between Armagnacs and Burgundians (allies of the English). ◇ 1408 *Les Très Riches Heures* (The Very Rich Hours) by the duke of Berry, a manuscript illuminated by the Limbourg brothers. ◆1415 Defeat by the English under Henry V at Agincourt. ◇ 1417 End of the Great Western Schism. ◆1418 Flight of the Dauphin to Bourges. ◆1419 Murder of John the Fearless. Philip the Good (Philippe le Bon) (1396 – 1467) becomes duke of Burgundy.
◆1420 Signature de la 'paix perpétuelle' de Troyes. Henri V recouvre la plus grande partie de la Normandie et est reconnu comme Régent de France et héritier de la couronne de France. ◆1422 Henri VI (1421 – 1471) succède à son père à l'âge de neuf mois. Bien que couronné roi de France en 1431, les territoires conquis par son père lui échappent peu à peu. ◆1423 Les Anglais, alliés aux Bourguignons, remportent la victoire de Verneuil sur les forces franco-écossaises.	◆1420 The 'perpetual peace' of Troyes is concluded. Henry has regained control of most of Normandy, and is recognized as heir to the French throne and Regent of France. ◆1422 Death of Charles VI. The Dauphin proclaims himself king and becomes Charles VII (1403 – 1461). ◆1423 An allied force of English and Burgundian troops defeat a French–Scottish army at Verneuil.
◆1431 Jeanne d'Arc (Joan of Arc) est brûlée vive. Toutefois son action avait mis fin à l'hégémonie des Anglais en France.	◆1429 Joan of Arc (Jeanne d'Arc) (1412 – 1431) fights in the siege of Orléans. Charles VII crowned at Reims. ◆1430 Joan of Arc is taken prisoner at Compiègne. ◆1431 Trial and execution of Joan of Arc.

English/Anglais	French/Français
	◆1435 Treaty of Arras which brings to an end the war between the Armagnacs and the Burgundians. Reconquest of France by Charles VII. ◇1440 Trial of Gilles de Rais or Retz (1400 – 1440): this comrade-in-arms of Joan of Arc is condemned and executed for having indulged in satanic worship.
◇1440 Henri VI fonde le collège d'Eton, 'public school' pour garçons. Mort de la mystique anglaise Margery Kempe (née v. 1373). Elle est l'auteur d'une des premières autobiographies, *The Book of Margery Kempe* (Le Livre de Margery Kempe), dictée entre 1432 et 1436.	
◆1445 Une épidémie de peste se déclare en Angleterre.	◇1445 *Portrait of Charles VII* by Jean Fouquet (1415 – 1480).
	◇1450 In Strasbourg, Johannes Gutenberg invents a mould for casting movable type, and the first printing press is born. ◆1453 End of the Hundred Years War, with the Battle of Châtillon. Only Calais (regained in 1558) and the Channel Islands remain English territories.
◆1453 La bataille de Châtillon met fin à la Guerre de Cent Ans. Les Anglais ne conservent que Calais (qu'ils perdront en 1558) et les îles de la Manche. ◇1453 Mort du compositeur anglais John Dunstable (né v. 1390). ◆1455 Début de la guerre des Deux-Roses, guerre civile en Angleterre, dont la cause est la lutte pour le pouvoir entre les deux branches rivales de la maison des Plantagenêts: la maison d'York qui a pour emblème la rose blanche, et la maison de Lancastre dont l'emblème est la rose rouge.	
1461 – 1485 Les Yorks	
◆1461 Henri VI est détrôné par Édouard IV de la maison d'York (1442 – 1483). ◇1471 Mort de l'écrivain anglais Sir Thomas Mallory. Son chef-d'œuvre, *Le Morte d'Arthur*, est une adaptation en prose de la geste d'Arthur. ◇1475 L'imprimeur et traducteur anglais William Caxton (v. 1422 – 1491) publie à Bruges le premier livre imprimé en anglais, *The Recuyell of the Historyes of Troye*. ◇1476 William Caxton établit une imprimerie à Westminster et publie le premier livre imprimé en Angleterre, *The Sayings of the Philosophers*.	◆1461 Reign of Louis XI (1423 – 1483). ◇1461 The *Testaments* by François Villon (1431 – 1463).
◇1480 Caxton imprime *The Chronicles of England* (Chroniques d'Angleterre). ◆1483 Le jeune Édouard V (1470 – 1483) occupe le trône pendant une courte période avant d'être emprisonné dans la Tour de Londres où il est probablement assassiné. ◆1483 – 1485 Règne du roi Richard III (1452 – 1485), dernier roi de la dynastie des Plantagenêts.	◇1476 Nicolas Froment (1425 – 1483) paints the *Triptyque du Buisson Ardent* (Moses and the Burning Bush). ◆1477 Acquisition of the duchy of Burgundy by Louis XI. ◆1483 Reign of Charles VIII (1470 – 1498).
1485 – 1603 Les Tudors	
◆1485 La bataille de Bosworth Field où Richard III, vaincu, trouve la mort, met fin à la guerre des Deux-Roses. Henri VII (1457 – 1509), le vainqueur, devient le premier souverain de la dynastie des Tudors. Pendant son règne, il réussit à rétablir la paix et la prospérité en Angleterre. ◆1490 Renouvellement de l'alliance franco-écossaise: en cas de guerre entre la France et l'Angleterre, l'Écosse s'engage à attaquer l'Angleterre. ◆1497 Jean Cabot, navigateur gênois au service de l'Angleterre, découvre les terres d'Amérique septentrionale (île du Cap-Breton et Nouvelle-Écosse).	◆1498 Reign of Louis XII of Orléans (1462 – 1515), cousin of Charles VIII. ◇1498 *Mémoires*, historical chronicles by Philippe de Commynes (1447 – 1511).

{ **1500** }

English/Anglais	French/Français
◇1500 L'ouverture d'une imprimerie par Wynkyn de Worde dans Fleet Street à Londres marque le début de la longue association entre cette rue et les métiers de l'imprimerie. ◆1509 Henri VIII (1491 – 1547) succède à Henri VII.	
◆1512 Henri VIII envahit la France et remporte la victoire des Spurs (1513). ◆1513 Les forces franco-écossaises sont vaincues à la bataille de Flodden.	◆1515 Reign of Francis I (François I) (1494 – 1547). Francis I wins the battle of Marignano (Marignan) and gains control of Milan for the French. ◇1516 Francis I brings Leonardo da Vinci (Léonard de Vinci) to the Court of France. ◇1519 Building of the château of Chambord (1519 – 1537), the last of the great châteaux of the Loire.
◇1516 L'humaniste et homme politique anglais Sir Thomas More écrit *Utopia* (L'Utopie). ◇1518 Le médecin et humaniste anglais Thomas Linacre (v.1460 – 1524) fonde le Royal College of Medecine (Collège Royal de médecine).	
◇1525 William Tyndale imprime à Cologne sa traduction en anglais du Nouveau Testament.	◆1525 The French army is defeated by the Spanish at the battle of Pavia: Francis I is taken prisoner (freed in 1526). ◆1530 Francis I founds the Collège de France, on the advice of Guillaume Budé (1467 – 1540). ◆1532 By the Edict of Union, Brittany is linked indissolubly with France. ◇1532 *Pantagruel*, by Rabelais (1494 – 1553). ◆1534 First voyage of Jacques Cartier (1491 – 1557) to Canada, on behalf of Francis I. France lays claim to Canada. ◇1534 *Gargantua*, by Rabelais.
◆1534 L'Acte de Suprématie (the Act of Supremacy) met fin à l'autorité du pape et établit le roi comme chef unique et suprême de l'Église d'Angleterre.	◆1535 The Frenchman John Calvin (Jean Calvin, 1509 – 1564) goes into exile in Basle. The Reformation begins in Switzerland. Second voyage of Jacques Cartier to Canada. Exploration of the Saint Lawrence river, which opens the way to French colonization of Canada. ◇1535 First Protestant bible in French. ◇1537 Requirement for every publisher to place a copy of every book in the royal Library (origin of the registration of copyright). ◇1539 Francis I signs the Edict of Villers-Cotterêts which confirms the primacy of French as official and legal language. ◆1541 Third voyage of Jacques Cartier to Canada. ◇1542 *Délie* (Delia), a collection of love poems, is published by Maurice Scève (1501 – 1560).
◆1540 La dissolution des monastères commence en Angleterre. ◆1545 – 1563 Le pape convoque le Concile de Trente qui se réunit en trois périodes pour examiner et redéfinir certains points du dogme. Ce concile fait partie de la Contre-Réforme.	◇1545 Ambroise Paré's (1509 – 1590) *Traité de chirurgie* marks the birth of modern surgery.

English/Anglais	French/Français
	◇1546 Francis I puts Pierre Lescot in charge of building the new Louvre (1546 – 1559). ✦1547 Reign of Henry II (1519 – 1559). ◇1549 *Fontaine des Innocents* (Fountain of the Innocents) by Jean Goujon (Paris). *Défense et illustration de la langue française* (Defence and Illustration of the French Language), by Joachim du Bellay (1522 – 1560).
✦1547 Édouard VI, fervent protestant, devient roi d'Angleterre. Sous son règne la Réforme se développe.	
✦1553 Lady Jane Grey monte sur le trône mais est renversée neuf jours plus tard par Marie Ière Tudor qui, fervente catholique, ramène l'Angleterre au catholicisme le plus intransigeant. Sa persécution des protestants lui vaut le surnom de 'Marie la Sanglante' (Bloody Mary). ✦1558 Élisabeth (1533 – 1603), demi-sœur protestante de Marie, devient reine. Son règne est marqué par l'essor général du pays ainsi que par une période de paix entre la France et l'Angleterre. ◇1558 Mort du mathématicien anglais Robert Recorde (né v.1510). Il est l'auteur des premiers manuels anglais d'arithmétique élémentaire et d'algèbre. C'est lui qui a introduit le signe d'égalité en mathématiques. ✦1559 Élisabeth devient chef de l'Église d'Angleterre. ✦1560 John Knox établit l'Église presbytérienne d'Écosse qui est restée l'Église nationale de cette province. ✦1562 Francis Drake et John Hawkins entreprennent le commerce des esclaves avec l'Amérique.	◇1552 *Les Amours* is published by Ronsard (1524 – 1585). ◇1555 Poet Louise Labé (1524 – 1566) publishes *Débat de folie et d'amour* (Debate Between Folly and Love).
◇1564 Naissance de Shakespeare, auteur dramatique, poète et acteur anglais (mort en 1616). ✦1567 Les nobles écossais emprisonnent Marie Ière Stuart, reine d'Écosse, au château de Loch Leven près de Kinross en Écosse. ✦1568 Mary Ière Stuart s'évade de Loch Leven et s'enfuit en Angleterre, où elle se fait emprisonner par Élisabeth.	✦1559 Reign of Francis II (François II) (1544 – 1560). The Treaty of Cateau-Cambresis ends the Franco-Spanish War. ◇1559 *L'Heptaméron* by the queen of Navarre, Margaret of Angoulême, sister of Francis I (1553 – 1615). ✦1560 Reign of Charles IX (1550 – 1574). Beginning of the regency of Catherine de Médicis (1519 – 1589). ◇1560 Jean Nicot (1530 – 1600) introduces tobacco into France. ◇1562 Massacre of the Protestants at Wassy. First War of Religion (1562 – 1563). ◇1564 Reform of the calendar; the year now begins on 1 January instead of 25 March.
◇1578 – 1580 Le romancier et auteur dramatique anglais John Lyly (v.1554 – 1606) écrit *Euphueus*, roman allégorique qui connaît un énorme succès. Le maniérisme du style, sa préciosité, ont donné naissance au terme 'euphuisme'. ◇1580 Francis Drake revendique la Californie pour l'Angleterre et revient dans son pays après avoir doublé le cap de Bonne-Espérance. ◇1582 Le pape Grégoire XIII introduit le calendrier grégorien qui ne sera adopté en Grande-Bretagne qu'en 1752. ✦1583 Sir Humphrey Gilbert prend possession de Terre-Neuve pour l'Angleterre. C'est la première colonie anglaise.	✦1572 On Saint Bartholomew's Eve (24 August), the Catholics massacre the Protestants in Paris and in the provinces (le massacre de la Saint-Barthélémy). Fourth War of Religion (1572 – 1573). ✦1574 Reign of Henry III (1551 – 1589). ◇1580 *Essais* (Essays) (1580 – 1588) by Michel de Montaigne (1533 – 1592).
✦1587 Élisabeth fait exécuter Marie Ière Stuart (1542 – 1587). ✦1588 Défaite de l'Invincible Armada, flotte envoyée par Philippe II d'Espagne avec pour mission d'envahir l'Angleterre. ◇1590 Publication des trois premiers livres de *The Faerie Queene* (La Reine des Fées), du poète anglais Edmund Spenser (v. 1552 – 1599). ◇1593 L'auteur dramatique anglais Christopher Marlowe (né en 1564) meurt poignardé au cours d'une rixe dans une taverne. Parmi ses œuvres, il faut citer *Tamburlaine the Great* (Tamerlan), *The Tragic History of Dr. Faustus* (La Tragique Histoire du docteur Faust) et *The Jew of Malta* (Le Juif de Malte). ✦1595 Sir Walter Raleigh s'embarque pour les Indes espagnoles d'où il ramène le tabac et la pomme de terre.	✦1585 Eighth War of Religion (1585 – 1598). **1589 – 1792 The Bourbons** ✦1589 Assassination of Henry III (without issue), last of the Valois. Accession of Henry IV of Bourbon (1553 – 1610), leader of the Protestants. ✦1590 Victory of Henry IV at the Battle of Ivry, near Evreux, on 14 March 1590, against the Holy Catholic League. ✦1593 Henry IV abjures Protestantism and enters Paris.
◇1599 Ouverture du Globe Theatre à Londres avec la représentation d'une pièce de Shakespeare, *Henry V*.	✦1596 Sully (1559 – 1641), counsellor to Henry IV, advocates the development of agriculture. ✦1598 Henry IV issues the Edict of Nantes (which allows freedom of worship to the Protestants) and so brings an end to the Wars of Religion and re-establishes peace in the kingdom.

1600

English/Anglais	French/Français
✦1600 Fondation de la Compagnie des Indes Orientales (East India Company). D'abord formée pour assurer à l'Angleterre le monopole du commerce avec les Indes, elle acquerra plus tard des pouvoirs territoriaux, y compris le droit de lever des impôts. ◇1600 Le médecin et physicien anglais William Gilbert (1544 – 1603) publie son traité sur le magnétisme terrestre *De Magnete*.	◇1600 Marriage of Henry IV and Marie de Médicis (1573 – 1642). ◇1600 The Grande Galerie du Louvre (1600 – 1608) is designed by the architect Jacques II Androuet du Cerceau (1550 – 1614). ◇1602 Henry IV founds the tapestry-making company Les Gobelins in Paris; Flemish artisans are invited to introduce new techniques.

1603 – 1649 Les Stuarts

English/Anglais	French/Français
✦1603 Jacques VI (James VI) d'Écosse, fils de Marie Stuart, devient également Jacques Ier d'Angleterre à la mort d'Elisabeth Ière, restée sans descendant. Sous son règne la Grande-Bretagne devient une réalité politique. ✦1605 Échec de la Conspiration des Poudres (The Gunpowder Plot), complot formé par des catholiques (dont Guy Fawkes). C'est le dernier complot catholique important. ✦1606 Adoption du drapeau britannique dit 'Union Jack' qui porte les croix des trois saints patrons de l'Angleterre, de l'Écosse et de l'Irlande. ◇1606 L'auteur dramatique anglais Ben Jonson (1572 – 1637) écrit *Volpone*. ✦1607 La Virginie devient la première colonie anglaise d'Amérique du Nord. ✦1611 Des colons anglais et écossais s'établissent en Ulster (nord de l'Irlande). ◇1611 Publication de la Bible anglaise *The Authorized Version* ou *King James' Bible*. ◇1614 Le mathématicien écossais John Napier (1550 – 1617) publie sa découverte des logarithmes dans son traité *Mirifici Logarithmorum Canonis Descriptio*. ◇1617 Le mathématicien anglais Henry Briggs établit les tables de logarithmes décimaux qui simplifient énormément les calculs numériques. ✦1620 Les Pères Pèlerins (Pilgrim Fathers), embarqués à bord du Mayflower, fondent la colonie de Plymouth en Amérique. ◇1621 Le mathématicien anglais William Oughtred (1575 – v. 1660) invente la première règle à calcul. Parution du premier journal anglais *The Corante*.	✦1608 French navigator and Governor of New France Samuel de Champlain (ca. 1570 – 1635) founds Quebec. ✦1610 Assassination of Henry IV. Louis XIII (1601 – 1643) becomes king of France. Regency of Marie de Médicis (1573 – 1642) and Concini (1575 – 1617). ◇1616 *Les Tragiques*, by Agrippa d'Aubigné (1552 – 1630), poem glorifying Protestantism. ◇1622 Marie de Médicis commissions from Rubens the paintings for the Gallery of the Luxembourg Palace in Paris.

English/Anglais	French/Français

◇1623 Sept ans après la mort de Shakespeare, deux acteurs de sa troupe, John Heminges et Henry Condell, rassemblent et publient 36 de ses pièces dans le *Premier Folio*.
L'auteur dramatique anglais John Webster (né v.1580 — mort v.1625) écrit *The Duchess of Malfi* (La Duchesse de Malfi).
✦1624 Les Hollandais chassent les Anglais de l'archipel des Moluques.
◇1624 Naissance de George Fox (mort en 1691), fondateur de la 'Société des Amis' ou secte des 'Quakers'.
✦1625 Charles Ier monte sur le trône.
La peste noire fait plus de 40 000 morts à Londres.
◇1626 Mort de Francis Bacon, philosophe et homme d'État anglais. Son ouvrage *Novum Organum* pose les principes d'une méthode inductive et expérimentale.
✦1627 L'Angleterre déclare la guerre à la France.
◇1628 Le médecin anglais William Harvey (1578 — 1657) publie son *Exertitatio Anatomica de Motu Cordis et Sanguinis* qui contient la première description de la circulation du sang.
✦1629 L'aventurier David Kirke prend possession de Québec pour la Grande-Bretagne.
✦1630 Début d'un fort courant d'émigration de l'Angleterre vers le Massachusetts.
◇1631 Mort du poète anglais John Donne (né v. 1572).
✦1632 Le traité de Saint-Germain-en-Laye rend Québec à la France.
◇1632 Naissance de Christopher Wren, architecte de la cathédrale de Saint Paul, du Royal Exchange et de l'Observatoire de Greenwich.
✦1635 Fondation de la colonie américaine de Rhode Island.
◇1635 Inauguration d'un service postal public entre Édimbourg et Londres.
✦1636 Fondation de la colonie américaine du Connecticut.
◇1637 En Écosse, l'Église d'Angleterre tente de s'imposer face à l'Église d'Écosse, presbytérienne et calviniste; la première lecture du *Revised Prayer Book* (nouvelle version du Livre de Prières des Anglicans) dans la cathédrale de St Giles, à Édimbourg, provoque de violentes émeutes.

✦1641 Des milliers de colons protestants périssent au cours d'un soulèvement en Ulster.
✦1642 – 1648 Guerre civile en Angleterre entre les Parlementaristes, inquiets de la croissance de l'absolutisme royal, et les partisans de Charles Ier.
✦1643 Batailles de Edgehill et de Newbury.
✦1644 Batailles de Marston Moor et de Naseby.

1649 – 1659 le Commonwealth ou Protectorat de Cromwell

✦1649 Exécution de Charles Ier d'Angleterre (né en 1600) et abolition de la monarchie. Oliver Cromwell (1599 – 1658) institue un nouveau régime, le Commonwealth.
Les niveleurs (the Levellers), républicains qui s'opposent aux tendances autoritaires de Cromwell et réclament une représentation populaire accrue, sont vaincus à la bataille de Burford.
◇1651 Le philosophe anglais Thomas Hobbes (1588 – 1679) expose ses théories philosophiques et politiques dans le plus important de ses ouvrages *Leviathan* (Le Léviathan).
✦1652 – 1674 Guerres anglo-hollandaises, trois guerres navales dues essentiellement à des rivalités commerciales et coloniales entre les deux pays.
✦1654 Annexation de l'Irlande. Le parti républicain irlandais s'oppose à la domination anglaise.

1660 – 1688 Restauration: retour des Stuarts

✦1660 Restauration de la monarchie. Charles II, de la maison écossaise des Stuarts, monte sur le trône.
◇1660 L'Anglais Samuel Pepys (1633 – 1703), fonctionnaire à l'Amirauté, commence la rédaction de son célèbre *Journal*.
◇1662 Le physicien et chimiste irlandais Robert Boyle (1627 – 1691) énonce la loi de Boyle, selon laquelle, à température constante, la pression d'un gaz est inversement proportionnelle à son volume.
✦1664 Les Anglais s'emparent de la colonie hollandaise de New Amsterdam qu'ils rebaptisent New York.
◇1665 Le poète anglais John Milton (1608 – 1674) termine *Paradise Lost* (le Paradis Perdu), son œuvre la plus célèbre.
✦1666 Le Grand Incendie de Londres (the Great Fire of London) éclate dans une boulangerie de Pudding Lane et, favorisé par les constructions en bois, fait de terribles ravages dans le centre de la ville. La cathédrale médiévale de St Paul est détruite.
✦1668 Sir William Temple (1628 – 1699) conclut la Triple Alliance (Grande-Bretagne, Hollande et Suède) contre la France.
◇1668 La nomination du poète John Dryden (1631 – 1700) au poste de 'Poet Laureate' inaugure la tradition des 'poètes officiels de la Cour'.
✦1670 Fondation de la Compagnie de la baie d'Hudson, établie pour le commerce des fourrures. Fondation des colonies de Caroline du Nord et du Sud en Amérique.
Signature des deux traités de Douvres, l'un secret et l'autre public, entre Charles II et Louis XIV. Charles II s'engage à se convertir au catholicisme, engagement qu'il ne tient d'ailleurs pas. Il est maintenant tenu de soutenir Louis XIV, en particulier contre les Hollandais.

✦1624 Richelieu (1585 – 1642) becomes minister of Louis XIII. His programme consists of reducing the power of the nobles, destroying the Huguenots and fighting Austria.

✦1628 Capitulation of La Rochelle, a Protestant refuge, after a year-long siege by Richelieu.

✦1630 Day of the Dupes: Richelieu triumphs over the supporters of Marie de Médicis.
◇1631 Théophraste Renaudot (1586 – 1653) founds the *Gazette*, which marks the beginning of journalism.
✦1632 The treaty of Saint-Germain-en-Laye returns Quebec to France.
◇1634 Richelieu founds the Académie Française.

◇1636 Corneille (1606 – 1684) publishes *le Cid*.
✦1637 Uprising of the Croquants (peasants) of the Limousin.
◇1637 Descartes (1596 – 1650) writes *Discours de la méthode* (Discourse on Method).
Claude Gelée, also known as Lorrain (1600 – 1682), paints *Port au soleil couchant* (Seaport at Sunset).
✦1638 The French take the island of Réunion.
✦1639 Uprising of the va-nu-pieds (Bare Feet) (1639 – 1641) in Normandy.
◇1640 Nicolas Poussin painter-in-ordinary to the king.
✦1642 Mazarin (1602 – 1661) becomes minister to Louis XIII.
✦1642 Building of the château of Maisons (Maisons-Laffitte) by François Mansart (1598 – 1666).
Pascal (1623 – 1662) invents a calculating machine.
✦1643 Reign of Louis XIV (1638 – 1715). Regency of Anne of Austria (1601 – 1666) and Mazarin.
◇1643 Molière (1622 – 1673) founds the Illustre Théâtre.
◇1645 Building of the Val-de-Grâce, by Mansart.
◇1647 Vaugelas (1585 – 1650) publishes *Remarques sur la langue française* (Remarks on the French Language).
✦1648 At the end of the Thirty Years War, the Treaty of Westphalia transfers to the king of France the rights of the Habsburgs in Alsace and proclaims the independence and neutrality of the Swiss Confederation.
✦1648 First Fronde (1648 – 1649) (insurrection) against Mazarin.
✦1650 Second Fronde (1650 – 53) led by parliament against Mazarin.

◇1654 Correspondence between Fermat, Pascal and Huyghens, on the origin of the calculation of probabilities.

◇1656 Pascal publishes *Les Provinciales* (Provincial Letters), a work in which he attacks the Jesuits and defends the Jansenists.
✦1659 Treaty of the Pyrenees: victory of France over Spain; France keeps among others Artois and Roussillon.
Creation of Saint-Louis, a French trading post in Africa (Senegal).
✦1661 Louis XIV reigns without a regent. Colbert (1619 – 1683) and Louvois (1639 – 1691) are ministers.
◇1661 The building of the palace of Versailles entrusted to Le Vau, Le Brun and Le Nôtre.
✦1664 Foundation of the Compagnie Française des Indes.
◇1664 Molière's *Tartuffe* is staged at Versailles and immediately banned.
◇1665 Molière writes *Dom Juan*.
La Rochefoucauld (1613 – 1680) publishes *Maximes*.

◇1667 Racine's (1639 – 1699) *Andromaque* is performed.
◇1668 Molière's *L'Avare* (The Miser) is performed. Jean de La Fontaine (1621 – 1695) publishes *Fables*.
◇1669 Molière's *Tartuffe* is finally permitted to be performed.
Racine writes *Britannicus*.
✦1670 Treaty of Dover creating an alliance between Louis XIV and Charles II.
✦1670 Pascal's *Pensées* is published posthumously.
✦1673 Expedition of Jolliet and Père Marquette up the Mississippi valley.
◇1673 Molière's *Le Malade imaginaire* (The Imaginary Invalid) is performed.

English/Anglais

◇1676 Inauguration de l'Observatoire de Greenwich conçu par Christopher Wren. Construit sur le méridien origine, il sert de base au temps solaire moyen de Greenwich.
♦1678 Sous la pression de l'opinion publique, Charles II conclut une alliance avec les Hollandais contre la France.
◇1678 L'écrivain anglais John Bunyan termine la première partie du *Pilgrim's Progress* (Le Voyage du Pèlerin).
Mort du poète et métaphysicien Andrew Marvell (né en 1621).
◇1680 L'astronome anglais Edmund Halley (1656 – 1742) prédit le retour d'une comète dont le passage au périhalie avait été observé en 1583 (comète de Halley) pour 1758, 1835 et 1910.
Introduction d'un service postal, le Penny Post, à Londres.
♦1681 Charles II octroie un territoire en Amérique à William Penn qui le nomme Pennsylvania en l'honneur de son père.
♦1684 Le mathématicien, physicien, astronome et penseur Sir Isaac Newton (1642 – 1727) expose sa théorie de la gravitation universelle dans *De Motu Corporum*.
♦1685 Jacques II d'Angleterre (Jacques VII d'Écosse) monte sur le trône.
◇1687 Isaac Newton publie son œuvre maîtresse *Philosophiae Naturalis Principia Mathematica* qui contient ses trois lois de la mécanique.

1688: La Révolution Glorieuse

♦1688 En Angleterre, la Révolution Glorieuse (The Glorious Revolution) oblige Jacques II à s'enfuir en France.
◇1688 Aphra Behn (1604 – 1689), sans doute le premier auteur féminin professionnel en Angleterre, publie son roman *Oroonoko*.
♦1689 Le protestant Guillaume d'Orange (Guillaume III d'Angleterre, Guillaume Ier d'Écosse) partage la couronne avec son épouse Marie II, fille de Jacques II.
◇1689 Mort du médecin anglais Thomas Sydenham (né en 1624). Ses ouvrages, avec leurs descriptions de maladies, seront traduits et réimprimés pendant tout le 18ème siècle.
Le compositeur anglais Henry Purcell (1659 – 1695) termine le premier opéra anglais, *Dido and Aeneas* (Didon et Enée).
♦1690 Guillaume d'Orange remporte la victoire de la Boyne en Irlande sur Jacques II qui s'enfuit en France.
◇1690 Le philosophe empiriste John Locke (1632 – 1704) publie son *Essay concerning Human Understanding* (Essai sur l'entendement humain).
♦1691 Guillaume d'Orange assiège Limerick, en Irlande. Traité de Limerick.
♦1692 À Glencoe, en Écosse, les Macdonald, partisans de Jacques II, sont massacrés par le clan rival des Campbell.
Jacques II et Louis XIV rassemblent des troupes en Normandie pour envahir l'Angleterre. Leurs tentatives échouent.
◇1692 Procès des sorcières de Salem dans la colonie du Massachusetts. Dix-neuf personnes sont accusées de sorcellerie et exécutées avant d'être reconnues innocentes.
♦1694 Après la mort de sa femme, la reine Marie, Guillaume d'Orange règne seul jusqu'à sa mort en 1702.
Création de la banque d'Angleterre.
◇1698 Le Parlement sanctionne la traite des Noirs. Entre 1680 et 1786, les marchands d'esclaves anglais transportent près de deux millions d'esclaves d'Afrique en Amérique où ils serviront de main d'œuvre dans les nouvelles plantations de sucre et de café.
◇1698 Thomas Savery (v. 1650 – 1715) invente la première machine utilisant la vapeur d'eau comme force motrice pour pomper l'eau dans les mines de charbon.

◇1701 L'agriculteur anglais Jethro Tull (1674 – 1740) invente la machine à semer en sillons.
♦1702 Anne, fille de Jacques II, devient reine d'Angleterre, d'Écosse et d'Irlande.
♦1704 Les Anglais s'emparent de Gibraltar, jusqu'alors possession espagnole.
◇1704 Le savant anglais Sir Isaac Newton publie *Opticks*.
♦1707 L'Acte d'Union unit l'Angleterre à l'Écosse.
◇1709 Le métallurgiste anglais Abraham Darby (v. 1678 – 1717) utilise pour la première fois le coke pour l'extraction du fer par fusion.
♦1713 Le Traité d'Utrecht établit la paix entre la France et la Grande-Bretagne et donne à celle-ci de vastes territoires au Canada.

1714 – 1901 Les Hanovre

♦1714 George Ier, roi protestant de la maison de Hanovre, devient roi de Grande-Bretagne et d'Irlande.
♦1715 Révolte des Jacobites (partisans de Jacques II et de la maison des Stuarts) en Grande-Bretagne contre la succession protestante hanovrienne.
◇1719 L'écrivain anglais Daniel Defoe (1660 – 1731) publie *Robinson Crusoe*.
♦1720 'The South Sea Bubble': l'effondrement des valeurs de la Compagnie des Mers du Sud après une période de spéculation effrénée entraîne une crise financière et la ruine de nombreux actionnaires.
◇1724 L'Anglais Thomas Longman fonde la maison d'édition qui porte toujours son nom.
◇1726 Jonathan Swift, pasteur et satiriste anglo-irlandais, publie *Gulliver's Travels* (Les Voyages de Gulliver).
♦1727 George II (1683 – 1760) devient roi de Grande-Bretagne et d'Irlande.
♦1733 La Géorgie devient colonie britannique par Charte Royale. C'est la dernière des 13 colonies anglaises d'Amérique du Nord à être fondée.
◇1733 La mécanisation de l'industrie textile progresse grâce à l'invention de la navette volante par John Kay (1701 – 1764).

French/Français

♦1678 Alsace becomes a French territory.
In the Treaty of Nimègues, Spain cedes Franche-Comté to France.
◇1678 Mme de La Fayette (1634 – 1693) writes *La Princesse de Clèves* (The Princess of Clèves), one of the first European novels.

◇1680 The Comédie-Française is founded.
Richelet publishes *Dictionnaire français des mots et des choses*, the first French dictionary.
♦1681 Strasbourg is annexed by France.
♦1682 Louis XIV moves the Court to Versailles.
René Robert Le Cavelier de La Salle (1643 – 1687) sails down the Mississippi and founds Louisiana in honour of Louis XIV.
◇1684 Furetière publishes *Essai d'un dictionnaire universel*.
♦1685 Louis XIV decrees the Revocation of the Edict of Nantes which leads to the exile of Protestants.
♦1686 De Troyes and Le Moyne D'Uberville take three English trading posts on James Bay, in Canada.

◇1688 La Bruyère (1645 – 1696) publishes *Les Caractères*, anthology of psychological and social portraits.
First report on the use of steam, by Denis Papin.

◇1690 François Couperin composes *Works for organ*.

◇1691 Racine writes *Athalie*.

◇1697 Charles Perrault (1628 – 1703) publishes his *Contes de ma mère l'oye*, the first collection of fairy tales in literature.
Pierre Bayle publishes his *Dictionnaire historique et critique*.

1700

◇1707 Denis Papin builds a boat propelled by paddle wheels.

♦1713 The Treaty of Utrecht establishes peace between Britain and France, and gives Britain large areas of what is now Canada.

♦1715 Reign of Louis XV (1710 – 1774). The French take Mauritius.
♦1718 Founding of New Orleans (La Nouvelle-Orléans).

◇1721 Montesquieu (1689 – 1755) writes *Lettres Persanes* (Persian Letters).
♦1723 Louis XV comes of age and rules without a regent.

◇1728 Abbé Prévost publishes *Manon Lescaut*.
◇1730 Marivaux publishes *Le Jeu de l'amour et du hasard* (Love in Livery).
◇1734 Voltaire (1694 – 1778) publishes *Lettres philosophiques*.
◇1735 Scientific voyage (1735 – 1744) of La Condamine and Bouger to South America to measure the length of a degree of meridian at the equator.

English/Anglais	French/Français

◇1739   Le philosophe écossais David Hume (1711 – 1776) publie A *Treatise of Human Nature* (Traité de la nature humaine).
◇1740   Le romancier anglais Samuel Richardson (1689 – 1761) publie *Pamela*, un roman épistolaire.
◇1742   Le compositeur allemand naturalisé britannique Georg Friedrich Haendel compose son *Messie* (Messiah).
✦1745   Deuxième révolte jacobite importante.
✦1746   La défaite des partisans de Jacques II face aux forces de George II (de la maison de Hanovre) à Culloden met fin aux ambitions jacobites. Début d'une campagne de répression féroce dans les Highlands d'Écosse, qui marque la fin du système des clans.

◇1750   Le philosophe écossais David Hume commence la rédaction des *Dialogues concerning Natural Religion* (Dialogues sur la religion naturelle).
◇1752   Adoption du calendrier grégorien en Grande-Bretagne.

✦1755   Au Canada, expulsion des Acadiens par les Anglais (Le Grand Dérangement). Certains d'entre eux s'installeront en Louisiane (les Cajuns).
◇1755   L'écrivain anglais Samuel Johnson (1709 – 1784) publie son *Dictionnaire de la langue anglaise*.
✦1757   Les forces britanniques conduites par Robert Clive (1725 – 1774) remportent la victoire de Plassey sur Siraj ud-Daula (v.1732 – 1757), nabab du Bengale. Cette victoire constitue une étape importante de l'acquisition du Bengale par la Grande-Bretagne.
✦1759   Le général britannique James Wolfe (1727 – 1759) l'emporte sur les Français aux Plaines d'Abraham, près de Québec.
✦1760   George III (1738 – 1820) accède au trône.
◇1760   Le peintre anglais Joshua Reynolds (1723 – 1792) exécute son *Portrait de Georgiana comtesse Spencer et sa fille*.
✦1763   Par le traité de Paris (marquant la fin de la guerre de sept ans), la France cède tout le Canada à la Grande-Bretagne et perd ses possessions en Inde à l'exception de cinq comptoirs.
◇1763   Les géomètres britanniques Charles Mason (1730 – 1787) et Jeremiah Dixon (mort en 1777) entreprennent la délimitation de la frontière entre la Pennsylvanie et le Maryland (Ligne Mason-Dixon). Cette frontière est considérée comme la ligne de démarcation entre le Nord et le Sud.
◇1764   L'Anglais James Hargreaves (1720 – 1778) invente la première machine à filer à plusieurs broches, dite 'spinning jenny'.
✦1765 – 1766   La crise du Stamp Act (Loi du Timbre) reflète le mécontentement grandissant des colons américains face aux exigences financières de la Grande-Bretagne.
◇1765   L'ingénieur écossais James Watt (1736 – 1819) perfectionne le moteur à vapeur.
◇1766   Le chimiste anglais Henry Cavendish (1731 – 1810) découvre l'hydrogène.

◇1770   Le capitaine James Cook (1728 – 1779), navigateur anglais, découvre Botany Bay en Australie.
◇1770   Le peintre anglais Thomas Gainsborough (1727 – 1788) exécute son célèbre *Blue Boy*.
✦1773   La 'Boston Tea Party': en réponse aux taxes instituées par la Grande-Bretagne, les colons américains jettent les cargaisons de thé de la Compagnie des Indes à la mer.
✦1774   Une communauté de chrétiens revivalistes, les 'Shakers', s'installe près d'Albany, dans l'État de New York.
◇1774   Le pasteur et chimiste anglais Joseph Priestley (1733 – 1804) découvre l'oxygène.
✦1775   Début de la Guerre d'Indépendance dans les colonies anglaises d'Amérique du Nord.
✦1776   Le Congrès continental américain adopte la Déclaration d'Indépendance qui rejette l'autorité du roi d'Angleterre le 4 juillet.

✦1778   La France et la Hollande soutiennent les colons américains et l'Angleterre déclare la guerre à la France.

✦1783   La Paix de Paris reconnaît l'existence de la République fédérée des États-Unis.
Le Second Pitt (William Pitt the Younger) (1759 – 1806) devient Premier ministre du Royaume-Uni. Son premier ministère est marqué par d'importantes réformes et une politique influencée par les théories libérales de l'économiste Adam Smith.
◇1785   Le pasteur anglais John Cartwright (1743 – 1823) invente le métier mécanique pour la filature du coton.
◇1786   Le poète écossais Robert Burns (1759 – 1796) publie ses *Poems, Chiefly in the Scottish Dialect* (Poèmes, pour la plupart en langue écossaise).
✦1787   George Washington devient le premier Président des États-Unis.
✦1788   Les premiers colons anglais débarquent à Botany Bay, en Nouvelle-Galles du Sud, en Australie.

◇1735   Rameau composes *Les Indes galantes*.
◇1736   Scientific voyage (1736 – 1739) of Maupertuis to Lapland to measure the length of a degree of meridian, leading to confirmation of Newton's theories on the flattening-out of the earth at the poles.
◇1737   Marivaux publishes *Les Fausses Confidences*.
◇1739   Le duc de Saint-Simon (1675 – 1755) begins his *Mémoires*.
◇1743   D'Alembert (1717 – 1783) publishes *Traité de dynamique*.

◇1751   Denis Diderot (1713 – 1784) begins the publication (1751 – 1772) of l'*Encyclopédie ou Dictionnaire raisonné des sciences, des arts et des techniques* (Encyclopedia, or Critical Dictionary of Sciences, Arts and Trades), which represents the full spirit of the Enlightenment.
◇1754   The architect J.A. Gabriel (1698 – 1782) builds the Place de la Concorde, the Royal Military Academy and the Petit Trianon at Versailles.
✦1755   Expulsion of the French population from Acadia by the English (the Grand Dérangement). Some of their descendants go on to settle in Louisiana and become the Cajuns.

✦1759   The British under the leadership of General James Wolfe (1727 – 1759) defeat the French on the Plains of Abraham, near Quebec.
◇1759   Voltaire writes *Candide*.
◇1762   Rousseau (1712 – 1778) writes *Emile* and the *Contrat social* (Social Contract).
✦1763   At the end of the Seven Years War, in the Treaty of Paris, France cedes Quebec with all of Canada to England, and the French Indies are reduced to five trading posts.

◇1770   Joseph Cugnot builds the first steam-powered vehicle.

✦1774   Reign of Louis XVI (1754 – 1793). Turgot (1727 – 1781) becomes Comptroller-General of Finance.
The English government grants Canada a statute (Quebec Act) which provides legislative and political guarantees for the French Quebecois, whilst reinforcing the authority of London.
✦1775   A terrible food shortage in Paris leads to the fall of the Minister of Finance, Turgot.
◇1776   Jouffroy d'Abbans (1751 – 1832) sails the first steam boat on the Doubs.
✦1777   The physiocrat Necker (1732 – 1804) becomes Comptroller-General of Finance.
◇1777   The chemist Lavoisier (1743 – 1794) explains the role of oxygen in the respiratory system.
✦1778 – 1782   France sends troops to fight against the British in the American War of Independence. General de La Fayette (1757 – 1834) plays a leading role in the war.
◇1781   Rousseau publishes *Confessions*.
◇1782   Choderlos de Laclos (1741 – 1803) publishes the novel *Les Liaisons dangereuses* (Dangerous Liaisons).
◇1784   Beaumarchais (1732 – 1799) writes the play *Le Mariage de Figaro* (The Marriage of Figaro).
Rivarol (1753 – 1801) publishes *Discours sur l'universalité de la langue française*.
✦1785 – 1786   The affair of queen Marie-Antoinette's diamond necklace, a swindle instigated by the adventurer Cagliostro, brings discredit upon the queen.
◇1785   Scientific expedition led by La Pérouse (1741 – 1788) in the Pacific Ocean. He is killed in 1788.
✦1788   Popular riots in Paris and the provinces. Calling of the Estates General.

1789: The French Revolution

✦1789   Beginning of the French Revolution.
The Estates General proclaim themselves a National Assembly. Parisians storm the Bastille on 14 July.
The abolition of Privileges is decreed (on the night of 4 August), and the Declaration of the Rights of Man and of the Citizen is passed. The property of the clergy is confiscated by the Nation.

English/Anglais	French/Français
	◇1789 David (1748 – 1825) paints *Le Serment du Jeu de Paume* (The Tennis Court Oath). ✦1790 Division of France into 83 departments. 14 July is established as the 'fête de la Fédération' (French national day). ◇1790 Jussieu (1748 – 1836) develops the Jardin des Plantes botanical gardens in Paris. ✦1791 Flight and arrest of the king at Varennes. Passing of the Constitution. In Canada, a constitutional bill separates Canada into two regions: French-speaking Quebec forms Lower Canada.

1792 – 1804 The First Republic

English/Anglais	French/Français
◇1792 Thomas Paine (1737 – 1809), auteur politique anglais, publie *The Rights of Man* (Les Droits de l'homme). ◇1793 L'Américain Eli Whitney (1765 – 1825) invente l'égreneuse qui sépare les graines des fibres de coton.	✦1792 Uprising in Paris and overthrow of the king. Abolition of royalty and proclamation of the First Republic on 21 September. Beginning of the king's trial. ◇1792 Rouget de Lisle (1760 – 1836) composes *La Marseillaise*. ✦1793 Execution of Louis XVI on 21 January. Promulgation of the 1793 Constitution known as Year II. France at war with England, Holland, Austria, Russia, Prussia, Spain and Portugal, who want to crush the revolution. Trial and execution of Marie-Antoinette.
✦1794 Publication de *Chants d'expérience* (Songs of Experience), du poète William Blake (1757 – 1827).	◇1794 Robespierre (1758 – 1794) has the Great Terror decreed, but his adversaries have it thrown out and he is guillotined along with his allies. ◇1794 Creation of the École Polytechnique. Creation of the National Archives. Creation of the École Normale Supérieure. French becomes obligatory in all public documents. ✦1795 Promulgation of the Constitution of Year III. Following an insurrection on 5 October (13 Vendémiaire in the revolutionary calendar), Bonaparte (1769 – 1821) crushes the royalists and establishes the Directory. ◇1795 Creation of the Écoles Centrales. Creation of the School of Oriental languages. Institution of the metric system.
◇1796 Le médecin anglais Edward Jenner (1749 – 1823) découvre le principe de la vaccination et réussit à immuniser un enfant contre la variole.	✦1796 Bonaparte, head of the French army in Italy, is victorious in the first Italy campaign at Lodi, Arcole, Rivoli and Mantua (1797). ◇1796 Laplace (1749 – 1827) publishes *Exposition du système du monde* (The System of the World), his nebular hypothesis of planetary origin. ✦1797 Bonaparte concludes his Italian victories by the Treaty of Campo Formio which sanctions the defeats of Austria. Belgium is ceded to France. ◇1797 Lamarck (1744 – 1829) publishes *Mémoires de physique*. ✦1798 Reuniting of Mulhouse and Geneva with France. The French give a constitution to Holland and to the Swiss Cantons.
✦1798 Échec d'un soulèvement en Irlande. William Pitt propose une union législative suivie de l'émancipation des catholiques. Victoire de Nelson contre Bonaparte à la bataille d'Aboukir. ◇1798 *Lyrical Ballads* (Ballades lyriques) de Coleridge et Wordsworth, véritable manifeste du romantisme.	Bonaparte leads the Egypt expedition: victorious in the battle of the Pyramids, he takes Cairo, but is defeated at the battle of Aboukir by Admiral Nelson, who destroys the French fleet. ◇1798 Bonaparte founds the Cairo Institute. ✦1799 Following his coup d'état on 9 November (18 Brumaire in the revolutionary calendar), Bonaparte becomes Consul for three years and promulgates the Constitution of Year VIII, which brings the French Revolution to an end and marks the beginning of the Consulate (1799 – 1804). ◇1799 Monge (1746 – 1718) publishes *Traité de géométrie descriptive* (Treatise on Descriptive Geometry).

1800

English/Anglais	French/Français
✦1800 Thomas Jefferson (1743 – 1826) est élu à la présidence des États-Unis (1800 – 1808). Il fut le principal auteur de la Déclaration d'indépendance en 1776. Les Anglais s'emparent de Malte.	✦1800 Foundation of the Bank of France. The second Italy campaign imposes peace on Austria through the Treaty of Lunéville (1801), concluded by the victory of Marengo. ✦1801 Bonaparte brings an end to the civil and religious wars by signing the Concordat with Pius VII (Pie VII). ✦1802 Bonaparte is appointed Consul for Life by plebiscite; he promulgates the Constitution of Year X. ◇1802 Chateaubriand (1768 – 1848) writes *Le Génie du christianisme* (The Beauties of Christianity or The Genius of Christianity). Bichat (1771 – 1802) publishes *Anatomie générale*: Bichat is the first anatomist to establish that each organ is composed of tissues. Creation of the Lycées and of the Legion of Honour.
✦1803 L'achat de la Louisiane à la France donne aux États-Unis le contrôle de toute la vallée du Mississippi.	✦1803 Napoleon sells Louisiana (which at the time represented a third of present-day America) to the United States. ◇1803 Jean-Baptiste Say publishes *Traité d'économie politique* (A Treatise on Political Economy).
✦1804 William Clark (1770 – 1838) et Meriwether Lewis (1774 – 1809) entament leur voyage d'exploration à l'ouest du Mississippi.	### 1804 – 1814 The Napoleonic Empire ✦1804 Promulgation of the Civil Code. Napoleon has himself proclaimed Emperor, and anointed by Pope Pius VII on 2 December. Promulgation of the Constitution of Year XII. Beginning of the First Empire. ◇1804 Cuvier publishes *Leçons d'anatomie générale* (Lessons of Comparative Anatomy).
✦1805 Bataille de Trafalgar. Nelson y remporte une éclatante victoire sur la flotte franco-espagnole mais y trouve la mort. ◇1805 J.M.W. Turner (1775 – 1851) peint *Shipwreck*.	✦1805 Third coalition (Anglo-Austro-Russian) against Napoleon. Resumption of the war with the English and defeat at Trafalgar by Nelson. The Grand Army crosses the Rhine. Napoleon is victorious over Austria and Russia at Austerlitz. ◇1805 Invention of the Jacquard loom (1752 – 1834). Chateaubriand writes *René*. ✦1806 Victorious in the battle of Jena over Prussia, Napoleon takes Berlin and Warsaw. ◇1806 Building of the Vendôme Column and start of the construction of the Arc de Triomphe on the Place de l'Étoile in Paris.

English/Anglais	French/Français

English/Anglais

◆1807   Abolition de la traite des esclaves dans l'ensemble de l'empire britannique, à la suite du mouvement lancé par le député réformiste William Wilberforce (1759 – 1834).
◇1807   Publication de *Ode on Intimations of Immortality*, de William Wordsworth (1770 – 1850).
Début de l'éclairage au gaz à Londres.
◆1808 – 1814   Guerre d'Espagne entre la France et la Grande-Bretagne pour le contrôle de péninsule ibérique.
◆1809   Défaite de la Grande-Bretagne face à la France à La Corogne.

◇1810   Le poète et romancier écossais Sir Walter Scott (1771 – 1832) publie *The Lady of the Lake* (La Dame du lac).
L'architecte britannique John Nash (1752 – 1835) entame la conception du Royal Pavilion de Brighton.
◆1811 – 1812   En Angleterre, des ouvriers de l'industrie textile (les Luddites) détruisent de nouveaux métiers à tisser en réaction contre les bas salaires et la menace du chômage.
◇1811   La romancière anglaise Jane Austen (1775 – 1817) publie *Sense and Sensibility* (Raison et Sensibilité).
◇1812   La publication du premier volume du chef-d'œuvre du poète britannique George Gordon, Lord Byron (1788 – 1824) *Childe Harold's Pilgrimage* (Le Chevalier Harold) connaît un vif succès. Childe Harold, personnage mélancolique et révolté, reste le type du héros romantique 'byronien'.
◇1813   Publication de *Orgueil et préjugé* (Pride and Prejudice), de Jane Austen.

◆1815   Battu à Waterloo par Wellington et Blucher, Napoléon abdique pour la deuxième fois et est déporté à Sainte-Hélène.
Le gouvernement de Lord Liverpool impose les 'Corn Laws', droits élevés sur les importations de blé étranger.
◆1818   Les États-Unis et la Grande-Bretagne décident de fixer la frontière entre le Canada et les États-Unis au 49ème parallèle.
◇1818   Publication de *Frankenstein*, de Mary Shelley (1797 – 1851).
◆1819   Sir Stamford Raffles (1781 – 1826) acquiert Singapour pour la compagnie des Indes Orientales.
Mort de onze personnes lors de l'intervention de la police au cours d'un meeting sur la réforme parlementaire à St Peter's Fields, à Manchester. Cet épisode est connu sous le nom de Peterloo Massacre (jeu de mots avec Waterloo).
L'Espagne vend la Floride aux États-Unis.
◇1819   Publication de *Prométhée délivré* (Prometheus Unbound), de Percy Bysshe Shelley (1792 – 1822).

◆1820   Le Compromis de Missouri: le parallèle 36 30 sépare les états esclavagistes des états non esclavagistes.
En Grande-Bretagne, George IV (1762 – 1830) accède au trône.
◇1820   Le poète anglais John Keats publie *Lamia and Other Poems* qui contient ses œuvres les plus connues, dont les *Odes*.
◆1821   Le physicien et chimiste anglais Michael Faraday (1791 – 1867) invente le moteur électromagnétique ainsi qu'une génératrice à courant continu.
◇1821   Le peintre paysagiste anglais John Constable (1776 – 1837) exécute *The Haywain* (La charrette de foin).
◇1822   Publication des *Confessions d'un mangeur d'opium anglais* (Confessions of an English Opium Eater), de Thomas de Quincey (1785 – 1859).
◆1823   La 'Doctrine de Monroe' affirme l'opposition des États-Unis à toute ingérence européenne sur le continent américain.
◇1825   Inauguration de la première ligne de chemin de fer avec traction à vapeur pour le transport des voyageurs, entre Stockton et Darlington, dans le nord-est de l'Angleterre.
◇1826   Publication du *Dernier des Mohicans* (The Last of the Mohicans), du romancier américain James Fenimore Cooper (1789 – 1851).
◇1828   Le lexicographe américain Noah Webster (1758 – 1843) publie *An American Dictionary of the English Language* (Dictionnaire américain de la langue anglaise).
◆1829   La totalité du territoire australien est déclarée dépendance britannique.
Le ministre de l'Intérieur Robert Peel fait adopter l'acte d'émancipation des catholiques; il crée la police londonienne (d'où les surnoms de 'Peelers' ou 'Bobbies' donnés aux policiers).
◇1829   Première course entre les universités d'Oxford et de Cambridge sur la Tamise.

◆1830   Guillaume IV (William IV) (1765 – 1837) accède au trône.
Les premiers colons américains s'installent en Californie, alors territoire mexicain.
◇1831   Le naturaliste anglais Charles Darwin (1809 – 1882) s'embarque à bord du Beagle. Il basera sa théorie de l'origine des espèces sur les observations qu'il effectuera au cours de son expédition.

French/Français

◆1807   Napoleon continues his conquests with victories over Russia at Eylau and Friedland and forces Tsar Alexander I to sign the Tilsit peace treaty. The Great Empire is established.
◇1807   Studies by Gay-Lussac (1778 – 1850) on the expansion of gases. David paints *Le Sacre* (Anointing of Napoleon).
◆1808   Creation of the imperial nobility. Conspiracy of Talleyrand (1754 – 1838) and Fouché (1759 – 1820).
◆1809   The 5th coalition against Napoleon, led by Austria, is defeated at Wagram. Repudiation of Joséphine de Beauharnais (1763 – 1814).
◇1809   J.B. Lamarck publishes *Philosophie zoologique* (Zoological Philosophy), the first great theory of the evolution of the species (Lamarckism).

◆1810   Marriage of Napoleon to Marie Louise (1791 – 1847), daughter of the Emperor of Austria. Publication of the Penal Code.
◆1811   Birth of the king of Rome, son of Napoleon and Marie Louise, nicknamed the Eagle (l'Aiglon). He is to die in 1832.
◇1811   J. Fourier (1768 – 1830) introduces the expansion of functions in trigonometric series.
◆1812   Napoleon marches on Moscow. After the taking of Vilna and Vitebsk and the victory of Borodino, the Grand Army has to retreat because of the winter which has reduced its ranks to one tenth their numbers: this is the rout of Berezina.
◇1812   Laplace publishes *Théorie analytique des probabilités*. Cuvier (1773 – 1838) starts writing his *Recherches sur les ossements fossiles*, the founding work of palaeontology.
◆1813   Napoleon is forced to retreat from Germany following defeat at Leipzig.

1814 – 1830   The Restoration of the Bourbon monarchy

◆1814   The France Campaign (January – March) ends in the invasion of the country and leads to the abdication of Napoleon and the restoration of Louis XVIII (1755 – 1824).
◇1814   Ingres (1780 – 1867) paints the *Grande Odalisque*. Ampère (1775 – 1836) discovers electromagnetism and invents the galvanometer and the electromagnet.
◆1815   The Hundred Days (from March to June). Napoleon leaves the Island of Elba and marches on Paris. After his defeat by Wellington and Blucher at Waterloo, he abdicates and is deported to Saint Helena, leaving Louis XVIII to reign over France until 1824.
At the end of the Battle of Waterloo, England conceives the plan of making Belgium a buffer state to contain the territorial ambitions of France: Belgium and the Netherlands are united and the Prince of Orange is called to the crown. But Belgium is Catholic whilst the Netherlands are Reformist (Calvinists).
The Federal Pact ratifies the membership of 22 Cantons of the Swiss Confederation, reproclaimed neutral and independent by the Congress of Vienna.
◇1816   The physicist Nicéphore Niepce (1765 – 1833) invents the technique of photography.
Benjamin Constant (1767-1830) publishes *Adolphe*.
◇1819   Théodore Géricault (1791 – 1824) paints *Le Radeau de la Méduse* (The Raft of the Medusa).

◆1820   After the assassination of the duke of Berry (1778 – 1820), heir to the throne, the Ultras (non-liberal royalists) return to power under minister Villèle (1773 – 1854) from 1821 to 1827.
◇1820   Lamartine (1790 – 1869) publishes *Méditations poétiques*. Ampère (1775 – 1836) discovers electrodynamics.
Arago (1786 – 1853) succeeds in magnetizing iron using electricity.
◆1821   Death of Napoleon at St Helena.
◇1821   Saint-Simon (1760 – 1825) develops in *Le Système industriel* a liberal version of industrial progress that is the precursor of an enlightened socialism, which will form the basis of Saint-Simonism.
◇1822   Champollion (1790 – 1832), the founder of Egyptology, deciphers the Egyptian hieroglyphs.
◇1823   Lamartine publishes *Nouvelles méditations*.
Saint-Simon publishes *Le Catéchisme des industriels*.
◆1824   The Chambre retrouvée: triumph of the Ultras at the legislative elections and reign of Charles X (1757 – 1836), who tries to restore the Ancien Régime.
◇1824   Arago (1786 – 1853) discovers the magnetism of rotation. Carnot (1796 – 1832) publishes his *Réflexions sur la puissance motrice du feu* (Reflections on the Motive Power of Fire), which is the foundation of thermodynamics.
◆1825   France recognizes the independence of Haiti.
◆1826   Having failed to re-establish the law of primogeniture, Charles X promulgates a more liberal Constitution.
◇1826   Brillat-Savarin (1755 – 1826) publishes his gastronomic treatise *Physiologie du Goût* (The Physiology of Taste).
◇1827   Victor Hugo (1802 – 1885) publishes his *Préface de Cromwell* (Preface to Cromwell), which marks the beginning of Romantic theatre, for which it is a manifesto.
◇1828   Berlioz (1803 – 1869) composes *La Symphonie fantastique*. Delacroix (1798 – 1863) paints *La Mort de Sardanapale*.

1830 – 1848   The July Monarchy

◆1830   The July Revolution (26 – 28 July) overthrows Charles X and heralds the reign of Louis Philippe I (1773 – 1850) of Valois.

1810

1820

1830

English/Anglais	French/Français

◇1832 William Chambers, auteur et libraire écossais, lance le *Chambers Edinburgh Journal* et peu après fonde avec son frère la maison d'édition W. & R. Chambers.
✦1833 Naissance de l'Oxford Movement (Le Mouvement d'Oxford), qui veut réformer l'Église anglicane en la rapprochant de la doctrine et des usages catholiques.
Abolition de l'esclavage dans l'empire britannique.
Le mathématicien anglais Charles Babbage (1792 – 1871) conçoit, sans la réaliser, une machine à calculer analytique qui peut être considérée comme l'ancêtre de l'ordinateur.
Des ouvriers agricoles du Dorset (les Tolpuddle Martyrs) organisent le premier syndicat. Ils sont condamnés à la déportation vers l'Australie.
◇1833 – 1834 L'homme de lettres écossais Thomas Carlyle publie son ouvrage de philosophie sociale 'Sartor Resartus'.
◇1835 Enregistrement du brevet du revolver Colt, de Samuel Colt (1814 – 1862).
✦1836 Début de la grande migration des Boers (The Great Trek) qui quittent la colonie du Cap pour échapper à la domination anglaise.
◇1836 Début de la publication par épisodes du premier roman de Charles Dickens (1812 – 1870), *The Pickwick Papers* (Les Aventures de M. Pickwick).
◇1837 Victoria (1819 – 1901) accède au trône.
◇1837 Sir Charles Wheatstone (1802 – 1875) fait breveter son télégraphe électrique.
Publication d'*Oliver Twist*, de Charles Dickens.
L'Américain Samuel Morse (1791 – 1872) invente le morse.
◇1839 L'inventeur américain Charles Goodyear (1800 – 1860) découvre la vulcanisation du caoutchouc.
L'Anglais William Fox-Talbot invente le calotype, procédé photographique qui fut le précurseur des procédés actuels car il donnait un négatif et permettait de tirer plusieurs positifs.
✦1839 Des émeutes éclatent en Grande-Bretagne, provoquées par le mouvement d'émancipation ouvrière des chartistes.

The ideas of the revolution in France open the way to the idea of Nation in Belgium: the States General proclaim the separation of the North and South, and the neutrality of Belgium, against the decision of the Congress of Vienna.
Beginning of the colonial conquest of Algeria. Taking of Algiers and Oran.
◇1830 Start of publication of the *Cours de philosophie positive* (1830 – 1848) by Auguste Comte (1798 – 1857), the founder of Positivism.
Lamartine (1790 – 1869) publishes *Harmonies Poétiques* (Poetical and Religious Harmonies).
Stendhal (1783 – 1842) writes *Le Rouge et le Noir* (Scarlet and Black).
Delacroix paints *La Barricade* and *La Liberté guidant le peuple* (Liberty Guiding the People).
✦1831 Revolt of the 'canuts' (silk workers) of Lyon.
The Independence of Belgium is ratified by the London Conference.
Léopold de Saxe-Coburg-Gotha is proposed as King of Belgium.
◇1831 Victor Hugo writes *Notre Dame-de-Paris* (The Hunchback of Notre Dame).
Michelet (1798 – 1874) publishes *Introduction à l'Histoire Universelle*.
◇1833 Guizot Law (1787 – 1874) on primary education paid for by the communes for the most impoverished. Ozanam founds the Saint-Vincent-de-Paul charity.
◇1833 Michelet publishes *Histoire de France* (1833 – 1867).
Balzac writes *Eugénie Grandet*.
Musset (1810 – 1857) writes *Les Caprices de Marianne*.
✦1834 In Algiers, the emir Abd-el-Kader (1808 – 1883) leads the resistance against the French conquest.
◇1834 Musset publishes *Lorenzaccio* and *On ne badine pas avec l'amour*.
Balzac writes *Le Père Goriot*.
Daumier (1808 – 1879) creates the lithograph *La rue Transnonain*.
✦1835 Failed assassination attempt against Louis Philippe.
Abd-el-Kader is defeated at the battle of Makta.
◇1835 Alexis de Tocqueville (1805 – 1859) publishes *De la Démocratie en Amérique* (1837 – 1840).
✦1836 Ministry of Adolphe Thiers (1797 – 1877). First attempted insurrection by Louis-Napoleon Bonaparte.
✦1837 Taking of Constantine in Algeria.
Revolts (1837 – 1838) in French-speaking Lower Canada (present-day Quebec) in favour of a parliamentary system. The revolts are harshly suppressed.
◇1837 Balzac publishes *Les Illusions perdues* (Lost Illusions).
Berlioz (1803 – 1869) composes his *Requiem*.
Chopin (1810 – 1849) composes *24 préludes opus 28*.
◇1838 L.J.M. Daguerre (1787 – 1851) produces the first daguerreotypes.

1840

✦1840 La Grande-Bretagne annexe la Nouvelle-Zélande.

✦1842 La Grande-Bretagne acquiert Hongkong.
✦1843 Les Britanniques s'emparent du Natal, alors tenu par les Boers.

✦1845 Entrée du Texas dans l'Union, ce qui provoque la guerre contre le Mexique (1846 – 1848).
✦1845 – 1851 Une famine causée par la maladie de la pomme de terre prive l'Irlande de la moitié de sa population, par mort ou émigration.

✦1846 Le Premier ministre Robert Peel abroge les Corn Laws, provoquant la scission de son parti. Benjamin Disraeli (1804 – 1881), adversaire de Peel, s'impose sur la scène politique.
◇1846 Fondation de la Smithsonian Institution, à Washington.

◇1847 Publication de *Jane Eyre*, de Charlotte Brontë (1816 – 1855).
Publication des *Hauts de Hurlevent* (Wuthering Heights), d'Emily Brontë (1818 – 1848).

✦1848 Ruée vers l'or en Californie.
Le parlement britannique abroge la loi qui interdisait l'usage du français au Canada.
◇1848 Le physicien britannique William Kelvin (qui deviendra Lord Kelvin) (1824 – 1907) établit une échelle théorique des températures (température absolue).
Création de la Confrérie des Préraphaélites, mouvement visant à renouveler l'art victorien.
Publication de *La Foire aux vanités* (Vanity Fair), de William Thackeray (1811 – 1863).

◇1840 France annexes Mayotte and Nossi-Bé (1840 – 1842) in the Comoros islands.
In the South Antarctic, Dumont d'Urville (1790 – 1842) takes possession of Adelie Land.
Act of Union of the two Canadas (present-day Quebec and Ontario) to form United Canada.
French ceases to be an official language in Canada.
◇1840 Pierre Joseph Proudhon (1809 – 1865), theoretician of socialism, publishes *Qu'est-ce que la propriété* (What is Property?).
◇1842 Eugène Sue (1804 – 1857) publishes *Les Mystères de Paris* in serial form.
✦1843 Taking of the retinue of chief Abd-el-Kader by the troops of the duke of Aumale (1822 – 1897).
Tahiti (Polynesia) becomes a French protectorate after conquest by Admiral Dupetit-Thouars (1793 – 1864).
✦1844 Franco-Moroccan war: bombing of Tangiers.
◇1844 Alexandre Dumas père (1802 – 1870) writes *Les Trois mousquetaires* (The Three Musketeers), an historical adventure story.
Prosper Mérimée (1803 – 1870) writes *Carmen*.
◇1846 Expedition of Père Huc (1813 – 1860) to Tibet and China.
✦1847 In Paris, the prohibition, during the electoral campaign, of banquets organized by the opponents to the regime of Louis-Philippe serves as a catalyst for the revolution that is to break out in 1848.
In Algeria, the surrender of Abd-el-Kader marks the beginning of French colonial rule.
The passing of a new Constitution transforms the Swiss Confederation into a genuine Federal State.
◇1847 Beginning of the publication (1847 – 1853) of Michelet's *L'Histoire de la Révolution Française*.
The painters Théodore Rousseau and Jean François Millet settle in Barbizon, where Corot and Courbet also spent periods of time. The Barbizon School is formed.

1848 – 1852 The Second Republic

✦1848 February French Revolution: the democratically and socially inspired popular Paris uprising brings about the fall of Louis-Philippe and the proclamation of the Second Republic (1848 – 1852) by a provisional government including figures such as Lamartine.
Decree on the abolition of slavery in the French colonies.
Canada: the British Parliament abrogates the article of the Act of Union that banned the French language.
Taking advantage of the Revolution, Louis-Napoleon Bonaparte (1808 – 1873) has himself made President of the Republic on 10 December and promulgates a new Constitution. From this moment, he methodically prepares the coup d'état which will make him Emperor of France.
◇1848 René de Chateaubriand (1768 – 1848) writes *Mémoires d'Outre-Tombe* (Memoires from Beyond the Tomb) (1848 – 1850).
Alexandre Dumas fils (1824 – 1895) writes *La Dame aux Camélias* (The Lady of the Camelias).

English/Anglais	French/Français
	◇1849 The physicist H. Fizeau (1819 – 1896) determines the speed of light and observes the infrared spectrum.

— 1850 —

English/Anglais	French/Français
◇1850 Publication de *David Copperfield*, de Charles Dickens. ◆1851 La Grande Exposition de Londres célèbre l'essor de l'industrie britannique. Elle se tient au Crystal Palace, construit à cette occasion. Ruée vers l'or en Australie. ◇1851 L'auteur américain Herman Melville (1819 – 1891) publie *Moby Dick* qui est considéré comme l'un des plus grands romans américains.	◇1850 At the 1850 Salon, Gustave Courbet (1819 – 1877) exhibits his painting *L'Enterrement à Ornans* (Burial at Ornans), the 'realism' of which scandalizes the critics. ◆1851 Coup d'état of the Prince-President Louis-Napoleon Bonaparte. ◇1851 Eugène Labiche's (1815 – 1888) *Le Chapeau de paille d'Italie* is performed (marking the birth of light comedy theatre). Claude Bernard (1813 – 1878) discovers the glycogenic function of the liver.

1852 – 1870 The Second Empire

English/Anglais	French/Français
◇1852 William Holman Hunt (1827 – 1910) peint *The Light of the World*. L'Américaine Harriet Beecher Stowe (1811 – 1896) publie *La Case de l'oncle Tom* (Uncle Tom's Cabin), roman qui contribuera à mobiliser l'opinion publique contre l'esclavage.	◆1852 Louis-Napoleon Bonaparte has himself proclaimed Emperor and becomes Napoleon III. He is to be deposed in 1870. ◇1852 The physicist Foucault (1819 – 1868) determines the velocity of light by the revolving mirror method. He goes on to demonstrate the rotation of the Earth with a pendulum. Establishment of the first department store in Paris, the Bon Marché on the left bank. ◆1853 Haussmann (1809 – 1891) is appointed prefect of the Seine. He revolutionizes the design of Paris and other cities of France with a view to modernizing the city and moving the working population away, largely to allow the police and army to exert control when needed. France occupies New Caledonia. Gobineau (1816 – 1882), diplomat and writer, sets forth in his *Essai sur l'inégalité des races* (The Inequality of Human Races) doctrines that are to become the inspiration of various racist theoreticians. ◆1854 Faidherbe (1818 – 1889) is appointed Governor General of Senegal (1854-1865).

}{

English/Anglais	French/Français
◆1854 – 1856 Guerre de Crimée: l'Angleterre et la France luttent aux côtés de la Turquie contre la Russie. ◆1854 Épisode de la charge de la brigade légère (the Charge of the Light Brigade). Florence Nightingale organise les hôpitaux de campagne. Victoires de l'Alma et d'Inkerman (avec les Français), et de Balaklava. ◇1855 L'auteur anglais Anthony Trollope publie *The Warden*, premier volume de sa Chronique des Barset. Walt Whitman (1819 – 1891) publie *Leaves of Grass* (Feuilles d'herbe). ◆1856 L'explorateur britannique David Livingstone (1813 – 1873) traverse l'Afrique d'Est en Ouest et 'découvre' les chutes qu'il baptise Victoria Falls (les chutes Victoria). ◇1856 L'Américain Elisha Otis (1811 – 1861) invente l'ascenseur. ◆1856 – 1858 Révolte des Cipayes ('the Indian Mutiny'): en Inde, les soldats indigènes recrutés par les Britanniques se soulèvent. La Compagnie des Indes Orientales transfère le contrôle de ses territoires à la Couronne. ◆1858 – 1864 Ruée vers l'or dans le Colorado et au Névada. ◇1859 Le philosophe utilitariste anglais J.S. Mill (1806 – 1873) publie *On Liberty* (La Liberté). Charles Darwin publie *The Origin of Species* (De l'origine des espèces au moyen de la sélection naturelle).	Crimean war: France and Britain fight alongside Turkey against Russia. A Franco-British coalition defeats the Russians at the battles of Alma and Inkerman. ◇1854 Gérard de Nerval (1808 – 1855) publishes his poems *Les Chimères*. Some of his work prefigures the surrealist experiments of the 20th century. ◆1855 Ferdinand de Lesseps (1805 – 1894) obtains permission to build the Suez Canal from the viceroy of Egypt. ◇1855 Paris Universal Exhibition. Courbet paints *L'Atelier du Peintre* (Studio of the Painter). ◇1857 Surrender of Kabylia (Algeria). Faidherbe founds the port of Dakar (Africa). French occupation of Canton (China). ◇1857 Gustave Flaubert (1821 – 1880) writes *Madame Bovary*. The anthology of poetry by Charles Baudelaire (1821 – 1867), *Les Fleurs du Mal* (Flowers of Evil), results in censorship and makes his name as a caustic and morbid critic of modern society. ◆1858 Creation of the first Ministry for Algeria in Paris. ◆1858 First aerial photograph (in a balloon) taken by F. Tournachon, known as Nadar (1820 – 1910). He goes on to immortalize the celebrities of his time. Visions of Bernadette Soubirous at Lourdes, which turn the town into a place of pilgrimage. ◆1859 War of Italy between Austria and Piedmont allied with France. Victories at the battles of Magenta and Solferino. Napoleon III and the Emperor of Austria sign the armistice of Villafranca, which completes the Austrian defeat. First French occupation of Saigon, which marks the beginning of its involvement in Indochina. Foundation of the bank Société Générale.

— 1860 —

English/Anglais	French/Français
◆1860 Robert Burke (1820 – 1861) et William Wills (1834 – 1861) dirigent la première expédition à travers l'Australie (du Nord au Sud). ◇1860 Publication du *Moulin sur la Floss* (The Mill on the Floss) de Mary Ann Evans (1819 – 1880), alias George Eliot. ◆1860 – 1861 Aux États-Unis, onze États du Sud qui s'opposent à l'abolition de l'esclavage font sécession et forment une Confédération. ◆1861 Abraham Lincoln, antiesclavagiste, est élu à la présidence des États-Unis. Début de la guerre de Sécession (American Civil War) entre le Nord et le Sud. À la première bataille de Bull Run, victoire sudiste sous le commandement du général Thomas 'Stonewall' Jackson. ◇1862 Herbert Spencer (1820 – 1822), philosophe évolutionniste adepte des théories de Darwin, publie le premier volume de son *System of Synthetic Philosophy* (Système de philosophie synthétique). C'est lui qui a forgé l'expression 'the survival of the fittest' (la survie du plus fort). L'Américaine Julia Ward Howe (1819 – 1910) écrit *The Battle Hymn of the Republic*, hymne nordiste. ◆1863 Aux États-Unis, Abraham Lincoln abolit l'esclavage. La victoire des nordistes à la bataille de Gettysburg marque un tournant décisif dans la guerre de Sécession. Sur les lieux de la bataille, Lincoln prononce son fameux discours, la Gettysburg address. ◇1863 Inauguration de la première ligne de métro à Londres. ◇1864 Henry Newman (1801 – 1890), théologien, cardinal et l'une des principales figures du Mouvement d'Oxford, publie son autobiographie spirituelle *Apologia Pro Vita Sua*. Le mathématicien écossais James Maxwell (1831 – 1879) publie ses recherches sur le lien entre lumière et électricité. ◆1865 Reddition des confédérés du général Lee aux troupes nordistes du général Grant à Appomattox, en Virginie. Fin de la guerre de Sécession. Assassinat de Lincoln dans un théâtre de Washington par John Wilkes Booth.	◆1860 In recognition of the French intervention in Italy, Piedmont cedes Savoy and Nice to France. In Lebanon, the French intervention against the Druze during the massacres of Damas leads to the first French occupation of Syria (1860 – 1861). ◇1860 Invention of the internal combustion engine by Lenoir (1822 – 1900). ◇1861 Charles Garnier (1825 – 1898) begins the building of the Paris Opera House (1862 – 1874). ◆1862 Annam (Indochina) cedes Cochin China to France which completes its conquest in 1867. French expedition to Mexico (1862 – 1867). ◇1862 Hugo publishes his novel *Les Misérables*. Flaubert publishes *Salâmmbo*. ◆1863 France imposes its protectorate on Cambodia. Foundation of the bank Crédit Lyonnais. ◇1863 Édouard Manet (1832 – 1883) paints *Déjeuner sur l'herbe* and *Olympia*. ◆1864 Foundation of the International Red Cross in Geneva (Geneva Convention), at the initiative of the philanthropist Henri Dunant (1828 – 1910). He is awarded the first Nobel Peace Prize in 1901. ◇1864 Alfred de Vigny (1797 – 1863) publishes *Les Destinées*. Gounod (1818 – 1893) composes the opera *Mireille*. Offenbach (1819 – 1880) composes the opera *La Belle Hélène*. Jules Verne (1828 – 1905) writes *Voyage au centre de la terre* (A Journey to the Centre of the Earth). ◇1865 Cl. Bernard (1813 – 1878) writes *Introduction à la médecine expérimentale* (Introduction to the Study of Experimental Medicine). ◇1866 Offenbach composes the opera *La Vie Parisienne* (Parisian Life). The *Grand Dictionnaire Universel du XIXème siècle* (1866 – 1876) is published by Pierre Larousse (1817 – 1875). ◆1867 Retreat of French troops from Mexico.

| English/Anglais | French/Français |

◇1865 Publication d'*Alice au pays des merveilles* (Alice in Wonderland), de Charles Dodgson (1832 – 1898), alias Lewis Carroll.
✦1867 Les États-Unis achètent l'Alaska à la Russie.
Création du dominion du Canada qui a désormais sa propre constitution.
✦1868 L'Anglais William Gladstone, chef du parti libéral, devient Premier ministre. Pendant son premier mandat il sépare l'Église de l'État en Irlande et généralise l'enseignement primaire.
Création du British Trades Union Congress (Congrès des Syndicats Britanniques).
◇1868 Publication du roman autobiographique *Les Quatre filles du Dr March* (Little Women), de la romancière américaine Louisa May Alcott (1832 – 1888).
✦1869 La jonction des voies ferroviaires des compagnies du Central Pacific et de l'Union Pacific établit la première ligne transcontinentale aux États-Unis.

Canada: coming into force of the Canadian Constitution. Article 133 gives French the status of official language in the Parliaments of Ottawa and Quebec and before the federal and Quebec courts.
◇1867 Gounod composes *Roméo et Juliette*. J.-F. Millet (1814 – 1875) paints *L'Angelus*.
J.-B. Clément's song *Le Temps des cerises* becomes an emblem of popular song.
Universal Exhibition in Paris.
◇1868 A. Daudet (1840 – 1897) publishes *Le Petit Chose* (Young What's His Name).
Discovery of the first remains of Cro-Magnon man at Eyzies-de-Tayac (Dordogne).
◇1869 Daudet publishes *Les lettres de mon moulin* (Letters from my Mill). Flaubert writes *L'Éducation sentimentale* (Sentimental Education).

—— 1870 ——

✦1870 Succeeding the Empire, the Government of National Defence headed by Léon Gambetta (1838 – 1882) proclaims the Third Republic (1870 – 1940), but is unable to prevent the Franco-Prussian War, which ends in the Defeat of Sedan and the Siege of Paris.
◇1870 Léo Delibes (1836 – 1891) composes *Coppelia*.

1871 – 1940 The Third Republic

◇1871 L'Américain James Whistler (1834 – 1903) peint le *Portrait de la mère de l'artiste* (Arrangement in Grey and Black — the Artist's Mother), influencé par l'art japonais.

✦1871 Government leader Adolphe Thiers signs the Frankfurt Peace Treaty which completes the French defeat with the loss of Alsace-Lorraine. The success of the monarchists in the legislative elections provokes the insurrection of the Commune in Paris (March to May), supported by the working classes. It is brutally repressed in the 'Semaine Sanglante' by the troops of the Thiers government from its seat at Versailles.
◇1871 Émile Zola (1840 – 1902) publishes his sociological novel, *La Fortune des Rougon* (The Fortunes of the Rougons), the first part of his novelistic work on the Rougon-Macquart family which forms the basis of naturalism in France.
✦1873 Marshall MacMahon (1808 – 1893), a legitimist, becomes President, but is forced to resign in 1879. Occupation of Hanoi by France.
◇1873 Arthur Rimbaud (1854 – 1891) publishes *Une saison en enfer* (A Season in Hell), poems in prose that are revolutionary both in spirit and tone.
Jules Verne publishes *Le Tour du monde en quatre-vingts jours* (Around the World in Eighty Days).
✦1874 At the Nadar studio, Claude Monet (1840 – 1926) exhibits *Impression, soleil levant* (Impression: Sunrise), which gives its name to the Impressionist movement.
Verlaine publishes the poems *Romances sans paroles* (Romances Without Words).
◇1875 Georges Bizet (1838 – 1875) composes the opera *Carmen*.
Camille Saint-Saëns (1835 – 1921) composes *Danse macabre*.
◇1876 Auguste Renoir (1841 – 1919) paints *Le Moulin de la Galette* (The Ball at the Moulin de la Galette).
Start of construction (1876 – 1912) of the Sacré-Cœur Basilica in Paris, built to atone for the Commune's revolt.
◇1877 Zola writes *L'Assommoir* (The Drunkard).
Saint-Saëns composes the opera *Samson et Dalila*.
✦1879 Jules Grévy (1807 – 1891) is elected President of the Republic (1879 – 1887).
◇1879 Pasteur (1822 – 1895) discovers the principle of vaccine by inoculating with microbes.

✦1874 – 1880 Benjamin Disraeli, conservateur, est Premier ministre. C'est pour la Grande-Bretagne une période de réformes sociales et de succès diplomatiques.
✦1875 La Grande-Bretagne achète le canal de Suez.
◇1875 Publication des *Aventures de Tom Sawyer* (The Adventures of Tom Sawyer), de Mark Twain (1835 – 1910).
✦1876 La reine Victoria est proclamée impératrice des Indes.
Bataille de Little Bighorn contre les Sioux de Sitting Bull: Custer et son régiment sont tués.
◇1876 L'inventeur américain d'origine écossaise Alexander Graham Bell (1847 – 1922) fait breveter son téléphone.
◇1877 Création de l'Armée du salut (The Salvation Army) à Londres par l'Anglais William Booth (1829 – 1912).
L'inventeur américain Thomas Edison (1847 – 1931) fait breveter le phonographe.
✦1879 En Afrique du Sud, défaite des Zoulous face aux Britanniques.

—— 1880 ——

✦1880 – 1881 En Afrique du Sud, la première guerre des Boers (guerre du Transvaal) contre la domination anglaise se termine par la défaite des troupes britanniques à Majuba Hill.
✦1880 Le hors-la-loi Ned Kelly (1854 – 1881) est exécuté en Australie.
◇1880 Adoption du temps solaire moyen de Greenwich en Grande-Bretagne.
✦1881 Le hors-la-loi 'Billy the Kid' (William Bonney (1858 – 1881)) est abattu au Nouveau-Mexique.
Fusillade à OK Corral à Tombstone, dans l'Arizona, dont Wyatt Earp (1848 – 1929) sort vainqueur.
◇1881 Publication d'*Un Portrait de femme* (Portrait of a Lady), de l'Américain Henry James (1843 – 1916).
✦1883 Paul Kruger (1825 – 1904) devient président de la république du Transvaal.
◇1883 Publication de *L'Île au trésor* (Treasure Island), de l'auteur écossais Robert Louis Stevenson (1850 – 1894).
Sir Hiram Maxim (1840 – 1916), Américain devenu citoyen britannique, invente le premier fusil automatique, le fusil Maxim.
◇1884 Parution de la première partie de l'*Oxford English Dictionary*.
✦1885 Fondation du Congrès National Indien, dont le but est d'affranchir le pays de la domination britannique.
Le général Gordon est tué à Khartoum, au Soudan, après avoir soutenu un siège de dix mois.
Le Britannique Cecil Rhodes (1853 – 1902) s'empare du Bechuanaland (aujourd'hui le Botswana), en Afrique australe.
✦1886 En Grande-Bretagne, le gouvernement de Gladstone essaie d'introduire le 'Home Rule' (projet de gouvernement autonome de l'Irlande). Le projet échoue et provoque la chute de Gladstone et la scission du parti libéral.
◇1886 La Statue de la Liberté (*La Liberté éclairant le monde*) cadeau de la France aux États-Unis, est installée dans le port de New York.

✦1880 Government of Jules Ferry.
◇1880 Guy de Maupassant (1850 – 1893) writes *Boule de Suif* (Ball of Tallow).
Zola writes *Nana*.
Rodin (1840 – 1917) completes the sculpture *Le Penseur* (The Thinker).
✦1881 Jules Ferry (1832 – 1893) has laws passed on freedom of assembly, of the press and trade union rights, and gives his name to educational legislation providing compulsory, free and non-religious primary schooling.
France establishes the protectorate of Tunisia, brought in by the Treaty of Bardo.
Ferdinand de Lesseps begins work on the Panama Canal.
◇1881 Édouard Manet (1832 – 1883) paints *Un bar aux Folies-Bergères* (A Bar at the Folies-Bergère).
The mathematician Henri Poincaré (1854 – 1912) discovers a general method for resolving differential equations.
✦1883 The second Jules Ferry cabinet (1883 – 1885) pursues a policy of colonial expansion, marked by the establishment of a French protectorate over Annam, the occupation of Madagascar and the foundation of Bamako (now Mali).
◇1883 Maupassant publishes *Une vie* (A Woman's Life).
The Egyptologist Gaston Maspéro (1846 – 1916) begins exploration of the Temple at Luxor and the Sphinx at Gîza.
✦1884 The Waldeck-Rousseau (1846 – 1904) law legalizes trade unions.
◇1884 Georges Seurat (1859 – 1891) radicalizes Impressionism with his painting *Un dimanche après-midi à la Grande-Jatte* (Sunday Afternoon on the Island of La Grande Jatte).
✦1885 Resignation of Jules Ferry following a setback in Tonkin.
The Republic resists as best it can the Boulangist crisis (1885 – 1889) instigated by the agitation of nationalists and monarchists led by General Boulanger (1837 – 1891) who is forced into exile in Belgium following an aborted attempt at a coup d'etat.
The Congo, personal property of Leopold II, becomes a Belgian possession. Universal suffrage is introduced in Belgium.
◇1885 Pasteur produces the first vaccine against rabies.

English/Anglais	French/Français

English/Anglais

◊1887 Publication de la première histoire de Sherlock Holmes, de l'Écossais Conan Doyle (1859 – 1930).
◊1888 L'industriel américain George Eastman (1854 – 1932) met au point le premier appareil photo portatif Kodak.
Le vétérinaire écossais John Dunlop (1840 – 1921) invente le pneu.

✦1889 Création de la Rhodésie (aujourd'hui la Zambie et le Zimbabwe) à partir de territoires occupés par la British South Africa Company de Cecil Rhodes.

———— 1890

✦1890 Massacre d'Indiens d'Amérique à Wounded Knee par l'armée américaine.
Première exécution à la chaise électrique aux États-Unis.
◊1891 Publication du Portrait de Dorian Gray (The Picture of Dorian Gray), de l'auteur irlandais Oscar Wilde (1854 – 1900).
L'auteur anglais Thomas Hardy (1840 – 1928) publie Tess of the d'Urbervilles (Tess d'Urberville).

✦1892 L'Écossais Keir Hardie (1856 – 1915) devient le premier député travailliste.

✦1893 Deuxième projet de loi sur le 'Home Rule' (voir 1896), adopté par la Chambre des communes mais rejeté par la Chambre des lords.

◊1894 Publication du Livre de la jungle (The Jungle Book), de Rudyard Kipling (1865 – 1936).

◊1895 Première représentation de The Importance of being Earnest (De l'importance d'être constant), pièce de l'écrivain irlandais Oscar Wilde.

◊1896 Publication d'Un Gars du Shropshire (A Shropshire Lad), du poète anglais A.E. Housman (1859 – 1936).

✦1898 À la fin de la guerre hispano-américaine, les États-Unis annexent Porto Rico et les Philippines.
Annexion de Hawaii.

✦1899 – 1902 Deuxième guerre du Transvaal en Afrique du Sud.
◊1899 Le compositeur anglais Edward Elgar (1857 – 1934) achève ses Enigma Variations.
✦1899 Un accord franco-anglais consacre le renoncement de la France sur le Nil en faveur des Britanniques.

———— 1900 ————

1901 – 1917 Les Saxe-Cobourg-Gotha

✦1901 La reine Victoria meurt après 64 ans de règne. Son fils aîné Édouard VII (Édouard Ier d'Écosse) lui succède. Il reste le seul souverain de la maison de Saxe-Cobourg. Malgré une conduite dissipée avant son accession au trône, il se montre habile diplomate.

French/Français

Zola publishes Germinal.
◊1886 Rodin sculpts Le Baiser (The Kiss).
Bartholdi (1834 – 1904) creates La Liberté éclairant le monde (Statue of Liberty) (a gift from France to the United States).
✦1887 Marie François Sadi Carnot (1837 – 1894) is elected President of the Republic.
Creation of French-English joint sovereignty over the New Hebrides.
Creation of the Union of Indochina.
◊1887 Gabriel Fauré composes Requiem.
✦1888 Issue of the first Russian loan in Paris.
◊1888 Vincent Van Gogh (1853 – 1890) paints La chambre de Vincent à Arles (Vincent's Room, Arles).
Opening of the Pasteur Institute.
◊1889 Henri Bergson (1859 – 1941) publishes Essai sur les données immédiates de la conscience (Time and Freewill).
The engineer Gustave Eiffel (1832 – 1923) builds the Eiffel Tower for the Paris World Exhibition.
Vincent Van Gogh paints Autoportrait à l'oreille coupée (Self-Portrait with Bandaged Ear).

✦1890 Establishment of a French-English colonial agreement over Madagascar, Zanzibar and the Sudan.
1 May is made international labour day at the congress of the second Socialist International in Paris.
◊1890 E.J. Marey (1830 – 1904) devises the first sequential photography, from which cinema develops.
Clément Ader makes the first aeroplane flight.
✦1891 The Panama financial scandal (1891 – 1893) gives rise to a wave of protests orchestrated by the opposition.
Strengthening of the labour movement, in spite of the bloody repression of a workers' strike in favour of the 8-hour day at Fourmies, on 1 May.
◊1891 First petrol-driven car built by R. Panhard and his partner É. Levassor.
Toulouse-Lautrec creates the poster La Goulue au Moulin-Rouge (Moulin Rouge, La Goulue).
'Scélérates' laws: repression of anarchist ideas and the anarchist movement.
◊1892 Toulouse-Lautrec paints Jeanne-Avril dansant (Jeanne Avril Dancing).
Paul Cézanne (1839 – 1906) paints Les Joueurs de cartes (The Card Players)
✦1893 Siam cedes the left bank of the Mekong to France. French protectorate over Laos.
◊1893 Marey builds the first cinema projector.
Émile Durkheim (1858 – 1917), one of the founders of sociology, publishes De la division du travail social (The Division of Labour in Society).
✦1894 President Sadi Carnot is assassinated by an anarchist.
Establishment of the French protectorate over Dahomey (now Benin).
The Dreyfus Affair: the officer Alfred Dreyfus (1859 – 1935) is unjustly accused of spying for Germany. He is dismissed and deported to Guyana.
✦1895 Félix Faure (1841 – 1899) becomes President of the Republic until 1899. Foundation of the national trades congress, the Confédération Générale du Travail (C.G.T.).
Organization of French West Africa consisting of Senegal, Mauritania, Sudan (Mali), Upper Volta (Burkina Faso), Niger, Ivory Coast and Dahomey. Annexation of Madagascar (1895 – 96).
◊1895 The Lumière brothers, Louis (1864 – 1948) and Auguste (1862 – 1954), invent cinematography: their first short films are L'Arrivée d'un train en gare de La Ciotat, L'arroseur arrosé.
✦1896 Departure of the Marchand expedition (1863 – 1934) to link the Nile with the Congo. J. B. Marchand reaches the Nile at Fashoda.
Madagascar becomes a French colony.
Constitution of French Indochina.
◊1896 Alfred Jarry (1873 – 1907) writes the play Ubu Roi, a forerunner of the Theatre of the Absurd.
Henri Becquerel (1852 – 1908) discovers radioactivity.
◊1897 Stéphane Mallarmé publishes the poem Un coup de dés jamais n'abolira le hasard (A Throw of Dice Will Never Abolish the Hazard).
André Gide (1869 – 1951) publishes Les Nourritures terrestres (Fruits of the Earth).
✦1898 Publication of J'accuse (I accuse): Émile Zola's plea on behalf of Dreyfus is published in the newspaper L'Aurore, and brings the affair into public debate. At the same time, the French extreme right founds Action Française.
◊1898 Pierre (1859 – 1906) and Marie (1867 – 1934) Curie discover polonium and radium.
Edmond Rostand (1868 – 1918) writes the play Cyrano de Bergerac.
✦1899 Émile Loubet (1838 – 1929) is President of the Republic (1899 – 1906). Formation of the Bloc des Gauches which pursues an anticlerical policy.
Second trial of Dreyfus, sentenced to ten years' imprisonment on 9 September, and pardoned on the 19th.
France concludes the agreement granting British authority over the Nile basin.

✦1900 The French gain possession of the Rabah Empire in Chad.
◊1900 Claude Debussy (1862 – 1918) composes Trois nocturnes.
Colette (1873 – 1954) publishes Claudine à l'école (first novel in the Claudine series).
World Exhibition and Summer Olympic Games held in Paris.
Opening of the Paris metro.

English/Anglais	French/Français

English/Anglais

Un acte du Parlement impérial crée le Commonwealth d'Australie avec pour capitale Canberra.
Le premier message transatlantique par télégraphie sans fil, la lettre 'S', est transmis de Cornouailles à Terre-Neuve.
◆1902 Victoire des Anglais contre les Boers lors de la seconde guerre du Transvaal.
◇1902 Le philosophe américain William James (1842 – 1910) publie *The Varieties of Religious Experience* (Les Variétés de l'expérience religieuse). La même année, son frère Henry James (1843 – 1916) écrit *The Wings of a Dove* (Les Ailes de la colombe).
Rudyard Kipling (1865 – 1936) publie un recueil d'histoires pour enfants *Just So Stories* (Histoires comme ça).
◇1903 Les frères Wright, Orville (1871 – 1948) et Wilbur (1867 – 1912), effectuent le premier vol mécanique à Kitty Hawk en Caroline du Sud.
◆1904 Signature de l'Entente Cordiale par la France et la Grande-Bretagne.
◇1904 Première représentation de *Peter Pan*, de J.M. Barrie (1860 – 1937). Première représentation de *Man and Superman* (L'Homme et le Surhomme) et *Major Barbara* (La Commandante Barbara) de George Bernard Shaw (1856 – 1950).
Les jeux Olympiques ont lieu à Saint Louis, aux États-Unis.

◇1905 Albert Einstein (1879 – 1947), physicien allemand naturalisé américain, publie un mémoire sur sa théorie de la relativité restreinte.

◆1906 Le British Labour Representation Committee adopte le nom de 'Labour Party'. La même année ce parti réclame le droit de vote pour les femmes.
Tremblement de terre et incendie de San Francisco.

◆1907 Triple Entente entre la France, la Grande-Bretagne et la Russie.

◇1907 La première représentation de la pièce *The Playboy of the Western World* (Le Baladin du monde occidental) de J.M. Synge (1871 – 1909) provoque des scènes d'émeute à Dublin.
L'Anglais Rudyard Kipling (1865 – 1936) remporte le prix Nobel de littérature.
◇1908 L'ingénieur automobile américain John Ford (1863 – 1947) lance son Modèle T, première voiture construite en série.
Le romancier anglais E.M. Forster (1879 – 1970) publie *A Room with a View* (Une chambre d'où l'on voit), œuvre dans laquelle il examine la bourgeoisie anglaise.
Les jeux Olympiques ont lieu à Londres.

◆1910 À la mort d'Édouard VII, son fils George V (1865 – 1936) lui succède.
L'Union d'Afrique du Sud (réunion de plusieurs provinces autonomes) devient un dominion.

◆1912 Naufrage du Titanic.
◇1912 L'explorateur anglais R.F. Scott entreprend une expédition dans l'Antarctique. Il atteint le pôle Sud où le Norvégien Amundsen l'avait devancé de 35 jours, mais périt avec ses hommes au retour de ce raid.

◇1913 *Sons and Lovers* (Fils), roman semi-autobiographique du poète et romancier anglais D.H. Lawrence (1885 – 1930) connaît un immense succès. Deux plus tard, l'auteur sera poursuivi pour obscénité après la publication de *The Rainbow* (L'Arc-en-ciel) qui examine les rapports amoureux du couple.

◆1914 Les troupes allemandes violent la neutralité belge garantie par le traité de Londres de 1839.
La Grande-Bretagne déclare la guerre à l'Allemagne et se bat aux côtés de la France.
Ouverture du canal de Panama. Construit par le corps des ingénieurs américains, il relie l'océan Atlantique au Pacifique.
◆1915 Échec de l'offensive franco-anglaise aux Dardanelles.
Torpillage du Lusitania.

French/Français

◆1901 Promulgation of the law allowing the creation of non-profit-making organizations with the exception of congregations.

◇1902 Debussy composes *Pelléas et Mélisande*.
Georges Méliès (1861 – 1938), *Le Voyage dans la lune* (A Trip to the Moon) (film).
First Lépine award, for inventors of all kinds.

◇1903 The first Tour de France cycle race.
Marie Curie wins the Nobel Prize for physics.

◆1904 Signature of the Entente Cordiale treaty between France and Great Britain.
◇1904 Monet paints *Vues de Londres* (Views of London).
Jean Jaurès founds the newspaper *l'Humanité*.
◆1905 Formation of the SFIO, the French socialist party founded by Jean Jaurès (1859 – 1914) and Jules Guesde.
Culmination of the anticlerical policy of the Bloc des Gauches, the law separating Church and State is promulgated.
◇1905 Rodin completes the sculpture *Victor Hugo*.
Appearance of the term fauvism to describe the paintings of Braque, Matisse, Vlaminck, Derain, Dufy and Van Dongen.
◆1906 Armand Fallières (1841 – 1931) is elected President of the Republic (1906 – 1913).
Georges Clemenceau (1841 – 1929), leader of the Radicals, becomes Prime Minister. Dreyfus' name is finally cleared by the Bloc des Gauches.
◇1906 Bergson publishes *L'évolution créatrice* (Creative Evolution).
Paul Claudel, *Partage de Midi* (play).
Opening of the Simplon tunnel in the Swiss Alps.
◆1907 Formation of the Triple Entente between Great Britain, France and Russia.
Law on freedom of worship in France.
◇1907 Picasso (1881 – 1973) finishes his *Demoiselles d'Avignon* (The Young Ladies of Avignon).
◆1908 Leopold II, King of the Belgians, cedes the Congo, his personal property, to Belgium.
◆1909 Aristide Briand (1862 – 1932) succeeds Clemenceau. The repressive policies of Clemenceau and Briand lead to disunity on the left and to ministerial instability.
◇1909 Louis Blériot (1872 – 1936) makes the first aeroplane flight across the English Channel.
Henri Matisse (1869 – 1954), leader of the Fauves, begins his fresco *La Danse* (Dance).
Foundation of the Ballets Russes by Sergei Diaghilev (1872 – 1929) in Paris.

◆1910 Organization of French Equatorial Africa (A.E.F.) which includes Gabon, Middle Congo (Congo), Ubangi-Shari (Central African Republic) and Chad.
◇1910 Raymond Roussel (1877 – 1933) publishes *Impressions d'Afrique* (Impressions of Africa), a novel that is to inspire surrealism.
Georges Feydeau (1862 – 1921) revives farce with *On purge bébé*.
Charles Péguy (1873 – 1914) publishes his poems *Le mystère de la charité de Jeanne d'Arc* (The Mystery of Joan of Arc's Charity).
◆1911 The Agadir Coup marks the second Moroccan crisis between Germany and France. The settlement of the crisis in favour of France leads to its occupation of Fez the same year.
◇1911 Marie Curie wins the Nobel Prize for chemistry.
◆1912 Raymond Poincaré (1860 – 1934) is Prime Minister. He establishes the French protectorate over Morocco.
Arrest of the criminals of Bonnot's gang, consisting of a group of anarchists specializing in organized crime.
◇1912 Claudel (1868 – 1955) writes the play *L'Annonce faite à Marie* (The Annunciation).
Anatole France publishes his novel *Les dieux ont soif* (The Gods will have Blood).
The choreography of Nijinsky (1889 – 1950) for Debussy's *L'Après-midi d'un faune* (Prelude to the Afternoon of a Faun) marks the beginning of modern ballet and causes scandal in the Paris press.
Marcel Duchamp (1887 – 1968) revolutionizes contemporary art with his *Nu descendant l'escalier* (Nude Descending a Staircase).
◆1913 R. Poincaré becomes President of the Republic (1913 – 1920).
◇1913 Marcel Proust (1871 – 1922) publishes *Du côté de chez Swann* (Swann's Way), the first section of *A la recherche du temps perdu* (Remembrance of Things Past) (1913 – 1927).
Guillaume Apollinaire (1880 – 1918) publishes the poems *Alcools*.
Alain-Fournier (1886 – 1914) publishes *Le Grand Meaulnes* (The Lost Domain).
Louis Feuillade (1873 – 1925) releases *Fantômas* (first in a series of five films).
In Gabon, Albert Schweitzer (1875 – 1965) founds the hospital of Lambaréné.
Roland Garros (1888 – 1918) makes the first aeroplane flight across the Mediterranean.
◆1914 On the same day as the assassination of Jaurès (31 July), Germany lays down its ultimatum to France. On 1 August France orders general mobilization. On 3 August Germany declares war on France.
The Sacred Union (l'Union sacrée) between the parties is urged by Poincaré.
The War begins with victory at the Battle of the Marne.
◆1915 Failure of the French and British Dardanelles naval expedition.

1910

[19]

English/Anglais	French/Français

◇1915 Sortie du film *The Birth of a Nation* (Naissance d'une nation) du réalisateur et novateur américain D.W. Griffith (1875 – 1948) qui marque une étape dans l'histoire du cinéma tant par la technique que par l'esthétique, en dépit d'une idéologie profondément raciste.
✦1916 Première utilisation du char de combat par les troupes britanniques pendant la bataille de la Somme. 420 000 soldats britanniques trouvent la mort au cours de cette série d'offensives et contre-offensives.
À Dublin, les nationalistes irlandais (Sinn Féin) s'insurgent contre la domination anglaise ('the Easter Rising'). Les rebelles proclament un gouvernement provisoire, mais le soulèvement est réprimé au bout de cinq jours et 14 de ses meneurs sont exécutés.

✦1916 Allied offensive on the Somme.
Pétain (1856 – 1951) wins the Battle of Verdun.
◇1916 In his novel *Le Feu* (Under Fire), Henri Barbusse (1873 – 1935) recounts the atrocities of trench warfare.
Foundation of the Dadaist movement in Zurich, around Tristan Tzara and Jean Arp.

1917 – Les Windsor

✦1917 L'entrée en guerre des États-Unis vient soulager la Grande-Bretagne, fortement éprouvée par la pénurie de vivres causée par la présence des sous-marins allemands.
Le Premier ministre britannique, Lloyd George, annonce un projet de loi pour donner le droit de vote aux femmes mariées âgées de plus de 30 ans.
Déclaration Balfour: le ministre des Affaires étrangères, Arthur Balfour (1848 – 1930) promet aux Sionistes la création d'un foyer national pour les Juifs en Palestine.
La famille royale britannique change son nom en 'Windsor', 'Saxe-Cobourg-Gotha' étant jugé trop germanique.
✦1918 Fin de la première guerre mondiale.
Les femmes votent pour la première fois aux élections législatives en Grande-Bretagne.
◇1918 En Grande-Bretagne, Marie Stopes (1880 – 1958) publie *Married Life* qui remet en cause la condition de la femme. Elle se battra toute sa vie pour les droits de la femme et l'accès à la contraception.
✦1919 La Société des Nations (the League of Nations) pour le maintien de la paix et de la sécurité naît du traité de Versailles. Elle a son siège à Genève. Ses membres fondateurs comprennent la plupart des Alliés victorieux mais les États-Unis n'en font pas partie.
◇1919 Les aviateurs anglais John Alcock (1892 – 1919) et Arthur Brown (1886 – 1948) effectuent le premier vol transatlantique. La même année, Alcock trouve la mort dans un accident d'avion.

✦1917 The failure of the Nivelle offensive at the Chemin des Dames propels Pétain to the rank of supreme commander. He restores the morale of the troops and prepares the counter-offensive of 1918.
◇1917 Paul Valéry (1871 – 1945) publishes the poems *La jeune Parque* (The Young Fate). His poetic and epistemological work is to lead to a chair of poetry being created for him at the Collège de France.

✦1918 The allied counter-offensives sound the German retreat. The Rethondes armistice is signed on 11 November, bringing the First World War to an end.
◇1918 Apollinaire (1880 – 1918) publishes *Calligrammes*, poems consisting of objects freely arranged on the page, the form of which represents the subject.
André Gide publishes *La Symphonie pastorale* (Two Symphonies).
✦1919 The Peace Conference meeting in Paris redraws the maps of Europe, and the signing of the Treaty of Versailles between Germany and the Allies reincorporates Alsace and Lorraine into France.
Creation of the League of Nations (la Société des Nations) which has its headquarters in Geneva.
◇1919 Roland Dorgelès (1885 – 1973) publishes *Les Croix de bois* (The Wooden Crosses), a novel about the horrors of trench warfare.
Marcel Proust publishes *À l'ombre des jeunes filles en fleurs* (Within a Budding Grove).

1920

◇1920 Publication posthume des *Poems* de Wilfred Owen (1893 – 1918), tué sur le front de l'Ouest une semaine avant l'armistice de 1918. Ces poèmes, édités par son ami Siegfried Sassoon, expriment toute l'horreur de la guerre des tranchées.
✦1921 Pour tenter d'apaiser la situation en Irlande, Lloyd George signe le traité de partage (the Irish Free State settlement) qui crée l'État libre d'Irlande. Six des neuf comtés de l'Ulster obtiennent une autonomie partielle et forment la province d'Irlande du Nord.
◇1922 Le logicien et philosophe anglais d'origine autrichienne Ludwig Wittgenstein (1889 – 1951) publie son *Tractatus Logico-philosophicus*, rédigé alors qu'il était dans l'armée pendant la première guerre mondiale. Cet ouvrage exercera une profonde influence sur la philosophie britannique du XXème siècle.
James Joyce (1882 – 1941), écrivain irlandais, publie *Ulysses* (Ulysse) à Paris. Cette œuvre va renouveler la structure du roman au XXème siècle. Toutefois, jugée obscène en Grande-Bretagne et aux USA, elle ne paraîtra dans ces pays qu'en 1936.
Publication de *The Waste Land* (La Terre gaste), de T.S. Eliot (1888 – 1965).
◇1923 Le poète et dramaturge irlandais W.B. Yeats (1865 – 1939) reçoit le prix Nobel de littérature.
✦1924 Élection du premier gouvernement travailliste avec à sa tête Ramsay MacDonald qui ne reste que onze mois au pouvoir.
Les Indiens des États-Unis obtiennent le droit à la citoyenneté américaine.
◇1924 L'Américain George Gershwin (1898 – 1937) compose sa *Rhapsody in Blue*, œuvre dont le romantisme s'exprime dans le style jazz.
◇1925 *The Great Gatsby* (Gatsby le magnifique) de Scott Fitzgerald (1896 – 1940).
The Gold Rush (La ruée vers l'or), de Charlie Chaplin (1889 – 1977).
L'auteur irlandais George Bernard Shaw (1856 – 1950) reçoit le prix Nobel de littérature.
✦1926 Par solidarité avec les mineurs qui protestent contre une diminution des salaires, le Trades Union Congress lance un appel à la grève générale. Cette grève est vite brisée, laissant les mineurs isolés.
◇1926 L'ingénieur et physicien écossais John Logie Baird (1888 – 1946) fait la première démonstration de transmission d'image télévisée.
◇1927 L'aviateur américain Charles Lindbergh (1902 – 1955) effectue le premier vol transatlantique sans escale, seul sur son monoplan 'The Spirit of St Louis'.
La compagnie Warner Bros produit le premier film avec passages parlants ou chantants *The Jazz Singer* (Le Chanteur de jazz).
La BBC reçoit le monopole de la radiodiffusion britannique.
To the Lighthouse (La Promenade au phare), de Virginia Woolf (1882 – 1941).
◇1928 Le bactériologiste écossais Alexander Fleming (1881 – 1955) découvre la pénicilline. Toutefois, son manque de connaissances en chimie ne lui permet pas d'isoler ce bactéricide et ce n'est que onze ans plus tard que deux de ses collègues en feront une étude qui mènera à la production industrielle de cet antibiotique.
D.H. Lawrence achève son roman *Lady Chatterley's Lover* (L'Amant de Lady Chatterley) qui fait scandale et sera interdit en Grande-Bretagne jusqu'en 1960.
✦1929 La crise financière déclenchée par le krach boursier de New York (the Wall Street Crash) entraîne une dépression mondiale (the Great Depression).

✦1920 At the Congress of Tours, the split between the socialists and communists is followed by the foundation of the French Communist Party (P.C.F.).
Syria and Lebanon are made French mandates by the League of Nations.
◇1920 In music, the critics create the term 'Les Six' for the new generation of young composers: Georges Auric, Arthur Honegger, Germaine Tailleferre, Darius Milhaud, Louis Durey and Francis Poulenc.
✦1921 The end of Belgian neutrality: French and Belgian troops occupy the Ruhr.
◇1921 Albert Calmette (1863 – 1933) and Camille Guérin (1872 – 1961) introduce the first vaccine against tuberculosis (BCG).
Coco Chanel creates the 'little black dress'.
◇1922 Charles Dullin (1885 – 1949) founds the Atelier theatre, and Firmin Gémier (1869 – 1933), the Théâtre National Populaire (TNP).
◇1923 Raymond Radiguet (1903 – 1923) publishes his novel *Le Diable au corps* (The Devil in the Flesh).
Louis de Broglie (1892 – 1987) sets out the principles of wave mechanics in physics.
Creation of the Le Mans 24-hour motor race.
✦1924 Election of the Cartel of the Left made up of Socialists, Communists and Radicals, opposed by the business and industry circles that constituted the Wall of Money.
◇1924 André Breton (1896 – 1966), along with Aragon (1897 – 1982), Soupault (1897 – 1990), Eluard (1895 – 1952) and Desnos (1900 – 1945), publishes *Le Manifeste du Surréalisme* (The Surrealist Manifesto), the founding deed of this literary and artistic movement.
The Summer Olympic Games are held in Paris, and the Winter Olympics in Chamonix.
◇1925 Blaise Cendrars (1887 – 1961) writes the novel *L'Or* (Sutter's Gold).
André Gide publishes *Les Faux-Monnayeurs* (The Counterfeiters).
✦1926 Birth of Algerian nationalism with Messali Hadj, leader of the Étoile du Nord movement.
In Paris, constitution of a government of national Union led by Poincaré (1926 – 29).
◇1926 Louis Aragon publishes *Le Paysan de Paris* (The Night Walker), the first surrealist novel conceived as a journey through Paris of the industrial era.
Paul Éluard publishes the poems *Capitale de la douleur* (The Capital of Pain).
✦1927 Building of the Maginot Line (1927 – 36), a defensive structure built on the north-east border of France. The Germans were to bypass it in 1940 when they invaded France through Belgium.
◇1927 François Mauriac (1885 – 1970) writes *Thérèse Desqueyroux*.
The film director Abel Gance (1889 – 1981) makes the silent film *Napoléon*.
Georges Bernanos (1888 – 1948) writes the novel *Sous le soleil de Satan* (Under Satan's Sun).
✦1928 In Paris, Poincaré devalues and stabilizes the franc, which becomes known as the Poincaré Franc.
◇1928 André Breton writes the surrealist novel *Nadja*. Marcel Pagnol (1895 – 1974) writes the play *Topaze*.
Maurice Ravel composes *Le Boléro*.
The Winter Olympic Games are held in St Moritz, Switzerland.
◇1929 Paul Claudel writes the play *Le Soulier de satin* (The Satin Slipper).

English/Anglais	French/Français

◇1929 *The Sound and the Fury* (Le Bruit et la fureur) de William Faulkner (1897–1962).

First appearance of the Tintin character created by the Belgian cartoonist, Georges Rémi, known as Hergé (1907 – 1983).

─── 1930 ───

◇1930 L'astronome américain Clyde Tombaugh (1906 – 1997) découvre Pluton, la plus petite planète du système solaire.
American Gothic, du peintre américain Grant Wood, portrait d'un fermier du Midwest et de sa fille.
L'Américain Sinclair Lewis (1885 – 1951) reçoit le prix Nobel de littérature.
◆1930–36 L'Américain John Dos Passos (1896 – 1970) publie sa trilogie *USA*.
◆1931 L'Afrique du Sud devient un état souverain au sein du Commonwealth.
Pour faire face à la crise qui s'abat sur la Grande-Bretagne, durement touchée par la dépression, Ramsay MacDonald forme un gouvernement d'Union nationale.
◆1932 Ouverture du pont du port de Sydney.
Publication du roman de l'auteur anglais Aldous Huxley (1894 – 1963) *Brave New World* (Le Meilleur des Mondes) qui exprime une vision pessimiste d'un avenir dans lequel les êtres humains sont créés en laboratoire.
Le romancier britannique John Galsworthy (1867 – 1933) reçoit le prix Nobel de littérature.
Jeux Olympiques d'été à Los Angeles, jeux Olympiques d'hiver à Lake Placid, aux États-Unis.
◇1934 Parution de *Tropic of Cancer* (Tropique du Cancer), roman de l'écrivain américain Henry Miller (1891 – 1980). Publié à Paris, ce roman fait scandale en Grande-Bretagne et aux USA où il est interdit.
◇1935 Le physicien écossais Robert Watson-Watt (1892 – 1945) met au point l'ancêtre du radar.
◆1936 Édouard VIII (Édouard II d'Écosse) (1894 – 1972) accède au trône mais abdique un an plus tard en faveur de son frère George VI (1895 – 1952) afin d'épouser Wallis Simpson, une Américaine deux fois divorcée.
Des mineurs et des ouvriers des chantiers navals frappés par le chômage organisent une marche de la faim (the Jarrow March) depuis le comté de Durham jusqu'à Londres pour protester contre la pauvreté qui règne dans le nord de l'Angleterre.
◇1936 La BBC, financée par la redevance, diffuse ses premières émissions télévisées.
L'architecte américain Frank Lloyd Wright (1867 – 1959) crée la maison de *Falling Water*.
Le dramaturge américain Eugene O'Neill (1888 – 1953) reçoit le prix Nobel de littérature.
◇1937 L'ingénieur aéronautique britannique Frank Whittle (1907 – 1996) invente le turboréacteur.
Sortie de *Snow White and the Seven Dwarfs* (Blanche-Neige et les sept nains) de Walt Disney (1901 – 1966); c'est le premier dessin animé de long métrage de l'histoire du cinéma.
◆1938 Conférence de Munich; la France et la Grande-Bretagne n'interviendront pas en faveur de la Tchécoslovaquie face à Hitler. De retour, le Premier ministre britannique Neville Chamberlain prononce son fameux 'I believe it is peace for our time'.
◇1938 La romancière américaine Pearl Buck (1892 – 1973) reçoit le prix Nobel de littérature.
◆1939 Début de la deuxième guerre mondiale: Hitler ayant envahi la Pologne, la France et la Grande-Bretagne déclarent la guerre à l'Allemagne.
1 200 000 personnes doivent quitter leur foyer pour échapper aux bombardements aériens.
◇1939 Sortie du western *Stagecoach* (La Chevauchée fantastique) de John Ford (1895 – 1973), premier grand rôle de John Wayne (1907 – 1979).
Victor Fleming (1889 – 1949) réalise *The Wizard of Oz* (Le Magicien d'Oz) et *Gone with the Wind* (Autant en emporte le vent).

◆1930 France promulgates a Constitution in Syria.
◆1931 Paul Doumer (1857 – 1932) is elected President of the Republic against Briand. He is assassinated the following year by a Russian émigré.
◇1931 Pierre Drieu La Rochelle (1893 – 1945) publishes the novel *Le Feu Follet* (The Fire Within).
◆1932 Albert Lebrun (1871 – 1950) becomes President of the Republic. In Africa, Upper Volta is divided between French Sudan (Mali), the Ivory Coast and Niger.
◇1932 Mauriac writes *Le Nœud de vipères* (The Vipers' Tangle). Louis-Ferdinand Céline (1894 – 1961) publishes *Voyage au bout de la nuit* (Journey to the End of Night), an iconoclastic novel shattering the myth of the heroism of war to show its atrocity and wretchedness.
◆1933 Rise in extremism of the right, including the Croix-de-Feu (Flaming Cross) movement of extreme right-wing militia, created by Colonel de La Rocque (1885 – 1946).
◇1933 André Malraux (1901 – 1976) publishes the novel *La Condition humaine* (Man's Estate).
◆1934 The Stavisky affair, named after the French financier who embezzled money and was found shot dead, causes a great stir and fuels the anti-parliamentarianism of the extreme right.
A violent demonstration by the extreme right on 6 February leaves 20 dead. In Belgium, King Leopold III supports Flemish nationalism.
◇1934 Irène (1897 – 1956) and Frédéric Joliot-Curie (1900 – 1958) discover artificial radioactivity.
Jean Vigo (1905 – 1934) makes *L'Atalante*, a film with Michel Simon.
◇1935 Jean Giono (1895 – 1970) writes the novel *Que ma joie demeure* (Joy of Man's Desiring).
Jean Giraudoux (1882 – 1944) writes the play *La Guerre de Troie n'aura pas lieu* (Tiger at the Gates).
◆1936 The Popular Front (1936 – 1938): Socialists, Communists and Radicals come together under the premiership of Léon Blum (1872 – 1950), heir to the French Socialist Party of Jaurès: wage rises, guaranteed trade union rights, 40-hour week, paid holidays, nationalization of armament factories.
◇1936 Georges Bernanos (1888 – 1948) publishes *Le Journal d'un curé de campagne* (Diary of a Country Priest).
◆1937 Creation of the SNCF, the French national railway company.
◇1937 Julien Duvivier (1896 – 1967) makes *Pépé le Moko*, a film with Jean Gabin.
Pablo Picasso (1881 – 1973) paints *Guernica*.

◆1938 Daladier government.
Munich conference and agreements: capitulation before Hitler. France and Britain will let Hitler invade Czechoslovakia.
◇1938 Malraux writes the novel *L'Espoir* (Man's Hope).
Jean-Paul Sartre (1905 – 1980) writes the novel *La Nausée* (Nausea).
Jean Cocteau (1889 – 1963) writes the play *Les Parents terribles*.
Marcel Carné's (1906 – 1996) film *Le Quai des Brumes* (Port of Shadows) is released.
◆1939 General mobilization (1 September).
Britain declares war on Germany, followed by France (3 September).
Beginning of the phoney war (la drôle de guerre).
◇1939 Jean Renoir's (1894 – 1979) film *La règle du jeu* (The Rules of the Game) is released.
Marcel Carné's film *Le jour se lève* (Daybreak) is released.
Nathalie Sarraute (1900 – 1999) publishes the novel *Tropismes* (Tropisms).

─── 1940 ───

◆1940 Évacuation de Dunkerque.
Sir Winston Churchill (1874 – 1965) forme un gouvernement de coalition qui siègera pendant toute la durée de la guerre. Churchill donne le ton de la résistance dans son célèbre discours 'Je n'ai rien d'autre à offrir que du sang, des efforts, des larmes et de la sueur' ('blood, toil, tears and sweat'). L'impôt sur le revenu est porté au taux record de 50% et le rationnement alimentaire est introduit.
Bataille d'Angleterre: la victoire de la RAF (aviation de chasse britannique) sur la Luftwaffe oblige Hitler à renoncer à sa tentative d'invasion de l'Angleterre.
◇1940 Ernest Hemingway (1899 – 1961) publie *For Whom the Bell Tolls* (Pour qui sonne le glas, sur la guerre d'Espagne).

◆1940 German invasion of the Netherlands, Belgium and Luxembourg, then of France.
Evacuation of Dunkirk (6 June).
Fall of Paris (14 June).
Beginning of the Occupation.
The government withdraws to the free zone (Tours, then Bordeaux and Vichy). Paul Reynaud (1878 – 1966) resigns from the Presidency of the Council.
17 June: Pétain calls for the cessation of fighting.
18 June: Call from General de Gaulle from London urging the French to continue fighting the enemy.
Small resistance groups are formed.
22 June: Signature of the French-German armistice. Marshal Pétain is elected by the National Assembly as head of the French State.
28 June: De Gaulle is recognized as the leader of Free France by Britain.
2 July: The State locates itself in Vichy.

July 1940 – Aug. 1944   The Vichy regime

◆10 July: Pétain is elected head of the government.
August: French Equatorial Africa and Cameroon join forces with General de Gaulle.
24 October: Pétain and Hitler meet at Montoire. Policy of collaboration.
30 November: Alsace-Lorraine is officially annexed by Germany.
◇1940 Chance discovery by two adolescents of prehistoric wall paintings in a cave in Lascaux (Dordogne).
◆1941 Admiral Darlan (1881 – 1942) is appointed leader of the Pétain government: he sets up a policy of collaboration with the occupying forces. The Free French Forces grant independence to Syria and Lebanon.

◆1941 L'attaque japonaise de la base navale américaine de Pearl Harbor aux îles Hawaii fait entrer les États-Unis dans la guerre aux côtés de la Grande-Bretagne et de la France.
◇1941 Sortie de *Citizen Kane*, chef d'œuvre du cinéma réalisé par l'américain Orson Welles (1915 – 1985).

English/Anglais	French/Français

French/Français column

◇1941 Robert Brasillach (1909 – 1945), director of the collaborationist journal *Je suis partout*, publishes *Notre avant-guerre*, a Nazi propaganda essay, whilst the composer Olivier Messiaen (1908 – 1992) writes a *Quatuor pour la fin du temps* (Quartet for the End of Time).

◆1942
17 April: Pierre Laval (1883 – 1945) becomes head of the Vichy government.
May: Requirement for Jews to wear the yellow star in the occupied zone.
21 – 22 July: The rounding up of Jews in the Paris Vélodrome d'Hiver: 13,000 Jews arrested by the French police.
8 November: Allied landings in North Africa.
11 November: The Germans occupy the free zone, in the south of France.
◇1942 Francis Ponge (1899 – 1988) publishes the poems *Le Parti pris des choses* (The Voice of Things).
Albert Camus writes *L'Étranger* (The Outsider).
Marcel Carné's film *Les Visiteurs du soir* (The Devil's Envoys) is released.

◆1943
January: Law setting up the Milice, to hunt down the Resistance.
February: Introduction of the STO (forced labour service).
Setting up of the National Council of the Resistance by Jean Moulin (1899 – 1943) who manages to unify the political movements around General de Gaulle.
The Teheran Conference between Churchill, Roosevelt and Stalin decides on the Allied landing in Provence.
De Gaulle visits Algiers; formation of the French Committee of National Liberation (CFLN).
◇1943 Jean-Paul Sartre publishes *L'Être et le Néant* (Being and Nothingness), the founding work of Sartre's existentialism.
Antoine de Saint-Exupéry (1900 – 1944) publishes *Le Petit Prince* (The Little Prince).
Henri-Georges Clouzot (1907 – 1977) makes *Le Corbeau* (The Raven), a detective film in which the subject and ambience reflect the atmosphere of the Occupation and its practices of denunciation.
Marcel Carné's film *Les Enfants du paradis* (Children of Paradise) is released.

June 1944 – 1946 Provisional Government of the French Republic

◆1944
6 June: Allied landings in Normandy in which the French Forces of the Interior (F.F.I.) take part.
19 – 25 August: Liberation of Paris by the forces under General Leclerc. Procession up the Champs-Élysées.
5 October: The right to vote is granted to women.
◇1944 First issue of the newspaper *Le Monde*, edited by Hubert Beuve-Méry (1902 – 1989).
Jean Anouilh (1910 – 1987) writes the play *Antigone*.
◆1945 Germany surrenders to the Allies.
Marshal Pétain's death sentence is commuted to life imprisonment.
Creation of the French Social Security system.
Ho Chi Min's Indochina and Laos declare their independence, which is not recognized by France.
Belgium is liberated.
◇1945 Foundation of the monthly *Les Temps Modernes* (Modern Times) by Jean-Paul Sartre, Simone de Beauvoir (1908 – 1986), Maurice Merleau-Ponty (1908 – 1961) and Raymond Aron (1905 – 1983).
The pro-Nazi writer Robert Brasillach is sentenced to death and executed in Febuary.

1946 – 1958 The Fourth Republic

◆1946 De Gaulle leaves the provisional government when the Constitution of the Fourth Republic is promulgated (1946 – 1958).
Creation of the French Union, which includes colonial possessions and creates the Overseas Départements (DOM).
Beginning of the conflict in Indochina (1946 – 1954) with the bombing of the Bay of Haiphong.
◇1946 Opening of the first Cannes International Film Festival.
Jean Cocteau and René Clément's film *La Belle et la Bête* (Beauty and the Beast) is released.
◆1947 Vincent Auriol (1884 – 1956) becomes President of the Republic (1947 – 54).
General de Gaulle founds the RPF (Rassemblement du peuple français).
France accepts the Marshall Plan for American aid in the reconstruction of Europe.
Insurrection in Madagascar.
In The Hague, signature of the customs protocol between Belgium, Holland and Luxembourg (Benelux).
◇1947 André Gide awarded the Nobel Prize for literature.
Albert Camus publishes *La Peste* (The Plague).
Aimé Césaire (1913 –), a poet from Martinique writing about black experience and culture, publishes the collection of poems *Cahier d'un retour au pays natal* (Notebook of a Return to my Native Land).
Jean Vilar (1912 – 1971) sets up the Festival of Avignon.
Édith Piaf (1915 – 1963) sings *La vie en rose*.
Le Corbusier (1887 – 1965) builds La Cité Radieuse, a housing complex in Marseille.
◇1948 Hervé Bazin (1911 – 1996) publishes the novel *Vipère au poing* (Viper in the Fist).
The Winter Olympic Games are held in St Moritz, Switzerland.
◆1949 Belgium signs the North Atlantic Treaty.
A world congress of the Peace movement is held in Paris, for which Picasso paints the dove of peace.
◇1949 Simone de Beauvoir publishes *Le Deuxième sexe* (The Second Sex), the founding text of feminism.
First issue of the magazine *Paris-Match*.

English/Anglais column

◆1942 La victoire britannique d'El Alamein (sous le commandement du Maréchal Montgomery), en Égypte, sur les forces allemandes de l'Afrikakorps marque un tournant dans la campagne d'Afrique du Nord, campagne qui avait débuté par l'invasion italienne de l'Égypte en 1940.
◇1942 Le physicien américain d'origine italienne Enrico Fermi (1901 – 1954) construit la première pile atomique. C'est en grande partie sous son influence que le gouvernement américain décide d'adopter l'énergie nucléaire.
Sortie du film *Casablanca*, de l'Américain Michael Curtiz (1888 – 1962).

◆1943 Conférence de Téhéran avec Churchill, Roosevelt et Staline. Projet de débarquement en Provence.

◆1944 Le débarquement de Normandie le 6 juin (D-Day) marque le début de la libération de l'Europe par les Alliés. Paris est libéré le 25 août.
◇1944 Première représentation de *The Glass Menagerie* (La Ménagerie de verre), de Tennessee Williams (1911 – 1983).

◆1945 L'Allemagne se rend aux Alliés en mai. En août, les bombes atomiques américaines lâchées sur Hiroshima et Nagasaki obligent le Japon à capituler.
En Grande-Bretagne, Clement Attlee (1883 – 1967) devient Premier ministre après la victoire travailliste aux élections; il entreprend la nationalisation des secteurs principaux de l'industrie et de l'énergie.
◇1945 L'auteur anglais George Orwell (pseudonyme d'Eric Blair) (1903 – 1950) publie *Animal Farm* (La Ferme des animaux), satire du totalitarisme stalinien.
Sortie du film *Brief Encounter* (Brève Rencontre) du britannique David Lean (1908 – 1991).
◆1946 Churchill prononce son célèbre discours de Fulton (États-Unis) dans lequel il parle du rideau de fer qui divise l'Europe.
Début de la Guerre froide.
◆1947 Le Président américain Harry Truman (1884 – 1972) promet l'aide économique et militaire des États-Unis aux pays menacés par le communisme (doctrine Truman).
La Nouvelle-Zélande acquiert son indépendance au sein du Commonwealth.
Le pilote d'essai américain Charles 'Chuck' Yeager (1923 –) effectue le premier vol à vitesse supersonique (1 078 km/h) à bord du Bell X-1, avion propulsé par un moteur-fusée.
◇1947 Création du festival international d'Édimbourg qui se déroule sur trois semaines en août-septembre (concerts, opéra, art dramatique). Durant cette période, le festival alternatif offre des milliers de spectacles moins prestigieux.
◇1947 – 1956 Le peintre américain Jackson Pollock (1912 – 1956) produit une série de toiles en utilisant la technique du dripping.
◆1948 L'Inde devient indépendante.
Création du National Health Service, financé par le gouvernement et les impôts locaux. Ce service de santé national promet la gratuité des soins et des médicaments.
◇1948 L'invention du transistor aux États-Unis améliore la réception des postes de radio et de télévision et constitue un événement d'importance majeure pour le développement de l'informatique.
L'Américain Alfred Kinsey (1894 – 1956) publie son rapport *Sexual Behaviour in the Human Male*.
Première représentation de *A Streetcar Named Desire* (Un Tramway nommé Désir), de Tennessee Williams (1911 – 1983).
Le poète américain T.S. Eliot (1888 – 1965) reçoit le prix Nobel de littérature.
Les jeux Olympiques ont lieu à Londres.
◇1949 George Orwell (1903 – 1950) publie son roman *1984*.
William Faulkner (1897 – 1962) reçoit le prix Nobel de littérature.
Sortie de *The Third Man* (Le Troisième homme) du cinéaste britannique Carol Reed (1906 – 1976) d'après un roman de Graham Greene (1904 – 1991).

English/Anglais	French/Français

─────────────────────── 1950 ───────────────────────

English/Anglais

◆1950 – 1953 Guerre de Corée. Les forces de l'ONU défendent la Corée du Sud contre l'invasion communiste de la Corée du Nord et de la Chine. Période du maccartisme.

◆1951 Winston Churchill est de nouveau Premier ministre.
◇1951 L'écrivain américain J.D. Salinger (1919 –) publie *Catcher in the Rye* (L'Attrape-Cœur). Son roman raconte les aventures d'un adolescent qui se rebelle contre un monde adulte et bourgeois.
◆1952 Premiers essais de la bombe à hydrogène aux États-Unis.
Mort de Georges VI. Élisabeth II (1926 –) devient reine du Royaume-Uni et chef du Commonwealth.
La Grande-Bretagne se dote de la bombe atomique.
◇1952 *High Noon* (Le Train sifflera trois fois), film de l'Américain Fred Zinnemann (1907 – 1997).
Le poète gallois Dylan Thomas (1914 – 1953) écrit *Under Milk Wood* (Au bois lacté).
Winston Churchill reçoit le prix Nobel de littérature.
◆1953 Dwight Eisenhower (1890 – 1969), rendu populaire par sa réussite de la difficile coordination des forces alliées, en particulier en Afrique du Nord, devient Président des États-Unis. La résistance au communisme et les contacts directs avec les chefs d'États étrangers sont les traits dominants de sa présidence.
◇1953 Découverte de la structure en double hélice de la molécule d'ADN par le biochimiste anglais Francis Crick (1916 – 2004) et le biologiste américain James Watson (1928 –) au laboratoire de Cavendish à Cambridge.
Première représentation de *The Crucible* (Les Sorcières de Salem), allégorie du maccartisme, du dramaturge américain Arthur Miller.
◇1954 *Lord of the Flies* (Sa Majesté des Mouches) de l'auteur anglais William Golding (1911 – 1993).
Kingsley Amis (1922 – 1995) publie son roman comique *Lucky Jim*.
Ernest Hemingway (1899 – 1961) reçoit le prix Nobel de littérature.
◇1954 – 1955 J.R.R. Tolkien (1892 – 1973) publie sa trilogie *The Lord of the Rings* (Le Seigneur des anneaux).
◆1954 – 1968 Lutte pour les droits civiques aux États-Unis.

◆1955 Anthony Eden (1897 – 1977), conservateur, succède à Churchill comme Premier ministre.
À Montgomery, dans l'Alabama, début du boycott des autobus organisé par Martin Luther King, à la suite de l'arrestation de Rosa Parks, une Noire qui s'était installée dans la section réservée aux blancs.
◇1955 *Rock Around the Clock* de Bill Haley (1925 – 1981) et les Comets est l'un des premiers grands succès de l'époque du rock and roll.
Rebel Without a Cause (La Fureur de vivre), de Nicholas Ray, avec James Dean (1931 – 1955).

◆1956 Crise de Suez. L'Égypte nationalise le canal de Suez; la France et la Grande-Bretagne, malgré les critiques, occupent la zone du canal, mais la crainte d'une intervention de la Russie et des USA les obligent à évacuer leurs troupes.
◇1956 Le philosophe britannique A.J. Ayer (1910 – 1989) publie *The Problem of Knowledge* (Le Problème de la Connaissance).
Première représentation de *Look Back in Anger* (La Paix du dimanche), pièce de l'auteur dramatique anglais John Osborne (1929 – 1994), chef de file des Angry Young Men (Jeunes Gens en colère).
Sortie de *Heartbreak Hotel*, grand succès d'Elvis Presley (1935 – 1977), devenu le chanteur le plus populaire aux États-Unis.
Première démonstration du magnétoscope par les ingénieurs américains Raymond Dolby (1933 –) et Charles Ginsburg.
Première représentation de *A Long Day's Journey into Night* (Long Voyage vers la nuit) du dramaturge américain Eugene O'Neill, qui remportera le prix Pullitzer l'année suivante.
Jeux Olympiques d'été à Melbourne, en Australie.
◆1957 Harold Macmillan (1894 – 1986), conservateur, devient Premier ministre en Grande-Bretagne. La popularité de ses mesures sociales et de sa politique étrangère lui vaudra d'être réélu en 1959.
◇1957 L'auteur américain Jack Kerouac (1922 – 1969) publie *On the Road* (Sur la route). Dans ce roman, il se fait le porte-parole de la 'Beat Generation' en révolte contre le conformisme bourgeois et la société de consommation.
◆1959 L'Alaska et Hawaï deviennent respectivement les 49ème et 50ème états des États-Unis.
◇1959 Vladimir Nabokov (1899 – 1977) publie *Lolita*, récit de la passion d'un quadragénaire pour une nymphette.
Some Like it Hot (Certains l'aiment chaud), film de l'Américain Billy Wilder (1906 – 2002) avec Marilyn Monroe (1926 – 1962).

French/Français

◆1950 Creation of the SMIG (guaranteed minimum wage).
Internationalization of the France-Vietnam conflict: the Americans provide support for the French against the Viet Minh forces and Ho Chi Minh.
◇1950 Eugène Ionesco (1912 – 1994) writes *La Cantatrice chauve* (The Bald Prima Donna), a play that marks the emergence of the Theatre of the Absurd.
◆1951 In Belgium, beginning of the reign of Baudoin I (1930 – 1993).
Treaty of Paris, establishing the European Coal and Steel Community (ECSC). Provided for by the Schuman plan, the ECSC is developed by R. Schuman (1886 – 1963) and Jean Monnet (1888 – 1979), the 'fathers of Europe'.
◆1951 Albert Camus publishes the essay *L'Homme révolté* (The Rebel): dispute with Sartre.
Jean Vilar takes over the management of the TNP.
François Mauriac wins the Nobel Prize for literature.
◆1953 In Morocco, France deposes sultan Mohammed V, who personifies the desire for independence of his country.
◇1953 Samuel Beckett's (1906 – 1989) play *En attendant Godot* (Waiting for Godot) is first performed. The English version is first performed in 1955.
Roland Barthes publishes *Le Degré zéro de l'écriture* (Writing Degree Zero).
◆1954 René Coty (1882 – 1962) becomes President of the Republic (1954 – 1958).
In Indochina, the disaster of Dien-Bien-Phu brings to an end the France-Vietnam war through the Geneva accords, which divide Vietnam into the democratic Republic in the North (governed by Ho Chi Minh) and the Republic of South Vietnam, led by Bao Dai, and confirm the independence of Laos and Cambodia.
In Algeria, insurrection in Kabylia and in the Aurès region, driven by the National Liberation Front (F.L.N.) founded by Ahmed Ben Bella, which marks the beginning of the War of Algeria (1954 – 1962).
◇1954 Françoise Sagan (1935 – 2004) publishes *Bonjour Tristesse*. This novel by the young French writer creates a scandal and meets with immediate success.
On the radio, Henri Groüès, known as Abbé Pierre (1912 –), launches an appeal on behalf of the destitute and homeless, helping them through the creation of the Companions of Emmaus community (1949).
Truffaut's *Manifesto* is published in the *Cahiers du cinéma*.
◆1955 End of the French protectorate in Morocco and reinstatement of Mohammed V.
Riots and violent repression in Algeria.
◇1955 Claude Lévi-Strauss (1908 –) publishes *Tristes Tropiques* (A World on the Wane), an autobiographical essay by the renowned anthropologist.
Pierre Boulez composes *Le Marteau sans maître* (The Hammer without a Master), based on words by the poet René Char.
Alain Resnais releases *Nuit et brouillard* (Night and Fog), a film about the Nazi concentration camps.
◆1956 Guy Mollet, President of the Council, goes to Algiers where he is met by a demonstration of Pieds-Noirs (French settlers in Algeria).
End of the protectorate in Tunisia; French trading posts are returned to India.
Creation of the Overseas Territories (Territoires d'outre-mer or TOM) prepared by Gaston Defferre (1910 – 1986), to lead to the independence of French West Africa and French East Africa.
The Suez crisis: France and Britain occupy the Suez Canal zone after it is nationalized by Nasser. They are forced to evacuate their troops after the operation is strongly condemned by both the USA and the USSR.
◇1956 Commander Jacques Cousteau (1910 – 1997) produces *Le Monde du silence* (The Silent World) with Louis Malle.
◆1957 Signature of the two Treaties of Rome setting up the European Economic Community (EEC), then known as the Common Market, and of Euratom. The founding countries form the Europe of the Six (France, West Germany, Italy, the Netherlands, Belgium and Luxembourg).
Declaration of independence by Morocco and Tunisia.
◇1957 Albert Camus wins the Nobel Prize for literature.
Samuel Beckett writes the play *Fin de partie* (Endgame).
Michel Butor (1926 –) publishes the 'new' novel *La Modification* (Second Thoughts).

1958 – The Fifth Republic

◆1958 The insurrection in Algiers brings General de Gaulle back to power. President of the Council, he is given emergency powers and goes to Algiers. By referendum (direct consultation of the citizens of France), he has the Constitution of the Fifth Republic approved and is elected President. The Community of French-speaking Africa succeeds the French Union. It is rejected by Guinea, which becomes independent.
◇1958 Marguerite Duras (1914 – 1996) publishes the novel *Moderato Cantabile*.
◆1959 De Gaulle is President of the Republic.
He announces a policy of self-determination in Algeria.
◇1959 Raymond Queneau publishes *Zazie dans le métro* (Zazie), a novel adapted for the cinema by Louis Malle in 1960.
François Truffaut's film *Les 400 coups* (The 400 Blows) is released.
Le Sacre du printemps (The Rite of Spring), choreography by Maurice Béjart (1927–), music by Igor Stravinsky.

─────────────────────── 1960 ───────────────────────

◇1960 Le physicien américain Theodore Maiman (1927 –) réalise le premier laser optique.
◆1960 John Updike (1932 –), romancier américain, publie *Rabbit, Run*.
Psycho (Psychose), d'Alfred Hitchcock (1899 – 1980).

◆1960 A week of street riots in Algiers fuelled by the opposition to self-determination of the population of French extraction.

English/Anglais	French/Français

English/Anglais column:

Les jeux Olympiques d'hiver ont lieu à Squaw Valley, en Californie.
◆1961 Devant l'opposition internationale à son régime de discrimination raciale (l'apartheid), l'Afrique du Sud se retire du Commonwealth et forme une république indépendante.
Élection de John F. Kennedy (1917 – 1963): il est le premier Président catholique des USA et le plus jeune. Parlant d'une 'nouvelle frontière', il met en place un programme de réformes sociales et d'intégration raciale.
◇1961 Le romancier américain Joseph Heller obtient un succès immédiat avec la publication de son roman *Catch 22* dont le titre est passé dans la langue pour désigner une situation sans issue.
◆1962 Crise des missiles de Cuba: la découverte de bases de fusées soviétiques à Cuba suscite une vive inquiétude internationale. Les États-Unis établissent le blocus de l'île. Kennedy finit par obtenir que l'URSS évacue ses fusées.
◇1962 Sortie de *Dr No*, premier d'une série de films à grand succès dont le héros est l'agent secret James Bond, rôle tenu à plusieurs reprises par Sean Connery.
Les Beatles obtiennent leur premier grand succès avec la chanson *Love Me Do*. Ils déclenchent un enthousiasme populaire quasi hystérique.
Le peintre américain Andy Warhol (1928 – 1987) réalise le *Marilyn Diptych*, photos colorées de Marilyn Monroe.
Le romancier britannique Anthony Burgess (1917 – 1993) publie *A Clockwork Orange* (Orange mécanique) dans lequel il dénonce la violence de la société moderne.
Le romancier américain John Steinbeck (1902 – 1968) reçoit le prix Nobel de littérature.
◆1963 John Kennedy est assassiné à Dallas, au Texas, à son arrivée en visite officielle. Lyndon Johnson (1908 – 1973), son Vice-Président, lui succède.
Martin Luther King prononce son discours 'I have a dream' au cours d'un rassemblement pour les droits civiques, à Washington.
Suite à la démission d'Harold Macmillan, Alec Douglas-Home (1903 – 1995) renonce à ses titres nobiliaires et devient Premier ministre du Royaume-Uni.
◇1963 L'Américaine Betty Friedan (1921 – 2006) publie son livre *The Feminine Mystique* (La Femme mystifiée), un des ouvrages phares du mouvement féministe.
Affaire Profumo en Grande-Bretagne: John Profumo, ministre de la guerre, démissionne à la suite de révélations concernant sa liaison avec une jeune femme également liée à un officier russe.
◆1964 Harold Wilson, leader des travaillistes, devient Premier ministre de Grande-Bretagne. Son programme économique est compromis par une grave crise financière.
Aux USA, Lyndon Johnson, poursuivant la politique d'intégration raciale de Kennedy, fait voter le 'Civil Rights Act' (loi sur les droits civils).
◆1964 – 1975 Les États-Unis envoient des troupes au Viêt-nam pour soutenir le régime anti-communiste du Sud contre ses adversaires communistes du Nord.
◇1964 Martin Luther King obtient le prix Nobel de la paix.
◆1965 Une loi électorale apporte une nouvelle amélioration au statut des Noirs américains.
◇1965 *The Sound of Music* (La Mélodie du bonheur), film de l'Américain Robert Wise (1914 – 2005).
◇1966 L'Angleterre gagne la Coupe du monde de football.
Cathy Come Home, film de Ken Loach (1936 –) qui traite du problème des sans-logis; c'est à la suite de sa diffusion que sera créée l'association d'aide aux SDF Shelter.
◇1967 En Afrique du Sud, le chirurgien Christian Barnard (1922 – 2001) réalise la première greffe du cœur. Le patient survivra 18 jours.
Sortie de l'album des Beatles *Sergeant Pepper's Lonely Hearts Club Band*.
◆1968 Martin Luther King est assassiné à Memphis, au Tennessee.
◇1968 *2001: A Space Odyssey* (2001: l'Odyssée de l'espace), film du cinéaste américain Stanley Kubrick (1928 – 1999).
◆1969 L'Irlande du Nord entre dans une période de violents affrontements entre catholiques et protestants. L'armée britannique envoie des troupes pour tenter de maintenir la paix.
Richard Nixon (1913 – 1994) est élu à la présidence des USA.
◇1969 L'astronaute américain Neil Armstrong, commandant d'Apollo 11, est le premier homme à mettre pied sur la Lune.
Premier vol du supersonique franco-britannique Concorde.
Festival pop de Woodstock, aux États-Unis.

— 1970 —

◆1970 Edward Heath (1916 – 2005), conservateur, est le nouveau Premier ministre en Grande-Bretagne.
◇1970 Publication d'une nouvelle version de la Bible, *The New English Bible*. Écrite dans un anglais littéraire moderne, elle tient compte des tout derniers travaux de recherche.
L'universitaire féministe australienne Germaine Greer publie *The Female Eunuch* (La Femme eunuque).
Le peintre britannique David Hockney (1937 –) présente *Mr and Mrs Clark and Percy*.
◆1971 Introduction du système décimal dans la monnaie britannique.
◆1972 Épisode du dimanche sanglant (Bloody Sunday) à Londonderry, en Irlande du Nord: 13 manifestants catholiques sont abattus par des soldats de l'armée britannique.
Visite de Nixon en Chine.
◇1972 *The Godfather* (Le Parrain), film du cinéaste américain Francis Ford Coppola (1939 –).
◆1973 La Grande-Bretagne et la République d'Irlande entrent dans la Communauté économique européenne.
Grève des mineurs en Grande-Bretagne.
Désengagement des troupes américaines au Viêt-nam sous la pression d'une opinion publique de plus en plus hostile à la guerre.

French/Français column:

The States of Africa which are members of the Community of French-speaking Africa or under French trusteeship become independent: Mauritania, Upper Volta, Niger, Chad, Senegal, Mali, Ivory Coast, Togo, Dahomey (Benin), Cameroon, Gabon, Congo, Central African Republic, Madagascar. Belgium proclaims the independence of Congo-Kinshasa (formerly the Belgian Congo, and now the Democratic Republic of Congo).
France has the atomic bomb.
Creation of the New Franc.
◇1960 The poet Saint-John Perse (1887 – 1975) wins the Nobel Prize for literature.
Jean-Luc Godard (1930 –), film critic for *Cahiers du Cinéma* and young filmmaker representative of the New Wave, films *À bout de souffle* (Breathless).
Pop music: start of the yé-yé wave around the magazine *Salut les copains*. Among its leading figures are Johnny Hallyday, Sylvie Vartan, Françoise Hardy, Claude François and Eddy Mitchell.
◆1961 After the proclamation by De Gaulle of the self-determination of the Algerian people, the French population of Algeria and army officers try to oppose it with an attempted coup d'état by senior army officers (which fails) supported by the OAS (Organisation Armée secrète), which commits several terrorist attacks in Algeria and France.
Canada: creation of the French language office (Office de la langue française).
◇1961 Jean Genêt (1910 – 1986) writes the play *Les Paravents* (The Screens).
Édith Piaf sings *Non, je ne regrette rien*.
◆1962 Amendment of the Constitution introducing the election of the President of the Republic by universal suffrage.
Death of eight people at the Charonne metro station during an anti-OAS demonstration. Signature of the Evian Agreements recognizing Algerian independence and bringing the war to an end. Mass exodus of French people from Algeria (the Pieds-Noirs).
Ruanda-Urundi (under Belgian trusteeship) becomes independent and splits into two States: Rwanda and Burundi.
◇1962 The Mont Blanc tunnel is built.
◇1963 Addis Ababa Conference, which sets up the Organization of African Unity (OAU).
◇1963 Jean-Luc Godard's film *Le Mépris* (Contempt), starring Brigitte Bardot, is released.
◆1964 France withdraws from the integrated military organization of NATO.
◆1964 Sartre refuses the Nobel Prize.
Jacques Demy's (1931 – 1990) musical film *Les Parapluies de Cherbourg* (The Umbrellas of Cherbourg) is released.
◆1965 Re-election of De Gaulle to the Presidency of the Republic.
Mehdi Ben Barka, leader of the forces of opposition to King Hassan II, is abducted and never seen again. This becomes known as the Ben Barka Affair.
◇1965 François Jacob, Jacques Monod and André Lwof receive the Nobel Prize for medicine for their work on the genetic code.
◇1966 Publication of *Écrits* (The Language of the Self: The Function of Language in Psychoanalysis) by Jacques Lacan (1901 – 1981), who reinterprets the theoretical approach of Freudian psychoanalysis.
Jean Genêt's *Les Paravents* (The Screens) is performed: the event of the theatre season.
Jean-Luc Godard's film *Pierrot le Fou* is released.
◆1967 De Gaulle travels to Canada where Quebec is experiencing a revival of French Canadian nationalism. In Montreal, he utters a resounding 'Vive le Québec libre!' (Long Live Free Quebec).
◆1968 In France, student demonstrations at the University of Nanterre spark off the May Events, leading to widespread social and political protests.
General strike on an unprecedented scale.
France has the H bomb.
◆1968 Albert Cohen (1895 – 1981) publishes the novel *Belle du Seigneur*.
The Winter Olympic Games are held in Grenoble.
◆1969 Resignation of General de Gaulle.
Georges Pompidou (1911 – 1974) is elected President of the Republic.
◇1969 First flight of the supersonic plane Concorde.
Marcel Ophuls (1927 –) makes *Le Chagrin et la Pitié* (The Sorrow and the Pity), a documentary about life in a French village during the Occupation.

◆1970 October crisis in Quebec: the Quebec Liberation Front kidnaps a British diplomat and a minister of the Quebec government, executing the latter. The army is brought in, as is the law on war measures.
Death of General de Gaulle.
◆1971 Creation of the Socialist Party at the Epinay Congress. François Mitterrand (1916 – 1996) is elected first secretary.
◇1971 Start of the building (1971 – 1975) in Paris of the Georges Pompidou Centre, by Renzo Piano and Richard Rogers.
◆1972 The left (François Mitterrand's Socialist Party, Georges Marchais' Communist Party, Robert Fabre's Radical Party) present a joint government programme.
◆1973 At the Lip watchmaking factory, striking workers decide in opposition to the management to resume work and to set up self-management of the factory.
◇1973 First issue of the newspaper *Libération*, under the aegis of Jean-Paul Sartre (edited by Serge July after 1974).
◆1974 Death of Georges Pompidou.
After the interim government of Alain Poher, Valéry Giscard-d'Estaing (1926 –) is elected President of the Republic (1974 – 1981).

English/Anglais	French/Français

English/Anglais column:

Nixon et Kissinger annoncent 'la paix dans l'honneur' et Nixon promet le versement de plus de 3 milliards de dollars en réparations au Viêt-nam, somme qui ne sera jamais payée.

Insurrection indienne à Wounded Knee, dans le Dakota du Sud, aux États-Unis.

La Cod War (Guerre de la morue), dispute entre la Grande-Bretagne et l'Islande à propos des zones de pêche.

◇1973 Le romancier américain Thomas Pynchon (1937 –) publie *Gravity's Rainbow*, roman controversé et d'un surréalisme obscur.

The Exorcist (L'Exorciste) de l'Américain William Friedkin (1939 –).

Le romancier australien Patrick White (1912 – 1990) reçoit le prix Nobel de littérature.

✦1974 Démission du Président américain Richard Nixon menacé d'impeachment' (mise en accusation) suite à l'affaire de Watergate. Gerald Ford (1913 –) lui succède, mais la 'grâce' qu'il accorde à Nixon le rend impopulaire.

Harold Wilson revient au pouvoir mais se heurte bientôt à de graves dissensions internes au sujet du maintien de la Grande-Bretagne dans la CEE.

En Angleterre, Lord Lucan, membre de la chambre des Lords, disparaît à la suite du meurtre de la nourrice de ses enfants.

Pendant environ deux mois, la semaine de travail est réduite à trois jours en raison d'une pénurie de carburant.

✦1976 Après la démission d'Harold Wilson, James Callaghan (1912 – 2005), nouveau chef des travaillistes, lui succède.

Fête du bicentenaire de l'Indépendance aux États-Unis.

◇1976 *Taxi Driver*, film de Martin Scorsese (1942 –) avec Robert De Niro (1943 –).

Le romancier Saul Bellow (1915 –) reçoit le prix Nobel de littérature.

Les jeux Olympiques ont lieu à Montréal.

✦1977 Élection du Démocrate Jimmy Carter (1924 –) à la présidence des États-Unis.

La Grande-Bretagne fête le Silver Jubilee de la reine d'Angleterre, marquant 25 ans de règne.

◇1977 Sortie de *Star Wars* (La Guerre des étoiles), superproduction de science-fiction réalisée par l'Américain George Lucas (1944 –).

Mort d'Elvis Presley 'Roi du rock and roll'. Il est pleuré par des millions de personnes.

✦1978 Série de grèves en Grande-Bretagne: le Winter of Discontent.

◇1978 Naissance en Grande-Bretagne de Louise Brown, premier 'bébé-éprouvette' (c.à.d. conçu par fécondation in-vitro).

Le romancier américain Isaac Bashevis Singer (1904 – 1991) reçoit le prix Nobel de littérature.

✦1979 Margaret Thatcher (1925 –), chef du parti conservateur, devient la première femme Premier ministre de Grande-Bretagne. Elle triomphera de nouveau aux élections législatives de 1983 et 1987. Durant ses trois mandats, elle poursuivra une politique générale de dénationalisation et de privatisation et diminuera le rôle des administrations locales. Sa personnalité et sa politique lui vaudront le surnom d''Iron Lady' (la dame de fer).

◇1979 *Apocalypse Now*, film de l'Américain Francis Ford Coppola (1939–), sur la guerre du Viêt-nam, avec Marlon Brando (1924 – 2004).

✦1979 – 1981 Crise des otages de l'Iran: des étudiants islamiques prennent en otage le personnel de l'ambassade des USA à Téhéran. Ils demandent en échange que le Shah en exil leur soit livré par les États-Unis pour être jugé par un tribunal islamique. Malgré des sanctions économiques, les 52 otages ne seront libérés qu'au bout de 444 jours de captivité.

━━━━━━━━━━ 1980 ━━━━━━━━━━

✦1980 Siège de l'ambassade d'Iran à Londres; un commando de l'armée donne l'assaut et libère les otages.

◇1980 John Lennon, auteur-interprète, ancien membre des Beatles, est assassiné à New York.

Représentation à Londres de la pièce de théâtre *Romans in Britain* de Howard Brenton (1942 –), une allégorie sur la présence de l'armée britannique en Irlande du Nord. Le metteur en scène Michael Bogdanov est poursuivi à cause du caractère sexuellement explicite de l'une des scènes.

Le poète américain Czeslaw Milosz (1911 – 2004) reçoit le prix Nobel de littérature.

Les jeux Olympiques d'hiver ont lieu à Lake Placid, dans l'État de New York.

✦1981 Ronald Reagan (1911 – 2004), est élu à la présidence des USA. Il lance un important programme de réformes économiques pour lutter contre l'inflation et réduire les dépenses publiques. Dans le domaine de la politique étrangère, il adopte une attitude résolument anti-communiste.

Grève de la faim de prisonniers catholiques membres de l'IRA en Irlande du Nord, qui revendiquent le statut de prisonniers politiques. Mort de dix d'entre eux, dont Bobby Sands, qui avait été élu député.

◇1981 Premier vol expérimental avec deux astronautes à bord de la navette spatiale américaine mise au point par la NASA. Lancée comme une fusée, cette navette réutilisable atterrit sur une piste commme un avion.

À Londres, première représentation de *Cats*, comédie musicale d'Andrew Lloyd Webber (1948 –).

✦1982 Guerre des Malouines (les Falklands en anglais). L'Argentine revendique cette colonie britannique. Suite à la rupture des pourparlers, elle occupe l'archipel. Les Britanniques attaquent la flotte argentine et après le débarquement de leurs troupes et deux mois de durs combats, ils obligent les Argentins à capituler. Cette victoire fait remonter l'indice de popularité du gouvernement.

'Canada Act': avec l'accord de Londres, la Constitution du Canada ne dépend plus que du gouvernement fédéral.

◇1982 *Blade Runner*, film de science-fiction de Ridley Scott, avec Harrison Ford (1942 –).

L'Américaine Alice Walker (1944 –) publie *The Color Purple* (La Couleur pourpre), et remporte le prix Pullitzer l'année suivante.

✦1983 Intervention américaine à la Grenade.

French/Français column:

The minimum voting age is lowered from 21 to 18. Simone Veil (1927 —), Minister of Health, secures the legalization of abortion in a law that bears her name.

◇1974 *Les Valseuses*, film by Bertrand Blier starring Gérard Depardieu, Patrick Dewaere and Miou-Miou.

✦1975 Declaration of the independence of the Comoros; only Mayotte chooses to remain French.

◇1975 Michel Colucci, known as Coluche (1944 – 1986), makes his debut at the Café de la Gare. Here he ushers in, with the group of comedians Le Splendid, a new style of comedy.

Bernard Pivot launches the literary television programme *Apostrophes*.

✦1976 At its 22nd Congress, the PCF abandons the doctrine of the dictatorship of the proletariat.

In Quebec, René Levesque's separatist party (Parti Québécois) attains power.

The Summer Olympic Games are held in Montreal.

◇1976 *Monsieur Klein* (Mr Klein), film by Joseph Losey with Alain Delon.

Michel Foucault (1926 – 1984) publishes *Histoire de la sexualité* (History of Sexuality).

✦1977 Belgium is divided into three regions: Wallonia, Flanders and Brussels.

The Republic of Djibouti (formerly the French Territory of the Afars and Issas) gains independence.

In Quebec, Law 101 establishes French as the official language.

◇1977 Opening of the Georges Pompidou Centre.

✦1978 The Swiss Confederation creates the canton of Jura, which combines three French-speaking regions.

◇1978 Oil slick in Brittany following the sinking of the Liberian tanker Amoco-Cadiz.

In *Le Monde*, Robert Faurisson publishes the article *Le problème des chambres à gaz, ou la rumeur d'Auschwitz* (The question of the gas chambers or the rumour of Auschwitz) which marks the beginning of revisionism, or denial of genocide.

Béate and Serge Klarsfeld publish the essay *Mémorial de la déportation des juifs de France*.

✦1979 The satirical newspaper *Le Canard enchaîné* publishes an article on the diamonds given by Emperor Bokassa (of the Central African Republic) to Valéry Giscard d'Estaing.

◇1979 First successful launch of the Ariane rocket.

Jean Fourastié (1907 – 1990) publishes *Les Trente Glorieuses*, a book about the thirty years of unprecedented economic prosperity in post-war France.

✦1980 In a referendum, the Quebecois vote against independence for the province.

◇1980 Attack on a synagogue in the rue Copernic in Paris.

The Belgian writer Marguerite Yourcenar (1903 – 1987) is elected to the Académie Française.

Le Père Noël est une ordure, alternative theatre success by the Le Splendid group of comedians.

Bernard Kouchner founds Médecins du Monde.

The first TGV (high-speed train) comes into operation.

✦1981 François Mitterrand is elected President of the Republic.

Abolition of the death penalty.

✦1982 Laws on nationalizations, decentralization, the 39-hour week and retirement at 60.

◇1982 Amandine, the first French test-tube baby, is born.

An antisemitic attack in the rue des Rosiers in Paris leaves 6 dead and 22 injured.

✦1983 The ex-Nazi Klaus Barbie, extradited from Bolivia, arrives in France where he is charged with crimes against humanity.

English/Anglais	French/Français
239 soldats américains sont tués dans un attentat à Beyrouth, au Liban. ◇1983 Le romancier britannique William Golding (1911–1993) reçoit le prix Nobel de littérature. ✦1984 Une bombe de l'IRA explose au Grand Hotel de Brighton pendant la conférence annuelle du parti conservateur, et fait quatre morts et de nombreux blessés. Grève des mineurs en Grande-Bretagne, menés par Arthur Scargill, en réaction à la fermeture annoncée de nombreux puits. Violentes confrontations entre grévistes et forces de l'ordre. ◇1984 Les jeux Olympiques ont lieu à Los Angeles. ✦1985 Émeutes raciales à Londres (Brixton et Tottenham) et à Birmingham (Handsworth). Drame du Heysel à Bruxelles: 41 personnes trouvent la mort au cours d'émeutes provoquées par les supporters de Liverpool. Les clubs britanniques sont exclus des compétitions européennes. Premiers cas d'encéphalopathie bovine spongiforme (maladie de la vache folle) en Grande-Bretagne. ◇1985 Mort de Robert Graves (1895–1985), poète et romancier anglais, auteur de *I, Claudius* (Moi, Claude), de *Claudius the God* (Le Dieu Claude), ainsi que de recueils de poèmes.	58 French soldiers are killed in a bomb attack in Beirut. ◇1983 Nathalie Sarraute publishes *Enfance* (Childhood). The tennis player Yannick Noah is the first French winner of the French Open since 1946. Professor Luc Montagnier (1932–) of the Pasteur Institute identifies the HIV virus responsible for AIDS. ✦1984 Laurent Fabius (1946–) becomes Prime Minister (1984–1986). Jacques Delors (1925–) becomes President of the European Commission. ◇1984 Marguerite Duras writes the novel *L'Amant* (The Lover). France wins the Football European Cup. ✦1985 Presentation of the Pisani Plan for a new more independent status for New Caledonia. The tiny extreme-left group, Action Directe, claims responsibility for the murder of René Audran, Director of International Affairs at the Ministry of Defence. On the initiative of Coluche, opening of the first Resto du cœur soup kitchen in Paris. Scandal of the Rainbow Warrior: the French secret services are implicated in the attack (in which one person dies) on a Greenpeace ship in New Zealand. ◇1985 Claude Simon (1913–2005) receives the Nobel Prize for literature. His best-known work is *La Route des Flandres* (The Flanders Road). *Shoah*, documentary film by Claude Lanzmann on the extermination of the Jews. Agnès Varda's film *Sans toit ni loi* (Vagabonde) is released. Beginning of the building of the Grande Arche at La Défense, by O. von Spreckelsen.
✦1986 Scandale de l'Irangate aux États-Unis: découverte de ventes secrètes d'armes à l'Iran — peut-être autorisées par le Président — pour tenter d'obtenir la libération d'otages américains détenus au Liban, et afin de financer la guerre et les opérations terroristes menées par les Contras contre l'état nicaraguayen dont les réformes économiques déplaisent à Washington. Des bombardiers américains basés en Grande-Bretagne bombardent la Libye à la suite d'attentats attribués au Colonel Khadafi. Explosion en vol de la navette Challenger. ◇1986 Avènement de l'ordinateur personnel Apple Macintosh. Mort d'Henry Moore, sculpteur anglais semi-abstrait. L'une de ses œuvres les plus célèbres, *Madonna and Child* (La Vierge et l'Enfant) se trouve dans l'église de St Matthew à Northampton. ✦1987 Début des travaux de creusement du tunnel sous la Manche (il sera terminé en 1994) entre Cheriton, près de Folkestone en Angleterre, et Sangatte, près de Calais. Nouveau krach boursier aux États-Unis. ◇1987 Le poète américain Joseph Brodsky (1940–1996) reçoit le prix Nobel de littérature. ✦1988 150 travailleurs trouvent la mort dans l'incendie de la plate-forme pétrolière Piper Alpha en mer du Nord. Un Boeing 747 de la Pan Am explose au-dessus de Lockerbie, en Écosse, provoquant la mort des 270 passagers et de 11 villageois. Bicentennaire de l'arrivée des premiers colons européens en Australie. ◇1988 *A Brief History of Time* (Brève Histoire du Temps), ouvrage de cosmologie du savant anglais Stephen Hawking (1942–) est un best-seller. Salman Rushdie publie *The Satanic Verses* (Les Versets sataniques), ouvrage jugé blasphématoire par de nombreux musulmans et qui lui vaut d'être l'objet d'une fatwa. Jeux Olympiques d'hiver à Calgary, au Canada. ✦1989 Le Républicain George Bush (1924–) accède à la présidence des États-Unis. Son mandat marque la fin de la guerre froide entre l'URSS et les États-Unis. Intervention américaine au Panama. En Angleterre, 95 supporters de Liverpool meurent écrasés au stade de Hillsborough, à Sheffield, à la suite d'un mouvement de foule non contrôlé. ◇1989 Mort du grand acteur et metteur en scène anglais Laurence Olivier (1907–1989). Célèbre avant tout pour son interprétation du théâtre shakespearien, il avait également mené une carrière d'acteur de cinéma et de télévision.	✦1986 Following the legislative elections, Jacques Chirac's RPR and Valéry Giscard d'Estaing's UDF obtain the majority of seats in the National Assembly; this is the start of the first 'cohabitation': Jacques Chirac (1932–) becomes Prime Minister (1986–1988). Assassination of Georges Besse, manager of the state-controlled car manufacturers Renault; responsibility is claimed by Action Directe. Series of fatal bomb attacks in Paris. ◇1986 Death of Coluche and Thierry Le Luron, the two most popular comedians of the decade. *L'Identité de la France* (The Identity of France), essay by the historian of human behaviour, Fernand Braudel. ✦1987 Arrest of the leaders of Action Directe. Trial of Klaus Barbie in Lyon where he lived during the Occupation; he is sentenced to life imprisonment for crimes against humanity. In response to the zero option (withdrawal of medium-range missiles in Europe) proposed by Mikhail Gorbatchev, President Mitterrand reasserts France's position on maintaining the nuclear deterrent. Referendum on self-determination for New Caledonia in favour of independence. ◇1987 Jean-Marie Lehn (1939–) wins the Nobel Prize for chemistry. The medieval historian Georges Duby (1919–1996), is elected to the Académie Française. Louis Malle's film *Au revoir les enfants* (Goodbye Children) is released. *Sous le soleil de Satan* (Under Satan's Sun) by Maurice Pialat wins the Palme d'or at the Cannes Film Festival. ✦1988 François Mitterrand is re-elected President of the Republic (1988–1995). Introduction of the RMI (minimum welfare payment funded by the wealth tax). Prime Minister Michel Rocard (1930–) negotiates the Matignon Accords in Paris with Jean-Marie Tjibaou (FLNKS, separatist party) and Jacques Lafleur (RPCR, against independence) on the future of New Caledonia. ◇1988 Maurice Allais (1911–) wins the Nobel Prize for economics. Monsignor Lefebvre (1905–1991) is excommunicated by Pope John Paul II, for having ordained four bishops without the authority of the Vatican. ✦1989 Assassination in New Caledonia of Jean-Marie Tjibaou and Yeiwéné-Yeiwéné (FLNKS). Third summit of French-speaking countries in Dakar: François Mitterrand announces the cancellation of part of the debt of 35 African countries to France. ◇1989 Celebration of the Bicentennary of the French Revolution. Opening of the Grand Louvre (with the glass pyramid).

—— 1990 ——

English/Anglais	French/Français
✦1990 L'introduction de la poll tax en Angleterre et au pays de Galles provoquent de graves émeutes, notamment à Londres. L'attitude 'eurosceptique' de Margaret Thatcher divise les Conservateurs. Elle démissionne lorsqu'elle n'obtient pas la majorité qualifiée lors du renouvellement statutaire du leader de son parti, cédant la place à John Major (1943–). En Afrique du Sud, libération de Nelson Mandela après 27 ans d'incarcération. Les équipes française et britannique opèrent la jonction du tunnel sous la Manche. De violentes tempêtes provoquent de graves dégâts en Angleterre et au pays de Galles. ✦1991 Guerre du Golfe: le Conseil de sécurité de l'ONU autorise l'intervention d'une force multinationale coordonnée par les Américains pour chasser les Iraquiens du Koweït. Destruction d'une grande partie des armements de l'Iraq. ◇1991 La romancière sud-africaine Nadine Gordimer (1923–) reçoit le prix Nobel de littérature. ✦1992 Graves émeutes à Los Angeles à la suite de l'acquittement d'un policier accusé d'avoir violemment battu un automobiliste noir. L'ouragan Andrew provoque d'importants dégâts en Floride. ◇1992 Michael Ondaatje (1943–), écrivain canadien d'origine sri-lankaise, obtient le prix Booker ex-aequo pour son roman *The English Patient* (Le Patient anglais).	✦1990 The two Eurotunnel construction sites meet beneath the Channel. ◇1990 Opening of the Opéra at Bastille. ✦1991 Beginning of the Gulf War to which France sends an armoured division. Vigipirate plan: enhanced measures to combat terrorist attacks. ◇1991 Scandal involving infected blood: the blood transfusion centre continued, knowingly, to use blood infected with the AIDS virus. ✦1992 Pierre Bérégovoy (1925–1993) succeeds Édith Cresson as Prime Minister (1992–1993). ◇1992 Infected blood affair: conviction of the managers of the blood transfusion organization. Georges Charpak (1924–) wins the Nobel Prize for physics. *Les Nuits fauves* (Savage Nights), a film by Cyril Collard makes AIDS a subject for mainstream cinema.

English/Anglais	French/Français

Le poète antillais de langue anglaise Derek Walcott (1930 –) reçoit le prix Nobel de littérature.
✦1993 Aux États-Unis, les Républicains cèdent la place aux Démocrates après 12 années au pouvoir. Le nouveau président, Bill Clinton (1946 –), promet le retour à la prospérité.
Une bombe explose au World Trade Center à New York; l'attentat est attribué à des fondamentalistes islamiques.
Fusillade et incendie meurtriers à Waco, au Texas, au cours de l'intervention armée du FBI contre la secte de David Koresh.
◇1993 L'artiste britannique Damien Hirst (1965 –) présente son œuvre *Mother and Child Divided*, une vache coupée en deux dans du formol.
La romancière américaine Toni Morrison (1931 –) reçoit le prix Nobel de littérature.
Jurassic Park, film de l'Américain Steven Spielberg (1947 –).
✦1994 Nelson Mandela (1918 –), condamné à la prison à vie en 1964 puis libéré en 1990, devient le premier président noir de l'Afrique du Sud.
Ouverture du tunnel sous la Manche.
✦1995 L'explosion d'une bombe dans un bâtiment du gouvernement fédéral à Oklahoma City fait 168 morts.
◇1995 Le poète irlandais Seamus Heaney (1939 –) reçoit le prix Nobel de littérature.
Toy Story, produit par les studios Disney et réalisé par John Lasseter, premier long métrage comprenant uniquement des images de synthèse.
✦1996 Bill Clinton est réélu à la présidence des États-Unis.
Les autorités britanniques annoncent qu'il existerait un lien entre le nouveau variant de la maladie de Creutzfeldt-Jacob et l'encéphalopathie bovine spongiforme. Début de l'embargo européen sur la viande bovine britannique.
◇1996 Sortie du film *Trainspotting*, du Britannique Danny Boyle (1956 –), d'après l'œuvre du romancier écossais Irvine Welsh (1961 –).
La romancière anglaise JK Rowling (1965 –) publie *Harry Potter and the Philosopher's Stone* (Harry Potter à l'école des sorciers). Cet ouvrage et les suivants sont des succès de librairie phénoménaux.
Les jeux Olympiques ont lieu à Atlanta, aux États-Unis. L'explosion d'une bombe fait une victime.
✦1997 Hongkong, qui avait été cédée à la Grande-Bretagne pour une période de 99 ans, est rendue à la Chine.
Élection des travaillistes en Grande-Bretagne, après 18 ans de pouvoir conservateur. Tony Blair est Premier ministre.
La princesse Diana est tuée dans un accident de voiture à Paris.
◇1997 Premier clonage d'un animal ('Dolly', une brebis) à Roslin, près d'Édimbourg.
Sortie du film *Titanic*, réalisé par l'Américain James Cameron (1954 –); plus gros succès commercial de l'histoire du cinéma à ce jour.
✦1998 Signature d'un accord de paix en Irlande du Nord (Good Friday agreement).
L'Écosse et le pays de Galles votent en faveur de davantage d'autonomie au cours de référendums.
L'ouragan Georges provoque d'importants dégâts en Floride.
◇1998 *The Angel of the North*, sculpture métallique géante du Britannique Anthony Gormley, est érigée à Gateshead, à côté de Newcastle.
◇1998 À la suite de sa liaison avec Monica Lewinsky, Bill Clinton devient le deuxième président des États-Unis à faire l'objet de procédures d'impeachment (le premier était Andrew Johnson en 1868). Il est accusé de faux témoignage puis acquitté.
✦1999 Inauguration du parlement écossais et de l'assemblée du pays de Galles.
L'ouragan Floyd dévaste les côtes de Caroline du Nord.
◇1999 Mort de Yehudi Menuhin, grand violoniste anglais né en 1916 aux États-Unis.

First broadcasts of Arte, Franco-German cultural television channel.
The Winter Olympic Games are held in Albertville.
✦1993 The defeat of the socialists in the legislative elections brings an RPR-UDF government back into power (1993 – 1995), with Edouard Balladur (1929 –) as Prime Minister; this is the beginning of the second period of 'cohabitation'.
In Belgium, a constitutional review transforms unitary Belgium into a federal State accompanied by decentralized powers. Albert II succeeds Baudoin I.
In Quebec, an amendment to Law 101 authorizes a limited use of English in advertising displays.
✦1994 Indictment of Ministers Georgina Dufoix, Edmond Hervé and Laurent Fabius for their involvement in the infected blood affair. Mme Dufoix declares herself to be responsible, but not guilty.
Paul Touvier, an official in the Pétain government, is sentenced to life imprisonment.
The Channel Tunnel is opened.
◇ 1994 The first map of the entire human genome is drawn up by the French Généthon team.
✦1995 Election of Jacques Chirac to the Presidency of the Republic (1995 – 2002). He calls on Alain Juppé (1945 –) as Prime Minister (1995 – 1997).
President Chirac acknowledges the wrongs committed by the French State against the Jews in the Second World War.
The Quebecois decide by a small majority against independence for the province.
◇1995 Cardinal Lustiger is elected to the Académie Française.
La Haine (Hate) is released, a film by Mathieu Kassovitz on the lives of three teenagers living in a deprived Paris suburb.
✦1996 Death of François Mitterrand on 8 January.
The Corsican issue is at the forefront of domestic French politics.
Assassination of seven French monks in Tibérine, Algeria.
Illegal Malian immigrants asking for asylum are taken in by the Saint-Bernard church in Paris: this marks the beginning of the affair of the 'sans-papiers' (people without work or residence permits).
✦1997 Massive mobilization in Europe against the French government's decision to close the Vilvorde Renault factory in Belgium.
President Chirac decides unexpectedly to dissolve the National Assembly, offering a victory to the left which makes Lionel Jospin (1937 –) Prime Minister.
Beginning of the Papon trial in Bordeaux: Maurice Papon, a former senior civil servant in the Vichy government, is accused of crimes against humanity.
◇1997 Claude Cohen-Tannoudji (1933 –) wins the Nobel Prize for physics.
✦1998 Beginning of the Elf affair: publication in the press of the investigation into the Elf affair, in which Roland Dumas, president of the Constitutional Council, is implicated.
Assassination of Claude Erignac, Prefect of Corsica, in Ajaccio.
Maurice Papon is sentenced to ten years' imprisonment.
The referendum on self-determination for New Caledonia achieves a 72% vote in favour.
◇1998 France (which is also the host country) wins the Football World Cup.
✦1999 Passing of the PACS (pacte civil de solidarité), a contract for people in a long-term relationship, which considerably extends the rights of unmarried couples and homosexuals.
Passing of the law on the 35-hour week.
◇1999 Violent storms cause considerable damage in France.

=== 2000 ===

✦2000 Élection controversée du Républicain George W. Bush à la présidence des États-Unis.
◇ 2000 Les jeux Olympiques ont lieu à Sydney, en Australie.
✦2001 Le Parlement britannique autorise le clonage d'embryons humains pour la recherche scientifique.
Grave épidémie de fièvre aphteuse dans toute la Grande-Bretagne.
Ré-élection du Premier ministre travailliste Tony Blair en Grande-Bretagne.
Le 11 septembre, des terroristes détournent plusieurs avions de ligne; deux d'entre eux percutent les tours jumelles du World Trade Center de New York, un autre s'écrase sur le Pentagone à Washington, un quatrième s'écrase en Pennsylvanie. Les attentats font environ 3000 morts.
Frappes américaines contre les Talibans en Afghanistan.
◇ 2001 La joueuse de tennis américaine Venus Williams (1980 –) remporte le tournoi de Wimbledon pour la deuxième fois consécutive.
Le romancier trinidadien VS Naipaul (1932 –) reçoit le prix Nobel de littérature.
✦2002 En Grande-Bretagne, décès de Sa Majesté la Reine Élisabeth, la Reine Mère, née Elizabeth Bowes-Lyon, à l'âge de 101 ans.
Golden Jubilee de la Reine Elizabeth II, célébrant 50 années de règne.
Le président George W. Bush crée un ministère de la Sécurité intérieure, le Department of Homeland Security, afin de prévenir les attentats terroristes ainsi que les catastrophes naturelles.
L'ancien président des États-Unis Jimmy Carter reçoit le prix Nobel de la paix.
◇ 2002 L'Américain Steve Fossett (1944 –) devient le premier homme à faire le tour du monde en ballon en solo.
Décès du poète, écrivain et comique britannique Spike Milligan à l'âge de 83 ans.

✦2000 In a referendum, a majority of voters declare themselves in favour of the five-year period for the presidency of the Republic.
◇ 2000 France wins the Football European Cup.
✦2001 Roland Dumas, former president of the Constitutional Council and foreign minister under Mitterrand, is sentenced to six months' imprisonment for accepting bribes from the oil company Elf.
End of National Service. The French army becomes entirely professional.
In September, an explosion at the AZF chemical factory in Toulouse kills 30 people and injures around 2,500, as well as causing considerable material damage.
French troops are sent to Afghanistan to fight the Taliban following the September 11 attack on the World Trade Center.
◇ 2001 French singer Charles Trenet dies aged 88.
Jean-Pierre Jeunet's film *Le Fabuleux Destin d'Amélie Poulain* (UK: *Amélie*, US: *Amélie from Montmartre*) is released.
The first football match between France and Algeria since Algerian independence takes place, but is interrupted by violent incidents involving young immigrants.
✦2002 The French franc is replaced by the euro.
After the first round of voting, the two candidates in the runoff for President are Jacques Chirac and National Front leader Jean-Marie Le Pen. Demonstrations against the Far Right ensue and Chirac is reelected President in a landslide victory.
Switzerland joins the United Nations.
The French centre-right party the UMP is created, replacing the RPR.
Former Vichy official and collaborationist Maurice Papon is released from prison on medical grounds.
France lifts its ban on British beef imports, imposed in 1996 due to fears of BSE.
◇ 2002 French sociologist Pierre Bourdieu dies aged 71.
French painter and sculptor Niki de Saint Phalle dies aged 71.

English/Anglais

◆2003 Mise en œuvre d'une taxe anti-embouteillages à Londres : les automobilistes désirant se rendre au centre-ville devront désormais payer.
En dépit de nombreuses manifestations, les États-Unis et la Grande-Bretagne lancent des frappes aériennes contre l'Iraq, suivies de l'invasion et de l'occupation du pays.
L'ancien culturiste et vedette de films d'action Arnold Schwarzenegger est élu gouverneur de l'État de Californie pour le Parti républicain.
Capture de Saddam Hussein par l'armée américaine à Tikrit.
◇2003 Décès de Johnny Cash, star de la country music, à l'âge de 71 ans.
Publication de The Da Vinci Code, de l'auteur américain Dan Brown, qui devient rapidement un best-seller international.
L'Angleterre remporte la Coupe du Monde de rugby à Sydney en battant l'Australie 20–17.
◆2004 Des photos de soldats américains maltraitant des prisonniers iraquiens dans la prison d'Abou Ghraib provoquent un scandale.
Ré-élection de George W. Bush à la présidence des États-Unis ; défaite du démocrate John Kerry.
Inauguration des nouveaux locaux du Parlement Écossais (Holyrood), à Édimbourg.
En Irlande, entrée en vigueur d'une loi interdisant de fumer dans tout lieu public.
◇2004 Le film Lord of the Rings: The Return of the King (Le Seigneur des anneaux: le retour du roi), du Néo-Zélandais Peter Jackson, remporte 11 Oscars.
Décès de l'acteur Marlon Brando à l'âge de 80 ans.
◆2005 Entrée en vigueur d'une loi interdisant la chasse à courre en Grande-Bretagne.
Tony Blair est élu Premier ministre pour la troisième fois consécutive.
À Londres, des attentats terroristes frappent plusieurs rames de métro et un bus, faisant 52 morts et de nombreux blessés.
L'ouragan Katrina frappe La Nouvelle-Orléans, provoquant d'immenses dégâts et des inondations dans de nombreux quartiers.
En Grande-Bretagne, entrée en vigueur d'une loi garantissant aux couples homosexuels la plupart des droits dont jouissent les couples mariés.
Mariage du Prince Charles et de Camilla Parker-Bowles à Windsor.
◇2005 Décès du dramaturge américain Arthur Miller à l'âge de 89 ans.
Le dramaturge anglais Harold Pinter (1930 –) reçoit le prix Nobel de littérature.
Décès du footballeur britannique George Best à l'âge de 59 ans, suite à de nombreuses années d'alcoolisme.
◆2006 Entrée en vigueur d'une loi interdisant de fumer dans tout lieu public en Écosse.
La Chambre des communes vote une loi interdisant de fumer dans tout lieu public en Angleterre.
En Grande-Bretagne, entrée en vigueur du Terrorism Act, qui interdit toute glorification du terrorisme sous peine de poursuites.
La reine Elisabeth II fête ses 80 ans.
◇2006 Décès de la romancière écossaise Muriel Spark, auteur de The Prime of Miss Jean Brodie, à l'âge de 88 ans.

French/Français

◆2003 February/March: France's anti-war stance causes tension with the USA.
8 March: a march organized by the women's group 'Ni putes ni soumises' (Neither Whores Nor Submissive) group ends in Paris: some 20,000 people demonstrate in the streets at violence against women in immigrant communities.
The heatwave sweeping Europe kills around 15,000 people in France, most of them elderly.
◇2003 Concorde's last commercial flight operated by Air France.
Belgian tennis player Justine Henin-Hardenne (1982 –) wins the women's title at Roland Garros.
Former French President Valéry Giscard d'Estaing is elected to the Académie française.
◆2004 A new law comes into effect in France banning the wearing of any religious symbols (including the Muslim headscarf) in public schools and state buildings.
◇2004 French photographer Henri-Cartier Bresson dies aged 95.
French writer Françoise Sagan dies in Paris aged 69. Her most famous novel is Bonjour Tristesse (1954).
The highest bridge in the world, the Norman Foster-designed Millau Viaduct in Southern France, is unveiled.
◆2005 Dominique de Villepin replaces Jean-Pierre Raffarin as French Prime Minister.
France votes against the proposed European Constitution in a referendum.
Serious rioting erupts in the Paris suburbs after two young immigrants die trying to escape from police; it spreads to other cities and a national state of emergency is declared.
Acquittal of all defendants in the 'Outreau Affair', a case involving a ring of alleged paedophiles in Boulogne. The case is dubbed 'a judicial disaster' by the government following five years of judicial error and miscarriage of justice.
French surgeons carry out the first human face transplant.
The Cadarache research centre in south-eastern France is selected as the site for the construction of the ITER nuclear fusion reactor.
◆2006 National protests in France against the government's proposed 'first employment contract' (CPE) for young people: demonstrations, strikes and occupation of university buildings. The government eventually backs down.
◇2006 The French football team is narrowly defeated by Italy at the World Cup final in Berlin.
French tennis player Amélie Mauresmo (1979 –) wins the women's title at Wimbledon.

French Communication Guide

Letters
Layout (31)
Beginnings (31)
Endings (32)
Addresses and postcodes (33)
Envelopes (33)

Model letters
Chatty letter to a friend or relative (34)
Postcards (34)
Greetings cards (35)
Letter of complaint (36)
Apologizing (37)
Making a reservation (37)
Letter of thanks to a friend or relative (38)
Invitations and replies (38)
Letter of condolence (41)
Asking for a brochure/information (42)
Letter to authorities: official statement (42)
Writing to a contractor (43)

Business correspondence
Business to business (general) (43)
Placing an order (44)
Replying to an order (44)
Informing a customer (45)
Letter of complaint (45)
Dealing with a customer complaint (46)
Invoice (46)
Reply to invoice (47)
Sales promotion letter (47)

Employment
Covering letter (48)
Replying to an advertisement (48)
Unsolicited application (49)
Asking for a work placement (49)
Curriculum vitae (50)

Abbreviations and acronyms: general correspondence (52)

Faxes
Business (53)
Booking a hotel room (53)

E-mail
Within a company (54)
Business to business (54)
To a friend (55)
Abbreviations and acronyms: e-mail and Internet (55)

Advertisements
Job advertisement (56)
Offering goods for sale (56)
Accommodation to rent (57)
Personal advertisement (57)

Telephone calls (58)

Letters

Basic principles

When sending a letter or other written communication, particular attention should be paid to the grammar and spelling as these are sensitive topics. Spelling mistakes and grammatical errors in a letter are considered very bad form, even in private correspondence.

The style should be simple and clear. It is a good idea to keep sentences short and to use active rather than passive verbs. Each paragraph should deal with one idea only. The idea is presented in the first sentence of the paragraph and is then developed. A new idea is expressed in a new paragraph.

Layout

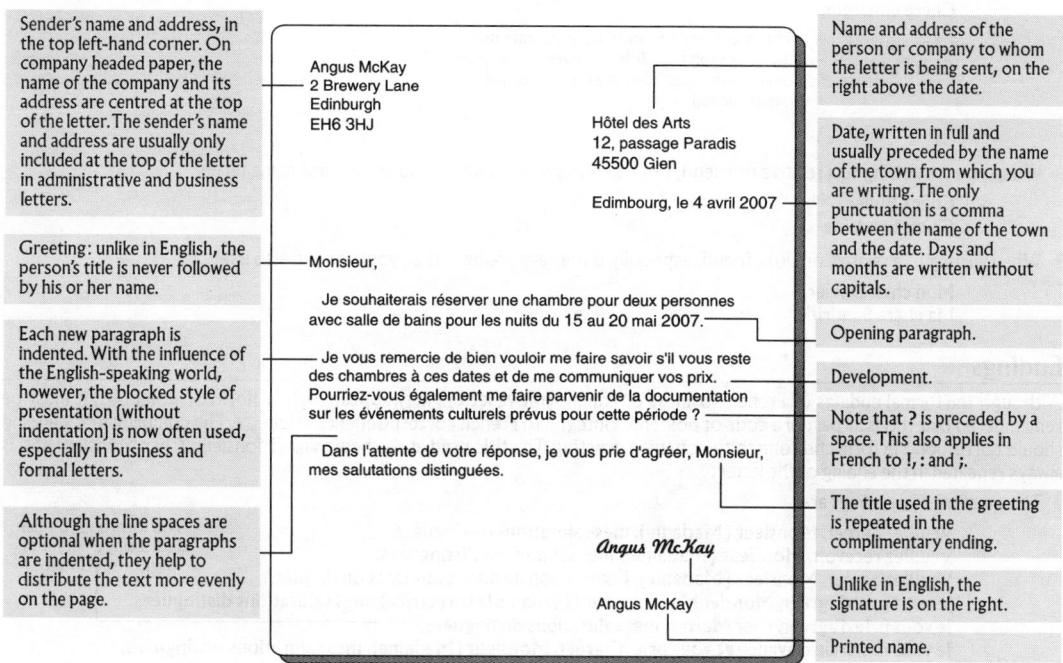

Sender's name and address, in the top left-hand corner. On company headed paper, the name of the company and its address are centred at the top of the letter. The sender's name and address are usually only included at the top of the letter in administrative and business letters.

Greeting: unlike in English, the person's title is never followed by his or her name.

Each new paragraph is indented. With the influence of the English-speaking world, however, the blocked style of presentation (without indentation) is now often used, especially in business and formal letters.

Although the line spaces are optional when the paragraphs are indented, they help to distribute the text more evenly on the page.

Name and address of the person or company to whom the letter is being sent, on the right above the date.

Date, written in full and usually preceded by the name of the town from which you are writing. The only punctuation is a comma between the name of the town and the date. Days and months are written without capitals.

Opening paragraph.

Development.

Note that ? is preceded by a space. This also applies in French to !, : and ;.

The title used in the greeting is repeated in the complimentary ending.

Unlike in English, the signature is on the right.

Printed name.

Letter content:

Angus McKay
2 Brewery Lane
Edinburgh
EH6 3HJ

Hôtel des Arts
12, passage Paradis
45500 Gien

Edimbourg, le 4 avril 2007

Monsieur,

Je souhaiterais réserver une chambre pour deux personnes avec salle de bains pour les nuits du 15 au 20 mai 2007.

Je vous remercie de bien vouloir me faire savoir s'il vous reste des chambres à ces dates et de me communiquer vos prix. Pourriez-vous également me faire parvenir de la documentation sur les événements culturels prévus pour cette période ?

Dans l'attente de votre réponse, je vous prie d'agréer, Monsieur, mes salutations distinguées.

Angus McKay

Angus McKay

Beginnings

The opening greetings and endings used in letters written in French follow certain well-established rules:

- If you do not know the person you are writing to, whether you know their name or not, or if you know them only slightly:

  Monsieur
  Madame
  > The greetings **Monsieur** and **Madame** are equivalent to 'Dear Sir' and 'Dear Madam' in English.

  Mademoiselle
  > **Mademoiselle** is used for an unmarried young woman. If in doubt, use **Madame**.

- When you are unsure whether the recipient of the letter is male or female:

  Madame, Monsieur

- When the letter is addressed to a company rather than to an individual:

  Messieurs

- When writing to the head of a company or institution:

  Monsieur le Directeur
  Madame la Directrice

  Monsieur le Président
  Madame la Présidente

- When writing to a minister, to the Prime Minister or the President:

  Monsieur le Ministre
  Madame le Ministre
  > The form **Madame la Ministre** is equally acceptable now.

  Monsieur le Premier Ministre
  Madame le Premier Ministre

  Monsieur le Président de la République
  Madame la Présidente de la République

- When writing to a lawyer or solicitor:

  Cher Maître
  > This form is used irrespective of whether one is addressing a man or woman in this context.

- When you know the person you are writing to and want to sound less formal:

> Cher Monsieur
> Chère Madame
> Chère Mademoiselle (for an unmarried young woman)

> These greetings are never followed by the name of the person. The equivalent of 'Dear Mr Allen' is **Monsieur** if you don't know him very well, or **Cher Monsieur** if you know him better and want to sound less formal. Always write the title in full and avoid abbreviations like **M.**, **Mme** and **Mlle.**

> If you are writing to more than one person, you need to repeat **Cher** before each title:
> **Cher Monsieur,**
> **Chère Madame,**

- When you are writing to a colleague you do not know or know only slightly:

> Cher collègue
> Chère collègue

> Cher confrère
> Chère consœur

> The titles **Cher confrère** and **Chère consœur** are used between professionals such as doctors and lawyers.

> Cher ami
> Chère amie

> The titles **Cher ami** and **Chère amie** are not used between friends but between colleagues or acquaintances. They are slightly formal and old-fashioned.

- When you are writing to a relative or friend, or to a colleague with whom you are on first name terms:

> Cher Olivier
> Chère Sandrine

- When writing to a relative or close friend, especially if they are younger than you, you can also use:

> Mon cher Olivier
> Ma chère Sandrine

Endings

Although the formal endings of French business or administrative letters may appear slightly florid or pompous, it must be remembered that this is all part of a code of politeness integral to French correspondence etiquette. The complimentary ending should correspond in form and tone to the opening greeting. The title used at the beginning (Monsieur, Cher Monsieur etc) is always repeated in the ending of the letter:

- The most neutral endings are:

> Veuillez agréer, Monsieur (Madame), mes salutations distinguées.
> Veuillez recevoir, Monsieur (Madame), mes salutations distinguées.
> Veuillez agréer, Monsieur (Madame), l'expression de mes sentiments distingués.
> Je vous prie d'agréer, Monsieur le Directeur (Madame la Directrice), mes salutations distinguées.
> Je vous prie d'agréer, cher Maître, mes salutations distinguées.
> Je vous remercie d'avance et vous prie d'agréer, Monsieur (Madame), mes salutations distinguées.
> Dans l'attente d'une réponse de votre part, veuillez agréer, Messieurs, nos salutations distinguées.

> This form is used when addressing a lawyer or solicitor specifically.

- If you want to end on a more respectful note, such as when writing to a superior:

> Veuillez agréer, Monsieur (Madame), l'expression de ma considération distinguée.
> Je vous prie d'agréer, Monsieur (Madame), l'expression de mon profond respect.
> Veuillez agréer, je vous prie, Monsieur le Président (Madame la Présidente), l'expression de ma respectueuse considération.

- If you want to show your gratitude:

> Veuillez agréer, Monsieur (Madame), l'expression de ma profonde gratitude.
> Veuillez agréer, Monsieur (Madame), l'expression de ma respectueuse reconnaissance.
> Croyez, Monsieur (Madame), à toute ma reconnaissance.
> Croyez, Monsieur (Madame), à ma sincère gratitude.

> As noted above, the expression **cher ami**, although more friendly, is still formal and should not be used for a friend.

- Although still formal, the following endings are more friendly:

> Veuillez agréer, cher Monsieur (chère Madame), l'expression de mes sentiments les plus cordiaux.
> Veuillez croire, cher Monsieur (chère Madame), à mon meilleur souvenir.
> Veuillez recevoir, cher ami (chère amie), mes plus cordiales salutations.
> Croyez, cher Olivier (chère Sandrine), à mon amical souvenir.

- Simplified and more informal endings are becoming more common. The following endings can be found more and more in everyday business letters, e-mails and faxes:

> Salutations distinguées.
> Cordialement. (more friendly)
> Bien à vous. (even more friendly)

- The following endings are used when writing to friends or relatives:

Polite:

> Amitiés.
> Amicalement.
> Bien amicalement.
> Bien affectueusement.
> Bien à toi.

Friendly:

> Je t'embrasse.
> À bientôt.
> Embrasse Pierre de ma part.

Informal:

> Grosses bises.
> Bisous.

Addresses and postcodes

▪ You might see the words "bis" and "ter" after the street number in a French address. For example:

> 3 bis, rue des Lilas
> 11 ter, avenue de Bernay

They indicate that there is more than one residence, whether in the form of a self-contained apartment or an annexe to the main house or premises, at the address in question. "Bis" is used to indicate that there is a second residential (or business) unit, "ter" a third. The examples above are equivalent to 3A and 11B in English.

▪ The first two numbers of a French postcode correspond to the administrative code number of the relevant "département". All postcodes for Paris begin with 75. This system also applies to vehicle licence plates. For example:

> 20, boulevard Arago
> 75013 Paris

In the example above, the first two numbers indicate the city of Paris while the last two figures indicate that the address is located in the thirteenth "arrondissement" (district) of the city. Note that in French addresses the postcode is usually written before the town, on the same line.

▪ The abbreviation "Cedex" is often found in French business addresses. For example:

> Société Delacour
> 77170 Fontainebleau Cedex

This is a special postcode ensuring rapid delivery of mail to businesses and certain institutions. The first two figures, as in other postcodes, denote geographical location but the following three figures denote an individual code assigned to the company in question.

▪ In Belgium addresses are often written with the building number coming after the street name. For an apartment or a house where there are more than three letterboxes it is usual to add the letterbox number (not the apartment number) after the street number. For example:

> Monsieur Luc Dujardin
> rue du Clocher 143, bte 12 ——— The abbreviation for **boîte**.
> 1040 Bruxelles

▪ Swiss addresses are also usually written with the street number appearing after the street name, and the postcode before the town. When writing from outside Switzerland the abbreviation CH (for "Confederatio Helvetica" or the Swiss Confederation) is often added. For example:

> Monsieur André Roux
> Avenue du Peyrou 4
> CH - 2000 Neuchâtel

▪ In Canada, it is usual to write the name of the town or municipality, followed by the province in which it is located, followed by the postcode, all on the same line. For example:

> Madame Chantal Lemoine
> 3567 rue Drummond
> Montréal (Québec) H3G 1M8 ———

> The name of the province is usually given in brackets after the name of the town or municipality. Alternatively an abbreviation can be used to designate the province: for example QC for **Québec**. If the abbreviated form is used then there is no need for brackets.

> The websites of the various postal services in French-speaking countries are a useful source of information regarding addresses and postcodes in particular.
>
> France: www.laposte.fr
> Belgium: www.post.be
> Luxembourg: www.pt.lu
> Switzerland: www.poste.ch
> Canada: www.canadapost.ca

Envelopes

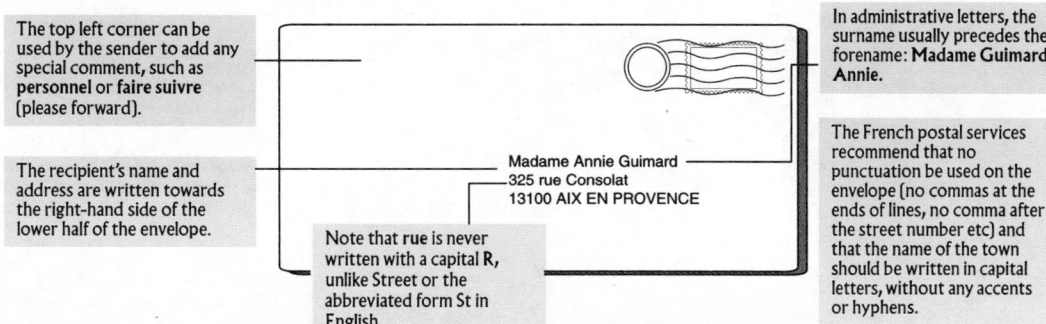

The top left corner can be used by the sender to add any special comment, such as **personnel** or **faire suivre** (please forward).

The recipient's name and address are written towards the right-hand side of the lower half of the envelope.

Note that **rue** is never written with a capital **R**, unlike Street or the abbreviated form St in English.

Madame Annie Guimard
325 rue Consolat
13100 AIX EN PROVENCE

In administrative letters, the surname usually precedes the forename: **Madame Guimard Annie.**

The French postal services recommend that no punctuation be used on the envelope (no commas at the ends of lines, no comma after the street number etc) and that the name of the town should be written in capital letters, without any accents or hyphens.

It is standard practice to write a return address on the back of the envelope at the top, in case the letter gets lost.

Model letters

Chatty letter to a friend or relative

When writing to friends and relatives, as in English, a more informal style is perfectly acceptable.

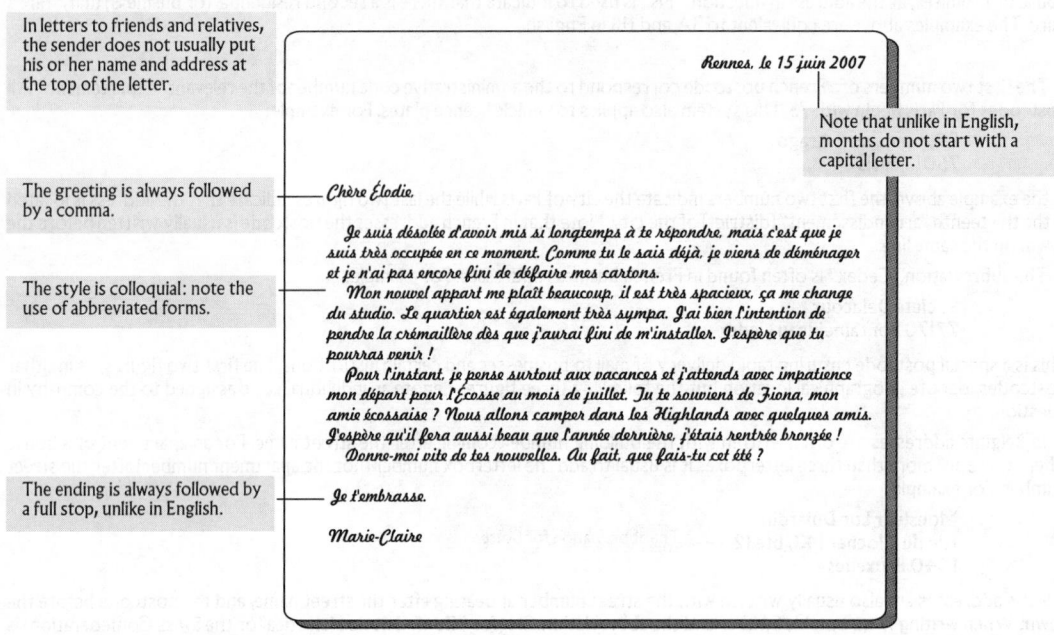

In letters to friends and relatives, the sender does not usually put his or her name and address at the top of the letter.

Rennes, le 15 juin 2007

Note that unlike in English, months do not start with a capital letter.

The greeting is always followed by a comma.

Chère Élodie,

The style is colloquial: note the use of abbreviated forms.

Je suis désolée d'avoir mis si longtemps à te répondre, mais c'est que je suis très occupée en ce moment. Comme tu le sais déjà, je viens de déménager et je n'ai pas encore fini de défaire mes cartons.

Mon nouvel appart me plaît beaucoup, il est très spacieux, ça me change du studio. Le quartier est également très sympa. J'ai bien l'intention de pendre la crémaillère dès que j'aurai fini de m'installer. J'espère que tu pourras venir !

Pour l'instant, je pense surtout aux vacances et j'attends avec impatience mon départ pour l'Écosse au mois de juillet. Tu te souviens de Fiona, mon amie écossaise ? Nous allons camper dans les Highlands avec quelques amis. J'espère qu'il fera aussi beau que l'année dernière, j'étais rentrée bronzée ! Donne-moi vite de tes nouvelles. Au fait, que fais-tu cet été ?

The ending is always followed by a full stop, unlike in English.

Je t'embrasse.

Marie-Claire

Postcards

It is not unusual in France to send a postcard in an envelope. Apart from the additional writing space this allows, it is a way of guaranteeing extra privacy. Your postcard will also arrive more quickly in an envelope with letter-rate postage.

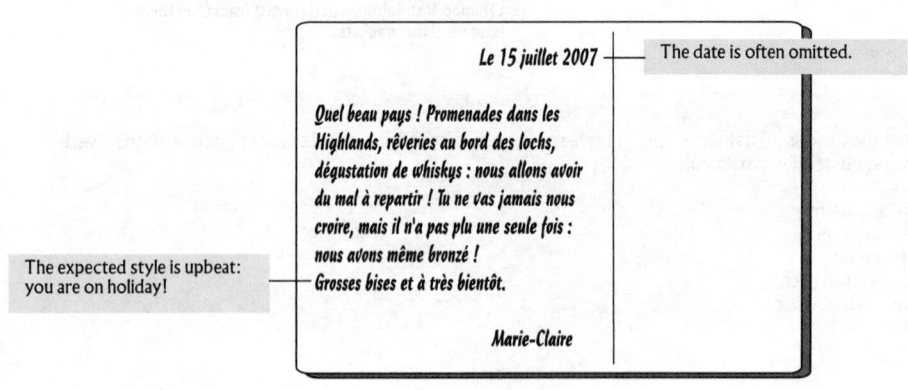

Le 15 juillet 2007 — The date is often omitted.

Quel beau pays ! Promenades dans les Highlands, rêveries au bord des lochs, dégustation de whiskys : nous allons avoir du mal à repartir ! Tu ne vas jamais nous croire, mais il n'a pas plu une seule fois : nous avons même bronzé !

The expected style is upbeat: you are on holiday!

Grosses bises et à très bientôt.

Marie-Claire

Greetings cards

■ Season's greetings

The use of greetings cards is not as widespread in France as in English-speaking countries. Greetings cards are usually sent for New Year rather than Christmas. You can send a New Year's card at any time from before Christmas until the end of January, although usually before the middle of January. They are mostly sent to friends and relatives who live far away and business acquaintances. They are always posted and are never handed to the recipient.

Bonne et heureuse année 2008 à tous les trois.

À très bientôt, j'espère.

Laurence

Cher Simon, chère Odile,

Tous nos vœux de bonheur pour l'année 2008 !

Bien à vous.

Vincent et Sylvie

Chère Mathilde,

Que cette nouvelle année t'apporte joie et bonheur et soit l'occasion de nous voir souvent !

Irène

Cher Jérôme, chère Nicole,

Nous vous remercions de vos vœux et nous vous souhaitons à notre tour une nouvelle année pleine de joie et de bonheur.

Affectueusement

Pascale et Jean-Pierre

■ Birthdays

Birthday cards are not as popular in France as in English-speaking countries. As with other types of greetings cards, they are mostly sent to friends and relatives who live far away rather than to people one sees regularly. Birthday cards are not usually handed directly to the recipient and presents are not systematically accompanied by a card.

Cher Thomas,

Bon anniversaire !
Dommage que nous ne puissions pas célébrer ensemble tes 30 ans.
Je penserai à toi dimanche en buvant un verre à ta santé !

Je t'embrasse.

Julie

Useful phrases:

Joyeux anniversaire !
Pierre se joint à moi pour te souhaiter un très bon anniversaire.

Congratulations

Written congratulations are usually sent after the announcement of a birth, engagement, wedding or promotion.

Grenoble, le 2 juillet 2007

Bravo ! Tes parents m'ont appris que tu as été reçu à tes examens. Quel soulagement, tu vas enfin pouvoir profiter de vacances bien méritées. Toutes mes félicitations et bon courage pour la suite de tes études !

Je t'embrasse.

Marie

Useful phrases:

- For an engagement/a wedding:
C'est avec grand plaisir que j'ai appris tes fiançailles avec Pierre.
Je te félicite, ainsi que Pierre, et vous présente mes meilleurs vœux de bonheur.
Je vous souhaite à tous deux joie et bonheur. (less formal)
Tous nos vœux de bonheur à tous les deux. (less formal)

- For a birth:
C'est avec joie que nous avons appris la naissance de Matthieu.
Félicitations à tous les deux et tous nos vœux de bonheur pour votre bébé. (less formal)

- For a promotion/success:
C'est avec grand plaisir que j'ai appris votre promotion/nomination au poste de...
Je vous adresse mes sincères félicitations, ainsi que celles de mes collègues. (formal)

Letter of complaint

If you want your letter of complaint to be effective, in French as in English, it is essential to remain polite and not simply to use the letter to give full vent to your anger.

For serious complaints, or if a first letter has been ignored, it is standard practice to send this type of letter by recorded delivery ("lettre recommandée avec accusé de réception").

Martine Fernet
Les Jardins du Bourg
74500 Thonon-les-Bains

Les Déménageurs Express
Service Clientèle
11 Haute Rue
74500 Thonon-les-Bains

Thonon-les-Bains, le 5 avril 2007

Monsieur,

Concise explanation of nature of complaint. —— Une de vos équipes vient d'effectuer notre déménagement et je suis au regret de vous annoncer que le travail a été exécuté de façon déplorable puisque certains de nos meubles et objets personnels ont été endommagés.

En effet, nous nous sommes rendus compte au déballage qu'un miroir avait été rayé, qu'une commode Louis XV avait perdu un pied et que le piano présentait une grande rayure sur sa partie inférieure. —— **Development.**

Demand for action. —— Très surprise par la négligence et le manque de professionnalisme de votre équipe, je me vois dans l'obligation de vous demander un dédommagement pour ces dégâts. Je tiens à vous rappeler que l'option que nous avions choisie nous garantissait un service haut de gamme, ce qui est loin d'avoir été le cas.

Dans l'attente d'une réponse de votre part, je vous prie d'agréer, Monsieur, mes salutations distinguées.

Martine Fernet

Martine Fernet

Apologizing

Even if you have already apologized by telephone, in some situations, for example if you have missed a formal appointment, a letter of apology is expected.

Apologize and recall briefly what happened.

Give the specific reason for the mishap.

End on a hopeful note: you hope the person you are apologizing to will excuse you.

> Ann Thorne
> 10, rue des Acacias
> 75017 Paris
>
> TECHNO-MEDIA
> À l'attention de Madame Dubreuil
> 14, rue du Vieux Marché
> 78100 Saint-Germain-en-Laye
>
> Paris, le 3 septembre 2007
>
> Madame,
>
> Je suis vraiment navrée de n'avoir pas pu me présenter à l'entretien que vous m'aviez fixé le lundi 3 septembre 2007, à 14 heures. En effet, ainsi que je vous l'ai expliqué lors de mon appel hier matin, aucun train ne circulait en direction de Saint-Germain-en-Laye, en raison d'une grève surprise du personnel de la SNCF.
>
> Je ne peux que vous renouveler mes excuses pour ce fâcheux incident indépendant de ma volonté. Vous serait-il possible de me proposer un nouveau rendez-vous, au jour et à l'heure qui vous conviendraient ?
>
> Je vous remercie à l'avance de votre compréhension et je vous prie d'agréer, Madame, l'expression de ma considération distinguée.
>
> Ann Thorne
>
> Ann Thorne

Making a reservation

The standard procedure is to make the reservation by telephone and then to confirm the booking in writing.

Specify all your requirements.

Mention that you expect a written response.

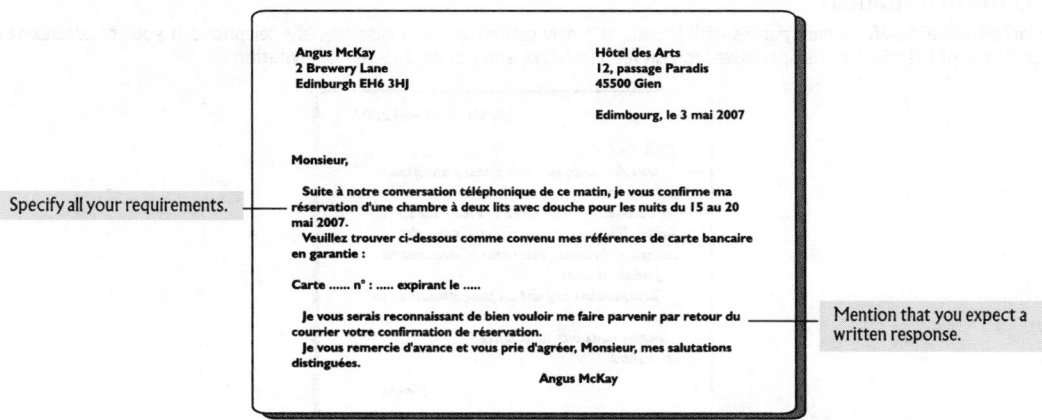

> Angus McKay
> 2 Brewery Lane
> Edinburgh EH6 3HJ
>
> Hôtel des Arts
> 12, passage Paradis
> 45500 Gien
>
> Edimbourg, le 3 mai 2007
>
> Monsieur,
>
> Suite à notre conversation téléphonique de ce matin, je vous confirme ma réservation d'une chambre à deux lits avec douche pour les nuits du 15 au 20 mai 2007.
> Veuillez trouver ci-dessous comme convenu mes références de carte bancaire en garantie :
>
> Carte ...... n° : ..... expirant le .....
>
> Je vous serais reconnaissant de bien vouloir me faire parvenir par retour du courrier votre confirmation de réservation.
> Je vous remercie d'avance et vous prie d'agréer, Monsieur, mes salutations distinguées.
>
> Angus McKay

Useful phrases:

Je vous confirme ma réservation de votre appartement... pour la période du...
Je souhaiterais réserver une chambre pour deux personnes avec salle de bains pour les nuits du... au... inclus.
Je vous remercie de bien vouloir me faire savoir s'il vous reste des chambres à ces dates et de me communiquer vos prix.
Veuillez trouver ci-joint comme convenu un chèque de... euros à titre d'arrhes.
Ci-joint un chèque de... euros, à valoir comme arrhes sur le montant total de la location, qui s'élève à... euros.
Dans l'attente de votre réponse...

Letter of thanks to a friend or relative

Although it is more common in France to thank your host by telephone, sending a thank-you letter after you have been staying at someone's house is always appreciated. A written thank-you letter is still considered obligatory for wedding or christening presents or for more formal situations.

This type of letter should be sent as soon after the event as possible.

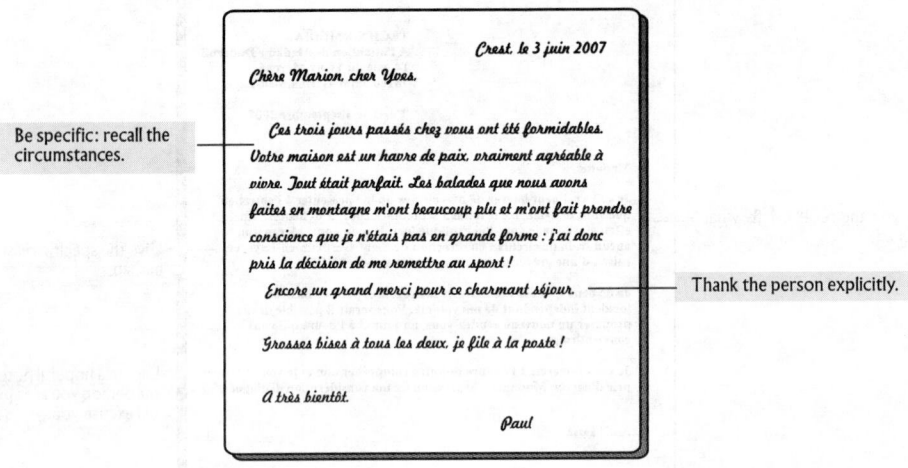

Be specific: recall the circumstances.

Crest, le 3 juin 2007

Chère Marion, cher Yves,

Ces trois jours passés chez vous ont été formidables. Votre maison est un havre de paix, vraiment agréable à vivre. Tout était parfait. Les balades que nous avons faites en montagne m'ont beaucoup plu et m'ont fait prendre conscience que je n'étais pas en grande forme : j'ai donc pris la décision de me remettre au sport !

Encore un grand merci pour ce charmant séjour. — Thank the person explicitly.

Grosses bises à tous les deux, je file à la poste !

À très bientôt.

Paul

Useful phrases:

Merci pour ton cadeau si généreux/pour ton aide si précieuse.
Merci pour cette magnifique écharpe qui m'a fait très plaisir.
Nous avons été très touchés de l'attention que vous nous avez témoignée avec ce magnifique service à thé.
Nous tenons à vous remercier pour la superbe ménagère en argent que vous nous avez offerte.
Nous vous remercions de tout cœur pour ce magnifique cadeau/de nous avoir si gentiment aidés.
Nous tenons à vous témoigner toute notre reconnaissance. (formal)
Permettez-moi de vous assurer de toute ma reconnaissance pour l'aide que vous m'avez apportée. (formal)

Invitations and replies

▪ Letter of invitation

Informal invitations, for dinner parties with friends or family gatherings, are made over the telephone. If you are organizing a party or want to invite friends or relatives to visit for a few days, you can send a letter of invitation.

Paris, le 25 mai 2007

Cher Andrew,

Que dirais-tu de venir passer quelques jours à la campagne ? Nous louons une maison en Normandie avec des amis du 7 au 15 juillet. Thomas nous a promis d'être des nôtres. Cela nous ferait très plaisir que tu te joignes à nous.

Tu trouveras ci-joint un plan détaillé de la région.

Donne-nous vite ta réponse !

À bientôt.

Pierre

Useful phrases:

À l'occasion du week-end du 1er mai, nous invitons quelques amis dans notre maison de campagne.
Pour fêter l'anniversaire de Simon, nous organisons une soirée le..., à partir de...
Nous comptons sur votre présence.

▪ Cards

More formal invitations or organized events are usually made with an invitation card or a visiting card.

These invitations are always written in the third person. You can reply either by a short handwritten note, in the first or second person, or on a visiting card, which always requires the use of the third person.

▪ Invitation on a visiting card

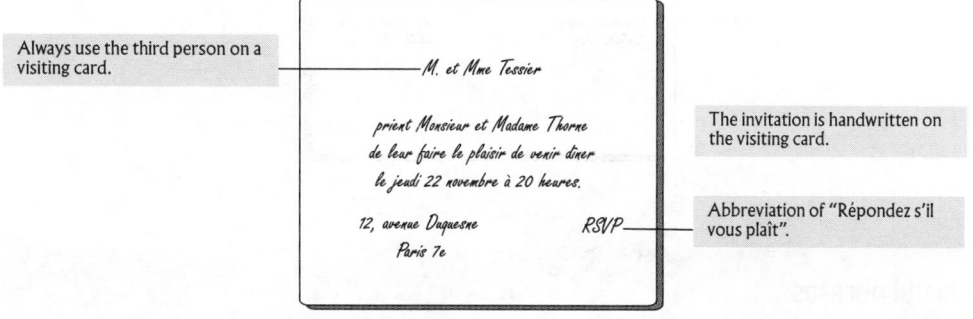

Always use the third person on a visiting card.

M. et Mme Tessier

prient Monsieur et Madame Thorne
de leur faire le plaisir de venir dîner
le jeudi 22 novembre à 20 heures.

12, avenue Duquesne
Paris 7e

RSVP

The invitation is handwritten on the visiting card.

Abbreviation of "Répondez s'il vous plaît".

Useful phrases:

M. et Mme X seront heureux de vous recevoir à l'occasion de...
M. et Mme X recevront la famille et les amis proches à l'occasion de...

▪ Invitation card

These are usually made by a printer, who can suggest standard formulas.

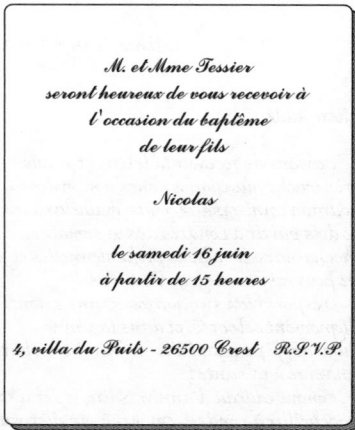

M. et Mme Tessier
seront heureux de vous recevoir à
l'occasion du baptême
de leur fils

Nicolas

le samedi 16 juin
à partir de 15 heures

4, villa du Puits - 26500 Crest   R.S.V.P.

Useful phrases:

Sophie Tessier recevra ses amis le... à partir de...
Jacques Tessier vous invite à venir assister à sa soutenance de thèse le... à partir de...
Nous organisons une soirée le... à l'occasion de... Nous serions très heureux si vous pouviez vous joindre à nous.

- **Wedding invitation**

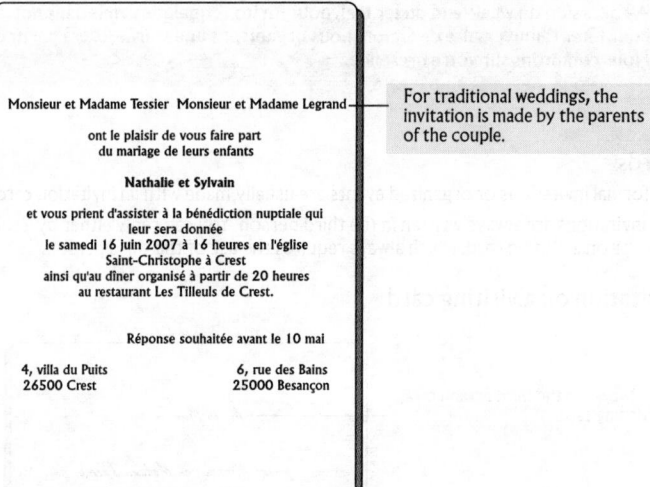

Monsieur et Madame Tessier Monsieur et Madame Legrand

ont le plaisir de vous faire part
du mariage de leurs enfants

Nathalie et Sylvain

et vous prient d'assister à la bénédiction nuptiale qui
leur sera donnée
le samedi 16 juin 2007 à 16 heures en l'église
Saint-Christophe à Crest
ainsi qu'au dîner organisé à partir de 20 heures
au restaurant Les Tilleuls de Crest.

Réponse souhaitée avant le 10 mai

4, villa du Puits   6, rue des Bains
26500 Crest   25000 Besançon

For traditional weddings, the invitation is made by the parents of the couple.

Useful phrases:

Monsieur et Madame X vous prient d'assister à la messe de mariage qui sera célébrée le... en l'église...
Monsieur et Madame X recevront à l'hôtel Les Tilleuls à l'issue de la cérémonie religieuse.
Nathalie Tessier et Sylvain Legrand sont heureux de vous annoncer leur mariage qui sera célébré le... à... à la mairie de Crest.
Un vin d'honneur sera servi à l'issue de la cérémonie à la salle des fêtes de Crest.

- **Declining an invitation**

Replies to invitations should be handwritten and sent as quickly as possible. If you are unable to accept the invitation, you need to give the reason.

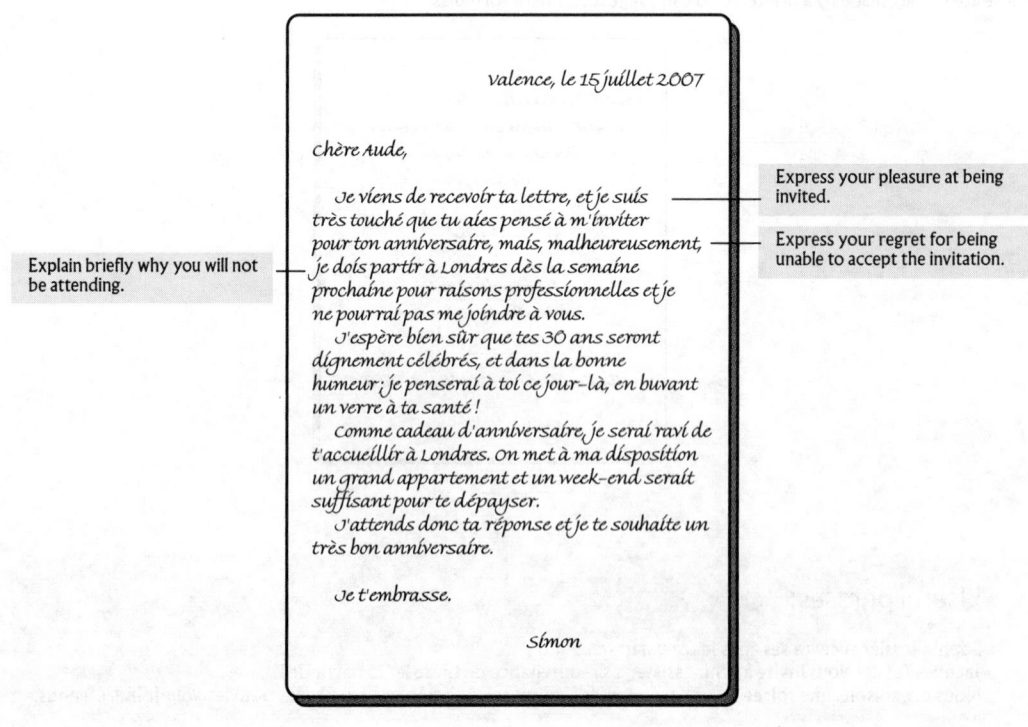

valence, le 15 juillet 2007

chère Aude,

Je viens de recevoir ta lettre, et je suis
très touché que tu aies pensé à m'inviter
pour ton anniversaire, mais, malheureusement,
je dois partir à Londres dès la semaine
prochaine pour raisons professionnelles et je
ne pourrai pas me joindre à vous.
J'espère bien sûr que tes 30 ans seront
dignement célébrés, et dans la bonne
humeur ; je penserai à toi ce jour-là, en buvant
un verre à ta santé !
Comme cadeau d'anniversaire, je serai ravi de
t'accueillir à Londres. On met à ma disposition
un grand appartement et un week-end serait
suffisant pour te dépayser.
J'attends donc ta réponse et je te souhaite un
très bon anniversaire.

Je t'embrasse.

Simon

Express your pleasure at being invited.

Express your regret for being unable to accept the invitation.

Explain briefly why you will not be attending.

Useful phrases:

Je suis vraiment déçu de ne pouvoir accepter mais je ne pourrai pas me libérer car des obligations professionnelles me retiennent à Paris à cette date.

J'aurais tellement aimé être présent à cette fête, mais malheureusement je suis déjà invité chez des amis/des raisons professionnelles m'en empêchent.

Nous regrettons de ne pouvoir nous libérer et nous espérons avoir très prochainement l'occasion de nous réunir.

Nous vous remercions de votre aimable invitation que nous avons le regret de ne pouvoir accepter, étant déjà retenus ce jour-là. (formal)

- **Accepting an invitation**

Express your pleasure at being invited.

Thank the sender for the invitation.

Nantes, le 14 janvier 2007

Cher Vincent,

Je viens de recevoir ta lettre et je suis ravi ! C'est vraiment gentil d'avoir pensé à moi. Ça faisait très longtemps que je rêvais de vacances et l'idée de faire du ski à Serre-Chevalier dans moins d'un mois me rend fou de joie !

J'irai à Briançon en train, et de là, je prendrai un taxi ou un bus, selon mon heure d'arrivée, pour rejoindre le chalet. Espérons qu'il continuera à neiger d'ici là !

Tout va bien ici. Mon nouveau travail me plaît énormément et l'équipe est jeune et sympa. Et toi ? Dois-tu repartir aux États-Unis avant les vacances de février ?

Je te téléphonerai bientôt pour préciser mon jour d'arrivée.

Je te remercie encore et je t'embrasse.

Michel

Useful phrases:

C'est avec grand plaisir que j'accepte votre invitation pour le.../que je me joindrai à vous le...

Je me réjouis à l'idée de vous revoir.

Nous nous faisons une joie d'accepter votre invitation.

Nous vous remercions de votre invitation au mariage de Sylvain, que nous acceptons avec joie/auquel nous viendrons avec grand plaisir.

Letter of condolence

There is no standard model for the expression of condolences, especially where friends and relatives are concerned. What matters most is to be sincere and to express your sympathy.

Name the person who died and, if you knew them, recall their qualities.

You can offer your support.

Toulon, le 3 décembre 2007

Cher Nicolas,

C'est avec beaucoup de peine que nous venons d'apprendre la triste nouvelle du décès de ton frère.

Nous savons à quel point vous étiez proches et nous imaginons ta douleur. Tout le monde appréciait Julien pour sa gentillesse et son enthousiasme. Il nous manquera beaucoup et nous ne l'oublierons pas.

Nous pensons beaucoup à toi. Si nous pouvons t'aider en quoi que ce soit dans ces moments difficiles, n'hésite pas à faire appel à nous.

Transmets à toute ta famille nos sincères condoléances.

Nous t'embrassons avec toute notre affection.

Olivier et Sandrine

Useful phrases:

C'est avec émotion que nous apprenons le malheur qui vient de vous frapper.
Nous sommes de tout cœur avec vous.
Nous prenons part à/Nous partageons votre peine.
Nous avons été bouleversés par ce deuil qui vous frappe.
Croyez, cher Nicolas, à l'expression de ma très sincère sympathie. (formal)
Croyez, cher Monsieur, à l'expression de mes sentiments attristés. (formal)
Je vous prie d'agréer, Monsieur, l'expression de mes sentiments profondément affligés/l'expression de mes très sincères condoléances. (formal)

Asking for a brochure/information

When asking for information, specify all your requirements in order to receive the relevant documentation.

Angus McKay
2 Brewery Lane
Edinburgh EH6 3HJ

Office du tourisme
11 place du Général de Gaulle
06600 Antibes

Edimbourg, le 4 avril 2007

Madame, Monsieur,

Souhaitant passer mes vacances (du 1er au 16 juillet) dans la région d'Antibes, je vous serais reconnaissant de bien vouloir me faire parvenir une liste des hôtels et des chambres d'hôte, à Antibes même ou dans les environs.
Pourriez-vous également me faire parvenir de la documentation sur les événements culturels prévus pour cette période ?
Je vous remercie d'avance et je vous prie d'agréer, Madame, Monsieur, mes salutations distinguées.

Angus McKay

Angus McKay

Useful phrases:

Je vous serais reconnaissant de bien vouloir me communiquer...
Pourriez-vous m'indiquer les propositions de locations pour la période du... au.../me communiquer la liste des appartements et villas à louer dans la région.
Je vous remercie de bien vouloir me faire parvenir ces renseignements.

Letter to authorities: official statement

This type of statement follows a set formula in French.

The adjective soussigné varies according to the gender: Je soussignée Madame X..., Nous soussignés...

It is important that the date is included.

The standard procedure is to give your name, occupation, date and place of birth, nationality and address.

Je soussigné Andrew Dixon, informaticien, né le 31/03/1962 à Glasgow, en Écosse, de nationalité britannique, demeurant 6 rue des Lilas à Paris (75019), certifie avoir été témoin de l'accident survenu à M. Charmier, le 20 novembre 2007 à 23 h 15, rue Léon Jouhaux à Paris.
Alors que je venais de garer ma voiture à la hauteur du 2 rue Léon Jouhaux, j'ai vu une 406 Peugeot blanche arriver à grande vitesse de la rue Beaurepaire et renverser M. Charmier qui traversait la rue Léon Jouhaux alors que le feu tricolore indiquait la priorité aux piétons.

Fait à Paris, le 2 décembre 2007.

Andrew Dixon

A precise statement of the facts should be given.

Writing to a contractor

Monsieur John Chandler
22, allée des Tilleuls
25000 Besançon

Entreprise Mercier et Cie
25, rue de la République
25000 Besançon

Besançon, le 3 septembre 2007

Monsieur,

J'ai obtenu vos coordonnées par l'intermédiaire de mes amis M. et Mme Sarlat qui m'ont recommandé vos services. Le toit de notre villa ayant été endommagé par la récente tempête, je souhaiterais que vous m'établissiez un devis pour les travaux de réfection. ⟵ Explain briefly the nature of the works.

Pourrions-nous convenir d'un rendez-vous dans le courant de la semaine prochaine afin que vous puissiez vous rendre compte sur place des travaux nécessaires ? Vous pouvez me joindre à mon bureau dans la journée (03 42 31 25 10) ou le soir à partir de 19 h à mon domicile (03 42 38 75 70).

Dans l'attente de vous rencontrer, je vous prie d'agréer, Monsieur, mes salutations distinguées.

John Chandler

Useful phrases:

Je souhaiterais faire installer le chauffage central dans ma maison de campagne.
Je vous serais très reconnaissant de bien vouloir me faire parvenir un devis dans les meilleurs délais.
Pourrions-nous convenir d'un rendez-vous afin que nous puissions discuter sur place des travaux à faire et de leur coût ?

Business correspondence

Business to business (general)

Business correspondence in French, although more and more influenced by the Anglo-Saxon style, still tends to be rather formal, as will be seen in the examples that follow.

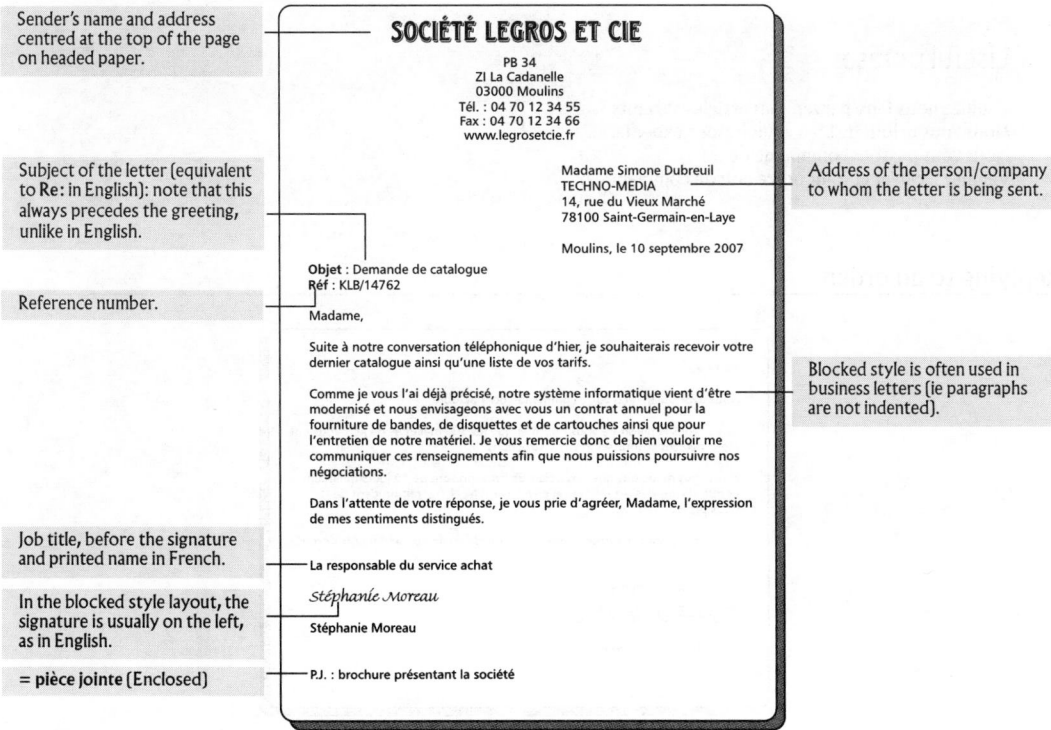

Sender's name and address centred at the top of the page on headed paper.

SOCIÉTÉ LEGROS ET CIE

PB 34
ZI La Cadanelle
03000 Moulins
Tél. : 04 70 12 34 55
Fax : 04 70 12 34 66
www.legrosetcie.fr

Madame Simone Dubreuil
TECHNO-MEDIA
14, rue du Vieux Marché
78100 Saint-Germain-en-Laye ⟵ Address of the person/company to whom the letter is being sent.

Moulins, le 10 septembre 2007

Subject of the letter (equivalent to **Re:** in English): note that this always precedes the greeting, unlike in English. ⟶

Objet : Demande de catalogue
Réf : KLB/14762

Reference number. ⟶

Madame,

Suite à notre conversation téléphonique d'hier, je souhaiterais recevoir votre dernier catalogue ainsi qu'une liste de vos tarifs.

Comme je vous l'ai déjà précisé, notre système informatique vient d'être modernisé et nous envisageons avec vous un contrat annuel pour la fourniture de bandes, de disquettes et de cartouches ainsi que pour l'entretien de notre matériel. Je vous remercie donc de bien vouloir me communiquer ces renseignements afin que nous puissions poursuivre nos négociations. ⟵ Blocked style is often used in business letters (ie paragraphs are not indented).

Dans l'attente de votre réponse, je vous prie d'agréer, Madame, l'expression de mes sentiments distingués.

Job title, before the signature and printed name in French. ⟶

La responsable du service achat

In the blocked style layout, the signature is usually on the left, as in English. ⟶

Stéphanie Moreau

Stéphanie Moreau

= pièce jointe (Enclosed) ⟶

P.J. : brochure présentant la société

Useful phrases:

En réponse à votre lettre du...,
Nous avons bien reçu votre lettre du... et nous vous en remercions.
Nous sommes tout particulièrement intéressés par...
Nous vous remercions de l'intérêt que vous portez à notre société et nous restons à votre disposition pour toutes informations complémentaires.

Placing an order

A letter placing an order needs to specify the items required, as well as the conditions of delivery and payment.

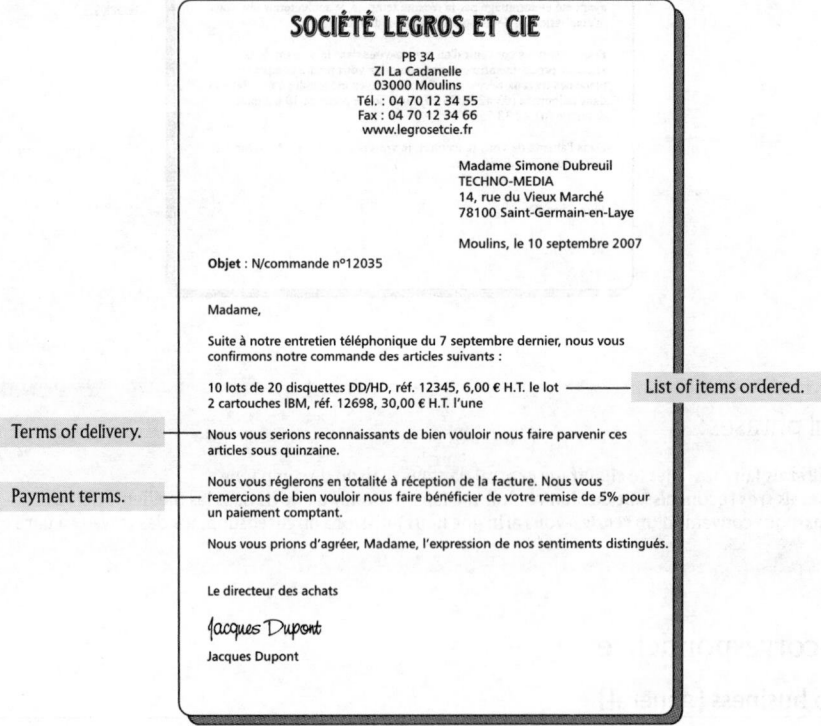

Useful phrases:

Veuillez nous faire parvenir les articles suivants...
Nous vous prions de bien vouloir nous expédier...
Nous vous passons commande de...
Veuillez trouver ci-joint notre bon de commande n°...

Replying to an order

Monsieur,

Nous avons bien reçu votre commande de 9 octobre.

Nous avons le plaisir de vous informer que les 300 mallettes de jeux vous ont été expédiées ce jour selon vos instructions.

Nous vous rappelons que nos délais de livraison sont de 10 jours minimum et que si vous désirez un nouvel envoi avant Noël, il serait prudent de nous prévenir par fax.

Nous vous prions d'agréer, Monsieur, l'expression de nos sentiments dévoués.

La directrice des ventes

Marie-Françoise Durand

Marie-Françoise Durand

Informing a customer

TECHNO-MEDIA
14, rue du Vieux Marché
78100 Saint-Germain-en-Laye
Tél. : 01 34 22 44 66   Fax : 01 34 22 44 67
http:\\www.technomedia.fr

Saint-Germain-en-Laye, le 10 septembre 2007

Monsieur,

Nous avons le plaisir de vous informer que vous pouvez désormais consulter notre catalogue et passer vos commandes sur notre site Web.

Notre site est entièrement sécurisé. Si vous souhaitez bénéficier de nos services en ligne, il suffit de vous enregistrer en vous connectant à :
http:\\www.technomedia.fr

Dans l'espoir que ce nouveau service vous donnera entière satisfaction, nous vous prions d'agréer, Monsieur, nos meilleures salutations.

La responsable du site Web

Sylvie Legrand

Sylvie Legrand

Useful phrases:

Nous vous informons que...
Nous vous annonçons que...
Nous tenons à vous signaler que...
Nous restons à votre entière disposition pour tous renseignements complémentaires.
Veuillez noter notre nouvelle adresse à partir du...
Notre magasin ouvrira ses portes le... à notre nouvelle adresse.

Letter of complaint

Madame,

Objet : Commande n° 2983

J'ai le regret de vous faire savoir qu'en ouvrant les colis que vous nous avez envoyés, nous nous sommes aperçus qu'il manquait 20 mallettes de jeux.

Cette situation nous plonge dans un profond embarras et nous vous prions d'effectuer immédiatement un nouvel envoi pour réparer l'erreur commise, faute de quoi nous serions obligés de nous adresser à un autre fournisseur.

Nous vous prions de croire, Madame, à l'expression de nos sentiments distingués.

Le directeur des achats

Jacques Dupont

Jacques Dupont

Concise explanation of nature of complaint.

Demand for action.

Dealing with a customer complaint

When replying to a customer complaint, it is necessary to give an explanation for what happened. If the complaint is justified, the company must apologize and offer a solution.

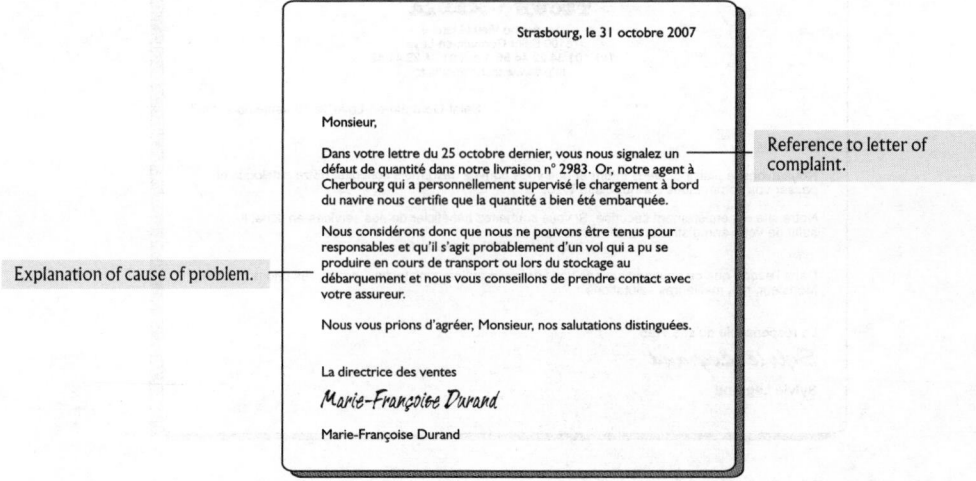

Strasbourg, le 31 octobre 2007

Monsieur,

Dans votre lettre du 25 octobre dernier, vous nous signalez un défaut de quantité dans notre livraison n° 2983. Or, notre agent à Cherbourg qui a personnellement supervisé le chargement à bord du navire nous certifie que la quantité a bien été embarquée.

Reference to letter of complaint.

Nous considérons donc que nous ne pouvons être tenus pour responsables et qu'il s'agit probablement d'un vol qui a pu se produire en cours de transport ou lors du stockage au débarquement et nous vous conseillons de prendre contact avec votre assureur.

Explanation of cause of problem.

Nous vous prions d'agréer, Monsieur, nos salutations distinguées.

La directrice des ventes

Marie-Françoise Durand

Marie-Françoise Durand

Useful phrases:

Nous vous prions de bien vouloir nous excuser pour cette regrettable erreur.
Veuillez accepter nos excuses pour le dérangement que nous avons pu vous causer.
Nous avons pris des mesures pour que cela ne se reproduise plus.
Nous espérons que ce contretemps n'aura pour vous aucune conséquence préjudiciable.

Invoice

A company is free to choose the layout of its invoices provided all the essential information is included.

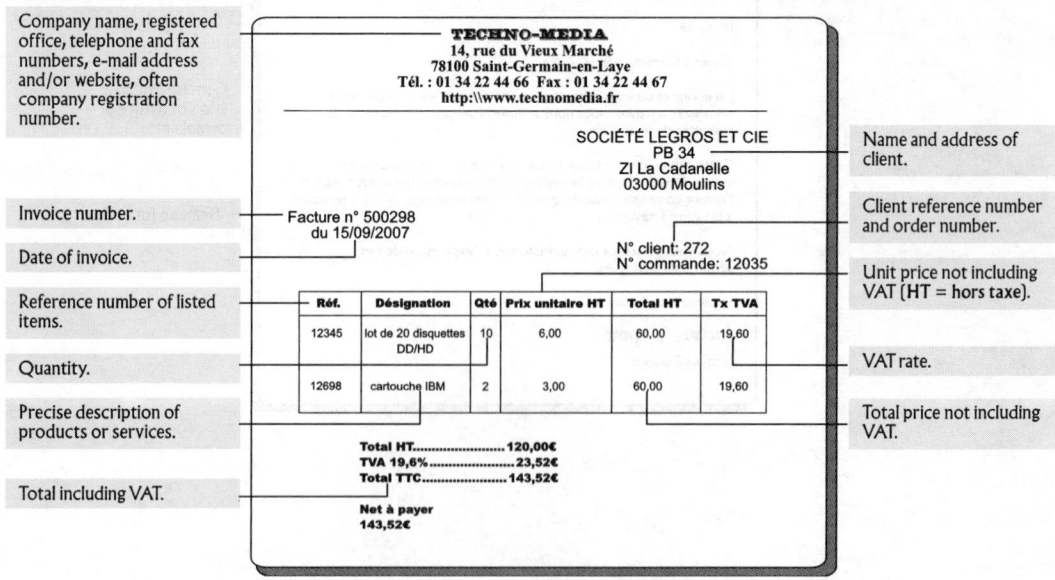

Company name, registered office, telephone and fax numbers, e-mail address and/or website, often company registration number.

TECHNO-MEDIA
14, rue du Vieux Marché
78100 Saint-Germain-en-Laye
Tél. : 01 34 22 44 66 Fax : 01 34 22 44 67
http:\\www.technomedia.fr

SOCIÉTÉ LEGROS ET CIE
PB 34
ZI La Cadanelle
03000 Moulins

Name and address of client.

Invoice number.

Facture n° 500298
du 15/09/2007

N° client: 272
N° commande: 12035

Client reference number and order number.

Date of invoice.

Reference number of listed items.

Unit price not including VAT (HT = hors taxe).

Réf.	Désignation	Qté	Prix unitaire HT	Total HT	Tx TVA
12345	lot de 20 disquettes DD/HD	10	6,00	60,00	19,60
12698	cartouche IBM	2	3,00	60,00	19,60

Quantity.

VAT rate.

Precise description of products or services.

Total price not including VAT.

Total HT......................... 120,00€
TVA 19,6%....................... 23,52€
Total TTC....................... 143,52€

Net à payer
143,52€

Total including VAT.

Reply to invoice

You only need to reply to an invoice if you are contesting it.

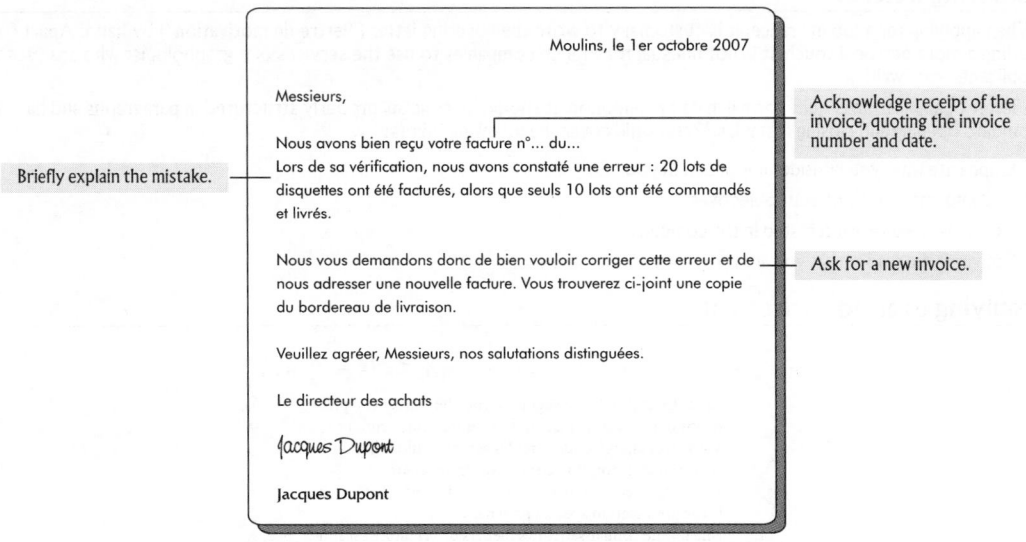

Briefly explain the mistake.

Acknowledge receipt of the invoice, quoting the invoice number and date.

Ask for a new invoice.

Moulins, le 1er octobre 2007

Messieurs,

Nous avons bien reçu votre facture n°... du...
Lors de sa vérification, nous avons constaté une erreur : 20 lots de disquettes ont été facturés, alors que seuls 10 lots ont été commandés et livrés.

Nous vous demandons donc de bien vouloir corriger cette erreur et de nous adresser une nouvelle facture. Vous trouverez ci-joint une copie du bordereau de livraison.

Veuillez agréer, Messieurs, nos salutations distinguées.

Le directeur des achats

Jacques Dupont

Jacques Dupont

Useful phrases:

Nous accusons réception de votre facture n°...
Les prix ne sont pas ceux qui ont été convenus lors de la commande, à savoir : ...
En vérifiant la facture que vous venez de nous faire parvenir, nous constatons que le montant ne correspond pas à notre commande.
Nous avons décelé l'erreur suivante : ...

Sales promotion letter

This type of letter, known as a "circulaire", is sent to many potential clients as part of a mailshot. The style is very direct and tries to sound as personal as possible. In addition to the standard greetings, various other greetings might be used : Cher client/Chère cliente, Cher Monsieur/Chère Madame etc.

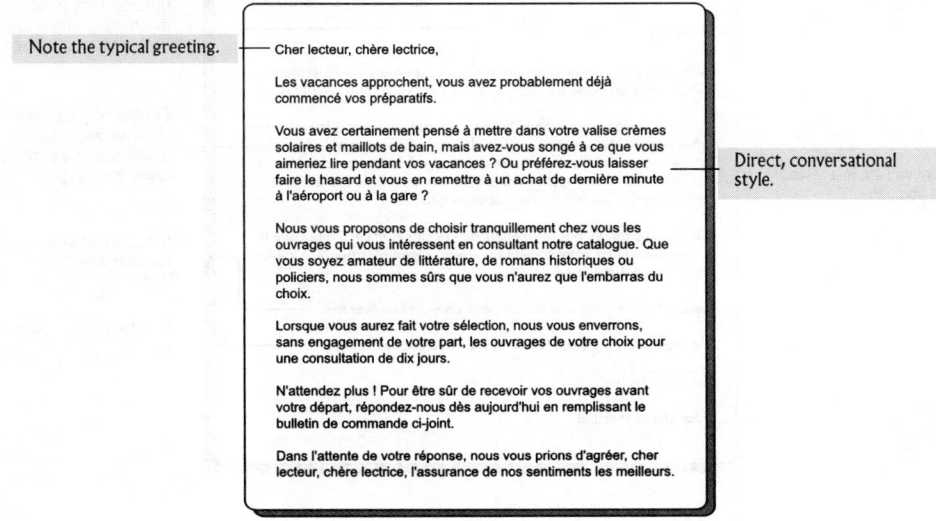

Note the typical greeting.

Direct, conversational style.

Cher lecteur, chère lectrice,

Les vacances approchent, vous avez probablement déjà commencé vos préparatifs.

Vous avez certainement pensé à mettre dans votre valise crèmes solaires et maillots de bain, mais avez-vous songé à ce que vous aimeriez lire pendant vos vacances ? Ou préférez-vous laisser faire le hasard et vous en remettre à un achat de dernière minute à l'aéroport ou à la gare ?

Nous vous proposons de choisir tranquillement chez vous les ouvrages qui vous intéressent en consultant notre catalogue. Que vous soyez amateur de littérature, de romans historiques ou policiers, nous sommes sûrs que vous n'aurez que l'embarras du choix.

Lorsque vous aurez fait votre sélection, nous vous enverrons, sans engagement de votre part, les ouvrages de votre choix pour une consultation de dix jours.

N'attendez plus ! Pour être sûr de recevoir vos ouvrages avant votre départ, répondez-nous dès aujourd'hui en remplissant le bulletin de commande ci-joint.

Dans l'attente de votre réponse, nous vous prions d'agréer, cher lecteur, chère lectrice, l'assurance de nos sentiments les meilleurs.

Useful phrases:

Nous sommes persuadés que...
Nous sommes sûrs de pouvoir vous donner satisfaction.
Nous espérons vivement vous compter bientôt parmi nos nouveaux clients.
Nous serons très heureux de vous compter au nombre de nos fidèles clients.

Employment

Covering letter

When applying for a job in France, it is customary to write the covering letter ("lettre de motivation") by hand. Apart from adding a more personal touch, it is not unusual for French companies to use the services of a graphologist who analyses the applicants' handwriting.

A letter of application is quite formal in its presentation. It should be concise, properly structured in paragraphs and have the standard opening and closing formulas. You should cover the following points:

- Emphasize what you consider important in your CV
- Add information about your objectives
- Explain why you are interested in the company
- Convince the reader that you are the right person for the job

Replying to an advertisement

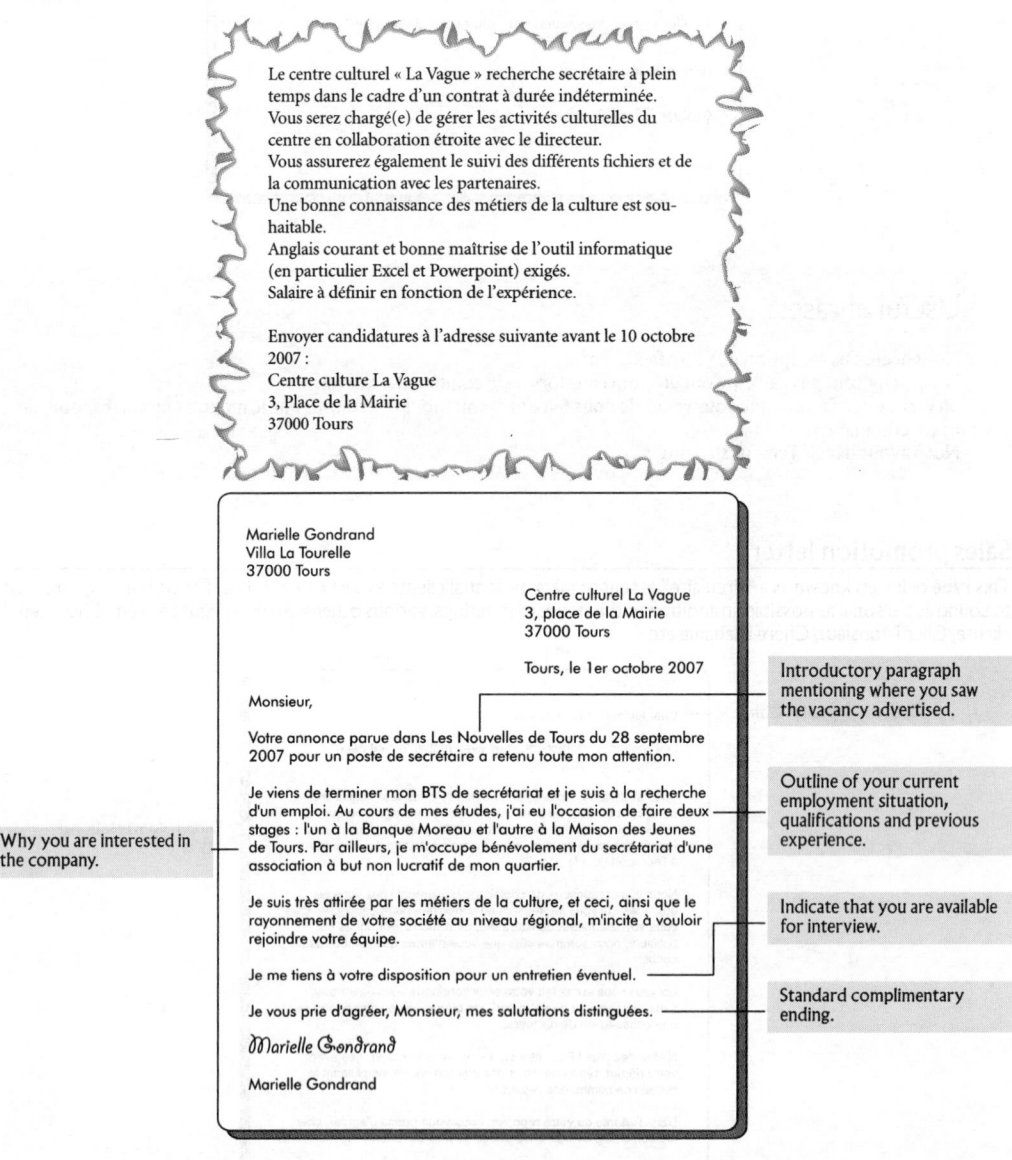

Le centre culturel « La Vague » recherche secrétaire à plein temps dans le cadre d'un contrat à durée indéterminée.
Vous serez chargé(e) de gérer les activités culturelles du centre en collaboration étroite avec le directeur.
Vous assurerez également le suivi des différents fichiers et de la communication avec les partenaires.
Une bonne connaissance des métiers de la culture est souhaitable.
Anglais courant et bonne maîtrise de l'outil informatique (en particulier Excel et Powerpoint) exigés.
Salaire à définir en fonction de l'expérience.

Envoyer candidatures à l'adresse suivante avant le 10 octobre 2007 :
Centre culture La Vague
3, Place de la Mairie
37000 Tours

Marielle Gondrand
Villa La Tourelle
37000 Tours

Centre culturel La Vague
3, place de la Mairie
37000 Tours

Tours, le 1er octobre 2007

Monsieur,

Votre annonce parue dans Les Nouvelles de Tours du 28 septembre 2007 pour un poste de secrétaire a retenu toute mon attention.

Je viens de terminer mon BTS de secrétariat et je suis à la recherche d'un emploi. Au cours de mes études, j'ai eu l'occasion de faire deux stages : l'un à la Banque Moreau et l'autre à la Maison des Jeunes de Tours. Par ailleurs, je m'occupe bénévolement du secrétariat d'une association à but non lucratif de mon quartier.

Je suis très attirée par les métiers de la culture, et ceci, ainsi que le rayonnement de votre société au niveau régional, m'incite à vouloir rejoindre votre équipe.

Je me tiens à votre disposition pour un entretien éventuel.

Je vous prie d'agréer, Monsieur, mes salutations distinguées.

Marielle Gondrand

Marielle Gondrand

Introductory paragraph mentioning where you saw the vacancy advertised.

Outline of your current employment situation, qualifications and previous experience.

Why you are interested in the company.

Indicate that you are available for interview.

Standard complimentary ending.

Useful phrases:

En réponse à votre annonce parue dans Les Nouvelles de Tours du..., je me permets de vous adresser mon curriculum vitae pour le poste de secrétaire.
Je dispose de plusieurs années d'expérience dans différentes entreprises.
Au cours de mes cinq années d'expérience auprès de la société X, j'ai acquis une bonne maîtrise de...
Je souhaite élargir mon expérience professionnelle tout en acquérant de nouvelles responsabilités et serais donc ravi d'intégrer une entreprise aussi dynamique et réputée que la vôtre.
En espérant que ma candidature retiendra votre attention, je vous prie d'agréer, Madame, Monsieur, l'expression de mes sentiments distingués.

Unsolicited application

Wilfrid Garnier
10, impasse des Petites Écuries
37000 Tours
Tél : 02 47 30 60 30
E-mail : wilf.garnier@free.fr

Tours, le 17 févier 2007

M. le Directeur des Ressources
Humaines
Supermarchés Guévara
Z. I. de la Gravière
37042 TOURS CEDEX

Monsieur,

Show what you have to offer. → Titulaire d'un BTS de gestion et après une expérience réussie en tant qu'assistant du responsable de la gestion des stocks de la société des Engrais Santic (voir CV ci-joint), je vous écris pour vous proposer mes services. Je souhaiterais désormais élargir mon expérience en utilisant mes compétences dans le domaine de la grande distribution. Ce secteur m'a toujours intéressé et je crois disposer des aptitudes nécessaires pour donner entière satisfaction dans toute mission que vous voudriez bien me confier.

Votre société m'intéresse particulièrement car elle jouit d'une réputation d'excellence sans pareil, et j'admire les efforts qu'elle a fournis pour le développement du commerce éthique. ← *Explain your interest in this particular company.*

Je me tiens à votre entière disposition pour vous fournir tout renseignement complémentaire.

Dans l'attente de vous lire, je vous prie d'agréer, Monsieur, l'expression de mes sentiments les meilleurs.

W Garnier

W Garnier

PJ : un CV avec photo

Asking for a work placement

Work placements are very popular in France and are a compulsory part of many courses. It is therefore advisable to send your request well in advance.

This type of letter is always handwritten in French (see Covering letter p.48).

Katherine Dixon
28 Fallowfield Road
COLCHESTER
Essex CM16 3JF

Cabinet d'urbanisme Alphacité
22 boulevard des Dames
33000 Bordeaux

Colchester, le 17 octobre 2007

Monsieur,

Mention your course. → Étudiante en licence d'urbanisme à l'Université de Colchester, je dois effectuer dans le cadre de mes études un stage en entreprise d'une durée de six semaines minimum, entre le mois de janvier et le mois d'avril 2008. Ce stage est destiné à enrichir l'enseignement reçu à l'université, d'une part en permettant à l'étudiant de se perfectionner *Explain what is expected from the placement.* → dans une langue étrangère, d'autre part en le mettant en situation réelle.

← *Specify the length of the placement and the dates.*

Très intéressée par la signalétique urbaine, et attirée par la réputation de votre cabinet, je souhaite mettre mes *Explain your reasons for choosing the company.* → compétences et mon savoir-faire au bénéfice de votre entreprise.

Dans l'espoir que ma candidature retiendra votre attention, je vous prie d'agréer, Monsieur, mes salutations distinguées.

Katherine Dixon

Katherine Dixon

Useful phrases:

Vous trouverez ci-joint mon curriculum vitae.
Je vous remercie de l'attention que vous porterez à ma demande et reste à votre disposition pour un entretien.
Je reste à votre disposition pour vous rencontrer et vous fournir tout autre renseignement.
En vous remerciant à l'avance de bien vouloir examiner ma demande, je vous prie d'agréer...

Curriculum vitae

The presentation of a CV in French is in many ways similar to an English or American CV. The following points should be noted.

- The title "Curriculum Vitae" should never be included in a French CV.
- Only mention hobbies if they add something personal to your profile or if they are particularly relevant to the job. It is assumed that everybody likes reading, going to the cinema, listening to music and travelling.
- Do not include referees on your CV: references are not commonly used in France apart from certain occupations where personal recommendation would be expected such as catering, cleaning, child care, building etc.
- Even if you do not complete your degree, you can mention the fact that you studied for it by using the word "niveau", for example "niveau licence".

- ### Experienced (British)

Mary Grant
198 Francis Avenue
LEICESTER LE4 9PQ
Grande-Bretagne
Tél : 00 44 1493 767 33 36   36 ans, célibataire
E-mail: mgrant@uk.net   Nationalité britannique

EXPÉRIENCE PROFESSIONNELLE

Depuis septembre 1994	Directrice des exportations, Gannett UK Ltd, Leicester (Fabrication et distribution de produits cosmétiques) » mise en place d'un réseau commercial (40 représentants et 10 agents) » négociations avec les points de vente » études de marché Augmentation du C.A. de 62 %
1990 - 1994	Responsable des exportations Europe, Simon & Co plc, Leicester (prêt-à-porter enfants) » prospection » contrôle des ventes » ouverture de deux nouveaux marchés (Espagne et Italie) Augmentation du C.A. de 53 % en 4 ans

FORMATION

1989 - 1993	MA (équivalent de la Maîtrise) en Gestion, Université d'Édimbourg
1989	A Levels (équivalent du baccalauréat) : économie, mathématiques, histoire et français (Lycée Harfield Comprehensive, Leicester)
1988	GCSE (premier examen de fin de scolarité) : anglais, mathématiques, français, économie, informatique et histoire (Lycée Harfield Comprehensive, Leicester)

AUTRES ACTIVITÉS

1993 - 1994	Séjour d'une année à Paris : enseignement de l'anglais commercial à la Chambre de commerce et d'industrie franco-britannique

LANGUES

Anglais : langue maternelle ; Bilingue français (mère française) ; Espagnol : lu, écrit, parlé

DIVERS

Bonne maîtrise de l'outil informatique sur PC et sur Mac
Chant choral

■ Experienced (American)

John Farmer
18 rue de Turenne
75004 Paris
Tél: 01 42 22 37 89
E-mail: jfarmer@nxl.fr

Né le 17 juin 1962
Marié, 2 enfants (11 et 14 ans)
Nationalité américaine

Directeur des ventes : 11 ans d'expérience

20 ans d'expérience dans la fonction commerciale

Connaissance approfondie du marché informatique

Depuis 1996 **Softlux France, Paris**
Directeur des ventes Europe
· Encadrement d'une équipe de 20 commerciaux
· Diversification et développement des marchés existants
· Ouverture de 3 nouveaux marchés (Grèce, Portugal, Espagne)
· Augmentation du chiffre d'affaires (+ 53 %)

1988-1996 **ICN Europe, Amsterdam**
Directeur commercial
· Responsable de la politique commerciale et du marketing
  opérationnel
· Recrutement et encadrement d'une équipe de 7 commerciaux
· Définition des objectifs commerciaux
· Dépassement des objectifs fixés: 1994:118 %, 1993: 110%,
  1992: 108 %

1984-1987 **Société ADB, Paris**
Ingénieur commercial grands comptes
· Responsable du développement des ventes pour le secteur de la
  grande distribution sur la région parisienne
· Ouverture de nouveaux comptes
· Atteinte des objectifs fixés

Formation
1988   MBA, Harvard Business School
1984   MS (équivalent de la maîtrise) en Économie et Gestion, Université de Harvard
1980   High school diploma (équivalent du baccalauréat)

Langues
Anglais : langue maternelle
Français : bilingue
Espagnol : notions

■ Recent graduate (British)

Stephen Forbes
81 Lincoln Walk
STEVENAGE
Herts SE19 2DN
Tél: 00 44 1283 456789
E-mail: sforbes@teaser.org.uk

22 ans, célibataire
Nationalité britannique

Formation
2002 - 2006   BSc (équivalent de la licence) en Biologie, Université de Swansea,
                 Grande-Bretagne.

2002   A Levels (équivalent du baccalauréat) : Mathématiques, Chimie, Biologie
                 et Français, Lycée Whitton Comprehensive, Bristol, Grande-Bretagne.

2000   GCSE (premier examen de fin de scolarité) : Anglais, Mathématiques,
                 Chimie, Biologie, Français, Histoire et Informatique, Lycée Whitton
                 Comprehensive, Bristol, Grande-Bretagne.

Expérience professionnelle
juillet - septembre 2006   Stage de 3 mois auprès du service d'hématologie de l'hôpital Frenchay de
                             Bristol : analyse de prélèvements sanguins.

octobre 2006 -   Enseignement de l'anglais langue étrangère, École de langues Babel, Osaka, Japon.
novembre 2007

Langues
Anglais : langue maternelle
Français : courant
Japonais : notions

Divers
Bonnes connaissances informatiques : animateur du club d'informatique d'une maison
des jeunes et de la culture (Bristol)

Titulaire du brevet de secourisme

■ Recent graduate (American)

Martha Jacobs
493 Huntington Avenue
Boston
MA 02575
États-Unis
Tél : (617) 267-1680
E-mail: mjacobs@totem.com

25 ans, célibataire
Nationalité américaine

Traductrice anglais/français/espagnol
Début de spécialisation en informatique

FORMATION

2005 - 2007   Diplôme de traducteur technique
Université McGill, Montréal

2002 - 2005   BA (équivalent de la licence) en français et espagnol, mention très bien
Université de Boston

2001   High school diploma (équivalent du baccalauréat)

EXPÉRIENCE PROFESSIONNELLE

2005 - 2006   **Éditions Dulis**, Montréal
Travaux de traduction en free-lance

juillet 2004 - septembre 2005   **Société AX Networks**, Boston
Stage de 3 mois dans le service de traduction : adaptation de logiciels
pour le marché européen

2003- 2004   **Lycée Dupuis**, Grenoble
Assistante de français

LANGUES
Anglais : langue maternelle
Français : bilingue (2 ans à Montréal, 1 an à Grenoble)
Espagnol : courant

CONNAISSANCES INFORMATIQUES
Word, Excel et Access (sur PC et Mac)

LOISIRS
Escrime, violoncelle

Abbreviations and acronyms: general correspondence

ac	argent comptant; année courante; acompte (ready money; current year; on account)	LCR	lettre de change relevé (bills of exchange statement)
AG	assemblée générale (General Meeting, GM)	LJM	livraison le jour même (same-day delivery)
arr.	arrondissement (district)	M	Monsieur (sir)
art	article (article)	Me	Maître (title applied to lawyers)
AV	avis de virement (transfer advice)	Melle(s)	Mademoiselle/Mesdemoiselles (Miss(es))
bd	boulevard	MM.	Messieurs (Messrs.)
BP	boîte postale (PO Box)	Mme	Madame (Madam)
CA	chiffre d affaires (turnover)	Mon, Mson	maison (firm)
C&A	coût et assurance (cost and insurance, C and I)	n.	notre, nos (our)
c-à-d.	c'est-à-dire (that is to say)	NB	Nota Bene
CAF	coût, assurance, fret (cost, insurance and freight, cif)	No	numéro (number, No.)
		N/Réf	notre référence (our ref)
c-c.	compte courant (current account)	p/c	pour compte
CCP	compte chèque postal (post office account)	P-DG	Président-Directeur Général (Chairman and Managing Director)
Cedex	courrier d entreprise à distribution exceptionnelle (postal code for business mail)	p.j.	pièce jointe (enclosure, enc)
Cie	compagnie (company)	PO	par ordre (by order)
cpt	comptant (cash)	p.p.	par procuration (by proxy)
CR	compte-rendu (minutes)	PTT	Postes, Télégraphes et Téléphones (General Post Office)
CV	curriculum vitae	réf	référence (reference, ref)
Dépt	département (administrative subdivision of France)	R.F.	République Française (French Republic)
Dest.	destinataire (recipient)	r.p.	réponse payée (reply paid)
DRH	Directeur(trice) des ressources humaines (Human Resources Manager)	R.S.V.P.	répondez, s il vous plaît (please reply, RSVP)
E.O.O.E	erreur ou omission exceptée (errors and omissions excepted)	S.A.	société anonyme (Limited Company)
		SARL	société à responsabilité limitée (limited (liability) company)
esc.	escompte (discount)	s.e. ou o.	sauf erreur(s) ou omission(s) (errors and omissions excepted)
Ets	établissements (factory; premises)		
Exp.	expéditeur (sender)	SS	Sécurité Sociale (social security)
Fres	Frères (brothers)	SVP	s'il vous plaît (please)
F.S.	faire suivre (please forward)	TEG	taux effectif global (annual percentage rate, APR)
hon.	honorée ('favour'; letter)		
HT	hors taxe (exclusive of tax)	Tél.	téléphone (telephone)
id.	idem (ditto)	T.S.V.P.	tournez s'il vous plaît (please turn over, PTO)
incl.	inclus (included)	v.	votre, vos (your)
j./jr(s)	jour(s) (day(s))	Ve; Vve	veuve (widow)
l/c	lettre de crédit (letter of credit)	V/Réf	votre référence (your ref)

Faxes

Faxes, which are by definition a form of rapid communication, can generally be drafted in a more casual and concise way than letters. The endings are usually short and simplified.

Business

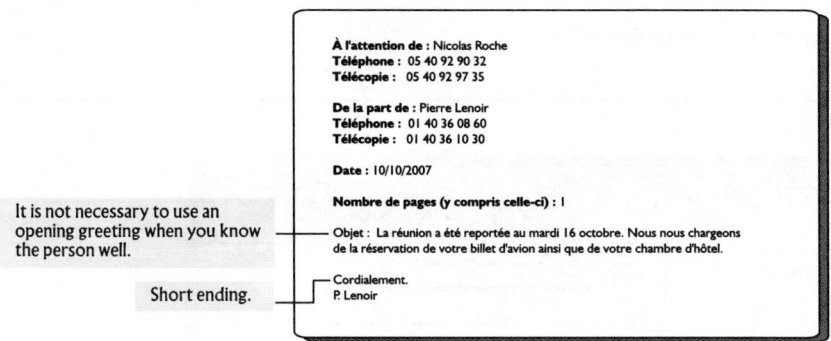

It is not necessary to use an opening greeting when you know the person well.

Short ending.

> À l'attention de : Nicolas Roche
> Téléphone : 05 40 92 90 32
> Télécopie : 05 40 92 97 35
>
> De la part de : Pierre Lenoir
> Téléphone : 01 40 36 08 60
> Télécopie : 01 40 36 10 30
>
> Date : 10/10/2007
>
> Nombre de pages (y compris celle-ci) : 1
>
> Objet : La réunion a été reportée au mardi 16 octobre. Nous nous chargeons de la réservation de votre billet d'avion ainsi que de votre chambre d'hôtel.
>
> Cordialement.
> P. Lenoir

Booking a hotel room

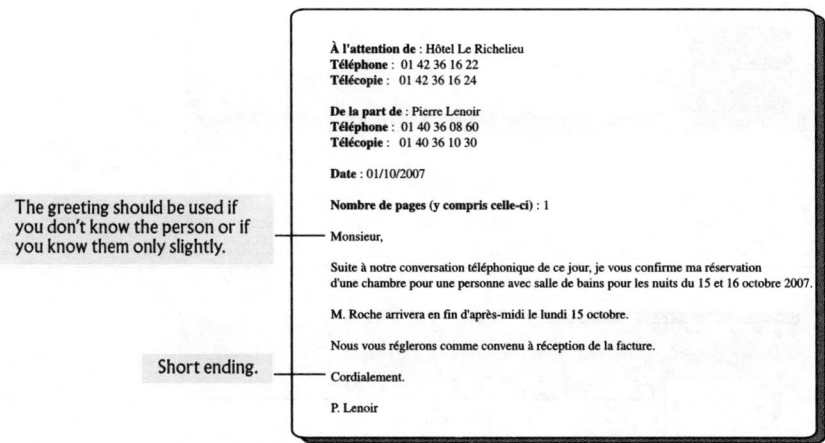

The greeting should be used if you don't know the person or if you know them only slightly.

Short ending.

> À l'attention de : Hôtel Le Richelieu
> Téléphone : 01 42 36 16 22
> Télécopie : 01 42 36 16 24
>
> De la part de : Pierre Lenoir
> Téléphone : 01 40 36 08 60
> Télécopie : 01 40 36 10 30
>
> Date : 01/10/2007
>
> Nombre de pages (y compris celle-ci) : 1
>
> Monsieur,
>
> Suite à notre conversation téléphonique de ce jour, je vous confirme ma réservation d'une chambre pour une personne avec salle de bains pour les nuits du 15 et 16 octobre 2007.
>
> M. Roche arrivera en fin d'après-midi le lundi 15 octobre.
>
> Nous vous réglerons comme convenu à réception de la facture.
>
> Cordialement.
>
> P. Lenoir

■ Alternative endings:

Salutations.
Salutations distinguées.
Bien à vous. (more friendly)

E-mail

■ Because of the nature of the medium, e-mails are not subject to the formal code of letter-writing that is prevalent in French.

■ E-mails in French are often written in slightly less telegraphic style than tends to be the case in English, this being mainly due to the fact that French contains fewer of the abbreviated forms that characterize so much of this type of communication in English. Endings are usually rather informal.

■ The same rules of "netiquette" apply as in English, so avoid typing entire words in capital letters as this is equivalent to shouting.

■ The symbol @ is pronounced [arobas] or [arobaz] in French.

Within a company

The headings are often in English as many French firms use American-manufactured software.

Informal greeting. It can also be omitted.

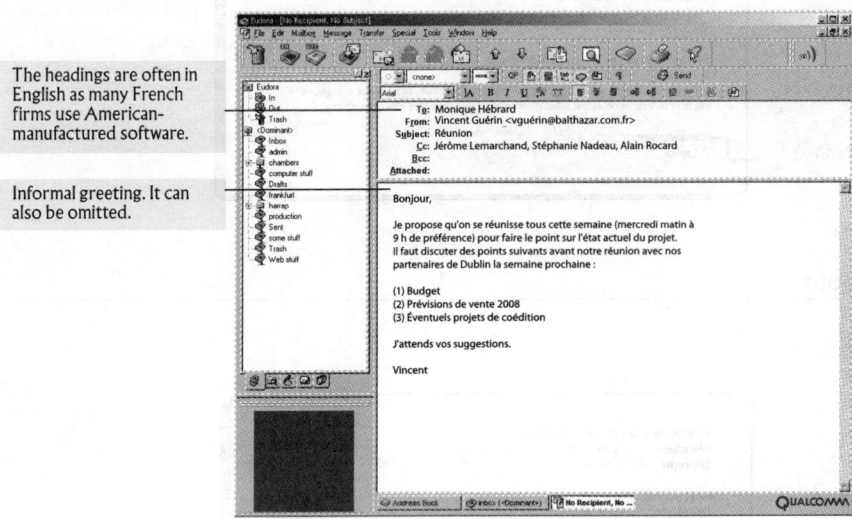

Business to business

Greetings are often omitted.

The ending is never as formal as in a letter.

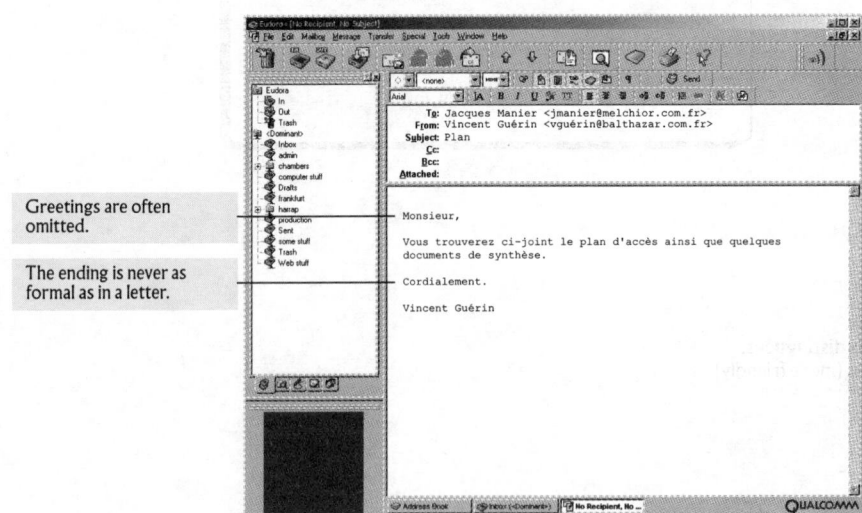

To a friend

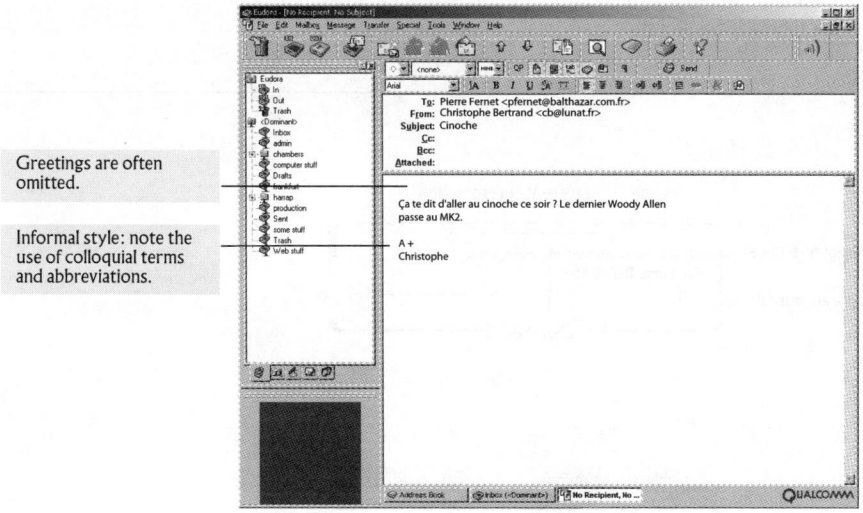

Greetings are often omitted.

Informal style: note the use of colloquial terms and abbreviations.

Abbreviations and acronyms: e-mail and Internet

Below is a list of French abbreviations that are used in e-mail correspondence, newsgroups and chatrooms. These abbreviations should only be used when you are sure that the person to whom you are sending the message understands what they mean. Some are familiar in register (labelled *Fam*) and therefore should only be used in casual correspondence with friends or very close colleagues.

Note that because English is the main language of the Internet, English abbreviations are much more well established than French ones.

A+ *Fam*	à plus tard (see you/talk to you etc later)	**impr.**	impression; imprimer; imprimante (printout; print; printer)
actu *Fam*	actualités (news, current affairs)	**info** *Fam*	information
alp *Fam*	à la prochaine (see you!; until we're next in touch!)	**Ltr**	lettre (letter)
ama *Fam*	à mon avis (in my opinion)	**m**	même (even; same)
amha *Fam*	à mon humble avis (in my humble opinion)	**Mdr** *Fam*	mort de rire (laughing out loud)
angl	anglais (English)	**MMS** *Fam*	mes meilleurs souvenirs (best regards)
BAL	boîte à lettres (mailbox)	**nvx**	nouveaux (new)
bcp *Fam*	beaucoup (a lot; many)	**p**	pour (for)
B.D.	base de données (database)	**pb, pbm**	problème (problem)
dc	donc (then, therefore)	**pr**	pour (for)
doc.	documents (documents, documentation)	**quoi 2/9** *Fam*	quoi de neuf ? (what's new?)
Doss	dossier (file)	**RAS** *Fam*	rien à signaler (nothing to report)
ds	dans (in)	**suiv.**	suivant (following)
envoy.	envoyer (please send)	**svt**	souvent (often)
err	erreur (error)	**urgt**	urgent
ex.	exemple (example)	**we**	weekend
fr	français (French)		

Advertisements

If you are not familiar with the abbreviations and style used, small ads can seem very cryptic.

Job advertisement

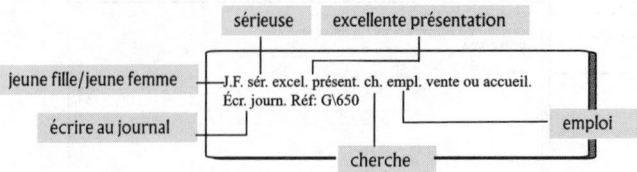

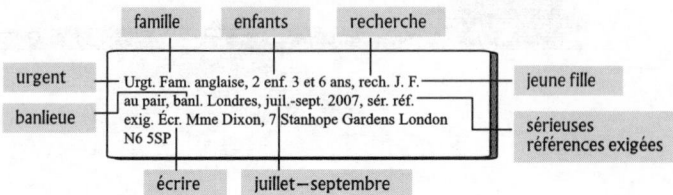

Offering goods for sale

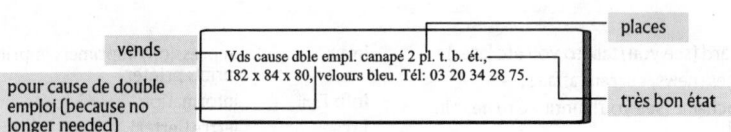

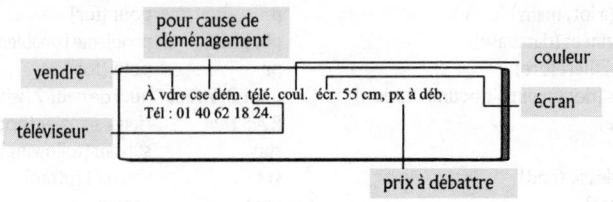

Accommodation to rent

Apartments in France are described in terms of the number of rooms (excluding the kitchen and bathroom). Advertisements also specify the total size of the property in square metres (m²). The rent may or may not include "charges" (monthly building maintenance charges).

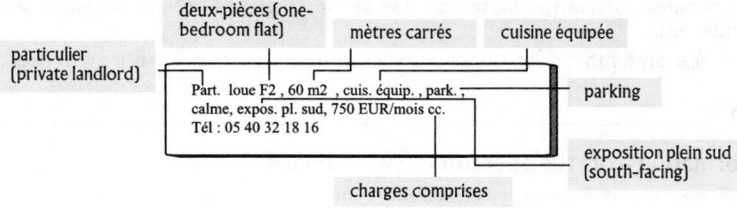

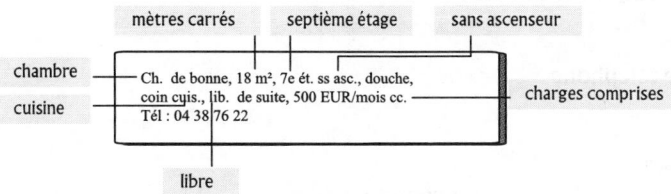

Personal advertisement

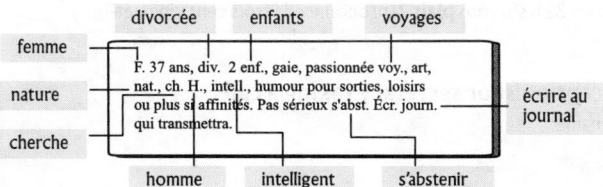

Common abbreviations:

à déb.	à débattre	park.	parking
appt.	appartement	pces.	pièces
balc.	balcon	px	prix
c.c.	charges comprises/chauffage central	rdc.	rez-de-chaussée
ch.	chambre/cherche	sdb.	salle de bains
compr.	comprenant	séj.	séjour
cuis.	cuisine	sér.	sérieux
env.	envoyer	tbe	très bon état
équip.	équipé	tt. conf.	tout confort
gar.	garage	se prés.	se présenter
gren.	grenier	Sté.	société

Telephone calls

Pronunciation of telephone numbers

When giving their phone numbers, French people say them two by two: 01 45 67 44 32: zéro un, quarante-cinq, soixante-sept, quarante-quatre, trente-deux.

This can be a little disconcerting for the English speaker and you may have to ask them to say it again one number at a time.

Typical Phrases

■ Asking for information from the operator or switchboard

Est-ce que vous pouvez me passer les renseignements, s'il vous plaît ?

J'essaie d'obtenir un numéro à Marseille.

Quel est l'indicatif pour le Maroc, s'il vous plaît ?

Comment fait-on pour appeler à l'extérieur ?

■ Answering the telephone

Informally:

Allô?

To which the caller replies:

Allô, (c'est) Georges? or Salut, Georges, c'est Christophe etc.

More formally:

Allô, Hélène Chapsal à l'appareil(, je vous écoute).

In a company or institution:

Déménagements Leclerc, bonjour.

Éditions Paoli, bonjour.

■ Asking to speak to someone:

Je voudrais parler à Monsieur Dupont.

Pouvez-vous me passer le service du/des ..., s'il vous plaît ?

Pouvez-vous me passer le poste 321, s'il vous plaît ? (pronounced "trois cent vingt-et-un")

■ Phrases used by a receptionist or secretary taking a call

When asking for the caller's name:

Qui dois-je annoncer ?

C'est de la part de qui ?

When putting a caller through:

Je vous le/la passe.

Ne quittez pas, je vous le/la passe.

When the caller cannot be connected immediately:

C'est occupé.

Il/Elle est en communication, voulez-vous patienter ?

Asking the caller if he or she wishes to leave a message:

Voulez-vous lui laisser un message ?

To which the caller may reply:

Pouvez-vous lui demander de me rappeler ?

■ Recorded messages

If you are put on hold, the standard recorded message while waiting is :

Nous vous demandons de bien vouloir patienter quelques instants. Nous allons donner suite à votre appel.

If you have to leave a message, you will hear the following standard set of sentences:

Vous êtes bien en communication avec ... Nous ne pouvons répondre à votre appel. Veuillez nous laisser votre nom et numéro de téléphone après le signal sonore et nous vous rappellerons dès que possible. Merci.

Nations of the World

Please note that the French name for the countries has been given in the second column. In order to find the French terms for the currencies and languages, please refer to the corresponding table in the French supplement.

Note also that the abbreviations given for currencies are the internationally recognised standard abbreviations established by the ISO and used in international financial transactions, rather than locally used abbreviations.

English name	French name	Local name	Official language(s)	Currency
Afghanistan	Afghanistan	Afghānestān	Dari, Pushtu	1 Afghani (AFA) = 100 puls
Albania	Albanie	Shqïpëri	Albanian	1 Lek (ALL) = 100 qindarka
Algeria	Algérie Algérie (French)	Al-Jazā'ir (Arabic),	Arabic	1 Algerian Dinar (DZD) = 100 centimes
Andorra	Andorre	Andorra Spanish	Catalan, French,	1 Euro (EUR) = 100 cents
Angola	Angola	Angola	Portuguese	New Kwanza (AOK) = 100 weil
Argentina	Argentine	Argentina	Spanish	1 Peso (ARS) = 100 centavos
Armenia	Arménie	Hayastani	Armenian	1 Dram (AMD) = 100 louma
Australia	Australie	Australia	English	1 Australian Dollar (AUD) = 100 cents
Austria	Autriche	Österreich	German	1 Euro (EUR) = 100 cents
Azerbaijan	Azerbaïdjan	Azarbaijan	Azeri (Azerbaijan)	1 Manat (AZM) = 100 gopik
Bahamas, The	Bahamas	Bahamas	English	1 Bahamian Dollar (BSD) = 100 cents
Bahrain	Bahreïn	Dawlat al-Bahrayn	Arabic	1 Bahrain Dinar (BHD) = 1,000 fils
Bangladesh	Bangladesh Bangladesh	Gana Prajatantri	Bengali	1 Taka (BDT) = 100 poisha
Barbados	Barbade	Barbados	English	1 Barbados Dollar (BBD) = 100 cents
Belarus	Biélorussie	Belarus	Belarussian	1 Rouble (BYB) = 100 kopeks
Belgium	Belgique	Belgique (French), Belgïe (Flemish)	Flemish, French, German	1 Euro (EUR) = 100 cents
Belize	Belize	Belize	English	1 Belize Dollar (BZD) = 100 cents
Benin	Bénin	Bénin	French	1 CFA Franc (XOF) = 100 centimes
Bhutan	Bhoutan	Druk-Yul	Dzongkha	1 Ngultrum (BTN) = 100 chetrum
Bolivia	Bolivie	Bolivia	Spanish	1 Boliviano (BOB) = 100 centavos
Bosnia-Herzegovina	Bosnie-Herzégovine	Bosnia-Herzegovina	Serbo-Croat	1 Dinar (BAD) = 100 paras
Botswana	Botswana	Botswana	English	1 Pula (BWP) = 100 thebe
Brazil	Brésil	Brasil	Portuguese	1 Real (BRL) = 100 centavos
Brunei	Brunei	Brunei	Malay	1 Brunei Dollar (BND) = 100 sen
Bulgaria	Bulgarie	Bǎlgarija	Bulgarian	1 Lev (BGL) (pl Leva) = 100 stotinki (sing stotinka)
Burkina Faso	Burkina	Burkina Faso	French	1 CFA Franc (XOF) = 100 centimes
Burma ▶ Myanmar	Birmanie			
Burundi	Burundi	Burundi	French, Kirundi	1 Burundi Franc (BIF) = 100 centimes
Cambodia	Cambodge	Preah Reach Ana Pak Kampuchea	Khmer	1 Riel (KHR) = 100 sen
Cameroon	Cameroun	Cameroon	English, French	1 CFA Franc (XAF) = 100 centimes
Canada	Canada	Canada	English, French	1 Canadian Dollar (CAD) = 100 cents
Cape Verde	Cap-Vert	Cabo Verde	Portuguese	1 Escudo Caboverdiano (CVE) = 100 centavos
Central African Republic	République centrafricaine	République centrafricaine	French, Sango	1 CFA Franc (XAF) = 100 centimes
Chad	Tchad	Tchad	French, Arabic	1 CFA Franc (XAF) = 100 centimes
Chile	Chili	Chile	Spanish	1 Chilean Peso (CLP) = 100 centavos
China	Chine	Zhongguo	Chinese	1 Renminbi Yuan (CNY) = 10 jiao = 100 fen

English name	French name	Local name	Official language(s)	Currency
Colombia	Colombie	Colombia	Spanish	1 Colombian Peso (COP) = 100 centavos
Comoros	Comores	Comores	French, Comorian	1 Comorian Franc (KMF) = 100 centimes
Congo, Democratic Republic of the	Congo, République démocratique du	Congo, République démocratique du	French, Lingala, Monokutuba	1 CFA Franc (XAF) = 100 centimes
Costa Rica	Costa Rica	Costa Rica	Spanish	1 Costa Rican Colón (CRC) (pl Colones) = 100 céntimos
Côte d'Ivoire	Côte d'Ivoire	Côte d'Ivoire	French	1 CFA Franc (XOF) = 100 centimes
Croatia	Croatie	Hrvatska	Serbo-Croat	1 Kuna (HRK) = 100 lipas
Cuba	Cuba	Cuba	Spanish	1 Cuban Peso (CUP) = 100 centavos; 1 Convertible Peso (CUC) = 100 centavos
Cyprus	Chypre	Kipros (Greek), Kibris (Turkish)	Greek, Turkish	1 Cyprus Pound (CYP) = 100 cents
Czech Republic	République tchèque	Česká Republika	Czech	1 Koruna (CZK) = 100 halřu
Denmark	Danemark	Danmark	Danish	1 Danish Krone (DKK) (pl Kroner) = 100 øre
Djibouti	Djibouti	Djibouti	Arabic, French	1 Djibouti Franc (DJF) = 100 centimes
Dominica	Dominique	Dominica	English, French, Creole	1 East Caribbean Dollar (XCD) = 100 cents
Dominican Republic	République Dominicaine	República dominicana	Spanish	1 Dominican Republic Peso (DOP) = 100 centavos
Ecuador	Équateur	Ecuador	Spanish	1 Sucre (ECS) = 100 centavos
Egypt	Égypte	Jumhuriyat Misr Al-Arabiya	Arabic	1 Egyptian Pound (EGP) = 100 piastres
El Salvador	Salvador	El Salvador	Spanish	1 Colón (SVC) (pl Colones) = 100 centavos
Equatorial Guinea	Guinée équatoriale	Guinea Ecuatorial	Spanish	1 CFA Franc (XAF) = 100 centimes
Eritrea	Érythrée	Eritrea	Tigrinya, Arabic	1 Ethopian Birr (ETB) = 100 cents
Estonia	Estonie	Eesti Vabariik	Estonian	1 Kroon (EEK) = 100 sents
Ethiopia	Éthiopie	Ityopiya	Amharic	1 Ethiopian Birr (ETB) = 100 cents
Faroe Islands	Îles Féroé	Faroyar/Faeroerne	Faroese, Danish	1 Danish Krone (DKK) (pl Kroner) = 100 øre
Fiji	Îles Fidji	Matanitu Ko Viti	English	1 Fiji Dollar (FJD) = 100 cents
Finland	Finlande	Suomen Tasavalta	Finnish, Swedish	1 Euro (EUR) = 100 cents
France	France	République française	French	1 Euro (EUR) = 100 cents
French Guiana	Guyane	Guyane française	French, French Creole	1 Euro (EUR) = 100 cents
French Polynesia	Polynésie française	Territoire de la Polynésie française	Polynesian, French	1 CPA Franc (XPF) = 100 centimes
Gabon	Gabon	République gabonaise	French	1 CFA Franc (XAF) = 100 centimes
Gambia, The	Gambie	Gambia	English	1 Dalasi (GMD) = 100 butut
Georgia	Géorgie	Sakartvelos Respublika	Georgian, Russian	1 Lari (GEL) = 100 tetri
Germany	Allemagne	Bundesrepublik Deutschland	German	1 Euro (EUR) = 100 cents
Ghana	Ghana	Ghana	English	1 Cedi (GHC) = 100 pesewas
Greece	Grèce	Elliniki Dimokratia	Greek	1 Euro (EUR) = 100 cents
Greenland	Groenland	Grønland (Danish), Kalaallit Nunaat	Danish, Greenlandic	1 Danish Krone (DKK) (pl Kroner) = 100 øre
Guatemala	Guatemala	Guatemala	Spanish	1 Quetzal (GTQ) (pl Quetzales) = 100 centavos
Guinea	Guinée	République de Guinée	French	1 Guinea Franc (GNF) = 100 centimes
Guinea-Bissau	Guinée-Bissau	Republica da Guiné-Bissau	Portuguese	1 CFA Franc (GWP) = 100 centimes
Guyana	Guyana	Guyana	English	1 Guyana Dollar (GYD) = 100 cents
Haiti	Haïti	République d'Haïti	French	1 Gourde (HTG) = 100 centimes
Holland ▶ Netherlands, The	Hollande			
Honduras	Honduras	Honduras	Spanish	1 Lempira (HNL) = 100 centavos
Hungary	Hongrie	Magyar Koztarsasag	Hungarian	1 Forint (HUF) = 100 fillér
Iceland	Islande	Ísland	Icelandic	1 Króna (ISK) = 100 aurar (sing eyrir)

English name	French name	Local name	Official language(s)	Currency
India	Inde	Bhārat (Hindi)	Hindi, English	1 Indian Rupee (INR) = 100 paisa
Indonesia	Indonésie	Republik Indonesia	Bahasa Indonesia	1 Rupiah (IDR) = 100 sen
Iran	Iran	Jomhoori-e-Islami-e-Iran	Farsi	1 Iranian Rial (IRR) = 100 dinars
Iraq	Irak	Jumhouriya al Iraquia	Arabic	1 Iraqi Dinar (IQD) = 1,000 fils
Ireland	Irlande	Poblacht na hEireann	Irish, English	1 Euro (EUR) = 100 cents
Israel	Israël	Medinat Israel	Hebrew, Arabic	1 Shekel (ILS) = 100 agora
Italy	Italie	Repubblica Italiana	Italian	1 Euro (EUR) = 100 cents
Ivory Coast ▸ Côte d Ivoire	Côte d Ivoire			
Jamaica	Jamaïque	Jamaica	English	1 Jamaican Dollar (JMD) = 100 cents
Japan	Japon	Nihon	Japanese	1 Yen (JPY) = 100 sen
Jordan	Jordanie	Al'Urdun	Arabic	1 Jordanian Dinar (JOD) = 1,000 fils
Kazakhstan	Kazakhstan	Kazak Respublikasy	Kazakh, Russian	1 Tenge (KZT) = 100 tiyn
Kenya	Kenya	Jamhuri ya Kenya	(Ki)Swahili, English	1 Kenyan shilling (KES) = 100 cents
Korea, North	Corée du Nord	Chosōn Minjujuũi In'min Konghwaguk	Korean	1 Won (KPW) = 100 chon
Korea, South	Corée du Sud	Taehan-Min'guk	Korean	1 Won (KRW) = 100 chon
Kuwait	Koweït	Dowlat al-Kuwayt	Arabic	1 Kuwaiti Dinar (KWD) = 1,000 fils
Kyrgyzstan	Kirghizistan	Kyrgyz Respublikasy	Kyrgyz	1 Som (KGS) = 100 tyiyn
Laos	Laos	Lao	Lao	1 Kip (LAK) = 100 at
Latvia	Lettonie	Latvijas Republika	Latvian	1 Lats (LVL) (*pl* Lati) = 100 santimi (*sing* santims)
Lebanon	Liban	Al-Lubnān	Arabic	1 Lebanese Pound/Livre (LBP) = 100 piastres
Lesotho	Lesotho	Lesotho	English, Sesotho	1 Loti (*pl* Maloti) (LSL) = 100 lisente
Liberia	Liberia	Liberia	English	1 Liberian Dollar (LRD) = 100 cents
Libya	Libye	Lībyā	Arabic	1 Libyan Dinar (LYD) = 1,000 dirhams
Liechtenstein	Liechtenstein	Furstentum Liechtenstein	German	1 Swiss Franc (CHF) = 100 centimes/rappen
Lithuania	Lituanie	Lietuva	Lithuanian	1 Litas (LTL) (*pl* litai) = 100 centai (*sing* centas)
Luxembourg	Luxembourg	Lëtzebuerg (Lëtz.), Luxembourg (French), Luxemburg (German)	French, German, Lëtzebuergesch	1 Euro (EUR) = 100 cents
Macedonia	Macédoine	Republika Makedonija	Macedonian	1 Denar (MKD) = 100 paras
Madagascar	Madagascar	Republikan'i Madagasikara	Malagasy, French	1 Malagasy Franc (MGF) = 100 centimes
Malawi	Malawi	Dziko la Malaẁi	Chichewa, English	1 Kwacha (MWK) = 100 tambala
Malaysia	Malaisie	Federation of Malaysia	Bahasa Melayu	1 Malaysian Dollar/Ringgit (MYR) = 100 cents
Maldives	Maldives	Maldives Divehi Jumhuriya	Divehi	1 Rufiyaa (MVR) = 100 laari
Mali	Mali	Mali	French	1 CFA Franc (XOF) = 100 centimes
Malta	Malte	Malta	English, Maltese	1 Maltese Lira (MTL) = 100 cents = 1,000 mils
Martinique	Martinique	Martinique	French, French Creole	1 Euro (EUR) = 100 cents
Mauritania	Mauritanie	Mauritanie (French), Mūrītāniyā (Arabic)	Arabic	1 Ouguiya (MRO) = 5 khoums
Mauritius	Île Maurice	Mauritius	English	1 Mauritian Rupee (MUR) = 100 cents
Mexico	Mexique	México	Spanish	1 Mexican Peso (MXN) = 100 centavos
Micronesia	Micronésie	Micronesia	English	1 US Dollar (USD) = 100 cents
Moldova	Moldavie	Republica Moldovenească	Moldavian	1 Leu (MDL) (*pl* lei) = 100 bani (*sing* ban)
Monaco	Monaco	Principauté de Monaco	French	1 Euro (EUR) = 100 cents

English name	French name	Local name	Official language(s)	Currency
Mongolia	Mongolie	Mongol Ard Uls	Halh Mongol	1 Tugrik (MNT) = 100 möngö
Morocco	Maroc	Mamlaka al-Maghrebia	Arabic	1 Dirham (MAD) = 100 centimes
Mozambique	Mozambique	República de Moçambique	Portuguese	1 Metical (MZM) = 100 centavos
Myanmar	Myanmar	Myanmar	Burmese	1 Kyat (MMK) = 100 pyas
Namibia	Namibie	Namibia	English	1 Namibian Dollar (NAD) = 100 cents
Nauru	Nauru	Naeoro (Nauruan), Nauru (English)	Nauruan, English	1 Australian Dollar (AUD) = 100 cents
Nepal	Népal	Nepal Adhirajya	Napali	1 Nepalese Rupee (NPR) = 100 paise/pice
Netherlands, The	Pays-Bas	Koninkrijk der Nederlanden	Dutch	1 Euro (EUR) = 100 cents
New Zealand	Nouvelle-Zélande	New Zealand	English	1 New Zealand Dollar (NZD) = 100 cents
Nicaragua	Nicaragua	Nicaragua	Spanish	1 Córdoba Oro (NIO) = 100 centavos
Niger	Niger	Niger	French	1 CFA Franc (XOF) = 100 centimes
Nigeria	Nigéria	Nigeria	English, French	1 Naira (NGN) = 100 kobo
Norway	Norvège	Kongeriket Norge	Norwegian	1 Norwegian Krone (NOK) = 100 øre
Oman	Oman	Saltanat 'Uman	Arabic	1 Omani Rial (OMR) = 1,000 baiza
Pakistan	Pakistan	Pākistān	Urdu, English	1 Pakistan Rupee (PKR) = 100 paisa
Panama	Panamá	Panamá	Spanish	1 Balboa (PAB) = 100 centésimos
Papua New Guinea	Papouasie-Nouvelle-Guinée	Papua New Guinea	English, Tok Písin, Hiri Motu	1 Kina (PGK) = 100 toea
Paraguay	Paraguay	Paraguay	Spanish	1 Guaraní (PYG) = 100 céntimos
Peru	Pérou	Perú	Spanish	1 New Sol (PEN) = 100 centavos
Philippines	Philippines	Pilipinas	Filipino, English	1 Philippine Peso (PHP) = 100 centavos
Poland	Pologne	Rzeczpospolita Polska	Polish	1 Zloty (PLN) = 100 groszy (sing grosz)
Portugal	Portugal	Portugal	Portuguese	1 Euro (EUR) = 100 cents
Puerto Rico	Porto Rico	Puerto Rico	Spanish, English	US Dollar (USD) = 100 cents
Qatar	Qatar	Dowlat Qatar	Arabic	1 Qatar Riyal (QAR) = 100 dirhams
Romania	Roumanie	Romănia	Romanian	1 Leu (ROL) (Lei) = 100 bani (sing ban)
Russia	Russie	Rossiya	Russian	1 Rouble (RUR) = 100 kopeks
Rwanda	Rwanda	Rwanda	(Kinya) Rwanda, French, English	1 Rwanda Franc (RWF) = 100 centimes
Samoa	Samoa	Samoa	Samoan, English	1 Tala (WST) = 100 sene
San Marino	Saint-Marin	San Marino	Italian	1 Euro (EUR) = 100 cents
Saudi Arabia	Arabie Saoudite	Al-'Arabīyah as Sa'ūdīyah	Arabic	1 Saudi Arabian Riyal (SAR) = 20 qursh = 100 halala
Senegal	Sénégal	Sénégal	French, Wolof	1 CFA Franc (XOF) =100 centimes
Seychelles, The	Seychelles	Seychelles	Creole French, English, French	1 Seychelles Rupee (SCR) = 100 cents
Sierra Leone	Sierra Leone	Sierra Leone	English	1 Leone (SLL) = 100 cents
Singapore	Singapour	Singapore	Chinese, English, Malay, Tamil	1 Singapore Dollar (SGD)/ = 100 cents
Slovakia	Slovaquie	Slovenska Republika	Slovak	1 Koruna (CSK) = 100 haléru
Slovenia	Slovénie	Republika Slovenija	Slovene	1 Tolar (SIT) =100 stotin
Solomon Islands	Îles Salomon	Solomon Islands	English	1 Solomon Islands Dollar (SBD) = 100 cents
Somalia	Somalie	Somaliya	Arabic, Somali	1 Somali Shilling (SOS) = 100 cents
South Africa	Afrique du Sud	South Africa	English, Afrikaans	1 Rand (ZAR) = 100 cents
Spain	Espagne	España	Spanish	1 Euro (EUR) = 100 cents
Sri Lanka	Sri Lanka	Sri Lanka	Sinhala, Tamil	1 Sri Lankan Rupee (LKR) = 100 cents
Sudan	Soudan	As-Sūdān	Arabic	1 Sudanese Pound (SDP) = 100 piasters

English name	French name	Local name	Official language(s)	Currency
Surinam	Surinam(e)	Suriname	Dutch	1 Surinam Guilder (SRG)/ Florin = 100 cents
Swaziland	Swaziland	Umbouso we Swatini	Swazi, English	1 Lilangeni (SZL) (*pl* Emalangeni) = 100 cents
Sweden	Suède	Konungariket Sverige	Swedish	1 Swedish Krona (SEK) = 100 øre
Switzerland	Suisse	Schweiz (German), Suisse (French), Svizzera (Italian)	French, German, Italian, Romansch	1 Swiss Franc (CHF) = 100 centimes/rappen
Syria	Syrie	As-Sūrīyah	Arabic	1 Syrian pound (SYP) = 100 piastres
Taiwan	Taïwan	T'aiwan	Chinese	1 New Taiwan Dollar (TWD) = 100 cents
Tajikistan	Tadjikistan	Jumkhurii Tojikistan	Tajik	1 Tajik Rouble (TJR) = 100 tanga
Tanzania	Tanzanie	Tanzania	(Ki)Swahili, English	1 Tanzanian Shilling (TZS) = 100 cents
Thailand	Thaïlande	Prathet Thai	Thai	1 Baht (THB) = 100 satang
Togo	Togo	Togo	French	1 CFA Franc (XOF) = 100 centimes
Tonga	Tonga	Tonga	English, Tongan	1 Pa'anga/Tongan Dollar (TOP) = 100 seniti
Trinidad and Tobago	Trinité-et-Tobago	Trinidad and Tobago	English	1 Trinidad and Tobago Dollar (TTD) = 100 cents
Tunisia	Tunisie	Tunisiya	Arabic, French	1 Tunisian Dinar (TND) = 1,000 millimes
Turkey	Turquie	Türkiye	Turkish	1 Turkish Lira (TRL) = 100 kurus
Turkmenistan	Turkménistan	Turkmenostan	Turkmenian	1 Manat (TMM) = 100 tenesi
Uganda	Ouganda	Uganda	English, Kiswahili	1 Uganda Shilling (UGX) = 100 cents
Ukraine	Ukraine	Ukraina	Ukrainian, Russian	1 Hryvna (UAK) = 100 kopiykas
United Arab Emirates	Émirats Arabes Unis	Ittihād al-Imārāt al-'Arabīyah	Arabic, English	1 Dirham (AED) = 100 fils
United Kingdom	Royaume-Uni	United Kingdom	English	1 Pound Sterling (GBP) = 100 pence
United States of America	États-Unis	United States of America	English	1 US Dollar (USD) = 100 cents
Uruguay	Uruguay	Uruguay	Spanish	1 New Uruguayan Peso (UYU) = 100 centésimos
Uzbekistan	Ouzbékistan	Uzbekistan	Uzbek	1 Sum (UZS) = 100 tiyin
Vanuatu	Vanuatu	Vanuatu	Bislama, English, French	1 Vatu (VUV) = 100 centimes
Vatican City	cité du Vatican	Citta' del Vaticano	Italian	1 Euro (EUR) = 100 cents
Venezuela	Venezuela	Venezuela	Spanish	1 Bolívar (VEB) (*pl* bolívares) = 100 céntimos
Vietnam	Vietnam	Viêt-nam	Vietnamese	1 Dông (VND) = 10 hào = 100 xu
Yemen	Yémen	Al-Yamaniya	Arabic	1 Yemeni Riyal (YER) = 100 fils
Yugoslavia	Yougoslavie	Jugoslavija	Serbo-Croat	1 New Dinar (YUN) = 100 paras
Zaire ▶ Congo, Democratic Republic of the	Zaïre			
Zambia	Zambie	Zambia	English	1 Kwacha (ZMK) = 100 ngwee
Zimbabwe	Zimbabwe	Zimbabwe	English	1 Zimbabwe Dollar (ZWD) = 100 cents

Administrative Divisions (French)

France

Region	Administrative centre
Alsace	Strasbourg
Aquitaine	Bordeaux
Auvergne	Clermont-Ferrand
Brittany (Bretagne)	Rennes
Burgundy (Bourgogne)	Dijon
Centre	Orléans
Champagne-Ardennes	Reims
Corsica (Corse)	Ajaccio
Franche-Comté	Besançon
Île-de-France	Paris
Languedoc-Roussillon	Montpellier
Limousin	Limoges
Lorraine	Nancy
Midi-Pyrénées	Toulouse
Nord-Pas-de-Calais	Lille
Normandy, Lower (Basse-Normandie)	Caen
Normandy, Upper (Haute-Normandie)	Rouen
Pays de la Loire	Nantes
Picardy (Picardie)	Amiens
Poitou-Charentes	Poitiers
Provence-Alpes-Côte d'Azur	Marseille
Rhône-Alpes	Lyon

Belgium

Province	Capital
Antwerp	Antwerp
Brabant	Brussels
E Flanders	Ghent
Hainaut	Mons
Liège	Liège
Limburg	Hasselt
Luxembourg	Arlon
Namur	Namur
W Flanders	Bruges

Switzerland

Canton	Capital
Aargau	Aarau
Appenzell Außer-Rhoden[1]	Herisau
Appenzell Inner-Rhoden[1]	Appenzell
Basle (Basel-Landschaft)[1]	Liestal
Basle (Basel-Stadt)[1]	Basel
Berne	Berne
Fribourg	Fribourg
Geneva (Genève)	Geneva
Glarus	Glarus
Graubünden (Fr: Grisons)	Chur (Coire)
Jura	Delémont
Lucerne (Luzern)	Lucerne
Neuenberg (Neuchâtel)	Neuchâtel
Nidwalden[1]	Stans
Obwalden[1]	Sarnen
St Gall (Sankt Gallen)	St Gall
Schaffhausen	Schaffhausen
Schwyz	Schwyz
Solothurn	Solothurn
Thurgau	Frauenfeld
Ticino	Bellinzona
Uri	Altdorf
Valais	Sion
Vaud	Lausanne
Zug	Zug
Zürich	Zürich

[1] Demi-canton — functions as a full canton.

French départements

All telephone numbers in mainland France and Corsica begin with a two-digit prefix; 01 for the Paris area, 02 for the north-west, 03 for the north-east, 04 for the south-east and 05 for the south-west. The right-hand column of the table below lists the number that prefixes all eight-digit telephone numbers for the respective départements.

Département	Code	Administrative centre	Region	Telephone code
Ain	01	Bourg-en-Bresse	Rhône-Alpes	4
Aisne	02	Laon	Picardie	3
Allier	03	Moulins	Auvergne	4
Alpes-de-Haute-Provence	04	Digne-les-Bains	Provence-Alpes-Côte d'Azur	4
Alpes (Hautes-)	05	Gap	Provence-Alpes-Côte d'Azur	4
Alpes-Maritimes	06	Nice	Provence-Alpes-Côte d'Azur	4
Ardèche	07	Privas	Rhône-Alpes	4
Ardennes	08	Charleville-Mézières	Champagne-Ardennes	3
Ariège	09	Foix	Midi-Pyrénées	5
Aube	10	Troyes	Champagne-Ardennes	3
Aude	11	Carcassonne	Languedoc-Roussillon	4
Aveyron	12	Rodez	Midi-Pyrénées	5
Belfort (Territoire de)	90	Belfort	Franche-Comté	3
Bouches-du-Rhône	13	Marseille	Provence-Alpes-Côte d'Azur	4
Calvados	14	Caen	Basse-Normandie	2
Cantal	15	Aurillac	Auvergne	4
Charente	16	Angoulême	Poitou-Charentes	5
Charente-Maritime	17	La Rochelle	Poitou-Charentes	5
Cher	18	Bourges	Centre	2
Corrèze	19	Tulle	Limousin	5
Corse-du-Sud	2A	Ajaccio	Corse	4
Corse (Haute-)	2B	Bastia	Corse	4
Côte-d'Or	21	Dijon	Bourgogne	3
Côtes-d'Armor	22	Saint-Brieux	Bretagne	2
Creuse	23	Guéret	Limousin	5
Dordogne	24	Périgueux	Aquitaine	5
Doubs	25	Besançon	Franche-Comté	3
Drôme	26	Valence	Rhône-Alpes	4
Essonne	91	Évry	Île-de-France	1
Eure	27	Évreux	Haute-Normandie	2
Eure-et-Loire	28	Chartres	Centre	2

(65)

Département	Code	Administrative centre	Region	Telephone code
Finistère	29	Quimper	Bretagne	2
Gard	30	Nîmes	Languedoc-Roussillon	4
Garonne (Haute)	31	Toulouse	Midi-Pyrénées	5
Gers	32	Auch	Midi-Pyrénées	5
Gironde	33	Bordeaux	Aquitaine	5
Hauts-de-Seine	92	Nanterre	Île-de-France	1
Hérault	34	Montpellier	Languedoc-Roussillon	4
Ille-et-Villaine	35	Rennes	Bretagne	2
Indre	36	Châteauroux	Centre	2
Indre-et-Loire	37	Tours	Centre	2
Isère	38	Grenoble	Rhône-Alpes	4
Jura	39	Lons-le-Saunier	Franche-Comté	3
Landes	40	Mont-de-Marsan	Aquitaine	5
Loir-et-Cher	41	Blois	Centre	2
Loire	42	Saint-Étienne	Rhône-Alpes	4
Loire (Haute-)	43	Le-Puy-en-Velay	Auvergne	4
Loire-Atlantique	44	Nantes	Pays de la Loire	2
Loiret	45	Orléans	Centre	2
Lot	46	Cahors	Midi-Pyrénées	5
Lot-et-Garonne	47	Agen	Aquitaine	5
Lozère	48	Mende	Languedoc-Roussillon	4
Maine-et-Loire	49	Angers	Pays de la Loire	2
Manche	50	Saint-Lô	Basse-Normandie	2
Marne	51	Châlons-en-Champagne	Champagne-Ardennes	3
Marne (Haute-)	52	Chaumont	Champagne-Ardennes	3
Mayenne	53	Laval	Pays de la Loire	2
Meurthe-et-Moselle	54	Nancy	Lorraine	3
Meuse	55	Bar-le-Duc	Lorraine	3
Morbihan	56	Vannes	Bretagne	2
Moselle	57	Metz	Lorraine	3
Nièvre	58	Nevers	Bourgogne	3
Nord	59	Lille	Nord-Pas-de-Calais	3
Oise	60	Beauvais	Picardie	3
Orne	61	Alençon	Basse-Normandie	2
Paris (Ville de)	75		Île-de-France	1
Pas-de-Calais	62	Arras	Nord-Pas-de-Calais	3
Puy-de-Dôme	63	Clermont-Ferrand	Auvergne	4
Pyrénées-Atlantiques	64	Pau	Aquitaine	5
Pyrénées (Hautes-)	65	Tarbes	Midi-Pyrénées	5
Pyrénées-Orientales	66	Perpignan	Languedoc-Roussillon	4
Rhin (Bas-)	67	Strasbourg	Alsace	3
Rhin (Haut-)	68	Colmar	Alsace	3
Rhône	69	Lyon	Rhône-Alpes	4
Saône (Haute-)	70	Vesoul	Franche-Comté	3
Saône-et-Loire	71	Mâcon	Bourgogne	3
Sarthe	72	Le Mans	Pays de la Loire	2
Savoie	73	Chambéry	Rhône-Alpes	4
Savoie (Haute-)	74	Annecy	Rhône-Alpes	4
Seine-Maritime	76	Rouen	Haute-Normandie	2
Seine-et-Marne	77	Melun	Île-de-France	1
Seine-Saint-Denis	93	Bobigny	Île-de-France	1
Sèvres (Deux)	79	Niort	Poitou-Charentes	5
Somme	80	Amiens	Picardie	3
Tarn	81	Albi	Midi-Pyrénées	5
Tarn-et-Garonne	82	Montauban	Midi-Pyrénées	5
Val-de-Marne	94	Créteil	Île-de-France	1
Val-d'Oise	95	Pontoise	Île-de-France	1
Var	83	Toulon	Provence-Alpes-Côte d'Azur	4
Vaucluse	84	Avignon	Provence-Alpes-Côte d'Azur	4
Vendée	85	La-Roche-sur-Yon	Pays de la Loire	2
Vienne	86	Poitiers	Poitou-Charentes	5
Vienne (Haute-)	87	Limoges	Limousin	5
Vosges	88	Épinal	Lorraine	3
Yonne	89	Auxerre	Bourgogne	3
Yvelines	78	Versailles	Île-de-France	1

Départements, régions et collectivités d'outre-mer

Département	Code	Administrative centre	Region
Guadeloupe	971	Basse-Terre	DROM
Martinique	972	Fort-de-France	DROM
Guyane	973	Cayenne	DROM
Réunion	974	Saint-Denis	DROM
Nouvelle-Calédonie	98	Nouméa	CS[1]
Wallis-et-Futuna	98	Mata-Utu	COM
Polynésie-Française		Papeete	COM
Terres australes et antarctiques françaises[2]			
Mayotte	976	Mamoudzou	CT
Saint-Pierre-et-Miquelon	97500	Saint-Pierre	CT

[1] 'Collectivité spécifique' — provisional status until its independence or otherwise is confirmed.
[2] French overseas territories with special status.

French Legal System

■ **Les tribunaux ordinaires : droit civil**
Ordinary Courts: Civil

Cour de cassation
Final court of appeal

Peut annuler les décisions rendues par les juridictions inférieures
Can overrule decisions from the lower courts

Cours d'appel
Courts of appeal

Examinent les appels de décisions civiles
Hear appeals in civil cases

Tribunaux de grande instance
Courts of first instance

Compétents en matière civile
Have general jurisdiction for civil cases and minor offences

Tribunaux d'instance
Small claims courts

Tribunaux de commerce
Courts hearing disputes over business contracts and commercial matters

Conseils de prud'hommes
Industrial arbitration courts dealing with disputes over employment contracts

Tribunaux des affaires de sécurité sociale
Courts hearing cases relating to social security matters

Tribunaux paritaires des baux ruraux
Courts hearing disputes over agricultural holdings

■ **Les tribunaux ordinaires : droit pénal**
Ordinary Courts: Criminal

Haute Cour de justice
High Court of Justice

Juge le Président de la République et les ministres du gouvernement pour crimes et haute trahison
Tries the President and government ministers for serious crimes and high treason

Cour de cassation
Final court of appeal

Peut annuler les décisions rendues par les juridictions inférieures
Can overrule decisions from the lower courts

Cours d'appel
Appeal courts

Examinent les appels de décisions pénales
Hear appeals in criminal cases

Cours d'assises
Assize courts

Jugent les crimes
Deal with serious crimes

Tribunaux correctionnels
Criminal courts

Jugent les délits
Deal with lesser offences

Tribunaux de police
Courts dealing with minor criminal matters

S'occupent des contraventions
Deal with petty offences

FRENCH LEGAL SYSTEM

■ **Les tribunaux administratifs**
Administrative Courts

Conseil d'État
Council of State

Juridiction suprême en matière administrative
Examine les appels concernant les élections et le gouvernement ; peut annuler les décisions rendues
par les juridictions inférieures ; conseille le gouvernement en matière législative
Supreme administrative court
Hears appeals on elections and government authority ; can overrule decisions from the lower courts on points of law ;
gives legal or legislative advice to the government

Cour des comptes
Audit court

Cours administratives d'appel
Administrative appeal courts

Cour de discipline budgétaire et financière
Budget and finance disciplinary court

Chambre régionale des comptes
Regional audit courts

Tribunaux administratifs
Administrative courts

S'occupent des plaintes portées
contre l'administration
Deal with complaints about
government agencies

Conseil constitutionnel
Constitutional Council

Compétent en matière de litiges concernant les élections législatives ou la constitutionnalité de nouvelles lois
Deals with disputes over parliamentary elections or the constitutionality of new laws

Tribunal des conflits

Décide de l'attribution des affaires à la juridiction civile ou administrative ; tranche les litiges
opposant des tribunaux ordinaires
Assigns cases to either the civil or the administrative court system ; resolves disputes between ordinary courts

Military Ranks

The classification and naming of military ranks varies considerably between different countries and languages. The following tables are designed to facilitate the translation of this terminologically complicated subject, and to allow comparisons to be made between the terms used in different English- and French-speaking countries. It should be stressed that precise word-for-word translation is not strictly possible, and that in all cases terms placed on the same line are the closest equivalents. Details of duties and roles will differ to a greater or lesser degree.

The dark blue line marks the division between commissioned and non-commissioned ranks. The alternating blue and white lines have been used simply to aid consultation.

Grades militaires

L'appellation des différents grades des armées varie considérablement en fonction des pays. Les tableaux suivants ont été conçus pour faciliter la tâche du traducteur s'aventurant sur le terrain miné des hiérarchies militaires. Ils lui permettront d'établir des correspondances entre les grades des armées des pays anglophones et francophones. Il faut noter qu'il est rare que les grades coïncident exactement d'un pays à l'autre, et à ce titre les termes figurant sur une même ligne constituent des équivalents plutôt que des traductions exactes.

La ligne bleu foncé sépare les grades d'officiers de ceux de sous-officiers. L'alternance de bleu et de blanc est destinée à faciliter la consultation des tableaux.

Air Force / Armée de l'air

RAF Armée de l'air britannique	USAF Armée de l'air américaine	RCAF - English Armée de l'air canadienne - anglais	RCAF - French Armée de l'air canadienne - français	Belgian Airforce Armée de l'air belge	French Airforce Armée de l'air française
Marshal of the Royal Air Force	General of the Air Force	Marshal of the RCAF	Maréchal de l'ARC		Chef d'état-major de l'Armée de l'Air
Air Chief Marshal	General	General	Général		Général d'armée aérienne
Air Marshal	Lieutenant General	Lieutenant General	Lieutenant-général	Lieutenant-général	Général de corps aérien
Air Vice Marshal	Major General	Major General	Major-général	Général-major	Général de division aérienne
Air Commodore	Brigadier General	Brigadier General	Brigadier-général	Général de brigade	Général de brigade aérienne
Group Captain	Colonel	Colonel	Colonel	Colonel	Colonel
Wing Commander	Lieutenant Colonel	Lieutenant Colonel	Lieutenant-colonel	Lieutenant-colonel	Lieutenant-colonel
Squadron Leader	Major	Major	Major	Major	Commandant
				Capitaine-commandant	
Flight Lieutenant	Captain	Captain	Capitaine	Capitaine	Capitaine
Flying Officer	First Lieutenant	Lieutenant	Lieutenant	Lieutenant	Lieutenant
Pilot Officer	Second Lieutenant	Second Lieutenant	Sous-lieutenant	Sous-lieutenant	Sous-lieutenant
Officer Cadet	Air Force Cadet	Officer Cadet	Élève-officier		Aspirant
Warrant Officer	Chief Master Sergeant of Air Force	Chief Warrant Officer	Adjudant-chef	Major	Major
	Chief Master Sergeant	Master Warrant Officer	Adjudant-maître	Adjudant-chef	Adjudant-chef
	Senior Master Sergeant	Warrant Officer	Adjudant	Adjudant	Adjudant
Flight Sergeant	Master Sergeant			Premier sergent-major	
	Technical Sergeant			Sergent-chef	Sergent-chef
	Staff Sergeant				
Sergeant	Sergeant	Sergeant	Sergent	Sergent	Sergent
Corporal	Senior Airman	Master Corporal	Caporal-chef	Caporal-chef	Caporal-chef
Senior Aircraftman	Airman First Class	Corporal	Caporal	Caporal	Caporal
Leading Aircraftman	Airman	Private	Soldat	1er Soldat	Aviateur de 1ère classe
Aircraftman	Airman Basic				Aviateur

MILITARY RANKS/GRADES MILITAIRES

Navy/Marine

Royal Navy (RN) Marine de guerre britannique	US Navy (USN) Marine de guerre américaine	Royal Canadian Navy (RCN) - English Marine de guerre canadienne - anglais	Royal Canadian Navy (RCN) - French Marine de guerre canadienne - français	Belgian Navy Marine de guerre blege	French Navy Marine nationale
Admiral of the Fleet	Fleet Admiral	Admiral of the Fleet	Amiral de la Flotte		Amiral de France
Admiral	Admiral	Admiral	Amiral		Amiral
Vice-Admiral	Vice-Admiral	Vice-Admiral	Vice-amiral	Vice-amiral	Vice-amiral d'escadre
Rear-Admiral	Rear-Admiral (upper half)	Rear-Admiral	Contre-amiral	Amiral de division	Vice-amiral
Commodore	Rear-Admiral (lower half)	Commodore	Commodore	Amiral de flottille	Contre-amiral
Captain	Captain	Captain	Capitaine de vaisseau	Capitaine de vaisseau	Capitaine de vaisseau
Commander	Commander	Commander	Capitaine de frégate	Capitaine de frégate	Capitaine de frégate
Lieutenant Commander	Lieutenant Commander	Lieutenant Commander	Capitaine de corvette	Capitaine de corvette	Capitaine de corvette
Lieutenant	Lieutenant	Lieutenant	Lieutenant de vaisseau	Lieutenant de vaisseau	Lieutenant de vaisseau
Sub-Lieutenant	Lieutenant Junior Grade	Sub-Lieutenant	Enseigne de vaisseau de 1ère classe	Enseigne de vaisseau de 1ère classe	Enseigne de vaisseau de 1ère classe
Sub-Lieutenant	Ensign	Acting Sub-Lieutenant	Enseigne de vaisseau de 2e classe	Enseigne de vaisseau de 2e classe	Enseigne de vaisseau de 2e classe
Midshipman	Midshipman	Naval Cadet	Aspirant		Aspirant
Warrant Officer	Warrant Officer	Warrant Officer	Adjudant	Maître principal chef	Major
Fleet Chief Petty Officer	Master Chief Petty Officer	Chief Petty Officer, 1st Class	Premier maître de 1ère classe	Maître principal	Maître principal
Chief Petty Officer	Chief Petty Officer	Chief Petty Officer, 2nd Class	Premier maître de 2e classe	Premier maître	Premier maître
	Petty Officer 1st Class	Petty Officer 1st Class	Maître de 1ère classe	Maître	Maître
Petty Officer	Petty Officer 2nd Class	Petty Officer 2nd Class	Maître de 2e classe	Second maître	Second maître
Leading Rate or Rating	Petty Officer 3rd Class	Master Seaman	Matelot-chef	Quartier-maître	Quartier-maître de 1ère classe
		Leading Seaman	Matelot de 2e classe		Quartier-maître de 2e classe
Able or Ordinary Rate or Rating	Seaman	Able Seaman	Matelot de 1ère classe	Matelot de 1ère classe	Matelot breveté
Junior Rate or Rating	Seaman Apprentice	Ordinary Seaman	Matelot 2e classe	Matelot	Matelot
			Matelot 3ème classe		

Army/Armée de la terre

British Army Armée de terre britannique	US Army Armée de terre américaine	Canadian Army - English Armée de terre canadienne - anglais	Canadian Army - French Armée de terre canadienne - français	French Army Armée de terre française	Belgian Army Armée de terre belge	Swiss Army Armée de terre suisse
Field-Marshal	General of the Army			Maréchal de France		
General	General	General	Général	Général d'armée		Général
Lieutenant-General	Lieutenant-General	Lieutenant-General	Lieutenant-général	Général de corps d'armée	Lieutenant-général	Commandant de corps
Major-General	Major-General	Major-General	Major-général	Général de division	Général-major	Divisionnaire
Brigadier	Brigadier-General	Brigadier-General	Brigadier-général	Général de brigade	Général de brigade	Brigadier
Colonel	Colonel	Colonel	Colonel	Colonel	Colonel	Colonel
Lieutenant-Colonel	Lieutenant-Colonel	Lieutenant-Colonel	Lieutenant-colonel	Lieutenant-colonel	Lieutenant-colonel	Lieutenant-colonel
Major	Major	Major	Major	Chef de bataillon, Commandant	Major	Major
					Capitaine-commandant	
Captain	Captain	Captain	Capitaine	Capitaine	Capitaine	Capitaine
Lieutenant	First Lieutenant	Lieutenant	Lieutenant	Lieutenant	Premier lieutenant	Premier lieutenant
Second Lieutenant	Second Lieutenant	Second Lieutenant	Sous-lieutenant	Sous-lieutenant	Lieutenant	Lieutenant
Officer Cadet	Officer Cadet	Officer Cadet	Élève-officier	Aspirant		
Warrant Officer 1st Class	Chief Warrant Officer 4-5	Chief Warrant Officer	Adjudant-chef	Major	Adjudant-major	Adjudant d'état-major
	Chief Warrant Officer 2-3	Master Warrant Officer	Adjudant maître	Adjudant-chef	Adjudant-chef	
Warrant Officer 2nd Class	Warrant Officer 1	Warrant officer	Adjudant	Adjudant	Adjudant	Adjudant
Sergeant Major	Sergeant Major	Sergeant Major	Sergent-major	Sergent-major	Premier sergent-major	Sergent-major
Staff Sergeant	Master Sergeant			Sergent-chef	Premier sergent	
	Sergeant 1st Class			Sergent (de carrière)		
	Staff Sergeant					
Sergeant	Sergeant	Sergeant	Sergent	Sergent	Sergent	Sergent
Corporal	Corporal	Master corporal	Caporal-chef	Caporal-chef	Caporal-chef	Caporal
Lance Corporal	Private 1st Class	Corporal	Caporal	Caporal, brigadier	Caporal	Appointé
				Soldat 1ère classe	Soldat 1ère classe	
Private	Private	Private	Soldat	Soldat	Soldat	Soldat

French Allusions

One of the innovations of this dictionary is that it includes explanations of allusions. An allusion has in this book been taken to mean a phrase that has immediate connotations for native speakers and forms part of their common cultural baggage. Such phrases can originate in high or low culture, from classical literature to television advertisements, but in all cases are used in modern speech or writing. A selection has been made of those judged to be the most common and interesting, and their origin and usage have been explained. The allusions included in the body of the dictionary have been grouped together below, to aid consultation.

ABSENT
Les absents ont toujours tort
This expression is used in two slightly different contexts. In the first, a speaker describes a delightful occasion that the listener has missed. The latter exclaims "If only I'd been there!", and the speaker rejoins **Les absents ont toujours tort**. This means literally "It is always a mistake to be absent" and more loosely "You really should have been there!". In the second usage, someone has failed to appear at a crucial gathering, where he had a role to play. By not attending, he has not only waived any right to criticize the proceedings, but laid himself open to blame if things go wrong. Here again, the literal meaning is "It is always a mistake to be absent", and more loosely in this context "The people who are not there always get blamed."

ADIEU
Adieu veau, vache, cochon, couvée
This is an allusion to *La Laitière et le pot au lait*, a fable by Jean de la Fontaine. The fable recounts the story of a dairymaid called Perrette, who is going to the nearby town to sell her milk. On the way she starts making all sorts of plans for the future, thinking that with the money from the milk she'll buy eggs which in time will turn into chickens that she'll then sell to buy a pig and then a cow and a calf... She gets so carried away that she skips in excitement and spills all her milk, putting an end to all her dreams of wealth and success, hence the words **Adieu veau, vache, cochon, couvée** ("Goodbye calf, cow, pig, brood"). The expression is used in situations where someone's rather unrealistic dreams have been dashed before anything has been accomplished.

AIMER
Je t'aime, moi non plus
The title of a Serge Gainsbourg song, made famous by Jane Birkin, and also of a film, this means literally "I love you, nor do I". It conveys the idea that people's feelings cannot be perfectly synchronized, and that love is a constant ballet of the emotions, with one party or the other being inclined to move on. In everyday conversation or journalistic use, this expression describes a situation where things are apparently not working out, or relationships (eg between two senior members of government) are starting to deteriorate. The English equivalent might be "The love affair is starting to cool down."

Qui m'aime me suive
This rousing battle-cry ("Let him who loves me follow me!") is attributed to Philippe VI of the House of Valois, in 1328. The expression has become part of everyday language: if one suddenly decides to rush off and do something, one might say this to the company at large, inviting them to come too ("Anyone like to join me?").

AMOUR
Amour, amour, quand tu nous tiens (on peut bien dire: Adieu Prudence!)
This is a quotation from La Fontaine's fable *Le lion amoureux* ("The lion in love"), which was addressed to Mme de Sévigné, with whom he was in love. In its entirety, the quo-

tation means "Love, when you have us in your power, well may we bid farewell to sense!" It is a reflection on the absolute sway of passionate love, which can cause near-insanity. The first two words of the quotation are often dropped, and La Fontaine's conclusion changed thus: **Argent, argent, quand tu nous tiens...** or **Pouvoir, pouvoir, quand tu nous tiens...**, the idea being that one can become utterly enslaved by wealth or power, and engaged in a frenzied pursuit of one's goal.

J'ai deux amours, mon pays et Paris
This is the title of a song made famous by Josephine Baker, the American-born music-hall artiste who was the darling of Paris in the 1920s and 1930s. The French public warmed to this declaration, which means "I have two loves, my own country and Paris", delivered in Josephine Baker's American-accented voice. In modern variants, people will substitute other terms, for example, **J'ai deux amours, la science et la voile** ("I have two loves, science and sailing").

ANNE
Anne, ma sœur Anne, ne vois-tu rien venir?
In Charles Perrault's story *Bluebeard*, Bluebeard's wife and her sister, Anne, are imprisoned in a castle, hoping their brother will come and rescue them. Each time Bluebeard's wife asks "Sister Anne, can't you see anything coming?", the answer is the same: "No, I can see only the high road shimmering and the green grass growing." In modern idiom, this expression is used jokingly while waiting for someone who is late, or for something which is late in starting.

ANNÉE
L'année de tous les dangers
The name of the Peter Weir film is also used allusively as an expression to describe any situation where everything is going wrong or when there are problems and potential risks ahead, for example **Pour l'équipe de France, c'est l'année de tous les dangers,** ie "Things are looking dangerous for the French team." Other words can be substituted for "année". In the example **Pour le pays, ce sont les élections de tous les dangers**, the meaning would be "These elections could be crucial for the country."

ANTAN
Mais où sont les neiges d'antan?
This famous refrain is from *La ballade des Dames du temps jadis* by François Villon (1431–63), an elegiac lament for passing time and fading beauty. It is translated into English as "Where are the snows of yesteryear?" In everyday conversation or newspaper articles, the expression is used to contrast a present-day state of affairs with a better one in times gone by. With Villon's refrain one can either express a truly nostalgic reaction or poke fun at others who are overly nostalgic, so the expression is used both sincerely and ironically. The word "neiges" can be replaced by another, eg **Où sont les grands sportifs d'antan?** ("Where are the great sportsmen of yesteryear?")

ARLÉSIEN
C'est l'Arlésienne
L'Arlésienne was a play by Alphonse Daudet, which Bizet turned into the better-known opera in 1872. The character known as l'Arlésienne ("the woman from Arles") never appears on stage at any point. The expression is used about someone or something that one believes may not exist at all, eg **Sa copine, c'est l'Arlésienne!** ("Does this much talked-about girlfriend really exist?") In addition, one can greet the re-appearance of a long-lost acquaintance by saying **C'est le retour de l'Arlésienne!**, ie "Well, well! It's the famous disappearing man/woman!"

ARROSEUR
C'est l'arroseur arrosé
This expression comes from a short silent film (1895) by the Lumière brothers. The title was *L'arroseur arrosé* (literally "the waterer gets soaked" but known in English as "Hoist by his own Petard") or alternatively *Le jardinier et le petit espiègle* ("the gardener and the little imp"). It is a comical vignette, in which a gardener, busy watering his plants, manages to turn the hose on himself and gets drenched to the skin within the space of a few minutes. The expression is used in contemporary French to describe a situation where the tables are turned on someone. For example, it could be used if a politician who had championed family values is revealed to be an adulterer, and is vilified by the press and his colleagues. The English expression "now the boot is on the other foot" conveys a similar idea; more rarely, one speaks of "the biter bit".

ATMOSPHÈRE
Atmosphère, atmosphère, est-ce que j'ai une gueule d'atmosphère?
In Marcel Carné's 1938 film, *Hôtel du Nord*, scripted by the Prévert brothers, the French actress Arletty plays the female lead (a prostitute). At one point, in a comical scene, Arletty's screen partner (her pimp) speaks of "feeling like a change of scene" ("vouloir changer d'atmosphère") from the dreary canal-side Parisian hotel where they are staying. She replies with this phrase "Do I look like an atmosphere?" because she doesn't know the word "atmosphère" and thinks it refers pejoratively to her. People will sometimes use this famous phrase **avoir une gueule d'atmosphère** for humorous effect and in an allusion to the film.

ATTENDRE
J'ai failli attendre
This is a quotation attributed to Louis XIV, and it means "I almost waited". According to the story, the king's coach arrived exactly on time, and this was his ironic comment. When one is kept waiting for something or someone, this is sometimes said; as a reproach to a friend who turns up late, it has the flavour of "So you finally decided to show up!"

AUTRE
Vincent, François, Paul et les autres
This 1974 Claude Sautet film starred Yves Montand, Michel Piccoli and Romy Schneider and was the story of several men in love with one woman. Listing names and ending

et les autres ("and the rest") caught on in popular speech; so people might say, for example, **Marx, Engels, Lénine et les autres**.

AVENIR
La femme est l'avenir de l'homme
Originally, this came from a Louis Aragon poem, and it means "Woman is the future of man". Aragon dedicated his 1963 collection of poems, *Le Fou d'Elsa*, to his wife, the writer Elsa Triolet. The poems were set to music and sung by Jean Ferrat. The cycle is a celebration of love, and speaks of its revitalizing effects. In modern French, any other term can be substituted for "la femme" and said to be the future of man: for example, **La science est l'avenir de l'homme** ("Science is the future of man").

BADINER
On ne badine pas avec l'amour
Alfred de Musset's play of this name was written in 1834, after the end of his affair with George Sand. De Musset suffered from his mistress's inconstancy, and the play's title is a warning that lovers have a responsibility to tread carefully, as people can get seriously hurt. In modern French, another word can be substituted for "l'amour", in alluding to anything that should be taken seriously.

BEAU
La belle et la bête
This expression means "Beauty and the Beast" in English, and is used in a similar way in the two languages. The 18th-century tale by Madame Leprince de Beaumont became a famous French film classic in the hands of Jean Cocteau (1946). The phrase is applied, somewhat unkindly, to an ill-assorted couple, one of whom appears more personable and charming at first sight.

Sois belle et tais-toi
This means "Look pretty and keep your mouth shut". Originally the title of a 1958 film by Marc Allégret, and a Serge Gainsbourg song, it was an archetypal male chauvinist expression. However, it is now used ironically to ridicule anyone who treats women as sex objects. One can substitute any other adjective for "belle", and use the phrase rudely to someone annoying.

BEAUF
The cartoonist Cabu invented a character he called "mon beauf" ("my brother-in-law"). This **beauf** is reactionary, narrow-minded, ultra-conventional and something of a redneck, and the sense has come to enter the French language in its own right. The word can be used as an adjective: for example, the idea that women should do all the cooking and child-care could be described as **beauf**.

BEAUJOLAIS
Le beaujolais nouveau est arrivé
This is an advertising slogan seen everywhere at the time of year when Beaujolais nouveau wine comes on sale; the campaign has even crossed the Channel. The slogan has been adapted, with other words substituted for **beaujolais nouveau**, and has become part of everyday French. Thus one might hear **L'impôt nouveau est arrivé** ("The new tax has come into force") or **Le Depardieu nouveau est arrivé** ("The latest Depardieu film is out").

BÉRÉZINA
C'est la Bérézina
In the disastrous Russian Campaign of 1812, Napoleon's army lost 30,000 men at the battle of the Berezina. The Russian winter inflicted terrible suffering on the troops. This expression was originally an allusion to the defeat itself and to the cold weather, rather as we still say in English, "It was like the retreat from Moscow". Today, however, the expression has become more jocular and describes any situation of total chaos and failure: "It's a complete disaster."

BÊTE
Bête et méchant
In 1960, a group of French cartoonists brought out a satirical magazine called *Hara-Kiri*, with the subtitle "un journal bête et méchant" ("a stupid and vicious publication"), which is itself an allusion to a Voltaire quotation ("en ville on devient bête et méchant"); in fact, it was caustic and original. The two adjectives are often run together and translated as "nasty" in English. Anything can be described as **bête et méchant** – a person, a situation or a story.

BIZARRE
Bizarre, bizarre, vous avez dit bizarre? Comme c'est bizarre...
This is a line of dialogue from Marcel Carné's 1937 film *Drôle de drame*. The actors Louis Jouvet and Michel Simon star in scenes that are now some of the most famous in French cinema. The allusion means "strange, strange, did you say strange? That's very strange", and has passed into everyday use, so the reaction to some strange occurrence might well be to murmur **bizarre, bizarre**...

BONJOUR
Chers amis, bonjour!
With this catchphrase, Lucien Jeunesse, radio game show host, introduced *Le Jeu des 1000 francs*, one of the longest-running French radio programmes and still going strong – albeit with a new host and the updated title *Le Jeu des 1000 euros*. A cheery greeting to all and sundry, it is still used today by anyone coming into a bar or café and seeing familiar friends.

Bonjour les dégâts
This was originally part of a slogan in a "don't drink and drive" campaign (the full slogan was **Un verre ça va! deux verres, bonjour les dégâts!** "One drink is fine, two means a mess!"). The shorter phrase is used today as a comment on any disastrous situation, whether used seriously or ironically.

BOTTE
Les bottes de sept lieues
The Charles Perrault fairy tale *Puss in Boots* tells the story of a cat with seven-league boots, which allow it to cover great distances in no time at all. In modern French, **chausser les bottes de sept lieues** ("to have one's seven-league boots on") means to have accomplished a great deal in relatively little time, or, more simply, to have got to a destination very quickly.

BRIOCHE
(S'ils n'ont pas de pain,) qu'ils mangent de la brioche!
This phrase ("Let them eat cake!" in English) is usually attributed to Queen Marie-Antoinette of France, who allegedly said it when told that a crowd of people outside the royal palace were complaining about the price of bread. However, the expression undoubtedly predates Marie-Antoinette and the French Revolution as it can be found in Rousseau's *Confessions*, where it is attributed to a princess. The expression literally means "if they don't have any bread, let them eat brioche" and it is used ironically to convey a lack of concern for and understanding of the plight of others, as anyone living in the real world would know that if you can't afford bread it is highly unlikely that you would be able to afford brioche. The phrase is essentially used to express one's (or comment on someone else's) indifference towards the hardship suffered by others.

CACHER
Un train peut en cacher un autre
At stations and level-crossings in France, this warning is a familiar sight: **Attention, un train peut en cacher un autre** ("Danger, one train may conceal another"). By analogy, the expression has expanded to give the idea that hidden danger may be lurking where we least expect it; for example **Une réforme peut en cacher une autre** suggests

that unwelcome legislation may be on the way. Used of the late Dame Barbara Cartland (**Une légende peut en cacher une autre**), the expression suggests the real person might be quite different from her public persona.

CALIFE
Vouloir être calife à la place du calife
A 1960s cartoon strip with a Persian flavour, *Iznogoud*, gave rise to this expression. In the cartoon, the grand vizir Iznogoud is obsessed with deposing the caliph and taking over his position. The expression is used today of someone who is displaying naked ambition and trying to oust his or her superior. For example, one might say of a pushy new recruit, **Regarde le nouveau, il veut être calife à la place du calife** ("Look at that new one, he's determined to push and shove his way to the top.")

CAMBRONNE
Le mot de Cambronne
At the Battle of Waterloo, the English called on General Cambronne to surrender; his comment was apparently **Merde!** ("Shit!"). Since "merde" is not used in polite society, **le mot de Cambronne** ("Cambronne's famous phrase") is used as a euphemism, as is "le mot de cinq lettres" – "the five-letter word".

CANDIDE
Jouer au/être le Candide
Candide, in Voltaire's story of the same name, is a naive young innocent, forced to experience all the horrors of human existence. This expression, which simply means "to play at being Candide" could be applied to anyone who knowingly plays the innocent in a given situation, usually with the aim of getting information or proving a point, or to anyone representing the point of view of the layman in a technical debate.

CARCASSE
Tu trembles, carcasse
This expression relates to an anecdote about Henri de la Tour d'Auvergne, vicomte de Turenne (1611–75), a doughty warrior. In old age, still fighting, the vicomte felt himself tremble with fear, and addressed his body as if it were a disobedient servant: "You tremble, feeble frame, but you would tremble even harder if you knew where I am taking you." This spirited remark is used today, out of context, whenever one shivers, or a person near one shivers.

CAUSER
Tu causes, tu causes, c'est tout ce que tu sais faire
The novel *Zazie dans le métro* (Raymond Queneau, 1959), filmed under the same title by Louis Malle in 1960, tells the story of a cheeky young girl who comes to Paris to visit her uncle. This quote "You talk and talk, but you don't actually do anything" is today used to someone as a reproach, and it can be loosely translated as "You just talk a lot of hot air."

CAVERNE
La Caverne d'Ali Baba
This expression means "Ali Baba's Cave". Although the story of Ali Baba and the Forty Thieves is equally familiar in English (Ali Baba seeing the thieves' treasure from his hiding-place in a jar), we are more apt to speak of a place where riches are displayed as an Aladdin's cave in English. The French will speak, for example, of a wonderful bookshop as **une vraie caverne d'Ali Baba** whereas we might speak of a "treasure-trove" in that context, reserving "Aladdin's Cave" for a display of something bright and glittering. In short, though the idea is similar in both languages, the usage varies slightly.

CHANGEMENT
Le changement dans la continuité
In 1969, Georges Pompidou used this slogan in his electoral campaign for the presidency. "Change, with continuity" was supposed to be a pledge that he would follow through on

various measures initiated by his predecessor. However, the expression is used ironically, the implication being that things will go on exactly as before.

CHATOUILLER
Ça vous chatouille ou ça vous gratouille?
This expression comes from a play by Jules Romains, *Knock, ou le triomphe de la médecine* (1923) about a very doubtful doctor, newly arrived in a village. The play was filmed with Louis Jouvet as Dr Knock. At one point, the doctor (who recalls Molière's doctors) asks a patient suffering with a cough to define his symptoms: **Ça vous chatouille ou ça vous gratouille?** ("Is it a tickly kind of cough or a scratchy kind of cough?") Today when people complain of vague symptoms, they can be teased with this question.

CHEZ
Chez de chez
This very generative colloquial expression imitates the wording used in French perfume advertisements, which give the name of the perfume followed by the name of the perfume house, for example "Coco, de chez Chanel". It indicates that whatever is being talked about possesses the quality discussed to an utmost degree, as in **Son costume est ringard de chez ringard** ("His suit is really, really tacky").

CIEL
Ciel! mon mari!
This is the classic cry of the unfaithful wife whose husband returns home unexpectedly, famous from a thousand farces and vaudeville plays featuring a love triangle: "Heavens! my husband!" In modern idiom people say this in situations where they have been surprised, and have to rush.

CINNA
Prends un siège, Cinna
Every French schoolchild has studied Corneille's play *Cinna* (1640) and is familiar with this phrase used by Auguste who wants to talk to Cinna. It means "Cinna, take a seat" and can be used jokingly today when inviting someone to sit down.

CIRCULER
Circulez, y'a rien à voir!
This was originally said by police when an accident or a disturbance in the crowd was making people slow down to stare: "Move along now, there's nothing to see." Comedians such as Francis Blanche and Coluche have used this phrase figuratively to mean "We won't dwell on that, will we?", particularly when there is an idea of cover-up, or information being swept under the carpet. In newspaper articles, the expression is used to suggest deliberate obfuscation on the part of the authorities, and means "They don't want us to know about this."

CŒUR
Le cœur a ses raisons (que la raison ne connaît point)
This celebrated saying from Blaise Pascal's *Pensées* (1658) is also well-known in English: "The heart has its reasons (of which reason knows nothing)." Pascal was pointing out that rational judgement was not always our invariably man's main motivating force. Today we say this when the logical motivation for behaviour, or for an attitude someone may hold, is not immediately clear to an outside observer.

Tu me fends le cœur
This expression was a coded reference to the suit hearts in cards. It comes from Marcel Pagnol's play *Marius* (1929), later a film with the actor Raimu in the leading role. In one scene, four people are playing cards and Marius is forbidden to speak to his partner. With this line, delivered in a strong Provençal accent, he tries to convey the crucial message "hearts!". The comic delivery of the line stuck in the public imagination, and so

Tu me fends le cœur ("You're breaking my heart") has a particular connotation.

Rodrigue, as-tu du cœur?
In Corneille's play *Le Cid* (1636) Don Diego ("Don Diègue" in French) is counting on his son Rodrigo ("Rodrigue" in French) to avenge an insult he has received. He asks him, **Rodrigue, as-tu du cœur?**, ie "Do you have the courage to do it?" Today these words can be used teasingly to someone who has to do something that requires a modicum of courage. In that context it means "Do you think you're up to it?" People may also use the phrase humorously as a pun during card games, when asking another player if he or she has any hearts.

COMPRENDRE
Je vous ai compris
In 1958 General de Gaulle visited Algiers, when Algeria was in the throes of the War of Independence. He opened his speech with these words: **Je vous ai compris. Je sais ce qui s'est passé ici. Je vois ce que vous avez voulu faire** ("I understand. I know what has happened here. I can see what you have been trying to do."). People sometimes use the phrase in connection with de Gaulle, parodying his stately delivery. When you want to convey the message that you have all the information you require and that no further explanation is necessary, you can say this, and it implies "Say no more."

COMPTE
Le compte est bon
This is a catchphrase from the very popular TV game show *Des chiffres et des lettres*, the French equivalent of the British show *Countdown*. In the "numbers" part of the show, when a contestant manages to get the right number, he or she has to say **Le compte est bon**, meaning here "It's the right number". One often hears this expression when buying something, as the seller counts out the small change; the meaning is simply "That's right, thank you."

COUR
C'est la cour du roi Pétaud
This is an expression from the sixteenth century. King Pétaud was a mythical figure whose court was said to be in utter chaos, full of noisy and ill-disciplined retainers. So today if one complains that some gathering is **la cour du roi Pétaud**, this means "It's like a madhouse."

COURIR
Rien ne sert de courir, il faut partir à point
In La Fontaine's fable, taken from Aesop, *The Tortoise and the Hare*, the two animals take part in a race. The over-confident hare keeps stopping for a rest, while the tortoise plods onward to win. This expression means "It's no use running, you must leave on time", and people say it when making a disparaging allusion to someone who appears too self-confident.

COURT
C'est un peu court, jeune homme
Cyrano de Bergerac, the hero of Edmond Rostand's play of the same name (1897), has an enormous nose and commensurate sense of honour. In one scene, Cyrano is taken to task by a Viscount who makes a weak attempt at an insult by stammering "Your nose is – er – er – very – er... big", to which Cyrano makes this rejoinder, "It's rather short, young man", referring to the man's statement, before launching into a long comic description of the nose, one of the best-known speeches in all of French drama. This expression is used today of a feeble and disappointing verbal performance, as a reproof to the speaker.

CULTIVER
Il faut cultiver notre jardin
This expression comes from the very end of Voltaire's *Candide, ou l'optimisme* (1759). The innocent young Candide has witnessed and

experienced every sort of horror in his quest for Princess Cunégonde. Finally forced to abandon the philosophy of Optimism, he and his companions, settled at last in one place, wonder how to carry on. Candide concludes "I know one thing, we must cultivate our garden." Much ink has been spilt over the interpretation of this celebrated expression; essentially it means "We must get on with the nearest practical task to hand, and do something useful." At the same time, however, it means "We must concentrate on things close to home, since we cannot make sense of the human condition." Today the expression is sometimes used in connection with retirement from public life, perhaps to a quieter existence.

DEGRÉ
Le degré zéro de...
This expression comes from the title of an essay by Roland Barthes, *Le degré zéro de l'écriture* (1953), and is used today to describe a total lack of whatever it might be. For example, one might speak of **Le degré zéro des droits des femmes dans certains pays** ("Women's rights being absolutely zero in some countries") or of **Le degré zéro de l'intelligence** ("Unadulterated silliness") when talking about a particularly inane TV game show.

DÉLUGE
Après moi, le déluge
This is a phrase expressing sublime indifference to the future. It is attributed to Madame de Pompadour, and means literally "After me, the Flood". Its true meaning is "what happens when I'm gone is none of my concern!"; in other words, the entire world could go to rack and ruin for all the speaker cares.

DEMAIN
À demain, si vous le voulez bien
This was the signing-off formula used by radio game show host Lucien Jeunesse, in his famous *Jeu des 1000 francs* (now known as *Le Jeu des 1000 euros*). It passed into everyday language to such an extent that if one friend says **À demain** ("See you tomorrow") the other may reply **Si vous le voulez bien** ("If that suits you").

DÉPEUPLER
Un seul être vous manque et tout est dépeuplé
This immortal line is from Alphonse de Lamartine's poem *l'Isolement*, from *Méditations poétiques* of 1823, a chef-d'oeuvre of French Romantic poetry. It means "One single being is missing, and the world is empty." So very famous is this line that it lays itself open to parody. It can be used in any context, eg **Si vous êtes philatéliste, un seul timbre vous manque, et tout est dépeuplé** ("If you're a stamp collector, you only need to be short of one stamp for it to seem like the end of the world").

DESSINER
Dessine-moi un mouton
This is possibly the most famous line of the most famous French children's book of all time, Antoine de Saint-Exupéry's *Le Petit Prince*. A pilot crashes in a desert, where he meets the naïve and charming Little Prince, who says to him **Dessine-moi un mouton** ("Draw me a sheep"). This innocent request is recalled whenever a French child asks "draw me this, draw me that", and the phrase is like an emblem of childhood.

DEUX
Les deux, mon capitaine
The origin of this expression is a joke from early 20th-century music-hall bawdy comedy in which a soldier learns by heart the answers to a set of questions that he is going to be asked by a captain. As the soldier character is very stupid, he gets mixed up in the sequence of answers (or the captain for once changes the order in which he asks his questions), as a result giving silly and outrageous answers to the officer's questions. The last

question is **Vous me prenez pour un con ou un imbécile?** ("What do you take me for, a twit or an idiot?"), to which the hilarious reply-cum-punchline is "**Les deux, mon capitaine!**" ("Both, sir"), which was supposed to be the answer to a completely different question. The phrase is used for humorous effect today whenever two statements equally apply to something, eg "**Livre d'histoire ou recueil de poésie? Les deux, mon capitaine!**" ("Both a history book and a poetry collection").

DIRE
Je dirais même plus!
Whenever someone says **Je dirais même plus** as a prelude to making virtually the same point as someone who has just spoken, they are making a reference to Dupond et Dupont, the bowler-hatted policemen in the Tintin cartoons (known in English as Thomson and Thompson), whose stupidity is legendary. It is simply a humorous way of saying that you agree with what has just been said. For instance, if someone says "Il fait froid aujourd'hui" (It's cold today), you could reply by saying "je dirai même plus: il ne fait pas chaud!" ("I'd even go as far as to say it's not warm"). In the English translations of Tintin, Thomson and Thompson use the phrase "to be precise", placed at the end of the sentence. For example, if one says "it's cold today", the other would reply "it's not warm, to be precise!"

DIVE
La dive bouteille
In Rabelais' *Cinquième Livre* of 1564, Panurge and his companions go to Chinon to consult an oracle named "l'oracle de la dive bouteille" ("the oracle of the divine bottle", ie of drink). During an initiation rite, the oracle makes its pronouncement: "trinch" ("drink!"). Today **la dive bouteille** simply means the pleasures of drinking.

DONC
Je pense donc je suis
This is the French translation of "Cogito, ergo sum", "I think, therefore I am", René Descartes' celebrated premise from the *Méditations métaphysiques* of 1640. In modern French, either half of the expression can be varied; for example **Je pense, donc je vote** ("I think, therefore I vote") or **Je mange, donc je suis** ("I eat, therefore I am"), or to quote Albert Camus, **Je me révolte, donc je suis** ("I rebel, therefore I am").

EAU
Que d'eau! Que d'eau!
This expression comes from a quotation attributed to the French President Mac-Mahon, when on a visit in 1875 to Toulouse to inspect the damage caused by floods in the area. With massive understatement, these words ("What a lot of water") were all he could manage to describe the scale of the damage. This phrase is used humorously and allusively today in many contexts, eg when it is pouring with rain, when the bath overflows, or when looking at the sea.

EMBRASSER
Embrassons-nous Folleville!
This is the title of a play by French playwright Eugène Labiche (1815–88). There is a passage in the play where a character called Folleville is about to challenge the father of the girl he wants to marry to a duel but changes his mind when the man benignly exclaims "Embrassons-nous Folleville!" ("Let me give you a hug, Folleville!"). The phrase is used allusively when speaking about the unexpected reconciliation of hitherto bitter enemies. For instance, when commenting on a meeting between two political enemies who have decided to work together, you could say **Cette rencontre a un air d'embrassons-nous Folleville**, suggesting that no one could have predicted a rapprochement between the two apparently irreconcilable parties.

ENFER
L'enfer, c'est les autres
This phrase, which has become famous in English too, as "Hell is other people", comes from Jean-Paul Sartre's *Huis Clos* (1944), a play in which three people are shut up together with no escape and find each other's presence unendurable. People use this expression today to complain about others, or about crowded conditions and lack of privacy.

ESPRIT
Les grands esprits se rencontrent
Voltaire used this expression, or to be exact **Les beaux esprits se rencontrent** ("Great minds think alike"), in a letter to Jean-Jacques Rousseau in 1760. The two did not always see eye-to-eye, but on this occasion at least, they did. The expression, which has become a proverb, is used in French exactly as in English.

EXISTER
Si Dieu n'existait pas, il faudrait l'inventer
One of Voltaire's most familiar "bons mots", this phrase (meaning "If God didn't exist, we would have to invent Him") comes from the *Épître sur les trois imposteurs* of 1768. In modern French, as indeed in English, the formula is simply used when speaking of something that we find indispensable or that we love (for example, beer or the Internet).

FACILE
C'est facile et ça peut rapporter gros
This slogan was invented by the French national lottery board in 1980 to encourage people to take part in the lottery. It means "It's easy and there are big prizes to be won." When you want to persuade someone to do something, or explain to them why you are going to do it yourself, you can say this in a joking way.

FAIRE
Fais ce que voudras
In François Rabelais' *Gargantua* (1534), this is the motto of the Abbey of Thélème: "Do what you please". The Abbey represents a Utopian society, based on Humanist values. The motto is often wrongly interpreted to mean "Do whatever you like", an invitation to excess. This motto is forever associated with the name of Rabelais.

FAUTE
C'est la faute à Voltaire
The Enlightenment philosophers Voltaire and Rousseau were viewed by the French clergy in the 19th century as the root of all evil. In Victor Hugo's novel *Les Misérables* (1862), a character named Gavroche sings a satirical song with the line **C'est la faute à Voltaire, c'est la faute à Rousseau** ("It's Voltaire's fault, it's Rousseau's fault"). In modern French, this expression is used sarcastically in a context where someone is being blamed for something, but is not there to defend himself. The English equivalent would be, "That's right, it's somebody else's fault."

FLACON
Qu'importe le flacon pourvu qu'on ait l'ivresse
This is a fragment of a couplet, from Alfred de Musset's *Il ne faut jurer de rien* of 1836, and its meaning is "What does the mistress matter? It's being in love that counts! What does the bottle matter? It's getting drunk that counts." In other words, it is the contents that matter, not the packaging. **Qu'importe le flacon** has become a very common expression in modern French when one wants to stress what is really most essential in a given situation.

FLEUR
Les jeunes filles en fleurs
This is a shortened version of the title of the second volume of Marcel Proust's *À la recherche du temps perdu*, *À l'ombre des jeunes filles en fleurs*. This volume deals with the narrator's adolescence, the girls in question

being Albertine and Gilberte, who will later play important roles in his life. When the phrase is used allusively today, it refers to the attractiveness of young girls in the first bloom of youth, at the stage when they suddenly blossom into young women with an awareness of their budding sensuality.

FORCE
La force tranquille
Advertising man Jacques Séguéla coined this slogan for François Mitterrand's 1981 successful presidential election campaign. It appeared on posters, with the candidate in the foreground and a background showing a typical French village set in a green and rustic landscape. This supposedly conveyed an image of solidity and serenity: **La force tranquille** ("Strength in tranquillity"). The expression stuck and people use it jokingly of themselves and others. It suggests "the strong, silent type" but the allusion to the Mitterrand poster remains strong.

FOU
Ils sont fous ces Romains
Obélix, the famous cartoon character from *Astérix*, makes this comment every time the Romans do something he does not understand. It means "These Romans are crazy!" When French people do not understand an unfamiliar aspect of a foreign culture (or when they disapprove of it), they will use this expression or a variant of it. For example, of the fact that the English put mint sauce on their lamb – **Ils sont fous ces Anglais!**

FRANÇAIS
Français, encore un effort
In the Marquis de Sade's *La Philosophie dans le boudoir* (1795), this allusion in its entirety reads **Français, encore un effort si vous voulez être républicains** ("A final effort, people of France, if you wish to become republicans"). Today, **Français, encore un effort** is frequently used as an encouragement to the nation, in articles about sport or the economic situation, for example.

FRÈRE
Si ce n'est toi, c'est donc ton frère
In La Fontaine's fable *Le Loup et l'Agneau* ("The Wolf and the Lamb"), a wolf sets out to kill a lamb. The wolf puts forward a series of false accusations, notably that the lamb has been speaking ill of him. When the lamb protests that he was not even born at the time, the wolf says: **Si ce n'est toi, c'est donc ton frère** ("Well, if it wasn't you, it was your brother"), drags him into the woods and kills him. The phrase is used today when two similar people or things are mistaken for each other, or when summary justice is meted out to an innocent person.

GALÈRE
Qu'allait-il faire dans cette galère?
This is a quotation from Molière's *Les Fourberies de Scapin*, act II, scene 7. A crafty, cheeky valet called Scapin is trying to get some money out of a character named Géronte by telling him that his son is a galley slave on a Turkish galley, and can only be freed on payment of a ransom. The miserly father cannot bear to think of paying up, and repeats several times **Que diable allait-il faire dans cette galère?** ("What the devil was he doing in the galleys?"), expressing exasperation rather than concern. Today the expression is used allusively when questioning how someone has got involved in something, eg **Mais qu'allais-tu faire dans cette galère?** ("Why on earth did you get mixed up in this?"). The word "galère" has itself taken on the sense of "mess", in the sense of a bad situation.

GRAVELOTTE
Tomber comme à Gravelotte
If people say **Ça tombe comme à Gravelotte**, they mean "It's raining cats and dogs", but the allusion is not altogether light-hearted. At the battle of Gravelotte (in the Moselle region), during the Franco-Prussian War in

1870, bullets and shells rained down in large numbers, causing heavy casualties.

GRENOUILLE
La grenouille qui veut se faire aussi grosse que le bœuf
This is the title of a La Fontaine fable *The frog who wants to become as big as the ox*. In this fable, a frog admires an ox for its size, swells up in an attempt to emulate it, and bursts. The expression is used of someone who appears overly ambitious, claims to be something they are not, or gives themselves airs.

HARPAGON
C'est un Harpagon
Harpagon is the name of the miser in Molière's play *l'Avare*, whose servants ultimately make a fool of him. Today, if someone is very tight-fisted or obsessed with accumulating wealth, one can say this of them.

IMPOSSIBLE
Impossible n'est pas français
In 1813, one of Napoleon's generals wrote to him to say that he was unable to carry out an order. Napoleon replied: "You write and tell me it is impossible; but impossible is not a French word". In other words, "There's no such word as can't": this English expression perfectly conveys Bonaparte's meaning.

INTERDIRE
Il est interdit d'interdire
This is a student slogan from the riots of May 1968. It means literally "It is forbidden to forbid", or "No saying no". The students saw French society as hedged about with all sorts of restrictions and stifled by convention. The expression is used today in a humorous way, when someone will not grant a request, or forbids a course of action; it is a jocular refusal to take "no" for an answer.

INVENTAIRE
Un inventaire à la Prévert
Jacques Prévert's poem "Inventaire" (from *Paroles*, 1946) consists of a long list of objects, apparently associated at random. This expression is used when describing a lot of miscellaneous items all together in one place, ie a mixed bag.

ITINÉRAIRE
Itinéraire d'un enfant gâté
This is the title of Claude Lelouch's hit film of 1988, starring Jean-Paul Belmondo and Richard Anconina. The expression is often used in newspaper articles. The translation is "The making of a spoilt child". In modern French, other words are substituted for **enfant gâté** in alluding to, for example, the career of a successful actor or politician. A French magazine article entitled **L'itinéraire d'un acteur comblé** might be translated "The making of a totally happy actor", and would chart his progress along the road to success.

LAPALISSADE
This word comes from La Palice, the name of a 16th-century Marshal of France. When he died, his soldiers composed a song in his honour containing the truism: **Un quart d'heure avant sa mort, il était encore en vie** ("A quarter of an hour before his death he was still alive"). It has since been used whenever somebody is only stating the obvious.

LEÇON
Cette leçon vaut bien un fromage
This is a line from La Fontaine's famous fable *Le Corbeau et le renard* ("The Fox and the Crow"). A fox wants a piece of cheese that a crow has in his beak. The fox flatters the crow by asking to hear him sing: the crow opens his beak, the cheese drops and the fox grabs it, pronouncing the moral of the story: **Mon bon Monsieur, apprenez que tout flatteur vit aux dépens de celui qui l'écoute; cette leçon vaut bien un fromage sans doute.** ("Let me tell you, dear Sir, that all flatterers live off the people they flatter; undoubtedly,

this lesson is well worth a piece of cheese.") People might quote this line from the fable when someone learns a hard lesson.

LIGNE
La ligne bleue des Vosges
In his will, the 19th-century statesman Jules Ferry expressed his wish to be buried in his native village of Saint-Dié in the Vosges: "I wish to be laid to rest… facing the blue line of the Vosges, whence rises the sad lament of the defeated to touch my faithful heart." Jules Ferry's allusion was to France's concession of Alsace-Lorraine at the end of the Franco-Prussian war, when the frontier was moved to run across the Vosges. Today, if one says of someone **Il a les yeux fixés sur la ligne bleue des Vosges**, it means that he is on the watch for a potential enemy so as not to be caught unawares. Sometimes, too, the expression is used quite out of context, to describe someone who is gazing absent-mindedly into space. In that case, it simply means "the far blue yonder".

LIMITE
Au-delà de cette limite votre billet n'est plus valable
The title of Romain Gary's 1975 novel, this is in fact a sign in the Paris metro on the exit doors. It means: "Your ticket is no longer valid beyond this point". The novel is about a man coming to terms with aging after an easy and pleasant life. People allude to the title when they feel they are no longer wanted, and generally seen as "past it". In English one might say wryly: "I'm past my sell-by date" or "I've had it"; in French one might murmur **Au-delà de cette limite…**

MADAME
Tout va très bien, Madame la Marquise
This expression is used ironically. It means "Everything is fine, Madam" and comes from a song by a French jazz band of the 30s and 40s, Ray Ventura et ses Collégiens. The Marquise in question is asking the servants, over the telephone, how everything is going on the estate. They reply with a list of disasters, but after describing each one add "But apart from that, Madam, everything is fine." When people say this today, it means the exact opposite: everything is going disastrously wrong.

MADELEINE
La madeleine de Proust
A madeleine is a small, individual Madeira cake, sometimes shell-shaped. Marcel Proust's novel *À la recherche du temps perdu* begins with recollections of childhood. When Marcel, the narrator, tastes a madeleine for the first time in many years, he is transported back to Combray, where he lived as a child. Anything that triggers a vivid memory of the past for someone can be spoken of as **la madeleine de Proust**.

MALADE
Un malade imaginaire
This phrase ("an imaginary invalid") comes from Molière's comedy *Le Malade imaginaire* about a grumpy hypochondriac with thousands of imaginary ailments. His servant Toinette decides to teach him a lesson by disguising herself as a doctor and playing tricks on him. Molière pinpointed the fixations of the hypochondriac so accurately that the play's title has become a familiar everyday phrase.

MAMELLE
Le labourage et le pâturage sont les deux mamelles de la France
This famous observation was made by the Duc de Sully (1559–1641), Henri IV's finance minister. It means "Ploughing and pasture; these are the two breasts that nurture France". A maxim well known by every French schoolchild, it not only sums up Sully's own view of the importance of agriculture, but has survived to this day because the French economy has always had a vital agricultural base, more so than in Britain

for example. This saying is often used, with variations, when one is discussing the characteristics of something, or itemizing attributes, eg **La pêche et l'élevage sont les deux mamelles de notre économie** – "Fishing and farming are the lifeblood of our economy."

MEILLEUR
Le meilleur des mondes possibles
In Voltaire's *Candide, ou l'optimisme*, Candide has a tutor, Pangloss, who constantly quotes the German philosopher Leibnitz and his fatalistic views. Distorting the doctrine of Optimism, Pangloss greets all the miseries of human life – atrocities, injustice, disasters – with the comment **Tout est pour le mieux dans le meilleur des mondes possibles** ("All is for the best in the best of all possible worlds"). To accept this idea – that all was part of a divinely ordained master plan – seemed to Voltaire to be wilful stupidity. The modern usage is almost always ironic. If one questions the value of something that others seem to accept uncritically, one can allude to **Le meilleur des mondes possibles**.

MIGNON
Mignonne, allons voir si la rose
This is the first line of a sonnet by Ronsard, from *Les Amours* (1552), dedicated to Cassandre. In the poem, the poet turns to the theme beloved of antiquity, *carpe diem* (ie "seize the day, enjoy the present"), and celebrates his lady as the inspiration for Platonic love. In this line, the poet invites his "darling" to come with him into the garden to look at a rose, to see how it has changed since the previous day. Today people use the expression jokingly, substituting words for **la rose**, when they propose doing something with a friend.

MOELLE
La substantifique moelle
In the prologue to *Gargantua* (1535), Rabelais uses this famous metaphor. He is speaking of how his reader can best grasp the text and understand it fully. **Rompre l'os et sucer la substantifique moelle** means "Crack open the bone and suck out the substantific marrow". The adjective was coined by Rabelais to mean the true inner philosophical message as opposed to the superficial appearance. Today, the phrase **la substantifique moelle** means "the true substance", as opposed to mere superficiality. This is one of the expressions forever linked with Rabelais' name. It is often used to encourage people to "dig deeper" and look beyond the outward appearance of things.

MONDE
Tout le monde il est beau, tout le monde il est gentil
This was the title of a film by Jean Yanne (1972) which made fun of contemporary society, progressive and "liberated" as it then was. The translation is "Everyone's gorgeous, everyone's great", and the idea is that one would have to be extremely optimistic and naïve to really think so. The expression is used in two ways: firstly, as above, as a warning about human nature; secondly, to reprimand someone who is being too judgemental and harsh about his fellow man, in which case one might say **Te fâche pas! Tout le monde il est beau…**, ie "Calm down! Everyone's gorgeous, everyone's great."

MONTAGNE
La montagne qui accouche d'une souris
This phrase was popularized by La Fontaine's fable *La montagne qui accouche* and other seventeenth-century French writers. Meaning literally "The mountain that brings forth a mouse", this expression is used allusively in sarcastic remarks about an undertaking that has been hyped up in advance but which does not live up to the grand claims made for it. It is similar in meaning to the English expression "to be a damp squib".

MOUCHE
Mouche du coche
This expression comes from La Fontaine's fable *The Stagecoach and the Fly*. In the fable, a stagecoach is being pulled up a steep hill by a team of labouring horses, while a fly buzzes around them. When at last the horses have pulled the coach to the top, the fly claims his share of the credit, saying he egged them on. When some people do all the work while others fuss around self-importantly, one speaks of **La mouche du coche** ("the stagecoach fly"), eg **Il est** or **il fait la mouche du coche** ("He's always buzzing around but he doesn't pull his weight").

MOUTON
Les moutons de Panurge
In Rabelais' *Quart Livre* (1552), Panurge wants to take revenge on a merchant called Dindenault. He has the idea of buying a sheep from him, then throwing it in the sea to get the other sheep to follow. The plan works perfectly, and the flock is lost. To call people **des moutons de Panurge** is to allude to them disparagingly as having a herd mentality, like a flock of sheep.

Revenons à nos moutons
In the fifteenth-century *La Farce de maître Pathelin*, a cloth merchant takes his shepherd to court, accusing him of stealing his sheep. In court, the merchant suddenly realizes that the shepherd's lawyer, Maître Pathelin, is the very man who has stolen something from him on an earlier occasion. Forgetting the matter in hand, the merchant starts to complain of the lawyer's dishonesty; but the judge intercedes with **Revenons à ces moutons** ("Let's get back to these sheep"). So when people get sidetracked from the central issue, one can say **Revenons à nos moutons** ("Let's get back to the point").

MOZART
C'est Mozart qu'on assassine!
Saint-Exupéry was the originator of this expression, which became the title of a novel by Gilbert Cesbron in 1966. The novel concerns the effects of divorce on the children involved. The meaning of the title is "We're killing off Mozart", the idea being that the potential of future generations is being jeopardized. The expression is used in the context of discussions about education, as a recommendation that we must uphold children's interests at all costs.

MULE
La mule du pape
This expression is a play on the word "mule" in the sense of "slipper". It is used in reference to a tale published by Alphonse Daudet in *Les Lettres de mon moulin* (*Letters from My Mill*), which features an episode in which an apocryphal Pope's mule is cared for by a man who treats the animal very kindly when the Pope is around but starts tormenting the poor beast as soon as the pontiff's back is turned. After an absence of seven years the man is reunited with the Pope and his mule, whereupon the animal, who recognizes its tormentor, gives him a painful kicking. If someone is compared to **la mule du Pape** ("the Pope's mule") it means that they are unforgiving and determined to get their own back, no matter how long after they have been slighted.

NOUVEAU
C'est nouveau, ça vient de sortir
This was a catchphrase of the comedian Coluche, whose sketches included comments on the news. It means "It's new, it's just come out". People say this when they suddenly hear about something new. When new regulations come into force without notice, the person announcing the change might say this, meaning "It's just been announced", while a person learning about the change might also say it, meaning "That's a new one on me".

ŒIL
T'as de beaux yeux, tu sais
This expression comes from the 1938 Marcel Carné film *Quai des brumes*, with a screenplay by Jacques Prévert, in which a deserter hiding in a French port meets and falls in love with a girl. The stars were Jean Gabin and Michèle Morgan and, in a legendary close-up, he tells her "You know, you've got beautiful eyes". The expression is used today lightheartedly, but still as a real compliment, by rather more ordinary lovers than Jean Gabin.

OMBRE
Tirer plus vite que son ombre
This expression comes from the Belgian comic strip character Lucky Luke. Lucky Luke is a cowboy with amazing shooting skills, so much so that he is said to be able to shoot faster than his own shadow ("Il tire plus vite que son ombre"). The phrase can be used when referring to people or things that possess amazing speed, for example **Alonso, l'homme qui conduit plus vite que son ombre** ("Alonso, the man who drives faster than the speed of light"), or when commenting on the fact that people are wasting no time in doing something, such as **le nouveau gouvernement privatise plus vite que son ombre** ("The new government is privatizing things like there's no tomorrow").

PARADIS
Le vert paradis des amours enfantines
This comes from a poem, *Moesta et errabunda*, from Baudelaire's *Les Fleurs du mal*, in which he evokes the lost world of happy childhood, which the expression now generally suggests. It means literally "the green paradise of our childhood loves".

Les paradis artificiels
In a prose poem of 1860 with this title, Baudelaire speaks of how taking drugs can make the user feel he is in paradise. The expression is still used today of a drug-induced state, but the more negative oblivion rather than euphoria is emphasized, eg **De nombreux jeunes en difficulté ont recours aux paradis artificiels** ("Many troubled young people turn to the oblivion of drugs").

PASCALIEN
Un pari pascalien
Blaise Pascal was both a mathematical genius and a Christian philosopher. One of the originators of probability theory, he suggested in his *Pensées* that if a man bets on the existence of God, he has everything to gain, and nothing to lose. In modern French, if one says **c'est un pari pascalien** it means that one has nothing to lose.

PATIENCE
Patience et longueur de temps font plus que force ni que rage
This is the moral of a La Fontaine fable, **Le Lion et le rat**. A lion spares the life of a passing rat, and when the lion is later caught in the mesh of a hunting net, the rat patiently gnaws through it to release him. The lion's strength is much less effective than the rat's patience in this situation. The expression means "patience and the passage of time do more than strength and rage". Where a French parent says to a child **Patience et longueur de temps**, it is the equivalent of using the English expression "All in good time!" to curb the child's impatience.

PATTE
Montrer patte blanche
In La Fontaine's fable **Le Loup, la chèvre et le chevreau** ("The Wolf, the Nanny Goat and the Kid"), a wolf overhears a password which should admit him to the nanny goat's house during her absence. When he comes to the door, and imitates the voice of a goat, the kid he is hoping to devour requires further proof of identity, telling him to **montrer patte blanche** ("show a white foot"). The wolf is foiled, his prey unscathed. **Montrer patte blanche** is used today to mean "to show that one has impeccable credentials"

or "to prove that one is bona fide", often in some sort of screening process.

PAVÉ
Sous les pavés, la plage
This slogan became famous during the student riots in Paris in May 1968. It means "Beneath the cobbles, the beach". The cobbles were the cobbles from the streets that were pulled up and thrown at the police, and "the beach" was the layer of sand in which they were set. Figuratively speaking, the cobbles represented the dreary society the students wanted to overthrow, centred round work and stuffy conformity, while sand, "the beach", represented a life of liberty and peaceful co-existence to which they aspired. The slogan is used today to describe the possibility of a better world, or simply to allude to the idealism of this time.

PEAU
Vendre la peau de l'ours (avant de l'avoir tué)
In La Fontaine's fable **The Bear and the Two Friends**, two impoverished friends try to negotiate the price of a bearskin without having even caught and killed the bear. The English equivalent of the moral here is "Don't count your chickens before they're hatched". La Fontaine's exact wording was, in fact, **Il ne faut jamais vendre la peau de l'ours qu'on ne l'ait mis à terre** ("You should never sell the bearskin before bringing down the bear").

PELLE
Les feuilles mortes se ramassent à la pelle
This line continues **les souvenirs et les regrets aussi**, and it means "Dead leaves are everywhere, memories and regrets too". The lines come from a song with words by Jacques Prévert, sung by Yves Montand, Juliette Gréco and others. The expression evokes autumnal melancholy and nostalgia. Since **se ramasser à la pelle** means literally "to be picked up by the shovelful" the expression is often changed and used in jokes. If a schoolchild says **Les mauvaises notes se ramassent à la pelle**, this means "Bad marks are coming thick and fast"; if a driver says **Les contraventions se ramassent à la pelle**, it means "I'm getting one ticket after another".

PERSAN
Comment peut-on être persan?
This expression means literally "How can one be Persian?" Montesquieu's *Lettres persanes* of 1721 poked fun at the French society of his day by presenting it through the eyes of a Persian visitor writing home with his impressions. At the time, nothing could have seemed more exotic than a Persian complete with turban and baggy trousers. At one point, the hero is quizzed by a Parisian: "Aha! So you are Persian, Sir! Amazing! And how exactly is one Persian?" This emphasizes the ignorance of the supposedly more civilized party. Today the expression is often varied, for example substituting **anglais** or **communiste**, but always with the intent of showing the limitations and bigotry of the speaker.

PILE-POIL
This expression comes from a satirical television programme *Les Guignols de l'Info* on Canal+, a French TV channel. This show is a take-off of a serious discussion programme, where media celebrities and politicians deal with serious issues. In the spoof, the people are replaced by puppets, **les guignols de l'Info** ("news puppets"), and the Jacques Chirac puppet is constantly saying **pile-poil**, which is supposed to mean "precisely" or "exactly". The word has now come to enter the French language with this meaning.

PLOMBIER
Qui c'est? c'est le plombier!
This phrase comes from a comic sketch written and performed by Fernand Raynaud involving a plumber and a parrot. The plumber

knocks on the door when no one is home, and the parrot cries out continuously, "Who's there, who's there?" The plumber, thinking the person inside is deaf, shouts louder and louder, "It's the plumber!" This sketch has given rise to parody, so if someone doesn't catch what one has said, one can imitate Fernand Raynaud's voice and screech, "It's the plumber". Similarly if someone doesn't catch the identity of a third party, and keeps asking who they are, one can reply, **C'est le plombier! c'est le plombier!**

POIGNÉE
Pour une poignée de dollars
The French title of Sergio Leone's famous spaghetti western is often adapted by journalists. It is sometimes used to describe touch-and-go situations; for instance, if a race is won or lost by a few hundredths of a second, newspaper headlines may describe the victory or defeat as **pour une poignée de centièmes**. It can also be used to describe the reasons behind people's actions. For example, if someone is disqualified from an election because of electoral fraud some journalists are bound to headline their article with **pour une poignée de bulletins** ("for a fistful of votes").

POT
C'est le pot de terre contre le pot de fer
In the La Fontaine fable *Le pot de terre et le pot de fer*, an earthenware pot suggests to a cast-iron one that they go travelling together. On the bumpy road, the two are thrown together, and the earthenware pot smashed to pieces; the weaker vessel, so to speak, is destroyed. The moral of the story is that one should associate with one's equals and not confront someone more powerful. The expression when used today refers to an unequal contest.

POTE
Touche pas à mon pote
In the early 1980s, the "Front national", an extreme right-wing political party, had a high profile in France. To combat its ideology, Harlem Désir founded a group called "SOS-Racisme", and this is its slogan ("Lay off my pal"). The expression caught on, and is used to express group solidarity when defending something from a threat, with the relevant word being substituted for "mon pote", for example **Touche pas à ma retraite!** ("Leave my pension alone!").

POULE
La poule aux œufs d'or
This is the title of a fable by La Fontaine, about a hen that lays a golden egg each day. The greedy owner kills her, hoping to find even more gold, but finds an ordinary chicken carcass instead. He has thus put paid to the source of all his wealth. In English we speak of the goose, rather than the hen, that lays the golden eggs; otherwise the expression works the same in both languages.

PROSE
Faire de la prose sans le savoir
In Molière's comedy *Le Bourgeois gentilhomme*, the social climber, monsieur Jourdain, tries to ape the aristocracy. He engages various teachers who are out to fleece him, and learns in one lesson that language can be divided into poetry or prose. The thought strikes him that he has been "talking prose without realizing it". In modern French, other words can be substituted for **prose** when people give signs of some natural aptitude not previously recognized, eg **Tu fais de la politique/de la philosophie sans le savoir, comme monsieur Jourdain faisait de la prose.** ("You were a politician/philosopher all along, you just didn't realize it.") There are echoes here of the English rhyme, "He's a poet and doesn't know it".

RAGE
Ô rage! Ô désespoir!
In Corneille's play *Le Cid* of 1636, Rodrigo ("Rodrigue" in French and better known as Le Cid) is a young nobleman intent on avenging an insult to his father (Don Diego, "Don Diègue" in French) by the father of the woman he loves. These words are uttered by Don Diego in a monologue where he bewails his own inability to right the wrong inflicted on him as he is an old man. Today, this is a mock-melodramatic cry: one might say, for example, **Ô rage! Ô désespoir! Jamais je n'aurai fini mon travail dans les délais**, the English equivalent being "Curses! I'll never get this work done on time."

RAISON
La raison du plus fort est toujours la meilleure
In La Fontaine's fable *The Wolf and the Lamb*, a wolf first tries to find some justification for killing and eating a lamb, and then decides to do it regardless, his superior strength being reason enough. The literal meaning of La Fontaine's line is "The will of the strongest always prevails", but the usual English translation is "Might is right". The expression is often used today as a wry comment on the ability of a powerful person or country to do whatever they want, without any need to justify their violent actions.

RALLIER
Ralliez-vous à mon panache blanc!
This was the rallying cry of Henry IV of France at the Battle of Ivry, near Évreux, on 14 March 1590, during the war of the Holy Catholic League. The meaning is "Rally round my white plume" (ie on the king's helmet). The phrase is used today allusively to rally one's friends and supporters around one (in somewhat grandiloquent language), meaning simply "Follow me!"

RAT
Le rat des villes et le rat des champs
This is the title of a La Fontaine fable (*The Town Mouse and the Country Mouse*). In this fable, a town mouse invites a country mouse to a lavish dinner but they are interrupted by some noise and have to run away. When they return, the country mouse suggests that instead the town mouse come to dine in the countryside the next day, when they could enjoy more humble fare but in peace. The expression is used today to emphasize the difference between people who live in the city and those who live in the countryside, and more generally between rich but stressful city life and frugal but peaceful country life.

RENCONTRE
Rencontre du troisième type
Steven Spielberg's 1977 film *Close Encounters of the Third Kind* gave rise to this expression. The phrase is used in French today, with allusive reference to the film, to refer to unexpected get-togethers between different sorts of people, or odd juxtapositions of disparate objects.

RÉPÉTER
Vous pouvez répéter la question?
This expression has its origin in a sketch by the French comedians Les Inconnus in which they parody general knowledge TV quiz shows where contestants have to correctly answer questions which are definitions. The sketch features a very stupid contestant who says "Can you repeat the question?" to every question, and then always gives the same answer: Stéphanie de Monaco (the princess beloved of sections of the French popular press). When one does not hear or understand a question, one can use this phrase in a mock-imbecile fashion, in an allusion to the Les Inconnus sketch.

RÉSISTANCE
Papy fait de la résistance
This is the title of a very popular French comedy film released in 1983 by director Jean-Marie Poiré. It is set during the Nazi occupation of France and tells the story of an apparently completely ordinary family who turn out to be secret Resistance fighters. The title, which means "Grandad is a Resistance fighter", can be adapted to suit most contexts where people are fighting back or resisting change. For instance, if the national football squad triumphs after losing several games, you may read **Les Bleus font de la résistance** ("The French team fight back") in the press. Or if workers are fighting the closure of their company, it is more than likely that some papers will use the headline **Les employés font de la résistance** ("The workers are fighting back").

ROSEAU
Le roseau pensant
One of the more unusual images of Blaise Pascal's *Pensées* is this one: **L'homme est un roseau pensant** ("Man is a thinking reed"). This seems a paradoxical observation, but Pascal's meaning is that although man is a weak creature, he is also an extraordinary one as he has the faculty of reason and has a sense of his own mortality. This very original phrase is still used with the same meaning, with a clear reference to Pascal.

ROULER
Rouler pour quelqu'un
French lorry-drivers decided to upgrade their image by displaying the slogan **Je roule pour vous** ("I'm driving for you") on their vehicles. The aim was to dispel the hostility of other road-users, by suggesting that the transport of goods was ultimately in their interest. **Rouler pour quelqu'un** came to mean "to serve someone's interests, to be backing someone". One could say of a French politician who seems to champion the "have-nots", **Il roule en fait pour les nantis**, ("He is actually serving the interests of the haves," or "He is on the side of the haves").

SAVOIR
Si j'aurais su, j'aurais pas venu
This expression comes from a novel by Louis Pergaud, *La Guerre des boutons* ("The War of the Buttons") (1912), adapted for the screen in 1961 by Yves Robert. It tells the story of two gangs of village urchins who go about snatching each other's buttons off and keeping them as trophies. One of the boys, known as Petit Gibus, keeps saying **Si j'aurais su, j'aurais pas venu.** By this he means "I wouldn't have come if I'd known" but the grammar is wildly inaccurate; it should read **Si j'avais su, je ne serais pas venu.** The phrase is used humorously and allusively today to express one's disappointment.

SCHMILBLICK
Faire avancer le schmilblick
In the early 1970s there was a popular radio quiz show presented by Guy Lux, in which contestants had to try and identify the **schmilblick**, a mystery object, by asking questions about it. **Faire avancer le schmilblick** means literally "to get the schmilblick moving", ie to ask a question which takes the contestant closer to identifying the object. The phrase is used today to mean "to make progress". A sketch by the famous comedian Coluche, making fun of the radio show, helped to fix the expression in people's minds.

SCIENCE
Science sans conscience n'est que ruine de l'âme
This famous maxim comes from Rabelais' *Pantagruel*, chapter 8, in which Pantagruel receives a letter from Gargantua, his father, on the subject of education. Gargantua says that learning should ideally go hand in hand with faith, reason and kindness to one's fellow-men. Today, this expression (which means literally "Knowledge without conscience is nothing but ruination of the soul") is used in support of the idea that there must be ethical constraints in the application of scientific discovery. For example, in the current controversy about genetically modified foods or cloning, this maxim might well be quoted today.

SEIN

Couvrez ce sein que je ne saurais voir

In Molière's *Tartuffe* (1669) Act III scene 2, Tartuffe says to Dorine, Mariane's maid, **Couvrez ce sein que je ne saurais voir. Par de pareils objets les âmes sont blessées, Et cela fait venir de coupables pensées** ("Cover that breast I cannot look upon. Such objects wound the soul and foster guilty thoughts"). The first sentence here is used allusively today, jokingly addressed to someone who is accidentally revealing rather more flesh than intended.

SÉSAME

Sésame, ouvre-toi

In English as in French, this quotation from *Ali Baba and the Forty Thieves*, "Open, Sesame", is eternally familiar. In the tale from the *Thousand and One Nights*, it is the password used to gain admission to the thieves' den with all its treasure. In French, however, **Le sésame, ouvre-toi** is used as a noun, meaning "the key to success" and can be applied to a person, thing or act.

SOUVENT

Souvent femme varie

This expression is attributed to François I of France who is alleged to have scratched the words on a window at the Château of Chambord after a disappointment in love. The full phrase is: **Souvent femme varie, et bien fol qui s'y fie** ("Woman is fickle, and only a fool puts his faith in her"). The saying is used allusively in modern French in a modified form to refer to anything that you believe to be unreliable. For example, in a newspaper one might read **Souvent sondages varient, bien fol qui s'y fie** ("Opinion polls vary, and only a fool puts his faith in them").

SPLENDEUR

Splendeurs et misères des courtisanes

This is the title of the sequel to Balzac's *Illusions perdues* published in 1843 and 1847. In it, we meet again the daughters of Père Goriot, a materialistic pair who have their ups and downs, both social and romantic. The title is used allusively in modern French, usually replacing **courtisanes** with another word, to refer to anyone or anything that has a sudden decline after a period of success.

TARTUFFE

Molière's play of 1669, originally banned as immoral, tells the story of a religious hypocrite named Tartuffe, who manages to worm his way into people's good graces. To call someone a Tartuffe is to call him a sanctimonious hypocrite.

TÊTE

Une tête bien faite vaut mieux qu'une tête bien pleine

This famous maxim comes from Montaigne's *Essais* (1580–95). It means "A mind that has been taught how to think is better than a mind crammed with facts". Montaigne was speaking of the education of young people, and the ideal qualities for a teacher. The expression is still used in debates about educational methods and goals.

TOMBER

Être tombé dedans quand on était petit

This is a very famous expression from the cartoon-strip *Astérix*, created by René Goscinny and Albert Uderzo in 1959. There is a magic potion which makes people invincible, and fortunately for Astérix's companion Obélix, **Il est tombé dedans quand il était petit** ("He fell into it when he was little"), thus acquiring its benefits by accident. The expression is used today of someone who is either naturally very talented, at music for example, or who has grown up in a certain environment from a young age, for example his/her parents were musicians. Thus, if one says of someone **Il est tombé dedans quand il était petit** It means "He's been doing it all his life, it's hardly surprising he's good at it".

TU

Tu quoque, fili!

According to Latin historians, these are the words (meaning "you too, my son!") spoken by Caesar when he was stabbed to death as he recognized his friend Brutus amongst his assassins. The phrase is used in literary French with somewhat facetious overtones to express surprised disappointment at the discovery that a friend has let you down. Sometimes the friend's name is used instead of "fili". The English equivalent, also in Latin, is "Et tu, Brute!", from Shakespeare's *Julius Caesar*.

VASE

Souviens-toi du vase de Soissons

This sentence is used with reference to a famous episode in French history. It is said that, while in Soissons (a city in northern France), Clovis – King of the Franks – ordered one of his soldiers to return a vase that had been given to him following the looting of a church, at the request of the Bishop of Reims. Rather than give the vase back, the aggrieved soldier broke it with his axe. Some time later, during an inspection of his troops, Clovis spotted the soldier, snatched his axe from his hands and threw it to the ground. As the soldier bent over to pick it up, Clovis smashed his head with his own axe, saying the words **Souviens-toi du vase de Soissons** ("Remember the vase of Soissons"). The sentence is used allusively when someone gets their revenge on someone who has wronged them.

VENIR

Si tu ne viens pas à Lagardère, Lagardère ira à toi

This expression comes from the swashbuckling novel *Le Bossu* by 19th-century writer Paul Féval and has been popularized by several film adaptations of the book. In it, a character called Lagardère vows to avenge the Duke of Nevers, who has been killed by a mysterious assassin when both men were set upon. As Lagardère slashes the hand of his friend's murderer, he says **Qui que tu sois, ta main gardera ma marque. Je te reconnaîtrai. Et, quand il sera temps, si tu ne viens pas à Lagardère, Lagardère ira à toi!** ("Whoever you are, your hand will bear my mark and, sooner or later, if you don't find me first, rest assured that I will find you!"). This expression is used in a wide variety of contexts, with the word "Lagardère" replaced to suit the situation. For instance, when writing about a travelling science show aimed at a wide public, commentators might use the slogan **Si tu ne viens pas à la science, la science ira à toi** ("If you don't come to science, science will come to you").

VERT

Ils étaient trop verts

La Fontaine's fable *The Fox and the Grapes* tells of how a fox sees some grapes which are too high for him to reach. Rather than admit defeat, he tells himself "They were too green, nobody civilized would touch them." The usage of **Ils étaient trop verts** in French is exactly like the expression "It's a case of sour grapes" in English.

VIE

La vie est un long fleuve tranquille

This enormously successful French film, made by Étienne Chatilliez (1987), tells the story of a respectable, churchgoing bourgeois French family. They would like to feel that, as the title says, "Life is a long quiet river", but instead they are subjected to all sorts of comical shocks and dramas. The film title is used ironically, to comment on a frenzied situation where we are at the mercy of circumstances. The expression can be varied, and different words substituted.

VOYAGE

Voyage au bout de la nuit

The writer Louis-Ferdinand Céline was a soldier in the 1914–18 war. Though decorated for his bravery, he could not subscribe to the heroic notion of war, and in his 1932 novel *Voyage au bout de la nuit* ("Journey to the End of Night") he recalled the true horror of his experiences. Today, the expression is used either in describing a situation where someone is pushed to an absolute extreme, perhaps staring death in the face, or, substituting another word for **nuit**, when a subject is treated in depth. For example, an in-depth TV documentary on drugs could be called **Voyage au bout de la drogue**.

Abréviations Français-Anglais/ French-English Abbreviations

A 1 *Élec* (*abrév écrite* **ampère**) A, Amp **2** *Météo* (*abrév écrite* **anticyclone**) anticyclone **3** (*abrév* **autoroute**) *Br* ≃ M, motorway, *Am* ≃ I, interstate **4** (*abrév écrite* **apprenti conducteur**) (*sur une voiture*) = indicates that the driver has recently obtained his or her licence, *Br* ≃ L

a (*abrév écrite* **are**) a

Å *Phys* (*abrév écrite* **Angström**) A, Å

A2 [adø] NF*Anciennement* (*abrév* **Antenne 2**) = French state-owned television channel (now France 2)

AAD *Électron* (*abrév écrite* **analogique analogique digital**) AAD

AB *Scol* (*abrév écrite* **assez bien**) = fair grade (as assessment of schoolwork), ≃ C+, ≃ B–

abdos [abdo] NMPL*Fam* (*abrév* **abdominaux**) **1** (*muscles*) abs, stomach *or* abdominal muscles▪ **2** (*exercices*) **faire des a.** to do exercises for the stomach muscles▪, to do abs

ABS [abɛɛs] NM INV *Aut* (*abrév* **Antiblockiersystem**) ABS

AC 1 (*abrév écrite* **appellation contrôlée**) appellation contrôlée (*official certification guaranteeing the quality of French produce, especially wines and cheeses*) **2** *Mktg* (*abrév écrite* **audience cumulée**) cumulative audience

ac 1 *Fin* (*abrév écrite* **argent comptant**) cash **2** *Compta* (*abrév écrite* **année courante**) current year

Acces [aksɛs] NF (*abrév* **association des chaînes du câble et du satellite**) = association of French cable and satellite channels

ACF [aseɛf] NM *Aut* (*abrév* **Automobile Club de France**) = French automobile association, *Br* ≃ AA, ≃ RAC, *Am* ≃ AAA

ACFAS [akfas] NF (*abrév* **Association canadienne-française pour l'avancement des sciences**) French-Canadian Association for the Advancement of Science

ach. (*abrév écrite* **achète, achètent**) (*dans une annonce*) **retraités a. maison en bord de mer** retired couple looking to buy seaside home

ACP [asepe] NM (*abrév* **Groupe des États d'Afrique, des Caraïbes et du Pacifique**) ACP Group

ACT [asete] NMF *Belg Rail* (*abrév* **accompagnateur de train**) ticket inspector

ACTH [aseteaʃ] NF INV *Biol* (*abrév* **adreno-cortico-trophic-hormone**) ACTH

ACV [aseve] NM *Méd* (*abrév* **accident cérébrovasculaire**) stroke, *Spéc* cerebrovascular accident

ADAC [adak] NM *Aviat* (*abrév* **avion à décollage et atterrissage courts**) STOL

ADAV [adav] NM *Aviat* (*abrév* **avion à décollage et atterrissage verticaux**) VTOL

ADD *Électron* (*abrév écrite* **analogique digital digital**) ADD

ADEME [adɛm] NF *Écol* (*abrév* **Agence de l'environnement et de la maîtrise de l'énergie**) = French public body responsible for environmental and energy management

ADM [adɛm] NFPL (*abrév* **armes de destruction massive**) WMD

ADN [adeɛn] NM *Biol* (*abrév* **acide désoxyribonucléique**) DNA; **A. mt** mtDNA; **A. recombinant** recombinant DNA

ADP [adepe] NF *Chim* (*abrév* **adénosine diphosphate**) ADP

adr. 1 (*abrév écrite* **adresse**) addr. **2** (*abrév écrite* **adresser**) addr.

ADSL [adeɛsɛl] NM *Ordinat & Tél* (*abrév* **Asymmetric Digital Subscriber Line**) ADSL; **est-ce que tu as l'A. chez toi?** have you got broadband at home?

AE [aɑ] NMF *Scol* (*abrév* **adjoint d'enseignement**) assistant teacher

A-EF [aɑɛf] NF (*abrév* **Afrique-Équatoriale française**) FEA

AELE [aɑɛlɑ] NF*UE* (*abrév* **Association européenne de libre-échange**) EFTA

AEN [aɑɛn] NF *Nucl* (*abrév* **Agence pour l'énergie nucléaire**) = French atomic energy agency, ≃ AEA

AF[1] **1** (*abrév écrite* **allocations familiales**) family allowance (*UNCOUNT*), child benefit (*UNCOUNT*) **2** *Suisse* (*abrév écrite* **Assemblée fédérale**) (Swiss) federal assembly

AF[2] (*abrév écrite* **Air France**) Air France

AFAT, Afat [afat] NF *Mil* (*abrév* **auxiliaire féminin de l'armée de terre**) = female member of the French army

AFB [aɛfbe] NF *Banque* (*abrév* **Association française des banques**) = French Bankers' Association

AFLS [aɛfɛlɛs] NF (*abrév* **Agence française de lutte contre le sida**) = French Aids research and care agency

AFME [aɛfɛmø] NF *Anciennement* (*abrév* **Agence française pour la maîtrise de l'énergie**) = French agency for energy management

AFNOR, Afnor [afnɔr] NF *Ind* (*abrév* **Association française de normalisation**) = French industrial standards authority, *Br* ≃ BSI, *Am* ≃ ASA

AF-P [aɛfpe] NF *Presse* (*abrév* **Agence France-Presse**) Agence France-Presse (*French national news agency*)

AFPA [aɛfpea] NF(*abrév* **Association pour la formation professionnelle des adultes**) = government body promoting adult vocational training

AFR [aɛfɛr] NF(*abrév* **allocation de formation reclassement**) = allowance paid to employees requiring further training or new qualifications

AG [aʒe] NF(*abrév* **assemblée générale**) GM

ag. (*abrév écrite* **agence**) agcy

AGC [aʒese] NM *Phot* (*abrév* **adaptateur graphique couleur**) CGA

AGCS [aʒesɛɛs] NM *Écon* (*abrév* **Accord général sur le commerce des services**) GATS

AGE [aʒeœ] NF (*abrév* **assemblée générale extraordinaire**) EGM

Aged [aʒɛd] NF (*abrév* **allocation de garde d'enfant à domicile**) = allowance paid to working parents who employ a childminder at home

Agétac [aʒetak] NM *Com* (*abrév* **Accord Général sur les Tarifs Douaniers et le Commerce**) GATT

AGO [aʒeo] NF (*abrév* **assemblée générale ordinaire**) ordinary general meeting

agrég [agrɛg] NF *Fam Univ* (*abrév* **agrégation**) = high-level competitive examination for teachers

Ah *Élec* (*abrév écrite* **ampère-heure**) ah

AHA [aaʃa] NM *Chim* (*abrév* **alpha-hydroxy-acide**) AHA

A.I., a.i. [ai] *Belg* (*abrév* **ad intérim**) ADJ (*président, trésorier*) interim (*avant n*), acting (*avant n*); (*secrétaire*) acting (*avant n*); (*gouvernement*) caretaker (*avant n*) ADVin a temporary capacity, temporarily

AID [aide] NF (*abrév* **Association Internationale de Développement**) IDA

AIDA [aidea] NM *Mktg* (*abrév* **attention-intérêt-désir-action**) AIDA

AIEA [aiɑa] NF *Nucl* (*abrév* **Agence internationale de l'énergie atomique**) IAEA

AIO [aio] NM*Mktg* (*abrév* **activités, intérêts et opinions**) AIO

AJ [aʒi] NF (*abrév* **auberge de jeunesse**) youth hostel

AJA [aʒia] NF *Agr* (*abrév* **aide aux jeunes agriculteurs**) = grant to young farmers

ALA [aɛla] NM *Biol & Chem* (*abrév* **acide alphalinolénique**) ALA

ALE [aɛlø] NF *Com* (*abrév* **Association de libre-échange**) FTA

ALENA [alena] NM *Com* (*abrév* **Accord de libre-échange nord-américain**) NAFTA

alloc [alɔk] NF *Fam* (*abrév* **allocation**) benefit▪; **les allocs** (*allocations familiales*) child benefit▪ (*UNCOUNT*)

alter [altɛr] NMF *Fam* (*abrév* **altermondialiste**) altermondialist

AM (*abrév écrite* **Assurance maladie**) health insurance

AME [aɛmø] NM *Écon* (*abrév* **Accord monétaire européen**) EMA

AMF [aemɛf] NF **1** (*abrév* **Association des maires de France**) = French association of mayors **2** *Bourse* (*abrév* **Autorité des marchés financiers**) = French Stock Exchange authority

AMI [aɛmi] NM*Fin* (*abrév* **Accord multilatéral sur l'investissement**) MAI

AMM [aɛmɛm] NF *Pharm* (*abrév* **autorisation de mise sur le marché**) = official authorization for marketing a pharmaceutical product

AMP [aɛmpe] NF**1** *Chim & Biol* (*abrév* **adénosine monophosphate**) AMP **2** *Méd* (*abrév* **assistance médicale à la procréation**) (*medically*) assisted conception

amphi [ãfi] NM *Fam* (*abrév* **amphithéâtre**) lecture hall▪ *or Br* theatre▪

ampli [ãpli] NM *Fam* (*abrév* **amplificateur**) amp

ANAH [ana, αenaaʃ] NF(*abrév* **Agence nationale pour l'amélioration de l'habitat**) = national agency responsible for housing projects and restoration grants

anar [anar] NMF *Fam* (*abrév* **anarchiste**) anarchist▪

ANASE [anaz] NF (*abrév* **Association des nations de l'Asie du Sud-Est**) ASEAN

ANC [aɛnse] NM(*abrév* **African National Congress**) ANC

anon. (*abrév écrite* **anonyme**) anon

ANP [aɛnpe] NM (*abrév* **assistant numérique personnel**) PDA

ANPE [aɛnpea] NF (*abrév* **Agence nationale pour l'emploi**) = national employment agency; **s'inscrire à l'A.** to sign on

ANRS [aɛnɛrɛs] NF (*abrév* **Agence nationale de recherches sur le sida**) = Aids research institute

ANSEA [ãsea] NF (*abrév* **Association des nations du Sud-Est asiatique**) ASEAN

AOC [aose] NF (*abrév* **appellation d'origine contrôlée**) appellation (d'origine) contrôlée (*official certification guaranteeing the quality of French produce, especially wines and cheeses*)

A-OF [aoɛf] NF *Géog* (*abrév* **Afrique-Occidentale française**) FWA

AP [ape] NF *Presse* (*abrév* **Associated Press**) AP

APD [apede] NF (*abrév* **Aide publique au développement**) ODA

APE [apøe] NF *UE* (*abrév* **Assemblée parlementaire européenne**) EP

APEC [apɛk] NF (*abrév* **Association pour l'emploi des cadres**) = agency providing information and employment and training opportunities for professionals

API [apei] NM *Ling* (*abrév* **alphabet phonétique international**) IPA
  NF (*abrév* **allocation de parent isolé**) = allowance paid to single parents

ap. J.-C. (*abrév écrite* **après Jésus-Christ**) AD

APL [apeɛl] NF (*abrév* **aide personnalisée au logement**) ≃ housing benefit

appt (*abrév écrite* **appartement**) apt.

apr. (*abrév écrite* **après**) after; **a. J.-C.** AD

APS [apeɛs] (*abrév* **advanced photo system**) ADJ INV (*appareil photo*) APS NM INV APS

AR¹ [aɛr] NM (*abrév* **accusé de réception**) acknowledgement (of receipt); **envoyer qch en recommandé avec AR** to send sth by *Br* recorded delivery *or Am* certified mail

AR² 1 (*abrév écrite* **arrière**) back 2 (*abrév écrite* **aller-retour**) R

ARC [ark] NF (*abrév* **Association de recherche sur le cancer**) = French national cancer research charity
  NM (*abrév* **Aids-related complex**) ARC

archi [arʃi] *Fam Archit* NF (*abrév* **architecture**) archit
  NMF (*abrév* **architecte**) archt

ardt *Admin* (*abrév écrite* **arrondissement**) 1 (*dans une ville*) = administrative subdivision of major French cities such as Paris, Lyons or Marseilles 2 (*au niveau départemental*) = administrative subdivision of a "département", governed by a "sous-préfet"

aristo [aristo] *Fam* ADJ (*abrév* **aristocratique**) aristocratic ▪
  NMF (*abrév* **aristocrate**) aristocrat ▪, *Br* toff; **les aristos** the upper crust, *Br* the toffs

ARN [aɛrɛn] NM *Biol* (*abrév* **acide ribonucléique**) RNA; **A. messager** messenger RNA; **A. de transfert** t-RNA

ARP [aɛrpe] NMF *Cin* (*abrév* **auteur-réalisateur-producteur**) writer-director-producer

arr (*abrév écrite* **arrondissement**) 1 (*dans une ville*) = administrative subdivision of major French cities such as Paris, Lyons or Marseilles 2 (*au niveau départemental*) = administrative subdivision of a "département", governed by a "sous-préfet"

arrdt (*abrév écrite* **arrondissement**) 1 (*dans une ville*) = administrative subdivision of major French cities such as Paris, Lyons or Marseilles 2 (*au niveau départemental*) = administrative subdivision of a "département", governed by a "sous-préfet"

arrt *Admin* (*abrév écrite* **arrondissement**) 1 (*dans une ville*) = administrative subdivision of major French cities such as Paris, Lyons or Marseilles 2 (*au niveau départemental*) = administrative subdivision of a "département", governed by a "sous-préfet"

ARS [aɛrɛs] NF (*abrév* **allocation de rentrée scolaire**) = allowance paid to parents to help cover costs incurred at the start of the school year

ART [aɛrte] NF *Tél* (*abrév* **autorité de régulation des télécommunications**) French telecommunications watchdog, *Br* ≃ Oftel

art. (*abrév écrite* **article**) art.

AS [aɛs] NF 1 *Sport* (*abrév* **association sportive**) sports club 2 (*abrév* **assistante (de service) sociale**) social worker

a/s (*abrév écrite* **aux soins de**) c/o

ASA, Asa [aza] NM INV *Phot* (*abrév* **American Standards Association**) ASA, Asa; **une pellicule 100 A.** a 100 ASA film

---

ASBL [aɛsbeɛl] NF (*abrév* **association sans but lucratif**) *Br* non-profit-making *or Am* not-for-profit organization

asc. (*abrév écrite* **ascenseur**) *Br* lift, *Am* elevator

ASCII [aski] NM *Ordinat* (*abrév* **American Standard Code for Information Interchange**) ASCII

ASE [aɛsø] NF *Astron* (*abrév* **Agence spatiale européenne**) ESA

ASI [aɛsi] NF (*abrév* **association de solidarité internationale**) international aid organization

ASS [aɛsɛs] NF (*abrév* **allocation de solidarité spécifique**) = allowance paid to long-term unemployed people who are no longer entitled to unemployment benefit

ASSEDIC, Assedic [asedik] NF (*abrév* **Association pour l'emploi dans l'industrie et le commerce**) = French unemployment insurance scheme, *Br* ≃ Unemployment Benefit Office, *Am* ≃ Unemployment Office; **toucher les A.** to get unemployment benefit

ASSU, Assu [asy] NF *Anciennement* (*abrév* **Association du sport scolaire et universitaire**) = former schools and university sports association

ater [atɛr] NMF *Univ* (*abrév* **attaché temporaire d'enseignement et de recherche**) = holder of, or candidate for, a doctorate with a temporary university teaching post, who must then sit a competitive entry examination to qualify for a full-time post

ATM [ateɛm] NM (*abrév* **asynchronous transfer mode**) ATM

atm *Phys* (*abrév écrite* **atmosphère**) atm

ATP [atepe] NF 1 *Tennis* (*abrév* **Association des tennismen professionnels**) ATP 2 *Biol & Chim* (*abrév* **adénosine triphosphate**) ATP
  NMPL (*abrév* **Arts et traditions populaires**) arts and crafts; **musée des A.** arts and crafts museum

AUD [ayde] NF (*abrév* **allocation unique dégressive**) = unemployment allowance that gradually decreases over time, the sum depending on age, previous salary and amount of national insurance paid

AUE [ayø] NM (*abrév* **Acte unique européen**) SEA

AV 1 *Banque* (*abrév écrite* **avis de virement**) (bank) transfer advice 2 (*abrév écrite* **avant**) front

Av., av. (*abrév écrite* **avenue**) Ave.

AVC [avese] NM *Méd* (*abrév* **accident vasculaire cérébral**) stroke, *Spec* cerebral vascular accident

av. J.-C. (*abrév écrite* **avant Jésus-Christ**) BC

AVS [aveɛs] NF 1 (*abrév* **auxiliaire de vie sociale**) ≃ social worker 2 *Suisse Assur* (*abrév* **assurance vieillesse et survivants**) = Swiss pension scheme

AWACS [awaks] NM *Aviat* (*abrév* **airborne warning and control system**) (*système*) AWACS; (*avion*) AWACS plane

AZT® [azɛdte] NM *Méd* (*abrév* **azidothymidine**) AZT

B

B 1 *Scol* (*abrév écrite* **bien**) = good grade (as assessment of schoolwork), ≃ B 2 *Phys* (*abrév écrite* **Bel**) B

B2B [bitubi] ADJ (*abrév* **business to business**) B2B

B2C [bitusi] ADJ (*abrév* **business to consumer**) B2C

BA [bea] NF *Fam* (*abrév* **bonne action**) good deed; **faire une BA** to do a good deed; **j'ai fait ma BA pour aujourd'hui** I've done my good deed for the day

bac [bak] NM *Fam Scol* (*abrév* **baccalauréat**) (*diplôme*) = final secondary school examination, qualifying for university entrance,

---

Br ≃ A-levels, *Am* ≃ high school diploma; **b. + 3** (*dans une annonce*) = three years of higher education required

BAFA, Bafa [bafa] NM (*abrév* **brevet d'aptitude aux fonctions d'animation**) = diploma for youth leaders and workers

BAL, Bal [bal, beaɛl] NF *Ordinat* (*abrév* **boîte aux lettres (électronique)**) e-mail

BALO [bealo] NM (*abrév* **Bulletin des Annonces Légales et Obligatoires**) = publication in which listed companies must make compulsory legal announcements, such as accounts and notice of annual general meetings

BAS [beaɛs] NM *Admin* (*abrév* **Bureau d'aide sociale**) welfare office

BAT [beate] NM (*abrév* **bon à tirer**) press proof, final corrected proof; **donner le B.** to pass for press

bât. (*abrév écrite* **bâtiment**) (*dans une adresse*) building

BBS [bebeɛs] NM *Ordinat* (*abrév* **bulletin board system**) BBS

BBZ [bebezɛd] NM *Compta* (*abrév* **budget base zéro**) ZBB

BCBG [besebeʒe, bɛsbɛʒ] ADJ INV (*abrév* **bon chic bon genre**) = term used to describe an upper-middle-class lifestyle reflected especially in expensive but conservative clothes; **elle est très B.** *Br* ≃ she's really Sloaney, *Am* ≃ she's a real preppie type; **ils ont une clientèle plutôt B.** they have a largely upper-middle-class clientele

BCE [besø] NF (*abrév* **Banque centrale européenne**) European central bank

BCG® [beseʒe] NM *Méd* (*abrév* **bacille Calmette-Guérin**) BCG®

bcp (*abrév écrite* **beaucoup**) many, a lot

BD [bede] NF 1 *Littérature* (*abrév* **bande dessinée**) (*dans un magazine*) comic strip, *Br* cartoon (strip); (*livre*) comic book 2 *Ordinat* (*abrév* **base de données**) dbase

bd (*abrév écrite* **boulevard**) Blvd.

bdc *Typ* (*abrév écrite* **bas de casse**) lc

BDF [bedeɛf] NF (*abrév* **Bibliothèque de France**) = the new French national library building

B. de F. NF (*abrév écrite* **Banque de France**) the Banque de France, = French issuing bank

BEE [beø] NM (*abrév* **Bureau européen de l'environnement**) EEB

BEI [beøi] NF (*abrév* **Banque européenne d'investissement**) EIB

BEP [beøpe] NM *Scol* (*abrév* **brevet d'études professionnelles**) = vocational diploma (taken after two years of study at a "lycée professionnel")

BEPC [beøpese] NM *Anciennement Scol* (*abrév* **brevet d'études du premier cycle**) = former school certificate taken after four years of secondary education

BERD, Berd [bɛrd] NF *Banque & UE* (*abrév* **Banque européenne pour la reconstruction et le développement**) EBRD

BF [beɛf] NF (*abrév* **Banque de France**) the Banque de France, = French issuing bank

BFCE [beɛfseø] NF (*abrév* **Banque française du commerce extérieur**) French foreign trade bank

BHL [beaʃɛl] NPR (*abrév* **Bernard-Henri Lévy**) = initials commonly used to refer to the philosopher and journalist Bernard-Henri Lévy

BHV [beaʃve] NM (*abrév* **Bazar de l'Hôtel de Ville**) = large department store in central Paris, now part of a nationwide chain

Bige® [biʒ] ADJ INV *Rail* (*abrév* **billet individuel de groupe étudiant**) **billet B.** = cut-price student travel ticket

BinHex *Ordinat* (*abrév écrite* **Binary Hexadecimal**) BinHex

bio [bjo] ADJ INV (*nourriture, aliment*) organic NF *Fam* 1 (*abrév* **biographie**) biog 2 (*abrév* **biologie**) biology ▪; *Scol & Univ* **faire de la b.** to do biology

BIOS [bjɔs] NM *Ordinat* (*abrév* **Basic Input/Output System**) BIOS

Bipe [bip] NM (*abrév* **Bureau d'informations et de prévisions économiques**) = French economic information and forecasting office

BIRD [bœrd] NF (*abrév* **Banque internationale pour la reconstruction et le développement**) IBRD

BIT [beite] NM (*abrév* **Bureau international du travail**) ILO

bld (*abrév écrite* **boulevard**) Blvd.

blog [blɔg] NM *Ordinat* (*abrév* **weblog**) blog; **b. vidéo** vlog, video blog

BM [beɛm] NF (*abrév* **Banque mondiale**) World Bank

BMPT [beɛmpete] NM *Beaux-Arts* (*abrév* **Buren, Mosset, Parmentier, Toroni**) **le groupe B.** the BMPT group

BMTN [beɛmteɛn] NM *Fin* (*abrév* **bon à moyen terme négociable**) MNT

BN [beɛn] NF (*abrév* **Bibliothèque nationale**) = the former French national library building, now containing only archive material and coins, medals etc

BNF [beɛnɛf] NF (*abrév* **Bibliothèque nationale de France**) = French national library, comprising the ''Bibliothèque de France'' and the ''Bibliothèque nationale''

BNP [beɛnpe] NF *Banque* (*abrév* **Banque nationale de Paris**) = the second largest French clearing bank

BNPA [beɛnpea] NM *Bourse* (*abrév* **bénéfice net par action**) earnings per share

BNT [beɛnte] NF (*abrév* **barrière non tarifaire**) NTB

BO [beo] NM *Admin* (*abrév* **Bulletin officiel**) = official listing of all new laws and decrees ▸ NF *Cin* (*abrév* **bande originale**) (*d'un film*) (original) soundtrack

bobo² [bobo] *Fam* (*abrév* **bourgeois bohème**) ADJ bobo ▸ NMF bobo

BOCE [beosea] NM *UE* (*abrév* **Bulletin officiel des communautés européennes**) = official listing of all new EC directives

BOF [beœf] NM *Hist* (*abrév* **Beurre, Œufs, Fromages**) = name given to black market profiteers during the Occupation of France

boul. (*abrév écrite* **boulevard**) Blvd.

BP [bepe] NF (*abrév* **boîte postale**) PO box

BPA [bepea] NM *Fin* (*abrév* **bénéfice par action**) EPS

BPAL [bepeaɛl] NF (*abrév* **base de plein air et de loisirs**) outdoor recreation centre

BPF *Anciennement Banque* (*abrév écrite* **bon pour francs**) = abbreviation printed on cheques and invoices before amount to be written in figures

BPI¹ [bepei] NF INV *Ordinat* (*abrév* **bits per inch**) bpi

BPI² [bepei] NF (*abrév* **Bibliothèque publique d'information**) = library at the Centre Pompidou in Paris

bpp [bepepe] NMPL *Ordinat* (*abrév* **bits par pouce**) bpi

bps [bepeɛs] NMPL *Ordinat* (*abrév* **bits par seconde**) bps

BRB [bɛrbe] NF (*abrév* **brigade de répression du banditisme**) organized crime division

BRGM [beɛrʒeɛm] NM *Géol & Minér* (*abrév* **Bureau de recherches géologiques et minières**) = French geological and mining research agency

BRI [beɛri] NF *Banque* (*abrév* **Banque des règlements internationaux**) BIS

BSPCE [beɛspeseə] NM *Bourse* (*abrév* **bon de souscription de parts de créateurs d'entreprise**) = stock option in a start-up company with tax privileges

BT¹ [bete] NM *Scol* (*abrév* **brevet de technicien**) = vocational training certificate taken at 17 after three years' technical training

BT² *Élec* (*abrév écrite* **basse tension**) LT

BTA [beteа] NM *Scol* (*abrév* **brevet de technicien agricole**) = agricultural training certificate (taken at age 18)

BTH [beteaʃ] NM *Scol* (*abrév* **brevet de technicien hôtelier**) = diploma in hotel and catering management

BTP [betepe] NMPL *Constr* (*abrév* **bâtiments et travaux publics**) = building and public works sector

BTS [beteɛs] NM *Univ* (*abrév* **brevet de technicien supérieur**) = advanced vocational training certificate (taken at the end of a two-year higher education course)

BTU [betey] NF (*abrév* **British thermal unit**) BTU

BU [bey] NF (*abrév* **bibliothèque universitaire**) university library

Buba [byba] NF *Banque* (*abrév* **Bundesbank**) **la B.** the Bundesbank

BVA [bevea] NF (*abrév* **Brulé Ville Associés**) = French market research company

BVP [bevepe] NM (*abrév* **Bureau de vérification de la publicité**) = French advertising standards authority, *Br* ≃ ASA

BZH (*abrév écrite* **Breizh**) = Brittany (as nationality sticker on a car)

C 1 (*abrév écrite* **Celsius, centigrade**) C **2** *Élec* (*abrév écrite* **coulomb**) C

c 1 (*abrév écrite* **centime**) c **2** (*abrév écrite* **con**) **c...** = abbreviation in polite texts for the word ''con''

CA [sea] NM **1** *Élec* (*abrév* **courant alternatif**) AC **2** *Com* (*abrév* **chiffre d'affaires**) turnover **3** (*abrév* **conseil d'administration**) board of directors **4** *Mil* (*abrév* **corps d'armée**) army corps **5** *Can* (*abrév* **comptable agréé**) *Br* ≃ CA, *Am* ≃ CPA ▸ NF (*abrév* **chambre d'agriculture**) = farmers' association

ca (*abrév écrite* **centiare**) sq. m.

CAC, Cac [kak] NM **1** *Bourse* (*abrév* **cotation assistée en continu**) automated quotation; *Bourse* **l'indice C.-40, le C.-40** the CAC-40 (index) (*Paris Stock Exchange Index*) **2** *Fin* (*abrév* **Compagnie des agents de change**) Institute of stockbrokers

CAD [seade] NM (*abrév* **Comité d'aide au développement**) DAC

c.-à-d. (*abrév écrite* **c'est-à-dire**) ie

CADA [kada] NF (*abrév* **Commission d'accès aux documents administratifs**) Commission for Access to Administrative Documents

CAEM [seaɛm] NM (*abrév* **Conseil d'assistance économique mutuelle**) Comecon

CAF [kaf] NF *Admin* (*abrév* **Caisse d'allocations familiales**) *Br* Child Benefit office, *Am* Aid to Dependent Children office ▸ ADJ INV *Com* (*abrév* **coût, assurance, fret**) cif ▸ ADV *Com* (*abrév* **coût, assurance, fret**) cif; **vente C.** sale on cif basis

CAHT [seaaʃte] NM *Com* (*abrév* **chiffre d'affaires hors taxes**) pre-tax turnover

cal (*abrév écrite* **calorie**) cal

CAO [seao] NM *Ordinat* (*abrév* **conception assistée par ordinateur**) CAD

CAP [seape] NM *Scol* **1** (*abrév* **certificat d'aptitude professionnelle**) = vocational training certificate (taken at secondary school), *Br* ≃ City and Guilds examination **2** (*abrév* **certificat d'aptitude pédagogique**) teaching diploma

Cap. (*abrév écrite* **capitaine**) Capt

CAPES, Capes [kapɛs] NM *Univ* (*abrév* **certificat d'aptitude au professorat de l'enseignement du second degré**) = secondary school teaching qualification, *Br* ≃ PGCE

CAPET, Capet [kapɛt] NM *Univ* (*abrév* **certificat d'aptitude au professorat de l'enseignement technique**) = secondary school teaching qualification for technical subjects

CARICOM [karikɔm] NF (*abrév* **Communauté des Caraïbes**) CARICOM

CAT [seate] NF (*abrév* **Confédération autonome du travail**) = French trade union ▸ NM (*abrév* **Centre d'aide par le travail**) = day centre which helps disabled people to find work and become more independent

cata [kata] NF (*abrév* **catamaran**) cat

CB¹ [sibi] NF *Rad* (*abrév* **citizen's band, canaux banalisés**) CB

CB² [sebe] NF *Banque* (*abrév écrite* **Carte Bleue®**) = bank card with which purchases are debited directly from the customer's bank account, *Br* ≃ debit card

CBV [sebeve] NM *Bourse* (*abrév* **conseil des bourses de valeurs**) = regulatory body of the Paris Stock Exchange

CC *Pol* (*abrév écrite* **corps consulaire**) CC

C/C [sese] NM *Banque & Compta* (*abrév* **compte chèque, compte courant**) C/A

cc 1 (*abrév écrite* **cuillère à café**) tsp **2** (*abrév écrite* **charges comprises**) inclusive of maintenance costs

CCB [sesebe] NM *Banque* (*abrév* **compte de chèque bancaire**) C/A

CCE [sesea] NF *UE* (*abrév* **Commission des communautés européennes**) ECC

CCI [sesei] NF **1** (*abrév* **Chambre de commerce et d'industrie**) CCI **2** (*abrév* **Chambre de commerce internationale**) ICC

CCNUCC [seseanysese] NF (*abrév* **Convention-cadre des Nations Unies sur les changements climatiques**) UNFCCC

CCP [sesepe] NM *Banque* (*abrév* **compte chèque postal, compte courant postal**) = post office account, *Br* ≃ Giro account, *Am* ≃ Post Office checking account

CCR [seseɛr] NM *Fin* (*abrév* **coefficient de capitalisation des résultats**) p/e ratio

CD¹ [sede] NM (*abrév* **Compact Disc**) CD; (*CD-ROM*) CD, CD-ROM; **CD audio** audio CD; **CD réinscriptible** CD-RW; **CD vidéo** CD video, CDV

CD² **1** (*abrév écrite* **chemin départemental**) minor road **2** (*abrév écrite* **comité directeur**) steering committee **3** (*abrév écrite* **corps diplomatique**) CD

cd *Phys* (*abrév écrite* **candela**) cd

CDD [sedede] NM (*abrév* **contrat à durée déterminée**) fixed term contract; **elle est en C.** she's on a fixed term contract

CD-E [sedea] NM (*abrév* **Compact Disc Erasable**) CD-E

CdF [sedeɛf] NMPL (*abrév* **Charbonnages de France**) = the French Coal Board

CDI [sedei] NM **1** (*abrév* **Centre de documentation et d'information**) ≃ school library **2** (*abrév* **contrat à durée indéterminée**) permanent (employment) contract; **elle est en C.** she's got a permanent contract

CD-I NM (*abrév écrite* **Compact Disc interactif**) CDI, interactive CD

CD-R [sedeɛr] NM (*abrév* **Compact Disc recordable**) CD-R

CD-ROM, CD-Rom [sederɔm] NM INV *Ordinat* (*abrév* **Compact Disc read-only memory**) CD-ROM; **C. d'installation** installation CD-ROM

CD-RW NM *Ordinat* (*abrév écrite* **Compact Disc Rewritable**) CD-RW

CDS [sedeɛs] NM *Pol* (*abrév* **Centre des démocrates sociaux**) = French political party

CDU [sedey] NF (*abrév* **classification décimale universelle**) DDC

CDV [sedeve] NM (*abrév* **Compact Disc Video**) CDV

CE [sea] NM **1** (*abrév* **comité d'entreprise**) works council **2** *Scol* (*abrév* **cours élémentaire**) = two-year subdivision of primary-level education in France (ages 7 to 9); **CE1** = second year of primary school, *Br* ≃ year 3; **CE2** = third year of primary school, *Br* ≃ year 4 **3** *UE* (*abrév* **conseil de l'Europe**) Council of Europe ▸ NF *UE* (*abrév* **Communauté européenne**) EC

CEA [seəa] NM (*abrév* **Commissariat à l'énergie atomique**) = French atomic energy commission, *Br* ≃ AEA, *Am* ≃ AEC

CEAM [seəaɛm] NF (*abrév* **Carte européenne d'assurance maladie**) EHIC

CEC [seəse] NF Pol (*abrév* **Confédération européenne des cadres**) CEC, European Confederation of Executives and Managerial Staff

CECA, Ceca [seka] NF UE (*abrév* **Communauté européenne du charbon et de l'acier**) ECSC

CECEI [seəseəi] NM (*abrév* **comité des établissements de crédit et des entreprises d'investissement**) = French public authority empowered to authorize suppliers of financial services

CEDEAO [sedeao] NF (*abrév* **Communauté économique des États d'Afrique de l'Ouest**) ECOWAS

CEDEX®, Cedex® [sedɛks] NM(*abrév* **courrier d'entreprise à distribution exceptionnelle**) = accelerated postal service for bulk users

CEDH [seədeaʒ] NF(*abrév* **Cour européenne des droits de l'homme**) ECHR

CEE [seəə] NF UE (*abrév* **Communauté économique européenne**) EEC

CEEA [seəaa] NF (*abrév* **Communauté européenne de l'enérgie atomique**) Euratom

CEG [seəʒe] NM Scol (*abrév* **collège d'enseignement général**) = former junior secondary school

CÉGEP, cégep [seʒɛp] NM Can Scol (*abrév* **collège d'enseignement général et professionnel**) = college of further education

CEI [seəi] NF (*abrév* **Communauté des États indépendants**) CIS

CEJ [seəʒi] NF (*abrév* **Cour européenne de justice**) ECJ

CEL [sɛl] NM Banque (*abrév* **compte épargne logement**) = savings account for purchasing a property

CEMAC [semak] NF (*abrév* **Communauté économique et monétaire de l'Afrique centrale**) CEMAC

CEN [seəən] NM UE (*abrév* **Comité européen de normalisation**) European Standards Commission

CEP [seəpe] NM Ancienneté Scol (*abrév* **certificat d'études primaires**) = basic examination taken at the end of primary education

CERC [serk] NM (*abrév* **Centre d'études sur les revenus et les coûts**) = government body carrying out research into salaries and the cost of living

CERES [serɛs] NM Ancienneté (*abrév* **Centre d'études, de recherches et d'éducation socialiste**) = the intellectual section of the French socialist party, now independent

CERN, Cern [sɛrn] NM (*abrév* **Conseil européen pour la recherche nucléaire**) CERN

CERS [seəɛrɛs] NF (*abrév* **Commission européenne de recherches spatiales**) ESRO

CES [seəɛs] NM 1 (*abrév* **collège d'enseignement secondaire**) = former secondary school 2 Ancienneté (*abrév* **contrat emploi-solidarité**) = short-term contract subsidized by the government

CESP [seəɛspe] NM(*abrév* **Conseil européen des syndicats de police**) CESP, European Council of Police Trade Unions

CET [seəte] NM 1 (*abrév* **compte épargne temps**) = scheme which allows employees to save up the hours of overtime they accumulate under the "RTT" system (see entry "RTT") for up to five years, eventually being compensated either financially or with additional holidays 2 Ancienneté (*abrév* **collège d'enseignement technique**) = technical school

C&A Com (*abrév écrite* **coût et assurance**) C&I

C&F Com (*abrév écrite* **coût et fret**) C&F

cf. (*abrév écrite* **confer**) cf

CFA [seɛfa] NF (*abrév* **Communauté financière africaine**) African Financial Community; **franc C.** = currency used in former French African colonies

NM (*abrév* **Centre de formation des apprentis**) = centre for apprenticeship training

CFAO [seɛfao] NF(*abrév* **conception et fabrication assistées par ordinateur**) CAD/CAM

CFC [seɛfse] NM 1 Chim (*abrév* **chlorofluorocarbure**) CFC 2 (*abrév* **centre de formation continue**) = centre for continuing education

CFDT [seɛfdete] NF (*abrév* **Confédération française démocratique du travail**) = French trade union

CFE–CGC [seɛfəseʒese] NF(*abrév* **Confédération française de l'encadrement–Confédération générale des cadres**) = French trade union for engineers and middle and lower management staff

CFES [seɛfɛs] NM Ancienneté Scol (*abrév* **certificat de fin d'études secondaires**) = school-leaving certificate

CFF [seɛfɛf] NMPL Suisse (*abrév* **Chemins de fer fédéraux**) = Swiss railways

CFL [seɛfɛl] NMPL (*abrév* **Chemins de fer luxembourgeois**) = Luxembourg railways

CFP [seɛfpe] NF 1 (*abrév* **Compagnie française des pétroles**) = French oil company 2 (*abrév* **Communauté française du Pacifique**) **franc C.** = currency used in former French colonies in the Pacific area
NM 1 (*abrév* **Centre de formation permanente**) = centre for ongoing training and education 2 (*abrév* **Certificat de formation professionnelle**) vocational training certificate

CFR [seɛfɛr] (*abrév* **cost and freight**) CFR

CFTC [seɛftese] NF (*abrév* **Confédération française des travailleurs chrétiens**) = French trade union

CGA [seʒea] NM Ordinat (*abrév* **colour graphics adaptor**) CGA

CGC [seʒese] NF(*abrév* **Confédération générale des cadres**) = French management union

CGI [seʒei] NM Admin (*abrév* **Code général des impôts**) general tax code
NF Ordinat (*abrév* **common gateway interface**) CGI

CGPME [seʒepeɛma] NF (*abrév* **Confédération générale des petites et moyennes entreprises**) = French small business employers' organization

CGT [seʒete] NF (*abrév* **Confédération générale du travail**) = major association of French trade unions (affiliated to the Communist Party)

CH(*abrév écrite* **Confédération helvétique**) = Swiss nationality sticker on a car

ch Aut (*abrév écrite* **cheval-vapeur**) hp

ch. 1 (*abrév écrite* **charges**) bills 2 (*abrév écrite* **chauffage**) heating 3 (*abrév écrite* **cherche**) architecte c. co-locataire architect seeks Br flatmate or Am roommate; **JH c. JF** male WLTM female

chap. (*abrév écrite* **chapitre**) ch

ch-l Admin (*abrév écrite* **chef-lieu**) = in France, administrative centre of a "département", "arrondissement" or "canton"

CHR [seaʃɛr] NM (*abrév* **centre hospitalier régional**) = regional hospital
NMPL(*abrév* **cafés, hôtels et restaurants**) = hotels, cafés and restaurants (*collectively*)

CHS [seaʃɛs] NM (*abrév* **centre hospitalier spécialisé**) = psychiatric hospital

CHSCT [seaʃɛsseete] NM (*abrév* **comité d'hygiène, de sécurité et des conditions de travail**) = health and safety committee

CHU [seaʃy] NM 1 (*abrév* **centre hospitalo-universitaire**) teaching hospital 2 (*abrév* **centre d'hébergement d'urgence**) emergency refuge

CI [sei] NM Fin (*abrév* **certificat d'investissement**) investment certificate

Ci Phys (*abrév écrite* **curie**) Ci

CIA [seia] NF (*abrév* **Central Intelligence Agency**) CIA

CIC [seise] NF (*abrév* **Confédération internationale des cadres**) CIC, International Confederation of Executives and Managerial Staff

CICR [seisɛr] NM (*abrév* **Comité international de la Croix-Rouge**) IRCC

CIDJ [seideʒi] NM (*abrév* **centre d'information et de documentation de la jeunesse**) = careers advisory service

Cidunati [sidynati] NM (*abrév* **Comité interprofessionnel d'information et de défense de l'union nationale des travailleurs indépendants**) = union of self-employed craftsmen

Cie (*abrév écrite* **compagnie**) Co

CIEP [seiəpe] NM(*abrév* **Centre international d'études pédagogiques**) = French centre for educational research

CIG [seiʒe] NF (*abrév* **Conférence Intergouvernementale**) IGC

CIJ [seiʒi] NF (*abrév* **Cour internationale de justice**) ICJ

CIO [seio] NM 1 (*abrév* **Comité international olympique**) IOC 2 (*abrév* **centre d'information et d'orientation**) careers advisory centre

CIP¹ [seipe] Com (*abrév* **carriage and insurance paid to**) CIP

CIP² [seipe] NM (*abrév* **conseiller d'insertion et de probation**) probation officer

CISL [seiɛsɛl] NF (*abrév* **Confédération internationale des syndicats libres**) ICFTU

CITES [sites] NF (*abrév* **Convention on the International Trade of Endangered Species**) CITES

CJAI [seʒiai] NF UE (*abrév* **Coopération concernant la justice et les affaires intérieures**) CJHA

CJE [seʒeə] (*abrév* **contrat jeune en entreprise**) = contract to help young unemployed people (aged 16–22) with few qualifications into the job market, under which employers must pay at least the minimum wage but receive government aid with employer contributions

cl (*abrév écrite* **centilitre**) cl

CLES, Cles [klɛs] NM (*abrév* **contrat local emploi-solidarité**) = community work scheme for young unemployed people

CLS [seɛlɛs] NM (*abrév* **contrat local de sécurité**) = list of measures to increase public safety within a town, involving all the official bodies who work together with the residents

CLT [seɛlte] NF (*abrév* **Compagnie luxembourgeoise de télévision**) = Luxembourg TV company

CM [seɛm] NF (*abrév* **Chambre des métiers**) Guild Chamber
NM (*abrév* **cours moyen**) = two-year subdivision of primary-level education in France (ages 10 to 11); **CM1** = fourth year of primary school, Br ≃ year 5; **CM2** = fifth year of primary school, Br ≃ year 6

cm (*abrév écrite* **centimètre**) cm; **cm²** sq.cm., cm²; **cm³** cu.cm., cm³

CMF [seɛmɛf] NF Bourse (*abrév* **Conseil des Marchés Financiers**) = regulatory body of the French stock market

CMH [seɛmaʃ] NM Méd (*abrév* **complexe majeur d'histocompatibilité**) MHC

CMJN Ordinat (*abrév écrite* **cyan, magenta, jaune, noir**) CMYK

CMP [seɛmpe] NM Fin (*abrév* **coût moyen pondéré**) weighted average cost

CMT [seɛmte] NF (*abrév* **Confédération mondiale du travail**) WCL

CMU [seɛmy] NF Admin (*abrév* **couverture maladie universelle**) = law introduced to ensure free health care for people on low incomes who have no social security cover

CMV [seɛmve] NM Méd (*abrév* **cytomégalovirus**) CMV

CNA [seɛna] NM Tech (*abrév* **convertisseur numérique-analogique**) DAC

CNAC [knak] NM(*abrév* **Centre national d'art et de culture**) = official name of the Pompidou Centre

CNAM [knam] NM (*abrév* **Conservatoire national des arts et métiers**) = science and technology school in Paris
NF Admin (*abrév* **Caisse nationale d'assurance maladie**) = French goverment

department dealing with health insurance and sickness benefit

CNAV [knav] NF (*abrév* **Caisse nationale d'assurance vieillesse**) = French government department dealing with benefit payments relating to old age

CNC [seɛnə] NM **1** (*abrév* **Conseil national de la consommation**) = consumer protection organization **2** (*abrév* **Centre national de la cinématographie, Centre national du cinéma**) = national cinematographic organization

CNCE [seɛnsə] NM (*abrév* **Centre national du commerce extérieur**) = national export organization

CNCL [seɛnseɛl] NF (*abrév* **Commission nationale de la communication et des libertés**) = former French TV and radio supervisory body

CND [seɛnde] NM INV *Ind & Tech* (*abrév* **Contrôle non destructif**) non-destructive control

CNDP [seɛndepe] NM (*abrév* **Centre national de documentation pédagogique**) = national organization for educational resources

CNE [seɛnə] NF **1** *Banque* (*abrév* **Caisse nationale d'épargne**) ≃ National Savings Bank **2** (*abrév* **contrat nouvelles embauches**) = open-ended employment contract for companies of up to 20 employees, under which employment can be terminated without justification within the first two years

CNEC [knɛk] NM (*abrév* **Centre national de l'enseignement par correspondance**) = national educational body organizing correspondence courses

CNED [knɛd] NM (*abrév* **Centre national d'enseignement à distance**) = national educational body organizing correspondence courses

CNES, Cnes [knɛs] NM (*abrév* **Centre national d'études spatiales**) = French national space research centre

CNI [seɛni] NM (*abrév* **Congrès national irakien**) INC

CNIL [knil] NF (*abrév* **Commission nationale de l'informatique et des libertés**) = board which enforces data protection legislation

CNIT, Cnit [knit] NM (*abrév* **Centre national des industries et des techniques**) = trade centre at la Défense in Paris

CNJA [seɛnʒia] NM (*abrév* **Centre national des jeunes agriculteurs**) = farmers' union

CNPF [seɛnpeɛf] NM *Anciennement* (*abrév* **Conseil national du patronat français**) = national council of French employers, *Br* ≃ CBI

CNR [seɛner] NM (*abrév* **Conseil national de la Résistance**) = central organization of the French Resistance founded in 1943

CNRS [seɛnerɛs] NM (*abrév* **Centre national de la recherche scientifique**) = French national organization for scientific research, *Br* ≃ SRC

CNSF–FNCR [seɛnsɛfɛfɛnsɛer] NF (*abrév* **Confédération nationale des salariés de France–Fédération nationale des chauffeurs routiers**) = French trade union representing lorry drivers and workers from other sectors

CNTS [seɛntees] NM (*abrév* **Centre national de transfusion sanguine**) = national blood transfusion centre

CNUCED, Cnuced [knysɛd] NF (*abrév* **Conférence des Nations unies pour le commerce et l'industrie**) UNCTAD

COB, Cob [kɔb] NF (*abrév* **Commission des opérations de Bourse**) = French Stock Exchange watchdog, *Br* ≃ SIB, *Am* ≃ SEC

Cobra [kɔbra] NM *Beaux-Arts* (*abrév* **Copenhague, Bruxelles, Amsterdam**) Cobra, CoBrA; **le groupe C.** the Cobra group, the Cobra artists

COD, C.O.D. [seɔde] NM *Gram* (*abrév* **complément d'objet direct**) direct object

CODEVI, codevi, codévi [kɔdevi] NM *Banque* (*abrév* **compte pour le développement industriel**) = type of instant-access savings account, money from which is invested in industrial development

COFACE [kɔfas] NF (*abrév* **Compagnie française d'assurances pour le commerce extérieur**) = export insurance company, ≃ ECGD

COI, C.O.I. [seoi] NM *Gram* (*abrév* **complément d'objet indirect**) indirect object

Col. (*abrév écrite* **Colonel**) Col

col. (*abrév écrite* **colonne**) col

coll. 1 (*abrév écrite* **collection**) coll **2** (*abrév écrite* **collaborateurs**) **et c.** et al

collabo [kɔlabo] NMF *Péj Hist* (*abrév* **collaborateur**) collaborationist

COM [kɔm] NF (*abrév* **collectivité d'outre-mer**) = French overseas collectivity

COMES, Comes [kɔmɛs] NM (*abrév* **Commissariat à l'énergie solaire**) = solar energy commission

COMESA [kɔmɛsa] NM (*abrév* **Common Market for Eastern and Southern Africa**) COMESA

compo [kɔ̃po] NF **1** *Fam Scol* (*abrév* **composition**) *(dissertation)* essay; *(examen)* test■; *(plus important)* exam■ **2** *Typ* (*abrév* **composition**) typesetting department; **partir en c.** to go to be typeset

condo [kɔ̃do] NM *Can* (*abrév* **condominium**) condo

conf. (*abrév écrite* **confort**) **tt c.** *Br* all mod cons, *Am* modern conveniences

COS [seoɛs] NM **1** *Gram* (*abrév* **complément d'objet second**) prepositional complement **2** *Constr* (*abrév* **coefficient d'occupation des sols**) plot ratio

courriel [kuriɛl] NM *Ordinat* (*abrév* **courrier électronique**) e-mail

CP [sepe] NM (*abrév* **cours préparatoire**) *Br* ≃ first-year infants class, *Am* ≃ nursery school

CPAM [sepeaɛm] NF *Admin* (*abrév* **caisse primaire d'assurance maladie**) = French Social Security department in charge of medical insurance

CPAS [sepeaɛs] NM *Belg* (*abrév* **centre public d'aide sociale**) welfare office *or* centre

CPE [sepeæ] NM (*abrév* **contrat première embauche**) = employment contract for people under 26 which could be terminated without justification in the first two years, proposed by the French government but abandoned under public pressure

CPGE [sepeʒeə] NF (*abrév* **classe préparatoire aux grandes écoles**) = preparatory class for the entrance examinations for the "grandes écoles"

cpl *Typ* (*abrév écrite* **caractères par ligne**) cpl

CPM [sepeɛm] NM *Com* (*abrév* **coût par mille**) cost per thousand

CPNT [sepeɛnte] NF *Pol* (*abrév* **Chasse, Pêche, Nature et Traditions**) = French political movement that promotes rural life, hunting, fishing and environmental protection

cpp *Ordinat* (*abrév écrite* **caractères par pouce**) cpi

cps *Ordinat* (*abrév écrite* **caractères par seconde**) cps

CPT [sepete] NM (*abrév* **carriage paid to**) CPT

cpt (*abrév écrite* **comptant**) cpt

CQFD [sekyɛfde] NM (*abrév* **ce qu'il fallait démontrer**) QED; **et voilà, C.!** and there you have it!

CR (*abrév écrite* **compte-rendu**) *(d'une réunion)* minutes

CRDP [seɛrdepe] NM (*abrév* **centre régional de documentation pédagogique**) = local centre for educational resources

CRDS [seɛrdeɛs] NF (*abrév* **contribution au remboursement de la dette sociale**) = income-based tax deducted at source as a contribution to paying off the French social security budget deficit

CRÉDIF, Crédif [kredif] NM (*abrév* **Centre de recherche et d'étude pour la diffusion du français**) = official body promoting use of the French language

Credoc [kredɔk] NM *Mktg* (*abrév* **Centre de recherche pour l'étude et l'observation des conditions de vie**) = large state-funded market research company in Paris

CREPS, Creps [krɛps] NM (*abrév* **centre régional d'éducation physique et sportive**) = regional sports centre

CRF [seɛrɛf] NF (*abrév* **Croix-Rouge française**) **la C.** the French Red Cross

croco [krɔko] *Fam* (*abrév* **crocodile**) NM crocodile■, crocodile skin■
□ **en croco** ADJ crocodile■ *(avant n)*, crocodile skin■

CROUS, Crous [krus] NM (*abrév* **Centre régional des œuvres universitaires et scolaires**) = student representative body dealing with accommodation, catering etc

CRS [seɛrɛs] NM (*abrév* **compagnie républicaine de sécurité**) *(policier)* state security policeman, *Br* ≃ riot policeman, *Am* state trooper; **les C. ont chargé les manifestants** the security police charged the demonstrators; **les C. responsables de la surveillance des plages** the security police responsible for keeping watch over the beaches

cs (*abrév écrite* **cuillère à soupe**) tbs, tbsp

CSA [seɛsa] NM (*abrév* **Conseil supérieur de l'audiovisuel**) = French broadcasting supervisory body

CSCE [seɛsseə] NF (*abrév* **Conférence sur la sécurité et la coopération en Europe**) CSCE

CSEN [seɛsaɛn] NF (*abrév* **Confédération des syndicats de l'éducation nationale**) = confederation of teachers' unions

CSG [seɛsʒe] NF *Fin* (*abrév* **contribution sociale généralisée**) = income-based tax deducted at source as a contribution to paying off the French social security budget deficit

CSM [seɛsɛm] NM (*abrév* **Conseil supérieur de la magistrature**) = French state body that appoints members of the judiciary

CSP [seɛspe] NF (*abrév* **catégorie socio-professionnelle**) socio-professional group

CT [sete] NF (*abrév* **collectivité territoriale**) = administrative division with a higher degree of autonomy than a "département"

Cte (*abrév écrite* **comte**) Count

Ctesse (*abrév écrite* **comtesse**) Countess

CTI [setei] NF (*abrév* **Confédération des travailleurs intellectuels de France**) = French trade union representing non-manual workers

CUB [kyb] NF *Anciennement* (*abrév* **Communauté urbaine de Bordeaux**) = syndicate of local authorities in the Bordeaux area

CUE [seyə] NM (*abrév* **Conseil de l'Union européenne**) CEU

CUS [kys] NF (*abrév* **Communauté urbaine de Strasbourg**) = syndicate of local authorities in the Strasbourg area

CV¹ [seve] NM (*abrév* **curriculum vitae**) *Br* CV, *Am* résumé; **ça fera bien dans ton CV** it'll look good on your *Br* CV *or Am* résumé

CV² *Aut* (*abrév écrite* **cheval-vapeur**) hp

CVG [seveʒe] NM *Bourse* (*abrév* **certificat de valeur garantie**) CVR

CVS [seveɛs] ADJ *Com & Écon* (*abrév* **corrigé des variations saisonnières**) seasonally adjusted

D¹ [de] NF **1** (*abrév* **route départementale**) = designation of secondary road **2** *Ftbl* (*abrév* **division**) Div; **D1/2/3** Div 1/2/3

D² *Météo* (*abrév écrite* **dépression**) cyclone, barometric depression, low

d (*abrév écrite* **déci**) = decilitre of wine

DA (*abrév écrite* **dinar algérien**) DA

da (*abrév écrite* **déca-**) da

DAB [dab] NM (*abrév* **distributeur automatique de billets**) *Br* cashpoint, *Am* ATM

DADS [deadɛɛs] NF *Admin* (*abrév* **déclaration annuelle des données sociales**) ≃ PAYE and NIC return

DAF [deaɛf] ADJ *Com* (*abrév* **delivered at frontier**) DAF

dal (*abrév écrite* **décalitre**) dal

dam (*abrév écrite* **décamètre**) dam

DAO [deao] NM (*abrév* **dessin assisté par ordinateur**) CAD

DARC [dark] NF (*abrév* **data radio channel**) DARC

DAS [deaɛs] NM *Com & Mktg* (*abrév* **domaine d'activité stratégique**) SBU

DAT [deate] NM INV (*abrév* **digital audio tape**) DAT

DATAR, Datar [datar] NF (*abrév* **Délégation à l'aménagement du territoire et à l'action régionale**) = regional land development agency

DB [debe] NF *Mil* (*abrév* **division blindée**) armoured division

dB (*abrév écrite* **décibel**) dB

DBO [debeo] NF *Écol* (*abrév* **demande biologique *ou* biochimique en oxygène**) BOD

DBS [debɛs] NM (*abrév* **direct broadcasting satellite**) DBS

DC [dese] NM *Fam* (*abrév* **directeur de la création**) creative director■

DCA [desea] NF *Mil* (*abrév* **défense contre les aéronefs**) AA, anti-aircraft

DCC [desese] NM (*abrév* **digital compact cassette**) DCC

Dchesse (*abrév écrite* **duchesse**) Duchess

DCO [deseo] NM *Écol* (*abrév* **demande chimique en oxygène**) COD

DCT [desete] NM *Méd* (*abrév* **diphtérie, coqueluche, tétanos**) DPT

DD [dede] *Ordinat* ADJ (*abrév* **double densité**) DD

NM (*abrév* **disque dur**) HD

DDA [dedea] NF (*abrév* **Direction départementale de l'agriculture**) = local offices of the Ministry of Agriculture

DDASS, Ddass [das] NF *Admin* (*abrév* **Direction départementale d'action sanitaire et sociale**) = Department of Health and Social Security; **un enfant de la D.** a state orphan

DDD *Électron* (*abrév écrite* **digital digital digital**) DDD

DDE [dedeə] NF (*abrév* **Direction départementale de l'équipement**) = local offices of the Ministry of the Environment

NM *Ordinat* (*abrév* **dynamic data exchange**) DDE

DDT [dedete] NM *Chim* (*abrév* **dichlorodiphényl-trichloréthane**) DDT

DE [deə] NM (*abrév* **diplôme d'État**) = recognized qualification

DEA [deəa] NM (*abrév* **diplôme d'études approfondies**) = postgraduate qualification which is a prerequisite for PhD candidates

dec [dek] (*abrév* **déconner**) **sans dec** ADV *Fam* **sans d.!** (*je t'assure*) no kidding!, *Br* straight up!, **sans d.?** (*est-ce vrai?*) no kidding?, yeah?, *Br* straight up

déco [deko] ADJ PL (*abrév* **décoratifs**) **arts d.** art deco

NF (*abrév* **décoration**) decor, decoration; (*métier*) (interior) decorating, interior design; **j'aime beaucoup faire de la d.** I love decorating

DECS [deəsɛs] NM (*abrév* **diplôme d'études comptables supérieures**) = postgraduate qualification in accounting

DECT [deəsete] NF *Tél* (*abrév* **digital enhanced cordless telecommunications**) DECT

DEFA, Defa [defa] NM (*abrév* **diplôme d'État relatif aux fonctions d'animation**) = diploma for senior youth leaders

DEL [deəl] NF *Électron* (*abrév* **diode électroluminescente**) LED

dép. 1 (*abrév écrite* **départ**) dep **2** (*abrév écrite* **département**) dept

DEPS [deəpɛɛs] NM *Com & Compta* (*abrév* **dernier entré premier sorti**) LIFO

dermato [dɛrmato] NMF *Fam* (*abrév* **dermatologiste**) dermatologist, skin specialist

DESS [deəsɛs] NM (*abrév* **diplôme d'études supérieures spécialisées**) = postgraduate diploma lasting one year

DET [deəte] NM *TV* (*abrév* **durée d'écoute par téléspectateur**) average viewing time

DEUG [dœg] NM (*abrév* **diplôme d'études universitaires générales**) = university diploma taken after two years

DEUST [døst] NM (*abrév* **diplôme d'études universitaires scientifiques et techniques**) = university diploma taken after two years of science courses

deuz, deuze [døz] *Fam* (*abrév* **deuxième**) ADJ second■; **je suis d.!** I'm second! NMF second■

dfc (*abrév écrite* **désire faire connaissance**) WLTM

DG [deʒe] NM (*abrév* **directeur général**) *Br* GM, *Am* CEO

NF (*abrév* **direction générale**) general management, senior management

dg (*abrév écrite* **décigramme**) dg

DGA [deʒea] NF (*abrév* **Délégation générale pour l'armement**) = section of the French armed forces responsible for building and testing armaments

NM (*abrév* **directeur général adjoint**) *Br* deputy managing director, *Am* vice-president

DGE [deʒeə] NF (*abrév* **dotation globale d'équipement**) = state contribution to local government capital budget

DGF [deʒeɛf] NF (*abrév* **dotation globale de fonctionnement**) = state contribution to local government revenue budget

DGI [deʒei] NF (*abrév* **Direction générale des impôts**) = central tax office

DGSE [deʒeɛsə] NF (*abrév* **Direction générale de la sécurité extérieure**) = arm of the Defence Ministry in charge of international intelligence, *Br* ≃ MI6, *Am* ≃ CIA

DH (*abrév écrite* **dirham**) DH

DHDO [deaʃdeo] NF (*abrév* **Dynamique Humaine et Développement de l'Organisation**) = postgraduate diploma in management

DHEA [deaʃea] NF (*abrév* **déhydroépiandrostérone**) DHEA

DI [dei] NF *Mil* (*abrév* **division d'infanterie**) infantry division

DIF [deiɛf] NM (*abrév* **droit individuel à la formation**) = law under which all salaried employees have the right to 20 hours' training per year

DIN, Din [din] ADJ *Élec & Phot* (*abrév* **Deutsche Industrie Normen**) DIN

DiREN [dirɛn] NF (*abrév* **Direction régionale de l'environnement**) = local government body in charge of environmental issues

dissert [disɛrt] NF *Fam Scol & Univ* (*abrév* **dissertation**) essay■

DIT [deite] NF (*abrév* **division internationale du travail**) international division of labour

DIVX [deiveiks] NM (*abrév* **digital video express**) DIVX

DJ [didʒi, didʒe] NM (*abrév* **disc-jockey**) DJ

DL [deɛl] NF *Anciennement Pol* (*abrév* **Démocratie Libérale**) = right-of-centre French political party

DLC [deɛlse] NF (*abrév* **date limite de consommation**) best-before date

DM *Anciennement* (*abrév écrite* **Deutsche Mark**) DM

dm (*abrév écrite* **décimètre**) dm

DN [deɛn] NF (*abrév* **distribution numérique**) numerical distribution

DNS [deɛnɛs] NM *Ordinat* (*abrév* **Domain Name System**) DNS

do (*abrév écrite* **dito**) do

DOC [dɔk] NM *Ordinat* (*abrév* **disque optique compact**) CD-ROM

doc [dɔk] NF *Fam* (*abrév* **documentation**) literature■, info; **est-ce que tu as de la d.**

sur les ordinateurs? do you have any literature *or* info about computers?

doc. (*abrév écrite* **document**) doc

DOM [dɔm] NM *Anciennement* (*abrév* **département d'outre-mer**) = French overseas "département"

DOM-TOM [dɔmtɔm] NMPL *Anciennement* (*abrév* **départements et territoires d'outre-mer**) = French overseas "départements" and territories

DON [dɔn] NM *Ordinat* (*abrév* **disque optique numérique**) digital optical disk

DOS, Dos [dɔs] NM *Ordinat* (*abrév* **Disk Operating System**) DOS

DP [depe] NM (*abrév* **délégué du personnel**) staff representative

DPE [depeə] NF (*abrév* **direction par exceptions**) management by exception

DPI [depei] NM *Méd* (*abrév* **diagnostic préimplantatoire**) PGD

dpi [depei] (*abrév* **dots per inch**) dpi

DPLG [depeɛlʒe] ADJ (*abrév* **diplômé par le gouvernement**) = certificate for architects, engineers etc

DPO [depeo] NF (*abrév* **direction par objectifs**) MBO

DQ (*abrév écrite* **dernier quartier de lune**) = last quarter

DR *Anciennement* (*abrév écrite* **drachme**) Dr

Dr (*abrév écrite* **Docteur**) Dr

dr (*abrév écrite* **droite**) R, r

DRAM [dram] NF *Ordinat* (*abrév* **dynamic random access memory**) DRAM

DRASS [dras] NF *Admin* (*abrév* **Direction Régionale des Affaires Sanitaires et Sociales**) = office administering health and social services at regional level

DRH [deɛraʃ] NF (*abrév* **direction des ressources humaines**) human resources department

NM (*abrév* **directeur des ressources humaines**) human resources manager

DRM [deɛrɛm] NM (*abrév* **digital right management**) DRM

DROM [drom] NM (*abrév* **Département et Région d'outre-mer**) = French overseas department and region

DSL [deɛsɛl] NM *Ordinat* (*abrév* **Digital Subscriber Line**) DSL

DSRP [deɛsɛrpe] NM (*abrév* **Document stratégique de réduction de la pauvreté**) PRSP

DST [deɛste] NF (*abrév* **Direction de la surveillance du territoire**) = internal state security department, *Br* ≃ MI5, *Am* ≃ CIA

DT [dete] NM *Méd* (*abrév* **diphtérie, tétanos**) = vaccine against diphtheria and tetanus

D.T.Coq. [detekɔk] NM *Méd* (*abrév* **diphtérie, tétanos, coqueluche**) = vaccine against diphtheria, tetanus and whooping cough

DTP [detepe], **DT-Polio** [detepoljo] NM *Méd* (*abrév* **diphtérie, tétanos, polio**) = vaccine against diphtheria, tetanus and polio

DTS [deteɛs] NMPL *Fin* (*abrév* **droits de tirage spéciaux**) SDRs

DTTAB [deteteabe] NM *Méd* (*abrév* **diphtérie, tétanos, tiphoïde A et B**) = vaccine against diphtheria, tetanus and typhoid

DTU (*abrév écrite* **dinar tunisien**) D

DUEL, Duel [dɥɛl] NM (*abrév* **diplôme universitaire d'études littéraires**) = university diploma gained after two years of arts courses, still existing in some French-speaking countries but replaced in France in 1973

DUES, Dues [dɥɛs] NM (*abrév* **diplôme universitaire d'études scientifiques**) = university diploma gained after two years of science courses, still existing in some French-speaking countries but replaced in France in 1973

DUT [deyte] NM (*abrév* **diplôme universitaire de technologie**) = diploma taken after two years at an institute of technology

DV [deve] NF (*abrév* **distribution valeur**) weighted distribution

DVB [devebe] NF (*abrév* **Digital Video Broadcasting**) DVB

DVD [devede] NM (*abrév* **Digital Versatile Disk, Digital Video Disk**) DVD; **D. réenregistrable** rerecordable DVD

DVD-R [devedeɛr] NM (*abrév* **Digital Versatile Disk-recordable**) DVD-R

DVD-ROM, DVD-Rom [devederɔm] NM INV (*abrév* **Digital Versatile Disk read-only memory**) DVD-ROM

DVD-RW [devedeɛrdubləve] NM (*abrév* **Digital Versatile Disk-rewritable**) DVD-RW

E (*abrév écrite* **est**) E

EAO [əao] NM (*abrév* **enseignement assisté par ordinateur**) CAL

EARL [aɛrɛl] NF *Écon* (*abrév* **Exploitation agricole à responsabilité limitée**) = farm registered as a limited company

EAU (*abrév écrite* **Émirats arabes unis**) UAE

EBIT [ebit] NM *Fin* (*abrév* **earnings before interest and tax**) EBIT

EBITDA [ebitta] NM *Fin* (*abrév* **earnings before interest, tax, depreciation and amortization**) EBITDA

EBS [əbeɛs] NF *Vét* (*abrév* **encéphalopathie bovine spongiforme**) BSE

EBV [əbeve] NM *Méd* (*abrév* **Epstein-Barr virus**) EBV

ECG [əseʒe] NM *Méd* (*abrév* **électrocardiogramme**) *Br* ECG, *Am* EKG

Ecofin [ekɔfin] NM *UE* (*abrév* **Economic Council of Finance Ministers**) Ecofin

écolo [ekɔlo] *Fam* ADJ (*abrév* **écologique, écologiste**) green

   NMF (*abrév* **écologiste**) environmentalist■

ÉCU, écu [eky] NM *Ancienne UE* (*abrév* **European Currency Unit**) ECU, ecu; **É. dur** hard ECU

éd. (*abrév écrite* **édition**) ed., edit

EDF [ədeɛf] NF (*abrév* **Électricité de France**) = French national electricity company

EDI [ədei] NM *Ordinat* (*abrév* **échange de données informatisé**) EDI

édit. (*abrév écrite* **éditeur**) publ.

EED [əəde] NM *Ordinat* (*abrév* **Échange Électronique de Données**) EDI

EEE [əəə] NM *Pol* (*abrév* **Espace économique européen**) EEA

EEG [əəʒe] NM *Méd* (*abrév* **électro-encéphalogramme**) EEG

EGA [əʒea] NM *Ordinat* (*abrév* **enhanced graphics adaptor**) EGA

ELSJ [əɛlɛsʒi] NM *UE* (*abrév* **Espace de liberté, de sécurité et de justice**) AFSJ

EMT [əɛmte] NM *Ancienne Scol* (*abrév* **éducation manuelle et technique**) = practical sciences

EN¹ [əɛn] NF *Ancienne Scol* (*abrév* **École normale**) = primary school teachers' training college

EN² (*abrév écrite* **Éducation Nationale**) (*ministère*) (French) Ministry *or* Department of Education; (*system*) state education (*in France*)

ENA [ena] NF *Admin & Pol* (*abrév* **École nationale d'administration**) = prestigious university-level college in France preparing students for senior posts in the civil service and public management

E-N-E (*abrév écrite* **Est-Nord-Est**) ENE

ENI [eni] NF **1** (*abrév* **École normale d'instituteurs**) = former primary school teachers' training college **2** (*abrév* **École nationale d'ingénieurs**) = one of five prestigious engineering schools throughout France

ENM [əɛnɛm] NF (*abrév* **École nationale de la magistrature**) = "grande école" for the judiciary

ENS [əɛnɛs] NF *Scol & Univ* (*abrév* **École normale supérieure**) = prestigious "grande école" for teachers and researchers

ENSA, Ensa [ɛnsa] NF *Univ* (*abrév* **École nationale supérieure agronomique**) = one of five competitive-entry agricultural engineering schools

ENSAD, Ensad [ɛnsad] NF *Scol & Univ* (*abrév* **École nationale supérieure des arts décoratifs**) = "grande école" for applied arts

ENSAM, Ensam [ɛnsam] NF (*abrév* **École nationale supérieure des arts et métiers**) = "grande école" for engineering

ENSBA *Scol & Univ* (*abrév écrite* **École nationale supérieure des Beaux-Arts**) = leading art school in Paris

ENSET, Enset [ɛnsɛt] NF *Scol & Univ* (*abrév* **École nationale supérieure de l'enseignement technique**) = "grande école" training science and technology teachers

ENSI, Ensi [ɛnsi] NF *Scol & Univ* (*abrév* **École nationale supérieure d'ingénieurs**) = competitive-entry engineering institute

env. (*abrév écrite* **environ**) approx.

EONIA [eonja] NM *Bourse* (*abrév* **Euro Overnight Index Average**) EONIA

EOR [əoɛr] NM *Mil* (*abrév* **élève officier de réserve**) military cadet

ephlet [eflɛ] NM (*abrév* **essai-pamphlet**) essay pamphlet

EPO [əpeo] NF *Physiol* (*abrév* **érythropoïétine**) EPO

eprom, EPROM [eprɔm] NF INV *Ordinat* (*abrév* **erasable programmable read-only memory**) EPROM

EPS [əpeɛs] NF *Scol* (*abrév* **éducation physique et sportive**) PE

   NM *Ordinat* (*abrév* **encapsulated PostScript**) EPS

E/S *Ordinat* (*abrév écrite* **entrée/sortie**) I/O

ESB [əɛsbe] NF *Vét* (*abrév* **encéphalopathie spongiforme bovine**) BSE

ESCP [əɛssepe] NF *Scol & Univ* (*abrév* **École supérieure de commerce de Paris**) = prestigious business and management school

E-S-E (*abrév écrite* **Est-Sud-Est**) ESE

ESEU [ezø] NM *Ancienne* (*abrév* **examen spécial d'entrée à l'université**) = university entrance examination

ESSEC, Essec [esɛk] NF *Scol & Univ* (*abrév* **École supérieure des sciences économiques et commerciales**) = "grande école" for management and business studies

ét. (*abrév écrite* **étage**) fl

ETA [ətea] NF *Pol* (*abrév* **Euskadi Ta Askatasuna**) ETA

etc. (*abrév écrite* **et cetera, et cætera**) etc

Ets *Com* (*abrév écrite* **établissements**) E. Legrand Legrand (& Co)

ETSI [əteɛsi] NM (*abrév* **European Telecommunications Standards Institute**) ETSI

ETTD, E.T.T.D. [ətetede] NM *Ordinat* (*abrév* **équipement terminal de traitement de données**) DTE

E-U (*abrév écrite* **États-Unis**) US

E-U A (*abrév écrite* **États-Unis d'Amérique**) USA

Euratom [øratɔm] NM *UE* (*abrév* **European Atomic Energy Commission**) Euratom

EURIBOR [øribɔr] NM *Bourse* (*abrév* **Euro Interbank Offered Rate**) EURIBOR

EURL [əyɛrɛl] NF *Com* (*abrév* **entreprise unipersonnelle à responsabilité limitée**) trader with limited liability

EV (*abrév écrite* **en ville**) by hand

eV (*abrév écrite* **électron-volt**) eV

ex. (*abrév écrite* **exemple**) eg, ex; **par e.** eg

exam [ɛgzam] NM *Fam* (*abrév* **examen**) exam■

exhibo [ɛgzibo] NMF *Fam* (*abrév* **exhibitionniste**) exhibitionist■

exo [ɛgzo] NM *Fam* (*abrév* **exercice**) exercise■

expo [ɛkspo] NF *Fam* (*abrév* **exposition**) exhibition■

expo-vente [ɛkspovãt] (*pl* **expos-ventes**) NF *Fam* (*abrév* **exposition-vente**) (*gén*) display■ (*where the items are for sale*); (*d'objets d'artisanat*) craft fair■

EXW [əiksdubləve] *Com* (*abrév* **ex-works**) EXW

F¹ [ɛf] NF *Sport* (*abrév* **Formule**) F; **la F1** F1

F² **1** (*abrév écrite* **franc**) F; **500 F** 500 F, F 500 **2** (*abrév écrite* **fahrenheit**) F **3** (*abrév écrite* **farad**) F **4** (*abrév écrite* **femme**) F

FAB [ɛfabe] ADJ INV & ADV *Com* (*abrév* **franco à bord**) FOB, fob

FAC [ɛfase] ADJ *Com* (*abrév* **franc d'avarie commune**) FGA, fga

   NM *Admin* (*abrév* **fonds d'aide et de coopération**) = French government fund which administers economic and social projects in former colonies

fac [fak] NF *Fam* (*abrév* **faculté**) university■, uni; **f. de droit/de lettres** faculty of law/arts■; **en f., à la f.** at university■ *or* college■, at uni; **être en f. d'allemand** to be studying German at uni

facob [fakɔb] NM *Assur* (*abrév* **traité facultatif obligatoire**) open cover

FAI [ɛfai] NM *Ordinat* (*abrév* **fournisseur d'accès à l'Internet**) IAP

famas [famas] NM *Mil* (*abrév* **fusil d'assaut de la manufacture d'armes de Saint-Étienne**) Famas rifle (*type of French assault rifle*)

FAO [ɛfao] NF **1** *Ind* (*abrév* **fabrication assistée par ordinateur**) CAM **2** (*abrév* **Food and Agricultural Organization**) FAO

FAP [ɛfape] ADJ *Assur* (*abrév* **franc d'avarie particulière**) FPA, fpa

FAQ [fak] *Ordinat* (*abrév* **frequently asked questions, foire aux questions**) FAQ

fax [faks] NM *Tél* (*abrév* **Téléfax**) **1** (*machine*) fax (machine); **par f.** by fax; **envoyer qch par f.** to send sth by fax, to fax sth; **numéro de f.** fax number; *Ordinat* **f. modem** fax modem **2** (*message*) fax; **f. sur papier ordinaire** plain paper fax

FB *Ancienne* (*abrév écrite* **franc belge**) BF

FBI [ɛfbiaj] NM (*abrév* **Federal Bureau of Investigation**) FBI

FC [ɛfse] NM (*abrév* **Football Club**) FC

FCA [ɛfsea] *Com* (*abrév* **free carrier**) FCA

f.c.é.m. [ɛfseeɛm] NF *Élec* (*abrév* **force contre-électromotrice**) cemf, bemf, opposing emf

FCFA (*abrév écrite* **franc CFA**) = currency used in former French colonies in Africa

FCFP (*abrév écrite* **franc CFP**) = currency used in former French colonies in the Pacific

fco *Com* (*abrév écrite* **franco**) franco

FCP [ɛfsepe] NM *Fin* (*abrév* **fonds commun de placement**) investment company *or* trust, mutual fund

FCPE [ɛfsepeə] NM *Fin* (*abrév* **fonds commun de placement d'entreprise**) company investment fund

FCPR [ɛfsepeɛr] NM *Fin* (*abrév* **fonds commun de placement à risques**) VCT

FDR [ɛfdeɛr] NM *Fin* (*abrév* **fonds de roulement**) working capital

FECOM [fekɔm] NM *Fin & UE* (*abrév* **Fonds européen de coopération monétaire**) EMCF

FED [ɛfəde] NM (*abrév* **Fonds européen de développement**) EDF

FEDER [fedɛr] NM (*abrév* **Fonds européen de développement régional**) ERDF

FEI [ɛfəi] NM (*abrév* **Fonds européen d'investissement**) EIF

FEN [fɛn] NF (*abrév* **Fédération de l'Éducation nationale**) = teachers' trade union, *Br* ≃ NUT

FEOGA [feoga] NM (*abrév* **Fonds européen d'orientation et de garantie agricole**) EAGGF

FF *Ancienne* (*abrév écrite* **franc français**) FF

FFA [ɛfɛfa] NFPL (*abrév* **Forces françaises en Allemagne**) = French forces in Germany

FFI [ɛfɛfi] NFPL *Hist* (*abrév* **Forces françaises de l'intérieur**) = French Resistance forces during World War II

FFL [ɛfɛfɛl] NFPL *Hist* (*abrév* **Forces françaises libres**) = free French Army during World War II

FFR [ɛfɛfɛr] NF (*abrév* **Fédération française de rugby**) = French rugby federation

fg (*abrév écrite* **faubourg**) suburb

FGA [ɛfʒea] NM (*abrév* **fonds de garantie automobile**) = fund financed through insurance premiums to compensate victims of uninsured losses

Fgaf [ɛfʒeaɛf] NF *Pol* (*abrév* **Fédération générale autonome des fonctionnaires**) = French civil servants' trade union

FGDS [ɛfʒedeɛs] NF (*abrév* **Fédération de la gauche démocrate et socialiste**) = former French socialist party

FGEN [ɛfʒeɛn] NF (*abrév* **Fédération générale de l'Éducation nationale**) = teachers' trade union

FIAC [fjak] NF (*abrév* **Foire internationale d'art contemporain**) = annual international contemporary art fair in Paris

FIF [ɛfif] NF (*abrév* **Fédération internationale du film**) FIF

FIFA [fifa] NF (*abrév* **Fédération internationale de football association**) FIFA

fig. (*abrév écrite* **figure**) fig.

FINUL, Finul [finyl] NF (*abrév* **Forces intérimaires des Nations unies au Liban**) UNI-FIL

FIP [fip] NF (*abrév* **France Inter Paris**) = Paris radio station broadcasting continuous music and traffic information

FIS [fis] NM (*abrév* **Front islamique du salut**) **le F.** the FIS, the Islamic Salvation Front

FIV [ɛfive] NF (*abrév* **fécondation in vitro**) IVF

FIVETE, fivete [fivɛt] NF (*abrév* **fécondation in vitro et transfert d'embryon**) GIFT; **une F.** a test-tube baby

FL (*abrév écrite* **florin**) Fl, F, G

fl. (*abrév écrite* **fleuve**) R

FLB [ɛfɛlbe] NM (*abrév* **Front de libération de la Bretagne**) = Breton liberation front
ADJ INV & ADV *Com* (*abrév* **franco long du bord**) FAS

FLE [flə] NM (*abrév* **français langue étrangère**) French as a foreign language

FLN [ɛfɛlɛn] NM *Hist* (*abrév* **Front de libération nationale**) = one of the main political parties in Algeria, established as a resistance movement in 1954 at the start of the war for independence

FLNC [ɛfɛlɛnse] NM (*abrév* **Front de libération nationale corse**) = Corsican liberation front

FLNKS [ɛfɛlɛnkaɛs] NM (*abrév* **Front de libération nationale kanak et socialiste**) = Kanak independence movement in New Caledonia

flops [flɔps] NM *Ordinat* (*abrév* **floating point operations per second**) FLOPS

FLQ¹ [ɛfɛlky] ADJ INV *Com* (*abrév* **franco long du quai**) FAQ

FLQ² [ɛfɛlky] NM (*abrév* **Front de Libération Québécois**) = militant political movement in favour of Quebec's independence in the 1960s

FM [ɛfɛm] NF (*abrév* **frequency modulation**) FM

FME [ɛfɛmə] NM (*abrév* **Fonds monétaire européen**) EMF

Fme (*abrév écrite* **femme**) F

FMI [ɛfɛmi] NM (*abrév* **Fonds monétaire international**) IMF

FMP [ɛfɛmpe] NM *Cin* (*abrév* **full motion picture**) FMP

FMV [ɛfɛmve] NM *Cin* (*abrév* **full motion vision**) FMV

FN [ɛfɛn] NM (*abrév* **Front national**) Front National (*French extreme right-wing political party*)

FNA [ɛfɛna] NF (*abrév* **Fédération nationale de l'artisanat automobile**) = French car mechanics' trade union

FNAC, Fnac [fnak] NF (*abrév* **Fédération**

nationale des achats des cadres**) = chain of large stores selling hi-fi, books etc

Fnap [fnap] NF (*abrév* **Fédération nationale autonome de la police**) = French police trade union

FNE [ɛfɛne] NM (*abrév* **Fonds national de l'emploi**) = state fund providing aid to jobseekers and workers who accept lower-paid work to avoid redundancy

FNEF, Fnef [fnɛf] NF (*abrév* **Fédération nationale des étudiants de France**) = students' union, *Br* ≃ NUS

FNGS [ɛfɛnʒeɛs] NM (*abrév* **Fonds national de garantie des salaires**) = national guarantee fund for the payment of salaries

FNI [ɛfɛni] NFPL *Mil* (*abrév* **Forces nucléaires intermédiaires**) INF

FNSEA [ɛfɛnsea] NF (*abrév* **Fédération nationale des syndicats d'exploitants agricoles**) = farmers' union, *Br* ≃ NFU

FO [ɛfo] NF (*abrév* **Force ouvrière**) = moderate workers' union (formed out of the split with Communist CGT in 1948)

FOB [fɔb, ɛfobe] ADJ INV *Com* (*abrév* **free on board**) FOB; **vente F.** FOB sale

foire-expo [fwarɛkspo] (*pl* **foires-expos**) NF *Fam* (*abrév* **foire-exposition**) trade fair ▪

FOR (*abrév écrite* **forint**) F, Ft

FORPRONU [fɔrprɔny] NF (*abrév* **Forces de protection des Nations unies**) UN-profor

FP (*abrév écrite* **franchise postale**) PP

FPA [ɛfpea] NF (*abrév* **formation professionnelle pour adultes**) adult education

FPLP [ɛfpɛlpe] NM (*abrév* **Front populaire de libération de la Palestine**) PFLP

FPU [ɛfpey] NF *Ordinat* (*abrév* **floating-point unit**) FPU

FR3 [ɛfɛrtrwa] NF (*abrév* **France Régions 3**) = former French state-owned television channel (now France 3)

FRBG [ɛfɛrbeʒe] NM (*abrév* **fonds pour risques bancaires généraux**) FGBR

FS (*abrév écrite* **franc suisse**) SFr

FSE [ɛfɛsə] NM **1** (*abrév* **foyer socio-éducatif**) ≃ community centre **2** (*abrév* **Fonds social européen**) ESF

FSM [ɛfɛsɛm] NF (*abrév* **Fédération syndicale mondiale**) WFTU
NM (*abrév* **Forum social mondial**) WSF

FSU [ɛfɛsy] NF (*abrév* **Fédération syndicale unitaire**) = French association of teachers' and lecturers' trade unions

FTP [ɛftepe] NM *Ordinat* (*abrév* **File Transfer Protocol**) FTP
NMPL *Hist* (*abrév* **Francs-tireurs et partisans**) = Communist resistance during World War II

FUNU, Funu [fyny] NF (*abrév* **Force d'urgence des Nations unies**) UNEF

FV (*abrév écrite* **fréquence vocale**) VF

G [ʒe] NM *Belg Fam* (*abrév* **GSM**) *Br* mobile, *Am* cell

g 1 (*abrév écrite* **gramme**) g **2** *Phys* (*abrév écrite* **gauss**) G **3** (*abrév écrite* **giga**) G **4** (*abrév écrite* **gauche**) L

G7 [ʒesɛt] NM (*abrév* **Groupe des Sept**) **le G7** G7

G8 [ʒeyit] NM (*abrév* **Groupe des Huit**) **le G8** G8

GAB [gab] (*abrév* **guichet automatique de banque**) *Br* ≃ Minibank, *Am* ≃ ATM

GAEC, G.A.E.C. [gaɛk] NM (*abrév* **groupement agricole d'exploitation en commun**) = farm run as a mini-cooperative

Gal (*abrév écrite* **Général**) Gen

GAO [ʒeao] NF (*abrév* **gestion assistée par ordinateur**) CAM, computer-aided management

GATT, Gatt [gat] NM (*abrév* **General Agreement on Tariffs and Trade**) GATT

GB, G-B (*abrév écrite* **Grande-Bretagne**) GB

gd (*abrév écrite* **grand**) lg.

GDB [ʒedebe] NF *Fam* (*abrév* **gueule de bois**) hangover ▪

GDF [ʒedeɛf] NM (*abrév* **Gaz de France**) = the French gas board

GEIE, G.E.I.E. [ʒeəiə] NM (*abrév* **groupement européen d'intérêt économique**) EEIG

GFU [ʒeɛfy] NM *Tél* (*abrév* **groupe fermé d'utilisateurs**) CUG

GHB [ʒeaʃbe] NM *Chim* (*abrév* **gamma-hydroxybutyrate**) GHB

GI, G.I. [dʒiaj] NM INV *Mil* (*abrév* **Government Issue**) GI

GIA [ʒeia] NM (*abrév* **Groupes islamiques armés**) GIA

GIC [ʒeise] NM **1** (*abrév* **grand invalide civil**) severely disabled person; **macaron G.** disabled sticker **2** (*abrév* **Groupe interministériel de contrôle**) interdepartmental regulatory committee

GIE, G.I.E. [ʒeiə] NM (*abrév* **groupement d'intérêt économique**) economic interest group

GIEC [geiəse] NM (*abrév* **Groupement intergouvernemental de l'étude du climat**) IPPC

GIF [geiɛf] NM *Ordinat* (*abrév* **Graphics Interchange Format**) GIF; **G. animé** animated GIF

GIG, G.I.G. [ʒeiʒe] NM (*abrév* **grand invalide de guerre**) = war invalid

GIGN [ʒeiʒeɛn] NM (*abrév* **Groupe d'intervention de la gendarmerie nationale**) = special crack force of the gendarmerie, *Br* ≃ SAS, *Am* ≃ SWAT

GM [ʒeɛm] NM **1** (*abrév* **gentil membre**) holidaymaker (*at Club Méditerranée*) **2** *Com* (*abrév* **grand magasin**) department store

GMS [ʒeɛmɛs] NFPL *Com* (*abrév* **grandes et moyennes surfaces**) large and medium-sized commercial outlets

GMT [ʒeɛmte] ADJ INV (*abrév* **Greenwich Mean Time**) GMT

GNL [ʒeɛnɛl] NM (*abrév* **gaz naturel liquéfié**) LNG

GO [ʒeo] NFPL *Rad* (*abrév* **grandes ondes**) LW
NM (*abrév* **gentil organisateur**) group leader (*at Club Méditerranée*)

Go NM *Ordinat* (*abrév* **gigaoctet**) GB

GODF [ʒeodeɛf] NM (*abrév* **Grand Orient de France**) = principal masonic lodge of France, *Br* ≃ United Grand Lodge of England

GPAO [ʒepeao] NF *Ordinat* (*abrév* **gestion de production assistée par ordinateur**) computer-aided production management

GPL [ʒepeɛl] NM (*abrév* **gaz de pétrole liquéfié**) LPG

GPRS [ʒepeɛrɛs] NM *Tél* (*abrév* **General Packet Radio Service**) GPRS

GPS [ʒepeɛs] NM *Tél* (*abrév* **global positioning system**) GPS

GQG [ʒekyʒe] NM (*abrév* **grand quartier général**) GHQ

GR® [ʒeɛr] NM (*abrév* **sentier de grande randonnée**) long-distance hiking path

gr (*abrév écrite* **grade**) grade, mark

GRETA, Greta [greta] NM (*abrév* **groupements d'établissements pour la formation continue**) = state body organizing adult training programmes

GRH [ʒeɛraʃ] NF (*abrév* **gestion des ressources humaines**) HRM

GSM [ʒeɛsɛm] NM *Tél* (*abrév* **global system for mobile communications**) **1** (*système*) GSM; **réseau G.** GSM network **2** *Belg* (*téléphone portable*) *Br* mobile phone, *Am* cellphone

GSS [ʒeɛsɛs] NF *Com* (*abrév* **grande surface spécialisée**) specialist superstore

Gud, GUD [gyd] NM (*abrév* **Groupe union défense**) = extreme right-wing student group

gynéco [ʒineko] NMF *Fam* (*abrév* **gynécologue**) gynaecologist ▪

H¹ [aʃ] NM INV *Fam* (*abrév* **haschisch**) hash, *Br* blow

H² (*abrév écrite* **homme**) M

h 1 (*abrév écrite* **heure**) hr; **2 h** 2 hrs; **à 2h** (*du matin*) at 2 am; (*du soir*) at 2 pm **2** (*abrév écrite* **hecto**) h

ha (*abrév écrite* **hectare**) ha

hab. (*abrév écrite* **habitants**) **50 000 h.** pop. 50,000

HALDE [ald] **NF** (*abrév* **Haute Autorité de Lutte contre les Discriminations et pour l'Égalité**) = independent authority set up to fight discrimination in France

hallu [aly] **NF** *Fam* (*abrév* **hallucination**) hallucination■; **je dois avoir des hallus!** I must be seeing things!

HCR [aʃeɛr] **NM** (*abrév* **Haut-Commissariat des Nations unies pour les réfugiés**) UNHCR

HD *Ordinat* (*abrév écrite* **haute densité**) HD

HD MAC [aʃdemak] **NM** (*abrév* **High Definition Multiplexed Analogue Components**) HD MAC

hdr (*abrév écrite* **heures des repas**) = at lunchtime or in the evening (*used in newspaper advertisements*)

HEC [aʃəse] **1 NF** (*abrév* **Hautes études commerciales**) = prestigious business school in Paris

2 NMF = graduate of the "HEC" business school

hecto [ɛkto] **NM** *Fam* **1** (*abrév* **hectogramme**) hectogramme■, hectogram■ **2** (*abrév* **hectolitre**) hectolitre■

hélico [eliko] **NM** *Fam* (*abrév* **hélicoptère**) chopper

hélio [eljo] **NF** *Fam* (*abrév* **héliogravure**) heliogravure■

héro [ero] **NF** *Fam* (*abrév* **héroïne**) smack, skag

hétéro [etero] *Fam* (*abrév* **hétérosexuel**) **ADJ** hetero, straight
NMF hetero, straight

HF *Tél* (*abrév écrite* **hautes fréquences**) HF

HIV [aʃive] **NM** (*abrév* **human immunodeficiency virus**) HIV; **être atteint du H.** to be HIV-positive

hl (*abrév écrite* **hectolitre**) hl

HLM [aʃɛlɛm] **NM OU NF** (*abrév* **habitation à loyer modéré**) (*immeuble*) *Br* ≃ block of council flats, *Am* ≃ public housing unit; (*appartement*) *Br* ≃ council flat, *Am* ≃ (apartment in a) public housing unit; (*maison*) *Br* ≃ council house, *Am* ≃ low-rent house

hm (*abrév écrite* **hectomètre**) hm

HO ADJ *Archit* (*abrév écrite* **hors œuvre**) out of alignment, projecting

homo [ɔmo] *Fam* (*abrév* **homosexuel**) **ADJ** gay
NMF gay

Horeca [ɔreka] **NM** *Belg* (*abrév* **hôtels, restaurants, cafés**) = hotels, cafés and restaurants (*collectively*)

HP¹ [aʃpe] **NM** *Fam* (*abrév* **hôpital psychiatrique**) psychiatric hospital■

HP² (*abrév écrite* **haut-parleur**) loudspeaker

HPA [aʃpea] **NF** *Aviat* (*abrév* **heure probable d'arrivée**) ETA

HPD [aʃpede] **NF** *Aviat* (*abrév* **heure probable de départ**) ETD

HR (*abrév écrite* **heures des repas**) = at lunchtime or in the evening (*used in newspaper advertisements*)

HS [aʃɛs] **ADJ** *Fam* (*abrév* **hors service**) (*appareil*) out of order■; (*personne*) *Br* knackered, shattered, *Am* bushed; **la télé est complètement H.** *Br* the telly's on the blink, *Am* the TV's on the fritz

HT ADJ *Com* (*abrév écrite* **hors taxe**) not including tax, exclusive of tax; **200 euros HT** 200 euros plus VAT
NF (*abrév écrite* **haute tension**) HT

HTML [aʃteɛmɛl] **NM** *Ordinat* (*abrév* **Hyper Text Markup Language**) HTML

HTTP [aʃtetepe] **NM** *Ordinat* (*abrév* **Hyper Text Transfer Protocol**) HTTP

hyper [ipɛr] **NM** *Fam* (*abrév* **hypermarché**) hypermarket■, superstore■

Hz (*abrév écrite* **hertz**) Hz

IA [ia] **NF** *Ordinat* (*abrév* **intelligence artificielle**) AI

IAC [iase] **NF** (*abrév* **insémination artificielle entre conjoints**) AIH

IAD [iade] **NF** (*abrév* **insémination artificielle par donneur extérieur**) DI, AID

IAO [iao] **NF** (*abrév* **ingénierie assistée par ordinateur**) CAE

IATA [jata] **NF** (*abrév* **Association internationale des transporteurs aériens**) IATA

ibid. (*abrév écrite* **ibidem**) ibid

IC [ise] **NM** *Math* (*abrév* **intervalle de confiance**) IC

ICBM [isebeɛm] **NM INV** (*abrév* **Intercontinental Ballistic Missile**) ICBM

id. (*abrév écrite* **idem**) id

IDA [idea] **NF** *Méd* (*abrév* **insémination par donneur anonyme**) = AID

IDH [ideaʃ] **NM** *Écon* (*abrév* **indicateur de développement humain**) HDI

IDHEC [idɛk] **NM** *Anciennement* (*abrév* **Institut des hautes études cinématographiques**) = former French film school

IDS [ideɛs] **NF** *Mil* (*abrév* **initiative de défense stratégique**) SDI

IED [iade] **NM** (*abrév* **investissement étranger direct**) FDI

IEP [iape] **NM** (*abrév* **Institut d'études politiques**) = "grande école" for political science

IFOP, Ifop [ifɔp] **NM** *Mktg* (*abrév* **Institut français d'opinion publique**) = French market research institute

Ifremer [ifrəmɛr] **NM** (*abrév* **Institut français de recherche pour l'exploitation de la mer**) = French research establishment for marine resources

IG [iʒe] **NM** *Méd* (*abrév* **index glycémique**) GI

IGEN [iʒeaɛn] **NM** *Scol* (*abrév* **Inspecteur général de l'Éducation nationale**) = high-ranking education inspector

IGF [iʒeɛf] **NM INV** *Anciennement* Fin (*abrév* **impôt sur les grandes fortunes**) wealth tax

IGH [iʒeaʃ] **NM** (*abrév* **immeuble de grande hauteur**) = very high building

IGN [iʒeɛn] **NM** (*abrév* **Institut géographique national**) = French national geographical institute, *Br* ≃ Ordnance Survey, *Am* ≃ United States Geological Survey

IGP [iʒepe] **NF** *Com* (*abrév* **indication géographique protégée**) = designation of a product which guarantees its authentic place of origin and gives the name protected status

IGPN [iʒepeɛn] **NF** (*abrév* **Inspection générale de la police nationale**) = police disciplinary body, *Br* ≃ Police Committee

IGS [iʒeɛs] **NF** (*abrév* **Inspection générale des services**) = police disciplinary body for Paris, *Br* ≃ Metropolitan Police Commission

IHS [iaʃɛs] **NM** *Rel* (*abrév* **Iesus Homimum Salvator**) IHS

ILM [iɛlɛm] **NM** (*abrév* **immeuble à loyer moyen**) = apartment building with low-rent accommodation (more expensive than an HLM)

ILN [iɛln] **NM** (*abrév* **immeuble à loyer normal**) = apartment building with low-rent accommodation

ILV [iɛlve] **NF** *Mktg* (*abrév* **information sur le lieu de vente**) point-of-sale information

IMA [ima] **NM** (*abrév* **Institut du monde arabe**) = Arab cultural centre and library in Paris holding regular exhibitions of Arab art

IMAO [imao] **NM** *Pharm* (*abrév* **inhibiteur de la monoamine-oxydase**) MAOI

IMC [iɛmse] **NM** *Méd* **1** (*abrév* **indice de masse corporelle**) BMI **2** (*abrév* **infirme**

moteur cérébral) person suffering from cerebral palsy
NF (*abrév* **infirmité motrice cérébrale**) cerebral palsy

IME [iɛmə] **NM** **1** *Écon* (*abrév* **Institut monétaire européen**) EMI **2** (*abrév* **Institut médico-éducatif**) special needs school

impro [ɛ̃pro] **NF** *Fam Mus & Théât* (*abrév* **improvisation**) improv

INA [ina] **NM** **1** (*abrév* **Institut national de l'audiovisuel**) = national television archive **2** (*abrév* **Institut national d'agronomie**) = "grande école" for agricultural studies

INC [iɛnse] **NM** (*abrév* **Institut national de la consommation**) = national institute for consumer advice, *Br* ≃ National Consumer Council

indé, -e [ɛ̃de] **ADJ** *Fam* (*abrév* **indépendant**) indie; **le rock i.** indie (rock)

INED, Ined [inɛd] **NM** (*abrév* **Institut national d'études démographiques**) = national institute for demographic research

INPI [iɛnpei] **NM** (*abrév* **Institut national de la propriété intellectuelle**) French National Patent Office

INR [iɛnɛr] **NM** *Belg* (*abrév* **Institut national de radiodiffusion**) = Belgian broadcasting company

INRA, Inra [inra] **NM** (*abrév* **Institut national de la recherche agronomique**) = national institute for agronomic research

INSEAD [insead] **NM** (*abrév* **Institut européen d'administration**) = European business school in Fontainebleau

INSEE, Insee [inse] **NM** (*abrév* **Institut national de la statistique et des études économiques**) = French national institute for statistical and economic studies

INSERM, Inserm [insɛrm] **NM** (*abrév* **Institut national de la santé et de la recherche médicale**) = national institute for medical research

interro [ɛ̃tero] **NF** *Fam Arg scol* (*abrév* **interrogation**) test■

intro [ɛ̃tro] **NF** *Fam* (*abrév* **introduction**) intro; (*musicale*) theme tune■

inv. (*abrév écrite* **invariable**) inv

IOM [ioɛm] **NM** *Pétr* (*abrév* **indice d'octane moteur**) MON

IOR [ioɛr] **NM** *Pétr* (*abrév* **indice d'octane recherche**) RON

IP [ipe] **NM** (*abrév* **indice de protection**) SPF

IPC [ipese] **NM** *Mktg* (*abrév* **indice des prix à la consommation**) CPI

IPP [ipepe] **NM** *Écon* (*abrév* **indice des prix à la production**) PPI

IPR [ipeɛr] **NM** (*abrév* **Inspecteur pédagogique régional**) = locally-based education inspector

IR [iɛr] **ADJ** (*abrév* **infrarouge**) IR

IRA [ira] **NF** (*abrév* **Irish Republican Army**) IRA; **l'I. provisoire** the Provisional IRA

IRBM [iɛrbeɛm] **NM** (*abrév* **intermediate range ballistic missile**) IRBM

IRC [iɛrse] **NM** *Ordinat* (*abrév* **Internet Relay Chat**) IRC

IRM [iɛrɛm] **NF** *Méd* (*abrév* **imagerie par résonance magnétique**) MRI

IRMf [iɛrɛmɛf] **NF** *Méd* (*abrév* **imagerie par résonance magnétique fonctionnelle**) fMRI

IRMN [iɛrɛmɛn] **NF** *Méd* (*abrév* **imagerie par résonance magnétique nucléaire**) NMRI

IRPP [iɛrpepe] **NM** (*abrév* **impôt sur le revenu des personnes physiques**) income tax

IRSM [iɛrɛsɛm] **NM** *Mktg* (*abrév* **impact sur la rentabilité de la stratégie marketing**) PIMS

ISA [iɛsa] **NM** *Mktg* (*abrév* **imprimé sans adresse**) mailshot

ISAF [izaf] **NF** (*abrév* **International Sailing Federation**) ISAF

ISBN [iɛsbeɛn] **NM** (*abrév* **International standard book number**) (numéro) I. ISBN

ISF [iɛsɛf] **NM** *Fin* (*abrév* **impôt de solidarité sur la fortune**) wealth tax

ISMH [iɛsɛmaʃ] **NM** (*abrév* **inventaire supplémentaire des monuments historiques**) register of listed buildings; **château classé I.** = château classed as a listed building

ISO [izo] NF Phot (abrév **International Standards Organization**) ISO

ISRS [iɛsɛrɛs] NM Pharm (abrév **inhibiteur sélectif de recapture de la sérotonine**) SSRI

ISSN [iɛsɛsɛn] NM (abrév **International standard serial number**) (**numéro**) **l.** ISSN

IST [iɛstɛ] NF (abrév **infection sexuellement transmissible**) STI

ITER [itɛr] NM Phys (abrév **International Thermonuclear Experimental Reactor**) ITER

ITP [itepe] NM (abrév **ingénieur des travaux publics**) civil engineer

IUFM [iyɛfɛm] NM (abrév **Institut universitaire de formation des maîtres**) = teacher-training college

IUP [iype] NM (abrév **Institut universitaire professionnel**) = business school

IUT [iyte] NM (abrév **Institut universitaire de technologie**) = institute of technology offering two-year vocational courses leading to the DUT qualification

IV [ive] ADJ Méd (abrév **intra-veineux**) IV

IVG [iveʒe] NF (abrév **interruption volontaire de grossesse**) termination (of pregnancy)

J¹ [ʒi] NM (abrév **jour**) day; Hist & Fig **le jour J** D-day

J² (abrév écrite **joule**) J

JAC, Jac [ʒiasɛ] NF (abrév **Jeunesse agricole chrétienne**) = Christian youth organization

JAPD [ʒiapede] NF (abrév **journée d'appel de préparation à la défense**) = day during which young people are introduced to issues connected with national security

JAT [ʒiate] ADJ (abrév **juste-à-temps**) JIT

J.-C. (abrév écrite **Jésus-Christ**) J.C.; **en (l'an) 180 avant/après J.-C.** in (the year) 180 BC/AD 180

JCR [ʒisɛɛr] NF (abrév **Jeunesse communiste révolutionnaire**) = Communist youth movement

JEC, Jec [ʒiəse] NF (abrév **Jeunesse étudiante chrétienne**) = Christian youth organization

JF, jf 1 (abrév écrite **jeune fille**) girl **2** (abrév écrite **jeune femme**) young woman

JH, jh (abrév écrite **jeune homme**) young man

JMF [ʒiɛmɛf] NFPL (abrév **Jeunesses musicales de France**) = association promoting music for the young

JO [ʒio] NM Admin (abrév **Journal Officiel**) = French government publication giving information to the public about new laws, parliamentary debates, government business and new companies, Br ≃ Hansard, Am ≃ Federal Register

NMPL (abrév **jeux Olympiques**) Olympic Games

JOC, Joc [ʒiose] NF (abrév **Jeunesse ouvrière chrétienne**) = Christian youth organization

JPEG [ʒipɛg] NM Ordinat (abrév **Joint Photographic Experts Group**) JPEG

JRI [ʒiɛri] NMF Presse (abrév **journaliste reporter d'images**) reporter-cameraman

JT [ʒite] NM (abrév **journal télévisé**) TV news

K Ordinat (abrév écrite **kilo-octet**) K

k (abrév écrite **kilo**) k

K7 [kasɛt] NF (abrév **cassette**) cassette; **radio-K7** radiocassette

Kb (abrév écrite **kilobit**) Kb

keV (abrév écrite **kiloélectronvolt**) keV

KF [kaɛf] NM Anciennement (abrév **kilofranc**) thousand francs; **son salaire annuel est**
de 100 KF he/she earns 100,000 francs a year

kg (abrév écrite **kilogramme**) kg

kHz (abrév écrite **kilohertz**) kHz

kilo [kilo] NM Fam (abrév **kilogramme**) kilo

kiné [kine] NMF Fam (abrév **kinésithérapeute**) physio

kJ (abrév écrite **kilojoule**) kJ

km (abrév écrite **kilomètre**) km

km/h (abrév écrite **kilomètre par heure**) kmph

KO [kao] NM Ordinat (abrév **kilo-octet**) K, KB; **une disquette de 720 KO** a 720K diskette

K-O [kao] (abrév **knock-out**) NM INV KO; **K. technique** technical knockout

  ADJ INV **1** Sport KO'd; **mettre qn K.** to knock sb out; **être K.** to be out for the count **2** Fam (épuisé) all in, dead beat, Br shattered; **mettre qn K.** to exhaust sb■

ko/s Ordinat (abrév écrite **kilo-octets par seconde**) kbps

KRD (abrév écrite **couronne danoise**) Kr, DKr

KRN (abrév écrite **couronne norvégienne**) Kr, NKr

KRS (abrév écrite **couronne suédoise**) Kr, SKr

kW (abrév écrite **kilowatt**) kW

kWh (abrév écrite **kilowattheure**) kW/hr

l (abrév écrite **litre**) l

labo [labo] NM Fam (abrév **laboratoire**) lab; **l. de langues** language lab; **l. photo** darkroom■

lat. (abrév écrite **latitude**) lat

LAV [ɛlave] NM Méd (abrév **lymphadenopathy associated virus**) LAV

l/c Banque (abrév écrite **lettre de crédit**) L/C

LCD [ɛlsede] NM Électron (abrév **liquid crystal display**) LCD; **écran LCD** LCD screen

LCE [ɛlseø] NM Univ (abrév **Langue et civilisation étrangères**) espagnol/anglais L. Spanish/English language and civilization

LCR [ɛlsɛɛr] NF **1** Fin (abrév **lettre de change relevé**) bills of exchange statement **2** Pol (abrév **ligue communiste révolutionnaire**) = militant Trotskyist organization

LDL-cholestérol [ɛldeɛlkɔlɛstɛrɔl] NM Méd (abrév **low-density lipoprotein-cholesterol**) LDL-cholesterol

LDR [ɛldeɛr] NM Électron (abrév **light dependent resistor**) LDR

LEA [ɛləa] NFPL Univ (abrév **langues étrangères appliquées**) = applied modern languages

LED [ɛlɛde] NF Électron (abrév **light emitting diode**) LED

LEP, Lep [lɛp] NM **1** Anciennement (abrév **lycée d'enseignement professionnel**) = former name for a "lycée professionnel" **2** Banque (abrév **livret d'épargne populaire**) = special tax-exempt savings account **3** (abrév **Large Electron-Positron collider**) LEP

LFAJ [ɛlɛfaʒi] NF (abrév **Ligue française des auberges de jeunesse**) = French youth hostel association

LICRA [likra] NF (abrév **Ligue internationale contre le racisme et l'antisémitisme**) = anti-racist movement

lidar [lidar] NM Tech (abrév **light detection and ranging**) lidar

Lieut. (abrév écrite **Lieutenant**) Lieut

Lieut.-col. (abrév écrite **Lieutenant-colonel**) Lieut.-Col

LIFO [lifo] NM Com & Compta (abrév **last in first out**) LIFO

lino [lino] NM Fam (abrév **linoléum**) linoleum■, Br lino -

LISP [lisp] NM Ordinat (abrév **list processing**) LISP

LIT (abrév écrite **lire italienne**) L, Lit

litho [lito] NF Fam (abrév **lithographie**) litho

LJM Com (abrév écrite **livraison le jour même**) same-day delivery

lm (abrév écrite **lumen**) lm

LMD [ɛlɛmde] ADJ Univ (abrév **licence, master, doctorat**) **système (européen) L.** European Bachelors, Masters, Doctorate system (aimed at standardizing university qualifications across the EU)

LMDS [ɛlɛmdeɛs] NM Tél (abrév **local multipoint distribution system**) LMDS

LMNH [ɛlɛmɛnaʃ] NM Méd (abrév **lymphome malin non hodgkinien**) NHML

LNH [ɛlɛnaʃ] NM Méd (abrév **lymphome non hodgkinien**) NHL

LNPA [ɛlɛnpea] NF Ordinat & Tél (abrév **ligne numérique à paire asymétrique**) ADSL

LO [ɛlo] NF (abrév **Lutte ouvrière**) = militant Trotskyist organization

LOA [ɛloa] NF Com (abrév **location avec option d'achat**) lease financing

loc. cit. (abrév écrite **loco citato**) loc. cit.

loco [loko] NF Fam (abrév **locomotive**) loco

long. (abrév écrite **longitude**) long

loran [lɔrã] NM (abrév **Long Range Aid to Navigation**) loran

LP [ɛlpe] NM **1** (abrév **lycée professionnel**) vocational high school **2** (abrév **Long Playing**) LP

LPG [ɛlpeʒe] NM Belg (abrév **Liquid Petroleum Gas**) LPG

LPO [ɛlpeo] NF (abrév **Ligue pour la protection des oiseaux**) = society for the protection of birds, Br ≃ RSPB

LSD [ɛlɛsde] NM (abrév **lysergic acid diethylamide**) LSD

LSI [ɛlɛsi] NF Ordinat (abrév **large scale integration**) LSI

lx (abrév écrite **lux**) lx

M 1 (abrév écrite **million**) M **2** (abrév écrite **masculin**) M **3** (abrév écrite **méga**) M **4** Mil (abrév écrite **Major**) M **5** Naut (abrév écrite **mile (marin)**) nm **6** Anciennement Élec (abrév écrite **maxwell**) Mx

m 1 (abrév écrite **mètre**) **60 m** 60 m **2** (abrév écrite **milli**) m

M. (abrév écrite **Monsieur**) Mr

Mo (abrév écrite **métro**) metro

MA [ɛma] NM Anciennement Scol (abrév **maître auxiliaire**) Br supply or Am substitute teacher

mac [mak] NM Fam (abrév **maquereau**) pimp, Am mack

macro [makro] NF Ordinat (abrév **macro-instruction**) macro

MAIF [maif] NF (abrév **Mutuelle assurance des instituteurs de France**) = mutual insurance company for primary-school teachers in France

MAL, Mal¹ [mal] NF (abrév **maison d'animation et des loisirs**) ≃ cultural centre

Mal² Mil (abrév écrite **maréchal**) marshal

MAN [ɛmaɛn] NMF Can Pol (abrév **Membre de l'Assemblée Nationale**) MNA

manif [manif] NF Fam (abrév **manifestation**) demo; **une m. lycéenne/étudiante** a student demo

MAS [mas] NF (abrév **Maison d'accueil spécialisée**) = nursing home for severely disabled people

maso [mazo] Fam (abrév **masochiste**) ADJ masochistic■; **t'es m. ou quoi?** you're a real glutton for punishment; **je ne vais pas lui dire la vérité tout de suite, je ne suis pas m.** I won't tell him/her the truth right away, I'm not a masochist; **t'es complètement m. d'avoir accepté!** you must be a masochist or a glutton for punishment if you agreed!

  NMF masochist■; **c'est un m.** he's a glutton for punishment or a masochist

MATIF, Matif [matif] NM **1** Bourse (abrév **Marché à terme international de France**) = body regulating activities on the French

stock exchange **2** *Fin* (*abrév* **Marché à terme des instruments financiers**) financial futures market; *Br* ≃ LIFFE, *Am* ≃ CBOE

MAV [ɛmave] NM *Mktg* (*abrév* **marketing après-vente**) after-sales marketing

max [maks] NM *Fam* (*abrév* **maximum**) **1** *(peine)* maximum sentence■; **il a écopé du m.** he got the maximum sentence *or Am* rap, *Br* he copped the full whack

2 *(locution)* **un m.** loads, lots; **ça va te coûter un m.** it's going to cost you a packet *or Br* a bomb; **on s'est éclaté un m.** we had a really fantastic time; **il débloque un m.** he's totally off his rocker; **il en a rajouté un m.** he went completely overboard; **assurer un m.** to do brilliantly; **sur scène ils assurent un m.** they really rock on stage; **un m. de fric** loads of money; **un m. de monde/de voitures** stacks *or* a ton of people/cars

max. (*abrév écrite* **maximum**) max

Mb *Ordinat* (*abrév écrite* **mégabit**) Mb

MBA¹ [ɛmbea] NF *Compta* (*abrév* **marge brute d'autofinancement**) cashflow, funds generated by operations

MBA² [ɛmbie] NM (*abrév* **Master of Business Administration**) MBA

Mbps *Ordinat* (*abrév écrite* **mégabits par seconde**) mbps

MCAC [ɛmsease] NM(*abrév* **Marché commun d'Amérique centrale**) CACM

MCCA [ɛmsesea] NM(*abrév* **Marché commun centraméricain**) CACM

MCJ [ɛmseʒi] NF (*abrév* **maladie de Creutzfeldt-Jakob**) CJD

MDD [ɛmdede] NF *Com* (*abrév* **marque de distributeur**) distributor's brand name, own brand

MDR *Ordinat & Tél* (*abrév écrite* **mort de rire**) LOL

Me (*abrév écrite* **Maître**) = title for lawyers

Mec Art, Mec'Art [mɛkart] NM *Beaux-Arts* (*abrév* **Mechanical Art**) Mec Art

MÉDAF [medaf] NM *Fin* (*abrév* **modèle d'évaluation des actifs**) CAPM

Medef [medɛf] NM (*abrév* **Mouvement des Entreprises de France**) French employers' association, *Br* ≃ CBI

MEG [ɛmɔʒe] NM *Méd* (*abrév* **magnétoencéphalographie**) MEG

MEM [ɛm] NF *Ordinat* (*abrév* **mémoire morte**) ROM

Mercosur [mɛrkosyr] NM *Écon* (*abrév* **Marché commun du cône sud**) Mercosur

MEV [mɛv] NF *Ordinat* (*abrév* **mémoire vive**) RAM

MeV (*abrév écrite* **méga-électronvolts**) MeV

MF¹ [ɛmɛf] NF *Rad* (*abrév* **modulation de fréquence**) FM

MF² *Anciennement* **1** (*abrév écrite* **mark finlandais**) Mk, Fmk **2** (*abrév écrite* **million de francs**) a million francs, one million francs; **10 MF** 10 million francs

Mflops *Ordinat* (*abrév écrite* **mégaflops**) Mflop

mg (*abrév écrite* **milligramme**) mg

Mgr. *Rel* (*abrév écrite* **Monseigneur**) Mgr

MHD [ɛmaʃde] NF *Phys* (*abrév* **magnétohydrodynamique**) MHD

MHz [ɛmaʃzɛt] NM (*abrév* **megahertz**) MHz

MIDEM, Midem [midɛm] NM (*abrév* **Marché international du disque et de l'édition musicale**) = trade fair for the music industry which takes place annually in Cannes

MIDI [midi] NM (*abrév* **musical instrument digital interface**) MIDI

MIME [mim] NM *Ordinat* (*abrév* **Multipurpose Internet Mail Extensions**) MIME

MIN [min] NM (*abrév* **marché d'intérêt national**) = wholesale market for agricultural produce

min (*abrév écrite* **minute**) min

min. (*abrév écrite* **minimum**) min

minimex [minimɛks] NM *Belg* (*abrév* **minimum de moyens d'existence**) *Br* ≃ income support, *Am* ≃ welfare

MINUK [minyk] NF (*abrév* **Mission d'administration intérimaire des Nations Unies au Kosovo**) UNMIK

MIPS [mips] NM *Ordinat* (*abrév* **million d'instructions par seconde**) MIPS

MIP-TV [miptevɛ] NF (*abrév* **marché international des programmes de télévision**) = trade fair for the television industry which takes place annually in Cannes

MIRV [mirv] NM *Nucl* (*abrév* **multiple independently targetable reentry vehicle**) MIRV

Mis (*abrév écrite* **Marquis**) Marquis, Marquess

Mise (*abrév écrite* **Marquise**) Marchioness

MJC [ɛmʒise] NF(*abrév* **maison des jeunes et de la culture**) community centre

MJPEG [ɛmʒipɛg] NM *Ordinat* (*abrév* **Moving Joint Photographic Expert Group**) MJPEG

ml (*abrév écrite* **millilitre**) ml

MLF [ɛmlɛf] NM (*abrév* **Mouvement de libération de la femme**) = women's movement, *Am* ≃ NOW

Mlle (*abrév écrite* **Mademoiselle**) Miss

Mlles (*abrév écrite* **Mesdemoiselles**) Misses

mm (*abrév écrite* **millimètre(s)**) mm

MM. (*abrév écrite* **Messieurs**) Messrs

Mme (*abrév écrite* **Madame**) *(femme mariée)* Mrs; *(femme mariée ou célibataire)* Ms

Mmes (*abrév écrite* **Mesdames**) Ladies

MMPI [ɛmɛmpei] NM *Psy* (*abrév* **Minnesota multiphasic personality inventory**) MMPI

MMS [ɛmɛmɛs] NM *Tél* (*abrév* **multimedia message service**) MMS

MNR [ɛmɛnɛr] NM (*abrév* **Mouvement National Républicain**) = right-wing French political party

MNS [ɛmɛnɛs] NM (*abrév* **maître nageur sauveteur**) lifeguard

Mo [ɛmo] NM *Ordinat* (*abrév* **mégaoctet**) MB, Mb

M-octet *Ordinat* (*abrév écrite* **mégaoctet**) MB, Mb

MONEP [mɔnɛp] NM *Bourse* (*abrév* **marché des options négociables à Paris**) MONEP *(Paris traded options exchange)*, *Br* ≃ LIFFE, *Am* ≃ CBOE

mops *Ordinat* (*abrév écrite* **mégaoctets par seconde**) MBps, Mbps

MOS [ɛmoɛs] NM *Ordinat* (*abrév* **métal oxyde semiconducteur**) MOS; **M. à canal N** NMOS; **M. à canal P** PMOS; **M. complémentaire** complementary MOS

mouv' [muv] NM *Fam* (*abrév* **mouvement**) **c'est dans le m.** it's dead hip, it's totally cool

MOX [mɔks] NM *Nucl* (*abrév* **mixte oxyde**) MOX; **combustible M.** MOX fuel

MPEG [ɛmpɛg] NM *Ordinat* (*abrév* **Moving Pictures Expert Group**) MPEG

MRAM [ɛmram] NF *Ordinat* (*abrév* **magnetic random access memory**) MRAM

MRAP [mrap] NM (*abrév* **Mouvement contre le racisme, l'antisémitisme et pour la paix**) = pacifist anti-racist organization

MRBM [ɛmɛrbɛɛm] NM(*abrév* **medium range ballistic missile**) MRBM

MRG [ɛmɛrʒe] NM (*abrév* **Mouvement des radicaux de gauche**) = left-wing political grouping of local councillors

MRJC [ɛmɛrʒise] NM (*abrév* **Mouvement rural des Jeunesses chrétiennes**) = Catholic youth movement in rural areas

MRP [ɛmɛrpe] NM (*abrév* **Mouvement républicain populaire**) = centre-right political group influential under the Fourth Republic

ms (*abrév écrite* **manuscrit**) ms

MSBS [ɛmɛsbeɛs] NM *Nucl* (*abrév* **mer-sol balistique stratégique**) SLBM

MS-DOS [ɛmɛsdɔs] NM *Ordinat* (*abrév* **Microsoft Disk Operating System**) MS-DOS

MSF [ɛmɛsɛf] NM (*abrév* **Médecins sans frontières**) = organization providing medical aid to victims of war and disasters, especially in the Third World

MSO [ɛmɛso] NM *TV* (*abrév* **multiple system operator**) MSO

MST¹ [ɛmɛste] NF (*abrév* **maladie sexuellement transmissible**) STD

MST² [ɛmɛste] NF *Univ* (*abrév* **maîtrise de sciences et techniques**) = master's degree in science and technology; **M. hôtellerie-restauration** = higher vocational qualification in hotel management and catering

MT (*abrév écrite* **moyenne tension**) MT

MTS [ɛmtɛes] NF *Can* (*abrév* **maladie transmissible sexuellement**) STD

m.t.s. *Anciennement* (*abrév écrite* **mètre, tonne, seconde**) M.T.S.

muscu [mysky] NF*Fam* (*abrév* **musculation**) body-building (exercises)■; **faire de la m.** to do body-building■, to pump iron

N 1 (*abrév écrite* **newton**) N **2** (*abrév écrite* **nord**) N

n 1 (*abrév écrite* **numéro**) no. **2** (*abrév écrite* **nano**) n

NAP [nap] (*abrév* **Neuilly-Auteuil-Passy**) ADJ *Br* ≃ Sloaney, Sloany, *Am* ≃ preppy

▸ NMF *Br* ≃ Sloane (Ranger), *Am* ≃ preppy type

NASA, Nasa [naza] NF (*abrév* **National Aeronautics and Space Administration**) NASA, Nasa

Nasdaq® [nasdak] NM *Écon* (*abrév* **National Association of Securities Dealers Automated Quotation**) Nasdaq®

Natel® [natɛl] NM INV *Suisse* (*abrév* **national Telefon**) *Br* mobile (phone), *Am* cellphone

NB (*abrév écrite* **nota bene**) NB

NBC [ɛnbese] ADJ *Mil* (*abrév* **nucléaire, biologique, chimique**) NBC

nbreuses (*abrév écrite* **nombreuses**) many

nbrx (*abrév écrite* **nombreux**) many

n.c. 1 (*abrév écrite* **non communiqué**) n/a **2** (*abrév écrite* **non connu**) n/a

N.-D. (*abrév écrite* **Notre-Dame**) OL

n.d. 1 (*abrév écrite* **non daté**) nd **2** (*abrév écrite* **non disponible**) n/a

NDA (*abrév écrite* **note de l'auteur**) = author's note

NDLR (*abrév écrite* **note de la rédaction**) Ed.

NDT (*abrév écrite* **note du traducteur**) translator's note

N-E (*abrév écrite* **Nord-Est**) NE

NEI [ɛnɔi] NM (*abrév* **Nouvel État Indépendant**) newly independent state, NIS

nemi [nemi] NM (*abrév* **nouvelle échelle métrique de l'intelligence**) = test which evaluates the mental age of children between the ages of three and twelve

NF [ɛnɛf] NF (*abrév* **Norme française**) = label indicating compliance with official French standards, *Br* ≃ BS, *Am* ≃ US standard

NGV [ɛnʒeve] NM *Naut* (*abrév* **navire à grande vitesse**) = high-speed boat

NICAM [nikam] NM INV (*abrév* **near instantaneously companded audio multiplex**) NICAM, Nicam

nida [nida] NM *Tech* (*abrév* **nid-d'abeilles**) honeycomb

NIP [nip] NM *Can Banque* (*abrév* **numéro d'identification personnel**) ≃ PIN (number)

NL (*abrév écrite* **nouvelle lune**) new moon

NN (*abrév écrite* **nouvelle norme**) = revised standard of hotel classification

N-N-E (*abrév écrite* **Nord-Nord-Est**) NNE

N-N-O (*abrév écrite* **Nord-Nord-Ouest**) NNW

NNTP [ɛnɛntepe] NM *Ordinat* (*abrév* **Network News Transfer Protocol**) NNTP

no., no (*abrév écrite* **numéro**) no.

N-O (*abrév écrite* **Nord-Ouest**) NW

NPF [ɛnpeɛf] NF (*abrév* **nation plus favorisée**) MFN

NPI [ɛnpei] NM (*abrév* **nouveau pays industrialisé**) NIC

▸ NMPL (*abrév* **nouveaux pays industrialisés**) NICs

N/Réf (*abrév écrite* **Notre référence**) our ref
NRF [ɛnɛʀɛf] NF (*abrév* **Nouvelle Revue française**) **1** (*revue*) = literary review **2** (*mouvement*) = literary movement
N.-S. (*abrév écrite* **Notre-Seigneur**) Our Lord
N.-S. J.-C. (*abrév écrite* **Notre-Seigneur Jésus-Christ**) = Our Lord Jesus Christ
NSP (*abrév écrite* **Notre Saint Père**) = Our Holy Father
NT Rel (*abrév écrite* **Nouveau Testament**) NT
NTI [ɛnei] NFPL (*abrév* **nouvelles technologies de l'information**) NIT
NTSC [ɛnteɛsse] NM (*abrév* **National television system committee**) NTSC
NVOD [ɛnveode] NM (*abrév* **near video-on-demand**) NVOD

O [o] (*abrév écrite* **Ouest**) W
OAA [oɑɑ] NF (*abrév* **Organisation des Nations unies pour l'alimentation et l'agriculture**) FAO
OACI [oɑsei] NF (*abrév* **Organisation de l'aviation civile internationale**) ICAO
OAS [oɑɛs] NF Hist (*abrév* **Organisation armée secrète**) OAS (*French terrorist organization which opposed Algerian independence in the 1960s*)
OAT [oɑte] NF Fin (*abrév* **obligation assimilable du Trésor**) = French government bond
OBSA [opsɑ] NF Fin (*abrév* **obligation avec bon de souscription d'actions**) bond with share warrant attached
OC Rad (*abrév écrite* **ondes courtes**) SW
OCA [osɑ] NF Bourse & Fin (*abrév* **obligation convertible en actions**) convertible bond, convertible
OCDE [osedǝ] NF (*abrév* **Organisation de coopération et de développement économiques**) OECD
OCR [osɛʀ] NF (*abrév* **optical character recognition**) OCR
ODE [odǝ] NF Mktg (*abrév* **occasion d'entendre**) opportunity to hear
ODV [odeve] NF Mktg (*abrév* **occasion de voir**) opportunity to see
OEA [oǝɑ] NF (*abrév* **Organisation des États américains**) OAS
OEB [oǝbe] NM (*abrév* **Office européen des brevets**) EPO
OECE [oǝsǝɑ] NF (*abrév* **Organisation européenne de coopération économique**) OEEC
OFCE [oɛfsɑ] NM (*abrév* **Observatoire français des conjonctures économiques**) = economic research institute
OFPRA [ɔfpʀɑ] NM (*abrév* **Office français de protection des réfugiés et des apatrides**) = government department dealing with refugees and stateless persons
OGM [oʒɛɛm] NM (*abrév* **organisme génétiquement modifié**) GMO
OHQ [oɑʃky] NM (*abrév* **ouvrier hautement qualifié**) skilled worker
OICS [oisɛs] NM (*abrév* **Organe international de contrôle des stupéfiants**) l'O. the INCB
OIRT [oiɛʀte] NF Anciennement (*abrév* **organisation internationale de radio-télévision**) = broadcasting organization of Eastern European countries merged in 1993 with the European Broadcasting Union
OIT [oite] NF (*abrév* **Organisation internationale du travail**) ILO
OJD [oʒide] NM (*abrév* **Office de justification de la diffusion des supports de publicité**) advertising industry watchdog
OLP [oɛlpe] NF (*abrév* **Organisation de libération de la Palestine**) PLO
OM [oɛm] NM Ftbl (*abrév* **Olympique de Marseille**) l'OM = the Marseilles football team
OMC [oɛmse] NF (*abrév* **Organisation mondiale du commerce**) WTO
OMCI [oɛmsei] NF (*abrév* **Organisation de la navigation maritime consultative et intergouvernementale**) IMCO

OMI [oɛmi] NF (*abrév* **Organisation maritime internationale**) IMO
OMM [oɛmɛm] NF (*abrév* **Organisation météorologique mondiale**) WMO
OMPI [oɛmpei] NF (*abrév* **organisation mondiale de la propriété intellectuelle**) WIPO
OMS [oɛmɛs] NF (*abrév* **Organisation mondiale de la santé**) WHO
ONF [oɛnɛf] NM (*abrév* **Office national des forêts**) the French Forestry commission, Br ≃ the Forestry Commission, Am ≃ the Forestry Service
ONG [oɛnʒe] NF (*abrév* **organisation non gouvernementale**) NGO
ONISEP [onisɛp] NM (*abrév* **Office national d'information sur les enseignements et les professions**) = national careers guidance service
ONN [oɛnɛn] NM (*abrév* **Office national de la navigation**) French national shipping and inland waterways office
O-N-O (*abrév écrite* **Ouest-Nord-Ouest**) WNW
ONU, O.N.U. [ony, oɛnuy] NF (*abrév* **Organisation des Nations unies**) UN, UNO
ONUDI, Onudi [onydi] NF (*abrév* **Organisation des Nations unies pour le développement industriel**) UNIDO
OP [ope] NM (*abrév* **ouvrier professionnel**) skilled worker
OPA [opeɑ] NF Fin (*abrév* **offre publique d'achat**) takeover bid; **lancer une O. (sur)** to make a takeover bid (for); **être l'objet d'une O.** to be the subject of a takeover bid; **O. amicale** friendly takeover bid; **O. hostile** ou **inamicale** ou **sauvage** hostile takeover bid
op. cit. (*abrév écrite* **opere citato, opus citatum**) op. cit.
OPCVM [opesevɛɛm] NM Bourse (*abrév* **organisme de placement collectif en valeurs mobilières**) collective investment fund, Br ≃ unit trust, Am ≃ mutual fund; **O. actions** ≃ equity-based Br unit trust or Am mutual fund
OPE [opeɑ] NF Fin (*abrév* **offre publique d'échange**) exchange offer, takeover bid for shares
OPEP, Opep [ɔpɛp] NF (*abrév* **Organisation des pays exportateurs de pétrole**) OPEC
OPHLM [opeɑʃɛlɛm] NM (*abrév* **Office public d'habitations à loyer modéré**) = main office responsible for the allocation of council housing
ophtalmo [ɔftalmo] NMF Fam (*abrév* **ophtalmologiste**) eye specialist■
OPJ [opeʒi] NM (*abrév* **officier de police judiciaire**) = police officer in the French Criminal Investigation Department
OPR [opeɛʀ] NF Fin (*abrév* **offre publique de retrait**) public buy-out offer
OPV [opeve] NF Fin (*abrév* **offre publique de vente**) public offering, public share offer
OQ [oky] NM (*abrév* **ouvrier qualifié**) skilled worker
ORA [oɛʀɑ] NFPL (*abrév* **obligations remboursables en actions**) redeemable bonds
ORL [oɛʀɛl] Méd NMF (*abrév* **oto-rhino-laryngologiste**) ENT specialist
NF (*abrév* **oto-rhino-laryngologie**) ENT
ORSEC, Orsec [ɔʀsɛk] ADJ (*abrév* **Organisation des secours**) **plan O.** = disaster contingency plan; **plan O.-Rad** = disaster contingency plan in case of nuclear accident
ORTF [oɛʀteɛf] NM Anciennement (*abrév* **Office de radiodiffusion télévision française**) = former French broadcasting corporation
OS [oɛs] NM (*abrév* **ouvrier spécialisé**) skilled worker
OSCE [oɛssǝɑ] NF (*abrév* **Organisation pour la sécurité et la coopération en Europe**) OSCE
OSI [oɛsi] NF (*abrév* **organisation de solidarité internationale**) international aid organization
O-S-O (*abrév écrite* **Ouest-Sud-Ouest**) WSW

OST [oɛste] NF Com (*abrév* **organisation scientifique du travail**) organization and methods, time and motion studies
OTAN, Otan [ɔtɑ̃] NF (*abrév* **Organisation du traité de l'Atlantique Nord**) NATO
OTASE [ɔtaz] NF (*abrév* **Organisation du traité de l'Asie du Sud-Est**) SEATO
OTM [oteɛm] NM Com (*abrév* **opérateur de transport multimodal**) multi-modal operator
OTSI (*abrév écrite* **Office du tourisme-syndicat d'initiative**) tourist office
OUA [oyɑ] NF (*abrév* **Organisation de l'unité africaine**) OAU
OUC [oyse] NF Rad (*abrév* **ondes ultra-courtes**) USW
Oulipo [ulipo] NM Littérature (*abrév* **Ouvroir de Littérature Potentielle**) l'O. = literary group concerned with experimental writing techniques, founded by Raymond Queneau and François Le Lionnais in 1960 and including the writer Georges Perec
Oupeinpo [upɛ̃po] NM Beaux-Arts (*abrév* **Ouvroir de Peinture Potentielle**) l'O. = artistic group founded by Jacques Carelman and Thierry Foulc in 1980, with the aim of applying mathematical principles to painting and inventing new art movements
OVNI, Ovni [ɔvni] NM (*abrév* **objet volant non identifié**) **1** (*objet volant*) UFO **2** Fig (*personne ou objet atypique*) **faire figure d'O.** to stand out, to break the mould; **lors de sa sortie, ce roman a fait figure d'O. dans le paysage littéraire de l'époque** when it was first published this novel really stood out from the literature of the time

p 1 (*abrév écrite* **pico**) p **2** (*abrév écrite* **page**) p **3** Scol (*abrév écrite* **passable**) = fair grade (as assessment of schoolwork), ≃ C **4** (*abrév écrite* **pièce**) room; **à louer: 2p** (*dans une annonce*) one-bedroomed Br flat or Am apartment to let
P. Rel (*abrév écrite* **Père**) F
P2P [pitupi] ADJ Ordinat (*abrév* **peer to peer**) P2P
Pa Phys (*abrév écrite* **pascal**) Pa
PAC, Pac [pak] NF UE (*abrév* **politique agricole commune**) CAP
PACA, Paca [paka] NF (*abrév* **Provence-Alpes-Côte d'Azur**) = region of south-eastern France
PACS, Pacs [paks] NM INV (*abrév* **Pacte civil de solidarité**) civil solidarity pact (*bill introduced in the French parliament in 1998 allowing unmarried heterosexual couples and homosexual couples to legally formalize their relationships*)
PAF [paf] NF (*abrév* **police de l'air et des frontières**) airport and border police
NM Rad & TV (*abrév* **paysage audiovisuel français**) French broadcasting
PAG [peaʒe] NF Com (*abrév* **procédure accélérée générale de dédouanement**) accelerated customs clearance procedure
PAL, Pal [pal] ADJ TV (*abrév* **Phase Alternation Line**) PAL
PAM [pam] NM (*abrév* **programme alimentaire mondial**) WFP
PAO [peao] NF (*abrév* **publication assistée par ordinateur**) Ordinat DTP
PAP [pap] NM (*abrév* **prêt d'accession à la propriété**) = loan for first-time home-buyers
parano [parano] Fam ADJ (*abrév* **paranoïaque**) paranoid■
NMF (*abrév* **paranoïaque**) (*personne*) paranoid person■; **c'est un/une p.** he's/she's paranoid
NF (*abrév* **paranoïa**) (*maladie*) paranoia■; **tu es en pleine p.!** you're being completely

paranoid!▪; **arrête ta p.!** stop being paranoid!▪

part. (*abrév écrite* **particulier**) **p. vend moto état neuf** private sale: brand-new motorbike

PAS [peɑɛs] NM *Pharm* (*abrév* **acide para-amino-salicylique**) PAS

PC [pese] NM **1** (*abrév* **parti communiste**) CP, Communist Party **2** (*abrév* **personal computer**) PC **3** (*abrév* **prêt conventionné**) = approved mortgage loan **4** (*abrév* **permis de construire**) building permit *or* licence, *Br* planning permission **5** *Mil* (*abrév* **poste de commandement**) HQ **6** (*abrév* **Petite Ceinture**) (*bus*) = bus following the inner ring road in Paris

  NF *Fin* (*abrév* **pièce de caisse**) cash voucher

pc (*abrév écrite* **pièce**) room; **à louer: 2 pc** one-bedroomed *Br* flat *or Am* apartment to let

PCB [pesebe] NM *Chim* (*abrév* **polychlorobiphényle**) PCB

pcc (*abrév écrite* **pour copie conforme**) certified accurate

Pce (*abrév écrite* **prince**) prince

pce (*abrév écrite* **pièce**) room; **à louer: 2 pce** one-bedroomed *Br* flat *or Am* apartment to let

Pcesse (*abrév écrite* **princesse**) princess

PCF [peseɛf] NM (*abrév* **Parti communiste français**) French Communist Party

PCG [peseʒe] NM *Compta* (*abrév* **plan comptable général**) chart of accounts

PCI [pesei] NM **1** (*abrév* **Parti communiste italien**) Communist Party of Italy **2** (*abrév* **Parti communiste international**) International Communist Party

PCP [pesepe] NF *Chim* (*abrév* **phencyclidine**) PCP

PCR [peseɛr] NF *Biol* (*abrév* **polymerase chain reaction**) PCR

PCS [peseɛs] NFPL (*abrév* **professions et catégories sociales**) socio-economic categories

PCV [peseve] NM *Tél* (*abrév* **à percevoir**) *Br* reverse-charge call, *Am* collect call; **appeler Paris en P.** *Br* to make a reverse-charge call to Paris, *Am* to call Paris collect; **je les ai appelés en P.** *Br* I reversed the charges when I called them, *Am* I called them collect

PDA [pedea] NM *Ordinat* (*abrév* **personal digital assistant**) PDA

  NF *TV* (*abrév* **part d'audience**) audience share

PDF [pedeɛf] NM *Ordinat* (*abrév* **portable document format**) PDF

P-DG [pedeʒe] NMF INV (*abrév* **président-directeur général**) *Br* ≃ MD, *Am* ≃ CEO

PDM [pedeɛm] NF *Com* (*abrév* **part de marché**) market share

PDV [pedeve] NM *Com* (*abrév* **point de vente**) POS

PEA [peɑa] NM *Fin* (*abrév* **plan d'épargne en actions**) ≃ investment trust, *Br* ≃ ISA

PEbd [peɑbede] NM INV (*abrév* **polyéthylène basse densité**) LDPE

PECO [peko] NM (*abrév* **pays d'Europe centrale et orientale**) CEEC

PED [peɑde] NM (*abrév* **pays en développement**) developing country

PEE [peɑa] NM (*abrév* **plan d'épargne d'entreprise**) company savings scheme

PEGC [peɑʒese] NMF *Scol* (*abrév* **professeur d'enseignement général de collège**) = teacher qualified to teach one or two subjects to eleven-to-fifteen-year-olds in French secondary schools

PEhd [peɑaʃde] NM INV (*abrév* **polyéthylène haute densité**) HDPE

PEL [peɑɛl] NM *Banque* (*abrév* **plan (d')épargne logement**) *Br* ≃ building society account, *Am* ≃ savings and loan association account

péno [peno] NM *Fam* (*abrév* **penalty**) penalty▪, *Br* pen (*in football*)

PEP [pɛp] NM *Banque* (*abrév* **plan d'épargne populaire**) = personal pension plan

PEPS [peəpɛs] NM *Com & Compta* (*abrév* **premier entré, premier sorti**) FIFO

PER [peɛr] NM **1** *Banque* (*abrév* **plan d'épargne retraite**) retirement savings plan *or* scheme **2** (*abrév* **price/earnings ratio**) p/e ratio

périph [perif] NM *Fam* (*abrév* **boulevard périphérique**) **le p.** the Paris *Br* ring road *or Am* beltway▪

perm [pɛrm] NF *Fam* **1** *Mil* (*abrév* **permission**) leave▪; **être en p.** to be on leave **2** *Scol* (*abrév* **permanence**) (*tranche horaire*) study period▪; (*salle*) study *Br* room *or Am* hall▪; **aller en p.** to go to the study *Br* room *or Am* hall

perme [pɛrm] NF*Fam Mil* (*abrév* **permission**) leave▪; **être en p.** to be on leave

perso [pɛrso] *Fam* ADJ (*abrév* **personnel**) personal▪, private▪

  ADV (*abrév* **personnellement**) **il joue trop p.** he hogs the ball too much

PESC [peɑɛsse] NF *UE* (*abrév* **politique étrangère et de sécurité commune**) CFSP

p. ex. (*abrév* **par exemple**) eg

PGCD [peʒesede] NM *Math* (*abrév* **plus grand commun diviseur**) HCF

pH [peaʃ] NM *Chim* (*abrév* **potentiel hydrogène**) pH; **savon/shampooing/***etc* **(à) p. neutre** pH balanced soap/shampoo/*etc*

phage [faʒ] NM *Biol* (*abrév* **bactériophage**) phage

PHARE [far] NM *UE* (*abrév* **Pologne Hongrie Aide à la Reconstruction Économique**) PHARE

philo [filo] NF *Fam* (*abrév* **philosophie**) philosophy▪

phonie [fɔni] NF *Tél* **1** (*abrév* **radiotéléphonie**) radiotelephony **2** (*abrév* **téléphonie**) telephony

phono [fɔno] NM *Fam Vieilli* (*abrév* **phonographe**) phonograph▪, gramophone▪

PIB [peibe] NM (*abrév* **produit intérieur brut**) GDP; **P. nominal** nominal income; **P. potentiel** potential GDP; **P. réel** real GDP

PIN [peiɛn] NM *Écon* (*abrév* **produit intérieur net**) NDP

PJ[1] [peʒi] NF*Fam* (*abrév* **police judiciaire**) *Br* ≃ CID, *Am* ≃ FBI

PJ[2] (*abrév écrite* **pièces jointes**) encl.

PL *Transp* (*abrév écrite* **poids lourd**) HGV

Pl., pl.[1] (*abrév écrite* **place**) Sq.

pl.[2] (*abrév écrite* **planche**) pl

PL/1 [peɛlɛ̃] NM*Ordinat* (*abrév* **Programming Language One**) PL/1

PLS [peɛlɛs] NF *Méd* (*abrév* **position latérale de sécurité**) recovery position

PLU [ply] NM(*abrév* **plan local d'urbanisme**) = local town planning scheme

PLV [peɛlve] NM*Mktg* (*abrév* **publicité sur le lieu de vente**) point-of-sale promotion

PM [peɛm] NF *Mil* **1** (*abrév* **préparation militaire**) pre-call-up training **2** (*abrév* **police militaire**) MP

  NM (*abrév* **pistolet-mitrailleur**) sub-machine-gun

PMA [peɛma] NF (*abrév* **procréation médicalement assistée**) assisted conception

  NMPL(*abrév* **pays les moins avancés**) LDCs

PmaC *Écon* (*abrév écrite* **propension marginale à consommer**) APC

PmaE *Écon* (*abrév écrite* **propension marginale à épargner**) APS

PME [peɛmə] NF INV(*abrév* **petite et moyenne entreprise**) small business; **les P.** small and medium-sized enterprises

  NM (*abrév* **porte-monnaie électronique**) electronic wallet, electronic purse

PMI [peɛmi] NF INV (*abrév* **petite et moyenne industrie**) small industry; **les P.** small and medium-sized industries

  NF (*abrév* **protection maternelle et infantile**) mother and child care (*including antenatal and postnatal clinics and family planning*)

PMO [peɛmo] NFPL (*abrév* **pièces et main-d'œuvre**) parts and labour

PmoC *Écon* (*abrév écrite* **propension moyenne à consommer**) APC

PmoE *Écon* (*abrév écrite* **propension moyenne à épargner**) APS

PMU [peɛmy] NM(*abrév* **Pari mutuel urbain**) = French betting authority, *Br* ≃ tote, *Am* ≃ pari-mutuel

PN (*abrév écrite* **Parc National**) National Park

PNB [peɛnbe] NM (*abrév* **produit national brut**) GNP

PNN [peɛnɛn] NM *Écon* (*abrév* **produit national net**) NNP

PNUD, Pnud [pnyd] NM (*abrév* **Programme des Nations unies pour le développement**) UNDP

PNUE, Pnue [pny] NM (*abrév* **Programme des Nations unies pour l'environnement**) UNEP

PO 1 *Rad* (*abrév écrite* **petites ondes**) MW **2** *Com* (*abrév* **par ordre**) by order

POP [peope] NM *Chim* (*abrév* **polluant organique persistant**) POP

porno [pɔrno] *Fam* ADJ (*abrév* **pornographique**) (*film, magazine, scène*) porn (*avant n*), porno (*avant n*); **des photos pornos** dirty pictures

  NM (*abrév* **pornographie**) **1 le p.** (*genre*) porn; (*industrie*) the porn industry **2** (*film*) blue movie, *Br* porno film

POS, Pos [pɔs] NM(*abrév* **plan d'occupation des sols**) = document detailing local land development plans

postprod [pɔstprɔd] NF*Fam Cin & TV* (*abrév* **postproduction**) postproduction

PP [pepe] ADJ (*abrév* **préventive de la pellagre**) **vitamine PP** niacin

pp 1 (*abrév écrite* **pages**) pp **2** (*abrév écrite* **par procuration**) pp

PPCM [pepeseɛm] NM*Math* (*abrév* **plus petit commun multiple**) LCM

PPE [pepeə] NF(*abrév* **prime pour l'emploi**) = tax credit awarded to low wage-earners, as an incentive to continue working and not claim benefit instead

ppm [pepeɛm] NFPL **1** *Chim* (*abrév* **parties par million**) ppm **2** *Ordinat* (*abrév écrite* **pages per minute**) ppm

PPP [pepepe] NM (*abrév* **partenariat public-privé**) PPP

ppp (*abrév écrite* **points par pouce**) dpi

PQ[1] [peky] NM*très Fam* (*abrév* **papier-cul**) *Br* bog roll, *Am* TP

PQ[2] **1** (*abrév écrite* **province de Québec**) PQ **2** (*abrév écrite* **premier quartier (de lune)**) = first quarter

PQR [pekyɛr] NF (*abrév* **presse quotidienne régionale**) local daily press

PR[1] [peɛr] NM (*abrév* **parti républicain**) = right-wing French political party

PR[2] (*abrév écrite* **poste restante**) PR

Pr (*abrév écrite* **professeur**) Prof

préampli [preɑpli] NM*Fam* (*abrév* **préamplificateur**) preamp

PréAO [preao] NF *Ordinat* (*abrév* **présentation assistée par ordinateur**) computer-assisted presentation

PRG [peɛrʒe] NM *Pol* (*abrév* **Parti radical de gauche**) = left-of-centre French political party

pro [pro] *Fam* (*abrév* **professionnel**) ADJ **1** (*émission, film*) professional▪ **2** *Sport* professional▪; **il est joueur p. maintenant** he's turned pro

  NMF pro; **c'est une vraie p.** she's a real pro; **passer p.** to turn pro; **ils ont fait un vrai travail de p.** they did a really professional job▪; **elle a fait ça en p.** she did it like a pro

prof [prɔf] NMF *Fam* (*abrév* **professeur**) **1** *Scol* teacher▪; **ma p. de maths** my maths teacher **2** *Univ* (*sans chaire*) *Br* ≃ lecturer▪, *Am* ≃ instructor▪; (*titulaire de chaire*) prof; **elle est p. de fac** ≃ she's *Br* a lecturer *or Am* an instructor **3** (*hors d'un établissement scolaire*) teacher▪, tutor▪; **ma p. de piano** my piano teacher

prox. (*abrév écrite* **proximité**) **p. commerces** near shops

PS[1] [peɛs] NM (*abrév* **parti socialiste**) = French socialist party

P.S., PS² [peɛs] NM (*abrév* **post-scriptum**) PS, ps

PSC [peɛsse] NM *UE* (*abrév* **Pacte de stabilité et de croissance**) SGP

pseudo [psødo] NM *Fam* (*abrév* **pseudonyme**) pseudonym

PS-G, PSG [peɛsʒe] NM *Ftbl* (*abrév* **Paris St-Germain**) = Paris football team

PSIG [peɛsiʒe] NM (*abrév* **Peloton de surveillance et d'intervention de la gendarmerie**) = gendarmerie commando squad

PSU [peɛsy] NM *Anciennement* (*abrév* **parti socialiste unifié**) = former French socialist party

PTA *Anciennement* (*abrév écrite* **peseta**) Pta, P

PTCA [petesea] NM *Transp* (*abrév* **poids total en charge autorisé**) = maximum authorized load

Pte 1 (*abrév écrite* **porte**) door **2** (*abrév écrite* **pointe**) pt

PTFE [petɛɛfø] NM *Chim* (*abrév* **polytétrafluoroéthylène**) PTFE

PTT [petete] NFPL *Anciennement* (*abrév* **Postes, Télécommunications et Télédiffusion**) = former French post office and telecommunications network

PU [pey] NM *Com* (*abrév* **prix unitaire**) unit price

PV [peve] NM *Fam* (*abrév* **procès-verbal**) (parking) ticket; **j'ai eu un PV ce matin** I got a ticket this morning; **mettre un PV à qn** to give sb a ticket

PVC [pevese] NM (*abrév* **polyvinyl chloride**) PVC; **un siège en P.** a PVC seat

PVD [pevede] NM (*abrév* **pays en voie de développement**) developing country

PVP [pevepe] NM *Com* (*abrév* **prix de vente publique**) public selling price

px (*abrév écrite* **prix**) **px à déb** offers

q (*abrév écrite* **quintal**) q

QCM [kyseɛm] NM (*abrév* **questionnaire à choix multiple**) multiple-choice questionnaire

QG [kyʒe] NM (*abrév* **quartier général**) HQ

QHS [kyaʃɛs] NM (*abrév* **quartier de haute sécurité**) high-security *or* top-security wing

QI [kyi] NM *Psy* (*abrév* **quotient intellectuel**) IQ

qsp (*abrév écrite* **quantité suffisante pour**) qs

QSR [kyɛsɛr] NM (*abrév* **quartier de sécurité renforcée**) high-security *or* top-security wing

quadra [kwadra, kadra] *Fam* (*abrév* **quadragénaire**) ADJ quadragenarian■; **être q.** to be in one's forties■

NMF (*personne*) person in his/her forties■; **c'est un q.** he's in his forties

quinqua [kɛ̃ka] *Fam* (*abrév* **quinquagénaire**) ADJ quinquagenarian■; **être q.** to be in one's fifties■

NMF person in his/her fifties■; **c'est un q.** he's in his fifties

R¹ [ɛr] (*abrév* **Renault**) **une R19/21/25** a Renault 19/21/25

R² 1 *Vieilli Phys* (*abrév écrite* **roentgen**) R **2** (*abrév écrite* **rand**) R

R., r. (*abrév écrite* **rue**) St

RAM, Ram [ram] NF *Ordinat* (*abrév* **random access memory**) RAM; **R. sur carte** onboard RAM

RAS [ɛraɛs] ADV *Fam* (*abrév* **rien à signaler**) nothing to report

RATP [ɛratepe] NF (*abrév* **Régie autonome des transports parisiens**) = Paris transport authority

RAU [ɛray] NF (*abrév* **République Arabe Unie**) UAR, United Arab Republic

RBE [ɛrbeə] NM (*abrév* **revenu brut d'exploitation**) gross profit

RBL (*abrév écrite* **rouble**) R, Rub

R-C (*abrév écrite* **rez-de-chaussée**) *Br* ground floor, *Am* first floor

RCS [ɛrsɛɛs] NM (*abrév* **Registre du commerce et des sociétés**) register of companies

R-D [ɛrde] NM (*abrév* **recherche et développement**) R & D, R and D

r.d. (*abrév écrite* **rive droite**) right bank

RDA [ɛrdea] NF *Anciennement* (*abrév* **République démocratique allemande**) GDR; **vivre en R.** to live in the GDR; **aller en R.** to go to the GDR

RDB [ɛrdebe] NM (*abrév* **revenu disponible brut**) gross disposable income

RDC [ɛrdese] NF (*abrév* **République démocratique du Congo**) **la R.** the DRC

RdC (*abrév écrite* **rez-de-chaussée**) *Br* ground floor, *Am* first floor

RDS [ɛrdeɛs] NM **1** *Fin* (*abrév* **remboursement de la dette sociale**) = contribution paid by every taxpayer towards the social security deficit **2** *Tech* (*abrév* **radio data system**) RDS

réa [rea] NF *Fam* (*abrév* **réanimation**) **être en salle de r.** to be in intensive care■ *or Am* the ICU

réf. (*abrév écrite* **référence**) ref

rem [rɛm] NM *Nucl* (*abrév* **roentgen equivalent man**) rem

RER [ɛrəɛr] NM *Rail* (*abrév* **Réseau express régional**) = Paris metropolitan and regional rail system

RES [ɛrəɛs] NM *Fin* (*abrév* **rachat de l'entreprise par ses salariés**) employee buy-out

RESA [reza] NF (*abrév* **réservation**) = TGV seat reservation ticket

résa [reza] NF (*abrév* **réservation**) reservation, booking

RF (*abrév écrite* **République française**) French Republic

RFA [ɛrɛfa] NF *Anciennement* (*abrév* **République fédérale d'Allemagne**) FRG, West Germany; **vivre en R.** to live in West Germany; **aller en R.** to go to West Germany

RFI [ɛrɛfi] NF (*abrév* **Radio France Internationale**) = French World Service radio station

RFO [ɛrɛfo] NF (*abrév* **Radio-télévision française d'outre-mer**) = French overseas broadcasting service

RG [ɛrʒe] NMPL (*abrév* **Renseignements généraux**) = secret intelligence branch of the French police, *Br* ≃ Special Branch, *Am* ≃ the FBI

r.g. (*abrév écrite* **rive gauche**) left bank

RH [ɛraʃ] NFPL (*abrév* **ressources humaines**) HR

Rh *Physiol* (*abrév écrite* **Rhésus**) Rh

RI [ɛri] NM *Mil* (*abrév* **régiment d'infanterie**) infantry regiment

NMPL (*abrév* **Républicains indépendants**) Independent Republicans (*conservative Gaullist party founded in the early 1960s*)

RIB [rib] NM (*abrév* **relevé d'identité bancaire**) = document giving details of one's bank account

RICE [ris] NM *Banque* (*abrév* **relevé d'identité de caisse d'épargne**) = savings account identification slip

RIP [rip, ɛripe] NM *Banque* (*abrév* **relevé d'identité postale**) = document giving details of one's post office account

RISC [risk] NM INV (*abrév* **reduced instruction set computer**) *Ordinat* RISC

riv. (*abrév écrite* **rivière**) river

RMC [ɛrɛmse] NF (*abrév* **Radio Monte-Carlo**) = independent radio station

RMI [ɛrɛmi] NM (*abrév* **revenu minimum d'insertion**) = minimum welfare payment paid to people with no other source of income, *Br* ≃ income support, *Am* ≃ welfare

RMN [ɛrɛmɛn] NF (*abrév* **résonance magnétique nucléaire**) NMR

RN [ɛrɛn] NF (*abrév* **route nationale**) *Br* ≃ A-road, *Am* ≃ state highway

RNIS [ɛrɛniɛs] NM *Ordinat* (*abrév* **réseau numérique à intégration de services**) ISDN; **envoyer qch par R.** to ISDN sth, to send sth by ISDN

ro (*abrév écrite* **recto**) first side *or* front of a page, *Spéc* recto

ROC [ɛrose] NF *Ordinat* (*abrév* **reconnaissance optique des caractères**) OCR

ROM [rɔm] NF *Ordinat* (*abrév* **read only memory**) ROM, Rom

RP¹ [ɛrpe] NFPL (*abrév* **relations publiques**) PR

NF (*abrév* **recette principale**) (*de la poste*) main post office; (*des impôts*) main tax office

RP² (*abrév écrite* **région parisienne**) Paris area *or* region

R.P. *Rel* (*abrév écrite* **Révérend Père**) Rev

RPR [ɛrpeɛr] NM *Anciennement Pol* (*abrév* **Rassemblement pour la République**) = right-wing French political party

RSFSR [ɛrɛsɛfɛsɛr] NF (*abrév* **République socialiste fédérale soviétique de Russie**) **la R.** RSFSR

RSVP (*abrév écrite* **répondez s'il vous plaît**) RSVP

RTB [ɛrtebe] NF (*abrév* **Radio-télévision belge**) = Belgian broadcasting company

RTC [ɛrtese] NM *Tél* (*abrév* **Réseau Téléphonique Commuté**) PSTN

rte (*abrév écrite* **route**) rd

RTGS [ɛrteʒeɛs] NM *Banque & UE* (*abrév* **Real-Time Gross Settlement**) RTGS; **système R.** RTGS system

RTL [ɛrteɛl] NF **1** (*abrév* **Radio-télévision Luxembourg**) = private broadcasting network based in Luxembourg **2** *Élec* (*abrév* **résistance transistor logique**) RTL

RTT [ɛrtete] NF (*abrév* **réduction du temps de travail**) = reduction of the working week in France from 39 to 35 hours, introduced by the government of Lionel Jospin in 1998 and phased in from 2000 onwards; **être en R.** to have time off (*because one has accumulated annual leave through the "RTT" system*)

RTVE [ɛrteveə] NF (*abrév* **Radio-télévision espagnole**) = Spanish broadcasting company

RU [ry] NM *Fam* (*abrév* **restaurant universitaire**) university cafeteria *or Br* canteen *or* refectory■

RUPI (*abrév écrite* **roupie indienne**) Re

RUPP (*abrév écrite* **roupie du Pakistan**) Re, Pre

R-V (*abrév écrite* **rendez-vous**) meeting, appointment

RVB [ɛrvebe] NM (*abrév* **rouge, vert et bleu**) RGB

RVE [ɛrveə] NF *Écon* (*abrév* **restriction volontaire des exportations**) VER

S (*abrév écrite* **Sud**) S

s (*abrév écrite* **seconde**) s

s/ (*abrév écrite* **sur**) on

SA [ɛsa] NF (*abrév* **société anonyme**) *Br* ≃ plc, *Am* ≃ Corp.; **une SA** a limited company

S.A. (*abrév écrite* **Son Altesse**) HH

SACD [ɛsasede] NF (*abrév* **Société des auteurs et compositeurs dramatiques**) = association of writers and performers founded by Beaumarchais in 1777 which protects copyright and ensures royalties are paid

SACEM, Sacem [sasɛm] NF *Mus* (*abrév* **Société des auteurs, compositeurs et éditeurs de musique**) = body responsible for collecting and distributing royalties, *Br* ≃ Performing Rights Society, *Am* ≃ Copyright Royalty Tribunal

SADC [ɛsadese] NF Écon (abrév **Southern African Development Community**) SADC

sado [sado] Fam (abrév **sadique**) ADJ sadistic ▪; **il est un peu s.** he's a bit of a sadist NMF sadist ▪

sado-maso [sadomazo] (pl **sado-masos**) Fam (abrév **sadomasochiste**) ADJ SM, S & M; **il a des tendances sado-masos** he's into S & M, he has S & M tendencies NMF sadomasochist ▪; **c'est un s.** he's into S & M

SAE [ɛsaə] (abrév **Society of Automotive Engineers**) ADJ INV SAE NF SAE

SAFER, Safer [safɛr] NF Agr (abrév **Société d'aménagement foncier et d'établissement rural**) = agency entitled to buy land and earmark it for agricultural use

SALT [salt] NM Mil (abrév **Strategic Arms Limitations Talks**) SALT

SAM [sam] NM (abrév **Sol-Air Missile**) surface-to-air missile, SAM

SAMR [ɛsaɛmɛr] NM Méd (abrév **staphylococcus aureus méticillino-résistant**) MRSA

SAMU, Samu [samy] NM (abrév **Service d'aide médicale d'urgence**) = French ambulance and emergency service, Br ≃ ambulance service, Am ≃ Paramedics; **appelez le S.!** call an ambulance!; **le S. social** = mobile medical and support service for homeless people

sana [sana] NM Fam (abrév **sanatorium**) Br sanatorium ▪, Am sanitarium ▪

S.A.R. (abrév écrite **Son Altesse Royale**) HRH

SARL, Sarl [ɛsaɛrɛl] NF (abrév **société à responsabilité limitée**) limited liability company; **Balacor S.** Br ≃ Balacor Ltd, Am ≃ Balacor Inc

S.A.S. (abrév écrite **Son Altesse Sérénissime**) HSH

satis [satis] NF Belg Fam Arg scol (abrév **satisfaction**) = minimum pass (grade)

SAV [ɛsave] NM (abrév **service après-vente**) after-sales service

saxo [sakso] NM Fam 1 (abrév **saxophone**) sax 2 (abrév **saxophoniste**) sax (player)

SBF [ɛsbeɛf] NF (abrév **Société des bourses françaises**) = company which runs the Paris Stock Exchange, Br ≃ LSE, Am ≃ NYSE; **le S. 120** = broad-based French stock exchange index

SBS [ɛsbeɛs] NF Méd (abrév **syndrome du bébé secoué**) SBS

SCA [ɛssea] NF Com (abrév **société en commandite par actions**) partnership limited by shares

SCH Anciennement (abrév écrite **schilling**) S, Sch

SCI [ɛssei] NF 1 (abrév **société civile immobilière**) property investment partnership 2 Écon (abrév **société de commerce international**) international trading corporation

SCOP [skɔp] NF (abrév **Société coopérative ouvrière de production**) = manufacturing cooperative

SCP [ɛssepe] (abrév écrite **société civile professionnelle**) professional or non-trading partnership

SCPI [ɛssepei] NF (abrév **Société civile de placement immobilier**) = company which owns and manages rented accommodation

SCS [ɛsseɛs] NF (abrév **société en commandite simple**) limited partnership

SCSI [ɛsseɛsi] NF (abrév **small computer systems interface**) SCSI

SCT [ɛssete] NM Méd (abrév **syndrome du choc toxique**) TSS

sdb (abrév écrite **salle de bains**) bathroom

SDECE [sdɛk] NM Anciennement (abrév **Service de documentation extérieure et de contre-espionnage**) = French Intelligence Service

SDF [ɛsdeɛf] NMF INV (abrév **sans domicile fixe**) homeless person; **les S.** the homeless

SDN [ɛsdeɛn] NF (abrév **Société des Nations**) **la S.** the League of Nations

S-E (abrév écrite **Sud-Est**) SE

S.E. (abrév écrite **Son Excellence**) HE

SEBC [ɛsəbese] NM Fin & Écon (abrév **Système Européen de Banques Centrales**) ESCB

SECAM, Secam [sekam] TV (abrév **séquentiel couleur à mémoire**) ADJ INV SECAM NM INV SECAM

Sécu [seky] NF Fam Admin (abrév **Sécurité sociale**) (système) Br ≃ Social Security ▪, Am ≃ welfare ▪; (organisme de remboursement) Br ≃ DWP ▪, Am ≃ Social Security ▪

SEITA, Seita [seita] NF (abrév **Société nationale d'exploitation industrielle des tabacs et allumettes**) = French government tobacco and matches monopoly

SEL [ɛsəɛl] NF (abrév **société d'exercice libérale**) = company practising a liberal profession

SEM [sɛm] NF Écon (abrév **société d'économie mixte**) = company financed by state and private capital

S.Em. (abrév écrite **Son Éminence**) HE

SEO [ɛsəo] Compta (abrév **sauf erreur ou omission**) E & OE

SEP [ɛsəpe] NF Méd (abrév **sclérose en plaques**) MS

SERNAM®, Sernam® [sɛrnam] NM (abrév **Service national des messageries**) = rail delivery service, Br ≃ Red Star®

SET® [ɛsəte] NF Ordinat (abrév **secure electronic transaction**) SET®

S.Exc. (abrév écrite **Son Excellence**) HE

SF [ɛsɛf] NF Fam (abrév **science fiction**) sci-fi, SF

SFI [ɛsɛfi] NF Fin (abrév **Société financière internationale**) IFC

SFIO [ɛsɛfio] NF Hist (abrév **Section française de l'Internationale ouvrière**) = the French Socialist Party between 1905 and 1969

SFP [ɛsɛfpe] NF TV (abrév **Société française de production**) = former state-owned television production company

SFS [ɛsɛfɛs] NM TV (abrév **service fixe par satellite**) SFS

SG [ɛsʒe] NM Pol (abrév **secrétaire général**) GS

SGAO [ɛsʒeao] NM Ordinat (abrév **système de gestion assisté par ordinateur**) computer-assisted management system

SGB [ɛsʒebe] NM Med (abrév **syndrome de Guillain-Barré**) GBS

SGBD [ɛsʒebede] NM Ordinat (abrév **système de gestion de base de données**) DBMS

SGBDR [ɛsʒebedeɛr] NM Ordinat (abrév **système de gestion de bases de données relationnelles**) RDBMS

SGDG [ɛsʒedeʒe] ADJ (abrév **sans garantie du gouvernement**) without government guarantee

SGEN [ɛsʒeən] NM (abrév **Syndicat général de l'Éducation nationale**) = teachers' trade union

SGML [ɛsʒeɛmɛl] NM Ordinat (abrév **standard generalized mark-up language**) SGML

SI [ɛsi] NM 1 (abrév écrite **syndicat d'initiative**) tourist (information) office 2 (abrév **Système International**) SI

SICAF, Sicaf [sikaf] NF Bourse & Fin (abrév **société d'investissement à capital fixe**) closed-end investment company

SICAV, Sicav [sikav] NF Bourse & Fin (abrév **société d'investissement à capital variable**) 1 (société) OEIC, Br ≃ unit trust, Am ≃ mutual fund; **S. actions** equity-based unit trust; **S. éthique** ethical investment fund; **S. mixte** split capital investment trust; **S. monétaire** money-based unit trust; **S. obligataire** bond-based unit trust 2 (action) = share in an open-ended investment trust

SICOB, Sicob [sikɔb] NM (abrév **Salon des industries du commerce et de l'organisation du bureau**) **le S.** = annual information technology trade fair in Paris

SICOVAM, Sicovam [sikɔvam] NF Bourse (abrév **société interprofessionnelle pour la compensation des valeurs mobilières**) = French central securities depository

SIDA, Sida [sida] NM Méd (abrév **syndrome immuno-déficitaire acquis**) Aids, AIDS; **S. déclaré** full-blown Aids

SIM [ɛsiɛm] NM 1 Mktg (abrév **système d'information marketing**) MIS 2 Tél (abrév **subscriber identity module**) SIM; **carte S.** (pour téléphone portable) SIM card

SIMM [sim] NM Ordinat (abrév **single in-line memory module**) SIMM

SIRPA, Sirpa [sirpa] NM Mil (abrév **Service d'information et de relations publiques des armées**) = French military services public information service

SIT [ɛsite] NM (Banque) (abrév **système interbancaire de compensation**) = interbank automated clearing system, Br ≃ CHAPS

SIVOM, Sivom [sivɔm] NM (abrév **Syndicat intercommunal à vocation multiple**) = group of local authorities pooling public services

SIVP [ɛsivepe] NM (abrév **stage d'initiation à la vie professionnelle**) = training scheme for young unemployed people

skin [skin] NM (abrév **skinhead**) skin, skinhead

SLBM [ɛsɛlbeɛm] NM (abrév **Submarine Launched Ballistic Missile**) SLBM

SLCM [ɛsɛlseɛm] NM (abrév **Submarine Launched Cruise Missile**) SLCM

s.l.n.d. (abrév écrite **sans lieu ni date**) = date and origin unknown

SM [ɛsɛm] NM (abrév **sado-masochisme**) S&M

S.M. (abrév écrite **Sa Majesté**) HM

SMAG, Smag [smag] NM Agr (abrév **salaire minimum agricole garanti**) = guaranteed minimum agricultural wage

SMCT [ɛsɛmsete] NM UE (abrév **soutien monétaire à court terme**) STMS

SME [ɛsɛmə] NM Écon 1 (abrév **Système monétaire européen**) EMS 2 (abrév **Serpent monétaire européen**) European currency snake

SMI [ɛsɛmi] NM Écon (abrév **Système monétaire international**) IMS

SMIC, Smic [smik] NM (abrév **salaire minimum interprofessionnel de croissance**) = index-linked guaranteed minimum wage

SMIG [smig] NM Anciennement (abrév **salaire minimum interprofessionnel garanti**) = index-linked guaranteed minimum wage

SMP [ɛsɛmpe] NF Mil (abrév **société militaire privée**) PMC

SMR [ɛsɛmɛr] NM Méd (abrév **service médical rendu**) = assessment of the medical benefits of a drug or treatment

SMS [ɛsɛmɛs] NM Tél (abrév **short message service**) SMS

SMUR, Smur [smyr] NM Méd (abrév **Service médical d'urgence et de réanimation**) = French ambulance and emergency unit

SNALC [ɛsɛnɑlse] NM (abrév **Syndicat national des lycées et collèges**) = teachers' union

SNC¹ [ɛsɛnse] NF Écon (abrév **société en nom collectif**) general partnership

SNC² (abrév écrite **service non compris**) service not included

SNCB [ɛsɛnsebe] NF Belg (abrév **Société nationale des chemins de fer belges**) = Belgian national railway company

SNCF [ɛsɛnseɛf] NF (abrév **Société nationale des chemins de fer français**) = French national railway company; **la S. est en grève** there's a (French) rail strike; **il travaille à la S.** he works for the (French) Br railways or Am railroads

SNE [ɛsɛnə] NF (abrév **Syndicat national de l'édition**) = French publishers' union

SNECMA [snɛkma] NF Aviat (abrév **Société nationale d'études et de construction de moteurs d'avion**) = aeroplane engine manufacturer

SNES, Snes [snɛs] NM (*abrév* **Syndicat national de l'enseignement secondaire**) = secondary school teachers' union

Sne-sup, Snesup [snɛsyp] NM (*abrév* **Syndicat national de l'enseignement supérieur**) = university teachers' union

SNG [ɛsɛnʒe] NM (*abrév* **satellite news gathering**) SNG

SNI [sni] NM *Anciennement* (*abrév* **Syndicat national des instituteurs**) = primary school teachers' union

SNJ [ɛsɛnʒi] NM(*abrév* **Syndicat national des journalistes**) = journalists' union

SNSM [ɛsɛnɛsɛm] NF (*abrév* **Société nationale de sauvetage en mer**) = national sea-rescue association

S-O (*abrév écrite* **Sud-Ouest**) SW

s.o. (*abrév écrite* **sans objet**) n/a

socialo [sɔsjalo] *Fam* (*abrév* **socialiste**) ADJ socialist ▪, leftie, lefty

NMF socialist ▪, leftie, lefty

SOFRES, Sofres [sɔfrɛs] NF (*abrév* **Société française d'enquêtes par sondages**) **la S.** = French market research company

sono [sɔno] NF *Fam* (*abrév* **sonorisation**) (*d'un groupe, d'une discothèque*) sound system ▪, sound; (*d'une salle de conférences*) public-address system ▪, PA (system) ▪

SOPK [ɛsopeka] NM *Méd* (*abrév* **syndrome des ovaires polykystiques**) PCOS

SOS [ɛsoɛs] NM (*abrév* **save our souls**) **1** (*signal de détresse*) SOS; **lancer un S.** to put *or* to send out an SOS

2 *Fam* (*demande d'argent*) **envoyer un S. à ses parents** to send an urgent request for money to one's parents

3 (*dans des noms de sociétés*) **S.-Amitié** = charity providing support for people in despair, *Br* ≃ the Samaritans; **S. médecins/dépannage** emergency medical/repair service; **S.-Racisme** = voluntary organization set up to combat racism in French society

sous-off [suzɔf] (*pl* **sous-offs**) NM *Fam Arg mil* (*abrév* **sous-officier**) non-commissioned officer ▪

SPA [ɛspea] NF (*abrév* **Société protectrice des animaux**) = society for the protection of animals, *Br* ≃ RSPCA, *Am* ≃ ASPCA

SPADEM [spadɛm] NF (*abrév* **Société de la propriété artistique et des dessins et modèles**) = organization set up to defend the interests of designers, photographers, artists etc

SPI [ɛspei] NMPL (*abrév* **Secrétariats professionnels internationaux**) ITS

SPOT, Spot [spɔt] NM (*abrév* **satellite pour l'observation de la Terre**) earth observation satellite

SPRL [ɛspeɛrɛl] NF *Belg* (*abrév* **société de personnes à responsabilité limitée**) limited liability company

sq (*abrév écrite* **sequiturque**) f

sqq (*abrév écrite* **sequunturque**) ff

SR [ɛsɛr] NM *Journ* (*abrév* **sécretaire de rédaction**) subeditor

SRAS [sras] NM *Méd* (*abrév* **syndrome respiratoire aigu sévère**) SARS

SRPJ [ɛsɛrpeʒi] NM (*abrév* **Service régional de la police judiciaire**) = French regional crime unit

SRS [ɛsɛrɛs] NM *Rad & TV* (*abrév* **service de radiodiffusion par satellite**) SBS

SS [ɛsɛs] *Hist* (*abrév* **SchutzStaffel**) NF SS

NM **un SS** a member of the SS; **les SS** the SS

S/S *Naut* (*abrév écrite* **steamship**) S/S

S.S. 1 *Admin* (*abrév écrite* **Sécurité sociale**) SS, *Br* ≃ DWP, *Am* ≃ SSA **2** (*abrév écrite* **Sa Sainteté**) HH

SSBS [ɛsɛsbeɛs] NM (*abrév* **sol-sol balistique stratégique**) ≃ MRBM

S-S-E (*abrév écrite* **sud-sud-est**) SSE

SSII [ɛsɛsii] NF (*abrév* **société de services et d'ingénierie en informatique**) = software and computing services company

S-S-O (*abrév écrite* **sud-sud-ouest**) SSW

SSR [ɛsɛsɛr] NF *Suisse TV* (*abrév* **Société suisse de Radiodiffusion et de Télévision**) = French-speaking Swiss broadcasting company

St (*abrév écrite* **saint**) St., St

st (*abrév écrite* **stère**) st

Ste (*abrév écrite* **sainte**) St., St

Sté (*abrév écrite* **société**) Co; **S. Leroux** Leroux

Stib [stib] NF *Belg* (*abrév* **Société des transports intercommunaux de Bruxelles**) = Brussels transport authority

STO [ɛsteo] NM *Hist* (*abrév* **service du travail obligatoire**) = compulsory labour service during the Second World War for which French workers were sent to Germany

stol [stɔl] NM INV *Aviat* (*abrév* **short take-off and landing**) STOL

stp (*abrév écrite* **s'il te plaît**) please

STS [ɛsteɛs] NF (*abrév* **section de technicien supérieur**) = two-year advanced vocational course, taken after the "baccalauréat"

SUD-PTT [sydpetete] NM (*abrév* **solidaires, unitaires et démocratiques-postes, télécommunications et télédiffusion**) = French post office and telecommunications trade union

SVP [ɛsvepe] (*abrév* **s'il vous plaît**) please

syphilo [sifilo] NMF *Fam* (*abrév* **syphilitique**) = person suffering from syphilis

sysop [sizɔp] NM *Ordinat* (*abrév* **Systems Operator**) SYSOP

T 1 (*abrév écrite* **tesla**) T **2** (*abrév écrite* **téra**) T

t (*abrév écrite* **tonne**) t.

t. (*abrév écrite* **tome**) vol.

TAA [teɑa] NM *Transp* (*abrév* **train autos accompagnées**) *Br* Motorail train, *Am* Auto Train

TAC [teɑse] NM *Transp* (*abrév* **train autocouchettes**) car sleeper (train), *Br* Motorail train (*with sleeping accommodation*)

TAI [teɑi] NM(*abrév* **temps atomique international**) IAT

TAO [teɑo] NF(*abrév* **traduction assistée par ordinateur**) CAT

TAT [teate] NM *Psy & Mktg* (*abrév* **thematic apperception test** *ou* **test d'aperception thématique**) TAT

TB, tb *Scol* (*abrév écrite* **très bien**) vg

TBE, tbe (*abrév écrite* **très bon état**) vgc

TBF [tebeɛf] NM *Banque* (*abrév* **transferts Banque de France**) = French automated clearing system

TCA [teseɑ] NF *Fin* (*abrév* **taxe sur le chiffre d'affaires**) sales *or* turnover tax

TCF [teseɛf] NM *Aut* (*abrév* **Touring Club de France**) = French motorists' club

TCI [tesei] NM *Com* (*abrév* **terme commercial international**) incoterm

TCP/IP [tesepeipe] NF *Ordinat* (*abrév* **transmission control protocol/Internet protocol**) TCP-IP

TCS [tesees] NM *Aut* (*abrév* **Touring Club de Suisse**) = Swiss motorists' club

TD [tede] NMPL *Univ* (*abrév* **travaux dirigés**) seminars

TdF [tedeɛf] NF *TV* (*abrév* **Télédiffusion de France**) = French broadcasting authority which controls both radio and TV networks

TDM [tedeɛm] NF *Méd* (*abrév* **tomodensitométrie**) CT

TEC [tɛk] NF *Belg* (*abrév* **société de transport en commun**) = Walloon public transport authority

tec [tɛk] NF INV (*abrév* **tonne d'équivalent charbon**) TCE

TEE [teəə] NM *Rail* (*abrév* **Trans-Europ-Express**) TEE

TEG [teəʒe] NM *Fin* (*abrév* **taux effectif global**) APR

tél. (*abrév écrite* **téléphone**) tel

TEMPÉ [teæmpe] NM *Bourse* (*abrév* **taux moyen pondéré en euros**) EONIA

TEP [teəpe] NM **1** *Théât* (*abrév* **Théâtre de l'Est parisien**) = theatre in Paris **2** *Com* (*abrév* **terminal électronique de paiement**) electronic payment terminal, PDQ

NF *Méd* (*abrév* **tomographie à émission de positrons**) PET

tep [tɛp] NF INV (*abrév* **tonne d'équivalent pétrole**) TOE

TER [teœɛr] NM *Transp* (*abrév* **transport express régional**) = French regional network of trains and coaches

TF1 [teɛfɛ] NF *TV* (*abrév* **Télévision Française 1**) = French independent television company

TG [teʒe] NF **1** *Fin* (*abrév* **trésorerie générale**) paymaster's office (*in a "département"*) **2** *Mktg* (*abrév* **tête de gondole**) aisle end display, gondola end

TGB [teʒebe] NF(*abrév* **très grande bibliothèque**) = the new French national library in the Tolbiac area of Paris

TGI [teʒei] NM *Jur* (*abrév* **tribunal de grande instance**) = court of first instance in civil and criminal matters

TGP [teʒepe] NM *Cin & TV* (*abrév* **très gros plan**) BCU

TGV [teʒeve] NM *Rail* (*abrév* **train à grande vitesse**) = French high-speed train

th (*abrév écrite* **thermie**) 10^6 calories

Thada [tada] NM *Méd* (*abrév* **trouble d'hyperactivité avec déficit de l'attention**) ADHD

thalasso [talaso] NF *Fam* (*abrév* **thalassothérapie**) seawater therapy ▪, thalassotherapy ▪

THG [teaʒe] NF *Chim* (*abrév* **tétrahydrogestrinone**) THG

THS [teaʃɛs] NM *Méd* (*abrév* **traitement hormonal substitutif**) HRT

TI [tei] NM *Jur* (*abrév* **tribunal d'instance**) = lowest-level court in French legal system, having limited jurisdiction

tiags [tjag] NFPL *Fam* (*abrév* **santiags**) cowboy boots ▪

TIBEUR *Fin* (*abrév écrite* **taux interbancaire européen**) EURIBOR

TIG [teiʒe] NM *Jur* (*abrév* **travail d'intérêt général**) ≃ community service

TIOP [tjɔp] NM *Banque* (*abrév* **taux interbancaire offert à Paris**) PIBOR

TIP [tip] NM*Banque* (*abrév* **titre interbancaire de paiement**) = payment slip for bills

TIPP [teipepe] NF (*abrév* **taxe intérieure sur les produits pétroliers**) domestic tax on petroleum products

TIR [teiɛr, tir] NM *Transp* (*abrév* **transport international routier**) TIR

TJJ [teʒiʒi] NM *Fin* (*abrév* **taux d'argent au jour le jour**) overnight *or* call rate

TLJ (*abrév écrite* **tous les jours**) every day

TMM [teæmɛm] NM *Fin* (*abrév* **taux moyen du marché monétaire**) money-market rate

TMT [teɛmte] NM (*abrév* **technology, media and telecommunications**) TMT

TNP [teɛnpe] NM *Théât* (*abrév* **Théâtre national populaire**) **le T.** the French National Theatre (*based at the Palais de Chaillot in Paris until 1972 and at Villeurbanne near Lyons since then*)

TNT [teɛnte] NM *Chim* (*abrév* **trinitrotoluène**) TNT

NF *TV* (*abrév* **télévision numérique terrestre**) digital television, DTT

TO *Aut* (*abrév écrite* **toit ouvrant**) sunroof

TOC [teose] NM (*abrév* **trouble obsessionnel compulsif**) OCD

TOM [tɔm] NM INV *Admin* (*abrév* **territoire d'outre-mer**) French overseas territory

TP [tepe] NMPL **1** *Scol & Univ* (*abrév* **travaux pratiques**) **avoir un TP de chimie** to have a practical chemistry lesson *or* a chemistry lab; **être en TP** to be in the lab **2** (*abrév* **travaux publics**) civil engineering

NM *Fin* (*abrév* **Trésor public**) **le TP** *Br* ≃

the Treasury, *Am* ≃ the Treasury Department

TPC [tepese] NF *Ordinat* (*abrév* **tierce partie de confiance**) TTP

TPE [tepeə] NF *Écon* (*abrév* **très petite entreprise**) very small business (*employing fewer than 20 people*)
  NM (*abrév* **terminal de paiement électronique**) pinpad

TPG [tepeʒe] NM *Fin* (*abrév* **trésorier-payeur général**) paymaster (*for a "département" or "région"*)

TPIR [tepeiɛr] NM *Jur* (*abrév* **Tribunal pénal international pour le Rwanda**) ICTR

TPIY [tepeiigrɛk] NM *Jur* (*abrév* **Tribunal pénal international pour l'ex-Yougoslavie**) ICTY

tpm [tepeɛm] NMPL *Tech* (*abrév* **tours par minute**) rpm

TPS [tepeɛs] NF *Can Fin* (*abrév* **taxe sur les produits et services**) GST

tps (*abrév écrite* **temps**) time

TPV [tepeve] NM *Mktg* (*abrév* **terminal point de vente**) point-of-sale terminal, POST

tr (*abrév écrite* **tour**) rev

trad. 1 (*abrév écrite* **traduction**) trans. **2** (*abrév écrite* **traducteur**) translator **3** (*abrév écrite* **traduit par**) translated by

Transilien® [trɑ̃siljɛ̃] NM (*abrév* **transport francilien**) = Paris suburban train network

trichlo [triklo] NM *Fam* (*abrév* **trichloréthylène**) trichlorethylene▪ (*used as a drug*)

trigo [trigo] NF *Fam Math* (*abrév* **trigonométrie**) trig, trigonometry▪

trim. *Scol & Univ* (*abrév écrite* **trimestre**) term

triso [trizo] *Fam Péj* (*abrév* **trisomique**) ADJ spazzy, *Br* mong
  NMF spaz, *Br* mong

tr/mn, tr/min *Tech* (*abrév écrite* **tours par minute**) rpm

3G [trwaʒe] NF *Ordinat & Tél* (*abrév* **troisième génération**) 3G

tr/s *Tech* (*abrév écrite* **tours par seconde**) revs/s

ts (*abrév écrite* **tous**) all

TSF [teɛsɛf] NF *Vieilli Tél* (*abrév* **télégraphie sans fil**) (*appareil*) wireless; (*procédé*) wireless telegraphy

TSVP (*abrév écrite* **tournez s'il vous plaît**) PTO

TT [tete] NM *Aut* (*abrév* **transit temporaire (autorisé)**) = registration for vehicles bought in France for tax-free export by non-residents

tt (*abrév écrite* **tout**) ADJ all
  ADV everything

TTC [tetese] ADJ *Com* (*abrév* **toutes taxes comprises**) inclusive of all tax, including tax

tt conf (*abrév écrite* **tout confort**) with all mod cons

tte (*abrév écrite* **toute**) all

ttes (*abrév écrite* **toutes**) all

TTL [teteɛl] ADJ *Phot* (*abrév* **through the lens**) TTL

TTX *Ordinat* (*abrév écrite* **traitement de texte**) WP

TU [tey] NM (*abrév* **temps universel**) UT, GMT; **à 0h TU** at 0h UT *or* GMT

TUC, Tuc [tyk] (*abrév* **travaux d'utilité collective**) NM = community work for unemployed young people; **faire un T.** to do community work
  NMF (*employé*) = person involved in a "TUC" scheme

TUE [teyə] NM *EU* (*abrév* **traité sur l'Union européenne**) TEU

TUP [typ] NM *Banque* (*abrév* **titre universel de paiement**) universal payment order

TV [teve] NF (*abrév* **télévision**) TV

TVA [teveɑ] NF *Fin* (*abrév* **taxe sur la valeur ajoutée**) *Br* ≃ VAT, *Am* ≃ sales tax; **exempt de T.** zero-rated; **soumis à la T.** ≃ subject to *Br* VAT *or Am* sales tax; **T. encaissée** output tax; **T. récupérée** input tax

TVHD [teveaʃde] NF (*abrév* **télévision haute définition**) HDTV

TVP [tevepe] NF (*abrév* **thrombose veineuse profonde**) DVT

UAP [yape] NF *Ind* (*abrév* **unité autonome de production**) autonomous production unit

UAS [yaɛs] NF *Mktg* (*abrév* **unité d'activité stratégique**) SBU

UCE [yseə] NF *Aut* (*abrév* **unité de contrôle** *ou* **de commande électronique**) ECU

UDF [ydɛɛf] NF *Pol* (*abrév* **Union pour la démocratie française**) = right-of-centre French political party

UDR [ydeɛr] NF *Anciennement Pol* (*abrév* **Union pour la défense de la République**) = right-wing French political party

UE [yə] NF (*abrév* **Union européenne**) EU

UEAPME [yəapeɛmə] NF *Écon* (*abrév* **Union européenne de l'artisanat et des petites et moyennes entreprises**) UEAPME, European Association of Craft, Small and Medium-sized Enterprises

UEFA [yəɛfa] NF *Ftbl* (*abrév* **Union of European Football Associations**) UEFA; **la coupe de l'U.** the UEFA cup

UEM [yəɛm] NF *Écon* (*abrév* **Union économique et monétaire**) EMU

UEMOA [yəɛmoa] NF *Écon* (*abrév* **Union économique et monétaire ouest-africaine**) WAEMU

UEO [yəo] NF (*abrév* **Union de l'Europe occidentale**) WEU

UER [yəɛr] NF **1** *Anciennement Univ* (*abrév* **unité d'enseignement et de recherche**) = former name for a university department **2** *Rad* (*abrév* **Union européenne de radiodiffusion**) EBU

UFC [yɛfse] NF (*abrév* **Union fédérale des consommateurs**) = French consumers' association

UFR [yɛfɛr] NF *Univ* (*abrév* **unité de formation et de recherche**) = university department

UFT [yɛfte] NF *Pol* (*abrév* **Union française du travail**) = French association of independent trade unions

UHF [yaʃɛf] NF *Phys* (*abrév* **ultra-haute fréquence**) UHF

UHT [yaʃte] ADJ (*abrév* **ultra-haute température**) UHT; **lait stérilisé U.** UHT sterilized milk

UIT [yite] NF *Tél* (*abrév* **Union internationale des télécommunications**) ITU

UJP [yʒipe] NF *Pol* (*abrév* **Union des jeunes pour le progrès**) = French political party

ULM [yɛlɛm] NM *Aviat* (*abrév* **ultraléger motorisé**) microlight

UMA [yɛma] NF *Écon* (*abrév* **Union du Maghreb arabe**) AMU

UME [yɛmə] NF *UE* (*abrév* **Union monétaire européenne**) EMU

UMP [yɛmpe] NF *Pol* **1** (*abrév* **Union pour un Mouvement Populaire**) = centre-right French political party, formed mainly from members of the former RPR party **2** *Anciennement* (*abrév* **Union pour la Majorité Présidentielle**) = former centre-right coalition, now renamed "Union pour un Mouvement Populaire"

UMTS [yɛmteɛs] NM *Tél* (*abrév* **Universal Mobile Telecommunications System**) UMTS

UNEDIC [ynedik] NF (*abrév* **Union nationale interprofessionnelle pour l'emploi dans l'industrie et le commerce**) = the department controlling the "ASSEDIC"

UNEF, Unef [ynɛf] NF (*abrév* **Union nationale des étudiants de France**) ≃ National Union of Students

UNESCO, Unesco [ynɛsko] NF (*abrév* **United Nations Educational, Scientific and Cultural Organization**) UNESCO, Unesco

UNICEF, Unicef [ynisɛf] NF (*abrév* **United Nations International Children's Emergency Fund**) l'U. UNICEF, Unicef

---

Unix® [yniks] NM *Ordinat* (*abrév* **Uniplexed Information and Computing System**) Unix®

UNR [yɛnɛr] NF *Hist* (*abrév* **Union pour la nouvelle République**) = former Gaullist political party

UNSA [ynsa] NF *Pol* (*abrév* **Union nationale des syndicats autonomes**) = French trade union representing civil servants and other workers

UPA [ypeɑ] NF *Pol* (*abrév* **Union professionnelle artisanale**) = French employers' organization for craft industries

UPI [ypei] NF *Presse* (*abrév* **United Press International**) UPI

UPU [ypey] NF (*abrév* **Union postale universelle**) UPU

URL [yɛrɛl] NF *Ordinat* (*abrév* **uniform resource locator**) URL

URSS [yrs, yɛrɛsɛs] NF *Anciennement* (*abrév* **Union des républiques socialistes soviétiques**) l'U. the USSR; l'ex-U. the former USSR

URSSAF, Urssaf [yrsaf] NF *Admin* (*abrév* **Union pour le recouvrement des cotisations de Sécurité sociale et d'allocations familiales**) l'U. = French administrative body responsible for collecting social security payments

US [yɛs] NF *Sport* (*abrév* **union sportive**) sports club *or* association; **l'US (de) Liévin** the Liévin Sports Association *or* SA

USA [yɛsa] NMPL (*abrév* **United States of America**) **les U.** the USA, the US, the States

USB [yɛsbe] NM *Ordinat* (*abrév* **universal serial bus**) USB

UTA [yteɑ] NF *Aviat* (*abrév* **Union des transporteurs aériens**) = French airline company

UV [yve] NF *Univ* (*abrév* **unité de valeur**) course credit *or* unit
  NM INV (*abrév* **ultraviolet**) UV; **faire des UV** to go to a solarium

UVA [yveɑ] NM INV (*abrév* **ultraviolet A**) UVA; **bronzage U.** sunbed tan

---

V (*abrév écrite* **volt**) V

V. (*abrév écrite* **voir**) see

v. 1 (*abrév écrite* **vers**) v (*verse*) **2** (*abrév écrite* **verset**) v (*verse*) **3** (*abrév écrite* **vers**) towards **4** (*abrév écrite* **voir**) see

VA (*abrév écrite* **voltampère**) VA

Val [val] NM *Rail* (*abrév* **véhicule automatique léger**) automatic urban train service

VAN [veaɛn] NF *Compta* (*abrév* **valeur actuelle nette**) NPV, net present value

var [var] NM *Élec* (*abrév* **volt-ampère-réactif**) var

vd (*abrév écrite* **vend**) **particulier vd...** for sale...

VDQS [vedekyɛs] NM (*abrév* **vin délimité de qualité supérieure**) = label indicating quality of wine

vds (*abrév écrite* **vends**) for sale

VF [veɛf] *Cin* NF (*abrév* **version française**) = indicates that a film is dubbed in French ❏ **en VF** ADJ dubbed in French; **voir un film en VF** to see a film dubbed in French

VGE [veʒeə] NPR (*abrév* **Valéry Giscard d'Estaing**) Valéry Giscard d'Estaing

VHD [veaʃde] NF (*abrév* **vidéo haute définition**) HDV

VHF [veaʃɛf] NF *TV & Rad* (*abrév* **very high frequency**) VHF

VHS [veaʃɛs] NM *TV* (*abrév* **video home system**) VHS

VI [vei] NF *Compta* (*abrév* **valeur d'inventaire**) balance sheet value, break-up value

VIH [veiaʃ] NM *Méd* (*abrév* **virus de l'immunodéficience humaine**) HIV

VIP [viajpi, veipe] NMF (*abrév* **very important person**) VIP

VL [veɛl] NM *Transp* (*abrév* **véhicule lourd**) HGV

VLF [veɛlɛf] NF *TV & Rad* (*abrév* **very low frequency**) VLF

VMC [veɛmse] NF *Constr* (*abrév* **ventilation mécanique contrôlée**) mechanical ventilation system

vMCJ *Méd* (*abrév écrite* **variant de la maladie de Creutzfeldt-Jakob**) vCJD

VMP [veɛmpe] NFPL *Bourse* (*abrév* **valeurs mobilières de placement**) marketable securities

VNO [veɛno] NM *Méd* (*abrév* **virus du Nil occidental**) West Nile virus

VO [veo] *Cin* NF (*abrév* **version originale**) = indicates that a film is in the original language and not dubbed
▫ **en VO** ADJ in the original version; **en VO sous-titrée** in the original version with subtitles; **voir un film en VO** to see a film in the original (language) version

vo (*abrév écrite* **verso**) vo.

VOD [veode] NF (*abrév* **video-on-demand**) VOD

vol. (*abrév écrite* **volume**) vol

VPC [vepese] NF (*abrév* **vente par correspondance**) mail-order (selling)

VRC [veɛrse] NF *Mktg* (*abrév* **vente par réseau coopté**) multilevel marketing, MLM

V/Réf (*abrév écrite* **Votre référence**) your ref

VRP [veɛrpe] NM *Com* (*abrév* **voyageur représentant placier**) sales rep; **V. multicarte** freelance rep (*working for several companies*)

vs *Ling* (*abrév écrite* **versus**) v, vs

VSAT [vesat] NM INV *Tél* (*abrév* **very small aperture terminal**) VSAT

VSD [veɛsde] NM *Presse* (*abrév* **vendredi samedi dimanche**) = French popular weekly news magazine

VSN [veɛsɛn] NM *Mil* (*abrév* **volontaire du service national**) = recruit who chooses to carry out his national service by doing voluntary service overseas

VTC [vetese] NM (*abrév* **vélo tout chemin**) hybrid (bike)

VTOL [veteoɛl] NM INV *Aviat* (*abrév* **vertical take-off and landing**) VTOL

VTT [vetete] NM (*abrév* **vélo tout-terrain**) mountain bike

Vve (*abrév écrite* **veuve**) widow

VVF [veveɛf] NM (*abrév* **village vacances famille**) = state-subsidized holiday village

vx (*abrév écrite* **vieux**) old

W 1 *Phys* (*abrév écrite* **watt**) W **2** (*abrév écrite* **ouest**) W

W3 [trwadublǝve] NM *Ordinat* (*abrév* **World Wide Web**) WWW

WAIS [wɛjz] NM *Ordinat* (*abrév* **wide area information service** *or* **system**) WAIS

WAP [wap] NM *Tél* (*abrév* **wireless application protocol**) WAP; **W. lock** WAP lock

Wb *Phys* (*abrév écrite* **weber**) Wb

W-C [vese, dublǝvese] NMPL (*abrév* **water closet**) WC

Wh *Phys* (*abrév écrite* **wattheure**) Wh

WIFI [wifi] *Ordinat* (*abrév* **wireless fidelity**) NM WiFi
ADJ WiFi

WWW [dublǝvedublǝvedublǝve] NM *Ordinat* (*abrév* **World Wide Web**) WWW

WYSIWYG [wiziwig] *Ordinat* (*abrév* **what you see is what you get**) WYSIWYG

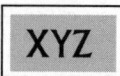

XMCL [iksɛmseɛl] NM *Ordinat* (*abrév* **Extensible Media Commerce Language**) XMCL

XML [iksɛmel] NM *Ordinat* (*abrév* **extensible mark-up language**) XML

Y (*abrév écrite* **yen**) Y

yougo [jugo] *très Fam* ADJ (*abrév* **yougoslave**) Yugoslav▪
▫ **Yougo** NMF (*abrév* **Yougoslave**) Yugoslav▪, = offensive term used to refer to a Yugoslav

ZA (*abrév écrite* **zone artisanale**) small industrial *Br* estate *or Am* park (*for craft-based businesses*)

ZAC, Zac [zak] NF (*abrév* **zone d'aménagement concerté**) = area earmarked for local government planning project

ZAD, Zad [zad] NF (*abrév* **zone d'aménagement différé**) = area earmarked for future development

ZCIT [zɛdseite] NF *Météo* (*abrév* **zone de convergence intertropicale**) ITCZ

ZEC [zɛk] NF *Can* (*abrév* **zone d'exploitation contrôlée**) = area in which hunting and fishing are restricted

ZEP, Zep [zɛp] NF **1** *Scol* (*abrév* **zone d'éducation prioritaire**) = designated area with special educational needs **2** *Écol* (*abrév* **zone d'environnement protégé**) = environmentally protected zone

ZI (*abrév écrite* **zone industrielle**) industrial *Br* estate *or Am* park

ZIF [zif] NF (*abrév* **zone d'intervention foncière**) = area earmarked for local government planning project

ZLEA [zɛdɛlǝa] NF *Com* (*abrév* **Zone de libre-échange des Amériques**) FTAA

ZUP, Zup [zyp] NF (*abrév* **zone à urbaniser en priorité**) = area earmarked for urgent urban development

Abbreviations Used in this Dictionary
Abréviations utilisées dans ce dictionnaire

gloss [introduces an explanation]	=	glose [introduit une explication]
cultural equivalent [introduces a translation which has a roughly equivalent status in the target language]	≃	équivalent culturel [introduit une traduction aux connotations comparables]
abbreviation	abbr, abrév	abréviation
accounting	Acct	comptabilité
adjective	adj	adjectif
administration	Admin	administration
adverb	adv	adverbe
agriculture	Agr	agriculture
American English	Am	anglais américain
anatomy	Anat	anatomie
antiquity	Antiq	antiquité
archaic	Arch	archaïque
archaeology	Archeol, Archéol	archéologie
architecture	Archit	architecture
slang	Arg	argot
article	art	article
insurance	Assur	assurances
astrology	Astrol	astrologie
astronomy	Astron	astronomie
Australian English	Austr	anglais d'Australie
cars	Aut	automobile
auxiliary	aux	auxiliaire
aviation	Aviat	aviation
Belgian French	Belg	belgicisme
biology	Biol	biologie
botany	Bot	botanique
British English	Br	anglais britannique
Canadian French	Can	canadianisme
carpentry	Carp	menuiserie
catholicism	Cathol	catholicisme
ceramics	Cer, Cér	céramique
chemistry	Chem, Chim	chimie
cinema	Cin	cinéma
commerce	Com	commerce
compound-forming noun	comp	nom à fonction adjectivale
comparative	compar	comparatif
accounting	Compta	comptabilité
computing	Comput	informatique
conjunction	conj	conjonction
building industry	Constr	bâtiment
continuous form	cont	forme progressive
cooking	Culin	cuisine
definite	def, déf	défini
ecology	Ecol, Écol	écologie
economics	Econ, Écon	économie
electricity	Elec, Élec	électricité
electronics	Electron, Électron	électronique
English	Eng	anglais d'Angleterre
entomology	Entom	entomologie
especially	esp	surtout
European Union	EU	Union européenne
euphemism	Euph	euphémisme
exclamation	exclam	exclamation
feminine	f	féminin
familiar	Fam	familier
figurative use	Fig	sens figuré
finance	Fin	finance
feminine plural noun	fpl	nom féminin pluriel
football	Ftbl	football
geography	Geog, Géog	géographie
geology	Geol, Géol	géologie
geometry	Geom, Géom	géométrie
grammar	Gram	grammaire
gymnastics	Gym	gymnastique
heraldry	Her, Hér	héraldique
history	Hist	histoire
horticulture	Hort	horticulture
humorous	Hum	humoristique
hunting	Hunt	chasse
fish	Ich	poissons
industry	Ind	industrie
insurance	Ins	assurances
indefinite	indef, indéf	indéfini
invariable	inv	invariable
Irish English	Ir	anglais d'Irlande
journalism	Journ	journalisme
law	Jur	droit
linguistics	Ling	linguistique
masculine	m	masculin
mathematics	Math	mathématique
medicine	Med, Méd	médecine
carpentry	Menuis	menuiserie
meteorology	Met	météorologie
metallurgy	Metal, Métal	métallurgie
meteorology	Météo	météorologie
military	Mil	militaire
mineralogy	Miner, Minér	minéralogie